Random House
Historical
Dictionary
of
American Slang

Random House Historical Dictionary of American Slang

Volume 2, H–O

J.E. Lighter, Editor

Assistant Editors

J. Ball

J. O'Connor

Jesse Sheidlower, Project Editor

RANDOM HOUSE
NEW YORK

 All inquiries should be addressed to Reference & Information Publishing, Random House, Inc., 201 East 50th Street, New York, NY 10022. Published in the United States by Random House, Inc., New York and simultaneously in Canada by Random House of Canada Limited.

Excerpts from the following works are from manuscript materials housed at the Kinsey Institute Collections, Bloomington, Indiana: "Sexual Vocabulary" by Henry N. Carey, "Jody Calls" by Paul Cameron, "Folklore of the U.S. Marine Corps" and "U.S.M.C. Marianas" Collection by Don Higginbotham, manuscript graffiti collection by John Del Torto, "Old American Ballads," "41st Fighter Squadron Songbook," and Erotic Verse to 1955."

Grateful acknowledgment is made to the following for permission to print unpublished material:

Collin Baker, D.R. Ladd, and Thomas Robb: Excerpts from "CUSS: College Undergraduate Slang Survey" by Collin Baker, D.R. Ladd, and Thomas Robb, written at Brown University in 1968 under the supervision of professor W. Nelson Francis. Reprinted by permission of the authors.

Dan Cragg: Excerpts from "Lexicon Militaris" by Dan Cragg and a personal letter to the author. Reprinted by permission of Dan Cragg.

Folklore Institute at Indiana University: Excerpts from various collections housed in the Folklore Archives at the Folklore Institute at Indiana University. Reprinted by permission.

University of Missouri–Columbia, Western Historical Manuscript Collection: Excerpts from the Peter Tamony Collection. Reprinted by permission of the University of Missouri–Columbia, Western Historical Manuscript Collection.

Library of Congress Cataloging-in-Publication Data
Historical dictionary of American slang / editor, J.E. Lighter
    p.   cm.
    Includes bibliographical references.
    ISBN 0-394-54427-7 (v. 1). 0-679-43464-X (v. 2).
    1. English language—United States—Slang—Dictionaries.
2. English language—United States—Obsolete words—Dictionaries.
3. Americanisms—Dictionaries.
I. Lighter, J.E. (Jonathan E.)
PE2846.H57 1994
427'.973'03—dc20   94-9721
                                            CIP

Visit the Random House Web site at: http://www.randomhouse.com/

Typeset and printed in the United States of America.

First Edition
0 9 8 7 6 5 4 3 2 1

ISBN 0-394-54427-7 (Volume 1)
     0-679-43464-X (Volume 2)

New York   Toronto   London   Sydney   Auckland

CONTENTS

ACKNOWLEDGMENTS

The appearance of this second volume of the *Random House Historical Dictionary of American Slang* affords me a welcome opportunity to reiterate my thanks to all those individuals and institutions acknowledged in Volume One of this work, whose influence here remains undiminished and has, in numerous cases, actually increased in the interim since its publication.

The continued enthusiasm of my associate Jesse Sheidlower, project editor of this dictionary at Random House, is reflected everywhere in this volume. His task, once again splendidly accomplished, has been to regularize and supplement its contents (for which he has my sympathy) even while keeping its production on an even keel (for which he has my special thanks).

Now to recognize the valued assistance of still more individuals and libraries.

At Random House, I thank Charles Levine, Phil Pfeffer, and Peter Bernstein on the executive level for their continued support of this project; and Jennifer Dowling, Joseph Vella, and Michele Purdue for their work in the managing and production of the book.

At the University of Tennessee, for unflagging interest and active encouragement, it would be hard to surpass Chancellor William T. Snyder, Vice Chancellor John Peters, and President Joseph E. Johnson, to all of whom I owe a special debt of gratitude. Similar thanks is owed to Professor D. Allen Carroll and to the trustees of the Hodges Better English Fund. Laura Curd, Lisa Lance, Sheri Stephens, and the indefatigable Linda Stooksbury deserve credit for innumerable tasks well done.

For their gracious responses to queries or for new and helpful information unselfishly supplied, grateful acknowledgment is hereby made to Sandy Ballard, Chris Barrett, Tom Beckner, Elizabeth Bogner, Carl Cobb, Tom Dalzell, Andrew Downey, Toney Frazier, Joan Hall and Luanne von Schneidemesser of the *Dictionary of American Regional English* for generous access to the *DARE* files and supplying prepublication galleys of Volume III of *DARE* in time to be incorporated into the present volume, Dean Harper, La Vinia Jennings, Gus Lee for clarifying several questions about slang in his novels, Thomas P. Lowry for several important citations, Kathy J. Lyday-Lee for her collection of student slang, Dan Mather, Wolfgang Mieder, Andy Newman, Julie O'Leary for her collection of student slang, Barry Popik, for tracking down a number of remarkable sources, Dirk Quirk of Knoxville Photocopy, Andrew Rappaport, William Safire, Fred Shapiro for his wizardry in tracking down valuable citations, Richard Weiner, and H. Bosley Woolf.

A special acknowledgment goes to Cullen Murphy and the *Atlantic Monthly* for granting me the opportunity to discourse upon specifics of American slang in the pages of that magazine.

In addition to all the libraries and institutions mentioned in Volume One, the following libraries, their Interlibrary Services in particular, handily provided hard-to-find source material for the present volume: the Birmingham, Alabama, Public Libraries; the library of Cambridge University; the Central Arkansas Library System, the Chicago Public Library System; the Drake University Library; the Duke University Libraries; the Eugene Shedden Farley

Library of Wilkes College; the Florida State University Library; the George C. Marshall Research Library, Lexingon, Virginia; the Irene Sullivan Ingram Library of West Georgia College; the Louisiana State University Libraries; the Middle Tennessee State University Library; the Southern Technical University Library; the Stanford University Libraries; the Library of the State Historical Society of Wisconson; the University of Florida Libraries; the University of Georgia Libraries; the University of Memphis Libraries; the University of Minnesota Libraries; the University of Wisconsin Libraries.

This dictionary has been made possible in great measure by support from the National Endowment for the Humanities, an agency that deserves not only my thanks but also general acknowledgment for its support of research in the humanities that enhances our understanding of our culture and thus the quality of American life.

SELECT ANNOTATED BIBLIOGRAPHY

The following notable books on slang have been published after Volume One of the present work went to press.

Allen, Irving Lewis. *The City In Slang: New York Life and Popular Speech*. New York: Oxford Univ. Press, 1993. Illuminates historical aspects of New York's mass culture through an examination of more than one thousand words and phrases, organized as "a time-walk through the historical city of the mind." The lexical items are eclectically drawn from glossaries, reportage, and social and historical treatments.

Dalzell, Tom. *Flappers 2 Rappers: American Youth Slang*. Springfield, Mass.: Merriam-Webster, 1996. Attractively produced, well-researched look chiefly at teen slang, giving significant attention to the popular culture that creates and disseminates it. Organizes decade-by-decade a colorful lexicon, drawn in large part from the Tamony Collection at the University of Missouri, Columbia.

Eble, Connie. *Slang and Sociability: In-Group Language among College Students*. Chapel Hill, N.C.: University of North Carolina Press, 1996. A readable sociolinguistic and rhetorical analysis of nonstandard vocabulary collected 1972–1993 from students at the Chapel Hill campus of the University of North Carolina. Emphasizes the use of novel, nonstandard vocabulary as an aid in the socialization process on campus through its structuring of shared perceptions of campus life. The first professional book-length study of American college slang.

Major, Clarence. *Juba to Jive: A Dictionary of African-American Slang*. New York: Penguin, 1994. The largest such compilation thus far, containing about 5,000 entries gleaned from oral and printed sources.

Smitherman, Geneva. *Black Talk: Words and Phrases from the Hood to the Amen Corner*. Boston: Houghton Mifflin, 1994. Glossary of current Black English including much material from hip-hop culture. Lively introduction addresses sociolinguistic features of Black English, seen as a source of cultural identity and a "counterforce to verbal deadness." Many entries were contributed by the author's students at three universities over a twenty-year period.

Guide to the Dictionary

Form and Order of Headwords

An entry always begins with the headword in boldface type. The headword is given in standard form and any exceptions are usually shown after the definition as variant forms. A headword can be followed immediately by a variant form if the variant is a common phonological or orthographical variant of the same lexeme. Examples:

> **hooch**[1] or **hootch**
> **-ass** or **-assed**

For further discussion, see *Variant Forms*, below.

Entries are listed in strict alphabetical order. Words that have the same part of speech and the same spelling except for capitalization are ordered by decreasing number of capital letters. Example:

> **BAM** *n.*
> **Bam** *n.*
> **bam**[1] *n.*
> **bam**[2] *n.*

Superscript homograph numbers are assigned to headwords that have identical spellings and identical parts of speech but different etymological origins. Senses stemming from the same source irrespective of semantic development are typically treated under the same headword. For instance, all senses of the noun *Joe* stem from the male given name *Joe*, a hypocoristic form of *Joseph*. Though the sense 'coffee' may derive from the title of the minstrel song "Old Black Joe," or from a shortening of JAMOKE, these derivations are tied to the name *Joe*, and the sense is listed under that entry. On the other hand, the noun *hooch* has several entirely different origins: one is a clipping of Tlingit *hoochinoo*, one is a clipping of HOOTCHY-KOOTCHY, and one is a pidgin borrowing from Japanese *uchi*. Each of these has been considered a different word, and therefore identified by a different homograph number.

Homographs are ordered by the date of the earliest citation.

Headwords with the same spelling but different parts of speech are ordered as follows:

> *n.*
> *pron.*
> *adj.*
> *adv.*
> *prep.*
> *conj.*
> *v.*
> *interj.*
> *art.*
> *(bound forms:)*
> > *prefix.*
> > *infix.*
> > *suffix.*
> > `comb. form.*

While this practice differs from that usually followed in historical dictionaries, it allows a reader to find a desired part of speech without focusing on the historical development of forms. Notes discussing issues of development are provided where necessary.

For entries entirely in brackets, see the discussion at *Definitions*, below.

Pronunciation

The pronunciation immediately follows the headword and is given in a broad International Phonetic Alphabet (IPA) transcription enclosed in virgules (//). Pronunciations are given for a very small number of words, usually only when a feature such as stress or vowel length is notably different from the usual pronunciation of the word. Also, pronunciations are usually given for pronunciation spellings such as *b'hoy* and for facetious variants such as /gɑrˈbɑʒ/ for *garbage*. No attempt has been to represent pronunciations for nonstandard varieties of English.

Part of Speech

Words are classified in this dictionary into the parts of speech listed above; however, pronouns, prepositions, conjunctions, and articles are extremely rare in slang and seldom occur in this dictionary. The part of speech is given immediately after the headword or after a pronunciation. The only other label used in this position is *n.pl.* to indicate plural nouns. Phrases are not usually labeled with part-of-speech designations.

Words that occasionally function as other parts of speech without any significant changes in meaning have this noted after the definition. For example:

> **noogie** *n.*....an act of rubbing or striking a person's head....Also as v.

In cases like these, where the changes in meaning result solely from differences in syntactic structure, a separate listings for the different part of speech is given only when justified by their frequency in the corpus.

Noun is used to classify all words with nominal function, including single words, compound or phrasal nouns, proper nouns, verbal nouns (when not treated under the verb), and nominalizations of verbs or verb phrases such as *make-out*. When attributive use of a noun seems frequent, this is noted; if it is especially prevalent or if the meaning is notably different, this usage may be pre-

sented separately as an adjectival entry.

Verbs are not usually labeled for transitivity; in most cases, the definition and the illustrative citations make clear whether or not the verb takes an object. When a distinction is necessary but the structure of a definition makes this impossible, it is noted in a comment or as an internal comment before a part of the definition. Other parts of speech formed from verbs, such as agentive nouns, verbal nouns, or participial adjectives, are normally treated at the verb; they may or may not be explicitly shown.

Combining forms are bound forms that are words in their own right. Thus *-o* is given as a suffix but *-happy* is a combining form. This label is used sparingly; combining forms that function as infixes are labeled as infixes, and nouns with one sense functioning as a combining form usually have a comment "usu. used in combs." for that sense, rather than separating the sense into a new entry.

Etymology

The etymology appears in square brackets. It is placed immediately before the sections of an entry to which it applies, so that an etymology referring to an entire word will follow the part of speech, but an etymology referring to a single sense will follow the definition number for that sense. The etymology should not be confused with the discursive note (see discussion at *Discursive Notes*, below), which is also in square brackets but which follows the definition and does not normally cover etymological ground; when an etymological comment is quite long, the discussion has sometimes been moved to or extended into the discursive note.

The majority of slang words are formed by semantic shifts from Standard English words. Etymologies are not supplied for the standard words, since these may be found in general dictionaries. The slang senses are only discussed when the semantic connection to the standard word might be obscure.

References to other languages are kept to a minimum. Words clearly borrowed from another language are usually traced to that language only, and not to the ultimate source. In some cases analogs in other languages are given where a sense development seems unusual; in these cases it is made clear whether the language may be a source of the English construction or merely provides an interesting parallel. Example:

> **daylight** *n*....[cf. L *lumen* 'eye', lit. 'light']...an eye.

Field Label

The field label appears in italics immediately before the definition. Note that the field label refers to the group, subculture, etc., of people who notably *use* the word, not necessarily to those to whom the word applies. Modifiers such as "Esp." or "Orig." may appear before a label, and one definition may have more than one label, such as "*Navy & USMC.*"

The decision to include field labels was made on the basis of citational evidence, and while in most cases this evidence is an accurate reflection of a word's range of use, the presence of a label should not imply that the word is used exclusively by the designated group, or that persons using such words have real ties to the designated group.

Definition

Definition numbers (or letters) are given in boldface type. Individual senses of a word are usually labeled with Arabic numerals; subdivisions of those senses are labeled with lowercase letters. In several complicated instances, an entry has been structured around a major division of senses. For example, the major senses of *bird* are divided into three groups: "senses referring especially to people," "senses referring to the physical representation of birds or to the ability of flight," and "other senses." These major divisions are labeled with uppercase Roman numerals.

The degree of precision possible in sense division depends greatly on the amount of available evidence. If the evidence for one sense is slight, this definition may be run into an existing one, preceded by a word such as "(*hence*)" or "(*also*)," even if the senses are not very close. In other cases, it has been possible to carefully divide and define much more closely related senses simply because the evidence is more abundant.

The reader should note that the extended context, in addition to that provided in a citation, has often facilitated the accurate placement of a citation, even though such placement may seem problematical at first glance. Users of this dictionary seeking full contexts of the citations are referred to the original works cited.

Certain comments can appear before or within a definition, in parentheses. The most common of these, which show the relationship between two parts of a definition, are (*hence*), which indicates that the second meaning logically and usually chronologically follows from the first; (*also*), which merely indicates that the second meaning is related to the first; and (*specif.*) and (*broadly*), which indicate respectively that the second meaning is a narrower or broader version of the first. Certain other comments, such as "(now *colloq.*)," "(*rare* in U.S.)," "(*trans.*)," or "(*hence*, as adj.)" can also appear internally when they affect only one part of the definition; their meanings are discussed elsewhere in this Guide.

In most cases, definitions are ordered by the date of the earliest citation. This also applies to lettered subdefinitions, but definitions are treated discretely. That is, if a word has definitions 1.a., 1.b., and 2., sense 1.b. will be later than sense 1.a., and sense 2 will be later than sense 1.a. but not necessarily later than sense 1.b. For dating purposes, bracketed citations (see discussion at *Citations*, below) are generally treated as relevant when they clearly point to the use under discussion. When a bracketed citation is simply an interesting parallel, it is discounted in the ordering of senses.

Because a strict historical presentation is the most accurate and the most helpful for the reader, very close relationships between senses are reflected by lettered subdivisions of definitions or by a breakdown within the definition itself.

There are two major exceptions to this chronological treatment. In a few cases where one sense is almost certainly the original, but a logically secondary sense is attested earlier, the senses have been given in the assumed logical order, rather than the chronological one. There is usually a note such as "despite the evidence of the dates, this meaning is undoubtedly the original." (When the development is less clear, the definitions have been left in chronological order with a note added, such as "prob. the original sense.") In a few instances, words usually used in combination have their senses divided based on the part of speech with which they are combined. The order of senses follows the order given above for parts of speech.

A definition, or very rarely a whole entry, can appear entirely in brackets. Here the brackets indicate that the word or sense under discussion has not been discovered in slang use in the United States. Usually this occurs either when a word or sense is attested only in British sources, but points to related uses in American slang (an example is JELLY, *n.*, 1), or when a sense has always been colloquial or dialectal but may have influenced the development of slang senses (an example is CHICKEN, 1.a.). There is always a note explaining the rationale behind the decision.

For the use of phrases within definitions, see discussion at *Phrases*, below.

Comments and Labels about Usage and Status

Certain definitions in this dictionary bear additional comments. These may consist of information about grammar, style, frequency, currency, and other aspects of usage. Most comments about usage are preceded by a dash, although others (such as "Now *S.E.*" or "*Joc.*") may be freestanding.

The abbreviation "usu.," meaning "almost always, though not inevitably," is used before a label to indicate that "mainstream standards" are flexible and are primarily based on situation and speaker-to-speaker relationships.

Ethnic and racial epithets are classic examples of the double lives led by some English words. What makes them epithets (or "slurs") is their willful use to demean or degrade. Yet, within the insulted groups, the same words may be used in mere derision or rough humor; in very recent use, some terms, such as *dyke*, *nigger*, and *queer* have been used self-referentially in an attempt to defuse their effect as epithets of hatred. It is such variation in intent and effect that warrants the use of "usu." with labels for these terms.

As used in this dictionary, "vulgar" carries the meaning 'coarsely offensive to mainstream standards of delicacy and taste'; the level of vulgarity can range from mild to extreme. Those entries marked "vulgar" typically refer to items of a sexual or scatological nature.

The words "derisively" and "contemptuously" are meant to convey their everyday meanings. "Derisively" implies an element of ridicule or banter that makes such terms less directly provocative than those entries marked as "contemptuous." Although many slang terms applied to human beings convey at least mild disrespect, only those senses conveying strong derision or contempt are so labeled. Labels are used only when the nature of the definition does not make its status clear; definitions of the sort "an idiot; fool" do not require labels such as "derisive" or "contemptuous."

The label "offensive" means that a term is likely to be considered offensive by the person, group, etc., to whom it refers. Used alone, it does not imply that any offense is intended by the person using the word. *Although the "offensive" label is not normally used for a word labeled as "derisive" or "contemptuous," such a word should be considered "offensive" nonetheless.* As with other labels, the "usu." has been applied to terms labeled "offensive" to account for the varying reception given to words by different individuals. Logically, the offensiveness lies in the context of the word's use, rather than inhering in the word itself.

Certain labels reflect the status of terms. A label of "Now *hist.*" indicates that as far as the editors can determine, a word is only used in historical contexts. This can mean that the referent of the word no longer exists (the *Blues* and the *Grays* of the Civil War, or the *flappers* of the Jazz Age) or that the word itself, while still remembered, is no longer in active use (the *Ameche* for a telephone, or a *flivver* for a cheap automobile). The "Now *hist.*" label does not necessarily mean that a word is rare or that it is no longer slang, although frequently used

terms of this sort often become Standard English. This dictionary does not necessarily include recent citations for words labeled "Now *hist.*," but the label itself indicates that the word may still be encountered, especially in historical writing.

The label "*Joc.*" indicates that a word is likely considered humorous by the person using the word, but should not be regarded as inherently amusing. Some terms may be used jocularly, but can be offensive nonetheless; such words, when not labelled as derisive or contemptuous, will always be labeled as offensive as well. An offensive word that is labelled "*Joc.*" should not be regarded as less offensive due to its jocular use; the "*Joc.*" label is not intended to mitigate the very real offense such terms can cause.

The labels "Now *colloq.*" and "Now *S.E.*" are used for words that have shaken off their slang status; the differences between colloquial and Standard English terms are discussed in the Introduction to Volume One of this dictionary. No systematic attempt has been made to supply recent citations for these terms. Such words should be regarded as being in reasonably frequent use unless otherwise indicated.

Labels of the sort "*Obs.*" or "*Rare*" are not shown when this information can be easily inferred from the citations. However, labels of the sort "*Obs.* [or *Rare*] in U.S." are used when there is evidence that a sense apparently obsolete or rare in America is still in use elsewhere, especially in Britain or Australia. These "obsolete" and "rare" labels do appear internally, to separate parts of definitions, since these distinctions are often difficult to determine from a quick glance at the citations.

Variant Forms

Variant forms, except for those given

directly after the headword (see *Form and Order of Headwords*, above), are found immediately after the definition in several different formats. In this dictionary, a "variant form" is any form other than that given at the headword: a different spelling or a different combination, a use as a different part of speech, and a derived form are all considered variants.

Different spellings appear in boldface type preceded by the word "Also." Only spellings with a reasonable currency are generally shown. The variety of often idiosyncratic spellings, especially for the early history of a word's use, for words not normally written down, or for words borrowed from other languages, can be great: *jalopy*, for example, has *jaloopy, jalupie, jaloppy, jaloppi, geloppy, jalopie, jollopi, julappi,* and *jollopy* as variants. Since it is not the purpose of this dictionary to catalog all spelling variations of a word, these variants are not listed individually, nor are cross references given at the different spellings. In most cases such an entry includes an "Also vars." label, which is the broadest label used for variants. Conversely, relatively minor variants appear in the citations without comment. Variants for such aspects as differing hyphenation, capitalization, or presence or absence of periods in abbreviation are almost never listed. The "Also" is used in addition for different combinations:

> **Mickey Mouse hat** *n.*....Also **Mickey Mouse helmet.**

As in other cases, such variants are combined when their independent currency is small.

For variant parts of speech, see the discussion at *Parts of Speech*, above. The form is "Also as adj." or the like.

A derived form is given after a definition (as opposed to as a new entry) when it has no large independent currency and when the derivation is quite clear. Such derived forms are shown in boldface immediately after the definition and are preceded by the word "Hence." Cross references to derived forms are not normally given.

> **ironhead** *n.* a blockhead. Hence **ironheaded,** *adj.*
>
> **leather-pusher** *n. Boxing.* a boxer. Hence **leather-pushing,** *n.*
>
> **mittflop** *v.* mittglom. Hence **mitt-flopper** mitt-glommer.
>
> **nautch** *n.* a brothel. Hence **nautch broad** a prostitute working in a brothel.

Discursive Note

The discursive note, in square brackets, is usually the last element preceding the body of citations. It may cover a variety of subjects depending on the needs of an entry, including etymological material. The following examples represent typical discursive notes:

> [Quots. ref. to WWII.]
>
> [See *OED* for closely related S.E. senses not recorded here.]
>
> [U.S. usage has app. arisen independently of 18th C. quots. given below.]
>
> [Typical of the "Valley Girl" fad of 1982–83.]
>
> [The sense intended in the 1840 quot. is not entirely clear.]
>
> [Farmer & Henley *Slang* erroneously dates *1789 quot. as "1781."]

Cross Reference

Words that are treated elsewhere in this dictionary are given in small capital type, followed by the part of speech when necessary and the definition number where possible; often a cross reference refers to several senses and it is not practical to specify every one. Example: Cf. LOAD, *n.*, 3.c.

Cross references to other senses of the same entry have the definition number in boldface type, in parentheses, with the word "above" or "below" to direct the reader to the proper spot. Examples: quot. at **(4.b.),** below; quot. at **(a),** above.

Phrases in cross references are given in italics, with the headword where the phrase is found given in small capitals. If the phrase is at the same entry, it will be followed by "above" or "below." Cross references normally cite only the base form of the phrase, even though variants for phrases are given at the actual entry. Examples: See *hell of a* s.v. HELL. Cf. *live large*, below.

Citations

Citations are ordered strictly chronologically. For a citation with a range of dates (see discussion at *Dating and Bibliographic Style*, below), the last date is the one used for ordering. Citations from the same year are ordered by exact date if this is available.

An asterisk (*) before the date indicates that a citation is from a non-North American source. However, an English book referring to an American usage or quoting an American author will not have an asterisk, and an American book quoting British usage will have an asterisk. The reader should also note that before *ca*1820, differences between British and American slang, as between British and American English in general, are far less marked (see the Introduction in Volume One for a discussion of this issue).

In this dictionary American and Canadian English are not differentiated—neither variety has an asterisk (see the Introduction in Volume One for a discussion of the relationship between Canadian and American slang). There is very little Canadian English in this dictionary; even the most notable exception—Thomas C. Haliburton—was writing in the voice of a Yankee.

A citation is placed in square brackets if it does not actually exemplify the slang use under discussion. The following are the most common reasons for a bracketed citation:

1. A citation has the same word as the slang sense but the relationship between the citation and the slang sense is unclear, or the bracketed example may be suspected of being poorly or erroneously defined in the original source. Example from the word JOE COOL 'a man who is extremely cool'; there is a discursive note commenting that "The 'Joe Cool' in 1949 quot. is a fictional character whose name is not explained":

   [**1949** W.R. Burnett *Asphalt Jungle* 20: Thank God for Joe Cool!]

2. A citation has the same word as the slang sense but in a different meaning. Example for a nonce usage of GOON apparently unrelated to the later sense 'stupid person':

   [**1921** F.L. Allen, in *Harper's Mag.* (Dec.) A goonish style is one that reads as if it were the work of a goon. It is thick and heavy...It employs the words "youth" and "lad," likes the exclamation "lo!" [etc.].]

3. A citation is a possible allusion, or perhaps simply an interesting parallel, to a slang sense. Example from GEESEFEATHERS 'snow':

   [**1912** in Truman *Dear Bess* 73: The heavenly geese are certainly shedding feathers around this neighborhood this morning.]

4. A citation exemplifies a use—perhaps a nonce use—closely related to the headword. Example from CHINA SYNDROME 'a meltdown of a nuclear reactor':

   [**1974** Widener *N.U.K.E.E.* 67: The core was in a run-away melt-down condition—the classic "China Accident."]

5. A citation is an unmistakable allusion to a slang sense without explicitly using the headword. Example from *wrote the book* s.v. BOOK:

   [**1906–07** Ade *Slim Princess* 52: "You have traveled a great deal?"..."Me and Baedeker and Cook wrote it."]

6. A citation is a euphemistic variant of a slang sense. Example from the slang

phrase *the sweat off (one's) balls* s.v. BALL:

[**1928** Dahlberg *Bottom Dogs* 130: You're keepin' up the old homestead by the sweat of your groins.]

Dating and Bibliographic Style

The task of assigning a precise date to a text is often difficult. Even the seemingly straightforward case of a novel published only once has a number of complications: Was it written at an earlier time but not published for several years? Was it written over a span of several years? Is a fictional character quoting an actual earlier source? Is the action set in an earlier period of which the author has personal experience?

The overriding concern has been to supply a date that most accurately reflects the time the word was used. In some cases the date of a citation is at variance with the publication date of a book. The bibliography in the final volume will be explicit about publication dates of books and dates of citations in those books, but the citations in the dictionary will only give the specific date of the specific citation and enough information about the edition used to allow the work to be tracked down. A number of different conventions have been adopted for determining the dating of a citation:

1. Use of *in* in citations.

    When a citation is known to have originated earlier than the work in which it is found, the date of the citation will be followed by *in*, followed by the bibliographical reference to the work itself. The range of possibilities is very large: citations quoted from other historical dictionaries (**1821** in *OED*); citations quoted from historical works or other works of scholarship (**1846** in H.L. Gates, Jr. *Sig. Monkey* 93); letters or diary entries, or collections thereof;

    The author of a citation is usually not given if the source is a magazine or a

historical dictionary. However, when an author being quoted is celebrated in his or her own right, the name is given before *in*, such as *****1739** H. Walpole, in *OED* or **1940** Z.N. Hurston, in *Amer. Mercury.*

If the source itself cites a date earlier than the publication date, but does not give the actual citation, the style is **1947** (cited in *W10*). If the source does give the actual citation but this dictionary does not quote it, the style is **1927** in Partridge *DSUE* 21.

2. Book written earlier than the publication date of the edition.

    Books published as current editions—that is, books that are not editions of earlier works, later publications of historical memoirs, etc.—can sometimes be shown to have been written earlier than the publication date. For instance, the first edition of Mencken's *American Language* is dated 1918 in this dictionary, even though the publication date is 1919. The preface is dated January 1, 1919, and therefore the book as a whole must have been written before that. Similarly, Edwin H. Sutherland's edition of *The Professional Thief,* by Chic Conwell, was published in 1937, but since Sutherland acknowledges in the preface that the manuscript was secured seven years previously, we have dated the book to 1930. In most cases the difference will be only a few years.

3. Citations dated with a range of years.

    Some citations have a range of dates spanning a number of years, rather than a single date. For instance, James Joyce wrote *Ulysses* from 1914 to 1922; it is therefore cited as *****1914–22** Joyce *Ulysses.* An article published in a 1944 issue of *American Speech* discussing a research project that began in 1942 is cited as **1942–44** *AS.* Entries in the *Dic-*

tionary of American Regional English often quote examples from the *DARE* survey, which largely took place from 1965 to 1970; when quoting these examples they are cited as **1965–70** in *DARE.*

4. Use of *a* and *ca*, especially in citations.

The abbreviation *a*, for Latin *ante* 'before', is used immediately before a date to indicate that the citation was written (or the event occurred) shortly before the date given, but it is not possible to be any more accurate. In all cases citations are dated no earlier than is defensible on the basis of evidence. In no case should *a* be assumed to refer to an indefinitely long period. For example, a nonhistorical dictionary such as *WNID3* may give a citation without giving the full source, and here the only possible reference is *a***1961** in *WNID3.*

The abbreviation *ca*, for Latin *circa* 'about', is used similarly but more broadly. It comes immediately before a date or age, and signifies only that the date or age is in a general but not a specific range. For example, *ca* is used when an actual composition date is impossible to determine, when a reference is too vague (such as "in the mid-1850's,...was the state of affairs"), in ages (as in oral citation, when the collector did not know the exact age of the informant), and so on. When any other information about the dating is available, it is supplied in bracketed notes.

5. Use of bracketed note with "ref. to" in citations.

If a citation explicitly refers to another era, a bracketed note such as "[ref. to WWII]" or "[ref. to 1891]" is often added immediately before the citation. This practice is followed when a word appears to be characteristic of its historical reference rather than the actual date

of the cited material, or when the source appears to be particularly trustworthy in depicting an earlier era from firsthand experience. For an earliest citation, it can indicate that a word was probably in use at an earlier date than is directly attested. For example, a term that was current during the Vietnam War may not be discovered in print until later, presumably an accident of the sampling process; this is borne out by the fact that veterans' memoirs are often not published until years after the events described. However, although the fallible evidence of recollection is allowed in the citations, boldface dates are never "backdated" on the basis of such evidence. Bracketed notes are supplied only when the information is notable in some way; no attempt was made to characterize the historical setting of each source when it does not illuminate an aspect of the word's use. Thus Conwell's *Professional Thief*, mentioned above, refers to the period 1905–1925, but we do not include this information in bracketed notes unless it is specifically relevant.

The bracketed note with "ref. to" is occasionally used for geographical or other designations when these are relevant or of special interest: "[ref. to Princeton University]".

Oral citations have not been specifically designated, but it will be clear from the lack of other bibliographical evidence if a citation is oral, as opposed to one taken from television, radio, print, or other sources. The usual form is **1976** N.Y.C. man, age *ca*38: [citation]. Any citation not personally collected by J.E. Lighter will give the name of the collector: **1995** N.Y.C. man, age *ca*28 (coll. J. Sheidlower): [citation]. The plan of the project has prevented any systematic search for oral citations, and the geographic distribution of informants is necessarily limited to the editors' personal experience. It is hoped that the wide range of print and broadcast sources used will go some way toward counterbalancing any unequal representation so introduced.

Detailed information about the nature and location of typescript or manuscript works will appear in the final volume of this dictionary.

Page references indicate the page on which the word under discussion appears, not where the extract begins. When quoting from alphabetical dictionaries or glossaries, volume and page numbers have usually been omitted. When quoting from an entry for a different word, the style is ***1812** Vaux *Vocab.* s.v. *cadge* (the entry under discussion is *game*). The abbreviation "unp.", for "unpaged," is used for texts that are not paginated. Occasionally chapter references rather than page references are given, especially for books that are easily accessible in differently paginated editions. When quoting drama or poetry (act, scene, and) line numbers are typically given rather than page references.

An author's name has been placed in brackets when a work was published anonymously or pseudonymously but the true name of the author is known. Thus, Thomas C. Haliburton is known to be the author of *The Clockmaker; or, The Sayings and Doings of Samuel Slick of Slickville*, but since this book (published in three series) was attributed to "Sam Slick," Haliburton's name is given in brackets. Authors known primarily by their pseudonyms have these names in double quotation marks: "Fab 5 Freddy," "M. Twain," "O. Henry." Authors known exclusively by their pseudonyms or changed names (Woody Allen, Bob Dylan) have these names given without comment. Names of musical groups are also given in double quotation marks as a convention.

Citations are recorded exactly as they appear in the source with several minor exceptions. Each citation begins with a capital letter and ends with closing punctuation. Citations have been conformed trivially to the modern American standards of punctuation. For example, single quotation marks are used inside double quotation marks, and commas and periods are placed inside a closing quotation mark. Lines of verse are separated with a virgule (/); the first word of a new line is capitalized. Spellings, use of italics (except as noted below), capitalization, etc., have not been changed.

Most importantly, when quoting from a dictionary, glossary, or other word list, the word or phrase being glossed has been placed in italics. When reading through a block of citations, it is easier to recognize a word or phrase with definition when the word is italicized. And on a practical basis, there are so many different conventions adopted by various sources—regular type, italics, boldface, small capitals, and indents and dashes of various sorts—that trying to represent them accurately would difficult. Some examples:

*1785 Grose *Vulgar Tongue: Aqua Pumpaginis,* Pump water.
1859 Matsell *Vocab.* 26: *Diver.* A pickpocket.
1934 Weseen *Dict. Slang* 334: *Flappers*—the ears.
1918 *DN* V 24: *To gip*..."to swipe" something.

Since the main concern has been to represent the meaning of the slang word, a source has often been quoted selectively, as by starting or finishing a quote in the middle of a sentence or by use of ellipsis, in order to save space and emphasize the slang use. Although the citation itself has never been altered (except as noted above), some of these abridgements may change the style or occasionally the meaning of an author's words. In no case should a citation be taken to represent the viewpoint of the quoted author.

Selection

Examples found naturally in running texts have been favored over those that only appear in word lists of dubious origin or reliability. Most words and phrases claimed as "slang" are nonce terms or "oncers," never to be seen or heard of again. Some become true "ghost words," recorded in slang dictionaries for many years but never demonstrably encountered in actual usage. We have felt no obligation to include such expressions in this dictionary. However, in certain cases words attested only in word lists have been included when the editors judged that the lists were an accurate reflection of usage and that additional evidence would be difficult to find due to the nature of the evidence.

The number of citations given does not necessarily correspond to an entry's actual frequency of usage. However, unusually common expressions are often accompanied by multiple citations. The additional citations are included for several reasons: first, to give some suggestion of the commonness of the sense; second, to indicate continuity through its history or intensity in one period of the usage; and third, to illustrate nuances that cannot succinctly be placed in the definition. The editors have tried to supply their own citations from primary sources wherever possible, rather than quoting from secondary sources; the interested reader may thus be able to find additional evidence by searching the *Oxford English Dictionary*, the *Dictionary of American Regional English*, the *Dictionary of Americanisms*, the journal *American Speech*, and other references of a general or specific nature.

In every case, the earliest citation per sense is the earliest that can be documented from the corpus. With language in general, and especially with slang, due to its oral nature, words and senses may be used regularly for quite some time before they are recorded in print. On a surprising number of occasions this dictionary has been able to provide antedatings of slang recorded in other historical dictionaries, notably the *Dictionary of American Regional English* and the second edition of the *Oxford English Dictionary*. However, it is likely that many terms in this dictionary were in use earlier than the earliest evidence herein, for such is the nature of the historical dictionary. It has not been possible to provide up-to-the-minute examples of every sense, but many senses lacking recent citational evidence retain currency nevertheless. Indeed, any well-attested entry with citations as late as the 1960's is probably still current.

Phrases

This dictionary organizes phrases under the main word of the phrase, usually the word least subject to variation. The editors feel that the increasingly common practice of locating phrases by the first word of the phrase (placing *have an edge on* under *have*, for example) is confusing and obscures the relationship of different phrases stemming from the same word. Also, slang phrases often have so many variants that the main word may be the only stable one of the phrase. Where there is potential for confusion, cross references have been added.

Phrases, which are always printed in boldface type, may appear in two places in an entry: as a run-on to an existing definition, or in a separate phrase section at the end of the standard definitions.

The phrase is given as a run-on to a definition if the phrase directly results from and is similar to that meaning, and often if the available evidence is insufficient to make it a separate phrasal entry. A run-on phrase also fits in with the development of other senses of the word. Examples:

bum *n....***3.** *Hobo.* an act of begging; usu. in phr. **put the bum on (someone)** to beg from (someone).

gonger *n.* [orig. unkn.] *Narc.* an opium pipe; in phr. **kick the gonger** to smoke opium.

Phrases appear in a separate section if their meaning is relatively independent of any sense in the definition section, or if the use as a phrase is significantly broader or more common than the use as a word alone. In potentially confusing cases there are cross references from the phrase section to the definitions and vice versa, and the reader is advised to look over the entire entry to be sure of finding a desired construction.

Phrases in the separate section are alphabetized by the first word of the phrase. In this case, no other method was practicable; furthermore, very few entries have so many phrases that finding any one would be difficult. The section itself is introduced by the symbol "¶" followed by "In phrases:". Each phrase is also preceded by the "¶" symbol for clarity.

The phrase section otherwise resembles a small entry in most respects. Sense division conforms to the same criteria as discussed above (see *Definition*); senses are ordered by date of first citation; each sense may have labels; etc. Variants of a phrase, are enclosed in square brackets, usually with "or" preceding the next element:

¶ **put** [or **tie**] **on the feedbag** to eat a meal.

¶ **chew** [**up**] **the scenery** *Theat.* to overact.

It is possible to have an "Also vars." note following a definition in the phrase section. We have not attempted to account for every possible variation in a phrase, for as much as a slang word itself may vary, the phrases in which it may be found may vary even more. As with many other elements in this dictionary, our description of variants is intended to be a general, not an absolute, guide to the possibilities.

PRONUNCIATION KEY

Vowels

ɑ	farm
æ	cat
ai	nice
au	shout
ɛ	set
ei	claim
ɛə	fair
ɪ	ship
i	keep
ɪə	hear
ɔ	pause
ɔi	boil
ou	rope
ʊ	good
u	rude
ʊə	poor
ə	about
ʌ	tub

Consonants

b	big
d	dog
ð	then
ʤ	jump
f	fun
g	get
h	hum
k	kit
l	love
m	me
n	no
ŋ	ring
p	pot
r	run
s	sip
ʃ	shore
t	tap
ʧ	chip
θ	think
v	violin
w	wish
z	zipper
ʒ	azure

Stress

ˈ primary stress
ˌ secondary stress

These are vertical stress marks that precede the stressed syllable.

LIST OF ABBREVIATIONS

This list does not necessarily include standard abbreviations.

*	(before the date of a citation, used to indicate a non-North American source); (*also*, in etymologies) (used to indicate an unattested or reconstructed form)
<	is derived from
>	from which is derived
a	ante (before)
abbr.	abbreviation, abbreviated
absol.	absolute(ly) (in grammatical sense)
acad.	academy
adap.	adaptation, adapted
adj.	adjective(s), adjectival(ly)
adv.	adverb(s), adverbial(ly); (*also*) advertisement
adver.	advertising
Afr	Africa(n)
alter.	alteration
AmE	American English
Amer.	America(n)
AmSp	American Spanish
anthol.	anthology
aph.	apheretic
app.	apparently
Apr.	April
arch.	archaic
AS	*American Speech*
assoc.	associated
astron.	astronomy
ATS	Berrey & van den Bark, *American Thesaurus of Slang*
attrib.	attributive(ly)
Aug.	August
Austral.	Australia(n)
av.	aviation

BDNE, BDNE2, BDNE3	Barnhart, Steinmetz, and Barnhart [*Second/Third*] *Barnhart Dictionary of New English*
bib.	bibliography
biog.	biographical, biography
Black E	Black English
BrE	British English
Brit.	British
C.	century
ca	circa (about)
Canad.	Canadian, Canadianism
cap.	capitalized
CB	citizen's band
cf.	*confer* (compare)
ch.	chapter
Chi.	Chicago
coll.	collect(or), collected (by)
collec.	collection
collect.	collective(ly)
colloc.	collocation
colloq.	colloquial(ism)
comb., combs.	combination(s)
comb. form	combining form
comm.	communication(s)
Confed.	Confederate, Confederacy
conj.	conjunction
contr.	contraction
constr.	construed
DA	Mathews, *Dictionary of Americanisms*
DAE	Craigie & Hulbert, *Dictionary of American English*
DARE	Cassidy, *Dictionary of American Regional English*
DAS	Wentworth & Flexner, *Dictionary of American Slang*
DAUL	Goldin, O'Leary, & Lipsius, *Dictionary of American Underworld Lingo*

Dec.	December	G	German (language)
def.	define(d), definition(s)	gamb.	gambling
der.	derived	gaz.	gazette
deriv.		Gk	Greek (language)
devel.	develop(ment)	Gmc	Germanic (languages)
dial.	dialect(al)	gram.	grammar, grammatical(ly)
dict.	dictionary		
dim.	diminutive		
DN	*Dialect Notes*	Heb	Hebrew (language)
docu.	document	Hiberno-E	Hiberno-English
DOST	Craigie & Aitken, *Dictionary of the Older Scottish Tongue*	hist.	history, historical
		hndbk.	handbook
		homosex.	homosexual(ity)
DSUE	Partridge, *Dictionary of Slang and Unconventional English*	hosp.	hospital
		hum.	humorous(ly)
Du	Dutch		
		ibid.	*ibidem*
		i.e.	*id est* (that is)
E	English (language)	illus.	illustrate(s), illustrated
ed.	edition, editor, edited (by)	imit.	imitative(ly)
EDD	Wright, *English Dialect Dictionary*	imper.	imperative(ly)
		Ind	Indian
e.g.	*exempli gratia* (for example)	infl.	influence(d)
elab.	elaborated, elaboration	interj.	interjection, interjectional(ly)
ellipt.	elliptical(ly)		
Eng.	English (in titles)	intrans.	intransitive(ly)
eques.	equestrian(ism)	Ir	Irish (language)
erron.	erroneous	It	Italian (language)
esp.	especially	IUFA	Indiana University Folklore Archives
et al.	*et alii, et alia* (and others)		
ety.	etymology, etymological(ly)		
euphem.	euphemism, euphemistic(ally)	*JAF*	*Journal of American Folklore*
		Jan.	January
ex., exx.	example(s)	Japn	Japanese (language)
exclam.	exclamation, exclamatory	joc.	jocular(ly)
expl.	explanation	Jour.	Journal (used in titles)
		journ.	journalism
		juve.	juvenile
F	French (language)		
F & H	Farmer and Henley, *Slang and Its Analogues*	L	Latin
Feb.	February	lang.	language
fem.	feminine, female	lit.	literal(ly); (*also*) literature
fig.	figurative(ly)		
fr.	from		
freq.	frequently; (*also*) frequentative(ly)	M	Middle (ref. to period of a language)

mag.	magazine	p., pp.	page(s)
Mar.	March	*PADS*	*Publication of the American Dialect Society*
masc.	masculine (grammatically)		
ME	Middle English	pap.	(in titles) papers
MED	*Middle English Dictionary*	pass.	passive
med.	medical, medicine	perh.	perhaps
MexSp	Mexican Spanish	Pg	Portuguese (language)
mil.	military	phr.	phrase(s)
mo.	month(ly)	pl.	plural
mod.	modern	pol.	politics, political
ModE	Modern English	pop.	popular(ized)
		poss.	possessive
		ppl.	participle, participial
N	North(ern)	p.ppl.	past participle
n.	noun	prec.	precede, preceding
NADS	*Newsletter of the American Dialect Society*	prep.	preposition, prepositional(ly)
N & Q	*Notes and Queries*	pres.	present
narc.	narcotics	pris.	prison
nat.	national	prob.	probable, probably
naut.	nautical	pron.	pronounce, pronunciation
NDAS	Chapman, *New Dictionary of American Slang*	pros.	prostitution
		prov.	proverb, proberbial(ly)
N.E.	Northeast		
nec.	necessary, necessarily	Qly.	Quarterly (used in titles)
N.O.	New Orleans	quot., quots.	quotation(s)
No.	North(ern)		
Nov.	November	RAF	Royal Air Force
N.Y.(C.)	New York (City)	redup.	reduplication, reduplica-tive(ly)
		ref.	refer(s), referring
obj.	object	reflex.	reflexive(ly)
obs.	obsolete	repr.	represent(s)
occ.	occasion, occasional(ly)	resp.	respelling
Oct.	October	rev.	revise(d), revision; (*also*) review
OE	Old English		
OED	Murray et al., *Oxford English Dictionary*	*RHD*	Stein, *Random House Dictionary of the English Language*
OEDS	Burchfield, *Supplement to the Oxford English Dictionary*	*RHD2*	Flexner, *Random House Dictionary of the English Language*, 2nd edition
OED2	Simpson & Weiner, *Oxford English Dictionary*, 2nd edition	R.R.	railroad
		Russ	Russian
OF	Old French		
opp.	opposite		
orig.	origin, original(ly)	S	South(ern)

sc.	scilicet (namely)	univ.	university
S.E.	Standard English	unkn.	unknown
sel.	selected	unp.	unpaged
Sept.	September	USAF	United States Air Force
sg.	singular	USMC	United States Marine Corps
Sks.	Sketches (used in titles)		
sl.	slang	usu.	usually
SND	Grant, *Scottish National Dictionary*	*UTSQ*	University of Tennessee Student Questionnaire
So.	South(ern) (used in labels)		
Sp	Spanish (language)	v.	verb
specif.	specific(ally)	var(s).	variant(s)
st.	stanza	vaud.	vaudeville, vaudevillian
stu.	student	vet. med.	veterinary medicine
suff.	suffix		
sugg.	suggest(ed)		
supp.	supplement	W	West, Western
S.W.	Southwest	*WDEU*	Gilman, *Webster's Dictionary of English Usage*
Sw	Swedish (language)		
syn.	synonym, synonymous	*WNID, WNID2, WNID3*	*Webster's New International Dictionary* [2nd, 3rd editions]
s.v.	*sub vocem* (under the word)		
		W9	Mish, *Webster's Ninth New Collegiate Dictionary*
theat.	theater, theatrical(ly)		
trans.	transitive(ly)	*W10*	Mish, *Merriam-Webster's Collegiate Dictionary*, 10th edition
transf.	transfer(red)		
		WWI	World War I
ult.	ultimately	WWII	World War II
uncap.	uncapitalized		
uncert.	uncertain	Yid	Yiddish
und.	underworld		

H *n.* **1.** (a partial euphem., in var. senses, for) HELL.

1861 in J.R. Lowell *Poetical Works* 225: An' give the nigger…a most H fired lickin'. **1862** in W.C. Davis *Orphan Brig.* 124: What in -H are you doing here? **1879** in W.A. Graham *Custer Myth* 326: A recent letter in which…[we] catch, well, Merry H. **1945** I. Brecher & F. Finklehoffe *Meet Me in St. Louis* (film): There'll be the H to pay if my family ever found out I called long distance. **1983** Leeson *Survivors* (film): Somebody's gonna tell me what the H is goin' on around here.

2. *Narc.* heroin.

1926 in *OEDS*: H, heroin. **1929** *Sat. Eve. Post* (Apr. 15) 54: Cocaine is C. Morphine is M. Heroin is referred to as H. **1932** Berg *Prison Doctor* 66: So the "junkies" cursed their "connection" for diluting their M or C or H with sugar of milk or acetanilid. **1952** Ellson *Golden Spike* 244: Junkie Main-liner Horsehead H-man. **1962** T. Berger *Reinhart in Love* 135: I never fool with H. **1962–63** in Giallombardo *Soc. of Women* 204: H-Joint. A place where heroin is sold to addicts. **1963** Uhnak *Policewoman* 30: The game is over. Hand over the "H." **1971** Contini *Beast Within* 60: Well, it's like that with me when I think of a needle full of "H." **1974** (quot. at HEAVY, *n.*, 8). **1989** Radford & Crowley *Drug Agent* x: He had the H at a house in Pasadena. *1993* I. Welsh *Trainspotting* 42: Keep oaf the H for mair thin ten minutes.

haba-haba, habba-habba see HUBBA-HUBBA.

habe *n.* *Law.* a writ of habeas corpus.

1974 *Time* (June 17) 59: *Habe:* writ of habeas corpus. **1974** G.V. Higgins *Cogan's Trade* 5: Remember them habes we had? **1979** Homer *Jargon* 77.

habit *n.* *Narc.* addiction to opium or an opiate such as morphine or heroin; (*also*) a craving for narcotics.—often constr. with *the*.

1881 H.H. Kane *Opium* 44: Thus, a man who smokes three times [a day] is said to have a "triple habit." **1887** in *AS* (1948) XXIII 246: May he continue to wage war against…[opium dens] until the habit has been swept entirely out of existence. **1892** Norr *China Town* 39: Fitz and I always had the habit, you know, and carried our layout with us. **1895** Townsend *Tenements* 224: "The habit" is the term the [opium] smokers use to express a recurrence of the craving for the drug. **1897** Townsend *Whole City Full* 153: The habit is on you. You wantee pipe. **1914** Jackson & Hellyer *Vocab.* 41: I feel my habit coming on. **1925–26** Black *You Can't Win* 161: The "habit" came on, and the necessity for a shot in the morning as a bracer. **1960** C.L. Cooper *Scene* 236: She's got exactly four dollars and a nickel in her wallet, and she's got a habit. **1963** Braly *Shake Him* 26: She's a veteran whore with a habit a mile long. **1972** P. Thomas *Savior* 7: Bobby got out of Riverside, where he went to kick the habit. **1978** Rascoe & Stone *Who'll Stop Rain?* (film): You've got a habit, Marge. How much? **1980** in Courtwright et al. *Addicts Who Survived* 91 [ref. to ca1920]: I used to see them chinks on the ground [in jail] breaking habits.

habitch *n.* *Law.* a habitual criminal.

1956 Fleming *Diamonds* 66: He's been in trouble all over the South, what they call a "little habitch" as opposed to a "big habitch"—habitual criminal. **1976** Schroeder *Shaking It* 24: My cell mate tells me he's an habitch.*…*A man being charged as an habitual criminal; such charges often carry an open-ended, indefinite sentence.

hachi *n.* [pidgin; see 1954 quot.] Orig. *Mil. in East Asia.* the penis; (see also 1965 quot.).—usu. in phr. **suck** [or **eat**] **a hachi** (used as a vulgar taunt). Also vars.

1954 in *AS* XXX (1955) 47: From the Far East to Germany, wherever the U.S. Army has soldiers, in fact, the phrase *suck a hachi* is heard…derived by folk etymology from the Japanese *shakuhachi* (literally, "one foot eight inches"), the Japanese name for the Chinese horn….The figurative sense of the phrase is *Go to hell*; the literal implication, to the GI, is sodomy. **1960** *AS* XXXV 121 [ref. to Korean War]: *Suckahachi* or *I've got your hachi*, "go to hell." **1962** W. Crawford *Give Me Tomorrow* 176 [ref. to Korean War]: The young man kept grabbing his crotch, screaming…"Merkah suck-a-hachi!" *Ibid.* 242: "Maleen, you

die!" "Suck-a-hachi you gook bastard!" **1965** Trimble *Sex Words* 97: *Hatchi* 1. The Vagina. 2. One particular female as a Sex Object. From the sound of the number eight in Japanese. **1967** *DAS* (Supp.) 690: *Hotchee*…the penis. *Armed forces use in Korea.* **1969** Bouton *Ball Four* 389 [ref. to ca1955]: But "eat a hodgy" must have been nationwide because Norm was saying "eat a hodgy" out on the coast while I was saying it in Bloom Township High in Chicago Heights. **1973** *TULIPQ* (coll. B.K. Dumas): Dick, peter, hotchie, chopper. **1980** Cragg *Lex. Militaris* 222: Hotchee. The penis. Widely used in Korea.

¶ In phrase:

¶ **never hachi** usu. /ˈnɛvə ˈhɑtʃi/ *Mil. in East Asia.* *never happen* s.v. HAPPEN. Also vars.

1952 Holles *Armourers* 164: The American was saying, "Ten bucks, you lousy little Nip…it never *hatchi!*" **1954** in *AS* XXX (1955) 47: *Suck a hachi* has united with the GI *nevah hoppen* to beget *nevah hachi* meaning precisely…"never happen." **1955** in *AS* XXXV (1960) 265: Never hatchie. **1960** *AS* XXXV 121 [ref. to Korean War]: *Nevah hachi*, or more emphatically, *nevah buckin' hachi*, "impossible" or "nevah-hoppen." **1980** McDowell *Our Honor* 198 [ref. to ca1952]: "Is that a hint?"…"Nebba hotchie, Joe," Krupke replied in the pidgin English common to veterans of Korea and Japan. *1982* Partridge *DSUE* (ed. 8) 786: *Never hachi.* Nonsense; "it never happened (or never will happen):" United Nations troops in Korea, ca1951–5; in the 1960s, sometimes heard in Hong Kong. *a1987* Bunch & Cole *Reckoning for Kings* 61: Never hachi. You got laundry?

hack[1] *n.* **1.** an attempt; try; CRACK, 7.a.

1836 "D. Crockett" *In Texas* 79: Better take a hack by way of trying your luck at guessing. **1863** in R.G. Carter *4 Bros.* 266: I will…try the "Johnnies" another *hack*. **1885** *Puck* (Apr. 29) 138: Jim said it was glanders, and we took a hack at that. **1897** Hamblen *General Mgr.* 238: It has always seemed to me that sometime I'd have a hack at it. **1899–1900** Cullen *Tales* 194: San Francisco people will take a hack at anything that gives them a whirl. **1902** Remington *John Ermine* 170: I think I will go to Saw-Bones and let him have a hack at me; I never was so sick before. **1903** Townsend *Sure* 72: Any wise guy who gets holt of a real interest for a play must keep it alive till all de odder play writers has had deir hack at it. **1906** Ford *Shorty McCabe* 37: Goin' to take a hack at the 'lixir business? **1906** in Bierce *Letters* 115: Let Robertson…have a hack at it. **1957** J.D. MacDonald *Death Trap* 78: There's a suntan job wants a hack at the young stuff. **1972** R. Barrett *Lovomaniacs* 105: I always wanted to have a real hack at that.

2. *Navy & USMC.* confinement to quarters as punishment, esp. for officers; officer's arrest.—constr. with *in* or *under*. [Early quots. ref. to WWII.]

[**1898** Green *Va. Folk Speech* 173: A person is said to be "under *hack*" when he is controlled and ordered by another. "She has her husband under *hack*."] **1944** in Morgan & Michalson *For Our Beloved Country* 363: Art…was restricted to his room (put in hack). **1946** Heggen *Mr. Roberts* 114: Ten days in hack means for an officer ten days confinement in his room. **1952** *Marine Corps Gaz.* (Nov.) 74: *Hack n.* Arrest, officer's; *to be in,* or *to be under arrest.* **1959** Cochrell *Barren Beaches* 41: "In hack for two weeks." Chick laughed and swore. "Got in a knife-fight with a couple pogey-bait Sixths, and the MPs turned me in. Gotta report to the OD every hour." **1960** MacCuish *Do Not Go Gentle* 360: You birds mess around, I'll toss ya in hack till yer brains cave in. **1961** Boyd *Lighter Than Air* 68: "Will you miss Lola Larue, being in hack?" asked Cooper. **1964** Hunt *Ship with Flat Tire* 48: You've got to get me out of this jam or I'll be in hack forever. **1966** Heinl *Marine Officer's Guide* 593: *Hack* (n): Arrest, officer's; *to be in or to be under…*: to be under arrest. **1967** Dibner *Admiral* 270: Could be you'll put me under hack for it, but, Captain, you never in your life saw such a waste of Navy time. **1971** Waters *Smugglers of Spirits* 13 [ref. to 1920's]: Officers and gentlemen, indeed! I've a good mind to give all of you a taste of hack (room confinement). *Ibid.* 46: Hack, in the old Coast Guard, was room confinement for an officer, a rather drastic form of punishment scarcely designed to future his career.

hack² *n.* **1.a.** [fr. earlier S.E. sense 'a hackney coach or carriage'] a taxicab.

1928 *New Yorker* (Nov. 3) 94: Hack—a familiar and affectionate term for a taxicab. **1942** *Pittsburgh Courier* (Sept. 19) 7: She parked her trim figure in the back of Charlie's "hack." **1953** *Pop. Science* (Dec.) 215: Road-tested practically every make of hack put together on these shores. **1954–60** *DAS*: Hack…A taxicab. **1961** Heinlein *Stranger* 19: It would take this hack two hours to get that far. **1970** *N.Y.C. cabdriver*: Driving a cab is usually called *pushing a hack*. **1976** Elman *Taxi Driver* 3: Right away I went down to the hack bureau to apply for a license. **1981** *Taxi* (ABC-TV): Is that your hack? **1996** *N.Y. Press* (Feb. 21) 22: As much as $300 a night, driving a hack.

b. [prob. an independent coinage based on **(a)**, above, rather than a survival of *OED* def. 3 'the driver of a hackney carriage' illustrated in *1687, *1713 quots. below] a cabdriver; HACKIE, 1.

*1687 in *OED*: [They] slipping through the Palsgrave, bilkt poor Hack. *1713 in *OED*: The happy minute…when our hack had the happiness to take in his expected fare. **1934** Appel *Brain Guy* 16: "Who is he?" "A hack." *Ibid.* 79: Hell, that hack must've figured you a big shot. **1935** Odets *Waiting for Lefty* 23: If I thought it would help us hacks get better living conditions, I'd let you walk all over me. **1939** Appel *Power House* 73: The tenner was the hack's split. **1984** *N.Y. Post* (Aug. 2) 42: Don't just complain about surly hacks—report 'em. **1988** T. Logan *Harder They Fall* 43: Not that he ever busted a hack for driving without a medallion. **1994** *TV Guide* (July 30) 10: We watch the correspondent trick one of these discriminating hacks.

2.a. a hearse.

1914 in *U. Mo. Studies* XV (1940) 333: They took him to that cemet'ry/In a rubber-tired hack. **1918** in Sandburg *Amer. Songbag* 444 ("The Hearse Song"): They'll take you away in a big black hack,/They'll take you away but won't bring you back. **1950** in *DARE*. *a*1961 *WNID3*. **1968–69** in *DARE*.

b. an old, slow, or dilapidated motor vehicle, aircraft, or ship; HEAP, 3. (R.R.) a caboose.

1916 *Editor* XLIII (Mar. 25) 343: Crummy, hack, dog house, van, caboose. **1918** in Rossano *Price of Honor* 201: Our old…hacks [airplanes] are almost ready now. **1927** Faulkner *Mosquitoes* 301: "Take the Studebaker," he added. "That old hack?…I'll take your Chrysler." **1928** Carr *Rampant Age* 118: I don't like to drive that hack of mine around at night when I'm tight. **1929** *Bookman* (July) 525: We're goin' so fast I can look back and see the door in the hack [caboose]. **1930** *AS* VI (Dec.) 132: Hack, n. Automobile. **1931** *Writer's Dig.* (May) 42: Hack—Another term for caboose. **1933** Stewart *Airman Speech* 69: Hack. A plane. **1936** Twist *We About to Die* (film): Just keep movin' this hack right ahead. **1938** *AS* (Dec.) 307: Hack. A designation for any bus. **1948** Seward & Ryan *Angel's Alley* (film): We oughta get at least two bills from Tony for this hack. **1956** in Harvey *Air Force* 63: We'll put a gun camera on that old hack of yours. **1966** Cassiday *Angels Ten* 145: Boy, they really ride them hacks hard, don't they? **1972** Cleaves *Sea Fever* 150 [ref. to 1920's]: We waited 'til we got this damn ol' hack into port.

c. a motorcycle sidecar; (hence) a motorcycle equipped with a sidecar.

1962 T. Jones *Stairway to the Sea* 32: And there was a cat with a sidecar who drove up and down the road outside, demonstrating the virtues of his combination to a prospective buyer who sat in the hack. **1969** *Pop. Science* (Dec.) 124: That included the sidecar, or the "hack" as the true enthusiast calls it. **1979** Frommer *Sports Lingo* 165.

3. *Und.* a watchman, security guard, or police patrolman; (now *usu.*) a prison guard or corrections officer.

1914 Jackson & Hellyer *Vocab.* 42: Hack…A night watchman; a night policeman or marshal. **1925** in Partridge *Dict. Und.* 316: Hack. A keeper in prison; a watchman; a policeman. **1928** Callahan *Man's Grim Justice* 82: There's only one night hack (cop) in the burg and he goes home at one in the morning. **1931** *AS* (Dec.) 108: Hack…1. A watchman; usually restricted to merchant-policemen and differentiated from the…police. 2. A pen guard. **1948** Mencken *Amer. Lang. Supp.* II 674: The guards are [called]…hacks. **1954** Lindner *50-Minute Hr.* 148: What're you gonna do if I don't? Call the hacks? **1955** Graziano & Barber *Somebody Up There* 122: I could tear apart any hack in the joint. **1960** C.L. Cooper *Scene* 268: It's the goddamn hack. **1961** Parkhurst *Undertow* 117: There's always a hack on guard at the

end of each row of cells. **1965** C. Brown *Manchild* 248: The hacks were always kicking his ass for no good reason. **1974** R. Carter *16th Round* 79: He was a young hack. **1983** *Reader's Digest Success with Words* 86: Black English…hack = …'prison guard'. **1985** *Harper's* (July) 24: Going to a guard was out of the question….One never went to a hack to work out one's problems.

4. [sugg. by journ. phr. *party hacks*] *Labor.* a labor organizer belonging to the Communist Party of the United States. Now *hist.*

1967 Raskin *True Course* 56 (ref. to 1940's): The dual role of the "hacks"—as the disciplined Communists came to be known among seamen—was going to create problems. *Ibid.* 57: Had the "hacks" prevailed, the immediate interests of the Soviet Union would have been the only consideration.

hack¹ *v.* **1.** to ride in a hackney coach (*obs.*) or taxicab.

1879 in *Century Dict.*: Are we more content to depend on street cars and walking, with the accustomed alternative of hacking at six times the money? **1923** *DN* V 209: *To hack around*…to drive about in a hack. **1947** Schulberg *Harder They Fall* 37: Hacking down Eighth Avenue, past the quick lunches, the little tailor shops, the second-hand stores [etc.]. **1958** in *DARE* [ref. to 1910's]: We're going to "hack it" (ride in a hack).

2. to drive a hackney coach (*obs.*) or taxicab as an occupation (occ. used trans.); (*also*) to drive (a person) in a taxicab.

1903 *Independent* (Apr. 2) 771: I've been thirty-five years at the hackin' business in Brooklyn an' Manhattan. **1928** in E. Ferber *One Basket* 322: Yeh, hackin', there's nothing in it. Too many cabs, see? *Ibid.* 324: You'll be hackin' when you're sixty. **1935** Macdonnell *Visit* 55: When will these cheap muzzlers…learn to hack like men? **1935** Odets *Waiting for Lefty*: He's probably been coming here every morning and laying you while I hacked my guts out! **1942** *Pittsburgh Courier* (Sept. 19) 7: So Charlie is still "hacking" away. **1947** Schulberg *Harder They Fall* 174: Hacking in Chi you c'n make yourself a buck. **1952** *New Yorker* (May 10) 23: We were being hacked about town. **1952** Brossard *Darkness* 221: The guy played the violin at night and hacked during the day. **1957** Mayfield *Hit* 89: What kind of garage had a dispatcher that had never hacked? **1961** Brosnan *Pennant Race* 201: Twenty-six years I been hackin'. **1968** *N.Y. Post* (Sept. 13) 24: It is necessary to buy out a retiring hackie in order to hack the streets of the city legally. **1981** WINS radio news (Dec. 10): The question is whether drivers who hack at night should be paid extra money. **1984** *All Things Considered* (Nat. Pub. Radio) (June 19): In a half a century of hacking, Sid has missed only three years behind the wheel for a hitch in the army in World War II. **1985** *Our Town* (N.Y.C.) (Aug. 25) 2: I'm not anti-cab. Known too many good guys who hack. **1986** Ciardi *Good Words* 176: The special situation of cabbies who hack radio cabs. **1996** *N.Y. Press* (Feb. 21) 22: I started hacking in 1984.

hack² *v.* **1.** *Stu.* to socialize idly; gad or fool about; waste time.—now usu. constr. with *around* or *off*.

1888 *Stag Party* (unp.): It is said we are all good at "hacking,"/Dancing, drinking, hugging, and smacking. **1923** *DN* V 209: *To hack around*…to ramble around. **1950** *New Yorker* (Aug. 26) 61: [The shirts are] extra special and not meant for hacking around a campus. **1957** *N.Y. Times* (Aug. 18) I 72: Much more time is spent hanging around and "hacking," as the young people called it. **1957** M. Shulman *Rally* 46: She was always hacking around and yocking up a storm. **1960** *Many Loves of D. Gillis* (CBS-TV): You don't hack around and rub elbows with the other fellows. **1965** *N.Y. Times Mag.* (Apr. 4) 99: "Hacking around" (which can be roughly translated as "fooling around" or "doing nothing") is a favorite teen-age pastime. **1968** Baker, Ladd & Robb *CUSS* 132: Hack off. Waste time, not study. **1968** in *Rolling Stone Interviews* 46: So I…hacked around for awhile and that was more of a drag. **1972** in *Playboy* (Jan. 1973) 240: I can't hack around the rest of my life with this goddamned thing, you know? **1974** Eble *Campus Slang* (Oct.) 2: *Hack around*—v., to waste time: I had two tests this week, and since then I've been hacking around. **1977** Sayles *Union Dues* 204: Then cut over to Revere Beach, hack around awhile, see if we can pick anything up.

2. to annoy, irritate, or anger; provoke; goad.—now often constr. with *off*. See also HACKED, 1.b.

1893 W. James *Maverick* 177: It would hack him to know that the cook knew more than to swallow all of his gags about St. Louis. **1908** *DN* III 318: We tried to hack the pitcher. **1909** *Sat. Eve. Post* (July 3) 6: Gosh, it hacks me! **1917** *DN* IV 413: That joke hacks Steve to this day. **1959** Farris *Harrison High* 194: Really hacks me. **1966** Cassiday *Angels Ten* 135: Get off your high horse, Fletch. Mills isn't hacking you. **1966** Walnut Ridge, Ark., high school student (coll. J. Ball): Man, that really hacks me off. **1971** Private, U.S. Army, Ft. Campbell, Ky. (coll. J. Ball): These mess sergeants really hack me. **1975** C.W. Smith *Country Music* 201: You could think of a dozen things off the bat that hacked you off about her. **1995** *CBS This Morning* (CBS-TV) (May 11): It didn't hack you off?

3.a. Now esp. *USAF.* to put up with; tolerate; endure.—often constr. with *it*, often without specific antecedent.

   1915 *DN* IV 275: *Hacking Her*…An expression of greeting, like "How are you?"…"Well, how are you hacking her?" **1945** in Gellhorn *Face of War* 160: Those P-47's. I don't hack their [slangy] talk. **1955** B.J. Friedman, in *Antioch Rev.* XV 378: Next time I come round I want the tire out here….One thing I don't hack is a man stealing. **1956** Heflin *USAF Dict.* 243: *Hack, v. trans.* To tolerate or put up with *something. Slang.* **1959** *Sat. Eve. Post* (May 2) 68: When you'd hacked a deal like that, you couldn't get too excited about a minor fluctuation in one propeller out of four. **1961** Baar & Howard *Missileman* 166: He had to be certain his officers and men were able to "hack it." **1964** Newhafer *Last Tallyho* 135: You need Barry for insurance, to take over in case Crowley can't hack it. **1967** Wolf *Love Generation* 153: I just couldn't hack the job scene any more. **1967** Michaeles *Suicide Command* 14: Don't you think I can hack it, Colonel? Do you think I'll freeze up and run? **1968** K. Cooper *Aerobics* 5: As the boys down on the flight line would say, "They just couldn't hack it." **1969** *CBS-TV News*: [I] Just can't hack that stuff all day. **1970** N.Y.U. student: If *I* were an elephant, they couldn't make me stay outdoors and hack the rain. **1971** WINS radio (Mar. 5): They could, in the old Princeton phrase, "hack it" in Laos. **1983** Univ. Tenn. instructor: I can't hack this shit one more minute. **1993** A. Lomax *Where Blues Began* 331: True democracy—if you could hack it. **1994** in *Reader's Digest* (Jan. 1995) 157: I just can't hack it anymore.

b. to accomplish or manage successfully; cope with.—usu. constr. with *it*, often without specific antecedent.

   1952 Randolph & Wilson *Down in the Holler* 250: *Hack: v.t.* To achieve, to accomplish something. "I cain't quite *hack* it" is an admission that some specific task is beyond the speaker's ability. *Hack the jimson* carries the same meaning. **1955** Scott *Look of Eagle* 244: He was in full sunlight when he saw land….He had it made. He'd hacked it. It was in the bag. **1956** in F. Harvey *Air Force* 50: Joe Hiltebrandt had trained a lot of approach controllers…and by now he knew which ones would be able to hack it. **1958** McCulloch *Woods Words* 28: *Can't cut 'er*—Said of a man who does not savvy the job, or is not strong enough to do it….*Can't hack 'er*—Same. **1959** Montgomery & Heiman *Jet Nav.* 119: I don't think he's going to be able to hack the B-52. **1959** *Sat. Eve. Post* (May 2) 68: Coming back to base at night, in blowing snow, with just enough fuel for one pass at the icy strip: When you'd hacked a deal like that, you couldn't get too excited about a minor [engine problem]. **1962** Tregaskis *Vietnam Diary* 20: He had gained his private pilot's license, but when it came to becoming a Marine Corps pilot, "I couldn't hack the physical." **1962** G. Olson *Roaring Road* 70: Dave found himself hoping…that Cole would accept Claude's challenge and succeed. "Come on, Cole….We can hack it." **1963** Boyle *Yanks Don't Cry* 145 [ref. to WWII]: Anyway, I got all set up to spend the rest of my tour with the gal, but the way things turned out I couldn't hack it. **1963–64** Kesey *Sometimes a Great Notion* 27: Maybe some fathers and sons talk to each other like that, but me and old Henry was never able to hack it. **1965** Adler *Vietnam Letters* 99: I'm afraid I'd never hack it though: too much math! **1966** Newhafer *No More Bugles* 30: "Think you could still hack it, Tom?" "Hell, yes…I'm not that old yet." **1966** Shepard *Doom Pussy* 2: I'm studying to be a gunner. Ought to hack it in two more weeks. **1968** W. Anderson *Gooney Bird* 50: Two quarts won't hack it. **1976** *Kojak* (CBS-TV): How do we hack this? **1980** Carlino *Santini* (film): You'll hack it or pack it! *a***1982** Medved *Hospital* 208: Then I was an incompetent woman who couldn't hack it in the real world. **1984–85** in Schneider & Schneider *Sound Off!* 30: All the other girls were going through what I was going through, and they were staying and hacking it.

4. to engage in amorous play or sexual activity.

   1943 *AS* XVIII 154: *Hacking.* Necking, petting, spooning, courting, depending on how old you are. **1954–60** *DAS*: *Hack*…To neck, pet, or

spoon. *c***1940**. *Not common.* **1964** R. Moore *Green Berets* 132: Sergeant Hanh…took them to the local whorehouse and let them take pictures of him hacking.

5. *Computers.* **a.** to work on or study (a computer component, program, etc.). Also intrans.

   1971 (quot. at HACKER², 3). **1976** in *OED2:* The compulsive programmer spends all the time he can…"hacking." **1983** Naiman *Computer Dict.* 68: This week I'm hacking the terminal driver. **1983** Steele et al. *Hacker's Dict.: Hack*…To work with a computer. **1984** *California* (Nov.) 135: He really wanted to get out of San Diego, hack games and be happy.

b. to gain or attempt to gain unlawful access to (a proprietary computer system) through the use of another computer. Also intrans.

   1983 *N.Y. Times* (Aug. 28) IV 20: Hackers…wouldn't…think of calling up on the telephone and saying, "Hi, I'm a bright young guy and I'd like to hack your computer." **1990** *Newsweek* (Apr. 30) 50: "Cyberpunk" [a rule book for a computer game] describes techniques for "hacking" into computers and encourages players to break into fictitious machines. **1990** *Larry King Live* (CNN-TV) (Mar. 23): There's a computer guy out there trying to hack you? **1993** *L.A. Times Mag.* (Sept. 12) 24: He hacked Pacific Bell computers to obtain "unpublished telephone numbers for the Soviet Consulate."

6. *Stu.* to vomit.

   1970–72 in *AS* L (1975) 60: *Hack vi* Vomit. "He makes me want to hack."

7. *Basketball.* (see 1977 quot.).

   1977 *Webster's Sports Dict.: Hack*…To strike the arm of an opponent with the hand. **1994** N. McCall *Wanna Holler* 54: I didn't hack you man! You just mad 'cause you losin'!

¶ In phrase:

¶ **hack the course** Esp. *USAF.* to accomplish a task at hand; succeed.

   1966 Shepard *Doom Pussy* 128: We need something for the lady reporter to wear to the jamboree tonight. Think you can hack the course? **1968** Broughton *Thud Ridge* 39: We were desperately short on flight leaders and the personnel pipeline just couldn't hack the course.

hack³ *v.* [perh. alter. of HAWK, *v.*] *Black E.* (see quot.)
   1971 H. Roberts *Third Ear:* To watch closely…"hack."

hack dog *n.* the assistant to a hackney driver.
   1915 H. Young *Hard Knocks* 233 [ref. to San Francisco, 1876]: I…became what he termed the "hack dog." *Ibid.* 234: This was where the part of the "hack dog" came in, as I was supposed to go to the assistance of the driver.

hacked *adj.* **1.a.** *So. & So. Midland.* dispirited; tired or disconcerted; embarrassed.

   1882 Watkins *Co. Aytch* 47: The boys were "hacked," nay, whipped. *Ibid.* 120: I felt so sorry for the yellow-hammer Alabamians, they looked so hacked, and answered back not a word. *Ibid.* 169: Sherman is getting cautious, his army, hacked. **1892** J.C. Harris *Uncle Remus & Friends* 349: When you once git 'em hacked dey er hacked fer good; dey des give right up. **1905** *DN* III 82: *Hack, v. trans.* To embarrass. "He was hacked."

b. angry or annoyed.—also constr. with *off*, rarely with *up*.

   1936 *AS* XI 368: *Hacked*…Annoyed; confused. **1958** F. Davis *Spearhead* 50 [ref. to 1945]: Bradlow's hacked because I got command of the task force and he didn't. **1958** *AS* (Oct.) 225: Annoyed…*hacked.* **1959** Farris *Harrison High* 294: The other guys would just get him hacked. **1959–60** R. Reiser *Jazz Titans* 157: *Hacked:* tired, irritated. **1962** W. Crawford *Give Me Tomorrow* 32 [ref. to 1951]: Linebarrier's so hacked he left home to eat breakfast. **1963** in H. Ellison *Sex Misspelled* 46: I was getting highly hacked by this scene. **1970** Grissim *Country Music* 103: I wouldn't be so hacked off about it if I didn't love Country music. *****1980** Leland *Kiwi-Yank. Dict.* 49: I'm so hacked off with this job that I'm ready to…piss off to the West Coast. **1984** *Psychology Today* (July) 17: Martina really babies me along if I'm in a hacked-up mood. **1985** *L.A. Times* (Jan. 21) III 16: Somebody hacked off at his wife who just wants to see how far he can go until he wishes he were back with her again.

2. *Und.* (of a place to be robbed) watched by a security guard.

1914 Jackson & Hellyer *Vocab.* 42: "The joint's hacked but not kipped," that is, watched but not occupied by a sleeper.

hacker[1] *n.* HACKIE, 1.

1938 R. Chandler, in *Dime Detective* (Jan.): A hacker asleep in his cab. **1949** in *DAS*: He enriched another hacker by an even $5000. **1963** *Wash. Post* (July 14) E6: As indicated by the spokesman for nine cab companies...hackers earn an average of only 78 cents an hour. **1963** *Wash. Post* (Oct. 30) B1: Checking taxicab manifests of a sampling of Government-employed, part-time hackers.

hacker[2] *n.* **1.a.** *Sports,* esp. *Tennis & Golf.* a player, often a beginner, demonstrating poor form or mediocre ability.

1949 Cummings *Dict. Sports* 192: *Hacker*...slang. A tennis player with poor form—who "hacks" at the ball instead of stroking it properly. **1953** *N.Y. Times* (May 31) VI 16: Most of that equipment...is used for very horrible golf because the hackers outnumber the experts. **1970** Scharff *Encyc. of Golf* 418: *Hacker.* An unskilled golfer. **1973** *Oui* (June) 109: Her bizarre strokes make her the international heroine of a million neighborhood hackers. **1976** T. Walker *Ft. Apache* 5: My name is Tom Walker. I'm a hacker. If you've ever played schoolyard basketball, I was the type of guy with limited ability who tried to win the best way he could: with elbows, hands, almost anything available. *a*1977 T. Barnett *Golf Is Madness* 65: Shots...any hacker can make if he tries often and hard enough. **1977** *Time* (June 6) 90: A mile run in eight minutes, which is a good hacker's pace. **1977** *Flightime* (June) 13: The largely-aluminum racquet...[is] perfectly legal and promises to grant even the happy hacker a crispness of delivery...beyond his Mittyesque imaginings. **1978** *N.Y. Times* (Apr. 24) C1: [Description of tennis racquet:] Vinyl tubing boon to hacker, overkill in hands of professionals. **1981** D.E. Miller *Jargon* 245: *Hacker.* An earnest but awkward amateur [tennis player]. *a*1989 P. Dickson *Baseball Dict.* 192: *Hacker.* A batter with poor form at the plate. **1994** N. McCall *Wanna Holler* 53: Most of the [pickup basketball] teams were really hoodlum squads, filled with hackers.

b. Esp. *Stu.* any person of ordinary or mediocre ability, motivation, etc. Also fig.

1968 Baker, Ladd & Robb *CUSS* 132: *Hacker.* A person [student] who always fools around. **1970** N.Y.U. prof.: So the lecture is actually being given on two levels—one for the physics majors, and the other for the ordinary hackers. But the hackers should get a lot out of it. **1974** *Business Week* (Feb. 23) 13: The authors classify companies.... There are the pros (including, incidentally, IBM and Xerox), par shooters, bogie shooters, hackers...and quitters. **1977** in L. Bangs *Psychotic Reactions* 213: This hacker from the New York *Post*...whipped up a book. *a*1989 Spears *NCT Dict. Slang* 167: *Hacker*...a generally unsuccessful person.

2. *Mil.* an especially competent individual. Cf. NON-HACKER.

1951 in Whitehouse *Fighters in Sky* 165: Mr. Briscoe...should have been a two-star guy....a hacker like Briscoe.

3. *Computers.* a computer enthusiast, esp. if highly skilled; (*specif.*) a hobbyist who attempts to unlawfully penetrate proprietary computer systems. [Among serious computer users, *hacker* is used solely in a positive sense; the term *cracker* is used for those who attempt to violate computer security. See, e.g., discussion in E. Raymond *New Hacker's Dictionary* (1991).]

1971 *How to Get Around MIT* (ed. 3) 169: *Hack*...A verb meaning to apply oneself very earnestly to something. Example: a computer hacker. Also connotes fanaticism. **1976** in *OED2*: The compulsive programmer, or hacker as he calls himself, is usually a superb technician. **1982** *Time* (Nov. 8) 92: *Hackers* (computer fanatics) at MIT and Stanford. **1983** *All Things Considered* (Nat. Pub. Radio) (May 8): A hacker is someone who...learns the rules of the computer system and abuses the hell out of it. **1983** *USA Today* (Aug. 2) 1D: *Hacker*—a technical expert skilled at searching out the possibilities of a computer. **1983** *N.Y. Times* (Aug. 13) 7: Dr. Weizenbaum recalled how a group of student computer enthusiasts, known as "hackers" in the academic community, recently managed to break through the security of a computer used by the University of California at Berkeley. **1983** *N.Y. Times* (Aug. 28) IV 20: There is a malicious or inquisitive hacker, or meddler, who would like to discover information by poking around. **1984** *Time* (May 14) 83: Hackers who crack security codes just for the fun of it. **1984** *Time* (Dec. 3) 76: Hackers, as most computer experts use the term, are distinguished not by their mischievousness but by their per-

sistence and skill. **1989** *USA Today* (Feb. 22) 3A: Hacker Heaven. Santa Monica, Calif., residents with personal computers can access 50 city agencies under a [municipal] program. **1989** *CBS This Morning* (CBS-TV) (Mar. 3): A Harvard professor...discovered the intrusion and helped track down the hackers.

hack hand *n.* a commercial driver.

1942 *AS* (Apr.) 103: *Hack hand.* Truck driver.

hackie *n.* **1.** a hackman or cabdriver.

1899 Gunter *M.S. Bradford* 31: Where shall I tell hacky to drive? **1926** Finerty *Crim.* 28: *Hackie*—a taxi or horse cab driver. **1928** O'Connor *B'way Racketeers* 64: He mentioned a nigger hackie that used to drive him home almost every night. **1934** in North *New Masses* 153: Say, did you ever see a hackie on duty wit' a soft hat? **1935** Odets *Waiting for Lefty* 11: And any other hackie that won't fight...let them all be ground to hamburger! **1941** H.A. Smith *Low Man* 117: Look at me. A hackie. **1946** Gresham *Nightmare Alley* 135: The hackie slid between a bus and a sedan...."G'wan, ya dumb son-of-a-bitch," he yelled back. **1948** Lait & Mortimer *New York* 137: You still find the hackies at 59th Street and Fifth Avenue, the last of their kind in the country. **1950** Maddow & Huston *Asphalt Jungle* 133: Keep out of this, hackie. **1955** R. Stout *3 Witnesses* 12: The hackie twisted his head around. **1957** Mayfield *Hit* 87: Or maybe he would like to work for one of those companies where they made the men shape up every morning and sometimes a hackie didn't get a car at all. **1961** in Yates *Loneliness* 206: I could ask any hackie if I didn't believe him. **1974** A. Bergman *Big Kiss-Off* 52: I'd heard people on the street say that, hackies, barbers, newsies, average Joes. **1984** *Washington Monthly* (Dec.) 49: Even though I'd gladly pay a hackie $5 to drive me 2.8 miles, I can't get a cab in Midtown.

2. *Navy.* (see quot.)

1958 Cope & Dyer *Petty Officer's Guide* (ed. 2) 349: *Hackie.* (Slang) A newly-rated chief petty officer (from his hat, which when new, resembles a cab driver's).

hack-pusher *n.* a cabdriver. Also (*West.*) **hack-skinner.**

*ca*1935 in Holt *Dirty Comics* 92: A smart hack-pusher sets him on the trail. **1938** *AS* (Dec.) 307: *Hackskinner.* A driver, usually of proved skill and competence. **1961** J. Jones *Thin Red Line* 270: There was no doubt in his hard hackpusher's mind. ***1966** Baker *Austral. Lang.* (ed. 2) 213: *Hack pusher;* a taxi driver.

hack rack *n.* a taxicab stand.

1972 in *AS* LI (1976) 287: Cab stand, taxi stand,...hack rack.

had[1] see s.v. HAVE.

had[2] *v.* var. HAT, *v.*

haddock *n.* money.

1865 *Harper's Mo.* XXX 606: Money...brads...dust...horse-nails...haddock.

haffies var. HALVIES.

hag *n.* Esp. *Stu.* a young woman, esp. if unattractive or sexually promiscuous; in phr. **hag [and stag] party** a party for women [and men].—usu. used disparagingly.

1928 T.A. Dorgan, in Zwilling *TAD Lexicon* 107: She hates dem hag and stag parties dey has at houses nowadays. **1932** Lorimer *Streetcars* 117: What do I want to go around with a lot of hags for? **1942** Hollingshead *Elmtown's Youth* 225: Certain activities, such as girls' "hag parties"...are organized on a single sex basis. **1942** *ATS* 356: *Hag* (any woman). **1946** Boulware *Jive & Slang* 4: *Hag*...Bad girl. ***a*1950** W. Granville *Sea Slang* 117: *Hags.* Women in general. (R.N. and W.R.N.S. officers' term.) "How many hags will be at the party?" **1952** Lait & Mortimer *USA* 116: Experienced, sophisticated hags...of eighteen.

ha-ha *n.* **1.** a laugh of ridicule or mockery; derision or scornful rejection.—usu. constr. with *give the* [*merry*].

1896 *Amherst Olio* 164: All the peops in chapel gathered, / Raised a shout of merry ha-has. **1896** Ade *Artie* 58: She just give him the ha-ha and says: "That'll be all right. *Ibid.* 84: Everything I done or said they give me the ha-ha. **1900** Remington *With Bark* 28: They would give them the merry ha-ha when they returned to the post. **1902** Townsend *Fadden & Mr. Paul* 46: De gang agreed...to give de Reformers de merry haha. **1902** K. Harriman *Ann Arbor Tales* 230: I gave him the "ha-ha" and passed him a con. about...how...*I* wanted it square. **1909** "Clivette" *Café Cackle* 74: We'll give the public a little run for their money and slip them the "ha-ha." **1913** *Sat. Eve. Post* (Mar. 8) 19: Here's the Clarion with a front-page column givin' us the merry ha-ha. **1913** J. London *Valley of Moon* 285: There was the two of 'em, givin' me the ha-ha. **1914** Ellis *Billy Sunday* 185: The devil will give you the ha! ha! until you're gray-haired. **1915** Howard *God's Man* 190: She took his dough and gave him the ha-ha. **1917** Depew *Gunner Depew* 86: Would I let myself croak so youse can give me the ha-ha? **1921** J. Conway, in *Variety* (Dec. 30) 97: I don't want to follow you into that can and get the ha! ha! from the harmonica players when I flop with it. **1928** Sharpe *Chicago May* 76: All the other boarders gave poor O'Reilly the merry Ha! Ha! **1928** *New Yorker* (Dec. 8) 28: Her past has...given her the Ha-Ha! **1929** Asch *Pay Day* 41: Give the bastard the merry ha-ha. **1933** D. Runyon, in *Collier's* (July 8) 9: Many citizens gathered to give him the ha-ha. **1948** *N.D. History* XV 233: I...told the men and they gave me the "ha-ha." **1936–75** Earp & Boyer *Wyatt* 64: Doc...made the fatal mistake of giving Johnny the "ha-ha" about it in public.

2. an object of ridicule; laugh.
1921 "M. Brand" *Black Jack* 107: As a peterman, he was a loud ha-ha.

3. *Narc.* marijuana.
1971 Hilaire *Thanatos* 313: You been blowing too much ha-ha. *1990 Thorne *Dict. Contemp. Slang* 229: *Ha-ha* n. British. marihuana or hashish.

¶ In phrase:

¶ **have the ha-ha on** to be in a position of scornful superiority over; have the laugh on.
1893 Hampton *Maj. in Washington* 101: When I get into a scrape, nobody has the ha-ha on me. **1903** Townsend *Sure* 22: I began to tink dat I'd have de ha-ha on shuffer [*sic*] when I got home.

ha-ha *v.* to deride.
1925 *Sat. Eve. Post* (Oct. 3) 21: Nobody ha-has a winner.

hail *n.* ice, as in a drink. Cf. HAILSTORM.
1935 in *AS* (Feb.) 43: *Hold the hail.* Coca-Cola without ice. **1945** *Calif. Folk. Qly.* IV 55: *Heavy on the hail:* Extra amount of ice in the drink(s)...*Hold the hail:* No ice in the drink(s).

Hail Columbia *n.* [sugg. by "Hail Columbia," patriotic song (1798) by Joseph Hopkinson] (a partial euphem. for) HELL (in fig. senses).
1854 in Thornton *Amer. Gloss.* I: The note in which he says we gave him Hail Columby. **1863** [Fitch] *Annals of Army* 639: He had already had one bout with the rebels, and given them "Hail Columbia." **1864** "E. Kirke" *Down in Tenn.* 199: Come on, boys! Give them Hail Columbia! **1869** in *DAE:* She occasionally...raises Hail Columbia **1893** *Confed. War Jour.* (July) 64: I'd give this feller hail Columbia. **1910** *DN* III 442: You'll get Hail Columbia when your mother comes. **1917–20** in J.M. Hunter *Trail Drivers* I 470: There are so many "spooks and ghosts" to play Hail Columbia with cattle. **1921** J. Conway, in *Variety* (Nov. 18) 29: Duffy was beltin hail columbia out of all the northern New York light-weights. **1928** Delmar *Bad Girl* 16: I'll get Hail Columbia if my brother's in. **1935** J. Conroy *World to Win* 255: I'll bet the heifers ketch hail Columbia tomorrow. **1955** N.Y.C. woman, age *ca*40: She starts all the trouble and I get Hail Columbia. **1969, 1968–70** in *DARE.*

Hail Mary *adj.* Esp. *Football.* (of a usu. high pass, shot, etc.) made in desperation, with a very small chance of success. Also as *n.* Also *fig.* [Figurative use of this phr. was popularized during the Gulf War by Gen. H. Norman Schwarzkopf, who compared a flanking maneuver to the football play in a Feb. 27, 1991, press briefing.]
1982 Considine *Lang. Sport* 146: *Hail Mary:* A low-percentage pass, one that would require a great deal of luck or the intercession of a "higher power" for completion. **1983** Goldaper & Pincus *How to Talk Basketball* 95: *Hail Mary* adj: the type of shot whose only chance to go in the basket is accompanied by devout prayer. **1983** *Chi. Sun-Times* (Nov. 21) 9: [In list of recent superlative football performances:] *Hailest Mary:* Atlanta's 47-yard touchdown pass...to beat San Francisco on the game's final play. **1983** *L.A. Times* (Dec. 7) V 1: Tuned in on the Ram [*sic*] game Sunday just in time to see that final "Hail Mary" pass, which failed so abysmally. **1989** "Fresh Air" Nat. Pub. Radio (Sept. 6): Staubach hurls a Hail Mary pass into the end zone. **1990** *Time* (Aug. 13) 34: The "Hail Mary" play in football. "With time running out and 80 yards to go...you throw the long one and pray." **1991** *New Yorker* (Sept. 16) 81: Davies saved one game point [in court tennis] with a Hail Mary lob. **1991** *Newsweek* (June 17) 21: The risky

"Hail Mary" flanking maneuver into southern Iraq was not surprised by a counterattack. **1993** T. Taylor *Lightning in Storm* 197: The "Hail Mary"...a desperate, last second play. **1995** *CNN Saturday Morning* (CNN-TV) (July 8): It would be the...equivalent of a Hail Mary pass.

hailstorm *n.* a mint julep or similar cocktail made with crushed ice.
1832 in *DA:* Recourse ought to be had to his Hail-Storms, which infallibly overcome the most sultry drought. **1838** in *DAE:* Sipping "mint-julaps" before breakfast, "hail-storms" at dinner, and "old Monongahela" at night. **1839** in *DAE:* Divine mint julep!...which is in the southern and western states denominated "hail-storm." **1843–45** T.G. Green *Tex. Exped.* 368: A "sherry cobbler,"...a "Tom and Jerry,"...a "hail storm." **1847** in *DAE:* Or may I never drink a hail-storm again.

haily-gaily *adj.* tipsy.
1813–18 Weems *Drunk. Looking Glass* 60: Damp—tipsy—fuddled—haily gaily.

haim var. HAME.

Haines *n.* ¶ In phrase: **My name is Haines!** I must leave!
1840 *Spirit of Times* (Apr. 18) 77/3: "My name is Haines" enjoys a popularity which no other slang or cant phrase has ever attained. "I'm o-p-h," "I must mizzle," "I must make myself scarce," are frequently used, but the expression which heads this article leaves them all out of sight.

hair *n.* **1.** *West.* a scalp taken as a trophy; in phr. **lift** [or **raise**] **hair** to scalp someone.—usu. constr. with possessive. Now *hist.*
1848 Ruxton *Far West* 8: I've "raised the hair" of more than one Apach. *Ibid.* 12: Hurraw, Dick, mind your hair. *Ibid.* 14: Hyar's a nigger lifted hair that spree. **1850** Garrard *Wah-to-yah* 64: But, running too great a risk of "losing his hair" (scalp) at the hands of the impetuous, *coup*-anxious braves, he sojourned awhile with the more friendly Sioux. *Ibid.* 163: This coon has "raised har" so often sence, he keers fur nothing now. **1852** in *DAE:* The red varmints want his hair bad. **1858** in M. Simmons *Santa Fe Trail* 58: A band of Pawnees had..."lifted their hair." *ca*1859 Chamberlain *My Confession* 270 [ref. to 1846]: He offered...one thousand dollars for the hair of the famous Apache chief Santana. **1870** Duval *Big Foot* 106: I noticed my friend Jeff..."lifting the hair" from the head of an Indian. **1872** "W. Dexter" *Young Mustanger* 32: Probably they got their hair lifted. **1873** Perrie *Buckskin Mose* 231: I'll have his darned hair. **1942** Garcia *Tough Trip* 99: He had 280 aboriginal relatives who would only be too willing to lift our hair. **1953** L'Amour *Hondo* 3: Young bucks out to lift some hair or steal horses. **1970** A. Cody *Outcasts* 40: They are in need of a good lesson—such as losing their hair!

2. [sugg. by prov. phr. *hair of the dog (that bit one)* 'liquor taken as a supposed curative for a hangover'] liquor, esp. whiskey, usu. as added to a nonalcoholic drink.
1848 in J.Q. Anderson *Bark On* 119: Having taken a couple of fingers of "har," he departed to see his friend Dr. B. **1976** Hayden *Voyage* 114: "Here"—he extended the bottle—"would you like to put a little hair in that coffee?"

3. (see quots.); in phr. **put down some hair** to engage in copulation.
a1890–93 F & H IV 247: *Hair*...generic for the [female] sex: e.g., *after hair* = in quest of a woman; *plenty of hair* = lots of girls; *hair to sell* = a woman with a price; *hair-monger*, a wencher; *bit of hair* = the sexual favour. **1966** S. Stevens *Go Down Dead* 63: When I laying you then we is balling it or putting down some hair. **1974** Miami Univ. student: *Hair* means sex. "Let's get some hair." Or it can mean girls, like "Look at that hair."

4. manly spirit; nerve; guts. See also *have hair on (one's) chest,* below.
1958–59 Lipton *Barbarians* 160: Organized church worship...is religion "shorn of its hair and balls," as Chuck Bennison will tell you. **1964** in *AS* XL (1965) 194: An athlete may be said to have *a lot of hair* or *show a lot of hair* if he plays aggressively and well in a game. A student criticizing his professor's pet thesis may also *show a lot of hair*. The phrase *no hair* thus connotes a lack of masculinity or guts; one may hear it at a football game where the home team is not showing enough "hustle." **1968** Baker, Ladd & Robb *CUSS* 133: *Hair.* Courage. **1969** *Current Slang I & II* 47: *Hair,* n. Courage; guts.—Male instructors,

South Dakota; Air Force Academy cadets. **1973** Sgt., U.S. Army Comm. Command—Taiwan (coll. J. Ball): But who has the hair to tell him that? I sure don't….If you've got any hair at all, you'll tell that girl you're married. **1974** Pfc., U.S. Army Comm. Command—Taiwan (coll. J. Ball): WOW! That bastard's got hair! **1977** Filosa *Surf. Almanac* 186: *Hair.* Nerve, fearlessness. **1979** Hiler *Monkey Mt.* 76: Come on….Let's show some hair. *a***1984** in Safire *Stand Corrected* 201: To "show hair" still for bodysurfers and the like means to display courage….A fellow who conquered…[big waves] "had hair" [in the 1960's]. **1984** McInerny *Bright Lights* 69: You never would have worked up the hair to hit on her.

5. *Baseball.* speed applied to a ball.

  1983 in P. Dickson *Baseball Dict.* 192: That one had a little hair on it.

¶ In phrases:

¶ **bad hair day** [extended fr. the recent literal sense 'a day on which one's hair looks unattractive', as in bracketed quots. below] a difficult or unpleasant day; a bad day.

  [**1991** *Seattle Times* (Jan. 25) Tempo 10: I told them I was having a bad hair day.] [**1991** *L.A. Times Magazine* (Feb. 3) 6: Some days are just bad hair days. A while back, for example, there was a hot, dry 30-mile-an-hour Santa Ana wind blowing, and I'd been driving around in a convertible. I looked like a feral Hungarian mop dog.] [**1993** *Glamour* (July) 134: "My hair has a mind of its own," complained one of the hundreds of readers who wrote in about their bad hair days.] **1993** *Science* (Aug. 27): If the director doesn't like it, he can just say the guy [doing the review] had a bad hair day [brackets in orig.]. **1993** *Time* (Sept. 27) 96: Robinowitz climbed down so fast he scorched his pants. "I was having a bad-hair day…and I'm totally bald." **1994** *Oprah* (synd. TV series): When life is bad hair days one after another maybe there's a physical problem. **1994** Atlanta, Ga., journalist, age 38: I can remember first hearing *bad hair day* in June 1991. We were laughing about it as hairstyle terminology, but after about an hour we were using it in the sense of just a day when everything goes wrong. **1995** *World News Tonight* (ABC-TV) (Nov. 20): It's probably booby-trapped with a mine underneath. And you got a bad hair day.

¶ **curl (someone's) hair** to shock or terrify.

  1896 Ade *Artie* 20: I put up a bluff that'd curl your hair. **1903** A. Adams *Log of Cowboy* 86 [ref. to 1880's]: I'm not hankering for the dramatic in life, but we had a run last night that would curl your hair. **1905** Belasco *Golden West* 332: Send him to me—I'll curl his hair for him! **1963** *Dick Van Dyke Show* (CBS-TV): He told me some things that would have curled your hair! **1983** K. Weaver *Texas Crude* 32: Don't that curl your short hairs?

¶ **get a [wild] hair up** [or **in**] **(one's) ass** to be or become angry, excited, or irritable; (*also*) to have an eccentric notion.—usu. considered vulgar. Cf. WILD HAIR.

  1952 Uris *Battle Cry* 129 [ref. to WWII]: Jesus, he sure got a wild hair up him. **1920–54** Randolph *Bawdy Elements* 82: To say that a man *has got a wild hair in his ass* means only that he's excited or distraught. **1962** E. Stephens *Blow Negative* 194: He had this wild hair up his ass about the true submersible and all that. **1963** Boyle *Yanks Don't Cry* 150: Something sure put a hair in his ass. **1973** R. Roth *Sand in Wind* 338: The Gunny's got a hair up his ass. **1975** S.P. Smith *Amer. Boys* 20: You never knew when he'd get a hair up his ass and do something weird. **1978** in Lyle & Golenbock *Bronx Zoo* 213: If we had won both, that really would have put some hair up Boston's ass. **1982** R.M. Brown *So. Discomfort* 70: Have you got a wild hair up your ass, or what, girl? **1983** N. Proffitt *Gardens of Stone* 337: Marvin also had a hair up his ass because he was an officer and Clell was only a noncom. **1986** J.J. Maloney *Chain* 191: You get a wild hair in his ass, you can't talk to him. **1989** D. Sherman *There I Was* 78: Some goddam sergeant major gets a wild hair up his ass about me. **1995** *Jerry Springer Show* (synd. TV series): He gets a wild hair and he goes off and leaves.

¶ **have a hair across (one's) ass** to be angry or irritable.—usu. considered vulgar.

  1968 Baker, Ladd & Robb *CUSS* 133: *Hair across your ass, have a.* Constantly complaining and irritable. **1966–80** McAleer & Dickson *Unit Pride* 69: What's eatin' you, Billy? You got a hair across your ass a mile wide today.

¶ **have hair on (one's) chest** [or (*vulgar*) **ass**] to have or show masculine courage, spirit, or toughness.—now usu. in negative contexts.

1916 H.L. Mencken, in Riggio *Dreiser-Mencken Letters* I 285: Take the advice of men with hair on their chests—not of women. **1918** F. Gibbons *They Thought We Wouldn't Fight* 344: "What do you think of the President of the United States?"…"Say,…that guy's—got hair—on his chest." **1933** Hammett *Thin Man* 223: "Jesus," he said admiringly, "there's a woman with hair on her chest." **1972** C. Gaines *Stay Hungry* 146: These kids now, they don't have a hair on their ass. I've done it all, man, glue, *mush*rooms,…*Nem*butal, [etc.]. **1973** Karlin, Paquet & Rottmann *Freefire Zone* 164: "But this harassment bullshit, these senseless details!"…"No hair on your ass, huh?" Warren held an innocent smile up for Billy's inspection. **1974** C.W. Smith *Country Music* 278: Heavy, you hadn't got a hair on your ass, you know that? Here you carried on to beat hell about this machine, but when it comes time to deliver, looks like you're a bit doubtful about it. **1978** Hasford *Short-Timers* 161 [ref. to 1968]: You ain't got a hair on your ass. **1978** J. Webb *Fields of Fire* 12: If he has a hair on his ass he'll sue Mister Baum. **1980** Conroy *Lords of Discipline* 178: Pig said I did not have a hair on my ass if I didn't publish it in the *Guidon*. *Ibid.* 198: Because of that poem, paisan….Because you've got hair on your ass. *a***1991** Kross *Splash One* 69: We'll see if Danforth has any hair on his ass. *a***1994** J. Boyle *Apache Sunrise* 3: The kind of team that any commander with hair on his ass would want his unit to be like. **1995** *Donahue* (NBC-TV): A guy who eats nails for breakfast and he's looking for a chance to show he's got hair on his chest.

¶ **have (someone) by the short hairs** [or **where the hair is short**] to have (someone) at a disadvantage.

  1861 in H. Lind *Long Road Home* 42: The next time i [*sic*] will have them wher [*sic*] the hair is short if they try any of their games. **1872** Burnham *Secret Service* 207: I knock under….You've got me where the ha'r is short! **1882** in Bunner *Letters* 71: Truly, this cold has caught us where the hair is short. **1883** *Life* (Feb. 8) 80: He would get the Drummer where the Hair was comparatively Short. **1885** B. Harte *Shore & Sedge* 50: You've got this crowd where the hair is short; excuse me, but it's so. *****1888** Kipling *Wee Willie Winkie* 67: Then they'll rush in, and then we've got 'em by the short hairs! **1902** in *Comments on Ety.* XXIV 1–2 (Oct.–Nov. 1994) 58: You got me where the hair is short. I'll swan you have. **1927** *AS* (May) 356: You certainly have him where the hair is short. **1942** Wilder *Flamingo Road* 215: We sure enough got 'em by the short hair. **1963** Boyle *Yanks Don't Cry* 29: The individual Japanese…always appeared to hold an American in awe—even when he had us where the hair was short. **1964** Pearl *Stockade* 101: He had *me* by the short hairs with that Keyes broad. **1965** Bryan *P.S. Wilkinson* 82: I've got you by the short hairs and I'll make an example of you that the officers and men of this unit will never forget. **1966** King *Brave & Damned* 82: They've got us where the hair is short and it's our own damned skin we're fighting for. **1968** Westheimer *Young Sentry* 339: "I had him by the short hairs," the colonel said deprecatingly. **1973** *N.Y. Post* (July 23) 27: It looks like this Sam Ervin has him by the short hairs now with these tapes. **1982** *Morning Line* (WKGN radio) (June 11): Public employee unions have you by the short hairs before they even sit down to bargain.

¶ **in (someone's) hair, 1.** attacking (someone).

  1839 in Blair & Meine *Half Horse* 65: And if any man dare doubt it, I'll be in his hair quicker than hell could scorch a feather. **1851** in *DA*: I shall depend on your honor…that you won't tell on me, cause if you did, I should have Hetty Gawkins in my hair in no time.

2. persistently annoying someone; in phr. **out of (one's) hair** no longer annoying. Now *colloq.*

  1880 "M. Twain" *Tramp Abroad*: What you learn here, you've got to know…or else you'll have one of these…old professors in your hair. **1929** J.M. Saunders *Single Lady* 15: He gets in your hair. **1935** S. Lewis *Can't Happen Here* 123: When Fascism begins to get into people's hair. **1948** in *DA*: That's three fellows we won't have in our hair for quite a few years. **1949** Gordon & Kanin *Adam's Rib* 20: I'd like to see her put away somewhere, that's all. Out of my hair. **1957** O'Rourke *Bravados* 46: Keep her out of my hair. **1981** D. Burns *Feeling Good* 62: Get out of my goddam hair!

¶ **keep your hair on!** don't get excited!

  1883 in *OED*: Keep your hair on, my young friend. **1885** B. Harte *Shore & Sedge* 212: "Keep yer hair on!" remonstrated the old man. *****1889** Barrère & Leland *Dict. Slang* I 442: Keep yer hair on, Lizer. **1903** *Pedagog. Sem.* X 379: Keep your shirt on. Keep your head on. Keep your hair on. **1924** *DN* V 290: *Keep your hair on*…Same as keep your shirt on. **1929** *Our Army* (Mar.) 19: Keep your hair on, Wilson. **1944** in Ryan *Longest Day* 39: Cut out that claptrap and keep your hair on. **1946** Steinbeck *Wayward Bus* 74: You'll find out, just keep your pretty hair on, little girl.

¶ **let (one's) hair down, 1.a.** Orig. *Theat.* to abandon restraint, esp. in becoming confidential or expressing (one's) true feelings.

*1850 in *OEDS*: I am well aware that a little ranting and "letting down the back hair" would have "told" upon the audience with more noisy effect. *1933 P.G. Wodehouse, in *OEDS*: No reporters present. We can take our hair down and tell each other our right names. **1937** Weidman *Wholesale* 3: "It's all right, Tootsie," I said. "You can let your hair down in front of me." **1940** S. Lewis *Bethel Merriday* 45: Let's let our hair down and be frank. **1940** Baldwin *Brother Orchid* (film): You turned out to be a real guy in my book, so I'm gonna let down my hair. **1971** Meggyesy *Out of Their League* 186: The Cardinal organization naively believed the players would let their hair down and openly discuss the contents of Olsen's article in front of the owners and coaches. **1973** *Playboy* (June) 80: I thought, when he was out of office, that he would let his hair down and say, "Well, there were some points where I think we went wrong; there were some things that I did that I wish…I hadn't done. **1995** *Donahue* (NBC-TV): She's fun, she lets her hair down….She's a lot of fun being around.

b. *Homosex.* to confide that (one) is homosexual.

1935 Pollock *Und. Speaks: He let his hair down*, admitted sexual perversion. **1941** G. Legman, in Henry *Sex Vars.* II 1168: *Hair, To let down one's* To drop all restraint in displaying one's homosexuality, or to admit being homosexual. The use of this phrase in common American slang, as meaning to drop all pretense or finally to tell the truth, seems to stem from the homosexual meaning. **1950** (quot. at HAIRPIN, *n.*, 3).

2. to become free and informal in behavior, esp. after work; relax. [The 1929 quot. is literal.]

[**1929** McEvoy *Hollywood Girl* 1: Well, pull up a chair and take down your hair, and tell us all about it.] **1937** Wexley & Duff *Angels with Dirty Faces* (film): Let your hair down, have a little fun. **1946** Dadswell *Hey, Sucker* 27: "Let down your hair," as the saying goes, and "be yourself." **1949** Maier *Pleasure I.* 178: Not a bad guy when he takes his hair down—but he doesn't take it down very often. **1977** J. Olsen *Fire Five* 118: Drink beer and orgle [*sic*] the broads and let our hair hang down. **1980** Freudenberger & Richelson *Burn Out* 212: Let your hair down. Have a good time.

¶ **May your hair never slip!** (used as a joc. toast).

1933 J.V. Allen *Cowboy Lore* 40: Here's to the cowboy, and "may his hair never slip."

¶ **part (someone's) hair** to hit (someone) over the head; (*also*) to shoot in the head; kill.

*ca*1910–18 Hoyt *Buckskin Joe* 116 [ref. to 1870's]: Dang your hide, Joe, I came nigh parting your hair. **1938** I. Shaw *Sailor off Bremen* 283: Join a union, get yer hair parted down the middle by the cops. **1958** Bard & Spring *Horse Wrangler* 119 [ref. to *ca*1900]: "There's one of the bastards. I'll part his hair for him." At that the Kid put a bullet through the head of the bedstead. **1980** Kotzwinkle *Jack* 166: Spider pulled out his rod. "I'll part his fuckin' hair." **1989** Zumbro & Walker *Jungletracks* 18: He coulda parted my hair real good with that [knife].

¶ **take the hair off** to be unendurable; exceed one's patience or forbearance.

1877 in FitzGerald *Dr.'s Wife* 297: It is rather rough on us to be roused out of our warm beds at 3, 4, or 5 a.m. It almost "takes the hair off," as they say.

¶ **that wears** [or **wore**] **hair** *West.* (of an unbroken horse) that exists (or ever existed).

1900 Fletcher *Up the Trail* 91: Cowboys…would contract to…ride any quadruped that wore hair. **1910** in C.M. Russell *Paper Talk* 79: You said there wasent nothing waring hair hoofs an hide from the Gulf of Mexico as fare north as grass grows that you couldent fork. **1915** H.L. Wilson *Professor* 298: I won't have this girl pestered by Jackson or by…any man that wears hair! **1963** in Woods *Horse-Racing* 21: There's nothing that wears hair can beat this colt! **1984** L'Amour *Son of Wanted Man* 7: You can ride anything that wears hair.

¶ **through (one's) hair** into (one's) mind.

1858 in G.W. Harris *High Times* 147: The thought got throu my har that hit were the ghostez ove some Frenchman.

¶ **whiskey in the hair** a hangover.

1865 Sala *Diary* II 313: When seltzer and sherry are taken, they are gulped down early in the morning, to cure the ailments known as "hot coppers" or "whisky in the hair."

¶ **put hair on your chest** (said of a strong drink).

1931 Buckingham & Higgin *Painted Desert* (film): Take a swig of this. It'll put hair on your chest. **1959** N.Y.C. man: That'll put hair on your chest. **1970** N.Y.U. student: It'll put hair on your chest. **1974** Loken *Come Monday Morning* 102: Take a little snort'a that. Put a little hair back on your chest. **1982–84** Safire *Take My Word* 34: When was the last time you heard *It'll put hair on your chest*?

hairbag *n.* **1.** *Police.* a veteran police officer; old-timer.

1958 *N.Y. Times Mag.* (Mar. 16) 88: Hair bag—A veteran policeman, especially knowledgeable about the inner workings of the Police Department. **1963** *True* (May) 104: Good man, real salty hairbag from the old school. **1973** Droge *Patrolman* 47: The old-timers, or "hairbags" as they're often called, had a rule of thumb. **1974** Radano *Cop Stories* 120: Sitting in the squadroom…is this first-grade detective—an old hairbag—and he asks my partner what's wrong….Later the hairbag comes over to me. **1975** V. Miller *Trade-off* 105: But I know where you stand on this. You're a hairbag from the word "go." **1980** W. Sherman *Times Square* 10: An older cop, a "hairbag,"…robbed a two-week-old corpse. **1985** M. Baker *Cops* 36: There wasn't a guy had less than fifteen years on the force, which is to say they were all hairbags and I was a rookie. **1987** Taubman *Lady Cop* 13: He was a real hairbag in Soph's first precinct. *Ibid.* 268: *Hairbag*: Derogatory term for an old-fashioned cop. **1994** *New York* (Oct. 17) 15: These hairbags are so scared….There's gonna be so many desk jobs lost, they're gonna have to get out there and do some work.

2. a disgusting or offensive person.

1978 S. King *Stand* 93: You got this comin outta the store, you hairbag. **1981** *Hill St. Blues* (NBC-TV): Police! You freeze it, hairbag! **1981–85** S. King *It* 23: Avarino could almost read this hairbag pussy's little mind. **1986** C. Stroud *Close Pursuit* 84: I don't want a bunch of hairbags from the Eighth…fucking things up.

hairball *n.* **1.** a difficult or messy situation. Cf. aviation sense of FURBALL, 1.

*a*1977 in S. King *Bachman* 110: Let's…get it done before this thing turns into a hairball.

2. a stupid or disgusting person.

1981 *Hill St. Blues* (NBC-TV): What's the matter, hairball? **1981** *Hill St. Blues* (NBC-TV): Move your leg, hairball. **1981** Wambaugh *Glitter Dome* 51: You two hairballs come up with a good idea once in a while. **1984** Mason & Rheingold *Slanguage: Hairball*, n. A loser. **1986** Calif. man, age *ca*19, on *Story of English* (PBS): Ugh! Hairball! **1988** *News Watch* (CNN-TV) (May 31): And if the inspectors find a violation, you're busted, hairball. **1989** *CBS This Morning* (CBS-TV) (Jan. 10): You hairball! I asked for a bad guy and I get Michael Jackson! **1989** *Newsweek* (Nov. 27) 79: Hey, Hairball! You're gone!

hairbrush *n.* a braided epaulette. Now *hist.*

1955 T. Blackburn *Legend of Davy Crockett* (film): You know, sometimes I wonder why they gave you them hairbrushes.

hairburger *n.* HAIR PIE; FURBURGER.—usu. considered vulgar.

1981 Spears *Slang & Euphem.: Hairburger*…The female genitals with reference to cunnilingus. *1990 T. Thorne *Dict. Contemp. Slang* 229: *Hairburger* an alternative form of *furburger*.

hair case *n. West.* a hat.

1922 Rollins *Cowboy* 105 [ref. to *a*1900]: These other [cowboy] names [for a hat] included…"hair case."

hair-curler *n.* liquor. *Joc.*

1857 Willcox *Faca* 184: Major June, Lieutenant Soldan and myself went downstairs to discuss the matter, over a little of the "hair curler." A sly joke of the Skipper's…over Jamaica spirits. **1975** (cited in Spears *Drugs & Drink*).

haircut *n.* **1.a.** a blow over the head. Cf. *part (someone's) hair* s.v. HAIR.

1896 Hamblen *Many Seas* 398: Come on now, me hearties!…Who's next for a hair cut?

b. (see quot.).

1962 Yablonsky *Violent Gang* 258: He was laughed at, ridiculed, and given a "haircut" (a verbal dressing down) by other old-time con men of the organization.

2. *Med.* a case of syphilis.

1935 (cited in Partridge *Dict. Und.* 317). **1972** *Nat. Lampoon* (July) 76: *Haircut* Syphilis. [Medical school slang].

¶ In phrase:

¶ **give a haircut** to cut down (crops or vegetation).

1948 Wolfert *Act of Love* 451 [ref. to WWII]: The artillery began giving the plantation "a haircut," as the phrase borrowed from the wheatlands had it.

haired *adj.* Esp. *N.E.* angry or annoyed.—usu. constr. with *up* or *off*. Cf. HAIR UP.

1904–14 in *DN* IV (1914) 73: *Haired…*Angry; vexed. **1929** in *Amer. Legion Mo.* (Jan. 1930) 10 [ref. to WWI]: Now don't get excited and all haired up about nothing. **1955** "W. Henry" *Wyatt* 156: Roaring like a haired up silvertip. **1968** Baker, Ladd & Robb *CUSS* 133: *Haired off.* Constantly complaining and irritable. **1989** R. Miller *Profane Men* 174: Getting the 'yards and the green beanies all haired off.

hair fairy *n. Homosex.* an effeminate male homosexual who wears long or carefully styled hair.—used derisively.

1966 *Time* (Jan. 21) 40: "Swish" bars…[cater to] the effeminates and "hair fairies" with their careful coiffures. **1966** H.S. Thompson *Hell's Angels* 82: They're a bunch of mean hair fairies, that's all. **1968** S. Harris *Puritan Jungle* 156: Here are the queens in female clothes and the "hair-fairies" not only in drag but with long, teased hair or wigs. *a***1972** B. Rodgers *Queens' Vernacular* 102: It's amazing what a hair fairy can do with a teaspoonful of dye.

hairhead *n.* a man, esp. a hippie, having long hair.—used derisively.

1971 Drill sgt., U.S. Army (coll. J. Ball): I bet you wish you was back on the hilltop smokin' dope with your fuckin' hairhead buddies. **1987** Pelfrey & Carabatsos *Hamburger Hill* 43 [ref. to Vietnam War]: Some hair-head has her on her back right now and is telling her to fuck for peace. *Ibid.* 182: And a hair-head is taking a leak in the john.

hair-hopper *n.* a woman who frequently changes her hair-style. *Joc.*

1987 J. Waters *Hairspray* (film): She's a hair-hopper, that's what she is!

hair out *v. Surfing.* to become afraid; CHICKEN OUT; lose (one's) composure.

*a***1984** in Safire *Stand Corrected* 202: A display of fear in the face of the ocean would be summed, "he haired out." **1993** *X-Files* (Fox-TV): I haired out.

hair pie *n.* oral (*rarely* genital) copulation upon a woman; the female genitalia as objects of cunnilingus.

*ca***1938** in Maurer *Lang. Und.* 116: Cunnilingus…*hair-pie.* **1941** G. Legman, in Henry *Sex Vars.* II 1168: *Hair-pie, To eat.* To perform cunnilinctus. **1952** in IUFA *Folk Speech:* "Hair pie" (i.e., female genitalia). **1952** H. Grey *Hoods* 88: He goes in for hair pie. **1965** Hersey *Too Far to Walk* 81: You want fi-buck or twenny-buck poontang?….They only got homemade hair pie round here. **1971** *Coming, Dear!* 50: He wants a piece of "hare pie"…where do we keep it? *1990** Thorne *Dict. Contemp. Slang* 229: *Hair pie…*heard in Britain but more widespread in Australia and the USA.

hairpin *n.* **1.** a fellow; person.—often used disparagingly.

1877 *Puck* #3 (March) 6: Say, pa,…wasn't Benedict Arnold a reg'lar snide?…A crooked hairpin, you know; a shark, a sort of a fraud generally? **1879** Wheeler *In Leadville* 11: That's the kind o' hair-pin Deadwood Dick is. **1879** Grant *Tin Gods* 6: That is the species of hair-pins that we are. *Ibid.* 8: That is the kind of a hair-pin that he is! **1882** C. Morris *Shadow Sam* 10: Jist…tell them what kind of a hair-pin he is. **1884** Peck *Boss Book* 40: The American boy…is not that kind of a hair-pin. **1885** *Puck* (May 15) 171: We do not want that kind of hair-pin to represent us. **1885** in Guerin *Mountain Charley* 64: They found to their chagrin that she was not "that kind of a hairpin," as she was pleased to express it. **1889** Barrère & Leland *Dict. Slang* I 442: *Hairpin* (American), a man. This odd expression became popular about 1880.…."That's the kind of *hair-pin* I am." **1931** in Goodstone *Pulps* 86: And the third hairpin is none other than our own Dishpan Charlie! **1934** Cunningham *Triggernometry* 392: And these hairpins would have gunned me right then. **1958** P. Field *Devil's R.* 106: There ain't a sign of gimp in that hairpin. *1965** S.J. Baker *Australian Lang.* (ed. 2) 177 [ref. to WWII]: *Hairpin,* derogatory reference to a male. **1965**

Borowik *Lions* 15: Even a smart hairpin like Morris Bartlett could forget the real truth. **1968** Brasselle *Cannibals* 123: This hairpin was still walking around—with a beautiful wife. **1970** L. Gould *Friends* 160: That's the kind of hairpin He is. **1973** Overgard *Hero* 89: He's the kind of a hairpin that gets deadly sick every time out. **1974** V.B. Miller *Girl in River* 43: Because some hairpin is hassling one of the pros.

2. a woman.

1920 in De Beck *Google* 97: Golly—if he's gonna bring any fancy hair-pins up here I ought to clean myself up a bit. **1927** *AS* (June) 387: A woman is a *hair pin.* **1929** *AS* IV (June) 341: *Hairpin.* A housewife; a woman. **1939** *Chi. Tribune* (Jan. 22) (Graphic Sec.) 9: Hijackers' Argot…*Hairpin*—a woman. **1953** W. Brown *Monkey on My Back* 158: "One more stop. There's a party going on—a hairpin joint." "A what?" "Hairpin joint—bow tie party—lesbians."

3. *Homosex.* an indication that one is homosexual; usu. (quots. at *drop hairpins* s.v. DROP, *v.*) in phr. **drop hairpins** to drop hints that one is homosexual.

1950 Vidal *Thirsty Evil* 166: Since then…we've let our hair down, as the saying goes, and the hairpins flew in all directions when we did. **1965–72** E. Newton *Mother Camp* 33: The process of sending out subtle cues or "feelers" is called "dropping the hairpin." (This phrase is also used when one has made an outright admission of homosexuality.)

hairpin *v. West.* to mount (a horse).

1922 Rollins *Cowboy* 65: He still lived on horseback, but regretfully, humiliatingly refrained from "hair-pinning" or "forking" at sight "anything on four hoofs." **1927** *AS* III 168: To mount a horse is to "hairpin"…him. **1944, 1959** in *DARE.*

hair-pounder *n. Logging.* a teamster who drives horses, oxen, or mules.

1930 *Amer. Mercury* (Oct.) 235: He next became a hairpounder, or teamster. **1930** Irwin *Tramp & Und. Slang: Hair Pounder.*—A teamster or mule driver. **1939** *Chi. Tribune* (Jan. 22) (Graphic Sec.) 9: *Hair pounder*—A teamster. **1942** *AS* (Dec.) 222: *Hair Pounder.* A horse teamster. **1948** J. Stevens *Jim Turner* 239: Pull on your rags, you timber beasts, you hair-pounders. **1958** McCulloch *Woods Words* 79: *Hair pounder*—A teamster, mule skinner, or in the old days, an ox driver.

hair-raiser *n.* something terrifying; (*specif.*) *Publishing.* an adventure story; thriller. Now *colloq.* or *S.E.*

*1897** in *OEDS:* The writer being put on his mettle merely to throw in what an American has felicitously called "hair-raisers" by the way. **1912** in Truman *Dear Bess* 79: Mamma read a hair raiser in *Adventure.* **1913** in *Ibid.* 110: This month's number sure contains some hair raisers. **1918** in Morgan & Michalson *For Our Beloved Country* 295: Have given the Frenchies many hair raisers on first sight. **1931** Reichenbach *Phantom Fame* 225: His first Broadway play was "Confession," a mystery-murder hair-raiser. *1936** Partridge *DSUE* 366: *Hair-raiser.* An exciting adventure story.

hair up *v.* to anger. Cf. HAIRED [up].

1935 Lorimer & Lorimer *Heart Specialist* 141: Don't never pay to hair up a voter. Those folks might…stay home.

hairy or **hairy-ass[ed]** *adj.* **1.a.** Orig. *Stu.* difficult; exacting or demanding. [The forms with *-ass[ed]* are usu. considered vulgar.]

*1848** A.H. Clough, in *OEDS:* He…never once had brushed up his *hairy* Aldrich. *1864** in *F & H* III 248: *Hairy* for difficult is a characteristic epithet. *a***1890–93** *F & H* III: *Hairy, adj.* (Oxford University)…Difficult. **1925** Dos Passos *Manhattan Transfer* 86: Let's see…A—the first of the vowels, the first letter in all written alphabets except the Amharic or Abyssinian, of which it is the thirteenth, and the Runic of which it is the tenth….Darn it that's a hairy one…. **1942** in C.R. Bond & T. Anderson *Flying T. Diary* 82: And when vultures get involved on the runway…things get even more hairy. *1946** in *OEDS:* There you go again using great long hairy words. **1955** R.L. Scott *Look of Eagle* 15: Boy! This one will sure be a hairy go. Point to point and no detours. **1962** *We Seven* 82: But if you happen to be pulling a lot of Gs…it might get a little hairy trying to manipulate the controls with all the finesse you'd like. **1964** Melchior & Higgins *Crusoe on Mars* (film): And here's the hairiest problem of all—isolation, being alone. **1965** Summers *Flunkie* 57: Les Miserables…was too long and has a lot of big hairy words. **1968** Schell *Military Half* 30: In tight situations, we put it in as close as four hundred or six hundred metres, but that's real hairy. That's the real danger zone. **1978** L'Amour *Prov-*

ing Trail 29: If I'd thought that trail was hairy before, I had no doubt of it now.

b. Esp. *Mil. Av.* scary; harrowing; dangerous.

1945 O'Sheel & Cook *Semper Fidelis* 131: I hauled back on the stick and roared up in a big hairy climb. *Ibid.* 135: There were four Corsairs coming down on me in a big hairy run. **1945** Hamann *Air Words: Hairy mission*: A raid in which tough, wild enemy opposition is encountered. **1951** [VMF-323] *Old Ballads* 8: The rail cuts are hairy, for close air [support missions] we pine. **1955** Ruppelt *Report on UFOs* 233: He...repeated some rather hairy stories of what he'd been through. **1956** Lay *Toward Unknown* (film): He flies all the hairiest [missions] himself. **1958** Johnson & Caidin *Thunderbolt* 169: Bill had a hairy time of it. **1959** R.L. Scott *Flying Tiger* 121 [ref. to WWII]: Nobody could blame drab delivery boys for wanting a friendly pat on the back after a hairy hour and a half of being shot at. **1960** MacCuish *Do Not Go Gentle* 185: Corpsman told me ya was in the Gavutu thing. Real hairy, huh? **1967** Halberstam *One Very Hot Day* 14: The war itself was not yet hairy enough to drive them into the arms of a chaplain. **1968** Kirk & Hanle *Surfer's Hndbk.* 140: *Hairy:* describes difficult, dangerous, fast, and big surf. **1969** Huffaker *Hellfighters* (film): What a hairy beast [sc. an oil well fire]! **1969** *N.Y. Times Mag.* (June 4) 119: Sort of eerie here, isn't it? Sometimes it really gets hairy out at these sites, when it's forty below zero and you think there might be someone here and you have to crawl through snow or woods. **1980** W.C. Anderson *Bat-21* 91: At best it was a hairy trip. This time, it had been hairy as an ape. **1984** Univ. Tenn. student: "That was a real *hairy* movie" means it was real scary. **1985** Heywood *Taxi Dancer* 5: It would be a straight-in, hairy-ass, steep, jinking dive from fifteen thousand feet. **1990** Berent *Steel Tiger* 224: "It's a hairy one."...He showed the pilots their target.

c. bad; poor; badly done; severe; very unpleasant or unsatisfactory.

1949 *Time* (Oct. 3) 37: While "frip" has replaced "lousy" in the South, "hairy" seems to be the coming word for it on the West Coast. **1951** [VMF-323] *Old Ballads* 8: Our catapult shots are quite hairy. **1952** Mauldin *In Korea* 145: He lets you know if you're too fast or too slow or if one wing is low, and if he thinks your approach is really bad, or "hairy," as these navy guys say, he waves you off and makes you try again until you're good or "fat." **1964** in *AS* XL (1965) 194: *Hairy*..."poor, mean, contemptible"..."unsatisfactory, displeasing"...; one of us recalls it in this sense from high school in the middle 1950s, but not since. ***1968** in *OEDS*: "Were you ever at one of his parties?"..."It wasn't my style really. In fact is was pretty hairy....Too many jumped-up gentry." **1970** Segal *Love Story* 74: It got a little hairy at the end when we drove him to the bus, however. I mean, the wet-eyes bit. **1972** M. Rodgers *Freaky Friday* 19: I couldn't think of anything more hairy than turning back into myself in front of McGuirk. **1979** Gutcheon *New Girls* 197: Somebody must have a hairy case of blue balls. **1980** *N.Y. Times* (Aug. 10) IV 5: Trips Are Hairier, Inspections Fewer On Commuter Rails. **1982** Corey & Westermark *Fer Shurr* (unp.): *Hairy*...irksome.

d. wild; crazy; (*hence*) unusual; weird.

1961 Terry *Old Liberty* 135: Everybody...played baseball on the green, and...it was a hairy riot. **1962** Mandel *Mainside* 76: I mean, it's all bound to get out, all this, and it was a pretty hairy night. **1964** Hill *One of the Casualties* 19: Not that Clay would listen to any hairy schemes to pull a raid, or anything, but he was a little curious to get a gander at the chicks. **1965** Summers *Flunkie* 107: It was the dumbest, hairyest, fruityest, and most disgustedest thing I ever read. *Ibid.* 108: No one but a bunch of hairy idiots would publish a pile of garbage like that. *Ibid.* 122: Jason said that he quite liked it even though it was "a bit hairy tasting." **1970** Cortina *Slain Warrior* 30: Hairy, huh? See, my grandmother had guilt feelings about my mother and my mother had guilt feelings about me. Kind of like some female penitenté ritual with me as the scourge. **1970** N.Y.U. student: When I saw all that grass [marijuana] going to waste, I went all hairy. **1971** N.Y.U. student: "It's enough to drive you hairy" is one of my all-time favorites. I heard it in Pittsburgh in 1967 or '68. ***1990** T. Thorne *Dict. Contemp. Slang* 229: The place was full of hairy-arsed builders.

2.a. big; large; impressive.—sometimes as a simple intensive.

*1892 Kipling *Barrack-Room Ballads* 127: 'Ave you 'eard o' the Widow at Windsor/With a hairy gold crown on 'er 'ead? **1955** *AS* XXX 117: *Hairy gaggle*...a relatively large number of planes. *a***1960** Federoff *Side of Angels* 155: One big hairy flop. **1978** Druck *Final Mission* 52 [ref. to WWII]: The Squadron is throwing a big, hairy, sloppy

party—and there will be women. **1980** D. Hamill *Stomping Ground* 245: I couldn't give a hairy rat fuck what happens. **1983** Curry *River's in My Blood* 259: It's no big hairy deal.

b. severe; intense.

[*a***1989** P. Dickson *Slang!* 29: *Hairy* Describing racetrack traffic that is thick and fast.] **1989** P. Munro *U.C.L.A. Sl.* 46: *Hairy*...intense. **1995** *Jerry Springer Show* (synd. TV series): We got into a hairy fight and almost broke up.

3. shrewd; clever. [The **1914 quot. is clearly misdefined in *OEDS*.]

*1914 J. Joyce *Dubliners* 60: She doesn't know my name. I was too hairy to tell her that. **1924** Garahan *Stiffs* 175: Then I leapt in with a real hairy idea.

4.a. (usu. of persons) virile and hirsute; (*hence*) hard-bitten; intrepid; tough.—sometimes used sarcastically. [Despite the nominal form, 1949 and 1958 quots. undoubtedly ref. to the adj. The forms with *-ass* or *-assed* are usu. considered vulgar.]

*1914 in *OEDS*: It's top-hole fun, with four hairy captains teaching us things. **1949** Algren *Golden Arm* 96: She...upbraided all the males in sight just for being males...."you godamned hairy-ass...booze bums." **1949** Monteleone *Crim. Slang* 111: *Hairy*...A he man. **1950–53** in *AS* XXXI (1956) 191: A marine who postures toughness is sarcastically labeled a *badass* or a *hairy-assed* marine. **1958** *N.Y. Times Mag.* (Mar. 16) 88: *Hairy*—A chesty or boastful cop. **1958** Talsman *Gaudy Image* 141: This is no place for two hairy-assed men. *****a***1961** Partridge *DSUE* (ed. 5) 1123: *Hairy-arsed*...Mature and hirsute and virile: Naval: since ca1947. A young servicemen's term...for a "type" of rugged masculinity and maturity. **1962** Tregaskis *Viet. Diary* 280: He was "a real hairy adviser" (in the sense of being eager and dynamic). *Ibid.* 286: He'll probably go in, all right. He's hairy enough. **1966** Braly *On Yard* 235: I'm going to...find some hairy-assed old bastard in there with me. **1967** Dibner *Admiral* 21: He knew he needed exercise, that good and clean and somewhat hairy American ritual. **1970–72** in *AS* L (1975) 60: *Hairy*...Extremely masculine. **1993** J. Watson & K. Dockery *Point Man* 76: We were big hairy frogmen and we could do what the Army couldn't.

b. (of a drink) strong.

1966 Braly *Cold* 113: Grove made her a drink. "A hairy one," he told her, "so you can catch up."

5. angry; provoked. Cf. HAIRED, HAIR UP, and phrs. with *wild hair* s.v. HAIR.

*1927 in *OEDS*: He got shirty or hairy. **1966–67** W. Stevens *Gunner* 165: Trueblow...appeared to be hairy for some reason. Deacon didn't particularly care what his problem was, but he asked. **1977** Torres *Q & A* 30: Don't ever make fun of his name. He gets very hairy about that.

6. stylish; (*also*) excellent.

1962 *Britannica Bk. of Yr. 1963* 855: *Hairy*...excellent. **1963** Braly *Shake Him* 123: Where'd you get the hairy fiddle [suit]? *a***1972** B. Rodgers *Queens' Vernacular* 102: *Hairy*...(dated, Ariz. teen sl., late '50s) satisfying, great. **1972** *N.Y. Post* (Nov. 30) 47: Today's youth might say, though, "Hey man what about 'heavy,' 'hairy,' 'funky,' 'fly' for sharp and 'foxy' for pretty, whattyasay man?"

¶ In phrase:

¶ **have a hairy canary** to have a fit of temper. [The ref. in 1946 quot. is to a representation of a literal hairy canary.]

[**1946** *Popeye the Sailor* (animated cartoon): Well, blow me down! A hairy canary!] **1969** in Partridge *DSUE* (ed. 8) 772: My mother would have a hairy canary if...I did that. **1987** *Larry King Live* (CNN-TV): If the Russians put a strategic force in Canada or Mexico we'd have a hairy canary.

hairy buffalo *n.* (see quots.).

1969 *Current Slang I & II* 47: Hairy buffalo, n. A popular drink used to loosen tight females at parties.—Air Force Academy cadets. **1980** Pearl *Pop. Slang* 66: *Hairy buffalo n.* a strong alcoholic beverage made with any combination of liquors mixed together.

hairy eyeball *n.* a glance, usu. of suspicion or hostility, made with partially lowered eyelids.—constr. with *the*.

1963 *N.Y. Times Mag.* (Nov. 24) 52: "He gave me the hairy eyeball" means that somebody was disapproving. **1970** Whitmore *Memphis-Nam-Sweden* 24: They're all giving us the hairy eyeball, but no one is saying a word. **1971** Sonzski *Punch Goes Judy* 75: I was tired of hairy eyeballs from white *and* black militants who thought I was a liberal jerk. **1972** M. Rodgers *Freaky Friday* 12: "What'll it be for you, lover boy?" I asked, crossing my arms and giving him the hairy eyeball. **1967–79** in S. King *Bachman Bks.* 217: They've been giving me the old hairy eyeball for the last hour or so. **1987** *GI Joe* (Sept.) 17: Why is this bozo giving us the hairy eyeball? **1989** *Donahue* (NBC-TV): I'd get…what I call a "hairy eyeball" kind of look.

hairy wolf *n. West.* a violent, dangerous, or formidable fellow. Also **hairy dog.**
  1926 Nason *Chevrons* 154 [ref. to 1918]: "Listen, you birds," began Jake, shaking his immense fist at the prisoners, "I'm a hairy wolf an' the direst descendant of a long line of catamounts! Never forget it!" **1967** "W. Henry" *Butch Cassidy* 109: He was a hairy dog of first reputation in the street-fighting folklore.

halatious var. HELLACIOUS.

half *n.* ¶ In phrase: **and a half** (used as an intensive); a notable example of; and more.
  *1636 in *OED2* s.v. *heart, n.*, 39b. **1832** J.K. Paulding *Westward Ho!* II i 7: Bushfield, too, was here in all his glory, and was not only a whole team, but a team and a half, good measure, as he asserted. **1836** *Davy Crockett's Almanac* (1837) 17: I'm first rate and a half and a lettle past common. **1867, 1897** in *DARE*. **1911, *1917, *1959* in *OED2*. **1989** P. Munro *U.C.L.A. Slang* 15: She's a bitch and a half. **1992** *Garfield & Friends* (CBS-TV): [This story]'s a snooze and a half. **1994** A. Heckerling *Clueless* 65: You are a snob and a half.

half-and-half *n.* **1.** a hermaphroditic or bisexual person. Also as adj.
  1935 *Amer. Mercury* (June) 229: *Half-and-half:* hermaphrodite. **1944** *PADS* (No. 2) 43: *Half-and-half: n.* and *adj.* A hermaphrodite; hermaphroditic. "De say he *half-and-half*."—Negro woman, 50. Charlotte Co., Va.…Generally used by Negroes. **1946** Dadswell *Hey, Sucker* 100: *Half and half,* a side-show performer who claims to be half woman, half man. **1967** in *DARE*: A womanish man…*Half-and-half.* **1970–72** in *AS* L (1975) 60: *Half-and-half n.* Bisexual.

2. *Prost.* oral copulation followed or preceded by vaginal intercourse. Also as adv.
  1937 Reitman *Box-Car Bertha* 178: Nowadays few men want it straight. They want it half and half. **1961** T.I. Rubin *In the Life* 58: "Anyway, I gave it to him half and half and he came around okay." "Half and half?" "You know, first I ate him, then I finished him off in the cash register [vagina]." **1966** Longstreet & Godoff *Wm. Kite* 67: I wanna stand treat in the best cathouse in Paris. Round-the-world, and half-and-half. **1967** Hersey *Algiers Motel* 91: A half-and-half for ten dollars. **1970** Winick & Kinsie *Lively Commerce* 150: Today a "straight" is $10, "half and half" (oral stimulation before coitus) usually costs $15, and a "French" (fellatio) $20. **1972** Carpentier *Flight One* 67: She can give you a "half-and-half" that'll curl your toes—permanently. **1978** E. Thompson *Devil to Pay* 151: Jacqueline…would give you a half-and-half in her dressing room for fifty dollars. **1980** R. Hammer *Don't Answer* (film): I'll give you a good deal on some half and half. **1990** L.B. Rubin *Erotic Wars* 131: So I had half and half. She gave me some oral sex, then we had intercourse. **1992** in Ratner *Crack Pipe* 69: Half-and-half, ten dollars!

half-ass *n.* a blockhead or bungler; (see also 1978 quot.).—usu. considered vulgar.
  1929–33 Farrell *Young Manhood* 398: He's the All-American-Half-Ass. **1948** Cozzens *Guard of Honor* 544: That half-ass would jump all right. **1978** Gann *Hostage* 46 [ref. to *ca*1930]: As my enrollment came during the middle of the year I would henceforth be known as a "half-ass," a caste in cadet society equivalent to a leper. *Ibid.* 47: You are a goddamned plebe and a half-ass at that. **1980** E. Sacks *Small Circle of Friends* (film): I figured out it was better to be an ass than a half-ass.

half-ass[ed] *adj.* **1.** contemptible; ridiculous; unsatisfactory; half-baked; stupid; (*also*) minor, puny, or insignificant.—often used as a generalized term of disparagement.—usu. considered vulgar.
  1863 in T.P. Lowry *Story Soldiers Wouldn't Tell* 47: There goes our half-assed Adjutant. **1917–20** Dreiser *Newspaper Days* 421 [ref. to 1893]: You'll…fuss around trying to make a half-assed living. **1932** *AS* VII (June) 333: *Half-assed*—mediocre; insignificant. **1932** V. Nelson *Prison Days* 25: They don't do a goddam thing for us except let us have

three half-arse meals a day and a cell to sleep in at night. **1934** Binns *Lightship* 284: That half-arsed Allen!…He's pumping *oil* overboard! *Ibid.* 345: If we do pull out of this, don't go saying it was your half-arsed sails that did it. **1934** in J. O'Hara *Selected Letters* 95: The L. of D. is something that a few half assed laymen and publicity-seeking priests put over. **1933–35** D. Lamson *About to Die* 154: Some no-good whining half-ass imitation of a man. **1935** Anderson *Winterset* 5: These…professors! Looking up their half-ass cases! **1939** *New Directions* 136: All these half-ass metaphysicals. **1942** McAtee *Supp. Grant Co. Dial.* 6 [ref. to 1890's]: *Half-assed*, adj., imperfect, unsatisfactory; "That's a — way of doing it." **1950** Hemingway *Across River* 237: "The pointers, a sort of half-assed billiard cue that they used for explanation."…"I don't know, even, what half-assed means." "Shortened, or abbreviated in an inefficient manner." **1954** E. Hunter *Blackboard Jungle* 21: Maybe Small is a good man after all, despite his half-assed jokes. **1957** in J. Steinbeck *Acts of K. Arthur* 359: Nothing is so dangerous as the theories of a half-assed or half-informed scholar. **1958** Frede *Entry E* 44: That's the kinda half-assed consolation I'd expect from you. **1963** Hayden *Wanderer* 146: This is no half-assed yacht. **1963** Fehrenbach *This Kind of War* 193: Some of the men told him they didn't mind fighting a big war.…But they had no interest in fighting a half-ass war like this one. **1966** "T. Pendleton" *Iron Orchard* 39: Them bosses got a lot to do, sendin' me a bunch half-ass kids, an' I'm supposed t'git a day's work done! **1967** J. Kramer *Instant Replay* 77: We are not going to have half-assed performances around here. **1969** Whittemore *Cop!* 88: Plus they got all them half-ass interns up there. They don't know what the hell is happening. **1970** in A. Sexton *Letters* 351: I even think I'm good at it in my kind of inarticulate half-assed manner. **1970** N.Y.C. man: And I see you people coming around taking pictures with your stupid half-assed cameras. **1973** G.C. Scott, in *Penthouse* (May) 62: I don't feel that my being a half-assed public figure gives anyone the right to intrude on me. **1980** McDowell *Our Honor* 6: As I was telling you half-assed clowns, we are your three Drill Instructors. **1984** J. McCorkle *Cheer Leader* 56: "Cute" is really a half-assed thing to say about someone. **1994** *New York* (Dec. 12) 33: Just how odd—and oddly half-assed—the official treatment of this case has been.

2. unenthusiastic; half hearted.—usu. considered vulgar.
  1936 Levin *Old Bunch* 89: They would get used to half-ass acceptance, squirming their way through life, never quite getting what they wanted. **1959** Brosnan *Long Season* 122: Or, he'll take a half-ass swing at a pitch, and you swear you had him fooled. **1962** E. Stephens *Blow Negative* 237: Why the half-ass smile? **1968** in Rowan & MacDonald *Friendship* 74: Am I then a half-assed Liberal, or merely a Centrist trying to be Modern? **1987** Santiago *Undercover* 90: Help me all the way, not this half-ass shit.

half-ass[ed] *adv.* half; halfway; half-heartedly; poorly.—usu. considered vulgar.
  1929–33 Farrell *Young Manhood* 327: If I plan to do something, I don't see any reason to do it half ass. **1947** Schulberg *Harder They Fall* 225: Never do nothin' halfass. **1961** Forbes *Goodbye to Some* 178: I wouldn't do it half-ass, like Frank. **1967** Mailer *Vietnam* 192: Grizzer…works a little half ass at covering the carcass over. **1971** Woodley *Dealer* 116: You can't do nothin throughout life half-ass. **1972** P. Thomas *Savior* 2: I cooled my role, half-ass comforting myself. **1968–77** Herr *Dispatches* 54: The machine [was] running half-assed and depressed. **1978** Selby *Requiem* 165: They looked around half assed but…they knew they couldn't do better. **1984** Riggan *Free Fire* 155: I kind of half-ass asked him. **1985** Bodey *F.N.G.* 206: I sort of half-ass offer it to him. **1985** Flowers *Mojo Blues* 70: Tucept was halfassed amused.

half-ass *v.* to prepare, carry out, etc., in a makeshift or half-hearted manner.—usu. considered vulgar.
  1948 Cozzens *Guard of Honor* 156: I've seen them. They go half-assing along, scaring the be-Jesus out of everyone. Telling you they're as good as they ever were, with so much rank hardly anybody can ground them. **1968** in *DARE*: It will never last—he just…*Half-assed it.* **1985** *Newsweek* (Apr. 15) 46: We knew eventually they were going to break it down.…So we half-assed a gallant last stand.

half-case *n.* [*half* + CASE[3], *n.*] a half dollar.
  1878 Pinkerton *Strikers* 55: The careless fellows will hang about the printing offices, hide about for printers in luck to borrow a "half-case" (a half-dollar) from them, and sun themselves in City Hall Square upon the benches until night.

half century *n.* [*half* + CENTURY] a fifty-dollar currency note. Also **half a century.**

1885 *Puck* (Apr. 29) 138: I didn't buy…an Eclectic [diploma] for a half-century. 1908 *Sat. Eve. Post* (Dec. 5) 17: No, none of these twenties are from the new batch,…but this half-century is one that we're all proud of. [1915 Bronson-Howard *God's Man* 281: Beau and me had beat him out of half-a-century.] 1931–34 in Clemmer *Pris. Community* 332: *Half a century*…a fifty-dollar bill. 1934 Weseen *Dict. Slang* 296: *Half century*—A fifty-dollar bill.

half colonel *n. Mil.* a lieutenant colonel.

1956 Chamales *Never So Few* 591 [ref. to WWII]: "You're late, Major," the half-colonel said. 1983 Beckwith & Knox *Delta Force* 100: "What's the SAS commanded by?" "A half colonel." "Well, we'll use a full colonel."

half-cut *adj.* see s.v. CUT, *adj.*

half-mast *n.* ¶ In phrase: **at half-mast** in a partially lowered position (now used esp. of trousers or the like). *Joc.*

1871 "M. Twain" *Roughing It* 50: He…hangs his tail at half-mast for a week. 1884 Hartranft *Sidesplitter* 71: A nautical friend says that ballet-dancers wear their dresses *at half mast*, as token of respect to departed modesty. 1905 Belasco *Girl of Golden West* 371: Nice company he keeps. One of them Cachuca girls with eye-lashes at half-mast, ha! 1919 Johnson *Heaven, Hell, or Hoboken* 10: You needed suspenders to keep your misfit breeches from falling to half mast. 1938 Epstein & Coffee *Four Daughters* (film): Your tie's at half mast. 1950 in *DARE.* 1966 J. Lewis *Tell It to Marines* 192: If the gooks attacked then, they'd have caught every man in this outfit with his pants at half-mast! 1971 Sonzski *Punch Goes Judy* 95: A girl hobbled by a pair of tights at half mast is like no girl at all. 1988 B.E. Wheeler *Outhouse Humor* 73: With his overalls at half-mast. 1995 *New Yorker* (Oct. 30) 70: Zack was still struggling at half mast [i.e., with a partial erection of the penis].

half-mast *v. Mil.* to lower (trousers or drawers); (*rarely,* of trousers or drawers) to be lowered. Also absol.

1957 Campbell *Cry for Happy* 129: All that hardware around his waist was about to half-mast his britches. 1961 Coon *Meanwhile at the Front* 207: You go there, half-mast, remast and leave. 1963 J. Ross *Dead Are Mine* 272: But particular whores. Their khaki drawers would never half-mast for the likes of a rifle slinger. *a*1982 Berry *Semper Fi* 275 [ref. to 1943]: "Like hell," she said, "I don't half-mast my skivvy drawers for no bellhop!" 1982 Cox & Frazier *Buck* 1: Bend over and halfmast your drawers.

half-nelson *n.* ¶ In phrase: **have a half-nelson on** to have a firm grip on or exclusive control of. *Joc.*

1896 Ade *Artie* 154: This thing got the half-Nelson on me before I know it. 1904 Ade *True Bills* 62: Harold had a Half-Nelson on Gertie and was trying to make it appear that he thought well of her. 1958 McCulloch *Woods Words* 72: *Got a half-Nelson on the payroll*—a man with relatives among the bosses of the company.

half-past-eight *adj.* sneaking; shady.

1984 in Terkel *Good War* 390: He was a kind of half-past-eight guy anyway. I don't know what the hell he was in there for, but he was supposed to be shot. I think he killed another GI.

half pint *n.* a short person; runt; (*joc.*) a child.—usu. used derisively.

1876 J. Miller *First Fam'lies* 182: Here's to the Little Half-a-pint! 1926 Maines & Grant *Wise-Crack Dict.* 9: *Half-pint*—stunted individual. 1928 W.R. Burnett *Little Caesar* 76: The half-pint's a good boy. 1931 Farrell *McGinty* 55: That half-pint p—k ain't no brother of mine. 1939 O'Brien *One-Way Ticket* 8 [ref. to *ca*1925]: That little half-pint's passed out cold under the torpedo tube. 1939 Attaway *Breathe Thunder* 35: It'll go all right if we don't have to be bothered with the half-pint. 1941 H.A. Smith *Low Man* 76: The half pint took a plane for New York. 1959 W. Williams *Ada Dallas* 71: Freddy was a grinning little half-pint who had shot and killed nine men after they had shot at him first. 1963 *Twilight Zone* (CBS-TV): On a horse you're a man. On the ground you're a half-pint. 1974 Radano *Cop Stories* 54: That half-pint son-of-a-bitch.

half-portion *n.* HALF PINT.

1914 T.A. Dorgan, in Zwilling *TAD Lexicon* 42: You—half portion I oughta. 1928 Havlin *Co. A* 87 [ref. to 1918]: He was a youngster of fifteen years, and was referred to as the "Half-Portion Boche." 1942 *ATS* 386: Small person…*half-portion.*

half seas over *adj.* rather drunk; inebriated. Also fig.

*1698–99 "B.E." Dict. Canting Crew: Half Seas over, almost drunk. *1714 in F & H III 251: Our friend the alderman was half-seas over before the bonfire was out. *1785 Grose Vulgar Tongue: Half seas over. Almost drunk. 1807 J.R. Shaw Autobiog. 138: Getting as usual about half seas over. 1821 Waln Hermit in Phila. 27: Half seas over, I fancy. 1823 J.F. Cooper Pioneers 399: Benjamin…was now in that state which by marine imagery is called "half-seas-over." 1833 Mil. & Naval Mag. of U.S. (Dec.) 218: No officer never seed me half-seas-over in my life. 1838 [Haliburton] Clockmaker (Ser. 2) 115: The whole on us were more than half-seas over. 1861 in Heartsill 1491 Days 4: Many of the boys are "Half sea's over." *1986 G. Brach Pirates (film): I'm half seas over with joy.

half-shot *adj.* see s.v. SHOT, *adj.*

half-smart *adj.* stupid; reckless. Also **half-slick.**

1927 in Hammett *Knockover* 322: Don't get the idea he's half-smart. He's dangerous. 1928 O'Connor *B'way Racketeers* viii: The half-smart egg…thinks he is three jumps ahead of Broadway himself. 1950 Riesenberg *Reporter* 47: Ogle gets some half-smart ideas, but he doesn't lie. *Ibid.* 216: Shut up, you half-smart flunky. 1961 Peacock *Valhalla* 108: Half-Slick Willy Woechowski, the marine with the number-ten-can nose. 1963 Braly *Shake Him* 11: He was more than half-slick.

half-step *v.* Esp. *Army.* to move slowly; hang back; do something half heartedly; (*broadly*) to loaf. Hence **half-stepper.**

1942 E. H. Hunt *East of Farewell* 173: Tonight's our last night of half-stepping.…After we've fueled we'll do twenty knots. 1971 Drill instructor, U.S. Army, Ft. Campbell, Ky. (coll. J. Ball): Come on! Assemble those weapons! Quit half-steppin'! 1972 Drill Instructor, U.S. Army Ft. Campbell, Ky. (coll. J. Ball): That goddam plowboy can sure half-step, but he sure as hell can't march. 1973 Staff sgt., U.S. Army Comm. Command—Taiwan (coll. J. Ball): So wake up the motor pool! Give those slopes something to do besides half-step. 1974 Specialist 4, U.S. Army Comm. Command—Taiwan (coll. J. Ball): He's got to be the only guy in the whole Army who'd half step on the way to a beer bust. 1975 S.P. Smith *Amer. Boys* 250 [ref. to 1967]: Me and Sergeant Wallace gettin' things set up so we can half-step all the time once you guys leave. 1979 R. Foster *Concrete Cowboys* (film): You ain't exactly half-steppin' when you're livin' down there. 1967–80 Folb *Runnin' Lines* 42: Don't come half-steppin', come fiendish. 1982 Goff, Sanders & Smith *Bros.* 49 [ref. to 1968]: Don't…start half-stepping; stay alert when you get to the Nam. *Ibid.* 130: When you half-step, it may be your last step. 1983 K. Miller *Lurp Dog* 7: We don't half step, and that's why we're still alive. *a*1984 in Terry *Bloods* 49: Stop half-steppin'. We gotta move. 1985 Bodey *F.N.G.* 131: So don't be fuckin' half-stepping. 1988 *CBS Sunday Morning* (CBS-TV) (Jan. 24): We do not come here to practice half-stepping. 1993 "Big Daddy Kane," in *Source* (July) 36: Ain't No Half Steppin'. *a*1994 in C. Long *Love Awaits* 90: I don't wanna have some half stepper with me.

half-shaved *adj.* see s.v. SHAVED, *adj.*

halfy *n.* **1.** (among beggars) a legless beggar or other person.

1918 L. Livingston *Delcasee* 43: *Halfy*…Train rider who lost both legs below knee. 1930 Irwin *Tramp & Und. Slang: Halfy.*—A beggar with both legs off at the hips; any legless individual. 1953 Gresham *Midway* 104: A lad who had been working as a "halfy" had an argument with another performer who was unwise enough to sneer at him.

2. *pl.* see HALVIES.

halibut *n.* a foolish or offensive person.

1905 Belasco *Girl of Golden West* 329: The darned old halibut!

Halifax *n.* (a euphem., in var. senses, for) HELL.

1807 in *DARE*: The victor…had thrown the worthless thing [*sc.* a U.S. Navy warship] back upon our hands, instead of sending it where he wished it had gone, to Halifax, or to the bottom. 1875 *N & Q* (Ser. 5) IV 66: *Go to Halifax.* This expression is sometimes used in the United States as a mild substitute for a direction to go to a place not to be named to ears polite. 1906 in *DARE*: I'll jist be diddle-de-diddle-de-daggon if I don't wish the dern corn wuz in Halifax and him with it! 1918 E.E. Rose *Cappy Ricks* 93: Oh, go to Halifax! 1948 in *DARE.* 1959 N. Nye *Long Run* 79: I'll blow you to Halifax. 1965–70 in *DARE* [many informants, joc. uses].

Hall *n.* (esp. among tramps) alcohol. Cf. DOCTOR HALL.

1925–26 J. Black *You Can't Win* 209: You probably thought I "smoked him off" because I was full of "Hall" (alcohol) and wanted to cut some crazy caper. 1927 *AS* (June) 389: Drinking has supplied its quota of words to the vag's lexicon. *Alki* and *hall* come from alcohol and explain themselves. Often *John Hall* is used. **1935** Pollock *Und. Speaks:* Hol, alcohol.

hall *n.* ¶ In phrase: **hire a hall!** (said derisively to a person expressing strong unpopular views).

  1877 Dacus *Great Strikes* 415: Her auditors listened good naturedly for fifteen minutes, but…[soon] she was advised to "hire a hall," and the chairman was advised to "fire her out." **1882** Peck *Peck's Sunshine* 115: O, go and hire a hall! **1883** Hay *Bread-Winners* 209: They would listen awhile, and then shout, "Give us a rest!" or "Hire a hall!" or "Wipe off your chin!" **1889** Barrère & Leland *Dict. Slang* I 413: *Go and hire a hall* (American)…It is addressed to a bore who talks a long time, or always on some special subject. **1891** Maitland *Slang Dict.* 141: *Hire a hall* (Amer.), advice offered to a man who talks too long to suit his audience. **1901** *Our Naval Apprentice* (June) 3: When these "chip in" to the war discussions they are told by the "Vets" to "go hire a hall," etc. **1908** in H.C. Fisher *A. Mutt* 131: "Can't you let a fellow sleep?"…"Aw! rent a hall!" **1918** F. Gibbons *Thought We Wouldn't Fight* 134: "Hire a hall!" shouted the gruffy top sergeant. **1922** Paul *Impromptu* 70: Oh, hire a hall, Ma. Where's your patriotism? **1922** Tully *Emmett Lawler* 255: "But it's no use to wake people up—the poor boobs…" "Hire a hall," said Whitey. **1926** Dunning & Abbott *Broadway* 220: Why don't you two hire a hall? **1957** N.Y.C. woman, age *ca*70: Tell her to hire a hall!

hallelujah *n.* (a partial euphem. for) HELL (in var. senses).

  1908 W.G. Davenport *Butte Montana* 28: I can…give them hallelujah.
  1993 in Tomedi *No Bugles* 100: We'd beat the hallelujah out of them.

Hall of Fame *n. Police & Und.* a rogues gallery. *Joc.*

  1902 Hapgood *Thief* 268 [ref. to 1898]: Whenever I square it and go to work I am nailed regularly, because my mug is in the Hall of Fame.

halo *n.* ¶ In phrase: **win a halo** to be killed. *Joc.*

  1970 Lincke *Jenny* 124: A wrong guess, however, and he'll win a halo.

halvies *n.* [var. of *halvers* (see *OED*)] Esp. *Juve.* a half-share.

  1927 *Sat. Eve. Post* (Mar. 5) 167 [ref. to 1918]: Nix. Halvies on what I get. **1936** Kingsley *Dead End* 705: Akey! Akey! Haffies! **1937** Kober *Having Wonderful Time* 135: Wanna go halfies, Chick? **1966** R.E. Alter *Carny Kill* 62: Help me knock off my hubby and I'll inherit the bundle and give you halvies.

halyards *n.pl.* ¶ In phrase: **swig** [or **pull**] **at the halyards** *Naut.* a bracing drink of liquor.

  *1805 J. Davis *Post-Captain* 191: And then we'll take a pull at the halliards together. **1849** H. Melville *White-Jacket* ch. xliii: He pronounces his grog basely *watered*,…*thinner than muslin*; he craves a more vigorous *nip at the cable*, a more sturdy *swig at the halyards*.

ham *n.* **1.a.** a stupid, clumsy, or worthless fellow; oaf; (*often*) an unskilled or untalented athlete, esp. a prizefighter.

  1863 in Wightman *To Ft. Fisher* 97: He [steals] one from some "green hams." **1864** in *Ibid.* 167: The poor hams…were incapable of making those nice discriminations. *Ibid.* 184: Our fellows politely invited the crestfallen "ham" to wait and see our officers give orders. **1888** in Farmer *Amer.*: He is a good fighter but will allow the veriest ham to whip him, if there is any money to be made by it. **1889** Barrère & Leland *Dict. Slang* I 444: *Ham* (American), a loafer. **1896** Ade *Artie* 19: Some o' them was dead tough and the others was hams. **1902** Clapin *Amer.* 220: *Ham*…Sporting slang for a loafer. **1907** *McClure's Mag.* (Feb.) 380: You hams standing around with wrinkles in your bellies sidestepping like a bunch of mules in the road. **1913–15** Van Loan *Taking the Count* 137: Those big hams?…I could lick 'em myself. **1915** *DN* IV 199: *Ham*, slow awkward base ball player. "He was a perfect *ham* running around the diamond." **1918** "Commander" *Clear the Decks!* 131: You poor ham…. What are you good for now? **1917–20** Dreiser *Newspaper Days* 630 [ref. to 1894]: We gotta keep mosta dese hams outa here. **1920** Witwer *Kid Scanlan* 38: All I hope is that he ain't no cheap ham! **1922** *Leatherneck* (Apr. 29) 5: *Ham*—An uncomplimentary epithet. Originally "ham-fatter," a low-grade actor. Possibly a corruption of Hamlet or from "The ham-fat man," a negro song much used by traveling minstrels. **1924** M. Anderson & L. Stallings *What Price Glory?* 68: A shambling bunch of hams that wouldn't salute anything under a general. **1924** Hecht & Bodenheim *Cutie* 14: What…did this big ham do for a living? **1925** in Hemingway *Selected Letters* 150: This Paolino they talk about is just a big ham that can hit. Just a woodchopper. **1927** C. McKay *Home to Harlem* 169: But I ain't gwine to worry 'cause mah buddy was a ham;/Ain't gwine to cut

mah throat 'cause mah gal ain't worf a damn. **1931** *AS* VI (Feb.) 204: *Ham:* one of unpolished manners. **1933** *AS* VIII (Oct.) 35: *Ham.* A poor fighter. **1939–40** Tunis *Kid from Tomkinsville* 161: Who ever told that ham he could hit? **1940** in Truman *Letters Home* 142: Mr. Stark is a ham, whether it is as governor, candidate, or judge. **1962** H. Simmons *On Eggshells* 30: Agh, that ham's just lucky. *a*1994 H. Roth *Mercy of Rude Stream* 49: A *dub*, a ham, he couldn't catch, he couldn't hit, he couldn't run.

b. [cf. earlier HAMFATTER] Orig. *Theat.* an untalented actor or variety performer, esp. one given to overacting.

  1881 *Wash. Post* (Mar. 13) 3: The "variety" player is looked down upon by the legitimate actor and is called a "ham." **1882** in *OEDS:* "Banjo Hams" are held up to scorn.…One writer proudly describes himself as "no ham, but a classical banjo player." **1885** *Puck* (Apr. 8) 90: Mr. Macready Ham, the Popular Actor, is Making Active Preparation for His Spring Tour Through the Country. **1891** Maitland *Slang Dict.* 136: *Hamfatter* (Amer.), or more briefly "ham," a tenth-rate actor or variety performer. **1899** Cullen *Tales* 132: There were twelve sad people on the platform. They were "hams." I can tell a ham two miles away. **1900** Ade *More Fables* 174: She was a Ham, and her Dress didn't fit her, and she lacked Stage Presence. **1906** *Variety* (Mar. 24) 8: The hams that can't make it anywhere think it's a walkover in vaudeville. **1908** in Sampson *Ghost Walks* 433: They…engaged about twenty of these "hams." **1908** *Hampton's Mag.* (Oct.) 456: There live the Up-to-Date Hustler, the Hopeless Ham,…the Man a Soul above Art and the Man with Art above a Soul. **1914** *DN* IV 122: *Ham*, from *hamfatter*. A third-rate actor. "Dramatic Club *Hams* in action." **1915–16** Lait *Beef, Iron & Wine* 235: There's another ham wants to move in here. **1929** *Bookman* (Apr.) 148: The word "ham" is almost exclusively identified with actors. **1931** Hellinger *Moon* 48: You ain't nothin' but a ham dancer and you ain't goin' no place.

c. a person given to self-consciously theatrical, often amusing, behavior; show-off. *Joc.* [Now the prevailing sense.]

  1933 Hecht & Fowler *Great Magoo* 129: *Julie.* There's room enough for you to write a book about yourself. *Weber.* Don't go ham on me. Don't go ham. **1950** A. Lomax *Mr. Jelly Roll* 6: The biggest ham of a teacher I've heard or seen since or before. **1957** in Marx *Groucho Letters* 122: I must say that I'm a bigger ham than I thought. **1967** J. Kramer *Instant Replay* 88: We always seem to play well for a large audience. We're big hams. **1974** Old Rhinebeck, N.Y., air show announcer: He's a real ham, ladies and gentlemen. He's a ham on rye. **1975** Lichtenstein *Long Way* 59: She was the most outrageous ham on the [tennis] circuit. **1994** N.Y.C. woman, age *ca*40: What a ham!

2. *Theat.* absurd overacting or verbal exaggeration; (*also*) a tendency toward this; a desire to play to an audience; (*broadly*) nonsense.

  1930 Bodenheim *Roller Skates* 192: She…picked up this ham slinger somewhere, just to serve as her escort. **1940** S. Lewis *Bethel Merriday* 283: You said my acting technique was all ham. **1941** H.A. Smith *Low Man* 65: Sally cries out in a voice redolent of ham, I'll sue! **1942** Pegler *Spelvin* 183: "Against the pale radiance of the moon the beautiful oval of her face—" Nope. Ham! **1942** in E. O'Neill *Letters* 526: It's the ham variety I detest—the phony and obviously pumped up, the putting on an act, exhibitionism which has nothing behind it but wind and a stupid vanity. **1943** R. Chandler *High Window* 441: Don't feed me the ham. I've been in pictures. I'm a connoisseur of ham. *ca*1942–50 in Getz *Wild Blue Yonder* I C-8: And we don't give a damn,/About the groundling's point of view,/And all that sort of ham. ***1959** in *OEDS:* What he says might apply equally well to ham acting. In fact, it sounds suspiciously like ham. **1981** Brenner & Nagler *Only the Ring* 79: TV brought out the ham in Ali. **1988** Frazier & Offen *W. Frazier* 156: In a sense, we were entertainers too. We had ham in us.

3. [perh. infl. by *am*ateur] *Communications.* a novice telegrapher; (*hence*) an operator of an amateur shortwave radio station; (*broadly*) an amateur (at any activity). Often attrib. Now *S.E.*

  1919 Darling *Jargon Book* 16: *Ham*—A student telegraph operator. **1922** in *OEDS:* In popular parlance one who has qualified and taken this "Radio Operator Amateur—First Grade" certificate is dubbed a "ham." **1929** *AS* (Oct.) 45: In the early days of radio, *ham* was a term of reproach. **1930** *Railroad Man's Mag.* II 470: *Ham*—A telegraph operator. Usually referred to one of a poorer variety. ***1936** in *OEDS:* Of course, the "hams" use the short wavelengths. **1960** Bonham *Burma*

Rifles 25: All ham outfits have been ordered shut down. **1967** Morris & Morris *Dict. Wd. & Phr. Orig.* II 126: As a one-time FCC-licensed radio telegrapher, I'm well aware that most radio hams today are not unskilled. **1973** Michelson *Very Simple Game* 6: I am even today a ham horticulturist. I love gardening. **1979** in Raban *Old Glory* 106: That's where he keeps all his equipment. Bob's a real big ham. **1981** Hofstadter & Dennett *Mind's I* 76: A radio ham listening to another ham broadcasting in Morse code. **1982** T.C. Mason *Battleship* 36: They bragged about the ham rigs they had built. **1989** Leib *Fire Dream* 401: You got through to a ham in the States who had a phone link.

4. the penis; in phr. **slam the ham** (of a man or boy) to masturbate. Cf. HAMBONE, n., 5. *Joc.*

1958 *Dangerous Dan McGrew* 1: With a sixteen inch ham for his job. **1971** *Nat. Lampoon* (Dec.) 37: Now, every time I'm by myself in my room, I can't seem to think about anything but slamming my ham. You know, pulling my pud. **1974** N.Y.C. social worker, age 26: *Slamming your ham* means jerking off. I heard that in the '60s. **1976** *Nat. Lampoon* (Aug.) 39: Some hot [photos]…you can slam the ham to.

5. [sugg. by BAM] *USMC.* (see quot.).—usu. considered vulgar. *Joc.*

1980 Manchester *Darkness* 179 [ref. to WWII]: They [female Marines] called the men "HAMs," for "hairy-assed Marines."

¶ In phrases:

¶ **ham and** an order of ham and eggs.

1884 in *AS* XX 71: "Beef and" and "ham and" were frequently heard, and the orders were filled with beef and beans and ham and eggs. **1905** in "O. Henry" *Works* 43: Acres of "ham and." **1908** in H.C. Fisher *A. Mutt* 61: Gans would still be dealing "ham and" off the elbow. **1909** M'Govern *Krag Is Laid Away* 137: The ham portion of "ham and." **1917** Oemler *Slippy McGee* 127: I dream…about the…ham-and and the jane that slings it. **1917–20** Dreiser *Newspaper Days* 631: I partook of "ham and" and coffee. **1920** Edwards *Doniphan to Verdun* 30: The British have a weakness for tea and jam where the American calls for coffee and "ham and." **1927** F. Thrasher *The Gang* 298: Cookie's passion for "ham and" was traditional. **1928** Callahan *Man's Grim Justice* 37: The Baltimore Dairy Lunch or some other "ham-and" joint. **1930** Buranelli *Maggie* 30: The chef…could not have put together a decent dish of "ham and." **1946** Veiller *Killers* (film): One ham and, one bacon and.

¶ **ham and motherfuckers** [or **mothers**] see s.v. MOTHERFUCKER.

ham *v.* **1.** *Und.* to go on foot; walk.

1914 Jackson & Hellyer *Vocab.* 42: *Ham*, Verb. General usage. To walk. Example: "If we get a tumble, it's a case a ham." **1929** Milburn *Hobo's Hornbook* 87: Down the track came a hobo, hamming,/And he said, "Boys, I'm not turning." *Ibid.* 150: We got ditched in Myno Junction, so we started to ham. *Ibid.* 285: *Ham*, to walk across country. From the traditional ham actor whose company gets stranded on the road, and who is forced to walk back to the city. **1935–62** in Ragen & Finston *Toughest Pris.* 802: *Ham*—To walk.

2. Orig. *Theat.* to overact; show off.—usu. in phr. **ham it up.** Also trans.

1930 *Scouting* (Jan.) 17: What you hamming about then? ***1933** in *OEDS*: Hamming. **1937** *Printers' Ink* (Apr.) 54: *Ham* it—overacts for emphasis—bluster. **1942** *ATS* 586: *Ham, ham it*…to act amateurishly or ineffectively. **1950** *New Yorker* (May 27) 19: The official was hamming up his signals for the benefit of the television audience. ***1955** A. Huxley, in *OEDS*: She dearly loved to ham it up. **1980** Kotzwinkle *Jack* 216: He hammed it up, got a few laughs. **1981** Patchett et al. *Great Muppet Caper* (film): You're overacting! You're hamming it up! **1991** Rudnick *I Hate Hamlet* 26: Hamming. Mugging. Over the top. **1994** N.Y.C. man, age *ca*45: OK, OK, quit hamming it up. **1994** *Space Ghost* (TV Cartoon Network): Was I hamming it up a little too much?

ham-and-egg *adj.* [perh. an elaboration of HAM, *n.*, 1] Orig. *Boxing.* unskillful; untalented. Also **ham-and-bean.**

1916 T.A. Dorgan, in Zwilling *TAD Lexicon* 42: Bat Nelson was a ham and egg fighter until he licked Eddie Hanlon. **1927** in Paxton *Sport* 122: Bill Brennan, a fighter of the ham-and-bean variety, who already had been knocked out by Dempsey while the latter was a mere pugilistic climber. **1939** C.R. Cooper *Scarlet* 88: Car hops,…dance contestants, ham-and-egg entertainers.

ham-and-egger *n.* **1.** Orig. *Boxing.* an amateur or semiprofessional boxer, esp. of mediocre skills; (*broadly*) an oaf; PALOOKA.

1919 Wilkins *Co. Fund* 10: Geweh! you hamandegger. **1920** Hicks *Three-Eleven* 11: "Marty," our Ham and egger from Pennsylvania. **1921** *Variety* (Feb. 25) 23: He told me…he was doin' my ham-and-egger a favor by not postponin' the fight. **1929** in Gelman *Photoplay* 127: He has made clinky the pockets of all sorts of ham-and-eggers who…[opened] schools of…elocution even though they themselves talked of "erl" wells and "moiders." **1931** Adamic *Laughing* 58: Joe…let him fight at the Club every other week, and before long Steve became known in the Williamsburg Bridge neighborhood as a pretty fair "ham-an'-egger." **1932** *AS* VII (June) 333: *Ham & egger*—a person who is below par; a "second rater." **1933** in R.E. Howard *Iron Man* 69: In the Barbary…the toughest ham-and-eggers of the West Coast display their wares. **1946–51** J. Jones *From Here to Eternity* ch. ii: The beans a ham and egger has to eat while he is trying to work up to the big time. **1960** (quot. at NUTCRACKER). **1978** Alibrandi *Killshot* 2: You kicked ass out of that limp-wristed ham-'n'-egger. **1985** *Newsweek* (Dec. 23) 60: Rocky was a club fighter of 30 at the time, a "ham-and-egger" by his own…estimate. **1988** Sayles *Eight Men Out* (film): There's that series [scheme] those ham-and-eggers pitched. **1993** *Beavis & Butt-Head* (MTV): You ham-and-eggers!

2. a short-order restaurant.

1970 E. Thompson *Garden of Sand* 345: On the corner in front of a brightly lit, steamy ham-and-egger, a cop…chatted with a…whore.

hambo *n.* **1.** HAM, 1.b.

1926 *Variety* (Dec. 29) 7: A "milkman" was a real hambo, who stole more bows than the applause warranted at the finish of his act. **1943** *New Yorker* (Apr. 17) 19: If I din know, some other flesh-peddler would grab him in a minute. I would wipe my hands fomm this hambo.

2. HAM, 1.c.

1980 Manchester *Darkness* 152: We scorned conscientious objectors and other hambos.

hambone *n.* **1.a.** HAM, 1.b.

*1893 in *OEDS*: Hambones! I told you so. I could vardy that when I heard them joggering. ***1905** in *OEDS*: Ham bones means them as pays to act, which they can't do, and so saves the manager engaging deserving actors. **1948** Mencken *Amer. Lang.* Supp. II 690: In the *Stage* (London), June 1, 1944, Edgar T. Hayes said that *hambone* meant an amateur [performer]. **1949** *Collier's* (Aug. 27) 26: A pampered hambone living in Hollywood. **1990** *Nat. Lampoon* (Apr.) 37: Could spell death for the Oscar-hustling hambone.

b. HAM, 2.

*1936 in Mencken *Amer. Lang.* Supp. II 690: I suppose [ham] is an abbreviation of what used to be called *hambone*. **1962** Serling *New Stories* 51: But heroics or hambone….in matters of the gun, [they] were as efficient as they were dedicated. **1963** *JAF* LXXVI 273: The breadth of vision which encompasses hambone to bluegrass in a potential unity. **1984** *Daily Beacon* (Univ. Tenn.) (July 31) 3: But my ham bone had already started to itch, so I took a drama course at New York University one summer. **1985** C. Busch *Vampire Lesbians* 54: Magda Legerdemain is a great artist….Madeleine Astarté: pure hambone.

c. HAM, 1.c.

1952 in *DAS*: Every hambone from the deep sticks was constrained to make a speech for the…cameras. **1955** *TV Guide* (Jan. 7) 18: They're real hambones, just like me. **1960** Keaton & Samuels *Slapstick* 13: Because I was also a born hambone, I ignored any bumps…I may have got at first on hearing audiences gasp. **1970** *Current Slang* V (Winter) 8: *Ham bone*, n. A sarcastic person; a "wise guy."—College students…Minnesota. **1972** in *Playboy* (Feb. 1973) 185: Tittle's the big hambone with the Gynts then, they all start calling Richie Y.A. Tittle. **1989** *48 Hours* (CBS-TV): What a bunch of hambones!

2. *pl.* knees; MARROWBONES.

1908 in J. London *Letters* 275: I have to get down on my hambones and beg forgiveness.

3. *Jazz.* a trombone. *Joc.*

1934 Weseen *Dict. Slang* 167: *Hambone*—A trombone.

4. *Naut.* a sextant.

*1938 in *OEDS*: What altitude have you got on that hambone, Stringer? **1961** Burgess *Dict. Sailing* 108: *Hambone.* A sextant. **1976** Hayden *Voyage* 410: Red Ruhl came up with his hambone and…started to shoot the sun.

5. *Black E.* the penis. Cf. HAM, *n.*, 4. *Joc.*
  1927 in *DARE:* Womens in Alabama/Going to let my hambone spoil. *ca***1945** "Muddy Waters," in A. Lomax *Where Blues Began* 85: These little women.../Gonna let my...hambone spoil. **1977** Dillard *Lexicon* 33: Other Black terms for the penis include...*Hambone.*

hambone *v.* **1.** to live as an itinerant performer.
  1921 *Variety* (Nov. 11) 4: Tomato would be hambonin' around the rest of his natural life knockin' over these local guys and never get his name in a New York newspaper.
2. to trick; swindle.
  *a***1961** Longman *Power of Black* 195: Or letting some lease hound hambone you into signing away your mineral rights.
3. to show off; HAM, *v.*, 2.
  1981 McKee & Chisenhall *Beale* 7: Soon all three were jiving, clapping hands, hamboning, scatting—making music out of nothing. **1984** WKGN radio (May 25): It's old-timers hamboning on Royal Street.

hamburger *n.* **1.** lacerated or mangled flesh or remains; (*hence*) cannon fodder; in phr. **Hamburger Hill** (see 1969 quots.). Rarely as *v.*
  [**1901** Ade *Mod. Fables* 285: After the kid had been carried out of the [Prize] Ring looking like a Hamburger Steak.] [**1928** R. Bradford *Ol' Man Adam* 125: I'm gonter make hamburgers outer yo' measly army.] **1943** Perrin & Mahoney *Whistling in Brooklyn* (film): This thing's gonna make hamburger out of us. **1945** R.J. Casey *Where I Came In* 176: Are they good troops or just hamburger? **1949** Shane & Cooper *City Across the River* (film): Drag him away from here before we turn him into hamburger. **1968** Kirk & Hanle *Surfer's Hndbk.* 140: *Hamburger:* a crash on rocks or pier. **1969** *Time* (May 30) 27: On military maps it is listed as Hill 937. Last week it acquired another name: Hamburger Hill...for the battle took the lives of 84 G.I.s and wounded 480 more. **1969** *Newsweek* (June 2) 42: Ap Bia...was a battle that chewed up so many men that the U.S. troops engaged came to call Ap Bia "Hamburger Hill."...The fight for Hamburger Hill began on May 10. **1972** Carr *Bad* 147: He'd beat you back into hamburger. **1973** Yount *Trapper's Last Shot* 19: You lucky you ain't hamburger. **1973** Roth *Sand in Wind* 424: All we found were parts of the radio...some hamburger. That was it. **1980** S. Fuller *Big Red* 348: The taking of the hill had chewed up so many of them that it was named Hamburger Hill. **1983** La Barge & Hold *Sweetwater Gunslinger* 233: Get your head out of your butt, or you'll be hamburgered [by a jet intake]. **1994** J. Shay *Achilles* 8: Even battles like Dak To and Ap Bia Mountain (Hamburger Hill) were American victories in the sense that Americans held the ground when the last shot was fired.
2. a stupid, offensive, or worthless individual.
  [**1947** *ATS* (Supp.) 15: Cook...*hamburger.*] **1949** in *AS* XXV (1950) 304: Dog racing circles...call a bad dog...a *hamburger.* **1950** *West. Folk.* IX 158: *Hamburger*...An ignorant, foolish, or uninitiated person. **1951** R.L. Richards *Air Cadet* (film): The Major thinks I've inherited a couple of hamburgers this time. **1959** Maier *College Terms* 1: *Hamburger*—This is a bad guy. **1961** Brosnan *Pennant Race* 8: One loudmouth cried, "Go write a book, you hamburger!" **1972** *Nat. Lampoon* (July) 80: I'll bet you're one of those hamburgers who strides into the boudoir with nothing on but a hard. **1972** W.C. Anderson *Hurricane* 37: I even like Babbitt Clark and those other screwy hamburgers I fly with. **1987** Robbins *Ravens* 264: "Hamburger" was the vogue word...to denote a swaggering, boastful John Wayne type. **1993** J. Watson & K. Dockery *Point Man* 53: Why don't you hamburgers try and set some sort of record for your class.

hamburgerhead *n.* MEATHEAD.
  1954 Bissell *High Water* 116: What a grand and glorious country of opportunity for hamburgerheads we got...here.

hamburger heaven *n.* [perh. sugg. by *Hamburger Heaven*, a chain of N.Y.C. restaurants] a diner or small eating place that serves mainly hamburgers.
  1944 Ruskin et al. *Andy Hardy's Blonde Trouble* (film): Joe's Place. It's a hamburger heaven with rug-cutting on the side. **1957** Myrer *Big War* 120: Some character...knocked over a hamburger heaven in town. **1954–60** *DAS.*

ham-chewer *n.* an amateur. *Joc.*
  1972 Grogan *Ringolevio* 275: More ham chewers trouped up to the mike and kept saying how wonderful it was with all that energy in one place at the same time.

hame *n.* *Black E.* a usu. unpleasant job. Also as *v.*
  1941 in Ellington *Music Is My Mistress* 179: Hame...job. **1955** in R.S. Gold *Jazz Talk* 119: *Hame:* job outside the music business. **1960** C. Cooper *Scene* 59: A haim is a job, but junkies don't bother with 'em. **1961** *N.Y. Times Mag.* (June 25) 39: *Hame*—Any unpleasant job, from mowing the lawn to playing trumpet in a Mickey Mouse band. **1967** Gonzales *Paid My Dues* 88: He knew he had to cop him a haym (job). **1972** Claerbaut *Black Jargon* 67: *Hame*...a job. **1974** in B. Jackson *Swim Like Me* 91: I know you got these things by hamin',/I'm willing to bet you got three, four jobs and spend your weekends lamin'. **1994** Smitherman *Black Talk* 130: Haim A Job.

hamfat *n.* **1.** a black person or persons.—used contemptuously.
  1903 in Porter & Dunn *Miami Riot* 5: Clean out the town [Miami, Fla.] of the hamfat, as the loafing, gambling negroes are called.
2. an amateur; HAMFATTER. Also **hamfat man.** Also attrib.
  1904–11 Phillips *Susan Lenox* I 251: His vanity had got savage wounds from the hoots and the "Oh, bite it off, hamfat," which had greeted his impressive lecture on the magic lantern pictures. **1918** in "M. Brand" *Coll. Stories of Max Brand* 30: But of all the tin-horn sports, the ham-fat, small-time actors, you're the prize bonehead. **1930** in *Comments on Ety.* (Jan. 1989) 11: [Andrew Jackson Leavitt's minstrel song "The Hamfat Man"] was taken up by the lowliest troupes until, as a term for all third-rate actors, "hamfat man," later abbreviated to "ham," entered the dictionary. **1938** in R.S. Gold *Jazz Talk:* The Harlem Hamfats grind out the tune. **1946** Mezzrow & Wolfe *Really the Blues* 51: A lot of beat-up old ham-fats who played and sang a commercial excuse for the real thing. *Ibid.* 306: *Hamfat:* ham performer, a nobody. **1967–69** Foster & Stoddard *Pops* 2: Uncle Wyatt was what we called a hamfat violin player—he wasn't so good and he wasn't so bad. **1973** Buerkle & Barker *Bourbon St. Black* 220: That's where this term "ham-fat" musician came from. It referred to some guys who, instead of takin' lessons, just picked up their instruments and started playin'.
3. *Black E.* (a euphem. for) HELL.
  1956 Childress *Like One of Family* 171: What the hamfat is the matter with you? Ain't you mad?

hamfatter *n.* an inept performer; HAM, 1.b.
  1879 *Nat. Police Gaz.* (May 31) 13: I don't pass ham-fatters nor beats in the "perfesh" or out of it. **1879** Sala *America Revisited* I 66: Every American who does not wish to be thought "small potatoes" or a "ham-fatter" or a "corner loafer," is carefully "barbed" and fixed up in a hair-dressing saloon every day. **1883** *Life* (Mar. 8) 118: The American actors are a lot of hamfatters, that's what they are. **1887** in *DAE:* The third-rate actor is called a hamfatter. **1889** *Century Dict.: Hamfatter*...a term of contempt for an actor of a low grade, as a negro minstrel. Said to be derived from an old-style negro song called "The Ham-Fat Man." **1891** *Nation* (Oct. 1) 262: The slang theatrical word *hamfatter* is fairly familiar to the readers of the New York journals. It is a contemptuous designation for actors of the grade of negro minstrels. **1902** Clapin *Amer.* 220: *Hamfatter.* In the fashionable quarters of New York City, and more especially in that part known as the "Tenderloin," a recent name applied to a second-rate dude or masher, or a low variety actor. **1928** Callahan *Man's Grim Justice* 25: Dese mugs...ain't grifters,...dey're eighteen-carat-ham-fattters, finks.

hamhead *n.* MEATHEAD.
  1925 in Nason *3 Lights* 135 [ref. to 1918]: Hey, ham-head. **1954** in J. Blake *Joint* 59: New Year's Day two hamheads picked me up.

Hamilton *n.* [fr. the portrait of Alexander *Hamilton* on the note] a ten-dollar currency note; ten dollars.
  1948 Manone & Vandervoort *Trumpet* 92: I stashed away those five Hamiltons. **1949** R. Smith *Big Wheel* (film): I have a Hamilton here. **1960** Bluestone *Cully* 99: Powers got two Hamiltons. All I got is Lincolns. **1967** Colebrook *Lassitude* 132: Ten Hamiltons a *week*, why with King I'd be bringing in a yard and a half a night. **1986** R. Campbell *In La-La Land* 1: Having counted ten Hamiltons...Lacy was about to do as requested. **1990** *New Yorker* (Sept. 10) 56: I wanna see *Hamiltons.* **1992** N. Cohn *Heart of World* 67: Joe...peeled off five Hamiltons.

hammer *n.* **1.** Now esp. *Black E.* the penis; in phr. **how's your hammer hanging?** (used as a coarsely joc. greeting, usu. between men).
  *1698–1707 in D'Urfey *Pills* IV 195: Her Husband she said, could scarce raise up his Hammer....Good Lad, with your Hammer, come hither tomorrow. **a1850* in R. Palmer *Brit. Ballads* 236: The musical

hammer of Darby O'Golicker. **1937** in Oliver *Blues Tradition* 213: I know how to hold my hammer and I drive it in. **1943** J. Mitchell *McSorley's* 201: Hello, Pop…how's your hammer hanging? ***1945** S.J. Baker *Austral. Lang.* 162: *Hammer.* The penis. **1949** (cited in Partridge *Concise Slang Dict.* 207). **1951** Kerouac *Cody* 109: They call their cocks "hammers," cunt's a "gash" and do the up-your-ass fingersign slapping finger down into palm. **1962** Killens *Heard Thunder* 292: Boy, I have gotten so much pussy in my day,…when I do die, they gon say, I died with my hammer in my hand. **1968** Myrer *Eagle* 545: How'd *you* like to have your scrotum slung up ahead of your hammer? **1969** Maitland *Only War* 189: How's your hammer hanging, Mellow? **1970** W.C. Woods *Killing Zone* 126: You can bet your sorry wilted hammer on that. **1974** N.Y.C. man, age 23: One guy says, "How's your hammer hanging?" Then you say, "Lower than a snake's belly." **1974** in J.L. Gwaltney *Drylongso* 160: A cow can take ten times as much hammer as any bull can throw. **1977** J. Olsen *Fire Five* 248: Hey, Chief….how's your hammer hanging? **1979** Hiler *Monkey Mt.* 331: All right, gunnie, how's your hammer hangin'? **1989** H. Bennett, in C. Major *Calling Wind* 519: How your hammer hanging, boy?

2. [sugg. by KNOCK, *v.*] unjust or carping criticism or a tendency toward this.
1898 Kountz *Baxter's Letters* 20: She could build the best battleship Dewey ever saw with her little hammer. **1908** McGaffey *Show Girl* 145: They would lay for the chance to get in a hammer. **1915** H.L. Wilson *Ruggles* 299: Is that any reason they should get out their hammers? Ain't she earned some right to a good time? **1926–35** Watters & Hopkins *Burlesque* 40: He's been goin' on [stage] stewed regular, and there's plenty o' hammers out for him. **1974** G.V. Higgins *Cogan's Trade* 80: I'm not putting the hammer on Mike….He's just expensive, is all.

3. a thug; gangster.
***1931** (cited in Partridge *DSUE*). **1981** R.B. Parker *Savage Place* 109: Rafferty…says he saw Sam Felton make a payoff to a hammer named Franco. *Ibid.* 110: That hammer…tried to kidnap you.

4. Esp. *Black E.* a sexually attractive woman; (*also*, in recent use) a sexually attractive man.
1968–70 *Current Slang* III & IV 64: *Hammer, n.* A girl.—Junior high school males, Negro, Iowa. **1970** *Current Slang* V (Fall) 8: *Hammer, n.* A pretty girl. **1970** D. Long *Nia* 12: Gang war gang war/zip guns and base ball bats/rap to the wrong hammer/and that's your ass. **1974** Beacham & Garrett *Intro 5* 66: Baxter's tried…to get "out of the way" with some of the young hammers when he thought no one would find out. **1975** S.P. Smith *Amer. Boys* 48: The hammer he got hung on was cool too…and she didn't come on with any phony shit. **1978** W. Brown *Tragic Magic* 123: Yeah, well, whatever I got I'm taking it out of here and seeing if any of these fine hammers wants any of it. **1988** "M.C. Hammer" (name of rap performer). **1994** Smitherman *Black Talk* 130: *Hammer* A good-looking woman; emerging as a term for a good-looking man also.

5. Esp. *Auto.* an accelerator.—constr. with *the*. Also fig.
[**1942** *ATS* 55: Act of running; rapid pace….*the hammer*.] **1974** D. & K. Price, in Bibb et al. *CB Bible* 73: Put the hammer down tight. **1975** *Nat. Lampoon* (Apr.) 26: He had the hammer down on Interstate 70 when the voice of God came over his C.B. **1975–76** Dills *CB* 13: *Back off the hammer*—slow down. **1975** *Atlantic* (May) 42: Let's put the hammer down on this thing. **1976** Whelton *CB Baby* 21: Those 18-wheelers can really shake you up, especially when you got the hammer down hard. **1976** Lieberman & Rhodes *CB* 127: *Drop the Hammer* ([or] *Put the Hammer Down*)—1. Accelerate to top speed. 2. Put the gas pedal to the floor. 3. Run at full speed. **1976** Adcock *Not Truckers Only* 42: I'm puttin' the hammer down to get the hell out of range. **1986** *ALF* (NBC-TV): I got the hammer down and I'm headin' for Andromeda. **1987** G. Hall *Top Gun* 48: He has the hammer down, "going for knots."

6. HAMMER MAN. Cf. *OED*, 1.b.
1989 *21 Jump St.* (Fox-TV): He's the hammer in the Zone.

¶ In phrases:

¶ **drop the hammer on** to take decisive action against; "lower the boom on."
[**1929–32** in *AS* (Dec. 1934) 290: *Throw one's hammer.* To show one's authority; said of a professor.] **1978** Diehl *Sharky's Machine* 100: So we go over, drop the hammer on about twenty of 'em, and poor old Mabel turns up in the lineup. **1985** Baker *Cops* 188: You shouldn't frat-

ernize too much with your subordinates, because sooner or later it's going to make it harder to drop the hammer on them.

¶ **put the hammer on, 1.** to take decisive action against; put an end to; stop.
1942 Freeman & Gilbert *Larceny, Inc.* (film): They put the hammer on his parole. **1970–71** Higgins *Eddie Coyle* 86: Somebody…put the hammer on him and he's looking to get back. **1978** Truscott *Dress Gray* 242: Maybe that would…put the hammer on his little operation.

2. to ask or demand money of.
1965–71 (quot. at HAMMER, *v.*, 1).

3. to criticize in a carping manner; claim unjustly to find fault with.
1984 *N.Y. Post* (Aug. 11) 37: Guys like to put the hammer on him [the pitcher of an opposing baseball team].

hammer *v.* **1.** (among beggars) (see quot.).
1965–71 in *Qly. Jour. Studies on Alcohol* XXXII (1971) 733: *Hammer.* To solicit money for drinks, to panhandle. Also *put the hammer on.*

2. to copulate vigorously with (a woman).—usu. considered vulgar.
1977 Bredes *Hard Feelings* 248: I should've hammered her right then, *that's* what's obvious.

3. to drink (usu. beer) rapidly.
1987 U. Chi. student, age 21 (coll. J. Sheidlower): Just lemme hammer this, and I'll come in a minute. **1989** Munro *U.C.L.A. Slang* 46: Paul hammered three beers as soon as he got home from school.

4. to punish.
*a***1989** R. Herman, Jr. *Warbirds* 7: Why do we get hammered for what we do on our own time?

hammer and saw *n.* [rhyming slang for *officer of the law*] a policeman.
1929 in Hammett *Knockover* 56: I cut for the [R.R.] yards. Down there I ran into a whole flock of hammer and saws and had to go overboard in China Basin, swimming up to a pier, being ranked again by a watchman there.

hammer back *v. Auto.* (see quot.).
1976 Lieberman & Rhodes *CB* 130: *Hammer Back*—Slow down.

hammered *adj.* [cf. HAMMERISH] drunk; highly intoxicated.
1954–60 *DAS*: *Hammered*….Drunk. *Not common.* **1961** H. Ellison *Memos* 86: There was pot circulating, and a few bottles, and everyone was just about hammered enough to forget where they were. **1965** in H. Ellison *Sex Misspelled* 348: They wrestled around the other side of the booth, each too hammered to do the other any harm. **1968** Baker, Ladd & Robb *CUSS* 133: *Hammered* Drunk. **1972** Nilsen *Slang at UNI* 3: *Hammered*: Drunk or on drugs. **1978** Hasford *Short-Timers* 49: Rafter Man was hammered, but so was I, so I couldn't stop him. **1984** Hindle *Dragon Fall* 70: Instead of pursuing females or getting hammered at somebody's party. **1989** C.T. Westcott *Half a Klick* 108: He's hammered, probably sleeping it off somewhere. **1991** Hasburgh *NYPD Mounted* (film): Some yokel must have got hammered.

hammerhead *n.* a blockhead; a stupid and stubborn individual; dolt.—now used esp. of horses and mules.
[***1581** in *OED2*: Your owne foolish lying wordes properly forged in that hammerhead of yours.] ***1628** in *OED2*: The Hammer-heads sate lately vpon like consultation. **1916** *Chi. Defender* (Sept. 30) 4: They sure are a bunch of hammer-heads. **1926** Nason *Three Lights* 137 [ref. to 1918]: Hey hammerhead! Hear any bubbles? **1937** Weidman *Wholesale* 166: The best way is for one of the three to be a hammerhead. **1938** Haines *Tension* 233: Clayton ain't a bad old hammerhead for a chief engineer. **1952** Steinbeck *E. of Eden* 307: The old hammerhead was free to drag his nose if he wished. **1958** Lindsay & Crouse *Tall Story* 30: There are other ways a hammerhead can break training. **1971** Curtis *Banjo* 11: From the barn, he could hear his father trying to gentle the hammerheads with sweet-talk nonsense. **1986** Columbia, S.C., woman, age 30: I said, "Where have you *been*, hammerhead?" **1986** Stroud *Close Pursuit* 133: Hey, hammerhead. Clean your face off.

hammerheaded *adj.* stupid; stupid and stubborn.—now used esp. of horses and mules.
***1552** in *OED*: Hammer headed knave. ***1600** in *OED*: Hammer-headed…clowns. **1854** in Dorson *Long Bow* 85: A hammer-headed, strong-sinewed chestnut. ***1855** C. Dickens, in *OED*: You hammer-

headed woman. **1954** in *DARE*: *Hammer-headed*, hard-headed. **1979** Decker *Holdouts* 182: You mean-natured, stump-sucking, hammer-headed, ram-nosed, ewe-necked, goat-withered, pigeon-toed, one-gutted, cat-hammed, cow-hocked, rat-tailed, ill-mannered sonofabitch. **1986** *Plus* (Sept.) 14: I love my husband, but he's as hardheaded as a mule....An ornery, balky, hammer-headed mule!

hammerish *adj.* drunk.
 1737 *Penna. Gaz.* (Jan. 6) 1: The Drinker's Dictionary... Hammerish.

hammer lane *n.* CB. the left or leftmost traffic lane on a highway. Cf. GRANNY LANE.
 1977–78 Dills *CB Slanguage* (ed. 4) 50: *Hammer Lane*: left lane; passing lane. **1986** (quot. at GRANNY LANE). **1993** *Newsweek* (Dec. 20) 10: We [*sc.* truckers] resent the four-wheeler, which is not on a schedule, clogging the passing or "hammer" lane.

hammer man *n.* Esp. *Black E.* a man who exercises authority over others. [In *1821 quot., a vigorously punching pugilist, a sense not found in the U.S.]
 [*1821 *Real Life in London* I 394: Tom [was] appointed to take up the prime hammer-man.] **1929–32** in *AS* (Dec. 1934) 288: *Hammerman*. Generally: anyone with more authority than the speaker. **1970** Major *Afro-Amer. Slang* 63: *Hammer-man*. An authoritarian figure. **1973** Andrews & Owens *Black Lang.* 112: *Hammer Man*—A person with authority over you.

hammers *adj.* *Und.* (see quot.).
 1807 Tufts *Autobiog.* 293 [ref. to 1794]: *I'm hammers to ye*...I know what you mean.

hammy *adj.* being or characteristic of a HAM, *n.*, 1; exaggerated in manner.
 1899 Cullen *Tales* 24: I remembered how "Rory O'More" went, all right, but I was the hammiest thing that ever happened when it came to doing it with a bow. **1929** T. Wolfe *Look Homeward* 367: With fat hammy sonority he welcomed them. **1939** *New Republic* (Jan. 11) 281: The acting is consistently hammy. **1941** *Time* (Sept. 1) 26: [Spencer Tracy's acting is] hammy when he chuckles fiendish "Heh, heh, hehs" at his lecherous face in the mirror. **1942** *AS* XVII (Apr.) 123: *Hammy*. Characteristic of a ham actor. **1944** C.B. Davis *Leo McGuire* 223: I thought it was a pretty hammy show. **1957** E. Lacy *Room to Swing* 133: Like somebody in a hammy play. **1959** in Cox *Delinquent, Hipster, Square* 74: MINISTER:...The world is not a playground for sex, Richard....RICHARD: Pretty hammy.

hamola *n.* [HAM, *n.* + -OLA] *Theat.* HAM, 1.b.
 1941 G.R. Lee *G-String* 279: What a couple of hamolas! What corn, right off the cob!

ham-rester *n.* an idler.
 1896 Ade *Artie* 77: His office hours is from 11:00 to 11:30 and he ain't nothin' but a ham-rester when he *is* there.

Hancock *n.* JOHN HANCOCK.
 1925 *Sat. Eve. Post* (Jan. 3) 14: Nothing goes into the picture without your Hancock.

Hancock *v.* *Journ.* to affix one's signature to.
 1928 in Paxton *Sport* 126: Sure, it's all right....Want me to Hancock it now?

hancty var. HINCTY.

hand *n.* [all these senses except for *shake hands with* and *throw hands* have their origin in card playing, esp. poker]
 ¶ In phrases:
 ¶ **fill (one's) hand** *West.* **1.** to draw a gun. [The 1889 quot. is literal.]
 [**1889** in *OEDS*: *To fill your hand*, to improve it by the draw.] **1929** "M. Brand" *Last Showdown* 87: You've done your shooting from in front and given your man a chance to fill his hand. *a*1944 R. Adams *West. Words*: *Fill your hand*. To draw a gun. **1959** W. Burroughs *Naked Lunch* 3: He...says, "Fill your hand, stranger" and hauls out an old rusty six shooter. **1982** *News-Sentinel* (Knoxville, Tenn.) (June 28) C-11: I've had enough o' you, mister....Fill your hand!
 2. to obtain cash.
 1893 in F. Remington *Sel. Letters* 156: I will see that you get the $100 as soon as I "fill my hand."
 ¶ **play a cold hand** to engage in unprofitable activity.

1887 Badger *Rustler Detective* 5: He's playing a cold hand for the Falcon Ranch.

¶ **play a cool hand** to act calmly and cunningly.
 1904–11 Phillips *Susan Lenox* II 162: You'll have Freddie eating out of your hand, if you play a cool hand.

¶ **play a lone hand** to act independently of others' aid or approval. [Used allusively in 1885 quot. The S.E. sense is attested fr. 1799; see *OED2* s.v. *lone, adj.*, 1.b.]
 1885 Harbaugh *Denver* 14: Woe to ther [*sic*] galoots who interfere with my lone hand. **1893** Hampton *Maj. in Washington* 160: As I am the only member of that Committee I'll play a lone hand. **1902** Hobart *Up to You* 31: I thought you were playing a lone hand? **1903** A.H. Lewis *Boss* 183: They were elected as "Fusion" candidates, an' they think that entitles 'em to play a lone hand. **1931** Grant *Gangdom's Doom* 115: He's not a dick. He's more like a crook. Works at night, and plays a lone hand. **1931** Lake *Earp* 45: Wyatt Earp's venture as a buffalo-hunter undoubtedly gave first rise to legends which picture him as invariably playing a lone hand. **1931** "M. Brand" *Ambush* 13: He may play a lone hand, and he may work with a gang. **1935** C.J. Daly *Murder* 255: The Flame's got to play a lone hand tonight, Race. **1940** Clemmer *Pris. Community* 118: He is the man who is almost always playing a "lone-hand." **1940** Meehan & Tugend *Seven Sinners* (film): That little lady's playin' a lone hand in these islands. **1986** *Miami Vice* (NBC-TV): I don't have time to play a lone hand.

¶ **shake hands with** to take up and use.
 1893 Frye *Field & Staff* 177: He hadn't shooken hands wid a piece o' soap for more'n a mont'. **1979** in R. Carson *Waterfront* 66: Shake hands with the goddamn preventer chain, will ya?

¶ **throw hands** to throw punches; to engage in a fistfight.
 1973 R. Roth *Sand in Wind* 463: You been drinking, man? Looks like you wanna throw some hands. **1978** Hasford *Short-Timers* 92: You and I are going to throw some hands. **1989** *CBS Summer Playhouse* (CBS-TV): All I can do, I can throw some hands.

hand *v.* **1.** to inflict (a kick or blow) upon; (*hence*) to impart to.
 *a*1881 G.C. Harding *Misc. Writings* 136: I...handed him a kick under the ear. **1907** in Fountain *Sportswriter* 86: When the umpire hands us one that puts us on the blink. **1914** E.R. Burroughs *Mucker* 53: The mucker had not hesitated to "hand them one." **1919** *Variety* (Mar. 28) 34: Gee, that handed me a laugh. **1941** D'Usseau & Collins *Lady Scarface* (film): We sure handed them a thrill.

2. to tell, esp. with intent to deceive or impose upon. Now *S.E.*
 1897 Ade *Pink Marsh* 130: 'At's sutny 'e hottes' thing you handed me yet. **1901** in *DA*: I told him he ought to give it to somebody else, and he handed me a lot of stuff about my experience. **1906** *Nat. Police Gaz.* (Aug. 11) 6: D'you fellers mean to hand it to me that you didn't know that this is a phony? **1907** in "O. Henry" *Works* 1610: I handed it to you on the level. **1908** *New Broadway* (July) 30: "Of course I know it," I handed him back. **1936** Twist *We About to Die* (film): The next guy that hands me a hard-luck story is gonna get a kick in the pants. **1970** N.Y.U. student: Don't hand me that bullshit. **1994** N.Y.C. man, age *ca*45: Don't hand me that crap.

¶ In phrase:
¶ **hand it to, 1.** to give deserved credit to. Now *S.E.*
 1902 in Blackbeard & Williams *Smithsonian Comics* 23: Well, you've got to hand it to me. I'm there wid Bills money. *ca*1906 in *OEDS*: You must hand it to the Jap. **1907** in H.C. Fisher *A. Mutt* 7: You have to hand it to A. Mutt for being a game lad. **1914** S. Lewis *Mr. Wrenn* 43: That's where you got to hand it to these street-corner shouters. **1913–15** Van Loan *Taking the Count* 172: I've got to hand it to you! It worked like a charm. **1916** *Variety* (Dec. 1) 2: You've Got to Hand It to the Golden West. **1920–21** Witwer *Leather Pushers* 21: I gotta hand it to Lefty Murray. **1935** D.H. Clarke *Regards to Broadway* 4: "You got to hand it to the Kid," Joe Green said. **1950** A. Lomax *Mr. Jelly Roll* 188: I'll have to hand it to him. That guy was prolific.

2. to inflict ridicule or punishment on; (*also*) to conquer; vanquish.
 1907 in Fountain *Sportswriter* 86: When the umpire hands us one that puts us on the blink. **1908** McGaffey *Show Girl* 84: Maybe those artful kidders didn't hand it to me. **1911** A.H. Lewis *Apaches of N.Y.* 23: "What was that shooting?" "Oh, a couple of geeks started to hand it to each other." *Ibid.* 100: He tells everybody he's goin' to hand it to

me—goin' to cook me on sight, see? **1923** in Eckstorm & Smyth *Minstrelsy of Maine* 150: He can hand it to Jack Dempsey in the ring. **1929–33** Farrell *Young Manhood* 424: He didn't hand it to the sheiks much, did he? **1943** Chandler *High Window* 465: I hand it to her. I'd like to hand it to her with an elephant gun, but my polite breeding restrains me.

handbook *n. Gamb.* **1.** a small bookmaker who takes bets esp. on horse races. In full, **handbook man.**
   1894 in *DA:* These "handbook" men. **1956** "T. Betts" *Across the Board* 135: Handbooks could be characters, too. **1954–60** *DAS: Handbook…*The owner or an employee of…[an illicit] betting business. **1972** Wambaugh *Blue Knight* 68: I thought that if this lifelong handbook…started crying, I'd flip.
   2. (see 1942 quot.).
   1914 in *DA:* I've known 'em to go as low as four a week for protecting a hand-book. **1942** *ATS* 692: *Handbook*…a place where bets are placed away from the track. **1946** in *DA:* The mob was…operating handbooks with full knowledge of your police department. **1949** in *DAS:* I was in a handbook near Loomis and Madison.

hand cannon *n.* a pistol; CANNON, 1.a. Also **hand artillery.**
   1929 L. Thomas *Woodfill* 58: So wild did it make that hombre that he ran amuck, pumpin' right and left with his hand artillery. **1934** Lomax *Amer. Ballads & Folk Songs* 89: Went on home an' I went to bed,/Put my hand cannon right under my head.

handcar *n.* ¶ In phrase: **ride the handcar** (of a man or boy) to masturbate.
   1967 Taggart *Reunion of 108th* 139 [ref. to 1941]: Course maybe he don't at all, maybe he jes' rides the old handcar.

handcuff *n.* an engagement ring. *Joc.* Cf. BALL AND CHAIN.
   [**1903** Hobart *Out for Coin* 20: If you only had nerve enough to lure that girl of yours away to a minister and have him rivet the handcuffs on!] **1926** Finerty *Criminalese* 30: *Handcuff*—Engagement ring. **1934** Weseen *Dict. Slang* 346: *Handcuff*—An engagement ring. **1936** Mencken *Amer. Lang.* (ed. 4) 560: The idea of calling an engagement-ring a *handcuff* did not occur to the young gentlemen of Harvard by mass inspiration; it occurred to a certain definite one of them…and he gave it to the rest and to his country.

handcuff volunteer *n. Mil.* a draftee. *Joc.*
   1944 Kendall *Service Slang* 7: *Hand cuff volunteer*….selective service draftee. **1980** McAleer & Dickson *Unit Pride* 37: This was to be a handcuff volunteer outfit. **1981** Sledge *Old Breed* 171 [ref. to 1944]: The drafted Marines took a good bit of kidding about being "handcuffed volunteers" from those of us who had enlisted into the Marine Corps.

handfuck *v.* (see quot.).—usu. considered vulgar.
   *a***1989** C.S. Crawford *Four Deuces* 48 [ref. to Korean War]: To find the break they wrap their hands around the telephone line…and let it run between their fists. That's what they call "hand-fucking" the line….They were out hand-fuckin' a line lookin' for a break in it.

handful *n.* **1.** *Pris.* a five-year prison sentence.
   1930 in *OEDS:* A five-year sentence is a "handful." **1932** *Writer's Digest* (Aug.) 46: The five-year servers have a "handful." **1942** *N.Y. Times Mag.* (Jan. 25) 30: *Handful*—five-year stretch. **1959** Behan *Borstal Boy* 151 [ref. to *ca*1940]: Laggin's and 'andfuls. "E'd give you five year like five bleedin' minutes, 'e would. *Ibid.* 345: *Handful.* Five years. ***1966** in *OEDS:* Going up for a handful (receiving a sentence of five years' imprisonment).
   2. five (of anything).
   1967 *AS* XLII 63: *Handful*…(before 1946) Five [of an order at a soda fountain].
   ¶ In phrase:
   ¶ **grab a handful of** Orig. *Hobo.* to steal or secure a ride on (usu. a freight train).
   1918 *DN* V 29: *To grab a handfull of rods*, vb. phr. To beat one's way on the freightbeams. **1927** *DN* V 448: *Grab a handful of cars*, n. To catch a freight. **1927** *AS* (June) 389: A *handful of box-cars*, nailing 'em on the fly and hitting the grit are common expressions. **1989** *Married with Children* (Fox-TV): I can go down to the bus station, grab me a handful of Greyhound, and get the hell out of Dodge.

hand gallop *n.* an act of masturbation. *Joc.*
   1970–71 G.V. Higgins *Friends of E. Coyle* 38: In Lewisburg he used to tell me he was saving it up, no hand-gallops for him, because when he got home he was going to have to account for every ounce he owned.

hand grenade *n.* **1.** *Army.* a meatball or hamburger. *Joc.*
   1919 Allen *33st Field Arty.* 349: We heartily enjoyed the first supper of macaroni and hand grenades, little thinking what was in store for us in that line. **1941** Kendall *Army & Navy Sl.* 7: *Hand grenades*….hamburgers. **1982** F. Hailey *Soldier Talk* 30: *Hand Grenade.* A hamburger sandwich on a round bun.
   2. *R.R.* a hand-fired locomotive.
   1937 *AS* (Apr.) 154: *Hand grenade.* Hand-fired locomotive. **1945** Hubbard *R.R. Ave.* 346: *Hand Grenade*—Engine without automatic stoker, which is hand-fired.

hand jig *n.* Esp. *Pris.* HAND JOB, 1. Also as v.
   1931–34 in Clemmer *Pris. Community* 332: *Hand jig*, v.i. To masturbate. **1935–62** in Ragen & Finston *Toughest Pris.* 802: *Hand jig*—self-abuse. **1962–68** in B. Jackson *In the Life* 421: They just give hand-jigs or they'll give blowjobs….They'll…give each other hand-jigs.

hand jive *n.* [fr. jazz sense, 'hand movements made in time to music'] HAND JOB, 1. Also as v.
   *a***1972** B. Rodgers *Queens' Vernacular* 116: *Hand jive*, male masturbation. **1973** *Oui* (June) 104: The kings are getting a little hand jive action. **1974** U.C.L.A. student: *Doing the hand jive* means jacking off. **1978** W. Brown *Tragic Magic* 112: With all that funky hand-jivin' between your legs you lucky your brains ain't scrambled more than they are.

hand-jive *v.* **1.** to slap one's hands together rhythmically, esp. in time to jazz music.
   1958 in *OED2:* There was no room for dancing but here and there couples were hand-jiving. **1975** Sepe & Telano *Cop Team* 56: The motions police call "hand jiving." This is a simple, sweeping slap of hands…universally practiced by sellers and buyers of narcotics on public streets. **1989** *Mystery Sci. Theater* (Comedy Central TV): I was *born* to hand-jive.
   2. see S.V. HAND JIVE, *n.*

hand job *n.* **1.** an act of masturbation, usu. by one person on another who is a male.—usu. considered vulgar.
   1937 Di Donato *Christ in Concrete* 107: Then…go into the cellar and do the hand-job!!! **1948** J.H. Burns *Lucifer* 377: Betsy Wagner's…gonna gimme a handjob before the evenin gets much older. **1962–63** in Giallombardo *Soc. of Women* 204: *Hand Job.* Digital stimulation of the genitals. **1963** T.I. Rubin *Sweet Daddy* 11: Through my pants—gives me a hand job. **1968** P. Roth *Portnoy* 20: If only I could cut down to one hand-job a day. **1968** Spooner *War in General* 103: Highway handjobs. What's this ol' Army comin' to? **1974** Terkel *Working* 585: So here was a guy gettin' a hand job. **1979** Gutcheon *New Girls* 293: Not what you'd call an affair, really, just the odd handjob. **1980** Kotzwinkle *Jack* 170: They gave everybody a handjob. **1992** G. Wolff *Day at the Beach* 107: The would-be loverboy…composed himself with the lexicon of…"huge huggers" and "hand jobs." *a***1993** in Ratner *Crack Pipe* 52: Finally, 30 percent of these men masturbated other men ("hand jobs").
   2. an act of insincere assuaging or assuring; flattery; blandishment.
   1972 J. Mills *Report* 122: Whoever the big shot is gets a hand job about how the department turned things upside down looking for his daughter. **1973** Flaherty *Fogarty* 232: Don't fall for that honky hand job….You'll become an indentured servant. **1984** Caunitz *Police Plaza* 190: Malone thought, you're giving me a handjob, Anderson.
   3. an obnoxious or hateful person; JERKOFF, 2.
   1986 Stinson & Carabatsos *Heartbreak* 88: What handjob had put on the wrong [shirt]? **1995** *N.Y. Press* (Sept. 27) 1: Handjob strolling up Broadway, cellphone to his biscuit.

hand-job *v.* to masturbate (another person, esp. a male).
   1969 Girodias *New Olympia Reader* 64: Juveniles swagger and brag Molly hand-jobbed twenty of them. *a***1981** in S. King *Bachman* 613: I can't fuck you over the telephone. I can't even hand-job you. **1985** *Nat. Lampoon* (Sept.) 42: I've…handjobbed two collaborators.

handkerchief head *n.* **1.** [see 1969 quot.] *Black E.* a black person, esp. if old or poorly educated, who is subservient to whites.
   1942 Z.N. Hurston, in *Amer. Mercury* (July) 95: *Handkerchief-head*—sycophant type of Negro; also an Uncle Tom. **1950** A. Lomax *Mr. Jelly Roll* 233: This corny old handkerchief-head would assert the Count Basie did not know piano. **1954** Killens *Youngblood* 202: Sure, I

know, we got Uncle Toms and handkerchief-heads among us. **1955** Mankiewicz *Trial* (film): You're a handkerchief-head! You're an Uncle Tom! **1959** Murtagh & Harris *Who Live in Shadow* 53: "Dig," I says. "I ain't no handkerchief-head square." **1961** H. Ellison *Gentleman Junkie* 250: He often damned himself for not being a "handkerchief-head," illiterate and content to let the white boss run his life. **1966** *Amer. Jour. Soc.* LXXII 142: There seems to be a tendency among lower-ranking Negro enlisted men…to view Negro NCO's as "Uncle Toms" or "handkerchief heads." **1967** Gonzales *Paid My Dues* 78: Why not cut out all the old-time "handkerchief head waitresses" and recruit all young college "foxes." **1969** Hannerz *Soulside* 35: The tied headcloth imputed to a "handkerchief head" is similarly symbolic of the lowly black servant woman's status in the Old South. **1971** S. Stevens *Way Uptown* 286: They looked just like any two handkerchief heads. **1985** *Newsweek* (Aug. 26) 11: Her 1939 role as that "silly, stupid handkerchief head" Prissy in David O. Selznick's "Gone With the Wind." **1994** N. McCall *Wanna Holler* 293: Although the [*Atlanta Journal-Constitution*] had its share of handkerchief-heads, many of the blacks were cool and down to earth.

2. a man who wears a turban.

  1970 S.J. Perelman, in *New Yorker* (Oct. 17) 40: I can never tell those handkerchief heads apart.

handle *n.* **1.a.** the penis. *Joc.*

  ***1710** in [J. Roberts] *Merry-Thought* I 26: And for want of his Handle,/[She] Made use of a Candle. ***1731** in [J. Roberts] *Merry-Thought* III 8: My dear, like a Candle,/Lights every one's Handle. **1969** M.F. Beale, in *New Amer. Rev.* #7 (Aug.) 194: Everyone joked about this one being another girl, but Darrell's father…said, "No, by God, this one's going to have a handle on 'im." **1976** Braly *False Starts* 300: "Come on, that's just a handle to turn you over with." "I've got your handle/Dangling low/And when you want it/Let me know."

b. the nose.

  1750/1 in Breslaw *Tuesday Club* 271: Furnished with very large handles to their faces….The orator Complimented his nose in particular. ***1811** *Lexicon Balatron.*: *The cove flashes a rare handle to his physog*; the fellow has a large nose. **1863** in *Jour. Ill. State Hist. Soc.* LVI (1963) 324: With a head the shape of a cocoanut, [and] a "handle" to his face large enough for the tongue of a bob-sled.

c. *pl.* the breasts.

  1980 Lorenz *Guys Like Us* 128: She wasn't bad, good legs, nice handles.

2.a. a personal name.

  1837 Neal *Charcoal Sks.* 116: They were satisfied that a sonorous handle [here a given name] to one's patronymic acts like a balloon to its owner, and that an…everyday cognomen…is a mere dipsey, and must keep a man at the bottom. **1849** Melville *Redburn* ch. vi 26: "What's your name, Pillgarlic?" "Redburn," said I. "A pretty handle to a man, that….haven't you got any other?" **1861** E.S. Ellis *N. Todd* 24: "What's your handle?" asked the trapper. **1877** Wheeler *Deadwood Dick, Prince of the Road* 79: "Is there a man among you, gentlemen, who bears the name of Hugh Vansevere?"…"That is my handle, pilgrim," said a tall, rough-looking customer. **1878** [P.S. Warne] *Hard Crowd* 6: Oh, almost any handle'll fit—Tom, Dick, or Jerry. **1879** Wheeler *In Leadville* 11: My handle is Calamity Jane. **1881** Ingraham *Buffalo Bill from Boyhood* 98: "I am named William Frederick Cody." "You has handle enough." **1885** Harbaugh *Denver Duke* 6: The handle doesn't suit yer. **1895** in J. London *Tramp Diary* 62: Charley wuz his handle? **1907** in "O. Henry" *Works* 1608: "Ruby Delamere." "That's a swell handle….Mine's McManus." **1908** *Hampton's Mag.* (Sept.) 293: Name's like the place; any old handle will do. **1923** Grey *Wanderer* 10: My handle's Merryvale. **1956** N. Algren *Wild Side* 61: The name is Kitty Twist—…not my real handle of course. **1960** Leckie *Marines* 8: "Jerry," I said, figuring the natives use only one handle and there wasn't any sense in loading her up with names. **1968** I. Reed *Yellow Back Radio* 41: What handle you go by Chief?

b. a title of rank, respect, or profession.

  1855 Brougham *Chips* 386: The…hepithet of *Reverend*….The owner of the title by the simple reason of having that 'ere handle…distinctly taxes us for our reverence. ***1855** in *F & H* III 258: She…entertained us with stories of colonial governors and their ladies, mentioning no persons but those who had *handles* to their names, as the phrase is. ***1857** "Ducange Anglicus" *Vulgar Tongue*: *Handle*, n. Title. Oh, you want a handle to your name. **1870** Duval *Big-Foot* 241: Such handles to my name would not be agreeable. **1886**

Pinkerton *Dyke Darrel* 16: "I seldom go out, Mr. Ruggles, or Professor Darlington Ruggles, I suppose." "Never mind the handle, madam." **1893** Hill *20 Yrs. at Sea* 102: He didn't have a handle to his name then. We were both in the forecastle. **1923** Riesenberg *Under Sail* 98 [ref. to 1897]: In many ships, captain and mates never fail to use their "handles" in addressing each other, and this was so on the *Fuller*; in fact there was…little familiarity aft, in the personal relations of our officers. **1929** T. Gordon *Born to Be* 109: "Well—ain't the white people up there got any handles to their names?"…"Sure. Henry, John, Edith."…"Naw, naw! I mean Miss and Mister." **1941** Roberts & Sanford *Honky-Tonk* (film): "Good evening, Reverend." "That ain't my handle." **1948** McHenry & Myers *Home Is Sailor* 165: They…pull out cards full of M.A.'s and Ph.D.'s and all sorts of other fancy handles. *a***1956** Almirall *College to Cow Country* 143 [ref. to *a*1918]: "Dad says it's O.K., Mr. Almirall."…"Handles on names…don't go. I'll be 'Al' to…all hands." *ca***1979** in J.L. Gwaltney *Drylongso* 145: You had to call these little prissy white boys master this and master that and give them long, fancy handles to their rotten names.

c. a sobriquet; nickname.

  1882 in Botkin *Folk-Say* 93: If I do say it, the handle [Billy the Kid] has fitted me right well. **1958** Talsman *Gaudy Image* 19: But Titania didn't know his name, not even his handle. ***1964** in *OEDS*: One was Toothless Annie….She had come by her "handle" when a hysterical grass-eater had kicked her teeth in.

d. *CB.* a usu. imaginative nickname used by the operator of a CB radio for identification during transmissions.

  1974 D. & K. Price, in Bibb et al. *CB Bible* 73: All my buddies got a handle. **1975** Dills *CB Slanguage* 39: *Handle*: code name CBer uses in transmission; e.g. "The Stripper"; "Jungle Jim"; [etc.]. **1975** *Atlantic* (May) 41: What's your handle, buddy, and where you comin from? **1976** Whelton *CB Baby* 17: My handle. My CB name. You got to have a handle if you want to talk on CB. **1976** Lieberman & Rhodes *CB* 130: *Handle*—Name or pseudonym used in identifying a particular CBer. **1994** Knoxville, Tenn., man, age *ca*50: Part of the fun of owning a CB is picking out a handle.

3. *pl.* muttonchop sidewhiskers.

  1914 Jackson & Hellyer *Vocab.* 42: *Handles*, Noun….Side-whiskers; "mutton chops."

4. *Gamb.* the total amount of money changing hands between players and the house in a gambling enterprise. Now *S.E.*

  1942 *ATS* 691: *Handle*, the amount of money paid into pari-mutuel or other betting pools. **1957** (cited in T.L. Clark *Dict. Gambling* 96). **1961** Scarne *Comp. Guide to Gamb.* 1: Note that this $500 billion is not the gambling industry income; it is the annual gambling *handle*. This means all the money handled; it is the total amount wagered. **1973** Haney *Jock* 177: *Handle*: Total money wagered on a race or an entire card.

5. a firm grip, as on a fielded ball; (*also*) a way of managing or understanding.—usu. in negative constrs.; in phr. **get a handle!** calm down! get ahold of yourself! Now *colloq.*

  1961 Ellison *Memos* 92: He was the weakest, most vulnerable kid I'd ever seen. He couldn't get a handle on life. **1970** N.Y. Yankees vs. Boston Red Sox (WPIX-TV): But he can't find the handle! He drops the ball! **1982** T. Considine *Lang. of Sport* 18: Plenty of time to throw out the runner, but the fielder couldn't find the handle. ***1986** in Partridge *Concise Slang Dict.* 208: The police have a handle on the mob problem. **1993** G. Lee *Honor & Duty* 191: Get a handle, man!

6. *pl.* LOVE HANDLES.

  1984 *Good Morning America* (ABC-TV) (June 12): That's good for the sides, if you got those handles on the sides. **1989** Munro *U.C.L.A. Slang* 46: *Handles* bulges of extra fat around the waist. **1993** *Mystery Sci. Theater* (Comedy Central TV): I think she touched my handles.

¶ In phrases:

¶ **fly off the handle** to become very excited; lose self-control; (now *esp.*) to become furiously angry; in phr. **off the handle** excited; out of control.

  1825 in *DA*: How they pulled foot, when they seed us commin', most off the handle, some o' the tribe, I guess. **1833** S. Smith *Pres. Tour* 58: Aunt Keziah was in such a pucker to have everything nice, I didn't know but she would fly off the handle. **1833** in [S. Smith] *Letters of Downing* 147: The doctors would think he was jest ready to fly off the handle. **1844** *Spirit of Times* (Mar. 16) 53: "I wouldn't fite a duel with narry man that ever lived!" "Oh,…don't fly off'n the handle that way." **1844** in *F & H* III 42: You never see such a crotchitical old critter as he is. He flies right off the handle for nothing. **1862** in J.R. Lowell *Works* 236: For growed-up folks like us 'twould be a scandle/When we git sarsed, to fly right off the handle. **1868** Macy *There She Blows!* 31: Well, now, don't be flyin' off de handle, altogedder. **1868** "W.J. Hamilton" *Maid of Mt.* 20: Darn it, man, yew fly off the handle tew easy, I think. **1870** Duval *Big-Foot* 171: As we grow older, we learn a thing or two, look some before we leap, and don't "fly off the handle" quite so easily. **1871** Schele de Vere *Americanisms* 195: If a fair lady…breaks the tender promise, she is said to *fly off the* handle, and the disappointment is as serious to the unlucky lover as a lost axe to many a settler. **1874** Pinkerton *Expressman* 45: Den Massa 'Roney…fly right off de handle. **1877** *Puck* (Aug. 8) 6: You're off your handle. Get away from here or I'll have you locked up. **1888** in *F & H* III 42: "I can't say that I am stuck on Sue Fitzpercy," remarked Amy. "She is liable to fly off the handle." **1901** *Chi. Tribune* (Aug. 25) 8: I don't like the way the lady flies off the handle about my company—and that after I am through with my work! **1909** Warner *Lifer* 65: I simply inquired what he meant, instead of flying off the handle, and denying having been connected with any hold-up. **1912** Lowrie *Prison* 282: I thought he'd fly off the handle, but he didn't. **1934** in Fenner *Throttle* 55: He's not likely to fly off the handle just because he gets snapped at. **1935** J. O'Hara *Butterfield 8* 266: Oh, now don't fly off the handle this way over a simple little telephone message. **1940** DeLeon *Tugboat Annie Sails Again* (film): I should not fly off the handle like this. I must learn to curb my temper. **1958** A. Drury *Advise & Consent* 12: "Fly off the handle!" the old voice roared. "Fly off the handle! Who's flying off the handle, Bob? Who's flying off the handle?" **1988** Shoemaker & Nagler *Shoemaker* 41: Don't fly off the handle. Let's see if we can straighten this thing out. **1988** M. Bartlett *Trooper Down!* 20: He'd be short-tempered, flying off the handle at the least little thing. **1995** *World News Tonight* (ABC-TV): Some Democrats flew off the handle.

¶ **go** [or **slip**] **off the handle, 1.** to die.
   1843 Haliburton *Attaché* (Ser. 1) ch. xxviii: If Old Cran. was to slip off the handle, I think I should make up to [his daughter]. **1843** "J. Slick" *High Life in N.Y.* 9: I thought…[he] would a gone off the handle, he larfed so. **1843** in *DAE*: The old woman would go off the handle if I should come back without you. **1871** Schele de Vere *Americanisms* 195: The New York *Home Journal* speaks of a poor man having succeeded to a large fortune from a distant relative, who "*went off the handle* in England rather unexpectedly." (July 21, 1867). **1872** O.W. Holmes *Poet* 282: My old gentleman means to be Mayor or Governor or President or something or other before he goes off the handle, you'd better b'lieve. **1877** Bartlett *Americanisms* (ed. 4) 784: To *slip off the handle* is to die.

2. to *fly off the handle*, above.
   1984–85 in Schneider & Schneider *Sound Off!* 137: Why am I any…more liable to go off the handle than a nurse?

¶ **pop off the handle** to jilt.
   1863 Brobst *Letters* 22: Well, Elsie has soured on me. She has popped me off the handle short as pie crust, and just imagine how I must feel.

¶ **to the handle** thoroughly; to the hilt.—usu. constr. with *up*.
   1833 in *OEDS*: He is determined to carry the contest, "to the handle." **1866** [H.W. Shaw] *J. Billings* 25: I beleave in femail eddikashun, clear up tu the handle. **1868** Macy *There She Blows!* 26: I know my duty, chock to the handle. **1870** *Overland Mo.* (Jan.) 85: Canvas and me saveyed hosses up to the handle. **1885** Harte *Snow-Bound* 20: You're likely to hev your ideas on this matter carried out up to the handle. **1887** Hinman *Cpl. Klegg* 110: He would volunteer to serve as the guard, and he would do his duty "right up to the handle."

¶ **with handles** to an extreme degree. Cf. syn. *on wheels* s.v. WHEEL, *n.*
   1949 in Hemingway *Selected Letters* 663: Marce I always thought…of as a bitch with handles.

handle *v.* to treat roughly; manhandle.
   1912 T.A. Dorgan, in Zwilling *TAD Lexicon* 108: Yer honor this man was assaulted while tryin' to collect a bill—Pipe the glim on 'im. Yes your honor they handled me. **1913** T.A. Dorgan (cited in Zwilling *TAD Lexicon* 108).

handlebar *n.* a handlebar mustache.
   1952 *Combat Forces Journal* (Aug.) 4: I'll wager that he does not sport that handlebar Stateside.

hand-mucker *n. Gamb.* (see quots.).
   1935 Pollock *Und. Speaks*: Hand mucker, card cheater who holds out playing cards without the aid of a hold-out machine. **1961** Scarne *Comp. Guide to Gamb.* 681: Hand-Mucker or Holdout Man. A card cheat who specializes in palming cards.

handout *n.* **1.** Orig. *Hobo.* a portion of food, money, or the like given at the door to a beggar. Now *S.E.*
   1882 Sweet & Knox *Tex. Siftings* 195: If I can't get a "hand-out" for it I can at least expatiate on its merits. **1885** "Lykkejaeger" *Dane* 45: All my capital squandered for a "hand out" far below the general average. **1887** M. Roberts *W. Avernus* 71: "Bummers" is American for beggars, and a "hand out" is a portion of food handed out to a bummer or a tramp at the door when he is not asked inside. **1891** Maitland *Slang Dict.* 136: Hand out…a cold lunch given to a tramp. **1893** in J.I. White *Git Along Dogies* 94: Unless I get a big hand-out,/I'm a cowboy that is broke. **1896** Ade *Artie* 32: I see barrelhouse boys goin' around for hand-outs that was more on the level than you are. **1899** "J. Flynt" *Tramping* 394: Hand-Out: a bundle of food handed out to a beggar at a back door. **1900** Kennedy *Adrift* 291: A "hand-out" is a parcel of food, which derives its name from being handed out through a half-opened door. **1902** "J. Flynt" *Little Bro.* 43: A few "hand-outs" that Blackie had saved from the noon hunt for dinner had sufficed for their supper. **1908** in Fleming *Unforgettable Season* 136: Yesterday a fireman in uniform was taking "handouts" at the Polo Grounds. **1913** in J. Reed *Young Man* 49: You t'ought just because you give me a hand-out, I'd do a sob-story all over you.

2. a line of insincere or offensive talk.
   1908 Hopper & Bechdolt *9009* 168: What sort of a hand-out is this you're giving me? Do I get in?

hand out *v.* to tell; say; impart by speaking or writing.—often with the implication of insincerity or imposition.
   1899 Ade *Fables* 28: He would have to hand out a little Guff. **1905** in Paxton *Sport USA* 23: I don't know whether Socrates or "Chuck" Connors ever handed this out before, but it is true. **1908** McGaffey *Show Girl* 25: What was that you handed out? Come again, please. **1920** Ade *Hand-Made Fables* 53: He was a Great Hand at reading Papers to the emancipated Suffs and they would almost get what he was Handing out. **1932** V. Nelson *Prison Days & Nights* 25: And the line of crap they hand out to the papers and the women's clubs.

hand queen *n. Homosex.* a male homosexual masturbator.
   1965 Trimble *Sex Words* 97: Hand queen…A male Homosexual who prefers to manually Masturbate his love partner. *a*1972 B. Rodgers *Queens' Vernacular* 116: Masturbator…*hand queen.*

handshake *v.* Esp. *Mil.* to curry favor [with].
   1917 in Lord *Boyd's Battery* 24: Handshake; v. intrans.…to suavely seek favor with authority. **1918** Rowse *Doughboy Dope* 9: Cyzerznski only ducked a spell in the jug by handshaking with the top-kick. **1918** *110th Field Arty. Mustard Roll* (Aug. 18) 1: Give Saint Pete an army grin,/Handshake him to let us in. *Ibid.* (Sept. 15) 7: He went and handshook with the Top. **1927–28** in R. Nelson *Dishonorable* 217: There won't be any prominent people left to handshake Queens. **1941** Hargrove *Pvt. Hargrove* 56: "Now this Corporal Gantt, when he first came in, was one of the greenest rookies in the bunch. But he snapped out of it and made corporal in four months." "Was that soldiering…or handshaking—as the Latins used to say, *mittus floppus*?" **1959** Ogburn *Marauders* 217: Now there….was a real handshaking son-of-a-bitch! I'll bet he made corporal the day they drafted him! **1962** Mandel *Wax Boom* 73: You don't have to be hand-shaking me, Proctor.

handshaker *n.* **1.** a usu. insincere person who makes a show of amiability and flattery; one who curries favor; BROWN-NOSE.
   1884 *Life* (Jan. 17) 33: Naw, we won't have no hand-shakers,/Nor no daisies what ain't straight. **1898** in S. Crane *War Dispatches* 193: The American soldier alludes to the natives here as handshakers. It is his way of expressing a cynical suspicion regarding all the "viva Americanos" business that he hears and sees in this city of Ponce. **1900** Ade *More Fables* 178: When he had to go out and Rustle for a Job he was a Busy Hand-Shaker once more. **1902** Mead *Word-Coinage* 166: A professional appreciator…is known as a "genial." "The handshaker" is another name for the "genial." **1917** Lord *Boyd's Btry.* 24: Handshaker n.—See Lily Presser, Mitt Wobbler, Dog Robber. **1919**

Cortelyou *Arizona* 101: When a new sergeant is made in an outfit all the corporals except the lucky one let out a wail and call him a "hand shaker" and everything else they can think of. **1919** *Our Navy* (Aug.) 68: Of course we had some "hand-shakers" in the detail and the only sacks they wrestled were sacks of Bull Durham. **1925** S. Lewis *Arrowsmith* 641: I'm a hand-shaker myself. I know less about medicine than Prof. Robertshaw. **1926** *Amer. Leg. Mo.* (Sept.) 9: He's a bootlicker, a handshaker, a natural born dog-robber, and if you don't do something about him, Grasby, you and I are going to have a falling out. **1938** Noble *Jugheads* 140 [ref. to 1918]: One thing the captain could never accuse me of being was a "handshaker."

2. a confidence swindler.

1892 Norr *China Town* 15: The men were of a familiar class, handsome, well-groomed fellows, known to Inspector Byrnes's men as expert "handshakers." **1896** Hamblen *Many Seas* 407: "Clear out, now, before I call a policeman and have ye locked up!...You are one of these handshakers; that's who you be!...I had been reading in the paper this morning, about the tricks of the handshakers, as they call them.

hand shoe *n.* [< G *Handschuh*] a glove. *Joc.*

1871 C.G. Leland *Breitmann's Ballads* 245: Hand-shoe, (Ger. *Handschuh*)—Glove. **1930** in *DARE*. **1931** *Writer's Dig.* (May) 42: *Hand shoes*—Gloves. **1932** *Editor* (Aug. 30) 131: The shack runs ahead to throw the switch from the siding on to the main line. As he travels he pulls on his hand shoes. **1958** McCulloch *Woods Words* 79: *Hand shoes*—Gloves. **1976** in *DARE*.

handsome *n.* ¶ In phrase: **do the handsome** to act generously or graciously.

*a1890–93 F & H III 259: *To do the handsome...*To behave extremely well; to be "civil." **1904** A.H. Lewis *President* 419: There's no pinch goes with it, and Mr. Brown's willing to do the handsome. **1908** W.G. Davenport *Butte & Montana* 236: London...did the handsome.

handspike *n.* an old musket.

1866 E.C. Downs *Scout & Spy* 245: I received in exchange for my "handspike" (musket) the Enfield that was promised to me.

handy wagon *n.* (see quots.).

1927 DN V 449: *Handy wagon*, n. The police patrol wagon. **1939** *Chi. Tribune* (Jan. 22) (Graphic Sec.) 9: *Handy Wagon*—A police patrol car.

hang *n.* **1.** *Horse Racing.* a fairly even race.

1840 *Spirit of Times* (Mar. 7) 6: Since the match begins to *squint* at something like "a hang," betting men are regarding the *chances* in Wagner's favor, with a kind of seriousness.

2. (in negative contexts) the least bit; a damn.

*1861 in *OED*: She looks as well as you by candlelight, but she can't ride a hang. ***1876** in *OED*: She don't care a hang what anybody says of her. **1971** J. Brown & A. Groff *Monkey* 45: He never gave the slightest indication...that he gave a hang.

3.a. [perh. related to syn. HAME] *Black E.* a job.

1950 in M. Daly *Profile of Youth* 235: Negro teen-agers on Chicago's South Side...[call] a job...a "hang." **1968–70** *Current Slang III & IV* 64: *Hang*, n. A job.—Watts [district of L.A.]. Have you found a hang yet? **1970** Major *Afro-Amer. Sl.*: *Hang*: a job, especially one taken or held grudgingly. **1971** H. Roberts *Third Ear*: *Hang*, n. a job. **1983** *Reader's Digest Success with Words* 86: Black English...*hang* = 'job, gig'.

b. an act of relaxing or socializing.

1995 N.Y. jazz musician, age 32 (coll. J. Sheidlower): A gig is "a hang," so you say things like "That was a good hang." But you use it in general too: "Do you want to have a hang tonight?" meaning just "Do you want to hang out?," or "That was a good hang" meaning "That was a pleasant evening." **1995** *Time Out N.Y.* (Oct. 18) 83 [personal ad]: SWF...seeks a male companion to drink, laugh, and do the hang with.

hang *v.* **1.** *Horse Racing.* to race in a closely matched competition (*obs.*); (*also*) (see *a*1951 quot.).

1841 *Spirit of Times* (Sept. 25) 354: I should like to see Blount and Mariner "hang." It would...make an interesting and betting race. *a*1951 in Maurer *Lang. Und.* 214: *Hang...*To keep up with the leaders or to maintain a slim lead to the finish.

2.a. to impose upon; inflict (upon or with); (*hence*) to make a criminal charge against.

1908 McGaffey *Show Girl* 19: He'd better...hang the curfew on a few of those town romps. **1915** in Grayson *New Stories* 561: Him and

the newspapers hung that name on me. **1925–26** J. Black *You Can't Win* 165: If I get six months they'll have to hang them on me. I ain't going to reach out an' grab them. **1928** Scanlon *God Have Mercy* 221 [ref. to 1918]: "Where did you get all the corporal stripes?" "They hung them on me just before Saint-Mihiel." **1930** Conwell *Pro. Thief* 10: So coppers are not a bit particular whom they hang a rap on. **1972** Carr *Bad* 88: They'd hung him with no less than forty counts of armed robbery. **1974** R.H. Carter *16th Round* 28: They hung some mean sport right on his black ass.

b. to fix blame for.—constr. with *on*.

1915–16 Lait *Beef, Iron & Wine* 169: I ain't no vag. But that captain'll hang it on me. **1927** DN V 449: *Hang something on one*, v. To convict on false evidence. **1927** Coe *Me—Gangster* 55: Nobody can really fix a killing if they hang it on you. **1928** Sharpe *Chi.* May 39: I felt quite certain the dicks couldn't hang anything on me. **1931** Grant *Gangdom's Doom* 85: We'll be in wrong if this is hung on us. **1935** Fortune *Fugitives* 157: Raymond did rob the Grand Prairie Bank and the bank at West. Clyde also had these two "hung on him," but told us he did not have anything to do with either. **1936** Washburn *Parlor* 40: In a getaway I left a set of tools and some soup (nitroglycerine) so they tried to hang the job onto me. **1938** Steinbeck *Grapes of Wrath* 24: Why do we got to hang it on God or Jesus? **1941** Halliday *Tickets for Death* 99: Trying to hang something on me? **1944** J. Paxton *Murder My Sweet* (film): They might try to hang a murder on your neck. **1954** Johnson *Black Widow* (film): Nancy Ordway was murdered and they're trying to hang it on me.

3.a. to remain; lie.

1923 in W.F. Nolan *Black Mask Boys* 67: I'll hang low until my lawyer has proven a case against this gang.

b. to loiter or idle, esp. in company; wait; (*hence*) to associate; socialize; HANG OUT, 2.

1941 *New Yorker* (Apr. 26) 22: *To hang...*means to loiter. "I used to hang in Forty-sixth Street, front of *Variety*," a small bookmaker may say. **1941** in Whyte *Street Corner Society* 267: I get bored sometimes hanging in Spongi's. **1953** Kramer & Karr *Teen-Age Gangs* 10: The Emeralds had driven a Negro soda jerk out of a drugstore in which they sometimes hung. **1954** Yablonsky *Violent Gang* 78: I hang in my hallway—the janitor yells. **1958** Schwitzgebel *Streetcorner Research* 47: You think you can hang with them kind of guys? **1958** *Jour. Social Issues* XIV (No. 3) 15: He don't hang with us. **1968** Johnson & Johnson *Count Me Gone* 139: That's one reason I hang in there sometimes. **1969** Postman et al. *Lang. in America* 201: "Whatcha doin'?" "I was hangin'." **1969** *Playboy* (Dec.) 100: When I'm not on a football field, I hang with whoever I want to hang with. **1972** *Nat. Lampoon* (Feb.) 6: For instance, yesterday we were just hanging in the dorm really zonked on some fantastic stuff. **1974** Stone *Dog Soldiers* 141: Quasi's is where we hang now. I guess it's a bar. **1973–76** J. Allen *Assault* 125: He went to this joint where a lot of homosexuals hang. **1977** Sayles *Union Dues* 182: She didn't want to go hang in the bars. **1981** Safire *Good Word* 80: I'll just hang this evening. **1984** Toop *Rap Attack* 23: I had to be in at eight, so I couldn't hang. **1985** Flowers *Mojo Blues* 8: You wanna hang with us, you got to do better. **1993** Mowry *Six Out Seven* 332: Hang a second, man. **1993** *New Yorker* (Nov. 15) 67: I'm going to hang with you for the anniversary! **1994** N. McCall *Wanna Holler* 42: It was viewed as a social thing among hanging partners. *Ibid.* 50: He s'pposed to be one of your hanging buddies.

c. (rarely used trans.).

1961 H. Ellison *Purgatory* 39: I hung the streets, shot some pool from time to time.

4. *Und.* to murder.

1959 W. Burroughs *Naked Lunch* 3: He...hauls out an old rusty six shooter and...hangs three fags before the fuzz nail him.

5. *Narc.* to slip into a drugged state; (*also*) to be in need of drugs.

1958–59 Lipton *Barbarians* 186: And he hits up the whole thing and he...starts nodding, you know, hanging. And this other guy,...he's hanging. **1966** Brunner *Face of Night* 232: *Hanging*—in distress for lack of narcotics. Also, "hung up."

6. *Sports.* to pitch or throw (a ball) so that it is easily hit or caught by an opposing player.

1961 Brosnan *Pennant Race* 107: How about if you hang a curve ball with the bases loaded and lose the game by one run? **1965** Borowik *Lions* 52: "Of course he does hang* a lot of them."...*To "hang" a pass is to throw it so that it can be intercepted. **1990** *TV Guide* (July 7) 26: I hung a screwball to Willie Mays…and he hit it out.

7. to execute (a turn), as in an automobile. See also LOUIE, RALPH.

1967 (quot. at LOUIE). **1966–68** *Current Slang I & II* 47: *Hang,* v. To turn.—College males, Kansas, South Dakota.—*Hang* a left. **1971** Dahlskog *Dict.* 30: *Hang a (left) (right)*, make a left, or a right, turn. **1972** Eble *Campus Slang* (Oct.) 3: *Hang a left*…go left. **1972** *West Village* 77: Straight ahead to Top's house…then hang a right and follow the river bank to the big coconut tree. **1972** N.Y.U. student: You can *hang* a right or a left or a U-turn. **1973** Lucas, Katz & Huyck *Amer. Graffiti* 27: Quick! Hang a right! **1977** Butler & Shryack *Gauntlet* 60: Six blocks down….Hang a left. **1985** Heywood *Taxi Dancer* 78: You…hung a one-eighty and found another way to get where you were going. **1995** *Radioactive Man Colossal* (No. 1) (unp.): Hang a left at the thirteen moons of Vimulon….If you hit the sun, you've gone too far.

8. [sugg. by *hang paper* s.v. PAPER] to pass (worthless checks, securities, etc.).

1973 N.Y.C. man, age 24: The guy was hanging bad checks all over town. **1975** *Business Week* (July 21) 10: They give instructions on how to "hang" stolen securities and counterfeit certificates.

9.a. [prob. shortened fr. *hang tough*, below] to remain steadfast; stay; *(hence)* to do well; succeed; accomplish.

1980 in Goss & Barnes *Talk That Talk* 478: Hang in there—hang till you graduate. **1989** Munro *U.C.L.A. Slang* 46: This is so stressful. I can't hang. **1989** S. Robinson & D. Ritz *Smokey* 17: Most cats would have run. Not Daddy; Daddy hung. **1990** *Star Trek: Next Generation* (synd. TV series): We can hang in a firefight a lot longer. **1992** S. Straight *Been in Sorrow's Kitchen* 255: What do you think about Mason? Can he hang? *Ibid.* 282: Y'all think you can hang fishin in the city instead a the swamp? *a***1994** N. McCall *Wanna Holler* 400: Turkey is hanging: Once he was hustling, now he's got a real job.

b. to act or behave.

1989 *ALF* (NBC-TV): All *right!* Way to *hang*, Willie boy!

c. to accept something posited; accept something as satisfactory.

1989 Munro *U.C.L.A. Slang* 46: Is that okay with you?—Yeah, I can hang.

¶ In phrases:

¶ **hang a B.A.** see s.v. B.A., *n.*, 3.

¶ **hang and rattle** *West.* to remain seated on a bucking horse; persevere.

1910 in C.M. Russell *Paper Talk* 77: Hang an rattle, Jimmy. **1936** in *DA*: Stay with him, Parson. Hang and rattle.

¶ **hang a pin** *Stu.* to give one's girlfriend one's fraternity pin to wear as a token of an exclusive dating relationship.

1930 in D.O. Smith *Cradle* 28: You had little respect for the real meaning of hanging a pin…and decided that hanging the pin would be a delightful gesture toward the Goddess Romance. **1934** Weseen *Dict. Slang* 184: *Hang a pin*—To become engaged to a girl and put a fraternity pin on her as a sign.

¶ **hang five** see s.v. *hang ten*, below.

¶ **hang in [there]** to remain steadfast; persevere. [The 1697 date adduced by *W9* does not apply to the present sense of the phr.]

[*a***1890–93** F & H III 261: *To hang in*…to get to work; to do one's best.] **1936** Monks & Finklehoffe *Brother Rat* 117: Go ahead…Hang in there. **1961** in J. O'Hara *Selected Letters* 366: Hang in there, pal. **1961** Brosnan *Pennant Race* 201: "When's the last time we had a day off?" "Tomorrow. Hang in there." **1971** Dahlskog *Dict.* 30: *Hang in*, v. To stick with it; not give up; to keep plugging, as: Hang in there, buddy. **1973** *Playboy* (Oct.) 172: My mother would have hung in there. **1974** *New York* (Mar. 18) 39: Rose Mary Woods is hanging in, but her friends say it has been difficult. *a***1982** Medved *Hospital* 13: Right away, I was in over my head, but I hung in there and I made it. **1994** Univ. Tenn. students: "How ya doin'?" "Hangin' in there."

¶ **hang iron** *Labor.* to be a structural ironworker.

1979 in Terkel *Amer. Dreams* 236: He hung iron for a while….My pa was a mill hand. *Ibid.* 239: I know a lot of guys that hang iron in South Chicago.

¶ **hang it all over** to surpass or outdo.

1913–15 Van Loan *Taking the Count* 11: I think Billy has hung it all over Brady so far.

¶ **hang [it] easy!** take it easy!

1951–53 in *AS* XXIX (1954) 97: See you later. Hang it easy! **1960** MacCuish *Do Not Go Gentle* 199: Hang easy, buddy.

¶ **hang it in your ass!** see s.v. ASS, *n.*

¶ **hang it on the limb** [or **on a bush**] *Pris.* to escape from prison.

1932 Burns *I Am a Fugitive* 63: Sam, I got six years; that's a long time, and I'm going to try to "hang it on the limb," and I need a little help. *Ibid.* 72: So you "hung it on the limb," eh?…He just hung six years on the limb. [**1948** Mencken *Amer. Lang.* (Supp. II) 674: To escape is…*to hang it, to be on the bush*.] **1954** in *West. Folklore* XIV (1955) 135: *Hanging it on a bush*. To escape from prison. **1959** Duffy & Lane *Warden's Wife* 146: For nearly a year…no convict had succeeded in "hanging it on a bush."

¶ **hang it out** [euphem. for *hang (one's) ass out* s.v. ASS, *n.*] to risk one's life or safety; run a risk.

1969 in R. Mains *Dear Mom* 224: If I do fly I won't be assigned a mission where I "hang it out" too much. *ca***1969** in Tuso *Vietnam Blues* 62: We hung it out at fourteen thou'—the burner going strong/The flak came flying by my bow, we can't hang out here long. **1971** Caillou *Evel Knievel* (film): I do as I please/Hang it out in the breeze. **1971** *N.Y. Times* (Mar. 7) 16: "Face it," said David Anderson, the 24-year-old pilot of a Slick, or troop-carrying chopper, "I'd rather hang it out for my own people—all of us would." **1982** Basel *Pak Six* 104: They took chances, hung it out a mile. **1987** Robbins *Ravens* 273: People were beginning to feel Chuck was hanging it out *too* much. **1989** *CBS This Morning* (CBS-TV) (Oct. 26): I always thought that being an actor was hanging it out there…and taking your chances. **1990** Berent *Steel Tiger* 246: In combat you got to hang it out if you want to do your job.

¶ **hang loose** to remain calm; take it easy. Cf. LOOSE, *adj.*

1955 Stern *Rebel Without a Cause* (film): Hang loose, boy. I'm warning you. *Ibid.* Hang loose, we got all night. **1955** in J. Blake *Joint* 110: Be happy, hang loose, keep the faith. **1958** Simonson & Phillips *Blob* (film): You gotta hang loose, like me. **1959** on *Golden Age of TV* (A & E): I can't hang loose in a room solo. **1960** MacCuish *Do Not Go Gentle* 218 [ref. to WWII]: Hang loose, hoss. **1961** L.G. Richards *TAC* 53: "Hang loose," Major Prevost orders. **1968** Ragni & Rado *Hair* 148: I'm hanging loose. **1970** *Odd Couple* (ABC-TV): I'm an artist. I hang loose. **1976–77** C. McFadden *Serial* 32: So he decided to hang loose and risk it. **1977** R.S. Parker *Effective Decisions* 27: It is a popular philosophy today to "hang loose, trust your feelings, do what you really want to do." **1984** Mason & Rheingold *Slanguage: (To) hang loose*…To take it easy; mellow out. **1993** N.Y.C. man, age *ca*45: OK, just hang loose.

¶ **hang one on, 1.** to deliver a sharp blow to; wallop.

1908 McGaffey *Show Girl* 200: Hauling off wifey hangs one on Alla's map. **1911** Bronson-Howard *Enemy to Society* 295: You call her a "dame" again, and I'll hang one on you right from my heel, un'stand? **1918** Lardner *Treat 'Em Rough* 16: The next time them wops try to slip me something…I will hang one on their jaw. **1928** MacArthur *War Bugs* 145: A Ritzy Hauptmann had one hung on his nose right in front of his men. His monocle was tossed up for grabs. **1934** Cain *Postman* 89: Next time I try to act smart, will you hang one on my jaw? **1948** Cozzens *Guard of Honor* 129: As soon as we got down, he walked over to the other plane and hung one on the pilot. **1956** I. Shulman *Good Deeds* 65: Suppose I hang one on you? **1957** Fuchs & Levien *Jeanne Eagels* (film): I would like to hang one on her!

2. to get very drunk. Cf. syn. *tie one on* s.v. TIE, *v.*

1945 Seaton *Billy Rose's Diamond Horseshoe* (film): The assistant stage manager hung one on last night. **1951** Styron *Lie Down* 32: "Say, you look real sick," she said. "You must of hung one on last night." **1952** Uris *Battle Cry* 77 [ref. to 1942]: You really hung one on. **1956** Yordan *Harder They Fall* (film): Come on. Let's hang one on. **1962** J.P. Miller *Days of Wine and Roses* (film): Really hung one on. **1965** Conot *Rivers of Blood* 39: Look at good old so-and-so hanging one on. **1980** "A. Landers," in *Santa Barbara News-Press* (July 25) B7: If you go to California, folks, and plan to hang one on, make sure the taxi driver is sober.

¶ **hang (one's) ass out** see s.v. ASS, *n.*

¶ **hang [out] cool** to remain calm or cool; take it easy.

1970 Ebert *Beyond Valley of Dolls* (film): Hang cool, teddybear. **1978** Selby *Requiem* 126: They had to hang cool, but tough. **1979** R. Foster *Concrete Cowboys* (film): I took some shekels from those dudes in Mississippi so we can hang out cool for a while. **1982** Least Heat Moon *Blue Hwys.* 102: But we gotta show the brothers they can do more than hang cool like meat in a locker.

¶ **hang out** [or **up**] **to dry** to punish or vanquish; overcome completely.

*a***1982** Medved *Hospital* 178: If you…voice your opinion too loud, then you're going to be hung up to dry. **1984** *N.Y. Post* (Aug. 13) 41: The old Panamanian smoothie hung Angel Cordero Jr. out to dry like the family wash. **1989** L. Roberts *Full Cleveland* 194: It was me that had to split before I got hung out to dry.

¶ **hang paper, 1.** see s.v. PAPER. Cf. PAPER HANGER.

2. *Circus.* to provide publicity; advertise.

1975 McKennon *Horse Dung Trail* 241: He…was sort of "hanging paper" for the kids.

¶ **hang (someone's) ass** see s.v. ASS, *n.*

¶ **hang ten** [or **five**] *Surfing.* to ride a surfboard with the toes of both feet [or of one foot] extended over the edge of the board.

*****1962** in *OEDAS* II 140. *****1963** in *OEDS: Hang ten*, ten toes over the nose of the board. *****1963** in *OEDS: Hanging five*, five toes over the nose of the board for maximum speed. **1964** *Look* (June 30) 55: *Hang Five*: five toes over nose. *Hang Ten:* ten toes hooked over nose of board. **1967** *Ladies Home Journal* (Oct.) 172: Five toes hanging over the edge is called "hanging five." "The ultimate in surfing is to hang ten." **1977** *L.A. Times* (July 24) IV 3: "What is surfing's hole-in-one?"…"Hanging 10.…riding the big wave with all 10 toes curled over the front end of your board." **1989** *TV Guide* (Mar. 4) 34: [He] had to wait until he attended college in Hawaii to really start hanging 10. **1995** *Sci-Fi Trader* (Sci-Fi Channel TV): When you hang ten through those cosmic wormholes! **1995** *Sky* (Dec.) 21: He learned to write and "hang ten" in more or less equal installments.

¶ **hang the landlady** (see quot.).

1902 Clapin *Amer.* 220: *Hang the landlady*. To decamp without payment, a phrase applied to "moonshining" practices of all descriptions.

¶ **hang tight** to sit tight; wait; remain calm under pressure.

1947 Overholser *Buckaroo's Code* 17: If you want to hang tight and get a dose of hot lead, it's your business. **1963** Boyle *Yanks Don't Cry* 78 [ref. to WWII]: We hung tight, and every man clung doggedly to the belief that the war would be over "tomorrow"—not next week and never next year or the year after that—but always "tomorrow." **1964** Crane *Sgt. & Queen* 88: Hang tight, Ben, while I send someone to check him out. **1966–67** Harvey *Air War* 25: Hang tight.…We'll pick you up in a couple of minutes. **1970** M. Thomas *Total Beast* 78: Charlie put his face between two of the bars. "Hang tight, Eddy." **1978** W. Brown *Tragic Magic* 16: I wanted to hang tight with my cap pistols and the vacant lot revivals of John Wayne and Randolph Scott Westerns. **1987** Santiago *Undercover* 81: No, I want you to hang tight tonight. **1968–90** Linderer *Eyes of Eagle* 183: He told us to hang tight. **1995** *Leeza* (synd. TV series): Could you hang tight with me here for a minute?

¶ **hang tough** to remain unyielding, steadfast, or defiant; (*also*, with weakened force) (used as a valediction). Also (*vulgar*) **hang tough tit**. [The meaning of *hang out tough* in 1867 quot. is not clear.]

[**1867** Clark *Sailor's Life* 268: "Well, here we are [guarding an empty ship]," said a friend at my elbow, "and likely to hang out tough. I expect they will do up all their farming before they sail."] **1936** Duncan *Over Wall* 329: How you coming, Dan?…Your fifteen years [of a prison sentence] still hanging tough? **1954** Voorhees *Show Me a Hero* 118: The chaplain looked back. "Hang tough, boy." **1958** W. Henry *Seven* 52: Their best chance was to hang tough. **1958** McCulloch *Woods Words* 80: *Hang tough tit*—To stick to a decision. **1962** Crump *Killer* 132: Yeah, I'll hang tough. **1963–64** Kesey *Sometimes a Great Notion* 38: G'by, Lee, hang tough. **1965–66** Pynchon *Crying* 137: "Hang tough," Oedipa advised. **1966** Elli *Riot* 235: All we've got to do is hang tough. **1970** E. Knight *Black Voices* 112: I…would caution him to be cool, to hang tough. **1972** *N.Y. Post* (July 1) 56: That's how the Mets have won four of their last five games. Somehow. They're hanging tough. **1980** WINS radio news (Mar. 18): They don't see how a

strike can be avoided if both sides hang as tough as they are. **1988** *Beauty & the Beast* (CBS-TV): You are going to have to hang *tough* now. **1989** *Cops* (Fox-TV): Just hang tough, partner. **1990** in N. George *Buppies, B-Boys* 150: The actor now hangs tough with the rapper in a potent linkage.

¶ **hang with** to put up with or accept.

1979 in Debrecht *Best Soul Songs* 59: If you can't hang with the feelin', [etc.]. **1987** *21 Jump St.* (Fox-TV): Guys like him don't hang with being humiliated. **1989** Munro *U.C.L.A. Slang* 46: She turned me down? Oh, well, I can hang with that. **1990** Knoxville, Tenn., attorney, age 36: I can hang with that. **1992** Straight *Been in Sorrow's Kitchen* 294: Major in Chemistry—I can't hang with all that math.

¶ **how are they hanging?** how are you doing?; *how's your hammer hanging?* s.v. HAMMER, *n.*, 1; also (*rarely*) with ref. to the mammaries.—usu. considered vulgar.

1928 J.M. March *Set-Up* 16: How they hankgink, Herman? **1932** Nicholson & Robinson *Sailor Beware!* 16: Yeah, but you can't say "Hi, kid, how they hangin'?" to a guy whose old man's just passed out. **1937** Weidman *Wholesale* 256: "Hello, Meyer," I said. "How are they hanging?" **1963** Morgan *Six-Eleven* 266: Hello, George.…How are they hanging? **1966** Gass *Omensetter's Luck* 96: How they hanging? **1969** Tynan *Oh! Calcutta!* 35: Hiya, buddy! How they hangin'? **1970** G. Walker *Cruising* 42: Lynch had seen [male] hustlers on the streets night and day, shaking their things, asking you how they're hanging today, man. **1978** Diehl *Sharky's Machine* 239: "How they hangin', Sergeant?" "Hangin' full, babe." **1980** W.C. Anderson *Bat-21* 36: How they hangin', Jake? **1984** Trotti *Phantom* 203 [ref. to Vietnam War]: Hello, Lunar.…How're you hanging? **1987** F. Ray & T. Lankford *Hollywood Chainsaw Hookers* (film): Girls, how's it hangin'? **1989** *21 Jump Street* (Fox-TV): How's it hangin', guy? **1991** *UTSQ: How's it hangin'?* or *How they hangin'?* means: How's it going? Refers to male anatomy and female breasts—depends on who you're addressing. **1993** Mowry *Six Out Seven* 322: So, how they hangin, Bilal?

¶ **how does that hang?** *Black E.* what is your impression of that?

1981 Safire *Good Word* 80: How do that hang?

¶ **how's your hammer hanging?** see s.v. HAMMER, *n.*, 1.

¶ **let it all hang down** see *let it all hang out*, below.

1994 *Mystery Sci. Theater* (Comedy Central TV): It's almost midnight. We're gonna let it all hang down.

¶ **let it all hang out** to abandon restraint, convention, propriety, etc.; to be completely candid; (*also*) to do one's best or utmost. [Usu. regarded as orig. having a phallic or mammary reference.]

1961 Brosnan *Pennant Race* 88: Let it all hang out now, Tits.…Don't hold back there. *Ibid.* 214: I let it *all* hang out on that one. *Ibid.* 218: Come on, Joe, let it all hang out. **1962** T. Berger *Reinhart in Love* 192: 55 m.p.h.…was what the Chevy could make with, in the jargon of the road, "everything hung out." **1962** E. Stephens *Blow Negative* 70: "Lets it all hang out." "Doesn't zip his pants?" "Talks too much. But…makes a lethal martini." **1964** Reuss *Field Collection* 178: Let's all get drunk and get naked.…And let it all hang out! **1967** Ragni & Rado *Hair* 23: Let It All Hang Out. Tell It Like It Is. **1968** Baker, Ladd & Robb *CUSS* 150: *Let it all hang out.* Go wild. **1968** in Rowe *5 Yrs. to Freedom* 303: *Mat* can't maintain tempo of attacks much *longer*—and he has it ALL hanging out—if only Sam has a big stick left. **1969** Bouton *Ball Four* 217: Up and at 'em. Fuck 'em all. Let it all hang out. **1970** Grissim *Country Music* 283: Oh what a hell of a mess…let it all hang out. **1973** World Series (NBC-TV) (Oct. 21): Kenny let it all hang out and did a superb job. **1974** Scalzo *Stand on Gas* 134: Let it all hang out today, Kenny.…I want you to win. **1977** *Amer. Dict. CB Slang* 44: *Let it all hang out*—Full speed ahead. **1978** in Lyle & Golenbock *Bronx Zoo* 194: I really enjoy watching him [smash and throw things]. When he goes nuts, he just lets it all hang out. **1980** in McCauley *Dark Forces* 441: I warned him that if he tried to stop me in court I'd let it all hang out—the jealousy, the drinking, everything. **1987** *Verbatim* (Summer) 12: With contraceptives being advertised openly on television, we seem to be letting it all hang out (if you will excuse the expression), and none of us is likely to be surprised by anything. **1988** *CBS This Morning* (CBS-TV) (Nov. 1): Did he wake up one morning and say, "I've got nothing to lose. I'm gonna let it all hang out." **1992** D. Burke *Street Talk* I 40: *To let it all hang out*…to wear skimpy clothing in order to show off one's body. **1993** A.

Lomax *Where Blues Began* 378: In these days of "letting it all hang out" it's hard to recall the prudishness of that…period.

hangar *n.* the fly of the trousers. *Joc.*
   1976 Knapp & Knapp *One Potato* 89: Your hangar's open.

hangar-flying *n. Av.* discussing flying or bragging about flying experiences. Hence **hangar-fly**, *v.*
   1918 H.E. Townsend *War Diary* 51: It is most interesting to listen to their "hangar flying"; the gossip and experiences told and recounted. **1933** Stewart *Airman Speech* 106. **1942** *Time* (Apr. 6) 50: Hangar flying (bull sessions to college students). **1944** *AAF* 368: *Hangar flying:* Conversation about flying and kindred subjects. **1959** R.L. Scott *Flying Tiger* 44: They were more adept at "hangar flying" and bragging in bars about past exploits than in actual performance in the air. **1960** Archibald *Jet Flier* 5: During some "hangar flying"…he'd heard that airline passengers had really "seen nothing yet." **1962** Tregaskis *Vietnam Diary* 84: All of them [were] engaged in a hangar-flying session. **1972** Facos *Silver Lady* 27 [ref. to WWII]: The men slouched around the tables…hangar-flying the day's raid. **1972** Carpentier *Flt. One* 29: Whether we like it or not, we're going to hangar-fly all over this sauna. **1975** in Higham & Siddall *Combat Aircraft* 12: A reputation embellished for shock effect during "hangar flying" bull sessions throughout the Air Corps. *a*1991 Kross *Splash One* 87: Spending three hours…"hangar flying," going over flying tactics and procedures on the ground.

hangar pilot *n. Av.* a nonaviator or a poor aviator who talks knowingly about flying.
   1941 Kendall *Army & Navy Sl.* 7: Hangar pilot….mechanic who talks a great flight. **1942** Gamet & Trivers *Flying Tigers* (film): Any of you hangar pilots topped that yet? **1944** *AAF* 368: *Hangar Pilot:* One who does his best "flying" in conversation.

hangar queen *n. Av.* an aircraft that is out of repair or obsolete.
   1943 Pyle *Here Is Your War* 115: Those condemned planes were towed to the engineering section, and there they gradually disappeared. Finally…they were picked bare by the salvaging mechanics. The salvage planes were nicknamed "hangar queens." **1944** in Newby *Target Ploesti* (frontispiece): Hangar Queen. **1946** Haines *Command Decision* 9: Security! Even the hangar queens patched up and gone today but I'm not supposed to know there's a mission out. **1956** *AS* XXI (Oct.) 228: *Hangar Queen.* An aircraft that spends large amounts of time out of commission; sometimes parts are taken from it to repair other aircraft. **1964** Lucas *Dateline* 66: They swear some helicopters become hypochondriacs….Such a chopper is called a "hangar queen." **1965** Le May & Kantor *Mission with Le May* 133: You couldn't tell: overnight a couple of airplanes might have decided to become hangar queens. **1973** W. Crawford *Gunship Cmndr.* 134: I've cannibalized every hangar-queen we've got. **1975** in Higham & Siddall *Combat Aircraft* 69: But where it had been one of the nimblest planes on the wing, it became…a hangar queen—a real "dog." *a*1984 in M.W. Bowman *Castles* 54 [ref. to 1943]: A B-17 that was under repair waiting for parts—a "Hangar Queen." **1985** Yeager & Janos *Yeager* 186: We called them "hangar queens" because that's where they sat while the engineers worked them over. **1995** Gingrich & Forstchen *1945* 368: A hangar-queen abortion of an aircraft that pilots loved to hate.

hangar rat *n. Av.* an airplane mechanic or other person who frequents an airplane hangar.
   1954 *N.Y. Times Mag.* (Mar. 7): *Hangar Rats*—Jet mechanics. **1955** *AS* XXX (May) 115. **1975** R.P. Davis *Pilot* 89: People around the airport—the hangar rats, rubbernecks—held a party…that afternoon.

hanger *n. Und.* (see quot.).
   1983 *N.Y. Times* (Sept. 6) B6: Other [pickpocket] terms include…"hanger," a wallet protruding visibly from a pocket or purse.

hangers *n.pl.* a woman's breasts.
   *a*1967 Partridge *DSUE* (ed. 6) 1166: *Hangers.* Female breasts: Australian raffish: since *ca*1930. **1976** Price *Bloodbrothers* 14: Chubby took in her jugs again. Nice big hangers. **1994** Usenet discussion group alt.binaries.pictures.erotica: [Description of erotic picture:] Heavy hangers.

hanging bee *n.* an occasion on which a criminal or criminals are publicly hanged.
   1836 in *DAE:* The chief topic of discourse seemed to be the "hanging-bee" at Trenton. **1882** Baillie-Grohman *Camps in Rockies* 365: Typical Western scenes—the audacious "road-agent," or grimly-

grotesque "hanging bee." **1900** in *DAE.* **1904** in *DAE:* Big hanging bee is now on in Chicago.

hanging Judas *n. Sailing.* (see quot.).
   1961 Burgess *Dict. Sailing* 109: *Hanging Judas.* (1) A rope or line hanging loose. (2) Anything suspended untidily.

hang-loose *adj.* very informal or relaxed; LAID-BACK.
   *a*1976 in *6,000 Words* 88: Adherence to the hedonistic hang-loose ethic….it's a hang-loose outfit….Nobody knows which end is up. *a*1982 Medved *Hospital* 219: He's a down-to-earth, hang-loose kind of person.

hangnail *n. Sports.* a minor injury.
   1970 Libby *Life in Pit* 93: The ordinary injuries we call "hangnails." We play with everything except broken bones.

hangout *n.* **1.** *Stu.* a feast or entertainment.
   1852 in B. Hall *College Wds.* (ed. 2) 247: I remember the date from the Fourth of July occurring just afterwards, which I celebrated by a "hang-out."

   2. a more or less disreputable place frequented by a particular person or persons; haunt; (*occ.*) one's place of residence. Now *S.E.* [Despite the form of the def., the 1859 quot. may have been intended to refer to the corresponding v. only; the verbal example is copied fr. an earlier dictionary, quoted at HANG OUT, *v.*, 1.]
   1859 Matsell *Vocab.* 40: *Hang Out.* The place one lives in. *"The cops scavey where we hang out,"* the officers know where we live. [**1892** L. Moore *Own Story* 251: They, too, had seen me there before, and thought that was my "hang-out place."] *a*1890–93 *F & H* III 262: *Hang out*…(*subs.*) a residence; a lodging. **1893** *Century* (Nov.) 105: They often have a "hang-out" on the outskirts of the town, where they camp quite unmolested. **1895** *Century* (Oct.) 943: Some thirteen boys appeared at the "hang-out." **1897** Hamblen *General Mgr.* 207: I went directly to the conductors' "hangout," a large waiting-room off the despatcher's office. **1899** "J. Flynt" *Tramping* 394: *Hang-Out:* the hobo's home. **1898–1900** Cullen *Chances* 28: I was in a Dearborn street hang-out for racing men one night. **1902** "J. Flynt" *Little Bro.* 32: They are given hobo names and…pass in and out of "hang-outs" unchallenged. **1903** Kildare *Mamie Rose* 83 [ref. to 1880's]: I have several times mentioned "hang-out." Most of these "hang-outs" were ginmills (saloons). **1907** in "O. Henry" *Works* 1606: "Rooney's"…[was] a tough "hangout." **1904–11** Phillips *Susan Lenox* II 248: She avoided the tough places, the hang-outs of the gangs. **1914** in Wendt & Kogan *Bosses* 310: The notorious Silver Dollar saloon, a hangout for low characters. **1917** Cahan *D. Levinsky* 140: He told me that I was a nuisance and bade me find another "hang-out" for myself. **1927** W.H. Wright *Canary Case* 128: The house he lives in is a pretty tough hang-out. **1928** Carr *Rampant Age* 176: We can go over to my hang-out and do 'em. **1929** Hotstetter & Beesley *Racket* 227: *Hang-out*—Place where criminals or tough characters congregate. **1929** *AS* IV (June) 341: *Hang-out.* Any recognized meeting place. **1927–30** Rollins *Jinglebob* 4: This sage-brush ain't as tony as the Ol' Man's hang-out, the Cheyenne Club. **1943** J. Mitchell *McSorley's* 68: The Jefferson Diner…is one of his hangouts. **1984** N. Stephenson *Big U.* 225: This is their hangout….They must like the music. **1987** Covin *Brown Sky* 240: Them white hangouts.

hang out *v.* **1.** to reside; dwell.
   *1811 Lexicon Balatron.: The traps scavey where we hang out; the officers know where we live. *1837 C. Dickens *Pickwick Papers* ch. xxx: "I say, old boy, where do you hang out?" Mr. Pickwick replied that he was at present suspended at the George and Vulture. *1851 H. Mayhew *London Labour* I 248: Where do you "hang out" in Sheffield?…I mean where do you *dos?* **1861** in S. Clemens *Twain's Letters* I 108: With a view to ascertaining her whereabouts—or, in simpler language, where she was supposed to live. **1865** Williams *Joaquin* 55: They "hang out" instead of live. **1868** "J.F. Henderson" *Two Trails* 30: "You don't mean to say that you hang out on that rock, way up yonder?"…"No Sam, I don't live there." **1866–71** Bagg *Yale* 45: *Hang out,* to occupy a room, to reside. **1883** Flagg *Versicles* 38: Warn't it Corinth, where our forefathers used to hang out? **1889** "M. Twain" *Conn. Yankee* 175: Where do they hang out?…Yes, where do they live? **1891** C.C. King *By Land & Sea* 129: Where yer hangin' out? **1892** Garland *Prairie Folks* 32: I reckon ye can hang out with me, 'f ye feel like ut. **1910** in O. Johnson *Lawrenceville* 198: "Where do you hang

out?" "Green House." **1920** in O'Brien *Best Stories 1920* 353: Here's where the doc hangs out.

2.a. to spend one's time (in a favorite place or along with others), esp. in an idle way; loiter; (*hence*) to consort or associate, esp. in public. Now *colloq.* or *S.E.*

   1867 Alger *Ragged Dick* 258: "Where do you hang out?"..."At Henderson's hat and cap store, on Broadway." **1888** Pierson *Slave of Circumstances* 131: I got down by the docks where he hangs out when he's in liquor. **1890* in *EDD* III 52: Don't hang out here, stops business. **1893** Frye *Field & Staff* 122: I went up to that club where the Fourth's fellows hang out. **1901** in "O. Henry" *Cabbages & Kings* 54: The consul told me you hung out at this caravansary. **1902** "J. Flynt" *Little Bro.* 139: [New] York....That's the place where the number one stiffs hang out. **1907** *Lippincott's Mag.* (May) 675: Them no-good kind hang out at the saloon. **1910** Hapgood *City Streets* 32: Tramps, town "bums," Bowery politicians of the most extreme character "hang out" there day and night. **1929** T. Gordon *Born to Be* 158: Also a tribe of Indians he hung out with. **1930** D. Runyon, in *Collier's* (Mar. 22) 20: If a guy hangs out with tough guys long enough he is apt to get to thinking maybe he is tough himself. **1934** *WNID2: Hang out*...to loiter idly. *Slang.* **1935** in *OEDS:* Where do you hang out? **1954–60** *DAS: Hang out*...To loaf or loiter in a recognized rendezvous, such as a bar, drugstore, or the like. *Very common.* **1970** J. Howard *Please Touch* 83: You're a sweet, sensitive kid who ought to hang out with kids your own age. **1975** Hinton *Rumble Fish* 11: I was hanging out in Benny's, playing pool. **1984** Kagan & Summers *Mute Evidence* 396: Pals....They hung out together. **1993** K. Scott *Monster* 71: We...made a pact and began to hang out together.

b. to idle away time, usu. with street companions; to play or loiter with friends during or after school or working hours.

   1958 *Jour. Social Issues* XIV (No. 3) 11: The term "hanging out" in lower class culture refers to extended periods of standing around, often with peer mates, doing what is defined as "nothing," "shooting the breeze," etc. **1965** C. Brown *Manchild* 102: I was thirteen, so now it was okay for me to hang out. **1968** in E. Knight *Belly Song* 13: Guys coming and going in to see their counselors, guys going home, and some guys just hanging out. **1968–71** Cole & Black *Checking* 96: There's a group of kids standing around just hanging out. **1973–76** J. Allen *Assault* 106: I was pretty much staying around the house and not hanging out. **1980** Wielgus & Wolff *Basketball* 11: If you don't play [basket]ball, you can't hang out. **1989** Univ. Tenn. instructors: "What do kids like to do most?" "Hang out."

3. to take (a chance); risk (someone or something). Cf. *hang it out* s.v. HANG, *v.*

   1978–86 J.L. Burke *Lost Get-Back Boogie* 104: I really went over the edge and hung one out. **1990** Bing *Do or Die* 6: How many of the kids...were going to hang themselves out in the name of reputation.

¶ In phrases:

¶ **hang it out** see s.v. HANG, *v.*

¶ **hang [out] cool** see s.v. HANG, *v.*

¶ **let it all hang out** see s.v. HANG, *v.*

hangtough *n.* one who hangs tough; tough character.

   1972 Wambaugh *Blue Kt.* 30: Most beat officers swagger....It shows the hangtoughs you're not afraid, and people expect it. *Ibid.* 33: I wish I hadn't never met that hangtough, Barty Mendez.

hang-tough *adj.* obdurate; stubborn.

   1965 Ward & Kassebaum *Women's Pris.* 49: Nineteen percent of the staff sample also approved of Smith's *hang tough* loyalty to other inmates. **1968** *Newsweek* (Dec. 2) 42: Washington is currently in a hang-tough mood vis-à-vis the Russians.

hang tough *v.* see s.v. HANG, *v.*

hang-up *n.* **1.** something provided on credit; in phr. **on hang-up** on credit.

   1906 Kildare *Old Bailiwick* 306: Now, there are more "hang-ups" than cash shines on this stand. *Ibid.* 313: I guess Nick will be shining your shoes for some time on "hang-up."

2. a cause of delay.

   1942 *ATS* 265: Delay; postponement...*Hang-up*,...*hold-up*. **1960** Partridge *DSUE* (ed. 5) 1125: *Hang-up*...Delay; frustration: Canadian jazz-lovers': since *ca*1956. **1968** N.Y.C. stock clerk, age *ca*50: What's the hang-up down there?

3.a. an inhibition, fixation, or other psychological or emotional problem.

   1952 J.C. Holmes *Go* 200: I'm being smothered...all these relationships, hangups, conflicts. **1952** Kerouac *Cody* 211: You'll never catch *him* goin off on some, ah, hangup. **1954** in Kerouac *Letters* 428: Biggest trouble is hangup on self, on ego-personality. **1955** in J. Blake *Joint* 100: Another hangup that paralyzes me in my writing is the daunting realization of my flimsy background and meager education. **1962** Kesey *Cuckoo's Nest* 165: Getting shut of her wouldn't be getting shut of the real deep-down hang-up that's causing the gripes. **1964–66** R. Stone *Hall of Mirrors* 195: I know it's a hang up. I can't help it. **1966** Little *Bold & Lonely* 189: You have a hang-up about me. **1966** *Look* (Dec. 27) 72: A few hang-ups were pulled out—sex and the church, fear of being unloved. **1966** Young & Hixson *LSD* 26: I wanted to become aware of my hang-ups and I felt LSD could help. **1968** O.H. Hampton *Young Runaways* (film): That's not your *bag*....That's your *hang-up*. **1971** *Inter. Jour. Add.* VI 358: Hang up—any neurotic manifestation. **1971** S. Miller *Hot Springs* 105: The only way to conquer this hang-up and break through to fuller human potential is by falling. **1975** Cohen *Jung & Sci. Att.* 4: The [Jungian] term "complex"...is the same thing we now popularly call a "hang-up." **1988** *Academe* (Jan.) 6: The reviewer obviously has a special "hang-up" with respect to Bellow. **1989** *Geraldo* (syndic. TV series) (May 15): How do I know what kind of hang-ups *you* have? **1995** Zabel *Official Denial* (film): I'm willing to accept that this is your hang-up and to help you work through it.

b. a difficulty, obstacle, irritation, hindrance, or cause for worry; problem.

   1952 A. Ginsberg, in Kerouac *Letters* 373: Taperecords are partly hangup, should be shortened and put in place after final trip to Frisco. **1958** A. King *Mine Enemy* 240: And that's the real hang-up. **1959** in *OEDS: Man*—Omnibus salutation extended to men, women, domestic animals—saves cool cat hangup of remembering names. **1960** in Bruce *Essential Lenny* 89: That being Protestant and Catholic and Jewish is a big hangup. **1964** E. Wilson *Wilson's N.Y.* 154: There's no hang-up....I don't have to worry about liquor licenses or whether a kid is eighteen or not. **1965** *N.Y. Post* (Dec. 1) 8C: You couldn't carry around an amplifier and electric guitar and expect to survive, it was just too much of a hang-up. **1974** Dubinsky & Standora *Decoy Cop* 177: The newscaster goes on to talk about a hangup in the Paris peace talks.

4. *Pris.* a suicide by hanging; a person who commits such a suicide.

   1974 *N.Y. Times Mag.* (Feb. 17) 14: Inside the Tombs a suicide is called a "hang-up."...A hang-up usually wets his bedsheet to keep it from ripping and ties it to crossbars above his head.

hang up *v.* **1.a.** to chalk up (a debt); to buy on credit.

   *1725 *New Canting Dict.: Hang-it-up*, speaking of the Reckoning at a *Bowsing-ken*, when the Rogues are obliged, for want of Money, to run on Tick. **1785* Grose *Vulgar Tongue: Hang it up.* Score it up: speaking of a reckoning. **1841* in *OEDS: Hang it Up*, to go on credit. **1873** Small *Pythias* 38: I furthermore swear that I will patronize every worthy Knight of Pythias, and never ask him to "hang it up" so long as I have a dollar's worth of personal property about me. **1873** "M. Twain" & Warner *Gilded Age* I 133: The Colonel muttered something to the barkeeper about "hanging it up." **1877** *Puck* (May) 4: Send me a few barrels of Robinson County—and "hang it up." **1902** Jarrold *Mickey Finn* 72: A man that dhrinks always has to borry, or hang up his liquor. **1940** E. O'Neill *Iceman* 101 [ref. to 1912]: He give me strict orders not to let Willie hang up no more drinks.

b. to request credit of.

   1882 in L. Levy *Flashes of Merriments* 280: But if they'd try to hang me up, the house was not to let. **1906** Kildare *Old Bailiwick* 70: Try and "hang him up" for two "tubs" until to-morrow, will you? **1927** T.A. Dorgan, in Zwilling *TAD Lexicon* 42: If we get our names in the papers we can hang up some hash joint for the hash.

c. to extend credit to.

   1909 in O. Johnson *Lawrenceville Stories* 20 [ref. to 1890's]: We're not asking you to hang us up this time, Al. **1942** S.H. Adams *Tambay Gold* 191: They hung me up for the parking fee.

2. to stop work; knock off (now *rare*); (*hence*) to stop or quit; give up; retire.—now usu. constr. with *it*.

   1845 in Eliason *Tarheel Talk* 276: Made 2 hauls & hung up [for the fishing season]. **1854** in *DAE:* When I came to that point I "was befogged, and hung up for the night." **1880** J.C. Harris *Uncle Remus* 132: 'En w'en I seed dat, I drap my axe, en I come in yer en sot flat down right whar youer settin' now, en I say ter myse'f dat it's 'bout time fer ole Remus fer ter hang up en quit. **1895** *DN* I 372: A mower, when rain was coming on: "I reckon we'll have to hang up for all day." **1936** Duncan *Over the Wall* 136: Hang it up. I didn't see you sticking your mitt out when I was living on bread and water in the Dark Hole—and I sure as hell don't need it now. **1959** O'Connor *Talked to a Stranger* 208: It's only the fools go around thinkin' about hangin' it up—killin' theirselves. ***1962** in Wilkes *Dict. Austral. Colloq.* 171: A shearer putting in a wet ticket, after a majority dry vote, can "hang up" and go to the huts without dismissal. **1966** Elli *Riot* 243: He's about ready to hang it up. **1969** B. Beckham *Main Mother* 54: Once you're over the hill, its [*sic*] all through...you might as well hang it up. **1970** *Playboy* (Sept.) 59: Any number of rock poets can hang it up now that Eugene McDaniels is out front with *Outlaw*. **1971** *Adam-12* (NBC-TV): Why don't we hang it up, Mac? *a*1972 *Urban Life & Culture* I 86: My little brother [was] sniffing glue, and I used to whip on him thinking he'll hang it up, man. **1973** H. Foster *Ribbin'* 8: If that's the best you can do, you better hang up. *a*1979 Pepper & Pepper *Straight Life* 83: Why don't you hang up that jive and get in a different groove? **1994** *Vicki* (synd. TV series): I was gonna clean teeth, marry a rich dentist, and hang it up.

3.a. (see quots.).

1872 Crapsey *Nether Side* 23: Those desperate thieves the police style "hangers-up"...steal upon a man in some private place, bind him hand and foot, and after robbing him leisurely and effectually go away, leaving him to loosen himself as best he may. ***1873** Hotten *Slang Dict.* (ed. 4): *Hang up*, to rob with violence, to garrotte. **1891** Maitland *Slang Dict.* 137: *Hang up* (Amer.), to rob with violence on the street. See *hold up*.

b. to set back in funds, esp. to charge exorbitantly.

*1886 in *EDD* III 52: I'm darned if I'll be a hanged up like this here. **1912** Field *Watch Yourself Go By* 285: Say, kid, how much are you going to hang me up for? **1953–58** J.C. Holmes *Horn* 55: So then this square cab driver hung me up for a buck getting over here to Geordie's.

c. to place under arrest.

1956 Resko *Reprieve* 235 [ref. to 1940's]: He's got to hang me up for using stuff...and I got to dummy up about all the studs I know on the kick.

4. to lodge; put up.

1874 in *OEDS:* You mou't get a place 'bout a mile furder on whar you could hang up for the night. **1886** Nye *Remarks* 169: Mr. George W. Mulqueen come there and wanted to engage the school at the old camp, where I hung up in the days when the country was new. **1908** Hopper & Bechdolt *9009* 174: Who's keepin' you? Who're you hanging up with?

5. to pawn.

1891 Maitland *Slang Dict.* 137: *Hang up*...to pawn. **1891** Campbell, Knox & Byrnes *Darkness & Daylight* 610: Ladies' dresses are "hung up," as they would be injured by folding. Hence arises the slang term of "hung up" for an article that has been pledged at the pawnbroker's. **1945** Hubbard *R.R. Ave.* 346: *Hanging Up The Clock—Boomer* term that meant hocking your railroad watch.

6. [fr. S.E. sense 'end a telephone call'] to cease talking; shut up.—now also constr. with *it.*—used imper.

1918 in "M. Brand" *Coll. Stories of Max Brand* 54: Cut it out, Freddie....Ring off. Hang up. **1934** Weseen *Dict. Slang* 347: *Hang up*—To cease talking. **1942** *ATS* 236: "Shut up"...*hang up* (*the line's busy*). **1965** Hersey *Too Far to Walk* 193: Oh, Wagner. Hang up. You're disturbed. **1966** Braly *On Yard* 136: "Hang up," Chilly broke in. [**1971** *Current Slang* (Winter) 6: *Hang it up*, v. (imperative) Forget it.] **1987** *Throb* (synd. TV): Oh, hang it up!

7. Esp. *Jazz.* to exasperate; frustrate; vex; plague; disconcert.

*ca*1953 Hughes *Lodge* 82: I had never had an orgasm in my life....And that of course hung me up a lot too because it was always the same old story. **1959–61** Kerouac *Pull My Daisy* 25: You guys have gotta act a little better on behavior there because you don't want to hang the bishop up you understand. **1961** R. Russell *Sound* 8: I mean, it really hangs me up.

8. *Pris.* to make an escape from confinement.—constr. with *it.*

1971 in J. Blake *Joint* 14: I could use [the sneakers] not only for working in, but they'll be handy when I hang it up.

¶ In phrases:

¶ **hang up (one's) fiddle** see s.v. FIDDLE.

¶ **hang up the gloves** [or **hang 'em up**] (orig. of prize-fighters) to quit one's career; retire.

1942 *ATS* 675: *Hang up the gloves*, to retire from boxing. **1957** M. Shulman *Rally* 20: Three squares and a flop...and a pension when you're ready to hang up the gloves. **1972** Bunker *No Beast* 36: No, I'm hanging up the gloves. I'm going to get a job and settle down. **1973** D. Morrow *Maurie* 165: I'm hanging them up last game of the season. **1976** Woodley *Bears* 132: My boys will want to hang up their gloves forever. **1981** Brenner & Nagler *Only the Ring* 77: He was all through and ready to hang them up.

¶ **hang up the spikes** *Sports.* to retire from baseball, football, etc.

1942 *ATS* 660: *Hang up the spikes*, to retire from baseball. **1986** Univ. Tenn. instructor: What does he do when he finally hangs up the spikes?

Hank Snow *n.* ¶ In phrase: **pull** [or **do**] **a Hank Snow** [alluding to country-western song "I'm Movin' On" (1950), words and music (and a popular phonograph recording) by Hank Snow (1914–)] to move on or clear out.

1962 W. Crawford *Give Me Tomorrow* 48 [ref. to Korean War]: A couple of Dodge's yo-bos pulled a Hank Snow and moved on the other night. **1974** *Playboy* (Apr.) 132: Sheriff T.J. Flournoy would...suggest...your rapid leave-taking. The wise or the prudent didn't pause....You just did a quick Hank Snow.

hankty var. HINCTY.

hanky-pank *n.* **1.** see HANKY-PANKY.

2. a pitchman.

1906 *Nat. Police Gaz.* (Aug. 18) 6: Hanky panks trying olives or caviare sandwiches for the first time. **1921** Sandburg *Sunburnt West* 25: "Feed it to 'em,/They lap it up,"/...Said a hanky-pank selling jumping-jacks.

hanky-panky *n.* [perh. of Romani orig.; see 1889–90, 1953 quots.] Also **hanky-pank.** **1.a.** clever trickery or deception; cheating; intrigue; (now *esp.*) sly misconduct or wrongdoing, often of a sexual nature.

*1841 in *OED:* Only a little hanky-panky. ***1847** in *OED:* Necromancy, my dear Sir—the hanky-panky of the ancients. ***1863** in T. Taylor *Plays* 211: So you've come out for a little hanky-panky with old Moss. ***1864** in *F & H* III 265: If there was any *hanky panky*, any mystery I mean, he'd always swear he was out. ***1877** in *F & H:* There's some hanky panky business going on among the men of No. 2 prison. [**1877** *Puck* (Mar.) 15: Yankee Pankee...For a long time past the issue of the presidential election has been involved in a Hayes.] ***1880** in *F & H:* He kept a pretty sharp look out to see that what he was pleased to term *hanky panky* was not carried on under his nose. ***1887** in *EDD:* None of your hanky-panky. **1889** *Century Dict.: Hanky-panky*...Jugglery; trickery; legerdemain. ***1889–90** Barrère & Leland *Dict. Slang* I 447: *Hanky-panky*, adroit substitution, palming, sleight-of-hand in legerdemain....In gypsy, *huckeny pokee*, or *ponkee*, means the adroit substitution by sleight-of-hand of a bundle containing lead or stones for another containing money or valuables. ***a1890–93** *F & H* III 264: *Hanky-Panky*...(1) legerdemain; whence (2) trickery; underhand work; cheating; any manner of double-dealing or intrigue. **1916** S. Lewis *Job* 254: Such feminine "hanky-panky tricks," he assured her, were the cause of "all these...divorces." **1945** in *DAS:* The good doctor was up to his neck in some extramarital hanky-panky. **1952** Bellow *Adventures of Augie March* 416: There wouldn't be any hanky-panky with the girl. **1953** Gresham *Midway* 114: Another Romany name for this [fortune-telling] dodge is *hakk'ni panki*, from which *hanky-panky*, as a synonym for trickery of any kind, probably stems. **1962** L'Engle *Wrinkle in Time* 138: If you want to see Murry you'd better come with me and not try any more hanky-panky. **1976–77** Kernochan *Dry Hustle* 124: Getting too old for the hanky-pank...don't you look the cute little tramp. **1979** Homer *Jargon* 207: *Hankypanky*...any type of sexual activity. **1981** Ehrlichman *Witness* 326: A lot of hanky-panky that we have nothing to do with ourselves. **1983** L. Barrett *Gambling with History* 457: But the collective hanky-panky detectable in this administration...was as hubcap theft is to bank robbery. **1983** WKGN radio news (Apr. 21): Word has leaked out about further hanky-panky at the

Environmental Protection Agency. **1984** *News-Sentinel* (Knoxville, Tenn.) (June 22) 1: This sends a very powerful signal to the other guy that you're not trying hanky-panky, that you're really serious about winding down [the arms race]. *a***1989** Micheels *Braving Flames* 94: One thing leads me to believe there was a little hanky-panky going on there. **1994** *Young & Restless* (CBS-TV): If you want to keep your hanky-panky secret, I suggest you soundproof those walls.

b. foolishness or silliness; silly talk; (*Carnival*) (see 1954–60 quot.).

1901 Ade *Modern Fables* 38: His Sense of Humor prevented him from getting down on his Knees and giving her any of this Mrs. E.D.N. Southworth Hanky-Pank. **1914** Jackson & Hellyer *Vocab.* 42: *Hanky Pank*, Noun. Current in polite slang circles. Insincere or trifling small talk. Flattery, garrulousness. See "Breeze," "Bull." **1920** Ade *Hand-Made Fables* 308: Every Whispering Order had a different kind of Grip, with much interlocking of Digits, pressure on the Wrist, and other Hanky-Pank. **1954–60** *DAS: Hanky-pank*...A carnival barker's urgings to get customers to take a chance in...a game; spiel. **1963** W.C. Anderson *Penelope* 134: Through all of this hanky-pank, the man...in the lounge chair had remained completely aloof. **1972** Meade & Rutledge *Belle* 96: This is a lot of hanky-panky to go through for a conference. **1974** Matthews & Amdur *My Race* 225: All this hanky-panky sounds exciting, except that...you have to enlist in the Army for two years.

c. *Carnival.* (see quots.).

1946 Dadswell *Hey There, Sucker!* 101: *Hanky-panky*...a trivial thing that is no good. **1954–60** *DAS: Hanky-pank*...Anything cheap and gaudy.

2. *Carnival.* any of various carnival games.

1883 E. Field *Tribune Verse* 200: Josep Wilson—half-past one—/Hanky-panky—lots of fun....Thinks of Hanky-panky then/Wishes he were back again. **1908** in Fleming *Unforgettable Season* 200: Even allowing the great American game of "Hanky Pank" to be played for a small limit. **1954–60** *DAS: Hanky-pank*...Any of several carnival games that cost 5¢ or 10¢ to play. **1970** A. Lewis *Carnival* 18: A hanky-pank is a game of skill, a group game, perhaps, where someone wins a prize every time. **1988** Gryczan *Carnival Secrets* 3: *Hanky-panks*—games operated so players are assured of walking away with some sort of cheap souvenir.

hanky-spanky *adj.* (see quots.).

***1889** in Barrère & Leland *Dict. Slang* I 447: *Hanky-spanky*...dashing, in dashing style; refers specially to garments. **1913** *DN* IV 24: *Hanky-spanky.* Dashing, stylish, nobby; specifically of well-cut clothes. Facetious. Used in Nebraska...."He's some *hanky-spanky* fellow that's been hangin' round here for quite a spell."

Hannah *n.* ¶ In phrases:

¶ **holy Hannah!** (used to express astonishment).

1982 Braun *Judas Tree* 29: Holy Hannah!...I just had a brainstorm! **1982** *World's Finest Comics* (Sept.) (unp.): Holy Hannah! The weight's all wrong!

¶ **so help me Hannah!** (used as an asseverative oath).

1924 *DN* V 269: *Hanna:* so help me ——. **1928** Bodenheim *Georgie May* 123: Ah'll cut mah throat befoah ah let them lug me back, so help me Hanna. **1960, 1966–9** in *DARE.*

¶ **that's what's the matter with Hannah** that is precisely the case.

1879 Rooney *Conundrums* 80: And that's what's the matter with Hannah! **1882** A.W. Aiken *Joe Buck* 7: Aha, a self-cocker, eh?...and that is what's the matter with Hannah! **1884** Peck *Boss Book* 40: American boys...know what is the matter with Hanner. **1888** in *AS* XXXVII (1962) 76: *That's what's the matter with Hannah* A flip rebuke to a person who has belabored the obvious. **1891** Maitland *Slang Dict.* 137: *Hannah*, "that's what's the matter with" (Amer.), an expression used to corroborate an asseveration, expressive of certainty.

Hanoi Hilton *n.* [sugg. by the international chain of *Hilton* hotels] Esp. *Mil. Av.* a North Vietnamese prison; confinement as a prisoner of war in North Vietnam. Now *hist.*

1966–67 Harvey *Air War* 148: Penicillin...isn't on the room-service list at the Hanoi Hilton. **1967** Mulligan *No Place to Die* 162: They might not have room service at the Hanoi Hilton. **1969** Broughton *Thud Ridge* 23 [ref. to 1966]: Those who made mistakes—and even many who did everything properly—are either dead or guests at the

Hanoi Hilton. **1972** *N.Y. Times Mag.* 11: Death, to the pilots, seems more remote than the actuality of "Hanoi Hilton," the sour fliers' name for a North Vietnamese prison camp. **1975** N. McDaniel *Another Voice* 14: We arrived at the infamous "Hanoi Hilton," the main NV prison camp where nearly all the captured U.S. flyers were processed. **1980** Santoli *Everything* 233: I think people have a tendency to call that Hoa Lo complex the Hanoi Hilton. **1980** W.C. Anderson *Bat-21* 15: Or maybe worse, being on his way to the Hanoi Hilton. **1992** *Santa Barbara News-Press* (Oct. 28) A12: The notorious Hanoi Hilton prison, where American fliers were tortured and interrogated during the Vietnam War, is being demolished. **1995** *Morning News* (CNN-TV) (Apr. 28): The old Hanoi Hilton, where American prisoners once were held, will become a real hotel.

hap or **haps** *n.* [short for HAPPENINGS] Esp. *Black E.* the latest occurrence; news; in phr. **What's the haps?** (used as a greeting).

1961 *N.Y. Times Mag.* (June 25) 39: *Haps*—An event, an occurrence. **1962** *Eng. Jour.* LI 325: *How's haps?*—How are you? What's new? **1970** A. Young *Snakes* 42: I like to...check out the haps. **1970** Landy *Underground Dict.* 98: *Hap n.* Occurrence of interest that is going on....*Where is the hap?* **1985** Heywood *Taxi Dancer* 13 [ref. to Vietnam War]: Hey, Lead, what's the haps? **1986** Stinson & Carabatsos *Heartbreak* 206: Hey, gunny, what's the hap? **1990** *Teenage Mutant Ninja Turtles* (CBS-TV): Hey, dudes! What's the haps? **1992** *Amer. Detective* (ABC-TV): What's the haps, Paps?

¶ In phrase:

¶ **no haps** *Black E.* no indeed.

1988 S. Lee *School Daze* (film): Rachel? No, no haps.

happen *v.* **1.** Orig. *Music Industry.* to meet with great success, popularity, or critical acclaim; to attract much attention or publicity.

1949 in *OEDS*: A song happens...when the preparatory work results in a successful bid for popularity. **1959** *Life* (Nov. 23) 45: *Happening*—a record making the charts. **1961** in Broven *Walking to N.O.* (photo. sec.): [Ad for phonograph record:] It's happening! breaking in Baltimore, Washington and Detroit. **1964** Rhodes *Chosen Few* 160: That's Jeeter up and down, and I mean t' tell ya, he's happenin'. **1966** R.E. Kent *Hot Rods to Hell* (film): It's what's happening around here. **1987** *Miami Vice* (NBC-TV): When he first started out, Tommy Lowe was happening—the greatest rock manager *ever.*

2. to be exciting or of significant interest; in phr. **where it's happening** where the interest, fun, or excitement is.— usu. constr. in progressive tenses. See also *what's happening?*, below. See also HAPPENING.

1955 *Down Beat* (July 13) 33, in Gold *Jazz Lexicon*: I don't think much of anything happens here. **1958** in Gold *Jazz Lexicon*: Well, like it's got to "funk" all the time...without it, nothing's happening. **1968** O.H. Hampton *Young Runaways* (film): It's where the action is....It's where it's happening, you dig? **1972** Wambaugh *Blue Kt.* 29: You and Sissy are the only ones. You're what's happening, baby. **1977** Flusser *Squeal Man* 176: The Upper East Side,...the place where everything is happening, where everything seems shimmering and new. **1977** Univ. Tenn. instructor: Milton's not what's happening these days in critical studies. The Beats are where it's at. **1984** Mason & Rheingold *Slanguage: Happening*, adj. "This place is happening." Approval and enjoyment of a place or situation. Ex: Restaurant, nightclub, party, or small town in Ohio. **1985** "J. Blowdryer" *Mod. Eng.* 8: *Cranking*...Something that is really happenin'. **1987** Univ. Tenn. student theme: A bar which is fairly crowded, busy, and seems to be popular and exciting may be called "hopping," "rocking," "rolling," "jumping," "happening," and "going." **1988** *Right On!* (June) 35: Missed out on an issue of *Right On!?* They're all hot and happening. **1988** *Rage* (Knoxville, Tenn.) (Sept.) 31: The miracle student who seems to always have just enough money to be where it's happening, every time. **1989** *Nat. Lampoon* (June) 50: This is where it's all happening—the girls, the sex,...the uninhibited madness. **1993** *Mystery Sci. Theater* (Comedy Central TV): This whole halter-top thing just isn't happening for him.

3. to make an appearance; show up; appear.

1980 Gould *Ft. Apache* 94: He was still proud of the pad, even if the bitches weren't happening. **1986** Clayton & Elliott *Jazz World* 173: I never chose these cats as "brothers"; they just happened.

4. to function properly; be in operation; work.

1988 *It's Garry Shandling's Show* (Fox-TV): Is the compass working? Is the altimeter still happening? **1989** *Sonya Live in L.A.* (CNN-TV) (May 19): The administrators are making the [existing, functioning] program happen.

¶ In phrases:

¶ **never happen** usu. /ˈnɛvʌ ˈhɑpən/ [orig. pidgin] Orig. *Mil.* it never will (or never did) happen; never; no indeed. Cf. *never hachi* s.v. HACHI, *n.*

1950 *N.Y. Times Mag.* (July 23) 42: Such new Army slang phrases as "never happen."...It means, roughly, "You must be crazy." **1953** in Valant *Aircraft Nose Art* 295: Never Hoppen. **1954** in *AS* XXX (1955) 47: *Suck a hachi* has united with the GI *nevah hoppen* to beget *nevah hachi*. **1959** Searls *Big X* 96: Never hoppen, Kato. Never hoppen. **1960** *AS* XXXV 262: *Nevah hoppen* (a negative response). **1961** Brosnan *Pennant Race* 6: "Bet he takes one pitch now."..."Never happen." Lynch came to swing." **1976** C.R. Anderson *Grunts* 50: "If you lived in Arlington you'd be home by now." "Nevah hoppen, GI." **1968–77** Herr *Dispatches* 26: He goes to me, "Take a little run up to the ridge and report to me," and I goes like, "Never happen, Sir." **1985** Flowers *Mojo Blues* 9: I'm not spending all my money in a hotel room. Never happen GI. **1989** *Married with Children* (Fox-TV): Never happen! **1989** T. Blackburn *Jolly Rogers* 249 [ref. to WWII]: In my best Waikiki beach-boy pidgin I answered, "Nevah hoppen."

¶ **not what's happening** *Black E.* not what one should do.

1966 I. Reed *Free-Lance Pall-Bearers* 2: Your father is a big fat stupid Kabalsa who is doin' one to five in Sing Sing for foolin' around with them blasted chickens. That is definitely not what's happening.

¶ **what's happening?** Esp. *Black E.* what's up? how are you?—used as a greeting. Cf. (2), above.

1955 in *Tenn. Folk. Soc. Bull.* XXI (1956) 23: "*What's happening, man?*"—A common greeting [among jazzmen]. **1956–60** J.A. Williams *Angry Ones* ch. xii: We cut in past the doorman. I couldn't resist saying, "What's happening, Dan?" **1966** in *Trans-action* IV (Apr. 1967) 11: The conventional greeting. "What's happening, Brother." **1968** K. Hunter *Soul Bros.* 153: Hands were raised in greeting as she passed. "Hey." "What's happenin'?" **1970** Landy *Underground Dict.* 196: *What's happening?*...what's going on, or how are you? *a*1971 in Bullins *Hungered One* 118: Hey, what's happenin', man? **1989** Univ. Tenn. student: Hey, Bill. What's happening?

happening *adj.* [extended fr. HAPPEN, 2] up-to-date; extremely fashionable; (*hence*) splendid. Cf. HAPPEN, 2.

1976–77 C. McFadden *Serial* 312: Marin's this whole high-energy trip with all these happening people...This is where it's at, you know? **1988** Wendy's, Inc., TV ad: First you get yourself a happening piece of equipment. **1988** N.J. electrical engineer, age *ca*25: That watch is *so* happening! **1988** *ALF* (NBC-TV): No way, man. I think these films are *happening!* **1988** *N.Y. Times Mag.* (Dec. 11) 22: *Happening*...is being used to mean *chic, in vogue, approved*...."He's a happening guy" or "That's a happening outfit." **1989** *ALF Tales* (NBC-TV): A happening blond dude....Let's turn this place into a happening amusement park! **1989** Wendy's, Inc., TV ad: My daughter said, "Dad! It's like a major totally happening cheeseburger." **1993** Bahr & Small *Son-in-Law* (film): "How are *you*?" "Happening!" **1994** *TV Guide* (July 30) 6: My pecs aren't my favorite, but my biceps are pretty happening.

happenings *n.pl. Jazz.* **1.** goings-on of any nature in one's surroundings, esp. those of immediate interest; SCENE.

1953 in R.S. Gold *Jazz Talk* 120: Later for the happenings, baby. **1958** in R.S. Gold *Jazz Talk*: Our two friends, standing in a corner, were diggin' the happenings. **1961, 1963** in R.S. Gold *Jazz Talk*.

2. illicit drugs.

1958 *AS* XXXIII 225: *Junk, gage, happenings, pod* and *tea* (all meaning narcotics).

happiness job *n. Mil. Av.* an easy combat mission.

1982 Basel *Pak Six* 124 [ref. to 1968]: Led a happiness job into Pak Three. Easy. Got good hits on a road segment and truck park.

-happy *comb. form.* (used in compounds implying the loss of one's restraint or good sense relative to the first element of the compound) -crazy; -crazed; intoxicated or dazzled by; preoccupied with; given to the excessive use of; made neurotic, insane, or eccentric by; terrified of. Also in more elliptical constructions. [The following quots. illustrate rare or unique compounds; more frequent compounds (e.g., SLAP-HAPPY, TRIGGER-HAPPY) appear as main entries in this dictionary.]

[**1930** in Oliver *Blues Tradition* 241: Soap is a nickel and the towel is free,/I'm pigmeat happy, now who wants me?] **1931** *Amer. Mercury* (Dec.) 449: I...saw again a beer-happy humanity...standing at the bar. **1938** Steinbeck *Grapes of Wrath* 307: Cop-happy....Fella was sayin'—he's bull-simple. **1941** Kendall *Army & Navy Sl.* 6: He's gear-happy....truck driver who shifts excessively. *Ibid.* 12: *Rate-happy*...a recently non-commissioned officer full of authority. **1942** *Yank* (Sept. 16) 6: Australian women...are Yank-happy. **1944** Kendall *Service Slang* 5: *Code-happy*....exuberant Radio school student. **1945** in *Calif. Folk. Qly.* V (1946) 377: Similarly, the radioman—affectionately known as *Sparks*—is *dit happy* or *code-happy* when he continuously taps off messages or practices frequently. **1948** Lowry *Wolf That Fed Us* 44: He looked at the load of furlough-happy soldiers he'd collected along the road from Bari. **1948** Cozzens *Guard of Honor* 592: You see, we're a little bit bomber-happy, Nat. That's our biggest trouble. **1950** Stuart *Objector* 214: All officers are whistle-happy. **1951** Spillane *Lonely Night* 14: When you're right you're a hero. When you're wrong you're kill-happy. **1951** Grant *Flying Leathernecks* (film): Don't get careless, or ace-happy. A live Marine's better than a dead hero. **1954** Gaddis *Birdman* 35: "That club-happy screw," Stroud said softly. **1958** *Life* (Apr. 14) 132: Youngblood was clothes-happy. **1959** A. Anderson *Lover Man* 150: They all said I was "music happy." **1959** Morrill *Dark Sea* 14: Her steering is yaw-happy. **1961** Boyd *Lighter Than Air* 98 [ref. to WWII]: All that he was sure of was that Burns had caught the well-known dread disease: He was Sub-happy. **1961** Coon *At the Front* 180: This lanky bastard was just as rank-happy as he is now. **1961** Clausen *Season's Over* 48: They were, to a man, "elephant-happy." Most of them spent almost twenty-four hours a day with the elephants....Once addicted to elephants they seldom left the show. **1961** Davis *Marine at War* 177: They're glory-happy enough to make a fire-fight out of a misfire. **1963** Huff & Smith *Defensive Football* 14: A bumper crop of pass-happy quarterbacks. **1972** Ramsay *No Longer on Map* 3: The conquistadores may have been gold-happy, but they were realists. **1972** *N.Y. Times* (May 7) 15: His willingness to talk about using nuclear devices left him an open target for Democratic efforts—not always scrupulous—to picture him as a bomb-happy warmonger. **1973** "Lady Sheba" *Witch* 60: A Witch can abuse the use of his astral....There is always the danger of becoming ASTRAL HAPPY. **1979** Kiev *Courage to Live* 28: The 1960s...that drug-happy decade. **1993** *Donahue* (NBC-TV): You're...sue-happy!

happy camper *n.* a person who is pleased or happy.—usu. used in negative contexts.

1981 in *N.Y. Times Mag.* (Dec. 25, 1988) 24: It is not a group of happy campers that gets off the bus. **1985** Eble *Campus Slang* (Oct.) 5: *Happy camper*—someone in a cheerful mood. "Give Kelley some ice cream and she's a happy camper." **1987** *Night Court* (NBC-TV): Is it just me, or is Roz not a happy camper? **1988** *Daybreak* (CNN-TV) (Dec. 4): And Bobby Knight is not a happy camper on this afternoon [because his team is losing]. **1988** *N.Y. Times Mag.* (Dec. 25) 8: Mr. Fuller has fought hard for the chief of staff's job and was described by one friend as "not a happy camper."..."You got a bunch of happy campers up here," an astronaut A-O.K.'d Mission Control. **1989** *CBS This Morning* (CBS-TV) (Jan. 2): I'm not real popular with [the tobacco industry] right now. They're not happy campers. **1989** Vice-pres. D. Quayle, in *Newsweek* (May 8) 13: You all look like happy campers to me....happy campers you will always be. **1990** *Wall St. Jour.* (Aug. 3) B1: Business is off 10% to 40% during the week. "We're not a bunch of happy campers right now." **1995** *N.Y. Times* (Oct. 10) A15: I am a happy camper doing what I'm doing, and hopefully I can get back to it soon.

happy dust *n. Narc.* a drug, as cocaine, morphine, or heroin, in powdered or crystalline form.

1914 in Terry & Pellens *Opium* 112: [Heroin] was variously termed "happy dust," "snow," etc. **1917** Oemler *Slippy McGee* 29: And I let the happy dust alone. Most dips are dopes, but I was too slick; I cut it out. **1919** Darling *Jargon Book* 16: *Happy Dust*—Cocaine. **1922** E. Murphy *Black Candle* 67: The boxes were found to contain cocaine, or "happy-dust." **1925** *Amer. Mercury* (Feb.) 198: He offers "happy dust" or "snow" [heroin] to the tyro. **1925** Van Vechten *Nigger Heaven* 243: Got any happy dust, Danny? *Ibid.* 285: Happy Dust. Cocaine. **1925** Heyward *Porgy* 83: Happy dus'!...Take dat t'ing away, nigger. **1927** *DN* V 449: *Happy dust*...cocaine. **1929** *AS* IV 341: *Happy dust*—Morphine. **1930** Irwin *Tramp & Und. Sl.*: *Happy dust.*—Cocaine or any other powdered narcotic. **1957** *Sat. Eve. Post* (Nov. 30) 95: "I don't keep anything behind my pictures but dust," he said. "As long as it's not happy dust, O.K." **1961** Peacock *Valhalla* 29: An overdose of her happy dust. **1962–63** in Giallombardo *Soc. of Women* 204: *Happy Dust.* Cocaine. **1964** Smith & Hoefer *Music* 145: We also had plenty of visits from Yellow Charleston, a dope fiend specializing in happy dust.*…*Cocaine. **1971** Curtis *Banjo* 214: Funny how that happy dust takes away your appetite. **1978** Maupin *Tales* 40: Happy dust. This stuff is an American institution. **1981** Sann *Trial* 23: Who also thought all the answers came in pills or the happy dust. ***1990** Thorne *Dict. Contemp. Slang* 232: *Happy dust*…has been applied to cocaine, PCP and amphetamines among others.

happy-duster *n. Narc.* a user of HAPPY DUST.
    1922 E. Murphy *Black Candle* 19: Indeed, the snuffers of cocaine are frequently designated as "happy-dusters" because of their sense of exhilaration and satisfaction. **1925** (cited in Partridge *Dict. Und.* 320). **1953** (cited in Spears *Drugs & Drink*).

happy farm *n.* FUNNY FARM. Occ. as adj.
    1972 N.Y.U. student: The *happy farm* is the nuthouse. Same as *funny farm.* **1985** M. Baker *Cops* 220: That stuff is happy farm. It's crazy.

happy grass *n. Narc.* marijuana. [The 1935 quot. is almost certainly a misprint for this.] *Joc.*
    [**1935** Pollock *Und. Speaks: Happy gas,* mariahuana.] **1967–80** Folb *Runnin' Lines* 241: *Happy grass.* Marijuana. **1980** Novak *High Culture* 181: Some…would be only too happy to toke Thai "happy grass."

happy hand *n.* GLAD HAND, 1.—constr. with *the.*
    1973 J.A. McPherson, in C. Major *Calling Wind* 362: D.B. Ferris…the same dude…that was gonna give me the happy hand.

happy hands *n.pl. Stu.* (of a man or boy) a propensity for making unwanted physical advances on a date. Hence **happy-hand,** *v.*
    1952–57 J. Jones *Some Came Running* 155: Please take your hand off my breast.…I don't like some joker happy-handing me in the back seat of a car just because I agreed to a party with him. **1955–57** Felder *Collegiate Slang* 3: *Happy hands*—a boy too insistent on necking.

happy harness *n.* jewelry. *Joc.*
    1908 *New Broadway* (July) 30: A real toppy mother and daughter who wore enough happy harness to stock a new Tiffany's.

happy hour *n.* **1.** *Navy.* a scheduled period for entertainment and refreshments on shipboard.
    1920 Belknap *Yankee Mining Sq.* 52 [ref. to 1918]: Boxing and wrestling were taken up by the individual ships and, generally speaking, one evening each week was given over to "happy hours," for bouts in the ring and on the mat. *Ibid.* 86: [The mines'] presence forbade moving pictures on board, restricted smoking, and limited the "happy hours" and similar forms of diversion. **1945** in J. Utley *Amer. Battleship* 133: *U.S.S. Tennessee* Happy Hour in Japan. Monday Oct 1st at 1400. **1946** Heggen *Mr. Roberts* 137: The crew held a "Happy Hour," devoted almost entirely to skits of the broadest and most animalistic sort. **1958** Cope & Dyer *Petty Officer's Guide* (ed. 2) 349: *Happy Hour.* Period of entertainment aboard ship, including refreshments. **1958** Plagemann *Steel Cocoon* 99 [ref. to WWII]: Ensign Cripps…felt that part of the noontime happy hour should be devoted to news broadcasts. **1969** Smith *USMC in WWII* 427 [ref. to 1942]: They are Americans, lads who came over on the boat with us, stood in line with us for chow, and laughed with us at "Happy Hour."

2. a time, usu. in the late afternoon, when a bar lowers the price of drinks or serves free snacks. Now *colloq.*
    1959 *Sat. Eve. Post* (Apr. 25) 24: Except for those who spend too much during "happy hour" at the bar—and there are few of these—the money mounts up fast. **1961** in *OED2*: Deprived of their happy hour at the cocktail bar. **1965** *Sat. Eve. Post* (July 17) 71: The period known as "happy hour," when pre-dinner cocktails cost only a quarter. **1965** *Air Officer's Guide* 437: *Happy hour*—cocktail hour, especially 5–6 p.m. Fridays at many officer's messes. **1967** Briscoe *Short Timer* 13: Another Happy Hour is in swing now, with the troops dancing and trying to forget that a war is going on. **1968** Moura & Sutherland *Tender Loving Care* 18: I'll see you at Happy Hour. **1969** Maitland *Only War We've Got* 162: We're gonna miss Happy Hour if they don't get here soon. **1969** in H.S. Thompson *Shark Hunt* 478: On Friday afternoons, from four-thirty to seven, they crowd into the officers' club bar

for the weekly "happy hour." **1970** N.Y.U. student: Happy hour is Friday from five to six. Drinks are two for one. **1975** *Business Week* (Feb. 17) 48: The law also forbids bars and restaurants from offering cut-rate drinks. So much for happy-hour. **1981** *L.A. Times* (July 5) VI 10: Survivors…of 1,001 popcorn and peanut-filled happy hours. "Drunks, losers."

happy house *n.* a psychiatric hospital. Also **happy home.**
    1966 R. Djivre "They're Coming to Take Me Away, Ha-Haaa!" (pop. song): They're coming to take me away…to the happy home. **1969** N.Y.C. editor: This kind of thing leads to the happy house. **1974** Widener *N.U.K.E.E.* 153: Ohmvolt had sprung him from his cushioned confines at a nearby "happy house" the same week.

happy hunting ground *n.* [perh. translated from a Native American language, but perh. more likely a naively imagined European concept] the afterlife; death. Also pl. *Joc.*
    [Orig. a literary phr. used in Native American contexts, as by W. Irving, but adopted allusively as slang, esp. by writers of Western fiction; E.W. Voegelin gives a succinct summary in M. Leach, cited below. Cf. *last round-up* s.v. ROUND-UP.]
    1837 W. Irving, in *DAE*: Then we killed at his grave fifteen of our best and strongest horses, to serve him when he should arrive at the happy hunting grounds. **1876** in *DAE*: Animals were hunted in the "happy hunting grounds" for amusement only, but were never killed. **1881** in Miller & Snell *Why West Was Wild* 145: Duff…sent the entire outfit to the happy hunting grounds. **1908** W.G. Davenport *Butte & Montana* 211: To cut a man short after he has been licking up…rotgut…means a trip to the happy hunting grounds. **1918** in "M. Brand" *Coll. Stories of M. Brand* 60: Before we're through flashin' guns, some of us are goin' to start out…for the happy huntin' grounds. *a*1949 E.W. Voegelin, in M. Leach *Dict. Folk., Myth & Legend* 479: *Happy hunting ground* A popular term for the hereafter in references by whites to American Indian concepts of life after death. That the Indians believed in such a concept is well attested, but their own descriptions of the activities which go on in such a land seldom include references to hunting.

happy juice *n.* high spirits derived from the use of liquor or drugs; (*hence*) liquor.
    1921 Benet *Beginning of Wisdom* 290: He was too full of happy-juice. **1952** in *DAS*: The increased taxes on happy-juice has cut the revenue from liquor sales. **1953** Paley *Rumble* 56: Pass on some of that happy juice to Sad Sack.

happy landings *interj.* Orig. *Av.* (used as a drinking toast).
    1918 I. Cobb *Glory of the Coming* 163: I saw them last…with…their glasses raised, wishing to us "Happy landings!" ***1934** in *OEDS.* **1949** Loos & Sales *Mother Is a Freshman* (film): Happy landings! **1953** in *OEDS.*

happy pill *n.* a pill or capsule containing a tranquilizer or stimulant.
    *1956 A. Huxley, in *OEDS*: The present mass-consumption of "Happy Pills," (Miltown-Equanil). **1957** *N.Y. Times* (Jan. 20) VI 56: Tranquilizing pills.…Whether "happy pills" can contribute to lasting improvement in canine behavior has yet to be explored. **1957** *Harper's* (Nov.) 10: Many physicians use these drugs rarely as "happy pills." ***1964** in *OEDS.* **1966** Asimov *Fantastic Voyage* 4: You've got that tranquilizer gleam in your eye, Doctor. I don't need any happy pills. **1967** *Star Trek* (NBC-TV): How did you arrange to touch her, Bones? Give her a happy pill?

happy rags *n.pl.* glad rags (s.v. GLAD RAG, 1).
    1928 Coe *Swag* 63: Take that note and get yourself some happy rags in the morning.

happy shop *n. Black E.* a liquor store.
    1967 Lit *Dictionary* 20: *Happy Shop*—Booze store. **1971** Dahlskog *Dict.* 30: *Happy shop, n.* A liquor store.

happy stuff *n.* HAPPY DUST.
    1929–31 (cited in Partridge *Dict. Und.* 320). **1974** Gober *Black Cop* 84: Wilson is always right there on time with the happy stuff.

happy talk *n. TV Journ.* light, informal human interest stories; (*also*) banter between newscasters included for its presumed audience appeal. Also attrib. [In later colloq. use, 'overly optimistic sentiments'.]

*1973 in *BDNE2:* What Happy Talk means in fact is that the consumer-listener-viewer gets an inverted perspective of the world in which he lives. **1976** in *BDNE2:* The happy talk, the newscasters in clown suits. **1978** *U.S. News & W.R.* (Nov. 20) 53: A serious focus on current events—a turnabout from the…"happy talk" delivery. **1982** Woodruff & Maxa *At White House* 91: Maybe I wasn't the fastest with the happy-talk quips. **1984** *Atlantic* (Aug.) 35: The spread of "happy-talk" formats in TV journalism in recent years. **1991** *New Republic* (Dec. 16) 50: Bring back Bill Moyers-style commentary on the evening news…turn their backs on "happy talk" and Q ratings. **1993** *N.Y. Times* (Aug. 1) E16: A world of whited-out newspapers, happy-talk TV, sex-free cinema and laundered literature.

Happy Valley *n. Navy.* the aircraft carrier U.S.S. *Valley Forge.* Now *hist.*

    1978 L. Davis *MiG Alley* 4 [ref. to 1950]: USS *Valley Forge*…"Happy Valley." *Ibid.* 5: We returned to the "Happy Valley" at about 0900. *a***1986** Hallion *Nav. Air War* 62 [ref. to 1950]: A "hot" landing…aboard the "Happy Valley."

harbor gasket *n. Navy.* a high collar and bow tie.

    1918 Ruggles *Navy Explained* 76: Men who wear high collars and white neckwear are referred to as wearing harbor gaskets. Officers and chief petty officers are the only men in the naval service who wear harbor gaskets. **1926** *AS* (Oct.) [ref. to 1898]: "Lookit, see that fella all rigged out in a harbor gasket and everything, like a parlor dunnigan."…One might ask scores [of sailors today]…the meaning of "harbor gasket" without getting the right answer.

hard *n.* **1.** hard cash, esp. coins; hard currency.—also constr. with *the.*

    [**1704** S.K. Knight *Journal* 22: Good hard money, as sometimes silver coin is termed by them.] **1830** in *OED:* Four hundred and thirty-three dollars counted out to me in the hard. **1859** *Spirit of Times* (Apr. 2) 88: All the…"filthy lucre,"…All the "hard" and all his funds. **1871** (quot. at JOHN). *a***1890–93** *F & H* III 267: (American)…Hard…= silver or gold as compared to cheques or *soft.* **1903** *Enquirer* (Cincinnati) (May 5) 13: *Hard*—Silver and gold money. **1942–49** Goldin et al. *DAUL* 91: The okus…is dry…and there's nothing but hard in his kick. **1987** *21 Jump St.* (Fox-TV): Check it out. [Opens suitcase filled with money.] Hard, boys. Hard.

2. *Pol.* an advocate of hard money as a national standard. Now *hist.*

    1843 in Sperber & Trittschuh *Amer. Pol. Terms* 187: The hards and the softs…have at last resorted to the keen weapons of wits! **1844** in *DAE:* The locofocos…are divided in that State [Missouri], and are known…[as] "Hards" and "Softs," in consequence of their views upon the currency question. **1847** in *DAE:* He has occupied the position of what is termed a "hard." **1848** Robb *Squatter Life* 91: Hards, softs, whigs and Tylerites were represented. **1855** in Meserve & Reardon *Satiric Comedies* 125: Being a *hard* himself, [he] does not intend an insult.

3. HARD CASE.

    1864 "Spectator" *Snoblace Ball* 65: The "hards,"…the fast demireps and men,/There, gambling.

4. *Restaurant.* an order of toast.

    1885 *Puck* (Mar. 11) 19: Two doomps wid hard on the side!

5. hard labor in prison.

    *a***1889** in Barrère & Leland *Dict. Slang* I 448: And then do his month's *hard* on his head. *a***1890** in *F & H* III 267: The certainty of seven days incarceration, with or without hard, would soon diminish the nuisance. **1906** H. Green *Boarding House* 350: Six years at "hard," up the river. **1912** H.L. Mencken, in Riggio *Dreiser-Mencken Letters* I 111: Both of us to the pen for a year's hard! **1966–67** W. Stevens *Gunner* 220: That's good for twenty years hard just by itself. **1981** Brenner & Nagler *Only the Ring* 111: He had been in numbers before doing four years hard for manslaughter.

6. an erection of the penis.—usu. considered vulgar. Cf. HARD-ON, *n.*

    *a***1890–93** *F & H* III 269: Bit of hard…The *penis* in erection. **1927** *Immortalia* 150: I thought his hard was on him. **1927** [Fliesler] *Anecdota* 28: He laughed so hard he laughed his hard off. **1944** E. Caldwell *Tragic Ground* 50: I'd hist my skirt and have the men poking hards at me all over this part of the world. **1954–60** *DAS.* **1964–66** Kirstein *Rhymes* 148: At hot hand strokes an aching hard. *a***1967** in *OEDS:* He pulled up her red woollen dress…but still no hard. **1969** Pharr *Numbers* 87: Dave's as scared of being poor as the average man is scared of

not being able to raise a hard some day. *a***1972** B. Rodgers *Queens' Vernacular* 103: All that dirty talk gave me a hard. *a***1973–87** F.M. Davis *Livin' the Blues* 84: I also got a whopping "hard." **1994** "G. Indiana" *Rent Boy* 30: If I feel I'm about to lose the hard I start fucking real mean. **1995** *N.Y. Press* (Apr. 26) 71: Both of us boys on her breasts…and we were both packin' hards.

7. hard cider; (*also*) hard liquor, esp. whiskey.

    1953–58 J.C. Holmes *Horn* 129: The grandiloquent county politician stumping the hustings with a barrel of "hard." **1985** Frede *Nurses* 249: Will you get me five fifths of the other kind of hard?

8. *Narc.* hard drugs.

    1967 [R. Beck] *Pimp* 64: You don't transport no "hard" in your "stomp," keep it in your mitt. **1979** D. Thoreau *City at Bay* 100: Tell me what you hear about the hard business lately.

hard *adj. Black E.* very fashionable or attractive; splendid; intensely enjoyable.

    1938 Calloway *Hi De Ho* 16: That's a hard tie you're wearing. **1944** Burley *Hndbk. Jive* 130: Solid! Man, Solid! Yo' sure layin' some hard jive. *Ibid.* 139: *Hard*—fine; excellent. **1947** *Tomorrow* (Aug.) 29: *Hard* has been introduced [into jazz circles] as a synonym for *sharp*, but has made less headway. **1959** *AS* XXXIV 155: *Hard cats* are well-dressed and very popular men. **1964** in B. Jackson *Swim Like Me* 90: I took her to my pad.…I always featured a pad as hard as this. **1965** in R.S. Gold *Jazz Talk* 120: I give this one three stars, because it's a hard tune. **1970** Major *Afro.-Amer. Sl.* 64: For black people "hard" has a positive connotation, *terribly* good. **1971** Dahlskog *Dict.* 30: *Hard*.…Great; excellent. **1985** Eble *Campus Slang* (Oct.) 5: *Hard*—anything good or favorable. "Hey, that movie was hard." **1988** *N.Y. Times* (Aug. 29) C15: Jive me them *hard* jams every time. **1993** P. Munro *U.C.L.A. Slang 2: Hard*…awesome, great, excellent, well done. *That shirt is hard. I gotta have it.*

¶ In phrase:

¶ **the hard way** *Craps.* (of the points 4, 6, 8, or 10) rolled as the sum of identical pairs.

    1930 D. Runyon, in *Sat. Eve. Post* (Apr. 5) 5: "Charley,…do you make it the hard way?"…two fives is the hard way to make a ten with the dice. **1941** Mahin & Grant *Johnny Eager* (film): Did you see me make the last eight the hard way? **1947** Schulberg *Harder They Fall* 268: "There it is, boys, the hard way!" someone called out. **1954–60** *DAS:* Thus, "6 the hard way" is made by two 3's. **1962** Olmsted *Heads I Win* 64: "Getting six the hard way" (that is by double threes). **1987** T.L. Clark *Dict. Gambling* 97: Hard way…In craps, the numbers 4, 6, 8, or 10 rolled in pairs of the numbers 2, 3, 4, or 5 respectively.

hard and lard *n. Mil.* (see quot.).

    1993 G. Lee *Honor & Duty* 417 [ref. to 1960's]: C-rations…included hard and lard (ham and beans).

hard ankle *n. So. Midland.* a coal miner.

    1938 in *AS* (Apr. 1939) 90: The hardancles [*sic*] have struck for higher wages. **1940** *AS* (Dec.) 447: *Hard Ankle.* Coal digger. "The hard ankles are on a strike."

hard artery *n.* an intransigent person.

    1964 Peacock *Drill & Die* 147: He's a hard artery, ace. He'll kill us all. Wait till you meet him.

hard-ass *n. Esp. Mil.* a strict, severe, intransigent, or recalcitrant person, usu. a man.—usu. considered vulgar. Cf. HARDTAIL, 2.

    [**1876** in *No. Dak. Hist.* XVII (1950) 176: Gen Custer [is called] "Long Hair" & Hard Back Sides [by Indians].] [*a***1890–93** *F & H* III 269: An abbreviation of *hard-arse.*] **1961** Crane *Born of Battle* 98 [ref. to Korean War]: Ain't he a real, genuine hard-ass. **1964** Howe *Valley of Fire* 197: The other kind are the hard-asses. The reactionaries. **1967** D. Ford *Muc Wa* 36: Courcey's a hard-ass. **1969** Crumley *Cadence* 102: Making me have to play the hardass. **1969** Ellis *Alcatraz* 147: Ok! You hard-asses.…Come out. **1970** M. Thomas *Total Beast* 10: "You still think you're a hardass?…Why you're liable to die in there, old Barnes!" **1980** *New York* (Nov. 10) 70: Her platoon leader, Captain Doreen Lewis…a grinning hard-ass who looks at Judy the way a shark looks at a bluefish. **1984** J. Dailey *Silver Wings* 57: I don't know why I ended up with such a hard ass for an instructor. **1985** Frede *Nurses* 248: He's a class-A hardass as a patient. *a***1989** C.S. Crawford *Four Deuces* 21: I don't promote fuck-ups or hard-asses. **1993** *New Yorker*

(May 17) 60: The sort of hard-ass who…would issue a speeding ticket to someone for driving just five miles over the limit.

¶ In phrase:

¶ **give the hard-ass** to hector; give a hard time to.—usu. considered vulgar.

    1974 Blount *3 Bricks Shy* 109: "You just piss people off."…"Bruce, you're always giving me the hard-ass."

hard-ass[ed] *adj.* strict, intransigent, or recalcitrant.—usu. considered vulgar. Also as adv.

    1903 F & H I (rev. ed.) 66: *Hard-arsed* = niggardly. **1961** Crane *Born of Battle* 85 [ref. to Korean War]: I'm Colonel Freedham, you hard-assed son of a bitch, and I'm just as tough and ten times as friggin' mean as you are. **1966** H.S. Thompson *Hell's Angels* 131: The original Oakland Angels were hard-ass brawlers. **1970** Woods *Killing Zone* 6: Old Sarge, hard-assed campaigner, professional soldier. **1970** Whitmore *Memphis-Nam-Sweden* 35: McDonald was strictly hard-ass military. **1970** *Rolling Stone Interviews* 422: Be hard-ass for four more years. **1975** H. Ellison *Gentleman Junkie* 40: He hadn't figured on running into a hard-ass senior editor like Neville. **1985–87** Bogosian *Talk Radio* 35: We were both hard-ass hippies. **1987** C. Joyner *Prison* (film): [He's] one hard-assed son-of-a-bitch. **1994** *New Yorker* (June 27) 142: The usual hard-ass lawman.

hard-ass *v.* **1.** to bully, harass, or treat with severity; hector; give a hard time to; (see also 1975 quot.); (*also,* in 1961 quot.) to be influenced by bullying.—usu. considered vulgar. Also absol. [Prob. the orig. sense.]

    1960 Loomis *Heroic Love* 165 [ref. to WWII]: Don't hard-ass me, Sarge….Ain't we goin' overseas to fight the war together? **1961** Braly *Felony Tank* 70: He hard-assed the captain. But the captain didn't hard-ass worth a damn. *ca***1962** in A. Lomax *Where Blues Began* 295 [ref. to 1940's]: If you gonna hard ass [in prison], you gotta have an iron ass, a brass belly, and a heart of steel. **1970** Ponicsan *Last Detail* 142: You think we're gonna stand here and be hard-assed because some dude in Norfolk forgot to endorse our orders? **1971** Hilaire *Thanatos* 98: Hard-ass them and you're in trouble. **1971** Rowe *5 Yrs. to Freedom* 359: It's stupid to put yourself in a worse spot by hard-assing him. **1975** McKennon *Trail* 17: The horses had all been "hard-assed" for three weeks in winter quarters…but three hours a day pulling…wagons…wasn't enough to get them in condition. *Ibid.* 497: *Hardass.* Working the big teams for several hours each day before a show. **1979–81** C. Buckley *To Bamboola* 106: And he kept calling me on the intercom….Hard-assing me, like he always does. **1981** Hathaway *World of Hurt* 127: All he did was hard ass you.

2. to endure through one's toughness of character.

    1955 Klaas *Maybe I'm Dead* 46 [ref. to WWII]: Shorty…managed to hard-ass it more than a hundred miles over the mountains into Czechoslovakia before the Gestapo caught him. *Ibid.* 357: Hard-assing at night and holing up in daytime. **1966** Braly *On Yard* 14: You did it the easiest way you could and hard-assed the difference.

hard-baked *adj.* (see 1981 quot.).

    1847 in *F & H* III 268: It's my opinion, these squirtish kind a fellars ain't perticular hard-baked. **1981 Macquarie Dict.*: Hard-baked…(of a person) toughened by experience, esp. outwardly.

hardball *n.* **1.** aggressive or ruthless competition, esp. in politics or business; in phr. **play hardball** or [as v.] **hardball it** to engage in such competition; to do whatever is necessary to prevail or succeed. Often attrib. Now *colloq.*

    1972 in Bernstein & Woodward *President's Men* 173: This is the hardest hardball that's ever been played in this town. We all have to be very careful, in the office and out. **1973** in *Submission of Pres. Convers.* 223: He is playing hard ball. He wouldn't play hard ball unless he were pretty confident that he could cause an awful lot of grief. **1975** *N.Y. Times* (Aug. 24) IV 19: Nixon was a mean, tough, hardball politician. **1979** Eble *Campus Slang* (Mar.) 4: *Hard ball*—tough, given to ruthless tactics: He's a real hard ball businessman. **1982** *L.A. Times* (Nov. 21) IA 6: Paul's really hard-balling it now….They're locked in a relatively high level for competition. **1983** *L.A. Times* (Oct. 26) I 6: [Sen. J. Biden] accused White House counselor Edwin Meese III…of deciding "to hardball it." **1983** W. Walker *Dime to Dance By* 68: The opposing counsel was serving notice that he intended to play hardball. **1987** *RHD2*: He wasn't ready for the hardball politics of Washington….

Reporters asked the president some hardball questions. **1988** Kienzle *Marked for Murder* 114: He plays hard ball.

2. an inflexible person; HARDNOSE.

    1987 Univ. Tenn. student theme: A hard or picky instructor is a "hard-ball."

hardball *v.* **1.** see s.v. HARDBALL, *n.,* 1.

2. SPEEDBALL.

    1982 *Santa Barbara News-Press* (Mar. 12) B8: An overdose of heroin and cocaine, a process called "hardballing."

hardballer *n.* one who excels in an atmosphere of HARDBALL; one who plays HARDBALL.

    1976 *Time* (Dec. 27) 52: Grodin plays the honcho as a hardballer. **1981** *Maclean's* (Jan. 12) 20: The political hardballers always seem to win in Ottawa. **1983** Wambaugh *Delta Star* 205: "Internal Affairs is gonna nail him one a these days." "Naw, he's a hardballer….A hardballer."

hardbody *n.* a trim, muscular person, esp. if young and sexually attractive.

    1984 S. Green, E. Alter, & M. Griffiths *Hardbodies* (film title). **1984** *N.Y. Post* (Aug. 3) 47: The hardbodies competition site is at West Tremont Avenue. **1984** W. Murray *Sweet Ride* 12: Del Mar…in the hot months teems with golden California hard-bodies of the kind Jay favors. **1985** in *Barnhart Dict. Comp.* IV 134: Product tie-ins and the cult of the hardbody intersect at the fashion model. **1988** *Rage* (Knoxville, Tenn.) I (No. 11) 41: Ideal Woman: Long legged hardbody with spirit and sense of humor. **1990** Thorne *Dict. Contemp. Sl.* 232: *Hardbody*…a young Californian male…interested in physical culture and body-building. A vogue term of the late 1970s and 1980s. **1991** B.E. Ellis *Amer. Psycho* 33: Hot number, big tits, great legs, this chick was a little hardbody. **1994** *N.Y. Times* (Sept. 11) (Styles) 63: He works…at Vail's chic Cascade Athletic Club and considers himself something of a hardbody.

hard-boiled *adj.* unyielding or ungenerous; unsentimental; inflexible; callous; cynical; tough; in phr. **hard-boiled egg** (obs.) a person of this sort. Now *colloq.* or *S.E.* [Discussed by P. Tamony in *AS* XII (1937), 258–61.]

    [**1886** "M. Twain," in *DA*: Hard-boiled, hide-bound grammar.] [**1899** F. Dumont *Witmark Amat. Minstrel Guide* 87: "What's the hardest thing to *beat?*" "A hard boiled egg."] **1904** Hobart *Jim Hickey* 85: There's a certain hard-boiled clam out that way who deserves our unbridled attention. **1906** Kildare *Old Bailiwick* 311: Now don't be talking like a hard-boiled egg. **1915** T.A. Dorgan, in *AS* XII (1937) 260: Hard boiled egg who wouldn't bid 90 on 100 aces. **1916** T.A. Dorgan, in *Ibid.*: He can stand longer at a bar and buy less than anyone I ever saw—one hard boiled egg. **1917** in Grider *War Birds* 15: I am sure every man on board was affected [by the music], no matter how hardboiled he was. **1918** in Truman *Letters Home* 53: I'm the hard-boiled captain of a shanty Irish battery. **1919** *DN* V 70: *Hard boiled egg,* a stingy person. "Every one calls him a hard boiled egg because he is so close with his boys." New Mexico. **1919** De Beck *Google* 43: Gosh—this is a hard-boiled neighborhood. **1919** in Pottle *Stretchers* 354: We are too hardboiled to make much of a demonstration. *Ibid.* 358: Two hardboiled Irish sergeants are terrorizing the barrack. **1921** E. O'Neill *Hairy Ape* 237: Huh! You're a hard boiled duck, ain't you! When you spit, it bounces! **1922** *Harper's* (Mar.) 526: Our basic idea of a hero is really a "hard-boiled egg." **1922** Tully *Emmett Lawler* 279: Think you can go the route with Blinky? He's a hard-boiled egg. **1924** M. Anderson & L. Stallings *What Price Glory?* 63 [ref. to 1918]: I'm here to keep you in hot water till you're hard-boiled. See? **1925** in Dreiser *Diaries* 423: I bawl the man out….He tells me not to get "hard boiled." **1926** in *AS* II (1927) 258: Jack Doyle…described a certain class of pool and billiard players as hard boiled eggs, meaning tight in their play, close in their finances, and in everything else. **1927** P. Wylie *Heavy Laden* 26: You think you're hard boiled. Well, you're a lot of old women. **1929** Bowen *Sea Slang* 63: *Hard Boiled.* Said in the U.S. Navy of an officer who is particularly strong on the regulations. **1931** Hellinger *Moon* 221: You would call her, I suppose, hard-boiled. **1932** C. McKay *Gingertown* 30: You wa'n't nevah hard-boiled enough to be a cabaret gal. **1938** Smitter *Detroit* 80: Go easy. You can't get hard-boiled with Riley. **1939** C.R. Cooper *Scarlet* 19: Prisoners don't make good records when they're hard-boiled. **1958** Chandler *Playback* 53: She put a hardboiled sneer on her face. **1965** Gary *Ski Bum* 191: He was a hard-boiled, practical realist.

1970 Boatright & Owens *Derrick* 77: A hardboiled gal, a former Regular Army nurse. **1994** *TV Guide* (July 23) 3: Hard-boiled private eye.

hard-boiled hat *n.* a stiff hat, such as a derby or top hat.

1903 A. Adams *Log of Cowboy* 127 [ref. to 1880's]: That fellow in front of the drugstore over there, with the hard-boiled hat on. **1906** *DN* III 139: Words from Northwest Arkansas…*hard-boiled hat*…A derby hat. **1922** P.A. Rollins *Cowboy* 106: Furthermore the Range knew that the city-dwellers wore "hard" or "hard-boiled" hats. **1954** Collans & Sterling *House Detect.* 100: Pictures typed the house officer as a poker-faced joker wearing a hard-boiled hat, a suspicious scowl and a well-gnawed cigar butt. **1968** R. Adams *Western Words* 140: *Hard-boiled hat*—A cowboy's name for a derby.

hard-boiled shirt *n.* a detachable starched shirt-front; dickey.

1916 in McManus *Bringing Up Father* 5: Gee! Do I have to put on the hard-boiled shirt?

hard-boiler *n.* (see quot.).

1917 *Call & Post* (S.F.) 11: As far back as 1885…a tightwad was called a Hard Boiler, and they'd hire guys to sit in [at faro] so that the Hard Boiler couldn't get a deal.

hardboot *n. Horse Racing.* a trainer or stable owner who is a Kentuckian.

1923 *Wash. Post* (Feb. 17) 19: I am stringing with the hard boots and their dough this afternoon. **1939** in *DARE*: Kentucky "hard boots" (chronic backers of Kentucky horses). **1942** *ATS* 684: *Hardboot*, a horseman of Kentucky. **1949** Cummings *Dict. Sports* 200: *Hardboot….Horse racing.* A Kentuckian. **1956** "T. Betts" *Across Board* 316: *Hardboot*—A bantering or derisive term for a Kentucky horseman. **1968** Ainslie *Racing Guide* 468: *Hardboot*—A Kentucky horseman of the old school, because of the legendary mud caked on his boots. **1973** in J. Flaherty *Chez Joey* 107: Churchill Downs….A fitting true church for hard boots. **1983** in *Time* (Jan. 2, 1984) 78: Hardboots can be sentimental about a horse on the lead.

hard-case *n.* **1.** a tough or hard-bitten individual, esp. a criminal. Occ. adj. Now *colloq.*

1836 in *OEDS*: A "hard case" called Emanuel Allen. **1842** in *DAE*: My host came after me to tell me a canoe full of "hard cases" (vagabonds) had passed up the river. **1849** Melville *Redburn* ch. iii: These city boys are sometimes hard cases. *a***1855** in *DAE*: Col. Crockett…[was] lugged into the calaboose, and kept there as an out-and-out "hard case." **1849–59** Bartlett *Amer.* (ed. 2): *Hard Case.* A dissipated, worthless fellow; a drunkard. **1891** in F. Harris *Conklin* 32: She had taken a likin' to him, though he was such a "hard case." **1899** Garland *Eagle's Heart* 64: I like you and I don't want you to think I'm a hard case. **1947** *Atlantic* (Oct.) 60: Cell Block 9…is the solitary block where they keep all the hard cases. **1947** Overholser *Buckaroo's Code* 45: Maxon never was anything but a hard case who drank too much [and] gambled away his big money. **1961** in Mjelde *Glory of Seas* 185: He didn't know how to be hard-case, not on the coast. **1961** H. Ellison *Memos* 83: I was a hardcase, there was no doubt about it. **1965** "R. Stark" *Tugger* 45: A young hardcase like you could take care of this problem of mine with no sweat. **1967** Spillane *Delta* 59: There were too many hardcases…inspecting the crowd…with hostile eyes their smiles couldn't conceal. **1976** Whelton *CB Baby* 138: I knew she was a hooker and probably a hard case in her own right. **1980** Hogan *Lawman's Choice* 46: Figured he was some hardcase heading for the border. **1992** J. Garry *This Ol' Drought* 137: I was in a poker game with a bunch of hardcases.

2. an Oregonian.

1845 in *DA*: The inhabitants of…Oregon [are called] Hard Cases.

hard-charger *n. USMC & Army.* a combat soldier of exceptional initiative. Hence, in nonmil. contexts, **hard-charging** *adj.* aggressive.

1960 Leckie *March to Glory* 175 [ref. to Korean War]: "Able, Able—hot to go!" That was their cry. They called themselves hard-chargers. They had a good skipper. **1961** Peacock *Valhalla* 456: Hey, hard charger. **1963** Boyle *Yanks Don't Cry* 234 [ref. to WWII]: If there's a whorehouse left standing in Osaka we'll find it! Come on, hard chargers, let's go! **1965** *Marine Officer's Guide* 593: *Hard-charger.* Aggressive, dynamic, zealous, indefatigable officer or enlisted Marine; one who is professionally keen. **1969** M. Herr, in *New Amer. Rev.* 7 (Aug.) 68: He was such a hard-charger that they gave him the EM Club to manage. **1980** Manchester *Darkness* 146 [ref. to WWII]: A tough fighter was [called] a *hard-charger*. **1982** *Business Week* (Sept. 20)

93: The crucial concern…remains keeping up with hard-charging IBM in mainframe developments. **1985** *U.S. News & W.R.* (Mar. 4) 62: The lifestyle of the hard-charging executive is not the family wrecker that popular myth says it is. **1988** Poyer *The Med* 149: Task Force 61 was led by a Hard Charger, a True Professional, someone who would accept nothing less than perfection. **1992** Democratic Nat. Convention (CNN-TV) (July 17): He's energetic, he's hard-charging, he's aggressive. **1995** *TV Guide* (June 24) 22: Hard-charging tennis legend Martina Navratilova.

hard cheese *n.* **1.** a difficult situation, state of affairs, etc. [In earlier Brit. use, 'bad luck'; see *OED2*.]

1981 *N.Y. Times* (Sept. 18) D2: It looks like hard cheese for labor…with stagnation and higher unemployment the only remedy in sight for inflation. *a***1989** R. Herman, Jr. *Warbirds* 209: That can be pretty hard cheese [flying] close to the ground.

2. *Baseball.* fastballs.

1987 in P. Dickson *Baseball Dict.* 195: He threw some good hard cheese up there.

hard colt *n.* var. HARD HORSE.

hardcore *adj.* **1.** *Mil.* unswervingly dedicated, esp. to military life. Now *colloq.* [The more general senses 'irreducible, unalterable, etc.' stem from this and have always been colloq. or S.E.]

[**1953** *Combat Forces Jour.* (Apr.) 10: The formation and instruction of a cadre which will serve as a base (or "hard core" as it is now known) and upon which a full unit can be formed.] **1964** in J. Lucas *Dateline* 67: A hard-core, professional Viet Cong battalion. **1966** in Steinbrook *Allies* 16: They are truly professional hard-core people. **1972** Haldeman *War Year* 18: The clubs open at six—that's 1800 for you hard-core types. **1983** Elting, Cragg & Deal *Soldier Talk* 146: *Hard-core…*Dedicated. **1990** Berent *Steel Tiger* 280: Hard-core NVA troops.

2. Esp. *Mil.* hardened; tough; pitiless.

1966 in J. Lucas *Dateline* 331: Yes sir, Sarge, you're hard core. **1972** Haldeman *War Year* 2: Tell 'em all about it, hard-core. *Ibid.* 24: Some guys like to act hard-core, scare the shit out of ya. **1973** W. Burroughs, Jr. *Ky. Ham* 21: You're gonna be one hard-core mother-fucker. **1980** M. Baker *Nam* 115: But you get so hardcore, you would just go through a stream and, if you get leeches, you wouldn't even bother with them. **1982** Goff, Sanders & Smith *Bros.* 29 [ref. to 1968]: We called him Hard-core….Just a real cold-blooded dude. *Ibid.* 58: So we was pretty damn hard-core ourselves. **1985** M. Baker *Police* 93: It's easy to be hard-core, to be the macho man. **1988** *Rage* (Knoxville, Tenn.) I (No. 11) 32: Campus cops are trying to be hard core these days. **1993** *CNN & Co.* (CNN-TV) (Aug. 17): Now the way is to be tough, to be hardcore.

hard crowd var. HARD LOT.

hard-cutting *adj. Black E.* extremely fashionable or attractive; HARD-HITTING.

1942 *Yank* (Dec. 23) 18: He was togged in some hard-cuttin' brown. **1946** Mezzrow & Wolfe *Really the Blues* 188: Lemme pick up on some of that hard-cuttin' jive. *Ibid.* 306: *Hard-cutting:* Powerful, very good.

hard daddy *n. Pris.* (among female convicts) a tough homosexual woman.

1962 in Ward & Kassebaum *Women's Pris.* 136. **1968** in Giallombardo *Impris. Girls* 76: I know there are some girls on campus, some of the *hard daddys* and they want to get out of the racket. *Ibid.* 146: The true butch…is sometimes referred to as "stone butch" or "big" or "hard daddy." *a***1972** B. Rodgers *Queens' Vernacular* 103: *Hard daddy*…the lesbian *husband* who sets up housekeeping with another woman.

hard dick *n.* a tough or recalcitrant fellow; HARDLEG, 1; HARD GUY.—usu. considered vulgar.

1975 Univ. Tenn. grad. student: A *hard dick* is a tough guy. I heard that in Texas in 1965 or so. **1983** P. Dexter *God's Pocket* 32: They'd pick a hard dick to keep an eye on the job. *Ibid.* 58: This neighborhood…even the old ladies are hard dicks. **1984** Hammel *Root* 351: Belmer, whom everyone called Hard Dick (after his own standard greeting, "Hey, how you doin', Hard Dick?").

hard duty *n. Mil.* a difficult task.

1833 J. Hall *Harpe's Head* 37: "Come," said General Armour…"tell us how the buck was taken, before you alight." "Hard duty, that."

hard five *n.* [short for HARD STRIPE E-5] *Army.* the rank of sergeant (enlisted pay-grade five); a sergeant of that grade.

1984 Riggan *Free Fire* 127 [ref. to Vietnam War]: He told me how soft we have it—easy rank. It took him years to earn hard five back in the old army.

hard guy *n.* a man who is tough or brutal, esp. a hardened criminal; tough guy.

1916 in C. Burton *Letters* 225: We have a "hard guy" Sergeant named Murphy here. **1918** "M. Brand" *Harrigan* 86: We're the best gang at bustin' up these hard guys that ever walked the deck of a ship. **1918** in *AS* (Oct. 1933) 27: *Hard guy* 1. Prisoner, officer, guard or anyone else who is unquestionably hardboiled. 2. Professional criminal or his understudy. **1927–28** Tasker *Grimhaven* 4: The Deputy removed the manacles from my wrists. "They'd think I was bringing in a hard guy if I left 'em on." **1929–30** Farrell *Young Lonigan* 77: Both were chewing tobacco, expectorating the juice like dyed-in-the-wool hard guys. **1952** Clayton *Angels* 173: I'm *really* goin' to fix Mr. Hard Guy. **1954** Lindner *Fifty-Minute Hour* 16: It consisted of the "hard guys," each of whom had won his right to belong by demonstrating qualities of cruelty, lack of sentiment, ability to withstand pain, sexual perversion, and proficiency at every kind of knavery and thievery the environment offered. **1972** N.Y.U. student: He comes on playin' the hard guy. **1973** Lucas, Katz, & Huyck *Amer. Graffiti* 67: Yeah, hard guy. **1976** G.V. Higgins *D. Hunter* 22: A couple hard guys show up to shoot him. **1987** Mamet *House of Games* (film): How'd you size me up that I'm not some hard guy who's gonna rough you up? **1992** G. Wolff *Day at the Beach* 115: Here are the hard guys, Billy Badass and his gang.

hard hat *n.* **1.** a person, now esp. a construction worker, whose occupation requires the wearing of a safety helmet. Now *colloq.* [The early nuance defined in 1942 quot. may be misleading.]

1942 *AS* (Dec.) 222: *Hard hat.* A safety engineer, because of these officials' attempts to get loggers to wear helmets while working. **1956** Newell *Hardhats* (title). **1958** McCulloch *Woods Words* 80: *Hard hat*— a. A metal or plastic safety hat….b. a logger who wears one. **1970** *N.Y. Times* (May 9) 24: The hardhats [were] long scornful of excesses by privileged longhairs on campus. **1970** *Time* (May 25) 20: [On May 8], a gang of 200 hardhats, equipped with U.S. flags and lengths of lead pipe, had waded into a crowd of antiwar students in Wall Street. Police…stood by as some 70 peace demonstrators were beaten….Almost overnight, "hardhats" became synonymous with white working-class conservatives. **1970** *Newsweek* (May 25) 34: To some, the hard hats raised the specter of violent right-wing reaction. **1970** *Sat. Review* (Oct. 10) 20: Not everyone joins in denouncing the hardhats. **1971** Trudeau *A Lot Smarter* (unp.): You hardhats are all the same. **1974** Dohan *Our Own Words* 300: *Hard-hat,* for a blue-collar man with, it is implied, programmed social attitudes. **1978** Shem *House of God* 268: Looking out the window into the face of a hardhat. ***1981** *Macquarie Dict.: Hard hat*…a construction worker, working in an area in which safety helmets must be worn. **1990** *CBS This Morning* (CBS-TV) (Dec. 31): You see a hardhat hangin' from a girder: "Hey, Mel! How ya doin'?"

2. *Mil.* (see 1983 quot.).

1965 *Time* (Aug. 6) 28: Of that total, some 50,000 [Viet Cong] are "hard-hats" (full-time fighters), another 100,000 are local guerrillas who can be ordered up from farm or village as needed. **1983** Elting, Cragg & Deal *Soldier Talk* 146: *Hard-hat*…A Vietcong or main-force soldier of the National Liberation Force Army. Pike attributes the term to the fact that these soldiers wore metal or fiberboard helmets. **1991** C. Roberts *Combat Medic* 136: The "hard hats" (the nickname we gave the NVA because of their distinctive brimmed sun helmets).

3. *Pol.* a person who clings stubbornly to a nationalistic political position. Cf. 1970 *Time* quot. at **(1),** above.

1971 *Time* (June 14) 41: Gradually,…[Mr. Nehru] became a hard-hat on the Tibetan border question.

hardhead *n.* **1.a.** *Midland.* a white native of the mountains of Tennessee or Kentucky.—used derisively.

1845 in Thornton *Amer. Gloss.* II 974: Hoosiers,…Buckeyes, Corncrackers,…Hard Heads, Hawk Eyes, Rackensacks [etc.]. **1846** Durivage & Burnham *Subjects* 110: Most of the passengers had disappeared for the night, and only a knot of "hard-heads" were left upon deck. These remained till day-light, amusing each other with long yarns.

1932 *AS* VI 267: *Oil Field Language…hard-head,* n. A man from Tennessee. **1946–51** J. Jones *Here to Eternity* 289: These Kentucky mountain hardheads cause a man more trouble than a regiment of niggers. **1954–60** *DAS: Hardhead…*A Southern hill mountaineer. *Dial.*

b. Esp. *Black E.* a pugnacious fellow; troublemaker. Cf. 1946–51 quot. at **(a),** above.

1942 Z.N. Hurston, in *Amer. Mercury* (July) 85: Whenever he was challenged by a hard-head…on the right of his title [etc.]. **1960** in T.C. Bambara *Gorilla* 48: The colored section was altogether unbelievable: outhouses, corner hard-heads,…junkyards,…poverty. **1963** Coon *Short End* 23: Every outfit has its hardheads, the guys who seem to like trouble. **1969** Kimbrough *Defender of Angels* 31 [ref. to a1918]: All right, you hardheads, let's get on the outside. **1966–80** Folb *Runnin' Lines* 241: *Hardhead.* See *bad-ass nigger.* **1990** "Boo-Yaa Tribe" *New Funky Nation* (rap song): I'm a hardhead and I'm down.

2. *Whaling.* a California gray whale.

1873 Scammon *Marine Mammals* 24: [The name] "Hardhead"…arose from the fact of the animals having a great propensity to root the boats when coming in contact with them, in the same manner that hogs upset their empty troughs. **1884** in *DARE.* **1889** *Century Dict.*

3. a mule; HARDTAIL.

1950, 1966–69 in *DARE.* **1983** Elting, Cragg & Deal *Soldier Talk* 146: *Hardhead* [1919–41]…A mule.

hard-hitter *n.* a derby hat. [Chiefly an Austral. term.]

*1895 in *OEDS:* White shirt, hard-hitter, tight trousers, etc. **1903** *Independent* (Dec. 31) 3105: He (the boss) had a red mustache, a redder face, a glad hand and a pleasant look, and wore a "hard hitter" well poised on the back of his bullet shaped head, just as it might have hung on a peg. ***1907, *1924** in *OEDS.* ***1926** (cited in Partridge *DSUE*).

hard-hitting *adj. Black E.* HARD.

1944 Burley *Hndbk. Jive* 139: *Hard-hitting*—Class, up-to-date, nice-looking.

hard horse *n.* a pugnacious, brutal, or unyielding fellow. Also **hard colt.**

1813–18 Weems *Drunk. Look. Glass* 77: Hurra, for me! a hard horse I am gentlemen, a proper hard horse, depend! may-be I an't a Roarer! **1834** in *DA:* The prisoner was what some people would call a "hard colt." ***1889** Barrère & Leland *Dict. Slang* I 448: *Hard horse* (nautical), a tyrannical officer. ***a1890–93** *F & H* III 268: A brutal mate or officer…*hard-horse.* ***1929** Bowen *Sea Slang* 64: *Hard Horse, A.* A tyrannical officer.

hard leg *n. Black E.* **1.** a man or boy, esp. if tough.

1946 Boulware *Jive & Slang* 4: *Hard Leg…*Boy. **1969** *Current Slang I & II* 49: *Hard leg,* n. Boy.—High school males, Negro, Michigan. **1970** A. Young *Snakes* 135: She was sitting on the sofa next to some curly-headed hard-leg I'd never seen before. **1971** H. Roberts *Third Ear: Hard legs* n. a man. **1983** *Reader's Digest Success with Words* 86: Black English…*hard leg* = (1) "a man" (2) "an ugly woman." **1985** Flowers *Mojo Blues* 47: Aint no hardleg getting shit of mine, she snarled.

2. an ugly or debauched woman; a hardened prostitute.

1967 [Beck] *Pimp* 177: She ain't no "hard-leg." **1970** Winick & Kinsie *Lively Commerce* 43: The old whore is a "hard leg"—she's got a million miles on her. **1970** Major *Afro-Amer. Sl.* 64: *Hardleg:* Any man or an ugly woman. **1983** (quot. at **(1),** above).

hard lines *n.pl.* hardship; misfortune.

*1824 Sir W. Scott, in *OED:* The old seaman paused a moment. "It is hard lines for me," he said, "to leave your honour in tribulation." ***1850** in *OED:* It will be "hard lines" upon him. ***1855** in *F & H* III 269: *Hard Lines.* Whence is this expression, so common, particularly among seafaring men, derived? ***1857, *1884, *1886** in *OED.* **1890** Janvier *Aztec Treasure House* 155: It's pretty hard lines on that jackass…leaving him behind down there. **1898** Brooks *Strong Hearts* 119: "That's hard lines, General," said sympathetic Jack. **1901** Ade *Modern Fables* 72: It is Hard Lines for a Sociable Girl to sit around the House and practise Finger movements. **1920** Ade *Hand-Made Fables* 50: It was Hard Lines for Effie, sitting in the little old Apartment for Hours at a Stretch.

hard lot *n.* a tough, recalcitrant, or pugnacious person. Also **hard crowd.**

1876 "M. Twain" *Tom Sawyer* ch. xxx [ref. to 1850's]: I'm kind of a hard lot—least everybody says so. **1884** "M. Twain" *Huck. Finn* ch. xi:

She told…all about pop and what a hard lot he was. **1886** E.L. Wheeler *N.Y. Nell* 8: My name is…New York Nell, news girl, spotter, detective, and hard crowd generally.

hard-luck *adj.* Esp. *Sports.* plagued by misfortune.—used prenominally. Now *colloq.*

　1899 Cullen *Chances* 48: It'll be a miracle if that hard-luck skate finishes at all. **1912** Lowrie *Prison* 213: Jake Oppenheimer is the hardest luck man I've ever known. **1922** Tully *Emmett Lawler* 196: But I'm the original hard luck guy. If it was rainin' soup I'd be out with a fork. **1941** *New Yorker* (July 26) 15: Boy, am I the original hard-luck guy!…I'm the hard-luck kid. **1941** Wald et al. *Navy Blues* (film): I'm a hard-luck dame. **1969** in Van Devanter & Morgan *Before Morning* 179: She's the original hard-luck kid. **1972** P. Fenty *Superfly* (film): You gonna give that hard-luck nigger a heart attack.

hardnose *n.* a strict, severe, unyielding, or pugnacious person; HARD-ASS.

　1944 Kendall *Service Slang* 24: *Hard nose*….an officer who doesn't get along with enlisted men. **1958** Meltzer & Blees *H.S. Confidential* (film): He's a hardnose. He wouldn't lend me money even when I begged for it. **1962** *AS* XXXVII 269: The Language of Traffic Policemen…*Hardnose*, n. A vindictive, abusive, offensively driving motorist. **1965** E. Franklin *Cold in Pongo-ni* 117: Such a hardnose. **1966** Elli *Riot* 13: They were on gossipy terms with the hardnoses—the guard haters and wheelers and dealers who spent most of their time in Isolation. **1966** Westlake *Busy Body* 122: I hate hardnoses. **1971** *Harper's* (Sept.) 72: Something of a hard-nose with an Irish talent for hotheadedness. **1978** Wharton *Birdy* 118: Why you want to be such a hard nose, kid? **1995** Foreman & Engel *By George* 13: Coach Bryant called me "Hard-nose," because nobody was tougher or more determined.

hardnose *v.* HARD-ASS.

　1958 *Time* (Jan. 20) 44: We weren't quite ready to hardnose with them so early. **1964** Newhafer *Last Tallyho* 66 [ref. to WWII]: If Crowley thinks he can wipe away that day at Midway by hard-nosing my air group, he's got another think coming.

hard-nosed *adj.* obstinate or unyielding; HARD-BOILED. Also (*rare*) **hardnose**.

　1927 in *AS* III (Feb.) 254: *Hard Nosed*—Stubborn. [**1927** *AS* II 276: *Hard-nosed cookie*—homely girl.] **1952** S. Bellow, in *New Yorker* (Dec. 27) 24: I didn't intend to be hard-nosed and difficult about the company's interests. **1959** Roger Kahn, in *N.Y. Times* (Apr. 5) VI 49: All the old, hard-nosed pro sports. **1959** Brosnan *Long Season* 12: Vinegar Bend Mizell's reaction to contract discussions was that of any shrewd, hard-nosed Alabama farmer who always got plenty of peanuts for his peanuts and why shouldn't the subsidy remain the same? **1960** Wohl *Cold Wind* 12: Hard-nosed old bitch. But you had to hand it to her. She didn't ask for any favors. **1961** R. Davis *Marine at War* 39 [ref. to WWII]: What did I tell you? He's hard nose. **1966–67** Harvey *Air War* 101: They're precisely trained and they know it. And they're absolutely hard-nosed. **1967** T. Wicker, in *N.Y. Times* (Sept. 3) IV 10: The Hard-Nose Phenomenon….The world puts high value on physical courage, strength and determination; in the grotesque Washington phrase, it is admirable to be "hard-nosed." **1967** J. Kramer *Instant Replay* 178: I went out and played hard-nosed football. **1974** R. Campbell *Chasm* 186: Various hardnosed teachers and approaches. **1982** "W.T. Tyler" *Rogue's March* 53: An aging European diplomat…wasn't "hard-nosed" enough to carry out the Moscow negotiations.

hard nut *n.* a tough, pugnacious, or recalcitrant person.

　1883–84 Whittaker *L. Locke* 170: I've been a captain at sea and handled just as hard nuts as you think yourself to be. **1908** *DN* III 319: *Hard nut*…Same as *hard case*. **1914** Z. Grey *Rustlers of Pecos Co.* 115: I always had you sized up as a pretty hard nut, a man not to be trifled with. **1922** *DN* V 165: *Hard nut*, n. Hard case. Alabama. Nebraska. **1931** Haycox *Whispering Range* 239: Those hard nuts have got the country speckled with eyes. ***1936** Partridge *DSUE*: *Hard nut*. Abbr. *hard nut to crack*: a dangerous foe; a "hard case"…from ca1875. ***1966** G.W. Turner *Eng. in Austral. & N.Z.* 121: A *hard shot* is a "hard case"…or a "hard nut."

hard oil *n.* (see quots.).

　1923 McKnight *English Words* 56 [ref. to WWI]: *Hard oil* for "butter." **1930** Irwin *Tramp & Und. Slang*: *Hard Oil*.—Butter. **1944** Burley *Hndbk. Jive* 139: *Hard-Oil*—Butter, oleomargarine, lard.

hard-on *n.* [by reanalysis of phr. *to get* (or *have*) *a hard on*; see

HARD, *n.*, 6] **1.a.** an erection of the penis.—usu. considered vulgar.

　1888 *Stag Party* 17: Home to-night. Big hardon. *a*1890–93 *F & H* III 351: An erection of the *penis*…hard-on (American). **1916** Cary *Venery* I 123: *Hard On*—Prick proud. An erection of the penis. ***1914–21** Joyce *Ulysses* 539: That gives you a hardon? **1926** in Randolph & Legman *Roll Me in Your Arms* 105 [song learned *ca*1900]: An' the sailor got a hard-on. **1927** [Fliesler] *Anecdota* 2: I've got an awful hard on. *Ibid.* 79: He had taken pills to give him a hard on. *Ibid.* 124: Them Turkish whores can't raise a hard on on us. **1929–30** Dos Passos *42d Parallel* 336: He got a hardon and couldn't sleep. **1936** Farrell *World I Never Made* 28: This was the end of that perpetual hard on. **1952** Uris *Battle Cry* 39: I ain't had a hard on since I been here. **1967** W. Crawford *Gresham's War* 47 [ref. to Korean War]: It was Hard-on Ridge, right? **1972** Pelfrey *Big V* 37: Feels like you're nine feet tall with a hard-on, don't it Henry boy? **1984** T. Kay *Dark Thirty* 110: He wadn't sixteen. Couldn't get him a pee hard on. **1988** *Donahue* (NBC-TV): What happens to the twenty-five men who have hard-ons after the performance? **1994** Berendt *Midnight in Garden* 118: Gettin' a hard-on in that position ain't no picnic.

b. sexual desire; (*hence*) foolish infatuation or naive eagerness.—constr. with *for*.—usu. considered vulgar.

　1971 in E. Lewis *Who Took Weight?* 32: Got me a hard on/for some/CRACKER/JACKS. **1976** C. Keane *Hunter* 244: What's this sudden hard-on you got for Mexico? **1977** Sayles *Union Dues* 144: They think it's an adventure story, they get a big hod-on for the boogies. They want to be like them, join up with them. **1980** S. Fuller *Big Red* 350: Then you could've asked her why she had a hard-on for Hitler. **1984** Caunitz *Police Plaza* 91: Why do you have such a hard-on for this case? **1988** Univ. Tenn. students: "She's really got a hard-on for you." "Yeah, she calls me all the time."

2. a fit of ill temper; (*also*) a grudge.—often constr. with *for*.—usu. considered vulgar.

　1931 Farrell *Gas-House McGinty* 40: He don't ride us much, only now and then, he gets a h— on and blows up. **1942–49** Goldin et al. *DAUL*: Every bull (policeman) in town has a hard-on for an ex-con. **1949** Monteleone *Crim. Slang* 113: *Hard On* (N[oun]…)…having [*sic*] a grievance against an individual. **1954** Killens *Youngblood* 347 [ref. to 1930's]: That cracker sure is got a hard-on for you. **1963** J. Ross *Dead Are Mine* 27 [ref. to 1944]: Now he's got a hard on for me. Has the idea I can't take orders and would very much like to see me in some other platoon. **1964** Peacock *Drill & Die* 7: Bizal's had a hard on for all of us for a long time….he hates your guts worst of all. **1966–67** W. Stevens *Gunner* 21: What've you got, a real hard-on this morning? **1970–71** Rubinstein *City Police* 322: You'd really have a hard-on for him. **1972** Pearce *Pier Head Jump* 22: He had a real hard-on for me….The grumpy old son of a bitch. **1978** in Lyle & Golenbock *Bronx Zoo* 105: Billy seems to have a hard-on for Andy, and I don't know why that is. **1982** Leonard *Cat Chaser* 188: The CIA had a hard-on for Castro. **1989** Care *Viet. Spook Show* 128: He's got a hard-on for anybody smarter than he is. **1994** N. McCall *Wanna Holler* 283: If I got a gun, it wouldn't take much for me to use it, especially against some Deep South ofay with a hard-on for blacks.

3. a doltish or despicable man.—usu. considered vulgar.

　1968 P. Roth *Portnoy* 119: You mean, miserable hard-on you. **1974** Price *Wanderers* 170 [ref. to 1960's]: You know what that hard-on did? **1976–77** Kernochan *Dry Hustle* 266: One poor hard-on got thrown out into the snow, and there was no one out there to beat up on. **1977** Bredes *Hard Feelings* 342: Gimme a break, you hard-on. **1964–78** J. Carroll *Basketball Diaries* 43: I can hear the other hardons…laughing. **1979** V. Patrick *Pope* 128: I'm glad I got the chance to see what a collection of first-class hard-ons I'll be working with for the next six months. *a*1986 D. Tate *Bravo* 20: "Miss Electric Fanny!" some high school hard-on had cackled. **1995** *New Yorker* (Feb. 20) 216: Palmer, ex-wise guy and general Mob hard-on, a shylock who gives loans at a hundred and fifty per cent.

4. a difficult or dangerous task; BALLBREAKER.—usu. considered vulgar.

　1985 Bodey *F.N.G.* 176: Walking point is the hardon….There is nobody else to rely on.

¶ In phrase:

¶ **die with a hard-on** (of a man) to die violently, esp. in disgrace or by hanging.—usu. considered vulgar.

1962 McKenna *Sand Pebbles* 427 [ref. to 1920's]: The ship's nickname was *Die Hard.* "I hope them chinchy bastards all die with a hard on!" Red Dog said. **1963** Hayden *Wanderer* 205 [ref. to ca1939]: Fourteen, goddam it, boys, fourteen she goes, or I hope to die with a hard-on! *a***1968** Legman *Rationale* 656: Until public hangings were discontinued at about the turn of the century, it was common lore…that the hanged man's penis would erect at the moment of death.…This…is the source of the phrase "*To die with a hardon,*" meaning to come to a bad end, and specifically to be hanged. **1970** Ponicsan *Last Detail* 168: Well, fuck you and I hope you die with a hard-on. **1992** N. Russell *Suicide Charlie* 82: We found an old man in there the day after the attack. Died with a hard-on.…Artillery round found him before we did.

hard-on *adj.* having an erection of the penis.—usu. considered vulgar.
　*a***1890–93** F & H III 270: *Hard-on adj. phr.*…Prick-proud. **1961** C. Cooper *Weed* 18: Fresh home and hard-on, he'd found…the address.

hard pan *n.* the basic or most fundamental level.
　1870 Medbery *Wall St.* 212: Hard pan is soon reached, and both old world and new are full of hard-pan capitalists. **1873** in *DA:* He's a realist,—believes in coming down to what he calls "the hard pan." **1875** H.B. Stowe, in *DAE:* Mr. Selby…had a genuine interest in coming to the real "hard pan" on which our social fabric is founded. **1883** in *OED:* But it [sc. a book] didn't appear to get down to hard-pan or to take a firm grip on life. **1901** Ade *Modern Fables* 5: It put a Sickening Crimp in his Visible Assets and moved him about three Notches nearer to Hard Pan. **1908** in *DAE:* It will be well for Springfield to get down to hard pan and realize [etc.].

hardrock *n.* a tough, pugnacious, or recalcitrant fellow; a hardened criminal.
　1945 J. Bryan *Carrier* 96: In any crowd of sailors, you'll always find a few "hard rocks" who cock their caps over their left eyebrows. **1950** in *Dict. Canadianisms:* He ran up against a hardrock from Spencer's Island, and when the fracas ended he had been completely thrashed. **1955** O'Connor *Last Hurrah* 372: The old will to live.…And your uncle's got it to spare. A real hard rock. **1959** N. Nye *Long Run* 84: There was eight fellers with me. Some of them hardrocks you got around you now. **1961** Scarne *Guide to Gambling* 681: *Hard Rock* (1) *Poker:* A tight player. (2) A gambler who refuses to lend money. (3) A player who is hard to beat. **1964** Peacock *Drill & Die* 108: I'm the hardest rock in dear old Chosen [Korea]. **1965** Capote *Cold Blood* 292: Dick was not the "hardrock" he'd once thought him: "pragmatic," "virile," "a real brass boy." **1968** Cuomo *Thieves* 126: Especially if they're going to be sending in two Negro hardrocks. **1976** Braly *False Starts* 356: The hardrocks and the psychos formed a wavering line…while an MTA issued them tranqs. **1977** N.Y. Mets telecast (WOR-TV) (Aug. 20): He's a hardrock. **1979** R. Carson *Waterfront* 1: I am known as Big Red, and I've worked ships for fifteen years, along with Flugo,…Shovel Mouth, and Hardrock. **1989** *Beachin' Times* 3: If you can't stand the heat, well, get out of the freakin' sun, Hardrock. **1991** Nelson & Gonzales *Bring Noise* 99: Heavy was at once a poet…and a hardrock.

hard-rock hotel *n.* a prison. Also **hard-rock.** [In 1970 quot., "*city*" is Cɪᴛʏ, 1.a.]
　*ca***1949** W. Guthrie *Dead or Alive* (song): I don't like your hard-rock hotel. **1954** Gaddis *Birdman of Alcatraz* 23 [ref. to ca1910]: He soon grew to hate "the hardrock hotels and the screws," and since these were the product of what he called the "Christian Society" outside, his rejection of religion increased. *a***1960** in A. Lomax *Folk Songs of N. Amer.* 428: If all the jails I been in was all put together, it would make a hard rock hotel as big as the Capitol building. **1970** E. Thompson *Garden of Sand* 409: Catch us with that stuff and it's hard-rock city.

hard-shell *n.* **1.a.** (usu. *cap.*) a member of the Primitive Baptist Church. Now *colloq.*
　1845 in *DAE:* A "Hard-Shell" recently turned a "Soft-Shell" out of church. **1848** in F & H III 270: The old hard-shell laid about him. **1851** in *DAE:* A Hard Shell Story. **1855** in *OEDS:* The claim of "Hard-Shells," touching their familiarity with the Bible. *a***1867** G.W. Harris *Lovingood* 51: Them hard shells over thar dus want me the wus kine. **1908** DN III 319: *Hardshell*…A Primitive Baptist. **1941** Nixon *Possum Trot* 37: The annual "foot-washing day" was a great day…for "Hardshells" for miles around.

　b. an obstinate, uncompromising, tough, or extremely

conservative person; (*specif.*, in 1850's) a conservative member of the New York State Democratic party.
　1853 in Bartlett *Amer.* (ed. 2): The difference between a *Hardshell* and a *Softshell* is this: one favors the execution of the Fugitive Slave Law and goes for a distribution of the offices among the Nationals, while the other is a stickler for Union and Harmony. **1854–55** in Sperber & Trittschuh *Amer. Pol. Terms* 188: A Whig…said…"I am a whole hog—I am a Hard-shell." **1858** in *DA:* We have, however, one or two specimens in our eye of the genus, *hard shell,* who still do as their *daddies* did. **1860** in Sperber & Trittschuh *Amer. Pol. Terms* 188: The Soft Shells and the Hard Shells of New York are terribly distressed just now. **1900** in *DAE:* The elder…observed…that certain of the "hardshells" were looking askance at the fiddle. **1916** H.L. Wilson *In Red Gap* 135: A grouchy old hardshell with white hair and whiskers whirling about his head. **1919** in *OEDS:* I've ridden up here from Tall Timber Junction to get acquainted with you hardshells. **1922–26** Scoggins *Red Gods* 26: And when work's done, you can get drunk, or play poker with a gang of homesick hardshells. *a***1956** Almirall *College to Cow Country* 227: His welcome to newcomers wasn't…a universal one. There were some "hardshells" around that cow country that envied the fact that others did what they couldn't. **1971** Keith *Long Line Rider* 144: They're bringin' a bunch in from Tucker. All hard shells. **1977** Coover *Public Burning* 60: I had to cool the barnburners, soften up the hardshells, keep the hunkers and cowboys in line.

　2. *Naut.* a sailor who has been initiated in a Crossing-the-Line ceremony; sʜᴇʟʟʙᴀᴄᴋ.
　1918 Ruggles *Navy Explained* 46 [ref. to 1910].

hard-shell *adj.* **1.** (usu. *cap.*) being a member of the Primitive Baptist Church. Now *colloq.*
　1838 in *OEDS:* Was introduced to Daddy Spraggins, a Hardshell Baptist preacher. **1853** in Glisan *Jour.* 123: His first two sermons sounded very much like good old hard shell baptist harangues. *a***1859** in Bartlett *Amer.* (ed. 2): An old Hardshell preacher, as they call them in Georgia. **1871** Schele de Vere *Amer.* 241: The *Hard Shell Baptists,* who call themselves *Primitive* Baptists, set their faces like flint—to use their own term…against all foreign evangelical missions. **1964–66** R. Stone *Hall of Mirrors* 17: Whose family was Hard Shell and temperance. **1987** Sayles *Matewan* (film): There's the missionary folks—they're hardshell Baptist.

　2. extremely conservative; uncompromising; intransigent.
　1859 Bartlett *Amer.* (ed. 2): Hardshell Democrats. **1867** in *DA:* The "real grit hard-shell" Democracy. **1889** Barrère & Leland *Dict. Slang* I 449: *Hard-shell* (American), thoroughly orthodox, unyielding, "hidebound" or conservative in religion or politics.…"Genuine hard-shell fanatics." **1900** in *DAE:* The old hard-shell Presbyterian of the old school. **1901** in *DA:* Now the schoolmaster and the manufacturer are fast getting the better of these "hardshell" types of men. **1958** J. King *Pro Football* 16: Of course the hardshell magnates of the NFL did not take their commissioner on faith. **1963** J.A. Williams, in *Provincetown Rev.* VI 12: His circle of hardshell addict friends grows smaller and smaller. **1981** G. Wolf *Roger Rabbit* 153: I'm strictly hardshell. Let them call me what they will.

hard stripe *n.* *Army.* **1.** one of the chevrons indicating the rank of a noncommissioned officer, as opposed to those of a specialist. Often attrib.
　1970 W.C. Woods *Killing Zone* 14: Four…platoon sergeants, sir: three staff and a hard-stripe E-5 draftee. **1977** U.S. Army MSG, Dugway Proving Ground, Utah (coll. J. Ball): Pretty soon all you specialists will be trading your eagle patches for hard stripes. **1980** M. Baker *Nam* 160: There were three other guys who were hard-stripe sergeants.

　2. a noncommissioned officer, as opposed to a specialist; (*also*) a noncommissioned rank.
　1973 U.S. Army sgt., STRATCOM-Taiwan (coll. J. Ball): Specialists are a bunch of fuckin' pussies and Uncle Sam knows it. That's why a hard stripe of the same grade has priority. **1984** Riggan *Free Fire* 104 [ref. to Vietnam War]: Make E-6 hard-stripe, some of them do, in two years.

hard-striper *n.* *Army.* ʜᴀʀᴅ sᴛʀɪᴘᴇ, 2.
　1983 Elting, Cragg & Deal *Soldier Talk* 147: A noncommissioned officer is referred to as a *hard-striper.*

hard stuff *n.* **1.** hard cash, esp. coins.
　1788 S. Low *Politician Out-witted* IV.i: Money trash! Ready Rhino trash! Golden…money! I'm sure he couldn't mean the hard stuff.

1889 Farmer *Amer.: Hard-stuff…*Money. *a***1909** Tillotson *Detective* 92: *Hard stuff*—Silver money. **1931** in D.W. Maurer *Lang. Und.* 48: *Hard stuff…*Metal money. **1942–49** Goldin et al. *DAUL: Hard stuff.* Coins; change as distinguished from bills. Stick the soft (bills) in your kick (pocket) and the hard stuff in the bag.

2.a. hard liquor, esp. whiskey.

[**1810** in *OEDS:* What could possibly have kept me from hard drink?] **1861** in *OEDS:* Order up some hard stuff to give them something to drink. **1884** in *OED:* Two or three kegs of the "hard stuff." **1889** Barrère & Leland *Dict. Slang* I 449: *Hard stuff* (up-country Australian), intoxicating liquors. **1938** Korson *Mine Patch* 39: But I'm off the hard stuff for life. **1949** Ellson *Tomboy* 98: We're going to drink hard stuff. **1954** G. Kersh, in Pohl *Star of Stars* 18: Scotch….I've laid off the hard stuff for…years. **1956** Metalious *Peyton Place* 71: I'll bet a nickel they don't even have any beer left, let alone hard stuff! **1966–69** Woiwode *Going to Do* 239: You're not going to drink hard stuff, are you? **1974** L.D. Miller *Valiant* 40: I went to the back porch for a drink of "hard stuff." **1979** Gram *Foxes* 165: They proceeded to knock back the beer, the wine and the few bottles of hard stuff. **1990** Crow Dog & Erdoes *Lakota Woman* 46: We went "uptown" to hustle some hard stuff.

b. strongly addictive drugs, esp. opiates.

1955 *AS* XXX 87: *Hard stuff.* Opium. **1958** Gilbert *Vice Trap* 5: *Hard Stuff*—heroin. **1964** "Doctor X" *Intern* 290: A few decks of reefers, plus a little of the hard stuff as well—heroin. **1970** Wexler *Joe* (film): Maybe we could stay off the hard stuff for a while and just smoke. **1983** *Hour Magazine* (ABC-TV) (May 9): Smoking grass? Hard stuff?

hardtack *n.* **1.** Orig. *Naut.* hard, unsalted, unleavened bread provided orig. to sailors as a standard ration. Now *S.E.* [The Civil War helped establish this as a standard term, replacing the earlier *ship bread, pilot bread,* and *ship biscuit.*]

1832 (quot. at SALT JUNK). **1833** (quot. at HORSE). **1836** in *OED:* That monkey there…knows how to do nothing but gnaw hard tack. **1847** M'Sherry *El Puchero* 25: *Hard tack,* i.e. pilot bread. **1861** in Beatty *Volunteer* 62: But at daybreak, when reveille is sounded, these wanderers must come trooping back again in time for "hardtack" and double-quick. **1873** Hotten *Slang Dict.* (ed. 4): *Hard tack,* ship biscuits. This is a term used by sailors to distinguish their ordinary sea-bread from that obtained on shore, which is called *soft tack,* or soft tommy. **1892** M.O. Frost *10th Mo.* 122: With a few "hard tacks," we started on. **1898** Bowe *13th Minn.* 24: Bean-soup, hard-tack, and red-horse.

2. (see quot.).

1894 *DN* I 397: *Hard tack.* Silver money, esp. dollars.

hardtail *n.* **1.** *Midland & Army.* a mule.

1917 Empey *Over the Top* (gloss.): *Hard tails*—mules. **1925** Nason *Three Lights* 112 [ref. to 1918]: Them hard-tails o' yours been fed yet? **1928–29** Nason *White Slicker* 6: Don't you know how to stop a hard-tail from lyin' down? **1929** L. Thomas *Woodfill* 78 [ref. to *ca*1905]: The only lingo the Missouri hardtail knows is the kind that fogs the atmosphere. **1929** *AS* IV (June) 341: *Hardtails*—Mules. **1930** "D. Stiff" *Milk & Honey* 207: *Hardtails*—Mules, usually old ones. So named because they show little response to the skinner's whip. **1936** R. Adams *Cowboy Lingo* 202: Mules were called "hard tails." **1936** *AS* (Oct.) 275: *Hard-tail.* Mule. "See him plow the hard-tail." **1942** *Mo. Hist. Rev.* XXXVII 341: The "Ard Tail," as the British soldiers learned to call the Missouri mule during the Boer War. **1944** *Collier's* (Feb. 5) 14: Ask any old jughead-rassler around a remount Army post what wins wars for us, and he'll tell you…"Jugheads. Hardtails. Mules." **1968** S.O. Barker *Rawhide Rhymes* 14: But ol' Kit Carson rode a mule and other pioneers/Sure viewed a heap of country over some ol' hard-tail's ears. **1982** F. Hailey *Soldier Talk* 31: *Hard tail.* Artillery (Mountain pack) mule.

2. an experienced fellow; man.

1933 "W. March" *Co. K* 182: Frank Halligan….Why, I hadn't thought of that old hard tail for years! **1978** *UTSQ:* A guy is called a *hardtail.* A girl is a *split tail.*

hard ticket *n.* **1.** a tough or recalcitrant fellow.

*ca***1855** [G. Thompson] *Rd. to Ruin* 71: Been in to see the prisoner, ma'am? Bad case, ma'am—hard ticket. *a***1877** Bartlett *Amer.* (ed. 4) 703: A "hard *ticket*," a man whom other people had better let alone; an unscrupulous man to deal with. **1904** in *OEDAS* II: Old Laban Simpkins…was a mighty hard ticket. Drank rum by the hogshead, pounded

his wife till she left him, and was a tough nut gin'rally. **1985** in *OEDAS* II: *Ticket,* a person, as in a hard ticket (a tough guy).

2. something difficult to obtain.

1985 T. Wolfe, in *Rolling Stone* (Feb. 28) 50: A table by the window…was not a particularly hard ticket at…two in the afternoon.

hard time *n. Pris.* a prison sentence that is especially long or otherwise severe; (*broadly*) time in prison.

1927 Murphy *Gray Walls* 50: He soon began doing what prisoners call "hard time," that is, brooding and worrying over his sentence. **1929** Hotstetter & Beesley *Racket* 227: *Hard Time*—A long sentence to prison. **1954** Gaddis *Birdman of Alcatraz* 154: I was in prison when they had the silence system. I know what hard time is. **1965** Bonham *Durango St.* 71: I'll give you odds most of them are doing hard time before Christmas. **1986** E. Weiner *Howard the Duck* 158: I'm gonna do hard time in the Big House! **1992** *Amer. Detective* (ABC-TV): They're lookin' at some hard time.

hard-time *v.* to haze or harass.

1963–64 Kesey *Great Notion* 398: Some of them might hardtime you a little. **1969** Sidney *For Love of Dying* 18: Mitchell hard-timed him. **1972** Pearce *Pier Head Jump* 98: Don't they hard-time you for bein' Porto Rican?

hard-timer *n. Pris.* a convict serving HARD TIME.

1986 *CNN News* (CNN-TV) (Oct. 9): All the hard-timers on Rikers Island.

hard-up *n.* a destitute or impoverished person.

1851 H. Mayhew *London Labour* 3: The cigar-end finders, or "hard-ups," as they are called,…collect the refuse pieces of smoked cigars from the gutters, and having dried them, sell them as tobacco to the very poor. **1857** "Ducange Anglicus" *Vulgar Tongue:* Hard-up, a poor person. **1874** Carter *Rollingpin* 94: Three parts of laziness and one of pride will make a genuine hard-up.

hard up *adj.* **1.** Orig. *Naut.* impaired, worn out, or in poor condition (*obs.*); in want or need; desperate; (*often specif.*) having little or no money; broke. Now *colloq.*

1818 (cited in Partridge *DSUE* (ed. 8)). **1821** *Real Life in London* II 55: Captain R---- is…rather what we call *hard up* just now. **1823** *Blackwood's Mag.* (Sept.) 276: They were in this hard-up and dreary way one dismal, rainy, and squally night. **1821–26** Stewart *Man-of-War's-Man* II 126: You'd see whether these old shattered trotters of mine, hard up as they are now, wouldn't do their duty. **1840** De Quincey, in *OED:* As hard up for water as the Mecca caravan. **1841** [Mercier] *Man o' War* 42: Well, shipmates, sailor-like, I went the whole figure while the cash lasted, not even buying myself a fit-out of clothes; and in a little time I was *hard up.* **1842** *Spirit of Times* (Oct. 29) 416: To back a friend hard up or face a foe. **1850** J.H. Greene *Tombs* 124: I could not trust the "hard-up" gamblers. **1849–59** Bartlett *Amer.* (ed. 2): *Hard Up.* In straits for want of money; short of funds. **1859** L. Barney *Auraria* 30: Being "hard up," [they] are anxious to sell a few [lots] to raise funds to improve the remainder. **1862** C.F. Browne *A. Ward* 117: Individooals, who git hard up, embark in the lekturin business. **1865** Byrn *Fudge Fumble* 161: He said if I was "hard up for money he could let me have what I wanted." **1865** in Schele de Vere *Amer.* 608: They are *hard-up* for political capital. **1868** Macy *There She Blows!* 8: The city rowdy…had run himself "hard up" on a spree, and, no longer able to raise the wind, had shipped for a sea voyage as a last resort. **1869** *Carmina Princetonia* 29: In the days when I was hard up, not many years ago. **1870** *Comic Songster* 35: However "*hard up*" for an offer,/Never marry a medical man! **1905** Sinclair *Jungle* 279: I'm hard up, too, my goo' fren'. **1908** in H.C. Fisher *A. Mutt* 47: If we get hard up we can hock the goat. **1910** in O. Johnson *Lawrenceville* 210: Doc is devilishly hard up. Offer him a couple of dollars and see. **1957** J.D. MacDonald *Death Trap* 154: It's a hell of a way to buy a ticket into Vicki's bed. You must be hard up. **1958** J. King *Pro Football* 2: Frequently as hard-up as a panhandler. **1986** S. Bauer *Amazing Stories* 175: All of us was hard up.

2. in need of sexual gratification; HORNY.

1938 "Justinian" *Amer. Sexualis* 25: *Hard Up.* adj. In need of sexual gratification. Said of both sexes, usually in derision or humorous belittlement. **1965** in Cleaver *Soul on Ice* 30: I'm hard-up enough to suck my grandmother's old withered tits. **1960–69** Runkel *Law* 235: I got hard up as hell….Yeh, I was real horny. **1973** Sesar *Catullus* xvi: His poems…[are] lewd and lascivious,/And can get somebody pretty hard-up, too. **1986** *NDAS:* He declared he was so hard up he'd fuck mud.

hardware *n.* **1.** hard liquor, esp. whiskey.

 1839 *Spirit of Times* (June 1) 153: "Cuff," said a Militia officer, to a negro at his side, as he prepared to swallow his fifth invoice of "hardware." **1840** *Spirit of Times* (July 4) 216: By dint of hard digging, hard swearing, and *hard-ware*, we managed to reach S— in five hours. **1846** Durivage & Burnham *Stray Subjects* 104: This child don't meddle with no more *hard ware* in this trap, *no how!* **1852** in *DA:* He was reckless and "extravagant;" that is, he spent all his money for "hardware." **1891** McCann & Jarrold *Odds & Ends* 34: I thought my gal would smell the hardware he'd been drinking. **1920** T.A. Dorgan, in *DARE:* Oh Cyril—oh-hoo—Got any hardware on the hip? **1929** Hotstetter & Beesley *Racket* 227: *Hardware*—Hard liquor; whiskey. **1932** *Writer's Digest* (Aug.) 47: If he wants hard liquor he says, "hardware." **1967** in *DARE:* General words…for any kind of liquor…*Hardware.*

2. coins; cash.

 1859 Matsell *Vocab.* 40: *Hardware.* False coin. **1942** *ATS* 535: Coins…*hardware.* **1962** G. Olson *Roaring Rd.* 119: Maybe pick up a little hardware and a lot of kicks on weekends in an MG race.

3.a. an edged weapon or firearm carried by an individual; (now *usu.*) a pistol; personal weapons collectively.

 1865 in *DAE:* Capt. Hammond…charged upon the rebels in his front, crying as he flew forward, "give them your hardware, boys!" **1881** Nye *Forty Liars* 69: The poor cucumber, with assorted hardware sticking out in all directions like the hair on a cat's tail,…yields up the victory. **1902** A.H. Lewis *Wolfville* 18: He puts up his hardware an' composes himse'f. **1902–03** Ade *People You Know* 182: He went home to oil up his Pocket Hardware. **1908** Raine *Wyoming* 77: The boys don't like seeing your hardware so prominent at a social gathering. **1911** Howard *Enemy to Society* 291: If we start tryin' to unload hardware…we're gone. **1914** Jackson & Hellyer *Vocab.* 42: *Hardware*…weapons; knives; razors. **1918** Swan *My Co.* 138: It was a laughable sight to see this moving-picture man marching behind the eight boches, all their "hardware" on him, and they carrying his moving-picture apparatus. **1919** *DN* V 34: *Hardware, n.* Slang for guns and pistols. **1954** Kibbee & Webb *Vera Cruz* (film): Little careless with your hardware, ain't ya? **1958** Simonson & Philips *Blob* (film): Tell him to bring every piece of hardware he can find in the police department. **1935–62** Ragen & Finston *Toughest Pris.* 802: *Hardware*—Weapons in general; knives, guns, or razors. **1972** Bercovici & Prentiss *Culpepper Cattle Co.* (film): Don't let your mouth overload your hardware, cowboy. **1979** Cassidy *Delta* 69: I notice you changed your hardware. **1980** Gould *Ft. Apache* 79: Murphy don't need no hardware….All he has to do is breathe on the suckers, and they give up without a fight. **1990** Vachss *Blossom* 237: Where'd you hear I was in the market for some hardware?

b. *Mil.* armament or munitions (now *S.E.*); (esp. in early use, now *rare*) bullets, shells, shrapnel, etc., usu. in flight.

 1865 Springer *Sioux Country* 54: Flannigan's Batterie 16th Kansas Cav. throwed them a piece of "hardware" over which scared them nearly into fits. **1873** *Custer's Yellowstone Exped.* 18: A large quantity of arms and ammunition was shipped to the [trading] posts as "hardware." These agencies sadly need investigation. **1876** J. Wilkinson *Blockade-Runner* 154: And bringing in "hardware," as munitions of war were then [1863] invoiced. **1897** in Congdon *Combat: Civil War* 250: The Eighth Indiana battery…suffered…severely from the rebel "hardware." **1918** *Forum* (Oct.) 409: They had our number where we were waiting in the woods and were dropping all the hardware in the world on us. **1919** *Lit. Digest* (Feb. 15) 86: It's the same way with captured guns and ammunition. One of the best sports I know of is tossing their own hardware back at them. **1950** *Life* (Sept. 4) 17: It also meant sending continuous reinforcements of troops and hardware—GI slang for guns, tanks and ammunition. **1961** in Galewitz *Great Comics* 282: You'd never make it without stopping hardware. **1961** *U.S. News & W. R.* (Oct. 23) 46: Until six months ago, this was an Army with "hardware" a decade behind the times.

4.a. *Mil.* military medals; (*also*) metal insignia; (*broadly,* as in 1990 quot.) any sort of medal or trophy. [Early quots. ref. to WWI.]

 1921 Wiley *Lady Luck* 21: Wildcat listened strong to the appeal made by the jingling hardware of heroism. **1927** Liggett *AEF* 268: Some men cannot take their medals or let them alone. "Hardware" is the Army's deprecating term for them, and our manly chests came to look like show windows on ceremonious occasions. **1930** *Our Army* (Aug.) 33: *Hardware.* Medals and decorations. **1941** Hargrove *Pvt. Hargrove* 84: *Chest hardware*—medals….*Shoulder hardware*—the shoulder insignia of a commissioned officer. **1944** in Galewitz *Great Comics* 270: I sohta hammuhed th' stah into a loo-tenint's hahdweah. **1945** *Yank* (Oct. 26) 15: You had all that hardware but no basic training. **1957** E. Brown *Locust Fire* 19 [ref. to 1944]: When that's over with, the adjutant starts reading the citations and Rogers is busier than a one-armed paper hanger passing out the hardware. **1965** Barrett *In Harm's Way* (film): These were my stars before I picked up this heavier hardware. **1967** Dibner *Admiral* 415: I'm seeing to it personally they get all the Air Medals and Flying Crosses and whatever else kind of Navy hardware tickles their fancy. **1990** *Maclean's* (May 7) 58: In the 25 years since the trophy's inception, pretenders have been permitted to carry away the hardware on all but eight occasions.

b. jewelry. *Joc.*

 1939 Trumbo *Sorority House* (film): Miss Fisher—I see you have some new hardware [*sc.* a fraternity pin]. **1945** in *OED2: Hardware,* flashy jewelry. **1951** I. Shaw, in *OED2:* When the rating goes up, I buy my hardware at Cartier's.

5. *Pris.* shackles.

 1977 Bunker *Animal Factory* 158: Whaddya think, I'm goin' somewhere in all this hardware?

hardware store *n. Army.* a heavy-caliber high-explosive shell.

 1918 in Cowing *Dear Folks* 223: Showers of shrapnel, whizz-bangs, Busy Berthas and German hardware stores. **1918–29** Nason *White Slicker* 211: A couple of hardware stores…came showerin' down.

hardwood *n. Theat.* tickets that have been paid for or distributed. [Contrasted with DEADWOOD, 3.]

 1934 Weseen *Dict. Slang* 143: *Hardwood*—Tickets for standing room; tickets given in exchange for higher priced ones. **1942** Liebling *Telephone* 164: Tickets that have been paid for—known in the trade as "the hardwood"—and…complimentaries, or "deadwood."

harker *n.* an ear.

 1856 *Ballou's Dollar Mo. Mag.* (Oct.) 326: And if my harkers ain't out of order, it's the ghost of Jack Brace, my old bunk mate. **1871** Banka *Prison Life* 146: First Round. Offense threw out a flanker and caught defense under the right hearker.

Harlem taxi *n. Police.* (see quot.).—used derisively.

 1961–62 in *AS* XXXVII 269: The Language of Traffic Policemen [in So. Calif.]…*Harlem taxi, n.* An oversized, tail-finned, flamboyantly colored passenger car.

harness *n.* **1.** marriage.—constr. with *the;* in phr. **in [double] harness** married.

 1838 in *DA:* We soon hitch'd traces to trot in double harness. **1900** Ade *More Fables* 146: Moral: As soon as he begins to Frequent the Back Rooms of the House, measure him for the Harness. **1926** C.M. Russell *Trails* 122: By spring we can pull off nearly as good a quarrel as civilized folks in harness. **1966–69** in *DARE* s.v. *double harness* [in various phr. for *double harness*].

2.a. costume or clothing; outfit; uniform, esp. a police uniform. Hence **harnessed up** dressed. Cf. *OED* def. 5, "Household and personal equipment;…apparel. *Obs.*"

 1853 G. Thompson *Gay Girls* 26: Wonder where she got her good harness? **1853** [G. Thompson] *Garter* 73: He ain't got a cent—look at his ragged harness. **1874** Carter *Rollingpin* 195: We buri'd 'em on Spar Island bar,/ With their fitin' harness on. **1883** Hay *Bread-Winners* 88: She took several days to prepare what she called "a harness" of sufficient splendor. **1891** "M. Twain" *What Is Man?* 225: At the Metropolitan in New York they sit in a glare, and wear their showiest harness. **1895** Townsend *Fadden* 5: Say, I knowed ye'd be paralyzed wen ye seed me in dis harness. *Ibid.* 243: I…furnished him with a suit of clothes—which he called a harness. **1899** Green *Va. Folk-Speech* 178: *Harness*…clothing, dress garments. **1905** in A. Adams *Chisholm Trail* 117: But in toggery, in my visiting harness, I looked like a rank tenderfoot. *a*1904–11 Phillips *Susan Lenox* I 245: Now, Vi, get busy and put her into harness. Make her a work of art. **1911** Bronson-Howard *Enemy to Society* 113: The transfer of Lieutenant Kneebreeks back to "harness," with a station somewhere in a lonely part of the Bronx. *Ibid.* 212: I got into that telephone "harness" again and went around…to ask 'em if the 'phones were working all right now. **1927** T.A. Dorgan, in Zwilling *TAD Lexicon* 43: The old woman sez I oughta give the moths some air so I gits myself harnessed up. **1930** *Railroad Man's Mag.* II 470: *Harness*—Passenger conductor's uniform. **1931** Uhler

Cane Juice 107: You look like all hell in this harness. **1938** Beebe *High Iron* 221: *Harness:* Dress uniform of a passenger conductor, blue tailcoat. **1966–68** in *DARE*.

b. *Army.* pack and equipments.

   1862 in M. Lane *Dear Mother* 90: So we put on our "harness" and hurried on over the worst of roads.

¶ In phrase:

¶ **in harness, 1.** see (1), above.

2. *Pros.* working as a prostitute.

   1951 G. Fowler *Schnozzola* 17 [ref. to *ca*1910]: Several waiters at Diamond Tony's had women "in harness," as the saying was, or "on the turf," and took most of their earnings. **1977** Sayles *Union Dues* 183: Inez been put out on the block again…gone back in *harness*.

harness *adj.* *Police & Und.* being a uniformed police officer.—used attrib.

   1903 *Enquirer* (Cincinnati) (May 9) 13: *Harnessed* [*sic*] *bull*—Policeman in uniform. **1903** A.H. Lewis *Boss* 262: [The] Captain sends along a couple of his harness bulls from Mulberry Street. **1904** *Life in Sing Sing* 256: *Harness bull*—Officer in uniform. *a*1909 Tillotson *Detective* 92: *Harness copper*—Uniformed policeman. **1914** E.R. Burroughs *Mucker* 12: Billy saw a harness bull strolling toward him. **1920** *Variety* (Dec. 31) 8: What were those odd looking lids the harness bulls were wearing—helmets! **1922** N. Anderson *Hobo* 154: The uniformed upholder of the law, the civil police, is given the uncomplimentary epithet, "harness bull." **1925–26** J. Black *You Can't Win* 31: The "harness cop"…went back to his beat. **1928** J. O'Connor *B'way Racketeers* 182: It looks as though every harness dick in the precinct was next to the racket. **1931** Wilstach *Under Cover Man* 1: An old-time harness bull. **1956** H. Ellison *Deadly Streets* 39: A cop…a harness boy. **1960** Himes *Gold Dream* 49: "Yeah, the inspector telephoned us you were coming," one of the harness bulls said. **1963** D. Tracy *Brass Ring* 360: The sergeant was…long a harness cop. *a*1979 Pepper & Pepper *Straight Life* 129: And the harness bulls, I think we had them licked, but then the detectives came over. **1986** C. Stroud *Close Pursuit* 25: Bitching about the bosses and ragging the harness guys.

harp *n.* **1.** *So.* a harmonica.

   1887 in *OEDS*: She displayed a flimsy red silk handkerchief and a child's harp. **1895** *DN* I 418: *Harp:* n. mouth organ. **1902** "O. Henry" *Works* 834: I stuck the harp up against his mouth. "If you can't pay—play," I says. **1905** *DN* III 82: *Harp, n.* Harmonica. **1919** Amerine *Alabama's Own* 23: One had invested a few "marks" in a harp and was playing familiar ragtime tunes. **1929** Botkin *Folk-Say I* 95: I have myself…sung and played on the harp. **1938** Natteford *Billy Returns* (film): You'll be sharp if you try this harp. **1951–59** F. Ramsey *Been Here* 49: I…went to blowin' the harp with the guitar. **1968** J.P. Miller *Race for Home* 4: He could be playing his harmonica (which he called a harp), a sad song about a jailhouse and the wings of an angel, or a happy song. **1970** Wohl & Brackett *Rio Lobo* (film): Neither do you unless you promise not to play that harp. **1982** A. Shaw *Dict. Pop/Rock* 66: A response is made by an instrument, "harp" or guitar. **1987** Carver *Amer. Reg. Dial.* 103: *Harp*…[is] used more often by blacks than whites. **1989** *New Yorker* (May 9) 7: My guess is Speedo's a harmonica player….A *harp* player, that's what you call it. **1988–93** Wilcock & Guy *Damn Right* 26: I'd play that…shit on the harp. **1993** A. Lomax *Where Blues Began* 14: He used to follow all these harp blowers, mandoleen and guitar players.

2. an Irish person.—sometimes used contemptuously. Also as adj.

   1898–1900 Cullen *Chances* 238: This Harp from Connemara … can't turn two of these tricks right after the other. **1904** *Life in Sing Sing* 249: *Harp.* An Irishman. **1911** A.H. Lewis *Apaches of N.Y.* 167: Th' sight av that grandstand full av harps, Hughey at th' head, almosht gives him heart failure. **1919** Tompkins *Rainbow Div.* 62: The old 69th New York—"The Fighting Harps." **1922** E. Paul *Impromptu* 12: "How many Harps?" "Four of 'em, but Grady is a Protestant." **1928** in E. Ferber *One Basket* 333: The big harp…starts bawling me out, see? **1934** H. Roth *Call It Sleep* 416: Shet up…yuh bull-faced harps. **1940** Goodrich *Delilah* 19: Maybe the big harp got sore and smacked him. **1943** in Tapert *Lines of Battle* 118: Mike Moran…a big harp if there ever was one. **1954** Schulberg *Waterfront* 171: You dumb harp, you must like gettin' hit in the head. **1960** Krueger *St. Patrick's* 167: Why do all these goddam harps head for a church when they get

loose? **1977** Dunne *True Confessions* 9: That big harp voice booming through the sanctuary. **1985** T. Wolfe, in *Rolling Stone* (Mar. 28) 108: Irish machismo—that was the whole game! They called themselves Harps and Donkeys! **1992** N. Cohn *Heart of World* 9: Friggin' Harps, straight off the friggin' boats. *a*1994 H. Roth *Mercy of Rude Stream* 258: A harp an' a Jew.

¶ In phrase:

¶ **play a harp** [alluding to conventional representations of the Christian heaven] to be dead. *Joc.*

   1927 in F.V. Mason *Fighting Amer.* 692 [ref. to 1918]: "Do you know where I'll be by nine o'clock day after to-morrow morning?" "You may be playing a harp." *a*1981 "K. Rollins" *Fighter Pilots* 185: "Really? What's the son doing now?" "Playing a harp." **1989** P. Benchley *Rummies* 254: Touch me once more, pal, you'll be playin' the harp with fuckin' stumps.

harpoon *n.* **1.** a harsh or ridiculing comment; ridicule or victimization, or a propensity for these.—usu. constr. with *the*.

   1896 Ade *Artie* 56: Mame's mother started to throw the harpoon into him….Sure, the stringin' business. **1903** A.H. Lewis *Boss* 196: He comes up for renomination within two months. He'd look well throwin' the harpoon into me right now, wouldn't he? **1908** W.G. Davenport *Butte & Montana* 35: [The card sharps] throw the harpoon into them with a straight flush in a cut-throat game of poker. **1913** Z. Grey *Desert Gold* 24: He kept ramming the harpoon into me till I just couldn't stand it. **1914** Paine *Wall Between* 204: "So they stuck th' harpoon into ye an thin twisted it," croaked the old main. **1923** *Atlanta Constitution* (Comics) (Feb. 4) 4: I t'rew the harpoon into him….I give him the razz. **1933** D. Runyon, in *Collier's* (Aug. 5) 7: He loves to heave the old harpoon into actors if they do not act to suit him….He is generally in there harpooning pretty good. **1935** D.H. Clarke *Regards to Broadway* 111: "He might have tried to throw the old harpoon into me," Arthur said…."He'd've harpooned you, all right, if he could, and if he could see he stood to gain anything by it." **1939** Wilbur & Niblo *Hell's Kitchen* (film): It's a frame I guess. The old harpoon. Somebody's got it in for Buck. **1945** Lindsay & Crouse *State of the Union* 477: She…spent the rest of the night tossing harpoons into him. **1945** Bryan *Carrier* 25: This morning Coop slipped a harpoon into the air group. **1959** *AS* (May) 155: The loser gets…*the maroon harpoon.*

2. *Esp.* *Narc.* a hypodermic needle.

   1938 in D.W. Maurer *Lang. Und.* 103: *Harpoon.* The hypodermic needle. **1939** (cited in Partridge *Dict. Und.* 322). **1947** *ATS* (Supp.) 28: *Harpoon line,* those [servicemen] receiving immunization inoculations. *a*1962 Maurer & Vogel *Narc. Add.* (ed. 2) 305: I can get you cut in if you can dig up a harpoon.

3. the penis.—usu. in Phr. **throw the harpoon in [to]** to copulate with. *Joc.*

   1960 in *DARE*: I'd shore like to throw the harpoon in her. **1966** in Legman *No Laughing Matter* 332: I'm going to…throw the harpoon into that blonde stewardess in the back cabin.

harpoon *v.* **1.** to victimize; (*also*) to ridicule.

   1840 *Spirit of Times* (Nov. 21) 440: She'll harpoon you yet, if you don't mind your eye. **1914** Jackson & Hellyer *Vocab.* 43: *Harpoon,* Noun. General currency. Used as a metaphor for lampoon. As a verb, it signifies to "give a person the worst of it." **1933, 1935** (quots. at HARPOON, *n.,* 1). **1974** Radano *Cop Stories* 60: Sergeant Heiden—was out to harpoon me. *Ibid.* 61: Anyone reading the complaint would assume the sergeant had harpooned a boozer.

2. to copulate with (a woman).

   1965 in Di Donato *Naked as Author* 92: I always have the feeling he'd like to "harpoon" me himself, the prissy bastard.

Harry *n.* *Narc.* heroin.

   1955 in Partridge *Dict. Und.* (ed. 2) 831: "Harry"…"horse"…Heroin. **1956** Nyswander *Drug Addict* 172: *Harry*…Heroin. **1969, 1972, 1980** (cited in Spears *Drugs & Drink*).

¶ In phrase:

¶ **by the Lord Harry** (used as a mild oath).

   *1687 Congreve, in *OED2*: By the Lord Harry he says true. *1708, *1821 in *OED2*. **1825** in *JAF* LXXVI (1963) 279: By the lord harry. **1900** Bacheller *Holden* 27: Lord Harry! here's honey bees.

Harry High School *n.* var. HIGH SCHOOL HARRY.

harsh *adj. Stu.* disagreeable or unfair; unfortunate; (*also*) harmful; disgusting.

 1984 Mason & Rheingold *Slanguage: Harsh* adj....unpleasant; undesirable..."My midterm exam was harsh." **1985** *Daily Beacon* (Univ. Tenn.) (Apr. 15) 5: *Harsh*—Mean, strict. Also something bad that happens, as in "That's harsh." **1989** P. Munro *U.C.L.A. Slang* 47: *Harsh* very bad, mean...I have a final on my birthday—that's harsh. **1990** Dickson *Slang!* 219: *Harsh*....bad. **1992** *Donahue* (NBC-TV): Alcohol is still a drug. It's harsh. **1994** Univ. Tenn. student: God that [*sc.* a horror film] was harsh! **1995** *X-Files* (Fox-TV): So this is the dude that died. That's pretty harsh, man.

harsh *v.* to ruin; damage, spoil.

 1993 Bahr & Small *Son-in-Law* (film): Your PC got harshed. **1996** *Suck* (Mar. 19): Who hasn't had their mellow harshed by an equally trivial...event?

¶ **Harsh me out!** *Stu.* "That's very unfair or disagreeable!"

 1984 Mason & Rheingold *Slanguage: Harsh me out*...Used to describe anything unpleasant.

¶ In phrases:

¶ **harsh on** *Stu.* to criticize; speak ill of.

 1990 P. Munro *Slang U.: Harsh on* to be hard on, be mean to...The professor really harshed on me when I was late for class. **1992** *Twentysomething* (ABC-TV special): I don't want to harsh on anybody's marriage. I've seen some good marriages. **1993** Haverford College alumnus, age 22 (coll. J. Sheidlower): I was tryin' to pick her up, but she was totally harshin' on me.

Harvy *n.* a Harvard student.

 1845 Ingraham *Alice May* 38: There was a good many of the "Harvies" in town.

hash[1] *n.* **1.a.** food; victuals.

 1861 in Herdegan & Beaudot *At Gettysburg* 77: Bless each of us and damn this hash. **1865** in Hilleary *Webfoot* 37: Returned to camp in time for hash (bean soup). **1867** S. Clemens, in *Twain's Letters* II 130: We liked four bells best, because it meant hash—*dinner*. **1868** in *DA*: Yesterday we dropped in at a popular restaurant...for our regular "hash." **1866–71** Bagg *Yale* 45: *Hash*, is sometimes used in a sense similar to *grub*, though as a noun only. **1871** *Overland Mo.* (July) 88: Us that has to rustle round on the outside for our hash, hain't got no time for foolishness. **1875** *Minstrel Gags* 10: Come, shut off de steam. It's time for hash. **1891** in *DAE*: I just sleep till the hash bell goes. **1910** J.A. Lomax *Cowboy Songs* 227: His bread it was corn dodger, his beef I could not chaw,/This was the kind of hash they fed me in the State of Arkansaw. **1914** Knibbs *Songs of the Outlands* 37: What we're needin' most is hash. **1925** Bailey *Shanghaied* 46 [ref. to 1898]: The negro...cooked our morning hash (breakfast). **1933** Ersine *Pris. Slang* 43: *Hash, n.* Food. **1946** in *DA*: It is better form, to keep your social standing among your fellow cynics, to call it "grub" or "hash."

b. *U.S. Mil. Acad.* (see quots.).

 1871 O.E. Wood *West Point Scrap Book* 338: *Hash.*—Supper cooked in room after taps. **1900** *Howitzer* (No. 1) 120: *Hash.*—A Cadet party held after taps, usually with the purpose of consuming boodle. [Obsolete.]

2. *Communications.* garbled transmission; background noise or interference; static.

 1949 in *OEDAS* II: The filter in the primary leads is used to prevent any "hash" (r-f disturbance) that might be created. **1958** Cooley *Run for Home* 294: There's a lot of hash I can't read. **1966** *Combat!* (ABC-TV): Nothing but hash. **1976** Dills *CB* 39: *Hash and trash*: background noise; signal unclear. **1978** Dills *CB* (ed. 4) 51: *Hash*: interference on the channel. **1983** Naiman *Computer Dict.* 71: *Hash*. Visual static on the screen. **1984** *U.S. News & W.R.* (Feb. 13) 62: Known as "hash" or "noise" to technicians, electromagnetic pollution is an unwanted byproduct of the electronic age.

¶ In phrases:

¶ **fix (someone's) hash** to do for; retaliate decisively against.

 1907 in *DA*: I've seen the mate and if you eat along them hogways he'll fix your hash.

¶ **settle (someone's) hash** to subdue, defeat, or overcome decisively; finish. Now *colloq.*

 *1803 in J. Ashton *Eng. Satires on Napoleon* 148: Why I think the *first round* will settle his hash. **1809** in *DAE*: We therefore mean to make a dash,/To settle fighting Europe's hash. *1825 in *OED*: The

hash of the Yankees he'll settle. *1829 Marryat *Frank Mildmay* 360: Don't you think they would settle his hash? **1839** *Spirit of Times* (Aug. 24) 294: I can settle his hash for him any day. **1844** "J. Slick" *High Life in N.Y.* 117: I'll settle your hash,...you mean old shote! **1857** in *DAE*. **1868** Macy *There She Blows!* 31: I'll settle *your* hash for you to-morrow. [**1871** Willis *Forecastle Echoes* 9: O Statesmen...Splice Canada and Mexico, and season Cuba's "hash."] *1873 Hotten *Slang Dict.* (ed. 4): "To settle his *hash*"...is equivalent to..."cook his goose" *i.e.*, to kill him. **1880** J.C. Harris *Uncle Remus* 40: "Well, den, I'll settle yo' hash right now," sez Brer Fox. **1882** C. Morris *Shadow Sam* 3: Just leave me to settle that burglar's hash. **1884** Blanding *Sailor Boy* 316 [ref. to Civil War]: If the old leather-head...does not behave himself, we will soon settle his hash. **1892** F. Harper *Iola Leroy* 29: You made him settle de oberseer's hash. **1927** Rollins *Jinglebob* 186 [ref. to 1880's]: That settled his hash for any ridin' a hoss. **1995** *Simpsons* (Fox-TV): Yeah, I'd like to settle his hash too.

¶ **settle the hash** to settle difficulties, esp. by decisive action.

 1807 in Thornton *Amer. Gloss.*: This settles all the hash. *1821 *Real Life in Ireland* 310: I settled the hash, merely to get rid of the bill. **1824** in Thornton *Amer. Gloss.*:The parties settled the hash, and retired to...quaff cogniac. **1833** in *DAE*. **1847** Downey *Portsmouth* 60: The English and Peruvians have had a muss, and the Old Admiral give 'em twenty four hours to settle the hash, or else he was going to open his fire on the Castle. **1848** *Life in Rochester* 24: They have been to see me, and want to settle the hash. **1859** "Skitt" *Fisher's River* 44 [ref. to 1820's]: Ax me no questions, else I'll settle the hash with you all quick.

¶ **sling hash, 1.** to serve or prepare meals for a work crew, military or prison mess, cheap eating place, or the like.

 1868, 1871, 1873 etc. (implied at HASH-SLINGER). **1906** in "O. Henry" *Works* 45: I guess she won't want to sling hash any more when she sees the pile of dust I've got. **1909** in *Everybody's Mag.* (Jan. 1910) 116: They dared him to take them up to where she slung the hash. **1918** in Dos Passos *14th Chronicle* 230: I have to coerce unwilling and half seasick soldiers to sling the hash. **1926** Nason *Chevrons* 47: I was slingin' hash in this man's army before he was pupped. **1927** C. McKay *Harlem* 145: If I had your edjucation I wouldn't be slinging no hash on the white man's chu-chu. **1936** Tully *Bruiser* 40: I'd sling hash a year for that much. **1947** Motley *Any Door* 206: She slings hash on North Clark Street. **1958** D. Stanford *Ski Town* 44: She slings hash...from four o'clock until midnight. **1960** Glemser *Fly Girls* 186: He used to sling hash for the cattlemen. **1965** in H.S. Thompson *Shark Hunt* 472: Tutoring, typing, clerking, car washing, hash slinging and baby sitting are all easy ways to make a subsistence income. **1992** N. Cohn *Heart of World* 61: Before slinging hash, she had been a truck driver.

2. to talk nonsense.

 1989 *Current Affair* (syndic. TV series): He looks so serious and he slings such hash, you know what I mean?

¶ **wrestle hash** to dine.

 1871 Hay *Pike Co. Ballads* 24: He'll wrastle his hash tonight in hell,/Or my name's not Tilmon Joy! **1876** B. Harte, in *Calif. Folk. Qly.* I (1942) 288: That woz a place wor yer hash ye might hev wrestled. **1881** A.A. Hayes *New Colo.* 92: A prominent gentleman...who came in on Billy Bullion's boss coach last night and wrastles his hash at the Occidental.

hash[2] *n. Mil.* HASH MARKS.

 1942–45 Caniff *Male Call* (unp.): Seagoin' gyrenes with hash to the elbows.

hash[3] *n. Narc.* hashish.

 1948 Schwartz *Blowtop* 147: No, this is brown. It's African. It might even be hash. **1951** *Neurotica* (Spring) 75: I don't push no hash no more. **1957** in W.S. Burroughs *Letters* 353: *Majoun*...hash. **1959–60** R. Reisner *Jazz Titans* 157: *Hash*: hashish. **1961** R. Russell *Sound* 16: "Hash" all through them Moslem countries, man. That's why the cats over there is so cool. **1965** Matthiessen *Fields of Lord* 77: Pot...or hash...or peyote. **1970** *N.Y. Post* (Mar. 18) 2: For two years she had been using drugs—"marijuana, goof balls, down, hash, nothing stronger...." **1976** J.W. Thomas *Heavy Number* 28: You ever blast good hash? **1989** Kienzle *Eminence* 291: He mixed booze and hash. *a*1990 E. Currie *Dope & Trouble* 76: I was selling weed, you know, hash. *1995 *Absolutely Fabulous* (BBC-TV): Have you ever smoked grass or...hash?

hash *v.* to work as a HASH-SLINGER.

 1899–1900 Cullen *Tales* 280: We can...get jobs hashin'—table waiters are always wanted at summer resorts. **1908** W.G. Davenport *Butte & Montana* 113: A good looking flusie is hashing in the kitchen. **1930** Graham & Graham *Queer People* 229: If I hadn't horned into her affairs, she'd still be hashing at Henry's. **1935** E. Anderson *Hungry Men* 224: I hope you...get me a job. I wouldn't mind learning how to hash. **1942** Hollingshead *Elmtown's Youth* 279: Being a waitress is rated as the lowest type of work a girl can do....She started to "hash" nights in Monk Café. **1984** *Santa Barbara News-Press* (June 24) D2: Although some food booths typically sell out...Hofmeister [a food supplier] makes sure his customers have extras. "They can hash right up to the end."

hash-burner *n.* *Army.* a mess cook.
  1919 *Twelfth U.S. Inf.* 81: Fortunate, indeed, is the Company that boasts a Cook who ranks above the average of "hash-burners." **1941** *AS* (Oct.) 166: *Hashburner.* Cook. **1944** Kober & Uris *In Meantime, Darling* (film): What this hut needs is a new hashburner.

Hashbury *n.* the Haight-Ashbury section of San Francisco.
  1967 *Time* (July 7) 19: Within the Hashbury circulate more than 25 undercover narcotics agents. **1967** Bronsteen *Hippy's Handbook* 14: *Hashbury* n. colloquial for Haight-Ashbury (hippy central in S.F.). **1967** in H.S. Thompson *Shark Hunt* 446: The "Hashbury" is the new capital of what is rapidly becoming a drug culture.

hash-driver *n.* HASH-SLINGER.
  1879 (quot. at POT-SLINGER).

hasher *n.* HASH-SLINGER.
  1908 W.G. Davenport *Butte & Montana* 90: A good looking...hasher from the Florence Hotel. **1916** *Editor* (Mar. 11) 297: *Hasher,* meaning waitress. **1918** *DN* V 25: *Hasher,* n. A waiter in a restaurant; usually a woman. General. **1923** O'Hare *In Prison* 28: She was a "hasher" in a "beanery" in St. Louis. **1936** *AS* (Feb.) 43: *Hasher.* Counterman. **1946** N. Nye *Breed* 26: The hasher's tired eyes revealed a shopworn interest. **1948** Chaplin *Wobbly* 251 [ref. to 1918]: I worked with the prison "hashers" for a couple of weeks, setting out plates and cups, carting them away, scrubbing the tables, and finally sweeping and mopping the floor. **1951** Pryor *The Big Play* 262: You still got a hasher for a wife. **1968** Swarthout *Loveland* 79: I don't mean to be personal, but how much do you make as a hasher? **1970** Boatright & Owens *Derrick* 81: Those hashers in those cafés....They made far more money in tips...those old boys did. **1981** *L.A. Times* (Apr. 12) (Home) 36: I worked...at everything from hasher at sorority houses to bartender at a country club.

hashery *n.* HASH HOUSE.
  1870 in *DA:* Having lately opened a hashery, I send you this, my rules and regulations. **1872** in *DAE:* The railroad hashery at Florence. **1877** in *DAE:* At the door of a cheap hashery in...Columbus, Texas. **1901** *Munsey's Mag.* XXIV 568: The salary was ten times what she was getting at the hashery. **1912** *Sat. Eve. Post* (July 13) 3: They sure don't call 'em hasheries when they cost you eight bones a day up! **1918** *DN* V 10: *Hashery.* Same meaning and use as *beanery.* **1953** in *DAS:* We'll...inhale a few hamburgers at some fashionable hashery! **1955** Kerouac *On Road* ch. x: To haunt her honest labors in the hashery. **1966** *Time* (Sept. 23) 53: Stopping off at a sleazy hashery for a cup of hot milk with a dash of coffee. **1986** S. Bauer *Amazing Stories* 74: It was a good honest hashery, with cheap thick coffee...and daily specials...for $2.35.

hash factory *n.* HASH HOUSE. Also **hash foundry.** *Joc.*
  1880 in M. Lewis *Mining Frontier* 130: Does it stand to reason that a bloke would feed upon corn husks when there was hash factories in the camp? **1904** Hobart *Jim Hickey* 36: We can't...leave the little woman and the kid alone in that hash foundry. **1913** T.M. Osborne *Pris. Walls* 308: You started something while in the hash foundry. **1937** *Lit. Digest* (Apr. 10) 13: He leaves behind him New York's "main stem" with its "hash foundry," flop-houses, and easy life.

hash hammer *n.* *Logging.* GUT HAMMER.
  1958 McCulloch *Woods Words* 81: *Hash hammer*—Same as gut hammer.

hashhead *n.* *Narc.* a habitual user of hashish.
  1959 W. Burroughs *Naked Lunch* 92: You bloody hash-heads, get out of here! **1969** *Time* (Jan. 31) 42: Morocco is a hashhead's delight. **1969** Geller & Boas *Drug Beat* 67: There are, in addition, other kinds of heads—"hashheads," who smoke hashish out of tiny pipes with long stems, aiming beyond the "buzz" and the high to the timeless "zonk."

1970 *Playboy* (Apr.) 36: It's not just another *disco* with hash-head decor. **1971** in L. Bangs *Psychotic Reactions* 6: A buncha...hashheads.

hash hook *n.* a hand; GRUB HOOK.
  1910 in Wilstach *Stage Slang* 46: Pull in your "hash-hook" and ask for what "eats" you desire. [**1927** *Columbia Jester* (Dec.) 10: Fork, hash hook used to pitch food into the mouth.]

hash hound *n.* CHOWHOUND.
  1915 T.A. Dorgan, in Zwilling *TAD Lexicon* 43: Dance Sunday night Crowley's Hash Hounds. **1941** Hargrove *Pvt. Hargrove* 90: Boy-oboy, are we going to give those hash hounds a holiday treat!

hash house *n.* Esp. *West.* a place where hash or other cheap or simple meals are served; (*obs.*) a boarding house; a cheap restaurant.
  1868 *Overland Mo.* (Nov.) 470: He...contemptuously classes all other restaurants than French, as "hash-houses." **1869** in *DA:* The Mayor proposes to double the tax on all "hash houses." **1871** Crofutt *Tourist's Gde.* 141: "Hash houses"—roadside restaurants. **1875** in *OEDS:* In the slang vernacular, an eating place is a "hash house." **1885** Byrn *Greenhorn* 45: Madame Chissel kept a one-horse boarding-house...; we went with her to get grub for a season....We give below the bill of fare at our hash-house. **1892** Garland *Spoil of Office* 297: Living in a hash-house ain't a guarantee of honesty any more than living in a four-story brown-stone is a sure sign of robbery, but it's a tolerably safe inference. **1905** *Nat. Police Gaz.* (Dec. 30) 3: The irreverent might refer to them as hash houses. **1918** *DN* V 25: *Hash-house,* n. a restaurant or boarding house. **1930** Graham & Graham *Queer People* 45: Whitey...slunk away to a hash-house across the street. **1935** deLeon & Thompson *Ruggles of Red Gap* (film): We ain't never had decent hash house here in Red Gap. **1958** McCulloch *Woods Words* 81: *Hash house*—a. Cookshack. b. A restaurant. **1958** S.H. Adams *Tenderloin* 75: Workin' in hash houses in the Northwest. **1969** Kimbrough *Defender of Angels* 52: When I entered that hash house, I was just another hungry joker. **1982** *Time* (Nov. 1) 78: Sequestering incompatible people...at roadside hash houses under duress is one of the hoariest devices known to drama. **1990** Murano & Hoffer *Cop Hunter* 229: All around me was the routine noise of the hash house.

hashhouse *v.* to defeat; *settle (someone's) hash* s.v. HASH[1], *n.*
  1911 in J. London *Short Stories* 508: Ward's a top-notcher....But he can't hashhouse Rivera in short order.

hash joint *n.* HASH HOUSE.
  1895 *Inlander* (Univ. Mich.) (Dec.) 116: *Hash-joint...*boarding-house. **1910** Service *Trail of '98* 34: A scullion in a third-rate hash joint. **1929–30** Dos Passos *42d Parallel* 89: He found himself passing the same Chink hashjoint for the third time. **1929–33** J. Lowell *Gal Reporter* 73: I was bus girl in a hash joint. **1940** Hartman & Butler *Rd. to Singapore* (film): Roamin' around, eatin' in hash joints. **1947** Schulberg *Harder They Fall* 118: Well, some of them hash joints, they don' want the music. **1957** Collins & Powell *My Gun Is Quick* (film): I met her in a hash joint. **1967** M. Howard *Call Me Brick* 100: A waitress in a hash joint. **1976–79** H.G. Duncan & W.T. Moore *Green Side Out* 169: A waitress at a local...hash joint. **1985** Briskin *Too Much* 143: I think of her slaving in that hash joint.

hash mark *n.* **1.** *Mil.,* orig. *Navy.* a service stripe. Also (*rare*) **hash bar.** Now *colloq.*
  1907 in *DA:* "Hash-marks" are the stripes showing the number of enlistments a man has served. **1908** *Bluejacket* (Jan.) 208: "Can't tell a man's service by the number of his hash marks," ruminates the sea-lawyer after taps. **1908** *Man-o'-Warsman* (Nov.) 39: The following is a list of some of the names which were suggested:...The Hash Mark Magazine. **1909** *Man-o'-Warsman* (Dec.) 24: First Sergeant John J. Maloney earned another hash-mark on November 24th. **1914** *DN* 150: *Hashmark.* n. A service stripe. **1918** Paine *Fighting Fleets* 354: Young men...directly in charge of chief gunner's mates and chief boatswain's mates with three or four "hash bars" on their sleeves. **1918** Ruggles *Navy Explained* 75: This red mark is called a hash mark, assuming that the man re-enlisted for his hash. **1941** Hargrove *Pvt. Hargrove* 77: An old thirty-year man with five or six hash marks on his sleeve will tell you that no matter how long you stay in the Army, you'll never find a battery that quite stacks up to the first battery in which you served.... **1942** *Leatherneck* (Nov.) 146: *Hashmark*—Service stripe; one for every four years of service. Also known as bean stripe. **1966** Gallery *Start Engines* 155: The Chief, with six gold hash-marks on his sleeve, obviously figured that...this was *his* ship. **1967** Dibner *Admiral* 89: Hash-

marks clean up to his elbow…. **1970** Ponicsan *Last Detail* 2: Three red hash marks slice diagonally down his forearm. **1972** Wambaugh *Blue Kt.* 75: He wore one five-year hashmark showing he had between five and ten years on [the police force]. *a*1995 M. Kelly *Proudly* 41: He was an old guy with hash marks all the way up to his neck.

2. *pl. Football.* (see 1977 quot.). Also **hash lines.**

1949 Cummings *Dict. Sports* 201: *Hash lines. Football.* The short lines intersecting each 5-yard line so as to divide the width of the field into three equal parts. **1954** Dodd *On Football* 195: From "hash mark to hash mark." **1965** Bonham *Durango St.* 135: Spot pass on the forty-yard hashmark! **1977** *Webster's Sports Dict.: Hash mark*…One of the sections of an inbounds line marked on the ground where it crosses a yard line. **1990** *N.Y. Post* (Jan. 2) 50: [A] chip shot from the right hash mark.

3. a narrow fecal stain, as left on underpants or sheets.

*a*1972 B. Rodgers *Queens' Vernacular* 141: Shit stains…*hash marks.* **1974** Univ. Tenn. student: He sleeps in the nude, got hash marks all over his sheets. **1980** Pearl *Pop. Slang* 68: *Hash marks n.* fecal stains left on underwear.

4. *Mil.* a red mark left by a spanking. *Joc.*

1976 Conroy *Santini* 437: If you don't I'm coming right home to put a dozen hashmarks on your butt.

hash-mill *n.* HASH FACTORY.

1907 McDermott-Stevenson *Lariat Letters* 30: You can cut a wider swath here than in any hash-mill I ever run up against before.

hash pile *n.* GRUB-PILE.

1891 in *DA:* "Hash-pile!"…was the signal that breakfast was ready.

hash-slinger *n.* a person who serves or prepares meals for a work crew, military or prison mess, cheap eating place, or the like.

1868 in *DAE:* The nice young man of Washoe may or may not be some kind of a clerk, a hash-slinger, or a check-guerrilla. **1871** Crofutt *Tourist's Guide* 141: "Hash houses"—roadside restaurants. Waiters are called "hash slingers." **1873** T.W. Knox *Underground* 636: The waiters are known by the elegant title of "hash-slingers." **1895** Coup *Sawdust* 83: After dinner they formed congenial knots and strolled around while the "hash slingers" washed the dishes and the men once more loaded up. **1899** Cullen *Tales* 164: Ringing basement door-bells and getting the quick chase from kinky-headed hash-slingers. **1904** *Life in Sing Sing* 256: *Hash-Slinger.* Restaurant waiter. **1908** Raine *Wyoming* 31: Did yo' ever hear about Soapy and that Caspar hash slinger? **1918** Stringer *House of Intrigue* 213: [The] Hash-slingers didn't know enough to stand still. **1936** N. Nye *No-Gun Fighter* 167: Got a date with that goldy-headed hash-slinger at the Santy Fe. **1943** Farrell *Days of Anger* 11: She was just another hash-slinger with feet of clay. **1946** Diamond & Kern *Never Say Goodbye* (film): Listen, you over-stuffed hash-slinger—if you're trying to make a chump out of me—. **1964** Hunt *Ship with Flat Tire* 146: Damn your hashslingers and damn your lousy soup. **1965** Hersey *Too Far to Walk* 80: He had gone to Emil, the hash-slinger, for advice. **1969** Marshe & Lifton *Centerfold* 37: It may be argued that the Bunny is just a waitress serving food and drink, just like tens of thousands of other hash-slingers. **1974** Terkel *Working* 536: If I were a hash slinger in the suburbs, they'd ask me to move out of the neighborhood.

hash stripe *n. Mil.* (see 1928 quot.). Now *colloq.*

1919 Small *Story of the 47th* 118 [ref. to 1918]: Every man had from two to eight "hash stripes" to his credit. **1928** Dolph *Sound Off!* 3: *Hash stripes:* Soldier slang for service stripes that are worn on the sleeve to indicate the number of enlistments completed. **1954–60** *DAS.*

hash town *n. Theat.* a small rural town.

1928 McEvoy *Show Girl* 3: I have been hopping around from one hash town to another.

hash up *v.* **1.** to dine; take a meal.

1887 *Lantern* (N.O.) (Mar. 26) 2: He even brought his girl to the market to hash up.

2. to make a botch or a hash of. Cf. *OED hash, v.,* def. 3 "To…mangle."

1930 Graham & Graham *Queer People* 132: It doesn't make any difference what you do, the director will hash it up anyway. **1942** *ATS* 271: Bungle; botch…*hash up.* **1986** *NDAS.*

hash wagon *n.* [sugg. by MEAT WAGON] *USAF.* a crash ambulance; MEAT WAGON.

1951 Burnett & Burnett *Story* 97 [ref. to WWII]: Runway's clear and waiting, boy, I've got the hash-wagon out for your gunner.

hassle *n.* **1.a.** a quarrel, dispute, or contentious disagreement.

1945 in *OEDS:* Building bands is getting to be a habit with Freddie Slack. He broke up his last few after booking hassels. **1946** *Sat. Eve. Post* (Aug. 31) 72: "Hassle" is a gorgeously descriptive word which lately has won wide usage in show business. It means a quarrel, a fuss, an argument, a struggle or a mess. **1948** Manone & Vandervoort *Trumpet* 46: These guys and me frequently got into a hassel over how the tune should be played. **1951** Algren *Chicago* 53: Who came out the truer Christian in a hassle like *that?* **1951** Sheldon *Troubling of a Star* 92: Well, said Braith, it was any body's hassel after that. **1952** in T. Williams *Letters* 272: Mr. Moon [is] putting in his two cents' worth whenever there is a hassle. **1955** Ruppelt *Report on UFOs* 6: The hassle over the word "proof" boils down to one question: What constitutes proof? **1956** Holiday & Dufty *Lady* 36: There was a real hassle before I could convince him Mom was really my mother, and only trying to help. **1957** McGivern *Against Tomorrow* 58: Nothing big….A little neighborhood hassle, some bad feeling all around. **1958** Drury *Advise and Consent* 83: I think he suspects…that you have designs on him if this thing gets into a real hassle. *Ibid.* 203: I hear Bob Munson and the others got into quite a hassle with our ambassadorial friends. **1964** Thompson & Rice *Every Diamond* 62: The hassle reached Rickey and he acted as peacemaker. **1972** *Glass House* (film): Now take that hassle that happened over there, that fight.

b. *Mil.* an armed encounter with an enemy force, esp. a dogfight between aircraft.

1953 in *History of Chaplain Corps USN* VI 187: We hope we are just through winding up another hassle that started early last night….These are the worst "clobbered" of any hassel since I've been out here. **1953** in Loosbrock & Skinner *Wild Blue* 469: Every time we vectored friendly fighters into a hassle that got a MIG, we'd celebrate. **1966** F. Elkins *Heart of Man* 52: Our fighters [were] hot for a hassle. **1968** Broughton *Thud Ridge* 67: It seems like every hassle we get wrapped up in pits us against light weight and highly maneuverable interceptors who always have the ability to outturn us and disengage at will. **1982** Basel *Pak Six* 98: I sat back and thought about the fight. What a hassle! *a*1984 in C.R. Bond & T. Anderson *Flying Tiger Diary* 160: The…Second and Third Squadrons got in a real hassle when the Japanese attempted to hit Loiwing with bombers and fighters. **1985** M. Brennan *War* 150 [ref. to 1967]: I don't know if it matters. Tomorrow we'll be in another hassle and might all be dead. **1995** Cormier et al. *Wildcats* 93: The MiGs pressed close enough for a hassle to develop.

2. that which is annoying or exasperating; vexation; annoyance; difficulty; inconvenience; struggle; bother. Now *colloq.*

1946 in R.S. Gold *Jazz Talk* 123: That'll be a hassel. **1946** (quot. at **(1.a.)**, above). **1950** in Kerouac *Letters* 237: Our plans to go live in Mexico…[will involve] money hassles and madness. **1951** in Kerouac *Letters* 276: All the hassles of foolish life. **1952** J.C. Holmes *Go* 140: I mean that's a real hassle, isn't it, baby? **1952** Mandel *Angry Strangers* 58: He's Mrs. Jenks' boy; what's the hassle? *Ibid.* 337: We don't need any guns to get us in a hassle. **1953** Wicker *Kingpin* 204: I've been in a hassle….Fred Pollock got himself in some girl trouble and I had to get him out of it. **1956** Reach *Teachers* 15: And it was quite a hassle. **1958** in R.S. Gold *Jazz Talk* 123: Jazz musicians…have been brought down by life's hassels. **1958–59** Lipton *Barbarians* 76: She's pregnant. So I just walked out of that hassle. **1959** A. Anderson *Lover Man* 58: You ever find yourself in a great big hassle and say to yourself, "This was just what I *thought* would happen"? **1961** in C. Beaumont *Best* 94: And then there's all the hassle of taking off your clothes and all. **1965** C. Brown *Manchild* 167: She was always getting down on me about bringing certain chicks to the house….It became a real hassle. **1967** *Esquire* (Sept.) 101: The hassle to drive here in rush hour. **1967–68** von Hoffman *Parents Warned Us* 86: It's a hassle….Hassles, gee, wow, are a bummer. **1974** Hejinian *Extreme Remedies* 122: A Bach cello suite touched the soul without human hassles. **1977** J.L. Dillard *Lex. Black Eng.* 177: Present-day teenage *hassle* "inconvenience" (the great fear of the modern American teenager!). **1984** "W.T. Tyler" *Shadow Cabinet* 128: Tell me about all this hassle you've been dishing out. **1994** *Parade* (Sept. 4) 18: You don't want the hassle. **1994** in *Reader's Digest* (Jan. 1995) 162: How to Make Christmas Happy and Hassle-Free.

3. (see quot.).

1953 *AS* XXVIII 143: Louisville, Kentucky, youth call any kind of party a "hassle."

hassle *v.* [earlier U.S. So. dial. *hassle* 'to gasp for breath, usu. as a result of exertion', a sense illus. (in the context of a quarrel) by 1939 quot.; cf. also U.S. and Eng. dial. *hassle* 'to saw or hack away [at]']

1.a. to engage in a quarrel or dispute; wrangle; argue.

[**1939** M.K. Rawlings, in *Sat. Eve. Post* (Nov. 25) 60: I don't want your man nor no other woman's man. Now you quit your hassling...and I'll carry you where you can see just what your husband's been a-doing.] **1953** *AS* XXVIII 143: Politicians *hassle* in Congress, in party conventions, in other public places. **1959** [Sabre & Eiden] *Glory Jumpers* 8: Inside the war room. Hassling with the general and his staff. **1959** in *OEDS*: The chief metaphysical bones hassled over in recent years concern such points as "biuniqueness." **1962** Kesey *Cuckoo's Nest* 25: They say I'm a habitual hassler. Like I fight some. **1965** Ward & Kassebaum *Women's Pris.* 171: I knew that you and your friend were hassling. **1967** *Esquire* (Sept.) 191: Some hassle for an hour before they buy. **1972** N.Y.U. professor: Socrates and Euthyphro are hassling over the concept of piety. **1974** Hejinian *Extreme Remedies* 117: I remember hassling....Just like now.

b. to settle (something) by discussion.—constr. with *out*.

1968 Baker, Ladd, & Robb *CUSS* 134: *Hassle it out.* Work out of a difficult situation. **1978** Wharton *Birdy* 99: We're hassling this out.

c. *Mil. Av.* to engage in an aerial dogfight.

1972–79 T. Wolfe *Right Stuff* 24 [ref. to 1950's]: Likewise, "hassling"—mock dogfighting—was strictly forbidden. **1983** Van Riper *Glenn* 135: "Hassling"—mock dogfighting—in planes costing millions of dollars. **1993** in Tomedi *No Bugles* 174: Their pilots were simply not as good as us....But once in a while you got a guy who could really hassle with you.

2.a. to contend or annoy oneself.—constr. with *with*.

1953 *AS* XXVIII 143: Hassling with "Hassle." *Ibid.* 144: *Hassle*...the current meaning [is] "to struggle," "to work hard at." **1970** N.Y.U. student: I haven't got time to hassle with the details. **1970** Major *Afro-Amer. Sl.* 64: *Hassle:* to...worry. **1987** *RHD2*: We don't want to hassle with all that waiting in line.

b. to concern oneself about.

1969 Mitchell *Thumb Tripping* 6: Don't hassle it, man.

3. to harass; provoke; annoy; pester.

1958–59 Lipton *Barbarians* 185: My old man and my old lady...hassle me all the time. **1962** Kesey *Cuckoo's Nest* 167: I got just as much to lose hassling that old buzzard as *you* do. **1968** Baker, Ladd & Robb *CUSS* 134: *Hassle.* Tease or annoy someone. **1970** Thackray *Thief* 264: You mean, a guy don't pay, so I go hassle him. Maybe stick a shank in him or something if he really figures to make a thing of it? **1974** in *Mad Super Special* (No. 64) 34: Okay, buddy. What's hassling you lately? **1977** Newman & Berkowitz *Take Charge* 22: You hassle yourself this way most every night. **1980** J. Carroll *Land of Laughs* 41: I've had one lousy day so far, okay? So don't hassle me! **1986** Philbin *Under Cover* 168: What the fuck you hasslin' me, mon? **1988** T. Robinson & B. Stainback *Extra Innings* 51: Obviously the cop knew we were players, and he wanted to hassle us. **1995** *Donahue* (NBC-TV): Effeminate men are hassled by both straight and gay men.

hasty banana *interj.* [alter. of Sp *hasta mañana* 'till tomorrow'] (used as a valediction). *Joc.*

1949 *Looney Tunes* (animation): Well, nice meeting ya. Hasty banana! **1949** *AS* (Oct.) 235: *Hasty banana*...is used widely by students as a manner of leave-taking.

hat *n.* **1.** Esp. *Und.* sexual gratification experienced by a man; a sexually promiscuous woman, esp. a prostitute; (*hence*) a young woman. Cf. OLD HAT, *n.*

a*1890–93 *F & H* III 277: Hat...The female *pudendum.* Generally *old hat*....(Scots').—A prostitute of long standing. ***1911 O'Brien & Stephens *Austral. Sl.* 71: *Hat, old:* a diggings and general nickname for sexual intercourse. **1942–49** Goldin et al. *DAUL* 91: *Hat*...A passive pederast...a loose woman. "Mickey's partner...turned out to be a hunk of hat in the big house." **1957** *N.Y. Times Mag.* (Aug. 18) 26: *Have you seen my hat?*—Have you seen my girl, chick, broad, rib? **1963** E. Horne *Hiptionary* 8: *Hat*—Girl, chick, wife. **1964** R.S. Gold *Jazz Lexicon* 140: *Hat*...obscene semantic development...some currency esp.

among Negro jazzmen since ca. 1940. **1967** Lit *Dictionary* 44: *Wear a Hat*—Have a girl friend; or to be married.

2.a. (see quot.).

1952 E. Brown *Trespass* 42 [ref. to 1940]: He had watched the stony-faced white floor bosses [at the post office], the "Hats," patrolling the aisles like walking doom.

b. *Army.* (see quot.).

1975 Univ. Tenn. ROTC trainee: A Green Beret—a paratrooper—is a *hat.* A nonparatrooper is a *leg.*

c. *USMC.* a drill instructor.

1989 M. Norman *These Good Men* 196 [ref. to *ca* 1971]: To become a drill instructor, or "Hat" as...[they] called themselves....For years the Hats ruled the island. [*sc.* Parris Island].

3. *Police & Und.* a cash bribe; in phr. **buy a hat** to bribe.

1970 Winick & Kinsie *Lively Commerce* 214: For some years people involved in prostitution spoke of handing out "hats" to police. **1971** *N.Y. Times* (Oct. 21) 52: *Hat*—An initial bribe to establish rapport. It comes from the expression, "Buy yourself a hat." **1972** *N.Y. Times* (May 7) 11: This finally was rejected because the policemen involved did not want to lose the $200 monthly bonus or "hat" for the dangerous job of making the pickups themselves. **1973** Breslin *World Without End* 88: When you bought a cop a hat it meant you gave him twenty dollars. **1984** Caunitz *Police Plaza* 81: When someone "wants to...give you a hat" that means that there is a payoff waiting for you if you overlook a violation of law.

4. *Black E.* a condom.

1988 "Boogie Down Productions" *Jimmy* (rap song): Wear your hat. **1993** Mowry *Six Out Seven* 361: I just want me some real black cunt, out no goddamn hat on my dick!

¶ In phrases:

¶ **bust (one's) hat** to get furiously angry; *blow (one's) top* s.v. TOP.

1979 in Terkel *Amer. Dreams* 196: I told him, "Mr. Smith, we only come to [register to vote]." He woulda bust his hat on that one.

¶ **come out of that hat!** (used to express derision, addressed esp. to a man wearing a stovepipe hat).

1864 in Gilbert *Confed. Letters* 36: "Come out of that hat," "get down and pull a root," "there goes another hog." **1867** [S.B. Putnam] *Richmond During War* 346: A suit of new broadcloth, or a new hat, or other article of dress of extraordinary neatness, would...subject the...wearer to the annoyances of the boys or soldiers on the street, who were wont to accost them in the slang of the army, with: "Come out of that broadcloth! Come out of that hat!" etc.

¶ **get** [or **grab**] **[a] hat** *Black E. & Mil.* to leave; get out; go.

1966 *Sat. Eve. Post* (July 16) 38: "Let's get hat"—a cavalryman's phrase meaning to depart in haste...."He got hit in the butt with a mortar fragment, got hat, and that's the last I saw of four hundred rounds of ammo." **1968** J. Lester *Look Out Whitey* 57: The slaves were free to "get hat." **1968** Stuard TS. (unp.): In Viet Nam the favorite phrase for all people who want some one to go with them somewhere is "grab a hat"...in lieu of "let's go." **1968–70** *Current Slang* III & IV 54: *Get hat*, v. To leave; to go.—Watts [district of L.A.]. **1971** H. Roberts *Third Ear: Get hat!* an imperative urging one to leave; get out!...*got hat*, v. left hurriedly. **1973** Karlin, Paquet & Rottmann *Free Fire Zone* 140: Where you goin', tiger?...Getting a hat. **1975** S.P. Smith *Amer. Boys* 40: He was...getting up from the back dining room, ready to get hat.

¶ **hang (one's) hat on** to depend upon.

1880 A.A. Hayes *New Colo.* 118: Why that's *my* preacher. I hang my hat on him every time.

¶ **hang** [or **hold**] **onto your hat!** prepare yourself for a shock.

1911 D. Runyon *Tents of Trouble* 82: Hang onter yer hat—th' cavalry's comin' through! **1937** Weidman *Wholesale* 8: "All right, then, Tootsie," I said. "Hold on to your hat." **1941** Schulberg *Sammy* 78: Hold your hats, boys and girls, I thought, here we go again. **1943** Hubbard *Gung Ho* (film): Hold onto your hat! **1950** Wouk *Caine Mutiny* 309: Hold on to your hat.

¶ **have** [or **put**] **a hat on (someone)** *Black E.* to single someone out for abuse or revenge.

1970 *Adam-12* (NBC-TV): According to the Captain, somebody's put a real hat on me....Somebody's accused me of blackmailing them.

1973 Layne *Murphy* (unp.): Word got out/That Lincoln had a hat on Ginzo./But Ginzo went shoppin' for Lincoln first.

¶ **in your hat!** (used to express derision and incredulity). Also (*vulgar*) **go shit in your hat!** Also vars.

[*ca***1784** in W. Blake *Complete Poetry & Prose* 451: I'll sing you a song said the Cynic. The trumpeter shit in his hat said the Epicurean & clapt it on his head said the Pythagorean.] **1926** Dunning & Abbott *Broadway* 236: In your hat! **1927** *Vanity Fair* (Nov.) 132: "In your hat" is equivalent to "applesauce," "boloney," "hooey," or "banana oil." **1930** in Perelman *Old Gang* 123: "In your hat, grandma," riposted Coralie. **1933** C.G. Sullivan *Men Must Fight* (film): "War in twenty-four hours." "War in five minutes." War—in my hat! **1934** Appel *Brain Guy* 39: "I resigned." "In your hat. You got fired." **1935** *Our Army* (Oct.) 17 [ref. to 1918]: In your hat! Gimme a chance…just once! **1936** Kingsley *Dead End* 701: In yuh hat, fat slob! **1937** Weidman *Wholesale* 210: All I have to say is: in your hat and over your ears; you look good in brown. **1947** Willingham *End As a Man* 37: Go shit in your hat. **1957** M. Shulman *Rally* 68: In your hat! **1958** Hersey *War Lover* 49 [ref. to WWII]: Go shit in your hat and call it curls! **1960** Wohl *Cold Wind* 42: "In your hat, Jack," Vito said. **1980** Garrison *Snakedoctor* 50: You tell 'im to go crap in his hat? *a***1982** Berry *Semper Fi* 192 [ref. to WWII]: If you were talking to a sailor, it was suggested that he defecate in his flat hat.

¶ **make (one's) hat** *Mil.* to make an escape or get out; *get hat*, above.

1978 J. Webb *Fields of Fire* 96 [ref. to 1969]: It's too late. They gotta make their hat most ricky-tick.

¶ **pin** [or **paste**] **it in your hat** be certain to remember it.

1891 in F. Remington *Sel. Letters* 113: Don't forget to paste Lieut. Casey's name on your hat. **1902** *N.Y. Eve. Jour.* (Dec. 3) 12: Pin this in your hat—that there will surely be something doing before the bout is long in progress. **1918** in Berry *Kaiser* 27: I want all loyal Americans to paste it in their hats that it was C Battery, 6th United States Field Artillery that fired that shot.

¶ **price of a hat** a gratuity of a few dollars.

1971 Horan *Blue Messiah* 608: Every time we shook hands I made sure they received "the price of a hat," for their extra trouble.

¶ **put the hat on (someone)** (see quot.).

1984 A. Pincus *How to Talk Football* 57: *Put the hat on*…to hit a ballcarrier so hard that your helmet leaves an impression.

¶ **spin (someone's) hat** to dazzle someone.

1941 Horman *Buck Privates* (film): Man, that really spins my hat!

¶ **talk through (one's) hat** to talk rubbish; speak without real knowledge or understanding.

1888 in *F & H* III 278: Dis is only a bluff dey're makin'—see! Dey're talkin' tru deir hats. **1893** S.F. Batchelder *Hamlet* 58: Madder than the maddest hatter/Talking through his hat. **1895** Townsend *Fadden* 75: I was dat crazy wid bein' foun' out dat I guess I was talkin' troo me hat. **1895** *DN* I 418: *Hat, Talk Through One's:* To talk nonsense. **1909** Krapp *Mod. Eng.* 211: "To talk through your hat" is slang, not only because it is new, but also because it is…grotesque. **1947** in Botkin *Sidewalks* 241: You were said to be "talking through your hat" when you appeared unfamiliar with your topic. **1966** Cassiday *Angels Ten* 156: Black doesn't just talk through his hat. **1970** in P. Heller *In This Corner* 43: I knew he was talking through his hat, because there's no such thing as a comeback.

¶ **to the hat** thoroughly.

1934 H. Miller *Tropic of Cancer* 47: He is fried to the hat.

¶ **under** [or **beneath**] **(one's)** [or **the**] **hat, 1.** in (one's) head or mind.

1885 in *OEDS*: Nuttie…was taking in all these revelations with an open-eyed, silent horror.…It was all under her hat, however, and the elder ladies never thought of her. **1899** "J. Flynt" *Tramping* 383: "Crippled under the hat" is also heard, but "bughouse" supplants this expression. **1899** Cullen *Tales* 79: This fellow's spiel got the horse bug to buzzing beneath the hat again, and that's when I thought out my scheme. **1904** in "O. Henry" *Works* 594: The governor man had a bit of English under his hat, and when the music was choked off he says: "Ver-r-ree fine." **1926** C.M. Russell *Trails* 77: From looks you'd say he didn't have nothin' under his hat but hair.

2. secret; to be held in confidence.—often constr. with *keep.*

1904 in "O. Henry" *Works* 1441: Don't ever tell nobody—keep it

under your hat. **1906** H. Green *Boarding House* 35: This under yer hat, a' course. **1918** in York *Mud & Stars* 60: He's got a mess of troubles on his mind/And likes to keep 'em underneath his hat. **1928** in J. O'Hara *Selected Letters* 36: This soul-unburdening letter is under the hat, hear? **1930** *Amer. Mercury* (Dec.) 415: Well, here it is, but it's strictly under the hat, see? **1938** "E. Queen" *4 Hearts* 11: Keep it under your hat, Alan. **1950** Schnee *Next Voice* (film): Keep it under your hat, will ya? **1951** Sheldon *Troubling of a Star* 160: Keep this under your hat, will you? **1965** Spillane *Killer Mine* 100: This is under the hat, Kid. The tip was made to our office.

¶ **where'd you get that hat?** [see *1977 quot.] (used to express derision).

1899 Dunne *Countrymen* 110: What is your opinion iv a hereafter? Where did you get that hat? **1914** Giles *Rags & Hope* 24: As I drew near I heard some fellow call out, "Where did you get that hat? Come down out of that, I know you are there! I see your feet a-wiggling!" *****1977** Partridge *Dict. Catch Phrs.* 247: *Where did you get that hat?* was very popular in Britain *c*1885–1914. From a well-known music-hall song.…The words of another song so titled, words by Joseph J. Sullivan, started in the US, in 1888 and inaugurated a vogue there too.

hat *v.* [sugg. by *get hat* s.v. HAT, *n.*] *Black E. & Mil.* to leave; get out; go.—usu. constr. with [*it*] *up* [or *out*]. Also (*rare*) **had.**

1970 *Current Slang* V (Fall) 8: *Hat*, v. To leave. **1970** Landy *Underground Dict.* 99: Hat it up…Leave; depart. **1970** Whitmore *Memphis-Nam-Sweden* 20: The man comes in the front; we had it up out the back, and vice versa. *Ibid.* 21: Otherwise you just have to had it up. Split. *Ibid.* 25: We had it down the road. *Ibid.* 97: Let's had it up, baby! **1971** in Sanchez *Word Sorcerers* 181: An then the *Chaplains* came hattin over across the grass. **1971** H. Roberts *Third Ear: Hat up!* an imperative urging one to leave. **1971** Dahlskog *Dict.* 30: *Hat up,* v. To leave; depart, as from a party. **1972** West *Village* 179: The next time the colonel comes by, I ding him and hat it out. *Ibid.* 226: Let's hat out. **1973** Huggett *Body Count* 341: We gotta hat up. Not much time. **1973** Andrews & Owens *Black Lang.* viii: I…hatted it out of L.A. to a new slave/at Cal State Hayward. **1974** Former USMC L/Cpl, N.Y.C. [ref. to 1967–69]: *Hat out* or *hat it up* meant to beat it. **1978** W. Brown *Tragic Magic* 12: The way they hatted up, you'd have thought we were the second coming of the Moors.

hatch *n.* **1. a.** a jail or prison; BOOBY HATCH, 1.—constr. with *the.*

1908 in H.C. Fisher *A. Mutt* 104: Put all troublesome judges in the hatch? **1910** *Variety* (June 18) 7: He was being…led to the hatch at the north end of the park by a blue-coated individual. **1914** Jackson & Hellyer *Vocab.* 43: *Hatch,* Noun. General currency. A calaboose; a prison; police station; a jail.

b. a psychiatric hospital; BOOBY HATCH, 2.—constr. with *the.*

1908 in Blackbeard & Williams *Smithsonian Comics* 58: The defendant was torn from his young wife and infant child and sent to the hatch. **1940** in W.R. Burnett *High Sierra* 251: Not counting screwballs, of course, who ought to be in the hatch. **1962** T. Berger *Reinhart* 397: Take Advantage of My Lunacy and Buy Quick Before I Am Hauled Off to the Hatch. **1974** R. Stone *Dog Soldiers* 251: So my status was weird because I'm just out of the hatch.

2. Orig. *Naut.* the throat or mouth; HATCHWAY; esp. in phr. **down the hatch!** (used as a drinking toast).

1924 Anderson & Stallings *What Price Glory?* 125 [ref. to 1918]: Close your hatch. **1932** M. Anderson *Rain* (film): Down the hatch! **1934** Appel *Brain Guy* 201: "Down the hatch."…The drink was strong and amiable. **1940** [W.C. Fields] *Bank Dick* (film): Here she goes. Down the hatch! *ca***1940** in Welsch *Got Yourself a Horse* 141: No one has had to hold me while they poured liquor down my hatch. **1943** *Time* (Mar. 22) 52: When two Americans are having a drink they no longer shout "Down the hatch!" They raise their glasses and say "Cheers" in modulated tones. **1943** Halper *Inch from Glory* 10: Come on, faster with the drink.…Down the hatch. **1944** Rodney *Cavalryman* 43 [ref. to *ca*1900]: Before night ye'll be holdin' both hands to your hatch to keep your meal below deck. **1948** *Neurotica* (Spring) 29: Well in your eye i said/And down the hatch she said. **1949** Maier *Pleasure I.* 32: "Down the hatch and into the bilge."…Halyard sipped the drink. **1953** R. Matheson, in Pohl *Star of Stars* 192: Come on…Down the hatch! **1953** R. Chandler *Goodbye* 136: I reached for my glass and dropped the contents down the hatch. **1958** J. Ward *Buchanan* 21: "Down the hatch," Buchanan coaxed, holding the coffee to the other man's lips. **1962** T. Berger *Reinhart* 29: No sooner did it go down your hatch than you rushed to the john, where it came right up again. **1982** W.R. Dunn *Fighter Pilot* 174: The pilot would toast "gumbay," meaning "down the hatch." **1984** *Tales from Darkside* (synd. TV series): Come on. Down the hatch! **1989** *Daywatch* (CNN-TV) (May 29): And the young lady *is* going to swallow the sword. Down the hatch! **1995** *My So-Called Life* (ABC-TV): Down the hatch, honey!

3. *Navy & USMC.* a door (of any sort). Cf. BULKHEAD.
   1991 J.T. Ward *Dear Mom* 5: The hatch (door) was flying open.

hatchet *n.* **1.** (used allusively in ref. to the female genitals).—usu. considered vulgar. *Joc.*
   1864 in R. Mitchell *Vacant Chair* 71: Some of the real women went, but the boy girls were so much better looking...no one could hav told wich of the party had fell on a *hatchet*. **1974** N.Y.U. student: *Where the Injun hit her with the hatchet* means her vagina.

2. [perh. sugg. by *hatchet-faced*; cf. BATTLE-AX] an ugly, unpleasant, or debauched woman.
   *1889 Barrère & Leland *Dict. Slang* I 451: *Hatchet* (tailors), a name vulgarly applied to a plain or ugly woman. **1935** Pollock *Und. Speaks*: *Hatchet*, an unappealing woman; lacking in sex appeal. **1958** S.H. Adams *Tenderloin* 26 [ref. to 1890's]: The raddled "hookers," "cruisers," and "hatchets" of the dim-lit side streets...were ostracized by the superior sisterhood. *Ibid.* 35: A lota those hatchets don't get more than two dollars a throw.

¶ In phrases:

¶ **bury the hatchet** [or (*obs.*) **tomahawk**] to put aside a usu. personal grievance. [S.E. in the sense 'to make peace', orig. used of hostilities with or between Native American tribes.]
   1807 in *DAE*: I had long been persecuted by the General, but wished to bury the hatchet. **1843** in *DAE*: Uncle John now proposed to bury the hatchet. **1871** Schele de Vere *Amer.* 36: Burying the hatchet...[was] soon used in conversation generally for the...amically arranging of difficulties of every kind. **1873** "M. Twain" & Warner *Gilded Age* ch. xlii: Shall we bury the hatchet and be good friends and respect each other's little secrets? **1890** Quinn *Fools of Fortune* 211: Often the proprietor...leaves...a substantial token of his readiness to "bury the hatchet." *a*1910 Bierce *Shapes of Clay* 376: "Let's bury the hatchet," said Miller to Platt. **1921** *DN* V 157: *Bury the hatchet* Or *bury the tomahawk*. **1957** Evans & Evans *Dict. Contemp. Usage* 76: *Bury the hatchet*...a cliché. It should be quietly buried in forgetfulness. **1958** Malden, Mo., police officer (coll. J. Ball): If you boys don't quit [fighting] and bury the hatchet right now, I'll have to tell your parents. **1962** Imboden, Ark., boy (coll. J. Ball): Come on! Bury the hatchet. He didn't mean it. **1963–64** Kesey *Great Notion* 230: Along with my decision to bury the hatchet. **1980** Lorenz *Guys Like Us* 81: Have a drink, bury the hatchet. **1989** *Star Trek: Next Generation* (Fox-TV): I came here to bury the hatchet with my son. **1994** *CBS This Morning* (CBS-TV) (Nov. 10): Burying the hatchet's actually a very good thing. They're doing it in Washington.

¶ **fling** [or **throw**] **the hatchet** to tell an exaggerated story. Also vars. *Rare* in U.S.
   *1789 G. Parker *Life's Painter* 94: Telling anecdotes, adventures, and the like, to a mode of the hatchet-flinging extreme. *1820–21 P. Egan *Life in London* 173: There is nothing "*creeping*" or "*throwing the hatchet*" about this description. **1841** [Mercier] *Man-of-War* 14: Garnet,...knowing the simplicity of his auditor, was now determined to *fling the hatchet*, as sailors call it. **1891** Maitland *Slang Dict.* 205: *Pitching the hatchet*, telling incredible yarns of the Munchausen order. *1893 in *F & H* III 279: She'd sling the hatchet to them, and tell them she was a poor lone widow left with five children.

hatchet *v.* to perform a HATCHET JOB on; be a HATCHET MAN, 1.
   1962 *Time* (Dec. 21) 18: He and/or his aides were out to hatchet Adlai. **1968** (quot. at HATCHET JOB). **1970** in *Atlantic* (Jan. 1971) 35: The description and fabrication of cold fact...was all *Time*'s not unusual procedure for hatcheting.

hatchet job *n.* an instance of character assassination, malicious distortion, or excessively harsh criticism.
   1944 *Time* (Oct. 23) 20: Exuberant hatchet jobs were...done on Foster Dulles because of his Wall Street connections. **1947** in J.P. Cannon *Notebook* 149: I noticed the hatchet job most of the critics of the big press were doing on the picture. *1959 in *OEDS*: His criticism was a hatchet job on every book. **1965** Horan *Seat of Power* 45: The

bum is good for any hatchet job...[City] Hall wants. **1968** Safire *New Lang. of Politics* 185: The work performed is called a "hatchet job" as well as "hatcheting." Harry Truman's assessment of the Republican party in the 1948 campaign: "Gluttons of privilege...all set to do a hatchet job on the New Deal." **1974** Strasburger *Rounding Third* 134: At least we'll leave one person pure at the end of this hatchet job. **1980** Berlitz & Moore *Roswell* 47: A "most unscrupulous journalist from San Francisco" who may have been paid off to do "the hatchet job" on Scully. **1980** Key *Clam-Plate* 108: Even a hatchet-job review would invite heat from the ad agencies. **1986** in N. George *Buppies, B-Boys* 310: As if he suspected I was out to do a hatchet job.

hatchet man *n.* **1.** *Pol. & Journ.* a loyal supporter who engages in HATCHET JOBS or similar activities on behalf of a particular candidate or cause.
   1941 in B.O. Davis, Jr. *Davis* 79: One other officer, the Hatchet Man, I am told. **1949** in *DA*: Truman's hatchetman...announces that he is sending organizing teams into the South to work for the defeat of Congressmen and Senators who oppose the Truman-CIO legislative program. **1951** *Sat. Eve. Post* (June 16) 130: Stalin might send his hatchet men to do away with a tool that could compromise him. **1957** Blumgarten *Mr. Rock & Roll* (film): Your hatchet man boss already told the truth—coast to coast! **1964** *Newsweek* (July 27) 27: He'll be the hatchet man,...just like Nixon was in '52. **1966** F. Harvey *Raiders* 100: Executive assistant ("hatchet man" was the term used in Washington). **1974** Bernstein & Woodward *President's Men* 24: Charles W. Colson, special counsel to the President of the United States, was the White House "hatchet man," he said. **1984** J. McNamara *First Directive* 210: They were administrative captains, hatchet men.

2. *Sports.* a particularly rough or violent player.
   1976 (quot. at HEADHUNTER, 4.c.). **1982** T. Considine *Lang. of Sport* 228: *Hatchetman*...A particularly rough or violent player [of ice hockey]. **1983** Goldaper & Pincus *How to Talk Basketball* 95: *Hatchet man*...a player whose specialty is fouling, often with the purpose of taking the opposing team's star out of the game.

hatching jacket *n.* a maternity blouse or dress. *Joc.*
   1967, **1965–70** in *DARE*. **1976** *N.Y. Folklore* II 240: *Hatching jacket*...maternity blouse.

hatch up *v.* to commit to a psychiatric hospital.
   1970 *N.Y. Times* (June 14) 1: With those crazy popping eyes and that bizarre speech pattern, the lady would be hatched up on sight.

hatchway *n. Naut.* the throat or mouth. Cf. HATCH, 2.
   *1823 Egan *Vulgar Tongue*: *Hatchway*...mouth. **1849** Melville *White Jacket* 371: See that white shark!...he'll have that man down his hatchway! **1886** P.D. Haywood *Cruise* 71: Ye mane...that I've taken that bloody ile down my hatchway? **1889** Barrère & Leland *Dict. Slang* I 451: *Hatchway* (nautical), the mouth.

hate *n.* [orig. a Brit. term, sugg. by the German "Hymn of Hate"] *Army.* a German bombardment. [Quots. ref. to WWI.]
   [*1915 *Punch* (Feb. 24) 150 (caption): Study of a Prussian household having its morning hate.] *1915 in *OEDS*: They drop their shells regularly, trying to catch our transport at night. We call it the "Evening Hate." **1918** *Sat. Eve. Post* (Mar. 23) 102: The regular "morning hate" of Fritz's artillery. **1918** Proctor *Iron Division* 42: The regiment went...through what was left of Pargny after its several days of German "hate." **1920** Acker *Thru the War* 82: However, no matter how quiet it might be thru out the day there is always the morning and evening "hate"—the morning and evening exchange of "courtesies" by the artillery. **1940** Carter *101st Field Artillery* 108: Such behavior was naturally unpopular with the infantry in the vicinity of the gun; left behind, they had to take the "hate" that came over.

¶ In phrase:

¶ **have** [or **take**] **a hate on** to dislike intensely; hate.
   1949 *Sat. Eve. Post* (Jan. 22) 100: The brightest boy in the class cannot get by forever if everyone takes a hate on him. **1992** *Likely Suspects* (Fox-TV): He had a hate on for Breen.

hat job *n. Pros.* HEAD JOB, 1.
   1975 Harrell & Bishop *Orderly House* 34: The term "Hat Job"...[means] a Full French.

hatrack *n.* **1.** an emaciated horse, mule, or cow.
   1907 *McClure's Mag.* (Feb.) 381: They wasn't horses. They were hat-racks! **1912** *Adventure* (July) 476: I thought you had your old hat-

rack all ready to gallop to Burke's? **1930** Fredenburgh *Soldiers March* 194 [ref. to 1918]: It's these hat-racks in harness that worry me. Look at 'em; every nose in the mud and sagging at the knees. **1935** *AS* (Dec.) 270: *Hatrack.* An old, thin cow. **1937** *AS* (Apr.) 103: An old cow is designated by such terms as *nellie, hatrack, skin, shell,* or *canner.* **1965–70** in *DARE.*

2. the head; the mind.

1929 Barr *Let Tomorrow Come* 27: Don't go haywire, Joe. Use your hatrack. **1963** in Clarke *Amer. Negro Stories* 298: If you spent half as much time tryin' to put something *inside* that worthless hat-rack as you did havin' your brains fryed—. **1965–70** in *DARE* [48 informants]. **1974** Univ. Tenn. student: Your *hatrack* is your head.

hat trick *n.* [orig. a term in cricket (1877 in *OEDS*), "the taking of three or more usu. successive wickets by a single bowler in one game; the bowler was often awarded a new hat for this accomplishment"]

1. *Horse Racing.* the winning by a single jockey of three races in one day.

1909 in *OEDS*: It is seldom that an apprentice does the "hat trick," but the feat was accomplished...on Soldier...Lady Carlton..., and Hawkweed. **1931 in Woods *Horse-Racing* 62: And then he began "pulling the hat trick," which means winning three races in one day. **1968** Ainslie *Racing Guide* 469: *Hat trick*—The winning, usually by a jockey, of three races on a single program.

2. *Sports.* the scoring by a single player of three goals in one game.

1949 Cummings *Dict. Sports* 201: *Hat trick*....In ice hockey it is achieved by a player scoring three goals in a game, and the term is used similarly in goal games such as soccer and lacrosse. **1967 in *OEDS*: Apart from a hat trick by our centre forward it wasn't much of a game. **1970** *Everett* (Wash.) *Herald* (May 4) 1C: Bucyk's three goals—his first hat trick in playoff competition. **1976** *Webster's Sports Dict.* 206: *Hat trick*...The term is widely used in hockey and soccer to indicate the scoring of 3 goals by one individual in a single game.

3. *Baseball.* (see 1982 quot.).

1949 Cummings *Dict. Sports* 202: *Hat trick*....In baseball it is sometimes applied to hitting for the cycle. **1950** *N.Y. Times* (Nov. 5) VII 3: He'll have hit for the hat trick.*...*In baseball, hitting a single, double, triple and home run in one game. **1982** T. Considine *Lang. Sport* 24: *Hat trick:* To hit in one game a single, double, triple, and home run.

4. *Broadly,* any remarkable accomplishment, usu. of three consecutive successes or achievements.

1951 *New Yorker* (Apr. 28) 64: Mr. Gaitskell...brought off a remarkable political hat trick. **1953** *N.Y. Times* (May 3) VII 8: A new...novel has an inside track with one of the big book clubs—and so Little, Brown may be coming up with a sort of "hat trick." **1962** *Time* (Nov. 2) 90: The auto industry is about to perform the hat trick by following zooming 1962 sales...with an even hotter 1963. **1988** Frazier & Offen *W. Frazier* 126: Hey, man, you got the hat trick [in a basketball game]. **1994** *New Yorker* (Oct. 3) 52: He conducted Berlioz's five-hour "Les Troyens" on a Thursday night and, two days later, a matinée of Verdi's "I Lombardi" and an evening performance of Strauss's "Electra"—a hat trick that few would dare to imitate.

haul *n.* **1.a.** a quantity, number, or amount, esp. a large amount of loot or financial profit, gained or secured at one time. Now *colloq.*

1776 in *OED*: I think we made a fine haul of prizes. **1821** Martin & Waldo *Lightfoot* 84: I proposed to go out and overtake the stage, and we should probably, make a *grand haul.* Ibid. 89: He...gave up his purse, which was a pretty rich haul. **1834** *Mil. & Naval Mag. of U.S.* (June) 248: I say, Captain, seeing I ha'nt no plunder (i.e. baggage) along, I reckon you thinks you won't make no great haul in me. **1848** Judson *Mysteries* 37: Lize made a big haul last night. **1850** Butler *Barnum's Parnassus* 21: I'm thinking that my next *haul* will be,/Upon the "liberal public." **1853** S. Robinson *Hot Corn* 80: What a glorious haul, boys. **1864** "E. Kirke" *Down in Tenn.* 11: We had on board...over four hundred thousand dollars...and the fellows might have made a rich haul. **1867** *Galaxy* (Mar. 15) 640: The parents look forward to the day when a "big haul" shall enable them to retire from the [thieving] business. **1872** McCabe *N.Y. Life* 220: Sometimes the drivers make a "haul" in a curious way. **1882** C. Morris *Shadow Sam* 5: I could put

any outsider in the way of making a nice haul. **1883** Needham *Arabs* 35: Sometimes we begs, sometimes we earns. When we get a haul it ain't so bad, but when we don't we ketch it. **1898** Norris *Moran* 66: Oh, it's a haul, son, it's a haul, an' you can lay to that. **1899** in "O. Henry" *Works* 522: Now half of this haul goes to me, and the other half the rest of you may divide. **1926** Lewisohn *Mr. Crump* 24: Once...he had "made a haul."

b. a robbery or theft.

1847 in Partridge *Dict. Und.* 323: Halloo! ain't somebody had a *go in,* or a *haul*...up your way? **1847–49 Bonney *Banditti* 82: They have made some pretty good *hauls* of late. **1853** G. Thompson *Garter* 40: I never missed a chance to make a *haul.* **1866** *Nat. Police Gaz.* (Apr. 21) 3: I suppose the Kingston "haul" and others down that way were productive, and amply repaid the "gonnoffs" for their exertion. **1896** in S. Crane *N.Y.C. Sketches* 179: No-Toe's made another haul. **1904** in "O. Henry" *Works* 835: The best haul I made was just seven years after the first one. **1909** Fletcher *Up the Trail* 110: I know of a good place to make a haul. **1928** Dahlberg *Bottom Dogs* 41: They ducked into the garden patch to make a little haul.

2. a roundup (of suspects, prisoners, etc.); seizure. Now *colloq.* or *S.E.*

1866 *Night Side of N.Y.* 40: We see before us the net proceeds of the "haul." Observe the self-possessed manner of nearly every one [of the prisoners]. **1872** Burnham *Secret Service* 395: Another Haul of Counterfeiters. The U.S. Secret Service Detectives made another important arrest of counterfeiters, and seizure of counterfeit plates and material yesterday.

haul *v.* **1.** Orig. *Naut.* to clear out; depart or go rapidly.—usu. constr. with *it.*

[The constr. with *it* is now often regarded as a euphem. for *haul ass,* below, but cf. earlier *haul (one's) freight* s.v. FREIGHT, 1; the *it* may be in origin no more than a dummy obj.]

1805 J. Davis *Post-Captain* 77: Then go!...Your behavior is so unlike that of an officer's lady, that the sooner you brace up and haul aft the better. **1907 Bush *Enlisted Man* 58: I wouldn't be a bit surprised if he had "hauled it" with the horses. **1919** T. Kelly *What Outfit?* 178: O.P.'s report that the Germans are hauling it fast. **1928** Fisher *Jericho* 155: I'm...haulin' it through the crowd. **1942** Z.N. Hurston, in *Amer. Mercury* (July) 95: Man! He cold hauled it! **1956** R. Ellison, in W. King *Black Antho.* 263: We better haul it outta these woods. **1960** Stadley *Barbarians* 13: No matter how fast they haul, he's right with 'em. **1962** Stone *Ride High Country* (film): Now haul it. You're leavin'. **1975** *UTSQ*: Going fast...*hauling.* **1995** *Action News* (Oct. 5) (WBIR-TV): So [Hurricane Opal] is *hauling.*

2. to extract (a tooth).

1880 *Harper's* (Nov.) 839: They think nothing of having fifteen or more fangs "hauled"—to speak technically—in order to substitute...a set of false teeth.

3. to take into police custody; *haul in,* below.

1936 Farrell *World I Never Made* 208: But I ain't done nothin' but smoke a cigarette. You ain't gonna haul me for that, are you?

¶ In phrases:

¶ **haul ass, 1.** to depart, get out, or flee; go; *(also)* to hurry.—usu. considered vulgar. Cf. *haul tail,* below, and HAUL-ASS.

1918 Noyes *MS* (unp.): To haul ass. Meaning "to leave," "to get out." No derivation. Usually used in the Imperative. **1918** in E. Wilson *Prelude* 274: Haul ass! Hurry up! **1923** in J. O'Hara *Selected Letters* 10: I'd better haul ass and get into a tub. **1935** J. Conroy *World to Win* 216: Haul ass outa here. **1939** O'Brien *One-Way Ticket* 143: I leave you, and you get up and haul ass? Uh-huh. **1940** Farrell *Father & Son* 11: I'm hauling ass home. **1950** Calmer *Strange Land* 193: You guys better haul ass up that slope. **1951** W. Williams *Enemy* 83: "All right," said the captain. "Start hauling ass." I started hauling. "All engines ahead full." **1953** M. Harris *Southpaw* 88: He would...work a week and then haul ass by bus as far as his money went. **1958** T. Berger *Crazy in Berlin* 137: Haul ass, kid. No riders. **1965** Gallery *Eight Bells* 134: The merchant sailors...saw their naval escorts haul ass for home, leaving them to their fate. **1969** H.R. Brown *Die Nigger Die* 36: So I turned around and hauled ass getting out of there. **1987** A.A. Shockley, in C. Major *Calling Wind* 485: Now y'all haul ass and git that stuff off'n my truck. **1986–91** Hamper *Rivethead* 187: This was a cue to haul ass. **1993** Dolly Parton, on *Donahue* (NBC-TV): I'm not sayin' I was fat, but when I hauled ass I had to make two trips.

2. to apply oneself energetically; work hard.—usu. considered vulgar.

> **1970** A. Young *Snakes* 125: About the only way I know to master this shit is to haul ass and study.

3. to be exceptionally successful.

> **1993** P. Munro *U.C.L.A. Slang: Haul ass*...to perform exceptionally well: to kick butt. *I hauled ass on that test.*

¶ **haul in** Orig. *Police.* to bring (someone) to a police station for questioning or esp. booking.

> **1927** C.J. Daly *Snarl of the Beast* 34: And that's often the reason the innocent bystander gets hauled in so much. **1933** Ersine *Pris. Slang* 43: *Haul in*...To arrest. **1942** *ATS* 464: Arrest...[*to*] haul in. **1949** *Life* (Oct. 24) 25: The police decided to haul them all in. **1958** Simonson & Philips *Blob* (film): You know I don't want to haul you in.

¶ **haul** [*or* pull] (one's) **freight** see s.v. FREIGHT, 1.

¶ **haul stakes** see s.v. STAKE, *n.*

¶ **haul tail** (a partial euphem. for) *haul ass,* above. Also vars.

> **1924** Stallings *Plumes* 5 [ref. to 1918]: You allee samee haul tail away from here pronto. **1926** *Sat. Eve. Post* (Sept. 25) 12 [ref. to 1918]: They're all haulin' tail back t' the other bridge we come over on. **1927** J. Stevens *Mattock* 2 [ref. to 1918]: Haul feet, you blue-cord son of an ape! **1927** C. McKay *Home to Harlem* 25: Come on, let's haul bottom away from here to Harlem. **1928** Fisher *Jericho* 29: I been haulin' furniture....but when they starts plantin' dynamite, this baby's gonna start haulin' hind-parts! **1945** Wolfert *Amer. Guerrilla* 12: We hauled tail the hell out of there. **1946** Michener *So. Pacific* 134: He was on the rock when Mussolini hauled tail, and on the rock Joe heard the news about Normandy. **1968** Baker, Ladd & Robb *CUSS* 134: *Haul butt.* Leave a place. **1969** *Current Slang I & II* 49: *Haul buns, v.* Move out, hurry. **1983** in "J.B. Briggs" *Drive-In* 190: You need to haul buns out of here. **1986** *Miami Vice* (NBC-TV): When you see that, you haul butt for the door.

¶ **haul taut** *Naut.* to finish what one is doing; quit.

> **1856** *Ballou's Mo. Mag.* (Oct.) 322: Just you haul taut and belay that jaw tackle of your'n, will yer? or your slack braced wit may carry away your brains in the slings.

¶ **haul the mail** see s.v. MAIL, *n.*

haul-ass *v.* to go rapidly; *haul ass* s.v. HAUL, *v.*—usu. considered vulgar.

[This form is generally distinguished from the verbal compound with HAUL by the attachment of inflectional ending to -*ass*; cf. parallel use of *drag [(one's)] ass* s.v. DRAG, *v.*, and DRAG-ASS, *v.*]

> **1958** Camerer *Damned Wear Wings* 26 [ref. to WWII]: Most...were haul-assing home. **1963** Hayden *Wanderer* 172: We'll haul-ass out of here around ten tomorrow morning.

haul down *v.* to earn (money).

> **1899** Cullen *Tales* 139: He told me that this was his last show on earth to haul down a few dollars. **1970** Quammen *Walk the Line* 142: I ain't hauling down any green.

haul-down promotion *n. Navy.* a promotion awarded a commissioned officer upon retirement.

> *a***1974** G.E. Wheeler *Adm. Pratt* 335: In...1929 he recommended ...that "haul-down promotions" be given to captains when they retired.

haul off *v.* **1.** *Naut.* to leave; withdraw.

> **1835** *Mil. & Nav. Mag. of U.S.* (Dec.) 295: I was just thinking of hauling off out of the smoke. **1870** *Galaxy* (June) 774: Bren, I say, why don't you haul off? That fellow's got the wind of you. It'll only be the harder by and by.

2. to draw back the fist before striking a blow; to withdraw slightly in preparation for some decisive action; (*hence*) to take any sort of sudden action; strike a blow. Now *colloq.*

> **1840** *Spirit of Times* (Jan. 25) 560: I hauled off, and took him in the burr of the ear. **1870** "M. Twain," in *Galaxy* (Oct.) 572: Suppose he should..."haul off" and fetch me with the butt-end of it? **1908** McGaffey *Show Girl* 200: And hauling off, wifey hangs one on Alla's

map. **1918** in Grider *War Birds* 137: He hauls off and stretches the long tall bird on the floor. **1923** Witwer *Fighting Blood* 44: He throws up his job, hauls off, and enlists. **1930** D. Runyon, in *Collier's* (Dec. 20) 32: Then Lily hauls off and gives me a big kiss. **1929–31** Farrell *Young Lonigan* 39: They gotta hell of a lot of nerve haulin' off on a guy just because they're priests or nuns. **1937** Kober *Having Wonderful Time* 177: I don't know why you didn't haul off and take a sock at me. **1942** Z.N. Hurston, in *Amer. Mercury* (July) 89: We hauled off and went to church last Sunday. **1963** J. Ross *Dead Are Mine* 48: Look at that smug bastard. I ought to just haul off and drive his teeth down his throat. **1990** *Essence* (Apr.) 26: Before you can stop yourself, you haul off and slap him.

haul up *v.* to call or hale to account before a legal or administrative authority.

> **1851** B. Hall *College Wds.*: In many colleges, one brought up before the Faculty is said to be *hauled up.* ***1882** in *OED*: They were all young officers...and probably at times require to be hauled up sharply. **1890** *Overland Mo.* (Feb.) 123: I want him hauled up. Can't ye make out the papers? **1925** Z. Grey *Vanishing Amer.* 131: I'll put you in jail....I'll haul you up for this. **1938** in Inman *Diary* 879: [The] bull...wouldn't haul me up in Petersburg because he said the courts dere didn't have nothin' against hobos.

hava-no [pidgin] *Mil. in Korea.* there is [*or* was] no; doesn't or don't [*or* didn't] have; unavailable.

> **1951** *Herald-Tribune* (N.Y.C.) (Dec. 16) II 5: *Hava no:* Don't have any, such as "hava no eggs for breakfast," or "hava no soap." ***1953** (cited in Partridge *DSUE* (ed. 8) 536). **1955** in *AS* XXXV (1960) 265: Cindy-san, watch hava-no....Time to stop hava-no. **1960** *AS* XXXV 122 [ref. to Korean War]: The GI may have known the Korean words *ye* and *ani,* "yes" and "no," but he usually preferred periphrastic constructions involving the phrase *hava-yes* and *hava-no. Ibid.* 263: Laundry hava-no. **1963** Fehrenbach *This Kind of War* 456 [ref. to Korean War]: Ammunition, except small arms, was "hava-no."

hava-yes [pidgin] *Mil. in Korea.* there is [*or* was]; have or has [*or* had]; available.

> ***1953** (cited in Partridge *DSUE* (ed. 8) 536). **1960** (quot. at HAVA-NO).

have *v.* **1.** to cheat or trick; (now *colloq.* or *S.E.*) to defraud.—used in pass. only.

> ***1770** in Partridge *Dict. Und.* 323: Above all, beware of betting or engaging in company you...have no knowledge of, for if you do, ten to one but you are *had,* a cant word they make use of, instead of saying, as the truth is, *we have cheated him.* ***1789** G. Parker *Life's Painter* 150: Imposed on, or...*to be had.* ***1818** in Partridge *Dict. Und.* s.v. *suit:* Not to be *had* upon any *suit* whatever. ***1820–21** P. Egan *Life in London* 252: Some of the *best judges* [of character] have [in this way] been "*had.*" ***1847** T. DeQuincey, in *OED*: The good señora...was not... to be had in this fashion. ***1879** in *OED*: There's not a real diamond among them. If you've advanced money on 'em, you've been had. ***1899** Whiteing *John St.* 205: He is ever haunted by the ungenerous suspicion that when working for fixed wages he is being "*had.*" **1909** *Sat. Eve. Post* (July 3) 7: Oh, Kirkpatrick, you've been had—Jove, how you've been had! **1928** R. Fisher *Jericho* 46: He knew that he simply couldn't be "had." [**1970** Horman & Fox *Drug Awareness* 463: *Been had*—arrested.]

2. Esp. *Mil.* to kill or injure.—used in pass. only.

> **1973** Andrews & Owens *Black Lang.* 74: *Had*...Beaten up. "That cat been *had.*" **1972–76** Durden *No Bugles* 147 [ref. to Vietnam War]: The place [*sc.* a morgue] where they try to fix up dudes who've been had. **1983** LaBarge & Holt *Sweetwater Gunslinger* 34: This is it. My ass is had now. **1987** E. Spencer *Macho Man* 59 [ref. to Vietnam War]: If you were the first to get it [be killed], you wouldn't even know what was happening until after you'd been had.

¶ In phrases:

¶ **have** [got] 'em [bad] to have the d.t.'s; (*hence*) be crazy or overly enthusiastic.

> *a***1867** G.W. Harris *Lovingood* 40: She went...down the mountain, tu git the purticulers, an' when she cum back she sed she *had em.* I thot she had myse'f. **1884** *Life* (July 31) 58: He is plunged at once into a painful quandary as to whether...he has...got 'em again. **1885** in Lummis *Letters* 256: The sight of running water...is so unusual that a man is cautious about speaking of it—he doesn't know but what he has got 'em again. **a***1890–93** *F & H* III 188: *Got 'em bad*...A superlative

of earnestness or excessiveness: *e.g.*, anyone doing his work thoroughly, a horse straining every nerve, a very sick person, especially a patient in the horrors, is said to have *got 'em bad. ca*1893 McCloskey *Across Continent* 82: You've got them bad. Don't come near me….I ain't been vaccinated. **1911* G.B. Shaw, in *OEDS:* You seem to have got it pretty bad. **1941** in *OEDS:* I got it bad and that ain't good. **1942** *ATS* 334: Be in love…*have it bad.*

¶ **have had it** Orig. *Mil. Av.* **1.a.** (ironically) to have missed or lost one's chance for a desired thing (specified or implied by context); to be too late. *Rare* in U.S.

    *1941 in *OEDS: To have had it,* to miss something pleasant, e.g. leave. **1943** *Time* (Mar. 22) 52: Some R.A.F. expressions wander into wondrous double talk. Example: "Can I get a taxi?" asked the American outside the Savoy. "You've had it," said the R.A.F. flyer, *i.e.,* "You haven't got it and you won't get it." **1945** E. Partridge, in *College English* VII 27: *You've had it* is ironic, for it means "You have not had it—and, what is more, you won't get it."…A few American airmen have adopted the phrase. **1946** G.C. Hall, Jr. *1000 Destroyed* 71: The first thing the Debden soldier did was to…order a scotch and soda. "Sorry," the barmaid would answer, "you've had it." "Had it, did you say? I just got here." Somebody would then explain that "had it" was RAFese for you're out of luck, or it's all gone there ain't no more.

b. to be fated, as to imminent death, destruction, failure, punishment, etc.; to be doomed.

    1944 Stiles *Big Bird* 34: The flak [was] behind us…."I thought we'd had it," somebody said. **1944** in Inks *Eight Bailed Out* 19: Number Two engine began coughing…."We've had it, men." **1946** G.C. Hall, Jr. *1000 Destroyed* 285: The Mustang plummet[ed] into the water, carrying Bunte. The tail section disappeared. "God, he's had it!" a pilot gasped. The impact of the plane on the water knocked Bunte unconscious. **1942–49** F.A. Johnson *One More Hill* 110: The next phase…promises to be one of those times, as the British say, when "we've had it." **1955** Comden & Green *Always Fair Weather* (film): Well, I guess we've had it. **1955** Salter *Hunters* 95: Well, damn if it didn't turn out to be the commandant's wife….The Doctor thought he'd had it, but she didn't get a good enough look at him. **1956** Heflin *USAF Dict.* 277: He's had it, the old man just heard of the ground loop. **1957** Ness & Fraley *Untouchables* 143: Well, right off I figure some bird has had it. **1957** Gurney & Martin *Invasion of Saucer Men* (film): Uh-oh. Looks like we've had it. **1961** *WNID3:* He's been cheating me badly for years but now he's had it. *a*1966 in *World Bk. Encyc. Dict.:* The B-47 is so much faster that if it starts flying you, you've had it. **1985** *Cheers* (NBC-TV): If I come home and find you've flushed the car keys again, you've had it! **1980–87 Collins Cobuild Dict.:* If you say that someone *has had it,* you mean that they will be in trouble because of something they have done. **1989** Knoxville, Tenn., man, age *ca*40: Man, if they don't do something to stop all the drugs and violence in this country, America has *had it!*

c. to have done, gained, or experienced whatever (usu. unsatisfactory) amount that conditions will allow; esp. in phr. **you've had it!** stop what you're doing at once! you're through!

    1946 G.C. Hall, Jr. *1000 Destroyed* 234 [ref. to WWII]: "I'm out of ammo [after a series of dogfights]."…"Guess we've had it now….we'd better go on back." *Ibid.* 340: You'll have to return to Debden. **1959** in Cox *Delinquent* 72: What are you doing on a swing, Beth?…You've had it. **1963** in L. Bruce *Essential Bruce* 126: And the most depressing thing, you know, there's nothing to do in these towns. You go to the park, you see the cannon, and you've had it. **1965** N.Y.C. mother, age *ca*40 (to child in playground): OK. You've had it. Let's go.

2. to have recently been shot down in an aircraft or otherwise killed in action; (*hence*) to die or be dead.

    *1942 in Partridge *DSUE* (ed. 3) 1073: "He's had it"…he's been killed. **1944** in Stiles *Big Bird* 49: You just say, Mac's gone, Mac went down, Mac's had it. **1946** G.C. Hall, Jr. *1000 Destroyed* 255: Hofer is N.Y.R. ["not yet returned"]…Afraid he's had it. **1949** Bartlett & Lay *Twelve o'Clock High* (film): Mac's had it….McKissen's dead. **1952** in I.M. Marks *Fear* 12: Poor guy, he must be dead. "You're dead, you've had it." **1952* N. Coward, in *OEDS:* Of course they're still alive, but I never see a telegram coming into the house without saying…"Sarah's had it!" **1959** *Twilight Zone* (CBS-TV): The doctor said I'd almost had it [in a car crash]. **1962* in Partridge *DSUE* (ed. 7) 1190: *To have*

had it [meaning to have been killed] originated in the Gulf Country of northern Queensland, where one of us heard it as early as 1929. **1965** Daniels *Moments of Glory* 10: I stepped over a soldier who'd had it. **1965** Beech *Make War in Madness* 122: "Where is he?" he demanded…."He's had it," the CIA man said gently, simply. **1968** Craig *Anzio* (film): He's had it.

3.a. to be at the point of mental or emotional collapse, esp. as a result of exposure to combat.

    1944 Pyle *Brave Men* 215: It was only when a man "had had it"—the combat expression for anyone who had had more than he could take—that he sat alone and didn't say much and began to stare. *ca*1944 in Craven & Cate *AAF in WW II* VII 405: He's edgy….I think he's had it….He won't be fit to fly for months. **1946** Sevareid *Wild Dream* 238: After a year you start talking to the lizards; after eighteen months you start talking to yourself; after two years you don't talk at all—and then you've had it. **1948** Wolfert *Act of Love* 433: Buster, you've had it. The bats are playing ping-pong with the bells in your belfry. **1952** Grant & Taylor *Big Jim McLain* (film): If you ask me, he's had it….A total nervous breakdown. **1953** Michener *Sayonara* 1: The Air Force doctor took one look at me and said, "Gruver, you've had it." **1960** *Twilight Zone* (CBS-TV): I've had it, huh? All my marbles are gone! **1966–67** W. Stevens *Gunner* 69: If Deacon thought he'd had it…the colonel wanted to [know]. **1967** Dibner *Admiral* 29: Oley's had it, he thought. Nutty as a fruitcake. **1973** Kiley & McDonald *"Catch-22" Casebook* 301: Yossarian…obviously had "had it"—the World War II phrase for combat fatigue.

b. to have had enough, esp. enough to make one angry, disgusted, or exhausted.—often constr. with *with.* [Early quots. ref. to WWII.]

    1949 Quigley *Corsica* 62: I'll tell you, Ed, I'm not going to fly any more. I've had it! **1950** Calmer *Strange Land* 159: I don't feel like blaming men who have been in combat. There are a lot of them here right now…they sure have had it. **1952** *I Love Lucy* (CBS-TV): That's all, brother. I've had it. **1952** in J. Blake *Joint* 51: I merely want to…leave the travails of Art to the younger and sturdier. I've had it. **1956** Chamales *Never So Few* 209: I've had it with Margaret. **1956** Yordan *Harder They Fall* (film): Gus has had it. He's punched out. **1959** Wurthman & Brackett *Rio Bravo* (film): I told you, Stumpy. I've had it. Don't let me tell you again. **1960** *Twilight Zone* (CBS-TV): I've had it, understand. I can't take this another day, another hour. **1961** *Car 54* (NBC-TV): I've had it with you two, do you hear me? I've had it up to here! **1966** Kenney *Caste* 233: I'm just doggone tired. I've had it, Mike. **1971** *N.Y. Times* (Aug. 22) 1: "I've had it with interviews," he grunted. **1975** Silliphant *Dr. Durant* (film): I think you'd better lie down. You've had it. **1977** Flusser *Squeal Man* 101: I've had it with you guys….You're bugging me. Now I've had it. **1981** Patchett et al. *Great Muppet Caper* (film): Well, you had it up to here. So what did you do? **1990** Alexander & Karaszewski *Problem Child* (film): I've had it with him! **1995** *Jerry Springer Show* (synd. TV series): Roommates who've had it with their freeloading friends.

4.a. (of things) to be no longer usable or serviceable; be beyond repair.

    1946 G.C. Hall, Jr. *1000 Destroyed* 266 [ref. to WWII]: "That ship won't fly anymore, lieutenant." "No, it's had it." **1959* in *OEDS:* He re-wound the cord and tried again: no spark. "It's had it, I think." **1961** *Twilight Zone* (CBS-TV): This building has had it. It's worn out, used up. **1967** N.Y.C. woman, age *ca*50: This dress has about had it. **1976 Heinemann Austral. Dict.:* His car *has* really *had it* (= is beyond repair). **1980–87 Collins Cobuild Dict.:* It's worn out, this piano. It's just had it.

b. to have had one's day, esp. one's period of youth, ability, fashion, or favor.

    1953 Eyster *Customary Skies* 101 [ref. to WWII]: Take me. I'm still young, but I feel I've had it. **1961** J.A. Williams *Night Song* 58: "He's had it," another musician said. "Ritchie Stokes has had his day." *a*1966 in *World Bk. Encyc. Dict.:* By twenty they had begun to fade, by twenty-five they have had it. **1966** *RHD:* He was a great pitcher, but after this season he'll have had it….Quiz shows have had it. **1981 Macquarie Dict.: Have had it*…to become out of fashion or no longer popular. **1985** Univ. Tenn. instructor: I'd say Shakespeare and Milton have pretty much had it as far as most students are concerned.

¶ **have had the course** Esp. *Mil.* **have had it**, above.

    1958 J. Davis *College Vocabulary* 2: "I've…had the course"—The worst has happened to me. **1966–68** *Current Slang I & II* 47: *Had the course…Exhausted; used up.*—Air Force Academy cadets.—This hat has *had the course*.

¶ **have had [up to here]** to have had more than enough of; be fed up with.

1941 Wead & Buckner *Dive Bomber* (film): Three weeks and I've had marriage up to *here*. ***1943** in *OEDS*: I've had the club. **1946** J.H. Burns *Gallery* 294: I've *had* Naples. O Mr. Roosevelt, can't I please go home? **1955** Salter *Hunters* 147: I've had this war. Ninety-seven missions and still looking for a damaged. What's the use? **1956** Bellow *Seize the Day* ch. i: After he had driven a painted flivver and had worn a yellow slicker with slogans on it, and played illegal poker, and gone out on Coke dates, he had *had* college. **1959** Mahin & Rackin *Horse Soldiers* (film): All right, section hand, I've *had* you! **1960** Kirkwood *Pony* 267: By the time we'd pawed over the pictures I'd "had" the book, but Sid was really mesmerized. **1961** Rossen & Carroll *Hustler* (film): I've *had* that kind of life. **1965** Hersey *Too Far to Walk* 7: John had just about had [his roommate] Flack.

¶ **have it off** to copulate. *Rare* in U.S.

***1937** in Partridge *DSUE* (ed. 3) 1073: *Have it off…is also used…by a man that has contrived to seduce a girl.* ***1962** in *OEDS*: My wife went to France and had it off with everyone in sight. **1972** Friday *Secret Garden* 101: Harry and Isobel are having it off and her husband's in the next room! **1986** R. Campbell *In La-La Land* 175: Some gazoony…having it off with Mary Fist.

¶ **have on** to hoax.

***1867** in *OEDS*: It looks as if somebuddy wur havin me on. **a*1890–93 *F & H* III 281: *To have on…*(colloquial).—To secure a person's interest, attention, sympathy: generally with a view to deceiving him (or her). ***1895**, ***1928**, ***1951** in *OEDS*. **1971** Sonzski *Punch Goes Judy* 103: "You're having me on," I said in British tones. **1981** *Nat. Lampoon* (Apr.) 6: How time flies when you're having people on! **1983** S. King *Christine* 8: Arnie, you're having me on, aren't you? **1981–85** S. King *It* 63: Trying to decide if Rich…was having him on.

¶ **I['ve] got your ——** Esp. *Mil. & Pris.* (used between men as a contemptuous retort).—often elaborated obscenely with *hanging, swinging*, etc.

1926 *Sat. Eve. Post* (Sept. 25) 13 [ref. to 1918]: "Them are ration dumps that Fritz is burnin' so we won't capture 'em."…"I got your old ration dumps right here!" **1958** Berger *Crazy in Berlin* 5: "I got your Roman ruins and your art right here," he would sometimes say, grabbing his clothes in the area of the scrotum. [**1960** Loomis *Heroic Love* 182 [ref. to WWII]: "Regulations!" He laughed harshly, stepped back, and seized his crotch, in an old city gesture of derision. "Here's your goddam regulations, you son-of-a-bitch!"] **1962** Killens *Heard the Thunder* 68 [ref. to WWII]: "Just cause you're the CO's pet you think your shit don't stink," Solly said offhandedly, "I got your CO's pet." **1966** Braly *On Yard* 78: I got your bramble patch hanging. **1970** Ponicsan *Last Detail* 43: "It's your goddam fault." "I gotch your goddam *fault*—dangling." *Ibid.* 167: I gotch your production, partner—swinging. **1973** Andrews & Owens *Black Lang.* 94: I got yo mama hanging low. If you want her, let me know. **1973** Goines *Players* 143: "Why, you black bitch!"…"I got your black bitch hanging," she said. **1975** S.P. Smith *Amer. Boys* 113: "Horseshit." "I got your horseshit hangin'." *Ibid.* 254: Hard-working Al Chase! I got your hard work hanging from the hairs on my ass. **1975** J. Jones *Dolemite* (film): "Well, goodbye, boy."…"I got your boy *hangin'*." **1972–76** Durden *No Bugles* 144: "I can't trust Whipple…with my pigs." "I got your fuckin' pig *hangin'*." I grabbed my crotch. "Here's your goddamn pig." **1989** S. Lee *Do the Right Thing* (film): I *got* your boycott swingin'.

¶ **let have it** to fire a gun or guns at; (*hence*) to attack or assault with great force, as by shooting, punching, or rebuking; (*often*) to shoot dead.

1823 [J. Neal] *Errata* I 62: I…"let him have it," as we say, into his face and eyes. **1823** J.F. Cooper *Pilot* 317: "Let them have it!" cried Griffith, in a voice that was heard in the remotest parts of the ship. **1833** J. Neal *Down-Easters* II 143: Employ a good lawyer, and *let them have it*. **1839–40** Cobb *Green Hand* II 32: Let 'um have it—fire! **1840** *Spirit of Times* (May 2) 97: I let him have it, right and left—bang! bang!—20 buck-shot in each barrel. **1843–45** T.J. Green *Tex. Exped.* 85: "Let them have it, boys!"…one hundred shots…were poured into them. **1877** in Miller & Snell *Why West Was Wild* 295: Shaw turned his battery upon the officer and let him have it in the right breast.

1925–26 Black *You Can't Win* 209: I let that Gold Tooth have it. **1931** Rouverol *Dance, Fools, Dance* (film): We can't let him have it here, and he's too wise to frame. **1937** Hoover *Persons in Hiding* 116: Let 'em have it!…Up went the rifle, flame spurting from its muzzle. **1950** A. Lomax *Mr. Jelly Roll* 133: Toodlum and Boar Hog waited for him at the place he always got off the street car…and let him have it. **1956** Neider *Hendry Jones* 82: That's the dead line brother. You cross that and I'll let you have it. **1958** A. Gibson *Be Somebody* 13: She had just got through calling me a pig-tailed bitch when I let her have it. **1962** *Leave It to Beaver* (ABC-TV): Now I'm *really* gonna let him have it! **1963** D. Tracy *Brass Ring* 315: The next time you call me Clarence…I'm going to let you have it right in the middle of your…kisser. **1968** Blackford *Torpedo Sailor* 131: Train your gun on that S.O.B., and if he casts off let him have it! *a*1982 Medved *Hospital* 35: He…really let me have it. He said, "You asshole. You insolent, lousy kid!"

¶ **not having any** not interested; disdainful.

***1918** Bishop *Winged Warfare* 164: We managed to have three short goes at different artillery machines in the course of half an hour next day, but they were not "having any," however, and turned away and fled toward home. ***1923** D.H. Lawrence *Studies in Amer. Lit.* 26: So H. St. J. de C. tried to put Nature-Sweet-and-Pure into his pocket. But nature wasn't having any, she poked her head out and baa-ed. **1950** G. Homes *Lawless* (film): They got tough and we weren't having any. *ca*1953 Hughes *Fantastic Lodge* 32: He was slightly more interesting but I still wasn't having any. **1958** Taradash *Bell, Book & Candle* (film): What's the use, Sid? He isn't having any. **1961** Sullivan *Shortest, Gladdest Yrs.* 283: Anson wasn't having any.

¶ **you can have ——!** (the thing or person named) is offensive, worthless, etc.

1929 Hammett *Maltese Falcon* 149: She's a tough racket. You can have it for mine. **1934** D. Runyon, in *Collier's* (Mar. 3) 8: You can have him. **1940** W.R. Burnett *High Sierra* 15: Not a trace of human habitation. Nothing but a…road…mountains…moonlight, and a chill wind. "Brother…you can have it!" **1941** Macaulay & Wald *Manpower* (film): I'm not gonna work up here in the rain with 230,000 volts poppin' around me. They can have it. **1942** in Tapert *Lines of Battle* 60: I always thought that "physical courage" was one overrated virtue and it sure is. You can have it if you want it. The guys who proved yellow were mentally yellow in the first place. **1986** B. Clayton & N. Elliott *Jazz World* 25: To hell with Bella Vista, Arkansas. You can have it.

hawbuck *n.* a lout; bumpkin.

***1805** J. Davis *Post-Captain* 6: The hawbuck has not rolled up a single hammock. **1835** *Knickerbocker* (Dec.) 562: One haw-buck dancer…came up to me with an impudent air.

hawk[1] *n.* **1.** a sharper or swindler.

***1698–99** "B.E." *Dict. Canting Crew: Hawk*, a Sharper. ***1785** Grose *Vulgar Tongue: Hawk…also* signifies a sharper, as opposed to a pigeon. ***1822** D. Carey *Life in Paris* I 54: Upon your guard against *hawks* and sharpers. **1859** Matsell *Vocab.* 41: *Hawk.* A confidence man; a swindler.

2. *Und.* **a.** a bailiff (*obs.*) or watchman; a police officer; (*also*) a prison guard.

***1785** Grose *Vulgar Tongue: Ware hawk*; the word to look sharp, a bye-word when a bailiff passes. ***1834** Ainsworth *Rockwood* 19: The game's spoiled this time, Bob Rust,…the hawks are upon us. **1845** *Nat. Police Gaz.* (Oct. 11) 58: It is certain that the hawks will puzzle themselves not a little to know where those inquiries came from. **1925** in Partridge *Dict. Und.* 323: *Hawk…*a detective, or other police officer. **1936** *AS* (Apr.) 122: *Hawks.* Guards in Federal prisons. **1966** R.E. Alter *Carny Kill* 121: The hawks are about.

b. a watcher or lookout.

1990 *Inside Edition* (synd. TV series) (June 12): There are spotters or "hawks" in public places who watch for [victims to be robbed].

3. the U.S. eagle insigne, esp. as represented on military badges.

1872 Beidler *Delegate* 67: A bird on the button that looked like a hawk. **1918** (quot. at CROW, *n.*, 5).

4. *Naval Av.* a dive bomber, esp. in formation.

1943 Mears *Carrier* 106: Then another group of "hawks" from the other carrier, this time accompanied by fighters, would dive to bomb and strafe. **1945** J. Bryan *Carrier* 42: A "chicken" is a fighter plane, a "hawk" is a dive bomber. **1964** Newhafer *Tallyho* 169 [ref. to WWII]: He called the dive bombers. "Charlie hawks, go in." **1967** Lord

Incredible Victory 100 [ref. to 1942]: Tallyho! Hawks at angels 12…supported by fighters.

5. *Black E.* HAWKINS, 1. —usu. constr. with *the*.

   1946 Mezzrow & Wolfe *Really Blues* 186 [ref. to 1930's]: Hawk's out here with his axe. **1959–60** R. Reisner *Jazz Titans* 158: *Hawk, The:* cold weather. **1968** *Newsweek* (Mar. 18) 28: The nights are cold—when it is really chill, the men say "the hawk is out." **1969** Bullock *Watts* 221: The "hawk" (wind) creeping into the tenement flat. **1970** Whitmore *Memphis-Nam-Sweden* 91: But when we hit Japan and the huge back doors of that plane swung open, the hawk came swooping in. That cold wind cutting like a razor blade. **1970** A. Young *Snakes* 105: It was one of those killer Decembers. The hawk was talking! **1973** *N.Y. Times* (Jan. 7) 1: The sun isn't up yet and the "Hawk," Chicago's cruel wind, lashes down on the thousands of workers huddled at bus stops. **1978** B. Johnson *What's Happenin'* 126: The hawk…sucked at the people scurrying along the sidewalks. **1981** Hathaway *World of Hurt* 49: Time to let in the hawk. **1985** Flowers *Mojo Blues* 14: Pulling his hood up against the hawk. **1989** WKXT-TV news (Apr. 11): Here comes the hawk, as they say in Chicago….Tonight, 28 degrees.

6.a. *Pol.* a person, esp. in public office, who advocates a warlike, aggressive, or deliberately confrontational national military policy. Now *S.E.* [Usu. contrasted with DOVE.]

   1962 *Sat. Eve. Post* (Dec. 8) 20: The hawks favored an air strike to eliminate the Cuban missile bases….The doves opposed the air strikes and favored a blockade. **1964** (quot. at DOVE). **1967** in J. Flaherty *Chez Joey* 7: The Hawks in May: A Day to Remember. **1973** *U.S. News & W.R.* (Aug. 27) 32: The "hawks" in the Soviet leadership are believed to be arguing that a quick military operation could solve all of these problems at a single stroke. **1981** *Time* (July 27) 11: If the Administration persists…, warn some of the most fervent hawks in Congress, the present consensus for heavy defense spending could evaporate. **1987** M. Hastings *Korean War* 186: In the eyes of the "hawks"…the change of mood in Washington represented a weakening of the American position. **1990** *Daily Beacon* (Univ. Tenn.) (Aug. 27) 4: The hawks are certain that American air power can virtually eliminate Iraq's air force. **1994** *New Republic* (July 4) 10: Celebrated by David Halberstam as the dove among the Vietnam hawks.

b. any person who advocates an aggressive policy in business, government, etc.

   1972 *Business Week* (Oct. 28) 39: The division's policies are being promoted by corporation "hawks carrying out a policy which might not be pleasing to higher-ups." **1976** *U.S. News & W.R.* (Dec. 27) 27: The Shah of Iran has been a price hawk in OPEC. **1981** *Business Week* (July 27) 40: The OPEC price hawks "have ruined the market and have made a mockery of Saudi Arabia." **1982** *U.S. News & W.R.* (May 10) 25: I'm a hawk on spending cuts.

7. *Stu.* (see quot.).

   1966–68 *Current Slang I & II* 49: *Hawk, n.* One who regularly studies hard.—College students,…Virginia.

8. a criminal, esp. a mugger, who robs at night.

   1971 S. Stevens *Way Uptown* 95: Then one night some hawks tried to steal my shoes in a alley on 115th Street and I beat one of 'em half dead.

9. *Homosex.* CHICKENHAWK, 1.

   *a***1972** B. Rodgers *Queens' Vernacular* 45: Chicken hawk…hawk (=older man whose lustful peculiarities are shared solely with young, unjaded boys). **1984** *All Things Considered* (Nat. Pub. Radio) (June 13): The men are known as *hawks*; the boys are known as *chickens. a***1986** in *NDAS*: The police believe he was acting the role of a "hawk," finding "chickens" (young boys) for older men. **1986** R. Walker *AF Wives* 131: He'd heard tales about how the chickens turned on the hawks.

¶ In phrase:

¶ **on the hawks** on the lookout.

   1961 in Algren *Chicago* 25: They're on the hawks, and will take whatever comes along first—a woman, money, or just the icy pleasure of kicking a queer's teeth down his neck. **1968** Algren *Chicago* 131: The cops would be on the hawks/Behind every tree/For people with sex on their minds. **1980** Algren *Dev. Stocking* 275: Had a fight with my old man….He's going to be on the hawks for me all over town.

hawk² *n.* [resp. (to represent regional pronun.) of HOCK] pawn.

   1928 Dahlberg *Bottom Dogs* 176: He expected to take it out of hawk soon.

hawk *v.* **1.** to watch, esp. closely; stare at; *(also) (obs.)* to tend or mind, as a child.

   1886 *Lantern* (N.O.) (Oct. 6) 2: And to keep solid home he hawks the baby. **1971** H. Roberts *Third Ear: Hawk…*v….to watch closely. **1983** *Reader's Digest Success with Words* 86: Black English…*hawk:* (2) (verb) "to pursue or watch closely." **1988** *N.Y. Times Mag.* (Dec. 11) 24 [ref. to 1960's]: If I remember correctly, we used to *hawk* when we were watching the passing throng. These days, students…*scope.* **1986–91** Hamper *Rivethead* 221: Sanders and Jackson…were beginning to hawk my every move. **1994** *Totally Unoffic. Rap Dict.: Hawk…*To look at something….To stare down someone. **1995** Stavsky, Mozeson & Mozeson *A 2 Z* 46: *Hawkin'*…admiring or checking out with the intent to steal: Don't you be *hawkin'* my chains.

2. *Naval Av.* to carry out an air attack upon.

   1943 Mears *Carrier* 33: On the offensive the dive bombers tuck 500-pound or 1,000-pound "eggs" behind their props and launch to "hawk 'em." *Ibid.* 73: At four o'clock our scouts and bombers, along with those from the other carrier, took off to intercept the Jap force. The boys were out to "hawk 'em." [**1954** *N.Y. Times Mag.* (Mar. 7) 20: "Jet-flight glossary"…*Hawk it:* Make a tight turn in flight.]

3. *Stu.* (see quot.).

   1966–68 *Current Slang I & II* 49: *Hawk, v.* To study intensely….College students,…Virginia.—Joe *hawked* all night for this physics test.

4. to pilfer; swipe.

   1981–85 S. King *It* 29: Or maybe somebody hawked it out of my pocket in the…playyard at school. **1994** *Mystery Sci. Theater* (Comedy Central TV): Coleman hawked all the good lines for himself.

hawker *n.* (see 1974 quot.).

   1974 N.Y.U. prof., age *ca*65: In Philadelphia in the 1920's a *hawker* meant phlegm hawked up and expectorated. **1981** C. Nelson *Picked Bullets Up* 122 [ref. to 1967]: Dragon Lady…spit out a…hawker. *a***1990** in *Maledicta* X 32: *Hawker* a chunk of sputum coughed up and expectorated.

hawker *v.* to cough up; hawk.

   1985 Bodey *F.N.G.* 55: He hawkers and a glob of snot lands on my boot.

Hawkeye *n.* a usu. white native or inhabitant of Iowa. Now *S.E.*

   1838 in *Iowa Jour. Hist.* IV (1906) 171: We propose that the Iowans take the cognomen of Hawk-eyes. **1839** in *DA:* Hawk-eye and Iowa Patriot [newspaper founded at Burlington, Sept. 5]. **1845** in Thornton *Amer. Gloss.* II 974: Pukes, Wolverines, … Hoosiers, … Buckeyes, … Hawk Eyes, Rackensacks [etc.]. **1850** P. Decker *Diaries* 240: A rather pretty little "Hawkeye" girl. [**1859** Bartlett *Dict. Amer.* (ed. 2): *Hawk-eye State.* The State of Iowa. It is said to be so named after an Indian chief who was once a terror to voyageurs to its borders.] **1865** in *Civil War Hist.* VIII (1962) 286: She declared she would marry a Hawk Eye or never marry. **1866** *Beadle's Mo.* (Jan.) 44: Ground was broken under a bedstead in a cabin occupied by Iowa officers, the "Hawk-eye Mess." **1878** Beadle *West. Wilds* 36: We was much skeered of each other as we was of the Hawkeyes. **1949** *AS* (Feb.) 26: Almost every American has heard…*Hawkeye* for an Iowan.

Hawkins *n.* [orig. unkn.] *Black E.* **1.** keen winds or bitter weather. Also **Mister Hawkins.**

   1934 *Baltimore Sun* (Dec. 21) 14: Hawkins is outside (is coming). **1944** Burley *Hndbk. Harlem Jive* 25: I tossed and rolled,/Trying to collar a wink as Hawkins blew cold. *Ibid.* 26: Mister Hawkins flapped it round like a hothouse fan. *Ibid.* 140: *Hawkins:* Cold winter wind. **1946** Boulware *Jive & Slang* 4: *Hawkins…*Cold weather. **1958** Hughes & Bontemps *Negro Folklore* 484: *Hawkins:* The wind, wintertime, cold weather, ice, snow. In February, Hawkins talks. **1964** R.S. Gold *Jazz Lexicon* 141: According to jazzmen, *Hawkins* has been current esp. among black jazzmen since *c*1900, *hawk* since *c*1935.

2. (see quot.).

   1995 *N.Y. Times* (July 30) XIII 10 [ref. to 1945–46]: "It's Hawkins in here." Don't know if musicians still use that phrase, meaning that business was bad at the club, but it fit the ambiance.

hawkshaw *n.* [the name of the detective in the play *The Ticket-of-Leave Man* (1863), by Eng. dramatist Tom Taylor; popularized in U.S. by the comic strip *Hawkshaw the Detective*, by U.S. cartoonist Gus Mager] a detective.—usu. used derisively.

[*1863 in T. Taylor *Plays* 167: Hawkshaw, the 'cutest detective on the force.] 1895 in H. Hutton *Vigilante Days* 239: Great detectives are the Hawkshaw Association. 1903 "H. McHugh" *Back to Woods* 59: The village Hawkshaw snapped the bracelets on his wrists. 1912 Stringer *Shadow* 57: You think you're the king of the Hawkshaws! 1920 Ade *Hand-Made Fables* 6: The Village Hawkshaws knew that a Relief Expedition would try to break through. 1925 in Hammett *Knockover* 166: I feared the Emperor of Hawkshaws would find the odor of such low blood distasteful to his elegant nostrils. 1933 Ersine *Prison Slang* 43: Hawkshaw....A bungling detective. 1938 O'Hara *Hope of Heaven* 133: You mean them gumshoe artists, Jim? Those hawkshaws? 1941 Riskin *Meet John Doe* (film): OK, Hawkshaw. Grab a pencil. 1957 McGivern *Against Tomorrow* 64: The local hawkshaw, Earl thought, with a pointless bitterness.

hawse *n.* ¶ In phrase: **cross** [or **come athwart**] **(someone's) hawse** *Naut.* to encounter or come into conflict with someone.

    *1805 J. Davis *Post-Captain* 180: If any land-privateer...should come athwart our hawse. *1829 (cited in Partridge *DSUE* (ed. 8) 539). 1834 *Mil. & Naval Mag. of U.S.* (Oct.) 116: Never mind shipmate—'case as how we happened to cross your hawse, it's no use to be sort o' down about it. 1908 *Hampton's Mag.* (Dec.) 768: Say "sir" to me when you cross my hawse, or I'll give you worse than the mate did.

hawse-hole *n.* ¶ In phrase: **come up through the hawse-hole** *Naut.* (of a ship's officer) to have been commissioned after service as an enlisted man. Also vars.

    *1829 Marryat *Frank Mildmay* 249 [ref. to *ca*1810]: The service had received serious injury by admitting men on the quarter-deck from before the mast; it occasioned there being two classes of officers in the navy—namely, those who had rank and connections, and those who had entered by the "hawse-holes," as they were described. 1846 Codman *Sailors' Life* 123: He "came in at the hawsehole," and by zeal and activity, had soon acquired...promotion. 1849 Melville *White Jacket* 37 [ref. to 1843]: In sea parlance, [the warrant officers]..."come in at the hawseholes." 1873 Scammon *Marine Mammals* 122: We are indebted to the...skill of those...who commenced the life of a sailor by "coming through the hawse-holes." 1933 Witherspoon *Liverpool Jarge* (unp.): I'm the mate....I come in through the hawse hole.

hawse-pipes *n.pl. Naut.* the throat.

    1863 in Gibbons *Tales That Were Told* 77: My hawse-pipes are so choked by smoke/I hardly know the nights from mornings.

¶ In phrase:

¶ **come up through the hawse-pipe** *Naut.* to *come up through the hawse-hole* s.v. HAWSE-HOLE. Also vars.

    1901 *Our Naval Apprentice* (Nov.) 10: Through Hawse Pipe to Ward Room. 1929 in Williams *Whaling Family* 250 [ref. to *ca*1875]: There were few captains at that time that had not started in the forecastle, or as the saying was "came in through the hawsepipe" and worked their way aft. 1936 Healey *Foc's'le & Glory-Hole* 40: In the navy and in the merchant marine, the man who is promoted from the forecastle to the officers' mess is said to have "come up through the hawse pipe." 1937 Thompson *Take Her Down* 22 [ref. to 1918]: Dobie has risen from the ranks—"come up through the hawse pipe," as the Navy puts it. 1959 Morrill *Dark Sea* 12 [ref. to 1942]: Stay away from the Old Man. He's a blue-chip sailor—up from the hawsepipe. He treats you fair. *a*1961 R.H. Dillon *Shanghaiing Days* 79: He came up "by the hawsepipe," the hard way. In the Navy he would have been called a "mustang." 1976 S. Lawrence *Northern Saga* 11: My first and second mate both came up through the hawse pipe. 1979–81 C. Buckley *To Bamboola* 69: He was...the only academy-trained officer aboard. The others had all come up through the hawsepipe, as the expression goes. 1986 Coonts *Intruder* 161: Bosun Muldowski was a warrant officer and had worked his way up from the enlisted ranks, "up the hawse pipe," as the expression ran. 1987 *Smithsonian* (Sept.) 120: Jay worked his way up through the ranks, "up through the hawsepipe," they call it, after the opening where an anchor line penetrates the hull.

hawse-pipe sailor *n. Naut.* a seaman, as opposed to an officer.

    1883 Russell *Sailors' Lang.* 66: "Hawse-pipe sailor."—A man before the mast. One who starts the profession from the forecastle.

hay *n.* **1.** a bed.—usu. constr. with *the*; in phr. **hit the hay** to go to bed or to sleep; in phr. **roll in the hay** an act of coitus. Also vars.

    1902–03 Ade *People You Know* 13: He crawled into the Hay at 9:30 P.M. 1905 in Paxton *Sport USA* 26: [The baseball player] has a language of his own. Going to bed for him is to "hit the hay." 1907 in H.C. Fisher *A. Mutt* 8: Now if I can duck up to the hay without bumping into a couple of collectors I'm O.K. 1908 McGaffey *Show-Girl* 118: The next morning while she was yet beating the hay, I...took it on the run away from there. *ca*1910 in Dolph *Sound Off!* 63: For you work all day/Till it's time to hit the hay. 1911 *Adventure* (Mar.) 903: I go to the hay, and my eyes are shut tight. 1912 in Davidson *Old West* 79: Mornin' is a mile away,/Never 'spect to hit the hay. 1915 Braley *Songs of Workaday World* 55: Loadin' all day an'/Unloadin' all night,/Hittin' the hay/By the dawn's early light. [*1921 *Jour. Irish Folk Song Soc.* XVIII 33: "Where have you been all the day,/My bonny blue-eyed Tommy, O?"/"I've been rolling in the hay,/With a lassie young and gay."] 1923 McKnight *Eng. Words* 49: Expressions such as *hit the hay, hop a rattler, pound one's ear,* need no translation. 1927 Rollins *Jinglebob* 75 [ref. to 1880's]: There remained naught to do but "hit the hay," this being the cowboys' figurative description of lying on hard ground [to sleep]. 1928 in E. Ferber *One Basket* 333: Guessed he'd call it a day and go home to...the hay. 1936 Monks & Finklehoffe *Brother Rat* 71: It would have been just as easy to put your hay up before. 1944 Busch *Dream of Home* 61: With a girl like that you didn't just go out and jump in the hay. 1945 in *OEDS*: He gets something out of it....Maybe just a good roll in the hay. 1947 Motley *Knock on Any Door* 275: Nick said, "Let's hit the hay." 1951 O'Hara *Farmers Hotel* 51: Just a short stroll, then back to the hay. 1951–52 Frank *Hold Back Night* 95: Sue had said..."Darling, when I want a toss in the hay I want it to be the real thing." 1952 Sandburg *Strangers* 170 [ref. to *ca*1890]: My guff to you is you beat it in the hay tonight. 1953 Chandler *Goodbye* 5: It might have been a hotel room rented for...a roll in the hay. 1968 Smart *Long Watch* 28: An extra bounce in the hay or bottle of liquor. 1980 Teichmann *Fonda* 111: He was expecting a good wrestle in the hay with one of these girls and he got nothing. 1992 Strawberry & Rust *Darryl* 192: That's all she wrote, and I hit the hay. 1993 Suddeth & Goldstein *Prehysteria* (film): Did you have a nice little role in the hay?

2. *Narc.* marijuana or hashish.

    1934 *N.Y. Times* (Sept. 16) 21: The...tins contain enough "hay" to make thirty or forty cigarettes, one of which is enough to intoxicate the smoker. 1935 Pollock *Und. Speaks:* Hay, mariahuna; hashish. 1943 (quot. at MARY JANE). 1946 Mezzrow & Wolfe *Really Blues* 145: We could at least get loaded on good hay. 1947 in W.S. Burroughs *Letters* 11: I would like some of that hay. 1951 *Sat. Eve. Post* (Mar. 17) 71: Hay, bush, tea...marijuana. 1959–60 Bloch *Dead Beat* 76: The guy's breath smelled of hay. Not the new-mown kind, either. 1960 *Esquire* (Mar.) 87: God *damn,* he thought, this is *some* hay. 1967 Rosevear *Pot* 158: Hay: Marihuana. 1993 "Us3" *Lazy Day* (rap song): I'm puffin' on the hay.

3.a. money. [Prob. the orig. sense.]

    1940 [W.C. Fields] *Bank Dick* (film): You can buy 'em for a handful of hay. 1943 *Darling Jitterbugs* (film): Ten thousand dollars is a lot of hay! 1956 Sorden & Ebert *Logger's* 18 [ref. to *a*1925]: Hay, money in a pay envelope. 1961 F. Brown *Geezenstacks* 69: A two-C suit with a white carnation in the lapel, expensive cigars...and a pocketful of hay. 1961 Scarne *Comp. Guide to Gambling* 681: *Hay* Money, chips, dough, sugar cabbage, lettuce. 1994 *N.Y. Times* (Nov. 20) I 42: Six stamp speculators who planned to make hay out of a misprint.

b. *Specif.,* a small amount of money; (*hence*) something to be disdained or ignored.—usu. in phr. of the sort **that ain't hay.**

    1936 *New Yorker* (Sept. 12) 13: Seventeen hundred dollars for one week in Cleveland....That is not hay. 1938 R. Chandler *Big Sleep* ch. xx: Real money, they tell me. Not just a top card and a bunch of hay. 1942 Liebling *Telephone* 175: Twenty-five thousand dollars...and that's not hay. 1942 *Yank* (Dec. 16) 18: Fifty bucks a month ain't hay. 1946 Veiller *Killers* (film): I'm out ten G's and that ain't hay for me these days. 1952 Himes *Stone* 162: "What the hell kind of a lousy school is this where you can get a degree in law for five hundred and eight bucks?" "Hell, you call that hay?" 1969 in *OEDS*: Executor's fees...won't be hay. 1994 *Sally Jessy Raphaël* (synd. TV series): Seven husbands! That ain't hay!

hayako *v.* [Japn *hayaku!* 'Go ahead!', 'Make it snappy!'] *Mil. in East Asia.* to hurry.

1977 Caputo *Rumor of War* 39 [ref. to 1965]: When that was done, hayako down to the company area. *Ibid.*: I told him to hayako his ass back to Schwab because we were going South.

haybag *n.* **1.** Esp. *Und.* a woman, esp. a prostitute or a vagrant, who is fat and usu. dissipated, dissolute, etc.; (*also*) a fat person.

　　*1851 H. Mayhew *London Labour* I 217: Hay-bag…A woman. **1863** in E. Marchand *News from N.M.* 69: Sarah has a good deal of trouble with Fathers old haybag and familly. *1873 Hotten *Slang Dict.* (ed. 4): *Hay bag*, a woman. **1908** W.G. Davenport *Butte & Montana* 107: one of them alluded to me [a man]…as a haybag, whatever that is. **1919** *DN* V 41: *Haybag.* A woman hobo. **1929** Barr *Let Tomorrow Come* 44: You get a hideful o' scat once in a while an' a flop with some old haybag. **1929–31** Runyon *Guys & Dolls* 89: She is nothing but an old haybag. **1935** Algren *Boots* 182: Girls who picked up drunks were called hay-bags, and straight-hookers wouldn't even talk to them. **1939** Abbott & Smith *Pointed Them North* 121: A woman they called Big Ox, who was one of those haybags that used to follow the buffalo camps. **1961** Carse *Moonrakers* 65: The various well-established doxies in shoreside brothels around the world were known as "haybags." **1966** Braly *Cold* 101: Maybe you can get some old hay bag to pick up your tabs. **1976** S. Lawrence *Northern Saga* 19: You know what you can do with Clara and the hay bags she digs up.

　　2. *Army.* a laundress on a military post; in phr. **haybag row** the laundresses' quarters.

　　1865 in Springer *Sioux Country* 52: We were…sparking and courting the "haybags" and "shirt-tail banders" at Fort Riley and Kearny and Laramie. **1918** Griffin *Ballads of the Reg't* 30 [ref. to 1890's]: She was queen of "soap-suds" row,/The ranking "hay-bag" you'd soon know./…"Mag" washed the "duds" of Comp'ny K,…/Abused the "hay-bags" on the row. **1925** in *OEDS* [ref. to 1877]: I asked a passing corporal the way to the haybag quarters. He was a married man and lived in haybag row.

hayburner *n.* **1. a.** a horse; (*hence*) any animal that consumes hay.—often used derisively.

　　1904 McCardell *Show Girl & Friends* 161: Trim…needs no urging to whack his hay burner. **1918** F. Gibbons *Thought We Wouldn't Fight* 102: All I do all day long is prod around a couple of fat-hipped hayburners. My God, I hate horses. **1926** Norwood *Other Side of Circus* 85: Elephants…eat all day….That's why you'll sometimes hear them called the "hay-burners." **1938** in *AS* (Apr. 1939) 90: *Hay burner.* A mule. "The hay burner is in the stall." **1940** O'Hara *Pal Joey* 74: The hay-burners stop running at Hialeah. **1948** J. Stevens *Jim Turner* 239: She's time to cuff and leather up the hay-burners! **1963–64** Kesey *Great Notion* 538: Get them hayburners up here and hooked on. **1968** Ainslie *Racing Guide* 469: *Hayburner*—Horse that fails to pay its own feed bill; "oatburner." **1971** Nichols (NBC-TV): Why, that old hayburner of yours'd finish third in a two-horse race. **1973** *N.Y. Times Mag.* (Apr. 1) 36: If the hayburner loses, the bookie…at least breaks even. **1980** Tenn. woman, age 30: Strictly speaking, a *hayburner* is a high-strung horse that's a poor keeper—he can't keep any fat on and his ribs are always showing. It doesn't necessarily mean a broken-down horse. A hayburner is wide-coupled.

　　b. *Army.* (see quot.).

　　1941 *Sat. Review* (Oct. 4) 9: *Hayburners.* Cavalry.

　　c. *Film.* a Western movie.

　　1948 in *DA*: "What is a hay-burner?"…"A horse opera….An oater, a Western."

　　2. *R.R.* a kerosene lantern.

　　1930 *Railroad Man's Mag.* II 470: *Hay-Burner*—Hand oil lantern. **1932** *The Editor* (Aug. 30) 132: Danger of fire is great, especially with oil cars or having the hayburner or lamp overturn in the caboose. **1970** *Current Slang* (Summer) 8: *Hayburner*, n. A kerosene burning trainmen's lantern. (No longer in use, but still referred to by older trainmen.)

　　3. [fr. HAY, 2] *Und.* a smoker of marijuana or hashish.

　　1935 Pollock *Und. Speaks*: *Hay burner*, a mariahuana fiend. **1943** *Life* (July 19) 85: The "snowbird" (cocaine sniffer) and "hay-burner" (marihuana smoker) are carried off into a state equivalent to deep alcoholic intoxication. *a*1986 in *NDAS*: About half the guys in the troupe were hay-burners.

hay foot *n.* **1.** Esp. *Army.* the left foot. Cf. STRAWFOOT.

　　1851 in *OEDS*: At company training and general training…it was all "hay-foot, straw-foot" with him. **1887** Hinman *Si Klegg* 104 [ref. to Civil War]: Hayfoot—Strawfoot! Hayfoot—Strawfoot! **1914** Nisbet *4 Yrs. on Firing Line* 17 [ref. to 1861]: Mark time! Hay-foot! Straw-foot! **1914** Knibbs *Outlands* 46: Hay-foot, strawfoot, that's my gait. **1948** A. Murphy *Hell & Back* 19: Then they send him to school to build up his brain till he can tell the hay-foot from the straw-foot.

　　2. a farmer; rustic.—used derisively.

　　1901 Palmer *Ways of Service* 198: I tried to treat the hayfoots and strawfoots they brought into the square to be drilled as if they was white. **1919** Darling *Jargon Book* 16: *Hay-foot*—A farmer. **1952** Malamud *Natural* 21: What's the matter, hayfoot, you scared?

hay-footed *adj.* rustic.—used derisively.

　　1886 B. Harte *Tasajara* 151: Harcourt…was dispensing "tanglefoot" and salt junk to the hayfooted Pike Countians of his precinct. **1889** B. Harte *Dedlow Marsh* 243: Fought pretty well for a hay-footed man from Gil-e-ad.

hayhead *n.* [fr. HAY, 2] *Und.* a smoker of marijuana or hashish.

　　1942 *ATS* 476: *Hay head*…a marihuana smoker. **1955** (cited in Partridge *Dict. Und.* (ed. 2) 829).

hay kicker *n.* a farmer; rustic.—used derisively.

　　1941 *Slanguage Dict.* 20: *Haykicker*…a farmer.

haymaker *n.* **1.** Esp. *Naut.* a farmer; rustic; (*hence*) a lubber; raw recruit. Hence **haymaking,** *adj.*

　　1847 in Leyda *Melville Log* 115: Pull, pull, you lubberly *hay-makers!* **1871** Willis *Forecastle Echoes* 15: The sailors set up a roar, and the officer called me a "hay-maker"…and ordered me up on the main-yard "to remain until some of the hay-seed had blown away from me." **1878** Shippen *30 Yrs.* 68: Oh, you hay-makers! Are you going to sleep there, you lubbers? *Ibid.* [ref. to 1861]: Another "blank" haymaker! **1884** Blanding *Sailor Boy* 84 [ref. to Civil War]: The "haymakers," as the new recruits were called, had to suffer that night. **1885** Johnson & Buel *Battles & Leaders* I 746 [ref. to 1862]: I…resolved that I, an "old haymaker," as landsmen are called, would stick to my ship as long as my officers. **1893** Lockwood *Drummer-Boy* 182: A camp of citizen hay-makers had been established down on the bank of the river. **1898** Stevenson *Cape Horn* 192: You're a haymaker, that's what you are! **1899** Hamblen *Bucko Mate* 10: I allus call fer brakes there…in case some hay-maker like you 'r stopped here ter git a jug o' buttermilk er sumthin'. **1904** *Our Naval Apprentice* (Oct.) 53 [ref. to *ca*1860]: No sailor likes to be called a "haymaker." **1908** *Hampton's Mag.* (Dec.) 720: Monsters of the deep were…constantly threatening dire things to those "landlubbers" and "hay-makers" who ventured to invade their domain. **1937** Records *Cherokee Outlet* 79 [ref. to *a*1900]: One rough old sea captain called out, "Say port, you haymaking son of a bitch!" **1941, 1950** in *DARE*.

　　2. the Sun.—usu. const. with *old.*

　　1862 in Bensill *Yamhill* 9: The ground was covered with snow which soon disappeared before "Old Haymaker." **1908** W.G. Davenport *Butte & Montana* 75: We must pounce upon our fellows…while the haymaker is unobserved in the heavens. **1920** Conklin & Root *Circus* 17 [ref. to 1870's]: I found that it bothered even the oldtimers to stay awake, although most of them did until light in the morning, but there was a saying among the show people that "nobody can keep awake after the old haymaker comes up."

　　3. *Boxing.* a hard swinging blow; (*hence*) a finishing blow. Also *fig.*

　　1902 T.A. Dorgan, in Zwilling *TAD Lexicon* 43: [Caption of panel showing fighter Rube Ferns:] Rube's "haymaker chop." **1906** *Nat. Police Gaz.* (Mar. 24) 10: One of those…fellows is going to get the "haymaker" over on your jaw. **1907** Siler *Pugilism* 192: *Haymaker*—swinging blow. **1910** *N.Y. Evening Jour.* (Feb. 17) 17: A haymaker in the eighth nearly stowed the popular Mr. Goodman away. **1911–12** Ade *Knocking the Neighbors* 87: Every time he landed a crushing Hay-Maker on her Family History she countered with a short-arm Jolt on his Personal Appearance. **1913** J. London *Valley of Moon* 78: He shoots a short hook to my head…a real hay-maker if it reaches my jaw. **1915–16** Lait *Beef, Iron & Wine* 264: He hangs a haymaker on the high guy's ear. **1922** Paul *Impromptu* 142: Now and then a loose rail landed a haymaker. **1925** Cobb *Many Laughs* 196: The Swede started a haymaker from his knees. **1928** *Amer. Mercury* (May) 1: David…had just hung his haymaker on Goliath. **1928** Springs *Bright Blue Sky* 129: The champion took a long right hay-maker swing. **1929–30** Dos Passos *42d Parallel* 355: He let fly another haymaker. **1938** Smitter *Detroit* 5: Somebody'll reach over and plant a haymaker right on the side of his jaw. **1940** *Batman* #1 (unp.): The Joker explodes a haymaker off the Batman's jaw!!! **1961** S. Baker *Practical Stylist* 26: John hit Joe…a real haymaker. **1978** *N.Y. Times* (June 25) V 3: The haymaker…was a grand slam home run by John Milner. **1978** Strieber *Wolfen* 130: It hit him like a haymaker. **1982** D. Williams *Hit Hard* 56: Johnson…smacked him with a haymaker right on the nose. **1986** J.J. Maloney *Chain* 68: Ernie swung a haymaker that bounced the Creeper's head off the steel bars. **1993** *Donahue* (NBC-TV): This is a haymaker of a question.

4. *Entertainment Industry.* a song or other performance that is especially profitable, popular, or effective.

1954–60 *DAS: Haymaker*…the best song, joke or performance of an entertainer's repertory. **1981** *N.Y. Times Mag.* (June 21) 16: Singers we haven't heard from in years [are] belting out the old haymakers, crooning the old smoothies.

haypile *n.* a bed or mattress.

1904 T.A. Dorgan, in Zwilling *TAD Lexicon* 108: Kind of bad just before hitting up the haypile. **1910** T.A. Dorgan, in *N.Y. Evening Jour.* (Mar. 11) 18: Oh you haypile and how I love you! **1918** Lardner *Gullible's Travels* 76: And oh, how grand that old hay-pile felt when I finally bounced into it! **1929** "M. Brand" *Beacon Creek* 9: Lead me to that hay pile, sheriff, will you?

haypitcher *n.* HAYMAKER, 1.

1888 *Farmer Amer.* 290. **1895** Barentz *Woordenboek* 144: Hay-pitcher…Hay-seed, prengel, boer, omnoozele bloed. **1917** in C. Mills *War Letters* 223: What do you think of me, a pen pusher, going to war with a crowd of hay pitchers? **1942** *ATS* 365: Rustic; bumpkin…*hay pitcher.*

hayrack *n.* HAYBAG, 1.

1881 Small *Smith* 41: I never saw the darned old hay-rack but once in my life.

hayraker *n.* HAYMAKER, 1.

1954 Overholser *Violent Land* 194: I'm not afraid of…a bunch of hayrakers. **1962** J.P. Miller *Wine & Roses* (film): That old hag? She's a hayraker.

hayrick *n. Naut.* a slow or unseaworthy vessel.

1883 *United Service* (Feb.) 203: That 'Merican frigate out thar to anchor would knock them ar two old·hay-ricks tew pieces in two minutes, although the dam'd things carry a hundred and twenty guns each.

hay rube *n.* RUBE; HAYSEED.

1900 *DN* II 40: Hay rube, n. Country man, farmer [Northwestern Univ.]. **1953–55** Kantor *Andersonville* 388: Hope you take him out of here tonight, Hay Rube. I'll Hay Rube you.

hayseed *n.* an ignorant rustic.—used derisively. Also as adj.

[**1834–40** Dana *2 Yrs. Before Mast* ch. xxv: The greater part of the crew were raw hands, just from the bush, and had not yet got the hayseed out of their hair.] **1851** Melville *Moby-Dick* ch. vi: Ah, poor Hay-Seed! how bitterly will burst those straps in the first howling gale. **1879** *Puck* (Oct. 22) 522: Say, hayseed, does yer clo'es fit yer? **1883** in *OEDS*: Where the hay seeds may work at their farming. **1892** Bierce *Beetles* 238: Hayseed…*a Granger.* **1894** *Harper's* (Oct.) 696: Cert'nly he's a hayseed. **1895** Wood *Yale Yarns* 11: In strolled a long, lanky, dusty hayseed Westerner. **1903** Merriman *Letters* 49: He looks more like a hayseed than a wheat king. **1910** in O. Johnson *Lawrenceville* 381: Don't act like a lot of hayseeds on a rail. **1914** D.W. Roberts *Rangers* 148: He…told them to look as near like "hay seeds" as they could, to keep down suspicion. **1914** Ellis *Billy Sunday* 24: I was bred and born…in old Iowa….I am a hayseed of the hayseeds. **1919** Z. Grey *Desert* 161: "Boss, the hay-seeds have run off," called the man from the flat car. **1928** *Amer. Mercury* (Aug.) 473: The hayseed firemen! They could get him out! **1931** Bontemps *Sends Sunday* 32: Barney was the city Negro's idea of a hayseed. **1960** *Chaparral* (Stanford Univ.) (Apr.) 25: I guess that shows him he's not dealing with some hayseed. **1974** A. Bergman *Big Kiss-Off* 173: A bus full of hayseeds gazed at us. **1975** T. Berger *Sneaky People* 202: You're sure a hayseed. **1980** J. Carroll *Land of Laughs* 104: We're the kind of place people joke about when they talk about hayseeds. **1984** Bane *Willie* 144: Something they've been told is hayseed all their lives, and they're finding out that maybe it's not so hayseed. **1984** Mason & Rheingold *Slanguage: Hayseed,* n. A person from the non-urban Midwest. Hayseeds often carry rifles in their cars and wear Cat Diesel or Redman caps. **1990** J. Leo, in *U.S. News & W.R.* (Apr. 16) 17: The two hayseeds in the Bartles & Jaymes TV ad.

hayseeder *n.* HAYSEED.

1891 in *DA* [ref. to 1830's]: These young swells scorned the waiting for the afterpiece, or farce, as vulgar; only the thing for "hayseeders"…to do. **1912** Siringo *Cowboy Detective* 485: The hayseeder replied: "I dunno."

hayshaker *n.* **1.** HAYMAKER, 1.

1924 Anderson & Stallings *What Price Glory?* 84 [ref. to 1918]: Don't be a hayshaker, Quirt. You can't play guardhouse lawyer in this country. **1927** (quot. at PLOW JOCKEY). **1929** *Our Army* (Nov.) 14. **1942** Lindsay & Crouse *Strip for Action* 225: All right, hayshaker. You never been out of Kansas and you know everything. **1955** O'Connor *Last Hurrah* 394: Out in the western part of the state he's a big wheel. He packs quite a wallop with the hay-shakers! **1964** Thompson & Rice *Every Diamond* 37: You must be a real hayshaker, coming from there. **1966** Jarrett *Private Affair* 90: This was peanuts compared with the clipping one girl got from an out-of-town hayshaker at a seed convention. **1972** Sherburne *Ft. Pillow* 69: And you, you simple-minded hay-shaker, if I ever see you lower your gun to load it during a bayonet charge again, I'll snatch you bald-headed! **1973** Ace *Stand On It* 43: Only the hayshakers wear socks at any time of day or night. **1980** Hogan *Lawman's Choice* 62: Every two-bit rancher and clodhopping hayshaker in the country.

2. HAYSEED.

1940–41, 1942, 1950, 1966–68, 1971, 1973 in *DARE.*

haytosser *n.* HAYMAKER, 1.

1904–11 Phillips *Susan Lenox* 210: She'll set the hay-tossers crazy! **1912** *Hampton's Mag.* (Jan.) 747: If all those hay-tossers who come to this town…were only as lamblike as you people imagine they are! **1913** *Sat. Eve. Post* (Mar. 15) 30: Me leave Chicago! Me be a rube! Me a haytosser! Me a farmer! Me a spinach-chin!

haywagon *n.* a sightseeing bus.

1931 Harlow *Old Bowery* 432 [ref. to *ca*1900]: "Haywagons" or "rubberneck wagons"…were now coming down from Times Square.

haywire *n.* flimsy or worthless material.

1928 *N.Y. Times* (Mar. 11) VIII 6: Slang of Film Men…*A Lot of Hay-wire*—Flimsy; unsubstantial.

haywire *adj. & adv.* [sugg. by *hay wire* 'light baling wire used for binding hay'] **1.** *Esp. Logging.* poorly equipped or hastily or poorly put together; slipshod; substandard; no good.

1905 in *DA: Haywire outfit.* A contemptuous term for loggers with poor logging equipment. **1921** *DN* V 109: *Hay-wire,* adj. Of no account,…ugly. **1923** in Kornbluh *Rebel Voices* 93: I…know that a system that is slung together in such a haywire manner has had some damn poor mechanics on the job. **1925** *AS* (Dec.) 139: She's a haywire rig. **1927** *DN* V 449: *Hay wire outfit,* n. One at which the workers are furnished with poor living facilities. **1938** Haines *Tension* 31: They was a little crank-and-cuss haywire telephone line running along the track by the station. **1941** *AS* (Oct.) 233: *Haywire.* A term used to denote anything and everything which is either poorly operated or poorly put together. **1944** V.H. Jensen *Lumber & Labor* 65: Small "family" operators, medium-sized "haywire" operators. **1958** McCulloch *Woods Wds.* 81: *Haywire*…Anything not up to snuff; a miserably poor outfit; anything broken or no good. **1979** Toelken *Dyn. of Folklore* 55: *Haywire outfit* any logging operation that uses lighter-gauge cable than the job demands; therefore…a company so parsimonious that it is willing to endanger the lives of its men.

2.a. out of order, proper condition, or control; awry; impaired; ruined; ill; unsound; amiss.—often constr. with *go.*

1920 *DN* V 82: *Hay wire.* Gone wrong or no good. Slang. **1925** in Hammett *Big Knockover* 206: A hombre that lets a bronc dirty him up three times hand-running and then ties into a gent who tries to keep him from making it permanent ain't exactly haywire. **1925** *AS* (Dec.) 139: "Haywire" has always been a common word among American camp men…."The outfit's gone haywire." "I feel haywire all over." These are expressions I have heard since boyhood. The loggers apply the word to everything from Calvin Coolidge to the calks in their boots. **1929** in *OEDS*: When some element in the recording system becomes defective it is said to have gone haywire. **1930** Botkin *Folk-Say* 106: I don't think me eyes were haywire, look some more. **1930** *AS* V (Feb.) 238: *Go hay-wire:* to get out of form. "The captain went haywire in his golf-game." **1931** Haycox *Whispering Range* 221: I think somethin's haywire in all this schemin'. **1935** Coburn *Law Rides Range* 110: There's some sort of an old adage about the plans of mice and men often going haywire. **1937** in Galewitz *Great Comics* 220: Our radio-phone has gone haywire, too. **1940** W.R. Burnett *High Sierra* 93: But if things go haywire or if anything should happen to me, just read the letter and you'll know what to do. **1941** in Boucher *Werewolf* 121: My reflexes are all haywire. **1951** Styron *Lie Down in Darkness* 39: Isn't it enough that I've got all this, without something else going haywire? **1953** Brossard *Bold Saboteurs* 134: Their plans went haywire. **1963–64** Kesey *Great Notion* 113: Something is really haywire with them. **1967** Moorse *Duck* 138: O'Grady…put us onto the idea about the end of the world. I mean, we figured something was pretty haywire, but we didn't quite know what it was. **1970** A. Walker *Copeland* 59: His life, as it was destined, had "gone haywire." **1983** *N.Y. Post* (Sept. 2) 46: My life seems to be going haywire. **1987** Pres. R. Reagan, on *NBC Nightly News* (Apr. 23): It's no secret that I wear a hearing aid. Last week it went haywire. **1995** *Jerry Springer Show* (synd. TV series): Once you don't communicate, then things can go haywire.

b. *Specif.*, mentally deranged; crazy.

[**1920** (quot. at HAYWIRED).] **1926** Finerty *Criminalese* 29: Haywire—Mental trouble. **1928** Hall & Niles *One Man's War* 47: Besides, there was a short-legged fellow in our platoon who was going "haywire." **1930** Lait *On Spot* 204: Haywire…Crazy. **1933** Hecht & Fowler *Great Magoo* 82: He hears Julie singing your sonata and goes haywire. **1936** R. Chandler, in Ruhm *Detective* 127: I've got an idea. It may be all haywire….But I'd like to try it out. **1938** Holbrook *Mackinaw* 3: He never looked inside [an almanac] and was sure that anyone who did was haywire. **1945** S. Lewis *C. Timberlane* 91: You're not *that* haywire! **1955** Archibald *Aviation Cadet* 127: I got a little haywire and forgot to report the emergency. **1967** Lockwood *Subs* 38: Gasoline fumes are…as intoxicating as 40-Rod Kentucky moonshine. Sniff enough and the whole crew will go haywire. **1976** Univ. Tenn. student: My God! I'm going haywire! *a***1989** in Kisseloff *Must Remember This* 535: The hungrier you get…the more haywire you become.

haywired *adj.* HAYWIRE, 2.b.

1920 in Hemingway *Selected Letters* 40: I tore my gut on a cleat…and had internal hemorrhages….They thought I was haywired tho for a while though.

haze gray *adj.* [in allusion to a standard naval camouflage color] *Navy.* (see 1971 quot.).

1971 Murphy & Gentry *Second in Command* 54: Gene H. Lacy, our chief warrant officer, was "haze gray"—all Navy. **1988** Schneider & Schneider *Sound Off!* 128: But many a woman, enlisted or officer, still struggles for sea duty, "haze gray and under way."

HCL *n. Journ.* high cost of living.

1917 *Lit. Digest* (Apr. 28) 1284: H.C.L. Baffled. **1920** *Amer. Leg. Wkly.* (July 16) 12: An undertaker in a Minnesota town fought the H.C.L. by taking the agency for a sewing machine. **1972** *CBS News* (WCBS-TV) (July 21): The HCL goes up less.

head *n.* **1.** the mouth (as a source of offensive or inappropriate talk).—constr. esp. with *open* or *shut*.

1848 *Life in Rochester* 85: If you see anything about it you don't like, you've got to keep your head shut, and not say a word about it. **1849** in *OEDS:* But don't you open yer head about it to no other indiwiddiwal. **1851** M. Reid *Scalp Hunters* 33: Who the h—l asked you to open your head? *Ibid.* 81: Shet up yur heads, an' wait. **1856** *Spirit of Times* (Mar. 8) 37: Shut your head. **1864** in Northrop *Chronicles* 30: Shut your heads, its nothing but a d—d nigger let a span of horses loose. **1873** Payne *Behind Bars* 175: Shut up your — head. **1880** *Harper's Young People* (Dec. 7) 82: I won't open my head if every one of 'em's bad. **1883–84** Whittaker *L. Locke* 147: Shut up your head. You're too cheeky by half. **1889** Harte *Dedlow Marsh* 11: Shut your head. Go to bed. **1892** Garland *Spoil of Office* 93: Every man stay at home and not open his head. **1893** F.P. Dunne, in Schaaf *Dooley* 48: An' he'll find it out th' next time he opens his head to me in that parnicious manner. **1898** Bullen *Cachalot* 87: Only yew keep yer head tight shut, an' nebber say er word, but keep er lookin', 'n sure's death you'll see. **1900** Johnston *Hus'ling* 339: Shut up! Shut up!…Don't you open your infernal head again. **1900** Hammond *Whaler* 382: Don't yeh open your head to me ag'in about no discharge. **1912** in Truman *Dear Bess* 89: If I'd only kept my head shut about K.C. **1927** Faulkner *Mosquitoes* 215: If he opens his head again, David, just knock him right out of the boat. **1928** Scanlon *God Have Mercy* 101 [ref. to 1918]: Hancock was shooting his head off about the Kaiser being the whore that sat on seven hills and caused the war. **1930** Sage *Last Rustler* 150: The old man

began to run off at the head in an unusual way. **1933** W.C. MacDonald *Law of .45's* 19: Tucson's runnin' off at the head again, Mr. Hayden. **1983** S. King *Christine* 284: Give me that bottle and shut your head.

2. a headache caused by overindulgence in alcoholic beverages; hangover; in phr. **have a head on** to have a hangover.

*****1869** A. Trollope, in *OEDS:* Don't you know how one feels sometimes that one has got a head? *****1888** R. Kipling, in *OEDS:* The "head" that followed after drink. *****1889** in *OEDS:* In the pleasing vernacular of the modern youth about town, he has a "head" on him. **1889** Bailey *Ups & Downs* 91 [ref. to *ca*1870]: He didn't show up until the last moment, and then he claimed that he had such a "head" on him that he was afraid of drawing attention at the bank. **1892** *Outing* (Mar.) 439: Curious-looking little apples, that when eaten in abundance made one dizzy and drunk and gave one a regular champagne "head" next day. **1896** Ade *Artie:* I've got a peach of a head. **1902** "J. Flynt" *Little Bro.* 121: He "had a head on" the morning they were brought before him for a hearing. **1921** Dos Passos *Three Soldiers* 39: "Gee, Bill, I've got a head," said Fuselli. "Ye're ought to have….I had to carry you up into the barracks." **1934** Weseen *Dict. Slang* 277: Head—After-effects of intoxication. **1956** Algren *Wild Side* 128: He had a big bad head and held it hard, mourning, "Oh, it drinked dandy but Lord the afterwards." **1954–60** *DAS: Head, have a.* To have a hangover; to feel as though one's head is swollen and throbbing, owing to overindulgence in alcoholic beverages. **1989** Spears *NCT Slang Dict.* 175: How do you get rid of a head so you can go to work?

3.a. a person; individual, without special reference to the mind.—usu. constr. with prec. adj. [Cf. *OED* def. 7.a.; modern usage is prob. abstracted from S.E. *old head* 'a person of much experience; old hand; old-timer', as in bracketed quots.]

[**1874** Flipper *Colored Cadet* 14: He says there are many "old heads" who believe Flipper will graduate with honor.] [**1877** Pinkerton *Maguires* 87: I am fully convinced you are all right, an "old head." *Ibid.* 91: You are too old a head not to understand.] [**1920** Bissell *63rd Inf.* 23: And there were "old heads" at the Presidio who were always willing to teach neophytes all the fine points.] [**1922** Tully *Emmett Lawler* 142: Take an old head's tip and do that.] **1924** in D. Hammett *Continental Op* 137: Wise head. Playing safe. **1928** Guerin *Crime* 85: Some of the "heads" had heard about me and took me off to Newmarket racing. **1943** R. Chandler *High Window* 445: Morny's a good head. **1945** in Kluger *Yank* 310: What a bunch of heads! **1942–49** Goldin et al. *DAUL* 92: *Head*…Any person. **1954** Mirvish *Texana* 128: That Nick is a right good head. **1955** *AS* XXX (May) 119: *New head, n. phr.* Man who has been in the outfit a relatively short time. **1958** Gilbert *Vice Trap* 8: They've got a new bunch of heads in here. **1958** J. Davis *College Vocab.* 5: *Bad head*—One who can't take a joke. *ca***1965** in Schwendinger & Schwendinger *Adolescent Subcult.* 191: A bitchen guy….He's a cool [i.e., likable] head….Acts like us. **1968** Maule *Rub-A-Dub* 37: "How is he?" "Seems like a pretty good head." **1973** Andrews & Owens *Black Lang.* 86: *Heads*—another name for dudes or cats. **1976** "N. Ross" *Policeman* 132: This particular month, we had a cushion of heads (that is,…a sufficient amount of arrests to coast the rest of the period). *Ibid.* 73: She'll give you a couple of heads, and those heads will give you more heads, until you find the main squeeze. **1978** Pici *Tennis Hustler* 7: So what kind of a head is he, Artie? **1979** *Easyriders* (Dec.) 6: My stepfather…happens to be a pretty cool [i.e., likable] head. **1988** Poyer *The Med* 65: You seem like a good head. **1993** P. Munro *U.C.L.A. Slang* 2: *Head* n. person. *A bunch of us heads chipped in ten bones each.* **1995** Stavsky, Mozeson, & Mozeson *A 2 Z* 46: *Head*…gang member: I knew there'd be trouble when I saw the ride full of heads pull over.

b. *Und.* an illegal immigrant.

1929–33 J. Lowell *Gal Reporter* 153: This is his racket. He runs "heads" in from Cape Verde Islands. *Ibid.* 164: That…gang of head runners are under arrest!

c. a young woman or girl; woman.—usu. used with prec. adj.

1933 Hammett *Thin Man* 302: She's a wise head—plenty smart. **1941** *New Yorker* (Apr. 26) 24: Morty meticulously refers to all youngish women as "heads," which has the same meaning as "broads" or "dolls" but is newer…."One head…used to claim to sell stockings…'Five o'clock,' this head said." **1951** H. Robbins *Danny Fisher* 304: Sam's secretary would be a good-looking head, and Sam hadn't changed a bit. **1958** Camerer *Damned Wear Wings* 218: She reminded Johnny of a finely bred Italian head in a Lake Como layout in *Harper's Bazaar*. **1963** T.I. Rubin *Sweet Daddy* 135: There were a couple nice heads....Yeah, a couple chicks. **1963** Cameron *Black Camp* 105: She wasn't a bad-looking head. **1968–70** *Current Slang III & IV* 66: *Head*, n. A woman with definite sex appeal. **1970** S.J. Perelman, in *New Yorker* (Oct. 17) 39: Some of those Chinese heads are pretty zoftick. **1978** Selby *Requiem* 22: No kiddin Angel, do ya ever get anything special in here, like some young good lookin heads? **1979** in Terkel *Amer. Dreams* 220: We got a couple of hookers. They were good-lookin' heads. **1982** Condon *Prizzi's Honor*: Ed copped a feel from a nice-looking young head standing just in front of him.

4. fellatio or cunnilingus; in phr. **give head** to perform fellatio or cunnilingus.—usu. considered vulgar.

1941 G. Legman, in G. Henry *Sex Vars.* II 1168: *Head*. A generic noun or predicate nominative referring to a fellator, as, e.g., "looking for head." Term reported from Montreal in 1940. **1956** in R.S. Gold *Jazz Lexicon* 142: She's wild, man! Gives the craziest head! **1962** in Wepman, Newman & Binderman *The Life* 47: I flipped when she gave me some head. **1964** Rhodes *Chosen Few* 174: She likes a little head once in a while, too...you ever eat any? **1965** Ward & Kassebaum *Women's Pris.* 99: What we call *giving some head* (oral-genital contact). **1968** *Playboy* (May) 64: "A man who refuses to "give head to his woman" denies her (and himself) an exquisite dimension of her sexuality. **1969** Tynan *Oh! Calcutta* 102: She gives me some head and then I give her some. **1969** L. Sanders *Anderson Tapes* 172: And no head in the morning. **1972** *Anthro. Ling.* (Mar.) 107: *Serve head*...To perform fellatio. **1976** Braly *False Starts* 160: Should I start swishing and putting out head? **1977** Corder *Citizens Band* 81: I hear she gives good head. **1977** *Rolling Stone* (Dec. 1) 23: When we first came to New York she gave us all head. **1991** B.E. Ellis *Amer. Psycho* 101: I'm on my knees giving her head. **1993** "Pansy Division" *James Bondage* (pop. song): Strapped to a four-poster giving him head. **1994** *Details* (July) 64: Madonna's iconography has equated cunnilingus with top-woman-ship....Demanding head was a way to be sexy.

5. [sugg. by S.E. sense, 'a shipboard lavatory'] Orig. *Naut. & USMC*. any lavatory; toilet.

1942 *Leatherneck* (Nov.) 146: *Head*—Latrine. In civil life, "the little boys' room." **1943** Sherrod *Tarawa* 38: That's why the Japs build their heads (toilets) over the water. **1944** Kendall *Service Slang* 24: *Head*....lavatory. **1944** Huie *Can Do!* 158: What few heads—Navy for latrine—they had built were nothing but shallow holes just outside their huts. **1951–52** P. Frank *Hold Back Night* 32: Running water, and real houses, and indoor heads. **1955–57** Felder *Collegiate Slang* 3: *Head*—the toilet. **1958** Frede *Entry E* 100: What brought him...was a trip to the head. **1961** Terry *Old Liberty* 16: I...went out in the hall and down to the head. **1963** Westlake *Getaway Face* 19: In the head, inside the diner. **1972** N.Y.U. student: Up at Rhode Island [U.], the guys always used to call the bathroom "the head." *ca*1933–74 E. Mackin *Didn't Want to Die* 174: What's the news from the "head"? **1981** C. Nelson *Picked Bullets Up* 47: Kurt, there's a head down the hall. Why don't you take a shower? **1993** J. Watson & K. Dockery *Point Man* 45: Tip acted as if he wanted to...flush me down the head. **1996** McCumber *Playing off Rail* 237: Did you knock that off the board while I was in the head?

6. [short for *head arrangement*] *Jazz*. an unwritten, esp. improvised, arrangement of a musical piece.

[**1946** Blesh *Shining Trumpets* 251: "Head" arrangement....A memorized, not written, arrangement, that leaves ample room for improvisation.] **1953–58** J.C. Holmes *Horn* 193: But maybe if we do a whole set of heads, old ones—. **1971** Wells & Dance *Night People* 23 [ref. to *ca*1935]: Because the music was a lot of "heads," and if it wasn't, some of Benny Carter's music was pretty rough, and you couldn't play it. *Ibid.* 117: *Head*, n. An oral [*sic*] arrangement. **1986** Clayton & Elliott *Jazz World* 43: So all we could do was to...play "heads" all night. Heads are arrangements made on the spur of the moment with no music.

7.a. *Narc.* a drug-induced state; HIGH, *n.*, 1.a.

1952 H. Ellson *Golden Spike* 194: The drug...got him a "head" and made him feel better. **1965–70** J. Carroll, in *Paris Rev.* (No. 50) 109: A nice codeine head. **1970** Wertheim & Gonzalez *Talkin' About Us* 45: Get some dope/Get a head. **1970** Cole *Street Kids* 83: It's not bad, it gives you a good head. It makes you feel like flying, and you see things like god and angels. **1970** Thackrey *Thief* 25: Pot is great stuff for just getting your head. But some things, you got to use the firewater. Right!

1980 Novak *High Culture* 190: Jamaican pot..."has a quick head," a dealer told me, which means that the high comes and goes fairly swiftly.

b. (one's) sense of emotional or mental well-being; way of thinking; state of mind.

1962 in Wepman et al. *The Life* 140: Brought some reefer and got my head up tight. **1966** Braly *On Yard* 180: I think he's trying to play with my head. **1966** in Wepman et al. *The Life* 69: This act alone shook their heads. **1969** Mitchell *Thumb Tripping* 184: Where's your head at now, Mr. Vic? Wow, just groove behind it. **1970** Southern *Blue Movie* 227: Exactly where Maude's *head* is at this particular moment—that is to say, the full extent of her mania. **1970** *Playboy* (Nov.) 77: My head is still a little crooked and I'm still very much motivated by my emotions. **1972** N.Y.U. student: Western civilization has been in this head for two thousand years and it's about time it got out of it. **1972** Kerr *Dinky Hocker* 82: Hasn't your own head ever been messed up? **1975** S.P. Smith *Amer. Boys* 76: Didn't have no year in no Fulda to get their heads all nasty. **1976** Price *Bloodbrothers* 147: Everybody's in a very heavy neighborhood head. **1977** Rutgers Univ. student: What kind of a head are you in? **1987–89** M.H. Kingston *Tripmaster Monkey* 48: Change one's head, change the universe. **1994** *My So-Called Life* (ABC-TV): Just to mess with your head.

8. [nominalization of -HEAD, *comb. form*, 1] *Narc.* a habitual user of psychotropic or hallucinogenic drugs. [The 1967 *Esquire* quot. is erroneously dated "1937" in E.L. Abel, *Marihuana Dict.*]

1953 Anslinger & Tompkins *Traf. in Narc.* 311: *Head*. A drug addict. **1957** Murtagh and Harris *First Stone* 52: No percentage, little girl, selling junk to other junkies. What you have to do is make a couple new heads. *Ibid.* 305: *Head*. A drug user or addict. **1957** H. Simmons *Corner Boy* 45: There was pod for the light heads, boy and girl for the mainliners and now snow for the sniffers. **1958–59** Lipton *Barbarians* 316: *Head*—A marijuana user, pot head. **1959** *Life* (Nov. 30) 116: ["Beat talk"] substitutes "Spade" for Negro, "head" for narcotic user, and utilizes the word "like" as a means of beginning almost any sentence. **1959–60** R. Reisner *Jazz Titans* 158: *Head*: old-time marijuana user. **1961** R. Russell *Sound* 16: If Hitler and Mussolini had of been heads, there never would have been no Big Scuffle on the other side. **1963** Coon *Short End* 146: I hadn't thought much about the fact that we had a lot of heads in the company. **1966** Goldstein *1 in 7* 11: He met all the campus "heads," or frequent pot users. **1967** Rechy *Numbers* 56: The bar...attracted exiles of every breed: dykes, queens, hustlers, "heads," even famous movie stars. **1967** *Esquire* (Sept.) 192: These were the real heads. **1972** Wambaugh *Blue Knight* 160: One of the other vice officers...looked like a wild young head, with his collar-length hair, and beard, and floppy hat with peace and pot buttons all over it. **1976** *Harper's* (Dec.) 94: All we know is pigs and heads. **1984** Mason & Rheingold *Slanguage*: *Head*, n....One who smokes a lot of marijuana and/or does a lot of drugs in general. **1985** T. Wolfe, in *Rolling Stone* (Feb. 28) 48: Eyeing the drunks and heads. **1994** *New Yorker* (Nov. 7) 213 [ref. to 1960's]: To the assorted heads and freaks who hung out there, it was the Mecca...of hippie chic.

9. [sugg. by S.E. *head [of the penis]* 'glans penis'] the erect penis; (*hence, rare*) sexual intercourse as experienced by a woman.—usu. considered vulgar.

1954–60 *DAS*: *Head*...the erect penis....*Head, give [her] some* (taboo). To have sexual intercourse with a girl. **1967** in Wepman, Newman & Binderman *The Life* 137: You better get down on your knees and slobber my head. **1968** Vidal *Breckinridge* 106: Having strapped on a formidable dildo because, as he said, "You got to have head," he was able to give her maximum pleasure. **1970** M. Thomas *Total Beast* 88: Another convict...clutched his own crotch with both hands. "I got it right here if you're a head feeler, Florence, baby!" **1971** Dahlskog *Dict.* 31: *Head, give (slide) (someone) some*, vulgar. To have intercourse with a girl.

10. facial appearance.—usu. constr. with *bad*.

1961 Brosnan *Pennant Race* 14: [She's got] choice wheels...but, ooh, a bad head. **1963** in P. Dickson *Baseball Dict.* 196: Men who are considered to have "the bad head" include Rocky Bridges, Don Mossi and Yogi Berra. **1967** *Lit Dict.* 2: *Bad head*—An ugly, ugly, ugly face.

¶ In phrases:

¶ **do something [standing] on (one's) head** to do (something) with ease.

*a1890–93 F & H III 285: To do on one's head…(thieves').—To do easily and with joy. *1896 G.B. Shaw, in OEDS: Of course, Mr. Waring does the thing on his head, so to speak. *1897 Conrad Nigger of Narcissus ch. i: It's a 'omeward trip.…Bad or good I can do it hall on my 'ed. 1911 A.H. Lewis Apaches of N.Y. 67: I could do it standin' on me head. *1922, *1923, *1944, *1968 in OEDS. 1994 Knoxville, Tenn., man, age ca50: You can do that standing on your head.

¶ **get (one's) head bad** [or **right**] Black E. to get intoxicated from liquor or drugs.

1962 in Wepman, Newman & Binderman The Life 47: We got our heads bad and left the pad. 1971 Black Scholar (Apr.) 35: That a baaaad nigger when he gets his head bad. 1975 S.P. Smith Amer. Boys 313: And I was just gettin' a little buzz. I want to get my head bad tonight. 1980 Eble Campus Slang (Oct.) 3: Get one's head right—Get high: "I guess I'll get my head right this weekend" (frequently used by blacks). a1984 in Terry Bloods 83: They had been drinking and…got their heads bad. a1994 N. McCall Wanna Holler 331: We gonna freak this skank when her head gets bad.

¶ **get (one's) head cut in** R.R. to begin thinking sensibly.

1942 Sat. Eve. Post (June 13) 27: You handle the valve like a cub does marbles. Why don't you get your head cut in? 1958 McCulloch Woods Words 80: Has his head cut in—A man who is a clear thinker; from the railroad slang to cut in the air brakes on a train, and thus have some control over it.

¶ **get (one's) head straight** to start thinking clearly or behaving normally.

[1970 Wexler Joe (film): If your head's on straight like yours is, it's a game.] 1970 in H.S. Thompson Shark Hunt 88: My head was not straight at that stage of the investigation. Two weeks of guerrilla warfare with Jean-Claude Killy's publicity juggernaut had driven me to the brink of hysteria. 1974 in Mad Super Special (No. 64) 34: Get your head straight and cool it, you dig? 1992 Sonya Live! (CNN-TV) (June 26): I was trying to get my head straight about who I was.

¶ **get (one's) head together** see TOGETHER, adv.

¶ **give head, 1.** see (4), above.

2. see (9), above.

3. to speak insincerely or flatteringly to. Cf. HEAD JOB, 2.

1965 C.D.B. Bryan P.S. Wilkinson 185: "Listen, you're not just giving me head about Charlie, are you?" "No. No, he really got married."

¶ **go soak your head!** (used as a sarcastic retort).

1870 in Leitner Diamond in Rough 102: A general hoot and a suggestion to "soak your head." 1882 Peck Peck's Sunshine 281: Said they were all [crazy], and had better soak their heads. 1911 Van Loan Big League 66: Aw, go soak your head! 1955 N.Y.C. schoolchildren: Aw, go soak your head! Go jump in the lake! 1972 Cleaves Sea Fever 55: Aw, go soak your head.

¶ **have (one's) head screwed on right** [or **straight** or **tight**] to have good sense.

*1820–21 P. Egan Life in London 221: A well-known dashing Prig, whose head was considered to have been screwed on the right way. 1864 in Horrocks Dear Parents 104: Right William. I thought you wanted your head screwing on tighter but I find it will do at present. *1936 Partridge DSUE 738: Screwed on right or the right way, have one's head. To be shrewd and businesslike; be able to look after oneself: coll.: mid-C. 19–20. 1973 in J. Jones Reach 352: His head is screwed on right, despite the semi-hippy exterior. 1975 McKennon Horse Dung Trail 240: The boy has his head screwed on right. 1984 McNamara First Directive 53: The kids…saw her as someone with her head screwed on right. 1989 CBS This Morning (CBS-TV) (May 22): The biggest challenge for someone with Peter's gifts is keeping his head screwed on right.

¶ **have (one's) head up and locked** [sugg. by have (one's) head up [or in] (one's) ass s.v. ASS, and up and locked '(of landing gear) fully retracted and secured'] Mil. Av. to be inordinately stupid or inattentive.

1944 in Howard & Whitley Island 225: A bottle of burning gasoline was thrown under a nearby P-47, the Hed Up 'N Locked. 1961 Forbes Goodbye to Some 153 [ref. to WWII]: The pride of Hamtramck with his head up and locked, as usual. 1964 Newhafer Last Tallyho 23 [ref. to WWII]: At the time your head was securely up and locked, a position most unbecoming to an air group commander. 1977 Baa Baa Black Sheep (NBC-TV): I guess my head was up and locked.

¶ **have (one's) head up** [or **in**] **(one's) ass** see s.v. ASS.

¶ **have (one's) head wedged** to be very stupid or mistaken.

1966 Time (June 3) 22: I believe that Johnson has his head wedged; the war is political suicide. 1968 Baker, Ladd & Robb CUSS 135: Head wedged, have your. To be mistaken or stupid. 1966–69 (quot. at GOONED).

¶ **have rocks in (one's) head** see s.v. ROCK, n.

¶ **off the head** Gamb. (see quot.).

1945–50 in D.W. Maurer Lang.Und. 187: Off the head means paid before expenses are deducted.

¶ **on (one's) head** very angry.

1938 T. Wolfe Web & Rock 42: Well, you don't need to go gettin' on your head about it.

¶ **pull** [or **get**] **your head out!** [fr. have (one's) head up [or in] (one's) ass s.v. ASS] Mil. start paying attention!

1942–44 in AS (Feb. 1946) 34: Pull your head out., v. "Pay attention to what you are doing." 1944 M. Hart Winged Victory (film): You better get your head out tomorrow night. 1985 Boyne & Thompson Wild Blue 68: Get your head out and get this clunker started. a1987 Bunch & Cole Reckoning for Kings 158: Get your head out and start worryin' less. a1987 Coyle Team Yankee 254: Waiting for…their commander to pull his head out and give them some orders. 1991–5 Sack Co. C 178: Let's go!…Pull your heads out!

¶ **put a head on** to administer a beating to; drub.

1868 in DA: One calls the other a "regular dead beat!" at which he, in return, threatens to "put a head on him." 1869 in DAE: The…proprietor…volunteered to "put a head" on the man who fired the pistol. 1870 Overland Mo. (Jan.) 86: They've got one bully boy there now—Custer—and he's puttin' a head on them Injuns. 1872 Burnham Secret Svc. vii: Put A Head On, to punish; to bruise (A new cant term). Ibid. 415: Oh, I wish you was here. I would put a head on you, bigger 'an a twenty-shillin' bean pot. 1872 Alger Phil 295: If you don't give it to me I'll put a head on you. 1878 Flipper Colored Cadet 297: "That's right, Clark; kill the d—d nigger," "Choke him," "Put a head on him." 1881 Small Farming 16: Whoop! Sind out yer ould woman, 'till I'd put a head on her, too. 1883–84 (quot. at SKIP, v.). 1885 Siringo Texas Cowboy 81: One of them finally "put a head on me"—or in grammatical words, gave me a black eye. 1891 Maitland Slang Dict. 213: Put a head on (Amer.), to punch or assault another. ca1894 McCloskey Across the Continent 72: I'll put such a head on you that yer mother wouldn't know ye. 1921 in DA: If you open your mouth again…I will put a head on you.

¶ **run (one's) head** to talk at length or out of turn.

1970 M. Thomas Total Beast 61: All you head-running bunch of punks think you can fuck with me,…huh? 1981 Easyriders (Oct.) 56: One of the things I liked about him, really, was that he didn't run his head all the time or fight his case twenty-four hours a day.

¶ **shrink (someone's) head** to administer psychotherapy, esp. psychoanalysis, to (someone). Cf. HEADSHRINKER.

1954 Sherdeman Them (film): I've already told those head-shrinkin' doctors four different times. 1961 Kanter & Tugend Pocketful of Miracles (film): I oughta have my head shrunk doin' a thing like this. 1971 Barnes Pawns 106: Oh, yeah…we gave him some pills and we shrunk his head. 1984 McNamara First Directive 154: Why don't they quit their crummy jobs…and get sane so they won't need their heads shrunk?

¶ **where (one's) head is** what mood (one) is in; (also) what (one) means or enjoys.

1971 Simon Sign of Fool 7: My attention slowly drifted back to what Richie was rapping about. I had a fair idea now of where his head was. 1973 R. Poole Mack (film): That's not even where my head is. I been trying to get away from shit like this.

head v. [fr. HEAD, n., 4] to perform fellatio or cunnilingus on.— usu. considered vulgar.

1975 Harrell & Bishop Orderly House 80: I suggest we head each other or sixty-nine. 1975–77 in Fine With Boys 172: Head me.…suck my willie.

¶ In phrase:

¶ **tell (someone) where to head in** to rebuke or admonish (someone).

1912 Field Watch Yourself Go By 410: I'll durn soon tell you whar to head in. 1914 Ellis Billy Sunday 252: He decided to go out and tell

Goliath where to head in. **1918–19** MacArthur *Bug's Eye View* 94: Kline Gray and his gang began telling all the officers where to head in. **1921** McAlmon *Hasty Bunch* 150: She hasn't the ginger to tell old Frank where to head in at. **1923** O'Hare *In Prison* 123: We mighty quick told them where to head in, and they soon got an earful and beat it. **1934** Boylan & Baldwin *Devil Dogs of the Air* (film): It's about time this mug learned where to head in. **1956** G. Green *Last Angry Man* 17: Why doesn't someone tell 'em where to head in?

-head *comb. form.* **1.** a person habituated or addicted to (a specified kind of alcoholic beverage or psychotropic drug or substance). See also citations at other headwords, as BASEHEAD, COKEHEAD, HASHHEAD, HOPHEAD, POTHEAD, etc.

    1930 in Leadbitter & Slaven *Blues Records* 475: Whiskey Head Man. **1936** Duncan *Over the Wall* 21 [ref. to 1918]: Canned heat stiffs, paregoric hounds, laudanum fiends, and…the veronal heads. **1949** *Harper's* (Aug.) 96: The heroin-head smiled virtuously. **1952** Mandel *Angry Strangers* 320: You're drunk like a sakihead missionary. **1955** in Leadbitter & Slaven *Blues Records* 8: Wine Head Woman. **1966** "Petronius" *N.Y. Unexp.* 37: Agreeable outer space mixture from nutmeg heads to missionaries from Zanzibar. **1992** *N.Y. Rev. of Bks.* (July 16) 23: That part of a basehead's time not actually involved in the preparation and ingestion of the drug is spent in the search for and acquisition of more of it.

2. a devotee or enthusiast of (something specified in the initial element). See also citations at other headwords, as DEADHEAD, METALHEAD, etc.

    1960 L. Buckley *Hiparama* 7: The Reed Heads, the Lute Heads, and the Flute Heads. **1966** "Petronius" *N.Y. Unexp.* 168: Dykes, comics,…pin-ball heads and many more. **1967** Wolf *Love Generation* 131: No, I'm sort of a Jap-head. I've got a lot of affinities toward what I've read about Zen and the discipline. **1972** *Playboy* (Sept.) 19: Happy Humping with Henry the Health-Head. **1976** *L.A. Times* (Oct. 21) VI 1: Americans who proudly refer to themselves as "chili heads." **1981** *Time* (Oct. 5) 43: Just as there are Bruce Springsteen heads, there now are Kamali heads. **1993** *Source* (July) 43: All hip-hop heads. **1995** *Newsweek* (Aug. 21) 51: A number of Deadheads over the years became Tourheads, following the band from gig to gig.

headache *n.* one's wife or girlfriend. *Joc.*

    1933 Hecht & Fowler *Great Magoo* 25: That little headache of yours with the honky-tonk eyes is trouble—plenty. **1936** *Esquire* (Sept.) 162: "Meet the headache" (meet the wife) … [is] among … [Jack Conway's] improvisations that are now standard in American slanguage.

headache *interj. Constr.* (used as a warning to beware of esp. falling objects).

    1944 *AS* XIX 231: Headache…a warning to look up and beware of objects moving overhead. **1947** *PADS* (No. 9) 32: Headache…A cry or shout from a mechanic who is working high around a [petroleum] distillery when he wishes to drop a heavy object, such as a wrench. **1949** *AS* XIV 33: In [oil] rig building the cry *headache* is a signal to run when something falls. **1961, 1967, 1968** in *DARE*. **1973** *Everett* (Wash.) *Herald* (June 9) 4A: He heard someone on the ground scream "Headache! Headache!"—a code word among tower workers meaning something's falling. **1979** Hurling *Boomers* 122: He opened his mouth to shout "Headache!" as the chipping gun fell out of his hands.

headache ball *n. Constr.* a wrecking ball. Cf. earlier sense in *DARE* 'heavy steel ball that hangs from the crane cable to keep it taut'.

    1979 Hurling *Boomers* 133: I signaled the crane operator to pick me up on the headache ball. *a*1981 H.A. Applebaum *Royal Blue* 24: The demolition ball was called a "headache" ball.

headache bar *n.* (see quot.).

    1991 Reinberg *In the Field* 103 [ref. to *ca*1970]: Headache bar…the protective safety bar in the roof over the driver's seat in a Rome plow.

headache post *n. Petroleum Industry.* (see 1937, 1944, 1947 quots.).

    1887 in *DN* II 341: Headache-post…Designed to save the driller a head-ache, or perhaps his life in case the wrist-pin should break. **1925** Dobie *Hunting Ground* 65: The…"headache post"…is…a big beam that goes up and down over a well that is being pumped. **1937** *AS* (Apr.) 154: Headache-post. Post to hold front end of walking beam from coming down into the rig. **1944** Boatwright & Day *Hell to Breakfast*

148: A post set under the walking beam to catch the sucker rods in case the pitman breaks on a standard rig is the "headache post." **1947** *PADS* (No. 9) 32: Headache post: n. Any type of protection for the head of a driver of a truck whose cab may be crushed by loads he receives or carries. **1951** Pryor *The Big Play* 74: The driller did not even have to glance at the log sheets or at the pegboard near the headache post which served as a scorekeeper. **1970** Boatright & Owens *Derrick Floor* xiii: The headache post…would keep [a beam] from falling on you when you was there at the throttle running the engine.

headache rack *n. Trucking.* a rack positioned over or behind the cab of a truck to prevent injury from shifting cargo.

    1969 in *AS* XLIV 205. **1971** Tak *Truck Talk: Headache rack:* the heavy meshwork grill on the rear of a cab that protects it from damage from a load that may shift forward. *a*1977 W.I. Little *Transp.-Logistics Dict.* 157: Headache rack. An extension of a holding rack over the cab from the trailer. Normally used for holding pipe or such freight. **1982** in *DARE*.

headache stick *n.* a stick used as a club; a billy club.

    1919 White *Negro-Amer. Folk-Songs* 361: I want to century [i.e., earn a hundred dollars] just one more time./I don't bother no man but the man with the headache stick. **1932** L. Berg *Prison Doctor* 111: His "headache stick" was both a scepter and an instrument of punishment. **1934** L. Berg *Prison Nurse* 57: You sure swing a mean "headache stick." **1972** Grogan *Ringolevio* 160: He didn't notice Kenny take the headache-stick away from his partner.

headbanger *n.* **1.** a fan of heavy-metal rock music; (*hence*) a heavy-metal musician. Also **headbang,** *v.* to dance to heavy-metal music.

    1979 in *OEDAS* II: This is where the fans keep in trim for concerts, practising the subtle art of headbanging. *1979 in *OEDAS* II: Their fans are long-haired headbangers. *1980 in Partridge *DSUE* (ed. 8) 541: Headbangers—the zombies' revenge. **1984** J. Green *Dict. Contemp. Slang* 134: Head-banger…a fan of…"heavy metal music," usu. a denim-clad, patch-bestrewn youth who plays a make-believe guitar and shakes his head violently as he watches or listens to his heroes. **1985** "J. Blowdryer" *Mod. Eng.* 18: Headbanger…Describes…rabid fans…of heavy metal music. **1986** B. Breathed *Bloom Co.* (syndic. comic strip) (Nov. 20): Welcome, fellow profit-minded headbangers. I'm only interested in experienced, down 'n' dirty, grim 'n' grimy heavy-metal musicians now. **1987** *Campus Voice* (Winter) 27: The Los Angeles-based band attracts everyone from headbangers and punks to students. **1988** *N.Y. Post* (June 21) 25: Inside Metal Mania. A mom's-eye view of rock's headbangers. **1990** *Current Affair* (synd. TV series): Guess who's coming to defend the heavy-metal headbangers? *a*1991 D. Weinstein *Heavy Metal* 130: Headbanging involves a downward thrust of the head with a gentler upthrust. **1992** *Northern Exposure* (CBS-TV): Who else's mom knew how to headbang?

2. a violent person. Cf. HEADBEATER.

    1991 McCarthy & Mallowe *Vice Cop* 196: Head-bangers…and… sleazeballs.

headbeater *n.* a brutal police officer who beats suspects with a nightstick; (*hence*) *Black E.* a police officer.

    1958 *Life* (Apr. 14) 127 [ref. to *ca*1950]: I take aim. Bam! Scratch one headbeater! *Ibid.* 128: The headbeaters would stop any group of five or more boys on suspicion of unlawful assembly. **1959** *Swinging Syllables: Head beater*—Policeman. **1970–71** Rubinstein *City Police* 279: There are policemen who develop reputations among their colleagues as "headbeaters" or "headhunters," but they are relatively rare. **1974** Gober *Black Cop* 106: You don't go callin' them red-neck headbeaters on your own kind.

headbone *n.* [earliest quot. reflects OE *hēofod bān;* no continuity of usage has been shown between ME and recent exx.] the skull; (*hence*) the mind.

    *a*1400 in *OED2*: He…Made the Sarazenes hede bones Hoppe. **1933** in Lomax & Lomax *Our Singing Country* 24: An' de neck bone jump to de head bone. **1952** in *DAS*: This boot you got stuck on yo' headbone…is gotta come off! **1967–72** Weesner *Car Thief* 67: You gonna get silly in the fuckin headbone, man. **1973** N.Y.U. prof.: That hypothesis is only valid if you make some sort of assumption about the human headbone. **1989** Spears *NCT Dict. Slang* 175: I got a nasty bump on my headbone.

head bucket *n. Mil.* a steel helmet. Cf. BRAIN BUCKET, 2.

    1942 E. Colby *Army Talk* 101: As soon as they began to be issued to the troops [in 1942], soldiers…gave the new name "head bucket" to the new article. **1944** *Slanguage Dict.* 51: *Head bucket*—deep steel helmet issued to soldiers.

headbuster *n.* **1.** a blackjack.

    1930 Mae West *Babe Gordon* 255: An' put dat head-buster away.

    2. HEADBEATER. Also **headbreaker.**

    1959 W. Miller *Cool World* 14: Why you think the headbreakers usen a Colt if it no good? **1961** Lehman *West Side Story* (film): Them headbusters ain't got no manners. **1965** Yurick *Warriors* 29: The General wanted to know if the driver wanted some hard-hand head-buster…to break a few against his beak. **1966** S. Harris *Hellhole* 148: She still ain't about to turn me in to the headbreakers. **1971** Horan *Blue Messiah* 237: Three generations of head busters! **1977** Torres *Q & A* 66: I've been a headbuster, I don't deny it. **1987** Blankenship *Blood Stripe* 232: I'll come back with some of the best head-busters in the MP's.

head-candler *n.* a psychotherapist. Hence **head-candling,** *n.* psychotherapy.

    1955 Reifer *New Words* 99: *Head-candler n. Slang.* A psychologist who examines people on a mass basis, as in the armed forces. **1964** Hill *One of the Casualties* 54: Sigmund is for the jaybirds.…That head-candlin jazz is okay for well-heeled nuts that can afford twenty bucks an hour couch rent, maybe, but I got a sneaky suspicion nobody comes out ahead but the head-shrinker.

head case *n.* a person undergoing or in need of psychiatric treatment; lunatic.

    *1966 P. Townshend *I'm a Boy* (pop. song: "The Who"): My name is Bill and I'm a head case. **1966** L. Heller *Flight of Phoenix* (film): They ain't gonna let no head case run a drillin' operation. **1982** Sculatti *Catalog of Cool* 58: A deranged head case. **1985** Va. man, age 26: Every one of 'em's a head case. **1986** *Miami Vice* (NBC-TV): You keep talkin' like that, you're gonna turn yourself into a head case. **1987** Blankenship *Blood Stripe* 133: Glory hunters. Drug addicts. Head cases. *a*1988 D. Smith *Firefighters* 137: Wally was a bit of a head case, though…without a hint of neurosis.

head check *n. Mil.* a psychiatric evaluation.

    1987 Blankenship *Blood Stripe* 150: The post psychiatrist gave him a head check and kicked him loose.

head cheese *n.* **1.** a boss; BIG CHEESE.

    1913 J. London *Valley of Moon* 175: The Head Cheese sizes me up…an' gives me an application blank.

    2. (see 1941 quot.).—usu. considered vulgar.

    1941 G. Legman, in G. Henry *Sex Vars.* II 1168: *Head-cheese.* The preputial smegma in the male. **1942** McAtee *Supp. Grant Co. Dial.* 6 [ref. to 1890's]: *Head-cheese,* n. cheesy matter collecting under the prepuce behind the glans of the penis. **1981** in *DARE.*

head cock *n.* a man in charge; boss.

    1972 Pendleton *Vegas Vendetta* 137: Who'd you say is the head cock out there?

head devil *n.* a person in charge; boss; ringleader.

    1844 in Oehlschlaeger *Reveille* 58: The "head devil" jumped into the middle with…a pigeon-wing. **1863** in Hay *Lincoln* 138: Delahay is here all alive with the idea that there is a Chase conspiracy about the President of which Pomeroy is one of the head devils. **1891** Rodenbough *Sabre* 345: *Coa-co-chee*…then became the *"head devil"* of the real Seminoles, and swore vengeance. **1911** Spalding *Base Ball* 126: I knew that the Boston crowd would consider me the head devil in this secession movement.

head doctor *n.* a psychotherapist.

    1953 F. O'Connor *A Good Man Is Hard to Find:* It was a head-doctor at the penitentiary said what I had done was kill my daddy. **1956** in *OEDS:* "What's the matter with this guy?" "Nothing that a head doctor couldn't cure." **1959** on *Golden Age of TV* (A&E-TV, 1988): You talk too much for a head doctor. *a*1970 in Nachbar *Focus on Western* 79: You oughtta go see a head doctor! **1974** Loken *Come Monday Mornin'* 50: Guess it's just like that head-doctor said. **1974** V.B. Miller *Girl in River* 77: I've been listening to a lot of those head doctors on the radio. **1989** *Capital Gang* (CNN-TV) (Sept. 2): Next—the PTL's Jim Bakker: Off to see the head doctors.

header *n.* **1.** a headlong dive, jump, or fall.

    *1849 in *OED:* A "header" from the bank through a thin coat of ice.

    *1859 in *OED:* Four blacks one after the other took a header into the boiling current. **1885** "Lykkejaeger" *Dane* 30: A "header" into deep water. **1885** Ingersoll *Crest of Continent* 290: Chum sings: "Now is the time for disappearing," and takes a header out of the side door. **1888** Bidwell *Forging His Chains* 85: A "header" out of a car window, and escape in irons. **1895** *Harper's* (Nov.) 961: So if…he took a header his brain wouldn't suffer. **1902** Bangs *Bikey* 15: I knew a boy once who took a header just as you did…and turned a beautiful Roman nose into a stub nose. **1921** *Variety* (July 1) 5: He always took a coupla headers to make the other guy think he was a set up. **1928** *AS* III (June) 408: "To take a header" is to fall headforemost, headfirst, or headlong. **1934** in Ruhm *Detective* 92: A couple of more headers like that and you'll get your face lifted. **1949** Algren *Golden Arm* 98: She took a header and he hollered, "Leave her lay! She oney fainted!" **1956** Arthur *Return of Texan* 129: Neck's busted. Musta taken a header off the stairs. **1958** S.H. Adams *Tenderloin* 5: Did you ever take a header from one of those five-foot machines? **1975** V.B. Miller *Deadly Game* 81: He took a header into the gravel path behind the man.

    2. a head-on collision.

    1973 (quot. s.v. *down the tube* s.v. TUBE).

    3. an act of oral copulation, esp. fellatio.

    1976 "N. Ross" *Policeman* 162: The state had our stoolie for shaking down a dude who was patronizing a prostitute and then forcing the broad to give him a header. **1966–80** McAleer & Dickson *Unit Pride* 177: "Want to get laid, Joe?" "How about a header instead?" **1980** S.E. Martin *Breaking & Entering* 145: Come on, I have a room. I want a header.

head fake *n. Sports.* a feint made by looking momentarily in a direction other than that toward which a player intends to throw or run.

    1967 Baraka *Tales* 3: Change speeds, head fake, stop, cut back. **1972** in W. King *Black Anthol.* 95: He had a head fake like Red Beans. *a*1989 P. Dickson *Baseball Dict.* 196.

head-feeler *n.* a psychotherapist.

    1942 Pegler *Spelvin* 141: The fad of Viennese mind-probing [began with]…the hope of dirty people that some head-feeler would tell them that they could cure their nervousness only…in a cabin…with some other man's girl.

headfuck *v.* to confuse, mislead, or the like, esp. deliberately; MINDFUCK.—usu. considered vulgar.

    1978 Price *Ladies' Man* 211: I feel like you're fucking with my head.…I feel head-fucked. **1985** Frede *Nurses* 287: I told you, Trina. Don't pull that headfucking with me.

headfucker *n. Narc.* a powerful hallucinogenic or psychotropic drug; MINDBENDER.—usu. considered vulgar.

    1975 in Spears *Drugs & Drink* 254: Headfucker ["a potent head drug"]. *a*1989 Spears *NCT Slang Dict.* 176: This stuff is a real headfucker. Stay away from it.

head game *n.* usu. *pl.* MIND GAME; in phr. **run a head game on** to fool; con.

    1979 "Foreigner" *Head Games* (pop. song): No time ever seems right/To talk about the reasons why you and I fight.…I can't take it anymore…don't wanna play the head games. **1984** Ehrhart *Marking Time* 45: No…women trying to play head games with you. **1988** Schneider & Schneider *Sound Off!* 24: A process often described by military women as a "mind game" or "head game." **1991** Marcinko & Weisman *Rogue Warrior* 188: I had no…excuse for playing malevolent head-games on my superiors. *a*1994 N. McCall *Wanna Holler* 114: I had to run a head-game on myself. I had to shut down my mind. **1994** *Bold & Beautiful* (CBS-TV): You're playing head games with me!…It's manipulation!

head gasket *n.* a condom. *Joc.*

    1964 in Fry TS: "Head gaskets for hot rods." Graffito scratched on prophylactic vending machine in small town in Texas, as reported to me by a sophomore at the University of Oklahoma. **1973** *TULIPQ* (coll. B.K. Dumas): Birth control methods: The pill, rubber, (head gasket for a hot rod). **1976** *N.Y. Folklore* II 240: A prophylactic, commonly called a condom, may be jokingly called a *head gasket.* **1983** K. Weaver *Texas Crude* 76: *Head gaskets.…Condoms.*

head honcho see s.v. HONCHO.

head-hunt *v.* **1.** *Boxing.* to try to punch an opponent's head repeatedly.

1960 Hoagland *Circle Home* 60: He head-hunted, Santos did, looked to hit the mouth. **1989** P. Heller *Bad Intentions* 155: You're head hunting....Body shots first, then the head.

2. *Business.* to seek out for the purpose of hiring; recruit.

1965 in *OED2*: A dozen "head-hunting" firms. **1966** *Harper's* (Dec.) 90: Now with state money, faculty salaries have been jacked up a good thirty per cent, and we can do some real headhunting. **1971** *Business Week* (Mar. 6) 84: The recruiting or head-hunting profession demands a broad knowledge of business. **1983** (cited in J. Green *Dict. Contemp. Slang* 134). *a***1989** Spears *NCT Slang Dict.* 176: He went to the conference to head hunt a new employee.

headhunter *n.* **1.** *Mil. Av.* (see quot.).

1918 Bishop *Winged Warfare* 44: And I had heard of German "head-hunters," too. They are German machines that fly very high and avoid combat with anything like an equal number, but are quick to pounce down upon a straggler, or an Allied machine that has been damaged and is bravely struggling to get home.

2.a. *Labor.* a person employed to report on the performance of subordinates.

1937–41 in Mencken *Amer. Lang. Supp. II* 724: *Headhunter.* An efficiency man [in an automobile plant]. **1992** *Donahue* (NBC TV): They think that I'm a headhunter and I'm going to get them fired.

b. *Police & Mil.* an investigative officer belonging to an internal affairs division; SHOOFLY.

1965 Conot *Rivers of Blood* 235: In order to insure good conduct, he operated an investigative section of 19 "head hunters," who circulate anonymously, monitoring the behavior of deputies. **1974** Weisman & Boyer *Triple Cross* 15: There was some talk in Traffic that he was going to join the Headhunters. **1975** Wambaugh *Choirboys* 155: I wonder if Lieutenant Grimsley and all them IAD headhunters get a finder's fee when they nail a cop? *Ibid.* 367: This boy isn't fit to be interrogated by *anyone*, especially not the headhunters. **1978** *New West* (June 5) SC 24: Complaints of false arrest and serious brutality are investigated behind closed doors by the "headhunters" of the LAPD's internal-affairs division. **1981** Wambaugh *Glitter Dome* 83: The headhunters … were … able to absolve Captain Woofer of any charge of misconduct. **1986** Coonts *Intruder* 268 [ref. to 1972]: I want to be the first to hear what you're gonna tell that Pentagon headhunter tomorrow at your hearing.

3. *Business.* a person whose job it is to recruit employees, esp. for high-level corporate positions.

1954–60 *DAS: Head hunter.* The owner or boss of an executive employment agency; a business executive in charge of recruiting new personnel. **1962** *Time* (Oct. 26) 93: U.S. business has known no more indefatigable head-hunter than David Karr. **1963** *Sat. Eve. Post* (July 27) 34: Du Pont headhunters roam the campuses in search of bright new scientific talent. **1965** *Time* (Apr. 9) 100: Training them so rigorously that they are eagerly courted by the headhunters of big international companies. **1970** *Time* (June 22) 78: You're hot and everything you do works and they're calling you for a job and the headhunters are crying for you. **1970** Della Femina *Wonderful Folks* 116: Now he starts with the headhunters and asks them to start setting up appointments for him. **1977** *N.Y. Times* (Aug. 4) C3: A number of D/R executives were once employed by Habitat, thanks to a headhunter. **1983** *United Airlines Mag.* (June) 45: Corporate headhunters regularly report no trouble persuading job candidates to move.

4.a. *Boxing.* (see 1982 quot.). Cf. HEAD-HUNT. [Prob. the orig. sense.]

1970 La Motta, Carter & Savage *R. Bull* 174 [ref. to 1940's]: He was...a headhunter—he was always going for the other guy's chin. **1982** T. Considine *Lang. of Sport* 108: *Headhunter:* A boxer who punches mainly to the head and rarely throws a body punch. **1991** McCarthy & Mallowe *Vice Cop* 30: I'm not a headhunter. If you know what you're doing, go for the body.

b. *Police & Pris.* a brutal police or corrections officer who uses a billy club freely against suspects or convicts.

1966 King *Brave & Damned* 52: He'd been a head hunter, one of those club swinging, nut cracking guards at some state pen. **1970–71** (quot. at HEADBEATER).

c. *Baseball.* a pitcher who deliberately aims pitches near a batter's head to intimidate him. Hence **headhunting,** *n.*

1969 *Everett* (Wash.) *Herald* (May 13) 1C: Pitcher Fred Talbot drew a warning and automatic $50 fine for headhunting in the same inning.

1974 Perry & Sudyk *Me & Spitter* 120: Headhunting, begun by players long forgotten, somehow endured as an unbreakable habit. **1982** Luciano & Fisher *Umpire Strikes Back* 124: There are certain pitchers who are known as headhunters, there are other pitchers who won't throw at anybody. **1984** *N.Y. Post* (Aug. 16) 6: Beanballers vs Headhunters. **1990** *ALF* (NBC-TV): "They call the pitcher on the other team The Headhunter." "What does that mean?" "It means Brian will get on base tonight."

d. *Ice Hockey & Football.* an unnecessarily rough or violent player.

1976 *Webster's Sports Dict.* 207: *Headhunter.* A player who engages in unusually rough and violent play for the sake of being violent. In ice hockey, such a player may also be called a *hatchetman.* **1982** T. Considine *Lang. of Sport* 145: *Headhunter:* A [football] player known for excessive roughness or violence. **1984** A. Pincus *How to Talk Football* 40: *Head hunter…*a rough player, usually a defensive player, who is looking to put his opponent out of the game each time he hits him. **1991** Lott & Lieber *Total Impact* 95: Shawn Collins is saying in the other locker room that you're a headhunter.

5. a person who aggressively and singlemindedly pursues a selfish goal, esp. to the detriment of other persons.

1986 R. Walker *AF Wives* 64: She was a head hunter, checking up on the captain's eligibility. **1989** *CBS This Morning* (CBS-TV) (June 2): You've got too many [Congressmen] in either party who are headhunters now.

head job *n.* **1.** an act of fellatio or cunnilingus; (*hence*) a performer of oral copulation.—usu. considered vulgar.

1963 Coon *Short End* 197: Pankari's first head job contest. **1966** H.S. Thompson *Hell's Angels* 92: Nothing to look forward to but the chance of a fight or a round of head jobs from some drunken charwoman. **1966** C. Ross *N.Y.* 121: So let's just hustle up to the roof for a fast head job. **1971** Rader *Govt. Inspected* 72: I was in no mood for a head job. **1972** Wambaugh *Blue Knight* 163: Anyway, Reba ain't just a good head job. **1973** Hirschfeld *Victors* 78: She's as good a head job as you can find on the East side. **1981** Wambaugh *Glitter Dome* 172: A hot head job with the foxy little chippie.

2. an insincere or lying line of talk.—usu. considered vulgar.

1973 Spec. 5, U.S. Army, STRATCOM-Taiwan (coll. J. Ball): He's only been here a week and he's already giving me that old head job about the whore saying she felt like she ought to be paying *him!*

head knock *n. Black E.* HEADKNOCKER, 1; (*also*) God.

1944 Burley *Hndbk. Jive* 22: Me, the Head Knock, was really drug. **1946** Mezzrow & Wolfe *Really Blues* 150: We were up near the Head Knock's territory. **1958** in *DARE.*

headknocker *n.* **1.** a person having primary authority; boss, foreman, etc.

1896 Ade *Artie* 51: I'm goin' to be the head knocker in the push. **1944** Boatright & Day *Hell to Breakfast* 141: The manager of a field is officially the District Superintendent, but the hands will refer to him as the "kingfish," "head roustabout," "head knocker," or "the Man." **1964** Brewer *Worser Days* 117: But de headknocker of de board confab wid de ol' granpappy like dis. **1973** Ellington *Music Is My Mistress* xi: Ben Webster used to tell people to "See the 'Head Knocker.'" **1977** in McKee & Chisenhall *Beale* 162: And the head knockers, see, they had barns set up all over, where they'd send the mens out from, on calls.

2. a person who employs force or violence in the exercise of authority; (*also*) HEADBEATER.

1966 H.S. Thompson *Hell's Angels* 53: Tiny, the Oakland chapter's sergeant at arms and chief head-knocker. **1980** *AS* (Fall) 197: Policeman...*fuzz...head knocker.*

headlamps *n.pl.* the eyes.

a*1858** A. Mayhew *Paved with Gold* 189: Ned waltzed out of the way, administering a "full stop" on Jack's "head-lamps." **1978** W. Brown *Tragic Magic* 29: I could feel the heavy wattage...from the head lamps of the dudes in the chow hall. **1986** *UTSQ:* Eyes...*head lamps.*

head-lanyard *n. Naut.* a queue.

1823 J.F. Cooper *Pioneers* 281: It would have been more shipshape to lower the bight of a rope...than to seize an old seaman by his head-lanyard; but I suppose you are used to taking men by the hair.

head-laundry *n.* a place where brainwashing is practiced. *Joc.*

1967 "M.T. Knight" *Terrible Ten* 186: In that case, let's drag them down to the head-laundry and start scrubbing their brains.

headlight *n.* **1.** usu. *pl.* an eye.

    1870 in Somers *Sport in N.O.* 163: [His strategy was] to shut off Allen's head-lights. **1899** Robbins *Gam* 154: Their head-lights stuck out so you could hang your hat on 'em. **1903** *Pedagog. Sem.* X 371: You'll get your headlights smashed in. **1967** *Lit Dict.* 20: *Head Lights*—Your eyes. **1985** Univ. Tenn. grad. student, age 35: I once heard a guy say, "I'm gonna hit you on the back of the head so hard it'll knock your goddam headlights out." He was an auto mechanic.

    2. an ostentatious gem, esp. in a stickpin.

    1899 A.H. Lewis *Sandburrs* 285: Of course, d' spark ain't d' real t'ing; only a rhinestone; but it goes in d' Bend all d' same for a 2-carat headlight. **1902** Cullen *More Tales* 150: A four-carat headlight in his shirt front. **1904** *DN* II 397: *Headlight*, n. A diamond scarf-pin. Slang. Ithaca. **1908** *DN* III 319: *Headlight*, n. A diamond, a solitaire. "I see she's got a *headlight* on her finger." Slang. **1949** in *DAS:* That headlight she wore on her finger is the size that poor people can't buy. **1958** Hynd *Con Man* 147: He swaggered through the streets in loud suits and headlight stickpins. **1978** *Gamblers* 54: A ruffled white shirt whose bosom sparkled with a huge stud—sometimes a diamond, sometimes a fake—called a "headlight."

    3. usu. *pl.* a woman's breast.

    *ca*1919 in Winterich *Mlle. from Armentières* (unp.): She waggled her headlights and caboose. **1942** H. Miller *Roofs of Paris* 44: You can't class the headlights she sports with the accessories that most women carry. **1943** in J. Gunther *D Day* 256: See the headlights on those girls; aren't they terrific? **1944** Kapelner *Lonely Boy Blues* 110: That's her, Harry! The one with the big headlights! **1949** Mende *Spit & Stars* 225: She got a pair of headlights on her that'll take your eyes out. **1954** Wertham *Innocent* 178: Her headlights are showing *plenty*. **1984** Mason & Rheingold *Slanguage: Headlights.* n. Nipples and/or breasts. **1987** F. Ray & T. Lankford *Hollywood Chainsaw Hookers* (film): He said that he was very happy with the headlights.

    4. *pl.* eggs. *Joc.*

    1927 *AS* (June) 389: Eggs are *headlights*.

head-peeper *n.* HEAD-CANDLER.

    1981–85 S. King *It* 418: See a doctor, Hanlon. The head-peeper kind of doctor.

headphones *n.pl. Med.* a stethoscope. *Joc.*

    1980 *AS* (Spring) 49.

head-piece *n.* **1.** the head; (*hence*) the mind. Orig. *S.E.*

    *1579 E. Spenser, in *OED:* In his headpeace he felt a sore payne. *1588 in *OED:* Not lurking in the obscure head-pieces of one or two loytering Fryers. *1613 in *OED:* The hurt...which was feared had somewhat crazed his headpiece. *1627 in *OED:* One...Hood doth fit the head-piece of divers Actors. **1671** in *DARE:* I have used my best skill & hedpes to discover anything that might tend to the hurt of o[u]r nation. *1677 in D'Urfey *Two Comedies* 181: His wit is hereditary. Ah! his father...had a notable head-piece. *1741 S. Richardson, in *OED:* You have an excellent head-piece for your years. **1806** Webster *Compendious Dict.: Headpiece...*understanding. *1821–26 Stewart *Man-of-War's-Man* I 17: Don't you think poor Ralph's headpiece is in a sad taking?...the little brain he ever had is leaving him fast. *Ibid.* II 171: It...[never] entered my head-piece. **1871** Small *Parson Beecher* 11: He...whistled Yankee Doodle...as well as his damaged head-piece would allow. *1899 Whiteing *John St.* 237: Whose head-piece does the plannin'? **1900** Willard & Hodler *Powers That Prey* 144: I got a head-piece on me, I have. **1901** Irwin *Sonnets* (unp.): I possessed a headpiece like a tack. **1910** Hapgood *City Streets* 327: You're a good guy, but your head-piece isn't right, or you'd know de reason why you can't git away from de Lane. **1924** in Hemingway *Sel. Letters* 137: He's got a headpiece so that when you tell him a thing once he does it. **1944** Busch *Dream of Home* 50: With a headpiece like you got, you...have to be afraid of...truant officers. **1965** E. Hopkins *Lower Depths* 15: My headpiece hums. **1967** in *DARE*. **1994** "Notorious B.I.G." *Gimme the Loot* (rap song): Don't let me throw my clip up in your back and head-piece.

    2. *Naut.* the face.

    1827 J.F. Cooper *Red Rover* 162: "Had he a thieving look?...was he a man that had the air of a sneaking runaway?" "As for his head-

piece...he had the look of one who had been kept, a good deal of his time, in the lee-scuppers."

head pin *n. R.R.* (see quots.).

    1930 *R.R. Man's Mag.* II 470: *Head Pin*—The head brakeman. **1945** Hubbard *R.R. Ave.* 346: Front brakeman on a freight train who rides the engine cab...*head pin*.

head push *n.* a person in charge. Cf. PUSH, *n.*

    1913 Jocknick *Early Days* 39 [ref. to 1870's]: Hartman...[was], practically, the "head push." *Ibid.* 85: Our wagon boss, the "head push," as we called him.

headquarters pimp *n. Army.* a headquarters clerk.—used derisively.

    1864 in Geer *Diary* 184: Had some trouble with Hd Qr. pimps in regard to the details.

head queen *n. Homosex.* (see 1972 quot.).

    1949 *Gay Girl's Guide* 11: *Head-Queen:* Homosexual whose chief operating areas are toilets. **1972** *Anthro. Ling.* (Mar.) 103: *Head queen...*A male homosexual who "cruises" public restrooms.

head-rails *n.pl. Naut.* the teeth. *Rare* in U.S.

    1767 "A. Barton" *Disappointment* 78: If one word goes through my head-rails, the devil blow me to jillkicker. *1785 Grose *Vulgar Tongue: Head Rails.* Teeth. *Sea Phrase.* *1805 J. Davis *Post-Captain* 161: "What a pair of top-lights!" "What head-rails, Harry!" *1829 Glascock *Sailors & Saints* II 197: It's not the first time Bob Brace has held on by his head-rails.*...*Teeth. *1854 in *F & H* III 288: Your head-rails were loosened there, wasn't they?

head-raping *n.* (see quots.).

    1956 H. Gold *Not With It* 108: "I've got a new specialty, Buddy boy. Head raping." "Phrenology?" "Tells the truth through contact with the spirits that live on dandruff." **1968** Poe *Riot* (film): You guys plannin' a head-rapin' [brainstorming] session, huh?

head-rigging *n. Naut.* **1.** a covering for the head.

    1858 [S. Hammett] *Piney Woods* 127: The Major made a grab at Pond's head-riggin' and away went...Pond's bandanna.

    2. the head or mind.

    1862 J.S. Warner *Albion* 92: What are you thinking of, Jim?...Something's got foul in your head-rigging.

head-set *n.* a state or frame of mind; pattern of thought; mood; mindset.

    1976 R. Price *Bloodbrothers* 243: Really, it's like a split wit' that whole head set. **1976–77** McFadden *Serial* 110: It brought back Spokane and that whole head-set. **1984** Univ. Tenn. instructor: You need to get into a very different head-set to understand where third-world people are coming from.

head shed *n. Mil.* a headquarters; (*also*) (see 1982 quot.).

    1963 E.M. Miller *Exile* 134: This move will soon get the large kiss of imprimatur from the Midget Men in the Head Shed at the Potomac Puzzle Palace. **1966–68** *Current Slang I & II* 50: *Head shed...*the superintendent's office.—Air Force Academy cadets. **1978** Buchanan *Shining Season* 107: I just follow the rules the head-shed hands down. **1980** Duncan & Moore *Green Side Out* 7 [ref. to 1957]: Monk...offered to...introduce me to some of the "Pogues in da head shed." **1980** W.C. Anderson *Bat-21* 59: We're lining up our ducks at the head shed. **1982** F. Hailey *Soldier Talk* 32: *Head shed.* Intelligence officer's interrogation tent (S-2). **1989** Zumbro & Walker *Jungletracks* 12: Who's your buddy up at the head shed?

headshrink *n.* HEADSHRINKER.

    1969 Girodias *New Olympia Reader* 67: Fuck headshrinks. **1973** Childress *Hero* 17: Social workers and head shrinks don't take kids home to their house after they get through plantin dumb ideas. **1980** M. Baker *Nam* 41: They made me go see two head shrinks. **1991** R. Brown & R. Angus *A.K.A. Narc* 146: I didn't have to be a head shrink to know that.

headshrinker *n.* a psychotherapist, esp. a psychoanalyst.

    1950 *Time* (Nov. 27) 19: During his early years in Hollywood, anyone who had predicted that he would end up as the rootin'-tootin' idol of U.S. children would have been led instantly off to a headshrinker.*...*Hollywood jargon for a psychiatrist. **1955** Stern *Rebel Without a Cause* (film): "You know if the boy ever talked to a psychiatrist?" "You mean a headshrinker." **1957** Laurents & Sondheim *West Side Story* 207: So take him to a headshrinker. **1958** T. Capote *Break-*

fast at Tiffany's 18: I know this idiot girl who keeps telling me I ought to go to a head-shrinker; she says I have a father complex. **1960** Wohl *Cold Wind* 13: What would a head-shrinker say about that? **1961** Grau *Coliseum St.* 194: I don't need a head shrinker….I'm not crazy. **1963** D. Tracy *Brass Ring* 305: I c'ld explain it like the goddam headshrinker inna hospital at Cannes did. **1968** W. Crawford *Gresham's War* 52: I am a psychiatrist, a headshrinker, very true. I also happen to be an officer in the United States Navy. **1973** Childress *Hero* 10: School-teachers, social workers and head shrinkers tag names on me and go to generalizin. **1978** I.M. Marks *Fear* 209: I wish the doctors and head shrinkers would get together and agree. **1995** *Leeza* (synd. TV series): There's my headshrinker! One of 'em! Hi!

headshrinking *n.* psychoanalysis; psychotherapy. Also attrib.

    1966 Samuels *Baby* 122: I charge fees for longer head-shrinkin'. **1970** *Harper's* (Feb.) 65: Those in New York with rooms of their own…being the support of an immense headshrinking industry. **1971** *Harper's* (Apr.) 104: They are right…to look beyond the conventional wisdom of the headshrinking trade.

head smack *n. Narc.* a dose of heroin inhaled through the nose. Also as v.

    1973 Browne *Body Shop* 5: *Head smack:* sniff of heroin. *Ibid.* 90: It's nights like these I wouldn't mind a head smack….In Nam, I was sniffing two vials a day. *a***1986** K.W. Nolan *Into Laos* 382: *Head smack:* To snort heroin through the nose.

head space *n.* mood; frame of mind.

    1996 Leicht *Co-Ed Call Girl* (film): It puts them in the right head space to tackle the student body.

heads-up *n. Pol.* a warning. Also attrib. Now *colloq.*

    1989 T. Clancy *Clear & Pres. Danger* 319: The shooters got a heads-up for an important job several days ago. **1990** Stoll *Cuckoo's Egg* 125: My boss wanted me to call our funding agency, the Department of Energy—"Give them a heads-up." *a***1991** Kross *Splash One* 254: Got a heads-up from the public information officer…about a negative story running in the States. **1994** *Time* (Aug. 1) 21: He gave White House officials a "heads up" briefing on the RTC probe. **1994** *N.Y. Times* (Nov. 6) IV 2: He took care, too, to send an early heads-up to his Pentagon and Congressional overseers. **1995** *New Yorker* (Apr. 17) 64: Commissioners were left to decide whether a document or a media contact or a political request required a heads-up to City Hall.

heads-up *adj. Esp. Sports.* wide-awake; alert. [The 19th-C. quots. are evidently to be taken literally, i.e., 'holding one's head erect'.]

    [**1834** Caruthers *Kentuckian in N.Y.* I 29: There I sat with my feet drawn straight under my knees, heads up, and hands laid close along my legs, like a new recruit on drill.] [****1838** Glascock *Land Sharks* II 24: In anything but a "head's up" posture.] **1934** Weseen *Dict. Slang* 211: *Heads-up ball*—Good baseball playing. **1939–40** Tunis *Kid from Tomkinsville* 184: I want this club to play heads-up, percentage ball. **1940** R. Buckner *Knute Rockne* (film): You played a great game all year—smart, heads-up football. **1944** F.G. Lieb *Cardinals* 164: Frisch always played hard-driving, heads-up baseball. **1951** Willingham *Gates of Hell* 32: Lanky had *not* been playing exactly a heads-up ball game. **1953** Sher *Kid from Left Field* (film): They used to play heads-up ball, but they don't anymore. **1970** Byrne *Memories* 87: I want you to play heads-up ball and hit the open man. **1975** Durocher & Linn *Nice Guys* 11: I don't call that cheating; I call that heads-up baseball. **1972–79** T. Wolfe *Right Stuff* 80: As all heads-up pilots knew. *a***1989** Micheels *Braving Flames* 93: If one heads-up guy had been there to say, "Hey, watch the wires."

heads up *interj.* look alive! watch out!

    1914 *Collier's* (Aug. 1) 7: Heads up, you guys!…We ain't licked yet. **1940** R. Buckner *Knute Rockne* (film): Jackie! Heads up! [warning of ball falling].

head trip *n.* **1.** Orig. *Narc.* a drug-induced reverie; (*hence*) a fantasy.

    1966 I. Reed *Pall-Bearers* 152: Avant-garde muggle-smoking and head trips. **1967–68** von Hoffman *Parents Warned Us* 40: Some users…want to go on a "head trip"—that is, spend the time they're high thinking about themselves. **1972** *N.Y. Times Mag.* (Oct. 1) 68: Crumb is creating a whole new way of thinking, a whole new head trip. **1978** J. Reynolds *Geniuses* 42: All these things are just headtrips, just intellectualizing. **1981** in D.K. Weisberg *Children of Night* 112:

[The] strange head trips people have. **1992** D. Burke *Street Talk* I 74: She's on a real head trip. She thinks she's the smartest person in class.

    2. a matter that requires or challenges thought; (*also*) MIND GAME.

    1971 Adelman *Generations* 47: I really don't know what particular thing they're into, but I know I'll get a chance to get into a heavy head trip. **1985** E. Leonard *Glitz* 196: They can tap their toes if they want, but it's a head trip too. **1992** *Vanity Fair* (Sept.) 304: The estrangements and head trips your family has put you through.

    3. deception or flattery.

    1986 *Stingray* (NBC-TV): You know that head trip you're tryin' to run on us? It ain't gonna work.

head-trip *v.* to indulge in fantasy.

    1972 Kopp *Buddha* 129: The breakdown of the social-expectation games and intellectual head-tripping. **1978** B. Johnson *What's Happenin'?* 40: He's just head-trippin', man.…We ain't goin' nowhere the way he's treatin' us. *a***1986** in *NDAS:* Man seeks companion for head-tripping, studying together, Scrabble, etc. **1987** Estes *Field of Innocence* 97: Can you dig the stars? Makes you just wanna kick back and head trip.

head-tripper *n.* a psychotherapist.

    1979 Alibrandi *Custody* 289: I'm not going to Dr. Stafford, or any other head-tripper!

headwhipper *n. Black E.* HEADBEATER.

    1974 R.H. Carter *16th Round* 62 [ref. to early 1950's]: Headwhuppers are people—cops. **1979** D. Glasgow *Black Underclass* 100: Police are seen as bandits, thugs, and "head whippers."

headworks *n.* Orig. *Naut.* the head; the mind.

    1823 J.F. Cooper *Pilot* 195: I believe the best man among them can't measure much over a fathom, taking him from his headworks to his heel. **1823** J.F. Cooper *Pioneers* 395: Ay! I know him, and if he hasn't got all the same as dead wood in his head-works, he knows sum'mat of me. *a***1899** in Paget *Poetry of Wit* 152: But something was the matter with my headworks.

healthy *n.* [short for *healthy swing*] *Baseball.* a powerful swing at a pitched ball.

    1914 in R. Lardner *Round Up* 343: Elliott takes his third healthy and runs through the field down to the clubhouse. **1922** in Bak *Turkey Stearnes* 86: A batter … took such a "healthy" that he fell down. **1939** in P. Dickson *Baseball Dict.* 197: He walked to the plate and took his healthy.

heap *n.* **1.** a large amount or number; "a ton." Also pl. Now *colloq.*

    a*1661** in *OED2:* A heap of castles. *****1741** in *OED2:* What a heap of hard names does the poor fellow call himself! **1810** in *DARE:* They say there is a *heap* of people moving this fall. **1821** Wetmore *Pedlar* 6: Massa wants one a heap. *Ibid.* 7: You've got a *heap* of larnin stranger. **1829** in M. Mathews *Beginnings of Amer. Eng.* 106: Heap. Much—a great quantity or number. *Southern and Western States.* As "it is a *heap* colder to day." A *heap* of pains, a *heap* of dollars. **1832** [M. St.C. Clarke] *Sks. of Crockett* 109: It made me feel in a heap better humour. **1848** [W.T. Thompson] *Jones's Sks.* 22: Wimmin…say a heap, jest to see what you'll say. **1850** *Spirit of Times* (Jan. 26) 581: It was…heap too good for him. **1855** in *Calif. Hist. Soc. Qly.* VIII (1929) 345: Italians and a heap of others. **1865** in S.C. Wilson *Column South* 298: She sends heaps of love. **1894** in Bierce *Letters* 35: I hope you are…having "heaps" of rest and happiness. **1925** *Sat. Eve. Post* (Oct. 3) 54: Spud looks a whole heap more fit than he did. *ca***1938** in Rawick *Amer. Slave* II (Pt. 1) 236: I heard 'bout them a heap.

    2. a large amount of money; PILE.

    *a***1834** in *OED2:* To go to church in New York in any kind of tolerable style costs a heap a-year. **1836** in Eliason *Tarheel Talk* 276: I would not be in their places for a heap. **1854** Soulé, Gihon & Nisbet *Annals of S.F.* 632: To labor lustily for so many months, accumulate another nice little "heap," then descend upon San Francisco, to leave it shortly afterwards upon steamer-day.

    3.a. a motor vehicle, esp. if old or slow; automobile.

    1921 *DN* V 114: *Heap, n.* An automobile, especially if old. A heap of junk. Machine shop; college students. **1927** in Hammett *Knockover* 311: Get that damned heap away from the front door. **1928** Hammett *Red Harvest* 37: I saw Mrs. Willsson's heap standing in the street. **1929** in Grayson *Stories for Men* 62: We got room in the heap. **1929** Booth

Stealing 196 [ref. to 1917]: You see, the "heap" is actually stolen in another state, but is registered in this one a *month* before it's reported missing in the other state. **1936** in Weinberg et al. *Tough Guys* 10: "They stole my heap!" the taxi-driver shrieked. **1938** Chandler *Big Sleep* 65: He's outside in my heap. **1951** O'Hara *Farmers Hotel* 67: I got two freezing broads out in that heap of mine. **1953** Felsen *Street Rod* 29: I didn't know this heap could go fast enough to slide on gravel. **1958** J.B. West *Eye* 8: A Caddy coupé.…Yeah. That was a real heap. **1959** *Twilight Zone* (CBS-TV): You're just like this heap! **1967** Spillane *Delta* 7: It took a punk kid in a stolen heap…to smash me through a store window. **1981** Graziano & Corsel *Somebody Down Here* 130: I give 'im my heap so he can ride in a classy car.

b. an old or slow vessel or aircraft.

   1941 Kendall *Army & Navy Sl.* 7: *Heap*.…an airplane. **1979–81** C. Buckley *To Bamboola* 71: How had this rotten old heap kept afloat so long?

heap of coke *n.* [rhyming slang] *Und.* BLOKE, 1.

   *****1851** H. Mayhew *London Labour* I 418: Have a touch of the *broads* with me and the other heaps of *coke* at my *drum*. **1919** T.A. Dorgan, in Zwilling *TAD Lexicon* 43: Its the rhyming slang…Heap o' coke that's a bloke. **1928** Sharpe *Chicago May* 288: *Heap of coke*—bloke. **1943** Holmes & Scott *Mr. Lucky* (film): You're a girl: *twist and twirl.* I'm a bloke: *heap o' coke. Ibid.:* The heap o' coke? Joe Baskopolous.

hear *v.* to understand fully; (*often*) agree with completely.

   1963 R. Serling *Seven Days in May* (film): "Mention that to General…Scott when he's up before you this morning." "I hear ya." **1967** Walnut Ridge, Ark., high school football coach & players (coll. J. Ball): "Get out there and score, or I'll have you doing wind sprints till noon tomorrow!" "We hear you." **1976–77** McFadden *Serial* 177: "Oh, man, I *hear* you," Ms. Murphy said. "I really, *really* hear you. Boy, I can just *imagine* the space you're in." **1977** in Rice *Adolescent* 273: I *hear* you—I understand completely. **1978** Univ. Tenn. students: "The Bama game's always wild." "I hear you." **1980** in *Barnhart Dict. Comp.* I (1982) 62: They say "I hear you," meaning "I understand what you're saying." **1987** *Miami Vice* (NBC-TV): "We're not gonna find it." "I hear that."

hearker var. HARKER.

hearse *n.* **1.** a gloomy, pessimistic person.

   1880 Grant *Frivolous Girl* 114: One girl had nicknamed him "the hearse," on account of his habitual pensive melancholy.

2.a. a police patrol wagon.

   1892 Norr *China Town* 51: I was just getting into the hearse after being sentenced when Ida ran up.

b. an old car.

   1920 T.A. Dorgan, in Zwilling *TAD Lexicon* 108: If they took longer than 10 minutes to put that hearse together that you have they were loafing on the job. **1938** *AS* XIII 315: *Hearse.* A high large old "crate." **1986** in *DARE.*

c. *R.R.* a caboose.

   1930 *R.R. Man's Mag.* II 470: *Hearse*—Caboose.

hearse driver *n.* **1.** a gloomy, pessimistic person.

   1894 in F. Remington *Selected Letters* 209: Well you old hearse driver.

2. *Faro.* a case-keeper. Now *hist.*

   *a***1943** in D.W. Maurer *Lang. of Und.* 137: *Hearse-driver.* The *case-keeper* in a faro game. **1979** E. West *Saloon* 48 [ref. to *a*1900]: A "case keeper," or "hearse driver,"…sat across the table with an abacus-like device that showed which cards had been played.

heart *n.* **1.** *Und.* a combination of audacity and recalcitrance, esp. in a criminal; nerve, esp. in defying the law or legal authorities. Cf. broader S.E. sense, 'courage or spirit'.

   1937 Hellman *Dead End* (film): Aah, you just ain't got any heart. You shoulda slugged her. **1939** Wald et al. *Roaring Twenties* (film): No heart, huh? **1942–49** Goldin et al. *DAUL* 92: *Heart.* A combination of courage and underworld loyalty. **1958** Horan *Mob's Man* 6: Me, the guy they said had more heart than any guy in the numbers racket. **1958** *Jour. Social Issues* XIV (No. 3) 25: "Heart" or courage in fighting is the most highly prized virtue.…To demonstrate "heart" it is not necessary to give the other fellow a decent chance or to show forbearance toward an outnumbered or defeated enemy. **1958** Salisbury *Shook-Up* 25: Heart, well, that's when a bop isn't afraid of anything or anybody.…He will do absolutely anything.…Chico has more heart than anybody I ever saw. He's crazy, that boy. *Ibid.* 34: They judge by

the same false standards of "heart" and "punking out." **1959** E. Hunter *Conviction* 198: "They all got heart," Big Dom said. **1966** J. Mills *Needle Park* 21: He had great skill and daring in burglaries—what junkies call "heart." **1966** in *Amer. Sociol. Rev.* XXXII (1967) 215: *Argot*:…Got heart. *Current Definition:* Has guts, bravery. **1972** J. Mills *Report* 93: They lost their heart. That's an expression on the street. You lose your heart. You're afraid then, because you know what can happen. **1973–74** in *Urban Life* VI 140: When you're a take off artist you have to be cold. You gotta show your heart. You gotta show you're not scared to…kill this person if he gives you any hassle. **1978–89** in Jankowski *Islands in Street* 49: We don't care nothing about whether he can fight or if he got no heart (courage). **1995** *Donahue* (NBC-TV): This young boy had a lot of heart, what we call "heart."

2. usu. *pl. Narc.* a roughly heart-shaped tablet, usu. of an amphetamine.

   1965 Verme *Helping Youth* 119: Benzedrine drugs…are also known as…"hearts." **1967** J.B. Williams *Narc. & Halluc.* 113: *Hearts*—"Benzedrine" or "Dexedrine" (brands of amphetamine sulfate and dextroamphetamine sulfate, Smith, Kline and French laboratories) heart-shaped tablets. **1970** *Sat. Rev.* (Nov. 14) 21: *Hearts.* Dexedrine tablets. **1971** *Go Ask Alice* 51: This heart will pep you up like tranquilizers slow you down. **1972** *Nat. Lampoon* (Oct.) 41: Benzedrine 10 mg. (heart). **1973** Gent *N. Dallas* 229: "Jake used to take codeine and hearts.".…Hearts were Dexedrine or Dexamyl tablets.

¶ In phrase:

¶ **have a heart!** show mercy! show some consideration!

   1917 (quot. at *for the love of Mike* s.v. LOVE). *****1917** in *OED2.* **1931** Farrell *McGinty* 169: Come on, Mac, have a heart. **1953** Paul *Waylaid* 170: "You have a way with women—of setting them off like Roman candles." "Have a heart," Finke said, gruffly. **1995** N.Y.C. woman, age 60 [to an annoying pet]: Lucy! Have a heart!

heart and lung *n.* [rhyming slang] (see quot.).

   1928 Sharpe *Chicago May* 287: *Heart and lung*—tongue.

heart attack *n.* In phrase: ¶ **serious as a heart attack** extremely or foolishly serious, esp. in demeanor.

   1970 in Van Peebles *Sweetback* 75: Shit Serious As A Heart Attack. **1982** *Time* (Nov. 8) 92: Two expressions have popped up this summer: *serious as a heart attack* and *That's Kool and the Gang.* **1984** Univ. Tenn. grad. student: Yes! He was serious as a heart attack. **1987** Lipper *Wall St.* 182: Money's as serious as a heart attack. **1995** *New Republic* (Mar. 13) 27: Newt [Gingrich] is not funny. Newt is as serious as a heart attack.

heartbeat *n.* **1.** *Stu.* HEARTTHROB.

   1935 Lorimer & Lorimer *Heart Specialist* 190: Hello, heartbeat, this your bag? **1938** Epstein & Coffee *Four Daughters* (film): Emma! Here comes your heartbeat!

2. a split second; usu. in phr. **in a heartbeat** without hesitation; immediately; (*hence*) unquestionably.

   1984–85 in Schneider & Schneider *Sound Off!* 24: Put on your PT things. You have a heartbeat to do it. *Ibid.* 214: If I was single I would stay in a heartbeat. **1988** Halberstadt *Airborne* 131: *Heartbeat:* a basic measure of time. **1990** *Essence* (Apr.) 26: You see your boyfriend flirting with another sister [woman] at a party, and in a heartbeat you march up to them and go off. **1991** *Sally Jessy Raphaël* (synd. TV series): "Could he be cheating on her?" "In a heartbeat." **1992** Gov. Bill Clinton, in *Time* (July 20) 24: He could stop this stuff [*sc.* negative campaigning]…in a heartbeat. *a***1994** N. McCall *Wanna Holler* 43: See you in a heartbeat.

Heartbreak Hotel *n.* [alluding to "Heartbreak Hotel," rock-and-roll song (1956) by Mae Boren Axton, Tommy Durden, and Elvis Presley] a prison.

   1984 Cunningham & Ethell *Fox Two* 39 [ref. to Vietnam War]: If it had gone off…they would have been eating pumpkin soup in the Heartbreak Hotel [in Hanoi] shortly thereafter. **1990** Crow Dog & Erdoes *Lakota Woman* 166 [ref. to 1973]: That jail with the goons jokingly called "Heartbreak Hotel."

heart burner *n.* (see quot.).

   1897 *Chi. Trib.* (July 25) 15: The Kansas Dialect.…*Heart Burner*—A drink of liquor—"Let us drop into a Topeka drug store and take a heart burner."

heartthrob *n.* a person with whom one is infatuated; (now *usu.*) a male entertainment celebrity adored by young women; (*broadly*) an extremely attractive young man.

1926 in Gelman *Photoplay* 94: Pola continued speedily on her exhilarating game of heart throbs. **1942** *ATS* 772: Sweetheart; lover...*heart throb.* **1943** in *OEDS:* She's a little too anxious to have it understood I'm her heart-throb. **1950** Bissell *Stretch on the River* 20: She was now the big heart throb with me. *a*1978 Cooley *Dancer* 45: What a heart throb! And I think he likes me. **1978** *News World* (N.Y.C.) (Sept. 16) 2A: Remember Fabian, the heart throb of millions of teenagers in the early '60s? **1985** *N.Y. Post* (Aug. 12) 3: They were rescuing one of Britain's biggest heart-throbs and Princess Diana's favorite pop singer. **1990** *CBS This Morning* (CBS-TV) (Dec. 31): Up next: the Australian heartthrob, Mel Gibson.

heart-to-heart *n.* a heart-to-heart talk. Now *colloq.*
   1910 in *DA:* Let's have a heart-to-heart, and find out where we stand. **1936** *Esquire* (Sept.) 160: An executive meeting is a *confab*, a *powwow*,...or a *heart-to-heart.* **1958** T. Capote *Breakfast at Tiffany's* 58: Things were pretty tense until I had a heart-to-heart with Mag. **1963** Gann *Good & Evil* 131: There was indeed a perfect place for a heart-to-heart. **1978** Diehl *Sharky's Machine* 227: You need to have a heart-to-heart with the kid.

heat *n.* **1.a.** a state of intoxication from the use of liquor or drugs (in 1904 quot., a drink of liquor); (*broadly*) a euphoric feeling.—constr. with *on.*
   1904 T.A. Dorgan, in Zwilling *TAD Lexicon* 43: (TAD Offers Jack Munroe A Few Hints That May Help In His Attempt To Lick Jeff) [Scene in a barroom:] Munroe might buy Jeff a "heat" before entering the ring. **1912** Lowrie *Prison* 77: A few years ago this dump was full of dope. Every other man y'r met had a heat on. **1930** D. Runyon, in *Collier's* (Mar. 22) 20: In comes Handsome Jack Maddigan with half a heat on. **1952** Uris *Battle Cry* 387: You ain't lived till you get a heat on with Manischewitz wine. **1963–64** Kesey *Great Notion* 264: If there was one thing...that I could get a good heat goin' on, it was music. **1967** *Amer. Sociol. Rev.* XXXII 708: A patrolman said to a man radiating an alcoholic glow on the street, "You've got enough of a heat on now; I'll give you ten minutes to get your ass off the street!"

b. a state of amorous or lustful excitement. Also attrib.
   1942 *ATS* 333: Be in love with...*have a heat on for.* **1963** T.I. Rubin *Sweet Daddy* 11: Going around with a big heat all the time. *Ibid.* 45: Each babe thinks I got a special heat on for her. *Ibid.* 54: Understand it wasn't a big heat dream.

c. intense sex appeal.
   1942 *ATS* 341: Have sex appeal...*carry plenty of heat.*

d. pornography.
   1965–68 E.R. Johnson *Silver St.* 43: "Got any dirty pictures for sale?"..."I've been selling heat on this corner for twenty years."

e. a state of anger or excitement.
   1986 Zeybel *First Ace* 260: He is in extreme heat over a fifth MiG. **1989** C.T. Westcott *Half a Klick* 52: Don't get inta heat, Narvel....They got us outnumbered. **1996** McCumber *Playing off Rail* 95: He, not his opponent, was being distracted by his anger, and he began to play even worse. This is known as "taking the heat," getting angry, often at yourself.

2.a. *Und.* intensive law-enforcement activity in the form of investigation, patrols, arrests, etc.; danger from or pursuit by police; (*hence*, proleptically in recent use) anything likely to prompt an intense police response.
   1925 *Collier's* (Aug. 8) 30: Police agitation is "heat." **1928** *Amer. Mercury* (May) 80: The greatest difficulty for such a mob was to avoid another's *heat.* **1930** Conwell *Pro. Thief* 79: So much heat developed around the Fifty-first Street subway station that the field was broadened. **1930** Pasley *Al Capone* 227: "Coppers," they figured, and decided to keep strolling around till "the heat" was off. **1931** *Sat. Rev.* (July 18) 978: *Heat Is On*—Prohibition officers in the neighborhood. **1935** Ersine *Pris. Slang* 43: *Heat*...Danger. "Blow, the heat is on!" **1935** *Amer. Mercury* (June) 229: *Heat:*...activity of the law. **1937** Reitman *Box-Car Bertha* 183: "The heat was on," and the police ordered the joint closed for a few hours. **1942–49** Goldin et al. *DAUL:* We can't grift...in this heat. **1993** *Sally Jessy Raphaël* (synd. TV series): The older pimps know that [teenage prostitutes] are heat.

b. Orig. *Und.* coercive or relentless pressure of any kind; trouble.
   1929 Hotstetter & Beesley *Racket* 235: *Put the heat on*—Bring heavy pressure to bear. **1930** *Amer. Mercury* (Dec.) 456: *Heat*, *v.:* Trouble.

"Either take our beer or it's plenty of heat for yours." **1931** D. Runyon, in *Collier's* (Apr. 25) 7: I am looking for plenty of heat when we start to go into the palace. **1931** in D.W. Maurer *Lang. Und.* 48: *Heat*...trouble. "He left a lot of heat behind him." "He was always in the heat." **1936** McCarty & Johnson *Great Guy* (film): I'll turn the heat on for anybody who threatens my men. ***1957** in *OEDS:* The moment seemed opportune to "turn the heat" on Turkey. **1961** *Twilight Zone* (CBS-TV): When the heat's on, you fold. **1972** N.Y.C. man, age *ca*35: There's an old saying, "If you can't stand the heat, get out of the kitchen." **1977** P. Wood *Salt Bk.* 163: I got him and put the screws to him—I mean the heat to him. And he [confessed].

c. censure or blame; (*hence*) taunting or sarcasm.
   1932–34 Minehan *Boy & Girl Tramps* 49: But it was my old man's cottage, so I got the heat. **1939** Polsky *Editor* 12: Everybody from the mayor down to the newest rookie cop has been getting plenty of heat from the big shots. **1947** Boyer *Dark Ship* 159: One guy, Stack, is takin' all the heat. **1951** in J.P. Cannon *Notebook* 254: The Police Department was "getting a lot of heat" then because of unsolved crimes. **1970** Rudensky & Riley *Gonif* 121: It was only natural the heat would pour on from the hill-billies. *Ibid.* 125: If you were outside and somebody gave you the heat, you couldn't fight back and slug them. **1983** L. Frank *Hardball* 17: This confidence in vocal expression is manifest in the willingness that players have to "give heat" [to]—taunt—both opponents and teammates. **1985** M. Baker *Cops* 270: Your wife or girlfriend will give you all kinds of heat about doing what you do for a living....They start giving you heat about being on this job. **1988** Dietl & Gross *One Tough Cop* 46: I just don't feel like running into that...heat—Fat Tony and Fish riding my ass about when...I'm gonna bring these guys in.

3.a. *Und.* a handgun; firearms collectively.
   1926 Finerty *Criminalese* 44: *Pull the heat*—Pull a gun. **1930** *Liberty* (July 5) 23: He packs no heat. *Ibid.* (Aug. 23) 32: My hand pulls out a heat with the hammer cocked. **1935** Algren *Boots* 171: Don't we need a heat or somethin'? **1936** Duncan *Over the Wall* 32: I acted as a car driver, while my companion handled the heat. **1938** Chandler *Big Sleep* 49: Don't kid yourself. I won't use this heat. **1954** *Harper's* (Nov.) 36: *A heat:* a pistol. **1958** *Life* (Apr. 14) 128 [ref. to *ca*1950]: We kept our jackets zipped up to cover the heats stuck into our waistbands. **1959** Horan *Mob's Man* 22: This is enough to buy a heat. **1961** J.A. Williams *Night Song* 85: That's what I'm gonna do...buy some heat. **1967** Gonzales *Paid My Dues* 41: We both reached for our heat at the same time. **1971** Woodley *Dealer* 146: But how many dudes would expect you to carry two heats? **1973** in H. Ellison *Sex Misspelled* 277: So I started packing the heat....I dug playing pistolero. **1993** *Young & Restless* (CBS-TV): Are you packing a gat, a heat, a rod—a gun? **1993** *TV Guide* (Nov. 6) 122: Celebrities Who Pack Heat.

b. *Und. & Mil.* gunfire; in phr. **give** [or **turn on**] **the heat** to fire a gun at someone.
   1930 Rosener *Doorway to Hell* (film): I oughta give ya a little of that heat just for luck. **1932** in *AS* (Feb. 1934) 28: *Turn on the heat.* To begin to shoot. **1932** Farrell *Guillotine Party* 181: Sure, if you'd believe her, we poke a gat into Marty's guts and say here get pie-eyed or we'll pump the heat into you. **1933** Duff & Sutherland *I've Got Your Number* (film): One more yip outta you and you'll get the heat! **1933** Ersine *Pris. Slang* 43: *Heat*...Gunfire. "Turn on the heat!" **1935** Pollock *Und. Speaks: Turn the heat on*, to shoot with a pistol. **1935** C.J. Daly *Murder* 162: It's Race Williams, the dick. Better give him the heat. **1987** E. Spencer *Macho Man* 55: The M-16...can...put out some heat in a hurry. *Ibid.* 64: The heat the lieutenant is taking is probably ours.

4. *Und.* **a.** a law-enforcement officer, esp. a policeman.
   1930 Conwell *Pro. Thief* 238: *Heat*, n.—...a policeman. **1958** Gilbert *Vice Trap* 9: That was before he'd become a narco heat. **1961** in L. Bruce *Essential Bruce* 247: And the one heat is cool. He said, You broke the law. **1966** H.S. Thompson *Hell's Angels* 64: We called that bike heat Terrible Ted because he really was bad, man.

b. law-enforcement officers; police collectively.—usu. constr. with *the.*
   1931 D. Runyon, in *Collier's* (Apr. 25) 7: Things are...bad...in Philly, what with investigations going on...and plenty of heat around and about. **1931–34** in Clemmer *Pris. Comm.* 332: A police car is a "load of heat." **1937** E. Anderson *Thieves Like Us* 95: There's plenty of heat behind us. **1942** Algren *Morning* 25: There wouldn't be no heat pullin' up 'n some flat-foot hollerin', "Pull over, you." **1947** Motley *Knock on Any Door* 160: "There's the heat," Butch said. "Riley and Big

Tim." **1958–59** Lipton *Barbarians* 110: I don't want the heat coming around. **1963** Williamson *Hustler!* 86: They goin' a draw heat—you know, bring the police. **1970** *Playboy* (Dec.) 122: I mean, the heat are only people. **1976** *Deadly Game* (film): How do I know you ain't the heat? **1993** *Newsweek* (July 26) 57: I saw uniforms, plainclothes, Secret Service, all the heat in Maryland coming right at me.

5. *Hobo.* canned heat that is drunk in solution as a substitute for liquor.

1934 Kromer *Waiting* 15: I can squeeze more alky out of a can of heat. *Ibid.*: When you have been swigging heat for a year. **1937** *Lit. Digest* (Apr. 10) 12: *Heat artists.* Canned heat drinkers. **1965–71** in *Qly. Jour. Studies on Alc.* XXXII (1971) 732: *Heat* short for *canned heat.*

6. *Baseball.* a fastball or fastballs; speed (on a pitch). Cf. HEATER, *n.*, 5.

[**1942** *ATS* 54: Swiftness; speed…*heat.*] **1973** *World Series* (NBC-TV) (Oct. 13): McGraw throwing heat out there. **1978** *Monday Night Baseball* (ABC-TV): Eckersley had some heat on that [pitch] too. **1983** Whiteford *Talk Baseball* 100: *Heat*…an exceptionally good fastball. **1988** *N.Y. Daily News* (June 9) 100: Bosox' Heat Wilts Yanks. **1990** *Simpsons* (Fox-TV): Here comes some real heat!

7. *Entertainment Industry.* strong audience appeal; great popularity; (*hence*) a strong audience response.

1979 on *Decades* (A&E-TV, 1989): Then as the heat starts to simmer down, the Cassidy pictures get smaller. **1980** *AS* (Summer) 145: The term for audience response generally [is] *heat.* In a good match…the wrestlers will *get heat.* **1989** *CBS This Morning* (Aug. 5) (CBS-TV): I think after a show's been on for a while it doesn't have the kind of heat that results in [an Emmy] nomination. **1989** *Newsweek* (Nov. 13) 8: *Heat:*…an artist's sex-appeal and box-office power. **1990** *Inside Edition* (synd. TV series): You have to make the decision at the right time, when the heat's on, as they say. **1990** T. Fahey *Joys of Jargon* 185: *Heat* (Entertainment) A performer's box-office power. **1990** in N. George *Buppies, B-Boys* 61: There's always a chance that the heat on him may cool—Hollywood is profoundly fickle. **1993** A. Adams & W. Stadiem *Madam* 11: A club's heat was directly proportional to the beauty of its distaff patrons. **1994** *CBS This Morning* (Apr. 19) (CBS-TV): Boy, he brought some heat to late night, didn't he? Arsenio.

8. nuclear radiation.

1987 S. Weiser *Project X* (film): Unless we can bring that reactor down it's just going to keep generating heat!

¶ In phrases:

¶ **at the speed of heat** *Mil. Av.* extremely fast.

1983 M. Skinner *USAFE* 51: *Speed-o-heat:* Very fast indeed. **1988** M. Maloney *Thunder Alley* 97: We got four bandits coming up on us, moving at the speed of heat. **1989** J. Weber *Defcon One* 5: These guys are closing at the speed of heat! **1990** Lightbody & Poyer *Complete Top Gun* 254: *Speed of heat.* Very, very fast.

¶ **give the heat, 1.** (see (3.b.), above).

2. to make strong sexual advances to.

1981 Eells & Musgrove *Mae West* 111 [ref. to 1930's]: And you gave the heat to another one…and he felt great.

¶ **in heat** *Gamb.* on a winning streak.

1919 Clover *Stop at Suzanne's* 97 [ref. to 1917]: He was the most fortunate crap shooter in the world when he was "in heat" as he called it. **1982** Hayano *Poker Faces* 61: They play in nearly every hand while they are "in heat."

heater *n.* **1.** an overcoat.

1913 *Sat. Eve. Post* (Mar. 15) 10: He had a brown heater and a stiff lid and patent-leather gums. **1935** Pollock *Und. Speaks: Heater,* an overcoat.

2. a cigar.

1918 T.A. Dorgan, in Zwilling *TAD Lexicon* 44: He can smoke anything.…Some of the heaters that he mooches would kill a horse. **1930** Lait *On the Spot* 204: *Heater*…cigar. **1938** Haines *Tension* 144: I found 'em walled up in Beckett's room with some cigars and whiskey.…I taken a heater and waved the whiskey off cause I had to go back to the yard later. **1949** *New Yorker* (Nov. 5) 84: He calmly begins puffin' on my four-bit heater. **1981** *N.Y. Post* (June 15) 16: He was a colorful…character who smoked "heaters" and who thought of women as "wonderful dolls" or "broads."

3. *Und.* a handgun; pistol.

1926 Finerty *Criminalese* 29: *Heater*—A gun. **1929** Barr *Let Tomorrow Come* 41: I'm packin' a heater, see, an' I don't wanta stand no frisk. **1930** Pasley *Al Capone* 242 [ref. to *ca*1925]: A revolver was a heater. **1939** Wald et al. *Roaring Twenties* (film): That heater of yours is gonna blast you right into the hot seat! **1940** R. Chandler *Farewell, My Lovely* ch. xxxviii: You'll put the heater up before we go through the door. **1954** J. Hayes *Desperate Hours* 64: You know what happens if one of those heaters goes off, don't you? **1959** W. Williams *Ada Dallas* 235: You shouldn't ought to have gone for the heater that way. **1969** Gordone *No Place* 449: Bet you ain't never held a heater in yo' han' like that in yo' life. **1972** Smith & Gay *Don't Try It* 203: *Heater.* Gun. **1987** *Perfect Strangers* (ABC-TV): Hold it right there! I'm packin' a heater!

4. *Und.* the vulva or vagina.

1935 Pollock *Und. Speaks: Peeping the heater,* a lewd act. **1965–66** in D.W. Maurer *Lang. Und.* 308: *Heater.* The female genitals.

5. *Baseball.* a fastball. Cf. HEAT, 6.

1977 Shem *House of God* 50: Luis Tiant…comes in with his heater. **1977** in Lyle & Golenbock *Bronx Zoo* 21: Goose…throws a 100-mile-an-hour heater. **1978** *N.Y. Post* (June 28) 110: Nolan Ryan is Nolan Ryan because he's got a 104-mile-an-hour heater and a 104-mile-an-hour deuce that drops off the table. **1984** *N.Y. Post* (Aug. 16) 70: Henderson, expecting another heater, choked up. **1993** *USA Today Baseball Wkly.* (Aug. 4) 6: The lack of a blazing heater.

heave *n.* **1.** a drink; swig.

1840 in *DA:* Joe took to drinking…and was always to be found hanging about where there was a chance of getting a heave.

2. *Navy.* a coal-passer.

1919 Battey *70,000 Miles* 302 [ref. to 1918]: A coal-passer is a "heave" and one who has worked up in that line to be a first-class fireman or a watertender is an "educated heave." Anybody in authority is "the man."

3. *Police.* a place resorted to by a police officer who illicitly leaves his beat; COOP, 2.b.

1958 (quot. at COOP, 2.b.).

4. HEAVE-HO.—constr. with *the.*

1968 N.Y.C. baseball fan: So there was a rhubarb and [the manager] got the heave. **1980** Lorenz *Guys Like Us* 220: Your friend gives me the heave. **1989** N.Y.C. woman, age *ca*50: He's waiting for his latest girlfriend to give him the heave.

heave *v.* **1.** to vomit.—occ. (*obs.*) constr. with *up.* Cf. much earlier S.E. sense 'to make an effort to vomit', in *OED* def. 17.

1832 Wines *2½ Yrs. in Navy* 57 [ref. to 1829]: But all the sympathy you get is a hearty laugh from every one who happens to hear you when you "heave up," accompanied perhaps with the still more provoking description of a copious use of salt water and raw pork. **1862** in *F & H* III 291: Stickin my hed out of the cabin window, I *hev.* **1906** *DN* III 140: *Heave, v. intr.* To vomit. **1911** *DN* III 544: *Heave, v.* Vulgar for vomit. **1942** *ATS* 159: Vomit…*heave,…puke,…throw up.* **1958** in C. Beaumont *Best* 70: Damn if I didn't heave all over the floor. **1963** Coon *Short End* 59: This bastard heaved on me. **1971** Jacobs & Casey *Grease* 21: Hey, Marty, Sandy's sick. She's heavin' all over the place! **1984** Algeo *Stud Buds* 6: To vomit…*heave.* **1995** Eble *Campus Slang* (Apr.) 5: *Heave*—vomit.

2. to lose (a game or contest) deliberately; THROW.

1865 in *DA:* We are going to "heave" this game and we will give you $300 if you like to stand in with us.

3. *Police.* to desert one's post or beat temporarily; COOP, *v.,* 2.

1954 in Botkin *Sidewalks* 442: The funeral parlor was this cop's "heaving hole." And policemen don't want anyone interfering with their ancient privilege of "heaving" on the late tours.

¶ In phrases:

¶ **avast heaving** *Naut.* to stop talking.—usu. as interj.

*1771 T. Bridges *Bank-Note* IV 5: Avast heaving, cousin Lovely. **1841** [Mercier] *Man-of-War* 20: "Avast heaving there, my honey," interrupted Bradley himself, who at this moment elbowed his way amongst the group. **1869** *Overland Mo.* (Apr.) 353: 'Vast heavin' and b'lay all for a while, till I tell you more'n you seem to know jes' now.

¶ **heave out and lash up** [presumably orig. in ref. to hammocks] *Navy & USMC.* to get out of bed quickly, make the bed, and be ready for duty.

1918 in Wallgren *AEF* (unp.): Heave out 'n lash up. Didn't youse hear reveille? **1924** Anderson & Stallings *What Price Glory?* I i [ref. to

1918]: You might just as well heave out and lash up. That bird could curse the hide off a whole Senegalese regiment. *Ibid.* II: All right. Heave out and lash up. Lively now. Rations are in. **1944** Kendall *Service Slang* 24: Heave out and lash up. **1958** Cope & Dyer *Petty Officer's Guide* (ed. 2) 349: *Heave out; Roll out.* "Rise and shine." Get out of bed.

¶ **heave the log** [punning on the naut. S.E. sense] *Naut.* to vomit.

1857 Willcox *Faca* 37: The lieutenant went above. "To heave the log," said one. "To cast up his accounts," said another.

¶ **heave to** *Naut.* to come to a stop; cease.

*1832 F. Marryatt, in *OED*: We must "heave-to" in our narrative awhile. **1848** in *AS* X (1935) 40: *Heave to!* Stop! *a*1953 in T. Coffin *Proper Bk.* 45: She...for me hove to.

heave-ho *n.* a tossing out; ejection, as from a public place; dismissal or rejection; jilting.—usu. constr. with *the [old]*. Also (*obs.*) **heave-o.**

1932 D. Runyon, in *Collier's* (Jan. 9) 8: A couple of big guys...give them the old heave-o out of the joint. **1932** in Runyon *Blue Plate* 361: How 'Lasses can ever give him the heave-o for such a looking guy...is...a mystery. **1933** D. Runyon, in *Collier's* (Oct. 28) 7: His newspaper will give him the heave-o. **1940** in W.C. Fields *By Himself* 381: Egbert does not expect to be greeted with the fatted calf upon his returns from the road. The audience knows he is going to get the old heave-ho...[from] his wife and mother-in-law. **1940** P. Gallico, in M.H. Greenberg *In Ring* 22: They give me the heave-o out of P.S. 191 and I hadda go to work. **1941** in Galewitz *Great Comics* 123: So you got the old heave-ho too, Willie. **1941** *Sat. Eve. Post* (May 17) 19: The Yankees' Jake Powell almost got the heave-o from Umpire Eddie Rommel. **1943** in W.C. Fields *By Himself* 477: The District Court of Appeals would give the old heave-ho to the verdict. **1950** Spillane *Vengeance* 90: The dawn began to break and she gave him the heave-ho. **1954** Collans & Sterling *House Detect.* 95: And being bouncer for a high-grade hotel is by no means the cinch you might expect it to be. It's much tougher than being the heave-o specialist in a bar or café. **1956** H. Gold *Not With It* 111: I did give him the boot and the heave-ho a couple months later. **1964** Thompson & Rice *Every Diamond* 23: I'm just a run-of-the-mill ballplayer and I get the heave-ho [from a baseball game]. **1980** *N.Y. Post* (June 21) 4: Navy weighs old heave-ho for eight "lesbian" sailors. **1980** in *Nat. Lampoon* (Jan. 1981) 80: I gave Freddy Four-Eyes the old heave-ho right into the jaws of some grateful killer sharks. **1994** *As World Turns* (CBS-TV): I hear you got the old heave-ho.

heave-ho *v.* to vomit; HEAVE.

1944 G. Fowler *Good Night* 176: It became expedient to heave-ho, and quickly. **1974** J. Rubin *Barking Deer* 256: He got him there just as Kim heaved-ho. **1988** Clodfelter *Mad Minutes* 27: But the fun soon turned sour as men began lining the sides of the ship to heave-ho.

heaven-disturber *n. Naut.* a sail set above a skysail. Also **heaven-tormentor.** Cf. ANGEL'S FOOTSTOOL; CLOUD-CLEANER. *Joc.*

1890 Erskine *Twenty Years* 286: I have heard of ships carrying many light sails, such as moonsails, star-gazers, sky-scrapers, and heaven disturbers, but the *Rainbow* carried nothing above her sky-sails. **1929** Bowen *Sea Slang* 65: *Heaven Tormentors.* One name for the moonrakers which were occasionally set above the skysails, although most stories of them are mythical.

heavy *n.* **1.** money.

1859 *Spirit of Times* (Apr. 2) 88: All the "gelt" and all the "heavy,"/All the "sweet pecuniary."

2.a. *Theat.* a serious or tragic role, esp. the lead in a drama or melodrama; an actor who plays such roles.

1875 *Minstrel Gags* 102: I was one of de heavies, den; used to play Richard and Otellar, and Macbeff. **1900** in Sampson *Ghost Walks* 215: Hogan, the basso, plays the heavy, a tough sport. **1904** McCardell *Show Girl & Friends* 116: The "Two Orphans" are the first heavy and the pianist. **1906** Ford *Shorty McCabe* 70: So far it's as good as playin' leadin' heavy in "The Shadows of a Great City." **1926** Tully *Jarnegan* 94: He told me I could play the heavy.

b. Orig. *Theat. & Film.* a villainous role; an actor who plays villains; (*hence*) someone or something held responsible for another's problems or unhappiness; villain; scoundrel.

1926 *AS* I 437: *Heavy*—The villain of the drama. **1930** Graham & Graham *Queer People* 131: I met a guy who used to be the heavy and

take tickets in a tent show I was in. **1935** O'Hara *Butterfield 8* 66: One of those gangster pictures, full of old worn-out comedians and heavies that haven't had a job since the two-reel Keystone Comedies. **1937** in Goodstone *Pulps* 9: The heavy grabbed the leading lady by the hair and dragged her across the scenery. **1939** in W.C. Fields *By Himself* 350: Page 50, shows what a dirty rat heavy I am. **1942** Chandler *High Window* 335: "What kind of lad is he? Tough?"..."I suppose he is....He used to be a screen heavy." **1946** Cooper & Kimble *Bamboo Blonde* (film): I suddenly feel like a heavy—causing trouble between you and your girlfriend. **1962** J.D. Salinger, in *OEDS*: I'm sick and tired of being the heavy in everybody's life. **1970** *Odd Couple* (ABC-TV): Why am *I* always the heavy? **1981** Ehrlichman *Witness* 173: When they needed someone to lean on him I often played the heavy as they, demanding help for our legislation, could not. **1982** *L.A. Times* (Feb. 14) VI 11: Make yourself out to be the heavy—don't criticize her. **1993** *N.Y. Times* (Apr. 18) (Wk. in Rev.) 4: If the international diplomacy is to achieve its stated goals, Washington may soon be called upon to play the heavy. **1994** *Newsweek* (Apr. 18) 25: Antonin Scalia, the court's right-wing heavy.

3.a. *Boxing.* a heavyweight boxer. Now *colloq.*

1899 *S.F. Examiner* (Mar. 8) 4: He even taken a shy at the "heavies." **1902** T.A. Dorgan, in Zwilling *TAD Lexicon* 44: (Jim Britt May Fight This Month) If Billy Madden comes to the Coast he would want to bring both of his heavies. *1913 in *OED2*: I remember in the finals of the heavies at the All-India Championship of 1909 [etc.]. **1914** E.R. Burroughs *Mucker* 12: Fourth-rate heavies and has-beens. **1929** Barr *Let Tomorrow Come* 151: An' 'e was a good heavy. **1930** in R.E. Howard *Iron Man* 15: Them that fought wide open didn't last no time, 'specially among the heavies. **1947** Schulberg *Harder They Fall* 3: Here's Jackson...the first of the heavies to get up on his toes.

b. a very large person.

1922 Paul *Impromptu* 332: When the girls [prostitutes] grew older and inclined toward stoutness, they were termed "heavies." Each house had a heavy, usually a friend of the landlady whom the latter did not have the heart to replace. It was understood that the "heavies," being less in demand, had to entertain the rough men, the freaks, and those who were so drunk they were hard to handle. **1946** Boulware *Jive & Slang* 4: *Heavey* ...Fat or large man.

c. *Und. & Police.* a hardened or professional criminal who commits crimes of violence; (*hence*) a person, esp. a thug, paid to employ coercion.

1930 *Amer. Mercury* (Dec.) 416: He done the same to a bunch of them horrible guiney heavies. **1933** Ersine *Prison Slang* 43: *Heavy, Heavyman. n.* A gunman, bank robber. **1949** W.R. Burnett *Asphalt Jungle* 19: He started packing heat....You're either a heavy or you're not. Joe wasn't. **1949** in *Harper's* (Feb. 1950) 72: The "heavy."...his techniques are based upon the use or threat of force. **1950** Maddow & Huston *Asphalt Jungle* 52: I know a very tough heavy, but I haven't seen him for some time. **1957** in Tamony *Americanisms* (No. 34) 13: If you'd like to be au courant along the Embarcadero, don't refer to musclemen as "goons." Among the cognoscenti they're "heavies." **1967** Taggart *Reunion* 100: Between 1945 and 1950, Henry Williams was a used-car salesman, "heavy" in a collection agency, retail grocery detailer, [etc.]. **1967** Spillane *Delta* 54: "Any heavies in the act?"..."Russo Sabin. He's a hatchet man for Carlos Ortega." **1974** A. Bergman *Big Kiss-Off* 171: Thugs, heavies, and free-lance muscle. **1976** *Urban Life* V 156: They disparage lesser criminal types (e.g., heistmen, muggers, burglars, and other heavies). **1983** *L.A. Times* (Feb. 23) I 1: Bookmakers, loansharks, and "heavies" from Chicago, New York and California.

4. *Stu.* one's steady sweetheart; one's escort on a HEAVY date; (*also*) a HEAVY date. Cf. HEAVY, *adj.*, 8.

1918 T.A. Dorgan, in Zwilling *TAD Lexicon* 108: Get the map on silly [*sic*] her heavy—Ain't it a riot. **1923** Revell *Off the Chest* 96: If you don't swear the night you've got a "heavy,"/And are informed it's your turn to relieve/...You'll not be a nurse—you'll be a saint, my child. **1926** Hormel *Co-Ed* 63: From the first Phil Moore was recognized by the sisters as Lucia's "heavy."..."He dated her solid" for the Symphony Series. **1927** Faulkner *Mosquitoes* 59: He said she couldn't go without him. He's her heavy, I gather.

5. *Und.* violent, profit-motivated crime, esp. safecracking or armed robbery.—constr. with *the.*

1925 *Collier's* (Aug. 8) 30: Yeggs....Their "racket" is known as "being on the heavy." **1927** in *AS* III (1928) 254: *On the heavy*—[Engaged in] holdup. **1931** D.W. Maurer, in *AS* (Oct.) 107: I fell for the heavy and drew a fin in Joliet. *1935* (cited in Partridge *Dict. Und.* 326). **1949** Monteleone *Crim. Slang* 166: *On the heavy*...Engaged in robbing banks. **1968** Algren *Chicago* 137: Some on the heavy and some on the hype.

6.a. a person (or, occ. a thing) of unusual ability, importance, influence, status, or power; BIG SHOT; *Mil.* (in recent use) a senior officer.

1925 *Collier's* (Aug. 8) 30: The [pickpockets'] mob chief is a "heavy" or "tool." **1932** in F.S. Fitzgerald *Corres.* 296: But it ought to be...[written] by a "heavy," not a reporter. **1944** Burley *Hndbk. Jive* 112: A Jiver puts down a Spiel for Two Heavies....The Big Educator and...the Social Worker. **1955** *AS* XXX 303: *Heavy, n.* Brilliant student. **1961** Scarne *Comp. Guide to Gambling* 681: *Heavy.* A bigtime racketeer. **1968** in *Rolling Stone Interviews* 67: Too amateurish; not enough good musicians, no real heavies. **1969** Walker *Rights in Conflict* 50: Between the cultural Yippies and the political activists, or "heavies" as they were called. *1973* in *Austral. Nat. Dict.*: This Fujita must be a real heavy....a very important man. **1974** *N.Y. Times* (Aug. 25) II 11: The unique characteristic of sci fi (the heavies object to this abbreviation, but let them) is that it deals in futures. **1974** *Odd Couple* (ABC-TV): Don't let these show biz heavies push you around. **1974** in H.S. Thompson *Shark Hunt* 344: The most obvious way...is to make some kind of a deal with the heavies in his own party. **1976** C.R. Anderson *Grunts* xiv [ref. to 1969]: High-ranking staff personnel and unit commanders, the *heavies. Ibid.* 49: Them fucking heavies back in their air-conditioned bunkers at Quang Tri. **1977** *San Francisco* (June) 111: A media heavy like the award-winning *Herald.* **1980** *Atlantic* (Feb.) 74: Second papers...must compete with the heavies, with the suburban press, and with television. **1981** Sann *Trial* 49: She was some kind of heavy in...Powell's...Church. *a*1989 R. Herman, Jr. *Warbirds* 83: The heavies [senior officers] would have fits if they found out. **1995** *Leeza* (synd. TV series): My agent or somebody—some heavy. **1995** Lormier et al. *Wildcats* 149: After the details were worked out, the air wing "heavies" assigned the mission pilots.

b. *pl.* important or profound ideas.

1992 in J. Mack *Abduction* 46: Now the heavies...now the serious part...now we think we can tell you things.

7. hard physical labor; *(pl.)* laborious physical tasks; in phr. **bust heavies** Esp. *Mil.* to work hard.

1942 *Sat. Eve. Post* (June 13) 27: His brakeman, or "shack," who performs more physical labor, is said to "do the heavy." **1976** C.R. Anderson *Grunts* xiv [ref. to 1969]: However, when the grunts said they were *busting heavies,* they were working hard. *Ibid.* 50: Christ—talk about busting heavies. **1977–81** S. King *Cujo* 39: Hubby is busting heavies at the office. **1984** Former spec. 5, U.S. Army: When I was in the service in the '70's I heard people talking about *having to do some heavies.* That meant hard work.

8. *Narc.* a strongly addictive drug or drugs, esp. heroin.

1952 W. Burroughs *Junkie* 14: *Heavy*...Junk, as opposed to marijuana. **1963** Braly *Shake Him* 95: But you look clean as far as heavy goes. That's where the real heat is. As for one pothead more or less.... **1968** *Seattle Times* (Apr. 21) 95: They don't attempt to change your viewpoint about the use of drugs except for the "heavies." **1969** Geller & Boas *Drug Beat* xix: *Heavy:* Narcotic drugs—morphine, cocaine, and heroin—as opposed to the psychedelic drugs—LSD, psilocybin, mescaline, peyote, marijuana. **1968–70** *Current Slang III & IV* 66: *Heavies, n.* Hard drugs.—College males, California. **1974** Lacy *Native Daughter* 122: My old man is an addict. On H, you know, the heavy. **1983** *N.Y. Post* (Sept. 5) 9: In the hospital they start out with the heavies, the Demerols and the morphines and so forth.

9. *Surfing.* a big wave.

1961 *Life* (Sept. 1) 51: "A good set of heavies" (big, rideable waves). *1962* in *Austral. Nat. Dict.*: *Heavy,* a big wave. **1968** Kirk & Hanle *Surfer's Hndbk.* 140: *Heavies:* big surf, big waves.

10. *pl. Mil.* heavy casualties.

1988 Poyer *The Med* 369: We just went patrol..., maybe a day back at battalion if you took heavies.

¶ In phrase:

¶ **do the heavy** to put on airs.

1884 in *OED:* Your ordinary thief, if he have a slice of luck, may "do the heavy" while the luck lasts. *a*1890–93 *F & H* III 292: *To come (or do) the heavy*...To affect a vastly superior position; to put on airs or frills. **1896** Ade *Artie* 3: I've got as much right to go out and do the heavy as any o' you pin-heads. If I like their show I'll help 'em out next time.

heavy *adj.* **1.** *Theat.* **a.** (of an actor) playing or accustomed to playing a tragic or serious role or roles.—used prenominally.

*a*1828 in *OEDS:* The Company consisted of a heavy man who played the tyrants in tragedy. *1860* in *OEDS:* There was no heavy lady for the Emilias or Lady Macbeths. **1870** in *OEDS:* In California she played all lines of business, from walking ladies to heavy, and juvenile leading.

b. (of a dramatic role) tragic or serious; melodramatic.—used prenominally.

1838 C. Dickens *Nickleby* ch. xxii: I played the heavy children when I was eighteen months old. *1868* in *OED:* As the heavy villain at the Surrey Theatre would say. **1877** Burdette *Mustache* 178: When I got into the heavy business, I was left. **1883** Needham *Arabs* 69: "Ah, that's only when we're playin'," returned the "heavy ruffian," his grinning face growing serious.

2.a. (esp. of persons) substantial, wealthy, powerful, or influential; prominent; consequential; (in recent use) popular.

1842 in *DAE:* The congregation is not numerous, but it is said to contain some "very heavy men," by which is meant wealthy. [Maine]. **1863** [Fitch] *Annals of Army* 459: He said, further, that Schwab & Co., a heavy firm in Nashville, had been engaged in smuggling. **1867** *Nat. Police Gaz.* (Oct. 26) 4: Griffin is wanted in [New York] for some pretty heavy jobs he has "put through." **1868** S. Clemens, in *Twain's Letters* II 167: It is with the heaviest publishing house in America, & I get the best terms. **1875** in *DAE:* A heavy merchant...went to Sonora to collect bills. **1883** in *DAE:* Truman B. Handy...has associated with him several heavy New-York capitalists. **1887** [C. McKenzie] *Jack Pots* 27: Her heavy father is a warden in the church. **1888** Gunter *Miss Nobody* 113: One of Boston's heavy capitalists, and heavy swells now. **1929** Hotstetter & Beesley *It's a Racket* 227: *Heavy guy*—Head of a "mob" or racket. **1968–70** *Current Slang III & IV* 67: *Heavy*...Significant; popular. High school students,...Ohio. **1971** in *Rolling Stone Interviews* 416: But the heaviest art form on the planet is certainly films. **1973** Childress *Hero* 84: People like you to be actin cool and powerful, like you a real heavy person, in charge of your situation at all times. **1979** D. Thoreau *City at Bay* 146: He's the only one heavy enough to make Yee come out in the open. **1988–93** Wilcock & Guy *Damn Right* 39: Jazz was very heavy down there at the time.

b. *Specif.* possessing much ready cash; flush. Also as adv.

1840 in *Amer. Qly. Church Rev.* (Jan. 1866) 552: You will go back heavier, I guess, than you came, by a plaguy long chalk. **1872** in Silber & Robinson *Songs of Amer. West* 97: At a poker game he was always thar,/And as heavy too, as bricks. [**1923** in W.F. Nolan *Black Mask Boys* 71: He's...dough-heavy.] **1933** Ersine *Pris. Slang* 43: *Heavy, adj.* Having plenty of money. "See John, he's heavy." **1966–67** W. Stevens *Gunner* 73: Got to get heavy for when we break out of this hole, got to get some so I can get some. **1970** S. Ross *Fortune Machine* 155: Take the kid to any bank he wants....He's holding heavy.

3.a. dangerous. [No continuity of usage can be shown between *1851 and later quots.]

1851 H. Mayhew *London Labour* I 313: Very "heavy" (dangerous). **1970** A. Young *Snakes* 127: Sound like he might be into some heavy shit....Cat better watch his step. **1977** P. King *Code Name: Diamond Head* (film): "We got a job [undercover]." "Heavy?" **1979** *Easyriders* (Dec.) 73: Goin' into a heavy neighborhood? Protect your valuables. **1984–88** Hackworth & Sherman *About Face* 802: These were not by-the-book, All-American, white-collar Army [intelligence] agents—these were very heavy guys. **1992** in N. George *Buppies, B-Boys* 70: Fly threads, groovy chicks, heavy dudes.

b. shocking or emotionally distressing.—usu. used predicatively. Cf. *OED* def. 25.

1936 R. Chandler, in Ruhm *Detective* 123: It's heavy....Get set....He's been bumped off—in his bed. **1969** Mitchell *Thumb Tripping* 84: Eating dope was always heavy for Gary: the act of swallowing was irrevocable. **1974** Hejinian *Extreme Remedies* 137: My old man...split. A heavy scene. **1976–77** McFadden *Serial* 123: Wow, this is so *heavy*, you know?…It's just terrible. **1978** *New West* (June 19) 34: "Pat, I have been *raped.*" It was heavy. **1983** *Chi. Trib.* (Mar. 5): You put yourself in the officer's place and—blowing away a 5-year-old kid, that's heavy. **1987** E. Spencer *Macho Man* 32: It is a very heavy place. My childhood leaves me at Khe Sanh. **1988** Univ. Tenn. student theme: In the late seventies we would have said, "That's heavy, man," if something was wrong. **1996** *New Yorker* (May 13) 82: And the heavy things she'd seen—abused children and illicit drugs and alcohol.

c. (in a weakened sense) characterized by strain upon the nerves or feelings; tense; provoking anxiety.

1967–68 von Hoffman *Parents Warned Us* 37: Oh, oh, oh, it's a heavy scene all over. There are three cats in a room at the Jeffrey-Haight, right now, with three guns. **1970** *N.Y. Times Mag.* (Nov. 29) 46: In Madison, Wis., this has been a tense autumn. November, said the students and the street people, looked heavy. "Heavy," as I understand it, means difficult, dull, ominous, without promise of laughter, ease or grace. Anyone new around with bell-bottoms and a beard can be F.B.I., they said. **1974** V.B. Miller *Girl in River* 88: I didn't want you to go make a heavy scene. **1977** B. Davidson *Collura* 38: Things are gettin' heavy in the city. **1979** *Mork & Mindy* (NBC-TV): Oh! Heavy vibes! What's wrong? **1984** *N.Y. Times* (Sept. 2) 36: She pressed for continued patrols. "We want to show the entire city we are there for you, no matter how heavy it gets." **1987** Tristan & Hancock *Weeds* (film): The heaviest thing about the joint [prison]?…I never really minded the joint that much. **1989** *21 Jump St.* (Fox-TV): If this gets too heavy, you bail.

4. remarkable in a positive or negative way; extraordinary. [Now subsumed by more recent senses; cf. (**7–13**), below.]

1863 in F.E. Daniel *Rebel Surgeon* 186: How this heaviest "heavy coon-dog"/Turned the ladies in the quadrille. **1864** in Patrick *Reluctant Rebel* 245: Everything is very *heavy*. If a man can do anything very well, they say he is very *heavy* on it. If the weather is cold or hot, very dry or very wet, it is quite *heavy*. If they see a…pretty woman, she is a *heavy* one. **1866–71** Bagg *Yale* 45: *Healthy* and *heavy*, are used as sarcastically complimentary epithets. **1895** Wood *Yale Yarns* 10: He told a heavy one [*sc.* a story] on Elias B.!

5. *Und. & Police.* involving, employing, or given to the use of violence, as in criminal activities.—used prenominally or in combs.; esp. in phr. **heavy man** a safecracker or armed robber.

1902 Hapgood *Thief* 54 [ref. to *ca*1885]: "Keep away from heavy workers," (burglars) she would say. **1924** (cited in Partridge *Dict. Und.* 327). **1925** *Collier's* (Aug. 8) 30: Bank burglars, stick-up men, mail robbers…are known as "heavy men." **1925–26** J. Black *You Can't Win* 302: It was the kind of safe that discourages the "heavy man" (safe breaker). **1926** in *AS* LVII (1982) 262: *Heavy-man.* Safe-blower; denotes the more violent [type]. **1928** Sharpe *Chicago May* 286: *Heavy Guys*—stick-up men, or safe-breakers. **1930** Conwell *Pro. Thief* 14: He may then become a beggar, a pimp, a steerer for some gambler, get into the heavy rackets, or try to grift single-handed. **1931** in D.W. Maurer *Lang. Und.* 62: *Heavy rackets,* n. Those…involving violence or the threat of violence to take money. **1933** Ersine *Pris. Slang* 43: *Heavyman*…A gunman, bank robber. **1933** in D. Runyon *More Guys* 8: He had joined up with a mob of heavy men, or safe blowers. **1931–34** in Clemmer *Pris. Comm.* 332: *Heavy man*…1. A safe blower. 2. A person who guards gambling houses, etc. 3. A bruiser or killer for a mob. **1937** in Conwell *Pro. Thief* 238: *Heavy,* adj.—Involving force or violence. **1937** Reitman *Box-Car Bertha* 72: Two of the "heavy men" (burglars) I met that night were killed by policemen soon after. **1942–49** Goldin et al. *DAUL* 92: *Heavy time*…Crimes of violence, as safe-blowing, armed robbery, etc. **1935–62** Ragen & Finston *Toughest Pris.* 803: *Heavy man*—Armed watcher in a gambling house. **1968** Beck *Trick Baby* 14: After all, I'm not a heavy gee. **1971** *N.Y. Times Mag.* (Nov. 28) 94: Special if you doing the heavy work (armed robbery, homicide with a gun). Then they kick ass.

6. insolent or belligerent.—constr. with *get.*

1907 Bush *Enlisted Man* 207: One of them "got heavy" with one of the sergeants and was put in the "crib" for the night.

7. (of money) significant or impressive in amount.—used prenominally.

[**1922–24** McIntyre *White Light Nights* 189: If he is "heavy sugared" they will find him out.] **1924** Wilstach *Anecdota Erotica* 6: I have now lots of money. Heavy money. **1926** Maines & Grant *Wise-Crack Dict.*

9: *Heavy sugar papa*—sweet old man with fat purse. **1927** *DN* V 449: *Heavy sugar guy,* n. A good spender. **1929** Bodenheim *60 Secs.* 230: The heavy-sugar men wanted a girl to treat them on the very first night. **1930** G. Schuyler *Black No More* 100: They ain't got a thin dime; it's this other crowd that's holding the heavy jack. **1930** Weaver *Collected Poems* 247: Then we begin to shoot for the heavy dough! **1930** in Blackbeard & Williams *Smithsonian Comics* 156: $25,000.00 Boy!!! That's heavy dough. **1943** in Steinbeck *War* 96: There's guys used to pay heavy dough for stuff like this and we get it for nothing. **1951** E.H. Hunt *Judas Hour* 46: He remembered Miami beach in '44, jammed with black-marketers, heavy-money boys, touts, bookies. **1956** *Sat. Eve. Post* (May 5) 149: Why did she walk out on a movie career that was paying her heavy money? **1959** in R.S. Gold *Jazz Talk* 125: Ya see, I'm not one of those cats who is always trying to break in on all the heavy loot. **1981** Graziano & Corsel *Somebody Down Here* 189: Pete…[sold]…the book to Hollywood for some heavy bucks.

8.a. *Stu.* (of a sweetheart) seriously involved in a romantic relationship; constant; steady.—used prenominally.

1923 T.A. Dorgan, in Zwilling *TAD Lexicon* 44: Lamping Della's heavy lover as he listens to salad talks while waiting to take her to dinner. **1926** in F.S. Fitzgerald *Stories* 297: From several sources he heard that she had a "heavy beau." **1934** Weseen *Dict. Slang* 185: *Heavy date*—A beau; a steady; a *fiancé* or *fiancée.*

b. (of a romantic date) pressing and much desired; raising or fulfilling romantic or amatory expectations. Now *colloq.* Cf. HEAVY, *n.,* 4.

1926 in *AS* II (1927) 202: He calls his evening with her a "heavy date." **1929–30** in *DAS*: A heavy date with a light lady. **1932** *AS* VII (June) 333: *Heavy date*—an important or exceedingly pleasant "date." Refers to the engagement or the person "dated." **1937** Kober *Having Wonderful Time* 119: Make it snappy, kiddies. I gotta heavy date. **1952** in *OEDS*: He has sort of a heavy date here with a girl named Janey. **1963** Gant *Queen St.* 16: Hot dates. Real heavy. Elvis Presley and Tab Hunter. **1967** *Zap Comix* (Oct.) 5: Shore glad it's payday. I kin *use* it! Got a heavy date tonight!

c. urgent or important. Now *colloq.*

1930 W.R. Burnett *Iron Man* 158: I got a heavy poker date for this afternoon. **1934** Jevne & Purcell *Joe Palooka* (film): I got a heavy message for you. **1953** W. Fisher *Waiters* 221: I don't wanna have to spoil the heavy play you puttin' down. **1969** Salerno & Tompkins *Crime Confed.* 36: There was going to be a "heavy" meeting tonight, with a bail bondsman and a judge present.

d. (of lovemaking, esp. kissing and caressing) extremely passionate. Now *colloq.*

1942 *ATS* 336: Caressing…*heavy love-making* or *necking,*…*hot lovin'* [etc.]. **1945** in *Calif. Folk. Qly.* V (1946) 385: Pitching heavy woo. **1954–60** *DAS*: *Heavy necking.* Extremely passionate necking; intimate caresses and kisses often including sexual foreplay but never actual coitus. **1960** in *OEDS*: What is called "heavy petting" in which frank exploration of each other's bodies is permitted. **1977** Univ. Tenn. student: It was pretty hot and heavy, let me tell you. **1995** *New Republic* (Feb. 20) 30: Fishburne and Barkin are having their hot and heavy sex.

9.a. Orig. *Black E.* profound in thought or content, esp. if also hard to understand; intellectually complex or difficult.—often (esp. ironically) as interj.

1934 G.W. Lee *Beale St.* 217: To Duke everybody is "fine as split silk," and whatever they say is "heavy stuff." **1944** Burley *Hndbk. Jive* 114: Ole man, that's a heavy spiel you're laying down…I don't see half your traction. **1970** A. Young *Snakes* 121: Take that last test in Spanish we had. Miss Van Camp hit us with all that heavy vocabulary and I threw it right back at her. **1970** Ark. State Univ. student (coll. J. Ball): "I don't care how red-white-and-blue you paint it—war kills!" "Heavy!" **1970** *Current Slang* V (No. 1) 20: *Heavy,* adj. Loaded with significance or hard to understand; complex. "That's a very *heavy* statement." "English 147 is a very *heavy* course." "*The Population Bomb* is a *heavy* book." **1970** *Time* (Aug. 17) 32: Some current hiplingua favorites…*Heavy:* deep and serious ("Marcuse is heavy stuff"). **1970** Landy *Underground Dict.* 101: He uses heavy words. **1971** N.Y.U. students: "So the whole point of Zen is the idea, What is the sound of one hand clapping?" "Heavy." **1972** in *OEDS*: Not heavy stuff about what is terrible or what should happen, but how to remake life and stay alive in the process. **1975** Sepe & Telano *Cop Team* 167: This case…isn't so heavy.…What have you got that warrants any further delay? **1975** *Atlantic* (Oct.) 37: Not only in *Science*, but in the *American Journal of Physiology, Scientific American,* and the *New England Journal of Medicine,* all very heavy. **1980** Pearl *Pop. Slang* 69: *Heavy*…profound. **1982** Rucker *57th Kafka* 34: He never stopped moving except when he wanted to say something heavy.

b. *Jazz & Rock.* (of music, esp. a single arrangement) complex or technically demanding.

1958 Blesh & Janis *All Played Ragtime* 117: *Victory Rag,* a "heavy" number of great difficulty, went on the market in 1921. **1970** in Dance *World of Swing* 23: In New York, they used to write heavier, more technical arrangements.…Yes, those arrangements were hard. **1973** *Atlantic* (Oct.) 64: An eight- or a nine-year-old isn't going to understand a fifteen-minute guitar lick in six-thirteen time. When the Beatles started getting more heavy and experimental, thousands of kids were left out. **1982** I. Carr *M. Davis* 175: It was really fancy with a lot of chords—you know, a really heavy tune.

c. Esp. *Black E.* (of persons) extremely intelligent; highly knowledgeable or well-educated; of intellectual or emotional depth.

1961 J.A. Williams *Night Song* 39: I don't mean an ordinary preacher. He had all that bullshit behind his name, B.D. and D.D. Went to some seminary at Harvard. A real heavy cat. *a***1962** Maurer & Vogel *Narc. Add.* (ed. 2) 305: *Heavy.* Intelligent or educated. **1962** H. Simmons *On Eggshells* 239: Like I know you're heavy and all that, but like this is my band. **1967** Spillane *Delta* 19: A lot of heavy minds went into screening any possible escape route. **1966–68** *Current Slang I & II* 50: *Heavy,* adj. Intelligent.—High school males, Negro, Washington, D.C.—Man, he's pretty heavy. **1967–68** von Hoffman *Parents Warned Us* 94: I used to say Leary has a guru complex, but…Leary's a heavy cat. **1968** K. Hunter *Soul Bros.* 10: Yeah, Fess is so heavy upstairs he don't even go to Southern High with the rest of us. **1970** A. Young *Snakes* 118: Donna Lee tells me her father has a lot of bks on jazz & on Langston Hughes that I could use for the paper I'm writing for Engl. Comp. Heavy little chick. **1971** *N.Y. Times Mag.* (Oct. 10) 94: Anybody who would blow up buildings was a nut, but he obviously had some respect for Sam as a heavy dude. **1972** Jenkins *Semi-Tough* 37: For one thing, he turned out to be a dog-ass Jet fan, and that was a dead giveaway right there that he wasn't too heavy to anybody outside of Queens. **1976–77** McFadden *Serial* 228: She's one heavy old lady, and we let her move in because we wanted to make a statement about ageism in America. **1994** Smitherman *Black Talk* 132: *Heavy*…Describes a person who is a profound thinker, or one with highly developed leadership skills.

d. concerned, often inappropriately, with sober or weighty matters; serious.

1968 O.H. Hampton *Young Runaways* (film): "You ought to take it back." "Hey, man, don't get *heavy* on me." **1978** *Rolling Stone* (Nov. 30) 52: We've become so serious, we get too heavy about all this—what everything means. **1979** Univ. Tenn. student: I don't want to get heavy, but where's the money for all this going to come from?

10. Esp. *Black E.* very impressive or affecting; amazing; *(also)* admirable, attractive, or superlative.

1944 Burley *Hndbk. Jive* 15: I dug a skull…putting down a spiel on a heavy hen on the main trill…a mellow, yellow wren. **1962** H. Simmons *On Eggshells* 190: Yeh, man, that's heavy. That's about as cool as you could ask for anything to be. **1967** *Lit Dict.* 40: *Heavy*—Out of sight; great; gone; gassed and groovy. **1968** J. Garrett, in Chambers & Moon *Right On!* 237: Thanks, Johnny. You're a heavy cat. **1969** Mitchell *Thumb Tripping* 170: It would be heavy, he promised. Heavier than the hash. **1968–70** *Current Slang III & IV* 67: The heavy music you are hearing is performed by Canned Heat.…He's a heavy talker. I like to hear him. **1970–72** in *AS* L (1975) 60: *Heavy*…Excellent, fine, very good. "This poster is heavy." *****1972** in Partridge *DSUE* (ed. 8) 544: Just the funkiest, heaviest set of girls…and complete with outstanding new back-up band. **1976** J.W. Thomas *Heavy Number* 6: On the ring finger of his left hand was a dark green stone…mounted in a heavy gold setting.…"That's a heavy ring, man." **1983** *Reader's Digest Success with Words* 86: Black English…*heavy*…(1) "nice, enjoyable" (2) "stylish, attractive." **1985** Swados & Trudeau *RapMaster Ronnie* 3: He's heavy.…He's cool.…The cat can swing. **1987** E. Spencer *Macho Man* 7: Nuns were heavy. They could get you to do things without saying a word. *a***1989** Spears *NTC Dict. Slang* 177: This is a real heavy thing you're doing for me.

11. *Narc.* (of drugs) strongly addictive. Cf. 1952 quot. at HEAVY, *n.,* 8.

1958–59 Lipton *Barbarians* 185: Myra's boast that she has been on horse since she was thirteen…is mostly a boast, because the heavy stuff is much too costly for a kid of her age. **1985** in N. George *Buppies, B-Boys* 318: I was never forced into dealing heavy drugs. *a***1990** E. Currie *Dope & Trouble* 113: I didn't start doing anything *heavy* until I was like thirteen.

12. strong, intense, or severe.

1963 in L. Bruce *Essential Bruce* 39: So that's some heavy propaganda, man. **1966** S. Stevens *Go Down Dead* 226: If we get Durango and Humper they going to be finish. They going have no heart for the heavy mix [gang fight] no more. **1970** Landy *Underground Dict.* 101: He gave us a heavy ultimatum. **1972** N.Y.U. student: Maybe he's into some heavy witchcraft scene. **1972** in *OEDS:* Where's the heavy dope scene now. **1976** *L.A. Times* (May 16) (Calendar) 75: There might be some heavy personality clashes. **1976** *S.F. Chronicle* (July 14) 38: There's a great deal at stake when a gun is involved. The consequences are very heavy. **1988** Terkel *Great Divide* 195: They're heavy bigots. They hate blacks just to look at 'em.

13. *Police.* in possession of illicit drugs or other contraband.

1975 Sepe & Telano *Cop Team* 177: He should be heavy around six o'clock.

heavy-breather *n. Publishing.* a popular romantic novel that includes numerous descriptions of passionate lovemaking.

1983 *USA Today* (Aug. 2) 1D: *Heavy breather*—a popular romance novel. [**1992** *Time* (May 25) 73: The film's heavy-breathing style…is too studied to be erotic.]

heavy cheer *n.* malt liquor; HEAVY WET.

1864 "Spectator" *Snoblace Ball* 69: Strong concocted German beer/And floods of other "heavy cheer."

heavy-duty *adj.* **1.** intense in degree; of serious import; serious. Cf. var. senses of earlier HEAVY, *adj.*

1935 Lorimer & Lorimer *Heart Specialist* 252: It's an extra-sized, overstuffed, heavy-duty headache. **1951** *Harper's* (June) 30: Ferdinand Eberstadt, who was then one of the most influential heavy-duty thinkers in Washington. **1957** *Time* (June 10) 15: In recent decades there has been a new, strong trend toward really heavy-duty thinking about the nature of God and man. **1976** Price *Bloodbrothers* 188: I mean I really did some heavy-duty thinkin'. **1978** G. Trudeau *Doonesbury* (synd. comic strip) (July 13): You're talking about some pretty heavy duty scam. **1984** Hindle *Dragon Fall* 106: I've got to get into some heavy-duty z's, y'know? **1984** J. McCorkle *Cheer Leader* 92: Your brother's got a heavy-duty conversation going on out on the steps. **1985** Heywood *Taxi Dancer* 235: Somebody was going to catch some heavy-duty flak over it. *a***1988** D. Smith *Firefighters* 40: We had some heavy-duty firefighting. **1988** *Right On!* (June) 21: Sheryl and I did some heavy-duty talking. **1989** *Donahue* (NBC-TV): It got to the heavy-duty boyfriend stage.

2. formidable; difficult to deal with; severe; dangerous.

1976 Price *Bloodbrothers* 115: Jamaica's a very heavy-duty place, very poor, especially Kingston. There's a lot of rough numbers goin' down there. **1980** in Safire *Good Word* 5: You are not a heavy-duty writer—too much sense of humor. **1981** *L.A. Times* (Nov. 26) I 1: There is "heavy-duty Soviet involvement" in the movement. *a***1982** Medved *Hospital* 306: He was a very close friend of mine, and [his death] was a heavy-duty number. *a***1988** D. Smith *Firefighters* 168: It was a heavy-duty accident. **1989** Leib *Fire Dream* 242: This is a heavy-duty trail.

3. splendid or attractive; first-rate.

1977 *Nat. Lampoon* (Aug.) 33: The pics were great and the words very heavy duty. *Ibid.* 34: If you've pulled off a really heavy-duty number, KICKZ wants to hear about it. **1986** Merkin *Zombie Jamboree* 99: "Were they cute?"…"Yeah, a couple of them were real heavy-duty."

4. thoroughgoing; habitual; deeply involved, committed, or the like. Also as adv.

1980 in Safire *Good Word* 5: "Earl Holding (the owner of Sun Valley) is a heavy-duty Mormon." "Eric Heiden is a heavy-duty skater." **1981** *New West* (May) 108: She was a "heavy-duty" student, a biology major. **1981** *N.Y. Post* (July 14) 22: My wife…had a heavy-duty gambler for a father. He was so addicted he'd gamble away the rent and food money. **1992** *N.Y. Observer* (Feb. 10) 5: He is a heavy-duty patron of call girls. **1997** *L.A. Times* (Apr. 3) E5: He's a digger…He's into this case heavy duty.

5. (of drugs) strongly addictive.

> *a*1982 Medved *Hospital* 36: I never did heavy-duty drugs.

heavy-foot *n.* **1.** (among itinerants) a plainclothes detective.

> **1932–34** Minehan *Boy & Girl Tramps* 19: His eyes automatically scan the men in the car for heavy-foots. *Ibid.* 265: *Heavy-foot*—detective wearing plain clothes but identifiable by his heavy shoes and large feet.

2. Esp. *Police.* a driver of a motor vehicle who habitually drives fast; LEADFOOT. [The 1959 quot., though defined as adj., prob. intends to define the n.]

> **1942** *AS* (Apr.) 103: *Heavy Foot.* Fast driver. **1958** *N.Y. Times Mag.* (Mar. 16) 88: *Heavy foot*—A speeder. **1959** *N.Y. Times* (May 24) VI 86: [Auto racing terms:] *Heavy foot*—Characteristic of fast drivers who keep the throttle as near the floorboard as they can. Also, lead foot.

heavy hitter *n.* [sugg. by the standard baseball term (1883: Nichols *Baseball Term.*), 'a batter who gets many hits'] **1.** a violent criminal, esp. a hired thug; dangerous malefactor.

> **1970** Gattzden *Black Vendetta* 66: He's a heavy-hitter—probably syndicate. **1978** *N.Y. Post* (Dec. 8) 13: The inmates were being transferred…to their cells, in a special area where officials house so-called "heavy hitters"—people charged with serious crimes. **1982** *U.S. News & W.R.* (Nov. 1) 48: We must make sure that the heavy hitters go to prison but that the lightweights get probation. **1985** *A-Team* (NBC-TV): *You* guys are supposed to be the heavy hitters from Chicago. **1985** M. Baker *Cops* 103: These guys are punks. But she's coming from a group of heavy hitters. They've been involved in…homicides. **1986** C. Stroud *Close Pursuit* 227: Hitler was a heavy-hitter if there ever was one. **1990** Murano & Hoffer *Cop Hunter* 18: A heavy hitter, a racketeer, a mobster.

2. a person or company having great influence, power, money, or ability; BIG SHOT.

> **1976** (cited in *W10*). **1981** P. Sann *Trial* 172: He was a very heavy hitter in this business. **1981** Graziano & Corsel *Somebody Down Here* 75: The part got turned down by two heavy hitters, John Garfield and Burt Lancaster. **1982** *L.A. Times* (Sept. 5) V 3: Heavy-hitters in the financial world who are interested in buying and selling big-ticket items. **1983** WINS radio news (Aug. 25): There's a good chance the Dow Jones will rally after Labor Day when the heavy hitters come back from the Hamptons. **1984** *Good Morning America* (ABC-TV) (July 30): She's making her debut…with so many heavy hitters in this movie. **1989** *National Review* (Dec. 22) 8: Such heavy hitters as Senator Malcolm Wallop, Ambassador Jeanne Kirkpatrick, and columnist William Safire. **1992** *N.Y. Times* (Feb. 16) (Wk. in Rev.) 1: In 1960, almost all the heavy hitters ran—Johnson, Symington, Humphrey, along with a much less senior figure named John F. Kennedy. **1994** *Nation* (Oct. 10) 379: The high-tech heavy hitters, like Microsoft, Apple, I.B.M. and Sun Microsystems.

3. [sugg. by *hit the bottle*] a person who drinks alcoholic beverages heavily.

> **1983** Flaherty *Tin Wife* 40: Boozer, heavy hitter, juicer, yes; but never alcoholic.

heavy man see s.v. HEAVY, *adj.*, 5.

heavy metal *n.* [after the S.E. sense 'heavily amplified, often harsh rock music'] *Mil.* heavy weaponry, esp. tanks.

> **1988** Halberstadt *Airborne* 113: The Air Force Spectre gunship begins to hose the defenders with its heavy metal magic. **1990** *CBS Morning News* (CBS-TV) (Dec. 7): M1A1 Abrams tanks—the Army's number-one heavy-metal killer. **1990** *CBS Evening News* (CBS-TV) (Dec. 27): The heavy metal of the massive build up ordered by the president. **1992** USAF TV commercial (CNN-TV): We offer a course in heavy metal. Aim high. Air Force. **1993** *Beavis & Butt-head* (MTV): In Operation Helping Hand, we used heavy metal to scare the enemy.

heavy swell *n.* a person who dresses in the height of fashion.

> ***1819** in *OED* s.v. *swell*: No heavier swell/Thy groaning pavement…vext. ***1830** in *OED*: Who's that heavy swell? **1836** *Spirit of Times* (July 16) 170: It is quite a *mania* among them, from the proprietor of the humble *donkey*, the natty kill-bull, up to the *Heavy Swell.* ***1883** in *OED*: Marry some heavy swell with heaps of coin. **1893** Hampton *Maj. in Wash.* 110: There's a lot of heavy swells around here that wear the Loyal Leegin button. **1901** in *DA*: Guess he must be a heavy swell where he comes from, and where all the fandangoes are

got up in gilt-edged style. **1917** in *DA*: Lewis…was afraid of his part, which he thought was to be played in the "heavy swell" manner.

heavyweight *n.* **1.** a person of exceptional ability, influence, power, or importance. Also attrib. Now *S.E.*

> **1879** in *DAE*: He is a heavyweight wherever he is. *a*1889 *Century Dict.*: *Heavy-weight*…a person of weight or importance; one of much influence. **1896** in J.M. Carroll *Benteen-Goldin Letters* 298: However, he can't get any heavyweights to war with on that threadbare subject. **1920** Ade *Hand-Made Fables* 241: He was joshing the Heavyweights…kidding the Millionaires. **1934** Weseen *Dict. Slang* 348: *Heavyweight*—An important person; an able person. **1942** *ATS* 19: Important…big,…big-time…*heavyweight*. **1972** Grogan *Ringolevio* 140: Othello was Charlie's partner and a heavyweight put-on artist. **1976** Univ. Tenn. grad. student: The test is going to cover six heavyweight critics—Kant, Schopenhauer, Rousseau—those guys. **1967–80** Folb *Runnin' Lines* 242: *Heavyweight* 1. Person whose ideas or observations have depth and meaning. 2. Person who has succeeded in life.

2. *Police & Und.* a violent criminal; thug.

> **1914** Jackson & Hellyer *Vocab.* 43: *Heavy weight.* Noun. Current amongst long-odds crooks. A desperate thief; a husky capable of delivering a dangerous attack in the event of a personal encounter; a yegg; a burglar; a "stick-up man." **1931** Wilstach *Under Cover Man* 116: Several blunt-nosed heavy-weights, in shiny business suits. **1975** *Kojak* (CBS-TV): He's no heavyweight—not one to plot an assassination.

3. (see quot.).

> **1970–72** in *AS* L (1975) 61: *Heavyweight n.* Overweight person, especially a female.

heavy wet *n.* (see **1821, *1889* quots.).

> ***1820–21** P. Egan *Life in London* 180: Heavy wet and spirits. ***1821** *Real Life in London* I 255: *Heavy wet*—a well-known appellation for beer, porter, or ale. ***1821** in *F & H* III 292: The soldiers…were seen tossing off the heavy wet and spirits. ***1828** in Barrère & Leland *Slang* I 455: And our cares we'll forget/In a flood of *heavy wet.* **1837** *Every Body's Album* II 125: Just tip the blunt to the dealer in *heavy vet* and *blue ruin*, and you'll be a intimate as if you had been acquainted for years. **1842** *Spirit of Times* (May 28) 154: The society for the suppression of drinking "heavy wet." **1849** in R. Moody *Astor Pl. Riot* 123: Innumerable pots of the "heavy wet." **1861** in F. Moore *Rebel. Rec.* I P18: Och! whin they get/Their heavy wet/They get as high as Haman. **1864** "Spectator" *Snoblace Ball* 65: Punch and…quarts of other, "heavy wet." ***1889** Barrère & Leland *Slang* I 455: *Heavy wet*…strong malt liquor; particularly used to describe porter, stout, or double stout.

Hebe *n.* [shortening of *Hebrew*] a Jew; (*Mil.*) an Israeli.—usu. used contemptuously. Also **Hebie.**

> **1926** in Lardner *Best Stories* 229: One [joke] about a Scotchman and some hotel towels and one about two Heebs in a night club. **1927** Thrasher *Gang* 196: A good many others…were eager for the fun of helping the "Hebes lick the Polocks." *ca*1929 in Longstreet *Canvas Falcons* 276 [ref. to 1917]: I don't want anybody saying the goddam Heeb, he's got a streak of yellow crap up his back. **1929–31** Farrell *Young Lonigan* 77: He should have been a nigger or a hebe instead of Irish. **1931–35** D. Runyon *Money* 241: A friend of mine by the name of Heeby Rosenbloom. **1939** in W.C. Fields *By Himself* 332: Remember those two…Hebes? **1941** Schulberg *Sammy* 11: Most of the Hebes I know drive me nuts because they always go around trying to be so gaddam kind. **1966** *Time* (May 20) 88: I'm only a little Hebe who was brought up in the gutters of Brooklyn. **1970** Corrington *Bombardier* 44: Stow it, hebe, Krepinski said. **1979** Gutcheon *New Girls* 144: I bet she's the Hebe. **1988** Dye *Outrage* 4: Hakim…got the Hebes to haul-ass while talking Arafat into leaving with his troops. **1995** *Harper's* (May) 43: If they can't call you a kike then they will say Jewboy, Judas, or Hebe.

heck *n. & interj.* [of dial. orig.] (a euphem., in var. senses, for) HELL.

> ***1887** in *OEDS*: What the heck are yŏ up to? **1895** in F. Remington *Sel. Letters* 272: Now I will get "heck." **1906** in A. Adams *Chisholm Trail* 200 [ref. to 1880's]: Dead as heck. **1928** E. Wilson *Twenties* 474: The heck you do! **1930** *Scouting* (Jan.) 31: Aw, heck….That's what he's always sayin'. **1935** Lorimer & Lorimer *Heart Specialist* 39: Well, heck, I'm a cameraman, not an author. **1943** P. Harkins *Coast Guard* 75: Say, who the heck does he think he is? **1944** Busch *Dream of Home* 128: So the heck with mooning about girls. **1945** F. Baldwin *Ariz. Star*

40: "Heck," said Sam, "why not?" **1948** Wouk *City Boy* 71: Aw, the heck with that old serial. **1954** Arnow *Dollmaker* 218: That's a heck of a lot for cigarettes. **1955** Frings *Shrike* (film): I flatter the heck out of him. **1957** Bradbury *Dandelion Wine* 130 [ref. to 1920's]: Out it comes on the wall, clear as heck. **1958** Hailey & Castle *Runway* 7: Heck, I shouldn't be smoking. **1962** T. Berger *Reinhart* 43: To heck with the next fellow. **1964** in *Social Problems* XII (Winter 1965) 291: Christ, what the heck can I believe. **1965** in A. Sexton *Letters* 264: When in heck do you ever get to sleep at night? **1969** Layden & Snyder *Diff. Game* 22: It certainly sounds like one heckuva great trick play. **1972** in *Dance World of Swing* 36: That…could have been a heck of a thing if they just could have gotten it together. **1976** Kassorla *All Together* 58: What the heck is wrong with you, Lady? **1977** *Bionic Woman* (ABC-TV): It was your duty as a motorist to get the *heck* out of the way! **1981** G. Wolf *Roger Rabbit* 13: What the heck,…let him. **1986** *Campus Voice* (Sept.) 50: Heck, they *want* snow. a**1988** in D. Smith *Firefighters* 32: The heck with this. **1989** Pres. G. Bush, on *CBS This Morning* (CBS-TV) (Aug. 29): We'll take [the fish] home and eat the heck out of him. **1989** *Mystery Sci. Theater* (Comedy Central TV): He may have choked the heck out of people at times, but kill them—never. **1991** in *Harper's* (Feb. 1992) 33: Her mom had to work like heck to get those curls set just right. **1994** *Newsmaker Saturday* (CNN-TV) (Dec. 31): The heck with it.

heckle *v. Mil. Av.* to harass with sporadic bombing from aircraft, esp. at night. Hence **heckler**, *n.* an airplane flying such missions.
  1945 in *Calif. Folk. Qly.* V (1946) 378: Planes sent out to annoy the enemy by causing them to lose sleep and setting their nerves on edge without staging a serious attack are *hecklers.* **1956** Heflin *USAF Dict.* 248: *Heckle, v. tr.* To harass enemy *troops, installations,* etc. Hence, *heckling mission.* **1958** Cope & Dyer *Petty Officer's Guide* (ed. 2) 326: *Hecklers.* Night bombing planes which harass enemy during darkness. **1980** *Air Classics: Air War over Korea* 45 [ref. to 1953]: The pilots referred to the night missions as "heckler hops."

he-coon *n. So. & West.* a prominent or influential man; BIG SHOT.
  1897 A.H. Lewis *Wolfville* 101: I takes it you're the old he-coon of this yere outfit. **1925** *Liberty* (Nov. 14) 45: Hey!…Who's the he-coon around here? **1928** R. Bradford *Ol' Man Adam* 52: Ev'y time I axes him yo' name he swells up and acks like a he-coon. *Ibid.* 151: Dat's ole Goliar.…De he-coon er de Philistines. **1955** "W. Henry" *Wyatt* 75: The old he-coon himself. **1971** *CBS Evening News* (CBS-TV) (Nov. 4): Bob Sykes, known as the "he-coon of the First District."

hedgehop *v. Av.* (see 1956 quot.). Now *S.E.*
  1918 P. Crowe *Pat Crowe* 138: Hedge-hopping is the fanciful name for flying low. **1941** in Wiener *Flyers* 45: *Hedge Hopping.* Flying too low. **1944** *AAF* 368: *Hedgehopping:* flying below level of obstacles and hopping over them. **1944** M. Brown *Walk in the Sun* 46: There was no anti-aircraft fire. The planes were too low, they had come too suddenly, hedgehopping, and any shrapnel from the anti-aircraft might have caught the men on the beach. **1956** Heflin *USAF Dict.* 249: *Hedgehop, v. Slang. intr.* 1. To fly close to the ground, rising up over hedges, trees, houses, or other obstacles as they present themselves. 2. In a less exact sense, to fly at a very low level. Hence, *hedgehopping, n.*

heebie-jeebies *n.pl.* [app. coined by Billy De Beck, U.S. cartoonist, 1923] **1.** a feeling of anxiety or apprehension; jitters. Also (*rare*) **heebie-jeebs.**
  1923 B. De Beck, in *N.Y. American* (Oct. 26) 9: You gimme the heeby jeebys! **1925** Dos Passos *Manhattan Transfer* 344: I'm going to walk up.…I've got the heeby-jeebies tonight. **1926** Boatright *Texas Folk* 217: She gives me the hebe-jebes (also, the heaves). **1926** (quot. at SCREAMING MEEMIES). **1927** Nicholson *Barker* 61: I just got the heeby-jeebies—I'll get over it. **1928** Wharton *Squad* 139 [ref. to 1918]: Can it, Mike, you give me the heeby-jeebies. **1928** Anderson & Hickerson *Gods of Lightning* 537: I hope they raid you and find enough Rights of Man around here to give the Department of Justice the heebie-jeebies. **1932** in E. O'Neill *Letters* 394: Anything in the way of a public occasion…bedevils me with heebie-jeebies. **1933** Odets *Awake & Sing!* 58: A guy with one leg—it gives her the heebie-jeebies. **1940** E. O'Neill *Iceman* 116: Dey give me de heebie-jeebies. **1946** Michener *So. Pacific* 132: It was the heebie-jeebies or the screaming meemies. **1966** Jarrett *Private Affair* 10: This is the type of situation that can give an escort operator a bad case of heebie-jeebies. **1971** Cole *Rook*

236: Catch *me* getting the heebie-jeebies over a bunch of stiffs! **1975** *Atlantic* (May) 42: He's a terminal case of the heebiejeebs, he's an overdose of strange. **1994** N. Karlen *Babes in Toyland* 211: Kat's mere presence…had given him the heebie-jeebies.

2. craziness; foolishness.
  1924 B. De Beck *Bughouse Fables* (syndic. comic strip) (Sept. 12): You've Got the Heebie Jeebies If You Think We Don't Know What It's All About!

3. delirium tremens.
  1926 Maines & Grant *Wise-Crack Dict.* 9: *Heebie-jeebies*—Alcoholic shimmy. **1935** Pollock *Und. Speaks: Hebe jebis,* delirium tremens. **1964** Hunt *Ship with Flat Tire* 156: The Executive Officer [was] locked up in his room with the screaming heebie-jeebies. **1966–69** in *DARE* [11 informants].

4. errors or irregularities; imperfections.
  1973 N.Y.U. prof., age *ca*50: On a take-home midterm you can edit out all the heebie-jeebies before you hand it in.

heebies *n.pl.* HEEBIE-JEEBIES, 1, 3.
  1926 in Perelman *Old Gang* 18: Then the frog made Dora feed him with her own spoon and she nearly got the heebies doing it. **1932–33** P. Cain *Fast One* 197: You started having the screaming heebies. **1946** Mezzrow & Wolfe *Really Blues* 306: *Heebies:* jitters. **1958** Hughes & Bontemps *Negro Folklore* 484: *Heebies:* Delirium tremens, the shakes. Cheap wine will give you the heebies. *1971 in *OEDS:* That little creep…gives me the screaming heebies. **1996** Alson *Ivy League Bookie* 118: I found myself looking at him…and I got the heebies.

heefus *n.* [orig. unkn.] sexual intercourse.
  1964 Howe *Valley of Fire* 202 [ref. to 1950's]: I'm starving to death and all I can think of is screwing!…A little old-fashioned heefus and a big glass of Dago Red after.

hee-haw *n.* loud or offensive laughter; (*hence*) derision; HA-HA.—constr. with *the.*
  1907 *Lippincott's Mag.* (May) 675: He…[got] the downright hee-haw. **1928** *New Yorker* (Dec. 8) 58: I gives him the hee-haw, and one word leads to another. **1939** Attaway *Breathe Thunder* 48: Cut the "hee-haw," and let's find somebody who knows when a freight pulls through here.

heehee house *n.* [Chinook jargon] *N.W.* a dance hall or other place of amusement.
  1922 Rollins *Cowboy* 79 [ref. to a1900]: A "heehee house" was any place of amusement.

heel *n.* **1.** *Und.* **a.** a sneak thief; (*also*) a petty thief.
  a**1909** Tillotson *Detective* 92: *Heel*—A sneak thief. **1911** Bronson-Howard *Enemy to Society* 330: I guess since the beginnin' of time there never was such a deep heel as this one, boys! **1914** (quot. at HEEL, *v.,* 1.c.). **1921** "M. Brand" *Black Jack* 107: As a heel or a houseman, well, them things were just outside her. **1930** Conwell *Pro. Thief* 6: Two heels (sneak thieves) had got into the stockroom of a high-class jewelry house. **1931** *AS* VI (Aug.) 439: *Heel.* A petty larceny thief. **1937** Reitman *Box-Car Bertha* 103: Later I found it was for being a sneak thief, a "heel" as they call it.

b. the practice of sneak thievery.—constr. with *the.*
  1911 Bronson-Howard *Enemy to Society* 235: I wasn't above usin' it…when I was out on the "heel." **1930** Conwell *Pro. Thief* 52: The jug heel is a special type of stealing from banks. *Ibid.* 238: *Heel, n.*—The racket of stealing by sneaking.

2.a. Orig. *Und.* a contemptible or despicable man (now *rare*); (*often*) a man who treats women cynically or cavalierly; cad.
  [**1903** T.W. Jackson *Slow Train* 47: The heading of another piece read like this, "Big shoe store burnt in the East. One thousand soles lost, all the heels were saved."] **1914** Jackson & Hellyer *Vocab.* 43: *Heel.* Noun. General currency. An incompetent; an undesirable; an inefficient or pusillanimous pretender to sterling criminal qualifications. **1918** *Chi. Sun. Trib.* (Feb. 17) V (unp.): If she tossed you becus you was no good…then you're a heel an' you oughta never get a girl to marry you again. **1923** *N.Y. Times* (Sept. 9) VIII 2: *Heel:* A performer who is disliked. **1926** *Clues* (Nov.) 159: I think some one single-duked us, but if so I'll shiv the heel. **1927** *Vanity Fair* (Nov.) 132: A "rat" or a "heel" is a double-crosser or a worthless person. **1928** *AS* III (Feb.) 219: *Heel*—A male student who is not a good fellow. **1928** Hecht & MacArthur *Front Page* 457: You dirty punks! Heels! Bastards!

1930 Mae West *Babe Gordon* 188: The double-crossin' heel! **1930** Graham & Graham *Queer People* 229: But it burned me up to see her with that heel, Blynn. **1929–33** Farrell *Young Manhood* 343: What a heel O'Brien had turned into. **1939** Attaway *Breathe Thunder* 109: Don't be a heel, c'mon. **1942** Liebling *Telephone* 44: Any time a heel acts prosperous enough to rent an office,...you know he's getting ready to take you. **1943** J. Mitchell *McSorley's* 21: That makes me feel like a heel. **1944** Butler & Cavett *Going My Way* (film): Never loan money to a church. As soon as you start to close in on them, everybody thinks you're a heel. **1944** in C. Gould *Tracy* 3: Most people who share cabs are swell citizens, but once in a while you run into a heel. *a*1992 Stern & Stern *Encyc. Pop Culture* 7: Alda just as often played a heel as a likeable guy. (In...*Jenny*, he marries...Marlo Thomas...to avoid the draft, then isn't kind to her.) **1993** *World News Tonight* (ABC-TV): The jury felt that Ted Briseraft, then isn't kind to her.) you

b. *Wrestling.* a professional wrestler who adopts a villainous persona.

1979 in Terkel *Amer. Dreams* 233: For many years he was a bad guy. We call him a heel. What makes a great heel in wrestling? Guts. **1980** *AS* (Summer) 144: A wrestler intensely disliked by the fans is called a *villain* or *heel.*

3. HEEL-TAP.

1965–71 (quot. at HEEL-TAP).

¶ In phrases:

¶ **cop a heel, 1.a.** *Und.* to rob or steal stealthily.—constr. with *on.*

1914 Jackson & Hellyer *Crim. Slang* 23: He copped a heel on the chip and glommed a century.

b. *Pris.* to assault stealthily.—constr. with *on.*

1935 Pollock *Und. Speaks: Cop a heel,* to assault from behind. **1938** (cited in Partridge *Dict. Und.* 147).

2. *Und.* to go away quickly or stealthily; escape.

1927 *AS* II (Mar.) 280: They "hot-foots" (hurry) it down the alley and..."cops a heel" (make a getaway). *Ibid.* 281: *Cop a heel*—To get away. **1968** Beck *Trick Baby* 41: That's why I copped a heel when you went to the phone.

¶ **stiff in the heels** well-provided with money; HEELED, 2.

1858 Pollard *Diamonds* 57: Dandified negroes...touch their hats to the "gem'men" who are "stiff in their heels," (*i.e.* have money).

heel *v.* **1. a.** to run; run away.—usu. constr. with *it;* (*Und.*) to flee or escape from (a place).

*1828 in *OED: Heeler,* a quick runner, active. **1843** *Spirit of Times* (Mar. 4) 7: The mighty African lion...tucks his tail and heels it like a scared dog. **1859** Matsell *Vocab.* 41: *Heels* [*sic*]. To run away. **1864** in A.P. Hudson *Humor of Old So.* 498: "Dead-blowed" with heeling it for the "fer corner." **1884** "M. Twain" *Huck. Finn* 202: Heel it, now, or they'll hang ye, sure! **1918** in *AS* (Oct. 1933) 27: *Heel.* To run away. **1935** J. Conroy *World to Win* 40: Dogface ran bellowing toward home....."My daddy'll cook *your* goose!" Dogface shouted as he heeled it. **1942–49** Goldin et al. *DAUL* 94: Let's grab a drag (freight train) and heel town. *a*1950 in *AS* XXVIII (1953) 116: *Heel* (a joint)....To leave without paying one's bill. **1966** *AS* XLI 281: We managed to heel that motel before they could give us the bill.

b. to walk rapidly or with determination.—usu. constr. with *it.*

*1843 in *DAE:* How...[the horse] would heel it snorting and showing his teeth. **1878** in *DAE:* We shambled and heeled it...down into the valley. **1952** Randolph & Wilson *Holler* 251: *Heel it: phr.* To walk rapidly.

c. *Und.* to walk, esp. stealthily or quietly; sneak; slip.

1911 A.H. Lewis *Apaches of N.Y.* 169: An' if we...can't heel in—we'll climb the fence. **1914** Jackson & Hellyer *Vocab.* 43: *Heel*...Used also in the sense of "sneak" as a noun and verb. **1927–28** Tasker *Grimhaven* 180: I was heelin' down to the [barber shop]. **1934** Appel *Brain Guy* 51: But me, I like Broadway, but McMann's always heelin' around Eighth like a cheap skate. **1935** Algren *Somebody in Boots* 48: He tried to heel out with mah ring. **1935–62** Ragen & Finston *Toughest Pris.* 803: *Heel*—To walk.

d. *Und.* to engage in sneak thievery.

1925 (cited in Partridge *Dict. Und.* 327). **1929** Booth *Stealing* 122 [ref. to *ca*1916]: I learned that he and his girl had been out "heeling"

on a store. She entered and occupied the clerk in conversation; Red sneaked behind the counter and stole the cash-box.

e. to cheat (a hotel) by allowing an unregistered guest to sleep in one's room or by sleeping in another's room as an unregistered guest; (*also*) to sneak (an unregistered guest) into a hotel room; (*broadly*) to cheat (an establishment).

1931 in D.W. Maurer *Lang. Und.* 31: (*To*) *heel a hotel*...To slip into the room of a friend who is staying at a hotel in a single room. **1942–49** Goldin et al. *DAUL: Heel a joint*...To cheat the landlord by allowing others to sleep in quarters where rent is paid for one or two. **1961** Clausen *Season's Over* 87 [ref. to *a*1945]: "We'll round up two more girls and heel it."..."Heeling," she explained, was a standard circus expression and practice—slipping extra, unregistered occupants into a hotel room or apartment. *Ibid.* 112: I wasn't sure how my roommates would react, or how we would "heel" Su Lan...past our apartment-house manager. **1974–75** Powledge *Mud Show* 146: One guy would...rent a room, and about fifteen or twenty of them would heel the joint. You know, all of them sleep there and only one pay [*sic*] for it. *Ibid.* 147: On the front of the lot there was a café. And all these guys [were] going in and heeling the joint, you know.

2.a. Esp. *West.* to provide (oneself) with a weapon, esp. a pistol.—now constr. with *up.* Cf. HEELED, 1.

[**1755* Johnson *Dict.: To heel*...to arm a [fighting] cock.] **1872** *Overland Mo.* (Jan.) 44: Go "heel" yourself! **1873** J. Miller *Modocs* 301: This was his signal to "heel" himself. **1876** J. Miller *First Fam'lies* 100: He's a heelin himself like a fighting-cock. **1877** in *DA:* His man had gone off to "heel himself," and there would soon be trouble. **1878** in M. Lewis *Mining Frontier* 125: Go an' heel yerself then. **1947** in *DA:* Carberry...told him to wait until he could "heel himself." **1942–49** Goldin et al. *DAUL* 94: We better heel up with chivs. **1962–63** in Giallombardo *Soc. of Women* 204: *Heel Up.* To arm oneself; especially to arm oneself with a razor.

b. (see 1909 quot.). Cf. HEELED, 2.

1902 Mead *Word-Coinage* 166: "To stake" and "to heel" mean to lend. **1909** *WNID: Heel*...to supply or equip, as with money. *Slang, U.S.* **1947** in D.W. Maurer *Lang. Und.* 170: To *heel the sticks.* To pass out money with which the shills are to bet as instructed.

3.a. to court or pursue servilely for financial, political, or social advantage; pay flattering attention to; (*Stu.*) to pledge a fraternity or other student society.

1879 Rooney *Conundrums* 63: The average California attorney...hanging around the city prison and "heeling the peelers" in order [to]...gobble up all the paying drunks and enjoy a monopoly of the business of the police court. **1912** O. Johnson *Stover at Yale* ch. ii: Society piffle.....Skull and Bones—Locks and Keys—...toe the line, heel the right crowd. **1934** Appel *Brain Guy* 160: Two men heeling two doll-like dames. **1950** *Time* (Mar. 13) 76: The hard-working team of freshman "heelers" who compete every year for the two dozen coveted positions on the *News* board....He couldn't hold a part-time job and still work the 10 to 12 hours a day that heeling calls for. **1950** *Sat. Eve. Post* (Aug. 26) 70: The clubhouse boys, drawn...by the heady smell of fresh money and patronage, are heeling the wards with faithful vigor. **1960** *Yale Record* (Oct.) 11: Marvin was a normal Yalie who...heeled the News. **1961** Sullivan *Shortest, Gladdest Yrs.* 63: One immortal heeler had chugalugged a pint of martinis. *Ibid.* 145: Think what good pals we've been. Ever since heeling.

b. *Und.* to follow or pursue (someone) closely and stealthily; shadow; (*hence*) to scout (a place to be robbed); CASE, 1.a.

1914 Jackson & Hellyer *Vocab.* 43: *Heel*...to stalk. **1931–34** in Clemmer *Pris. Community* 332: *Heel, vt.* To investigate, or to look up; "to heel the joint"; to shadow, to follow.

heel-and-toe *n.* the act of running or stepping rapidly, esp. away; in phr. **take it on the heel-and-toe** to run away; escape.

*ca*1870 in Fowke *Canadian Folk Songs* 17: See how they play that "heel and toe"!/See how they run from their Irish foe. 239: *Heel and Toe, get on the.* To hurry. "Come on, Charlie, let's get on the heel-and-toe or we'll be late!" **1936** Duncan *Over the Wall* 185: I figured on walking out of the burg; not because I liked it on the heel-and-toe, but because it was too dangerous to steal a car. **1963** Braly *Shake Him* 101: Providing you don't take it on the heel and toe. **1966** Elli *Riot* 63: They'd take it on the heel-and-toe if it came to a fight. **1976–77**

McFadden *Serial* 133: He did a fast heel-and-toe out to the Volvo. **1979** *Easyriders* (Dec.) 8: I took it on the heel and toe 5½ years ago.

heel-and-toe *v.* to run or walk rapidly.—usu. constr. with *it*.

> **1893** Frye *Field & Staff* 32: I'll heel-and-toe it over this blossoming path until we land in the middle of next week. **1952** *N.Y. Times* (Dec. 28) VII 16: The selections he wanted played while he heeled-and-toed it around the track. **1968** Spradley *One Drunk* 43: I make move to heel and toe. He, "Hold it. You're not going nowhere." **1977** in Lyle & Golenbock *Bronx Zoo* 11: John Dennai...used to be an Olympic walker, and on special nights Dennai would stand at first base in his Olympic uni and would heal-toe [*sic*] it from first.

heel-and-toe watch *n. Navy.* a deck watch that alternates with an equal period off watch.

> **1922–37** Gleaves *Admiral* 11 [ref. to *ca*1878]: Standing a strict "heel and toe" watch at night. **1945** Wolfert *Amer. Guerrilla* 44: I set a heel-and-toe watch for Pierson and myself, four on and four off. **1958** Cope & Dyer *Petty Officer's Guide* (ed. 2) 350: *Heel and Toe.* A period of duty (watch) alternating with a period of rest. Also called *watch and watch.*

heeled *adj.* **1.** [perh. orig. an allusion to the sharpened spurs used in cock-fighting] Orig. *West.* armed, esp. with a pistol.

> **1866** in "M. Twain" *Letters from Hawaii* 86 [ref. to 1860]: He...would lay his hand gently on his six-shooter and say, "Are you heeled?" **1871** Crofutt *Tourist's Guide* 132: To be well armed and ready for a fight is "to be heeled." **1881** in A.E. Turner *Earps Talk* 63: Mr. Earp said, "Are you heeled or not?" **1882** D.J. Cook *Hands Up* 301: We are well heeled, and if you don't stop, we'll kill you. **1883** Sweet & Knox *Mustang* 15: They said that he "always went heeled, toted a derringer, and was a bad crowd generally." **1883** in *OED*: The ratio of "heeled" citizens increased...the meekest-looking individual having one [revolver]. *ca*1895 McCloskey *Across Continent* 111: How is any nigger heeled? Got a razor. **1897** A.H. Lewis *Wolfville* 228: I wants to note what he's like an' how he's heeled. **1904** *Life in Sing Sing* 249: *Heeled.* Armed. **1921** Casey & Casey *Gay-Cat* 76: He's not even heeled now. **1922** Rollins *Cowboy* 41: The average puncher was unwilling to encumber himself with more than one gun, and often failed to "go heeled" (armed) to the extent of "packing" (carrying) that unless conditions insistently demanded. **1933** Young & Wylie *Island of Lost Souls* (film): I'm already heeled. **1947** Boyer *Dark Ship* 10: I take my forty-five because I want him to see I'm heeled and not to horse around. **1958** S.H. Adams *Tenderloin* 289: "But keep 'em up." "I ain't heeled." **1960** Roeburt *Mobster* 50: You were heeled with a gun, so as to save yourself. **1971** *Adam-12* (NBC-TV): If the woman's right, he's heeled to the teeth. Twelve-gauge shotgun and four boxes of ammunition. **1982** in S. King *Bachman* 792: If you're heeled, drop it down. **1991** R. Brown & R. Angus *A.K.A. Narc* 135: I'll be heeled so we're covered.

2. provided with money; wealthy; usu. in phr. **well heeled.** Now *colloq.* Cf. *stiff in the heels* s.v. HEEL, *n.*

> **1873** Beadle *Undevel. West* 351: Stage fare increases at even a greater ratio....To travel long out West a man must be, in the local phrase, "well heeled." **1880** *DA:* His friends want him to go "heeled." **1882** Steele *Frontier Army Sketches* 316: What his occupation was, nobody precisely knew or cared; but they " 'lowed" he was "well-heeled" and "had a little tucked away somewhere." **1887** Francis *Saddle & Moccasin* 120: Ain't we struck it big, eh? ain't we just eternally heeled? **1887** DeVol *Gambler* 146: They were a pretty tough lot, but appeared to be well-heeled. **1896** Hamblen *Many Seas* 310: Again I was in London, and "well-heeled" financially once more. **1902** Mead *Word-Coinage* 167: "Well-heeled" is a term borrowed from the cockpit, and means to have plenty of money. **1904** *Life in Sing Sing* 249: *Heeled....*having plenty of money. **1929** Hotstetter & Beesley *It's a Racket* 228: *Heeled...*supplied with money. **1936** Anderson *High Tor* 76: You go well-heeled/when you go mountain-climbing. Is it real? **1943** *Amer. Mercury* (Nov.) 554: Everybody is *heeled* (solvent) again. **1949** in W.S. Burroughs *Letters* 53: Tell Neal to come too if he is heeled. I have to watch the $. **1949** *New Yorker* (Oct. 8) 23: He was well heeled as a young man and...his...inventions have made him better heeled. **1961** Rossen & Carroll *The Hustler* (film): "Well heeled, partner?" **1988** R. Robertson & J. Wynorski *Earth* (film): Swell joint. You must be pretty well heeled.

3. equipped; provided; supplied; prepared.

> **1873** Beadle *Undevel. West* 190: As it was my first visit to Washington, I was but poorly "heeled" for the work. **1877** in J.M. Carroll *Camp Talk* 106: I bought a pair of German socks...& buffalo moc-

casins, so I am "heeled" for cold. **1878** Hart *Sazerac* 45: I always used to go heeled with bread and 'lasses...for fear of accidents. **1880** "M. Twain" *Tramp Abroad* ch. xxxii: Her stripling brought an armful of aged sheet-music from their room—for this bride went "heeled" as you might say. **1881** in *OED*: We ain't much "heeled" for chairs. **1882** Watkins *Co. Aytch* 35: It was pretty heavy, but Pfifer was "well heeled." **1883** J.C. Harris *Nights* 167: Dey'd fine out terreckly dat de ole .nigger heel'd wid rabbit foot. **1885** S.S. Hall *Gold Buttons* 3: I war a fool...ter glide up range without bein' well heeled, fur es red-eye is consarned. **1892** *DN* I 230: Kentucky Words...to be *heeled* = to be prepared for an undertaking. (So *to be well heeled*, Massachusetts.) **1928** MacArthur *War Bugs* 200: German prisoners invariably were well heeled with such items as salmon and hardtack.

4. *Narc.* (see 1970 quot.).

> **1968, 1969** (cited in Spears *Drugs & Drink*). **1970** Landy *Underground Dict.* 101: *Heeled...*Having drugs...*holding.*

heeler *n.* [fr. *heel* '(of a dog) to follow at the heels'; cf. HEEL, *v.*, 3] **1.** Orig. *Und.* a usu. unskilled accomplice of a swindler, thief, or other criminal; a hired thug; a servile supporter or backer; hanger-on.

> **1859** Matsell *Vocab.* 41: *Heeler.* An accomplice of the pocket-book dropper. The heeler stoops behind the victim, and strikes one of his heels as if by mistake; this draws his attention to the pocket-book that lies on the ground. **1881** in Partridge *Dict. Und.* 328: A Bowery dive heeler. **1891** Maitland *Slang Dict.* 139: *Heeler*, the backer of another, as of a gambler or a striker. A heeler also "stakes" gamblers who are "dead broke." *a*1890–93 *F & H* III 298: *Heeler...*(American).—A bar or other loafer; anyone on the lookout for shady work. **1900** *DN* II 40: *Heeler...*One who accompanies the musical or athletic clubs and pays his own expenses [Princeton Univ.]. **1902** Hapgood *Thief* 116 [ref. to *ca*1888]: A certain "heeler" put me on to a disorderly house where we could get some stones. **1904** *Life in Sing Sing* 249: *Heeler...*a toady; a "bouncer." *a*1904–11 D.G. Phillips *Susan Lenox* II 153: The proprietor's heeler of Finnegan's.

2. *Pol.* a hanger-on or adherent of a politician or political party who usu. carries out the orders of political bosses in the hope of personal aggrandizement.—used contemptuously. Now *rare* except as (now *S.E.*) **ward-heeler.**

> **1876** in *AS* XXVII (1952) 165: As the crowd dispersed...a gentleman happened to say that the gang in the room was composed of Tammany "*heelers*," when a Tammany retainer taking umbrage at the epithet knocked the gentleman down. *a*1877 in Bartlett *Amer.* (ed. 4): Wirt Sykes as a journalist would make as good a consul as Wirt Sykes the politician, who has been a heeler about the capital, or Wirt Sykes the army bummer. **1884** T. Fortune *Black & White* 131: Demagogues, tricksters, and corruptionists who figure in the newspapers as "bosses," "heelers," and "sluggers." **1886** T. Roosevelt, in *Century Mag.* (Nov.) 78: The "heelers"...stand at the polls. **1888** in *F & H* III 298: A band...preceded a lot of ward heelers and floaters. **1888** in *OED*: By degrees he rises to sit on the central committee, having...surrounded himself with a band of adherents, who are called his "heelers," and whose loyalty...secured by the hope of "something good," gives weight to his words. **1900** J.R. Spears *Amer. Slave Trade* 4: He was what ward politicians would call a "heeler" of the Earl of Warwick. **1901** *Chi. Trib.* (July 28) 38: Ward captains and others known in politics as "heelers." **1903** in *DA:* The local man, often called a "heeler," has his body of adherents. **1904** in "O. Henry" *Works* 513: We get the heelers out with the crackly two-spots. **1904** *Life in Sing Sing* 249: *Heeler*—A politician in a small way. **1909** *WNID: Heeler...*One who follows at the heels; *specif.*, a subservient hanger-on of a political patron. *Polit. Cant, U.S.* **1915** *DN* IV 201: *Heeler*, a political fellow ready to do dirty work. **1917** U. Sinclair *K. Coal* 210: The foreman of the jury [was] a saloon-keeper, one of Raymond's heelers. **1943** in *Dict. Canadianisms:* Judges...are all political heelers or they would not be judges. **1944** E.C. Smith & A.J. Zurcher *Dict. Amer. Pol.* 151: *Heeler.* A party worker who runs errands for a district or precinct leader, distributes literature, canvasses for votes, arranges for open or disguised bribery of individual voters, and gets out the vote on election day. **1942–49** Goldin et al. *DAUL: Heeler...*Any ward politician whose tactics are those of a ruffian. **1950** P. Green *Peer Gynt* 101: A thief and a heeler come in at the right front.

3. *Und.* (see quots.). Cf. HEEL, *v.*, 1.d.

> **1931** in D.W. Maurer *Lang. Und.* 49: Sneak thief...West Coast, *heeler.* **1968** "H. King" *Box-Man* 87: A heeler is a hotel prowler.

heel-tap *n.* a small quantity of liquor remaining in a glass or bottle, esp. after a toast has been drunk.

*1780 in *OED2:* He was saluted with a call of "No heeltaps!" *1788 Grose *Vulgar Tongue* (ed. 2): A person having any liquor in his glass, is frequently called upon by the toast-master to take off his heel-tap. *1795 in *F & H* III 298: Briskly pushed towards me the decanter containing a tolerable bumper, and exclaimed, "Sir, I'll buzz you; come, no heel-taps!" *1805 J. Davis *Post-Captain* 164: Get rid of your heeltaps. *1821 *Real Life in London* I 91: I mix'd the heel-taps all in one bottle. *1841 in *F & H:* Empty them heeltaps, Jack, and fill out with a fresh jug. 1860 Shipley *Privateer's Cruise* 11: "Here's success to the *Arrow*—no heel-taps." The toast was drunk with a huzza. 1889 Barrère & Leland *Dict. Slang* I 456: *Heel-tap,* a small quantity of liquor left in the glass by anyone who drinks...the honour of a proposed toast. This was held in the ultra convivial days of our not very remote ancestors to be a mark of disrespect or of effeminacy, and was often met by the warning of "No heel-taps." Also the fag-end of a bottle. 1905 R. Grant *Orchid* 48: "All up!" cried the master....."No heel taps!"...they drained their glasses. 1930 *Amer. Mercury* (Dec.) 435: Member...must drink three martinis...absolutely no heel-taps allowed. 1965–71 in *Qly. Jour. Studies on Alc.* XXXII (1971) 732: *Heel Dregs* in the lower corner (or heel) of a tilted bottle. Also **heel taps.**

heel up *v.* see HEEL, *v.,* 2.a.

heifer *n.* a girl or woman, esp. if plump.—used disparagingly or jocularly.

1835 Longstreet *Ga. Scenes* 45: I'll lick him till he learns you better manners, you *sassy* heifer you. 1836 in Haliburton *Sam Slick* 77: She warn't a bad lookin' heifer at that. 1839 Briggs *H. Franco* I 207: And now he's got another reg'lar nice young heifer. 1862 in Hicken *Ill. in Civil War* 78: Why sir the Haughty Stinking heiffers here in Huntsville will go and Draw there grub of us and with their mouth filled with our bread treat us with utter Scorn and Contempt. 1863 C.F. Browne *Ward: Travels* 191: The old gentleman is present...with a large number of wives. It is said he calls them his "heifers." *1865 in *Comments on Ety.* (Jan. 1995) 27: That pretty Scotch heifer in Dundee has "kidded" me into it. 1867 G.W. Harris *Lovingood* 82: Ole Adam married that heifer, what wer so fon' ove talkin tu snaix. 1871 "M. Twain" *Roughing It* 35: I reckon I'm a pretty sociable heifer after all. 1879 Burt *Prof. Smith* 102: Who's your heifer now, Felix? 1889 in Davidson *Old West* 80: Bunch the heifers in the middle! 1895 F.P. Dunne, in Schaaf *Dooley* 277: With that out thripped a heifer, Jawn, that ye niver see th' likes iv. I'll not tell ye what she had on, though I cud without detainin' ye. She was pretty, I'll say that. 1900 Wister *Jimmyjohn Boss* 118: What's the heifer speakin' this trip? 1904 *Life in Sing Sing* 249: *Heifer.*—A woman. 1922 Rollins *Cowboy* 170: Say, boys, Bill Smith that used to be down at the Two-Star Ranch has roped a heifer for life. 1938 Steinbeck *Grapes of Wrath* 90: Five hundred folks there, an' a proper sprinklin' of young heifers. 1965 Hernton *Sex & Racism* 58: Do you want to git yoself lynched! Messing round wit a *white* gurl! A little, trashy white heifer. 1965 C. Brown *Manchild* 202: Yeah, that was good for that old heifer, that old no-good whorish hussy. 1974 Univ. Tenn. student: Heifers are fat cows. So fat chicks are *heifers.* Real fat chicks. 1980 Univ. Tenn. student: God, she's a heifer [i.e., very fat]! 1990 P. Dickson *Slang!* 219: *Heifer.* Fat girl. 1994 Smitherman *Black Talk* 133: *Heifer*...any female; used by males or females; a fairly neutral term. 1994 A. Heckerling *Clueless* 28: I'm such a heifer, I had two bowls of "Special K" this morning.

heifer dust *n.* **1.** (a joc. euphem. for) BULLSHIT; nonsense.

1927 in *OEDS:* Even if they do get pinched, they always have some heifer dust ready about laying a trap for a ship. 1929 in Leadbitter & Slaven *Blues Records* 231: Heifer Dust. 1933 J. Conroy *Disinherited* 41: "Heifer dust!" snorted Ben. *1941 S.J. Baker *Pop. Dict. Austral. Slang* 35: *Heifer dust.* Nonsense, "bullsh." 1950 in *DARE.* *1955 in Wilkes *Dict. Austral. Colloq.* 173: All they could do was take his money and string him a line of heifer dust as long as your arm. 1985 in *DARE:* Heifer-dust is what girls say when they mean bullshit.

2. Bull Durham (brand of) tobacco; chewing tobacco or snuff.

1927 *AS* II (Oct.) 25: Among other things it sells bacon—"sow bosum" and snuff—"rest powder" or "heifer dust." 1931 Haycox *Whispering Range* 198: I've tried to...[roll cigarettes] one handed and wasted three sacks of heifer dust.

heifer-prodder *n.* *West.* a cowboy. *Joc.*

1941 *So. Folklore Qly.* 218: You, you fat head of a heifer-prodder, are going to eat that other chop.

Heinie[1] *n.* [< G *Heine,* hypocoristic form of *Heinrich* (equiv. to E *Henry*)] **1.** Esp. *Mil.* a German.—used disparagingly. Often attrib. and hence as adj.

1904 *Life in Sing Sing* 249: *Hiney.* A German. 1916 in Roy *Pvt. Fraser* 208: Two dead Heinies. *Ibid.* 212: A Heinie dress helmet. 1917 in Morgan & Michalson *For Our Beloved Country* 276: Now go get Hiney! *1917 W. Lewis, in Materer *Pound/Lewis* 78: Three or four English planes hove in sight, and Heine [*sic*] pushed off. (Heine is a good new name for the stinking foe.). 1919 Duffy *Duffy's Story* 312: It was a rare thing to hear a soldier in a combat division talk about "Huns." It was always the "Heinies," the "Jerries," the "Boches," or simply the "Germans." 1919 in Cornebise *Amaroc News* 2: German presses operated by Heinie personnel. 1929 Springs *Bright Blue Sky* 227: Those yellow-bellied Heinies can't kill you. 1930 in H. Miller *Letters to Emil* 36: The waiters invariably mistake me for a Heinie or a Swede. 1937 *Pic* (May) 17: He is giving the Nazi salute...in the approved Heinie manner. 1940 W.C. Williams *In the Money* 44: That little Heinie's pretty smart, J.W., and he sure knows the ropes. 1943 Lawson & Korda *Sahara* (film): Boy, I'd give plenty to see the expression on that Heinie's face. *a*1945 Windolph *With Custer* 4 [ref. to 1870's]: They used to call me "Dutchy." And some of the boys called me "Sauerkraut," and then once in a while I'd get called "Heinie." 1948 Lay & Bartlett *12 O'Clock High!* 49: That Heinie navigator, Zimmermann, went up to help him. 1950 Calmer *Strange Land* 89: If the British don't get control of that dam, the heinies can flood this whole Haenl valley. 1954 Schulberg *Waterfront* 121: You Heinie bastard. 1958 A. King *Mine Enemy* 151: Not one of these learned Heinies was able to suppress his patronizing sneer for Frenchmen, for Englishmen, for Americans. 1979 McGivern *Soldiers* 169: It happened when the Heinies were sending guys from here to Poland. 1980 *Nat. Lampoon* (Apr.) 83: By the way, Beethoven means "beet garden" in heinie talk.

2. *Mil.* the German armed forces.

1915 in Roy *Pvt. Fraser* 32: I asked him how far away Heiny was. "75 yards," he uttered. 1917 in *OEDS:* The Canadians call their enemy Heine [*sic*] and not Fritz. 1918 *Sat. Eve. Post* (Feb. 9) 45: Pretty soon our own boys were out hunting for Heinie in the dark of the moon. 1918 R. Casey *Cannoneers* 243: He ain't dead. Heinie's got him. 1919 Prentice *Padre* 243: As nothing more happened, the guns apparently had ceased firing, and "Heinie" had evidently taken his leave. 1925 Thomason *Fix Bayonets!:* Boy, ain't Heinie gettin' it now! *ca*1933–74 E. Mackin *Didn't Want to Die* 41 [ref. to 1918]: Heinie wanted that outpost and meant to get it back.

3. the German language.

1942 *Yank* (Sept. 9) 18: "Schwimmerflugzeug" (Heinie for "seaplane.").

Heinie[2] *n.* a Heineken (brand of) beer.

1977 *Sat. Night Live* (NBC-TV): How 'bout a Heinie, honey? 1982 L. Glass *Valley Girl* 27: *Heinies.* Heineken beer. 1992 Mowry *Way Past Cool* 88: This last Heinie.

heinie *n.* var. HINEY[2].

heinous *adj.* *Stu.* unpleasant, objectionable, unattractive, etc.; awful. [The intended sense of the 1970 quot. is apparently 'grievous or severe', and is most likely merely catachrestic.]

[1970 *Black Studies* (Sept.) 43: Today our struggle is in some ways less heinous but far more complex. What about black studies today?] 1982 Univ. Tenn. student: The party shouldn't be too heinous. 1984 Algeo *Stud Buds* 7: A person who wears unusual clothing or has an unusual hair style [is referred to as]...*banous* [*sic*]. *a*1986 D. Tate *Bravo* 168: This heinous hill. 1986 Eble *Campus Slang* (Mar.) 5: *Heinous*—anything bad, ugly, or negative. Usually refers to a female: "That girl you were with was really heinous." 1988 Univ. Tenn. student theme: "Haneous"...is often used instead of gross or disgusting. 1989 P. Munro *U.C.L.A. Slang* 48: *Heinous*...ugly, unattractive. 1989 C. Matheson & E. Solomon *Excellent Adventure* (film): Bogus, heinous, most nontriumphant! 1992 *Melrose Place* (Fox-TV): Both are equally heinous propositions in this town. 1992 *Middle Ages* (CBS-TV): That fast food is heinous. I think I'm gonna blow chunks.

Heinz *n.* [sugg. by "Heinz 57 Varieties," a trademark of Heinz Corp.] a mongrel. Also **Heinz dog, Heinz 57.** *Joc.*

1950 in *DARE:* A dog of mixed breed...*Heinz*...*Heinz dog.* 1965–70 in *DARE* [many informants]. **1974** Univ. Tenn. student: A mongrel dog's a Heinz 57. **1977–81** S. King *Cujo* 302: He's a Heinz. Fifty-seven Varieties. **1982** Knoxville, Tenn., woman, age *ca*50: Now the mother's a German Shepherd and the poppa's a Heinz. **1987** *Wkly. World News* (July 21) 30: Jasper is of the collie variety with some Heinz 57 thrown in.

heist *n. & v.* see s.v. HOIST, *n., v.*

heist artist *n. Und.* a thief, esp. an armed robber.
     1949 W.R. Burnett *Asphalt Jungle* 24: They're offering a thousand-dollar reward for the capture of this heist artist. **1950** Spillane *Vengeance* 76: You a heist artist? **1977** M. Franklin *Last of Cowboys* 41: Heist artists don't use trailer rigs for getaway cars.

heister *n.* see s.v. HOISTER.

heist man *n. Und.* a man who is an armed robber. Also **heist guy.**
     1931 *AS* VI (Aug.) 439: Hist man, n. A hold-up man. **1932** Burns *I Am a Fugitive* 145: Jack Martin, killer, heist guy, pete man and jail breaker extraordinary. **1931–33** in Clemmer *Pris. Community* 332: Heistman, n. A highway robber. **1940** Burnett *High Sierra* 36: Running around with a couple of ten-cent heist guys. **1949** in *Harper's* (Feb. 1950) 70: Holdup-men—"heist-men" in the underworld argot. **1967–68** von Hoffman *Parents Warned Us* 107: Junior heistmen hid in the darkness. **1970** Terkel *Hard Times* 180: I been a con man, a heist man—you name it.

helen see s.v. MILIHELEN.

heligoflipter *n.* (see quot.). *Joc.*
     1986 R. Zumbro *Tank Sgt.* 53 [ref. to 1967–68]: Supply was still by helicopter (Sergeant Bell called them "heligoflipters").

helium brain *n. Stu.* a silly or empty-headed person; AIRHEAD. Hence **helium-brained,** *adj.*
     1955 *Science Digest* (Dec.) 70: "He's helium-brained" used to be a slur of the day [prior to World War II]. **1984** Algeo *Stud Buds* 3: A rather stupid person…*helium brain.*

helium head *n.* **1.** *Navy.* (see quot.).
     1952 Cope & Dyer *Petty Officer's Guide* 260: Helium Heads. (Slang). Men who fly lighter-than-air aircraft.
     2. HELIUM BRAIN.
     1960 Leckie *Marines!* 129 [ref. to WWII]: I'm gonna teach you helium-heads how to shoot mortars. **1980** Eble *Campus Slang* (Oct.) 3: *Helium head*—Synonym for *Airhead.* *a*1989 Spears *NCT Dict. Slang* 178: Well, what's that helium head done now?

hell *n.* **1.a.** (used with *as, like,* and *than* for emphatic comparison). [Bracketed quots. show its orig. in allusive S.E. similes.]
     [*1511 in Tilley *Prov. in Eng.* 306: It is…derke as hell.] [*1563 in Tilley *Prov. in Eng.:* As blacke as hell.] *1619 in Tilley *Prov. in Eng.:* As false as hell. [*1640 in *OED:* He sets out sin (most lively) black as hell.] *1676 in D'Urfey *Two Comedies* 61: And yet she's false as Hell! [*1780 W. Cowper, in *OED:* Delusions strong as Hell shall bind him fast.] **1768–70** in Mead *Shanties* 112: Got Drunk as all Hell. **1773** H. Kelly *School for Wives* 112: 'Tis false as hell! **1775** in Whiting *Early Amer. Provs.* 209: Hungry as hell. *1813 in W. Wheeler *Letters* 117: He was retiring when one of our men observed to him "That it was Chelsea as dead as H—l." **1813–18** Weems *Drunkard's Looking Glass* 61: He continues to bawl out that you are a "d—d clever fellow," and swears by his Maker, that "he loves you like h—l." *1829 Marryat *Frank Mildmay* 234: Stinks like h—! **1837** Strong *Diary* I 77: Us Democrats licked the Whigs like hell. **1840** *Spirit of Times* (Mar. 7) 8: "Here's at you for a quarter."…"Good as hell." **1841** [Mercier] *Man-of-War* 267: Yes, yes, I marked that morning well,/I mind, too, 'twas cold as h—l. **1843** Field *Pokerville* 62: 'Tis false as hell! **1844** Porter *Big Bear* 133: Presently I hearn him cummin, *blowin* like a steamboat, and mad as hell. **1858** in *N. Dak. Hist.* XXXIII (1966) 307: Jeff shouted out "run like hell." *ca*1863 in Wiley & Milhollen *They Who Fought* 57: The meat stinks like hell. **1864** in Bensill *Yamhill* 172: Sept. 5, 1864. Clear. Dull as Hell. **1866** Dimsdale *Vigilantes* 70: If we ever hear a word from one of you, we'll kill you surer than h—l. **1877** Draper *King's Mountain* 247 [ref. to 1770]: Here they are, my brave boys; *shout like h—l and fight like devils!* **1907** S.E. White *Ariz. Nights* 16: They crawled along…hotter'n hell with the blower on. **1917–20** in J.M. Hunter *Trail Drivers* I 287: Quicker'n hell can scorch a feather. **1925** Kelly *Craig's Wife* 185: You know, he was always as jealous as hell of her. **1929** "C. Woolrich" *Times Sq.* 6: The emergency ward.…Drive like

hell! **1931** *AS* (Aug.) 433: It's colder'n hell on them prairies. You're crazier'n hell, Kid.…I hate like hell to do this. **1935** C.J. Daly *Murder* 10: He was…deader than hell. **1936–38** in Yetman *Voices from Slavery* 41: He say us all am free as hell. **1938** R. Chandler, in *Dime Detective* (Jan.): Sorry as all hell and so on. *Ibid.:* You look cuter than all hell. **1941** in J. Jones *Reach* 15: I'm sleepy as hell. **1946** in J. O'Hara *Sel. Letters* 198: I am trying like hell to be fair to all concerned. **1945–51** Salinger *Catcher in Rye* ch. viii: She sounded interested as hell. *Ibid.* ch. ix: Suave as hell. **1953** R. Chandler *Goodbye* 5: He was…polite as hell. **1985** L. Iacocca, in *Newsweek* (Dec. 23) 11: I may not know the secret to success, but I sure as hell know the secret to failure—and that's to keep trying to please everybody. *a*1987 Bunch & Cole *Reckoning for Kings* 176: Darker'n hell's hinges. **1993** A. Lomax *Where Blues Began* 7: Moonshine…as fiery as the 4th of July in West Hell.
     b. *Specif.,* in phr. **look** [or **feel**] **like hell** to look [or feel] dreadful.
     1898 Kountz *Baxter's Letters* 25: I feel like h—l. **1918** Grider *War Birds* 76: We looked like hell in our little khaki jackets. **1960** N.Y.C. man: I know I must look like hell.…I really feel like hell about what happened. **1984** J.R. Reeves *Mekong* 225: You guys look like hell warmed over.

     2.a. (used interjectionally to express anger, irritation, contempt, etc., or (with weakened force) surprise, resignation, or unconcern). [Often elab., esp. in early use; *hell and damnation!* is the most freq. collocation.]
     *1605 B. Jonson *Eastward Ho!* IV i: What! Landed at Cuckold's Haven! Hell and damnation. *1676 in D'Urfey *Two Comedies* 127: Oh Hell! Hell! Hell! Were ever hopes so frustrated? *1678 J. Dryden, in *OED:* Hell, death! This eunuch pandar ruins you. *ca*1680 in Horne *Marriage Poems* (unp.): Marry'd! O Hell and Furies! Name it not. *1688 Shadwell *Squire of Alsatia* IV i: Death and Hell, 'tis my Father. *Ibid.* V i: Hell and Damnation! We are all undone. *1688 Shadwell *Woman-Captain* ii: Hell and confusion!…Hell and Devils! *1693 in Congreve *Comedies* 82: Hell, and the Devil! Does he know it? **1836** *Spirit of Times* (July 23) 182: Oh hell!…It's all over now. **1841** [Mercier] *Man-of-War* 73: Hell, I thought 'twas twice the place it is. **1843** Field *Pokerville* 60: "Oh, h—l!" contemptuously blurted out Mr. Walters. **1847** Downey *Portsmouth* 59: Oh Hell, then we shan't get it these six months. **1851** M. Reid *Scalp-Hunters* 177: H—l!…I thort so. **1862** in Rosa *Wild Bill* 56: [A newspaper reported General McCulloch's last words to be] "Oh Hell!" **1908** Hopper & Bechdolt *9009* 194: "Oh, hell!" he said—and he lay down on his back again. **1953** Wicker *Kingpin* 81: Hell, I'm loaded too. Want to see my checkbook? *1975 M. Marshall *Bozzimacoo* 78: O Hell is a pretty lightweight oath these days. **1983** J. Hughes *Nat. Lampoon's Vacation* (film): Hell, yes! I'm fine. I'm having a ball. **1994** in *Reader's Digest* (Jan. 1995) 134: Hell,…I'm just glad he's not calling collect anymore.
     b. (used as a usu. postpositive interjection to express irritation, incredulity, irony, or scorn).
     1845 in Blair & McDavid *Mirth* 80: "Fayette is yet in its youth…" "Youth, Hell!" **1855** W.G. Simms *Forayers* 100: "We've lost him, I reckon."…"Lost h—l!" **1856** Olmstead *Slave States* 631: "They are having a protracted meeting there."…"Hell they are!" **1879** [Tourgée] *Fool's Errand* 197: "An' he wouldn't do it?"…"Do it! Hell!" **1879** in R.L. Stevenson *Across Plains* 45: "I only asked you to pass the milk."…"Pass! Hell! I'm not paid for that business." **1893** Casler *Stonewall* 27: "Cease firing, you are firing on friends!"…I know I remarked, "Friends, hell!" **1899** Hamblen *Bucko Mate* 9: "Did somebody wake you up so soon?"…"Wake me up H—l!" **1928** W.C. Williams *Pagany* 245: And to tell you about my baby.…—You want a baby, hell. **1963** Stallings *Doughboys* ch. v [ref. to 1918]: Neville…replied, "Retreat, hell. We just got here."
     c. a damn.
     *a*1950 P. Wolff *Friend* 92 [ref. to WWII]: Do I give one holy hell what happens? **1968** in J. Flaherty *Chez Joey* 56: And who gave a hell about winning?

     3. (used usu. in possessive in various interjectional phrases to indicate irritation or incredulity). See also HELL'S BELLS, *interj.*
     1832 in *DA:* "Liberty!—why hell sweat"—here I slipped out at the side door. **1903** A. Adams *Log of Cowboy* 108: "Hell's fire and little fishes!" said Joe Stallings. **1904** Hobart *Jim Hickey* 12: Hells delight! *1914–21* J. Joyce *Ulysses* 234: Hell's delights! She has a fine pair, God

bless her. **1925** in E. Wilson *Twenties* 221: Hell's teeth—Christ's foot! **1928** Nason *Sgt. Eadie* 52: Hell's terbaccer! *a*1930 in Tomlinson *Sea Stories* 550: Hell's delight! Fat chance I got...now! **1935** T. Wolfe *Time & River* 71: Hell's pecker!...Let's see the world now! **1937** Kyner & Daniel *End of Track* 78: Hell's fire!...This ain't no spellin' school! **1942** *ATS* 225: Hell's peckerneck! **1951** J. Wilson *Dark & Damp* 227 [ref. *ca*1920]: Hell's pecker, Dode, can't we have some box music? **1958** Frankel *Band of Bros.* 120: Hell's molasses.

4. (used as an intensifier after verbs); the daylights, stuffing, etc.—constr. with *out of*, often with prec. *the*.

1845 *Nat. Police Gaz.* (Oct. 11) 57: They raked hell out of the race [at the bottom of the creek] for the lush. **1866** Dimsdale *Vigilantes* 32: I nearly frightened the h—l out of a fellow over there. **1887** W.P. Lane *Advent.* 61 [ref. to 1848]: Clark...had proposed to "whale h—l out of him" if he said another word. **1893** F.P. Dunne, in Schaaf *Dooley* 272: I could whale hell out iv anny man fr'm Haley's to th' bridge. **1899** J.S. Wise *End of Era* 428 [ref. to Civil War]: He said that the enemy had "knocked hell out of Pickett." **1906–07** Mulford *Bar-20* 66: Plug h—l out of them. **1918** in Asprey *Belleau Wood* 191: Our people have knocked hell out of them and they are running. **1919** Wallgren *AEF* (unp.): I rank hell outa you, teacher. **1924** Anderson & Stallings *What Price Glory?* II: I was kidding hell out of you. **1931** Adamic *Laughing* 89: I'll punch the livin' hell out of you. **1957** Anders *Price of Courage* 117: I admire hell out of the guy. **1964** Newhafer *Tallyho* 29: I'm going to miss hell out of you, Barry. **1978** Truscott *Dress Gray* 35: I've always liked the hell out of him.

5. HELL BOX, 1.

1849 G.G. Foster *Celio* 47: The "hell" I used to have nailed to my case in the shape of an old shoe, into which all battered and broken type were indiscriminately thrown.

6. a formidable or astonishing person. Now esp. *Black E.*

1893 in F. Remington *Sel. Letters* 202: I have always thought I would be "hell on a black charger" if I ever got at Hindoo Koosh or Siam. **1906** *Nat. Police Gaz.* (May 5) 3: I'll put you up against the game, for you always were hell when it came to no limit play. **1929–32** in *AS* (Dec. 1934) 288: [Black student slang] *A hell*...Anyone who excels at something. **1938** R. Chandler, in *Dime Detective* (Jan.): Hell with women—these fliers. **1954–60** *DAS: Hell*...A person who excels. *Some Negro and jive talker use.* **1994** C. Major *Juba to Jive: Hell*...impressive person.

7. ¶ (used in other phr. of obvious meaning, often occ. vars. of those entered hereinunder).

1776 J. Leacock *Fall of Brit. Tyranny* IV.vii: My poor marines stood no more chance with 'em than a cat in hell without claws. **1809** in Whiting *Early Amer. Provs.* 210: Kick up hell and leetle Tom[m]y. **1814** B. Palmer *Diary* (July 9): My prayer is that our Government may send the prisoners in the states to Hell, Hackney or New Orleans. **1820** in Whiting *Early Amer. Provs.* 210: Long ago it was said when a man left other States, he is gone to hell, or Kentucky. **1845** Hooper *Simon Suggs* 49: H-ll and scissors! who ever seed the like of the books! **1850** *Spirit of Times* (Feb. 23) 1: H—l and scissors, stranger! **1851** M. Reid *Scalp-Hunters* 112: We'll hew start enough to carry us from h— to Hackensack. **1862–64** Noel *Campaign* 32: Here it was that I was made to see happy h—l. **1866** Shanks *Personal Recollections* 101 [ref. to Civil War]: I am in possession of Knoxville, and shall hold it till hell freezes over. **1868** in G.W. Harris *High Times* 304: The durndest, scaley heeled, rule-a-roost 'oman, atwix h—l, an' breakfast time. **1881** in A.E. Turner *Earps Talk* 74: I wouldn't last longer than a snowball in hell if I should do that! **1883** Sweet & Knox *Mustang* 17: I can make the biggest man of them eat dirt, *I* can. I'm hell on the Wabash, *I* am. **1885** in Lummis *Letters* 273: My one quart bottle lasted no longer, to use a western simile, than a snowball in h—l. [**1887** C. McKenzie] *Jack Pots* 113: I want $5,000 quicker 'n Hades can scorch a feather.] **1899** Boyd *Shellback* 93: I've had hell and Tommy enough for one day. [**1896** Lillard *Poker Stories* 89: I want $5,000 quicker than Hades can scorch a feather.] [**1899** Kountz *Baxter's Letters* 50: They will stumble over a live wire, and then it will be pay-day on the Wabash.] **1902** L.J. Wilson *Confed. Soldier* 187 [ref. to Civil War]: We'll fight them till h—l freezes over and then meet them on the ice. **1904** in Paxton *Sport U.S.A.* 12: "A snowball in h—l," he said curtly to his assistant. **1906** M'Govern *Sarjint Larry* 134: Almost as scarce as long-tailed icycles in hell. **1907** S.E. White *Ariz. Nights* 139: Smelt like hell on housecleanin' day. **1908** W.G. Davenport *Butte & Montana* 367: The nerve...and lack of judgment...reminds us of a

fool celluloid dog starting to chase an asbestos cat through...hell. **1911** B. Duke *Remin.* 132 [ref. to Civil War]: Well, d—n my eyes to ze deep blue h—l. **1917–20** in J.M. Hunter *Trail Drivers* I 201: I told him I'd fight him till hell froze over, an' then skate with him on the ice, before I'd pay one cent. *Ibid.* 287: Quicker'n hell can scorch a feather. **1920** Mayo *That Damn Y* 321: We'll have about as much chance as a cat in hell without claws. **1923** M. Cowley, in Jay *Burke-Cowley Corres.* 144: How in hell's name are we going to live? **1926** Nason *Chevrons* 113: There'll be happy hell jumpin' here in another minute. **1926** C.M. Russell *Trails* 11: Between the smoke, the barkin' of the guns an' the bellerin' of the bear, it's like hell on a holiday. **1927** Nason *Top-Kick* 286 [ref. to 1918]: Their chance would be less than that of a celluloid cat pursued by an asbestos dog [in hell]. **1927** in Hammett *Knockover* 348: Blue hell!...What good's all that? **1928** F.R. Kent *Pol. Behavior* 102: That "Hell and Maria" stuff of Mr. Dawes before the Senate Committee in 1922 was pure showmanship and extremely effective too. **1930** Botkin *Folk-Say* 49: Here she come from the west like a ball out of hell. **1931** *AS* (Aug.) 435: As much chance as a snowball in hell. **1935** O'Hara *Butterfield 8* 239: She might fool him and say no; there was that chance. "A celluloid cat's in hell," he assured himself, but a chance. **1947** K. Roberts *Lydia Bailey* 38: I'll raise such a dust in all New England that you and your jail and your judges will be blown to Hell, Hull, and Halifax! **1947–52** R. Ellison *Invisible Man* 486: Ride 'em, cowboy. Give 'em hell and bananas. **1953** *JAF* LXVI 293: As little chance as a blind calf in a cane brake, as a snowball in hell on an August afternoon, or as a celluloid cat chasing an asbestos dog in hell. **1955** Childress *Trouble in Mind* 170: While you give me hell-up-the river, I'm supposed to stand here and take it with a tolerance beyond human endurance. ***a*1956** Almirall *College to Cow Country* 93: I could still hear the red-faced old cowman giving me hell an' maria. **1962** A. Stevenson, on news special report (CBS-TV) (Oct. 23): I am prepared to wait for an answer till hell freezes over. **1968** N.Y.C. man: This is a hell of a way to run a railroad [i.e., to do things]. ***1972** in *OED2*: Poor Robert's empirical doubts don't stand a snowflake's chance in hell. **1974** "A.C. Clark" *Death List* 18: I'll bet my front seat in hell, man, that he put out that contract on Billy. **1980** Garrison *Snakedoctor* 175: I might get...blown to Hell and Texas. **1986** *Miami Vice* (NBC-TV): Those guys'd charge hell with a bucket of water. *a*1988 in Safire *Look It Up* 207: A hell of a way to run a railroad. [Includes anecdotal orig. of phr.]. **1988** *Daily Beacon* (Univ. Tenn.) (Mar. 31) 8: It's hell in a handbag trying to read a lot of those students' handwriting in the blue books. **1989** Joss *Strike* 2: Hotter than the hubs of hell or colder than charity...savage extremes [of weather]. **1988–92** R. Mains *Dear Mom* 184: Just what in hell's name do you think you're doing firing that thing? **1993** Carhart *Iron Soldiers* 207: They were ready to charge hell with a bucket of water.

¶ In phrases:

¶ **all over hell** everywhere; all over; in all directions. Also in elab. vars.

1942 *ATS* 44: Everywhere...*all over hell*. **1956–60** J.A. Williams *Angry Ones* ch. xii: Unread manuscripts piled all over hell. *a*1960 N.Y.C. man: There's no point running all over hell for it. **1973** F. Carter *Outlaw Wales* 29: He's got mobs after us all over hell and Sunday...I ain't totin' ye all over hell's creation. **1974** Univ. Tenn. student: They've had me running all over hell and half of Georgia. **1984** Kagan & Summers *Mute Evidence* 81: We had cars scattered all over hell.

¶ **all to hell** [extended fr. *to hell*, below] thoroughly.

1981 *Magnum, P.I.* (CBS-TV): Well, *pardon me* all to *hell!*

¶ **beat hell** to surpass everything, esp. in degree of astonishment.

1837 *Spirit of Times* (June 10) 132: Well now, the lawyer beats hell amazingly. **1893** in Remington *Sel. Letters* 200: I can talk English to beat hell. **1903** A. Adams *Log of Cowboy* 229: Well, wouldn't that beat hell! **1906–07** Mulford *Bar-20* 131: Well, don't that beat hell? **1916** L. Stillwell *Common Soldier* 229 [ref. to Civil War]: Well, don't that beat hell! **1939** "L. Short" *Rimrock* 38: Well, don't that beat hell. **1960–69** Runkel *Law* 152: A peace officer with my record. If that don't beat hell out of the punchin' bag.

¶ **catch** [or **get**] **hell** to suffer severe punishment; (with weakened force) to get a harsh scolding or reprimand.

1857 Willcox *Faca* 86: The offenders preferred to "catch" their "hell" outside, and be strung up to the rigging. **1864** in S.L. Foster *Cleburne's Command* 125: Don't follow us, if you do you will catch

H–ll. **1876** in S.L. Smith *Sagebrush Soldier* 101: I now expected to git hell all a round. **1883** Larison *Silvia Dubois* 65: If I was a little saucy...I'd catch hell again. **1933** Hecht & Fowler *Great Magoo* 24: Forgot all about it...till five minutes ago. Will I get hell! **1935** Odets *Waiting for Lefty:* I smacked a beer truck today. Did I get hell! ***1938** in *OED2:* So then you got hell, I suppose. **1942** in F.A. Johnson *One More Hill* 128: Our 1st Battalion is catching hell [in a German attack]. **1987** J.B. Harris *Cop* (film): Daddy's gonna catch hell. **1995** *Donahue* (NBC-TV): You would catch holy hell.

¶ **cut up hell** to *raise hell,* below.

1857 in *Calif. Hist. Soc. Qly.* IX (1930) 157: Cut up hell, had several wrestles and done some fancy sparking.

¶ **for the hell of it** out of a spirit of sheer mischief or perversity; for fun; for the mere sake of doing it.

*1934 in *OED2:* The mischievous type that misbehaves just for the hell of it. **1939** R. Chandler, in *Sat. Eve. Post* (Oct. 14) 74: I wouldn't be telling you just for the hell of it. **1945–51** Salinger *Catcher in Rye* ch. ix: I'd put on my red hunting cap...just for the hell of it. *a***1987** in *World Bk. Dict.:* The guy who runs the gadget...sent everything into motion just for the hell of it. **1989** *New Republic* (Dec. 18) 4: For the hell of it, I searched for the phrase "essential reading" in...newspaper and magazine articles.

¶ **from hell** Esp. *Stu.* (used as an intensive); formidable, effective, or extraordinary (esp. in a negative way); bad or offensive; good or pleasing.

1965 in W. King *Black Anthol.* 305: Mac's copping me a number from hell for a nickel! **1980** Carlino *Great Santini* (film): Expectin' her to look like horseshit from hell. **1984** N. Stephenson *Big U.* 6: The screaming-guitars-from-Hell power chords. **1988** *Lame Monkey* (Knoxville, Tenn.) (Aug. 22) 7: [The professor is] the biggest goddamned bitch from hell at this university. **1989** *Village Voice* (N.Y.C.) (Apr. 11) 47: You know the guy, schmuck from hell, he'd joke about abortions. **1989** *CBS This Morning* (CBS-TV) (Aug. 30): You've got a schedule this year that's a schedule from hell. **1989** Univ. Tenn. student theme: "From hell"—Anything that is really great *or* really awful...."Draft is the beer from hell." **1991** *New Republic* (Jan. 28) 42: The recent curriculum revision craze has introduced the faculty meeting from hell. **1991** *Simpsons* (Fox-TV): Psychedelic paint job from hell! **1994** *New York* (Feb. 14) 17: His bid for Paramount had turned into "the deal from hell."

¶ **from hell to breakfast, 1.** everywhere; from end to end; thoroughly.

1862 in Wiley *Billy Yank* 78: Scattered from Hell to Breakfast. [**1908** W.G. Davenport *Butte & Montana* 263: He has evidently been up and down the line from Pluto's realm to breakfast.] **1926** Tully *Jarnegan* 168: I've rambled over this world from hell to breakfast— I've drilled over the roads of Spain. **1928** Dobie *Vaquero* 160 [ref. to *ca*1880]: I told my hostess that I understood now what was meant by "riding from hell to breakfast." **1928** C. Sandburg, in *Amer. Mercury* (Aug.) 388: They...left it busted from Hell to breakfast. **1928** Raine *Texas Man* 94: You sure go through from hell to breakfast. **1930** in D.O. Smith *Cradle* 72: They formed us into two sections that stretched from "hell to breakfast." *ca***1943** in L'Amour *Over Solomons* 47: This country has been prospected from hell to breakfast. **1944** *Collier's* (Feb. 12) 70: You outrank me from hell to breakfast time. **1963–64** Kesey *Great Notion* 26: We'll whup this swamp from hell to breakfast. **1978** Rascoe & Stone *Who'll Stop Rain?* (film): I'm layin' wire from hell to breakfast. **1984** J.R. Reeves *Mekong* 76: God damn you from hell to breakfast, you worthless shit-eatin' dog!

2. from far off.

1938 Steinbeck *Grapes of Wrath* 14: When you been in stir a little while you can smell a question comin' from hell to breakfast.

¶ **get hell** see *catch hell,* above.

¶ **get hell in (one's) neck** to become disorderly or intransigent.

1863 in Wiley *Johnny Reb* 140: But when they get Hell in their Neck I cant do any thing with them.

¶ **give hell** to inflict punishment or injury on; let have it; (*hence*) to defeat; vanquish; (*often*) to rebuke severely.

1836 in J. Long *Duel of Eagles* 242: Come on, boys,...we'll give them *Hell.* **1837** *Spirit of Times* (June 10) 132: Jim Cole gave a fellow hell....Jim was on him like a duck on a junebug. **1840** *Spirit of Times*

(May 9) 109: We're giving them other squads hell, I tell you. **1841** [Mercier] *Man-of-War* 33: I've got a noble brush....'twill give a hammock clear hell. **1843–45** T.J. Green *Tex. Exped.* 122: Aha! white man, dey cotch you now; dey gib you hell! **1847** in H.C. Lewis *Works* 115: Well, I guess thar given on her h—l! She yells powerful. **1848** Judson *Mysteries* 356: Go it, Mose! Give him hell! **1856** Olmstead *Slave States* 48: If they ever saw him in those parts again, they would "give him hell." **1861** Wilkie *Iowa First* 113: Now, boys, keep cool, aim low, and give 'em hell. **1861** in H. Holzer *Dear Mr. Lincoln* 47: Give those South Carolina villians [*sic*] h--l and we will support you. **1863** in Boyer *Naval Surgeon* I 169: He gives me particular h—l for the shortness of my letters. **1862–64** Noel *Campaign* 17: Would have give us particular h—l. *ca***1875** in Aswell *Humor* 346: I gave myself some unshredded hell in some of those arguments. **1877** Draper *King's Mountain* 443 [ref. to 1780]: Huzza for Brother Bob!—that's right, give 'em h—l! **1905** W.S. Kelly *Lariats* 118: "Give 'em hell! Give 'em hell!" Now the troops rush toward the fortress, the Spanish fired a terrible volley. **1905** in E.M. Steel *Mother Jones* 55: I give Rosefelt H— about that Commission. **1911** *JAF* (Oct.) 359: The niggers up town givin' cocaine hell. **1923** *Poems, Ballads, & Parodies* 29: And Julius was set to give Jane hell,/But when you're past fifty you never can tell. **1934** Faulkner *Pylon* 187: That blanket will give that skinned place hell. **1946** Steinbeck *Wayward Bus* 23: They were so mad they gave Alice hell about the pie. **1948** (Sept. 17) Pres. H.S. Truman, in *New Yorker* (Apr. 1, 1991) 63: I'm going to give 'em hell! **1979–81** C. Buckley *To Bamboola* 29: The press was much amused and gave her all sorts of hell. **1991** *N.Y. Times* (Mar. 24) (Nippon [adv. supp.]) 7: Persevere, hustle, knuckle down, concentrate on what you're doing, don't let the other guy psych you out, hang in there, give 'em hell.

¶ **go to hell** (used as an imprecation or, later with weakened force, as an expression of disbelief). Now *colloq.* [The imprecatory imper. is undoubtedly much older than the available direct evidence suggests.]

[***1596** Shakespeare *Merchant of Venice* III ii: Let Fortune go to hell for it, not I.] **1788** S. Low *Politician Out-witted* I.i: De ansare vas (excuse moy, monsieur), "go to h-ll, if you be please." **1797** Brackenridge *Mod. Chivalry* 264: Let him gae to hell for me. **1813** in Howay *New Hazard* 137: Mr. Gale...told him to go to hell. ***1816** in *OED2:* Gentlemen, you may go to H-ll. ***1821** *Real Life in Ireland* 249: Go to Hell...the scoundrel is dreaming or mad. **1833** J. Neal *Down-Easters* I 97: Well then you-go to hell, as the Frenchman said. **1843** [W.T. Thompson] *Scenes in Ga.* 27: Oh go to h-ll, will you? **1846** W.H. Richardson *Jour.* 46: Our interpreter cut short his harangue by telling him to "go to hell and bring on his forces." **1847** Robb *Squatter Life* 151: Well, go to h-ll, then. **1850** in *Amer. Neptune* XXI (1961) 72: Telling master-at-arms to go to hell—6 lashes with the colt. **1857** in *Calif. Hist. Soc. Qly.* IX (1930) 140: I sent him word to go to Hell. **1863** in Rowell *Artillerymen* 155: Pat told him to "go to hell" as impudently as possible. **1865** in G.W. Harris *High Times* 162: I ventured tu surjest tu him tu go tu hell. **1886** L. Wood *Geronimo* 33: Go to Hell, I don't speak Spanish. **1887** DeVol *40 Yrs. a Gambler* 18: I walked up to him and asked him what he was doing. He told me to go to h—l. **1905** W.S. Kelly *Lariats* 262: "Go to hell," she hissed. **1908** J. London *M. Eden* 400: You can take that laundry an' go to hell. **1913–14** J. London *Elsinore* 75: Aw, go to hell, you old stiff. **1995** M. Murray *Visitors of Night* (film): "Get in the car!" "Go to hell!" "You go to hell!"

¶ **go to hell on a shutter** *West.* to die by violence.

1922 Rollins *Cowboy* 55: Consequently, each "bad man" sooner or later would "go out of the territory for his health or to hell on a shutter." **1924** Raine *Desert's Price* 53: Someone's going to hell on a shutter one o' these days. **1936** R. Adams *Cowboy Lingo* 171: Perhaps it was said of the deceased that he..."went to hell on a shutter."

¶ **hell afloat** *Naut.* **1.** a vessel having brutal officers or conditions.

*1837 Marryat *Diary in America* 263: I have often heard the expression "Hell afloat" applied to very uncomfortable ships in the service. ******a***1867** Smyth *Sailor's Wd.-Bk.:* Hell-afloat, a vessel with a bad name for tyranny. **1887** Davis *Sea-Wanderer* 100 [ref. to 1830's]: The *Columbus* achieved a most unenviable notoriety, and was not infrequently referred to as the "hell afloat."

2. a steamboat.

1869 J.L. Peyton *Over Alleghanies* 70: A small screw boat,...one of those boats commonly called "out West" "Hells Afloat."

¶ **hell a mile** *hell on wheels*, below.
   1883 Sweet & Knox *Mustang* 247: It's hellamile when you come to tradin' lead with the Indians. **1928** Callahan *Man's Grim Justice* 59: They were astonishingly devout and reverent on Sundays, but from Monday morning till Saturday night they were "hell a mile." *Ibid.* 189: The New York dicks were hell a mile, the toughest gang of man hunters and man-breakers that God Almighty ever created.

¶ **hell and gone** (used as an expletive); distant; godforsaken. See also *since hell and gone, the hell and gone,* and *to hell and gone,* below.
   1919 V. Lindsay *Golden Whales* 21: The hellangone. **1989** "Capt. X" & Dodson *Unfriendly Skies* 11: The two of them sent off to some hell-and-gone airport neither one of them had ever seen before.

¶ **hell and** [or **or**] **high water** nearly insuperable obstacles; in phr. **come hell or high water** no matter what obstacle or difficulty comes; no matter what.
   1915 in *OED2:* He'll be one of us in spite of hell and high water. **1948** *N.Y. Times* (Oct. 7): Coercing and compelling the jury to return some sort of indictment, come hell or high water. **1956** N.Y.C. woman, age *ca*70: And he'll do it, come hell or high water. **1980** W.C. Anderson *Bat-21* 186: I've spent a week and a half with the guy, through hell and high water. **1992** *N.Y. Times* (Oct. 4) (Sports) 9: We were going to make it happen come hell or high water.

¶ **hell for, 1.** intent or insistent upon.
   1832 in Huntingdon *Songs Whalemen Sang* 3: Lay on Captain Bunker/I'm hell for to dart. **1855** W.G. Simms *Forayers* 20: Willie Sinclair is all h—l for a charge! *a*1961 in *WNID3:* He was hell for efficiency and made life miserable for any man who could not fulfill his duties. **1963** Walnut Ridge, Ark., man (coll. J. Ball): He's really hell for Chevies....He's really hot hammered hell for her.

2. exceedingly.
   1958 McCulloch *Woods Wds.* 84: *Hell for*—Exceedingly; as, "hell for strong." **1975** McCaig *Danger Trail* 59: I got me a crew of men that's hell for tough and ready for anything. *a*1979 Toelken *Dyn. of Folklore* 189: It ain't much for purty, but it's hell for stout.

¶ **hell in harness** tremendously powerful or formidable. [Both quots. ref. to railway locomotives.]
   1834 in *AS* XXVIII (1953) 143: When they asked him what scared his horses, he said he did not jist know, but it must be hell in harness. **1839** in Strong *Diary* I 108: As to the engine, the most pithy and expressive epithet I ever heard applied to it is "Hell-in-Harness."

¶ **hell is popping** [or (*obs.*) **flopping**] hell is breaking loose.
   1876 J. Miller *First Fam'lies* 159: Hell's a poppin', I tell yer. **1887** Francis *Saddle & Moccasin* 147: There'll be hell a-popping whenever they do come together. **1887** DeVol *Gambler* 145: I must have my money back, or h—l will flop around here mighty quick. **1893** Hampton *Maj. in Wash.* 9: If I was home now there'd be h—l a poppin' in our neighborhood. **1908** Kelley *Oregon Pen.* 12: Then hell commenced to pop. **1915** H.L. Wilson *Ruggles* 93: Hell begins to pop. **1916** E.R. Burroughs *Return of Mucker* 198: At the ranchhouse, "hell was popping." **1918–19** MacArthur *Bug's-Eye View* 35: Then, the Uhlans were coming down the track, and there would be hell popping. **1922** Hough *Covered Wagon* 237: Hell's a-poppin' now! **1929** "E. Queen" *Roman Hat* 19: Move fast, Mr. Panzer, before hell pops. **1938** Steinbeck *Grapes of Wrath* 41: Hell musta popped here. **1972** *Harper's* (Sept.) 100: Flashing film shots in the background, hellzapoppin sound effects, [etc.].

¶ **hell of** the most bedeviling, vexatious, or surprising feature of.—constr. with *the.*
   ***1903** R. Kipling, in *OEDS:* And that is the perfectest Hell of it! **1913** J. London *J. Barleycorn* 6: And that is the perfectest hell of it. **1921** Dos Passos *3 Soldiers* 77: The hell of it was we got so excited about the race we forgot about the sergeant an' he fell off an' nobody missed him. *a*1961 in *WNID3:* The hell of the plan is that it works. *a*1967 K. Cook *Other Capri* 56: And the hell of it is, we're not getting as much fighter opposition as we used to.

¶ **hell of a** a hellish or extraordinarily unpleasant example of (a thing specified); (*hence*) a poor specimen of (a thing specified); (*later*) an extraordinary or notable example, often in a favorable context. Also **helluva.** Cf. similar colloq. use of *devil of a* in *OED*, def. 14.

*ca***1680** in Burford *Bawdy Verse* 172: It's grown such a Hell of a calling. **1776** J. Leacock *Fall of Brit. Tyranny* IV.vii: Damn it, don't let us kick up a dust among ourselves, to be laugh'd at fore and aft—this is a hell of a council of war. ***1805** J. Davis *Post-Captain* 160: And you was always a h-ll of a fellow to carry sail. **1806** in *DAE:* I've had a hell of a time in your service. ***1810** in *OED:* They all knew what a hell of a row had been kicked up. ***1811** *Lexicon Balatron.* s.v. *article:* She's a devilish good piece, a hell of a *goer.* ***1821** *Real Life in London* I 145: What a h-ll of a light there is! **1831** Seabury *Moneygripe* 63: A hell of a temper. **1833** A. Greene *Duckworth* I 135: Master Switchem gin him one hell of a licking. **1840** *Spirit of Times* (July 4) 216: Well, the piece is going like smoke—somebody's making a hell of a hit—must repeat this another night. **1844** *Spirit of Times* (Mar. 2) 1: *Dear Romeo,* —I have just taken hellebore, and a hell of a bore I find it. **1846** in Oehlschlaeger *Reveille* 131: Telling "a h-ll of a yarn!" **1858** in G.W. Harris *High Times* 87: I have seen...a h—l of a sight smaller breakfasts than this. ***1851–61** H. Mayhew *London Labour* II 224: I...got a h— of a clouting. **1863** in Rowell *Artillerymen* 87: Sir, it is nondescript. A hell of a place the soldiers say. **1863** in T. Whitman *Dear Walt* 23: And a hell of a lot of other things. **1866** E.C. Downs *Scout & Spy* 102: I "was a h—l of a fellow" [and]..."had got a d—d good horse." **1867** in W.H. Jackson *Diaries* 179: We had a h—l of a time crossing. **1874** Pinkerton *Expressman* 68: Och, mine Got, dis ish von h—l of a blace! **1882** Triplett *Jesse James* 40: We'll go to Texas and have a h—l of a time. **1890** Langford *Vigilantes* 439: No passengers, no treasure-box, no *nothing*. This is a —— of an outfit. **1893** F.P. Dunne, in Schaaf *Dooley* 191: Thin they was dinner, a hell iv a dinner, iv turkey, or goose with bacon an' thin a bottle iv th' ol' shtuff with limon an' hot wather, an' toasts was drunk to th' la-ads far away. **1895** Sinclair *Alabama* 169: Why, you'll go on shore, have a h—l of a drunk...and ship again for the Indies. **1900** S.E. White *Westerners* 311: "That was a hell of a performance last night," said Lafond brutally, "and it don't go again." **1904** Hough *Law of Land* 334: Hell of a joke, ain't it? **1905** W.S. Kelly *Lariats* 19: Oh! we'll have a hell of a time....We'll make Mrs. Wilson feel proud of her new home. **1908** W.G. Davenport *Butte & Montana* 35: [That] don't make it wrong by a hellovasite. **1921** Dos Passos *3 Soldiers* 58: But we got to some hell of a town or other. **1924** Anderson & Stallings *What Price Glory?* I i: It's a hell of a war, but it's the only one we've got. **1937** Jeter *Strikers* 9: Polk's a helluva superintendent, anyway. **1941** Hargrove *Pvt. Hargrove* 25: Let's not burden the Army when it has a helluva job already. **1979** *L.A. Times* (May 9) III 1: The month I had was a step in my career. It was a helluva month. **1988–89** L.D. Levine *Bird* 240: He's one hell of a competitor. **1994** *Newsweek* (Nov. 14) 20: Having a hell of a time.

¶ **hell of a note** an extraordinarily unpleasant piece of news.
   1871 Banka *Prison Life* 415: Pardoned! that's a "hell" of a note! **1897** in S. Crane *War Dispatches* 51: This is a heluva note. Wanta shoestring? This is a heluva note. **1900** Hammond *Whaler* 270: Wa-al, *that's* a —— of a note, *that* is. [**1902** "J. Flynt" *Little Bro.* 223: This is a devil of a note.] **1909** in "O. Henry" *Works* 1604: Say, Shack, ain't that a hell of a note? **1914** in J. Reed *Young Man* 101: And now comes an order from Villa to discharge all the Americans in the ranks and ship 'em back to the border. Ain't that a hell of a note? **1921** Dos Passos *3 Soldiers* 46: They're having an inspection. It's a hell of a note. **1931** *AS* (Aug.) 434: Got away! Well, that's a hell of a note. **1941** Cain *Mildred Pierce* 125: Well say, this is a hell of a note. **1994** *My So-Called Life* (ABC-TV): *That's* a hell of a note. **1995** *Harper's* (Nov.) 55: He had more expensive stuff to worry about. Ain't that a hell of a note.

¶ **hell on, 1.** very fond of; concerned with; (*also*) a capital hand at.
   1850 in Thornton *Amer. Gloss.* I 244: Mammy has always been hell on dignity. **1857** *Spirit of Times* (Dec. 26) 544: I know but d—d little law, but I am *h—* on jestice. **1865** in Sala *Diary* II 336: To be h—— on anything means to be what we call a "dab" at it. **1872** Marcy *Reminiscences* 151: But what the old man wants you particularly for is to dive for oysters, for he's h—l on oysters. **1873** Small *Grangers* 42: "I'm hell on pork!" said he, as he started for the hog pen. **1920** Conklin & Root *Circus* 25: He "was hell on figures." **1966** Walnut Ridge, Ark., high school student (coll. J. Ball): He [the coach] is really hell on pass plays.

2. very hard on, effective against, or detrimental to; (*also*) opposed to.
   1944–61 D.K. Webster *Para. Inf.* 15: Don't let the general catch

you in a wool-knit cap!…The general's hell on wool-knit caps! *a*1961 in *WNID3:* Such a life was hell on his digestion. **1961** Forbes *Goodbye to Some* 50: Swede Engelson is hell on this form of celebration. **1972** U.S. soldier, Taiwan (coll. J. Ball): The CO's really hell on new guys. **1985** Briskin *Too Much* 125: The steep grade…was holy hell on the big rig's brakes.

¶ **hell on wheels** hellish; most formidable, savage, or aggressive; ungovernable; relentless. Also vars. Also as interj.

1843 in *DA: Hell-upon-Wheels!* now if that ain't the most appropriate name for that craft, you may blow me. **1845** Carleton *Logbooks* 188: H–ll upon *trucks!* what upon earth is to pay now! **1868** in *DA:* It is a most aggravated specimen of the border town of America, not inaptly called "Hell on Wheels." **1885** in Lummis *Letters* 228: In general letting us know what a hell of terror he was on wheels. **1893** in S. Crane *Complete Stories* 110: It was hell on roller skates. **1908** in *DA:* A mule…[whose] name was Hell-on-wheels. **1918** in Grider *War Birds* 274: Tubby Ralston…reports hell on roller skates. **1925** T. Boyd *Points* 258: Those West Pointers think they're hell on wheels. **1932** Ellsberg *S-54* 266: Our skipper was hell on wheels, wit' no more regard fer a groggy sailor 'n ye might have fer a sick alley cat. **1936** Dos Passos *Big Money* 195: The plant's been hell on wheels all week. **1942–43** C. Jackson *Lost Weekend* 73: Do you know what a good woman is? They're hell on wheels. **1949** R. MacDonald *Moving Target* 11: He can be hell on wheels. **1954** Mirvish *Texana* 56: But from what I've been told he's no hell on wheels. **1960–61** Steinbeck *Winter of Discontent* 176: I won't allow the kids to make my free two weeks a hell on wheels. **1970** Grissim *Country Music* 286: If I could play a guitar like B.B. King, I'd be President of the United States. I'd be hell on wheels. **1982** Braun *Judas Tree* 50: Palmer was a hell-on-wheels lawman. **1982** *L.A. Times* (Sept. 15) V 6: He [*sc.* William Saroyan] was someone to reckon with.…And hell on wheels to have as a father. **1991** McCoy & Mallowe *Vice Cop* 201: He thought I was hell on wheels. **1996** *Donahue* (NBC-TV): My son's hell on wheels. He'll take a piece of steel and bend it around.

¶ **hell's broke loose in Georgia** *So.* hell has broken loose.

1882 Watkins *Co. Aytch* 158 [ref. to Civil War]: Afterward I heard a soldier express himself by saying that he thought "Hell had broke loose in Georgia, sure enough." **1931** *PMLA* XLVI 1305: Hell's broke loose in Georgy! (A fight has commenced.)

¶ **hell's mint of** a great quantity [of].

1873 "M. Twain" & Warner *Gilded Age* ch. i: He's come back…with a hell's-mint o' whoop-jamboree notions. **1887** Francis *Saddle & Moccasin* 123: There's a hell's mint of soap-weed killed these Indian times. **1909** in "O. Henry" *Works* 1656: He'll ask you a hell's mint of questions.

¶ **hell's own** very much of a; a *hell of a*, above.

1893 F.P. Dunne, in Schaaf *Dooley* 68: He'll be th' 'ell's own man, won't he though? **1926** Hemingway *Sun Also Rises* 54: You've got hell's own drag with the concierge now. **1926** in Hemingway *Sel. Letters* 190: And I think you're making hell's own strides as a poet. **1929** J.M. Saunders *Single Lady* 228: It's hell's own shakes of a place for officials. *1968 in *OED2:* I had hell's own time changing the wheel. **1968** W. Crawford *Gresham's War* 40: I…agreed he must have been hell's own fine pilot.

¶ **hell to pay** dire consequences to be faced.

*1807 in *OED2:* There has been hell to pay between the Dukes of York and Cumberland. **1850** in Blair & McDavid *Mirth* 105: There was all the folks, there was the snake, and…hell to pay! **1878** in *Seal & Salmon Fisheries* IV 6: Thereafter the town and Indian village would be flooded and —— would be to pay. **1906–07** Mulford *Bar-20* 118: Get yore hands closer to yore neck or they'll be h—l to pay! **1942–49** in F.A. Johnson *One More Hill* 69: It's hell to pay and no hot pitch on the seventh. **1969** Stern *Eagles* 313: Hell to pay and no pitch hot.

¶ **hell-west and crooked** [or **winding**] into complete disarray, disorder, confusion, etc.; in every direction.

1878 Hart *Sazerac* 147: We're blowed hellwest and crooked. **1907** S.E. White *Ariz. Nights* 176: This event sure knocks me hell-west and crooked. **1914** Nisbet *4 Yrs. on Firing Line* 154: One of their shells…[exploded] sending our dishes and dinner "hell-west-and-winding." **1928** in Grayson *New Stories* 217: He's knocked him hell west and crooked. *1951 in *Austral. Nat. Dict.* 308: One big stampede to unnerve them, and the cattle are off every night, "hell, west, and crooked." *1966, *1970 in *Austral. Nat. Dict.*

¶ **hell with the lid off** that which is exceptionally difficult to deal with or bear.

1893 M. Philips *Newspaper* 219: The late James Parton said that Pittsburgh at night reminded him of "hell with the lid taken off." **1925** Bailey *Shanghaied* 166 [ref. to 1899]: He'll be Hell with the lid off in the mornin'! *ca*1969 *Gunsmoke* (CBS-TV): It was hell with the lid off.

¶ **holy hell!** (used to express astonishment, frustration, or the like). Cf. **(2.c.)**, above, and *raise hell*, below.

1927 in Hammett *Big Knockover* 288: "Holy hell!" she gasped, and was gone. *1931 Hanley *Boy* 75: Well, Holy Hell! **1965** Pollini *Glover* 96: Holy Hell, man! **1966** F. Elkins *Heart of Man* 33: Holy hell, who just went by me?

¶ **hope** [or **wish**] **to hell** to hope [or wish] intensely.

[**1884** in Lummis *Letters* 17: I wish to misery, I could find some water…fit to drink.] *1891 in *F & H* III 300: I hope to H—— the horse will break his neck and his rider's too. *a1890–93 *F & H:* To hope (or *wish*) *to hell*…To desire intensely. **1929–31** Farrell *Young Lonigan* 50: I wish to hell you'd lemme alone. **1939** in *Army Song Book* 8: I…hope to h—— for once he's right. *1962 in *OED2:* I wish to hell I was out of it.

¶ **I'll be go to hell!** Esp. *Midwest & West.* (used to express astonishment).

1938 Haines *Tension* 140: I'll be go to hell.…What does it weigh, Margrave? **1952** Uris *Battle Cry* 171: I'll be go to hell, that's great. **1957** Leckie *Helmet for My Pillow* 78: Well I'll be go-to-hell! **1962** G. Ross *Last Campaign* 94: "Well, I'll be go to hell!" Benfield said in mock surprise. **1963** J. Ross *Dead Are Mine* 196: "Well I'll be go to hell!" Terry softly exclaimed. **1982** Braun *Judas Tree* 55: I'll be go to hell! **1978–86** J.L. Burke *Lost Get-Back Boogie* 134: I'll be go-to-hell if I should have done any such thing.

¶ **in [the] hell** *the hell*, 1, below.—used after interrogatives only.

1847 Buhoup *Narrative* 16: Fellow Sogers: what in the h-ll is these things they call haversacks? **1861** in *Jour. Ill. Hist. Soc.* XVIII (1926) 817: Who in the hell is that fellow anyhow? **1861** in *Iowa Jour. of Hist.* LVII (1959) 102: Why in the Hell don't you holler fire. **1873** J. Miller *Modocs* 78: What in hell are you doing here anyhow? **1877** Hayes *Diary* 72: Why did the Devil never learn to skate? [Answer.] How in Hell could he? **1890** in F. Remington *Sel. Letters* 103: What in the h—did you…buy one for? **1902** L.J. Wilson *Confed. Soldier* 52: Where in the h—ll are you going? **1902** in *OEDS:* Then why in hell didn't you say so! **1913–14** J. London *Elsinore* 20: Who in hell's the old stiff annyways? **1922** P. Rollins *Cowboy* ch. iv: How in hell can a man keep from dropping out a cuss word now and then…? **1931** *AS* (Aug.) 433: Where in the hell are you going? **1944** Sherrod *Tarawa* 5: Where in the hell am I going to put them? **1958** in C. Beaumont *Best* 212: How in the holy hell did you know about this? **1967** Schaefer *Mavericks* 69: What in holy hell you doin' without a hat? **1973** Gent *N. Dallas* 297: Who in Great God's Hell do you think you are? **1973** C. Ozick, in *Ms.* (Spring): What in hell was going on? **1976** Machlin *Pipeline* 437: How in the hell did they get it out? **1994** C. Bradley *Aleutian Echoes* 256: Why in all hell are you burning these sleeping bags?

¶ **kick up hell** see *raise hell*, below.

¶ **like hell, 1.** see (1), above.

2. (used sarcastically or ironically to express strong negation or incredulity).

*1892 in Kipling *Works* XIX 66: "Hit, old man?" "Like hell," he said, and went on biting his unlit cigar. **1921** Dos Passos *3 Soldiers* 16: Like hell he did. **1924** Anderson & Stallings *What Price Glory?* III: Like hell I am. **1929** Asch *Pay Day* 72: Like hell you don't. **1937** Jeter *Strikers* 148: Like hell I am. **1947** Roberts *Lydia Bailey* 46: "Perhaps things might be worse."…"Like hell they might!" **1945–51** Salinger *Catcher in Rye* ch. xi: Like hell you are.…Cut the crap. **1972** R. Barrett *Lovomaniacs* 408: The day would come when he would.…*Like hell!* **1989** Univ. Tenn. instructor: He told me to move my car, and I said "Like hell!"

¶ **play hell [and Tommy]** to create a disturbance; make trouble; create havoc or ruin. Cf. earlier S.E. *play the devil*, in *OED* s.v. *devil*, def. 22k.

1780 in F. Moore *Songs of Revolution* 301: Know that some paltry refugees…/Are playing h—l amongst the trees. **1792** Brackenridge *Mod. Chivalry* 261: I am not afraid of the devil; I could…play hell with him. *1803 in *OEDS:* I'll be good to the landlord but I'll play hell with his wife! [*1805 J. Davis *Post-Captain* 116: The Frenchman's shot is playing at hell and turn-up-jack there!] *1815 in J. Ashton *Eng. Satires on Napoleon* 415: I'll play Hell with them all. *1832–34 T. De Quincey, in *OED:* Lord Bacon played Hell and Tommy when casually raised to the supreme seat in the council. **1835** Longstreet *Ga. Scenes* 45: They're playing h—l with her there, in Zeph Atwater's store. **1838** [Haliburton] *Clockmaker* (Ser. 2) 148: Plunder 'em, and tax 'em,…and play hell and Tommy with them. **1843** Field *Pokerville* 68: Mr. Waters had come into town, alone, "rearin' up and playin' hell." **1855** W.G. Simms *Forayers* 74: Ef you wants to play h-ll wid de crop, da's jist de way for do um. *1879 in *OED:* I've played hell-and-tommy already with the lot of them. **1893** in Remington *Sel. Letters* 175: Jim is playing hell on a scweeaky old fiddle. **1918** in Grider *War Birds* 100: The Hun has played hell with the troops in France. **1928** Harlow *Sailor* 1: "We could have picked you up after the squall had passed." "You'd play hell doing it," said the mate. **1938** T. Wolfe *Web & Rock* 206: He's just an ass! He's just gone and played hell, that's what he's done! **1944** in Tapert *Lines of Battle* 145: The flack was bad, and the Jerry fighters sure played hell. **1979** Cassidy *Delta* 223: This is just going to play hell with our beautiful platonic relationship. **1984** N. Stephenson *Big U.* 31: The Worm…began to play hell with things.

¶ **raise** [or **kick up**] **hell** to create havoc or a disturbance, esp. in revelry or merrymaking; create an uproar. Also in elab. vars., esp. with *holy* or *merry.*

1796 in *DA:* Nor any other hell-kicking treaty member. **1815** B. Palmer *Diary* (entry for June 7): Then there was Hell Kicked up. Sure enough. [*1821 *Real Life in London* I 195: So drunk, that they keep *merry hell* in a roar.] **1845** in Oehlschlaeger *Reveille* 117: Jake was off a raisin' h-ll. **1858** in G.W. Harris *High Times* 138: I hed suckseedid in raisin' h—l generally. **1862** in M. Lane *Dear Mother* 128: James Howell…has raised and pitched and kicked up hell. **1866** "E. Kirke" *Guerillas* 77: The Cunnel will raise — with all on us, ef ye doan't. **1875** in F. Remington *Sel. Letters* 11: The fellows raise H— with him. **1900** S.E. White *Westerners* 110: I feels jest like raisin' hell and puttin' a chunk under it! **1906–07** Mulford *Bar-20* 352: The prettier they are, th' more h—l they can raise. **1904–11** D.G. Phillips *Susan Lenox* II 279: To have merry hell raised with us. **1922** Rollins *Cowboy* 46 [ref. to 1889]: Rise up, you murderous devils, and raise immortal hell for the ladies. **1924** Anderson & Stallings *What Price Glory?* I i: There's a drunken Mick named Mulcahy raising hell outside. *ca*1926 in *OED2:* We don't get drunk to…kick up merry hell. **1931** *AS* (Aug.) 434: We'll raise hell and put a block under it. **1929–33** Farrell *Young Manhood* 310: You…raised all holy hell. **1937** Kober *Having Wonderful Time* 53: But they're raisin' holy hell with me! **1954** E. Hunter *Runaway Black* 7: Some big boy upstairs would raise six kinds of hell if this sort of thing went on. **1965** Linakis *In Spring* 108: I expected Mama to raise merry hell about the screaming. **1970** Thackrey *Thief* 419: So I raised hell and stuck a prop under it. **1990** *U.S. News & W.R.* (Dec. 17) 90: I said I was going to raise hell on the field and off.

¶ **send to hell** to kill (someone).

1839 in Eliason *Tarheel Talk* 104: Should they conclude you were a pidgeon no longer worth the plucking there are many of them who would willingly send you to Hell to pump thunder at 3 cts. a clap. **1857** Gladstone *In Kans.* 47: I'd send him to hell pretty quick. **1873** J. Miller *Modocs* 120: Keep your distance, you Sydney duck,…or I will send you to hell across lots in a second. **1962** C. Ryan *Longest Day* (film): Send 'em to hell!

¶ **since hell and gone** since before anyone can remember.

1929–33 Farrell *Young Manhood* 194: He hadn't had a fight since hell-and-gone.

¶ **smell hell** to face, endure, or sense great danger, trouble, or hardship.

1834–40 R.H. Dana *Before the Mast* ch. xxx: You may see Boston, but you've got to "smell hell" before that good day. **1841** [Mercier] *Man-of-War* 15: We'll double the cape in…November…and if you don't smell h-ll, then my name aint Garnet. *1881 (cited in *EDD*). **1981–89** R. Atkinson *Long Gray Line* 30: Tom could "smell hell" as he waddled into the corridor.

¶ **the hell, 1.** (used as an intensifier to express irritation, anger, impatience, etc.; orig. after interrogatives, later also with certain usu. imperative verb-adverb combinations

[esp. with *get*], now also with greater syntactical flexibility); in phr. **what the hell!** (used to express resignation or cynical acceptance); so what! Cf. similar, earlier uses of *the devil* (*OED*, def. 20), infl. by **(4),** above.

*1829 Marryat *Frank Mildmay* 22: What the h— brought you back again, you d—d young greenhorn? *1837 C. Dickens, in G. Hughes *Swearing* 152: Demanded in a surly tone what the—something beginning with a capital H—he wanted. **1840** Dana *Before the Mast* [ref. to 1836] 235: Who the hell are you? **1842** in Barnum *Letters* 18: Now how the hell to keep anything from the damned traitors. **1845** in Robb *Squatter Life* 62: "What the h—l are you doin' in *disguise*?" says the old man—he swore dreadfully. **1848** G.G. Foster *N.Y. in Slices* 120: Who de —— guv yer de extra shillin'? **1855** Wise *Tales for Marines* 311: Why, who the hell be you? **1857** Rivors *Murders* 63: What the bloody hell is the use of keeping me here just waiting on you? **1864** Armstrong *Generals* 253: Who the h—l ever heard of a sutler being entitled to any justice? *1872 "G. Eliot," in *OEDS:* But what the hell! the horse was a penny trumpet to that roarer of yours. **1878** McElroy *Andersonville* 116: What the hell does Key want with me? **1892** F.P. Dunne, in Schaaf *Dooley* 42: He's been down to see Grover. What th' 'ill! He's as good as Grover anny day. **1902** Bell *Worth of Words* 219: *To get solid with…To bet your sweet life*…and *What th' 'ell, Bill?* are all strong slang phrases. *a*1904–11 D.G. Phillips *Susan Lenox* II 257: Get the hell out.…I want to sleep. **1913** A. Palmer *Salvage* 76: Why the h— are you snivelling, Rose? **1916** T. Dreiser, in Riggio *Dreiser-Mencken Letters* I 259: Which the h—— is it? **1918** Grider *War Birds* 173: I saw a Hun two-seater away the hell and gone over Roulers. **1918** in Hemingway *Sel. Letters* 8: Anyway my girl loves me and she believes I am going to be a great newspaper man and says she will wait for me, so What the Hell Bill. **1921** Dos Passos *3 Soldiers* 76: Where the hell's Nantes? *Ibid.* 79: Well, I've got to get the hell out of here. *Ibid.* 81: How the hell did she get here? **1922–24** White *Light* 31: She cries throatily, after the manner of Ethel Barrymore: "I'm all the hell there is, there isn't any more." **1928** Anderson & Hickerson *Lightning* 535: Will you get the hell out? **1929** Hammett *Maltese Falcon* 43: "What the hell?" Spade's surprise was genuine. **1930** in E. O'Neill *Letters* 367: So what the hell, Bill, what the hell? **1929–33** Farrell *Young Manhood* 452: Red…told him to get the hell out of the place. **1938** *Amer. Mercury* (Oct.) 146: We have only forty more blocks to go, so what the hell? **1943** in M. Curtiss *Letters Home* 21: Hello and how the hell are you? **1948** Cozzens *Guard of Honor* 260: Way the hell up [in the sky]. **1949** Robbins *Dream Merchants* 10: George…how the hell are yuh? **1945–51** Salinger *Catcher in Rye* ch. vi: No wonder you're flunking the hell out of here. **1956–60** J.A. Williams *Angry Ones* ch. i: Let's get the hell out of here. *a*1960 Common in N.Y.C.: It's way the hell across town someplace.…Shut the hell up!…Stay the hell away from there!…Leave me the hell alone!…Get your hands the hell off of my stuff!…I wish the hell you'd shut up. **1966** F. Harvey *Raiders* 200: Get the hell ready! **1967** J. Herndon *Spozed to Be* 53: What the hell good was it? **1975** Kennedy *Train Robbers* (film): "We're not stayin'." "How the hell come?" **1978** Groom *Better Times* 460: And you'd better the hell keep a respectful attitude. **1980** Hillstrom *Coal* 50: You'd better the hell get on out. **1986** *Night Court* (NBC-TV): I just want him to *get* the *hell* out of my *life!* **1989** *It's Garry Shandling's Show* (Fox-TV): Get the hell out of the store! **1992** C. Lucas *Prelude to a Kiss* (film): Who the hell is she, anyway?

2. (used sarcastically or ironically to express disbelief or contempt). Cf. similar use since early ModE of *the devil* (*OED*, def. 21).

1843 [W.T. Thompson] *Scenes in Ga.* 32: The h-ll you is! **1844** *Spirit of Times* (Mar. 16) 27: "Mr. President, the Capitol is on fire," said a Senator. "The hell it is!" said the President. **1845** Hooper *Simon Suggs* 159: The Grand Jurors of the State of Alabama…upon their oaths present—the h—l they do!—that Simon Suggs [etc.]. **1847** in McClellan *Mex. War Diary* (Jan. 2) 29: "Holloa there," says the Colonel "you man there, you don't know how to file." "The h—l I dont," yells the man "d—n you, I've been marching all day, and I guess I'm tired." **1854** in G.W. Harris *Lovingood* 34: The hell yu did! **1866** E.C. Downs *Scout & Spy* 96: A prisoner? the h—l you are! **1882** D.J. Cook *Hands Up* 51: "The hell you do!" he exclaimed, showing that he took in the situation at a glance. **1886** in *Mil. Essays & Recoll.* I 145: "I've often heard Colonel Ruggles speak of you.…" "The h—l! do you know Ruggles?" **1893** Casler *Stonewall* 192: "Digging a gun-pit," I replied. "The h—l you are...you are digging potatoes." **1893** F.P. Dunne, in Schaaf *Dooley* 64: Th' 'ell he has. **1910** Z. Grey *Heritage of Desert* 107: "The h—l you did!" shouted Snood. **1931** Bontemps *Sends Sunday* 32: "Tha's a ignorant damn lie." "De hell it is." **1937** Jeter *Strikers* 87: "I'd almost decided there wasn't much we could do." "The hell there ain't."

¶ **the hell and gone** (used after *away* as an intensifier). Cf. *hell and gone* and *since hell and gone*, above, and *to hell and gone*, below.

   1918 (quot. at *the hell*, 1, above). **1926** Springs *Nocturne* 71: It was way the-hell-and-gone from Piccadilly.

¶ **the hell with** see *to hell with*, below.

¶ **the hell you say!** (used to express surprise or incredulity at another's words). Also vars.

   1864 in W.C. Davis *Orphan Brig.* 235: "Surrender, you dam Rebels."..."The H—l you say." **1866** Marcy *Army Life* 373: The he-e-e-ll you say, stranger! **1867** Duke *Morgan's Cavalry* 161: "The h-ll you say," responded a member of Co. A; "Don't you think Morgan's men need praying for as well as Woolford's?" **1877** *Puck* (Apr.) 2: The h-ll you say! **1902** L.J. Wilson *Confed. Soldier* 79 [ref. to Civil War]: "I...am trying to reach home to refit for the war." "The h—l you say, come back, comrade, have a drink, and tell us of the 'foit.'" **1922** Rice *Adding Machine* 117: The hell yer say! **1924** W. White *Fire in the Flint* 101: Th' hell you say! **1924** *Adventure* (Mar. 30) 161: The —— you preach! **1934** Cain *Postman* 53: The hell you say. Getting tough with me, hey? **1942** *Inf. Jour.* 156 [ref. to 1918]: The hell you pipe! **1959** A. Anderson *Lover Man* 116: "Yeah." "The hell you preach." **1961** O. Davis *Purlie* 303: The hell you preach!

¶ **to hell, 1.** to ruin or destruction; (*hence*) to pieces. Also in elab. vars.

   [**1776** J. Leacock *Fall of Brit. Tyranny* IV.iii: Blast 'em, if they come within a cable's length of my hammock, I'll kick 'em to hell through one of the gun ports.] **1820** Durand *Able Seaman* 65: I wished that Captain and every Englishman I knew had been on board the *Guerriere* to be blown to hell with her. **1827** in *JAF* LXXVI (1963) 294: Thare's a thousen dollers gone tu hel. **1841** [Mercier] *Man-of-War* 119: Have that old jacket to h-ll, and put up something worth looking at. [**1861** *Mo. Army Argus* (Nov. 30): If everybody is, in fact, goin to the old Nick in a hand gallop, let the Croaker Division be made an advanced guard.] **1881** in F. Remington *Sel. Letters* 30: Husted will be "cut to hell" [in the election]. **1892** in F. Remington *Sel. Letters* 151: Miles is the only...[one] who is worth the powder to blow him to hell. *a***1890–93** *F & H* III 300: *All to hell* (or *gone to hell*)...Utterly ruined. **1905** D.G. Phillips *Plum Tree* 23: Otherwise what becomes of the party? Why, it goes to hell, and we've got anarchy. **1912** *DN* III 577: He's runnin' with Josh Sanders—goin' to hell in a wheelbarrow. **1913–14** London *Elsinore* 11: The merchant service is all shot to hell. **1918** in "M. Brand" *Coll. Stories of Max Brand* 37: I'll go to hell and slave for you as long as I live....Tell me again that you love me and you'll be a man! **1922–24** McIntyre *White Light Nights* 226: What do you expect me to do?...Ride to hell in a hack? **1924** Anderson & Stallings *What Price Glory?* I i: We've gone to hell for chow since he left. *Ibid.* II: Right arm torn all to hell. **1928** J.M. March *Set-Up* 41: Dere goes duh goddamned shoe-string t' hell! **1931** Rynning *Gun Notches* 104: The dam had gone to hell schooner-rigged. **1929–33** Farrell *Young Manhood* 379: Then he left school and he just went to hell. **1937** Barry *Clowns* 554: You know if you don't watch her like a hawk she'll go to hell in a hack. **1938** Steinbeck *Grapes of Wrath* 86: A wicketer, cussin' er man never lived. He's goin' to hell on a poker, praise Gawd! **1941** Randolph *Church House* 130: The Government was going to hell in a handbasket. **1942** *ATS* 10: Ruined...*all to hell.* **1942** Algren *Morning* 104: His kid won't be goin' to hell on *that* handcar. **1952** Sandburg *Young Strangers* 169 [ref. to *ca*1890]: The first time I heard about a man "going to hell in a hanging basket" I did a lot of wondering what a hanging basket is like. **1952** Steinbeck *E. of Eden* 217: Each happily believed all the others were bound for hell in a basket. **1953** Wicker *Kingpin* 60: The old American backbone and spirit...are just about shot to hell. **1958** J. Jones *Pistol* 33: The world was rocketing to hell in a bucket. **1965** Longstreet *Real Jazz* 36: Again some say "the classic blues period is gone to hell in a hack." **1965** LeMay & Kantor *Mission* 311: The whole outfit will go to hell in a handbasket, and so will that particular operation. **1966** Longstreet & Godoff *Wm. Kite* 83: I tell you creation is

going to hell in a handcart. **1970** N.Y.U. student: The world is going to hell in a hack. **1972** *Maude* (CBS-TV): The country is going to hell on a toboggan. **1972** Pendleton *Boston Blitz* 153: The rest of you guys can go to hell in a basket for all I care. **1983** S. King *Christine* 421: Let him go to hell in his own handcar. **1985** Briskin *Too Much* 291: As far as I'm concerned, this marriage is going to hell in a bucket. **1989** *CBS This Morning* (CBS-TV) (Nov. 8): We'll be going to hell in a bucket. **1994** *Donahue* (NBC-TV): His grades went to hell. **1996** *Donahue* (NBC-TV): We better start working together, or we're going to go to hell in a handbasket.

   2. far away; far off; (*also*) *the hell*, 1, above.

   1833 Ames *Old Sailor's Yarns* 216: We ketch'd one of these thundering Levanters, and was druv 'way to h-ll, away up the Gulf of Venus. [**1895** J.L. Williams *Princeton* 11: Dash it! I wish to dash you fellows would dash quickly get to dash out of here.] **1904** *Independent* (Mar. 24) 658: I heard the Old Man call out to them to get to 'ell for'ard. **1908** in J. London *Short Stories* 310: You've got to get to hell outa here. **1929** Asch *Pay Day* 67: And then why to hell meet her?

¶ **to hell and gone, 1.** to utter ruin or destruction.

   1863 in H. Lind *Long Road Home* 151: Tom the sailor [a prizefighter] knocked him to hell and gone. **1865** in Hilleary *Webfoot* 132: Lots of it [has] blown to hell and gone. **1887** Francis *Saddle & Moccasin* 228: [The gamblers] played him to hell and gone in a very short time. **1916** in J. London *Short Stories* 677: I'll bust the whole outfit to hell and gone.

   2. to, at, or in a distant place; very far away. Cf. *hell and gone*, above.

   1908 Paine *Stroke Oar* 142: If they take you to hell-and-gone, obey my orders. **1914** in R. Lardner *Round Up* 257: They'll ship me to Hellangone. **1916** *Sat. Eve. Post* (Feb. 12) 8: Away to hell-and-gone, on the other side of town! **1927** in F.V. Mason *Fighting Amer.* 698 [ref. to 1918]: We're scattered to hellangone. **1927–28** in R. Nelson *Dishonorable* 112: Out to hellangone on that interview. **1935** Lindsay *Loves Me Not* 16: I...beat it to hellandgone. **1937** Binns *Laurels Are Cut* 124: We got iced up and driven away to-hell-and-gone into the Pacific. **1943** Coale *Midway* 30: Damn it—I'm ordered to hell-an-gone down under. **1961** Himes *Pinktoes* 21: Now it's to hell and gone in all directions, north, east, south, and west, from the Harlem River to the Hudson. **1961** in A. Sexton *Letters* 130: I...have been giving readings around hell and gone. **1967** Edson *Fast Gun* 117: Before all the horses spooked to hell-and-gone.

¶ **to** [or (*later*) **the**] **hell with** (used in imprecations or as an expression of irritation or anger).

   1846 *Nat. Police Gaz.* (June 27) 353: To hell with you! you bloody hound! **1849** in *Calif. History* LXIII (1984) 316: To H-ll wid you and yer Childer. *****1851** H. Mayhew *London Labour* I 55: If this here is free trade, then to h——with it, I say! **1865** in Glatthaar *March to Sea* 184: To h—l with your reveille. **1896** F.P. Dunne, in Schaaf *Dooley* 238: All in favor'll say "Aye." To 'ell with th' noes. **1900** in J. London *Letters* I 170: To hell with foundations. **1913** in *OEDS*: To hell with 'em. **1918** in Grider *War Birds* 144: To hell with all expense! **1918** Mencken *Amer. Lang.* 128: Early in 1918, when a patriotic moving-picture entitled "To Hell with the Kaiser" was sent on tour under government patronage, the word *hell* was carefully toned down, on the Philadelphia billboards, to h——. **1919** I. Cobb *Life of Party* 32: Aw, to hell with you and your troubles! **1933** Hecht & Fowler *Great Magoo* 194: To hell with it!...No Mr. Kuntzmiller for me! **1936** Farrell *World I Never Made* 168: Well, the hell with it all! **1937** Kober *Having Wonderful Time* 38: I say the hell with him! **1938** R. Chandler in *Dime Detective* (Jan.): To hell with guys like you guys. **1974** R. Fitzgerald *Iliad* 215: To hell with him, Zeus took his brains away! **1980** *N.Y. Times* (June 22) IV 11: Join with me in saying: standard English—the hell with anything else! **1984–85** in Schneider & Schneider *Sound Off!* 128: Well, I've got mine. The hell with you.

hell *v. West.* to gallop or go noisily. Cf. earlier HELL AROUND.

   *a***1951** in A. Lomax *Folk Songs of No. Amer.* 371: He's a-helling and a-yelling as he drifts by. *a***1956** Almirall *College to Cow Country* 350 [ref. to *a*1918]: The...cow ponies...couldn't go hellin'.

hella- *prefix* [sugg. by HELLACIOUS, *hell of a, s.v.* HELL, etc.] *Stu.* exceedingly; MEGA-; extraordinary. Also as adj., many; much.

   1989 *Life* (July) 27: "He's so *tender*," she tells a friend. "He's *hella-fine.*"...At parties he'd get *messed up* or *hella-high.* **1989** P. Munro *U.C.L.A. Slang* 48: You should see that new movie; it's hella cool.

*a*1990 E. Currie *Dope & Trouble* 75: She was like *hella* big. **1990** Thorne *Dict. Contemp. Sl.* 239: *Hella* prefix…The most popular device in the combination "hellacool," heard among American teenagers in 1987 and 1988. **1991** in *RapPages* (Feb. 1992) 58: To create hella collages. **1993** P. Munro *U.C.L.A. Slang* 2: *That movie was hella good.*…adj. a lot of, many: *There are hella people here.* **1993** "Snoop Doggy Dogg" *Murder was the Case* (rap song): Havin' money and blowin' hella chronic smoke. **1997** *N.Y. Times* (Jan 5.) ("metro") 25: New York City was hella cold last year.

hellacious *adj.* [alter. of *hellish*] *So. & West.* extraordinarily good, bad, intense, violent, severe, etc. Hence **hellaciously,** *adv.*

 1929 Botkin *Folk-Say I* 53: It was a hellashus fight, too. **1929–32** in *AS* (Dec. 1934) 289: *Hellacious.* Outstanding. **1943** in Ruhm *Detective* 313: You got a hellacious style if you don't mind my sayin' so. **1963** W.C. Anderson *Penelope* 113: That thing sho' is hellacious. **1965** Adler *Vietnam Letters* 99: There did ensue the most HELLACIOUS downpour ever witnessed by civilized man! **1969** Bouton *Ball Four* 264: Yup. Great Knuckleball. Hellacious. **1971** Keith *Long Line Rider* 121: But Screamin' John was one hellacious yardman. **1982** *N.Y. Post* (May 30) 54: He has added some hellacious moves facing the basket. **1986** Ciardi *Good Words* 141: *Halatious.*…Swell. Great. Groovy.…Since *ca*1965. **1989** Knoxville, Tenn., attorney: They're predicting a hellacious thunderstorm for tonight. **1991** *Bill & Ted's Excellent Adventure* (Fox-TV): I am hellaciously bummed. **1994** *Newsweek* (Jan. 31) 50: He risked his neck to witness some of the most hellacious battles of the war. **1994** *N.Y. Times Mag.* (July 17) 40: With traffic hellacious and accidents on the rise.

hell-all *n.* DAMN-ALL. Also **hell-in-all.**

 1969 Sidney *Love of Dying* 84: You think you bein' a sergeant means hell-all here? *ca*1933–74 E. Mackin *Didn't Want to Die* 118 [ref. to 1918]: You don't amount to hell-in-all up here.

hell around *v.* to create a disturbance; *(also)* gallivant.

 1897 Wister *Lin McLean* 60: A man was liable to go sporting and helling around till he waked up. **1927** Faulkner *Mosquitoes* 299: Here I've had to pay a man two days just because you were off helling around somewhere. **1931** *AS* (Aug.) 434: O, he's hellin' around with a tough crowd from the South Side slums. **1949** *Sat. Eve. Post* (Oct. 8) 95: I'd always helled around with older men. **1951** *Time* (Apr. 2) 21: Things besides drinking and helling around. **1960** in Marx *Groucho Letters* 147: Massa Nunnally Johnson is hellin' around with Ava Gardner. **1961** *Time* (June 23) 48: We'll keep them so busy studying they won't have time to hell around. **1972** Pendleton *Boston Blitz* 92: That bastard would still go on helling around looking for them. *a*1985 in C. Williams *So. Mountain Speech* 86: *Hell around*…to cause trouble; to raise cain.

hell-bender *n.* something or someone that is especially formidable, aggressive, or outrageous; *(specif.)* (now *colloq.*) the menopeme or American salamander.

 1812 in *DAE:* Memoir concerning an Animal of the Class Reptilia or Amphibia, which is known by the name of Alligator and Hellbender. *a*1877 Bartlett *Amer.* (ed. 4) 283: Jack has been on a perfect hellbender of a spree. *a*1890–93 F & H III 301: *Hell-bender*…(American). —A drunken frolic; a tremendous row. **1895** Coup *Sawdust* 124: Among the rare animals which I had one season were some Memiponias, or tiny deerlets—"hell benders," as they were commonly called. **1933** Weseen *Dict. Slang* 348: *Heller*—A very daring, aggressive or active person…*Hellbender* is a variant. **1964** Deutsch *Unsinkable Molly Brown* (film): The biggest high-toned hell-bender of a party.

hell-bending *adj.* hellish; arduous.

 1890 Kerbey *War Path* 273 [ref. to 1860's]: We went along here at a hell-bending trot. **1989** S. Hugill, at Mystic Seaport Museum, Conn.: It was hell-bending work [on shipboard].

hellbent *adj.* unshakably or recklessly determined. Also as adv. Now *colloq.*

 1835 in *DA:* A large encampment of savages…"hell-bent on carnage." **1840** *Spirit of Times* (Aug. 8) 276: A chap comes in…h—l bent for woodin' up the hull bar-room. **1853–60** Olmsted *Texas* 23: He's *hell-bent* on this boat now, aint he. **1860** in "M. Twain" *Letters:* To use an expression which is commonly ignored in polite society, they were "hell-bent" on stealing some of the…oranges. **1894** F.P. Dunne, in Schaaf *Dooley* 155: An' up he gets on it an' goes hell bent down th' road. **1938** Smitter *Detroit* 32: It gave a man a headache to try and keep them off the track where they were all hell-bent on standing.

1942 in D. Schwartz *Jours.* 17: Hell-bent for Hell in a hack. **1950** *Harper's* (Oct.) 196: A super-highway goes hell-bent. **1951** Pryor *The Big Play* 14: The tool pusher had to admit this was an expert crew, doubly valuable in this crowded, hell-bent, rampaging new oil field. **1960** *Sat. Eve. Post* (Jan. 30) 90: A considerable group of growers think that Mosher is hell-bent for ruining the orchid business with his mass production. *a*1978 Cooley *Dancer* 166: He's hell bent to do concerts first. **1995** *New Republic* (Feb. 6) 8: Hell-bent on bringing down House Speaker Jim Wright over suspicious book royalties.

¶ In phrase:

¶ **hellbent for election** [or **leather** or **breakfast** or **Georgia**] HELL FOR LEATHER; HELLBENT. Occas. as adj.

 1899 in S. Crane *Stories* 630: One puncher racin' his cow-pony hell-bent-for-election down Main Street. **1919** T. Kelly *What Outfit?* 199: Listen to that hell-bent-for-election noise. **1924** *Adventure* (Dec. 10) 106: We run on to a 77 th' Germans had beat it away from —bent for breakfast. **1931** in *DA:* I was going lickety-split, hell-bent for breakfast, trying to head off a gotch-eared stallion. **1932** Z. Grey *Robbers' Roost* 118: You come ridin' hell-bent for election. **1940** F. Hunt *Trail from Tex.* 27: To ride hell-bent-fer-election after them four-legged snakes. *1949 Granville *Sea Slang* 121: *Hell-bent for election.* Steaming at full speed. **1965** *Ski* (Dec.) 70: Jimmy coming hell-bent-for-leather out of a slalom gate before he was ten years old. **1972** Swarthout *Tin Lizzie* 90: Hell-bent for election, into the Rio Grande. **1975** McCaig *Danger Trail* 140: Ride for the train hell-bent for election. **1976** G.V. Higgins *D. Hunter* 119: Up comes the guy comes out of the ditch on his tractor, hell-bent for leather and hollering like a banshee. **1977** in Curry *River's in My Blood* 42: He was hell-bent for Georgia to go down the river. *a*1987 Coyle *Team Yankee* 51: They were hell-bent for leather to break through. **1987** *Big Story* (CNN-TV) (Sept. 13): Our morality is going hell-bent for leather to catch up with our creativity. **1990** Ruggero *38 N. Yankee* 207: They'd be blowing through hell-bent-for-leather.

hell-boot *v.* to go at top speed.—constr. with *it.*

 1918 in D. York *Mud & Stars* 36: A line o' transports, crazy lined,/…Hellbootin' it for France.

hell box *n.* **1.** *Printing.* a box for holding broken or damaged type.

 *1888 Jacobi *Printers' Vocab.* 59: *Hell box.*—A receptacle for battered or broken letters.—in olden times a box was used. *1889 Barrère & Leland *Dict. Slang* I 458: *Hell-box*…the receptacle for bad, broken, or "battered" letters, which are eventually melted down. **1909** "M. Twain" *Is Shakespeare Dead?* 73: Here, devil, empty the quoins into the standing galley and the imposing stone into the hell-box. **1912** in Alter *Utah Journ.* 95: All are fit subjects for the "hell-box." **1931–34** Adamic *Dynamite* 391: In a print-shop in Kansas City the men, instead of distributing expensive type, dumped it into the so-called "hell box." *ca*1940 in Botkin *Treas. Amer. Folk.* 552: [In] the hell box…there's a lot of dross lino metal. **1983** *Business Week* (May 16) 7: Has a mad scientist of typography taken over the tiller? Every rule I ever learned to make the reader keep reading has apparently been tossed in the hell-box.

2. *Naut.* a galley stove.

 1929 Bowen *Sea Slang* 66: *Hell Box.* The galley stove, used most frequently in the Canadian and American ships.

3. *Mil.* an infrared imaging device used for firing at night or in limited visibility.

 1986 Zumbro *Tank Sgt.* 233 [ref. to 1968]: Roman fired the gun with a hellbox.…We couldn't see through the…dust and smoke.

4. *Mil.* a detonator.

 1992 Lehrach *No Shining Armor* 383 [ref. to Vietnam War]: *Hell box.* Firing mechanism used to detonate explosives, e.g. C-4 or dynamite. **1993** J. Watson & K. Dockery *Point Man* 102 [ref. to 1960's]: Bill got down into position with the hell box (detonator)…hollered, "Fire in the hole!…" and twisted the firing handle.

hell buggy *n. Army.* a battle tank. *Joc.*

 1941 *Army Ordnance* (July) 79: *Hell buggy.*…Tank. **1941** *Nat. Geo.* (July) 4: Iron Bulls, Steel Turtles, Hell Buggies. **1942** Sanders & Blackwell *Fighting Forces* 205: *Hell Buggy*…A tank…("Peek Magazine," November, 1940).

hell-buster *n.* HELL-RAKER.

 1918 *Everybody's* (Jan.) 41: If this world is as big the other way as 'tis the way we've come, she's a reg'lar hell-buster, ain't she? *1929 J.B. Priestley, in *OED2:* They're all damned good, but the last two are real hell-busters.

hellcat *n.* **1.** a person, esp. a woman, who is uncontrollable or incorrigible, esp. in wickedness, spite, ferocity, etc. Now *colloq.* or *S.E.*

  *a1605 in *OED2:* The whorson old hellcat would have given me the brain of a cat. *1632 in *OED2:* We cannot be too bitter, she's a hell-cat. *1698–99 "B.E." *Dict. Canting Crew:* Hell-cat, a very Lewd Rake-helly Fellow. *1785 Grose *Vulgar Tongue:* Hell Cat. A termagant, a vixen, a furious scolding woman. *1837 F. Marryat, in *OED2:* A hell-cat, who hates me as she does the devil. 1851 Ely *Wanderings* 29: She has been called by them a perfect hell-cat. 1858 J. Clemens *Mustang Grey* 238: We can weaken him by cutting his *hell-cats* to pieces. 1862 H.J. Thomas *Wrong Man* 54: What's kept the h—l-cat sneaking round here these two days? 1905 W.S. Kelly *Lariats* 52: Don't fire until yer sure you can kill one of the God damned hell-cats. 1939 Appel *People Talk* 308: Those God damn bears are...hellcats when they're hungry.

  2. *pl. U.S. Mil. Acad., U.S. Nav. Acad.* a fife-and-drum corps (*obs.*); a drum-and-bugle corps.

  1908 *Howitzer* (U.S. Mil. Acad.) (No. 9) 325: *Hell-cats,* n....The fife and drum corps. 1918 *Scribner's* (July) 12: Led by the drummers and buglers—"Hell Cats" of the "Bungle Corpse." 1920 *341st F.A.* 41: Band concerts were the social events of the life there. The "Hell Cats" put in their appearance at Castelnau. 1928 *AS* III (Aug.) 453: *Hellcats.* The bugle corps. 1929 *Our Army* (Nov.): "Hell Cats" is West Point for the drummers and buglers in action at reveille. 1936 *Nat. Geo.* LXIX 790: Presently, we marched off to music played by the "hellcats," as the midshipmen drum and bugle corps is called by the Regiment.

hell-clinking *adj.* HELL-ROARING.

  1917 C.E. Van Loan, in Woods *Horse-Racing* 290: If this here Bismallah is such a hell-clinkin' good race horse, how come they ain't *all* bettin' on him?

hell-dodger *n.* a zealous or sanctimonious Christian; DEVIL-DODGER, b.

  1908 *Howitzer* (U.S. Mil. Acad.) (No. 9) 325: *Hell-dodger,* n. One in constant attendance at the Y.M.C.A. 1966 Kenney *Caste* 101: That hell-dodger would enjoy your corny sermon.

heller *n.* **1.** an especially formidable, difficult, exciting, or unmanageable person or thing.

  1895 Gore *Stu. Slang* 9: *Heller. n.* A remarkable person. "He is a heller at foot-ball." 1896 *DN* I 418: *Heller:* a remarkable person. "He's a *heller* to win." 1923 *DN* V 210: *Heller,* n. A thing or person possessing extreme characteristics. "He's a heller fer work." "That storm was a heller." "This ax shore is a heller." 1933 *AS* VIII 81: *Heller*—One who is unusually daring or aggressive, intensified usually as *a regular heller.* 1938 Smitter *Detroit* 9: He could be a heller with women if he wanted to. 1939 Steinbeck *Grapes of Wrath* ch. viii: Ain't he a heller? 1949 *PADS* XI (Apr.) 22: *Heller: n.* A big tough one, hard to handle—a person or a thing. 1950 in Inman *Diary* 1515: The year 1950...has been a nonpareil heller. 1971 Le Guin *Lathe of Heaven* 68: In fact, that dream was a heller, wasn't it? 1970–72 in *AS* L (1975) 61: *Heller n.* Exciting, activity-filled party.

  2. a person who raises hell.

  1933 Weseen *Dict. Slang* 348: *Heller*...a person who indulges in immoral, illegal, or questionable practices. 1950 J.D. Salinger, in *New Yorker* (Apr. 8) 29: With the deadpan expression of a born heller, he methodically went about annoying his governess. 1960 *Heller in Pink Tights* (film title). *a1987 in *World Bk. Dict.:* His father was a lazy farmer, a local heller who loved his booze.

hellfighter *n.* a firefighter specially trained to fight fires in gas or oil wells. Hence **hellfighting,** *n.*

  1968 Huffaker *Hellfighters* (film). 1985 *TV Guide* (Nov. 23) A94: MacGyver...turns "hellfighter" to help a friend cap an oil-well fire. 1985 *MacGyver* (ABC-TV): You mean you gave up hellfightin' for this?

hell-fired *adj.* damned. Also **hellfire.** Cf. ALL-FIRED.

  *1756 in *OED2:* Sir...he is a h-ll-fir'd good creature. *1781 G. Parker *View of Society* II 108: There was not such a hell-fire old cat living. *1821 *Real Life in Ireland* 227: He was a "hell-fire dog" and lived by gambling. 1833 J. Neal *Down-Easters* I 79: See what a hell-fired noise it makes! 1860 in H. Holzer *Dear Mr. Lincoln* 340: Old Abe Lincoln God damn your god damned old Hellfired god damned soul to

hell...and god damnation. 1917–20 in J.M. Hunter *Trail Drivers* I 286: There is going to be some hellfired racket here. 1929 *AS* V (Dec.) 119: A man who had done something dishonest was "pretty small potatoes" or "ought to be prosecuted," or "ought to have a cow hiding," or was a "hell-fired cuss." 1983 *Nat. Lampoon* (Apr.) 58: Why are you in such a hellfire rush?

hellfire stew *n. Army in Civil War.* a stew concocted of any available ingredients. Now *hist.*

  *ca*1880 Bellard *Gone for a Soldier* 122 [ref. to Civil War]: One of our dishes was composed of anything that we could get hold of. Pork or beef, salt or fresh, was cut up with potatoes, tomatoes, crackers, and garlic, seasoned with pepper and salt. This we called Hish and Hash or Hell fired stew. 1958 *Civil War Hist.* IV 88: Army flapjacks, "skilly-galee,"..."scouse," and the conglomerate hell-fired stew....Hell-fired stew incorporated everything edible available. 1987 J.I. Robertson *Blue & Gray* 69: The resultant concoction was "hellfire stew."

hell-for-breakfast *adv.* HELL-FOR-LEATHER. See also *hellbent for election* [or *leather* or *breakfast* or *Georgia*] s.v. HELLBENT.

  1943 *Reader's Digest* (Dec.) 115: She and the cans went snorting out, hell-for-breakfast after the sub. *a1956 Almirall *College to Cow Country* 33: That calf's old lady...had come hell-for-breakfast in response to her baby's bawl. 1972 Pendleton *Boston Blitz* 70: Probably had them running hell-for-breakfast all over the place.

hell-for-leather *adv.* at full speed; all-out; recklessly. Also as adj. See also *hellbent for election* [or *leather* or *breakfast* or *Georgia*] s.v. HELLBENT.

  *1889 Kipling, in *OED2:* Ride hell-for-leather. 1908 (quot. at SPLIT, v.). 1939 in *DARE:* Hell-for-leather—In great haste. "Ridin' hell-for-leather" suggests very hard use of leather (i.e., whip). 1938–40 W.V. Clark *Ox-Bow* 63: I saw that kid Greene...come by here hell-for-leather half an hour ago. 1942 in *DARE:* It has been a turbulent, rip-snorting, hell-for-leather past. 1950 *N.Y. Times* (Oct. 1) I 11: There is some criticism of the "hell-for-leather" way the Marine Commanders led the campaign. 1950 *Time* (Oct. 9) 22: Douglas, not up for election himself, was campaigning hell-for-leather for his colleague, Senator Scott Lucas. 1979 J. Morris *War Story* 297: They flew hell for leather toward our LZ. 1981 L. Heinemann, in *Harper's* (Aug.) 59: With the chopper pilot hauling ass hell-for-leather. 1982 Braun *Judas Tree* 110: He...galloped hell-for-leather toward Virginia City. 1992 in *Harper's* (Jan. 1993) 86: Going hell for leather in his Toyota.

hell-hole *n.* **1.** a drinking and gambling den.

  1828 Bird *Looking Glass* 6: There's an ass of a sailor, in citizen's clothes, that gets into all the decent hell-holes in town.

  2. *Av.* a wheel well or other accessible space beneath the flooring of an aircraft.

  [1967–69 in *DARE:* A small space anywhere in a house where you can hide things or get them out of the way...Hellhole.] 1976 Fuller *Ghost of Flt. 401* 55: Repo, getting ready to go down in the "hell hole" where the landing gear was, paused a moment....There was room enough for a man to stand down there. 1983 R.C. Mason *Chickenhawk* 56 [ref. to 1960's]: The cargo deck [of a Bell UH-1 helicopter] was U-shaped because of the intrusion of the hell-hole cover that enclosed the transmission and hydraulics directly under the mast. *Ibid.* 84: Cramming sticks down the hell-hole. 1983–88 J.T. McLeod *Crew Chief* 29: Hell Hole—Hole in the bottom of a Huey where the cargo hook sticks out. It is directly under the transmission, very oily and barely large enough for one man to fit in from the waist up. 1991 Linnekin *80 Knots* 237: An under-the-fuselage "hellhole" access door.

hellifying *adj.* HELLACIOUS.

  1971–73 Sheehy *Hustling* 50: Legs is what a man looks for...and you got one *hellifying* pair of legs.

hell-in-all see s.v. HELL-ALL.

hell-jelly *n. Mil. Av.* napalm.

  1946 De Chant *Devilbirds* 163 [ref. to WWII]: The Napalm "hell jelly," ironically, was mixed with captured Japanese gasoline stores. 1962 Leckie *Strong Men Armed* 366: Some planes were dropping napalm bombs, those tanks of jellied gasoline which the fliers accurately called "hell-jelly." 1987 Nichols & Tillman *Yankee Sta.* 25: Napalm....We refrained from using "hell-jelly" in North Vietnam, which was too bad.

hell night *n. Stu.* the night when pledges are hazed and initiated into a fraternity or sorority. Cf. HELL WEEK.

1947 in *DA:* Last Wednesday…was "Hell" night for the girls at the 55th Street beach. *ca***1965** in Schwendinger & Schwendinger *Adolescent Subcult.* 213: And on the "Hell night" we take the pledge to Hollywood and give him a round of swats in front of the show. **1982** D.J. Williams *Hit Hard* 164: As if I were a college freshman pledged to a Greek-letter fraternity and about to go on hell night.

hello /typically pronounced with strong stress and falling intonation on ultimate syllable/ *interj.* (used to call attention to the foolishness of an idea, comment, etc.).

1985 Gale & Zemeckis *Back to Future* (film): Hello? McFly? **1990** P. Munro *Slang U.* 106: *Hello!* [means] I can't believe this! What's going on here! **1994** A. Heckerling *Clueless* 63: "You were totally sprung on me."…"Hello, don't you mean Tai?" **1995** *Business Week* (Dec. 4) 13: He boldly predicts…that hundreds of entrepreneurs will start businesses to create programming and content for the Net. Hello? Maybe readers have heard of Netscape Communications. **1995** in *Premiere* (Jan. 1996) 114: Scandal? Bitchy? *Moi? HEL-LO!* **1996** J. Sheidlower, in *Esquire* (Mar.) 35: Snort derisively and scoff, "Can I quote you on that?" "Good one!" or "Hel-*lo*?" **1996** *N.Y. Times* (June 25) C17: You like actually come out in favor of uniforms? Hell-o? That is not so cool.

hello-girl *n.* a female telephone operator.

1889 "M. Twain" *Conn. Yankee* 177: The humblest hello-girl along ten thousand miles of wire could teach gentleness, patience, modesty, manners, to the highest duchess in Arthur's land. **1936** Steel *College* 39: Since when'd you take up being a hello-girl? **1975** Reader letter in RHD files: *Hello-girl:* used to be verbal shorthand for a telephone operator.…I remember the New Haven *Register* on sports page referred to SNETCO's gal [basketball] players as "Hello Girls."

Hell-on-the-Hudson *n. U.S. Mil. Acad.* the U.S. Military Academy at West Point, N.Y.

1969 Searls *Hero Ship* 208 [ref. to WWII]: West Pointers from Hell-on-the-Hudson called Annapolis the Country Club on the Severn. **1987** D.O. Smith *Cradle of Valor* 1 [ref. to 1930]: This is the United States Military Academy, commonly known as Hell-on-the-Hudson.

hell-raking *adj.* characterized by great violence, tumult, or (*later*) excitement; rip-roaring. Hence **hell-raker** a violent or rip-roaring person or thing. *Obs.* in U.S.

*1606 in *OED2:* Whose Hell-raking, Nature-shaking Spell. ***1816** Sir W. Scott, in *OED2:* A' thae hell-rakers o' dragoons wad be at his whistle in a moment. **1877** Burdette *Mustache* 177: An old hell raker of a piece. ***1960** in *OED2:* Hellraking times at Balliol.

hell-roaring *adj.* roaring furiously; (*hence*) wild; uncontrolled; rip-roaring. Hence **hell-roarer,** *n.*

1878 Hart *Sazerac* 26: There come up one of them hell-roarin' big snow-storms. **1883** Topping *Yellowstone* 63: He was asked what kind of a stream the next creek was. "It's a hell roarer," was his reply, and Hell Roaring is its name to this day. **1894** in F. Remington *Sel. Letters* 255: I want to make some pictures of the ponies going over the hell roaring mal-pais. **1918** Beston *Full Speed Ahead* 104: What do you think you are anyway—Hell-Roaring Jack the Storm-King? **1922–24** McIntyre *White Light* 48: The feverish energy of the "hell-roaring" gold camp. **1928** Ritchie *Forty-Niners* 233: The hell-roarin' days of the Argonauts. **1934** Cunningham *Triggernometry* 28: I'm that hell-roaring Bill Longley you've heard so much about. **1935** Algren *Somebody* 169: Ah'm a Texas hell-roarer! **1942** Garcia *Tough Trip* 440: The Bitterfoot Valley…was a hell-roarer and fit only for an Injun. **1944** Huie *Can Do!* 25: A hell-roaring Seabee, mounted on a 20-ton bulldozer. **1947** J. Lomax *Ballad Hunter* 74: The deep-drinking, hell-roaring, "hard case" Michigander lumberjack. **1967** W. Decker *To Be a Man* 46: This [nightmare] was a real hell-roarer, too.

hell-robber *n.* a Christian evangelist.

1936 Mencken *Amer. Lang.* (ed. 4) 150: Hard-shell…circuit-rider…hell-robber…to get…religion. **1981** Sann *Trial* 25: The…evangelists you always called Hell-robbers who were getting rich saving lost souls.

hell-rooster *n.* HELLCAT.

1894 S. Crane *Red Badge* 77: Th' boys fight like hell-roosters.

hell's bells *n.* the daylights; the stuffing; HELL, 3.

1886 Leman *Old Actor* 299 [ref. to 1863]: Leman, old boy, I'm sorry to hurt your feelings, but we've got great news from Vicksburg, and Pemberton's knocked h—l's bells out of Grant's wheel-houses.

¶ In phrase:

¶ **like hell's bells** HELL'S BELLS, *adv.*

*1819 [T. Moore] *Tom Crib* 36: These Swells/Are soon to meet…To chime together, like "*hell's bells.*" **1928** Dahlberg *Bottom Dogs* 271: Lorry…ran like hell's bells out.

hell's-bells *adj.* rowdy; wild.

1923 Ornitz *Haunch, Paunch & Jowl* 76: You got a crust, bringing me a lot of sissies to do turns in a hell's-bells spielers' parlor.

hell's bells *adv.* with great power or speed; headlong.

1930 Botkin *Folk-Say* 49: The wind [was] just blowin hell's bells out of the west. **1977** Coover *Public Burning* 414: What a wind! It come rippin' hell's bells outa the north. **1986** *Moonlighting* (ABC-TV): You just can't fly hell's bells into the most important decision of your life.

hell's bells *interj.* (used to express irritation or incredulity). Occas. as *n.*

*1832 in Lover *Legends & Stories* 144: They all swore out, "Hells bells attind your berrin',…you vagabone." **1847** in Oehlschlaeger *Reveille* 161: "H-ll's bells!" exclaims the musician. **1897–1900** "M. Twain" *Mysterious Stranger Mss.* 38: Hell's bells! did you think I was lying? **1912** in *OED2:* Goshity gosh, helzbelz, there ain't no such animile. **1918** *Sat. Eve. Post* (Nov. 16) 15: "Hell's bells!" ejaculated Captain Bill. **1925** Nason *Three Lights* 18 [ref. to 1918]: "Hell's bells and the devil to ring 'em," groaned Nell. **1925** Mullin *Scholar Tramp* 42: "Why, hell's bells!" shouted Frisco scornfully. "You talk as if you was doin' 'em a favor." **1925** Dos Passos *Manhattan Transfer* 222: But hell's bells what's the use when this goddam Yankee takes the whole front page! **1934** Randolph *Who Blowed Up the Church House?* 11: As for the stove, hell's bells! We can cook in the fireplace! **1947** Willingham *End as a Man* 295: What in the name of hell's bells is going on down there. **1957** Mayfield *Hit* 176: Well, hell's bells! **1967** Lockwood *Subs* 35: Hell's bells, when it comes to submarines, this man's navy hasn't seen anything yet. **1971** N.Y.U. student: Well, hell's bells. Hell's bells, man. **1986** C. Lewis *Revenge* (film): Well, hell's bells, Bailey! You think you're the only one who wants to get ahead in this world? **1989** Munro *U.C.L.A. Slang* 49: Hell's bells! That was a hard test!

hell's delight *n.* **1.** a furious commotion or absolute chaos.

*1823 "J. Bee" *Slang* 95: Kicking up hell's delight. ***1835** in *OED2:* She said if I went out, she would kick up *hell's delight.* **1976** Hayden *Voyage* 306: This Garden of Hell's delight.

2. HELL, 3.

1912 Field *Watch Yourself* 23: Ef ye had my spunk, ye'd hev knocked hell's delight out of some of 'em.

3. see s.v. HELL, 4.

hell's grist *n.* a large amount; bunch.

1855 in *Calif. Hist. Soc. Qly.* VIII (1929) 345: Found a hell's grist of them at the lower end of the Bar.

hell's half acre *n.* a wild, desolate, or dangerous place.

1864 "E. Kirke" *Down in Tenn.* 130: I come ter de place whar dey fit so two days arterwuds—dey call it "Hell's-half-acre." **1874** McCoy *Cattle Trade* 210: The keepers of those "hell's half acres" find some pretext arising from business jealousies…to suddenly become belligerent. **1884** in Roe *Army Letters* (Aug.) 322: We were leaving the woods by "Hell's Half Acre." **1891** Kipling *Amer. Notes* 74: And they called the place [in Yellowstone Park] Hell's Half-Acre…Hell's Half-Acre…is about sixty acres in extent. **1910** *Harper's Wkly.* (Mar. 5) 16: These [songs] have helped to banish from many a "Hell's half-acre" that obsessing desire for personal safety which at times attacks even the bravest. **1912** Siringo *Cowboy Detective* 24: In the slums, or what should be called "Hell's Half Acre." **1919** McKenna *Btty. A* 36: So often was Jones I shelled and gassed that the position became known throughout the [Toul] sector as "Hell's Half Acre." **1917–20** in J.M. Hunter *Trail Drivers* I 38: To the right of Fort Worth just about where Hell's Half Acre used to be. **1924** Tully *Beggars of Life* 130: I druv stakes wit' Barnum's circus all over Europe, Aziah, Aferca, and hell's half acre. **1942** *ATS* 49: Slum district…*hell's (half) acre.* **1948** J. Stevens *Jim Turner* 118 [ref. to *ca*1910]: I tracked along with them to the "Hell's Half Acre" of cribs. **1966** Hicken *Ill. in Civil War* 117 [ref. to 1862]: Other regiments were sent to Hazen's support during that commander's stubborn defense of "Hell's Half Acre," or the "Round Forest." **1966** King *Brave & Damned* 159: We can't stay here on hell's half acre. **1976** *Dallas Morning News* (Dec. 5) 1A: Teresa has been across hell's half-acre. **1991** Reinberg *In the Field* 104: *Hell's Half Acre* nickname for an area just north of Cu Chi [during Vietnam War].

¶ In phrase:

¶ **all over hell's half acre** everywhere.

1930 Sage *Last Rustler* 251: The cattle was…scattered all over hell's half acre. **1953** Felsen *Street Rod* 97: Some guy with a big car does something wrong, and the cops beg his pardon all over Hell's half-acre for stopping him. **1958** Swarthout *They Came to Cordura* 101: We might get through the mouth, but in the dark we would be scattered all over hell's half acre. **1966** F. Harvey *Raiders* 144: I drove old Gannon all over hell's half acre lookin' for the other guy. **1970** Thackrey *Thief* 412: Got to wander all over hell's half-acre until you almost say it *for* them. **1971** *U.S. News & W.R.* (Aug. 16) 53: You won't have so much paper being moved all around hell's half acre. *a***1987** Bunch & Cole *Reckoning for Kings* 325: Looks like it went…all over hell's half acre.

hell-ship *n. Naut.* a ship characterized by hellish conditions, esp. brutal officers. Now *S.E.*

1898 Stevenson *Cape Horn* 363: The offensive name of "Yankee hell-ship." **1913–14** London *Elsinore* 204: The hell-ship *Elsinore!* ***1929** Bowen *Sea Slang* 66: *Hell Ship.* The worst type of ship to be found, with brutal officers. Borrowed from the Americans. **1940** *Life* (Nov. 18) 4: The naval transport *Chaumont* (a hell-ship if I ever saw one). **1947** W.M. Camp *S.F.* 6: Barnes secured the conviction of a couple of officers of another "hellship," the *Crusader.* **1956** Lockwood & Adamson *Zoomies, Subs & Zeroes* 18: Men don't stow away aboard unhappy ships, often called "hell ships." **1980** Valle *Rocks & Shoals* 25: In the years immediately following the War of 1812, she was the reputed "hell ship" of the Fleet.

hell's kitchen *n.* **1.** the hottest part of hell; (*hence*) any markedly unpleasant or dangerous place.

1834 Crockett *Tour to No. & Down East:* But these are worse than savages; they are too mean to swab hell's kitchen. **1837** in N. Hawthorne *Amer. Notebooks* 54: He…swore fervently of driving the British "into hell's kitchen," by main force. [**1873** T.W. Knox *Underground* 257: He would take me to…"Hell's Kitchen" [a disreputable establishment].] **1917** H.L. Mencken, in Riggio *Dreiser-Mencken Letters* I 304: Avoid the Chesapeake shore.…It is hell's kitchen. **1981** *Maclean's* (Feb. 2) 43: In the hell's kitchen of Canadian weather—the storm-brewed north Pacific.

2. *cap.* a violent city slum district; (*specif.* and *usu.*) such a slum on the West Side of Manhattan (formerly) in New York City.

1879 *Snares of N.Y.* 68: Nearer Eleventh avenue, there are a number of shanties on the rocks. This is known in the neighborhood as "Hell's Kitchen." **1891** Campbell, Knox & Byrnes *Darkness & Daylight* 154: "Hell's Kitchen," and many another nest of infamy. **1893** Riis *Nisby* 34: Now its rays…lighted up the windows of the tenements in Hell's Kitchen and Poverty Gap. **1894** *Harper's Mag.* (July) 223: Just at the edge of Hell's Kitchen. **1905** in "O. Henry" *Works* 1415: The Stovepipe Gang borrowed its name from the sub-district of the city called the "Stovepipe," which is a narrow and natural extension of the familiar district known as "Hell's Kitchen." **1911** Ovington *Half a Man* 37: Here and down by the river at Hell's Kitchen the rioting in 1900 between the Irish and the Negro took place. **1918–19** Sinclair *Higgins* 265: Grady…had left a wife and three children in a tenement in "Hell's Kitchen," New York. **1959** N.Y.C. woman, age *ca*70: Tenth Avenue in the Forties—that's Hell's Kitchen. *a***1989** in Kisseloff *Must Remember This* 170: There was no organized-crime stuff, not like in Hell's Kitchen. *They* were killers. **1991** McCarthy & Mallowe *Vice Cop* 31: Bill…was born…on March 6, 1945…in Hell's Kitchen on the West Side.

hell-snorting *adj.* RIPSNORTING.

1880 in M. Lewis *Mining Frontier* 98: Amerriky's a hell-snortin' big piece of land.

hell-stick *n.* a sulphur match. *Joc.*

1900 *DN* II 40: *Hell-sticks,* n. Matches [at five colleges]. **1968** R. Adams *West. Words* (ed. 2) 145: *Hell stick.* What the cowman sometimes called the sulphur match…; when struck it really gave him a "whiff of hell."

hell-to-split *adv.* at breakneck speed; lickety-split. Also **hell-to-toot.**

1814 B. Palmer *Diary* (entry for May 24): Old Hell to Split Miller. **1867** in *DA:* The firemen…came "hellety split." **1871** Hay *Pike Co. Ballads* 14: And hell-to-split over the prairie/Went team, Little Breeches and all. **1912** Raine *Brand Blotters* 100: Jim Little saw her cutting across country…hell-to-split. **1948** in *DAS:* I piled after her hell to split. **1965** D.G. Moore *20th C. Cowboy* 119: They were going in every direction, "hell-to-toot."

hell-wagon *n. Naut.* HELL-SHIP.

1923 Riesenberg *Under Sail* 146 [ref. to 1897]: The next day out to sea for us in this bloody hell wagon. **1934** Binns *Lightship* 185: "What kind of a ship is this?" "A hell wagon, bound for Australia."

hell week *n. Stu.* (see 1970–72 quot.); (*hence*) any period of intense harassment.

1930 in D.O. Smith *Cradle* 14: It's much like "hell week" at the Sigma Nu house. **1930** in *DA:* They were strongly in favor of eliminating "Hell Week" from fraternity procedure entirely. **1950** in M. Daly *Profile of Youth* 111: I kind of got respect for myself, too, for getting through Hell Week okay. **1951** *N.Y. Times* (Dec. 2) I 1: The traditional "hell week," when fraternity and sorority pledges are hazed. **1966** Fariña *Down So Long* 20: Wear a propeller-topped beanie during Hell Week, pull a quacking toy to class. **1970–72** in *AS* L (1975) 61: *Hell week n.* Period of confinement and hazing for pledges prior to initiation into the fraternity. **1983** *Texas Monthly* (Nov.) 140: The last night of Hell Week, when we were blindfolded with Kotexes, dragged down to the basement, and made to crawl about on our hands and knees. **1984** Ehrhart *Marking Time* 73: We don't do any hazing here. We don't have a Hell Week. **1988** *21 Jump Street* (Fox-TV): Gentlemen, welcome to hell week. **1993** *New Yorker* (Apr. 19) 46: After the Miami *Herald* rushed into print with the results of its stakeout of Hart's town house, on Capitol Hill, "Hell Week" began for the campaign. **1993** J. Watson & K. Dockery *Point Man* 40 [ref. to 1960]: In our [naval commando] class the loss rate was 86 percent.…Later on, just before Hell Week, the twenty-five or so of us that were left were pretty close.

hell-whooping *adv.* ¶ In phrase: **go hell-whooping** to go wildly or at great speed.

1939 in G.E. Wheeler *Adm. Pratt* 21 [ref. to 1890's]: I would have let her go hell whooping to the eastward unless you ordered me to change course.

helo *n. Av.* a helicopter.

1965 *L.A. Times* (July 30) I 22 [a Navy pilot in Vietnam]: Then they told me on the radio that the helo (helicopter) was on the way. **1966–67** F. Harvey *Air War* 176: I waved the helo off. **1972** Kaplan & Hunt *Coast Guard* 125: The "helo" had been involved in a rescue mission of its own. **1973** Huggett *Body Count* 113: Well, *we*…are going on some helo op and nobody knows where. **1977** Langone *Life at Bottom* 53: Like that helo pilot who parked his bird on the top of Erebus and took a piss into the crater. **1980** Millett *Semper Fidelis* 510: Three observation squadrons with light helos. **1981** Mersky & Polmar *Nav. Air War in Viet.* 216: Two helos were shot down. **1984** Hammel *Root* 71: Young helo pilots. **1989** Joss *Strike* 45: Lifesaving SH-3 helo alights for mere seconds.

helo *v.* to fly by helicopter.

1966 Lucas *Dateline* 305: We heloed in.

helpers *n.* usu. *pl. Narc.* an amphetamine pill.

1963 Braly *Shake Him* 73: But I had a little help tonight. Some nutty little helpers. Redbirds. **1965** Vermes *Helping Youth* 119: Benzedrine drugs…are also known as "helpers," "co-pilots," "hearts," "footballs," and "blackjacks."

hemo *n.* [short for HEMORRHOID] *Stu.* an annoying or obnoxious person; HEMORRHOID.

1984 Univ. Tenn. student: A guy who's a *hemo* is a real pain in the butt. It's short for hemorrhoid. **1985** Univ. Tenn. student theme: Teachers who…are difficult graders are [called] "hemos" (short for hemorrhoids). [They] are definitely a pain in the butt.

hemorrhage *n.* ketchup. *Joc.*

1915 Poole *Harbor* 50 [ref. to *ca*1900]: It was our habit, in our new-found manliness, to eat with our hats on, shout and sing, and speak of our food as "tapeworm," "hemorrhage," and the like. **1936** *AS* (Feb.) 43: *Hemorrhage.* Ketchup.

¶ In phrase:

¶ **have a hemorrhage** to become furiously angry; become unduly excited.

[**1902** Corrothers *Black Cat Club* 183: You *must* le'be me talk er I'll take a hemorrhage!] **1927** in Hammett *Knockover* 349: Don't have a hemorrhage.…This is just another of the things you don't know about. **1928** Hecht & MacArthur *Front Page* 446: Walter sounded like he was having a hemorrhage. **1930** Botkin *Folk-Say* 107: It was more than a Christ-fearing man could gulp, even old Job hisself would of had a hemorrhage. **1932** *AS* VII (June) 333: *Have a haemorrhage*—to be exceedingly agitated or angry. **1936** Levin *Old Bunch* 97: Harry Perlin nearly had a hemorrhage. **1943** in Truman *Dear Bess* 503: But the *Post-Dispatch* couldn't have as serious a hemorrhage over him as over Finnegan. **1954** Ellson *Owen Harding* 41: My dad has seventeen hemorrhages when he finds them gone. **1957** Kohner *Gidget* 59: My folks had almost six hemorrhages apiece. **1957** M. Shulman *Rally* 190: Okay, okay....Don't get a hemorrhage. **1977** Langone *Life at Bottom* 178: Well, the old man had a fucking hemorrhage, and I don't know how they finally settled that one. **1977–81** S. King *Cujo* 147: Okay, don't have a hemorrhage.

hemorrhage *v.* [fr. *have a hemorrhage* s.v. HEMORRHAGE, *n.*] to react with shock or anger.
     1994 *My So-Called Life* (ABC-TV): Patty like hemorrhaged the first time she saw it.

hemorrhoid *n.* an annoying or vexatious person or thing; *pain in the ass* s.v. PAIN.
     1969 in J.C. Pratt *Viet. Voices* 129: You know what's wrong with this fouled-up hemorrhoid of a war? **1975** Wambaugh *Choirboys* 33: "How about...[the word] Hemorrhoids?" "Everybody uses that [as a term of abuse]." **1984** S. King *Cat's Eye* (film): Forget the cat, you hemorrhoid! Get the gun! **1985** M. Baker *Cops* 153: There's two hemorrhoids standing inside. *Ibid.* 154: That poor hemorrhoid just knew he was dead now. **1986** Stinson & Carabatsos *Heartbreak* 25: Ease off, hemorrhoids, or I'll send you back to the asshole you popped out of. **1988** Univ. Tenn. student theme: This Todd character is a major hemorrhoid. **1989** C.T. Westcott *Half a Klick* 16: Get this fuckin' hemorrhoid [car] moving. **1993** P. Munro *U.C.L.A. Slang II: Hemorrhoid...*obnoxious, annoying person.

hemp *n.* **1.** *Narc.* marijuana. [In early use (*ca*1870), S.E. for 'hashish'; see *OED2*.]
     1883 *Harper's Mag.* (Nov.) 948: Smokers from different cities, Boston, Philadelphia, Chicago, and especially New Orleans, tell me that each city has its hemp retreat. **1931** in Abel *Marihuana Dict.* 50: Restrictions respecting the smoking of "hemp." **1952** Mandel *Angry Strangers* 126: Now, smoking hemp, she let out the laughter she'd choked back. **1954** in Wepman, Newman & Binderman *The Life* 39: We sat there...blowing on our hemp. **1961** Russell *Sound* 17: The hemp was starting to take over. **1964** Howe *Valley of Fire* 218: Tea! Hemp! **1974** Angelou *Gather Together* 143 [ref. to *ca*1950]: They won't let you smoke hemp, though. **1985** Univ. Tenn. student theme: Marijuana [is called]...*hemp, herb,* etc. **1993** *Village Voice* (N.Y.C.) (June 22) 28: The wonderful world of hemp, as marijuana is currently called by discerning smokers.

2. the hair of the head.
     1902 Cullen *More Tales* 41: My crooning friend with the blue-gray lamps and grayish curly hemp. *Ibid.* 99: Youse is got hay in y'r hemp, dat's wot!

3. a cheap cigar.
     1947 Schulberg *Harder They Fall* 9: It ain't the hemp. It's the headaches I got. **1954–60** *DAS*: *Hemp...*A cigar....*Not common.*

4. *Baseball.* a line drive; FROZEN ROPE.
     1979 in P. Dickson *Baseball Dict.* 198: Hisle was laying out some hemp.

¶ In phrase:

¶ **pull** [or **stretch**] **hemp** to be executed or commit suicide by hanging.
     1843 in A. Johnson *Papers* I 124: That kind of sympathy that a crowd of spectators would feel for a culprit about to "pull hemp without foot-hol't." **1856** in WPA *S.F. Songster* 64: If one was found a rascal then,/Men took his case in hand, sir,/And made him go to pulling hemp,/Or drove him from the land, sir. **1862** [W.G. Stevenson] *Rebel Army* 23: We'll show him a new trick, how to stretch hemp, the cursed Yankee. **1863** "E. Kirke" *So. Friends* 261: Thet d—d Yankee 'ooman shud pull hemp fur thet. **1865** Byrn *Fudge Fumble* 21: Before twelve o'clock they had all "pulled hemp," and swung dead in the air. *Ibid.* 119: It was almost enough to make a man "pull hemp" and almost choke himself in an other world. **1892** L. Moore *Own Story* 311: They, too, would be sent over the line, with a fair prospect of pulling

hemp. *a*1956 Almirall *College to Cow Country* 58: Others...ended up...by stretching hemp (hanging).

hemp *v.* to execute by hanging; (*Und.*) to choke to death.
     1857 Gladstone *In Kans.* 264 [ref. to 1855]: "This infernal scoundrel will have to be hemped yet," writes the editor of one of the Missouri journals. **1859** Matsell *Vocab.* 41: *Hemp.* To choke. *Hemp the flat.* Choke the fool. **1863** in C.H. Moulton *Ft. Lyon* 163: The treacherous citizens...should be ferreted out...and immediately "hemped."

hemp cravat *n.* a hangman's noose; HEMP NECKTIE.
     ca*1785 in *F & H* III 297: Your hemp cravats,...your Tyburn miser. **1856 *Ballou's Mo. Mag.* (Oct.) 322: [I came] within the twinkling of a topsail sheet block of getting my neck stretched out like a giraffe, with a hemp cravat slung to a Java Dutch gallows.

hemp fever *n.* execution by hanging. Also **hempen fever.**
     1785 Grose *Vulgar Tongue*: A man who was hanged, is said to have died of a hempen fever. **1839 in *F & H* III 302: Three of her husbands died of hempen fevers. **1938 E.J. Mayer et al. *Buccaneer* (film): They said I'd give them hemp fever.

hemp necktie *n.* a hangman's noose. Also **hempen necktie.**
     *ca*1862 in Dannett *Civil War Humor* 162: The Valentine most meet for you,/Is a *Neck-tie made of Hemp.* **1864** Armstrong *Generals* 156: Here's to the blessed Union as it will be, after all the d—d Rebels are either under the sod or swinging in hemp neck-ties about ten feet above it. **1882** A.W. Aiken *Joe Buck* 8: Or a hempen neck-tie warranted to fit. **a*1890–93 *F & H* III 302: *Hempen necktie...*The hangman's noose. **1912** Beach *Net* 298: You'd have voted for eleven hemp neckties, eh? **1930** Stallings & MacArthur *Billy the Kid* (film): All they'll give you is a hemp necktie. **1940** in *DA*: We wanted to lynch Frank Canton, and if we had been allowed to hand him a hemp necktie right then, it would have saved a heap of good men.

hemp party *n.* a public hanging, esp. a lynching.
     1892 in *DA*: If the incendiarist is found, a hemp party may result.

hen *n.* **1.** a woman or girl (now *rare*); (now *usu.*) an unpleasant older woman.
     ca*1626 in *OED2*: One of the soldiers...sayes th'are dainty Hennes. **1632 in *OED2*: Are you the Cockbawd to the Hen was here? **1785 Grose *Vulgar Tongue*: *Hen.* A woman. **1821 Martin & Waldo *Lightfoot* 34: We met with none but petty farmers and *old hens,* who carried no change about with them. **1823 "J. Bee" *Slang Dict.*: In Black-boy Alley I've a...saucy...moon-eyed hen. **1889** Barrère & Leland *Dict. Slang* I 458: *Hen* (American), a wife or mistress, girl or woman. **1891** Maitland *Slang Dict.* 140: *Hen convention* (Am.), a gathering of women for political or social purposes. **1900** *DN* II 40: *Hen,* n. A woman student. General at co-educational institutions. *Hen-medic,* n. A woman studying medicine. **1935** G.W. Henderson *Ollie Miss* 36: Th' ol' hen gits mad when you take her lard, Ollie. **1939** in Botkin *Sidewalks* 289: Here's these hens sittin' in the cab. **1941** in Ellington *Music Is My Mistress* 179: *Sport my hen...*show off my girl. **1941–42** Gach *In Army Now* 168: They're a bunch of bags....a lot of goddam hens! **1958** *AS* XXXIII 224: The *cat* (or *stud*)...[has] *eyes* to *make the scene* with his *chick* (or *hen*). **1962** T. Berger *Reinhart* 90: "Mr. Humbold, a person to see you."..."Hen or rooster?" **1964** in Gover *Trilogy* 318: Some john pick you outa that mob a hens. **1978** Truscott *Dress Gray* 250: So I take her up to the Waldorf with the rest of these hens and their dates.

2. [sugg. by EGG, *n.,* 2.a.] *Mil. Av.* a bombing plane.
     1944 Ind *Bataan* 313: "We're missing one hen....Is she in some other roost?"....A hen was an egg-carrying airplane.

¶ In phrases:

¶ **a hen is on** something very important is planned or happening.
     1878 in *DA*: Keep cool, boys, there's a hen on. **1883** *Life* (Aug. 30) 104: Go easy: there's a hen on in these parts. **1890** in P. Dickson *Baseball Dict.* 198: From what Ewing says there is no longer any doubt that there is a very large National League hen on. **1896** Ade *Artie* 60: Miller,...I got a hen on. **1908** McGaffey *Show Girl* 211: Something has gone wrong, or there is a big hen on. **1937** Parsons *Lafayette Escadrille* 153: There was no question but that there was a big hen on, but nobody knew what it was to be. **1946** *Calif. Folk. Qly.* V 231: *She's got a hen on.* She is hatching up some scheme.

¶ **in a hen's ass** not at all.—usu. considered vulgar.
     1966–80 McAleer & Dickson *Unit Pride* 189: In a hen's ass,

O'Hara. I ain't goin' for that shit. *Ibid.* 352: "Were they drunk or
weren't they?" "In a hen's ass they were."

hen apple *n.* an egg. Cf. HEN FRUIT. *Joc.* Also **hen berry.**
  1938 in *AS* (Apr. 1939) 90: *Hen Apples.* Eggs. "I eat scrambled hen
  apples for breakfast." *ca*1960 in *DARE.* **1960** in *DARE: Hen
  berries*...Once used humorously for eggs. **1966** in *DARE* [both forms].
  1976 *N.Y. Folklore* II 238: Eggs are called *cackleberries* or *hen apples.*

henchman *n.* a friend.
  1958 Meltzer & Blees *H.S. Confidential* (film): We're good henchmen, you and me. **1959** R. Smith *Girls Town* (film): How'd you like to
  be my henchman?...You know, buddies. Pals. **1959–60** R. Reisner
  Jazz Titans 158: *Henchmen:* friends.

hen college *n.* a college for women.—used derisively.
  1922 S. Lewis *Babbitt* 18: Oh, ain't we select since we went to that
  hen college! **1940** S. Lewis *Bethel Merriday* 32: You'd never expect to
  find her in a hen college. **1942** *ATS* 774.

hen-coop *n.* **1.** *pl. Naut.* a ship's gratings.
  1882 *United Service* (Sept.) 298: Mrs. Cringle was at the helm and
  the captain asleep on the "hen coops."
  2. *Stu.* a women's dormitory.
  1900 *DN* II 40: *Hen-coop,* n. Dormitory for women students. **1906**
  DN III 140: *Hen-coop, hen-house,* n. Young women's dormitory.

hen frigate *n. Naut.* a ship whose captain is unduly influenced by his wife, who is also aboard.
  [*1695** W. Congreve, in *OED2* s.v. *hen-pecked:* I believe he that marries you will go to Sea in a Hen-peck'd Frigat.] *1785** Grose *Vulgar
  Tongue: Hen frigate*...a sea phrase...applied to a ship the captain of
  which had his wife on board, supposed to command him. *a*1867**
  Smyth *Sailor's Wd. Bk.: Hen-frigate.*—A ship wherein the captain's wife
  interfered in the duty or regulations. **1883** Russell *Sailors' Lang.* 68:
  Hen-frigate:—A ship was so called when the captain's wife influenced
  the routine, &c.

hen fruit *n.* an egg or eggs. *Joc.*
  1854 in *DA:* A young lady is said to have asked a gentleman at the
  table of a hotel "down East" to pass her the "hen fruit." She pointed to
  a plate of eggs. **1873** in *OED2:* Their "hen fruit," as it is elegantly
  termed in America. **1885** in Guerin *Mountain Charley* 91: The boys
  were soon very agreeably occupied in roasting the "hen-fruit" in the
  ashes. **1900** *DN* II 40: *Hen-fruit,* n. Eggs. **1903** *DN* II 316: *Hen-fruit,*
  n. Eggs. Formerly used facetiously, but now used seriously by many
  country people. **1909** *Miss. A&M Reveille* 150: Never discuss the
  future production of hen fruit until the process of incubation has thoroughly materialized. **1918** Beston *Full Speed Ahead* 200: Of course,
  sometimes the "hen fruit"...gives way to *soi disant* buckwheat cakes.
  1919 Piersbergen *Aero Squad* 13: Over-ripe hen fruit was laid before
  them. **1922** *Leatherneck* (Apr. 29) 5: *Hen Fruit:* Eggs. **1923** Frank Silver & Irving Cohn *Yes! We Have No Bananas* (sheet music, N.Y.: Skid-
  more Music Co.) 2: We got those hen fruit, have you tried 'em? **1927**
  Amer. Leg. Mo. (Apr.) 25: So what's the use of breakin' your neck over
  a lotta hen-fruit. **1951** Pryor *The Big Play* 9: If we've got to have
  boiled hen fruit every day, why can't they put in a little salt? **1981** G.
  Wolf *Roger Rabbit* 190: He must have been made of sterner stuff than
  your normal hen fruit.

hen hawk *n. Lacrosse.* an underhand shot.
  1976 *Webster's Sports Dict.* 210.

henhouse *n.* a women's residence; *(also)* a women's prison.
  [*1785** Grose *Vulgar Tongue: Hen house.* A house where the woman
  rules.] *1889** Barrère & Leland *Dict. Slang* I 458: *Hen-house* (old), a
  house for soldiers' wives. **1906** (quot. at HEN-COOP, 2). **1939** Howsley
  Argot 24: *Henhouse*—jailer's term for the female section; a prison for
  women.

hen out *v.* CHICKEN OUT.
  1964 Hill *One of the Casualties* 168: We kin git ol Milt loaded an
  maybe he won't hen out on this deal.

hen party *n.* a social gathering of women only. Also fig. Cf.
  STAG PARTY.
  *1887** in *OED2:* It was a "hen party" to which his wife had gone.
  *1889** Barrère & Leland *Dict. Slang* I 459: Hen-party. **1898** Norris
  Moran 2: "Might have known it would be a hen party till six, anyhow,"
  he muttered. **1906** *DN* III 140: *Hen party*...A party at which only
  women or girls are present. **1907** S.E. White *Arizona* 143: It was one
  continual round of...afternoon hen-parties. **1959–60** Bloch *Dead Beat*

65: Min invites a bunch of women over for a hen party. **1965** Graham
& Block *What's Her Name* 3: This was one hen party that didn't lay an
egg. **1981** Carpi *Escape 2000* (film): [To a group of men:] Hey, what is
this? A hen party? Shape up! We got a job to do! **1982** R.M. Brown
So. Discomfort 177: "What do you mean?" "Hen party."

hen pen *n.* (see quots.). *Joc.*
  1943 *School & Soc.* LVIII 169: *Hen-pen:* private girls' school. **1947**
  ATS (Supp.) 19: Servicewomen's quarters...*hen pen.*

Henry *n.* [after *Henry* Ford] a Ford automobile. Also **Henry J.**
  1917 Ford *Cheer-Up Ltrs.* 100: I discovered a "miss" in the Henry.
  1918 *Radiator* (May 30) 2: There were half a dozen "Henrys" around
  the corner to carry off the casualties. **1920** Acker *Thru the War* 133
  [ref. to 1918]: Every vehicle does its duty religiously as a "Henry" and
  with less rattle. **1927** [Fliesler] *Anecdota* 60: "Why is a Ford car called
  a Henry in Detroit and a Lizzie in New York?" "Because by the time it
  gets to New York it loses its nuts." **1939** Eldredge *Death for Surgeon*
  63: If that damned Packard ahead would move over and give my
  Henry a chance. **1966–68** in *DARE.* **1982** in *Nat. Lampoon* (Feb.
  1983) 85: On the New Jersey turnpike in a stolen "Henry J."

hen's age *n.* a very long time; DOG'S AGE.
  *a*1867** in G.W. Harris *Lovingood* 149: George, that wer the fust
  spessamin ove a smokin mad gal I've seed in a hen's age.

hens and chickens *n.pl. Army.* lice.
  1863 in *Civil War Hist.* X (1964) 43: Some of the boys in camp have
  got "hens and chickens."

hen-skin *n. West.* a feather quilt; *(also)* a very thin blanket;
  (see also 1958 quot.).
  1902 in *DA:* Why don't you burn these henskins and get you a
  decent bed? **1910** in *DA:* None of the usual jest and badinage over
  "hen-skin blankets"...a cold morning usually inspired. **1917–20** in
  J.M. Hunter *Trail Drivers* I 62 [ref. to 1880's]: One sugan, a hen-skin
  blanket, and a change of dirty clothes. **1936** R. Adams *Cowboy Lingo*
  36: Heavy comforts...stuffed with feathers were called "hen skins."
  1939 Abbott & Smith *Pointed Them North* 98 [ref. to 1880's]: Them
  henskins...wouldn't cast a shadow on the ground if you'd hang them
  up. **1958** McCulloch *Woods Words* 84: *Henskin*— a. Thin soled shoes
  not stout enough to take calks. b. Light underwear. **1977** in *DARE*
  [logger lingo]: *Hen skins*—Light summer underwear.

hen tailor *n.* a designer of women's fashions.
  1867 in G.W. Harris *High Times* 177: Hits true the hen tailors, an'
  sich cattil, hev invented a substitute [for women].

hen tracks *n.pl.* awkward or illegible handwriting; CHICKEN
  TRACKS; GOOSE TRACKS.
  1878 Huftalen *Diary* 22: I am perfectly ashamed of my journal
  there are so *many* blob[s] & goose tracks (or as pa calls them hens
  tracks) all the way through. **1928, 1950, 1951,** etc., in *DARE.*
  1965–70 in *DARE* [41 informants].

he-one *n.* In phrase: ¶ **the old he-one** the largest or most
  important person or thing.
  1885 in Lummis *Letters* 246: Give 'em time, and they'll both catch
  up with "the old he one" [the largest canyon in the area]. **1904** in *AS*
  XLI (1966) 23: The Gen'ral had to go...to the old He One.

hep *n.* hepatitis.
  1967 Wolf *Love Generation* 135: The Communications Company
  printed up a thing about serum hep, that lays it right there, that lays
  the information out. **1973** *Oui* (Feb.) 112: But of course it's more in
  context than American hep, it's *jaundice* and don't worry.

hep *adj.* [orig. unkn., cf. HIP, *adj.* and HIPPED; the form *hept* is
  the earliest known in print; alteration of the vowel from /ɛ/
  to /ɪ/ is phonologically perhaps more likely than the
  reverse, but both *hip* and *hep* appear in print at about the
  same time. Discussed by P. Tamony, *Americanisms* (No. 17)]
  Also **hept, hepped, Joe Hep[t], Johnny Hep.**
  1. fully aware of what is planned or happening; in the
  know; cognizant; familiar; in phr. **put hep [to]** to inform
  (of), alert, or introduce (to); **be hep** to understand.
  1903 *Enquirer* (Cincinnati) (May 9) 13: Modern Slang
  Glossary...*Hept*—To get wise or next. **1904** T.A. Dorgan, in Zwilling
  TAD Lexicon 44: Take it easy now fellers, one of you stay behind so that
  no one will get hep. **1905** in Tamony *Americanisms* (No. 17) 10: Ain't
  hep that he's a pretty important bloke....Why I'm hep to a few things

about you meself. **1906** Hobart *Skiddoo* 53: Rush hither to your happy little home in Harlem, where the mosquito…stingeth not like a serpent, are you hep? **1906** H. Green *Actors' Boarding House* 31: "I'm hep," said Terence briefly. **1907** *McClure's Mag.* (Feb.) 381: He got hep that he had a crowd of the real things under him. **1907** *Reader* (Sept.) 346: I was hep in a minute.…He was a coward. **1908** in "O. Henry" *Works* 692: I don't want 'em hep just yet to the fact that I'm pounding the asphalt for another job. *a***1909** Tillotsen *How to Be a Detective* 86: One thief will say to his pal, "Are you hept" or "Are you joseph" or "Are you jo hept?" His pal will say, "I'm wise." The expression was given its fame from the characteristic of an old circus man who was famous. He would always say that he knew just what to do or what was being said.…Finally when anyone contemplated an act or expression around the show grounds, the gang would say, "Yes, you are the same as Joe Hept." **1911** A.H. Lewis *Apaches of N.Y.* 75: When it's one of me friends, I puts 'em hep, see? **1911** T.A. Dorgan, in *N.Y. Eve. Jour.* (Jan. 11) 12: Can you put me hep to anyone who's in right? **1912** *Hampton's Mag.* (Jan.) 844: I'm hep to you like a neighbor. **1912** Mathewson *Pitching* 151: We will arrange a set of signs that I can give if we think they are "hep" to yours. **1913** London *Valley of Moon* 81: An' he knows the trick. He's hep. **1912–14** in E. O'Neill *Lost Plays* 170: "Discretion is the better part of valor"—any well-bred Mexican flea is hep to that. **1914** Jackson & Hellyer *Vocab.* 43: *Hep*…"next;" on. Derived from the name of a fabulous detective who operated in Cincinnati, the legend has it.…"Chop the skirmish; he's hep." **1915–16** Lait *Beef, Iron & Wine* 265: Next day the kid gets hepped to who it was pulled that there rod. **1916** E.R. Burroughs *Return of Mucker* 140: It was a skirt tipped it off to me.…Now are you hep? **1918** *Stars & Stripes* (May 10) 4: *But to myself I am not hep.* **1921** Casey & Casey *Gay-Cat* 208: I meant on'y I was Jerry, Johnny Hep, wise, yuh know. **1924** Marks *Plastic Age* 195: Wake up and, as you would say, "get hep to yourselves." **1928** Bodenheim *Georgie May* 19: His woman, now, she's sweet on me but he ain't hep to it. **1928** Hammett *Red Harvest* 33: "Whisper's hep," the burly man told the chief. "He phoned Donohoe that he's going to stay in his joint." **1931** Wilstach *Under Cover Man* 9: I ain't hep yet to this burg. **1931** Hellinger *Moon* 178: Get hep, baby. This ain't no night for grandpas to be chasin' around. **1932** L. Berg *Prison Doctor* 229: But I'm hep now and I'm through playing a sucker's game! **1939** Attaway *Breathe Thunder* 47: Aw, the guy was hep to us all the time. **1940** D.W. Maurer, in *AS* XV 119: *Joe Hep* or *Hep.* Smart, or "wise" to what is happening. Probably so called from one Joe Hep, a proprietor of a saloon in Chicago where *grifters* had their headquarters. **1944** Burley *Hndbk. Jive* 120: They all were hep, that St. Nick ain't nowhere. **1944** Sturges *Conquering Hero* (film): You're happy, she's happy, and nobody's hep to nothing. **1960** C.L. Cooper *Scene* 233: She probably knows someone there who's hep on what she's doing. **1963** Williamson *Hustler!* 46: After I got hep to it myself, I'd make them stand in the line. **1965** Himes *Imabelle* 35: And there you is, ain't got hep yet that you been beat. **1972** D. Dalby, in Kochman *Rappin'* 180: Hep, hip,…hepcat.…Cf. Wolof *hepi, hipi,* "to open one's eyes, be aware of what is going on"; hence *hipi-kat,* "someone with his eyes open, aware of what is going on." **1976** Braly *False Starts* 136: In time,…everyone was hep, even the dimmest of friendly guards.

2.a. worldly-wise; shrewd; sophisticated; smart. [The basis for the nickname in 1912 quot. is uncertain.]

[**1912** Stringer *Shadow* 88: Hep Roony saw Binhart this mornin'.] **1921** Casey & Casey *Gay-Cat* 146: Wunst I knowed a expert shoplifter name o' Detroit Mamie that was Mis' Johnny Hep. **1922** S. Lewis *Babbitt* 172: Something doing, boys. Listen to what the Hep Bird twitters. **1931–33** in Clemmer *Pris. Community* 332: Hep cop, n. An officer who knows what is going on about him. **1944** Burley *Hndbk. Jive* 121: Ain't no cat so hep as me. **1942–49** Goldin et al. *DAUL: Hep*…Experienced in the underworld; sophisticated; having underworld wisdom. [*hence*] *hep broad,…hep ghee.* **1954** L. Armstrong *Satchmo* 25: By running with the older boys, I soon began to get hep. **1961** R. Considine *Ripley* 185: Ripley yielded to the clamor of his nautically hep guests. **1970** Cortina *Slain Warrior* 28: Oh, no, I wasn't that hep. **1971** D. Berg *Sick World* 70: Hey, Pauline, you're a hep chick. I gotta hand in this composition for English. You tell me if it's any good. **1975** Sepe & Telano *Cop Team* 70: You guys are hepped. **1977** J.L. Dillard *Lexicon of Black Eng.* 73: Young [white] adults of the 1930s…prided themselves on being "hep" (NB: not hip). **1966–80** McAleer & Dickson *Unit Pride* 422: He didn't seem very hep. **1980** *N.Y. Daily News* (Sept. 9) 17: Mayor Koch, Sen. Moynihan and Gov. Carey—sometimes referred to by hep Democrats

as the Gang of Three. **1996** Knoxville, Tenn., attorney, age 43: She is *hep* politically in every way.

b. in fashion; fashionable and up-to-date, esp. keenly appreciative of the very latest styles in music, dress, or social behavior; fashionably smart or sophisticated. [Associated chiefly with the swing-music era, *ca*1935–50; now generally supplanted by HIP.]

1942 *Pittsburgh Courier* (Aug. 1) 13: My students…have acquainted me with the "hep" language. **1942** in *Great Music of D. Ellington* 69: It's a real "hep" treat. **1942** *ATS* 567: Hep…with an understanding of "swing." **1946** in Tamony *Americanisms* (No. 17) 7: If you say "hep,"…you ain't hip. **1946** H.A. Smith *Rhubarb* 29: "I can tell," she said, "I can tell—he's hep." **1950** C.W. Gordon *High School* 114: Positively rated persons are "hep," "rite," and "george." **1953** W. Fisher *Waiters* 143: Some hepped chick's walked off with my old man. *ca***1953** Hughes *Lodge* 182: She was very musically hep. ****1957** in *OED2*: Where can I get a shirt like that?…It's hep. **1958** *PADS* (No. 30) 40: In the swing period "hep" was widely used by musicians to mean…"possessed of good taste." **1962** E.A. Smith *Amer. Youth Culture* 12: A costly cashmere sweater was viewed as "hep" by the girls. **1962** Crump *Killer* 170: Yeah, what's wrong with dying young and hep? **1971** N.Y.U. student: White people just aren't hep. **1972** J.L. Dillard *Black Eng.* 119: It is…a commonplace of the jazz language that *hep* is a white man's distortion of the more characteristically Negro *hip*. **1976** T. Walker *Ft. Apache* 157: "It's not Heaven, baby," the spirit's voice offered. I had to restrain myself from laughing again.…I didn't know spirits were this hep [in their language]. **1978–86** J.L. Burke *Lost Get-Back Boogie* 143: They memorize all kinds of ep phrases for every life situation. *a***1986** H. Gold, in *NDAS:* But I'm hep, man; for example, I had my vasectomy already. **1989** *Married with Children* (Fox-TV): Sammy Davis…is one hep black cat. **1989** N.Y.C. woman: When I was in high school [*ca*1950], "He's *hep*" meant that he was involved in all the latest things like music and hotrods.

3. enthusiastic; excited; HIPPED[1], 3. See also HEPPED UP.

1938 "R. Hallas" *You Play the Black* 62: You're both hepped on this Ecanaanomic gag. **1940** *New Yorker* (Nov. 16) 21: When she gets hepped on a subjeck she can keep on and on till a person feels she's gonna bust or something. **1973** Michelson *Very Simple Game* 41: She wasn't really hep to my going. I mean, she wasn't crazy about the idea. **1984** N.O. woman, age 35: You could tell she wasn't real hep on the idea.

¶ In phrase:

¶ **hep** [or **hip**] **to the jive** *Jazz.* in the know; fashionable; etc. Cf. *hipped to the jive* s.v. HIPPED[3], 2.b.

1940 in Oliver *Meaning of Blues* 320: I've got to sell from this bin, everybody's getting hip to the jive. **1944** *Slanguage Dict.* 59: *Hep to the jive*—in the know. **1947** *ATS* (Supp.) 5: Up-to-date; fashionably knowing…*hep to the jive.* **1954** L. Armstrong *Satchmo* 192: As the days rolled on I commenced getting hep to the jive. I learned a good deal about life and people. **1976** *Muppet Show* (CBS-TV): That was great. Really hep to the jive. **1982** Sculatti *Catalog of Cool* 118: Increasing numbers of Chicanos are getting hep to the jive.

hep *v.* [prob. back formation of *hepped,* var. of HEP, *adj.,* or functional shift of HEP, *adj.*] to make informed; WISE UP.—usu. constr. with *up.*

1921 J. Conway, in *Variety* (Nov. 18) 29: I pulled a new one the other night for I had a hunch that too much of the knock em dead stuff might hep em up. **1942** *ATS* 229: Inform; give inside information…*hep, hip,…give the dope.* **1942–49** Goldin et al. *DAUL* 94: Ain't that ghee…ever going to get hepped up?…Hep Tuttie up that the bulls…are on his pratt.

hepcat *n.* [HEP + CAT] a person, esp. a man, who is HEP; (*specif.*) *Jazz.* a keen devotee of swing music. Now mainly *hist.*

1938 *S. F. Chronicle* (Mar. 13) (Tamony Coll.): A "hepcat"…is a person with decided tastes in both classical and modern music. **1938** C. Calloway *Hepster's Dict.:* Hep cat—a guy who knows all the answers, understands jive. **1939** in A. Banks *First-Person* 242: Don't you hear them hep cats call? **1942** "E. Queen" *Calamity Town* 19: Square dances and hepcat contests. **1943** Darling *Jitterbugs* (film): To her he's a real hepcat. Right in the groove. **1943** in Inman *Diary* 1164: Girls and boys danced wildly to its ululating rhythms. "They're hepcats," a red-headed girl explained. **1943** A. Scott *So Proudly We Hail!* (film): I'da made a real hepcat out of you [a woman]. **1946** Boulware *Jive & Slang* 4: *Hep Cat*…Man who knows the jive. **1948** Manone & Vandervoort *Trumpet*

172: A solid hepcat is a fella who knows the gracious way of living. **1951** in Leadbitter & Slaven *Blues Records* 257: A Hep Cat's Advice. **1954** L. Armstrong *Satchmo* 238: After that the hep cats would have to look out, for he would blow one whale of a trombone. **1970** A. Young *Snakes* 140: Now, you wouldnt try to lay a hype on an old hepcat like me, would you? **1971** Torres *Sting Like a Bee* 93: My father is a hep-cat....He is a hep fella—fifty-seven years old crazy about the girls. **1972** (quot. at HEP, *adj.*, 1). **1972** Chipman *Hardening Rock* xiv: Chuck Berry...was *the* mythmaker for millions of hepcats and dungaree dolls. **1980** *N.Y. Times Mag.* (Sept. 7) 112: Not...all men are shearing their tresses. Two glaring exceptions are "the hippies, or the hep cats," says Louis Natole...[a barber]. **1981** O'Day & Eells *High Times* 73: I was the toast of all the hep (hip came later) musicians and hepcats in the city.

hep kitten *n.* a woman who is a keen devotee of swing music.
    1974 E. Thompson *Tattoo* 87: A gum-chewing hep kitten who could really jive.

hepped up *adj.* excited or agitated; (*hence*) intoxicated by liquor or drugs.
    1939 M. Levin *Citizens* 141: The union boys got all hepped up. **1942** *ATS* 123: [Drunk:] *Hepped up...pifflicated* [etc.]. **1950** F. Brown *Space on Hands* 119: What are they hepped about? **1951** E. Wood, Jr. *Violent Years* (film): Nothing to get so hepped up about. **1952** Bellow *Augie March* 71: The whole race was hepped-up about appliances. **1953** R. Wright *Outsider* 6: One time he was all hepped-up over one writer and the next time he was through with 'im and was gone on to another. **1955** T. Anderson *Own Beloved Sons* 43: Two of their rear emplacements got attacked....Major's all hepped up about it. **1958** H. Ellison *Deadly Streets* 92: I don't know why you're so hepped-up about this. **1968** Baker, Ladd & Robb *CUSS* 136: *Hepped up* Eager for or looking forward to something or someone. Tense at the last minute. **1983** *Nat. Lampoon* (Mar.) 41: A boxcar of hepped-up rattlers. **1986** F. Walton *Once Were Eagles* 159: I was real hepped up to get assigned to the Black Sheep. **1994** *Simpsons* (Fox-TV): The guy's hepped up on goofballs!

hepster *n.* HIPSTER. Now *hist.*
    1938 C. Calloway *Hepster's Dict.* [title]. **1941** *Pittsburgh Courier* (Mar. 22) 20: They know...you're a "hepster." **1944** Burley *Hndbk. Jive* 120: Then one hepster arose. **1947** *Tomorrow* (Aug.) 27: *Hepsters* who wanted a token that they were *hepper* than other *cats* sharpened it to *hip*. **1950** in *DAS*: The hundred hepsters joined in the chorus. ***1958** in *OED2*: An egghead minority of hepsters.

Herb *n. Stu.* a clumsy or stupid person; GEEK, *n.*, 1.a.; (*hence*) *Und.* a victim; SUCKER. Also attrib.
    [***1990** T. Thorne *Dict. Contemp. Slang: Herb...a* street urchin.] **1993** Univ. Tenn. prof., age 49: A *Herb* is a geek. **1993** in *Parade* (Jan. 2, 1994) 8 [college slang]: *Herb*—geek. **1994** *N.Y. Times Mag.* (Aug. 14) 28: The search for easy victims is called "catching a Herb." *Ibid.* 30: If the Herb was reluctant about giving up his money, one of them would grab the Herb in a choke hold. **1994** Graffito in N.Y.C. subway (coll. J. Sheidlower): John Dewey is a herb high school. **1995** *N.Y. Press* (July 26) 8: Wright was something of a loser—excuse me, Herb. **1995** Stavsky, Mozeson, & Mozeson *A2Z: Herb...an* easy victim.

herb *n. Black E.* marijuana. Also (rare) **herbs**.
    1962 in Wepman, Newman & Binderman *The Life* 31: A pocket full of money and a head full of herb. **1968** Heard *Howard St.* 98: You been smokin' herb at Two-Day's. **1973** Huggett *Body Count* 93: "How 'bout we smoke some shit?" "You got herb?" **1974** Blount *3 Bricks Shy* 56: A paper bag in which he said he had some "herbs and wine." **1974** in D.C. Dance *Shuckin' & Jivin'* 282: A good stick o' herb. **1973–76** J. Allen *Assault* 61 [ref. to 1950's]: Smoking herb and drinking wine and fighting and stealing. **1976** *N.Y. Post* (Sept. 10) 3: We were sitting around playing cards, drinking, smoking a little herb. **1980** Novak *High Culture* 255: I have to smoke Hawaiian or Thai herb to do this. **1985** Flowers *Mojo Blues* 9: Wine and some herb. **1994** *N.Y. Newsday* (May 2) A27: Like smoking cigarettes and experimenting with herb and alcohol it was an act of rebellion.

herd *n. Esp. USMC.* a platoon of trainees; (*hence*) platoon; small unit.—usu. used contemptuously.
    1957 Barrett *D.I.* (film): You people are not even a mob. A mob has a leader. You're a herd. *Ibid.:* I'll stake my herd against any of 'em. **1973** Layne *Murphy* (unp.): You don't learn very fast, herd. **1976** C.R. Anderson *Grunts* 93 [ref. to 1969]: Third platoon, called "Third Herd," had been considered...the weakest in the Company. **1978** J. Webb *Fields of Fire* 108: And in five minutes the Third Herd had a

new Papa Sierra. Like it or not. **1978** Hasford *Short-Timers* 5: Am I correct, herd? **1985** Dye *Between Raindrops* 256: Not much to say to my newly-acquired herd. **1989** D. Sherman *There I Was* 43: Third herd, saddle up. **1990** Helms *Proud Bastards* 44: I have one highly motivated and squared-away herd.

¶ In phrase:

¶ **ride herd on** *Orig. Cattle Industry.* to watch over; oversee; tend.
    1897 A.H. Lewis *Wolfville* 29: "Cherokee makes me tired," says Peets, who's ridin' herd on the play. **1908** McGaffey *Show Girl* 116: I was, figuratively speaking, riding herd on him. **1925** in Hammett *Big Knockover* 213: I gone and got me another job—riding herd on law and order. **1929** McEvoy *Hollywood Girl* 14: I've been...riding herd on a movie director. **1931** Rynning *Gun Notches* 41: Monte was some relation to the famous Tombstone sheriff of that name who rode herd on southern Arizona years later. **1938** Haines *Tension* 157: But ride herd on him and Florabelle we can't hardly do. **1958** in J. Jones *Reach* 262: We sort of rode herd on him for a few days, father-sitting we call it. **1975** *L.A. Times* (Nov. 21) II 7: For years he tried to persuade the Senate to set up some effective machinery to ride herd on the Central Intelligence Agency. **1982** *U.S. News & W.R.* (Jan. 18) 10: Riding herd on the up-front feature is Deputy Editor John Gibson.

herd *v.* **1.** *Esp. Labor.* to superintend the work of (scabs or convicts).—used contemptuously. Hence **herder**, *n.*
    1887 in Barrère & Leland *Dict. Slang* I 459: I found large gangs of Chinamen at work in different places, in charge of a white man who was called the *herder.* **1914** in [J. Chase] *Mil. Occup. Coal Zone* 113: Some called to me "Baldwin-Feltz Thug," others Scab-Herding Son-of-a-bitch. **1930** *Amer. Mercury* (Dec.) 456: *Herder, n.* A guard in a penal institute. "That herder's strictly wrong." **1934** in E. Levinson *Strikes* 292: Down with the scab-herder Bergoff! **1987** Sayles *Matewan* (film): Yellow scab-herders!
    2. to drive (a motor vehicle) or pilot (an aircraft).
    1933 Stewart *Airman Speech* 71: *Herd.* A term used in the West; to "herd" a plane is to fly it. **1939** Fessier *Wings of Navy* (film): And it takes a darned sight better man to fly one than to herd one of your fighting doodlebugs. **1943** *Yank* (Sept. 3) 7: I'm herding a 6 by 6. **1945** in Rea *Wings of Gold* 268: I have my hands full herding [the F4U] along. **1963** J. Ross *Dead Are Mine* 90 [ref. to 1944]: By the way, can you herd a jeep? **1971** Tak *Truck Talk* 82: *Herd*—To drive a truck. **1973** Gwaltney *Destiny's Chickens* 7: Every loafer present would be wondering who was herding this snappy red pickup.

herd call *n. Theat.* CATTLE CALL.
    1969 Gordone *No Place to Be Somebody* 414: Melvin...Gabe had an audition today. Gabe. I said it was a herd call, Melvino Rex!

herder *n. R.R.* a man who guides trains or engines in a railroad yard.
    1930 *R.R. Man's Mag.*, in *DARE: Herder*—A man who couples engines on and takes them off. **1931** *Writer's Digest* (May) 42: *Herder*—A man who couples engines on and takes them off. **1970** *Current Slang* V (Summer) 8: *Herder, n.* A railroad employee who guides trains and engines to and from the main track, and through yards. **1990** L. Nieman *Boomer* 2: Don't worry about the herder. *Ibid.* 250: *Herder.* Switchman who guides engines and trains in and out of a yard.

Hereford *adj. West.* (see quots.). *Joc.*
    *ca*1889 Newspaper clipping in N.Y.P.L. copy of Matsell *Vocab.*: A white shirt [the cowboy] calls a Hereford shirt because Hereford cattle have white faces. Similarly he calls anything Hereford that is white, for example, Hereford dishes and Hereford hats. Carrying this fancy still further, a "white" man is known as a Hereford man. **1916** *Editor* (Mar. 11) 297: *Hereford Shirt.* A stiff-bosomed white shirt.

Herk *n. Mil. Av.* HERKY BIRD. Also **Herc.**
    1981 Mersky & Polmar *Nav. Air War in Viet.* 135: Marine "Herks"...provided air-to-air fueling of tactical aircraft. **1988** M. Maloney *Thunder Alley* 215: Prop job....It's got to be a Herc.

Herky Bird *n. Mil. Av.* the Lockheed C-130 Hercules transport and tanker airplane. [Quots. ref. to Vietnam War.]
    1980 Cragg *Lexicon Militaris* 217: *Herky Bird.* The C-130 ("Hercules") cargo aircraft. **1984** Trotti *Phantom* 249: C-130 Hercules (Herky Bird). *a*1990 R. Herman, Jr. *Force of Eagles* 121: How else you expect to get there before the Herky Birds?

herky-jerky *adj.* **1.** jerky or awkward; extremely uneven.

1943 in I. Hawks *B-17s* 67: Herky Jerky II. **1944** *Yank* (Jan. 21) 8: The crew of the *Herky Jerky.* **1957** (cited in *W10*). **1965** *N.Y. Times* (Oct. 17) II 1: Her adaptation of a French play is as herky-jerky and self-conscious as her performance of the title role. **1976** Rosen *Above Rim* 48: Even Quinton's herky-jerky pigeon-toed gait was transfigured into a smart reggae beat. **1978** Pici *Tennis Hustler* 107: Moving herky-jerky fashion. **1980** Schruer *Blondie* 149: The song pulls out of its herky-jerky rhythm. **1988** Frazier & Offen *W. Frazier* 95: He's got too much herky-jerky in his game, giving too many moves and fakes he doesn't need to do. **1989** *TV Guide* (Mar. 25) 31: Another herky-jerky season. **1991** D. Anderson *In Corner* 62: Nobody thought he would make a fighter. He was too herky-jerky.

2. silly; foolish.
    1977 Shem *House of God* 50: He gives you all this herky-jerky stuff. **1988** Dye *Outrage* 163: And one more thing…all this herky-jerky bullshit aside.

Herman *n. Mil.* a German plane.
    1945 in Gellhorn *Face of War* 160: We sure clobbered the Herman.

hernia bar *n.* a bar or lever that is difficult to operate.
    1987 Nichols & Tillman *Yankee Sta.* (photo section): Ordnancemen strain a "hernia bar" to load bombs on the racks of an A-6…in May 1972. **1991** Linnekin *80 Knots* 361: A virtual "hernia bar."

hero gear *n. USMC.* battle souvenirs. *Joc.*
    1961 R. Davis *Marine at War* 172 [ref. to 1945]: "I swap the pastry to the troops for hero gear" (battle souvenirs) "and I swap the hero gear to the swabbies for pogey bait" (candy).

herp *n.* genital herpes.—constr. with *the.*
    1978 Univ. Tenn. student: Guess who's got the herp? **1987** Knoxville, Tenn., attorney, age *ca*35: As long as she hasn't got AIDS or the herp, she qualifies.

herped *adj.* carrying the virus that causes genital herpes.—usu. constr. with *up* or *out.*
    1983 *Nat. Lampoon* (Apr.) 62: You're herped out to the max. **1983** *Nat. Lampoon* (Aug.) 4: Slutball herped-to-the-max swingles. *a*1989 Spears *NCT Dict.*: They say all those frat guys are herped up.

herring *n.* **1.** a worthless, foolish, or offensive person. [The sense intended in 1859 quot. is uncertain.]
    *1821 *Real Life in Ireland* 44: I was brought…to catch a Dublin Bay herring, a soft-roed fellow, but fat. **1840** *Spirit of Times* (May 2) 99: I hear o' your braggin', you miserable spint herrin', that has neither the heart or appointments of a man. [**1859** Matsell *Vocab.* 41: *Herring.* All bad, all alike.] **1889** Barrère & Leland *Dict. Slang* I 459: *Herring* (American)…a man who is exactly like all his associates, a narrow-minded, average sort of person, who has been packed away as it were among others. *a*1919 in J.A. Lomax *Cattle Trail* 180: Some high-col-lared herrin' jeered the garb that I was wearin'. **1919** Ashton *F,63* 75: No, ya herring, I lugged it all over Frogland so's t' make you a present of it. **1928** Levin *Reporter* 27: If you want me to speak to that herring, I will. **1951** J. Reach *My Friend Irma* 15: I'd even settle for a little herring like the Professor. **1975** *Urban Life* IV 211: "B.C., there's a herring in the joint." (Look out, don't say anything, there's a suspicious-looking guy asking too many questions.).

2. dollars; FISH[1], *n.,* 2.a.
    1933 Deleon & Martin *Tillie & Gus* (film): May I remind you ecclesiastically that the pot was shy two hundred and twenty-five herring?

¶ In phrase:

¶ **dead herring** GONE GOOSE.
    1869 J.L. Peyton *Over Alleghanies* 58: You'll be a dead herring in less than an hour.

herring box *n.* a big shoe. *Joc.*
    1884 P. Montrose *Clementine* (pop. song): Herring boxes without topses/Sandals were for Clementine. **1895** Foote *Coeur D'Alene* 11: Show her me "herring-boxes."…And your own little shlippers wid the hobnails.

herring-choker *n. Naut.* a herring fisherman; (*hence*) a native of the Canadian maritime provinces or of Scandinavia; (*also*) a vessel from one of these places.—used derisively or disparagingly.
    1899 in *OED2*: I am down among the "herring chokers" and "blue noses" for a few weeks. **1919** Duffy *G.P.F. Book* 109: Does this "her-ring-choker" come to attention for the Colonel now? **1923** in Eck-storm & Smyth *Minstrelsy of Maine* 149: He's…a regular herring chok-er. **1924** *Adventure* (June 20) 163: This guy's one o' them Aroostook

potato-bugs….He's a frog. Potato-bugs and lumberjacks, this regi-ment's full of 'em. 'N herrin' chokers. **1926** *Writer's Mo.* (Mar.) 197: A "P.I.," "Bluenose" or "Herrin'-choker" means a Prince Edward's Islander, or any man from "the Provinces, down East." *1929 Bowen *Sea Slang* 66: *Herring-Joker* [sic]. A Nova Scotian man or ship, used as an alternative to *Bluenose.* **1936** Mencken *Amer. Lang.* (ed. 4) 296: Scandinavian…*squarehead…herring choker.* **1950** in *DARE: Herring choker*—Norwegian…Scandinavians. **1973** Flaherty *Chez Joey* xiii: I was born in 1936, in Brooklyn,…to John Flaherty of the County Gal-way ("herring-chokers") and Maggie Casey of the County Tipperary ("stone-throwers"). **1973** Beck *Folklore & the Sea* 66: Herring chokers are men from Nova Scotia. **1976** Hayden *Voyage* 146: You'd best fetch a bucket of water for that herring choker. **1976** *Nat. Lampoon's Book of Funnies* 2: Some herring-choker college dean whose area of specializa-tion is glandular diseases in fish.

herring-gutted *adj.* starved-looking; emaciated. Also (*obs.*) **heron-gutted.**
    *1726 in *OED2*: Meagre, Herring-gutted wretches. *1811 in *OED2*: Lank-jawed, herring-gutted plebeans. *1811 *Lexicon Balatron.*: *Herring gutted.* Thin, as a shotten herring. **1893** Hampton *Maj. in Washington* 155: Lantern-jawed, heron-gutted, fish-blooded, pink-liv-ered fools. **1899** Boyd *Shellback* 294: You—herring-gutted Bluenose.*…*Bluenose is the name given to the natives of Nova Sco-tia. **1968** Ainslie *Racing Guide* 469: *Herring-gutted*—a poor doer with practically no depth of abdomen.

herring machine *n.* a person from Cape Hatteras.—used derisively.
    1858 in G.W. Harris *High Times* 123: Thar sot astraddle ove a limb ove a big red Oak, a long bony speciment ove a regular herrin mer-sheen, in his shuttail.

herring-pond *n.* the sea or ocean, esp. the North Atlantic Ocean.—constr. with *the.* Cf. POND. *Joc.*
    *1686 in *OED2*: I'le send an account of the wonders I meet on the Great Herring-Pond. *1689 in *OED2*: My sometime Friends and Allies on the other side of the Herring-pond. *1729 in *OED2*. **1766** in Whiting *Prov. Phrs.* 211: On the other side of the great herring pond. *1824 in *OED2*. **1840** *Spirit of Times* (Apr. 25) 90: All have crossed the "herring pond." **1892** Stevens *Sailor Boy's Experience* 91: The trip across the "Herring Pond" was all that could be desired. *1929 Bowen *Sea Slang* 66: *Herring Pond.* The Atlantic. *ca*1944 in A. Hopkins *Front & Rear* 48: They sailed across the Herring Pond.

herring-snapper *n. Naut.* HERRING-CHOKER.
    1930 *AS* V (June) 391: *Herring-snapper.* A Newfoundlander or Nova Scotian, sometimes an inhabitant of Maine.

Hershey bar *n.* [named for Gen. Lewis B. *Hershey,* director (1941–70) of the U.S. Selective Service System, with pun on *Hershey bar* 'a bar of Hershey's chocolate'] *Mil.* (see 1955 quot.).
    1945 *Yank* (Aug. 31) 9: A theater ribbon and a three-inch strip of Hershey bars. **1946** *Amer. N & Q* (Feb.) 168: *Hershey Bar:* soldier's gold sleeve insignia denoting six months' overseas duty; named for the Selective Service director. **1955** Reifer *New Words* 100: *Hershey bar. Mil. Slang.* A gold-colored bar, worn on the left sleeve, representing six months of overseas service. **1956** Heflin *USAF Dict.* 250: *Hershey bar.* (After Maj. Gen. Lewis B. Hershey (1893–).) An overseas bar. *Slang.* **1988** Coonts *Final Flight* 265: Hershey-bar lifer pricks.

Hershey Highway *n.* [ref. to *Hershey's,* trademark for a brand of chocolate, alluding to the similarity in color of choco-late and feces] the rectum. *Joc.* Also **Hershey Road.**
    1973 *TULIPQ* (coll. B.K. Dumas): Hershey highway. **1974** Dubin-sky & Standora *Decoy Cop* 105: These two guys [were] doin' the Her-shey Road number. **1980** D. Hamill *Stomping Ground* 290: Gonna take you for a ride up the Bosco Boulevard. Then down the Hershey High-way. **1985** "J. Blowdryer" *Mod. Eng.* 70: Anal orifice…*Hershey High-way.* **1988** R. Snow *Members of Committee* 4: What do you [male homosexuals] use to describe the physical act of making love?…"Up the Hershey Highway." **1988** Univ. Tenn. student theme: Diarrhea….A person can [refer to] "Hershey highway." **1989** P. Munro *U.C.L.A. Slang* 71: *Ride Hershey Highway* to have sex (of homosexual males).

Hershey squirts *n.pl.* [see note at HERSHEY HIGHWAY] diar-rhea. *Joc.*
    1972 Sgt., U.S. Army, STRATCOM-Taiwan (coll. J. Ball): Mack

had to leave suddenly. You know, Gimo's revenge, the Hershey squirts, the splatters. **1973** *TULIPQ* (coll. B.K. Dumas): *Hershey squirts* (diarrhea). **1974** Univ. Tenn. grad. student: My friend used to call the shits the *Hershey squirts* back in New York in the late '50's. **1977–81** S. King *Cujo* 222: By tomorrow morning I'll probably have the Hershey-squirts. **1984** Mason & Rheingold *Slanguage:* The hershey squirts. **1985** *Maledicta* VI 96: Modern student slang, *Hershey squirts* [for diarrhea] is phonetically and visually vivid. **1985** Dye *Between Raindrops* 311: Stopped by a bad case of Hershey Squirts.

he-shark *n.* a ferocious man.
   1846 in G.W. Harris *High Times* 64: He was cut short…by the approach of the old *he shark, gun* in hand.

he-she *n.* an androgynous, cross-dressing, transsexual, or homosexual person.—used derisively.
   ***a*1871** in Hindley *Curios. Street Lit.* 141: Tom the He She barman. **1962–63** in Giallombardo *Soc. of Women* 56: The he-shes. **1968** Baker, Ladd & Robb *CUSS* 135: *He-She.* An effeminate male. **1974** R. Carter *16th Round* 170: These vicious, gutter-sniping he-shes were…deadly. **1976** G. Kirkham *Signal Zero* 125: "He-shes"…abounded on West Allison. *a*1990 C. Fletcher *Pure Cop* 115: [Male transvestites] are also known as "he/she's." **1992** Hosansky & Sparling *Working Vice* 220: They arrested "he-shes"—transvestites. **1995** *N.Y. Times* (July 16) XIII 3: The Shantytown of the He-Shes [headline].…By gender they are male, but by profession they are ladies of the evening. **1995** *Jerry Springer Show* (synd. TV series): I'm not gonna deny it because she's a he-she!

het *n. Homosex.* a heterosexual person.
   *a*1972 B. Rodgers *Queens' Vernacular* 190: *Straight* (n)…heterosexual…*het.* ***1982** in M. Amis *Moronic Inferno* 108: Nervous hets among Vidal's readers. **1992** *Sonya Live* (CNN-TV) (Mar. 30): Heteros hate us, and all we can do is get in the hets' faces. **1995** *N.Y. Press* (Apr. 26) 71: I'm a partially-reformed 28-year-old het who learned that two males can have as much fun…as a male and female can.

hetero *n. & adj.* [a] heterosexual. Now *colloq.* Also **heter.**
   *1933 in *OED2:* The odd thing…is that…I should be so purely "hetero" in spite of lack of opportunity. **1951** in W.S. Burroughs *Letters* 89: A neurotic heter with…queer leaning. **1955** in C. Beaumont *Best* 171: He didn't look like a hetero. **1959** in Russell *Perm. Playboy* 333: *Wipe out the heteros!* **1962** in J. Blake *Joint* 315: He is as howling a hetero as they get. **1966** "Petronius" *N.Y. Unexp.* 40: Most run-of-the-mill heteros [have] been run out by the freaks. ***a1968** [ref. to 1918] (quot. at HOMO, *adj.*). **1968** *N.Y.P.D.* (ABC-TV): Establishment type. Straight.…Hetero. **1969** Moynahan *Pairing Off* 33: But what I don't get is why you're so straitlaced about keeping your homo and hetero acquaintances segregated. **1992** *N.Y. Times* (May 5) A19: Anyone who dares to oppose them gets labeled as part of the white, hetero, patriarchal hegemony.

het up *adj.* [*het* (dial. var. of *heated*) + *up*] excited.
   1909 *DN* III 398: *Het, v.* pret. and pp. Heated. "He got putty *het up* by the argument." **1921** in Cornebise *Amaroc News* 163: All "het up" over a new book called *Three Soldiers.* **1923** *DN* V 210: *Het up* = angry. **1921–26** Santee *Men* 135: Old Buck was all het up about the news. **1927** *AS* III (Dec.) 139: They spoke of being "het up" (angry). **1929** *AS* V (Dec.) 123: The frequent expressions "mad as a hornet,"…"het-up,"…need no explanation. **1926–35** Watters & Hopkins *Burlesque* 34: I can't get as het up about this New York thing as you and Bonny are. **1942** *Pittsburgh Courier* (Feb. 21) 11: He sure looks het up! **1950** *PADS* (No. 14) 36: *Het:* adj. past part. Heated; angry; excited. Usually with *up.* **1968** Baker, Ladd & Robb *CUSS* 136: *Het up, be all.* Angry. **1984** N. Bell *Raw Youth* 32: We're all het up. **1990** *Inside Edition* (synd. TV series): They are so het up…that any remark could make them shoot.

hewgag *n.* [orig. (1850: *OED2*) 'a toy musical instrument similar to the kazoo'; ult. orig. unkn.] **1.** a bugle or trumpet; (*hence*) a battle cry. *Joc.* Also **gugag.**
   1864 in Heartsill *1491 Days* 223: The "Hu-gag" (as Briggs calls the Bugle) has sounded and we are off west. **1877** Lee *Fag-Ends* 24: The meal is o'er, but stomachs still are void,/The "gugag" in the hall doth blow. **1906** *Army & Navy Life* (Oct.) 498: The bugle has been changed in the midshipmen's vocabulary to the *gugag.* **1977** Coover *Public Burning* 448: Deeds, not words: that was Ike's hewgag.

   2. (see quot.).
   1866–71 Bagg *Yale* 45: *Hewgag,* a what-d'ye-call-it, a thingumbob.

hey *n.* [euphem. for HELL] ¶ In phrase: **what the hey** what the hell.
   [**1932** Lorimer & Lorimer *Streetcars* 154: What the hi!] **1966** Longstreet & Godoff *Wm. Kite* 343: Hello, you ol' cooter! What the hey! **1974** V.B. Miller *Girl in River* 88: "What the hay?" she says. **1980** Lorenz *Guys Like Us* 81: Why don't we give those bags a call? What the hay. **1983** in "J.B. Briggs" *Drive-In* 118: But what the hey, it wasn't any *Mr. Ed.* **1983** *Muppet Show* (CBS-TV): Hey—what the hey?! **1987** *Spring Break Guide* 3: So what the hey, let's give the kid a shot. **1988** *N.Y. Newsday* (June 28) 25: But what the hey? By the time the payments balloon, you could be history! **1994** TV ad for MCI: My luggage is on the wrong flight? What the hey!

hey *interj.* (used affectedly for emphasis within a sentence, esp. after *but*). Now *colloq.* [Esp. common during 1980's and '90's; discussed with cites in *AS* 61:4 (Winter 1986) PP. 365f.]
   1974 N.Y.C. man, age *ca*25: But, hey, that's the kind of guy I am. **1977** *Nat. Lampoon* (Aug.) 9: But, hey, I don't hate life. **1984** in "J.B. Briggs" *Drive-In* 282: After that, hey, it's a free country. **1989** Brooks & Pinson *Working with Words* 168: Avoid what Joseph Epstein calls "the California Hey"—*hey* inserted needlessly in a sentence. **1994** Ad for Dewar's Scotch whisky (N.Y.C.): It's not easy at first, but hey, neither are a lot of things.

hey-joe *n.* [fr. phr. *Hey, Joe!*; see 1985 quot.] *Mil.* a native shop or street vendor in an overseas country.
   1985 Petit *Peacekeepers* 102 [ref. to 1983]: The Hey Joe was a small store run by some enterprising Lebanese.…It was the Hey Joe because that's what the Lebanese called us when they wanted to sell us something. **1983–86** G.C. Wilson *Supercarrier* 252: [In Naples] Hey Joes hawking sleazy wares displayed on car hoods and on the sidewalk…did a brisk business. **1986** Coonts *Intruder* 113 [ref. to Philippines, 1972]: The Hey-Joe kids [were] begging money or selling glass necklaces. **1988** Dye *Outrage* 145: The Americans called all merchants and vendors "Heyjoe."

hey-rube *n.* [fr. phr. *Hey, Rube!*, used to summon help; see RUBE; cf. CLEM] *Circus.* a brawl, esp. between circusmen and townsmen; (*hence*) an uproar; argument.
   1899–1900 Cullen *Tales* 280: The circus had got mixed up in a "Hey, Rube!" battle a couple of towns up the line. **1922** *Variety* (Aug. 11) 8: A grand Hey Rube started. **1935** *Amer. Mercury* (June) 229: *Heyrube:* general uprising of spectators. **1939** in A. Banks *First-Person* 204: A "Hey Rube" is practically unknown today. **1946** Gresham *Nightmare Alley* 67: The Ackerman-Zorbaugh Monster Shows had never had a "Hey-rube" since Stan had been with them. **1951** G. Fowler *Schnozzola* 103: I stay and try to pacify people in this Hey Rube, and I only got the arms and legs God give me to protect myself. **1956** H. Gold *Not With It* 6: We found ourselves with an old-fashioned hey-rube and obliged to move the show that night. **1961** Clausen *Season's Over* 197: Minnie ain't so young anymore and we have a "Hey, Rube" every time I talk to a broad. **1974** Blount *3 Bricks Shy* 8: In Pittsburgh they call a brawl a "hey-rube." **1995** *CBS This Morning* (Sept. 26) (CBS-TV): They decided after this hey-rube to give the shirts away!

hick *n.* **1.** [formerly a hypocoristic form of *Richard*] an unsophisticated country person; bumpkin; yokel; (*Und.*) (*obs.*) a victim; (*broadly,* now *rare*) a fool. [The 1565 quot. in *OED* does not precisely illus. the present usage.]
   *1669 *New Acad. of Compliments* 191: The eight is a Bulk,/That can Bulk any Hick. ***1676** in Partridge *Slang* 268: But when…the merry hick we meet,/We bite the Cully of his Cole/As we walk along the street. ***1698–99** "B.E." *Dict. Canting Crew:* Hick, any Person of whom any Prey can be made, or Booty taken from; also a silly Country fellow. ***1702** R. Steele, in *OED2:* Richard Bumpkin! Ha! A perfect Country Hick. ***1698–1706** in D'Urfey *Pills* IV 323: You would sware she was a Hick,/And no common Brim. ***1713** in *OED2:* That not one hick spares. ***1720** in *F & H* III 307: Among whom was a country farmer…which was not missed at all by the Country Hick. ***1737** in W.H. Logan *Pedlar's Pack* 143: The eighth is a Bulk, that can bulk any hick. ***1754** in *F & H* III 307: A gamester…sees the Hick. ***1785** Grose *Vulgar Tongue:* Hick. A country hick; an ignorant clown. *Cant.* **1904** Ade *True Bills* 91: One of the Joys of his Childhood was to get together a Gang of Hicks and throw Stones at the Brakemen. **1908** H. Green *Maison de Shine* 54: That hick thinks he's killed right now. **1908** *Sat. Eve. Post* (Dec. 5) 16: He's an educated

Hick...and I got him out of the heart of the hay-fever district. **1917** Lardner *Gullible's Travels* 26: I don't want her marryin' none o' them Hoosier hicks. **1917** Appleton *With the Colors* 20: A year or so ago they called us "hicks".../An' joshed the farmer and his hired man! **1918** R.J. Casey *Cannoneers* 107: This is the Eighteenth Infantry, Buddy, and we're going to knock your block off, you hick. **1919** S. Lewis *Free Air* 102: These were not peasants, these farmers. Nor, she learned, were they the "hicks" of humor. **1921** Benchley *Chips* 150: *Agricola* means "farmer," and so does *hic*, or, as it has come down to us in English, "hick." **1921–25** Gleason & Taber *Is Zat So?* 81: You're just...a common West Side hick! **1929** *AS* IV (June) 341: *Hick*. A farmer; a dumbbell. **1929** W.R. Burnett *Iron Man* 66: I'll show you smart New York hicks a fighter. A gong to gong fighter. **1938** I. Shaw *Sailor off Bremen* 224: Lissen, you dumb Philadelphia hick. **1949** in *DAS:* The automobile largely nullified the outward distinctions between hick and city slicker. **1975** N.Y.C. man, age *ca*22: We don't have "rednecks" up North, but we do have "hicks," and they're about the same thing. **1983** Moranis et al. *Strange Brew* (film): Looks like LeRose picked up those two hicks. **1994** *TV Guide* (Apr. 2) 30: When I heard I was going to this rural town with only 500 people,...my first thought was, "They'll just be a bunch of hicks I won't be able to talk to."

2. a Puerto Rican person.—used contemptuously.

    1967 *DAS* (Supp.) 689: *Hick*...A Puerto Rican. **1970** Cole *Street Kids* 134: One of the white boys called out, "Hey you hicks."

hick *adj.* like or characteristic of a yokel or bumpkin; unsophisticated; provincial.—usu. used prenominally.

    1908 McGaffey *Show Girl* 138: These hick towns. **1913** T.A. Dorgan, in Zwilling *TAD Lexicon* 44: At last they put a plank over the puddle—gee. these [*sic*] hick towns are the limits on improvements. **1918–19** MacArthur *Bug's Eye View* 104: A typical hick town. **1920** Witwer *Leather Pushers* 216: His...features wasn't bad looking in a hick way. **1921** Casey & Casey *Gay-Cat* 147: They goes with them shows inter little hick towns. **1924** H.L. Wilson *Prof.* 257: Some...hick college. **1929** Millay *Agst. the Wall* 55: The idea of stoppin' at all those little hick towns! **1936** Dos Passos *Big Money* 426: They think there's something hick about patent medicines. **1946** Veiller *Killers* (film): It'll be mud up to the axles on them hick roads. **1952** in Brookhouser *Our Years* 148: Daughters looked hick in calico. **1977** S. Gaines *Discotheque* 82: Sometimes you're very hick, very uncool.

hickey *n.* **1.a.** THINGUMABOB; DOOHICKEY; (in 1902–03 quot.) an odd person.

    1902–03 Ade *People You Know* 112: He heard a Hickey in a Striped Sweater tell a red-headed Man that Josie Jinks [a racehorse] would roll in. **1913** *DN* IV 58: *Hickey*. Heard at Parksville [Tenn.], among laborers from Rock Hill, S.C., where it is common. "Hand me that *hickey*." **1920** Ade *Hand-Made Fables* 58: You wear...that narrow white Hickey inside the Vest. **1937** in D. Runyon *More Guys* 216: He...puts a hickey in his keyhole. **1965** O'Neill *High Steel* 271: *Hickey*. Anything at all; in electrical work, a long-handled tool used for bending pipe. **1968, 1970** in *DARE.* **1982** E. Leonard *Cat Chaser* 247: Looks like your standard nine-millimeter Smith Parabellum except for that hickey sticking out.

b. the penis.

    1942 *ATS* 147: Male pudendum...*hicky, jock,* [etc.]. **1968** Brasselle *Cannibals* 119: No broad would ever put a ring in your nose or lead you around by the hickey. **1994** Crumb (film): Leading me around by the hickey.

2.a. a mole, pimple, or boil, esp. on the face.

    1918 *DN* V 25: *Hickey,* n. A pimple on the face. General. **1935** *Louisville & Nashville* (Apr.) 22: Your correspondent had a "hickey" on the back of his neck last month; was treating it for a boil and it turned out to be a carbuncle. **1935** E. Anderson *Hungry Men* 101: I wish I didn't have these hickeys on my face. **1936** in Goodstone *Pulps* 34: He's got such an *awful* lot of hickies, you sort of don't want to see him. **1948** J.H. Burns *Lucifer* 172: A hundred girls in kimonos, gouging at their hickies or plucking winkers from their eyelids. **1963** W.C. Anderson *Penelope* 39: I have a little hickey just above my right buttock. It's hardly even noticeable, but I thought you ought to know. **1977** Laxalt *Nevada* 102: He couldn't stand the slightest blemish on his face. He would run to the doctor if he had a hickey.

b. *Stu.* a discolored mark on the skin caused by biting or sucking during lovemaking.

    1942 *ATS* 337: *Hicky*...a red mark caused by sucking or biting. **1956** H. Gold *Not With It* 235: Tall...skinny, big blue hickie on the face. **1966** in IUFA *Folk Speech: Hickey:* A mark left on the body from kissing and drawing blood to the surface. **1968** Baker, Ladd & Robb *CUSS* 136: *Hickey.* Redness of skin caused by affectionate nibbling. **1971** Jacobs & Casey *Grease* 38: Yeah, but I got disqualified 'cause I had a hickey on my neck. **1974** *Happy Days* (ABC-TV): Course it doesn't look like a hickey. Can't walk around with teethmarks on your neck. **1978** Pilcer *Teen Angel* 116: What's that on your face? A hicky? **1981** Crowe *Fast Times* 142: He tried to get Doug mad by giving me a hickey. **1983** W. Safire, in *N.Y. Times Mag.* (Aug. 7) 6: A *hickey's* primary meaning today is that telltale red mark left on your neck...[as] a souvenir of passion. **1988** *Wkly. World News* (Feb. 9) 20: It got to the point where he'd come to see me with hickies on his neck from kissing other girls. **1992** S. Straight *Been in Sorrow's Kitchen* 289: Them damn girls never even had a hickey on their necks.

c. *So.* a bump or bruise.

    1969 Weals *Hillbilly Dict.* 4: *Hickey*—Lump; knot. She knocked a hickey on his head. **1973** I. Reed *La. Red* 118: We bopped the bushwa nigger who was running it, and he had a big hickey on his head. **1984** Sample *Racehoss* 151: Hickeys and scars on...bald heads. **1985** in Safire *Look It Up* 164: New Orleans has its own dialect. *Hickey* is a term for a knot on the head.

3. *Printing.* **a.** (see quots.).

    1940 in *OED2: Hickey,* printer's slang for ornament. *a***1984** J. Green *Newspeak* 120: *Hickey*...any ornament in the type.

b. an imperfection on a printed page.

    1982 N.Y.C. editor, age *ca*40: A *hickey* is a spot of dirt that shows up on a page. *a***1984** J. Green *Newspeak* 120: *Hickey*...a blemish in the printing or in the engraving of an illustration. **1988** *Print & Graphics* (Oct.): *Hickies* Defects in print appearing as specks of ink surrounded by a white halo.

hickory oil *n.* a whipping, as with a hickory switch. Cf. *oil of birch* and vars. s.v. OIL.

    1940 *AS* (Apr.) 215: But she talked a lot about giving me *hickory-oil.*

hickory tea *n.* HICKORY OIL.

    1905 *DN* III 82: *Hickory tea, n.* whipping. "You'd better watch out, or you'll get a dose of *hickory tea.*" **1938** in *AS* (Apr. 1939) 90: The school teacher feeds hickory tea to the bad boys.

hickory towel *n.* a hickory switch or club.

    1834 Caruthers *Kentukian in N.Y.* 30: If I ever caught him on my trail, I would wipe him down with a hickory towel. **1855** W.G. Simms *Forayers* 119: I thought of giving him a wipe with a hickory towel more than once.

Hicks see s.v. JIMMY HICKS.

Hicksville *n.* [HICK, 1 + -SVILLE] a HICK town.—used derisively. Also **Hickville.** Later (usu. lower-case, infl. by -SVILLE) also as adj.

    1942 *ATS* 44: Imaginary "hick" town...Hickville. **1952** Himes *Stone* 112: The toughies who had nothing but their outside reps got their throats cut by hicksville punks who had never heard of them. **1963** *Twilight Zone* (CBS-TV): Hicksville! I don't see how they stand it in these small burgs. *a***1966** Levenson *Everything But Money* 217: Sentiment is "corny." Deep feeling is "square." Great...spiritual moments are "from Hicksville." **1976** Conroy *Santini* 60: This town is hicksville. **1983** Ehrhart *VN-Perkasie* 391: "Never thought I'd be so happy to see Perkasie."..."It's still Hicksville." **1989** Radford & Crowley *Drug Agent* 41: His new job wasn't the...legitimate...operation he'd been used to in Hicksville.

hicky *adj.* HICK.

    1942 *ATS* 172: Boorish; rustic...*hicky.* **1968–71** Cole & Black *Checking* 118: I mean the girls were hickey and shit but they were all right. **1980** M. Baker *Nam* 34: I'm from Bakersfield. It's pretty hicky, but a lot of America is pretty hicky.

hid *n.* (see quot.).

    1889 Barrère & Leland *Dict. Slang* I 460: *Hid* (American), an abbreviation of hideous, used as a noun. Used chiefly by girls. "She's a perfect hid."

hide *n.* **1.** the human skin (now usu. used contemptuously, esp. in imprecations or in hyperbolic expressions denoting a severe scolding or rebuke); (*hence*) (one's) personal safety or well-being; (*occ.*) self. [S.E. until the 17th C.; see *OED*.]

*1607 in *F & H* III 307: A skubbing railer...Grating his hide, gauling his starued ribs. *1645 J. Milton, in *OED:* Who could have beleevd so much insolence durst vent it self from out the hide of a varlet? 1864 in D. Chisholm *Civil War Notebook* 45: We was working to save our *hides.* 1871 Banka *Prison Life* 137: I'll have you cut all to pieces! I'll loosen up yer hide fer ye, sir! *a1873 in *OED2:* The poor fellow meant only to save his own hide. 1900 Hammond *Whaler* 217: Blessh y'r old hide an' tallur, Pete. 1901 J. London *God of His Fathers* 16: Do you value your hide? 1903 McClallen *He Demons* 168: She goes...to get her old hide full of "Booze." 1912 Siringo *Cowboy Detective* 108: Charlie Siringo....I would know your hide in a tan yard in h—l. *Ibid.* 109: Why Charlie, you can't fool me. I would know your hide in a tan-yard. 1926 E. Springs *Nocturne* 266: The general took advantage of our embarrassment and took our hides off. 1929–30 Dos Passos *42d Parallel* 45: Goddam your hide, I want my money. 1930 Fredenburgh *Soldiers March!* 206 [ref. to 1918]: Simmons ripped the hide off Wilder this morning for pulling a boner in a report to Brigade. 1934 Appel *Brain Guy* 134: Duff, you won't risk your hide. 1951 [VMF-323] *Old Ballads* 3: Hope to hell you sizzle well, God damn your hides. 1959 in R. Russell *Perm. Playboy* 339: Better Miss Irvine peeling off a little of his hide than Nancy yatting at him about the damn Olds. 1975 Julien *Cogburn* 73: Damn your murdering hides.

2. [**a.** the vulva or vagina.—usu. considered vulgar. [Not attested in U.S., but related to **(b)**, below.]

*1720 D'Urfey *Pills* VI 93: For I have been tanning of a Hide,/This long seven years and More Sir;/And yet it is hairy still.]

b. a woman or women regarded as sexual objects; (*also*) a dissipated or sexually promiscuous woman; (*hence*) copulation with a woman.—used contemptuously.—usu. considered vulgar.

1916 Cary *Venery* I 129: *Hide*—The human skin. In America, generic for women. *ca*1945 in Dundes & Pagter *Alligators* 58: The shoemaker gets his hide every day. 1942–49 Goldin et al. *DAUL* 95: *Hide*...Loose women; prostitutes;..."A piece of hide"—sexual intercourse. 1968–70 *Current Slang* III & IV 67: *Hide, n.* A girl.—New Mexico State. 1983 K. Weaver *Texas Crude* 70: Aw, some ol' hide over at the Skid Row Lounge fell in love with me. 1992 Lincoln Memorial Univ. student: When I'm on the phone talking to my girlfriend, my husband asks, "Are you still talkin' to that old hide?" *a*1994 H. Roth *Mercy of Rude Stream* 102 [ref. to *a*1920]: Piece of hide, piece of ass, pussy, cunt.

3. *Und.* a leather pocketbook, billfold, or wallet.

1932 in *AS* (Feb. 1934) 26: *Hide.* A pocketbook. 1966 Braly *On the Yard* 27: "Get twenny outa your hide."..."What's a hide?" "A billfold." 1973–76 J. Allen *Assault* 187: [They] put all their hides, all their wallets, in one pile. 1980 in Courtwright et al. *Addicts Who Survived* 212 [ref. to 1940's]: After I hit their hide, I'd...clean it out and put it back on his hip. 1983 *N.Y. Times* (Sept. 6) B6 [pickpocket terms]: "Hide," a wallet.

4. a horse.—usu. used disparagingly.

1934 D. Runyon, in *DAS:* While it is a cheap race, there are some pretty fair hides in it. 1934 *Journ. Qly.* (Dec.) 352: *Hide, n.* (racing)—race horse. 1937 in D. Runyon *More Guys* 101: He blows a hundred and sixty thousand betting on a hide called Sir Martin to win the Futurity. 1968 E.M. Parsons *Fargo* 10: Virg, these hides won't last 'til noon.

5. *pl. Jazz.* drums; in phr. **hide-beater** a drummer.

1939 Calloway *Swingformation:* Hides...are a set of...drums. 1946 Mezzrow & Wolfe *Really Blues* 128: The tricky points of the hide-beating art. 1957 *N.Y. Times Mag.* (Aug. 18) 26: *Hides*—Drums. 1961 in R.S. Gold *Jazz Talk* 127: Still beating his hides and winning all the polls. 1971 Curtis *Banjo* 220: He heard it from a hide-beater hophead.

¶ In phrases:

¶ **get under (someone's) hide, 1.** to irritate, anger, or vex (someone).

1925 W. James *Drifting Cowboy* 61: It didn't get under your hide like the other did in time. 1927 J. Stevens *Mattock* 127 [ref. to 1918]: I knowed it would get under his hide, but I never had any idea it would make him so crazy mad. 1932 Halyburton & Goll *Shoot and Be Damned* 213 [ref. to 1918]: I have a feeling that we can get under his hide. 1947 Overholser *Buckaroo's Code* 69: This [guy] has got under my hide once too often.

2. to affect or endear oneself to (someone).

1933 *Newsweek* (Mar. 11) 2: You have a...style that is bound to get under a man's hide.

¶ **tan (someone's) hide** to whip, thrash, or trounce (someone). Now *colloq.*

1714 in Meserve & Reardon *Satiric Comedies* 34: Four Dozen dragons Hides he Tann'd,/Of Giants eke Four Score. *1731 in *F & H* III 307: Come and spin, you drab, or I'll tan your hide for you. *1803 in J. Ashton *Eng. Satires on Napoleon* 160: I'll tan his vile hide. *1842 in *OED2:* One who...tanned the hide of a poor pigmy. 1858 in G.W. Harris *High Times* 149: Ef he lef home, sum neibor's dog tanned his hide, an ef he staid at home, I was allers arter hit tu tan hit. 1872 G. Gleason *Specter Riders* 68: I better tan yer hide a trifle, jist to show you what opinion I have of you. 1906 *DN* III 160: *Tan one's hide, v. phr.* To punish one. 1909 *DN* III 379: *Tan one's hide, v. phr.* To give one a whipping, flog. 1928 Dahlberg *Bottom Dogs* 135: She'd tan his young hide till he was black and blue.

hide *v.* to eat eagerly. *Joc.*

1929 Cruze *Great Gabbo* (film): I could hide some hot dogs without any trouble.

¶ In phrase:

¶ **[play] hide the weenie** [or **salami**] to engage in sexual intercourse.—usu. considered vulgar. *Joc.* Also vars. See also *hide the baloney* s.v. BALONEY, *n.,* 3.

1918 in M. Carey *Mlle. from Armentières* II (unp.): The drivers went to St. Nazaire/To hide the weenie anywhere. *ca*1935 (quot. at GASH-HOUND). 1940 Farrell *Father & Son* 114: Haven't you ever played hide the weenie with the girls out here at night? 1942 Algren *Morning* 209: Ain't you gonna play Hide-the-Weenie, Hon? 1979 Dallas man, age *ca*38: I'm going to spend the weekend with my wife playin' hide the weenie. 1980 Conroy *Lords of Discipline* 222: I'd love to play hide the sausage with [her]. *Ibid.* 467: The upper classes like to play hide the banana when they get away from their wives. 1983 in "J.B. Briggs" *Drive-In* 142: Wanna play Hide the Salami? 1985 Petit *Peacekeepers* 89: I know you want to...play a little hide the sausage. 1986 Merkin *Zombie Jamboree* 95: Trying to play hide-the-salami with Corinne was Bad Idea Number Ten. 1988 D. Boyd *Chillers* (film): His secretary might play hide the salami in the back office. 1989 S. Lee *Do the Right Thing* (film): All Sal wants to do is hide the salami.

hide-jerker *n. West.* a buffalo-skinner.

1899 in Remington *Own West* 207: Have a drink on the Army. Kem up, all you hide-jerkers.

hideout *n. Und.* a person in hiding; fugitive.

1942 *ATS* 428: Fugitive....*hideout,* one who is in hiding. 1995 Alicea & DeSena *Air Down Here* 38: He's a hideout, with no place to go.

hideout gun *n.* a concealed pistol.

1972 Wambaugh *Blue Knight* 146: He was one of those creeps that carried an untraceable hideout gun and bragged how if he ever killed somebody he shouldn't have, he'd plant the gun on the corpse and claim self-defense.

hideout money *n. Gamb.* money held back for an emergency.

1970 in P. Heller *In This Corner* 113 [ref. to 1930's]: I figure this is "hideout" money.

high *n.* **1.a.** an intoxicated or euphoric state induced by drugs or alcohol. Now *S.E.*

1944 La Guardia Comm. *Marihuana* 145: The smoking of one or two cigarettes is enough to bring on the effect known as "high." 1951 *Conf. on Drug. Add.* 10: The *high* is similar to the alcoholic *high.* The opiate *high* is really a lethargy. 1951 Kerouac *Cody* 89: Walking forth from D's the real high began. 1953 W. Brown *Monkey on My Back* 115: I realized that he had a "high on." 1955 H. Ellson *Rock* 30: A high on wine is good enough for me. 1956 H. Gold *Not With It* 252: He was permitted to think of Grack in his dreamy high next door. 1965 C. Brown *Manchild* 104: Now we wanted to get some highs off horse. 1966 Brunner *Face of Night* 233: *High*—...Noun: the state of exhilaration caused by taking drugs. 1966 Goldstein *1 in 7* 19: Many point out that the heroin "high" is depressive, while marijuana is a stimulant. 1963–70 in *Paris Rev.* (No. 50) 94: One of the finest cheap highs you can get. *a*1993 Ratner *Crack Pipe* 83: He done wore your high off anyway.

b. a feeling of elation, exhilaration, or excitement.

[The 1915 quot., unique in its period, undoubtedly alludes to the phr. *how's that for high?* s.v. HIGH, *adj.,* 2; its resemblance to the current sense is undoubtedly coincidental.]

[**1915** in J.A. Lomax *Cattle Trail* 106: It's the best grand high that there is within the law,/When seven jolly punchers tackle "Turkey in the Straw."] **1970** *N.Y. Post* (July 1) 30: And Bob would tell them what a high it gave him to see this gook step on a mine he'd put out the night before: "He just blew himself away." **1975** in Higham & Siddall *Combat Aircraft* 17: I was on an unbelievable "high"—keenly alert and filled with boundless energy. **1981** *N.Y. Times Mag.* (Aug. 9) 26: Acting is like boxing, you know. It gives you the same type of high.

2. something, esp. a drug, that induces an intoxicated or euphoric state.

   1962 H. Simmons *On Eggshells* 156: Whisky was a lame high. **1967** [R. Beck] *Pimp* 221: Cocaine sure chills you. I guess you picked the right high for you. **1971** *Playboy* (June) 216: Motor racing....it's one of the great highs of all time. **1988** Santiago *Undercover* 106: Crack was the latest high on the street.

high *adj.* **1.a.** intoxicated by alcohol or (later *esp.*) by drugs. Now *colloq.* or *S.E.*

   *****1627** in *OED2*: He's high with wine. *****1639** in *OED2*: At the banquet...high in our cups. **1811** in Howay *New Hazard* 48: Lang and Jack got high....Armourer and Jack had a squabble. **1813–18** Weems *Drunk. Looking Glass* 60: Boozy—groggy—blue...cut in the craw...high. **1833** J. Hall *Soldier's Bride* 124: He [was]...*a little high.* **1845** Corcoran *Pickings* 63: "You is high," said the watchman. **1847** N.J.T. Dana *Monterrey* 179: All got high. **1852** Furber *Ike McCandliss* 12: Kelly was "high" surely. **1854** Avery *Laughing Gas* 130: The Moon Getting "High." **1856** Hall *College Wds.* (ed. 2) 254: *To get high*, i.e. to become intoxicated. **1861** in F. Moore *Rebel. Rec.* I P18: Och! whin they get/Their heavy wet/They get as high as Haman. **1931** D. Redman *Reefer Man* (recording): He smokes a reefer, he gets high,/And he flies up to the sky. **1932** in *AS* (Feb. 1934) 26: *High*, Under the influence of a narcotic. **1935** J. Conroy *World to Win* 157: He kept drinking until he had to feel his way out of the place, but he never appeared to get high. **1939** Goodman & Kolodin *Swing* 238: Jazz musicians who got loaded on weed or high on liquor. **1944** La Guardia Comm. *Marihuana* 13: The smoker determines for himself the point of being "high." **1947–52** R. Ellison *Invisible Man* 80: He's high as a Georgia pine. **1954** G. Kersh, in Pohl *Star of Stars* 31: A fat old drunk...higher than a kite. **1955** Q. Reynolds *HQ* 332: The addict, who was "riding high," slashed at Martin with a switch-blade knife. **1966** Jarrett *Private Affair* 171: I wasn't sure whether they were drunk or "high." **1967–68** T. Wolfe *Kool-Aid* 48: There is no other earthly reason to have these...plants except to get high as a coon. **1971** Wells & Dance *Night People* 67: Your breath don't smell like no bed of roses either. You're always as high as a Georgia pine. **1989** *Harper's* (June) 54: Testy old Slim is high now.

b. (formerly also constr. with *up*).

   1844 Porter *Big Bear* 56: Ain't you never seen a man here in Featte, when he gits *high* up, just pulls out his knife, and goes to chawin' it as if he'd made a bet he could bite it in two? **1847** Furber *Volunteer* 203: They came to camp at night "high up" and noisy;—for, although but few of them had any money, yet, as it was known that the regiment would soon be paid, there were many in town who would trust them for liquor.

c. *Broadly*, elated, enthusiastic, or exhilarated; thrilled; (*also*) interested; keen. Cf. *OED2* defs. 14b, 16a.

   1937 in D. Runyon *More Guys* 105: He is very high indeed on this mare, and in fact I never see anybody any higher on any horse. **1944** in Himes *Black on Black* 198: But I was so high off'n them dreams I let it pass. **1947** in J. Jones *Reach* 93: I am working fine now and feeling high. **1951** Robbins *Danny Fisher* 187: Champion! I was as high as a kite. The feeling stayed with me all the way down to the dressing room. **1958** J. King *Pro Football* 90: They wanted to go for broke. They were high, and I went along with them by changing the play. **1958–59** Lipton *Barbarians* 78: I have always been able to get high on poetry, music, or sex stimulation. **1959–60** R. Reisner *Jazz Titans* 158: *High*: to be in a blissful, euphoric state induced by drugs, sex, alcohol, or any stimulant. **1961** H. Ellison *Gentleman Junkie* 58: I heard Arville Dreiser drop the beat for a second, which he *never*, so I knew they were all pretty high on the kid. **1964** in Gover *Trilogy* 262: He's high on what he's sayin. **1965** Summers *Flunkie* 18: Frankly I am not too high on skool. **1965** Spillane *Killer Mine* 58: René still feeling pretty high when he got killed? **1976** Kassorla *All Together* 190: He said I looked "high" and asked me what happened during the day. **1976–77** C. McFadden *Serial* 18: Kate wasn't really high on chest hair because

it seemed to collect deviled egg...at stand-up parties. **1980** *Nat. Lampoon* (Aug.) 68: The whole organization is very high on you, Barry, very high. **1981** Patchett et al. *Great Muppet Caper* (film): Steppin' out with a start and feelin' high! **1983** *Hour Magazine* (ABC-TV) (Apr. 20): After you jog, you're high as a kite on endorphins. **1992** *CBS This Morning* (CBS-TV) (Oct. 21): "He must be high as a kite because the cars are good." "He's happy."

2. impressive; splendid; superlative; fancy; attractive; (*occ.*) in phr. **how's that for high?** what do you think of that?; **high as nine** very splendid or superlative. Also as *adv.*

   1839 J.S. Jones *Solon Shingle* I.i: And the way I'll take the shine out of some of the boys will be high. **1848** G.G. Foster *N.Y. in Slices* 120: I say, Jim! ain't this high? **1848** Baker *Glance at N.Y.* 14: When he takes out dat sword, and comes down to de front and says something—ain't dat high? *Ibid.* 30: Say, Lizey, ain't this high? **1849** Doten *Journals* I 17: They received our boat's company in fine style and "treated them as high as nine." **1850** "N. Buntline" *G'hals of N.Y.* 38: Aint that *h-i-g-h!* *Ibid.* 72: "Isn't that pleasant?" "It's *h-i-g-h!*" **1855** G.G. Foster *N.Y. Naked* 149: A fast horse and a "high" gal are the two great earthly beatitudes of the New York b'hoy. **1868–71** C.G. Leland *Breitmann's Ballads* 11: De rowdies...saidt dat de fun vas "high." **1873** Bailey *Danbury Newsman* 64: His neighbors...facetiously enquired, "How's that for high?" **1880** in M. Lewis *Mining Frontier* 127: Who is he? Well, now, if that ain't the boss play for high. **1887** Francis *Saddle & Moccasin* 315: "How's that for high, boys?" concluded the narrator, when he had told his tale. "That's on top....That takes the cake." **1898** Bullen *Cachalot* 289 [ref. to 1875]: Sending his lance quivering home all its length into the most vital part of the leviathan's anatomy....he shouted exultingly, "How's dat fer high?"—a bit of slang he had picked up, and his use of which never failed to make me smile. **1916** MacBrayne & Ramsay *One More Chance* 230: Such a concert for over an hour. How is that for high? Some concert, believe me. **1947** in Botkin *Sidewalks* 240: "How's that for high?" was a bid for commendation.

3. HIGHBALL, *n.*, **2.**

   1961 J. Flynn *Action Man* 42: Ask the barman for a ginger high.

¶ In phrases:

¶ **how's high?** how are you?

   1877–88 in J.W. Crawford *Plays* 113: Hello...how's high?

¶ **how's that for high?** see **(2)**, above.

high-and-tight *n. Mil.* a kind of military haircut having the back and sides of the head shaved and the remaining hair cropped extremely short.

   [**1969** in J.T. Ward *Dear Mom* 38: The sides are "high and tight." That means short.] **1984** Hammel *Root* 57: Chanting Marine marching chants, sporting the "high-and-tight" haircuts that Marines...wear. **1985** Petit *Peacekeepers* 74: The style was called a "high-and-tight," and only Marines who were extremely gung-ho wore it. **1986** Stinson & Carabatsos *Heartbreak* 88: The sun was reflecting off all those shiny "high and tights." **1987** D. da Cruz *Boot* 218: But this haircut is different: it's a "high-and-tight."...Only the hair on the side of the head is shorn to the scalp; the hair on the crown is left intact, giving a rakish Mohawk Indian effect...The "high-and-tight" symbolizes the senior status of Third Phase recruits.

high-ass *adj.* haughty.—usu. considered vulgar.

   1931 in H. Miller *Letters to Emil* 76: I don't want any of your high-ass Russian variety. **1968** Gover *JC* 126: Hey Odessa, ain't you never comin back an see us no more? You gone highass?

high-ass *v.* HIGHTAIL.—usu. considered vulgar.

   1964 Allen *High White Forest* 242 [ref. to WWII]: I mean everybody high-assed it down the road like they'd never stop this side of St. Louis.

highball *n.* **1.a.** *Orig. R.R.* a signal given (as to a locomotive) to start, or to proceed at high speed. Also *fig.*

   1897 in *DA*: "Milk trains"...have "rights" over the rails and get nothing but "high balls." **1908** W.G. Davenport *Butte & Montana* 267: Boobies so devoid of reason that it is necessary to give 'em the highball to get 'em in out of the rain. **1913** *DN* IV 11: The conductor gave the engineer the *high-ball* to go ahead. **1916** *Editor* XLIII (Mar. 25) 343: *Highball*. The hand, flag, or lantern signal for departure. **1941** in Fenner *Throttle* 173: His order board was red, and as the extra approached, he swung his lantern in a highball, notice to the engineer that he had an order that would clear the board. **1958** P. O'Connor *At*

Le Mans 61: Worm let out the clutch, a flagman gave him the highball, and he shot off down the track.

b. *Army.* a hand salute, esp. if smartly given.

1918 *Wadsworth Gas Attack* (Feb. 2) 22: We trust it will not be long before we hand them the "highball." **1919** *307th Field Arty.* 155: We gave a "highball" and said "yes, sir." **1927** *Amer. Leg. Mo.* (June) 46: Watch me knock his eye out with a snappy comeback when he throws me a highball. **1945** *Stars & Stripes* (Shanghai ed.) (Oct. 13): When the flag came abreast I gave it the best salute I could muster, and I was sort of sorry I was a little out of practice in the highball business. **1958** *N.Y. Times Mag.* (Mar. 16) 88: Highball—Also *slam.* A salute. **1961** *N.Y. Times Mag.* (Aug. 13) 8: A lieutenant…demonstrates the proper way to throw…a highball. **1963** Cameron *Black Camp* 43: Flint threw the officer a contemptuously correct highball. **1969** Broughton *Thud Ridge* 63: He stepped smartly back and threw you the sharpest salute you have ever seen. There was no baloney in the way that highball was rendered and returned.

c. *R.R.* (see 1942 quot.).

1934 Weseen *Dict. Slang* 71: Highball…a fast freight. **1942** *ATS* 726: Fast train; express…*highball.* **1982** D.A. Harper *Good Company* 45: He gets that mail and jumps back on that diesel *high*ball.

2. a drink of whiskey mixed with club soda or ginger ale and served with ice in a tall glass; (*hence*) (*joc.*) a dose of salts. Now *S.E.* Cf. BALL, *n.*, 8; LOWBALL, *n.*

1898 Kountz *Baxter's Letters* 16: I…licked up about four high-balls. **1898** in *DA:* Evening dress and khaki talked much sport and a little war over "high balls." **1899** Ade *Doc' Horne* 11: Lush…drank two magnificent "high balls." **1908** McGaffey *Show Girl* 27: I feel like a highball. **1918** in *St. Lawrence Univ. in the War* 8: I have been to the doctor a couple of times and got what he calls a camp highball. So am quite well. **1918** Mencken *Amer. Lang.* 85: Whiskey-and-soda. The Americans…at once gave it the far more original name of *high-ball.* **1944** Busch *Dream of Home* 114: He…put liquor in the glass, adding seltzer.…Cliff handed him the highball.

highball *v.* **1.a.** *R.R.* to signal to proceed.

1912 *R.R. Man's Mag.* XVII 493: The con high-balled and the manifest freight/Pulled out on the stem behind the mail. **1927** *DN* V 449: *Highball*…To signal for a train to move. **1970** in *DARE.*

b. to wave or signal to; (*hence*) to alert; give the go-ahead to; (*rarely*) point out.

1928 Callahan *Man's Grim Justice* 284: Eddie "high balled" me. "Lay off that cooking stuff, kid.…I'll do the cooking." **1930** "D. Stiff" *Milk & Honey* 53: Often they highball the cops and you get raided. **1931** Bontemps *Sends Sunday* 6: The steamboat man had high-balled Little Augie! **1940** S. Longstreet *Decade* 357: Don't highball any hideout for this lug. He's hot, this lamster. **1942–49** Goldin et al. *DAUL:* *Highball*, v. To signal; to give the okay; to summon; to greet.

c. *Mil. & Police.* to greet with a hand salute.

1970–71 Rubinstein *City Police* 449: There are some supervisors who demand to be "highballed," and their wish is grudgingly granted.

2.a. *Orig. R.R.* to come or go at top speed.—also constr. with *it.*

1912 in *DARE:* She whistled twice and high-balled out,/They were off—down the Gila Monster Route. **1918** Mills *War Letters* 343: Highballing it back home through the air lanes. **1918** Sherwood *Diary:* I "high-balled" in, organized the detail and got in all the wire possible. **1919** Johnson *Heaven, Hell, or Hoboken* 7: The cats "high-balled" for safer quarters. **1926** Nichols & Tully *Twenty Below* 84: I'm highballin' out o' here. **1938** Holbrook *Mackinaw* 181: To *highball* is to hurry. **1938** in A. Banks *First-Person* 47: He'd high-ball for shallow water…and head up into some mangrove swamp. **1952** in Fenner *Throttle* 17: I want to be back in Hannibal before the special highballs. **1961** Himes *Pinktoes* 72: The last she ever seen of him he was highballing it toward Erie with a big hole burnt in the ass of his pants. **1977** Sayles *Union Dues* 257: This villager, this woman, she come high-ballin' acrost the fields towards us, screamin to wake the dead. **1982** D.A. Harper *Good Company* 6: The train highballs and the tracks are bad. *Ibid.* 10: And they highball out of the yards so's you can't hardly grab him on the run. **1989** *Harper's* (June) 58: A high-balling, top-priority, double-decker train.

b. *Orig. R.R.* to drive (orig. a locomotive) at high speed.

1945 in *OED2:* He highballed the big locomotive down the tracks. **1952** in Fenner *Throttle* 16: He highballed Number 23 from the Han-

nibal yards through morning mist from the Mississippi. **1978–86** J.L. Burke *Lost Get-Back Boogie* 47: I highballed the pickup all the way.

3. *R.R.* to pass by.

1942 *ATS* 732: *Highball the switch*…not to slow down for the brakeman to close the switch, leaving this to a switchman. **1970** *Current Slang* (Summer) 8: *Highball*, v. To pass by, leave undone.—Highball the work at Marysville. Highball the switch. (Don't bother to operate it.).

highball artist *n. R.R.* a locomotive engineer.

1921 in Kornbluh *Rebel Voices* 313: He was an excitable high ball artist. **1930** *R.R. Man's Mag.* II 470: *Highball artist*—A locomotive engineer who is noted for fast running.

highball camp *n. Logging.* (see 1925 quot.).

1925 in *Amer. Mercury* (Jan. 1926) 67: *Highball-camps* are those where work is speeded up by a superintendent or foreman or by *straw-bosses.* **1941** *AS* (Oct.) 233: A "high ball camp" is a hurry-up affair.

highballer *n. Logging.* (see quot.).

1963–64 Kesey *Great Notion* 286: A highballer, see, is a old loggin' term for a guy who did about twice as much work as the others.

high-banker *n. Logging.* a pretentious person.

*a***1904** in *DA:* Come on, Jimmy. Don't be a high-banker. **1908** in *DA:* Are you going to let that old high-banker walk all over you?

high beak *n.* [high + BEAK², *n.*] *Und.* (see quot.).

1859 Matsell *Vocab.* 41: *High Beak.* The first judge; the president; the governor; the head official.

high bicycle *n.* a celebrated or self-important person.

1931 Lorimer & Lorimer *Streetcars* 3: Here was Lysbeth, a high bicycle at fourteen if ever there was one. **1933–34** Lorimer & Lorimer *Stag Line* 6: What gets me down is losing out to a high bicycle like Buckmaster.

highbinder *n.* [in pl., app. orig. the name of a criminal gang, as in 1806 quot. below, but the reason for its choice is unkn.] **1.a.** *N.Y.C.* a violent criminal; thug; (with weakened force) a rowdy.

1806 in *DA:* There has for some time existed in this city, in and about George and Charlotte Streets, a desperate association of lawless and unprincipled vagabonds, calling themselves "Highbinders." **1835** *Knickerbocker* (July) 65: Benjamin Smith…was a…loafer.…I was surprised…that he never was sent to the Legislature; for he was one of our distinguished "high-binders," and deserved…office. **1859** Bartlett *Amer.* (ed. 2) 192: *Highbinder.* A riotous fellow. New York slang. **1916** H.L. Wilson *Somewhere in Red Gap* 21: So I left these two lady highbinders. **1916** E.R. Burroughs *Return of Mucker* 58: Some…[Mexican] highbinder's bound to croak you.

b. *Police.* a member of a secret Chinese criminal organization, esp. an assassin. Now *hist.*

1876 in *OED2:* Refined ladies could no longer submit to be jostled at the church door by the Mongolian *chiffonier* or high-binder. *a***1877** in Bartlett *Amer.* (ed. 4) 785: (*Ques.*) What do you mean by *high-binders?*… *Ans.* I mean men who are employed by the China companies here to hound and spy upon the Chinese, and pursue them. I have often heard it applied to bad men. Sometimes they are employed to assassinate Chinese. **1879** in *DA:* It is shown by the testimony that coolies attempting to evade their debt contracts are subjected to violence by a special class of Chinese known as "Highbinders." **1892** in *OED2:* The Italian Mafia is a dangerous enemy to law and order, like the Chinese "highbinders" of California. **1898** L.J. Beck *Chinatown* 122: The "highbinder" is an American designation applied to a class of Chinese immigrants whose business is crime and violence. **1909** Chrysler *White Slavery* 84: Every pig-tailed highbinder…carries a heavy caliber Colt's revolver. *a***1940** Riesenberg *Golden Gate* 165: Their membership…included the feared highbinders, or hatchetmen, as they were better known, who…[brought] swift punishment to any who opposed their tong. **1947** A. McLeod *Pigtails & Gold Dust* 228: The word "highbinder" was used to designate the individual members who carried out blackmailing and murder orders for the tong.

2. *Pol.* an unscrupulous politician or political intriguer. [The 1835 quot. at **(1.a.)**, above, either anticipates or plays upon this sense.]

1890 in *OED2:* *Highbinders*…applied to…political conspirators and the like. **1903** A.H. Lewis *Boss* 136: Them…high-binders at the top o' Tammany. **1920** Ade *Hand-Made Fables* 72: Tax Dodgers and amateur High Binders. **1920** in Safire *New Lang. Politics* 415: A lot of old highbinder standpatters who haven't had an idea since the fall of Babylon. **1942** *ATS* 787: Political intriguer. *Highbinder.* **1952** in *DAS:* The *AFL-News Reporter* covered the winter meeting of the grand inner circle of high-binders at Miami Beach.

high bob *n.* [perh. *high* + *Bob*] a HIGHFALUTIN fellow.
    1881 C.M. Chase *Editor's Run* 134 :There is no criticism of personal conduct, no standard of…respectability, no "high bobs," no fanatics, nobody to dictate…how to…behave.

highboy *n.* HIGHBALL, 2.
    1902 Cullen *More Tales* 116: I was letting the rickeys and the high boys trickle into Hennessy.

highbrow *n.* [alluding to the *high* forehead once frequently regarded as a sign of superior intellect] a person who is, or has pretensions of being, intellectually, culturally, or artistically superior; an intellectual; (*hence*) a snob. Now *colloq.* Cf. LOWBROW, MIDDLEBROW.
    1907 in Bierce *Letters* 131: So your colony of high-brows is re-establishing itself at the old stand. **1908** in *DA:* High-brows and reformers. **1910** T.A. Dorgan, in *N.Y. Eve. Jour.* (May 25) 20: Bonehead Barry was a high brow compared to you. **1913** *DN* IV 11: Most of the faculty are high-brows. **1914** Atherton *Perch* 49: Her dreaded reputation as a "high-brow." **1914** E.R. Burroughs *Mucker* 147: You're a highbrow, so youse gotta live on Riverside Drive. **1919** *DN* V 62: She tries to be a high-brow, but she doesn't slip anything over me. **1926** in *DA:* No selected group of highbrows can inflict a classic on mankind. **1928** Harlow *Sailor* 127: Dare's nobody but th' high-brows aft thet ye'll be after a-callin' Mister. **1935** S. Lewis *Can't Happen* 205: You highbrows—you stinking intellectuals! **1948** in *DAS:* My husband, Will Irwin, invented both the terms highbrow and lowbrow. He used them in a series of articles in the N.Y. *Morning Sun*, circa 1902–03. **1981** *N.Y. Times Bk. Rev.* (Jan. 4) 14: As defined by Brander Matthews: "a highbrow is a person educated beyond his intelligence."

highbrow *adj.* being, characteristic of, appealing to, or involving a highbrow. Now *colloq.* Also as *adv.* Cf. LOWBROW. [The uniquely early date of the "1884" quot. may sugg. a later editorial alteration; the book was published in 1966.]
    1884** in Troubridge *Among Troubridges* 169: Went with a not very exciting party to the Healtheries Exhibition.…Mr. Hope…suggested that we would be at some highbrow part of the Exhibition—looking at pictures I think, but…we were [eating a snack]. **1909** Chrysler *White Slavery* 5: Some of the highbrow authors will find a million faults with this book, especially if it has a big sale. **1911** Bronson-Howard *Enemy to Society* 182: So much of this high brow stuff in the theatres this month. **1911** in Truman *Dear Bess* 48: I like high-brow shows sometimes, but I like the Orpheum all times. **1914** S. Lewis *Mr. Wrenn* 180: She was—oh, awful highbrow. **1913–15** Van Loan *Taking the Count* 125: De gall of him—pullin' dat highbrow stuff on Riley! **1919** Hedges *Iron City* 112: Well, Mr. Sociologist, if you are in such a high-brow mood, let's go and see the paintings. **1920** E. Hemingway, in *N.Y. Times Mag.* (Aug. 18, 1985) 61: This is the genuine high-brow stuff. **1923** in H. Miller *Letters to Emil* 10: My stuff looks good—only a bit too high-brow. **1930** G. Schuyler *Black No More* 165: This crowd thinks they're too highbrow to come in with the Knights of Nordica. **1930–33** T. Wolfe *Time & River* 14: You'll be gettin' so educated an' high brow here before long that you won't be able to talk to the rest of us at all. **1940** *Current Hist. & Forum* (Nov. 7) 22: [Don't] talk highbrow. **1947** in *DAS:* Nearly all agreed the program was too highbrow. **1963** M. Shulman *Victors* 83: He had long ago mentally dismissed her as a "highbrow dame." *a1974** Toll *Blacking Up* 4: Almost inevitably, entertainment in America fragmented into "highbrow" and "lowbrow," elitist and popular. **1977** Ruhm *Hard-Boiled* xii: From 1908 to 1912 Chandler contributed sketches, verse, and anonymous paragraphs to highbrow weeklies, like the *Spectator* and Lord Alfred Douglas' *The Academy.* **1984** Blumenthal *Hollywood* 111: This picture is too highbrow—it's got no appeal to the kids.

highbrow *v.* HIGH-HAT.
    1930 Sage *Last Rustler* 128: They highbrowed me as if I didn't have any right on there with an accident.

high brown *n.* a black person, esp. a woman, having medium- or light-brown skin.—usu. regarded as offensive. Also as adj. Cf. HIGH YELLOW.
    1915 in Handy *Blues Treasury* 89: I want to talk to that High Brown

of mine.…Sunday night my beau proposed to me. **1927** C. Sandburg, in *DARE:* Then come all you rounders, an' all you high-browns too. **1929–33** Farrell *Young Manhood* 320: You know he went for a high brown…and, boy, I thought we'd get our throats slashed. **1936** (quot. at HIGH YELLOW). **1938** *AS* (Dec.) 314: Step aside, coal car, and let a high brown pass. **1962** W. Faulkner, in *DARE:* That gold-tooth high-brown seen it. **1965–70, 1970, 1986** in *DARE.*

high card *n.* a preeminent person.
    1903 Ade *Society* 106: He could put in an Afternoon with five or six boulevard Netties and make every one of them think that she was the High Card. **1903** Hobart *Out for the Coin* 77: I don't do no sneak till I pull off a meeting with the High Card.

high cotton *n.* ¶ In phrase: **in high cotton** in an easeful or advantageous position. [This phr. is already entered as a var. of *in tall cotton* s.v. COTTON, in *HDAS* I; the following quots. provide additional evidence, and the first three quots. antedate the entry in *HDAS* I.]
    1942 in *DARE:* We frequently, if less delicately, refer to times of great prosperity as those in which we were defecating "in high cotton." **1912–43** *Frank Brown Collection* I 550: *High cotton, to be (walk) in: phr.* To be prosperous; in good social standing.—General. **1945** *AS* (Apr.) 83: That fellah sure thought he was in high cotton. **1984** Jackson & Lupica *Reggie* 17: To this day, if someone gets up and cooks me breakfast, I just feel like that's *high* cotton.

high-dive *v. Und.* to pick (a pocket). Hence **high-diver**, *n.*
    1930 "D. Stiff" *Milk & Honey* 207: High diver—Yegg who picks pockets. **1979** Edson *Gentle Giant* 65: He could not hope to "high dive" her reticule without being detected.

high-end *adj.* expensive; advanced; of high quality; top-of-the-line.
    1977 *New Yorker* (June 6) 96, in *OEDAS* II: It stands to reason that "high end" means expensive. **1977** *Pop. Science* (Aug.) 99: To learn how these high-end superdecks compare with other machines on the market, [etc.]. **1977** *N.Y. Times* (Sept. 16) D11: Tobacco, liquor, high-end stereo, imported cars, [etc]. **1979** *Rolling Stone* (Jan. 25) 68: Rappaport's success is due to the boom in high-end audio. **1983** *Business Week* (Nov. 7) 44: Honeywell will continue to offer new high-end computers. **1988** *People's Court* (ABC-TV): We do very high-end jewelry. **1990** *Newsweek* (Aug. 13) 46: The most impressive gains in Japan have been made by high-end automakers.

higher see s.v. HIGHER-HIGHER.

higher-higher *n. Mil.* **1.** higher headquarters. Also **higher.** [Quots. ref. to Vietnam War.]
    1982 Del Vecchio *13th Valley* 208: Higher-higher sent us to one bad ass AO. **1983** K. Miller *Lurp Dog* 213: Someone in Higher targeted the place for…a B-52 strike. **1985** Bodey *F.N.G.* 123: Higher-higher said there oughta be a bunch of dead dinks out there.

2. a senior officer.
    1985 Bodey *F.N.G.* 148 [ref. to Vietnam War]: We'll get even with them fuckin' Higher-highers.

highfalutin *n.* a pompous air or affectation; bombast.
    1848 in Bartlett *Amer.* (ed. 2) 195: A regular built fourth-of-July—star-spangled banner—times-that-tried-men's-souls—Jefferson speech, making gestures to suit the highfalutens. **1858** in *DA:* Judge Freelon appeared on the part of the defence, and wasted a great deal of hyfalutin on Grecian mythology. **1859** Bartlett *Amer.* (ed. 2) 195: *Highfaluten.* High flown language, bombast. This word is in common use in the West and bids fair to spread over the country. **1864** in *DAE:* It is a curious jumble of American sense and Southern highfaluting. *a***1889** in Barrère & Leland *Dict. Slang* I 461: A paper in Cincinnati was very much given to *high falutin'* on the subject of "this great country." **1903** in *DA:* A high-erected vein which not seldom reaches to tall talk and highfalutin.

highfalutin *adj.* [orig. unkn.; prob. infl. by *high-flown*] pompous or bombastic; high-flown; arrogantly pretentious. Now *colloq.* or *S.E.*
    1839 in *DA:* Them high-faluting chaps. **1841** *Spirit of Times* (Oct. 30) 409: I expect "Loo"…to introduce me to all the "high faluting" actresses, and come the "high flung" over the green 'uns. **1856** in *DAE:* Upon the whole, the production was on the "highfaluten" order of eloquence. **1857** Gladstone *In Kans.* 43: One of the boys, I reckon?…No highfaluten airs here, you know. **1857** *Spirit of Times* (Dec.

26) 544: A "hifalutin" strain about the injuries which his unfortunate client has sustained already. **1868** in *DAE:* The Border State Convention of Colored Men...adopted the following highfalutin address. ***1870** in *F & H* III 309: A driveler of tipsy, high-flown, and high-falutin' nonsense. ***1884** in *F & H:* It is the boast of high-falutin' Americans that theirs is a country "where every man can do as he darn pleases." **1871** Schele de Vere *Amer.* 271: An after-dinner *high-faluting* speech. **1902** W.N. Harben *Abner Daniel* 72: Some highfalutin crowd o' worshippers that kneel down on soft cushions an' believe in scoopin' in all they kin in the Lord's name. **1905** *DN* III 11: *Highfalutin*, adj. High flown. **1912** in *DN* III 578: None of your high-fallootin' talks counts here. **1913** *DN* IV 24: *Highfalutin*...Pompous, stuck-up...."We don't want any of your highfalutin ideas." **1920** in *DAS:* Ideas less "high falutin." **1941** in *OED2:* And then hear some announcer in his highfaluting voice, telling her summer was coming. **1958** Bard & Spring *Horse Wrangler* 105: Some of their high-falutin' parties. **1980** J. Quinn *Amer. Tongue* 15: We know you're against teaching this highfalutin stuff called calculus. **1990** *New Yorker* (May 7) 24: "It's not a highfalutin name," says Julia Wolfe.

high five *n.* [elab. of *five* as in *slap five* s.v. FIVE, *n.*; see 1989 quot.; an undocumented date of "1966" alleged in J. Green *Neologisms* (1990) appears to be unreliable] Orig. *Sports.* a form of congratulation or greeting in which one person slaps another's palm as it is held above eye level.
    1980 in *OEDAS* II: What they do now is reach high and bang hands up there ("The high five, man"). **1982** *Time* (May 3) 80: Dusty Baker thought the San Diego hand-slapping (high fives, low fives) a little elaborate. **1982** *N.Y. Times* (June 22) Slapping high fives with his friends along the sideline. **1984** Nettles & Golenbock *Balls* 41: They were giving high-fives all over the field. **1984** *Paper Chase* (CBS-TV): I thought you two guys were gonna give each other high fives! **1984** McCrimmon, Trimmer & Sommers *Writing with Purpose* (ed. 8) 137: Some people receive "high fives," some just congratulations. **1986** N.Y.C. bus ad: Give him the high five! **1986** Cosby *Fatherhood* 116: He can give high fives until his palms bleed. **1987** *Daily Beacon* (Univ. Tenn.) (Oct. 29) 9: The players waved to the crowd...and leaned out of the cars to give "high fives" to those lucky enough to get close. **1989** P. Dickson *Baseball Dict.* 199: *High five*...The origin of the gesture and the term were claimed by Derek Smith of the University of Louisville basketball team, which won the NCAA championship in the 1979–80 season. Smith was quoted [widely]...to the effect that he and two fellow Georgians on the Louisville squad, Wiley Brown and Daryl Cleveland...[created the] high five during preseason practice and introduced [it] to the nation in 1979. **1991** B.E. Ellis *Amer. Psycho* 19: I laugh. We slap each other high-five.

high-five *v.* Orig. *Sports.* to congratulate or greet with a HIGH FIVE. Also absol.
    1981 in *OEDAS* II: Jumping and high-fiving it, hair flapping. **1982** *L.A. Times* (Apr. 24) III 3: What a pathetic and spiteful attitude for him to get upset because the Padres high-five. **1983** *L.A. Times* (Aug. 31) I 16 [caption]: Sergio Herra...and Antonia Meze, both 8, high-five each other in their...classroom. **1987** *N.Y. Newsday* (July 31): The two of them started laughing and they high-fived and then low-fived. **1988** *N.Y. Times* (Feb. 29) C7: She high-fived and low-fived with her coach. **1988** *Rage* (Univ. Tenn.) (Mar. 30) 31: He...high-fives the bros as he takes her outside to talk. **1989** *TV Guide* (June 17) 23: He high-fives the guys and kisses the gals. **1992** *L.A. Times* (Oct. 31) F2: Police high-fiving after arrests.

high-flier *n.* a brash, extravagant, or daringly unconventional person, esp. one who makes a display of high or fast living; (*often*, in early use) a fashionable prostitute. Now *colloq.*
    *1663 S. Pepys, in *OED2:* He...would have me...to look him out a widow....A woman sober, and no high-flyer, as he calls it. ***1698–99** "B.E." *Dict. Canting Crew: High Flyers*, Impudent, Forward, Loose, Light Women; also bold Adventurers. ***1708** in D'Urfey *Pills* I 79: A Pox of your race of high Flyers,/That late on the Battlements stood. **1792** Brackenridge *Modern Chiv.* 16: Better to trust a plain man...than one of your high flyers. ***1821** in *F & H* III 310: As you have your high-fliers at Almack's, at the West End, we have also some "choice creatures"...in the East. ***1823** "J. Bee" *Slang Dict.: High-flyers*—women of the town, in keeping, who job a coach, or keep a couple of saddle-horses at least. *ca***1855** [G. Thompson] *Outlaw* 44: One of the upper-crust night-walkers, I suppose....Now Miss Highflyer,...please to keep your

mouth shut. **1859** Matsell *Vocab.* 41: *Highflyer.* An audacious, lewd woman. *a***1860** Hundley *So. States* 143: His master was one o' them raal ole fashion' Virginny high-flyers—proud, Sir, proud! kept mighty fine liquors, played high, bet high. **1862** M.V. Victor *Unionist's Dtr.* 105: She's game, that girl is, and one of your real highflyers too. **1863** "E. Kirke" *So. Friends* 74: I knows jest the feller...one o' yer raal highflyers; rich's a Jew...lives like a prince. **1883** Hay *Bread-Winners* 80: We've got to have a set of gold spoons, I guess. These will never do for highfliers like us. **1888** *Stag Party* 16: The tony saloons where dudes and high-flyers congregate. ***1892** in *F & H* III 310: That 'ighflyer, 'Arry.

high-go *n.* a frolic or bout of merriment.
    *1825 in *OED2:* Our volatile high-go's were troublesome enough to everybody. **1840** R.H. Dana *2 Yrs.* ch. xxvii: The last night they...were getting into a high-go when the captain called us off. **1844** in B. Hall *College Wds.* (ed. 2) 253: He it was who broached the idea of a high-go to give us a rank among the classes in college. **1856** B. Hall *College Wds.* (ed. 2) 254: *High Go.*...This word is now seldom used.

high-grade *n. Mining.* **1.** see s.v. HIGH-GRADER.
    2. stolen high-grade ore.
    1956 Crampton *Deep Enough* 36: Wages were good, but there was no high-grade to help out.

high-grade *v. Mining.* to steal (high-grade ore) from a mine; (*broadly*) to steal, esp. in small increments.
    1904 in *DA:* Many miners...continue to work and to "high grade." **1910** in *Dict. Canadianisms:* Red Meekins...went on high-grading. **1927** *AS* (June) 391: *Highgrade, promote, clout, snare* and *glahm* are synonymous verbs and mean to take what does not legally belong to one. **1929** *AS* IV (June) 341: *Higrade:* To procure something illegitimately. **1930** Sage *Last Rustler* 91: My rope itched for that old pony....Well, I knowed it wouldn't do to high-grade him right now. **1942** *Calif. Folk. Qly.* I 43: An excuse invented to account for the possession of ore "high-graded" from Hunter Valley. **1949** in *DA:* Highgrading...was prevalent. **1963** in *Dict. Canadianisms:* Some Timmins stores have been known to accept high-graded ore in payment for grocery bills. **1977** *L.A. Times* (Nov. 30) I 3: When a man steals from the depths of a mine, pocketing such ore that legally belongs to the mine owner, that is called high grading.

high-grader *n. Mining.* a person who steals high-grade ore from a mine, esp. in small increments. Also **high-grade.**
    1904 in *DA:* One of the pests of gold mining in Colorado is the high-grades, which is a polite term for the ore thief...high-grades...steal only high-grade ore. **1904** in *DA:* Throughout this camp are men known to rumor as "high graders," in other words ore stealers. **1908** W.G. Davenport *Butte & Montana* 212: Highgraders like Heinze break in...and steal. *Ibid.* 217: The "high grader"...steals millions in the courts. **1938** in A. Banks *First-Person* 80 [ref. to 1880's]: Highgrade men...the men who steal it are known as highgraders. **1948** *Sat. Eve. Post* (Nov. 13) 38: High-graders...enter other people's mines and help themselves. **1963** in *Dict. Canadianisms:* The heat was supposed to be on Timmins' high-graders, the men who steal, refine, and sell gold from the local mines. **1980** *Atlantic* (July) 44: High-grade ore is the kind that is rich enough to steal as it is, and the men who steal it are known as high-graders.

high gun *n. Shooting.* the best marksman of several; top gun.
    1982 Downey *Losing the War* 79 [ref. to WWII]: There was great prestige for being "high gun" and platoons made up a money-pool to be won by the best shot.

high guy *n.* BIG SHOT.
    1896 (quot. at SPIEL). **1900** Ade *More Fables* 156: He was the K.G. of one Benevolent Order and the Worshipful High Guy of something else. **1903** Ade *Society* 98: Accordingly the Young Fellow put in an Application with a large Wholesale Concern. The High Guy called him in and gave him a Talk. **1911** A.H. Lewis *Apaches of N.Y.* 111: [Dress suits] make it so you can't tell th' high-guys from th' waiters. **1970** Terkel *Hard Times* 136: The vast majority got fucked up by the high guys.

high hat *n.* **1.** *Narc.* a large pellet of opium, as prepared for smoking.
    1896 in S. Crane *N.Y.C. Sks.* 144: The $1 smokers usually indulge in high hats, which is the term for a large pill. **1933** in Partridge *Dict. Und.* 330: He told me he would cook me a "high hat."
    2. HIGHBALL, 2.
    1906 *Nat. Police Gaz.* (Dec. 8) 6: It'd take two hunnerd high hats t'

keep me tonsils from dryin' up. **1955** Post *Little War of Pvt. Post* 59 [ref. to 1898]: In his hand were two tall glasses of the kind that the Bowery made famous years ago and known as "high hats."

3. a person, esp. a man, who is aristocratic, wealthy, snobbish, or conceited.

    1923 *N.Y. Times* (Sept. 9) VIII 2: *High Hat:* Swelled head....*Just a high hat.* See...all wet. **1926** in Smith & Hoefer *Music* 136: To see the "high hats" mingle with the native stepper is nothing unusual. **1927** (quot. at SILK STOCKING). **1927–28** in R. Nelson *Dishonorable* 218: That special investigatin' grand jury o' prominent high-hats. **1930** Mae West *Babe Gordon* 211: He's the original high-hat. **1962** Perry *Young Man Drowning* 141: He sure ain't no high-hat with a swelled up head!

¶ In phrase:

¶ **give** [or **put on**] **the high hat** to act snobbishly or haughtily (toward).

    1923 *Nashville Banner* (Jan. 14) II 1: Putting on the "high hat," huh? **1925** Weaver *Collected Poems* 128: And when he gives you the high hat, all the time—. **1934** O'Hara *Appt. in Samarra* ch. iv: Trying to give me the old high hat. The old absent treatment. **1965–70** in *DARE*. **1994** *Mystery Sci. Theater* (Comedy Central TV): Are you giving me the high hat?

high-hat *adj.* snobbish; haughty.

    [**1922** in *DN* V 147: *High hatty*—conceited, aloof, exclusive.] **1924** P. Marks *Plastic Age* 12: The Nu Delts. Phew! High-hat as hell. *Ibid.* 149: Christmas Cove's...not so high-hat as Bar Harbor. **1928** F.R. Kent *Pol. Behavior* 21: Those who participate [in politics] on the very highest intellectual levels and in the most "high-hat" way. **1928** Sharpe *Chicago May* 109: I got high-hat and demanded that they come with it to me. **1930** J.T. Farrell *Calico Shoes* 52: She looks pretty high-hat. **1931** McConn *Studies* 30: Half the chapter flunked out last June, but they're too dam high hat. **1931** Hellinger *Moon* 54: She developed the reputation of being slightly high hat. **1935** Clarke *Regards to Broadway* 112: You've gone high hat and don't speak to anybody any more. **1936** in Galewitz *Great Comics* 22: Did she go high hat all of a sudden! **1941** in Truman *Dear Bess* 458: I found this high-hat stationery in my bag and thought maybe you'd appreciate hearing from a United States Senator. **1944** Micheaux *Mrs. Wingate* 153: I've often wondered if he's "high-hat." **1952** J.C. Holmes *Go* 12: I'm just fed up with these goddamn, high-hat publishers, that's all! *a***1989** in Kisseloff *Must Remember This* 580: There was nothing high-hat about him.

high-hat *v.* to act snobbishly or haughtily toward; snub. Now *colloq.* [Since Wilson uses the v. in the 1923 quot., the 1922 usage is presumably the v. also.]

    1922 in E. Wilson *Twenties* 116: Upstage. Lousy. Highhat. **1923** in E. Wilson *Twenties* 136: You can't try to high-hat everybody and fall off chairs at the same time. **1923** *N.Y. Times* (Oct. 7) VIII 4: *High Hatting:* One artist patronizing another. **1926** Walrond *Tropic Death* 91: To the lovely young ladies in question it was a subject to be religiously highhatted and tabooed. **1927** H. Miller *Moloch* 14: Don't try to high-hat me. **1927** Mayer *Between Us Girls* 241: You can put a crest on your note-paper and high-hat everybody. **1928** F.R. Kent *Pol. Behavior* 151: The other mistake is in "high hatting" the voters. **1929** W.R. Burnett *Iron Man* 166: Don't high-hat me. **1944** Bontemps & Cullen *St. Louis Woman* 33: You tryin' to high-hat me. I ain't gonna have it! **1945** MacDougall *Mildred Pierce* (film): I'm fed up with the way she high-hats me. **1963** D. Tracy *Brass Ring* 122: You think I'm high-hatting that bunch back there, huh? **1972–79** T. Wolfe *Right Stuff* 157: Some of the boys felt that rocket pilots like Crossfield were high-hatting them. **1985** Briskin *Too Much* 132: And I'm sick of being high-hatted.

high-hatter *n.* HIGH HAT, 3.

    1929 W.R. Burnett *Iron Man* 268: Damn dressed-up highhatter!

high-heeled *adj.* haughty; arrogant; often in phr. **have on (one's) high-heeled shoes** [or **boots**] to be haughty or arrogant.

    1843 [W.T. Thompson] *Scenes in Ga.* 137: Major Bangs...fixed his fierce gaze upon the fire, and remained silent. "Never mind, gentle-*men*,...the major's got his high-heeled boots on to-night." **1859** Bartlett *Amer.* (ed. 2) 195: To say of a woman that she "has on her *high-heeled shoes*" is to intimate that she is..."stuck up." **1872** Burnham *Secret Service* vi: *High-Heeled Boots.* Triumphant, confidant [*sic*] appendages! **1877** Bartlett *Amer.* (ed. 4) 286: A proud, haughty person is said to "have on his high-heeled boots." **1895** J. Fox *Cumberland* 45: They air bigoted 'n' high-heeled, 'n' they look down on us. **1903** J.

Fox *Little Shepard* 380: Bein' so high-heeled that you was willin' to let him mighty nigh bust his heart. **1912** Raine *Brand-Blotters* 190: You're mighty high-heeled to-day.

high-heeler *n.* (among beggars) a woman; a female beggar. Also **high heels.**

    1925 in Partridge *Dict. Und.* 331: *High heels.* **1929** Zombaugh *Gold Coast* 111: A "high-heeler" is a female beggar who works with a squawker.

high hook *n. Angling.* the most successful or proficient fisherman in a fishing party. Cf. HIGH LINE.

    1848 in *DAE:* High hook, the one who catches the largest or the greatest quantity of fish. **1899** in *DAE:* When we met to...compare notes...and make up the fish stories for the year, Beekman was almost always "high hook." **1939** in *DA:* Mr. James Wood...is..."high hook" of Nantucket.

high iron *n. R.R.* main or high-speed railroad track.—constr. with *the.*

    1930 Irwin *Tramp & Und. Slang:* High iron...a main line track. **1934** Weseen *Dict. Slang* 71: *High iron*—A main track; a main line. **1937** *AS* (Apr.) 154: *High iron.* High-speed track. **1958** in *DARE:* The last steam passenger train on the "high iron"—the main lines—chugged into memory in July. **1989** *Harper's* (June) 49: I'm up here riding the high iron.

highjack var. HIJACK.

high-jive *v.* [*high* + JIVE] to tease; JIVE.

    1938 *New Yorker* (Mar. 12) 36: "Boo's high....Don' high-gyve Boo."..."High-gyve" is conversational baiting, or teasing a [marijuana] smoker. **1952** Mandel *Angry Strangers* 30: They'll highjive you till you get hooked *with* them. **1970** Southern *Blue Movie* 122: Teasing, cajoling, flattering and high-jiving the enchanted Pamela.

high-life *n.* carbon disulfide.

    1906 *DN* III 140: *High life, n. phr.* Bi-sulphide of carbon. **1911** *Adventure* (Mar.) 831: 'Tis really an acid, but in the Southwest we call it "high-life." **1947** in *DA:* Fumigate corn with carbon disulphide (high life) about two weeks after it is put into the crib.

high line *n. Angling.* the person or vessel that makes the best haul in a given time; (*also*) the best catch. Cf. HIGH HOOK.

    1856 Nordhoff *Whaling & Fishing* ch. xviii: Several had at different times been "high line" from Harwich. **1864** in *DA:* Captain Aleck was determined to fish for "high line" out of Chatham. **1885** in *DA:* The emulation to be "high line" for the day and for the season is extreme.

high lonesome *n. Midland & West.* a drinking spree. Also fig.

    1883 Sweet & Knox *Mustang* 257: He was a cowboy, who, being on a "high lonesome," entered the saloon, and incontinently began discharging his six-shooter at the lamps and mirrors behind the bar. **1901** Ade *Modern Fables* 93: So they went on a Toot of the High-Lonesome Variety. **1934** Cunningham *Triggernometry* 41: The Sabine River they found "on a high lonesome," as the punchers say. **1942** *AS* (Apr.) 130 [Indiana]: *High lonesome* (a drunken spree). **1958** J.D. Horan *Wild Bunch* 102: The boys...looked as if they were coming in to go on a high lonesome, and who knows what a man will say when he's liquored up? *Ibid.* 115: Kid Curry was "on a high lonesome" and became so loud they locked him in the kitchen. **1970** in *DARE. a***1985** C. Williams *So. Mtn. Speech* 87: *High lonesome*...a drunken spree.

high-maintenance *adj.* (of persons) demanding, esp. emotionally. [Pop. by film *When Harry Met Sally* (1989).]

    1989 Ephron *When Harry Met Sally* (film): "I want things the way I want them." "Yeah, high-maintenance." **1990** Eble *Campus Slang* (Fall) 3: *High maintenance*—requiring a lot of time, effort, or money. "Rob's girlfriend is extremely high maintenance." **1994** Denver architect, age 25: Girlfriends are often referred to as "high-maintenance." It's like annoying or demanding. **1995** *Donahue* (NBC-TV): She's a little too high-maintenance. She never walks out of the house without makeup. **1995** *Getting Healthy* (TV Food Network): He's a high-maintenance son. **1995** *Leeza* (synd. TV series): I was always very aggressive and 'untrainable.'" "High-maintenance lady!" **1996** Patchett & Fusco *Project: ALF* (film): This ambassador's pretty high-maintenance. **1996** *New Yorker* (Apr. 8) 68: They're a perfect match—she's high-maintenance, and he can fix anything.

high micky-doodle *n.* HIGH MUCKAMUCK.

    1918 McNutt *Yanks Are Coming!* 170: The head professor and all-round high-micky-doodle of the packer's school is Jim Keneely.

high muckamuck, high muckety-muck, etc. see s.v. MUCKA-MUCK

high muldoon *n.* HIGH MUCKAMUCK.
>   **1905** W.S. Kelly *Lariats* 7: It was a high muldoon Spaniard and a feller from thur East.

high noon *n. Craps.* a throw of twelve.
>   **1982** in T. Clark *Dict. Gambling* 99.

high octane *n.* highly intoxicating liquor; (*also, joc.*) caffeinated coffee.
>   **1992** *Herman's Head* (Fox-TV): Fill up her tank [i.e., a woman's stomach] with high-octane [*sc.* liquor]. **1995** Knoxville, Tenn., professionals, age *ca*43: "Would you like some coffee?" "High-octane or low?" "Uh…" "High-octane is caffeine, low is decaf." **1996** *As World Turns* (CBS-TV): I'm on my second cup of high-octane.

high-octane *adj.* dynamic; high-powered; (*specif.*) (of alcohol) highly intoxicating.
>   **1980** *Maclean's* (Feb. 11) 22: Last year's high-octane effort to woo workers had only limited success. **1985** *California* (Feb.) 36: Sustained, high-octane acting is beyond him. **1992** *Rolling Stone* (Apr. 30) 64: Catch Gallagher's Levy—an incisive portrait of high-octane guile. **1994** *Mystery Sci. Theater* (Comedy Central TV): High-octane suds.

high one *n.* TALL ONE.
>   **1919** Darling *Jargon Book* 17: High One—a glass of beer.

high overcast *n. USAF.* a meteorologist. *Joc.*
>   **1955** R.L. Scott *Look of Eagle* 17: The forecaster, whom everyone in the Air Force always dubbed High Overcast, even when he was a runt, stood up in front. *Ibid.* 137: The weather was as perfect as the Elmy High Overcast had so arrogantly predicted.

highpockets *n.* **1.** a tall, usu. lanky, man.
>   **1912** *DN* III 578: See what a *high-pockets* he is, anyhow. **1926** Norwood *Other Side of Circus* 58: Then there's one that wears a Norfolk jacket a couple of sizes too small. They dubbed him "High Pockets." **1929** Connelly *Green Pastures* 204: Ain't his pockets high from de ground? Ol' High-Pockets. **1937** C.B. Davis *Anointed* 21: I have had lots of names…like…Highpockets. **1937** Lay *I Wanted Wings* 50 [ref. to 1932]: HIGHPOCKETS: The term applied by the B Company Misters to those of A Company, who are taller. The original definitions of these two terms [*highpockets* and *sandblower*], which must be learned verbatim by each Dodo, lend themselves readily to omission here. **1938** R. Chandler *Big Sleep* 84: Get busy and spin that wheel, highpockets. *ca*1939 in A. Banks *First-Person* 91: Highpockets…came into the mill room. **1945** in Truman *Letters Home* 196: Mr. DeGaulle was here last night. He's a real "high pockets." 6 ft. 6 in. tall. **1952** *Life* (Aug. 25) 73: Highpockets Cooper in "High Noon." **1953** Manchester *City of Anger* 120: I'm happy when you're happy, highpockets. **1954** R. McGill *Fleas* 18: Well, Highpockets, I guess I just got tired. **1955** Graziano & Barber *Somebody Up There* 254: Think about Harvey and all the highpockets from out West. **1977** Monaghan *Schoolboy, Cowboy* 40 [ref. to 1908]: Each stride covered at least six feet.…The boys called him High-Pockets.

2. a supercilious or haughty person.
>   **1972** D. Newman & R. Benton *Bad Company* (film): Highest pockets in the U.S.A. Probably gonna be governor some day.

high-power *n.* (see quot.).
>   **1928** Dobie *Drinkin' Gou'd* 50: "High-powers" are officials of high rank in the company controlling the [oil] drilling.

high-powered *adj. Black E.* stylish; attractive.
>   **1944** Burley *Hndbk. Jive* 140: *High-powered*—Up-to-date, nicelooking. **1953** W. Fisher *Waiters* 38: She's high-powered.…Everybody falls for her. *Ibid.* 82: Those high-powered 'partment houses.

high-pressure *adj.* HEAVY-DUTY; (*also*) high.
>   **1860** in Dana *2 Yrs.* (Kemble ed.) II 455: Steamer is Mississippi style, high pressure.…Prices are "high pressure," also.

high-pressure cap *n. Naut.* a gold-braided uniform cap worn by a ship's officer. Also **high-pressure hat.**
>   **1942** *ATS* 90: *High-pressure cap* or *hat*…A ship officer's cap. **1945** in *Calif. Folk. Qly.* V (1946) 387: The officer's dress cap…is frequently referred to as the *high-pressure* cap. **1972** Pearce *Pier Head Jump* 8: He had only a towel wrapped around his ass and this high-pressure cap on his head with all this gold braid on it. **1976** S. Laurence *Northern Saga* 252: He'd sport a high-pressure hat and have gold braid on his arm.

high private *n. Mil.* an ordinary private soldier. *Joc.* Now *hist.*
>   **1834** (quot. at CAITIFF). **1836** in J. Long *Duel of Eagles* 191: High private. **1845** *Recollections* 162: I reckon you never heern me tell how I 'scaped on that horriferous tramp I took to W—, in 1831. I war a "high private" in them days. **1848** *High Private* 29 [ref. to 1846]: Sergt. O'Reilly…was reduced to "high private," and ordered to leave the fort in one hour. **1859** Tayleure *Boy Martyrs* 13: If ebber I has a chance at de boss sojer dat ordered his high priwates to lick me—. **1863** in Patrick *Rebel* 116: Clarence was a *high private.* **1864** in Eppes *Eventful Yrs.* 234: We call him High Private Wilson. **1873** Badger *Two-handed Mat* 10: First as a drummer-boy, then as a "high private," he had worn the gray. **1876** J. Wilkinson *Blockade-Runner* 25: The fastidious young captains, and the equally sensitive "high privates." **1882** Watkins *Co. Aytch* 19: I only give a few sketches and incidents that came under the observation of a "high private" in the rear ranks of the rebel army. **1899** Thayer *Co. K.* 114: I had much rather be a high private in the rear rank. **1916** C.C. Davis *Olden Times* 19: I was…enrolled as a "high private" in Company D, 44th Iowa Volunteers. **1933** *15th Inf. Sentinel* (July 1) 12: High Privates Pasuda and Booth have also gone as instructors. **1952** Sandburg *Young Strangers* 405 [ref. to 1898]: Now along with others like myself I could say when asked my rank and position, "I'm a high private in the rear rank."

high-res var. HI-RES.

high-rider *n.* Esp. *Calif.* a usu. young working-class man who drives a car modified so that its back end is much higher than its front. Cf. LOW-RIDER.
>   **1982** Corey & Westermark *Fer Shurr!* (unp.): *Hi-rider*…male individual who jacks up the rear end of his vehicle for no apparent reason, often found in parking lots at the beach.

high-roll *v.* to behave boldly or aggressively. Also trans.
>   **1982** D.A. Harper *Good Company* 73: I'm goin' to high-roll to do it.…You got to high-roll to get those good days.…run up and down that ladder like a fuckin' monkey. *That's* high-rolling. **1996** McCumber *Playing off Rail* 106: I asked him if he'd like to play some for twenty or thirty a game, and he tried to high-roll me, and said, "Well, I'll play you a set for five hundred."

high roller *n.* **1.a.** a person who spends or gambles money freely and who often makes a display of fast living; (*hence*) a wealthy individual.
>   **1881** in *DAE*: California's Speculators who invest large sums are called "high rollers." **1887** DeVol *Gambler* 142: There was more money on board than I ever saw in my life before, and all the men were "high rollers." **1887** Francis *Saddle & Moccasin* 145: He's a high roller, by gum!—when he's got it! **1891** Powell *Amer. Siberia* 47: Joseph Alston…had at one time been quite rich and what is familiarly termed a "high-roller." **1891** Maitland *Slang Dict.* 141: *High-roller* (Amer.), a fast-liver; one who gambles freely and for large sums. **1898** *Cosmopolitan* (Mar.) 551: He's a high-roller and Dan is laying for him today. Dan won't do a thing to him but get his bank roll. **1899** Garland *Eagle's Heart* 242: She's a pretty high roller, as they call 'em back in the States, but she helps the poor, and pays her debts…and it's no call o' mine to pass judgment on her. **1899** Townsend *Perils* 14: Kenneth Marston?…The eighteen-year old high roller? **1903** A.H. Lewis *Boss* 184: I'd like to learn how you moral an' social high-rollers reconcile yourselves to things. **1905** *Nat. Police Gaz.* (Nov. 18) 3: A pool room…not frequented by the high rollers—two dollar bets are big here. **1922** S. Lewis *Babbitt* 190: Babbitt…didn't care a fat hoot for all these highrollers, but the wife would kind of like to be Among Those Present. **1952** Felton & Essex *Las Vegas Story* (film): The high roller next to her. That's her husband. **1966** Terkel *Division St.* 285: I'm a high roller.…If I walk into a bar and I see three guys and they're with ten people, I buy everybody a drink. I always leave a deuce or three bucks tip.…That's a high roller. **1977** Shah *Mackin* 144: High rollers are big tippers. **1987** *N.Y. Daily News* (July 2) 2: Elegantly dressed Oriental high rollers bet with the banker. **1993** K. Scott *Monster* 72: "High roller" is Crip terminology for a ghetto-rich drug dealer; "baller" is the equivalent in Blood language.

b. an expensive prostitute; HIGH-FLIER.
>   **1976** G. Kirkham *Signal Zero* 172: "We've got a bunch of high rollers…working out of some of the better downtown hotels.…A high roller is a prostitute [who charges]…maybe a hundred and fifty bucks a shot.

2. *Black E.* a kind of wide-brimmed hat often worn by gamblers.

> **1931** Bontemps *Sends Sunday* 25: His high-roller had tiny naked women worked in eyelets in the crown.

high-rolling *adj.* being a HIGH ROLLER, 1.a.

> **1890** McBallastir *Society* 11: [She] would have been a high rolling Nob, but for a few impediments. **1892** Bierce *Beetles* 220: The high-rolling…hallelujah-lad.

high school Harry *n. Stu.* a male student at a high school or college who behaves with notable immaturity. Also **Harry High School.**

> **1953** M. Shulman *Affairs of Gillis* (film): A high school Harry. **1959** *AS* XXXIV 155: *High-school Harrys* are perpetual show-offs, especially when they drive their cars recklessly, spinning the tires and screeching the brakes. **1966–69** *Current Slang I & II* 49: *Harry high school*…A high school student who does not intend to attend college. **1975** Univ. Tenn. student: That's all high school Harry stuff. **1987** Horowitz *Campus Life* 181: The high school Harrys…dominated athletics and publications.

high school hop *n. Baseball.* (see quot.).

> **1964** Thompson & Rice *Every Diamond* 141: *High school hop:* A big high bounce, easy to field.

high shot *n.* HIGH ROLLER, 1.a.; BIG SHOT.

> **1925** in D. Runyon *Poems for Men* 13: One o' the high shots, Mister, a cold, cold clammy guy,/He'd roll those bones to a blister with never a word or sigh. **1926** Maines & Grant *Wise-Crack Dict.* 9: *High shot*— Rich fellow. **1930** D. Runyon in *Collier's* (Mar. 22) 20: Handsome Jack is quite a high shot in this town. **1970** Thackrey *Thief* 311: Big fucking hoodlums. High-shot stickup-men. Let's stop at a motel, Tony baby, so we can split our loot up.

high side *n.* ¶ In phrase: **go over the high side** to lose one's good sense or composure; *go off the deep end* s.v. END.

> **1990** Niemann *Boomer* 151: I was going over the high side. I had no control.

high-side *v. Black E.* to clown or show off.

> **1965** Cleaver *Soul on Ice* 38: High-siding. Cutting up; having fun at the expense of others. **1966** Braly *On the Yard* 210: So call yourself lucky and knock off the highsiding. **1973** *Oui* (Mar.) 70: The high-sidin' players here could actually be a look into our own future. **1973** Schulz *Pimp* 65: I'm out high-siding with my friends and I got somebody like Gloria on my arm.

high sign *n.* **1.** a usu. surreptitious signal, as of recognition, warning, approval, etc.

> **1899** in "O. Henry" *Works* 521: Dat man…is a dead ringer for Boston Harry. I'll try him wit' de high sign. **1902** T.A. Dorgan, in Zwilling *TAD Lexicon* 44: Rube Waddell gave Dunleavy the "high sign" when he came to bat. **1903** McCardell *Chorus Girl* 111: I gave him the high sign, but he passed me up. **1905** in W.C. Fields *By Himself* 30: Be ready to "git" when I give the "high sign." **1908** McGaffey *Show Girl* 235: I…gave the high sign to the steward to kick in with a few refreshments. **1909** Irwin *Con Man* 30: He gave me the high-sign of the profession to show he was all right. **1918** E.E. Rose *Cappy Ricks* 118: She'll be right on top…the moment I give the high-sign! **1918** Jones *Huns* 278: I gave them the "high sign" to let it go. **1923** in W.F. Nolan *Black Mask Boys* 56: Larkin gives me the high sign. **1931** Armour *Little Caesar* (film): You'll be in the lobby to give us the high sign that everything is on the up-and-up. **1962* L. Deighton, in *OED2:* He gave us the high sign with thumb touching forefinger. *a1985* C. Williams *So. Mtn. Speech* 87: He gave me the high sign. **1996** McCumber *Playing off Rail* 197: Someone Tony knew…winked at him.…The guy who gave Tony the high sign told us he had overheard one of the observers give the order: "Find their fuckin money."

2. FINGER, 4.a.—constr. with *the.*

> **1965** Summers *Flunkie* 21: Sherman shot me the finger (you know—the high sign!) three times while you rode on the blackbored. **1968** Baker, Ladd & Robb *CUSS* 137: *High sign*…gesture with the middle finger.

high-sign *v.* **1.** to signal, esp. surreptitiously.

> **1925** Cohan *Broadway* 46: And Josie started high-signing me again to quit "butting in." **1957** in *OED2:* I high-signed the barkeep for mine. **1962* in *OED2:* I high-signed him to follow.

2. *Black E.* HIGH-SIDE.

> **1973** Andrews & Owens *Black Lang.* 86: When someone acts like they're better than everyone else, even themselves, they *high signin.* **1967–80** Folb *Runnin' Lines* 109: To *high sign*…to show off or upstage others.

high-stepper *n.* a proud, fashionable, or spirited person, esp. a young woman.

> **1860* in *OED2:* [The beauty] which makes a woman be called, when young and in good action, "showy" and "a high-stepper." **1885** B. Harte *Shore & Sedge* 124: He's a regular high-stepper, you bet. **1888** Gunter *Miss Nobody* 104: She's English and a high-stepper. **1889** Barrère & Leland *Dict. Slang* I 462: *High stepper*…a well-dressed girl, who has a good figure and is handsome, a swell of any kind. **1892** Gunter *Miss Dividends* 103: Ain't the Cap a high stepper! **1904** in "O. Henry" *Works* 674: She was one of the genuine high-steppers. You could tell by the way her clothes fit and the style she had that Fifth Avenue was made for her. *a1904–11* D.G. Phillips *Susan Lenox* II 142: I saw you were a high stepper the minute I looked at you. **1912** *DN* III 578: *High-stepper,* n. One who lives a high life, especially one who spends money freely. *a1957* McLiam *Pat Muldoon* 39: A…boffo flick with Marilyn Monroe or any of these high-steppers.

high-strikes *n.pl.* [intentional malapropism] hysterics. *Joc. Obs.* in U.S.

> **1834** Caruthers *Kentuckian in N.Y.* I 27: An old woman would have sworn I had the high-strikes. **1835** in Eliason *Tarheel Talk* 71: Now dont you think such is enough to give me the *high strikes.* **1887** Call *Josh Hayseed* 10: T'other story teller nigh had a fit of highstrikes. **1914** Atherton *Perch* 204: If you don't get us out of here quick I'll have high-strikes. **1922, *1945, *1957* in *OED2.*

hightail *v.* to run or go at top speed; run away.—usu. constr. with *it.*

> **1919** Farrell *1st U.S. Engrs.* 119: Then down to the stables and feed those damn mules,/And "high-tail" to the chow line. **1921** Dienst *353rd Infantry* 223: Beat it down along this wall, chase yourself across that opening and high-tail up to that building with the stone steps. Now be damned quick about it. **1925** *AS* I 149: "I high-tailed out of there"…"High-tail" comes straight from the plains where a mustang, when startled, erects his tail in a sudden, quick gesture and runs like the wind. **1927** Saunders *Wings* 100: If you get separated or lost, hightail it for home. **1932–34** Minehan *Boy & Girl Tramps* 16: We…"high-tail" down the…road to camp. **1937** *Rev. of Reviews* (June) 43: *High tailing*—Speeding behind another truck. **1965** A. Arthur *Zebra in Kitchen* (film): We hightailed it over there. **1970** W.R. Woodfield *S.F. International* (film): Hang up that phone and hightail it out of there. **1988** Kienzle *Marked for Murder* 87: We hightailed it back here. **1994** Donahue (NBC-TV): So you're hightailing it after him.

high-tension whiskey *n.* very potent whiskey.

> **1934** Lomax & Lomax *Amer. Ballads* 208: Drink yo' high-tension whisky, babe,/An' let yo' cocaine be.

high-ti *n.* (see quot.).

> **1856** B. Hall *College Wds.* 254: *High-Ti.* At Williams College, a term by which is designated a showy recitation.

high-ticket *adj. Business.* costing or involving much money; BIG-TICKET. —used prenominally.

> **1970** Della Femina *Wonderful Folks* 125: Don't take on a lot of accounts, just a few high-ticket, very large accounts.

high-tone *v.* to treat haughtily.

> **1917** in Grider *War Birds* 35: He got hightoned by the Colonel and lost his head and indulged himself in an orgy of bootlicking. **1925** in Truman *Ltrs. Home* 75: They can't high-tone me anyway.

highty-tighty var. HOITY-TOITY.

high-water *adj.* (of trousers) of insufficient length; short. *Joc.* Hence **highwaters,** *n. pl.* trousers of insufficient length.

> [**1856** "M. Twain," in *DARE:* Then some soldiers with bob-tailed tin coats on (high water coats we used to call 'em in Keokuk) come in, then some gals (with high-water dresses on).] **1902** in *DARE:* High-water-pants boys, who take their college education and make some fellow's business hum with it. **1922** Dean *Flying Cloud* 92: O'Brien in His High-Water Pants. **1932** Hecht & Fowler *Great Magoo* 61: He is dressed in a very old suit of an era that went in for wasp waists and high-water pants. **1942** *ATS: High-water pants*…trousers shorter than the fashion. **1978** Katz *Folklore* 27: When a person wears pants so short they'd be good for wading home in a downpour, have you heard them

teasingly called *floods* or *high water britches?* **1978** Sopher & McGregor *Up from Walking Dead* 176: His pants were always too short, like high-water britches. **1982** Sculatti *Catalog of Cool* 116: Worn cuffless at "high-water" levels, exposing…sock…between shoe top and pant bottom. **1981–89** R. Atkinson *Long Gray Line* 101: Cadets guilty of "high-water trou"—trousers that rode too high on the ankle. **1987–89** M.H. Kingston *Tripmaster Monkey* 5: Highwaters or puddlecuffs. *a*1994 N. McCall *Wanna Holler* 292: High-water khakis.

highway *n.* ¶ In phrase: **it's my way or the highway** "do things as I direct or leave."

   1986 Knoxville, Tenn., attorney, age *ca*33: I'm just gonna tell this bitch—it's *my* way or the *high*way. **1988** Frazier & Offen *W. Frazier* 17 [ref. to 1970]: All through my basketball career, my coaches had been disciplinarians. You did it their way. "His way or the highway," we used to say. **1991** *Brooklyn Bridge* (CBS-TV): "It's my way or the highway," she used to say. **1995** *Ricki Lake Show* (synd. TV series): He says, "It's my way or the highway!"

highwayman *n. Naut.* a ship's purser.

   1830 Ames *Sketches* 201: The purser…is frequently called in American ships, "the highwayman," and…is allowed by our sapient government, twenty per cent. profit upon "slops"…and his *own* profit upon all other [items].

highway mopery var. MOPERY.

high yellow *n.* a black person having light-brown skin.—usu. considered offensive. Also **high yaller.** Also as adj. Cf. HIGH BROWN.

   1923 J. Dos Passos, in *OED2*: Ought to see them high yallers down there if you're stuck on girls. **1925** Von Vechten *Nigger Heaven* 8: A high yellow boy. *Ibid.* 30: The managers…are looking for high yallers. **1930** Mae West *Babe Gordon* 164: A high yellow…was loving up three brown-skinned women. **1932** C. McKay *Gingertown* 11: When a high-yaller queen joined the company. **1936** Mencken *Amer. Lang.* (ed. 4) 296: The American Negroes have many words of their own to designate shades of color, e.g. *brown-skin, high-brown,* and *high-yellow.* **1977** Blockson & Fry *Black Genealogy* 119: An admiration for those with skin naturally light enough to earn the label "high yellow." **1978** Diehl *Sharky's Machine* 236: Almost like a high yellow, only he's white. **1987** in *N.O. Review* (Spring 1988) 49: This high yaller with her pear-shaped self and her big ball of whiffy hair. *a*1989 in Kisseloff *Must Remember This* 295: She was not black, but she was not white either. She was a high yaller. **1993** Mowry *Six Out Seven* 146: There were several "mulattos" at school. A dirty-sounding word like the label high-yellow, which implied low-black and which nobody used. **1994** Berendt *Midnight in Garden* 327: I ain't got nothing against high yellas. Their color ain't their fault.

hijack *n.* [orig. uncert.; perh. fr. *Hi,* JACK!, as addressed to an unsuspecting victim, as in 1925 quot.; perh. *high* (with uncert. meaning) + *jack* 'to hunt' (see *DA*); cf. 1912 quot.] Also **highjack, hyjack. 1.** *Und.* a holdup man; armed robber; HIJACKER.

   [**1912** *DN* III 580: *Kick up high jack, v. phr.* To cause a disturbance; to have a "hot time." "They are goin' over to the school-house tonight and will just *kick up high jack.*"] **1920** E. Hemingway, in *N.Y. Times Mag.* (Aug. 18, 1985) 23: Get some cheap hyjack if you want a sloppy job. **1922** N. Anderson *Hobo* 24: He is a hi-jack caught in the act of robbing a fellow who was sleeping, a greater crime in the jungle than an open hold-up. **1923** in Kornbluh *Rebel Voices* 90: So as not to interfere with the beneficent work of the High-jacks. [**1925** in *Amer. Mercury* (Jan. 1926) 63: The popular *hijack*…has reached wide circulation since the advent of Volsteadism.…It comes from "High, Jack!," a command to throw up the arms, and originated among the gangs of small crooks which used to traverse the harvest belt at the close of the wheat season.] **1926** *AS* I 651: *Highjack*—traveling hold-up man.

   2. a hijacking. Now *colloq.*

   1933–35 D. Lamson *About to Die* 235: The victims of the hi-jack and the pay-off. **1965** Spillane *Killer Mine* 62: This guy who pulled the hijack was waiting when the driver holding the loot came out of his motel, stuck a gun in his ribs, made him drive to a spot where he had a car parked, belted him cold, took the money and ducked out. **1968 in *OED2*: Our airline has been hit harder by hijacks than any other. **1971** "R. Stark" *Lemons* 61: It's left over from a hijack.

hijack *v.* **1.a.** to commit armed robbery against; hold up.

   1922 N. Anderson *Hobo* 20: Jungle crimes include…"hi-jacking," or robbing men at night when sleeping in the jungles. **1928** M. Sharpe *Chicago May* 279: I thought the baby had been hi-jacked and thrown into the Detroit River, or maybe arrested. **1933** in R.E. Howard *Iron Man* 118: I craves nothin' except a proper respeck from a yegg which has just tried to hi-jack me! **1939** Wald et al. *Roaring Twenties* (film): United States Government Warehouse Number 7 was hijacked last night. **1948** Chaplin *Wobbly* 88 [ref. to *ca*1908]: He was still in danger of being "hijacked" or "rolled" by professional thieves who made a practice of "harvesting the harvesters." **1953** Cain *Galatea* 143: You should have thought of it when you hijacked the filling station. **1970** Boatright & Owens *Derrick Floor* 70: I never heard of a man getting highjacked in Sour Lake in early boom days.

   b. to subject to extortion or violent coercion.

   1925 in *Amer. Mercury* (Jan. 1926) 63: They close in on a gondola or box-car full of scissorbills and by threats of violence *hijack* them into paying initiatory fees. **1927** *DN* V 450: *Hijack*…(1) To commit pederasty upon a boy forcibly. (2) To force membership of the I.W.W. upon hoboes. **1937** in Galewitz *Great Comics* 217: I'll *teach* you to hi-jack passengers, you rat! **1938** Connolly *Navy Men* 46: They tried to hi-jack President Roosevelt on the price. **1943** Wakeman *Shore Leave* 36: She paid twenty-one dollars a month for this place, but she had hijacked the landlord into painting it "her way," so she felt she had a bargain.

   2.a. to stop and steal the cargo of (a vehicle or its drivers); (*hence*) to steal or commandeer (a vehicle, vessel, or aircraft). Now *S.E.*

   1923 *Lit. Digest* (Aug. 4) 51: I would have had $50,000…if I hadn't been hijacked. **1924** H.L. Wilson *Professor* 62: We nearly got hijacked. **1929** E. Sullivan *Look at Chi.* 11: Hi-jacking is a stiff way to make a living. **1931** Wilstach *Under Cover Man* 29: Dan's fleet to hi-jacked speed boats of competitors. **1936 in *OED2*: I still don't see how we're going to high-jack Groom's men. **1961** *Chi. Daily Trib.* (Aug. 12) 5: An Eastern Electra airliner was hijacked July 24 and flown to Cuba. **1968 in *OED2*: One of our planes with 35 on board was hi-jacked and flown to Cuba. **1970–71** Rubinstein *City Police* 329: A man hijacks a plane and the visible power of the state is mobilized to suppress the crime. **1985** Petit *Peacekeepers* 162: I hope the plane isn't hijacked.

   b. to steal (cargo in transit) (now *S.E.*); (*hence*) to steal.

   1926 *Amer. Mercury* (June) 242: *To hijack* is…now apparently used exclusively in reference to road-robbery of illicit liquor. **1929** E. Sullivan *Look at Chicago* 99: In many cases, too, the prohibition agent…will decide to hi-jack the carload of booze. **1930** Lavine *3d Degree* 165: Some even get a few pals and hijack the truck and its contents by pretending to be rival beer or hard liquor runners. **1941** *Slanguage Dict.* 21: *Highjack*.…to steal another's sweetheart. **1964** Westheimer *Von Ryan* 37: They'll report you for hijacking their prisoner. **1968** Cleaver *Soul on Ice* 178: The "Yeah! Yeah! Yeah!" which the Beatles highjacked from Ray Charles. **1970** Boatright & Owens *Derrick Floor* 70: They didn't have to highjack it, because they was taking it fast enough with those crooked dice and crooked cards. **1970** Rudensky & Riley *Gonif* 63: A guard accused me of hi-jacking another con's shipment of cigarettes. **1979** F. Thomas *Golden Bird* 35: It was Dowson's gang that had hijacked the Bird. **1994** *CBS This Morning* (Dec. 14) (CBS-TV): They've been in the business of hijacking a lot of our ideas since the election.

   3.a. to transfer (a person) against his will; SHANGHAI, 2.

   1928 Callahan *Man's Grim Justice* 251: The big boy immediately highjacked me out of Detroit to one of the branch manufacturing plants. **1973** D. Chandler *Captain Hollister* 47: My older sister got knocked up when she was sixteen and the parents found out too late to do anything about it so they hijacked her to New York. **1979** J. Morris *War Story* 222: He was the man who hijacked me into the PLO job in the first place. **1980** Manchester *Darkness* 85: Runners like me were transients, subject to hijacking by any commander who needed an extra hand.

   b. to take hostage or kidnap, esp. in the course of a hijacking.

   1967 in *OED2*: The aerial hijacking of Moise Tshombe was commissioned…by the Congolese Government. **1974 Barwood & Robins *Sugarland Express* (film): I believe our man is hijacked. **1982** "W.T. Tyler" *Rogue's March* 40: Tell him no one is going to hijack him.

hijacker *n.* one who HIJACKS. Now *S.E.* [A putative date of "1866" for a quot. in L. Anders, *21st Missouri* (1975), p. 253, is erroneous.]

   1922 *Sat. Eve. Post* (Mar. 4) 106: There has been developed a company of superthieves known as high-jackers.…They…hold up the bootleggers, usually the truckmen who are taking it about the country.

1923 in *OED2*: *Highjackers* (an oil region term for murderous robbers). **1924** Henderson *Keys to Crookdom* 407: *Highjacker*—One who robs bootleggers and liquor smugglers of whisky and wine. **1925** Dos Passos *Manhattan Transfer* 320: Prohibition agents nutten, goddam hijackers. *Ibid.* 323: I've just seen a fight between bootleggers and hijackers. **1925** in Faulkner *N.O. Sketches* 197: They wasn't only one thing we had to worry about—hi-jackers. **1926** *Amer. Mercury* (Apr.) 108: The word *hijacker*, used to designate an outlaw bootlegger who holds up and robs respectable members of the profession,…is in none of the dictionaries, yet I find it in the newspapers almost every day. **1926** *Amer. Mercury* (June) 241: [Before 1919] *hijacker*…meant the same as a footpad or road-agent. **1927** *AS* II (June) 387: The *hi-jacker*…originated in the wheat district, where, during the harvest season, individuals and gangs harvested the harvesters at the point of the *rod* or *Roscoe* (gun). **1928** O'Connor *B'way Racketeers* 252: *Hijacker*—One who robs bootleggers. **1929** Bowen *Sea Slang* 66: *High-Jacker.* A 20th century pirate preying on the American rum runners. **1929** E. Sullivan *Look at Chicago* 10: A hi-jacker…waylays a bootlegger and takes his carload of liquor away from him. **1930** "D. Stiff" *Milk & Honey* 207: *High jacker*—Yegg who robs hobos with a gun or by brute strength. **1951** in *DAS*: A highjacker who looted a truck. **1955** *PADS* (No. 24) 93: The individual [pickpocket] using very rough techniques is called a *hijacker.*

hike¹ *n.* [orig. unkn.] (see quots.).
   1896 in *DA*: The average Pennsylvanian contemptuously refers to these immigrants as "Hikes" and "Hunks." The "Hikes" are Italians and Sicilians. **1898** in *DA*: The Italians are termed Hikes.

hike² *n.* ¶ In phrase: **take a hike** to get out; walk away; leave.—usu. used imper.
   1961 Brosnan *Pennant Race* 44: Go take a hike, both of you. **1962** *Eng. Jour.* LI 325: Get lost; beat it; take a hike. **1974** Coppola & Puzo *Godfather II* (film): Take a hike, girls. **1977** Hamill *Flesh & Blood* 115: I made you an offer and you took a hike. Now take another hike. **1979** in R. Carson *Waterfront* 38: Take a fuckin' hike, you old goat. **1982** *N.Y. Post* (Sept. 21) 52: Players Take A Hike. **1982** Braun *Judas Tree* 57: He might tell you to take a hike! **1988** Sayles *Eight Men Out* (film): I told 'em to take a hike! **1994** *News Hour* (CNN-TV) (Apr. 1): No comment! Take a hike!

hike *v.* **1.** to go, esp. hurriedly; (*hence*) to get out or get away; depart. Cf. S.E. sense.
   *1724 in Partridge *Dict. Und.* 333: My *Boman* he hick'd away…Her *Rogue* had got away. *1728 in Partridge *DSUE* (ed. 7): He *hyk'd* off with the *Cly.* *1744 in Partridge *Dict. Und.* 333: Hyke up to the Gigger and undubb it…Go up to the Door, and unlock it. *1745 in C.H. Wilkinson *King of Beggars* 120: *Bampfylde* bid the Ghost *hike* to the *Vile.* *1788 Grose *Vulgar Tongue* (ed. 2): *To hike off*; to run away. **1859** Matsell *Vocab.* 42: *Hike.* Run away. "Hike; the cops have tumbled to us," run; the officers have seen us. **1898** (quot. at *hit the road* s.v. HIT). **1905** *DN* III 62: Hike, v. Hurry. **1908** Whittles *Lumberjack* 15: I'll have to join—or hike. **1912** Siringo *Cowboy Detective* 75: Dan…"hiked" back to America [from London]. **1914** Ellis *Billy Sunday* 86: Take your helpers and hike. You are hurting our business. **1914** E.R. Burroughs *Mucker* 115: Here's where de ginks…hiked fer.
   2. to trick or defraud.
   1951 *N.Y. Times* (June 15) 14: They're in such a hurry to hike someone out of some money.

hiker *n.* **1.** (among tramps) a small-town law officer.
   1902 Hapgood *Thief* 86 [ref. to *ca*1880]: "Get on to the Hiker," (countryman) said Patsy to Joe, and they both laughed. **1926** *AS* I (Dec.) 651: *Hiker.* Town marshal. **1937** *Lit. Digest* (Apr. 10) 12: The *hiker.*—Small town marshal.
   2. a person's leg.
   1927 J. Stevens *Mattock* 184: So…here I am, in the Brennes hospital with my right hiker missing.

hill *n.* **1.** *Baseball.* a pitcher's mound.—usu. constr. with *the.*
   1908 *N.Y. Eve. Jour.* (Mar. 11) (cited in P. Dickson *Baseball Dict.*). **1915** [Swartwood] *Choice Slang* 75: On the hill with nothing but a glove and a prayer. **1934** *Journ. Qly.* (Dec.) 352: *Hill*, *n.* (baseball)—pitcher's mound. **1948** L. Allen *Reds* 270: Walters was…one of the best fielders of his position that ever took the hill. **1966** in P. Dickson *Baseball Dict.*: I was interested to see you out there on the hill in the ninth.
   2. *Naut.* the horizon at sea.—constr. with *the.*
   1936 Mulholland *Splinter Fleet* 60 [ref. to 1918]: But we made a great show of energetically dashing back and forth, rushing out to the

dim horizon, where "over the hill," we pretended our supernatural sight had detected the possibility of a lurking enemy.
   3. the position of needing one game to win a contest.
   1996 McCumber *Playing off Rail* 15: Han was two sets ahead and "on the hill," having won four games and needing just one more win in the third set. *Ibid.* 22: He won four games in a row to tie the set at six apiece—"hill-hill." One game left to decide the set. *Ibid.* 215: He made it [*sc.* a shot in pool] to tie the match at ten games apiece—hill-hill in the race to eleven.
   ¶ In phrases:
   ¶ **go over the hill, 1.a.** *West.* to run away; abscond.
   1912 Siringo *Cowboy Detective* 168 [ref. to 1892]: It was Dallas and his gang searching for me.…After they had looked at the face of each man Dallas remarked: "The —— must have gone over the hill."
   b. *Mil.* to desert; (*also*) to go absent without leave.
   1917 in Judy *Diary* 46: — —, my orderly, went over the hill. **1918** O'Reilly *Roving & Fighting* 76 [ref. to 1899]: "One of two things has happened," said the corporal. "Denny has deserted and gone over the hill, or some gu-gu has killed him." **1918** *Sat. Eve. Post* (Jan. 19) 17: What's on your mind this evening? Going over the hill? **1919** Emmett *Give 'Way* 274: We would "go over the hill" for a visit to a nearby village. **1926** Nason *Chevrons* 9: Sick to death of…the replacement camps…[they] had…gone over the hill and were trying to rejoin their organizations. **1940** McCullers *Golden Eye* 28: He had occasionally seen the same queer habit in young soldiers who have grown homesick for the farm and womenfolk, and who plan to "go over the hill." **1942** *Leatherneck* (Nov.) 148: Over-the-hill—Deserted…the penalty is fatal. **1945** Windolph *Custer* 42 [ref. to 19th C.]: We'd come back here and get rich. We might even "go over the hill." **1957** Leckie *Helmet* 117: Don't give me that.…You went over the hill, didn't you? **1971** *Nat. Lampoon* (Aug.) 27: That afternoon all 6 went over the hill. **1981** R.O. Butler *Alleys* 145: Why'd you go over the hill, anyway? **1995** *Space: Above & Beyond* (Fox-TV): I went over the hill. I took the aircraft.
   c. *Pris.* to escape from penal confinement.
   1918 in *AS* (Oct. 1933) 27: *Go over the hill*…Escape from prison, especially by running away from a [work] gang. **1927** *DN* V 448: *Go over the hill*, v. To escape from prison. **1935** E. Anderson *Hungry Men* 182: I told him to go to hell and walked out of the place and went over the hill. **1970** Rudensky & Riley *Gonif* 14: The…cons nearby knew we were going over the hill.
   2. to become insane.
   1968 C. Victor *Sky Burned* 128: Never, never could he have imagined himself going over the hill, cracking up.
   ¶ **on the hill** pregnant.
   1957–64 Selby *Last Exit* 85: When Suzy told Tommy she was on the hill I guess he was a little surprised. **1968–70** *Current Slang III & IV* 89: *On the hill*, adj. Pregnant.—High school and college males, Florida.

hill ape *n.* HILLBILLY.—used contemptuously.
   *ca*1965 IUFA *Folk Speech*: Kentuckians are called Hill Apes or Briar Hoppers in Indiana.

hillbilly *n.* [*hill* + *billy* 'fellow' (dial.), fr. *Billy*, hypocoristic form of *William*] Orig. *So.* an uncouth person from a mountainous region, esp. the southern U.S.; (*broadly*) any person from a remote area.—usu. used disparagingly.
   1900 in *DA*: In short, a Hill-Billie is a free and untrammelled white citizen of Alabama, who lives in the hills, has no means to speak of, dresses as he can, talks as he pleases, drinks whiskey when he gets it, and fires off his revolver as the fancy takes him. **1902** W.N. Harben *Abner Daniel* 102: By hunkley, Uncle Ab, you don't mean to tell me you don't know what that passle o' hill-Billies is a goin' to do with you…at meetin'? **1904** *DN* II 418: *Hill billy*, n. Uncouth countryman, particularly from the hills. "You one-gallused *hill billies*, behave yourselves." **1904** W.N. Harben *Georgians* 87: You scalawags!…you lazy hill-billies, you yaps. **1923** *DN* V 210: *Hill billy*, n. A resident of the hills in contradistinction to an inhabitant of the lowlands or valleys. Also expressive of contempt, or meaning ignorant. **1926** *Variety* (Dec. 29) 1: "Hill-Billy" Music. **1938** Arthur & Musselman *Ky. Moonshine* (film): What in tarnation's a hillbilly? **1939** *AS* XIV (Feb.) 23: The Charleston cadets have only the hackneyed term *hillbilly* for their "up-country" classmates. **1939** McIlwaine *So. Poor-White* XV: "Hill-billies"…has become a popular misnomer for mountaineers. **1947** Paxton *Crossfire* (film): He's a dumb hillbilly. **1949** *AS* XXIV (Feb.) 26:

The rest were *hillbillies* from the creeks of Appalachia. **1952** Randolph & Wilson *Down in the Holler* 252: Congressman Dewey Short, Galena, Mo., describes himself in public speeches as a *hillbilly*, but many hill-folk regard it as a fightin' word. John O'Neill shot and killed Elmo McCullars, of St. Louis, in 1934 because the latter called him a *hillbilly*. **1958** *AS* XXXIII (Dec.) 265: Pejorative Designations of Rural Dwellers in the Upper Midwest....*hillbilly*. **1962** *The Beverly Hillbillies* (CBS-TV) [title]. **1966** Cassiday *Angels Ten* 237: No Arkansas hillbillies. **1970** *Black Scholar* (Nov.) 13: Many blacks sit together in enlisted men's clubs, scorning "hillbilly" and "country and western" music. **1970** R. Vasquez *Chicano* 78: They laugh and say we're Mexican hillbillies. **1975** Gainer *Folk Songs* XV: To true West Virginia mountaineers the term "hillbilly" is highly derogatory. It is as insulting to us as such terms as "nigger," "hunkie," "kike," and "wop" are to other people. **1988** Terkel *Great Divide* 316: I heard lots of others say bad things about mountain people: dumb hillbilly, lazy hillbillies....Am I dumb? Am I lazy? *Ibid.* 317: This...woman said, "I always heard that hillbillies were drunks and the men beat their wives." I said I heard the same thing about [other groups].

hill-cat *n.* (see quot.).
    1860 in *DA*: If they see any mountaineers (Hill-Cats, as they call them) descending towards their valley, they immediately raise the war-cry.

hilljack *n. Calif.* HILLBILLY.—used contemptuously.
    1992 Hosansky & Sparling *Working Vice* 69: Appalachians...had to face prejudice and were called "hilljacks."

himbo *n.* a young man who is attractive but unintelligent; a male BIMBO[2], 2.
    1988 *Wash. Post*, in *OEDAS* II: The macho himbo who strutted the Croisette wearing a 16-foot python like a stole around his shoulders and neck. **1994** *Wash. Post* (Feb. 26) D6: Male-ogling has been a staple of other media for some time, of course. The "himbo" shows up regularly in film, in calendars, in print ads from Calvin Klein. **1994** *N.Y. Times* (Sept. 25) (Styles) 52: "Himbos are straight, good-looking men who read Hampton's magazine and chase models around SoHo on their Harleys."...Its use can be traced from the June issue of Entertainment Weekly to Vogue and The Village Voice in September. **1995** *N.Y. Press* (Jan. 3, 1996) 12: Both were branded as model-dating "himbos." **1996** *YM* (Apr.) 80: He's blond and he's on *Baywatch*, but is David Chokachi a himbo? Hardly!

himmel *n.* [< G *Himmel* 'heaven'] (see quot.).
    1900 *DN* II 40: *Himmel*, n....Topmost gallery in a theater. (Reported from six colleges and universities.).

hincty *n. Black E.* a HINCTY person.
    1952 E. Brown *Trespass* 141: He say he want to see where you hangin' out with all these hinkties. **1970** in *DARE*.

hincty *adj.* [orig. unkn.] *Black E.* **1.** snobbish; haughty; conceited; aloof; fastidious. Also vars.
    1924 in Handy *Blues Treasury* 144: Well I am hinkty and I'm low down too. **1934** L. Hughes *Ways of White Folks* 58: She wasn't a bit hinkty like so many folks when they're light-complexioned and up in the money. **1945** Drake & Cayton *Black Metropolis* 444: One of the most general criticisms of Negro merchants is the charge that "they are stuck up," or "hincty." As one customer complained: "The average Negro in business will frown and become very haughty at the least thing." **1948** Manone & Vandervoort *Trumpet* 10: Sometimes we worked in places so hincty the men's can...looked like the annex to a king's palace. **1952** in W.S. Burroughs *Letters* 129: I am not being hincty, Allen. **1952** E. Brown *Trespass* 14: Course, he wasn't talking now about no real hinkty folks. Nobody like you find on Park Avenue. **1959** A. Anderson *Lover Man* 118: If I hit on her the first time around she'd get all hinckty and say no. **1962** T. Berger *Reinhart* 121: And that hincty little chick...give you many a bad time. **1963** Parks *Learning Tree* [ref. to 1920's] 10: "That thing's dirty!" "You picked a hell of a time to get hinkty, boy." **1964** Rhodes *Chosen Few* 115: Hincty, fancy-talking northern niggers. **1970** Knight *Black Voices from Prison* 101: By this time the other guys were getting hincty and cursing her, so I drove off.

2. *Und. & Police.* wary or extremely cautious; feeling suspicion. Also vars.
    1929 T. Gordon *Born to Be* 135: I was hinkty as hell for more than one reason. First, I had been bilked by the gal I was in love with. Second, cause I was down South, and third, cause I loathed the sight of him....I was kinda hinkty and thought to myself, a fine, deceitful lot, getting ready to can me and not telling me anything about it until the

time came. **1932** in *AS* (Feb. 1934) 26: *Hinkty.* Suspicious. **1935** Pollock *Und. Sp.*: *Hincty*, suspicious. **1938** (cited in Partridge *Dict. Und.*). **1962–68** B. Jackson *In the Life* 122: I don't know if she was hankty (suspicious) or what. *a*1972 B. Rodgers *Queens' Vernacular.* 107: *Hincty*...paranoid; afraid of being arrested or beaten.

hind gearing *n.* the legs.
    1851 in A.P. Hudson *Humor of Old So.* 302: The way he made his hind gearin' play the ear, was beautiful.

hindpaw *n.* a foot. Cf. FOREPAW.
    *1785 (quot. at FOREPAW). **1859** Matsell *Vocab.* 65: *The hind paw*, foot.

hindsights *n.pl.* the posteriors.
    1849 *Spirit of Times* (Nov. 10) 452: The dogs...'gan to chaw at his hide and kinder tickle the hind sights of the varmint.
    ¶ In phrase:
    ¶ **knock the hindsights off** to destroy, ruin, or defeat; (*also*) to surpass greatly. Also vars.
    1834 Caruthers *Kentuckian in N.Y.* 21: And as sure as you saw the fire at the muzzle of his gun, so sure he knocked the creter's hind sights out. **1836** *Spirit of Times* (July 9) 162: Oh! my Grapevine, tear the hind sites off him, you'll lay him cold as a waggontire—roll your bones—go it you cripples. **1850** Garrard *Wah-to-yah* 199: Wagh!...this knocks the hind sights off of Touse. I'se drunk. *ca*1851 in J. Anderson *Bark* 134: She's a raal screamer—enough to knock the hind sights right off a feller what's got no old woman of his own. **1871** Eggleston *Hoosier Schoolmaster* 87: Ef it's rendered right, it'll knock the hind sights off of any rheumatiz you ever see. **1892** in *DAE*: The American producer...can knock the hind sights off the producer anywhere else on the face of the earth. **1903** Benton *Cowboy Life on Sidetrack* 46: I reckon she could just knock the hind sights off anybody when it came to singing. **1950**, *ca*1960 in *DARE*.

hind tit see s.v. TIT, *n.*

Hindu *n.* **1.** *Calif.* a member of the Know-Nothing Party.
    1855 in *Calif. Hist. Soc. Qly.* IX (1930) 41: The anti-Catholic test, which here in California the Hindoos (Know Nothings) profess to repudiate.

2. a person who has a seemingly magical ability with or is noteworthy for (something specified); a "wizard."
    1908 in H.C. Fisher *A. Mutt* 27: You're a Hindoo with that gat, Pa. *Ibid.* 47: You're a Hindoo at pickin' 'em, kid. Go to it. **1916** T.A. Dorgan, in Zwilling *TAD Lexicon* 109: Down in Kentucky they say he's a hindoo at pinochle. **1916** T.A. Dorgan, in *Ibid.*: Don't be trying to look cute Andrew—You're no hindoo for looks.

hiney[1] var. HEINIE.

hiney[2] *n.* [prob. fr. *hinders* or *hindparts*] the buttocks; BUTT, *n.*—also in phrs. corresponding to those at ASS, *n.* Also vars., esp. **heiny.**
    1921 E. O'Neill *Hairy Ape* 233: Gee, pipe de heine [*sic*] on dat one! Say, youse, yuh look like de stoin of a ferry-boat. **1929** T. Gordon *Born to Be* 40: Most of the kids realized what they had done and hauled their hinies for home. **1948** in Legman *Limerick* 133: Its heiny/Will stretch quite as big as a house. **1958** Frankel *Band of Bros.* 14: We'll have to knock these fellers on their hi-neys. **1969** Marshe & Lifton *Centerfold* 38: Dressed in an outfit cunningly designed to accentuate and then reveal a deep cleavage and half her hindy. **1970** Baraka *Jello* 25: I bet this really burns your li'l hiney up, don't it. Haha. **1971** *Blushes & Belly-laffs* 7: Know the difference between a male and a female flea? The female flea has a tiny heinie and the male has a teenie weenie. **1971** G. Davis *Coming Home* 47: Your hinnie is a little too big for your legs. **1971** in Sanchez *Word Sorcerers* 121: I kicked her fat hiney with the side of my foot. **1975** C.W. Smith *Country Music* 79: Bobby Joe could use a swift kick in his little hiney! **1978** in Fierstein *Torch Song* 42: Someone's got his hand on my heiney. **1981** Luagner *Incredible Shrinking Woman* (film): I'd slip and slide and slimy/Over everybody's hynie. **1986** Watterson *Calvin* 31: Girls have more delicate heinies. **1990** G. Lee *China Boy* 221: Getchur heinie in the goddamn door. **1991** Nelson & Gonzales *Bring Noise* 127: He's knockin' hiney.

hinge *n.* a look.
    1935 Wald & Epstein *Stars over Broadway* (film): Take a good hinge at yourself. **1938** Baldwin & Schrenk *Case of Murder* (film): With a look on his pan like a hungry tramp taking a hinge at a lunch room. **1940** O'Hara *Pal Joey* 194: It is a good thing I only write you letters

instead of getting a hinge at yr holy kisser so I could hang a blooper on it. **1940** in Goodstone *Pulps* 112: Everybody wanted a hinge at the hero. **1941** Mahin & Grant *Johnny Eager* (film): Maybe it just looks dead. Let's take a hinge. **1947** Schulberg *Harder They Fall* 56: I take one hinge at the boy and I see he's got something. **1972** R. Barrett *Lovomaniacs* 149: Get a hinge at Vanni. **1973** *Chase* (NBC-TV): Take a hinge at this.

hinkty var. HINCTY.

hinky *adj.* [var. HINCTY] Orig. *Black E.* **1.** HINCTY, 1.
   1967 *Lit Dict.* 21: *Hinky*—Very cheap and petty.
   2.a. HINCTY, 2; *(hence)* nervous or jumpy.
      1956 Resko *Reprieve* 55: The guy was hinky on talking and I figured him for a shrewd apple or an out-and-out chump. *Ibid.* 244 [ref. to 1940's]: The hipsters…had a word for Mac—hinkey. He was not suspicious…he was careful, hinkey. **1966** Brunner *Face of Night* 38: But James is real hinkey. He's probably been looking you over for the last ten minutes. *Ibid.* 233: *Hinkey*—suspicious. **1970** Wambaugh *New Centurions* 127: They make you hinky. What's their secret? You always wonder. **1971** *Adam-12* (NBC-TV): I've been working this guy for three weeks, but he's hinky. **1972** R. Barrett *Lovomaniacs* 420: Bankers…those guys are always a little hinky about short-term money. **1974** *Police Woman* (NBC-TV): He's still not hinky. **1981** *Hill St. Blues* (NBC-TV): He's gettin' hinky, babe. He'll be clammin' up on us soon. **1990** C.P. McDonald *Blue Truth* 11: Yeah, you know, hinky…acting nervous.
   b. *Police.* arousing suspicion.
      1975 Wambaugh *Choirboys* 107: "Driver of the pimpmobile looks hinky."…"Let's bring him down. Might have a warrant." **1985** M. Baker *Cops* 154: There's something hinky about this. They may be thinking about doing a robbery. *a***1986** in *NDAS:* Something hinky is going down. **1986** Stroud *Close Pursuit* 245: Gonna look pretty hinky on his performance profile.
   3. refractory.
      1987 *21 Jump Street* (Fox-TV): This one kid got real hinky. Had to subdue him.

hinky-dink[y] *adj.* [nickname of Michael "Hinky Dink" Kenna (1858–1946), longtime alderman and political boss of Chicago's First Ward; cf. DINKY, 2] **1.a.** little; DINKY, 2.
   [**1894** in Ade *Chicago Stories* 48: In the "Hinky Dink" precinct he was standing apart watching the barrel-house delegation put in enough ballots to offset the entire school-teacher vote.] **1909** Chrysler *White Slavery* 211: A long talk with "Hinky Dink" Kenna. **1943** Wendt & Kogan *Bosses* 74 [ref. to 1870]: "Kenna's my name.…Michael Kenna, from over on Polk Street." "That's a good Irish name," Medill replied, "but I'm going to call you Hinky Dink because you are such a little fellow."
   b. RINKY-DINK.
      1967 J. Kramer *Instant Replay* 65: There's a second-class bowl game, and it's a hinky-dinky football game, held in a hinky-dinky town, played by hinky-dinky football players.
   2. excellent; tiptop.
      1913 *DN* IV 24: *Hinky-dinky.* Excellent; first-rate. Facetious. Used in Nebraska.…"That's just *hinky-dinky,* it suits me fine." **1935** *AS* (Feb.) 17 [ref. to *a*1910]: *Hinky-dink*…Excellent; having class or quality.

hip[1] *n.* [spelling var. of *hyp,* abbr. of *hypochondria*] low spirits; blues.—often constr. with *the.* Also vars. Orig. *colloq.*
   *ca***1705** in *OED2:* Hyps and such like unaccountable things. *****1710** J. Swift, in *F & H* III 387: Will Hazzard has got the Hipps, having lost to the Tune of Five Hundr'd Pound. *****1738** J. Swift, in *F & H:* I warrant it put her into the hipps. *****1762** in *OED2:* That…sentimental strain gives me the hip. **1763** in Whiting *Prov. Phrs.* 212: After you left this our old Lodgings became vacant, which has almost given me the hip. **1775** in R.M. Lederer *Colonial Eng.* 113: Mrs. Green is better, but Miss Beatty says she has the hipp. **1788** in W. Dunlap *Diary* 22: His very looks give gentlemen the Hip. *****1811** *Lexicon Balatron.:* Hyp. The hypochondriac: low spirits. *****1825** in *OED2:* I was dying there of hyp! **1902** Clapin *Amer.* 228: Hips (to have the). To be restless at night and unable to sleep.

hip[2] *n.* usu. *pl.* (used as a euphem. for ASS, esp. in fig. senses).
   *a*****1890–93** *F & H* III 316: Hip, (in pl.)…Conventional—as in the proverb, "Free of her lips, free of her hips"—for the buttocks. **1908** (implied by HIP-PEDDLER). **1914** Jackson & Hellyer *Vocab.* 44: I can't see you tonight; I've got a Jane on my hip. "What's the use of taking more

on your hip?"…"Don't round, we've got somebody on our hip." **1918** in Niles *Songs Mother Never Taught* 221: Said I ought to lay the Kaiser's hips to rest. **1928** W.R. Burnett *Little Caesar* 34: It's our hips for this. **1934** L. Hughes *Ways of White Folks* 57: And me working my hips off keeping 'em fed and lickered up. **1934** W. Smith *Bessie Cotter* 84: You can peddle your hips for it while I'm away. **1937** Hemingway *Have & Have Not* 175: She's too old to peddle her hips now. **1959** W. Williams *Ada Dallas* 18: He put my mother out in her younger years to support him by, his expression was, peddling her hips. **1964** H. Rhodes *Chosen Few* 129: I'm takin' my boys t' th' flick t'morra night, if they don't rip their hips durin' th' day." *Ibid.* 148: Man, when you rip your hip, you do it five big ways, don'cha?…Long, deep, wide, again and again."

¶ In phrases:

¶ **lay the hip** *Narc.* to smoke opium.
   1930 Mae West *Babe Gordon* 268: Dey're layin' duh hip. **1930** Lait *On the Spot* 206: Lay the Hip…Smoke opium. **1953** Anslinger & Tompkins *Traf. in Narc.* 311: Lay the hip. To smoke opium. **1971** Tamony *Americanisms* (No. 29) 7: Clendenyn may have been the first white to *lay the hip* in the U.S.A. but ingestion of opium must have been common in those decades.

¶ **on the hip** [fr. a S.E. wrestling sense; *OED* cites lit. examples fr. the 15th C. onward] **1.** near defeat; in a finishing position; fully under one's mastery or control.
   *****1596** Shakespeare *Merchant of Venice* IV i: Now infidell I have thee on the hip. *****1602** in *OED2:* When Dauid seem'd, in common sence, already on the hip. *****1604** Shakespeare *Othello* II i: I'll have our Michael Cassio on the hip. *****1617** in *F & H* III 316: If he have us at the advantage, on the hip as we say, it is now great matter then to get service at our hands. *****1635** in *OED2:* The Divell hath them on the hip, he may easily bring them to anything. *****1677** in D'Urfey *Two Comedies* 209: The rogue has me upon the hip. *****1698–99** "B.E." *Dict. Canting Crew: Upon the Hip,* at an Advantage, in Wrestling or Business. **1701** in Whiting *Prov. Phrs.* 212: He then hath them upon the hip. *****a*1755** S. Johnson *Dict.:* To have on the Hip. (A low phrase.) To have an advantage over another. It seems to be taken from hunting, the *hip* or *haunch* of a deer being the part commonly seised by the dogs. **1798** in Whiting *Prov. Phrs.* 212: The Directory have us "on the hip." **1815** in Whiting *Prov. Phrs.:* We've got the daring vaunters on the hip. **1838** [Haliburton] *Clockmaker* (Ser. 2) 23: You got me on the hip, and I can't help myself; say fifty dollars, and I will. **1899** B.W. Green *Va. Folk-Speech* 261: He had him *on the hip.* **1899** Hamblen *Bucko Mate* 110: They think I'm their meat, but I'll soon have 'em on the hip. **1900** in J. London *Letters* 92: You had me on the hip, and scored hard. **1928** Callahan *Grim Justice* 23 [ref. to *ca*1900]: In the vernacular of the institution I had the dungeon on the hip. I had conquered it. *Ibid.* 36: I will firt…[with] the sap. When I think I've got him on the hip, I'll give you the tip. **1940** E. O'Neill *Iceman* 134 [ref. to 1912]: I'm telling you, Ed, it's serious this time. That bastard, Hickey, has got Harry on the hip. **1978** H. Cosell, on *ABC Monday Night Baseball* (ABC-TV) (July 3): In the first inning it appeared they had Eckersley on the hip.

2. *Narc.* engaged in smoking opium.
   1921 *Variety* (Aug. 12) 4: If you get an idea while you're on your hip some night, wrap it up and shoot it along. **1933** Hammett *Thin Man* 267: Some of the boys and girls were celebrating upstairs and…he wasn't off his hip…all afternoon. **1936** *AS* (Apr.) 123: *To lie on the hip.* To be smoking opium. **1945** Bryan *Carrier* 32: Radio Tokyo got on its hip with an opium pipe and dreamed up this one tonight. **1942–49** Goldin et al. *DAUL* 95: *Hip, on the*…Smoking the opium pipe. **1964** Larner & Tefferteller *Addict in the Street* [ref. to 1930's]: Instead of dancing, we enjoyed ourselves just lying on the hip. **1967** Colebrook *Cross of Lassitude* 174: But Clara sure was hittin' it on the hip. Ah had to send her up to Paragoula for a rest cure. **1972** Kopp *Buddha* 199: "To be on the hip"…was…a bit of opium-smoking argot. The smoker lies on his hip, off in his inner world. **1980** in Courtwright et al. *Addicts Who Survived* 87 [ref. to 1930's]: That's what they call…"taking it on the hip."

3. (of liquor) in a hip flask on one's person.
   1914 *DN* IV 74: *Hip, to have suthin' on yer*…To have a bottle of liquor. **1916** R. Lardner, in *Sat. Eve. Post* (Feb. 19) 36: "Got anything on the hip?"…"I'm drier than St. Petersgrad." **1931** Wilstach *Under Cover Man* 43: I've something good on the hip. **1942** *Pittsburgh Courier* (Jan. 17) 13: Say, Mag,…have you got anything on your hips?

hip[3] *n.* **1.** the quality of being HIP, *adj.*, 2.b.; stylish sophistication.

1956 N. Mailer, in *Village Voice* (N.Y.C.) (Apr. 25) 5: Hip is an exploration into the nature of man, and the emphasis is on the Self rather than Society. **1959** in Cox *Delinquent, Hipster, Square* 21: In the language of "hip," they think these others are too square. **1968** Gover *JC* 70: It doesn't pay to blow your cool—hip is *in*. **1975** *Oui* (Mar.) 51: Hip died the night you glanced up and noticed that Ed Sullivan had let Elvis Presley into the room. **1986** *N.Y. Review of Bks.* (May 29) 30: Why Japan for this story of love and anxiety...? Maybe it's just for the hip of being on location. **1994** *Time* (Aug. 8) 48: Hip was a notion roomy enough to describe flower children in tie-dye as well as bikers in leather.

2. *Journ.* a person who is HIP, *adj.*, 2.b.; (*specif.*) HIPPIE, 2.

1967 McNeill *Moving Through Here* 82: The real battle today is between the hips and the squares. **1967–68** von Hoffman *Parents Warned Us* 10: Down on Parnassus Avenue where the rich hips lived. **1973** Buerkle & Barker *Bourbon St. Black* 30: What are their attitudes toward themselves, "squares," "hips," narcotics and God?

hip *adj.* [orig. unkn.; cf. ety. note at HEP, *adj.*; also cf. HIPPED[3], 2.b.; *hip* has been the dominant form nationally since *ca*1960, but much earlier among blacks, esp. jazz musicians]

1. fully aware; in the know; HEP, 1.

1902 T.A. Dorgan, in Zwilling *TAD Lexicon* 45: (Light and Shadow In The Police Court) [Sign carried by boy in cartoon panel:] Joe Hip/For Congress/Son of old man Hip. **1904** Hobart *Jim Hickey* 15: Say, Danny, at this rate it'll take about 629 shows to get us to Jersey City, are you hip? **1908** in H.C. Fisher *A. Mutt* 149: Oh, I'm so glad you got hip to yourself at last! **1912** in *DN* IV 28: *Put one hyp*...To put one "wise to"; to inform. **1916** "A. No. 1" *Snare of the Road* 83: You got hip to my presence. **1919** Darling *Jargon Book* 43: *Hip To It*—To get wise or understand about a thing. **1926** Dunning & Abbott *Broadway* 218: Say, sweetheart, why don't you get hip to yourself? **1935** Pollock *Und. Speaks: Hip-to-it*, thoroughly understands the situation or proposition. **1938** Lawes *Invisible Stripes* 255: I think we guys oughta get hip to ourselves. **1956** E. Hunter *Second Ending* 349: "She a real music lover....what I mean, a *real* one." "I'm hip....What about an intro?" **1958** Ferlinghetti *Coney Island* 10: He is hip/to who made heaven/and earth. **1958** *AS* XXXIII (Oct.) 223: The shibboleth in jazz circles is the word *hip* (meaning knowledgeable, full of understanding, taste, and sympathy). To use *hep* (the older form of the same adjective) or the noun *hepcat* instead of *hipster* dates a man among hipsters in pretty much the same way that those who still call fools *saps* date themselves among the rest of us. **1958** in R.S. Gold *Jazz Talk* 128: The correct word is "hip." It comes from a story of a fisherman warning young fishermen never to wade in deep water without hip boots on because they could run into trouble. So, when you hear the words "I'm hip" or "I'm booted" it's said to let you know they have no fear of trouble or that they understand what's shaking. **1959** A. Anderson *Lover Man* 161: "I been looking for you."..."I'm hip." **1959** E. Hunter *Matter of Conviction* 203: You're hip to the car aerials, huh? **1965** Tavel *Lady Godiva* 184: Leofric...has levied a heavy tax on the local inhabitants....You hip? **1970** *Playboy* (Dec.) 279: "Yeah," Stevie said, "I'm hip." **1970** Southern *Blue Movie* 173: "Nicky thinks it's a swell idea." "I'm hip he does." **1972** (quot. at HEP, *adj.*, 1). **1979** R. Salmaggi, WINS radio (June 22): I'm hip it's supposed to be a screwball comedy. **1992** *CBS This Morning* (CBS-TV) (Sept. 11): People are starting to get hip now and they're reading the side nutritional labels. **1993** *Seinfield* (NBC-TV): "Excuse me. I'm going to the bathroom." "I'm hip."

2.a. *Broadly,* shrewd; sophisticated; smart; HEP, 2.a. [The sense of the 1927 quot. is unclear.]

[**1927** in *AS* III (1928) 255: Crook Argot...*Hip gee*—Wise money.] **1938** Calloway *Hi De Ho* 16: *Hip* (adj.): wise, sophisticated, anyone with boots on [i.e., in the know]. **1944** Burley *Hndbk. Jive* 22: The cooking up of real hip plays [schemes]. *Ibid.* 53: I'm a hip kitty from New Yawk City. **1946** Mezzrow & Wolfe *Really Blues* 306: *Hip:*...worldly-wise, clever, enlightened, sophisticated. **1948** Seward & Ryan *Angel's Alley* (film): You can't pull the wool over this lamb's eyes: she's hip. **1951** O'Hara *Farmers Hotel* 66: "You're pretty *hip* for your set."..."They're not all stupid." **1952** Ellson *Golden Spike* 3: Angel was too smart, too hip. **1952** Mandel *Angry Strangers* 238: Like—you too hip, you don' get hooked. **1965** C. Brown *Manchild* 107: I was older and bigger and hipper now. **1967–80** Folb *Runnin' Lines* 242: Hip 1. Knowledgeable. 2. Street-wise. 3. Self-possessed. 4. Articulate.

b. in fashion; up-to-date; HEP, 2.b.

1944 Burley *Hndbk. Jive* 106: I'm so hip it hurts, I'm so sharp I figure I'll cut myself on these creases. *Ibid.* 122: Root boots with hip tips. **1946** in Tamony *Americanisms* (No. 17) 9: If you say "hep,"...you ain't hip. **1952** J.C. Holmes *Go* 130: They studied each other ceaselessly, drinking very little, smoking with pinched lips, and deciding who among the new arrivals was "hip." *ca*1953 Hughes *Lodge* 84: I dressed hip, I talked hip. **1959* in *OED2*: He...uses hip endearments as "angel-cake" and "gorgeous." **1962** McDavid *Mencken's Amer. Lang.* 231: "He's from *squaresville*" [is] considered somewhat more *hip* than simply calling some out-of-date person a *square*. **1965** C. Brown *Manchild* 206: It was a hip thing to do. **1966** Young & Hixson *LSD* 10: The "hip" U.S. campus set prefers to try flashing lights...along with hypnotic staring at specialized works of art. *Ibid.* 12: The "hip" phrase, "It's what's happening, Baby." **1966–67** P. Thomas *Mean Streets* 162: I really dig her. She ain't hip and that's what I like. **1967** J.B. Williams *Narc. & Hallucin.* 113: Hip, hep...opposite of square. **1970** Major *Afro-Amer. Slang* 66: Hip...in fashion. **1973** Jong *Flying* 21: When he felt he'd been attacked, he became nasty and threw in a four-letter word to show how hip he was. *a*1976 Roebuck & Frees *Rendezvous* 144: They speak in a hip vernacular, a composite jargon spoken by musicians, show-biz people, drug addicts, and criminals. **1984** Blumenthal *Hollywood* 34: Taking high tea...is an ultra hip thing to do. **1986** Cosby *Fatherhood* 116: No matter *how* he talks, a father cannot sound hip to his children. **1989** *Harper's* (Dec.) 47: Doing lines of cocaine hasn't been hip for at least five years.

c. Esp. *Black E.* splendid; fine; enjoyable.

1944 Burley *Hndbk. Jive* 22: The brook, old man, was also hip. **1945** Hartman & Shavelson *Wonder Man* (film): That's a hip chick. **1959** Lederer *Never Steal Anything Small* (film): *Love* is a soap that's really hip. **1965** C. Brown *Manchild* 428: I dig it. It sounds like a pretty hip life. **1967** L. Jones, in C. Major *Calling Wind* 271: "We figured it'd be better than 3-D." "Yeh? That's pretty hip." **1971** Giovanni *Gemini* 138: Sitting on the john was hip. **1974** *Black World* (Nov.) 60: Hey, it's been hip. **1973–76** J. Allen *Assault* 91: "After you're here for a while and you learn the recipes, then we will talk about a raise." So I said, "Well, that's hip." **1978** *Watch Your Mouth* (WNET-TV): Oh, wow! This is really hip! You're not *old*! *a*1979 Pepper & Pepper *Straight Life* 104: That was the hippest shit in town. **1988** *Right On!* (June) 59: The [film] clip is hip.

d. insolent.

1942 *ATS* 554: *Hipchick*, a "snooty" girl. **1944** Burley *Hndbk. Jive* 96: Don't get too hip, 'cause/You I might clip with this righteous chib. **1955** E. Hunter *Jungle Kids* 3: When somebody's trying to give you advice, don't go hip on him.

3. infatuated; excited; HIPPED[3], 1.—constr. with *be*.

1948 in Kerouac *Letters* 166: My brother-in-law's all hip on the idea. **1967** Hamma *Motorcycle Mommas* 34: They wanted to see if we were with it, and we wanted to show them we were hip to anything they could dream up. *a*1968 in Haines & Taggart *Ft. Lauderdale* 22: I wasn't too hip about going down, but two of my closer friends were going. **1974** *Nat. Lampoon* (Feb.) 66: "Well, what do you say?" "Suits me!" "I'm hip." **1984** *News-Sentinel* (Knoxville, Tenn.) (Mar. 18) F1: Her surgeon is hip on early discharge. **1987** *RHD2*: We explained our whole plan, and she was hip.

hip *v.* **1.** to put in a finishing position; ruin. Cf. HIPPED[2], 1.

1900 Hammond *Whaler* 204: The critter missed us by jest a scratch and that was all—he was mighty nigh to hippin' us that time.

2.a. Esp. *Black E.* to inform or alert; make aware; tell. Cf. HIPPED[3], 2.a.

1932 in *AS* (Feb. 1934) 26: *Hip* (or *hep?*) To give information. **1942** *Yank* (Dec. 23) 18: Hip us, Santa, just what ya got. **1944** Burley *Hndbk. Jive* 18: Uncle is hipping a whole lot of cats as to what to do. **1944** L. Armstrong, in Hodes & Hansen *Sel. from Gutter* 79: So I jus' tell him, hip this cat to what I want him to do. **1945** T. Anderson *Come Out Fighting* 25: We gotta...hip some of them unhepped cats on the other side. **1947** *Tomorrow* (Aug.) 27: Let me hip you to this. **1952** Mandel *Angry Strangers* 233: I hipped who I could 'n I oney hope the word got around. **1964** in B. Jackson *Swim Like Me* 97: Will you hip him, baby, to who I am? **1967** Heard *Howard St.* 161: Thanks for hippin' us, baby. **1968** in *Trans-action* VI (Feb. 1969) 27: The man's friends "hip" (inform) him to what's going on. **1974** Gober *Black Cop* 199: Don't pull your [gun] until I hip you, you dig? **1978** Selby *Requiem* 232: We were hipped to a dude thats holding some weight. **1967–80** Folb *Runnin' Lines* 97: Man, dat ain't too cool, lemme hip you to what's happ'nin'.

b. to render HIP, *adj.*, 2.b.

   1982 Goff, Sanders & Smith *Bros.* 29: A guy from the city....I figured he could really hip me. **1994** *Time* (Aug. 8) 48: The original Woodstock...a giant step toward the hipping of the world at large.

hip agent *n.* a bootlegger. *Joc.*

   1926 *Detective Fiction Wkly.* (Jan. 16) 640: I sashayed for a legger an' run into a rube hip agent with a bottle and some jake.

hip boots *n.pl.* ¶ In phrase: **have (one's) hip boots on** *Jazz.* to be HIP, *adj.*, 2.a.

   [**1938** (quot. at HIP, *adj.*, 2.a.).] **1939** Attaway *Breathe Thunder* 47: Aw, the guy was hep to us all the time....Yessir, he had his hip boots, all right. **1942** *Pittsburgh Courier* (Jan. 3) 7: My mother...[was] putting my hip boots on when she told me. **1953** *ATS* (ed. 2) 162: "Knowing"; "hep." (Manifesting knowledge of what is proper or fashionable.)...hep, hip,...with the hip boots on.

hipcat *n.* [prob. HIP + CAT, *n.*, 3.b. or var. of HEPCAT, but cf. 1972 quot. at HEPCAT] *Black E.* HEPCAT.

   [**1936–40** in McDonogh *Fla. Negro* 32 [ref. to Civil War]: We mostly used hippecat (ipecac) for medecine.] **1944** Burley *Hndbk. Jive* 64: I thought you were a solid hipcat. **1944** in C. Himes *Black on Black* 199: I'm a hipcat from way back. **1946** Mezzrow & Wolfe *Really Blues* 193: The hip cat plays the game with his tongue almost coming through his cheek. **1952** in Kerouac *Letters* 346: A Mexican hipcat named Enrique. *1959 in *OED2*: It was like getting a hip cat into a symphony concert. **1970** Major *Afro-Amer. Slang* 66: *Hippie*...a would-be hipcat.

hipp *n.* **1.** *Circus.* a hippopotamus.

   1895 Coup *Sawdust* 28: Of all fierce, ungovernable, lusty brutes, the hippopotamus with young is the very worst; and whenever we start off to get a baby "hip" we calculate to come back with one or more men missing. **1926** Norwood *Other Side of Circus* 65: A hipp's nostrils are a good deal the same as a camel's.

   2. (*cap.*) *Theat.* the Hippodrome (as the name of various theaters).

   1908 McGaffey *Show Girl* 166: He is kept busy looking after the animals at both the Hip. and the circus. **1916** in T. Lewis *H. Crane's Letters* 12: Last night I went to the Hipp. with Bill Wright. **1919** *Variety* (Mar. 28) 4: "Joy Bells" Opens at Hip. **1939** in Botkin *Sidewalks* 290: I happened to cruise by the Hipp once.

hipped[1] *adj.* [HIP[1], *n.* + *-ed*] **1.** affected with hypochondria or low spirits; dejected; bored. Orig. *colloq.* Also vars.

   *ca***1710** in *OED2*: Allmost half of them are Hypt (as they call it), that is, disordered in their brains. *1712 in *F & H* III 317: I cannot forbear writing to you, to tell you I have been to the last degree hipped since I saw you. *1784 in *OED2*: It was the common opinion among his friends that he was hyp'd. *1796 Grose *Vulgar Tongue* (ed. 3): He is hypped; he has got the blue devils, &c. **1806** in *U. Mo. Studies* XV (1940) 47: One whose spirets were very low and much hiped. **1816** Paulding *Letters from South* I 197: It...[is] a great piece of assurance in one man to tell another that he [is] *hipped*, as the phrase is. *1821 *Real Life in London* I 42: You are a merry fellow....We should have been hipped without you. **1833** H.W. Longfellow, in *OED*: What with his bad habits and his domestic grievances, he became completely hipped. **1841** in Bleser *Secret & Sacred* 58: I am badly hypped...and I feel like giving up. *1864–65 C. Dickens *Mutual Friend* 515: You are a little hipped, dear fellow....You have been too sedentary. Come and enjoy the pleasures of the chase. *1873 Hotten *Slang Dict.* (ed. 4): *Hipped*, bored, offended, crossed, low-spirited, &c. **1900** Willard & Hodler *Powers That Prey* 47: It's jus' a general case o' grouch. I get hipped ev'ry now an' then jus' as I used to.

   2. drunk. [The citations for this sense found in Weseen *Slang Dict.* and *ATS* are prob. borrowed from the *DN* quot. below and do not represent independent usage.]

   1926 *DN* V 387: *Hipped*...Drunk (same as tight). Common [in Maine].

hipped[2] *adj.* **1.** defeated; done for; in a finishing position; *on the hip*, 1, s.v. HIP[2].

   1904 *Life in Sing Sing* 249: *Hipped*.—At a disadvantage; stranded; indigent. **1924** in Tamony *Americanisms* (No. 17) 13: If the plans for committing a burglary are discovered by officers beforehand they refer to it as a "rumble" or "hipped." If informed on they call it

"tipped." **1935** D.W. Maurer, in *AS* (Feb.) 17 [ref. to *a*1910]: *Hipped*. 1. Caught napping; whipped. 2. To be covered with a gun.

   2. *Und.* carrying a gun on one's hip; armed; (in 1920 quot.) carrying whiskey in a hip flask.

   1920 *Variety* (Dec. 31) 8: But what about that drink thing? It was a great idea, but where were they gonna get it unless the college boy was hipped? He sure was—the real old stuff. **1942** *ATS* 81: Armed...*heeled, hipped*. **1946** M. Shulman *Amboy Dukes* 120: All you boys were hipped except you and Frank. What's the matter? Get scared after Mr. Bannon was knocked off?

hipped[3] *adj.* **1.** infatuated (with); enthusiastic, excited, or fanatic (about).—usu. constr. with *on*.

   1895 Wood *Yale Yarns* 262: It's because you are so hipped on a girl you think you see one behind every bush! **1910** *Everybody's Mag.* (May) 592: He...got a drag with our Old Man who was always hipped on helping along "ambition." **1925** Dreiser *Amer. Tragedy* 647: But I do know that he is still hipped over this second girl. **1935** McCoy *They Shoot Horses* 124: You're hipped on the subject of waves....That's all you've been talking about for a month. **1936** in Dos Passos *14th Chronicle* 491: He retorted that all these articles had been drawn from his book, too, so I think he may be a little bit hipped. **1943** J. Laughlin, in Witemeyer *Williams-Laughlin* 91: He is sort of hypped on various things, but a good boy. **1947** M. Hart *Gentleman's Agreement* (film): You're getting a little hipped on this series, too. **1947** Riskin *Magic Town* (film): She's hipped on changing the town. **1950** *Sat. Eve. Post* (Apr. 1) 75: He is...a little more hipped on the exhibitionistic charm routine. **1952** "Dr. Seuss" *5,000 Fingers* (film): My mother is really hipped on the piano. **1962** G. Olson *Roaring Road* 58: Hardin's hipped on injectors. Okay, it's his money. **1962** Shepard *Press Passes* 81: He was hipped on the subject of Cuban women's honor. **1963** Coon *Short End* 57: But he was hipped on this prejudice bit. **1970** G. Walker *Cruising* 98: Unlike some talkers, Dave wasn't really hipped on anything. It was all small talk, like leaving the radio on. **1972** Friday *Secret Garden* 267: Type B was very hipped on books and reading.

   2.a. aware (of); informed (about).—constr. with *on*.

   1920 F.S. Fitzgerald *Paradise* 238: Oh, just one person in fifty has any glimmer of what sex is. I'm hipped on Freud and all that, but it's rotten that every bit of *real* love in the world is ninety-nine per cent passion and one little soupçon of jealousy. **1927** in *DA*: "New York," as the manager of one of the largest hotels remarked lately, "is badly 'hipped' on dining in public."

   b. HIP, 1, 2; in phr. **hipped to the jive** [or **tip**] *hep to the jive* s.v. HEP, *adj.*

   1938 *AS* (Dec.) 314: *Hipped to the jive*. Well informed on the latest slang expressions. **1940** *Current Slang & Forum* (Nov. 7) 22: Convicts are *hipped to the jive* (know lies when they hear them)....You're *hipped to the tip*. **1944** Burley *Hndbk. Jive* 19: That zoot-suit action...wasn't hipped. *Ibid.* 32: They were hipped to the Jive, I swear. *Ibid.* 116: You'll get booted to what's hipped and what's unglamorous. **1946** Boulware *Jive & Slang* 4: *Hipped To...Wise. Hipped To The Jive*...Know the latest....*Hipped To The Tip*...Understand everything. **1947** *Esquire* (Apr.) 76: "Are there any squares in this outfit?" "No, man, we're all hipped." **1953** W. Fisher *Waiters* 9: Atta boy. He's hipped.

hip-peddler *n.* a prostitute, esp. a streetwalker.

   1908 W.G. Davenport *Butte & Montana* 269: The...herd of speckled spinsters, hip peddlers,...old hens,...rough necks, [etc.]. **1942** *ATS* 471: Prostitute...*hip peddler*.

hipper-dipper *n.* [of fanciful origin] *Football.* complicated, unconventional play on offense.

   1949 Cummings *Dict. Sports* 208: *Hipper-dipper. Slang. Football.* Fancy and complicated offensive maneuvers.

hippie or **hippy** *n.* **1.** *Jazz.* a person who is or attempts to be HIP.—often used derisively.

   1952 Mandel *Angry Strangers* 379: Every junky and hippie came to sit around her table. **1957** *N.Y. Times Mag.* (Aug. 18) 26: *Hippy*— Generic for a character who is super-cool, over-blasé, so far out that he appears to be asleep when he's digging something the most. **1958** in R. Russell *Perm. Playboy* 358: Upper Bohemia, tired of Van Gogh, Italian movies, charades, and sex, and so ready to try anti-art, anti-sex, anti-frantic non-movement. These latter comprise the Madison Avenue hippies...[and] a host of Ivy League symbol-manipulators. **1959** *Swinging Syllables: Hippy*—One who feels he is hip when in reality way in (square). **1959–60** R. Reisner *Jazz Titans* 158: *Hippie:* a young person who is trying to put on hip airs, but doesn't quite make it. **1961** Wolfe *Magic of Their Singing* 125: For example, the hippies in this circle peppered all their choppy, laconic sentences with the word "like," as though they lived in a world not of events but of similitudes. **1963** in Bruce *Essential Bruce* 150: Fifteen thousand Nalline testing stations, loop-o meters, and they got four dopey junkies left, old-time 1945 hippies. **1963** in Clarke *Amer. Negro Stories* 309: The hippies ran for girls. **1964** Gold *Jazz Lexicon* 147: *Hippie.* A would-be hipster— one who affects awareness, sophistication, wisdom, but is deficient in these qualities.…current since c. 1945. **1965** in W. King *Black Anthol.* 304: The Rocks have hippies such as Sweet Mac. **1965** Hentoff *Jazz Country* 93: If it is true, like some of the hippies say, that Fred has been trying to be white all his life…that's because of me. *Ibid.* 110: Even those hippie disc jockeys on FM are afraid to play my record. **1966** I. Reed *Pall-Bearers* 23: He's a real hippy. Reads *Evergreen Review* and eats cheese blintzes at *Max's Kansas City*, a place where all the artists hang out downtown. **1966** Manus *Mott the Hoople* 63: Leroy went off, diddledybopping along like the Harlem hippie he was. **1966** *Sat. Eve. Post* (July 2) 22: In my son's eyes, rock is my kind of music; he probably tells the other kids that Daddy is a hippy, and he will probably grow up thinking of rock as a curious relic of olden days. **1967** Baraka *Tales* 9: Where are you now, hippy, under this abstract shit?

2. a usu. young, longhaired person who dresses unconventionally, holds various antiestablishment attitudes and beliefs, and typically advocates communal living, pacifist or radical politics, and the use of hallucinogenic drugs.—usu. used disparagingly. Now *S.E.*, chiefly *hist.* Also as adj. [This nuance seems to have arisen through media coverage of the teenage drug scene in New York and San Francisco during late 1966.]

1966 Young & Hixson *LSD* 8: The poundage of LSD swallowed by college "hippies" is…a minuscule amount. *Ibid.* 63: Harvard "druggies"—that label being preferred in Cambridge to the Western term "hippies." **1966** Goldstein *1 in 7* 73: Ah, the Harvard hippie. I knew him well. Ready to prove that Kennedy and Dostoevsky and Holden Caulfield have not lived in vain. He defies his parents by sleeping with his girl friend, his neighbors by letting his hair grow, and his university by smoking pot. *Ibid.* 121: The real hippies—I mean the ones that matter under the purple sun-glasses—go in for stronger stuff. **1967** Tamony *Americanisms* (Mar.) (No. 17) 15: After late December, 1966, news stories and column comment on the San Francisco *hippies* appear daily in the *San Francisco Chronicle* and almost daily in the *San Francisco Examiner.* **1967** J. Flaherty, in *Village Voice* (N.Y.C.) (May 18): Hippies are not un-American. **1967** in J. Flaherty *Chez Joey* 7: If your hair was slightly too long, your chin foliated, your dress too hippy,…you were best off south of…Sixty-second Street. **1967** Brelis *Face of S. Vietnam* 100: "The music is good. Real American. Hippy." "What's hippy?" "The latest. Modern." **1983** Leeson *Survivors* (film): Take that little hippie girl with you. **1986** Stinson & Carabatsos *Heartbreak* 31: Man, there ain't been any hippies around for centuries. **1987** WINS radio news (June 20): Summer begins tomorrow and a group of British hippies plan to celebrate it at Stonehenge. **1989** *Daily Beacon* (Univ. Tenn.) (July 11) 4: If some hippy is gonna burn the flag in front of me, I'll kill the…. **1989** *Murphy Brown* (CBS-TV): You talkin' about the wimpy guy in the hippie outfit? **1993** *News-Sentinel* (Knoxville, Tenn.) (July 20) B1: You have to wonder how many hippies travel with nail polish.

hippodrome *n. Sports.* a horse race or other sporting contest whose outcome has been prearranged; (*broadly*) a fraud.

1866 in *DA*: As for the general belief that no one but Alexander could mount him, that's a hippodrome, or a stall, as Mike Walsh used to say. **1880** *N.Y. Clipper Almanac for 1881* 44: *Hippodrome*—A race that aims for gate money only, while professing to be for a stake, purse, or prize. **1887** in *DAE*: No one calls the affair a hippodrome. The fight was to be for points.…A number in the audience pronounced the affair a hippodrome. **1889** *Century Dict.*: *Hippodrome*…In *sporting slang,* a race or other athletic contest in which it is arranged beforehand that a certain contestant shall win. **1915** in *DA*: They…turned the game into a hippodrome before the inning was over.

hippodrome *v. Sports.* to prearrange the outcome of a horse race or other sporting event; put on a mere show of fair competition.—usu. as vbl.n. **hippodroming.**

*a*1867 in *OEDS*: An arrangement was entered into by means of which the former and Lancet travelled together, to trot for purses and

divide the profits. It was a new sort of thing, and was…called "Hippodroming." **1868** in *DAE*: [A mare] was hippodromed with a good deal.…"Hippodroming" has come more and more into fashion. **1875** *Chi. Tribune* (Oct. 15) 1: The ninth game between the Chicagos and the Philadelphians…was a disgraceful, hippodroming affair. **1886** in *Century Dict.*: There never has yet been the slur of hippodroming cast upon any college contest. **1896** in *DA*: The Boston club defeated the Clevelands in the next four games, thereby utterly depriving the enemies of the professional class of any chance to cry "hippodroming." **1923** *Nashville Banner* (Jan. 3) 6: [The boxing referee] must be able to detect hippodroming or faking.…A set of "hippodromers" goes out. **1948** in *DA*: Cynics argue there is a great deal of hippodroming [in ice hockey].

hippy-dippy *n.* HIPPIE, 2.—used derisively. Also as adj.

1978–86 J.L. Burke *Lost Get-Back Boogie* 62: We'll watch the hippy-dippy from Mississippi here do his Ernest Tubb act. **1988** M. Maloney *Thunder Alley* 54: You were picked up by some hippy-dippy people— Manson Family people. **1987–89** M.H. Kingston *Tripmaster Monkey* 45: I look like a…hippy-dippy.

hips *n. Black E.* HIPSTER, 1.

1964 R. Kendall *Black School* 216: It scares the life outta her, that crazy mixed up hips.

hip spoon *n.* a shovel. *Joc.*

1947 Carter *Devils in Baggy Pants* 59: The shovel! that hip-spoon! It'll have to do!

hipster *n.* **1.** a person who is or attempts to be HIP, esp. a fan of swing or bebop music; (*often*) BEATNIK.

1940 *Current History & Forum* (Nov. 7) 22: A *hipster* never teaches a *square* anything (a wise guy never helps out the inexperienced inmate). **1942** *Pittsburgh Courier* (May 9) 7: This is the way two Hipsters meet. **1942** *Yank* (Sept. 23) 14: A Harlem hipster. **1944** Burley *Hndbk. Jive* 101: I'm a hustler, a rustler, the solid hipster they all boost. **1945** in Tamony *Americanisms* (No. 17) 14: Harry "the Hipster" Gibson…in Hollywood. **1949** in Kerouac *Letters* 197: A…Hipster smoking a weed. **1952** *Life* (Sept. 29) 67: *Hipster:* modern version of hepcat. **1952** J.C. Holmes *Go* 7: She kept yelling across the room to some hipster. **1956** Ginsberg *Howl* 9: Angelheaded hipsters burning for the ancient heavenly connection/to the starry dynamo in the machinery of night. **1960** R. Reisner *Jazz Titans* 158: *Hipster:* one who is aware, as opposed to one who is square. **1970** in H.S. Thompson *Shark Hunt* 181: A local businessman and ex-hipster named Craig. **1972** Kopp *Buddha* 198: I was a Hipster…in the Forties. **1979** Gram *Blvd. Nights* 29: He took on a slight hipster swagger. **1989** *TV Guide* (Nov. 11) 17: But will Middle America dig a 5-foot-tall hipster pixie…who's never done comedy?

2. usu. *pl.* a hip boot.

1981 *WKRP in Cincinnati* (CBS-TV): The only way to break in these hipsters is to wear 'em.

Hiram *n.* [considered to be a typical rustic name; cf. ALVIN, ELMER, HICK, RUBE] an uncouth country fellow; male yokel.

1930 Irwin *Tramp & Und. Sl.: Hiram.*—The districts populated by farmers or, traditionally, "Hirams." **1932** W. Faulkner, in *DARE*: You better go back to the farm, Hiram. **1942** *ATS* 365: Rustic; Bumpkin…*Hiram.*

hi-res *adj.* [fr. *high resolution* (used to describe image quality on a video monitor)] fine; well. Also vars.

1938–85 McCrum, Cran & MacNeil *Story of English* 37: She's *high res.* (She's on the ball.) **1986** Eble *Campus Slang* (Nov.) 5: *Hi rez*…feeling good: "I'm ready for that test. Strictly *Hi rez* today." *a*1989 Spears *NTC Dict.* 180: This is a real high-res day for me. **1996** Idaho woman, age *ca*21 (coll. J. Sheidlower): *Hi-res* means "cool." There's a bunch of computer terms used as slang now.

hi si *n.* high society.

1957 M. Shulman *Rally* 173: She's real hi-si, see, and if word ever got out about this, she'd be ruined with the Four Hundred.

Hisso *n. Av.* a motor manufactured by the Hispano-Suiza Corporation; (*hence*) a plane with such a motor. Now *hist.*

1926 *Writer's Mo.* (Nov.) 395: *Hisso*—A training plane equipped with a Hispano-Suiza motor. **1929** Springs *Carol Banks* 182 [ref. to 1918]: Try starting with a Hisso motor on a cold morning. **1940** Hartney *Up & At 'Em* 283 [ref. to 1918]: Some thirty feet behind me, he was already in his machine with his "Hisso" taking over. **1955** in

Loosbrock & Skinner *Wild Blue* 32: Wing wires and…Mercedes and Hisso engines. **1970** Lincke *No Lady* 40: A few variations mounted the horrendous Hispano-Suiza, nicknamed the "Hisso," which was crammed with 100, 150, 200, or 300 hp.

history *n.* ¶ In phrase: **be history** [infl. by S.E. *[ancient]* history 'that which should be forgotten or left to the past', e.g.: "After twelve hours…[a printed newspaper] is ancient history [to journalists]" (M. Philips, *Making of a Newspaper* (1893), p. 6)]

1. to be completed; (*hence*) to be doomed or dead; be no longer present, active, relevant, etc.

 1978 T. Sanchez *Zoot-Suit* 220: Five more strikes and this game is history. **1980** J.S. Young *Rumor of War* (film): Forget me! I'm history! **1983** *Night Court* (NBC-TV): One pull of the trigger and I'm history! **1982–84** (quot. at (2), below). **1984** *Miami Vice* (NBC-TV): One move and you're history, buster! **1987** Lipper *Wall St.* 155: I guarantee you this place is history tomorrow. **1987** *21 Jump Street* (Fox-TV): No fast moves or you're history! **1987** *Sable* (ABC-TV): If I go out that door, I'm history. **1988** *Supercarrier* (ABC-TV): "I got a [radar] lock." "He's history!" **1990** *New Yorker* (Aug. 13) 28: Now that "Nausea: The Picture" is history, I have to say that it's hard to believe it ever happened. **1991** *N.Y. Times* (Nov. 15) A31: Anyone naïve enough to think that racism was history in this country. **1992** *Time* (Mar. 16) 29: In another year, against a stronger field, Tsongas may already be history.

2. to be leaving.—used in farewell, constr. with *I* or *we*.

 1980 L. Birnbach, ed. *Preppy Hndbk.* 223: Exit Lines…"Let's cruise."…"Let's bolt."…"We're history." "We're out of here." **1982–84** in Safire *Take My Word* 113: Here's a farewell I picked up…in L.A. which is gaining wide usage in Adspeak circles: "I'm history." It's also an effective meeting-ender as in "Are we history? Terrific." **1984** Algeo *Stud Buds* 4: To leave a place, go away…*we're history, I'm history*. **1984** in "J.B. Briggs" *Drive-In* 224: I'm out of here. I'm history. **1986** *T.J. Hooker* (ABC-TV): You wanna stick around here and play kid's games…that's fine. But I'm history.

hit *n.* **1.** an instance, attempt, or time.

 1807 *Port Folio* (Aug. 8) 125: To nimming Ned I went to bed,/Who look'd but queer and glumly,/Yet every hit, he brought the bit,/And then we spent it rumly. **1971 H.S. Thompson *Las Vegas* 139: That circuit of second-rate academic hustlers who get paid anywhere from $500 to $1000 a hit for lecturing to cop-crowds. **1979** Gram *Blvd. Nights* 136: C'mon, man. We'll take a hit. She looks interested.

2.a. Orig. *Theat.* a performance, performer, play, song, etc., that is a great success; (*broadly*) something or someone that is a great popular success. Now *S.E.*

 1811 C. Mathews, in *OEDS*: Maw-worm [a character in a play] was a most unusual hit, I am told. **1811 in Mathews & Yates *Life of C. Mathews* 157: "Bartlemy Fair" was as great a hit as the other.…No farce ever went off so well on a first night in Dublin. **1820–21 P. Egan *Life in London* 8: Admired hero of the stage, teach me to make a *hit* of so *Kean* a quality that it may…be long remembered in the metropolis. **1829 in *OED2*: Mr. Peel seems to have made a hit in the chief character of Shiel's play. **1844 in Barnum *Letters* 30: It will be the biggest hit in the universe, see if it ain't! **1867** in Sampson *Ghost Walks* 6: Her character song is one of the greatest "hits" ever made. *ca*1899 in Sampson *Ghost Walks* 192: Flo Irwin's Latest "Hit,"…Words and Music by Walter Hawley. **1903** Ade *Society* 131: The Automobile was a Hit until some of the New Machines began to pass me. **1908** in *OEDS*: Orchestra selections…"Broadway Hits." **1917** in *DAS*: "Hit" is still regarded by conservative lexicographers as a bit of theatrical slang. **1927** *AS* III 21: In theatrical parlance a play is never a success or a failure, it is either a "hit" or a "flop." **1927** W. Winchell, in *Bookman* (Dec.) 381: If the song is usable, the writer is persuaded to permit the firm to pattern it along the lines of a "hit." **1932** *AS* VII 252: The motto of the song-writers is…"A hit is not an aesthetic triumph, it is something that sells."

b. a wonderfully favorable impression; usu. in phr. **make a hit.** Now *colloq.*

 1835 C. Dickens, in *OEDS*: The insertion of another Prison Paper would decidedly detract from the "hit" of the first. **a1845 T. Hood, in *F & H* III 318: Nor yet did the heiress herself omit/The arts that help to make a hit. **1861 "Citizen" *Southern Chivalry* 5: Muses…/…tune my banjo while I sit/And strike, that I may make a hit. **1862** C.F. Browne *A. Ward* 44: Bill Shakspeer had made a great

hit with old Bob Ridley. **1882** in Bunner *Letters* 73: Really, it…has made a hit. **1897** F.P. Dunne, in Schaaf *Dooley* 147: They made a big hit in New York. **1900** Johnston *Hus'ling* 333: Well, Doctor, you made a big hit. **1905** in Opper *H. Hooligan* 59: We're making a big hit in London. **1925** Dos Passos *Manhattan Transfer* 154: I'll tell yer Jim it's Irene Castle that makes the hit wid me.…To see her dance the onestep juss makes me hear angels hummin'.

3. *Gamb.* a winning number or series of numbers in a lottery or in numbers gambling; (*also*) an instance of winning. [Orig. jargon; cf. *OED* def. 3a.]

 1818 in Partridge *Dict. Und.* 334: Hit…a winning number in a lottery. **1847** in *DA*: Some of my heaviest players are getting discouraged.…It would be a good idea…[to] let them get a hit, in order to keep their custom. **1865** *Rogues & Rogueries* 10: He may come in for a second, tenth, or twentieth "hit." **1875** *Chi. Tribune* (Nov. 21) 13: Players win but rarely, and they seldom make a "hit" large enough to pay back to them the money they invested in tempting fortune. **1943** Whyte *Street Corner Soc.* 115: Unable to pay off on large "hits" (winnings). **1954–60** *DAS*.

4.a. the sudden euphoric or stimulant effect of taking a drug; RUSH; KICK.

 1913 J. London *J. Barleycorn* 249: I had to get the kick and the hit of the stuff [alcohol]. **1960** C.L. Cooper *Scene* 84: Getting the first hit of the narcotics, feeling her belly warm over. **1969** Geller & Boas *Drug Beat* xix: Hit: the drug's effect on the consciousness, sometimes called a "buzz." To get a *hit* is to experience a concrete pleasurable sensation as a result of using the drug. **1988** *thirtysomething* (ABC-TV): Let me get you some coffee. I haven't had a caffeine hit in fifteen minutes. **1989** Strieber *Majestic* 162: I recall cigarettes that could really give you a hit.

b. *Narc.* a dose of a narcotic or psychotropic drug; (*hence*) a tablet or capsule containing such a drug; crack crystal.

 1952 Ellson *Golden Spike* 159: Do you think you can get a hit? **1963** Braly *Shake Him* 17: You want a hit?…Good stuff. Schmeck. **1967** Kolb *Getting Straight* 112: I laid the hit [of LSD] on him myself. **1970** Landy *Underground Dict.* 104: Hit…*n.*…Injection of a narcotic. **1972** Grogan *Ringolevio* 268: All the street people were handed five hits of LSD apiece. **1972** R. Barrett *Lovomaniacs* 178: I didn't know you were going to let the poor sad cat drop a whole eight-way hit. **1976** Arble *Long Tunnel* 173: Here's two hits of orange mescaline. **1974–77** A. Hoffman *Property of* 97: I'm carrying my last hit. **1976–77** Kernochan *Dry Hustle* 33: He thrust the mirror and a cocktail straw under my nose. "Have a hit, dear." **1989** *Daily Beacon* (Univ. Tenn.) (Nov. 22) 3: With $10 you can buy a hit of crack cocaine. **1991** *CBS This Morning* (July 25) (CBS-TV): You can get about a thousand hits of acid on the head of a pin. **1994** *My So-Called Life* (ABC-TV): I know she took Ecstasy. Two hits. **1995** *Donahue* (NBC-TV): Five hits would last some people…about a [*sic*] hour.

c. Orig. *Narc.* a draw on a marijuana cigarette; TOKE; (*hence*) a draw on a tobacco cigarette.

 1952 Mandel *Angry Strangers* 241: Take harder hits on it; don't sip it like you're scared. *Ibid.*: Give me a couple hits, Dinch. **1962** H. Simmons *On Eggshells* 175: He took a couple of more long hits. **1967** Wolf *Love Generation* 241: If somebody hands you a joint and you don't take a hit off of it, it's like sticking out your hand and not having someone shake it. **1970** *Playboy* (Dec.) 287: I took another long, luxurious hit. **1971** *Essence* (Sept.) 23, 74: Inhalation from a "joint" or "square": *Hit*. **1985** Flowers *Mojo Blues* 67: Tucept took a long hit on the joint. **1985** J. Schumacher & C. Kurlander *St. Elmo's Fire* (film): Like stopping smoking. I go as long as I can and I just gotta have a hit.

d. a drink, swallow, or sip; SWIG.

 *ca*1970 in D. Rose *Black Street Life* 207: Give me a hit [from a wine bottle]. **1973** *Oui* (May) 88: I took nine hits.…It's the most I've ever done off tequila. **1976** Univ. Tenn. student: Gimme a hit off that Schlitz. **1977** Univ. Tenn. student: Give me a hit off that [can of Coca-Cola]. **1979** G. Wolff *Duke of Deception* 170: Boys who liked to sneak a coffin nail or a hit off a bottle of Four Roses. **1981** Hathaway *World of Hurt* 145: Have a hit of Scotch? **1982** Rucker *57th Kafka* 243: He took a hit of tequila, a pull of beer, and lit one of the reefers. **1983** Univ. Tenn. student: Let me have another hit off that wineskin. **1987** *ALF* (NBC-TV): Drilling holes so I can put straws in these coconuts. Want a hit?

e. *Narc.* (see quot.).

1971 *N.Y. Times* (May 17) 12: G.I.'s sit smoking the mixed tobacco-and-heroin cigarettes called "hits."

5. *Narc.* a successful purchase of a narcotic drug; SCORE.

1936 D.W. Maurer, in *AS* (Apr.) 122: *Hit*....used when delivering dope to an addict....it signifies in general that the sale is consummated. **1951** in *OED2*: They are anxious to make a "connection," "score," or "hit." **1953** Anslinger & Tompkins *Traf. in Narc.* 310: *Hit.* A meeting with a drug peddler.

6. *Pris.* a sentence of imprisonment; (*also*) a denial of parole.

1949 Monteleone *Crim. Slang* 118: *Hit*...A prison term. **1966–67** P. Thomas *Mean Streets* 264: I think I got a hit, maybe a year. *Ibid.* 289: Pops Hills...came in jail in 1927 to serve out a five-year hit.

7.a. Orig. *Und.* an underworld killing; RUBOUT; (*hence*) an order for such a killing.

1950 Rackin *Enforcer* (film): It was a hit. I had the contract. **1960** Roeburt *Mobster* 74: The next time we go, *I* make the hit. **1962** Perry *Young Man Drowning* 205: They are trying to recall all the details of the hit to see if there were any slip-ups anywhere. **1966** S. Stevens *Go Down Dead* 26: He is the executioner for the Playboys. The one what makes the hit. **1967** *Star Trek* (NBC-TV): I'll give you just eight hours...or I'll put the hit on your friends. **1967–68** von Hoffman *Parents Warned Us* 73: There's a bunch of us going...to make a hit on Useless. **1975–76** T. McNally *Ritz* 75: Frankie...is gonna put a hit out on you. **1979** Kilian, Fletcher & Ciccone *Who Runs Chicago?* 67: Gangland murders are done by pros....And that's why we have problems solving hits. **1985** WINS radio news (Dec. 16): The hit could be the beginning of a crime war for control of the underworld. **1987** Levinson & Link *Terrorist* (film): He put out a hit and five people got killed. **1988** *McCall's* (May) 88: Little is known about the case except that it looked like a "hit." **1989** Courtwright et al. *Addicts Who Survived* 92: Louis "Lepke" Buchalter...coined the word "hit" as a euphemism for contract murder. **1992** *TV Guide* (Knoxville, Tenn., ed.) (Aug. 29) 91: A nightclub owner is suspected of buying a hit on a rival. **1995** *Leeza* (synd. TV series): It wasn't a carjacking, it was a hit.

b. *Und.* the intended victim of a killing or an assault.

1950 Rackin *Enforcer* (film): A murder is a contract. The hit is the sucker that gets killed. **1966** Braly *On the Yard* 212: The hit moved in a limited pattern. **1970–71** Rubinstein *City Police* 359: Frequently [muggers] carry no weapon, wandering about for a hit—a woman, a drunken man, anyone they think can be overpowered. **1972** Sapir & Murphy *Death Therapy* 98: "I don't hate my patients." "I rarely hate my hits." "How many people have you killed, Mr. Donaldson?"

c. *Police.* an arrest or police raid.

1966 Young & Hixson *LSD* 13: Police have accomplished little more in the long run than to drive the price of LSD temporarily higher in the area where a "hit" is made. **1970** Horman & Fox *Drug Awareness* 467: *Hit*...an arrest.

d. *Und.* a raid carried out against a rival gang. [In 1882 quot., S.E. for 'an attack'.]

[**1882** in Thrapp *Crook & Sierra Madre* 84: I need not repeat the General's anxiety that your troops shall make a hit [upon the Apaches].] **1967** *Star Trek* (NBC-TV): What's the matter? You guys never saw a hit before? **1972** *N.Y. Post* (June 26) 26: Then the rival clique retaliates with a "hit," a swift foray into enemy territory to collect some denim trophies of its own. **1972** *N.Y. Post* (June 27) 39: A "hit," explained city youth worker Dino Rodriguez, "means that you grab a member of the other gang, beat him up and take away his clothes." **1995** *N.Y. Times* (Mar. 1) B4: A rival gang began selling [crack] on Wild Cowboy turf. "What definitive action did you take?"..."I put a hit on them," Mr. Sepulveda said, referring to the Dec. 16, 1991 killing of one rival gang member.

e. *Und. & Police.* a theft or violent crime.

1962–68 B. Jackson *In the Life* 55: We'd just made a hit that afternoon and we had about $10,000 in this drawer in the bedroom. **1970** Rudensky & Riley *Gonif* 95: The big hit was developing. **1973–74** in *Urban Life* VI (1977) 147: Mugging "making a hit," "scoring," "getting down," "robbing," [etc.]. **1975** Sepe & Telano *Cop Team* 114: All the other hits [rapes] were in Linden. **1983** Helprin *Winter's Tale* 601: He had been pulled in without a charge, just before a hit at Delmonico's. **1987** Tine *Beverly Hills Cop II* 186: The robberies, the hit at Adriano's....Dent doesn't need the money. **1994** *Eyewitness News* (WABC-

TV) (Apr. 25): The so-called Silver Gun Carjacker...has terrorized Queens recently with eight hits.

8. *Blackjack.* the act of dealing an additional card to a player.

1981 D.E. Miller *Jargon* 298: I'll take another hit. **1982** (cited in Clark *Gambling & Gaming*).

9. *Tennis.* (see quot.).

1975 Lichtenstein *Long Way* 37: "It's just like they're going out to have a good hit."..."Having a hit" meant either practicing, or having a fun game with someone.

10.a. *Mil.* a wound or injury.

1863 in *E. Tenn. Hist. Soc. Pub.* XLV (1973) 108: Capt. Harris was wounded—he "staid in" till he got a severe hit. **1987** E. Spencer *Macho Man* 19: He showed me his hit....The scar went from his gut to his neck.

b. blame, reversal, or setback; a blow; in phr. **catch a hit** *Mil.* to be rebuked.

1987 *N.Y. Times* (July 10) A1: He was willing to take the hit. He was ready to be dropped like a hot rock. **1987** D. da Cruz *Boot* 297: *Catch a hit* get dressed down, chewed out, told off. **1987** *Big Story* (CNN-TV) (Oct. 4): The sports market on TV is going to take a real hit on this. **1987** Lipper *Wall St.* 30: I don't have the bread, Dad; especially after today's hit. **1988** *Daily News* (N.Y.C.) (June 23) 4: "My people are not going to take the hit for us," said Queens Borough President Claire Shulman. **1989** *Donahue* (NBC-TV): You have taken as much of a media hit as anybody.

hit *v.* **1.a.** to use or consume (usu. drugs or alcohol); indulge in, usu. excessively.—usu. constr. with *the*. See also *hit the pipe*, below.

1841 in *AS* XXVI (1951) 183: John set the decanter and after seeing us hit it to our satisfaction went to show us [etc.]. **1889** in *DA*: His own appetite for hitting the booze. **1894** *Harper's* (Oct.) 700: Yank's been hitting the bottle till he was crazy. **1897** *Harper's Wkly.* (Jan.) 90: Men who drink too much and too frequently are said to suffer from "hitting the bottle." At first it was said of the opium-smokers that they "hit" the pipe—as all pipe-smokers do, to cleanse the instrument—so that hitting anything has come to signify an abuse of the habit with which the article thus "hit" is intimately connected. **1899** Kountz *Baxter's Letters* 52: After I had hit three [drinks], I could see waving green fields and fruit-laden orchards. **1902** Hapgood *Thief* 108: Perhaps if I had never hit the hop I would not have engaged in the dangerous occupation of a burglar. **1904** W.N. Harben *Georgians* 88: I hit the booze. **1914** Ellis *Billy Sunday* 207: If there is a father that hits the booze, he doesn't want his son to. **1925** W. James *Drifting Cowboy* 87: It was high time we hit our soogans. **1930** Shaw *Jack-Roller* 161 [ref. to *ca*1920's]: He repaid me by telling me of his experiences in life, and how he started to "hit M" (morphine). **1939** in *AS* (1942) XVII 206: Bill is hitting cigarets some. **1946** Mezzrow & Wolfe *Really Blues* 306: *Hit the jug*: drink heavily, often from the bottle; have a drink. **1942–49** Goldin et al. *DAUL* 97: *Hit the needle.* To take a hypodermic injection of drugs; to be addicted to drug injections. **1952** H. Grey *Hoods* 277: He's hitting the needle again. **1969** L.L. Foreman *Last Stand Mesa* 36: He...was hitting the jug. **1965–71** in *Qly. Jour. Studies on Alc.* XXXII (1971) 733: *Hitting the wine* Drinking wine. **1973** J.R. Coleman *Blue-Collar* 35: Gus saw me try to lift one of the lengths [of sewer pipe] and fail...."Better hit the Wheaties, John." **1980** Santoli *Everything* 207: When I hit Dexedrine I'd just turn into a pair of eyeballs and ears. **1994** *Simpsons* (Fox-TV): She hit the bottle pretty hard and lost her job.

b. to arrive in or at, reach, esp. suddenly, energetically, or for a brief stay; (*also*) (constr. with *the*) to take to or resort to (a place or location), go to (as one's bed); (*hence*) to be mentioned prominently in or on. Now *colloq.* Cf. *OED* def. 11.

1887 (quot. at *hit the flat*, below). **1888** in Farmer *Amer.*: Professor Rose, who hit this town last spring, is around calling us a fugitive from justice. **1896** Ade *Artie* 74: A little more weather like this and we'll be hittin' the park. **1906** Tomlin *H. Tomlin* 197: As soon as he "hit the bed" that night I began. *ca*1910 in T. McCoy *Remembers* 36: I'd like to hit the bunk and sleep the clock around. **1910** in *DA*: He hit the desk at ten o'clock [to start work]. **1922** Hisey *Sea Grist* 201: I hit the bunk shortly after. **1924** Marks *Plastic Age* 289: I think that's why she's been hitting the high spots. **1927** in Hammett *Knockover* 306: When we hit the street, we split. **1932** Harvey *Me and Bad Eye* 151: Everybody has bowel trouble and we have to hit the latrine about every half an hour.

1932 V. Nelson *Prison Days & Nights* 23: And we're the poor slobs that hit the big house—you and me are the suckers....Steal a million and you'll never hit the can. **1932–34** Minehan *Boy & Girl Tramps* 59: You can always return and hit the missions for a meal. **1934** Weseen *Dict. Slang* 257: *Hit the headlines*...to gain notoriety. **1935** Pollock *Und. Speaks: Hit the pavement*, out of jail. **1936** Mackenzie *Living Rough* 240: Hit the farmhouses in daytime for a big feed. **1941** Kendall *Army & Navy Sl.* 20: *Hit the pavement*....go ashore. **1945** in Bradbury *Golden Apples* 82: Play ball or hit the showers! **1946** Mora *Trail Dust* 38: Cowboys hitting town after the long drives. **1946** *Amer. Mercury* (Apr.) 467: Boose had barely hit town and had not yet had time to set up his flag and his soapbox. **1950** L. Brown *Iron City* 106: I only got five more months to pull [in prison] before I hit the street. **1953** Dodson *Away All Boats* 308: I'm going to hit the cot for an hour or so. **1953** W. Brown *Monkey on My Back* 52: Is Hector going to hit the papers? **1955** Q. Reynolds *HQ* 236: If he were a pickpocket, he reflected, he'd hit the Canarsie pier. **1956** in *DAS*: We'll be in Russia 20 days,...hitting Leningrad, Odessa, Kiev. *a*1961 R.H. Dillon *Shanghaiing Days* 193: Sailors just paid off would hit the hurdy-gurdy houses. **1970** N.Y.U. student: Time to hit the library. **1973** N.Y.U. student: Instead of saying somebody died, I like to say they "hit the obits." **1973** N.Y.U. student [ref. to 1961]: In the Army in Berlin, when we were going on a pass or something, we'd say, "When do we hit the Strasse?" or "Let's hit the Strasse." **1975** V.B. Miller *Trade-Off* 13: We draw our communications gear and hit the street. **1975** Wambaugh *Choirboys* 348: She'll be damn glad not to be hitting the slammer so she won't be asking any questions of me. **1978** Truscott *Dress Gray* 40: He was getting ready to hit the computer center down in the basement of Thayer Hall. **1980** Univ. Tenn. instructor: Do that and you'll hit the front page in no time. **1982** Flexner *Listening to America* 518: The workers...have to *hit the asphalt*, 1909,...to look for another job. **1989** *Daily Beacon* (Univ. Tenn.) (Aug. 4) 4: As soon as I hit Hollywood, I felt like an investigative reality. **1992** S. Straight *Been in Sorrow's Kitchen* 278: Let's hit the flicks.

c. to go at vigorously; in phrs. **hit the books** to spend time in study; **hit a brace** *Mil.* to come rigidly to attention.

1924 P. Marks *Plastic Age* 238: If I don't hit that eccy, I'm going to be out of luck. **1926** in *AS* II (1927) 276: *Hit the books*...study. **1944** E.H. Hunt *Limit* 157: But in the winter you hit the books. **1958** Johnson & Caidin *Thunderbolt* 39 [ref. to WWII]: Hit a brace, Mister! **1958** J. Davis *College Vocab.* 14: *Hit the books*—Study. **1977** Univ. Tenn. instructor: Time to hit those test papers. **1979** *L.A. Times* (Sept. 5) IA 1: Stretching bucks will be as important to school officials as hitting the books will be for students.

d. [prob. sugg. by colloq. or S.E. sense 'to carry out a military attack against'] to commit a crime against; break into, attack, rape, steal from, etc. Now *colloq.* Also *absol.*

1927 in Hammett *Big Knockover* 280: They hit the two banks at ten sharp. **1934** Appel *Brain Guy* 119: Why call on him just the day Metz got hit? **1955** Q. Reynolds *HQ* 317: The 14th Squad collared two men hitting a liquor store late last night. **1959** Horan *Mob's Man* 23: We decided to hit only Chinese laundries and Chinese-American restaurants. **1965** Linakis *In Spring* 30: We'd...hit every Yank plane on the field, taking chutes, val-packs, and everything that wasn't bolted down. **1966** J. Mills *Needle Park* 59: But last year, during winter, I was out working; hitting cabs. **1967** *Star Trek* (NBC-TV): "Krako hit us, boss."..."Then you hit him back, you hear?" **1974** Terkel *Working* 147: I was called one weekend on a restaurant job. They felt it was being hit. **1975** Sepe & Telano *Cop Team* 156: That rapist. He's just hit another one. **1980–86** in Steffensmeier *Fence* 15: Some of the burglars I dealt with were hitting something fierce,...four and five times a week. *a*1989 in Kisseloff *Must Remember This* 159: We used to steal the coal. We'd hit all the private brownstones. **1990** Bing *Do or Die* 26: They hit an army base for some guns and stuff.

e. *Police.* to raid (an illegal establishment); (*hence*) to visit (a place or a person) for the purpose of investigation.

1955 Q. Reynolds *HQ* 227: Wait until they come out and then grab them, and we'll hit the place. **1977** P. Wood *Salt Bk.* 151: Whenever we hit a place, I always seemed to be the guy that was first. **1988** Dietl & Gross *One Tough Cop* 68: They hit three such locations, then came back to the stationhouse to see if anyone had had better luck.

2. to ask (someone) (for something, esp. money or the like); beg from; make a request of; ask; accost.—also constr. with *up*.

1894 *Century* (Feb.) 518: You can't hit a bloke for a dime in the streets without a bull seein' ye and chuckin' ye up for fifty-nine days in Utica jail. **1896** *DN* I 418: Can I hit you for a V? **1899** Cullen *Tales* 19: I...hit up some people there for a job. **1907** London *Road* 28 [ref. to 1894]: A freezing fog was drifting past, and I "hit" some firemen I found in the round-house. They fixed me up with the leavings from their lunch-pails. *Ibid.* 137: Hitting for a "light piece" on the street. **1919** in Wallgren *AEF* (unp.): You want to get up courage...to hit the boss for a loan. **1922** S. Lewis *Babbitt* 79: How to lay a proposition before the Boss, how to hit a bank for a loan. **1928** Bodenheim *Georgie May* 77: You got to hit *me* up, sistah, ah'm sitting purty now. **1928** Santee *Cowboy* 26: I figgered that now was as good as any to hit him for a job. **1935** E. Anderson *Hungry Men* 59: I hit those Mexicans up, and I couldn't even rate a cigarette. **1937** *Esquire* (Feb.) 80: I do not say that city dwellers cannot be "hit" with success. **1962–63** in Giallombardo *Soc. of Women* 204: *Hit*: To make a proposal of homosexual marriage. **1964** Redfield *Let. from Actor* 229: The same beggar who hit you twice will hit you again. **1965** Spillane *Killer Mine* 78: Reese was going to hit me up for a bundle. **1968** Gover *JC* 17: Gonna have t'hit somebody jes t'eat. **1993** K. Scott *Monster* 10: "Hittin' people up" means asking...which gang they are down with.

3. *Stu.* to pass (a course or examination) with a high grade.

1897 *Lucky Bag* (U.S. Nav. Acad.) (No. 4): *Biff*—To do a thing well....*Hit*—Same as "Biff." **1900** *DN* II 41: In other phrases a *hit a written*, pass a written examination easily. **1906** *Army & Navy Life* (Nov.): *Hit.* Means to do something well...synonymous with *biff* and *Frap* and *Frappe*. **1924** P. Marks *Plastic Age* 36: Would he hit Math I in the eye? He'd knock it for a goal. **1928** *AS* III (Feb.) 219: *Hit a quiz*, v. phr.—To acquit oneself creditably in an examination. "I sure hit old Rosenow's quiz yesterday." **1966** Brunner *Face of Night* 162: "I might as well go to class for a change," he said. "I got to hit those finals coming up next week." **1970** *Room 222* (ABC-TV): You've still got your mid-semester test. Why don't you try to really hit that?

4.a. Orig. *Blackjack.* to deal a card to. Now *colloq.*

1924 Anderson & Stallings *What Price Glory?* 126 [ref. to 1918]: Hit me again. **1932** (quot. at **(b)**, below). **1939** I. Baird *Waste Heritage* 65: Hit me one but make it soft. **1962** Olmsted *Heads I Win* 46: "Hit me"...deal me another card. **1970** Major *Afro-Amer. Slang* 66: To say "hit me" while playing cards...is to ask for a card from the deck. **1976** *Las Vegas Today* (Feb. 18) 9: An unfair advantage in deciding whether to stand or hit his hand.

b. to serve or provide (someone), esp. with a drink.—also constr. with *up*.

1932 Harvey *Me and Bad Eye* 21 [ref. to 1918]: The men hold out their mess kits and say, Hit me hard, or hit me light, like in blackjack. **1953** Paxton *Wild One* (film): Hit us with a couple of beers. **1962** *Esquire* (Dec.) 66: He signaled the bartender. "Hit us again." **1962** J.P. Miller *Days of Wine & Roses* (film): Louis, hit me again! **1972** *Nat. Lampoon* (June) 45: Why don't we go in there and eat something. Then I can hit you up with some funds. **1988** T. Logan *Harder They Fall* 189: "Hit me again," he told the bartender.

5.a. *Gamb.* to win, esp. in an illegal lottery.

1930 Mae West *Babe Gordon* 130: Must have hit the numbers. **1931** B. Niles *Strange Bro.* 27: You must have hit the numbers to-day, Ira, the way you're spending money! **1932** R. Fisher *Conjure-Man* 137: Hit for a dollar, you get six hundred minus the ten percent that goes to the runner. **1941** Brecher & Kurnitz *Shadow of Thin Man* (film): Maybe somebody hit the daily double. **1943** Whyte *Street Corner Soc.* 117: The customer who "hits" receives odds of 600 to 1 on a three number play. *a*1945–50 in D.W. Maurer *Lang. Und.* 187: To *hit*: To win [at dice]. **1977** Dillard *Lex. of Black Eng.* 92: The chances of "hitting" are about 1 in 1,000.

b. to return a large profit, esp. suddenly.

1969 L. Sanders *Anderson Tapes* 144: I have this hustle planned....If I hit, it means a lot of money. **1987** Lipper *Wall St.* 148: I'll park some money in your account, and if it hits, you get a good cut.

6. *Entertainment Industry.* to be a popular or financial success; be a hit.

1934 Weseen *Dict. Slang* 143: Theater...*Hit*—A success; to succeed. **1942** *ATS* 584: Be a hit...*click*,...*hit*,...*score a smash*. **1945** Fay *Be Poor* 87: But, with or without talent, to those who did and will "hit," money in Hollywood comes in bundles. **1971** in Bangs *Psychotic Reactions* 8: The Yardbirds...hit with "I'm a Man." **1989** S. Robinson & D. Ritz

Smokey 214: Motown…started hitting. **1997** *New Yorker* (Mar. 17) 78: I'm telling you…this is going to hit.

7. (of drugs or alcohol) to begin to have an effect; have an effect.

1936 D.W. Maurer, in *AS* (Apr.): *To be hit.* To begin to feel the effects of a narcotic injection. **1940** R. Chandler *Farewell, My Lovely* ch. xvii: Gin's cheap. It hits.

8. to switch on or off; apply (brakes, etc.). Now *S.E.*

1942 *ATS* 754: *Hit 'em,* to turn on all the lights. **1964** N.Y.C. man: Don't hit the brakes too hard. **1965** N.Y.C. high school student: Who hit the lights? **1980** W. Sherman *Times Square* 3: "Hit it."…An electrician…threw a switch. **1982** "J. Cain" *Commandos* 353: Hit the red lights.

9. *Und. & Police.* to murder, esp. by agency of a hired killer.

1942–49 Goldin et al. *DAUL* 267: Maybe we [should] hit (shoot) this fink. **1960** Roeburt *Mobster* 78: Maybe you're not the torpedo that hit Mickey. *Ibid.* 81: There was no damned reason to hit him! **1962** *Untouchables* (ABC-TV): Bad news, Elliott. Somebody just hit Danny Coogan. **1962** Perry *Young Man Drowning* 160: You already know we're going to hit somebody over there. **1970** Conaway *Big Easy* 118: I want to know who hit the jockey? Who murdered Littlebit? **1983** *N.Y. Post* (Sept. 5) 1: "Wrong man" hit in Village rubout. **1984** J. McNamara *First Directive* 267: Why would the mob start hitting cops? It's not their M.O. **1995** *Strange Luck* (Fox-TV): I think I know who you're supposed to hit.

10. *Narc.* **a.** to administer an injection to; inject (a drug). Also *absol.* [Prob. the orig. sense.]

1949 Algren *Golden Arm* 57: Hit me, Fixer. Hit me. **1952** Ellson *Golden Spike* 32: Let me hit you. **1958** Motley *Epitaph* 151: When you hit yourself with it you'd know it wasn't any good. **1958–59** Lipton *Barbarians* 186: This other guy hits up but he only hits half of it. **1964** Larner & Tefferteller *Addict* 34: [Needle] tracks…[come] from hitting in the same place so much. **1971** Goines *Dopefiend* 160: Big Ed…was standing in front of a mirror trying to hit in the neck. **1976** Chinn *Dig Nigger Up* 187: Do you think you can hit me? The stuff and works are in that drawer. **1979** Alibrandi *Custody* 216: "Hit me," she begged.

b. to take a drag (on a cigarette, esp. a marijuana cigarette).

1947 *AS* (Apr.) 121: *Hit on.* To take a drag on a cigaret.

c. to cut or adulterate (drugs).

1963 Braly *Shake Him* 141: She hit again. **1969** Smith & Gay *Don't Try It* 105: The *kilo connection* pays $20,000 for the original kilogram, and gives it a one and one cut (known as *hitting it*), that is, he makes two kilos out of one by adding the common adulterants of milk sugar, mannite…and quinine. **1975** V. Miller *Trade-Off* 6: He takes his supply and hits it one and one, doubling it. **1978** E. Goode *Deviant Behavior* 192: Both heroin and cocaine are "hit," "cut," or "stepped on" with cheap, nonactive fillers. **1980** Gould *Ft. Apache* 207: The shit's good, man….You can hit it seven, eight times, and them junkies'll still be comin' to you with their hands out.

11. to copulate or copulate with (a woman).

1959 Morrill *Dark Sea* 111 [ref. to WWII]: Wow, I'll bet you can't wait to hit the old lady that first time. **1970** E. Thompson *Garden of Sand* 176: They called fucking "hitting" in ordinary conversation.

12. to *hit on all cylinders,* below.

1980 DiFusco et al. *Tracers* 38: Everybody was up. Everybody was hyper. Everybody was hittin'.

¶ In phrases:

¶ **hit in the palm** to press a tip into the palm of.

1972 Jenkins *Semi-Tough* 29: We'll get a good table from…Ugo, as much as me and Shake have hit…[him] in the palm when he was a captain waiter at La Scala.

¶ **hit it, 1.a.** to go fast; get going; (*hence*) (usu. *imper.*) to begin one's performance; get busy.

1911 in *DA*: They nabbed us for speeding….Said we were hitting it at fifty an hour. **1928** in Farrell *Guillotine Party* 23: They kept hitting it along at about thirty miles an hour. **1930** Lait *On the Spot* 90: "Hit it!" called Goldie. With a lunge the limousine leaped forward. **1937** Kober *Wonderful Time* 64: Now…everybody sing! Hit it [i.e., start the music], Sammy! **1942** *ATS* 60: Depart, esp. hurriedly; "beat it."…*hit it. Ibid.* 610: *Hit it*…start the broadcast. **1945** T. Anderson *Come Out Fighting* 25: Now, look here, ya cats, we gotta hit it down the main drag, and hip some of them unhepped cats on the other side. **1966** Braly *On the Yard* 73: Hit it, punk.

b. to drink heavily; carouse.

1974 Loken *Come Monday Mornin'* 100: He was out hittin' it las' night.

c. to engage in copulation.

1993 "Tribe Called Quest" *Electric Relaxation* (rap song): Let me hit it from the back, girl. **1994** in C. Long *Love Awaits* 103: It's like yeah, yeah, yeah, you're a nice female and all, but how soon can I hit it? *Ibid.* 114: I would much rather you tell me you just wanted to hit it.

2. to go to bed; *hit the sack* s.v. SACK, *n.*

1959 W. Bernstein *That Kind of Woman* (film): Hit it, kid. You're going to need all the sleep you can get. **1975** S.P. Smith *Amer. Boys* 293: I better hit it, Orville. Can't handle all that beer.

3. Esp. *Navy & USMC.* to jump to one's feet, esp. out of bed; *hit the deck,* 1, s.v. DECK, *n.*

1963 in Clarke *Amer. Negro Stories* 325: Don't mean it ain't time to get up….Hit it, Ty! **1970** Flanagan *Maggot* 43: Outa those racks, people! Hit it! Hit it! Hit it! **1972** Ponicsan *Cinderella Liberty* 16: Let's *hit* it! **1972–76** (quot. at GUNHAWK).

¶ **hit it up** see s.v. HIT UP.

¶ **hit on, 1.a.** to make a sexual proposition to; (*broadly*) to make any sort of romantic advance to. [The 1931 quot. prob. illus. the colloq. sense 'to find by chance'. The present sense became widely current in the late 1960's.]

[**1931** L. Zukofsky, in Ahearn *Pound/Zukofsky* 90: And like one well-fed stud bustin' his harness runs like mad thru Central Park wanting to get drunk, hits on a couple of swell truck horses, sure he's got "it."] **1954** in Wepman, Newman & Binderman *The Life* 38: Go hit on one of them Indian bitches. **1959** A. Anderson *Lover Man* 118: She looked so good I felt like hitting on her right then. **1959–60** R. Reisner *Jazz Titans* 158: Hit on, to: Attempt seduction. **1963** Williamson *Hustler!* 150: That was an old prostitute neighborhood. It's impossible for a man to walk through that neighborhood and not get hit on. **1965** Ward & Kassebaum *Women's Pris.* 122: One week they're my brother and the next week they're hitting on me. **1967–68** von Hoffman *Parents Warned Us* 183: If you hit on a chick who doesn't want to, you don't. **1970** A. Young *Snakes* 95: Do you want some pussy?…Didnt you come up here to hit on me, or what? **1970** Landy *Underground Dict.* 104: *Hit on someone*…Flirt with. *a*1971 in Bullins *Hungered One* 24: He could see she was hitting on him. **1982** E. Leonard *Cat Chaser* 14: I suppose a lady as attractive as your wife has guys hitting on her all the time. **1988** *21 Jump St.* (Fox-TV): Judy's a beautiful woman. Somebody's always hittin' on her. **1994** *Donahue* (NBC-TV): The high school girls were hitting on him.

b. to approach in an attempt to swindle or victimize.

1967 Colebrook *Cross of Lassitude* 104: Don't let those pimps hit on you. **1970** Landy *Underground Dict.* 104: *Hit on someone*…Trick…con.

2. Esp. *Black E.* to ask (someone); HIT, 2, above.

1957 Simmons *Corner Boy* 80: I'm going to hit on Monk for the same deal in J City. **1959–60** R. Reisner *Jazz Titans* 158: Hit on, to: to request money. **1960** in T.C. Bambara *Gorilla* 48: So what's this high-yaller Northern bitch doin' hittin' on evil ole Ham? **1962** H. Simmons *On Eggshells* 221: Lobo hit on him about…forming a band again. **1964** in B. Jackson *Swim Like Me* 90: I hits on her to be my girl. **1965** in W. King *Black Anthol.* 303: I had intentions to hit on him for a…sandwich. **1966** Brunner *Face of Night* 233: *Hit on*—to approach in any way, but especially for the purpose of buying narcotics.

¶ **hit on all cylinders** [or **all six**] to perform with the greatest energy or effectiveness; be in excellent form. Also vars.

1912 Mathewson *Pitching* 269: So the best infielder takes time to fit into the infield of a Big League club and have it hit on all four cylinders again. **1920** in De Beck *Google* 101: The sweet woman is hittin on all six. **1922** *Variety* (July 28) 5: The beauty parlor…is now hittin' on all six. **1923** in Hammett *Knockover* 146: My luck was hitting on all cylinders. **1928** *Sat. Eve. Post* (Mar. 10) 127: Modern science offers you a natural means to keep you "hitting on all six"—every minute of the day. **1930** Sage *Last Rustler* 152: Some must have figured I was hitting on all six cylinders. **1934** Weseen *Dict. Amer. Slang* 350: *Hit on all six*—To work efficiently; to work at full force. **1936** in H. Gray *Arf* (unp.): Gee, the boss sure is hittin' on all twelve cylinders today—

never saw him so active. **1972** *Nat. Lampoon* (July) 81: If she strokes it like a Siamese cat, you're hittin' on eight. **1985** Resnick *Maxie* (film): Now I'm hittin' on all sixes. **1987** *Crossfire* (CNN-TV) (Feb. 24): Although he may not be *legally* insane, he still isn't hitting on all six. **1987** Whiteley *Deadly Green* 45: My mind wasn't hitting on all fours. **1989** Knoxville, Tenn., attorney, age 35: You're goin' along, feelin' fine, hittin' on all cylinders. **1994** *CBS This Morning* (CBS-TV) (Dec. 14): I'd like to know if something's not quite right, if I'm not hitting on all eight cylinders.

¶ **hit the beach** see s.v. BEACH, *n.*

¶ **hit the bottle** see **(1.a.),** above.

¶ **hit the breeze** see s.v. BREEZE, *n.*

¶ **hit the bricks** see s.v. BRICK.

¶ **hit the ceiling** [or **roof**] see s.v. CEILING and ROOF.

¶ **hit the deck** see s.v. DECK, *n.*

¶ **hit the dirt** to throw oneself to the ground. Now *colloq.*

   1902 in "O. Henry" *Works* 833: "Jump overboard, son," I said, and he hit the dirt like a lump of lead. **1908** in Fleming *Unforgettable Season* 114: Titus did not slide to the plate in the first inning and the failure to hit the dirt cost him $25. **1911** Spalding *Base Ball* 306: Base stealing,…sprinting and "hitting the dirt." **1918** in Asprey *Belleau Wood* 323: The other [shell] hit within twenty feet of my sergeant and myself, but we had heard it coming and had hit the dirt (as they call it in baseball) into a ditch, so all was well. **1919** *Twelfth Inf.* 96: The only limitation that the reader need place upon his comprehension of our feelings toward what is known as "hitting the dirt" is his own imagination. **1935** in *Americans vs. Germans* 33: Don't be afraid to hit the dirt!

¶ **hit the fan** [sugg. by the anecdote alluded to in 1936 quot.; cf. vulgar syn. *when the shit hits the fan* s.v. SHIT, *n.*] (of trouble, scandal, etc.) to erupt with suddenness or intensity; in phr. **the egg has hit the fan** the trouble has begun.

   [**1936** Sandburg *People, Yes* 155: The joker who threw an egg into the electric fan soon was stood/on his tin ear.] **1945** in M. Chennault *Up Sun!* 136: Sounds like the stuff was about to hit the fan. **1949** McMillan *Old Bread* 30: Ninety per cent of the men would have sworn that the stuff was going to hit the fan right on the beach. [**1953** "L. Short" *Silver Rock* 88: Don't go off half-cocked. Once you do, the pie has hit the fan.] **1961** Forbes *Goodbye to Some* 108 [ref. to WWII]: Something hit the fan. **1962** E. Stephens *Blow Negative* 92: It had all hit the fan. **1962** W. Robinson *Barbara* 296 [ref. to WWII]: This time the Krauts really have run into something: this time the egg has really hit the fan. **1962** H. Simmons *On Eggshells* 197: Yeh, the stuff's gonna hit the fan in 1964. **1963** Breen *PT 109* (film): What happened? Somethin' hit the fan? **1963** J. Ross *Dead Are Mine* 222 [ref. to WWII]: The idea being that whoever handled the body would not notice the booby trap…and then the egg would hit the fan. **1964** Gallant *Friendly Dead* 47 [ref. to WWII]: It's hit the fan good. **1966** Newhafer *Bugles* 166: If the Old Man was here, then something was surely destined to hit the fan. **1966** "T. Pendleton" *Orchard* 250: In 1954 (in the technical language of the trade) it really hit the fan when the Supreme Court handed down a decision that in effect said just that. **1967** "M.T. Knight" *Terrible Ten* 78: When the cops show up…it'll really hit the fan. **1972** *M.A.S.H.* (CBS-TV): This is when the whole thing hits the fan. **1974** Sann *Dead Heat* 160: Everything hit the fan in the horse parlors. **1974** A. Bergman *Big Kiss-Off* 169: When they see you go in, that's when it'll hit the fan. **1976** T. Walker *Ft. Apache* 57: Hey, Lou…every time you work, it really hits the fan. **1984** Holland *Let Soldier* 75: *Everything* has hit the fan. **1987** Pres. R. Reagan, in *N.Y. Times Mag.* (June 28) 6: I told you the truth that first day…after the—everything hit the fan.

¶ **hit the flat** *West.* to take to the prairie; (*hence*) to get out of town.

   1887 in Westermeier *Cowboy* 45: Hit the flat. **1889** Barrère & Leland *Dict. Slang* I 464: *Hit the flat* (cowboys), to go out on the prairies.

¶ **hit the grit, 1.** to go; move on; (*also*) to tramp.

   1888 in *AS* XXXVII (1962) 76: *Hit the grit.* Get going; get out of here. **1902** Bell *Worth of Words* 209: One running in…extreme earnestness is well described as *hitting the grit*. **1926** *AS* I (Dec.) 651: *Hitting the grit*—"hiking" or walking on foot. **1935** Coburn *Law Rides Range* 73: Get yore horses and hit the grit.

2. *R.R.* to leap or be thrown from a moving train.

1927 *DN* V 450: *Hit the grit, v.* To be thrown off a train. **1935** Algren *Boots* 85: You…best hit the grit now, whilst you still got a chanst.

3. to get busy; work hard.

   1984–87 Ferrandino *Firefight* 125: Says you had too much ghost time in the hospital while the rest of us been hittin' the grit.

¶ **hit the ground** [or **gravel**] to leap or fall to the ground, esp. from a moving train.

   1893 *Century* (Nov.) 106: Well, hit the gravel! I can't carry you on this train. **1902** in "O. Henry" *Works* 832: "Hit the ground," I ordered, and they both jumped off. **1966** Coppola et al. *Property Is Condemned* (film): Here she is—Dodson. Get ready to hit the ground runnin'.

¶ **hit the hay** see s.v. HAY.

¶ **hit the pike** see s.v. PIKE, *n.*

¶ **hit the pipe, 1.** to smoke opium.

   1881 H.H. Kane *Opium* 11: The likely chance of having to pay $20 in the Police Court…[as a fine] has made the white smokers find other means of hitting the pipe. **1884** Costello *Police Protectors* 517: A number of the denizens…were caught…"hitting the pipe." **1886** T. Byrne *Prof. Crim. Amer.* 385: Joe did not "hit the pipe." *Ibid.* 386: I "hit" my first pipe, as the slang goes, about four o'clock one afternoon. **1887** in Courtwright *Dk. Paradise* 78: There are few second or third class lodging houses…where…"hitting the pipe" is not practiced. **1890** Quinn *Fools of Fortune* 395: "Hitting the pipe" at last brought him to his death. **1891** Campbell, Knox & Byrnes *Darkness & Daylight* 569: How long have you been hitting the pipe? **1892** Norr *China Town* 3: I am probably better qualified to write about the subject than any other newspaper man, having for years "hit the pipe" in Chinatown. **1894** Gardner *Doctor & Devil* 36: Don't you want to hit a pipe? **1904** in "O. Henry" *Works* 81: He hits the pipe every night. **1904** *Life in Sing Sing* 256: *Hitting the pipe*, smoking opium. **1951** in W.S. Burroughs *Letters* 83: You can hit the pipe that often with no risk of a habit. **1954** N. Johnson *Night People* (film): Burnsy must be hittin' the pipe these days.

2. to smoke a tobacco pipe.

   1895 Wood *Yale Yarns* 128: They let out the sail, threw off their coats, "hit" their pipes.

¶ **hit the pot** [or **pots**] to drink to excess; *hit the bottle*, above.

   1908 Sullivan *Crim. Slang* 13: *Hitting the pots.*—Excessive drinking. **1935** *AS* (Feb.) 17 [ref. to a1910]: *To Hit the Pot.* To get drunk.

¶ **hit the rack** see s.v. RACK, *n.*

¶ **hit the road** to be on one's way; move on; get out. Also vars. with syns. for *road*; see also *hit the steel* and *hit the ties*, below. [The nuance in 1893 quot. is 'to walk at a brisk pace'.]

   [***1893** in *OED2*: I have been hitting the road something to get here quick.] **1897** in *DA*: Men can pass out the church door, shoulder their packs of general cussedness, and unconcernedly hit the trail to the lower [regions]. **1898** in *Dict. Canadianisms*: It is now clearing so I must "mush on," hike or hit the trail, in hieroglyphist parlance. **1899** "J. Flynt" *Tramping* 394: *Hit the Road*: to go tramping. *ca***1875–1903** *DN* III 316: I must hit the road for home. **1904** in *DAE*: The delegates were…summarily ordered to hit the pike by the national committeemen. **1904** London *Faith* 74: Whoever wins can be hitting the trail for God's country this time to-morrow morning. **1904** *Life in Sing Sing* 256: *Hitting the Road.*—Traveling. **1905** *DN* III 62: *Hit the pike…road…trail…*Go; move on. **1908** Beach *Barrier* 116: Well, I'm ready to hit the trail. **1912** Siringo *Cowboy Detective* 139 [ref. to 1890's]: Told to "hit the road" and never return at the peril of their lives. **1912** *DN* III 578: When they began talking money, I hit the pike. **1914** Z. Grey *West. Stars* 43: An' Gene Stewart hit the trail for the border. **1915** *DN* IV 244: *Hit the…trail…*to set off on the road, usually walking. **1926** Nichols & Tully *Twenty Below* 74: All the same, guess we'll hit the trail. **1929** Caldwell *Bastard* 54: We'd better be hitting the road, hadn't we? **1953** Gresham *Midway* 15: You better turn in the stuff and hit the road after we close tomorrow night. **1953** R. Chandler *Goodbye* 100: Hit the trail, sweetie. Buzz off fast. **1978** Strieber *Wolfen* 198: OK, kids, let's hit the road. We've got work to do. **1984** Algeo *Stud Buds* 4: To leave a place, go away…*hit the highway.* **1986** Knoxville, Tenn., attorney: Guess I'll be hitting the road. **1986** Stinson & Carabatsos *Heartbreak* 105: Hit the road, Jack! **1987** *Night Court* (NBC-TV): I told him that sounded like sexual harassment and he said, "Hit the road." **1996** *Montel Williams Show* (synd. TV series): So she finally told you to hit the road.

¶ **hit the sack** see s.v. SACK, *n.*

¶ **hit the sheets** to go to bed.

*a***1972** B. Rodgers *Queens' Vernacular* 137: *Hit the sheets* (les[bian] sl[ang]) to be passive to the overtures of another woman. **1977** Dills *CB Slanguage* (ed. 4) 53: *Hit the sheets:* go to bed. **1987** N.Y.C. woman, age *ca*45: Just because they were in the house together doesn't mean they hit the sheets.

¶ **hit the shit** see s.v. SHIT, *n.*

¶ **hit the silk** see s.v. SILK, *n.*

¶ **hit the skids** see s.v. SKIDS.

¶ **hit the slats** to go to bed.

1915 *DN* IV 244: *Hit the slats*…To go to bed.

¶ **hit the steel** *Logging.* (see quot.).

1958 McCulloch *Woods Wds.* 86: *Hit the steel*—In the days of railroad logging, to walk the track away from camp, either because fired, or quitting the job.

¶ **hit the stem** see s.v. STEM, *n.*

¶ **hit the ties** (among itinerants) to walk along a railway track.

1907 in Service *Complete Poems* 40: The choice is thine…/To hit the ties or drive thy motor-car. **1927** *DN* V 450: *Hit the ties,* v. To walk along the railway. **1936** in F. Brown *N.C. Folklore* III 430: But, I fear, in a year or two,/I'll be hitting the ties again.

¶ **hit the wall** see s.v. WALL, *n.*

¶ **hit up** see HIT UP.

¶ **how are you hitting them?** how are things going? how are you? Also vars.

1897 Kipling *Capts. Courageous* 7: "Say, Mac,…how are we hitting it?"…"Vara much in the ordinary way." **1898** L.J. Beck *Chinatown* 158: "Hello, Harry; how did you hit them lately?" "Oh, fairish." **1933–35** D. Lamson *About to Die* 37: "How you hitting?"…"All right, I guess." **1970–71** Higgins *Eddie Coyle* 135: Hey, Wanda,…how you hitting them? **1971** Coffin *Old Ball Game* 60: "How are ya' hittin' 'em?" "Real good now." **1974** Loken *Come Monday Mornin'* 49: "How you hittin' 'em, Russ?" "Can't complain." **1988** T. Harris *Silence of Lambs* 355: How're you hittin' 'em, Starling?

hit car *n. Und. & Police.* (see 1969 quot.).

1969 Salerno & Tompkins *Crime Confed.* 162: "Hit car" (slang for an automobile used to make a getaway from the scene of a murder or to carry a kidnaped victim to the place where he is to be killed). **1976** R. Daley *To Kill* 3: I belong in the hit car.

hitch *n.* **1.a.** a particular time; in phr. **this hitch** this time.

1835 in *DAE:* Their favorite…expression [is]…"We shall clear up three loads this hitch." **1835** in *Dict. Canadianisms:* At last he said, which way are you from, Mr. Slick, this hitch. **1835–3** [Haliburton] *Clockmaker* (Ser. 1) 169: She'll mind her stops next hitch, I reckon. **1842** in *DAE:* Put the leak into them this hitch. **1845** J. Hooper *Suggs* ch. x: They're badly lewed this hitch!

b. *Mil.* a period of duty or service; (*specif.*) a period of enlistment.

*ca***1905** in Dolph *Sound Off!* 64: But before I'd serve again in Zamboanga, I'd rather serve a hitch in hell. **1906** Beyer *Amer. Battleship* 83: "Hitch"—an enlistment. **1906** M'Govern *Bolo & Krag* 29: I had a little sunstroke when I was over here last hitch. **1907** *McClure's Mag.* (Feb.) 379: Casey…had just reënlisted for his fifth "hitch." **1907** *Army & Navy Life* (July) 779: If ever I get this "hitch" in /…I'll hang this coat upon a peg and with it I'll give o'er/Every thought of martial glory. **1914** *Collier's* (June 6) 5: Come to me when ye've served ye're hitch. **1914** Paine *Wall Between* 6: Now, what about your re-enlistment?…Are you going to take on another hitch? **1917** Depew *Gunner* 23: Murray was an ex-garby—two hitches (enlistments), gun-pointer rating. **1918** Ruggles *Navy Explained* 75: A four-year term considered a hitch or a cruise. **1918** in D. York *Mud & Stars* 6: It is then we'll hear St. Peter tell us loudly with a yell,/"Take a front seat, you soldier men, you've done your hitch in hell." *Ibid.:* When we die we're bound for Heaven, 'cause we've done our hitch in Hell. **1918** in Straub *Diary* (entry for Oct. 1): We have to put on a guard over this place so that no one can get in before our battery comes so I stood the first "hitch." **1918** in Cowing *Dear Folks* 195: The last time we came

out from a "hitch" we had only enough time to wash our feet before we had to serve in another sector. **1919** *Inf. Jrnl.* (Mar.) 707: A Hitch in the Trenches. **1920** Acker *Thru the War* 16: After the [Civil] war he served four "hitches" in the regular army. **1928** Wharton *Squad* 167 [ref. to 1918]: Mike, take the first hitch on the Chauchat. **1928** Weaver *Collected Poems* 200: Back there in nineteen-ten, after/My hitch in the cavalry, I worked two years/In…Los Angeles. **1963** Coon *Short End* 15: In the regular Army drawing a hitch in Korea is just a little worse than a general court-martial. **1964** Hunt *Ship with Flat Tire* 50: The rest of my three-year hitch. **1991** LaBarge *Desert Voices* 161: I got a two-year hitch with the Corps now.

c. *Pris.* a term of imprisonment.

1923 in W.F. Nolan *Black Mask Boys* 85: A one-to-fourteen-year hitch. **1927** in Hammett *Knockover* 324: Her brother's doing a hitch up north now—Johnny the Plumber sold him out. **1929** Barr *Let Tomorrow Come* 88: Take an old vic, fer instance…that's done half a dozen hitches in somebody's bighouse. **1929** Hammett *Maltese Falcon* 127: He did a short hitch in Joliet for pistol-whipping another twist. **1930** "D. Stiff" *Milk & Honey* 207: *Hitch*—Prison term. **1930** *Amer. Mercury* (Dec.) 456: He's inside with a ten space hitch. **1932** L. Berg *Prison Doctor* 243: I've got a one-year hitch and I'm eligible [for parole] at the end of ten months. **1955** Reynolds *HQ* 43: Practically everyone had served a hitch or two in Sing Sing. **1964** Larner & Tefferteller *Addict in the Street* 96: I just came back last November from doing a hitch at Elmira. **1966** Elli *Riot* 29: You just signed up for another hitch when you grabbed Andy Gump. **1992** *Weekly World News* (Aug. 11) 21: A hitch in the hoosegow.

2. a lift given to a hitchhiker. Now *colloq.*

1928 Dahlberg *Bottom Dogs* 194: Walking the Lincoln Highway…he was unable to get a hitch. ***1955** in *OED2.* **1965** *Harper's* (July) 95: A young…newlywed he had given a hitch was looking for a home.

3. *Narc.* a scar resulting from repeated hypodermic injections.

1953 W. Brown *Monkey on My Back* 106: There was a row of "main-line hitches" along the soft inner flesh of his left thigh.

hitch *v.* **1.a.** to marry; wed.—usu. in passive, occ. constr. with *up.* [Prob. the orig. sense.]

1846 in Blair & McDavid *Mirth* 89: A'ter the varmint got Sophie hitched, he told the joke all over the settlement. **1856** in Dorson *Long Bow* 75: Wen we're hitched…by Parson Crout. **1862** C.F. Browne *A. Ward* 60: If you mean gettin hitched, I'm in! **1867** in G.W. Harris *High Times* 178: Arter we were hitched in, an' an hour or so spent in passin round vittils. **1872** in *DAE:* The justice could hitch them by virtue of his office. **1873** Hotten *Slang Dict.* (ed. 4): *Hitched.* An Americanism for married. **1879** Maitland *Sensations* 247: Once they're hitched they're going up the lakes for a bridal tower. **1881** Small *Smith* 25: If she wants to get hitched, I'm her door knob. ***1892** in *F & H* III 319: "We've come to get hitched," said the man, bashfully. **1892** Norr *China Town* 10: I wantcher to get hitched fair and square. **1902** in *DAE:* I've got a notion that you and I ought to be hitched. **1926** Dunning & Abbott *Broadway* 233: Listen, honey, how about getting hitched up? **1930** Conselman *Whoopee!* (film): Her old man wouldn't let them get hitched. **1936** in H. Gray *Arf* (unp.): If you still think you want to hitch yourself to a pauper….When shall we plan to get married? **1938** in Inman *Diary* 884: I wasn't gonna get hitched up to no sloppy wife. **1947** Schulberg *Harder They Fall* 36: No kidding, you should get yourself hitched. **1953** in *DAS:* Now that you two is practically hitched. **1954** L. Armstrong *Satchmo* 158: We went straight down to City Hall and got hitched. **1955** Stout *Three Witnesses* 63: I don't bother with those who are already hitched. **1958** Talsman *Gaudy Image* 62: Then we're hitched. **1976** S. Lawrence *Northern Saga* 19: A guy could hitch up with a lot worse than her. **1994** *TV Guide* (July 23) 3: Estes is happily hitched to…Josie Bissett. **1995** *TV Guide* (Oct. 28) 174: Guess Who's Gettin' Hitched?

b. to get married—also constr. with *up.*

1880 in *DAE:* Ef yer on the marry…, jist squeal an' we'll hitch. **1902** Harben *A. Daniel* 195: About the time you an' Betsey fust hitched together. **1910** Hapgood *City Streets* 38: But I booze too much and I may hitch up sometime. **1931** Hellinger *Moon* 314: You'll have a cinch if you'll hitch up with him. **1934** H. Miller *Tropic of Cancer* 155: Hitch up!…You have nothing to lose! **1983** *Rolling Stone* (Feb. 3) 23: New Year's Eve saw Steve Van Zandt hitching for keeps with longtime steady Maureen Santora. **1986** *Daily Beacon* (Univ. Tenn.) (June 3) 4: I'm all in favor of growing up before hitching up.

c. to become partners; team up.—constr. with *on* or *up*.

1830 in [S. Smith] *Letters of Downing* 33: So sure as you get hitched on the Jackson party or the Hunton party. **1884** in Lummis *Letters* 174: I don't know of any other place that is as anxious for my company, and Golden and I will have to hitch. **1899–1900** Cullen *Tales* 212: You're broke ain't you?…So'm I. So we'll have to hitch up, and do something.

2. to fight; tangle.

1874 Carter *Rollingpin* 144: These Bungtown and Scripville boys never kin hitch. *Ibid.* 193: You orto've seen 'em hitch.

3. to hitchhike.—also constr. with *it*. Now *S.E.*

1929 Zombaugh *Gold Coast* 95: Then when times are lean, he "hitches" his way to New York. **1937** L. Hellman *Dead End* (film): There's plenty of places to hitch to. *a***1938** Adamic *My America* 510: I…began to hitch—California, here I come! **1940** in T. McGrath *New & Sel. Poems:* He gets the night freight for Denver. She hitches out for Billings. **1940** in Mailer *Ad. for Myself* 72: "Been hitching, huh?" "Yeah, walked the last three miles." **1948** Lowry *Wolf That Fed Us* 101: "Let's hitch," Joe said. **1955** Graziano & Barber *Somebody Up There* 203: I hitch home on the trucks. **1955** Stern *Rebel Without a Cause* (film): "How did you get here?" "I hitched." **1962** Perry *Young Man Drowning* 24: Let's go hitching out to Prospect Park. **1967** *Zap Comix* (Oct.) 16: He invited me to hitch it with him out to the Coast.

¶ In phrases:

¶ **hitch on** to strike up an acquaintance or a romance with a young woman.

1860 J.G. Holland *Miss Gilbert* 209: "Have you hitched on anywhere yet?" "I don't understand you."…"I mean have you got a girl?…Don't go to hitching on to Joslyn's oldest girl.…She belongs to me."

¶ **hitch teams** to get married.

1864 Alcott *Picket* 5: Come, reel off a yarn and let's hear houw yeou hitched teams.

hitchhiker *n.* **1.** *Logging.* (see quot.).

1958 McCulloch *Woods Wds.* 86: *Hitchhiker*—A log caught or entangled but not choked with the turn, hauled all or part way to the landing.

2. *Computers.* an unauthorized person who gains access to a computer system.

1979 Homer *Jargon* 145.

hitch on *v.* to understand.

1885 B. Harte *Shore & Sedge* 123: I reckon I don't hitch on, pardner.…security what for?

hit lady var. HIT WOMAN.

hit list *n.* **1.** a list of persons, projects, or the like, singled out for special attention, esp. for opposition or elimination.

1972 (cited in *W10*). **1973** *Seattle Times* (Dec. 16) E3: The hotel is indeed high on the University of Washington's hit list for redevelopment. **1976** *New Times* (Jan. 23) 30: A "hit list" of 4,300 hoods Kennedy had designated for harassment and prosecution. **1977** *U.S. News & W.R.* (Aug. 1) 29: No. 1 on Moscow's political "hit" list of those accused of splitting Communist world. **1978** Cleaver *Soul on Fire* 21: We were at the top of [J. Edgar] Hoover's hit list. **1980** Manchester *Darkness* 199: Australia itself was on the Jap hit list. **1980** *Daily News* (N.Y.C.) (Dec. 24) 14: A "hit list" of current U.S. ambassadors to be fired [by the new administration]. **1982** *N.Y. Post* (Aug. 13) 18: TA Makes Up Hit-List of Subway Crooks. **1989** *New Yorker* (Aug. 7) 65: She was already on Miami's "hit list," suspected of smuggling cocaine into Fort Lauderdale.

2. *Specif.* a list of persons to be murdered or assassinated.

1976 *Time* (Jan. 5) 46: One intelligence official…labeled *Counterspy's* roster of CIA agents as nothing more or less than a "hit list." **1977** *Harper's* (Sept.) 99: The Red Brigades issued a "hit list" of thirty prominent anti-Communist journalists and editors. **1980** WINS radio news (Aug. 25): What other baseball owner ever got on the hit list of the…Symbionese Liberation Army? **1982** *N.Y. Times* (Jan. 10) E5: Candidate rolls would simply become "hit lists" for the paramilitary murder squads.

hit man *n.* **1.** *Orig. Und.* a man who is a hired killer.

1963 (cited in Partridge *Dict. Und.* (ed. 3) 831). **1967–68** von Hoffman *Parents Warned Us* 81: A hit man for the syndicate. **1971** *Newsweek* (Mar. 8) 20: Through its cavernous courtrooms have passed generations of Chicago's outlaws and outcasts—a faceless succession of bootleggers, bookies, hit men, drifters, thieves, whores, petty Mafiosi.… **1971** H.S. Thompson *Las Vegas* 195: And that guy sitting next to him

is a hit-man for the Mafia. **1977** P. King *Code Name: Diamond Head* (film): A contract hit man for East German Intelligence. **1977** L. Jordan *Hype* 212: Sharon seemed to be holding her own with the hit man. **1979** *N.Y. Post* (Sept. 10) 3: Top Protestant hit-men are reportedly in training in Northern Ireland to assassinate Pope John Paul II when he visits Dublin at the end of this month. **1982** *N.Y. Post* (Aug. 30) 9: We can't see him as a hellbent hitman. **1994** G. Siskel, on *CBS This Morning* (CBS-TV) (July 29): Standard-issue faceless mob hit men.

2. *Ice Hockey & Football.* a player who tries to foul or injure members of the opposing team.

1974 in *AS* LV (1980) 55: Hockey's Hit Men Track the Flyers. **1976** *Reader's Dig.* (Mar.) 34: Every team employs swashbuckling "hit men" and "enforcers." **1990** *N.Y. Post* (Jan. 2) 48: And he'll be concerned with the knees of…hit man Reyna Thompson.

3. (see quot.).

1989 Hynes & Drury *Howard Beach* 276: I also chose Boyar as my designated "hit man," the attorney to crack any witnesses sympathetic to the defense.

hit parade *n.* Orig. *Journ.* a listing or grouping of favorite popular recordings; (*hence*) a listing or grouping of any favorites.—now often used ironically.

1937 Ropes & Ornitz *The Hit Parade* [film title]. **1940** Ropes *Hit Parade of 1941* [film title]. **1943** F. Gill *Hit Parade of 1943* [film title]. **1948** Lay & Bartlett *12 O'Clock High* 14: The 918th has already made Goering's hit parade. **1948** Manone & Vandervoort *Trumpet* 44: My Sunday gal was strictly Number One on my Hit Parade. **1959** Gault *Drag Strip* 53: Arky Banning wasn't on their hit parade; that much seemed certain. **1970** G. Walker *Cruising* 79: The good professor had become number one on Stuart's Hit Parade. **1979** Story *Guardians* 9: Leading the hit parade is an ex-hotel manager…the irrepressible Erich von Däniken—who has become…one of the most successful authors of all time.

hit squad *n.* Esp. *Journ.* a group of underworld assassins or political terrorists.

1969 Salerno & Tompkins *Crime Confed.* 284: Murder, Incorporated was simply the "hit squad" of the New York Syndicate. **1976** in *OED2*: Apart from the attempts to kill Major Muhayshi in Tunisia, a Libyan hit squad sought him out in London in February. **1976–77** McFadden *Serial* 285: He…started gibbering about this international conspiracy of women, and how…they had a hit squad that offed his cat. **1978** in *BDNE2*: They are a self-appointed hit squad for a revolution none of them have yet been able to articulate. **1980** *U.S. News & W.R.* (Aug. 11) 31: Islamic hit squads have carried out assassinations of Iranian exiles. **1989** *Village Voice* (N.Y.C.)(Aug. 15) 36: A Sunday service disrupted by a three-man hit squad shooting up four parishioners. **1995** *X-Files* (Fox-TV): Last night we were chased by some kind of hit squad.

hit team *n.* **1.** HIT SQUAD.

1978 *Time* (Nov. 13) 37: Dellacroce dispatched hit teams of his own toward Danbury. **1989** *Daily Beacon* (Univ. Tenn.) (Aug. 29) 6: American killed by hit team.

2. *Mil.* a small task force.

1987 *Time* (July 13) 24: "Ollie was always talking about hit teams" to strike at terrorists, says one colleague. **1989** Halberstadt *Army Av.* 54: The smart thing to do is to send in the spies.…Then you can send in a hit team.

hitter *n.* **1.a.** *Orig. Und.* a hired killer; ENFORCER.

1959 (quot. at STONE, *adj.*). **1969** Salerno & Tompkins *Crime Confed.* 102: The "hitters"…will do the shooting or break the arms and legs required. **1970** R. Sylvester *Guilty Bystander* 240: In gangster terms, a "hitter" is a fellow who does heavy work like killing people. **1977** Torres *Q & A* 52: These two…walk into the joint like two hitters on a contract. *a***1981** in S. King *Bachman* 508: Or did you want to buy a hitter to knock off your wife or your boss? **1984** *Miami Vice* (NBC-TV): How'd the hitter know where to find him? **1985** *Lady Blue* (ABC-TV): They got some high-class hitter right off the boat. **1990** Vachss *Blossom* 113: I'm looking for the real hitter. **1995** *O.J. Trial* (E!-TV) (July 13): A Colombian drug hitter.

b. a rowdy usu. working-class white youth.

1972 N.Y.U. student: There's too many hitters in the playground.…Guys who punch you out [if you beat them in basketball]. **1987–91** D. Gaines *Teenage Wasteland* 104: The "hitter chicks" we used to idolize. **1991** D. Gaines *Teenage Wasteland* 57: In another age they'd be hitters or greasers or hippies or heads or freaks.

2. *Und.* a firearm; HEATER.

    1980 Pearl *Pop. Slang* 71: *Hitter n.* (Crime) a gun.

hit up *v.* **1.a.** HIT, 1.b.

    1899 Cullen *Tales* 44: My two ducks had a bottle apiece with 'em to keep out the cold, and they were hitting them up pretty hard. *Ibid.* 59: We couldn't hit up warm beer, so we did the other thing. **1903** A.H. Lewis *Boss* 272: He hits up th' bottle pretty stiff at that. **1906–07** Ade *Slim Princess* 80: Hitting up just one small libation. **1920–21** Witwer *Leather Pushers* 179: That was the first and last time the kid hit up the red-eye. **1925** in Moriarty *True Confessions* 29: Frankie was a good boy, but he got to hitting that stuff up, and went to the dogs for fair. **1928** Heyward *Mamba's Daughters* 258: "Hit her up, Sister."…"What is it—whisky?"

b. to visit.

    1903 Ade *Society* 78: She wanted to get out and hit up the High Spots and dazzle the Public with her A1 Exhibit of Precious Stones. **1986** Merkin *Zombie Jamboree* 14: We're probably going to…hit up the movie theater. You know what's playing there?

2. *Narc.* to SHOOT UP.

    1958–59 Lipton *Barbarians* 186: So we get this horse and…we jump in and Muzzy hits up.…And he hits up the whole thing. **1976** in L. Bangs *Psychotic Reactions* 198: Tying off, hitting up, sterilizing my works with alcohol. **1987** Estes *Field of Innocence* 196: Oh, God, hit me up. Come on, hit me up.

3. see HIT, 2.

¶ In phrase:

¶ **hit it up** to go or work vigorously or fast; (*hence*) to drink heavily; carouse.

    1893 W.K. Post *Harvard Stories* 146: When you are doing better than three and a half [miles an hour] you are hitting it up pretty well. **1895** J.L. Williams *Princeton* 52: "Have you poled up Billy's history for the written recitation?"…"No, but I expect to…hit it up until three o'clock to-night." **1900** Willard & Hodler *Powers That Prey* 19: On occasions, particularly if he had been "hitting it up," he made no attempt to explain or to excuse. **1903** Fox *Little Shepherd* 67: Hit her up! Hit her up—*Now!* **1930** B. King *Son of Gods* (film): She's been hitting it up. Running wild. **1931** Wilstach *Under Cover Man* 228: He's been hitting it up all day. **1929–33** Farrell *Young Manhood* 310: "He's getting skinnier than a rail." "Yeah, he's hitting it up."

hit woman *n.* a woman who is a hired killer. Also **hit lady.**

    1974 Mimieux *Hit Lady* [film title]. **1977** *TV Guide* (Dec. 10) A7: Of course he's got to be assassinated and an international hit woman is hired. **1978** *Wonder Woman* (ABC-TV): Violet used to be our number-one hit lady. **1980** in *BDNE2*: Blanche Wright, accused "hit" woman. **1984** *Fall Guy* (ABC-TV): You're gonna love this one—a deadly hit lady. **1986** *Head of the Class* (ABC-TV): I became a hit lady for the mob.

hive *n.* *U.S. Mil. Acad.* (see 1978 quot.). Cf. HIVE, *v.*, 3 and HIVEY.

    1978 Truscott *Dress Gray* 388: The "hives," the cadets who really dug in and *studied.* **1981–89** R. Atkinson *Long Gray Line* 122: Jack personified the "hive," a man diligent in his studies. **1993** G. Lee *Honor & Duty* 214: Goats are supposed to study with hives. *Ibid.* 257: I'm looking for a…hive.

hive *v.* *U.S. Mil. Acad.* **1.** to take or pilfer; (*also*) to capture.

    1864 in Lyman *Meade's HQ* 124: Do not, for a moment, look for the "annihilation," the "hiving," or the "total rout" of Lee. **1871** O.E. Wood *West Point Scrapbook* 339: *To hive.*—To appropriate; to take without permission. **1878** Flipper *Colored Cadet* 53: "To hive."…Also, to take, to steal. **1895** in J.M. Carroll *Goldin-Benteen Letters* 234: I haven't a doubt but Gen Miles "hived them" from the scouts by whom they were sent.

2. to catch or discover (someone) in the act.

    1871 O.E. Wood *West Point Scrapbook* 338: *To get hived*—To get caught in a scrape. **1878** Flipper *Colored Cadet* 53: "To hive."—To detect, in a good and bad sense. *ca***1890** Averell *10 Yrs.* 38 [ref. to 1854]: All [were] "hived" absent for an hour by inspections. **1894** C. King *Cadet Days* 157: Messrs. Ferguson and Folliott…had been "hived" absent at inspection after taps. **1900** *Howitzer* (U.S. Mil. Acad.) (No. 1) 120: *Hive.*—To catch in the act. **1909** J. Moss *Officers' Manual* 283: *Hive*—to discover, to catch.

3. to discover by mental effort; understand; (*also*) to study intently. Cf. HIVE, *n.* and HIVEY.

1983 Elting, Cragg, & Deal *Soldier Talk* 152: *Hive* (At least as early as 1900; West Point)…To understand, to study, to comprehend. **1993** G. Lee *Honor & Duty* 150: You will hive 'til the Rhodes Committee sings your praise! *Ibid.* 253 [ref. to 1960's]: I've hived the answer to a victory in Vietnam.

hivey *adj.* *U.S. Mil. Acad.* quick-witted or studious.

    1931 in D.O. Smith *Cradle* 156: Math…is full of hivy men. **1944** in *DAS*: Everyone was surprised that a file-boner as hivey as Cunningham was D in math. **1947** *ATS* (Supp.) 28: *Hivey*, smart (West Point). **1983** Elting, Cragg & Deal *Soldier Talk* 152: *Hivey*…bright and clever.

HN *n.* (see quot.).

    1982 A. Shaw *Dict. Pop/Rock* 156: *HN.* Abbreviation of "house nigger," the latest black term for an Uncle Tom.

HNIC *n.* [initialism of *head nigger in charge*] *Black E.* a black person in a position of authority.

    1972 R.L. Williams *BITCH* 4: *HNIC.* Head Nigger In Charge. **1973** Andrews & Owens *Black Lang.* 81: *H.N.I.C.*—Head Nigger In Charge. Sometimes *N.I.C.* Nigger In Charge. *a***1979** Gillespie & Fraser *To BE* 41 [chapter heading]: H.N.I.C. **1990** *All Things Considered* (Nat. Pub. Radio) (Dec. 26): He needs an HNIC—a head black in charge.…Mr. Bush talks and listens, but he must do more than listen. **1993** *Time* (June 7) 62: There's a part of him that wants to be the next H.N.I.C. It's not just white folks holding him up. **1994** Smitherman *Black Talk* 134: *HNIC* Head Nigger in Charge; a Black person put in charge by whites, usually not in charge of anything meaningful.

ho *n.* [resp. of *whore* to represent a Black E pron.] Esp. *Black E.* **1.a.** a whore; prostitute. [Prob. the orig. sense.]

    1965 in W. King *Black Anthol.* 303: Most of the hip whoes [*sic*] around the city eat at Joe's. **1965** in B. Jackson *Swim Like Me* 157: Then Smilin' Moe, he went for the who'. **1966** Elli *Riot* 171: They're always talkin' about their "white hoes" like every white whore on the streets is hustlin' for a shine. *ca***1969** Rabe *Hummel* 80: That ain't no dead Ho jus' 'cause she layin' so still. **1970** A. Young *Snakes* 42: I might…talk some old nickel ho into runnin round with me. **1971** Giovanni *Gemini* 17 [ref. to 1950's]: "*Ho*" was always a favorite [insult].…Yo' mama's…a "ho!" **1972** Pfister *Beer Cans* 23: Them hos in them doors/watchin' & wishin'. **1972** in *Playboy* (Feb. 1973) 182: You want to get a good ho and get laid. **1974** Angelou *Gather Together* 137: When you turn the first trick, you'll be a 'ho. A stone 'ho. **1974** in D.C. Dance *Shuckin' & Jivin'* 228: In walked this ho. **1977** Bunker *Animal Factory* 3: Nigger calls himself a pimp…an' ain't nuthin' but a shade tree for a ho. *a***1979** Pepper & Pepper *Straight Life* 337 [ref. to 1965–66]: I got this white "ho." **1981** *Penthouse* (Mar.) 157: Players don't socialize with *ho's.* **1984** Sample *Raceboss* 25: Where there's hoes and boozin, there's sho to be gamblin. *a***1986** in *NDAS*: The bar was a hangout for players and hos. **1992** Hosansky & Sparling *Working Vice* 132: His bondsmen knew the judge that sent one of his ho's to the workhouse for sixty days. **1993** Mowry *Six Out Seven* 53: Most dudes just say she a ho.

b. Esp. *Black E.* a sexually promiscuous woman.—sometimes used with reduced force to mean simply 'woman'.

    1958–59 in Abrahams *Deep Down in Jungle* 263: *Main Who'* (pronounced like "hoe")—Best girlfriend. **1988** *Village Voice* (N.Y.C.) (Jan. 19) 36: What makes a girl a ho? Because she won't give you none? **1989** *Life* (July) 27: Now he's *getting together* with a girl who sleeps around, a real *ho.* **1990** *Village Voice* (N.Y.C.) (Aug. 7) 80: She threatens to smack a "ho" who "gets out of hand." **1993** Ephron et al. *Sleepless in Seattle* (film): She's a ho! My dad's been captured by a ho! **1993** *Newsweek* (Nov. 29) 62: A ghetto world where the men sling dope and tote firearms, and the women are bitches or "hoes." **1994** *Santa Barbara* (Calif.) *News-Press* (Feb. 19) D1: Frank's use of "broad" and "chick" were, for a tamer time, the equivalent of today's "bitch" and "ho." **1994** *Newsweek* (Oct. 17) 64: You put on something nice, they call you a 'ho.…They say, "She's oversexed—she's no virgin." **1995** *Jerry Springer Show* (synd. TV series): She's not a prostitute, [but] she's a *ho!*

2. a sexually promiscuous man.

    1993 "Tribe Called Quest" *Electric Relaxation* (rap song): She simply said, "No," labeled me a ho. **1995** *Jerry Springer Show* (synd. TV series): You guys are ho's.

hobble *v.* **1.** *Und.* to arrest (a person); (*also*) to steal (an object).

    ****1718** in Partridge *Dict. Und.* 335: Bound or hobbled, *alias* Taken. ****1789** G. Parker *Life's Painter* 172: *Hobbled*, a term when any of the gang is taken up, and committed for trial, to say, such a one is *hobbled.*

1791 [W. Smith] *Confess. T. Mount* 19: To take, *to hobble. Ibid.* 21: His golden chain I hobbled first.

2. to restrain.

1870 Duval *Big-Foot* 118: While it was firing off the men dodged behind everything that was handy, some of them hallooing, "Hobble the thing," "Rope it," "Pitch it into the creek," etc. **1903** A. Adams *Log of a Cowboy* 284 [ref. to 1882]: Will you kindly hobble your lip?

hobby *n. Stu.* an English translation of a foreign-language text; PONY.

1851 B. Hall *College Wds.* 162: *Hobby.* A translation. Hobbies are used by some students in translating Latin, Greek, and other languages, who for this reason are said to ride, in contradistinction to others who learn their lessons by study, who are said to *dig* or *grub.*

hobbyhorse *v.* (of a boat) to rock rapidly fore and aft.

1979 G. Wolff *Duke of Deception* 147: I looked sharp, saw the boat hobbyhorsing a little.

hobnail express *n. Army.* the act of marching across country. [Quots. ref. to WWI.]

1918 in *Chrons. of Okla.* LXV (1987) 24: Left Minot by hobnail express. **1919** Jacobsen *Blue & Gray* 52: Seeing France on the "Hobnail Express." **1919** Roth *Co. E* 72: That part of the A.E.F. which tours France by the hobnail express. **1919** Thompson *310th Infantry* 109: None dreamed that the Argonne, seemingly so far distant, was our ultimate destination; proceed "without delay" via the "Hob-Nail Express." **1936** Reddan *Other Men's Lives* 137: From this point on we were very much like a "barnstorming" circus making one or two day stands, marching at night with such sleep as we could catch during daylight hours, touring France via "hobnailed express."

hobo *n.* [orig. unkn.; the plausible ety. suggestions are these: *hoe-boy* 'a hoehand' is reasonable on phonological as well as semantic grounds, but is unrecorded by lexicographers; HO-BOY, *n.*, is poorly documented, though sense 2 (reported from a single source decades after the event) comes from the same geographical area—the Pacific Northwest—as the 1889 quots. of *hobo.* The relevance of HO-BOY, *v.,* is uncertain; see the note there for discussion. An assimilated form of HOEBUCK has not previously been conjectured. See also Mencken, *Amer. Lang. Supp. II,* p. 679; *AS* II (1927) 386, XLVII (1972) 303–04; Allsop, *Hard Travellin'*, pp. 103–05]

1. a tramp; *(hence)* a usu. homeless vagabond or itinerant who, typically stealing rides on freight cars, alternately travels and works, esp. at seasonal or unskilled occupations. Now *S.E.* [The precise date of the *ca*1885 quot. is not known, though it occurs in a parody of the song "The Regular Army O!" (*ca*1875) by the vaudevillians Harrigan & Hart. The parody's reference to Indian warfare in Arizona argues for the assigned date, but a rather earlier or later origin cannot reasonably be ruled out.]

*ca*1885 in Dolph *Sound Off!* 9: When we [Irish recruits] got out to Fort Hobo they run us in the mill. **1889** in *DA:* The hobo crop is more plentiful than ever before. **1889** in *DA:* The tramp has changed his name, or rather had it changed for him, and now he is a "Hobo."...One constable recently laid the blacksnake on a quintette of hobos who refused to work. **1891** *Contemporary Rev.* (Aug.) 255: The tramp's name for himself and his fellow is *Hobo,* plural *Hoboes.* **1891** in Brunvand *Readings in Folklore* 293: Come join in the chorus and sing of its fame,/You poor hungry hoboes that's starved on the claim. **1893** Griggs *Lyrics* 263: The origin of *Hobo,* the term now so generally applied to the railroad grader, is unknown, but is generally supposed to have come from the salutation of "Ho, boy!" which was shouted by one workman to another....The Hobos are enlisted...by labor agents in the larger...western cities and shipped, in carloads, to the points where wanted. **1893** in *Independent* (Nov. 21, 1901) 2761: He said you was seeking information from the fraternity of Haut Beaus. **1894** *Atlantic* (Sept.) 318: He...had been a well-known "hobo" (beggar) out West some years before. **1894** in S. Crane *Complete Stories* 139: By the time he had reached City Hall Park he was...completely plastered with yells of "bum" and "hobo." **1894** O. Wister, in Remington *Wister* 90: A hobo is a wandering unemployed person, a

stealer of rides on freight trains, a diner at the back door, eternally seeking honest work, and when brought face to face with it eternally retreating. **1897** in *DAE:* The men who do the most important work [in the threshing season]—are transient laborers....Men of this character are not "hoboes." **1899** "J. Flynt" *Tramping* 394: *Hobo:* a tramp. Derivation obscure. **1899** H. Garland *Eagle's Heart* 341: She's too high class for a hobo like me. **1902** in "O. Henry" *Works* 430: Chicken Ruggles...was a "hobo." *a*1909 Tillotson *Detective* 65: He was a common, ordinary "hobo." **1913** in *DAE:* Hobo is a much misunderstood word. It should not be confused with tramp or vagrant. It means a casual, migratory worker, either unskilled or jack-of-all trades. One who works at seasonal occupations or on construction projects. **1923** H.L. Foster *Beachcomber* 171: I was beginning to feel a peculiar satisfaction in being a hobo. **1927** *DN* V 450: *Hobo and tin can route,* n. The Houston and Texas Central Railway. **1930** Irwin *Tramp & Und. Slang* 100: *Hobo.*—A migratory worker, especially one who will work whenever he finds an opportunity; a tramp who works. **1937** Reitman *Box-Car Bertha* 142: I found a hobo over in Union Square. She's on the bum and sick. **1967** Allsop *Hard Travellin'* 28: All the official agencies informed me that...the hobo was extinct. **1982** D.A. Harper *Good Company* 94: The man on skid row...that's the true bum. The hobo will work.

2. [perh. short for **hobo cell*] (see 1907 quot.).

1903 J. London *Abyss* 234: As a vagrant in the "Hobo" of a California jail, I have been served better food and drink than the London workman receives in his coffee-houses. **1907** J. London *Road* 109 [ref. to *ca*1894]: From the office we were led to the "Hobo" and locked in. The "Hobo" is that part of a prison where minor offenders are confined together in a large iron cage. Since hoboes constitute the principal division of the minor offenders, the aforesaid iron cage is called the Hobo.

3. [pun on *provost*] *Army.* (see quot.).

1907 Moss *Officers Manual* 243: *Hobo.* The provost sergeant.

4. *S.W.* the penis.—usu. considered vulgar.

*ca*1910 in Logsdon *Whorehouse Bells* 40: I tried his courage all night long but his hobo wouldn't stand. *Ibid.* 65: Woke up one mornin' on the old Chisholm Trail,/With my hobo in my hand and a heifer by the tail.

5. *Trucking.* (see quot.).

*a*1977 W.I. Little *Transp.-Logistics Dict.* 159: *Hobo.* Tractor that is transferred from one terminal to another.

hobo *v.* to live or travel as a hobo.—also used trans. Now *S.E.* [The relevance of the 1848 quot. at HO-BOY, *v.,* is uncertain; see note there.]

[**1848** (quot. at HO-BOY, *v.*).] **1905** Sinclair *Jungle* 31: One could go out on the road and "hobo it," as the men phrased it, and see the country, and have...an easy time riding on the freight cars. **1907** Peele *N.C. to S. Calif* 32: "Been hoboing?" asked the darkey. *Ibid.* 60: To hobo the [rail]roads successfully, one has to give up all thought of life or death. **1908** J. London *M. Eden* 158: I can hobo, all right, all right. **1916** (quot. at PIKER). **1918** Livingston *Delcassee* 48: Every one of these...beggars...came to the trimming of his anatomy while hoboing trains. **1923** H.L. Foster *Beachcomber* 183: Having hoboed my way thus far, I could afford to travel as a passenger the rest of the way. **1950** A. Lomax *Mr. Jelly Roll* 134: No, I can't hobo. I tried that once. **1983** Curry *River's in Blood* 162: He "hoboed" part of the route. **1994** *Nation* (Oct. 3) 353: Women were not supposed to hobo, sleep around or drink.

hobo coffee *n.* (see quot.).

1987 E. Spencer *Macho Man* 71 [ref. to 1968]: Gunny always has a pot of hobo coffee brewed....Hobo coffee is coffee grounds boiled in water without filters.

hobo pullman *n. R.R.* SIDE-DOOR PULLMAN.

1939 Attaway *Breathe Thunder* 1: We were seated in the doorway of...our "hobo pullman."

ho-boy *n.* **1.** (see 1859 quot.).

1857 in Bartlett *Amer.* (ed. 2) 197: Degraded to the occupation of a *haut-boy.* **1859** Bartlett *Amer.* (ed. 2): *Ho-boy,* or *Haut-boy.* A nightman. New York.

2. (see quot.).

1920 *DN* V 86: "Hobo"...The following story...is vouched for by a relative of mine who was working on the Oregon Short Line railroad in the 1880's. The mail carriers on the Oregon Short Line used the call "Ho, boy!" when they were delivering mail. Gradually these men came to be called "hoboys." Then those who travelled along the tracks, not carrying mail, came to be so called. In its final stage of development, the *-y* was dropped and the word used indiscriminately to designate vagrants.

ho-boy *v.* [orig. uncertain; see note] to go; travel. [The orig. of this word, and its relevance to HOBO, *n.* or *v.*, are unknown. Though it would seem to be an Anglicization of a putative MexSp word *¡jopo!* 'get out!', cited in *DN* V [1927] 450, this word, while called "familiar" in that source, is otherwise unattested. Though it fits in well with HOBO, *v.*, that word is so much later that any connection must be conjectural.]
　　1848 *New Orleans Picayune* (Aug. 19) 2: A year's bronzing and "ho-boying" about among the mountains of that charming country called Mexico.

hobs *n.pl. Army.* hobnailed shoes.
　　1918 Straub *Diary* (entry for May 26): I drew another new blouse and a pair of American "hobs" from our Q.M. **1919** in Cornebise *Amaroc News* 121: Clad in O.D. from head to hobs. **1920** Acker *Thru the War* 163: A Dutch handmaiden…even wipes the dust from my other pair of "hobs."

Ho Chi Minh *n. Mil. in Vietnam.* a sandal fashioned from tire treads or inner tubes, worn by the Viet Cong. Now *hist.* Also **Ho Chi.**
　　1985 Bodey *F.N.G.* 13: They all have on the sandals made out of tires, "Ho Chis." **1988** Clodfelter *Mad Minutes* 135: "Ho Chi Minh" rubber tire sandals. **1968–90** Linderer *Eyes of Eagle* 144: [The trail] was covered with fresh Ho Chi Minh tracks.

Ho Chi Minh's revenge *n. Mil. & Journ. in Vietnam.* dysentery or diarrhea contracted in Vietnam. Also **Ho Chi Minhs.** Cf. MONTEZUMA'S REVENGE, PHARAOH'S REVENGE.
　　1968 Brass *Bleeding Earth* 124: VD, a few fevers and colds, now and then a run of the Ho Chi Minhs (gastro-enteritis is known in South Vietnam as "Ho Chi Minh's Revenge") make up most of the medical cases we get in the ward. **1968** W.C. Anderson *Gooney Bird* 187: I'd just as soon have malaria as Ho Chi Minh's Revenge for two days after each pill. **1973** Huggett *Body Count* 207: It wasn't malaria. Only Ho Chi Minh's revenge in triplicate, maybe dysentery. **1977** Caputo *Rumor of War* 220: For Christ's sake, sir, I've got Ho Chi Minh's revenge. **1981** C. Nelson *Picked Bullets Up* 339: Caught a nasty case of Ho Chi Minh's revenge. *a*1991 J.R. Wilson *Landing Zones* 172: What the medical people called "Ho Chi Minh's Revenge."

hock¹ *n.* usu. *pl.* a person's foot or (in 1965 quot.) leg; (*occ.*) a shoe; in phr. **rattle (one's) hocks** *West.* to get moving. Also **huck.**
　　*1785 Grose *Vulgar Tongue: Hocks.* A vulgar appellation for the feet. You have left the marks of your dirty hocks on my clean stairs; a frequent complaint from a mop-squeezer to a footman. **1859** Matsell *Vocab.* 42: *Hocks.* The feet. **1894** (quot. at *hit the breeze* s.v. BREEZE, *n.*). **1900** in *AS* XLI (1966) 24: They make ye peel your hucks in the street and walk to the bar in your stocking feet. **1907** Cook *Border & Buffalo* 88: As the cowboys would say, "I fairly rattled my hocks." **1926** *Writer's Mo.* (Mar.) 199: "Hucks" are feet, and "huckin' it" is "riding Shank's mare." **1929** Barr *Let Tomorrow Come* 147: Sit down and rest your hocks. **1935** Coburn *Law Rides Range* 25: Rattle yore hocks. You too, Peg Leg. **1936** R. Adams *Cowboy Lingo* 190: Pull off yo' shoes an' smell of yo' socks,/An' grab yo' a heifer an' rattle yo' hocks. **1941** L. Breslow *Great Guns* (film): Now, rattle your hocks! **1945** Hubbard *R.R. Ave.* 357: *Rattle her hocks*—Get speed out of an engine. **1958** P. Field *Devil's R.* 128: On your hocks, mister—you're comin' with me. **1961** Peacock *Valhalla* 340: Stay off my hocks! **1965** in B. Jackson *Swim Like Me* 158: She had long curly locks and big fine hocks. **1968** J.P. Miller *Race for Home* 284: Well, you better *git* in the mood, boy, and rattle yo' hocks, 'cause ole Dawg here he li'ble to commence to *biting.*

¶ In phrase:

¶ **on the hocks** (see quot.).
　　1930 Irwin *Tramp & Und. Slang* 137: *On the Hocks.*—Literally standing. Impoverished.

hock² *n.* [< Du *hok* 'hutch, kennel, prison, (hence) debt']

¶ In phrases:

¶ **catch in [the] hock** *Gamb. & Und.* to catch in the act of cheating or wrongdoing.

　　1859 Matsell *Vocab.* 42: *Caught in hock;* caught by the heels. "*If the cove should be caught in the hock he won't snickle,*" if the fellow should be caught in the act, he would not tell. *Ibid.* 113: When one gambler is caught by another…and is beat, then he is in hock. Men are only caught, or put in hock, on the race-tracks, or on the steamboats down South. **1872** Burnham *Secret Service* vi: *In the hock,* in the act of commission; on the spot. *Ibid.* 82: This notorious villain…on this occasion was fairly "nabbed in the hock."

¶ **in hock, 1.** Esp. *Und.* in custody; in prison.
　　1859 Matsell *Vocab.* 113: Among thieves a man is in hock, when he is in prison. **1860* in Partridge *Dict. Und.* 336: In about ten minutes…we had them "in hock" (the cells). **1882** in Sonnichsen *Billy King* 60: That accounts for your not being taken out of "hock" before. **1887** Walling *N.Y. Chief of Police* 286: She has sent money to defend a man "in hock" to the uttermost parts of the United States. **1899** A.H. Lewis *Sandburrs* 152: His breakin' out of hock that time is some luck, but mostly 'cause Joe himself is a dead wise guy an' onto his job. **1902** Harben *Abner Daniel* 234: I determined to have it by hook or crook, ef it killed me, or put me in hock the rest o' my life. **1927** in *AS* III (Feb. 1928) 255: *In Hock.* In prison. **1944** in Gould *Tracy* 50: Now we can get that ham actor out of hock before he falls apart on us.

2. in pawn. Now *S.E.*
　　1883 in *OED2*: We deeply regret that our india-rubber armor is in hock. **1884** in *DA*: My other coat's in hock. **1896** Ade *Artie* 94: They go back home and leave all their stuff in hock. **1898** in J. London *Letters* 7: I…got my watch out of hock. **1898** in *DAE*: His burros were in hock and so were his blankets and his very cooking utensils. **1900** Flandrau *Freshman* 102: I haven't been able…even to get my watch out of hock. **1907** in H.C. Fisher *A. Mutt* 7: With the old cannon in hock, he is still at it. **1908** McGaffey *Show Girl* 37: I had everything in hock but my self-respect. **1925** Faulkner *N.O. Sketches* 69: It's in hock for two dollars and a half. **1937** Asch *The Road* 204: Everything he had was in hock to the banks. **1953** *Mr. & Mrs. North* (CBS-TV): The first time this has been out of hock in some time.

3. in debt.
　　1900 Ade *More Fables* 138: She took him out of Hock. **1903** A.H. Lewis *Boss* 135: The Chief has got that jurist in hock to him. **1916** Marcin *Cheaters* 9: We're in hock to Lazarre for the coin to plant ourselves in this house. **1925–26** J. Black *Can't Win* 390: I was in hock to friends who saved me from a heavy sentence. **1949** *New Yorker* (Nov. 5) 86: He is so much in hock, specially with the feed bill. **1950** *Best Army Short Stories* 88: If he ever gets out of hock he should run for sheriff. **1953** W. Fisher *Waiters* 36: You gonna be in hock all your natural life. **1956** Holiday & Dufty *Lady Sings Blues* 1: She worked her way out of hock in the hospital. **1961** Rossen & Carroll *Hustler* (film): What's the kid in hock for so far? **1962** in A. Sexton *Letters* 150: I'm still in hock to him. **1968** Simoun *Madigan* (film): He and his nitwit wife were in hock to a loan association. **1988** P. Beck & P. Massman *Rich Men, Single Women* 286: I'm in hock up to my ears. **1991** "R. Brown" & R. Angus *A.K.A. Narc* 41: That would have put me in hock for the *next* two months.

4. in trouble.
　　1970 Vance *Courageous & Proud* 70: We're going north to help the Vietnamese Army get their goddam ass out of hock. **1973** Overgard *Hero* 115: And if any son-of-a-bitch fucks up and puts the rest of us in hock, then I will personally kick his asshole into his throat. **1976** Sgt., U.S. Army, Dugway Proving Ground, Utah (coll. J. Ball): Miss P.T. one more time and your ass is in hock.

hock³ *n.* HOCKEY¹, 2.
　　1948 Wolfert *Act of Love* 130: It's just a crock, just a crock of it, just a crock of hock. **1966** "T. Pendleton" *Iron Orchard* 139: But I jus' wanta tell you this one thing, an' no more hock, see?

hock¹ *v.* [sugg. by *in hock,* 2, s.v. HOCK, *n.*] **1.** to pawn. Now *S.E.*
　　1878 in *DA*: To soak—*to hock*—Yer upper benjamin at yer uncle's to get the "sugar" for a good square meal. **1880** Sala *Amer. Revisited* II 133: "Hock my sparks," "soak my gems," and "Walker my rainbows"—to use the American euphemisms for the act of pawning your jewellery. **1893** *Life* (Feb. 2) 70: When you vamoose dis ranch, don't hock yer Bibles, but…read dem an' buzz wid yer neighbor on religion. **1895** F.P. Dunne, in Schaaf *Dooley* 169: I'll hock me coronet. **1896** in Cather *Short Fiction* 557: Got anything left you can hock? **1907** in H.C. Fisher *A. Mutt* 7: If I hadn't hocked my gun I'd take the short

cut. **1925** in Hammett *Knockover* 73: Myra...came into his joint...and hocked a lot of stuff. **1930** Bodenheim *Roller Skates* 133: Better not hock your skin, Terry. *Ibid.* 280: Hock your skin...Make a difficult promise. **1939–40** O'Hara *Pal Joey* 3: I finally...hocked my diamond ring. **1948** in *DA:* I hocked all my possessions...and was on a train to Grainbelt City.

2. to steal; (*hence*) to secure for oneself.

1934 Appel *Brain Guy* 77: Was the guy planning to frame him? How many years in the coop for a hocked car? *Ibid.* 163: It's a good car. I hocked it from a rich guy. **1959** Farris *Harrison High* 140: Where'd you hock the beast, Griffo? *Ibid.* 208: Just a little driving....An easy way to hock a gee. **1971** *Current Slang* V (Spring) 14: Hock, v. To steal. **1973** *TULIPQ* (coll. B.K. Dumas): *Hock*...steal or swipe. **1976** Rutgers Univ. grad. student: When I was a kid in Kalamazoo, we always used *hock* to mean steal something. Always. I didn't even know it meant to pawn something until I went to Notre Dame.

3. to advertise; hawk.

1977 Shem *House of God* 163: The Yankee Clipper is hocking instant coffee on TV these days.

4. [by confusion with *hawk*] *Juve.* to hawk up (phlegm). Cf. HOCKER.

1992 *Down the Shore* (Fox-TV): I think you hocked up your gallbladder. **1993** *Beavis & Butt-head* (MTV): Would you let her hock a loogie on you?

hock² v. to prevaricate or exaggerate. Cf. HOCKEY¹, *n.*, 2.

1966 "T. Pendleton" *Iron Orchard* 139: Don' think I'm hockin' ol' son, 'cause I never had a brother, but if I did, you'd be him, an' I mean it.

hock³ v. [prob. sugg. by HOCK¹, *n.*] to kick.

1974 Strasburger *Rounding Third* 109: A guy gets hocked in the jock, and then stuffs a guy in on the rebound.

hocker n. *Juve.* a gob of phlegm (or, broadly, any substance) expelled from the mouth. Cf. HOCK¹, *v.*, 4.

1966 in IUFA *Folk Speech: Hocker*—Nasal mucus and spit all rolled up into one. **1968–70** *Current Slang III & IV* 68: *Hocker,* n. Phlegm expelled from the throat.—University of Kentucky. **1970** Wakefield *Going All the Way* 107: One guy spit a big hocker into the cinders. **1981** *Nat. Lampoon* (July) 55: Drop a big hocker in the cream. **1990** *Simpsons* (Fox-TV): One hocker coming up. **1992** Strawberry & Rust *Darryl* 64: Buddy...opened his mouth and spit a full hocker of chewing gum all over his shoe.

hockey¹ n. 1. excrement.

1886 in *DARE: Hockie* is used in East Tennessee among little children, which may be connected by the original word "cacky." **1923** *DN* V 210: *Hockey,* n. Dung. [**1931** *N.Y. Sun* (Oct. 30): There is a game that they play on the ice in the North which we who were brought up in the South almost instinctively blush at the mention of.] **1935** Hurston *Mules & Men* 215: Dat lie you told is po' as owl harkey. **1942** McAtee *Supp. Grant Co. Dial.* 6 [ref. to 1890's]: *Hockey,* n., human excrement. **1948** in Randolph *Pissing in Snow* 53: He went out to the privy and filled two big capsules with fresh hockey. **1961** Forbes *Goodbye to Some* 106: Someone pitched a lot of hocky in there again last night. *1966 Shaw & Spiegl *Scouse* 45: *Ockey* excrement.

2. untruths; nonsense; foolishness; BULLSHIT, 1.a.

1930 Schuyler *Black No More* 78: Oh, that's a lotta hockey. **1945** Himes *If He Hollers* 70: Don't hand me that hockey. **1945** *AS* (Dec.) 263: The *hockey team* are those [officer candidates at Ft. Benning, Ga.] who, because of their general deficiencies, are most often called upon to act as leaders in tactical problems....*Hockey team* originates in a pun upon *hockey,* the game, and *hockey*...a synonym for dung. **1947** Willingham *End as a Man* 78: Don't you try and hand *me* any of that hocky about being a white man! **1959** Cochrell *Barren Beaches* 49: The whole outfit stays here till chow goes unless you snap out of your hockey. **1969** *N.Y. Post* (May 17): A lot of hockey.

hockey² n. usu. *pl.* [HOCK¹, *n.* + *-ey*] a person's leg.

1945 *Best from Yank* 62: Notice the young lady, or frail...[and] her distracting legs, or hockeys.

hockey v. to defecate.

1902 *DN* II 236: *Hawky,* or *hockey*....Child's word for go to stool. **1923** *DN* V 210: *Hockey*...To evacuate the bowels. **1935** J. Conroy *World to Win* 40: Well, why ya standin' there shiverin' like a dog hockeyin' peach seeds? **1942** McAtee *Supp. Grant Co. Dial.* 6 [ref. to 1890's]: *Hockey*...v., to defecate.

hockey box n. the buttocks.

1979–82 Gwin *Overboard* 119: Willy, just look at the hockey box on this 'un.

hockey puck n. [introduced *ca*1963 by Don Rickles, U.S. comedian] a stupid or useless person.

1963 D. Rickles, on *Dick Van Dyke Show* (CBS-TV): You hockey puck! **1988** *TV Guide* (Mar. 26) A-4: Come on, Bob, you hockey puck. **1990** *Current Affair* (synd. TV series): Then some hockey puck came up to me. **1995** *N.Y. Times* (Dec. 22) B7 (adv.): Find out when and where all your favorite movies are playing. You can even buy tickets. So don't be a hockey puck. Call 777-FILM. **1995** Whedon et al. *Toy Story* (film): What are *you* looking at, ya *hockey puck?*

hock shop n. a pawnshop. Now *colloq.* or *S.E.*

*1871 in *OED2:* That piece I dropped in the *hock* shop. **1879** *Nat. Police Gaz.* (Sept. 13) 14: Sending out rings and watches to "hock-shops." **1886** *Lantern* (N.O.) (Sept. 22) 2: Take the bed too, and run it into a hock shop. **1898** Riis *Mulberry St.* 190: Wait till I send round to the hockshop. **1899** Cullen *Tales* 27: At a hock shop, for a couple o' dollars. **1902** in *DA:* As a last resort, fell into a hock-shop. **1902–03** Ade *People You Know* 96: It meant...the Pianola to the Hock-shop. **1906** *Nat. Police Gaz.* (Aug. 18) 6: This isn't a hock shop. **1906** A.H. Lewis *Confessions* 66: Do you know Lazarus, who keeps the hock shop in Chatham Square? **1908** in H.C. Fisher *A. Mutt* 33: The Mutt family parrot which the police found in a hock shop. **1919** *DN* V 65: *Hock-shop,* a pawn shop. I just got my watch back from the *hock-shop.* New Mexico. **1925** in Hammett *Knockover* 73: A hockshop dealer came in this morning. **1956** M. Levin *Compulsion* 53: Years ago he ran a fancy hock shop.

hocky adj. [sugg. by HOCKEY¹, *n.*] (see quot.).

1974 Eble *Campus Slang* (Oct.) 2: *Hocky*—adj., (a general derogatory term) disagreeable, unpleasant: What a hocky place!; That was a hocky dinner we had.

hocus n. *Und.* **1.** a stupefying drug; (*hence*) (see 1938 quot.).

*1823 "J. Bee" *Slang: Hocus.*—A deleterious drug mixed with wine, &c. which enfeebles the person acted upon. *1865 in *Comments on Ety.* XVII (Oct. 1, 1987) 16: Folkestone...was afraid she might "tumble" to the "hocus" before drinking it. **1938** in D.W. Maurer *Lang. Und.* 103: *Hocus.* A ration of cocaine, morphine, or heroin in solution, ready for injection. **1953** Anslinger & Tompkins *Traf. in Narc.* 310: *Hokus.* Opium. **1971** *Inter. Jour. Add.* VI 359: *Hocus.* morphine.

2. see HOCUS-POCUS.

hocus v. 1. Esp. *Und.* to stupefy with drugs; to drug (liquor). [The sense given in the bracketed quots. is apposite, but unrecorded in U.S.]

[*1725 *New Canting Dict.: Hocus,* disguised in Liquor; drunk.] [*1785 Grose *Vulgar Tongue:* He is quite *hocus;* he is quite drunk.] *1821 in Partridge *Dict. Und.* 336: To *hocus* a man, is to put something into his drink, *on the sly,* of a sleepy, stupifying [*sic*] quality, that renders him unfit for action. *1831 in *OED2:* [A witness] saw May put some gin into Bishop's tea. He said, "Are you going to hocus (or Burke) me?" *1836 in *F & H* III 324: For that we hocussed first his drink. *1837 C. Dickens *Pickwick Papers* ch. xiii: "What do you mean by 'hocussing' brandy-and-water?"..."Puttin' laud'num in it," replied Sam. *a1839 T. De Quincey, in *OED2:* The landlord they intended to disable by a trick then newly introduced amongst robbers, and termed hocussing. **1855** Wise *Tales for Marines* 157: But I larned as 'ow he 'ad designs to peach, and so I hokussed his drink. **1859** Matsell *Vocab.* 42: *Hocus.* To stupify. "Hocus the bloke's lush, and then frisk his sacks," put something into the fellow's drink that will stupify him, and then search his pockets. **1880** in Tamony *Americanisms* (No. 29) 4: Randall...was hocussed....To "hocus" a man is to put something in his drink of a narcotic quality, that renders him unfit for action. **1887** Walling *N.Y. Chief of Police* 464: It is quite possible to "hocus" beer by its mixture with a few grains of opium. *1892 in *OED2:* The bribing of jockies and the "hocussing" of horses. *a1961 R.H. Dillon *Shanghaiing Days* 210 [ref. to *a1900]: A wily fellow tried to "hocus" him...[with] whiskey dosed with knockout drops.

2. *Gamb.* (see quot.).

*a1945–50 in D.W. Maurer *Lang. Und.* 187: To *hocus:* To alter fair dice to crooked dice.

hocus-pocus n. [pun on syn. POKE, *n.*] *Und.* (Esp. among pickpockets) a small bag or purse (*obs.*); (*hence*) a wallet, pocketbook, or billfold. Also **hocus, okus.**

   ca1640** in *OED:* His very fingers cryed "give me the gold!" which...he put into his hocas pocas, a little dormer under his right skirt. **1933** Ersine *Prison Slang* 44: *Hocus, n.* A pocketbook, leather. "Sock him and grab his *hocus.*" **1935** Pollock *Und. Speaks: Hokus-pocus,* a pocketbook. **1942** *True Detective* (Mar.) 73: *Okus.* **1942–49** Goldin et al. *DAUL* 148: *Okus.* (Chiefly Mid-West pickpockets' jargon) A wallet. *a1955** in D.W. Maurer *Lang. Und.* 243: *Hocus* or *hocus-pocus. n.* See *poke.*

hod *n.* *Naut.* a ship.

   1972 Cleaves *Sea Fever* 28 [ref. to 1920's]: The old hod's dry as a drum, Captain....Anyhow, if she makes water now her boilers won't blow hell out of her. *Ibid.* 101: That bloody coal hod.

hodad *n.* [perh. alter. of *hodag* 'a kind of grotesque imaginary beast of Wisconsin' (see Dorson, *Man and Beast in American Comic Legend,* pp. 38–44, and *DARE*); but this is made unlikely by the California orig. of the present term; perh. fr. "Ho, dad" as form of address]

Orig. *Surfing.* an obnoxious or offensive nonsurfer who frequents surfing beaches; (*hence*) any obnoxious or offensive person. Also **ho-daddy, hodag.**

   1961 *Life* (Sept. 1) 48: "Ho-daddy" (intruding wise guy). "If you're not a surfer,...you're not 'in.'" ***1962** in *OED2: Ho-dad,* anyone who annoys board-riders while they surf. **1963** *Time* (Aug. 9) 49: They climb a 12-ft. wall of water...till the wave carries them in to the hot white shore where gremmies, ho-dads and wahines watch in wonder. **1963** Rusoff *Beach Party* (film): Where the gremmies and the hodads never go. **1964** *Look* (June 30) 55: *Hodad:* objectionable non-surfing hanger-on. **1968** Kirk & Hanle *Surfer's Hndbk.* 129: Hodads are great for slapping homebrew bleaches on their heads to give them that so-called "surfer-look." *Ibid.* 140: *Hodad, hodaddy:* usually a non-surfer; wise guy; loudmouth; beach bum; beach hood. **1973** *Urban Life & Culture* II 147: At many schools, the "surfers" came into conflict with the lower stratum, whom they labeled "hodadies" or "hodads." **1979** Gram *Foxes* 99: And Susan Halpern and all her spiffy hodaddy friends down at Newport. **1982** Corey & Westermark *Fer Shurr!: Hodad*...cretin, clown, wimp, phony. **1985** Schwendinger & Schwendinger *Adolescent Subculture* 103: The metaphor, Hodad, was derived from the Surfer peer greeting: Ho! Dad! **1988** *S.F. Chronicle* (Aug. 15) (Punch 7): Somebody who doesn't surf but constantly points out surfers' mistakes is called a "hodad." **1989** Univ. Tenn. student theme: That guy is such a hodag! **1990** *Mystery Sci. Theater* (Comedy Central TV): Come on, you hodaddies!

hodgy var. HACHI.

hoebuck *n.* [var. of Eng. dial. *hawbuck*] a country bumpkin.

   1836 *Davy Crockett's Almanack* (1837) 36: I suppose you think I'm a hoebuck, because I'm on a keel, and have not got a good coat on; I'm a real tar, and by G—d I'll whip any body with a good coat on.

hoe down *v.* to defeat utterly; *clean out* s.v. CLEAN, 2.

   1841 *Spirit of Times* (Feb. 13) 595: He gets hoe'd down by being a *few* too much against the winner.

¶ In phrase:

¶ **hoe it down** [or **off**] to dance energetically or riotously; dance a hoedown. Hence (orig. *colloq.,* now *S.E.*) **hoe-down,** *n.*

   [**1807** W. Irving, in *DA:* As to dancing, no Long-Island negro could shuffle you "double trouble," or "hoe corn and dig potatoes" more scientifically.] **1835** in *DA:* "Pooh," replied his panting rib, hoeing it off like a regular Juba. **1850** Doten *Journals* I 80: I'm thinking of how they will "hoe her down" in old Pilgrim hall this evening. **1851** F.B. Mayer *Pen & Pencil* 40: The fiddle scrapes a merry jig, a "ho-down" follows. **1867** Clark *Sailor's Life* 322: "Go in there, Sal." "Hoe her down, Molly." **1874** McCoy *Cattle Trade* 209: His eyes lit up with excitement, liquor, and lust, he plunges in and "hoes it down" at a terrible rate in the most approved yet awkward country style. **1942** in *DA: Hoe down*...to dance vigorously.

hoe in *v.* *Stu.* (see quot.). Cf. syn. GRUB, 2.

   1851 B. Hall *College Wds.* 162: *Hoe In.* At Hamilton College, to strive vigorously.

hog *n.* **1.a.** a shilling; (*hence*) any small silver coin.

   ***1673** in *OED2:* Shilling, *Bord* or *Hog.* ***1698–99** "B.E." *Dict. Cant-*

ing Crew: Hog...a Shilling....*Will you fence your Hog in the next Boozing-ken,*...Will you Spend your Shilling at the next Alehouse. ***1773** in Partridge *Dict. Und.* 337: Because we could not three hog pay. **1807** Tufts *Autobiog.* 293 [ref. to 1794]: *Hog*...a pistareen. ***1809** in *F & H* III 327: "It's only a tester or a hog they want your honour to give 'em...," said Paddy...."all as one as an English shilling." ***1812** Vaux *Vocab.: Hog:* a shilling; five, ten, or more shillings, are called five, ten, or more *hog.* ***1821** *Real Life in Ireland* 6: A hog and a penny (fourteen pence). ***1851** H. Mayhew *London Labour* I 473: In speaking of money, the slang phrases are constantly used by the street lads; thus a six pence is a "tanner," a shilling a "bob," or a "hog." **1859** Matsell *Vocab.* 42: *Hogg.* A ten-cent piece. ***1875** in *OED2:* What's half a crown and a shilling? A bull and a hog.

b. a dollar. Also **hoggie.**

   1941 Kendall *Army & Navy Sl.* 7: *Hoggie*....a dollar. **1957** in *DARE:* "It cost a hundred"...Hogs. **1954–60** *DAS: Hogs*...Dollars, usu. just a few dollars, never a large amount....*Had minor pop. with some bop groups, c1945.*

2. pork or bacon; in phr. **hog and hominy** *So.* pork or bacon with hominy grits or cornbread. Also (esp. *Naut.*) (*obs.*) **old hog.**

   1776 in *DA:* That I might...eat my Hogg & Hominee without anything to make me afraid. **1853** Delano *Life on Plains* 37: We...relished...our "hog and hominy" fare. **1852–55** C.G. Parsons *Inside View* 80: Corn-bread and bacon..."hog and hominy." **1864** in McKee *Throb of Drums* 190: Got a...little cold hog and hardtack for dinner. **1896** "M. Twain," in *Harper's Mag.* (Sept.) 522: They kept him loaded up with hog and hominy. **1903** *Independent* (Nov. 26) 2794: On the passage out we had been fed on the regulation diet of old hog, old horse and hardtack. **1917** *Independent* (Sept. 29) 503: The original scale of provisions served out to American seamen until...1898...consisted chiefly of old horse, old hog, and hard tack. **1942** *ATS* 101: Pork...*hog. a***1994** N. McCall *Wanna Holler* 241: This stuff has...hog in it.

3. *R.R.* a railway locomotive, esp. if unusually large or powerful.

   1888 in *DA:* A gigantic "hog" engine...was taken up the road Wednesday....The "hog" will haul nine loaded cars up the heavy A1 to grade, while the ordinary road engine had a hard tussel to haul four or five. **1903** *Sci. Amer.* (May 23) 392: In anthracite drifts steam locomotives of a small and peculiar type known as "hogs" haul the trains. **1923** McKnight *English Words* 44: Hog for locomotive. **1925** in *AS* I (Jan.) 250: The heaviest type of engine, "battleship"; lighter types, "hog." **1927** *AS* (June) 389: An engine [is] a *hog.* **1930** Irwin *Tramp & Und. Sl.: Hog.*—A locomotive; a "hog" for fuel. **1942** *Sat. Eve. Post* (June 13) 27: That hog we had couldn't pull the hat off your head. **1964** Fielder *R.R.s of the Black Hills* 124: Their crews looked at the Deadwood Central narrow-gauge hog and found they had one thing in common. **1970** *Current Slang* V (Summer) 8: *Hog, n.* Locomotive. **1972** *Urban Life & Culture* I 374: "Hog" now generally refers to any locomotive; in some locations in the old days, it also referred to any steam engine.

4. *Logging.* (see quots.).

   1898 in *OED2:* The big slab grinding hog for grinding up slabs, edgings and mill refuse into fuel. **1904** *DN* II 398: *Hog*...a machine for grinding logs. **1930** *DN* VI 88: *Hog,* the machine that grinds up slabs for fuel in the furnaces. **1956** Sorden & Ebert *Logger's Wds.* 18: *Hog,* A machine which makes fuel out of lumber slabs or refuse to make steam power for saw mills. **1969** in *OED2:* Waste blocks...are often chuted...on to a conveyor which automatically takes them to a refuse hog.

5. (often *cap.*) **a.** *Av.* (see 1973–74 quot.). [Presumably the earliest sense; cf. **(b),** below.]

   1973–74 in *West. Folk.* XXXVII (1978) 97: *Hog*...a poor flying aircraft. **1983** M. Skinner *USAFE* 74 [ref. to Vietnam War]: They got shot up...and brought that hog [A-1 Skyraider] back without any sweat.

b. [sugg. by the short, barrel-like fuselage] *Naval Av.* a Chance-Vought F4U Corsair fighter-bomber. Now *hist.*

   1943 in T. Blackburn *Jolly Rogers* [plate 7]: Big Hog [inscribed on Corsair cowling]. **1944** in J. Sullivan *F4U Corsair* 58: Thundering Hog II [inscribed on Corsair cowling]. **1969** Searls *Hero Ship* 149 [ref. to WWII]: I got ten thousand hours...in them things. Fighters, torpeckers, hogs, flying boats—everything but balloons. **1989** T. Blackburn *Jolly Rogers* 43: By [1943] the Corsair had earned a servicewide soubriquet.…[Because it was] "as cooperative as a hog on ice"…the F4U was known for a long time as the Hog. **1991** Linnekin *80 Knots* 130 [ref. to *ca*1950]: I was about to meet the Corsair—the "Hog."

c. *USAF.* a Republic F-84 Thunderjet interceptor. Now *hist.* Cf. SUPERHOG, ULTRAHOG.

1961 R.L. Scott *Boring Holes* 222: The "big hog," as the boys called the F-84. **1961** L.G. Richards *TAC* 149: The F-84.…The Hog's cruising speed [was] 450 knots. **1973** M. Collins *Carrying the Fire* 11: The F-84 was Republic's first production jet, and it was affectionately referred to as the "Hog"—apparently because it was not as lean, trim, or swift as some of its contemporaries. A swept-wing version was promptly dubbed the "Super-Hog," and when the F-105 appeared, what else could it be but the "Ultra-Hog"? **1979** L. Drendel *A-10 in Action* 2: The F-84 Thunderjet was called the *Hog*. **1982** W.R. Dunn *Fighter Pilot* 220: These were the straight-wing F-84s, nicknamed "Hogs."

d. *USAF.* an A-10 Thunderbolt II strike fighter.

1983 M. Skinner *USAFE* 75: Hog drivers don't have to worry…about…SAMs. *a*1984 T. Clancy *Red Oct.* 207: The A-10 was called…the Warthog or just plain Hog by the men who flew her. **1990** *Crisis in the Gulf* (CNN-TV) (Oct. 26): The men who fly them call them Hogs. They in turn are called Hog-drivers.…The A-10 Warthog.

6. *Black E.* a large luxury automobile, esp. a Cadillac.

1960 C. Cooper *Scene* 223: Yeah, I got a Hog.…A Cadillac. *Ibid.* 308: *Hog*: any large automobile. **1967** Gonzales *Paid My Dues* 88: There were ten "hogs" (Cadillacs) double parked. **1970** in *Black Scholar* (Jan. 1971) 41: He bought him a "Hog" with all the accessories on it. Man, this Cadillac had air-horns, white-walls, power windows, power brakes, power steering, power's mamma! **1970** Landy *Underground Dict.* 104: *Hog*…Big car, especially the '55 or '56 Buick. **1971** S. Stevens *Way Uptown* 134: You see him driving 'round Harlem in his pink hog. **1972** Carr *Bad* 37: Right away I had to get…my outfit and my hog. *Ibid.* 80: We got in his hog (a chopped-down '56 Buick). **1973** J.A. McPherson, in C. Major *Calling Wind* 360: They called him "Eldorado" because that was the kind of hog he drove. **1974** V. Smith *Jones Men* 91: That's all they got to do, ride around in the Hogs and talk shit. **1974** Goines *Eldorado* 211: Drives a light blue '73 hog. **1967–80** Folb *Runnin' Lines* 242: *Hog*…Cadillac. **1992** Majors & Billson *Cool Pose* 81: The hustlers call them hogs…Cadillacs.

7. (*pl.*) *Sports.* the University of Arkansas Razorbacks.

1963 Ark. football fans (coll. J. Ball): Woooo pigs, soooie! Go hogs! **1982** *N.Y. Post* (Dec. 30) 44: Florida Wary of Hogs' Defense.

8. a large, powerful motorcycle, esp. a Harley-Davidson 74.

1965 *Sat. Eve. Post* (Nov. 20) 35: A motorcycle is a "hog."…The Harley Davidson 74 is the favorite. **1966** H.S. Thompson *Hell's Angels* 5: Hell's Angels…on big "chopped hogs." **1967** W. Murray *Sweet Ride* 93: I figured I was lucky and I haven't been able to get on one of those hogs since. **1968** L. Downe *She-Devils* (film): We got a whole bunch o' horny hog-riders. **1979** Gram *Foxes* 107: Ten or eleven hogs—Harleys and big Hondas—flashed along in single, double and triple file. **1979–82** Gwin *Overboard* 7: Bar-rooms…collect swarms of Harley hawgs around their front doors. **1985** Jenkins & Jenkins *Road Unseen* 171: He used to ride one of the original "hawgs," an old Harley Davidson 74. **1988** *21 Jump St.* (Fox-TV): "What do you drive, Douglas?" "A hog." "He has a motorcycle." **1990** Vachss *Blossom* 62: Three bikers went by on chopped hogs. **1995** *New Yorker* (July 10) 68: Hogs—that is, Harleys, especially old Harleys—are fat, wide, and difficult to handle. **1996** *World News Sunday* (June 16) (ABC-TV): A herd of Harley hogs heading for Amarillo.…It's heaven on a hog.

9. *Mil.* a helicopter gunship; (*specif.*) a UH-1 gunship.

1964 J. Lucas *Dateline* 131: The "Hog" is the biggest of the armed Cobras. It totes 48 deadly rockets.…The Viet Cong respect it. **1966** Mulligan *No Place to Die* 144: "Hogs"…D-model Huey helicopters capable of carrying seven fully equipped infantrymen. **1966–67** F. Harvey *Air War* 103: When a Huey Hog lets loose with all its armament, you feel as if you were inside an exploding ammo factory. **1971** T. Mayer *Weary Falcon* 20: I was flying a Huey Bravo gunship, a Hog, the type we had before Cobras. **1972** Pelfrey *Big V* 18: Hogs.…They ain't nothin. Wait till you see the Cobras work out. **1983** T. Page *Nam* 17 [ref. to Vietnam War]: Occasionally you get to ride a hog gunship.…I knew a hog driver who flew on acid. **1984** Doleman *Tools of War* 36: Illustrated here is a…UH-1B "Hog."

10. a shotgun; (*Army*) a machine gun; in phr. **hog-60** an M-60 machine gun. Cf. HOG-LEG.

1972 N.Y.U. student: "Down South they call a sawed-off single-barreled shotgun a *hog*. It's the kind of gun you keep behind a bar in case you have to mess up a whole lot of people." "Where did you hear it?" "In Georgia." **1986** "J. Cain" *Suicide Squad* 105 [ref. to Vietnam War]: A Hog-60. *Ibid.* 109: Now we put the Hog to work.

11.a. a large motor vehicle or aircraft that requires great quantities of fuel.

[**1930** (quot. at **(3)**, above).] **1975** *Atlantic* (May) 45: Now Imo…fill this old hog of mine up. **1975** Wambaugh *Choirboys* 49: These hogs probably only top out at a hundred ten, so you push it very long you'll probably…blow the engine. **1978** S. King *Stand* 85: We don't even have enough cash to fill this hog's gas tank. **1985** Heywood *Taxi Dancer* 89: When you were low on fuel, nothing looked so good as a big gray hog wallowing along above the clouds. *Ibid.:* After I slow this hog down, my fuel's going to be in pretty good shape.

b. *Esp. USMC.* an amtrac or other armored, tracked vehicle.

1974 L/cpl., USMC, age 24 [ref. to 1968]: We called tank retrievers *hogs*—because they literally ate hydraulic oil. You'd fill 'em up with 200 gallons a day. So we called 'em *hogs* and *pigs*. *a*1982 Dunstan *Viet. Tracks* 148: Amtracs…were…called by Marine infantry "hogs," or "gators" after their Second World War predecessor, the Alligator. **1984** Hammel *Root* 41: Amphibian assault vehicles (known variously as AAVs, amtracs, and hogs). *Ibid.* 128: A column of three hogs rolled past the building.

12. the penis; in phr. **beat** [or **belt**] **the hog** to masturbate.—usu. considered vulgar.

[*ca*1925 in Logsdon *Whorehouse Bells* 142: And I had a dozen shankers on my root, hog, or die.] *a*1968 in Haines & Taggart *Ft. Lauderdale* 13: So I started off by pulling down my fly and pulling out my hog. **1968** Baker et al. *CUSS* 137: *Hog*…Male sex organ. **1970–71** G.V. Higgins *Eddie Coyle* 145: No, I think they go home and beat the hog over them. **1974** G.V. Higgins *Cogan's Trade* 42: I'll take care my own hog. **1977** Bredes *Hard Feelings* 270: I'm giving you five seconds to get your cheesy old hog over here or I'm gonna cut it off. **1977** Dunne *Confessions* 40: Weeny flashers. Panty sniffers.…The guy who belts his hog on the Number 43 bus there. **1986** *UTSQ*: Penis…*hog*.

13. *Esp. USMC.* a recruit undergoing basic training.—used contemptuously.

1968 Mares *Marine Machine* 30: If you hogs win seven streamers, you become a Superior Platoon. **1970** Whitmore *Memphis-Nam-Sweden* 48: "Seventy-eight hogs, all present and accounted for, sir." "What did you say, Marine? I see seventy-eight Marines in front of me. I have no hogs in my platoon." **1973** R. Roth *Sand in Wind* 78: You're hogs now, but when I get through with you you'll be Marines or you'll be dead. *Ibid.* 81: Any of you hogs that have been to college take one step forward. **1987** Estes *Field of Innocence* 10 [ref. to 1968]: Hogs, I want you to file in squad formation inside the receiving station.

14. *Esp. Mil.* a coarse but sexually complaisant woman; PIG.—used contemptuously.

1961 L.E. Young *Virgin Fleet* 76 [ref. to WWII]: Is she a pig, slut, beast, hog, skunk, seagull or just plain garbage scow? [**1968** Baker et al. *CUSS* 139: *Hog*…An ugly person, female.] **1971** *Current Slang* V (Spring) 14: *Hog runner*, n. One who takes out girls mainly for sex. **1973** Sgt., USAF, Taiwan (coll. J. Ball): Hiya, hogs! **1974** (quot. at HOG BOARD). **1983–86** G.C. Wilson *Supercarrier* 80: Many of the sailors would be "hog-hunting," looking for easy women to be bed down with during liberty. **1987** Fine *With Boys* 175 [ref. to 1977]: Instead of calling girls "mutts," the Iowan male subculture calls these creatures "hogs."

15. *Pris.* a tough or muscular fellow; TUSH-HOG.

1969 Hopper *Sex in Prison* 115: A hog is able to "take it" and to maintain a stoic integrity in the face of privation. **1972** Carr *Bad* 177: I fell in with these dudes who were called the "hogs." They let me into the club which was limited to guys who could bench press three hundred pounds.

16. (esp. among radical political groups) a police officer; PIG.—used contemptuously.

1970 *N.Y. Post* (July 10) [ref. to 1968]: Sure, I've been to Nam (Vietnam), and I'd rip off (attack) a hog (policeman) in a minute. **1972** Smith & Gay *Don't Try It* 203: *Honda Hogs.* Division of San Francisco Tactical Squad that rides little Honda motorcycles. **1978** *UTSQ* (terms for police): Watch out for the *pigs, hogs, heat.* **1967–80** Folb *Runnin' Lines* 242: *Hog(s), the.* Police. **1980** *AS* (Fall) 197.

17. *Narc.* phencyclidine piperidine HCl; PCP; ANGEL DUST.

1970 Landy *Underground Dict.* 104: *Hog*…Phenanthrene. **1974** Hyde *Mind Drugs* 174: Sernyl…and Benaktyzine are coming back under the name of Hog. **1978** Petersen & Stillman *PCP Abuse* 77: In 1968 [PCP]…surfaced on the East Coast under the guise of "Hog."

¶ In phrases:

¶ **call hogs** to snore loudly.

1912 in *DARE: Call hogs*…To snore. **1946** Mezzrow & Wolfe *Really Blues* 303: *Call some hogs:* snore. **1965–70** in *DARE* I 517.

¶ **caught by the hogs** *R.R.* (see quot.).

1942 *Sat. Eve. Post* (June 13) 27: "Getting caught by the hogs" is a briefer way of saying that the crew was on duty sixteen hours and couldn't work longer because of the Federal law, or "hog law."

¶ **cut a hog** Esp. *Black E.* to make oneself look foolish, esp. by attempting something beyond one's capacity; (*hence*) to make a mistake.

[**1912** *DN* III 574: *Cut a big hog in the mouth with a small knife*…To attempt something beyond one's capacity.] **1928** C. McKay *Banjo* 221: You won't be able to stand them drunk or sober. I know it. You'll cut a hell of a hog before you know what's happening. **1937** Hurston *Watching God* 149: B'lieve Ah done cut a hawg, so Ah guess Ah better ketch air. **1947** *AS* XXII 299: You'll cut a hog in two studying law. But if you are bound to stick to law, you can see what you can do. **1967–69** Foster & Stoddard *Pops* 101: If you cut a hog in a record in those days, you had to stop and start over on a whole new wax.

¶ **get a hog in** (see quot.). Cf. HOG IN.

1962–68 B. Jackson *In the Life* 348: 'Cause the first thing they want to do is try to get a hog in (put pressure) on you. "If you don't…cooperate…you're gonna be in trouble."

¶ **go the whole hog** to go or commit oneself all the way; do a thing thoroughly or unrestrainedly. See also WHOLE-HOG, *adv.*

1828 in *OED2:* [Andrew Jackson] will either go with the party, as they say in New York, or go "the whole hog," as it is phrased elsewhere. **1830** Ames *Sketches* 31: The cook shops…"go the whole hog." **1833** Paulding *Lion* 27: There's no back out in my breed—I go the whole hog. **1836** *Spirit of Times* (July 16) 169: "I'll go the whole hog," says he, and with that he sprawled whole length in the gutter. **1838** [Haliburton] *Clockmaker* (Ser. 2) 34: Go the whole hog, and do the thing genteel. **1841** [Mercier] *Man o' War* 263: I guess I then went the whole hog/In eating up you sailors' prog. *ca*1844 in H. Nathan *D. Emmett* 326: She went de hog wid a perfec swine. **1852* in *OED2:* When a Virginian butcher kills a pig, he is said to ask his customers whether they will "go the whole hog," as, in such case, he sells at a lower price than if they pick out the prime joints only. **1938** Lawes *Invisible Stripes* 133: He might as well go the "whole hog" and wear a uniform. **1938** "E. Queen" *4 Hearts* 179: Only we smear it on. Go the whole hog, see? **1976** Braly *False Starts* 29: She kissed me hard, then drew back to ask, "Would you really have gone the whole hog?" **1978** Gribbin *Timewarps* 162: Roger Zalazny…goes the whole hog in avoiding such complications.

¶ **in a hog's valise** [or (*vulgar*) **ass**] not at all; emphatically not. Cf. similar phrs. at PIG, *n.*

1877 in J.M. Carroll *Camp Talk* 81: Yes, in a hog's valise he'll do it! **1924** Wilstach *Anecdota Erotica* 44: In a hogs a— you did!

¶ **on the hog [train], 1.** living and traveling as a tramp or hobo; (*hence*) destitute; broke.

1894 C. Lawlor & J. Blake *Sidewalks of N.Y.* (pop. song) st. 3: Others they are on the hog, but they all feel just like me. **1896** Ade *Artie* 88: A man gets two or three times as much coin—[but he's] always on the hog, and goin' around lookin' like a tramp. **1896** F.P. Dunne, in Schaaf *Dooley* 175: Here's th' pa-aper. Let me see. McKinley at Canton….Bryan on th' hog train. **1897** in J. London *Reports* [ref. to 1892]: The "Road," the hog-train, or, for brevity's sake, the hog: it is a realm almost as unexplored as fairyland. **1899** Cullen *Tales* 29: I'm temporarily on the hog, but I'm hanging on to that violin all right. **1900** *DN* II 41: "On the hog"…Out of money. **1906** *DN* III 141: "He come on the *hog-train*" (i.e., "He stole a ride on a train.") "I'll have to go on the *hog*, if I get there." **1911** *JAF* (July) 270: "On a Hog"…means the condi-

tion of a "broke ho-bo" or tramp. *Ibid.* 271: Jes' come here to git off'n dat hog. *ca*1912 in Kornbluh *Rebel Voices* 72: Louie was out of a job,/Louie was dead on the hog. **1914** in Handy *Blues Treasury* 78: Seen him here an' he was on the hog…not a jitney on him. **1921** "M. Brand" *Black Jack* 107: I'm on the hog for fair, as a matter of fact. **1926** *AS* I (Dec.) 652: *On the hog*—penniless. **1927** Sandburg *Songbag* 191 [ref. to *ca*1900]: And I'm still on the hog train flagging my meals,/Ridin' the brake beams close to the wheels. **1930** Irwin *Tramp & Und. Slang* 137: *On the Hog.*—Penniless; down and out; forced to accept anything, much as a hog roots for whatever it can find. **1942** Coleman & Bregman *Songs* 71: Ah come to life an' slung mah dogs,/Look fo' sho' lak Ah'm on de hog!*…*Down on one's luck. **1964** J.M. Brewer *Worser Days* 59: So he write his mammy an' pappy an' ask 'em to please sen' him some money to come home on, dat he up dere in New York City on de "Hog."

2. in a bad way or condition; (*hence*) inferior or undesirable; no good.

1896 Ade *Artie* 29: On the hog, that's all. Been feelin' rotten all day. **1899** A.H. Lewis *Sandburrs* 188: D' fam'ly was on d' hog for fair when Bridgy gets there. *Ibid.* 288: His ratty eyes—one of 'em on d' hog, as I states. **1899** Thayer *Co. K* 77: "Unmilitary," "Rotten,"…"Mediocre," "On the hog,"…"On the bum." **1900** *DN* II 41: "On the hog"…Very poor, bad…At a disadvantage. **1904** *Life in Sing Sing* 256: On the hog. No good. **1905** *DN* III 91: *Put on the hog train, v. phr.* To mislead, to get the better of in a bargain. **1906** *DN* III 141: That's kin'er on the *hog.* **1907** London *Road* 17 [ref. to 1892]: Salinas is on the "hog," the "bulls" is "horstile." **1909** M'Govern *Krag Is Laid Away* 95: Why sure, that danged tailor has put these pants on the hog. **1912** in Kornbluh *Rebel Voices* 76: Things are dull in San Francisco,/On the hog in New Orleans,/Rawther punk in cultured Boston. **1958** McCulloch *Woods Wds.* 126: *On the hog*—haywire, broken down, out of order.

¶ **root hog, or die** see s.v. ROOT, *v.*

¶ **try it on the hog** (see 1903 quot.). Cf. DOG TOWN.

[*a*1890–93 *F & H* III 327: *Hog*…(American)—An inhabitant of Chicago.] **1903** Merriman *Ltrs. from a Son* 104: Billy Poindexter says that in the east they speak of "trying it on the hog," when they produce a new play in this town [Chicago], and that if the animal squeals and shows signs of displeasure, they know the thing will be a great success in New York.

¶ (used in var. self-explanatory prov. phrs.).

1857 in *DA:* He's "as independent as a hog on ice!" **1889** Farmer *Amer.: Hog in togs,* a well-dressed loafer. **1903** *DN* II 316: *Like a hog to war,* adv. Sideways. "The horse was feeling gaily and went *like a hog to war* much of the time. **1914** *DN* IV 68: *Accommodatin' as a hog on ice,* adj. phr. Extremely disagreeable and unobliging. **1917** *DN* IV 394: *Independent as a hog on ice,* adv. phr. Very independent. **1923** *DN* V 221: *Since the hogs et up m' brother,* adv. phr. A very long time. **1927** *AS* III (Dec.) 169: When there is room for doubt about his knowledge he is said to know as much about it as a "hog does a side saddle." **1929** *AS* V (Oct.) 75: One who is slow is "slow as a snail climbin' a slick hog." **1941** in Hemingway *Sel. Letters* 529: As tight about money as a hog's ars in flytime. **1942** Hurston *Dust Tracks* 136 [ref. to *ca*1917]: The baritone started teasing me the first day. I jumped up and told him to stop trying to run the hog over me! **1944** *PADS* (No. 2) 9: *Since the hog et grandma (my little brother):* Expressive of great amusement. "I haven't laughed so much since the hog et grandma." Ala. Low popular. (Also, reported from S.C.). **1948** *Time* (Aug. 9) 18: Its rank & file…like to think of themselves as independents—independent as a hog on ice. *a*1950 P. Wolff *Friend* 41: He went out to crap and the hogs et him. **1953** Wicker *Kingpin* 280: I wouldn't hit a hog in the ass with Harry Watts, but I felt sorry for him that morning. **1977** Olsen *Fire Five* 144: "You threatening me, Fireman?" "Do a hog shit on Tuesday?" **1983** R.C. Mason *Chickenhawk* 57: He was happier than a dead hog in the sunshine. **1989** (quot. at (**5.b.**), above).

hog *v.* **1.** Orig. *Und.* to defraud or cheat; bamboozle.

1859 Matsell *Vocab.* 42: *Hogging.* To humbug. **1865** C.F. Browne *Ward: Travels* 70: "Go, my son, and hog the public!" (he ment, "knock em," but the old man was allus a little given to slang). **1880** in *DA:* The chief has made gambling an expensive luxury to the many professionals of both the square and "hogging" games.

2.a. to steal or pilfer; CRIB, 1.—also constr. with *up.*

1867 in A.K. McClure *Rocky Mtns.* 246: A few parties "hogged up" the whole of the pay-claims. **1884** "M. Twain" *Huck. Finn* ch. xxvi: So, says I, s'pose somebody has hogged that bag on the sly? **1896** "M. Twain," in *Harper's Mag.* (Aug.) 350: I says to myself, I'll hog them di'monds the first chance I get. **1900** *DN* II 41: *Hog,* v.t. to get from another without work. **1928** Weseen *Dict. Grammar* 125: *Hog,* to crib or plagiarize. **1936** N. Nye *No-Gun Fighter* 28: You tryin' to hog this spread with no guns? **1966** Kenney *Caste* 98: Our flatheaded pal's hogged some other guy's play and is blowin' himself out on it. **1973** in *OED2*: The inquiry could go on without hogging the headlines from him.

b. to greedily take more than one's share of; selfishly appropriate or dominate.—also constr. with *up.* Now *colloq.* or *S.E.*
   1887 in Farmer *Amer.*: If the crook is obstinate enough to hog it all. **1888** in Farmer *Amer.*: To hog whatever there was in the business for themselves. **1894** in *DN* VI 347: The Creator never meant that we should "hog" it all, or we would have been made with snouts. **1896** in *DAE*: It would give them a chance to say I was hogging everything and giving no-one else a chance. **1909** *WNID*: *Hog*…To take selfishly: as, to *hog* all one can get. *Slang.* **1915** *DN* IV 221: *Hog,* take more than one's share. "Yes and you let Jack La Rue *hog* sixty feet in one scene." **1923** Southgate *Rusty Door* 116: In the tracks of the sea-hoggin' liners. **1927** *AS* III (June) 367: If one actor tries to get before the camera to the disadvantage of his fellow-worker he is "hogging the camera." **1931** Wilstach *Under Cover Man* 196: The big ones were hogging things. **1942** *ATS* 588: Steal the center of attention…*hog the limelight* or *spotlight, hog the stage* or *act.* **1955** "W. Henry" *Wyatt* 38: Hogging the middle of the road. **1989** *Crossfire* (CNN-TV) (Aug. 10): You think I'm gonna let you hog up this show? **1989** *ALF* (NBC-TV): I don't want to hog all your time.

3. *Pris.* to subject to physical assault, esp. homosexual rape.
   1962–68 B. Jackson *In the Life* 419: "Him and this other boy hogged this Mexican that wasn't a punk."…"What happened to the guy that got hogged?"

hogan *n.* **1.a.** usu. *pl.* a woman's breast. [Prob. the orig. sense.]
   1967 Dibner *Admiral* 216 [ref. to WWII]: He admired the mound of her breast in splendid isolation. *With hogans like that,* he thought, *who needs the Taj Mahal?* **1968** Baker et al. *CUSS* 137: *Hoagons.* The female breasts. **1993** G.V. Higgins *Bomber's Law* 145: That junior cheerleader with the gorgeous hogans on her.

b. *Stu.* (see quots.). *Joc.*
   1966–69 *Current Slang I & II* 51: *Hogen,* n. Unit of measurement equal to one mouthful.—Air Force Academy cadets. **1987** *Nat. Lampoon* (Oct.) 100: Bending over so that great cubic hogans of boze [breast] were displayed. **1989** *UTSQ*: *Hogan*—a unit of volume. Cubic mouthfuls, most often used in reference to Women's Breasts…."I'll bet they'd go to about 8–10 hogans a piece."

2. a young woman.
   1962 Quirk *Red Ribbons* 80 [ref. to 1940's]: I pulled that [ribald joke] on some Hogans when I was an enlisted man.

hog board *n.* *USMC.* (see quots.). Also **hoggie board.**
   1974 Former 1/cpl., USMC [ref. to 1967]: At Parris Island the DI's made everybody bring in a picture of their girlfriend to put up on the bulletin board so everybody could make fun of them—the board was the *hoggie board* and the girls were always referred to as *hogs.* **1987** D. da Cruz *Boot* 98: To show his displeasure…one S.D.I. will take away privileges…or clear the "hog board" of pictures of sweethearts and parents. *Ibid.* 301: *Hog board* bulletin board on quarterdeck on which are posted photos of family and Suzies.

hog bosom *n.* SOW BOSOM. *Joc.*
   1905 in *DA*: 'Bout to-morrer evening we'll be eating hog-bosom on Uncle Sam.

hog-caller *n.* a loudspeaker or bullhorn.
   1944 *PM* (Sept. 17) 32. **1948** Heym *Crusaders* 323: Bing dropped a package on the chair. "Why, the hog-caller!" exclaimed Troy.…"My God, you haven't brought those damned loudspeakers again." [**1967** Sadler *I'm a Lucky One* 77: There is also instruction in radio broadcasting, tape recording, and the use of "hog-calling" loudspeakers.]

hog down *v.* **1.** to eat or drink (something) voraciously.
   1932 D.H. Lawrence, in *OED2*: The only way to eat an apple is to hog it down like a pig. *a*1961 in *WNID3*: Hogged down his dinner and rushed out. **1980** Lorenz *Guys Like Us* 33: Hogging down Old

Styles. **1989** Knoxville, Tenn., man, age *ca*35: I'm fixin' to hog down a few cheeseburgers and fries.

2. *Stu.* HOG OUT.
   1989 *Daily Beacon* (Univ. Tenn.) (Aug. 31) 1: Hog down!

hog-drunk *adj.* very drunk.
   1955 Abbey *Brave Cowboy* 48: Got hog drunk and hit the floor. **1964** J. Thompson *Pop. 1280* 48: You were out here hog-drunk, just about too stupid to appreciate what a good thing you had.

hog-eye *n.* **1.** (sense uncertain; see quots.). [Though of uncertain meaning, these are the earliest citations.]
   1853 in W.L. Rose *Hist. Slavery in No. Amer.* 504 [ref. to 1840's]: Who's been here since I've been gone?/Pretty little gal wid a josey on./Hog Eye! Old Hog Eye. **1864** in H. Nathan *D. Emmett* 372: De [slave] trader rode upon a mule /…The "hog-eye" kept his temper cool./…He gib de word to go ahead!/Den crack his whip an say "nuff sed."

2. *Calif.* a kind of barge. Now *hist.*
   *a*1870 in Whall *Sea Songs* 94: Oh, the hog-eye men are all the go,/When they come down to San Francisco. **1925** Bailey *Shanghaied* 39 [ref. to 1898]: Senn was trying to make his getaway by the last hog-eye (barge). **1910–27** Whall *Sea Songs* 93 [ref. to *a*1872]: [Around San Francisco] there was a great business carried on by water, the chief vehicles being barges, called "hog-eyes." The derivation of the name is unknown to me.

3. the vulva or vagina.—usu. considered vulgar.
   *a*1910 in Lomax & Lomax *Amer. Ballads* 432: She could smile, she could chuckle,/She could roll her hog eye. **1938** J. Colcord *Songs of Sailormen* 99: "The Hog-Eye Man"…Terry hints at hidden obscenity in the name itself; but if this were the case, the originators have taken their knowledge with them. **1942** *ATS*: Female pudendum…*hog-eye,… monkey,…twat* [etc.]. **1944** S.P. Bayard *Hill Country* 75: [In] Greene County [Pa.]…"Hog Eye" has an indecent meaning…. "All she had to give me was a hog-eye and a 'tater."…"I stepped right up and kissed her sweet/And asked her for some hog-eye meat." **1920–54** in Randolph & Legman *Blow Candle Out* 788: The female sex organ…*cunt,…hog-eye,… snatch* [etc.]. **1966** Longstreet & Godoff *Wm. Kite* 368: The female pudendum, called jelly-roll and hog-eye by Billy Brunswick.

3. *R.R.* HOGGER, 1.a.
   1940 (quot. at HOG JOCKEY).

hogger *n.* **1.** *R.R.* **a.** a locomotive engineer.
   1914 in N. Cohen *Long Steel Rail* 369: His friends around him closely pressed to hear the hogger's last request. **1916** *Editor* (Mar. 25) 343: *Hogger*—engine driver. **1919** Warren *Ninth Co., 20th Engineers* 29: His one desire, to become a hogger. **1927** Sandburg *Songbag* 186: A hogger on his death-bed lay. His life was oozing fast away. **1927** Shay *Pious Friends* 15: All the switchmen knew by the engine's moans,/That the hogger at the throttle was Casey Jones. **1931–35** T. Wolfe *Time & River* 71: Come on, you hogger, let's see the great plains and the fields of wheat! **1952** in Fenner *Throttle* 14: Frank, the youngest hogger on the line, was taken down a peg or two.

b. a locomotive; HOG, 3.
   *a*1940 in Lanning & Lanning *Texas Cowboys* 20: Those big eastern engines were a heap different from the little old hoggers Texas had in them days.

2. *Stu.* a homely, esp. fat, young woman.—used contemptuously.
   1969 *Current Slang Cum. I & II* 51: *Hogger,* n. A fat, ugly girl.—College males, Minnesota. **1971** *Current Slang* V (Spring) 14: *Hogger,* n. A girl.

3. the penis; HOG, 12.—usu. considered vulgar.
   1981–85 S. King *It* 303: Scariest thing I've seen lately was Mark…takin a leak….Ugliest hogger you ever saw.

hoggineer *n.* [HOG(GER) + en*gineer*] *R.R.* HOG JOCKEY. *Joc.*
   1940 (quot. at HOG JOCKEY).

hoghead *n.* *R.R.* a locomotive engineer.
   1906 *McClure's Mag.* (Nov.) 17: What is a hoghead, that he must pride it an' take the rise of you an' me? **1907** in *OED2*: The anxious gaze of the hoghead (*Anglice:* engineer). **1914** in N. Cohen *Long Steel Rail* 369: A hoghead on his deathbed lay, his life was ebbing fast away. **1916** *Editor* XLIII (Mar. 25) 343: *Hog-head.* Engine driver. **1919** *Lit. Digest* (Feb. 22) 95: They had a caboose full of old "hog-heads" (slang for engineers). **1927** Sandburg *Songbag* 186: "Hogger" is railroad

slang for an engineer or "hoghead." **1929** *AS* IV (June) 341: *Hoghead*. An engineer on the railroad. **1930** *Danger Lights* (film): I'd have made a good hoghead. **1965** D.G. Moore *20th C. Cowboy* 13: That...son-of-a-bitching hog head couldn't run his aunt's sewing machine without tearing it to pieces! **1970** *Current Slang* V (Summer) 8: *Hoghead*, n. Railroad engineer. **1976** Hayden *Voyage* 455: Th' old hoghead what swiped the train oncet. **1990** L. Nieman *Boomer* 32: The hoghead was from Oregon.

hog heaven *n. Esp. So. & West.* a state or condition of usu. foolish bliss; (see also 1944 quot.).

   1944 Wheeler *Steamboatin' Days* 77 [ref. to *ca*1890]: In cold weather they liked to sleep under the boilers. This space was known among the rousters as "hog heaven." **1945** *AS* (Apr.) 83: Look at ol' Billie Bob over there. He thinks he's in hog-Heaven. **1973** M. Collins *Carrying the Fire* 307: Chuck Berry was in hog heaven. Here he had been waiting nearly a decade for someone in flight to solicit his advice. **1973** Gent *N. Dallas* 254: All I need now is a moon pie...and halftime would be hog heaven. **1974** Carr *Bad* 214: And I was pregnant—we were both in hog heaven about that. **1985** *Time* (Apr. 15) 104: For any connoisseur of...pop culture, pro wrestling in its latest guise is like a trip to hog heaven. **1986** N.Y. State Lottery TV ad: If you win, you'll be in hog heaven. **1987** Pedneau *A.P.B.* 229: Whit Pynchon's in hog heaven. *a*1991 Ethell & Sand *Ftr. Command* 16: It was "hawg heaven."

hog hole *n. So.* a disgusting or filthy place; DOGHOLE, 1.a.

   1872 in Blockson *Underground Railroad* 159: The "cage" he denounced as a perfect "hog hole," and added, "it was more than I could bear."

hog holiday *n.* HOG HEAVEN.

   1983 Ehrhart *VN-Perkasie* 180: I ain't had a cheeseburger in eight months. This is hog holiday!

hog in *v.* HORN IN. Cf. *get a hog in*, s.v. HOG, *n*.

   1964 *Rawhide* (CBS-TV): There's another marshall up at the summit. He might want to hog in.

hog jockey *n. R.R.* HOGGER, 1.a.

   1940 *R.R. Mag.* (Apr.) 46: An engineer may be called a *hogger, hoghead, hogmaster, hoggineer, hog jockey, hog eye, pig mauler*, etc.

hog-killing *n.* a sudden or enormous profit or success; financial killing.

   1898–1900 Cullen *Chances* 8: They had just pulled off a swell hog-killing up in Toronto and had two or three thousand each in their clothes. **1911** *Adventure* (Apr.) 958: A Gigantic Hog-Killing. We have Inside Information of a Long Shot that should Win To-morrow at 10 to 1.

hog-killing *adj. West.* violent; disorderly; (*hence*) wildly enjoyable. Also as *n.*

   1864 in Wiley & Mulhollen *They Who Fought* 264: As the saying is, we made a hog-killing business of it. **1903** A. Adams *Log of Cowboy* 194 [ref. to 1880's]: According to their report the boys had had a hog-killing time, old man Don having been out with them all night. **1905** "W. Hale" *Cowboy & Ranchman* 33: December came and then Xmas. Me and Tom had a hog-killing time. Mr. Rily had an eggnog and a fine dinner and lots of whiskey and wine. **1919** *Variety* (Mar. 28) 40: Tuesday, parade day, was a hog killing for the restaurants. **1923** J.W. Raine *Saddle-Bags* 102: "We had the *hog-killin'est* time"...any lively occasion. **1927** in *OED2*: When I ask my friends to have a hog-killing-time with me, I foot all bills. **1933** *AS* VIII 49: *Hog-killing*. Any sort of hilarious celebration or jollification. "We-all shore did have a hawg-killin' time over t' th' dance t' other night."

hog law *n. R.R.* (see 1930 quot.).

   1930 Irwin *Tramp & Und. Slang* 101: *Hog Law*.—The Federal Sixteen-Hour Law prohibiting railroad workers from working more than that time without suitable rest. The expression, "The hog law's got me," properly means that the speaker is unable to work until he has had some rest, or that he is completely worn out. **1934** Weseen *Dict. Slang* 72: *Hog law*—A statute that forbids railroad companies to use a trainman more than sixteen consecutive hours. *ca*1940 in Botkin *Treas. Amer. Folk.* 534: He thinks the hog law is going to catch us, we're making such bad time.

hog-leg *n.* **1.** *West.* a large pistol. Also **hog's leg**.

   1919 in J.M. Hunter *Trail Drivers* I 260 [ref. to 1880's]: The kind of a machine the cow-puncher had was sometimes called a "cutter," and sometimes was called a "hog-leg," but it was better known as a six-shooter gun, and we frequently had a use for it. **1926** C.M. Russell

Trails 118: He knows this hog-leg that's hangin' on Bowles' hip ain't no watch chain. **1928** Dobie *Vaquero* 128 [ref. to *ca*1880]: Joe plunged in, spurs, leggins, "hog-legs," and all. **1936** McCarthy *Mosshorn* (unp.): *Hog-leg.* Another term for a six-shooter. **1940** F. Hunt *Trail from Tex.* 25 [ref. to *ca*1880]: Maybe that ole hawg leg you got there'll come in right handy. **1940** Chandler *Farewell* 171: A plainclothesman with his coat off and his hog's leg looking like a fire plug against his ribs. **1952** Randolph & Wilson *Down in the Holler* 99: When a hillman says "I *roostered* my old hog-leg" he means that he cocked his revolver. **1963** Grant *McClintock!* (film): Drago, drag out that hog-leg. Get me some attention. **1970** Thackrey *Thief* 29: He kept a hogsleg behind the counter. **1972** Pendleton *Boston Blitz* 100: He had the Beretta and the AutoMag hawgleg. **1979** *Young Maverick* (CBS-TV): You'd best take your hand off that hog-leg. **1992** G. Wolff *Day at the Beach* 127: I keep a loaded hogleg on the night table.

2. a shotgun.

   1987 E. Red & K. Bigelow *Near Dark* (film): You havin' some trouble with your hog-leg? **1991** "R. Brown" & R. Angus *A.K.A. Narc* 102: No one carrying a badge would ever haul out a hog's leg like that sawed-off!

hogmaster *n. R.R.* HOG JOCKEY.

   1940 (quot. at HOG JOCKEY).

hog out *v.* PIG OUT.

   1986 Knoxville, Tenn., attorney, age 33: I've been hoggin' out lately. **1988** Univ. Tenn. student: We were hogging out totally.

hog-poker *n.* (see quot.).

   1985 *Civil War Times Illus.* (Mar.) 23: The Dutchman soon had his farmboys learning the drill for their "hog-pokers," as many Texans called the lances.

hog ranch *n. West.* a disreputable saloon or dance hall where prostitutes are usu. available. Now *hist.* [The sense of the 1869 quot. is perh. ambiguous.]

   1869 in *DA*: Another trail...follows up the divide...joining the first-named trail at the "Hog Ranch." **1885** in *DARE*: The Priest girls, who live at what is known as "the hog ranch" in the southwest part of the city. **1897** Wister *Lin McLean* 128: [At] the hog ranch, whiskey and variety awaited. **1900** Forsyth *Soldier* 140: These shacks soon became known as "hog ranches" and...held whisky by the barrel...possibly a faro layout...one or three bedrooms...and two or three of the most wretched and lowest class of abandoned women. **1902** Wister *Virginian* 75: He was spending a little comfortable money at the Drybone hog-ranch. **1907** S.E. White *Arizona Nights* 84: I had to quit the main street and dodge back of the hog-ranch. **1912** Siringo *Cowboy Detective* 60 [ref. to 1887]: The "Hog ranch" (a tough saloon and sporting house). **1915** H. Young *Hard Knocks* 99 [ref. to 1870's]: There were many of these...in the vicinity of the post and they were called "Hog Ranches." Why...I could not say...but think that perhaps it had reference to the girls as they were a very low, tough set. **1926** C.M. Russell *Trails* 85: But we're all peaceful enough till the sport that runs this hog-ranch objects to the noise I'm makin'. **1931** Bisbee *Four Amer. Wars* 178 [ref. to *ca*1867]: Oaths, "hog ranch" vernacular and brawling wildness prevailed throughout the night. *a*1940 in Lanning & Lanning *Texas Cowboys* 24: Old Dad Guest had a hog ranch at Fort Chadbourne along in the early seventies. [**1956** Vaughn *Rosebud* 7: There had been little to amuse Crook's men at the post with the exception of the *Hog Pasture*, a rip-snorting, bawdy saloon and dance hall located across the river a mile to the north.] **1964** Twist *Distant Trumpet* (film): That hog ranch on wheels. **1978** T.A. Larson *Hist. of Wyoming* 203: Many "soiled doves" could be found in Wyoming towns and at rural "hog ranches."

hog-rich *adj.* extremely wealthy.

   1983 R. Thomas *Missionary* 49: The Keatses went from dirt-poor to hog-rich to banker-stuffy in one generation.

hogshead *n.* **1.** a clumsy or stupid person. *Rare* in U.S.

   ca*1515 in *OED*: Some couched a hogges heed under a hatche. **1586 in *OED2*: If you delight in a Pigs-nie, you may by receiving of him be sure of a Hogs-head. **1619 in *OED2*: Their Parish Priests (as those hogs-heads terme him). **1645 J. Milton, in *OED2*: Such an unswill'd hogshead. **1919 Hedges *Iron City* 164: No, you hogshead, I'm not afraid of you. **1945** Yates & Mankiewicz *Spanish Main* (film): So I am, hogshead!

2. *R.R.* HOGHEAD.

   1923 McKnight *Eng. Words* 44: *Hogger* or *hogshead* for "engineer."

hogswallow *v. West.* to confound.

   1927 Rollins *Jinglebob* 134 [ref. to 1880's]: Likely what hogswallowed 'im was too much gloatin' over the money he'd thought he'd won.

hogwash *n.* **1.** weak or inferior liquor or beer.

   *****1712** in *OED2:* Your butler purloins your liquor, and the brewer sells you hogwash. **1883** in B. Harte *Writings* IV 79: He had "had enough of that sort of hog-wash ladled out to him for genuine liquor." **1923** T. Boyd *Through Wheat* 36: Wine? You call that red hog-wash wine? **1930** Lait *On Spot* 23: An' when he swills up a bellyful o' that hogwash, he goes cookoo. **1935** Pollock *Und. Speaks:* Hog-wash, beer. **1966–70** in *DARE.*

   2. arrant or offensive nonsense; lies or misrepresentation; bosh. Now *S.E.*

   1882 in B. Harte *Writings* III 313: "You don't mean to say that's the sort of hog wash the old man serves out to you regularly?" continued Lance, becoming more slangy in his ill temper. **a*1890–93 *F & H* III 329: *Hog-wash*…(journalists').—Worthless newspaper matter: *slush, swash,* and *flub-dub.* **1907** J.C. Lincoln *Cape Cod* 103: The reg'lar hogwash about the "breath of old ocean." **1912** *DN* III 578: Hog-wash, n. Tommyrot. "All that he had to say was just plain *hog-wash.*" *****1912** G.B. Shaw, in *OED2:* Exactly the same "hogwash." **1938** "R. Hallas" *You Play the Black* 88: Not hogwash without guts like these Hollywood authors write. **1949** Gresham *Limbo Tower* 20: Sounds like hogwash to me. **1961** Kohner *Gidget Goes Hawaiian* 26: I am here to expose this Chamber of Commerce bilge as just so much hogwash. **1962** J. Clifford *Carnival of Souls* (film): Hogwash! All of us imagine things. **1971** *Ramparts* (Aug.) 22: It's hogwash. It is a political opiate and a psychological crutch. **1977** *Amer. Dict. CB Slang* 38: Hog Wash—An untruth. **1994** *TV Guide* (July 16) 72: And Aaron Spelling couldn't squeeze in *one* minority actress? Hogwash!

hog-wild *adj.* completely unrestrained; out of control.—usu. constr. with *go.*

   1904 *DN* II 419: Hog wild, adj. Wildly excited…."They went *hog wild.*" **1912** Mathewson *Pitching* 130: He is a "hog wild" runner. **1918–19** MacArthur *Bug's Eye View* 98: Gosh, I'll bet their [*sic*] hogwild back home. **1926** C.M. Russell *Trails* 23: The red hoss…goes hog-wild. **1931** Haycox *Whispering Range* 49: The buzzards will go hog-wild. **1955** L. Shapiro *6th of June* 137: You've gone hog-wild over the war. **1956** Fleming *Diamonds* 61: And then for one month—August—the place goes hogwild. **1963** D. Tracy *Brass Ring* 7: The ebullient Colonel Franklin went hog-wild. **1972–76** Lynde *Rick O'Shay* (unp.): He jes' went hog-wild an' snake crazy! **1980** Lorenz *Guys Like Us* 89: She's just afraid you'll go hog-wild and spend it all. **1989** *N.Y. Times Mag.* (Oct. 8) 18: The decorator went kind of hog-wild.

hog-wrestle *n.* a dancing party marked by rough or vulgar conduct; *(also)* a difficult or tangled situation.

   1915 *DN* IV 233: Hog-wrastle, n. A modern dance. **1919** Wilkins *Co. Fund* 25: The gink writing this copy didn't see any more of the hog-rassle than the law allowed. **1926** *DN* V 387: Hog wrestle (—rassle) n. phr. Contemptuous term for a cheap or vulgar dance. "The dance last night was a regular hog wrestle." **1928–29** Nason *White Slicker* 70 [ref. to 1918]: They don't know what's going on in this gigantic hog wrastle! **1933** *Leatherneck* (Feb.) 29: Jimmy Lowery, who rarely misses a hawg-rassle, hasn't been to a dance in a coon's age. **1940** Nason *Approach to Battle* 28 [ref. to 1918]: I cursed my horse and my own folly for letting myself in for any such hog wrastle.

hog-yoke *n. Naut.* a quadrant.

   1839 Olmstead *Whaling Voyage* 83: A *quadrant* receives the very undignified and unphilosophical name of a "hog-yoke." **1893** Barra *Two Oceans* 62: He couldn't handle the "hog yoke," as the sailors call the quadrant. **1897** Kipling *Capts. Courageous* 140: The old…quadrant they called the "hog-yoke." **1899** Robbins *Gam* 16: Now it was my duty to take the hog-yoke on deck at eleven o'clock. **1923** Riesenberg *Under Sail* 133: Our first officer came aft…carrying an ancient "hog yoke." **1923** Southgate *Rusty Door* 110: Well, there was no course-layin' in thim days—hog-yokes and Waterbury clocks.

hoist or **heist** *n.* [see note at HOIST, *v.*] **1.a.** *Und.* the practice of burglary (*obs.*), shoplifting, picking pockets, or robbery.

   *****1714** in Partridge *Dict. Und.* 338: He pursued his old Courses of going on the *Top* or *Hoist,* that is, breaking into a house…by getting in at a Window one Story high, which they perform by one Thief standing on the Shoulders of another. *****1777** in Partridge *Dict. Und.* 337: The *Lift* or *Hoist.* *****1797** in Partridge *Dict. Und.:* Lift, or *hoist,* shop-lifting or robbing a shop. *****1812** Vaux *Vocab.:* The *game* of shop-lifting is called *the hoist;* a person expert at this practice is said to be *a good hoist.* **1914** Jackson & Hellyer *Vocab.* 44: Hoist…the profession of shoplifting. **1930** *Amer. Mercury* (Dec.) 455: The mutts bang up on foolish powder an' go on the hist. **1934** in *Jour. Abnormal Psych.* XXX (1935) 359: *Go out on the hoist*—To commit a robbery. **1940** Clemmer *Pris. Comm.* 289 [ref. to 1920's]: Eventually, to continue his accustomed scale of luxurious living, he went on the "heist." Several robberies netted large returns. **1956** Resko *Reprieve* 183: A guy that goes out on…the heist now. *****1958** in *OED2:* My old woman's still out on the hoist now. **1996** McCumber *Playing off Rail* 235: What a five-star place for a heist.…carjacking, mugging, robbery, fuckin homicide, you name it.

   b. Orig. *Und.* a theft, esp. a hijacking or holdup; in phr. **put the heist on** to steal or rob. [In this and the following senses, *heist* and /haist/ are now the only forms in general use in the U.S.]

   1930 *Liberty* (July 5) 18: *Street heist*—a hold up committed on the street. **1930** E.D. Sullivan *Chi. Surrenders* 229: Any such giant "heist." **1931** *Sat. Review* (July 18) 978: Crooks…speak of a…hold-up as a "hoist," which must come from hoisting the hands at the point of a gat. **1933** Ersine *Pris. Slang:* Heist…A stickup, daylight robbery. **1935** Algren *Boots* 254: Ah aint told yo' half what ah done since that butcher shop hoist. **1936** Duncan *Over the Wall* 32: I suppose they give guys medals for a heist job. **1937** Reitman *Box-Car Bertha* 158: He…did a bit in the pen for a hoist (theft). **1952** Mandel *Angry Strangers* 236: Like—he pulls a little hyste 'n lives off it. **1955** "W. Henry" *Wyatt* 71: The…McLowrys handled the rustling; Stilwell…the stage hoists. **1967** [R. Beck] *Pimp* 116: Some louse put the heist on your [cheap jewelry]. **1968** R. Beck *Trick Baby* 99: You'd rather put the heist on Fort Knox. **1972** Kopp *Buddha* 216: It was to be one of those professional heists of the Topkapi genre. *a***1982** in Berry *Semper Fi* 396: Then it was Cape Gloucester and the great beer hoist. **1987** *Mighty Mouse* (CBS-TV): It was destined to go down as the biggest heist in the history of Mouseville! **1988** Mays & Sahadi *Say Hey* 26: Gangsters…discussed some heist. **1990** *Evans & Novak* (CNN-TV) (Aug. 11): Saddam Hussein seized Kuwait—put the heist on it, like a bank.

   c. the proceeds of a theft.

   *a***1961** *WNID3:* Heist…*slang:* something (as money, jewels) acquired by robbery or theft. **1973** D. Morrow *Maurie* 29: Our next heist is yours. **1978** Smullyan *What Is the Name* 67: The criminal…took the heist away in a car.

   d. a thief; HEIST MAN.

   *ca***1963** in Schwendinger & Schwendinger *Adolescent Subculture* 290: The Heist comes to me with the merchandise and says, "Sell it on the street."

   e. *Und.* a place to be robbed.

   1977 Caron *Go-Boy* 43: The heist was a combination post office and grocery store.

   2. a sudden tripping or fall; *(also)* a kick or prod.

   1837 Neal *Charc. Sks.* 74: I'm sure to get a hyst. *Ibid.:* Put not your trust in politicianers or you'll get a hyst. **1859** in *DAE:* "He got a deuce of a hist," meaning a fall. **1868** Chisholm *So. Pass* 108: The Buffalo…gave the mule one "hyst" with his horn and sent him kiting. **1916** in *DARE.* **1942–49** Goldin et al. *DAUL* 94: "A heist in the keister"—a boot in the rear with the knee. **1966–67** in *DARE:* "He slipped on the steps and took quite a"…Heist…Hoist.

   3. a favorable mention; boost.

   1878 Hart *Sazerac* 152: [He requested] us to "give her a h'ist in the paper," as he "wanted to attract the attention of capitalists."

   4. a raise or increase.

   1940 O'Hara *Pal Joey* 81: The owner…gave me a quick hist in pay. **1942** *ATS* 26: Increase.—n….heist, histe, hike,…raise.

hoist or **heist** /hɔist/ or /haist/ *v.* [The pron. /haist/ (represented most recently by the spelling *heist*) has been common for centuries in regional speech, yet was rarely represented orthographically before the early 19th C.; thus some of the quots. with the spelling *hoist* presumably represent the /haist/ pron. Since the 1920's the spelling *heist* has become almost exclusively associated with the various underworld senses of the term and is now popularly perceived as a different word. The pron. /hɔist/ in these senses is virtually obs. in the U.S. but survives elsewhere.]

1. *Stu.* (see 1851 quot.). Cf. *OED, hoist, v.,* def. 1.c.

1773 in *DA:* I was histed…for eating before the Scholars came in. **1851** B. Hall *College Wds.* 162: It was formerly customary at Harvard College, when the Freshmen were used as servants, to report them to their Tutor if they refused to go…on an errand; this complaint was called a *hoisting,* and the delinquent was said to be *hoisted.*

2.a. *Und.* to shoplift; *(hence)* to steal. Cf. earlier quots. of HOISTER, 1.

*1815 Vaux *Memoirs* 82: *Hoisting*…Shop-lifting. **1866** *Nat. Police Gaz.* (Nov. 3) 2: Polly Smith, the Tenth ward "lifter," has been doing considerable business lately among the down town silk and ribbon houses in the "hoisting" way. **1867** *Nat. Police Gaz.* (Oct. 26) 2: Mrs. Elkin…got five years in Sing Sing for "hoisting." **1904** *Life in Sing Sing* 260: *Hoisting a slab of stones.* Stealing a tray of diamonds. **1929** in Partridge *Dict. Und.* 337: We'll just hoist his stuff and what the hell will he do about it? **1932–34** Minehan *Boy & Girl Tramps* 190: I just heists it off the Wop's stand and tucks it under my coat. **1940** R. Chandler *Farewell, My Lovely* ch. xxxvi: Sending boys out to heist jewels off rich ladies. **1947** S.J. Perelman *Westward Ha!* 123: He discovered that his new ball-point fountain pen…had been heisted by the attendants. **1949** in *Harper's* (Feb. 1950) 71: Jewelry heisted from Aga Khan last fall. *1962 in *OED2:* I know where we can hoist a car. **1967** in M.W. Klein *Juve. Gangs* 65: The "heisting" of Christmas trees for "Mom" was frequently reported. *a*1989 Spears *NCT Dict.* 178: Lefty heisted a car. **1989** *Guiding Light* (CBS-TV): To her it's no trouble…heisting the kid.

b. *Und.* to commit an armed robbery against; hold up.— occ. constr. with *up.*

1927–28 Tasker *Grimhaven* 159: Jockey…went up to the big house for hysting a dice game. **1928** Panzram *Killer* 64 [ref. to 1911]: I was sizing up the youngest…of the two and figuring when to pull out my hog-leg and heist 'em up. **1929** Hotstetter & Beesley *Racket* 228: *Hoist*—To rob with a gun. **1930** *Liberty* (July 19) 22: My four men and I heist seven guys in succession. **1930** *Amer. Mercury* (Dec.) 456: *Hist*—to hold up; to hyjack. "We hist the mutt's plant for fifty cases of skee." **1935** Pollock *Und. Sp.:* Hist, to hijack. **1935** Algren *Boots* 168: Me an' Nub got to hoist a joint somewheres. **1935** *Chi. Tribune* (Jan. 22) (Graphic Sec.) 9: *Heist*—to hold up. **1949** in *DAS:* They hoisted the place. **1951** Pryor *The Big Play* 30: "You've never been heisted," Ball said. **1961** *Twilight Zone* (CBS-TV): No, it's just Santa Claus tryin' to heist the joint. **1971** Horan *Blue Messiah* 267: Screw 'em all you want but don't heist 'em! **1974** Andrews & Dickens *Over the Wall* 61: We're going to heist a gas station. **1986** S. Bauer *Amazing Stories* 178: Some…street thug wants to hoist me up.

c. *Gamb.* to take advantage of; defeat soundly and take the money of.

1973 N.Y.C. pool player, age 24: Like for example if I challenge you to a game of pool for money, I could say I'd *heist* you at pool because you'd probably be so bad.

3. to drink (beer or liquor).—in early use usu. constr. with *in.*

1862 C.F. Browne *A. Ward* 128: I thowt I'd hist in a few swallers of suthin strengthin. **1865** C.F. Browne *Ward: Travels* 26: In a state of mind which showed that he'd bin histin' in more'n his share of pizen. **1883** Sowell *Rangers and Pioneers* 60: Well, boys, we will all die together, I have *histed* in what you left. **1883** Peck *Bad Boy* 314: A father that is in the habit of hoisting in too much benzine. **1890** McBallastir *Society* 43: My Nobs…did not ask him to "hist in a few." **1891** Devere *Tramp Poems* 19: So put up yer "leather," thar, Ole Men/An' hoist in some licker with me. **1897** in Hoppenstand *Dime Novel Detective* 72: You've been "histing" it a little too heavily of late. **1903** (quot. at PIE-EYED). **1936** A. Adams *Cowboy Lingo* 228: To take a drink was to "h'ist one." **1939** "E. Queen" *Dragon's Teeth* 72: We sat on the terrace and hoisted a few, and she got very, very chummy. **1948** McHenry & Myers *Home Is Sailor* 67: Heading for the first speak…to hoist a few against the cold. **1956** Neider *Hendry Jones* 112: We hoisted in a cargo of aguardiente. **1957** J. Jones *Some Came Running* 35: We can hoist a few brews and just talk. **1958** Traver *Anatomy* 26: You know I'd like to stay and heist a few more with you and keep the vigil. **1983** Stapleton *30 Yrs.* 70: He figured he'd hoist a few, watch a skin show [etc.]. **1987** *New Leave It to Beaver* (TBS-TV): Let's not go to work today! We'll hoist a few, shoot some pool—.

4. to kick or knock (someone) down; *(hence)* to thrash (someone).

1894 F.P. Dunne, in Schaaf *Dooley* 110: I thought me frind Casey'd

be taken up f'r histin' a polisman f'r sure, though…I niver knowed him to do but wan annychist thing. **1912** Field *Watch Yourself* 209 [ref. to *ca*1890]: She'll hist him higher then Gilroy's kite.

5. *Poker.* to raise the bet of (an opponent).

1887 [C. Mackenzie] *Jack Pots* 10: Was hoisted, called, lost, and was $40 out. *Ibid.* 48: The man…hoisted him a blue stack. **1905** *Nat. Police Gaz.* (Dec. 2) 6: "I'll have to h'ist you, I reckon," so he…threw in $10 more.

¶ In phrase:

¶ **hoist tail** to get going.

1944 H. Brown *Walk in Sun* 19: He started to work his way towards the stern of the boat. "Hoist tail," he said over and over again. "Hoist tail." **1944–46** in *AS* XXII 55: *To hoist tail.* To take off, move out, leave.

hoister or **heister** *n.* [see note at HOIST, *v.*] **1.** *Und.* a housebreaker *(obs.),* shoplifter, pickpocket, or robber. [*Heister* and /'haistər/ are now the only forms in general use in the U.S.]

*1708 in Partridge *Dict. Und.* 338: *Hoisters.* Such as help one another upon their Backs in the Night-time to get into Windows. *1790 in *OED2: Hoister,* a shoplifter. *1847–50 in *F & H* III 330: A *hoyster* is a pickpocket. **1859** Matsell *Vocab.* 42: *Hoister.* A Shop-lifter. *1865 in *Comments on Ety.* XVII (Oct. 1, 1987) 16: Among those in front of the bar was Uxbridge Jack, the "heister." **1890** Roe *Police* 388: A "hoister" or male shop-lifter. **1899** "J. Flynt" *Tramping* 394: *Hoister* or *Hyster:* a shoplifter. **1902** in "O. Henry" *Works* 1091: The article, we will say, is written by a *typical* train hoister. **1904** *Life in Sing Sing* 249: *Hoister.*— Shoplifter, wagon thief. *a*1909 Tillotson *Detective* 92: *Hoister*—A shoplifter. **1911** A.H. Lewis *Apaches of N.Y.* 128: She could bring home th' bacon, if any of them hoisters could. **1927** *DN* V 449: *Heister*…A shoplifter. **1928** Sharpe *Chicago May* 286: *Boosters,* or *Hoisters*— shoplifters. **1929** Hotstetter & Beesley *Racket* 228: "Hoister"—robber. **1947** Helseth *Martin Rome* 79: He was just a small-time heister without the brains of a school kid. **1968** R. Beck *Trick Baby* 14: You have almost a week to find a heister or safecracker to share your Christmas sentiments. **1971** in *OED2:* Cop slang. A hoister is a pickpocket or shoplifter.

2. a heavy drinker. Cf. BOOZE-HOISTER.

1889 Barrère & Leland *Dict. Slang* I 468: A *hoister* means…a sot. **1940** Goodrich *Delilah* 409 [ref. to 1917]: But the Captain of the Yard, despite his being a "hoister" from way back, never even would go on the parties to Grande. **1942** *ATS* 110: Drunkard…*heister, hister, hoister.*

hoist in *v.* **1.** *Naut.* to accept as true.

*1805 J. Davis *Post Captain* 27: She says she loves him dearly.…I can hardly hoist it in, sir! **1841** [Mercier] *Man o' War* 154: "Bowser, I don't know how to swallow that yarn," cried Flukes, "I know Dick was pretty wide-awake, but I can't hoist that *gas* in no how." **1868** Macy *There She Blows!* 130: You haven't got tobacco enough to make me hoist in either. **1899** Hamblen *Bucko Mate* 39: The idea…was almost more than he could "hoist in."

2. see HOIST, *v.,* 3.

hoisting engineer *n.* a heavy drinker. *Joc.*

1929–31 Farrell *Young Lonigan* 120: "He's a hoisting engineer," said Swan, who accompanied his statement with the appropriate drinking gesture.

hoity-toity *adj.* haughty; snobbishly disdainful; pretentious. Also **highty-tighty.** Also adv. Cf. *1749 quot. at HOITY-TOITY, *interj.*

*a1720 in D'Urfey *Pills* I 255: The Frowzy Browzy,/Hoyty Toyty,/*Covent*-Garden Harridan. *1820 J. Keats, in *OED2:* See what hoity-toity airs she took. **1840** *Spirit of Times* (July 18) 229: Them *highty tighty* sort of tunes he sung. *1848 W.M. Thackeray *Vanity Fair* ch. xviii: La, William, don't be so highty-tighty with us. We're not men. **1889** Nye *Western Humor* 178: He sails round in a highty-tighty room with a fire in it night and day. **1899** F.H. Smith *Other Fellow* 50: But dey sent Miss Rachel to a real highty-tighty school, dat dey did, down to Louisville. **1900** Ade *More Fables* 166: They…went to see the Hity-Tity Variety and Burlesque Aggregation. **1919** S. Lewis *Free Air* 198: Needn't be so hoity-toity about it, "He's my father, madam!" **1925** S. Lewis *Arrowsmith* 902: But what I can't understand is how after living with Leora, who was the real thing, you can stand a hoity-toity skirt like Joycey! **1929** "E. Queen" *Roman Hat* 75: A little respect now and then from some of our hoity-toity legal lights. **1944** L. Smith *Strange Fruit* 1: Stuck up like Almighty Nonnie Anderson.…holding her head so highty-tighty. **1952** in *DAS:* In the hoity-toitiest of the Fifth Avenue shops…the mink coat…arouses…talk. **1958** S.H. Adams *Tenderloin* 328: That highty-tighty pal of yours. **1978** A. Rose *Eubie Blake* 61: At the hoity-toity Royal Poinciana Hotel in Palm Beach.

hoity-toity *v.* (see quot.).

　　1871 Schele de Vere *Americanisms* 488: *Hity-tity*…is here also used as a verb. "She expects to be *hitied-titied*, that is, to be made much of."

hoity-toity *interj.* [app. via reduplication of obs. *hoit* 'to indulge in madcap or prankish behavior'; var. spellings reflect dial. prons. for which cf. note at HOIST, *v.*] (used to express surprise or disdain).

　　*1695 W. Congreve, in *OED:* Hoity toity, what have I to do with his Dreams or his Divination? ***1747** in *OED:* Heyty titey, very fine truly. ***1749** H. Fielding *Tom Jones* Bk. VII ch. viii: Hoity toity!…madam is in her airs. **1788** S. Low *Politician Out-witted* IV.i: Then hoity-toity, whisky frisky, &c. **1833** A. Greene *Duckworth* I 168: Hoity-toity! Mister—he's my own hoss! ***1835** Marryat *Midshipman Easy* 38: Highty-tighty, what ails Susan? **1939** Osborn *Morning's at Seven* 355: CORA. None of your business. ARRY. Hoity-toity! **1952** Uris *Battle Cry* 113: Oh, hidy tidy, Christ almighty,/Who in the hell are we,/Zim, zim, *God Damn,*/The fighting Sixth Marines!

Ho-Jo *n.* **1.** a Howard Johnson's motor inn or restaurant.

　　1963 in A. Sexton *Letters* 191: I have become a lover of french fries (not frozen, not Ho-Jo). **1970–71** G.V. Higgins *Eddie Coyle* 97: You could get something to eat.…There's a Ho-Jo about six miles back. **1979** N.Y.C. woman, age 24: We stayed at Ho-Jo's and then at Travelodge. **1980** L. Fleischer & C. Gore *Fame* 58: She could have her breakfast in the HoJo on Times Square. **1982** Sculatti *Catalog of Cool* 75: [The characters] hole up in Ho-Jo's. **1989** Radford & Crowley *Drug Agent* 180: Nine thirty, Hojo's service area.

2. a take-out meal purchased from a Howard Johnson's restaurant.

　　1988 T. Logan *Harder They Fall* 139: He sent me out to get some HoJo's and some wine.

hoke *n.* Orig. *Theat.* HOKUM, 1.

　　1921 *Variety* (July 1) 17: Before the softest hoke audience in the metropolis they went strongly. **1921** *Variety* (Dec. 16) 10: All of the hoke and standards were present. **1921** *Variety* (Dec. 30) 4: They hand me a lot of cans to play where I ruined them with the old hoke. **1925** *Sat. Eve. Post* (Jan. 3) 14: What do you mean, U.S.A.? Flag waving hoke? **1929** *Variety* (Oct. 30) 5: Four Big Theatres Worry Over What To Give Them Extra. Toss 'Em Hoke Bait.…Hoke is propagandaed in the butcher shops to get them in. **1926–35** Watters & Hopkins *Burlesque* 19: You gotta make up your mind, Bonny, that I'm a hoak comic. **1942** in *DAS:* You know, the usual hoke. **1952** A. Green & B. Comden *Singin' in the Rain* (film): My grandfather said go out and tell 'em a joke/But make sure it's got plenty of hoke.

hoke *v.* **1.a.** Orig. *Theat.* to employ or infuse with HOKUM, 1; treat (a role, subject, etc.) in an exaggerated, usu. comic or sentimental, way so as to appeal to a popular, unsophisticated audience; falsify in this manner.—usu. constr. with *up.*

　　1925 *Sat. Eve. Post* (Feb. 14) 47: Among the more outspoken of the profession the process is called hoking it up. **1928** in W.C. Fields *By Himself* 82: It's hokum. But…Fields…doesn't "hoke." **1938** M. McCarthy, in *Partisan Rev.* (Jan.) 48: It is well known that actors who have been playing for a long time in the same play will…"hoke" their performances more and more. A giggle becomes a laugh; a catch in the throat, a sob; a tremor, a spasm. **1939** *AS* XIV (Dec.) 318: It's all right to hoke the incident but not the theme. **1940** *Sat. Review* (June 15) 24: To hear Beatrice Kay sing "Waiting at the Church" was a return to our youth—but don't *hoke* it too hard. **1940** S. Lewis *Bethel Merriday* 289: Mr. Nooks had…overplayed—"hoked" is the technical word—the role of the Apothecary, which is a pretty easy role for anyone to hoke, if he has been born a…ham. **1941** Schulberg *Sammy* 254: One of them is to make a newspaper picture—only not the usual drunken reporter and madcap heiress crap. The real thing—the way you and I know it. Hoked up of course. **1942** in *DAS:* I should apologize for hokin' up your number. **1948** I. Shulman *Cry Tough!* 66: You've been seein' too many hoked up movies. **1990** W.T. Anderson *Reality* 11: The story of Gaia, an ancient Greek myth hoked up anew in the guise of science. **1994** E. Goode & N. Ben-Yehuda *Moral Panics* 32: Panics need not be hoked up or fabricated by cynical, manipulative agents scheming for their own advantage.

b. to alter or devise so as to deceive.—usu. constr. with *up.*

　　1942 *ATS* 709: Hoke (up)…to arrange or prepare, as dice, to facilitate cheating. **1973** Lanham *Style* 15: How can I believe in a thesis obviously hoked up for English?

2. to flatter or hoax.

　　1935 Pollock *Und. Speaks:* Hoke, to string along; to jolly; to ridicule. **1971** *Life* (June 11) 66: To hoke sales still higher, Stuart teased the press into columns of speculation about the real identity of the author.

hokey[1] *n.* ¶ In phrase: **by [the] hokey** (used as a mild oath).

　　*1825 Jamieson *Scot. Dict.:* Hoakie…Used as a petty oath. *By the hoakie.* **1838** in *DARE:* By the hokey! **1844** Stephens *High Life in N.Y.* 71: By the living hokey, I never seen anything like it! **1859** in Botkin *Treas. Amer. Folk.* 588: By hokey! **1874, 1906, 1912, 1984** in *DARE.*

hokey[2] *n.* **1.** a person who employs HOKUM, 1, 2.

　　1951 M. Berle, in *DAS:* I can be a hokey, I can do a straight line. **1967** J. Kramer *Instant Replay* 123: We've got the hokies this week, huh? We've got a bunch of patsies…huh?

2. HOKUM, 2.

　　*a***1989** C.S. Crawford *Four Deuces* 113: I didn't need any of that kind of hokey.

hokey *adj.* being or characterized by HOKUM; artificial; meretricious; pretentious; CORNY.

　　1927 *Variety* (June 29) 31: This mixed couple have the makings of a good hokey act. **1945** *N.Y. Times* (Aug. 19) 3: The dull films, the tasteless, hoky confections that public taste ought to repudiate. **1964** *Dick Van Dyke Show* (CBS-TV): You and that hoky jacket you're wearing. **1965** S.J. Perelman, in *New Yorker* (Aug. 28) 28: Hokey old sketches like "Irish Justice," routines like "Flugel Street." **1966** "Petronius" *N.Y. Unexp.* 11: She'll come across without the hokey BS. **1971** *Rolling Stone* (June 24) 31: A closing piece [on a record], "Sometimes," is embarrassingly hokey. **1973** *Penthouse* (May) 40: There is a basic honesty about even the hokiest country song. **1980** Grizzard *Billy Bob Bailey* 40: He didn't like clichés, nor anything that was "hokey." **1989** *Daily Beacon* (Univ. Tenn.) (Aug. 30) 4: Will younger fans reject the clothing as being too old-fashioned and/or hokey?

hokum *n.* [prob. blend *hocus*-pocus + bunk*um*] **1.** Orig. *Theat.* obvious or familiar elements of low comedy, melodrama, sentimentality, or the like, designed to appeal strongly to an unsophisticated audience. Now *S.E.*

　　1908 McGaffey *Show Girl* 214: Honest, to hear him spring that sure-fire hokum you would have thought he believed it. **1917** *Lit. Digest* (Aug. 25) 28: "Hokum" [means]…low comedy verging on vulgarity. **1918** R. Casey *Cannoneers* 227: Nobody takes it very seriously. Whoever wrote the book put too much hokum in it. **1923** *N.Y. Times* (Sept. 9) VIII 2: *Hokum:* Old and sure-fire comedy. Also tear-inducing situations. **1923** in *AS* IV (1928) 159: I…and my father…learned the word hokum from the Negroes on my grandfather's plantation [in North Carolina] and from those of Southern Maryland. From them it was carried by…the old-time minstrel troupes…to the stage. **1922–24** McIntyre *White Light Nights* 206: [George M. Cohan] was the first to dramatize the flag—revealing his insight into "hokum." **1926** *AS* I (May) 437: Hokum is not always comedy; sometimes it borders on pathos. **1926** Tully *Jarnegan* 134: He did not discuss art. "Give them the old hokum…they love it." **1928** *N.Y. Times* (July 8) VIII : This word hokum has been in general use in the theatre for half a century or more.…Among actors hokum has meant solely and definitely the repetition of a joke or piece of business which has proved "sure-fire." Hokum is merely old stuff which…has been found to "get over." **1933** *Newsweek* (Mar. 4) 28: Hokum, if it's good hokum produced with the tongue placed at the proper angle in the cheek, can be hugely entertaining. ***1987** Carr et al. *Jazz* 374: A jazz-based vaudeville act featuring Shields's fine playing interspersed with clarinet hokum.

2. claptrap; flattery; falsehoods; nonsense. Now *S.E.*

　　1921 (quot. at GOULASH, 1). **1923** in *AS* IV (1928) 159: That's all hokum." Here it replaces the obsolescent "bull." **1924** G. Henderson *Keys to Crookdom* 408: Hokum. Unreliable talk, line of bull, bull con. **1927** *AS* II 276: Hokum—buncombe. **1928** *N.Y. Times* (Mar. 27) VIII 8: *Hokum*…has been picked up and used as being synonymous with…hooey…and bologna. **1928** Hall & Niles *One Man's War* 334: Did you really go to Russia, or was that all hokum? **1928** Benchley *20,000 Leagues* 144: They scribbled on their conference-pads some slight heresy against the hokum of business. **1929** Ferber *Cimarron* 270: The slang words hokum and bunk were not then [1898] in use, but even had they been they never would have been applied, by that appreciative crowd, at least, to the flowery and impassioned oratory of the Southwest Silver Tongue, Yancey Cravat. **1929** in R.E. Howard *Book* 84: The glory road leads only to disappointment and hokum. **1931** Grant *Gangdom's Doom* 55: But he fell for some line of hokum, or he wouldn't be there now. **1932** Lawes *20,000 Yrs.* 315: It sounds like hokum, but it's true. **1981** D. Burns *Feeling Good* 36: All that stewing…was just a lot of self-imposed hokum. **1983** Curry *River's in My Blood* 127: Most pilots now claim to disregard such "hokum."

hold *n. Naut.* the belly; stomach. *Joc.*

 1854 Sleeper *Salt Water Bubbles* 80: The shark…carefully stows him away in the lower hold, whenever he has a chance. **1877** Lee *Fag-Ends* 52: But we'd both be blowed,/if we'd either be stowed/In the other chap's hold, do you see?

¶ In phrase:

¶ **(one's) best** [or **strong** or **main**] **hold** (one's) forte or best course of action. Also (pron.-sp.) **holt.**

 1862 C.F. Browne *Artemus Ward* 132: Fassinatin peple is her best holt. **1866** Locke *Round the Cirkle* 48: Compermises wuz our best holt. **1874** Carter *Rollingpin* 220: Perlitical meetins wer hiz very best holt. **1882** Pinkerton *Bank-Robbers* 73: My best hold…is in the beer-gardens with "wine, women and song." **1885** (quot. at TAFFY). **1889** Field *Western Verse* 165: "Ben Bolt"/…wuz regarded by all odds ez Vere de Blaw's best holt. **1890** Quinn *Fools of Fortune* 374: I asked him…what was his "strong-hold" in the line of a professional card sharper. **1894** in *DN* VI 347: He drew a picture of…the beauties of the springtime there. That is his best hold. **1901** (quot. at COME-ON, 1). **1907** in C.M. Russell *Paper Talk* 55: Writing aint my strong holt. **1926** C.M. Russell *Trails* 7: Walking aint my strong holt and these boulders don't help me none.

hold *v.* **1.** usu. as **holding,** *ppl.* **a.** Esp. *Gamb.* to possess ready money; in phr. **hold heavy** to possess ready money in large amounts.—sometimes used trans.

 *1889 Barrère & Leland *Dict. Slang* I 468: *Hold, do you* (London slang), have you any money to lend or stand treat with? **1918 Bodleian Qly. Rec.* II 153: Soldiers' War Terms…"Are you holding?", i.e. Have you any money? **1920** *Variety* (Dec. 24) 5: If she had jack and held heavy you could label him as a male gold digger. **1924* in Wilkes *Dict. Austral. Colloq.* 174: *Holdin'.* Possessing money. **1933** Ersine *Pris. Slang* 44: *Holding heavy.* Having much money. "Abe should be holding heavy; he just pulled a big job." **1934** Kromer *Waiting* 28: Does he think I would sleep in that lousy building if I was holding anything? **1937** in D. Runyon *More Guys* 215: "Is this ex-king holding anything?"…"Not a quarter." **1948** McHenry & Myers *Home Is Sailor* 57: Billy never felt embarrassment about accepting pieceoffs from sailors who came ashore holding heavy. **1966** Braly *Cold* 66: "He looks like he's holding." "He's not." "Maybe he's got something we can pawn." **1968** Maule *Rub-A-Dub* 17: Seems like I remember some pretty wild stories he told [for sympathy] when he ain't holding. *Ibid.* 136: "You holding?"…"I'm broke." **1970** Terkel *Hard Times* 37: They wanted money….My mother wasn't holding that day. So she had to wait for the customers to come in and borrow it from 'em. **1965–71** in *Inter. Jour. Stud. Alcohol* XXXII (1971) 737: *How much are you holding?* How much money do you have? **1976** "N. Ross" *Policeman* 113: This time he was holding pretty good. He offered me $200, and I took it.

 b. *Narc.* to possess drugs, esp. for illicit sale.—also used trans.

 1935 Pollock *Und. Speaks* s.v. *are*: Are you holding? Have any dope to sell? *Ibid.* s.v. *I'm*: I'm holding, I have dope to sell. **1955** E. Hunter *Jungle Kids* 114: You want the Law to know we're holding? **1956** E. Hunter *Second Ending* 138: "You holding?" Andy asked suddenly. **1958** Motley *Epitaph* 117: The Wolf was…holding…a ounce. **1959–60** R. Reisner *Jazz Titans* 158: *Holding:* to have marijuana on one's person. **1963** Coon *Short End* 178: If we really smoked pot it was because somebody older was holding. **1967** Wolf *Love Generation* 6: I was holding when I was busted, and I had to drop inside the Berkeley jail. **1971** Dibner *Trouble with Heroes* 206: You holding?…Speed? Pot? **1974–77** A. Hoffman *Property Of* 97: I could be holding in less than half an hour if I could get a ride into the city.

 c. *Und.* armed.

 1971 S. Stevens *Way Uptown* 177: Sure he's holding, but she don't use it on nothin' like you. **1980** (quot. at FLAKE, *n.*, 4).

 2. to omit (an ingredient) from a usual order of food or drink (usu. *imper.*; now *S.E.*); (*hence*) to refrain from describing, uttering, etc.

 1942 *ATS* 765: *Hold the cow,* an order of coffee without cream. **1945** *Calif. Folk.* IV (Jan.) 55: *Hold the hail:* No ice in the drink(s). **1954–60** *DAS:* Lettuce and tomato salad, hold the mayonnaise. **1962** N.Y.C. high school student: I'd like a hamburger. Hold the onions. **1982** Huttmann *Code Blue* 79: Don't tell us all that yucky stuff….Hold the gore! **1989** Univ. Tenn. instructor: Hold the flattery.

¶ In phrase:

¶ **hold the bag** [or **sack**] see s.v. BAG, *n.,* and SACK, *n.*

hold down *v.* to occupy (a place); (among tramps) to ride atop (a freight car).

 1891 in *DA:* Jumping an east bound freight…I managed to hold it down or keep on it till I got to…Alameda. **1894** in London *Tramp Diary* 31: We held her down all night till we arrived in Truckee. *ca*1894 in *Independent* (Jan. 2, 1902) 28: Some of them will go into a city or town and stay there "holding down the town" H.B.'s call it, until the Police…Run them out. **1903** A.H. Lewis *Boss* 205: I s'ppose I can hold down a hearse as good as th' next one. **1914** Graham *Poor Immigrants* 116: I'm holding down a bed in the hospital.

holding see s.v. HOLD, *v.,* 1.

hold out *v.* to live; HANG OUT.

 1855 in *DA:* Is this the place where the phrenologist "holds out?"

hold over *v.* to hold a clear advantage over.

 1871 "M. Twain" *Roughing It* 249: You ruther hold over me, pard. I reckon I can't call that hand. **1882** in *DAE:* [We] supposed the Boston bean must hold over every other bean. **1889** in *DA:* Do we hold over bowers?

hold-up *n.* **1.a.** an armed robbery. Now *S.E.*

 1878 in Roe *Army Letters* 206: The driver is their only protector, and the stage route is through miles and miles of wild forest, and in between huge boulders where a "hold-up" could be so easily accomplished. **1880** in *DA:* Now he hath joined a hold-up outfit on the overland stage route. **1881** C.M. Chase *Editor's Run* 134: This business game of this element is "Hold up." **1885** *Harper's Mag.* (Apr.) 695: The streets [of Albuquerque] were brightly illuminated…, a particularly gratifying change from the…darkness of former days, into which one ventured with grave apprehensions lest a "hold-up" might be in waiting for him. **1890** in *DAE:* No more hold-ups have been reported. **1896** in *OED2:* The prisoner confessed to a hold-up. **1909** *WNID: Holdup,* n. *Slang, U.S.*…An assault on a traveler or passenger for the purpose of robbery,—orig. on traveling parties in the western United States. **1924** G. Henderson *Keys to Crookdom* 104: After they have committed the holdup, they "ditch" the stolen motor vehicle.

 b. an instance of extortion or overcharging. Cf. *S.E. highway robbery.*

 1908 in *OED2:* The people insisted on electing a desperado to the presidential office—they must take the hold-up that follows. **1910** in *DA:* Our house…cost twenty-five thousand dollars, exclusive of the plumber's little hold-up and the Oriental rugs. **1914** in *DAE:* Libel suits are generally "hold-ups." **1919** in De Beck *Google* 28: This is a hold-up joint—I'll go some place else. **1939** in *OED2:* It's a hold-up, and God help the poor bastards who have to take it at that price.

 2. an armed robber. [The 1885 quot. at **(1.a.),** above may actually illus. this sense.]

 1888 in *F & H* III 331: He…ran against a party of *hold-ups.* **1897** A.H. Lewis *Wolfville* 160: I'm due to down the first hold-up who shoots across any layout of mine. **1906** A. Adams *Cattle Brands* 6: The attacked party…opened fire on the hold-ups. **1909** *WNID: Holdup…*n., *Slang, U.S.*….a highway robber. **1911** in C.M. Russell *Paper Talk* 85: Here's to the holdup an' hoss thief/That loved stage roads an' hosses too well. **1914** D.W. Roberts *Rangers* 122: Next came the professionals, burglars, cracksmen, robbers and "hold-ups" of every description. **1926** C.M. Russell *Trails* 113: When the hold-up gets through trimmin' us he…grabs the old lady's roll. **1928** Levin *Reporter* 173: That's where we get our hold-ups, thieves, prostitutes, criminals.

hold up *v.* **1.** to lean against. *Joc.*

 1845 in G.W. Harris *High Times* 47: Two fine lookin galls was standin in the door, face to face holdin up the door posts with their backs, laffin. **1968** Gover *JC* 58: Here is, my ole man. Holdin up the hotel, waitin on me.

 2.a. to halt and rob; commit an armed robbery against. Now *S.E.*

 1851 in *DA:* At St. Louis he *held up*…several men and got more or less money. **1879** in *DA:* Later they took a jug of whisky away from a granger...and "held up" two men for their money. **1881** C.M. Chase *Editor's Run* 135: A pair of roughs..."holding up" a tenderfoot. **1882** Triplett *Jesse James* 72: The knights of the road...used often to "hold up" the coach...from London. *Ibid.* 114: We mean to hold you up, G— d— you! **1888** in *F & H* III 331: One man *held up* six stage passengers in Arizona the other day and robbed them of $2,000. *a***1889** in Barrère & Leland *Dict. Slang* I 468: Two thieves were caught in New York...mistaking two detectives for persons in their own line of business, they invited them *to hold up* a man. **1890** Messiter *Sport* 365: Two ambulances...had been "held up," as it is called, which means stopped by "road agents." **1893** in B. Matthews *Parts of Speech* 188: Slang...[includes] violent metaphors, like *in the soup, kicking the bucket, holding up* (a stage-coach). *****1894** in *OED:* At noon yesterday four unmasked men "held up" a Texas Pacific train near that place. **1900** *Webster's International Dict.* (Supp.) 97: Trains [in South Africa] are not stopped and robbed; coaches are not "held up." **1901** "J. Flynt" *World of Graft* 20: Worington...and...Kennedy...held up an elderly gentleman at the corner of Western Avenue and Sixteenth Street, taking away the man's watch and a few dollars. **1918** Mencken *Amer. Lang.* 306: Brander Mathews...thought *to hold up* slang; it is now perfectly good American. **1923** McKnight *Eng. Words* 193: Hold up. In its origin...short for "hold up your hands," it comes to be used as a noun naming the action of a highwayman, and then the noun in turn is converted into a verb..."hold up a train." **1935** Horwill *Mod. Amer. Usage* 167: Although it is the victims that actually hold up their hands....the expression *hold up* has curiously come to be applied to the action of the criminals. "The gang of outlaws had planned to hold up the westbound express." **1957** Evans & Evans *Dict. Contemp. Usage* 475: In America the armed robbery of persons is more and more being called a *hold-up,* and the perpetrators *hold-up men, robbers* being restricted more to those who steal goods.

b. to make a demand of someone (for something); (*hence*) to charge (someone) an exorbitant price. [The earliest quot. is defined by Barrère & Leland as meaning 'to take into custody', but no independent confirmation of such usage is available.]

[*a***1889** in Barrère & Leland *Dict. Slang* I 468: Didn't I give you fifty dollars for leaving my place alone when it was on your beat? You can't *hold me up* now.] **1890** in *DAE:* Cattle inspectors of New Mexico were holding up trail herders for one and one-half cents per head for all cattle admitted into the territory. **1896** Ade *Artie* 16: A fellow holds me up for the price of a ticket to a dance up on North Clark Street. **1911** *N.Y. Eve. Jour.* (Jan. 14) 8: Only this morning he held me up for a quarter. **1922** in Hemingway *Dateline: Toronto* 118: The Red Mill holds him up worse than we did. **1958** S.H. Adams *Tenderloin* 163: Suppose the Grand Jury holds you up for names, dates and places.

hole *n.* **1.** the anus.—usu. considered vulgar.

*****ca***1387** Chaucer *Milleres Tale* l. 3732: And at the wyndow out she putte hir hole. *****1607** in *OED2:* There are seven crosse ribs in his neck, and seven from his reins to his hole. *****1614** B. Jonson *Bartholomew Fair* V iv 130: A pox o' your manners, kiss my hole here and smell. *****1744** in Baring-Gould *Mother Goose* 25: Little Robin red breast,/Sitting on a pole./Niddle, Noddle/Went his head,/And Poop went his Hole. [**1888** *Stag Party* 17: My first is a vowel, my second a stove, and you can suck my whole.] *****a***1890–93** *F & H* III 332: Hole...(common).—The *rectum....Suck his hole* = a derisive retort upon an affirmative answer to the question, "Do you know So-and-So?" *****1909** in J. Joyce *Selected Letters* 185: A lot of tiny little naughty farties ending in a long gush from your hole. *****1911** O'Brien & Stephens *Austral. Sl.* 126: Suck, or suck-hole, or suck-arse: a low-down cringing sycophant. Workmen's epithet for a tale-bearer or informer who ingratiates himself with foreman or master by doing informing or other dirty work. "He would suck the boss's hole if he asked him to." **1934** H. Roth *Call It Sleep* 251: Wadda stink!...Who opened his hole? *Ibid.* 291: I like bedder poinds....Give a bedder kickinna hole! **1966** in *OED2:* Shove it up your occult hole. **1972** R. Wilson *Forbidden Words* 199: *Up your hole with a ten-foot pole* is a taunt among New York schoolboys. **1973** Sesar *Catullus* xv: With catfish...rammed up your hole. **1980** D. Hamill *Stomping Ground* 134: We could say up-your-hole-with-a-Mello Roll to the courts.

2.a. *Pris.* a dungeon or punishment cell; solitary confinement.—constr. with *the.*

*****1535** in *OED2:* Wee have gart bind him with ane poill,/And send

him to the theif is hoill. *****1607** in *OED2:* He is deni'de the freedome of the prison,/And in the hole is laide with men condemn'd. *****1657** in *F & H* III 332: Next from the stocks, the hole, and little-ease. *****1666** Pepys *Diary* (July 2): He was clapped up in the Hole. **1863** in *War of Rebellion* (Ser. 2) vi: He was taken to the "hole" and not even permitted to take a blanket with him. **1871** Banka *Prison Life* 25: In the basement is the dungeon, or "black hole," as it is called. **1912** Lowrie *Prison* 65: The rule was that a man should go to the "hole" on bread and water. **1914** Spencer *Jailer* 24: The "hole"...is a small cell located in the basement of the jail building. It is eight feet wide and nine feet long. **1918** in *AS* (Oct. 1933) 27: Hole (the). Place of solitary confinement. **1929** Tully *Shadows of Men* 124: Before long Eddie was put in "the hole"—solitary confinement for forty-eight hours. **1958** J. Thompson *Getaway* 44: You'd probably have to do the rest of your time in the hole. **1986** J.J. Maloney *Chain* 114: He was glad to be in the hole.

b. a subway station or tunnel; subway system.—constr. with *the.*

1933 Ersine *Pris. Slang* 45: Hole...A subway. **1953** W. Burroughs *Junkie:* Working the hole. **1958** *N.Y. Times Mag.* (Mar. 16) 88: Hole— The subway. **1994** *N.Y. Observer* (Oct. 24) 14: Cops sometimes refer to the subway as "the hole."

c. *Mil.* an operations room or headquarters built underground.—constr. with *the.*

1946 Haines *Command Decision* 80: I'll be in the hole with Colonel Martin.

3.a. the vagina.—usu. considered vulgar. [Though accepted by *OED2,* the 1592 quot. may not illus. this specific sense.]

*****1592** Shakespeare *Romeo & Juliet* II iv 94: This driveling Love is like a great Naturall, that runs lolling vp and downe to hid his bable in a hole. *****ca***1600** in Burford *Bawdy Verse* 49: That fittes to stopp a Maydens hole. *****a***1649** in *F & H* III 332: Fair nymphs, in ancient days, your holes, by far,/Were not so hugely vast as now they are. *****a***1661** in Ribton-Turner *Vagrants* 619: *The Tinker*...goes about, from house to house, to stop the good wifes hole. *****1719** T. D'Urfey, in *F & H* III 332: It has a head much like a Mole's,/And yet it loves to creep in Holes. **1923** *Poems, Ballads & Parodies* 28: He strolled right into the lady's hole. **1930** *Lyra Ebriosa* 20: Her hole...fit most any pole. **1934** Lomax & Lomax *Amer. Ballads* 193: My chuck grindin' every hole but mine. **1935** Algren *Boots* 214: Fact is I kind o' like niggers. We all come out of a hole, didn' we? **1938** "Justinian" *Amer. Sexualis* 25: Hole. n. The female pudend....*to hide it in the hole,* to grant the sexual favor (of a woman). **1946–51** J. Jones *Here to Eternity* 438: Like a couple dry hole old maids. **1954–61** Peacock *Valhalla* 180: He who eats the hole will eat the pole. **1960–69** Runkel *Law* 119: I could find her hole by radar. **1971** *Blushes & Bellylaffs* 17: She married a fighter pilot and soon had an ace in the hole. **1967–80** Folb *Runnin' Lines* 242: Hole— Vagina. **1992** N. Baker *Vox* 83: I felt him slide slowly up my...hole.

b. copulation with a woman.—usu. considered vulgar.

*****1936** Partridge *DSUE:* Hole...coition or women viewed as sexual potentialities or actualities, as in "He likes a, *or* his, bit of hole" or "Hole means everything to that blighter." **1962** Folklore—Poems and Songs, TS. in files of Inst. for Sex Research: Did you ever see a fat man trying to get a piece of hole? **1986** *NDAS.* *****1994** R. Doyle *Snapper* (film): You've had your hole.

c. (used as an abusive or dysphemistic term for a woman); (*often*) a prostitute.—usu. considered vulgar.

1942 *ATS* 770: College men's names for girls...babe,...bimbo,...hole. **1952** E. Brown *Trespass* 116: Who you callin' a common old hole? **1966** M. Terry *Keep Tightly Closed* 178: Don't call me Ava! I hate that hole! She can't even act. **1968** Gover *JC* 136: Doc says I's a healthy hole. **1970** Standish *Non-Stand. Terms* 15: Who's that hole I saw you with? **1970** Winick & Kinsie *Lively Commerce* 118: You think I take it easy? I have to take care of my hole, keep her away from other guys, get her welfare check.... **1970** Cain *Blueschild Baby* 38: And the hole, she be goofing this sucker too, laughing and pulling on my dick. **1972** Carr *Bad* 74: He had three top-notch holes, homos who looked like beautiful women, whom he was pimping. **1980** Gould *Ft. Apache* 91: I put the chick to work....And she used to be the main hole on the set. **1984** Riggan *Free Fire* 79: The dude gets his hole to write him a letter sayin' she's leavin.

4. the mouth.—usu. in phr. **shut (one's) hole.**

*a***1867** in G.W. Harris *Lovingood* 147: The ole Sock, never alterin the shape ove the hole tore in his face, sed, mity sneerin like, "Yu is hosspitabil." **1933** Ford & Tyler *Young & Evil* 155: Shut your hole. **1935** S. Anderson *Winterset* 14: Shut that hole in your face! **1946** I. Shulman *Amboy Dukes* 19: Shut your hole about my old man. He's a hell of a lot smarter than you. **1952** Mandel *Angry Strangers* 235: Aw, shut your big hole! **1957** E. Brown *Locust Fire* 174: "Shut your hole," Mossi told him. **1967** Dibner *Admiral* 243: Shut your hole, Fatty. **1977** Stallone *Paradise Alley* 42: Shut ya hole! **1981** T.C. Boyle *Water Music* 22: He told her to shut her hole. **1983** S. King *Christine* 40: That's all I hear comin out'n your hole. **1993** *Simpsons* (Fox-TV): Shut your hole!

5. *Police.* a place where a patrolman may sleep while on duty; in phr. **in the hole** sleeping on duty.
  1929 Merriam *Chicago* 39: Restaurants, pool rooms, laundries, bakeries and other similar places may be found to be convenient "holes" for officers who were presumably...watching over the sleeping public. **1972** Wambaugh *Blue Knight* 109: Or when you're "in the hole" trying to hide your radio car, in some alley where you can doze uncomfortably for an hour.

6. Esp. *Stu.* one's room, as in a dormitory.
  1929–32 in *AS* (Dec. 1934) 290: *Open up your hole!* Usually a command to the occupant of a room to open the door. **1986** M. Paseornek & B. Kesden *Meatballs III* (film): Ditch your gear in your hole.

7.a. a space or position to be filled by something or someone; slot.
  1942 *ATS* 682: Position in a race...*hole,...slot.* **1972** in Terkel *Working* 221: I could spin a car with one hand and never miss a hole. **1974** *N.Y. Times* 29: Thus the paper's "news hole"—the amount of space given to news—will remain about the same. **1984** W. Murray *Dead Crab* 10: He's in the one hole and could get pinned on the rail.

b. (see quot.).
  1942 *ATS* 721: Gears....*hole,* a shift position.

¶ In phrases:

¶ **hole in (one's) head** a lack of good sense. See also *need like a hole in the head,* below.
  1928 Dahlberg *Bottom Dogs* 46: Wolfe...never had anything in his head but mick's holes. **1946** *Sat. Eve. Post* (July 20) 22: Amateurs with holes in their head. **1950** Stuart *Objector* 21: All right, hole in the head,...let's go. **1951** in Cassill *Writing Fiction* 73: You got holes in your head.

¶ **hunt (one's) hole** to run away; CLEAR OUT.
  1863 in E. Marchand *News from N.M.* 55: We will make...[the] Copperheads hunt their holes as we say out here. **1864** in C.W. Wills *Army Life* 291: At the opening yell they all "hunt their holes," in army slang, take position in their works. **1885** Siringo *Texas Cowboy* 27: A policeman punched me in the ribs and told me to "hunt my hole." **1887** Peck *Pvt. Peck* 31 [ref. to 1864]: If I could have been close to Grant, and given him some pointers....the Confederates would be hunting their holes. **1908** in "O. Henry" *Works* 1588: Thomas McLeod's [whistling]...made the biggest flutes hunt their holes. **1919** *Our Navy* (Sept.) 60: Yep, you Jireens were sure wonderful fighters and you sure did make 'em hunt their holes.

¶ **in the hole, 1.** in debt; (*hence*) in trouble. [Initial quot. refers to a receptacle under a poker table where players must deposit chips to cover the house's percentage on called hands.]
  [**1890** Quinn *Fools of Fortune* 219: It is only a question of time before all the player's chips will go into the "hole."] **1890** in *OED2:* His failure leaves a number of our local dealers in the hole for amounts ranging from $200 down. **1892** L. Moore *Own Story* 268: He had been put in the "hole" seven hundred and fifty dollars. **1903** Ade *Society* 39: Hiram came home as Pale as a Ghost and broke the News that he was in the Hole. **1909** in O. Johnson *Lawrenceville Stories* 110: I'm in an awful hole. *ca***1910–18** Hoyt *Buckskin Joe* 72: It was a hard trip, a cold one, and we were always in the hole. **1925** W. James *Drifting Cowboy* 137: I was still a hundred and thirty dollars in the hole to the outfit. **1954–60** *DAS*.

2. *Baseball.* **a.** (see 1982 quot.).
  1908 in Fleming *Unforgettable Season* 180: So old Joe has him in the hole right off the reel. **1912** Mathewson *Pitching* 15: I had him in the hole all the time, and I struck him out three times. **1982** T. Considine *Lang. Sport* 27: *In the hole*...At a disadvantage to the batter with a count of more balls than strikes....At a disadvantage to the pitcher with two strikes in the count.

b. being the batter after the on-deck batter.
  1910 in O. Johnson *Lawrenceville Stories* 214: Brown to the bat, Stover on deck, Satterly in the hole. **1982** T. Considine *Lang. Sport* 27: At bat, on deck, in the hole. **1984** Jackson & Lupica *Reggie* 113: I was "in the hole." The guy in the hole is the batter after the man on deck.

3. *R.R.* (of a train) on a siding.
  1931 *Writer's Digest* (May) 42: *In the Hole*—On a siding. **1944** in N. Cohen *Long Steel Rail* 472: That mean that Rock Island line train's got to go in the hole. **1970** *Current Slang* V (Summer) 8: *Hole,* n. Siding.—We went in the hole to meet the passenger.

¶ **need like a hole in the head** to need not at all; be better off without.
  1944 in *Best from Yank* 69: The Partisans need chowchow like they need a hole in the head. **1950** Sheekman *Mr. Music* (film): We need [that] like a hole in the head. **1950** in F. Brown *Honeymoon* 38: You need a drink like I need a hole in my head. **1953** Paul *Waylaid* 36: You need me like a hole in the head. **1958** Frede *Entry E* 8: I need you...like a hole in the head. **1977** T. Jones *Ice* 161: "You like writing forms, eh, Tristan?" "Yeah, like a hole in the head."

hole *v.* **1.** to fire a bullet into (a person); BORE, 3.
  *****1847** A. Trollope, in *OED2:* We'll hole him till there ar'nt a bit left in him to hole. **1862** M.V. Victoria *Unionist's Daughter* 127: They were determined to "hole" the hated Bell. *****a1882** A. Trollope, in *OED2:* Keep yourself from being holed as they holed Muster Bingham the other day.

2. HOLE UP.—also constr. with *in.*
  1931 Wilstach *Under Cover Man* 43: Good we have a nice dump like this to hole in. **1948** Lait & Mortimer *N.Y. Confidential* 18: Long Island, where...he might hole in for a day or two.

hole card *n.* [fr. the poker term] an effective final resource; *ace in the hole* s.v. ACE, *n.*
  1926 C.M. Russell *Trails* 71: Course ye can't tell what an Injun's got for a hole-card by readin' his countenance. **1941** *Pittsburgh Courier* (May 24) 11: He was her best "hole card"...so she called him "Ace." **1944** *Collier's* (Jan. 15) 50: My hole card is my knowledge of his background in junk. **1974** in H.S. Thompson *Shark Hunt* 343: And [President] Nixon has two extremely heavy hole cards. **1977** Bunker *Animal Factory* 82: He kept his hands exposed to show he wasn't armed—though he wouldn't have put his hand under his clothes even if he was; that showed the hole card.

¶ In phrase:

¶ **peep (someone's) hole card** *Gamb.* to discover (someone's) true character, limitations, or intentions.
  1954 in Wepman, Newman & Binderman *The Life* 39: I peeped your hole card, you're a funny-time lame. **1964** Rhodes *Chosen Few* 222: I thought that tech was tryin' t' burn him...'til Blood peeped his hole card. **1968** Heard *Howard St.* 74: I done peeped you old cats' hole card. **1975** S.P. Smith *Amer. Boys* 254: But that's how you assholes keep going isn't it? Someone peeps your hole card you send them to jail. **1984–87** Ferrandino *Firefight* 163: He nicked you that time. He done peeped your hole card. **1989** *Village Voice* (N.Y.C.) (May 9) 29: I...wanted to beat him until he realized that I had peeped his hole card...and that shit didn't work anymore.

hole in the wall *n.* **1.** a small, usu. shabby or disreputable dwelling place or business establishment; (in early use, *usu.*) a one-room drinking or gambling den. Now *colloq.*
  *****1822** in *OED2:* I had heard Mr. James Simpkins...when the character of the *Hole in the Wall* was brought in question, observed—"The house is a very good house, and the company quite genteel." **1856** in *DA:* A "grocery"—a "doggery"—a "hole in the wall"—is an odious damned spot in any community. **1896** in *DA:* Many lived in "dugouts," which they called "holes in the wall." **1908** W.G. Davenport *Butte & Montana* 285: The establishment of both pigs and holes-in-the-wall. *ca***1921** Sandburg *Slabs of Sunburnt West* 41: In a hole-in-a-wall on Halsted Street sits a gypsy woman. **1924** Woollcott *Enchanted Aisles* 138: His first piano...stood in the sawdust of a dilapidated Bowery hole-in-the-wall. **1931** R.G. Carter *On the Border* 314: There was a "hole in the wall" booze shop at the station. **1956** Holiday & Dufty *Lady Sings the Blues* 74: One time we stopped at a dirty little hole in the wall, and the whole band piled in. **1958** Cooley *Run for Home* 27:

They opened the door and walked into the oppressive air of the hole-in-the-wall joint. **1959** Tevis *Hustler* 68: He found [a poolroom] on a street named Parmenter, a hole in the wall called Wilson's Recreation Hall, the kind of place with green paint on the windows. **1982** P. Michaels *Grail* 168: Are you hungry, Father?…There are several holes-in-the-wall around here.

2. *Naut.* a cove.

1845 J.H. Barnum *Life* 20 [ref. to *ca*1805]: [The pirates] held a council, and agreed to go back to their old home, and begin a settlement in the "hole in the wall," as they styled it.…They run to the "hole in the wall," and then sailed for New Providence. **1940** Riesenberg *Golden Gate* 212: For the shipping of lumber, small brigs and brigantines were in wide use at first, craft that could go into the "holes in the wall" along the ragged Pacific Coast.

3. *CB.* a highway tunnel.

1976 Lieberman & Rhodes *CB* 130: *Hole In the Wall*—A tunnel. **1976** Whelton *CB Baby* 8: Can you give this guy a steer toward the hole in the wall? **1977** *Sci. Mech. CB Gde.* 172: There's a fender bender in that hole in the wall.

-holer *comb. form.* Orig. *Mil.* (used to designate outhouses and latrines according to the number of seats provided).

1945 *Yank* (Apr. 6) 5: A brand-new eight-holer had been constructed. **1952** *ATS* (ed. 2) 83: *One-holer, two-holer* &c., an outhouse distinguished by the number of toilet seats. **1962** Mahurin *Honest John* 160 [ref. to WWII]: Because porcelain toilet facilities were nonexistent, we had a standard eight-holer which was used by all officers. **1972** West *Village* 207: The dirty chores, like clearing out the two-holer. **1975** V.B. Miller *Trade-Off* 61: The men's room. It's a "two-holer." **1979** Edson *Gentle Giant* 76: There's a "four-holer" to the left. **1986** in *DARE*: [Widespread throughout Gulf Region]. **1988** B.E. Wheeler *Outhouse Humor* 18: One-holers, two- and three-holers.

hole-up *n. West.* a place of refuge for fugitives; hideout.

1937 E. Anderson *Thieves Like Us* 53: We got a good hole-up in this joint, though. **1956** Pence & Homsher *Ghost Towns* 56: It was a rendezvous for outlaws, a hole-up for killers, a hurdy-gurdy for the madams.

hole up *v.* Orig. *West.* to isolate oneself or go into hiding. Now *S.E.*

1875 in *DAE*: Only five days was I compelled to "hole up" in my stateroom. **1912** in *OED2*: Go slow, Tex; mebby he's holin' up on us, like he did on Buck. **1922** Rollins *Cowboy* 52: In the eighties some "rustlers" "holed up" in a cabin at the outlet of Jackson Lake in Wyoming. **1929** Hammett *Red Harvest* ch. xviii: Thaler's holing up there. **1932–34** Minehan *Boy & Girl Tramps* 265: *Hole up*—remain for the winter, as comfortable as possible.

-holic see **-AHOLIC**.

holiday *n.* **1.** Esp. *Naut.* an area left neglected or untouched during work, esp. a gap on a surface to be painted, coated, or scrubbed; (*hence*) an unusual or undesirable gap in a line of objects.

*1785 Grose *Vulgar Tongue*: A holiday is any part of a ship's bottom, left uncovered in paying [*sic*] it—*Sea Term*. **1899** Robbins *Gam* 5: He would have tarred the rigging from the fore-royal stay to the topping lift (and left no "holidays.") **1909** *WNID*: *Holiday…Chiefly Naut.* a neglected piece of work. *Slang.* **1929** Bowen *Sea Slang* 67: *Holidays.* Patches missed when painting or tarring down, also gaps left between slung hammocks or clothing left up to dry. **1941** Maryland WPA *Gde. to Naval Acad.* 151: *Holiday*—A poor job; interstices on a paint job. **1945** in *Calif. Folk. Qly.* V 388: A man who leaves holidays* in his work.…*Not free time, but an unfinished portion of work, as a spot left unpainted. Even in minesweeping, a portion of the ocean left unswept is a *holiday.* *1949 Granville *Sea Slang* 122: *Holiday.* A space left when painting the ship's side or scrubbing the decks. "Get on with that job and mind, no bloomin' 'olidays." Also, a gap in a line of caps on the hooks in a cloak-room. **1987** D. da Cruz *Boot* 301: *Holiday*, gap in painting, or in swabbing deck.

2. *Av.* a bright patch visible in an overcast sky.

1955 R.L. Scott *Look of Eagle* 244: Those fighting wisps of moisture…joined hands, and fought back to close the "holidays"; lightning leaped from layer to layer.

¶ In phrase:

¶ **give (something) a holiday** to refrain from; "give it a rest."

1872 G. Gleason *Specter Riders* 68: Give that [talk] a holiday, you pesky lyin' imp.

holler *n.* **1.a.** a cry of protest; (*hence*) a complaint.

1896 Ade *Artie* 83: I couldn't stand for that. I put up a holler right at the jump. **1901** *Chicago Tribune* (Aug. 25) 3: All this time there was a holler from headquarters that this man was all right and should be let go. **1903** Townsend *Sure* 8: It's to be run by machinery, and warranted to make no holler, even if de ghost don't walk and all de press notices is roasts. **1914** Lardner *You Know Me Al* 131: I says I guess you have got no holler comeing on the way I spend my money. **1921** Conklin & Root *Circus* 157: At rare intervals some fellow would put up a real "holler" about his knife, but a few shafts of rough wit from Spaf and the jeers of the amused crowd soon silenced him. **1933–35** D. Lamson *About to Die* 188: So the wife makes a big holler to the bulls. **1957** Campbell *Cry for Happy* 28: If you don't like the chow, make your holler to Chiyoko.

b. *Specif.* (*Und.*) a complaint or report made to the police.

1894 (cited in Partridge *Dict. Und.* 339). **1900** Willard & Hodler *Powers That Prey* 82: Will you square the hollers? **1906** *Nat. Police Gaz.* (June 9) 6: After a touch had been made there and a "holler" ensued. **1914** Jackson & Hellyer *Vocab.* 45: Did the sucker make a holler? **1924** *N.Y. Times* (Aug. 3) VIII 16: We got it from a reliable source that the holler was legit. **1926** Clark & Eubank *Lockstep* 174: *Square hollers*—"fix" a case, to escape trial. **1956** "T. Betts" *Across the Board* 13: He was smart enough not to make a sucker's holler. **1974** Radano *Cop Stories* 37: If you make a holler about this, the next time we meet I'll kill you.

2. a cause for laughter; HOOT.

1941 G. Fowler *Billy the Kid* (film): Ha! That's a holler.

3. a call made on a telephone, CB radio, or the like.

1975 Dills *CB*: Give me a holler next time you're on the ol' channel. **1976** Whelton *CB Baby* 58: The whole Council was waiting to get a holler from you before they came over. **1976** Adcock *Not Truckers Only* 4: The day will come when you…pick up the mike and "make your first holler."

holler *v.* **1.** to cry uncle; admit defeat; give up.

1843 in *DARE*: Who hollered? Which gave up? *a*1846 in *DAE*: Jist to save his time I hollered. *a*1859 in Bartlett *Amer.* (ed. 2): Tige…had done whipped me; but pshaw! I never did *holler.* **1859** Bartlett *Amer.* (ed. 2): To *Holloo* (Pron. *holler.*) To give up; to quit; to yield.…I once heard a Western man say he had "*hollered* on drinking," meaning that he had quit the practice. **1925–26** J. Black *Can't Win* 43: Holler before you're hurt; that's my motto.

2. to complain. Now *colloq.*

1899 Ade *Horne* 206: I ain't hollerin', but I want to tell you that Gracie Watson didn't have no more license to beat Dido that day than I've got to walk backwards from here to Milwaukee and beat the limited. **1904** *Life in Sing Sing* 249: *Hollar*, complain. **1923** Hough *North* 55: If we do the best we can fer you, you'll never holler? **1932** Harvey *Me and Bad Eye* 20: Inspection again, but you don't dare to holler about it. **1967** in *OED2*: Everyone hollers about the damage to the children if the schools are shut one day because of a teacher-school committee disagreement. **1987** R.M. Brown *Starting* 73: Don't then turn around, Mr. Elected Official, and squeal and holler that voter turnout is low.

holler guy *n. Baseball.* a spirited player or coach who shouts encouragement to his teammates on the field. Cf. BENCH JOCKEY.

1941 *Sat. Eve. Post* (May 17) 86: Fresco Thompson [was]…the wittiest and most imaginative of the holler guys. **1941** in Tamony *Americanisms* (No. 7) 7: Crosetti Has Lost Position But He's Still Holler Guy. **1950** Cleveland *Great Mgrs.* 83: As a manager, Jennings was a holler guy. **1954** Dodd *On Football* 55: The center needs to be a "holler guy" and full of enthusiasm for his assigned task. **1980** Lorenz *Guys Like Us* 228: You're looking at the holler guy.

hollow *adv.* [semantic development unkn.] completely; decisively; utterly.—formerly often constr. with *carry*, now solely with *beat.* Now *colloq.* Now usu. **all hollow.**

1668–71 in *OED*: He carried it Hollow, *Luculenter Vicit vel Superavit,*…credo dictum quasi "he carried it *wholy.*" *1759* in *F & H* III 334: Crab was beat *hollow.* *1762* in *OED*: You succeeded?…Yes, yes, I got it all hollow. *1767* in *OED*: He set up for the County of Middlesex, and carried it hollow, as the jockeys say. *1785* Grose *Vulgar*

Tongue: All Hollow, He was beat all hollow, i.e. he had no chance of conquering: *it was all hollow,* or *a hollow thing;* it was a decided thing from the beginning. ***1814** in *F & H* III 334: Squire Burton won the match *hollow.* **1815** J. Adams, in *DAE:* Burr...said, "Now I have him all hollow." **1824** W. Irving, in *DAE:* Her blood carried it all hollow; there was no withstanding a woman with such blood in her veins. **1834** *Davy Crockett's Almanack* (1835) 6: She preferred me all holler. **1836** *Davy Crockett's Almanack* (1837) 20: Of all the rivers on this airth, the Mississippi beats all holler. ***1837** in *F & H* III 334: His lines to Apollo/Beat all the rest hollow. **1846** *Nat. Police Gaz.* (Oct. 17) 41: Dead men tell no tales, and that's a rule that beats the lawyers all hollow. **1848** *Life in Rochester* 13: You'll bluff Dan and Grattan all hollow. **1867** in Schele de Vere *Amer.* 440: In this matter we *beat* the English *all hollow,* and we mean to do the same in everything else. ***1871** in *F & H* III 334: It licks me hollow, sir. **1875** J. Miller *First Fam'lies* ch. xx: Well, that bangs me all hollow! **1877** Bartlett *Amer.* (ed. 4) 8: *All-holler.* To beat one *all-holler,* or *all hollow,* is to beat him thoroughly.

hollowhead *n.* a blockhead; AIRHEAD.
    1834 (quot. at WOLVERINE). **1928** Dahlberg *Bottom Dogs* 64: If ther's gonna be any work-out, I'll take ker of it, get me, hollerhead? **1957** Anders *Price of Courage* 20: Ol' Hollow Head just about got us all kilt. **1981** Eble *Campus Slang* (Oct.) 4: *Hollowhead*—person with little common sense: He can sometimes be a real hollowhead. **1984** Algeo *Stud Buds* 7: An absent-minded or inattentive person...*hollowhead.*

hollow leg *n.* **1.** a remarkable capacity for consuming liquor or *(rarely)* eating. Hence **hollow-legged,** *adj.*
    1929 Springs *Carol Banks* 253 [ref. to 1918]: Does he drink?...He's got a hollow leg. **1935** in Weinberg et al. *Tough Guys* 194: I think you're a hollow-legged souse. **1947** Overholser *Buckaroo's Code* 170: His appetite grew until Santiam said, "You sure got a hollow leg." **1956** I. Shulman *Good Deeds* 96: A skirt who concentrated on filling her hollow legs with six-per-cent. **1969** Pharr *Numbers* 359: Make up your mind, a girl with a hollow leg is one who drinks and drinks and never gets drunk. **1972** Pearce *Pier Head Jump* 27: I figured he was tryin' to signal me that this broad had a hollow leg. **1974** J. Robinson *Bed/Time/Story* 13: He was a heavy drinker...one of those men with a hollow leg. ***ca1977** in Partridge *DSUE* (ed. 8): *He's got hollow legs....*I first heard it ca. 1904. **1988** *L.A. Law* (NBC-TV): I gotta go empty out this hollow leg.
    2. a person having such a capacity.
    1926 Norwood *Other Side of Circus* 50: Mister Willie Hollow-legs Carr...can...eat more than any agent ahead of the show. **1958–65** Alfred *Hogan's Goat* 25: For the goose that lays gold eggs/Lays no more for hollow legs. **1973** W. Crawford *Gunship Cmndr.* 48: You couldn't possibly drink all that, not even a hollow-leg like you. ***1984** Partridge *DSUE* (ed. 8): *Hollow-legs.*

Hollyweird *n.* Hollywood, Calif. *Joc.*
    1979 Gram *Foxes* 42: "Where's she going?" "Holly-weird." **1982** A. Lane & W. Crawford *Valley Girl* (film): I heard there's something really groaty about the air in Hollyweird, you know. **1984** Blumenthal *Hollywood* 163: Nicknames for "The Coast": *Hollyweird,...Tinseltown.* **1987** R.M. Brown *Starting* 59: Tinkering with individual words is always a good exercise....How about Hollywood to Hollyweird? **1989** *Reporters* (Fox-TV): Hollyweird—that's what I call this place. **1990** *Nat. Lampoon* (Apr.) 98: This is Hollyweird, babe-ola! **1995** *TV Guide* (Aug. 12) 26: Growing Up in Hollyweird.

Hollywood *adj.* Esp. *Mil.* characterized by show but not truly effective, empowered, authentic, etc. Also as adv.
    1941 Hargrove *Pvt. Hargrove* 84: *Hollywood corporal*—an acting corporal. **1956** Hargrove *Girl He Left* 82: Hanna's gonna make him a Hollywood sergeant. **1957** Anders *Price of Courage* 89: "Felty, have your people fix bayonets."..."Isn't that being kinda Hollywood?" **1961** Baar & Howard *Missileman* 132: Called "Hollywood hard"—because they looked hardened but actually were not—these [launch] pads did offer some protection. **1971** Rowe *5 Yrs. to Freedom* 61 [ref. to 1961]: Day jumps, night jumps, jumps with combat equipment, "Hollywood jumps" with only a helmet and cartridge belt. **1974** Merchant marine captain, ca60, N.Y.C.: A *Hollywood sailor* is a sailor who doesn't know his job. **1988** Halberstadt *Airborne* 50: The first is a "Hollywood jump," a daylight jump without combat equipment.
    ¶ In phrase:
    ¶ **go Hollywood** see s.v. GO, *v.*, 7.

Hollywood Marine *n. USMC.* A U.S. marine trained or stationed at San Diego, Calif.—used derisively.
    1949 McMillan *Old Breed* 4: By 1940 the First [Marine Brigade] was being called "The Raggedy-Ass Marines;" the Second, which occasionally furnished men for movie productions, became "The Hollywood Marines." **1952** Uris *Battle Cry* 270 [ref. to 1942]: Sounds like the Hollywood Eighth Marines. **1957** Leckie *Helmet for My Pillow* 90: The Eighth Marine Regiment—the "Hollywood Marines"—had reached our shores. **1958** Frankel *Band of Bros.* 6: Looks like a recruitin' poster....A Hollywood marine if I ever saw one. **1962** Gallant *Valor's Side* 20 [ref. to 1941]: Those who lived on the other side of this great dividing line went to boot camp at San Diego, California, and were labeled "Hollywood Marines" by Parris Island graduates, who envied the rumored luxury in which these boots were supposed to be trained. *a***1984** in Terry *Bloods* 3: I was a Hollywood Marine. I went to San Diego, but it was worse in Parris Island. **1987** D. da Cruz *Boot* 161: "Hollywood Marines," graduates of Parris Island boot camp derisively term those produced in...the Marine Corps Recruit Depot, San Diego.

Hollywood shower *n. Navy.* a shower bath lasting more than three minutes.
    1984–85 Schneider & Schneider *Sound Off!* 131: The ship makes its own water....You take a Hollywood shower...and just let the water run; or a Navy shower, a three-minute shower.

Hollywood stop *n.* CALIFORNIA STOP.
    1986 (quot. at CALIFORNIA STOP).

Hollywood wound *n.* (see quot.). Now *hist.*
    1988 Fussell *Wartime* 254: One just severe enough to send one home...without amputation or disfigurement...[was in WWII] called a *Hollywood wound.*

hols *n.pl. Stu.* holidays. *Rare* in U.S.
    ***1905** in *OED2:* The governor pointed that out last hols. **1963** D. Tracy *Brass Ring* 8: He closed the school extremely early for the Thanksgiving "hols."

holy [for interjections beginning with *holy,* see under the principal noun of the phr.]

Holy Ground *n.* a red-light district; *(also)* a slum area.—used as a proper name.—usu. constr. with *the. Obs.* in U.S.
    1787–89 Tyler *Contrast* 57: I went to a place they call Holy Ground....a young gentle-woman called me...honey, just as if we were married. **1807** J.R. Shaw *Autobiog.* 67 [ref. to 1782]: Hell Street [in Carlisle, Pa.]...in this street was kept the "holy" ground, where all sorts of pastimes were carried on. ***1960** Hugill *Shanties from 7 Seas* [song learned *a*1920] 435: And we'll drink one toast to the Holy Ground, and the girl that we adore. *Ibid.* 434: The "Holy Ground" is a poor quarter of Cobh, inhabited mainly by fishermen. ***1965** O Lochlainn *More Irish Ballads* 220: Cork men maintain that "The Holy Ground" is the waterfront at Cobh (Queenstown), but others hold that it is Swansea dockland, and others still that it is part of New York harbour.

Holy Joe *n.* **1.** Esp. *Mil.* a clergyman, esp. a chaplain. Also *(obs.)* **Holy John.**
    1864 in K.E. Olson *Music & Musket* 109: The best meeting I ever attended in the Army, at Holy Jo's tent. **1868** in Boyer *Nav. Surgeon* II 22: The Holy Joes (parsons) delivered their sermons in grand style. ***1873** Hotten *Slang Dict.* (ed. 4): *Holy Joe,* a sea-term for a parson. **1878** Willis *Our Cruise* 25: What d'ye think ov that cuffee that Holy Joe spun us yesterday? ***1881–84** Davitt *Prison Diary* I 167: Holy Joe....Oh! that is our chaplain. **1885** Clark *Boy Life in USN* 67: There's the chaplain, we call him "Holy Joe." **1892** C.C. King *Soldier's Secret* 111: "Holy Joe," as the parson had been termed. **1894** *Lucky Bag* (U.S. Naval Acad.) I 67: *Holy Joe...*The Chaplain. **1899** Robbins *Gam* 147: They're spliced by some sky-pilot or Holy Joe or other. **1900** Benjamin *Naval Acad.* 271: Pretty soon the youngster decided that he was not to be referred to as a "Holy Joe" or a "Sky Pilot." **1906** J. Moss *Officers' Manual* 243: *Holy Joe*—the chaplain. **1918** Griffin *Ballads of Reg't.* 16: He pulls a strong wire with the post's "Holy Joe." **1941** Hargrove *Pvt. Hargrove* 84: *Holy Joe*—the chaplain. **1949** Pirosh *Battleground* (film): The chaplain....Holy Joe's gonna pray for us at the Christmas service. **1956** Wier & Hickey *Navy Wife* 103: *Holy Joe.* The Chaplain. **1959** Wiley & Milhollen *They Who Fought* 198: Chaplains were known to [Civil War] soldiers...as "Holy Joes" and "Holy Johns." **1969** L. Hughes *Under a Flare* 130: I ran across a lot of chaplains in South Vietnam. Many were run-of-the-mill Holy Joes living the life of an officer, completely detached from their men.

2. a sanctimonious or zealously religious fellow.—used disparagingly.

    1889 Barrère & Leland *Dict. Slang* I 469: *Holy Joe* (prison and nautical), the chaplain or any religious person. **1901** King *Dog-Watches* 254 [ref. to 1886]: Togerson, a sailor in the forecastle, was…ridiculed and buffeted by almost everybody, called "Holy Joe" and the "Psalm Singer." **1905** *Independent* (Nov. 2) 1022: We diligently…besought the gullible Holy Joes at the Seamen's Institute for relief tickets and handouts. **1940** Raine & Niblo *Fighting 69th* (film): I don't go for that Holy Joe stuff. **1948** McIlwaine *Memphis* 365: Commissioner "Holy Joe" Boyle. **1951** Longstreet *Pedlocks* 111: In the East they're all holy Joes and teach in Sunday schools. A new kind of pirate. **1952** Viereck *Men Into Beasts* 68: He threw through our bars his tracts and leaflets with Biblical quotations. The boys called him Holy Joe. **1956** Gold *Not With It* 169: Holy joes and petes are usually trouble; they don't like the carnies. **1962** Mandel *Wax Boom* 119: Since when are you such a Holy Joe? **1966** Neugeboren *Big Man* 49: He finishes with all this Holy Joe stuff. **1971** Flanagan *Maggot* 97: A young dumb kid. A mama's boy. A holy joe. **1976** *Urban Life* V 145: Nobody is going to say nothing about what I'm doing. No boss, no holy Joes. No wife. **1986** R. Walker *AF Wives* 419: Nothing worse than a holy Joe.

Holy Joe *interj.* (used to express surprise).

    1933–34 Lorimer & Lorimer *Stag Line* 159: Holy Joe, look at that! **1996** *Simpsons Comics* (No. 22) (unp.): Holy Joe! Dagnabbit's spooked!

holy roller *n.* **1.** (often *cap.*) a member of a Pentecostal church.—usu. used disparagingly. Orig. *S.E.*

    1841 in *DA* s.v. *Sweezyite*: A new sect of Religionists, so called, has sprung up in Yates County, New York, called the Sweezyites, or Holy Rollers; an appellation applied on account of their exercises being those of rolling upon the floor. **1842** in *DA*: It is a new species of religion, which sprang up…contemporaneously with the enthusiasm of the "Holy Rollers." **1893** in *DAE*: When the Holy Spirit seized them…the Holy Rollers…rolled over and over on the floor. **1909** in *DAE*: The 300 or more members of "The Latter Reign of the Apostolic Church," who called themselves "True Immersionists," and are popularly known as "Holy Rollers." **1918** Mencken *Amer. Lang.* 113: The English…get on without…*holy rollers*…and other such American *ferae naturae*. **1927** in *OEDS*: You'd make a good Methodist of the Holy Roller variety. **1928** *Amer. Mercury* (Oct.) 183: The Holy Rollers…date back less than fifty years as a separate denomination. **1947** in *DA*: I get awfully tired of people who keep saying that we have to like the Negroes or the Jews or the Mongolians or the Holy Rollers. **1958–59** Southern & Hoffenberg *Candy* 69: He had begun to shout again, carried away like a holy-roller preacher. **1969** *New Yorker* (June 14) 78: It would be chic to be a black militant.…They sound like fire-and-brimstone preachers in Holy Roller churches. **1993** *New Yorker* (May 17) 64: Many congregations…once endured the stigma of being "Holy Rollers" on the poor side of town.

2. a sanctimonious or zealously religious person.—used contemptuously.

    1975 N.Y.C. editor, age 24: Those people are such holy rollers. **1979** D. Milne *Second Chance* 40: Hey, what's the holy roller doing around here? **1985** M. Baker *Cops* 49: All these really holy roller Hassids. **1988** Univ. Tenn. student paper: I get so tired of these judgmental holy rollers who can do no wrong. **1988** LaLoggia *Lady in White* (film): Don't be such a holy roller! **1990** Steward *Bad Boys* 30: The usual holy-roller stuff of the far-right fundamentalist kind.

hombre *n.* [< Sp 'a man'] **1.** *S.W. & Mil.* a Mexican man; (*often*) a Mexican soldier.

    1846 in Magoffin *Santa Fé Trail* 93: Not only the children, but *mujeres* and *hombres* swarmed around me like bees. **1847** in *West. Penna. Hist. Mag.* LII (1969) 240: Our loss is very heavy but a much greater number of Umbries fell. **1847** in *Jour. Ill. Hist. Soc.* XLVIII (1955) 377: Had…not…Lt. Ridgway's horse [thrown] him…there would have been *Hombres* killed or captured. **1847** in Peskin *Vols.* 81: Got a glimpse of the enemy's works, hombres heads above the breastworks. *Ibid.* 83: Quite a quantity of dead hombres. **1848** I. Smith *Remin.* 60: Capt. Reid…fearlessly rushed upon…the enemy,…causing many *hombres* to bite the dust. **1848** in Peskin *Vols.* 234: They were stoned by the hombres when in pursuit. **1852** in [Clappe] *Shirley Letters* 195: Half a dozen…miners, and one hatless *hombre*. **1894** *DN* I 324: man. Often used to call Mexican *tamele* men or candy peddlers on

the street. **1962** in *DARE: Person of Mexican origin…Hombre…*tend[s] to be less popular in the younger groups. **1970** in *DARE*.

2. Esp. *S.W.* a man; character; fellow; customer.—occ. used in direct address.

    1853 Downey *Filings* 119: Most…have since become…distinguished "hombres" in this state. **1854** in Overdyke *Know-Nothing Party* 62: Friends of that ubiquitous *hombre*. **1856** in *Calif. Folk. Qly.* I (1942) 277: This hombre will vanish for Pike. **1859** in C.A. Abbey *Before the Mast* 229: An hombre of my description. **1883** *Overland Mo.* (Mar.) 263: Who is that *hombre?* **1885** *United Service* (Mar.) 284: All ready old fellow! All ready, hombre! *ca*1902 in *Harper's Wkly.* (Mar. 5, 1910) 17: I'd be a savez hombre and I'd know a great lot. **1914** *Collier's* (May 23) 9: "Listen to that, hombre," said the marine; "that's real music!" **1914** D.W. Roberts *Rangers* 126: I knew he was a bad "hombre." **1918** *Stars & Stripes* (Apr. 12) 7: Occasionally one hears a little Mex talk—a man referred to as a good *hombre*. **1918** in *AS* (Oct. 1933) 28: [A] slick hombre. **1921** Casey & Casey *Gay-Cat* 113: He's a bad hombre. **1925** L. Thomas *World Flight* 67: These Alaskan fishermen are the burliest, toughest, shaggiest-bearded *hombres* I have ever seen. **1926** Norwood *Other Side of Circus* 52: You're a smart hombre. **1928** Ruth *Baseball* 23: There's one cagey hombre, that McGraw. **1929** Ferber *Cimarron* 80: Say, he's a bad hombre, that fella. **1929–30** Dos Passos *42d Parallel* 285: This guy Moorehouse, the big hombre from New York. **1946** Kober *That Man Is Here Again* 5: A smart hombray, that Sandy. **1962** Halleran *Boot Hill Silver* 68: He's a right smart hombre. **1965** Hersey *Too Far to Walk* 4: Hey, look at that hombre. **1982** *Contact P.M.* (WKGN radio) (July 5): That's no easy job out there in the oilfields. You got to be a real tough hombre to make it out there. **1993** G. Lee *Honor & Duty* 193: That's it for me, hombres.

home *n. Black E.* HOMEBOY, 1; (*hence*) BUDDY, 1.—used esp. in direct address.

    1944 Burley *Hndbk. Jive* 109: Well, Home,…you'd better get on it if you want it. **1969** B. Beckham *Main Mother* 148: I'm talking to you, home. **1970** Major *Dict. Afro.-Amer. Slang* 66: *Home:* (rare) a term of address used by two black people either from the same Southern state or simply from the South (Southern use). **1970** *Current Slang* V (Fall) 8: *Home,* n. A person from the same town or state. **1973** N.Y.C. man, age *ca*35: So you see what I'm saying to you, home? **1974** Matthews & Amdur *My Race* 117 [ref. to *ca*1966]: "Hey, home, I'm back here." The term "home" was used to describe anyone from your hometown or neighborhood. **1978** W. Brown *Tragic Magic* 144: Excuse me, home,…but has anyone ever told you, you resemble Slick Swanson, the disc jockey? **1981** Eble *Campus Slang* (Mar.) 4: *Home*—clipping of *Home Boy*—a good friend, usually used by and about males. **1983** Spottiswood *48 Hrs.* (film): You come in here often, home? **1985** Milicevic et al. *Runaway Train* (film): It's me, home. **1984–87** Ferrandino *Firefight* 148: That's square business, home. **1989** *Miami Vice* (NBC-TV): Time is on *my* side, home.

¶ In phrase:

¶ **nobody** [or **no one at**] **home** (used to denote a person with no intelligence, emotions, or consciousness). See also *the lights are on but nobody's home* s.v. LIGHT, *n.*, 3.

    1914 T.A. Dorgan, in Zwilling *TAD Lexicon* 59: No he has no sense—nobody home nobody home. **1915** "High Jinks, Jr." *Choice Slang* 41: A weak minded person. "Nobody home." **1919** *DN* V 73: *Nobody home*, a stupid, dull condition. **1923** Ornitz *Haunch, Paunch, & Jowl* 196: She would have sized up the situation succinctly—"nobody home." **1953** *ATS* (ed. 2) 167: Insane; crazy.…*no one at home, nobody home. Ibid.* 170: Inattentive; absent-minded…*nobody home, no one at home.* **1990** G. Lee *China Boy* 167: Mr. Lewis would look into the eyes of a kid who was KO'd, to see if anyone was still home. **1994** *New Republic* (Jan. 9, 1995) 32: She looks, moves, sounds just like a human being, except that nobody is home.

home bird *n. Mil.* FREEDOM BIRD.

    1971 *Playboy* (Aug.) 212: As my home bird jets me toward back in the world, I have one overriding thought.

homebody *n.* Esp. *Black E.* HOMEBOY, 1.

    1991 Nelson & Gonzales *Bring Noise* xvii: Hiding out in front of…the local candy store…with my homebody, Darryl.

homeboy *n.* **1.** Orig. *Black E.* a male from one's hometown or neighborhood; (*broadly*) a male friend; (*also*) (now *rare*) an unsophisticated or rustic male. Cf. S.E. *homefolks.*

    1899 *Colored American* (Nov. 25) 3: The "home-boys" with the

Williams and Walker aggregation were sore over the frost they met with in…Washington. **1927** (cited in *W10*). *ca***1930s** Randolph *Pissing in Snow*, in *DARE*: There was a fellow from Oklahoma a-telling jokes down at the store.…The home boys all laughed like hell when they heard that [joke about incest in Arkansas families], but there was a big farmer from Arkansas come in the store just then, and he got mad. **1942** Z.N. Hurston, in *Amer. Mercury* (July) 87: Youse just a homeboy, Jelly. **1954** L. Armstrong *Satchmo* 235, in *DARE*: "Is this my home boy?" she asked.…Filo and we sat around and talked ourselves silly about New Orleans. *a***1964** "Malcolm X" & Haley *Autobiog.* [ref. to 1940's]: You Shorty's homeboy? **1967** *AS* XLII 238: *Home boy* is a slang expression particularly in vogue among students at Southern Negro colleges.…*Home boy* and…*home girl*…denote individuals who come from the same hometown as the speaker. **1974** Matthews & Amdur *My Race* 117 [ref. to *ca*1966]: "What's happening, home boy?"…Most everyone on the bus had a "home boy" they had run against in high school or who came from their same area. *a***1974–78** J.W. Moore *Homeboys* 99: Prisoners routinely watch the bus bringing new prisoners and immediately identify a barrio carnal (homeboy). **1984** Toop *Rap Attack* 158: *Homeboy:* a close friend or someone you grew up with. **1985** J. Hughes *Breakfast Club* (film): Hey, homeboy! Why don't you close that door? **1987** in *DARE*: The man I worked with called me "home boy."…He thought I didn't have any street smarts.…He thought I was too "country," you know, a hick. **1987** *Newsweek* (Mar. 23) 61: He wasn't going to bump along from one minimum-wage job to another like some of his homeboys. **1993** K. Scott *Monster* 25: My homeboys became my family—the older ones were father figures.

2. a young black or Hispanic man, esp. a member of a street gang.

1979 Gram *Blvd. Nights* 13: Raymond…look[ed] as much American Indian as Chicano homeboy. **1982** Sculatti *Catalog of Cool* 95: It's published right there in San Jose, *Califas*, where lots of the homeboys hang out. **1985** "J. Blowdryer" *Mod. Eng.* 64: Homes, homeboy…A gang member,…an ally. **1986** C. Stroud *Close Pursuit* 9: Home boys with…the threat coming off them in waves. **1989** *21 Jump Street* (Fox-TV): Every homeboy in the Zone'll be tryin' to kill ya. **1991** N. Krulik *Hammer & Ice* 6: The Oakland homeboy is proud of the successes he's had. **1995** *Wash. Post* (Aug. 22) C1: He alienated the city's police by befriending and ministering to the Latino gang members ("gangbangers," "homeboys" or "homies").

homebrew *n. Sports.* an athlete who plays or competes in the area in which he was raised.

1976 *Webster's Sports Dict.* 216.

home-brewed *n. Boxing.* blood drawn during a prizefight.

1870 *Putnam's Mag.* (Mar.) 301: The combatants struck each other…upon…the nose…drawing the blood, the claret, the ruby, the crimson, the home-brewed.

homegirl *n.* Orig. *Black E.* a female from one's hometown or neighborhood; (*broadly*) a female friend; (*also*) a young black or Hispanic woman, esp. a member of a street gang. Also **home chick.**

1934 Wilder *Heaven's My Destination* 53, in *DARE*: Snappiest little home-girl in Oklahoma. **1967** (quot. at HOMEBOY, 1). **1983** *L.A. Times* (July 27) I 20: I tell people I'm from East L.A. And they tell me, "Wow, man, you must have been a *chola*. Or you're my homegirl." **1985** "J. Blowdryer" *Mod Eng.* 64: Homegirl…Is the female version [of homeboy]. **1988** Norst *Colors* 42: Did he sense…that she was a homegirl? **1990** Bing *Do or Die* xiii: In South Central with a sixteen-year-old homegirl. **1990** *Village Voice* (N.Y.C.) (May 1) 91: Salt-n-Pepa are homegirl nationalists, cultural rather than radical feminists. **1990** *L.A. Times* (July 21) B7: The homegirls will come around asking for coffee cans and pickle jars. **1991** *N.Y. Times* (nat. ed.) (Feb. 5) A12: Ms. Youngblood and her 13 closest "homegirls." **1996** *Dangerous Minds* (ABC-TV): I think you got that covered, home chick.

home guard *n.* [in ironic ref. to the volunteer companies of *home guards* organized during the Civil War] (among itinerants) a person, esp. a tramp or sidewalk pitchman, who remains in a particular locality year-round; a nonmigratory worker; a local resident.

1903 *Enquirer* (Cincinnati) (May 9) 13: Homeguard—A fellow who has never left his native city. **1903** *Independent* (July 23) 1722: There are "home guards" in the town who take care of all the surplus cash

floating around. **1922** N. Anderson *Hobo* 7: South Street is the rendezvous of the vagabond who has settled and retired, the "home guard" as they are rather contemptuously referred to by the tribe of younger and more adventurous men who still choose to take to the road. **1925–26** J. Black *You Can't Win* 219: The gangs are made up of natives and "home guards," and some of them are not above snitching on you. **1929** *AS* IV (June) 341: *Home guard.* Native; one who remains in the same place year after year. **1929** *Sat. Eve. Post* (Oct. 12) 29: *Home guard:* A pitchman who works only in his home city. **1935** J. Conroy *World to Win* 57: [I] got to be a home guard, I guess, the balance o' me days. **1938** Holbrook *Mackinaw* 181: A *homeguard* is a long-time employee of one certain company. **1942** *Sat. Eve. Post* (June 13) 27: And joining the "home guards" means that he's tired of changing jobs and wants to stay put. **1945** Hubbard *R.R. Ave.* 347: *Home Guard*—Employee who stays with one railroad, as contrasted with *boomer.* **1949** in Botkin & Harlow *R.R. Folklore* 165: Leaving the "home guards" (company men) to face the music. **1970** Terkel *Hard Times* 307: The home guard. The fellows who weren't migratory workers. **1982** D.A. Harper *Good Company* 104: It's the homeguard goin' up there.…If he's a homeguard, he's no tramp, no hobo.…You might call him a town bum.

home piece *n.* Esp. *Pris.* (see 1974 and 1980 quots.); (*also*) a close friend; HOMEBOY, 1.

1974 Piñero *Short Eyes* 124: *Home piece* An inmate with whom one hung out before going to prison. **1980** Pearl *Pop. Slang* 72: *Home piece n.* (Prison) a fellow inmate who was one's friend before imprisonment. **1985** in N. George *Buppies, B-Boys* 47: Yo home piss.…You ready to serve these Israelis? **1995** Univ. Tenn. student: *Home piece* is the same as *home boy* or *home girl.* Like, "Yo, home piece!"

home plate *n.* **1.** home. *Joc.*

1908 W.G. Davenport *Butte & Montana* 135: One fifteenth of the population of this state enrolled in a school 2,500 miles from home plate. **1942** *Pittsburgh Courier* (Jan. 3) 7: "Home" was playing games away from home plate.

2. *USMC & Naval Av.* an aircraft carrier or air base where an aircraft is stationed.

1957 (quot. at SPLASH, *v.*). **1983** LaBarge & Hold *Sweetwater Gunslinger* 5: Home Plate. This is Gunslinger 201. **1984** Trotti *Phantom* 134 [ref. to 1960's]: Pigeons to homeplate two-six-five for sixty-two. *a***1989** R. Herman, Jr. *Warbirds* 271: Head straight for home plate, Thunder; let's get the hell out of Dodge. *a***1990** Poyer *Gulf* 55: Home plate dead ahead.

homer *n.* **1.** *Sports.* an official whose decisions consistently favor the home team.

1888 *N.Y. Press* (June 3) (cited in Nichols *Baseball Term.*). **1921** J. Conway, in *Variety* 7: The guesser [i.e., referee] was a homer, and told us we would wear five-ounce gloves or forfeit the fight. **1932** *S.F. News* (Nov. 13), in Dickson *Baseball Dict.*: Referee Arthur Badenock is an out and out "homer." He cost Stanford a game and did his best to take the UCLA game away from the Gaels. **1959** Brosnan *Long Season* 271: *Homer.* To umpires, an insulting word inferring partiality is being given to the home team. Sometimes used by ballplayers who wish to be thrown out of the game. **1964** Thompson & Rice *Every Diamond* 141: *Homer:* Umpire who appears to favor the home team. **1969** Layden & Snyder *Diff. Game* 46 [ref. to 1920's]: Again I complained bitterly about the "homer," as we used to call home-favoring officials. **1976** Rosen *Above Rim* 114: You homer!…You asshole! You've been screwing up all night! **1983** L. Frank *Hardball* 67: One of the worst things an umpire can be called is a "homer," someone who is favoring…the home team.

2. HOME RUN.

1963 Blechman *Omongo* 58: I hear she's been knocked for a homer.

3. HOMEBOY; HOMEGIRL.

1988 *N.Y. Newsday* (July 6) 9: Now the homers from Flatbush know that Franklin [Avenue] is major money. **1991** G. Trudeau *Doonesbury* (synd. comic strip) (Mar. 11): Any homers still holed up in K-City?

home run *n.* Esp. *Stu.* an act of seduction culminating in sexual intercourse. Cf. *get to first base, get to second base,* and *get to third base,* all s.v. BASE; and SCORE, *v.*

[**1961** Gover *$100 Misunderstanding* 80: Nex, homerun! Yeah! Boff us pop like the forff of July!] **1963** (implied by HOMER, 2). **1974** Lahr *Trot* 16: French kiss…Hickie…Hand job…Blow job…Home run. **1988** *Cheers* (NBC-TV): First base nothing. I bet I could hit a home run with her. **1988** *Wonder Years* (ABC-TV): How far you gonna go, Kev? Gonna try for a home run, huh?

homes *n. Black E & Mil.* HOMEBOY, 1; *(hence)* BUDDY, 1.—used in direct address.

 1971 Wells & Dance *Night People* 117: Homes, n. A nickname for someone from your hometown. **1983** S. Wright *Meditation* 116 [ref. to Vietnam War]: Homes!…yeah, you. My man. **1983** J. Hughes *Nat. Lampoon's Vacation* (film): Excuse me, homes. What it is, bro. **1985** *Miami Vice* (NBC-TV): Everybody knows about that, homes. **1988** *Newsweek* (Mar. 28) 20: Hands on the car, homeboy!…Where you been, where you going? Answer me, homes—I'm talkin' to YOU! **1988** M. Schiffer *Colors* (film): That dude was fly, homes. **1989** Sandor & Gough *Tarzan in Manhattan* (film): Hey, homes, who taught you how to drive, man? **1989** *21 Jump Street* (Fox-TV): This is bull, homes. Change the channel. **1989** *L.A. Times* (June 25): It was "Holmes [*sic*], this" and "Homeboy, that."

homeside *adj. & adv. Navy.* STATESIDE.

 *a***1988** W.J. Dunn *Pacific Microphone* 211 [ref. to WWII]: Charcoal grills produced "genuine home-side" hamburgers.

home skillet *n.* HOMEBOY, 1.

 1993 P. Munro *U.C.L.A. Slang II* 51: Home skillet/home slice *n.* close friend. **1994** *Parade* (Jan. 2) 8: *Homeskillet*—good friend. **1994** Univ. Tenn. prof.: I heard on the *Today* show that *home skillet* means a good friend. **1995** Eble *Campus Slang* (Apr.) 5: Home skillet—friend.…"I'll see you later, home skillet." From African American.

homeslice *n.* HOMEBOY, 1.

 1984 Mason & Rheingold *Slanguage: Holmie*…A person who is a good friend. Also holmes, homeboy and homeschlice [*sic*]. **1984** Eble *Campus Slang* (Spring) 4: Holm [*sic*] slice…black male.…What's up, Holm slice? After Larry Holmes, heavy-weight champion. **1991** Nelson & Gonzales *Bring Noise* 112: After hearing his homeslice is dead, Ice packs real lethal weapons. **1993** (quot. at HOME SKILLET). **1994** G. Smitherman *Black Talk* 136: Home slice…See homey.

homeward-bounders *n.pl. Navy.* whiskers allowed to grow during a ship's homeward voyage.

 1841 [Mercier] *Man o' War* 184: So come all you with faces bare,/Of *homeward-bounders* raise a pair. **1849** Melville *White Jacket* 228 [ref. to 1843]: You can't raise a pair of whiskers yet; and see what a pair of homeward bounders I have on my jowls! *Ibid.* 332: There they anticipated creating no small impression by their immense and magnificent *homeward-bounders*—so they called the long fly-brushes at their chins.

homework *n.* lovemaking, esp. with one's spouse. *Joc.*

 1931 Farrell *McGinty* 186: My wife and I want a kid, and we do plenty homework, but…I just can't connect. **1935** in Atkinson *Dirty Comics* 143: Why Casper, you can't even do your homework. I'll bet Buttercups can satisfy a girl quicker than you. **1971** *Black Scholar* (Nov.) 7: You got to keep up your homework.…If you don't, somebody else'll be doing it for you. **1974** Terkel *Working* xxxvi: I'll read [pornography] at work and go home and do my homework. (Laughs.) That what the guys at the plant call it—homework.

homey or **homie** *n. Esp. Black E.* HOMEBOY, 1, 2.

 1944 Burley *Hndbk. Jive* 140: *Homey*—One newly arrived from the South, a person from one's home-town, one who isn't fully aware of what is going on. **1946** Mezzrow *Really the Blues* 334: *Homey:* form of greeting between people from the same place. **1942–49** Goldin et al. *DAUL: Homey.* (South; rare elsewhere except among Negroes) A person from one's neighborhood, home town, or state. **1970** *Evergreen Rev.* XIV (Apr.) 77: "Is this guy a homeie?" asked Smith, pointing to me. **1974** Piñero *Short Eyes* 26: Look out for your homey, Shoe. *Ibid.* 125: *Homey* A fellow prisoner from one's neighborhood or home town. **1976** Chinn *Dig Nigger Up* 60: Now and then I would see and talk to a homie. **1979** Gram *Blvd. Nights* 130: We take care of the homies, you know that. **1981** in *West. Folklore* XLIV (1985) 7: *Homeys.*…From the same city as you are. **1984** S. Hager *Hip Hop* 109: *Homey*—short for homeboy. **1986** *Miami Vice* (NBC-TV): If any of his homeys are there, we're made. **1994** G. Smitherman *Black Talk* 137: *Homey*…A person from one's own neighborhood. **1995** (quot. at HOMEBOY, 2).

homicide *n.* something or someone that is especially formidable; MURDER.

 1956 Resko *Reprieve* 235: This stuff is homicide, man!

homie see s.v. HOMEY.

homing device *n. Mil.* a furlough leave.

 1942 *Randolph Field* 131: What makes you think you rate a homing device, Mister?

homing pigeon *n. Mil.* a military discharge button.

 1945 in *AS* XXI (1946) 153: *Homing pigeon*…not as widely used as "ruptured duck." I have heard more sailors use it than soldiers. **1946** *Newsweek* (Mar. 18) 34: "Ruptured duck": GI for the discharge button which ex-servicemen wear in their lapels; also, "homing pigeon" and "screaming eagle." **1946** *Amer. Legion Mag.* (May) 26 [ref. to WWII]: Also, besides being a "ruptured duck," the discharge emblem was a "homing pigeon."

homo *n.* a person, esp. a male, who is homosexual.—usu. used contemptuously.

 1922 N. Anderson *Hobo* 145: Some "homos" claim that every boy is a potential homosexual. **1925** in J. Katz *Gay/Lesbian Almanac* 424: There is something "not quite right" with the male or female homo. *a***1927** in P. Smith *Letter from Father* 158: Homos often came to Neil's parties. **1927** H. Miller *Moloch* 135: To be literary, a fellow thinks he must be either a hobo or a homo. **1929** Zombaugh *Gold Coast* 96: A group of "homos" from the South Side also came in. **1933** Ford & Tyler *Young & Evil* 144: You homos don't like each other. **1933** in Mencken *New Ltrs.* 286: I have long had a rule against stories about homos. **1938** Lawes *Invisible Stripes* 94: But nobody had any use for homos. **1947** Willingham *End as a Man* 159: He acts…as if he was a homo. **1948** Lait & Mortimer *New York* 74: Most female homos' hangouts are in Third Street. *ca***1953** Hughes *Lodge* 183: These chicks…were homos and faggots. **1958** A. King *Mine Enemy* 19: He was a homo and, like most pansies, had few of the virtues of men, and all the little weaknesses of women. **1965** Yurick *Warriors* 162: The homo asked, "What's your name?" **1971** Le Guin *Lathe of Heaven* 45: The plaintiff was actually a terrific repressed homo. **1979** Gutcheon *New Girls* 33: He looks like a homo. **1982** M. Mann *Elvis* 93: The homos sicken me. **1993** *N.Y. Times* (Dec. 8) A18: They spit on me and threw things at me and called me faggot, homo. **1995** *Jerry Springer Show* (synd. TV series): She thinks she can take *me*—a homo—and turn me into the perfect man!

homo *adj.* homosexual.—usu. used contemptuously.

 1933** in *OEDS*: Round about six, fifteen and twenty are the recognized "homo" ages in women. **1941** G. Legman, in Henry *Sex Vars.* II 1168: *Homo*…homosexual, used as a noun and (predicate) adjective. **1949** De Forest *Gay Year* 23: It didn't make him homo. ***1957** in *OEDS*: Sometimes they muttered to each other that he was "homo." **a1968** Ackerly *Father & Myself* 117: Almost the first…question he shot at me [in 1918] was "Are you homo or hetero?" I had never heard either term before.

honch *n.* [prob. short for an unattested sense or fig. use of HONCHO] *Narc.* heroin.

 1970 Conaway *Big Easy* 127: I mean smack. Horse, honch, duji, H, snow, heroin—it's all the same animal.

honcho *n.* [< Japn *hanchō* 'squad leader'] *Orig. Mil. in Japan.*
1. a boss, chief, leader, etc.; person in charge.—often constr. with *head* or *top.*

 1947 (cited in *W10*). **1955** *Life* (June 27) 153: The C.O.—we called him "the Honcho," the GI's Japanese for "boss" or "chief." **1955** Salter *Hunters* 24 [ref. to Korean War]: If it's really one of their *honchos* back there, you're just out of luck. **1964** Peacock *Drill & Die* 50: But Schale won't be honcho of this division forever. **1968** in Morgan & Michalson *For Our Beloved Country* 420: I went to a G-4 meeting…for all the supply honchos in the Division. **1970** Ponicsan *Last Detail* 20: "Okay, Buddusky," says the chief, "you're the honcho." **1970** Southern *Blue Movie* 285: His head-honcho, as it were. **1974** *Gunsmoke* (CBS-TV): Which one o' you's the top honcho? **1985** Boyne & Thompson *Wild Blue* 169 [ref. to 1953]: We'd call the few tough aggressive [Communist] pilots "honchos" and the rest "students."

2. a person of influence or importance; BIG SHOT.

 1958 in Harvey *Air Force* 13: He'd knocked down eight MIGs in Korea. The Japanese had a name for men like George: *honcho*, boss man. **1972** Hannah *Geronimo Rex* 37: We'd watch her collar some cheerleader…and start chattering away…making out to have crucial deals going with the honchos of the school. **1972** West *Village* 156: All the village honchos are here. **1984** *Hardcastle & McCormick* (ABC-TV): He's a honcho with Denco Motor Parts. **1987** M. Hastings *Korean War* 262 [ref. to 1952]: His growing reputation as a "honcho"—a top pilot. **1994** N. Karlen *Babes in Toyland* 71: Carr exhaled gratefully after the Warners honchos met the band.

3. a fellow; HOMBRE, 2.

1961 McMurtry *Horseman* 70: You honchos want to go? **1967** W. Crawford *Gresham's War* 22 [ref. to 1953]: One sound and you are a headless honcho. Understand? **1970** Ponicsan *Last Detail* 97: He's one smart honcho, that's for sure. **1972** C. Gaines *Stay Hungry* 143: There are a few bad honchos around, but none of them started out that way. **1974** *Nat. Lampoon* (Feb.) 64: Any of you honchos lose something? **1988** in G. Tate *Flyboy* 121: There was some linebacker- and tight-end-sized honchos with headsets.

4. *Mil.* a Korean person.

1964 Howe *Valley of Fire* 191 [ref. to Korean War]: It was…an understood code when dealing with the Ofays or the honchos. *Ibid.* 218: The honcho farmers use it for makin' their clothes.

honcho *v.* to oversee; boss.—occ. used intrans.

1955 *AS* (May) 118: *Honcho*…A man in charge.…2. To direct a detail or operation. **1956** Heflin *USAF Dict.* 253: *Honcho, v.*, to boss a job. **1958** Frankel *Band of Bros.* 84 [ref. to 1950]: Skipper's going to honcho when we jump off.…You see Skinhead down there honchoin' the company? **1962** Blake *Heartbreak* 28 [ref. to 1953]: You've got to *honsho* a truckload of GI's.

hondoo *n. S.W.* the vagina.—usu. considered vulgar.

*ca***1915** in Logsdon *Whorehouse Bells* 54: He…opened her hondoo.

honest Injun *interj.* honestly; truly.—now sometimes considered offensive.

1851 in *DA*: He will…nod his head interrogatively, and almost pathetically address you with the solemn adjuration, "Honest Indian?" **1876** "M. Twain" *Tom Sawyer* 21: Ben, I'd like to, honest injun. **1877** Burdette *Mustache* 258: "Honest injun," "pon my nonner," and "cross my heart." **1881–82** Howells *Modern Instance* 98: "No, honest Injian, now," protested Kinney. **1882** A.W. Aiken *Joe Buck* 3: "Is *that* so?" "Honest Injun!" **1890** Bunner *Short Sixes* 90: Hope to die—Honest Injun—cross my breast! **1903** C.E. Stewart *Uncle Josh* 48: Now look here, honest injun, did you give me that five-dollar bill? **1915** Poole *Harbor* 317: I'm sorry! Honest Injun! **1925** Z. Grey *Vanishing Amer.* 289: "You'll go off alone and stay alone?"…"Honest Injun." **1929** A. Smedley *Daughter of Earth* 103: "Well, whatdye say to gettin' married?" "Sure!" I replied. "Honest Injun?" **1982** R.M. Brown *So. Discomfort* 92: No I don't. Honest injun. **1988** *Geraldo* (WNBC-TV): How many of you guys—honest Injun—actually have drugs somewhere in the background? **1991–95** Sack *Co. C* 111: His name, honest Injun,…was Bushyhead.

honest John *n.* an honest man; (*Und.*) a law-abiding fellow.

[**1807** W. Irving *Salmagundi* 9: The whole corps [of actors] from the manager…to honest *John* in his green coat and black breeches.] **1884** Hartranft *Sidesplitter* 148: Never did Paddy utter a better bull than did an honest John, who, being asked by a friend, "Has your sister got a son or a daughter?" answered, "Positively I do not yet know whether I am an *uncle* or an *aunt.*" **1903** *Pedagog. Sem.* X 376: Honest John. **1933** Guest *Limey* 31: The gangsters…are…exploiting the decent burghers, or "honest Johns." **1933–35** D. Lamson *About to Die* 191: The honest-johns get soaked plenty because they're honest an' green an' don't know the business.…An' the judge throws the book at 'em. **1936** Duncan *Over the Wall* 175: A gaunt, bewhiskered Honest John had just stooped over a pile of neatly stacked cordwood. **1949** Bezzerides *Thieves' Market* 166: They're standing around to hand [money] to you, all the honest Johns. **1955** Graziano & Barber *Somebody Up There* 358: All these famous Honest Johns I meet up, they like me. **1968** M.B. Scott *Racing Game* 49: The major distinction between trainers is that of "honest johns" and "manipulators." The former are non-betting trainers. **1980** McAleer & Dickson *Unit Pride* 36: He said scum like me shouldn't be safe in jail,…an honest Johns gettin' killed to protect me. **1980** *M*A*S*H* (CBS-TV): Uncle Lou is one honest John.

honest-to-God *n.* the complete and utter truth.—constr. with *the.* Also **honest-to-John.**

1929 Hammett *Maltese Falcon* 121: What's the honest-to-God on this guy, Sam? **1933** *Amer. Mercury* (Feb.) 204: The sure-thing boys came round offering me dough to give me the honest-to-John.

honey *n.* **1.** semen; (*also*) the precoital secretion of the vagina; (*hence*) (also constr. with *piece of*) copulation.—usu. considered vulgar.

1719 (implied by HONEYPOT, 1). **a***1890–93** *F & H* III 338: *Honey*…(venery).—The *semen*. **1909** in *JAF* XXVIII (1915) 190: Rain, come wet me! Sun come dry me!/Gal got honey, an' she won't come nigh me. **1927** C. McKay *Home to Harlem* 13: Take it from me, buddy, there ain't no honey lak to that theah comes out of our own belonging-to-us honeycomb. **1929** in Oliver *Blues Tradition* 218: But the way he spreads his honey, he will make me lose my mind. **1930** Farrell *Calico Shoes* 150: Not if ah had to give up mah honey. No, sir, ah couldn't go without getting mahself a piece of honey now and then. *Ibid.* 151: Nevah…turn down a piece of honey that drifts your way. **1940** Del Torto TS.: She kept saying…Oh dear, suck it good I want to come all over you, don't waste the honey. **1952** Mandel *Angry Strangers* 380: Hotstick cats who had to dip into her honey. **1961** Gover *$100 Misunderstanding* 80: This sweet bumblebee got him jes bout all the honey he kin get fer now. **1975** *Nat. Lampoon* (Sept.) 39: Where else could grandma get her honey dipped? No white man fucked doggy style until 1923. **1986** C. Stroud *Close Pursuit* 103: Thinking about spreading some fine white legs and getting some of that uptown honey on his fingers. **1992** Madonna *Sex* (unp.): Honey poured from my…gash. **1995** *N.Y. Press* (May 31) 17: It's all subtext and hushed porn lingo: the…dark-meat honey-lapper made to look respectable and nice.

2. money. Cf. syn. SUGAR.

1859 Matsell *Vocab.* 43: *Honey.* Money. **1906** A.H. Lewis *Confessions* 202: I drew the honey from his poke.

3. something (*occ.* someone) that is especially noteworthy, effective, pleasing, etc.; something of excellence.

1888 in *F & H* III 338: Dave is a honey. **1890** *DN* I 61: *Honey:* good. "That's a honey strike." Western Ohio. **1928** MacArthur *War Bugs* 69: We laid a box barrage around a couple of regiments in the Bois des Chiens that was a honey. **1933** *Chi. Sun. Trib.* (Nov. 5) (Comics) (unp.): That haircut was a honey, Trixie. **1933** *AS* VIII 35: *Bear-cat,* an excellent fighter, a *honey.* **1934** Duff & Sauber *20 Million Sweethearts* (film): I've got a perfect honey of an idea. **1935** Wead *Ceiling Zero* (film): Gee, your landing was a honey. **1936** Tully *Bruiser* 29: A good fellow, Joe—shady as a woods—but a honey if he's on your side. **1938** Smitter *Detroit* 14: I think the machine weighed sixty tons. "She's a honey." **1938** "E. Queen" *4 Hearts* 22: A honey of a human int'rest story. **1938** Steinbeck *Grapes of Wrath* 172: Cars from all over the country.…Sure some honeys on the road. **1945** J. Bryan *Carrier* 85: The F6 is a honey. **1945** in F. Brown *Angels & Spaceships* 110: Here's the press—a honey of a little Miehle. **1946** Boulware *Jive & Slang* 2: *A Honey*…Anything pretty. **1947** Perelman *Westward Ha!* 32: A dame with a honey of a shape. **1950** F. Brown *Space on Hands* 110: Willem has…a little lathe that's a honey. **1950** *Sat. Eve. Post* (May 6) 142: Didn't you see that honey of a right? **1951** Mannix *Sword-Swallower* 166: They had dreamed up a rope-tie that was a honey. **1953** Gresham *Midway* 90: The show was called *Stepping Stones*; it was the debut of Fred's daughter, Dorothy, and it was a honey. **1968** in *OEDS*: A real honey, automatic power steering, power brakes, radio. **1978** in T. O'Brien *Things They Carried* 172: There's still the seven medals.…Seven honeys.

4. human excrement; night soil. See also HONEY BUCKET, HONEY-DIPPER, HONEY WAGON, etc.

1930 Nason *Corporal* 172 [ref. to WWI]: The busiest bee that ever buzzed would have nothing on you as a honey gatherer! **1950** *Amer. N & Q* (Feb.) 172 [ref. to *ca*1900]: He told me he was "movin' de honey from de garden house." **1961** Coon *At the Front* 148: She pushed a dung barrow/Singing "Dung balls and honey/All fresh from the throne." **1966–80** McAleer & Dickson *Unit Pride* 176: He…landed right in the honey vat.

5.a. an attractive young woman. Also (*obs.*) **piece of honey.** [The bracketed quots. illustrate the colloq. sense '(one's) sweetheart'.]

[**1863** in Boyer *Naval Surgeon* I 181: Billy and his "honey," as he calls his wife, almost bursted with joy.] [**1903** in "O. Henry" *Works* 1195: This Rafael seems to be her honey.] [**1908** W.G. Davenport *Butte & Montana* 42: Balance all and swing your honies.] [**1926** in Truman *Dear Bess* 320: These birds…lose all respect by going over the hill to see their honeys.] **1930** Farrell *Calico Shoes* 151: Git yourself a piece of honey that's plump and willing and nice, and don't evah let it bother you. **1932** R. Fisher *Conjure-Man* 51: I asked…what this honey's name was. **1935** *AS* (Feb.) 17: *Honey*…any attractive girl. **1939** R.A. Winston *Dive Bomber* 27: Local girls....There are some real honeys down here. **1951** in Mailer *Ad. for Myself* 119: Do you think that crazy honey is really serious? *a***1976** Roebuck & Frese *Rendezvous* 82: Look at Charlie over there with two fine honeys. **1977** in L. Bangs *Psychotic Reactions* 242: I...ask him if he ever hies any of the local honeys up to bed. **1991** *Houston Chronicle* (Oct. 8) 2D: *Honey*—A female, especially a good-looking one.

b. (see quots.).

1970–72 in *AS* L (1975) 60: *Honey*...Handsome or sexy male (female use). **1994** *Totally Unofficial Rap Dict.*: *Honey*...Person, generally attractive.

honey barge *n. Naut.* a garbage scow. Also **honey boat.**

1941 Maryland WPA *Guide to U.S. Naval Acad.* 151: *Honey Barge*—For refuse only. **1941** Kendall *Army & Navy Sl.* 20: *Honey barge*...comes alongside for garbage. **1945** in *Calif. Folk. Qly.* V (1946) 381: Refuse from the meals is loaded on the *honey barge* and *given the deep six.* **1947** *ATS* (Supp.) 38: *Honey boat,* a garbage barge. **1961** L.E. Young *Virgin Fleet* 31 [ref. to 1941]: Honey barge coming alongside. **1962** McKenna *Sand Pebbles* 76: It was from a passing string of barges taking liquid Hankow sewage back to the fields that fed Hankow. Sailors called them *honey barges.* **1966** Noel & Bush *Naval Terms* 179: *Honey barge:* Garbage scow.

honey bucket *n. Rural & Mil.* a can used for collecting human excrement or similar wastes; (*hence*) a toilet receptacle.

1931 Brophy & Partridge *Songs & Slang* 318 [ref. to WWI]: *Honey-Bucket.*—Latrine—receptacle for excreta. Canadian. *ca***1944** in Kaplan & Smith *One Last Look* 53: Our latrine (with running water instead of the usual "honey buckets") is next door. **1951** [VMF-323] *Old Ballads* 23: 'Twas built of honey buckets, so they named it Pusan U. **1963** W.C. Anderson *Penelope* 52: They carry [human fertilizer] around in wooden barrels called "honey buckets." **1965** Linakis *In Spring* 347 [ref. to WWII]: The only times I came out was when the guard took me to the last cell where they kept the honeybucket. **1976** Braly *False Starts* 115: A brief visit once a day to feed us and change our honey buckets. **1984** Tiburzi *Takeoff!* 54: You don't have to open up the airport, you don't have to...carry the bags, empty the honey buckets.

honey cart *n.* **1.** HONEY WAGON, 1.a.

1929 Barr *Let Tomorrow Come* 140: You ought to be drivin' a honey-cart somewhere. **1942** *Leatherneck* (Nov.) 146: *Honey-Cart*—Garbage wagon or barge. **1943** in Stilwell *Papers* 164: The honey carts scatter pollution. **1963** Boyle *Yanks Don't Cry* 119 [ref. to WWII]: Honey carts—the second step in Japan's crop fertilizing program—are flat wagons fitted out with several large wooden barrels that are pulled through the streets by a horse or an ox, and sometimes by a man or a woman whose status in life is lower than that of a *ninsoku.* **1964** Crane *Sgt. & Queen* 82 [ref. to Korean War]: Ben...whipped the remodeled jeep around a lumbering honey cart. *****1971** in *Austral. Nat. Dict.*: A honey cart is the dear little vehicle that the airlines use to empty the aircraft lavatories.

2. HONEY WAGON, 2.

1953 in *Western Folk.* XIII (1954) 10: The "powder room," of both genders, portable, for [use on filming] locations, is the "honey cart."

honey-cooler *n.* [orig. unkn.] an extraordinary person or thing.

1868 in *DN* VI 349: Make [this Indian] your friend, for he is a good one. Do the square thing by him and he is a honey-cooler. Do anything mean to him...and he will get even. **1902** Remington *John Ermine* 110: Say, it's a honey-cooler. You will fall dead when you see it. **1905** "H. McHugh" *Search Me* 82: That boy Bunch is a honey-cooler all right.

honey-digger *n.* HONEY-DIPPER.

1950 (quot. at HONEY WAGON, 1.a.).

honey-dipper *n.* a worker who collects and removes excrement or raw sewage.

1961 J. Jones *Thin Red Line* 220: Despite his career in life as a honeydipper in Cambridge Mass. **1963** D. Tracy *Brass Ring* 447: A record that would scare off a honey-dipper needing a helper. **1968** Lockridge *Hartspring* 151: You've been through more crap this year than a honey-dipper at a sewage plant. **1972** L.J. Anderson [letter to J.E.L., June 20] [ref. to 1918]: Latrine workers were called "honey dippers." **1968–77** Herr *Dispatches* 14: The VC got work inside all the camps as shoeshine boys and laundresses and honey-dippers, they'd starch your fatigues and burn your shit and then go home and mortar your area. **1983** Neaman & Silver *Kind Words* 51: *Honey dipper* was a common term for a latrine cleaner during the Vietnam War. **1988** B.E. Wheeler *Outhouse*

Humor 21: In England honey-dippers were called "rakers" or "gongfermors," and their honey wagons were called "lavender carts."

honey-dipping *n.* the removing of excrement or raw sewage.

1926 *AS* I (Dec.) 651: *Honey Dipping.* Odorless excavating. **1930** "D. Stiff" *Milk & Honey* 207: *Honey-dipping*—Working as a *shovel* stiff in a sewer, or any kind of unpleasant shovel work. **1988** B.E. Wheeler *Outhouse Humor* 21: Honey-dipping was always done at night.

honey-do *n.* [fr. imper. phr. beginning with "Honey, do..."] a household chore. *Joc.* Also **honeydew.**

1990 *Senior World of Central Coast* (Calif.) (June) 1: Most of his chores and "honey-do's" are done. **1991** *Lompoc* (Calif.) *Record* (Oct. 7) A7: The projects were "honey dos." **1991** Marcinko & Weisman *Rogue Warrior* 145: A...list of "honeydews"—house and yard maintenance chores. **1992** Knoxville, Tenn., plumber, age *ca*55: That's what I call a "honey-do." "Honey, do this, Honey, do that." **1996** *Donahue* (NBC-TV): We have a...honey-do list when he gets home. [*Laughter from audience.*]. **1997** *L.A. Times* (Feb. 13) E5: Our home became badly nelgected because he was unable to do all the "honey do's" he had taken care of prior to his surgery.

honeyfuck *n.* a sexy young woman.—usu. considered vulgar.

1970 E. Thompson *Garden of Sand* 295: Come on...honeyfuck. **1979** L. Heinemann, in *Tri-Quarterly* (Spring) 184: The snazziest hotto-trot honey fuck to hit the mainland since the first French settlers.

honeyfuck *v.* [prob. alter. of HONEYFUGGLE, *v.,* 3] to engage in unusually gratifying copulation.—also used trans.—usu. considered vulgar.

1954–60 *DAS: Honey-fuck*...v.i., v.t. To have sexual intercourse in a romantic, idyllic way; to have intercourse with a very young girl...*honey-fucking*...extremely gratifying and slow intercourse. **1980** L. Heinemann, in *Harper's* (June) 64: She's honey-fucking the everlasting daylights out of some guy. **1986** Merkin *Zombie Jamboree* 121: We were honey-fuckin', real slow and low, takin' our time.

honeyfuggle *n.* cajolery.

1929 in *AS* VI (1931) 255: What is "baloney" to Alfred E. Smith is "honeyfogle" in Missouri's Senate. As explained by Senator McCawley, the word is used to denote cajolery or subterfuge by sweet-sounding phrases.

honeyfuggle *v.* [var. of E dial. *connyfogle*] **1.a.** to deceive or cajole; take in by flattery, promises, or pleasing talk; impose upon; (*occ.*) to obtain (something) in this manner.

1829 in *DAE: Honeyfuggle,* to quiz, to cozen. **1852** *Knickerbocker* (Dec.) 548: A neighbor...had honey-fackled him in the matter of a heap of logs. **1855** in *DAE:* They were...determined no longer to endure such imposition, no longer to be honey-fuggled by promises made only to be disregarded. **1856** in *OED2:* They go cavorting out, honey-fuggling their consciences. **1858** *Harper's Mag.* (July) 270: "It's all honey-fuggling."..."What's honey-fuggling?" "It's cutting it too fat over the left." **1858** in Bartlett *Amer.* (ed. 2) 200: I will wager that he will so beautifully *honey-fuggle* both South and North, that the people will pronounce him one of the best Presidents we have ever had. **1859** Bartlett *Amer.: Honey-fogle.* To humbug, swindle, cheat. West and South. **1862** in M. Lane *Dear Mother* 99: We have been honey-fuggled worse than almost any other regiment. **1864** C.H. Smith *Bill Arp* 119: I don't know much about banking nor financing, nor the like of that, but I can't be honeyfuggled as to how my money comes and how it goes. **1868** in *DN* VI 349: The design of that letter...was to "honeyfuggle" Mr. Seward and Mr. Johnson. **1888** in *DAE:* He acts like a man that's got a deadfall all sot, un is a-tryin' to honey-fugle the varmint to git 'im to come underneath. **1890** in *DN* VI 349: You propose to put one arm around his neck and "honey-fugle" him, and get him to vote for the Republican ticket. **1894** *DN* I 331: [New] Jerseyisms....*honey-fogle:* to allure by traps. **1902** Harben *Abner Daniel* 157: He's been tryin' to honeyfuggle the old man into a trade. **1905** S.G. Phillips *Plum Tree* 278: Posting to make peace on whatever terms he could honeyfuggle out of my conciliation-mad candidate. **1906** *DN* III 141: *Honey-fuggle*...To cajole, flatter. "He can't *honey-fuggle* him." **1912** *DN* III 578: [Western Indiana]...*honey-fuggle,* v.t. To win with sweet promises. **1941** *Time* (May 26) 16: [The president now has] power to do legally things which Bernard M. Baruch had to wangle by what he called "buttering and honey-fuggling."

b. to refuse to commit oneself; hedge.

1906 *Nation* (Feb. 22) 149: As to the present officers, he thought they had no excuse for not submitting to full investigation. "Don't honey-fugle," he advised the committee, "but go to the bottom in any way possible."

2. to ingratiate oneself, esp. for a deceptive, self-serving, or dishonest purpose.

1856 in *DAE:* Pardon me for using the word; but Sharp "*honey-fug-gled*" around me. **1887** *Courier-Journal* (Louisville, Ky.) (May 7) 4: The modern practices in politics of pandering to this sentiment and that;...and of honey-fuggling with rascals instead of hitting them a death blow between the eyes. **1888** in Farmer *Amer.:* Noonan's companion objected to this honey-fugling by knocking the demonstrative stranger down.

3. to engage in kissing and hugging, esp. with a very young girl.

1871 Schele de Vere *Amer.* 205: Susan B. Anthony...uses *honey-fugling* for "kissing," in her lectures on Women's Rights. **1898** B. Harte *Light & Shadow* 191: Wot's this yer I'm hearin' of your doin's over at Red Pete's? Honeyfoglin' with a horse-thief, eh? **1934** P. Wylie *Finnley Wren* 101: He and Doris had lain together for a full hour stark naked....Doris was only seven and sexual exposure might have damaged her. He...was keenly aware of mysterious pains and penalties attached to what Floyd Binger called "honey-fuggling." **1969–70** in *DARE: When people make too much of a show of affection in a public place...Honeyfugglin'.* [**1970** *Nat. Lampoon* (Apr.) 56: Constance Honeyfuggle and her Electric Banana or "What's a Joint Like This Doing in a Girl Like You?"]

honey house *n.* a privy.

1915 *DN* IV 233: College Slang...*honey-house*, n. = water closet.

honey pit *n.* a pit for the burial of excrement.

1958 Frankel *Band of Bros.* 9 [ref. to Korean War]: You mean yer gonna stick yer paw in that honey pit?

honeypot *n.* **1.** the vagina.—usu. considered vulgar.

***1719** in *OED2:* For when you have possession got,/Of Venus Mark, or Hony-pot. **1958–59** Southern & Hoffenberg *Candy* 91: Concealing her honeypot from the prying eyes of Dr. Dunlap. **1969** in Girodias *New Olympia Reader* 630: You can bite the lips of the honey pot a little, but very gently. **1972** J. Pearl *Cops* 14: Dreaming of your honey pot, eh? **1972** *Nat. Lampoon* (July) 82: We come at last to the honeypot at the end of her rainbow. **1973** *TULIPQ* (coll. B.K. Dumas): Female sexual organ...*Snatch, honey pot.* **1987** Covin *Brown Sky* 241: One o' the sweetest honey-pots I ever dipped into.

2. HONEY BUCKET.

1954 in *AS* XXX (1955) 47: The American in Japan speaks of *honey buckets, honey wagons*...and even *honey pots.* **1960** J. Algeo, in *AS* XXXV 118 [ref. to Korea, 1953]: These conveyances were known as *honey-carts, honey-wagons,* or *honey-pots.* **1971** Vaughan & Lynch *Brandywine's War* 6: Drag the honey-pots from beneath the latrines.

honey shot *n. TV.* a camera shot of an attractive female spectator, as during a sporting event.

1968 *Newsweek* (Oct. 28) 71: Three "honey shots" (ABC lingo for prolonged looks at female spectators). **1974** *Sports Illustrated* (Feb. 11) 14: A honey shot...is a quick camera glimpse of a girl in the stands. **1990** T. Fahey *Joys of Jargon* 185: *Honey shot* (Entertainment) Brief shot of a pretty girl at a sporting event.

honey up *v.* to talk to in a flattering or blandishing way.

1853 Doten *Journals* I 168: [We tried] to honey up to some of the squaws, but couldn't come it. **1955** E. Hunter *Jungle Kids* 105: He's honeying her up, come on doll, open the door, and all that kind of crap.

honey wagon *n.* **1.a.** a truck, cart, or wagon used in the collection, disposal, or treatment of human waste; (*broadly*) a garbage truck.

1923 H.L. Foster *Beachcomber* 283: The "honey wagons," as the carts are called by European residents [of Japan]. **1930** *AS* V (June) 384 [ref. to 1917]: *Honey wagon.* French manure cart. **1941** Hargrove *Pvt. Hargrove* 84: *Honey wagon*—the garbage truck. **1945** *Yank* (Nov. 9) 18: I need a couple men for honey-wagon detail. **1945** Beecher *All Brave Sailors* 43: Here the "honey-wagons" used to go, collecting the accumulation from thousands of privies. **1950** *Amer. N & Q* (Feb.) 172: Before the days of improved plumbing in Petersburg (Va.) [*ca*1900], the squad that cleaned privies at night was known to boys as the "honey-diggers" and the night wagon was the "honey-wagon." Adults occasionally used the term; but my father cautioned me against using it in the presence of ladies. **1960** MacCuish *Do Not Go Gentle*

123 [ref. to WWII]: Aw, c'mon, what is it—permanent garbage detail? The honey-wagon boys—that's us. **1966** F. Harvey *Raiders* 112: They'd have to call the honey wagon...to carry the stuff away. **1983** E. Dodge *Dau* 18 [ref. to Vietnam War]: Hutch...was busy pumping out the...toilets and checking the gauges on the side of the large, yellow honey wagon. **1986** Spears *Drugs & Drink* 265: *Honey wagon*...a septic tank pumping truck. **1986** Clayton & Elliott *Jazz World* 72 [ref. to China, 1934]: We called them "honey wagons" and they would be drawn by old men and old women who I guess couldn't find any other kind of work. **1995** *N.Y. Times* (Aug. 20) II 15: [Movie jargon:] A "honeywagon driver" is the person who drives the portable toilets.

b. (see quot.).

1971 *Current Slang* V (Spring) 14: *Honey wagon,* n. A manure spreader.

2. a movable outdoor toilet.

1942 *ATS* 801: *Honey wagon,* a rolling toilet. *a*1976 *6000 Words* 93: *Honey wagon*...a portable outdoor toilet.

Hong Kong dong *n.* [*Hong Kong* + DONG, 1] *Mil. in E. Asia.* gonorrhea. *Joc.*

1972 Medic, U.S. Navy, Hqs. Support Group–Taiwan (coll. J. Ball): And you'll learn Chinese, too. Damn near every G.I. learns "Hong Kong dong" the first weekend out. **1974** Spec. 4, U.S. Army STRAT-COM–Taiwan (coll. J. Ball): I'll kill that bitch—she gave me the Hong Kong ding! **1975** Spec. 5, U.S. Army, U.S. Taiwan Defense Command (coll. J. Ball): Mac's not drinking for a while—says he's on the wagon—but I says it's Hong Kong dong.

honk[1] *n.* **1.** a wild goose.

1800 in *DAE:* Wild-geese...during their annual migrations, constantly utter a cry, resembling *Cohonc....* The animals themselves, by natural onomatopoeia, were also called *Honc.*

2. speech or conversation.

1903 A. Adams *Log of Cowboy* 81 [ref. to 1880's]: I hung up my gentle honk before his eyes and ears and gave him free license to call it.

3. a drinking party; spree.

***1959** (cited in Partridge *DSUE* (ed. 8)). **1969** M. Williams *Reading Matter* (unp.): One sip could wipe out the memory of last night's honk.

4. a laugh; HOOT[1], 2.

1964 Hill *One of the Casualties* 169: As for the door signs, he said Gatos was the Mexican word for cats. Milt and Speck got a honk out of that.

5. the penis.—usu. considered vulgar.

1969 *Zap Comix* (No. 4) (unp.): The servant girl began suckin' on the Prince's honk.

6. country-western or honky-tonk music.

1973 *Penthouse* (June) 42: The rough magic of Sahm's singing encompasses every style from country honk to scat blues.

7. *Narc.* an inhalation of cocaine, heroin, etc.; SNORT.

*a*1987 Bunch & Cole *Reckoning for Kings* 23: Right under his nose I took a honk.

honk[2] *n. Black E.* HONKY[2].—usu. used contemptuously.

1973 W. Burroughs, Jr. *Ky. Ham* 16: He was black obviously, but even us honks gotta know our p's and q's. **1977** Univ. Tenn. student: Start shaping up, honk. **1978** Diehl *Sharky's Machine* 44: Whatsa matter, honk, got the chills? **1986** Knoxville, Tenn., painter, age 32: Outta my sight, honk!

honk *v.* **1.** *Jazz.* (see 1936 quot.).

1936 in *AS* (Feb. 1947) 46: *Honk.* To play a note in the lower register with force and in a definite rhythmic pattern. Used of reed instruments only. **1961** in R.S. Gold *Jazz Talk* 131: Shavers screams, the Hawk honks, and only Bryant and Duvivier show any real sense of proportion. **1967** Kolb *Getting Straight* 93: "You gonna holler this next set?" "No thanks. You can honk without me."

2. *Esp. Av.* **a.** to pull or yank; (*specif.*) to abruptly change the direction of (an aircraft in flight); (of an aircraft) to bank sharply.

1946 G.C. Hall, Jr. *1000 Destroyed* 11 [ref. to WWII]: A Mustang...honking its...nose up in a peel-off. *Ibid.* 62: Gentile suddenly honked his ship up and stood it on his prop. **1955** *AS* XXX (May) 117: *Honk it*...Make a tight, fast turn. **1967** H.M. Mason *New Tigers* 98: The nose is honked up to forty or fifty degrees of pitch and the stick moved hard to the left. **1978** Katz *Folklore* 27: Have you ever heard a parachutist talk about *honking on the toggles*? *a*1989 R. Herman, Jr.

Warbirds 209: Jack…honked back on the stick…for a smooth pullout. **1989** T. Blackburn *Jolly Rogers* 103: The leader…honked his Zeke around in a tight, tight climbing turn. *Ibid.* 139: His wingman honked around in a tight level…turn.…I honked back hard. **1989** G. Hall *Air Guard* 91 [caption]: HC-130…honks into a steep turn.

b. to switch (power on or off).

    1984 Trotti *Phantom* 128 [ref. to 1960's]: The student tries to salvage things by honking off all the power and racking the airplane up into a 90-degree angle of bank.

3. to talk loudly; brag.—also quasi-trans.

    1963 Boyle *Yanks Don't Cry* 85 [ref. to WWII]: Those Red Cross people are probably playing this one for the grandstand so they'll have something to honk about the next time they come around for a donation. **1968** Gover *JC* 63: But with simple-ass Cholly robot honkin the wig off me here, I gets the urge t' be gone.

4. *Stu.* to be highly offensive or disagreeable; SUCK.

    [*a***1966** S.J. Baker *Austral. Lang.* (ed. 2) 139: To stink, *to honk*.] *Ibid.* 426: Offensiveness…*honk* (or *hoot*) *like a gaggle of geese.* **1978** *UTSQ*: Unattractive male…[He] *honks loudly.* **1989** Univ. Tenn. student: To *honk* is to act in a gooby fashion. He really *honks*.

5. *Narc.* to take by inhalation; SNORT.

    1968 H. Ellison *Deadly Streets* 107: A few were honking their cocaine. **1976–77** Kernochan *Dry Hustle* 33: You're supposed to be selling that coke, not honking it.

6. *Stu.* to vomit. [Pop. in U.S. by the "Wayne's World" sketch on NBC's *Saturday Night Live* and the eponymous 1992 film based on it.]

    ****1967** (cited in Partridge *Concise Dict. Slang* 221). **1992** M. Myers et al. *Wayne's World* (film): What if he honks in the car? **1993** P. Munro *U.C.L.A. Slang II* 51: *Honk*…to vomit.

7.a. to drive or go very fast; in phr. **honk it on** to go at top speed.

    1968–70 *Current Slang* III & IV 69: *Honk*, v. To go fast (in a car).—College males, Minnesota. **1970** *Current Slang* V (Winter) 8: *Honk*, v. To move fast (both figuratively and literally). **1974** Scalzo *Stand on Gas* 154: Listen, you dumb bastards, I warned you about going honking into that corner like that. **1976** PFC, U.S. Army, Dugway Proving Ground, Utah (coll. J. Ball): Fast? Shit! You should have gone with us to Idaho—man, we were honkin'! **1984** Trotti *Phantom* 70 [ref. to Vietnam War]: OK, Asp, nose to the horizon and honk it on! SAMs in the air at four and seven. *a***1990** P. Dickson *Slang!* 29: Boy, was I honking!

b. to go away; get out.—also constr. with *off*.

    1970–72 in *AS* L (1975) 61: Why don't you honk on out of my life? **1976** Univ. Tenn. student: *Honk off* means about the same as *fuck off! shove it!*

8. to grab or squeeze the penis or breast of. Cf. HONK JOB.

    1970 Wambaugh *New Centurions* 186 [ref. to 1962]: If it looks like he's making a move to honk you, just grab his hand and he's busted. **1975** Wambaugh *Choirboys* 279: He knew that he had just been "honked," as the vice squad called it, in a public place and that Scuz had said something about honking being a misdemeanor. **1979** Univ. Tenn. student: Man, I thought that good-lookin' one was gettin' ready to honk me right there on the street.

9. *Und.* to kill (someone).

    1970 J. Anderson, in *N.Y. Post* (Sept. 14): If brothers get mad at each other, they should go out and honk (kill) a pig (policeman) and then shake hands.

honk around *v. Av.* (see quot.).

    1969 Cagle *Naval Av. Guide* 394: *Honk around.* To fly aimlessly; to "bore holes."

honkatonk var. HONKY-TONK.

honked [off] *adj.* [perh. alter. of HACKED (OFF)] *Stu.* angry. Hence **honk off**, *v.* to anger.

    1958 J. Davis *College Vocab.* 8: *Honked off*—Angry. **1959** Maier *College Terms* 5: *Honked off*—mad. **1970** *Nat. Lampoon* (Aug.) 6: I just saw Mike Wadleigh's *Woodstock* at the thee-ay-ter, and boy, am I honked off. *Ibid.* (Sept.) 55: Well, because I watched Ed Sullivan, she wouldn't let me have a fruit cup, which as you can imagine, really honked me off at the old bitch. **1972** R. Barrett *Lovomaniacs* 153: I was honked at her. **1973** *Luke Cage—Hero for Hire* (comic) (Feb.) 5: D.W.'s uncle gonna be honked off enough as it is—. **1976** Univ. Tenn. student: He

was pretty honked off. **1980** *Bosom Buddies* (ABC-TV): You know what really honks me off? I could do the job better than she could! **1980** Lorenz *Guys Like Us* 24: It was…to honk off the Major who, he knew, would be watching. *Ibid.* 54: Let me say, gentlemen, that I am honked. **1986** Merkin *Zombie Jamboree* 40: That's what I was so honked off about. **1994** *Simpsons Comics* (No. 2) 4: Wow! Principal Skinner is really honked this time!

honked up *adj. Stu.* excited.

    1968–70 *Current Slang III & IV* 54: *Get honked up*, v. To become excited or agitated.—College students…New Hampshire. **1973** *Penthouse* (May) 111: I'm really honked up over a girl.

honker *n.* **1.** Esp. *Hunting.* a goose, esp. a wild goose.

    *a***1841** in *DAE*: We have killed wild geese…a glorious gaggle of honkers. **1884** in *DAE*: My First Honker. **1888** in *OED2*: *Branta canadensis*…Honker or Old Honker in recognition of its hoarse notes or "honking." **1926** Norwood *Other Side of Circus* 151: I've been training the old honkers there for going on twenty years. **1948** in *DA*: Honkers were winging their way south in high Vs. **1962** Kesey *Cuckoo's Nest* 86: Canada honkers up there. **1974** Loken *Come Monday Mornin'* 111: The big honkers headin' home. **1979** Hassler *Simon's Day* 5: Shot four big honkers that year. **1991** *Wkly. World News* (Apr. 23) 19: Baby geese…Orphaned honkers.

2.a. a person's nose, esp. if large.

    1942 *ATS* 150: Nose…*honker.* **1973** (quot. at SNOT-BOX). **1981** *Taxi* (ABC-TV): Nose? I've got a honker here that won't quit. **1985** Ark. man, age *ca*35: I'm gonna bash your honker. **1985** B. Breathed, in *Daily Beacon* (Univ. Tenn.) 7: I must've slept on my honker wrong. **1986** R. Campbell *In La-La Land* 179: She got a honker like a bugle. **1987** *Golden Girls* (NBC-TV): The air is free so you might as well have a big honker and suck up all you can. *****1994** Lackey, Marcil et al. *Trashcan* (unp.): Fix me honker. **1996** *N.Y. Observer* (May 20) 19: They've…readjusted their noses, or "honkers," in the words of one [plastic] surgeon.

b. the penis, esp. if large.—usu. considered vulgar.

    *a***1972** B. Rodgers *Queens' Vernacular* 211: *Penis immensus*…honker. **1986** *UTSQ*: Penis…*honker.*

c. usu. *pl.* a woman's breasts, esp. if large.

    1974 N.Y.C. banker, age 27: At Princeton we used to say, "She's got some honkers." This was in 1965–69. **1988** *Wonder Years* (ABC-TV): She's got honkers out to here! **1991** *Married with Children* (Fox-TV): A long-legged Nordic beauty with big honkers. **1994** *Wash. Post* (June 9) C10: Whenever a smart, independent woman tries to gain the respect she deserves, all anyone can think of is to comment on her honkers.

3. *Jazz.* a brass player, esp. if unskilled.

    1963 Braly *Shake Him* 17: "These cats are honkers," he said mockingly. *Ibid.:* I'm not going to blow with honkers. **1972** Hannah *Geronimo Rex* 167: You could get B.B. King and a lot of other fine pluckers and honkers on it. **1972** in *OED2*: Others in the R & B field…are just dismissed as "honkers."

4. a very fast vehicle.

    1975 *Sing Out!* (July) 8: There's nobody there now, they are all on this honker. **1976** *Webster's Sports Dict.* 217: *Honker. Drag Racing* an especially fast car. **1980** Pearl *Pop. Slang* 72: *Honker n.* (auto racing) a particularly speedy car.

5. *Stu.* an offensive or unattractive person.

    1978 *UTSQ*: [Unattractive male]…dog,…*honker.* **1982** Pond *Valley Girl* 58: *Honker*—Someone weird. **1982** L. Glass *Valley Girl* 58: Shine that…honker. *a***1989** Spears *NTC Dict.* 185: Merton is a classic honker. *a***1990** Univ. Tenn. student: A *honker* is a socially unpleasant individual.

6. a gob of expelled phlegm or mucus; HOCKER.

    1981 *Easyriders* (Oct.) 82: She snorted a green honker into my trusty headrag. *a***1990** in *Maledicta* X 32: *Honker*…a chunk of sputum coughed up and expectorated. **1991** Marcinko & Weisberg *Rogue Warrior* 55: "Honker?" I'd clear my nose into his cup.

7. *Black E.* HONKY.[2]—usu. used contemptuously.

    1982 Heat Moon *Blue Hwys.* 103: Two honkies sit watchin'. I ask if the machine was broke, and one honker says it takes thirty cents now.…Other honker says, [etc.].

honking *adj.* [prob. sugg. by HONK, *v.,* 6] very drunk.

    a*1984** Partridge *DSUE* (ed. 8). **1987** Univ. Tenn. student theme: *Honking,* inebriated, wasted.

honk job *n.* the act of squeezing another's penis.—usu. considered vulgar. cf. HONK, *v.*, 8.

> **1974** Kingry *Monk & Marines* 169: Snoopy was giving a honk job to Bartholomew.

honk-out *n. Stu.* (see quot.).

> **1931** *AS* VI 204: *He's a honk-out:* he's a failure.

honky[1] *n. Hunting.* a wild goose.

> **1929** *AS* (Oct.) 73: "Canadian Honkies" are geese from Canada.

honky[2] *n.* [dial. pron. of HUNKY, l.b.] *Black E.* a white person.—usu. used contemptuously. [The second 1946 quot. is presumably either an overly specific def. or a reflection of HUNKY, l.a.]

> **1946** Mezzrow & Wolfe *Really Blues* 185 [ref. to 1930's]: Man, I'm down with it, stickin' like a honky. *Ibid.* 306: *Honky:* factory hand. **1958** Douglas & Smith *Defiant Ones* (film): [You're a] nigger....I'm a honky. You don't have to argue me out of it. **1967** *Time* (Aug. 4) 17: Damning Lyndon Johnson for sending "honky* cracker federal troops into Negro communities to kill black people," Brown called the President "a wild mad dog, an outlaw from Texas"....*Honky, or honkie, is a black-power word for any white man, derived from the derogatory "Hunkie"—Hungarian. **1968** Gover *JC* 122: Them honkies come on like some kinda mad dogs. **1968** G. Edwards *Urban Frontier* 20: It was only a logical step from this premise to the advocacy of hatred of "whitey" or "the honkies." **1969** Linn & Pearl *Masque of Honor* 189: Get the honkies! **1970** *Nat. Lampoon* (Apr.) 12: In white suburbia, the kids are happily helping honkey dad polish up the Country Square and the brass flamingo. **1970** in *BDNE:* Even the name Indian is not ours—it was given us by dumb honky. **1971** *Black Scholar* (Sept.) 41: Why didn't you knock that honky mothafucka out? **1971** Wynn *Glass House* (film): He's a honkie. **1974** N.Y.C. security guard, age *ca*22: [In St. Louis in the early 1960's] *honky* meant a dirty, low-down white man. *Honky* or *peckerwood,* same thing. **1978** *NBC's Saturday Night* (NBC-TV): He's my favorite honky. **1967–80** Folb *Runnin' Lines* 242: *Honky, honky beast.* White person (especially derogatory). **1980** L. Fleischer & C. Gore *Fame* 180: Some middle-aged honkie with a gut made of blubber. *a*1981 D. Travis *Black Chicago* 42 [ref. to 1930's]: My father or his brother Joe...would have advised me to "punch the honkies in the mouth." *Ibid.* 64: I wouldn't have hit that honky if he hadn't threatened to beat my black ass. *a*1982 Naylor *Women of Brewster Place* 51: You couldn't trust those honky lawyers. **1985** *Diff'rent Strokes* (ABC-TV): So long, honky! **1990** Helms *Proud Bastards* 81: Hell, they call us "crackers" or "honkies." **1990** Crow Dog & Erdoes *Lakota Woman* 9: In a free-for-all with honkies I can...do real damage. **1996** McCumber *Playing off Rail* 174: They like honkies like you up there, want to play pool for big money.

honky-tonk *n.* [rhyming compound of imit. orig.; the Suffolk dial. *honky-donks* 'hobnailed shoes' (E. FitzGerald, *Medley* (1869), p. 87) is prob. a coincidence] **1.** Orig. *West.* a disreputable, usu. small, establishment where liquor, gambling, and (*esp.* in early use) prostitutes are available; a cheap dance hall, casino, or saloon; (*hence*) a tawdry bar or nightclub. Now *S.E.* Also (*obs.*) **honkatonk.**

> **1894** in *DA:* The honk-a-tonk last night was well attended by ballheads, bachelors and leading citizens. **1899–1900** Cullen *Tales* 353: Youse ain't bin rolled none aroun' dis honkatonk. **1911** Bronson-Howard *Enemy to Society* 119: The honkatonk-postgraduate course of "singing waiter." **1917** in Rudwick *Race Riot* 210: Aunt Kate's Honkytonk. Something Doing Every Hour. **1918** *Variety* (Apr. 5) 10: In 1916 flamboyant violations of various honky-tonks attracted the attention of the newspapers to the cabaret situation. **1927** Kennedy *Gritny People* 44: Y'all take my house for a honky tonk? **1927** Sandburg *Amer. Songbag* 232: It was moaned by resonant moaners in honky tonks of the southwest. **1928** M. Sharpe *Chi. May* 287: *Honky-tonk*—gaudy saloon with back-room hangout. **1929** Hostetter & Beesley *Racket* 228: *Honky tonk*—Low place of amusement; any place where entertainment can be had and liquor purchased. **1930** Graham & Graham *Queer People* 8: A tempestuous Mexican girl who had lately abandoned a Tia Juana honky-tonk for a career on the screen. **1931** Lake *Wyatt Earp* 71 [ref. to 1880's]: The frontier bordellos—honky-tonks or hurdy-gurdies, they were called. **1931** *AS* VII (Oct.) 29: *Honkytonk...n.* A disorderly house. **1935** Pollock *Und. Speaks* (unp.): *Honkey tonk,* an underworld dance hall in which female entertainers are employed. **1936** R. Adams *Cowboy Lingo* 179: Some of the women

were not exempt, especially those of the honkatonks and resorts. **1938** Abbott & Smith *Pointed Them North* 26 [ref. to *a*1880]: I told him I was keeping a girl at one of the honky-tonks for a mistress. **1949** Gruber *Broken Lance* 8: I've kissed better'n her in honky-tonks. **1950** A. Lomax *Mr. Jelly Roll* 50: These honkey-tonks ran wide open twenty-four hours a day and it was nothing for a man to be drug out of one of them dead. **1954** Lindner *50 Min. Hr.* 41: Here, on both sides of the street, for a quarter of a mile, the gin mills and honky-tonks even at this early hour literally shook with activity. **1960** Archibald *Jet Flier* 32: Times Square and the honky-tonk stretch of West Forty-Second Street. **1970** Boatright & Owens *Derrick* 90 [ref. to 1920's]: They had what we called a honky-tonk down there....They had about fifteen or twenty girls. **1978** in Curry *River's in Blood* 173 [ref. to 1920's]: What it was built for was a honky tonk. Every time a boat came by...the girls would come out, and they'd heist their dresses up and shake it up for us...as we went by. **1990** Steward *Bad Boys* 21: The honkytonk section...was a real skidrow.

2. *Theat.* a small, usu. disreputable, vaudeville or burlesque theater.

> **1925** *AS* I 36: "I was playin' the sticks...the honky-tonks," explains Ovinda, modestly. **1927–29** W.N. Burns *Tombstone* 31: Nightly the Bird Cage Opera House offered "stupendous attractions," and nightly the famous old honky-tonk was packed to the doors. **1965** Bonham *Durango St.* 170: Bibbs's street was...lined with pawnshops and honky-tonk theaters.

honky-tonk *adj.* second-rate; RINKY-DINK.

> **1978** Pici *Tennis Hustler* 166: Not running off to every honky-tonk [tennis] tournament.

honky-tonk *v.* to frequent HONKY-TONKS, 1.

> **1958** *Jour. Social Issues* XIV (No. 3) 11: "Honky-tonkin'"; "goin' out on the town"; "bar hoppin'." **1963–64** Kesey *Great Notion* 142: Hank ain't above honky-tonking some. **1972** *Playboy* (Dec.) 164: A yellow-haired wife who had honky-tonked one time too many. **1973** Gent *N. Dallas* 216: We're goin' honky-tonkin'.

honky-tonker *n. West.* a woman employed in a HONKY-TONK, 1.

> **1966** "T. Pendleton" *Iron Orchard* 132: He looked upon honky-tonkers as harpies who preyed on lonely sex-starved oil-field hands and gave nothing in return.

honyock var. HUNYAK.

honyocker *n.* [*honyock,* var. of HUNYAK + *-er*] *No. Plains.* **1.** a homesteader or nester; (*broadly*) a yokel; boor.—used contemptuously. Also vars.

> **1912** in Brunvand *Readings in Folklore* 301: Don't ask me my name, a honyocker I am. **1919** S. Lewis *Free Air* 106: I got plenty of money!...I could buy out half these Honyockers! **1922** *DN* V 181: *Honyocker,* n. A Dakota cattleman. **1941** *Sat. Eve. Post* (June 7) 29 [ref. to *ca*1877]: "Honyocks," the Yankee neighbors called them. "Honyocker" came to be a name generally applied to any farmer who tries to raise grain and livestock in the high prairies of the Northwest. **1958** H.B. Allen, in *PADS* (No. 30) 8: Occurring...only [in] the western Dakotas—is the invidious term *honyocker,* applied some 70 years ago to the incoming homesteaders by the resentful cattle ranchers. It is probably related to *honyock,* a pejorative found also in the eastern United States but here in the Upper Midwest...it designates a boorish or uncouth farmer of foreign background. *Honyocker* (rarely *honyock*) was applied...to anyone who fenced in the open range....New Englanders..., for example, were so called by the cattlemen. **1958** Bard & Spring *Horse Wrangler* 160: Some of the Honyockers were riding work horses....Some of the calves belonged to Honyocker cows. **1979** Jenison *Kingdom in Sage* 15: Listen, honyocker,...Mr. Brett's told you you ain't wanted in here. **1996** *New Yorker* (May 20) 70: "Honyockers!" Mr. Brown laughed....What [the word] effectively does is to travesty the word "homesteader" syllable by syllable, and render the homesteaders themselves as ridiculous oafs, saps, and dimwits. It gathers up all the anger and contempt that the [Montana] ranchers felt for the newcomers.

2. HUNYAK, 1.

> **1949** (quot. at HUNYAK, 1).

hooch[1] or **hootch** *n.* [< Tlingit *hoochinoo,* a distilled liquor made by the Hoochinoo Indians of Alaska] **1.** illicitly distilled whiskey; (*broadly*) any alcoholic beverage, esp. if homemade.

> [**1869** in *Seal & Salmon Fisheries* IV 60: The natives manufacture by distillation from molasses a vile, poisonous life and soul destroying

decoction called "hoochenoo."] **1897** Hayne *Klondyke* 91: The manufacture of "hooch"...is undertaken by the saloon-keepers themselves. **1898** in J. London *Short Stories* 17: Hain't fergot the *hooch* we-uns made on the Tanana. **1913–15** Van Loan *Taking the Count* 158: Synthetic hooch, made of something almost as good. **1915** H.L. Wilson *Ruggles* 99: It would help...to...get a few shots of hooch under their belts. **1918** *Radiator* (Aug. 15) 2: John Barleycorn, my hooch. **1922** Colton & Randolph *Rain* 60: Well, now that it's settled where I flop, let's all have a shot of hooch. **1922** S. Lewis *Babbitt* 116: I found a place where I can get all the hooch I want at eight a quart. **1921–25** Gleason & Taber *Is Zat So?* 49: Uncle Eddie's old man *died* from too much *bum hooch.* **1927** Niles *Singing Soldiers* 126: When I had only five francs left, I spent it fur a bottle of cheap hooch. **1928** Heyward *Mamba's Daughters* 258: Can't you even take a drink o' hooch? **1946** Wead & Sheekman *Blaze of Noon* (film): I won't have anyone spillin' hooch on it. **1951** Pryor *The Big Play* 23: I know a joint where the hooch ain't *pure* fusil oil—jest about half. **1953** Nickerson *Ringside Jezebel* 73: Can't you stay off the hooch for a night? **1959** Cochrell *Barren Beaches* 141: Roger. Go on in and I'll fetch the hooch. **1960** Jordan & Marberry *Fool's Gold* 68 [ref. to 1899]: A well-known citizen was arrested for selling hooch to the Eskimos. **1984** Trotti *Phantom* 132: Failure to do so is an automatic bottle of hootch for the LSO. **1989** *Dream Street* (NBC-TV): You don't have a weakness for the hooch, do you? **1991** G. Trudeau *Doonesbury* (synd. cartoon strip) (Mar. 14): We've been drinkin' hooch made of glass cleaner. *a*1994 H. Roth *Mercy of Rude Stream* 250: They're gettin' the hooch out.

2. nonsense.

   1920–21 Witwer *Leather Pushers* 5: Gettin' a occasional line of hooch about you in the papers. **1970** in *DARE: When you think that the thing somebody has just said is silly or untrue: "Oh, that's a lot of"...Hooch.*

3. Esp. *Stu.* marijuana; (*broadly*) any illicit drug.

   1972 Eble *Campus Slang* (Oct.) 3: *Hooch*—marijuana. **1977** (cited in Spears *Drugs & Drink* 266). **1988** *N.Y. Times* (June 4) 36: Reefer...weed...*hooch*...grass...[mean] marijuana. **1992** N. Russell *Suicide Charlie* 75 [ref. to Vietnam War]: Sergeant Miller was smoking hootch with some blond-haired...American mama-san. **1994** *Newsweek* (Dec. 19) 45: Five pounds of cocaine...had been crudely implanted in the [dog's] abdomen....A New Jersey man...tried to claim the hooch-filled pooch.

hooch² or **hootch** *n.* **1.** HOOTCHY-KOOTCHY, 1.—usu. used attrib.

   1915 *Variety* (June 4) 5: You can get a better hootch...on State Street. **1926** Tully *Jarnegan* 203: The old boy had wanted the little girl to do the hootch dance for him. **1927** W. Winchell, in *Bookman* (Dec.) 378: [Broadway] is a sublimated Coney Island or county fair, with its...peep shows,...skating rinks, hooch dances, freaks and fol-de-rol. **1929** E. Caldwell *Bastard* 28: And we...engaged a hooch dancer for a little private performance....A little hooch, you know—that's the first thing. **1944** Micheaux *Mrs. Wingate* 269: Edrina was now doing an imitation of the hootch which...*stopped the show.* **1986** M. Howard *Expensive* 192: The cops have caught her hooch show operating without a license.

2. HOOTCHY-KOOTCHY, 2.

   *a*1986 *NDAS: Hooch*...Sexual activity.

hooch³ or **hootch** *n.* [pidgin < Japn *uchi* 'house'] *Mil. in E. Asia.* **1.** a usu. small Asian house or dwelling; (often *specif.*) a peasant shack or hut. Orig. **hoochie.**

   *ca*1952 in O. Brand *Out of the Blue* (LP recording): When you're in Seoul City, whatever your plan,/Stay away from Lee's hootchie; sit flat on your can. **1953** in Cray *Erotic Muse* 133: I went to her *hootchie.* **1955–56** in *AS* XXXV (1960) 264: Taksan years ago, skoshi Cinderella-san lived in hootchie with sisters,...hava-no social life. *Ibid.* 265: Cindy-san...rush off to Seoul to hootchie of...prince. **1962** Tregaskis *Viet. Diary* 253: A lot of hooches (native huts or houses). **1964** *Time* (Oct. 16) 48: A Hooch is Not a Home....The G.I. gets his "key money" back at the end of his tour by selling the hooch, complete with furniture and moose [prostitute] to an incoming soldier. **1964** in *DAS* (Supp.) 690: *Hooches*—The huts woven from banana leaves and roofed with straw or corrugated tin that are the standard housing for Vietnamese outside the cities. **1966** *N.Y. Times Mag.* (Oct. 30) 102: You have hootch (house)? **1968** Cameron *Dragon's Spine* 151: Nearby hootches on their bamboo stilt legs. **1969** *Newsweek* (Dec. 8) 33: We had about seven or eight people that we was gonna put into the hootch (hut). **1977** Natkin & Fume *Boys in Co. C* (film): We'll search and clear all the hooches, all the rice piles,

everything. **1980** Santoli *Everything* 207: So when we would go in, I'd be barefoot, I would move up to a hootch....they're not expecting Americans. **1980** W.C. Anderson *Bat-21* 62: They were heading directly for the nearest hooch at the edge of the village. **1982** Del Vecchio *13th Valley* 7: Villages with thousands of children and hundreds of peasant hootches. **1983** Ehrhart *VN-Perkasie* 183: It was really a small walk-up hooch made of plywood....The outhouse was built on high stilts. **1984** J. Fuller *Fragments* 143: Tuyet's hootch was the sixth in line. **1984–87** Ferrandino *Firefight* 39: The detail poured gas on the hooches.

2.a. any small, usu. makeshift structure used, esp. for sleeping and shelter, by troops in the field; a dugout, tent, roofed emplacement, etc., esp. one's own. Orig. **hoochie.**

   1952 in *OED2:* The "hoochie" is a GI term for a bunker or a prepared defensive position. *1952–53 in Forty War in Korea* 113: The hutchie [was] a square hole...just long enough for a bedroll, and two feet wider. Within...was a drip-fed fire...and a chimney of...ammunition cases. *Ibid.:* The men who had been told to stay under cover, in case the enemy shelled the area, sat in the doorways of the "Hoochies"...waiting for the guns to start. *1953 in Partridge DSUE* (ed. 7): *Hoochie* or *hoochy* [a temporary shelter]. *1954 in OED2:* In its final stages, the war in Korea yielded a number of new terms, among them the British soldier's name for a dugout—a *Hoochie.* **1966** in Russ *Happy Hunting Ground* 46: The wind blew down several hootches (pup tents). **1978** J. Webb *Fields of Fire* 413: A Marine poncho hootch. **1984** Hammel *Root* 126: Between the blast wall and the command hooch. **1985** Bodey *F.N.G.* 30: A hooch is a hole. Its upper sides and roof are layers of sandbags....On these walls lie timbers. **1984–87** Ferrandino *Firefight* 168: "We gotta make some kind of a hooch."...They snapped ponchos together and tied the hoods tight. **1987** D. da Cruz *Boot* 301: *Hootch* two-man field tent. **1984–88** in Berry *Where Ya Been?* 211 [ref. to 1951]: I dug a hole where I put the machine gun. Then I started to dig a hooch for myself. **1988** von Hassell & Crossley *Warriors* 165: A poncho stretched between two trees as a primitive rain shelter is also a hootch.

b. a military Quonset hut, barracks tent, or usu. semipermanent barracks; (*hence*) a soldier's living quarters; (*broadly*) any more or less temporary military structure.

   1960 in *Sat. Review* LI (Oct. 26, 1968) 35: Twas the night before Christmas, and all through our hootch/Not a creature was stirring, not even the pooch. **1960–63** in *AS* LX (1985) 372: *Hooch honcho,* the NCO in charge of a barracks. **1963** *Sat. Eve. Post* (July 27) 25: A house or barracks is still called "hooch" (from the Japanese word for house, *uchi*). Not one GI in 10 knows the origin. **1964** in *DAS* (Supp.) 690: *Hooches*....Some Americans have appropriated the term for their own quonset-styled barracks. **1965** Bryan *P.S. Wilkinson* 31: He would be at the major's hooch if he was needed. "Well, Wilkinson," Major Sturgess said as Wilkinson came into his rooms. "It's nice of you to join us." **1967** Ford *Muc Wa* 38: The chow hall, like all the hooches in camp..., was an airy building with a high-pitched tin roof, a concrete floor, and walls that were sand-bagged to shoulder height. **1968** *Sat. Review* (Aug. 28) 35: "Hootch"...is used universally here in Vietnam to describe any dwelling, including our own. **1970** *Black Scholar* (Nov.) 14: 60 per cent wanted to live in all-black hootches or barracks. **1973** Karlin, Paquet & Rottmann *Free Fire Zone* 177: Joshua glanced around at the interior of the hootch. Ten evenly lined cots under bare tin walls. **1978** Hasford *Short-Timers* 62: I meet...Daytona Dave...at the...enlisted men's hootch. **1982** Del Vecchio *13th Valley* 49: The hootches were all the same....The standard [plywood] building was sixteen feet wide and thirty-two feet long. **1982** Goff, Sanders & Smith *Bros.* 93: We saw the CO come down from the colonel's hootch. **1983** Groen & Groen *Huey* 12 [ref. to 1970]: Each officer [in the makeshift barracks] lived in his own eight-by-ten cubicle called a hootch. Hootches were furnished with single beds and...wooden wardrobes. **1984** Riggan *Free Fire* 7: I've been assigned to his hooch, a large tent stretched over a wooden frame that serves as sleeping quarters. **1991** *N.Y. Times* (nat. ed.) (Jan. 29) A4: Soldiers in their bunkers and prefabricated "hooches."

hooched *adj.* drunk.

   1922 Colton & Randolph *Rain* 60: "Not that you'll need it, Sadie," said he, "you were born hootched." **1942** *ATS* 123: Drunk...*hooched (up),...hopped (up),* [etc.].

hooch girl *n. Mil. in Vietnam.* a young Vietnamese woman working as a maid or laundress at a military base camp. Now *hist.* Also **hooch honey.**

    1981 Former U.S. Navy yeoman, age 32 [ref. to 1970]: The *hootch honeys* were the Vietnamese girls who used to do cleaning and stuff. **1985** J.M.G. Brown *Rice Paddy Grunt* 75: The hootch girls...worked for the Americans...at Phu Loi, doin' laundry an' cleaning. **1992** N. Russell *Suicide Charlie* 120 [ref. to 1968]: Hootch girls, cold beer, swimming pools.

hoochie[1] see s.v. HOOCH[3].

hoochie[2] *n.* [prob. HOOCH,[1] 3 + *-ie*] *Stu.* marijuana.

    1973 *TULIPQ* (coll. B.K. Dumas): Marijuana—*hoochie*. **1977** in Rice *Adolescent* 273: *Hoochie*—pot, grass, weed.

hoochie[3] var. HOOTCHIE.

hood[1] /hʊd/ or (esp. Midwest) /hud/ *n.* **1.** HOODLUM, 1.

    1880 in *AS* XLIX (1974) 298: The "hood" who had perpetrated the outrage—a young man of twenty—was pointed out, and the steward went forth...to give him battle. **1929** Hostetter & Beesley *Racket* 228: *Hood*—Hoodlum; tough character, a criminal with or without a record, or one of criminal tendencies or associations. (Pronounced "Hōōd.") **1930** G. Rosener *Doorway to Hell* (film): Hood [pron. /hud/]. **1930** Pasley *Al Capone* 241: A hoodlum was a hood, the oo pronounced as in fool. **1930** *Amer. Mercury* (Dec.) 456: Hood, n.: A criminal. "None of those St. Louis hoods are going to cut in here, see?" **1931** *Sat. Review* (July 18) 978: Crooks speak of an ordinary thief as a "hood." This is undoubtedly short for hoodlum. **1933–35** D. Lamson *About to Die* 195: It's part of your business to know them things if you're a hustler or a thief or a hood. **1935** in R. Nelson *Dishonorable* 243: Don't you call those boys hoodlums!...And I suppose Giuseppe is a hood. **1938** Bellem *Blue Murder* 15: But I wouldn't hire out to croak anybody in cold blood. I'm no hood. **1950** E. Felton *Narrow Margin* (film): What kind of a dame would marry a hood? **1951** in Kriegel *Myth of Manhood* 178: They were high-school hoods. **1955** Q. Reynolds *HQ* 51: The way to treat those young hoods is to throw them in the can. **1959** Farris *Harrison High* 12: He looks like a hood to me. **1966** in *Amer. Jour. Soc.* LXXII (1967) 462: "Hoods" are the sort of people who do not care about their grades, about their personal appearance, about morals, etc. **1972** Singer *Boundaries* 416: Somehow I feel on the side of the officers, yet I help the hoods. *a*1988 D. Smith *Firefighters* 129: Some young hoods stole a rig from a fire scene. **1991** J. Dwyer *Subway Lives* 135: A gang of school-age hoods ran a robbery ring in the Bronx.

    2. *West.* (see quot.).

    1933 J.V. Allen *Cowboy Lore* 61: *Hood.* Man who drives the "Hoodlum" wagon.

hood[2] *n.* Esp. *Black E.* a neighborhood, esp. in a city.

    1967 (cited in *W10*). **1968** in *Trans-action* VI (Feb. 1969) 27: He come back over to the hood (neighborhood). **1970** Quammen *Walk the Line* 54: Greedy ol' cracker holdouts who seen their 'hoods go but wouldn't give up their house to no niggers. **1971** in E. Leacock *Culture of Poverty* 303: A strange youth comes into the school or "hood" (neighborhood). **1972** Grogan *Ringolevio* 54: There was this guy in the hood. **1986** *Miami Vice* (NBC-TV): Man, you can't be from his hood and *not* know how to mix it up. **1986** *Stingray* (NBC-TV): The trash don't care nothin' for a brother from the hood. **1988** *Harper's* (Aug.) 28: We come back to our 'hood and we be talking about how much fun we had. **1992** S. Straight *Been in Sorrow's Kitchen* 275: My hood called the Jungle. **1992** S. Elkin, in *Harper's* (Jan. 1993) 72: This one guy, this neurologist who lived in the hood. **1993** M. Brooks *Robin Hood* (film): Everything turned out good. King Richard's on the throne and Robin's back in the hood.

hoodie *n. Black E.* a hooded shirt or sweatshirt. Also **hoody.**

    1993 in A. Sexton *Rap on Rap* 18: Boo in the blue silk hoody pops up. **1993** *N.Y. Times* (Apr. 13) B6: He spent money on gold chains with crucifixes, rings,...an assortment of Russell hooded sweatshirts called hoodies, gang dues, [etc.]. **1994** *Totally Unoff. Rap Dict.* (vers. 7.21.94): *Hoodie* (n) T-shirt with hood attached to it.

hood-lifter *n.* an automotive mechanic. *Joc.*

    *a*1977 W.I. Little *Trans.-Logistics Dict.* 160: *Hood lifter.* A mechanic.

hoodlum *n.* [< G dial. *Hudellump, Hodalump,* etc. 'a ragamuffin or good-for-nothing'; see J.T. Krumpelmann, "Hoodlum," in *Modern Language Notes* L (1935), pp. 93–95]

1. Orig. *Calif.* a young loafer or street ruffian; (*also*) (esp. in recent use) a thug or gangster. Now *S.E.*

    1871 *Daily Union* (San Diego, Calif.) (Apr. 27) 1: Kelly and Dunn, San Francisco "Hoodlums,"...were arrested at San Jose...Sunday last. *Ibid.* (Aug. 3) 1: Judge Sawyer...sentenced Joseph King, a hoodlum, to a year in the County Jail for stabbing a man named Bennett. **1872** in M.S. Goldman *Gold Diggers* 61: Boys attending [this theater] regularly will surely become hoodlums. **1872** in *F & H* III 339: All the boys to be trained as...polite loafers, street-hounds, hoodlums, and bummers. **1876** W. Wright *Big Bonanza* 359: A "hoodlum" went into a cigar store in Virginia City one day. **1877** in Bartlett *Amer.* (ed. 4) 293: You at the East have but little idea of the hoodlums of this city [San Francisco]. They compose a class of criminals of both sexes, far more dangerous than are to be found in the Eastern cities. They travel in gangs, and are ready at any moment for the perpetration of any crime. **1877** in *Ibid.*: The stoning and beating of Chinamen, long time a popular recreation among young hoodlums. **1878** Pinkerton *Strikers* 410: The "hoodlums" had fired the Pacific Mail docks. **1879** *Courier-Journal* (Louisville, Ky.) (Jan. 28) 4: Mr. Williamson as the "hoodlum"...and Mrs. Williamson as *Biddy* demonstrated their unusual versatility. **1881** in *DA*: The hoodlums of San Francisco are young embryo criminals—regularly organized gangs of boys and girls. **1881** in Leitner *Diamond in Rough* 130: No San Francisco hoodlums could have made a worse showing, on the same ground. ***1886 in *OED2*: A miscellaneous assortment of hoodlums and corner men, anxious to profit by the excitement generated in Trafalgar-square. **1890** in Ownby *Subduing Satan* 133: The heathenish hoodlums began shooting their pistols. **1898** in J. London *Letters* 7: A bunch of brute hoodlums on a street corner. **1891–1900** in Hoyt *Five Plays* 123: Some pack of hoodlums in that next room! **1913** J. London *Valley of Moon* 8: An' a lot of young hoodlums makin' eyes at you. **1914** T.P. Bailey *Race Ortho.* 197: The typical hoodlum "grows" in the town. **1941** Mahin & Grant *Johnny Eager* (film): One hoodlum more or less doesn't matter anyway. **1945** I. Brecher & F. Finklehoffe *Meet Me in St. Louis* (film): "She's such a sweet little thing." "Sweet? She's a hoodlum!" **1968** "H. King" *Box-Man* 5 [ref. to *ca*1915]: I was affiliated with a crew...called the Hoodlums—the hoods. They lived south of Market Street in San Francisco. **1973** P. Heller *In This Corner* 20: He is credited with eliminating much of the hoodlum element from California boxing.

    2. HOODLUM WAGON, 2.

    1909 in *DA*: The outfit was engaged in packing the chuck-wagon and the hoodlum.

hoodlum wagon *n.* **1.** a police patrol wagon.

    1893 in Dreiser *Jour.* I 161: That gentleman was carted off...in a hoodlum wagon. **1936** Moffitt & Solkow *Murder with Pictures* (film): Take me to headquarters. I want to ride in your hoodlum wagon. **1943** Guthrie *Bound for Glory* 357: A big long black hoodlum wagon drove up and fifteen or twenty big cops fell out with all of the guns and sticks and clubs it would take to win a war. **1965–67** in *DARE*.

2. *West.* an auxiliary wagon used to carry supplies, as on a cattle drive; (*also*) (see 1935 quot.).

    1908 in *DA*: The jolting of the hoodlum wagon now focused the herd's attention. **1920** J.M. Hunter *Trail Drivers* I 299: A second wagon for carrying the extra beds and bringing wood and water into camp...is called the hoodlum wagon. **1932** in *AS* (Feb. 1933) 29: *Hoodlum wagon.* A wagon in addition to the chuck wagon for carrying wood, water, and extra supplies. **1933** J.V. Allen *Cowboy Lore* 12: The hoodlum wagon [is] loaded with spare saddles, ropes, branding irons, tools, tents, and the men's blanket rolls. **1935** J. Conroy *World to Win* 73: Leo had to jump to dodge hoodlum wagons, trucks with two large wheels in the center and a small one on each end, pushed by men with their heads down.

hoodoo[1] *n.* [perh. var. of *hoedown*] *West.* a lavish celebration or drinking party. Now *hist.*

    1880 in M. Lewis *Frontier* 129: But in all public hoodoos it is a parliamentary rule for anybody as wants to ax questions to rise up an' fire them off. **1882** Beadle *West. Wilds* 558: If you can find an Indian tradition to match it, your "hoodoo" is complete. **1979** E. West *Saloon* 64 [ref. to 1870's]: He might...open the spring mining season with a "hoodoo" featuring whiskey on the house.

hoodoo[2] *n.* [app. alter. of *voodoo*] **1.** a malign spell; curse; (*hence*) a run of bad luck; WHAMMY.—also used attrib. Now *S.E.*

    1883 (cited in P. Dickson, *Baseball Dict.* 210). **1889** in *Century Dict.*:

The prospect of pleasing his party and at the same time escaping a hoodoo must be irresistibly attractive. **1889** in *OED2*: Friday, September 13…that hoodoo date. **1894** in *OED2*: Superstitious persons are likely to think that T.J. starts in his race against B. with a heavy handicap, or "hoodoo" in the language of the street. **1896** in *OED2*: Means to exorcise the hoodoo which makes so much trouble for the battleship Texas. **1906** *Nat. Police Gaz.* (Aug. 11) 6: Famous French Beauties…Who Have Hoodoos. **1929–33** J. Lowell *Gal Reporter* 25: The hoodoo that has pursued Gloucester fishing schooners once they…indulge in racing for money. **1933** Saunders & Hanemann *Ace of Aces* (film): "There goes another new pilot." "What do you want to bet he won't come back?" "Shut up! Do you want to put the hoodoo on him?" **1956** Moran & Reid *Tugboat* 107: They remembered the hoodoo of sailing on Christmas. **1972** in P. Dickson *Baseball Dict.* 210: Cuellar Authority on Whammies and Hoodoos. **1994** *Fresh Air* (Nat. Pub. Radio) (June 9): When someone tries to put a hoodoo on me and make me back off, it adds fuel to my fire.

2. a bringer of bad luck; jinx.—also used attrib.

*a***1889** *Century Dict.*: Hoodoo…a person supposed to bring bad luck: opposed to *mascot*. **1893** in B. Matthews *Parts of Speech* 208: A *mascot*, meaning one who brings good luck, and a *hoodoo*, meaning one who brings ill fortune, are terms invented in the theater, it is true. **1900** E.L. Thayer, in M. Gardner *Casey* 33: Flynn…was a hoodoo. **1900** Dunbar *Gideon* 124: If you don't turn out a hoodoo, you're a winner, sure. **1900** Garland *Eagle's Heart* 226: I'm a hoodoo, Cory; nobody is ever in luck when I'm around. **1901** in *DA*: If it's a hoodoo, as you thought, why not throw it away? **1904** in *DA*: It is hard to find a crew for a "hoodoo" ship. Men desert from a vessel with an uncanny reputation. **1911** in Truman *Dear Bess* 58: We ought to take out a little fire insurance though because he's a hoodoo on fires. He was at the Coates when it went up. **1916** in T. Lewis *H. Crane's Letters* 9: We had *English* today and Latin and Geometry are due tomorrow. They are my hoodooes and so I am not a little worried…about the out come. **1924** in *Dict. Canad.* 344: Jake got it into his head that Jacko was a "hoodoo," as he called it. **1932** Hecht & Fowler *Great Magoo* 7: I don't want him loitering around here. He's a hoodoo!

3. *Naut.* a lubberly seaman.

1925 Farmer *Shellback* 106 [ref. to 1890's]: Hoodoo and Shellback have often been represented as grovelling counter-jumpers who never hit back. *Ibid.* 109: They were men who had recently arrived in the country and were seeking employment. These were the "hoodoos." **1929** Bowen *Sea Slang* 68: Hoodoos. Under sail, useless hands who had been shanghaied by the crimps as A.B.'s.

hoodoo *v.* **1.** to bewitch, esp. to afflict with ill luck or disaster; hex.

1886 in *DA*: The surest way to provide against being "hoodooed," as American residents call it, is to open one's pillow from time to time. **1887** in E. Ellis *Dooley's Amer.* 29: Mr. Handy…set himself to the task of hoodooing the Chicago Club with his wit. **1888** in *DAE*: Which is sufficient to hoodoo the organization for the balance of the season. *a***1889** in Barrère & Leland *Dict. Slang* I 470: I'm hoodooed sure as eggs are eggs. I've been training to do that [stage] death all summer, and…now Lil has gone and gobbled my business. **1896** in *OED2*: The coterie of Democrats that hoodooed the Wilson bill. **1902** in Kipling *Traffics & Discoveries* 8: 'Twould have hoodooed my gun for all time. **1908** in Fleming *Unforgettable Season* 114: Something turned up to hoodoo the season. **1912** in Truman *Dear Bess* 71: She would think her visit was hoodooed sure. **1930** Sage *Last Rustler* 27: He either likes this place powerful well or you've got him hoodooed. **1938** "R. Hallas" *You Play the Black* 51: I figured the wheel was hoodooed and the black would come up forever.

2. to swindle; hoodwink.

1897 in *DARE*: Hoodoo…to deceive or cheat in a blustering manner. **1919** R.G. Carter *Ca.G. Carter* 86: The people have been "fooled," "flim-flammed," "hoodooed," or "buncoed" ever since the world begun. **1966–67, 1976** in *DARE*.

hoodoo wagon *n.* *Black E.* HOODLUM WAGON, 1.

1911 *JAF* (Oct.) 359: Carried him off in hoo-doo wagon,/Brought him back wid his feet a-draggin'.

hoody *n.* see s.v. HOODIE.

hoody *adj.* being, resembling, or typical of a hoodlum.

1966 in *Amer. Jour. Soc.* LXXII (1967) 462: "Hoody" life styles. **1980** M. Baker *Nam* 29: There was a part of town where there were a few hoody guys, but I always kept my distance. **1977** *AS* XLIX 299: Certain Chicago phrases like *hoodie boots*, black Oxford shoes with a black suede saddle, or *hoodie clothes* that "greasers" or other small-time hoodlums might wear (both riming with *foodie*). **1980** Rimmer *Album* 29 [ref. to 1965]: Who's that guy, he looks so hoody. **1981–85** S. King *It* 227: A kind of hoody strut.

hooey *n.* [orig. unkn.] **1.** utter nonsense; rubbish. Cf. HOY. See also HORSE HOOEY.

1912 in Kornbluh *Rebel Voices* 76: Same old hooey in St. Looie. **1923** in J. O'Hara *Sel. Letters* 10: I might not like to take hooey from some half-boiled freshman. **1924** P. Marks *Plastic Age* 100: Aw…my prof's full of hooey. **1927** Benchley *Early Worm* 238: Now this is a lot of hooey and I told my father so. **1928** in E. O'Neill *Sel. Letters* 312: Of course I expect this, knowing the original source of all such hooey. **1928** Rice *Street Scene* 577: T' hell wit' all dat hooey! **1929** Millay *Agst. the Wall* 402: What a lot of hooey that was. **1933** Young *Over the Top* 52 [ref. to 1918]: Oh that is a lot of huey. **1934** H. Miller *Tropic of Cancer* 183: That's all hooey. **1934** Cain *Postman Rings Twice* 101: It's just a lot of hooey, that this guy thought up so he could fool the judge. **1942** in F. Brown *Angels & Spaceships* 49: It sounded like a lot of big words to me, and hooey at that. **1946** Hecht *Notorious* (film): It's a lot of hooey. **1971** *Newsweek* (Oct. 25) 84: "I used to be inclined to dismiss Christ as hooey," said Rice. **1974** in *Time* (Jan. 6, 1975) 66: It's all hooey. Columbus never reported seeing white water in the area. **1988** *N.Y. Times Mag.* (Dec. 25) 10: My observation about the reported attacks by Thomas Hoving on the Getty [Museum] is that it's hooey. **1992** *Guiding Light* (CBS-TV): Astrology isn't just a bunch of hooey. **1993** *X-Files* (Fox-TV): UFOs.…Bunch of hooey if you ask me. **1993** G. Lee *Honor & Duty* 212: This is a lot of horse hooey.

2. excrement.

1987 Thain *Cold as Banker's Heart* 86: Hooey is also another term for *road apples* [horse dung].

hoof *n.* a person's foot; (*rarely*) a person's leg or shoe. [Uniquely in *****1675 quot., 'a hand'.]

*****1598** Shakespeare *Merry Wives* I iii: Goe, Trudge; plod away ith' hoofe: seeke shelter, packe. *****ca***1645** in *OED*: The Secretary was put to beat the hoof himself, and Foot it home. [*****1675** in Duffett *Burlesque Plays* 74: With Princely hoof I knock'd.] *****a***1687** in *F & H* III 340: I…bang the hoof incognito. *****1797** in Partridge *Dict. Und.* 341: Hoof, the foot. *****1821** *Real Life in Ireland* 51: Propelled by the…hoof of Brian Boru. *****1834** in *OED*: Contriving…to tread heavily on my toes with his own hoofs. **1839–40** Cobb *Green Hand* I 148: I will slip a noose over his hoof. **1849** Melville *White Jacket* 68: You, Jim, take your hoof off the cloth! **1855** Wise *Tales* 119: The use of those sprawly hoofs and flippers that the devil has given ye. **1874** Carter *Rollingpin* 193: They ramm'd their heads into the beans,/And their hoofs into the hash. **1881** in Sweet *Texas* xvii: "Well, you see," said Bill, putting both hoofs on the table. **1884** in Lummis *Letters* 176: Strips of canvass…supplemented the shoes and kept my hoofs warm. **1884** Baldwin *Yankee School Teacher* 65: When 't comes ter treadin' on a moc'sin wid my bare huf, ole Lucindy'll run like ole Satan hisself. **1895** in J.I. White *Git Along Dogies* 66: I don't see why a cowboy can't get there with both hoofs. **1899** in Davidson *Old West* 154: We could…pound the floor till our hoofs were sore a swingin' the dance house dames. **1917** Oemler *Slippy McGee* 29: Ever hear of a one-hoofed dip? **1925** *Sat. Eve. Post* (Jan. 3) 14: He's tricked out from hat to hoof. **1928** Haycox *Guns Up* 48: I'll drop your horse and leave you on your hoofs. **1929** Booth *Stealing* 180: Stick your hoof up here, Eighteen, an' I'll turn you loose. **1934** H. Roth *Call It Sleep* 338: Give us yer hoof. **1962** T. Berger *Reinhart in Love* 196: "Izzat right," asked the guy, jerking his artificial hoof. **1970** *Current Slang* III & IV 69: *Hoofs*, n. Shoes, feet—College females, New Hampshire. **1983** Kaplan & Smith *One Last Look* 171: If you bums hadda been taught by us how to use parachutes, you mighta had fewer broken hooves. **1991** *Married with Children* (Fox-TV): I shoved her hoof into a shoe.

¶ In phrases:

¶ **on the hoof** *Restaurant.* (of meat) cooked rare.

*a***1983** Mariani *Dict. Food & Drink* 239: On the hoof. Meat done rare. **1985** N.Y.C. woman, age *ca*50: I always order my meat *very* rare. One time [*ca*1963] when I was eating at a lunch counter the waitress called out the order "on the hoof!" **1994** N.Y.C. man, age 59 (coll. J. Sheidlower): *On the hoof* meant "very rare" when I worked at a lunch counter in the late '40's, early '50's. I still hear it all the time.

¶ **pad the hoof** to walk; walk away. Cf. earlier syn. *beat the hoof (ca*1645–1794) in *OED.*

   *1838 C. Dickens *Oliver Twist* ch. ix: Charley Bates expressed his opinion that it was time to pad the hoof. **1866** *Nat. Police Gaz.* (Nov. 17) 3: He watched his opportunity and "padded the hoof." ***1903** J. London *Abyss* 100: "Paddin' the 'oof"…is walking. **1927** *DN* V 457: *Pad the hoof, v.* To walk.

¶ **sling** [or **fling** or **shake**] **a hoof** to dance.

   1847 *Spirit of Times* (Feb. 27) 2: By the catemount! doesn't Suze fling a hoof to the whole compass? **1888** Gordon & Page *Befo' De War* 86: An' dance! Lord, you jes' orter see what a huf/Dat 'ar lame nigger slings, when he tries sho' enuf! *a*1919 in J.A. Lomax *Cattle Trail* 15: A-shakin' our hoofs with the dance hall dames. **1925** S. Lewis *Arrowsmith* 899: How's chances on dragging her out to feed and shake a hoof with Uncle Clif? **1929** in R.E. Howard *Book* 64: Let's shake a hoof, baby.

hoof *v.* **1.** to go on foot; walk or run.—usu. constr. with *it.*

   *1641 in *OED:* I am sorely surbated with the hoofing already. ***1685** in *OED:* I must hoof it away. ***1698–99** "B.E." *Dict. Canting Crew: Hoof it*…to walk on Foot. ***1728** in *OED:* Neither are their women and children (many of which hoof it over those Desarts…) very apt to lag behind. ***1772** in *F & H* III 340: I…must hoof/Up to the poet yonder. ***1785** Grose *Vulgar Tongue:* He hoofed it…every step of the way from Chester to London. **1842** C. Mathews *Puffer Hopkins* 288: The prettiest heifer that ever hoofed it down the Third Avenue. **1865** in Morgan & Michalson *For Our Beloved Country* 201: In preference to hoofing it. **1871** "M. Twain" *Roughing It* 362: They sport the economical Kanaka horse or "hoof it" with the plebeians. **1877** E. Wheeler *Deadwood Dick, Prince of the Road* 78: The remainder of the company rode in the wagons or "hoofed it," as best suited their mood. **1877** in Miller & Snell *Why West Was Wild* 327: Jackson "hoofed it" the balance of the way to the camp. **1884** Baldwin *Yankee School Teacher* 64: I'll hoof it down ter King's an' fill my bag. **1885** in *F & H* III 340: These busted theatrical people…are hoofing it back to Detroit. **1885** Siringo *Texas Cowboy* 8: I had to hoof it up there every morning. **1887** Hinman *Si Klegg* 581: Marching was [called] "hoofing it." **1895** Clurman *Nick Carter* 76: Cash Brazen is the worst cuss as hoofs it. **1901** Ade *Modern Fables* 3: When they went out to a Party, he always remarked that it seemed to be a Pleasant Evening and they might as well hoof it. *a*1909 Tillotson *Detective* 92: *Hoof*—To walk. **1910** in O. Johnson *Lawrenceville* 188: Hoof it: you're due at the Doctor's in half an hour. **1918** Witwer *Baseball to Boches* 103: Well, Joe, we hoof it along the roads singin'. **1929–31** Farrell *Young Lonigan* 30: Coady…hoofed it after the dog. **1948** Manone & Vandervoort *Trumpet* 129: Then we started hoofing up the street. **1969** Spetz *Rat Pack Six* 56: C'mon people, on your feet. We gotta get hoofing again. **1973** *N.Y. Times* (Jan. 1) 17: You gotta be jivin' man—you mean from now on we gotta hoof it! **1974** Dubinsky & Standora *Decoy Cop* 89: We hoof it over.

   2. *Theat.* to dance, esp. to tap-dance before an audience.—occ. constr. with *it.* See also HOOFER, 2.

   1916 (implied by HOOFER, 2). **1920** *Variety* (Dec. 31) 8: He glimmed a bare-legged ballet pulling some neat classical hoofing on the floor. **1925** Cohan *Broadway* 71: I…"hoofed" myself blue in the face trying to get their attention. **1925** *AS* I 36: A "hoofing act" is entirely made up of step dancing. **1925** Van Vechten *Nigger Heaven* 13: Le's hoof, Ruby urged. **1926** Dunning & Abbott *Broadway* 218: Hoofing in cabarets. **1927** (quot. at HOOFER, 2). **1927** "S.S. Van Dine" *"Canary" Murder* ch. xvi: I'm apt to be back hoofing it in the chorus again. **1928** McEvoy *Show Girl* 13: Sammy Lee didn't think my hoofing was so hot. **1939** Saroyan *Time of Your Life* I: Harry is hoofing better than ever. **1944** Breslow & Purcell *Follow the Boys* (film): They hired me to hoof in the background. **1959** in Cannon *Nobody Asked* 162: The old Paradise, where Rita hoofed, is no more. **1977** Stallone *Paradise Alley* 21: Y'know, you're a snappy dish. Why're ya still hoofin' at that joint?

hoof-and-mouth disease *n.* a propensity for putting one's foot in one's mouth. Cf. FOOT-IN-MOUTH DISEASE.

   1945 Hubbard *R.R. Ave.* 112: One of their number, Bud McDaniels, had what is sometimes known as "hoof and mouth disease"; he gallivanted around and talked too much. **1963** E.M. Miller *Exile* 227: Damn fool Winsted suffers from hoof-and-mouth disease. Runs around and talks too much.

hoof-covers *n.pl.* boots or shoes. *Joc.* Also **hoof-coverings.**

   1882 *Judge* (Dec. 19) 7: No public shining of hoof-covers. **1899** Stratemeyer *Under Otis* 218: Them's American-made hoof coverin's.

hoofer *n.* one who HOOFS, *specif.:*

   1. a tramp.

   1885 "Lykkejaeger" *Dane* 117: It was a "cold day" for the "hoofer" when he did not transfer a quarter from my pocket to his own dirty fist.

   2. Orig. *Vaudeville.* a dancer, usu. a professional performer such as a tap-dancer.

   1916 *Milwaukee Jour.* (Nov. 3) 18: *Don't you suppose he's hep to the hoofer you were featuring?* Don't you suppose he knew the dancer you had with you? **1915–17** Lait *Gus* 46: Tell that dyin' hoofer she gets the…wine. **1917** *N.Y. Times* (Dec. 23) IV 6: "Hoofer," meaning a dancer.…"It's now in general use, but I heard Billy Emerson use it thirty years ago," said Cressy. **1919** *Variety* (Apr. 4) 23: He was a cabaret hoofer out of a job. **1923** *N.Y. Times* (Sept. 9) VIII 2: *Hoofer:* A dancer; also a heel-beater. **1925** Cohan *Broadway* 145: The expert "hoofers" used to laugh at the idea of anyone saying that I was a good dancer. **1926** Dunning & Abbott *Broadway* 229: Well, hoofer, I guess you'll be looking for a new partner. **1927** *Vanity Fair* (Nov.) 132: The word "hoofer" is show business for dancer. Entertainers who "hoof" used to "hop the buck." **1936** Parker *Battling Hoofer* (film): He's not an actor—he's a hoofer. **1941** Schulberg *Sammy* 82: Sammy looked at us the way a hoofer looks at his audience as he finishes his routine. **1971** *N.Y. Post* (Feb. 16) 49: Jane…said, "Ruby Keeler's a hell of a hoofer." **1994** *New Republic* (Jan. 9, 1995) 40: Among the…hoofers, he was smitten by Rita Greene, who became his dancing partner.

hoogie *n.* [perh. a phonetic spelling of a var. of HOOJAH; perh. directly an alter. of HOOSIER] *Black E.* a white person.—usu. used contemptuously.

   *ca*1970 in *DARE* s.v. *hoosier* 1.b. **1975** G. Jones, in C. Major *Calling Wind* 375: My daddy hate hoogies (up north I hear they call em honkies). **1988** *AS* 63 (Summer) 134: Prison talk.…*Hoojie n.* White inmate (used by black inmates). **1996** Message on Amer. Dialect Soc. electronic mailing list: I have recently heard a word I presume to be Black English:…huji /hoojie? It is supposed to refer to whites.

hoo-ha *n.* [< Yiddish *hu-ha* 'a hullabaloo; uproar'] **1.a.** an uproar or commotion.

   *1931 Brophy & Partridge *Songs & Slang* (ed. 3) 318 [ref. to WWI]: *Hoo-Ha.*—An argument, trouble, hubbub, an artillery "demonstration." "There's a hell of a hoo-ha going on over there." **1959** in *Dict. Canad.* 344: Today there was a hoo-haw about chairs. **1967** *Time* (Mar. 24) 68: The present hoo-ha is simply proportionate to the prize. **1974** *Atlantic* (June) 104: A monument to…its own inadequacies and corporate hooha. **1982** *Harper's* (June) 64: In the ensuing hoohah…Sontag's question was sidestepped. *a*1988 in Terkel *Great Divide* 60: He really expected to get drafted…over this last hoo-ha with Libya. **1992** *Crier & Co.* (CNN-TV) (Apr. 6): Making a lot of hoo-ha about that.

   b. *pl.* intense nervous anxiety; HEEBIE-JEEBIES.—constr. with *the.*

   1932 T.S. Eliot *Sweeney Agonistes* 30: You've had a cream of a nightmare dream and you've got the hoo-ha's coming to you.

   2. empty talk; HOOEY, 1.

   1979 Gutcheon *New Girls* 55: It seemed like so much smug hoohah to me. **1991** *Newsweek* (Jan. 21) 29: Schwarzkopf calls it "a bunch of hoo-hah."

   3. an important or self-important person.

   1984 *Hardcastle & McCormick* (ABC-TV): A bunch of hoo-has who want to make nice-nice with Mario Andretti. **1992** Knoxville, Tenn., woman, age 38: Some big hoo-ha from Washington is coming down to look things over.

hoo-ha *adj.* GAGA, 1.

   1932 Lorimer *Streetcars* 195: He was Stanley Hughes, the handsomest man that ever breathed, that all the girls were who-ha about.

hoojah *n.* [prob. alter. of HOOSIER] *Black E.* a Southern white person; CRACKER, 1.—usu. used contemptuously. Cf. HOOGIE, which may be a var. of this.

   1928 C. McKay *Banjo* 190: The froggies treat you better than the hoojahs, eh?

hoojie see s.v. HOOGIE.

hook *n.* **1.** a fellow.—constr. with *old.* Now *hist.* Also in phr. **whole hook** a good or reliable fellow.

   1827 in Shackford *Crockett* 81: The old hook is going ahead electioneering.…I am…for your father and am a whole hook. *a*1950 in

Shackford *Crockett* 35 [ref. to *ca*1815]: Old hook, from no on *I'll* do the grunting around here.

2.a. usu. *pl.* a finger; (*hence*) a hand or fist.

*1829 in *OED2*: To his clies my hooks I throw in. **1849** Melville *White Jacket* 304: But how did you feel, Jack, when the musket-ball carried away one of your hooks there? **1877** in Asbury *Gem of Prairie* (opp. 144): Provided Long Jerry will keep his hooks out of the Sour-krout until after the "Amen" is reached. ***1881–84** Davitt *Prison Diary* I 111: The "lady" is always provided with a dress having long and wide sleeves, within which she can easily move her hand and "hooks" (fingers) when standing or sitting close to the individual whose pocket she is anxious to explore. **1887** Davis *Sea-Wanderer* 290: Occasionally some member of the watch on deck would try his hooks on the duds (milk the cow), by way of proving that he had not forgotten his farm lessons ashore. **1890** Bunner *Sixes* 13: He's dead stuck on my hooks, an I have to keep 'em lookin' good. **1896** F.P. Dunne, in Schaaf *Dooley* 175: Now ye can't tell him that ye spint th' summer with wan hook on th' free lunch an' another on th' tickertape. **1905** Phillips *Plum Tree* 27: He's...found a way of sinking his hooks in the head devil of the Reformers and Ben Cass' chief backer, Singer. **1918** *Everybody's* (Nov.) 20: And I'm a son of a sea cook if I don't plant me hooks in his dead-lights for it, too! **1927** Finger *Frontier Ballads* 136: He was handy with his hooks, he was orn'ry in his looks. **1933** Witherspoon *Liverpool Jarge* (unp.): He wouldn't 'a' told 'em if he'd been where I could lay my hooks into him. **1955** Blackburn *Legend of Davy Crockett* (film): I'd sure like to get my hooks on him. **1956** G. Green *Angry Man* 287: Keep your hooks off me, you cheap bum. **1956** *Looney Tunes* (animation): Get your cotton-pickin' hooks offa me! **1957** Myrer *Big War* 178: Derekman clenched his fists....."I believe in these two hooks right here." **1975** McCaig *Danger Trail* 20: The Sioux and Cheyennes would give their eagle feathers to get their hooks on that. *ca*1979 in J.L. Gwaltney *Drylongso* 127: Hooks do not deceive me,...my man. **1989** *Life Goes On* (ABC-TV): Get your greasy hooks off me. **1989** P. Dickson *Baseball Dict.* 210: A "good pair of hooks" on an adept fielder.

b. a person's foot.

1846 *Spirit of Times* (Apr. 18) 85: "Take away your hooks!" to which the wife replied..."Ah!...when we were first married...you used to say..."take away your little hootsy footsy tootsys!"

c. *pl.* riding spurs.

*1911 O'Brien & Stephens *Australian Sl.* 73: Hooks, spurs. ***1921** *N & Q* (Dec. 10) 466 [ref. to 1918]: Hooks. Spurs. Chiefly to recruits. "You've forgotten your hooks, lad!" **1936** A. Adams *Cowboy Lingo* 36: [Cowboys referred to spurs as] "hooks," "gut-hooks," [etc.]. *a*1956 Almirall *College to Cow Country* 39: I hung my hooks into Hotfoot's barrel. **1983** Elting, Cragg & Deal *Soldier Talk* 155: Hooks...spurs. *To put your hooks* into a horse was to spur him vigorously.

3. *Und.* a pickpocket; (*broadly*) a thief.

*1863 in *OED2*: The party who picks the pocket while the "stiff-dropper" is attracting the victim's attention is called "the hook." ***1881–84** Davitt *Prison Diary* I 25: Manchester "hooks" (pick-pockets)...boast of being the rivals of the "Cocks," or Londoners, in the art of obtaining other people's property without paying for it. **1914** Jackson & Hellyer *Vocab.* 45: *Hook* means a thief. **1919** *Bookman* (Apr.) 208: A certain hook...getting rap to it, maces A and B for a split. **1919** *DN* V 41: *Hook,* n. A "crook." **1929** Booth *Stealing* 192: It don't make any difference to a guy that's not stealing, but, being a hook, you can't even stand an investigation. **1929** Barr *Let Tomorrow Come* 153: It's dif'ernt if a hook is on a rap with a mob. *Ibid.* 267: *Hook*—a pickpocket. *a*1929 in Milburn *Hobo's Hornbook* 267: [They] were all in stir for thinking they was hooks. **1930** Conwell *Pro. Thief* 28: A hook (pickpocket who takes the money from the pocket of the victim) who has now retired. **1942** Algren *Morning* 78: You're a jack roller....You're a strong-arm bandit. You're a hook. **1955** Q. Reynolds *HQ* 235: The third member, known as the hook, will walk behind the victim. ***1968** in *OED2*: We've nothing on him. But then we've nothing on half the hooks in Eastport. **1983** *N.Y. Times* (Sept. 6) B6: "Dip, hook, mechanic and tool," all meaning pickpocket.

4.a. a concealed drawback; catch. Cf. early figurative quots. in *OED* def. 2.b.

*a*1889 *Century Dict.*: Hook...A catch; an advantage. (Vulgar.) ***a*1890–93** *F & H* III 341: Hook...(common).—A catch; an advantage; an imposture. **1928** in Tuthill *Bungle Family* 60: Listen! here's the hook! **1980** *Bosom Buddies* (ABC-TV): What's the hook? **1983** *TalkNet* (NBC radio) (Oct. 28): Well, here's the catch. Here's the hook.

b. Now esp. *Adver. & Entertainment Industry.* an inducement; (*hence*) a specific element or stratagem intended to excite the interest of the public; gimmick; angle.

*1895 in *OED2*: We often...have a perfectly visible hook offered to us, in a young lady, a speculation...or what not. **1937** *AS* (Apr.) 101: *Hook* is that part of the *commercial* which urges you to send in the box tops. **1956–60** J.A. Williams *Angry Ones* ch. xv: The approach I used was integration. Everyone was interested in it, of course, but Crispus had nothing about it in his book....But you always need a hook and that was the one I chose, phony as it was. **1977** in L. Bangs *Psychotic Reactions* 233: Oh, so is that gonna be the hook for your story, then? **1982** D. Weissberg *Music Making* 56: What are called "hooks" in the music business. A hook is a recurring lyric or musical phrase that is designed to get the listener involved with a song. Often the hook is also the title of the song. **1987** in *Black Teen* (Jan. 1988) 10: "I always think of the hooks and he thinks of the verses." That hook is the mysterious addiction which makes us want to hear a song repeatedly. **1989** *ALF* (NBC-TV): Arm wrestling for the captured mating stock is really a good hook. **1989** Hynes & Drury *Howard Beach* 58: Searching for what prosecutors call a "hook" upon which to hang the case. **1989** S. Robinson & D. Ritz *Smokey* 120: You buried your hook. Bring it up at the end, man.

5. a sharp pang of emotional distress inflicted by another; (*hence*) a vicious criticism.—constr. with *the*; in phr. **throw the hooks into** to subject to harsh criticism or abuse.

1896 Ade *Artie* 35: But to think of that stiff turnin' on me because I spoke to him. That's what put the hooks into me. I won't forget it. **1899** Kountz *Baxter's Letters* 54: Literally forced me to drink that punch, gets me ripened up, and then throws the hooks into me. **1903** Ade *Society* 103: Those who are very Bright often marry into the families of the vulgar Rich, thus acquiring the Means to go Abroad and, at the same time, throw the Hooks into their Native Land. **1911** T.A. Dorgan, in *N.Y. Eve. Jour.* (Jan. 11) 12: On first class paper and in a first class manner [he] slipped the hooks to Mr. B. Nelson of Hegewisch. **1920** Ade *Hand-Made Fables* 29: [They] would loll in front of the [fire] and give the Hook to most of the People being featured in the Society Column. **1922** Colton & Randolph *Rain* 75: What did the Government know or care about me until you went and hauled your hooks into me? **1928** Carr *Rampant Age* 171: I just can't get over the feelin' of there bein' some big guy up above the clouds who can throw the hooks into you if you get too damn cocky. **1946** Sevareid *Wild Dream* 72: Christ, do they have to throw in the hook even after he's dead?

6. *Naut.* an anchor; in phr. **ride** [or **swing on**] **the hook** to ride at anchor.

*1902 Masefield *Salt-Water Ballads* iii: *Hooker*—A periphrasis for ship, I suppose from a ship carrying *hooks* or anchors. **1902** J. London *Dazzler* 193: Break out ze hook. **1919** *Our Navy* (May) 53: We dropped our hook off Sassnitz. **1923** in O'Brien *Best Stories of 1923* 4: Stand by to drop the hook. **1937** *Esquire* (Feb.) 115: We're due to drop the hook off Diamond Head about eight o'clock. **1945** *Newsweek* (Mar. 19) 46: Why do they make the "hook" out of steel? **1945** Huie *Omaha to Okinawa* 148: Some of [the ships]...had been "riding the hook" for four months! **1951** W. Williams *Enemy* 153: She's dropped her hook, Cap'n. **1956** Wier & Hickey *Navy Wife* 103: Hook, the. The anchor. **1959** J. Simms *Killer Shrews* (film): Break out the heavy-weather hook. **1961** L.E. Young *Virgin Fleet* 9: We're supposed to get off this tub when she drops the hook. **1969** Bosworth *Love Affair* 198: On the coast of Chile, the *Essex* dropped the hook long enough to put boats ashore and shoot wild pigs, a welcome change from salt horse. **1969** Searls *Hero Ship* 47: The ship had dropped the hook. *a*1974 G.E. Wheeler *Adm. Pratt* 61: After five months of "swinging on the hook" off the Puget Sound Navy Yard, Pratt was detached from *St. Louis* on 2 April 1910. **1980** Teichmann *Fonda* 168: The *Curtis* no longer "swung on the hook." **1979–81** C. Buckley *To Bamboola* 154: We dropped the hook (anchor) in the afternoon.

7.a. [in ref. to the long, hooked pole formerly used to pull untalented vaudeville performers off stage and into the wings; the hook was reportedly introduced in 1903 at Harry Miner's Bowery Theater in New York City. (See Harlow, *Old Bowery*, p. 471)] *Orig. Theat.* immediate removal, ejection, or discharge.—constr. with *the*; in phr. **get the hook!** get that performer off stage!

1907 in H.C. Fisher *A. Mutt* 13: Have you anything to say for yourself before I give you the hook? **1908** in Blackbeard & Williams *Smithsonian Comics* 58: Dr. McGetthehook, County Boob Inspector. **1910** *N.Y. Eve. Jour.* (Feb. 8) 12: They had to nail Paris and give Helen the hook. **1911** in Truman *Dear Bess* 62: I have an idea that Mr. Mac got the hook. **1912** in Robinson *Comics* 51: The hook for this guy! **1914** *Collier's* (May 16) 12: They will give you the hook if you don't learn to cook. **1914** Dale *Songs of Seventh* 96: "I'll get wet feet sure," he gurgled. Some one hollered "get the hook." **1915** [Swartwood] *Choice Slang* 74: Umpire Bait....Take him out, get the hook, the hook. **1916** S. Lewis *Job* 264: I've been fired!...Canned....Got the hook thrown into me. **1948** Hargrove *Got to Give* 37: Give him the hook! **1955** Mankiewicz *Trial* (film): I remember the first time *I* got the hook....His contract isn't being renewed. **1964** Allen *High White Forest* 326: Give him the hook! **1977** Bredes *Hard Feelings* 243: Richard got the big hook. Out a month for hitting [the teacher]. *a***1988** C. Adams *More Straight Dope* 12: Since the name that comes first gets priority, apatasaurus [sic] and brontosaurus got the hook. **1991** *Beetlejuice* (ABC-TV): Get the hook!

b. an instance of treachery; a double cross.—constr. with *the.*

1908 in H.C. Fisher *A. Mutt* 39: Baby Jack...testifying that he had been given the hook by the prosecution. The witness claimed that...he had been promised immunity and that now they were renigging on him.

8. *Und.* STEERER.

1906 Wooldridge *Hands Up* 106: The "steerers," "cappers," "coin separators," "outside hooks" and "come-ons" begin to surge toward the street.

9. *Baseball.* a curve ball.

1910 (cited in Nichols *Baseball Termin.*). **1912** *American Mag.* (June) 203: *Hook*—A fast overhand curve that breaks downward at an unusually sharp angle. **1914** in Lardner *Round Up* 259: The hook couldn't be no worse'n the fast one. **1927** in *AS* V (1930) 279: A curve ball is almost always a "hook." **1983** Whiteford *How to Talk Baseball* 103: *Hook*...a curve ball. **1984** *N.Y. Post* (Aug. 18) 44: Krukow...owns "one of the best hooks in this league."

10.a. *Constr.* a mobile crane.

1916 *Editor* XLIII (Mar. 25) 343: *Hook.* the wrecking crane. **1934** *AS* (Feb.) 73: *Big hook.* Wrecker, so called because of the large hook supported by the crane. **1942** *Amer. Mercury* (June) 741: *Big hook*—wrecking crane. **1942** *Sat. Eve. Post* (June 13) 27: The wrecking crane, or "hook," cleared the lead track that connects the yard tracks. **1965** O'Neill *High Steel* 272: *Hook.* a crane. **1970** *Current Slang* V (Summer) 4: *Big Hook*, n. The steam-driven mobile crane (railway) used to pick up derailed cars and engines.

b. *Av.* a flying crane, esp. the Sikorsky S-64 Skycrane or the Chinook.

1968 in Morgan & Michalson *For Our Beloved Country* 434: I'm in a "hook" to go back now. **1970** Flood *War of Innocents* 54: All done by helicopter. Everything—food, ammo, mail. For the artillery they sling the guns under the big ones. They call 'em Hooks. **1971** Vaughan & Lynch *Brandywine's War* 31: The "hooks" come in to pick them up. **1989** Zumbro & Walker *Jungletracks* 221: Yo, Gator, we're bringing in two hooks with fuel and ammo. **1983–90** L. Heath *CW2* 32: We couldn't get a Hook. *Ibid.* 367: *Hook*—Chinook. **1993** T. Taylor *Lightning in Storm* 309: Three 'hooks, northbound over EA.

11. HOOKER³, 1.

1918 *DN* V 25: *Hook*, n. A harlot. **1972** Jenkins *Semi-Tough* 91: There were these three spade hooks in attendance. **1975** R.P. Davis *Pilot* 167: There were always a few hookers around...first-class hooks.

12. *Pris.* a straight razor or knife used as a weapon.

1918 in *AS* VIII (1943) 28: Man, Ah'd like to catch dat screw outside some day when Ah had mah hook right handy! **1944** *Papers Mich. Acad.* XXX 599: *Hook*, a knife or razor. **1942–49** Goldin et al. *DAUL* 100: *Hook*...A straight razor. **1935–62** Ragan & Finston *Toughest Pris.* 803: *Hook.* A razor.

13. Esp. *N.Y.C.* an influential patron or associate; political influence.

1931 Wilstach *Under Cover Man* 160: You're a good hook, Jones. **1968** Radano *Walking Beat* 134: If your hook is big enough you can get any job. **1971** N.Y.U. student: They say, "you gotta have a hook. That guy's got a long hook around here." It means influence, pull, somebody you know. **1972** J. Mills *Report* 99: Oh, she got in on a

hook. **1973** Schiano & Burton *Solo* 23: You gotta have a hook. You gotta know the mayor or some senior officer to get in something like that. **1973** Droge *Patrolman* 57: Near the end of March all the probies called their "hook." A hook is a person who claims he can get you the exact assignment you want, and sometimes he can. In the telephone company we called him a "rabbi." **1978** Strieber *Wolfen* 107: That's their whole career, that and figuring out who has the biggest hook, who *is* the biggest hook for that matter. **1983** Flaherty *Tin Wife* 286: I used a hook to get my kid off a felony. **1987** Taubman *Lady Cop* 268: *Hook:* Someone of higher rank who can bring someone up, provide references for better assignments or even order transfers on their own authority. **1991** McCarthy & Mallowe *Vice Cop* 52: Gussman became McCarthy's "hook," his "rabbi."

14. *Mil.* a chevron indicating an enlisted grade.

1941 *AS* XVI 166: *Hooks.* Chevrons. ***1941** in S.J. Baker *Australian Lang.* 154: *Hooks.* Chevrons. **1943** Steinbeck *Once There Was a War* [entry for July 25]: I'd take the hooks for a job like this, but I don't want to tell a bunch of men what to do. **1944–46** in *AS* XXII 55: *Hooks.* Chevrons.

15. Esp. *Mil.* a hypodermic injection.—constr. with *the.*

1941 Kendall *Army & Navy Sl.* 7: The hook....any one of the three injections a soldier receives. **1942** Kahn *Army Life* 16: "Watch out for the hook." The "hook" is a term used to describe hypodermic injections of either a typhoid or tetanus preventative. **1959** Lay & Gilroy *Gallant Hours* (film): Watch out for the hook, sir! **1965** Linakis *In Spring* 213: "You get the hook tomorrow morning."..."For a busted kidney?...I thought you got it for clap."

16. *Poker.* a jack or a seven.

1949 G.S. Coffin *Winning Poker* 179: Hook—Any jack or any seven, so called because the J or 7 is hook-shaped. **1968** F. Wallace *Poker* 217: *Hook*—A jack.

17. *Narc.* a drug addiction.

1954 in Partridge *Dict. Und.* 832: He thought he could avoid "the hook" (addiction) by "spacing his shots." **1972** P. Thomas *Savior* 7: I mean this was his first hook and...he made it to...the "kick factory."

18. *Stu.* an academic grade of C.

1964 in *Time* (Jan. 1, 1965) 56: A's are *aces*, C's are *hooks.* **1965** *Esquire* (July) 45: The aces and hooks on the suburban teen's report card didn't exist for them. **1966–68** *Current Slang I & II* 51: *Hook*, n. A grade of "C."—Air Force Academy cadets; College females, New York. **1968** Baker, Ladd & Robb *CUSS* 138: *Hook.* The grade "C." **1968–70** *Current Slang III & IV* 70: Well, at least I got a hook. **1976** Eble *Campus Slang* (Nov.) 3: The grade C...I got a hook on the test.

19. *Surfing.* the crest of a breaker.

1965 (quot. at SOUP).

20. *Communications.* a radiotelephone hookup.—constr. with *the.* [Earliest quots. ref. to Vietnam War].

1976 C.R. Anderson *Grunts* 90: Six on the hook, Sir. **1982** Del Vecchio *13th Valley* 231: Brown was on the hook to the artillery on the firebase. **1983** Eilert *Self & Country* 17: Get Match on the hook. **1988** Dye *Outrage* 108: Corporal Mallory!...Six callin' for you on the hook.

21. *Und.* police.—constr. with *the.*

1994 *Mich. v. Todd & Hardy* (Court TV) (Apr. 7): The hook...."Yeah, I'm the hook. What are you doing out here?"...The hook has got to operate. **1994** G. Smitherman *Black Talk* 138: *Hook*...the police.

¶ In phrases:

¶ **and a hook** *Army.* and a trip back to the United States at the end of one's tour of duty. Cf. WAKE-UP.

1986 Dye & Stone *Platoon* 74 [ref. to Vietnam War]: You're lookin' at a double-digit midget, man! Ninety-two and a hook! DEROS April 17, man!

¶ **get the hook!** see (7.a.), above.

¶ **hooks and crooks** letters; writing.

1804 Brackenridge *Mod. Chivalry* 368: A great part of their learning, is but the knowledge of *hooks* and *crooks.*

¶ **in the hooks** (sense uncertain; see quot.).

1827 in Shackford *Crockett* 81: Old Maj. Henry has cut out for Orleans in the hooks.

¶ **off the hook** *Rap Music.* wonderful; exciting; impressive.

1996 *New Yorker* (Feb. 12) 27: Everyone else is at some party that's off the hook (incredible). **1996** N.Y.C. man, discussing rap performance (coll. J. Sheidlower): I thought LL [*sc.* "L.L. Cool J"] was off the hook. **1997** *Dangerous Minds* (ABC-TV): This book you gave me is off the hook, man!

¶ **off the hooks, 1.** in or into a state of madness or intense excitement; crazy, angry, or vexed; unhinged. *Rare* in U.S.

*1612 in *OED*: Agrippina began…to flye off the hookes: and coming to Nero himself threatened to take his Empire from him. *1662 Pepys *Diary* (Apr. 28): [His son's attitude] is one thing that hath put Sir Wm so long off the hookes. *1665 Pepys *Diary* (May 26): The Duke of Albemarle…I found mightily off the hooks that the ships are not gone out of the River. *1676 in T. D'Urfey *Two Comedies* 54: The truth is, my brothers a little off o' th' hooks. *1698–99 "B.E." *Dict. Canting Crew*: *Off the Hooks*, in an ill Mood or out of Humour. *1824 Sir W. Scott *St. Ronan's Well* ch. xxx: Everybody about this St. Ronan's business is a little off the hooks—…in plain words, a little crazy. **1914** Atherton *Perch* 108: Oh, I'm not saying you'll go off the hooks,…but if the man comes along you'll fall in love all right.

2. dead.—constr. with *go, knock, drop*, etc., in phr. meaning 'to die' or 'to kill'. *Rare* in U.S.

*1831 in Partridge *DSUE* (ed. 8) 567 [ref. to 1815]: The French…opened fire on us, which knocked many a poor fellow off the hooks. **1834–40** R.H. Dana, Jr. *2 Years Before Mast* 236: What's that?…Has the bloody agent slipped off the hooks? *1840 in *OED2*: No man was ever able to write his own life complete. He's certain to go off the hooks before he has finished it. *1842 in *OED2*: Our friend…has popp'd off the hooks. **1870** *Galaxy* (July) 122: Fears were entertained of his "going off the hooks" by the short cut his father took. **1870** Greey *Blue Jackets* 25: Mother's gone off the hooks. *1872 in *F & H* III 342: S'pose the odds are against Jerningham going off the hooks between this and the first spring-meeting. *1873 Hotten *Slang Dict.*: "Dropped off the hooks," said of a deceased person. **1908** W.G. Davenport *Butte & Montana* 201: Now take a shot and get braced up. You don't want to go off the hooks feeling tough. *1921 J. Galsworthy, in *OEDS*: Old Timothy, he might go off the hooks at any moment. I suppose he's made his Will.

¶ **on (one's) own hook** on (one's) own initiative; by (oneself). Now *colloq.*

1812 in Thornton *Amer. Gloss.*: They forget that Rodgers himself says that he went upon his own hook. **1836** *Davy Crockett's Almanack* (1837) 6: A daring Tennessean…seemed to be fighting "on his own hook." **1840** in Strong *Diary* I 122: He's going…to do it on his own hook without the help of the rascally booksellers. **1845** in Robb *Squatter Life* 65: Made every hair stand "on its own hook." **1845** in Eliason *Tarheel Talk* 277: She told me she was very economical…since she was…going *upon her own hook.* **1847** Robb *Squatter Life* 23: In poured the subscribers to the dinner…and in poured John "on his own hook." **1850** Garrard *Wah-to-yah* 18: Mr. St. Vrain and companions brought in the choice parts of a buffalo, and every person was busied in cooking on their "own hook" and swallowing the tender meat. **1853** W.W. Brown *Clotel* 32: I…commenced business on my "own hook." *1858 in Franklyn *Rhyming Sl.* 195: If he does anything on his own responsibility, he does it on his own "hook." **1864** in H. Johnson *Talking Wire* 130: Emigrants are going through on their own hook. **1869** Logan *Foot Lights* 236: Never mind the old woman, girls; *go it on your own hook!* **1884** Bruell *Sea Memories* 55: Why,…they will all fight on their own hook. **1890** E. Custer *Guidon* 20: They've been hunting on their own hook again. **1913** [W. Dixon] *"Billy" Dixon* 51: I was lucky enough to kill several "on my own hook." **1929** Hammett *Maltese Falcon* 136: You're sore because she did something on her own hook, without telling you. **1980** McAleer & Dickson *Unit Pride* 114: I joined the army on my own hook. **1989** "Capt. X" & Dodson *Unfriendly Skies* 97: They're on their own hook now. They're so close to the ground, there are no instructions for them.

¶ **on the hook, 1.** by or engaging in theft.

1865 in Glatthaar *March to Sea* 129: [Unauthorized foraging was called] foraging on the hook. *a1890–93 *F & H* III 341: *On the hook*…(common)….On the thieves; *on the cross.*

2. absenting oneself from school; playing HOOKY[1].

1906 in McCay *Little Nemo* 71: And other desperadoes, who/Had been on many "hooks,"/Now came to school in model style,/Each bringing all his books. **1934** H. Roth *Call It Sleep* 249: "Well, w'y aintchjis in school?"…"He's onna hook." **1946** I. Shulman *Amboy*

Dukes 22: The only thing he didn't like about going on the hook was that after he came out of the show he didn't know what to do or where to go.

3. *West.* belligerent.

1924 Raine *Desert's Price* 138: Don't get on the hook. **1942** *ATS* 330: Belligerent…*on the hook.*

4. addicted to (a drug); helplessly dependent upon.

1952 Mandel *Angry Strangers* 238: Dinch, you get kids on the hook for Buster? **1953** W. Brown *Monkey on My Back* 12: It is inevitable that many youngsters will experiment with these drugs and that some of them will land "on the hook." *Ibid.* 52: You knew he was on the hook? **1963** D. Tracy *Brass Ring* 257: There was no danger that Kelly would get on the hook to booze.

5. in debt.

1957 *Sat. Eve. Post* (Aug. 10) 69: So you'll go on the hook for some new tweeds, one of those eighty-dollar sports-car coats and a ten-dollar cap. **1960** E. Wood, Jr. *Sinister Urge* (film): You're on the hook to me for plenty. **1971** B.B. Johnson *Blues for Sister* 124: He and Curly told me I was on the hook to the company almost two hundred thousand.

¶ **play the hook** to play HOOKY[1].

1988 DeLillo *Libra* 4: He'd played hooky again,…playing the hook, they called it here.

¶ **sling (one's) hook** Esp. *Naut.* to depart; (*hence*) to sign aboard ship. *Rare* in U.S.

*1873 Hotten *Slang Dict.* (ed. 4): "Sling your hook," a polite invitation to move-on. *1892 in *F & H* III 342: I…wos quietly slinging my 'ook. *1899 Whiteing *John St.* 48: An' blow me if I sha'n't be sold up, too, if I don't soon sling my 'ook an' git some more. **1908** *Independent* (Apr. 23) 907: "Old Summer Time" and I slung our hooks on board an English topsail schooner or "jackass bark," bound to the Mediterranean.

¶ **throw the hooks, 1.** *Und.* to inveigle victims.

1887 DeVol *Gambler* 91: I called the passengers around a table, and began to throw the hooks. **1927** *AS* (June) 390: In the northwest, *chopping a limb* and *throwing the hooks* are phrases used in begging.

2. see **(5)**, above.

hook *adj. Black E.* sexually attractive. Cf. HOOKED, *adj.* 2.

1988 "Biz Markie" *Pickin' Boogers* (rap song): She was dressed real def and her body was hook.

hook *v.* **1.** to steal; filch. [The *1615 quot. seems to ref. to the use of an actual hook in the commission of the theft.]

[*1615 in *OED*: Picking of locks, or hooking clothes at windows.] *1785 in R. Burns *Selections* 215: For monie a pursie she had hooked. **1821** Martin & Waldo *Lightfoot* 118: I went about the small villages, to see if I could *hook* anything. **1834** Hoffman *Winter in West* II 88: Plundering Indian property, under the innocent phrase of "Hooking from Uncle Sam." **1841** [Mercier] *Man o' War* 179: Dat dere Flukes is de slickest feller at *hooking* any ting dat ever I seed in all my born days. **1841** in Angle *Prairie State* 199: They even hook (or steal) timber to build meeting houses of! **1845** in Oehlschlaeger *Reveille* 64: The propriety of "hooking" a bier for the occasion. **1847** Buhoup *Narrative* 17: Who in the h-ll has been hooking the stirrups off my saddle? **1847** in H.C. Lewis *Works* 115: The bank! Is that where they ruins the widows and hooks orphans' dimes, stranger? **1861** O.W. Holmes, Jr., in M.D. Howe *Shaping Yrs.* 93: The artillerymen hooked his pigs, geese, &c. **1862** in Bear *Letters* (Dec. 17) 12: When Soloman and I was in town Soloman hooked two large Sweet Potatoes. **1866** G.A. Townsend *Non-Combatant* 189: I did hook this hoss, but you wan't the party. **1866** in Hilleary *Webfoot* 204: They steal his whiskey…, hide his clothing, hook his pie. **1910** in O. Johnson *Lawrenceville* 206: Why, that beats hooking signs all hollow. **1927** Shay *Pious Friends* 50: Railroad Bill led a mighty bad life,/Always hookin' some other man's wife. **1934** Appel *Brain Guy* 113: The Metz robbery proved his lousiness. Of all places to hook. **1965** Bonham *Durango St.* 160: I'll hook a bottle while you guys tip over his garbage can. **1975** T. Berger *Sneaky People* 177: Somebody hooked my bike.

2.a. to snare, entice, or swindle (a victim); inveigle; trick. Cf. earlier S.E. *hook in* (OED def. 9).

*ca1730 *Country Spy* 40: Having thus hooked the *Chub*, I said…I desire no Recompense. *1758 *Jonathan Wild's Advice* lxiii: Thieves…are as simple and easy to be hooked as the creatures they prey upon. *a1800 in *OED2*: He was anticipating…the young spendthrifts whom he hoped to hook at the gaming table. *1821 *Real Life in*

London I 142: The odds were…that Bob would be *hook'd* [by a prostitute]. **1873** Beadle *Undevel. West* 93: The … "cappers" … have … "hooked a gudgeon." **1920** Bissell *63d Inf.* 72: Men nudged one another…and nodded affirmative replies. In the argot of the "spieler" or "barker" of a very different sphere, many were already "hooked!" **1927** Webster *Best of H.T. Webster* 17: Trying To Think of Something Funny About Poker When You've Been Hooked For $150 The Night Before. **1931** Hellinger *Moon* 203: Each time she hooks a new sucker, she evidently hooks him for plenty. **1939** Appel *Power-House* 297: We want to hook a union man to tip us off about the union. **1942–49** Goldin et al. *DAUL* 100: Hook…To swindle; to trick; to defraud. "I hooked him with readers (marked cards) and he's gonna stay hooked." **1978–86** J.L. Burke *Lost Get-Back Boogie* 144: How much did they hook you for the bottle? **1995** *Calif. v. Simpson* (Court TV) (Feb. 24): I'm not trying to hook a guy.

b. to catch or apprehend by law; arrest; NAB.

　1928 W.R. Burnett *Little Caesar* 102: My cab driver got hooked for speeding. **1974** G.V. Higgins *Cogan's Trade* 47: Then I got hooked and they try me. *a***1986** D. Tate *Bravo Burning* 7: The U.S. Army…hooked him. **1988** Norst *Colors* 37: We're going to do one thing—hook and book. **1990** *Cops* (Fox-TV): You were hooked for prostitution and you just got out an hour ago? **1995** *N.Y. Times Mag.* (Jan. 22): The street, where it used to be hooking and booking…now it's driving and waving.

c. to secure (a ride) for oneself, as by hitchhiking; steal a ride on (a train).

　1930 Irwin *Tramp & Und. Sl.: Hook.*—To steal.…Even the boys who catch rides on the back of drays and wagons referring to the practice as "hooking" a ride. **1939** C.R. Cooper *Scarlet* 157: They "hooked" numerous rides from soft-hearted motorists. **1958** in *Dict. Canad.* 344: I had to hook a ride home. **1980** Bruns *Knights of Road* 24: You can't hook a train on the go anymore. **1989** in *DARE: Hook rides.*…This was popular with school boys…with the meaning, "To solicit and obtain free rides from motorists."

3.a. to run away; clear out.—usu. constr. with *it*, occ. with *them*.

　*ca***1776** in Silber *Songs of Independence* 78: It scared me so I hooked it off. ****1835** in Partridge *DSUE* (ed. 7) 1201: Hook it, you b------s. ****1850** in Partridge *Dict. Und.* 341: A male voice said, "So help me God, Bill, it is the *copper, hook* it!"—*copper* means policeman, and *hook it*, make your escape. ****1851** H. Mayhew *London Labour* II 123: There was a regular fight…[but] he slipped from her and hooked it. ****1855** in Hindley *Curios. Street Lit.* 101: We must now all hook it without more delay. **1865** Darley *Yankee Doodle* 8: It scared me so, I hooked it off,/Nor stopped as I remember;/Nor turned about till I got home,/Locked up in mother's chamber. **1919** MacGill *Dough-Boys* 212: "They're hookin' it," Sullivan laughed.…"They've had enough iv it!" **1962–68** B. Jackson *In the Life* 92: You all better hook 'em (take off). **1971** Dahlskog *Dict.* 32: Hook it!…An order to someone to make himself scarce, to leave, get out, or get lost. **1983** *All Things Considered* (Nat. Pub. Radio) (Apr. 23): "That's why you left." "That's why I'm hookin' it." **1985** M. Baker *Cops* 63: We're hooking. We're getting the fuck away from these fuckers.

b. to play truant from.—also used intrans. (occ. constr. with *off*). [Infl. by *play hooky* s.v. HOOKY[1]; cf. *hook Jack*, below]

　1890 *DN* I 25: To hook off, to play truant. **1946** in Mencken *New Ltrs.* 569: [In Baltimore] *To play hookey* is always *to hook school.* **1956** Holiday & Dufty *Lady Sings* 17: There were about a hundred girls there, mostly for stealing and hooking from school. **1973–76** J. Allen *Assault* 20: If you continued to steal or hook school, then you're coming back. **1981** *Film Comment* (May) 30: Movies…which I immediately hooked school to go see. **1984** Algeo *Stud Buds* 1: To not go to class…hook. *a***1994** N. McCall *Wanna Holler* 31: Hook school and go shoot some pool. **1996** *Montel Williams Show* (synd. TV series): You've hooked from school.

4.a. Orig. *Narc.* to make a drug addict of; (*broadly*) to addict.—usu. as **hooked**, *adj.* Now *colloq.*

　1922 Murphy *Black Candle* 243: He does not use morphine for any pleasure it affords, but because he suffers when it is taken away. To use the correct jargon, it has "hooked him." **1925** *Writer's Mo.* (June) 486: *Hooked*—to become a drug addict. **1928** *AS* IV 20: My observations have led me to believe that the drug addict is "hooked" by "dope" talk as well as by the "dope" itself. **1929** E. Booth *Stealing* 282: I tell the damn little fool that using so much stuff [morphine] will make a bum out of

him, but Billie—that twist he's with—got him hooked. **1932** L. Berg *Pris. Dr.* 63: "Gees" stay off two, three, even ten years and then get hooked again. **1936** Dai *Opium Add.* 118: From that time on she was "hooked." **1946** Mezzrow & Wolfe *Really Blues* 208: I had…a terrible yen for hop.…Nothing else mattered. I was hooked. **1951** *New Yorker* (Nov. 10) 46: A substantial percentage…have got hooked—become addicted, that is. *ca***1953** Hughes *Lodge* 110: Even if it were hooking you know, even if it were possible to be hooked by girl [cocaine]. **1979** W. Cross *Kids & Booze* 52: He got hooked on booze and…he was an alcoholic. *a***1989** Spears *NTC Dict.* 185: The constant use of bicarb hooked him to the stuff. **1995** *News Day* (CNN-TV) (Feb. 18): [They] manipulated nicotine content of cigarettes to hook smokers.

b. to make helplessly enamored; captivate.—usu. as **hooked**, *adj.* Now *colloq.* [The 1839 quot. illustrates the S.E. sense 'to secure as a spouse'.]

　[**1839** in Strong *Diary* I 116: I suppose I shall be hooked some of these days, and I'd like to have some foreknowledge of the where and the when.] **1927** H. Miller *Moloch* 72: He is hooked. **1928** W.R. Burnett *Little Caesar* 15: "Has old Seal Skin got The Greek hooked yet?" "Well…he spends a lot of jack on her." **1929** in Runyon *Guys & Dolls* 64: By this time Miss Billy Perry is taking her peeks back at him and Waldo Winchester is hooked. **1930** Farrell *Guillotine Party* 251: Look at him! And that bitch has got him hooked! **1938** in Hammerstein *Kern Song Bk.* 189: I'm sold! I'm hooked! ****1965** in *OED2*: You are hooked the very first time you step out of Lime Street Station to be confronted by…St. George's Hall.

5. [infl. by HOOKER[3], 1 and HOOK SHOP] to work as a prostitute. Cf. ***1821 quot. at **(2.a.)**, above.

　[**1949** Partridge *Dict. Und.* 342: In *hook shop*…the ref. is to *hooking*, successfully inveigling men.] **1959** "E. McBain" *Killer's Wedge* 57: She's been in the city almost a year, Pete. Hooking mostly. **1965** C. Brown *Manchild* 252: It's the drugs that make them look so wasted, more than the night life or going around hooking. **1966** "Petronius" *N.Y. Unexp.* 79: The quality of the colored girls who hook has gone down. **1971** *Ramparts* (Dec.) 25: I had orgasms…and that is why I continued hooking. **1971** in Boydell et al. *Deviant Behaviour* 540: Most of the strippers hooked part time to supplement their income. **1971–73** Sheehy *Hustling* 167: So I taught her how to hook. **1985** M. Baker *Cops* 49: They were buddies and they hooked together. **1989** *Geraldo* (CBS-TV) (Feb. 24): "That's where you were based when you were hooking." "I was a call-girl." "Oh. Sorry." **1993** *Donahue* (NBC-TV): You began hooking when you were at a modeling agency. **1994** *Newsweek* (June 27) 10: A young woman who did not look as if she were hooking.

6. *Stu.* to receive a grade of C on or for.

　1976 Eble *Campus Slang* (Nov.) 3: Hook—v., n. to make the grade C: I hooked the test. **1980** Eble *Campus Slang* (Oct.) 3: Hook—n.,v. The grade C: "Well, I hooked another test today."

7. *Stu.* to engage in kissing, petting, or sexual intercourse; MAKE OUT. Cf. HOOK UP.

　1989 Eble *Campus Slang* (Mar.) 5: Hook—to kiss passionately. "You can hear them upstairs hookin'." **1990** Eble *Campus Slang* 5: Hook…Engage in sexual activities. "I hear that Dave hooked with three different chicks from that mixer." **1994** J. O'Leary *Univ. Del. Slang* 1: Hooking…To engage in kissing with another. *Ibid.* 15: Hooking to make out, kiss, etc. I saw Sue & Mike hooking at the party last night.

¶ **In phrases:**

¶ **get hooked** to get married. Cf. 1839 quot. at **(4.b.)**, above.

　1910 T.A. Dorgan, in *N.Y. Eve. Jour.* (Feb. 23) 17: It costs mazuma to get hooked. **1914** in Lardner *Round Up* 342: I'm stickin' here because o' that series dough, so's I can get hooked.

¶ **hook in** to put into close touch or association with; (*hence*) to direct to a source of.

　1918 *Chi. Sun. Trib.* (June 16) V (unp.): Weyer [a reporter] was "hooked in" on a story of monumental importance. **1970–71** G.V. Higgins *Coyle* 30: You hooked in with the goddamned Mafia or something? **1988** H. Gould *Double Bang* 14: Bearer bonds.…I can hook you into some gilt-edged motherfuckers too.

¶ **hook Jack** *N.E.* to play truant.

　1877 Bartlett *Amer.* (ed. 4) 294: *Hook Jack.* To play truant. New England. **1890** Erskine *Twenty Years* 3: I was sent to school, but very seldom went,—in fact, I "hooked Jack" nearly all the time. **1892** *DN* I 216: In all the period from 1840 to 1850 the current phrase among the boys [in Boston] was *to hook Jack*. The phrase *to play hookey* never greeted my eye or ear before I opened the "Dialect Notes." **1905** in *DA:* The boy "hooked Jack" for a whole day.

hook-block *n.* ¶ In phrase: **by the [big] hook-block** *Naut.* (used as a mild oath).

　　1833 N. Ames *Yarns* 309: By the hook-block! how our two snowballs of cooks will swear! **1867** Clark *Sailor's Life* 307: By the big hook-block, I'm in earnest!

hooked *adj.* **1.** see s.v. HOOK, *v.,* 4.

　　2. HOOKED UP, 2. Cf. slightly earlier HOOK, *adj.*

　　1990 Eble *Campus Slang* (Spring) 4: *Hooked*—attractive, well put together: Her hair was hooked. **1994** G. Smitherman *Black Talk* 138: *Hooked* Describes something or someone that is attractive, tastefully put together, upscale.

hooked up *adj.* **1.** see s.v. HOOK UP.

　　2. well put together; (*hence*) well-dressed or intelligent.

　　1933 Duff & Sutherland *I've Got Your Number* (film): Maybe you're not hooked up right. **1974** Scalzo *Stand on Gas* 4: But if the car handles well, or is "hooked up" as the mechanics and drivers say, no one laughs. **1974** Andrews & Dickens *Big House* 29: You are without a doubt the hooked-up-est dude I have ever seen. **1978** Sopher & McGregor *Up from Living Dead* 257: The Legal Aid attorney...is a young cat who's really hooked up. **1986** Eble *Campus Slang* 6: Oh, you're hooked up today. What's the occasion?

hook-em-up *adj. S.W.* married.

　　1972 Jenkins *Semi-Tough* 104: Your gonna have to stay hook-'em-up the rest of your life.

hooker¹ *n.* [orig. 'a Dutch fishing vessel', < Du *hoecker-schip*] *Naut.* a sailing vessel; ship.

　　****1821** *Blackwood's Mag.* (Nov.) 417 [ref. to *ca*1812]: Agreeing as well with each other as the old hooker does to her course with the wind all round the compass. **1823** J.F. Cooper *Pilot* 191: I spent the better part of another week in search of some hooker on board which I might work my passage across the country. ****1821–26** Stewart *Man-of-War's-Man* I 46: It has pleased the Lords Commissioners of the Admiralty, my lads, to bestow the command of this hooker on me. **1833** Ames *Yarns* 218: Why, there couldn't have been no sailors aboard the hooker. **1846** Codman *Sailors' Life* 95: She was a small hooker. **1858** in C.A. Abbey *Before the Mast* 151: Bloody old Hooker. **1868** Macy *There She Blows!* 105: I've only been four months on this hooker. **1873** F. Whittaker *Sea Kings* 58: It'll be like my luck if he sinks the hooker before I get to shore. **1884** Blanding *Sailor Boy* 318: This old "Hooker" will not last long in a blow. **1894** Henderson *Sea-Yarns* 10: This hereschooner...were a wall-sided old hooker an' a regular church for carryin' sail. **1896** Hamblen *Many Seas* 42: Ned...said he had not had a decent meal of victuals since he came aboard of the "d— hooker." **1900** in Foner *Labor Songs* 187: They damned the hooker as they fell. **1908** Paine *Stroke Oar* 180: The old man has told me to make this old hooker take a pilot in ten days from now if she carries away half her spars and strains her seams wide open. **1913–14** London *Elsinore* 272: On this hooker...it's going to be like old times. **1918** *DN* V 16: *Hooker,* n. A boat, especially of an inferior sort. "It was real rugged out there for his old *hooker.*" **1918** King *Bk. of Chanties* iii: Some "old Hookers" leaked considerably. **1930** F. Shay *Here's Audacity* 18: That ol' hooker jes' rolled about like she was beam to the wind. **1937** C.B. Davis *Anointed* 198: Say, do you know this hooker's listing to port? **1954** G. Kersh, in Pohl *Star of Stars* 32: That hooker...was called the *Harry.*

hooker² *n.* [orig. Scots dial.] a drink of liquor, esp. if copious.

　　****1833** in *OED2*: Ye'll be nane the waur o' a hooker after yer fricht. ****1865** in *OED2*: Sandy liket a hooker. **1887** *Lantern* (N.O.) (Oct. 1): Where the juice of the corn is retailed at so much a hooker. **1887** in *OED2*: A pretty stiff hooker each. **1897** A.H. Lewis *Wolfville* 34: The old man 'pears like he's mighty sick that away, so thar's nothin' for it but to give him another hooker, which we does accordin'. **1899** A.H. Lewis *Sandburrs* 48: It's gettin' late an' I'll just put me frame outside another hooker an' then I'll hunt me bunk. **1905** *Nat. Police Gaz.* (July 29) 3: Mitchell took a hooker himself and it eased his wounds. **1919** Darling *Jargon Book* 17: *Hooker*—A drink of whiskey. **1920** Huneker *Veils* 236: It was not the first "hooker" she had drunk that day. **1928** Benchley *Under the Sea* 13: With a good hooker of rye inside him, a whippet might not really be running fast but he would think that he

was, and that's something. **1933** Clifford *Boats* 287: One more hooker, then. **1938** "E. Queen" *4 Hearts* 51: Mr. Queen sighed over a hooker of aged brandy. **1959** J. Lee *Career* (film): She could start a war on a hooker of bourbon. **1963** in A. Sexton *Letters* 188: Could have used a triple hooker of whiskey. **1961–64** Barthelme *Dr. Caligari* 138: Hookers of grog thickened on the table. **1964** Faust *Steagle* 215: Did you know a stiff hooker of champagne the morning after is a marvelous pick-me-up? **1970** Gattzden *Black Vendetta* 118: I'm gonna get me a good, stiff hooker.

hooker³ *n.* [HOOK, *v.* + *-er*] **1.** a prostitute; (*specif.*) a streetwalker. Now *colloq.*

　　1845 in Eliason *Tarheel Talk* 277: If he comes by way of Norfolk he will find any number of pretty Hookers in the Brick row not far from French's hotel. **1859** Bartlett *Amer.* (ed. 2) 201: *Hooker.* A resident of the Hook, i.e. a strumpet, a sailor's trull. So called from the number of houses of ill-fame frequented by sailors at the Hook (i.e., Corlear's Hook) in the city of New York. **1865** Sala *Diary* I 75: The American...opined that the lady in ermine was a "hooker"—that is to say, an improper person. **1889** Barrère & Leland *Dict. Slang* I 471: *Hooker*...(American), a woman of easy virtue, generally one who plies her trade on the streets. **1914** Jackson & Hellyer *Vocab.* 45: *Hooker*...A prostitute. **1918** in O'Brien *Wine, Women & War* 29: N— and A— had brought the two hookers into the adjoining room, leaving them for some reason, and they wandered into our room. **1925** Dos Passos *Manhattan Transfer* 123: Last night I wanted to go with a hooker. **1927–28** in R. Nelson *Dishonorable* 170: Why put me in with those hookers? **1935** (quot. at HAYBAG). **1940** Goodrich *Delilah* 71: So he went out again and walked into the hooker district, where he searched around until he found the lowest dive in the place. **1942** Garcia *Tough Trip* 57 [ref. to 1880's]: Their scheme was to get a hooker, or harlot, of the town, and go visit the Shinnick place. **1942** Wilder *Flamingo Road* 6: People look at you as though you were a half-dollar hooker every time you step off the lot. **1989** *Geraldo* (CBS-TV) (July 6): Anthony, you're a hooker. **1995** *Jerry Springer Show* (synd. TV series): I'm *not* a hooker. I'm a call girl.

　　2. *Und.* a warrant for arrest or re-arrest.

　　1934 in *Jour. Abnormal Psych.* XXX (1935) 363: *Hooker*—a warrant. **1942–49** Goldin et al. *DAUL* 100: *Hooker*...A warrant for re-arrest pending one's release from prison.

　　3. *Labor.* (see 1937 quot.).

　　1937 in Mencken *Amer. Lang. Supp.* II 777: *Hooker.* An operative who inveigles union men into acting as spies on their fellows and keeps them *hooked* by threatening to expose them to the union. **1939** Appel *Power-House* 338: You're a hooker, a stoolie. We don't want you in our union!

　　4. a trick or concealed drawback; catch.

　　1966 Derrig *Pride of Green Berets* 115: "But here's the hooker, son," Fowler said disgustedly. **1970** Cortina *Slain Warrior* 3: But that's the hooker, isn't it, just what you said, "If you don't use." **1971** *Current Slang* V (Spring) 14: *Hooker,* n. A difficult question on an examination. **1987** J. Thompson *Gumshoe* 274: But there's an enormous hooker in all this....The embassy has already made inquiries.

　　5. *Adver. & Entertainment Industry.* an element or inducement intended to stimulate the interest of a reader, audience, customer, etc.; HOOK, 4.b.

　　1968 (cited in *BDNE2*). **1972** in *BDNE2*: A television program...should have a hooker, a teaser and a conclusion. **1977** Urdang *Dict. Ad. Terms* 81: *Hooker*...a particularly attractive feature of a package deal. **1977–81** S. King *Cujo* 25: The copy set in bold-face was the real hooker. **1987** R.M. Brown *Starting* 47: You have to snare the reader with the first line (called a "hooker" in our trade).

hooknose *n.* a Jewish person.—used contemptuously.

　　*a***1867** in G.W. Harris *Lovingood* 140: Murd'rs, 'dult'rs, hook-nose Jews, suckit-riders. **1883** *Life* (June 14) 281: The detective found the wax mask av that hooknose corpse in a corner....the hooknose corpse...an' sivinty-sivin hooknose mourners. **1908** W.G. Davenport *Butte & Montana* 71: Keep 'er up, young hooknose. **1929–31** Farrell *Young Lonigan* 138: Two hooknoses...did come along. **1942** *ATS* 359: Jew...hook-nose. **1968–69** in *DARE*. **1967–80** Folb *Runnin' Lines* 242: *Hook nose*...Jew.

hook shop *n.* a brothel.

　　1889 Barrère & Leland *Dict. Slang* I 473: *Hook shop* (American), a brothel, "hooker" being a prostitute. Much used by English residents in China. **1904–11** D.G. Phillips *Susan Lenox* II 277: Unlawful goods of any kind from opium and cocaine to girls for "hook shops." **1916** Miner *Slavery of Prostitution* 19: There they had the hook-shops. **1916** Cary *Venery* I 135: Hook Shop—A brothel. **1918** *DN* V 16: *Hook-shop,* n. A house in the restricted district. **1930** Mae West *Babe Gordon* 11: She could bring down big money in the high-class hook-shops. **1934** W. Smith *B. Cotter* 28: You'd think I was running one of them cheap West Side hook-shops. **1940** E. O'Neill *Iceman Cometh* 162 [ref. to 1912]: We had one hooker shop in town, and, of course, I liked that, too. **1942** Sonnichsen *Billy King* 61: Around in the cribs and hookshops. **1944** Busch *Dream of Home* 61: The Mexican hook-shops were better. **1956** H. Gold *Not With It* 281: Nancy ran an advanced hookshop.

hookshop *v.* to visit brothels.
  1979 L.T. Carter *Eubie Blake* 48 [ref. to ca1905]: The two men would, as Eubie puts it, go out "hookshopping."

hook-up *n.* **1.** a joining of forces; (*hence*) a political or other connection. Now *colloq.*
  1903 A.H. Lewis *Boss* 116: It'll put us in line for a hook-up with th' reform bunch in th' fight for th' town next year. **1928–30** Fiaschetti *Gotta Be Rough* 139: That was interesting, provocative....Wasn't there a hook-up somewhere? **1930** Lait *On the Spot* 30: You know what hook-ups he's got. You know the precin't captains...are in with him. **1957** Ness & Fraley *Untouchables* 13: They could be brought in from other cities...to insure that they had no hookup with the Chicago mobsters.

  2. *Specif.* a romantic or sexual relationship; (*hence*) the person with whom one has such a relationship.
  1987 in T. McMillan *Breaking Ice* 120: Our relationship...didn't exactly start out to be one of those everlastin' hookups. **1994** J. O'Leary *Univ. Del. Slang* 7: *Hook-up*...the person you make out with....Did you see Jen's hook-up? What a freak.

hook up *v.* **1.a.** to meet and join (a person or persons). Now *colloq.* [Prob. the orig. sense.]
  1906 Ford *Shorty McCabe* 11: So I hooks up with Leonidas. **1908** in H.C. Fisher *A. Mutt* 22: We'll hook up and enter the race of life as a stable entry. **1909** W. Irwin *Con Man* 32: I hooked up with an old professional whom we called "Neversweat." **1916** E.R. Burroughs *Return of Mucker* 84: I'm hooked up with this Pesita person now an' I guess I'll stick. **1935** Sherwood *Idiot's Delight* 134: If you're hooking up with me, its only for professional reasons—see? **1949** Algren *Golden Arm* 132: Frankie had been his wall and the wall was gone, leaving him as defenseless as he had been in the years before he'd hooked up with the dealer. **1969** Whittemore *Cop!* 12: A guy comes into this job...and if by perchance he manages to hook up with a couple of guys who may not be conscientious about their jobs, they do a job in a lackadaisical manner. **1995** *Jenny Jones Show* (synd. TV series): Then we hooked up together after we graduated.

  b. to marry or get married.
  1902–03 Ade *People You Know* 69: Then he hooked up with Laura so as to get a real Home. **1904** Ade *True Bills* 36: Some of them hooked up merely to get a Whack at the Finery. **1911** in Truman *Dear Bess* 52: He is going to get hooked up on the twenty-eighth. **1922** in W. Burnett *Best* 115: I wouldn't get hooked up unless I could give my wife the best of everything. **1944** C.B. Davis *Leo McGuire* 63: You're plumb nuts to get yourself hooked up before you're twenty-one. **1962–68** B. Jackson *In the Life* 162: Well, I can dig it, buddy, 'cause I'm hooked up myself, I got a dough-roll (wife) and two crumb-catchers (children), you know. *a*1994 N. McCall *Wanna Holler* 239: Marriage....hooking up like there was nothing to it.

  c. to become romantically or sexually involved.
  [**1985** Eble *Campus Slang* (Apr.) 5: Hook up with...to pick someone up at a party.] **1986** Eble *Campus Slang* (Mar.) 6: Hook up—to date seriously. [**1987** Eble *Campus Slang* (Fall) 5: Hook up with—leave a social gathering with a member of the opposite sex. "I can't believe she hooked up with Brad last night."] **1988** Eble *Campus Slang* (Fall) 5: *Hook up*...Become amorously involved with a person...for at least the duration of the evening...."Did you hook up with Debbie last night?" **1989** Eble *Campus Slang* (Fall) 4: Hook up with—meet someone, often for the purpose of noncommittal sex. *a*1990 P. Dickson *Slang!* 220: [Teen slang:] *hook-up*. To begin a [romantic] relationship. **1994** *21st Century Slang Dict.* 135: Hook up...to launch a romantic or physical relationship. **1994** *Midtown Resident* (N.Y.C.) (June 24) 17: There are

a lot of guys, and there are a lot of girls, and they're all trying to hook up. **1994** C. Long *Love Awaits* 13: I'm into soft passion and I think that's because I was once hooked up. **1995** *Montel Williams Show* (synd. TV series): I wanted to hook up with him [as his girlfriend].

  2. to provide (someone).—usu. constr. with *with.*
  1983 Eble *Campus Slang* 3: Hook me up with some bills. **1990** Eble *Campus Slang* (Fall) 5: What do you need? I'll hook you up. **1993** Bahr & Small *Son-In-Law* (film): Zack hooked me up with last month's issue. **1993** P. Munro *U.C.L.A. Slang* II 51: Hook up...to give (something) to (someone)...*Can you hook me up with some beer?...Hook me up with a discount.* **1995** *Martin* (Fox-TV): Why don't you hook a brother up with a Rolex watch! **1995** *Ricki Lake Show* (synd. TV series): We're hooking you up [i.e., fixing you up on a date]! Surprise! **1995** *Noonday* (WKXY-TV) (Dec. 20): Bill...can hook you up with a nice dulcimer.

  3. *Stu.* to engage in kissing, petting, or (*usu.*) sexual intercourse.
  1993 *Wkly. World News* (July 13) 13: To hook up...To make out. **1993** Eble *Campus Slang* (Fall) 3: Hook up...Kiss, engage in heavy petting: "Leonard hooked up with Maria...after the Florida State game." *Ibid. Hook up (with)*—have sexual intercourse, usually casually with no commitment: "The only thing she was looking for was to hook up." **1994** *UTSQ: Shack, hook up,* spend the night w/ someone of the opposite sex. They hooked up last night. **1994** J. O'Leary *Univ. Del. Slang* 9: *To hook up*...to have sex. Jane and Tom hooked up the other night after the party. *Ibid.* 11: *Hook-up* (v) kiss, heavy petting; *not* meaning sex. Did you hear that Jen hooked-up with Matt last Saturday? *Ibid.* 21: *Hook-up* (v) to be intimate with the opposite sex, from kissing to intercourse. I think Fred hooked up with Ginger. **1994** in C. Long *Love Awaits* 140: There's a behavior for when you want to hook up with us. There's a change in behavior for after you hook up. **1995** *USA Today* (Mar. 13) 1D: A few women insist they never go out with the intention of "hooking up," or having sex. **1995** *CNN & Co.* (CNN-TV) (Oct. 19): The kids see shacking up and hooking up as the equivalent of marriage.

  4. *Police.* to handcuff.
  1995 *Calif. vs. Simpson* (Court TV) (July 18): "*Hook him up*...[means] *cuff him*."..."You 'hooked him up'?" "I placed him in handcuffs, yes, I did." **1996** *N.Y. Times* (Jan. 6) (Wk. in Rev.) 5: The officer is...apprehending a perp [and] hooking him up.

hooky[1] *n.* [perh. sugg. by Dutch *hoekje (spelen)* 'hide-and-seek'; see J.R. Sinnema, "The Dutch Origin of *Play Hookey,*" *AS* XLV (1970), pp. 205–09; the sugg. that it derives fr. *hook it* s.v. HOOK, *v.,* 3.a. is unlikely due to the later attestation of that term in U.S.]
  ¶ In phrase: **play** *hooky* to play truant; skip school. Now *S.E.*
  1848 Bartlett *Amer.:* Hookey. To "play hookey" is to play truant. A term used among schoolboys, chiefly in the State of New York. **1862** H.J. Thomas *Wrong Man* 33: Why wasn't you at school yesterday? I'm afraid you played *hooky.* **1868** Aldrich *Bad Boy* 156: I never played truant ("hookey" we called it) in my life. **1887** DeVol *40 Yrs. a Gambler* 9: When my parents thought me at school, I was playing "hookey" with other boys. **1890** *DN* I 25: To *play hookey*..., to play truant. **1914** *Collier's* (Aug. 1) 24: Look what's here, playing hookey from the graveyard! **1923** Revell *Off the Chest* 287: I had helped kids play "hookey" to go fishing. **1931** Dos Passos *1919* 259: Let's play hookey and have a swell time. **1937** in Truman *Dear Bess* 397: I played hookey from the Appropriations Committee this morning. **1963** G. Abbott *Mr. Abbott* 10: Arthur was forgiven for playing hooky. **1988** (quot. at *play the hook* s.v. HOOK, *n.*).

hooky[2] *n. Und.* a thief.
  1931–34 in Clemmer *Pris. Comm.* 124: He...doesn't intend to be a "hooky" (to steal) when he gets out.

hooky *v.* to play truant. Cf. HOOKY[1], *n.*
  1984 Algeo *Stud Buds* 2: To not go to class...*hook, hookey, play hookey.* **1993** E. Richards *Cocaine True* 126: When I first hookey school...[I] had fifty dollars.

hooley *n.* [orig. unkn.] a worthless person.
  1964–66 R. Stone *Hall of Mirrors* 304: That knock-nose hooley made a hobo of me.

hooligan *n.* (see quot.).
  1980 Pearl *Pop. Slang* 73: *Hooligan*...(Auto Racing) a race of secondary importance held for competitors not qualifying for a major race.

Hooligan Navy *n.* **1.** *Navy.* the U.S. Coast Guard.—used derisively.

    1922 L. Hisey *Sea Grist* 7: "Haven't even been in the Hooligan Navy? Just land lubbers."...Whatever the Hooligan Navy was, we had not been in it, we were sure of that. **1943** *Amer. Mercury* (Nov.) 555: *Hooligan navy*—the Coast Guard. **1953** Dibner *Deep Six* 204: Like the goddamn hooligan Navy. **1983** Curry *River's in My Blood* 251: That's the Hooligan Navy, the Coast Guard. **1989** *New Yorker* (Aug. 7) 46: The Coast Guard of [the 1970's]...—in its appearance, anyway—had all too often deserved its nickname the Hooligan Navy.

2. *Naut.* any fleet of small or auxiliary vessels.—used derisively.

    1930 *Our Army* (Dec.) 21: Enlist in this Hooligan's Navy again? **1947** Morison *Naval Ops. in WWII* I 268: Civilian in its origin and always informal, the [Coastal Picket Patrol] was affectionately known to its personnel as the "Hooligan Navy"; the official Coast Guard title, "Corsair Fleet," was little used. *Ibid.* 275: But the "Hooligan Navy" ceased to be on 1 October 1943. **1962** Farago *10th Fleet* 119: Thus was born [in 1942] the Coastal Picket Patrol or, as the Coast Guard called it, the Corsair Fleet. Its own personnel...preferred to refer to it as the "Hooligan Navy," calling themselves the "Hooligans." **1963** Breen *PT109* (film): He doesn't like this hooligan navy much better than he does the Japanese Navy. **1965** Schmitt *All Hands Aloft!* 225 [ref. to 1918]: With that damn Hooligan Navy crew of cadets she has aboard, anything might have happened. **1982** T.C. Mason *Battleship* 168 [ref. to WWII]: Why don't they ship 'em to the Hooligan Navy—the goddam flattops?

hoolihan *n. West.* **1.** (among cowboys) (see 1985 quot.).

    1910 in Lomax & Lomax *Amer. Ballads* 384: I am a-riding old Paint, I am a-leading old Dan,/I'm goin' to Montan' for to throw the hooli-han. **1985** H. Cannon *Cowboy Poetry* 138: *Hoolihan* backhand thrown loop for roping horses.

2. an exciting or extraordinary event.

    1973 F. Carter *Outlaw Wales* 182: Seen him take on five pistoleros. He got three of 'em before they cut him down....It was a real hoolihan.

¶ In phrase:

¶ **throw the hoolihan** [fr. sense of **(1)**, above] (among cowboys) to celebrate riotously.

    1944 R. Adams *Western Words*: *Hoolihan, throw the*...to paint the town red.

hoolihan *v.* [perh. obscurely fr. *Houlihan*, Irish family name] *West.* to bulldog (a steer) by bringing it to the ground without twisting its neck.

    1925 W. James *Drifting Cowboy* 105: I hoolyhanned him on the jump and busted him right there. **1933** J.V. Allen *Cowboy Lore* 12: *Hoolihaning* is the act of leaping forward and alighting on the horns of a steer in bull-dogging in a manner to knock the steer down with-out...twisting the animal down with a wrestling hold. Hoolihaning is banned at practically all recognized contests. **1936** McCarthy *Mosshorn* (unp.): *Hoolihaning*. The old-time practice of bulldogging.

hoop *n.* **1.** Now *Und.* a finger ring. Orig. *S.E.* [*OED* gives clearly S.E. quots. fr. 1507 to 1857.]

    1856 in Dorson *Long Bow* 75: Dang it, ef I don't...buy the hoop what'll dew for Sall's finger. **1859** Matsell *Vocab.* 43: *Hoop.* A ring. **1895** in J. London *Tramp Diary* 62: Didn't he sport a little hoop...I mean a ring. **1903** *Enquirer* (Cincinnati) (May 9) 13: Modern Slang Glossary...*Hoop*—A ring. **1904** *Life in Sing Sing* 249: *Hoop.*—A ring. **1912** D. Runyon *Firing Line* 116: [A] Hoop I gives ter Katie when I useter call 'er mine! **1918** in *AS* (Oct. 1933) 28: I'd like t' have de rock (diamond) de colonel wears in dat hoop! **1922** *Variety* (Aug. 18) 5: She...handed him back a diamond hoop that the champ had staked her to. **1926** Clark & Eubank *Lockstep* 173: *Hoop*—ring. **1929** *Sat. Eve. Post* (Oct. 12) 29: *Hoops*: Rings. **1968** Brasselle *Cannibals* 33: I stuffed the hoop in my inside pocket. **1980** Bruns *Knights of Road* 202: *Hoop chisler.* Peddler of worthless rings and watches. **1986** *Miami Vice* (NBC-TV): No necklaces, no wristwatches, no hoops.

2. *Boxing.* a person's rib.

    1898 Dunne *Mr. Dooley in Peace & War* 166: "Hurl yer maulies into his hoops," she says. "Hit him on th' slats!"

3. *Pris.* anal copulation.—usu. considered vulgar.

    1935 Pollock *Und. Speaks*: *Hoop*, sodomy (prison).

4. Esp. *Auto. Industry.* an automobile tire.

    1941 in *AS* XVI 240: *Hoop.* Tire. **1947** in *Look* (Jan. 6, 1948) 26: *Hoop*...auto tire.

5. *Basketball.* **a.** a goal; basket; in phr. **shoot hoops** to shoot baskets.

    1942 *ATS* 660: Basketball...Goal...*hoop*...; *shower of hoops*, a number of baskets. **1967** in *OED2*: Jim Small scored the first hoop of the game. **1972** N.Y.U. student: Let's shoot some hoops. **1975** S.P. Smith *Amer. Boys* 98: Any nigger...sho 'nough could run. Shoot hoops, too. **1976** Price *Bloodbrothers* 118: An' he bops outta the room like he just finished shootin' hoops. **1984** *N.Y. Post* (Dec. 12) 78: The Knicks' only hoop in the past four minutes came on a courageous follow by Walker.

b. the game of basketball; in phr. **shoot hoop** to play bas-ketball. Also *pl.*

    1970–72 in *AS* L (1975) 61: *Hoop, shoot some*...Play basketball. **1977** Sayles *Union Dues* 277: Shooting a righteous game of hoop just when the sport was swinging into popularity didn't hurt any either. **1980** Eble *Campus Slang* (Mar.) 5: *Shoot some hoop*—play basketball. **1983** WINS radio (Dec. 19): And the news in college hoop. **1988** *N.Y. Newsday* (July 20) 7: [He] wore a long-sleeved wool sweater as he played hoops. *a***1989** Spears *NTC Dict.* 186: Welcome to another evening of college hoops. **1989** *Daybreak* (CNN-TV) (Mar. 12): An amazing day of hoop. **1992** *Rolling Stone* (Apr. 30) 65: Sidney...the black hoop master. **1994** *CBS This Morning* (CBS-TV) (Aug. 31): The legislation actually encourages shooting hoops.

¶ In phrases:

¶ **roll (one's) hoop** to go away; get out.

    1899 Kountz *Baxter's Letters* 52: I am told...to roll my hoop out of that house forever. **1908** McGaffey *Show Girl* 30: My goodness, I've got to roll my hoop. **1927** S. Lewis *Elmer Gantry* 12 [ref. to *ca*1902]: Now go roll your hoop. **1927** in Hammett *Knockover* 306: When we hit the street, we split....You roll your hoop, we'll roll ours. **1934** Halper *Foundry* 202: "Go roll your hoop," he said...and his voice was not the one of brotherhood. **1936** in R.E. Howard *Iron Man* 163: Go roll your hoop, you toe-dancin' four-flusher! **1937** Steinbeck *Mice & Men* 87: Maybe you just better go along an' roll your hoop. **1939** Bessie *Men in Battle* 171: Go on, roll your hoop. **1947** Helseth *Martin Rome* 62: Go roll a hoop! **1958** S.H. Adams *Tenderloin* 243 [ref. to 1890's]: Roll your hoop, Jerry.

¶ **take to the hoop** [fr. the basketball sense 'drive toward the basket'] to confront successfully; confront.

    1979 D. Thoreau *City at Bay* 210: That nigger never could take me to the hoop. *a***1994** N. McCall *Wanna Holler* 367: We were both ready to take it to the hoop and see where it led.

hoop¹ *v.* [shift of HOOP, *n.*, 5.b.] to play basketball.—also con-str. with *out* or *down.* Hence **hooper**, *n.*

    1980 in Safire *Good Word* 213: To "hoop out" is to play basketball, but actually playing is "hooping down." **1988** *Rage* (Knoxville, Tenn.) (Mar. 30) 19: He has a pair of Nike Air Revolutions and can't hoop a lick! **1992** *CBS This Morning* (CBS-TV) (Nov. 21): She's a hooper!

hoop² *v.* [alter. of WHOOPS] to vomit.

    1986 C. Stroud *Close Pursuit* 161: One of the guys from Emergency Services hooped into his boots over it.

hooping boots *n.pl.* (see quot.).

    1985 Univ. Tenn. student theme: Basketball shoes [were] always referred to as *hoopin' boots.*

hoople¹ *n. Und.* a finger ring; HOOP, 1.

    [**1848** Bartlett *Amer.* 180: *Hoople.* (Dutch, *hoepel.*) The boys in the city of New York still retain the Dutch name *hoople* for a hoop.] [**1911** *DN* III 544: *Hoopel*, n. Occasional variant of *hoop*.] **1928** O'Connor *B'way Racke-teers* 252: *Hoop* or *Hoople*—A finger ring. **1930** Irwin *Tramp & Und. Slang*: *Hoople.*—A ring, more frequently used by pitchmen selling "slum."

hoople² *n.* [perh. orig. in ref. to Major *Hoople*, cartoon char-acter featured in "Our Boarding House," syndicated comic strip originated by Gene Ahern in 1923 and still appearing (drawn by Bill Freyse) in the 1960's]

a foolish, ridiculous, or worthless person; idiot. [The 1970 def. may be erroneously overspecific.]

    1928 *N.Y. Times Mag.* (Nov. 11) 21: One of the strangest terms used by [N.Y.C. taxi] drivers is used to describe one who does not wish to work definite hours on schedule. A driver of this sort is called by his mates a "hoople." [**1952** in Kerouac *Letters* 369: An old…Major Hoople idiot.] **1966** Manus *Mott the Hoople* [title]. **1970** *Current Slang* V (Fall) 8: *Hoople,* n. A white person. **1971** *Inter. Jour. of Addiction* VI 360: *Hoople,* an alcoholic eccentric. **1977** Hamill *Flesh & Blood* 225: These hooples don't even have dressing rooms. **1980** *AS* (Fall) 200: Hayseed…hick…hillbilly…hoople…old bum…yokel. **1988** H. Gould *Double Bang* 28: All these hooples [were] just dying to make a major assault on one crooked cop.

hooplehead *n.* HOOPLE², *n.*
    *a***1994** H. Roth *Mercy of Rude Stream* 216 [ref. to *ca*1920]: Mock-solemn, Irish chaffering. They called each other hoople-head and satchel-back.

hoopster *n. Sports Journ.* a basketball player.
    1934 Weseen *Dict. Slang* 257: *Hoopster*—A basketball player. **1995** *TV Guide* (Apr. 18) 38: Brown was an All-Ivy League hoopster.

hoopty *n.* [orig. unkn.; cf. slightly earlier syn. *hoopy* in *DARE*] Orig. *Calif.* an automobile. Also vars.
    1968–70 *Current Slang* III & IV 70: *Hoopty, whoopty,* n. A car.—Watts. **1970** Landy *Underground Dict.* 105: *Hoopdee*…Latest-model car. **1985** "J. Blowdryer" *Mod. Eng.* 64: *Hoopry* [*sic*]…a car. **1986** *Morning Call* (Allentown, Penn.) (Aug. 18): [Court slang:] *Hoopty:* Car. **1988** Norst *Colors* 209: The Man everywhere, like four to a hoopty. **1990** "Sir Mix-A-Lot" *My Hooptie* (rap song): My hooptie rollin'. **1995** *UTSQ: Hooptie,* a big, older model ('76) car. He was driving his grandmother's hooptie.

hoorah¹, hooraw vars. HURRAH.

hoorah² *n.* a damn.
    1984 *Agronsky & Co.* (Mutual Radio Net.) (July 22): I don't think there are 80,000 people out of 80 million voters who give a hoorah about who's the Democratic national chairman.

hoose *v.* [sugg. by HOOSEGOW] to jail.
    1922 *Variety* (June 30) 6: They…were lucky to get out of town without gettin' hoosed.

hoosegow *n.* [< MexSp *juzgao* (var. of *juzgado*) 'jail' < Sp 'courtroom'] Esp. *West.* a jail or other place of confinement; lockup.
    1908 in H.C. Fisher *A. Mutt* 52: Mutt…may be released from the hooze gow. **1909** T.A. Dorgan, in Zwilling *TAD Lexicon* 46: I sentence you to 10 years in the hoozegow breaking rock. **1911** Bronson-Howard *Enemy to Society* 295: No thanks for th' little lady savin' th' bunch of you from th' "hoose-gow." *ca***1919** in Sandburg *Smoke & Steel* 59: I locked myself up and nobody knew it./Only the keeper and the kept in the hoosegow/Knew it. **1921** *Ohio Doughboys* 86: I took my camera to Venice—and landed in the Dago Hoosgow. **1922** Rice *Adding Machine* 115: But what I'm thinkin' of is that I went to the hoosegow on account of him. **1924** T. Boyd *Points of Honor* 51 [ref. to 1918]: I suppose they socked you in the hoosegow? **1926** *Amer. Leg. Mo.* (Sept.) 12: Corporal Meany, take this boot-lickin'…guard house lawyer down to the hooze-gow and tell the officer of the guard he is confined at the captain's orders. **1928** Hammett *Red Harvest* 74: "Oh, it's you," he said, as if it made any difference who took him back to the hoosegow. **1929** L. Thomas *Wood-fill* 98 [ref. to 1906]: "Nothin' doin'," we'd reply, "catchem whiskey for you and we get put in the hoosegow!" **1948** in *DA:* The bonafide stranger gets a summons and shows up at the hoosegow and is let go with a kindly warning. **1955** "W. Henry" *Wyatt* 16: He took the guns off Henry Plummer and elbowed him into the Dodge City hoosegow. **1935–62** Ragan & Finston *Toughest Pris.* 804: *Hoosegow*—A jail. **1989** "Capt. X" & Dodson *Unfriendly Skies* 131: When the FBI came and hauled him off to the hoosegow, they found quantities of drugs stuffed down under his seat cushion. **1993** *Newsweek* (Jan. 11) 54: Connick spent a night in the hoosegow and faces up to a year in jail.

hoosegow *v.* to jail.
    *ca***1923** in Hecht *Charlie* 69: Weber was hoosegowed.

hoosier *n.* [orig. unkn.; the most cogent discussion remains that of J.P. Dunn, *Indiana and Indianians,* II (1919), pp. 1121–55, but his conclusion that the origin lies in BrE (Cumberland) dial. *hoozer* '(said of anything large)' (*EDD*), is made dubious by the poor degree of attestation of *hoozer* (in a single word list of 1899) and the absence of any U.S. quots. in a clearly parallel sense (the meaning intended in the 1832 citation given by *DA* under its def. 1b is more

probably 'Indiana native'). Also discussed by R.I. McDavid, Jr., "Word Magic: Or, Would You Want Your Daughter to Marry a Hoosier?" (1967), rpt. in *Dialects in Culture* (Univ. Alabama Press, 1979) 254–257.]

1. (now usu. *cap.*) a native or inhabitant of Indiana.—often used attrib. Now *S.E.* [The 1826 quot. may belong to **(2.a.),** below.]
    1826 in *Chi. Tribune* (June 2, 1949) 20: The Indiana hoosiers that came out last fall is settled from 2 to 4 milds [*sic*] of us. **1832** *Indiana Democrat,* in *DAE:* Ask for our "hoosiers" good plantations. **1833** in Hoffman *Winter in West* I 210: There was a long-haired "hooshier" from Indiana, a couple of smart-looking "suckers" from…Illinois. *Ibid.* 226: The term "Hooshier," like that of Yankee, or Buckeye, first applied contemptuously, has now become a soubriquet that bears nothing invidious with it to the ear of an Indianian. **1833** in *Indiana Qly. Mag.* I (1905) 56: I'm told, in riding somewhere West,/A stranger found a Hoosier's Nest. **1834** (quot. at WOLVERINE). **1834** in *Indiana Mag. of Hist.* XXVIII (1932) 209: Before…[Indiana] was regularly surveyed—many families located and were called squatters…the surveyor on finding one of these would ask who's here, and place the name on their map…."Who's here"…eventuated in the general term of Hoosiers. **1835** A.A. Parker *Trip* 87: Those of Michigan are called *wolverines;* of Indiana *hooshers.* **1844** Porter *Big Bear* 17: "Where did all that happen?" asked a cynical-looking Hoosier. **1847** Robb *Squatter Life* 19: He shaped his way for the Hoosier state. **1855** in W. Whitman *Leaves of Grass* 40: A boatman over the lakes or bays or along coasts….a Hoosier, a Badger, a Buckeye. **1861** in Beatty *Volunteer* 56: The entire Fifteenth Indiana sprang to arms….The Hoosiers again returned to their couches. **1879** Pinkerton *Gypsies* 160: A queer, quaint Hoosier town is Bloomington. *ca***1885** in Hough *Soldier in West* 85: Thus I lost my Colonelcy because I was not a Hoosier. **1887** E. Custer *Tenting* 44: He…gave us his native state (Indiana) in copious…supplies…this tall Hoosier. **1900** Nicholson *Hoosiers* 12: William M. Chase, the artist, [was] also a native Hoosier. **1946** in *Harper's* (Jan. 1947) 67: Other Hoosiers ridicule them as hillbillies. **1968** E.A. Leary *Indiana Almanac* 107: Hoosier…connotes a warm, friendly, gracious, strong and self-reliant people with a sense of the past and a firm grip on the future.

2.a. Esp. *So. Midland.* an uncouth countryman; yokel. [The assertion made in the 1948 quot., though hardly improbable, is unsupported by documentation; but cf. note at **(1),** above.]
    1836 *Spirit of Times* (Oct. 15) 278: After waiting almost as long as the Hoosier did for salt river to run by that he might pass over dry, I at last caught an opening. **1837** *Spirit of Times* (July 1) 153: He may get his steam up some night so as to burst his boiler, which would be apt to mix the gentlemen and ladies in the dress circle with the snow drops and hooshiers of the gallery [in La.]. **1840** *Spirit of Times* (Nov. 14) 438 [ref. to 1836]: Let me portray to thee a [Georgia] *hoosier*…six feet six, without his shoes,—articles with which his feet had never been acquainted. **1840** in *DAE:* One of them cornfed Connecticut Hooshur gals, that you'll see sot a-straddle on every fence in Ohio. **1842** J.L. Scott *Missionary* 70: A company of "Hoosiers" (a term applied to the lower class in [Indiana]) came for dinner, and their common language was that of profane songs, vulgar jokes, and low ribaldry. **1845** Corcoran *Pickings* 46: An original character is your genuine hoosier…such an one as has all the attributes that peculiarly belong to the back woodsmen of the West. **1852** in *AS* XXX (1955) 172: We found the decks crowded with 60 or more Alabama housiers who are employed in stowing the cotton. **1853** in *Mo. Hist. Review* XXXVII (1942) 513: Pickles "green as a hoosier, and sharp as a shrew." **1857** in *DAE:* The mere "cracker" or "hoosier," as the poor [Southern] whites are termed. **1864** in *Ala. Review* X (1957) 218: Mr. Stimpse [is] a good, easy, ignorant, mountain hoosier [of E. Tenn.]. **1885** Siringo *Texas Cowboy* 35: The old gentleman introduced me to his wife as a little Texas hoosier that had strayed off from home….I wanted a broad brimmed hat and star top boots, but she said I would look too much like a hoosier with them on. **1902** W.N. Harben *Abner Daniel* 164: Yo're nothin' but a rag-tag, bob-tail mountain Hoosier, an' he's a slick duck from up North. **1902** in *Indiana Qly. Mag.* I (1905) 88: The word "hoosier" in Tennessee and North Carolina seemed to imply…an uncouth sort of rustic. **1912** Field *Watch Yourself* 156: They was nearly all "mountin hoosiers." **1926** Siringo *Riata & Spurs* 5 [ref. to 1870's]: The good lady thought boots would make me look to [*sic*] much like a "hoosier." **1927** J. Stevens *Mattock* 147: You big

Kansas Hoosier. **1935** *Amer. Mercury* (June) 229: *Hoosier:* countryman; hick. **1943** in *AS* XIX (1944) 104: Sailor's language....A *hoosier,*...any sort of farmerish chump. **1948** Dick *Dixie Frontier* 310: Before it was used to designate the citizens of Indiana, the term "Hoosier" was used in the South to describe a rough or uncouth person. **1949** *Chi. Tribune* (June 2) 20: Alabama hoosiers. **1956** Resko *Reprieve* 130: A Hoosier...in prison lingo meant that he hailed from some place other than New York City and therefore was not...as hep as we city cons. **1978** *UTSQ:* Country bumpkin...*clod, redneck, hoosier.* **1979** in Raban *Old Glory* 272: Buffalo, Iowa....Is that some kind of hoosier place?

b. *Gulf Coast.* a flatboatman or longshoreman.

1841 (quot. at GREEN, *n.,* 1). *ca*1845 in *Indiana Qly. Mag.* I (1905) 97: We do love to see a Hoosier roll along the levee with the proceeds of the plunder of his flatboat in his pocket. **1852** (see quot. at **(2.a.),** above. **1932** Bone *Capstan Bars* 85: The term "hoosier" in the song refers to a man, white or coloured, employed in loading a ship in the Southern States....Oh! a dollar a day is a hoosier's pay. /An' ship for more is what they say.

c. *Gamb. & Und.* a gullible or credulous person, esp. a naive law-abiding citizen; SUCKER.

1843 J. Greene *Gambling* 75: A gambler got to playing with a man whom he mistook for a green Hoosier, that knew nothing of playing scientifically. **1843** in G.W. Harris *High Times* 19: A right *verdant* Hoosier stepped up to me. **1899** "J. Flynt" *Tramping* 370: Them hoosiers couldn't see the thing in that way. *Ibid.* 394: Everybody who does not know the world as the hobo knows it is to him a "farmer," "hoosier," or outsider. **1931** *AS* VI (Aug.) 439: *Hoosier.* An outsider; a prison visitor. **1954** Chessman *Cell 2455* 89: The squares with dough—the hoosiers, the marks, the chumps—would have to look out for themselves. **1961** Braly *Felony Tank* 24: You didn't let a hoosier off with a fair price. **1964** in *IUFA Folk Speech: Hoosier.* Common law abiding person, those free outside of prison. **1962–68** B. Jackson *In the Life* 267: Well, where in hell are those hoosiers? They gotta be somewhere. **1986** J.J. Maloney *Chain* 41: These hoosiers around here want something they can understand.

d. an incompetent amateur or novice.

1874 in *DAE:* "Greenhorns" and hoosiers as the regular hunters call such fellows,...always...cry, "Down! down! Here comes a duck!" **1925** in *Amer. Mercury* (Jan. 1926) 64: The word *hoosier* is applied to anyone who is incompetent. **1940** Clemmer *Pris. Comm.* 295: There seems to be a distinction between the "elite class," the middle class, and the "hoosiers." **1941** *AS* (Oct.) 233: *Hoosier.* A newcomer without knowledge of logging work. **1944** *Amer. N & Q* III (Mar.) 188: During the I.W.W. strike...a number of Indianans who knew little or nothing about the lumbering business [came to work in Idaho]; hence the word *hoosier* in the lumber trade came to mean "a man who doesn't know his job." **1951** Haines & Burnett *Racket* (film): This is not smart, Nick. This is hoosier stuff. **1935–62** Ragan & Finston *Toughest Pris.* 804: *Hoosier*—An inefficient worker. **1980–82** in Courtwright et al. *Addicts Who Survived* 379: *Hoosier*—an addict who is not street-smart or experienced.

hoosieroon *n.* [HOOSIER, 1 + *-oon* (of obscure orig.)] an Indianian. *Joc.*

1833 in *Ind. Qly. Mag.* I (1905) 56: Half a dozen Hoosheroons/With mush and milk, tincups and spoons. **1834** in *DAE:* A few remote Kentuckians, or Indiana Hoosheroons. **1853** in Thornton *Amer. Gloss.:* He looks like a Hoosieroon; all he lacks is a chunk of gingerbread in his fist. **1889** Barrère & Leland *Dict. Slang* I 475: I can remember that in 1834, having read of hoosiers, and spoken of them, a boy from the West corrected me, and said that the word was properly hoosieroon.

hoosier up *v. Logging.* to slow down the pace or efficiency of one's work.

1925 in *Amer. Mercury* (Jan. 1926) 64: When a crew of workmen purposely *hoosier up* on the company, it means what experts in sabotage term a "conscious withdrawal of efficiency." **1941** *AS* XVI 233: [Logging terms:] *Hoosier.* To frame up [a] plot for slowing down work. **1964** Kornbluh *Rebel Voices* 253: But, instead of doing a full day's work, they would "hoosier up," that is, act like "greenhorns" who had never seen the woods before. **1976** *Atlantic* (Apr.) 76 [ref. to *a*1920]: Resolved to do "poor work for poor pay, poor food and poor conditions" and to "hoosier up," that is, to work like green farm boys who had never seen the woods before.

hoot[1] *n.* **1.** the least bit; a whit; a damn. Also in elab. vars., as **hoot in hell.** Cf. HOOTER[1].

1878 Beadle *Western Wilds* 615: I got into my reaper and banged down every hoot of it before Monday night. [**1898** Stevenson *Cape Horn* 386: You're no more good than a hoot down a dumb-waiter shaft.] **1912** in Truman *Dear Bess* 81: I really do not care a hoot what you do with my letters so long as you write me. **1921** Dos Passos *Three Soldiers* 14: I didn't give a hoot in hell what it cost. **1925** Fraser & Gibbons *Soldier & Sailor Wds.* 120 [ref. to WWI]: I don't care two hoots in hell. **1927** Mayer *Between Us Girls:* I honestly think it is absurd to spend a lot of money...for people you do not give a hoot in hell about. **1927** Kyne *They Also Serve* 49: He didn't care two hoots in a hollow. **1929–30** Farrell *Young Lonigan* 16: He didn't know what they were saying, and anyway, he didn't give two hoots in hell. **1933** Howard *Yellow Jack* 467: I don't give a hoot in hell how it spreads. **1938** "E. Queen" *4 Hearts* 132: [I] don't give a hoot. **1941** Hargrove *Pvt. Hargrove* 11: You weren't destined to be worth a hoot as a public relations man. **1942** E.S. Gardner *Drowning Duck* 67: I don't think *she'll* care a hoot about that. **1942** Liebling *Telephone* 221: It is not certain that Herbert Pulitzer gave a hoot. **1947** Riskin *Magic Town* (film): The rest of 'em ain't worth a hoot in a holler. **1948** Cozzens *Guard of Honor* 110: I don't give a hoot in hell about Bullen! **1962** L'Engle *Wrinkle in Time* 40: They don't give a hoot about me. **1967** Schaefer *Mavericks* 113: I don't give a hoot in hell how much work it is. **1978** B. Johnson *What's Happenin'* 73: If they don't give a hoot, I'm in trouble. **1988** M. Felsen *Anti-Warrior* 108: She doesn't give a hoot in hell for me.

2. a cause for laughter; source of fun.

1921 *DN* V 141: *Hoot,* n. An absurdly funny person, thing, or occurrence. "My dear, she's such a hoot!" **1942** *ATS* 288: Something humorous...*hoot.* *1969 in *BDNE* 211: It's going to be an absolute hoot! **1972** N.Y.U. student: It was a hoot, let me tell you. **1983** Flaherty *Tin Wife* 268: That would be a hoot. **1987** J. Hughes *Ferris Beuller* (film): Call the police. This will be a hoot.

hoot[2] *n.* HOOTENANNY, 2.

1943 *New World* (Seattle) (July 15) 3: "Hoots" will Honor Birth on July 31st. **1957** *Sing Out!* (Fall) 2: At the first hoot I went to, about three years ago, I was very impressed with the fact that here were songs whose lyrics at least had some meaning. **1968** Sebald *Adolescence* 252: *Hoot*—a wild party.

hoot *v.* to carouse.

1966 Susann *Valley of Dolls* 84: I'll want to stay up late and hoot. And I can't hoot the night before a matinee.

hootch, etc. var. HOOCH.

hootchie or **hoochie** *n.* [prob. ult. fr. HOOTCHY-KOOTCHY] Esp. *Rap Music.* a young woman, esp. if sexually promiscuous. Also **hootchy mama.** Cf. HOOTCHIE-PAP. [Though the written examples for this form show the spelling *hoochie,* we have placed the entry here based on the presumed etymological origin.]

1992 *L.A. Times* (Aug. 18) E1: A mac daddy was scamming on a fly hoochy. **1993** P. Munro *U.C.L.A. Slang II* 51: *Hoochie*...female....*Look at that hoochie* dressed like a tramp. *Ibid.* 51: Get that hoochie-mama off your lap! *a*1994 Smitherman *Black Talk* 137: *Hoochie* A sexually promiscuous female. **1995** Stavsky, Mozeson & Mozeson *A 2 Z* 49: *Hoochie, hoochie mama*...a promiscuous girl: A *hoochie mama* is gonna break your heart. **1995** *Martin* (Fox-TV): You turn your head and men look at every hootchie in town. **1995** *CBS This Morning* (CBS-TV)(Sept. 12): She's a hip-hop hootchie from the Bronx. **1995** *Jerry Springer Show* (synd. TV series): 'Cause she ain't nothin' but a troublemaker and a hoochie mama. **1996** *Street Talk II* 3: "She a straight up hoochee." [means] She's easy.

hootchie-pap *n.* [orig. unkn.] *Black E.* copulation.

1925 Van Vechten *Nigger Heaven* 208: Out fo' a little hootchie-pap, Ah *pre*-sume. *Ibid.* 286: Hootchie-pap: see boody.

hootchy-kootchy *n.* [orig. unkn.; the relationship between the use illustrated in the 1890 quot. and later usage is unclear; see G. Cohen, "Towards the Origin of *Hoochie-coochie*," *Comments on Etymology* XVIII (1989), 4, pp. 11–14]

1. a sinuous, suggestive dance, usu. in crude imitation of a belly dance, performed by a woman, esp. as a carnival attraction.—often used attrib. Also vars.

[**1890** in *OEDS:* I have been told that one night "Hoochy-Coochy" Rice, the minstrel man—they always call Billy "Hoochy-Coochy" because he invariably says that whenever he comes on stage—entered Hoyt's room…and stole a new song.] **1895** in Lloyd *Amer. Heritage Songbook* 186: She never saw the streets of Cairo [at the World's Columbian Exposition];/On the Midway she had never strayed;/She never saw the kutchy-kutchy. **1896** Walker *Amherst Olio* 34: Ide and Ward entered the one mile hoochee coochee. **1898** F.P. Dunne *Peace & War* 2: He's seen th' hootchy-kootchy an' th' Pammer House barber shop an' th' other ondacint sights iv a gr-reat city. **1904** Hobart *Jim Hickey* 84: We could make sandwich money in front of a hootchy-kooch palace. *a***1919** in J.A. Lomax *Cattle Trail* 99: They all swear you beat a circus /Or a hoochy-koochy dance. **1930** Farrell *Grandeur* 204: Just give me a fling at a hootchie kootchie like that one. **1931** "D. Stiff" *Milk & Honey* 155: Enlivening them with the vitality of a hoochy-coochy dancer. **1933** D.O. Stewart *Going Hollywood* (film): What are you doing? A hootchie-kootch? **1937** *Fortune* (Dec.) 143: The Midway,…where Little Egypt once danced the hootchy-kootchy for the raucous [Chicago] World's Fair crowds of 1893. *a***1940** in Lanning & Lanning *Texas Cowboys* 189: Some [horses] are just natural pitchers and can do the hootchy-kootchy while in the air. **1973** in L. Bangs *Psychotic Reactions* 124: Cruise out on the midway and stop to watch the hoochiekoo dancer. **1975** Mostert *Supership* 128: I can dance the hootchy-kootchy. **1984** J. McCorkle *Cheer Leader* 36: She did a hoochie koochie dance to "Ahab the Arab." *a***1973–87** F.M. Davis *Livin' the Blues* 94: Even if he promised to show me the Statue of Liberty doing the hootchy-kootchy. *a***1988** M. Atwood *Cat's Eye* 64: Salome was a dancer, she did the hoochie kootch.

2. sexual activity; HANKY-PANKY. Cf. earlier OOTCHIMA-GOOTCHI.

*a***1986** *NDAS:* Hootchie-coochie…Sexual activity = *ass:* He propositioned her for a little hootchie-coochie. **1993** P. Munro *U.C.L.A. Slang II* 51: Hoochie-coochie…sexual activity; fooling around. *They were engaging in hoochie-coochie.* [influenced by the M.C. Brains song "Oochie-Coochie."] [brackets in orig.].

hooted *adj.* drunk.—also constr. with *up.*

1899–1900 Cullen *Tales* 196: I got back, pretty well hooted up. **1927** (quot. at POTTED). **1934** Weseen *Dict. Slang* 277: Hooted—intoxicated.

hootenanny *n.* [orig. unkn.] **1.** a comparatively small thing whose name is unknown or forgotten; a whatchamacallit; gadget; (hence, *rarely*) an inconsequential person.

1929 *AS* V 151: Hootenanny—the same as gadget. **1934** Weseen *Dict. Slang* 352: Hootenannie—An indefinite substitute name for any appliance or device. **1942** *AS* (Dec.) 222: Hoot-Nanny. A gadget used to hold a crosscut saw when a log is sawed from underneath. **1962** *We Seven* 94: That's just the hootenanny valve on the whatchamacallit fluttering a little. **1966** Longstreet & Godoff *Wm. Kite* 306: Chuck, that hootenanny, he's happy because he's not spendin' no money on nothin' here. **1977** *New West* (Oct. 10) 77: That damn hootenanny in the window is giving me a sick headache.

2.a. any sort of informal social event; party.

1940 *Washington New Dealer* (Seattle) (July 25) 4: The New Dealer's Midsummer Hootenanny…Dancing. Refreshments. Door Prizes. **1981** K. Pollitt, in *Mother Jones* (Dec.) 56: The disdain of an Orthodox rabbi for an Ethical Culture hootenanny. **1988** *Rage* (Knoxville, Tenn.) (Mar. 30) 3: Sigma Chi and MDA…presents The Derby Days Hootenanny Jamboree.

b. a performance of folk music, esp. by a number of artists with a degree of audience participation. Now *colloq.*

1957 P. Seeger, in *Sing Out!* (Winter) 34: Another took a tape recorder with her and set up small hootenannies in country stores, and recorded the singing. ***1960** Seeger & MacColl *Singing Island* 1: The kind of songs which are delighting audiences at concerts and hootenannies up and down Great Britain. **1963** P. Tamony, in *West. Folklore* (July): Under four sponsorships, over seventy-five programs of folk song were presented [in New York City] under the "Hootenanny" title between 1941 and 1960. **1975** Greer *Slammer* 39: I suppose that means guitars and hootenannies in my chapel. **1988** B.E. Wheeler *Outhouse Humor* 14: I was singing at a "hootenanny."

3. a confused or turbulent situation; commotion.

1987 *21 Jump St.* (Fox-TV): Tell the cops. 'Cause after last night's hootenanny they're gonna be crawlin' all over this place.

hooter[1] *n.* [orig. unkn.] the least bit; a whit; HOOT.

1839 in Thornton *Amer. Gloss.:* Now the Grampus [a vessel] stopt and didn't buge [budge] one hooter. *ca***1849** in *DAE:* What cares he about the "honor of the nation?"…—Not a hooter. **1859** Bartlett *Amer.* (ed. 2) 202: Hooter. Probably a corruption of *iota.* Common in New York in such phrases as "I don't care a *hooter* for him," "this note ain't worth a *hooter.*" *a***1889** in Barrère & Leland *Dict. Slang* I 474: Ah, Billy, you and your sword-cane can't do a *hooter* among the girls. **1889** in *DAE:* It has not harmed the Republican cause in Ohio a hooter. **1896** *Harper's Mag.* (Apr.) 784: Whiskey.…now I can have all I want, [so] I don't care a *hooter!* **1900** in *DA:* "Do you mean that you don't know anything about the matter at all?"…"Not a hooter."

hooter[2] *n.* **1.** HOOKER[2].

1899 Green *Va. Folk-Speech* 191: Hooter, n. A dram; a drink; from a tin cup from which the drink was taken. **1899–1900** Cullen *Tales* 151: I poured out a very small one—I wanted a hooter, but I was looking for effect, not joy.

2. a person's nose.

***1958** in *OED2:* He held it [a handkerchief] up to his face as though he was going to blow his hooter. ***1960** Partridge *DSUE* (ed. 5) 1136: Hooter…Nose: low jocular: since *ca*1940. **1973** *M*A*S*H* (CBS-TV): That's quite a hooter. **1981** *Nat. Lampoon* (Nov.) 18: Hey, you've got a big woogie hanging out of your hooter! **1984** N. Bell *Raw Youth* 41: You really think I've got a big hooter? **1986** *UTSQ:* Nose…hooter. **1988** *ALF* (NBC-TV): This Cyrano guy had a jumbo hooter.

3.a. usu. *pl.* a woman's breast.

1975 K. Hall *Sisters* (film): Did you see the hooters on this babe? **1979** G. Wolff *Duke of Deception* 181 [ref. to 1950's]: Went the distance last night with that babe from Walker's, huge hooters. **1980** *Maclean's* (Feb. 4) 51: Ali MacGraw screaming her hooters off. **1981** in *Nat. Lampoon* (Jan. 1982) 32: Knockers Breasts Mammaries Hooters. **1982** in "J.B. Briggs" *Drive-In* 13: Women…should be judged by the size of their hooters. **1987** *Cheers* (NBC-TV): She's got a great set of hooters. **1987** *Newhart* (CBS-TV): Your wife has great hooters. **1994** *Harper's* (Oct.) 41: Is one…a gorgeous blonde with big hooters or something?

b. a young woman having large breasts.

1985 Univ. Tenn. student theme: Ladies who are blessed with big breasts are called "hooters." **1983–86** G.C. Wilson *Supercarrier* 5: The aviators and their ladies—called Hooters—at the party followed.

4. a telephone; HORN, 6.a.

1977–81 S. King *Cujo* 195: Trenton got on the old hooter.

5. *Stu.* a marijuana cigarette; (*also*) marijuana.

1984 (cited in Spears *Drugs & Drink* 267). *a***1986** *NDAS:* Hooter…a marijuana cigarette. *a***1990** P. Dickson *Slang!* 116: Hooter. Marijuana.

6. [cf. Austral slang *hoot* 'to stink'] a breaking of wind.

1986 Univ. Tenn. students: "Man, it stinks in here." "Did you pop off a hooter?"

hoot-owl [shift] *n.* Esp. *Coal Mining.* a late-night work shift.

1947 *PADS* (No. 9) 33: Hoot owl: n. One name for the 12 midnight to 8 morning shift. **1958** McCulloch *Woods Wds.* 89: Hoot owl shift—Any early morning job. **1972** (quot. at GRAVEYARD). **1976** Arble *Long Tunnel* 37: This was the last night of the hoot-owl shift, 11 P.M. to 7 A.M. *Ibid.* 40: This was the last night of hoot owl and the fatigue caught up with me. *Ibid.* 57: We all work hoot owl every third week. **1977** Sayles *Union Dues* 32: The men of the hoot-owl shift are already there on benches in coal-grimed work clothes. *a***1986** D. Tate *Bravo* 132: I don't dig working this hoot-owl shift. **1987** Pedneau *A.P.B.* 1: He was the only unit working the hoot owl.

hoot-owl trail *n. West.* ¶ In phrase: **ride the hoot-owl trail** to lead the life of an outlaw.

1968 S.O. Barker *Rawhide Rhymes* 42: Bill Doolin led an outlaw clan /and rode the hoot owl trail. **1975** Julien *Cogburn* 36: You have ridden the "Hoot Owl Trail" and tasted the fruits of evil.

hooty *adj.* angry.

1929 Milburn *Hobo's Hornbook* 150: Now I was feelin' salty and I glued Squire Grimes' hat,/When the town clown got hooty, and he flailed me with his bat. *Ibid.* 260: Next day the justice he was hooty. *Ibid.* 285: Hooty, angry.

Hoover *n.* [fr. *Hoover,* trademark for vacuum cleaners, in ref.

to the sound of the engines] *Naval Av.* a Lockheed S-3 Viking antisubmarine patrol aircraft.

1986 M. Skinner *USN* xiii: *Viking*—S-3 ASW aircraft; the "Hoover." *Ibid.* 42: The peculiar vacuum-cleaner sound the S-3 makes around the ship has earned it the nickname "Hoover." **1989** Joss *Strike* 99: Lockheed's...S-3. Properly the Viking, dubbed the Hoover (hear its twin turbofans and you understand the nickname instantly).

hoover *v.* [sugg. by *Hoover,* a trademark for vacuum cleaners; used as v. meaning 'to vacuum' in BrE since 1927] **1.** to take (cocaine or the like) by inhalation.

1980–82 in Courtwright et al. *Addicts Who Survived* 379: *Hoover*—to snort [drugs] greedily. **1984** McInerny *Bright Lights* 42: There are dances to be danced, drugs to be hoovered. **1986** N.Y.C. man, age 37: You could be a jet-setter, hoovering coke.

2.a. to consume (food or drink) greedily; devour.

*a***1986** in *NDAS:* Instead of the moussaka and lamb that everyone else was hoovering. *****1986** in T. Thorne *Dict. Contemp. Sl.:* We laid out a spread and they hoovered it up in minutes. **1989** *ALF* (NBC-TV): I never thought I'd miss the sound of him hoovering down his food. **1992** *Closer Look* (NBC-TV): People who have eaten next to Diana say that she kind of hoovers it up.

b. to snatch up greedily. Also fig.

*a***1990** P. Dickson *Slang!* 61: *Hoovering.* Acquiring stocks as if one were sucking them up with a vacuum cleaner. **1993** *Time* (Feb. 8) 80: The [artworks] were hoovered up. **1997** *New Yorker* (Apr. 7) 86: The same mechanism that hoovers the hip into the mainstream.

3. to fellate vigorously.—usu. considered vulgar. *Joc.* Also as *n.*

*a***1986** in *NDAS:* Will you hoover me immediately, before I pay any attention to you? **1988** H. Gould *Double Bang* 59: She had a Hoover like a tornado.

Hoover blankets *n.pl.* [see note at HOOVERVILLE] newspapers wrapped around oneself for warmth. Now *hist.*

1948 (quot. at HOOVER HOG).

Hoover flags *n.pl.* [see note at HOOVERVILLE] (see quot.). Now *hist.*

1977 Johnson & Williamson *Whatta-Gal* 77 [ref. to 1932]: Empty pockets turned inside out were "Hoover flags."

Hoover flush *n.* [see note at HOOVERVILLE] *Poker.* an incomplete or "busted" flush.

1933–35 D. Lamson *About to Die* 206: Hell-bent on fillin' Hoover flushes.

Hoover hog *n.* [see note at HOOVERVILLE] a wild rabbit or armadillo, or its meat. *Joc.* Now *hist.*

1940 *AS* XV 447: *Hoover hog.* Rabbit. **1945** in *DA:* He might resort to eating "Hoover hogs," which was the name given to rabbits by the valley farmers. **1948** in Brookhouser *Our Years* 313: Old newspapers were called "Hoover blankets," jack rabbits "Hoover hogs," and the shanties of starvation rising on outskirts of cities "Hoovervilles." **1976** *N.Y. Folklore* II 238: Wild game rabbits are frequently referred to as *Hoover Hogs.* **1977** Johnson & Williamson *Whatta-Gal* 77 [ref. to 1932]: Stringy jackrabbits that hungry farmers were often forced to eat were called "Hoover hogs." **1978** Katz *Folklore* 34: "Hoover Hogs" What...my maternal grandparents, used to call the rabbits they were able to trap during the Depression years. **1982** Heat Moon *Blue Hwys.* 147: Poor whites ate...[armadillos]...during the Depression and called them "Hoover hogs" or "Texas turkeys." **1983** W.A. Owens *Tell Me a Story* 24: Armadillos, "Hoover hogs," they called them, furnished meat for those who could stomach them.

Hoover hotel *n.* (see quot.).

1931–34 Adamic *Dynamite* 423: The flophouses—or "Hoover hotels," as they were called—were overcrowded with strong, jobless men.

Hooverville *n.* [Herbert Clark *Hoover* (president of the U.S. at the beginning of the Great Depression) + *-ville*] a collection of small shacks inhabited by the homeless.

1933 in *DA:* Hoovervilles are in a separate nation, with separate codes. **1938** Steinbeck *Grapes of Wrath* ch. xix: There was a Hooverville on the edge of every town. **1949** *Sat. Review of Lit.* (Aug. 6) 116: They called them "Hoovervilles" [during the Depression]. Evicted families lived in tin-and-cardboard shacks. **1958** Horan *Mob's Man* 42: Men who had once been respectable family men were living

in Hooverville, a collection of shacks on the edge of the Bowery. **1966** Braly *Cold* 97: You don't remember when people lived in Hoovervilles, do you? **1967** Raskin *True Course* 12: Long patient breadlines; apple sellers; Hoovervilles. **1970** Terkel *Hard Times* 32: Every place I went, Hoovervilles—they were raided. **1983** S. Wright *Meditations* 110: The shabby, dispossessed look of a Depression-era Hooverville. **1987** *N.Y. Times* (Dec. 23): The Hooverville that is jerrybuilt nightly down below the glittering South Bank arts center.

hoozie *n.* [perh. orig. a blend of *hussy* + FLOOZIE, but cf. HOSIE[1]] a sexually promiscuous woman, esp. a prostitute.

1974 Terkel *Working* 240: "You look like a hoozy." But today all girls look like hoozies.

hop[1] *n.* **1.** a dancing party. Now *colloq.* or *S.E.*

*****1731** in *OED:* Near an hundred people of both sexes...dancing to the musick of two sorry fiddles...it was called a three-penny hop. **1757** in *DAE:* She had no notion at her age of sacrificing all the dear pleasures of routs, hops, quadrille for a philosophical husband. *****1821** *Real Life in London* I 95: *Hop*—A dance. **1849** in *DAE:* It is very common...to give weekly "hops," as they are called, which are neither more nor less than dancing parties divested of some of the usual ceremonies of such assemblages. **1859** in L. Barney *Letters* 31: Some fifty males and seven females graced the "hop." **1860–61** R.F. Burton *City of Saints* 254: The proportion of the sexes at "hops" rarely exceeds one to seven. **1869** W.H.H. Murray *Adv. in Wilderness* 44: Here they have civilized "hops," and..."operatic singing." **1870** *Comic Songster* 26: In a lager-bier garden, where they had a sort of "hop." **1877** in J.M. Carroll *Camp Talk* 106: There will be a "Hop" at the Trader's to-morrow night. **1884** in Lummis *Letters* 174: These comical "hops" come around as often as the natives can crowd them in. **1894** in A. Charters *Ragtime Songbk.* 46: Last night I went to colored hop. **1904** in "O. Henry" *Works* 29: Few strangers could boast of having shaken a foot at the regular hops. **1908** Ade *In Babel* 173: They move the chairs out of the dining-room every two weeks and have a "grand hop." **1918** McKay *Little Pills* 9: I never knew why it was called a hop instead of a dance, but it was always so designated in the army. **1973** Ellington *Music Is My Mistress* 20: We are going over to Ina Fowler's house and have a hop.

2.a. BELLHOP, 1.

1930 (quot. at JIGABOO). **1951** Elgart *Over Sexteen* 142: He tipped the 'hop generously to insure against that worthy letting the news leak out that they were newlyweds. **1958** R. Chandler *Playback* 104: And with that amount of baggage a hop came up with him naturally. **1958** Bard & Spring *Horse Wrangler* 169: The hop says, "I can fix you up O.K." **1980** in Courtwright et al. *Addicts Who Survived* 168: He couldn't smoke opium on a hop's salary.

b. CARHOP.

1975 C.W. Smith *Country Music* 228: The hop came striding down the median in answer to his persistent honks.

¶ In phrase:

¶ **take it on the hop** to run away or get out; CLEAR OUT.

1968 Heard *Howard St.* 51: Take it on the hop, man. I don't wanna hear that shit. **1966–80** McAleer & Dickson *Unit Pride* 272: Take it on the hop, creeps.

hop[2] *n.* [prob. sugg. by HOP-TOY; less prob. a pidgin form of Mandarin *ho ping* (Cantonese *nga pin*) 'tranquility, bliss, peace; (hence) opium'] Orig. *Narc.* **1.a.** occ. *pl.* opium.—often constr. with *the.*—often used attrib.

1886 in Courtwright *Dk. Paradise* 74: Another feature of the "hop" fiend is his absolute aversion to the society of everybody, save and except the fiend or Chinaman. **1887** *Lantern* (N.O.) (May 14) 4: So long as a smoker can obtain his "hop," so long will we have opium joints in our midst. **1896** F.P. Dunne, in Schaaf *Dooley* 246: All a man wants is a nice room in th' back iv a Chinese laundhry an' a lung full iv hop an' he can make a monkey out iv the la-ad that wrote th' arithmetic. **1896** in S. Crane *N.Y.C. Sks.* 146: Who ever heard of a man committing murder when full of hop. **1898** L.J. Beck *Chinatown* 149: This process is known as "cooking" the "hop" or opium. **1904** in "O. Henry" *Works* 81: Wish I knew the brand of hop that he smokes. *a***1909** Tillotson *Detective* 92: *Hop*—Opium. **1914** London *Jacket* 143: I guess that is what all the novel-writers do—hit the hop so as to throw their imagination into the high gear. **1918** in *AS* (Oct. 1933) 28: *Hops.* Opium or other intoxicating drug. **1929** T. Gordon *Born to Be* 35: We were surprised to learn that he was putting up all the fuss about some girl stealing his hop-pipe in Helena. **1950** A. Lomax *Mr.*

Jelly Roll 25 [ref. to 1890's]: I would…bring back several cards of hop. **1965** Himes *Imabelle* 161: Hank's on hop and Jodie on heroin. **1971** Horan *Blue Messiah* 35: You're smoking hop, Nick. **1974** Angelou *Gather Together* 95 [ref. to 1940's]: Marijuana, cocaine, hop (opium) and heroin. **1984** *Prairie Home Companion* (Nat. Pub. Radio) (Oct. 22): Down-on-their luck piano players strung out on hop in Hong Kong.

b. occ. *pl.* morphine or heroin; (*broadly*) any narcotic or stimulating drug.—often constr. with *the*.

1907 in H.C. Fisher *A. Mutt* 11: He may last 'till Monday, Doc, if we shoot a little hop into him. **1908** in H.C. Fisher *A. Mutt* 25: This plug is so used to the hop that he don't mind it. *ca***1910** in Lomax & Lomax *Amer. Ballads* 185: He bought a million dollars' worth of hops to smoke. **1918** T. Smith *Biltmore Oswald* 6: Hospital apprentice treated me to a shot of Pelham "hop"…taken through the arm. **1919** *DN* V 41: *Hops*, n.pl. Dope. **1925–26** Black *You Can't Win* 162: Given a sufficient quantity of hop, no fiend is ever at a loss for a sound reason for taking a jolt of it. **1930** Graham & Graham *Queer People* 220: Blynn put the poor kid on the hop. **1931** Hellinger *Moon* 239: I often suspected that he was on the hop. **1937** Schary & Butler *Big City* (film): Or a maniac full of hop. **1943** Chandler *High Window* 419: So they drag him over to the hospital ward and shoot him full of hop. **1962** Riccio & Slocum *All the Way Down* 62: Joey Boy was on the hop, but he went the entire night without a fix. **1980** in Courtwright et al. *Addicts Who Survived* 298: I paid forty-five dollars for a tin of hop [heroin] in 1940. *a***1990** E. Currie *Dope & Trouble* 44: It's the heroin, the hop, whatever you want to call it.

c. Esp. *Mil.* a state of dreamy inattention or idle distraction; reverie.

1918 Noyes *MS.* (unp.): *To Snap out of one's Hop* = to get out of one's hammock on the jump. Generally used in the imperative. Derivation unknown. **1919** Ashton *F,63* 52: Riddle pretended to be a Colonel and had the driver stop several times on the way out and snapped a few M.P.'s out o' the hop. **1924** in T. Boyd *Points of Honor* 72: Come out of your hop, Wainwright.…There's no use lyin' when the real dope's bad enough. **1941** Kendall *Army & Navy Sl.* 20: *To put in a hop.*…befuddled.

2. stuff; nonsense. Cf. syn. DOPE, 10.

1912 *Adventure* (June) 245: On the level…human nature is funny hop. **1940** E. O'Neill *Iceman* 156 [ref. to *ca*1912]: Jess, dat Cora sure played you for a dope, feedin' yuh dat marriage-on-de-farm hop!

3. HOPHEAD, 1.a.

1916 MacBrayne & Ramsay *One More Chance* 125: In police circles these unfortunates are known as "dope fiends" or "hops." *Ibid.* 135: The criminal…may have become a criminal only after he became a "hop." **1918** in *AS* (Oct. 1933) 28: *Hop, Hophead.* A drug-addict. **1929** Barr *Let Tomorrow Come* 151: You talk like one o' these hops when they're charged up.

¶ In phrases:

¶ **full of hop[s]** thinking or behaving as though stupefied by a drug; devoid of common sense.

1911 Bronson-Howard *Enemy to Society* 148: Oh, you're full of hop. **1914** Lardner *You Know Me Al* 133: The recruit pitchers that is along with our club have not got nothing and the scout that reckommended them must of been full of hops or something. **1926** in *AS* II (1927) 276: *Full of hops* (or *beans*)—crazy. **1928** Burnett *Little Caesar* 141: I wasn't even in that end of town the night Courtney was bumped off. That dame's full of hop.

¶ **in a hop** very angry.

1935 Lorimer & Lorimer *Heart Specialist* 129: Well, I was just in a hop.

hop¹ *v.* **1.** to attack or assault; (*Av.*) to attack from the air; JUMP.—also (*obs.*) constr. with *on*. Also (*vulgar*) **hop (someone's) ass.**

1833 J. Hall *Soldier's Bride* 226: The other had *hopped on him* without provocation. **1847** in Eliason *Tarheel Talk* 153: He got mad & I thought he would "hop me" as granny says. **1899** Cullen *Tales* 107: When we showed 'em our sole remaining six bits we were hopped. **1920** Clapp *17th Aero Squadron* 50: Later, on the same day, the 148th "hopped" the Blue-Tails, or what remained of them, and cleaned up six of them. **1943** in Cundiff *Ten Knights* 78: We were hopped by Zeros. **1943** W. Simmons *Joe Foss* 98: I…was afraid of being hopped by Zeros and shot down. **1945** J. Bryan *Carrier* 32: Frank Onion got hopped yesterday…and took some bullets in his engine. **1956** Heflin *USAF Dict.* 254: *Hop*, v. In slang usage…To attack an *aircraft* from the

air. **1983** Flaherty *Tin Wife* 222: Breaking up drunken domestic brawls and hopping the asses of neighborhood rowdies.

2. to mount and copulate with.—usu. considered vulgar.

*ca***1929** *Collection of Sea Songs* 29: So he hopped her. **1962** T. Berger *Reinhart* 345: They made Abelard a bullock for hopping Héloise. **1968** Westheimer *Young Sentry* 152: They act like you'd hopped their mother or something. **1973–74** M. Smith *Death of Detective* 8: He'll hop you like a German shepherd, Mary. **1994** *Wash. Post* (Aug.; day not known) G6: 21 Black Jacks slinging cocaine/21 Black Jacks hip to hop Jane.

3. to leave (town) hurriedly; SKIP.

1942–49 Goldin et al. *DAUL* 101: *Hop town.* To flee a city or town, especially when wanted by police. **1984** Algeo *Stud Buds* 1: To not go to class…*hop town.*

4. *Av.* to carry or fly (passengers) in an aircraft.

1954 in Loosbrock & Skinner *Wild Blue* 15: "Hopping passengers" was as popular in the early days of ballooning as it was later to be in the youth of the airplane. **1956** Heflin *USAF Dict.* 254: *Hop*, v. In slang usage…To take *a person* on a hop.

5. to work as a bellhop.

1959–60 Bloch *Dead Beat* 76: Sometimes I do a little hopping when we have a rush.

¶ In phrases:

¶ **hop bail** to forfeit one's bail by fleeing the jurisdiction of a court.

1902 Cullen *More Tales* 90: They hopped the bail and it was a long time before O'Brien was nailed again. **1942–49** Goldin et al. *DAUL* 101: I'da hopped bail if I knew the D.A. could settle me for mopery.

¶ **hop bells** see s.v. BELL.

¶ **hop it** to get going; be off.

*****1914** W. Owen, in *OED2*: I should hop it, immejit. **1953** Paley *Rumble* 31: "You wanna work, don't you?…Hop it." **1954–60** *DAS*: *Hop it* To go away; beat it.

¶ **hop the twig, 1.** to depart suddenly or hurriedly; abscond.

*****1785** Grose *Vulgar Tongue*: To *Hop the Twig.* To run away. *Cant.* *****1789** in *F & H* III 347: *Hop the twig*…means to depart suddenly. *****1803** in J. Ashton *Eng. Satires on Napoleon* 148: Promise not to hop the twig to Hanover. **1821** Waln *Hermit in Phila.* 25: It's time to *hop the twig; I'll draw in my horns.* *****1830** in *F & H* III 347: The lady bird—has hopped the twig. *****1884** in *F & H*: They got too numerous and strong, and then we hopped the twig. **1903** in "O. Henry" *Works* 141: I'll make him hop the twig.

2. to die. *Rare* in U.S.

*****1797** in *OED2*: [He] kept his bed three days, and hopped the twig on the fourth. **1859** Matsell *Vocab.* 43: *Hopped the Twig.* Hung. *****1870** in *OED*: If old Campbell hops the twig. **1944** Burley *Hndbk. Jive* 140: *Hop a twig*—Die.

hop² *v.* [shortened from HOP UP, 1] *Horse Racing*. (see 1968 quot.).

[**1942** *ATS* 698: "Dope" a horse…*hop up.*] *a***1961** *WNID3*. **1968** Ainslie *Racing Guide* 469: *Hop*—To drug a horse illegally.

hoper *n.* a person who is hopeful of something; (*specif.*) a prospective guest or passenger awaiting accommodations as a result of a cancellation.

1954 Collans & Sterling *House Detect.* 219: *Hoper.* Prospective guest without registration, waiting for cancellation.

hop-fiend *n.* a person addicted to opium or opiates. Cf. FIEND, *n.*, 1.

1886 (quot. at HOP², *n.*, 1.a.). **1898** L.J. Beck *Chinatown* 139: The number of "hop fiends," as opium smokers are called, is far greater in New York than people have any idea of. **1909** Chrysler *White Slavery* 89: Opium smokers, "hop fiends" or "hop heads" as they are called. **1914** (quot. at FIEND, *n.*, 1). **1915** Bronson-Howard *God's Man* 376: I told you what always happened to these little hop-fiends if they kept lying on their side. **1928** Callahan *Man's Grim Justice* 32: The hop fiends were shouting as Kelly and I fell and stumbled over the "layouts."

hop-fighter *n.* an opium smoker.

1915 Bronson-Howard *God's Man* 392: Well, that's a hop-fighter's dinner, you know.

hophead *n.* **1.a.** a person addicted to the use of opium or a similar drug; drug addict.

1901 T.A. Dorgan, in Zwilling *TAD Lexicon* 46: Hophead Hank has a dream. **1907** in H.C. Fisher *A. Mutt* 16: I've been after you hop heads for some time. **1909** (quot. at HOP-FIEND). **1911** A.H. Lewis *Apaches of N.Y.* 248: It can't be some hop-head has blown out the gas? **1912** Lowrie *Prison* 87: Every third or fourth prisoner entering San Quentin at that time was a "hop-head." **1914** Spencer *Jailer* 110: Drug fiends, or as they are better known, hop-heads, are those addicted to the use of morphine, cocaine, marihuana, opium, and yen-she. **1918** in H.W. Morgan *Addicts* 85: Another "hop head," loaded with morphine. **1922** Murphy *Black Candle* 29: Here…lay four opium debauchees or, as the police designate them, "hop-heads." **1923** O'Hare *In Prison* 52: The next was a "hop head" arrested for peddling "dope." **1927** McKay *Harlem* 79: He's the biggest hophead I ever seen. Nobody can sniff like him. **1930** Lavine *3d Degree* 152: If the woman is a "hophead," the matter is easy; merely deprive her of her drug. **1930** Deitrick *Parade Ground* 144: That stuff was doped. The bitch is a hophead! **1946** I. Shulman *Amboy Dukes* 72: He's becoming a regular hophead. **1958** T. Capote *Breakfast at Tiffany's* 90: That ro-ro-rovolting and de-de-degenerate girl. I always knew she was a hop-hop-head. **1966** Fariña *Down So Long* 58: New Mexico, man,…right where every hophead in the country figured he'd be. **1970** R. Vasquez *Chicano* 217: I can tell a hophead a mile off. **1985** Grave *Fla. Burn* 10: A pair of ragged Puerto Rican hopheads.

b. *Specif.*, a user of cannabis.

1964 Harris *Junkie Priest* 127: With marijuana, sometimes I couldn't think straight. So I kept staying with the junkies rather than the hopheads. **1990** *New Yorker* (Sept. 10) 77: There was marijuana around, but it was associated with visiting bandleaders, "hopheads."

c. *Horse Racing.* (see quots.).

1949 Cummings *Dict. Sports* 212: Hophead. Slang.…A horse that runs well only when illegally stimulated. **1951** *PADS* (No. 16) 36: Hop head…A horse which has been given a drug before a race to alter his speed.

2. a foolish or crazy person.

1966 van Italie *Really Here* 41: Well, I must admit I do look a little like a hophead with that nutty grin on my funny little face and those goopy stars in my peepers.

3. a drunkard.

1970 Boatright & Owens *Derrick* 146 [ref. to *ca*1920]: One old hophead says, "What line's that?"

hop joint *n.* **1.** an opium den. Now mainly *hist.*

1887 *Lantern* (N.O.) (June 4) 5: The police…raided the "hop joints." **1890** in Dobie *Rainbow* 160: I knocked her down on the hop-joint floor. **1899** *Nat. Police Gaz.* (Mar. 25) 3: I never saw such a bunch of knockers in a hop joint in all my life. **1900** *Blue Book* (unp.): The contents of this book are fact and not dreams from a "hop joint." **1908** in H.C. Fisher *A. Mutt* 77: United Hop Joint. **1912** in D. Runyon *Firing Line* 103: A layin' in a hop joint an' a smokin' of yen-shee. **1914** *Amer. Mag.* (June) 31: My friend suggested a visit to a "hop-joint." **1914** in *Univ. Mo. Studies* XV (1940) 333: She went into a hop joint,/And she didn't go for fun. **1935** in *Calif. Folk. Qly.* II 46: In a hop joint on Dupont street. **1936** Duncan *Over the Wall* 27: Opium dens or hop joints were hidden away behind Chinese laundries.

2. a cheap barroom.

1915 *DN* III 226: West Texas…hop-joint, n. A saloon. **1954–60** *DAS*: Hopjoint…A cheap saloon. **1979** Erdoes *Saloons of West* 44: The western saloon was known by many names:…whiskey mill,…hop joint,…doggery [etc.].

hop juice *n.* beer.

1896 Ade *Artie* 49: Last night when I was sloppy I thought she was the best ever. That just goes to show what the hop-juice'll do for you.

hop off *v.* [cf. *hop the twig*, s.v. HOP¹, *v.*] **1.a.** to die. *Rare* in U.S.

***1797** in *OED*: Must look in upon the rich old jade before she hops off. ***a1890–93** F & H III 347: To die…To hop off. **1942** *ATS* 132: Die…hop off.

b. *Und.* to kill (a person).

1928 Sharpe *Chicago May* 43: As I have said, the skunk was hopped off. The killer was tried and acquitted.

2. *Army.* to initiate an attack; jump off.

1918 Swan *My Co.* 109: He "hopped off" with a couple of squads from the Bois de Ramieres with orders to bring back some prisoners.

Ibid. 136: A regiment of Infantry was to "hop off" early in the morning, going over to take a certain town.

3. to depart hurriedly.

1935 Algren *Boots* 185: It's time to scram. Hop off, beat it.

hopped *adj.* **1.** HOPPED-UP, 1.a.

1921 Benet *Beginning of Wisdom* 289: I couldn't take her through the window, hopped like she was. **1929** *AS* IV (June) 341: Hopped. Under the influence of a powerful drug. **1937** in Partridge *Dict. Und.* 344. **1953** E. Hunter *Jungle Kids* 29: I thought Turk was just hopped and talking through the top of his skull. **1965** Himes *Imabelle* 92: "You think she's drunk?"…"Either that or hopped." **1970** *Current Slang* V (Winter) 9: Hopped, adj. Intoxicated on drugs.—College students…California.

2. drunk.

1934 Appel *Brain Guy* 47–49: The men passed the whisky bottle.…"You're hopped." "Maybe gettin' hopped's smartest."

hopped-up *adj.* [HOP², *n.*, 1.a. + *-ed* + *up*; cf. HOP UP] **1.a.** Orig. *Narc.* under the influence of a psychotropic drug; doped; (*broadly*) intoxicated or addicted.

1918 in *AS* (Oct. 1933) 28: Hopped up. In a stupor from drugs. **1924** Henderson *Keys to Crookdom* 408: Hopped up—Intoxicated on opium. **1927** Coe *Me—Gangster* 43: They are all hopped up with dope. **1930** Lavine *Third Degree* 227: "Coked" or "hopped up" gunmen. **1952** "R. Marsten" *So Nude, So Dead* 127: Dirty, hopped-up liar. **1955** O'Connor *Last Hurrah* 42: A bunch of hopped-up coons in purple suits blowing horns at a mob of high-school nitwits. **1935–62** Ragan & Finston *Toughest Pris.* 804: Hopped up—Under the influence of opium or of any narcotic. **1966** S. Harris *Hellhole* 89: Anyhow, I couldn't go out on the street or go with tricks unless I was hopped up. **1975** Hinton *Rumble Fish* 24: "He's been poppin' pills."…Now, I hate fighting hopped-up people. They're crazy. **1982** Knoxville, Tenn., woman, age *ca*60: So many people are just hopped up on dope and mean as the devil. **1992** N. Russell *Suicide Charlie* 151: I would have to be hopped up to even think about it. **1995** *Wall St. Jour.* (Feb. 6) A1: People today are sick.…They're hopped up on drugs, sex, food.

b. excited, esp. full of enthusiasm; impatient or eager (to act).

1920 T.A. Dorgan, in Zwilling *TAD Lexicon* 46: We gotta new editor an' the boys are kinda hopped up. **1920–21** Witwer *Leather Pushers* 18: Du Fresne…will be all hopped up to make a terrible flash in the openin' canto. **1922** J. Conway, in *Variety* (Feb. 24) 9: The skirt had him all hopped up that he was the makins of a second Jolson. **1925** *Collier's* (Sept. 19) 8: I couldn't seem to get hopped up over Mother Mooney's Thrifty Tip-offs for Young Brides. **1930** in D.O. Smith *Cradle* 108: Everyone is hopped up over the New York trip. **1935** in Galewitz *Great Comics* 256: Don't get so hopped up! He's still dynamite! **1936** Miller *Battling Bellhop* (film): I really should be all hopped up. You were a sensation. **1938** I. Shaw *Sailor off Bremen* 228: He's all hopped up. His friends keep yelling what a great guy he is, so he believes it. **1946** Mezzrow & Wolfe *Really Blues* 74: That kid could get as lively and hopped-up as anybody you ever saw. **1955** Scott *Look of Eagle* 204: Steve had thought Atlas was "hopped up" on the extra shot of adrenaline nature supplies the human for such excitement. **1957** Margulies *Punks* 46: Man, take it easy.…You're hopped up. **1961** Clausen *Season's Over* 48: She knows what to do to get 'em all hopped up, too. **1967** J. Kramer *Instant Replay* 104: I was all hopped up, the adrenalin flowing the way it always does for several hours after a game. **1973** Droge *Patrolman* 171: He was really getting me hopped up about the idea. **1979** Haas & Hunter *Over the Edge* (film): You're in such a hopped-up hurry to get out of the city.

2.a. (of an engine, automobile, etc.) having increased power; supercharged; unusually fast.

1941 Schulberg *Sammy* 85: With a special hopped-up motor. **1941** Coldewey *Lady Gangster* (film): These squad cars are hopped up plenty. **1945** *AS* (Oct.) 226: Hopped up. Applied to a plane built for speed. Taken from the "hopped up" automobiles of the high-school set. **1951–53** in *AS* XXIX 98: Hopped up…"souped up"; said of a car with any added speed equipment. **1957** Bradbury *Dandelion Wine* 67: A walk on a spring morning is better than an eighty-mile ride in a hopped-up car. **1960** Kirkwood *Pony* 159: You all pile into these hopped-up cars and drive out to the desert looking for kicks. **1968** Gomberg *Breakout* (film): Now the jeep is hopped up. It's gonna be a rough ride. **1984** Kagan & Summers *Mute Evidence* 316: Kagan imagined a very fast, hopped up red convertible. **1993** Carhart *Iron Soldiers*

25: Our new, hopped-up sabot round with the depleted-uranium penetrator.

b. enlivened, embellished, or intensified, esp. in a cheap or meretricious way.

1942 *ATS* 255: Lively; spirited; "peppy."...*hopped up*,...*jazzed up*. **1950** in *DAS:* One of those hopped-up novels in which passion is named but not felt. **1952** "E. Box" *Fifth Position* 125: The pianist...played a hopped-up version of *Swan Lake*.

hopper *n.* **1.** BELLHOP, 1.

1926 Finerty *Criminalese* 28: Hoppers—Hotel bell-boys.

2. a toilet commode.

1974 G.V. Higgins *Cogan's Trade* 19: They'd look in the tanks of all the hoppers. **1987** S. Stark *Wrestling Season* 14: Roses are red, violets are blue, flush the hopper when you are through. **1988** *Cheers* (NBC-TV): We didn't catch you on the hopper, did we?

hopper-arsed *adj.* having large buttocks.—usu. considered vulgar.

***1698–99** "B.E." *Dict. Canting Crew:* Hopper-arst, when the Breech sticks out. ***a1720** in D'Urfey *Pills* VI 351: And there'll be hopper-ars'd *Nancy.* **1752** in Breslaw *Tues. Club* 349: Till they become Swagg bellied & hopper-ars'd, like the members of an ancient drunken Club at Babylon. ***1785** Grose *Vulgar Tongue: Hopper-arsed.* Having large projecting buttocks; from their resemblance to a small basket, called a hopper...worn by husbandmen for containing seed corn, when they sow the land.

hopping *adj.* [short for colloq. *hopping mad*] furiously angry.

1887 Call *Josh Hayseed* 60: It made me feel hoppin'. **1892** in Thompson *Youth's Companion* 404: Don't it make you hoppin' to have anybody pat you on the head? **1895** Clurman *Nick Carter* 95: Weren't the deacon hoppin', when he found out we'd watched 'em? **1917–20** Dreiser *Newspaper Days* 137 [ref. to 1893]: He'll be hopping!

hoppin' John *n. So.* a dish consisting of meat, esp. bacon or pork, rice, and peas cooked and seasoned with red pepper. Now *colloq.*

1838 in *DA* 833: Hopping John. **1856** in *DA.* **1879** Stroyer *My Life* 9: The mixture was called by the slaves "hopping John." **1932** R. Fisher *Conjure-Man* 231: Pigtails an hoppin'-john. **1963** in T.H. Clarke *Harlem* 61: Black eyed peas, often cooked with rice and bacon to form the popular "hopping John." **1967** in Bambara *Gorilla* 73: A pan of hopping john and a gallon of Gallo. **1973** Ellington *Music Is My Mistress* 393: They served the world's best Hoppin' John. **1992** S. Straight *Been in Sorrow's Kitchen* 65: Hoppin John—...rice...cowpeas and bits of ham and pepper.

hoppy *n.* **1.** a lame person.—used derisively.

1891 Campbell, Knox & Byrnes *Darkness & Daylight* 124: "Hoppy," a little lame boy. **1904** *Life in Sing Sing* 249: Hoppy. A cripple.

2. a drug addict; HOPHEAD, 1.a.

1907 *Lippincott's Mag.* (Feb.) 285: Hoppy-eyed an' full of hash-sheesh till his skin was like to crack. **1922** Murphy *Black Candle* 114: The Chinese here still furnish a large percentage of the "hoppies." **1924** Henderson *Keys to Crookdom* 403: Drug addict....hoppy, gutter hype,...coke-blower, on th' stuff. **1927** Coe *Me—Gangster* 212: Lots of hoppies get that trick. **1953** W. Brown *Monkey on My Back* 72: I ain't no hoppy. **1954** E. Hunter *Jungle Kids* 64: This what you come down after, Hoppy? This it? **1959** Hecht *Sensualists* 126: And, oh what a bitch she was. A crazy hoppie. **1971** Curtis *Banjo* 227: I know a lot of hoppies.

hops *n.* **1.** beer. Now *rare* in U.S. Cf. HOP JUICE.

1902 Mead *Word-Coinage* 167: "Hops"...beer. **1903** *Enquirer* (Cincinnati) (May 9) 13: Hops—Beer. **1903** Jarrold *Bowery* 17: Drink yer hops, pet, while yer waiting. **1908** in "O. Henry" *Works* 306: A chloral hydrate and hops agency in a side street...off Broadway. **1908** McGaffey *Show Girl* 106: Anything from a glass of hops to a Merry Widow cocktail. **1966** H.S. Thompson *Hell's Angels* 178: My own taste for the hops is very powerful, and I had no intention of spending a beerless weekend in the withering sun. ***1969** in *Austral. Nat. Dict.:* When Gus was on the hops he smashed everything in sight. **1972** Claerbaut *Black Jargon* 69: Hops, n. beer: *He'll buy the hops.*

2. *Pris.* tea.

1904 *Life in Sing Sing* 249: Hops.—Tea.

hop stick *n.* an opium pipe; (hence) a cigarette containing marijuana or an opiate.

1936 *AS* (Apr.) 122: Hop Stick. An opium pipe. **1936** Hoerl *Tell Yr. Children* (film): Keep feeding him those hop sticks.

hop talk *n.* foolish or exaggerated talk such as might be occasioned by indulgence in opium.

1899–1900 Cullen *Tales* 199: You were giving us a hop-talk last night about walking back to 'Frisco. **1908** Sullivan *Criminal Slang* 12: Hop talk—Drawing the long bow; bragging. **1965** Spillane *Killer Mine* 86: What kind of notion have you got in your head that you're going out and shoot up somebody? That's hop talk, guy.

hop toad *n. R.R.* (see 1958 quot.).

1930 Irwin *Tramp & Und. Sl.:* Hop Toad.—A derailing device on a railroad. **1930** *Railroad Man's Mag.* II 471: Hop toad—Derail. **1932, 1938** in *DARE.* **1958** McCulloch *Woods Words* 89: Hop toad—A derailer on a railroad switch to prevent cars from running out on the main track.

hop-toy *n.* [Anglo-Cantonese pidgin, perh. lit. 'bliss container'] *Narc.* a small container of opium.

1881 H.H. Kane *Opium* 35: A box of buffalo-horn to contain the opium (*hop-toy*). **1887** in *AS* XXIII (1948) 246: The roller dips his yenhook into the shell or hoptoy, and conveys the opium over the lamp to cook it. **1898** L.J. Beck *Chinatown* 158: The opium for the common smoker does not come in the hop-toy. **1925–26** J. Black *Can't Win* 238: The little horn container, the "hop toy," is empty.

hop-up *n. Auto.* (see 1942 quot.); (hence) HOT ROD.

1942 *ATS* 682: Hop-up, a racing car that has been speeded up by special equipment. **1945** (quot. at HOT ROD). **1950** Felsen *Hot Rod* 7: The hours that others spent with mothers, fathers, sisters or brothers, Bud spent with his homemade hop-up.

hop up *v.* [back formation from HOPPED-UP] **1.** to excite or stimulate by or as by the use of drugs; drug.

1942 *ATS* 478: [To] dope...hop up. **1945** Huie *Omaha to Okinawa* 27: They were hopping themselves up, preparing for their last...drunken...charge.

2. to increase the power of (an engine or automobile); supercharge.

1942 *ATS* 35: Hop up...to increase or intensify, as the action of a motor or in electrical potential. **1953** *New Yorker* (Mar. 7) 23: How to Hop Up Your Chevrolet. **1978** Wharton *Birdy* 44: Maybe hopping up cars and tearing them apart. **1982** Del Vecchio *13th Valley* 142: Ah've ordered me a Super Sport ta hop up when Ah get back home.

horizontal *adj.* ¶ In phrase: **get horizontal** to lie down to sleep; (hence) to drink oneself into a stupor.

1975 Dills *CB* (1976 ed.) 35: *Get horizontal:* sleep; go to bed. **1977** *Sci. Mech. CB Gde.* 170: I'm going to get horizontal at the next rest-um up. **1990** *UTSQ: Get horizontal*—get drunk. "Let's go out to the Strip Friday night and get horizontal." **1993** J. Davis *Buzzwords* 24: *Get horizontal* Naptime.

horizontal dance [for vars. with specific dances, see s.v. HORIZONTAL REFRESHMENT]

horizontal engineering *n. Mil.* sleep. *Joc.*

1942–44 in *AS* (Feb. 1946) 34: *Horizontal Engineering;* To nap. **1956** Boatner *Military Customs* 114: Bunk fatigue Bed rest, "sack time," "horizontal engineering," etc. **1958** Frede *Entry E* 65: You out and out bastard, the only engineering *you* ever did was horizontal.

horizontal exercise *n. Mil.* sleep. *Joc.*

1918 Ruggles *Navy Explained* 75: When a sailor is caulking off on the deck he is taking his horizontal exercise. **1931** *Leatherneck* (Aug.) 25: Well, I guess I'll put away the scrapbook, and do a little "horizontal exercise"—just like the "Old" and "New" Marine Corps. (we call it "bunk fatigue" now—Ed.).

horizontal fatigue *n. Mil.* sleep. *Joc.*

1930 Fredenburgh *Soldiers March!* 279 [ref. to 1918]: "I'm going to do a little horizontal fatigue," said Geary....."That four-to-six morning watch sure breaks into my beauty sleep."

horizontal fever *n.* a feeling of vertigo or faintness. *Joc.*

1928 W.H. Dixon *West. Hoboes* 85: That thread of a stream a mile, or probably only 500 feet below, gave me an acute attack of "horizontal fever." *Ibid.* 88: Never again did "horizontal fever" attack us virulently.

horizontal refreshment *n.* [cf. earlier F *horizontale* 'a prostitute'] sexual intercourse. *Joc.* Also vars., now esp. with names of dances.

***1889** Barrère & Leland *Dict. Slang* I 475: *Horizontal refreshments* (common), carnal intercourse with a woman. **1918** Grider *War Birds* 128: I'd be willing to guarantee that no one had indulged in any horizontal refreshments here. **1935** L. Hughes *Little Ham* 83: Gilbert warn't no good for nothing but what my white actress lady where I used to work calls "horizontal refreshment." **1959** Morrill *Dark Sea* 37 [ref. to WWII]: Ever see a society broad that didn't play horizontal polo? **1980** Birnbach *Preppy Hndbk.* 220: *Horizontal rumble...*Sexual relations. **1988** Nyswaner *Prince of Penn.* (film): Yes. Horizontal dancing. **1989** Eble *College Slang 101* 81: Intercourse...*horizontal bop, horizontal mambo, horizontal twist and shout.* **1993** *Time* (Oct. 11) 82: Clark, you can do the horizontal rhumba with the entire Metnet cheerleading squad if you want. **1994** *UTSQ*: Hey, babe, what say you and I get together and do the horizontal polka? **1995* Scottish folksinger in N.Y.C.: This is a song about a soldier and a lady. Well, not really a lady—let's say a "purveyor of horizontal refreshment." **1995** *New Yorker* (Oct. 30) 114: Demi Moore's woodland gallops and horizontal barn dancing.

horizontals *n.pl.* sexual intercourse. *Joc.*
   1929–33 Farrell *Young Manhood* 389: Besides, the black boys were happiest when engaged in the horizontals. That meant an increased birth-rate amongst them.

horizontal worker *n.* [cf. earlier F *horizontale* 'a prostitute'] a prostitute. *Joc.*
   1870 in Rosa & Koop *Rowdy Joe* 24: Horizontal worker.

hork *v.* [perh. alter. of *hawk*] to steal; swipe.
   1983 Moranis et al. *Strange Brew* (film): Somebody horked our clothes! *Ibid.* There's those guys who horked our clothes! **1989** P. Munro *U.C.L.A. Slang* 50: I couldn't believe he horked my notes right before the test. **1990** Eble *Campus Slang* (Fall) 5: *Hork*—steal...(often a beer). "Hey, you hoser, you horked my beer." From the...movie *Strange Brew*. **1993** P. Munro *U.C.L.A. Slang II* 51: I horked six bagels from the cafeteria this morning.

hormone queen *n. Homosex.* a male transvestite who takes estrogen to enhance his feminine appearance.
   1965–72 E. Newton *Mother Camp* 27: There are no feminine counterparts of the male...hormone queens.

hormones *n.pl.* nerve; BALLS, 4.c.
   1986 *L.A. Law* (NBC-TV): You've got a lot of *hormones*, lady!

horn *n.* **1.a.** an erection of the penis; (*hence*, of either sex) a state of sexual excitement (usu. constr. with *the*, occ. *pl.*); (*broadly*) the penis.—usu. considered vulgar. [The Shakespearian quots., usu. taken as simple allusions to the horns of cuckoldry, seem equally to lend themselves to the present interpretation; the bracketed quots. may likewise be ambiguous.]
   *1594 Shakespeare *Taming of Shrew* IV i: *Curtis.* Away you three-inch foole! I am no beast. *Gremio.* Am I but three inches? Why thy horne is a foot and so long am I at the least. **1599* Shakespeare *Much Ado* V iv: Prince, thou art sad, get thee a wife, get thee a wife, there is no staffe more reuerent then one tipt with horne. **1669* *New Academy of Complements* 216: He'l [*sic*] be content with a hard piece of Horn. *Ibid.* 217: For a Horn, they can tell,/Was always a friend to the night. **1671* in Adlard *Forbidden Tree* 62: Have you...e'er a fair maid /That would be a nun?...Hark how my merry horn doth blow/Too high, too low. Too high, too low. [**1728* in *F & H* III 354: A profane, obscene meeting called the *horn-order*.] [**1785* (quot. at HORN COLIC).] **1850** Melville *Moby-Dick* ch. xxxii: The Earl of Leicester, on bended knees, did...present to her highness another horn. **1864** in J.I. Robertson *Blue & Gray* 121: The older the Buck the Stifer the horn and the women, some of them, seem to have the same disease. **1882* *Boudoir* 237: "Who'll take the horn out of me?" he exclaimed. **1889* Barrère & Leland *Dict. Slang* I 475: "To have the *horn*," to be in a state of sexual desire. **a1890–93* *F & H* III 351: *Horn*...An erection of the *penis*. (Properly of men only: but said of both sexes). *Ibid.: Horn*...The penis. **1909* in Joyce *Sel. Letters* 190: Before I could get a horn stiff enough even to put into you. *Ibid.* 191: Does it give you [his wife] the horn? **1928** in Randolph & Legman *Roll Me in Your Arms* 40: And right below the navel I bored her with my horn. *ca*1929 *Collection of Sea Songs* 2: The Queen prefers my rival /Because my horn is short. **1932** in Read *Lexical Evidence* 20: [Urinal inscription] Bulls with short/horns stand up close. **1937** in Oliver *Meaning of Blues* 144: Mama, I'm gone, with a horn long as your right arm. **1938** "Justinian" *Amer. Sexualis* 25: To have [a] *horn* or *get a horn* is to have a priapism, often said of the

female as well as the male. **1950** in Randolph & Legman *Roll Me in Your Arms* 325 [song learned *ca*1910]: Liza come a-runnin' and she grabbed me by the horn. **1953** in Randolph *Pissing in Snow* 92: "Now stick the horn in me," she says. *a*1972 B. Rodgers *Queens' Vernacular* 109: I can't walk around LA without gettin' the horns. **1972** McGregor *Bawdy Ballads* 47: She gazed with scorn at the steaming horn as it rose from his hairy thighs. **1974** J. Robinson *Bed/Time/Story* 192: Hey, listen, I am getting these incredible horns. Can I pick you up and we'll go to the hotel? **1974** G.V. Higgins *Cogan's Trade* 182: She's really something. I could've beat up five guys with the horn I had on.

b. a strong or lustful desire; LETCH.
   1988 *Miami Vice* (NBC-TV): He's got a horn for hookers.

2. *pl.* **a.** a derisive, inimical, or insulting gesture made by holding the fist with two fingers (now usu. the first and fourth) extended like a pair of horns.

[The orig. force of the gesture was to suggest cuckoldry, as in *OED* def. 7.a.; among persons of Italian descent the gesture is usually identified as the Mediterranean sign of the evil eye. The gesture is not common in the U.S. Cf. FINGER, *n.*, 4.a., which is regarded as far more contemptuous and offensive.]
   [**1602* T. Campion, in *F & H* III 352: Mock him not with horns, the case is altered.] **1607* Dekker & Webster, in *F & H*: If a man be deuorst...whether may he have an action or no, gainst those that make horns at him? **1652* in *OED*: Denmark was so disguised, as he would have lain with the Countess of Nottingham, making Horns in Derision at her Husband. **1708* in *F & H* III 354: Sometimes his dirty paws she scorns,/While her fair fingers show his horns. **a1812* Ireland & Nichols *Hogarth's Wks.* 278: This *water-wit* the abandoned young man returns by holding up two fingers [to his own brow] in the form of horns. **1957** N.Y.C. children: "Jimmy's making horns [behind the head of another child]!" "*Horns* mean the person getting them is stupid. He looks like a donkey." **1978** Pici *Tennis Hustler* 56: "That lady'll put the hex on you *Malocchio!*" And she made the horns with her fingers and thrust them at me. **1984** J. McCorkle *Cheer Leader* 12: She's the one doing horns over Lisa Helms.

b. in phr. **put the horns on** Esp. *Italian-Amer.* to jinx.
   1942–49 Goldin et al. *DAUL* 170: *Put the horns on* 1. To cheat. 2. To jinx...."Someone's puttin' the horns on us. We get a rumble...every trick...we go on." **1945–50** in D.W. Maurer *Lang. of Und.* 190: To *put the horns on:* To give a player bad luck. **1981** Graziano & Corsel *Somebody Down Here* 5: Somebody musta t'rown the horns in on our house before I was born.

3. a drink (of liquor); dram.
   *1814 in Wetherell *Adventures* 258: We...took...a stiff horn of Cogniac. **1820–21* P. Egan *Life in London* 93: And a horn or so of humming stingo! **1824** in Nevins & Weitenkampf *Cartoons* 33: A *small* horn of rotgut. **1828** in *JAF* LXXVI (1963) 300: I...give him a thrippyny horn. **1830** in *DA:* Tipplers call their idol..."a slug of blue fishhooks," "a horn of gunpowder," "essence of lockjaw." **1833** *Mil. & Naval Mag. of U.S.* (Apr.) 106: They amicably pledged each other in a horn of old Jamaica. **1834** *Davy Crockett's Almanack* (1835) 4: He grew as savage as a meat-axe, for he had been taking a few horns, and was in a good condition to make the *fur* fly. **1837** *Almanack of Wild Sports in the West* I (No. 4) 13: I was...taking a horn of midshipman's grog...first a draught of whiskey, and then one of river water. **1839** Briggs *Franco* I 22: Then you shall take a horn, so come along. *ca*1840 Hawthorne *Privateer* 146 [ref. to 1813]: He had no objection to *taking a horn* whenever he could get it. **1841** [Mercier] *Man o' War* 188: And just before he backed his horse,/He took another *horn*. **1846** in Harlow *Old Bowery* 191: I only takes a extra horn,/Observing, "Let her went!" **1850** Garrard *Wah-to-yah* 167: How are ye?...come in and take a "horn"—a little of the *arwerdenty*—come—good for your stomach. **1851** in Windeler *Gold Rush Diary* 132: When I got home, I took a good horn of Coffee & Brandy. **1856** in Derby *Squibob* 44: He kant drink mor an 3 hornes 'thout gittin tite. **1858** in G.W. Harris *High Times* 139: A horn ove tanglelaigs whisky. **1865** in Hilleary *Webfoot* 111: He then pressed me to come in and "take a horn." *ca*1900 *Buffalo Bill* 204: He used to be a judge of "horns," when poured in a tin cup. **1908** Thorp *Songs of Cowboys* 17: Think a horn of whiskey will help the thing along. **1944** Busch *Dream of Home* 229: Just a short horn before you go? **1964** *AS* (Oct.) 281: *Horn, n.* A drink. **1971** Curtis

Banjo 210: Zirp swore every morning over his horn of white lightning that Gus Gilpin would die.

4. the nose.

[***1823** "J. Bee" *Dict. of Turf: Horney*—a nose; one that resounds in expectoration.] **1843** in *DARE:* The most awful clearing of throats, *hawking*, and horn-blowing. **1845** Corcoran *Pickings* 67: There was a purty polthogue I got just between the lug and the horn, where the Connaughtman sthruck his ass. **1859** Avery *Comical Stories* 90: A strapping young Hoosier, "blew his horn."…"Did you blow your nose, sir?" **1891** McCann & Jarrold *Odds & Ends* 35: I'd like to put a bunch of fives under that feller's horn. *a***1890–93** *F & H* III 351: *Horn*…The nose. **1899** Thomas *Arizona* 9: I…used to shine up my horn this way [He catches his nose with one hand and pretends to polish it vigorously with the other.] Whenever she began her lecture. **1914** Lardner *You Know Me Al* 146: Then I come with my fast ball right past his nose and I bet if he had not of ducked it would of drove that big horn of hisn clear up in the press box where them rotten reporters sits and smokes their hops. **1932** *AS* VII 401: *Horn*, n. Nose. **1933** Ersine *Pris. Slang* 45: *Horn*—A man's nose. **1937** in D. Runyon *More Guys* 223: A big horn indicates character, and a mustache is good luck. **1971** Horan *Blue Messiah* 51: With a horn that size and color…I figger he puts away a quart a day. **1973** (quot. at SNOT-BOX). **1986** *UTSQ:* Nose…*horn*. **1983–88** J.T. McLeod *Crew Chief* 301: But with a horn like this, I can't blame anybody but my old man.

5. (one's) voice or conversation; in phrs. **blow (one's) horn** to speak or sing, usu. out of turn; **hear (one's) horn** to hear and give due weight to what (one) is saying.

1848 Baker *Glance at N.Y.* 22: *Lize.*…If it wasn't for bein' in the street, I'd sing it for you. *Mose.* It's too early in de mornin' for many folks to be out—so you're safe. Blow your horn. **1858** in G.W. Harris *Lovingood* 94: I'm gwine back, do you hear my horn? **1859** "M. Twain," in *OED:* Permit me to "blow my horn." *a***1860** Hundley *So. States* 259: Tell yer what, I'm goin' ter make tracks fer dad's—yer heer my horn toot! **1866** in G.W. Harris *Lovingood* 270: Say, George, I dusent much like the soun' ove that ar ho'n; I smell a slur in hit. **1887** J.W. Nichols *Hear My Horn* 169: We can git as many of you as you can of us and the first man that crosses that fence is my meat. Now you hear my horn.

6.a. telephone.—constr. with *the*.

1941 *Slanguage Dict.* 28: *On the horn*….on the telephone. **1945** Shelly *Jive Talk Dict.* 31: *On the horn*—Telephoning. **1956** Heflin *USAF Dict.* 255: *Horn*…A telephone. *Slang*. **1957** Berkeley *Deadly Mantis* (film): Get the old man on the horn, will you, Pete? **1958** Lindsay & Crouse *Tall Story* 9: Eddie, you're wanted on the horn. **1959** Zugsmith *Beat Generation* 41: That's Dave on the horn. **1971–72** Giovannitti *Medal* 63: Get the lieutenant on the horn and tell *him* the situation. **1983** *Morning Contact* (WKGN radio) (May 27): I thought I'd give you a buzz first, but I'm going to get right on the horn to them. **1988** D. Sandefur *Ghost Town* (film): Get on the horn to Livie and tell her to call everybody in. **1994** *X-Files* (Fox-TV): I'm going to hike down to the truck [and] get on the horn. **1995** *JAG* (NBC-TV): Skipper's on the horn for you, sir.

b. *Communications*. (see quot.).

1982 Connors *Mass Media Dict.* 121: *Horn*. microwave antenna.

7. a dollar.

1958 Swarthout *Cordura* 104 [ref. to 1916]: I can sure use the extra two horns a month.

¶ In phrases:

¶ **around the horn** [prob. alluding to Cape *Horn*] **1.** *Police & Und.* (see quots.).

1926 Clark & Eubank *Lockstep* 85: Ask any old-time thief about his trip Around the Horn and he will…shudder. *Ibid.* 173: *Around the horn*—a trip around the circuit of city police stations for the purpose of being identified by victims. **1942–49** Goldin et al. *DAUL* 19: *Around the horn, to ride one.* To move an arrested criminal suspect from one police station to another to prevent him from seeing an attorney.

2. having experienced long service and hard treatment.

1942 *AS* (Apr.) 102: *Been Around the Horn.* Truck with a high mileage on the speedometer. **1973–77** J. Jones *Whistle* 68: No, not me. I been around the Horn before.

3. *Baseball.* around the infield, esp. from third base (or the shortstop) to second to first.

1956 in Dickson *Baseball Dict.* 14: And the Seals pull a twin killing around the horn. **1973** N.Y. Mets vs. Chicago Cubs (WOR-TV) (Sept. 30): So the Mets get two [outs]. Around the horn. **1980** McBride *High & Inside* 25: The infield ball-tossing ritual and the 5-4-3 double play are both referred to as "around the horn." **1987** in Dickson *Baseball Dict.* 14: Two 'round-the-horn double plays.

¶ **between the horns** in the center of the forehead; in the head.

1930 F. Marion *Big House* (film): You stick your head out there and I'll put a slug between your horns! **1975** Wambaugh *Choirboys* 314: Was ready to bust a cap between his fuckin horns. **1982** Sculatti *Catalog of Cool* 130: All I have to do is whack him one between the horns and it'd be over. **1984–88** Hackworth & Sherman *About Face* 28: When the defender came up…, he'd be shot between the horns. **1984–88** in Berry *Where Ya Been?* 212: Just an inch or so higher and it would have got me right between the horns.

¶ **bust (someone's) horns** to goad or annoy (someone).

1984 D. Smith *Steely Blue* 326: You can bust my horns if you want to, but don't embarrass the badge, you know. Because I'll have to take a poke at you.

¶ **come out at the little** [or **small**] **end of the horn** to be bested or defeated; fail. [Cf. BrE prov. *to be squeezed through a horn* (OED s.v. horn def. 2.f.).]

1833 Neal *Down-Easters* II 40: He nebber come out o' de little eend o' de horn yet. **1840** Porter *Big Bear* 37: Why, colonel, I see you have had a skrimmage. How did you make it! You didn't come out at the little *eend* of the horn, did you? **1864** in Brobst *Civil War Letters* 86: I will write you a little about our big fight on the first of this month, and on the fifth, and on the seventh. The rebs came out at the small end of the horn every time. **1891** Maitland *Slang Dict.* 168: *Little end of the horn*, "to come out at the," to fail in an undertaking. **1943** Pyle *Here Is Your War* 98: If two Lightnings and two Messerschmitt 109s got into a fight, the Americans were almost bound to come out the little end of the horn, because the Lightnings were heavier and less maneuverable.

¶ **in a [hog's] horn** not at all; no, indeed; (used to indicate disbelief or refusal).

1840 *Spirit of Times* (Mar. 7) 7: Duane was sold after the first heat…for $12,000 ("in a horn!"). **1840** *Spirit of Times* (Apr. 11) 61: The unfamiliar duty of penitential psalm-singing—("in a horn")—at sea. **1840** in *DAE:* The Baltimore Clipper tells the following story "in a horn." **1848** Judson *Mysteries* 460: "Yes, sir," said Frank, but as soon as he got outside the door he added, "*in a horn*." **1858** in Bartlett *Amer.* (ed. 2) 203: I have mentioned before the innumerable comforts—*in a horn*—of the old White Sulphur Springs. **1864** Armstrong *Generals* 292: "Mine private property," he replied.…"In a horn," said one of the Grey-backs, pointing to the U.S. on the shoulder of the beast. **1864** in Babcock *Letters & Diaries* 74: "Has he any command nowadays?" "Oh Yes. He commands the department of the Gulf." I did not say "in a horn." **1866** in *Nebr. Hist.* XLVI (1965) 299: I concluded to go with them…—in a horn. **1869** Carleton *Kaleidoscope* 17: Oh, yes, he'll bring it back in *a horn*. **1878** in A.P. Hudson *Humor of Old South* 484: I wish that you would go—…in a horn, Tom. **1882** Watkins *Co. Aytch* 66: It was the generals that everybody saw charge such and such, with drawn sabre, his eyes flashing fire, his nostril dilated, and his clarion voice ringing over the din of battle—"in a horn," over the left. **1889** Barrère & Leland *Dict. Slang* I 475: *Horn* (American). "Yes, in a horn." This is uttered as an expression of disbelief or refusal. "In a hog's *horn*," as hogs have no horns.

¶ **scrape** [or **cut**] **(one's) horns** (of a man) to engage in sexual activity, esp. after a period of abstinence.—usu. considered vulgar.

1966–68 *Current Slang I & II* 77: *Scrape*…*horns*, v. To indulge in heavy petting after a lapse of sexual activities.—College males, Arizona; Air Force Academy cadets. **1976** Conroy *Santini* 285: Now, I know all you boys got the hot pants cause I was young myself and I had to cut my horns like everyone else. But…this is no time to be screaming about some cheap piece of poontang.

horn *v.* **1.a.** to force (someone)—usu. constr. with *off* or *out*.

1850 in *DA:* Sutter is wanting to horn out some squatters off what he calls his property. **1851** in *F & H* III 354: You horned me off to get a chance to get gaming witnesses out of the way. **1870** Duval *Big-Foot* 219: They succeeded in "horning me off." **1881** in Thornton *Amer.*

Gloss.: MacVeagh is trying…to horn Blaine out of the Cabinet herd, just as young buffalo bulls horn out the old ones. **1912** Mathewson *Pitching* 52: He's tryin' to horn my friend Bill out of a job.

b. see HORN IN.

2. GOOSE, 2.a.

1928 Dahlberg *Bottom Dogs* 128: The railroad-hand feeling his way thru the dark tried to horn her going up the steps.

3. *Narc.* to take (cocaine or heroin) by inhalation; SNORT.

1967 J.B. Williams *Narc. & Halluc.* 113: Horning—Sniffing narcotics by nose. **1970** Horman & Fox *Drug Awareness* 467: Horn—to sniff powdered narcotics into nostrils. **1973** *Zap Comix* (No. 6) (unp.): Wanna horn some coke, Merle? **1978** Selby *Requiem* 32: So tiny horns a little just to be cool, an he gets wasted jim. *a***1979** Pepper & Pepper *Straight Life* 83 [ref. to 1950]: She came over…and offered me some stuff, just to horn it, sniff it.

hornbug *n.* (see quot.).

1956 in Hitchcock *Skeleton Crew* 170: "I don't like his looks. He acts like a Horn Bug." "You mean one of those sex maniacs?" *Ibid.* 173: Nothing's wrong unless Fat Boy *is* a Horn Bug.

horn colic *n.* an erection of the penis, esp. when painful due to sexual stimulation without ejaculation; (*hence*) sexual desire.—usu. considered vulgar.

*****1785** Grose *Vulgar Tongue: Horn cholick.* A temporary priapism. **1912** in *DARE: Horn-colic*…Pain caused by priapism. **1930** in *DARE: Horn colic*—Pain said to be caused by suppressed sexual desire. **1954** in Randolph *Pissing in Snow* 149: A fellow named Taylor come down with the horn colic one night, but he didn't have the two dollars.

horndog *n. Stu.* a lustful or sexually aggressive person; (see also 1985 quot.). Also as *v.*, to letch.

1984 Algeo *Stud Buds* 5: A male who is known for his aggressive…sexual behavior…*horndog.* **1985** "J. Blowdryer" *Mod. English* 18: *Horndog*…some creep who is always trying to hunch in on other people's territory, whether it be their leg or their social group. **1986** *NDAS: Horndog*…a dedicated fornicator. **1993** *Real World* (MTV): Thought I was a little horndog just because I was looking at his boxer shorts. **1993** P. Muro *U.C.L.A. Slang II* 51: He is such a horndog—he was all over me during that movie. **1994** *Wild Oats* (Fox-TV): Are you horndoggin' tonight or you just here for the show? **1996** *Married with Children* (Fox-TV): That horndog of a bear.

horned-up *adj.* sexually excited.—usu. considered vulgar.

1968 Baker, Ladd & Robb *CUSS* 138: *Horned up.* Sexually aroused. **1974** Loken *Come Monday Mornin'* 23: He remembered seein' [mares]…so horned up they'd try to mount the stallion. **1991** Nelson & Gonzales *Bring Noise* 250: He's one of the horned-up masses.

hornety *adj.* ill-tempered; angry.

1834 in *DA:* The Gineral got as hornety as all nature at this.

hornies *n.pl.* sexual desire.—constr. with *the.*

1973 Gwaltney *Destiny's Chickens* 16: When I git the hornies, you'll faint dead away before you give me comes enough. *Ibid.* 41: She's got the hornies for you, boy! **1976** Univ. Tenn. student: Your only problem is you're suffering from the hornies. **1981** C. Nelson *Picked Bullets Up* 298: Having a bad case of the raging hornies. **1986** C. Horrall & C. Vincent *Wimps* (film): It's just a case of the hornies, Charles.

horn in *v. Esp. West.* to intrude oneself; interfere; BUTT IN, 1.

1911 T.A. Dorgan, in Zwilling *TAD Lexicon* 46: Hughey Campbell picked this up in the park and wants to horn in on it. **1912** Mathewson *Pitching* 213: Many of them try hard to "horn in" with the men who have made good as Big Leaguers. **1913–15** Van Loan *Taking the Count* 26: See what you get for horning in? **1916** Lait *Beef, Iron & Wine* 128: He'll horn in the White House an' he'll call off the war. **1920** E.M. Rhodes *Stepsons* 150: If we'd only known we might have horned in. **1921** *DN* V 119: *Horn in, v. phr.* Slip in. West. **1922** Rollins *Cowboy* 304: They merely had a dread of "horning-in." **1922** *DN* V 147: *Horn in*—to get into a place without an invitation. **1923** Hough *North* 74: Don't you come horning in. **1923** *DN* V 211: *Horn in, v. phr.* To interrupt a conversation. **1930** Mulford *Eagle Ranch* 79: We are…hornin' right in to plenty of trouble. **1930** Irwin *Tramp & Und. Sl.: Horn In.*—To intrude; to edge one's way into a party or a discussion. **1931** *AS* VII (Oct.) 109: (*To*) *horn in, v. phr.* To muscle in. **1935** in Fife & Fife *Ballads of West* 82: An outlaw come a-hornin' in and asked who I might be. **1941** Haycox *Trail* 69: You horn in, and he's one more man on your trail. **1949** *PADS* XI 7: *Horn in on: v.i.* To

force oneself into a place in which he is not wanted. "I didn't like his horning in on our conversation." **1958** "W. Henry" *Reckoning* 117: They would have had their fair trial…if you hadn't of horned in. **1967** L'Amour *Matagorda* 27: I got no right to expect you to horn in on my fight. **1976** Haseltine & Yaw *Woman Doctor* 145: How can you horn in on those GYN cases, after all? **1989** Zumbro & Walker *Jungletracks* 221: You think we can get…up there in time to horn in on the fracas, sir? **1995** Ex-pres. G. Bush, on *Today* (NBC-TV) (June 13): Bosnia?…Why horn in, as mother would say?

horn-mad *adj.* HORNY, 1.a. *Obs.* in U.S.

1726 in *William & Mary Qly.* (Ser. 3) XXXVIII (1981) 273: As horn-mad as a Buck in Rutting time. **a***1890–93** *F & H* III 356: *Horn-mad*…Sexually excited; lecherous: *musty* (q.v.). Also, *horny.* *****1951** in *OED2:* The evil-minded and horn-mad levantine.

hornrim *n. Business.* (see quot.).

1979 Homer *Jargon* 28: *Polling the hornrims* is referring the proposal to the staff intellectuals.

hornswoggle *n.* deception; nonsense.

1864 Hotten *Slang Dict.* (ed. 3): *Hornswoggle*, nonsense, humbug. Believed to be of American origin. **1877** Bartlett *Amer.* (ed. 4) 786: *Hornswoggle.* Foolery, deception. Western. *****1980** *New Statesman* (Jan. 25) (cited in Partridge *Concise Dict. Slang* 223).

hornswoggle *v.* [orig. unkn.] **1.** to embarrass or perplex; (*hence*) to fool; take in; bamboozle; swindle; deceive. Also vars.

1829 in M. Mathews *Beginnings of Amer. Eng.* 107: *Hornswoggle.* "To embarrass irretrievably." *Kentucky.* **1840** *Spirit of Times* (Oct. 24) 398: He looks tired of his bargain already, what you call fairly onswaggled. **1877** Bartlett *Amer.* (ed. 4) 786: *Skullduggery*…Its best Eastern equivalent is *shenanigan*, although…*hornswoggling* rather directly translates it. **1889** Barrère & Leland *Dict. Slang* I 476: *Hornswoggle, to* (American), to humbug, delude, seduce, etc. **1894** in Dreiser *Jour.* I 223: You can't hornswaggle me. **1900** Dreiser *Carrie* 49: A truly deep-dyed villain could have hornswoggled him. **1904** in *DAE:* One practical working theory in advertising circles is that the ad's chief function is to hornswoggle the consumer. **1920** Ade *Hand-Made Fables* 71: People were being thimble-rigged and hornswaggled and shortchanged. **1930** F. Shay *Here's Audacity* 17: It makes me pretee mad when I see some of the hornswogglers of today. **1934** in Botkin *Treas. Amer. Folk.* 557: It would be a shame to miss an opportunity to hornswoggle the public. **1935** (quot. at RUNNING GEAR). **1953** Chandler *Goodbye* 240: I'd just have to pick a name at random and probably get hornswoggled. **1956** Neider *Hendry Jones* 49: You'll hear people say Dad Longworth was…a greater fighter than the Kid. That's hornswoggling. **1960** L'Amour *Sacketts* 168: Fooled us…hornswoggled us. **1963** in *Uncle Scrooge* (May 1977) (unp.): I have to borrow your winning ways long enough to hornswoggle my old enemy, McDuck! *****1990** Thorne *Dict. Contemp. Sl.* 251: *Hornswoggle*…to swindle or bamboozle…familiar worldwide through its use in Western movies. **1994** Knoxville, Tenn., graphic artist, age 40: You better not get hornswoggled by that guy [a used-car salesman].

2. to curse or confound; darn.—used in mild or humorous oaths, in passive only.

1834 Caruthers *Kentuckian* I 61: I wish I may be horn swoggled, if ever I thought to live to see the day. *a***1866** C.H. Smith *Bill Arp* 133: I'll be hornswaggled if the talkin…has got to be done…any longer. **1880** Bailey *Danbury Boom* 29: Well, may I be hornswoggled! **1881** Small *Smith* 44: I'll see her eternally hornswoggled first. **1901** H. Robertson *Inlander* 284: Well, I be hornswoggled! **1914** Ellis *Billy Sunday* 304: I will be hornswaggled if they did not owe him $400 then. **1933** H. Stephenson *Glass* 157: Well, I be hornswoggled…if that ain't the midway at the World's Fair! **1959** *Nation* (Apr. 11): The raising of said question did outrage, irritate, embarrass, hornswoggle, and otherwise demoralize certain knaves, thugs, punks, poltroons, [etc.]. **1987** C. Chiodo & S. Chiodo *Killer Klowns* (film): I'll be hornswoggled! **1994** *Simpsons Comics* (No. 2) 4: Well, I'll be hornswoggled!…I guess he doesn't wear a toupee after all!

horney *n. Und.* a constable or sheriff.

*****1753** in Partridge *Dict. Und.* 344: *Horney.* *****1789** G. Parker *Life's Painter* 173: *Hornies.* Constables, watchmen, and peace officers. **1791** [W. Smith] *Confess. T. Mount* 19: A constable, *a horney.* **1807** Tufts *Autobiog.* 293 [ref. to 1794]: A horney's a coming…a sheriff is coming. *****1874** in Ribton-Turner *Vagrants* 494: A constable [is] a horny. *****1912** J. Stephens *Crock of Gold* 30: I'll teach you how to play Horneys and Robbers.

horny *adj.* **1.a.** sexually excited; (*also*) lustful. Also in prov. phrases. Cf. earlier HORN-MAD.

1826 in Bleser *Secret & Sacred* 5: [Feeling] so horny. **1864** in *Manuscripts* XXX (1978) 194: Don't let that horseradish make you horney for I am not there you know. **1888** E. Field *Socratic Love* (st. 2): It was the usual thing for horny Greeks to diddle/This gummy vent. **1889** Barrère & Leland *Dict. Slang* I 476: *Horny* (American, also English), lecherous, in a state of sexual desire, in rut. *a***1890–93** F & H III 351: *Horny*…disposed to erection. **1916** Cary *Venery* I 142: *Horny*—Disposed to an erection of the penis or clitoris. **1918** *DN* V 25: *Horny*, adj. Amative. **1923** McAlmon *Companion Volume* 50: God, I feel horny tonight. **1927** H. Miller *Moloch* 63: General Grant was just a horny gaffer. **1933** J. Conroy *Disinherited* 75: We're all getting pretty horny, for one thing. **1934** [J.M. Hall] *Anecdota* 93: Why you little bitch!…I didn't know you were so goddam horny! **1936** Levin *Old Bunch* 152: Horny, always horny. **1943** J. Mitchell *McSorley's* 44: He's so horny he doesn't know what's taking place. **1959** De Roo *Wolves* 63: "I feel real groovy tonight," she whispered. "Downright horny." **1964** R. Moore *Green Berets* 130: Ling was still as horny as a bag of toads. **1968** M.B. Scott *Racing Game* 21: It is…believed that "common horses"…are "horny" or lustful animals. **1968** "R. Hooker" *M*A*S*H* 29: "I'm hornier than a three-balled tom cat," agreed Hawkeye. *Ibid.* 101: Ah'm hornier than a bitch in heat. **1969** Searls *Hero Ship* 200: All these guys…are horny as hoot owls. **1972** Wambaugh *Blue Knight* 144: He was…so horny he'd mount a cage if he thought there was a canary in there. **1983** LaBarge & Holt *Sweetwater Gunslinger* 91: I'm so horny that the crack of dawn could turn me on. **1983** Eilert *Self & Country* 206 [ref. to 1968]: I'm hornier than a ten-dicked billy goat. **1983** C. Rich *Advisors* 107: I am hornier than a three-balled tomcat. *Ibid.* 122: I'm hornier than a hoot owl. **1987** Zeybel *Gunship* 96 [ref. to Vietnam War]: By then Wexford was so horny he honked. **1991** Nelson & Gonzales *Bring Noise* 24: I'm so horny I'll fuck the crack of dawn. **1993** G. Lee *Honor & Duty* 217: Hornier than a Texas toad.

b. obsessively eager or desirous.

1982 Hayano *Poker Faces* 34: He got "horny" for Poker.

2. provoking sexual desire; lewd; erotic.

1930 Irwin *Tramp & Und. Sl.*: *Horny*…lewd. *a***1960** Federoff *Side of Angels* 227: He had seen the ads in the horny men's magazines. **1961** Forbes *Goodbye to Some* 139: I am due for a nice horny reply to the nice horny letter I wrote my girl. **1969** *N.Y. Times* (Mar. 23) II 1: I have nothing against horny pornography, either. **1973** in Flaherty *Chez Joey* xiv: The Brooklyn *Tablet*…was our invaluable guide to what we supposed were horny movies. **1974** Terkel *Working* xxxvi: I don't do that much reading from Monday through Friday. Unless it's a horny book. **1976** *Nat. Lampoon* (Aug.) 39: Some hot, horny hole-shots you can slam the ham to while you're tooling down Interstate 80. *a***1977** in S. King *Bachman* 133: You gotta listen to this.…Boy, is it horny. **1977** Langone *Life at Bottom* 194: You know, they show these films of chicks on the screen, and they got music playin' with it, and it's a real horny show.

horrendioma *n.* [*horrendo*us + *-i-* + *-oma*, suff. used to form names of tumors] *Med.* an especially dangerous medical condition, usu. cancer; (*hence*) a patient having such a condition. Also **horrendoma, horrenderoma.**

1977 Shem *House of God* 195: I began to get bogged down with the lonely horrendomas. **1980** E. Morgan *Surgeon* 18: Jim tells me you had a horrendioma last night.…There was no way you could have saved him. He was a bloody disaster. **1981** in Safire *Good Word* 154: Horrendioma. **1990** T. Fahey *Joys of Jargon* 22: Or an internist [may] call you a *horrendeoma*, a patient with many complications—or worse. *a***1991** in *Atlantic* (Oct.) 139: A golf-ball-sized mass in his frontal lobe, most probably a lymphoma but possibly some other terrible *horrenderoma*.

horrendoplasty *n. Hosp.* (see quot.).

1972 *Nat. Lampoon* (July) 76: *Horrendoplasty* A difficult operation, often lasting eight or nine hours. Very hairy.

horriblectomy *n. Med.* (see quot.). Also **horridzoma.**

*a***1987** in K. Marshall *Combat Zone* 7 [ref. to Vietnam War]: We used to call [treatments for cases of extreme burns] horriblectomies and horridzomas.…Horriblectomies were when they'd had so much taken out or removed. Horridzoma meant the initial grotesque injury but also the repercussion of the injury—the tissues swelling and all that.

horrors *n.pl.* delirium tremens; (*hence*) *Narc.* withdrawal sick-ness.—usu. constr. with *the*. [In earlier (1768) colloq. use, 'a fit of horror or depression', see *OED*.]

1839 Briggs *Harry Franco* I 188: The delirium tremens, or, as the sailors called it, the horrors. **1848** Cowen *Alcohol the Great* 221: In *horrors blue* my case I rue. **1865** in Hilleary *Webfoot* 57: He seemed to be affected with the "horrors." **1872** Hobbs *Wild Life in Far West* 62: He was nearly dead with the horrors. **1878** Shippen *30 Yrs* 165: One of the crew…was declared by the mate to have "a bad case of horrors." **1882** Campbell *Poor* 52: Trembling with weakness and incipient "horrors." *****1903** in Kipling *Traffics & Discoveries* 60: I don't get the horrors off two glasses o' brown sherry. **1930** Irwin *Tramp & Und. Sl.*: *Horrors*…delirium tremens. **1946** Gresham *Nightmare Alley* 7: Nothing scares a real rummy like the chance of a dry spell and getting the horrors. **1949** R. Rose *Mighty Joe Young* (film): Has he got the horrors! **1965–71** in *Inter. Jour. Stud. Alcohol* XXXII (1971) 732: *Horrors.* Delirium tremens. **1989** P. Benchley *Rummies* 96: The…shakes and the horrors.

horror show *n.* an occasion or experience that is embarrassing, disgusting, frightening, disastrous, or the like.

1959 *Swinging Syllables: Horror Show*—Anything unpleasant. **1969** *Current Slang I & II* 52: *Horror show*, n. The process whereby one makes a fool of himself.—College females, New York. **1974** Dubinsky & Standora *Decoy Cop* 95: It's a Goddamned horror show. **1978** C. Miller *Animal House* 11: Getting incredibly drunk with the guys, for instance, and participating in some kind of horror show. **1981** in Safire *Good Word* 124: The advance-decline figures on the New York Stock Exchange are a horror show. **1982** Del Vecchio *13th Valley* 73: The rear ain't what it's cracked up ta be. It's a real horror show.…I'm more scared back here than I was out there. **1986** Merkin *Zombie Jamboree* 23: She starts speaking that dumb stuff, and it's just a horror show. *a***1987** Coyle *Team Yankee* 208: He wasn't sure if he could deal with another horror show like the last one.

horse also **hoss** *n.* **1.** *Printing.* work charged for but not yet done, or work done but not yet charged for. Cf. DEAD HORSE.

*****1770** in *OED2*: If any journeyman set down in his bill on Saturday night more work than he has done, that surplus is called Horse. *****1841** W. Savage *Dict. Art of Printing* 322: *Horse*…is not always deducted in the next bill. **1859** Bartlett *Amer.* (ed. 2) 247: *Live Horse.* In printers' parlance, work done over and above that included in the week's bill. **1909** *WNID*: *Horse*…Work paid for in advance. *Slang.*

2.a. a strong or athletic fellow; (*hence*) (now *rare*) a person who is formidable, admirable, unequaled, extremely capable, etc.; a good fellow. [In earlier S.E. use, a term of contempt much like *ass* or *mule*; see *OED* def. 4.]

1808 C. Schultz *Travels* II 145: One said, "I am a man; I am a horse; I am a team. I can whip any man *in all Kentucky*, by G-d." The other replied, "I am an alligator; half man, half horse; can whip any *on the Mississippi*, by G-d." **1813** Weems *Drunkard*: Hurra for me! a hard horse I am gentlemen, a proper hard horse, depend! may-be I an't a *Roarer!* **1821** Waln *Hermit in Phila.* 29: They all agreed that she was *half-horse, half-alligator, and a little bit of a steam-boat.* **1832** in *DA* s.v. *team:* Whoop! Aint I a horse? **1832** J.P. Kennedy *Swallow Barn* 42: When the old woman's mad, she is a horse to whip! **1833** Paulding *Lion* 25: Aha, says I, you may be a screamer, but perhaps I'm a horse! **1838** in Botkin *Amer. Folk.* 28: To sum up all in one word *I'm a horse.* **1844** in *DAE:* "Huzzah! Huzzah!" went round the crowd, while Jeptha's particular friends swore he was "a horse." **1845** in Oelschlaeger *Reveille* 226: "That's the talk!" "You're a horse, Judge!" **1845** in G.W. Harris *High Times* 49: Misses Spraggins, you're a hoss! **1847** Robb *Squatter Life* 70: None of your stuck-up imported chaps from the dandy states, but a real genuine westerner—in short, a *hoss!* **1847** in Blair & Meine *Half Horse* 89: The officer was a clever fellow, and "a small *hoss* in a fight." **1859** Bartlett *Amer.* (ed. 2): Even of a prominent lady a Western eulogist will say, "she is a *hoss*," that is, a sort of Pandora or nonsuch. *a***1860** [J. Jones] *Marie* 51: Well, Bob Rainsford, you ar' [a] hoss among the gals, anyhow. **1873** [J.S. Williams] *Old Times in West Tenn.* 176: Carroll is a statesman, Jackson is a hero, and Crockett is a *horse!!* **1874** Pinkerton *Expressman* 17 [ref. to 1858]: Can you send me a man—half horse and half alligator? **1899** Hamblen *Bucko Mate* 260: "Colonel Snodgrass, you're a horse!" exclaimed Phil, shaking his hand ardently. **1900** *DN* II 41: *Horse*…A student of remarkable ability. **1935** *N & Q* CLXIX (Nov.) 365: *Horse*—Strong and with great capacity for work. A man held in high esteem. **1938** in

Rawick *Amer. Slave* II (Pt. 1) 286: You is de jiggin hoss. *ca*1939 in Mencken *Amer. Lang. Supp.* II 753: *Horse.* A fast, expert carver or upholsterer [of furniture]. **1977** in Lyle & Golenbock *Bronx Zoo* 21: The Pittsburgh Pirates…had some real horses, Roberto Clemente, Willie Stargell, Al Oliver, to name a few.…We didn't have the sluggers Pittsburgh had. **1980** Pearl *Pop. Slang* 73: *Horse*…(Sports) a strong offensive player. **1984** Algeo *Stud Buds* 3: A college athlete…*hoss.* **1989** P. Munro *U.C.L.A. Slang* 50: Gary is such a hoss. His biceps are bigger than my quadriceps. **1990** in Wimmer *Schoolyard Game* 12: Kentucky put in a big quick old horse named Allen Feldhaus. **1994** Bainbridge & Cragg *Top Sgt.* 26: You can throw a grenade maybe twenty yards, thirty if you're a real hoss. **1995** *CNN Sports Tonight* (CNN-TV) (June 18): He's the kind of guy who can be a horse.

b. a fellow; man.—usu. used in direct address, esp. constr. with *old.*

1834 in Hoffman *Winter in West* II 198: "Halloo, horse!" said old Boniface, slapping on the shoulder a broad-backed fellow that stood in the doorway. **1839** J.S. Jones *Solon Shingle* I.i: Mr. Winslow, you are the head horse in the temperance team, and as I—. **1843** *Spirit of Times* (Sept. 9) 326: What luck, old horse? **1843** Field *Pokerville* 23: Put it into him, hoss! **1844** Porter *Big Bear* 81: I never seed any thin' hold on so—takes an amazin' site of screwin, hoss, to get 'em out. **1846** in *Ark. Hist. Qly.* XII (1953) 305: Old Horse, damn your soul, if you give such orders I will shoot you for certain. **1846** in G.W. Harris *High Times* 62: He'll jist give you goss in a minit, little hoss! **1847** in H.C. Lewis *Works* 128: Come quick! dear Doctor! That's a good old hoss! **1847** in Blair & Meine *Half Horse* 90: You aint arter me, are you, hoss? **1848** Ruxton *Far West* 8: Hyar's a hoss as'll make fire come. **1850** J. Greene *Tombs* 100: Wonder if we can get some old hoss to give us a preach? **1851** *Spirit of Times* (Nov. 8) 453: My early edication was sooperintended by a larned ole hoss named Dorsey. **1853** Lippard *New York* 92: "Come, hoss, there's no use of that." "Hoss! Do you apply such words to me," indignantly echoed the merchant prince. **1858** [S. Hammett] *Piney Woods* 93: I believe you're bluffing me, hoss. **1858** Pollard *Diamonds* 102: I say, big hoss, I hope you didn't disgrace Ole Virginny. **1861** Guerin *Mountain Charley* 26: Here's at you, old hoss! **1863** in Benson *Civil War Bk.* 48: Well, old hoss, we've had another *turrible* march, and nobody knows whether it's over yet. **1878** Mulford *Fighting Indians* 11: A recruit…detailed in the Adjutant's Office…is respected by all the "old hosses," as he now has—or thinks he has—a way of knowing the plans and intentions of all the officers in the whole army. **1882** Ellis *Huge Hunter* 116: Yer can't fool this yar hoss in that style. **1883** *United Service* (Feb.) 207: No, sirree, horse; I'm none of them kind. **1887** Willett *Sandy* 24: Don't be too sart'in of that, ole hoss. **1904** Harben *Georgians* 148: Went back on us, ole hoss. **1915** H.L. Wilson *Ruggles* 46: Well, old horse!…Who'd ever expected to see you here, darn your old skin! **1933** Duff & Sutherland *I've Got Yr. Number* (film): Joe, old horse. **1961** Trosper & Willingham *One-Eyed Jacks* (film): Do somethin'? Not this horse. **1961** Terry *Old Liberty* 56: How you feel, hoss? **1964** Caidin *Everything But Flak* 138: I just don't see what your problem is, old hoss. **1969** R. Stone, in *New American Review* (No. 6) 200: Everyone called each other "hoss" and chuckled…country-style. **1972** Jenkins *Semi-Tough* 161: You hosses get a lot of rest these last few hours. **1972** Ponicsan *Cinderella Liberty* 25: And it *hurts*, hoss. **1973** Yount *Trapper's Last Shot* 14: Yore last price was a quarter, Hoss. **1995** Knoxville, Tenn., attorney, age 42: How's it goin', hoss?

c. Esp. *Naut.* a strict or tyrannical officer; (see also**a*1867 quot.).

1840 R.H. Dana *2 Yrs.* ch. xxii [ref. to *ca*1835]: Though "a bit of a horse"…he was generally liked by the crew. **1851** Ely *Wanderings* 71: Yes, and you are a horse. **1860** in C.A. Abbey *Before the Mast* 272: The mate…knows his duty &c &c but he's a rascal, or to use a sea phrase ("a regular Horse"). **a*1867 Smyth *Sailor's Wd.-Bk.*: *Horse*…is a term of derision where an officer assumes the grandioso, demanding honour where honour where not his due. Also, a strict disciplinarian, in nautical parlance. **1896** Hamblen *Many Seas* 317: The second-mate of a packet-ship is supposed to be a "horse," and Mr. MacDonald filled the bill to perfection. The man who would give him a fight was the man he loved.

d. (one's) husband.

1858 in G.W. Harris *High Times* 119: I told you, George, that Sicily an her hoss, ole Clapshaw, warn't gwine ter pull well in the same yoke.

e. a fine or remarkable specimen.—usu. constr. with *of.*

1858 in G.W. Harris *High Times* 95: I allers sed you wer a hoss ov a doctor; you cured Davy with itims what dont either puke or purge. **1876** J.M. Reid *Old Settlers* 160: The people…at the funeral declared that he was "a hoss of a feller." **1955** Shapiro *Sixth of June* 134: I want personally to thank each and every one of you. This section has done a horse of a job. **1972** Hannah *Geronimo Rex* 256: That "Charlemagne" [a musical piece] is really a horse. That's the best thing I ever heard on the march. **1995** Eble *Campus Slang* (Apr.) 5: *Hoss*—someone or something that exhibits extraordinary ability at something: "That 1978 Chevy truck is a hoss."

3. Esp. *Naut. & Mil.* SALT HORSE.—often constr. with *old,* later with *canned.*

[**1839** Briggs *Harry Franco* II 168: Another said the beef was part of an old horse, and swore he found a horse's hoof, with the shoe on it, in the cook's coppers.] **1856** in C.A. Abbey *Before the Mast* 44: Give us that "'orse" & the "spuds." **1871** Gould *Maine Regt.* 44: The beef was tougher than the "old hoss" which the sailors say came from "Saccarapp to Portland Pier." **1883** Russell *Sailor's Lang.* xi: "Old horse" is the sailor's term for his salt beef. **1884** Blanding *Sailor Boy* 66: Our salt junk we used to call "old horse." **1898** Markey *Iowa to Philippines* 125: That mummified product, canned corn beef, known to the boys as "canned horse." **1899** Skinner *4th Ill.* 126: Cold beans and "canned hoss." **1900** *DN* II 41: *Horse,* n. Corned beef. **1906** Moss *Officers' Guide* 243: *Canned Horse,* canned beef. **1920** Mozley *Miracle Bttry.* 9 [ref. to 1918]: The food was very poor, usually, and consisted of rice, prunes, fish, or "horse." **1933** Palmer *With Own Eyes* 199: We still had some "canned horse," two crackers apiece, and coffee left in our stores. **1935** (quot. at GREASE, *n.,* 1). **1936** Reddan *Other Men's Lives* 44 [ref. to 1918]: Canned horse, gold fish, slum, bullets, etc.

4.a. *Gamb.* (in policy gambling) a selection of four numbers to be played simultaneously.

1872 Crapsey *Nether Side of N.Y.* 106: A player has a "saddle" when any two of the numbers he selects are drawn,…and a "horse" when the four appear. **1882** McCabe *N.Y.* 551: Four numbers make a "horse," and win $640. **1949** *AS* XXIV (Oct.) 192: *Horse.* A type of play in policy in which the individual wagers on four numbers to appear in the drawing.

b. (see quot.).

1931 *Amer. Mercury* (Nov.) 352: [Circus words:] *Horse,* n. One thousand dollars.

5. *Gamb.* (in monte) (see quot.).

1885 Siringo *Texas Cowboy* 127: I put…thirty-five dollars, on the Queen, or "horse," as it is called, being the picture of a woman on horseback.

6. *Stu.* (see 1909 quot.).

*a*1889 *Century Dict.: Horse*…A translation or similar forbidden aid used by a pupil in the preparations of his lessons; a "pony"; a "trot"; a "crib": so called as helping the pupil to get on faster. **1896** Walker *Amherst Olio* 169: [There was] No horse to Latin and German was too hard. **1900** *DN* II 41: *Horse,* n. A literal translation used in preparing a lesson. **1902** Mead *Word-Coinage* 187: I say Dick, pawn me your horse for half an hour. I must do a…[lesson] with which Doolicks has stuck me. **1909** *WNID: Horse*…*Student slang*…A translation or other illegitimate aid in study or examination;—called also *trot, pony, Dobbin.*

7. an unexpected turn of fortune (against someone); (*also*) a rough joke at someone's expense.—constr. with *on.*

1889 Field *Western Verse* 101: When we get played for suckers, why, that's a horse on us! **1891** Townsend *Negro Minstrels* 39: A hoss on you. **1891** Maitland *Slang Dict.* 145: *Horse on me* (Am.), one against the speaker. **1895** *DN* I 418: "That's a *horse* on him," the laugh is on him. N.Y. **1895** Wood *Yale Yarns* 2: Make him come up and tell that horse on his chum's dad last summer. **1897** A.H. Lewis *Wolfville* 35: This is a hoss on us, an' no doubt about it. **1900** *DN* II 41: *Horse*…A joke especially broad or humiliating. **1902** Townsend *Fadden & Mr. Paul* 99: "De horse is on me, me dear," I says. **1915** in White *Amer. Negro Folk-Songs* 203: Hawse slipped up an' fell on de flea./Flea says, "Dat's a hawse on me." **1923** Dobie *Sugar in Gourd* 49: If one darkey is a point ahead he says, "I'm a hoss on you"; if behind, "that's a hoss on me." **1931** Perelman & Johnstone *Monkey Business* (film): The bicycle will never replace the horse. On the other hand, the horse will never replace the bicycle. Which is quite a horse on the bicycle if I ever saw one. **1935** J. Conroy *World to Win* 25: Reckon that's a hoss on *me!* **1938** Natteford *Billy Returns* (film): You know, Roy, this whole thing is a horse on me. **1960**

Simak *Worlds* 32: If the Fivers had expected to sneak in and catch the camp confused and thus gain a bit of face, it was a horse on them. **1972** Sherburne *Ft. Pillow* 61: Well, boys, I reckon this is a horse on me. **1977** J. Olsen *Fire Five* 254: My fault. A horse on me.

8. *pl. Craps.* misspotted dice used for cheating. In full, **horse dice.**

1894 (quot. at RING IN). **1897** (quot. at LITTLE JOE). **1936** in Partridge *Dict. Und.* 345: "Tops and bottoms" or "horses" are mis-spotted dice with which it is impossible to make certain losing combinations. **1961** in *DAS* (Supp.): Karnov explained the use of "horses," mismatched dice that turn up only certain combinations.

9. *Stu.* horseplay; fun.

1895 J.L. Williams *Princeton* 42: They had great horse calling each other "Blamed Neo-Platonists" and "Doggoned Transcendentalists." *Ibid.* 65: Wow!...I haven't had so much horse since sophomore year. **1909** *WNID: Horse...Student slang...*Horseplay; tomfoolery; monkeyshines.

10.a. arrant nonsense; rubbish; HORSESHIT, 2.a.

1903 A. Adams *Log of Cowboy* 179 [ref. to 1880's]: From then on, the yarning and conversation was strictly *horse.* **1929–33** J.T. Farrell *Manhood of Lonigan* 210 [ref. to ca1920]: "Listen, punk, there's plenty of stuff left in Barney Keefe!" "Horse," said Paulie. **1939** Polsky *Curtains for Editor* 11: "What *is* your first name?" "Haven't any." "Horse." **1942** *ATS* 177: Nonsense...(*a lotta*) *horse.*

b. *pl.* (used as an interjection to express anger or disappointment); HORSESHIT, 2.b.

1927–28 in R. Nelson *Dishonorable* 109: *Miller* (Staring at his beaten hand): Horses!

11. usu. *pl.* horsepower.

*1904 R. Kipling, in *OED:* It was a big, black,...twenty-four horse Octopod. *1931 in *OED2:* Each of them with a few "horses" in reserve. **1939** R.A. Winston *Dive Bomber* 16: None of your thirty-horse put-puts for us. **1943** in J. Gunther *D Day* 245: How many horses does she pack? **1954** in D. McKay *Wild Wheels* 95: Mr. Hardtop...had plenty of horsepower, but Joel had horses too. **1966** *New Yorker* (Dec. 31) 30: It's got 350 cubes with 295 horses. **1975** *Wond. World of Disney* (NBC-TV): "It's more horses than we need." "I ain't stealing no engine!" **1983** Ford Motor Co. ad (CBS-TV) (Aug. 8): Twenty-six more horses ahead of its nearest competition. **1986** Thacker *Pawn* 232: "How many horses?"..."Fifty-six." **1994** Pontiac ad (WQXR-FM): Traction control, 225 supercharged horses, [etc.]. **1996** *Mystery Sci. Theater* (Comedy Central TV): Powered by a twenty-horse Evenrude.

12. *Trucking.* a tractor truck.

1942 *AS* (Apr.) 104: *Loose horse.* Tractor without trailer. **1951** *AS* XXVI (Dec.) 308: *Horse, n.* A tractor. **1955** *AS* XXX 92: *Horse, n.* A tractor or power unit. **1961** *AS* XXXVI 272: It is common to call a tractor a *horse* and a trailer a *semi.*

13. a motorcycle.

1942 *ATS* 83: Motorcycle...*horse.* **1961–62** in *AS* XXXVII 269: *Horse...*A motorcycle.

14. *Narc.* heroin.

1950 *Time* (Aug. 28) 4: Heroin...H, horse, white stuff. **1951** *N.Y. Times* (June 13) 24: Heroin....We called it "horse" and "H." **1951** *New Yorker* (Nov. 10) 51: Shortly after Charlie became sixteen,...he started on heroin or "horse." **1952** "R. Marsten" *So Nude, So Dead* 23: To shoot a deck of horse into his arm for...two bucks. **1953** Paley *Rumble* 124: Some coke? Little horse? **1956** E. Hunter *Second Ending* 252: A deck of hoss might cost you a dollar, or it might cost you five. **1960** in Tyler *Org. Crime* 271: About $18,000 worth of hoss (heroin). **1962** T. Berger *Reinhart in Love* 122: They always...needin' a quick fix and I tell you horse ain't gettin' cheaper. **1965** Spillane *Killer Mine* 103: It's only a weed....an invitation to ride the horse that comes later. **1973** Childress *Hero* 36: Hey, man...you gonna let him ride the horse? **1974** Charyn *Blue Eyes* 103: Look at those marks. The cholos put her on horse. **1976** *S.W.A.T.* (NBC-TV): I've seen his pushers turning 11-year-old kids on to horse. **1980** D. Hamill *Stomping Ground* 168: Enough money for a sack of horse. **1984** Hindle *Dragon Fall* 71: Horse, reds, acid, kinky sex, and worldwide fascism. **1985** M. Baker *Cops* 254: About one out of every three times, you'd catch him holding some horse. **1994** *N.Y. Observer* (Oct. 24) 3: Coke makes them talk....With horse, they just sit there.

15.a. a person, as a prostitute or athlete, who works as a member of a "stable."

1925 *Sat. Eve. Post* (Oct. 3) 52: The fight's off...if that's all you think of your horse. **1957** Murtagh & Harris *Cast First Stone* 305: *Horse...*One of a group of girls in a pimp's stable...*new horse* A new girl taken on by a pimp. **1978** Alibrandi *Killshot* 238: I'd like to challenge your horse. One match. Two grand to the winner. *Ibid.* 248: Coldiron's horse had whipped nearly every player listed. **1978** Pici *Tennis Hustler* 182: I've heard you're looking for fresh horses for your stable. *Ibid.* 248: Dalton...was...playing a new horse. **1996** McCumber *Playing off Rail* 26: I had made arrangements to launch myself and my "horse," Mr. Tony Anigoni, on an ambitious international road trip.

b. *Pol.* (see quot.).

1989 *Newsweek* (Oct. 2) 8: A horse is a congressman who introduces or supports a lobbyist's bill.

16. *Und.* a person who has been bribed, paid, or duped into delivering contraband, esp. illicit drugs.

1966 Braly *On the Yard* 73: Just hang tough until I find a horse to put in the line. *a*1987 J. Green *Jargon* 287: *Horse...*(US) (Prisons) a guard who has been bribed to smuggle extra supplies—drugs, tobacco, etc.—into a jail, and to take letters out.

17. *CB.* (see quots.).

1975 Dills *CB* (1976 ed.) 40: *Horse:* Ford Mustang or Colt. **1977** *Amer. Dict. CB Slang* 38: *Horse*—Specific brand car—Mustang.

¶ In phrases:

¶ **hold (one's) horses** to check (one's) impulsiveness; be calm.

1842 *Spirit of Times* (May 21) 135: Hold your horses! What'll you have to drink? **1845** Corcoran *Pickings* 48: Oh, hold your horses, Squire. **1846** in Blair & McDavid *Mirth* 87: Well, hold your hoss for a minute, and I'll sweeten the tin with a speck more. **1847** Robb *Squatter Life* 24: Hold on fellars...jest hold your hosses, boys—he'll come out directly. **1848** *Life in Rochester* 67: Hold your horses, there; one at a time, *if* you please. **1880** J.C. Harris *Uncle Remus* 46: Hole yo' hosses, Sis Cow, twel you hear me comin'. **1903** *Pedagog. Sem.* X 371: Hold your horses. **1930** Stallings & MacArthur *Billy the Kid* (film): Aw, hold your horses, Ballenger. I'll get him out. **1940** *New Yorker* (Nov. 16) 20: Will you kindly holdja horses fa two seconds so's I can talk awready? **1945** Rodgers & Hammerstein *Carousel* 112: Hold yer horses! **1953** in C. Beaumont *Best* 38: Kid's just acting up is all. Hold your horses. **1979** Kunstler *Wampanaki Tales* 8: Hold your horses. I'll be right there. **1996** *Politically Incorrect* (Comedy Central TV): Hold your horses, Bill.

¶ **horse and horse** Esp. *Gamb.* dead even.

1846 in *DARE:* "Hoss and hoss!" "Yes; 'hoss and hoss,' and my deal!" *a*1859 in Bartlett *Amer.* (ed. 2) 204: I sot down to old sledge along with Jake Stebbins. It was horse and horse, and his deal. *a*1890–93 F & H III 358: *Horse and horse...*(American).—Neck and neck; even. **1905** *DN* III 11: *Hoss and hoss* means the same as *neck and neck* or *six to half a dozen.* **1908** in *DAE:* It was horse and horse between the professors. **1928** Weseen *Dict. Grammar* 310: *Horse and horse.* Gambling slang meaning on even terms or "all square." **1959** in Partridge *DSUE* (ed. 5) 1137: When shaking dice, best two out of three, if the first two throws result in a tie, the players...are *horse and horse.*

¶ **horse to horse** (see quot.).

1942–49 Goldin et al. *DAUL* 102: *Horse-to-horse.* Everything being equal...."Horse-to-horse, we can muscle...that mob out of the grift."

¶ **[get] on (one's) horse** to get moving; hurry up.

1942 Casey *Torpedo Junction* 19: Found call from Navy telling me to collect my orders and get on my horse. **1944** Gamet et al. *Tampico* (film): Get on your horse. Beat it. **1956** G. Green *Last Angry Man* 24: You'd better git on your horse, kid. **1957** Bannon *Odd Girl* 49: Well, we'd better be on our horses, children. **1962** Quirk *Red Ribbons* 128: Jack, Military Police Headquarters is your best bet. On your horse. **1963** G. Abbott *Mr. Abbott* 207: Never mind all that crap, you just get on your horse and get busy. **1975** in G.A. Fine *With the Boys* 169: *Get on your horse...*Run fast. **1977** P. Rizzuto, on N.Y. Yankees Baseball (WPIX-TV): Mickey Rivers is gonna get on his horse...and he's there [to catch a fly ball].

¶ **play horse, 1.** to play the fool or engage in horseplay; (*hence*) (constr. with *with*) to tease, annoy, or make merry with.

1892 S. Crane, in *DA:* Curious faces appeared in doorways, and whispered comments passed to and fro. "Ol' Johnson's playin' horse agin." **1896** Ade *Artie* 57: Mame's mother tried to jolly the crowd up by playin' horse with Tommy. *Ibid.* 92: Do you think I'm goin' out ridin' with her and have a lot o' cheap skates stoppin' to play horse with her everywhere we go? **1900** S.E. White *Westerners* 290: I'm jest as willin' to play "horse" as anybody. **1900** *DN* II 49: *Play horse with*…1. To ridicule or make sport of. 2. To tease or annoy. **1907** "O. Henry," in *DN:* I'll drop the tanglefoot and the gun play, and won't play hoss no more.

2. to confound, defeat, or take advantage of.—constr. with *with*.

1900 *DN* II 49: *Play horse with*…To overcome easily.…To confuse. **1904** in *DAE:* You've got to have some well-matured plan…if they try to play horse with you again.

¶ **straight from** [or **out of**] **the horse's mouth** (of information) from an inside source; reliable. Now *colloq.* Cf. earlier syn. *from* [or *out of*] *the feed box* [or *bag*] s.v. FEED BOX. [Aldington's 1943 assertion that the phrase originated during the Napoleonic Wars lacks evidentiary support.]

[**1917** in Woods *Horse-Racing* 290: This tip comes straight from the barn.] **1928** P.G. Wodehouse, in *OED2:* The prospect of getting the true facts—straight, as it were, from the horse's mouth—held him…fascinated. *1939 N & Q* CLXXVII (Dec. 30) 484: A saying current in recent years, in racing and betting circles…[is] "straight from the horse's mouth." It indicates that the tipster believes (or pretends) he has specially inspired information…on the ability of a given horse to win a race. **1942** *ATS* 502: *Straight from the horse's mouth*, of turf information, direct from dependable sources. *1943 Aldington *Duke* 125: The clique of old generals headed by the Duke of York at the Horse Guards…exercised a despotic…control of the army, dating their foolish ukases from "Stable Yard," whence the saying: "Straight from the Horses' mouth." **1947** *Amer. N & Q* (Nov.) 121: "Out of the horse's mouth."…I have heard it used often since I moved to Ohio.…in the sense of quotation from an unimpeachable source. **1964** N.Y.C. high-school student: This comes straight from the horse's mouth. **1966** Boatner & Gates *Dict. Idioms:* They are going to be married. I got the news straight from the horse's mouth—their minister.

horse *adj.* (a partial euphem. for) HORSESHIT.

1961 Brosnan *Pennant Race* 155: "I've been pretty lousy—lately," I said.…"All of us have been horse, Professor." *Ibid.* 175: Or you might say that he looked horse—as if he shouldn't get anybody out.

horse also **hoss** *v.* **1.** to copulate or copulate with (a woman).—usu. considered vulgar. [In ME and later, '(of a stallion) to cover a mare'; see *OED.* The recent U.S. quots. may be factitious; cf. **(5.c.)** below.]

*1614 B. Jonson *Bartholomew Fair* IV iii: Say'st thou so, filly?…I'll horse thee myself. **1958–59** Southern & Hoffenberg *Candy* 69: Horsing on the floor! Humping under the bed! *a1986 NDAS:* They caught him horsing his secretary.

2.a. to flog; whip; (*also, fig.*) to treat roughly. Cf. *OED* def. 2.b.

1775 in R.M. Lederer *Colonial Eng.* 115: You published…that Mr. Fithian horsed me for Staying out all night. *1822 in *OED:* A judicious teacher, when he is compelled to punish a wicked boy, horses him (as the phrase is) on the back of a dunce. **1862** Sill *Journal* 74: The wind [and sea]…tumbled us and tossed us…and…"hossed" us.

b. Esp. *Naut.* to bully or tyrannize into hard work or extra effort.

*1867 in *F & H* III 356: To *horse* a man, is…to work down the other man. **1879** Shippen *30 Yrs.* 20: The world appeared to me to be peopled with men more or less yellow or brown, and a few white men to take command and "horse" them, as we sailors say. **1882** Miller & Harlow *9'-51"* 20: This Midshipman he was inclined "to horse."…"I am the boss, and I intend to 'hoss'/You youngster." *a1889 Century Dict.: Horse…Naut.* to "ride" hard; drive or urge at work unfairly or tyrannically: as, to *horse* a ship's crew. **1908** Stirling *Midshipman* 12: He isn't much liked by the middies because he "horses" us so much,

but the captain swears by him. **1918** Riesenberg *Under Sail* 240 [ref. to 1898]: We were horsed about unmercifully at the washdown. **1976** Hayden *Voyage* 20: [The] second mate…was horsing the…crew from downhauls and clewlines to buntlines and braces, under a hail of oaths.

3. (see quots.).

*1857 in *OED:* A workman "horses it" when he charges for more work than he has really done. *a1889 Century Dict.:* To horse a bill, to try to get pay for work not yet done. (Printers' slang).

4. *Stu.* (see quots.).

*a1889 Century Dict.: Horse…To make out or learn by means of a translation or other extrinsic aid: as, to *horse* a lesson in Virgil. (School and college slang). **1900** *DN* II 41: *Horse*, v.t.…To study with the help of a translation.

5.a. to trick or deceive; (*also*) (occ. constr. with *around* or *up*) to hoax, bluff, flatter, lie to, etc.

1891 *United Service* (June) 646: Well, I horsed the "old man" pretty bad, and, when at last he opened a jackpot, he was about cleaned out. **1895** Wood *Yale Yarns* 235: I don't believe the professor has ever been horsed by it. **1900** *DN* II 42: *Horse*, v.t.…To swindle or beat. **1908** W.G. Davenport *Butte & Montana* 213: After allowing his manager to horse poor Gans around the way he did. **1932** *AS* VII (June) 333: *Horse*—v.—to cheat; to give a "raw deal"; to hoax. **1932** Harvey *Me and Bad Eye* 40: Slim says, Don't horse us, sailor, probably the cook…opened a can of sardeens and throwed it overboard. **1935** E. Anderson *Hungry Men* 43: Don't let him horse you.…He reads all the time. **1939** Rossen *Dust Be My Destiny* (film): Bank robbers! You tryin' to horse me around? **1940** Wald & Macauley *They Drive by Night* (film): You can't horse me. **1941** Macaulay & Wald *Manpower* (film): Don't horse me, mister. **1945** Wolfert *American Guerrilla* 86: "Nuts," he said, "you're just trying to horse me up." **1956** Heinlein *Door* 44: But who worded those documents you horsed me into signing? You?

b. to tease or make sport of; bait; kid.

1900 *DN* II 41: *Horse*, v.t.…2. To joke someone. **1901** in *OED2:* He developed the idea that we had no interest in the work and were trying to "horse" him. **1909** *WNID: Horse*…To make (one) the object of horseplay. *Slang, U.S.* **1928** in *OED2:* Always playing jokes on each other, they began to "horse" each other cryptographically. **1933** in Weinberg et al. *Tough Guys* 114: This jane's horsing us. Come on; let's fan the joint. *a1961 in *WNID3:* If there was nothing else to do, you could horse the newspaper vendor.

c. to indulge in rough jokes or horseplay; fool around; (*hence*) to waste time in trifling activity; fool; (*broadly and euphemistically*) to philander.—now usu. constr. with *around.* Now *colloq.*

1900 S.E. White *Westerners* 118: Moroney can do such elegant horsing. **1919** Johnson *Heaven, Hell or Hoboken* 157: This time the petite little waitress "horsed around a bit," so to speak. **1926** in *AS* II (1927) 276: *Horsing around*—engaging in horse play. **1926** *AS* II (Oct.) 45: Animal comparisons in Indiana.…*To horse*—"to play, to be in horse play." **1927** in *AS* III (1928) 219: *Horse around*, v. phr. To indulge in ill-timed trifling or horse-play. "Quit horsing around, will you? Can't you see I'm busy?" **1930** *AS* V (Apr.) 305: *Horse around*—About the same as "monkey around." "Where is Smith?" "O I don't know—out horsing around somewhere." **1931** *AS* VI 204: *Horsing around:* acting foolish, awkward and unpleasant. **1935** J. Conroy *World to Win* 230: The girl at the soda fountain always had a bunch of sheiks horsing around. **1938** Sherman & Sherman *Crime School* (film): Maybe we'd better quit horsin' around. **1938** Smitter *Detroit* 58: Stop horsin' around—she's gettin' cold! **1942** Wilder *Flamingo Road* 41: That fellow…an' Pete…were horsin' around in a booth. **1943** in Ruhm *Detective* 301: Why horse around?…You opened the man's letter—why not admit it? **1945** Kanin *Born Yesterday* 220: I don't think he'll like you horsin' around with his girl in the middle of the night. **1949** G.S. Coffin *Winning Poker* 179: *Horse*—To make a silly play whose only virtue is cheapness. **1954** "W. Henry" *Death of Legend* 32: Dingus was really mad about it; he wasn't just horsing now. **1956** Longstreet *Real Jazz* 67: This is a respectable band…and there ain't goin' to be any immoral horsin' goin' on. Whoever you start sleepin' with this trip, that's how you end the tour! **1967** H. Nemerov, in J.P. Hunter *Norton Intro. Poetry* (ed. 2) 237: Where Justice, after considerable horsing around,/Turns out to be Mercy. **1970** Benken *Apache Raiders* 73: Whatever I say, that's what you do without asking questions or horsing around. **1972** in *Playboy* (Jan. 1973) 146: You're serious, is it?…You think I'm just horsing around? **1979** Hofstadter *Gödel* 106: I would be rather wary of horsing around with these strange liquids. **1994** *Court TV* (June 21): Claim he and Manning were just horsing around.

d. to impose on contemptuously.—usu. constr. with *around.*

1938 Bezzerides *Long Haul* 21: "You've been horsing me around long enough." "You've got me all wrong, Nick. Why should I horse you?" **1940** DeLeon *Annie Sails Again* (film): You can't horse me around like that! **1940** Wald & Macauley *They Drive by Night* (film): You been horsin' us around long enough. **1965** Linakis *In Spring* 318: Will you stop horsing me around? Am I on the roster or aren't I? **1974** Sann *Dead Heat* 25: I don't want to be horsed around any more.

e. *Craps.* to shoot (dice) idly for no stakes.

1946 G.W. Henderson *Jule* 113: Don't horse dice. Shoot for something! Don't like to see nobody horse dice!

6. to walk or go quickly.—also constr. with *it.*

1895 Wood *Yale Yarns* 273: Paige said it was time to "horse to likker" (referring to the Benedictine). **1968–70** *Current Slang III & IV* 70: *Hoss it,* v. To walk hurriedly.—University of Kentucky. "He *hossed it* over to the Union."

7.a. to haul; *(Angling)* to attempt to haul in (a hooked fish) through violent effort.

1905 in *DARE: Horse logs, to.*…to drag stranded logs back to the stream by the use of peaveys. **1916** in R.C. Brown *Hard Rock Miners* 170: They "horse" [logs] over muck piles with the most apparent ease. **1940** Hartman & Butler *Rd. to Singapore* (film): I think I can horse him [a swordfish] in. **1984** H. Gould *Cocktail* 134: We horsed the bar onto the service elevator. **1985** J.G. Hirsch *Richard Beck* (film): Don't horse him [a hooked fish]! Don't horse him! Take it easy!

b. to jerk (a throttle) so as to change direction abruptly; change the direction of (a locomotive, aircraft, or motor vehicle) abruptly; *(hence)* to drive (a heavy vehicle).—usu. constr. with specifying adv.

1937 in *DARE: Horse her over*—Reverse. **1939** R.A. Winston *Dive Bomber* 79: Horsing back on the stick during the pull-out. **1939** in Galewitz *Great Comics* 235: Nothing happens when I horse back the yoke.*…*Pull back control column to raise tail flippers. **1941** Kendall *Army & Navy Sl.* 8: Horsing 'er down.…swooping to scare pedestrians. **1943** *AS* XVIII (Oct.) 166: *Horse her over.* To put an engine into reverse. **1956** Heflin *USAF Dict.* 255: *Horse,* v. In slang usage: 1. *To horse the controls,* to yank savagely on the controls of an airplane. 2. *To horse an airplane,* to jerk an airplane about in flight. **1956** *AS* XXXI (Oct.) 228: *Horse it off. v. phr.* If the aircraft has not attained sufficient flying speed on reaching the end of the runway on take-off, the pilot must use considerable back pressure on the control column, or "horse it off." **1982** Basel *Pak Six* 97: I horsed the plane wildly to the right. **1991** R. Brown & R. Angus *A.K.A. Narc* 173: Two of Townsend's boys would horse the semi while he rode with me in my Caddy.

8. *Publishing.* (see quots.).

1969 Kent *Lang. of Journ.: Horse* to read proof alone, comparing it directly with copy; and without the aid of a copyholder. **1982** Connors *Mass Media Dict.* 121: *Horse*…to read proofs singlehanded, comparing them directly with manuscript or copy.

horse apple *n. & interj.* [cf. G syn. *Pferdapfel*] **1.** a ball of horse dung.

[**1924** Anderson & Stallings *What Price Glory?* 74 [ref. to 1918]: He's seen Cooper pulling a fag at reveille this morning. What's Cooper doing now? Boy, following the ponies…*He's* out collecting apples.] **1929–31** J.T. Farrell *Young Lonigan* 109 [ref. to 1916]: Studs felt uncomfortable, as if maybe Leon had horse apples in his hands. **1934** in Legman *No Laughing Matter* 697: Here, let me kick them horseapples offa there. **1940** H.L. Mencken, in *AS* (Feb. 1952) 46: Unfortunately, the brakemen…mistook the horse apples for rocks. *ca*1940 in Botkin *Treas. Amer. Folk.* 536: A man had better get him a tin bill and pick horse apples with the chickens. **1958** Gilbert *Vice Trap* 37: I won't kick any horse apples down the street. **1968** C. Victor *Sky Burned* 67: For want of a horseapple my kingdom was lost. **1982** Braun *Judas Tree* 119: No one would poke around beneath a pile of horse apples. **1983** S. King *Christine* 2: A load of dried horseapples from the…stables.

2. usu. *pl.* HORSESHIT, 2.

1929–30 J.T. Farrell *Young Lonigan* 40: Schools are all so much horse apple. **1933** J.T. Farrell *McGinty* 12: That's my opinion!…Horse

apples! **1966** "T. Pendleton" *Iron Orchard* 82: "I reckon that's why they pay you experts fifty thousand a year. To make the right decisions." "Horse-apples!" said Wakely. **1982** Heat Moon *Blue Hwys.* 206: People get emotional about mustangs because they think they're wildlife. Horse apples. Half are strays. **1986** Ware & Morrill *Alamo* (film): Horse apples!

horseback *adj.* tentative and based on informed speculation.—used prenominally. Now *colloq.*

1879 in *DA:* I am not here as a judicial authority or oracle. I can only give horseback opinion. **1972** R. Barrett *Lovomaniacs* 243: Just as a horseback guess. **1984** T. Wicker, in *N.Y. Times* (Dec. 30) E13: But horseback analysis…is all too often wishful thinking.

horse blanket *n.* **1.** Esp. *Mil.* a heavy overcoat.

1918 O'Reilly *Roving & Fighting* 16 [ref. to 1898]: Why any man should be tempted into military life by "thirteen dollars and a horse blanket," was never explained. **1939** O'Brien *One Way Ticket* 13: Look at that stupid leatherneck.…Twenty-one bucks a month and a horse blanket. **1944–48** A. Lyon *Unknown Station* 74: Why don't you get rid of your overcoat? You can't keep up with that goddamn horse blanket on. **1969** *Current Slang I & II* 53: *Horse blanket,* n. Cadet issue overcoat.—Air Force Academy cadets. **1970** Major *Afro-Amer. Sl.* 67: *Horse blanket:* (1940's) an overcoat.

2. *Logging.* a pancake. *Joc.*

1958 McCulloch *Woods Wds.* 89: *Horse blankets*…Flapjacks.

horsechips *n.pl.* HORSESHIT, 2.a.

1968 Johnson & Johnson *Count Me Gone* 68: Fred said that was a lot of horsechips.

horsecock *n.* **1.** Esp. *Navy.* sausage, esp. bologna or salami.—usu. considered vulgar. [Prob. the orig. sense; cf. the semantic devel. of syn. BALONEY.]

1942 *ATS* 91: Bologna…*horse cock.* **1947** Matthews *Assault* 18: Supper was…horsecock (cold cuts, that is). **1951** W. Williams *Enemy* 164: "How about a horse-cock sandwich, Whitey?" Horse cock was the trade name for bologna meat. **1957** Herber *Tomorrow to Live* 61: We had horse cock again. **1961** Forbes *Goodbye to Some* 206: You'll all be home eating fried horse cock…long before us. **1966** "T. Pendleton" *Iron Orchard* 10: Tasty, if you happen to like horse-cock and stale bread. **1971** Lavalle *Event 1000* 55: Chow down.…Horsecock and cheese. **1977** Langone *Life at Bottom* 111: It is near midnight and the menu is cold cuts—the Navy calls it horse-cock. **1991** Killingbeck *U.S. Army* 44 [ref. to 1953]: This is horsecock. Now use a slicing machine to slice it thin.

2. arrant nonsense.—usu. considered vulgar. Cf. syn. BALONEY, 2.

1925 in Hemingway *Sel. Letters* 143: Don said it was all horse cock except they didn't want to lead off with a bunch of short stories no matter whether good or not.…That will probably end in horsecock too. **1934** "J.M. Hall" *Anecdota* 16: Whoops my dear,/Horsecock! **1942** H. Miller *Roofs of Paris* 109: She was…teaching the students…to draw swastikas…the old primitive horsecock. **1953** Eyster *Customary Skies* 66: Horsecock, Oakie. Nobody can.

3. HORSE'S ASS; PRICK, 2.—usu. considered vulgar.

1927 [Fliesler] *Anecdota* 81: "He's a horse cock."…"Now, now,…don't call him that. He's really a nice fellow." **1970** R. Sylvester *Guilty Bystander* 287 [ref. to WWII]: "American horse cock sons of bitch," he screamed.

horsecollar *n.* **1.a.** a zero, esp. as a score in sports; GOOSE EGG.

1900 *DN* II 42: *Horse-collar,* Another name for the cipher when indicating the score of a game or the mark of a student. **1907** in Nichols *Baseball Term.* ix: The horsecollars on the Yankee's scorecard were much more in evidence than those marks that count.

b. *Baseball.* an instance of a batter failing to get a hit during a game.

1928 Ruth *Baseball* 46: Burns went hitless against Zachary the other day. Up three times for a horse-collar. **1929** *N.Y. Times* (June 2) IX 2: A string of "goose eggs" in the hit column is termed a "horse collar."…When he [goes hitless five times] the other players say that "so-and-so got a horse collar, size five." **1940** in P. Dickson *Baseball Dict.* 211: Joe DiMaggio didn't get a hit. It was his first "horse collar" in six games. *a*1982 T. Considine *Lang. of Sport* 26: To "wear the horsecollar" is to go without a hit for the game.

2. nonsense; HORSEFEATHERS.

1923 Bellah *Sketchbook* 41: Horse collar! **1935** J. Conroy *World to Win* 112: "Horsecollar!" scoffed Alan. **1958** Camerer *Damned Wear Wings* 141: Kept shooting him the old horse collar about team spirit. **1961** Bosworth *Crows* 11: Never mind the horse collar, Mac—the babes and the beer are waiting.

3. a man's high collar; (*hence*) a clerical collar.

1942 *ATS* 94: *Horse collar,* a large collar. **1958** in *Dict. Canadianisms* 347: The passenger...was a clergyman, as could be seen from his horse collar.

4. *Av.* a rescue sling lowered from a helicopter.

1969 Cagle *Naval Av. Guide* 109: One of the primary uses of helicopters is in the rescue of downed pilots. Here [is] a UH-2 Seasprite prepared to hoist a pilot aboard. He has just received the rescue sling, sometimes called the "horsecollar." **1983** LaBarge & Hold *Sweetwater Gunslinger* 83: The Russian didn't protest as the American pulled him into the horsecollar. **1983–86** G.C. Wilson *Supercarrier* 91: Rockel gave the hand signals to the helicopter to lower the horse collar. *a***1990** Poyer *Gulf* 161: Number three in the horse collar, sir.

horse-collar *v.* **1.** *Baseball.* to keep (a batter) hitless during a game.

1941 *N.Y. Herald Tribune* (June 7) 17: He...was horse collared...by a couple of high hard ones. **1943** *AS* (May) 105: If he has a bad day at the plate, he may *get O-for-four* (no hits in four times at bat) or *be horse-collared.*

2. *Sports.* to render scoreless; shut out.

1973 Flaherty *Fogarty* 146: He had them horse-collared...before he even threw a puck.

horse cop *n.* a mounted police officer.

1942 *ATS* 418: *Horse cop*...a mounted policeman. **1952** Lait & Mortimer *USA* 302: Horse cops are a common sight all over midtown New York. **1972** N.Y.U. student: They used to have a lot more horse cops than they do now.

horsecrap *n. & interj.* HORSESHIT, 2.—sometimes considered vulgar.

1934 in North *New Masses* 93: They had him in their fancy parlors, talking their horse crap, did they? **1935** Algren *Boots* 182: That was horsecrap, Nora knew. **1960–61** Steinbeck *Discontent* 7: Now there's a bunch of horse crap for you. **1968** Lockridge *Hartspring* 124: Why all that horsecrap about principle? **1976** Conroy *Santini* 28: What kind of happy horsecrap have you been feeding Karen while I've been gone?

horse dookie *n. & interj.* HORSECRAP. Cf. DOOKIE.

1973 Yount *Last Shot* 78: Horse dookie....I'm not talking about gambling, man.

horsefeathers *n. & interj.* [joc. euphem. for HORSESHIT] nonsense; rubbish.

1927 T.A. Dorgan, in Zwilling *TAD Lexicon* 46: The cashier's department—Bah—Horsefeathers. He wouldn't give you a ticket to see Halley's comet. **1928** *AS* IV (Dec.) 98: Described in the vernacular to which it belongs, *horsefeathers* at this moment of slang history may be said to be the *snake's hips* as an expression denoting *apple sauce*...Answering my inquiry, Mr. William De Beck, the comic-strip comedian responsible for "Barney Google," assumes credit for the first actual use of the word *horsefeathers*. **1929** McEvoy *Hollywood Girl* 35: They can see...I'm not handing them a lot of horsefeathers. **1932** *AS* VII (June) 333: Horsefeathers—an expression of incredulity or disgust. **1933** in Spectorsky *College Years* 115: Listen, fella, if we let horsefeathers like that go here, half the freshman class wouldn't be wearing freshman caps right now. **1944** in Stillwell *Papers* 261: Pat told him "Horsefeathers." **1948** Cozzens *Guard of Honor* 508: "Horse feathers!" Captain Wiley said. **1969** Turner *Mayberly* 74: "Horsefeathers," Aunt Sue said. **1970** Thackrey *Thief* 389: I went right on running the bar after all the hay and horsefeathers about the Melchior score died down. **1983** *Good Morning America* (ABC-TV) (Oct. 28): Well, that may be true, but in my own observation it's horsefeathers. **1986** S. Bauer *Amazing Stories* 157: "Horsefeathers!" the old man said. **1996** *Good Morning America* (ABC-TV) (July 4): Horsefeathers!

horse-fly *n.* **1.** a fellow; (*occ.*) a scamp. Also **hoss-fly.**

1846 in *DA*: Sure of dat, hoss-fly? **1848** Judson *Mysteries* 504: Lookee here, hoss-fly, if you say that 'ere agin, I'll have to do su'thin' that goes aginst my grain. **1850** *Spirit of Times* (Jan. 26) 581: Did you ever hear how that hoss fly died? **1853** in *Western Folk.* VII (1948) 22: Here, take it, ole hossfly. **1854** *Spirit of Times* (Feb. 4) 604: Yes, sir-ee,

old hossfly, you ain't comin' none o' your big locks over this crowd. **1859** "Skitt" *Fisher's River* 240: Yes, horse-fly, I'm happy. **1865** Browne *Ward: Travels* 97: Yes, I have, old hoss-fly. *a***1870** *Coon-Hunt* 16: He was the durndest, cantankerous hoss-fly that ever clum a tree! **1870** Duval *Big-Foot* 318: No, sir-ee, horse-fly, Bob. **1930** Sage *Last Rustler* 34: Hello there, you little horse-fly.

2. *Army.* a cavalryman.

1926 *Marine Corps Gaz.* (Dec.) 244: Yuh know the Horse Flies has races each year, and I told 'em that they's fixed them races.

horsefuck *v.* to copulate with (a woman) from behind; DOG-FUCK.—usu. considered vulgar.

1972 Wambaugh *Blue Knight* 114: Sexy little twist....I'd like to break her open like a shotgun and horsefuck her. **1977** Univ. Tenn. student: Horsefuckin' is the best position.

horse-fucking *adj.* huge.—usu. considered vulgar.

*a***1968** in Legman *Rationale* 549: Two great horse-fucking volumes.

horsehead *n.* [HORSE, *n.*, 14 + HEAD] a heroin addict.

1952 Ellson *Golden Spike* 68: They knew he was on drugs, a real horsehead who hit the main. **1956** E. Hunter *Second Ending* 249: There's always a will when you're a horsehead.

horsehide *n.* a baseball.

1895 (cited in Nichols *Baseball Termin.*). **1907** S. White *Colored Base Ball* 108: Again the pitcher raised his arm,/Again the horse-hide flew. **1934** Weseen *Dict. Slang* 212: Horsehide—A baseball. **1943** *AS* XVIII (May) 108: The ball is the *old apple,* the *orange, pill, pellet* or *horsehide.* **1983** Whiteford *How to Talk Baseball* 103: Horsehide...The baseball. Balls are covered with either horsehide or cowhide. **1985** *Cheers* (NBC-TV): Wouldn't you like to see Sam flinging the old horsehide again?

horse hockey *n. & interj.* HORSECRAP.

1964 Howe *Valley of Fire* 180 [ref. to Korean War]: I think conventions and rules in war...to horse-hockey in wars. **1965** Hardman *Chaplains* 159: Horse hockey. **1966** E. Shepard *Doom Pussy* 21: There sure is a lot of horse hockey in the papers about pickets and guys that don't think we belong over here. **1980** W.C. Anderson *Bat-21* 187: A hero, Colonel? Horse hockey! **1988** *Crossfire* (CNN-TV) (Nov. 4): That's a lot of horse hockey. **1991** *CBS This Morning* (CBS-TV) (Aug. 26): This sounds like so much horse hockey.

horse-holder *n. Army.* an uninfluential or sycophantic aide or executive officer. Also **horse-handler.**

1982 F. Hailey *Soldier Talk* 33: *Horseholder.* An *aide-de-camp.* (One who serves in direct support of a general officer). **1983** Elting, Cragg & Deal *Soldier Talk* 155: "Lt. Col. Jones is General Smith's horse holder" means that Jones tags along, runs errands, and caters to the general's every whim. **1983** Beckwith & Knox *Delta Force* 114: It goes up to his horse-holder (executive officer). **1984–88** Hackworth & Sherman *About Face* 577: A horse handler immediately [was] dispatched to fill his glass. **1989** *Newsweek* (July 24) 4: *Horseholder:* Executive assistant to a top officer. **1993** T. Taylor *Lightning in Storm* 41: Cody...would have been...a horse holder with other lieutenant colonels if he were to attend the briefing at all.

horse hooey *n.* HORSESHIT, 2.

1989 *Knoxville* (Tenn.) *Jour.* (Dec. 8) 1: Little green men and all that horse hooey. **1993** G. Lee *Honor & Duty* 212: This...is a lot of horse hooey.

horse jiggler *n. West.* a horse-wrangler.

1930 Sage *Last Rustler* 114: The Kid held down the duties around the ranch as a horse jiggler.

horse jockey *n.* a hard taskmaster.

1851 Ely *Wanderings* 40: They call Capt. B. "the blow hard," "Old Assassinator," "Old Flogag," "Old Horse Jockey," "Typhoon Jack," etc.

horse johnny *n.* a stableboy.

1892 Moore *Own Story* 142: Then I spoke to the horse Johnny.

horse laugh *n.* ¶ In phrase: **give the horse laugh** to mock or deride.

1896 Ade *Artie* 84: When they see me they all give me the horse-laugh, even the hired girl. **1914** Ellis *Billy Sunday* 347: You are afraid of the horse-laugh the boys will give you. **1920–23** in J.M. Hunter *Trail Drivers* II 861: The boys gave him the "horse laugh" and he pulled out for home.

horse-mackerel *n. Naut.* a dolt.

1823 J.F. Cooper *Pilot* 157: What's that you're grumbling there, like a dead northeaster, you horse-mackerel?

horse manure *n. & interj.* arrant nonsense; rubbish; HORSE-SHIT, 2.

1928 Dahlberg *Bottom Dogs* 165: That was all horse-manure. **1934** in North *New Masses* 91: All they talked about was horse manure. **1937** Weidman *Wholesale* 45: The blow must have cleared the horse manure out of his head. **1944** C.B. Davis *Leo McGuire* 159: Don't give me that old horse manure, kid. **1954** E. Hunter *Blackboard Jungle* 57: That's all so much horse manure. **1958** A. King *Mine Enemy* 9: Horse manure! **1962** Killens *Heard the Thunder* 260: That is unadulterated horse manure. **1970** Newman & Benton *Crooked Man* (film): Horse manure. There's nothin' wrong with your heart. **1976** Berry *Kaiser* 207: Well, that was a lot of horse manure; he hadn't helped us one damn bit. **1979** *N.Y. Post* (Sept. 10) 2: Democratic National Chairman John White says reports of President Carter stepping aside in favor of Ted Kennedy are "pure horse manure." **1994** *X-Files* (Fox-TV): This…is a lot of horse manure.

horse marine *n. Naut. & Mil.* a lubberly or clumsy fool; dolt.

1823 J.F. Cooper *Pilot* 278: "Now, a'n't ye a couple of old horse marines!" again interrupted the young sailor. **1839–40** Cobb *Green Hand* I 58: It's only as a punishment for insinuating a hint that my high reputation as a boatswain can…be worked upon by a horse-marine like yourself. **1840** *Spirit of Times* (Apr. 4) 49: Horse Marines. **1849** Melville *White Jacket* 123: The officers sent the midshipmen…to find out who those "horse marines" and "sogers" were. *Ibid.* 352: To call a man a "horse marine" is, among seamen, one of the greatest terms of contempt. **1864** in O.W. Holmes *Poetical Works* II 136: Belay y'r jaw, y' swab! y' hoss-marine! **1871** *Overland Mo.* (Feb.) 169: If I don't make it all right with you, call me a horse marine! **1876** J. Wilkinson *Blockade-Runner* 36: I should contrast…all this efficiency and discipline with the…crew of "horse marines" which I had just left. **1887** Peck *Pvt. Peck* 35 [ref. to 1864]: He said something about my being a Horse-Marine and sent me back to my company.

horsemeat *n.* corned beef.

1927 in F.V. Mason *Fighting Amer.* 703: Where's that can of horse meat you've been boasting about?

horse nails *n.pl.* cash; money.

1859 Hotten *Slang Dict.*: Horse nails, money. **1859** *Spirit of Times* (Apr. 2) 88: All the "dimes" and all the "horse-nails,"/All the "brass" and all the "needful."

horse opera *n.* **1.** an entertainment featuring trained horses; (*hence*, disparagingly) a circus or carnival.

[**1857** in *DA*: The denizens of the Bowery, who prefer the equine opera, will do well to make the most of present opportunities.] **1864** in *DA*: Those fond of "horse opera"—and who is not?—will have an opportunity to gratify themselves—by visiting the Pavilion. **1867** in *DA*: Of course all our people, old and young, will visit the "horse opera." **1931** *Amer. Mercury* (Nov.) 352: Horse opery, n. Jocular for any circus. **1946** Dadswell *Hey There, Sucker!* 101: Horse opera…[carnival] show using horses.

2. a cowboy film, esp. if undistinguished; (*hence*) a radio or TV western.

1927 in *OEDS*: Horse Opera…is an opus of the West where men are cowboys. **1928** *N.Y. Times* VIII (Mar. 11) 6: Horse Opera—a western cowboy picture. **1928** Wilstach *Motion Picture Sl.* (unp.): "A hoss opera" is the term applied to Western pictures. **1929** McEvoy *Hollywood Girl* 201: They specialize in horse opera. **1935** Wald & Epstein *Stars over Broadway* (film): It's from a horse opera, professor. It's a cowboy song. **1936** *Esquire* (Sept.) 64: Horse opera…a western film. **1938** "E. Queen" *4 Hearts* 10: I was brought out here to do the story and dialogue on a horse opera. **1939** West *Locust* 322: He worked occasionally in horse-operas and spent the rest of his time in front of a saddlery store on Sunset Boulevard. **1963** Cameron *Black Camp* 16: I was in a couple of horse operas out on the coast. **1982** Connors *Mass Media Dict.* 121: Horse opera…[radio or TV] program with strong emphasis on fighting, gunplay, chases, etc. **1987** *Time* (July 13) 68: It's not that *Star Wars* is less worthy of satire than horse opera or gothic horror. **1991** Logsdon *Cowboy Songs* 1: In 1935 a new movie genre, starring singing cowboys and called the "horse opera," was created for Gene Autry. **1994** *TV Guide* (Dec. 31) 39: A made-for-video horse opera.

horse piss *n.* weak or unpalatable beer.—usu. considered vulgar.

[**1920** H.L. Mencken, in Riggio *Dreiser-Mencken Letters* II 388: "Mike…have you ever tasted horse-piss?" "No," said the friend. "Well,…you ain't missed much."] **1965–70** in *DARE: Nicknames…for*

beer…Horse piss. **1986** Coonts *Intruder* 39: Cheap booze and horse-piss beer.

horsepower *n.* Esp. *Navy.* power; influence; (*hence*) rating or rank.

1939 O'Brien *One-Way Ticket* 39 [ref. to 1920's]: My name's Joel. I'm the chief machinist's mate in charge of the engine room. What's your name, rate, and horsepower? **1939** I. Baird *Waste Heritage* 242: There's more horse-power to a sit-down than all the riots…ever staged. **1968** Blackford *Torp. Sailor* 36 [ref. to 1916]: I realized that someone "with plenty of horsepower" must have wanted the ship to sail that morning.

horse pucky *n. & interj.* HORSE HOCKEY.

1975 Stanley *WWIII* 176: Legend. Scuttlebutt, you mean. Horse pucky. **1982–84** Chapple *Outlaws in Babylon* 8: We can't afford the usual horse pucky. **1990** Westcott *Half a Klick* 158: Horse pucky.…You goin' hippie on me! **1991** Marcinko & Weisberg *Rogue Warrior* 81: Don't give me any of your "aye-aye" horse puckey either.

horse-pusher *n. West.* a stockbreeder's representative sent to accompany a rail shipment of horses.

1922 (quot. at BULL NURSE).

horseradish *n. & interj.* arrant nonsense; rubbish; HORSESHIT, 2.a.

1924 *DN* V 270: Horse radish! [indicates disgust]. **1925** *Adventure* (Dec. 10) 85: "Horse radish!" blared Corrigan. **1927** Saunders *Wings* 175: "Horse-radish," said Johnny roughly.…"That's a lot of horse-radish." **1930** Botkin *Folk-Say* 106: "You want to deceive them, lie to them."…"Horse-radish." **1930** in W.F. Nolan *Black Mask Boys* 108: "Horseradish!" she said. **1968** Saunders & Harkins *UFOs* 155: We suspected from the start that the Snippy case was horse radish.

¶ In phrase:

¶ **stronger than horseradish** very strong.

1909 Chrysler *White Slavery* 63: I will give you a little proof that is "stronger than horseradish."

horse's ass *n.* a stupid or contemptible person, usu. a man.—usu. considered vulgar.

*a***1865** in J.I. Robertson *Blue & Gray* 128: [He is a] horse's ass. **1888** *Stag Party* 12: Yer not a horse but yer a horse's arse. **1894** in Rose *Storyville* 27: Vic Demornelle told the officer that he was a horse's —. The officer was not pleased at being termed that part of a horse's anatomy that is under his tail. **1913** Jocknick *Early Days* 22 [ref. to 1870]: Calling the agent by opprobrious names, such as "Old Stiff," "Cabbage Head," "Horse's Ass," etc. [**1917** M. Cowley, in Jay *Burke-Cowley Corres.* 44: I am now perhaps…fluent.…Now at last I know merdre, cocu, con, ordure, foutu, grand morceau de cul de cheval.] **1925** in Hemingway *Sel. Letters* 143: Don says not to be a horse's ass and starve to death in a place with a name like Schruns. **1930** *Lyra Ebriosa* 8: We'll drink another glass to the latest horse's arse. **1933** Buckley *Squadron 95* 69: Mademoiselle, Cosgrain est le premier horsesass Américain. **1933** E. Caldwell *God's Little Acre* 32: "You did, you big horse's ass," Darling Jill said. "What's the matter with you? Can't you see anything?" **1934** in J. O'Hara *Sel. Letters* 90: I met her father-in-law, a pompous horse's ass. **1937** Weidman *Wholesale* 121: I had a chance to call myself as many different kinds of a horse's ass as I could think of. **1942** McAtee *Supp. Grant Co. Dial.* 6 [ref. to 1890's]: *Horse's-ass*, n., an undesirable citizen, a fool. Euphemized in directional expressions, as "the north end of a horse going south." **1948** Lay & Bartlett *12 O'Clock High!* 79: I'll admit you made a horse's ass of yourself. **1952** in Sandburg *Letters* 481: Also I have known horses-asses who monkey-doodled with my copy wherefore I make it explicit that there are to be no changes or deletions. **1959** Brosnan *Long Season* 4: His machine-like chatter would talk the ears off a donkey, and I wasn't about to let him make a horse's ass out of me. **1965** Bryan *P.S. Wilkinson* 388: Congress?…Those horses' asses. The only thing they're worried about is whether this call-up is going to help them or hurt them. **1969** N.Y.C. business executive: He's such a horse's ass. **1988** *21 Jump St.* (Fox-TV): I wasn't always such a horse's ass. **1989** *Alien Nation* (Fox-TV): Do you have…a fondness for being a horse's ass?

horse's cock *n.* HORSECOCK, 3.—usu. considered vulgar.

1974 G.V. Higgins *Cogan's Trade* 134: You horse's cock.

horse-shed *v.* **1.** *Law & Pol.* to attempt to influence individual voters, witnesses, or jurors, esp. while feigning impartiality.

1846 J.F. Cooper *Redskins* 240: This "horse-shedding" process…is well-known…and extends not only to politics, but to the administration of justice. Your regular "horse-shedder" is employed to frequent taverns where jurors stay, and drop hints…touching the merits of causes known to be on the calendar.…It is true there is a law against doing anything of this sort. **1856** B. Hall *College Wds.* (ed. 2) 258: *Horse-Shedding.* At the University of Vermont, among secret and literary societies, this term is used to express the idea conveyed by the word *electioneering.* **1901** in *DN* VI (1933) 369: There was no opportunity, as Mr. Lincoln used to say, to "horse-shed" [the witnesses] before they were brought in. **1914** *DN* IV 108: We don't expect to horseshed any witnesses.

2. to negotiate informally with a buyer or seller.

1888 in *DAE*: Incipient steps [were] taken toward purchases or trades.…seller and buyer…would talk, saying, "If it was tomorrow, what and so." This was generally…known as "horse-shedding."

horseshit *n. & interj.* **1.** horse dung.—usu. in proverbial or semiproverbial phrs.—usu. considered vulgar. [Prob. the orig. sense.]

1925 McAlmon *Silk Stockings* 53: Been as common as horseshit all my life, I have. **1956** in Kerouac *Letters* 563: He's all over Oregon like horseshit. **1962** G. Ross *Last Campaign* 149 [ref. to 1950]: "Well," said Seymore sagely, "let's wait and see how the horse shit falls." **1968** Westheimer *Young Sentry* 17 [ref. to *ca*1944]: "God Almighty!" he cried. "It goes down like razor blades and horseshit!" **1966–80** McAleer & Dickson *Unit Pride* 421: Sir, they're like horseshit, all over the place. *a*1982 in Berry *Semper Fi* 374: We're going to stick close to you like flies on horseshit. **1986** Coonts *Intruder* 111: Doesn't know horseshit from peanut butter. **1990** *UTSQ*: Let's make like horse shit and hit the dusty trail.

2.a. offensive rubbish; arrant nonsense or lies.—usu. considered vulgar. [Usu. more expressive of contempt than syn. BULLSHIT, 1.a.]

1923 in J. O'Hara *Sel. Letters* 9: Frankly, I think that stuff is horseshit. **1926** in Hemingway *Sel. Letters* 187: When you say you are the greatest living judge of poetry etc. that is just horse-shit. **1927** [Fliesler] *Anecdota* 33: And the moral…is, that when you're full of horseshit, don't chirp too much! **1929** in E. O'Neill *Letters* 330: He was…just another English sparrow—cocky and full of horseshit! **1934** H. Roth *Call It Sleep* 251: Aw, hosschit. **1938** H. Miller *Trop. Capricorn* 19: It was a tempting offer, even if it was wrapped up in a lot of horseshit. **1938** Steinbeck *Grapes of Wrath* 361: Well, they're tired of bein' rich. Horseshit! **1939** Bessie *Men in Battle* 302: It published too much "horse-shit" about how-to-win-the-war and we-must-keep-our-morale-up. **1947** Mailer *Naked & Dead* 456: Aaah, horseshit. **1960** H. Selby, Jr., in *Provincetown Rev.* III 76: Don't give us any of that horseshit. **1961** B. Wolfe *Magic of Their Singing* 16: "Hoyt Fairliss majors in advanced horseshit," Endicott said. **1965** Gary *Ski Bum* 15: Lenny hated the whole damn sentimental crap of it, it was pure horseshit anyway. **1969** Whittemore *Cop!* 12: "You'll soon get used to this horseshit," Kettle offered. **1972** *N.Y. Times Mag.* (Mar. 12) 113: You know, this is horse—. **1973** Krulewitch *Now You Mention It* 27 [ref. to 1917]: Marching backwards, facing the company, [the drill sergeant] screamed, "Who said that *last* horseshit?" He was known as Horsh ever after. **1981** *Harper's* (Feb.) 6: It is full of liberal intellectual horseshit. **1993** R. Peters *Flames of Heaven* 205: "And I've never interfered in your private life." "Horseshit." **1995** *New Yorker* (Nov. 6) 14: Still peddling the same old horseshit?

b. (used as an exclamation of disgust, disappointment, etc.).—usu. considered vulgar.

1965 C.D.B. Bryan *P.S. Wilkinson* 84: "Oh, horseshit!" the major said. **1978** Pici *Tennis Hustler* 13: Dawkins dropped his racket and swore, "Horse shit!"

3. a damn.—usu. considered vulgar.

1947 Willingham *End as a Man* 45: Do you think I give a horse-shit?

4. daylights.—usu. considered vulgar.

1973 Gwaltney *Destiny's Chickens* 3: Poppa slapped the bejesus horseshit out of him.

¶ In phrase:

¶ **happy horseshit** Esp. *Mil.* foolish stuff.—usu. considered vulgar.

1971 Sheehan *Arnheiter* 142: What the hell was all that happy horseshit about? **1972** Pelfrey *Big V* 6: I need your next of kin and some other happy horseshit. **1972–76** Durden *No Bugles* 250: No hollerin' or any of that happy horseshit. *a*1977 in S. King *Bachman Bks.* 7: Flowerbeds or baby pine trees or any of that happy horseshit. **1989** D. Sherman *There I Was* 23: Or any such happy horseshit. **1990** Ruggero *38 N. Yankee* 262: "No more Vietnams," and all that happy horseshit.

horseshit *adj.* **1.a.** contemptible or pretentious; worthless; offensive; unsatisfactory.—usu. considered vulgar.

1939 *New Directions* 138: Get down off that horseshit New York wise-guy stuff. **1949** in Kerouac *Letters* 207: These here brittle, horseshit New York mannequins. **1958** Gardner *Piece of the Action* 27: Do me a favor and stop smoking those horseshit green cigarettes. **1964** Newhafer *Tallyho* 195 [ref. to WWII]: You claimed a plane that Anders shot down, and that is about as horseshit as a man can get out here. **1972** *Playboy* (Sept.) 12: Never…have I read a piece of fiction that…[was] such a horseshit waste of time. **1975** Univ. Minn. student: This is a horseshit recording. **1977** in G.A. Fine *With the Boys* 110: Would taste awful horseshit. **1979** in Terkel *Amer. Dreams* 241: I hear guys saying about how horseshit medicine is in this country. **1980** *N.Y. Post* (June 17) 64: "A horse— game, just horse—," said Alex Trevino, who was picked off first *and* second base. **1984–88** in Berry *Where Ya Been?* 265: This was one horseshit bed.

b. *Sports.* inept; unskillful; clumsy.—usu. considered vulgar.

1969–71 Kahn *Boys of Summer* 108: Someone stole two bases. Someone made a horseshit pitch.…Whatever the hell. **1973** Wagenheim *Clemente!* 64: I be going horseshit, I mean horse*shit*—I can't hit, I can't do nothin'. **1977** in Lyle & Golenbock *Bronx Zoo* 8: I don't get upset when a club would try to do something to you, like trading you or telling you how horseshit you are. **1984** Nettles & Golenbock *Balls* 64: He'll say, "I'm going as horseshit as anyone," but all he can do is keep trying. **1986** P. Markle *Youngblood* (film): May I ask you a question? How'd you get so horseshit in one day?

2. *Mil.* overly concerned with the enforcement of petty regulations; CHICKENSHIT, 1.b.—usu. considered vulgar.

1959 Groninger *Run from Mtn.* 46: I think it's the horseshit position they're always forcing you into. **1961** Coon *Meanwhile at the Front* 161: I believe I will become horse shit. We will start running this squad by the book. **1982** T.C. Mason *Battleship* 130 [ref. to WWII]: "How come the old bastard's so horseshit then?" "He's Old Navy.…and he wants you…to know who's boss."

horseshit *v.* to lie to; (*hence*) to flatter; BULLSHIT, *v.*, 1.—occ. used absol.—usu. considered vulgar.

1955 O'Hara *Ten North Frederick* 67: Mike, you don't have to horseshit me. **1964** in Bruce *Essential Bruce* 106: Now look, I'm not horseshittin you.…You think I'm horseshittin? **1965** Linakis *In Spring* 225: Don't horseshit me, Al. **1966** Longstreet & Godoff *Wm Kite* 378: We're too old to horseshit each other with denials and penitence. **1991** R. Brown & R. Angus *A.K.A. Narc* 141: We can horse shit the lab's location out of this guy.

horseshit luck *n.* unexpected extraordinary good luck.—usu. considered vulgar.

1970 La Motta, Carter & Savage *Raging Bull* 24: "Christ, he hit it!" "Horseshit luck if I ever saw it!"…It was plain horseshit luck that ever got us through this.

horseshoe *n.* a propensity to have good luck.

1912 Mathewson *Pitching* 113: You were shot full of horseshoes to get that one. **1927–28** in R. Nelson *Dishonorable* 111: *Pratt:* Nobody gets a chance. *Miller:* He's got a horseshoe.

¶ In phrase:

¶ **set of horseshoes** a horse. *Joc.*

1882 Baillie-Grohman *Rockies* 29: He has "found a set of horseshoes" (horse-thieving).

horse-skinner *n.* one who drives horse teams; teamster.

1954 in *Dict. Canadianisms* 348: Either bull whacker or horse skinner had to be able to make his whip talk. **1956** Sorden & Ebert *Logger's* 19 [ref. to *a*1925]: *Horse-skinner,* Nickname for a teamster.

horse's neck *n.* [**1.** a kind of cocktail. [Colloq. or S.E. as a cocktail name, but prob. related to **(2)**, below.]

1908 T. Dreiser, in Riggio *Dreiser-Mencken Letters* I 18: I will take you to a place where they sell horses necks as long as my arm. **1909** *WNID*: *Horse's neck*…A beverage of ginger ale flavored with lemon peel, sometimes with whisky added. **1913** J. London *J. Barleycorn* 224:

I drank horse's necks. **1962** E. Stephens *Blow Negative* 292: It takes real imported brandy for a horse's neck.]

2. (a partial euphem. for) HORSE'S ASS.

1928 Carr *Rampant Age* 11: Come on, Buck, yuh ole horse's neck. **1934** in Ruhm *Detective* 107: Old Nonsplit Tom Flannery, the great horse's neck. **1935** T. Wolfe *Time & River* 635: Since when did you staht callin' him a horse's neck? **1944** Kober & Uris *In Meantime, Darling* (film): The skipper must think I'm a horse's neck. **1971** *Nichols* (NBC-TV): Don't be a horse's neck. Did you think we were guests?

horse's ovaries *n.pl.* [intentional malapropism] hors d'oeuvres. *Joc.*

1935 Pollock *Und. Speaks: Horse's ovaries*, hors d'oeuvres. **1972** N.Y.U. student: My brother calls *hors d'oeuvres* "horse's ovaries."

horse's patoot *n.* (a partial euphem. for) HORSE'S ASS. Also **horse's patootie.**

1983 in "J.B. Briggs" *Drive-In* 160: You start to act like a horse's patoot. **1988** *Night Court* (NBC-TV): Why, you creepy, sleazy, slimy, two-faced horse's patootie!

horse thief *n.* a dishonest person; crook; (*hence*, affectionately) rascal.

1929 Paramore & Estabrook *Virginian* (film): "You ornery low-down horse thief, you." "I only said it'd be funny." **1931** in Gottfried *Boss Cermak* 205: *Chicago Tribune* called him a horse-thief, now they say elect a thief. **1932–33** Nicholson & Robinson *Sailor, Beware!* 68: Hello, you old horsethief! **1935** de Leon & Thompson *Ruggles of Red Gap* (film): Let the old horse thief tell you about his trip in his own way. **1940** (quot. at KNEE-HIGH). **1972** Cleaves *Sea Fever* 28: Put that back, you horse thief. **1981** Graziano & Corsel *Somebody Down Here* 210: How you like that address for an old horse thief?

hose *n.* **1.a.** the penis.—usu. considered vulgar.

1928 in Read *Lexical Evidence* 59: Ajust the distance according to your hose. *ca***1930** G. Legman, in *F & H* I (rev. 1966 ed.) lxxi: Another cooled her Hot-box with his hose. **1941** in Peters *Wisc. Folk Songs* 266: I pulled out my clothes and he pulled out his hose. **1942** H. Miller *Roofs of Paris* 93: I'm going to suck his...hose! *ca***1944** in A. Hopkins *Front & Rear* 53: They never, never seem to tire/Of pulling their hose. **1947** Guthrie *Born to Win* 60: This hose, this dong, dick, this stick and rod and staff of birth. **1952** Larson *Barnyard Folklore* 81: Penis...prong, dong, baloney, prick, cock, pecker, pud, jock, club, knob, hose, pencil; old stiff, sprinkler, stud-horse, Indian root, Adam's whip, tally-whacker; drip, spigot, faucet, gun, rod, staff, joy-stick. **1968** Tauber *Sunshine Soldiers* 178: I just gotta give her the hose where she wants it. **1971** *Coming, Dear!* 101: Why is a fire engine red?...If your hose was hanging out you'd be red too! **1984** Mason & Rheingold *Slanguage* (unp.): *Hose. n.* Male sex organ. *a***1994** A. Radakovich *Wild Girls Club* 97: He held his hose.

b. *Pros.* a prostitute's protector or manager; pimp.

1968 Gover *JC* 97: Remind me a them mens hangs out at the Paradize—we calls 'em hozes. *Ibid.* 124: Here come four sheens fulla holes an hozes. What we calls 'em, crowd I hangs out with. *Ibid.* 137: I was kiddin them holes an hozes bout how I'm all squared up here.

c. *Stu.* a boyfriend.

1984 Mason & Rheingold *Slanguage* (unp.): *Hose*...boyfriend. ex. Is that Jane's latest hose?

2. *Baseball.* a strong pitching or throwing arm.

1964 Thompson & Rice *Every Diamond* 141: *Hose:* The throwing arm. **1969** Bouton *Ball Four* 272: Hose is arm. **1983** L. Frank *Hardball* 52: "I've seen better hoses in a garden!"...hose is a slang term [for a player's throwing] "arm."

3. *Stu.* HOSEBAG.

1989 P. Munro *U.C.L.A. Slang* 50: *Hose* female who sleeps with lots of guys.

¶ In phrase:

¶ **hit the hose** to drink to excess.

1903 Hobart *Out for the Coin* 32: Whenever I hit the hose the first thing I do is...get the hot air busy.

hose *v.* **1.** *Mil.* **a.** to riddle with automatic-weapons fire; (*occ.*) to bombard heavily.

*****1917** in Lee *No Parachute* 138: The tracer was hosing him fine, but he must have been wearing an iron suit, for nothing happened. [**1935** Pollock *Und. Speaks: Turn the hose on*, to attack with a machine gun.]

1941 Wead & Buckner *Dive Bomber* (film): You hose him with eight machine guns and a cannon. **1945** in Gellhorn *Face of War* 161: We say, "hose the Hun, of course." **1948** Wolfert *Act of Love* 520: It's a log....Let's hose it for luck. **1955** Salter *Hunters* 138: "Hosed 'em," he said. "That's the important part, isn't it?" **1965** *Air Officers' Guide* 437: *Hose* (*down*)—to shoot full of holes. **1966–67** Harvey *Air War* 104: I ran that little mother all over the place hosing him with guns. **1968** Coppel *Order of Battle* 55 [ref. to 1944]: Harry was just hosing the area, the way he always did, probably overheating his gun barrels, and I was about to tell him to use shorter bursts. **1974** Stevens *More There I Was* 54: FAC to fighter jocks...Guess who gets hosed? **1977** Univ. Tenn. prof.: They hosed the whole area with artillery.

b. to direct (bullets or missiles).—occ. used absol.

1937 Parson *Lafayette Escadrille* 99 [ref. to WWI]: They got him in a cross fire and hosed lead at him from all angles. **1948** Wolfert *Act of Love* 432: I can't do more than hose while moving. *a***1967** K.F. Cook *Other Capri* 11 [ref. to WWII]: Hose away at him if he's in range. **1968** Broughton *Thud Ridge* 67: They could hose a missile at you, but if you keep thundering, they couldn't quite get the edge they wanted.

2. *Stu.* to curry favor with.

1927 in *AS* III (Feb. 1928) 219: *Hose.* To flatter, to cajole. A student who *hoses* the prof is one who tries to get a grade out of him by means of some personal contact. "I see Caffey was hosin' old Crawford again today."

3. Orig. *Police & Und.* to beat with a rubber hose; (*hence*) to punish or defeat decisively; drub.

1929 Hotstetter & Beesley *Racket* 228: *Hose*—To hose; to beat a suspect...with a piece of rubber hose. **1942** *ATS* 318: Beat; thrash...hose. **1946** I. Shulman *Amboy Dukes* 121: You guys are really giving us a hosing. Why don't you let us alone? **1942–49** Goldin et al. *DAUL* 102: *Hose*...To subject to unduly severe punishment. *a***1970** *Webster's New World Dict.*: *Hose*...(slang) to beat as with a hose. **1971** Faust *Willy Remembers* 227: Champ Clark got some hosing in 1912. **1980** in Safire *Good Word* 304: I got hosed on the midterm.

4.a. (of a man) to copulate with.—also used intrans.—usu. considered vulgar.

1935 (cited in Partridge *Dict. Und.* 345). *ca***1936** in Atkinson *Dirty Comics* 77: Tee-hee. You firemen know your hoseing. **1941** G. Legman, in G.V. Henry *Sex Vars.* II 1169: *Hose.* To pedicate....also used heterosexually of the copulation of a man with a woman, e.g. *to give her a good hosing.* **1942** *ATS* 342: Copulate...hose, hump, jazz [etc.]. **1951** [VMF-323] *Old Ballads* 39: Hose her I did. **1954** Ellison *Owen Harding* 166: I think she needs a good hosing. **1959** Zugsmith *Beat Generation* 37: Many women were...shocked by a day-time hosing. **1962** Mandel *Mainsode* 219: He laugh again and he axe am I hosin' some girls. **1963** Horwitz *Candlelight* 83: The girls were going to be taken up in the B-17s and L20 charged for the privilege of hosing in the clouds. **1968** J.P. Miller *Race for Home* 294: Caught 'im hosing a cow.

b. to cheat or victimize.—usu. used in passive.

1940 Zinberg *Walk Hard* 35: I guess I'll get a hosing in the end. **1942–44** in *AS* (Feb. 1946) 34: *Hose, v.t.* To cheat. **1956** Resko *Reprieve* 264 [ref. to 1940's]: They're tryin to make it look good while they give everybody a hosin. **1963** Cameron *Black Camp* 137: Ok. So you got hosed....That any reason to hose guys like...me? **1964** in *Dict. Canadianisms* 348: I'm sick and tired the way the Rangers get hosed by the officials in this league. **1966** *AS* XLI 281: *Hosed*...Cheated. **1973** *Oui* (Mar.) 13: And we're getting *hosed* on cobalt. **1978** *NBC's Saturday Night* (NBC-TV): You guys have been hosed, baby....Tricked. **1986** *NewsWatch* (CNN-TV) (Nov. 21): Insider trading—that's when we all get hosed. **1990** *CBS This Morning* (CBS-TV) (May 25): I'm a red-blooded American. And I think we're being hosed.

hosebag *n.* *Stu.* DOUCHEBAG, 1, 2.

1978 in *Maledicta* VI (1982) 25: Prostitute...*hose bag.* **1979** Eble *Campus Slang* (Mar.) 4: *Hosebag*—a sexually promiscuous female: She's a hosebag...! (derogatory, disapproving—often used by females). **1981** Eble *Campus Slang* (Oct.) 4: *Hosebag*—weak or unattractive person. **1986** Univ. Tenn. student: A *hosebag* is a slut. That's a real common expression. **1987** Oak Ridge, Tenn., high school teacher, age 27: *Hosebag* was in common use in my high school in Washington, D.C. [in 1977–78]. It usually meant a whore, but it could also refer to anybody you didn't like. It was about the same as *douchebag*. **1987** *Rage* (Knoxville, Tenn.) I (No. 2) 16: Now...he's trying to get lucky with some hosebag. **1988** *It's Garry Shandling's Show* (Fox-TV): You scum!

Swine! Hosebag! **1991** Univ. Tenn. student paper: "She's a hose bag." She sleeps around.

hosebeast *n.* HOSEBAG; HOSE MONSTER.
   1994 *Newsweek* (Apr. 11) 72: Steve Albini...referred to the meddlesome Love as a "psycho hosebeast."

hosed-out *adj.* exhausted by fatigue; WASHED OUT.
   1969 Jessup *Sailor* 298: Never seen a crew hosed out like them.

hosehead *n. Stu.* a dolt.
   1983 Moranis et al. *Strange Brew* (film): OK, hosehead. **1983** S. King *Christine* 407: Off my case, hose-head. **1985** "J. Blowdryer" *Mod. Eng.* 22: *Hoser, hosehead*...A name that jocky, collegey beer drinkers call other jocky, collegey beer drinkers.

hose job *n.* an act of fellatio.—usu. considered vulgar.
   1978 C. Miller *Animal House* 97: Get any? Hah? Little hose job? Hah? Hah? **1986** C. Stroud *Close Pursuit* 33: Looks like the hooker was doing a hose job on one of the truckers. *Ibid.* 332: *Hose job.* Street slang for oral sex.

hoseman *n.* COCKSMAN.
   1977 J. Olsen *Fire Five* 43: Plummer's specialty is ginch...."One of the department's finest hosemen," his F.D. biography says.

hose monster *n. Stu.* a lecherous or sexually promiscuous person.
   1984 Mason & Rheingold *Slanguage* (unp.): *Hosemonster.* **1984** Algeo *Stud Buds* 5: A male who is known for his aggressive...sexual behavior...*hose monster.* **1987** Univ. Tenn. student: My roommate's from Virginia and he calls real horny women *hose monsters.* **1987** Aykroyd et al. *Dragnet* (film): Who knows what thrill-seeking hose monster he's got in there! **1988** *Nat. Lampoon* (Apr.) 26: Women: Slits, hosemonsters, slutbags, [etc.].

Hose Nose *n. Mil. Av.* a Vought F4U (or Goodyear FG-1) Corsair fighter-bomber. Now *hist.*
   *a***1977** R. Abrams *Corsair* 150 [ref. to Korean War]: One of the problems unique to the Corsair was the length of its nose, thus giving rise to its popular nickname—the Hose Nose. **1988** in Bowman & Bunce *Thunder in Heavens* 124 [ref. to WWII]: An elongated fuselage forward of the cockpit...earned the aircraft the nickname "Hosenose." **1989** G. Hall *Air Guard* 42: The F-4U "hose nose." **1991** Linnekin *80 Knots* 130 [ref. to *ca*1950]: The Corsair—the..."Hose Nose." **1991** *First Flights* (A&E-TV): The cockpit was moved further to the rear, giving her a longer nose and the nickname "the Hose Nose."

hose off *v.* to get out; go away.—usu. used imper.
   1987 (quot. at HOSER, 1). **1987** Univ. Tenn. student: *Hose off* means get lost!

hose-out *n. Stu.* a useless person; WASHOUT.
   1932 Lorimer *Streetcars* 141: I was the leading lady and...loathing the hose-out they'd picked for hero.

hose queen *n. Stu.* a sexually promiscuous woman.
   1984 McInerny *Bright Lights* 6: You suddenly realize that he has already slipped out with some rich Hose Queen. **1988** *Rage* (Knoxville, Tenn.) (Mar. 30) 15: Q. What do New York City and a hosequeen have in common? A. Flatbush....Q. How many frat boys does it take to satisfy a hose queen? A. Five. Four to commit unnatural acts and the other to give her his pin.

hoser *n.* [perh. sugg. by HOSEHEAD] **1.** a stupid, crude, or annoying person; lout. [Orig. Canadian slang; pop. by "Bob and Doug McKenzie," loutish Canadian characters created by Rick Moranis and Dave Thompson on the TV show *SCTV*.]
   1982 *MacLean's* (Apr. 12) 8: The Nylons are a lily-whitewashed, gosh-golly, hoser version of an authentic music form developed in the black ghettos of American urban centres. **1983** *Time* (Sept. 12) 70: Dave Thomas and Rick Moranis...of *SCTV*...stumbled into celebrity impersonating a couple of Canadian oafs named Doug and Bob McKenzie. These Two Stooges...sprawled about in parkas...guzzling...Molson's and calling each other "hosers." **1983** Moranis et al. *Strange Brew* (film): Don't wreck our movie, you hoser. **1984** Mason & Rheingold *Slanguage* (unp.): *Hoser*...1. A simpleton. 2. Somebody annoying. 3. Somebody who lets you down. 4. A Canadian person. **1984** Algeo *Stud Buds* 2: An extremely dull teacher...*hoser.* **1984** Eble *Campus Slang* (Sept.) 4: *Hoser*—jerk: That hoser put shaving cream in my shoes. **1985** "J. Blowdryer" *Mod. Eng.* 22: Hey, you hoser! Bring that beer in here, Jeff! **1987** Univ. Tenn. student: A *hoser* is a kind of a

nuisance or stupid person. When I lived in Wisconsin in 1981 and '82, people were into Canadian expressions and that was one we used a lot. *Hose off* meant go away, get out of here. **1988** *N.Y. Post* (June 22) 3: You hoser. **1993** *Mystery Sci. Theater* (Comedy Central TV): Knock it off,...hoser! **1995** Eble *Campus Slang* (Apr.) 5: *Hoser*—one whose behavior is wimpy, cowardly, or ignoble. Also *loser.* **1996** Joseph & Schepps *Encino Woman* (film): Cretins! Wannabes! Hosers!
   2. an uncultivated Canadian person. *Joc.*
   1984 (quot. at (1), above). *a***1986** in *NDAS:* Unavailable to us hosers, but can be bought down south. *Ibid.* Unlike their hoser cousins. **1995** Univ. Tenn. student: I'm from Toronto...A *hoser* isn't just a Canadian; it's more like a Canadian redneck, like the McKenzie brothers on *SCTV* [see first 1983 quot. at (1), above].

hosie[1] *n.* HOSEBAG.
   1978 in *Maledicta* VI (1982) 25: Prostitute...*hosie.*

hosie[2] *n. Fire Dept.* a firefighter belonging to an engine company.
   1983 Stapleton *30 Yrs.* 240: *Hosie*—Jake [i.e., fireman] assigned to an engine company.

hosp *n.* a hospital.
   1942 *ATS* 507: Hospital...*hosp.* **1948–51** J. Jones *Here to Eternity* [ref. to 1940's]: It was during the month after Angelo had gone to the hosp.... **1966** Kenney *Caste* 84: No other hosp in this area is as well equipped. **1984** *Daily News* (N.Y.) (Aug. 20) 7: Bus flip leaves 1 in hosp.

hospital *n. Army.* an incapacitating wound.
   1913 R.G. Carter *4 Bros.* 391 [ref. to 1864]: One of our...officers...expressed the wish that he might get a slight wound, a "hospital," or "thirty days' scratch."
   ¶ In phrase:
   ¶ **in the hospital** *Und.* in prison.
   1908 Sullivan *Criminal Slang* 13: In hospital—In jail. **1927** in *AS* III (Feb. 1928) 255: Hospital, in the: In prison.

hospital ball *n. Football.* (see quot.).
   *a***1982** T. Considine *Lang. of Sport* 147: *Hospital ball.* A short pass lofted over the middle that forces a receiver to leap and catch it, leaving himself unprotected and vulnerable to injury from a hit by a defensive back.

hospital hold *n. Labor.* an unsafe hold on a piece of equipment.
   1983 K. Weaver *Texas Crude* 94: *A hospital hold.* An unsafe grip on a pipe with a pipe wrench.

hospital pimp *n. Army.* HOSPITAL RAT. Now *hist.*
   1916 L. Stillwell *Common Soldier* 154 [ref. to Civil War]: The idea was intolerable that the other boys should be...marching and fighting, while I was in the rear, playing the part of a "hospital pimp."

hospital rat *n. Army.* a chronic malingerer. Now *hist.* [Quots. ref. to Civil War.]
   1862 in Jackman *Diary* 24: The hospital rats commenced bundling up and "shoving out." **1863** in Cumming *Kate* 134: I have heard...brave men and patriots...called by the ignominious name of "hospital rats." **1864** in *War of Rebellion* (Ser. 1) XLII (Pt. 1) 903: Two men deserted from Gracie's brigade to the enemy. General Gracie says, however, that they were hospital rats, and but little injury is done to the country by their desertion. **1865** in Neely, Holzer & Boritt *Confed. Image* 38: The Hospital Rat. **1878** Benson *Civil War Book* 52: I remember very well on going through the camps, before reaching my own, being hailed with continuous cries of "Hospital Rat! Hospital Rat!" **1899** F.E. Daniel *Rebel Surgeon* 130: A "hospital rat" as the chronic stayers were called. **1914** Nisbet *4 Yrs. on Firing Line* 81: There were officers and men who were forever feigning disability, that they might avoid the march and the battle. "Hospital rats," these, and objects of contempt. **1988** *Smithsonian* (July) 71: The [Union] prisoners freely admitted that their lines were being held by "counter jumpers, hospital rats and stragglers."

hoss var. HORSE, *n. & v.*

hot *n.* **1.** a hot meal; in phr. **three hots and a cot** three hot meals and a cot or bed. [The 1902 quot. is in the colloq. sense 'hot cakes', as in 1942 *ATS* 761.]
   [**1902** T.A. Dorgan, in Zwilling *TAD Lexicon* 46: [Man calling out order in restaurant kitchen:] How's them hots comin.] **1927** Shoup *Marines in China* 30: The regular three "hots" a day. **1942** Z.N. Hurston, in *Amer. Mercury* (July) 86: He might have staked him...to a

hot. **1946** Boulware *Jive & Slang* 2: *Collar A Hot*…Eating a meal. **1947–51** Motley *We Fished* 248: In the army I got my three hots a day. *ca*1962 A. Lomax *Where Blues Began* 289 [ref. to 1940's]: We gets three hots a day and our s— washed away [in jail]. **1968** Myrer *Eagle* 132: You look as though you ain't getting your three hots per. **1970** Libby *Life in Pit* 18: Three hots and a cot. That's the way we put it [in the 1950's]. **1971** Faust *Willy Remembers* 57: But as long as we had three hots and a flop, who cared. **1973** *N.Y. Post* (Dec. 4) 3: Three hots and a cot, that's what I gotta find. **1977** Dunne *Confessions* 239: Hundred a week, three hots and a cot. **1977** in Curry *River's in My Blood* 21: Man gave me a job during the Depression for two dollars a day and three hots and a flop. **1984–88** Hackworth & Sherman *About Face* 244: We got "hots" for breakfast and dinner. *a*1994 N. McCall *Wanna Holler* 177: Guaranteed three hots and a cot.

2. copulation. [The def. below is prob. inaccurate.]
    1916–22 Cary *Sex. Vocab.*: *Bit of hot.* The vulva.

3. [prob. a back formation from *hot-walker* 'person who cools down horses after exercise'] usu. *pl. Horse Racing.* a horse that has just completed a run.
    1939 *Sat. Eve. Post* (Apr. 1) 33: "Cooling out hots"…means walking horses around the barn until there is no fear they will stiffen. **1976** Calloway & Rollins *Moocher & Me* 42: I was a nigger kid walking hots out at Pimlico. **1988** Shoemaker & Nagler *Shoemaker* 28: I was still walking hots.

¶ In phrase:

¶ **on the hot** *Und.* on the run; as fast as possible.
    1930 *Liberty* (July 5) 25: *On the hot*—Quickly; "burning up the pavement." **1942–49** Goldin et al. *DAUL.*

hot *adj.* Also (*emphatically*) **red-hot.**

1.a. sexually aroused; (*also*) lustful; (of animals) in heat. [Besides conveying its literal sense, *hot* in early English commonly meant 'excited, excitable, passionate or ardent in any way'; thus it is not difficult to find Middle English quots. that are more or less congruent with the specific senses grouped together here. Yet with the gradual disappearance in ordinary speech of the tendency to apply the word in such a broad manner, these specific senses have become decidedly slangy. See *OED* and *MED* for additional, less clear-cut quots.]
    *?a***1300** in *MED:* Ich wes hot and am kold. *ca***1387–95** G. Chaucer, in *MED:* As hoot he was and lecherous as a sparwe. *?ca***1425** in *MED:* He were froted and made hote wiþ alle pynges þat maken hote and exciten. *ca***1450–1500** in *MED:* Morgain…was the most hotest woman of all Bretaine. *ca***1597** Shakespeare *I Henry IV* I ii: And the blessed sunne himselfe a faire hot wench in flame-couloured taffata. *1598** B. Jonson *Every Man in His Humour* IV viii: Dost not thou shame,/When all thy powers in chastity is spent,/To have a mind so hot? And to entice…a lustful woman? *1604** Shakespeare *Othello* III iii: As prime as Goates, as hot as Monkies,/As salt as Wolues. *1614** B. Jonson *Bartholomew Fair* II i: You look as you were begotten a'top of a cart…when the whelp was hot and eager. *a***1693** in Dryden *Poetical Works* 402: Nor mares, when hot, their fellow-mares desire. *1708** *Modern World Disrob'd* 101: For she is as hot and amorous as a Pigeon in Seed-Time. *1719** in *F & H* III 362: He laughs to see the girls so hot. *1797** in *OED2:* I took a female rabbit, hot, (as the feeders term it) that is, ready to be impregnated. *1882** *Boudoir* 4: I believe all really warm-constitutioned women get hotter the older they are. *a***1890–93** *F & H* III 361: *Hot*…Of persons: sexually excitable; lecherous…*Hot as they make them* = exceedingly amorous. **1926** in *AS* II (1927) 202: A "red-hot mama" is a girl "strong for lovin'" and who is always ready for a "necking party." **1926–27** in *AS* III (1927) 220: She looks hotter than a little red wagon. **1928** Edmonds *Rome Haul* 36: He's crazy as a hot bitch. **1929** Asch *Pay Day* 30: She's a good, hot kid, and willing. **1931** Wilstach *Under Cover Man* 43: Her hair was brushing against his cheek, and he could hear her breathing rapidly.…"This is no time to go hot on me." **1932–34** Minehan *Boy & Girl Tramps* 52: He was pretty hot for me too. **1944** Micheaux *Mrs. Wingate* 30: That gal's dynamite…she's as *hot* as hell. Needs a man, plenty of him. **1948** Mencken *Amer. Lang.*

Supp. II 646: A good deal of this slang comes close to being obscene, e.g., the *hot mamma* of a few years ago. **1935–62** Ragan & Finston *Toughest Pris.* 804: *Hot*…amorous. **1965** in Legman *New Limerick* 367: Though she looks and acts hot/Free twat she gives not. **1968** J.W. Wells *Taboo Breakers* 124: [She's] hot as a stove. **1972** *Urban Life & Culture* I 269: Then she said, "Oh wow, you sure have got me hot." **1980** Rimmer *Album* 10: Bet she uses those pictures to get hot over. **1985** J. Hughes *Breakfast Club* (film): She's only a tease if what she does gets you hot.

b. zealous or keen (often excessively so); intent; (*hence*) eager or enthusiastic. [In earliest use, usu. in ref. to one's nature or personality (see quots. in *MED* and *OED*); in modern use, solely in ref. to specific, usu. temporary, desires, interests, aims, etc.]
    *ca***1593** Shakespeare *Richard III* I iii: I was too hoat to doe some body good,/That is too cold in thinking of it now. *a***1598** Shakespeare *Two Gent. Verona* II v: I tell thee, my Master is become a hot Louer. *1603** B. Jonson *Panegyre:* [He] was not hot, or covetous to be crown'd. *1667** Pepys *Diary* (July 12): But the design is, and the Duke of York says he is hot for it, to have a land army, and so to make the government like that of France. *1758** J. Wesley, in *OED* s.v. *red-hot:* A red-hot Predestinarian, talking of God's "blowing whole worlds to hell." *1819** in J. Keats *Poems* 578: The Emperor on this marriage is so hot,/Pray Heaven it end not in apoplexy! **1841** [Mercier] *Man-of-War* 136: He's as hot as Chili pepper on anything that touches…his state. **1873** Perrie *Buckskin Mose* 243: Tom…occasionally assisted him in a way which in the East might have been stigmatized as "red-hot" charity. **1928** Dahlberg *Bottom Dogs* 41: Doc's office, which the guys weren't so hot about. **1936** Miller *Battling Bellhop* (film): The public's hot for it. **1937** C.B. Davis *Anointed* 110: Wunsdorf was red-hot to be a skipper. **1945** Wolfert *Amer. Guerrilla* 141: What MacArthur wants is intelligence. He's red-hot on that. He's got a one-track mind on that. **1951** W. Williams *Enemy* 60: Maybe you're not so hot about being out of Norfolk. **1951–53** in *AS* XXIX (1954) 99: Phil's…[racing car] looks hot to go. **1956** Childress *Like One of Family* 23: I ain't so hot on goin' on no picnic. **1957** Bradbury *Dandelion Wine* 18: Ate six hundred peaches, eight hundred apples. Pears: two hundred. I'm not hot for pears. **1963** Holzer *Ghost Hunter* 8: Still, it shows I was hot on the subject, even then! **1970** N.Y.U. classics professor: If you're so hot for Virgil, wait till he comes around in graduate school. *a***1978** Cooley *Dancer* 15: I'm gonna cool you off, little job stealer.…You're gettin' too hot for yer own good! **1979–82** Gwin *Overboard* 173: They were hot for Enlightenment. **1987** R.M. Brown *Starting* 93: One man to another about a business deal: "They're hot. Let's slip them the meat." **1988** Dietl & Gross *One Tough Cop* 32: You got me all hot over a fuckin' hunch?

c. (of persons) angry; in phr. **hot enough to fuck** (*vulgar;* with pun on **(a)**, above) furiously angry. See also *hot under* [or *in* or *around*] *the collar,* below.
    *ca***1594** Shakespeare *Comedy of Errors* II i: She is so hot because the meate is cold. *a***1849** in C. Hill *Scenes* 175: First that…rascal puts me in a rage, and when I get over that,…[my] daughter…pipes me hot again. **1849** *Spirit of Times* (Nov. 10) 452: I was hot, I tell *you.* **1866** Dimsdale *Vigilantes* 75: He was away for two hours, and the proprietor was "as hot as a wolf," when he came back. **1891** De Vere *Tramp Poems* 71: I am terrible hot, I will go for his nibs. **1893** in Dreiser *Jour.* I 221: I'm hotter than a four-pronged purgatory fork, and I won't cool down. **1900** *DN* II 42: *Hot*…Angry. **1904** Bowers *Chip* 45: Old Man was sure hot about that. **1953** W. Fisher *Waiters* 227: Naw,…I'm jus' hotter than a chicken with the pox. **1966** Braly *On Yard* 201: The doc was hot enough to fuck. **1971** Wells & Dance *Night People* 69: I couldn't have heard him because I was hot as a bad girl's dream. **1974** Millard *Thunderbolt* 50: Kee-rist! No wonder you're hotter than a two-dollar pistol. **1966–80** McAleer & Dickson *Unit Pride* 358: Miller's gonna be hot enough to fuck before this mess is over. **1988** Dietl & Gross *One Tough Cop* 15: Well, I got real angry. I left there and I'm telling you I was hot. **1995** *Donahue* (NBC-TV): I was pretty hot.…I was definitely not this calm. **1996** McCumber *Playing off Rail* 328: He even got hot at Francisco for leaving me a couple of shots.

2. (of times, places, etc.) characterized by feverish, bustling, boisterous, or uncontrolled activity.
    *1614** B. Jonson *Bartholomew Fair* I i: 'Twas a hot night with some

of us last night, John.…We were all a little stained last night, sprinkled with a cup or two. **1693** in Congreve *Comedies* 83: Come not near that House, that Corner-house—that hot Brothel. **1864** in Cate *Two Soldiers* 232: February 1st…waiting for orders to be relieved; acting as rear guard;…wagons all in and we start for camp some 4 miles away; hot time. **1885** Siringo *Texas Cowboy* 187: I found El Paso to be a red-hot town of about three thousand inhabitants. **1889** O'Reilly & Nelson *50 Yrs. on Trail* 180: Denver at this time was "red-hot." It was full of gambling hells and grog shops, and a lively place for murders. ***1893** in *F & H* III 362: I started life in a training stable, and a hot life it was for a boy. *a***1929** in Stratton *Pioneer Women* 218: The quiet little village of a few months before became a "red-hot town" with a street designated as "Red-Hot Street."

3.a. dangerous or distressing, esp. so as to compel one to desist, get away, etc. (orig. *S.E.*); (*hence*) *Und.* unsafe for criminal activity.

*1618 in *OED:* Caesar Augustus thought good to make that practice too hot for them. ***1660** in *OED:* 'Ere they make the Island too hot for the English. ***1726** A. Smith *Mems. of J. Wild* 133: *Cady* came strait to *London*, but fearing…that it would be too hot to hold him, to avoid being apprehended by a *Hue* and *Cry*, he did not stay above an Hour before he rid as fast as he could for *Scotland*. ***1771** in *OED:* The share he had in your honour's intrigue…soon made this city too hot for poor Ned. ***1830** in *F & H* III 362: This place is now too hot for me, captain. Bills overdue and bailiffs in full chase, have driven me to a hasty leave of my home. **1830** in [S. Smith] *Letters of Downing* 30: There's a hot time ahead. I almost dread to think of it. **1844** in Taylor & Whiting *Proverbs* 193: I begun to think York was a going to be rather too hot to hold me. **1859** Matsell *Vocab.* 43: The cove had better move his beaters into Dewsville, it is too hot for him here. **1872** Crapsey *Nether Side* 60: I suppose that you have wondered how I got away and where I am things was so hot I had no time to let you know before. ***1879** *Macmillan's Mag.* (Oct.): When I got there I found it so hot (dangerous), because…there was a reeler [policeman] at almost every double [turn in the road]. **1930** Pasley *Al Capone* 151: Chicago in 1927 and 1928 was tagged in underworld jargon as "hot" for any outsiders who had no business there, so well had Capone consolidated his gains. **1930** Conwell *Pro. Thief* 28: But a mob never breaks up because a racket gets too hot (dangerous). **1982** D.A. Harper *Good Company* 10: The only hot yards [for hoboes] are those old U.P. yards in Portland, but you can beat those too.

b. *Mil.* (of a place) under heavy fire; (now *also*) defended or occupied by an enemy combat force.

1864 in D. Chisholm *Civil War Notebk.* 135: The Picket lines is pretty hot all the time. **1887** Hinman *Si Klegg* 696 [ref. to Civil War]: Some regiments were fortunate enough in occupying the less exposed positions in battle, while others, which had the "hot" places, were, not infrequently…almost annihilated. **1917** in Dos Passos *14th Chronicle* 98: We…landed in the hottest sector ambulance ever ambled in. **1918** Casey *Cannoneers* 65: "You'll have to ride fifty meters apart on this road," he cautioned us. "It's hot—what I mean." **1926** Nason *Chevrons* 57: "Ah," said Eadie. "Is this a hot sector?" **1944** H. Brown *Walk in the Sun* 138: It was too hot a place, much too hot. "Go back," he yelled. "Patrol back." **1961** Forbes *Goodbye to Some* 15 [ref. to WWII]: When I know the sector is hot, I spend the night calculating the risks we must run. **1962** Robinson *Barbara* 145 [ref. to WWII]: You could count on the radio to go out when you needed it most, in the middle of a hot town. **1970** Hersh *My Lai* 45 [ref. to 1968]: One of the helicopter's pilots had reported that the LZ was "hot," that is, Viet Cong were waiting below. **1982** D.J. Williams *Hit Hard* 247 [ref. to WWII]: That next village. I think it's going to be hot. *a***1991** J.R. Wilson *Landing Zones* 49: Yeah, that village we're going to is hot, man. You'd better be ready. **1995** *Space: Above & Beyond* (Fox-TV): Sending your people and Army personnel into a hot LZ.

c. *Naut.* (of a vessel) characterized by strict or brutal discipline.

1883 Keane *Blue-Water* 206: I've been in a few regular scorching hot packets, both Yanks and blue-nosers, but this puts the capper on the lot. **1896** Hamblen *Many Seas* 319: Howly Moses, but this is a red-hot ship. **1899** Hamblen *Bucko Mate* 42: "The Black Ball Line"…holds the record to this day, in the memories of old sailors, as being the "hottest" ships afloat. *Ibid.* 51: She had been so infernally

"hot" that even her officers left her. *a***1930** in Hugill *Shanties & Sailors' Songs* 144: The Limey packets got too hot. **1939** O'Brien *One-Way Ticket* 38: She looks plenty hot to me.…Shined bunks, varnished locker tops, snow-white tables. **1941** *Amer. Mercury* (May) 594: The *Crockett* [was] a "hot ship" and no two ways about it.

d. *Und.* (of a place to be robbed) occupied during the commission of crime.

1924 G. Henderson *Keys to Crookdom* 409: *Hot joint.* Tenanted house located for robbery. If not hot, it is a "cold slough." **1927** *DN* V 451: *Hot joint*…A house to be robbed while the occupants are in it. **1935–62** Ragan & Finston *Toughest Pris.* 804: *Hot joint*—A house or store to be robbed while occupied or while business is being conducted.

e. *Police.* (of a suspect or prisoner) likely to resist arrest or otherwise to become violent.

1944 *Pap. Mich. Acad.* XXX 592: *Hot*…likely to cause trouble. **1970** Rudensky & Riley *Gonif* 49: They treated me as if they believed I was the hottest piece of humanity since John Wilkes Booth. Anyway, they had five guards in the escort party. **1972** Wambaugh *Blue Knight* 241: So damn many policemen got shot or thumped by guys who practiced coming out of that spread-eagled position.…I put hot suspects on their knees or bellies.

4. tipsy; drunk.

[***1610** Shakespeare *Tempest* IV i: I told you Sir, they were red-hot with drinking.] *ca***1720** in Rankin *Piracy* 110: A great deal of Liquor…kept the Company hot, damned hot, then all Things went well again. ***1814** in Wetherell *Adventures* 231: They had made…free with…old cogniac, so…he set them all hot for drill. **1845** in G.W. Harris *High Times* 46: Two "bits" for what corn-juice you suck…and a bed too in the hay, if you git too hot to locomote. *a***1856** in B. Hall *College Wds.* (ed. 2) 461: A few of the various words and phrases…in use, at one time or another, to signify some stage of inebriation:…half seas over, hot, high, corned, [etc.]. **1899** B. Green *Va. Folk-Speech* 192: *Hot*, adj. Half drunk. **1914** *DN* IV 74: *Hotter'n a skunk, hotter'n love in hayin' time*…Extremely intoxicated. **1927** *AS* III 136 [ref. to *a*1900]: Intoxication was indicated by such terms as "tight," "full," "hot," "liquored up," [etc.].

5. *Med.* **a.** affected with venereal disease or pubic lice.

[***ca1680** in Marvell *Poems & Letters* I 219: But now Yorkes Genitalls grew over hot/with Denham and Coneig's infected pot.] ***1731** [J. Roberts] *Merry-Thought* III 6: But then, if Cl-ps proceed from Love,/How hot are all the Gods and Goddesses above! **a***1890–93** *F & H* III 362: *Hot*…(venery).—Infected; venereally diseased. **1952** Viereck *Men into Beasts* 14 [ref. to 1943]: Brown cheerfully offered to supply me with an ointment if I was "hot." By "hot" he meant if I played host to the little animals known as crabs.

b. seriously infected.

1952 *ATS* (ed. 2) 499: *Hot appendix*, an appendix dangerously near rupture. **1968** "J. Hudson" *Case of Need* 55: She has a history of a primary luetic oral lesion…and five episodes of hot tubes. **1972** B. Harrison *Hospital* 16: On that same day a chest surgeon…was grabbed to remove a hot appendix because there were no other surgeons available. **1977** Shem *House of God* 200: A hot [appendix], ready to pop.

6.a. highly adept, skillful, or capable, now esp. in a reckless or ostentatious way.

1845 in G.W. Harris *High Times* 52: I am a *hot* hand at the *location* of capital letters and punctuation. ***1888** in *OED2* s.v. *red-hot*: You take the fellows in town that make their living after dark.…There's some red-hot ones up—you know where—in Piccadilly. **1897** Ade *Pink Marsh* 143: He ain' such a hot readeh. **1905** in "O. Henry" *Works* 35: A fly guy…a hot sport. **1907** Cook *Border & Buffalo* 425: Major, here is my old friend Rees, one of the hottest Indian Trailers I ever met. ***1917** in Lee *No Parachute* 118: He was a pretty hot pilot, for he holed most of the Pups, but nobody could get a bead on him. **1922** Paul *Impromptu* 134: What a hot soldier. Letting a four-foot coon take his hat away. **1942** Z.N. Hurston, in *Amer. Mercury* (July) 86: You was beatin' up your gums…about how hot you was. **1944** *AAF* 368: *Hot pilot.* fighter pilot whose ability is recognized as superlative; fighter pilot show-off or braggart. **1947** Willingham *End as a Man* 80: You're so smart!…You think you're so hot! **1958** P. O'Connor *At Le Mans* 72: All right.…You're a hot driver, better than I am, maybe. **1963** D. Tracy *Brass Ring* 4: He had fancied himself a real red hot quarterback.

1968 M.B. Scott *Racing Game* 83: Well, actually Comiskey [a trainer] is pretty hot with first starters. **1972–74** Hawes & Asher *Raise Up* 99: Son, you hot. I came down to hear you. **1975** May *Courage to Create* 4: What masquerades as courage may simply turn out to be simply a bravado used to compensate for one's unconscious fear and to prove one's machismo, like the "hot" fliers in World War II. **1976** in G.A. Fine *With the Boys* 94: Tim…says sarcastically…after Steel strikes out, "Steel thinks he's so hot." *a***1989** Micheels *Braving Flames* 108: I was fast, I was good, I was hot, I was there. **1995** *Smithsonian* (Sept.) 2: A hot pilot means a cold, cold B-29.

b. (of statements, notions, jests, etc.) highly amusing, esp. if ludicrous or ironic; clever or intended to be so.—usu. constr. with *one.*

   1845 in G.W. Harris *High Times* 45: He says Knoxville is 200 miles from each of the places above named. Now *that's hot!* **1846** in G.W. Harris *High Times:* Wall, now, if that aint hot, I'm d-a-r-n-e-d. **1903** *Enquirer* (Cincinnati) (May 9) 13: *Hot one*…a verbal roast. **1903** *Pedagog. Sem.* X 374: That's a hot one. **1906** *Nat. Police Gaz.* (Sept. 1) 7: I had to stand for some hot ones from a titled Englishwoman once. **1912** *Hampton's Mag.* (Jan.) 842: Say…here's a hot one! Remember the Portsmouth Fat?…You know what that guy's doing? Well, he's sheriff of the county next to this. **1913** *DN* III 11: He told a *hot one* at the dinner table. **1915** in Lardner *Round Up* 196: Here's another hot one..…Can you imagine that? **1919** *Variety* (Apr. 4) 16: He shot over a hot one…about the darky billeted in a…French chateau. **1920** Ade *Hand-Made Fables* 88: George W. Fresh was carrying on with the Footlight Favourite and exchanging Hot Ones with Jimmy the Sport. **1922** Rice *Adding Machine* 125: So you thought you were all through, did you? Well, that's a hot one, that is. **1925** Gross *Nize Baby* 201: 'At's a hot one! Me income tax! **1925** B. Conners *Patsy* 12: Well, this is a hot one. What a wonderful home-coming this turned out to be! **1928** in Segar *Thimble Th.* 20: Haw! Haw! That's hot! **1929** Perelman *Ginsbergh* 185: You thought you pulled a hot one when you [jilted me], didn't you? **1948** I. Shaw *Young Lions* 53: We rob her? That's hot. It's just the other way around, Brother. **1957** Sale *Abandon Ship!* (film): Lucky! That's a hot one.

c. absolutely first-rate; splendid; (with weakened force) good or well, fashionably attractive; in phr. **not so hot** not very good or not very well. Also as adv. [After *ca*1910, esp. in negative or ironic contexts.]

   1866 [H.W. Shaw] *J. Billings* 173: I dreamed a good-sized, hot dream. **1869** in P. Murray *Proud Shoes* 212: Our Hides are all stamped with the name of our firm on them and they look hot. **1866–71** Bagg *Yale* 46: *Red hot*, excellent, perfect, magnificent. Sometimes abbreviated to *hot*, and usually used with some tinge of sarcasm. *ca*1875 in Fauset *Folklore from N.S.* 122: An' I was the gayest little darky in the land,…/I'se a red hot, hunky-dory contraband. **1879** Rooney *Conundrums* 85: Their frequent exclamations of delight—such as "Red hot, you bet!" "Ain't it fruit, though?" "Houp-la," etc., plainly indicated that they were enjoying themselves. **1887** *Lantern* (N.O.) (Feb. 19) 6: A red-hot newsy journal. **1895** in *Comments on Ety.* (Nov. 1995) 8: That's a Hot One [fashionable overcoat]. *ca*1895 McCloskey *Across Continent* 81: "Johnnie, how are you?"…"I'm red hot and still a-hottin'." **1897** Ade *Pink Marsh* 166: I need one of 'em hot lettehs to squaih it. **1899** Dunne *Hearts of Countrymen* 13: That was a hot pome an' a good wan! **1900** *DN* II 42: [College slang] *hot*…Tip-top, excellent.…Of good quality…often ironical. **1901** A.H. Lewis *Croker* 61: If he lives, he'll be a hot monarch. **1902** Dunbar *Sport* 78: D'jever hear "Baby, You Got to Leave"? I tell you, that's a hot one. **1919** *DN* V 70: *Hot one*, used as a term of disgust. "You're a hot one I must say." New Mexico. **1924** P. Marks *Plastic Age* 112: I didn't flunk out but my record isn't so hot. **1927** in E. Wilson *Twenties* 354: Not so good—not so hot. **1929** in Segar *Thimble Th.* 48: How do you like me new shirt, Cap'n? Ain't she hot, Cap'n? **1932** Miller & Burnett *Scarface* (film): That [bathrobe]'s pretty hot. **1936** Kenyon & Daves *Petrified Forest* (film): Poetry. That's pretty hot. **1938** in W. Burnett *Best* 496: Gee, I wish I was a writer. I bet I could write a hot story. **1943** Wendt & Kogan *Bosses* 10: Hot chance we'd have electing The Clock to anything. **1946** Kober *That Man Is Here Again* 4: Whose talents are, what you might say, a little on the not-so-hot side. **1946** J. Adams *Gags* 50: Some of the shows were "not so hot" and the customers walked out. **1953** Bradbury *Fahrenheit 451* 23: You don't look so hot yourself.

1953 "L. Padgett" *Mutant* 20: That thought wasn't so hot. **1960** Bannon *Journey* 124: Not feeling so red hot. **1963** Zahn *Amer. Contemp.* 5: What is there so hot about Pomona? **1963** D. Tracy *Brass Ring* 46: I dunno what I've done that's so hot—great, I mean. **1967** W. Crawford *Gresham's War* 107: You don't look too redhot your ownself, Miles. *a***1968** in M.B. Scott *Racing Game* 90: At first I didn't do too hot, barely breaking even. **1969** C. Brown *Mr. Jiveass* 51: "Hey, man, how's Paris."…"Hot, man, hot. It was a very heavy and beautiful scene." **1979** T. Baum *Carny* 128: Out of seeazight.…Totally heeazot. **1982** S. Black *Totally Awesome* 77: A totally hot metallic brown Firebird with a bitchen stereo. **1983** S. King *Christine* 325: A felony rap for interstate transport of unlicensed cigarettes and alcohol wouldn't look all that hot on his college application, would it? **1984–88** Hackworth & Sherman *About Face* 664: His chances…wouldn't be red-hot.

d. wonderfully lively or exciting. [As applied to jazz, now S.E.]

   1887 Walling *N.Y. Chief of Police* 467: "Golly! it was red-hot!" said a little boot-black…who was asked to describe the fight. **1894** in F. Remington *Sel. Letters* 212: Just back from Chicago—mob and soldiers—hot stuff. **1896** J. Hayden & T.M. Metz *A Hot Time in the Old Town Tonight* [pop. song title]. **1905** W.S. Kelly *Lariats* 259: Give me er [tune on the piano], Marian, as hot as yer can sling it. **1917–20** Dreiser *Newspaper Days* 579: Bright straw hats,…canes,…"hot" socks. **1924** in R.S. Gold *Jazz Talk* 133: This "hot" septet hails from Chicago. **1927** *AS* III (Feb.) 220: *Red hot*, adj.—Lively, peppy, pleasing. "The Kappas sure did throw a red hot party." **1927** Hemingway *Men Without Women* 80: "This is a hot town," said the other. "What do they call it?" **1933** *Fortune* (Aug.) 47: England and France have magazines strictly devoted to *hot* music. **1936** *Harper's* (Apr.) 570: The *hot* performance is the heart and soul of jazz. **1938** O'Hara *Hope of Heaven* 33: Their idea of something hot was to be a brakeman on the railroad and have a regular run. **1939** Fessier *Wings of Navy* (film): Once around the bay, and make it plenty hot. **1951** in *DAS*: A "hot" magazine is one that's sizzling and bubbling with vitality. **1977** in L. Bangs *Psychotic Reactions* 246: The Clash's set is brisk, hot, clean. **1986** *I'll Buy That!* 110: Chevrolet's advertising slogan that year [1956] was "The Hot One's Even Hotter." **1987** R.M. Brown *Starting* 67: Knock out *is*, *are*, *was*, etc., and insert something hot. Strong verbs are always hot.

e. (of people) exuberant, flamboyant, or daring in the pursuit of pleasure; uninhibited; wild.

   1888** in *F & H* III 362: You're a red-hot member! **a*1889** in Barrère & Leland *Dict. Slang* I 477: She's so *hot* that when she takes a walk out in November all the coal merchants shut up shop, fancying it is June. ***1889** Barrère & Leland *Dict. Slang: Hot*…exuberant in spirits, rowdy, full of extravagance and fun, "a warm one." A *hot* 'un, a fast man or woman. One who goes the pace.…a *hot* member of society is a man or woman who…sets most rules of decorum and morality on one side. **1897** Ade *Pink Marsh* 198: I jus'…listened to some of 'em hot boys th'ow lang'age at each otheh. **1900** (quot. at HOT BABY). **1903** Kildare *Mamie Rose* 227: I still considered myself a "red-hot sport." **1905** in Opper *H. Hooligan* 66: The Duke is a hot sport. **1925** *Sat. Eve. Post* (Feb. 14) 56: I don't know who you are, but you're a hot sport underneath. **1928** Fisher *Jericho* 88: Talk about one red-hot mamma! *Ibid.* 181: This red hot papa. **1928–29** Faulkner *Sound & Fury* 286: Them telling the new ones up and down the road where to pick up a hot one when they made Jefferson. *a1966** in *Social Problems* XIII 444: It has to do with being a swinger or hip. Going out and more or less cheating on your boyfriend or carousing around with a fast crowd and looking hot.…I won't do it. **1969** *Esquire* (Aug.) 141: He had a rep as hot as a ticket. **1989** P. Munro *U.C.L.A. Slang* 51: *Hot*…wild, slutty (of a female).

f. (of books, entertainment, etc.) sexually stimulating; erotic.

   1892** in *F & H* III 362: As most of our plays are now cribbed from the French, wy they're all pooty hot. ***1908** in *OED2*: Publishing firms…discovered that money was to be made out of what they called "the hot novel." **1928** C. McKay *Banjo* 133: Show you all the sights of Marseilles. Hot stuff in the quarter. Tableaux vivants and blue cinema. ***1930** Brophy & Partridge *Songs & Slang* 130 [ref. to WWI]: *Hot Stuff*…a book, a picture, or a theatrical entertainment not blatantly obscene but toying with impropriety. **1929–35** Farrell *Judgment Day* ch. xvi: A burlesque show. The hottest ones were south of Van Buren. **1942** *ATS* 497: *Hot book*, a pornographic book.…*hot mag*, a…pornographic magazine. **1965** N.Y.C. high school student: Are there any hot parts? *a1984** in E. Goode *Deviant Behavior* (ed. 2) 168: It's something hot for me to jerk off to in the middle of the night. **1986** Churcher *N.Y. Confidential* 177: An emporium advertising "the hottest live sex acts in America." **1990** *TV Guide* (May 11) 64: He tries to get as much sex…as he can. There are some scenes…which…are pretty hot.

g. urgent; pressing; important (often with an implication of some danger).

1896 Ade *Artie* 29: They had to make a hot touch…so as to get the price of a couple o' sinkers. **1911** Ferber *Dawn O'Hara* 301: I'll give you the hottest assignment on my list. **1938** in *AS* XVII (1942) 103: *Hot one.* Special delivery. **1943** Coale *Midway* 32: Well, today we got a hot [military assignment]. **1942–44** in *AS* XXVII (1952) 70: *Hot,* adj. A priority message. **1947** *ATS* (Supp.) 34: *Hot mission*…, a dangerous bombing or strafing operation with stiff opposition. **1950** O'Brien & Evans *Chain Lightning* (film): You want to fly a hot mission over Germany? **1955** *AS* XXX 92: *Hot load,* n. An emergency shipment of cargo. **1956** Heflin *USAF Dict.* 256: *Hot*…slang…Of information, papers, messages, etc.: Urgent; extremely important.…*Hot target.* An important target, or a target requiring immediate attack. *Slang.* **1958** Cromie *Chi. Fire* 42: Charley,…this is hot! **1963** *AS* XXXVIII 44: *Hot load*…Freight which must be moved or delivered rapidly. **1968** Broughton *Thud Ridge* 48: I liked to fly and I was in a position to outrank him on the hot missions. **1975** Schott *No Left Turns* 25: Most of the special inquiries…were considered "hot" because they had short deadlines. **1979–81** C. Buckley *To Bamboola* 6: A very hot, top secret shipment. **1981** G. Wolf *Roger Rabbit* 130: What makes it such a hot item in your book? **1988** Dietl & Gross *One Tough Cop* 3: Bo turned on the siren and smacked the dome light on the roof as if he were on a hot run, as if there were still some chance to save the [victim]. **1989** Berent *Rolling Thunder* 52: How the day had gone—no hot missions; how the weather was—lousy. **1989** *Newsweek* (Dec. 11) 10: *Hot mail.* Mail that gets preferential treatment, such as first-class and priority.

h. Orig. *Horse Racing.* (of information, esp. advance information) significant, confidential, and reliable.

1904 in Blackbeard & Williams *Smithsonian Comics* 59: Hot tip. Kitty Clyde [a racehorse]. Cinch. **1907** in H.C. Fisher *A. Mutt* 6: A. Mutt Overhears a Couple of Hot Tips. **1942** *ATS* 690: Tip on the races…*hot tip.* **1949** Monteleone *Crim. Slang* 125: *Hot tip*…An important piece of inside information. **1956** Heflin *USAF Dict.* 256: *Hot*…slang…having a high security classification. **1968** M.B. Scott *Racing Game* 95: The importance of *inside* (or *hot*) *information.* **1987** Lipper *Wall Street* 18: You said your printer gave you a hot tip to buy CQS? *a***1989** Spears *NTC Dict.* 341: I've got the hot skinny on Mary and her boyfriend. **1989** *Newsweek* (Sept. 25) 8: A slew of mysterious phone calls and hot tips.

i. Esp. *Journ.* (of news, information, evidence, etc.) arousing or intended to arouse intense public interest or controversy; (*often*) creating or likely to create scandal, outrage, or similar repercussions; sensational. Cf. **(d)**, above.

1914** in *OEDS:* "Hot news"…must be provided for the people, and thus we learn [falsely] from the Vienna "Abendblatt" that General French is a prisoner. **1931** Reichenbach *Phantom Fame* 105: It took three weeks [of clever publicity] to make "Three Weeks" the hottest book in the government mail bags. The Post Office Department began to receive protests against the book from all parts of the country. **1931** B. Morgan *Five-Star Final* (film): What's so hot about that [news story]? **1936** Riskin *Mr. Deeds Goes to Town* (film): Falling into a fortune is hot copy. **1941** *Pittsburgh Courier* (Oct. 25) 7: Too "Hot" for the Dailies to Handle. ***1944** Koestler *Twilight Bar* 29: Look, there is no minute to waste…News? You bet it is news…Hot? You bet it is hot. Burning like a…volcano. **1948** *Sat. Eve. Post* (Oct. 9) 54: You're the hot news, Farmer. **1950** *AS* XXV (Feb.) 37: *Red-Hot.* Filled with scandal. **1956** "T. Betts" *Across Board* 36: As one politician said of the slush fund, "It's hotter than the Lindbergh ransom money." **1968** N.Y.C. man, age *ca* 25: The *real* story is usually too hot for the papers to handle. **a1987** *Collins-COBUILD Dict.:* The tapes had existed but they were too hot to preserve and had been destroyed. **1989** Univ. Tenn. instructor: An alien landing would be the hottest story of all time—except for the Second Coming.

j. (of news, information, theatrical material, etc.) latest; novel; fresh. Cf. *OED* def. 9.a.

[**1908** "O. Henry," in *OED2:* To-day's news…served hot to subscribers.] ***1925** (cited in Partridge *DSUE* (ed. 1) 408). **1930** in W.F. Nolan *Black Mask Boys* 121: I got some hot dope on this guy. **1930** in *AS* (Feb. 1931) 204: *Hot stuff:* new, up-to-date material or new incidents; approved as being startling or the "latest." **1931** *AS* VII 439: *Hot wire*…late information. **1942** *ATS* 231: *Hot dope* [or] *news*…, the latest news or information. *Ibid.* 497: *Hot copy,* a late news item. **1953** Manchester *City of Anger* 226: Gimme the hot dope, hip gee, what's the word today? **1959** Morrill *Dark Sea* 109 [ref. to WWII]: "What's hot, Roaney boy?" he yawned at me. **1967** Dibner *Admiral* 65: Here's the hot dope, Oley.

k. sexually attractive; sexy. [Orig. applied only by men to women.]

1929–31 J.T. Farrell *Young Lonigan* 114: They saw one hot dame, in clothes that must have cost a million bucks. **1929–33** J.T. Farrell *Young Manhood* 216: The time to come when your wife wouldn't be a hot hunk any more. **1934** Weseen *Dict. Slang* 186: *Hot mamma*—An attractive girl with plenty of sex appeal. **1979** Gram *Foxes* 112: You sure used to think he was hot. **1982** Corey & Westermark *Fer Shurr!* (unp.): *Hot*…sexy. **1983** Lane & Crawford *Valley Girl* (film): Check out those pecs!…He's hot! **1985** Dillinger *Adrenaline* 103: Jillions of hot young guys. **1987** Eble *Campus Slang* (Apr.) 4: *Hot*—sexy. **1992** *Heights* (Fox-TV): They've got very hot waitresses at Bennings. **1994** *Friends* (NBC-TV): I met this really hot single mom at the store.

l. fast; having or conferring unusual speed, power, or performance, esp. if also requiring unusual skill in operation; (*specif.*) *Av.* (of an airplane) designed so as to land at high speed.

1934 Kromer *Waiting* 120: She [a freight train] is too hot to catch on the fly. **1942** *ATS* 82: Fast car…*hot* or *peppy crate.* **1943** *Amer. Mercury* (Nov.) 556: *Hot crate*…a fast plane. **1944** Pyle *Brave Men* 305: The B-26…had a bad name—it was a "hot" plane which took great skill to fly and killed more people in training than it did in combat. **1953** Felsen *Street Rod* 91: If we give 'em a track, it will look like we're telling them to build hot cars. **1955** in Loosbrock & Skinner *Wild Blue* 42: Crude wing flaps and brakes were tried in efforts to shoehorn "hot" ships into short fields. **1959** Montgomery & Heiman *Jet Nav.* 90: Well, just hang on, boy, because this B-52 is a hot job. **1962** E. Stephens *Blow Negative* 60: Red Whipple was helping Phil Harwyn tinker with the hot engine. **1964** Caidin *Everything But Flak* 39: The Mosquito was one of the hottest machines ever to fly in the war, and its pilots drove the Germans crazy by being able to outrun the best of the German fighters. **1969** in *I'll Buy That!* 110: [Sports car ad:] We made it hot.…You can make it scream! **1975** in Higham & Siddall *Combat Aircraft* 11: An aircraft that landed at an unusually high rate of speed was referred to as "hot." **1978** Ardery *Bomber Pilot* 45: The B-24s seemed only slightly "hotter"—that is, they landed a little faster and were slightly more difficult to handle. **1982** D.A. Harper *Good Company* 27: There's three times the trains, and they're hot ones. **1987** *Daily Beacon* (Univ. Tenn.) (May 1) 2: I guess hot cars and rock 'n' roll just go together. **1988** Hynes *Flights of Passage* 82: Corsairs…were said to be very hot, very hard to fly.

7.a. *Mining.* especially rich in minerals or other deposits; profitable.

***1855** in *OED:* As to the "hot-lode" at the United Mines…the discovery of which sent up shares from £40 to £450 each—both the heat of the lode and the ardour of the shareholders have considerably declined. **1949** in *DA:* Two new [oil] developments on Tejon ranch yesterday sent that region into the picture as one of the hottest areas in the State. **1957** in *Dict. Canadianisms* 349: Economically "hot" mineral areas…have become focal points for mining booms. **1958** in *Dict. Canadianisms:* Its properties are located *in the "hottest" mining district in Canada to-day*…an area that is commanding the attention of speculators both in Canada and the United States.

b. Orig. *Horse Racing.* backed by or generating heavy betting; (*hence*) likely to win. Now *colloq.*

***1882** in *OED2* s.v. *red-hot:* The first-named won three races…and was each time a "red hot" favourite. ***1889** in Clark *Dict. Gambling* 105: *Hot,* and sometimes *Warm.*—Backed for a great deal of money. A horse is said "to come *hot*" in the betting when he is suddenly backed for a large amount. ***1894** in *OED:* The possessor of one of the hottest favourites on record. **1923** *Washington Post* (Feb. 17) 19: Sea Cove is "hot," should prove the contender. **1931–35** Runyon *Money* 167: He generally knows about some horse that is supposed to be hotter than a base-burner, a hot horse being a horse that is all heated up to win a horse race. **1949** *AS* (Oct.) 192: *Hot number.* A number [in policy gambling] that is being heavily played by the public. **1951** *PADS* (No. 16) 36: *Hot horse…*A horse that, although not a favorite, has been touted until odds drop very low. **1953** W. Fisher *Waiters* 71: Cap'n Logan limited his play on a "hot [policy] number." **1968** M.B. Scott *Racing Game* 58: When a horse gets "hot," as bookies term it, they lay off bets. **1980** Lorenz *Guys Like Us* 54: Let's go to the track….I got some hot ones.

c. exciting great interest or demand or having great popularity, esp. among audiences, investors, purchasers, etc.; *(often)* commercially very successful; *(hence,* esp. in 1980's) enjoying a great vogue; at the height of fashion.

1909 Chrysler *White Slavery* 162: Jones and Smith are the hot favorites. About every other name is Jones or Smith. **1933** Martin *Int'l House* (film): One of Broadway's youngest and hottest stars—Baby Rose Marie! **1942** *ATS* 538: *Hot number,* a fast-selling piece of merchandise. **1952** A. Sheekman *Young Man with Ideas* (film): He's already hot at three studios. "Hot" is a professional term. It means they're real interested. **1953** in Perelman *Don't Tread on Me* 149: *Réalités* [is] the hot magazine here now. *a***1961** *WNID3*: *Hot…*of merchandise or securities: readily salable: enjoying current popularity <*hot* items in women's wear>. **1965** *World Bk. Dict.*: *Hot…Slang.* fashionable because exciting, novel, etc. *a***1970** *WNWD*: *Hot…*currently very popular (a *hot* recording). **1971** W. Murray *Dream Girls* 109: The studio *has* been known to renegotiate a better deal for someone who gets real hot. **1977** *Scribner-Bantam Dict.*: *Hot…*much in demand, popular. **1980** Rubin *Reconciliations* 40: Then…someone mentioned a "hot young conductor" who was looking for an orchestra. **a***1981** *Macquarie Dict.*: *Hot…*fashionable and exciting. **1981** *Rolling Stone* (Sept. 17) 1: He's hot, he's sexy, and he's dead. **1982** Connors *Mass Media Dict.* 121: *Hot…*publishing: denoting a title moving well. **1984** Blumenthal *Hollywood* 44: Sure, she's unknown *now,* but give me two years and she'll be red-hot. **1986** Churcher *N.Y. Confidential* 89: Religion…is hot with the upwardly mobile. **1987** *Atlantic* (Sept.) 65: Ticks are "hot" [in research] now, because of Lyme disease. **1987** Horowitz *Campus Life* 9: A rising flood of applicants competing for scarce places in the "hot" colleges. **1989** *TV Guide* (Oct. 28) 20: I see myself [a TV actor] hot for the next seven years at least. **1989** *CBS This Morning* (CBS-TV) (Nov. 10): Poetry is so hot now….Everybody in Los Angeles has decided to write poetry in the last six months. **1989** *TV Guide* (Nov. 11) 26: Occasionally you hear someone say that it's considered hot to be Hispanic now.

d. exceptionally promising.

*****1936** Partridge *DSUE* 408: *Hot…*In C-20 insurance s[lang], applied to a very likely insurer, a promising "prospect." **1942** *ATS* 514: *Lead,* a clue or opening for a sale, a prospective sale; *hot lead,* a good "lead." **1952** in W.S. Burroughs *Letters* 105: Hot prospects to buy my current work. **1963** N.Y.C. man, age *ca*25: The Mets figure Kranepool for a hot prospect. **1975** Sepe & Telano *Cop Team* 19: We've got something [a lead] hot here. **1978** Pici *Tennis Hustler* 79: Every hot young player in the country migrates down for [the tournament]. **1988** Dietl & Gross *One Tough Cop* 56: We got a hot suspect. **1990** *Newsweek* (May 14) 23: He emerges as a hot prospect for '92.

8.a. *Und.* known to or easily identifiable by police; *(also)* under police surveillance.

1859 Matsell *Vocab.* 43: *Hot.* Too well known. **1928** *Amer. Mercury* (Aug.) 476: The Buick…was too "hot" to be used for a week or so. **1929** Booth *Stealing* 292 [ref. to *ca*1920]: You know I'm hot, here in town—and we're right in front of the police station. **1931–34** in Clemmer *Pris. Community* 333: *Hot…*in a state of being watched [by authorities]. **1935** Pollock *Und. Speaks*: *Hot dough,* marked money paid to kidnapers. **1944** *Pap. Mich. Acad.* XXX 592: *Hot…*under observation by an officer. **1958** Hughes & Bontemps *Negro Folklore* 484: That watch is hot, and so is this bar.

b. *Und.* wanted by police, esp. for a crime recently committed; (in 1954 quot.) being sought for retribution by criminals.

1928 *Amer. Mercury* (May) 80: The old time peter-mobs…often referred to being hot. "He came out of K.C. *hot* from that P.O. blast." **1930** Irwin *Tramp & Und. Sl.*: *Hot…*"Wanted" by the police for some

crime but lately committed. **1929–31** Runyon *Guys & Dolls* 129: Big Jule is really very hot, what with the coppers…looking for him….In fact, he is practically on fire. *Ibid.* 136: You are hotter than a firecracker but they can't prove a thing. **1932** Binyon & Bolton *If I Had a Million* (film): I've read the newspapers and you're hot, hot as a stove. **1935** Pollock *Und. Speaks: Hot as a 45,* wanted by the police. **1939** Rossen *Dust Be My Destiny* (film): I'm hot. The law's after me. **1944** N. Johnson *Woman in Window* (film): It's the bodyguard who's hot now anyway. **1952** M. Chase *McThing* 49: The cops are out like flies. I'm hotter than a firecracker but they can't prove a thing. **1952** Mandel *Angry Strangers* 159: You're hot like stoves….Fuzz is hangin' by his house. **1954** Schulberg *Waterfront* (film): You're hot. You oughta be glad we're followin' you. **1955** Q. Reynolds *HQ* 140: Is this guy you're after real hot? **1956** *Daily News* (N.Y.C.) (Nov. 16) 5: The people uptown say get this kid out of town; he's red hot. **1961** J.A. Williams *Night Song* 15: "I killed my wife," he said…."You hot?" "No. Car accident." **1970** Thackrey *Thief* 216: "Whether the guard dies or not," he said then, "you're hotter than a two-dollar pistol." **1970** R. Vasquez *Chicano* 223: Canto's been sneaking around like a ghost, he's so hot. **1986** J.J. Maloney *Chain* 156: You hot again.

c. Orig. *Und.* stolen.

1924 G. Henderson *Crookdom* 117: Pawnshops…establish a reputation for handling "hot stuff" and there are very few…that will refuse to buy from a known thief. **1925** *Collier's* (Aug. 8) 30: Stolen bonds are "hot paper"; stolen diamonds "hot ice." **1926** in *Sat. Eve. Post* (Mar. 18, 1950) 56: Birger has two hot cars. **1927** Thrasher *Gang* 267: *Hot stuff*—stolen goods. **1930** *AS* V 236: *Hot one*—a car stolen within the previous twenty-four hours, the loss of which has perhaps been reported to the police. **1931** Wilstach *Under Cover Man* 168: Some red hot ice. **1933** Milburn *No More Trumpets* 26: Me and another kid was riding out in a Studie that was hot—that we had stole. **1937** Hellman *Dead End* (film): Here. It's hot. Be careful where you spend it. **1962** T. Berger *Reinhart* 398: I can prove this isn't a hot car. **1963** Williamson *Hustler!* 36: He had been sellin' hot shit*….*Stolen items. **1980** Freudenberger & Richelson *Burn Out* 5: We don't cheat on our taxes or buy hot typewriters. **1993** *New Yorker* (Jan. 11) 80: Daquan had bought it "hot" for fifty dollars.

d. *Und.* (of money, checks, documents, etc.) counterfeit, forged, worthless, or illicitly altered.

1922 in *DA*: Hot Check Artist En Route Ardmore. **1942** Wilder *Flamingo Road* 198: We ain't bothering with hot money retail…He sent five grand of the cold for twenty-five grand of the hot. **1942–49** Goldin et al. *DAUL* 102: *Hot dough.* Counterfeit money. *Ibid.* 103: *Hot paper…*Forged checks or instruments; counterfeit or stolen stocks or bonds; marked playing cards….*Hot stickers…*Counterfeit…stamps. **1961** McMurtry *Horseman* 116: You're a hot-check-writing bastard! *a***1962** Maurer & Vogel *Narc. Add.* (ed. 2) 306: *Hot money…*counterfeit money. **1995** Nashville, Tenn., man, age *ca*30: Gas stations don't like checks 'cause lots of them turn out to be hot.

e. Esp. *Pris.* contraband or illicit; *(hence)* in possession of contraband or illicit articles.

1933 Ersine *Pris. Slang* 45: *Hot stuff…*1. Stolen goods. 2. Contraband. **1942–49** Goldin et al. *DAUL* 103: *Hot stove…*A contraband stove for cooking. **1947** *PADS* (No. 9) 33: *Hot oil*: n….oil that is illegally possessed or transported. **1961** Parkhurst *Undertow* 125 [ref. to 1951]: Anythin' that we weren't supposed to have [in prison], we always called "hot." **1935–62** Ragan & Finston *Toughest Pris.* 804: *Hotter than a pistol*—A prisoner…who has extremely contraband articles in his possession. **1962–63** in Giallombardo *Soc. of Women* 205: *Hot.* Anything illegally made [in prison]. **1993** *NewsHour* (CNN-TV) (Nov. 30): Hot goods…[are] goods produced under illegal conditions.

f. *Horse Racing.* (of a horse) illicitly stimulated by a drug before a race.

1935 Pollock *Und. Speaks: Hot,* a racehorse doped up. **1951** *PADS* (No. 16) 36: *Hot horse…*A horse that is stimulated by drugs.

g. *Med.* testing positive, as for indications of illicit drugs in the blood or urine.

1989 G.C. Wilson *Mud Soldiers* 207: A lot of guys have come up hot on their piss tests.

9. *Baseball.* sharply hit or thrown. Now *S.E.*

1865 (cited by Nichols *Baseball Termin.* 35). **1868** in *DAE*: Hot

Balls.—This term is applied to balls sent very swiftly to the hands from the bat, or thrown in swiftly. **1870** *Putnam's Mag.* (Mar.) 301: The ball being a hot one, Pearce failed to hold it. **1872** Chadwick *Dime Base-Ball* 27: A "hot" ball is one which is either thrown or hit to a fielder with great speed. **1874** Ewert *Diary* 70: McCort...received a "red hot one" from pitcher McCurry right square in the eye. **1885** Chadwick *Fielding* 5: A hot "liner" is handsomely caught on the fly. **1893** *Chi. Daily Tribune* (Sept. 3) 7: Lange beat out a hot grounder in the second. **1908** in Fleming *Unforgettable Season* 219: Caroming a hot one off Herzog's shoe, filling the bases. **1942** *ATS* 659: *Too hot to handle,* said of a ball too swift to be caught. **1983** (quot. at HOT CORNER). **1989** *Tracey Ullman Show* (Fox-TV): You tired of throwing breaking balls? You want to throw some hot stuff?

10.a. *Gamb.* (of persons) enjoying good luck; (of dice and other equipment) favorable or lucky.

1890 *DN* I 60: *To be hot:* to have a run of luck. **1931** Wilstach *Under Cover Man* 82: Rolling...[the dice] in his hands, trying to make 'em hot. **1929–33** Farrell *Manhood of Lonigan* 205: The dice get hot for a guy like this maybe once in his whole life. **1935** Fowler & Praskins *Call of Wild* (film): Well, the hot seat [at a gaming table] went cold. **1941** Rossen *Blues in Night* (film): We got some fresh dice. Nice and hot. **1944** Busch *Dream of Home* 93: I was hot...hotter than a pistol. **1953** Manchester *City of Anger* 276: That end of the table must be hot. **1962** Olmsted *Heads I Win* 65: Another player is "hot" (lucky).

b. currently (usu. temporarily) performing exceptionally well or meeting with unusual success in a sport or other competition.

1941 *Sat. Eve. Post* (May 17) 86: Melton, a twenty-game winner in his first big-league season, was hot. **1942** *Yank* (July 1) 22: But the Dodgers are hotter than the Yankees. **1942** *ATS* 684: *Hot jockey,* one enjoying a winning streak. **1943** *Amer. Mercury* (Nov.) 556: *Hot pilot*—a fighter pilot who is having success against the enemy. **1944** Olds *Helldiver Sq.* 51: His...[pilots] already had won the reputation of being a "red hot" outfit. **1949** Leahy *Notre Dame* 130: When an individual back is "hot," use him as much as possible. **1950** Cleveland *Great Mgrs.* 181: It made no difference that Heath was "hot" or that he might be a better hitter. **1969** Hirsch *Treasury* 90: Which is better to follow: a "hot" jockey or a "hot" trainer? **1978** Northport, L.I., man, age 31: When you're hot, you're hot; when you're not, you're not. **1987** in Dickson *Baseball Dict.* 211: He's so hot he could fire a gun up into the air and kill a fish. **1990** *N.Y. Post* (Jan. 2) 36: Malone is...a streak shooter: when he's hot, he's very hot. Even when he's cold, he's still lukewarm.

11.a. (of microphones or other electronic equipment) in operation; turned on.

1929 *AS* V 48: *Hot*—[of a radio] to be at high potential. **1937** *Printer's Ink* (Apr.) 54: *Hot mike*—A microphone in which the current is flowing. A live microphone. **1941** *Amer. Mercury* (Oct.) 581: *Hot mike*—microphone which is turned on. **1946** Sevareid *Not So Wild a Dream* 65: The task was to keep...the microphones hot. **1950** A. Lomax *Mr. Jelly Roll* xiii: The amplifier was hot. The needle was tracing a quiet spiral on the spinning acetate. **1961** L.G. Richards *TAC* 73: "Too late," Montague murmured into his hot mike. **1966** Shepard *Doom Pussy* 58: He crooned into the hot mike of his Canberra on the way to a target. **1989** J. Weber *Defcon One* 232: Let's arm 'em up. Switches hot, and goin' combat spread.

b. dangerously charged with electricity; at high voltage; (*hence*) not grounded. Now *S.E.* Cf. HOT SEAT, 1.

1930 in *OEDS: Hot,* electrically charged, particularly when dangerous. **1938** Haines *Tension* 226: These tracks are eleven thousand volts; hot enough to melt the gold in your teeth. We don't try to work 'em hot. **1982** Connors *Mass Media Dict.* 121: *Hot*...not grounded, as in "that wire is hot."

c. (of a firearm) loaded with ammunition and ready for firing; (*Mil.*) involving the firing of live rounds.

1958 in Harvey *Air Force* 20: I'd like to...meet him at 40,000 feet over the lake—hot guns. **1960** Caidin *Black Thurs.* 66: A coal-black night-fighter cruises on patrol, the cannon and guns "hot." **1984** Trotti *Phantom* 130 [ref. to 1960's]: The armorers smirkingly insert the ammo pans for the "hot" flights, [knowing]...that...[only] about one student in seven...succeeds in piercing the [target] banner with so

much as a single round. **1986** *Mystery of Capone's Vault* (WGN-TV): The safety is off and the weapon is hot....OK. Safety off. Weapon hot. **1986** Former SP4, U.S. Army: *Hot* means loaded and ready to fire, especially automatic fire. I heard that frequently on the firing range in basic training [1971]. *a***1989** R. Herman, Jr. *Warbirds* 49: The pilot...[threw] the sequence of switches that activated his gun and made it "hot." **1989** J. Weber *Defcon One* 232: We're hot and moving out. *Ibid.* 320: Report weapons hot.

d. *Mil.* (of ammunition) live; (of ordnance) armed.

1962 Mahurin *Honest John* 159 [ref. to WWII]: "Captain...are those bombs hot?" Rush...didn't know that "hot bombs" meant those that were active and could be used for combat. **1977** J. Wylie *Homestead Grays* 71: Are you carrying any hot ammo? **1983–86** G.C. Wilson *Supercarrier* 211: They flipped a lot more switches to make their bombs hot. **1987** Robbins *Ravens* 13 [ref. to Vietnam War]: "Hot" meant that the guns and ordnance on a fighter should be armed.

e. *Entertainment Industry.* (of a stage set, etc.) ready for or in use and not to be disturbed.

*a***1984** J. Green *Newspeak* 124: *Hot* (radio) a notice placed on a tape machine to indicate that the tape wound on to it is being edited and...[must] be left there. **1985** Ensign & Knapton *Dict. Television & Film* 115: *Hot set.* A completely finished set ready for shooting in every detail including placed props.

12. *Narc.* (of an injection or a drug) causing or likely to cause death. See also HOT SHOT, *n.,* 4.

1936 (quot. at HOTSHOT, *n.,* 4). **1960** C. Cooper *Scene* 207: Maybe one of 'em slipped the hot pill in Hodden's fix. **1977** *Kojak* (CBS-TV): We got an epidemic of hot smack in the East Village....We're talkin' about hot smack, Sonny. It killed seven people.

13. *Finance.* likely to rise or fall suddenly in value, or to be reinvested on short notice; financially volatile.

1936 (cited in *W9*). **1953** W. Fisher *Waiters* 134: Too much "hot" money riding on a possible winning combination. **1959** in *Britannica Bk. of Year* (1960) 752: *Hot issue.* A stock issue which will increase in price when sold to the public. **a***1981** *Macquarie Dict.: Hot money*...money in a money market or foreign exchange market which is likely to be withdrawn hastily following small changes in market conditions. **1983** Pessin & Ross *Words of Wall St.* 106: *Hot stock*...Securities that rise rapidly in price on the initial sale date. *a***1988** D.L. Scott *Wall St. Wds.* 167: *Hot stock* A stock having large price movements on very heavy volume. *Ibid.: Hot money.* Funds controlled by investors seeking high short-term yields that are likely to be reinvested somewhere else at any time.

14. *Transport.* (of a carrier) ready to leave or go, esp. ahead of schedule; (*hence*) (of an aircraft) inspected and ready for flight.

1938 in *AS* XVII (1942) 103: *Hot.* Ahead of schedule. **1941–42** Kennerly & Berry *Eagles Roar* 213: As I crawled into the...cockpit, my mechanic sung out his customary, "She's hot and ready, Sir." **1947** Boyer *Dark Ship* 6 [ref. to 1941]: "She's feeding, she's sleeping, she's hot."...The ship was offering meals and quarters to the crew, something not always done until the vessel sails, while "hot" indicated that she would leave soon.

15. radioactive, esp. dangerously contaminated by radiation. Now *S.E.*

1942 in *OED2:* Almost all the "hot" sodium was in the form of NaOH. **1946** in *AS* XXIV (1949) 75: A large part of Bikini lagoon remained..."hot" with radioactivity. **1947** *Time* (Nov. 10) 82: "Hot" (radioactive) atoms have already caused plenty of trouble in laboratories. **1950** *Western Folklore* (May) 160: *Hot stuff.* Radioactive material. **1951** Landau *Lost Continent* (film): We're over something hot. **1955** Yates & Smith *It Came from Beneath Sea* (film): Nothing hot in here. **1956** Heinlein *Door* 21: And those "hands" they use in atomics plants to handle anything "hot." **1956** Heflin *USAF Dict.* 256: *Hot*...slang...Radioactive, esp. highly radioactive. **1959** in Loosbrock & Skinner *Wild Blue* 531: The plane...employed the "hot" reactor to test radiation effects. **1972** Barker & Lewin *Denver* 54: AEC representatives argue that the "hot" dust was so widely disseminated it was rendered harmless. **1983** *News-Sentinel* (Knoxville, Tenn.) (Jan. 17) 1: Brown's Ferry "Hot" Leak Minor. *a***1984** T. Clancy *Red Oct.* 131: The officers had just checked the "hot" compartments with radiation instruments.

16. *Av.* (of an aircraft) attempting to land in a disabled condition.

> **1978** Nemec & Blankfort *Fire in Sky* (film): Alert San Diego. Tell 'em they got a hot one coming their way.

¶ In phrases:

¶ **get hot** to get to work, get busy, get going, etc.—usu. used imper.

> **1928** McEvoy *Show Girl* 50: Whoopie! Get hot! **1932** Pagano *Bluejackets* 99 [ref. to 1926]: Lasky stepped over to the Victrola…and putting on a record, boisterously shouted "Get hot! Let's dance baby!" **1932** Mankiewicz & Myer *Million Dollar Legs* (film): It's terrific when I get hot! **1939** C.R. Cooper *Scarlet* 15: I said Scotch 'n' soda. How the hell are you ever going to get hot on [*sc.* get going] ginger ale? **1947** Carter *Devils in Baggy Pants* 278: Get hot! Draw your K rations and D bars. **1961** Brosnan *Pennant Race* 2: Go ahead.…Get hot. And try to go farther than I did last year. **1961** L. Sanders *Four-Year Hitch* 199: You better get hot on it. **1963** J. Ross *Dead Are Mine* 58: Okay you people, let's get hot. **1964** Brown *Brig* 66: Draw cold water from the head and make all the glass in the house sparkle. Let's get hot. **1978** Univ. Tenn. student: We've got to get hot on that boat, too. **1983** Eilert *Self & Country* 285: Let's get hot, Eilert. **1988** Poyer *The Med* 384: Let's get hot. We only got about four hours to get this sucker back together.

¶ **get the hot end of it** to be victimized.

> **1909** Chrysler *White Slavery* 44: See that she does not get the "hot end of it" (cheated).

¶ **hot and heavy** see s.v. HOT, *adv.*

¶ **hot to trot** ready for action; (*specif.*) extremely eager, esp. for sexual activity.—usu. used predicatively.

> *ca***1951** in Tomedi *No Bugles* (plate 2): Hot To Trot/2d B. 7th Reg/Fox Co. **1961** J. Flynn *Action Man* 71: She's hot to trot and mad at me. **1963** (quot. at SEXPOT). **1963** E.M. Miller *Exile* 50: Your own ship's on the line, hot to trot. **1964** Howe *Valley of Fire* 181 [ref. to Korean War]: Sure, you've got a few hot-to-trot elements in the army.…Hot-to-trot.…It means: anxious, eager. **1965** W. Crawford *Bronc Rider* 155: Have to check. I'm hot to trot, but not to get shot! **1969** Lynch *Amer. Soldier* 193 [ref. to 1953]: You're one of those real anxious soldiers, aren't you? All hot to trot down there to see where the real action was? **1969** Tynan *Oh! Calcutta!* 187: THE WIFE is still on her back bare-assed and hot to trot. **1970** Wakefield *Going All the Way* 81: Sounds like she's hot to trot. **1972** N.Y.U. student: *Hot to trot* means very anxious for, something or very ready. It also means *horny.* **1974** R. Carter *Sixteenth Round* 8: I was hot-to-trot to fight some more. **1978** Barry *Ultimate Encounter* 145: We just happened to run into him out at the search.…He was certainly hot to trot and everything. **1979** D.K. Schneider *AF Heroes* 35: Hell, we're airborne and hot to trot. **1986** *Penthouse* (Aug.) 32: [Headline:] Hot-to-Trot Cop…I would like to have a fling…I feel that life is passing me by. **1991** *Vanity Fair* (Oct.) 256: They're hot to trot and having a lovely time; sex was never so good. **1993** D. Gabor *Speaking Your Mind* 162: Especially if you are being pursued by a persistent romantic who is "hot to trot."

¶ **hot under** [or **in** or **around**] **the collar** angry; (*also*) uncomfortable.

> **1880** Nye *Boomerang* 90: And the elder son kicked even as the government mule kicketh, and he was hot under the collar. **1893** in Wister *Out West* 198: *Hot in the collar* angry. **1894** *Harper's* (Oct.) 697: If Yank Hurst gets on to that, he'll be hot in the collar. **1895** in *OED2*: He would storm erround dat room an' git hot under de collar. **1902** Wister *Virginian* 199: He got hot under the collar…and raised his language to a high temperature. **1903** A. Adams *Log of Cowboy* 81: It makes me hot under the collar to think of it. **1905** Riordon *Plunkitt* 23: It makes me hot under the collar to tell about this. **1906** Hobart *Skiddoo* 11: And I'd like to tell it right now while I'm good and hot around the collar. **1906** in J. London *Letters* 217: He got me rather hot in the collar. **1942** "E. Queen" *Calamity Town* 52: Goodness, you men get so hot under the collar. **1966** Boatner & Gates *Amer. Idioms* 164: Mary gets hot under the collar if you joke about women drivers. **1978** Druck *Final Mission* 357: I was getting hot under the collar

about this time. **1990** *New Republic* (Dec. 24) 23: Sununu got "hot under the collar" when peppered with budget questions.

hot *adv.* **1.a.** with great force or speed.

> **1869** in Williams & Duffy *Chi. Wits* 50: He would send the…ball hot to…Hatfield, on the short stop, [but]…he couldn't make it so hot that Brother H. wouldn't stop it.

b. *Transport.* ahead of schedule.

> **1938** in *AS* XVII (1942) 103: *Hot.* Ahead of schedule. **1972** *Urban Life & Culture* I 341: He got the all clear sign from a northbound and ran through Waverly three minutes hot.

c. *Av.* at high or dangerous speed. Also as adj.

> **1939** R.A. Winston *Dive Bomber* 31: I made a "hot" landing by coming in with excess flying speed.…In rough water, a hot landing is suicide. **1940** *PM* (Dec. 6) 14: The ship came in hot.…[i.e.] "too fast for a safe landing." **1944** *Sat. Eve. Post* (June 24) 80: PV's can outrun all but the fastest of Jap fighters, but they pay for their speed by landing hot. **1955** Archibald *Aviation Cadet* 7: He had just come away from the ramp after coming in with a T-6 trainer, too high and too hot. **1956** Heflin *USAF Dict.* 256: *Hot, adv.* In a fast manner. Slang. **1963** Dwiggins *S.O. Bees* 25 [ref. to WWII]: It's murder on a carrier landing. You come in too hot, you bounce clear over the barrier. **1963** E.M. Miller *Exile* 241: He landed hot and blew two tires. **1966–67** Harvey *Air War* 11: It lands hotter than anything else—about 165 knots at touchdown. **1984** Trotti *Phantom* 100: I was still at 110 as I passed…midfield…, too hot to touch the brakes yet. **1990** G. Simmons *Miracle Landing* (film): Paradise 243—you're coming in pretty hot.

2. *Mil.* with one's guns or rockets firing.

> **1967** Mulligan *No Place to Die*: The "guns" came in "hot," meaning with their rockets and machine guns firing. **1970** Hersh *My Lai* 43: We came in hot [firing], with a cover of artillery in front of us, came down the line, and destroyed the village. **1988** *Tour of Duty* (CBS-TV): We're goin' in hot.

¶ In phrase:

¶ **hot and heavy** vigorously, rapidly, passionately, or in great number or amount. Now *colloq.* Also as adj.

> **1841** [Mercier] *Man-of-War* 9: The rough and tempestuous weather…came on as our tars express it, "hot and heavy," though *cold* and heavy would…have been a more appropriate expression. **1864** in J.W. Haley *Rebel Yell* 144: From 4 o'clock we were into it all along the line, hot and heavy. **1864** in Redkey *Grand Army* 119: The loss in our brigade was "hot and heavy." **1884** F.R. Stockton *Lady or Tiger?* 82: We put off, hot and heavy, arter that ar 'coon, and hard work it was too. **1918** in Rossano *Price of Honor* 211: Then we had it out, hot and heavy. **1959** R.L. Scott *Tiger in Sky* 56: We learned to carry a drag chute and "pop" it for added brake control when we landed hot and heavy. **1966** Boatner & Gates *Amer. Idioms:* Fred got it hot and heavy when his wife found out how much he had lost at cards.…The partners had a hot and heavy argument. *a***1968** in Haines & Taggart *Ft. Lauderdale* 141: They started going at it hot and heavy. **1979** Univ. Tenn. student: We were goin' at it hot and heavy by midnight. **1984–88** Hackworth & Sherman *About Face* 118: The war stories…came hot and heavy. **1988** B.E. Wheeler *Outhouse Humor* 78: The boy went on a-courting hot and heavy.

hot air *n.* empty, exaggerated, or boastful talk; in phr. **hot-air artist** one given to such talk. Also (*rare*) **hot wind.** [Despite its acceptance by earlier dictionaries, the bracketed quot. in its full orig. context clearly does not exemplify the slang sense of this phr.]

> [**1873** "M. Twain" & Warner *Gilded Age* ch. xliv: The most airy scheme inflated in the hot air of the capital only reached in magnitude some of his lesser fancies.] **1899** Kountz *Baxter's Letters* 68: Bud gave us a lot of hot air about his mother's cousin. **1899** Ade *Fables* 58: He talked what is technically known as Hot Air. **1902** K. Harriman *Ann Arbor Tales* 65: I'm on—up to the game…no hot air goes with me. **1903** Benton *Cowboy Life* 20: We had been getting hot air from the railroad livestock agents…for some time. **1904** in "O. Henry" *Works* 106: He…tried his hot air again. **1905** Phillips *Plum Tree* 32: I was developing some talent for…dispensing "hot air" from the stump. **1910** *Sat. Eve. Post* (July 2) 13: "Hot-air artists" was a phrase

uncoined; the farmer called them "jawsmiths." **1911** *N.Y. Eve. Jour.* (Jan. 11) 12: What fighter is the biggest hot air shooter? **1912** Siringo *Cowboy Detective* 197: How much of this story was "hot air," I had no way of knowing. **1914** Ellis *Billy Sunday* 204: I'm not here to explode hot air and theories to you. **1925** *English Jour.* (Nov.) 704: Another form that is nearly...obsolete is..."hot air." **1926** Cushing *Devil in the Cheese* 68: Let me give you a tip—it takes more than gall and hot air to marry for money! **1927** in Robinson *Comics* 67: Oh what a bunch of hot air! **1931** Farrell *McGinty* 298: He's all hot air. **1948** Lay & Bartlett *12 O'Clock High!* 83: You think I was talking a lot of hot air. **1952** Chase *McThing* 51: Oh, what hot air he peddles! **1959** Zugsmith *Beat Generation* 84: For the sake of melodrama, that hot-air artist would call his own brother a rapist. **1966** in Steinbrook *Allies* 98: They're really full of hot wind. **1984** *Good Morning America* (ABC-TV) (July 2): Is political advertising just a lot of hot air? **1985** D. Steel *Secrets* 140: Sabina, you are full of hot air. **1986–89** Norse *Memoirs* 315: That's baloney!...A lot of hot air! **1995** *Earth Matters* (CNN-TV) (Apr. 16): Others say it was just a lot of hot air.

hot-air *v.* to flatter or deceive.
  1902–03 Ade *People You Know* 90: He would hot-air the Ladies until they flushed Crimson from the Joy of being hot-aired.

hot-and-cold *n. Narc.* a combination of heroin and cocaine.
  1970 Landy *Underground Dict.* 106: *Hot and cold n.*...Heroin and cocaine. **1981** (cited in Spears *Drugs & Drink*).

hot-ass *v.* HOTFOOT.—usu. considered vulgar.
  1975 Betuel *Dogfighter* 170: So he hot-asses it up here and drives for three fucking hours.

hot-assed *adj.* (of a woman) sexually excited; lustful.—usu. considered vulgar.
  ***1682–83** in Partridge *DSUE* (ed. 7): Hot-arsed. ***a1890–93** *F & H* III 363: *Hot-arsed*...Excessively lewd. (Of women only). **1938** "Justinian" *Amer. Sexualis* 25: *Hot-assed*, sexually excited (of a woman). **1948–51** J. Jones *Here to Eternity* ch. xiv: Went on the bum, instead of finding him a good hotassed wench and settling down like he should of. **1959** P. Marshall *Brown Girl* 33: If he din had every hot-ass girl 'bout the place he din have one.

hot baby *n. Stu.* (see quot.).
  1900 *DN* II 42: [College slang:] *hot-baby*...1. One very good in certain things, as "He is a *hot-baby* in Greek." 2. One inclined to be fast.

hot bed *n.* a bed that is rented two or more times in a day, or that is occupied in shifts by different persons.—often used attrib.
  1940 Ottley & Weatherby *Negro in N.Y.* 267: He would occupy a bed in the day that would be rented out at night....This was described as the "hot bed." **1944** Burley *Hndbk. Jive* 140: *Hot bed*—A bed used by three or four persons sleeping in relays in eight hour shifts, for...25 cents. *a***1945** in Osofsky *Harlem* 139: Hot-Bed System. **1945** in *OED2*. **1953** Paley *Rumble* 44: I got a face like an angel, the girls in the hotbeds say when they kiss me. **1957** Murtagh & Harris *Cast First Stone* 305: *Hot-bed hotel* A hotel in which the rooms are rented over and over for an hour or less [for purposes of prostitution]. **1959** Oliver *Meaning of Blues* 210: The "hot-bed" apartment....The "hot-bed" is an apartment which is rented to three separate groups of tenants each of whom use the flat for eight hours of the day or night. **1968** Hawley *Hurricane Yrs.* 49: This crummy little motel, nothing but a hotbed joint, a hideaway for drunks. **1970** Wambaugh *Centurions* 178 [ref. to 1962]: Apartments six, seven, and eight all have hot beds in them now. **1972** A. Kemp *Savior* 169: We talked ourselves right into a hot-bed hotel ($4.50 plus $1.00 deposit on the key). **1976** Pileggi *Blye* 39: The other places...are known as "hot bed" joints....Some of these motels have a whole section that they turn over to the hot-bed people and other rooms set aside for legitimate all-night guests....Also, hot bed motels are not necessarily crummy places at all. **1983** Wambaugh *Delta Star* 74: I know their hustlin tricks. I don't keep no rooms with hot beds. **1994** Bak *Turkey Stearnes* 131 [ref. to 1920's]: It didn't take much to open up a brothel: a couple of "hot beds"...and perhaps some complimentary rotgut.

hotbedding *n.* (see quot.).
  1978 *N.Y. City News* (Sept. 3) 3: Support proposed City Council

legislation to outlaw "hot-bedding," or renting the same room more than twice in a 24-hour period.

hot biscuit *n.* something that is especially popular or exciting.
  1989 *Newsweek* (July 24) 4: *Hot biscuit.* A promising research program...."That new gas laser is a real hot biscuit."

hot book *n.* a pornographic book or booklet. Cf. HOT, *adj.*, 6.f.
  1942 *ATS* 497: *Hot book*, a pornographic book. **1957** Gelber *Connection* 81: Cowboy was reading some kind of hot book. **1968** P. Roth *Portnoy* 206: Does she wrap them around your ass like in the hot books? **1980** Kotzwinkle *Jack* 52: He's sellin' hotbooks....Ever see one?

hot box *n.* **1.** *Naut.* a ship commanded by brutal officers; BLOOD BOAT.
  1903 Sonnichsen *Deep Sea Vagabonds* 53: Paid off from a dam' Yankee hot-box—the Henry Hyde.

  2. (see 1965 quot.).—usu. considered vulgar.
  1965 Trimble *Sex Words* 104: *Hot box*...A nymphomaniac or very passionate female. **1969** Pharr *Numbers* 145 [ref. to *ca*1930]: These Hot Springs hot boxes are not gonna pass up a chance at a N'Yawk man...if he's young.

  3. *Sports.* a steam cabinet for weight-reducing.
  1969 Hirsch *Treasury* 47: They might...hit the hotbox first, ride their race, and then come back and have a sandwich or a bowl of soup before their next mount. *Ibid* 48: Fifty percent or more of all jockeys reduce regularly in the hotbox or steam room. **1974** Terkel *Working* 360: They could lose seven pounds in three hours...in the hot box.

hot bunk *n.* Orig. *Naut.* (see quot.). Cf. HOT BED.
  1972 G. Bradford *Mariner's Dict.* 130: *Hot bunks*, those occupied by successive watches below...when the crew outnumbers the bunks available.

hot-bunk *v.* Orig. *Naut.* (see quots.). Cf. HOT BED, *n.*
  1945 Trumbull *Silversides* 143: Burlingame strongly disapproved of "hot bunking"—alternate use of the same bunk by men who are on separate watches. **1956** Lockwood & Adamson *Zoomies* 181: If extra officers or men were carried...cots or hammocks had to be rigged, or "hot bunking" was resorted to. **1959** Anderson *Nautilus 90 North* 53: On conventional fleet submarines sailors often share bunks, a practice known as "hot-bunking." *a***1984** J. Green *Newspeak* 124: *Hotbunk v.*...RN ratings term for crowded accommodation on cramped submarines: those off duty sleep in the bunks just vacated by the active watch. *a***1987** Coyle *Team Yankee* 86: They hot bunked with Bannon using Folk's sleeping bag tonight. It was a normal practice in a tactical environment.

hot button *n.* something that provokes a strong emotional response.—also used attrib.
  1975 (cited in *W10*) **1980** Freudenberger & Richelson *Burn Out* 39: "Dead" was a hot button to Ambrose. **1982** *Business Week* (Oct. 25) 92A: The point of the survey is to find out "what people's hot buttons are for buying videotex." **1983** *Working Woman* (Sept.) 52: It was a combination of knowing people's personalities and what they're afraid of, and anticipating their questions, knowing their hot button. **1987** *Atlantic* (Aug.) 88: *Hot button*...A concern, factor, or interest known to have key influence on decision-making....Our citations...go back to 1981. **1988** *This Week with David Brinkley* (ABC-TV) (Jan. 10): What happens when hot buttons like abortion and school prayer don't energize people? **1991** *Nation* (Jan. 7) 3: Trendy words ("empowerment," "responsibility," "choice") and hot buttons (racial quotas, Congressional paralysis, cultural permissiveness). **1994** *N.Y. Times* (May 9) D7: The power to galvanize a segment of public opinion on hot-button topics from Zoë Baird's taxes to homosexuals in the military.

hot card *n.* **1.** an amusing, lively, or notable person.
  1899 Cullen *Tales* 97: Met all the hot cards including the member of Congress from the district. *Ibid.* 226: "You're four-flushing...," said this hot card with the penetrating eye.

  2. *Entertainment Industry.* an act or performer that draws large audiences.
  1920 *Variety* (Dec. 31) 15: She...was now a "hot card," guaranteed to head any bill and "hold up."

hot-cha[-cha] *n.* [elab. of HOT, *adj.*] **1.** Esp. *Entertainment Industry.* excitement or lively spirit; (*also*) flashiness or showiness.

1931 Perelman & Johnstone *Monkey Business* (film): I want gaiety, laughter, hot-cha-cha! **1933** *Newsweek* (Feb. 17) 26: George White Forgets Hot-cha in Tuneful "Melody." **1938** Epstein & Coffee *Four Daughters* (film): I suppose you'd like this house to be filled with jazz and swing and crooners and hotcha! **1940** Zinberg *Walk Hard* 245: I'm a low-down dog with music in my legs and hotcha in my eyes. **1969** *Playboy* (Dec.) 236: Publisher Bernard Geis, a virtuoso of hotcha.

2. an attractive young woman.

1993 D. Lum, in J. Hagedorn *Chan Is Dead* 291: She was one hot-cha-cha.

hot-cha[-cha] *adj.* Esp. *Entertainment Industry.* flashy, showy, or exciting; HOT, *adj.,* 6.c., d., e.

1933 *Newsweek* (Feb. 17) 26: The name of George White suggests lovely women stooping to scandal, wide and handsome stepping, hot-cha music. **1935** Lindsay *She Loves Me Not* 45: It is a frenetic wooing in the terms of "hot-cha" dancing. **1935** Fortune *Fugitives* 51: I'm quoting…to refute the stories that…Bonnie was notorious in Dallas' night life, and the biggest "hotcha" girl in town. **1938** Chandler *Big Sleep* 31: It seems he run Sternwood's hotcha daughter…off to Yuma. **1939** Appel *Power House* 24: There were night clubs and hotcha dames. *Ibid.* 377: But you got to do things in a hotcha way if we're going to get new business. **1942** Davis & Wolsey *Madam* 16: You know after all he's conservative. Bob doesn't like hotcha stuff. **1947** Schulberg *Harder They Fall* 14: He finally had a blowout on that hotcha motorcycle of his.

hot-cha[-cha] *interj.* Esp. *Entertainment Industry.* (used to express enthusiasm).

1931 in K. Bloom *American Song* I 111: Ha! Cha! Cha! **1932** L. Brown & R. Henderson *Hot-cha* [title of musical comedy]. **1932** in *OEDS*: With a hey, nonny nonny, and a ha cha cha! **1933** Milburn *No More Trumpets* 279: Hot cha! Boo-pa-doop! I'll see you in my dreams! **1934** in Ruhm *Detective* 99: Hotcha!…I always thought that guy would wind up like this. **1949** R.D. Andrews *Bad Boy* (film): Hot-cha-cha! I got a million of 'em! **1957** W.C. Williams, in Witemeyer *Williams-Laughlin* 221: (Five!) specimens including me are to be examined. Hot cha! **1994** *CBS This Morning* (CBS-TV) (Dec. 12): *Told* you I was gonna nail it on the air! Hotcha!

hot chair *n.* Pris. HOT SEAT, 1.

1926 in *OED2*: I never shot nobody.…That's one thing I try to dodge—the hot chair. **1927** *DN* V 451: *Hot chair,* n. The electric chair. **1935–62** Ragan & Finston *Toughest Pris.* 804: *Hot chair*—The electric chair. **1962** Crump *Killer* 385: Dat ol' hot chair'll be filled wit' life once mo'.

hotchee, hotchie, hotchy var. HACHI.

hot cock *n.* USMC. latest news or information.—usu. considered vulgar.

1956 *AS* XXXI (Oct.) 193: Hot Cock, n. News. [*1966 S.J. Baker *Austral. Lang.* 189 [ref. to WWII]: *Hot cock,* nonsense, boasting, empty talk.] **1968** W. Crawford *Gresham's War* 75 [ref. to 1953]: "Gen. Intelligence. Information." "Oh. Dope. Scoop. Hot cock." **1989** Rawson *Wicked Words* 90: What's the hot cock?

hot corner *n.* Baseball. the third-base position.—constr. with *the.*

[**1852** Doten *Journals* I 133: God eternally damn him to the hottest of all the hot corners in hell.] **1889** in J. McBride *High & Inside* 58: The Brooklyns had Old Hicks on the hot corner all afternoon and it's a miracle he wasn't murdered. **1937** (cited in Nichols *Baseball Termin.*). a**1948** in Mencken *Amer. Lang. Supp.* II 736: *Hot corner.* Third base. **1957** N.Y.C. schoolboy, age 9: The "hot corner" is third base. **1976** Woodley *Bears* 25: I'm supposed to try third.…The Hot corner. **1983** Whiteford & Jones *How to Talk Baseball* 103: *Hot corner*…the third base position, a common expression that refers to the frequency of hot line drives and grounders that assault the third baseman.

hot damn *interj.* [prob. alter. of *goddamn*] (used to express excitement or astonishment). Also (*So. & West.*) **hot dang.**

1930–33 T. Wolfe *Time & River* 367: Hot damn! Thataway, boy! **1936** Steinbeck *In Dubious Battle* 90: Hot-damn, listen. **1953** Kantor *Andersonville* 283: Hot damn! **1957, 1971** in *OED2*. **1978** Abernethy *Paisanos* 25: Hot dang, he must've been big as a bear.

hot diggety [dog] *interj.* (used to express excitement or enthusiasm). Also vars.

1923 T.A. Dorgan, in Zwilling *TAD Lexicon* 46: Hot diggerty dog. **1922–24** McIntyre *White Light* 103: Hot diggedy dog! **1924** *DN* V 270: Hot diggity. **1927** Benchley *Early Worm* 142: Hot dickety-dog! **1933** Benchley *Chips* 102: Hot dickety! It must be fun to have a horn. **1942** Oppenheimer & Houser *Yank at Eton* (film): Hot diggety dog! **1991** *Bill & Ted's Adventures* (CBS-TV): Oh, boy! Wow! Hot diggety dog!

hot dog *n.* **1.** Orig. *Stu.* a cocky and proficient individual, now usu. a competitive athlete; (*also*) one who behaves, performs, or dresses in a flashy, conceited, or ostentatious manner; a mere show-off.

1894 in *Comments on Ety.* (Nov. 1995) 19: Two Greeks a "hot dog" freshman sought./The Clothes they found, their favor bought. **1897** in *Comments on Ety.* (Nov. 1995) 18: "Brown's a hot dog, isn't he?" "Yes, he has so many pants." **1899** Kountz *Baxter's Letters* 34: A Messe de Mariage seems to be some kind of a wedding march, and a bishop who is a real hot dog won't issue a certificate unless the band plays the Messe. **1900** *DN* II 42: [College slang:] *hot-dog*…One very proficient in certain things.…A conceited person. **1903** Ade *Society* 184: "Do you know, I sometimes suspect that I am not qualified to be a Hot Dog," said Herbert. **1948** Manone & Vandervoort *Trumpet* 120: I put on the [record] label "Barbecue Joe and His Hot Dogs." **1959** Brosnan *Long Season* 221: He may be a Hot Dog but I don't know where Scheffing would be without him. **1960** in Wagenheim *Clemente!* 78: Opposing players call him a "hot dog" and say he can be intimidated by fast balls buzzing around his head. **1962** in Rawson *Wicked Words* 202: Crybabies and "hot dogs," or show-offs, always earned…[a baseball umpire's] contempt. **1970** Wambaugh *Centurions* 188 [ref. to 1962]: They're the things that happen to young hot dogs like Ranatti and Simeone. **1972** Ponicsan *Cinderella Liberty* 133: Don't be a hot dog about this, please. **1973** Ace *Stand on It* 56: I know that you're a hot-dog and all that. **1977** *Baa Baa Black Sheep* (NBC-TV): Now you ain't gonna be a hot dog, are ya, sonny? **1978** in Lyle & Golenbock *Bronx Zoo* 128: Tito Fuente…has been one of the most renowned hot dogs in baseball history. **1983** Whiteford *How to Talk Baseball* 104: In the late 1940s and 50s, Cuban players began to call each other hot dogs and the expression spread. **1985** in Safire *Look It Up* 109: *Hot dog*…goes back nearly twenty years, at least in Philadelphia.

2.a. [a natural development of syn. DOG, 7] a frankfurter, esp. when cooked and served on a soft bun. Now *S.E.*

[**1895** *Yale Record* (Oct. 5), in *Comments on Ety.* (Nov. 1995) 6: But I delight to bite the dog/When placed inside a bun.] **1895** *Yale Record* (Oct. 19), in *Comments on Ety.* (Nov. 1995) 1: How they contentedly munched hot dogs. **1900** *DN* II 42: [College slang:] *hot-dog*…A hot sausage [current in at least 13 states]. **1900** *Howitzer* (U.S. Mil. Acad.) (No. 1) 120: *Hot Dog.*—A mess-hall sausage. **1900** Patten *Merriwell's Power* 80: "Permit me to loan you a nickel." "The price of a single hot dog." **1903** Merriman *Letters* 28: The Afro-American gentleman…sells hot corn and "hot dogs" in Harvard Square. **1906** T.A. Dorgan, in Zwilling *TAD Lexicon* 46: (Where They Sell Frankfurters Under The Ring) Hot Dog On/A Roll/A Dime. **1908** in "O. Henry" *Works* 300: We ate seven hot dogs. **1913** in *Comments on Ety.* (Dec. 1995) 13: They dined on that well known Coney Island dish, a "hot dog" and a roll. **1914** Hawthorne *Brotherhood* 186: I was succumbing to the influences of prison hash and "hot dog." **1915** T.A. Dorgan, in *Daily News* (N.Y.C.) (Aug. 1, 1984): Say, gimme a hot dog that didn't spend last summer at Coney, will ya? **1919** *Twelfth U.S. Inf.* 80: Their tone changed when they beheld platters piled high with wienies. "Hot dogs again," muttered everyone. **1939** *Pittsburgh Courier* (July 15) 2: Must Quit Holding Court in Rear of "Hot Dog" Stand. **1939** Appel *People Talk* 299: Their arms reach out for the platters of hot dogs and sauerkraut, fried crisp potatoes, brown beef in gravy, [etc.]. **1995** N.Y.C. woman, age *ca*60: To me a *hot dog* usually means the kind cooked and ready to eat on a hot dog bun. Without the bun, like still in the package, or with beans, it's still a hot dog, but I think I'd usually call it a *frank* or a *frankfurter.*

b. *Mil.* a kite balloon; sausage. *Joc.*

1918 Kauffman *Our Navy at Work* 151: Observation Balloons…

Hot-Dogs. **1918** in Janis *Big Show* 169: They looked so useless—great big "hot dogs" hanging there.

c. the penis.—usu. considered vulgar.

1925 in Legman *Dirty Joke* 52: Mama, Johnny put his hot dog in my bun! **1927** [Fliesler] *Anecdota* 182: Why is it so many young girls who marry old men leave them?…They prefer hot dog to cold tongue. **1927** in Leadbitter & Slaven *Blues Records* 133: I Wanna Hot Dog For My Roll. **1936** in P. Oliver *Blues Tradition* 234: Mama, I got a hot dog and it ain't cold,/It's just right for to fit your roll. **1968** in Bronner *Children's Folk.* 41: Do you have a license to sell hot dogs? (*To a boy with an open zipper*).

hot-dog *adj.* **1.a.** Orig. *Stu.* splendid or exciting.

1895 in *Inlander* (Jan. 1896) 148: Hot-dog, good, superior. "He has made some hot-dog drawings for —." **1928** McEvoy *Show Girl* 98: He's as cute as a little red wagon and writes beautiful and I think he's hot dog.

b. *Pris.* erotic.

1966 Braly *On Yard* 130: These were…hotdog books heavy with sex. **1972** Carr *Bad* 139: The homo convinced him to bring in *Playboy* and every other hot-dog magazine imaginable.

2. flashy; flamboyant; ostentatious; given to showing off one's abilities.

1923 *Amer. Leg. Wkly.* (Mar. 23) 11: This one I knew to be a hot-dawg admiral too. He could be counted upon on each and every occasion to outadmiral any other admiral in the Navy. **1923** Ornitz *Haunch, Paunch & Jowl* 74: He was dressed in what Sam called hot-dog clothes. **1966** *New Yorker* (Dec. 31) 28: He's a hot-dog surfer. **1966** Reynolds & McClure *Freewheelin Frank* 124: All the fine women of this hotdog street. **1969** Bouton *Ball Four* 146: "Oh, that hot dog son of a bitch." Sure he's a flashy umpire and sure he does a lot of showboating. **1972** Wambaugh *Blue Knight* 121: Why don't you…let those young coppers…do the hotdog police work? **1990** *Car & Driver* (Oct.) 167: His flying fingers [on a camera] will struggle to stay with the hot-dog drivers.

hot dog *v.* Esp. *Surfing, Skiing, & Skateboarding.* to display one's skills ostentatiously; show off. Hence **hot dogger,** *n.* [The sense in 1946 quot. is app. 'eating hot dogs'.]

[**1946** Werris et al. *If I'm Lucky* (film): There'll be some hotdoggin', leapfroggin', cotton candy and pink lemonade.] **1961** *Life* (Sept. 1) 48: Almost every wave carries a "hot dogger" doing tricks or…dressed in outlandish garb. **1963** *Time* (Aug. 9) 49: "Hot dogging" is either class-A surfing or show-off stuff. **1964** *Look* (June 30) 55: *Hot Dogger:* surfer skilled at stunts. **1967** W. Murray *Sweet Ride* 48: I mean, the surf, it's different there. It's big, real big. You can't do any hotdogging. **1968** Kirk & Hanle *Surfer's Hndbk.* 140: *Hotdog, hotdogger, hotdogging:* great and showy performer or performance; an expert surfer who does tricks on the board and takes calculated chances; also, a stunter or show-off. **1972** *Five Boroughs* (Nov.) 16: It is good for beginners [in skiing] to practice downhill racing and intermediates to develop their hotdogging virtuosities. **1973** *Urban Life & Culture* II 149: "Hot dogging," a surfing style characterized by sharp turns, "walking," "nose riding," and other radical maneuvers. **1991** Reebok ad (Fox-TV): I may hot-dog. But this is no bull.

hot dog *interj.* (used to express pleasure, surprise, approval, etc.). Also **hot doggies.** Cf. HOT DAMN.

1906 *DN* III 141: Hot dog, interj. phr. Bravo! **1921** Carter *A Marine, Sir!* 48: Hot dog! **1921** *Variety* (Sept. 30) 17: When he told how good looking his gal was, the little member drew a big laugh by snapping out "hot dog." **1921** in Kimball & Balcolm *Sissle & Blake* 105: Hot dog, my soul, goin-a knock 'em cold. **1924** Marks *Plastic Age* 26: Ray! Ray! Atta girl! Hot dog! **1928** Treadwell *Machinal* 497: Hot dog! Why ain't it? **1943** Schrank *Cabin in Sky* (film): Very good, sir. And hot *dog!* **1979** Kunstler *Wampanaki Tales* 108: "Hot doggies!" Bobby cried.

hot-dog board *n.* *Surfing.* (see quots.).

1963 in *OED2:* He always owns two boards at any one time, one "hot dog" board and a "big gun" (which is a foot or so longer). ***1965** S.J. Baker *Austral. Lang.* (ed. 2) 254: *Hot dogging,* turning quickly back and forth across the face of a wave; *hot dog board,* a surfboard used for this practice.

hotel *n.* a jail or prison. *Joc.*

1845 *Nat. Police Gaz.* (Nov. 8) 92: "Billy McCully, or Cullough's" late residence was our "Hotel" at Sing Sing. **1864** in C.W. Wills *Army Life* 228: Lieutenant Miller…was captured by the enemy, and is now on his way to the "Hotel de Libby." **1865** in Blackett *Chester* 298: The Hotel de Libby is now doing a rushing business. **1865** H.S. White *Pris. Life* 60: The prisoners of the "Hotel de Libby," at Richmond. **1873** Sutton *N.Y. Tombs* 92: "Do you keep a hotel?" "I do…The Tombs!" **1880** Martin *Sam Bass* 145: He would have pulled me into Uncle Hub Bates' hotel. **1882** *Judge* (Dec. 30) 7: I know a beautiful hotel…in the middle of the East River. **1901** *Naval Apprentice* (Oct.) 3: That is only the proprietor of the "Hotel de Brig" asleep. **1912** Lowrie *Prison* 40: Allus look out f'r y'r fingers when dey slams dat main entrance t' dis hotel. **1936** Twist *We About to Die* (film): Some day I'm gonna get some decent grub in this hotel if I have to hang for it. **1952** Viereck *Men Into Beasts* 56: The "hotel" at which I was an involuntary guest was more generous. **1963** T.I. Rubin *Sweet Daddy* 2: It's an okay hotel but a habit of it I don't want to make.

Hotel de Gink *n.* [*Hotel de* + GINK] (orig. among itinerants) (see 1930 quot.); (*hence*) (*joc.*) (see first 1944 quot.).

1930 "D. Stiff" *Milk & Honey Route* 208: *Hotel de Gink*—A charitable or municipal lodging house. **1933** Barks Bros. (MGM short subject): Partner, I'll be seeing ya at de Hotel de Gink. **1944** *Amer. N & Q* (Feb.) 166: *Hotel de Gink:* The often primitive "hotels," run by the Army Air Transport for visiting dignitaries are so called. **1944** *Life* (May 29) 67: He sketched Balchen in the transient officers' "Hotel de Gink" in Iceland. **1948** Wolfert *Act of Love* 437: Anyway…it's better than the Hotel de Gink that Craik runs. **1980** Ciardi *Browser's Dict.* 153: *Hotel de Gink* A generic name for a flophouse.

hotel-de-loose *n.* [pun on *hotel de luxe*] a brothel. *Joc.*

1888 *Stag Party* 15: He made arrangements at a hotel-de-loose.

hot enchilada *n.* HOT TACO.

1978 1st Lt., U.S. Army, Dugway Proving Ground, Utah (coll. J. Ball): I wish I had your job—driving up to Salt Lake twice a week alone with a hot enchilada like that.

hotfoot *n.* [functional shift of S.E. *hot-foot, adv.*] **1.** prompt action; haste.

1869 in *OED2:* The honorable Senator…admonishes us of the importance of hot-foot in this business.

2. *Police.* the action of a policeman tapping or beating on the soles of a sleeping vagrant's feet with a nightstick as a signal to move on.

1894 in Ade *Chicago Stories* 97: He was getting the "hot-foot." A heavy policeman was pounding the sole of his shoe. **1899** Cullen *Tales* 124: I distinctly recall the…skill with which the cop gave me the hot foot. **1906** A.H. Lewis *Confessions* 32: Ready to give my gentleman the "hot foot"…by smartly beating the soles of his feet…with [my] nightstick. **1925** Mullin *Scholar Tramp* 54: The bull in Mount Morris Park who gave me the hot-foot as a tingling eye-opener [explained] half apologetically…that the most seductive targets conceivable for a policeman's night-stick are the…feet of a sleeping bum.

3. a practical joke in which a match is inserted between the sole and upper of the victim's shoe and then lit; in phr. **give a hotfoot** *Mil.* to direct liquid flame or napalm against.

1934 D. Runyon, in *OED2:* The way you give a hot foot is to sneak up behind some guy…and stick a paper match in his shoe between the sole and the upper…and then light the match. **1935** E. Levinson *Strikes* 178: "Hotfoot," insertion of the lit end of a match between the soles and uppers of a sleeping fink's shoe, is always in order. **1942** *Pittsburgh Courier* (Aug. 29) 7: Swirling through his opponents like a hurricane with a hot-foot. **1949** Brown & Grant *Sands of Iwo Jima* (film): OK, Mac, give 'em a hotfoot. **1965** in Mersky & Polmar *Nav. Air War in Viet.* 31: [Inscribed on napalm canister in photo:] Hot Foot. Do You Need This or What? **1988–89** in Safire *Quoth Maven* 67: One of the most blazing hotfoots on record.

4. *Sports.* a fast runner.

1939–40 Tunis *Kid from Tomkinsville* 62: That hotfoot out there in short…picked up that liner.

¶ **In phrases:**

¶ **do a hotfoot** to run or hasten away.

1897 *Pop. Sci. Mo.* (Apr.) 833: To run from a police officer is *to do a hot foot.* **1900** *DN* II 36: "To do a hot *foot,*" to absent one's self from recitation. **1904** Hobart *Jim Hickey* 119: To-morrow we do a hot-foot for the West. **1906** H. Green *Boarding House* 60: Many's the time he gimme the office to do a hotfoot in the old days. **1915** H.L. Wilson *Ruggles* 27: We'd better report to her before she does a hot-foot over here.

¶ **give (someone) the hotfoot** to run out on.

1902 "H. McHugh" *Back to Woods* 66: Did somebody give you the hot-foot and make a quick exit?

¶ **on the hotfoot** as quickly as possible.

[***1827** in *OED2:* If your honour's in a hurry, I can run on hot-foot and tell the squire that your honour's galloping after me.] **1926** in Partridge *Dict. Und.* 346: I went on th' hot-foot. **1929** Coe *Hooch* 241: Come down here on the hot foot. **1966–80** McAleer & Dickson *Unit Pride* 99: He ran right in on the hotfoot to the Old Man.

hotfoot *v.* **1.** to run; hasten.—usu. constr. with *it.*—also used fig.

1896 Ade *Artie* 19: There was nothin' else in sight so I hot-foots up to the dance. **1900** Ade *More Fables* 163: He...Hot-Footed up to see the Boss. **1906** *DN* III 141: *Hotfoot it, v. phr.* To hasten. "He *hotfooted* it home." **1909** "Clivette" *Café Cackle* 31: By the time you "hot-foot" it back the coffee is cold. **1913** in Butterfield *Post Treasury* 152: They cut the telephone wire and...hot-footed back to town. **1916** in Hall & Niles *One Man's War* 214: The other [German plane] was hotfootin' back to Germany with my comrade on his tail. **1920** Bishop *Marines Have Landed* 133: Say, Joe, where do you suppose that marine was hot-footing it to? **1928** Barry *Holiday* 459: And in the meanwhile what? Hot-foot it around the world with a maid and a dog? **1934–41** in Mellon *Bullwhip Days* 67: We kept hot-footin' it till we gits ter Chattanooga. **1941** Epstein *Bride* (film): It's a cinch her pop will come hot-footin' in here. **1954** Armstrong *Satchmo* 39: The boys would hot foot back to the home when they heard the mess call. ***1970** in *OED2:* She hotfoots to Mexico. **1982** *Business Week* (Nov. 8) 54: Sales of Brazil's Hipoppatamus high-fashion shoes have hotfooted from $3.5 million in 1980 to more than $40 million this year.

2.a. to drive or chase away.

1915–16 Lait *Beef, Iron & Wine* 113: They's a lot o' smart suckers what kicks us an' hotfoots us every time we stops to rest. **1916** Livingston *Snare* 16: We roughly routed them from their hiding places and then hot-footed them to the boundaries of the village. **1927** in Dundes *Mother Wit* 200: Yes, boy, but suppose des white folks hot-foot you off des cars?

b. to dispatch urgently.

1926 Norwood *Other Side of Circus* 90: He hot-footed an agent to Liverpool.

hot hand *n.* [fr. HOT, *adj.,* 10.b.] *Basketball.* a period of unusual success in scoring.—usu. constr. with *the.*

1976 *Webster's Sports Dict.* 220: *Hot hand*...The ability to shoot [a basketball] well above one's average for a relatively short period of time. *a***1982** T. Considine *Lang. of Sport* 67: Had a hot hand for the three games he's played....A temporary heightened ability to accomplish or perform a task or activity. (Got the hot hand at picking winners today). **1988** *It's Garry Shandling's Show* (Fox-TV): You had the hot hand. **1993** *NewsHour* (CNN-TV) (Apr. 6): Williams had the hot hand again....He would score seventeen points in the second half.

hot item *n.* a romantically involved couple. Cf. ITEM, 2.

1981 *Daily Beacon* (Univ. Tenn.) (Feb. 26) 2: Friend, hell! We used to be a hot item. *a***1989** Spears *NTC Dict.* 188: Sam and Mary are quite a hot item lately.

Hotlanta *n.* [*hot* + At*lanta*] Atlanta, Georgia.

1975 Dills *CB* (ed. 2) 40: *Hot Lanta:* Atlanta, Georgia. **1976** S. Jones *CB Joke Bk.* (unp.): *Hot Lanta,* the CB name for Atlanta, G.A. **1985** *Maledicta* VIII 266: Atlanta, GA: *Hotlanta.* **1988** Headline News network (July 20): In keeping with the city's nickname of "Hotlanta." **1989** Univ. Tenn. student.: Atlanta is *Hotlanta.* **1994** *Daily Beacon* (Univ. Tenn.) (Aug. 5) 6: The Point, one of Hotlanta's premier venues.

hot line *n.* Orig. *Mil.* a direct telephone or telecommunications connection. Now *S.E.* [The derivative sense 'a tele-

phone number to be dialed for special information, as in an emergency' has always been S.E.]

1955 (cited in *W10*). **1956** Lasly *Turn Tigers Loose* 129 [ref. to Korean War]: The Old Man...was wanted on the "hot" line from Fifth Air Force. **1956** Heflin *USAF Dict.* 256: *Hot line.* A communication channel providing instantaneous communication without switching. **1957** Berkeley *Deadly Mantis* (film): I've got CONAD on the hot line, Colonel. **1962** *Newsweek* (Nov. 5) 30: Now the Pentagon kept hot lines open to the Strategic Air Command, the Air Defense Command, combat-ready divisions, and the U.S. Navy. **1964** *Newsweek* (July 27) 21: Then Barry picked up the "hot line" phone to his...Cow Palace command post. **1964** J. Lucas *Dateline* 97: Kelly had a hot-line phone by his bunk, and he answered personally. *a***1967** Bombeck *Wit's End* 148: She is buzzing the "hot line" to her president every two days. **1968** Safire *New Language of Politics* 193: *Hot line:* direct teletype link between world leaders, designed to prevent "accidental war." **1970** Grocery store mgr., N.Y.C.: The boss is on the hot line! **1971** *N.Y. Times Mag.* (Feb. 21) 67: The popularity of the "hot line" [emergency counselling service for drug addicts] has grown tremendously in the past few years, and by now there are probably hundreds of them in large and small communities across the country, supported by school systems, religious groups, [etc.]. **1971** *Drug Forum* I 49: Incidentally, there was a red telephone ("hot line") in the exhibit which the Ask Me staff used to call a center near the student's home to arrange for a first-step meeting. **1978** R. Rogers *Insiders* 47: It was the direct "hot line" from Howard Hansen's office.

hot-lips *n.* a person noted for passionate kissing.—usu. used as a nickname. *Joc.*

1924 *DN* V 270: Hot lips. **1929** in J. Katz *Gay Amer. Hist.* 72: Hot Lips. **1938** Mast *Bringing Up Baby* 230: Do you mind if I say goodbye to hot-lips before I go? **1945** Drake & Cayton *Black Metropolis* 719: "Hot Lips," twenty-five years of age and a native of St. Louis, burst out defiantly: "I bet all the colored folks was afraid to walk around." **1968** "R. Hooker" *M*A*S*H* 105: Stop these beasts...from addressing me as Hot-Lips. **1995** Spot ad for tabloid TV show (CBS-TV) (Sept. 12): Hollywood's Hot Lips on "Kissin' and Tellin'"!

hot load *n.* a high-power or explosive cartridge for a firearm.

1975 *Police Story* (NBC-TV): And you're the great white hunters with hollow-points and hot loads!...You were using hot loads, Armstrong. **1976** G. Kirkham *Signal Zero* 122: I hear Angie's got you carrying hot loads and wearing a vest. **1979** *TriQuarterly* (Spring) 302: They might as well have shot him...with a hot load. **1991** Marcinko & Weisberg *Rogue Warrior* 4: Hollow-point...hot loads that could...blow a man's head off.

hot-lot *v.* to rush; hasten.—constr. with *it.*

1972 Grogan *Ringolevio* 207: Two police patrol cars came hotlotting it up to the front of the house.

hot mamma *n. Navy.* HOT PAPA.

1959 Searls *Big X* 239: Behind their armored plate the fueling crew loitered, four of them swathed in the asbestos "hot mamma" suits they used to handle the vicious liquid oxygen, the rest in white Norco overalls.

hot member *n.* a lively, attractive, or passionate person; (see also 1916 quot.).

1896 Ade *Artie* 9: "Oh, but they was hot members! **1897** Ade *Pink Marsh* 133 "Little ol' Miss Lo'ena's [a] hot membeh" [*i.e.,* a pretty girl]. **1916** Cary *Venery* I 145 *Hot Member*—(1) a harlot; (2) a whore-monger...; and (3) the penis.

hot minute *n.* a moment.

1932 R. Fisher *Conjure-Man* 263: Can you give the law a hot minute? **1946** Mezzrow & Wolfe *Really Blues* 88: The muta made him fly right for a hot minute. **1977** Bunker *Animal Factory* 134: Man, you're goin' to the streets in a hot minute. *Ibid.* 180: Naturally they got busted in a hot minute when they started running amok outside. **1978** Sopher & McGregor *Up from Walking Dead* 61: For a hot minute it looked as though I was going to be [released]. **1984** Cameron & Hurd *Terminator* (film): I'll have a [police] car there in a hot minute.

hot number *n.* Orig. *Stu.* a lively or superior person; (specif., now *solely*) a sexy or sexually passionate person, esp. a young woman; (*also*) such a person's telephone number, esp. as written on the wall of a phone booth. Cf. NUMBER, *n.*

1896 in A. Charters *Ragtime Songbk.* 55: Say gal, you're sure a red hot number. **1919** *DN* V 70: *Hot number*, used [ironically] as a term of disgust [for a person]. New Mexico. **1929** Perelman *Ginsbergh* 186: And to think of some of the hot numbers that I've turned away on account of you! **1930** in *AS* (Feb. 1931) 204: *Hot number*: an up-to-date co-ed. **1942** *ATS* 755: *Hot number*, a young woman's telephone number. **1942** in Cheever *Letters* 84: A hot number in an evening gown singing "White Christmas." **1968** Standish *Non-Stand. Terms* 6: A gentleman walks into a House of ill repute whereupon he meets the madam. He states that he would like a real hot number tonight. **1972** B. Harrison *Hospital* 48: Nick also found time for himself, and for the neighborhood girls—the good girls and the girls they called hot numbers. **1991** (quot. at HARDBODY).

hot nuts *n.pl.* (esp. of a man) urgent sexual desire; (*hence*) wild eagerness.—usu. considered vulgar.

   *ca***1935** in Barkley *Sex Cartoons* 65: I knew the old bastard had hot nuts. *ca***1939** "M. Hunt" *Vulnerable* 155: He had "hot nuts." **1942** *ATS* 340: Passion; lust...*hot nuts*. **1945–48** *Marianas Coll.* (unp.): He was afraid that he would get hot nuts and try to fuck her. **1952** Kerouac *Cody* 206: I was all hot nuts to get to L.A. **1962** Killens *Heard the Thunder* 338: Man, her sister is prettier than she is, and she really got hot nuts for you. **1970** Southern *Blue Movie* 158: He's got hot nuts for you, kid. **1980** Kotzwinkle *Jack* 82: Fuckface has hot nuts.

hot oil *n.* a predicament; HOT WATER.

   1960–69 Runkel *Law* 268: Well, how are you? Good enough considerin' the hot oil I'm in.

hot pants *n.* **1.a.** strong sexual desire.

   1929 McEvoy *Hollywood Girl* 36: A sensational secret diary...all perfume and hot pants. **1934** O'Hara *Appt. in Samarra* ch. vi: I gotta...get up there and give these butter and egg men hot pants. **1934** (quot. at PETE). **1935** J. Conroy *World to Win* 210: She's got hot pants and she likes the way you handle it. **1936** Steinbeck *In Dubious Battle* 75: Every time the sun shines on my back all afternoon I get hot pants. **1937** Weidman *Wholesale* 208: Yet there I'd be...with my hot pants to remind me that I wasn't dreaming. **1940** Zinberg *Walk Hard* 74: I can always tell when I get hot pants—all the dames look prettier. **1942** H. Miller *Roofs of Paris* 218: The mother must have hot pants too. **1945** in Inman *Diary* 1250: She doesn't know what self-discipline is....And she has hot pants. *a***1952** M. Wolff *Back of Town* 300: You this hard up for a man, or you got a special case of hot pants just for me? **1953** Paley *Rumble* 17: He's ripe, Jimmy—soused and hot pants. **1954** Chessman *Cell 2455* 95: A sexy bitch, with hot pants. **1955** in Marx *Groucho Letters* 250: I had hot pants for a girl named Pearl. **1966** Shepard *Doom Pussy* 87: Seems she's giving *you* a harrowing dose of hot pants. **1973** Wideman *Lynchers* 37: She got hot pants behind that action I put on her. **1978** Wharton *Birdy* 11: She really had hot pants for you, buddy.

b. excessive eagerness.

   1966 Brunner *Face of Night* 212: You figure it's Richards, that's why you got hot pants. **1977** *Time* (May 30) 42: Americans...are too eager. We have hot pants for an agreement.

2. a woman who is excessively lustful for sexual activity.

   [**1931** in Goodstone *Pulps* 135: Know what they used to call me at school...? "Little Hot Rompers"—I went for the boys in such generous style.] **1938** R. Chandler *Big Sleep* 51: That goddamned little hot pants! **1951** Willingham *Gates of Hell* 163: Your wife is nothing but a little hot-pants. *****1966** in *OED2*. **1968** *Playboy* (July) 20: He...seduces a luscious hot-pants.

3. Orig. *Fashion Industry.* very brief shorts marketed for women beginning in 1970. Now *S.E.*

   1970 in *OED2*: As for hot pants, we haven't seen anything in the market....They're going to have to be styled very imaginatively. **1971** *N.Y. Post* (Feb. 16) 79: Hope also remembered when hot pants, now a fashion thing, was unmentionable in polite society, which was not so many years ago, come to think of it. **1971** W. Murray *Dream Girls* 123: Hef's steady girl, a pixie in hot pants. **1977** S. Gaines *Discotheque* 147: Two black girls in hot pants and high heels.

hot-pants *adj.* excessively eager for sexual activity.—usu. used prenominally.

   1927 Nicholson *Barker* 112: When you had him all hot-pants you married him. **1942** *ATS* 341: Passionate; amative; lustful...*hot-pants*

[adj.]. **1953** Brossard *Bold Saboteurs* 215: Herr Goering himself was one of her flush-faced, hot-pants victims. **1956** Ross *Hustlers* 124: You crazy hot-pants bastard, you. **1967** "M.T. Knight" *Terrible Ten* 146: There's plenty of hookers and hot-pants tourists. **1967** Talbot *Chatty Jones* 89: Oh, maybe Chatty's a hot-pants kid who'd get a bang out of some heavy necking.

hot papa *n. USMC & Naval Av.* (see 1956 quot.).

   1933 Stewart *Airman Speech* 106: *Hot Papa.* A sailor, part of the rescue squad on an aircraft carrier, encased in an asbestos suit so that he can work close to burning planes. **1951** Morison *Naval Ops. in WWII* VII xxxvii: Immediately the craft is surrounded by a swarm of men led by asbestos-clad characters who look like old-fashioned teddybears; these are the fire-fighters, known as the "hot papas." **1956** Heflin *USAF Dict.* 256: *Hot papa.* An asbestos-clothed crew member on an aircraft carrier whose duty is rescuing persons from any burning aircraft on the carrier's flight deck. **1966** Noel & Bush *Naval Terms* 180: *Hot poppa*: Man wearing asbestos suit trained to rescue crews of burning aircraft.

hot patootie *n.* [alter. of HOT POTATO] HOT POTATO, 1 (*obs.*); (*also*) a vigorous and attractive young woman. Cf. PATOOTIE.

   1919 *Lit. Digest* (Mar. 8) 59: "The Colonel?" chuckles a dusky dough-boy..."Some hot patootie!"...Sez he, "We're goin' through these or hell—we don't come back" "Some hot patootie!" **1927** in *AS* (Feb. 1928) 259: What do we call our women of today?..."hot patootie,"..."sweet mama." *ca***1929** *Hot Patootie Wedding Night* [song title] (cited in J. Burton *Blue Book of Broadway Musicals*) (Tamony Coll.). **1935** *Nation* (May 15) 562: He calls the object of his affection a "hot patootie." **1941** H.A. Smith *Low Man* 160: Lupe Velez, the hot patootie. **1970** *Playboy* (Aug.) 162: Hey, hot patootie, let's you and me take a little spin on the dance floor. **1978** *M*A*S*H* (CBS-TV): Your Major Houlihan is one hot patootie.

hot-pillow *adj.* being or relating to an establishment that rents cheap rooms for very short periods, as to prostitutes, adulterous lovers, etc.—used prenominally.

   1954 Collans & Sterling *House Detect.* 219: *Hot-pillow House.* Cheap hotel which rents a room several times a night. **1963** Boyle *Yanks Don't Cry* 10: Most of the old time sergeants had a vocabulary spiced heavily with earthy, four-letter words, and their idea of a good time was grabbing a case of beer and heading for the nearest hot pillow joint. **1967** Talbot *Chatty Jones* 5: Just let the meeting with Chatty take place in a hot-pillow joint or maybe in a lovers' lane. **1982** L. Block *Eight Million Ways* 192: I don't mean a hot-pillow joint, I mean a decent hotel. **1984** WINS radio news (Dec. 20): The landlords were turning the buildings into hot-pillow joints with two-hour rates. **1986** *Smithsonian* (Mar.) 134: The motel as a locale for sin was a standard part of its image. This side of the business was called "hot pillow" or "Mr. and Mrs. Jones trade." **1986** R. Campbell *In La-La Land* 160: In some hot pillow joint...fifty bucks bought the works.

hot place *n.* hell.—constr. with *the*.

   1839 *Spirit of Times* (Dec. 21) 498: He can out-pull any kivering horse this side of the hot place. **1921** in *DARE*: To the hot place with your city,/ Where they herd like frightened rats. **1936** Kenyon & Daves *Petrified Forest* (film): He doesn't give a hoot in the hot place about me. **1942** *ATS* 322: Hell...*hot place.* **1960, 1965–70** in *DARE*.

hotpot *n. Black E.* (see quot.).

   1929 T. Gordon *Born to Be* 100: She told me that the authors of *Didn't He Ramble* stole the theme from the sweetbacks and hotpots of Chicago....A sugar-man came in and demanded money from his hotpot to gamble with. *Ibid.* 236: *Hotpot*: A lewd woman.

hot potato *n.* **1.** a person who is energetic, clever, self-assured, or the like. Cf. HOT PATOOTIE.

   1887 Call *Josh Hayseed* 62: Don't you think I'm a greenhorn...becuz if you do you'll find me a plaguey hot pertater to handle. **1899** A.H. Lewis *Sandburrs* 63: It was to be a corker; for the McSweens were hot potatoes and rolled high. **1901** Ade *Modern Fables* 181: I have told myself...that I was a fairly Hot Potato, but if any one asked me to define Algebra, I couldn't make a sound. **1902–03** Ade *People You Know* 29: When I have taken my Degree then I will be the human *It*. My scholarly Attainments and polished Manner will get me...into the Inner Circle of Hot Potatoes. **1942** A.C. Johnston *Courtship of A. Hardy* (film): If he's such a hot potato himself he'll probably show up wearing his shirts. **1990** McDonalds, TV ad: You are one hot potato!

2. [sugg. by colloq. phr. *to drop (something or someone) like a hot potato*] a difficult, embarrassing, or controversial task or subject; (*also*) an unwanted person. Now *colloq.*

1950 in *DAS:* Everyone can see how the boss looks when he handles a hot potato. **1952** M. McCarthy *Academe* 257: It was a very hot potato…I chose to ignore the question. **1968** C. Victor *Sky Burned* 14: This was all his baby. The hot potato was all his. **1978** Shem *House of God* 382: Guilt's a hot potato—whoever holds onto it gets burned. **1979** F. Thomas *Golden Bird* 150: As our American cousins might say—we have a hot potato here. **1979** in Terkel *Amer. Dreams* 244: This is a hot potato. **1993** A. Adams & W. Stadiem *Madam* 210: You'll have a big life, but you're a hot potato now.

hot prowl *n.* [fr. HOT, *adj.*, 3.a.] *Und. & Police.* a housebreaking or burglary conducted while occupants are on the premises.

1933 Ersine *Prison Slang* 45: Hot prowl. The prowling of a house while the occupants are awake. **1965** Kastle *Hot Prowl* [title]. **1972** Wambaugh *Blue Knight* 25: I'd rather catch a hot-prowl guy than a stickup man any day. And any burglar with balls enough to take a pad when the people are home is every bit as dangerous as a stickup man. **1994** *L.A. Times* (Dec. 19) B8: Examples of "Copspeak"…Hot prowl—a prowler in an occupied home.

hot puppy *interj.* HOT DOG. Also **hot puppies.**

1924 *DN* V 270: Hot pup,—puppie ([indicates] joy). **1969** Beard & Kenney *Bored of Rings* 23: Swell!…Hot puppies, *grub!*

hot-rack *v. Navy.* (see quot.); HOT-BUNK.

1995 Former Navy submariner, Knoxville, Tenn. [ref. to 1982–84]: Hot rack, a verb: sharing beds on a sub, usually according to a schedule that allows one at a time, also [with reference to] homosexuality.

hot rail *n. & interj.* (*Hobo.*) (see quots.).

1938 *AS* XIII 70: Hotrail. "A train is coming; clear the track!" **1982** D.A. Harper *Good Company* 105: A hot rail…[is a] train comin' down the track. When it's in sight you call it a "hot rail."…It's dyin' out.

hot rock *n.* [prob. sugg. by HOT ROCKS] **1.** Orig. *Mil. Av.* an aggressive and proficient pilot; (*also*) a brash or conceited fellow; HOTSHOT.

1945 *Yank* (Aug. 10) 9: Major Bong and several other hot rocks. **1945** Hamann *Air Words* 31: Hot rock (1) A flyer who brags. (2) A flyer who can fly well and doesn't make any bones about it. **1945** in *AS* (Dec. 1946) 310: Hot rock. A show-off pilot. **1952** Sperling & Sherdeman *Retreat, Hell!* (film): Tell me, hot rock, just what are you trying to prove? **1954** *AS* XXIX 237: My first contact with *hot rock* was in the AAF in 1942, where the term was in wide use.…[It] indicates real excellence. **1956** Heflin *USAF Dict.* 256: Hot rock. In *slang* usage. 1. A hot pilot. 2. A skillful, industrious person. **1963** Breen *PT109* (film): Another hot rock. **1965** Harvey *Hudasky's Raiders* 28: Some hot rock who can fly upside down under a bridge while licking his ice cream cone. **1978** E. Thompson *Devil to Pay* 192: I've got a drawer full of applications from hot-rocks out of journalism schools looking for a job. **1985** Boyne & Thompson *Wild Blue* 164: Your husband is…a hot rock in the best outfit there is. *a***1991** Ethell & Sand *Fighter Command* 14: This hot rock shows real fighter pilot savoir faire.

2. a high-performance vehicle. Cf. HOT ROD, 1.

1954 Coleman *Relativity* 47: If the father tells him to keep his hot rock under 1000 miles an hour, the boy might reply…"Relative to what, Daddy?"

3. a strong desire. Cf. HOT ROCKS, 1.

1968 E.M. Parsons *Fargo* 31: You been talkin' it around you got a hotrock to take Judson's place.

hot-rock *adj.* Orig. *Mil. Av.* proficient and aggressive; (*also*) flashy or conceited.

1948 Lay & Bartlett *12 O'Clock High* 17 [ref. to WWII]: He's only acting C.O. until some hot-rock general from the Pentagon shows up. **1958** H. Ellison *Deadly Streets* 123: I make ya into a hot-rock bunch, an' ya got more jack in ya pocket than now. **1958** D. Stanford *Ski Town* 20: Now *there* goes a real hotrock skier!

hot rocks *n.pl.* [*hot* + ROCKS 'testicles'] **1.** (esp. of a man) strong sexual desire.—usu. considered vulgar. [Prob. the orig. sense.]

1947–51 Motley *We Fished All Night* 168: I've got hot rocks.…Let's

get layed. **1962** Quirk *Red Ribbons* 14: "This simple tool's Hot Rock Bennett."…"I didn't get the name flying. I've got hot rocks." [**1980** Manchester *Darkness* 393 [ref. to 1945]: [Mt.] Suribachi [was] prophetically encoded "Hotrocks."] **1982** Eells & Musgrove *Mae West* 111 [ref. to 1930's]: I said to her, "…You got hot rocks for some joker. It didn't work out."

2. *Stu.* something or someone that is wonderful or exciting. Also as adj.

1928 Carr *Rampant Age* 10: Snoot Hartman says she's the ole hot rocks. *Ibid.* 26: Thought you was the big shieks [*sic*] who was gonna see the hot-rocks bags [girls] over to Linville tonight? *Ibid.* 28: He…muttered that cryptic phrase of approbation, "Hot rocks!" *Ibid.* 32: It's the hot rocks inside, all right. *Ibid.* 82: Gee, wasn't that hot rocks the way that guy in the pitcher show jumped off that bridge and landed in that row boat?

3. HOTSHOT.—used derisively in direct address.

1950 Bissell *Stretch on the River* 115: Listen, hotrocks,…whadda you think we're doing out there, playing duck on a rock? **1952** Haines & Krims *One Minute to Zero* (film): All right, hot rocks, let's get with it.

hot rod *n.* **1.a.** a car whose engine has been modified or replaced for increased speed and whose chassis and body are often radically altered. Now *S.E.*

1945 *Life* (Nov. 5) 87: A "hot rod," also called a "hot iron," or a "hop-up" or "gow job," is an automobile stripped for speed and pepped up for power until it can travel 90 to 125 mph. **1946** *Sat. Eve. Post* (Sept. 14) 14: A hot rod is a hopped-up…flivver used by teenagers to terrify parents and frustrate the police. **1949** R. Smith *Big Wheel* (film): Wanna buy yourself a hot rod? **1950** *Life* (July 10) 20: Either these pilots were hot-rod jockies with jets, or else we Americans were again directly involved in…war. **1953** Felsen *Street Rod* 30: You don't call this a hot rod, do you? Man, it's more like a warm stick. **1954** *AS* (May) 89: [In] the late 1920s,…building "hot rods" first became popular. **1972** Hall & Nordby *Individual & Dreams* 151: In another dream, the dreamer was speeding in a "hot rod" to a racetrack when he was stopped by the police. **1974** *Black World* (Nov.) 55: The hot rod had come to a screeching freeze in the…intersection. **1986** Oddo *Street Rod Hndbk.* 7: Southern Ascot race track,…in Los Angeles, decided to run stock bodied "hot roadsters" one Sunday a month beginning in May 1939. The advertising of such events led to the term *hot rod*.…By the end of World War II, *hot rod* was used to describe any old car owned by a young person and modified for greater speed.

b. *Av.* a high-performance aircraft, esp. a single-seat jet fighter; in phr. **Heinemann's hot rod** [see 1962 quot.] the Douglas A-4 Skyhawk.

1959 R.L. Scott *Tiger in Sky* 105: He should have been thinking of leaving the flying of the aerial hot-rods to the fuzzy-faced lieutenants. **1962** Harvey *Strike Command* 155: The Douglas A-4-D Skyhawk…designed by…Ed Heineman…was…once known as "Heinemann's Hot Rod."…So small is the Hot Rod that its pilots are known as "Tinker Toy drivers." **1985** Boyne & Thompson *Wild Blue* 133: Did you ever look at the front end of these little hot rods? **1986** Zeybel *First Ace* 97: We had the F-86 Sabre, a real hot rod, built primarily for air superiority. **1989** T. Holmes *Fallon* 23: The uprated…engine gives "Heinemann's hot rod" an even hotter performance. **1990** Lightbody & Poyer *Complete Top Gun* 116: The "Hot Rod," as the A-4 was quickly nicknamed.

2. an aggressive, flashy, or undisciplined young fellow, now usu. the driver of a hot rod; HOTSHOT. [The sense of the 1947–53 quot. is frankly sexual.]

[**1942** *ATS* 427: Gunman…*hot rod*.] **1951** *New Yorker* (Sept. 8) 81: Guy your age gets ahold of one of these cans and right away he thinks he's a hot-rod. **1947–53** Guthrie *Seeds* 103: Now, how do you like this for a bed, Sir Longpole Guthrie? Sir Hotrod? **1953** J.L. Mahin *Mogambo* (film): You're turning into the original African hotrod. **1955** Reifer *New Words* 102: Hot rod.…By extension, any aggressive and undisciplined male adolescent. **1958** Landau *Violent Road* (film): Look, hot rod, what you tryin' to prove? **1959** Searls *Big X* 39: There's nothing worse than a hot-rod test pilot who thinks he's an engineer. **1973** in H.S. Thompson *Shark Hunt* 290: The New York Times…called in hotrods from its bureaus all over the country to overcome the Post's early lead. **1984** Knoxville, Tenn., waitress, age *ca*60:

And what can I bring you, hotrod? **1989** G.C. Wilson *Mud Soldiers* 176: The roof hatch was closed and a hot-rod was driving up front.

hot-rod *adj.* energetic, aggressive, proficient, etc.—used prenominally.

    1954 *Looney Tunes* (animation): Dese hot-rod kids! **1971** Mayer *Weary Falcon* 69: And these are supposed to be hot rod troops by Vietnamese standards.

hot-roll *n. West.* a bedroll.

    1907 McDermott-Stevenson *Lariat Letters* 34: I half wished I'd brought my hot roll along when it came to bunkin'. **1932** in Botkin *Treas. Amer. Folk.* 509 [ref. to 1891]: We crawled into our "hot-rolls." **1933** *AS* (Feb.) 29: Hot-Roll. A roll of camp bedding. **1933** J.V. Allen *Cowboy Lore* 7: Every cowboy furnishes his own…bedding, known as "hot roll."

hot roller *n. Police.* a moving vehicle that has been stolen.

    1972 J. Pearl *Cops* 13: He had spotted the "hot roller" in a stream of Sunday traffic. **1994** *L.A. Times* (Dec. 19) B8: Examples of "Cops-peak"…Hot roller—stolen car on the move.

hots *n.pl.* sexual desire; (*hence*) excessive desire of any sort.—constr. with *the*.

    1947 in *DAS*: I'd never get the deep undying hots for that rah-rah collitch [boy]. **1951** W.H. Auden, in *OED2*: George…has the hots for Jack. **1956** Holiday & Dufty *Lady Sings* 87: These poor bitches grow up hating their mothers and having the hots for their fathers. **1957** M. Shulman *Rally* 190: You ain't in love with Angela.…You just got a case of the hots. **1958** Gilbert *Vice Trap* 58: Where's this scam bank your friend's got the hots for? **1960** Sire *Deathmakers* 177: There's this gorgeous babe, see, that I got the hots for. **1961** Terry *Old Liberty* 69: They had the secret hots for one another. **1962** Quirk *Red Ribbons* 236: That girl's got the hots for you. **1963** Boyle *Yanks Don't Cry* 57: "She's probably got the hots for me," Lashio answered. "Just look at her stare!" **1966** Moran *Faster, Pussycat* (film): You really do have the hots for the long green. **1970** *Playboy* (Nov.) 248: She had a serious case of the hots for Brewster. **1973** Gwaltney *Destiny's Chickens* 125: He's one of them that's got their hots for this guy Tay Hogg. *a***1977** M. French *Women's Room* 65: She found some guy with the hots for her…and screwed him. **1981** *L.A. Times* (June 1) VI 8: He has the hots for sultry singer Lane Ballou. **1996** *Jenny Jones Show* (synd. TV series): Surprise! I've got the *hots* for you.

hot seat /ˈhɑtˌsit/ *n.* **1.** *Pris.* an electric chair; (*hence*) death by electrocution.

    1925 *Sat. Eve. Post* (Aug. 29) 18: A newspaper reporter said he heard the lad announce that he was not afraid to die "in the hot seat." **1926** Finerty *Criminalese* 29: Hot seat—Electric chair. **1928** Lawes *Life & Death* 166: Their accomplices…would also get the "hot seat." **1930** E. Caldwell *Poor Fool* 126: They had you all set for the hot-seat. **1944** C.B. Davis *Leo McGuire* 198: It isn't going to be touched until your trial is over and you're on the way to the hot seat. **1946** Petry *Street* 271: He gives up his life in the hot seat. **1947** Grant, Rinaldo & Lees *Buck Privates* (film): The electric chair. That's the hot seat. **1962** Perry *Young Man Drowning* 72: I don't want to sit in the hot-seat for a forty-buck haul. **1971** Cameron *First Blood* 85: It wouldda meant the hot seat! **1992** G. Wolff *Day at the Beach* 214: I felt like a death-row prisoner strapped in the hot seat.

2. an actual or figurative seat that is a position of embarrassment, anxiety, great responsibility, or the like; (*esp.*) a state of being under close questioning or scrutiny.

    1935 Pollock *Und. Speaks*: Hot seat…the next convict seated on a bench waiting to appear before the prison board. [**1938** M. Brooks et al. *Radio City Revels* (film): Brother, let me get off this hot seat!] **1942** *Time* (Apr. 6) 49: We are an entire nation of people who are trying to wage a war and everyone is trying, himself, to keep out of the hot seat. **1951** in Paxton *Sport* 399: A year ago I was occupying a hot seat as the coach of a football team that was supposed to win its conference championship. **1953** Wicker *Kingpin* 65: You get off one hot seat onto another. **1966** King *Brave & Damned* 160: What the hell do you want us to do? We're on a hot seat. **1968** in E. Knight *Belly Song* 14: Then the second man was called to sit in the "Hot Seat" [before going into the office of the parole board]. **1973** in *Submission of Pres. Convers.* 80: At present I hesitate to send Stans. They would give him a hot seat.

1977 in Newbold *Black Preaching* 45: Some doctors of the law and Pharisees sought to put Jesus on the "hot seat." **1981** *U.S. News & W.R.* (Apr. 27) 13: With Congress about to start writing a tax-cut bill, the man in the hot seat is Treasury Secretary Donald Regan. **1995** *Montel Williams Show* (synd. TV series): We got Montel's posse up here in the hot seats. **1995** *Good Morning America* (ABC-TV) (Apr. 20): You have been in the hot seat for the past couple of weeks.

3. *Mil. Av.* an ejection seat.

    1950 *Nat. Geographic* (Sept.) 311: "Hot seat"…refers to the ejection seat, used in jet fighters. **1955** *AS* XXX (May) 118: Hot Seat, n. phr. Pilot ejection seat. **1955** Reifer *New Words* 102: Hot seat. Air Force *Slang*. A device which forcibly expels a pilot from a jet plane.

4. (see quot.).

    1976 T. Walker *Ft. Apache* 152: The "hot seat"…is a device connecting the five passenger seats of the cab with the meter. If you weigh 20 pounds or more and sit on that seat for approximately 15 seconds, the meter flicks on.

hot session *n.* an exciting time; (*specif.*) (see *a*1961 quot.).

    1931 Rouverol *Dance, Fools, Dance* (film): Oh boy, wasn't that a hot session down there at the garage? *a***1961** Partridge *DSUE* (ed. 5) 1138: Hot session. Coïtion: since *ca*1920.

hot sheet *n.* **1.** *Police.* an official list of stolen automobiles or other stolen items; (*also*) an official list of crimes being investigated.

    1926 Finerty *Criminalese* 29: Hot sheet—Record of stolen autos. **1949** "R. MacDonald" *Moving Target* 64: What does the hot sheet say? **1970** *Adam-12* (NBC-TV): It's not on the hot sheet. **1970** Wambaugh *Centurions* 292: Dugan…was driving slowly checking license numbers against the hot sheet. **1974** Kurtzman *Bobby* 120: Everytime you use a card…you go in before and check their hot sheet to see if the person's got on it yet. **1983** "J. Cain" *Dinky-Dau* 75: Another day and he'd be on the hot sheets as a deserter.

2. a bedsheet used in a HOT-SHEET establishment.

    1970 Sargent *Walk the Line* (film): Whatcha need's a place around here with hot sheets.

hot-sheet *adj.* HOT-PILLOW.

    1952 Lait & Mortimer *USA* 42: There are motels that do not go in for the hot sheet trade. **1965** Longstreet *Sportin' House* 94: Whore houses, hot sheet hotels (rented by the hour) [etc.]. **1982** L. Block *Eight Million Ways* 228: They get cheaters, the hot-sheet trade, take a room for two hours. **1989** S. Robinson & D. Ritz *Smokey* 94: A quick night at a hot-sheet motel in Detroit. **1990** *Flash* (CBS-TV): You taught me a real lesson when you zoomed into that hot-sheet hotel.

hot shit *n.* **1.** HOT STUFF, 3.—usu. considered vulgar. Cf. HOT SPIT. [The remarkably early 1895 quot. is potentially a euphem. for this term; the 1959 quot. is clearly euphem.]

    [**1895** Gore *Stu. Slang* 20: Hot-slop…Same as…hot-stuff.…"How do you like your new instructor?" "He's hot-stuff."] **1959** Morrill *Dark Sea* 47 [ref. to WWII]: "You're hot crap, Joe," one of them said. **1954–60** *DAS*: He thinks he's hot shit.…*mainly student and young adult use.* **1969** C. Brown *Mr. Jiveass* 123: Everybody thought that was hot shit. But it ain't nothing and you know that. **1971** "R. Stark" *Lemons* 18: He was supposed to be such hot shit down there in Texas. **1971** in *Rolling Stone Interviews* 458: Lookit these big shots, they think they're such hot shit. **1972** N.Y.U. student [ref. to early 1960's]: When we were kids we used to say, "You think you're hot shit but you're just lukewarm diarrhea." **1972** A.K. Shulman *Ex-Prom Queen* 56: You don't seem to care who you step on to be a guy. You think you're pretty hot shit. **1974** C.W. Smith *Country Music* 258: Thinking I'm hot shit on a stick with my car because these guys are seniors and I'm just a sophomore. **1974** Loken *Come Monday Mornin'* 73: He really thought he was hot shit till he fumbled the first hand-off he had a crack at. **1975** Keane *Maximus Zone* 28: When I was a kid about your age, I thought I was hot shit. **1978** Pilcer *Teen Angel* 99: You think you're hot shit on a silver platter. **1980** in *Penthouse* (Jan. 1981) 164: She…probably thought drinking cocktails on a patio was hot shit.

2. a brash, self-assured person; HOTSHOT, 1.b.—usu. considered vulgar.

    1968 Cuomo *Thieves* 226: Mainly to give them enough chances to congratulate each other all the time on what hot shits they were. **1968** A. Hoffman *Revolution* 17: Billy sure was a hot shit in those days. **1972** C. Gaines *Stay Hungry* 72: You think you can catch big ones, hot shit? **1977** Langone *Life at Bottom* 200: And she was a hot shit, I'll tell you, about forty and she knew all the angles. *a***1981** in S. King *Bachman* 553: Then they had a big party and some hot-shit cut a ribbon. **1982** D.A. Harper *Good Company* 130: You got to let the people see you like you're a hot shit. **1983** W. Walker *Dime to Dance* 245: Here you were, the big hot shit in high school while I was just another nobody. **1986** Stinson & Carabatsos *Heartbreak* 8: Show some maturity, hot-shit, some dignity. **1978–89** in Jankowski *Islands in Street* 255: He wants to be some hot shit like governor.

hot-shit *adj.* **1.** splendid or exciting.—often used ironically.—usu. considered vulgar.

> **1962** in *AS* (Oct. 1963) 173: Most superlative…*hot shit.* **1965** Linakis *In Spring* 81 [ref. to WWII]: Be hot shit if I really couldn't remember afterwards. **1970** Quammen *Walk the Line* 201: It's a fuckin' hot-shit town. **1970** W.C. Woods *Killing Zone* 177: I thought you were such a hot-shit computer man. **1977** S. Gaines *Discotheque* 14: To be in that famous TV commercial…was a hot shit thing for Dick and Annie. **1978** C. Miller *Animal House* 94: She was the hottest shit woman he'd ever met. **1979** Gram *Blvd. Nights* 152: And fuck your hot-shit job. **1989** *Newsweek* (June 19) 62: We can…get a hot-s— guitar player.

2.a. offensively self-assured; conceited; HOTSHOT, 1.b.—usu. considered vulgar.

> **1970** Thackrey *Thief* 379: You know, the hot-shit parole officer? **1978** W. Wharton *Birdy* 110: He's not being hot-shit or anything, he's just…interested. **1978** Pici *Tennis Hustler* 127: Hot-shit hustler, huh? Where you from? Jersey? **1978** Maupin *Tales* 286: She's got an old man now. A hot-shit celebrity. **1982** W. Wharton *Midnight Clear* 80: Lousy, hot shit Nazis laughing at us. **1982** E. Leonard *Cat Chaser* 165: These guys kill me, all the hot-shit dealers.

b. very keen or enthusiastic.—constr. with *for.*—usu. considered vulgar. Cf. HOT ZIGGETY.

> **1970** Whitmore *Memphis-Nam-Sweden* 87: They were supposed to be hot shit for the Army.

hot shit *interj.* (used to express excitement or enthusiasm).—usu. considered vulgar.

> *ca***1940** in Atkinson *Dirty Comics* 169: Hot shit! There's Carole Bombard! **1962** in Rosset *Evergreen Reader* 478: I dig you, *Deep*, dad, all the way! Hot shit! **1963–64** Kesey *Great Notion* 352: Haw…haw…hot *shit*! **1964** Faust *Steagle* 114: "Hot shit," Mendy squealing, "a sangwich." **1965** Pollini *Glover* 93: Man in orbit. Hot shit. **1966** Cassiday *Angels Ten* 239 [ref. to WWII]: Hot shit! Look at that son of a bitch burn! **1973** P. Benchley *Jaws* 301: Brody now felt ebullient, gleeful, relieved.…He yelled, "Hot shit!" **1967–79** in S. King *Bachman Bks.* 216: "Hot shit," Gerraty said.

hot shoe *n.* *Drag Racing.* a successful or flashy racing car driver.—also used attrib.

> **1962** G. Olson *Roaring Road* 30: Wait'll the hot shoes get a look at the car.…the hero drivers. *Ibid.* 31: National dirt track champion…a real hot shoe back in the old days. **1976** *Webster's Sports Dict.* 221: *Hot shoe*…a top driver. **1980** Pearl *Pop. Slang* 74: *Hot shoe* (Auto Racing) an excellent racing driver. **1988** *Comic Strip* (WKCH-TV): Moose the Loose is one hot shoe. **1994** *CBS This Morning* (CBS-TV)(Sept. 2): Both are real hot-shoe drivers.

hotshot *n.* [sugg. by S.E. *hot shot* 'a bullet or piece of shot that is hot from firing'] **1.** [a. *Mil.* a hot-tempered, undisciplined fellow; a troublemaker. [Not attested in U.S., but prob. related to other senses below.]

> ***1600** in J. Marston *Plays* 208: By gor me am a hot shot. ***1604** in J. Marston *Plays* I 176: Amongst a hundred French-men, fortie hot shottes. ***1659** in Tilley *Dict. Proverbs in England* 328: You are a hot-shot indeed. A speech spoken in slighting derision. [***1678** in Tilley *Dict. Proverbs in England:* He is a hot shot in a mustard pot when both his heels stand right up.] [***1821–26** Stewart *Man-of-War's-Man* II 219: "What a red-hot shot of a fellow, that this Allen must be, surely!—Why, d—n me if he didn't bounce off like a Congreve rocket!"—"Bah!…a saucy, conceited, chitter-chattering fool."]]

b. a brash, often skillful, enterprising, or successful fellow;

a self-important, flashy, or cocky young man or (*later*) woman. [Continuity of usage with **(a)**, above, cannot be assumed; for attrib. use, see HOTSHOT, *adj.*]

> **1927** in Dobie *Tex. & S.W. Lore* 100: Men who are either slow or lazy are given such names as…"Hot Shot"…"Lightning," and "Speedy." **1929** in Mezzrow & Wolfe *Really Blues* 162: Eddie Condon's Hot Shots. **1931** Grant *Gangdom's Doom* 28: Hot shots, ha-ha!…Guess they got cold feet when they saw the Homicide Twins. **1933** Ersine *Pris. Slang* 45: Hot Shot…A flashily dressed person. **1933** *AS* (Oct.) 35: Hot shot. A champion, a leading contender. **1936** R. Chandler, in Ruhm *Detective* 142: Okey, hot shot.…Ceiling zero. See if you can reach it. **1939** Fessier *Wings of Navy* (film): In me you behold…a Navy hotshot. **1941** Schulberg *Sammy* 230: Good old Sammy! He sure was a hot-shot, that Sammy! I always said he'd sock the jackpot, but I sure never thought he'd get his in the movies. **1942** Hollingshead *Elmtown's Youth* 190: He's one of our wise guys. He thinks he's a hotshot. **1943** Farrell *Days of Anger* 95: The Burma girls don't get a chance at two Chicago hot shots like us every day in the week. **1945** Hamann *Air Words: Hot shot*…Anyone who is good at his job. **1953** Peterson *Take a Giant Step* 60: You know—hot shot—you got remarkable powers of persuasion there. **1959** E. Hunter *Matter of Conviction* 71: You're wasting my time, hotshot, and my time is valuable. **1959** Tevis *Hustler* 27: I can't give every hot shot I come heads up with two balls in a bank pool game. **1959** W. Williams *Ada Dallas* 114: I took on extra duties, came up with new ideas. I was the top newscaster in town; I had a weekly program called *Magazine of the Air* on which I fearlessly investigated, sensitively probed, dramatically presented.…I was a real hot-shot. **1960** in Oliver *Conversations* 86: In 19 and 24 at Lambert, Mississippi, a feller found me by the name of Hot Shots and I was playin' at a juke down there. *a***1977** T. Barnett *Golf Is Madness* 71: Old pros [and] young hot-shots. **1979–83** W. Kennedy *Ironweed* 6: Marcus played bridge with the bishop and knew all the Catholic hotshots. Some hotshot ran Saint Agnes Cemetery. **1994** *CBS This Morning* (CBS-TV) (July 19): Loved your interview with Jamie Lee Curtis. What a hotshot!

2. a cutting or sarcastic remark or rejoinder; wisecrack.

> [**1863** in Wightman *To Ft. Fisher* 101: Witticisms flew round like hot shot.] **1894** Gardner *Dr. & Devil* 61: "Hot shot, Doctor," I remarked to myself…"and an admirably aimed one." **1894** in J.M. Carroll *Benteen-Goldin Letters* 227: The hot-shot I threw in protesting against Custer's ugly phiz being shown in front of book, is having its effect. **1898** *Billboard* (Mar.) 12: [Caption over sarcastic letter from reader: Hot Shot]. **1908** W.G. Davenport *Butte & Montana* 85: Hot Shot at Our Rivals. **1928** MacArthur *War Bugs* 194: To buy champagne 'most every day. [There's a hot shot]. [brackets in orig.] **1964** Tamony *Americanisms* (No. 5) 11: Ted Cook, in his column "Cook-coos" (*S.F. Examiner,* August 26, 1933, p. 16), writes that "Don't Kid me, Kid McCoy" was a *hotshot* (i.e., wisecrack) of 1910.

3. *R.R.* a fast train, esp. an express train; (*hence*) an express vehicle.

> **1925** *Writer's Mo.* (June) 486: Hot Shot—A fast freight. **1926** *AS* I 651: *Hot-shot*—a fast freight of perishable merchandise. **1927** *DN* V 451: Hot shot, n. A fast train. **1929** *Bookman* (July) 524: I've got Forty-four and she's a hot-shot. **1930** "D. Stiff" *Milk & Honey* 207: Hot shot—A fast freight or passenger train. **1936** in Fenner *Throttle* 136: George figured he'd eat as soon as the hot shot got out of town. **1973** Mathers *Ridin' the Rails* 16: You know that Santa Fe's a hotshot. **1973** *Sing Out!* (July) 3: Yeah, 8797 is a hotshot going West. **1982** D.A. Harper *Good Company* 3: A main line…carries the hotshot out of Chicago through Minneapolis to the West. **1989** *Harper's* (June) 60: On the hotshot blasting across North Dakota.

4. *Narc.* an injection of heroin, morphine, or the like that is fatal or nearly fatal because it is poisoned or excessively pure.

> **1936** *AS* (Apr.) 122: Hot shot. Cyanide or other fastworking poison concealed in dope to do away with a dangerous or troublesome addict. **1953** W. Brown *Monkey on My Back* 10: She had died of a "hot shot"—an overdose of heroin. **1958** Motley *Epitaph* 150: Fear is what rules them.…Of getting a hot shot. **1959** Trocchi *Cain's Book* 243: That creepin bastard Fink!…someone's goin to slip him a hotshot. **1959** W. Burroughs *Naked Lunch* 2: He is due for a hot shot. *a***1979** in P. Goldstein *Prost. & Drugs* 107: I'd probably give her a hotshot (fatal

dose of narcotics). **1981** O'Day & Eells *High Times* 210: And you're likely to get a hot shot and end up in the morgue. **1986** Stroud *Close Pursuit* 332: *Hot shot* An unexpectedly potent and therefore lethal hit of heroin. **1994** "G. Indiana" *Rent Boy* 87: Homicide....A part-time addict that would only need a hot shot.

5. *Rodeo.* an electric animal prod.

1936 in *DARE: Hot shot.* An electrical charge used to make the tamest horse buck when being ridden by an amateur. **1939** in A. Banks *First-Person* 199: These steers and horses were plenty wild. They didn't have to use a hot-shot (an electric cattle prod) on those babies. **1955, 1967–68** in *DARE.*

6. *Police.* (see quot.). Cf. quots. at HOTSHOT, *adj.*, 3.

1995 *Calif. vs. Simpson* (Court TV) (Jan. 31) [ref. to 1989]: A "hot-shot" means [a 911 call requiring] an emergency response.

hotshot *adj.* **1.** [orig. attrib. use of HOTSHOT, *n.*, 3.] (see 1943 quot.).

1941 *Sat. Eve. Post* (Feb. 1) 13: Its hot-shot service over the Rockies is tops in trucking. **1943** *AS* XVIII 150: *Hotshot*...offering through or non-stop service (a truck-freighting term from about 1929).

2. [orig. attrib. use of HOTSHOT, *n.*, 1.b.] being, resembling, or characteristic of a HOTSHOT, esp. conceited, ostentatious, reckless, etc.; snappy.—usu. used derisively.

1941 *Sat. Eve. Post* (Feb. 8) 22: A hot-shot job as works manager of Superaviation Motor Company. **1943** J. Mitchell *McSorley's* 85: Joseph Ferdinand Gould, Hot Shot Poet from Poetville. **1944** in *DAS*: A young, hot-shot second lieutenant. **1945** W.C. Williams, in Witemeyer *Williams-Laughlin* 119: A hot shot agent who might take me on. **1957** M. Shulman *Rally* 114: If you're such a hotshot patriot, why didn't you re-enlist? **1971** Giovanni *Gemini* 7: I considered myself a hot-shot canasta player. **1973** P. Benchley *Jaws* 196: Where's this hotshot shark?...The shark that's killed all them people. **1981** *Rod Serling's Mag.* (Sept.) 18: I take all this money I save and stick it in a hotshot scheme to pay for my boy's education....I lose my freakin' shirt! **1984–88** Hackworth & Sherman *About Face* 303: A Ph.D. from some hotshot eastern university. **1995** *CBS This Morning* (CBS-TV) (March 22): A hotshot rookie [is] turning heads on and off the [tennis] court.

3. *R.R.* on an express schedule; (hence, esp. *Police*) urgent; emergency.

1929 Milburn *Hobo's Hornbook* 68: I snagged a hot shot freight. **1942** *AS* (Apr.) 103: *Hot Shot.* Through schedule. **1958** Kerouac *Subterraneans* 29: The hotshot passenger train...balls by. **1975** Wambaugh *Choirboys* 287: Radio cars, motorcycles, plainclothes units. Five separate hotshot calls had gone out. **1987** D. Barnes *Deadly Justice* 46: Link keyed his radio with the hotshot call. **1991** K. Douglas *Viper Strike* 80: It hadn't been coincidence which had led CAG to assign the hotshot mission to Tombstone Magruder.

hotshot *v.* **1.** *Narc.* to give (a drug user) a HOTSHOT, *n.*, 4.

1963 Braly *Shake Him* 148: Why would he hotshot me? **1988** H. Gould *Double Bang* 230: I hotshotted him, slipped him some of this Mexican smack, pure.

2. to behave like a HOTSHOT, 1.b.

1989 G. Hall *Air Guard* 10: The visceral thrill of military hotshotting ten or fifteen days a month.

Hotshot Charlie *n.* [the name of a cartoon character introduced by Milton Caniff in his aviation comic strip "Terry and the Pirates," June 25, 1944]

Esp. *Av.* (a derisive nickname given to) a brash or egotistical fellow.

1944 M. Caniff, in Galewitz *Great Comics* 271: Haven't you heard of Hot Shot Charlie, the little boy with the big smile? **1945** in *AS* (Dec. 1946) 310: *Hot shot Charlie.* An egotist. **1974** Stevens *More There I Was* 87: Let's see what Hotshot Charlie can do on one engine.

hot sketch *n.* an amusing or attractive person or thing.

1914 T.A. Dorgan, in Zwilling *TAD Lexicon* 47: She's a hot sketch. **1918–19** MacArthur *Bug's-Eye View* 45: Ward Kilgore and Bill Donaldson wore the crossed cannon of the first-class private on their sleeves, which was considered to be a Hot Sketch by the rest. **1921** Witwer *Leather Pushers* 176: This Roberts is a hot sketch for a fighter,

anyway! **1926–27** in *AS* III (1927) 220: *Hot sketch,* n.—A pretty girl who has...sex appeal. **1927** H. Miller *Moloch* 151: You're a hot sketch. **1929–30** Dos Passos *42d Parallel* 343: He's a hot sketch. **1935** Pollock *Und. Speaks: Hot sketch,* an unusually attractive girl.

hot spit *n.* HOT STUFF, 3. Cf. syn. HOT SHIT, 1.

1931 Stevenson *St. Luke's* [ref. to ca1910]: Gus would praise me up, talk science to me and make me feel I was pretty hot spit. **1942** *ATS* 29: Something excellent...*hot spit.* a**1986** *NDAS: Hot spit* = hot shit.

hot spot *n.* a popular nightclub, cabaret, cocktail lounge, etc. Now *colloq.*

1929 (cited in *W10*). [**1930** Irwin *Tramp & Und. Sl.: Hot Spot.*—A good location for business.] **1933–35** D. Lamson *About to Die* 205: Hangin' around clip joints, an' flashin' a big roll in hot spots. **1940** in H. Gray *Arf* (unp.): The Green Gander, eh? Of course, everybody knows it's our flashiest hot spot. **1943** Mears *Carrier* 27: We adjourned to the bar—or, rather, to join the ladies, for the cocktail lounge was crowded with them, most, in the terms of hot-spot owners, "unescorted." **1944** in Erdoes *Saloons of West* 49: The "Klondyke" ... was the village hot spot and had larger mirrors and bigger hanging lamps. **1944** in *Combat* 41: He...played the maracas and drums in a Greenwich Village hot spot. **1948** Kingsley *Detective Story* 325: Been doing the hot spots? **1950** Spillane *Vengeance* 32: She'd drag him around the hot spots with him footing the bill. *Ibid.* 42: What guy wouldn't take in a hot spot with a babe? **1954** Collans & Sterling *House Detect.* 26: They still get away with expensive coats at certain fashionable hotspots. **1961** Hemingway *Islands* 60: I guess you've spent the biggest part of your life in cafes and saloons and hot spots. **1988** *Rage* (Univ. Tenn.) (Dec.) 13: Tell them...you're late to meet other friends at the local hot-spot.

hot squat *n. Pris.* an electric chair; HOT SEAT, 1.

1928 McEvoy *Show Girl* 180: I ought to get something for that don't you think? The chair maybe—better known as the hot squat. **1932** Lawes *20,000 Yrs. in Sing Sing* 327: He...would...teach the condemned how to withstand the entire voltage of the "hot squat." **1936** Steel *College* 62: "Lottery for what, Hank?"..."For the hot squat." **1942** Wylie *Vipers* 98: Fear of the hot squat...is not deterrent to anti-social behavior. **1947** Helseth *Martin Rome* 7: I want to see him in the hot squat, roasting. He killed a cop. **1960** I.H. Freeman *Out of the Burning* 120: You can't get sent to the hot squat, either, or the Big House. **1963** Gant *Queen St.* 151: "Then where'd we be?"..."In the hot squat....We'd fry." **1974** Andrews & Dickens *Over the Wall* 151: Give it up, clown! You can't outlast the hot-squat!

hot squat *interj. Juve.* (see quot.).

1976 Knapp & Knapp *One Potato* 74: "Hot Squat!" we drawled in the thirties, meaning, "So, what's the big deal?"

hot stick *n.* an electric animal prod. Cf. HOTSHOT, *n.*, 5.

1944 Adams *West. Words: Hot stick*—A charged rod used in stockyards to prod cattle. **1966–70** in *DARE.* **1978** Ponicsan *Ringmaster* 8: Practically had to fry them with the hot stick to get them to do anything.

Hot Stove League *n.* Orig. *Baseball.* sports enthusiasts who continue to discuss their sport during the off-season. Also **stove league.**

[**1886** *Spirit of Times* (Mar. 20) (Tamony Coll.): The sleighing has gone, and most of the trotting is done around the hot stove at present.] **1912** *N.Y. Tribune* (Sept. 13), in P. Dickson *Baseball Dict.*: O'Day decided to try some of his new material which will win the pennant sometime in February in the Hot Stove League. **1914** in *DA* s.v. *stove*: The "stove league" season was in full blast. **1915** in *DA*: Banner Day for Hot Stove Baseball League. **1918–19** MacArthur *Bug's-Eye View* 16: The Hot Stove League would...allow that Number 1 man was sure to get killed first. **1945** *Yank* (Oct. 19) 23: Hot-Stove League. **1948** L. Allen *Reds* 270: Currently it is a favorite hot stove league question in the Queen City to ask, "Now, who was better in his prime, Derringer or Walters?" **1973** H. Peterson *Man Who Invented Baseball* 75: The winter of 1845–46 qualifies as the first Hot Stove League season ever. **1980** P. Rizzuto, on N.Y. Yankees Baseball (WINS) (Sept. 6): What a good Hot Stove League discussion this would make. **1981** W. Safire, in *N.Y. Times Mag.* (June 27) 7: Here is a survey from the Hot Stove League of the effect of baseball on the American language.

hot-streak *v. Gamb.* to enjoy a streak of good luck.

1980 Santoli *Everything* 83: 'Cause I was hot-streaking, boy, rollin' them sevens.

hot stuff *n*. **1.** *Mil.* bullets or shells; gunfire.

*1759 in Fowke et al. *Canada's Story* 46: And ye that love fighting shall soon have enough:/Wolfe commands us, my boys; we shall give them Hot Stuff. **1957** Anders *Price of Courage* 220: Can you squirt some hot stuff on that…[target]?

2. spiced rum; (*also*) strong liquor.

1840 *Spirit of Times* (Sept. 26) 360: Contoit [a theater manager] also, has disposed of more "hot stuffs" than ice creams for the last three weeks. **1853** in *DA:* Refreshing himself with about a pint of hot-stuff. **1880** Bailey *Danbury Boom* 189: He invited several of his fellow clerks to spend the evening at his house, the program embracing euchre and "hot stuff." **1925** McAlmon *Silk Stockings* 80: It's the real hot stuff you know, Steve. Some I brought from Ireland—pre-war.

3. anything or anyone unusually good, exciting, proficient, etc.; (*often*) a sexually passionate young woman or women; (*also*) erotic material.—often (esp. in direct address) used ironically. See also HOT, *adj.*, esp. 6.a.–k., 7.c.

1884 in Lummis *Letters* 22: I will tell you in my next about the cow-boys I saw at Junction City, Abilene and Salina. They are "hot stuff." **1889** in *OED2:* "Miss Middleton's Lover." Were there room for two words in that last line, "Hot Stuff" might be appropriate. **1893** Frye *Field & Staff* 176: Oh, 'twas hot stuff! **1895** in A. Charters *Ragtime Songbk.* 37: The judge asked me what had I done, Baby!…Hot Stuff! **1896** *Yale Record* (Feb. 1), in *Comments on Ety.* (Nov. 1995) 9: "I'm hot stuff," growled the dog. "That's all right," hissed the coffee-pot, "I've got more tin [*sc.*, money]." **1897** in Dreiser *Letters* I 43: Verily the said paintings…are hot stuff. **1897** Norris *Vandover* 440: I'm right in it with Beale; he thinks I'm hot stuff. **1899** F.E. Daniel *Rebel Surgeon* 116: That certainly *was* the much talked of "hot stuff." **1899** Ade *Fables* 29: This [sermon] is certainly Hot Stuff! **1900** *DN* II 42: Hot-stuff…A person of good quality; often ironical. **1902** Townsend *Fadden & Mr. Paul* 8: Say, dose ottermobiles he was telling of is hot stuff, too. *1916 J. Joyce *Dubliners* 93: I've been to all the Bohemian cafés. Hot stuff! Not for a pious chap like you, Tommy. **1921** T.A. Dorgan, in Zwilling *TAD Lexicon* 47: Dye get Bull showing that arm to Eddie? Hot stuff ain't he? **1924** Marks *Plastic Age* 28: I never had a better time. It was sure hot stuff. **1927** Aiken *Blue Voyage* 47: She looked to me like hot stuff. **1928** Dahlberg *Bottom Dogs* 137: A pimp…asked him…if he wanted some hot stuff for only two bucks a shot. **1928** Weseen *Dict. Grammar* 125: *Hot stuff.* Anything enjoyed. **1928** Segar *Thimble Th.* 22: I'm no coward. What there is of me is hot stuff. *1930 Brophy & Partridge *Songs & Slang* 130 [ref. to WWI]: *Hot Stuff.*—A woman willing to forgo the usual sexual reticences in conversation and perhaps in behaviour. But not applied to a professional harlot. The expression was also used of a book, a picture, or a theatrical entertainment not blatantly obscene but toying with impropriety.…Also used of any special application of skill, e.g. "He's hot stuff at the piano." **1935** L. Hughes *Little Ham* 59: I'm gonna buy my gal a hot stuff dress right straight from Fifth Avenue. **1938** "Justinian" *Amer. Sexualis* 25: *Hot stuff*, a fast, morally lax, or hypersexual female. **1939–40** Tunis *Kid from Tomkinsville* 55: Oh, yeah, I thought I was hot stuff, but they soon showed me I didn't have an idea what it was all about. **1970** Della Femina *Wonderful Folks* 170: I'll bet they really think they're hot stuff because they don't get to go to lunch because they're working so hard. **1984** Trotti *Phantom* 12 [ref. to 1966]: Well, I wouldn't worry about it too much, hotstuff, we've still got five more runs to work on your technique. **1991** Rudnick *I Hate Hamlet* 46: Hey—big night! Hot stuff!

4. insolent talk.

1927 in Dundes *Mother Wit* 200: Spit right square in his eyes if he tries to give you any *hot stuff* about your rights.

hotsy *adj.* HOTSY-TOTSY.

1929 Sullivan *Look at Chicago* 117: Business will pick up…and everything will be irretrievably hotsy. **1930** Mae West *Babe Gordon* 149: The Hotsy Club.

hotsy-totsy *n.* an attractive or amative young woman. Also **hotsy.**

1928 MacArthur *War Bugs* 245: Field clerks getting stewed in Paris and tipping their hats to hotsy-totsies. **1934** Weseen *Dict. Slang* 186: *Hotsie-totsie*—An attractive girl. **1942** *ATS* 376: Passionate young

woman; "hot mama"…*hotsy, hotsy-totsy*. **1959** Zugsmith *Beat Generation* 43: Never before had he put the blocks to a fuzz's hotsy.

hotsy-totsy *adj. & adv.* [joc. elab. of HOT, *adj.*] **1.** wonderful; delightful.—often used ironically.

1926 Dunning & Abbott *Broadway* 239: Everything is hotzy-totzy. **1927** Coe *Me—Gangster* 219: Everything looked hotsy-totsy, as the saying is. **1928** in Tuthill *Bungle Family* 45: Brown…is going to make everything hotsy-totsy. **1930** G. Schuyler *Black No More* 193: Everything's hotsy totsy. **1932** Hecht & Fowler *Great Magoo* 52: But everything's hotsy totsy, 'cause I got you. **1934** Garrett & Mankiewicz *Manhattan Melody* (film): Everything is just hotsy-totsy. **1956** Chamales *Never So Few* 44: He's not so hotsy-totsy. **1960** Barber *Minsky's* 142: If you're convinced you're such a hotsy totsy attraction all by yourself, Feef, why don't you prove it? **1968** P. Roth *Portnoy* 5: A hotsy-totsy free weekend in Atlantic City. **1990** Univ. Tenn. instructor: Things are really going hotsy-totsy.

2. pretentiously fashionable.

1984 *N.Y. Daily News* (Aug. 20) 12: At Frost's, one of Dallas' hotsy-totsy stores.

hot taco *n.* a passionate young woman, esp. of Hispanic descent. Cf. HOT TAMALE.

1974 Univ. Tenn. student: She looks all right. She might be a hot taco. **1978** 1st Lt., U.S. Army, Dugway Proving Ground, Utah (coll. J. Ball): I'll bet she's one hot taco!

hot-tail *v.* HOTFOOT; HIGHTAIL.

1986 Stinson & Carabatsos *Heartbreak* 45: Got to hot-tail, men. Late for pre-scuba diving school.

hot tamale *n.* **1.** a spirited, capable, or brash person.—often used ironically.

1895 in J. London *Tramp Diary* 61: Yer wants ter ast me a few questions? Den fire away. I'se yer red hot tamale. **1898** in Pierce *Co. L* 53: There'll be h— for every Spaniard/When the Eighth begins to scrap,/For we are the hot tamales/And we never give a rap. **1899** Cullen *Tales* 43: "How many for the pair of us?" asked the hot tamale that had hailed me. **1900** *DN* II 42: [College slang:] *Hot-tamale*…A clever fellow…One having merit…One who excels in anything. **1901** *DN* II 149: *Hot tamale*…In Otsego Co., N.Y., Dayton, O., applied to a clever person; may be ironical or jocular, usually the latter. **1904** in "O. Henry" *Works* 1428: Go it, you blamed little…hot tamales. **1931** Wilstach *Under Cover Man* 114: These hot tamales who want to hold back.

2. an attractive or amorous young woman.

1897 Ade *Pink* 197: 'At Belle's a hot tomolley. She no mo' got 'at Meth'dis' 'ligion 'an you have. **1925** in Leadbitter & Slaven *Blues Records* 316: Hot Tamale Molly. **1929** McEvoy *Hollywood Girl* 25: Your little Hot Tamale won't like it. **1954–60** *DAS:* *Hot tamale*…A sexy girl. **1972** Swarthout *Tin Lizzie* 19: A hot tamale in a white blouse. **1974** *Sonny & Cher Comedy Hour* (CBS-TV): I can be a hot tamale or a cool cucumber. **1976** Rosen *Above Rim* 98: Wayne called her his "hot tamale." **1979** Kunstler *Wampanaki Tales* 179: He had a date with a hot tamale. **1996** *Politically Incorrect* (Comedy Central TV) (Jan. 31): Shelley Winters was quite a hot tamale at one point.

hot tamale *interj.* (used to express excitement or enthusiasm).

1942 *ATS* 283: Interj.…of pleasure…*hot tamale! hot ziggety!* [etc.]. **1970** E. Thompson *Garden of Sand* 37: H-h-hot tamale!

hot ticket *n.* **1.a.** *Theat.* a successful show for which tickets are in great demand; (*hence*) a very popular and successful performer.

1936 Washburn *Parlor* 46: The Everleigh Club was, in the lingo of the Broadway ticket brokers, a "hot ticket." The show was a bona-fide hit. **1942** *ATS* 584: Successful show; hit…*hot ticket.* **1981** *N.Y. Times Mag.* (June 21) 26: We were hot tickets; we played all the campuses, society parties, the works. **1991** Lott & Lieber *Total Impact* 253: The current hot ticket [for groupies] is backup quarterback Steve Young. **1993** A. Adams & W. Stadiem *Madam* 4: This party was the hot ticket of the season.

b. anything that is currently popular.

1978 Shem *House of God* 47: "Social Medicine" was a hot ticket.

1990 *Cosmopolitan* (July) 94: A handsome, tall, charming bachelor is a hot ticket these days.

2. a clever or capable individual.—usu. used ironically.

1968 Baker, Ladd & Robb *CUSS* 140: *Hot ticket.* A quick or witty person. *a***1979** in S. King *Bachman* 215: "He's some hot ticket." … "Don't let him get under your skin." **1980** Eble *Campus Slang* (Oct.) 3: *Hot ticket*—Cool, in the know (usually used sarcastically).

hottie *n.* Esp. *Rap Music.* an attractive or sexually promiscuous person of the opposite sex, usu. a woman.

1991 Nelson & Gonzales *Bring Music* 177: After jivescamming on the hotties…they wanna be serious loverboys. **1991** in P. Munro *U.C.L.A. Slang II* 52: *Hottie*…promiscuous woman. **1993** Bahr & Small *Son-in-Law* (film): She is a *hottie!* **1993** P. Munro *U.C.L.A. Slang II* 52: *Hottie*…very attractive person (male or female). **1995** Stavsky, Mozeson & Mozeson *A 2 Z* 50: If you such a ladies' man, why ain't you coolin' with a *hottie?* **1995** Eble *Campus Slang* (Apr.) 6: *Hottie*—someone sexy, male or female. **1996** Lyday-Lee *Elon College Coll.* (Spring) 3: *Hottie* We passed this real *hottie* on the beach earlier and I wish we had stopped to talk to him. (noun) a very handsome, attractive man.

hot tomato *n.* a clever or spirited person.

1926 Finerty *Criminalese* 27: *Hot tomato*—A real smart fellow. **1936** in Hammerstein *Kern Song Bk.* 173: We should be a couple of hot tomatoes,/But you're as cold as yesterday's mashed potatoes.

Hot Town *n. CB.* Atlanta, Georgia. cf. HOTLANTA.

1976 (quot. at SHAKE).

hot up *v.* [in colloq. sense 'to heat', orig. dial.; see *OED2*] to make or become HOT (in various esp. slang senses).

*****1923** P.G. Wodehouse, in *OED2*: The atmosphere was…more or less hotted up when Cyril…breezed down centre. *****1928** in *OED2*: This car…is not in any sense a "hotted up" Morris six-cylinder. *****1936** P.G. Wodehouse, in *OEDS*: It did not need a razorlike intelligence to show me that things were hotting up, and that flight was the only course. **1955** Reifer *New Words* 102: *Hot up. v. Slang.* To accelerate, as a motor. **1956** in A. Gibson *Be Somebody* 102: Miss Althea Gibson has proved that baseline tennis, when "hotted up," is supreme. *a***1970** *Webster's New World Dict.* (ed. 2): *Hot up* (Slang) to heat or warm up. **1972** *Nat. Lampoon* (July) 76: Remember how "Dr. Kildare" and "Ben Casey" used to hot you up for medical school? *a***1987** in *World Bk. Dict.*: Next evening, Jimmy McPartland's gang, with George Wettling on drums, will start hotting it up.…The economic cold war in Rhodesia is to be abruptly hotted up. **1984–88** Hackworth & Sherman *About Face* 263: Only when it hotted up did we "stand to."

hot water *n.* trouble.—usu. constr. with *in.* Now *colloq.*

*****1537** in *OED2*: If they be to be had, I will have of them, or it shall cost me hot water. *****1765** in *OED*: We are kept, to use the modern phrase, in hot water. **1835** in Paulding *Bulls & Jons.* 20: After this he was always in hot water with his neighbours. **1853** "P. Paxton" *In Texas* 226: It war enuff to keep him in hot water all the time. **1860** J.G. Holland *Miss Gilbert* 454: Here I am, getting into hot water again! **1867** in Rosa *Wild Bill* 34: A gang of desperadoes…who kept us in the mountains in hot water whenever they were around. **1878** [P.S. Warne] *Hard Crowd* 5: What's that? Pistols!…Somebody's in hot water. **1879** Thayer *Jewett* 126: Like tea, his real strength was proved by being in "hot water." **1887** *Lantern* (N.O.) (May 7) 3: Johnnie Grears is in hot water. **1929** "E. Queen" *Roman Hat* ch. vi 76: Mr. Morgan is in deucedly hot water. **1974** Perry & Sudyk *Me & Spitter* 135: He was already in hot water over some disparaging remarks about black and Latin players.

hot wheels *n. R.R.* an express train; (*also*) great speed.

1970 *Current Slang* V (Summer) 9: We caught the hot wheels from Roseville to Garber.…This train has hot wheels.

hot wind var. HOT AIR.

hot wire *n.* **1.** a fresh bit of important news.

1931 *AS* VI (Aug.) 439: *Hot wire, n.* Good news; late information. "You can bet that he told everyone about the hot wire he had received."

2. *Mil.* HOT LINE.

1960 Rankin *Rode Thunder* 31: The information…had come into Marine Corps Headquarters over a special "hot wire." **1962** *Sat. Eve. Post* (Oct. 13) 58: A telephone link between the American President and the Premier of the Soviet Union. It had promptly been labeled the "hot wire." **1963** *Book Week* (Oct. 27) 4: A direct "hot-wire" telephone between the President and Khrushchev.

hot-wire *v.* Orig. *Police & Und.* to start the engine of (an automobile or other vehicle) by short-circuiting the ignition, usu. in order to steal the vehicle.—also used fig.

1954 *Time* (Aug. 2) 36: They showed how to "hot wire" a car (*i.e.*, bypass the ignition lock). **1962** *AS* XXXVII (Dec.) 269: *Hot-Wired, adj.* Designating a motor vehicle which has had the ignition switch short-circuited by a thief. **1970** E.S. Gardner *Cops* 121: I knew…how to hot-wire the car past the ignition. **1968** Brautigan *Pill vs. Springhill* 17: You hotwire death, get in, and drive away. **1971** Sanders *Family* 203: It was rumored that she could hot-wire a vehicle in thirty-seconds flat. **1973** Lucas, Katz & Huyck *Amer. Graffiti* 141: We only need a foot to hot-wire it. **1974** Verona & Gleckler *Lords of Flatbush* (film): I can hotwire any car in the world. **1977** Caron *Go-Boy* 16: I had no trouble breaking into a car and hot-wiring it. **1982** WINS radio news (Aug. 16): A prankster hotwired a bulldozer and took it on a joyride. **1989** P. Benchley *Rummies* 105: People…having their balls hot-wired in Argentine jails. **1993** *New Yorker* (Aug. 9) 21: Everything Sinatra does here is electrically nuanced, as if Preminger had hot-wired the star's eyes, vocal cords, and facial muscles.

hot ziggety *adj.* excessively keen or intent.

1931 J.T. Farrell *McGinty* 349: He was just hot ziggedy on savin' time.

hot ziggety *interj.* HOT DIGGETY [DOG]. Also vars.

1909 *DN* III 398: Hotzickity. **1915** *N.Y. Eve. Jour.* (Aug. 15) 9: They're off. Odzigity!!! **1924** *DN* V 265: Hot ziggety damn! **1933** in Galewitz *Great Comics* 34: Hot ziggety! **1949** H. Robbins *Dream Merchants* 202: Dames…hot zig! **1953** W. Fisher *Waiters* 255: Hot ziddity!

Houdini *n.* [after Harry *Houdini*, stage name of Erich Weiss (1874–1926), U.S. conjurer and escape artist] a man who is adept at escape or avoidance, esp. of work. *Joc.*

1955 Graziano & Barber *Somebody Up There* 26 [ref. to *ca*1930]: They call me Houdini.…My old man…said he never seen no kid disappear so fast when there's work or trouble around. **1979** Former USAF mech.: A *Houdini* is a guy who disappears whenever there's work to do. I had a real Houdini working for me in Vietnam. He could *smell* work coming and he'd just—vanish!

¶ In phrase:

¶ **do** [or **pull**] **a Houdini** [**act**] to escape or abscond in a sudden or mystifying manner.

1907 in H.C. Fisher *A. Mutt* 6: A. Mutt Overhears a Couple of Hot Tips and Does a "Houdini." **1924** *Sat. Eve. Post* (July 12) 15: *Doing a Houdini*—getting out of a tight place. **1933** Ersine *Prison Slang* 46: *Houdini, n.* A clever get-away trick. **1946** Mezzrow & Wolfe *Really Blues* 152: We…started to do a Houdini out of the neighborhood. **1985** *Miami Vice* (NBC-TV): Your boys are pullin' a Houdini act. **1985** WUOT-FM radio (Oct. 6): She'll be doin' a Houdini now any day.

hound *n.* **1.** a devotee, enthusiast, frequenter, seeker, etc.—usu. used in combs.

1911 (quot. at BOOZEHOUND). **1914** T.A. Dorgan, in Zwilling *TAD Lexicon* 47: How is that gardner I sent over to fix up your place?…That man's a hound for work ain't he? **1918** (quot. at GOLD-DIGGER, 1). **1920** Ade *Hand-Made Fables* 3: Many a visitor being led out of the select Road-House and gently steered toward the car would remark that, as a Host, good old Fred was a Hound. **1921** *Variety* (Feb. 25) 39: Jimmie has always been a regular "publicity hound." **1921** Benet *Beginning of Wisdom* 295: Bumming cigarettes…had once settled upon him the nickname of "Fag Hound." **1926** Hormel *Co-Ed* 17: That old boy's a reg'lar hound for the highbrow stuff! Simply laps it up! **1926** *AS* II 45: *Comma hound*—Applied to teachers of English composition. **1928** *N.Y. Times Mag.* (Nov. 11) 21: [A taxi driver] who searches diligently and gets trade is called "a hound." **1928** in *OED2*: Publicity hounds. **1933** J. Lowell *Gal Reporter* 17: Once I started I'd be known as Joanie the Scoop Hound. **1934** Peters & Sklar *Stevedore* 58: One of them poker hounds. **1938** "E. Queen" *4 Hearts* 136: A club for every hooch-hound in town. **1938** in Leadbitter & Slaven *Blues Records* 407: Reefer Hound Blues. **1941** Schulberg *Sammy* 70: The boys in the office across the hall told me Pancake was a credit hound, one of those writers who practically have convulsions over sole screen credits. **1945** Crow & Crow *Teen-age* 305: A girl should not be a "hound" for dates. **1951** Haines & Burnett *Racket* (film): He's a publicity hound. **1955** Jessup *Case for UFO* 11: Astronomers…being conscientious data hounds, were not content with merely seeing things move in space. **1955** T. Anderson *Beloved Sons* 58: Ain't many warhounds like you and Stanley, though….Ordinary sane people don't wanna go on Stanley's patrols much. **1961** Kohner *Gidget Goes Hawaiian* 29: They had nothing on Lord Gallo or Sexhound. **1986** F. Walton *Once Were Eagles* 71: Rusty was a book hound. *Ibid.* 72: He was the squadron's jive hound. **1991** Marcinko & Weisman *Rogue Warrior* 242: The Stallion was…a real pussy hound. *a***1994** A. Radakovich *Wild Girls Club* 74: Packed with fun-worshipping kegger hounds determined to party until they puked.

2. (usu. *cap.*) Esp. *Black E.* a bus of the Greyhound Corporation.—constr. with *the*. Cf. DOG, *n.*, 24.

    1959 *Swinging Syllables: Hound*—Bus. **1964** Chuck Berry *The Promised Land* (pop. song): The Hound broke down and left us all stranded/In downtown Birmingham. **1970** Gattzden *Black Vendetta* 172: I gotta catch a hound for New York. **1978** Dills *CB Slanguage* (ed. 4) 55: *Hound:* Greyhound bus. **1981–85** S. King *It* 24: He would get on a 'hound and see how things looked down in Florida. *a***1990** Westcott *Half a Klick* 15: Come in on the midnight 'hound, huh?

3. daylights.

    1963–64 Kesey *Great Notion* 542: I'll…kick the hound outa him. **1964** Brewer *Worser Days* 132: A. I drove de hound out of dat car. B. She made de hound out of dat dress. C. He beat de hound out of dat nigger.

hound *adj. Pris.* cowardly.

    1967 Salas *Tattoo* 313 [ref. to *ca*1951]: "Maybe the guys will think I'm hound if I use a blade?" "They'll think you're hound if you don't try and get 'im."

houndface *n. USMC.* a member of the U.S. Army; DOGFACE, 2.

    1962 W. Crawford *Give Me Tomorrow* 34 [ref. to 1951]: Evans, if we had a points rotation system like the houndfaces, where'd you be now?

hour-mill *n.* a clock. *Joc.*

    *a***1867** in G.W. Harris *Lovingood* 46: He changed sides every uther lunge, clar over Stilyards, an' his hour-mill tu.

house *n.* **1.** a brothel.

    1851 Doten *Journals* I 92: We took a turn about town—Went to some of *the houses*, saw *some of the senoritas*. **1893** in A. Rose *Storyville* 27: There was the devil to pay at 41 Basin Street, the well-known house kept by Kitty Reed. **1909** Chrysler *White Slavery* 190: I called for all the fellows I knew who were running houses and said they would have to pay $20 a month. **1910** Roe *Panders* 55: Her name is Myrtle—and she runs a "house" down there. **1929** T. Gordon *Born to Be* 19: Big Maude…made me page and cash boy in her new house on the sporting line. **1937** Reitman *Box-Car Bertha* 56: A girl friend of hers had a job in a "house." **1970** in P. Heller *In This Corner* 42: The second wife was a bum right out of a house. **1977** Dunne *True Confessions* 28: The problem was the car was registered to a woman named Brenda Samuels and Brenda Samuels ran three houses in his division. *a***1978** A. Rose *Eubie Blake* 19: At Gipsy Schaefer's "house," for instance.

2.a. *Police.* a police stationhouse; (*also*) a police precinct. Cf. HOUSE, *v.*, 1.

    1909 in *Comments on Ety.* (Apr. 1996) 2: You can…lead them around to the "house" and they'll never beef. **1970** Landy *Underground Dict.* 106: *House*…Jail. **1973** Whited *Chiodo* 51: We'd better lock her up, kid….I'm calling the house. **1987** Taubman *Lady Cop* 40: The dumb comments the guys in the house are making aren't helping matters. *Ibid.* 268: *House:* Stationhouse, precinct. **1988** H. Gould *Double Bang* 79: A busy house in the West Bronx where they'd be up to their eyeballs in ghetto squeals. **1991** McCarthy & Mallowe *Vice Cop* 50 [ref. to 1960's]: A "C" house is very quiet….no real crimes….And all of my precincts were "A" houses during the riots.

b. *Pris.* a cell.

    [**1970** (quot. at (**a**), above).] **1990** Crow Dog & Erdoes *Lakota Woman* 230: The punks…stood before Leonard's "house," taunting him.

3. *Printing.* a caret-like mark placed over a comma that is to be inserted into a text; DOGHOUSE, 1.

    1982 *Chicago Manual* (ed. 13) 55.

¶ In phrases:

¶ **in the house** Esp. *Rap Music.* excellent; popular; successful.

    1989 "N.W.A." *Compton's In tha House* [rap song title]. **1992** in A. Sexton *Rap on Rap* 224: The South is in the goddamn house! **1994** *Our Town* (N.Y.C.) (June 30) 46 (personal ad): Gorgeous…wildly creative diva is in the house!! (That's slang, guys. It means I'm single, glamorous, artistic and avant garde.). **1994** Eble *Campus Slang* (Apr.) 5: *In the house*—popular, cool: "That new band is really in the house." **1995** Stavsky, Mozeson & Mozeson *A 2 Z* 53: *In the house*—the place to be; successful or happening…: She's cool—she's *in the house*; With the release of their new album, Public Enemy is *in the house*. **1995** *Village Voice* (N.Y.C.) (May 23): The gangsta is in the house, for sure.

¶ **play house** to cohabit.

    1959 Russell *Permanent Playboy* 419: You don't drink with him at all. You ask him does he want to play house or not? **1960** Swarthout *Where the Boys Are* 151: Should a girl or should she not under any circumstances play house before marriage? **1961** L.E. Young *Virgin Fleet* 82: I'm not playing house or having any more romantic interludes. **1964** Mosel *Dear Heart* (film): I shook the old man, Squeaky. Let's play house.

house *v.* **1.** *Police.* to escort (an arrested person) to the stationhouse; arrest and jail.

    1929 Hotstetter & Beesley *It's a Racket!* 229: *House*—To arrest; to put in jail. **1976** "N. Ross" *Policeman* 141: "An' th' motha' fuckin' police…they fuckin' wif me." "How? Been getting housed lately?" "Naw, I ain't got busted in a month."

2. *Rap Music.* **a.** to take for oneself; steal.

    1986 "Beastie Boys" *Rhymin' & Stealin'* (rap song): I got your money and your honey…[I'm] housin' all girlies from city to city. **1990–91** *Street Talk* 4: *Housin'* taking[.] "I'm housin that chain." "I'm keeping it." **1994** Smitherman *Black Talk* 140: *House*…To take something from somebody.

b. to outdo; outshine; defeat.

    1987 in N. George *Buppies, B-Boys* 78: Give him another great record and he'll house all these m.f.'s. **1990** in N. George *Buppies, B-Boys* 126: These Hollywood dudes aren't gonna house us! **1997** *N.Y. Times* (Jan. 5) ("Metro") 25: *House:* to defeat. "Evander Holyfield housed Mike Tyson in their last fight."

c. [perh. sugg. by phr. *bring the house down*] to excite and impress (an audience).

    1988 "EPMD" *I'm Housin* (rap song): I'm…just pleasing/All partygoers,…/Who like the fast slow flow of rhymes…'cause I'm housing. *a***1990** P. Dickson *Slang!* 220: *House*…To bring down the house—a common rap term. **1991** N. Krulik *Hammer & Ice* 22: You'd get to…go around the country housin' every crowd!

d. (see quot.). Cf. ROUGHHOUSE.

    1992 "Fab 5 Freddy" *Fresh Fly Flavor* 33: *House*—To attack someone violently. [**1997** (quot. at (**b**), above).]

house ape *n.* a small child. *Joc.*

    1968 Gover *JC* 137: A bunch a blue-eyed spade house apes inta the bargain. **1976** J.W. Thomas *Heavy Number* 58: It couldn't be the neighborhood house apes. **1978** Selby *Requiem* 15: The goddamn house apes yelling and fightin about whose piece of meat is bigger and…whats for dessert. *a***1990** P. Dickson *Slang!* 220: *House ape.* Small child.

housecat *n. Army.* a member of a noncombat unit.—used derisively. [Quots. ref. to Vietnam War.]

    1974–77 Heinemann *Close Quarters* 31: Down the company street where the housecats—the vehicle mechanic and radio mechanics and cooks and clerks—held reveille. **1980** Cragg *Lex. Militaris* 222: *Housecats.* Combat service support personnel. **1985** J.M.G. Brown *Rice Paddy Grunt* 271: The pet monkey…another housecat dude had.

houseman *n. Und.* a man who is a house burglar.

    1904 *Life in Sing Sing* 255: *Houseman.* A burglar. **1921** "M. Brand" *Black Jack* 107: As a heel or a houseman, well, them things were just outside him. **1938** (cited in Partridge *Dict. Und.* 348).

house mouse *n.* **1.** *USMC & Army.* a room orderly or platoon clerk; (*also*) *Police.* a desk officer; (see also second 1969 quot.).

    1968 Mares *Marine Machine* 28: But the most important job, in the DI's eyes, is that of "house mouse." His formal duty is to care for the "house," a cubicle with bathroom where the drill instructor on duty stays. **1969** Crumley *One to Count Cadence* 45: "Yes sir, I'll get the shit-house mouse on it right away."…"I'd prefer if you didn't refer to the Operations orderly in that manner, Sgt. Krummel." **1969** *Current Slang* I & II 52: *House mouse*, n. House mother.—College females, South Dakota. **1971** Flanagan *Maggot* 39: The house mouse, the recruit who woke the D.I.s in the morning, ran errands and cleaned the hut. **1971** Jeffers & Levitan *See Paris* 38: The tightly made bunk prepared by the DI's "house mouse," whom the DI's had picked to do their housekeeping chores for them. **1988** Dye *Outrage* 130: Does that make him my full-time house mouse, sir? **1989** G.C. Wilson *Mud Soldiers* 148: "House Mouse!"…Russell…got his nickname from being platoon clerk. **1995** S. Moore *In the Cut* 47: They took his gun and his shield and put him on restricted duty. He's a housemouse now, filing papers. *Ibid.*: "What are housemouses?"…"Guys who put their balls in a drawer. Guys who take promotion tests. Guys who don't want to be in the street. Guys who are lazy. Or scared."

2. a person who rarely goes out; homebody.

　1968 Baker, Ladd & Robb *CUSS* 140: *House Mouse.* A person who studies a great deal. **1986** *New Gidget* (syndic. TV series): Listen! She's a house mouse! The romance is gone. **1995** (quot. at (1), above).

house nigger *n. Black E.* a black person who acts subserviently toward a white employer.—used contemptuously.

　*ca***1970** in J. Mills *On the Edge* 44: A prisoner yells, "Hey! What's goin' on, house nigger?" The guard keeps walking. **1972** A. Kemp *Savior* 17: Not to mention Dr. Calvin Lovell's hymn-singing house niggers. **1974** Heard *Cold Fire* 26: How much she payin' you, *house nigga?* **1986** *L.A. Law* (NBC-TV): I'm not going to be your house nigger any more. **1989** Chafets *Devil's Night* 173: I didn't come here to see the house nigger. **1995** Stavsky, Mozeson & Mozeson *A 2 Z* 50: *House nigga*…a traitor or self-hating Uncle Tom. **1995** *New Republic* (Oct. 23) 21: Before he can finish, a black man sitting in front of me interrupts: "House nigger," he shouts. "Uncle Tom."

House of D *n. Pris.* a house of detention.

　1964 J. Harris *Junkie Priest* 42: She had served one more stretch in the House of D. **1966** S. Harris *Hellhole* 91: Because that's a good reason to be a call girl, you know—you'll never get into the House of D. unless you're walking the streets or going with men in cars or some other low thing like that. **1966** J. Mills *Needle Park* 168 [ref. to 1964]: Like he could have stood up for her with the plainclothesman, but she's been booked now, she's in the House of D right now, so what can he do? **1974** A. Davis *Autobiog.* 61: At least ninety-five percent of the women in the House of D. were either Black or Puerto Rican. **1978** Fisher & Rubin *Special Teachers* 31: She had to spend a month in the House of D. **1980** D. Hamill *Stomping Ground* 339: In the Brooklyn House of Dee. **1984** Toop *Rap Attack* 159: After five weeks in the House of D, I'm ready to chill hard.

house pig *n. Army.* a member of a home-guard organization.—used derisively.

　1865 C. Davis *Diary* 21: Yet I would not if I could recall the twelve months' service in Colonel McAnerny's battalion of "house pigs" for "home defence only."

houseplant *n.* a homebody.

　1917 in Truman *Dear Bess* 227: We are all as happy as can be expected for a bunch of house plants. **1989** P. Munro *U.C.L.A. Slang* 51: *House plant* person who does nothing but sit around the house.

housewife time *n. TV & Radio.* (see quot.).

　1980 Pearl *Pop. Slang* 75: *Housewife time* n. (Broadcasting) late morning and early afternoon hours when the radio and television audience is composed largely of housewives.

how *n. Army.* a howitzer.

　***1915** in *OEDS:* The boom in the distance from one of our "hows." **1920** Crowell *313th Field Arty.* 64 [ref. to 1918]: A battery of 8 inch "Hows" made life miserable for us. **1943** *Yank* (Jan. 20) 18: A guy…who pushes around the end of a How. **1950** Leland *Shell Hole to Chateau* 95 [ref. to 1918]: There was one battery of six inch "hows" concealed in the ruins of a farmhouse. **1962** F. Downey *Indian Wars* 213: The "hows" had a considerable recoil. **1982** Cox & Frazier *Buck* 27: The shiny tubes of the bigger 155 Hows stood out.

how-able *v.* [former mil. communications alphabet *How* 'H' + *Able* 'A'] (a partial euphem. for) HAUL ASS.

1951 Sheldon *Troubling of a Star* 14: "I'll watch the gooks. The minute they show signs of hearing us we'll take plan How Able." "Plan what?" "How Able—haul ass, brother. And fast." **1956** Boatner *Military Customs* 119: *How able.* To pull out of a position or location in a hurry. Implies a lesser degree of panic than "bugging out." "How able" is old phonetic alphabet for "H.A.," meaning to "haul" something unprintable. **1985** in Safire *Look It Up* 158: G.I.'s…will point out that the operative term for retreat is *how able*.

how-come-you-so *adj.* tipsy; drunk. *Joc.* Also *-ye-*.

　1813–18 Weems *Drunk. Look. Glass* 60: Groggy…tipsy…how came you so…cut. **1827** J.F. Cooper *Red Rover* 160: Your husband was, like some others I can name…a little of what I call how-come-ye-so. **1832** [M. St.C. Clarke] *Sks. of Crockett* 121: I could see many a man who was "how come you so?" **1835** in Eliason *Tarheel Talk* 133: If on trying to read this you should come to the false conclusion that I must have been a little how come you so, when it was written, be assured that I have not drank more than half a pint of ardent spirits this whole day. **1843** "J. Slick" *High Life in N.Y.* 93: They got a leetle how-come-you-so. **1845** *Spirit of Times* (Nov. 15) 446: He had been drinking and *cavorting* mightily the whole day; so when night came on he was pretty much "how came you so?" **1864** Hill *Our Boys* 122: Gaskill was moderately "how come ye so." **1867** in W.H. Jackson *Diaries* 124: Some of the boys were considerably "how come you so." **1877** in "M. Twain" *Sketches* 348: They were pretty how-come-you-so by now, and they begun to blow. **1899** Dunne *Hearts of Countrymen* 135: Well, he was feelin' how-come-ye-so, an' he dhrifted over to where we was holdin' a fair. **1911** in *DARE.* **1968** in *DARE:* When they got pretty well how-come-you-so, why, they didn't always know just exactly what they were doing.

howdy doody *interj.* [extension of colloq. *howdy-do?*, reduction of *how do you do?* infl. by *Howdy Doody*, television marionette introduced on NBC's *Puppet Playhouse*, Dec. 27, 1947] how do you do?; hello. Also as v., to greet.

　1956 M. Wolff *Big Nick.* 129: "Howdy doody," she said gayly.…"How are things in Glocca Morra?" **1963** M. Shulman *Victors* 118: Howdy-doody, Corporal. I'll buy you a drink. **1987–89** M.H. Kingston *Tripmaster Monkey* 57: A salesman howdy-doodied her.

how-fare-ye *adj.* HOW-COME-YOU-SO.

　1851 in Dorson *Long Bow* 107: I was going home, a very leetle "how fare ye."

howgozit *n.* [pron. spelling of *how goes it?*] *Av.* a graph or similar notation plotting an aircraft's rate of fuel consumption or the like.

　1945 Hamann *Air Words:* Howgozit curve. **1956** Heflin *USAF Dict.* 256: *Howgozit, n.* ("How goes it.") A graph sometimes kept aboard an airplane, indicating fuel consumption and distance flown. **1961** L.G. Richards *TAC* 40: Our form 21a, our howgozit chart, is not looking so very good. This is a sort of a fever chart…maintained…by every jet pilot on every flight. **1964** Newhafer *Last Tallyho* 287 [ref. to WWII]: He consulted his how-goes-it chart. **1969** Cagle *Naval Av. Guide* 394: *Howgozit.* A chart which shows relationship between some or all of the fuel (used/remaining), time (elapsed/to go), and distance. **1984** Trotti *Phantom* 67: The key…lay in maintaining an ongoing record of where you were, and when, and what you'd done since. It's called a "howgozit."

howitzer *n.* a big pistol or revolver. *Joc.*

　1874 McCoy *Cattle Trade* 205: An affront or a slight, real or imaginary, is cause sufficient for him to unlimber one of [*sic*] more "mountain howitzers" invariably found strapped to his person. **1903** in "O. Henry" *Works* 959: What are you gunning for with that howitzer? **1909** in McCay *Little Nemo* 165: Our beautiful princess awaited the voice of Bill's trusty howitzer. **1964** Whitehouse *Fledgling* 30: I got…that "howitzer"…and pulled the trigger.

howl *n.* **1.** a loud objection or complaint; uproar.

　1871 Schele de Vere *Americanisms* 289: But Radicalism raised such an infernal howl [that]…the organization was finally abandoned. **1879** Burt *Prof. Smith* 18: I care not whatever howl it may raise in the country. **1908** in J. London *Letters* 256: I am just writing you a howl. **1913** T.M. Osborne *Pris. Walls* 309: You immediately put up a howl. **1913** in Pound *Letters* 23: There'll be a *howl*. They won't like it. **1914** Ellis *Billy Sunday* 73: It takes a big man to see other people succeed without raising a howl. **1921** Marquis *Carter* 150: This isn't a howl, it's merely an explanation. **1926** "M. Brand" *Iron Trail* 197: The owner of that pony will be making quite a considerable howl about losing him. **1938** Steinbeck *Grapes of Wrath* 39: You don't kick up a howl because you can't make Fords. **1942** in Stilwell *Papers* 31: GHQ...[is] fed up with the howls and a letter has been sent...telling them politely to shut up. **1971** J. Brown & A. Groff *Monkey* 22: I didn't put up too big a howl, either. **1971** Lavallee *Event 1000* 32: There would be one hell of a public howl.

2. a cause for hilarity; HOOT, 2.

1932 Lorimer *Street Cars* 175: A howl. **1942** in Stilwell *Papers* 30: What a howl! **1954–60** *DAS*. **1991** *Night Court* (NBC-TV): "Isn't that a hoot?" "That's better than a hoot. It's a howl."

¶ In phrase:

¶ **on the howl** on a spree.

1868–71 C.G. Leland *Breitmann's Ballads* 195: He vent at it on de howl.

howl *v.* to celebrate riotously.

1900 (quot. at BITTER CREEK). **1902** Wister *Virginian* ch. xiv: Some one was reciting "And it's my night to howl." "We'll all howl when we get to Rawhide," said some other one; and they howled now. **1908** Raine *Wyoming* 89: It may be their night to howl. **1935** *Bedroom Companion* 102: This is her night to howl. **1941** *Pittsburgh Courier* (Mar. 22) 7: This would be her night to "howl." **1951** Waggner *Operation Pacific* (film): Now everything's cleared up and you want someone to howl with. **1961** *Many Loves of Dobie Gillis* (CBS-TV): There's a full moon tonight, and we're gonna howl!

¶ In phrase:

¶ **make (someplace) howl** to celebrate riotously in; in phr. **make Rome howl** to create an uproar. Also **make them howl** to celebrate riotously.

1861 in C.H. Brewster *Cruel War* 71: When Col Briggs returns and finds out what they have been doing...he will make Rome howl. **1878** Willis *Our Cruise* 45: Both crews were allowed two days liberty on shore, during which we squandered the spoils won in the contest, and, quoting the words of Tom Harning, "made Nagasaki howl." **1882** Peck *Peck's Sunshine* 222: She made Monterey howl. **1887** *Lantern* (N.O.) (May 14) 2: When they get together they literally make Rome howl. **1889** E. Field *Western Verse* 23: And starting out to prowl, sir,/You bet he made Rome howl, sir. **1912** Siringo *Cowboy Detective* 78: Jacky and I made "Rome howl" every night at the dance hall. **1950** Schnee *Next Voice* (film): Remember the nights we used to make 'em howl?

howler *n.* **1.** a blatant error; an enormous blunder. Cf. slightly earlier BrE *come a howler* 'to come to grief' (1875 in *OED*). Now *colloq.*

*1885 in *F & H* III 368: What undergraduates call *howlers*, or grievously impossible blunders. **1891* in *F & H*: We wondered yesterday how many of our classical readers would see the howler—or the joke. **1894* in *OED*: The specimens of schoolboy blunders which, under the head of "Howlers," are so popular in our journals. **1915** in E. Pound *Letters* 71: I thought the standards of criticism in the number good, and without the howlers that so often annoy me. **1934** Weseen *Dict. Slang* 353: Howler—A laughable mistake, especially a bad blunder in the use of language. **1949** in *DAS*: Howlers Recently Noted....It is obvious that the writer...had no idea...what the word nuptial means. **1963** D. Tracy *Brass Ring* 76: I always thought they'd pulled a howler.

2. an expert or adept.

1938 in A. Lomax *Mr. Jelly Roll* 51: He was a howler, I'm telling you, the best there was...when it came to playing the blues.

3. a siren.

1959 *Sat. Eve. Post* (May 2) 67: With a Daggerjet you didn't fiddle around....when the howler blew, you took it on the dead run. **1986** Univ. Tenn. grad. student: A *howler* is a police siren. Howlers and lights.

howling *adj.* [prob. sugg. by phr. *howling wilderness* (Deuteronomy 32:10), literally, a place filled with the howling of wild beasts; later a loosely applied cliché] extreme; utter; thoroughgoing; very great. Also as *adv.*

*1865 in *OED2*: To risk a very vulgar phrase, a Nawab is "a howling swell" in the East. **1867** Williams *Brierly* 14: There were at this gathering, swells of the "howling" category, in the correctest of evening

dress. **1881** H.H. Kane *Opium* 12: Some men...go on howling drunks. **1885** *Puck* (June 3) 210: There's Ichabod howling drunk again. **1888** Pierson *Slave of Circumstances* 26: He was a regular howlin' swell....drove as fine a team of horses as you ever see in your life, and lived in high old style up by Central Park. **1889** (quot. at JAG, *n.*). **1894** Bridges *Arcady* 88: Meredith is a howling optimist. **1904–11** Phillips *Susan Lenox* II 125: Why you could pretend to be a howling fashionable swell. **1922** Dean *Flying Cloud* 33: The man was right in telling me I was a howling jay. **1938** Steinbeck *Grapes of Wrath* 348: They et green grapes. They all five got the howlin' skitters. **1979** J. Morris *War Story* 266: Listen, you howling, fucking idiot. **1980** Teichmann *Fonda* 40: We were a howling hit.

hoy *n.* HOOEY, 1.

1916 in E. Wilson *Prelude* 165: Hoy, bull [nonsense]. **1917** in Bowerman *Compensation* 45: This story is very probably "hoi" but it is very possible. **1918** *Wadsworth Gas Attack* 8: If I have to listen to any more hoy about 'at gal I'll desert.

H.P. *n.* [fr. *hot pilot*] *Mil. Av.* an unusually brash or skillful pilot.

1941 Kendall *Army & Navy Sl.* 7: An HP...a hot pilot. **1942** *Life* (June 1) 14: Buzz is an H.P. [hot pilot]. **1942** *Randolph Field* 131: H.P.—A Hot Pilot, in his own estimation. **1944** Wiener *Flyers* 41: The h.p. is a show-off. He takes unnecessary chances. **1947** *AS* (Apr.) XXII 112: An *H.P.* represents in all three air forces a *hot pilot*, a smart-alec aviator of inferior ability. Originally, the term indicated an excellent and daring pilot. **1955** *AS* XXX (May) 118: Hot Pilot; H.P.; Space Cadet, n. phr. Good pilot who indulges in daring feats of flying, or is over-confident; a show-off. **1957** *Time* (Apr. 1) 18: I was certainly not in the H.P. [Hot Pilot] category.

H Town *n.* (a nickname for) a city whose name begins with an initial *H*.

1976 Dills *CB Slanguage* (ed. 2) 38: H Town: Hopkinsville, Kentucky. **1995** Stavsky, Mozeson, & Mozeson *A 2 Z* 51: H-town...Houston, Texas: It's got an H-town vibe.

hub[1] *n.* [orig. in allusion to 1858 quot. below and similar metaphors] (*cap.*) Now *Journ.* Boston, Massachusetts.—constr. with *the.*

[**1858** O.W. Holmes *Autocrat* ch. vi: Boston State-House is the hub of the solar system.] [**1862** in F. Moore *Rebellion* V 600: As he left the metropolis and journeyed eastward to the "Hub of the Universe."] **1864** in *DAE*: Codfish aristocracy of "the Hub." **1869** in *F & H* III 369: A quintette of amateurs...from the Hub. **1872** in Barnum *Letters* 169: The cosy way they have of doing things at the "Hub." **1877** Bartlett *Amer.* (ed. 4) 301: "The Hub" is a term applied to Boston. **1879** in *Harper's Mag.* (Jan. 1880) 317: A town within twenty-five miles of "the Hub." **1884** Blanding *Sailor Boy* 23: We...marched to the Providence and Boston depot, where we took the train for the "Hub." **1888** in *F & H* III 369: The typical girl of the Hub has been much written about. **1978** Dills *CB Slanguage* (ed. 4) 56: *Hub:* the greater Boston, Massachusetts, area. **1989** Radford & Crowley *Drug Agent* 47: Two busy...Hub cocaine dealers.

¶ In phrase:

¶ **up to the hub** up to the limit; thoroughly; to the hilt.

1800 in *DAE*: This is not a half measure...this bill you will allow is up to the hub. **1827** in *DAE*: He was a Jackson man up to the hub. **1864** in R.B. Browne *Lincoln-Lore* 135: He had found it a Clay State up to the hub. **1865** Byrn *Fudge Fumble* 172: I am up to the hub in love with you. *ca*1865 O.W. Holmes, Jr., in M.D. Howe *Shaping Yrs.* 105: I was shot in the breast doing my duty up to the hub. **1868** J.R. Browne *Apache Country* 462: Pop, he's Union to the hub. **1884** "M. Twain" *Huck. Finn* ch. xx: I'm in, up to the hub, for anything that will pay.

hub[2] *n.* HUBBY.

1879 in J.M. Carroll *Camp Talk* 120: I am devotedly yr. hub.

hubba *n.* [orig. unkn.] *Narc.* crack cocaine; a pellet or lump of crack cocaine.

1988 *Newsweek* (Apr. 25) 64: Jennifer...is smoking hubbas, or rocks of crack. *a*1989 Spears *NTC Dict.* *a*1990 E. Currie *Dope & Trouble* xxv: Hubba. Crack cocaine. *Ibid.* 3: Crack is usually sold in small chunks or "rocks," also called "hubbas."

hubba-hubba *n.* **1.** lively or competitive spirit; energetic action. Also **hab[b]a-hab[b]a, hava-hava.**

1940 in Tamony *Americanisms* (No. 7) (1965) 1: There's more than a new coach…at St. Mary's.…Yep, the Gaels looked great in spring practice. Lots of the old haba-haba and what have you. But spirit alone does not win football games. **1940** in *Ibid.:* St. Mary's looked swell. The boys gave Gonzaga that old "hava hava," as Red said they would. **1945** *AS* XX 261: *Hubba-hubba*…now means the spirit of double-time and eagerness; it is…a noun. **1953** in Tamony *Americanisms* 7: The crowd doesn't boo or yell and the players don't talk it up. There's no "ol habba habba." **1959** "D. Stagg" *Glory Jumpers* 100: Hubba-hubba on it—they'll be hitting us soon.

2. utter nonsense.

1946 in *OED2:* I suppose you think that's a lot of hubba-hubba.

hubba-hubba *interj.* [cf. earlier forms *haba-haba* and *hava-hava* with *have a life* s.v. LIFE; alleged derivation from Chinese *hao³-pu⁴-hao³* is shown by A.F. Moe (*AS* XXXVI [1961], 188–94) to be untenable, as are those sugg. by A.D. Weinberger (*AS* XXII [1947], 34–39), repeated in *NDAS.* See esp. discussion by P. Tamony (*Americanisms* (No. 7) 1965).]

1. hurry up!, get busy!, look alive!, etc.; (*hence*) used to express excitement and approval, esp. at the sight of an attractive young woman or man. Also **hab[b]a-hab[b]a.**

1941 in Tamony *Americanisms* (No. 7) (1965) 2: Red's cheery battle call from baseball, "Habba, Habba" sung out as he entered the dressing room. **1944** in *AS* XXII (1947) 35: The cry "Haba-Haba" is spreading like a scourge through the land. **1945** in *AS* 34: That girl sitting in the front row…*hubba-hubba.* **1945** *Here Come Co-Eds* (film): We play for Bixby! Hubba-hubba! Yay!/For our side—hooray! **1945** in O. Cary *War-Wasted Asia* 90: You must surely remember the same attitude on Okinawa toward the "gooks" at whom the marines would shout "habba-habba." **1945** in *Calif. Folk. Qly.* V (1946) 385: *Haba haba*…is said to be a Micronesian native greeting. To the sailor it means hurry, haste, expedition, speed. **1946** *Popeye the Sailor* (animated cartoon): I'm just butter in his hands! Hubba hubba hubba hubba! **1947** *AS* XVII 35: *Hubba-hubba.*…I myself heard it…in the early summer of 1943 during a softball game at…Madison, Wis. The manager, a nonplayer, would clap his hands and call out a string of *hubba-hubbas* whenever it was the turn of his team to take the field. **1947** Spillane *Jury* 62: Okay, Mike. I'll watch the angles, you watch out for the curves. Huba huba. **1955** T. Anderson *Own Beloved Sons* 21: Get moving, now. Hubba-hubba. **1963** *Mad* (Jan.) 31: "Wanna lift?" "Hubba-hubba!" "Man, I go ape over freckles!" **1965** Tamony *Americanisms* (No. 7) 4: During the 1940's I discussed "hubba-hubba" with…Joe Devine, Pacific Coast scout of the New York Yankees. Devine remembered the expression from the 1920's, and verified earlier usage through C.E. "Truck" Eagan, who infielded around San Francisco principally.…Robert D. Buckley of Palo Alto, who played with Notre Dame in the late 1890's…instantly associated the expression as one of the hollers used by Bobby Edgar, an infielder of the 1906 Los Angeles team. **1965** Tavel *Godiva* 203: "The Life of Lady Godiva"…Hubba hubba! **1970** *Playboy* (Aug.) 108: Hubba-hubba! Hey, cutie-pie, what do you say you and me cut a rug? **1971** Sorrentino *Up from Never* 40: Hubba, hubba.…Get a gander o' those gams. **1975** *Daily Beacon* (Univ. Tenn.) (Feb. 6) 2: This is when the chanting [at a panty raid] climaxes. "Oh, boy, she's gonna do it!"…"Hubba-hubba!" The bloomers drift downward. **1976** J. Lee *Ninth Man* 167: A trio of young women lounging near a box hedge whispered as he approached. One of them winked and mouthed the words, "Hubba, hubba." **1981** Patchett et al. *Great Muppet Caper* (film): [To girl:] Hubba hubba! **1988** *Pee-Wee's Play House* (CBS-TV): Hubba hubba hubba hubba! Get a load of Dixie! **1990** *CBS This Morning* (CBS-TV) (Feb. 14): The Southeast—hubba-hubba! We're showin' off today: [temperatures in the] 70's and 80's!

hubby *n.* a husband.—now usu. used derisively. Orig. *colloq.*

*1688 in *OED:* Oh my hubby, dear, dear, dear hubby. *1772 in Farmer *Merry Songs* V 211: What could *Hubby* do then? *1798 in *F & H* III 370: The wife…Scarce knows again her lover in her hubby. *1811 in *F & H:* Now, madam, this once was your hubby. **1839** in

Essex Inst. Hist. Coll. LXXXIV (1948) 219: I did not want her hubby to get jealous. *a*1889 in Barrère & Leland *Dict. Slang* I 479: You…/Come across her hubby at the door. **1892** *Nat. Police Gaz.* (Oct. 15) 5: She licked her Mongolian hubby. **1908** McGaffey *Show Girl* 163: She had given hubby the slip. **1912** Siringo *Cowboy Detective* 18: No doubt they thought their "hubbies" had…stirred up a hornet's nest. **1939** *Pittsburgh Courier* (July 15) 3: Kills Hubby With Icepick. **1949** *Sat. Eve. Post* (Jan. 22) 49: I'll have your hubby bring you your breakfast. **1954–60** *DAS:* Hubby…A husband. **1990** *Daybreak* (CNN-TV) (Jan. 21): Just four days after her divorce from hubby number one became final. **1990** *U.S. News & W.R.* (Mar. 5) 68: As expected, hubby didn't sign and started divorce proceedings.

hubcap hands *n.pl. Baseball.* (see quot.). *Joc.*

1983 L. Frank *Hardball* 79: [A poor fielder] has "bad" or "hubcap" hands (since the ball bounces off of them as if they were metal).

huck *n.* [fr. HUCK(LEBERRY)] **1.** a fellow; HUCKLEBERRY, 2.

*ca*1910 in Rosa *Wild Bill* 194 [ref. to *ca*1870]: In a flash I had the other huck by the throat.

2. *Black E.* a black person.

1929 T. Gordon *Born to Be* 220: So when this spade tried to find the other two hucks they couldn't be found anywhere. *Ibid.* 236: *Spade, Huck, Dinge*…Nicknames for Ethiopians. **1935** L. Hughes *Little Ham* 79: Girl, my new man bought me the prettiest velveteen evening coat you ever seen yesterday from a hot selling huck. **1937** in *DARE* s.v. *huckleberry:* Huck—a Negro's name for Negro.

huck *v.* to huckster.

1971 Sloan *War Games* 46: It had been his pleasure to huck a few bonds in time of national trial.

huckleberry *n.* **1.** a minuscule amount; bit; in phr. **a huckleberry above (one's) persimmon** rather beyond (one's) abilities; superior to (one).

1832 in *DA:* Within a huckleberry of being smothered to death. **1835** in *DA:* Orson…is nothing to him—not a circumstance—not a huckleberry. [**1835** in Paulding *Bulls & Jons.* 35: In a state to which plague, pestilence, and starvation, are no more than "a huckleberry to a persimmon," as they say…down South.] **1840** *Spirit of Times* (Mar. 7) 1: We present…our new volume, in a new dress that is a huckleberry over anybody's persimmon. **1840** *Spirit of Times* (Apr. 25) 90: The time [will be] "a huckleberry" finer than was ever made in New Jersey. **1846** in Bartlett *Amer.* (ed. 2) 207: The way he and his companions used to destroy the beasts of the forests was [a] huckleberry above the persimmon of any native in the country. **1859** in Botkin *Treas. Amer. Folk.* 590: I'm danged…ef that don't take the huckleberry off of my 'simmon. **1859** "Skitt" *Fisher's River* 47 [ref. to 1820's]: But I'll show him I'm a huckleberry over his 'simmon, sartin. **1873** in Bunner *Letters* 18: By the way, a young Virginian told me the other day that "Wagner was a huckleberry above *his* persimmons!"…Wagner is, I guess, a huckleberry above most people's persimmons. So? **1890** Janvier *Aztec Treasure House* 250: A front door of solid gold is a huckleberry above Jay Gould's biggest persimmon. **1984** Wilder *You All* 151: *Huckleberry over my persimmons*…that's more than I can take; it's beyond one's knowledge, comprehension.

2. a fellow; character; boy; (in 1870 quot.) a good fellow; in phr. **(one's) huckleberry** (*obs.*) the very person for a particular job.

1868 in *DA:* Now then, my huckleberry, look sharp! You're wrong! **1870** "M. Twain," in A.L. Scott *Twain's Poetry* 79: Cap,…you air my huckleberry! **1877** Wheeler *Deadwood Dick, Prince of the Road* 83: Squar' ninety tens, my huckleberry, an' all won fa'r, you bet. **1883** Hay *Bread-Winners* 115: "I like a man that can hold his tongue." "Then I'm your huckleberry." **1887** Walling *N.Y. Chief of Police* 351: That's the kind o' huckleberry he is, is it? *a*1889 in Barrère & Leland *Dict. Slang* I 479: Dat's wot kind of a huckleberry 'Liger was. **1891** McCann & Jarrold *Odds & Ends* 79: That's the kind of a huckleberry I am, an' that's the kind of a raspberry you are. See? **1893** in J.I. Robertson *Blue & Gray* 7: I'm your huckleberry. **1899** Hamblen *Bucko Mate* 234: All right, sir; we're your huckleberries. **1914** Giles *Rags* 56 [ref. to Civil War]: "All right," said Mr. Bailey, "I'm your huckleberry." **1936** Tully *Bruiser* 49: Well, I'm your huckleberry, Mr. Haney. **1961** Forbes *Goodbye to Some* 184: I'm your huckleberry. **1987** Weiser & Stone *Wall St.* (film): It's yourself you gotta be proud of, huckleberry.

3. bad treatment.—constr. with *the*. Cf. RASPBERRY.

1883 *Century Mag.* (June) 280: He got the huckleberry, as we used to say in college, on that particular text. **1970** *Current Slang* V (Winter) 9: *Huckleberry*, n. Bad treatment, the "shaft."—College students...California.—"She really gave him the huckleberry."

4. a foolish, inept, or inconsequential fellow.

1889 "M. Twain" *Conn. Yankee* 340: Sir Persant of Inde is competent, intelligent, courteous, and in every way a brick....Sir Palamides the Saracen is no huckleberry himself. **1906** in *DA:* You know the whites—Welshmen, Cornishmen, and a good sprinklin' o' "huckleberries." **1947** Overholser *Buckaroo's Code* 81: We don't like you huckleberries no more than a little. **1974** Brasch & Brasch *Monikers* 10: "Huckleberry" did come to have the connotation of the country bumpkin personality and gave rise to the saying, "He's just a 'huckleberry.'" **1977** P. Rizzuto, on NY Yankees Baseball (WPIX-TV): That was a firecracker....Some huckleberry let one go out there right amongst the fans. **1987** *Prime News* (CNN) (Jan. 21): We can defend ourselves from the huckleberries up there.

¶ In phrase:

¶ **above** [or **beyond**] **(one's) huckleberry** beyond (one's) abilities; beyond (one).

1839–40 Cobb *Green Hand* I 261: A jack's hide and bull's tripe, dished up in mud, is a hash beyond my huckleberry. **1871** Schele de Vere *Americanisms* 577: *Above one's bend* means, above one's power of bending all his strength to a certain purpose....In the South the phrase is apt to expand into "above my *huckleberry*."

huckleberry train *R.R.* (see quot.).

1878–81 W.G. Marshall *Through Amer.* 65: A "huckleberry train" [is] one that stops at every station.

huddle *v. Police.* (see quot.).

1973 Maas *Serpico* 63: The fine art of "cooping," or sleeping on duty, a...police practice that in other cities goes under such names as "huddling" and "going down."

Huey *n.* **1.** [orig. unkn.] *Und.* the *National Police Gazette.*

1859 Matsell *Vocab.* 43: *Huey.* The National Police Gazette. **1866** *Nat. Police Gaz.* (Nov. 3) 3: She figured in the "huey" some time ago. **1867** *Nat. Police Gaz.* (Oct. 26) 4: Let the readers of the "Huey" know all about it. **1871** Banka *Prison Life* 493: Police Gazette,...*Huey.*

2. *Mil.* a Bell UH-1 (formerly HU-1) Iroquois helicopter.

1962 Tregaskis *Viet. Diary* 150: The new HU1A (called "Huey"). **1964** in J. Lucas *Dateline* 16: He was a gunner on a UH-1B—the helicopters they call Hueys. **1968** in B.E. Holley *Vietnam* 70: Yesterday we had sixteen choppers—ten Hueys and six Cobras. **1981** Mersky & Polmar *Nav. Air War in Viet.* 137: The name Iroquois was officially assigned, but the helicopter was always called "Huey," the name derived from the pre-1962 designation letters HU. **1982** Del Vecchio *13th Valley* 235: A huey slick approached...the LZ. **1984** Apostolo *Encyc. Helicopters* 47: Bell HU-1A...Iroquois....Delivery of the first...100 (...known by the unofficial name of "Huey") was not completed until June 1961. **1988** von Hassell & Crossley *Warriors* 131: In the Huey, the seat belt is not long enough to fit around me. **1992** Cornum & Copeland *She Went* 5: [The] UH-60 Black Hawk...is the utility and assault helicopter designed to replace the old "Huey" of Vietnam fame. **1995** *CNN Breaking News* (Apr. 19) (CNN-TV): Some Huey helicopters were brought in from Fort Sill.

3. see U-IE.

huff *v. Narc.* to inhale the vapors of, as a method of becoming intoxicated.—also used absol. Hence **huffer, huffing,** *n.*

1969 in *Crime & Delinquency* (Jan. 1970) XVI 5: Gasoline sniffers ("huffers") more frequently sniff directly from...[fuel] tanks, and other direct sources. **1968–70** *Current Slang* III & IV 53: *Huffer,* n. A person who sniffs glue.—High school students...Colorado. **1970–71** J. Rubinstein *City Police* 165: They're probably talkin' about where they can steal some glue to huff. *Ibid.* 202: They were up there huffin'. They always huff up in the yard. **1971** Guggenheimer *Narcotics & Drug Abuse* 27: *Huffer.* user of volatile chemicals, glue sniffer. **1978** *Nat. Lampoon* (Oct.) 4: Sniffing nitrous oxide...and huffing industrial solvents. **1982** Knoxville, Tenn., law student, age *ca*29: I had to drive a guy to the emergency room because he'd been huffing paint thinner. **1990** *CBS This Morning* (CBS-TV) (Dec. 17): Changes to look for if

you think your child is "huffing."...Three kids had been huffing Scotchgard out of their socks. **1993** E. Richards *Cocaine True* 114: Taiwal for two dollars to the "huffers" who wanted a quick, breathy high. **1993** *L.A. Times* (Apr. 27) E1: It is this use of inhalants, called "huffing" among kids, that has a growing number of drug abuse experts worried. **1996** *Geraldo* (synd. TV series): Are you still huffing paint?

huff-duff *n.* [sugg. by abbr. *HF/DF*] *Av.* a high-frequency radio direction finder. Now *hist.*

1946 *Amer. N & Q* (Feb.) 168: *Huff Duff*: high-frequency direction finding device. **1952** Morison *Naval Ops. in WWII* 226: Radar furnished the convoys with a cat's eyes, sonar with its ears, while the high-frequency direction-finders (HF/DF, pronounced "Huff Duff")...acted as a highly sensitive and elongated cat's whiskers. **1961** Hemingway *Islands* 225: And a pigeon probably has his Huff Duff in that incrustation above his beak. **1965** Gallery *Eight Bells* 161 [ref. to 1943]: By this time we had a network of radio direction finder stations (called "Huff-Duffs") in England, Iceland, Greenland, Canada, the U.S., and the Atlantic Islands.

huffer *n.* **1.** see s.v. HUFF, *v.*

2. *Mil. Av.* an auxiliary power unit.

1989 Joss *Strike* 126: Slim gets an engine start from the "huffer," or APU (auxiliary power unit) rolled up next to the bird.

hug-and-squeeze *n.* an attractive young woman.

1934 Boylan & Baldwin *Devil Dogs of the Air* (film): You don't mean that cute little hug-and-squeeze down at the—.

huge *adj.* wonderful; grand; great; IMMENSE; (*hence*) popular. [No continuity of usage from earliest example is evident.]

*a*1865 in W.C. Davis *Orphan Brig.* 51: Had a "huge" time in town. **1992** Crowe *Singles* (film): We're huge in Europe this year. **1992** *Seinfeld* (NBC-TV): This is major! This is huge! **1993** P. Munro *U.C.L.A. Slang II* 52: *Huge*...amazing; wonderful...: *That basketball game was just huge.* **1993** Bahr & Small *Son-in-Law* (film): You have no idea how huge you are on the college circuit! **1994** *New Yorker* (June 20) 6: Richter's goaltending is *huge.* **1994** *New York* (Sept. 12) 41: Hollywood men were equally impressed by...*Fatal Attraction*'s worldwide grosses. She's scary! She sells! She's huge! **1995** Eble *Campus Slang* (Apr.) 6: *Huge*—dominant, superlative.

hugger-mugger *n. Police.* a streetwalker who acts as a decoy for a mugger, or one who herself assaults pickup victims.

1970 Wambaugh *New Centurions* 188 [ref. to 1962]: Maybe battling some hugger mugger's pimp in some dark hotel lobby. *Ibid.* 196: She not just a whore, she's a booster and a hugger mugger and everything else. **1970** Gattzden *Black Vendetta* 52: Some hugger-mugger with a body. **1972** *Village Voice* (Nov. 9) 12: The huggermuggers pounce on their victims and then escape into the shrubbery of the darkened park. **1972** Wambaugh *Blue Knight* 11: I could drive down Main Street any time and see hugger-muggers, paddy hustlers, till-tappers, junkies, [etc.]. **1987** R. Miller *Slob* 12: Even the affluent yuppie suburbs had their fair share of raincoat flashers, hugger-muggers, dong danglers, and wienie waggers.

huggy-bear *n.* a cuddly person; in phr. **play huggy-bear** to hug and kiss. *Joc.*

1964 in IUFA *Folk Speech:* Huggy bear means necking. **1964** in *Time* (Jan. 1, 1965) 57: The same as playing *huggy-bear, smacky-lips, smash-mouth,* and *kissy-face.* **1968** Baker, Ladd & Robb *CUSS* 140: *Huggy Bear* (Noun). To neck [*sic*]. **1981** Univ. Tenn. student: Just a big huggy-bear. **1987** J. Kent *Phr. Book* 154: A huggybear.

hulk *n.* **1.** *Naut.* (one's) body or corpse.

1839–40 Cobb *Green Hand* I 147: If my old hulk isn't hogged by the morning, it will be no fault of the breakers underneath. **1853** [J. Jones] *Jack Junk* 27: Oh, I wish this old hulk of mine was in proper trim. **1893** Griggs *Lyrics* 28: They said if I didn't hoist it in,/They'd load my hulk with lead.

2. [sugg. by the Incredible *Hulk,* comic-book character created (1962) by Stan Lee and Jack Kirby, U.S. cartoonists; later a CBS-TV series, 1978–82] a big, muscular, often violent man; giant. Cf. *OED* def. 4.

1984 H. Gould *Cocktail* 97: A hulk with an extra chromosome who looked like he smothered rabbits on his coffee break. *Ibid.* 115: It was the inebriated hulk from Toomey's. *a*1987 Bunch & Cole *Reckoning for Kings* 144: Rosa had three hulks for brothers. **1988** M. Bartlett *Trooper Down!* 41: Her boyfriend, The Hulk, rises up to get me too. **1988** Dietl & Gross *One Tough Cop* 166: He's coming at me, like a fucking hulk.

hulkeys *n.pl.* the legs.

   1842 *Spirit of Times* (Nov. 5) 421: Gabriel relaxed his manly frame upon his "hulkeys."

hull *n.* **1.** *Naut.* a person's body or build. Now *hist.*

   *1805 J. Davis *Post-Captain* 42: The hull of his lordship could never withstand them. **1831* Trelawny *Adv. Younger Son* ch. xix: The bullets and the gout/Have…knocked his hull about. **1849** Melville *White Jacket* 303 [ref. to 1843]: We dragged his hull to one side. **1855** Brougham *Chips* 393: Bless his benevolent ould hull. **1863** in Gibbons *Tales That Were Told* 77: Before my time-worn figure-head/Was ever soiled by dust or powder,/My fins employed to shovel coal,/My hull by steam boiled into chowder. **1872** Thomes *Slaver* 97: Isadora, looking beautiful as Venus, entered the room.…"Say, Robert," the captain exclaimed…"what a figure-head and hull! Blast me if she ain't a full-rigged clipper, and no mistake. What a run, and what counters!" **1964* Hugill *Shanties & Sailors' Songs* 213 (folksong learned *ca*1925): She set fire to me riggin', as well as me hull,/An' away to the lazareet I had to scull.

   2. *West.* a saddle.

   1916 *Editor* XLIII (May 20) 535: *Hull*—A saddle. **1917–20** in J.M. Hunter *Trail Drivers* I 112 [ref. to 1871]: I…threw my "hull" on and galloped around the herd. **1931** Rynning *Gun Notches* 21: Hull was used as often as the word saddle. In those early days [*ca*1882] some of the punchers called a saddle a caque (pronounced kak), but, wherever it come from, that name never got to be used as much as the other two. *a*1956 Almirall *College to Cow Country* 63 [ref. to *a*1918]: Tom climbed back into his hull.

hull out *v. So.* to depart hurriedly. Cf. SHELL OUT.

   1851 Paine *Ga. Prison* 151: Well, well, Tony; that will do. Now hull out to work! **1944** Boatright & Day *Hell to Breakfast* 140: When you are in a big hurry, you "hull out" or "gin" (gin a bale).

hum[1] *n.* a humbug or deception; hoax; lie.

   *1751 in *OED2*: What a delightful *Hum* we had about a poor man's getting into a quart bottle. **1753* in *OED2*: 'Twas all a hum. **1756* in *F & H* III 376: Only a hum (as I suppose…) upon our country apes. **1767** "A. Barton" *Disappointment* 47 Hum [the name of a fraud in a comic opera]. **1799* S.T. Coleridge, in *OED*: The Bristol Library is a hum, and will do us little service. **1803* in J. Ashton *Eng. Satires on Napoleon* 225: This little Boney says he'll come/…But that I say is all a hum. **1820–21* P. Egan *Life in London* 226: To whom *past fetes* are little better than a *hum*. **1823* "J. Bee" *Slang Dict.*: *Hum.*—A whispered lie. **1837* in *F & H* III 376: It's "all a Hum!" **1854** St. Clair *Metropolis* 85: All a "hum," was it not? **1856** Melville *Confidence-Man* ch. xv: Cant, gammon! Confidence? hum, bubble! **1885, *1892* in *F & H* III 376.

hum[2] *n.* (a partial euphem. for) hell.

   1940 *AS* XV 221: What the hum do you mean? **1982** in *DARE*: *Hum*—euphemism for *hell*. To give someone hum. To catch hum.

hum[3] *n.* a mild state of drug intoxication; BUZZ, 2.a.

   1979 D. Glasgow *Black Underclass* 96: To get a "hum" and a little "high." [**1981** (cited in Spears *Drugs & Drink*): *Humming*…drug intoxicated.]

hum[4] *n.* HUM JOB.

   1985 *Nat. Lampoon* (Sept.) 8: So always look for the Union Labia/When you are buying a hump or a hum.…Prostitutes' Local #69.

hum *v.* **1.** to HUMBUG, 1.

   *1785 (quot. at HUMBUG, *v.*, 1). **1813* in J. Ashton *Eng. Satires on Napoleon* 359: The Corsican Munchausen humming the Lads of Paris. **1835** in Paulding *Bulls & Jons.* 16: They soon devised a scheme to hum John a little.

   2. *Und.* to arrest on a HUMBLE, 1.

   1965–68 McCord et al. *Life Styles in Black Ghetto* 242: The police…stopped Panther cars; hummed Panthers in (arrested them on spurious charges).

humble *n.* [prob. alter. of HUMBUG] **1.** *Und.* a false or trivial charge; HUMMER, 2.

1940 *Current Hist. & Forum* (Nov. 7) 22: He runs the risk of *being locked up on a humble* (sent to disciplinary company for talking back to a guard). **1965** C. Brown *Manchild* 142 [ref. to 1950's]: It was a jive tip, but there were a whole lot of cats up there on humbles. *a*1994 N. McCall *Wanna Holler* 360: It was a drug tip. Got busted on a humble. Judge gave me twenty years. I took the rap for two other dudes. **1994** *Homicide* (NBC-TV): Man, I can't take a humble like this.

   2. *Black E.* an effort or action that is foolish, harmful, self-defeating, or the like. Also **hummel.**

   1959 F.L. Brown *Trumbull Pk.* 385: The nobodies. The no-bread squares. The cats on a humble. The lushes. **1964** Rhodes *Chosen Few* 118 [ref. to *ca*1950]: It don't make sense t'get fucked up on a humble and one little peahole ain't worth it. *a*1967 in *Social Problems* XV (1968) 389: At Essexfields, a boy is said to be "sent home on a humble" when he is released…to probation although the group feels he has not really earned his way out. **1979** J.L. Gwaltney *Drylongso* xvi: *Hummel, humble*—a fruitless course; a misguided effort. *Ibid.* 213: He's living from day to day on a hummel!

   3. *Pris.* a fight or altercation; HUMBUG, 2.b.

   1978 W. Brown *Tragic Magic* 37: I wound up knockkneed in a jive humble.

humbug *n.* [orig. unkn.; see note in *OED*] **1.a.** Orig. *Stu.* a hoax or imposition; sham; imposture; fraud; pack of lies; (*broadly*) nonsensical pretense; rubbish; foolishness. Now *S.E.*

   *1751 in *OED*: That exalted species of wit which is now practised by gentlemen of the brightest parts under the elegant denomination of a Humbug. **1754* in *OED*: *Humbug*…[a] new-coined expression, which is only to be found in the nonsensical vocabulary, sounds absurd and disagreeable, wherever it is pronounced. **1785* Grose *Vulgar Tongue*: *Humbug*…a jocular imposition, or deception. **1832** in W. Dunlap *Diary* 633: [They] rail at the *Humbug* as they call it. **1832* B. Hall *Voyages* (Ser. 2) I 68: He was undergoing the operation well known afloat and ashore…[as] "the game of humbug." *a*1839 Nack *Earl Rupert* 158: This was an action in plea of humbug. **1842** in Bleser *Secret & Sacred* 90: This is all humbug and acting. **1845** Corcoran *Pickings* 106: The law is a humbug and so is the chairman. **1854** in Barnum *Letters* 79: I am about acting on your hint to write a lecture on the science of humbug. **1857** in Still *Underground R.R.* 144: The talk of cold in this place is all a humbug. **1858** in Doten *Journals* 458: End of the Frazer River "humbug." **1860** J.G. Holland *Miss Gilbert* 223: They know I won't stand any of their humbug. **1862** in J.M. Williams *That Terrible Field* 88: Camp rumors…invariably turn out all humbug. **1863** in Tapert *Bros.' War* 132: I must not enumerate the humbugs and impositions practiced upon the army and from which we suffer repeated disasters and defeats. **1865** *Harper's Mo.* (Oct.) 578: I allers told 'em it was a d—d humbug. **1875** Yelverton *Teresina* 250: Shucks! all humbug! **1918** *DN* V 69: Dialect Speech of [New Mexico] High School Pupils…*humbug*, a fraud or deception. **1929** *AS* IV (Apr.) 330: To this list of popular contemporary terms may be added the older "poppycock," "humbug," "slush," "fudge," [etc.]. *ca*1938 in Rawick *Amer. Slave* II 175: Marse Gregg…say: "It's a damn humbug" and drop dead.

   b. Now *Black E.* anything unpleasant, useless, or offensive.

   1861 in M. Lane *Dear Mother* 19: [The] bed tick…is of no use, as straw is not always convenient and it's humbug anyhow. **1865** in Hilleary *Webfoot* 80: I think that roll call on this expedition is a humbug anyhow. **1875** in Chesnutt *Journals* 63: And if I'm not down in a trice/She rings the old brass Humbug [i.e., annoying breakfast bell] twice. **1970** Major *Dict. Afro-Amer. Slang* 68: *Humbug:* anything perplexing or complicated or both. *a*1973 in Maurer *Lang. of Und.* 297: Anything which is boring or unpleasant…*hum bug.*

   c. *Und. & Police.* a false or trivial charge or arrest; HUMMER, 2.

   1972 Wambaugh *Blue Knight* 241: Sheee-it, this is a humbug, we ain't done nothin'.

   2.a. Now esp. *Black E.* a bother or predicament; useless exercise; (*hence*) unpleasantness; trouble.

   1852–57 [Strother] *Old South* 28: I pronounce the expedition a failure and a humbug. **1862** in C. Brewster *Cruel War* 84: We have to go out and sleep in the woods…for no possible purpose.…It is a perfect humbug. *ca*1870 in Mackenzie *Ballads from Nova Scotia* 337: O what a nice humbug he got us in/If it hadn't been for the cane end of me stick! **1927** in *DARE:* Don' try an' raise no humbug late in de night like dis. **1960** in Oster *Country Blues* 135: Well, okay, Buddy, but it's gonna be a little humbug there. **1962** Crump *Killer* 97: Ya got to use fi-ness, be diplomatic. Why, man I ain't never had no humbug with them guys down there. **1981** in *DARE:* [Hawaiian pidgin:] *Humbug…*Bother, hassle. "Real humbug fo' do all dees ovah, you know!"

b. *Black E.* (*Specif.*) a fight; brawl.

1962 Crump *Killer* 167: What about our humbug at the railroad crossing? **1971** H. Roberts *Third Ear* (unp.): *Humbug,* n…a fight.

3. a foolish or no-account person; (in 1869 quot.) a poseur. [Weakened from the earlier sense 'an imposter or practitioner of deception', which has evidently always been S.E. (*1804 in *OED*).]

1867 S. Clemens, in *Twain's Letters* II 108: I had an article partly written about the Quaker City humbug. *Ibid.* 117: Am hob-nobbing with these old Generals & Senators & other humbugs for no good purpose. **1869** "G. Ellington" *Women of N.Y.* 118: Madam Vere de Vere…is a humbug and everybody hates her. **1877–88** in J.W. Crawford *Plays* 97: He's gone to ax dem Mormon humbugs 'bout de road.

4.a. *Black E.* a blunder or misunderstanding; (*also*) a trifling matter that leads to trouble.

1968 J. Garrett, in Chambers & Moon *Right On!* 237: Ain't no use in you cuttin' out on a humbug. You blowin' too much soul. **1971** H. Roberts *Third Ear* (unp.): *Humbug* n….an unimportant trifle; e.g. They started to fight on a humbug. **1973** Andrews & Owens *Black Lang.* 104: *Humbug*—A lightweight happening that turned out to be trouble. *a***1986** D. Tate *Bravo* 47: Eyes play tricks.…I sure don't wanna see somebody get all shot up on 'count some humbug.

b. Esp. *Black E.* a cruel twist of fate; mischance; fiasco. [Quots. ref. to Vietnam War.]

1984–87 Ferrandino *Firefight* 34: The humbug is the one fucking thing there's no protection from. I'll be damned if it don't fly up and bite you on the ass the minute you think things are cool. *Ibid.* 101: What a humbug…after all the bullshit, to be gunned down…by some…lunatic. **1992** L. Chambers *Recondo* 105: If things turned bad, this could quickly turn into a real humbug.

humbug *v.* **1.** to impose upon or lie to; deceive; take in; fool. Now *S.E.*

1751** in *OED2*: "Did you observe how the Colonel Humbug'd his Grace last night?" "These theatrical managers humbug the town damnably!" ***1751** Smollett *Peregrine Pickle* ch. lxxxv: Taking his departure with an exclamation of "Humbugged, egad!" **1754** in Breslaw *Tues. Club* 522: I think this is the rankest Instance of *Humbugging* (to use the modern phraze) that ever I have met with. **1767** "A. Barton" *Disappointment* 103: Fait', and we're all humbugged. ***1785** Grose *Vulgar Tongue: To Hum, or Humbug.* To deceive, or impose on one by some story or device. **1793** Brackenridge *Modern Chivalry* 185: He but humbugs. ***1802** in J. Ashton *Eng. Satires on Napoleon* 117: Our People are very uneasy lest you should be Humbugging us. **1807** in W. Irving *Salmagundi* 13: Macbeth…[was] confoundedly humbugged by an aërial dagger. ***1821** *Real Life in London* II 217: Here the friend and the brother/Meet to *humbug* each other. ***1826** in *F & H* III 379: We would not have the reader believe we mean to humbug him—not for a moment. **1833** J. Neal *Down-Easters* I 50: Was he not humbugging a brother yankee? **1842** in Bleser *Secret & Sacred* 98: He…has humbugged them also, as he has done us. **1848** [W.T. Thompson] *Jones's Sks.* 27: Some travellers…takes pains to humbug their readers. **1848** in Barnum *Letters* 39: I get all the curses for humbugging the public with that critter. **1854** G. Thompson *H. Glindon* 18: I have humbugged you most completely. **1857** in Dressler *Pioneer Circus* 69: The people are poor and tiard of being humbuged. **1859** in Hafen & Hafen *Reports from Colo.* 97: The men…has been humbuged. **1863** in Tapert *Bros.' War* 132: Abused, humbugged, imposed upon and frequently half-starved and sick, he sees himself made a mere tool for political speculators to operate upon. **1866** Dennett *South as It Is* 309: He…had been humbugged. *a1889** F. Kirkland *Anec. of Rebellion* 256: The soldiers…were delighted to see the rebels so completely humbugged into wasting their time as well as powder.

2. Esp. *Naut.* to struggle more or less fruitlessly; fool around or waste time.

1840 Dana *Two Years* 270 [ref. to 1836]: We were all the watch bracing the yards, and taking in and making sail, and "humbugging" with our flying kites. *Ibid.* 321: For several days we lay "humbugging about" in the horse latitudes. **1853** [G. Thompson] *Garter* 68: Ye'd better take us to yer place at once, without any more humbuggin'. **1856** in C.A. Abbey *Before the Mast* 58: We have been "humbugging" about within 2 days sail of Port for a week. **1862** in J.M. Williams *That Terrible Field* 81: All is vanity saith the preacher.…Of all the humbugging that ever I went through, my last three or four days experience has beat all. **1907** in *AS* XXXVII (Dec. 62) 253: We pitchpoled and humbugged about in them latitudes till the Cap'n and all the rest-part aboard was sick and tired of the whole business. ***1922** in T.E. Lawrence *Mint* 86: Humbugging About. **1933** in *OED2*: For several days we were kept humbugging about with light variable breezes. *a***1977** Spec. 5, U.S. Army, Dugway Proving Ground, Utah (coll. J. Ball): Oh, he's always coming around here, humbugging around.

3. *Black E.* to fight or dispute.

1968 in *Trans-action* VI (Feb. 1969) 27: And they start humbuggin (fighting) in there. **1971** *Black Scholar* (Sept.) 42: He stopped humbugging when she fell. **1971** H. Roberts *Third Ear* (unp.): *Humbugging …* being or acting tough; fighting, especially in a group. *a***1972** Claerbaut *Black Jargon* 69: *Humbuggin'* v. fighting; brawling: The cats got to humbuggin', man.

humdinger *n.* an impressive or extraordinary example. Now *colloq.*

1905 *DN* III 62: *Hum-dinger,* n. Term of admiration. "She's a humdinger." **1912** *DN* III 579: *Hum-dinger,* n. Something very remarkable. **1913** *DN* IV 16: That dress is a *humdinger.* **1916** "B.M. Bower" *Phantom Herd* 100: That pit'cher's a humdinger! **1918** *Ladies' Home Jour.* (May) 21: The storm last night was certainly a humdinger. **1918** *Sat. Eve. Post* (Nov. 2) 22: He was a humdinger. **1927** *AS* III (Dec.) 131: He announces his opinion of the social and intellectual gifts of a fellow student in terms like: "keen stuff," "an oak,"…"a humdinger," [etc.]. **1936** Dos Passos *Big Money* 16: Miss Humphries, I think you're a…humdinger. *a***1956** Almirall *College to Cow Country* 428: The winter…was a "humdinger." **1974** R.H. Carter *16th Round* 168: They had some mean mister humdingers out there in those boxing gloves. **1981** Hogan *Doubtful Canyon* 133: Was a humdinger of a sandstorm going on. **1992** *Mystery Sci. Theater* (Comedy Central TV): Is it a sassy, brassy, musical humdinger? **1995** *N.Y. Times* (Nov. 5) XI 1: One guy called the Spyder [a sports car] a humdinger, a word I don't think I've heard before in actual conversation. "That is a real humdinger," he said, ho-hoing and shaking his head.

humdinging *adj. & adv.* extraordinary; extraordinarily.

1940 in *DAS:* A humdinging good tale. **1943** Wolfert *Tucker's People* 150: A real, humdinging comer.

hum job *n.* (see 1970 quot.).

1964 in Cray *Erotic Muse* 254: My true love gave to me/A hum job in a pear tree. *a***1968** in Haines & Taggart *Ft. Lauderdale* 106: A hum job.…one girl…took my testicles into her mouth and hummed. **1970** Landy *Underground Dict.* 106: *Hum job…*Oral copulation. Can be by putting another's testicles in one's mouth and humming. **1973** Huggett *Body Count* 315: A little hum-job might be nice. **1978** C. Miller *Animal House* 97: Get one off? Hah? Hum job? **1986** Thacker *Pawn* 241: So how about a little hum-job?

humma-humma *n.* controversy; uproar.

1989 *Donahue* (NBC-TV): So there was a lot of humma-humma for what? For nothing.

hummel var. HUMBLE, 2.

hummer *n.* **1.** an extraordinary person or thing; HUMDINGER.

1681** in Otway *Works* II 101: I gad, says he, she's a hummer, such a *bona Roba* ah-h-h. ***1698–99** "B.E." *Dict. Canting Crew: Hummer,* a loud Lie, a Rapper. ***1701** in *OED:* Odd! she's a Hummer! ***1748** in *F & H* III 380: *Hummer…*a great, monstrous, or notorious lie. **1879** Burdette *Chimes* 203: "Now you're shoutin'!" he cried with enthusiasm: "that's the hummer! Fast time and crowds of passengers!" **1882** *Puck* (Dec. 27) 261: Ten Commercial drummers going out to drum./All these little Hummers reckoned they were "some." *a1889** in Barrère & Leland *Dict. Slang* I 479: "Isn't she a swell?"…"C'rect, Cholly; she's a *hummer!*" **1894** *Harper's* (Dec.) 104: It's got to be a hummer from Humtown, doctor. **1895** Wood *Yale Yarns* 9: He was a hummer…and put down…five whiskey cocktails, six beers, three Manhattans, and a bottle of fizz. **1900** Hammond *Whaler* 260: Wa-al, he's a hummer, anyway. **1905** *Nat. Police Gaz.* (Dec. 9) 7: Next week's [story] will be a hummer. **1907** Mulford *Bar-20* 229: She's a hummer—…a whole lot prettier than that picture. **1917** in Baldwin *Canteening* 25: This week has been a hummer and I have scarcely stopped to breathe. **1923** Z. Grey *Wanderer* 129: She's a hummer in July. **1971** Dahlskog *Dict.* 32: *Hummer, n.* A sexually promiscuous girl. **1989** Radford & Crowley *Drug Agent* 220: This…red hummer is specked for over 180 mph.

2. *Und. & Police.* an arrest on a false or petty charge. Cf. *1698–99, *1748 quots. at **(1),** above.

1932 in *AS* (Feb. 1934) 26: *Hummer.* A false arrest. **1931–34** in Clemmer *Pris. Community* 333: *Hummer*…An arrest on a false charge. **1949** "R. MacDonald" *Moving Target* 56: The conspiracy rap was a hummer. All they could prove was I needed it myself. **1966** Braly *Cold* 153: If he didn't count the hummer over in L.A., and he didn't. That was a meatball beef. **1966** Bullins *Goin' a Buffalo* 171: Yeah, we know it was hard, baby, but you can't afford to lose your old man by his gettin' busted behind a jail visit. That would be a stone trick, Mamma. Nothin' but a hummer…Right? **1970** Wambaugh *New Centurions* 175: "You know the lieutenant doesn't want any hummer pinches." "Aw, it was no hummer, Jake…she just went for old Rosso here." **1971** H. Roberts *Third Ear* (unp.): *Hummer*…a "bum rap." **1980** S.E. Martin *Breaking & Entering* 95: Many policeman are…critical of fellow officers who make "hummers" (avoidable arrests for behavior that offended the officer rather than violated the law in any but a minor and/or technical sense).

3. *Baseball.* a fastball.

1942 *ATS* 652: Fast ball…*hummer.* **1959** Brosnan *Long Season* 185: He obviously didn't want the old hummer. Why not? It ain't hummin' tonight? **1964** Thompson & Rice *Every Diamond* 140: *Hummer*…fast ball. **1973** *World Series Coverage* (NBC-TV) (Oct. 13): Back to the hummer and it just misses the outside corner. **1982** in Dickson *Baseball Dict.* 215: At age 59, if that's what he was, Satch had lost the hummer. **1983** Whiteford & Jones *How to Talk Baseball* 105: *Hummer*…[a] fastball, named because of the humming sound produced by the ball rocketing toward the plate.

4. *Black E.* something that is erroneous, inconsequential, deceptive, or unprofitable.

1959–60 R. Reisner *Jazz Titans* 158: *Hummer:* A minor mistake, something that shouldn't have happened. **1963** in J. Blake *Joint* 359: You put me on a hummer. **1966** I. Reed *Pall-Bearers* 96: It all turned out to be a plot. What a hummer that was, man. **1970** Landy *Underground Dict.* 107: *Hummer*…A phony; a fake. **1971** H. Roberts *Third Ear* (unp.): *Hummer*…an unimportant or insignificant event.

5. *Stu.* an offensive or oafish person.

1968–70 *Current Slang III & IV* 71: *Hummer, n.* An idiot; a backward person.—University of Kentucky. **1971** H. Roberts *Third Ear* (unp.): *Hummer*…a nothing person. **1972** N.Y.U. student: A *hummer* is a real dope. Somebody who's not only stupid, but he hams things up.

6. HUM JOB; (*also*) a performer of a hum job.

1970 Landy *Underground Dict.* 107: *Hummer*…One who engages in oral copulation of the testicles by putting them in the mouth and humming. **1972** PFC, U.S. Army STRATCOM-Taiwan (coll. J. Ball): I'm gonna go out and get me a hummer! **1979** T. Baum *Carny* 118: You know what to do if the marks [at a carnival strip show] can't get it up?…You know what a hummer is? **1994** *Details* (July) 62: The predictable hummers in the back of the tour bus.

7. a drinking bout; in phr. **have a hummer going** to be very drunk.

1965–71 in *Qly. Jour. Stud. Alcohol* XXXII (1971) 732: *Hummer.* Drinking bout. **1974** Univ. Tenn. student: "He's got a hummer going" means he's drunk. I've never heard it used any other way.

8. an object or device; GIZMO, 1.a.

1982 "J. Cain" *Commandos* 258: See to it that you keep that hummer in your possession at all times from now on. **1983** M. Skinner *USAFE* 50: *Hummer:* Any ingenious device whose proper name the fighter pilot can't recall. **1987** G. Hall *Top Gun* 96: *Hummer*—Any ingenious machine—plane, car, weapon—whose actual name can't be

recalled. **1992** *CBS This Morning* (CBS-TV) (Dec. 18): How much would one of these hummers cost me?

9. (*cap.*) [sugg. by the vocalization of official designation *HMMWV* 'high-mobility multipurpose wheeled vehicle'] *Mil.* a military vehicle that combines the features of a Jeep with those of a light truck. [Now a trademark of American Motors Corporation; formally ref. to as "Hum Vee."]

1983 Willinger & Gurney *Amer. Jeep* 91: The new vehicle, dubbed the HMMWV (High-Mobility, Multipurpose wheeled vehicle), or Hummer, will solve many of the army's tactical problems. **1985** *Morning Edition* (Nat. Pub. Radio) (Nov. 28): The HUMV is…designed to replace the Jeep.…Soldiers…are calling it the *Hummer.* **1986** De Sola *Abbr. Dict.* (ed. 7) 454: *Hummer.* high-mobility multi-purpose wheeled vehicle. **1989** *NewsWatch* (CNN-TV) (Dec. 23): The streets are filled with Hummers—the vehicle that replaced the jeep.

10. (*cap.*) *Mil. Av.* (applied to various aircraft).

1984 Trotti *Phantom* 152 [ref. to 1969]: Mostly I flew the group's C-117—the Hummer. **1987** G. Hall *Top Gun* 96: The E-2 Hawkeye early-warning aircraft is also nicknamed the Hummer, in reference to the sound of its turbo-prop engines. **1989** J. Weber *Defcon One* 3: The [Grumman E-2C] Hawkeye early warning aircraft, nicknamed Hummer.

¶ In phrases:

¶ **hit the hummer** to *hit the road* s.v. HIT.

1908 McGaffey *Show Girl* 58: Then I hit the hummer for…Kansas.

¶ **on the hummer** in a bad way, esp. at a disadvantage or without money or a job.

*ca*1900 in Sandburg *Songbag* 191: Been on the hummer since ninety-four,/Last job I had was on the Lake Shore,/Lost my office in the A.R.U./And I won't get it back till nineteen-two. **1912** *DN* III 584: *On the hummer*…At a disadvantage. "I've got him *on the hummer* and he knows it." **1917** *DN* IV 346: *On the hummer*…Slang. Going to the bad. New Orleans. **1918** in E. Wilson *Prelude* 206: He's sorta on the hummer—he's got ague, that bird! **1919** Darling *Jargon Book* 45: *On the Hummer*—Broke and out of a job. **1948** McHenry & Myers *Home Is Sailor* 19: I've been on the hummer for a week. I've been…flopping on the docks. *a*1961 *WNID3: On the hummer*…not in working order…not well. **1979–83** W. Kennedy *Ironweed* 72 [ref. to 1930's]: The world'll be on the hummer.

hummingbird *n. Pris.* a form of torture using electricity.—constr. with *the.* [Def. in 1931–34 quot. is perh. erroneous.]

1899 A.H. Lewis *Sandburrs* 27: D' Hummin' Boid is what dey does to a guy in d' pen to teach him not to be too gay.…It's d' same t'ing as d' chair at Sing Sing, only not so warm. **1926** Clark & Eubank *Lockstep* 70 [ref. to 1890's]: They also had what was known as the humming bird. A man would be stripped and blindfolded and an electric battery applied to different parts of his body. **1928** Panzram *Killer* 76: The Humming Bird…made of steel, water, wire, a sponge and a little electricity.…That doesn't sound as tho it held such a hell of a torture as it did. **1931–34** in Clemmer *Pris. Community* 333: *Hummingbird*…The electric chair.

humongous /hju'mʌŋgəs/ *adj.* [sugg. by *huge* and *monstrous*, with stress pattern of *tremendous*] *Stu.* huge; tremendous. Also **humungous, humongoid, humongo.**

1968 Baker, Ladd & Robb *CUSS* 141: *Humongous* [amount]. A great deal. **1969** *Current Slang I & II* 53: *Humangous*, adj. A unit of measure one size larger than *monjorious*.—Air Force Academy cadets. **1972** N.Y.U. student: *Humongus* means like *gigunda*, only bigger. **1974** Reader letter to RH dictionary staff: I have been using the following word for years.…This past summer I heard it in California, New York, Massachusetts, and Maine.…The word is: "humongous" meaning excessively large. **1976–77** Kernochan *Dry Hustle* 286: Her humongous belly strained and peeked out all the wrong parts of her peekaboo nightie. **1978** Price *Ladies' Man* 215: I sat across the room from an old guy with a humongous belly. **1981** N.Y.C. Dept. of Traffic radio ad (June 29): Gridlock's a *humongous* traffic-jam! **1981** *Film Comment* (May) 27: Divine impersonates the humongous Francine Fishpaw. **1983** Wambaugh *Delta Star* 54: Two humungous pimples. **1984** *TriQuarterly* (Spring) 313: It was the humungous kick Maggie just gave it. **1985** N.Y.C. editor, age *ca*35: I recall a teacher I had in 1969 who used *humongous* and *bodacious* as examples of words to be avoided. **1985** Sawislak *Dwarf* 91: One of those humungous big machines. **1992** M. Myers et al. *Wayne's World* (film): Will you still love me when I'm an incredibly humongoid star? **1994** *Newsweek* (Dec. 26) 127: The chain of 13 humongous home-furnishing stores. **1995** Publishers' Clearing House TV ad: A humongo check. **1996** *Good Morning America* (ABC-TV) (Mar. 19): A comet is nothing but a dirty, humongoid snowball.

hump *n.* **1.a.** copulation; an act of copulation.—usu. considered vulgar.

　1918 Noyes MS. (unp.): *Hump=Jazz=Cunt.* **1924** Wilstach *Anecdota Erotica* 9: The 'ore is familiar with him and the Englishman finally says, "If you don't stop that familiarity this 'ump is off." *a***1927** in P. Smith *Letter from Father* 57: The nigger mill hands were usually in hock to the company store for calico with which they had paid for their "hump." **1930** in H. Miller *Letters to Emil* 49: The lowest dives where the Algerians and Arabs get their hump. **1934** "J.M. Hall" *Anecdota* 109: All mankind insists/On its tri-weekly hump. **1958** Cooley *Run for Home* 157: After the second hump you wind up with yer cock in a sling. *Ibid.* 424: A little gin and a good hump never made anybody feel bad. **1962** Perry *Young Man Drowning* 46: Say, I bet you ain't even had your first hump yet! **1966** Susann *Valley of Dolls* 439: I'll stand for you giving your wife a hump now and then. **1966** "Petronius" *N.Y. Unexp.* 6: A fleeting hump [is] the only practical reality. **1965–68** E.R. Johnson *Silver St.* 41: I'm not looking for any free hump. **1970** Whitmore *Memphis-Nam-Sweden* 45: I fucked her. She knows how to throw some hump on my dick. **1972** R. Barrett *Lovomaniacs* 202: Balling. Just plain old hump—it's friendly and it's natural. **1973** Toma & Brett *Toma* 15: The hump marketplace is open for business. **1986** Bozzone *Buck Fever* 18: There's a woman who can throw a good hump. **1988** H. Gould *Double Bang* 23: He'd been thinking about throwing her a hump. *a***1994** A. Radakovich *Wild Girls Club* 41: Make this last hump so enjoyable that your ex will forget how much he hates your guts. **1995** S. Moore *In the Cut* 80: I laid on top of her and I screwed her....I gave her a good hump.

b. a person, usu. a woman, regarded as a sexual partner.—occ. used collectively.—usu. considered vulgar.

　[**1918** Noyes MS. (unp.): *Hump.* refers, also, to one's physical popularity. "You're hump!" "She's hump."] **1925** in E. Wilson *Twenties* 240: Look at her lookin' at him all starry-eyed. She don't yet know he's a bum hump. **1927** "Fliesler" *Anecdota* 110: I didn't know then that she was hump! **1961** *New Directions* 17 220: I hear she's good hump. **1963** Horwitz *Candlelight* 60: She's a good hump. **1966** Bogner *7th Ave.* 20: Very definitely an easy hump, but where? **1966–67** W. Stevens *Gunner* 56: The hump'll be lined up a mile to...kiss our medals. **1968** P. Roth *Portnoy* 151: And now you want to treat me like I am nothing but some hump, to *use.* **1973** Toma & Brett *Toma* 138: She's an ex-movie star. What a hump! She...wants me to come over and take care of her. **1983** Stapleton *30 Yrs.* 66: I'm the best hump you'll ever have.

c. one's self; ASS (esp. in figurative senses, esp. ASS, 4); in phrs. **bust (one's) hump** to exert (oneself) to exhaustion; **break** [or **bust**] **(someone's) hump** to harass, vex, or overcome (someone).

　1928 C. McKay *Banjo* 26: Come on, fellahs; let's get outa this. Let's take our hump away from here. **1934** H. Roth *Call It Sleep* 415: G-go peddle yer h-hump, h-he says—. **1937** Di Donato *Christ in Concrete* 219 [ref. to *ca*1928]: These flats break your hump; you're either laying brick down on your face or a foot over your head. **1939** O'Brien *One-Way Ticket* 38 [ref. to 1925]: These guys don't seem to be breakin' their hump. Look at 'em. Just loafin' along. **1942** Lindsay & Crouse *Strip for Action* 12: We been here every night, breaking our humps, policing up the place. **1953** Paley *Rumble* 17: If they see the three of us knocking around, they gonna break our hump. **1957** Myrer *Big War* 285: I've been busting my hump for seven days trying to keep my name *out* of the God-damned papers. **1957** Mulvihill *Fire Mission* 16 [ref. to WWII]: I don't like to break hump; I'll just sit here and watch. **1964** Faust *Steagle* 208: Flo you cock tease you broke my hump with your adding machine tits and armor plate ass. **1966** Elli *Riot* 233: Hell, we're not bustin' our humps. **1968** D.L. Phillips *Small World* 93: We began to feel sorry for him—the poor guy breaking his hump for a nickel, while we just sat riding along. **1970** E. Thompson *Garden of Sand* 53: You got a good body on yuh. All legs and high little nigger

hump. **1971** Horan *Blue Messiah* 297: We're breakin' our hump on the roads up in Westchester. **1972** Ponicsan *Cinderella Liberty* 169: Nobody busting your hump and it's open gangplank every night if you want to come downtown for a beer. **1973** Herbert & Wooten *Soldier* 35: Those of us who've given our humps to the Army know there are still quite a few great [leaders] around. **1975** T. Berger *Sneaky People* 174: I got to work my hump off or I'll be on my uppers. **1977** Torres *Q & A* 81: Decent people breaking their hump trying to see their way through. **1981** C. Nelson *Picked Bullets Up* 25: He busted his hump...caring for his patients. **1986** J. Hughes *Ferris Beuller* (film): It really busts my hump, ya know....It makes me mad. **1990** *Night Court* (NBC-TV): We'd really have to bust our hump to get through these cases by midnight. **1995** *Critic* (Fox-TV): Move your humps!

d. Esp. *N.E.* a contemptible person, esp. a man. [The 1904 quot. is equivocal; the addressee is named Humphrey, and this quot. may simply be an insulting variant.]

　[**1904** J. London *Sea-Wolf* ch. iv: Grab hold something you—you Hump!] [**1935** Kingsley *Dead End*: Ah, shut up, yuh fat bag a hump!] **1963** Hayden *Wanderer* 163 [ref. to *ca*1933]: You're gonna make out, kid, don't ever forget it neither. You ain't like the rest of us humps. **1965** Petrakis *Pericles* 204: You the only hump at the hill don't scare when toby talks. **1973** Droge *Patrolman* 70: He just got here himself, the hump....he sounds like a real ballbuster. **1977** Torres *Q & A* 35: You hump, think I'm asleep? **1978** W. Green *Sorcerer* (film): Up against the wall, ya humps!...What are you gonna do with all that money, ya hump? **1978** Price *Ladies' Man* 175: And then you know what I suggest for *you*, you fucking hump? **1980** Whalen *Takes a Man* 147: You're lying, you hump! **1985** Cook *Out of Darkness* (CBS-TV movie): Like why didn't you knock the hump off the bar stool when you had the chance? *a***1989** Micheels *Braving Flames* 191: You hump!...You have no pride in yourself! **1991** McCarthy & Mallowe *Vice Cop* 48: But I was the hump who wouldn't give them back their pocketbooks. **1996** Alson *Ivy League Bookie* 82: That hump. I'd break him like a twig.

2. *Whaling.* a humpback whale.

　*a***1900** in F.P. Harlow *Chanteying* 220: We cruised about the Southern Seas/For sperm and humps as well.

3.a. Orig. *R.R.* a hill, ridge, mountain range, or mountain; (usu. *cap.*) the Continental Divide.—usu. constr. with *the.*

　1901 McGonnigle *Went West* 148: Away off to our left some forty miles could be seen the "Hump." **1914** *Sat. Eve. Post* (Apr. 4) 10: There ain't a kid like him this side of the Hump. **1918** Casey *Cannoneers* 161: We proceed over the hump into the valley of the Meuse without further incident. **1924** *Marine Corps Gaz.* (Mar.) 62: Crossed the "hump" (Rocky Mountains) at 12,000 feet and discovered what Arctic exploring in an undershirt is like. **1925** Mullin *Scholar Tramp* 301 [ref. to *ca*1912]: What was that guy's name? He went over the Hump with us two years ago. **1930** "D. Stiff" *Milk & Honey* 43: West over the Rockies, called "The Hump." *Ibid.* 208: "Over the hump" means to cross the mountains to the West Coast. **1933** Stewart *Airman Speech* 72: To fly a plane over the hump is to fly it over the mountains. **1938** Holbrook *Holy Old Mackinaw* 41: Then they would pack their turkeys on their backs and hit out over the Hump. **1945** O'Rourke *E Co.* 123: The British were coming up from the east, and the Americans were driving in across the hump. **1947** W.M. Camp *S.F.* 19: A curiosity to see what lay over the hump set the pioneer on his way. **1973** Mathers *Riding the Rails* 58: I traveled from Boston across the Continental Divide (the hump). **1977** *Sci. Mech. CB Gde.* 173: You can put the hammer down when you clear the hump. **1980** Bruns *Kts. of Road* 97: The Blue Mountain "hump" in Oregon became notorious territory for yegg highwaymen.

b. (*cap.*) *USAF.* the Himalayas; (*hence*) the air supply route to China over the Himalayas during World War II.—usu. constr. with *the.* Now *hist.*

　1942 in M. Chennault *Up Sun!* 133: We took off from Dinjam and flew over the Hump into Kunming, China....The Hump is the worst airline route in the world....Every day, scores of transport planes fly the Hump. **1943** *Yank* (Jan. 13) 13: Flying the Hump. **1943** in Stilwell *Papers* 177: We have lost six over the Hump. **1944** in Loosbrock & Skinner *Wild Blue* 243: The crews start their return trip to Assam where more supplies and new crews are waiting to fly the Hump.

1950 *Commentary* X 313: His brother was in the air force and was killed while flying the Hump. **1968** W.C. Anderson *Gooney Bird* 27: She flew the hump in Burma, she flew the Berlin Airlift, she saw action in Korea. **1975** Higham & Siddall *Combat Aircraft* 36: C-46 Commando over the first ridge of the Hump en route to China, 1944.

4.a. Esp. *Circus.* a camel. [Presumably the orig. sense.]

 1926 Norwood *Other Side of Circus* 65: We call the camels the "humps" and the zebras the "convicts." **1931** *Amer. Mercury* (Nov.) 352: *Hump…*A camel. *1978 in *Austral. Nat. Dict.* 318: A pair o' camels; it was the first time he'd ever had humps.

b. (*cap.*) *Mil. Av.* a Sopwith Camel pursuit aircraft.

 1919 Law *2nd Army Air Service Book* (unp.): Fly A Hump!…the Flopwith Camel. The Hospital Hounds' Delight! **1935** Archibald *Heaven High* 87 [ref. to 1918]: A Sopwith Camel…was known as the "Hump."

c. a Camel cigarette.

 1920 *Amer. Leg. Wkly.* (May 7) 14 [ref. to 1918]: One Carton Humps equal two weeks' board and lodging. **1921** Benet *Beginning of Wisdom* 295 [ref. to 1918]: Got a hump? **1923** McKnight *Eng. Words* 65: *Camel* cigarettes become *humps.* **1927** J. Stevens *Mattock* 115 [ref. to 1918]: "Got a hump, anybody?" I gave him a Camel. **1933** Milburn *No More Trumpets* 28: Say, buddy, you ain't got another hump there, have you? **1941** Kendall *Army & Navy Sl.* 20: *Have you got a hump on you?*…stake me to a cigaret. **1990** Univ. Tenn. prof.: When I worked in a drugstore in Omaha [1944–45] customers used to come in and ask for "a pack of humps," meaning Camels.

5. a fit of vexation or mood of discouragement—constr. with *the;* in phr. **with a hump on** angry.

 *1873 Hotten *Slang Dict.* (ed. 4): A costermonger who was annoyed or distressed about anything would describe himself as having "the hump." *1897 in *OED:* Well, my boy, you've evidently got the hump. **1926** Finerty *Criminalese* 30: *Hump, to get the*—Discouraged, despondent. **1988** S. Lee *School Daze* (film): She sure left with a hump on.

6. *Gamb.* a playing card whose edges or ends have been shaved to facilitate cheating.

 1890 Quinn *Fools of Fortune* 197: Humps. **1942** in D.W. Maurer *Lang. Und.* 118: *Humps.* Cards…which have been trimmed so that the dealer may locate and manipulate them at will. **1961** (cited in Partridge *Dict. Und.* 833).

7. *Surfing.* a big wave suitable for riding.

 1957 Kohner *Gidget* 11: Down to San Onofre or Tressle where the real big humps come blasting in. *Ibid.* 31: The whole bunch of them, waiting for an occasional hump.

8. *Army & USMC.* a wearying or laborious walk or tramp through rough country; (*specif.*) an infantry combat patrol. [The earliest quots. are Australian; the term gained currency in the U.S. armed forces during the Vietnam War.]

 *1863 in *OED2:* It was a precious hump [over the hill for provisions]. *1890 in *Austral. Nat. Dict.:* We get a fair share of exercise without a twenty-mile hump on Sundays. **1971** *Newsweek* (Sept. 13) 40: The hump to the proposed landing zone was an easy one. Only about 1 kilometer, compared with the average daily hike of 3 or 4 kilometers. **1972** Pelfrey *Big V* 141: Sixty days' hump tomorrow, what a fucking bummer. **1976** C.R. Anderson *Grunts* 43 [ref. to 1969]: The first day's hump was to be of moderate length, 6000 meters or six "clicks." **1978** Hasford *Short-Timers* 38: The way human beings look after they've survived a long hump in the jungle. **1980** M. Baker *Nam* 291: After a hump, you were wasted. **1985** Bodey *F.N.G.* 165: Four Squad and One are out on humps. **1988** Clodfelter *Mad Minutes* 20: Deathly wearying humps through the never ending bush. **1991** LaBarge *Desert Voices* 33: The grunts would have PT…three times a week and they would have to go on humps.

¶ In phrases:

¶ **break** [or **bust**] **([some]one's) hump** see **(1.c.),** above.

¶ **get a hump on** to hurry; get a move on.

 1892 *Harper's* (Feb.) 487: "We went fast enough then." "We do seem to be gittin' a little less hump on oursel's than we did then."

¶ **get (one's) hump up** to become touchy or combative.

 *1860 Hotten *Slang Dict.* (ed. 2): "To have one's *hump up,*" to be

cross or ill-tempered—like a cat with its back set up. **1870** in *N.Y. Folk. Qly.* XXIX 170: The camel he got up his hump and swallowed the blue-tail fly, sir. **1880** J.C. Harris *Uncle Remus* 236: W'en freedom come out de niggers sorter got dere humps up, an' dey staid dat way, twel bimeby dey begun fer ter git hongry, an' den dey begun fer ter drap inter line right smartually.

¶ **go over the hump** [sugg. by *over the hill* s.v. HILL] *Mil.* to desert or go absent without leave.

 1933 *Leatherneck* (June) 43 [ref. to 1918]: I went over the hump from the hospital three weeks ago and I've been lookin' for my outfit ever since. **1957** Myrer *Big War* 147 [ref. to WWII]: You people—you think you can calk off and get out from under by going over the hump. **1965** Linakis *In Spring* 29 [ref. to WWII]: Being AWOL was the most important thing to the army.…Everybody that was over the hump wasn't like Bill. No one had to tell you why Al had taken off.

¶ **on the hump** on the go; on the move.

 1948 Guthrie *Born to Win* 86: If I am made of dirt it's sure dirt on the move because I'm always on the hump and the go all the time.

¶ **over the hump** beyond the midpoint or most difficult part.

 1914 Jackson & Hellyer *Vocab.* 46: *Hump.…*the half-way point in a prison sentence.…"How long have you got yet on your bit? I'm just over the hump." **1919** in Acker *Thru the War* 186: We went over the "hump" last night and it is all down hill the rest of the way. **1927** *AS* (June) 390: A mountain is called a *hump.* To be *over the hump* and going *downgrade* is to be more than half-through with something,—a stretch of work or incarceration. **1935** in H. Gray *Arf* (unp.): The worst is over—We're over the hump—It'll be down-grade from now on. **1941** Schulberg *Sammy* 112: I'm over the hump.…From now on I can write my own ticket. **1941** H.A. Smith *Low Man* 58: I didn't stay to see whether she got over the hump on the second time around. **1942** in T. Williams *Letters* 51: The script was pretty near "over the hump" and more work will be on the right side. **1962** T. Berger *Reinhart in Love* 138: He was over the hump towards twenty-two. **1984** M. Groening *Love Is Hell* (unp.): 13 big chapters! 7 done! 6 to go! Over the hump! **1992** L. Chambers *Recondo* 273: *Hump*—The midpoint in a soldier's overseas combat tour.

hump *adj.* HEP, 1.

 1918 Noyes MS. (unp.): *Hump.* meaning "wise." "You're hump!"

hump *v.* **1.a.** to copulate or copulate with.—usu. considered vulgar.

 *1785 Grose *Vulgar Tongue:* Hump. To hump; once a fashionable word for copulation. *ca1800 in Holloway & Black *Later Broadside Ballads* 224: Keep your wife at home, for humpers will be at her. *1911 O'Brien & Stephens *Australian Sl.* 74: Hump /vulgar/ to cohabit with a woman. **1923** McAlmon *Village* 61: I know a couple who'll really give a guy a little humping if you coax 'em enough. **1936** Le Clercq *Rabelais* 144: "Let the clot hump her," Gargantua replied. **1951** [VMF-323] *Old Ballads* 15: He humped a girl from our town. **1961** Heller *Catch-22* 131: The girls had shelter and food for as long as they wanted to stay. All they had to do in return was hump any of the men who asked them to. **1966** I. Reed *Pall-Bearers* 81: Your mama must have humped a whole bunch of anteaters for you to have a snout like that. **1968** J.P. Miller *Race* 280: Come on over to Moose's barn, Laddy. Ole Moose gonna hump a cow. **1971** *Go Ask Alice* 99: Her mother…had humped with who knows how many men in between. **1972** *N.Y. Times Mag.* (Nov. 26) 102: This sex revolution thing. Everybody's supposed to be humping and jumping. *a1994* A. Radakovich *Wild Girls Club* 166: I still end up getting humped and dumped.

b. (used as a partial euphem. for *go fuck (yourself)* s.v. FUCK); curse.—constr. with *go.*—usu. considered vulgar.

 1949 H. Robbins *Dream Merchants* 248: An' if they don't like it, they can go hump 'emselves.

c. to victimize; SCREW.—usu. considered vulgar.

 1962 T. Berger *Reinhart* 398: He will hump you on the price, and if you holler, blow the whistle to the cops. **1973** Breslin *World Without End* 97: "How long did he go around saying his case was killed?" "Year." "Then what happened to him?" "He got humped." "Six months in the slam." **1977** Torres *Q & A* 166: They're trying to hump me. **1987** C.J. McElroy, in C. Major *Calling Wind* 468: You don't watch it, Touti, they hump you like some ol' stray dog. Take your stuff…when your back is turned.

2.a. to exert (oneself); (*reflex.*) to hurry or run.

*ca*1835 in *F & H* III: He was…humpin' himself on politics. **1844** Porter *Big Bear* 134: "Hump yourself," says I, and we both darted. **1856** *Spirit of Times* (Feb. 16) 1: There are two things upon which Uncle Sam especially "humps himself"—his Hotels and his Horses. **1870** in "M. Twain" *Stories* 62: He would now proceed to hump himself. **1873** Bailey *Danbury Almanac* (unp.): Then is the time for you to "hump yourself" for the house. **1880** J.C. Harris *Uncle Remus* 246: You ain't seed no nigger hump hisse'f like dat nigger. He tore down de well shelter and fo' pannils er fence. **1883** Peck *Bad Boy* 339: You get up and hump yourself and go feed the pigs. **1885** in Lummis *Letters* 227: Siddown and hump yerself as much as ye damplease. **1906** in "O. Henry" *Works* 132: They humping themselves in a mighty creditable way. **1974** Cherry *High Steel* 76: *Likes the work?…*All you do is hump yourself blue in the face.

b. to go fast; get moving.—usu. constr. with *it*, also (*vulgar*) with *ass.*

1853 "P. Paxton" *In Texas* 161: Ain't the river a humping it though? **1858** [S. Hammett] *Piney Woods* 66: We war a humpin' it like a quarter horse. **1864** in *Univ. Mo. Studies* XV (1940) 370: General Logan played a trump/Which made the Rebels hump. **1884** "M. Twain" *Huck. Finn* ch. xxix: I never hunted for no back streets, but humped it straight through the main one. **1889** Meriwether *Tramp at Home* 98: Ef you wanter go, you'd better hump. **1891** Rodenbough *Sabre* 156: "Uncle Billy" simply made us "hump it," until we reached our destination. **1935** in *Kans. Hist. Qtly.* VIII (1939) 44: Believe me, neighbor, he could hump and run. **1971** H. Roberts *Third Ear: Humping…*walking rapidly. **1984** Glick *Winters Coming* 128: The fuckin' point man can't keep a steady pace, so we hump ass to keep up. **1987** B. Hauser & D. DeCoteau *Creepozoids* (film): Now, let's hump it! **1989** P. Benchley *Rummies* 41: I gotta hump back and collect a lady lawyer coming in from Pasadena.

c. (esp. among itinerants) to tramp or trudge; march; go on foot.—usu. constr. with *it*; (*hence*) *Army*. to walk (a post).

*1891 in *Austral. Nat. Dict.* 318: I packed my clothes in a rough kind of "swag," or bundle, and "humped" it down to Albury. **1899** Johnson *Negro Soldiers* 33 [ref. to *ca*1890]: The Ogalallas would…pick out a spot for passage that was patrolled by a white "post-humper" [sentry]. **1899** Cullen *Tales* 107: "Want to hump it along with me?" "Not by a damned sight.…When I go East I'm going to ride in a sleeper." *1902 in *Austral. Nat. Dict.* 318: He'll have to "hump it" off "Home" again as they are doing. **1913** J. London *Valley of Moon* 210: A big rube that's…come a humpin' to town for the big wages. *1925 in Fraser & Gibbons *Soldier & Sailor Wds.* 122 [ref. to WWI]: *Hump it, To:* To march with full kit. To tramp on foot.

d. to pursue closely.

1895 *Harper's* (Feb.) 345: Them rats from the bolt-factory was a-humpin' him, too! Guess if the freight hadn't come along they'd a-ketched him.

e. to work hard; get busy.

1897 in *OED2*: Grit makes the man, the lack of it the chump; Therefore, young man, take hold, hang on, and hump. **1915** *DN* IV 233: College Slang…*hump, v.t.* and *i.* To study diligently. **1920** Weaver *In American* 30: Keepin' it goin'll keep me humpin', see? **1931** J.T. Farrell *McGinty* 312: From now on, you're gonna hump. **1936** Levin *Old Bunch* 120: But on the whole, everybody was humping. **1949** Schaefer *Shane* 33: In a week he'll be making even me hump or he'll be bossing the place. **1956** Hargrove *Girl He Left* 43: You'll get up at four o'clock in the morning, and you'll go to bed at nine, and from morning till night you will keep a-humpin'. **1971–72** Giovannitti *Medal* 63: Shit, what you humping for—sergeant stripes? **1973** in Fowler *UFOs* 281: I am going to school full-time at Southern Illinois University and, believe me, I really have to hump in order to keep up with these kids today. **1974** Cull & Hardy *Types of Drug Abusers* 193: *Hump*—To work. **1974** R.H. Carter *16th Round* 55: Talk about it, baby!…We're ready to hump! **1987** E. Spencer *Macho Man* 37: The new man is one tough, brave, humping guy. **1987** Norst & Black *Lethal Weapon* 35: Get humping on it.

f. *Army & USMC.* to patrol in rough or hostile country, esp. while laden with much equipment.—also used trans.

1966 *Sat. Eve. Post* (July 16) 37: You hump through the boondocks all day, sweating like a horse. **1969** in Lanning *Only War* 211: Headed east—Bad humping. **1969** in B. Edelman *Dear Amer.* 63: Humping these mountains is bad news. **1971** *N.Y. Post* (Jan. 6) 50: The Huey will insert the riflemen and extract six tired grunts who've been humping the bush for two days. **1971** Jury *Vietnam Photo Book* 102: We were out humping the boonies (patrolling) when the pointman got hit. **1971** T. Mayer *Weary Falcon* 29: I assumed he had learned to fly because he had gotten tired of humping the boonies. **1972** Pelfrey *Big V* 113: Alpha's gonna hump awhile…gonna be out sixty days before they come in. **1973** R. Roth *Sand in Wind* 25: The humping around here is murder.…Marching with packs on. **1976** C.R. Anderson *Grunts* 197: The grunts had been humping the hills and getting caught in ambushes. **1980** Di Fusco et al. *Tracers* 37: We'd been humpin' all day. **1990** Ruggero *38 N. Yankee* 21: Their feet still sore from humping the hills in South Korea.

g. to labor over or in.

1970 Grissim *Country Music* 174: Sold about two million records. And hell, there I went again, humpin' that pop field. **1977** Sayles *Union Dues* 110: On the tit, they said, like it wasn't work humping a typewriter all day and playing cop with the wives and asshole parents that come in.

h. *Army & USMC.* to lead (infantrymen) on patrol.

1982 Goff, Sanders & Smith *Bros.* 58 [ref. to Vietnam War]: The company commander…[would] hump us from can't-see in the morning till can't-see in the evening.

3. Esp. *Mil.* to lift or carry upon one's back or shoulder; (*hence*) to carry (something heavy) in any manner; lug. [Earliest quots. are Australian.]

*1851 in *Austral. Nat. Dict.* 318: Those who have not paid may be seen "humping" their cradles to some secluded spot. *Ibid.:* Having to hump (carry) them principally on our backs. *1853 in *OED2*: He "humped his swag; in diggers' phrase, that is, shouldered his pack. *1863 in *OED2*: We humped our swag containing our house, our bed, our grub. *1864 in *OED2*: It is very hard work humping your blankets and tucker. *1889 in Barrère & Leland *Dict. Slang* I 480: And you may often have to "hump your own swag." **1894** C. King *Capt. Close* 8: Well, hump it abawd, 'n' be quick about it. **1898** Doubleday *Gunner* 242: Coal humping. **1902** in Kipling *Traffics & Discoveries* 12: He said if you stretched a man at his prayers you'd have to hump his bad luck before the Throne as well as your own. **1903** Sonnichsen *Deep Sea Vagabonds* 43: The Californian, Andy, was a nondescript sort of a fellow. He had humped lumber on the coast for years. **1920** *Amer. Leg. Wkly.* (Aug. 13) 6: It was mules as humped the rations. *1925 in Fraser & Gibbons *Soldier & Sailor Wds.* 122 [ref. to WWI]: *To Hump:* To lift; to carry. **1966** *Sat. Eve. Post* (July 16) 46: All a trooper should have to hump is his weapon, ammo, water, first-aid kit and entrenching tool. **1966** in J.A. Williams *Beyond Angry Black* 163: I humped enough ammunition…on Peleliu. **1971** D. Smith *Engine Co.* 4: I am right behind humping the hose. **1973** R. Roth *Sand in Wind* 52: Be glad you don't have to hump a radio, like me. **1977** Caputo *Rumor of War* 99: I can hack it. I can hump my own gun. **1978** Matthiessen *Snow Leopard* 97: Slowly, he puts down the load that he has humped two thousand feet uphill. **1982** Del Vecchio *13th Valley* 20: Back in the bush, humping a ruck. **1985** J.M.G. Brown *Rice Paddy Grunt* 61: Humping a rifle in the jungle. **1986** Churcher *N.Y. Confidential* xii: One money launderer humped $3,409,230 in cash [in cardboard boxes] to a…currency exchange on lower Broadway. **1996** McCumber *Playing off Rail* 32: We humped our luggage into the cab.

Hump Day *n.* [sugg. by *over the hump* s.v. HUMP, *n.*] the day that is at the midpoint in a given period of work; (*often*) Wednesday, the middle of the work week. Similarly, **Hump Night.**

1955 *AS* XXX 226: *Hump Night…*Wednesday night, which is over the hump of the week. *ca*1965 in *DARE*: *Hump day* was used by counselors at summer camp to mean Wednesday. *ca*1970 in *DARE*: Hump day is Wednesday, the middle of the working week. **1974** Univ. Tenn. student: I don't even think I can get past Hump Day. **1977** Langone

Life at Bottom 202: Some of the parties in midwinter, that's when you're over the hump, Hump Night they called it, halfway home. **1983** WKGN radio (Jan. 26): It's Wednesday—Hump Day—and I'm Jack McCracken with the Hump Day edition of WKGN's Community Calendar. **1983** Van Devanter & Morgan *Before Morning* 166: Hump day, the exact middle of my tour when I would be "over the hump." **1987** Local radio broadcast, Knoxville, Tenn. (Nov. 18): Today is Hump Day, and we'll be celebrating Hump Day with you all evening. **1990** Headline News network (July 14): On Wednesdays they become the Hump Day Honeys. **1993** *Martin* (Fox-TV): Gina, you got it on Monday. Tommy, you got it on Tuesday. Pam, you got it on Hump Day.

humped *adj.* [sugg. by *get (one's) hump up* s.v. HUMP, *n.*] irritated; angry.
    1878 B. Harte *Drift* 60: Spose...that chap, feelin' kinder humped, goes up some dark night and heaves a load of cut pine over his fence.

humper *n.* **1.** an annoying object; FUCKER, 3.
    1972–76 Durden *No Bugles* 243: Yeah, here's the humper.

    2. a hard-working person.
    1976 C.R. Anderson *Grunts* 106 [ref. to 1969]: "Hey, you see that new second looey?" "Yeah, a real humper, eh?"

Hump-happy *adj.* *USAF.* made eccentric or neurotic by flying missions over the Himalayas. Now *hist.*
    1944 *Yank* (Feb. 11) 10: Hump Happy: The GI Musical Comedy Covers the India Circuit by Air. **1944** *Time* (June 19) 59: It was named from a form of war neurosis peculiar to the region where the hazards of flying the Hump are in every man's mind—*Hump Happy*. **1944** *Life* (Sept. 11) 88: They are declared to be "Hump happy," a phrase loosely used to describe any number of neurasthenic disorders. **1978** T.H. White *In Search* 141 [ref. to WWII]: Sometimes cracking under the strain they said made men "hump-happy." ("Yonder lies Tibet," they would say, pointing out snow-topped landmarks.).

humphead *n.* a blockhead.
    1986 Philbin *Under Cover* 264: You...shitface humphead.

hump-house *n.* a brothel.
    1921 in Cray *Erotic Muse* 194: Frankie she worked in a hump house.

humping *adj.* (a partial euphem. for) FUCKING.
    1944 Brooks *Brick Foxhole* 12: That's the best humpin' thing about this base. **1965** N.Y.C. man, age *ca*45: I'm sick of every humpin' one of 'em. **1972** Hannah *Geronimo Rex* 241: Six inches of black humping air!

hump-nutty *adj.* obsessed with copulation.—usu. considered vulgar.
    1925 in E. Wilson *Twenties* 240: Why, he's hump-nutty!

humpty *n.* HUMPTY-DUMPTY, 1.
    1973 Ace *Stand On It* 142: Man, those humpties and hayshakers all over the South just love demolition derbies and they sit up there in the stands and just get wet to the knees watching those big cars crash.

humpty *adj.* HUMPTY-DUMPTY.
    1995 *As World Turns* (CBS-TV) (May 5): That humpty music coming from the music box.

humpty-dumpty *n.* **1.** Esp. *Sports.* an incompetent person; oaf.
    1950 Roeder *J. Robinson* 102: Here I've been with humpty-dumpties at first base all spring. **1952** W. Brown *Sox* 141: It is improbable if the White Sox before or since were ever outfitted with a quainter collection of baseball's "humpty dumptys" than those to which Fonseca fell heir. **1972** DeLillo *End Zone* 95: This isn't another humpty-dumpty outfit. This is a squad that's big and mean....They're practically evil. **1975** Durocher & Linn *Nice Guys* 44: In baseball, the humpty-dumpties, the substitutes, come out early to take their batting and fielding practice. *Ibid.* 45 [ref. to 1920's]: Get out of here, you humpty-dumpty!...Get lost! **1980** Pearl *Pop. Slang* 75: *Humpty dumpty n.* (Politics) a candidate doomed to lose. **1984** "W.T. Tyler" *Shadow Cabinet* 171: He's like all these Humpty Dumpties around here.

    2. an egg. *Joc.*
    1957 in *Tom & Jerry* (Dec. 1969) (unp.): Here's your humpty-dumpties. Catch!

humpty-dumpty *adj.* inferior; (*also*) foolish or ridiculous.
    1920 in De Beck *Google* 84: He's certainly got his office in a humpty dumpty neighborhood. **1921** *Variety* (Nov. 18) 19: After a retort or two, the leader wants to know how [such] humpty-dumpty actors as

they are ever got in the business. **1940** in H. Gray *Arf* (unp.): The old car runs fine...after that humpty dumpty kettle-tinker brought it back from the garage. **1963** Hecht *Gaily, Gaily* 74 [ref. to *ca*1915]: "This is the most Humpty Dumpty prattle I ever read," said Mr. Mahoney. **1969** Sidney *Love of Dying* 58: A humpty-dumpty man he was, in a humpty-dumpty world. **1972** N.Y.U. professor: I'm not going to bother you with humpty-dumpty details. **1979** Homer *Jargon* 41: When a speech is called *Humpty Dumpty*, it's filled to the brim with flapdoodle signifying nothing.

humpy *n.* a person having a hunchback.
    1744 A. Hamilton *Gentleman's Progress* 109: Hump-back'd, and the tallest humpy I ever saw.

humpy *adj.* *Homosex.* sexually attractive.
    1978 Maupin *Tales* 189: Could you BUHLIEVE the pecs on that humpy number? **1981** C. Nelson *Picked Bullets Up* 265: There is good news: Half the men are humpy.

humungous var. HUMONGOUS.

Hun *n.* **1.** a Central European; a Magyar or Slav.—used contemptuously. Now *hist.*
    1887 "Zor" *Breaking Chains* 101: They have secondly imported the cheap Chinese from the west and the Huns and like cheap labor from the east. **1890** in *OED*: The Huns who are here [Pennsylvania] said to be creating a widespread dissatisfaction. They are engaged chiefly as labourers in the mines and ironworks. **1893** in F. Remington *Sel. Letters* 157: I want to see the Dutch in maneuver. Might tackle the Hun's but not in a canoe. **1894** O. Wister, in Remington *Wister* 80: You will not find many Poles or Huns or Russian Jews in that district. **1904** in "O. Henry" *Works* 1430: It's just landed. It must be a kind of a Dago or a Hun or one of them Finns, I guess. **1908** W.G. Davenport *Butte & Montana* 194: Through the gates of Castle Garden pour the unwashed hordes of lousy Huns and anarchistic ignorami of Sicily, Italy, and Russia. **1907–10** in Dillingham *Reports of Immigration Comm.* I 248: The modern Magyars or "Hungarians" are wrongly called "Huns" in America. **1914** Graham *Immigrants* 231: I came on a gang of Wops and Huns loading bridge-props. *a*1985 Stolarik *So. Side* 63 [ref. to *ca*1900]: Native Americans began to refer to Slovaks as "Huns."

2.a. *Journ. & Mil.* a German; the German armed forces.—also used attrib. Now *hist.*
    [The nickname took its inspiration from a speech by Kaiser Wilhelm II, delivered on July 27, 1900, in which he encouraged German troops being sent to Beijing to behave toward the Chinese "like the Huns a thousand years ago"; see *OED2* for quot.]
    1910 Balch *Slavic Citizens* 414: To be a German is not a thing to be ashamed of...."I ain't no Hun, I'm an American," expresses their reaction to the situation. **1918** in Truman *Dear Bess* 264: Then we hope to shoot some Huns. **1918** in *Ark. Hist. Qly.* XVIII (1959) 12: Seldom do we find any Huns that will fight....Once in a while flying low the Hun Infantry opens up. **1918** O'Brien *Wine, Women & War* 160 [diary entry for Aug. 2]: Passing through town which had been occupied by Hun. **1918** in Truman *Letters Home* 51: I shall be happy if I can only get to order my battery to fire one volley at the Hun. **1925** Z. Grey *Vanishing Amer.* 242: The Huns are licked. **1931** in Gottfried *Boss Cermak* 206: Tony, the German-hater, called the German-Americans Huns. **1932** T.S. Eliot *Sweeney Agonistes* 18: I'll tell the world we got the Hun on the run. **1936* C. Lewis *Sagittarius Rising* 26: We always referred to...the enemy as "Huns," just as the Infantry knew them as "Fritz" or "Jerry," and nothing derogatory was...intended. **1944** *N.Y. Times* (Mar. 12) 25: Old pilots warn, "The Hun is an opportunist and is quick to charge his approach." **1944** in *N.Y. Folk. Qly.* (Autumn 1949): Thanks for the memory,/Of flights to Germany,/Across the cold North Sea,/With blazing guns,/We fought the Huns/For air supremacy./How lucky we were! **1962** Farago *10th Fleet* 13 [ref. to WWII]: I'm...[letting] the Huns know that we are ready for them. **1982** W.R. Dunn *Fighter Pilot* 2: No, we will not forget....A new generation of Huns does not suddenly make them "good guys."...We fighter pilots regarded [this axiom] as absolute truth—"Beware of the Hun in the sun." **1982** W.R. Dunn *Fighter Pilot* 2: We fighter pilots regarded [this axiom] as absolute truth—"Beware of the Hun in the sun." **1985** Sawislak *Dwarf* 114: If we can require Jap cars sold in this country to have American parts, we can

oblige the Huns to use American grain in their beer. **1986** C. Freeman *Seasons of Heart* 86: A group of older men was swapping tales of World War I trench exploits against the "Huns." **1988** Terkel *Great Divide* 248: Right after World War Two, my aunt said, "Jean is going to marry a Hun." I thought, what the hell is a Hun? My husband's of German descent. **1993** Ebbert & Hall *Crossed Currents* 7: The idea of taking up arms against the "Huns" was popular [in 1918].

b. a German plane or ship. Now *hist.*

     1918 in Rossano *Price of Honor* 128: His tracers went way under the Hun. **1944** Mellor *Sank Same* 119: It was a sub...and it had to be a Hun. **1944** *N.Y. Times* (Mar. 12) 25: "Beware of the Hun in the sun," is what they say about "the sneak attack." **1945** in Gellhorn *Face of War* 161: Hose the Hun. *a***1991** Ethell & Sand *Fighter Command* 136 [ref. to WWII]: When I came out, the Hun wasn't there any longer.

hun[1] *n.* **1.** a hundred; a hundred dollars.

     1895 *Harper's* (Nov.) 962: Fact is, just got my wheel...pneumatic tires, tool-chest, cyclometer, lamp—all for a hun. **1895** Townsend *Fadden* 89: Dey gets two hun., tree hun., five hun., an', dis is straight, sometimes er tousan' plunks. **1901** T.A. Dorgan, in Zwilling *TAD Lexicon* 110: Sam Hildreth casting a sorrowful glance at Owensbora who cost him "Five Hun." **1916** E.R. Burroughs *Return of Mucker* 41: Youse don't tink we'll get any o' dat five hun, do youse? *a***1987** Bunch & Cole *Reckoning for Kings* 444: I could go four hun a day.

2. (*cap.*) [prob. infl. by HUN] *USAF.* the Republic F-100 Super Sabre fighter-bomber. [Quots. ref. to the Vietnam War.]

     1978 in Higham & Williams *Combat Aircraft* 3: An F-100 pilot with more than 1,000 hours in the "Hun." *Ibid.* 12: Quite a switch from the long snouts of the "Hun" and the "Thud." **1979** D.K. Schneider *AF Heroes* 56: In South Vietnam, the "Huns" were often scrambled from ground alert to support friendly troops in contact with the enemy. **1989** Berent *Rolling Thunder* 52: Hun drivers from Bien Hoa.

hun[2] *n.* HONEY, 3.

     1896 Ade *Artie* 73: "Look at the new hat on her."..."It's a hun."

hunch *n.* **1.** a nudge; (*hence*) a piece of advice or inside information; hint; tip; suggestion.

     1849 in *AS* XXVI (1951) 183: Another piece [of writing] gave a few hunches to the inexperienced freshman, warning them against [etc.]. **1896** Lillard *Poker Stories* 197: Didn't you know I was working? Didn't I give you the hunch? **1901** "H. McHugh" *John Henry* 57: The reason it's so good is because I took my hunch from Rud. Kipling's style. **1903** *Enquirer* (Cincinnati) (May 9) 13: *Hunch*—A tip. **1903** Ade *Society* 102: I might give you a Hunch on the Q.T. **1908** in H.C. Fisher *A. Mutt* 24: Curses! I simply must get a hunch some place. **1914** Z. Grey *West. Stars* 135: Take a hunch from me. **1923** Z. Grey *Wanderer* 11: So, son, if you're askin' me for a hunch, let me tell you, drink little an' gamble light an' fight shy of the females! **1926** C.M. Russell *Trails* 9: So, takin' Baldy's hunch, we unsaddle.

2. a presentiment or premonition; a suspicion. Now *S.E.*

     1888 E. Field *Sharps & Flats II* 3: We men of the world do not call them premonitions; we call them "hunches." **1899** *S.F. Examiner* (Jan. 26) 4: He had a hunch that William was a very good thing to tie to. **1899** in J. London *Short Stories* 46: It's only a "hunch," Kid,...but I think it's straight. **1902–03** Ade *People You Know* 28: He had a secret Hunch that it would be no Disgrace for him to go out and do the best he could. **1903** *Enquirer* (Cincinnati) (May 9) 13: *Hunch*—...an inspiration. **1905** in "O. Henry" *Works* 1271: The old woman has got a hunch that she wants a peach. **1907** in H.C. Fisher *A. Mutt* 11: "There's only one chance. We must move him to where he can get the sea air." "Sea Air? That's a horse's name. That's a hunch." **1913** A. Palmer *Salvage* 144: Gus himself never once suffered from cold feet, or, as professional parlance puts it, he never had a "hunch." **1914** S. Lewis *Mr. Wrenn* 142: I've got a hunch he'll be back here in three or four months. **1919** Hedges *Iron City* 123: A hunch is a hunch, you know. Just can't do it. **1927** Rollins *Jinglebob* 164: Don't say nothin' or do nothin' that'll give Jackson any hunch. **1929** in R.E. Howard *Book* 62: The minute I stepped ashore from the *Sea Girl*, merchantman, I had a hunch that there would be trouble. **1934** Cunningham *Trigger-nometry* 85: They "had a hunch" and stayed away. **1941** D'Usseau & Collins *Lady Scarface* (film): I think you've got a hunch on this case and I'm going to let you follow it through. **1941** in Ruhm *Detective*

263: Call it a hunch. **1944** in C. Gould *Tracy* 7: You fellows agreed it was a great hunch. **1952** W. Fisher *Waiters* 67: Dreams an' hunches don't mean nothin' in my life.

hunchbrain *n.* LAMEBRAIN.

     1979 in M. Adler *Drawing Down the Moon* 310: In the year 1166 B.C., a malcontented hunchbrain...got it into his head that the universe was as humorless as he.

hundred-mile coffee *n. Trucking.* strong coffee that can presumably keep a driver awake for the time it takes to drive one hundred miles.

     1976 *Nat. Lampoon* (July) 56: Got that free cup of hundred mile coffee. *a***1977** W.I. Little *Transp.-Logistics Dict.* 162: *Hundred mile coffee* strong coffee. **1978** Wheeler & Kerby *Steel Cowboy* (film): Hundred-mile coffee! **1979** J.H. Thomas *Long Haul* 134: Gallons of strong "hundred-mile coffee" are consumed by truckers for the caffeine content.

hundred-pounder *n. Narc.* (see quot.).

     1988 Univ. Tenn. student theme: Demerol [is] known on the street as a "dem," a "rol," or a "hundred-pounder" (a 100 mg. tablet of Demerol).

hung *adj.* **1.a.** (of a male) having large genitals.—usu. considered vulgar. Earlier **hanged.** [The "1785" quot. cited in *OED* is nonexistent; presumably the 1811 quot. below (fr. a later edition of the 1785 work) is the one intended.]

     *ca***1600** Shakespeare *Twelfth Night* I iv: MARIA....My lady will hang thee for thy absence. CLOWN. Let her hang me. He that is well hanged in this world needs to fear no colors. *ca***1610** Rowley *Woman Never Vext* (unp.): You must be well-hang'd e'r you can be as I am. *****1641** in *OED2*: Hung tuppes are such as have both the stones in the codde. *****ca***1645** in *OED2*: They say he was hung like an ass. *****a***1673** Rochester *Poems* 43: Had she picked out, to rub her arse on,/Some stiff-pricked clown or well-hung parson. *****1681** Dryden *Poems* 117: And therefore, in the name of dulness be/The well-hung Balaam and cold Caleb, free. *****1730** N. Bailey *Dict.* s.v. *cully:* Fools are said to be generally well hung. *****1811** *Lexicon Balatron* s.v. *well-hung: The blowen was nutts upon the kiddey because he is well-hung;* the girl is pleased with the youth because his genitals are large. **1855** Whitman *Leaves of Grass* 22: Will it help breed one goodshaped and wellhung man, and a woman to be his perfect and independent mate? *****ca***1866** *Romance of Lust* 150: I was too heavy hung. **1916** Cary *Venery* I 148: *Hung*—pertaining to the male genital organs. *a***1938** T. Wolfe *Web & Rock* 41: Let's find out how well he's hung. **1951** Longstreet *Pedlocks* 373: Stop robbin' the cradle, kid, and meet a well-hung man. **1952** Randolph & Wilson *Holler* 105: The preterite *hung* must be used with caution in elegant backwoods talk, because it has a sexual meaning in many wisecracks and anecdotes. **1965** Herlihy *Cowboy* 119: You think 'cause you're hung you can get away with this crap? **1968** J.W. Wells *Taboo Breakers* 108: Joe's hung like a bull. **1960–69** Runkel *Law* 262: He was hung better than a Rembrandt etching in the Washington National Gallery! **1969** Searls *Hero Ship* 171: "Forget *him*," Ape murmured audibly, "he's hung like a stud mosquito. Look at *me*." **1970** Graffito, N.Y.U.: Ed is hung. **1975** Wambaugh *Choirboys* 282: He's hung like a hummingbird....He's some kinda freak! **1982** Downey *Losing the War* 183: Joe...was hung like a Spanish mule. **1987** Taubman *Lady Cop* 201: A guy that looked like he was hung like a bull elephant. **1993** A. Lomax *Where Blues Began* 125: The most lavishly hung of all animals is the male donkey, or jack.

b. (of a woman) having large breasts.

     [*****1685** in *OED2*: A large Hound Bitch...pretty well hung, all white.] **1950** in M. Daly *Profile of Youth* 233: Boy, is she hung! **1962** *Mad* (Oct.) 29: **Kim Novak's favorite Chinese dish: Kim Sum Hung Chick. **1971** S. Stevens *Way Uptown* 244: I seen her a few times, she was tall and heavy hung and just a outasight kid. **1971** *Current Slang* V (Spring) 14: *Hung*, adj. Well-endowed (male and female). **1971** *N.Y. Times* (Sept. 5) 1: Women today are better hung than the men. **1993** *Beavis and Butt-head* (MTV): That chick is really *hung*!

2. suffering from a hangover; HUNG OVER.

     1947 Schulberg *Harder They Fall* 13: What's the matter? Hung? **1956** P. Moore *Chocolates* 107: We were hung, you see. That's why we had to eat, to feel better. **1960** J.A. Williams *Angry Ones* 2: I woke up angry, hung as hell, but alive. **1966–67** W. Stevens *Gunner* 171: He's still hung, sweetheart. **1968** "J. Hudson" *Case of Need* 139: I was hung over from a party after the game. Really hung. Too hung. **1970** Gaffney *World of Good* 208: "You look hung," Donelli remonstrated. **1990** P. Munro *Slang U.*: *Hung* hung over.

3. *Orig. Jazz.* **a.** desperate; stymied; poorly provided with; HUNG UP, 2.

> *ca***1953** Hughes *Lodge* 119: Cats who are sick and hung and without loot. **1955** in J. Blake *Joint* 110: I was really hung for something to read. **1963** in L. Bruce *Essential Bruce* 174: Vell, I'm a little hung for bread now. **1982** Sculatti *Catalog of Cool* 214: He's really hung for bread. **1984** W. Gibson *Neuromancer* 78: "Who am I?" "You got me hung, Jack. Who…are you?"

b. obsessed or infatuated; HUNG UP, 3.c.—*occ. constr.* with *out*.

> **1950** in Kerouac *Letters* 249: "The strange red afternoon light" Wolfe also was hung on. **1952** Kerouac *Cody* 39: I mean bleak, sad, really mated, hung, like Bull with June. **1960** Wohl *Cold Wind* 149: You know, like I'm hung on him. Is that a gas? **1965** Hentoff *Jazz Country* 1: Although he didn't play anything himself, he had a lot of records and he was almost as hung on jazz as I was. **1966** Susann *Valley of Dolls* 96: That's the…way a guy shows he's hung on you. **1968** McNeill *Moving Through Here* 168: Violence was the whole pattern of the Free Store. They were hung on violence. **1968–70** *Current Slang* III & IV 72: *Hung out,* adj. In love.—Watts [section of Los Angeles]. **1967–80** Folb *Runnin' Lines* 243: *Hung out.* 1. Addicted to. 2. Obsessed with.

c. depressed or upset; HUNG UP, 3.b.

> **1955** in Kerouac *Letters* 509: All complicated drug requests I [am] too hung to perform on. **1958** *AS* (Oct.) 225: Annoyed…*bugged, dragged,…hung.* **1965** Hardman *Chaplains* 4: Well, this poor lady, Peter Pan, was real hung…."Come now, children," she wheedles, "why, don't you know every time a little boy says he doesn't believe in fairies that a fairy somewhere falls down dead?" **1966** Fariña *Down So Long* 54: "You all right?" "Hung, man. And constipated." **1970** *Playboy* (Sept.) 96: But here was this cat, *totally* hung because he was convinced he had to be black in all things and he's a militant leader, man, *militant.* **1994** *New Yorker* (Sept. 5) 107: Even the hyperkinetic visual style is soothingly familiar, from music videos…nothing to get hung about.

hunger *n.* ¶ In phrase: **from hunger, 1.** *adv.* emptily, foolishly, or ineptly; (*occ.*) to a dismaying degree.

> **1934** Jevne & Purcell *Joe Palooka* (film): I'm not talkin' from hunger! **1935** in *DAS: Playing* [music] *from hunger:* similar to "corny," meaning playing in a style to please the uneducated masses. **1939** N. West *Locust* 284: There proved to be little demand for his talents, however. As he himself put it, he "stank from hunger."

2. *adj.* most unsatisfactory, unappealing, untalented, unattractive, etc.; no good.

> **1939** "E. Queen" *Dragon's Teeth* 29: That theatrical lead is strictly from hunger, I tell you! **1939–40** O'Hara *Pal Joey* 10: Two months ago, Joey was strictly from hunger as they say. **1942** Liebling *Telephone* 69: The singers are from hunger….the performers are from hunger and every day…saps pay for [music and acting] lessons so they can be from hunger too. **1944** Kapelner *Lonely Boy Blues* 96: She's too good for him! He's from hunger! **1944** *Slanguage Dict.* 61: *Strictly from hunger*—a jerk. **1948** I. Shulman *Cry Tough!* 29: She was strictly from hunger. **1949** *Always Leave Them Laughing* (film): "How y'all like it?" "It's from hunger!" **1953** Paley *Rumble* 236: Fuller is from hunger. **1971** *N.Y. Times* (Aug. 22) 13: This Poem Is From Hunger. **1993** *TV Guide* (Feb. 20) 44: Jeff Jarvis's criticism of *The Hat Squad* is from hunger. **1995** *N.Y. Times* (July 12) C2: How come the men I date are from hunger?

hung over *adj.* suffering from a hangover. Now *S.E.*

> **1942** *ATS* 125: Suffer from the effects of a debauch. *Be (a bit) hung-over.* **1950** in *OED2*: Brafferton just came in, looking as hung over as you can get. **1961** L. Sanders *Four-Year Hitch* 87: I'm just hung over. **1977–81** S. King *Cujo* 11: Bawling at a resigned (and often hung-over) George Meara. **1991** Jenkins *Gotta Play Hurt* 9: Listen, I'm kind of hung over.

hungries *n.pl.* hunger, esp. for snacks. Cf. earlier So. & Black E *hungry* 'hunger'.

> **1970** *Playboy* (Dec.) 122: The stoned hungries are merciless.

1972–76 Durden *No Bugles* 11: The screaming hungries hit us about an hour after we'd smoked….I thought I'd die. But that's the screamin' hungries as best as I can describe 'em. **1988** Baby Ruth candy TV ad (Jan. 1): Baby Ruth! Big B! No more hungries!

hungry *adj.* **1.** [narrowing of fig. S.E. sense (*OED* def. 5)] single-mindedly intent upon fame, victory, success, or profit; (*now often*) seeking bribes. Rarely (as in 1929 quot.) as *n.*

> **1862** in *Civil War History* VIII (1962) 378: But nothing could withstand the charge of our troops….They were *hungry* and MAD and *desperate* and fought like tigers. **1929** Botkin *Folk-Say* I 111: A *hungry* is a [taxi] driver who, anticipating the tip, can never produce change for a passenger. **1949** W.R. Burnett *Asphalt Jungle* 178: But sometimes guys get hungry…and then they get themselves in a lot of trouble. **1955** Graziano & Barber *Somebody Up There* 177: Money talked….This can had real hungry guards. **1957** Ness & Fraley *Untouchables* 39: I was to be the "hungry" one, although actually it made no difference as the money was to be marked and turned over to the district attorney as evidence. **1961** in Cannon *Nobody Asked* 143: Fight managers is just a pack of hungry guys. **1963** *Time* (Mar. 29) 54: I ain't fightin' for no high ideals….I'm a hungry fighter, man, very hungry. **1973** Palmer & Furlong *Go for Broke* 73: When I was young and "hungry," I never coveted money…for its own sake. **1976** Conroy *Santini* 299: You could have scored forty tonight. But you just weren't hungry enough. **1978** D. Evans (Boston Red Sox) (WINS radio) (Sept. 8): This is a funny, funny game. It's not that we weren't hungry—but they were hungry too….They got 21 hits in the ballgame and that's doing something. **1982** WINS news (Aug. 25): A hungry fighter is the most dangerous kind.

2. full of holes. *Joc.*

> **1863** Hosmer *Color-Guard* 159: My boots, as boys say, are hungry in many places.

Hungry Joe *n.* a man who is a beggar.

> **1901** A.H. Lewis *Croker* 64: I'd dig for a "twenty"…every time one of those Hungry Joes come near me.

Hungry Liz *n.* [sugg. by TIN LIZZIE] *Mil. Av.* (a nickname for) the crash ambulance stationed at a flying field. Also **Hungry Lizzie.**

> **1918** Bruno *Flying Yankee* 49 [ref. to 1917]: We fell about four miles away from the camp and "Hungry Lizzie," the white Packard twin six ambulance which was always on the field, had gone sixty miles an hour to the place where we fell. **1919** *N.Y. Times Mag.* (Mar. 30) 4: When we landed they had to take the Kiwee away in hungry Liz, the ride had scared him so. **1920** *Amer. Leg. Wkly.* (Jan. 30) 17: I got the engine going again, just as I thought it was a sure crash and hungry Liz had me.

hung up *adj.* **1.** delayed or hindered (orig. *dial.* or *colloq.*); (*hence*) stymied; bewildered.

> ***1876** in *EDD* III 52: [*Hung up*] To be delayed or hindered, as in hay-making or harvest, from bad weather or want of hands. ***1887** in *EDD*: "He is quite hung up," so circumstanced that he is hindered from doing what otherwise he would. ***1904** Kipling *Traffics* 324: The Guard is hung up: distinctly so. Old Vee will have to cut his way through. **1909** Ware *Passing Eng.* 156: *Hung up,* from the American—where personal catastrophe is referred to by this phrase. **1938** Steinbeck *Grapes of Wrath* 220: Look out for the desert. See you don't get hung up. Take plenty water, case you get hung up. **1945** Shelly *Hepcats Dict.* 21: *All hung up*—completely bewildered. **1946** Steinbeck *Wayward Bus* 204: I don't know if I could get through or not….If we get hung up I don't want to be to blame. **1966–67** P. Thomas *Mean Streets* 52: Momma looked like she was hung up tight, then said something. **1972** Claerbaut *Black Jargon: Hung up*…to be stymied; unable to progress: *He's got himself hung up on that one.* **1980–84** Shue *Nerd* 12: I got hung up at the zoo with Pinky and the kids.

2. in trouble; desperate; HARD UP. [The sense of the Eng. dial. quot. in brackets is 'poorly provided'.]

> [***1875** in *EDD* III 52: I was so hung up for time all last week I couldn't come.] ***1909** Ware *Passing Eng.* 156: *Hung up* (Soc[iety], 1879). Said where in lower classes stuck up [defined as "moneyless"] would be used. From the American—where personal catastrophe is referred to by this phrase. **1938** Steinbeck *Grapes of Wrath* 199: He'd be findin' out how bad you're hung up, an' how much jack ya got. **1952** Mandel *Angry Strangers* 196: "I'm the one who's stuck with it,

Diane. You're free." "Not as long as you're hung up." *ca*1953 Hughes *Lodge* 205: I was really hung up. On top of everything else, not to have a cigarette! **1954** *Harper's Mag.* (Nov.) 36: *Hung up:* in trouble, as left in the lurch by a girl. **1959** *Swinging Syllables: Hung up*—In trouble, plans fouled up. **1963** *N.Y. Times Mag.* (Nov. 24) 52: "I'm hung up"…[means] everything is ruined. **1969** L. Sanders *Anderson Tapes* 96: We had some expenses and we're hung up.

3. Orig. *Jazz.* **a.** afflicted with emotional problems; neurotic, repressed, anxiety-ridden, etc. [presumably the orig. sense.]

1952 J.C. Holmes *Go* 28: Her name's Georgia. She's all hungup, but what the hell. **1957** Gelber *Connection* 79: She was hung up in her head like everyone else I know. **1953–58** J.C. Holmes *Horn* 215: A goddamn bunch of creepy, hung-up kids. **1958–59** Lipton *Barbarians* 116: Now don't go getting hung up behind the scene, Tanya. **1961** Sullivan *Shortest, Gladdest Years* 27: Hamlet was hung up. **1965** B. Jackson, in *Atlantic* (Jan. 1966) 52: The men who become prisoners are the most obvious criminals: clumsy, stupid, impulsive, hung-up. **1972** Claerbaut *Black Jargon* 69: The fox is really hung up!

b. unhappy; depressed.

1948 *Neurotica* (Spring) 33: They are hungup, groggy from last night's gage. **1951** in Kerouac *Letters* 318: I get as much hung up, man, as you ever did in your most hungup days and at a time after I really wrote a great book. **1952** Brossard *Darkness* 251: At the end of my rope is right, Jack. I'm really hung up. **1952** Mandel *Angry Strangers* 9: You don't have to be hung up; you don't owe me anything. **1958** Mayes *Hunters* (film): I'm sorry. I'm all hung-up. Everybody's been giving me the business. **1958** Ginsberg *Kaddish* 57: They had slow hung-up talks at midnight. **1972** Friday *Secret Garden* 39: I used to be very hung-up about being flat-chested—I'm over that now.

c. obsessed or fixated; preoccupied; infatuated; (*also*) addicted.—constr. with *on*.

1950 in Kerouac *Letters* 244: If only you weren't so hung up and could save yourself a few…years and come with us. **1952** Kerouac *Cody* 126: Oh he was always hungup on his firewood you know, he was always talking about firewood. **1952** J.C. Holmes *Go* 37: It was inhabited by people "hungup" with drugs and other habits, searching out a new degree of craziness. **1954** in W.S. Burroughs *Letters* 215: You would get a habit on one shot and be hung up for life. **1961** L. Sanders *Four-Year Hitch* 102: It's a hell of a thing to be hung up on one incident of your life and not be able to enjoy the rest of it. **1961** in Bruce *Essential Bruce* 15: The reason I don't get hung up with, well, say, integration, is that by the time Bob Newhart is integrated, I'm bigoted. **1963** Stearn *Grapevine* 41: She was hung-up on her butch. Like the French say, she had her under her skin. **1961–64** Barthelme *Caligari* 98: Bobby…is hung up on sports cars, a veteran consumer of *Road & Track*. **1966–67** P. Thomas *Mean Streets* 200: I thought about being hung up on *tecata*. **1969** *Social Problems* XVII 60: But to get "hung-up" on a drug—to *need* to take drugs—is seen as losing "cool." **1976** R. Price *Bloodbrothers* 25: There was something about him that really had her hung up on the boards. **1990** *Guiding Light* (CBS-TV) (Mar. 21): She ain't hung up on money. **1994** *Gordon Elliott Show* (Fox-TV): I think she's a little too hung up on herself. **1994** in *Reader's Digest* (Jan. 1995) 138: When we get so hung up on getting our own way that we won't concede on *any* point, we do ourselves a real disservice. **1995** *Calif. vs. Simpson* (Court TV) (Sept. 6): He's so hung up on rules and stuff.

d. unpleasant; trying or tedious.

1958 in Hogan & German *Chronicle Reader* 45: Life is a drag, man.…Everything's all hung up, man.…Rugged, you know?

hungus *adj. Stu.* HUMONGOUS.

1983 Naiman *Computer Dict.* 74: *Hungus*…Unmanageably huge.

Hunk *n.* [prob. fr. *Hungarian,* infl. by HUNK, 1.b.] **1.a.** HUNKY, 1.a.

1896 *N.Y. Herald* (Jan. 13) 3: The average Pennsylvanian contemptuously refers to these immigrants as…"Hunks.".…"Hunks" is a corruption for Huns, but under this title the Pennsylvanian includes Hungarians, Lithuanians, Slavs, Poles, Magyars and Tyroleans. **1923** Ornitz *Haunch, Paunch & Jowl* 155: Hunks, Wops, Squareheads. *a*1927 in Finger *Frontier Ballads* 54: Dutchmen, Frenchmen, Hunks, and Jews. **1927** [Fliesler] *Anecdota* 31: An Armenian was being examined by the draft board. The physician [was] looking over the hunk's penis. **1938** *JAF* LI 67: "Hunk"—a Bulgarian laborer.

b. HUNKY, 1.b.

1969 Rodgers *Black Bird* 37: Muthafuckas/…pigs and hunks and negroes who try to divide and/destroy our moves toward liberation.

2. HUNKY, 2. Cf. HUCK.

1928 R. Fisher *Jericho* 301: *Hunk, Hunky* See *boogy*.

hunk *n.* **1.a.** HUNKS.

1856 A.O. Hall *Christmas Trot* 214: All [will] be paid by the old Hunk you speak of.

b. a heavy-set muscular fellow, esp. if dull or clumsy; LUMMOX.

1882 *Harper's* (Sept.) 646: *You* heered me, you ign'ant, you hunk. **1905** *DN* III 119: *Hunk, n.* A worthless person. "He's an ornry hunk." **1917** in Rossano *Price of Honor* 54: Every one of them is a gentleman, a wonderful soldier, and a great big hunk. **1917** in Bowerman *Compensations* 4: Poor Bill is laid low with sea sickness and occaisons [*sic*] much laughter, there is always something extremely funny in seeing a big hunk laid low by such a disease. **1945** Shelly *Hepcats Dict.* 13: *Hunk*…stalwart male. **1950** in Weinberg et al. *Tough Guys* 373: The actor.…All that hunk has to do is…give them a look at both sides of the profile. **1956** Moran & Reid *Tugboat* 46 [ref. to 1880's]: Why, you big clumsy hunk.…He's just lucky enough to be a big hunk and me too small.…That hunk over there don't speak up 'cause he has nothin' to speak up about. **1965–70** Karlen *Sexuality & Homosexuality* 534: My boss…was a real hunk, a real football-player type. **1990** Univ. Tenn. prof., age *ca*55: "He's a hunk" means he's kind of dull and slow-witted.

2.a. an act of copulation; PIECE; (*hence*) a person, usu. a woman, regarded as a sexual partner.—usu. considered vulgar.

1929–33 J.T. Farrell *Manhood of Lonigan* 216: The time to come when your wife wouldn't be a hot hunk anymore. **1931** J.T. Farrell *McGinty* 194: Say, I'll bet he never had a decent hunk in his life.

b. copulation; HUMP, 1.a.—usu. considered vulgar.

1942 *ATS* 341: Copulation…*Ass,…hunk, hump,…piece* or *hunk of tail,…-ass,* or *butt,* [etc.]. **1984** De Palma *Body Double* (film): I was gettin' good hunk for sixteen years.

3.a. a very attractive specimen (of a man or woman).—constr. with *of*.

[**1852** Doten *Journals* I 121: I…weighed 170 pounds…quite a hunk of a boy.] **1944** *Yank* (March 10) 15: The broken down old duffer…and the streamlined "beautiful hunk of man." **1944** *Slanguage Dict.* 60: *Hunk of man*—the current "big moment." **1947** *ATS* (Supp.) 1: Fellow. *Hunk of man.…Girl…hunk of woman.* **1948** *Looney Tunes* (animation): What a hunk of feminine pulchritudy! **1951** J. Reach *My Friend Irma* 35: What a lovely hunk of masculinity he was. **1957** H. Simmons *Corner Boy* 53: Isn't Gregory Peck the sweetest hunk of man? He really sends me. **1960** Kirkwood *Pony* 113: And she was what you call "a real hunk of woman."

b. (esp. among young women) a sexually attractive, esp. athletic, man. [The term gained national currency during the 1970's and 1980's.]

1947 *ATS* (Supp.) 2: "Smooth" fellow…*hunk*. **1963–64** Kesey *Great Notion* 575: To Hank the Hunk; a gorgeous Hunk of male. **1968** Baker, Ladd & Robb *CUSS* 141: *Hunk*. A sexually attractive person, male. **1969** *Esquire* (Aug.) 71: As They Used to Say in the 1950's…She might come across if he were…the living end. Cute. Neat.…A hunk. **1972** *Nat. Lampoon* (July) 49: Women have been calling me Casanova, Valentino, a hunk. **1972** N.Y.U. student: A *hunk* is a guy who's real handsome and athletic and well-built. It's complimentary. **1973** *TULIPQ* (coll. B.K. Dumas): He's a real hunk. **1987** *Magical World of Disney* (NBC-TV): Isn't he a *hunk*? **1991** *Time* (Sept. 23) 44: Rippling hunks wield electric guitars like chainsaws.

c. (among men) a sexually attractive woman.

[**1929–33** (see quot. at (**2.a.**), above).] **1949** *New Yorker* (Nov. 5) 82: Galvinatin' [*sic*] around town with a…well-stacked hunk blond special. **1971** *Playboy* (July) 186: Irish, you were a knockout tonight, babe. Turning 'em on like crazy.…you beautiful hunk. **1976** Univ. Tenn. student: This chick was a *hunk*. And she was all over him. **1978** *UTSQ*: [Attractive] young woman…*doll, angel, hunk, fox.* **1978** Diehl *Sharky's Machine* 118: She was a real hunk, Shark. A real hunk.

hunk *adj. & adv.* in a good or safe position; satisfactory; all right; fine; O.K.—usu. constr. with *all*.

   1843 Field *Pokerville* 50: Well, I allow you're just *hunk*, this time, then…for we have got the sweetest roaster for dinner you ever *did* see. **1850** G.G. Foster *Gas-Light* 74: You are here—you pay your shilling at the door—and you are "hunk." **1856** in Bartlett *Amer.* (ed. 2) 208: And now he felt himself all *hunk*, and wanted to get this enormous sum out of the city. **1859** Bartlett *Amer.* (ed. 2) 208: *Hunk*…(Dutch *honk*.) Place, post, home. A word…much used by New York boys in their play. "To be *hunk*," or "all *hunk*," is to have reached the goal…without being intercepted… to be all safe. **1862** in Frank & Reaves *Seeing Elephant* 172: If we can clean this gang out we will be all hunk. **1864** in G. Whitman *Letters* 114: If I have some one to look out for my grub, I shall be all hunk. **1865** Williams *Joaquin* 42: I'm hunk. Of course, I ain't hit if you're not. **1869–71** C.G. Leland *Breitmann's Ballads* 75: I'fe heard of miragles pefore,/Boot none so hunk ash dis. **1876** in *PADS* (No. 52) 41: Feel all Hunk. **1889** in F. Remington *Sel. Letters* 75: If I can only keep it down to this size I am all hunk. **1891** Wm. Devere *Tramp Poems* 17: We…closed up the shanty all hunk. **1894** *Harper's* (Dec.) 106: Now, if *you'll* listen to me, Miss Ericson, I'll be all hunk. **1903** A.H. Lewis *Boss* 181: The proposition's all hunk.

¶ In phrase:

¶ **get hunk** to get even; recoup losses; (*hence*) to take revenge.

   1842 *Spirit of Times* (Nov. 5) 421: Revenge.…an opportunity to "get hunk" out of Miss Bunk. **1845** *Spirit of Times* (May 24) 146: Those who lost their money on Fashion had two or three chances to "get hunk," especially on the last day. **1889** in F. Remington *Sel. Letters* 73: I told him I'de get *hunk* with him—d— him. **1899–1900** Cullen *Tales* 363: If you want to get hunk, all you've got to do is just wait. **1902** Mollineux *Room with Little Door* 121: Do you want to get "hunk"? **1902** Cullen *More Tales* 94: When my little chance came along…I got hunk and relieved of the burden at the same time. **1903** A.H. Lewis *Boss* 93: It's up to us to get hunk an' even on th' play. **1904** *Life in Sing Sing* 249: *Hunk*—Revenge. **1906** Kildare *Old Bailiwick* 137: I'm going to get hunk on him—or me friends is.…You see if I don't get hunk on that guy. I'll do him the minute I get out. **1908** H. Green *Maison de Shine* 231: I s'pose he lose a couple bets, an' done this to get hunk. **1922** Rollins *Cowboy* 312 [ref. to 1890's]: Rustling [was occasionally]…a means of "getting hunk" of some well-to-do but hated rancher. **1925** Cohan *Broadway* 71: The piano player…was having the time of his life getting "hunk" with me. **1927** P.A. Rollins *Jinglebob* 212 [ref. to 1880's]: Some Injuns ain't yet through gettin' hunk with white men. **1941** *Washington* (D.C.) *Daily News* (Feb. 19) 12: "Get Hunk With Hitler" at His Own Expense. **1958** Cooley *Run for Home* 64: But if you take advantage of what I just told the bosun and use it as an excuse to get hunk with him, *I'll* break your head before he has a chance to.

Hunker *n. Pol.* a member of the conservative element of the New York State Democratic party; (*hence*) a politically conservative person. Now *hist.*

   1843 in *DAE*: Let the "Hunkers" and "Barn-burners" contend. **1849** in Bartlett *Amer.* (ed. 2) 208: He is now the leader of the hunkers of Missouri. **1853** P.H. Myers *Emigrant Squire* 10: There are the Hunkers and the Barnburners. **1863** in R.G. Carter *4 Bros.* 345: Too many *hunkers* present, who voted what they believed rather than what the merits of the debate established. **1864** J.R. Browne *Crusoe's Island* 52 [ref. to 1849]: I'm a [manifest-]destiny-man myself.…I'm none of your old Hunkers. **1977** (quot. at BARNBURNER, 1).

hunks *n.* a miser; (*hence*) a disagreeable or sour-tempered individual.

   *1730** N. Bailey *Dict.*: *Hunks*, a Miser, a covetous niggardly Wretch. *1803** in J. Ashton *Eng. Satires on Napoleon* 161: And grind him as close as—Old Hunks keeps his money. **1821** Wetmore *Pedlar* 33: There is a passport,…old Hunks. **1838** [Haliburton] *Clockmaker* (Ser. 2) 20: When old Hunks thought we was abed. **1851** Melville *Moby-Dick* ch. i: What of it, if some old hunks of a sea-captain orders me to get a broom and sweep down the decks? **1860** J.G. Holland *Miss Gilbert* 220: Cussed old hunks, how shall we manage him? **1872** *Myself* 57: Good riddance, old hunks! **1883–84** Whittaker *L. Locke* 181: I'm glad you whipped old Skinner, anyway, the old hunks. **1919, 1969** in *DARE*.

hunks *adv.* ¶ In phrase: **go hunks** to take equal shares.

1891 Campbell, Knox & Byrnes *Darkness & Daylight* 163: We'll go hunks, an' whatever I have you shall have the same. [**1981** *AS* LVI 27: A child…could claim a share of anything by shouting *hunks!* The possessor would have to yield part of the loot unless he or she had already shouted *fen hunks!*]

hunkum-bunkum *adj.* HUNKY-DORY.

   1842 *Spirit of Times* (Nov. 5) 421: Everything was hunkum-bunkum for immediate flight. **1908** *DN* III 332: *Hunkum-bunkum*…Very fine, excellent, good, etc. **1913** *DN* IV 24: What hunkum-bunkum bread you have to-day!

Hunky *n.* [HUNK + *-y* (hypocoristic)] **1.a.** a person of Eastern European ancestry, esp. a Hungarian or Slav, often a manual laborer.—also used attrib.—usu. used contemptuously. Also **Hunkie.** Cf. HUN; HUNYAK.

   1909 in *JAF* LXXIII (1960) 204: They are only Hunkies. **1909** in Sinclair *Plays* 145: The man was only a poor Hunkie, and there was no one to know or care. **1907–10** in Dillingham *Reports of Immigration Comm.* I 255: *Magyar*…"Huns" and "Hunkies" are names…incorrectly applied to this race and to Slavs indiscriminately in some parts of America. **1910** Fitch *Steel Workers* 147: A "Hunky" is not necessarily a Hungarian. He may belong to any of the Slavic races. **1914** Graham *Poor Immigrants* 126: Hungarians are "Hunkies." **1914** Jackson & Hellyer *Vocab.* 47: *Hunkie*…current in areas where North European laborers abound. A corruption of Hungarian, but employed to signify a Continental European who is unwashed and unnaturalized. **1918** in Lindner *Letters* 15: My mates are hunkies from Pittsburgh. **1928** Wylie *Laden* 17: Polacks and Hunkies, Negroes and wops. **1932** Halyburton *Shoot & Be Damned* 229: You God-damned dirty Hunky! **1935** O'Hara *Dr.'s Son* 42: Because you couldn't be in business…without learning Hunkie names. **1935** S. Lewis *Can't Happen* 130: My dad was French and my mother a Hunkie from Serbia. **1939** M. Levin *Citizens* 100: Men of the kind they called hunkies—white men too, but mostly Polish and Italian by birth. **1943** W. Simmons *Joe Foss* 22: He was proud of his "Hunky" ancestry. **1951** Longstreet *Pedlocks* 366: A cluttering collection of what were known to the schoolboys as Polacks, Hunkies, Micks, and Shines. **1986** R. Walker *AF Wives* 89: I'm from Pennsylvania.…I'm a Polack. Hunkies they call us at home. **1987** C.M. Carver *Amer. Reg. Dials.* 80: In the Inland Eastern North a *hunky* is an East European, especially one who is an unskilled laborer. **1989** Ramis & Aykroyd *Ghostbusters II* (film): You're sweet on this Hunky stud.

b. *Black E.* a white person.—used contemptuously. Cf. syn. HONKY[2]. [In speech, as in 1987 quot., the precise quality of the central vowel is often difficult to distinguish from that of HONKY[2].]

   [**1952** Himes *Stone* 208: Convicts whose minds had gone and who had never had any to start with, one-armed black greasy niggers and one-legged pock-marked hunkies; convicts from the dirty gutters of cheap cities…degenerate and crazy.] **1959** F.L. Brown *Trumbull Pk.* 186: Boy, I have never seen a bunch of hunkies scatter so fast in all my life! **1964** *PADS* (No. 42) 31: Negro terms for Caucasian…*hunky*. **1967** Baraka *Tales* 104: Crackers. Hunkies. **1968** Millea *Ghetto Fever* 113: Those hunkies called us every foul name under the sun. **1969** Gordone *No Place to Be Somebody* 421: I put him in here when none'a these other hunkies 'roun' here would hire him. **1969** Rodgers *Black Bird* 10: U gon die and go tuh HELL/and i sd i hoped it wudn't be NO HUNKIES there. **1971** Thigpen *Streets* 17: Don't give me shit/Hunky/Cause I'll take/Black Power. **1972** in W. King *Black Anthol.* 97: He was a black man. There shouldn't be no hunkies at his funeral. **1973** "A.C. Clark" *Crime Partners* 57: Kill the hunky. That's our rally cry. Death to Whitey. **1987** Tristan & Hancock *Weeds* (film): It's a symbol for…hunky death culture. **1994** Smitherman *Black Talk* 137: *Honky*…Also *hunky*.

2. a black person.—used contemptuously.

   1928 R. Fisher *Jericho* 301: *Hunky*. See boogy. **1980** in Curry *River's in My Blood* 263: They don't know the—as we call 'em—hunkies, the colored people that stole from us, in Pittsburgh.

hunky[1] *adj.* [prob. HUNK, *adj.*, + *-y*] **1.** fine; splendid; satisfactory. Also as adv.

   1861 C.F. Browne, in *DA*: He (Moses) folded her to his hart, with the remark that he was "a hunkey boy." **1862** C.F. Browne *A. Ward*

30: Hunky boy! Go it, my gay and festiv cuss! **1863** *Beadle's Dime Comic Speaker* 55: It was a hunky watch—a family hair-loom. **1864** in D. Chisholm *Civil War Notebook* 6: I have a hunky time. *Ibid.* 7: I have a good fire and feel all hunky. **1865** O.W. Holmes, Jr., in M.D. Howe *Shaping Yrs.* 240: I killed four [rabbits]—hunky boy! **1865** C.F. Browne *Ward: Travels* 44: Both were hunky boys, and fit nobly....It was one of the hunkiest things ever done in the military line. **1865** Sala *Diary* II 29: I dare say, the "hunky girls of '76" were complimented on their determination to abstain from British imported tea. **1866** *Night Side of N.Y.* 68: New York might claim him for one of the "hunkiest" of her sons. **1867** Clark *Sailor's Life* 20: She is a gay boat and hunkey in every strand. **1867** Alger *Ragged Dick* 156: "How do you like it?" "It's hunky." I don't believe "hunky" is to be found in either Webster or Worcester's big dictionary; but boys will readily understand what it means. **1868** Williams *Black-Eyed Beauty* 36: "All hunky!" said he, returning. **1873** Hotten *Slang Dict.* (ed. 4): *Hunky*, an American term....."everything went off hunky." **1875** *Minstrel Gags* 36: O, we's all hunky fellers. **1878** B. Harte *Drift* 38: She's all hunky, and has an appetite. **1883** in J.M. Carroll *Camp Talk* 139: So we are "huncky" on the servant question. **1885** S.S. Hall *Gold Buttons* 3: All hunky, pard. **1897** A.H. Lewis *Wolfville* 245: Billy...allows...it's the hunkiest baby in Arizona. **1900** Hammond *Whaler* 23: If we don't have to be in at the same lick we c'n git along all hunky. **1903** in "O. Henry" *Works* 1655: All right, hunky. *ca***1905** in Logsdon *Whorehouse Bells* 72: Come all you hunky punchers that follow the bronco steer. **1920** Ade *Hand-Made Fables* 129: Everything was Swell, Elegant, and Hunky. **1941–42** Marquand *Last Laugh* 36: That's fine....Everything's going to be hunky—hunky-dory. *****1970** Partridge *DSUE* (ed. 7) 1208: *Hunky*...Good: since ca. 1945.

2. ingratiated; friendly.

1899 in S. Crane *Dispatches* 153: He...began to get "hunky" with all those people who had been plugging at him. **1906** J. London *White Fang* ch. xix: He's all hunky with the officials. The Gold Commissioner's a special pal of his. **1910** *Sat. Eve. Post* (July 16) 15: I want to get hunky with the Sanitary boss.

hunky[2] *adj.* [HUNK, 3.b. + -*y*] (esp. among young women and homosexual men) virilely attractive; muscular and handsome.

1972 B. Rodgers *Queens' Vernacular* 110: Tall and handsome; answer to a queen's prayer...hunky ('71, fr. *hunk*). **1978** Maupin *Tales* 181: A perfect HBU. Hunky But Uptight. **1985** J. Dillinger *Adrenaline* 25: One of those hunky, hyper-macho...models. **1989** *Daily Beacon* (Univ. Tenn.) (Mar. 31) 7: It's unfair that I'm not as hunky as Tom Cruise. **1989** *TV Guide* (Sept. 16) 53: Hunky Gregory Harrison and droll John Larroquette. **1994** *Esquire* (Apr.) 143: Large blowups of hunky nudes wrestling in the garden.

hunky-doodle *adj.* HUNKY-DORY.
1905 *DN* III 62: *Hunky dory, hunky doodle*, adj. All right.

hunky-dory *adj.* [elaboration of HUNKY[1], presumably as explained in 1877 quot.] splendid (*obs.*); fine; completely satisfactory; all right; very well. Also as adv. Also vars.

1866 *Galaxy* (Oct. 1) 275: I cannot conceive on any theory of etymology...why anything that is "hunkee doree"...should be so admirable. **1868** in L. Levy *Flashes of Merriment* 89: I'm hunkadora how are you. *a***1869** in Bartlett *Amer.* (ed. 4) 304: Oh, the noble class of '68 is just old hunkédoré;/It's bound to cover Hamilton, likewise itself, with glory. **1869** in Boyer *Naval Surgeon* II 148: Today I can call myself hunky-dory again. *ca***1870** in *AS* IX (1934) 154: Cries, as he rakes the pile,/Oh! ain't I Hunkydory? **1871** Schele de Vere *Americanisms* 492: *Hunky Dory*,..."Well, and in good spirits." **1872** Burnham *Secret Service* vi: *Hunky-dory*, on the right side; everything agreeable. *Ibid.* 66: And having obtained such information...as satisfied him that he was all "hunky-dory," in certain quarters, he rested. **1875** *John Kelly...Against...Wallis* 32: Kent and Parsons, Greenleaf, Story,/Put the matter hunkey-dory. **1877** Bartlett *Amer.* (ed. 4) 304: *Hunkidori.* Superlatively good. Said to be a word introduced by Japanese Tommy [a popular variety performer *fl.* 1865], and to be (or to be derived from) the name of a street, or a bazaar, in Yeddo. **1879** R. Wheeler *In Leadville* 12: My...shrewdness will get me into the Queen's favor, after which I am all hunki-dori. **1891** Maitland *Slang Dict.* 147: *Hunki-dori* (Amer.), all right. **1900** Wister *JimmyJohn Boss* 210: You're all right, and the spot is hunky-dory. **1905** London *White Fang* 9: Go to sleep

an' you'll be all hunkydory in the mornin'. **1908** W.G. Davenport *Butte & Montana* 11: Am getting along hunkydory. **1912** Field *Watch Yourself* 93: "We're all hun-ki-dora now"—a slang phrase in those days [1860's] signifying "all right." **1929** "C. Woolrich" *Times Sq.* 265: "Hunky-dory," agreed Fay. **1927–30** Rollins *Jinglebob* 33 [ref. to 1880's]: We'll light out hunkydory with 'em for Montana. **1929–30** Dos Passos *42d Parallel* 58: Ain't this hunkydory? **1938** *Sat. Review* (July 23) 22: I had a hunky-dorry time. **1940** R. Wright *Native Son* 106: "Say, how was it, Bigger?"..."Honky dory." **1944** Micheaux *Mrs. Wingate* 127: Everything is hunky dory, Eddie. **1949** Gordon & Kanin *Adam's Rib* 11: Lots of things a man can do and in society's eyes it's all hunky-dory. A woman does the same things...and she's an outcast. **1952** Vonnegut *Player Piano* 248: Everything hunky-dory in my little old home, eh? **1958** A. King *Enemy* 84: So everything had gone off hunky-dory. **1968** P. Roth *Portnoy* 190: Why don't we go back to Russia where everything is hunky-dory? **1975** Harington *Ark. Ozarks* 22: It was hunky-dory....Scrumdoodle. Galuptious. Splendiferous. Humdinger. Slopergobtious. Bardacious. Yum-yum. Swelleroo. Gumptious. Danderoo. Superbangnamious. **1980** *N.Y. Times Mag.* (Feb. 10) 10: "Copacetic"...means..."hunky-dory; cool." **1982** Knoxville, Tenn., woman, age *ca*40: Used to, when a teenage girl got pregnant, she got shipped out of town to have the baby and then she came back and everything was hunky-dory. **1984** Hindle *Dragon Fall* 79: Look, you and Eric get along just hunky-dory. **1991** *Yo! MTV Raps* (MTV): I'm feelin' hunky-dory.

hunky-dunky *adj.* HUNKY-DORY.
1955 Ruppelt *Report on UFOs* 119: Our vast files of reports are in tip-top shape; and in general things are hunky-dunky. **1981** Louisville, Ky., man, age *ca*50: Now everything looks hunky-dunky.

Hunland *n. Mil. Av.* German-held territory. Now *hist.* Cf. HUN, 2.a.
*****1917** Lee *No Parachute* 10: The Lys runs eastward to Armentières and on into Hunland. **1918** Biddle *Fighting Airman* 137: The scrap ended three or four miles in Hunland. **1918** Bishop *Winged Warfare* 26: I may say here, in passing, that in the [Royal] Flying Corps a German is seldom anything but a Hun, and the territory back of his lines is seldom anything but Hunland. **1918** *Lit. Digest* (Aug. 24) 36: You gave it to them until the Heinies went back to Hunland. **1918** Roberts *Flying Fighter* 195: I noticed we were swinging back over Hunland. **1926** Springs *Nocturne Militaire* 87: We had been up for perhaps an hour when I saw a speck above the clouds over by Armentières, twenty-five miles in Hunland. **1982** W.R. Dunn *Fighter Pilot* 121: We departed Hunland for our home base in England.

hunting license *n. Pol.* exceptional license to take unauthorized action against individuals, proposals, programs, or the like.
1979 Homer *Jargon* 41: But don't mess with the Sanitation Commissioner—he has a *hunting license.*

hunyak or **honyock** *n.* [if *hunyak* is indeed the orig. form, perh. alter. of HUN, 1 + -*y*- + (Po)LACK] *Midwest.* **1.** an immigrant from Central or Southern Europe, usu. a Magyar or Slav.—also used attrib. —used contemptuously. Also vars.
1907–10 in Dillingham *Reports of Immigration Comm.* I 255: *Magyar*...Hungarian, Hun, or Hunyak in popular language. **1919** Hedges *Iron City* 21: Guy Street, the thoroughfare of "hunyocks." *Ibid.* 171: There are too many ignoramuses in that shop to join the union, honyocks and niggers. **1922** J.J. Davis *Iron Puddler* 220: A poor bunch of striking hunyaks. **1925** Mullin *Scholar Tramp* 167 [ref. to *ca*1912]: His vocabulary consisted of only two words that I could understand, "Hunyak" and "goddamn." I take it that he was an unskilled Hungarian laborer. **1929** in Perelman *Old Gang* 72: The Berbers had attacked the Hunyoks near Spanish Flats. **1934** W. Smith *Bessie Cotter* 17: She'd throw Violet right out on her can...and she'd go back to them four-bit Hunyok joints where she belongs. **1936** Farrell *World I Never Made* 219: A young fellow who looked like he might be a dago or a hunyock. **1938** "E. Queen" *4 Hearts* 14: He was tossing away the stockholders' dough like a hunyak on Saturday night. **1949** *PADS* (No. 11) (Apr.) 23: *Hunyack, hunyacker*...A foreign workman, one of non-English descent, usually Italian or other Southern European. *a***1961** *WNID3*: *Hunyak*...*hunyock*...*honyak*...*honyock*...*hunky*—usu. used disparagingly. **1963** D. Tracy *Brass Ring* 117: Some foreigner, a polack or a slovak...this big, ugly hunyock was going to make a crack.

1963 Coon *Short End* 91: Folk dances are funny. It's my understanding that they're supposed to bring rain or make the rice grow, or make the big good-looking Hunyak from the next prefect get the hots for you.

2. an ignorant homesteader or farmer; yokel; lout. Also vars.

1927 J. Stevens *Mattock* 4 [ref. to 1918]: The Hunyoks never wanted to fight in the first place, or they'd of enlisted in the infantry and not in no ditch-diggin' outfit. **1932–33** Nicholson & Robinson *Sailor Beware!* 71: "There she is, Chet...that's her." "Who's the hunyak with her?" "Search me." **1938** W. James *Flint Spears* 62: Besides, that hawnyawk's mare was missing. **1942** *ATS* 368: Terms of disparagement...*hunyak,...lummox,* [etc.]. **1943** in *DAS*: Speaking as a pure-bred hon-yock out of the Middle West. **1958** Bard & Spring *Horse Wrangler* 160 [ref. to 1890's]: There were several dry farmers or Honyocks at the wagon along with the TL cowboys. **1958** *AS* XXXIII (Dec.) 265: Pejorative Designations of Rural Dwellers in the Upper Midwest....*honyock....honyocker.* **1965** De Vries *Let Me Count* 160: It was a kind of protest—the passionate outcry of honyocks everywhere. **1969–71** Kahn *Boys of Summer* 64: Then he said harshly, "Come on. Let's go see the Hun-yaks." "Hun-yaks?" "The people you're down here to write about. The ball players." **1971** *Current Slang* V (Summer) 14: *Honyok, n.*...One who shovels manure (derogatory, person who is lazy or out of touch).

hurdy *n. West.* HURDY-GURDY, 1.b.

1865 in M.S. Goldman *Gold Diggers* 115: 4 hurdies arrived...from Downieville—hurdy houses started this evening. **1866** Dimsdale *Vigilantes* 11: As a rule, however, the professional "hurdies" are Teutons, and, though first-rate dancers, they are with some few exceptions the reverse of good-looking. **1876** W. Wright *Big Bonanza* 438: He it is that...patronizes the Hurdies.

hurdy-gurdy *n.* **1.** *West.* **a.** a dance hall. Now *hist.* In full, **hurdy-gurdy house.**

1866 Dimsdale *Vigilantes* 9: One "institution," offering a shadowy and dangerous substitute for more legitimate female association, deserves a more peculiar notice. This is the "Hurdy-Gurdy" house. **1891** Bourke *Border* 386: Close by these [gambling dens] were the "hurdy-gurdies," where the music from asthmatic pianos timed the dancing of painted, padded and leering Aspasias, too hideous to hope for livelihood in any village less remote from civilization. **1913** in Rosa & Koop *Rowdy Joe* 52: The Lion's Den, a Hurdy-Gurdy of the blackest dye. **1958** "W. Henry" *Reckoning* 103: Three obvious brothels, some eight hurdy-gurdy houses, eleven open-front saloons. **1963** R.W. Paul *Mining Frontiers* 16 [ref. to 1850's]: Hotels and restaurants, brothels, and "hurdy-gurdy houses." The latter were dancehalls.

b. a woman employed as a dancer in a dance hall. Now *hist.* In full, **hurdy-gurdy girl.**

1866 Dimsdale *Vigilantes* 9: Beyond the barrier sit the dancing women, called "hurdy-gurdies," sometimes dressed in uniform, but more generally habited according to the dictates of individual caprice, in the finest clothes money can buy, and which are fashioned in the most attractive styles that fancy can suggest. **1868** J.R. Browne *Apache Country* 340: Hurdy-gurdy girls are singing bacchanalian songs in bacchanalian dens. **1963** R.W. Paul *Mining Frontiers* 16 [ref. to 1850's]: "Hurdy-gurdies" were not necessarily prostitutes. They, the courtesans, and a few actresses...were the principal feminine society accessible to most miners. **1968** I. Reed *Radio* 79: Come over here and look up my dress, said one of the hurdy gurdy girls from the Rabid Black Cougar.

c. a dance held at a dance hall.

1867 in A.K. McClure *Rocky Mtns.* 213: To attend a ball or a "hurdy-gurdy."

2. *Navy.* (see quot.).

1906 Beyer *Battleship* 84: "Hurdy-gurdy"—a sewing machine turned by hand.

hurl *v.* to vomit. [Pop. in Australia by the comedian Barry Humphries and later in the U.S. by the film *Wayne's World* (1992).]

***1964** B. Humphries, in *Austral. Nat. Dict.*: I've had liquid laughs in bars/And I've hurled from moving cars. ***1967** in *Austral. Nat. Dict.*: The many euphemisms for vomit include...spue,...hurl, the big spit. ***1986** J. Green *Slang Thesaurus* 34: *To vomit*...barf...boot...hurl.

***1990** T. Thorne *Dict. Contemp. Slang: Hurl...*to vomit. A usage common in Australia and to a lesser extent in Britain. **1992** MTV (Feb. 17): I feel like I'm gonna hurl. **1992** *Heights* (Fox-TV): He rides up on his bike: "Plenty of room on the back, babe!" I almost hurled. **1994** *Weird Science* (USA-TV): I think I'm gonna hurl! **1994** A. Heckerling *Clueless* 26A: DIONNE Maybe we should fix him up with someone. CHER NO WAY! Don't make me hurl.

hurler *n. Baseball Journ.* a baseball pitcher.

1908 *Baseball Mag.* (Nov.) 21 (cited in Nichols *Baseball Terminology*). **1926** in *OED2*: Thirteen hurlers appeared [in a ball game].

hurrah *n.* an uproar, row; (*hence*) a spree. Also **hoorah.**

1834 Caruthers *Kentukian in N.Y.* 36: I don't somehow believe in all these little hurrahs the women kicks up just for pastime. *a***1881** G.C. Harding *Misc. Writings* 91: The Mexicanized German is "on the hurrah." He gets drunk like an American...and scatters money. **1887** *Lantern* (N.O.) (Aug. 27) 2: Willie Jeffreys was on a great hurrah some days ago and hardly able to walk. **1912** Siringo *Cowboy Detective* 96 [ref. to 1880's]: That night he and I got on a big "hurrah" and I spent money freely. **1923** *DN* V 211: Whut's all the hoorah about? **1940** *Sat. Eve. Post*, in *DARE*: Talbot had raised a hooray at the cabin because Bud wouldn't trade him a jug. **1988** Norst *Colors* 193: Maybe you hear some hoo-rah about a war coming.

hurrah *adj. Esp. West.* lawless or wildly disorderly; (*also*) unrestrained. Also **hoorah.**

1883 Sweet & Knox *Through Texas* 257: What is called, in the classic vernacular of the country, "a hoorah place." **1905** *N.Y. Times* (May 2) 9: The New Yorks got off the mark in hurrah fashion. **1912** Siringo *Cowboy Detective* 118: One night on our rounds in the "hurrah" part of the city. **1920** Ade *Hand-Made Fables* 115: It was to be wide-open and Hoorah. **1934** Cunningham *Triggernometry* 262: He was very successful in law-enforcement in this "hurrah" town. *Ibid.* 334: Fremont County's "hurrah" cow capital. *a***1942** Alderson & Smith *Bride Goes West* 21: Miles City...was a pretty hoorah place.

hurrah *v. West.* to harass, vandalize, taunt, or intimidate. Now esp. *hist.* Also **hoorah, hooraw.**

1928 Lake *Earp* 144: Any attempt to hurrah stores, gambling-houses, or saloons along the Plaza was good for a night in the calaboose. *ca***1969** *Gunsmoke* (CBS-TV): He'll twist and turn that tooth and then he'll try to hoorah me. First he'll call me a muttonhead. *a***1973** in Bontemps *Old South* 49: You're too young a boy to hurrah a woman as old as me. **1974** E. Thompson *Tattoo* 477: They stood...like two gunslingers come to hurrah a sodbuster. **1975** Swarthout *Shootist* 36: "We've got five railroads here and they'll be glad to sell you a ticket to any damn where." "I won't be hurrahed." *Ibid.* 89: I should of badged some good men and tied your legs under a burro and hurrahed you out of town the day you showed. **1980** Hogan *Lawman's Choice* 43: You and your bunch are through hoorawing this town. *a***1973–87** F.M. Davis *Livin' the Blues* 38 [ref. to *ca*1920]: We also learned how to "hooraw," a vocal pastime consisting of poking fun at another boy's physical peculiarities. **1992** J. Garry *This Ol' Drought* 96: You know how cowboys hoorah one another.

hurrah's nest *n.* a tangle, mess, or commotion.

1829 H.W. Longfellow, in *DAE*: With a head like a "hurra's nest." **1830** Ames *Sketches* 53: Your intestines are twisted...into what sailors, when speaking of a *melange* of entangled ropes, call a "hurra's nest." **1834–40** Dana *Before Mast* ch. ii: There was a complete "hurrah's nest," as the sailors say, "everything up and nothing at hand." **1849** Melville *White Jacket* 228: What's this hurrah's nest here aloft? **1883** Russell *Sailors' Lang.* xiv: A hurrah's nest, everything at top and nothing on bottom, like a midshipman's chest. **1965–70** in *DARE*. **1976** Hayden *Voyage* 204: We'd have such a hurrah's nest the Old Man has to run into some port.

hurricane deck *n.* the back of a horse or mule. *Joc.* Now *hist.*

1864 Kirke *Down in Tenn.* 193: He journeys on the hurricane deck of a mule. **1885** Siringo *Texas Cowboy* (title page): Fifteen Years on the Hurricane Deck of a Spanish Pony. **1903** A. Adams *Log of a Cowboy* 380: McCann was transferred to the hurricane deck of a cow horse. **1976** Hayden *Voyage* 304: Holding down the hurricane deck of a jackass.

hurry-buggy *n.* HURRY-UP WAGON.

*a***1926** in *AS* I (Dec.) 651: *Hurry-buggy.* patrol wagon. **1939** *Chicago Trib.* (Graphics) 9: *Hurry buggy*—a patrol wagon.

hurry-up *n.* **1.** a request for money; in phr. **on the hurry-up** begging on the street; (*hence*) a romantic proposition; COME-ON.

> **1902** Hapgood *Thief* 52 [ref. to *ca*1885]: It was only when I was on the "hurry-up," however, that I worked alone. **1908** Beach *Barrier* 143: No more hard-luck stories and "hurry-ups" for me....No busted miners need apply. **1948** Maresca *My Flag* 30: Boy! And I thought I'd heard everything in the way of a hurry-up pitch.

2. HURRY-UP WAGON.

> **1956** Algren *Wild Side* 233: Oh, that Smitty, suppose to be watchin' that whore in the Hurry-Up, instead he's showin' off he's a tackle now for L.S.U.

hurry-up wagon *n.* PADDY WAGON.

> **1893** W.K. Post *Harvard* 118: The manager...told him to send for a hurry-up wagon, and run us all in. **1894** F.P. Dunne, in Schaaf *Dooley* 160: It took two polismen to hold him till th' hurry up wagon come. **1900** Ade *More Fables* 120: He...[was] slammed into the Hurry-Up Wagon. **1903** A.H. Lewis *Boss* 263: Dey rings for d' hurry-up wagon. **1912** Siringo *Cowboy Detective* 19: I had a...free buggy ride in the "hurry up" wagon and was put behind steel bars. *a*1928 in Shay *More Pious Friends* 201: Dey brought Bill home wid his toe-nails draggin',/Dey was taking Bill home in de hurry-up wagon. **1956** Algren *Wild Side* 186: And knew, Mama knew that soon or late...the hurry-up wagon would haul girls with pride and girls with none...to that cellar below the cells. **1967–69** in *DARE.* *1990 Thorne *Dict. Contemp. Slang* 257: *Hurry-up wagon* a black maria. Now dated...from the 1950s.

hurt *n.* Esp. *Mil.* trouble or suffering, esp. deliberately or callously inflicted; in phr. **a world of hurt** great trouble or suffering. See also *put the hurt on,* below.

> **1971** Drill instructor, U.S. Army, Ft. Campbell, Ky. (coll. J. Ball): It's only fair to tell you all that Sgt. Hatcher's been saving up a shitload of hurt to lay on someone special. **1983** N. Proffitt *Gardens of Stone* 342: Routine dust-off. And I run smack into a world of hurt. **1981–85** S. King *It* 22: Next time/I see him he's going to be in serious hurt. *a*1987 Bunch & Cole *Reckoning for Kings* 354: Man, I have my gun, I could put max hurt down that trail. *Ibid.* 425: We gone put these gooks in a world of hurt. **1989** R. Miller *Profane Men* 75: They're gonna show us some heavy-duty hurt before this...is over. **1991** U.S. soldier, on *War in Gulf* (CNN-TV) (Jan. 31): If we don't deal with Saddam right here...we're all gonna be in a world of hurt.

¶ In phrases:

¶ **in the hurt bag** [or **locker** or **seat**] in trouble or at a disadvantage; in bad shape; HURTING, 1.a.

> **1968** Baker, Ladd & Robb *CUSS* 141: *Hurtbag.* An unfavorable situation. **1971** Drill instructor U.S. Army, Ft. Campbell, Ky. (coll. J. Ball): I'm gonna put you in the hurt seat and leave you there! **1978** J. Webb *Fields of Fire* 2 [ref. to Vietnam War, 1969]: Ahhh, Lieutenant....More gooners than I ever seen. We would really be in the hurt locker tonight. *Ibid.* 151: Don't let it get to you, Lieutenant. If you start crying, we're in the hurt locker. **1982** S.P. Smith *Officer & Gentleman* 64: Now if your mug wasn't in the hurt locker, you'd be in good shape. **1983** Ehrhart *VN-Perkasie* 36 [ref. to 1966]: The Marine Corps will hate you forever and ever. And then you'll be in the hurt locker, ladies, and you won't like that at all. **1986** *America: Nissan* (Spring) 25: No, man, you learn that you don't have any limits....You never wind up in the hurt bag because you know you can handle whatever the environment dishes out. *Ibid.* 26: It's the ones who aren't smiling that will end up in the hurt bag. **1989** R. Miller *Profane Men* 212: Heading...toward the big green hurt locker out beyond. **1989** D. Sherman *There I Was* 168: We put his ass...in the hurt locker.

¶ **put the** [or **a**] **hurt** [or **hurting**] **on** [or **to**] Esp. *Black E.* to injure, beat up, victimize, or defeat.

> **1961** in Broven *Walking to N.O.* 162: She Put the Hurt On Me. **1967** "Iceberg Slim" *Pimp* 102: Yeh, Preston, you sure got the "hurt" put to you....You are overdue for a break. **1970** Wertheim & Gonzalez *Talkin' About Us* 132: All six began to put the hurt on....After beating him they all stabbed him. **1971** Drill instructor, U.S. Army, Ft. Campbell, Ky. (coll. J. Ball): I'm gonna put the hurt on you trainees! Straighten them shoulders! **1973** Wideman *Lynchers* 134: The man sure put a hurt on you. **1974** Lacy *Native Daughter* 78: I'm gonna put

a hurtin' on that jive motherfucker. **1974** S. Stevens *Rat Pack* 111: That man could put a hurt on you so bad you wake up dead. **1975** *Black World* (June) 76: Pop...would be too tired to put any kind of hurtin on me. **1976** *Urban Life* V 234: [The lazy worker] was...seen as deliberately "putting the hurt on" the other men. *a*1978 J. Carroll *Basketball Diaries* 29: This is the same dude that put the hurtin' on him. **1989** Headline News network (Feb. 21): Dallas put the hurt on the Spurs. **1991** *Saturday Newswatch* (CNN-TV) (Mar. 9): Duke put the hurt to North Carolina [in a basketball game]. **1994** *Early Prime* (CNN-TV) (Dec. 20): She put the hurt on *him.*

hurt *v.* to complain unjustifiably; whine.

> **1946** Haines *Command Decision* 90: "Quit hurting," said Dennis sharply. "You've had this coming."

hurting *adj.* **1.a.** in distress or at a disadvantage; in trouble; in a bad way. Also (*emphatically*) **hurtin' for certain.**

> [**1929** in Longstreet *Canvas Falcons* 273: I pressed off half a drum right into him, and the sonofabitch didn't seem to hurt at all.] [**1937** Hemingway *Have & Have Not* 68: I'm shot. And I'm hurting bad.] **1950** Stuart *Objector* 275: Stafford...was chewed up by a machine gun. We're hurting, kid. **1959** W. Williams *Ada Dallas* 335: He *is* hurting. **1967** Gonzales *Paid My Dues* 17: I wasn't hurting financially. **1971** S. Stevens *Way Uptown* 12: He said he was sorry 'bout the accident but he was hurtin' too 'cause his car goin' cost a lotta money to fix up. **1971** Drill instructor, U.S. Army, Ft. Campbell, Ky. (coll. J. Ball): You all make me look bad, you gonna be hurtin' for certain. **1972** Ponicsan *Cinderella Liberty* 178: "How're you doing, hoss?" "Four-point-oh, Smitty, how about you?" "Hurtin' for certain." **1978** S. King *Stand* 142: That was one monkey who was hurtin for certain. It was a hard old world. **1980** Eble *Campus Slang* (Oct.) 4: *Hurtin'*—Heavily intoxicated: "She was really hurtin' last night at the party." **1980** Syatt *Country Talk* 25: He's hurtin' for certain. **1987** Estes *Field of Innocence* 147: "He's hurtin' for certain." "Yeah, that dude is double fucked up."

b. *Specif.* short of money; in need of cash.

> **1943** *Amer. Mercury* (Nov.) 554: Nobody is *hurtin'* (broke) and everybody is *heeled* (solvent). **1944** Kendall *Service Slang* 8: *I'm hurtin'*....broke. **1967** *Lit Dictionary* 50: *Hurtin'*—Without money. **1971** "L. Short" *Man from Desert* 148: You've got to have a stack to run those games, so I'd say he wasn't hurtin'. **1982** in S. King *Bachman* 797: Besides, we can use the money. This is a hurtin family. **1986** R. Walker *AF Wives* 473: Look, brudda, I'm a little short and I'm really hurting.

2. *Black E.* very unattractive. Also (*emphatically*) **hurtin' for certain.**

> **1973** Andrews & Owens *Black Lang.* 69: *Hurtin'*...Ugly. **1975** Wambaugh *Choirboys* 220: There's one that's hurtin for certain. **1967–80** Folb *Runnin' Lines* 243: *Hurtin' for certain.* Ugly. *a*1989 Spears *NTC Dict.*: *Hurting*...in pain from ugliness.

hus var. HUZ or HUSS.

hush *n.* hush money.

> *1726 A. Smith *Mems. of J. Wild* 26: Now *Jonathan Wild* hearing this Robber was possess'd of a round sum of ready *Rhino,* gave him to understand he expected a Pair of Gloves, by way of *Hush.* **1938** R. Chandler *Big Sleep* 57: You got your pictures and you got your hush.

hush puppy *n.* *Mil.* a pistol equipped with a silencer; (*hence*) a silencer.

> **1991** Marcinko & Weisman *Rogue Warrior* 129: I carried a 9mm pistol with a hush-puppy—silencer. **1993** J. Watson & K. Dockery *Point Man* 274: Since the [silencer-equipped] pistol was intended to silence [barking Vietnamese] dogs....[it] was named the Hush Puppy. Because of that name, after a while, all silencers came to be called Hush Puppies.

Huskers *n.pl.* the University of Nebraska Cornhuskers.

> **1982** *N.Y. Post* (Dec. 30) 45: The Huskers went on to defeat the Rainbows 30–17.

Husky *n.* an Inuit.—used derisively.

> **1899** in J. London *Short Stories* 8: A sensible name like ... Siwash or Husky.

huss[1] *n.* [prob. clipping of HUSTLER] *Black E.* **1.** fellow.—used in direct address.

> **1959** A. Anderson *Lover Man* 157: Ain't nothing shaking, huss.

2. a very stylish suit of men's clothes. Also **hus.** Also as adj.

1965 *Esquire* (July) 44: *Hus*—for hustler—vines. Hus vines are baggy pants, "long-collar" shirts, the kangaroo shoes worn by hustlers....The addition of...long-toe shoes...makes a thing hus. An Ivy hus would be a natural-shoulder suit, cuff-link shirt, and those shoes.

huss[2] *n.* [clipping of HUSTLE] **1.** Esp. *USMC.* a favor; break; act of assistance; in phr. **cut a huss** to do a favor, aid. Also **hus.** [Quots. except for 1976 Eble ref. to Vietnam War.]

1976 C.R. Anderson *Grunts* xiv: Whenever possible, the grunts *cut each other a hus*, did favors for each other, to relieve the adversity. *Ibid.* 38: If they gotta put down their cold beer for five minutes to cut somebody a hus they won't do it. *Ibid.* 88: How about paying me back that hus I cut you on your R & R. **1976** Eble *Campus Slang* (Nov.) 2: *Cut someone a huss*—do someone a favor: The drunk asked the cop to cut him a huss and not take him to jail. **1978** Hasford *Short-Timers* 43: Come on, Joker, cut me a huss. *Ibid.* 85: You need a huss with that? *Ibid.* 163: Cut me a huss with my pack. **1983** Eilert *Self & Country* 206: You cut me a huss tonight, I'll catch you later. **1985** Dye *Between Raindrops* 169: They need every huss they can get. **1989** Care *Viet. Spook Show* 206: We could...give some of these guys a huss. **1989** D. Sherman *There I Was* 118: I'm cutting you a hus by not making you hump with the rest of us.

2. (*cap.*) *Mil.* a Sikorsky Seahorse helicopter.

*a*1982 Dunstan *Viet. Tracks* 133: A UH-34D "Huss" of MAG-16 evacuates casualties...1965.

hustle *n.* **1.** initiative; ambitious spirit; (*Sports*) alert and aggressive competitive play. Now *colloq.*

1898 in *OED2*: With characteristic "hustle," excursions in the United States have already been organised to Hawaii. **1905** *Sporting Life* (Sept. 2) 2 (cited in Nichols *Baseball Terminology*). **1906** in *DA*: What is popularly known as American "hustle"—the ability to go right to the point, to decide quickly, to act aggressively by means of simple and direct methods. **1923** *Nation* (Sept. 26) 313: A country with no "pep," no "hustle." **1924** LeFèvre *Stockbroker* 30: The family gumption and...spirit of hustle. **1942** *ATS* 54: Swiftness; speed...*hustle. Ibid.* 255: Animation; spirit; vim; initiative; enterprise...*hustle.* **1944** F.G. Lieb *Cardinals* 166: Their hustle...put them in the World's Series. **1953** Sher *Kid from Left Field* (film): You're doin' all right, kid. You got lots of hustle. **1978** Shefski *Football Lang.* 58: *Hustle.* Spirited movement of a team...enthusiastic attitude of players. **1978** T.H. White *In Search* 26: In Hebrew school, I learned about the God of the Jews. In the street school, other Jews were learning the American "hustle." **1981** D.E. Miller *Jargon* 231: "Good hustle" is an accolade that signifies a high-energy effort. **1983** *Faces of Culture* (WSJK-TV): I want to see a lot of hustle out there, a lot of howling, a lot of screaming. **1987** G.A. Fine *With the Boys* 63: Coaches treat defeat as prima facie evidence of lack of effort or "hustle." **1988** Ross & Spielberg *Big* (film): Nothing wrong with a little hustle. **1993** Fountain *Sportswriter* 133: Complacency and a lack of hustle...cheated the fan.

2.a. a line of insincere talk or other form of deception.

1942 Algren *Morning* 64: Don't gimme that hustle, Bicek. Don't gimme that executive hustle. **1976** Whelton *CB Baby* 6: He was the guy who had tried to put the hustle on me outside the Essco Building. **1995** *Harper's* (Dec.) 47: He's not wanted for anything. All Ivankov's doing is working a hustle, and he's not going to get busted for that, because everyone wants to believe it.

b. Orig. *Und.* an unlawful or unethical stratagem, esp. such a method of getting money; (*often*) RACKET.

1943 *Time* (July 19) 54: Are ya layin' down the hustle [selling marijuana]? **1944** Burley *Hndbk. Jive* 140: Hustle—Unconventional action of some sort. **1952** W. Fisher *Waiters* 110: Dave was really hot and bothered over the loss of his single-action hustle. **1951–53** in *Social Problems* V (1957) 4: A hustle [is any nonviolent means of] making some bread. **1963** in J.H. Clarke *Harlem* 199: A few "community associations" are but thinly-veiled "hustles"—the operators pocket the dues and assessments. **1966** in *Amer. Sociol. Rev.* XXXII (1967) 215: *A hustle.* Any illegal means of making money. **1968** Carey *College Drug Scene* 2: The "cat" not only has his distinctive "hustle," but also his distinctive "kick" which disavows the regulation of conduct in terms of future consequences. **1969** in Cannon *Nobody Asked* 88: Baseball...should be a boy's dream but it has become a fast-dollar hus-

tle. **1969** L. Sanders *Anderson Tapes* 117: My cousin Gino had a hustle planned. *Ibid.* 137: That is our price for financing his hustle. **1970** *Playboy* (Apr.) 170: A common golf hustle...is one on which the mark is allowed the option of playing three balls to the hustler's one, taking the best score on each hole. **1971** "R. Stark" *Lemons* 57: Everybody's got a hustle. **1978** Pici *Tennis Hustler* 9: I had more hustles with a [tennis] racket than Bobby Riggs ever dreamed of. **1989** E. Goodman, in *Boston Globe* (Oct. 31): America turns every achievement into a hustle and every achiever into a hustler. **1995** *Donahue* (NBC-TV): His hustle was to lure men for sex, then rob them.

c. *Black E.* a means of earning a living; occupation.

1944 Burley *Hndbk. Jive* 95: The Jive Julius Caesar Act I, Scene I...*Marullus*:...You, stud hoss, what is thy hustle? **1954** L. Armstrong *Satchmo* 94: It was hard work shoveling coal and sitting behind my mule all day long....So any time I could find a hustle that was just a little lighter, I would run to it like a man being chased. *a*1955 in Maurer *Dict. Und.* 243: Hustle...Any occupation. **1959** A. Anderson *Lover Man* 66: When I lost my hustle she took to bringing me little snips and snaps from Mrs. Charlie's kitchen, you dig? *Ibid.* 67: I didn't have no bread or nothing and I couldn't find me a hustle. **1965** *Esquire* (July) 44: A job is usually called a *hustle* [by teenagers].

d. a proposal or suggestion of sexual intimacy; PASS.

1970 A. Young *Snakes* 92: Both the other chicks...must have been out laying down hustles. **1978** Pici *Tennis Hustler* 124: Are you putting a hustle on me?...I hope so.

¶ In phrases:

¶ **get a hustle on** to get going; hurry.

1902 Harben *Abner Daniel* 19: I...told 'em to git a hustle on the'rse'ves. **1902** Corrothers *Black Cat Club* 171: You young niggahs ought to git a hustle on yo' se'ves! **1902** K. Harriman *Ann Arbor* 120: Let's get a hustle on and end this. **1931** Lubbock *Bully Hayes* 16: Get a hustle on!

¶ **on the hustle** *Und.* engaged in hustling (s.v. HUSTLE, *v.*).

1942–49 Goldin et al. *DAUL* 105: Hustle, on the...engaging in any criminal racket. **1951–53** in *Social Problems* V (1957) 4: [Women who are] on the hustle. **1959** on *Golden Age of Television* (A&E-TV) (1987): "Are you on the hustle?" "Do those look like the hands of a hustler?"

hustle *v.* **1.** to find, obtain, or secure quickly, cleverly, or with some difficulty.—also constr. with *up*; (*hence*) to secure by aggressive or dubious means.

1840 *So. Lit. Messenger* VI 414: Can't you go out to the woodpile and hustle me up a few chips to start this fire? **1894** *Century* (Feb.): He "ought to hustle better togs." **1894** *Atlantic* (Sept.) 322: Cig, you'd better run out 'n' hustle some beer. **1910** in "O. Henry" *Works* 921: You stay here and try to hustle some grub. **1911–12** J. London *Smoke Bellew* 151: What you must do is get out to-night and hustle dog-teams....Sitka Charley has eight Malemutes he's asking thirty-five hundred for. **1928** in Inman *Diary* 358: Think of all the...millions a' brains engaged in hustlin' a livin'. **1948** in *DA*: She hustled circulation, advertising and news for the weekly newspaper. **1949** *New Yorker* (Nov. 5) 82: Tryin' to hustle me a fast buck. **1952** Ellson *Golden Spike* 27: "I've been busy hustling."..."Hustling what?" "Money." **1955** Graziano & Barber *Somebody Up There* 6: I remember when I was even younger...hustling nickels with shoeshines. **1960–61** Steinbeck *Discontent* 29: He's trying to hustle some of our business. **1967** J. Kramer *Instant Replay* 81: Finally, I hustled up eight tickets to the game. **1970–71** Rubinstein *City Police* 383: I think he was just trying to hustle some information. **1991** *Week in Review* (CNN-TV) (June 16): Yeltsin hit the Soviet campaign trail to hustle votes.

2. to work or exert oneself energetically; (*often*) to hurry. Now *colloq.*

1887 *Courier-Journal* (Louisville, Ky.) (Feb. 16) 6: The snort of the iron horse now awakens the echoes of that hustling little town. **1888** in F. Remington *Sel. Letters* 50: The work I have in hand will be enough to keep me "hustling." **1889** in *DA*: He says he can't begin to hustle as his father did. **1890** in *DAE*: Feeders will being hustling for steers and they should go up another point. **1893** S. Crane, in Baym et al. *Norton Anthol.* II 716: You've gota git out an' hustle. I ain't goin' t' support yeh. **1907** in McCay *Little Nemo* 80: Down the steps quick! Oooh! Hustle! *a*1911 in Spalding *Base Ball* 299: The Orioles will hustle for the annual championship. **1958–59** Lipton *Barbarians* 75: "But what do I have to do to get loot? I got to hustle." Hustle is a word Itchy always uses for work, any kind of paid-for work. *Ibid.* 317: *Hustle*—To engage in any gainful employment. **1959–60** R. Reisner *Jazz Titans* 159: *Hustle:* to work at a job. *a*1982 Medved *Hospital* 98: While they goofed off I was hustling. I had to study all the time to stay at the top of the class. **1987** R.M. Brown *Starting* 47: The competition is tough. You hustle or you starve. **1988** F. Robinson & B. Stainback *Extra Innings* 49: I hear you don't always hustle.

3. to hawk, sell, make available, or serve to patrons, esp. in an aggressive way; in phrs. **hustle drinks** to serve drinks as a bar girl or cocktail waitress; **hustle hash** to work as a waiter or waitress; **hustle sheets** to hawk newspapers; **hustle shoes** to shine shoes on the street. [In 1942 quot., with location as obj.]

  1887 in *OED2*: She hustled the hash at Gilhooley's on Blank St. **1910** Roe *Panders* 130: I could hear the girls coax the men to buy drinks....I could just see in the part where they hustled drinks. **1929** *AS* IV (June) 341: *Hustlin' sheets*—Selling newspapers. **1931** *AS* (June) 332: Johnny's hustling gummy now. **1931** D. Runyon, in *Collier's* (Nov. 14) 7: He...has a lot of assistants hustling duckets around these different events. **1937** Reitman *Box-Car Bertha* 307: *Skin hustling*—Selling fake fur. **1939** Wald *Roaring Twenties* (film) [ref. to 1919]: I only use my cab nine hours a day. You can hustle it the rest of the time. **1940** S. Lewis *Bethel Merriday* 29: Get a nice job hustling hash. **1942** *ATS* 766: Wait on tables...*hustle tables....Hustle cars*, to wait on cars at a drive-in stand. **1945** Hellman & Kern *Horn Blows at Midnight* (film): May I hustle you some grub? **1960** Roeburt *Mobster* 77: Why is she out there hustling tickets? **1969** N.Y.C. literary agent: You are no longer a member of the book-buying public; you're now a member of the book-hustling public. **1970** Terkel *Hard Times* 30 [ref. to 1930's]: He picked apples in Washington, "hustled sheets" in Los Angeles, and worked on road gangs all along the coast. **1970** in P. Heller *In This Corner* 99: After I'd get through hustling papers, I'd go down to the bowling alley to set pins till twelve o'clock. **1974** Hejinian *Extreme Remedies* 30: I met him...in a bar....Where I was hustling drinks. **1936–75** Earp & Boyer *Wyatt* 7: I liked the traveling sort of man better than the kind that...hustled dry goods or groceries. **1976** Calloway & Rollins *Moocher & Me* 17 [ref. to *ca*1925]: I'd hustle shoes....There was a stand...where I'd shine shoes until around eight or nine o'clock. **1978** Ponicsan *Ringmaster* 12: I'll hustle popcorn for you, I'll sell it all. **1981** O'Day & Eells *High Times* 65 [ref. to 1930's]: Hustling drinks....The routine was simple. I'd take an order, give it to the bartender who mixed the drink, handed it to me, and I served and collected for it. **1983** *N.Y. Post* (Aug. 17) 29: Unlike the girls you find at topless bars...these are nice girls who don't hustle drinks. **1989** A. Cross *Roe vs. Wade* (film): Some chick hustlin' insurance. **1992** *Fate* (Sept.) 40: These individuals did not form cults, hit the lecture circuit, or hustle books.

4.a. to work or seek customers as a prostitute.—also used trans.; (*hence*) to solicit customers in (a place). [The bracketed quot. illustrates a sense not otherwise recorded.]

  [*a*1890–95 F & H III 386: *Hustle*...To copulate.] **1895** in Dobie *Rainbow in Morning* 166: Luluh...is in Kansas a-hustlin' in the cole ice and snow. **1911** in Reckless *Vice in Chicago* 39: We went to saloons hustling for prostitution....I hustled at this place for two weeks. **1913** Kneeland *Commercialized Prostitution* 88: The pimp shows her the way, provides places for her to solicit or "hustle" on the streets or in the vice resort. *Ibid.* 90: The girl is "hustling" for one of them. **1916** Miner *Slavery* 101: She would be sent "to hustle on the streets."..."A little kid...was going out that night to hustle." **1923** W.I. Thomas *Unadjusted Girl* 141: She will then be put on the street to "hustle," or in a house, and her earnings collected. **1929–30** Dos Passos *42d Parallel* 355: There's only one feller in this world gets it for nothin' and you ain't him....I don't hustle when he's in town. **1930** Mae West *Babe Gordon* 69: I'll get you picked up for hustling. **1932** V. Nelson *Prison Days & Nights* 103: They had been going out on the "racket" known as "hustling fags."...One of the men...lures the pervert into some pre-arranged position, where he can be safely beaten and robbed. **1934** G.W. Lee *Beale St.* 76: Each...had from one to three women "hustling" for him. **1937** Reitman *Box-Car Bertha* 157: In fact, most girls who hustle in a joint live some place else. **1940** E. O'Neill *Iceman* 100

[ref. to 1912]: I fix the cops fer dem so's dey can hustle widout getting pinched. **1958** in Cannon *Nobody Asked* 324: There were a lot of streetwalkers hustling the place. **1963** Stearn *Grapevine* 220: They were hustling you....They thought you were a John. **1964** Harris *Junkie Priest* 1: And the trick you hustled was a cop. **1967** Rechy *Numbers* 25: Is this why I've come back? To prove to myself I can still hustle? **1970** Winick & Kinsie *Lively Commerce* 174: Just stagger into the night and you'll be hustled. **1974** Angelou *Gather Together* 41: Lesbian prostitutes!...I had never heard of women hustling other women.

b. to make sexual advances toward.—occ. used intrans.

  1942 *ATS* 783: Court...*give the rush,...hustle (a dame)*. **1959** Farris *Harrison High* 166: Looks like someone's hustling your chick, McCalla. **1966** H.S. Thompson *Hell's Angels* 15: She wouldn't have none of me hustlin anything else while she was around. *a*1968 in Haines & Taggart *Ft. Lauderdale* 54: We...decided there was plenty of time to "hustle" the rest of the days. *Ibid.* 56: It eased Marty's conscience not to go out "hustling" alone. **1968** "J. Hudson" *Case of Need* 159: He was off hustling a nurse when it happened. **1974** *Time* (Jan. 14) 45: Some chicks come here to be hustled, others to fall in love. **1974** Univ. Tenn. student: "Let's go hustle some girls." It means "let's find some girls, let's pick some up." **1975** *S.W.A.T.* (NBC-TV): You're hustling my girl, Jack. Why don't you take a walk?

5.a. *Und.* to practice swindling, theft, or other unlawful activities, esp. in a small way. [The bracketed quot. may be indirectly related to the sense in question.]

  [*1823 "J. Bee" *Slang: Hustling*—Forcible robbery, by two or more thieves seizing their victim round the body, or at the collar.] **1903** Kildare *Mamie Rose* 134 [ref. to *ca*1895]: I was not yet fully able to "hustle" very much, and still stuck to the sheltering shadow of Steve Brodie's back room. **1907** "O. Henry" *Heart* 118: I'm tired of hustling. You and me have been working hard together for three years. Say we knock off for a while, and spend some of this idle money we've coaxed our way. **1924** *N.Y. Times* (Aug. 3) VIII 16: We was a mob of cannons hustling up in Connecticut. **1926** Clark & Eubank *Lockstep* 62 [ref. to 1890's]: Innsbruck made me a proposition to hustle for him outside of Toledo. *Ibid.* 173: *Hustle*—go to work, usually meaning theft. **1929–31** Runyon *Guys & Dolls* 77: He hustles some around the race tracks and crap games and prize fights. **1933–35** D. Lamson *About to Die* 198: I been hustlin'...ever since I was a punk kid....Jail time don't mean nothin'. **1970** *Playboy* (Apr.) 170: Hustlers and hustling techniques vary markedly not only from sport to sport but with any individual sport. **1973–76** J. Allen *Assault* 1: Hustling was their thing: number running, bootlegging, selling narcotics, selling stolen goods, prostitution.

b. (among tramps) to beg; (*also*) to beg from.

  1902 "J. Flynt" *Little Bro.* 98: Only last winter I had a beute of a kid as far as mug goes, but the little devil couldn't hustle worth a damn. **1953–58** J.C. Holmes *Horn* 49: I'll hustle strangers, I'll hit everybody I can think of. **1993** *CBS This Morning* (CBS-TV) (June 2): Poor and homeless people can survive only by hustling [i.e., begging].

c. *Und.* to practice theft or swindling at or in (a place).

  1915 Bronson-Howard *God's Man* 128: I was hustling the match with Joe Deane, and we took a Big Swede...for the works. **1918** in *AS* (Oct. 1933) 28: *Hustling shorts:* Gang-stealing (of small sums of money, personal effects) on a street car. **1961** C. Cooper *Weed* 29: Told myself I wasn't gonna hustle the poolhalls no more.

d. to exploit (a game such as pool) for the purpose of swindling one's opponents by initially concealing one's expert level of skill or deception.

  [**1928** O'Connor *B'way Racketeers* 15: Dice cheaters, pay-off mobs, pool hustlers and what not.] **1928** Caldwell *Bastard* 63: He lived on the town hustling pool. **1961** Rossen & Carroll *Hustler* (film): You want to hustle pool, don't you?

e. to inveigle (an unskillful player) into betting on a competition, esp. at pool.

  1932 D. Runyon, in *Collier's* (June 11) 7: Frank is...partial to...hustling a sucker around Mike's pool room...for Frank is an excellent pool player, especially when he is playing a sucker. **1959** Tevis *Hustler* 36: I don't never hustle people who carry leather satchels in poolrooms. **1992** *Heights* (Fox-TV): Well, I've been hustled.

f. to swindle or deceive; CON.

1933 D. Runyon, in *Collier's* (Feb. 11) 8: I will just as soon try to hustle Santa Claus as Professor Woodhead. **1954** Johnson *Black Widow* (film): "You think she was hustling the Amberleys?" "Why not? A rich family in Boston?" **1961** Rossen & Carroll *Hustler* (film): You hustling me? **1966** Bullins *Goin' a Buffalo* 157: Awww…Curt, man…don't try and hustle me. **1979** D. Glasgow *Black Underclass* 90: *Being hustled*—being taken advantage of by someone else. **1989** Kanter & Mirvis *Cynical Amer.* 49: Cynical companies give their recruits the come-on in much the same way that they hustle their customers and deceive the public. **1989** *Dream Street* (NBC-TV): We just got hustled! **1995** *Great Defender* (Fox-TV): Let me give you some advice. Never hustle a hustler.

hustle-buggy *n.* HURRY-BUGGY.

1929 Milburn *Hobo's Hornbook* 226: Hello, 2005—the Hoosegow? Send the hustlebuggy. **1932–34** Minehan *Boy & Girl Tramps* 265: *Hustle buggy ride*—A ride in a squad car.

hustle bumps *n.pl. Baseball.* (see quot.). *Joc.*

1964 Thompson & Rice *Every Diamond* 141: *Hustle Bumps:* Marks and bruises on a player's body.

hustler *n.* **1.** an energetic, hard-working, or ambitious person. Now *colloq.*

1885 in Lummis *Letters* 262: Two eastern hustlers came out there a year ago…and now have about 20 acres of fine land cleared. **1886** *Lantern* (N.O.) (Oct. 6) 3: Mike was a hustler from the start, and where a dollar was to be earned, he made it. **1886** in *DAE:* Young man, a "hustler" in every respect, wants a strictly first-class position with a "live" book house. **1888** in Alter *Utah Journal* 172: Charlie is a hustler; he was formerly a "rustler," but the name may have painful memories for him. **1891** Maitland *Slang Dict.* 148: *Hustler* (Am.), one who is energetic and pushing in business. Otherwise a *Rustler*. **1893** in Dreiser *Jour.* I 112: Imboden is a hustler, and he knows this country better than anybody. **1914** Atherton *Perch* 106: He's a good chap and a born hustler. **1915–16** Lait *Beef, Iron & Wine* 110: I got a gang o' harvest hustlers here an' we kin use more.

2.a. a racetrack tout.

1892 *Outing* (July) 265: From the many times millionaire in the members' stand to the coatless, penniless "hustler" in the infield, all were animated by one universal, common thought: "Who will win?" **1917** C.E. Van Loan, in Woods *Horse-Racing* 290: and suppose now that this fellow wasn't even a gambler. Suppose he was a hustler—a tout—but he'd asked the girl to marry him without telling her what he was.…He was a hustler, too, and a pal of mine. **1931–35** Runyon *Money* 234: Hot Horse Herbie is what is called a hustler around the race tracks, and his business is to learn about these horses…and then get somebody to bet on them.

b. a crooked gambler or small-time confidence swindler; crook.—esp. in phrs. **pool hustler, card hustler, dice hustler.**

1896 C. King *Garrison Tangle* 260: But when the Indians drew away and sought the shelter of the agencies, the "hustler" and the horse-thief began to infest the land. **1906** *Nat. Police Gaz.* (July 28) 6: The hustler…has no established business [unlike the bookmaker or casino owner]…and can hunt for his prey.…He is about on a par with a confidence man.…As a rule, a hustler is a thief who is afraid to steal. **1925** *Writer's Mo.* (June) 485: Crooks and hobos (and "hustlers" in general) defy grammarians. **1926** Finerty *Criminalese* 30: *Hustler*— Racketeer; professional criminal. **1928** O'Connor *B'way Racketeers* viii: The fellow who nibbles at the hustler's bait generally has a streak of larceny hidden somewhere in his own system. **1929** *AS* IV (June) 341: *Hustler*—One who lives by his wits and illegitimately. **1933–35** D. Lamson *About to Die* 197: The cheap crooks, the petty larceny guys, the shoplifters an' con guys an' two-bit gamblers an' hustlers. **1935** Sistrom *Hot Tip* (film): The cheap hustler. I know his breed. **1938** Ky. WPA *Songs Collected* (unp.): Go get six rolling dice hustlers,/Seven black-headed women to sing a song. **1954** L. Armstrong *Satchmo* 198: On Saturday nights hustlers loved to wear their jumpers and overalls to hustle in.…The hustlers thought this outfit brought good luck to them and their whores. **1956** Fleming *Diamonds* 62: The nomadic hustlers…travelled the gambling circuit. **1956** *Honeymooners* (syndic. TV series): If anybody had told me you was a pool hustler, I'da

laughed at him. **1960** Jordan & Marberry *Fool's Gold* 188 [ref. to 1899]: A [card] cheat in Alaska was called a hustler or a philosopher, or a Greek. **1961** Rossen & Carroll *Hustler* (film): Big John, you think this boy is a hustler? **1963** Morgan *Six-Eleven* 120: Is it possible there's another little hustler working the smoker? **1969** Smith & Gay *Don't Try It* 113: *Flatfooted hustler* is a term used on the street for one who will commit almost any kind of crime for money, depending upon the opportunities. **1971** H. Roberts *Third Ear: Hustlers don't call showdowns*, an expression almost equivalent to "beggars can't be choosers." **1971** Woodley *Dealer* 11: Jimmy is a full-time hustler, whose specialty is cocaine, which he deals on a scale that might bring him $5000 in a good week. **1972** Kopp *Buddha* 200: Gamblers, petty criminals, dope-pushers,…hookers and other hustlers.

3.a. a prostitute (of either sex).

1924 Henderson *Crookdom* 408: *Hustler*—prostitute. **1929** Hammett *Red Harvest* ch. iii: Dinah Brand…A soiled dove…a de luxe hustler, a big-league gold-digger. **1934** W. Smith *Bessie Cotter* 20: She's one of the busiest hustlers in the Hall. **1936** Dai *Opium Addiction* 182: Almost all of her women associates are "hustlers" and drug users. **1936** Kingsley *Dead End* 717: Wha da yuh mean? Francey ain' no hustlah! **1937** Asch *The Road* 250: I ain't a hustler.…You come home with me. **1945** Drake & Cayton *Black Metropolis* 193: Most of these girls are hustlers, and if they start any trouble they get put in jail. **1952** E. Brown *Trespass* 98: I could read "hustler" in her eyes. **1959** W. Burroughs *Naked Lunch* 125: Male Hustler: "What a boy hasta put up with in this business."

b. Orig. *Homosex. Specif.*, a male prostitute with homosexual clients (usu. as distinguished from HOOKER, a female prostitute). [The distinction between this sense and **(a)**, above, became widespread during the early 1970's.]

1936 Terman & Miles *Sex & Personality* 312: His chief source of income has been prostitution; is still an active "hustler." **1941** G. Legman, in W. Henry *Sex Variants* II 1169: *Hustler* A male prostitute to homosexuals, especially so called if he is himself heterosexual. **1953** in W.S. Burroughs *Letters* 151: Rolled by the local hustler.…I did lay him at least. **1956** Reinhardt *Sex Perversions* 48: *Hustler*…Male homosexual prostitute. **1957** H. Danforth & J. Horan *D.A.'s Man* 309: Barrow was a male "hustler" who sold himself and who savagely beat and robbed the homosexuals who picked him up. **1959** in *Amer. Jour. Psychotherapy* XXI (1967) 184: The "Hustler" in Chicago. **1966** in E. Newton *Mother Camp* 13: He…is living in a cheap hotel with Bunny (another street impersonator) and others (including a "hooker"—female whore—and a male hustler). **1983** *Rolling Stone* (Feb. 3) 18: Mann was a hustler—a career which began as a summer job…but one that…proved too…lucrative to quit.

c. (among street vendors) a hawker or pitchman.

1931 *AS* (June) 332: *Hustler*…A peddler or pitchman who…"hustles" anything that another pitchman will pay him for. **1931** D. Runyon, in *Collier's* (Nov. 14) 7: They are top-notch ducket hustlers. **1974** *Sociol. Symposium* XI 26: The term "hustler" is often used [by pitchmen] synonymously with "peddler."

hustling broad *n. Und.* a female prostitute. Also **hustling gal, hustling woman.**

1936 Dai *Opium Addiction* 153: The women were mostly hustling "broads" or whores. *ca*1950 in *AS* XXVIII (1953) 117: *Hustling broad*, n. A prostitute. **1954** L. Armstrong *Satchmo* 91: Harry Tennisen was killed by a hustling gal of the honky-tonks called Sister Pop. **1963** Braly *Shake Him* 164: You couldn't make a hustling broad out of her in a hundred years. **1962–68** B. Jackson *In the Life:* She was a hustling gal, but she had squared up. **1994** Calt *Rather Be Devil* 67: Crabtree had a large stable of "hustling" women.

hutch *n.* a police station.

1943 R. Chandler *High Window* 420: So we come back here to the hutch and phone Palermo.

hutzpah var. CHUTZPAH.

huz *n.* husband. Also **hus.**

1839 *Spirit of Times* (Nov. 23) 445: Why, huz, I've settled on Peter. **1863** in Mead *Shanties* 495: You want to take this man for your hus.

hydrant *n.* tears; weeping.

1905 in "O. Henry" *Works* 1416: "Turn off the hydrant," said the

Kid, one night when Molly, tearful, besought him to amend his ways. **1944** Ruskin et al. *Andy Hardy's Blonde Trouble* (film): Turn off the hydrant and give me back my money.

hyena *n.* a lazy, stupid, or coarse person. Cf. *OED* def. 2.

    1866 "E. Kirke" *Guerillas* 43: [Fetters] for this young hyena! **1912** Siringo *Cowboy Detective* 144: A one-eyed…Irish hyena from…Butte City. **1918** Ruggles *Navy Explained* 27: If there are certain duties to be done and a man is a little slow his officer or petty officer will tell him, "bear a hand with that, now boy." The old-timers used to say, "Shake a leg, you hyenie." **1919** *DN* V 70: "If I ever make a hyena of myself, I wish you would tell me." New Mexico. **1922** Evarts *Settling of Sage* 78: Don't you claim no relationship with me, you sorrel hyena. **1931** Buckingham & Higgin *Painted Desert* (film): He's too young to know what a pig-headed old hyena you are. **1952** Uris *Battle Cry* 193 [ref. to 1942]: "Now jest take it slow and easy, pard. We'll meet them hyenas in plenty of time." "Hey, Tex—same two beasts as last time?" "Yep." "I hear they call them sisters the witches of Wellington."

hyjack var. HIJACK.

Hymie *n.* [generic use of hypocoristic form of *Hyman*, male given name] a Jewish man or boy.—used derisively. Also as adj.

    1973 S. Roth *Sand in Wind* 81: *What are you trying to do to* MY MARINE CORPS, *Hymie?* [**1980** D. Hamill *Stomping Ground* 5: A Puerto Rican Jew….A regular Hymie Rodriguez.] **1984** *Washington Post* (Feb. 13) A5: In private conversations with reporters, Jackson has referred to Jews as "Hymies" and to New York as "Hymietown." **1984** T. Wolfe, in *Rolling Stone* (Aug. 2) 19: Yo, Goldberg! Yo, Hymie! **1985** *Nat. Lampoon* (May) 16: I'd rather fight Parkinson's/Than that ugly Hymie. **1986** C. Stroud *Close Pursuit* 101: Hymie…Jewboy. **1989** in *Nat. Lampoon* (Feb. 1990) 61: Evil Hymie influence. *****1990** Thorne *Dict. Contemporary Slang* 257: *Hymie*…a Jew. An unaffectionate, if not strongly offensive term…used in British English since the 1950s.

hymie *n.* [orig. unkn.] a surreptitious signal; HIGH SIGN.

    1938 Steinbeck *Grapes of Wrath* 66: Show 'em that Nash while I get the slow leak pumped up on that '25 Dodge. I'll give you a Hymie when I'm ready.

Hymietown *n.* New York City.—used disparagingly.

    1984 (*Wash. Post* quot. at HYMIE). **1984** T. Wolfe, in *Rolling Stone* (Aug. 2) 19: Yo, Goldberg! Go back to Hymietown! **1986–87** K.G. Wilson *Van Winkle's Return* 60: But great parts of society today will never forgive the use of an ethnic slurword such as *nigger* or *hymietown*, however inadvertent. **1987** Stroud *Close Pursuit* 227: What does he think about the Jews, Eddie? What about "Hymie Town"? **1990** Chetwynd *So Proudly We Hail* (film): Hymietown, here we come.

hynie var HINEY².

hype *n.* [fr. *hypo*dermic; (2) and (3) may reflect a different etymon] **1.a.** Esp. *Narc.* a hypodermic needle or syringe; (*also*) a hypodermic injection.

    1910 *Adventure* (Nov.) 183: I turned to give another hyp. *Ibid.* 186: I was filling a hyp. with a new solution. **1918** in *AS* (Oct. 1933) 28: *Hype.* Hypodermic injection. **1936** *AS* XI 122: *Hype.* The hypodermic needle used to inject narcotics. **1973–76** J. Allen *Assault* 169: I saw the second hype laying there, and for some reason felt like I had to shoot it.

b. *Police & Und.* a person addicted to the injecting of drugs, esp. heroin or morphine.

    1924 G. Henderson *Keys to Crookdom* 306: Next down the list is the "hype" or morphine-user. Morphine is taken by hypodermic injections. **1930** Mae West *Babe Gordon* 10: Jenny wanted Babe to get her "hype" customers. **1936** Duncan *Over the Wall* 21 [ref. to 1918]: The needles or hypes—morphine users. *Ibid.* 248: What have you got there?…Looks like a hype. **1953** Manchester *City of Anger* 119: Some hypes carried their own needles. **1958–59** Lipton *New Barbarians* 317: *Hype*—A heroin user. **1960** Stadley *Barbarians* 32: He's on junk and no hype can keep his mouth shut. **1965** *Sat. Eve. Post* (Dec. 4) 23: The "hype," police slang for a heroin addict, was a middle-aged man. **1968** *Adam-12* (NBC-TV): Probably a hype with a big habit, and he can't afford to take the day off without a fix. **1970** Thackrey *Thief* 361: He's a hype—and he's a fink. I mean, an *informer.* **1995** *Calif. vs. Simpson* (Court TV) (Aug. 30): Fresh blood from the scab of a hype.

2.a. *Und.* a shortchange swindle; (*hence*) a swindle or confidence game of any kind.

    1925 in Partridge *Dict. Und.* 351: *Hype.*—A short-change game. **1926** *Writer's Mo.* (Dec.) 541: *Out on the Hype*—A short-change man. **1930** Conwell *Pro. Thief* 74: The hype is a method of short-changing cashiers….Many angles of cross-fire are used to confuse the cashier at this moment of transaction so that the original bill together with its change are returned to the thief. **1931** in Partridge *Dict. Und.* 351: Hype artist. **1933** Ersine *Pris. Slang* 23: *Bundle hype.* A short-change method in which several folded bills are used. **1942** *ATS* 311: A cheat; swindle….*gyp,…hipe, hype,…shakedown.* **1957** Simmons *Corner Boy* 132: That hype couldn't last forever. Sooner or later somebody was gonna get wise. **1959** W. Burroughs *Naked Lunch* 13: Itinerant short con and carny hype men have burned down the croakers of Texas. **1965** Linakis *In Spring* 47: You've got a real cool hype going for you….I just wish I had your nerve. I'd pull it myself. **1966–67** P. Thomas *Mean Streets* 166: Brew and I looked at each other, wondering if this could be a hype.

b. an exorbitant, usu. temporary, increase in retail price.

    1926 Maines & Grant *Wise-Crack Dict.* 9: That place has a hype on this week. **1946** Dadswell *Hey There, Sucker!* 100: *To put on the hype*…to increase prices over and above normal as often is done by hotels during fair week.

c. deception; fraud; a false or exaggerated story; lies.

    1938 Calloway *Cat-alogue*: *Hype* (n., v.): build up for a loan, wooing a girl, persuasive talk. **1944** Burley *Hndbk. Jive* 27: Please believe me, Cholly Hoss, I'm laying no hype. **1945** Himes *If He Hollers* 68: It just got me for a chick like you to go for a hype like that. **1946** Mezzrow & Wolfe *Really Blues* 115: But that Danny laid down a super hype. *Ibid.* 306: *Hype*…n., a build-up, a phony story. **1953–58** J.C. Holmes *Horn* 85: I mean this town's a drag this year anyway, a hype. **1959** A. Anderson *Lover Man* 127: Meanwhile he's laying a line of hype on me so thick you couldn't dent it with an electric drill. **1959** "D. Stagg" *Glory Jumpers* 18: Just enough brains to see around that glory hype they lay on you. **1959–60** R. Reisner *Jazz Titans* 159: *Hype:* deception. **1961** B. Wolfe *Magic of Their Singing* 25: It needs wardrobe, Prosp. This is no hype. **1970** in Van Peebles *Sweetback* 145: The hype I'm layin' down to them people inside, it ain't dangerous. **1970** A. Young *Snakes* 95: Just dont be wastin my time…with some old chickenshit hype about how old you are and who your girlfriend was and first one thing and another. **1978** B. Johnson *What's Happenin'?* 24: Forget the press release hype. **1980** Schruers *Blondie* 35: We're just a media hype anyway, y'know? It doesn't really exist. **1983** *Rolling Stone* (Feb. 3) 18: Gay men…dismiss AIDS as a "media hype." **1983** *Reader's Digest Success with Words* 86: Black English…*hype* = "scheme, deception, phony situation." **1994** Smitherman *Black Talk* 141: *Hype* Deceptive, propagandistic statements or stories, particularly European American propaganda.

d. *Specif.,* extravagant, undue, or inflated promotion or publicity; (*also*) a publicity stunt or misleading advertising technique.

    1953–58 J.C. Holmes *Horn* 40: But he ain't good enough any more to justify this kind of hype. **1970** in H.S. Thompson *Shark Hunt* 98: No freaky hypes or shoestring promotion campaigns. **1971** E. Sanders *Family* 162: The hype was similar to other groups including Manson's. **1981** *N.Y. Times Mag.* (June 21) 70: Some people don't believe that the Beatles avalanche was a natural phenomenon, but rather was one of the greatest hypes in the annals of popular music. **1981** Hofstadter & Dennett *Mind's I* 70: We're bombarded with advertising hype. **1983** Aronson *Hype* 15: Hype can be most usefully defined as the merchandising of a product…in an artificially engendered atmosphere of hysteria, in order to create a demand for it or to inflate such demand as already exists. **1984** Blumenthal *Hollywood* 37: Hype…is simply the unrestrained use of hyperbole, embellishment, or deception for the purpose of self-promotion. **1984** Kagan & Summers *Mute Evidence* 230: Issuing scare headlines and "hype." **1988** in *N.Y. Times Mag.* (Jan. 1, 1989) 13: If you believed the hype, the show would be so fast-paced, so dazzlingly new, that it would define television for the 1990's. **1991** in *Rap Masters* (Jan. 1992) 22: Gangstas got the hype….Girls like that kind of hype, so brothers…wanna do it.

3. *Und.* a shortchange swindler.

    1926 in *OEDS*: *Hype*, short change artist. **1931** *Broadway Brevities*

(Oct. 5) 14: *Hype,* n. A specialist in short-changing. **1935** Pollock *Und. Speaks: Hype,* a short-change artist; a person who does not give the correct amount of change to a customer.

hype *adj.* **1.** fraudulent; PHONY.

   *a*1978 J. Carroll *Basketball Diaries* 144: You're the weasel that beat me with this hype acid last weekend.

2. *Rap Music.* splendid, exciting, or attractive. Also **hyped.**

   1989 *Village Voice* (N.Y.C.) (June 20) 39: Dressing up, not dressing down, is the hype move and these shoes are leading the way. **1989** *Spin* (Aug.) 12: If Milli Vanilli was hype, this was cool. **1989** *Yo! MTV Raps* (MTV): I'm nitro and I'm hype!...As I get older I get hyper! *a*1990 P. Dickson *Slang!* 220: *Hype.* Great. **1990** *Kid 'n Play* (NBC-TV): Come down to the hypest new spot in town. **1990** *N.Y. Newsday* (Sept. 10) II 7: I finally got to see the hottest, hypest hip-hop comedy of the year. **1992** *Martin* (Fox-TV): I mean, he is *too* hype! **1993** *Roc* (Fox-TV): We got a brand-new opening. It's hype, it's slammin', and it's cool. **1993** "Us3" *I Got It Going On* (rap song): Yo, check it out, I got a hype rhyme for ya. **1994** in Stavsky, Mozeson & Mozeson *A 2 Z* 51: I heard rap music and how *hyped* the beats was.

hype *v.* **1.a.** *Und.* to shortchange or overcharge; (*broadly*) to swindle or defraud; cheat.

   1914 (quot. at HYPER, *n.*). **1926** Maines & Grant *Wise-Crack Dict.* 9: *Hype*—To overcharge. **1930** Irwin *Tramp & Und. Slang* 99: *Hipe.*—To cheat or short-change. **1937** *New Yorker* (Aug. 7) 19: The chump is being consigned to a further "hyping." "Hyping," derived from "hypodermic,"...applies to all the steps in the Midtown's high-pressure technique of obtaining the maximum price for the minimum value. **1937** Reitman *Box-Car Bertha* 263: I made my money by panhandling, strong-arming, hyping, and by various kinds of chiseling. **1942** *ATS* 312: Cheat; defraud....gyp,...hipe, hype. *ca*1953 Hughes *Lodge* 82: I accumulated quite a sum of money....I'm an excellent hyper. *Ibid.* 116: You hype him too much....You need a certain amount of square junkies, the ones that can be hypped out of bread and so forth. **1972** P. Thomas *Savior* 119: That jive smooth-talking salesman...tried to hype us.

b. to blandish or cajole; fool.

   1938 Calloway *Cat-alogue: Hype* (n., v.): build up for a loan, wooing a girl, persuasive talk. **1945** Shelly *Hepcats Dict.* 13: *Hype* (v.)—To try a trick. **1946** Mezzrow & Wolfe *Really Blues* 306: *Hype:* v., to deliver a phony but convincing line, to build up a sucker for the kill, to lay the groundwork for a scheme. **1952** E. Brown *Trespass* 140: Look, boy, don't try to hype this gal. **1953–58** J.C. Holmes *Horn* 68: Who you trying to hype or something? **1959** A. Anderson *Lover Man* 127: But I couldn't hype him. He was a hipster from *way* back. **1961** J. Baldwin *Another Country* 353: He didn't seem to be trying to hype me, not even when he talked about his wife and his kids—you know? **1968** Heard *Howard St.* 183: They hyped the public against smokin' pot so they could kill 'em...with cancerous cigarettes. **1970** *Time* (Aug. 17) 32: *Hype:* to con. ("Don't hype me, pig"). **1984–85** in Schneider & Schneider *Sound Off!* 137: They've hyped the public into picturing your mother out there...[in combat] with a rolling pin. **1991** in *Rap-Pages* (Feb. 1992) 51: The white kids was hyped by that shit.

2. *Narc.* to inject hypodermically; (*also*) to drug by hypodermic injection.—often constr. with *up.*

   1938 in *OED2:* Y' gotta lay off the wimmin, an' don't hype y'rself up till y' goes out t' heist a joint. **1958–59** Lipton *Barbarians* 83: Trying to do himself in, lushing,/hyping, insane fucking, no sleep. **1971** E. Tidyman & J. Black *Shaft* (film): A lot o' hyped up black people gave you that money you're spendin', pimp. **1973** Peterson *Sicilian Slaughter* 19: Fighting the effects of the unknown drug Byron'd hyped him with, he staggered across the room to the single window. **1978** Buchanan *Shining Season* 121: And I've got to be fully responsive to them, not hyped up....No shots, for now.

3.a. to make more exciting or powerful.—also constr. with *up.*—also constr. with dummy obj. *it.*

   1942 *ATS* 562: *Hipe up,* to stimulate the playing [of music] by artificial devices. **1946** H.A. Smith *Rhubarb* 40: We could revolutionize horse-racing. Now, here's my idea: Hype up that long wait between races. **1975** Durocher & Linn *Nice Guys* 93: He had built it with a hyped-up outboard motor.

b. to make excited or enthusiastic; agitate.—usu. as **hyped-up,** *adj.* Cf. HYPO, 2.b.

   1946 Mezzrow & Wolfe *Really Blues* 52: Rapp was a little hyped-up Italian guy, with pop-eyes. **1956** E. Hunter *Second Ending* 252: You're hyped up one minute, and you're ready to nod the next. **1968** Gover *JC* 22: Whitie so hyped on shootin an killin, bomb-droppin an the like, he needs that shit. **1971** S. Stevens *Way Uptown* 240: Tiger was really hyped on 'em and he couldn' see what I was dealing. **1980** Eble *Campus Slang* (Oct.) 4: *Hyped*—Nervous, anxious in anticipation. **1984** Riggan *Free Fire* 210: We never got as hyped about another film. *a*1984 in Terry *Bloods* 17: I wasn't sleepy. I was still hyped up. **1985** M. Baker *Cops* 150: When you get all hyped up everything is like slow motion. **1989** "Public Enemy," in B. Adler *Rap!* 63: I'm ready and hyped. *a*1994 N. McCall *Wanna Holler* 374: Seeing how hyped and uptight I was, she prescribed some medication to chill me out.

4.a. to increase, enhance, inflate, or heighten.—often constr. with *up.* Cf. HYPO, 2.a.

   1947 *Tomorrow* (Aug.) 27: "A denunciation...might [actually] hypo [record] sales." *Hypo* and *hype,* from "hypodermic," are not new. **1950** in *DAS:* No fireworks [in this movie], no fake suspense, no hyped-up glamour. **1966** H.S. Thompson *Hell's Angels* 85: The hyped-up heel-grinding contempt for a man who tries and fails to deal with them on their own terms. **1981** O'Day & Eells *High Times* 141: My unadvertised appearance hyped business until July. **1983** Aronson *Hype* 209: For the hyping up of language has the same consequence as the inflation of money: It makes the coin worth less. **1988** "Kid 'n' Play" *Rollin' with Kid 'n Play* (rap song): We can get funky with the best,/ We're hypin' it up! **1989** Kanter & Mirvis *Cynical Amer.* 53: Cynical managers "hype up" people's hopes with promises of a fast track to success.

b. *Specif.* (*Carnival*) (see quot.).

   *a*1950 in *AS* XXVIII (1953) 117: *Hype,* v. and n. To raise the price of carnival merchandise above that regularly established; such a raise.

c. Esp. *Entertainment Industry.* to promote or publicize aggressively.

   1959 *Life* (Nov. 23) 45: *Hyping a platter*—overselling a record. **1982** Savitch *Anchorwoman* 94: The singer...was promoted, hyped, used, abused, and propelled into stardom. **1983** Aronson *Hype* 26: Marilyn Monroe's nude calendar was...dug up...and leaked to the press by producer Jerry Wald to hype his Monroe movie *Clash by Night.* **1984** Blumenthal *Hollywood* 37: Studios hype their films, agents hype their clients,...you can hype yourself. **1996** *N.Y. Times* (Sept. 8) "Sports" 13: Everybody hypes Tyson as being the man.

hyper *n.* [HYPE, *v.* + *-er*] (see quots.).

   1914 Jackson & Hellyer *Vocab.* 47: *Hyper*...Current amongst money-changers. A flim-flammer. **1930** Irwin *Tramp & Und. Slang* 106: *Hyper.*—A "short change" artist.

hyper *adj.* [fr. *hyper*active] excited; agitated; frenetic.

   1942 *ATS* 280: Overzealous; fanatic...*hyper.* **1968** Baker, Ladd & Robb *CUSS* 141: *Hyper.* Eager or looking forward to something or someone. **1971** *CBS News* (CBS-TV) (Feb. 17): He was "hyper"—psyched up. **1972** Harper College student: *Hyper* is the same as all excited. **1977** Sayles *Union Dues* 231: He's outa control, he is. Fuckin hyper. **1995** *Jerry Springer Show* (synd. TV series): They get all hyper and want to fight all the time!

hyper *v.* *N.E.* to bustle or hurry; run. [The *a*1903 quot. may have been written as early as *ca*1865.]

   1877 Bartlett *Amer.* (ed. 4) 307: *Hyper.* To bustle. "I must *hyper* about an' git tea." *a*1903 in Botkin *Treas. N.E. Folklore* 83: We ran down threw the school yard as fast as we cood hiper. **1946** R. Gordon *Years Ago* 91: Get them duds off an' hyper down to the railroad station and turn back your parlor-car ticket or it ain't goin' to be no good. **1953** R. Gordon *Actress* (film): Come on, hyper out from under there!

hyper down *v.* to calm down.

   1981 *Nat. Lampoon* (Oct.) 46: I still haven't hypered down over the heaviosity of my brain storm yesterday.

Hyper-Hog *n.* [sugg. by ULTRA-HOG] *USAF.* the Republic F-105 Thunderchief fighter-bomber aircraft.

   1975 in Higham & Siddall *Combat Aircraft* 86: In 1960 the F-105 ... had various ... nicknames such as "Squat Bomber" or "Hyper Hog."

1983 M. Skinner *USAFE* 56: Derisive nicknames [for the F-105]—Hyper-hog, Ultra-hog, Iron Butterfly, Squash Bomber, ... Thud.

hypestick *n.* (see quot.).
   1918 in *AS* (Oct. 1933) 28: *Hypestick.* Hypodermic needle.

hypo[1] *n.* [fr. *hypo*chondria] Also **hipo, hippo.**
   1. low spirits. Occ. *pl. Cf.* HIP[1].
      *1711 in *OED2:* A Treatise of the Hypochondriack and Hysterick Passion vulgarly call'd the Hypo in Men and Vapours in Women. **1800** in Trumbull & Trumbull *Season in N.Y.* 49: Here we are at Mr. Butlers all in good *trim*, and Harriet has quite got over her *heighpo* and feels very well. **1811** in E. Fletcher *Letters* 29: That disease called hypo. **1817** in Royall *Letters from Ala.* 83: [This] anecdote...will cure you of the *hypo*. **1850** Melville *Moby-Dick* I i: My hypos get the upper hand of me. **1864** in McKee *Throb of Drums* 299: I will have the hippo. **1869** Stowe *Oldtown Folks* 333: Alleging...that "t'would bring on her hypos."
   2. a hypochondriac.
      1896 (quot. at STILL). **1938** "E. Queen" *4 Hearts* 75: He's the healthiest man of his years I know. Damn all hypos! **1960** N.Y.C. woman, age *ca*45: You're turning into a regular hypo.

hypo[2] *n.* [fr. *hypo*dermic] **1.** a hypodermic syringe or injection. [Presumably the orig. sense.]
      *ca*1905 in Spaeth *Read 'Em & Weep* 105: "What's the charge?" the judge then said,/"Hittin' up the hypo," and the fiend dropped dead. **1908** McGaffey *Show Girl* 236: I eat so much I couldn't have crowded any more in me with a hypo. **1911** in Courtwright *Dark Paradise* 98: Three or four instances of exclusive hypo users,...morphine-fiends. **1918** in Semmes *Portrait of Patton* 64: One of my captains came into a first aid station and saw a chaplain leaning over him and a man with a big hypo sticking stuff into his stomach. **1921** in Murphy *Black Candle* 212: He gets angry with me and breaks my hypo. **1936** Dai *Opium Addiction* 131: She caught her roommate using the "hypo." **1962** McElfresh *Jill Nolan* 91: I'm going to give you a hypo.

2. *Narc.* a person addicted to the hypodermic injection of a drug, esp. morphine or heroin.
   1904 in *OED2:* The "Hypo" [caption to picture showing a morphine addict]. **1914** Spencer *Jailer* 111: There was brought into the jail one night a hop-head known as Hypo Bob. **1925** in Hammett *Knockover* 232: I found Dr. Haley in his house. A minute later he was carrying a charge over to the hypo. **1925–26** J. Black *You Can't Win* 159: Vag these two "hypos." **1927–28** Tasker *Grimhaven* 159: His friends among the hypos were many. **1929** E. Booth *Stealing* 67: Them damn hypos give me a pain. **1962** Crump *Killer* 93: Look, hypo, I said move.

3. (see quot.).
   1978 *Adolescence* XIII 499: A car with a lot of horsepower was called a "hypo."

hypo *v.* **1.** to administer a hypodermic injection to.
   1925 in *OED2: Hypo*, to use a hypodermic syringe. **1942** *ATS* 514: Give hypodermic; vaccinate....*hypo.* **1948** Lait & Mortimer *New York* 8: There crime and vice and con games and watering whiskey and hypoing horses are hatched.

2.a. to increase or enhance (business or the like).
   1937 *AS* (Dec.) 317: *Hypoing.* stimulating or increasing business. **1947** (quot. at HYPE, *v.*, 4.b.). **1967–68** von Hoffman *Parents Warned Us* 65: The drug's incredible power to hypo every kind of stimulus. **1987** R. Miller *Slob* 231: You also can't use the First Amendment as a shield for malicious...misrepresentations of relationships done to hypo circulation, or—.

b. *Entertainment Industry.* to stimulate the enthusiasm of.—also constr. with *up*.
   1936 *Esquire* (Sept.) 160: Professional M.C.'s...hypo the guests. **1969** Thompson *They Shoot Horses* 142: After we get rolling we'll throw in some wrinkles to hypo up the crowds.

hypped var. HIPPED.

I *n.* idea.—constr. with *the.*

1919 *Amer. Legion Wkly.* (Aug. 8) 26: "What's the big I," I asks him, getting sore? "Maybe you don't think I can get another job?" **1922** S. Lewis *Babbitt* 145: That's the i.! And another thing we got to do…is to keep these damn foreigners out of the country.

I and I *n. Mil.* (see quots.). *Joc.* Cf. A AND A, B AND B, R AND R.

1960 *AS* XXXV (May) 121 [ref. to Korean War]: Periodically the Korean GI could expect to be sent to Japan for R&R…frequently renamed *I&I,* "intercourse and intoxication." **1962** Blake *Heartbreak* 24 [ref. to 1953]: I&I, for "Intercourse and Intoxication." **1962** Butterworth *Court-Martial* 54 [ref. to Korean War]: It was officially R&R, but among the troops it was known as I&I, standing, in case you're unaware, for Intercourse and Intoxication. **1965** Beech *Make War in Madness* 39: R&R was Rest and Recuperation Leave. Troops were flown from Korea to Japan for a week's rest. It was known, more accurately by the troops, as I&I—Intercourse and Intoxication. **1969** Moskos *Enlisted Man* 89: Inevitably, R&R has come to be termed "I&I" (i.e., intercourse and intoxication) or "L&L" (i.e., liquor and love). **1978** Karl *13th Outpost* 37 [ref. to 1953]: I'm not going on R&R. I'm going on I&I. Intoxication and Intercourse.

I.C. *n.* [pun on *I see,* perh. infl. by *I.C.,* abbrev. for *Illinois Central* (Railroad)] ¶ In phrase: **on the I.C.** *Und.* on the lookout.

1930 in D.W. Maurer *Lang. Und.* 51: He was on the I.C. for the law.

IC[1] *v.* [functional shift of quartermaster's abbrev. *I/C, IC* 'inspected and condemned'] *Army.* to declare unfit for military use; (*hence*) to transfer or remove for unfitness. Now *hist.*

1863 in Mohr *Cormany Diaries* 358: 12 prs spurs IC'd. [**1906** J. Moss *Officer's Manual* 243: *I.C.*—condemned by an inspector.] **1930** *Amer. Legion Mo.* (Mar.) 31 [ref. to 1918]: Your bunk? I thought they'd "I.C.'d" you out of here. **1942** *Yank* (Dec. 30) 20: Mules and horses which cannot meet these tests…are "ICed": inspected and condemned. **1983** Elting, Cragg & Deal *Soldier Talk* 160: In 1946 the Philippine Scouts were ordered I/C'd trucks, while new trucks stood…all around Manila. **1986** Willeford *About a Soldier* 4 [ref. to 1939]: So if Old Raz had been I.C.'d, why were we putting new shoes on him?

I.C.[2] *v.* [sugg. by *I.C., n.,* perh. infl. by *IC*[1], *v.*] *Und.* to see; observe; watch.

1931 in D.W. Maurer *Lang. of Und.* 43: They I.Cd. Timber…in a pill-joint.

ice *n.* **1.** *Und.* money; (*specif.*) money paid or gained illicitly, as bribe money, an unethical premium or commission (as upon theater tickets), protection money, etc.

1887 DeVol *Gambler* 36: I came up with the ice and bet $250 before the draw. **1907** Corbin *Cave Man* 285: "He is kept in cold storage…[through] blackmail!" "He calls it my ice-bill." *Ibid.* 323: I'm getting tired of the little matter of the ice-bill. **1927** *N.Y. Times* (Oct. 30): *Ice*—Commissions formerly paid to box office men. **1929** Bodenheim *60 Secs.* 225: You're wasting your ice in this boiler. **1937** *Sat. Eve. Post* (May 22) 34: Money paid to the police for protection is "ice." **1945** D. Runyon, in *Collier's* (Sept. 29) 11: Ice…is a way of saying premiums….Sometimes Willie asks for more ice than the face value of the tickets. **1952** *Time* (May 19) 26: A list of bookies who were paying "ice." **1955** Deutsch *Cops* 44: The "ice man" [bribe-collector]—ice being a euphemism for graft. **1957** H. Danforth & J. Horan *D.A.'s Man* 39 [ref. to 1935]: Good setup. What's the ice? **1961** Scarne *Comp. Guide to Gambling* 11: This graft or protection money, known as *ice,* enables some police chiefs to own rows of apartment buildings. **1970** Thackrey *Thief* 104: To operate in L.A. a book had to be putting out some pretty heavy ice to the law, and would expect protection for that. **1994** *N.Y. Times* (May 1) (Wk. in Rev.) 17: Mr. Koppell's job is to find out where all those tickets go, and how they get there. Few in the theater doubt that ice plays a major role.

2. an icy or hostile reception; cold treatment; the cold shoulder.—usu. constr. with *the.*

[**1896** Ade *Artie* 71: Gee! you've got that icehouse stare o' yours down pat.] **1903** Hobart *Out for the Coin* 77: I was trying to cook up a chance to hand a line of talk to de Main Stake, but old Santa Claus gave me de ice. **1923** Witwer *Fighting Blood* 300: The Board of Trade puts on the ice for me and my partners. **1927** *Vanity Fair* (Nov.) 134: "Gave me the ice" is "ritzed me" or…"hi-hatted me." **1934** Duff & Sauber *20 Million Sweethearts* (film): Every office I go into they give me the ice. **1954** L. Armstrong *Satchmo* 142: Kid Ory and I noticed all those stuck-up guys giving us lots of ice. They didn't feel we were good enough to play their marches. **1963** T.I. Rubin *Sweet Daddy* 12: You know, turn on the ice—like I'm not there. **1968** Brasselle *Cannibals* 88: I gave Virgil ice. *Ibid.* 167: I gave him the ice. **1972** [V.M. Grosvenor] *Thursdays* 12: My ice would get her. **1989** *21 Jump St.* (Fox-TV): Freeze me. Look right through me. Give me ice! Ice me!

3. Orig. *Und.* diamonds or (*occ.*) other gems.

1905 in Paxton *Sports USA* 27: [The baseball player] has a language of his own….Diamonds—and every professional loves to flash them—he calls "ice." **1906** *Nat. Police Gaz.* (Aug. 11) 6: Nothin' doin' in the ice line just now. Stop your kiddin'. *Ibid.* (Aug. 18) 6: A big three-stoner, all white ice…."I'll just buy this ice from you outright." **1910** *N.Y. Eve. Jour.* (May 4) 15: The dame…wore two pieces of ice on her forefinger. **1911** A.H. Lewis *Apaches of N.Y.* 237: "Did youse lamp th' ice on them dames?"…Sop had an eye for diamonds. **1929** Barr *Let Tomorrow Come* 33: Where's the ice? **1930** Lavine *3d Degree* 20: A thief, hard-up for ready cash, may risk "hocking a piece of ice." **1946** J. Adams *Gags* 179: She was bedecked with an armful of "ice." **1952** Chase *McThing* 49: There's ice in this town but it's all behind plate glass. **1969** L. Sanders *Anderson Tapes* 118: He hit some East Side apartment for a bundle. Ice, mostly. *ca*1978 *Rockford Files* (NBC-TV): I'm looking for half a million dollars in hot ice. **1983** *Time* (May 2) 59: Hot Ice: Sotheby's loses a diamond.

4. *Gamb.* COLD DECK, 1.

*a*1943 in D.W. Maurer *Lang. Und.* 138: *Ice.* A stacked deck. **1968** F. Wallace *Poker* 217: Ice—A cold deck.

5. [sugg. by COOL, *adj.,* 3.a., COLD, *adj.,* 4.b., etc.] Esp. *Black E. & Rap Music.* something superlative. Also cf. use in pseudonyms of rap musicians, as Ice Cube, Ice-T, Vanilla Ice, etc. [As 1967, 1992 quots. suggest, this term may be construed as an *adj.,* but in the absence of unmistakably adjectival quots., placement here appears to be justified.]

1967 *DAS* (ed. 2) 691: *Ice*…Good; very fine; great. **1991** N. Krulik *Hammer & Ice* 49: Aw man, that's ice! A cold rap! **1992** "Fab 5 Freddy" *Fresh Fly Flavor* 35: *Ice*—cool.

6. *Narc.* **a.** cocaine, esp. in block form. Cf. earlier ICED, *adj.,* 2; SNOW.

1971 *Inter. Jour. Addiction* VI 360: *Ice* cocaine. **1974** Cull & Hardy *Types of Drug Abusers* 193: *Ice*—Cocaine. **1981** Jenkins *Baja Okla.* 180: He's got the best flake….He keeps blocks of ice, he's not a street guy.

b. methamphetamine prepared in crystalline form for smoking.

1989 *Prime News* (CNN-TV) (Sept. 7): It's called *ice*….The drug first surfaced in Hawaii….*Ice* is beginning to find its way to West Coast cities….Basically, ice is methamphetamine…crystals [that are smoked or inhaled]. **1989** *N.Y. Times* (Sept. 16) 1: The use of smokable methamphetamine…has reached major proportions here [Hawaii]….Experts on substance abuse fear that use of the drug, called ice, could grow. **1989** *CBS This Morning* (CBS-TV) (Nov. 13): Now, looming on the horizon—the new drug *ice* on them make the nineties even deadlier. **1990** *Reporters* (Fox-TV) (Feb. 3): It's a smokable form of speed called *ice*….It's worse than crack…Honolulu has earned itself the dubious honor of the ice capital of America…. **1990** *New Yorker* (Sept. 10) 85: New York dealers [are] trying to prevent the incursion of Asian dealers selling a smokable form of methamphetamine known as ice. **1994** *Reader's Digest* (Feb.) 89: In the '70s, a…more potent form of crystallized meth called "ice" came out of South Korea and Taiwan.

¶ In phrases:

¶ **cut ice** see s.v. CUT, *v.*

¶ **on ice, 1.** in readiness or reserve; in phr. **big thing on ice** an astonishing thing.

1862 *Campfire Songster* 48: There's a big thing coming, boys,/ "A big thing on ice;"/There's a big thing coming, boys,/Wait a little longer. **1868–71** C.G. Leland *Breitmann's Ballads* 59: Und de vay dese Deutschers vent to vork vos von pig ding on ice. **1894** in *DA:* They say she's never been able to find a man good enough for her, and so she's keeping herself on ice.

2.a. away; in abeyance; out of consideration; out of the way; out of use; temporarily deferred.

1875 in R.L. Wright *Irish Emigrant Ballads* 595: Old man, you're getting too fresh,/And we'll soon have to put you on the ice. **1888** Gunter *Miss Nobody* 231: In the hall, prominently posted up by a wag, under new memberships, is a notice: For Election: Gussie P. Van Beekman...*On ice!* **1891** Maitland *Slang Dict.* 136: *Hang it up,* to obtain credit. Equivalent to "put it on the slate" or on the ice. **1899–1900** Cullen *Tales* 294: Just charge it up to Hogan....Put the check on ice. **1900** Ade *More Fables* 132: So they took the High School Oration and put it on the Ice. **1913** Jocknick *Early Days* 31 [ref. to *ca*1871]: Next, he went to W.A. Smith (town marshal), to whom he showed the order..., and was only laughed at. Said he: "You put that order on ice." Major Thompson retorted: "I'll put you where there ain't any ice." **1930** Farrell *Calico Shoes* 151: Keeping your cherry on ice is what gets plenty of those guys put in the booby hatch. **1932** *AS* VII 335: *Put it on the ice*—"forget about it." To intentionally forget about something, usually a debt. **1949** Huggins *Lady Gambles* (film): Everything's on ice till Saturday. **1954** J. Hayes *Desperate Hours* 72: I had to put him on ice for a while, Hilliard. So he'd learn who was boss around here. **1960** Bluestone *Cully* 6: "Keep it on ice till I get back," one sharpie...told the fading skyline. **1969** Pendeton *Death Squad* 98: Don't get too shook up, either. We'll have this guy on ice soon enough. **1976** Price *Bloodbrothers* 98: If you can give her half the look you're giving me now, that should put her on ice for six months. **1978** *U.S. News & W.R.* (Aug. 7) 33: The proposal was put on ice earlier this year.

b. in the morgue; dead, esp. having been murdered.

1929 M.A. Gill *Und. Slang: On ice*—In the morgue. **1935** (quot. at ZAP, *v.*). **1937** in H. Gray *Arf* (unp.): Well, with that smart guy, "Blinkey," on ice, I guess our case is in th' bag. **1960** Roeburt *Mobster* 81: You wanted Beringer on ice so you could surprise Beaumont. **1964** in Wepman, Newman & Binderman *The Life* 133: The first and last bet he lost put him on ice. **1974** A. Bergman *Big Kiss-Off* 13: I figure Fenton was shaking someone else down....It made sense to put him on ice. **1978** Diehl *Sharky's Machine* 225: Somebody put this Domino on ice about four hours ago.

c. incarcerated or in police custody; (*Pris.*) in isolation.

1931 *Sat. Review* (July 18) 978: *On Ice*—In the penitentiary. **1933** Ersine *Pris. Slang* 46: Jake is on ice for a jim. **1939** C.R. Cooper *Scarlet* 327: Mae is "on ice" right now as a guest of the Federal Government on a White Slave Traffic charge. **1941** Coldewey *Lady Gangster* (film): She's liable to be on ice for a long time. **1955** Q. Reynolds *HQ* 190: "We've got Quinn on ice."...Quinn was picked up...on a West Side dock. **1956** Neider *Hendry Jones* 67: What good will it do to keep him on ice like that? **1967** Campbell *Hell's Angels on Wheels* (film): I might have to put you on ice for a couple of days. **1967** "M.T. Knight" *Terrible Ten* 85: Max is on ice for keeps, the Supreme Court turned down his last appeal cold. **1970** M. Thomas *Total Beast* 140: I put his ass on ice, too. **1974** J. Mills *One Just Man* 11: They pronounce isolation ice-o-lation. They say they're on ice. **1976** Whelton *CB Baby* 220: Try anything funny and I'll have your ass on ice for five years. **1977** Sayles *Union Dues* 201: He used to come over there to Roslindale, the detention center, when I was on ice.

d. in hiding, esp. from the law; in seclusion.

1937 *Sat. Eve. Post* (May 22) 34: When a criminal goes into hiding, he is said to be "on ice." **1956** Ross *Hustlers* 120: Get him, put him on ice, hold him till the heat's off. **1958** S.H. Adams *Tenderloin* 275: Willie Frye and his side-kick may have put him on ice somewhere. **1970–71** Higgins *Eddie Coyle* 107: I been on ice once or twice, but never as nice as this. **1974** Cull & Hardy *Types of Drug Abusers* 197: *On Ice*...To lie low or go out of sight temporarily. Wanted by the law.

3. certain to be won, achieved, or completed successfully.

1910 *N.Y. Eve. Jour.* (Apr. 1) 19: A timely tap would have put the game on ice, but the wallopers failed to biff. **1932** *AS* VII 334: To have

a game on ice is to be certain of winning. **1935** Lorimer & Lorimer *Heart Specialist* 28: They have the [tennis] doubles on ice. **1936** in *OED2:* I figured that and the record of the telephone call would be enough to put the case on ice. **1945** MacDougall *Mildred Pierce* (film): You're in the clear, Mrs. Beragon. The case is on ice. **1949** Davies *Happens Every Spring* (film): He ain't got this game on ice yet.

4. to the utmost degree.—constr. with *stink* or *smell.*

1927 in E. Wilson *Twenties* 416: It smells on ice! **1943** *Yank* (June 18) 14: Sgt. Flump stinks on ice. **1946** Kober *That Man Is Here Again* 12: Tellin him his work stinks even on ice. **1976** Elman *Taxi Driver* 17: I guess she thinks you stink on ice just for watching such pictures. **1981** Brooks *Mel B.'s Hist. of World* (film): "Your Highness, the people are revolting." "You said it. They stink on ice." **1987** *Perfect Strangers* (ABC-TV): The police department is incompetent...and stinks on ice.

ice *adj.* see ICE, *n.,* 5.

ice *v.* **1.a.** Orig. *Sports.* to assure victory in (a game); (*hence*) to clinch (a victory or an agreement).

1908 in Fleming *Unforgettable Season* 58: The Giants ought to have had yesterday's game done up and iced for Youngster Crandall. **1934** *AS* (Oct.) 238: Then came the play that *iced* the game. **1958** J. King *Pro Football* 153: Pat Harder connected from the 46 to "ice" a win for Detroit 17–7. **1978** N.Y. Yankees vs. Milwaukee Brewers (WINS radio) (June 28): A home run by Ben Ogilvie iced the victory for the Brewers. **1988** *Daily News* (N.Y.) (June 9) 100: Reliever Lee Smith came on to ice the 4–3 victory. **1989** Horwitt *Call Me Rebel* 35: Cermak had an answer that iced the deal. *a*1994 S. James et al. *Hoop Dreams* (film): A chance to ice the victory. **1995** Headline News network (Feb. 19): To ice a 73-70 victory.

b. *Boxing.* to knock out.

1942 Algren *Morning* 13: He'd ice the jig with a punch. **1987** Oates *On Boxing* 74: Opponents are not merely defeated...but are..."iced," "destroyed," "annihilated."

c. to put the finishing touch to; complete. [Infl. by standard phr., *the icing on the cake* 'the finishing touch'.]

1980 *Quest 80* (Oct.) 49: Its celebrity was iced with a controversial National Book Award in 1972. **1984** Kagan & Summers *Mute Evidence* 124: Howe's sepulchral narration iced the effect with serious tones worthy of Walter Cronkite or Mike Wallace.

d. *Sports.* to defeat.

1983 Mutual Radio network news (Apr. 11): The Islanders iced Washington. *a*1986 in *NDAS:* Nebraska iced Kentucky 55 to 16. *a*1994 D. Frey *Last Shot* 109: We ice 'em every time.

2.a. to treat or receive coldly; snub; slight.—occ. used intrans., constr. with *on.*

1932 L. Berg *Prison Doctor* 258: He glad hands me. "Hello, Wolf! When did you get back?" I'm leery and ices him. *a*1972 *Urban Life & Culture* I 85: He will be "iced" (kept at a safe distance and ignored). **1972** Claerbaut *Black Jargon* 69: She really iced me, man! **1973** Childress *Hero* 89: I iced on Nigeria when he teamed up with Cohen and turned me in. *a*1986 in *NDAS:* How women were "iced" by peers during corridor conversations.

b. to shun or exclude; FREEZE OUT, 1.—usu. constr. with *out.*

1970 in *BDNE* 218: When a lady is...getting herself dumped from someone's guest list [in Washington]..., it is not the same as getting herself iced out in New York or Chicago. **1972** Claerbaut *Black Jargon* 69: *Iced* v....to be isolated by virtue of being ignored. **1987** B. Hauser & D. DeCoteau *Creepozoids* (film): I've been iced out of some major decisions.

c. to fail to keep an appointment with; stand up.

1989 P. Munro *U.C.L.A. Slang* 42: *Get iced* to get stood up, get let down. **1991** *Donahue* (NBC-TV): I was planning on going to the movie but my friend iced me.

3. *Pris.* to imprison or place in isolation.—also constr. with *down.*

1933 Ersine *Pris. Slang* 46: *Ice. v.* To imprison. "The judged iced the whole mob." **1970** R. Sylvester *Guilty Bystander* 27: All they had to do was ice him away with no junk until he broke. **1981** Wambaugh *Glitter Dome* 147: If they iced down everybody who smoked a couple of lids a week they'd have half of Hollywood in the cooler. **1983** *Reader's Digest Success with Words* 86: Black English...*iced, be*..."to be imprisoned." **1995** *Burden of Proof* (CNN-TV) (Dec. 21): Claims he was iced by his pastor...who, he claims, was wearing a wire [and]...acting as agent for the police.

4. Esp. *Und.* to pay bribe or protection money to. Cf. ICE, *n.*, 1; ICED, *adj.*, 1.

1937 *Sat. Eve. Post* (May 22) 90: Able to furnish protection to their patrons without "icing" the police.

5.a. Orig. *Und.* to kill, esp. to murder.

1941 in D. Runyon *More Guys* 308: It is not nearly as nice as icing Buttsy for him. **1953** in Wepman, Newman & Binderman *The Life* 118: And in making my exit, I iced a cop. **1967** in T.C. Bambara *Gorilla* 79: The cat's just another angry dude that iced his wife. **1968** "H. King" *Box-Man* 69: He's...been iced. **1972** P. Fenty *Superfly* (film): Before somebody ices me. **1975** V.B. Miller *Deadly Game* 45: You think the number two man iced him? **1977** T. Berger *Villanova* 33: Teddy, we're gonna ice you. **1983** Sturz *Wid. Circles* 16: Yeah. I'm interested in not gettin' leaned on or iced. I don't want nobody walkin' on my head. **1989** *Star Trek: Next Generation* (Fox-TV): Cuzo's the guy who iced Marty O'Farren. **1990** *Simpsons* (Fox-TV): A guy who iced a bear with his bare hands. **1993** *N.Y. Times* (Dec. 9) A31: Maybe they will ice some pathetic walk-on who misheard their question. **1994** *Mystery Sci. Theater* (Comedy Central TV): I might have iced her myself.

b. to take finishing action against; destroy; cancel.

1979 Homer *Jargon* 42: "Let's *ice* this bastard" is Congressional jargon for "Let's see if we can get the goods on this guy." **1980** *New West* (July 28) 28: There was a draft for a master plan for Yosemite that was iced because it turned out to have been exclusively a collaboration between the bureaucrats...[and] the conglomerate. **1982** *Business Week* (Oct. 11) 31: Will Interior's offshore drilling plan be iced? **1988** M. Maloney *Thunder Alley* 213: You guys iced that Skyhawk?

c. to put out of sight; hide.

1992 Mowry *Way Past Cool* 210: Best we be keepin [the gun] iced long's we can.

6. *Black E.* to cease; COOL, 4.a.; (*hence*) to resolve.—usu. used imper.

1962 Crump *Killer* 226: Let's ice that action for tonight. **1971** H. Roberts *Third Ear:* Ice that noise, fellows! **1971** Dahlskog *Dict.* 33: *Ice it (that)! Interj.* An expression commanding someone to quiet down, slow down, or stop doing something. **1974** S. Stevens *Rat Pack* 151: "Ice that man!" "Keep it down, man." **1990** *New Yorker* (Sept. 10) 69: I had a beef with 'em one time, but it was iced, it was over.

iceberg *n.* an emotionally cold, unexcitable, or unresponsive person.

*1840 in *OED:* Captain Thelwal is a perfect iceberg. **1896** in Ade *Chicago Stories* 177: Oh, you iceberg! I don't believe you'd become enthusiastic over anything in the world. **1912** Beach *Net* 131: I am an iceberg! I never get excited. **1924** Marks *Plastic Age* 149: "I wish she wasn't so cold."..."Guess you picked an iceberg." **1928** Levin *Reporter* 95: At the start she's an iceberg. She doesn't let you even touch her hand until about the sixth time. **1933** in R.E. Howard *Iron Man* 57: To the managerial care of "Iceberg" Grondon. **1935** Fowler & Praskins *Call of Wild* (film): That female iceberg. **1941** Schulberg *Sammy* 137: "You're not the iceberg you'd like to have us think you are," I said.

icebox *n.* **1.** an emotionally unresponsive person, esp. a woman; ICEBERG.

1896 in Rose *Storyville* 128: We are about to be deprived of the presence of dear Josephine Icebox and Lillian Blodgett, who will leave for San Francisco in December. **1909** in J. London *Short Stories* 419: When a freshman he had been baptized "Ice-Box" by his warmer-blooded fellows. **1936** Farrell *World I Never Made* 78: But that wife of his, she was an icebox, not a woman for Lorry. **1962** Crump *Killer* 103: She comes by herself and leaves the same way. A real icebox, you dig? **1963** *AS* XXXVIII 173: *Icebox,* a co-ed...who refuses to date at all while at college. **1970** in Brooks & Warren *Modern Rhetoric* 96: Not only are you...a terrible date...you're an icebox—and this is the sin unforgivable.

2. a morgue.

1928 (quot. at DANCEHALL, 1). **1930** in Grayson *Stories for Men* 161: The dead men in the prison "ice box" were beyond admitting a single word. **1932** *Writer's Digest* (Aug.) 46: The coroner's office is...the "ice box." **1938** in *OED2:* Scavengers...cart them to the "ice box," as the morgue is known in prison. **1980** *AS* (Spring) 49: *Ice box...* Morgue (slang).

3. *Pris.* **a.** an isolation cell; punishment cells.

1928 *AS* III (Feb.) 255: *Icebox.* Special or solitary confinement cell. **1931** *AS* VI (Aug.) 439: *Icebox.* The isolation cells of a prison. **1934** Berg *Prison Nurse* 123: The correction cells...were known variously as the "bin," "hole," "dungeon," "ice box,"—and "cooler" as well as by a few more vulgar titles. **1970** *Playboy* (Feb.) 220: Dr. McNamee told about the "icebox," a special punishment facility of six cages set on a concrete slab in the open.

b. a prison.

[**1932** in *AS* (Feb. 1934) 27: *Icebox.* A life sentence.] [**1934** in *Jour. Abnormal Psych.* XXX (1935) 363: *Ice box*—an upstate [N.Y.] prison known for its severe climate.] **1938** Chandler *Big Sleep* 31: The sister...had Owen heaved into the icebox. **1953** Chandler *Long Goodbye* 96: He has so far stayed out of the icebox.

ice bunny *n.* [sugg. by BEACH BUNNY, SKI BUNNY, BUNNY, 3] *Ice Skating.* a novice ice skater or one who poses as an ice skater, esp. a young woman.

1991 *Beverly Hills 90210* (Fox-TV): Real skaters as opposed to ice bunnies.

ice cream *n. Narc.* cocaine, morphine, or heroin in crystalline form.

1928 Asbury *Gangs of N.Y.* 199: Lowest of all were the ice cream eaters, who chewed the crystals of cocaine, morphine, or heroin. **1951** in *AS* (Feb. 1952) 27: *Ice cream man,* n. Seller of drugs, usually opium derivatives. **1988** *TV Guide* (Knoxville-Chattanooga ed.) (Jan. 9) A-70: An "ice-cream" dealer's murder catapults O'Brien and Giambone...into a minor-league drug war.

ice-cream pants *n.pl.* a man's trousers, very light in color, for summer wear.

1908 *Sat. Eve. Post,* in *DARE:* Johnny ambled up, decorated with a blue coat, white vest an' ice-cream pants, an' his hair all slicked down. **1940** Faulkner, in *DARE:* White flannel trousers....A frightened and battered man in a pair of ruined ice cream pants. **1942–44** in *AS* (Feb. 1946) 34: *Ice cream pants,* n. Pearl gray colored trousers and slacks worn by seniors. **1950** *N.Y. Times* (Sept. 19) VI 44: His "ice cream pants." These, the sort of striped flannels that in his youth used to go with a blazer, [etc.]. **1982** in Terkel *Good War* 234: Girls in their pretty dresses and young men in their ice-cream pants.

ice-cream suit *n.* **1.** a man's lightweight suit, very light in color, for summer wear.

1890 in *DA:* Dragging a light colored ice cream suit into the ides of November with its chilling blasts. **1958** in R. Bradbury *Melancholy* 49: They will freeze...when they see you in the cool white summer ice cream suit. *Ibid.* 61: Buy us a nice white panama hat and a pale blue tie to go with the white ice cream suit. **1962** *New Yorker* (Apr. 7) 147: Ice-cream suits, for such ordeals as birthdays and Sunday school, are of a nubbly beige silk-and-rayon. **1965** in W. King *Black Anthol.* 305: Them cats with the cowboy hats and ice cream suits. **1970** R. Sylvester *Guilty Bystander* 6 [ref. to 1928]: My suit was almost white and of a heavy, hairy material. It was called an "ice cream" suit. The buttons were of leather, and...resembled sliced golf balls. **1984** "W.T. Tyler" *Shadow Cabinet* 67: What my dad used to call an ice cream suit, with a little bow tie. **1991** *All Things Considered* (Nat. Pub. Radio) (Aug. 18): Truman came out in his white ice-cream suit, as they called them.

2. *Navy.* a dress-white uniform.

1982 S.P. Smith *Officer & Gentleman* 99: You rich college boys struttin' around in your ice cream suits like you owned the goddamn place.

iced *adj.* **1.** *Und.* made secure or certain through the payment of graft or protection money. Cf. ICE, *n*, 1; ICE, *v.*, 4.

1937 *Sat. Eve. Post* (May 22) 34: The place where [the criminal] seeks safe refuge is said to be "iced."

2. intoxicated, esp. by cocaine.

1953 R. Chandler *Goodbye* 24: Dead drunk, paralyzed,...iced to the eyebrows. **1974** Gober *Black Cop* 47: The bitch had been snorting coke....She wasn't completely iced. She was just mellow.

icehouse *n.* (see quot.). Cf. ICEBOX, *n.*, 3.

1961 in Rose *Storyville* 151 [ref. to N.O., ca1905]: The woman who lived next door tol' me she just went to the "ice house" (popular term for the isolation hospital) for medicine.

iceman *n.* **1.** *Und.* **a.** (see 1942–49 quot.).

1926 Finerty *Criminalese* 31: Ice men—Diamond thieves. **1931** in Partridge *Dict. Und.* 352: His professional moniker of Larry the Iceman. **1942–49** Goldin et al. *DAUL* 106: *Ice-man*…A buyer of stolen diamonds.…A jewel thief. **1953** W. Brown *Monkey on My Back* 89: Pepe had confided in me that Rico was one of the "icemen."

b. (see quot.).

1961 Scarne *Guide to Gambling* 83: The machine boss has his *iceman* who collects protection payoffs.

c. HIT MAN.

1972 Pendleton *Boston Blitz* 13: "Whatta you want here with me?" "Figure it out," the ice man suggested. *ca***1982** *Benson* (ABC-TV): They got hit men, icemen, button men. *a***1986** *T.J. Hooker* (ABC-TV): Go play iceman.

2. a man who shows no emotion, esp. under stress; *(also)* a cold, calculating man.

1941 in *DAS*: An iceman, in racetrack slang, is a gambler who never loses his head. **1946** in D. McKay *Wild Wheels* 40: Even iceman Jimmy Hale lost some of his poker-faced look. **1958** Mayes *Hunters* (film): He's an iceman…no feelings, no nerves, no fear. **1967** *Lit. Dictionary* 50: *Ice Man*—An extremely cool and confident person during times of excitement. **1968** M.B. Scott *Racing Game* 26: A jockey who possesses this attribute is said to always "keep his cool," "to ride like an ice man," or to have ice in his veins. **1978** Pici *Tennis Hustler* 193: The guy's an iceman…no wonder he wins one hundred thou a year. **1989** "Capt. X" & Dodson *Unfriendly Skies* 110: While there are about 5,000 lives that seem to be hanging in the balance up there, this iceman…will be talking to a friend about what happened on a fishing trip yesterday.

3. *Trucking.* a refrigeration technician.

1971 Tak *Truck Talk* 88: *Ice man:* a Thermo King mechanic or any refrigeration man who works on reefer trailers.

ice princess *n.* ICE QUEEN.

1989 *Good Housekeeping* (Feb. 1990) 150: They'd heard she was an "ice princess."…I think they expected an aloof, cool character. **1993** *N.Y. Times* (Oct. 31) (Arts & Leisure) 33: She's blond, beautiful, smart, impeccably dressed, ice-princess cool and very direct. **1994** *New Yorker* (June 6) 54: Chatfield-Taylor's shy, sometimes aloof manner can give the impression that she's "an ice princess." **1996** *N.Y. Press* (Jan. 3) 23: Another glamorously unknowable ice princess, Catherine Deneuve.

ice queen *n.* a woman who shows no emotion; an aloof woman. Cf. ICE MAN, 2.

1980 Schruers *Blondie* 129: Not the ice queen some media people would make her out to be. **1981** *Time* (Sept. 14) 77: To the public, she seemed cool and haughty.…"I was the ice queen and they wanted to see me melt." **1982** in G. Trudeau *Doonesbury Dossier* (unp.): The ice queen's dismantled the whole enforcement team. **1985** *Newsweek* (Dec. 9) 8: As the "Ice Queen"…tells it in scathing terms, she did nothing wrong; she was a smart, hardworking Reagan loyalist victimized by scores of incompetents. *a***1989** Spears *NTC Dict. Slang* 192: Molly is not exactly an ice queen, but comes close. **1992** *Rolling Stone* (June 25) 41: She…retains her singular persona—an ice queen thirsting to be melted by love. **1994** *N.Y. Times* (Jan. 16) (Arts & Leisure) 18: Sally is a powerful woman, another ice queen whose roiling emotions remain contained. **1994** *N.Y. Times* (June 19) (Styles) 6: "Lack of sexual desire" was last on the list [of reasons for sexual abstinence]…shattering the image of the virgin ice queen.

ice wagon *n.* **1.** a lumbering, slow-moving vehicle or person.

1895 *DN* I 419: To be an *ice-wagon*, to be very slow. **1907** in *Comments on Ety.* (Mar. 1994) 12: Slide, Andy, you—ice wagon! **1909** in O. Johnson *Lawrenceville* 35: Now then, old ice-wagon—get your nose in it. **1914** Ellis *Billy Sunday* 274: He's an ice wagon on the bases, they say. **1923** *Nashville* (Tenn.) *Banner* (Jan. 13) 7: Ta ta old ice wagon [street car].

2. *Trucking.* a refrigerator truck or trailer.

1938 in *AS* (Apr. 1942) 103: *Ice wagon.* Refrigerator truck. **1971** Tak *Truck Talk* 88: *Ice wagon:* a refrigerated trailer.

Ichabod *interj.* (used as a mild oath).

1856 in K.E. Olson *Music & Musket* 3: But—Ichabod!—the glory has departed.

ichiban *adj. & interj.* [< Japn] Esp. *Mil. in Japan.* first-rate; perfect.

1900 Belasco *Madame Butterfly* 16: I tell you, she's just "ichi ban." **1951** *N.Y. Herald Tribune* (Dec. 16) II 5: Ichi-ban (Japanese) means No. 1, the best, superior. **1956** Lasly *Turn Tigers Loose* 73: Thomas

grinned and formed a circle with thumb and forefinger. "Ichi-ban, sir." **1965** *Air Officer's Guide* 437: [Air Force slang:] Ichi-ban (Jap.)—no. 1, first class. **1980** *Daily News Tonight* (N.Y.) (Sept. 18) 5: Ah, so—"Shogun" ichi-ban (No. 1).

ick *n.* ICKY, 1.

1942 *ATS* 558: *Ick*…a devotee of "sweet" music. **1943** M. Shulman *Barefoot Boy* 79: An evening with those icks would make anybody crazy. **1969** Coppel *Little Time for Laughter* 35 [ref. to *ca*1940]: What girl would be caught with such an ick?

ick *adj. & interj.* ICKY, 1.

1967 Crowley *Boys in the Band* 821: I don't think I could get through that morning-after ick attack. **1967** in *OEDAS* II: "Be quiet…or I shall serve hot oatmeal every morning.".…"Oatmeal, ick." **1978** Pilcer *Teen Angel* 160: Oh, ick! **1983** Nelkin & Brown *Workers* 161: Some stuff is just downright ick. **1985** J. Irving, in *OEDAS* II: Blood, people leaking stuff out of their bodies—ick.

icky *n.* **1.** Esp. *Jazz.* an unpleasant, unsophisticated, or old-fashioned person, often a devotee of sentimental-sounding music.

1937 *AS* (Oct.) 183: *Ickies.* The opposite of jitterbugs. **1938** in *OED2*: *Icky*, one who is not hip but thinks he is. **1939** Goodman & Kolodin *Swing* 73: "Bix"…preferred to go off with a few of the fellows to some quiet place where there weren't a lot of ickeys crowding around. **1940** in *Amer. Jour. Sociol.* XLVIII (1943) 570: The jiver…The flycat or icky…The cat. **1942** *Time* (Apr. 27) 16: Gates, cats and ickies were hurt good. **1942** in *Great Music of D. Ellington* 69: A rhythm that scares an "ickie." **1942** Davis & Wolsey *Call House* 216: Some smart icky trapped our clothes. **1944** in Himes *Black on Black* 196: We was at the Creole Breakfast Club knockin' ourselves out when this icky, George Brown, butts in. **1944** *Slanguage Dict.* 60: *Ickies*—intellectuals; upper crust. **1945** Hellman & Kern *Horn Blows at Midnight* (film): Bounce that icky out! **1946** J. Adams *Gags* 181: The "hicks" and "ickies" became sophisticated. **1947** *Tomorrow* (Aug.) 29: *Ickie*, meaning one ignorant of swing,…[has] become passé in a brief space of years. **1950–52** Ulanov *Hist. Jazz* 351: *Icky:* a "cornball," one who doesn't "dig," who isn't "hip" (in the argot of jazz just before and through the first years of swing; afterward rare).

2. *pl.* a feeling of apprehension or sickness; creeps.—constr. with *the.*

1959 Lipton *Barbarians* 19: It's horrifying, it really gives me the ickies.

icky *adj.* **1.** Orig. *Juve.* unpleasantly sticky or sweet; *(hence)* unpleasant; repulsive; ill. Also as adv. See also earlier ICKY-POO.

1929 Cruze *Great Gabbo* (film): When I drop my lollipop it gets all over icky. **1943** *School & Soc.* LVIII 169: *Icky:* no good. **1957** Kohner *Gidget* 129: One of those icky desert winds we call the Santa Ana. **1958–59** Lipton *Barbarians* 20: I mean, it's equivalently ickie. **1960** N.Y.C. schoolboy: I feel icky. **1960** Barber *Minsky's* 324: Having to redye her shoes…was a smelly, icky job. **1966** Fariña *Down So Long* 149: "These are different swamps."…"Not the icky kind?" **1967** Head *Mr. & Mrs.* 53: Singing some icky "why don't you love me" song. **1968** Lockridge *Hartspring* 152: Your veins…get all icky with cholesterol. **1968** Hudson *Case of Need* 251: The food tastes icky. **1968–70** *Current Slang* III & IV 72: *Icky, adj.*…ill. (Drug users jargon). **1970** L. Gould *Friends* 100: Just don't tell me how you hate sanitary belts and how *icky* it all is. **1977** *Maledicta* I 2: Proctologists, urologists and gynecologists handle feces, urine, rectal openings, diseased or otherwise icky genitals. **1978** Maupin *Tales* 163: Her hair drab and icky in a thick coat of Vaseline. **1982** Whissen *Way with Wds.* 44: Jelly beans are *icky.* **1982** Abodaher *Iacocca* 194: The minute he was named vice-president…an icky kind of ego seemed to mushroom overnight. **1983** *Green Lantern* (July) 8: That icky substance covering the creature's insides some kind of saliva. **1987** M. Mayfield *Thinking for Yourself* 67: I don't want to eat my carrots. They taste icky. **1988–90** M. Hunter *Abused Boys* 183: He's being kind of icky sweet. **1993** *Mystery Sci. Theater* (Comedy Central TV): You guys are icky. **1995** *CBS This Morning* (CBS-TV) (Apr. 28): I think it's a little icky to talk about it.

2. Orig. *Jazz.* lacking in sophistication; *(also)* foolishly sentimental.

1935 *Vanity Fair* (Nov.) 71: If the straight music is also oversweet, the term *icky*…is frequently employed to denote this. **1937** *New Yorker* (Apr. 17) 27: Those not up on current idioms are *corny, on the cob,* or…if their playing is oversweet, *icky.* **1971** Hilaire *Thanatos* 52: I just get icky for a guy.

icky-poo *adj.* [prob. ICKY + *-poo* (of unkn. orig.), despite the slightly earlier attestation of this form] ICKY, 1. *Joc.* Also **icky-boo.**

   ***1920** in *OED2*: Can it be that my little pet is feeling icky-boo? Face going green—slight perspiration—collar tight. **1964** *Sat. Eve. Post* (Apr. 11) 79: "Ickypoo" is a new addition to its [*sc. Women's Wear Daily's*] lexicon, as in: Ickypoo (i.e., nauseating) colors. **1965** *New Yorker* (Feb. 13) 134 [quoting *Women's Wear Daily*]: When Chanel has to use ickypoo colors she combines them with dark blouses. **1970** *New Yorker* (Nov. 14) 55: If any...engine conkouts, or fires make you feel icky-poo, you just come and tell. **1980** Birnbach et al. *Preppy Hndbk.* 220: *Icky*...Also "ickypoo."

icy *adj.* COOL, 2.
   1947 *ATS* (Supp.) 4: *Icy*,..."smooth." **1989** *Life* (July) 27: Her last boyfriend was *massively gorgeous*—and the *iciest* dancer.

icy mitt *n.* [sugg. by antonymous GLAD HAND, 1] a cold or hostile reception; rejection; show of indifference.—usu. constr. with *the.* Cf. CHILLY MITT. Also **icy mitten.**
   1897 in *DARE*: *Icy mitten:* cool refusal. **1906** London *Moon Face* 74: Gave you the icy mit, eh? **1908** Sullivan *Criminal Slang* 13: *Icy mitt*—The shake from your best girl. **1914** S. Lewis *Mr. Wrenn* 18: I'm sure you didn't intend to hand me the icy mitt. **1928** C. Sandburg in *Amer. Mercury* (Aug.) 389: The poker face...the icy mitt. **1968** in *DARE*.

ID *n.* **1.** identification, usu. in the form of a document; an identification card.—often used attrib. Now *S.E.*
   1941 in D.W. Maurer *Lang. Und.* 124: I had...plenty I.D. **1942** *ATS* 227: *I.D.*, identification card. **1947** *ATS* (Supp.) 11: *I.D. bracelet*, an identification bracelet. **1961** Kohner *Gidget Goes Hawaiian* 62: I...hoped...they would serve me a drink without me showing any I.D. **1962** E. Stephens *Blow Negative* 9: Let's see your I.D. card. **1963** Pynchon *V* ch. xiii: Pig was...trying simultaneously to salute, produce ID and liberty cards. **1967** Spillane *Delta* 110: Get him here and let him try to make a positive i.d. on me. **1985–87** Bogosian *Talk Radio* 59: Gotta break for a little station I.D. here. **1990** *Current Affair* (Apr. 5) (synd. TV series): The use of fake ID.

   2. *Stu.* an examination question requiring the identification of a name, date, quotation, or the like. Now *S.E.*
   1965 N.Y.C. high school teacher: The test will be multiple-choice and ID's. **1990** Univ. Tenn. student: How many ID's will there be?

ID *v.* to make a certain identification of. Now *colloq.*
   1944 in M. Chennault *Up Sun!* 120: ID'd a Jap airfield under construction at Q35 R36. **1984** J. McNamara *First Directive* 255: I had rather quickly ID'd Richard Stead. **1984** Caunitz *Police Plaza* 7: Has he [a victim] been I.D.'d? **1986** Cogan *Top Gun* 10: I'll ID him, you hook 'em. **1989** Zumbro & Walker *Jungletracks* 242: Two of the NVA are tentatively I.D.'d.

idea pot *n.* the head or mind.
   ***1785** Grose *Vulgar Tongue: Idea pot.* The knowledge box, the head. **1821** (quot. at KNOWLEDGE BOX).

idiot badge *n. Army.* the Combat Infantryman's Badge. *Joc.*
   1962 Blake *Heartbreak* 77 [ref. to 1953]: The Idiot Badge...combat infantry badge. **1978** Karl *13th Outpost* 120 [ref. to 1953]: The Idiot Badge—this Combat Infantry Badge.

idiot board *n.* IDIOT CARD, 1; (*hence*) the pane of a TelePrompTer.
   1952 *Newsweek* (Aug. 4) 51: The Republicans and Democrats got their "idiot boards" free. **1955** *Sat. Eve. Post* (Sept. 24) 29: "Idiot boards" are held out of camera range to prompt forgetful performers. Girls who hold them up are called "idiot girls."

idiot box *n.* **1.** a television set; (*hence*) television (as a medium).
   *ca***1955** (cited in *W10*). ***1959** in *OED2*: When my very existence depended on the magic idiot box. **1965** Hersey *Too Far to Walk* 70: Something's burning. Turn the TV off. There must be something gone in the idiot box. **1970** *N.Y. Times Mag.* (Apr. 12) 124: The idiot box processes the life of man into polarities of mindlessness. **1971** *All in the Family* (CBS-TV): What's on the idiot box? **1974** Abdul *Black Entertainers* 35: Some people call it "The Idiot Box." **1976** *NBC's Saturday Night* (NBC-TV): This cat is too wigged out for the idiot box. **1978** *Barney Miller* (NBC-TV): They just sit and watch that idiot box. **1980** Freudenberger & Richelson *Burn Out* 100: Television, that much maligned "idiot box." **1993** *Simpsons* (Fox-TV): Are you squandering the precious gift of life by sitting in front of the idiot box?

1995 *Critic* (Comedy Central TV): I have no intention of dancing on the idiot box.

   2. *Av.* **a.** any of various boxlike training devices.
   1958 in Loosbrock & Skinner *Wild Blue* 535: Here he learns to diagnose the complexities of high-speed, high-altitude flight, in those...million-dollar "idiot boxes" which can simulate the effect of winds up to 300 knots and speeds up to 1,500 nautical miles per hour. **1960** Archibald *Jet Flier* 97 [ref. to WWII]: Then there was the reflex test machine that reminded them all of a pinball machine....At Fort Worth it was known as the "idiot box."

   b. an automatic navigational or tactical device aboard an aircraft.
   1961 L.G. Richards *TAC* 235: She's stuffed full of idiot boxes. Her gizzard is crammed with miles of wires.

idiot card *n.* **1.** *TV.* a cue card.
   1957 *Sat. Eve. Post* (Sept. 7) 64: William Maitland goggled a moment like a TV performer caught without his idiot cards. **1958** *Time* (Feb. 3) 64: Mamie asked for an "idiot card" to cue her. **1964** *N.Y. Times* (Apr. 19) II 13: "As long as you're going to wear an idiot card, why don't you have my lines on it?" An "idiot card" is used to prompt actors. **1966** Susann *Valley of Dolls* 294: Tomorrow she'd have to use the "idiot cards." **1969** *N.Y. Times* (Mar. 9) II 21: Idiot card. **1969** *New Yorker* (Sept. 27) 86: We had all the written questions put on idiot cards, and then the people read them before the camera.

   2. *Av.* (see quot.).
   1991 Linnekin *80 Knots* 343 [ref. to 1960's]: "Idiot cards" (checklists) for various airplanes.

idiot girl *n. TV.* a woman who holds up cue cards for a television performer. Now *hist.*
   1955 (quot. at IDIOT BOARD).

idiot ink *n.* any of various white or colored liquids used to correct typed or written errors; correction fluid.
   1984 Univ. Tenn. student: Got any idiot ink?

idiot juice *n.* (see quots.).
   1974 Cull & Hardy *Types of Drug Abusers* 193: *Idiot Juice*—Nutmeg and water mixed for intoxication, largely used in prisons. **1976** *N.Y. Folklore* II 239: Liquor is called *idiot juice, joy juice*, or *booze.*

idiot light *n.* **1.** a small light that turns on automatically to indicate that power is being generated through an electrical system.
   1967 *Pop. Sci.* (Nov.) 205: You can, of course, get an idea of what's going on in your charging circuit by observing the idiot light or the ammeter mounted on your instrument panel. **1971** Tak *Truck Talk* 88: *Idiot light:* a small light sometimes found on the front end of a tractor, the light turns on when the ignition is started. **1979** Univ. Tenn. grad. student: An idiot light is a little light that comes on to tell you something is working.

   2. a small warning light, esp. on a dashboard or instrument panel.
   1968 in *OED2*: He watched the idiot lights in the dashboard. **1969** *Pop. Science* (Dec.) 116: Its thin strip-type speedometer and idiot lights instead of gauges. **1971** Tak *Truck Talk* 88: *Idiot lights:* the lights on a truck's dash. **1976** *Business Week* (May 31) 24: Competing POS terminals give similar help, through fixed "idiot lights" that are less versatile. **1979** Univ. Tenn. grad. student: When I had driver's ed in 1967 they used idiot lights on the driving simulator. A little light would come on to tell you when you should have braked but didn't. **1980** *Harper's* (June) 86: Oil pressure will fall so low that the "idiot" light on the dashboard will flash. **1983** S. King *Christine* 187: The oil and amp idiot lights came on. **1993** Headline News network (Apr. 3): Like red idiot lights going off simultaneously with something terrible happening to your car.

idiot loop *n. Mil. Av.* an Immelmann maneuver used when dropping a bomb from an aircraft.
   1961 L.G. Richards *TAC* 190: The High Angle LABS maneuver—essentially the old World War I Immelmann. This "idiot loop" can be executed...by any fighter-bomber pilot who can...find his target. **1969** Cagle *Naval Av. Guide* 394: *Idiot Loop.* A method of delivering a weapon using a modified loop maneuver.

idiot mount *n. Army.* a hatch mount for a machine gun on a tank turret.
   1986 R. Zumbro *Tank Sgt.* 204 [ref. to 1967–68]: I still had the

"idiot-mount" .50 to work around, but now...I could see without chancing sudden decapitation.

idiot pills *n.pl.* strong sedative pills.
> **1953** *ATS* (ed. 2) 497: *Idiot pills*, phenobarbital sleeping pills. **1965–66** in D.W. Maurer *Lang. Und.* 312: *Idiot pills.* Barbiturates. **1971** *Inter. Jour. Addiction* VI 360: *Idiot pills* sedatives.

idiot seat *n. Av.* a copilot's seat.
> **1955** *AS* XXX (May) 118: *Idiot seat.* Copilot's seat in multiplace aircraft. **1972** R. Barrett *Lovomaniacs* 29: The kid...asked Malnic if there'd be any chance of his sitting in the idiot-seat for a while.

idiot sheet *n.* IDIOT CARD, 1.
> **1956** G. Green *Last Angry Man* 478: He did not want them...reading it from an "idiot sheet." **1960** in *N.Y. Times* (Jan. 1, 1961) VI 33: There are some hard, new decisions which must be reached without a musical score or even a TV "idiot sheet" to guide him. **1962** in *OED2:* When cue cards first came into use for full script purposes, they were known derisively as "idiot sheets."

idiot spoon *n. Labor.* a shovel.
> **1947** *PADS* (No. 9) 34: *Idiot spoon*...Same as *idiot stick* [shovel]. **1948** A. Murphy *To Hell and Back* 89 [ref. to WWII]: A shovel...An idiot's spoon, that's what it is. **1966** "T. Pendleton" *Iron Orchard* 49: The two set to work, in tandem, with pick and shovel, driving their picks into the chalky caliche rock, then scooping out the rubble with their long-handled "idiot spoons."

idiot stick *n.* **1.** *Labor.* **a.** a shovel or similar implement for digging or the like.
> **1930** in *DARE: Idiot stick:* A shovel. **1936** in *AS* (Feb. 1937) 74: *Idiot-stick*—shovel, pick, axe. **1945** Huie *Omaha to Okinawa* 22: Manipulating an "idiot stick"—a shovel. **1953** T. Runyon *In for Life* 107: A shovel...which he referred to from the corner of his mouth as an "idiot stick." **1958** McCulloch *Woods Words* 93: *Idiot stick*—A large scoop shovel. **1958** in D. McKay *Wild Wheels* 153: These mitts of mine like the feel of an idiot stick.

b. any of various sticklike tools or utensils.
> *a***1958** in *AS* XXXIV (1959) 78: Logger Lingo...*Idiot stick, n.* A peeling bar. **1961–68** in *AS* XLIV (1969) 18: *Idiot stick*...A felt roller [and stick] used to apply paint.

2. *Army.* a rifle.
> **1962** Blake *Heartbreak* 40 [ref. to 1953]: Idiot stick bearer...Rifleman. **1971** Drill instructor, U.S. Army, Ft. Campbell, Ky. (coll. J. Ball): Pick up your idiot sticks and fall in! Your rifles, damn it! **1983** Elting, Cragg & Deal *Soldier Talk* 160 [ref. to WWII]: *Idiot stick*...Primarily a rifle, sometimes a shovel. **1990** Cawthon *Other Clay* xv [ref. to WWII]: I was authorized to wear the...infantry insignia of crossed rifles—proudly depreciated [*sic*] as "idiot sticks"—on the lapels.

3. *pl. Med.* (see quot.).
> **1964** "Doctor X" *Intern* 128: The baby was only about three and a half pounds, but it was alive, and the woman was doing okay, too, and after a while I quit shaking enough to hold onto the idiot sticks (retractors) and get a look at what was going on.

idiot-tickler *n.* a shuttlecock.
> **1959** Knowles *Separate Peace* 27: This idiot-tickler, the only thing it's good for is eeny-meeny-miney-mo.

idiot transmission *n. Trucking.* (see quot.).
> **1971** Tak *Truck Talk* 88: *Idiot transmission:* the five-and-two transmission with an overdrive gear...."Only an idiot would put fifth low in front of fourth high."

idiot tube *n.* television; IDIOT BOX, 1; BOOB TUBE.
> **1968** Lockridge *Hartspring* 64: Not Idiot-tube executives in hours and hours of trying. **1971** N.Y.U. professor: So you switch on the idiot tube and right away there's somebody trying to get your money or your vote. **1976** C. Keane *Hunter* 99: Watching the idiot tube.

ig *n. Black E.* a snub; rebuff.—used in phr. of the sort **put the ig on** to ignore; snub.
> **1963** in Clarke *Amer. Negro Stories* 302: And they kept leanin' over to one another, talkin' confidential—puttin' the ig' on the silks scattered amongs' 'em. **1970** *DARE* files, in *AS* 57:3 (Fall 1982) 177: If a man asks a woman to marry him and she refuses...."Gave him the igg." **1977** G. Smitherman *Talkin and Testifyin* 259: *Put the ig on*...to ignore somebody, act like you don't know them when you do.

ig *v. Black E.* to ignore; snub.
> **1946** Mezzrow & Wolfe *Really Blues* 25: For a long time the waiter

igged us. *Ibid.* 306: *Igg:* ignore. **1959** A. Anderson *Lover Man* 150: The chick iggs him completely. **1963** in *DARE: Ig:* to ignore. **1973** Claerbaut *Black Jargon* 69: *Ig,* v. to ignore; disregard. **1973** Childress *Hero* 12: I...tryin to show my respeck by iggin her. **1973** Andrews & Owens *Black Lang.* 104: *Ig*—ignore. *ca***1974** in J.L. Gwaltney *Drylongso* 20: Sam just igged 'em. **1983** *Reader's Digest Success with Words* 86: Black English...*igg* = "to ignore, disregard, reject." *a***1994** N. McCall *Wanna Holler* 132: I igged her like I usually did. I acted like I didn't even hear her.

iggie *n.* [fr. *ignore* + -*ie*] ¶ In phrase: **play the iggie** to avoid or ignore.—also constr. with a prep.
> **1961** Clausen *Season's Over* 153 [ref. to *ca*1945]: Dope! I was trying to tell you to play the iggie....To play the iggie means to play dumb—clam up. **1974–75** Powledge *Mud Show* 187: They play the iggie to you and get by. **1981** D.W. Maurer & A. Tutrell, in *AS* 57: 248: But she plays the iggie for him.

iggy *adj.* ignorant.
> **1918** Straub *Diary* (July 7): At 7:30 Major Wainright and several "iggy" Lieutenants came up and now General Bruning is helping them win the war with the scissors. *Ibid.* (Aug. 5): With me went four of the Third Division men; they sure have never been on a real live front before and they sure are "iggy" boys.

igno *n.* a fool; ignoramus.
> [**1979** *Rolling Stone* (Feb. 8) 40: We watch two creative ignoroids stuff black rifle powder and rags down the muzzle of their homemade cannon.] *****1979** Cleese, Chapman et al. *Life of Brian* (film): "Weirdo!" "Igno!" **1986** N.Y.C. woman, age *ca*50: But after talking with him, I realized he was just another igno. **1992** *Down the Shore* (Fox-TV): Do the words "snotty, tactless igno" mean anything to you?

ignorant end *n.* the end (of a tool) to be grasped by the human user.
> **1956** Lasly *Turn Tigers Loose* 152: Lasly started work in the oil fields, "beginning...on the ignorant end of a pair of pipeline tongs."

ignorant oil *n. Esp. Black E.* whiskey or wine.
> **1954** in Hayakawa *Use & Misuse of Lang.* 158: One finds in the blues comments on many problems...for example, the problem...of alcoholism, as in the song "Ignorant Oil." **1971** Wells & Dance *Night People* 2: I had a cousin called Curly who liked his ignorant oil....If you didn't have the money, just get him high and he would break the wildest stud in town. **1972** Claerbaut *Black Jargon* 69: *Ignorant oil*...wine...whiskey. **1976** N.Y.C. cabdriver, age *ca*30: I'm swearin' off that ignorant oil and stickin' to reefer. **1978** *Nat. Lampoon* (Oct.) 4: Myself, I favor juice....What you call your "ignorant oil."

ignorant stick *n.* a shovel or hoe; IDIOT STICK, 1.
> **1957** in Algren *Lonesome Monsters* 133: Well, play me a tune on that ignorant stick you got there. **1976** *N.Y. Folklore* II 240: The cotton hoe is called an *ignorant stick.*

ignorant stripe *n. Army.* a service stripe. *Joc.*
> **1947** *ATS* (Supp.) 21 [ref. to WWII]: *Ignorant stripe*, a hash mark. *a***1972** Spec. 4, U.S. Army, Ft. Campbell, Ky. (coll. J. Ball): Those little hash marks mean you're dumb enough to stay in longer than you had to. They're ignorant stripes. **1980** Cragg *Lex. Militaris* 226: *Ignorant Stripe.* A hash mark.

IHTFP *Army.* (see 1969 quot.).
> **1969** Crumley *One to Count Cadence* 27: All the way back to the barracks he explained why I too would soon adhere to the motto IHTFP or I Hate This Fucking Place. **1983** Elting, Cragg & Deal *Soldier Talk* 161: *IHTFP*...gained wide currency during the Vietnam War, when it was...seen...[inscribed] on helmet camouflage covers or cardboard placards.

Ike *n.* **1.** a fellow, esp. if uncouth or rustic.—usu. used in combs.
> **1896** *DN* I 419: *Ike*...an uncouth fellow. "He's an awful Ike." **1902** W.N. Harben *Abner Daniel* 72: He's a big Ike in some church in Atlanta. **1905** "W. Hale" *Cowboy & Ranchman* 134: The Mormon ikes began to crowd in. **1911–12** Ade *Knocking the Neighbors* 49: There is but one thing for a Wise Ike to do. **1919** *DN* V 64: *Crazy-boob, -ike, -mutt, -snoop,* all used in speaking of a foolish, stupid person. "He is such a *crazy-boob,* I don't like him." California. **1920** (quot. at COKE²). **1928** MacArthur *War Bugs* 242: The green Ikes scattered all over the place like Rhode Island Reds. *ca***1955** in *DARE:* Country Ike. **1965–69** in *DARE:* Smart Ike...Crazy Ike. **1986** in *DARE:* Country Ikes.

2. *Navy.* the aircraft carrier USS *Dwight D. Eisenhower.*
> **1989** Joss *Strike* 7: With *Ike's* return to the East Coast. **1990** R. Dorr *Desert Shield* 31: *Ike* was in the wrong body of water to be imme-

diately helpful. **1990–93** M. Moore *Woman at War* 23: The helicopter disgorged us onto the bustling deck of the *Ike*.

Ike jacket *n.* [a style associated with Gen. Dwight D. "Ike" Eisenhower] Orig. *Army.* a waist-length uniform jacket. Also **Ike coat.**

    1956 Heflin *USAF Dict.* 263: *Ike jacket.* An Eisenhower jacket. **1965** Linakis *In Spring* 119: I took off the Ike jacket and hooked it over the back of the chair. **1972–74** Hawes & Asher *Raise Up* 42: Ike jackets were very cool, and air force suntans. **1982** W.E.B. Griffin *Lieuts.* 58: The "Ike" jacket...now [in 1944] authorized for wear by both officers and enlisted men. **1983** Elting, Cragg & Deal *Soldier Talk* 161: The Ike jacket [was abolished] in the early 1950s. **1988** M. Bartlett *Trooper Down!* 33: Each cadet receives...an "Ike" coat (named after President Eisenhower, who made waist-length jackets popular during World War II).

Ikey *n.* [dimin. of male given name *Isaac*, regarded as a typical Jewish name] a Jewish man or boy.—used derisively.—also used attrib.

    *1864 Hotten *Slang Dict.* (ed. 3): *Ikey,* a Jew "fence." **1889** Barrère & Leland *Dict. Slang* I 481: *Ikey* (popular), a Jew. **1900** *DN* II 42: *Ikey,* n. A Jew. **1903** Ade *Society* 48: I got into a Poker Game with two of them Ikey Drummers on the Train and trimmed them for 87 Samoleons. **1931** Stevenson *St. Lukes* 28 [ref. to *ca*1910]: Soon Max was being called Ikey. **1950, 1956** in *DARE.* **1980** Ciardi *Browser's Dict.* 220: When I was a boy in Boston in the early 1920's *Ikey* (from Isaac) and Jew were synonyms.

ill *adj.* [prob. sugg. by S.E. *ill* 'suffering from mental illness; (hence, colloquially) markedly demented; "sick"'] *Rap Music.*
  1.a. crazy; offensive; rowdy; aggressive; (*broadly*) bad.

    1979 "Sugar Hill Gang," in L.A. Stanley *Rap* 325: Act civilized or act real ill. **1985** "Run-DMC" *My Adidas* (rap song): Now me and my Adidas do the illest thing, We like to stamp out pimps....It's time to get ill. **1986** "Beastie Boys" *Rhymin' & Stealin'* (rap song): Most illin'est B-boy....I am most ill. **1987** "EPMD" in B. Adler *Rap!* 67: No need to act ill....You gots to chill. **1991** Nelson & Gonzales *Bring Noise* 197: "Times Are Gettin' Ill" used live rhythm guitar. **1992** in N. George *Buppies, B-Boys* 68: Where rugged individualism has corroded into survival of the illest. **1994** in C. Long *Love Awaits* 52: Disrespecting a Black woman is some ill shit. That...ticks me off.

  b. unexpected; weird.

    1995 *Spin* (May) 14: Dude, you don't even know how ill it was....One second I was crashing on my agent's couch, then in one month it [*sc.* my business and popularity] exploded.

  2. excellent; CRAZY.

    1991 Nelson & Gonzales *Bring Noise* 91: Jazz...it's like real ill, and...it'll put you in a mood. *Ibid.* 140: Dressed to kill, her physique is ill. **1994** in Stavsky, Mozeson & Mozeson *A 2 Z* 53: Aside from the shit that he writes, his voice is what's so *ill* about him. **1996** *New Yorker* (Aug. 26) 88: All they cared about was how dope, how ill, how phat was the vibe.

  3. (see quot.).

    1993 Eble *Campus Slang* 4: *Ill*—angry, frustrated, disgusted. Also *pissed off.*

ill *v.* [fr. ILL, *adj.*; see also ILLING] Esp. *Rap Music.* **1.** to think or act wildly, irrationally, or crazily.—also used trans. [It is often not possible to distinguish this verb used in progressive tenses fr. ILLING, *adj.*, used predicatively; all but the unmistakably verbal exx. have been placed at ILLING, *adj.*]

    1986 "Beastie Boys" *Licensed to Ill* [rap album title]. **1987** "Schooly D" *Saturday Night* (rap song): I wanted to chill....She wanted to ill. **1988** "Slick Rick" *Treat Her Like a Prostitute* (rap song): The ho starts to ill;/She says, "I love you, Harold," and your name is Will. **1990** *New Yorker* (Sept. 10) 68: A girl...had made fun of a disabled boy, calling him a cripple. He "illed" her in return.

  2. (see 1995 quot.).

    1992 in Stavsky, Mozeson & Mozeson *A 2 Z* 53: Moe was out in Brooklyn *illin'.* **1995** Stavsky, Mozeson & Mozeson *A 2 Z: Illin'*...performing superbly.

illegit *adj.* illegitimate. Occ. as n.

    1945 Drake & Cayton *Black Metropolis* 610: Policy is technically "on the illegit," but it is a protected business. *Ibid:* On the illegit—illegal. **1952** H. Grey *Hoods* 16: Don't you know everybody's a crook? Everybody's illegit? **1954** Collans & Sterling *House Detect.* 34: The real problems were the female of the species, the Legits and the Ille-

gits. **1959** Goffman *Presentation of Self* 215: Con men...in what they call the "illegit" world. **1980–86** in Steffensmeier *Fence* 20: The legit helps the illegit, and vice versa.

illing *adj.* [see note at ILL, *v.,* 1] Esp. *Black E.* **1.** acting or thinking wildly, irrationally, or crazily; crazy. See also ILL, *v.,* 1. Usually as pron.-spelling **illin[']**.

    1986 "Run-D.M.C." *You Be Illin'* [rap song title]. **1986** Eble *Campus Slang* (Mar.) 6: *Illing*—problemsome or troublesome: "George said bad things about Claude last night. George is illing bad." **1987** P. Munro *U.C.L.A. Slang* 18: *Illin'*—stupid. **1988** S. Lee *School Daze* (film): "I'm gonna cut her loose."..."You illin' man." **1988** LeMay et al. *Facts on File Dict. New Words* 60: Illin is gaining widespread usage with the verb "be," as a slang term for crazy: "You is illin, turning down a deal like that." *a*1990 P. Dickson *Slang!* 220: *Illin'.* Stupid. **1991** *Village Voice* (N.Y.C.) (Nov. 19) 44: Some extremely illin' bouncers wore surgical gloves, no doubt to protect themselves from any tragic traces of fabulousness. **1992** "Fab 5 Freddy" *Fresh Fly Flavor* 35: *Illin'*—Acting wild and crazy. **1995** *House of Buggin'* (Fox-TV): Make as much mad, crazy, illin' noise as you want.

  2. unhappy; displeased. Usually as pron.-spelling **illin[']**.

    1988 *Daily Beacon* (Univ. Tenn.) (Jan. 19) 6: I said my main man Bif got a bump on the head./We were really illin cause we thought he was dead. **1989** P. Munro *U.C.L.A. Slang* 18: He was illin' when he found out he didn't pass his philosophy class.

illume *n. Mil.* illumination rounds.

    1971 *Playboy* (Aug.) 212: The 105s have run out of illume. **1983** Ehrhart *VN-Perkasie* 74: That's a roger on the illum, One. **1984** Hammel *Root* 209: Ferraro's grenadier popped the illume.

imaginitis *n.* [*imagine* + -ITIS] an overactive imagination.

    1955 N.Y.C. man, age *ca*70: I think you got imaginitis. **1966** Bogner *Seventh Avenue* 32: "He's got imaginitis," Al said, giving Jay a fishy look.

I-man *n. Trucking.* (see 1971 quot.).

    1938 in *AS* (Apr. 1942) 103: *I-men.* I.C.C. investigators. **1971** Tak *Truck Talk* 81: *I-men:* investigators from the Interstate Commerce Commission. **1978** Wheeler & Kerby *Steel Cowboy* (film): What with the D.O.T. and I-men and the Highway Patrol not makin' things any easier.

imby *n.* an imbecile.

    1981 Sann *Trial* 47: The imby blew it. *Ibid.* 116: Hey, imby....You gotta straighten up and fly right.

immense *adj.* perfectly splendid; wonderfully exciting.

    *1762 in *OED2:* Here's cream—damn'd fine—immense—upon my word! **1771* in *F & H* IV 2: Dear Bragg, Hazard, Loo, and Quadrille, Delightful! extatic! immense! **1856** Wilkins *Young N.Y.* 33: She's an immense brick, that woman. **1863** in Whitman *Corres.* I 82: It is immense, the best thing of all, nourishes me of all men. **1864** Kirke *Down in Tenn.* 88: Long Tom...is an incorrigible wag, and "immense" at telling a story. **1877** in F. Remington *Sel. Letters* 17: I am reading "Great Expectations"...and its immense. If he hadn't started off with something bout soldiers I never would have read it. **1881** in *Mo. Hist. Review* XXXVII (1942) 263: That game of ball...must have been immense. **1883** Peck *Peck's Bad Boy* 248: Pa said it [*sc.* the plan] was immense. **1885** Ingersoll *Crest of Continent* 292: And as for wheat, sir,—wheat? why it's immense! **1889** "M. Twain" *Conn. Yankee* 415: Ah, well, it was immense; yes, it was a daisy. **1890** Munroe *Orders* 25: That's an immense plan. **1895** Gore *Student Slang* 20: *Immense*...Fine, enjoyable. "The show was immense." **1899** in S. Crane *Complete Stories* 632: It's immense! Come on over! **1901** Bull *Flashes* 34: Everything seems under full headway; it's immense! **1902** in Kipling *Traffics & Discoveries* 6: Laughtite's immense; so's the Zigler automatic. **1906** Kildare *Bailiwick* 92: That is where O'Dowd was voted "immense."

immies *n.pl.* [fr. a type of playing marble] the eyes.

    1947 S.J. Perelman *Westward Ha!* 18: You certainly ought to set Singapore aflame with those immies in your head. **1981** Graziano & Corsel *Somebody Down Here* 37: Junked up to where his immies turn into little beads.

immortal *n. U.S. Mil. Acad.* a cadet near or at the bottom of his class.

    1878 Flipper *Colored Cadet* 288 [ref. to 1874]: In going over this course again he stood very high in his class, but when it was finished he began going down gradually until he became a member of the last section of his class, an "immortal," as we say, and in constant danger of being "found." **1889** Jayne *On Trail of Geronimo* 8: He vibrated between the first and second section, but was haunted by the continual horror of landing at the bottom among "the immortals." **1894** Putnam *Offensive* 38: Nearly all of them graduated somewhere about the immortals.*...*The word is applied at West Point to cadets who lag at the foot of their class. **1900** (quot. at GOAT, 2.b.).

immortal *adj.* splendid; wonderful.
    1846 (quot. at TILE).

implement *n.* a weapon. *Joc.*
    1870 Duval *Big Foot* 114: "You ought, by all means, to have your implements with you," (meaning, of course, a rifle and revolver).

import *n.* Esp. *Stu.* a date brought from another location to attend a dance or party.
    1926 Hormel *Co-Ed* 19: Six weeks after, Lucia made her appearance in university circles as an "import." **1968** Baker, Ladd & Robb *CUSS* 142: *Import.* Date from another school. **1969** Bouton *Ball Four* 272: And if a player, coach or manager should bring a girl with him to another city, she's called an *import*. If an import is a *mullion*, she may have to pay her own way.

improv *n. Theat.* improvisation; improvising.—also used attrib.
    1982 Sculatti *Catalog of Cool* 170: A black-turtlenecked improv actor. **1984** Heath *A-Team* 114: We're going to have to do some fast improv here, and we'll need all the props we can get. **1994** Advertising flyer for comedy group: Atomic Pile...Winner of the New York Improv Festival for best improv group in the city.

in *n.* **1.** *Und.* an entrance, as to a place to be robbed.
    1930 in D.W. Maurer *Lang. Und.* 49: Where's the in to this joint?

2. *Specif.*, a means of access, esp. to an influential person; *(also)* influence or special favor with such a person.
    1929 in Hammett *Knockover* 51: She didn't mean anything to him but an in to the old man's pockets. **1929** E.D. Sullivan *Look at Chicago* 21: His strong "in" with police. **1930** Lait *On the Spot* 205: I've got an in with the Chief. **1935** C.J. Daly *Murder* 238: But I've got an "in" with the Count. **1935** Sistrom *Hot Tip* (film): It's the missus I got my in with. **1939** Goodman & Kolodin *Swing* 68: He had an "in" at the hotel. **1943** Wolfert *Tucker's People* 106: Leo had no "in" downtown. He knew no one who could do business for him there. **1946** Steinbeck *Wayward Bus* 55: And if her cousin was Clark Gable, why, that was an "in" you couldn't beat. **1947** Schulberg *Harder They Fall* 10: If the kid is good, smarter managers with better "ins" always steal him away. **1956** Resko *Reprieve* 181: It would give us an immediate and solid "in" in the chaplain's office. **1957** E. Lacy *Room to Swing* 154: You have the "in" and I have the outfit. **1994** A. Heckerling *Clueless* 78: I'm new but maybe you've got an in with the heavy clambakes [i.e., parties]. **1995** N.Y.C. man, age 27 (coll. J. Sheidlower): I think I can get you an in with [an important magazine].

in *adj.* **1.** exhausted; ALL IN, 1.
    1922 *Variety* (July 28) 5: Eddie has been consolin' her and tellin' her that he ain't in, and will stage a comeback.

2. having intimate understanding; in the know; *(hence)* esoteric.
    1960 *Many Loves of D. Gillis* (CBS-TV): "Are you in?" "The innest." **1960** in *OED2*: Vegas (as we "in" people call Las Vegas). ***1969** in *OED2*: Its idiomatic "in" vocabulary.

3. extremely fashionable or sophisticated.
    ***1961** in *OED2*: In N.Y....the in-thing to do is to pronounce Broadway. **1962** Quirk *Red Ribbons* 155: The sons of top people envied the athlete. Swimming was "In" at Yale. **1963** *N.Y. Times Mag.* (Nov. 24) 50: The currently popular (or "in") children's slang. **1966** Susann *Valley of Dolls* 438: Her large parties drew all the "in" people. **1968** in L. Williams *City of Angels* 40: A new "in" place at every corner. **1971** *Love Youth & Drug Problem* 66: For these kids it is "the in thing to do." **1977** Flusser *Squeal Man* 179: The "in" discotheques of the 1960's. **1979** W. Cross *Kids & Booze* 43: They can look pretty cool to kids. *In*, I mean. **1984** *Kate & Allie* (CBS-TV): Americana is very in. **1986** P. Welsh *Tales Out of School* 102: Mark was moving with the "in" white crowd. **1986** B. Clayton & N. Elliott *Jazz World* 13: Jazz was just beginning to become the "in" thing. **1987** Ford & Chase *Awakening* 34: It was the "in" way to travel. **1993** *New Yorker* (Nov. 15) 107: "Right now cute Jewish is 'in,'" Tom Snyder commented...to explain the popularity of "Seinfeld."

in *adv.* [Certain of the following senses approach adjectival force.]

1. to or into prison.
    [**1848** Thompson *House Breaker* 30: "What are you *in* for?" "Stealing a door-mat," answered the Captain, disposed to be jocose.] **1903** A.H. Lewis *Boss* 19: I say they're both to go in. **1976** *Deadly Game* (ABC-TV movie): We got a case. You're goin' in.

2. assured of or having achieved success in a particular endeavor. See also *in like Flynn* s.v. FLYNN, an intensive var. of this sense.
    1907 in H.C. Fisher *A. Mutt* 3: S-h-h-h. Not a woid. This one's "in."...Put 500 on Serenity. **1939** "E. Queen" *Dragon's Teeth* 19: "He forgot his fountain-pen." "We're in that much, anyway." **1944** F.G. Lieb *Cardinals* 165: The New York club was considered "in" to such a degree that a national magazine...had the Giants battling the Detroit Tigers in the Series. **1960** Simak *Worlds* 22: Those gadgets sold like hot cakes and we knew we were in!

3.a. in a special or protected relationship, as with the authorities, esp. as a result of political influence or corruption.—often constr. with *right*; in phr. **in and in** emphatically so.
    1908 Sullivan *Crim. Slang* 13: "In right."—A man getting an easy living by political methods. **1908** in H.C. Fisher *A. Mutt* 45: Atty. Hash is now more confident than ever that Tobasco has the judge already "in." **1909** Chrysler *White Slavery* 21: I would like to locate [a brothel] here, but I want to get in "right." **1911** (quot. at HEP, *adj.*). **1920** *Variety* (Sept. 10) 5: They don't stand for everybody up there. And I'm in right. **1921** *Variety* (Nov. 25) 9: Despite Being "In," Shore Pulled Out in Police Raid....It was understood Shore was "in" with the administration. **1924** G. Henderson *Keys to Crookdom* 408: *In right.* Properly protected from the authorities. **1925–26** Black *You Can't Win* 131 [ref. to 1890's]: That's why you are declared "in and in" with the works.

b. (of persons) accepted or in favor socially.
    1929 Zombaugh *Gold Coast* 49: A constant struggle on the part of those who are not "in" to break into the circles of those who are. **1949** *Ladies' Home Jour.* (Nov.) 120: In one school, to be Polish American is to be "in," to be Italian American is to be "out." **1950** C.W. Gordon *High School* 55: You had to be in good with the major part of the school. *Ibid.* 121: People who are not "in" pay no attention [to fashions in shoes]. **1961** *Life* (Sept. 1) 48: "If you're not a surfer," explains one high school surfer, "you're not 'in.' If you're a good surfer, you're always in. All you've got to do is walk up and down the beach with a board and you've got girls." **1986** Clayton & Elliott *Jazz World* 194: The guys who are "in," to the extent that they play golf with all of the principal buyers. **1994** *Sally Jessy Raphaël* (synd. TV series): She wasn't part of the *in* crowd.

¶ In phrases:

¶ **get [it] in** to achieve intromission of the penis; *(hence)* to engage in sexual intercourse.—usu. considered vulgar. Cf. earlier *get into* s.v. INTO, *prep.*
    [**ca*1775 *Frisky Songster* 37: O then, says Jenny, I fear you'll be in me.] **1929** in E. Wilson *Twenties* 524: Her brother-in-law...always used to be asking, "Well, did Mr. Wilson get it tonight?—Why don't you let poor Mr. Wilson get it in?" **1947** Schulberg *Harder They Fall* 267: Maybe I got a dirty mind, but if Toro isn't getting in, Ruby's not the girl I've heard she is. **1951** Sheldon *Troubling of a Star* 72: If she likes you, and everything clicks, you can probably get in. **1952** Ellson *Golden Spike* 29: "I just went to see her."..."You get in?" "She ain't that kind." **1957** Laurents & Sondheim *West Side Story* 141: ANYBODYS: Riff, how about me gettin' in the gang now? A-RAB: How about the gang gettin' in—ahhh, who'd wanta! **1958** Appel *Raw Edge* 287: Ten-to-one you'd have to get in with dynamite. **1963** in Ellison *Sex Misspelled* 44: But don't lie to me, did he get in? **1970** G. Walker *Cruising* 43: What a man wanted was to get *in*. He didn't want anyone getting into *him*. **1972** A.K. Shulman *Ex-Prom Queen* 60: In the five months I had been going with Joey he'd come closer to "getting in" than anyone else, but I had always managed to resist. **1989** Berent *Rolling Thunder* 54: Silk Screen Sam, the ladies' man / If he can't get in, no one can.

¶ **in bad** see s.v. BAD.

¶ **in for** eager or ready for.
    1855 Doten *Journals* I 213: After supper all hands were "in for a bender." **1901** S.E. Griggs *Overshadowed* 156: Bully, Lanier, bully. I am in for it....I want a little fun....Yes, I am in for it.

¶ **in tough** *Horse Racing* (see quot.).
    1968 Ainslie *Racing Guide* 469: *In tough*—Of a horse entered with animals it is unlikely to beat.

¶ **in wrong, 1.** in disfavor or trouble.

1906–07 Ade *Slim Princess* 55: This is a shine country, and you're in wrong, little girl. **1911** A.H. Lewis *Apaches of N.Y.* 48: I never squealed to nobody. Do youse think I'd put poor Johnny in wrong? **1929** Hammett *Maltese Falcon* 127: Dixie got in wrong with the rest of the boys over some debts he couldn't…pay off. **1928–30** Fiaschetti *Gotta Be Rough* 33: Dopey Joe's in wrong with the Orchard Street gang. **1931** Wilstach *Under Cover Man* 219: All they do is get the police in wrong. **1958** S.H. Adams *Tenderloin* 110: I don't want to see a square-shooter like you get in wrong.

2. mistaken; at fault.

1913 J. London *Valley of Moon* 38: We don't want a row. You're in wrong. They ain't nothin' doin' in the fight line. **1918** *Chi. Sun. Trib.* (Mar. 17) V (unp.): But I'm afraid you're in wrong.—I mean you're makin' a mistake. **1921–25** J. Gleason & R. Taber *Is Zat So?* 13: Now don't go crabbin' when you're in wrong.

in *prep. Gamb.* **1.** in debt to. Cf. *be into,* 1.b., s.v. INTO, *prep.*

1925 *Collier's* (Sept. 19) 8: That egg's in me for two grand. **1929** in Segar *Thimble The.* 53: You're in the house for ten thousand an' we've only been shootin' three minutes. **1965** Twist & Susak *None But the Brave* (film): You're already in me for a thousand bucks.

2. in the position of creditor to.

1934 L. Berg *Prison Nurse* 100: The mob was "in him" for a buck sixty and he hadn't kicked in.

¶ In phrases:

¶ **in it, 1.** worthy of comparison or notice; (*hence*) capable; splendid.—usu. constr. with *not.*

1864 in Mohr *Cormany Diaries* 484: Genl. Sheridan is having glorious victories and we are "not in it" with him and our Cavalry Boys. But here is our post of duty, and we are obeying orders. **1891** Clurman *Nick Carter* 24: I kin stand knifin' a man…but when it comes to windin' that cord o' yourn 'round a feller's throat…I ain't in it. **1894** Bunner *More Short Sixes* 71: He…told him a string of stories of such startling novelty, humor and unfitness for publication that…the recent Drummers' Convention could not be said to be "in it" with the old man. **1895** J.L. Williams *Princeton* 48: He'll be in it all right some of these days. **1896** in Robinson *Comics* 161: Barnum ain't in it. **1901** *Our Naval Apprentice* (July) 3: Say, Schappa isn't in it with some of them. **1901** in Bierce *Letters* 46: You are leaving my other "pupils" so far behind that they are no longer "in it." **1902** Mead *Word-Coinage* 180: "Isn't in it" is a term borrowed from the turf. ***1904** Kipling *Traffics* 284: We're told off to 'em in rotation. A wilderness of monkeys isn't in it. **1910** Hapgood *City Streets* 59: By these friends he is greatly respected, particularly by his old father who is not "in it" so thoroughly. **1912** in Truman *Dear Bess* 68: The *strawberry* blond isn't in it with you when you wear that dress. **1914** Dale *Songs of Seventh* 86: But no matter what his voice, it wasn't in it with his snore. **1948** Wouk *City Boy* 170: A billy goat ain't in it with Clever Sam. **1962** *English Journal* (May) 325: *In it*—(adj.) Conforms to your ideas and doings.

2. Orig. *Sports.* having a reasonable chance to win or succeed. Now *colloq.*

1889 Barrère & Leland *Dict. Slang* I 481: A horse on publication of a handicap is said, in describing his prospective chance, to be *in it,* "not *in it,*" or "right bang *in it,*" according to the…judgment of the speaker. **1891** *Nat. Police Gaz.* (Sept. 26) 2: Gibbons was simply not in it. Jack Mauliffe virtually had him whipped from the start. **1891** Maitland *Slang Dict.* 190: *Not in it,* said of a person not likely to succeed, as "Jones is not in the race." **1906** *Independent* (Nov. 29) 1258: FATHER:…The football game did not last so long as last year, I take it? SON: No. Oh—they just weren't in it! That's all!

3. in trouble.

1923 T. Boyd *Through the Wheat* 47: Now we are in it for sure. **1935** H. Cobb *Paths of Glory* 22: You were up to your neck in it at Souchez. **1968** Simoun *Madigan* (film): Come on. Be a sport. I'm up to here in it!

¶ **in (one's)** in (one's) life; for (one's) portion.

1864 in H. Johnson *Talking Wire* 127: We would like to have a little texas or mexico or salt Lake in ours. *Ibid.* 136: I don't want any more Col Collins in mine if I can help it. **1865** in D. Chisholm *Civil War Notebk.* 74: Talk about southern Chivalry I don't want any of it in mine. **1866** in W.H. Jackson *Diaries* 81: A good many…will Bull whack up to Virginia City. Not any in mine, thank you! **1867** in A.K. McClure *Rocky Mtns.* 211: When a Western man declines any proposition…"none of that in mine" is his answer. **1873** *Overland Mo.* (Feb.)

113: He didn't want any more of that in his. **1873** in Applegate & O'Donnell *Talking on Paper* 71: I want no more Indian fighting…in mine. **1882** Peck *Peck's Sunshine* 42: She didn't want any Norwegian literature in hers. **1892** *Outing* (Aug.) 409: No more borrowed dog in mine! **1896** in J.M. Carroll *Benteen-Goldin Lets.* 266: "Custer is trying to keep…his brother Tom…from going to South Carolina." But Tom had to take S.C. in his! **1904** in "High Jinks, Jr." *Choice Slang* 35: Dere'd be no art galleries in mine. **1911** Van Loan *Big League* 176: None of that scandal stuff in mine! **1945** Bellah *Ward 20* 62: I don't want any gimp girls in mine.

¶ **in there** Esp. *Black E.* admirable; doing well; *in the groove* S.V. GROOVE.

1942 *Pittsburgh Courier* (Sept. 19) 7: Charlie felt then that he was "right in there," as the lads who wear the "zoot suits" would say. **1944** Burley *Hndbk. Jive* 60: Listen, Babes, you're really in there, understand? **1955** Shapiro & Hentoff *Hear Me Talkin to Ya* 106: The Lincoln Gardens was…still in there. **1964** R.S. Gold *Jazz Lexicon* 159: *In there*…Of a musician, playing superbly; of anyone, possessing sophistication or wisdom; of any thing or place, exciting or interesting.

in-and-outer *n. Sports.* an inconsistent player or competitor.

1893 in Ade *Chicago Stories* 10: He's an in-and-outer. I wouldn't lay a cent on him. **1898–1900** Cullen *Chances* 67: If ever there was a rank in-and-outer, that horse was Strathmeath. **1949** Cummings *Dict. Sports* 220. **1952** in *DAS:* Reynolds has 30 knockouts among his 52 victories but he has been an in-and-outer.

incest *n.* malicious treatment of one's colleagues for the advancement of one's own career.

1973 W. Crawford *Gunship Cmndr.* 147: You've run with them…and kiss-assed them so much you've come to practice incest just like they do. *Ibid.* 148: The whole army…filed charges against everybody in sight, good old fuck-your-brother week. Tell me that's not incest.

indescribables *n.pl.* [sugg. by *unmentionables*] trousers. *Joc.*

*1794 in *OED2:* Fashion has already begun to sport its vernal variety of indescribables. ***1837** Dickens *Pickwick* ch. xvi: Mr. Trotter…gave four distinct slaps on the pocket of his mulberry indescribables. **1840** *Spirit of Times* (Dec. 12) 487: Old "suckers" of fifty who have just parted with the buttons from their indescribables.

Indian *n.* **1.a.** an uncouth or unruly person; troublemaker; (in 1972–76 quot.) an enemy soldier.—now usu. considered offensive.

[**1843** "J. Slick" *High Life in N.Y.* 10: I don't believe such a lot of white Inguns ever got together before.] **1849** in Chittick *Roarers* 248: Git up, you lazy Injun. **1896** Ade *Artie* 30: Yes, but this guy's an Indian. He won't do. He don't belong.…That Indian's got to keep clear off o' that street. **1903** in F. Remington *Sel. Letters* 340: Say—you indian—I am working like hell here. **1909** in O. Johnson *Lawrenceville* 35 [ref. to 1890's]: Jump, you Indian, jump! **1930** Graham & Graham *Queer People* 96: The only way to save it is to send for some liquor and let these Indians drink and fight. **1937** *Rev. of Reviews* (June) 43: *Indian*—A speeder. **1968** Algren *Chicago* 124: To where Honest Cop/ Was throwing the night's last Indian out of the last bar/Left unlocked. **1972–76** Durden *No Bugles* 123: Cambodia? There's more fuckin' Indians there than there is here.

b. a person; in phr. **big Indian** a person of importance.—now often considered offensive. Also as quasi-adj.

1861 in C.W. Wills *Army Life* 37: I have four men a day to guard the prisoners and two orderlies to send errands for me, so I play big injun strongly. **1862** in *Jour. Ill. Hist. Soc.* XVIII (1926) 831: Sonny,…are you sesesh or friendly Ingins. **1867** in W. Morgan *Amer. Icon* 117: [He is a] big Ingin. **1874** Ewert *Diary* 66: Ree [remained] a big Injun all the evening. **1876** J.M. Reid *Old Settlers* 112: Augustus Caesar Dodge…was the big injin of the Democratic party. **1880** in Rosa *Gunfighter* 41: Meeting an eligible candidate for a place in his graveyard he emits his stereotyped oath and "blazes away." This…is termed…"getting the drop on his Injun"…"getting the bulge on the bloke." *a***1881** G.C. Harding *Misc. Writings* 323: Col. Burke was the "big Injun" of Camp Pratt. **1881** Crofutt *Gde. to Colo.* 101: Grant [Colo.] is not as "Big Injin" as the Grant for whom it is named. **1882** *United Service* (July) 107: There's a dead Injian anyhow, 'cause I thort he went clean through the boat's bottom. **1898** Riis *Mulberry St.* 77: General Ely S. Parker was the "big Indian" of Mulberry street in a very real sense. **1898** in S. Crane *Stories* 413: You Indians better go home. **1905** Belasco *Golden West* 324: Ha! I'm your Injun. **1908** J. London *M. Eden* 160: He's a good Indian, that boy….A good Indian. **1911** A.H. Lewis *Apaches of N.Y.* 106: Hippomenes [is] a fly Indian. **1913** *Sat. Eve. Post* (July 5) 4: He's a pretty wise Injun. **1922** E. Murphy *Black Candle* 70: Incorrigible or feeble-minded girls think, by indulging in these drugs they are "good Indians" and "playing the game." **1926** Dunning & Abbott *Broadway* 244: Besides, maybe I saved you from getting shot up by this Indian. **1972** Jenkins *Semi-Tough* 16: There ain't no smoke come off these Indians yet. **1977** Univ. Tenn. student: Look at that Indian go! **1987** Lipper *Wall St.* 162: Cromwell's a dead Indian.

2. whiskey.

1889 Barrère & Leland *Dict. Slang* I 487: Invitations to drink (American)…*Try a little Indian?*

3. (one's) anger or temper.—now often considered offensive. Cf. similar use of Dutch, Irish, etc.

1889 Barrère & Leland *Dict. Slang* I 487: *Irish, Indian, Dutch* (American), all…are used to signify anger or arousing temper. But to say that one has his "*Indian* up" implies a great degree of vindictiveness. **1893** in *DARE*: My "old Injun" was up, and I had "sailed in" for a fight. **1893** in *DA:* It woke Colonel John Forney up to very highest pitch of his fighting "Injun," or, as they say in Pennsylvania, his "Dutch." **1942** Garcia *Tough Trip* 152: Old Gabriel got his Injun up too and started into the tepee to get his gun to kill the buck that had said that. **1994** *Donahue* (NBC-TV): I was mad. The Indian came out in me.

4. [sugg. by the Indian head formerly appearing on pennies] a penny.

1893 Macdonald *Prison Secrets* 311: The borrowed penny…inherits the twelve "Indians" in the "pot."

¶ (In usu. vulgar prov. phrs.).

1939 O'Brien *One-Way Ticket* 9 [ref. to *ca*1925]: The wind blowin' like a bat outa hell and snow ass-deep to a tall Indian. **1953** *Jour. Amer. Folklore* LXVI (Oct.) 291: Hence a thing could be said to be three inches less than hip-deep to a tall Indian. *a***1956** Almirall *College to Cow Country* 399 [ref. to *a*1918]: Out…where the snow lies waist deep on a tall Indian and the wind howls. *Ibid.* 410: The snow gets hip-high on a tall Indian, hereabouts. **1956** N. Algren *Wild Side* 153: "How tall *are* you, Shorty?"…"About ass-high to a tall Indian." **1958** McCulloch *Woods Words* 86: *Hip deep to a tall Indian*—A measure of snowfall, or mud. **1963** Boyle *Yanks Don't Cry* 25 [ref. to WWII]: And those babies are headed for this rock just as straight as a tall Indian going for a crap! **1963** Rifkin *K. Fisher's Rd.* 150: I'm headin' for a drink straightern' an Indian goin' to shit. **1972** *Nat. Lampoon* (June) 4: A…thingie that bears more than a passing resemblance to wear [*sic*] the Indian hit Mom with his hatchet [i.e., the vagina]. **1988** Dietl & Gross *One Tough Cop* 31: I never saw so many bosses. All chiefs and no Indians.

Indiana pants *n. Horse Racing.* hobbles.

1949 Cummings *Dict. Sports* 221. **1979** Cuddon *Dict. Sports & Games* 464.

Indian burn *n. Juve.* brief redness and pain inflicted on someone, usu. another child, by grasping his forearm with both hands and twisting the skin sharply in opposite directions. Also as v.

1956 N.Y.C. schoolboys: Give him an Indian burn! **1960** in *DARE*: He began twisting her arm one way with one hand, the other way with the other, Indian-burning. **1967** G. Green *To Brooklyn* 235 [ref. to 1930's]: They subjected him to "Indian wrist-burn," grabbing his arms and twisting the skin in opposite directions. **1980, 1981, 1985, 1988** in *DARE* [ref. to 1950's]. **1994** S. Johnson, C. Marcil et al. *Ensucklopedia* (unp.): *Indian burn*—Kinda like, when you spank some dude's arm for him? **1995** N.Y.C. woman, age 61: Indian burns really used to hurt!…Nasty kids. I got one when I was six or eight [1940–42].

Indian country *n.* **1.** *Mil.* enemy-held territory.—now usu. considered offensive. Also **Indian territory.**

1945 R.J. Casey *Where I Came In* 48: At 4:00 P.M. we were off Cape Finistère, not a very long distance from Brest, and, presumably, in Indian country. **1945** J. Bryan *Carrier* 17: 0830. Underway for Indian Country. **1946** Wallace *Patton* 61: As we neared a woods in "Indian country" we would look the situation over carefully first. **1967** *Time* (May 26) 15: Deep in "Indian country," the Viet Cong's jungled heartland. **1969** Yates & Roberts *Bridge at Remagen* (film): That's Indian country out there. Loose Germans everywhere. **1973** Huggett *Body Count* 116: This is fucking Injun country. Ain't nothin' between us and

North Vietnam except a couple of hills and the Ben Hai River. **1988** F.C. Berry *Chargers* 116: This was true "Indian country," the stronghold of NVA units for years. **1991** *Village Voice* (N.Y.C.) (Aug. 27) 53: Middle-aged generals…referred to Iraqi-occupied Kuwait as "Indian country." **1993** Carhart *Iron Soldiers* 230: We're flying over…real "Indian country" [in Iraq, 1991]. **1996** *JAG* (NBC-TV): Indian territory. That's what we used to call the bush in Nam.

2. *Av.* general aviation air space, where many private aircraft may be encountered.—now usu. considered offensive.

1989 "Capt. X" & Dodson *Unfriendly Skies* 69: A space that's reserved for "general aviation." Among airline pilots, we refer to this as "Indian Country."

Indian drawers *n.pl. Mil.* (see 1983 quot.).—now often considered offensive. *Joc.*

1961 Garrett *Which Ones Are the Enemy?* 21 [ref. to *ca*1950]: The G.I. undershorts get all wrinkled and crawly—"Indian drawers," the old-timers called them—when you sweat a lot. **1983** Elting, Cragg & Deal *Soldier Talk* 359: *Indian drawers* (1930s; Marines) A type of issue underwear that would "creep up on you and cut you."

Indian rub *n. Juve.* Dutch rub. Cf. Indian burn.

1989 *Mystery Sci. Theater* (Comedy Channel TV): They'd…give you an Indian rub, like this.

Indian sign *n.* Esp. *Sports.* a decisive advantage or malevolent power over someone; hex or jinx; certainty of defeat.—now often considered offensive.

[**1850** Garrard *Wah-to-yah* 333: A California Indian…ran…far out toward the foiled enemy, making the Indian sign of insult and derision; and, in Spanish, abusing them most scandalously.] **1908** H. Green *Maison* 212: He's got the Injun sign on that dame. **1908** in H.C. Fisher *A. Mutt* 46: To have one's goat is to have one buffaloed, or the Indian sign on one's contemporaries. **1908** in Fleming *Unforgettable Season* 284: He seems to have the Indian sign on the [batters] from Coogan's Bluff. **1911** Van Loan *Big League* 134: They've got half the umpires scared, and they'll try to hang the Indian sign on you. **1912** Mathewson *Pitching* 6: Five hits out of five times at bat.…He's just got the Indian sign on you. That's all. **1914** *Collier's* (Aug. 1) 6: Kernohan can make monkeys out of most of the batters in this league, but Speck Adams has got the Indian sign on him. **1914** Patten *Lefty* 69: He's got the Injun sign on you off-side sluggers. **1915** "High Jinks, Jr." *Choice Slang* 50: *Indian sign*—A sign of being overawed, intimidated, or "buffaloed." **1922** *Sat. Eve. Post* (June 3) 130: That boy sure has the Indian sign on our lads. **1928** Bodenheim *Georgie May* 60: Don' be putting no Indeeun sign on me—. **1930** Graham & Graham *Queer People* 91: This old girl…must have the Indian sign on me. **1933** W.C. MacDonald *Law of .45's* 43: I've got the Injun sign on you from now on. **1939** Fessier *Wings of Navy* (film): I've got the Indian sign on that kid. **1939** Swerling & Presnell *The Real Glory* (film): What's the Indian sign you got on those other kids anyway? **1944** R. Adams *West. Words* 83: To put the Indian sign on someone meant to hex or curse him with some kind of witchcraft, also to get him where you want him. **1947** Nolte *Law of the Lash* (film): You're to blame for this. You put the Indian sign on us when you stole that woman's rings. **1961** Plantz *Sweeney Squadron* 233: "You sure must have the Indian sign on him, the way he recommended you—." **1994** *Time Trax* (synd. TV series): He's a burr up your butt.…He's got the Indian sign on you.…He's got you psyched out.

Indian talk *n. Trucking.* (see quot.). *Joc.*

1971 Tak *Truck Talk* 89: *Indian talk:* diesel smoke coming from a smokestack or exhaust pipe.

indie *n.* Esp. *Entertainment Industry.* an independent business, esp. a motion picture or record production company.—also used attrib.

1928 *N.Y. Times* (Mar. 11) VIII 6: *Indies*—Independent producers of pictures. **1936** *Esquire* (Sept.) 160: Indie duals. **1943** *Billboard* (June 26) 6: An indie press agent (not connected with network, station, or ad agency). **1967** *L.A. Times* (Mar. 3) IV 17: Then the indies began to fight the giants on their own terms: reruns of network shows. **1973** *Pop. Science* (Apr.) 163: The "indies" don't make their own gas; they buy it from the major companies' refineries. **1981** *Rod Serling's Mag.* (July) 35: A zombie will get dozens of indies to book *Strange, Isn't It?* **1987** *Campus Voice* (Winter) 31: Since we're on an indie label, we need money. **1987** *Newsweek* (Apr. 6) 64: "Indies" make more movies than the studios. **1992** *Rolling Stone* (Jan. 23) 41: Nirvana is the first of the slew of indie bands that made the jump to a major label.

Indo *n.* an Indonesian.

    ***1965** S.J. Baker *Australian Lang.* 368 (ed. 2): *Indo*, Indonesia (n). This word was mainly used by Australia's "yellow press," beginning in 1958, to fit headings. **1974** *N.Y. Post* (Jan. 16) 16: Indos Riot for 2d Day Vs. Tanaka. **1977** *N.Y. Post* (Dec. 21) 22: Indos free 10,000.

indo *n.* [prob. a clipping of *Indo*nesia] *Black E.* marijuana.

    1993 "Snoop Doggy Dogg" *Ain't No Fun* (rap song): I'd never have no motherfuckin' indo to smoke. **1993** "Snoop Doggy Dogg" *Gin & Juice* (rap song): Rollin' down the street, smokin' indo, sippin' on gin and juice. **1994** *Street Terms: Indo*—marijuana, term from Northern CA. **1995** Stavsky, Mozeson & Mozeson *A 2 Z* 53: *Indo*—n. Indonesian marijuana: I can smell that *indo* from across the street. **1995** *N.Y. Press* (Dec. 13) 25: The future's in marijuana…."Money's in indo," one of the younger guys who lives in that building told me. **1995** Alicea & DeSena *Air Down Here* 62: Walking down the street smoking indo.

indoor golf *n.* the game of craps. *Joc.*

    1927 Thrasher *The Gang* 90: Crap-shooting, or "indoor golf," which has been called the African national game, is learned by gang boys, both white and colored, as soon as they are old enough to handle the dice. **1952** H. Grey *Hoods* 166: Where can we play an interesting little game of indoor golf?

industrial-strength *adj.* extremely powerful, formidable, or oppressive. Cf. HEAVY-DUTY. *Joc.* [Popularized in its literal sense *ca*1969 by television commercials for Janitor In A Drum (trademark of Texize Chemicals, Inc.), advertised as "the industrial-strength floor cleaner."]

    1976 Univ. Tenn. student: I guess she's not ready for my industrial-strength love. **1980** *L.A. Times* (July 16) VI 1: Boy, Sam Fuller is what you call an *industrial strength* film maker. **1987** *Seventeen* (Nov.) 156: This…seems to throw a lot of people into an industrial-strength tizzy. **1988** Univ. Tenn. freshman paper: I blew the speaker in my bass cabinet. Industrial-strength bummer. **1989** R. Miller *Profane Men* 10: An industrial-strength nightmare. **1989** *Time* (June 26) 80: I said I'd never direct again. I had industrial-strength angst. **1990** Nike Air TV ad (Aug. 30): His industrial-strength lungs. **1995** WBIR-TV spot ad (Oct. 27): On your industrial-strength football station—Channel 10!

infant *n. Mil.* an infantryman. *Joc.*

    1861 in J.M. Williams *That Terrible Field* 16: It is more to my interest to remain here with my old "infants."

infit *n.* [in joc. contrast to *outfit*] *Naut.* (see quot.).

    1928 Tilton *Cap'n George Fred* 22 [ref. to 1870's]: I was taken up to Richardson's and there fitted out with an in-fit, which means a suit of shore clothes.

info *n.* information.

    [**1907** H.C. Fisher *A. Mutt* 3: Absorbing a little of the "inside infor."] **1907** T.A. Dorgan, in Zwilling *TAD Lexicon* 48: Now, this is the best "info" you ever got in your life. **1908** in H.C. Fisher *A. Mutt* 23: A piece of "inside info" came his way. **1911** *N.Y. Eve. Jour.* (Jan. 6) 17: Here's the ten, now slip me the info. **1920** *Variety* (Dec. 31) 8: Them was some wicked joints, according to my info. **1921** *Pirate Piece* (Apr.) 3: Some pretty good info on the 2nd B'n. **1930** Lavine *3d Degree* 11: He…is going to…get some "info" on a job. **1930** *Variety* (Jan. 8) 123: "They do worse than that," said the big info man. **1930** Biggers *Chan Carries On* 40: Dig up your own info. **1945** Seaton *Junior Miss* (film): Wait, I'll get the info. **1948** in Steiger *Blue Book* 55: Flight Service advised negative on the aircraft and took the other info, requesting our CO to verify the story. **1962** Shepard *Press Passes* 219: I was delighted at the prospect of getting inside info. **1979** *Rolling Stone* (Jan. 25) 107: He includes info on year of release, original running time, director, [etc.]. **1989** Hiaasen *Skin Tight* 6: Thanks for the info.

ing-bing *n.* [cf. WINGDING] a fit.

    1929 *Sat. Eve. Post* (Apr. 13) 50: If [a convict] goes insane, he *blows his top* or *throws an ing-bing*. **1943** R. Chandler *High Window* 450: "She threw an ing-bing."…"And just what is an ing-bing, Mr. Marlowe?"…"A case of the vapors, they used to call it." **1969** Angelou *Caged Bird* 251 [ref. to 1940's]: She threw her "ing bings" (passionate explosions guaranteed to depilate the chest of the strongest man) and was sweetly sorry (only to me) after.

inhale *v.* to eat or drink, esp. voraciously.

    1884 *Life* (Jan. 10) 18: One of the most powerful tribes that ever stampeded a mule corral or inhaled fire-water. **1902–03** Ade *People*

You Know 21: He sat there and pitied all those who were inhaling it [liquor]. **1904** Ade *True Bills* 41: They…inhaled the Scotch until they were all Pie-Eyed. **1908** McGaffey *Show Girl* 31: A nice gentleman invited me out to inhale a young table d'hote. **1908** in Fleming *Unforgettable Season* 273: Only those who have inhaled said sandwiches know how thin [they are]. **1914** in Lardner *Round Up* 328: Well, they took him in the dinin' room and they tell me he inhaled about four meals at once. **1915** T.A. Dorgan, in *N.Y. Eve. Jour.* (June 17) 14: Your wiff…says that you started inhaling the suds again. **1923** in J. O'Hara *Sel. Letters* 11: I had imbibed some White Rock but not at the same time as I inhaled the hootch. **1937** in Galewitz *Great Comics* 42: "Two sodas—one of which will be for you to inhale."…I could inhale a row of hamburgers. **1971** *N.Y. Times* (Dec. 19) 21: While Garner inhaled lunch, I inquired about "The Caine Mutiny Court-Martial." **1972** Jenkins *Semi-Tough* 55: Eight chili cheeseburgers.…And he inhaled ever one of them cats. **1977** Olsen *Fire Five* 31: A fireman that don't inhale suds is a misfit right away. **1993** *N.Y. Times* (Dec. 1) C6: Chefs do not merely eat—they inhale food. **1996** Nabisco TV ad: Wheat Thin Air Crisps…Inhale 'em!

ink *n.* **1.** a black person.—usu. considered offensive.

    1915 *DN* IV 227: West Texas…*ink*, n. a negro. "We've got a new *ink* for a cook." **1925** (cited in Partridge *Dict. Und.* 354). **1928** Fisher *Jericho* 301: Ink. See *boogy*. **1929** T. Gordon *Born to Be* 220: He had gone into some kind of a manufacturing business with two other inks.

    2.a. cheap red wine; RED INK.

    1917 Imbrie *War Ambulance* 115: Wine was "ink." **1929** in *OEDAS*: *Ink*, wine. This use was restricted to red wine. **1938** *New Yorker* (Mar. 12) 36: Wine is an aid to the hashish smoker and all the pads sell cheap local "ink." **1952** Steinbeck *E. of Eden* 510: Get loaded with ink and they go nuts.

    b. *USMC.* (see quot.).

    1922 *Leatherneck* (Apr. 29) 5: *Ink:* Worcestershire sauce.

    c. bitter coffee.

    1925 Ranck *Doughboys' Book* 14 [ref. to WWI]: They found that "petit dejeuner" consisted of unbuttered war bread with a pot of the "ink" that the Frenchman naively calls coffee. **1927** *AS* (June) 389: Other names for coffee are *ink*, *mud*, *alkali* and *embalming fluid*. **1941** Kendall *Army & Navy Slang* 1: Battery acid…coffee, also known as ink. **1945** *Sat. Rev.* (Nov. 24) 14: *Ink*—coffee.

    3. *Journ.* publicity, esp. in print media; press coverage.

    1953 Wicker *Kingpin* 7: Tucker himself was contemptuous of the *Capital Times'* triumphant ink. **1967–68** von Hoffman *Parents Warned Us* 203: Politicians…were getting a certain amount of cynical ink…by refusing the license. **1970** Libby *Life in Pit* 114: Ink means money, too—better contracts, more and better outside offers. **1974** Dubinsky & Standora *Decoy Cop* 48: The common gripe I hear from cops is that they never get "good ink." **1976** R. Daley *To Kill* 174: Well, they certainly had a lot of ink recently. **1968–77** Herr *Dispatches* 7: Amazing what some of them would do for a little ink. **1983** Stapleton *30 Yrs.* 99: They had captured the imagination of the entire country and were getting all the ink. **1986** *New Yorker* (Mar. 31) 24: I could have gotten him so much more ink than he gets now on his solo number. **1993** *N.Y. Times* (Oct. 17) (Business) 13: A public relations move that helped squeeze a little extra ink out of the splashy deal.

    4. a tattoo or tattoos.

    1984 C. Crowe *Wild Life* (film): I got some new ink. Don't touch. **1995** *New Yorker* (July 10) 72: A prejudice against bikers or people adorned with what bikers call ink.

¶ In phrase:

¶ **sling** [or **splash**] **ink** *Journ.* to write with a pen. Cf. INK-SLINGER, INK-SPLASHER.

    1879 *Puck* (Oct. 22) 522: I can sling ink like a bald-headed hyena of journalism. **1882** Baillie-Grohman *Rockies* 24: Anything will do for them inkslinging tenderfeet. **1888** in *Amer. Heritage* (Oct. 1979) 21: Then the Judge, "My dear boy,/I decidedly think/That you have been slinging/Of late too much ink." **1902** Corrothers *Black Cat Club* 23: 'Tain't evahbody splashes ink lak dat. **1917–20** Dreiser *Newspaper Days* 356 [ref. to 1890's]: You think you're a hell of a feller, dontcha, because you can sling a little ink?

ink *v.* **1.** *Journ.* to sign or persuade to sign. Now *colloq.*

    1940 *Variety*, in *OEDAS* II: William A. Seiter inked a deal to produce and direct two features for Universal. **1940** *AS* XV 204: *Inked*. Signed (of a contract). **1954–60** *DAS: Ink*…v.t. To sign a contract.

1968 G. Vidal, in *OEDAS* II: He promptly inked a multiple nonexclusive contract. **1984** in Dickson *Baseball Dict.* 220: One might...wonder...if Ripken hasn't also inked a contract with the devil. **1988** *N.Y. Post* (June 7) 63: Blues ink Merrimack ace.

2. to tattoo.
> **1987–91** D. Gaines *Teenage Wasteland* 188: Piercing your ears [and] getting inked.

inkbug *n.* a black person.—used derisively.
> **1856** [Burwell] *White Acre* 112: "Sa-hay! ink-bug!...give us a bra-hake down!" *Ibid.* 113: Joe Grant hadn't ought to call him an "ink-bug." It was so unfeeling.

ink-jerker *n.* INK-SLINGER, 1.
> **1865** *Harper's Mag.* (May) 683: This rattle-brained scribbler, this miserable ink-jerker, was about to become a candidate for Congress from the Territory of Nevada! **1915** *DN* IV 207: *Ink-jerker*...a scribbler.

ink pot *n. N.E.* a drinking party in a saloon; (*also*) a disreputable place; DIVE, 1.
> **1903** Kildare *Mamie Rose* 24 [ref. to *ca*1875]: The whisky bottle...was kept well filled....These occasions—no one knows why—are called "ink pots." **1904** *Life in Sing Sing* 256: Ink pot—Resort for low characters.

ink-slinger *n.* **1.** a writer of any kind; (*specif.*) a journalist.
> **1877** Bartlett *Americanisms* 786: *Ink-Slinger.* One who habitually writes for publication; particularly an editor or reporter of a newspaper. **1889** Barrère & Leland *Dict. Slang* 102: "Ink-slinger," a writer. **1891** Maitland *Slang Dict.* 149: *Ink-slinger* (Am.), a writer or editor. **1895** Gore *Student Slang* 20: *Ink-slinger*...a writer. **1902** Cullen *More Tales* 135: A good ink-slinger...kin spread good chin music on paper. **1909** "Clivette" *Café Cackle* 101: I know I can stand off the paper for the advertising as I am a "beauty bright" with ink slingers. **1936** Steel *College* 342: I never trust you inkslingers. **1936** Mackenzie *Living Rough* 11: I just don't happen to be an able enough ink-slinger to describe Alaska. **1966** Kenney *Caste* 98: Yeah, that'll fix that flatheaded ink-slinger. **1976** Hayden *Voyage* 177: A crowd of coal heavers and cranks and ink slingers. **1994** *Perspectives* (Knoxville, Tenn.) (July) 7: Ink Slingers: A reader's review.

2. *Labor.* a clerk or office worker.
> **1889** Barrère & Leland *Dict. Slang* I 484: *Inkslinger* (common), a clerk, a journalist or reporter. *1909** Ware *Passing Eng.* 157: *Inkslinger* (Navy). Purser's clerk. Term of sovereign contempt. **1913** *DN* IV 3: A clerk in a lumber camp...*ink slinger.* **1925** *AS* II (Dec.) 35: The "inkslinger"...keeps the camp's records and conducts the commisary, the railroaders and the cook. **1936** in Botkin *Treas. Amer. Folk.* 221: The fellow tells him he's Johnny Inkslinger and those are figures. **1942** *AS* (Dec.) 222: *Ink Slinger.* A logging camp timekeeper. **1950** *Western Folk.* IX 118: *Ink slinger.* A timekeeper, bookkeeper, or other office worker.

ink-splasher *n.* INK-SLINGER.
> **1908** Whittles *Lumberjack* 77: The clerk is the "ink splasher." **1920** *Our Navy* (Jan.) 8: When Jules Verne wrote "Twenty Thousand Leagues Under the Sea," his most ardent admirers possibly classified him as an irresponsible ink-splasher with an overdeveloped imagination.

inkspot *n.* a black person.—sometimes used derisively.
> **1910** *N.Y. Eve. Jour.* (May 7) 10: You *love* that little ink-spot. **1931** Bontemps *Sends Sunday* 18: Glossy ... fillie ... with little ink-spot jockeys ... resplendent in bright shirts and shining boots. **1966** in *DARE* s.v. *ink.*

ink stick *n.* (among pitchmen) a pen.
> **1942** *ATS* 196: *Ink stick*...a pen. **1943** *Sat. Eve. Post* (Sept. 25) 37: There are the ink-stick workers like Fred the Fountain-Pen Man. **1946** in *DAS*: At 15, Nellie was "making a pitch" with inksticks.

inkwell *n.* the vagina.—usu. considered vulgar.
> **1974** Radano *Cop Stories* 70: And then every once in a while a dab at the old inkwell.

in-law *n. Pros.* a prostitute working for a particular pimp. Cf. WIFE-IN-LAW.
> **1963** T.I. Rubin *Sweet Daddy* 86: She wasn't even one of my chicks.... She was no in-law.

innie *n. Juve.* (see 1973 quots.).
> **1973** *Odd Couple* (ABC-TV): Belly-buttons—there are two kinds—the kind that go in and the kind that go out. I want an outie! No, no! I want an innie! *1973** *Playboy* (June) 64: There's more, but it applies primarily to indented navels—innies. **1974** *N.Y.C.* social worker, age

---

26: Are you an innie or an outie? Does your belly-button go in or out? **1984** J. McCorkle *Cheer Leader* 24: Her navel [is] an "inny." **1989** *Cheers* (NBC-TV): Today my belly-button turned from an innie to an outie. **1989** *Tracey Ullman Show* (Fox-TV): Can you just adjust [your shirt] so that we can't tell if you're an innie or an outie?

-ino *suffix.* -ERINO.
> **1911** in O. Johnson *Lawrenceville Stories* 458: Two brutal sluggerinos who played professional feet-ball in...Chicago.

ins *n.* inside information.
> **1967** Salas *Tattoo* 207 [ref. to *ca*1951]: Rattler, ole buddy, ole shuck, tell me what come down when I out pickin' up Mis-tuh Dixon's busted he-ed? Gimme some ins, ma-han.

insane *adj.* astonishingly good or impressive; CRAZY.
> **1955** in *Tenn. Folk. Soc. Bull.* XXII (1956) 22: *Insane*—very, very good. **1959–60** R. Reisner *Jazz Titans* 159: *Insane:* very good. **1985** J. Dillinger *Adrenaline* 175: He does this Yugoslavian goulash that's really insane.

insect *n. Navy.* an ensign.—used disparagingly.
> **1920** *Atlantic Monthly* (Feb.) 219: Do you know, I think they *started* calling ensigns insects on this ship.

inside *n.* inside information; LOWDOWN.
> **1922** *Variety* (July 14) 5: Scouts...begun pussyfootin' around, tryin' to get the inside on the kid. **1931** Wilstach *Under Cover Man* 5: How to bore into the real inside? **1943** Kurnitz *They Got Me Covered* (film): You gotta give me the inside. **1958** S.H. Adams *Tenderloin* 204: The Big Boy in Mulberry Street knows the inside. **1958** Horan *Mob's Man* 31: All we need is a Chink to give us the inside. **1965** in H. Ellison *Sex Misspelled* 344: We want the truth, the inside. **1983** Olympic Stain ad (WKGN radio) (May 14): We've got the inside on outside protection. **1994** CBS *This Morning* (CBS-TV) (Apr. 21): Can you give us a little inside?

inside *adv. Und.* in or to prison. Occ. as *n.*
> *1888** in *OED2*: A once member of the dangerous classes, who has been "inside" many a time and oft. **1930** *Amer. Mercury* (Dec.) 456: *Inside, v.:* To be incarcerated. "He's inside with a ten space hitch." **1968** in L. Williams *City of Angels* 155: They don't actually put you inside for twenty, or gas you. **1974** Sann *Dead Heat* 55: The bagman...had to go inside but the Mayor himself came out...smelling like a...rose. **1974** R. Novak *Concrete Cage* 125: You mean you'd rather spend the rest of your life inside? **1976** *Deadly Game* (ABC-TV): Now I'm carryin' dope. I been inside before. And I ain't goin' again. **1980** McLendon *Macon's Run* 21: We're squeezing every stooge Inside. **1982** D.A. Harper *Good Company* 1: Two-hundred-forty [dollars] in sixteen months? You been on the *inside*? **1984** Caunitz *Police Plaza* 6: I have no intention of going inside.

inside track *n.* a position of special influence, favor, advantage, or access. Now *S.E.*
> **1872** Burnham *Secret Service* vi: *Inside Track*, the weather-gage; a clear advantage. *Ibid.* 105: He found little difficulty in getting the "inside track"...among the men who were zealously "shoving the queer" in his neighborhood. **1877** Bartlett *Amer.* (ed. 4) 786: *Inside Track.* Some advantage peculiar to the person in connection with whom the expression is used; as, "Robinson had the *inside track* in the whole speculation." **1897** Ladue *Klondyke* 27: Canadians...have emphatically the "inside track" to their own gold fields. **1958** S.H. Adams *Tenderloin* 173: I hear Hardwick has got the inside track with Mrs. C.

instant *adj.* hastily appointed or trained; in phr. **instant NCO** *Army.* a noncommissioned officer appointed after attending an eight-week training course.
> **1965** Bonham *Durango St.* 175: Anyway, you've got these instant cops to keep the peace, haven't you? **1972** T. O'Brien *Combat Zone* 76: The NCO's who go through a crash two-month program to earn their stripes are called instant NCO's; hence the platoon's squad leaders were named Ready Whip, Nestle's Quick, and Shake and Bake. **1985** J.M.G. Brown *Rice Paddy Grunt* 217: "Instant NCOs"...had become sergeants by going to a "shake 'n bake" school back in the world.

intel *n. Mil.* military intelligence; intelligence reports.
> **1972** T. O'Brien *Combat Zone* 143: Intel says this place is bad. **1979** Cassidy *Delta* 117: I've also got an intel written up on the information. **1981** Hathaway *World of Hurt* 107: Wells's got some intel about a VC company down there. **1989** Zumbro & Walker *Jungletracks* 198: Intel...from border sources often "jelled" puzzles up at Division. **1991** La Barge *Desert Voices* 34: They had intel. **1995** *Newsweek* (Nov. 13)

34: A military man who believes so fervently in the importance of accurate "intel."

intense *adj. & interj. Stu.* **1.** deeply satisfying; delightful.

> **1973** U.C.L.A. student: Man, this is intense! **1980** Birnbach *Preppy Hndbk.* 220: *Intense adj.* Anything *really* fun. **1983** Breathed *Bloom Co.* 82: I simply *love* yer car! Oh, it is absolutely *intense!* **1989** P. Munro *U.C.L.A. Slang* 52: Intense...really good, excellent...*Intense!* Wow!

2. (see quot.).

> **1989** P. Munro *U.C.L.A. Slang* 52: Intense...hard, difficult.

international flag *n.* a banknote. *Joc.*

> **1936** Reddan *Other Men's Lives* 31: I found the simplest way was to get around to the back of these food stalls, wave a small piece of the International Flag (dollar bill), thereby keeping from starving to death.

into *prep.* ¶ In phrases:

¶ **be into, 1.** *Gamb.* **a.** to win money from.

> **1894** in Ade *Chicago Stories* 99: "Pink"...had been "got into" for 30 cents. **1902–03** Ade *People You Know* 141: The Poker Players were into him and he began to suspect that he needed a Guardian.

b. to be in debt to.

> **1893** Hampton *Maj. in Washington* 38: "Herk" is into me to the extent of $75. **1908** W.G. Davenport *Butte & Montana* 367: Heinze was "into" the State Savings Bank at one time to the tune of $900,000. **1950** Hecht *Where Sidewalk Ends* (film): You're nineteen grand into us. **1953** Paul *Waylaid* 33: She's into us for $800 already. **1959** on *Golden Age of Television* (A&E-TV) (1988): I know we're already into you for three-fifty. **1967** W. Murray *Sweet Ride* 113: I was into him for a little over two C-notes. **1996** Pool hustler in N.Y.C. (coll. J. Sheidlower): He was into some bookies for some five, six grand.

2. to be interested in, or involved with, curious about, in favor of, etc.; *(often)* to enjoy very much. [In sense 'energetically involved in', the phr. occ. appears as a colloquialism in 19th-C. works; see bracketed quots. Current usage established itself only in the late 1960's.]

> [**1862** C.F. Browne *A. Ward* 45: My frends I've bin into the show biznis now goin on 23 years.] [**1871** "M. Twain" *Roughing It* 328: Well, bye an' bye, up comes this yer quartz excitement. Everybody was into it—everybody was pick'n' 'n' blast'n'.] **1965** *Esquire* (July) 44: Getting involved is *getting into something* and, if you're really into something, naturally you...*take care of business.* **1966** Fariña *Down So Long* 282: You're not into the monkey is why. **1967** Baraka *Tales* 106: Brother, what you in to?...Aw, I aint into shit, man. **1967** in *Rolling Stone Interviews* 23: I'm too far into my guitar to pack it up. **1969** *Newsweek* (Dec. 29) 18: She's gotten into tarot cards. **1970** A. Young *Snakes* 62: Champ say they musicians so they must be into *somethin.* **1970** *Time* (Aug. 17) 32: Into: to be deeply involved ("He's really into acid"). **1970** *Playboy* (Dec.) 122: I got more and more into this dude. **1972** Kopp *Buddha* 222: I had been deeply into reading ancient Chinese poetry. **1985** B.E. Ellis *Less Than Zero* 60: We brought fruit and these cinnamon cookies Blair was really into. *a***1988** Hess, Markson & Stein *Sociology* 209: She must really be into you. You'll score big. **1988** Barbie doll TV ad: We're into Barbie! **1989** *Reporters* (Fox-TV): He was really into getting away from these men. **1992** *House of Style* (MTV): I've always been very into, like, hip-hop and the whole rhythm scene. *****1992** W. Nash *Jargon* 161: Into, to be...a quick fix for smart talkers, used by people who have no time for "have an interest in," or "be an enthusiast for," or "take up as a hobby."

¶ **get into** to effect intromission of the penis into; *(hence)* to succeed in copulating with.—usu. considered vulgar.

> **ca***1866** *Romance of Lust* 62: Why, I am getting into you. **a***1890–96** *F & H* IV 13: To be (or get) *into a woman*...To possess a woman carnally. **1916** Cary *Slang of Venery* I 107: *Getting Into*—To occupy a woman. *Getting Into a Woman*—To possess her. **1941** G. Legman, in Henry *Sex Vars.* II 1167: *Get into.* To pedicate; also, to copulate with a woman. **1954** in Holm & Shilling *Dict. Bahamian Eng.* 86: Well, I love dat goil, so this is the only possible chance that I could get into her. *ca***1967** in *New Yorker* (Jan. 28, 1991) 28: She's wild, that one, I was into her three times. **1976** "N. Ross" *Policeman* 140: You will try to make the waitress....This is the type that you will first try to get into.

intro *v.* to introduce.

> **1986** E. Weiner *Howard the Duck* 3: Intro'd by me.

invite *n.* an invitation. Orig. *S.E.* Now *colloq.*

> *****1659** in *OED2*: Bishop Cranmer...gives him an earnest invite to

England. *****1778** in *OED2*: Everybody bowed and accepted the invite but me. *****1818**, *****1825** in *OED2*. **1834** Caruthers *Kentuck.*, in *DARE*: The whole company stared at me as if I had come without an invite. *ca***1840** in L. Levy *Flashes of Merriment* 17: As oft as I can I decline their invite. **1845** in Robb *Squatter Life* 105: In course, I got an invite. *****1873** Hotten *Slang Dict.* (ed. 4): *Invite*, an invitation—a corruption used by stuck-up people of mushroom origin. Often used, also, by people who know better, from their desire for slang of any kind. **1888** Gunter *Miss Nobody* 232: If poor Van Beekman went to one of these upon Lord Bassington's invite, I—. **1892** Bierce *Beetles* 265: Used to allers git invites.

iodine *n.* bitter coffee.

> **1929** M.A. Gill *Und. Slang: Iodine*—coffee. **1958** McCulloch *Woods Wds.* 95: *Iodine*...Strong coffee.

iodine-slinger *n. Mil.* (see quot.). *Joc.*

> **1922** *Leatherneck* (Apr. 29) 5: *Iodine Slinger*—A member of the Medical Corps. Extract from a book of instructions for Hospital Corpsmen—"When in doubt paint with iodine."

ipsydinxy *n.* whiskey. *Joc.*

> **1849** in Chittick *Roarers* 250: Thar's a few drinks of the *ipsydinxy* left.

Irish *n.* ire; *(hence)* fighting spirit, esp. in an Irish person. Cf. DUTCH, INDIAN, etc.

> **1834** Caruthers *Kentuckian in N.Y.* I 63: It raised the Irish in me pretty quick...for I jumped up and kicked the table over. **1834** in Hendrick & Hendrick *Ham Jones* 126: I dont care a...flint...when my Irish is up. **1849** P. Decker *Diaries* 90: Some one throwed it away which raised his *Irish*. **1872** Bigler *Chronicle* 25: This raised Colonel Smith's Irish a little. **1891** (quot. at *get (someone's) Dutch up* s.v. DUTCH, *n.*). **1906** Ford *Shorty McCabe* 69: One day she gets her Irish up. **1935** Algren *Boots* 147: An' he sure kin scrap all right wunst he gets his Irish up. **1958** Frankel *Band of Bros.* 91: Patrick sure had his Irish up. **1966** Farrar *N.Y. Times Crosswords* 36: Temper: Colloq....*Irish.* **1972** J. Pearl *Cops* 39: His Irish was getting up. **1987** *Wkly. World News* (July 21) 13: The Gipper got his Irish up when he found out that Nancy received a mysterious bouquet of pink carnations from an unknown admirer. **1991–95** Sack *Co. C* 160: His Irish [was] still up.

Irish ambulance *n.* a wheelbarrow.—now usu. considered offensive. *Joc.*

> **1931** Gallegher *Battle of Bolts & Nuts* 109 [ref. to 1918]: I do not think that since the invention of modern methods to move dirt, has ever such a gigantic project been undertaken to move as much dirt as was dug with a pick, shoveled with a hand shovel and moved in an Irish ambulance, as was moved on that job.

Irish apple *n.* a potato.—now usu. considered offensive. *Joc.*

> **a***1890–96** *F & H* IV 14: *Irish-Apple*...A potato. **1950** in *DARE*. **1958** McCulloch *Woods Wds.* 95: *Irish apples*—Potatoes. **1965** E. Hall *Flotsam, Jetsam and Lagan* 311: Aboard ship, potatoes are referred to as Irish apples, and when mashed, they become Irish applesauce. **1968** Spradley *Owe Yourself a Drunk* 31: Supper: terrific—baby beef, dressing, mashed "Irish Apples," [etc.]. **1977** in *DARE*.

Irish applesauce *n.* mashed potatoes.—now usu. considered offensive. *Joc.*

> **1965** (quot. at IRISH APPLE).

Irish apricot *n.* a potato.—now usu. considered offensive. *Joc.*

> *****1785** Grose *Vulgar Tongue: Irish apricots.* Potatoes. *****1846** in *OED2: Irish apricots*, potatoes. **1891** (quot. at IRISH LEMON).

Irish baby buggy *n.* a wheelbarrow.—now usu. considered offensive. *Joc.*

> **1919** Davis *Battery C* 123: Remember?...The Irish baby buggy? **1942** *ATS* 83: Wheelbarrow...*Irish baby-buggy.* **1969** in *DARE*.

Irish banjo *n.* a shovel.—now usu. considered offensive. *Joc.* Cf. BANJO, 2.

> **1941** in *DAS*: Guess we'll set you to strumming an "Irish banjo." **1962** *Western Folk.* XXI 30: *Irish banjo*—a shovel...(Los Angeles, 1960). **1964** Hill *Casualties* 319: Playin' an Irish banjo for the city water department all summer. **1973** B. Phillips *Good Though* [LP recording]: A short-handled shovel they called an Irish banjo.

Irish bouquet *n.* (see quot.).—now usu. considered offensive. *Joc.*

> **1972** R. Wilson *Playboy's Forbidden Words* 16: A stone or rock or any other implement suitable for cracking skulls...*Irish bouquet.*

Irish buggy *n.* a wheelbarrow.—now usu. considered offensive. *Joc.*

> **1928** Panzram *Killer* 53 [ref. to 1907]: My part was...to pack my lit-

tle iron pill and my tools into the Irish buggy and wheel it all back to the prison. **1929** *AS* IV 341: The Vocabulary of Bums...*Irish buggie*—A wheelbarrow. **1936** in *AS* (Feb. 1937) 74: *Irish buggy*—wheelbarrow. **1994** *Smithsonian* (Dec.) 70 [ref. to 1930's]: We called the wheelbarrows "Irish buggies."

Irish caviar *n.* a meat stew.—now usu. considered offensive. *Joc.*
    1937 Wexley & Duff *Angels with Dirty Faces* (film): C'mon, give out with this Irish caviar.

Irish channel *n.* the throat. *Joc.*
    1908 McGaffey *Show Girl* 189: Well, here's down the Irish channel.

Irish chariot *n.* IRISH BUGGY.—now usu. considered offensive. *Joc.*
    1945 Mencken *Amer. Lang. Supp. I* 604: A wheelbarrow was an *Irish chariot* or *buggy*, and there was a stock witticism to the effect that it was the greatest of human inventions, since it had taught the Irish to walk on their hind legs.

Irish cherry *n.* a carrot.—now usu. considered offensive. *Joc.*
    1935 in *AS* (Feb. 1936) 43: *Irish cherries*. Carrots.

Irish chicken *n.* pork.—now usu. considered offensive. *Joc.* Cf. IRISH TURKEY.
    1981 Univ. Tenn. professor: When I was a kid in Albany [N.Y., *ca*1925–30] my mother used to call pork *Irish chicken*. And rocks that the Irish kids used to throw we called *Irish confetti*.

Irish clubhouse *n.* a jail or police station.—constr. with *the*.—now usu. considered offensive. *Joc.*
    1904 *Life in Sing Sing* 256: *Irish Club House*. Police Station....*Ibid.* 259: *He got whipped back to the Irish club house*. He was remanded to the police station. **1925** Mullin *Scholar Tramp* 20 [ref. to *ca*1912]: When you get to the end o' the run, a bull comes round, opens a door, and escorts you politely to the hoosegow—or Irish Club-house, if you prefer a chummy word. **1935** Pollock *Und. Speaks*: *Irish club house*, a police station.

Irish cocktail *n.* a drugged drink.—now usu. considered offensive. *Joc.*
    1980 Ciardi *Browser's Dict.* 248: Mickey Finn...*Irish cocktail.*

Irish confetti *n.* stones or bricks, as thrown in a street brawl.—now usu. considered offensive. *Joc.*
    1913 T.M. Osborne *Pris. Walls* 312: I am personally acquainted with a party who could throw a piece of Irish confetti up in the air, and who, if he didn't duck, would get it on his conk and be reminded of old times. **1917** in Battey *70,000 Miles* 298: "Irish confetti" is the proper name on our ship for bricks. **1918** in Kauffman *Lost Squadron* 68: Kindly check all cabbages, Irish confetti, and decayed henfruit at the door. **1927** Thrasher *Gang* 212: Among the Irish, fighting has been described as a sort of national habit. Bricks are popularly known as "Irish confetti." **1935** Pollock *Und. Speaks*: *Irish confetti*, bricks. **1936** Connie Mack, in Paxton *Sport U.S.A.* 5 [ref. to 1884]: Our ball yard was just a vacant lot littered with Irish confetti—tin cans, plug-tobacco tags and shoe-finding scraps. **1960** *Jour. Amer. Folk.* LXXIII 208: *Irish Confetti*. A synonym for bricks, widely used in the San Francisco building trades by bricklayers and hodcarriers....I have heard bricklayers state that the term also applies to cobblestones lifted from the streets and thrown during riots and strikes. **1981** (quot. at IRISH CHICKEN). **1991** *Houston Chronicle* (Dec. 11) 11B: The [N.Y.C.] cops called these bone-breaking showers "Irish confetti."

Irish dividend *n.* a fictitious or nonexistent profit; deficit; assessment.—now usu. considered offensive. *Joc.*
    1867 A.D. Richardson *Beyond Miss.* 375: Many [mining] companies after immense expenditure reap only assessments, which in this region are termed "Irish dividends." **1868** *Overland Mo.* (July) 53: Some shareholders fell out by the way, discouraged and dismayed at the "Irish dividends," and one by one withdrew in great disgust. **1874** in G.M. Gould *L. Hearn* 37: Whether the Publishing Company will declare "Irish Dividends" in six months, or not, does not concern us. **1881** *Harper's Mag.* (May) 805: Members found themselves in debt and obliged to declare an "Irish dividend" to make the accounts balance. **1890** (quot. at IRISH NECKTIE). **1931–48** in Mencken *Amer. Lang. Supp. II* 773: *Irish dividend*. An assessment on stock. **1967** in *DARE.*

Irish fan *n.* a spade or shovel.—now usu. considered offensive. *Joc.*
    1922 *DN* V 181: *Irish fan*, n. A shovel. Miners in northern Idaho. **1965** O'Neill *High Steel* 272: *Irish fan*: a shovel.

Irish football *n.* a potato.—now usu. considered offensive. *Joc.*
    1971 D. Smith *Engine Co.* 17: Yessir, men, Mrs. O'Mann is cooking

Irish footballs tonight, and she requests that you clean off the tables. *Ibid.* 29: I have lost any hope of being satisfied with a dried-out Irish football.

Irish go-cart *n.* IRISH BUGGY.—now usu. considered offensive. *Joc.*
    1936 *Our Army* (Sept.) 22: Old Bill...is the official driver of those one-wheeled vehicles variously dubbed Georgia Buggies, Irish go-carts or wheelbarrows.

Irish goose *n.* a dish of codfish.—now usu. considered offensive. *Joc.*
    1866 *Night Side of N.Y.* 79: "Give us a plate of Tennessee..." means...hot corn bread, and "Irish goose" is codfish, baked or boiled.

Irish grape *n.* a potato.—now usu. considered offensive. *Joc.*
    1941 Hargrove *Pvt. Hargrove* 83: Potatoes become *Irish grapes*. **1979** in *DARE* s.v. *Irish apple.*

Irish hint *adj.* a broad or unmistakable hint; (*also*) a threat.—now usu. considered offensive. *Joc.*
    1769 in Whiting *Amer. Prov. Phrs.* 234: I believe there will not be the least danger of my getting an Irish hint as they call it. **1834** in *DAE*: Various young men...intimated, in what might be called Irish hints, that they had spied the worthy Mr. Hunt. **1842, 1989** in *DARE.*

Irish horse *n. Naut.* old salted meat.—now usu. considered offensive. *Joc.*
    *1748 Smollett *Roderick Random* ch. xxxiii: Our provision consisted of putrid salt beef, to which the sailors gave the name of *Irish horse*. **1889** *United Service* (Sept.) 274: "Irish horse" is old and tough beef. *a*1914 *Century Dict.* (rev. ed.) s.v. *horse*: *Irish horse*, old pickled beef. (Sailors' slang).

Irish hurricane *n. Naut.* a flat calm at sea. Earlier **Irishman's hurricane.**
    1803 in Whiting *Amer. Prov. Phrs.* 235: "It is almost like an *Irishman's* hurricane." "Right up and down." **1823** J.F. Cooper *Pioneers* 363: The wind has been at all them there marks this very day and that's all round the compass, except a little matter of an Irishman's hurricane at meridium, which you'll find marked right up and down. **1827** J.F. Cooper *Red Rover* 406: It...blew great guns...for the matter of a week. After which there was an Irishman's hurricane, right up and down, for a day. **1840** Dana *Before Mast* 271 [ref. to 1836]: We had, for the most part, what the sailors call "an Irishman's hurricane—straight up and down." This day, it rained nearly all day. **1883** Russell *Sailors' Lang.* xv: An Irishman's hurricane—right up and down; a calm. **1899** Robbins *Gam* 115: The wind...had died out to a calm. It was an Irishman's hurricane, straight up and down. *1929 Bowen *Sea Slang* 72: *Irish hurricane.*—A flat calm with drizzling rain. **1946** Sawyer *Gunboats* [ref. to 1899]: The explanation was given him that an Irish hurricane is the Navy term for a flat calm. **1948** Shay *Amer. Sea Songs* 71: An Irish hurricane was rain and fog on a calm sea. **1975** J. Gould *Maine Lingo* 142: An "*Irish* hurricane" is a "*flat-arse* calm."

Irish inch *n.* an erect penis.—usu. considered vulgar. *Joc.*
    1980 Gould *Ft. Apache* 33: "I wanna find out what they eat to make their tits grow so I can feed it to my wife." "They eat the Irish inch."

Irish lace *n.* cobwebs.—now usu. considered offensive. *Joc.*
    [*1909 Ware *Passing Eng.* 158: *Irish draperies* (Peoples', England). Cobwebs.] **1950, 1968–70** in *DARE.* **1975** N.Y. man, age *ca*20: That's what you call Irish lace. **1985** Miss. woman, age *ca*40: "The corners are filled with Irish lace!" I've known that expression forever.

Irish lasses *n.pl.* [rhyming slang] glasses. *Rare* in U.S.
    1928 Sharpe *Chicago May* 287: *Irish lasses*—glasses.

Irish lemon *n.* a potato.—now usu. considered offensive. *Joc.*
    1891 Maitland *Slang Dict.* 150: *Irish apricots* or *Irish lemons*, potatoes. *a1890–96 F & H* IV 14: *Irish-Lemon*...A potato.

Irish local *n.* a railway handcar; (*also*) a wheelbarrow.—now usu. considered offensive. *Joc.*
    1900 *DN* II 45: "*Irish local*," a hand-car. **1935–40** in Mencken *Amer. Lang. Supp. II* 773: *Irish local*. A wheelbarrow.

Irish man-o'-war *Naut.* a barge.—now usu. considered offensive. *Joc.*
    *1929 Bowen *Sea Slang* 72: A barge...*Irish Man-of-War*. **1948** Shay *Amer. Sea Songs* 71: Sailors liked to refer to a large and unwieldy barge that had to be towed as an Irish man-of-war.

Irishman's coat-of-arms *n.* (see quot.).—now usu. considered offensive. *Joc.*

1807 J.R. Shaw *Autobiog.* 37: I soon gave Mr. Airton an Irishman's coat of arms, i.e., two black eyes and a bloody nose.

Irishman's hurricane var. IRISH HURRICANE.

Irishman's reef *n. Naut.* a knot or tie made in the head of a sail.

> **1961** Burgess *Dict. Sailing* 121: *Irishman's reef.* The head of a sail tied up or knotted.

Irish necktie *n.* a rope.—now usu. considered offensive. *Joc.*

> **1890** *United Service* (Apr.) 442: I should have known what is meant by an "Irish dividend" or an "Irish necktie" if I had never been aboard a vessel of war.

Irish nightingale *n.* a bullfrog.—now usu. considered offensive. *Joc.*

> **1901** *DN* II 142: *Irish nightingale*, n. Bull frog. Newburgh, N.Y.

Irish parliament *n. Naut.* PORTUGUESE PARLIAMENT.—now usu. considered offensive.

> **1904** J.A. Williams, in *Independent* (June 23) 1432: Passing one of the many saloons which grace the waterfront, we were attracted by a boisterous Irish parliament within....In the bar-room a jolly crowd of excited mariners were holding forth all at once, everybody talking and nobody listening. **1947** Boyer *Dark Ship* 151: When exchanges become too warm between members of the staff, Joe sometimes says, "Let's not have an Irish parliament here!" **1965** Schmitt *All Hands Aloft!* 187 [ref. to 1918]: The Finn, seated beside him, after several vain attempts to make himself heard, gave up and shouted, "Yust lak God dam' Irish Parl'ment, everybody talkin', nobody lis'nin'!"

Irish pennant *n.* **1.** *Naut.* a dangling end of a rope or line; (see also 1962 quot.). Also (*obs.*) **Irish pendant.** *Joc.*

> **1840** Dana *Before Mast* ch. xxii [ref. to 1834]: There was no rust, no dirt, no rigging hanging slack, no fag-ends of ropes or "Irish pendants" aloft. **1869** *Overland Mo.* (Apr.) 354: Their riggin' was full of Irish pennants. **1883** Russell *Sailors' Lang.* 73: *Irish pennants*—fag-ends of rope, rope-yarns, &c. flying about. **1889** *United Service* (Sept.) 274: "Irish pendants" hang from the yards and rigging of untidy ships. **1890** *United Service* (Apr.) 442: When a rag, tatter, or bit of rope was seen dangling in the rigging, a man would be ordered to go and take off that Irish pennant. **1908** J.R. Williams, in *Independent* (Apr. 23) 908: Don't see no "Irish pennants," nor "dog's ears," nor "flyin' tassles" aloft, do yer? **1931** Erdman *Reserve Officer's Manual* 441: *Irish Pendant* (The "d" is not pronounced). Any piece of line, loose or adrift. Considered very unseamanlike. **1937** Rose *Brittany Patrol* 34 [ref. to 1918]: Deckhands were flemishing down lines on the forecastle and hauling aboard all Irish pennants. **1950** Morison *Naval Ops. in WWII* VI 271: No taut ship puts to sea with "Irish pennants" such as trailing lines and dangling fenders. **1962** *Western Folk.* XXI 31: *Irish pennants*—rags or laundry hung up to dry on board ship....U.S. Navy, *ca*1945.

2. Esp. *Navy & USMC.* a loose thread, strap, or end as on a uniform; the hem of a woman's slip visible beneath a uniform skirt; a dangling end of a sheet or blanket. *Joc.*

> **1941** Kendall *Army & Navy Sl.* 20: *Irish pennants*....sloppy loose ends which should be tucked in. **1944** *N.Y. Times Mag.* (Sept. 17) 32: *Irish pennant*—Spar designation for slip. **1945** in *Calif. Folk. Qly.* V (1946) 388: A man...who has *Irish pennants** dangling from his bunk....*Untidy loose ends of blankets or sheets. **1971** Flanagan *Maggot* 30: "That give you the right to wear Irish pennants?" Midberry dangled the green thread before Waite's eyes. **1973** Krulewitch *Now That You Mention It* 31 [ref. to USMC, 1917]: Carefully lacing leggings, folding in the slacks, regulation style, and guarding against Irish pennants, I checked out with the sergeant. **1981** Sledge *Old Breed* 218 [ref. to WWII]: Loose straps on a Marine's pack were called "Irish pennants"—why Irish I never knew—and resulted in disciplinary action or a blast from the drill instructor. **1982** S.P. Smith *Officer & Gentleman* 63: He...pulled a tiny piece of lint off Daniels' shoulder. "Irish pennant, boy....Improper uniform." **1988** von Hassel & Crossley *Warriors* 165: *Irish pennants.* Loose thread or fiber on a uniform. *a*1990 Poyer *Gulf* 4: You've got Irish pennants on the quarter. **1995** *L.A. Times* (Sept. 1) A3: At the police academy, he...was marked down whenever his uniform showed any tatters, strings or snags. In Marine lexicon used by academy sergeants, such imperfections had for decades been called "Irish pennants."

Irish promotion *n.* a demotion.—now usu. considered offensive. *Joc.*

> **a1890–96** *F & H* IV 17: *Irish Promotion*...A reduction in position. **1932** Ward *Big Parades* 86: He has been made the recipient of an

"Irish" promotion. That is, a reduction in grade from lieutenant colonel down to that of major.

Irish pullman *n. R.R.* a handcar.—now usu. considered offensive. *Joc.*

> **1989** *CBS This Morning* (CBS-TV) (Nov. 3): This is a railroad handcar, also called an "Irish pullman."

Irish root *n.* a potato.—now usu. considered offensive. *Joc.*

> **1853** in M. Lewis *Mining Frontier* 49: Now hunger makes "his bowels yearn,"/For "yams" or "Irish roots."

Irish rose *n.* a stone or brickbat.—now usu. considered offensive. *Joc.*

> **1930** Nason *A Corporal Once* 240 [ref. to WWI]: "Here's an Irish Rose for ye, ye blagyard!" muttered Dugan, and hurled a stone at the shadowy form.

Irish spoon *n.* a shovel or spade.—now usu. considered offensive. *Joc.*

> **1862** in Norton *Army Letters* 73: I can hear them calling the roll in some of the other companies, and one company just passed armed with "Irish spoons," going out to work in the trenches.

Irish toothache *n.* (see quots.).—now usu. considered offensive. *Joc.*

> **1882* *Boudoir* 2: That girl has given me the Irish toothache [an erection]. **a1890–96* *F & H* IV 14: *Irish-toothache*...An erection of the penis. **1926** Maines & Grant *Wise-Crack Dict.* 10: *Irish toothache*—Punch in the jaw. **1965–70** in *Qly. Jour. Stud. Alcohol* XXXII (1971) 732: *Irish toothache* (1) A thirst for liquor. (2) Hangover.

Irish turkey *n.* corned beef; corned beef and cabbage.—now usu. considered offensive. *Joc.*

> [**1866** *Night Side of N.Y.* 79: Hash is known to all the rounders as "boned turkey."] **1915** "High Jinks, Jr." *Choice Slang* 86: New York Bowery Slang...*Irish turkey*—Corned beef. **1920** Crawford *360th Field Arty.* 14 [ref. to WWI]: For dinner we had canned Irish turkey, Tomatoes and Hard-tack. **1927** *DN* V 451: *Irish turkey*, n. Corned beef and cabbage. **1929** *AS* IV (June) 341: *Irish turkey.* Corn beef and cabbage. **1935** in *AS* (Feb. 1936) 43: *Irish turkey.* Corned beef and cabbage. **1966, 1994** in *DARE*.

Irish wind *n. Naut.* IRISH HURRICANE.

> **1902** *Our Naval Apprentice* (Feb.) 14: The wind being an "Irish one"—up and down—we have made an average of two knots an hour on the passage.

iron *n.* **1.a.** *Mil.* artillery projectiles, bullets, shrapnel, etc.

> **1823** J.F. Cooper *Pilot* 7: Boy, never be so foolish as to trust a long shot. It makes a great smoke and some noise, but it's a terrible uncertain manner of throwing old iron about. **1863** in J.W. Haley *Rebel Yell* 103: The air seethed with old iron. **1884** Blanding *Sailor Boy* 289: The rebs are going to dose us again with their blarsted iron. **1887** Hinman *Si Klegg* 481 [ref. to Civil War]: I'd a mighty sight ruther go ahead...'n' pitch inter them fellers than ter lay here like a log while they're heavin' their old iron 'round so promisc'us like. **1919** Ellington *Co. A* 113: *Iron*—Projectories from American Artillery. **1919** Farrell *1st U.S. Engrs.* 111: The third day in Broyes Fritz tossed over a sample of his iron and caught our chow-line right in the middle. **1928–29** Nason *White Slicker* 31: Where did he stop his iron?...I don't see no blood!

b. exercise weights; in phr. **pump** [or **push**] **iron** to exercise with weights.

> **1965** in Cleaver *Soul on Ice* 52: And sometimes I go out to the weight-lifting area...and push a little iron for a while and soak up the sun. **1966** Braly *Cold* 36: Well, Big One, you still pushing iron? **1971** *Black Scholar* (Sept.) 39: The cat that lifts all that iron on the yard. **1972** C. Gaines *Stay Hungry:* What are you doing down here, Blake? Rich as cream and down here grunting and pumping iron like a poor man. **1975** S.P. Smith *Amer. Boys* 123: He looked as if he'd pushed iron at the gym every night. **1976** Braly *False Starts* 156: I'm going to push some iron. **1983** Goldman & Fuller *Charlie Co.* 206: Fifty-five new pounds of muscles from pumping iron. *a*1984 in *AS* LIX (1984) 200: *Iron* n. Weights used for training. **1984** Knoxville, Tenn., attorney, age 30: I gotta get back into pumping some iron. **1988** *CBS This Morning* (CBS-TV) (Dec. 16): The freshman football team is pumping iron. **1991** N. Krulik *Hammer & Ice* 24: After pumping iron, the dancers get down on the ground for...300 sit-ups!

2. [a development of the S.E. sense 'an iron shackle or fetter' (*OED* def. 7a)] *Police.* a set of steel handcuffs.—often constr. in pl.

1929 "E. Queen" *Roman Hat* ch. xi: The more I hear about Field the more I dislike putting the irons on the fellow who did away with him. **1975** Wambaugh *Choirboys* 314: Francis...tried to lay the iron on his wrists after the dude had went upside Momma's head.

3. the penis.—usu. considered vulgar.

*1698–1706 in D'Urfey *Pills* IV 195: Red-hot grew his Iron as both did desire. *ca***1937** in Holt *Dirty Comics* 50: Heave to a'fore I rams this iron up around yer gizzard. *ca***1939** "M. Hunt" *Vulnerable* 117: Giving a forward push to their irons. **1979** *Penthouse* (Mar.) 178: I pumped my iron deep within her cleavage.

4.a. money. Cf. IRON DOLLAR.

*1785 Grose *Vulgar Tongue: Iron.* Money in general. **1906** in *OED2:* The iron you're goin' to give me. **1923** McKnight *Eng. Words* 60: [Money:] Kale, *iron,*...jack,...dough, [etc.]. **1925** *Writer's Mo.* (June) 485: Bucks, Dough, Iron—Money. **1929** Barr *Let Tomorrow Come* 153: 'Is mouthpiece makes 'im for the iron an' lays 'im flat. **1966** Young & Hixson *LSD* 8: The Mafia has had trouble deciding whether the game is worth their iron. **1966* in *OED2:* He was earning a bit of iron. **1983** Whiteford *How to Talk Baseball* 52: *Iron* (money)....“That's where the iron is.” *a***1990** P. Dickson *Slang!* 216: *Drop some iron.* To spend some money.

b. a dollar; IRON MAN, 3.a.

1906 T.A. Dorgan, in Zwilling *TAD Lexicon* 49: There was a deck scrubber named Tom Sharkey who had a drag on Uncle Sam's roll for about nine irons a month. **1911** T.A. Dorgan, in *N.Y. Eve. Jour.* (Jan. 14) 8: There goes my kelly that cost me five irons last night—darn the luck.

5. a firearm, esp. a pistol; a gun or guns; in phr. **drag iron** (*rare*) to draw a gun.

[**1836* in *OED2:* Take care and have the marking irons in your pocket.] **1838** *Crockett Almanac* (1839) 7: Well, I hadn't time to load my iron. **1839** in Blair & Meine *Half Horse* 66: Davy Crockett's hand would be sure to shake, if his iron was pointed within a hundred mile of a she-male. **1840** *Spirit of Times* (Dec. 19) 499: Spang went the boy's iron, and down went one Indian. **1845** in Robb *Squatter Life* 131: Come, boys,...you all know that this old iron's *certain,* so give the varmint this chance. **1850** Garrard *Wah-to-yah* 211: I took my gun—that ar iron (pointing to his rifle, leaning against a tree), an' pops Blue over the head. **1858** J.C. Reid *Tramp* 226: He advanced to within ten steps of the game and “held out his iron.” **1860** E. Ellis *Bill Biddon* 62: “You going to shoot them?”...“Cain't tell yit. Jest see that yer irons is ready.” **1861** in W.H. Russell *My Diary* 130: The way the boys touched oft their irons at me...was just like a running fight with the Ingins. **1867** *Galaxy* (Dec.) 991: He was a “Texan Ranger” and knew how to use his irons. **1871** Hay *Pike Co. Ballads* 27: Blood drawed iron at last, and fired. **1879** Dacus *Frank & Jesse* 127: I'd go fur him with these 'ere irons. **1895** Wood *Yale Yarns* 277: I was in my peddler's disguise...and was armed with a “lead stick,” and had “iron in my boot,” as they say; that is one revolver, and a loaded cane. **1922** F.L. Packard *Doors of Night* 57: Leave me your gun....I might need your iron. **1928** Sharpe *Chicago May* 50: You, and that iron, don't go out of this office. **1938** R. Chandler *Big Sleep* 45: See if this bird is wearing any iron. **1947** Overholser *Buckaroo's Code* 21: Let that iron slide back. Put your hands on the table, Red. **1957** Margulies *Punks* 183: We only four, but four with two irons. **1966** *Dick Van Dyke Show* (CBS-TV): I can still handle these irons. **1970–71** Rubinstein *City Police* 293: Shit, man, he's got an iron. **1971** Nichols (NBC-TV): You're wearin' iron, ain't ye? *a***1987** Bunch & Cole *Reckoning for Kings* 416: Three of them made the mistake of dragging iron. **1989** Zumbro & Walker *Jungletracks* 53: Let this ol' butter bar plop himself down behind the iron [a machine gun]. **1993** *N.Y. Times* (Dec. 9) A31: Her last doubt about gun ownership had just been eliminated....Others were similarly deciding to go buy themselves an iron.

6. *West.* a stockbreeder's brand, as on cattle. Cf. S.E. sense 'a branding iron', fr. ME.

1912 Siringo *Cowboy Detective* 490: They had to be branded with my own “iron,” which had just been recorded. **1926** C.M. Russell *Trails* 6: “Neighbor, you're a long way from your range.”...“How did you read my iron?”...“It's your ways.” *a***1940** in Lanning & Lanning *Texas Cowboys* 18 [ref. to 1880's]: The iron was made like this. **1964** Brister *Renegade Brand* 35: I'd worked for this iron pretty near a year, and figured to keep workin' for it, at least until I had a look at the new owner. **1965** D.G. Moore *20th C. Cowboy* 184: I put the crew to

branding out this bunch in the Porter iron. **1979** Jenison *Kingdom in Sage* 29: That iron doesn't belong to any outfit in *this* country.

7.a. an automobile; motor vehicle.—also used collectively.

1935 in *OED2:* “Iron” is the dealer's name for an obsolete [automobile]. **1942** *ATS* 718: *Hot iron*...a fast car. **1949** R. Smith *Big Wheel* (film): But Reno, this is the fastest iron in the business. *Ibid.:* You don't know a guy with a hot iron who needs a new chauffeur? **1951–53** in *AS* (May 1954) 99: *Iron,* n. a “beat-up” car; a heavy, newer car. **1958** Frees *Beatniks* (film): We didn't mean to bend that pretty iron of yours. **1961** *Leave It to Beaver* (ABC-TV): I saw that big glamorous hunk of iron parked in the driveway. **1971** Tak *Truck Talk* 90: *Iron:* any old truck. **1974** E. Thompson *Tattoo* 410: He could see Cadillacs, Lincolns, Packards, Buicks and Chryslers lined up...a million dollars' worth of ice-cream and candy-colored iron. **1986** *CNN News* (CNN-TV) (Aug. 9): So why does the government continue to trash all that expensive iron [in safety tests]?

b. a motorcycle.

1966 H.S. Thompson *Hell's Angels* 60: By 1947 the state was alive with bikes, nearly all of them powerful American-made irons from Harley-Davidson and Indian. **1966** Reynolds & McClure *Freewheelin Frank* 28: Tiny's iron is...a three-wheeler. **1973** *Zap Comix* (No. 6) (unp.): Only time I work on ma' iron is onna Sunday.

c. *Av.* aircraft collectively; in phr. **push iron** to fly aircraft.

1985 Boyne & Thompson *Wild Blue* 556 [ref. to *ca*1973]: What the hell are we doing still pushing iron at our age? *a***1988** Lewin & Lewin *Thesaurus of Slang* 12: Airplane...*big iron* (multi-engine), *big iron fever* (desire to fly big aircraft). **1989** Berent *Rolling Thunder* 94: Flying fighter iron didn't make one a fighter pilot. *a***1991** Kross *Splash One* 117 [ref. to Vietnam War]: Paint your names on the planes. Own the iron together—as a team.

¶ In phrases:

¶ **draw iron** *Basketball.* to hit the rim of the basket, esp. without scoring.

1982 T. Considine *Lang. of Sport* 60: *Draw iron:* To hit the rim of the basket on a shot. Chick Hearn, broadcaster for the Los Angeles Lakers, popularized the expression in the late 1960s. **1989** Univ. Tenn. student: The shot didn't even draw iron. **1993** *Sports Close-Up* (CNN-TV) (Mar. 6): He didn't even draw iron.

¶ **lay iron** *Jazz.* to tap-dance.

1946 Mezzrow & Wolfe *Really Blues* 187 [ref. to 1930's]: Sonny Thompson...can lay some iron too. *Ibid.* 307: *Lay some iron:* tapdance. **1944** C. Calloway *New Hepster's Dict.: Lay some iron*... to tap dance.

¶ **work** [or **use**] **(someone's) old iron up** *Naut.* to harass or persecute (someone), usu. with hard work; haze.

1841 [Mercier] *Man of War* 164: I tell you, *Johnny Crapeau* is no slouch at killing a whale; he's worked that fellow's *old iron* up in as pretty a style as any Nantucketer could do it. **1849** in Windeler *Gold Rush Diary* 27: Our second mate is trying to work up our old iron, but he can't Shine. **1871** Thomes *Whaleman* 38: He turned away, muttering most terrible threats of “using up their old iron for 'em;” but the meaning of that term I did not know at the time. **1883** Russell *Sailors' Lang.* xv: “Working their old iron up,” “long togs,” for shore-going clothes, “ride a man down like the maintack,” to go on punishing him with plenty of hard work. **1887** Davis *Sea-Wanderer* 109: Just let me catch 'em making a fuss over it, and I'll work up their old iron in a way to open their eyes!

iron ass *n.* Esp. *Mil.* a person, esp. a military officer, who is strict, stubborn, unyielding, etc.—usu. considered vulgar.—usu. as a disparaging nickname. Also (*euphem.*) **iron pants.**

1942 *Time* (Apr. 27) 15: He was “Old Ironpants.” **1943** *Life* (Aug. 9) 85: Lieut. General “Iron Pants” Patton. **1942–45** in Campbell & Campbell *War Paint* 44: Iron Ass. **1947** *ATS* (Supp.) 16: *Iron ass,* a strict officer. **1958** Camerer *Damned Wear Wings* 183 [ref. to WWII]: Alongside, *Old Iron Ass* [a bomber] held her position. **1959** Morrill *Dark Sea Running* 135: He had woofed at them like a regular old Iron Ass. **1960** MacCuish *Do Not Go Gentle* 322: A real iron ass, eh? **1963** Dwiggins *S.O. Bees* 91: Old iron ass is upset. **1973** "J. Godey" *Pelham* 15: Are you not the officer they call Captain Ironass? **1976** Hayden *Voyage* 451: Here comes old Ironpants now. **1977** *Time* (May 30) 6: U.S. SALT Negotiator Paul Warnke and his Soviet counterpart, Vladimir (“Iron Pants”) Semyonov. **1980** Syatt *Country Talk* 20: He's so stubborn, we just call him old iron ass. **1982** W.J. Dunn *Fighter Pilot* 128 [ref. to 1944]: Below the cartoon were painted the words “Posterius Ferrous”...“Iron Ass.” **1985** Sawislak *Dwarf* 121: Give old Ironpants Swift a call. **1985** Boyne & Thompson *Wild Blue* 514: In *Twelve O'Clock High*, Gregory Peck just gets to be an iron ass, and everything is cured.

iron-ass[ed] *adj.* Esp. *Mil.* unbending, tough, or disciplinarian.—usu. considered vulgar. Also **iron-butt.** [Early quots. ref. to WWII.]
　　1948 Lay & Bartlett *Twelve O'Clock High!* 90: That iron-assed general has been chewing their tails up there. **1968** Westheimer *Young Sentry* 207: "I should have busted him one," Lang said doggedly. "Man, you've sure got ironass all of a sudden, ain't you?" **1968** Coppel *Order of Battle* 137: May the good Lord protect me from officers who were once enlisted men. Almost without exception they were iron-assed pricks. **1969** Coppel *Little Time for Laughter* 185: It was only a suggestion, sir. You don't have to get iron ass about it. **1982** Abodaher *Iacocca* 193: In today's business…you've got to be pretty iron-butt, bash in a lot of heads and kick a lot of asses. **1985** Dye *Between Raindrops* 37: Thought I was an iron-assed potential lifer.

iron balls *n.* Esp. *Mil.* a fearless, aggressive man, esp. a military officer.—usu. used as a disparaging nickname.—usu. considered vulgar.
　　1968 Legman *Dirty Joke* 375: The American [nickname] *Ironballs* for a tough general—euphemized to "Tuffypants" (!) in a newspaper version. **1969** L. Sanders *Anderson Tapes* 262: Don't tell me that's "Iron Balls" Delaney. **1987** Averill *Mustang* 264 [ref. to ca1955]: He chuckled and asked me if I knew what the troops called me…."Iron Balls— Old Iron Balls!" I had been called worse. **1987** Lipper *Wall St.* 14: Some of the younger traders nicknamed Lou "iron balls," a grudging accolade to his ability to ride out cycles and trends.

iron-bender *n. Logging.* (see quot.).
　　1958 McCulloch *Woods Wds.* 95: *Iron bender*—a. A camp blacksmith. b. A railroad brakeman. **1962** *AS* XXXVII 133: *Iron bender*…A railroad brakeman.

iron bird *n. Av.* an aircraft. Also **iron beast.**
　　1945 in Rea *Wings of Gold* 268: Flying the "Iron Beast" [*sc.* F4U Corsair] is one whale of a thrill. **1959** Montgomery & Heiman *Jet Nav.* 4: I think I have that iron bird mastered. **1988** Clodfelter *Mad Minutes* 53: Before the whirling iron bird bearing the red cross could fly him to the hospital.

iron bomb *n. Mil.* a high-explosive bomb (as opposed to a nuclear bomb).
　　1962 Harvey *Strike Command* 3: Rockets, napalm, little "iron bombs," and multi-megaton H-bombs. **1984** Sweetman *Phantom* 37: A pre-1968 "iron bomb" F-105 might have carried up to a dozen 750 lb. bombs. **1983–86** G.C. Wilson *Supercarrier* 207: The bomb's laser guidance system…was hooked into an old-fashioned iron bomb. **1991** Dunnigan & Bay *From Shield to Storm* 181: An old-fashioned "iron bomb" (a steel casing filled with explosive).

iron-bound *adj.* (of clothing) stitched with ornamental silver or gold lace.
　　*1785 Grose *Vulgar Tongue: Iron-bound;* laced. *An iron-bound hat; a* silver-laced hat. **1834** *Mil. & Naval Mag. of U.S.* (Sept.) 27: A Quaker once called an officer's coat, which was much stiffened with lace, an *iron-bound* coat.

iron boy *n.* a dollar; IRON MAN, 3.a.
　　1915 "High Jinks, Jr." *Choice Slang* 51: *Iron boys*—Silver dollars. **1918** Breddan *Under Fire* 45: It cost him just fifty iron boys. **1926** Nason *Chevrons* 183: Well, I earned a dollar yesterday an' I'll earn another one today. I'll remark they'll be the toughest two iron boys I ever made in my life.

iron-burner *n. Logging.* a blacksmith.
　　1942 *AS* (Dec.) 222: *Iron Burner.* A camp blacksmith. **1956** Sorden & Ebert *Logger's Wds.* 19 [ref. to a1925]: *Iron-burner,* The camp blacksmith. **1958** McCulloch *Woods Words* 95: *Iron burner*—A blacksmith.

iron candy *n.* hard candy. *Joc.*
　　1922 Rollins *Cowboy* 191: Got a little piece of iron candy for you.

iron cigar *n. Army.* an artillery shell. *Joc.*
　　1918 Adler *77th Div.* 45: The "traveling salesmen" or Corps Artillery…moved from place to place in the sector.…A "traveling salesman"…was "selling iron cigars," as he put it. **1960** Mason *Amer. Men at Arms* 78 [ref. to 1918]: The Germans decided to give these replacements a noisy welcome. All day they threw "ashcans," "iron cigars," "Minnies," and the "88's" which the men called whizzbangs.

ironclad *n.* **1.** *Army.* a hardtack biscuit; (*also*) a baked pie with a hard crust. Now *hist.* Also **ironclad pie.**
　　1864 in *Ark. Hist. Qly.* XII (1953) 360: The Federals issued to us [Confederate prisoners] 4 or 5 "ironclads" a piece (but no meat). **1889** Barrère & Leland *Dict. Slang* I 488: *Ironclads,* baked pies, so called from the armour-plated consistencies of the outside crust. Of American origin. **1914** *Confed. Vet.* XXII 307 [ref. to Civil War]: Some wagons came into camp loaded with iron-clad pies and other foodstuff, which, of course, went like hot cakes.…One of my men [had] a stack of twenty-two iron-clads piled up in his arms. **1958** *Civil War Hist.* IV 76: Encamped at Harrisburg, the First Wisconsin could get only "iron-clad pies," coffee, and "sowbelly" roasted on a stick. [***1974** in *OED2:* "Iron clads" are the…term for day-old Chelsea buns.] **2.** (see quots.).
　　1869 in *Jour. Ill. Hist. Soc.* XLVIII (1955) 395: I saw you when you first took command of the "iron-clads" [seasoned troops]. **1889** Barrère & Leland *Dict. Slang* I 488: During the [U.S.] Civil War, *ironclad* was applied to everything well defended or hard.…A severely virtuous girl was an *ironclad.*

ironclad *adj. Army.* **1.** difficult to chew.
　　1863 in Glazier *Fed. Cavalry* 317: The repast consisted of muddy water, rusty salt-pork, and half a hard cracker, termed by us "an iron-clad breakfast." **2.** invulnerable.
　　1891 Rodenbough *Sabre* 134 [ref. to Civil War]: I had always been considered iron-clad, and bomb-proof.

iron compass *n. Av.* railroad tracks used as a visual navigational aid by the pilot of an aircraft.
　　1933 Stewart *Airman Speech* 73: *Iron compass.* Railroad tracks. ***1934** (cited in Partridge *DSUE* (ed. 8)). **1965** Gallery *Eight Bells* 83 [ref. to 1926]: When you *had* to fly through soupy weather your best "instrument" was the "iron compass," i.e., railroad tracks. They always led somewhere. **1974** Stevens *More There I Was* 11: Ye Olde Iron Compass. **1986** *Good Morning America* (ABC-TV) (Sept. 17): "I'm going to be navigating the same way that Cal Rodgers did seventy-five years ago, and that's called the 'iron compass.'" "What's that?" "The railroads."

iron cow *n. Mil.* TIN COW. *Joc.*
　　1942 in *Yank* (Jan. 6, 1943) 18: A sailor…calls the canned milk "iron cow." **1972** Davidson *Cut Off* 120 [ref. to WWII]: "Iron cow" (cans of evaporated milk).

iron derby *n. Army.* a trench helmet. *Joc.* [Quots. ref. to WWI.]
　　1920 *304th Field Signal Battalion* 27: Those "iron derbies" were hard. **1925** Nason *Three Lights* 162.

iron dollar *n.* a dollar in cash. Also vars.
　　1903 in "O. Henry" *Works* 155: I had a t'ousand iron dollars saved up. **1904** Ade *True Bills* 5: Mrs. Gillespie had tapped the Bank for seven large, Iron Dollars. **1908** J. London *M. Eden* 405: With big iron dollars…in my jeans. **1911** *Adventure* (Jan.) 444: Sixty big iron dollars! **1911–12** J. London *Smoke Bellew* 261: Twenty-one hundred good iron dollars. **1916** E.R. Burroughs *Return of Mucker* 140: I'll bet an iron case she's a-waitin' for you. **1921** *Pirate Piece* (Apr.) 4: Two and one half iron bucks.

iron eye *n.* a hard, unfriendly glance.—constr. with *the.*
　　1941 J. Thurber, in Paxton *Sport* 297: We stand there givin' 'em the iron eye, it bein' the lowest ebb a ball-club manager'd got hisself down to since the national pastime was started. *Ibid.* 298: I give him the iron eye, and he finely got on the train.

iron foundry *n. Army.* a German heavy-artillery projectile.
　　1918 (quot. at DAISY-CLIPPER, 2). **1919** *307th Field Arty.* 148: On the morning of October 15th, the Dutchmen sent over a few "iron foundries." ***1919** Downing *Digger Dialects* 29: *Iron foundry.* A very heavy shell.

iron freak *n.* a weightlifting enthusiast. Cf. FREAK, 2.
　　1966 Braly *On Yard* 240: Iron freaks. Stick dismissed them with contempt. **1976** Arble *Long Tunnel* 143: Aldo is an iron freak along with handling cinder blocks all day. **1979** Crews *Blood & Grits* 70: He must have been an iron freak. Muscles…rippled and slid, ridged and quivered.

iron gaiters *n.pl.* leg irons. *Joc.* Also **iron garters.**
　　*1817 Sir W. Scott *Rob Roy* ch. xxii: Ye'll find the stane breeks and the airn garters, ay, and the hemp cravat for a' that. **1855** Wise *Tales* 312: You have a chance for a pair of twenty pound iron gaiters on your shanks.

iron hat *n.* a derby hat.

    1914 T.A. Dorgan, in Zwilling *TAD Lexicon* 49: (…Coming to work with last winter's iron hat) Where did you get that boiler? **1929** M.A. Gill *Und. Slang: Iron hat*—Derby hat. **1931** J. Gleason *Beyond Victory* (film): If you'd only take off that iron hat. **1935** Pollock *Und. Speaks: Iron hat*, a derby. **1939** "E. Queen" *Dragon's Teeth* 114: The other was the house dick. Big boy with an iron hat and a .38 in his fist.

ironhead *n.* a blockhead. Hence **ironheaded,** *adj.*

    1916–17 in McManus *Bringing Up Father* 8: That big iron-head hit me with a shovel once! **1941** LeMay, Bennett & Lasky *Reap Wild Wind* (film): No one but an ironheaded one. **1973** J.R. Coleman *Blue-Collar* 38: The trouble with you guys is you're all ironheads. You don't think. **1975** Durocher & Linn *Nice Guys* 186: Why, you big ironhead you—.

iron horse *n.* **1.** *Army.* an armored vehicle. *Joc.*

    1918 in *Acotank* 210: I'll say he missed the old Iron Horse considerable. **1941** *Army Ordnance* (July) 79: *Iron horses*…Tanks.

    2. *Journ.* IRON MAN, 1.

    1929 *N.Y. Times* (June 2) X 2: He's the iron horse among the sprinters.

    3. (applied to various types of machines; see quots.).

    *a*1940 in Mencken *Amer. Lang. Supp. II* 775: *Iron horse.* A loom. *a*1948 Mencken *Amer. Lang. Supp. II* 717: The modern automatic [telegraph] sending machine is an *iron horse.*

iron house *n.* a jail or prison.

    1927 *DN* V 451: *Iron house,* n. Jail. **1927** in *AS* III (Feb. 1928) 254: *Iron house, klink*—Jail. **1929** M.A. Gill *Und. Slang: Iron house*—Prison. **1975** J.P. Smith *Amer. Boys* 211: Could have reported the clown and got him sent to the iron house or the funny farm.

iron idiot *n.* *Army.* (see quot.).

    1986 R. Zumbro *Tank Sgt.* 110 [ref. to 1967–68]: Each tank used its ranging computer (iron idiot) to designate specific targets and areas of responsibility.

iron-jawed *adj.* (of a horse) unresponsive to the bit.

    1912 Z. Grey *Riders* 40: He's unruly…this horse is an iron-jawed devil. **1952** Holmes *Boots Malone* (film): When you want to stop some iron-jawed, cement-headed ox [etc.].

iron jenny *n.* *Army.* an armored reconnaissance car.

    1962 Houk & Dexter *Ballplayers* 37 [ref. to WWII]: The 89th Cavalry Reconnaissance Squadron of the Ninth Armored Division had horsepower but no horses. I trained painstakingly with Iron Jennies for the great assault on Hitler's Europe.

iron kelly *n.* *Mil.* a steel helmet.

    1942 (quot. at KELLY).

iron louie *n.* a dollar.

    1896 Ade *Artie* 50: I just fed eight big iron louies into that game last night.

iron man *n.* **1.** a man, esp. an athlete, of extraordinary stamina. Now *colloq.* or *S.E.*

    [*1617 in *OED*: They draw, like Loadstones, Iron-men.] **1902** (cited in Nichols *Baseball Term.*). **1905** *N.Y. Times* (May 29) 7: The "Iron Man" [Joe McGinnity] had been asked…to pitch for them. **1905** in Spalding *Base Ball* 257: The [Japanese] pitching wonder, "Iron Man" Kono…pitches every day, never seems to weaken. **1905** in Paxton *Sport USA* 24: Joe McGinnity….The "Iron Man" made an unprecedented record. He pitched and won three double-headers…. He then proceeded to win twelve games in succession. **1911** Van Loan *Big League* 234: Iron Man McFinnerty. Why, he just about won that pennant for the Giants last year. **1915** in Grayson *New Stories* 556: They tell me you're an iron man. **1934** Weseen *Dict. Slang* 213: *Iron man*—A pitcher who pitches two full games in succession. **1937** *Time* (Apr. 26) 25: Larruping Lou Gehrig…Baseball's "Iron Man." **1940** Ottley & Weatherby *Negro in N.Y.* 151: Battling Nelson, the famous "Iron Man."

    2.a. *Labor.* (applied to various automatic devices).

    *1897 in *OED*: In some of the thin seams of that district [Yorkshire coalfield], the coal-cutting has for some time been done by machine—by the "iron man." **1937** *AS* (Apr.) 154: *Iron man.* Stoker for mechanically feeding coal. **1938** Smitter *Detroit* 137: One company had a machine called the "Iron Man" that welded gas tanks. It was a spot welder—fully automatic….Four of these did the work of two hundred and fifty hand welders. **1945** Hamann *Air Words: Iron man.* Automatic pilot.

    b. *Horse Racing.* a parimutuel machine. Now *hist.*

    1942 *ATS* 692: Pari-mutuel machine. *Iron man.* **1951** in D.W. Maurer *Lang. of Und.* 216: *Iron men*…Pari-mutuel machines (obsoles-

cent except in such phrases as "to battle the *iron men*"). **1961** Scarne *Comp. Guide to Gambling* 47: Racing fans began referring to the Clickers as "iron men" as they began making their appearance in other racing centers [*ca*1910].

    3.a. a dollar in cash.

    1908 H. Green *Maison de Shine* 45: A feller…shells out his six iron men every week. **1916** Lewis *Job* 198 [ref. to *ca*1908]: I knock down more good, big, round iron men every week than nine-tenths of these high-brow fiddlers. **1919** Lewis *Free Air* 340: Well, the first thing I'm going to do is to borrow ten ironmen and a pair of pants. **1921** Wiley *Lady Luck* 141: Eight hund'ed iron men. **1922** *Iowa State College Bomb* 407: Later he found an Iron Man to be the minimum. **1925** Dos Passos *Manhattan Transfer* 72: "Twelve thousand iron men," gasped Gus. **1928** Hammett *Red Harvest* 63: I win myself six hundred iron men. **1930** Dos Passos *42d Parallel* 149: I got a hundred iron men in my pocket. **1940** R. Chandler *Farewell, My Lovely* ch. xx: Hundred dollars….Iron men. Fish. Bucks. **1956** Ross *Hustlers* 118: We picked up a…linen thing for five iron men. **1972** R. Barrett *Lovomaniacs* 8: Six million iron men…I hear he's got sunk in that [movie]. **1979** Edson *Gentle Giant* 18: I've got twenty lil ole iron men here's says they *can* and *will.*

    b. a thousand dollars.

    1962 Crump *Killer* 66: Eight grand, eight big iron men all shot to hell and gone.

Iron Mike *n.* [sugg. by IRON MAN, 2] **1.** *Naut. & Av.* an automatic piloting device.

    *1926 in *OED2*: He will be jealous indeed of the praise bestowed on Iron Mike, an eight-foot high iron box, with complicated electrical "innards," for the Captain of the liner on which Gyro-pilot—Iron Mike's Sunday name—was tried, stated that the ship saved eight or ten miles a day by superior steering. **1945** Hamann *Air Words: Iron Mike.* Automatic or gyropilot. **1959** Sterling *Wake of the Wahoo* 185: They evidently had the plane on "iron mike" or automatic gyro control. **1986** M. Skinner *USN* 23: It's not uncommon for commercial vessels to cruise at night on "Iron Mike"—automatic pilot.

    2. *Baseball.* an automatic pitching machine.

    1959 Brosnan *Long Season* 28: At one end of this cage stands a pitching machine…This is Iron Mike, and he throws rubber baseballs in the general direction of a plate sixty feet away. **1980** Wielgus & Wolff *Basketball* 22: The guy in the batting cage…gets sick of Iron Mike after a while.

iron out *v.* to kill (someone).

    1928–29 Nason *White Slicker* 158: We got a bunch of prisoners up there! Eight of 'em. They was in the old trench, so we couldn't iron 'em out like we intended. **1933** Ersine *Pris. Slang* 46: Two hoods ironed out a cop in Gary. **1984–88** Hackworth & Sherman *About Face* 103: Our big worry…was that we'd get ironed out by our own artillery.

iron pants *n.pl.* **1.** water-resistant trousers.

    1948 J. Stevens *Jim Turner* 123 [ref. to *ca*1910]: His iron pants and high boots [looked] too big for him.

    2. see s.v. IRON ASS.

iron pot *n.* *Army.* an artillery shell.

    1862 in *R.I. Hist.* XXXIX (1980) 120: Thay send…over one or two of them iron pots as the rebels call them.

iron rations *n.pl.* *Army.* bombs or shells. *Joc.*

    1918 *Texas Review* (Oct.) 79: On a bombing expedition, the aviator drops the machine's "iron rations" or "eggs." **1919** Thompson *310th Inf.* 144: Each night "iron rations" were served to the Huns in the Bois des Loges for the double purpose of providing him with entertainment as well as giving firing practice to the newer men of the auxiliary weapons platoons. **1931** Ottosen *Trench Artillery* 177: [Fired] a few iron rations over to Jerry. **1933** Young *Over the Top* 18: The Jerry birdmen liked to visit and drop a few iron rations, which they did almost every night. *1944 in *Best from Yank* 61: The Kraut threw over some stuff. "Here come his iron rations."

iron skull *n.* *R.R.* (see quot.).

    1930 *Railroad Man's Mag.* II 471: *Iron Skull*—A boiler maker.

iron triangle *n.* *Mil.* an area bounded by railway lines on three sides.

    1962 W. Crawford *Give Me Tomorrow* 46 [ref. to 1951]: And ask Ramsey if he'd ever heard of Chorwon and the Iron Triangle where the Army had been plenty busy. **1963** Fehrenbach *This Kind of War* 476 [ref. to 1951]: The original Iron Triangle—so called because the steel rails connecting the cities formed a rough triangle on that map—had had Hwach'on as one base, but when Hwach'on fell to the Eighth Army, the correspondents so liked the phrase that the town of P'yong-gang, farther north, was put in Hwach'on's place. **1966** in Steinbrook *Allies* 20: War Zone D, the Iron Triangle. **1966–67** Harvey *Air War* 107: It was a B-52 saturation drop or "carpet raid" into the Iron Triangle. **1968** Tiede *Coward* 97: This is our division's immediate area of responsibility....Its official name is the Iron Triangle. It's been home for several thousand Viet Cong for over a decade.

irrigate *v.* to drink liquor.
1856 "J. Phoenix" *Phoenixiana* 104: [He] was invited by the urbane proprietor to irrigate. **1875** in E. West *Saloon* 18: It is a custom of some of the b'hoys to "irrigate" to a considerable extent, when they strike a big bonanza. **1881** A.A. Hayes *New Colo.* 120: "Stranger, do you irrigate?" "If you mean drink, sir, I do not." **1883** in M. Lewis *Mining Frontier* 147: I admire a man who gives right in without arguing when he knows he's wrong. Come along and irrigate. **1885** S.S. Hall *Gold Buttons* 7: We'll irrigate as soon as the investigators arrive. **1899** Garland *Eagle's Heart* 239: Come, boys—irrigate and get done with it. **1900** *DN* II 42: *Irrigate,* v.i. To drink to excess. *1911 in *OED2*. **1912** Siringo *Cowboy Detective* 461: We three went into a saloon to "irrigate."

ish *n.* **1.** *Publishing.* an issue (of a periodical).
1967 in S. Lee *Son of Origins* 66: In order to defeat the Grey Gargoyle last ish, Iron Man was forced to drain his transistorized armor's life-giving energy! *a1972 B. Rodgers *Queens' Vernacular* 114: Did you get the last ish of Gayzette? *a1990 P. Dickson *Slang!* 125: Ish...In the world of science fiction literature, this means issue.
2. a political issue.
1992 *Donahue* (NBC-TV) (Jan. 28): It can be *an* ish, but don't let it be *the* ish.

ish kabibble *n. & interj.* [orig. unkn., perh. ult. of Jewish orig.; cf. Abie *Kabibble,* the name of a character featured in the comic strip "Abie the Agent," created (1914) by Harry Hershfield]
"I don't care"; (see also 1980 quot.). [Popularized as the name of a character played by Merwyn Bogue (1907–94) on *Kay Kyser's College of Musical Knowledge,* radio show fr. 1930's.]
1913 T.A. Dorgan, in Zwilling *TAD Lexicon* 49: Ish ki bibble. **1915** "High Jinks, Jr." *Choice Slang* 50: *I should worry*—I don't care. "Ish ka bibble." **1919** S. Lewis *Free Air* 339: So I say "ish kabibble," and I sneaks onto the blind baggage, and bums my way west. **1926** *AS* II 92: We read on the sport's arm band and the flapper's pennant "Ish kabib-bul" or "Ishkabibble"—or "I should worry." Through that expression all youth declared its independence. **1936** Levin *Old Bunch* 108: Arms conference in Washington, but ishkabibble, kiddo. **1963** E.M. Miller *Exile* 138: Ishkabibil, Turk said to himself. **1980** Ciardi *Browser's Dict.* 204: *Ish kabibble* 1. Meaningless nonsense spoken by immigrant Jews. 2....Any stupid chatter.

island fever *n. Mil.* restlessness, ill-temper, or the like caused by being stationed on a remote island.
1977 Caputo *Rumor of War* 28: The battalion was suffering from an epidemic of island fever when I joined it in January 1965....Their boredom was compounded by isolation.

island-happy *adj. Mil.* crazy or eccentric from overlong service on an island or islands.
1944–46 in *AS* XXII 55: *Island Happy.* A state of mind ascribed to any GI who has been on an island longer than two weeks. **1946** Michener *So. Pacific* 132: It was rock-jolly, or island happy, or G.I. fever, or the purple moo-moo. **1961** Davis *Marine at War* 141 [ref. to 1944]: When you start talking like that, you *should* go home. You're island-happy.

Isles *n.pl. Ice Hockey.* the New York Islanders of the National Hockey League.
1984 *N.Y. Post* (Dec. 12) 78: Devils Stun Isles, 7–5.

Isro *n.* [*Is*rael + Af*ro*] a full, rounded hairstyle similar to an Afro, worn by a Jewish person.
1975 *Oui* (Mar.) 134: Blair Sobol...used to wear microskirts and an Izro haircut. **1977** *L.A. Times* (Oct. 11) IV 6: To dye the few gray hairs in her soft, brown Isro, a Jewish Afro hair style. **1978** *Penthouse* (Apr.) 126: Three guys in aviator glasses and Isros squint through the glass front into the bar. **1978** Shem *House of God* 192: A tall...Sephardic Jew with a frizzy Isro Afro. *a1992 Stern & Stern *Encyc. Pop Culture* 5: Art

Garfunkel was another white boy who grew what was soon being called an "Isro."

I-suppose *n.* [rhyming slang] nose. *Rare* in U.S.
*1859 "Ducange Anglicus" *Vulgar Tongue:* I gave him a blow...on the *I-suppose.* *1917 *Living Age* (Nov. 10) 378: When it comes to calling the nose "I suppose" or the arm a "false alarm," one feels that the line has been crossed into idiocy. **1928** Sharpe *Chicago May* 287: *I sup-pose*—nose. **1943** Holmes & Scott *Mr. Lucky* (film): Wait till I powder my I-suppose and fix my Barnet Fair.

is-was *n. Navy.* (see 1966 quot.).
1937 Thompson *Take Her Down* 178 [ref. to 1918]: Scotty worked the "Is Was" (our name for a weird device for figuring out the attack). **1958** Grider *War Fish* 80 [ref. to WWII]: I...crouched near the top of the control-room ladder, manipulating a small device known as an "is-was"—a sort of attack slide rule used in working out distances and directions. **1966** Noel *Naval Terms* 190: *Is-was.* Slang: any crude or improvised measuring or calculating device. **1967** Lockwood *Subs* 97 [ref. to 1918]: Another new gadget was one called an "Is-Was." This we had got from British boats. It had two concentric dials marked in angles and speeds and with a pivoted arm. These were maneuvered to set up the enemy course and speed, our own angle on the enemy's bow, and desired track angle...It was a very clever device and led to improved calculators in our own Navy. *a1995 Gallantin *Sub. Admiral* 34 [ref. to 1930's]: The "IS-WAS"...assisted in determining courses to steer for desired torpedo attack angles.

it *pron.* **1.** copulation.—used without antecedent and usu. uttered with weak stress.
*1599 in Shakespeare *Comp. Works* 886: Had women been so strong as men,/In faith you had not had it then. *1611 Cotgrave *Dict.: Fretiller.* To...itch, lust to be at it. *1698–1720 in D'Urfey *Pills* V 271: Yet rather than Daughter shall want it, she Pimps. *1896 Farmer *Vocab. Amatoria* 118: *Faire*...to copulate; "to do it." **1929** in E. Wilson *Twenties* 532: She wanted it right away—lost no time. **1929–33** Farrell *Manhood of Lonigan* 185: She made him want it like he almost never wanted it before. **1930–33** T. Wolfe *Time & River* 119: It's the widder. She's let him have a little of it. **1936** Levin *Old Bunch* 254: He would tell how he had had it for the first time the first night in Paris. **1951** Willingham *Gates of Hell* 68: She'd only been doing "it" for about two months. **1952** Himes *Stone* 258. She ruined me for other women. She never got enough; she wanted buckets of it. **1956** in R. Russell *Permanent Playboy* 80: There are two distinct kinds of men: those who get it often and easily, and those who don't. **1957** J.R. MacDonald *Price of Murder* 26: Damn! She's really built for it. **1961** Forbes *Goodbye to Some* 29: Likes to insist that his girl...is a real love goddess and wild for "it" practically any hour of the day or night. **1973** Hirschfeld *Victors* 227: "How many times you had it?" "I don't understand." "How many times you been banged, boffed, laid?" *a1976 Roebuck & Frese *Rendezvous* 176: But we're not in the street...selling it [prostituting themselves]. **1992** *New York* (June 8) 36: Four duos were doing *It* in the balcony. **1993** *N.Y. Observer* (Sept. 27) 14: Those awful stories that used to circulate in college about couples clenching up mid-"it" and having to be borne off to the hospital.
2. the penis or vagina.—used without antecedent.
1846 N.J.T. Dana *Monterrey* 144: She...had not even the decency to put her hand before it. *ca1863 in Rable *Civil Wars* 55: Put it in the whole length....[I] will keep it closed fore you when you come home...it will be as tight as the first time you tried it. *a1890–96 F & H IV 17: It...The female *pudendum.* **1919** in Dreiser *Diaries* 297: He's got me down & he's putting it to me. **1979** C. Martin *Catullus* 21: You'd like to slip it into my beloved!
3. a stupid or offensive person.
1895 *DN* I 419: *It.* A worthless fellow. "An awful *it.*" **1900** *DN* II 42: *It,* n. 1. A word of contempt expressing that one is something less than a human being; hence an idiot, a dolt. **1903** McClallen *He Demons* 74: They'll come and stand out in a drizzling rain...to see this or that Royal "IT." **1903** *Pedagog. Sem.* X 371: You big *it.* **1925** *AS* I 103: *It* means simpleton or booby.
4. a focus of favorable interest or attention; the most superior or desirable person or thing.
1896 Ade *Artie* 4: I didn't do a thing but push my face in there about eight o'clock last night, and I was "it" from the start. **1898** *Survival of Fittest* (unp.): Noah...communed gleefully with himself, saying, "Verily, I am It!" **1902** K. Harriman *Ann Arbor Tales* 164: You've

got 'em goin'. Greeny, *you're it!* **1902** Townsend *Fadden & Mr. Paul* 37: He wasn't a has-been, nor a will-be, but he was an izzer. He was it. **1903** *Our Naval Apprentice* (May) 20: Baseball is "it!" **1905** Brainerd *Belinda* 31: She was IT; she was up to her eyebrows in romance. **1909** in O. Johnson *Lawrenceville Stories* 93: You're a wonder. You're great. You're it. **1911** *Baseball Mag.* (Feb.) 108: "And now," said the girl who was wise, "this is It —/ That pitcher is there with a pretty good spit." **1913** in Pound *Letters* 16: We've got to be IT, first in the hearts of our countrymen, etc. **1957** Bannon *Odd Girl* 28: Bud was Emmy's flame— Bud was "it." **1961** Parkhurst *Undertow* 163: When I first met her, I wanted her to think I was "it" but she was never impressed.

5. money.—used without antecedent.

1898–1900 Cullen *Chances* 138: He was covered with gig lamps and he had it in every pocket. **1958** Gardner *Piece of the Action* 231: You must really be raking it in. **1977–81** S. King *Cujo* 94: Fuck you, you're rolling in it.

6.a. whatever qualities, often including good luck, are required for or will guarantee success; (*often*) charm or personal magnetism.—usu. constr. with *have* and/or *got*.

1901 Ade *Modern Fables* 63: In the Commercial Agencies he was Rated AA plus A1, which meant that he had it in Bales. ****1904** Kipling *Traffics* 393: 'Tisn't beauty...nor good talk necessarily. It's just It. Some women'll stay in a man's memory if they once walk down a street. **1927** Shoup *Marines in China* 39: I was well aware that any 2d Lt. is not overloaded with "it" in the eyes of his superiors. **1928** (quot. at **(b)**, below). **1935** Wead *Ceiling Zero* (film): Dizzy Davis was a good guy when he had *it*. **1951** Robbins *Danny Fisher* 64: I'd see 'er 'f I was you. She's really got it. **1959** Sterling *Wake of the Wahoo* 76: Some guys sure have got it. **1970** N.Y.U. student: Some guys got it, and some guys ain't. **1975** Univ. Tenn. instructor: Some have it, and some don't. **1975–76** T. McNally *Ritz* 69: I mean, you have "it"...or you don't. **1987** E. Spencer *Macho Man* 102: All the bullshit that's been told about the black guy not having it. **1996** N. George, in *Village Voice* (N.Y.C.) (Sept. 24) 28: Onscreen he had that intangible "it."

b. *Specif.* sex appeal.—usu. said with emphatic stress. [Popularized by Elinor Glyn's 1927 novel.]

1927 Glyn *"It"* 10: He had that nameless charm, with a strong magnetism which can only be called "It." **1928** *N.Y. Times* (Mar. 11) VIII 6: *It*—Elinor Glyn's name for S.A. **1928** *AS* III (June) 436: The regular college slang for "sex appeal" or for magnetic personal qualities in general is now "it," writes G.H. Danton of Oberlin, Ohio. **1930** F. Marion *Big House* (film): How I miss my great big boy! You have *it!* **1980** L. Fleischer & C. Gore *Fame* 238: That's beautiful. Oh, yes, you've got it all. *a***1992** Deuterman *Scorpion* 25: You've got "it," kid....You're just going to have to learn to live with it.

¶ In phrase:

¶ **full of it** [euphem. for *full of shit*] (usu. of persons) spouting nonsense; entirely, often complacently, in error; lying.

1955 N.Y.C. schoolboy: Aaah, you're full of it! **1960** Matheson *Beardless Warriors* 193 [ref. to WWII]: Well, he's full of it. **1966** Bullins *Goin'a Buffalo* 201: Oh, man, you're full of it! **1966** Neugeboren *Big Man* 112: I tell him he's full of it, he says it's the truth. **1992** *60 Minutes* (CBS-TV) (Apr. 5): At first I was like, "This guy's full of it, man." **1993** *Real World* (MTV): You're full of it. **1993** *Sally Jessy Raphaël* (synd. TV series): That's *full* of it!

Italian salute *n.* a vulgar or obscene gesture in which the elbow is bent and the fist and forearm are abruptly jerked upward while the opposite hand grips the forearm or bicep; (see also 1975 quot.).

*a***1967** K. Cook *Other Capri* 42: That's an Italian salute....It means "screw you, Jack," or worse. **1972** Boston man, age *ca*20: Give 'em the old Italian salute. **1975** Durocher & Linn *Nice Guys* 311 [ref. to 1950's]: Sal was so mad he waited until I got back into the dugout so that he could give me the Italian salute...with his hand on his crotch. **1979** McGivern *Soldiers* 260 [ref. to WWII]: "An Italian salute to your mother, too," Larkin yelled back at him. **1987** Philmont, N.Y., man, age *ca*60, on Headline News network (July 8): I give the old Italian salute to those Congressmen! [*Gestures*.] *a***1989** C.S. Crawford *Four Deuces* 94 [ref. to Korean War]: I was giving the gooks on Hill 1052...the Italian "fuck you" salute, hitting my right elbow with a cupped hand, bouncing up my right forearm. **1990** Murano & Hoffer *Cop Hunter* 41: The Italian salute—the palm of one hand snapping

loudly upon the biceps of the other, upraised arm. This was the...counterpart to..."the finger."

italicize *v.* to knock out of shape. *Joc.*

1887 Peck *Pvt. Peck* 270: I will italicise his nose so he will look so cross-eyed that he can't draw his pay.

item *n.* **1.** a person.

1958 J. Davis *College Vocab.* 12: *Sick item*—...a person with a hangover. **1987** Stroud *Close Pursuit* 11: Woody Allen is saying this to some item he's trying to hustle.

2. a romantically involved couple.

1981 (quot. at HOT ITEM). **1984** *L.A. Times* (Aug. 6) I 12: Taylor and Burton were spending long hours in each others' dressing rooms; they were constantly together off the set;...they were An Item. **1987** in *Nat. Lampoon* (Feb. 1988) 32: What's this...about you and that Foster girl no longer being an item? **1988** *Golden Girls* (NBC-TV): We happen to be an item. **1989** *TV Guide* (Aug. 5) 20: The next evening, they went on a "real" date...and were quickly an item. **1990** C.P. McDonald *Blue Truth* 198: Everybody thought you two would be an item. **1995** *Strange Luck* (Fox-TV): Didn't you used to be an item?

Itie *n. & adj.* Esp. *Mil.* Italian; EYETIE.—often used derisively.

****1941** (cited in Partridge *DSUE* (ed. 7) 1216). **1942** *Yank* (June 17) 16: "Ities," Cassidy calls them. **1942** *Yank* (June 24) 1: U.S.—R.A.F. Cripple Itie Fleet.

-itis *suffix.* (used to create nonce forms indicating a fear of or obsession with that named in the initial element).

1912 Lowrie *Prison* 142: Skirtetis is a bad bug t' do time with. **1917** *Sat. Eve. Post*, in *DARE*: He had even talked golf to his wife—which is the last stage of incurable golfitis. **1927** *AS* II 245: Blueitis, bookitis, Charlestonitis,...crosswordpuzzleitis, danceitis [etc.]. **1954** McGraw *Prison Riots* 270: *Shortitis:* Nervousness of a prisoner who is short. **1981** Luagner *Shrinking Woman* (film): I think you've got a bad case of self-pity-itis. **1983** Groen & Groen *Huey* 15 [ref. to 1970]: Instructors warned you about check-ride-itis, the fear that kept you from doing as well as you were able. *a***1990** P. Dickson *Slang!* 145: *Hospitalitis.* Malaise of patients who have been in the hospital too long. **1995** Cormier et al. *Wildcats* 159: A severe case of "get-aboard-itis."

Itlo *n.* a person of Italian descent, esp. an Italian-American.

1981 *TV Guide* (June 13) 35: While I would have preferred a profile of William Paca (who signed the Declaration of Independence), the first so-called Itlo I met on the tube was Al Capone.

itzy house *n.* an insane asylum.

1931 Harlow *Old Bowery* 493 [ref. to 1890's]: Me in Congress!...To the itzy house with youse!

Ivan *n. Mil.* **1.** a Soviet or Russian man or boy; (*hence*) a Soviet plane.

[****1925** Fraser & Gibbons *Soldier & Sailor Wds.* 129 [ref. to WWI]: *Ivan:* The everyday name in the Russian Army, at any rate down to 1916, for a private soldier, equivalent to our "Tommy Atkins."] **1944** *Amer. N & Q* (June) 48: The [U.S. shuttle] airmen themselves...began to refer to every young Russian aide as "Ivan." **1963** Fehrenbach *This Kind of War* 39: When asked how he had outwitted the Ivans, Peavey would only smile gently. **1964** Caidin *Everything But Flak* 96: Two hundred pounds of ex-Marine "accidentally" slammed into the solar plexus of the falling Ivan. **1989** G. Hall *Air Guard* 38: Our flight will concentrate on the closer-in Ivan.

2. the Soviet Union; Soviet armed forces.

1950 *Time* (Sept. 18) 33: The mark and memory of Ivan's bestiality had set Berliners apart from their fellow Germans. **1969** *Russia in the Mediterranean* (NBC news special): Ivan's out there. **1972** Sapir & Murphy *Death Therapy* 113: John Bull and Ivan are the only holdouts. **1976** Atlee *Domino* 154: We're hours away from a head-on confrontation between Ivan, ourselves, and the mainland Chinese. *a***1984** T. Clancy *Red Oct.* 71: If Ivan was looking to play hardball, that *Yankee*'d be heading south. **1984** W. Gibson *Neuromancer* 35: Turkey shoot for Ivan. **1988** *Supercarrier* (ABC-TV): It's Ivan, Captain. A MiG-28 with a brand-new suit of clothes.

ivory *n.* **1.** usu. *pl.* a tooth.—also used collectively; in phr. **chip** [or **pound**] **the ivory** [or **ivories**] to talk or complain.

****1782** in *F & H* IV 17: Don Sancho, who...complains of the toothache, to make you believe that the two rows of ivory he carries in his head, grew there. ****1785** Grose *Vulgar Tongue* s.v. *flash*: To flash one's *ivory;* to laugh and shew one's teeth. ****1819** [T. Moore] *Tom Crib* 22: The Adonis

would ne'er *flash his ivory** again....**show his teeth.* **1821** Waln *Hermit in Phila* 27: Looks as if he had been fed with a fire shovel; always *sporting his ivory.* ***1831** Trelawny *Adv. of Younger Son* ch. xxi: The dislocation of his jaw, and loss of ivory. **1841** *Spirit of Times* (Feb. 13) 596: Drawing back his lips until his ivories appeared quite distinct. **1853** W.W. Brown *Clotel* 124: His little ivories shine. **1853** S. Robinson *Hot Corn* 76: Shut pan, or I'll chuck your ivory into your bread-basket. **1854** Sleeper *Salt Water Bubbles* 65: He looked as if he could have bitten off the but-end of a marlinspike without...blunting his ivories. ***1860** Hotten *Slang Dict.* (ed. 2): *Ivories*, teeth; "a box of *ivories*," a set of teeth, the mouth; "wash your *ivories*," i.e., "drink." **1866** Williams *Gay Life in N.Y.* 88: Another, was a noted pugilist who "queered the ogles;" "tapped the claret;" "smashed the ivories;" and "pounded the bread basket;" of many an adversary. **1867** (quot. at KISSER). **1891** *Puck* (Jan. 14) 355: Mulberry Bend: I've lost my ivories. English: Old, or Toothless. **1891** Maitland *Slang Dict.* 151: *Ivories*, teeth. A set of teeth is a box of "Ivories" or "Dominoes." "Rinse your ivories" means take a drink. **1944** Kendall *Service Slang* 19: *Beating the gums*....Also referred to as pounding the ivory, knashing the choppers or chipping the pickets. **1945** in *Calif. Folk. Qly.* V (1946) 376: A...skivvy-waver and a...bellhop were chipping the ivories. **1968** Lockridge *Hartspring* 102: She smiled. Hard, white ivories. **1984** D. Smith *Steely Blue* 5: Real men...put five big ones between the ivories to shut someone's mouth up.

2. [because orig. made of ivory] **a.** *pl.* dice. Cf. much earlier syn. BONE[1], 1.
    ***1830** in *OED2*: Suppose we adjourn to Fish lane, and rattle the ivories! ***1873** Hotten *Slang Dict.* (ed. 4): *Ivories*...dice. **1938–39** Dos Passos *Young Man* 82: He'll take your money away if he gets to rollin' the ivories. **1986** C. Freeman *Seasons of Heart* 285: Haven't rattled the ivories since college.

b. usu. *pl.* a poker chip.
    1887 [C. Mackenzie] *Jack Pots* 48: He deposited his last ivory on the ace. **1889** Barrère & Leland *Dict. Slang.* **1936** R. Adams *Cowboy Lingo* 230: [Poker] Chips were called "ivories." [**1973** in T.L. Clark *Dict. Gambling & Gaming* [for specifically white chips].]

c. *pl.* billiard balls.
    ***1888** in *F & H* IV 18: On new premises...where erstwhile the click of ivories was heard. **1889** Barrère & Leland *Dict. Slang* I 490: *Ivories*...(Billiards) the balls. **1955** Archibald *Aviation Cadet* 94: At the next table a pair of Norwegian cadets were clicking the ivories.

d. usu. *pl.* a piano key; a piano; in phr. **tickle the ivories** [and vars.] to play the piano.
    [***1818** J. Keats, in *OED2*: She plays the Music without one sensation but the feel of the ivory at her fingers.] **1891** De Vere *Tramp Poems* 9: And when he hit them ivories we all knowed he was in it. **1895** Outcault *Yellow Kid* 138: First his fingers jist did a dog trot all up an' down der ivories. **1899** (quot. at PROFESSOR). **1906** *Nat. Police Gaz.* (May 5) 3: Hitting up the ivories at swell concerts. **1913** W. Herzer *Tickle the Ivories* [ragtime composition]. **1924** *Pirate Piece* (Aug.) 3: I am still "spanking the Ivorys" with the "Ches Davis Revue." **1926** in *AS* II (Mar. 1927) 277: *Itch a mean ivory.* Play piano well. **1929** L. Thomas *Woodfill* 74: But in those days he...was still livin' in the Klondike ticklin' the ivories in some...saloon. **1931** Wilstach *Under Cover Man* 36: Do you pound the ivories? **1936** Miller *Battling Bellhop* (film): Louie, get busy on those ivories. **1938** in Inman *Diary* 878: Gees, dat guy could tickle the ivories. **1945** in Galewitz *Great Comics* 51: Y' like to get away from th' ivories for a day. **1965** Oliver *Conversations* 9: The singer's injunctions of "speak to me, guitar," "tell 'em, ivories" and similar modes of address to his instrument are evidence of the conception of the strings as an eloquent second voice. **1970** Boatright & Owens *Derrick* 147: He went over there and pounded the ivory. *a***1978** A. Rose *Eubie Blake* 19: An adroit manipulator of the ivories.

3. the head (of a stupid person). Cf. IVORY DOME.
    1918 in Bliss *805th Pioneer Inf.* 211: With a tin hat over your ivory,/With a rifle clutched in your fist. **1930** *Scouting* (Jan.) 21: He will learn what you are trying to inject into the "ivory."

ivory *adj.* racially white; Caucasian.
    1991 Nelson & Gonzales *Bring Noise* 14: These ivory B-boys bounce rhymes off one another.

ivory-bender *n.* a piano player.
    1922–24 McIntyre *White Light* 49: There is little flubdubbery among the "ivory benders."...Any number of them have never had a music lesson.

ivory dome *n.* the head of a dunce; a dunce; blockhead. Also **ivory nut, ivory top.**

1911 *Baseball Mag.* (Oct.) 32 (cited in Nichols *Baseball Term.*). **1912** *Adventure* (June) 242: Say, you big ivory-nut!...do you think I'm doing this for a joke? **1919** *DN* V 62: *Ivory-dome*, a dull, stupid fellow. "Doyle seems to be an *ivory-dome* in history class." New Mexico. **1919** *Amer. Legion Wkly.* (Aug. 22) 12: I said how May was no ivory top and would most likely guess it anyway. **1921** in Kornbluh *Rebel Voices* 248: A bright idea penetrated into my "ivory dome" as Red calls it. **1926** *Jour. Applied Psych.* X 254: *Ivory dome* means...bonehead.

ivory-domed *adj.* stupid; blockheaded.
    1912 *Adventure* (May) 51: I would offer the red-headed and ivory-domed prospector aid and comfort. **1929–31** J.T. Farrell *Young Lonigan* 88: Even ivory-domed Andy Le Gare.

ivory float [rhyming slang; prob. sugg. by the advertising slogan of Ivory soap, "It floats"] a coat.
    1928 Sharpe *Chicago May* 288: *Ivory float*—coat.

ivory hound *n.* a piano player.
    1935 Pollock *Und. Speaks: Ivory hound*, a piano player.

ivory-hunter *n. Journ.* a talent scout. Hence **ivory-hunting,** *n.* Also **ivory-sorter.**
    1922 *Sat. Eve. Post* (July 29) 12: McGrath, the ivory sorter, broke excitedly into Heenan's office at the Blue Sox park. **1942** *ATS* 646: *Ivory hunter*, a baseball scout who secures players for major-league teams. **1950** *Time* (Oct. 2) 36: He organized the Cardinal farm system, and reduced "ivory hunting" (*i.e.*, talent scouting) to a business basis. **1959–60** Bloch *Dead Beat* 50: Hell, there were a lot of ivory hunters...dragging down fancy loot in the plush joints out there.

ivory-pounder *n.* a piano player.
    1903 *Enquirer* (Cincinnati) (May 9) 13: *Ivory pounder*—Piano player. **1946** W.A. White *Autobiog.* 154: What we ivory-pounders and catgut squeezers used to scorn as classical music. **1972** *Life* (Oct. 27) 26: He was a real down ivory-pounder and blues-shouter.

ivory-thumper *n.* a piano player.
    1928 (quot. at OILED). **1941** Cain *Mildred Pierce* 235: She takes lessons from some cheap little ivory-thumper over in Glendale.

ivory-tickler *n.* a piano player.
    1911 in Truman *Dear Bess* 23: A pretty good piano player. Ivory tickler, as Shorty Short says. **1947** Goffin *Horn* 247: Ivory-ticklers like Earl don't grow on trees in Chicago. **1982** Braun *Judas Tree* 39: An ivory-tickler was pounding an upright piano. **1990** *Wkly. World News* (May 1) 12: The billionaire biker and the swishy ivory-tickler.

ivy pole *n.* [sugg. by *IV* 'intravenous'] *Hosp.* a rack from which a container of intravenous solution is suspended.
    1981 in Safire *Good Word* 158: "Ivy pole"...IV rack.

I.W.W. [authorized abbrev. of *Industrial Workers of the World*, an American syndicalist labor organization 1905–20] (interpreted in var. facetious ways; see quots.). Now *hist.*
    1922 N. Anderson *Hobo* 235: The I.W.W. is little understood by society in general. The public believes it is an organization of "tramps who won't work," and that the initials stand for "I Won't Work," or "I Want Whiskey." **1928** Dahlberg *Bottom Dogs* 116: Mush Tate...had become an I won't worker. **1929–30** Dos Passos *42d Parallel* 349: The boss said he'd have no goddam I Won't Works in this outfit. **1931** Farrell *Gas-House McGinty* 33: I.W.W.'s, so lazy, they all stink. I Won't Work, and I Want Whiskey bastards. **1951** J. Wilson *Dark & Damp* 175 [ref. to 1916]: You're one of these "I won't work" bastards. **1971** Curtis *Banjo* 54: He sounds very much like an anarchist, like one of those I Won't Work people.

ixnay *v. & interj.* [pig Latin] NIX.
    1929 Goulding & Mason *Broadway Melody* (film): Ixnay! Ixnay! **1930** Creelman *Half Shot* (film): Ixnay! Ixnay! **1933** in Ruhm *Detective* 78: Ixnay. I like trouble. **1946** J.H. Burns *Gallery* 283: If she says ixnay I tell her to get the hell out. **1951** J. Reach *My Friend Irma* 78: Ixnay! **1952** Malamud *Natural* 91: Roy Hobbs, El Swatto, has been ixnayed on a pay raise. **1956** Levin *Compulsion* 91: "Hey, ixnay." Artie gestured for him to drive on. **1966** R.E. Alter *Carny Kill* 8: Ixnay, soldier. **1979** T. Baum *Carny* 46: Ixnay....The meeazarks. **1981** *WKRP in Cincinnati* (CBS-TV): Ixnay on the "little guy" stuff. **1985** *Amazing Stories* (NBC-TV): Ixnay! Don't jinx the last round trip. **1989** *Murphy Brown* (CBS-TV): If he asks you to slow-dance near a window—ixnay, baby, ixnay. **1993** *CBS This Morning* (CBS-TV) (Jan. 25): Ixnay on the arriagemay.

J

J *n.* **1.** *Naval Av.* a North American SNJ Texan training plane. Now *hist.*

    1944 in Rea *Wings of Gold* 204: The J…is the SNJ-5,…the best known training plane in the Navy. *Ibid.* 220: There are hundreds of J's sitting out on the line. **1991** Linnekin *80 Knots* 48: The SNJ….The "J" was close to an unrestricted airplane for maneuvers.

2. [fr. JOINT] a marijuana cigarette. Also **jay.**

    1967 Rosevear *Pot: J, jay:* Marihuana cigarette. **1968** *N.Y. Post* (July 15) 12: The sergeant smoked a jay while he talked. Jay is military slang for a joint, but either way it's marijuana. **1970** *Look* (June 16) 72: They would begin with marijuana, or "J's," as the joints were nicknamed. **1972** *N.Y. Post* (Apr. 8) 25: "J's," joints or cigarets fashioned from marihuana and magazine paper, already have been passed around. *a***1977** in S. King *Bachman* 133: The j came around to me. **1980** Lorenz *Guys Like Us* 24: To take a few hits on the jay Ferd had slipped him. **1979–82** Gwin *Overboard* 7: Dock-boys [were] passing jays to one another. **1982** Del Vecchio *13th Valley* 178: A gallon a bourbon [and] a deck a Js. **1992** *Donahue* (NBC-TV): He said, "Let's smoke a J." **1993** "Snoop Doggy Dogg" *Gin & Juice* (rap song): A fat-ass J of some bubonic chronic [*sc.* marijuana] that made me choke. **1991–95** Sack *Co. C* 201: Young rolled a J and…took a toke.

3. *Basketball.* a jump shot. Also **jay.**

    1976 Rosen *Above Rim* 82: Jeremy Johnson's jump shot swished through the net….Bang! Another jay from twenty feet. **1978** B. Johnson *What's Happenin'* 32: I been stopping at the top of the lane and shooting my little jay. **1980** Wielgus & Wolff *Basketball* 54: The J (*n*) The jump shot. **1983** Goldaper & Pincus *How to Talk Basketball* 98: The player who has a good one can "shoot the J." **1987** *Academe* (July) 56: Stick to swishing the J's against me. **1988** in N. George *Buppies, B-Boys* 264: Johnny "Got-a-J-and-Know-How-To-Use-It" Newman. **1990** in Wimmer *Schoolyard Game* 103: Shoot the J.

jab *n.* **1.** (see quot.). Cf. syn. STAB.

    1900 *DN* II 43: *Jab*, n….An attempt at anything.

2. *Narc.* a hypodermic injection, esp. of a narcotic.

    1914 Jackson & Hellyer *Vocab.* 48: *Jab*, Noun Current amongst morphine and cocaine fiends. A hypodermic injection. **1922** E. Murphy *Black Candle* 128: They take their first "jab" or "sniff." **1927** in R.C. Allen *Horrible Prettiness* 278: She needed a jab. She's been taking heroin and morphine by the barrels. **1996** *Newshour with J. Lehrer* (PBS-TV) (Aug. 11): I'm gonna go get [the dog] some jabs today.

3. an act of copulation.—usu. considered vulgar. Cf. JAB, *v.,* 2.

    1989 (quot. at JAB, *v.,* 2).

jab *v.* **1.** *Narc.* to inject with (a drug). —also used absol.

    1908 McGaffey *Show Girl* 129: She either does that or jabs, though it don't show on her arm. **1926** in *OED2*: Coke don't need any jabbin'. **1938** *AS* XIII 186: *To Jab.* To take drugs hypodermically. **1956** Longstreet *Real Jazz* 114: Not all jazz-players smoke marijuana…or jab a vein. **1959** J. Laughlin, in Witemeyer *Williams-Laughlin* 229: He lets the local man jab him with…vitamins.

2. to copulate with (a woman).—usu. considered vulgar.

    *ca***1929** *Collection of Sea Songs* 11: My dear I've been jabbed by a stud. *****1959** in *OED2.* **1965** Trimble *Sex Words* 112: *Jab*…v.t. To copulate. *****1972**, *****1973** in *OED2.* **1989** P. Munro *U.C.L.A. Slang* 52: He jabbed her….I knew what was the matter. She needed a jab.

jabber *n.* (see quot.).

    1904 *Life in Sing Sing* 250: *Jabber.* Prize fighter.

jaboney var. JIBONEY.

jabongoes *n.pl.* [expressive formation; cf. sim. forms such as BAZONGAS] a woman's breasts.

    1961 Terry *Old Liberty* 32: A little wife with nice jabongoes to kiss me hello every night.

jack[1] *n.* [fr. *Jack*, hypocoristic form of male given name *John*] **1.** (usu. *cap.*) **a.** a seaman. Now *hist.* [The 1659 quot. appears to be a chance collocation.]

    [*****1659** in *OED:* The English…laid it most sadly upon Jack-Sailors breech.] *****1706** in *OED:* Here he and his Brother Jacks lie pelting each other with Sea-Wit. *****1821–26** Stewart *Man-of-War's Man* I 182: A fellow who is hardly ever sober, and who I am certain, were he a common jack, would never have his shank-painters clear of the grimmets. **1827** J.F. Cooper *Red Rover* 167: It is as bold as it would be in a foremast Jack to tell his officer he was wrong. **1841** [Mercier] *Man-of-War* 275: Two or three *reefers*, and eighteen or twenty *common Jacks.* **1847** Downey *Portsmouth* 132: A party of Marines was now detached…and the remainder, with the Jacks, marched off for their boats. *Ibid.* 141: A good law for…the Jacks, but not binding on the Officer. **1847** W.H. Richardson *Jour.* 73: But Jack knocked him down and broke his sabre in pieces. **1849** Doten *Journals* I 55: Very scientific "fiddling" performed by an old Jack. **1854** in McCauley *With Perry* 93: Last night a sympathising Jack, kindly put them in the coppers. **1863** J.S. Warner *Black Ship* 63: Well, sir, it's a failing we Jacks have. *****1867** in *F & H* IV 22: The old brigadier ordered the Jacks to storm. **1868** Macy *There She Blows!* 19: The whalemen criticised us as "half-Jack half-gentlemen." *Ibid.* 43: I obeyed orders…like a true Jack. **1873** in R.H. Dillon *Shanghaiing Days* 181: Day by day, we swung at our anchors…trying to coax a crew aboard. Not a Jack would come. **1913–14** London *Elsinore* 282: Fifty-six men before the mast, and the last Jack of 'em an able seaman. *a***1924** A. Hunter *Yr. on Monitor* 152 [ref. to Civil War]: A sergeant…greeted [me] with: "Hello, Jack! What brought you away up here?"

b. (a name used in familiar address to a man whose real name is unknown); MAN; in phr. **damn** [now usu. (*vulgar*) **fuck**] **you, Jack, I'm all right** (an expression of glib, self-satisfied contempt). [In early use perh. restricted to seamen, as 1823, ***1870 quots.; but cf. *OED* def. 2, "a low-bred or ill-mannered fellow, a 'knave'," reflected in bracketed quot. below.]

    [*****1632** B. Jonson *Magnetic Lady* I (chorus): *Dam.* Why so my peremptory Jack? *Boy.* My name is *John*, indeed.] **1823** [J. Neal] *Errata* I 146: Damn it, Jack, fair play! *a***1849** in C. Hill *Scenes* 169: "Oh, darn it all, don't git mad, Jack."…"You mind dat my name am not Jack, I is Bill Brown." *****1870** Greey *Blue Jackets* 26: Wot's the matter with *you*, Jack? *****1879** in *EDD:* Every farming lad, also, whose name is not known, is familiarly called Jack. "Well! Jack, borh!" *a***1889** *Century Dict:* *Jack*…A familiar term of address used among sailors, soldiers, laborers, etc. **1889** Barrère & Leland *Dict. Slang* I 490: *Jack* (American). It is common among schoolboys in Philadelphia to address a stranger as *Jack*, and also to speak of a blunderer or stupid fellow as a *Jack*—an abbreviation of *jackass.* **1894** *Century* (Feb.) 519: It's not in us to fool round a jerk town like this un too long. It's tiresome, Jack. *ca***1895** McCloskey *Across Continent* 78: "Come, Jack, you'd better accept my proposition."…"My name isn't Jack—my name is Johnnie." **1899** Young *Remin. & Stories* 432: Private soldiers are known as either Jack or Pete to their comrades. Any of them will answer to either name. **1904** *Life in Sing Sing* 17: "Jack"—all convicts are "Jack,"—"do you smoke?" **1905** *Independent* (Mar. 2) 486: The distinguishing trait of the twentieth century substitute sailor is selfishness, a habit never acquired by the genuine old timers. "D—n you, Jack, I'm all right," is being gradually adopted by the lords of the forecastle and quarter deck alike in place of the old time motto of generous consideration that was world famous, "Remember Your Shipmates." **1905** Sinclair *Jungle* 222: They call all foreigners and unskilled men "Jack" in Packingtown. *Ibid.* 223: Say, Jack, I'm afraid you'll have to quit. **1907** in Tamony *Americanisms* (No. 19) 8: Hey, Jack, do you see the shack?…Hey, Jack, what bug is dis guy got? **1918** E. Wilson *Prelude* 201: Holland's bon mot for the military system: "You go to hell, Jack: I'm all right!" *****1921** *N & Q* (Nov. 19) 417 [ref. to WWI]: The selfish would be rebuked with, "It's all '—you, Jack, I'm in the lifeboat' with you." **1927** in Fitzgerald *Stories* I 362: Suit yourself, Jack. **1931** in H. Miller *Letters to Emil* 79: And fuck you, Jack! **1933** "W. March" *Company K* 38 [ref. to 1918]: The bloody doctor laughed. "Are you still with us, 'Gentle Annie'?" he asked. "———Jack!" I said. *****1936** Partridge *DSUE* 304: F**k you, Jack, I'm all right! A [catch phr.] directed at callousness or indifference: nautical (late C. 19–20); hence military in [Great War] and after. **1941** in Ellington *Music Is My Mistress* 179: *Jack*…name for any fellow. **1950–52** Ulanov *Hist. Jazz* 351: *Jack:* equivalent of "Mac" or "Bud" in American slang; means of address to a male; in later years sometimes replaced by "Jim." **1973** P. Benchley *Jaws* 91: It was an "I'm all right, Jack" attitude. **1974** Blount *3 Bricks Shy* 171: People are yelling, "Fuck you, Jack." **1967–80** Folb *Runnin' Lines* 243: *Jack* Form of address among black males (used emphatically or as verbal punctuation). **1990** *Garfield & Friends* (CBS-TV): Hit the road, Jack. **1993** Mowry *Six Out Seven* 51: That a fact, jack? **1994** Knoxville, Tenn., man, age 41: Fuck you, Jack.

c. Now *Black E.* a boy or man. Cf. *OED* def. 2 (1548–1746). See also NEW JACK. [No continuity of usage is evident between early and current usage.]

1744 A. Hamilton *Gentleman's Progress* 14: That I may be in a trim to box the saucy jacks there [in Maryland]. **1943** *N.Y. Times* (May 9) II 5: Dig, my Jacks and Jills. **1947–53** Guthrie *Seeds* 379: You men, you two jacks, you can sleep up here on this roof. **1971** H. Roberts *Third Ear: Jack*...a male person. Syn. see CAT. **1976** Calloway & Rollins *Moocher & Me* 182: Dizzy Gillespie was a past master at hip talk, but even he would admit that Professor Calloway himself was the hardest jack with the greatest jive in the joint. **1988** *Spin* (Oct). 47: *New jack* n, rapper who got started after whoever is speaking. **1989** *Village Voice* (N.Y.C.) (June 20) 39: On B-boys, new jacks, or house servants, they're a sign of just how far we've traveled. **1992** N. Cohn *Heart of World* 101: One of the Jacks from the projects, Leavell Robinson,...[was] sporting a brand-new pair of Air Jordans. **1993** *Source* (July) 52: I learn about life from the old jacks.

2. *Pol.* a Jacksonian Democrat. Cf. earlier Brit. pol. sense, 'a Jacobite', as in bracketed quot.

[*a1720* in D'Urfey *Pills* I 28: Ye *Jacks* of the Town,/And *Whiggs* of renown.] **1830** in *DA*: The masons, as the antis say, are clearly unfit for office—the Jacks are just as bad.

3.a. a flapjack.

1832 J.P. Kennedy *Swallow Barn* 56: She was usually occupied in paring apples to be baked up into tough jacks for our provender. **1850** in *DAE*: [I soon] set to work upon the "jacks." **1944** E.H. Hunt *Limit* 19: Only one jack for me.

b. Esp. *N.J.* applejack or raisinjack.

1894 *DN* I 331: In Salem, Sussex, and Burlington counties [N.J.], where apple whiskey is made, it is commonly called "jack." **1940** in *DARE*: Jerseymen truncate "applejack" to "jack." **1946** in *DARE*: A side of beef and a gallon of jack to wash it down. **1946** McPhee *Pine Barrens* 59: Applejack...is known as jack [in So. N.J.]. **1982** Downey *Losing the War* 173 [ref. to WWII]: Everyone had different ideas on what good "jack" required for superior taste.

4. [fr. *jack*ass] **a.** a blockhead; jackass; JERK², 1.a.

a1867 in G.W. Harris *Lovingood* 108: An' he wer a jack, ove the longes' year'd kine. *a1889* in Barrère & Leland *Dict. Slang* I 490: Have the judges...awarded the prize to the biggest Jack? **1895** Wood *Yale Yarns* 142: You'll never see either hat or box again—you jack! **1905** Dey *Scylla* 63: Well, I ain't quite such a jack as all that, miss. **1979** D. Milne *Second Chance* 61 [ref. to 1950's]: This'll teach those jacks a lesson. *Ibid.* 69: That'll teach those jacks to mess around with us. **1982** Least Heat Moon *Blue Hwys.* 98: They're more likely from Northern jacks comin' down here messin' where it ain't their concern. **1989** *Newsweek* (Aug. 7) 6: *Jack:* Has no intention of buying a car, yet insists on test-drive, etc. Possibly lonely and looking for conversation.

b. *Stu.* a translation; PONY.

1900 *DN* 43: *Jack*, n. 1. A translation. 2. Concealed notes for use in examination or recitation. **1906** *Univ. Tenn. Vol.* (unp.): The trade in "Jacks"/Doth ever wax. **1906** *DN* III 142: He always gets his Latin with a *jack*. **1926** *AS* (Oct.) 46: Indiana...*jack*—"A literal translation." **1946** *PADS* (No. 6) 18: *Jack*...a small-sized, small-type translation of the classics....In a number of schools and colleges in N.C.

c. *R.R.* a locomotive.

1919 in Brown *N.C. Folklore* III 266: All aboard on the southern jack! **1919** in N.I. White *Amer. Negro Folk-Songs* 280: I got a southern jack;/First thing I do, shovel in the coal,/Next thing I do, watch the drivers roll. **1930** *Railroad Man's Mag.* II 471: *Jack*—Locomotive. **1941** in Fenner *Throttle* 183: The big jack took up her deep belly laugh as the blast of the hotshot died. **1945** Hubbard *R.R. Ave.* 349: *Jack*—Locomotive. (A term often confused with the lifting device, hence seldom used). **1948** McIlwaine *Memphis* 19: Such idols as "Casey" Jones...leaning out of the cabs of their roaring "jacks." **1968** in *DARE*: *Jack* is the name given to the locomotive by the Negro folk.

5. *West.* a jackrabbit.

1864 in *Kans. Hist. Qly.* VII (1938) 9: Followed some deer tracks. Started one "jack" and a flock of chickens. **1887** in *DAE*: The "jacks" is thicker'n tumble-weeds on the prairie. **1923** in *Dict. Canadianisms* 389: The jacks o' the prairies is twice the size. *a1956* Almirall *College to Cow Country* 19: Jack rabbits or "jacks." **1964** in *Dict. Canadianisms* 389: The jack's ears flop back in annoyance.

6. *Logging.* a lumberjack.

a1900 in Rickaby *Shanty-Boy* 97: Every jack's a cant-hook man. **1908** Whittles *Lumberjack* 134: The Jacks are crying like fiends for more. **1918** in Kornbluh *Rebel Voices* 268: But nary a jack will carry a pack/After the First of May. **1921** in Eckstorm & Smyth *Minstrelsy of Me.* 148: The saw-log Jacks...hev passed away. **1930** *Amer. Mercury* (Oct.) 237: One old jack wrote me not long ago that he heard he was dead. **1936** Murfin & Furthman *Come & Get It* (film): Free drinks for all the jacks! **1938** Holbrook *Holy Old Mackinaw* 65: Often a jack blew her in, every cent. **1939** Appel *People Talk* 300: A middle-aged jack. **1944** V.H. Jansen *Lumber & Labor* 22: The jacks were coarse and rough and extreme individualists. **1947** Lomax & Lomax *Folk Song U.S.A.* 203: The cook, if he was man enough, would slap a jack off his seat for "speaking over his victuals." **1950** *Amer. Mercury* (Mar.) 336: It was so cold that Paul [Bunyan] told him to pass water. He did, it froze, and the jack slid down on the icicle. **1963–64** Kesey *Great Notion* 41: We could sure use us another jack. **1976** N. Maclean *River Runs Through*, in *DARE* [ref. to 1927]: If he doesn't like a jack because the jack has the bad manners to talk at meal time, the cook goes to the woods foreman and the jack goes down the road.

7. money. [The form *jacks* is unique to the 1890 quot.; the sense prob. derives from *make (one's) jack*, below, infl. by *jackpot* (orig. spelled as two words).]

1890 in *OED2*: The...verbal wealth of the United States language is illustrated in an inquiry for a loan of money; by using any of the following words in conjunction with the inquiry. Have you any...Jacks, [etc.]. **1905** *Bluejacket* (May) 230: E.Z. Jack [title]... C.F. Brandon...loaned $160 to a "pick up" friend [who disappeared with it]. **1918** Ruggles *Navy Explained* 102: The sailormen of the navy probably coin more words for money than any other body of men....Sheckles, iron men, washers, clackers, jack, cart wheels, simoleons, kopex, mazuma, palm grease, evil metal, oro, jingles, liberty bait, gilt, sou, armor plate, holy stones, joy berries, and many others. **1918** R. Lardner *Treat 'Em Rough* 69–70: I was the only one that passed up all that jack to work for Uncle Sam at $30.00 per mo. **1918** in *AS* (Oct. 1933) 28: *Jack.* Money. **1917–19** J. Boyle *Boston Blackie* 38: Every day they wanted...more jack (money). **1923** Witwer *Fighting Blood* 8: I ain't got enough jack to get back to Boston. **1923** Ornitz *Haunch, Paunch & Jowl* 73: I got an idea how to get a lot of jack this summer. **1925** Gross *Nize Baby* 196: I could sooner tie on a bill an' go out pickin' woims wid de chickens an' make more jack! **1928** Wharton *Squad* 19 [ref. to 1918]: Ah've got enough jack to sit here all night. **1938** R. Chandler *Big Sleep* ch. xx: First off Regan carried fifteen grand....That's a lot of jack. **1961** T.I. Rubin *In the Life* 7: There's times I made so much jack I didn't know what to do with it. **1968** A. Walker *Once* 72: Five wads of jack. **1971** N.Y.U. student: On that mercantile question? I said, "Ef you ain' got de jack, you ain' as good as de other cat." Dig it? **1972** Claerbaut *Black Jargon* 69: *Jack*...money. **1982** in "J.B. Briggs" *Drive-In* 5: Trying to hustle up enough jack so they can move to Atlantic City. *a1990* Cundiff *Ten Knights* 33: That was a lot of jack in those days. **1993** *Mystery Sci. Theater* (Comedy Central TV): If you want to hit the big jack, this is the place to go. **1993** *Cool Like That Christmas* (Fox-TV): You know what kinda jack *that* is!

8. the penis.—usu. considered vulgar.

a1890–96 F & H IV 22: *Jack*...An *erectio penis*....The *penis*. *a1927* in *Immortalia* 9: But Pete war thar with every tack,/And kept a-lettin' out more jack.

9. *Gamb.* a jackpot.

1913 Jocknick *Early Days* 155 [ref. to 1870's]: Confident...that at the headwaters of another...creek we would strike "our everlasting Jack."

10. *Mining.* zinc.

1916 in Truman *Dear Bess* 206: Jack and lead are still worth enough to make lots of money. *Ibid.* 211: We made two tons of lead and two of jack on Monday.

11. a blackjack.

1918 T.A. Dorgan, in Zwilling *TAD Lexicon* 111: I had to bounce a jack over the guy's noodle before he'd loosen up. **1921** J. Conway, in *Variety* (Sept. 2) 5: The referee reaches into his blouse, brings out a jack and saps Tomato on the dome, droppin him like a log. **1931–35** D. Runyon *Money* 203: Brannigan is known to carry a blackjack…and…to boff guys on their noggins with this jack. **1965** in J. Mills *On Edge* 2: I'll go with the stick or the jack, and if I have to, I'll use my gun. **1970–71** Rubinstein *City Police* 179: I popped him with my jack, just a tap to put him out. **1971** Horan *Blue Messiah* 253: He tried to get out a blade and I let him have my jack. **1985** M. Baker *Cops* 58: There are jack marks…where they have been literally assaulted with blackjacks.

12. *Und.* JACK-ROLLER.

    1922 N. Anderson *Hobo* 52: Scarcely a day goes by on Madison Street but some man is relieved of a "stake" by some "jack" who will perhaps, come around later and join in denouncing men who will rob a workingman.

13. syrup.

    1939 *AS* XIV (Feb.) 32: At V.M.I the term for syrup is *jack*.

14. (*cap.*) Jack Daniel's brand of sour-mash whiskey. Also **Jack's.**

    1972 in L. Bangs *Psychotic Reactions* 108: My fifth of Jack's. **1977** *Nat. Lampoon* (Aug.) 9: Glass of Jack. **1984** W.M. Henderson *Elvis* 134: Gimme a shot of Jack there, sonny. **1984** Glick *Winters Coming* 276: Scotch'n soda and a double Jack rocks. **1985** *Nat. Lampoon* (Sept.) 39: A crew of Jack-swillin'…bros. **1995** *JAG* (NBC-TV): That's the third bottle of Jack you owe me.

15. the least bit; anything; JACK SHIT; (in non-negative constrs.) nothing.—usu. used in negative constrs.

    *a*1973 PFC, U.S. Army, U.S. Taiwan Defense Command (coll. J. Ball): Them new guys don't know jack! **1982** in "J.B. Briggs" *Drive-In* 80: He doesn't do jack about it. **1984** *Buckaroo Banzai* (film): You're not getting jack from me. **1986** Kingsport, Tenn., man, age 32: My father's said, "He doesn't know jack" for as long as I can remember. **1986** *Miami Vice* (NBC-TV): You don't know jack about this. **1987** *Nat. Lampoon* (June) 44: He didn't say jack. **1989** S. Lee *Do the Right Thing* (film): I ain't boycottin' *jack*! **1993** P. Munro *U.C.L.A. Slang II*: I got jack for my birthday….We didn't do jack today.

16. facts.—constr. with *the*.

    1988 M. Maloney *Thunder Alley* 55: I'll drag his ass in front of them and let him tell them the straight jack.

¶ **In phrases:**

¶ **forty ways from the jack** Orig. *Gamb.* in every way. Also vars.

    1907 Siler *Pugilism* 38: There is a man named Ferguson…that has got you skinned forty ways from the jack. **1908** H. Green *Maison* 137: She's there four ways from the jack. **1915** H.L. Wilson *Ruggles* 26: I got to eat a continental breakfast…but I got that game beat both ways from the Jack. **1920** Ade *Hand-Made Fables* 293: He's got it on us forty ways from the Jack! **1931** Rynning *Gun Notches* 39: Those Comanches' red rags had set the trail herd racing forty ways from the jack. **1937** Hecht *Nothing Sacred* (film): Oliver Stone is worse than radium poisoning four ways from the jack. **1945** Windolph *With Custer* 3: I'm not what they call an anti-Custer man, but I'm for Benteen all the ways from the Jack. **1961** Considine *Ripley* 163: With Rip, uniqueness beat artistic beauty ten ways from the Jack. **1962** Fraley & Robsky *Last Untouchables* 100: "He thinks she'd be willing to play it two ways from the jack, whatever that means." "He means…she'd be willing to take their money and sell us information too."

¶ **full of jack** full of mischief or high spirits. Cf. *tear up jack*, below.

    1872 in S. Hale *Letters* 96: Mr. Holmes…and James Lowell were full of Jack, chaffing each other and going on, and it was very nice.

¶ **jump back, Jack!** see s.v. JUMP, *v*.

¶ **make (one's) jack** to make (one's) fortune; (*also*) to achieve success.

    1778 in *DA*: My greatest pleasure here is thinking I shall make my Jack here if I can preserve my Night-Cap. **1807** in Eliason *Tarheel Talk* 279: She said…he'd make his Jack for a few years and then the mill would be done. **1817** in Royall *Letters from Ala.* 95: I will try to beguile the time in amusing myself with "mine host" and hostess, who I dare say, expect to make their Jack out of me—"Old Feginny begging!" **1851** in Blockson *Underground Railroad* 156: The united rewards for them would amount to from six…hundred [to] a thousand dollars. These were the times if I was a traitor to my brethren…when I could have made my jack. **1853** in *Mo. Hist. Review* XXXVII (1942)

257: These are the prices now paid by our citizens.…Dealers in pork are determined to "double" even before barreling. We are inclined to think now is the time for them to make their "jack," for, unless we are greatly mistaken, there will be some "falling off" before many moons. **1859** "Skitt" *Fisher's River* 122 [ref. to 1820's]: I…'cluded that was the time to make my Jack. **1877** Bartlett *Amer.* (ed. 4) 378: *Made his Jack.* Carried his point; was fortunate in his undertaking. **1889–90** Barrère & Leland *Dict. Slang* II 37: *Made his Jack* (American), got what he aimed at, attained his point, got into office, or became somebody of consequence. **1901** H. Robertson *Inlander* 25: So you see my advice is disinterested. You've come here to make your jack, and…a good way to do that is to dress as if you'd already made it.

¶ **pack of jacks** *Gamb.* a pack of playing cards.

    1864 in Northrop *Chronicles* 147: I have not known people here to buy a book, except some blank, or half-written diary, or a "pack of Jacks" some Yankee didn't heave away in going to battle. It is a superstition of soldiers that it would not be well with them to go to battle with cards on them.

¶ **tear up jack** to make a commotion or create a disturbance; raise Cain. Also vars. [The form *turn up Jack*—from the game of all-fours—is app. the earliest form.]

    [**1726 A. Smith *Mems. of J. Wild* 110: The Game…was *All-Fours*; and at any time when he turn'd up *Jack*, he would cry, *There's travelling Charges.*] **1805 J. Davis *Post-Captain* 116: The frenchman's [*sic*] shot is playing at hell and turn-up-jack there! **1845** in *DAE*: The girls always tear up Jack, in my absence. **1863** in Mohr *Cormany Diaries* 351: The men "tore up Jack in general." **1864** in H. Johnson *Talking Wire* 140: We are tearing up jack generally here, we have built a stable and corral…and are now building another house to live in ourselves. **1867** in S. Hale *Letters* 23: Ali brings coffee in little cups.…The street is…full of Arabs raising Jack all the time. **1882** Watkins *Co. Aytch* 50: There he began to cut up jack generally. He began to curse Bragg, Jeff. Davis…and all the rebels at a terrible rate. **1886** Nye *Remarks* 170: Didn't go to school to learn but just to raise Ned and turn up Jack. **1908** *DN* III 304: *Cut up Jack.…*To do mischief, romp around and tear things up. *Ibid.* 327: *Kick up jack.…*To raise a disturbance, cause a commotion, disarrange things. **1940, 1942,** *ca*1960, **1967–68** in *DARE*. **1985** in *DARE*: You kids quit messin' and gommin' and tearin' up Jack!

jack² *n.* [sugg. by JACK UP, *v.*, 4] *Und. & Police.* a holdup or mugging, esp. if violent.—also used fig. Also **jack move** an aggressive move to rob or assault.

    1988 "NWA" *Straight Outta Compton* (rap song): Ain't no tellin' when I'm down for a jack move. **1989** *Reporters* (Fox-TV): They're showing me just how a *jack*—a mugging—is done. **1989** *Cops* (Fox-TV): This is a jack! **1990** "C.P.O." *Ballad of a Menace* (rap song): Pumpin' sounds that I earned doin' a jack move. **1991** *Source* (Oct.) 4: And nothing is more simple than Hollywood's jack move against the…new Black films.

jack¹ *v.* [prob. clipping of JACK OFF] **1.a.** JACK OFF, 1.a.—usu. considered vulgar.

    *ca*1937 in Atkinson *Dirty Comics* 106: Drink two pints of moonshine every morning and jack yourself before every meal. **1940** in Logsdon *Whorehouse Bells* 273: So she skinned my peter back, and that bitch began to jack. **1951** Del Torto TS.: Jack me. **1960–69** Runkel *Law* 88: Then we got t' jackin' one another. **1971** Hilaire *Thanatos* 280: The bastard was jacking to a picture of the kid's ma. **1984** Sample *Raceboss* 252: When we got back I nelly jacked mysef to death. **1985** Eble *Campus Slang* (Spring) 5: Although they don't like to admit it, most guys jack.

b. to trifle or fool around; mess.—constr. with *with*.—usu. considered vulgar.

    1962–68 B. Jackson *In the Life* 233: I can't jack with [Dilaudid] and not get hooked. **1983** in "J.B. Briggs" *Drive-In* 183: Munkar decides to kill the Stalker, but he can't jack with him because the Stalker has the magic sword. **1984** D. Jenkins *Life Its Ownself* 235: Somebody's done jacked with his brain. **1983–90** L. Heath *CW2* 338: "Don't jack with me," he growled.

c. to maneuver cleverly or unfairly; deceive or taunt; JACK AROUND, 1.

    1956 "T. Betts" *Across the Board* 42: Racing officials were still getting themselves jacked into law courts. **1969** *Current Slang I & II* 55: *Jack*, v. To tease; to lie.—College males, Idaho. **1976** C.R. Anderson *Grunts* 29 [ref. to 1969]: "We'll go to the library?" "To the what? Who in the fuck you trying to jack anyway?" **1987** Stroud *Close Pursuit* 138:

They've gone into chambers to jack their way around the Fourth. **1988** R. Robertson & J. Wynorski *Earth* (film): You gotta be jackin' me. **1994** *Newsweek* (June 6) 45: He tried to please The Man, and The Man still jacked him in the end.

d. *Police & Und.* to harass; JACK UP, 2. Cf. JACK³, *v.*, 2.
   1988 Norst *Colors* 190: "That [policeman] jacking up the esseys, too." "Jacking the whole fucking town."

e. (see quot.).
   1991 Nelson & Gonzales *Bring Noise* 179: Contorting his face and jacking his body.

2. to *jack (one's) jaw*, below.
   1985 *Campus Voice* (Apr.) 43: He and the other…members enjoy jacking with reporters.

¶ In phrase:

¶ **jack (one's) jaw** [or **jaws**] *So.* to talk volubly and to no purpose; chatter. Also (*vulgar*) vars. with **jack off**.
   1960 Bluestone *Cully* 16: Guys who had nothing better to jack their jaws about. **1966** Braly *On Yard* 252: I thought you were just jacking off your jaw. **1970** M. Thomas *Total Beast* 186: A man's got somebody he wants to kill…he don't sit around and jack his jaws about it! *a*1972 B. Rodgers *Queens' Vernacular* 117: *Jack the jaws* or *jack the jaws off* to talk without making a point; to beat the gums. **1968–90** Linderer *Eyes of Eagle* 77: He pranced around…jackin' his jaws…in Spanish.

jack² *v.* [shift of JACK¹, *n.*, 4.b.] *Stu.* to use a translation in order to pass (a foreign-language course).—also used absol.
   1900 *DN* II 43: *Jack*, v.i. To use a translation. **1906** *DN* III 142: He *jacks* his Greek. **1908** *DN* III 323: He *jacked* his way through the entire Latin course.

jack³ *v.* [fr. HIJACK] **1.** *Orig. Und.* to steal; HIJACK. Cf. S.E. *jack* 'to hunt or fish illegally at night'.
   1930 *Amer. Mercury* (Dec.) 454: Two loads jacked. That's the blow off. You're through. **1931** C. Ford *Coconut Oil* 94: Somebody's hijacked another giraffe.…That's the third giraffe they jacked offen us today. **1959** Farris *Harrison High* 137: The only way to make any money out of cigarettes is to jack a carload. *Ibid.*: But jacking is no way to earn your dough. **1986** *Morning Call* (Allentown, Pa.) (Aug. 18) D3: *Jack*: Hijack. **1991** *Toxic Avenger* (Dec.) (unp.): Can't tell where we're heading'. Guess I'm jacked, for the duration. **1991** *CBS This Morning* (CBS-TV) (Sept. 6): On the streets it's simply called *car-jacking*—the theft of a car with the driver still in it.…It's armed robbery. **1993** *Funny Times* (Apr.) 17: And have you heard about all this "car-jacking" going on? My brother's Jag got jacked in January. **1993** P. Munro *U.C.L.A. Slang II*: *Jack*…to steal. *I'll jack his walkman.* **1993** *L.A. Times* (Aug. 11) B8: I'm gonna jack this car.

2. *Und.* to hold up; MUG.—also used intrans. Cf. JACK UP, 4.
   1982 in "J.B. Briggs" *Drive-In* 14: Now he was trying to jack me for a dollar. **1988** "N.W.A." *Fuck tha Police* (rap song): I'm tired of the motherfuckin' jackin'. **1988** *Harper's* (Aug.) 26: I used to "jack" people…just catch 'em and go into their pockets. **1989** *Reporters* (Fox-TV): You're out jackin' tourists. **1989** *Cops* (Fox-TV): We got little kids out there jackin' people. **1993** K. Scott *Monster* 193: G.C. and I had jacked a civilian [*i.e.*, non–gang member] for his car one night. *Ibid.* 251: You either jacked for money or you sold dope.

jack⁴ *v.* [fr. black*jack*] **1.** *Police & Und.* to strike with a blackjack.—also constr. with *up*. Cf. JACK UP, 4.
   1931 *AS* VI 439: *Jackin'*…A beating with a blackjack by the police. **1945** D. Runyon, in *Collier's* (Sept. 29) 70: Big Boy is jacked because he is about to start wrecking the joint. **1966–67** P. Thomas *Mean Streets* 264: Trusty blackjack and all, probably.…Well,…I don't have to be jacked up. **1971** Sorrentino *Up from Never* 4: Shut up, scumbag, before I jack ya head in right here. **1985** M. Baker *Cops* 58: I killed a gas pump. I jacked it and then I stomped it. **1988** H. Gould *Double Bang* 66: Even mutts he had jacked in the back of the car would…say hello, opening their mouths to show where he had knocked their teeth out.

2. to assault (a person).
   1993 *Martin* (Fox-TV): I got jacked.…They bum-rushed me.

jack⁵ *v.* [perh. alter. of syn. SHAKE] *Pris.* to serve (time in prison).
   1966 in B. Jackson *Swim Like Me* 52: "I'm only gonna give you ten years' hard time."/Said, "Gee, judge, that's no time,/I got a brother on Levenworth [*sic*] jackin' ninety-nine."

jack⁶ *v.* [clipping of JACK UP] **1.** to raise or increase.

1942 *ATS* 27: Increase…*V. tr.*…hike (up), *jack* (up). **1973** "A.C. Clark" *Crime Partners* 47: That…bastard jacks the price every time we buy from him. *a*1981 in S. King *Bachman* 536: He…turned on the TV and jacked the volume.

2.a. to push or shove (into position); in phr. **jack it up (someone's) ass** (*vulgar*) to punish or victimize.
   1961 Peacock *Valhalla* 309: He jacked a round into the chamber. **1980** Conroy *Lords of Discipline* 201: I'll jack it up your ass every time there's a room inspection. **1988** M. Bartlett *Trooper Down!* 39: He just jacked the shell in the chamber. **1968–90** Linderer *Eyes of Eagle* 189: Dozer jacked another round in his shotgun.

b. *Narc.* to inhale (a drug).
   1976–77 Kernochan *Dry Hustle* 36: I [saw him] jack a hit up his nostril.

3. *Baseball.* to hit (a pitched ball) squarely, usu. for a home run.
   1977 L. Nelson, on *N.Y. Mets Baseball* (WOR-TV) (Aug. 20): It was an 0-2 [pitch] and he just jacked it out of here. It wasn't a fly by any means. **1983** Whiteford *How to Talk Baseball* 105: *Jack*…to hit the ball a great distance. "He jacked one." **1989** P. Dickson *Baseball Dict.* 226: *Jack one*…To hit a ball a great distance. **1993** Headline News network (July 25): Barry Bonds jacks number twenty-one out of the park.

Jack and Jill *n. Army.* salt and pepper shakers. *Joc.*
   1920 *Amer. Leg. Wkly.* (Feb. 13) 15 [ref. to 1918]: No one knew he meant the salt and pepper when he asked for "Jack and Jill."

jack around *v.* **1.a.** to fool around.
   1962 in *AS* (Dec. 1963) 276: *Jack around* means "to engage in horseplay." *a*1968 in Haines & Taggart *Ft. Lauderdale* 75: He was always jacking around. **1968** Baker, Ladd & Robb *CUSS* 144: *Jack Around* Waste time, not study. **1972** Jenkins *Semi-Tough* 293: Shake Tiller's off jacking around somewhere, acting like he's Mr. Mysterious. **1977** Olsen *Fire Five* 12: He don't joke or jack around. **1979** Alibrandi *Custody* 189: But she blew it by jacking around…mixing reds and booze. **1982** Least Heat Moon *Blue Hwys.* 12: That's before people started jacking around with it. **1994** K. Costner, on *CBS This Morning* (CBS-TV) (June 28): I see people jackin' around on the weekends in the mountains going skiing and…I wish I could do that. **1995** *Calif. vs. Simpson* (Court TV) (June 21): "Mr. Simpson will not have opportunity to jack around with us.…" "The term 'jack around' is entirely inappropriate." "I agree."

b. to dodge about quickly or unpredictably; JINK.
   *a*1991 Kross *Splash One* 99: All this jackin' around better fool the flak radar computers.

2. to treat harshly, deceitfully, or with contempt.
   1968 Baker, Ladd & Robb *CUSS* 144: *Jacked Around.* Treated unfairly. **1972** Jenkins *Semi-Tough* 15: I don't think I'd let the world jack me around so much if I was a spook. **1979** J. Morris *War Story* 104: These Vietnamese officers will jack them around every time. **1990** *Wash. Post* (Oct. 6) A4: [He] described his constituents as "damned angry" and said federal workers are "getting jacked around."

jackass *n. Naut.* a hawse-bag.
   *a*1889 *Century Dict.*: *Jackass*…Same as *hawse-bag*. **1906** Beyer *American Battleship* 168: Some ships have sections of rubber which fit over the anchor-chain links. One end is tapered, and when drawn into the hawse-pipes they form a tight joint and thus keep out the sea water. These sections of rubber are called "jackasses." **1907** Mahan *Sail to Steam* 95 [ref. to *ca*1858]: The absurd-sounding, but legitimate, message to have the jackasses put in the hawse-holes.…To prevent [a rush of water through the hawseholes] conical stuffed canvas bags were dragged in from outside. These were called "jackasses." **1918** Riesenberg *Under Sail* 29 [ref. to 1897]: "Jackasses" were then bowsed into the hawse holes *for fair*. *Ibid.* 445: *Jackasses*—Heavy canvas cones stuffed with oakum and fitted with rope tails. These are used to plug up the hawse pipes at sea. **1948** de Kerchove *Inter. Maritime Dict.* 368: Jackasses are most effective method of making hawseholes watertight in ships using stocked anchors.

jackass battery *n. Army.* a battery of mountain artillery; (*broadly*) any unit employing mules for the transport of equipment.—used derisively. Now *hist.*
   1862 in Gould *Maine Regt.* 152: They had along with them the mountain howitzer or "Jackass" battery. **1863** in Rowell *Artillerymen* 60: Boys at work fixing ammunition for the "Jackass Battery" as the howitzers are called. **1864** in *Jour. Ill. State Hist. Soc.* LVI (1963) 335: The Militia, Jack Ass Battery, etc., have all gone out. *a*1881 G.C.

Harding *Misc. Writings* 313 [ref. to Civil War]: The Jackass battery [was] in front. **1893** Hampton *Maj. in Washington* 110: I'm in like a jackass battery. **1897** in Congdon *Combat: Civil War* 240: The rebels had what we used to call a "jackass battery," which replied feebly from time to time. **1906** M'Govern *Sarjint Larry* (gloss.): *Jack-Ass Battery:*—Mountain Artillery. **1919** Roosevelt *Average Americans* 46: Following them in turn [came] the machine-gun companies, or "jackass batteries," as they were called by our men, the mules finely currycombed and the harness shining. **1949** *N.D. History* XVI 78: He and his mule-riding companions were dubbed "the jackass battery" at that time [1876].

jackass brandy *n.* strong homemade or bootleg brandy.
    1920 in *OED2*: Intoxicating liquors, to wit, one pint bottle of jackass brandy. **1921** *DN* V 109: *Jackass brandy,* n. A home-made brandy with a powerful "kick." **1922** *Sat. Eve. Post* (Mar. 4) 105: How to…produce white-mule whisky or jackass brandy. **1923** in *OED2*: A still in operation and a stock of jackass brandy close by. **1968–70, 1974** in *DARE.*

jackass frigate *n. Naut.* a small or second-class frigate.—used derisively.
    *****1833** Marryat *Peter Simple* 89: "What do you mean by a jackass frigate?"…"I mean one of your twenty-eight gun ships, so called, because there is as much difference between them and a real frigate, like the one we are sailing in, as there is between a donkey and a race horse." **1833** N. Ames *Old Sailor's Yarns* 380: An English "jackass frigate." *****1851** in *OED*: The skipper looks anxiously toward the man of war, a jackass frigate, lying lower down the harbour. **1879** *United Service* (Oct.) 579: The latter was what used to be called a second-class or "jackass" frigate, to carry thirty-two guns. **1907** Mahan *Sail to Steam* 23: "Jackass"…was formerly used for a class of so-called frigates which intervened between the frigate-class proper and the sloop-of-war proper,…[sharing] more in the defects than in the virtues of either.

jackass lieutenant *n.* [sugg. by JACKASS FRIGATE] *Navy.* (see quot.).
    1907 Mahan *Sail to Steam* 23 [ref. to 1850's]: [After 1854] there was established a reduced pay for those [lieutenants] whose recent promotion made them in excess. For them was adopted, in naval colloquialism, the…term "jackass" lieutenants.

jackass rig *n.* [sugg. by *jackass-rigged* '(of a schooner) square-rigged forward but having no main topmast'] *Naut.* improper or ridiculous dress. *Joc.*
    1918 Ruggles *Navy Explained* 83: Any man improperly dressed, especially with two different colors of clothing, is in a jackass rig.

jack boy *n. Police.* a holdup man.
    1989 *TV Guide* (June 17) 18: Others flock here [*sc.* Broward Co., Fla.] too: Jamaican Jack-boys—rip-off artists armed with MAC-10 submachine guns.

jack brandy *n.* JACKASS BRANDY.
    1928 W. Rogers *Chews to Run* 28: A couple of swigs of "Jack Brandy" revived 'em.

jack bumps *n.pl.* acne supposedly caused by masturbation.—usu. considered vulgar.
    1967 G. Moore *Killing at Ngo Tho* 14: Cuts, bites, and abrasions, some infected, some healed or healing, gave him a look, he thought, of some senile teen-ager with jack bumps. **1967–69, 1990** in *DARE.*

Jack D *n.* Jack Daniel's brand of sour-mash whiskey.
    1983 Goldman & Fuller *Charlie Co.* 331: They downed the Jack D at a single draught apiece. **1992** Mowry *Way Past Cool* 140: A whole…quart of Jack D.

jack-dandy *n. & adj.* JIM-DANDY.
    1859 Matsell *Vocab.* 44: *Jack Dandy.* A little impertinent fellow. **1933** J.T. Farrell *To Whom It May Concern* 77: Ruth, you always see to it that everything is just jack-dandy for Sunday dinner.

jack-deuce *adv.* having one side set higher than the other; ACE-DEUCE, *adj.*, 2.
    1932 D. Runyon, in *Collier's* (Dec. 10) 7: He has a brown hat sitting jack-deuce on his noggin.

jacked *adj.* **1.a.** *Narc.* under the influence of a drug; HIGH; (*hence*) excited or exhilarated.—usu. constr. with *up.*
    1935 Pollock *Und. Speaks: Jacked-up,* under the influence of mariahuana [*sic*]. **1963** in Chipman *Hardening Rock* 39: On Friday we'll be jacked up on the football game and I'll be ready to fight. **1966** Reynolds & McClure *Freewheelin Frank* 134: We thought it was a

hitching post we were so jacked up. **1969** *Black Panther* (Oakland, Calif.) (Jan. 4): Your wife is jacked up on birth control pills. **1965–71** in *Qly. Jour. Studies on Alcohol* XXXII (1971) 733: Moderately intoxicated…*half-jacked-up.* **1973** Eble *Campus Slang* (Nov.) 2: *Jacked*—emotional (excited, happy, angry, etc.): I got jacked before the ball game. **1979** Hiler *Monkey Mt.* 254: So Gladieux comes haulin' ass over and gets all jacked up, cussin' up a storm when they make it back over the side. **1981** Crowe *Fast Times* 13: All the parents [were] jacked up on coffee. **1985** J. Dillinger *Adrenaline* 27: Guys [who were] jacked up on speed. **1987** E. Spencer *Macho Man* 84: Guys are jacked, like sharks just off a feeding frenzy. **1987** Univ. Tenn. student theme: A few [synonyms] are *hyped, wired,*…*keyed* [or] *jacked.* **1988** Norst *Colors* 75: I used to get all jacked up, too. Figured I needed the edge.

b. angry.—constr. with *out.*
    1980 Birnbach *Preppy Hndbk.* 220: *Jacked out*…Angry, pissed off.

2. afflicted; in trouble; at a finishing disadvantage.—constr. with *up.*
    1956 "T. Betts" *Across the Board* 122: He got himself jacked up with income-tax trouble. **1969** *Current Slang I & II* 55: *Jacked up,* adj. Ruined.—College males, Michigan. **1973** Andrews & Owens *Black Lang.* 120: *Jacked Up*—Immobile. Someone is *jacked up* when they are in a position where they can't get away, can't deny what you're saying and have to make good on their word.

3. anxious; nervous.—constr. with *up.*
    1970 Landy *Underground Dict.* 111: *Jacked up*…Overly excited and nervous. **1982** Sculatti *Catalog of Cool* 214: *Jacked up*…Upset, anxious…"I got jacked up over my rent. I'm hung for the dough and can't make it."

jacked-off *adj.* extremely eager.—usu. considered vulgar.
    1984 D. Jenkins *Life Its Ownself* 328: We're gonna be jacked-off like a housecat.

jacker *n.* **1.** *Gamb.* a jackpot.
    1884 Carleton *Poker Club* 12: I'se winned all de jackers and mos' ob de stray tussels. **1887** *Courier-Journal* (Louisville, Ky.) (Jan. 24) 2: Finally they played a jacker in which the opener was promptly raised $500. **1895** in *DA: Jacker*—Jack-pot.

2. HIJACKER.
    1984 *N.Y. Daily News* (Aug. 3) 2: Jackers yield & free 46.

jacket *n.* **1.a.** the skin of a human being; in phrs. **line (one's) jacket** to eat or drink (one's) fill; **dust (someone's) jacket** to give (someone) a beating; **under (one's) jacket** in (one's) belly.
    *****1611** Cotgrave *Dict.: Accoustrer*…He stuffes himself soundly, hee lines his jacket thoroughly with liquor. *****1687** in *OED*: I'll substantially thrash your jacket for you. **1834** Caruthers *Kentuckian in N.Y.* I 22: Hang me if he can ever put the pluck of a white man under a yellow [*i.e.,* Indian's] jacket. *Ibid.* 188: He'd go to Congress…as easy as I could put a gin sling under my jacket. **1840** *Spirit of Times* (Nov. 21) 447: I should have tanned his jacket for him. *****1845** in *F & H* IV 28: I'll dust your jacket if you do that again. **1847** (quot. at JOLLY). **1847** J.C. Neal *Charcoal Sks.* (Ser. 2) 40: It's no use sending me to school for the old man to cure his dyspepsy by dusting my jacket.

b. skin or peel, esp. of a potato. Now *colloq.* or *S.E.*
    *****1856** in *OED*: Potatoes…boiled unpeeled—or as we say, "in their jackets." *****1878** R.L. Stevenson, in *F & H* IV 28: Some potatoes in their jackets. **1919** Cortelyou *Arizona* 27: Pretty soon some potatoes with the jackets on were brought down to us in a big dirty looking pan. **1919** (quot. at DOG BISCUIT, 1). **1937** Thompson *Take Her Down* 35: Boiled spuds with their jackets on. **1961** Boyd *Lighter Than Air* 218: We got about twelve potatoes boiled with the jackets on.

2.a. Esp. *Mil. & Pris.* a dossier, as kept in a stiff paper folder.
    1944 in Rea *Wings of Gold* 240: Today our jackets (records) went before the squadron board. **1945** Hamann *Air Words: Flight jacket.* A humorous term for a horribly thorough record of a pilot's ups and downs. **1951** Morris *China Station* 11: His service jacket, stuffed with 267 other jackets into a bulging cabinet in the ship's office, was more expansive. **1958** Frankel *Band of Bros.* 10: See from your jacket you've had no combat experience. **1964** Newhafer *Tallyho* 31: He's got a good flight jacket, but this is his first time in a fight. *a***1965** B. Jackson, in *JAF* LXXVIII (1965) 326: *Jacket,* to the prison administration, means one's official records; to the inmates it means one's reputation; to some people it is an article of clothing. **1971** Keith *Long Line Rider* 180: Go get their jackets an' read 'em to me. **1971** *N.Y. Times Mag.* (Oct. 10) 21: Once you have a "jacket"—a dossier with all the past details of

your life, all the detrimental ones they can put together, that is…you are a *criminal*. **1989** Leib *Fire Dream* 282: In six months you will have a jacket the envy of any jaygee in the Navy. **1993** J. Watson & K. Dockery *Point Man* 63: My service jacket (military records).

b. *Police.* a criminal record.

    1951 Algren *Chicago* 102: We'll pick you up…'n fit you for a jacket. **1994** *L.A. Times* (Dec. 19) B8: Examples of "Copspeak"…*Jacket*—a criminal record.

c. *Pris.* a (usu. unfavorable) reputation. [Presum. a development of the earlier senses, despite the evidence of the dates.]

    1935 Pollock *Und. Speaks: Hot potato jacket*, a chiseling, selfish, worthless person. **1963** Braly *Shake Him* 11: You wouldn't want to be a chicken thief, would you? That's a hell of a jacket to carry. **1966** Elli *Riot* 220: And don't be hangin' a bum jacket on the guy. Skinny's a good-head. **1972** Wambaugh *Blue Knight* 174: You won't get a jacket. He'll never know you told me. **1968–73** Agar *Ripping & Running* 74: A *junkie* who is *busted* and reappears—with no charges is said to be *wearing a jacket* or *wearing a coat* (i.e., openly advertising his cooperation with the *man*). *a*1979 Pepper & Pepper *Straight Life* 143: If somebody didn't like you, they'd just make up a false jacket. There were always people…hanging false jackets. **1984** *Miami Vice* (NBC-TV): We're gonna set you loose in a Federal pen with a snitch jacket! **1996** *Leeza* (synd. TV series): The population has a tendency to put a jacket on some people.

3. a condom.

    1962 Ark. high school student (coll. J. Ball): I got me a pocket full of jackets so I ain't worryin' about nothin'. **1965** Trimble *Sex Words* 112: *Jacket*…A Condom. **1972** R. Wilson *Forbidden Words* 148: *Jacket*. A condom. **1985** Former Sp5, U.S. Army, age 35: Prophylactics in the service were often called *jackets*. I remember one guy just saying, "The only time I wear a jacket's when I get hot."

jacket *v.* **1.** *Und.* to identify as a suspect or criminal.

    [****1812** Vaux *Vocab.*: To *jacket* a person…is…applied to removing a man by underhand and vile means from any berth or situation he enjoys, commonly with a view to supplant him.] **1859** Matsell *Vocab.* 44: *Jacket.* To show one up; point one out. The fly cops pulled him and allowed the flat cops to jacket him. **1866** *Nat. Police Gaz.* (Nov. 17) 3: Joe…has kept himself…shady since he was "jacketted" and had his "mug" taken. **1866** (quot. at MOLL).

2. *Pris.* to give an unfavorable reputation to.

    1977 Bunker *Animal Factory* 110: It's the next worse thing to being jacketed as a stool pigeon. All a man in prison has is his name among his peers.

jackhandle *n.* the erect penis.—usu. considered vulgar.

    1960–69 Runkel *Law* 279: She was already playin' with my jackhandle.

jack-jaw *v.* JAW-JACK.

    1977 Corder *Citizens Band* 36: She's been jack-jawin' for two days straight.

Jack Johnson *n.* [fr. *Jack Johnson* (1878–1946), U.S. heavyweight boxing champion of the world] *Mil.* a German heavy-artillery shell.

    ****1914** in *OED*: The German "Jack Johnson" siege-guns. **1917** Depew *Gunner Depew* 84: The black smoke from the "Jack Johnsons" rolled over us, and probably there was gas, too, but you could not tell. **1917** Empey *Over the Top* 61: Sometimes whole platoons would disappear, especially when a "Jack Johnson" plunked into their middle. **1917** *Inf. Jour.* XIV (Nov.) 320: In the Civil War they didn't need trenches that would stop a Jack Johnson. **1918** *Sat. Eve. Post* (Jan. 19) 65: Well, we hadn't hardly passed them when Blewey!—a big old Jack Johnson hit in the ditch. **1919** Tomlinson *Sgt. Ted Cole* 86: *Jack Johnson*. A big shell which bursts with a cloud of black smoke. **1920** *Hicoxy's Army* 110: Jack Johnsons are plopping—/Machine-guns a-popping. **a*1925 Fraser & Gibbons *Soldier & Sailor Wds.* 129 [ref. to WWI]: *Jack Johnson*: The familiar name…for any heavy German shell giving off a dense black smoke in bursting. In allusion to the celebrated negro boxer Jack Johnson. (A name for him in America was "The Big Smoke"). **1930** *Our Army* (Dec.) 8 [ref. to 1918]: They throwed everything they had at us: sea-bags, Jack Johnsons, whiz-bangs, Lord only knows what.

Jack Ketch *n.* [S.E. *Jack Ketch* 'an executioner'] *Navy.* a master-at-arms.

    1833 N. Ames *Old Sailor's Yarns* 58: The master-at-arms and ship's corporal [are] familiarly called throughout the service "Jack Ketch and

his mate"; but in this…ship…they received the more apposite title of ship's "turkey buzzards."

jack lawyer *n.* [prob. clipping of *jackleg lawyer*] *S.W.* an unscrupulous attorney.

    1891 Bourke *On Border* 236: Murderers…were defended by shrewd "Jack lawyers," as they were called, and under one pretext or another escaped scot free.

jackleg *n.* an untrained, poorly trained, or unqualified practitioner; incompetent.

    1853 (quot. at JACKLEG, *adj.*, 1). **1864** in S. Clemens *Twain's Letters* I 312: Whether I was a literary "jackleg" or not. **1891** *Harper's Mag.* (June) 160: Why, once I was called a jack-leg and shyster—epithets calculated to goad any self-respecting lawyer almost to madness. **1972–74** Hawes & Asher *Raise Up* 1: My father wasn't one of the jacklegs. *ca*1979 in J.L. Gwaltney *Drylongso* 62: I'll say one thing for that jackleg, he's a nervy ass!

jackleg *adj.* [perh. orig. applied to unskilled carpenters fr. *jackleg* knife 'a jackknife'] **1.** *So. & Midland.* untrained, poorly trained, or unskillful; unqualified; (*broadly*) self-taught. Now *colloq.*

    [**1786** in Eliason *Tarheel Talk* 279: Jackleg knife.] **1837** *Spirit of Times* (Mar. 4) 22: He is no more to be compared to Osceola than a jack-leg lawyer to Cicero. **1839** in *DA*: That party contains no *jack-legged pettifogging* lawyers. **1850** in *DA*: Headed by what is there [in Texas] known as a "jack-leg" lawyer. **1853** "P. Paxton" *In Texas* 284: In the Texan vocabulary, all men who have a mere inkling of any trade or profession are called "jack-legs." You will hear of "jack-leg" lawyers, "jack-leg" preachers, and "jack-leg" actors. These men were "jack-leg" carpenters. **1898** Green *Va. Folk-Speech* 202: *Jack-leg, adj.* Used to signify a poor specimen in any trade or profession: "a *jack-leg* carpenter"; "a *jack-leg* doctor." **1900** Dunbar *Gideon* 312: Dey ain't no…Jack-leg doctors…gwine to save huh. **1905** *N.Y. Times* (May 28) III 7: A jack-leg carpenter is what we cullud folks calls a carpenter who ain't a fust-class carpenter. **1900–10** in *PADS* (No. 6) 18: *Jack-leg*, adj. Inferior, inefficient. "He's a *jack-leg* carpenter." **1913** *Sat. Eve. Post* (Jan. 4) 8: Virgil Custard was merely a jackleg amateur of theology. **1913** in Truman *Dear Bess* 120: Some jackleg lawyer will leave a flaw in the will. **1940** Ottley & Weatherby *Negro in N.Y.* 252: Harlem calls them "jackleg preachers." **1965** C. Brown *Manchild* 24: Mrs. Rogers…was also a jackleg preacher (she did not have a church). **1971** "L. Short" *Man from Desert* 86: That jackleg lawyer says that I can't. **1973** Wideman *Lynchers* 247: Regular, long standing employees, not just some jackleg kid working after school. **1974** in D.C. Dance *Shuckin' & Jivin'* 206: I know your reputation as some kind of a jackleg poet—at least you have some knowledge of the English language. *ca*1974 in J.L. Gwaltney *Drylongso* 22: They sent some Band-Aids and a jackleg doctor over there. **1980** Teichmann *Fonda* 134: He's a young jack-legged lawyer from Springfield. **1982** Braun *Judas Tree* 136: How come you put so much faith in what a jackleg lawyer has to say? **1983** Curry *River's in My Blood* 243: Jack-leg pilots, just out of that training school in Helena there. **1981–85** S. King *It* 438: Ted Dawson was a pretty good jackleg carpenter.

2.a. contemptible; poor; shoddy; (*also*) unscrupulous. [The *a*1881 quot. more likely illustrates **(1)**, above.]

    [*a*1881 G.C. Harding *Misc. Writings* 287: Jack-leg-lawyers and quack doctors.] **1942** in *DARE*: I…repair presses and linotype (jackleg repairing). **1966–70** in *DARE*: *To do a clumsy or hurried job of repairing something*…jackleg job. **1985** *Lady Blue* (ABC-TV): That jackleg creep. **1986** Norell *Barnum* (film): "What is your name, sir?" "Roberts, you jackleg pirate!" **1987** C.M. Carver *Amer. Regional Dials.* 259: *Jackleg* = (usually said of a preacher or lawyer) unprofessional; unscrupulous; dishonest. **1988** *Atlantic* (Oct.) 100: He did a *jackleg* job repairing the table.

b. hastily thrown together; ragtag.

    1989 Zumbro & Walker *Jungletracks* 126: Seems they like being a part of this jackleg outfit.

c. [infl. by JAKE-LEG] illicitly distilled; BOOTLEG, 1.

    1992 J. Garry *This Ol' Drought* 55: There had been a rash of poisoning from jackleg whisky. (…the sort of improperly distilled whisky that could seriously injure or even kill the drinker. Blindness was one of the most common reactions.).

jackleg *v.* to contrive, esp. for temporary use.

    1918 in *DA*: After an hour of what he called "putterin' and jackleg-gin'," he hung it [the timepiece] up again. **1956** Heinlein *Door* 33: With a machinist or two to help me jackleg new gadgets.

jack locker *n. Naut.* a place, such as a pocket or purse, where cash is kept.

  1918 Ruggles *Navy Explained* 82: His pocket...is often known as the jack locker.

Jack Mormon *n.* a man sympathetic to Mormon rights.—used contemptuously (now *rare*); (*hence*) a nominal or non-practicing Mormon.

  1845 in *DA:* Jack Mormons, and sympathizers abroad may croak and groan over the poor Mormons to their heart's content. **1847** in *DAE:* The county contained a goodly number of inhabitants in favor of peace....These were stigmatized by the name of "*Jack Mormons.*" **1875** in Alter *Utah Jour.* 161: For its Jack-Mormon proclivities. **1878** Beadle *Western Wilds* 505: The jury...consisted of nine Mormons, three Gentiles, and one "Jack-Mormon." **1913** Jocknick *Early Days* 10: An impecunious "Jack Mormon" possessing but one wife. **1947** *Time* (July 21) 21: The number of backsliding "jack-Mormons" is increasing. **1967** "W. Henry" *Alias* 112: In walks a Jack Mormon from Spanish Forks. **1986** P. Welsh *Tales Out of School* 188: She occasionally would describe herself as a "Jack Mormon"—the kind who smokes and drinks on social occasions.

Jack Nasty-Face *n. Naut.* a common seaman. Now *hist.* Cf. *Jack Nasty* in *OED.*

  ***1796** Grose *Vulgar Tongue* (ed. 3): *Jack Nasty Face.* A sea term, signifying a common sailor. **1855** in Leyda *Melville Log* 122: We had a shipmate once, whom we called "Jack Nastyface," from the fact that his face was as rough as a MacAdemized road. **1856** *Ballou's Dollar Mo. Mag.* (Nov.) 421: While here stand I, who...am as good as the best of you, nothing but a poor, continually-to-be-sneezed-at Jack Nastyface. **1889** *United Service* (Sept.) 276: An assistant to the paymaster is called "Jack-of-the-dust," and a cook's assistant, "Jack nasty-face." **1895** Sinclair *Alabama* 121: Here you have an old "Jack nasty-face." He is almost sure to be a quartermaster or boatswain's mate. ***1929** Bowen *Sea Slang* 73: *Jack Nasty Face.* In the old Merchant Service, the cook's assistant, but latterly anybody who happens to be ugly.

jack-of-clubs *n.* a fine fellow.

  ***1803** in Wetherell *Adventures* 44: Lieutenant Barker or in other words the bold Jack of Clubs...half drunk as usual. **1864** "E. Kirke" *Down in Tenn.* 109: Tom, you *are* a trump—the very Jack of clubs. **1866** Shanks *Personal Recollections* 307: Sheridan used to be called by the card-playing soldiers the "Jack of Clubs," and Logan was known as the "Jack of Spades." **1896** F.P. Dunne, in Schaaf *Dooley* 260: That grand ol' jack iv clubs, th' Hon. Jawn Im Pammer.

jack-off *n.* [cf. JERK-OFF] **1.a.** *Juve.* a masturbator.—used contemptuously.—usu. considered vulgar.

  1938 (quot. at JAG-OFF, 1). **1980** Kotzwinkle *Jack* 84: But then...the druggist would know you were a jack-off.

  b. an act of masturbation.—usu. considered vulgar. [The quot. is figurative.]

  1952 A. Ginsberg, in Kerouac *Letters* 374: Cut out the comedy and crap and personalia jackoffs.

  2. a dolt; idiot.—usu. considered vulgar.

  1938 (quot. at JAG-OFF, 1). *ca*1949 in Holt *Dirty Comics* 174: Ha, ha, look at you, you big jack-off! **1964** in Bruce *Essential Lenny Bruce* 108: I was in the service, too, you jack-offs, what are you provin'? **1964–66** R. Stone *Hall of Mirrors* 70: This jackoff was really *incredibly* bad news. **1966** Elli *Riot* 250: If I want any advice from you jack-offs...I'll let you know. **1968** Tamony *Americanisms* (No. 19) 5: But...during the 1930's, *jack-off*, an allusion to masturbation, became synonymous with *square*, one who is not *hep* or *hip*. **1972** in *Urban Life & Culture* III 231: To let some jackoff...know who told on him. **1982** Hayano *Poker Faces* 59: He's always been a jack-off. **1986** Thacker *Pawn* 144: Some jack-off put saccharin pills in the Lomotil jar.

jack off *v.* **1.a.** [cf. syn. JERK OFF, 1.a.] to masturbate.—usu. considered vulgar.

  1916 Cary *Venery* I 153: *Jack off*—To masturbate. **1921** McAlmon *Hasty Bunch* 147: That's why he was so scared this morning, wondering if all the things the book said about the dangers of jacking-off were true. **1927** in Hemingway *Sel. Letters* 248: But you thought up a swell subject that wouldn't be any form of jacking off for me to write on at all. **1927** *Immortalia* 105: I caught her by the railroad track/Jacking off

with a coupling-pin. **1942** McAtee *Supp. Grant Co. Dial.* 6 [ref. to 1890's]: *Jack off*...v. phr., masturbate. **1946** in J. Jones *Reach* 84: After I came home...I...jacked-off. **1948** in Randolph & Legman *Roll Me in Your Arms* 234 (song learned *a*1910): I saw her *ass* she hurried down the sidewalk/To see her brother *Jack off* on the train. **1952** J.C. Holmes *Go* 137: I'm almost ready to...start jacking off. **1958–59** Southern & Hoffenberg *Candy* 92: You've an ocean of drowned impulses to jack off! **1959** A. Anderson *Lover Man* 84: What the hell do you do? Jack off? **1959** Kerouac *Dr. Sax* 40: He jumped around jacking himself off the whole day. **1961** McMurtry *Horseman* 49: You boys ain't jackin' off, are you? **1969** Marshe & Liston *Centerfold* 6: I don't know what to call her but a *thing*, a thing to be ogled, lusted over, and, let's face it, jacked off over. **1970** A. Young *Snakes* 85: I turned on my side and jacked off. **1980** Key *Clam-Plate* 15: I spent an entire day at the Playboy Tower talking about *jacking off.* *a*1973–87 F.M. Davis *Livin' the Blues* 35 [ref. to *ca*1918]: Boy, do you jack off? **1980–89** Cheshire *Home Boy* 91: Jacking off is a mortal sin.

  b. to rub or handle nervously.—usu. considered vulgar.

  1978 Wharton *Birdy* 180: Weiss has stopped jacking off his pencil.

  2. to fool around, idle, loaf, etc.—usu. considered vulgar.

  1949 Bezzerides *Thieves' Market* 20: If you'd cut out jacking off all night, maybe you could get up in the mornings and get to work on time. **1954** Schulberg *Waterfront* 10: He's been seen going in and out of the Court House where they sit around jacking off or whatever they do. **1961** Gover *$100 Misunderstanding* 16: Give her a chance t'jackoff an piss round while us other cats go on workin. **1964** Gelber *On Ice* 289: You'll probably jack off here for a few days, get in our way. **1989** Rawson *Wicked Words* 214: *Jack off*...also means to goof off.

  3. to take advantage of, deceive, stall, or impose upon (someone).—usu. considered vulgar.

  1964 in Gover *Trilogy* 340: Everybody jackin off somebody else, tryin t'keep off the shiddy end a the stick. *a*1968 in Haines & Taggart *Ft. Lauderdale* 124: I figured she was just jacking me off. **1986** R. Campbell *In La-La Land* 116: That gazoony just jacked us off.

  4. to tease or taunt.—usu. considered vulgar.

  1973 Wagenheim *Clemente!* 146: It got to a point where every time a strange sports writer came into the clubhouse, someone...would holler, "Fight! Fight! He's got a knife."...They jacked those sports writers off all year about that.

jack-off flare *n. Mil.* a hand-held signal flare.—usu. considered vulgar. [Quots. ref. to Vietnam War.]

  1987 E. Spencer *Macho Man* 96: We light our LZ with jack-off flares, which are formally referred to as Flares Hand-held Illumination. **1988** "J. Hawkins" *Riverine Slaughter* 330: *Jackoff flare* A hand-held flare.

Jack-of-the-dust *n. Naut.* a sailor appointed to assist the purser's steward or paymaster's yeoman in issuing provisions or other stores; (*obs.*) USMC (see 1920 quot.). Earlier **Jack-in-the-dust.**

  ***1821** Stewart *Man-of-War's Man* I 32: From his worship the skipper, down to Jack in the dust. ***1829** Glascock *Sailors & Saints* I 177: Did you ever sarve as a Jack-i'-the-dust in a guard ship? **1834** *Mil. & Naval Mag. of U.S.* (July) 367: And master "Jack in the dust"—alias purser's steward's assistant. **1879** Shippen *30 Years* 66: The purser's steward and his assistant, the "jack of the dust." **1882** *United Service* (Mar.) 260: There is no greater idler aboard the ship than the "Jack of the Dust." **1882** Miller & Harlow *9'-51"* 177: A jack-of-the-dust gazed up at the tree. **1885** Clark *Boy Life in USN* 67: We have names for everybody on board a man-of-war, from the captain down to Jack-of-the-dust. **1906** Beyer *Amer. Battleship* 66: Jacks-of-the-Dust are detailed from apprentice seamen. They are attached to the pay department and assist in issuing small stores, rations, etc. **1918** in Battey *Sub. Destroyer* 303: A seaman...detailed to issue provisions from the commissary hold is "Jack of the Dust." **1920** *Our Navy* (Mar.) 37: Kitchen police [in the Marine Corps] are "jacks o' the dust." **1968** Blackford *Torp. Sailor* 56 [ref. to 1916]: Partly filled with alky and canned fruit stolen by the Jack-o'-the-dust. **1973** Lott *Bluejackets Man.* 174: *Jack o' the Dust* This man is in charge of the provision issue room.

jack pine savage *n. Upper Midwest.* an uncultivated woodsman or backwoodsman.—used derisively.

  1957 in *DARE.* **1958** *AS* XXXIII 265: Pejorative Designations of Rural Dwellers in the Upper Midwest...*jack pine savage.* **1968, 1971**

in *DARE*. **1975** Univ. Minn. student: *Rednecks in the South are jack pine savages in Minnesota.* **1990** in *DARE*.

jackpot *n.* **1.a.** Esp. *West.* a predicament; dangerous situation; disaster.

1887 DeVol *Gambler* 117: We devoted ourselves to studying how to get out of the "Jack-pot" we had got into. **1889** Field *Western Verse* 151: There hadn't been no grand events to interest the men/But a lynchin', or a inquest, or a jackpot now an' then. **1902** in *OED2:* On the occasion of his getting into a "jackpot" (some trouble) he had hunted Nome after me for some legal advice. **1904** "B.M. Bower" *Chip of Flying-U* 44: Don't get me into another jackpot like that! **1914** Jackson & Hellyer *Vocab.* 48: *Jackpot…*A dilemma; a difficult strait; a retribution; trouble; an arrest. **1918** *Sat. Eve. Post* (Jan. 19) 66: You will get into a jackpot sure. **1922** Rollins *Cowboy* 79 [ref. to 1890's]: Poker's "jack-pot" signified either a general smash-up or else a perplexing situation. **1926** C.M. Russell *Trails* 85: I ain't goin' into no details, but I'm with a trail outfit when I get into this jackpot. **1928** Santee *Cowboy* 156: If it hadn't been for Joe an' Jim I'd have been in a fine jack-pot. **1927–30** Rollins *Jinglebob* 32 [ref. to 1880's]: Forgot 'bout it in the jackpot. **1931** Rynning *Gun Notches* 14: We told him what kind of a jack-pot we was in. *Ibid.* 37: The only thing to do in a jack-pot like that…is try to keep the steers circling. **1942** Garcia *Tough Trip* 49: La Brie would have to scout on ahead to see if everything was all right so we wouldn't run into any jackpots. *Ibid.* 366: I gave Susie the dickens for getting us into a jackpot like this. **1947** in Cannon *Nobody Asked* 24: LaRocca got in a jackpot with the law. **1966** Olsen *Hard Men* 41: I don't fancy hard-nose questions off a man I pulled out of a jackpot. **1970–71** Rubinstein *City Police* 382: When he "gets in the jackpot," when he is in trouble. **1973** Breslin *World Without End* 45: Do you think I'd put anybody decent into a jackpot? **1981** O'Day & Eells *High Times* 34: Everybody's in close contact in a jackpot like this. **1990** Vachss *Blossom* 50: He got himself in a jackpot in Indiana.

b. *Logging.* a messy pile of logs; a botch.

1905 in *DARE: Jackpot…*an unskillful piece of work in logging. **1939** in *DARE:* Jackpots of wind-downed balsam that were ten feet high. **1958** McCulloch *Woods Words: Jackpot*—A bunch of logs crisscrossed and messed up in a bunch….Also logs felled every which way.

2. a windfall; in phr. **hit the jackpot** to gain extraordinary riches. Now *colloq.*

1896 Ade *Artie* 64: He don't do a thing…except travel around with some more o' them handy boys and lay for jack-pots. **1944** *Newsweek* (Dec. 25) 67: The "Vick's Vaper" had indeed hit the jack-pot.

¶ In phrase:

¶ **cut up jackpots** Orig. *Gamb.* to reminisce together; *(hence)* to chat.

1943 *Sat. Eve. Post* (Sept. 25) 37: They cut up jackpots or pipes— that is, exchange gossip. **1956** H. Gold *Not With It* 16: All right, so let's cut up a jackpot. How long you been grifting? **1966** Newhafer *No More Bugles* 6: I'd like to see Dusane again. Cut up some old jackpots. **1971** P. Hamill, in *N.Y. Post* (Apr. 1) 45: Oh, maybe they didn't call themselves the Mafia when they were sitting around cutting up jackpots. **1983** *TalkNet* (NBC radio network) (Oct. 28): Hi, I'm Bruce Williams and welcome to *TalkNet*. We're here to cut up some jackpots and talk about your life.

jackpot *v.* **1.** *Gamb.* (see quot.).

1935 *Amer. Mercury* (June) 229: *Jackpot:* to induce a player to continue to play—and pay—by raising the percentage of possible payoff; figuratively, it applies to the condition of a married man or a partner in business.

2. *Pris.* to make trouble for or get even with.

1971 Keith *Long Line Rider* 88: He wanted to jackpot ya fer what happened over theah with thet other shotgun man. *Ibid.* 144: Let's jackpot the bastard.

3. *Und.* to reminisce or gossip.

1975 *Urban Life* IV 203: For the elderly street hustlers, fantasy takes the form of reminiscing over past exploits and accomplishments (participants refer to this practice as "jackpotting").

jackrabbit *n.* **1.** a mule.

1898 *Chicago Record's War Stories* 181: The sextet of black "jack rabbits" refused to respond promptly to his call to "get ap." **1904** in "O. Henry" *Works* 557: The "jack-rabbit line" could mean nothing else than the mule-back system of transport. **1950, 1967–69** in *DARE*.

2. *Pris.* an escaped prisoner.

1980 McLendon *Macon's Run* 107: A lesson "jackrabbits," escapees, learned in the dark.

jackrabbit *v.* to run, esp. to flee.

1942 *ATS* 664: *Jack-rabbit…*to weave in and out through the opposition [football team]. **1944** Ind *Bataan* 297: Forced to accomplish some agile jack-rabbiting when they came back unexpectedly. **1977** Caron *Go-Boy* 13: Your best bet is to jackrabbit, and I mean tonight!

jack-ready *adj.* ready and eager.

1972 Bunker *No Beast* 19: I'm jack-ready for freedom.

jack-roll *v.* Orig. *Und.* to rob (a drunken or sleeping person); *(broadly)* to pick the pocket of or rob (an individual); ROLL; MUG.

1915–16 Lait *Beef, Iron & Wine* 160: Firs' I jackrolled a couple o' drunks. **1922** N. Anderson *Hobo* 41: Begging, stealing, and "jack-rolling." *Ibid.* 51: "Jack rolling" may be anything from picking a man's pocket in a crowd to robbing him while he is drunk or asleep. **1928** Bodenheim *Georgie May* 11: She wouldn't help him jack-roll a fat greenhorn. **1951** D. Wilson *Six Convicts* 94: But she forgits the guys we used to jackroll. **1965** Wallace *Skid-Row* 30: The police often use this as a handy reason for locking up a drunk: that he will freeze, be jack-rolled, or otherwise endangered. **1985** (quot. at JACK-ROLLER). **1977** Carabatsos *Heroes* 173: I was jack-rolled. *a*1988 in Giamo *On Bowery* 184: Once, when we were drinking at the Old Dover, a friend of mine got jackrolled by some guys out on the street. He got beaten up real bad. **1990** Steward *Bad Boys* 116: They beat up the "goddamned queers" after they jackrolled them. *Ibid.* 120: Hustling the queers and jackrolling the girls he went with.

jack-roller *n.* Police & Und. a thief who steals from drunken or sleeping individuals.

1922 N. Anderson *Hobo* 5: Here the professional gambler plies his trade and the "jack roller," as he is commonly called, the man who robs his fellows, while they are drunk or asleep. **1947** Motley *Knock on Any Door* 162: Everybody knew that he was tough and clever and a jack-roller. **1969** Whittemore *Cop!* 145: Yeah, but them dudes up there are being asleep! That's for them jack-rollers, you know. They'd have to be *awake* before *I* bother 'em. I don't bother nobody that's asleep. **1982** D.A. Harper *Good Company* 13: They ain't no tramps. We call them jackrollers. **1985** *Lady Blue* (ABC-TV): That's for them jack-rollers….Jack-rollin' don't take no skill.

jack shit *n.* **1.** the least amount; a damn.—usu. used in negative constrs.—usu. considered vulgar.

1969 in Estren *Underground* 67: Huh? Wha? I cunt see jackshit. **1972** Eble *Campus Slang* (Oct.) 4: *Jackshit*—a minimum; nothing: I didn't do jackshit this weekend. *a*1973 PFC, U.S. Army, U.S. Taiwan Defense Command (coll. J. Ball): I didn't know jack shit when I first came here. **1974** Cherry *High Steel* 32: I don't know jack shit about burning. **1977** Butler & Shryack *Gauntlet* 81: I didn't do jack-shit. **1978** Truscott *Dress Gray* 426: You haven't got jack-shit on me, Mr. Beatty. **1981** Hathaway *World of Hurt* 210 [ref. to 1960's]: And none of them knew jack shit about small unit tactics. **1981** C. Nelson *Picked Bullets Up* 106: That forty-five ain't worth jack-shit. **1982** R.M. Brown *So. Discomfort* 45: I don't give Jack Shit about the French Revolution. **1982** Goff, Sanders & Smith *Bros.* 66: Carl…didn't have Jack shit together. **1986** Univ. Tenn. instructor, age *ca*40: I first heard "He doesn't know jack-shit" absolutely no later than 1965.

2. nonsense; BULLSHIT, 1.a.—usu. considered vulgar.

1978 J. Webb *Fields of Fire* 239 [ref. to 1969]: And if he gives you any of his jack-shit you say, "Senator, you got a point."

3. a stupid or despicable fellow.—usu. considered vulgar.

1978 *UTSQ:* "That guy's a real Jack Shit" = asshole.

jackshite *n.* [app. JACK[1], 1.a. + *shite* 'shit', patterned on *Jack Tar*] *Naut.* a seaman.

[**1883 Russell *Sailor's Lang.* xiii: The merchant seaman…does not apparently blush to figure as "Jack Muck" and "Shellback."] **1910** (quot. at GOB[3]). **1914** *DN* IV 150: Navy slang…*jackshite, n. = gob* ["A bluejacket"]. [**1929 Bowen *Sea Slang* 73: *Jack Muck.* A merchant seaman, a term now obsolete.] *a*1966 in Hugill *Sailortown* 283 [song learned *ca*1925]: Julia slings she-oak at the bar,/An' welcomes Jack-shites from afar.

Jack's house *n.* a prison.

1851 [Byrn] *Ark. Doctor* 40: Should we be caught and the law enforced, we would both go to "Jack's house" for the term of three years.

Jackson *n.* [elab. of syn. JACK[1], 1.b.] **1.** Esp. *Jazz.* (a name used in direct address to a man); BUDDY, 3.

1941 *AS* (Oct.) 166: *Jackson.* Form of address for any soldier. **1942** in *Great Music of D. Ellington* 68: Don'tcha start relaxin', Jackson. **1942** Tugend *Star-Spangled Rhythm* (film): Jackson, hurry on back! **1943** Pyle *Here Is Your War* 37: My own special bomber crew arrived shortly after I landed in Africa....It was the one known as the House of Jackson—the one where everybody in the crew called everybody else "Jackson." **1945** *Merrie Melodies* (animated cartoon): Come on, Jackson! Cut yourself a slice of rug! **1947** G. Homes *Out of the Past* (film): Can you bust this for me, Jackson? **1970** *Playboy* (Aug.) 108: Solid, Jackson! **1982** Rucker *57th Kafka* 237: "Easy, Jackson."..."My name's Alvin, actually." **1985** *Miami Vice* (NBC-TV): You got the wrong brother, Jackson! **1993** *Garfield & Friends* (CBS-TV): "Thanks, Jackson." "My name is Wade."

2. [fr. the portrait of Andrew *Jackson* on the note] a twenty-dollar currency note.

1969 R. Beck *Mama Black Widow* 114: A Jackson frogskin! **1977** Sayles *Union Dues* 181: Take a load of Jacksons and Grants get you off my shit list, girl. **1992** N. Cohn *Heart of World* 66: How much?...A Jackson, a Franklin? **1993** Rebennack & Rummel *Under Hoodoo Moon* 219: He peeled off a Jackson, slipped it into my shirt pocket.

Jack Spaniard *n. Naut.* a Spanish vessel.

1829 J. Hall *Winter Eves.* 97 [ref. to 1800]: You had better advise Jack Spaniard to keep a greater offing.

jack squat *n.* [JACK (SHIT) + SQUAT] (a partial euphem. for) JACK SHIT.

1984 Ehrhart *Marking Time* 72: They don't mean jack squat. **1980–89** Chesire *Home Boy* 129: I don't know jack squat about it. **1989** R. Miller *Profane Men* 128: You won't have jumping jack squat.

jackstrap var. JOCKSTRAP, *n., v.*

Jack Tar *n.* [JACK[1], 1.a. + *tar*] a seaman. Now *hist.*

***1781** G. Parker *View of Society* I 53: Our house...was chiefly supported by Jack-Tars. ***1785** Grose *Vulgar Tongue: Jack Tar.* A sailor. ***1822** C. Lamb, in *F & H* IV 33: Displays before our eyes a downright concretion of a Wapping sailor—a jolly warm-hearted Jack Tar. ***1832** B. Hall *Voyages* (Ser. 2) I 8: The mere jack tar...is, and ought to be, pretty nearly a machine. **1835** [Ingraham] *South-West* I 52: A jack-tar, whom I questioned. **1841** [Mercier] *Man-of-War* 189: He soon was rigged *a la Jack Tar.* **1846** in Griffin *Dr. Comes to Calif.* 48: The Jack tars seemed highly delighted playing soldier. **1852** Hazen *Five Years* 47: Mates, second mates, boat-steerers, and common jack tars. **1862** in *Jour. Ill. Hist. Soc.* XVIII (1926) 832: A Lieutenant from our gunboats came up, a jolly jacktar of a fellow. **1865** in Woodruff *Union Soldier* 84: I was much amused at Nig. sentinel taking a "Jack Tar" to the "Lock up." ***1873** Hotten *Slang Dict.* (ed. 4): *Jack Tar,* a sailor. **1876** J. Wilkinson *Blockade-Runner* 32: Nor were the "jack tars" themselves willing to exchange camp life for...the naval service. **1884** Blanding *Sailor Boy* 17: Two...seamen...clinched the infuriated "jack tar" and bore him away. **1918** E.E. Rose *Cappy Ricks* 43: Get that, Skinner!—a jack-tar going into business! **1931** Lubbock *Bully Hayes* 7 [ref. to 1890's]: And what about the Jack Tars? **1965** R.H. Dillon *J.R. Browne* 9: To secure an improvement in the jack-tar's lot.

jack-up *n. Und.* an instance of harassment or jacking-up. Cf. JACK UP, 2.

1988 Norst *Colors* 106: Not even some peewees standing around on the edges of this jack-up.

jack up *v.* [fig. extension of lit. sense 'to raise up by means of a jack'] **1.** to increase; raise (usu. a price). Now *colloq.*

1904 in *OED2*: The management thought it saw a chance to jack up rents, and made a sudden announcement of a raise. **1928** (quot. at *take it on the chin* s.v. CHIN, *n.*). **1930** in E. O'Neill *Letters* 375: We may be able to jack them up to a bigger price. **1934** L. Berg *Prison Nurse* 109: The price of dope is jacked up and they can't buy enough of the stuff. **1944** in Loosbrock & Skinner *Wild Blue* 345: I jacked up the RPMs and gave it full throttle. **1953** W. Fisher *Waiters* 190: He could jack up the rentals. *a***1959** in *Thirty-One Stories* 130: The minute he found I wanted it, he jacked the price up. **1961** Brosnan *Pennant Race* 110: He might jack his club up right into the pennant race. **1967** Talbot *Chatty Jones* 141: Daisy would be able to jack up the fee. **1993** K. Scott *Monster* 284: The trustees had also jacked up the price of donuts.

2.a. to rebuke, upbraid, or call to account.

1896 Ade *Artie* 63: He was goin' to clean the streets and jack up the coppers and build some schoolhouses. **1900** Ade *More Fables* 163: The Main Works of a Wholesale House was Jacking Up the Private Secretary. **1902** Stone *2 Yrs.* 112: We never went into their quarters except that we were...called in...to get a "jacking up." **1905** *DN* III 83: *Jack up*...To reprove severely. **1907** Bush *Enlisted Man* 40: The sixth captain was "jacking up" a couple of his men about something. **1927** in Dundes *Mother Wit* 203: It's a bitter pill for white folks to be jacked up by black folks. **1927** *AS* II (May) 358: *Jacking-up.* n. A reprimand. "I got a good jacking-up when I went home." **1931** B. Morgan *Five-Star Final* (film): Randall needs a good jacking up. **1932** Parker *30 Yrs. in Army* 42: Every time he saw him he would "jack him up" about something. **1936** Tully *Bruiser* 53: He's always jackin' me up like I was some stumble bum, an' not a comin' champeen. **1950** Calmer *Strange Land* 209: Will I catch Hoyt-Purves before he goes back to his headquarters? He needs jacking up fast. **1983** P. Dexter *God's Pocket* 6: But I see him over there jackin' up Old Lucy, and it ain't going to end.

b. to fine or take disciplinary action against.

1897 Hamblen *General Mgr.* 132: The master mechanic had firemen "on the carpet" daily, jacking them up for a week or ten days on account of their inability to make steam. *Ibid.* 298: The engineer was...discharged; and the head brakeman...was jacked up for thirty days.

c. *Police & Und.* to stop and question or search.

1966 Braly *On Yard* 30: The fuzz...gave me star billing on their hit parade. I got jacked up and shook down. **1967** J.B. Williams *Narc. & Halluc.* 113: *Jacked up*—To be interrogated or arrested. **1972–74** Hawes & Asher *Raise Up* 135: The police had been jacking people up* there....*Harassing. **1985** M. Baker *Cops* 254: This dope dealer—like every time he saw him, Nat jacked Benny up to see what he was holding.

d. *Police.* to place under arrest or charge with a felony. Cf. JERK UP, 1.

1967 (quot. at (c), above). **1967** in *DARE: Jacked up for*—charged with. "A man jacked up for murder." **1970** in Foner *Panthers* 118: Hundreds of our Party members have been jacked-up on highly political charges. **1977** Caron *Go-Boy* 236: Say, heard you were jacked up on a beef out of Toronto? **1982** "J. Cain" *Commandos* 353: Would *you* stick around if they were gonna come and jack your ass up on murder charges? *a***1990** E. Currie *Dope & Trouble* 86: The police came, about twenty police cars. Started jacking everybody up.

3.a. to inspirit; encourage.

1914 S.H. Adams *Clarion* 100: I think I'll jack up our boys in the city room by hinting that there may be a shake-up coming under the new owner. **1914–16** *DN* IV 324: *Jack up*...To urge, incite...."They get careless and need to be *jacked up* every so often." **1929–34** Farrell *Judgment Day* 471: If he didn't jack himself up and quit mooning. **1953** LeVier & Guenther *Pilot* 123: This only served to jack you up and get you back on the ball. **1967** H.M. Mason *New Tigers* 83: The first task he set himself...was to jack up the mess officer and the cooks...whose performance was borderline.

b. [infl. by JACK[1], *n.*, 4.b.] *Stu.* (see quot.).

1915 *DN* IV 233: *Jack up*...To tutor (one) weak in studies.

c. to exhilarate; excite. Cf. JACKED, *adj.*, 1.a.

1966 Reynolds & McClure *Freewheelin Frank* 55: LSD...jacks you up stimulant-wise. **1996** *New Yorker* (July 15) 53: My boys are jacked up by...movies....They get used to feeling nothing but excitement.

4. to ruin; spoil; botch; FUCK UP, *v.*, 1. [The first 1970 quot. may instead belong at **(5.b.)**, below, where it is placed by *DARE*.]

1963 *AS* XXXVIII 44: *Jack up*...To wreck a truck or make a sudden stop. **1970** in *DARE: Joking or sly expressions...women use to say that another is going to have a baby*...[She's] Jacked up. **1970** in *DARE: To make an error in judgment and get something quite wrong*...Jacked it up. **1996** *Martin* (Fox-TV): Remember I told you they jacked up her hair at the beauty parlor?

5. [infl. by JACK[3] and JACK[4] *v.*] *Black E.* **a.** to beat up, assault, or injure; (*also*) to hold up; MUG; (*rarely*) to steal.

1965 *Esquire* (July) 45: They jacked him up in a hallway. **1967** Colebrook *Lassitude* 287: "Jacking up" a lady with a knife and stealing her car keys. **1969** H.R. Brown *Nigger* 18: Up come some high school dudes who'd jack you up and take the little dime your mama had given you. **1971** H. Roberts *Third Ear: Jack up*, v. to rob; to steal; to hold up and beat up. **1971** Woodley *Dealer* 116: You think you're making a fly move [in a football game], but you are really out there fuckin around, and you get jacked up. Gotta be alert...'cause you'll get jammed. **1971** in E. Leacock *Culture of Poverty* 303: "Dusting" or "jacking up" (i.e., fighting) the stranger. **1972** Claerbaut *Black Jargon* 69: *Jack up* v. 1. to rob or hold up someone. 2. to beat someone up: *I'll jack up the dude.* **1979** D. Milne *Second Chance* 66: Maybe you wanna get jacked up right now, huh? **1967–80** Folb *Runnin' Lines* 243: *Jack up* (one)...Physically assault. **1983** *Reader's Digest Success with Words* 86: Black English...*jack up* =..."to rob or steal." **1985** Dye *Between Raindrops* 86: Pissed-off Marines apparently jacked them up a little on the way back to the CP. Bruised and swollen faces. **1978–89** in Jankowski *Islands in Street* 207: He really jacked up (beat up) an old guy from the community.

b. to copulate with. [*DARE* places the 1970 quot. at **(4)**, above, at this sense, but it does not seem to belong here.]

    1966–80 Folb *Runnin' Lines* 152: The same terms used to characterize physical assault are also used to connote sexual intercourse—voluntary or otherwise—such as...*to jam, to jack up,* [etc.].

6. to vomit.

    1993 E. Richards *Cocaine True* 42: I would be jacking up, I'd be vomitting [*sic*] even from water.

jacky *n.* [dim. of JACK[1], 1.a.] a naval seaman; sailor. Now *hist.* Also **jackie.**

    ***1821–26** Stewart *Man-Of-War's Man* II 149: It...caused me to strut the decks for the whole following day, as lofty and proud as e'er a quarterly-account Jackey in the service. **1893** in *OED: Jacky,* a sailor. **1897** *Outing* XXX 358: A warm clasp of the hand...from the wealthiest owner as well as from the poorest "Jackey" in port. **1898** Doubleday *Gunner* 9: We became full-fledged "Jackies." **1906** Beyer *Amer. Battleship* 163: There is not a bluejacket in the Navy to-day that likes to be called a Jackie. The name seems repulsive in every respect. **1907** *Lippincott's Mag.* (Oct.) 501: They was a bunch of jackies from the Olympia under a lieutenant on the sidewheeler. **1909** B.C. Hoomes *The Jackies of the U.S.N.* [pop. song] [N.Y.: Hoomes & Dennis, 1909]. *a*1917 Hard *Banners* 35 [ref. to 1898]: The "Jackies" were very friendly and accommodating. **1918** Kauffman *Our Navy at Work* 55: The Rue de Siam is the street there [Bordeaux] which our jackies, remembering the Brooklyn Navy Yard, have named Sand Street. **1919** Griffith *Broken Blossoms* (film): Just a sociable free fight for the Jackies. **1917–20** Dreiser *Newspaper Days* 380: I was as humble in his presence as a jackie in the presence of an officer. *a*1924 A. Hunter *Yr. on Monitor* 148 [ref. to Civil War]: Here's a "Jacky" from the fleet, give him a nip....*Every Jacky drinks liquor!* **1927** E. Stockwell *Pvt. Stockwell* 164 [ref. to Civil War]: We brought up two big guns off a gunboat and the Jackies came with them to operate them. **1931** Dos Passos *1919* 17: I thought you looked more like a jackie than a merchant seaman, Slim. **1934** Weseen *Dict. Slang* 127: *Jackie*—A sailor in the vocabulary of outsiders but not of the sailor himself. *Gob* is his name.

jacky thin-soul *n.* a very thin fellow.

    1839 *American Joe Miller* 119: Having held a long conversation with a "jacky-thin-soul" merchant there, [he] made a bow to his cane in the corner, and, seizing the merchant by the head, walked off with him instead of the stick.

jadroney see s.v. JIBONEY.

jadrool *n.* [orig. unkn.; cf. JIBONEY] Esp. *Ital.-Amer.* a stupid, foolish, or offensive person; JIBONEY.

    1968 Brasselle *Cannibals* 362: A *jadrool*...is the Italian equivalent of the Yiddish *schlep.* **1988** *It's Garry Shandling's Show* (Fox-TV): I'm sittin' in here like some lonely jadrool.

Jag *n.* a Jaguar automobile.

    1953 *New Yorker* (Mar. 7) 23: Do you have a dual manifold for a Jag? **1956** M. Wolff *Big Nick* 51: I think it's that red Jag I parked up the hill. **1958** P. O'Connor *At Le Mans* 17: The Jags, Mercedes, and the rest of them are still selling. **1961** in Algren *Lonesome Monsters* 53: My Jag hit a small stone. **1962** G. Olson *Roaring Road* 99: Cads and Lincolns and Jags. **1977–81** S. King *Cujo* 13: Vic walked around to the back of his Jag. **1990** *Newsweek* (Aug. 13) 46: Japan's new rich drive Jags and BMWs and shop at the world's poshest designer boutiques.

jag *n.* [fr. Eng. dial. *jag* 'a load'] **1.a.** a state of drunkenness or (*later*) drug intoxication.

    ***1678** in *OED2*: Proverbiall Periphrases of one drunk...He has a jagg or load. ***1872** in *OED2*: He has got his jag, i.e. as much drink as he can fairly carry. **1887** in *DARE*: The three respectable ladies had "jags" on last night. **1889** Field *Western Verse* 143: Ye kyng was carried

from ye hall with a howling jag on him. *Ibid.:* Taking what ye tipplers call too big a jag on board. **1891** in F. Remington *Sel. Letters* 125: I...got a "jag on." **1891** Maitland *Slang Dict.* 153: *Jag* (Am.), a decided and emphatic drunk; a load. **1892** L. Moore *Own Story* 481: He must have had a heavy "jag" on. **1893** in *Harper's Mag.* (Jan. 1894) 226: Why, she teetered along jest like a chicken with a jag. **1893** F.P. Dunne, in Schaaf *Dooley* 192: An' lade me father to his room with his jag upon him singin' "Th' Wearin' iv th' Green" at th' top iv his voice. **1893** in B. Matthews *Parts of Speech* 202: Mr. Brown was...carrying a...jag. **1894** Gardner *Doctor & Devil* 39: A Chinaman...was freely getting his opium "jag." **1895** Wood *Yale Yarns* 62: Hurlburt was under a frightful jag. **1891–1900** in Hoyt *Five Plays* 144: I know everybody else was on a toot, so I filled up! Three very pretty jags we three gentlemen had! **1905** White *Boniface* 297: Radford had added not a little to a comfortable "jag" he had acquired before the meeting. **1920** E. Hemingway, in *N.Y. Times Mag.* (Aug. 18, 1985) 21: In vino veritas....These revealed [drunken] conditions were denominated in order—laughing, sloppy, crying, and fighting jags. **1933** Young *Over the Top* 31: He...always came back with a jag on. **1943** J. Mitchell *McSorley's* 78: I can walk up and down in front of a gin mill for ten minutes, breathing real deep, and get a jag on. **1943** *Time* (July 19) 54: Two or three puffs usually suffice to produce a light jag. The smoker is then said to be "high" or "floating." **1946** Mezzrow & Wolfe *Really Blues* 307: *Jag*: a state of extreme exhilaration produced by marihuana or some other stimulant. **1952** Sandburg *Strangers* 121 [ref. to *ca*1880]: I got a jag on,/I got a jag on,/I got it down in Danny Flynn's saloon.

b. a drinking spree; binge.

    1892 in J.M. Carroll *Benteen-Goldin Letters* 212: I've been on a slight "jag," so am not in good trim for writing. **1893** in J.I. White *Git Along Dogies* 85: I used to be a wild one/And took on big jags. **1894** Putnam *Offensive* 31: The whole garrison has been on a jag. **1895** Foote *Coeur D'Alene* 13: A jag picnic in the rain isn't just the thing to ask your daughter to. **1929** W.R. Burnett *Iron Man* 170: He's been on a four day jag. **1994** *My So-Called Life* (ABC-TV): Like any minute I'm going to go on some jag or something.

c. a foolish notion (*obs.*); (*also*) a brief period of uncontrolled indulgence or activity of a specified sort; fit; spree.

    *a*1889 in Barrère & Leland *Dict. Slang* I 493: He's got a *jag* that there's money buried in his place. **1909** Irwin *Con Man* 102: His curse was big, prolonged spending jags. **1913** J. London *Valley of Moon* 119: Aw, it's only one of his cryin' jags. **1915–16** Lait *Beef, Iron & Wine* 161: Chiggers an' me goes on a ice-cream jag. **1923** Witwer *Fighting Blood* 335: Books is one thing I can't get enough of and I go on regular reading jags. **1924** P. Marks *Plastic Age* 213: A few had drunk too much and were sick; one had a "crying jag." *Ibid.* 254: A girl got a "laughing jag" and shrieked with idiotic laughter until her partner managed to lead her protesting off the floor. **1930** Graham & Graham *Queer People* 18: Don't get on one of your fighting jags. **1931–34** Adamic *Dynamite* 372: He and Dolly were out on a spending jag. **1934** S. Anderson *No Swank* 45: You went on a writing jag—didn't you, George? **1951** Leveridge *Walk on Water* 53: I feel a talking jag coming on. **1956** M. Wolff *Big Nick* 212: I think I feel the beginnings of a talking jag. **1958–59** Lipton *Barbarians* 79: A funny crack...sent her into an uncontrollable laughing jag. **1974** Lahr *Hot to Trot* 101: If Irene goes on one of her jags, she's had it. In the Age of Aquarius, there's no time for lamentation. **1975** C.W. Smith *Country Music* 254: She lit out on her cussing jag again. **1977** Hassler *Staggerford* 6: She sometimes broke out in a talking jag. **1987** Headline News network (Dec. 14): She went on a fourteen-month spending jag. **1987** B. Raskin *Hot Flashes* 239: She begins to cry....She's off on a jag. **1988** P. Beck & P. Massman *Rich Men, Single Women* 71: To dissolve into another laughing jag.

d. *Police.* (see quot.).

    1955 Q. Reynolds *HQ* 273: He led them to an apartment where a "jag" (narcotics party) was being held.

e. a thrill of pleasure; in phr. **on a jag** elated as if by drink.

    1951 Robbins *Danny Fisher* 187: I went back to my corner grinning. Champion!...I was on a jag, walking on air. **1971** Curtis *Banjo* 132: I heard he was a cutter....Gets a big jag offa cuttin' a man.

f. *West.* a drink of whiskey.

    *a*1913 in R.M. Wright *Dodge City* 41: Not a-knowin' whether/To swig another jag. **1934–43** F. Collinson *Life in Saddle* 6: They were half-drunk then and went down to their quarters to have another jag.

2. a drunken person.

    *a*1890–96 F & H IV 34: *Jag*...(Amer.). A drunkard. **1901** *Chi. Tri-*

bune (July 21) 44: It is the mission of jags to hold up lamp posts. **1911** *Adventure* (Mar.) 906: The screw brought in a jag—a laughing jag—a guy with his snoot full of booze and who laughed like he'd just found a lot of money. **1929–33** Farrell *Manhood of Lonigan* 183: "Six cheers for the Scandinavians," whooped a jag.

3. a peculiar or inept fellow. Cf. JAG-OFF, 2.
    1906 in "O. Henry" *Works* 1328: "You're a queer jag," said he curiously. **1942–49** Goldin et al. *DAUL* 109: *Jag.* (Carnival). An inept person; a dolt. **1994** *Mystery Sci. Theater* (Comedy Central TV): What a jag you are!

jag *v.* to copulate with (a woman).—usu. considered vulgar.
    1960 Bluestone *Cully* 159: You could…jag a million Loreleis.

jag factory *n.* GIN MILL.
    1893 in *Harper's* (Jan. 1894) 226: Say! ain't they a jag-factory somewheres round here? Come in and have one with me.

jagged *adj.* intoxicated by liquor or drugs.—also constr. with *up.*
    1737 *Penna. Gaz.* (Jan. 13) 1: He's Jagg'd. **1889** Barrère & Leland *Dict. Slang* I 491: (American)…"jagged", drunk. **1895** Wood *Yale Yarns* 9: If he hadn't been somewhat jagged, he never would have given it away. **1895** "J. Flynt", in *Harper's* (Oct.) 782: We was both jagged, 'n' the copper served a paper on us. **1899** Cullen *Tales* 45: "Come 'long then," my jagged passenger said. **1899** "J. Flynt" *Tramping* 367: I didn't wanter say very much, I was so jagged. **1904** in "O. Henry" *Works* 1438: A…man that slugs you when he's jagged. **1921** Dos Passos *3 Soldiers* 79: Both of us [were] sort of jagged up. **1936** in Pyle *Ernie's Amer.* 148: They like to get all jagged up on marijuana. **1938** in Himes *Black on Black* 175: She made him smoke pot…[until] he got jagged. **1952** Himes *Stone* 248: Christmas morning we took some more blue boys with our breakfast coffee and were wonderfully jagged when we went over to the show. **1953** Anslinger & Tompkins *Traf. in Narc.* 311: *Jagged up.* Drug-exhilarated.

jagger *n.* **1.** a drunkard.
    *ca*1910 in A. Adams *Chisholm Trail* 279: He was a boozer from Boozerville, a jagger from Jaggertown.

2. Esp. *Carnival.* a tattoo artist, esp. if unskilled.
    1947 Dadswell *Hey There, Sucker!* 101: *Jagger*…tattoo artist. **1990** Steward *Bad Boys* 16: Here were the implements of the "jagger's" (a very derogatory term) trade at its worst. *Ibid.* 58: I wouldn't tattoo the hand, but many unscrupulous jaggers up the street would.

Jaggie *n. Army.* judge advocate general.
    1918 in Sullivan *Our Times* V 328: *Jaggie:* The Judge Advocate General. Chiefly officer slang.

jaggy *adj.* tipsy.
    1906 in *Montana* (Winter 1974) 45: He felt so good he had to get "jaggy" and I don't suppose he touches the stuff two times a year.

jag juice *n.* strong liquor.
    1918 Griffin *Ballads of the Reg't.* 69: He drank up all the "jag juice" that the whisky man would sell.

jaglets *n.pl.* [orig. unkn.] NIBS.
    1892 Norr *China Town* 60: I wonder if I could hang his jaglets over there for a beef stew?

jag-off *n.* **1.** a masturbator.—usu. considered vulgar.
    1938 "Justinian" *Americana Sexualis* 26: *Jagoff (Jackoff).* n. A man who is presumed to masturbate excessively. Any male disliked because of his idiosyncrasies or unconventional social habits. Low coll., C. 19–20, indigenously U.S. **1971** Dahlskog *Dict.* 34: *Jack-off, jag-off.*…One who masturbates; a disliked person; an ignorant, confused or simple person.

2. a dolt.—usu. considered vulgar.
    1938 (quot. at **(1)**, above). **1952** Bellow *Augie March* 101: Beat it, you little jag-offs, there's a sick person here. **1955** Abbey *Brave Cowboy* 114: *Cabrones!* You swipes, you crumbs, you bloody jag-offs—stay in line there. **1970** Landy *Underground Dict.* 111: *Jag off.*…Inept or stupid person. **1974** Blount *3 Bricks Shy* 18: There was an iron imperative not to be accounted a Jagov. The word is "jack-off" but in Pittsburgh it sounded like a Russian name. **1974** Terkel *Working* 225: Boy, you guys are all alike, you're a bunch of jagoffs. *Ibid.* 484: Teacher, he said a bad word.…He said, "Jagoff." **1979** Crews *Blood & Grits* 112: He doesn't want to talk to every Tom, Dick, and jag-off sent by some newspaper or magazine to interview him. **1983** J. Hughes *Nat. Lampoon's Vacation* (film): "He's always been a jag-off." "Watch your language." **1993** *Mystery Sci. Theater* (Comedy Central TV): "Jag-off." "*What's* that?"

jag off *v.* [var. of JACK OFF, prob. infl. by JAG, *n.*] **1.a.** to masturbate.—usu. considered vulgar. [Unquestionably the orig. sense.]
    1971 Dahlskog *Dict.* 34: *Jag off, v. Vulgar.* To masturbate. **1973** *Nat. Lampoon* (Aug.) 32: If you jag off…hair will sprout on the palm of the hand you jag off with. **1979–82** Gwin *Overboard* 37: So po' we had to jag off de dog to feed dat ol' cat.

b. to inject a drug.
    1958 Motley *Epitaph* 158: Again he injects into his arm, jagging-off, getting, getting a second sensation. **1966** Brunner *Face of Night* 197: You're the one that jagged off with it, not me. *Ibid.* 233: *Jag off*—to inject drugs slowly, a little at a time.

2. to fool around, idle, loaf, etc.—usu. considered vulgar.
    1976 "N. Ross" *Policeman* 63: "C'mon, quit jagging off!" I said; I was irritated.

3. to taunt or deceive.—usu. considered vulgar.
    1974 Blount *3 Bricks Shy* 18: Are you just jagging me off, or do you mean that?

jag parlor *n.* a barroom.
    1906 Ford *Shorty McCabe* 225: I never let 'em put my name over the door of any Broadway jag parlor.

jag snakes *n.pl.* hallucinations accompanying delirium tremens.
    1896 in Robinson *Comics* 161: A fine collection of jag snakes—come see em—den quit.

jail *n.* ¶ In phrase: **put under the jail** *So. & Black E.* to imprison under the severest conditions, esp. for life. [Rhetorically contrasted to simply putting someone *in* jail.]
    *a*1972 P. Dean, in W. King & R. Milner *Black Drama Anthol.* 304: I hope they catch that thing an' put his behind under th' jail. **1995** Univ. Tenn. instructor, age 30: If he's guilty, they oughta put him *under* the jail!

jail *v. Pris.* to serve time in jail or prison.
    1971 *Black Scholar* (Apr.) 30: The institutionalized inmate…no longer questions the…guard's command; all he does is "jail." **1974** *Parade* (Aug. 18) 26: I've been jailing since I was 14, in and out. **1978** Sopher & McGregor *Up from Walking Dead* 211: I started jailing in the forties. **1978–86** J.L. Burke *Lost Get-Back Boogie* 114: I don't like jailing with no queer. **1994** *New York* (Oct. 10) 30: Stop frontin', Leo. You jailin' too long for that.

jailbait *n.* **1.a.** a girl who is under the legal age of consent for sexual intercourse.—also used collect.
    1930 in Farrell *Calico Shoes* 48: "She's jail bait," Jack said. **1929–33** Farrell *Young Manhood* 351: Half of the broads here look like jail bait. **1935** McCoy *They Shoot Horses* 48: She's jail bait.…She's only about fifteen. **1946** Shulman *Amboy Dukes* 25: But he didn't want Alice fooling around with a kid who was definitely jail bait and on the make. **1952** Mandel *Angry Strangers* 9: You're wasting your time, Gran'pa, I'm jailbait. **1953** Eyster *Customary Skies* 291: Look, even if I wasn't on the level, yuh think I'd be stupid enough to mess with jail bait? **1959** W. Miller *Cool World* 37: She laugh an say, "I be 16 soon. You afraid of jail bait Big Man?" **1967** P. Welles *Babyhip* 16: The poor slob must feel very foolish, but that's what he gets for trying to pick up jailbait, hip chicks and all like that. **1993** *Sally Jessy Raphaël* (synd. TV series): Don't they have any laws there for men fooling around with jailbait? *a*1994 A. Radakovich *Wild Girls Club* 67: I hea[r]d a forty-seven-year-old guy named Herman searching for jailbait.

b. a sexually provocative woman, irrespective of age, whose behavior is likely to lead to sexual assault.
    1937 Steinbeck *Mice & Men* 36: I never seen no piece of jail bait worse than her. *Ibid.* 57: She's a jail bait all set on the trigger.

c. a charge of statutory rape.
    1961 Hemingway *Islands* 25: I was telling Tom I didn't know what they got you on but that it wasn't jailbait. **1971** E. Sanders *Family* 51: To ward off possible jail-bait charges, the young Miss Lansbury carried around with her a to-whom-it-may-concern letter from her mother, OK-ing association with C.M.

2. a person, esp. a youth, who is likely to be sent to jail; a troublemaker wanted by the law.
    1934 in O'Brien *Best Stories 1935* 206: He thinks you're a railroad dick and if he answers he's jail bait. **1942** Root & Fortune *Mokey* (film): Beat it,…jailbait. **1942** "D. Ormsbee" *Sound of American* 156: A

sense of the inevitable among us jail-bait. **1952** Bellow *Augie March* 115: I'm not going to sit by and let you turn into "jailbait." **1952** in *Qly. Jour. Stud. on Alcohol* XIV (1953) 474: Another resident may "tip him off" that his new acquaintance is a "bum" or "jail bait." **1957** Laurents & Sondheim *West Side Story* 70: Lissen, jail bait, I licked you twice and I can do it again. **1965–71** in *Qly. Jour. Stud. Alcohol* XXXII (1971) 732: *Jail bait.* Men who are certain to be arrested.

3. anything likely to lead to one's arrest.

1954 Gordon & Wood *Jail Bait* (film): You know that gun is jail bait. I won't go bail for you again.

jailbird *n.* a convict or exconvict. Orig. *S.E.*

*****1618–61** in *OED2: Servitia* and *Ergostala*, in Florus, signify Slaves and Gaol-Birds. *****1698–99** "B.E." *Dict. Canting Crew: Jayl-birds*, Prisoners. *****1796** Grose *Vulgar Tongue* (ed. 3): *Jail Birds*. Prisoners. *****1819** [T. Moore] *Tom Crib* 77: Makes the *Jail-bird** uneasy.... *Prisoner. **1838** [Haliburton] *Clockmaker* (Ser. 2) 47: Homocides and regecides,—jail-birds and galley-birds. **1877** in Miller & Snell *Why West Was Wild* 31: Ford County's Only Jail Bird. *****1879** in R. Browning *Poetical Works* 889: I'll to the jail-bird father, abuse her to his face. *Ibid.* 892: The grace that such repent is any jail-bird's due. **1905** Sinclair *Jungle* 206: He knew that Jurgis was a "jail bird" by his shaven head. **1916** MacBrayne & Ramsay *One More Chance* 81: Too often he feels that the mark of "jail bird" has been placed upon him. **1927** "S.S. Van Dine" *"Canary" Murder* ch. xxiv: They certainly weren't the kind that would be mixed up with a jailbird like Skeel. **1930** "D. Stiff" *Milk & Honey* 208: *Jail bird*—A fellow who brags about his *vag* record. **1965** Ward & Kassebaum *Women's Pris.* 9: The other degrading labels of prisoner, inmate, and "jail bird." **1967** Colebrook *Cross of Lassitude* 18: Yeah...he's nothin' but a jailbird! **1984** "W.T. Tyler" *Shadow Cabinet* 107: The guy's a jailbird, a record as long as your arm.

jailhouse daddy *n. Pris.* an older convict who protects and exploits a younger one in a homosexual relationship. Also **jailhouse daddy-o.**

1951 in J. Blake *Joint* 24: He is simply the brass-brained, muscle-bound Golden Boy who appointed himself my jailhouse Daddy-o. **1963** Stearn *Grapevine* 193: The butches, dominating the femmes, were known as Jailhouse Daddies, and they liked their girls jailhouse sharp.

jailhouse lawyer *n.* [sugg. by GUARDHOUSE LAWYER] a contentious prisoner with some knowledge of legal technicalities; (now *usu.*) an inmate who devotes himself to the study of law while imprisoned. Also **jail lawyer.**

1925–26 Black *You Can't Win* 114: "Soldier Johnnie" was something of a jail lawyer and agitator for his and his friends' rights. **1952** Viereck *Men into Beasts* 22 [ref. to 1943]: He was what is known as a jailhouse lawyer. He knew every legal technicality, every trick that could pry open the bars. **1970** L. Johnson *Devil's Front Porch* 203: All prisons have a goodly array of "jailhouse lawyers," and Lansing is no exception. **1970** E. Knight *Black Voices from Prison* 115: Since I was not only "cell boss" but also father-confessor and jailhouse lawyer, I thought at first he wanted to talk about his own case. **1985** Westin *Love & Glory* 313: A general amnesty, which some of the jailhouse lawyers argue is almost sure to follow. **1990** *Inside Edition* (synd. TV series): He has become one of the best jailhouse lawyers in the country.

jailhouse salute *n. Pris.* ITALIAN SALUTE.

1978 Nolan & Mann *Jericho Mile* (film): You can give the whole world the jailhouse salute.

jailhouse turnout *n. Pris.* a prisoner who is forced into homosexual acts or who becomes homosexual in prison.

1965 Ward & Kassebaum *Women's Pris.* 76: Those who are introduced to homosexuality in prison, the *jailhouse turnouts*. **1966** S. Harris *Hellhole* 234: Therefore, many inmates who are not practicing homosexuals outside of the jail, and who, in fact, are repelled by homosexuality, seek it out here. They are known as "j.t.'s" jailhouse turnouts.

jailie *n. Pris.* a jailer.

1936 (quot. at SMEAR).

jake[1] *n.* [var. of S.E. *jakes*, of unkn. orig.] a privy; lavatory.

*****1570** in *OED2:* Iake, *forica*. **1679** in R.M. Lederer *Colonial Eng.* 124: By reason of Jaques, Dunghills and excrementitious stagnations. **1900** *DN* II 43: *Jake*, n. Water-closet for men. **1935** *Esquire's Bedroom Companion* 95: They moved the jake to the second floor. **1955** in J. O'Hara *Sel. Letters* 246: I can't remember what it was called at Niagara Prep Sch., but at Fordham it was The Jakes. **1968** T. Wolfe *Kool-Aid* 57: Wild Weste Roughing It, motoring friends, But Sanitized jake

seats. **1977** *Esquire* (Dec.) 134 (Tamony Coll.): The basement lavatory (where, it turns out, the jakes are placed in stalls that lack doors, open with primitive simplicity to the airs).

jake[2] *n.* [fr. male given name *Jake*, hypocoristic form of *Jacob*; cf. ALVIN, ELMER, HICK, RUBE, etc.] **1.a.** an uncouth or ignorant countryman.—usu. constr. with *country*.

*a***1854** in *OEDS:* You're a pooty looking country jake...to advertise for a dog. **1884** "M. Twain" *Huck. Finn* 131: These country jakes won't ever think of that. **1884** in *DARE:* A masher, like many of the Jakes of the present day. **1885** Siringo *Texas Cowboy* 22 [ref. to *ca*1870]: There's a country Jake that I'll bet can lick any two boys of his size in the crowd. **1887** DeVol *Gambler* 190: The greenest sort of a country jake. **1890** Quinn *Fools of Fortune* 532: I walked up like a country jake. **1894** C.C. King *Cadet Days* 54: The greenest "country jake" from Indiana or Dakota. **1899** Ade *Fables* 36: Lyford had continued to be a rude and unlettered Country Jake. **1901** H. Robertson *Inlander* 30: I reckon he meant a country jake from Tennessee. **1915** *DN* IV 199: He's no jake even though he did come from a Nebraska farm. **1926** Norwood *Other Side of Circus* 160: We've got a sure-enough Jake—young fellow that joined out a couple of days ago. **1927** E. Stockwell *Pvt. Stockwell* 27: Gaping around like the country Jake I was. **1946** Gresham *Nightmare Alley* 69: I won that fin and I could of handled them two jakes. **1966–70** in *DARE.*

b. a fellow; GUY, 2.a.

1923 McKnight *English Words* 62: The girls' list of names for members of the other sex is nearly as rich. Noncommittal in general are: *dude, goof, john, jake, raspberry, yap, guy, kid.* **1942** Davis & Wolsey *Call House Madam* 96: From the time when he was a little jake in knee pants.

c. *Boston.* a firefighter.

1983 Stapleton *30 Yrs.* 7: His old man was still a jake in Boston. *Ibid.* 8: You wanna be a jake, this is part of it. *Ibid.* 239: Boston fire fighters are usually called "Jakes."

d. *N.Y.C.* a uniformed police patrolman.

1987 Stroud *Close Pursuit* 111: A blue-and-white with a pair of jakes pulled up to the curb. *Ibid.* 159: They call cops "jakes" on the street. *Ibid.* 333: *Jakes* Uniform [*sic*] police officers.

2. [infl. by *Jamaica*] an extract of Jamaica ginger used as an alcoholic beverage. Also **jakey.**

1923 in Eckstorm & Smyth *Minstrelsy of Me.* 149: His hide's well steeped with jakey,/And he's getting kind o' shaky. **1925** (implied by JAKEHEAD). **1926** Finnerty *Crim.* 32: *Jake*—Jamaica ginger. **1927** *AS* (June) 389: *Jake* is an intimate name for Jamaica Ginger. **1929** *AS* IV (June) 341: *Jake* n. Jamaica ginger. **1929** in Leadbitter & Slaven *Blues Records* 106: Jake Liquor Blues. **1935** E. Anderson *Hungry Men* 259: It's better than jake. **1937** E. Anderson *Thieves Like Us* 29: The druggists were fixing up the cheap trade with jake and orange peel and hair tonics. **1938** *Amer. Mercury* (Nov.) 320 [ref. to *ca*1920]: "Jake," as the stuff soon came to be known, was nothing but pure-grain alcohol with a dash of ginger and...was hotter than the traditional depot stove. **1986** Ciardi *Good Words* 160: Especially in the South, jake was the old toper's sneaky Pete.

3. [see **1980** McBride quot. at JAKE, *v.*] *Baseball.* (see quot.). Cf. JAKE, *v.*

1927 *Sun* (N.Y.C.) (July 18): *Jake*—One who stalls, and the derivation of it is the name of the one-time first-baseman of the Red Sox, Jake Stahl.

4. coffee; JAVA; JOE.

1977 Dunne *True Confessions* 27: You want some jake, you use Crotty's coffee pot. **1978** *Nat. Lampoon* (Aug.) 93: From the trashing of Grayson Kirk's office to the dousing...of Jane Pauley with a cuppa jake.

jake *adj.* [orig. unkn.] **1.** *Und.* aware; WISE.

1914 Jackson & Hellyer *Vocab.* 48: *Jake*...General currency among cosmopolitan crooks..."hep," "joe." Example: "You're making a boob of yourself; he's Jake to the whole works." **1916** *Milwaukee Jour.* (Nov. 3) 18: I was Jake to his play. **1922** J. Conway, in *Variety* (Jan. 6) 7: If they don't get jake to the knucks...Tomato will have a record of kay-ohs that will look like the box office reports from the battle of Chateau-Thierry.

2. satisfactory; acceptable; splendid; O.K.; safe; in phr. **sitting jake** safe; well-off; sitting pretty. Also as quasi-adv.

1914 Jackson & Hellyer *Vocab.* 48: As an adjective "jake" means good; satisfactory; acceptable; all right. **1917** *Editor* (Feb. 24) 153: *Jake*—good; as, a Jake town, a good town. *****1917** Coningsby *Carry On:* If it pleases them it's *Jake*—though where Jake comes from nobody knows. *1917 *Literary Digest* (Oct. 27) 66: *Jake*—Universal [British] army term to express satisfaction. If a girl is pretty she is "jake."…If anything is right it is "jake." Probably an Anglicization of "chic." 1918 Ruggles *Navy Explained* 83: *Jake*. The navy man's way of saying a thing is good. If it is a jake with him it is all right. "I had a jake time," is commonly heard. 1918 *Stars & Stripes* (Apr. 5) 4: "We're jake now," says Red. 1918 in York *Mud & Stars* 133: When you're a first-class private/And you know you're sitting Jake. 1918 in Guttersen *Granville* 9: I passed [my exams] "jake." 1918–19 T.W. Koch *Books in War* 59: If a girl is pretty, she is "jake"; if a stew tastes good, it is "jake." It is presumably an anglicization of "chic." *a1919 Downing *Digger Dialects* 29: *Jake*. Correct. 1919 Garrett *Trench Ballads* 34: And with this *tout ensemble* you can see I'm sitting jake. *Ibid.* 131: *Sitting Jake* means the same thing as "Sitting on the World"; i.e. everything salubrious and "breaking" just right. 1919 Wilkins *Company Fund* 45: Très jake. *1924 in *Austral. Nat. Dict.*: "Jake" was in use before the [1914–18] war, in Australia by drivers & others to indicate that the load and harness were secure and everything ready for a start. It was also used to indicate that all was well with the speaker. 1925 Dos Passos *Manhattan Transfer* 89: Nutten'll be jake till you stop playin' the ponies. 1935 E. Anderson *Hungry Men* 55: A man like him can just put in a word for you, see? and you're sittin' jake. 1938 R. Chandler *Big Sleep* ch. xix: Just keep your nose clean and everything will be jake. 1943 in Stilwell *Papers* 187: Everything will be jake. 1944 Kapelner *Lonely Boy Blues* 42: If it's okay with you it's Jake with me. 1949 R. Rose *Mighty Joe Young* (film): Everything's jake now. 1955–57 Felder *Collegiate Slang* 3: *Jake!*—Great! 1957 M. Berkeley *Deadly Mantis* (film): Weather Four made contact with them at 0813. Everything was jake. 1978 Wheeler & Kerby *Steel Cowboy* (film): I don't want to get mixed up in anything that isn't jake, if you know what I mean. 1980 *Daily News Tonight* (N.Y.) (Aug. 21) 12: TV ad pitch called jake by D'Amato. 1990 G. Lee *China Boy* 303: I figger it's jake fer ya ta do it. 1991 Brown & Angus *A.K.A. Narc* 107: Other than that everything's just jake.

jake *v.* [fr. JAKE², *n.*, 3] *Baseball.* to feign illness or injury; hang back during play.—also constr. with *it*. Hence **jaker.**

1946 in J. McBride *High & Inside* 60: [A] "jaker" [is a] ballplayer who stalls, or fakes sickness to keep from playing. 1959 Brosnan *Long Season* 114: Maz hit a fly ball…that Cimoli…should have gobbled up. But Gino broke late, then quit on the ball, and it went over his head. The winning run scored from third. "That jakin' bastard!" I yelled. 1964 Thompson & Rice *Every Diamond* 141: *Jaker:* Player consistently out of lineup with real and imaginary ailments. 1978 in Lyle & Golenbock *Bronx Zoo* 247: A couple of days later the pain left….They made a big joke about it. Made it sound like I was jaking. 1980 J. McBride *High & Inside* 59: According to nickname researcher Thomas P. Shea, "jaker" (or "jake") dates back to Garland ("Jake") Stahl, a famous player-manager of the early 1900s. Stahl, unwilling to play first [base] for the 1913 Red Sox because of a bad foot, was chastised by his teammates as a loafer. 1980 in P. Dickson *Baseball Dict.* 226: They were saying that he was "jaking," that he could have played but didn't want to, that he was letting down his teammates. 1987 *N.Y. Times* (Aug. 13) A26: The players…think he overstated the charge that Piniella said Henderson was "jaking it."

jakehead *n.* [JAKE², 2 + HEAD] a habitual drinker of Jamaica ginger. Now *hist.* Also **jakehound.**

1925 *Writer's Mo.* (June) 486: *Jake-Head*—A drinker of Jamaica ginger. 1929 *AS* IV (June) 341: *Jake hound*. A drinker of Jamaica ginger. 1975 McKennon *Horse Dung* 499: *Jake head:* An addict of Jamaica ginger during prohibition days.

jake-house *n.* JAKE¹.

1914 *DN* II 43: *Jake-house*, n. Water-closet.

jake-leg *n.* [JAKE², 2 + LEG; discussed in K.B. Harder, "The Jake Leg," *Tennessee Folklore Society Bulletin* XXVII (1961), pp. 45–47] loss of motor control over the arms and legs from the consumption of poisonous bootleg liquor; (*hence*) (see 1987 quot.).—also constr. in pl. [Bader, p. 200, notes that fifteen thousand cases of jake-leg were reported nationally in 1930, the result of the consumption of bad Jamaica ginger that had been manufactured from denatured alcohol.]

[1926 Finerty *Criminalese* 31: *Jake leg*—Liquor doped for immoral purposes.] 1931 in Leadbitter & Slaven *Blues Records* 183: Jake Leg Blues. 1938 *Amer. Mercury* (Nov.) 321: "Jake leg"…swept through the Southland [in 1931]. 1940 in *DARE:* The Lord ain't been kind to moonshiners nohow.…I never saw so many men walkin on canes with the jakeleg. 1954, ca1960 in *DARE.* 1986 R.S. Bader *Prohib. in Kans.* 200: Called "multiple peripheral neuritis" by physicians and "jake-leg" by the man in the street, the condition could result in the loss of motor control of the arms and legs for weeks, months, or years, or as in several hundred instances, in death. 1987 C.M. Carver *Amer. Reg. Dials.* 168: Delirium tremens…is sometimes known as *jake-legs* in the Upper South. During Prohibition, this expression applied…to a paralysis of the legs caused by drinking Jamaica ginger.

jake-leg *v.* to deceive playfully; pull the leg of.—constr. with *around.*

1991 J. Weber *Rules of Engagement* 211: "Harry, if you're jake legging me around.…" "I'm not kidding you."

jakeloo *adj.* [JAKE, *adj.*, 2 + *-loo*, orig. unkn., but cf. -EROO] eminently satisfactory; fine. *Rare* in U.S.

*a1919 Downing *Digger Dialects* 29: Jake-a-loo. *1919 W. Hastings *Jakerloo Jazz* [fox trot] [London: Francis, Day & Hunter, 1919]. 1938 Chandler *Big Sleep* 106: Everything is jakeloo.

jalopy *n.* [orig. unkn.; early forms *jaloopy, jalupie*, etc., are insufficiently attested] **1.** a cheap, old, or broken-down motor vehicle or (*occ.*) aircraft; (*broadly*) an automobile. Now *colloq.* or *S.E.* Also vars., esp. in early use.

ca1925 in Wentworth *ADD: Jaloopy. Jalupie.* 1926 Finerty *Crim.* 32: *Jaloppy*—An automobile. 1928 (cited in *W10*). 1929 Hotstetter & Beesley *It's a Racket!* 229: *Jaloppi*—A cheap make of automobile; an automobile fit only for junking. 1931 *Writer's Digest* (May) 40: *Geloppy*—A 12-passenger plane. 1932 Binyon & Bolton *If I Had a Million* (film): A fine-looking jalopy. Looks like a cement-mixer. 1935 in Wentworth *Amer. Dial. Dict.* 326: *Jalopie*, an old airplane or car. 1936 *Steel College* 249: Sure you can drive that jaloppi? 1936 Steinbeck *Dubious Battle* 90: You drive the gillopy. 1936 *AS* (Dec.) 306: A *jalopy* is an old, battered automobile. The word was used in Chicago about 1925.…The Chicago 1925 usage was limited to old Fords.…Recent testimony reached me concerning *jaloopy* or *jalupie*, used orally of old cars a decade or more ago. 1937 *Time* (June 7) 2: Sirs: Where did you get the word "jalopy" for junked auto?…[Ans.] "Jalopy," "jaloppi"—or "jollopy"…—has for years been the name used by U.S. second-hand car dealers and taxi drivers for an exhausted automobile. 1937 *Life* (June 7) 92: Regarding this picture of a Pomona student under his jaloppi. *Ibid.*(July 26) 6: The word "jalopy"…is most likely…the first three syllables of the Italian word for dilapidated—namely, *dilapidato.* 1938 *Sat. Eve. Post* (Oct. 8) 8: At the Red Arrow Hangar…teaching beginners how to hoist a couple of training jalopies around the field. 1939 *Pop. Science* (Feb.) 98: Jallopies Race On the Desert. 1941 Epstein *Bride Came C.O.D.* (film): I've been wasting my whole afternoon fixing up that jalopy of yours. 1941 Root & Burnett *Get-Away* (film): We'll take your jalopy and leave you in the mud. 1942 Algren *Morning* 18: Where we goin'? Whose jollopi? 1943 *College English* IV 439: The *Winston* dictionary notes that sports writers are said to have used the word in 1924, first in the form *julappi*, later *jelote* [sic]. The editor of the Winston writes that his information came from journalists, who were apparently the only users of the word in its early days. 1944 H. Brown *A Walk in the Sun* 112: Did you get a good look at that jalopy [German armored car]? 1950 in M. Daly *Profile of Youth* 228: Dallas teeners paint jalopies in polka dots and stripes. 1955 R.L. Scott *Look of Eagle* 187: He couldn't help but…feel pleasure at their flying together again, even in the truck-like cabin of a creaking jalopy. 1968 K.H. Cooper *Aerobics* 121: This teenage jalopy comes tearing out of a side street and crashes into your car. 1972 Singer *Boundaries* 193: He gathers his friends together in his jalopy and heads for the rock festival three states away. 1972 Rossner *Any Minute* 38: We should be able to get some kind of jalopy. 1982 *N.Y. Times* (Sept. 5) 32: He drove his jalopy, a 1964…convertible. 1990 Crow Dog & Erdoes *Lakota Woman* 44: It was incredible how many people they could cram into one of their jalopies. 1993 A. Lomax *Where Blues Began* 385: Sam and his folks careened around the Midwest in their jalopy.

2. a worthless or unattractive person or thing.

1936 Kingsley *Dead End* 715: And they socked that young jalopee in the eye. Yeah. I got that much myself. 1936 in Wentworth *ADD* 326: *Jollopy*, orig. a stout woman. W. Winchell in *Daily Mirror.* 1940 S. Lewis *Bethel Merriday* 103: He's…not so young that you can excuse him for falling for an old jalopy like Nile, who'll be playing Irish grandmothers in Hollywood in another year. 1946 Dadswell *Hey, Sucker* 29: All carnivals are not "hanky-pank jallopies."

jam¹ *n.* **1.** *Esp. N.E.* a large social gathering or party. Cf. **(3.c.)**, below.

   1827 H.W. Longfellow, in *DAE*: I have been several times to her evening jams; but as it was Lent, there was no dancing. *a***1845** N. Willis *Dashes* 64: The ice has been broken with a "jam," echoed by one musical *soiree*. **1851** in *DA*: Party succeeds to party, from a quiet little "social" to the pretending and fashionable "Jam," where "wheeling about and turning about is the order of the evening." *a***1860** Hundley *So. States* 171: An occasional "perfect jam" of a party when parties are in season. **1889** in *DAE*: We left at ten-thirty, and might have gone on to Mrs. Secretary Whitney's jam. **1929** Perelman *Gimsbergh* 119: She did NOT know Paul Whiteman personally....And she COULDN'T...whistle snatches of the "Rhapsody in Blue." So one night she went to a jam and met...Izzy Workman.

2.a. a predicament; tight spot; dangerous position. Now *colloq.*

   1894 in A. Charters *Ragtime Songbk.* 51: If you fool with me, you'll get in a jam. **1906** Wooldridge *Hands Up* 457: Myrtle was caught in the "jam,"...and I suppose must suffer. **1911** *Adventure* (Mar.) 903: I've been in jams where guys were after me good and strong. **1911** Van Loan *Big League* 148: If you get into a jam...I'll fine you a month's salary. **1913–15** Van Loan *Taking the Count* 76: He might think of some way to get us out of this jam. **1918** F. Gibbons *They Thought We Wouldn't Fight* 200: I'm telling you it was a real jam. **1929** *AS* IV (June) 341: *Jam.* A tight place; in trouble. **1933** Duff & Sutherland *I've Got Yr. Number* (film): This will help square the other jam. **1953** Gresham *Midway* 15: And if he's on morphine, he'll turn himself inside out to keep from getting "in a jam"—caught short without a dose. **1983–89** K. Dunn *Geek Love* 180: What kind of a jam are you in?

b. a dispute; altercation; fight. [Perh. the orig. sense; cf. 1894 quot. at **(a)**, above.]

   1927 Hemingway *Men Without Women* 68: "Did he have a jam with Soldier?" "Not a jam....He just told him to go back to town." **1934** Weseen *Dict. Slang* 357: *Jam*—A disagreement;...an argument. **1936** Sandburg *People, Yes* 12: They shot it out in a jam over who owned/One corner lot.

3.a. *Orig. Jazz.* a jazz passage during which all the instruments improvise together; (*hence*) JAM SESSION.

   1929 in *OED2*: There are many variations on this rhythm...which make excellent breaks—or "jams" as they now call them when they are taken by the whole band. **1935** *Vanity Fair* (Nov.) 71: Extremely hot ensemble improvisations are *jams*. **1941** *AS* XVI 29: This pastime has nothing in common with our present-day "Jam Party." **1944** Calloway *Hepster's Dict.*: *Jam*...(n.): improvised swing music....."That's swell jam." **1944** Burley *Hndbk. Jive* 141: *Jam*—Spontaneous swing music. **1952** Mandel *Angry Strangers* 451: They got some Sunday jam at Nelson's. Let's do go listen to some good ole music. **1956** Longstreet *Real Jazz* 104: Later, when almost everyone had gone home, Bix and the boys would blow it free and the jam was on. **1974** *Rolling Stone* (Mar. 14) 17: Rumors [of] a "superstar jam" in New York, the likely jammers being the four ex-Beatles, Leon Russell, Mick Jagger, and a few other "friends."

b. *Esp. Black E.* swing or other popular music; (*hence*) a musical recording, esp. of swing, rock, or rap music; (*broadly*) a song; (*later*) a music video.

   1937 Kalmar et al. *Life of Party* (film): Who brought the jam to old Jamaica?/Who made them swing in Singapore? **1944** Breslow & Purcell *Follow the Boys* (film): About the jam and jive. **1957** H. Simmons *Corner Boy* 36: Dig this crazy jam, I bet you never heard this. *Ibid.* 37: "What's the name of the jam?" "Sweety Pie." **1960** C.L. Cooper *Scene* 6: He could lie around up in his crib...and listen to jams. **1962** H. Simmons *On Eggshells* 193: We can put on some jams, talk about old times. **1970** A. Young *Snakes* 44: You say you wanna pay me back for some of them jams I'mo bring you to hear? **1971** *Essence* (Sept.) 74: Black language for "record"...*jam*. **1971** in L. Bangs *Psychotic Reactions* 55: The MC5 might have put you "flat on your back" with...[their] jams. **1973** *Oui* (June) 28: Lengthy jams like *Morning Dew*, nifty country-and-western cuts like *Tennessee Jed*. **1978** Price *Ladies' Man* 85: I threw an Al Green jam on the stereo. **1979** Univ. Tenn. student theme: Driving up to the [rock] concert was really fun, but experiencing a jam that long and well performed was excellent. **1980** M. Baker *Nam* 51: But I liked listening to her. She put on some good jams. **1982** Eble *Campus Slang* (Fall) 3: Put some jam on the stereo. **1985** Dye *Between Raindrops* 85: I'm gettin' me a...tape recorder...and listen to some jams. **1989**

Beachin' Times 2: Great food,...hot jams, games, prizes and...fun. **1993** P. Munro *U.C.L.A. Slang* II: *Jam*...song. *This jam's number one right now.*

c. a dancing party with jazz, rock, or rap music. Cf. 1929 quot. at **(1)**, above.

   1950 *New Yorker* (Feb. 4) 34: I got into a jam by attending a jam recently—one of those phonograph-record jams, or platter parties, to which each guest brings his or her favorite hot or blues recording. **1966** Sack *M* 21: Amaker...really intended to be in Harlem that afternoon digging the jams there. **1970** Quammen *Walk the Line* 84: The Book be going to a jam. **1971** in E. Leacock *Culture of Poverty* 303: "Jam" means party and a "boss-jam" is a very good party. **1971** *Essence* (Sept.) 74: Black language for "record," might also be a party: *jam*. **1983** Sturz *Wid. Circles* 60: She...spent her days at "jams" in the park instead of attending school. *Ibid.* 405: *Jam*, a disco with improvisations, often held in the street. **1987** "Public Enemy" *Raise the Roof* (rap song): This jam is packed so I just figure/All we need is the house to get bigger. **1988** S. Lee *School Daze* (film): They haven't had fun in so long, a jam will be on. **1994** *Comedy Central's Super Bowl Jam* [title] (Comedy Central TV).

d. a performance of jazz, rock, or rap music; (*hence*) a dance routine to accompany a rap performance.

   1991 Nelson & Gonzales *Bring Noise* 127: The jam starts off with our man slyly tilting his head. **1991** N. Krulik *Hammer & Ice* 25: Planning new jams for that night's show.

e. *Narc.* cocaine.

   *a***1972** Milner & Milner *Black Players* 272: *Jam* cocaine....*Jam House* an apartment where pimps and hustlers gather to buy cocaine from the "host" and then to "snort" it in company. **1972** Smith & Gay *Don't Try It* 203: *Jam.* Cocaine. **1984** (cited in Spears *Drugs & Drink* 286). **1995** W. Lasher *Hostile Witness* 110: That was his last chance aphrodisiac. Any hunter in town knows enough to pack some coke if he's really looking. If all else fails, you'll always pull in something with free jam.

f. something exciting, enjoyable, or attractive; something splendid.—usu. constr. with *the*.

   1984 Mason & Rheingold *Slanguage*: (The) *jam*...Anything that is really good or together. As in "Her shoes are the jam." **1985** Eble *Campus Slang* (Apr.) 5: *Jam*—something fun or enjoyable: "The mixer was a real jam." **1988** *Spin* (Oct.) 47: *The jam* n, a good record. **1989** P. Munro *U.C.L.A. Slang* 52: *Jam*...good song....That's a jam on the radio. **1990** P. Dickson *Slang!* 220: *Jam.* In the world of rap,...a good time.

¶ In phrase:

¶ **kick out the jams** to abandon restraint; (*hence*) to celebrate.

   [**1970** Major *Afro-Amer. Slang* 70: *Jams*: real and imaginary prisons.] **1971** H.S. Thompson *Las Vegas* 156: The big-beat sound of a dozen 50-year-old junkies kicking out the jams on "September Song." **1971** in L. Bangs *Psychotic Reactions* 7: Just waitin' for somebody to come along and kick out the jams. **1972** Burkhart *Women in Pris.* 224: Kick out the Jam. **1978** De Christoforo *Grease* 139: I just needed to kick out the jambs, you know what I mean? **1984** *N.Y. Post* (Sept. 3) 17: With the Giants stalled on their own 23 and protecting that eight-point lead, Haji-Sheikh was called upon to kick out the jams. **1985** Dye *Between Raindrops* 92: Kick out the jams, motherfuckers. Got this little box up in Hué City. **1987** *Nat. Lampoon* (Dec.) 12: I'm now able to kick out my jams riding on my own lunatic streak. **1994** *Radioactive Man* (No. 3) (unp.): Welcome, brothers and sisters! Kick out the jams for our beloved guru, his holy cosmicness.

jam² *n.* **1.** a young woman (*rare* in U.S.); (*also*) (*vulgar*) copulation with a woman. Cf. JELLY, 2.a., 3, JELLY ROLL.

   ca*1880** in *F & H* IV 35: When he called me his jam,/His pet and his lamb. *****1884** *Randiana* 10: I Ascertain the Meaning of "Real Jam."...She laughed, and opening her legs, answered me without saying a word. **ca***1886** in *F & H*: There were three bits of jam stepping out of the tram. *****1889** Barrère & Leland *Dict. Slang* I 493: Girls of the lower orders sometimes apply the term *jam* to sexual intercourse. **a***1890–96** *F & H* IV 36: *Jam*....The female *pudendum*: whence *To have a bit of jam* = to copulate. **1935** Pollock *Und. Speaks*: *Jam*, a sweetheart (prison). **1967–80** Folb *Runnin' Lines* 150: I'm gonna get me some *jellyroll*...[or] *jam*. *Ibid.* 243: *Jam*...1. Female's genitalia. 2. Attractive female.

2.a. (among hawkers and pitchmen) small cheap, shoddy, or stolen articles offered for sale; in phrs. **jam worker, jam man** a hawker of such articles. Cf. JAM², *adj.*

   1929 *Sat. Eve. Post* (Oct. 12) 29: *Jamb.* Any form of illegitimate selling....The jamb worker is rarer than when I was a med-show man. **1931** *AS* VI 332: *Jam-man*, n. A pitchman who has no professional ethics. **1931** *AS* VI (Aug.) 439: *Jam, n.* Stolen small articles, such as rings, watches. **1938** in A. Banks *First-Person* 189: The jam-man is the best pitchman of all. **1942–49** Goldin et al. *DAUL* 109: *Jam…*Petty stolen goods, as inexpensive watches or costume jewelry.

b. a huckster's sales pitch; SPIEL.

1987–89 M.H. Kingston *Tripmaster Monkey* 14: Doc Woo is giving the pitch amd jam:…You hurt? You tired?…This medicine for you.

3. *Homosex.* (see quots.). Cf. JAMPOT, 1.

1941 G. Legman, in Henry *Sex Vars.* 1164: *Eat jam* To perform anilinctus. *a***1972** B. Rodgers *Queens' Vernacular* 117: *Jam…*feces.

jam¹ *adj.* **1.** splendid; first-rate; satisfactory. Also as adv. [Current usage arises from var. contemporary senses of JAM, *n.* & *v.*]

1832 in *DA*: Do you like jam spruce beer, Miss? **1836** in Haliburton *Sam Slick* 59: A-ridin' about, titivated out rael jam, in their go-to-meetin' clothes, a-doin' nothin'. **1838** [Haliburton] *Clockmaker* (Ser. 2) 75: It's no skimmilk story, but upper crust, real jam. **1838** in *DAE*: There was something jam about Nance, that they couldn't hold a candle to. **1839** in *DAE*: Say no more, that's a jam gal. **1847** in Dolph *Sound Off!* 405: Young Texas came ob age quite jam,/And den she married Uncle Sam. **1989** R. Miller *Profane Men* 157: Hot damn, Sam, I am jam.

2. *Homosex.* heterosexual. Also as *n.*

1935 Pollock *Und. Speaks: Jam,* one who knows all about a sexual pervert but who does not tell. **1940** in T. Williams *Letters* 17: Have to play jam here and I'm getting horny as a jackrabbit, so line up some of that Forty-Second Street trade for me when I get back. **1941** G. Legman, in Henry *Sex Vars.* II 1169: *Jam…*A non-homosexual male (the term is said to be an abbreviation of *just a m*an, but this derivation may be merely a *camp*). **1942** in Legman *Limerick* 94: A quean from Siam/Said, "My dear, you're not jam!" **1947** in J. Katz *Gay/Lesbian Almanac* 622: Possibly the only "jam" recipient of your first issue. **1948** Vidal *City & Pillar* 246 [ref. to 1943]: A man who could not be had, who was normal, was called "jam." **1949** *Gay Girl's Guide* 11: *Jam*—Adjective synonymous with *butch.* **1955** Lindner *Must You Conform?* 62: Therein they can find the tolerance denied them by the "jam" or straight world. **1963** Stearn *Grapevine* 5: A "straight" was a heterosexual, a straight attitude "jam" and a "swinger," an object of admiration, could handle any lesbian situation. **1965** Trimble *Sex Words* 112: *Jam cat…*A Heterosexual. **1972** *Anthro. Linguistics* (Mar.) 104: *Jam* (adj.): Heterosexual, as in "jam people."

jam² *adj.* [orig. attrib. use of JAM², *n.,* 2] (among hawkers and pitchmen) involving or engaged in the sale or auction of cheap, sometimes shoddy or stolen, small articles.

1929 (quot. at JAM², *n.,* 2.a.). **1933** Ersine *Pris. Slang: Jam auction…*An auction, usually in a pawnshop…The crowd is a favorite one with *dips.* **1942** Liebling *Telephone* 15: A jam joint is a traveling auction store. **1942** *AS* XVII 91: Pitchmen's Cant…Auction stores are [called] jam stores. **1970** A. Lewis *Carnival* 254: My auctions may be jam, but they're run legitimately.

jam *v.* **1.** *Und.* to execute by hanging; (*hence*) to kill or murder.

*****1735** in Partridge *Dict. Und.* 360: I know I shall be *cast,* but I shan't be *jamm'd;* for I have good Friends who will save me. *****1788** Grose *Vulgar Tongue* (ed. 2): *Jammed.* Hanged. *Cant.* **1859** Matsell *Vocab.* 46: *Jammed.* Killed; murdered; hanged.

2.a. to beset with difficulties; cause trouble for; put into difficulty or danger.—usu. constr. with *up.*

1836 in Haliburton *Sam Slick* 73: The vessel will jam him up tight for repairs and new riggin'. **1887** *Lantern* (N.O.) (Jan. 22) 3: But jes de same I t'ink de collars could jam him for somethin' else. **1925** *DN* V 334: *Jam,* v.t. To get into trouble; perplex; puzzle; bother. **1927** Coe *Me—Gangster* 137: He's jammin' [himself] up with the big boss, the fool! **1930** Graham & Graham *Queer People* 19: He hates newspapermen because they sort of jammed him up when he got tight and drove into a streetcar a little while ago. **1950** *Time* (Jan. 16) 56: Ranger Coach Lynn Patrick had found a way to jam Detroit's high-velocity forward line. **1957** E. Lacy *Room to Swing* 43: A joker who had jammed himself years ago but seemed to have straightened out. **1971** *Who Took Weight?* 186: You gonna let that girl *jam* you? Sho'nuff *jam* you. **1988** Norst *Colors* 168: I get jammed if you put me with Crips. *Ibid.* 190: When Rocket jammed somebody, that body could wind up dead, fast. **1989** P. Munro *U.C.L.A. Slang* 52: *Jam up* to put on the spot./Jane had a talk with Maria about her behavior and really jammed her up.

b. Esp. *Und.* to harass; (*hence*) to threaten or put at a finishing disadvantage.—also constr. with *up.*

1971 Woodley *Dealer* 30: Yeah, well, some people…planned to bother me. They were going to jam me up. **1972–74** Hawes & Asher *Raise Up* 29: But it was only the cops jamming* brothers.…*Harassing. *Ibid.* 113: That's a standard number they do to jam* you.…*Coerce you into becoming a police informer. *Ibid.* 137: The management said the police were jamming them.**1976** *L.A. Times* (Mar. 5) IV 7: He had heard the student was show-boating through the halls, jamming (confronting) friends and giving teachers a hard time. **1983** *California* (Aug.) 135: Some of the boys from the park had "jammed" him earlier that day. **1988** *U.S. News & W.R.* (Jan. 18) 34: And…you take your gun…and you jam him. You got the cash, his jewelry, and the merchandise. **1989** *Cops* (Fox-TV): We can jam 'em here.

c. *Black E.* (see quot.).

1971 H. Roberts *Third Ear: Jam…*to fight.

d. Esp. *Black E.* to overcome or defeat decisively.—also constr. with *up* or *on.*

1967–80 Folb *Runnin' Lines* 243: *Jam (one up)…*Beat severely…Overpower. **1982** Eble *Campus Slang* (Fall) 3: Carolina will jam on Texas in El Paso. **1986** Eble *Campus Slang* (Fall) 5: The Heels were *jammin'* on Duke.

3. to work hard; (*rarely, trans.*) to work hard at.

1893 in F. Remington *Sel. Letters* 168: [I am] Jamming away on Cossacks. **1944** Burley *Hndbk. Jive* 122: Thine has really been jammin' with a heavy slave session. **1950** *New Yorker* (May 13) 55: Hemingway sat down on the couch with Mr. Scribner and began telling him that he had been jamming, like a rider in a six-day bike race. **1983** Eble *Campus Slang* (Spring) 4: *Jam…*to work hard at some activity. **1995** *N.Y. Press* (Aug. 30) 17: The bulky…physique of a guy who jams weights a couple times a week.

4. (among hawkers and pitchmen) to sell (usu. shoddy or stolen merchandise) to.—also used absol. Cf. JAM², *n.,* 2.a.

1903 *Independent* (July 23) 1720: It will be easier to say one was "jammed." *Ibid.*: Just try to stick to the sharpeners. Don't you "jam" or work "slum" without paying the regular tariff. It's $10 a day for jamming and $5 for slum. **1938** in A. Banks *First-Person* 189: I've seen women jamming in Texas, Oklahoma, Missouri, and Illinois, but only once in North Carolina. **1942** *AS* XVII 91: Pitchmen's Cant…*Jamming.* Selling to a whole crowd at once rather than to an individual.

5.a. Orig. *Jazz.* to improvise jazz in ensemble, esp. in an informal setting (now *S.E.*); (*broadly*) to play jazz or other popular music, esp. informally (now *colloq.*).—occ. used trans.

1935 in R.S. Gold *Jazz Talk* 141: *Jam:* to improvise hot music, usually in groups. **1936** *Harper's* (Apr.) 574: "Jamming"…is used to best advantage in conjunction with the solo.…When each instrument has had its say then the jamming begins. **1937** *New Yorker* (Apr. 17) 32: They jam until they are tired, or until the swing enthusiasts—the alligators—permit them to stop. **1937** *AS* (Oct.) 182: *Jam.* To play in the hottest style and without any written music; to improvise completely and intensely. **1939** Floyd Ray & His Orchestra *Jammin' the Blues (Tamin' the Blues)* [Decca phonograph record 2618]. **1939** Goodman & Kolodin *Swing* 89: We used to spend a lot of time there after work, drinking and jamming. **1940** in Handy *Blues Treasury* 171: But when he jams, with the bass and guitar/They holler, "Aw, beat me, daddy, eight to the bar." **1946** Mezzrow & Wolfe *Really Blues* 111: There…was drinking and jamming and fooling around. **1948** in Asimov, Greenberg & Olander *Sci. Fi. Short Shorts* 32: Then…the two players began to jam. **1948** Manone & Vandervoort *Trumpet* 20: Two colored bands…battled it out, with the one that jammed the best getting the crowd. *Ibid.* 26: Our way sounded better, so we'd jam it again. **1962** Charters & Kunstadt *Jazz* 271: The rest of them "jammed" in a hotel room until sunrise. **1971** Wells & Dance *Night People* 23: When you got through in a strange town, you went out and jammed. *Ibid.* 117: *Jam,* v. To improvise, usually after hours. **1988–93** Wilcock & Guy *Damn Right* 23: I asked him about playing with me, and we jammed for a good while.

b. *Jazz.* to play (a musical piece) in jazz style.—also constr. with *up.*

1939 (quot. at BARRELHOUSE, 2). **1948** Manone & Vandervoort *Trumpet* 113: A jammed-up version of that corny old tune "A Bicycle Built for Two." **1987** *RHD2: Jam…*to…jazz up; *to jam both standard tunes and the classics.*

c. Esp. *Black E.* to play music in an exciting manner; (*hence*) to do exceptionally well; excel.—occ. used trans.

1970 Major *Afro-Amer. Slang* 70: *Jam…*to make exciting music. **1982**

Eble *Campus Slang* (Fall) 3: *Jam*...to do something well...I *jammed* on my homework last night. **1984** Mason & Rheingold *Slanguage*: To *jam* means to dance or play music in an exceptionally good manner. **1984** in P. Munro *U.C.L.A. Slang* 52: *Jam*...to do something very well. **1984** Univ. Tenn. student: *Jammed it* means you did well on a test. You aced it. **1985** Eble *Campus Slang* (Apr.) 5: *Jam*—to do something especially well: "Michael Jordan jams on the basketball court." **1985** Eble *Campus Slang* (Oct.) 6: *Jam*—to do extremely well at a task. "Our floor's hockey team's gonna jam!" **1991** Nelson & Gonzales *Bring Noise* 148: Jamming hot tracks in seamless overlays on twin turntables. **1993** P. Munro *U.C.L.A. Slang II*: I really jammed on that test.

d. to enjoy oneself intensely, esp. at a party; have fun; (*hence*) *Narc.* to indulge in drug-taking.

1970 Major *Afro-Amer. Slang* 70: *Jam*...to have a good time socially; to "party." *a***1972** Milner & Milner *Black Players* 272: *To Jam* to sniff cocaine, e.g. "We been jamming all night." Perhaps related to the musical (jazz) meaning. *a***1972** *Urban Life & Culture* I 90: He...digs "jamming" with "girl" (cocaine). **1974** Univ. Tenn. student: Let's go jam! **1986** Eble *Campus Slang* (Fall) 5: We were really *jammin'* at the beach last weekend.

e. *Black E.* to talk, esp. forcefully or in a group.

1971 S. Stevens *Way Uptown* 112: There was Barbara jamming with Abner Goldstein. *Ibid.* 144: A East Village fox was jamming to me about it. **1967–80** Folb *Runnin' Lines* 242: *Jam*...Talk forcefully. **1989** *Village Voice* (N.Y.C.) (May 9) 35: All this week teen boys have...asked to jam on what makes them so frightening.

f. to dance or move one's body in time to music.—occ. constr. with *back* or *on*.

1972 Claerbaut *Black Jargon* 70: *Jam*...to dance: *Gonna jam a little.* **1976** Eble *Campus Slang* (Nov.) 3: *Jam*...to dance. **1983** *Reader's Digest Success with Words* 86: Black English...*jam back* = "to dance." **1984** Univ. Tenn. student: Do you like to jam?...Yeah, dance. **1986** Univ. Tenn. student theme: We went "jammin" at all the local "hot spots,"...dancing and partying at the local bars. **1987** Univ. Tenn. student theme: If a person wants to dance, he wants to *jam.* **1991** N. Krulik *Hammer & Ice* 22: You'd get to jam on Hammer's raps.

g. (esp. of music or popular entertainment) to be delightful or exciting; SWING.

1989 N.Y.C. teenager: It [a movie] jams—it totally jams. **1990** P. Dickson *Slang!* 220: *Jammin'.* Music that sounds good. **1992** *Donahue* (NBC-TV): Rock 'n roll was jammin' [on the stereo].

6. to spoil.

1946 Steinbeck *Wayward Bus* 105: Louie and that nigger was gonna split them up a couple half centuries and I guess I jammed it for them.

7. to copulate with (a woman).—occ. used absol.—usu. considered vulgar.

1968 I. Reed *Yellow Back Radio* 166: I miss...chug-a-lugging fine brandy with the gang and jamming some strumpets. **1972** R. Wilson *Forbidden Words* 149: I'd like to jam that chick. **1967–80** Folb *Runnin' Lines* 243: *Jam*...Engage in sexual intercourse....Rape. **1980** Eble *Campus Slang* (Spring) 3: *Jam*...to have sex. **1981** *Nat. Lampoon* (July) 85: I tried to take her out onto the beach...and maybe jam her while she was high. *a***1986** in *NDAS*: Did what? Jammed. **1994** N. McCall *Wanna Holler* 42: A train was...what happened when a bunch of guys got together and jammed the same girl.

8. to go at full speed.—usu. constr. with *it;* (*hence*) to leave; (now occ. constr. with *off,* also used trans.) go, esp. in a hurry. [The intended sense of the uniquely early 1896 quot. is prob. 'to rush in a crowd'.]

[**1896** Wister *Red Men* 35: I could see the hostiles jamming back home for dear life. They was chucking their rifles to the squaws, and jumping in the river...to wash off their war-paint.] **1965–66** Maurer & Vogel *Narc. & Add.* (ed. 3) 367: *Jam*...To leave the scene. **1966** H.S. Thompson *Hell's Angels* 97: Nothing on the road...can catch an artfully hopped-up outlaw 74 as long as there's room to "jam it"...and take advantage of the huge engine. **1970** Landy *Underground Dict.* 111: *Jam*...Depart; leave. **1975** Wambaugh *Choirboys* 286: I think you better jam off, baby. Leave those little girls alone. **1982** Pond *Valley Girls' Gde.* 59: When you jam your class you've got to leave fast. **1982–84** Safire *Take My Word* 109: Gotta go...Gotta split...Gotta jam. **1983–84** in P. Munro *U.C.L.A. Slang* 52: *Jam*...hurry. **1985** "Blowdryer" *Mod. Eng.* 32: Get on your bike, and let's jam to the tattoo parlour. **1985** *Miami Vice* (NBC-TV): Maybe we could jam on up

to 128th Street. **1986** *New Gidget* (syndic. TV series): Well, I gotta be jammin'. **1986** Wilson & Maddock *Short Circuit* (film): Come on, Stephanie! We be jammin'! **1987** *Rage* (Knoxville, Tenn.) I (No. 2) 13: *Jamming*—moving fast. **1989** Waters *Heathers* (film): Can we please jam now? *a***1990** E. Currie *Dope & Trouble* 110: When I was little, my mom jammed to Chicago. **1993** P. Munro *U.C.L.A. Slang II*: *Jam*...to leave quickly...*I've really got to jam, guys. I'm late.* **1994** *My So-Called Life* (ABC-TV): We gotta jam before anybody gets here.

9. *Black E.* to upset deeply.

1971 (quot. at JAMMED, 3).

10. to pressure; coerce.

1994 *L.A. Times* (Jan. 31) B3: The district is so big and powerful and influential that we can jam the state and the federal government to get things for us.

¶ In phrases:

¶ **jam a gear** [sugg. by GEAR-JAMMER] *Trucking.* to drive a truck or other large motor vehicle.

1986 Thacker *Pawn* 81 [ref. to 1970]: Franelli, can you jam a gear?

¶ **jam it [up your ass]** SHOVE IT.—usu. considered vulgar. Also vars.

1936 J.T. Farrell *World I Never Made* 312: Let them stick their help up where I'd like to see them jam it. **1941** Brackett & Wilder *Ball of Fire* (film): Jam it!...I didn't mean to say it. I'm sorry. **1943** Hersey *Bell for Adano* 186: "You can jam it up your ass for all I care," Sergeant Frank said harshly. **1945** in *Best from Yank* 214: They can take their apology and jam it and cram it. **1950** J. Barr *Quatrefoil* 205: Take this mess and jam it up your tail for all I care. **1952** Uris *Battle Cry* 122: Every time we pass a good-sized tree it blocks reception. I think we should jam them up the Navy's ass sideways...sir. **1959** O'Connor *Talked to a Stranger* 79: Well, you can take social agencies and jam 'em. **1966** Braly *Cold* 9: "Your free gift certificate." "Jam it!" **1974** in Mack *Real Life* (unp.): "Ain't dis a flip! One little stupid [toy] bicycle for $5.00." "They can jam it!" *a***1979** in S. King *Bachman* 273: You take your Joliet...and your mills and you jam them. Jam them crossways, if they'll fit. **1982** Savitch *Anchorwoman* 53: "I came back for one reason, honey," she told me. "I want to jam it up their asses." **1986** *L.A. Law* (NBC-TV): 150K? Is he kidding? Tell him to jam it! **1992** *Mystery Sci. Theater* (Comedy Central TV): Aah, jam it, ya crummy prole!

¶ **jam it [in]to** to victimize; treat unfairly; take advantage of; SHAFT.

1960–69 Runkel *Law* 139: Plenty of people jammed it into me for being scrawny. **1995** *CNN Saturday Morning* (CNN-TV) (July 6): He was so obviously trying not to jam it to O.J.

jambone *adj.* [see note at JIBONEY] contemptible; worthless.

1988 B. Dragin & R. McDonnell *Twice Dead* (film): "Very polite." "Especially for some jambone motherfucker."

jamboree *n.* [orig. unkn.; earlier (1864) as a term in euchre (see *DAE* and *Century Dict.*)] **1.a.** a boisterous celebration; (*obs.*) a carousal or drinking spree. Now *colloq.*

1868 in *DA*: The Seventh regiment has gone on a jamboree to Norwich, Connecticut. **1872** in *F & H* IV 36: There have not been so many dollars spent on any jamboree. *a***1877** in Bartlett *Amer.* (ed. 4) 320: Case was...drunk clear through. He was having a good deal of *jimboree* [sic], and defied the police to take him. *Ibid.*: G.B. went on a regular *jamboree* on Thursday night. Filling himself up with bad liquor, he raised a row and was taken up by the police. **1878** *Nat. Police Gaz.* (May 18) 14: Hyer had gone on a jamboree, and he found him in a saloon. **1878** in *OED2*: He enjoyed a drinking bout or a jamboree. **1884** in *DAE*: It is very creditable to Mr. O'Brien that he did not open a jamboree at the Parker House on the night of his election. *a***1889** *Century Dict.*: *Jamboree*...A carousal; a noisy drinking-bout; a spree; hence, any noisy merrymaking. (Slang). **1898** Atherton *Californians* 201: The first cocktail, and I'd be off on a jamboree. **1912** Siringo *Cowboy Detective* 138: That night I got on a big "jamboree," and spent my wages freely. **1915** *DN* IV 227: *Jamboree*, n. A boisterous entertainment. **1921** in H. Cannon *Cowboy Poetry* 19: I'm a ring-tailed he-gorilla on a hell-bent jamboree. **1927** Kyne *They Also Serve* 2: "I'd be inclined to join you in a...jamboree." "If there was only a good *estaminet* around here." **1929** *AS* V 75: A "shindig" at which there is much drinking of liquors might become a "jamboree." **1936** Sandburg *People, Yes* 56: Lumberjack payday jamborees. **1961** Kohner *Gidget Goes Hawaiian* 57: I was determined to make this evening...a giant jamboree.

b. a row or disturbance.

1871 Schele de Vere *Amer.* 611: *Jamboree*, a row, a disturbance…is genuine American slang. **1877** (quot. at COOP, 3.a.). **1896** in M. Simmons *Santa Fe Trail* 44: It was a motley scene…a general "jamboree" of noise, commotion, odor, and color. **1922** Rollins *Cowboy* 77: For instance "jamboree" might indicate, among other things, an innocent dancing party, a drunken debauch, or an active event, whether the last were a pistol fight or a stampede of animals. **1927–30** Rollins *Jinglebob* 31 [ref. to 1880's]: Almos' forgot about 'im in the jamboree with the rabbits.

2. lot; number.—constr. with *whole*.

1976 Hayden *Voyage* 551: The whole friggin' jamboree that works for wages has got to be Red.

jam box *n.* a portable combination stereophonic radio and cassette player; BOOM BOX.

1982 Eble *Campus Slang* (Nov.) 3: *Jambox*—a radio with a tape player: Bring the *jambox* to the beach. **1984** Univ. Tenn. student: I wanted to kick the jam box into the pool. **1985** N.Y.C. man, age *ca*30: I like 'at jam box she carryin'. **1991** *Drexell's Class* (Fox-TV): Why would you take my jam box?

jam-buster *n. R.R.* (see quot.).

1938 Beebe *High Iron* 222: *Jam buster:* Assistant yardmaster.

jam can *n.* (see quot.).

1918 *Sat. Eve. Post* (Nov. 23) 53: We could only obtain the crudest implements with which to bake them; we had a small stove commonly known as a "Jam Can"; removed the top and in its place put a large piece of sheet iron which served as a griddle.

James *n. Und.* (see quots.). *Joc.*

1812 Vaux *Vocab.: Jemmy*, or *James:* an iron-crow. **1858** A. Mayhew *Paved with Gold* 382: The "james"—a short crowbar—…soon cleared away the obstruction of the shutter. *a*1909 Tillotson *Detective* 92: *James*—A jimmy; a small crowbar.

James-dandy *n.* JIM-DANDY. *Joc.*

1896 Ade *Artie* 72: Ain't this a James-dandy of a night? **1901** Irwin *Sonnets* (unp.): The sonnet is…/A James P. Dandy.

jam fag *n. Homosex.* (see quot.).

*a*1954 in Krich *Homosexuals* 93: *Jam fags* are brilliant male homosexuals. Many…have pseudo-names, as Queen Mary, Princess Wee-Wee, [etc.].

jammed *adj.* **1.** intoxicated.

1922 in *DN* V 147: He got jammed.…*Jammed*—intoxicated, also shot, shellacked, canned, out like a light, potted, tanked, cuckooed, etc.

2. Esp. *Und.* in serious difficulty, esp. with the law; (specif.) arrested.—usu. constr. with *up*. Cf. JAM¹, *n.*, 2.

1925–26 J. Black *You Can't Win* 43 [ref. to 1890's]: The next time you get jammed up say something before you get thrown in. **1927** Coe *Gangster* 50: That guy would know us if we ever git jammed up over this. **1935** Pollock *Und. Speaks: Jammed*, arrested. **1939** Howsley *Argot* 27: *Jammed, Jammed Up*—in trouble, difficulty. **1940** *Batman* (No. 1) (unp.): All in all, he was badly jammed up, so he decided to kill himself. **1942–49** Goldin et al. *DAUL* 109: *Jammed up*. Arrested; in serious trouble. **1955** Margulies *Punks* 178: And get us all jammed-up, answering a million questions? **1963** Braly *Shake Him* 95: Refusal to cooperate with the police. You're jammed right. **1965** Linakis *In Spring* 139: "Are you jammed?" "What?" "Trouble." "Not yet." **1972** *N.Y. Post* (Dec. 20) 39: It's for jammed-up cops and for cops who never took a dime.…to guys jammed up with the wrong women. **1981** in Spears *Drugs & Drink* 286: *Jammed*…Arrested. **1986** J.J. Maloney *Chain* 75: I heard you got pretty jammed up. How'd it happen? **1990** C.P. McDonald *Blue Truth* 48: We don't want to get jammed up over…this…do we?

3. deeply upset.

1971 Woodley *Dealer* 110: I asked him how it affected him when his mother died.…"I'd just rather not talk about it. It jammed me up. I'm still jammed because of that."

jammer *n.* **1.** (among hawkers and pitchmen) a seller of various small, cheap items. Cf. JAM², *n.*, 2.a.

1939 in A. Banks *First-Person* 189: You can tell a jammer the minute he starts a block away.

2. GEAR-JAMMER.

1986 Thacker *Pawn* 81 [ref. to 1970]: And he was a good jammer too.

-jammer *comb. form.* player.

1989 *Beachin' Times* 16: Portable CD jammer.

jammie var. JAMMY.

jammies *n.pl. Juve.* pajamas; JAMS², 2.

*a*1967 Bombeck *Wit's End* 46: I've laid out your jammies and your bow wow. **1987** S. Stark *Wrestling Season* 127: Lay you odds Ma's still in her jammies. **1983–89** K. Dunn *Geek Love* 96: I got him into his jammies and tucked him into bed.

jamming *adj.* Esp. *Black E.* exciting; wonderful; great.

1983 Eble *Campus Slang* (Spring) 4: Have you heard that jammin' new song by Rush? **1984** Mason & Rheingold *Slanguage:* Good or together.…"The party was really jamming." **1984** Algeo *Stud Buds:* What terms do you use to describe something that is very good?…awesome,…great,…jamming, [etc.]. **1984** Eble *Campus Slang* (Spring) 4: Your new shoes are jammin'. **1986** Eble *Campus Slang* (Mar.) 6: *Jamming*…very good. "That's a jamming song." **1989** *Nat. Lampoon* (June) 29: He used to call himself the Jammin' Jersey Juggler. **1989** P. Munro *U.C.L.A. Slang* 52: *Jamming* neat, cool. That guy is just the coolest person, I think he is a jamming dude. **1992** *Melrose Place* (Fox-TV): That [food] was jammin'. It was so good! **1992** S. Straight *Been in Sorrow's Kitchen* 282: "I know I need a break." "Jammin."

jammy *n.* [orig. unkn.; Cf. JIMMY] *Black E.* a gun; (broadly) a thing; item. Also **jammie.**

1986 "Beastie Boys" *Rhymin' & Stealin'* (rap song): I'll pull out the jammy and squeeze off six. **1986** "Beastie Boys" *Slow Ride* (rap song): I got the jammy with the ammo inside my sock. **1990–91** *Street Talk!* 4: *Jammy* gun. "Yo, I'm gonna get this jammy." **1992** in N. George *Buppies, B-Boys* 69: There always seemed to be a new Fred Williamson jammie, something like [the film] *The Legend of Nigger Charley.* **1992** "Fab 5 Freddie" *Fresh Fly Flavor* 36: *Jammy*—A firearm. **1993** P. Munro *U.C.L.A. Slang II: Jammie* n. gun. **1995** S. Moore *In the Cut* 63: *Jammie*, n., gun.

jamoke *n.* [clipping of *jamocha*, fr. *Java + Mocha*, sources and types of coffee beans] **1.** Esp. *Naut. & Und.* coffee. Also **jamocha.**

1895 in Tisdale *Behind Guns* 13: "You will take to it like you take to your Jimokey!" I asked him what Jimokey was, and he seemed surprised that I did not know it to mean Jamaica—coffee. *Ibid.:* Then back to our Jimock—a cup of coffee taken standing. **1899** Markey *Iowa to Philippines* 290: It hustled the "Jamocha King" [the cook] to supply the demands placed upon him. **1921** Casey & Casey *Gay-Cat* 187: There ain't nothin' stronger in the booze line than pure alky mixed with jamocha. **1922** *Leatherneck* (Apr. 29) 5: *Jamoc'*—Coffee. **1927** in Botkin *Sidewalks* 308 [ref. to 1918]: De jamocha is rotten. De goddam chuck dey hands yer is rotten. **1928** *AS* III 451: Black coffee is *jamoke* to the Midshipman. *a*1929 in Milburn *Hobo's Hornbook* 57: Hand over a shot of that good jamoke. **1931** *AS* VI 439: Convicts' Jargon…*jamoke*, n. Coffee. **1931–34** in Clemmer *Pris. Community* 333: *Jamoke*…Coffee. **1942** *Life* (May 25) 58: Red is taking on a bowl of jomoke (coffee) and shootin' the breeze about a blonde in Newport. **1945** J. Bryan *Carrier* 22: It's not the jamoke. **1948** Wolfert *Act of Love* 234: How good that first cup of hot jamocha is going to taste. **1958** Cooley *Run for Home* 108: Let's go get a cup of "jamoke." **1982** T.C. Mason *Battleship* 75: I don't recall hearing the word *jamoke* as slang for coffee in a navy ship, although it appeared regularly in the columns of *Our Navy* magazine.

2. a stupid, objectionable, or inconsequential fellow; JOKER. [In 1924 and 1928 quots. (ref. to USMC, in WWI), an unexplained nickname.]

[**1924** in D. Hammett *Continental Op* 49: Fred Rooney, alias "Jamocha."] [**1928** *Our Army* (Oct.) 12: Ja-Moch. [a soldier's nickname].] **1946** "J. Evans" *Halo in Blood* 32: If I was going to find out what kind of jamoke Marlin was. **1972** in *Playboy* (Jan. 1973) 244: I don't think bringing in them jamokes was such a hot idea.…Those're hard Harps…They are very tough guys. **1977** J. Olsen *Fire Five* 160: When it comes to housework, she can dust the ears off any of these jamokes. **1983** Flaherty *Tin Wife* 143: She had it rough with Billy and Eddie, plus that jomoke in the zoo just now. **1989** *Dream Street* (NBC-TV): These jamokes ya run with. They tell me things. **1991** C. Fletcher *Pure Cop* 195: The poor jamoke…doing thirty miles an hour…gets broadsided by the guy doing seventy-five. **1995** N.Y.C. man, age *ca*30 (coll. J. Sheidlower): Don't bring any of your jamoke friends this time.

3. the penis.—usu. considered vulgar.

1966 Rimmer *Harrad Experiment* 34: I can see your jamoke, and it's sticking in the air.

jam-o-matic *n. Shooting.* an automatic weapon that often jams. *Joc.*

    1979 in Terkel *Amer. Dreams* 392: Throw this goddamn gun away, this is a jam-o-matic.

jam out *v. Jazz.* to dress up.

    1948 Manone & Vandervoort *Trumpet* 36: Cats…all jammed out in sharp suits. *Ibid.* 121: A drawing of some jammed-out swells.

jampot *n.* **1.** the vulva or vagina; (*Homosex.*) the anus.—usu. considered vulgar.

    ***a1890–96** *F & H* IV 37: *Jampot*…The female *pudendum.* **1941** G. Legman, in Henry *Sex Vars.* 1169: *Jam-pot* The anus. **1965** Trimble *Sex Words* 112: *Jam pot*…The fleshy part of the vulva.

    2. *Army.* a kind of German hand grenade; POTATO-MASHER. Now *hist.*

    1929 Cole *37th Div.* II 143 [ref. to 1918]: Pvt. Bradbrook started his automatic and sent a volley into the surprised enemy who began to yell and retreat, throwing "jam pots" as they went. *Ibid.* 145: Suddenly a "jam pot" hit on the bank near Red Griffin's automatic when it exploded, throwing the rifle out of his hands and loosening the rear assembling bolt, causing a jam.

jams[1] *n.pl.* **1.** decompression sickness; bends.—constr. with *the.*

    1873 T.W. Knox *Underground* 424: We have all had the jams…a feeling like the flesh a tearin' of off our bones.

    2. JIMJAMS.—constr. with *the.*

    1888 in Farmer *Americanisms:* My fader's de best doctor in Boston, an'…keeps de medicine to stave off de jams ready mixed. **1894** O. Wister, in *Harper's Mag.* (July) 208: That's the kind of clock gives a man the jams. Sends him crazy. **1908** Kelley *Oregon Pen.* 14: He had the jams. His eyes were bloodshot from booze.

jams[2] *n.pl.* [fr. *pajamas*] **1.** (now a registered trademark) loose knee-length swimming trunks.

    1966** in *OED2:* It's the season of the hubba hubba jams—and that's…a patio fashion stopper. **1968** *N.Y. Times* (Jan. 22) 36: Swim trunks and surfers' "jams," knee-length trunks with draw-string waists. **1968** Kirk & Hanle *Surfer's Handbook* 141: *Jams:* long, flowered, baggy shorts—like cut-off pajamas. **1970** *New Yorker* (Mar. 17) 34: He wore His-'n-Hers flowered at-home jams. **1973** *Playboy* (June) 113: Balloon-seated boxer trunks and John L. Sullivan-type Baggies and jams. **1980** Lorenz *Guys Like Us* 7: [A] T-shirt and a pair of surfer jams. **1986** Univ. Tenn. student theme: Preps dress in polo shirts, jams, Duckhead pants, and Hobi t-shirts. **1989** *Beachin' Times* 16: Hip jams [for beach-wear]. **1992** *CBS This Morning* (CBS-TV) (Jan. 30): Jams are hotter than ever this season because of the new prints. *a1994** D. Frey *Last Shot* 39: A new pair of cotton basketball jams.

    2. pajamas.

    1973 Kingry *Monk & Marines* 64: I took Mai's jams and covered her nakedness. **1986** De Sola *Abbrev. Dict.* (ed. 7) 510: *Jams* pajamas.

jam session [JAM[1], *n.*, 3.a. + *session*] **1.** Orig. *Jazz.* an informal and typically impromptu session of jazz music; (*broadly*) an informal meeting of musicians to play for enjoyment.

    1933 *Fortune* (Aug.) 90: Not unlike the jazz musicians' *jam sessions* where the players vie with one another in *hot solos.* **1936** *Harper's* (Apr.) 574: Thus in a typical "jam session" one instrument will lead off with a slightly modified form of the general melody, the other instruments "faking" the harmony. **1936** Benny Goodman and His Orchestra *Jam Session* [Victor phonograph record VIC 25497]. **1937** *AS* (Oct.) 182: *Jam session.* An after hours' gathering of musicians of the hot persuasion…for relaxation…and to jam a few numbers. **1939** in L. Patterson *Negro in Music* 59: In these early "jam sessions"…individual musicians would compete with one another. *ca***1945** in Driggs & Lewine *Black Beauty* 86: World Premiere, National Swing Concert and Jam Session!…The Country's Leading Instrumentalists *Together!* **1946** Mezzrow & Wolfe *Really Blues* 307: *Jam session:* a musical get-together in which all the playing is collectively improvised. **1950** in *DAS:* When they were holding jam sessions in the Onyx Club. *a***1981** in McKee & Chisenhall *Beale* 149: We'd go around and have a jam session, see if we could out-sing the other. **1988** T. Logan *Harder They Fall* 118: Sitting alone at a table in Maxie's Restaurant, listening to a blues jam session. **1989** *Rolling Stone* (Oct. 19) 53: Jam sessions in which records, cassettes, drum machines and all the technology of modern recording serve as the ensemble's instruments.

    2. an informal group discussion; RAP SESSION.

    1993 *UTK Library Record* (Univ. Tenn.) 2: Our librarians are Internet experts, teaching seminars on its use, holding "jam" sessions about its intricacies.

jam-spunky *adj.* JAM-UP.

    1863 in R. Mitchell *Civil War Soldiers* 243: Iowa is a jamspunky fine little state.

jam-up *adj.* splendid; first-rate; BANG-UP, 1.b. Also as adv.

    1823 [J. Neal] *Errata* II 175: Run agin me, run agin a snag…jam up. **1841** *So. Lit. Messenger* VII 54: The jam-up little company. **1842** J.L. Scott *Missionary* 62: If they conceive a good quality in anything, they say, "It's jam up." For instance, "That's a jam up friend or a jam up dinner," &c. **1850** J. Greene *12 Days in Tombs* 100: Give us a jam-up prayer. **1852** Hazen *Five Years* 262: I asked him how he got on in his new station. "Jam up—would'nt [*sic*] give the little craft for two old *Columbus'.*" *Ibid.* 274: "What sort of a character did this man bear in the *Columbus?*"…"Jam-up." **1862** in Wightman *To Ft. Fisher* 70: Made a "jam up" supper. **1873** *Slang & Vulgar Forms* 15: *Jam up*…a low barbarous phrase…signifying *good, very excellent;* as "His credit is *jam up.*" "These apples are *jam up.*" **1891** Maitland *Slang Dict.* 153: *Jam up,* good, prime. Same as "bang up" or "slap up." **1905** *DN* III 12: *Jam up*…First rate. **1927** in Dundes *Mother Wit* 202: We got to hit the ball, you know, and give 'em some service jam-up. **1946** Mezzrow & Wolfe *Really Blues* 14: I got my first chance to play in a real man size band, with jam-up instruments. **1962** Killens *Heard the Thunder* 69: She's…doing a jam-up job. **1962–68** B. Jackson *In the Life* 88: All them guards thought I was a jam-up old gal because I'd be down there rain or shine. **1968** Brasselle *Cannibals* 33: "How's the wife?"…"Jam up." **1969** Kimbrough *Defender of Angels* 191: These Mexican gals do a jam-up job. **1996** McCumber *Playing off Rail* 241: He heard you're playin jam up and he says he's off his game. *Ibid.* 288: John Bear plays jam-up…and you know it. **1993** Rebennack & Rummel *Under Hoodoo Moon* 44: We all became jam-up partners.

Jane *n.* **1.** a girl or woman; girlfriend. Also **jane.**

    1865** Sala *Diary* II 87: If this crazy Jane in a red jacket had uttered her nonsense in some Dissenting chapel…this plea might hold good. **1906** *DN* III 142: Going to take your Jane to the show? **1908** McGaffey *Show Girl* 240: Two of the Janes put up a horrible holler about it being a friendly game. **1909** Chrysler *White Slavery* 34: He plays for the "swell Janes." **1913** *Sat. Eve. Post* (July 5) 4: As soon as this jane finds out. **1915** "High Jinks, Jr." *Choice Slang* 51: *Jane*…A rather coarse appellation for a girl or young lady. **1917** (quot. at HAM-AND). **1918** Ruggles *Navy Explained* 82: *Jane*—The best girl is the Jane, widder, skirt, calico, the old lady, weezel, broad, judy, dame, tomatoe, wax doll, jelly bean, fair one, or wench. There is no vulgar thought in using the above mentioned words and they are characteristic of the present-day sailormen. **1918** *DN* V 25: *Jane, n.* A girl picked up on the street; the word has a good sense also. **1918** in "M. Brand" *Coll. Stories* 54: In the States a jane could pull that line now and then. **1922** in *DN* V 147: His regular jane had given him the air. **1924** Marks *Plastic Age* 149: I met a bunch of janes down at Bar Harbor. **1954** J. Berman & I. Silber, in *Sing Out* (Winter 1955) 34: Yes, I am the man, the very brave man, who names the hurricanes./It was me that thought of the brilliant idea of naming them after "janes." **1966** Kenney *Caste* 94: She's a good jane. **1969** B. Beckham *Main Mother* 139: We saw babes, chicks, janes, mamas, foxes. **1972** Grogan *Ringolevio* 83: His date was a cocky jane with a petulant mouth. *a1973–87** F.M. Davis *Livin' the Blues* 42: I had far better luck with jazz than with the janes.

    2. [sugg. by JOHN] a women's lavatory.

    1955 Nabokov *Lolita* 155: A great user of roadside facilities…Lo would be charmed by toilet signs—Guys-Gals, John-Jane, Jack-Jill, and even Buck's-Doe's. **1954–60** *DAS: Jane*…A (usu., but not necessarily, public) restroom, bathroom, or toilet as used by women. **1994** *New Yorker* (June 13) 38: I'm sitting on the john in a jane.

    3. *Narc.* MARY JANE.

    1971 Dahlskog *Dict.* 39: *Jane, n.* Marijuana. **1989** Leib *Fire Dream* 288: He, you know, *finds* this box he says is Jane.

Jane Q. Public *n.* [modeled on JOHN Q. PUBLIC] *Journ. & Pol.* the general female public; a woman who is typical of the general public. Also **Jane Q. Citizen.**

    1977 *Aviation Week and Space Technology* (May 9) 70 (Nexis): Those of us who have watched the Apollo or Viking projects financially and technically struggle…may have a different perspective on our numerous space accomplishments than does the general public, be they John Q. or Jane Q. Public. **1986** *NDAS: Jane Q Citizen* (or *Public*)…Any woman, esp the average or typical woman. **1995** *N.Y. Times* (June 14) A20: Mr. Perot has invited all members of United We Stand and also John and Jane Q. Public to this three-day conference.

JANFU *n.* [joint *a*rmy-*n*avy *f*uck-*u*p] *Mil.* (see 1945 quot.). *Joc.* [explanations 1944 quots. are euphem.]
> **1944** *Newsweek* (Feb. 7) 61: *Janfu:* Joint Army-Navy foul-up *Jaafu:* Joint Anglo-American foul-up. **1944** in *AS* XX 148: *JANFU.* Joint army-navy foulup. **1945** in *Verbatim* XVI (Autumn 1989) 6: *Janfu*…"joint army-navy fxxx up." A failed amphibious military operation considered badly planned and/or executed. **1946** *AS* (Feb.) 72: JANFU (Joint Army-Navy FU)…became fairly common in [the Pacific] theater, especially around the time of the Saipan operation.

jangles *n.pl.* JITTERS.
> **1962** Houk & Dexter *Ballplayers* 129: Like me, Ralph had taken to chewing tobacco to get rid of his jangles.

JAP /ˈdʒæp/ *n.* [*J*ewish-*A*merican *P*rincess] Esp. *Stu.* JEWISH PRINCESS.—usu. considered offensive; (with weakened force) a young American Jewish woman.—sometimes considered offensive. [Discussed in G.V. Zito *The Death of Meaning* (1993), pp. 65–69.]
> **1972** Selzer *"Kike!"* xv: It's the JAP, the Jewish-American Princess. *ca*1973 (cited in *W10*). **1977** Silver Spring, Md., man, age 35: She was a real JAP—a Jewish-American princess. **1978** *N.Y. Post* (July 17) 28: Do not be offended. The writer is a self-proclaimed J.A.P., and you'll hear from her later. **1980** in *Penthouse* (Jan. 1981) 173: Brenda Wilks had never put out for him—was probably a JAP dyke. **1983** "B. Knott" *Truly Tasteless Jokes* III 20: What's a JAP's idea of perfect sex? Simultaneous headaches. **1985** *Campus Voice* (Apr.) 28: Discussion looks at pros, cons of term "JAP." **1985** B.E. Ellis *Less Than Zero* 77: "A couple of hysterical J.A.P.'s" in Bel Air…talk of a werewolf. **1987** B. Raskin *Hot Flashes* 287: What does a good JAP make for dinner? Reservations. **1993** G. Zito *Death of Meaning* 66: The JAP of the late 1960s and early 1970s became a target for ridicule for her lack of good taste. *Ibid.* 67: Most Jewish students I have interviewed do not see JAP as [an especially racist term]. **1993** Adams & Stadiem *Madam* 54: Go be the JAP you always wanted to be. **1994** *Declarations* (PBS-TV): I still look like a JAP!

Jap *n.* **1.a.** Orig. *Naut.* a Japanese person.—often used contemptuously.—usu. considered offensive.
> **1854** in McCauley *With Perry* 100: The Commo: gives a grand dinner to the Japs on the 27th. **1859** in R.H. Dana *2 Yrs.* (Kemble ed.) II 430: "Boy Jap" to take care of stock. "You Jap"—"Kangaroos had no hay" [etc.]. **1868** *Galaxy* (May) 609: A daily hot bath is almost a religious duty with "Jap" and the American could not refuse a nightly boil. **1868** in Boyer *Naval Surgeon* II 29: The Mikado is the Great I am of all the Japs. *Ibid.* 34: The Japs have a high opinion of Americans—call us No. 1 (icheban). **1871** *Overland Mo.* (July) 44: One Jap, more or less, didn't matter. **1881** *United Service* (Aug.) 148: The Japs are young, too. **1893** in Dreiser *Jour.* I 136: Turks, Arabs, Hindoos, Japs, Egyptians. **1894** in Norris *Novelist* 61: I came into breakfast…and saw the Jap. plunged in the Herald. **1903** *Independent* (Nov. 26) 2794: The Japs are eager, intelligent workers and most amiable people. **1906** *Nat. Police Gaz.* (July 14) 3: The voice of the Jap came from the other room. **1908** in H.C. Fisher *A. Mutt* 41: The Jap has already received numerous offers for theatrical engagements. **1929** E. Wilson *Daisy* 109: The Japs did not kiss. **1932** Hecht & Fowler *Great Magoo* 183: He's as stoical as a Jap. **1944** Sherrod *Tarawa* 3: Are they going to invade the Jap-held islands so soon? **1946** K. Archibald *Shipyard* 103: In coat lapels appeared buttons with "Registered Jap Hunter" and "Open Season on Japs." **1958** T. Capote *Breakfast at Tiffany's* 7: The little Jap knew it was her the minute he saw her. **1977** Bunker *Animal Factory* 58: Stoneface is gonna be mad as a Jap. *Ibid.* 76: He'll be madder 'n a Jap if we don't show pretty soon. **1979** in Terkel *Amer. Dreams* 164: The drugstore on our corner would not serve "Japs," even in uniform. **1991** Jenkins *Gotta Play Hurt* 48: We stood in line for an hour behind Finns, Japs, Frenchmen, Italians, Swedes. **1993** G. Zito *Death of Meaning* 66: The students I interviewed [*ca*1970] could not understand why *Jap* was understood as a term of opprobrium for the Japanese, since it simply abbreviated their name. **1995** N. Schwarzkopf, on *CBS This Morning* (CBS-TV) (May 8): When I was in elementary school [during WWII], the worst thing you could call anyone was a *Jap.*

b. the Japanese language.—usu. used contemptuously.—usu. considered offensive.
> **1932** M. Anderson *Rain* (film): That's "I should worry" in Jap, buttercup. **1943** J. Mitchell *McSorley's* 190: What in hell would be the use of talking Jap to you? **1945** Huie *Omaha to Okinawa* 56: That's all the goddam Jap I need to know. **1954** Voorhees *Show Me a Hero* 20: Means Number One in Jap. **1960** J.D. MacDonald *Slam the Big Door* 13: They didn't give me a copy written in Jap. **1962** Gallant *Valor's Side* 294: I told you we had somebody who could speak Jap. **1976–83** Glimm *Flatlanders* 127: Said he could talk Chink, Wop, Jap, an' lots more.

c. an Asian person (of any nationality); (*Mil.*) an Asian who is an enemy.—usu. considered offensive.
> **1940** R. Chandler *Farewell, My Lovely* ch. xiv: A trade article that might have cost thirty-five to seventy-five cents in any Oriental store, Hooey Phooey Sing—Long Sing Tung, that kind of place, where a nice-mannered Jap hisses at you, laughing heartily. **1993** Watson & Dockery *Point Man* 13 [ref. to Vietnam War]: We [Navy SEALs] were deep into Jap country.…A legacy from the UDT [underwater demolition teams] of World War II, enemies in Asia were "Japs." *Ibid.* 163: Get the Japs! **1996** *N.Y. Times* (Nov. 27) B4: "Being Chinese-American is a factor of major importance in my life."…She remembered the pain of being called "Chink, Jap or flat-face" in school.

2. *Und. & Sports.* a black person or a mulatto.—usu. considered offensive.
> **1887** [C. Mackenzie] *Jack Pots* 80: Dars a couple of Japs up at de room now, waiting fur a game. **1904** *Life in Sing Sing* 249: *Jap.*—A colored person. [**1907** in Chalk *Pioneers of Black Sport* 56: Andrew "Jap" Payne.] **1928** R. Fisher *Jericho* 301: *Jap.* See *boogy.* **1942–49** Goldin et al. *DAUL* 110: *Jap* (Chiefly among carnival and transient grifters) A Negro.

3.a. (among teenage gangs) a surprise blow or attack, esp. a raid on a rival gang.—usu. considered offensive. Cf. JAP, *v.*
> **1955** Yablonsky *Violent Gang* 46: *Second* kind is a "Jap." That's when a group of guys, two guys or three guys, go down to a different club's territory, get in fast, beat up one or two guys and get out. **1971** Sorrentino *Up from Never* 153: It was just to get more leverage for his "jap," as sneak punches were called. **1979** D. Milne *Second Chance* 67 [ref. to 1950's]: We had a name for this kind of sneak attacker—"Jap-artist," in memory of Pearl Harbor.

b. *Stu.* an unannounced test; (*hence*) a ruinous surprise.—also used attrib.—usu. considered offensive.
> **1967** Vrooman *Good Writing* 68: The student…remarks that the grade on his [term paper] was a *jap.* **1968** Baker, Ladd & Robb *CUSS* 144: *Jap*…Surprise test. **1980** *AS* (Winter) 277: A *Jap* is a pop quiz or an unexpectedly difficult examination. **1984** Algeo *Stud Buds & Dorks:* An unexpected test…*Jap test.*

Jap *adj.* **1.** Japanese.—often used contemptuously.—usu. considered offensive.
> **1869** in Boyer *Naval Surgeon* II 201: Jap coal is worse than our bituminous coal at home. **1895** in *OEDS:* Plain colored Habutai Jap silk. **1918** Streeter *Dere Mable* 7: A troop of Jap akrobats. **1944** W. Duff *Marine Raiders* (film): It's an old Jap trick. **1987–89** M.H. Kingston *Tripmaster Monkey* 71: Holly's jap landlord.

2. sneaky; in phr. **Jap cuff** a surprise blow with the fist.—usu. considered offensive.
> **1966** Reynolds & McClure *Freewheelin Frank* 15: "How about a Jap cuff?"—swinging his arm off and jabbing into the air. **1967** Riessman & Dawkins *Play It Cool* 64: She told me not to talk about the old man—as if it was jap or something.

jap *v.* [orig. alluding to the surprise Japanese attack on Pearl Harbor, Dec. 7, 1941] **1.** to attack or assail suddenly or without warning; (*broadly*) to take by surprise.—usu. considered offensive.
> **1942** in W.C. Fields *By Himself* 186: The fellows…in Pearl Harbor…were caught napping, by the Japs Japping. **1942** Casey *Torpedo Junction* 260: If we are going to get Japped I think the dust-up will come between 11:30 and 1 P.M. **1957** *New Yorker* (Sept. 21) 135: "They japped us," a third boy said, meaning that the Cherubs had taken them by surprise. **1959** W. Miller *Cool World* 25: One time 3 Wolves japped me in my own building. **1960** Hoagland *Circle Home* 230: I know you haven't any tie-ins here to jap me. **1962** Riccio & Slocum *All the Way Down* 48: The crews didn't rumble for a time, but they "japped" each

other incessantly for weeks. **1964** "Dr. X" *Intern* 347: He was doing fine, and looked like a complete recovery coming up unless something japs us that I can't foresee. **1965** Yurick *Warriors* 24: Don't let them jap you, Brother. **1967** P. Thomas *Mean Streets* 61 [ref. to 1945]: Look out! Ya gonna get japped! **1969** *Current Slang I & II* 55: I got really japped by that quiz. **1971** Sorrentino *Up from Never* 61: Ya know ya gonna be in a fight or else look like a punk so ya might as well jap the other man. **1977** *Baa Baa Black Sheep* (NBC-TV): We'll jap him when his tanks are dry. **1980** Kotzwinkle *Jack* 18: They're no good, to Jap a guy that way. **1980** *AS* (Winter) 277: Man, that exam really Japped me!

2. to sneak.—usu. considered offensive.

　1964–66 R. Stone *Hall of Mirrors* 302: What are you doin' jappin' around my truck?

3. Esp. *Stu.* to renege or fail to appear.—usu. constr. with *out*.—usu. considered offensive.

　1968 Baker, Ladd & Robb *CUSS* 144: Japped out [on a date]. **1969** *Current Slang I & II* 55: Jap out…To fail to keep an appointment or a date.—College males, New York. **1972** N.Y.U. student: To jap out means to back out or chicken out. **1982** N.Y. man, age 34: Looks like he japped out on us. **1986** Eble *Campus Slang* (Oct.) 4: *Jap*—back out on an obligation: Marie was supposed to go to the mixer with us, but she japped.

Japanee *n. & adj.* [back formation of *Japanese*; cf. CHINEE, 1] a Japanese person; Japanese.—now usu. considered offensive.

　1863 in W. Whitman *Correspondence* I 105: I wore it three days, & carried a fan & an umbrella (quite a Japanee). *ca*1900 in Doerflinger *Shantymen* 118: There was Rooshian Finns…an' Japanees galore. **1961** Peacock *Valhalla* 25: A cold Japanee quart of beer. *a*1965 Shirota *Lucky Come Hawaii* 4: Stoopid Japanee!

Japanese liner *n. Baseball.* TEXAS LEAGUER.

　1938 Nichols *Baseball Term.* 39: *Japanese liner.* See "Texas leaguer;" used in Pacific Coast leagues. **1971** Coffin *Old Ball Game* 56: Few ball-players refer to a weak fly, "a Texas Leaguer," as "a banjo" or "a Japanese liner" anymore.

Japanese roller skate *n.* a compact car built by a Japanese corporation. *Joc.*

　1976 Adcock *Not Truckers Only* xi: The first thing I did was purchase a good CB radio. I slapped it into my "Japanese roller skate" (Toyota) and began listening.

Japland *n.* Esp. *Mil.* Japan.—used contemptuously.—usu. considered offensive.

　1919 F.K. Russell *Japland* [pop. song] [Waco, Tex.: Floyd K. Russell, 1919]. **1951** Thacher *Captain* 77: That's getting right up there by Jap-land, ain't it? **1951** Jones *Face of War* 122: Send us to Jap land for guard duty.

Jappo *n.* [JAP + -*o*] a Japanese person.—used contemptuously.—usu. considered offensive. Also **Jappy.**

　1942 Gamet & Trivers *Flying Tigers* (film): I hear the Jappos glow in the dark like bugs. **1956** Lockwood & Adamson *Zoomies* 256: Each time…the Jappy's would stop shooting.

Jap-slap *v.* to slap (someone) sharply and suddenly.—also used fig.—usu. considered offensive.

　1989 C. Bianchi *Dancing with Charlie* 115: Jackson Jap-slapped them so fast they didn't know what hit them. **1990** Rukuza *West Coast Turnaround* 217: He dropped two gears and stomped the floor with the accelerator, jap-slapping the governor silly with excessive Rs.

jar *n. Mil.* JARHEAD, 3.b.

　*a*1990 Westcott *Half a Klick* 53 [ref. to 1972]: You jars want to move that thing?

jar *v.* ¶ In phrases:

　¶ **jar loose** to release one's grip; (*hence*) to get going.

　1899 in Davidson *Old West* 76: Gi' me some red-eye—that's the stuff—/Jar loose an' let her run. **1903** A. Adams *Log of a Cowboy* 243: The…man…monopolized our guest. Nor did he jar loose until we reached water. **1906** H. Green *Actors' Boarding House* 336: Jar loose from six bucks. **1908** W.G. Davenport *Butte & Montana* 48: Jar loose, spit it out. *Ibid.* 56: You've just got to jar loose with five bucks. **1911** *Adventure* (Jan.) 447: When you have to jar loose actual money you begin to take an interest in how it is spent. **1918** in *Papers Mich. Acad.* (1928): At reveille…[the sergeant] routs the men out with such remarks as these: "Jar loose, you guys!" "One foot on the floor!" "Burning daylight!" "Where do you think you're at, a Granger's picnic?" **1929** T. Gordon *Born to Be* 203: But I made them jar loose with

a few fresh jokes from the sticks. **1942** Garcia *Tough Trip* 76: I had to call him twice before he would jar loose. **1945** O'Rourke *E Co.* 86: We just wanted to jar you loose.

　¶ **wouldn't that jar you?** isn't that enough to anger or exasperate you? Also vars.

　1897 in *DARE: Jar*…to surprise or shock, as, "Doesn't that jar you?" **1899** Norris *McTeague* 239: Whoever thinks of buying Nottingham lace nowadays? Say, don't that jar you? **1904** "O. Henry" *Cabbages & Kings* 306: Wouldn't it jar you? **1913** J. London *Valley of Moon* 33: Now wouldn't that jar you? **1919** Darling *Jargon Bk.* 50: *Wouldn't That Jar You?*—Don't that surprise you? **1933** Ford & Tyler *Young & Evil* 186: Wouldn't that jar your mother's preserves?

jarber var. JERVER.

jarhead *n.* [cf. JUGHEAD] **1.** *So. & Army.* a mule.

　1918 *DN* V 18: *Jarhead*, a mule. **1918** in Freidel *Over There* 172: For, when others may take to the dugouts, [the mule-driver] must remain with his "jar-heads," exposed to view. **1919** Farrell *1st U.S. Engineers* 119: When the thing is over, to our "Jarr-heads" we go,/And we groom till the black ones look whiter than snow. **1930** Nason *Corporal* 32 [ref. to 1916]: Move out, Jar-head! **1933** Clifford *Boats* 125: Lookee them jar-heads *travel.* **1938** in *AS* (Apr. 1939) 91: *Jar Head.* A mule. "He rides the jar head to town." **1941** Nixon *Possum Trot* 89: Steel mules are invading the cotton fields…and displacing the "hard-tail," or "jar-head" variety. **1965–70** in *DARE.*

2. *Petroleum Industry.* a cable-tool driller.

　1932 *AS* VII 267: *Jar head*, n. A cable-tool driller. **1951** Pryor *The Big Play* 16–17: Tom was a cable-tool man, a jarhead. **1972** Haslam *Oil Fields* 105: *Jar Head*, n. A cable-tool driller (called this by rotary workers).

3.a. [perh. alluding to the mule mascot of Army football teams and **(1)**, above] *USMC.* a member of the U.S. Army.

　1933 *Leatherneck* (May) 38: [Marine] Sergeants Kramer, Green and Carrick sure gave the Army the run around on the USAT *Republic.* Upon embarking they moved into the second class cabins, and it took three days and a squad of "jarheads" to get them and their baggage moved to the troop class. *Ibid.* 52: Withdrawal of West Coast Army from future football competition leaves only the San Diego Marines and West Coast Navy to battle for the coveted President's Cup next fall. The Jarheads…have had to abandon the sport because of financial difficulties.

b. *Mil.* a member of the U.S. Marine Corps.

　1943 Hubbard *Gung Ho* (film): You silly jarhead. When are you gonna learn to fix a pack? **1944** *Reader's Digest* (Sept.) 76: A "jar-head" is a Marine, but he's a "boot" if a recruit. **1947** *ATS* (Supp.) 35: *Jarhead*, a Marine. **1960** Leckie *March to Glory* 20: The "Jarheads," as the swab-jockies called them in this brand-new war. **1961** J. Flynn *Action Man* 100: The jarheads had…[used the] same vests in Korea. **1962** Mandel *Mainside* 205: I knows jes what them jarhead Marines is goin' to ack like. **1963** Serling *7 Days in May* (film): If it isn't my favorite jarhead himself. **1964** Howe *Valley of Fire* 36: They think I'm a rear-rank jarhead. **1966** Shepard *Doom Pussy* 73: And then the pickets at home scream bloody murder when the jarheads don't hold their fire. **1980** McDowell *Our Honor* 115: I always thought you was a gung-ho jar head. **1982** Downey *Losing the War* 73 [ref. to WWII]: You jar-heads had too much liberty? **1985** *Alfred Hitchcock Presents* (CBS-TV): One more step, jarhead, and it's a body bag! **1989** J. Weber *Defcon One* 15: Thought you "jar heads" were s'posed to be the first to fight. **1994** *Esquire* (Mar.) 111: *Dogfight*, in which Phoenix played a marine. "After *Dogfight* I remember thinking he was being a real jarhead asshole."

4. Esp. *Black E.* an ordinary or foolish fellow.

　1942 *Pittsburgh Courier* (July 18) 7: When a jar-head lightly speils…just listen…and just Wait. **1942** Z.N. Hurston, in *Amer. Mercury* (July) 94: *Jar head*—Negro man. **1969** Spetz *Rat Pack Six* 72: Not the company, jarhead, just us. **1971** *Current Slang VI* (Winter) 7: *Jar head*, n. A fool; or idiot. **1984** Algeo *Stud Buds*: A studious classmate…*jar head, jerk*, [etc.].

jarvey *n.* [app. fr. *Jarvey*, hypocoristic form of male given name *Jarvis*; semantic devel. unkn.] **1.** *Und.* a jacket or vest. Also (erroneously?) **jarvel.** Cf. JERVE.

　1807 Tufts *Autobiog.* 291 [ref. to 1794]: *Jarvel*…a jacket. **1848** *Ladies' Repository* VIII (Oct.) 315: *Jarvey*, A waistcoat; vest.

2. a coachman.

　[*1796 Grose *Vulgar Tongue* (ed. 3): *Jarvis.* A hackney coachman.] *1820 in *OED*: To see him through the jar of jarvies pushing. **1837** in Jackson *Early Songs of Uncle Sam* 44: My name's honest Jarvey…the railroads has ruin'd us. **1859** *Spirit of Times* (Apr. 2) 88: The jarvey answered, "May your honor long be abled, but seldom willing." **1859** Matsell *Vocab.* 46: *Jarvey.* A driver.

jasm *n.* [var. of JISM] spirit; energy; vigor. [The sense intended in 1964 quot. is not clear; cf. JISM.]

1860 J.G. Holland *Miss Gilbert* 350: "She's just like her mother....Oh! she's just full of *jasm!*" "You've got the start of me....Now tell me what 'jasm' is."..."If you'll take thunder and lightning, and a steamboat and a buzz-saw, and mix 'em up, and put 'em into a woman, that's jasm." **1871** *Scribner's Mo.* II 433: When a man has genuine "jasm" and irrepressibility...we are apt to wink at his processes and praise his pluck. **1886** *Harper's Mag.* (Sept.) 579: The mos' shif'less creeter I ever see. Willin', but hain't no more jas'm than a dead cornstalk. **1964** Baraka *Dead Lecturer* 26: "Jism" in white chalk on the...garage...."Jasm" the name the leader [of the motorcyclists] took.

jasper *n.* [fr. the male given name *Jasper,* taken as a typical rustic name; cf. ALVIN, HICK, RUBE, etc.] **1.a.** a yokel; rustic; (*hence*) an odd or inconsequential fellow.

1896 Ade *Artie* 64: If I had his face I'd start out sellin' them gold bricks to Jaspers. **1896** in *OED2*: There were a lot of "Jaspers" sitting around the stove, chewing tobacco and swapping lies. **1911–12** Ade *Knocking the Neighbors* 14: He...moved out to Jasper Township and tackled Intensive Farming. **1922** *Variety* (Sept. 22) 7: They will permit the "Jasper" to place his coin on the Bible. **1923** *N.Y. Times* (Sept. 9) VIII 2: *Jasper:* A man from the country. **1928** Fisher *Jericho* 49: That jasper's got mo' bucks 'n you got freckles. **1944** C.B. Davis *Leo McGuire* 72: This particular jasper had his glass fully insured. **1952** Lait & Mortimer *USA* 86: All the jaspers in the Midwest look like Truman. **1958** in C. Beaumont *Best* 66: They never would have found out I killed that jasper...if it hadn't been my black Irish luck. **1958** J. Ward *Buchanan* 84: Couple of jaspers rode into town one Monday morning. Bearded gents. **1965** D.G. Moore *20th C. Cowboy* 158: A...sandy-haired jasper who appeared to be nearing thirty. **1976** N. Meyer *West End Horror* xiii: He got a bundle on it from some jasper in New Mexico. **1989** P. Benchley *Rummies* 10: Beat it, Jasper. **1990** G. Lee *China Boy* 94: You'se stupid as a jasper.

b. *Black E.* a black man. Cf. syn. JAZZBO, 2.

1929 T. Gordon *Born to Be* 220: Do you know what was the matter with that Jasper? *Ibid.* 236: Spade, Huck, Zigaboo, Dinge, Jasper; Nicknames for Ethiopians.

2. *Black E.* a homosexual or bisexual woman.

1954 in Wepman, Newman & Binderman *The Life* 110: There was a jasper named Nora. **1962** Crump *Killer* 61: Shelley was a "jasper." **1967** C. Cooper *The Farm* 96: She was a musclebitch, and I got a little hint of jasper. **1967** Fiddle *Shooting Gallery* 304: But the other one was a colored broad that was a Lesbian, jasper, you know? **1967** Colebrook *Cross of Lassitude* 103: I'll go freak off with another jasper. Both of us go for what we know. **1962–68** B. Jackson *In the Life* 188: A "jasper broad"...is bisexual, she likes both men and women....She can entice other prostitutes to work for you....She was a jasper and very intellectual.

jass var. JAZZ, *n., v.*

jassack *n.* a jackass. *Joc.*

1845 in G.W. Harris *High Times* 46: He lied a jassack to death in two hours! **1906** in *AS* LVIII (1983) 250: Why, that's our jassack, Uncle. **1919** in *Ethnomusicology* XII (1968) 379: This unusual trio came to be called the Jassacks Band, the name being the popular inversion of the jackass, the famous solo singer of the Southern States. **1968** S.O. Barker *Rawhide Rhymes* 13: But jassacks simply don't believe in takin' any chance.

java *n.* coffee beans grown in Java (*obs.*); (*broadly* and *usu.*) coffee.

1850 Garrard *Wah-to-yah* 60: To secure the good will and robes of the sensitive men we had to offer our dear-bought Java at meal time. **1853** *Harper's Mag.* VII 276: Sh'd be glad to sell you a lot of damag'd Java at 7 cts. per lb. **1886** *Harper's Mag.* (Sept.) 578: I should admire to know what your coffee is made of. Reel old Javy don't make no brown stain. **1891** Garland *Main-Travelled Roads* 135: They called that coffee Jayvy...but it never went by the road where government Jayvy resides. I reckon I know coffee from peas. **1907** London *Road* 28: I got out of them nearly a quart of heavenly "Java" (coffee). **1907** in "O. Henry" *Works* 188: When the fooling was ended all hands made a raid on Joe's big coffee-pot by the fire for a Java nightcap. **1914** *DN* 151: *Java.* n. coffee. **1913–15** Van Loan *Taking the Count* 124: Den he orders a steak, medium, hashed brown, an' Java. **1918** Ruggles *Navy Explained* 22: Coffee is always "Java." **1927** C. McKay *Harlem* 92: First a great platter of fish and toma-

toes, then pork chops and mashed potatoes, steaming Java and best Borden's cream. **1935** O'Hara *Butterfield 8* 10: One cup of piping hot javver for the gentleman in the blue suit. **1942** S. Johnston *Queen of Flat-tops* 278: From these pots any man can draw himself a mug of "Java" at any hour. **1943** Furthman *Outlaw* (film): Let's have a cup of java. **1952** Kahn *Able One Four* 49: Thanks for the java. **1967** P. Roth *When She Was Good* 51: Coffee...he called "hot joe," or "hot java." **1975** *Nat. Lampoon 199th Birthday Book* 171: Twelve cups of Brazilian java! **1977** Monaghan *Schoolboy, Cowboy* 2 [ref. to 1908]: Coffee beans (called "java") [were] packed in burlap bags weighing eighty pounds each. *a*1989 C.S. Crawford *Four Deuces* 29: A lot of us were calling it "java," because, I think, it sounded tougher that way. **1993** *Living in '90's* (CNN-TV) (Nov. 22): A rich mug of piping-hot java. **1995** *Science News* (Feb. 4) 72: A strong cup of java can do more than give the heart a jolt.

jaw *n.* **1.a.** talk, esp. if complaining or insolent; chatter; in phr. **hold** [or **keep**] **(one's) jaw** to hold (one's) tongue; refrain from speaking.

***1748** Smollett *R. Random* ch. iii: "None of your jaw, you swab,"...replied my uncle. **1749–50** in Breslaw *Tues. Club* 191: All this Jargon and Instructive Jaw. ***1751** Smollett *P. Pickle* ch. xxxii: Desiring him to do his duty without farther jaw. ***1789** G. Parker *Life's Painter* 138: Let's have a *chaunt,* and no more jaw about [hanging]. ***1796** Grose *Vulgar Tongue* (ed. 3): *Jaw.* Speech, discourse. *Give us none of your jaw;* let us have none of your discourse. **1813** in Howay *New Hazard* 154: If I hear any more of your jaw I'll confine you. **1823** J.F. Cooper *Pioneers* 366: Howsomnever, they didn't come to facers, only passed a little jaw fore and aft. ***1821–26** Stewart *Man-of-War's Man* I 51: Fa the deyvel d'ye think's gaun to stand your jaw? ***1831** Trelawny *Adv. Younger Son* ch. vii: Stopper your jaw, or I'll hand ye...over to the doctor. **1833** J. Neal *Down-Easters* I 79: He's...all jaw like a sheep's head. **1841** [Mercier] *Man-of-War* 97: Some old *sea-lawyer* may by dint of *jaw,*/Find in his accusation some small flaw. **1852** Stowe *Uncle Tom's Cabin* ch. viii: Stop that ar jaw o' yourn. **1853** Ballantine *Autobiog.* 73: Hold your d—d jaw. **1862** [P. Davis] *Young Parson* 252: He...was induced...to "keep his jaw." **1869** Stowe *Oldtown* 80: I wasn't a-goin' to hear no sich jaw. **1880** J.C. Harris *Uncle Remus* 260: You come a slingin' yo' jaw at a man. **1884** in Lummis *Letters* 170: Most of the boys were...swapping jaw at Emmett's. *a*1889 *Century Dict.:* To hold one's jaw, to cease or refrain from talking. (Vulgar.). **1960** N.Y.C. woman, age *ca*70: It's nothing but jaw. **1991** H. Reid *Steel-Drivin' Man* [Woodpecker Records 107 band 4]: He loved the ladies, hated the law;/Just wouldn't take nobody's jaw.

b. a discussion, esp. if wrangling or contentious; a talk. [The form *jam* in 1857 quot. is unquestionably a written error for this.]

1810 in Howay *New Hazard* 4: The mates had a jaw at 4 P.M., not over at 8 P.M. Iverson struck Sampson with a handspike. ***1838** Glascock *Land Sharks* II 20: Join the jollies...in a jaw. **1857** in *Calif. Hist. Soc. Qly.* IX (1930) 154: Horse began to limp...I got him home and had a little jam [*sic*] with Darneill because he was lame. **1864** in J.W. Haley *Rebel Yell* 198: Keeping up an incessant jaw with the Rebs in front of them. **1873** Ballantyne *Black Ivory* 42: After we'd had our jaw out, I goes off...to think. ***1874** in *F & H* IV 41: Dora, I and my father have had a jaw. **1929** W.R. Burnett *Iron Man* 170: We ain't had a good jaw together since you left. ***1934** Yeates *Winged Victory* 259: We had a damned good jaw about old times. ***1961** V.S. Pritchett, in *New Yorker* (Sept. 23) 59: They're upstairs having a jaw.

c. a scolding.

1811 in Howay *New Hazard* 16: Captain at Iverson—a severe jaw.

2.a. *pl. So.* the vaginal labia.—usu. considered vulgar.

1945 in Randolph & Legman *Roll Me in Your Arms* 205: The jaws of her twat. **1966** in B. Jackson *Swim Like Me* 151: Lil had jaws on her pussy that would make a dead man come. **1984** Sample *Racehoss* 252: Dem britches she had on wuz so tight I could see the jaws! Had lips as fat as...boxin gloves.

b. copulation with a woman.—usu. considered vulgar.

1975 N.C. man, age *ca*25: I worked on a lobster boat on Chesapeake Bay in 1968, and some of the old lobstermen used to talk about getting some *jaw.* It meant *pussy.* I thought it was a pretty weird term.

3. *pl.* anger.—constr. with *the.*

1970 *Current Slang* V (Summer) 16: *Jaws*...Anger or frustration, (derived from: It really tightens my *jaws* that...). **1982** F. Hailey *Soldier Talk* 29: Got the jaws. Uptight and extremely "Teed off." **1987** *Tour of Duty* (CBS-TV): Just lookin' at you pukes gives me a real bad case of the jaws. **1966–88** Willson *REMF* 295 [ref. to 1967]: Everything I do gives them the jaws. Especially when I do nothing.

¶ In phrases:

¶ **flap (one's) jaw** [or **jaws**] to talk idly.
    1938 in Kober *That Man Is Here Again* 122: So we sits aroun', flappin' our jaws about this, that, the other thing. **1984** *Nat. Lampoon* (Dec.) 66: We wuz settin' on the back porch…jes' flappin' our jaws.

¶ **grind (someone's) jaw** to *tighten (someone's) jaws,* below.
    *a*1990 Westcott *Half a Klick* 154: Hey, you are grindin' my jaw, know that?

¶ **sling (one's) jaw** to speak impudently, angrily, or out of turn.
    1880 J.C. Harris *Uncle Remus* 260: You k'n go roun' yer an' sass deze w'ite people, an' maybe dey'll stan' it, but w'en you come a slingin' yo' jaw at a man w'at wuz gray w'en de fahmin' days gin out, you better go an' git yo' hide greased.

¶ **tighten (one's) jaws** *Black E.* to make (one) angry.
    1968 in Cade *Black Woman* 52: I thought the babe was gon kill me, her jaws was so tight. **1970** A. Young *Snakes* 42: Shee-it, [it] tighten my jaws! **1970** Landy *Underground Dict.*: My jaws are tight…Expression meaning I'm angry. **1973** *All in the Family* (CBS-TV): This chump tightens my jaws.

jaw *v.* **1.** to talk, esp. at length or to little purpose; *(also)* to argue. Also *(vulgar)* **jaw-ass.**
    *1748 Smollett *R. Random* ch. xxiv: And they jawed together fore and aft a good spell. *1760 in *OED*: Will you stand jawing here? *1771 in *F & H* IV 41: Though I cannot well jaw. **1791** in *DAE* s.v. *blatherskite*: A Blatherskite Irishman…kept constantly jawing to & teasing the girl all the way. **1811** in Howay *New Hazard* 5: Iverson and Gale jawing. *1843 in *F & H* IV 41: Why should four waiters stand and jaw…instead of waiting on the guests? **1855** Thomson *Doesticks* 127: When they jawed religion at him, he could jaw back. **1871** Hay *Pike Co. Ballads* 25: The neighbors…ca'mly drinked and jawed. **1907** *DN* III 223: *Jaw,* v.i. To converse. **1942** N. Nye *Trigger Talk* 33: So pretty quick I quit jawin'. **1949** S.J. Perelman, in *DAS*: Can't stand here jawing with you all day. **1958** Talsman *Gaudy Image* 38: Why don't you stop by the room? We can jaw. **1961** H. Ellison *Gentleman Junkie* 57: I invited the kid to sit down and jaw with me for a couple minutes. **1966** Garfield *Last Bridge* 43: You *do* have shovels down there, don't you, Lieutenant? Then God damn it, quit jaw-assing over this telephone and get your balls in gear. **1976** Whelton *CB Baby* 4: They were jawing back and forth about traffic conditions. **1985** McMurtry *Lonesome Dove* 84: He had surely jawed with Gus long enough. **1985** Briskin *Too Much* 47: Listen, ain't it bad enough you dropped your order and mosta mine, do you have to stand here jawing at rush hour? **1989** *21 Jump St.* (Fox-TV): They always talkin'. They was jawin' it up just a couple days ago. **1992** S. Straight *Been in Sorrow's Kitchen* 66: This must be what them boys was jawing about all last month.

2. to reprove or abuse loudly or at length; scold; (with weakened force) to talk to, esp. with rough jocularity.—also used absol.
    *1810 in *OED*: He was then very abusive and noisy; he kept jawing us. **1811** in Howay *New Hazard* 4: Iverson jawed Gale for letting reefs out. *1821–26 Stewart *Man-of-War's Man* II 173: We've other fish to fry than the standing up here listening to you two jawing each other. **1831** in [S. Smith] *Letters of Downing* 66: If they get…mad, they…talk and jaw one another. *1833 Marryat *Peter Simple* ch. xi: I have been jawed for letting you go. **1837** Neal *Charcoal Sketches* 68: They coaxed all my pennies out of me; coaxed me to take all the jawings, and all the hidings. **1862** C.F. Browne *A. Ward* 115: Otheller jaws him a spell & then cuts a small hole in his stummick with his sword. **1864** Fosdick *Frank on a Gun-Boat* 118: Don't go to jawin' her, now, 'cause yer ketched. **1864** in Malone *Whipt 'Em Everytime* 100: A Yankey Sergt. named Young shot one of our Officers for jawing him. **1867** Clark *Sailor's Life* 128: I've heard enough of you lubbers jawing that Yankee youngster. **1869** Stowe *Oldtown* 80: When they wasn't let in, you never heerd sich a jawin'. **1888** in Farmer *Amer.*: She'll lick both of us and jaw father all the evening. **1896** Hamblen *Many Seas* 60: I…got a "jawing" from the old man for going in the boat where I had no business. **1906** *DN* III 142: He jawed me a long time but I didn't buy anything. **1907** J.C. Lincoln *Cape Cod* 160: We set round in the shade and fought flies and jawed each other. *1908 K. Grahame *Wind in Willows* ch. xi: Toad…never minded being jawed by those who were his real

friends. **1904–11** Phillips *Susan Lenox* I 294: A girl of his own class…probably would have "jawed" him. **1924** Marks *Plastic Age* 118: I've been jawed until I don't know anything. **1927** Rollins *Jinglebob* 47: If anybody jaws you for drivin' them animals, say I tol' you to do it. **1934** Rhodes *Beyond Desert* 182: Them young things are sure goin' to jaw you about missin' that dance. **1952** J. Schaefer *First* 120: I didn't want him jawing me when I stepped out for a little fun. **1960** *Father Knows Best* (CBS-TV): What got into us? We've never jawed at each other like that before. **1978** S. King *Stand* 97: You still jawing this poor boy? **1991** Lott & Lieber *Total Impact* 98: I would still be jawing and bitching at them.

jaw action *n.* idle talk.
    1985 Univ. Tenn. prof., age *ca*45: That kind of jaw action is cheap.

jawblock *v. Black E.* to talk.
    1946 Mezzrow & Wolfe *Really Blues* 30: I used to see Scarface around there and jawblock with him sometimes. *Ibid.* 115: We were just jawblocking to pass the time.

jawbone *n.* **1.a.** a castanet.
    1844 in *DA*: Dancing and playing the *jaw bones* or Castanets.

b. a Jew's harp. Also **jawbone lute.**
    1845 in *DA*: The frequent sound of the violin, banjo, or jaw-bone lute. **1869** in *DA*: I can play the old jawbone, and can use the fiddlebow.

2. *West. & Mil.* credit.—also used attrib.
    1862 in Hotten *Slang Dict.* (ed. 4): We have a few…individuals who, in [California] digger's parlance, live on *jawbone* (credit), and are always to be found in saloons. **1891** Maitland *Slang Dict.* 153: *Jawbone,* credit. To live on jawbone is to "stand off" one's creditors. **1900** *Nation* (Oct. 4) 270: A common slang among American soldiers [in Luzon] for the word "credit" is "jawbone."…The soldier asks the native keeper of the little *tienda* to sell him a bottle of beer or a package of cigarettes "on jawbone." **1913** *Sat. Eve. Post* (May 10) 13: I know you're all right, but I can't do business on jawbone. **1922** *Leatherneck* (Apr. 29) 5: *Jawbone*—Credit. **1944** Kober & Uris *In Meantime, Darling* (film): If you lose, don't come to me for any jawbone. **1970** Boatright & Owens *Derrick* 124: He'd trust anybody. Made lots of jawbone trades.

3.a. talk or conversation; *(often)* empty talk.
    1873 *Overland Mo.* (Feb.) 108: The interlopers…signified their intention of "camping right there until the Doctor was prepared to come down with a little jaw-bone!" **1898** in *DA*: Jawbone is cheap, and there is plenty of it. Backbone is rare. **1947** Willingham *End as a Man* 70: McKee and Poley. Two jawbone experts. **1966** Braly *On Yard* 174: He didn't waste time on jawbone. **1978** Safire *Pol. Dict.* 346: President Nixon…in early 1969…said the economy needed more backbone, not more jawbone. **1990** C. Fletcher *What Cops Know* 36: Ninety-nine percent of this job is jawbone. You've got to know how to talk to people.

b. *Pol.* the practice of persuasion rather than compulsion as a means of accomplishing political goals.—constr. with *the.* Cf. JAWBONE, *v.,* 2.b.
    1969 *Business Week* (Mar. 15) 29: The Nixon Administration is being driven toward using the jawbone to supplement monetary and fiscal restraints against inflation. **1979** *Business Week* (Nov. 12) 32: Volcker's use of the jawbone to keep the prime down has a precedent.

jawbone *adj.* **1.** Esp. *Mil.* (of a wager) made orally as a pastime and for which the winner expects only a token payment; (of a game of cards or dice) allowing only such wagers.
    1891 Bourke *On Border* 298: Bets as high as five and ten thousand dollars were freely wagered. These were of the class known in Arizona as "jawbone," and in Wyoming as wind; the largest amount of cash that I saw change hands was twenty-five cents. **1926** Nason *Chevrons* 114 [ref. to WWI]: Jake and Baldy were shooting jawbone crap for their next month's wages. **1930** Nason *Corporal Once* 3: "I ain't got no money." "Jawbone game—come on," urged the horseshoer. **1947** Carter *Devils in Baggy Pants* 143: Five to one, jawbone, that he never comes up. **1963** Boyle *Yanks Don't Cry* 32: Small jawbone bets were made on what ship we would catch. **1984–88** Hackworth & Sherman *About Face* 168: He owed me about five hundred bucks from jawbone poker.

2. *Mil. & Pris.* for which credit is or will be granted; in phr. **jawbone time** time served before conviction and sentencing that will be subtracted from the total sentence imposed.
    1918 in *AS* (Oct. 1933) 28: *Jawbone time.* Time spent in the guardhouse pending trial and sentence. **1947** *ATS* 33: Air Corps…*jawbone*

mission, a [flying] mission for which credit is received. **1956** Algren *Wild Side* 14: Good time…jawbone time.

3. *Mil.* **a.** (of rank) temporary or acting.

1921 *15th Inf. Sentinel* (Jan. 21) 10: He'd more than likely be made a jaw-bone corporal. **1926** Nason *Chevrons* 71 [ref. to WWI]: The jawbone major sent me back with a message. **1928** Nason *Sgt. Eadie* 3 [ref. to WWI]: No cook, huh, and a jawbone mess sergeant, and no mess fund. **1930** Nason *Corporal Once* 87: A jaw-bone non-com is one who holds his grade by word of mouth alone, and not by a duly issued warrant. **1933** *Leatherneck* (Aug.) 30: Our "Jaw Bone" Corporals. **1941** in Cannon *Nobody Asked* 316: I knew he was a jawbone sergeant because he wore his red stripes on a blue arm band. That means he hadn't been issued his Warrant and he couldn't draw the pay of a sergeant. **1941** Hargrove *Pvt. Hargrove* 44: *Jawbone* is an apt word meaning "credit." A jawbone corporal is an acting corporal, who has neither the rating nor the pay of a corporal. **1942** *Time* (May 18) 63: During the [First World] war he held a "Jawbone" (temporary) commission as first lieutenant. **1959** "D. Stagg" *Glory Jumpers* 34: I need an assistant, Nolan. You're a jawbone corporal, as of now. **1982** F. Hailey *Soldier Talk* 34: All promotions not of a permanent nature were once referred to as "Jawbone promotions."

b. imitation or inferior.

1933 Clifford *Boats* 247: We're part of a jawbone, second-rate group in a forgotten world.

4.a. *Mil.* arranged solely by oral agreement and without official authorization.

1929 L. Thomas *Woodfill* 44 [ref. to 1899]: There were a few others [soldiers] likewise who had what we called a "jawbone" wedding—meaning just a verbal agreement without any padre to fix 'em up. **1967** Lockwood *Subs* 42 [ref. to 1914]: Sometimes, in getting repairs done or parts made, we had to resort to "jawbone" requisitions. This was the name given to the gentle art of wheedling work orders out of Navy Yard shops.

b. *Pol.* persuasive but noncompulsory. Cf. JAWBONE, *v.*, 2.b.

1959 *N.Y. Times* (Feb. 8) IV E3: A "jawbone" attack on the private forces, which takes the form of an appeal for restraint by business and labor. **1961** *N.Y. Times* (Oct. 1) IV 6E: Some of the President's less reverent aides call this the "jawbone approach" to price stabilization—one that relies on conversation, rather than compulsion. **1969** *U.S. News & W.R.* (Apr. 28) 46: Q Are you saying the "jawbone" approach is dead for this Administration? A Yes, if you mean trying to preach people into forgoing wage or price changes that market conditions encourage. **1978** (quot. at JAWBONE, *v.*, 2.b.).

jawbone *adv. Mil.* on credit; with merely a promise to pay.

1926 *AS* I 564: To buy something which is to be paid for on pay day is to "buy jawbone." **1930** Nason *Corporal Once* 87 [ref. to 1918]: If one buys anything jawbone, he buys it with a promise to pay later. **1961** Peacock *Valhalla* 50: It's damn near all jawbone, see? **1965** D.G. Moore *20th C. Cowboy* 81: She sold the Gisela Ranch to the Hazelton family practically "jawbone."

jawbone *v.* [orig. pidgin] **1.** *Mil.* to bargain for credit; (*also*) to extend credit to; to sell or obtain on credit.

*ca*1905 in Military Order of Carabao *Hist. Sketch* 144: Come you back, you *malo* soldier, come you back from o'er the sea,/Come you back and pay your jaw-bone; *por que* you jawbone me? **1918** *N.Y. Times Mag.* (Aug. 4) 10: Without any delay or "red tape" we sent $5000 worth of canteen supplies to the men and "jawboned" the entire battalion. "To jawbone" means, in the doughboy vernacular, "to trust." **1921** *15th Inf. Sentinel* (Feb. 4) 16: I jaw-boned two packages of New Yorks and smoked them all. **1929** *Marine Corps Gaz.* (Dec.) 281 [ref. to 1899]: I came to see if I could "jawbone" the boys and to look out for Dryden. **1922** *Leatherneck* (Apr. 29) 5: *Jaw-bone*—Credit. To buy on credit. **1952** in *DAS*: He jawboned enough thousands of dollars to set up an office and hire his personnel. **1956** Hargrove *Girl He Left* 45: They'll jawbone [the haircut], young soldier….You've always got credit at the barber shop. **1954–60** *DAS*: *Jawbone*…To carry on sincere, rational talk that leads to establishing financial credit or trust.

2.a. to talk or discuss; converse; JAW, 1.

1953 *Sat. Eve. Post* (June 6) 54: One day a man came into the shop, tried to jawbone the boss out of a D-Four tractor with an arch. **1966** *N.Y. Times* (Jan. 2) IV 2: Every price increase that happens to catch the public's eye must be "jawboned" to death by the Government. **1972** *Seattle Times* (Dec. 10) C4: Kissinger, cued by Metternich, can also jaw-

bone with them for hours on end. **1976** Conroy *Santini* 301: Are they fighting again?…Let me mop the floor with them. Then there won't be no more jawboning. **1980** in McCauley *Dark Forces* 260: He had always thrived on conversation, jawboning, even aimless chatter. **1982** Braun *Judas Tree* 69: Wish I had more time to jawbone. **1985** C. Busch *Times Sq. Angel* 48: I've had enough jawboning with you. **1988** D. Sandefur *Ghost Town* (film): Best not jawbone the boy to death, Grace. **1991** *Newsweek* (Aug. 12) 63: No idle jawboning. *a*1994 N. McCall *Wanna Holler* 175: He'd stop and jawbone with a group of the guys.

b. Esp. *Pol.* to admonish or persuade, esp. to urge voluntary compliance upon. Cf. corresponding and slightly earlier JAWBONE, *adj.*, 4.b.

1965 *N.Y. Times* (Oct. 24) IV E7: What is perhaps irreverently known in some circles as Presidential "jawboning"—that is, the attempt on the part of any White House occupant to persuade the citizenry to do, for the good of the country, what the President thinks is right. **1969** *Time* (Sept. 19) 36: Since June, Feather has been jawboning his union chiefs on the virtues of labor discipline on the shop floor. **1969** *U.S. News & W.R.* (Dec. 1) 8: The Administration's most ambitious effort yet to "jawbone" businessmen into supporting its anti-inflation campaign. **1974** *U.S. News & W.R.* (July 22) 87: All that the Government can do is "jawbone"—attempt to get voluntary co-operation from labor and management in holding down wage settlements. **1974** *Business Week* (Aug. 10) 8: The "jawboning" by congressmen of the $850-million Citicorp floating rate note issue…is another obvious attempt by the government to intervene and manipulate the free market to the detriment of borrowers, savers, and investors. **1978** Safire *Pol. Dict.* 346: *Jawboning*. The use of presidential admonition as a tool of incomes policy. "The jawbone method" was the phrase used by Walter Heller, chairman of the Council of Economic Advisers in 1962, to describe guidelines set down to restrain prices and wages. **1979** *N.Y. Times* (June 24) 1: The Department of Energy has been jawboning oil companies into increasing their production and sales of gasoline. **1983** *Morning Line* (WKGN radio) (Mar. 23): Now the President's jawboning the banks about interest rates. **1983** *Newsweek on Campus* (May) 19: Some schools have consciously stiffened standards—simply jawboning professors can help. **1989** *CBS This Morning* (CBS-TV) (Feb. 28): The President will weigh in with a little old-fashioned jawboning and even some arm-twisting.

jawbone payday *n. Army.* (see quots.).

1919 *Hist. 12th Inf.* 89: There is what is known in the Army as "Jaw-Bone Pay Day." This means Canteen-checks drawn against next month's salary. **1947** *ATS* (Supp.) 29: *Jawbone payday*, the day on which Post Exchange credit coupon books are issued.

jaw cove *n.* [JAW, *n.*, 1.a. + COVE] *Und.* (see quot.).

1859 Matsell *Vocab.* 46: *Jaw Coves.* Auctioneers, lawyers.

jaw exercising *n.* extended talking; conversation.

1994 B. Maher *True Story* 216: A day of rigorous jaw exercising began with the debate.

jawfest *n.* an extended talk; conversation.

1915 *DN* IV 353: The citizens of "Little Russia" got together for a *jawfest*. **1927** *DN* V 451: *Jaw fest, n.* Telling stories around the *jungle* fire. **1930** Irwin *Tramp & Und. Slang* 108: *Jaw Fest.*—A long talk; conversation.

jaw-flapping *n.* empty or voluble talk; chatter.

1956 Metalious *Peyton Place* 184: "Goddamn it!" roared the Doc. "Stop your jaw-flapping and do as I say!" **1979** Edson *Gentle Giant* 53: All that fancy jaw-flapping.

jawing-tackle *n. Naut.* JAW-TACKLE.

*1821–26 Stewart *Man-of-War's Man* II 169: He's got his jawing tackle hauled aboard, and could prate you there for a month of Sundays. **1859* in *OED*: Ah, Eve, my girl, your jawing-tackle is too well hung. **1899** Robbins *Gam* 125: If ever a seaman was rigged with self-acting jawing tackle, it's that same lubberly coward of a stormy Jones! **a*1950 Granville *Sea Slang* 133: *Jawing tackle.* The tongue. (Lower-deck.) **1961** Burgess *Dict. Sailing* 123: Anyone using his capacity for spinning yarns at length is said to have his jawing tackle on board.

jaw-jack *v. So.* to talk volubly and to no purpose; chatter.

1962 B. Jackson *In the Life* 163: And I'm sitting up here jawjacking with this other tramp. **1970** Whitmore *Memphis-Nam-Sweden* 87: So of course the two of us were always jaw-jacking about whose outfit was better. **1976** Lieberman & Rhodes *CB* 131: *Jaw Jacking*—Talking. **1976** C. Keane *Hunter* 74: And everybody talks about his specialty.

The word for it is "jawjacking." **1992** D. Burke *Street Talk* II 239: We jaw jacked on the phone for an hour.

jaw music *n.* CHIN MUSIC.

    1925 S. Lewis *Arrowsmith* 631 [ref. to *ca*1910]: Gosh, Clif, you cern'ly got a swell line of jaw-music.

jaw rope *n. Naut.* JAW-TACKLE.

    1866 Sleeper *Rowland* 30: Clap a stopper on your jaw rope, if it veers out such stuff as that.

jawsmith *n.* a contentious or voluble talker.

    1886 (cited in *Century Dict.*). **1887** in *DA*: George Schilling, Socialist and jawsmith. *a*1889 *Century Dict.: Jawsmith*…One who works with his jaw; especially, a loud-mouthed demagogue: originally applied to an official "orator" or "instructor" of the Knights of Labor. **1899** Prentiss *Utah Vols.* 53: The "jawsmiths" of the camp became transformed, as if by magic. **1909** *WNID: Jawsmith*…A professional talker; demagogue. *Low U.S.* **1910** (quot. at HOT AIR).

jaw suit *n.* a heated argument. *Joc.*

    1927 E. Stockwell *Pvt. Stockwell* 186 [ref. to Civil War]: We told them about the "jaw suit."

jaw-tackle *n.* Esp. *Naut.* the mouth, tongue, or speech organs generally; (*broadly*) needless or annoying talk.

    *1831 Trelawny *Adv. Younger Son* ch. xxxvi: Van would have countermanded this, had I not clapped my hand as a stopper on his jaw-tackle. **1837** *Spirit of Times* (June 17) 143: You haul taught your jaw tackles, and be d—d. **1839–40** Cobb *Green Hand* I 88 [ref. to 1815]: "I'll bet two to one, the Fifer's jaw-tackle is longer than his coat-tail is at present." "Toggle his tongue with a paint brush." *Ibid.* II 141: A Frenchified whelp, who lives by dealing out so many yards of cross-grained jaw-tackle per minute. *Ibid.* 145: The month's advance these chaps claim for dealing out jaw-tackle. **1844** Ingraham *Midshipman* 59: His jaw-tackle's wrong set in the first place. **1849** Melville *White Jacket* 228: Clap a stopper on your jaw-tackle, will you? **1871** Willis *Forecastle Echoes* 10: And having "filled the order" our jaw-tackle we'll belay. **1875** Sheppard *Love Afloat* 72: I spect I better keep my jaw-tackle belayed, though. First luff'll be down on me like a gull on a minner. **1883** Hay *Bread-Winners* 211: He looked like he had never worked a muscle in his life except his jaw-tackle. **1884** Blanding *Sailor Boy* 15: Belay that jaw-tackle of yours. **1887** Davis *Sea-Wanderer* 102: Haul in the slack of your jaw-tackle and lay on deck. *a*1889 *Century Dict.: Jaw-tackle*…The mouth. Also *jawing-tackle.* (Slang.)—*To cast off one's jaw-tackle*, to talk too much. (Fishermen's slang). **1904** J.H. Williams, in *Independent* (June 23) 1432: That put a stopper on my jaw tackle at once. **1905** Dey *Scylla* 53: I agreed to cast off my jaw-tackle for your benefit. **1918** *Scribner's Mag.* (Jan.) 29: Bugs that ain't big enough to see she gives names to that 'ud bust your jaw-tackle.

jaw-tackle fall *n.* [JAW-TACKLE + *fall* '(in tackles) the part of a rope between the free end and the pulley, or between pulleys'] *Naut.* one's propensity for JAW, 1, *n.*; (*broadly*) the organs of speech; tongue.

    1833 Ames *Old Sailor's Yarns* 264: You may all of you just pipe belay with your jaw-tackle-falls. **1904** J.H. Williams, in *Independent* (Mar. 24) 660: I…received strict orders to hold onto my jaw tackle fall, and get to 'ell for'ard. *Ibid.* (June 23) 1430: A smile that threatened to part his jaw tackle fall.

Jax *n. Local.* Jacksonville, Fla.

    1936 Dos Passos *Big Money* 323: Driving down from Jax to Miami the sun was real hot. **1945** J. Bryan *Carrier* 141: Jax (…Jacksonville). **1945** in Rea *Wings of Gold* 262: Spent the night at Jax. **1952** Pyles *Words & Ways* 185: *Jax* (local for Jacksonville, Florida, also the name of a brand of beer made there). **1960** J.D. MacDonald *Slam the Big Door* 91: It was Miami and Jax only. **1991** Linnekin *80 Knots* 95: The carrier qualification program at "Jax."

jay[1] *n.* a stupid, gullible, or contemptible fellow; (*also*) a rustic; greenhorn.

    1884 Dougherty *Stump Speaker* 12: They said he was a Jay. If he was such a *Jay* how did he get all the *Gould?* **1884* in *OED2*: The intending larcenist will strike up a conversation with a likely looking Jay in a public conveyance…and win his friendship. **1885* (quot. at FLAP, *v.*, 1). **1886** Field *Sharps & Flats* II 79: [They] mulct the callow jay. **1887** Peck *Pvt. Peck* 170 [ref. to Civil War]: He called me a "jay" and a "substitute," and a "drafted man," when I came to the regiment. *a*1889 *Century Dict.: Jay*…A general term of contempt applied to a stupid person: as, an audience of *jays.* In *actor's slang*, an amateur or a poor actor.

*1889 in Ware *Passing Eng.* 158: Professional gamblers and their J.'s. *Ibid.:* Think of the jays who offered about ten times the market price. **1890** Bunner *Short Sixes* 92: "Got a quarter from them jays," whispered the showman. **1891** Maitland *Slang Dict.* 153: *Jay* (Am.), a countryman or greenhorn. **1893** *Life* (Feb. 2) 70: Any one o' yer wot thinks he's got a soft snap with the devil, an takes 'im fer a jay, is a goin' to get left ev'ry time. **1893** W.K. Post *Harvard* 153: Will yer look at der jay?…He ain't nothin' but one o' them stoodent jays. **1894** in A. Charters *Ragtime Songbk.* 48: So don't you play me for a jay. **1894** in S. Crane *Comp. Stories* 145: I hope ter die b'fore I git anudder ball if there wasn't a jay wid a hully, bloomin' white nightshirt! **1895** Clurman *Nick Carter* 115: He has flown, the cunning jay. **1895* in S.J. Baker *Australian Lang.* 116: Don't you poke borak at me, you old jay! **1896** Hamblen *Many Seas* 271: Just as he was in the act of drawing the trigger, some jay in the rear sneezed. **1896** Ade *Artie* 4: I see the measliest lot o' jays—regular Charley-boys—floatin' around with queens. **1924** F.P. Adams *Velvet* 55: I think you're a hick and a jay!

jay[2] var. J.

jay *adj.* gullible; foolish; (*esp. of a town*) provincial; (*broadly*) contemptible.

    1889 in *OED2*: Smith has a poor opinion…of St. Joseph, which he alludes to as a "jay" town of the worst description. **1890** Bunner *Short Sixes* 91: You jay pill-box. **1894** in *DAE*: When I fixed myself all up to please him, he thought I looked jay,—and…wouldn't let me go down to dinner. **1894** in Ware *Passing Eng.* 159: In the United States…A *jay* town is a *country* town. **1899** Ade *Fables* 6: Moral: *Never Live in a Jay Town.* **1904** Hobart *Jim Hickey* 14: Stranded, here in this jay town! **1904–11** D.G. Phillips *Susan Lenox* II 23: You know, the buyers are men. Gee, what awful jay things we work off on them sometimes! They can't see the dress for the figure. **1912** in *DAE*: From the jayest county in Indiana. **1914** S. Lewis *Mr. Wrenn* 25: Tells how two confidence men fooled one of those terrible little jay towns. **1916** H.L. Wilson *Somewhere in Red Gap* 348: Them jay New York newspapers would fall for it. **1917** in Truman *Dear Bess* 228: When he moves out I'll have a store that will make Emery, Bird's look like a jay-town store. **1918** in "M. Brand" *Coll. Stories* 18: Two dollars for ham and—in a jay dump.

jaybird *n.* **1.a.** JAY[1].

    1886 Field *Sharps & Flats* II 79: From the land of logs and peaches/Came a callow jay-bird dressed/In homespun coat and breeches/And a gaudy velvet vest. **1902** Bell *Worth of Words* 211: *Jay-bird* is an epithet of mild ridicule or contempt, according to circumstances. **1918** Wagar *Spotter* 41: You've been a bird, alright, but of that class known as jay-birds. **1924** in Clarke *Amer. Negro Stories* 24: Where you find all the jaybirds when they first hit Harlem—at the subway entrance. **1980** Hogan *Lawman's Choice* 157: Tell these jaybirds they'd best…throw down their guns. **1985** Boyne & Thompson *Wild Blue* 97: I've got one jaybird out there…apparently lost.

    b. (with diminished force) an amusing or eccentric person.

    1982 Knoxville, Tenn., waitress, age *ca*55: You doin' all right, jaybird? **1986** Coonts *Intruder* 194: You two jaybirds get to fly the B.

    2. *Narc.* a marijuana cigarette; J, 2.

    1984–87 Ferrandino *Firefight* 45 [ref. to 1960's]: Wanna doodle-oo a jaybird?

¶ In phrase:

¶ **naked as a jaybird** stark naked.

    [**1893** James *Mavrick* 27: He will have the humbug qualifications of cow-boy stripped from his poor worthless carcass so quickly that he would feel like a jay bird with his tail feathers gone.] **1922** in *DARE*: I gwi' strip nakit ez a jaybu'd befo' 'e fedduh' grow! **1925** Mullin *Scholar Tramp* 65 [ref. to *ca*1912]: Why, she's naked as a jay-bird; no clothes on her a-tall! **1930** Riggs *Green Grow the Lilacs* 145 [ref. to *ca*1905]: Plumb stark naked as a jaybird! **1933** Caldwell *God's Little Acre* 48: And Will Thompson was as naked as a jay-bird, too. Ain't that something, though? **1940** De Leon *Annie Sails Again* (film): He's naked as a jaybird! **1941** *AS* (Feb.) 23: *Naked as a jaybird.* **1943** *AS* (Feb.) 67: *Naked as a jaybird.* S.C., La. **1952** Randolph & Wilson *Down in the Holler* 178: *Bare as a bird's butt* is understandable, but *naked as a jaybird* is not, since the jay is well-feathered. **1971** Flicker *Nichols* (NBC-TV): You wanta walk around nekkid as a jaybird, go right ahead.

jaybird *adj. So. Midland.* **1.** contemptible; inferior; JAY.

    1887 *Courier-Journal* (Louisville, Ky.) (May 2) 6: The man who has one or more good mares to breed can…make a very ridiculous ass of himself…in using some jay-bird stallion to breed them to. **1960** in *DARE:* Calla was sixteen, with a bullet head and jaybird heels. **1967, 1992** in *DARE.*

2. JAYBIRD-NAKED. Also as adv.

1974 Univ. Tenn. student: Like you can *go jaybird* or go swimming *jaybird.*…Or you could say, "Holy cow! She's jaybird!" **1985** Ark. man, age 35: "He went *jaybird.*" It's the same as *naked as a jaybird.* I heard that as a boy [*ca*1960].

jaybird-naked *adj.* stark naked.

1942 Wilder *Flamingo Road* 104: Stark, jaybird naked. **1960–61** Steinbeck *Discontent* 4: Don't think that lets you lie jaybird naked with a married man. **1983** Goldman & Fuller *Charlie Co.* 292: Jaybird-naked in a padded cell.

jayhawk *n.* [cf. JAYHAWKER] **1.** JAYHAWKER, 2.a.

1858 in *Coll. Kans. Hist. Soc.* V 552: I detached them in small posses, sent in different directions to watch the movements of the "Jay-hawks," as they are termed.

2. an ignorant rustic. Also as quasi-adj.

1906 *Nat. Police Gaz.* (July 7) 6: The jayhawk watertank towns of the South and Southwest. **1907** C.D. Stewart *Partners of Providence* 269: We was just jayhawks and greenhorns that had been picked up everywhere and didn't know nothing about war. **1951** Twist *Fort Worth* (film): Figured you'd jumped the fence with some jayhawk. **1958** *AS* XXXIII 265: Pejorative Designations of Rural Dwellers in the Upper Midwest…*jayhawk, jayhawker.* **1960** *PADS* (No. 34) 52: A more credible example of folk speech, probably also jocular, is the eastern Colorado *jayhawk* "a rustic."

3.a. a mythical bird used as an emblem of Kansas.

1919 V. Lindsay *Golden Whales* 19: Oh the long horns from Texas,/The jay hawks from Kansas,/The plop-eyed bungaroo and giant giassicus. **1944** in *DA:* We [in Kansas] have Jayhawk theaters, Jayhawk restaurants, Jayhawk lumber yards; the fabulous Jayhawk is the insignia not only of our state university, but of scores of other concerns. **1971** in Coffin & Cohen *Parade of Heroes* 523: The mascot…of Kansas University at Lawrence is the jayhawk. **1993** Carhart *Iron Soldiers* 120: Jayhawk Six, this is Iron Six.

b. JAYHAWKER, 3. Cf. 1919 quot. at **(a),** above.

1936 Mencken *Amer. Lang.* (ed. 4) 552: *Jayhawks* [are natives of] Kansas. **1948** in *DA:* Allen was "all wet" when he said the Jayhawks were suffering from a lack of experience.

jayhawk *v.* **1.a.** to raid or harry as a JAYHAWKER, *n.*, 2.b.; plunder. Now *hist.*

1861 in Gaeddart *Birth of Kans.* 139: Jayhawking was the only system that could reach the villains. **1875** in *DA* [ref. to 1858]: On the three following days and nights several persons in Linn county are jayhawked. *a*1889 *Century Dict.: Jayhawk*…v.t.….To harry as a jayhawker. (Slang, U.S.). **1988** Fellman *Inside War* 35: On November 12, 1861, Margaret J. Hayes was jayhawked on her farm near Kansas City.

b. *Army.* to operate as a raider or guerrilla soldier. Now *hist.*

1863 [Fitch] *Annals of Army* 520: They…returned to Kansas, where they jayhawked for a month or two. **1885** in *DA:* Legislative action…brought the territorial jayhawking era substantially to a close. **1912** I. Cobb *Back Home* 94: He was jayhawkin' back and forth along the State line here, burnin' folks' houses down around their heads. **1975** L. Anders *21st Mo.* 252: "Jayhawking" guerrillas…seized the steamer *Lily.*

2. to steal; carry off; (*Army in Civil War*) to obtain by foraging. Now *hist.*

1861 in *Jour. Ill. State Hist. Soc.* LVI (1963) 152: Yesterday we marched to Independence and jayhawked about fifty horses and mules. **1861** in S.Z. Starr *Jennison's Jayhawkers* 111: We…live quite well…from…what we jayhawked…that means when we come to the home of some…secesh…we take his horses and property, burn his house, &c, or as we say, clean them out. **1862** in S.Z. Starr *Jennison's Jayhawkers* 71: [I] jayhawked some silver cupps and sent them to Illinois. *Ibid.* 113: About 10 of us went out jayhawking. **1863** Hollister *Colo. Vols.* 34: We jayhawked pork, beef, and mutton, wherever we could successfully. **1863** in C.W. Wills *Army Life* 200: Understand that not a farthing's worth of the above was "jayhawked." **1862–65** C. Barney *20th Ia.* 73: I'll teach you to leave your company and "jayhawk" turnips, you villains! *Ibid.* 104: "Jayhawking" from rebels was preferable to starvation. **1865** in Glatthaar *March to Sea* 140: The man that does the most jay hawking is considered the most loyal for them. **1873** Beadle *Undeveloped*

West 210: "Jayhawking" was adopted into the language as a delicate euphuism for taking what you really needed when you couldn't pay for it. **1874** in *DA:* George Jones jayhawked a turkey from a stall on South Clark street yesterday. **1886** Johnson *Soldier's Reminiscences* 363: The "jay-hawking" manner in which much of the business of western cities is carried on is calculated to rob not only labor, but capital, of fair compensation. **1887** Peck *Pvt. Peck* 65 [ref. to Civil War]: In war times, everybody steals.…The soldier will not go hungry if he can jayhawk anything to eat. *Ibid.* 271: I did not secure the horse for the purpose of sawing it off on the chaplain. I jayhawked it and…thought I would trade it to some officer with gall. **1901** in *DA:* The greater portion of it [lumber] was "jayhawked" by a wagon master who had a shop near by. **1962** Castel *Quantrill* 36: Why not…jayhawk the slaves of Morgan Walker?

3. to harass or attempt to intimidate (a person).

1884 "Craddock" *Where Battle Was Fought* 48: Brennet fixed his eyes…[with] searching brilliancy, upon his friend, and replied not a word. The silence shook Travis's equilibrium. "Say something, Brennet," he cried angrily. "There's no use in jay-hawking me. You seem to hold me responsible for your disappointment."

4. *Naut.* (see quot.).

1972 G. Bradford *Mariner's Dict.* 138: *Jay hawking,* using a tender to tow a sailboat in a calm.

jayhawker *n.* [orig. unkn.; see W.A. Lyman, "Origin of the Name 'Jayhawker,'" *Coll. Kans. Hist. Soc.* XIV (1915–18), pp. 203–07] **1.** (of uncertain meaning; see 1915–18 quot.). Cf. 1875 quot. at **(3),** below, in light of 1915–18 quot. at this def.

1849 in *Coll. Kans. State Hist. Soc.* VIII (1903–04) 17: Jayhawkers. **1915–18** *Coll. Kans. State Hist. Soc.* XIV 203: It is well known that…as early as 1849 a party of Argonauts from Illinois made the overland journey to California and called themselves "Jayhawkers."

2.a. an ardent or violent Kansas abolitionist during the Free-Soil conflict of 1857–60. Now *hist.*

1858 in *Coll. Kans. Hist. Soc.* V 559: Mr. Fosset also stated that two of the "jayhawkers" [abolitionists] stayed all night with him…that he was afraid to refuse the "jayhawkers" to stay. **1858** in A.D. Richardson *Beyond Miss.* 125: Found all the settlers justifying the "Jayhawkers," a name universally applied to Montgomery's men, from the celerity of their movements and their habit of suddenly pouncing upon an enemy. **1860** in *DAE:* By the term "Jayhawkers" is here [Mound City, Kans.] understood the active, fighting abolitionists. **1861** in S.Z. Starr *Jennison's Jayhawkers* (dust-jacket photo of recruiting poster): Independent Kansas Jay-Hawkers. Volunteers are wanted for the 1st Regiment of Kansas Volunteer Cavalry to serve our country During the War.…Aug. 24, 1861. **1861** in *Ibid.* 38: I am authorized by the "Southern Kansas Jay-Hawkers" to tender you the…thanks of the company, for a beautifully wrought specimen of the American flag. **1868** in Rosa *Gunfighter* 36: The term "Jayhawker" was applied by the pro-slavery men to mean "thief" and after it became of general use, they ceased using any other term than "Jayhawkers" to all the Free State people of the territory. **1915–18** *Coll. Kans. State Hist. Soc.* XIV 203: In July, 1857…there existed in Linn county an organization known as the "Jayhawkers," brought together for mutual defense against the incursions of parties known as border ruffians of Missouri. **1940** Gaeddart *Birth of Kansas* 9: The leaders were active abolitionists who called themselves Vigilantes, but their enemies called them Jayhawkers. They operated in southern Kansas as early as 1857. **1953** Breihan *Jesse James* 76: Quantrill's only brother had been murdered by Jayhawkers. *a*1962 Strother *Underground R.R. in Conn.* 176: Free Soil "jayhawkers" with Sharps rifles rushed in from Northern states.

b. a member of any band of lawless mounted raiders or marauders during or following the Civil War; (hence) (during the war) an irregular or guerrilla soldier. Now *hist.*

1861 in Gaeddart *Birth of Kans.* 139: Jayhawkers from both sides of the [Kansas-Missouri] line. **1862** in *DA* s.v. *copperhead:* That faction of the Democracy who sympathise with the rebels are known in…Illinois as "guerrillas," in Missouri as "butternuts," in Kansas as "jayhawkers," in Kentucky as "bushwhackers." **1863** in *Confed. Vet.* XXVIII (1920) 11: The Tories (Jayhawkers) in the mountains before here and Tuscumbia have organized into a band of marauders and rob all who travel that route. **1863** in *Ark. Hist. Qly.* XXXVII (1978) 315: There are too many jayhawkers between here and home to make it safe for a few men. **1865** Duganne *Camps & Pris.* 317: Some say it wor jayhawkers got him. **1871** Schele de Vere *Amer.* 282: The *Jayhawkers*…[combined] murder with marauding, and were famous before the war already, during the bloody strife…in Kansas.…They fought in Kansas often side by side with the equally ill-famed *Border Ruffians*. **1882** Triplett *Jesse James* 8 [ref. to Civil War]: Woe to the jayhawkers who lay dreaming of easy victories over helpless women and children! **1886** in Womack *Mighty Men* 336: During the war the country [Tennessee] was overrun with guerillas and jayhawkers. **1887** E. Custer *Tenting* 165 [ref. to 1866]: Jayhawkers, bandits and bushwhackers had everything their own way for a time [in Texas]. *a*1889 in Barrère & Leland *Dict. Slang* I 495: The bandits…the "jay-hawkers," as they…dubbed themselves. **1907** Hough *Story of Outlaw* 344: Quantrell…border ruffian and jayhawker [for the Confederacy]. **1920** J.M. Hunter *Trail Drivers* I 148: A Kansas jay-hawker had been…exacting toll from the herds. **1926** Branch *Cowboy* 128: At Baxter Springs, Kansas, he learned that jayhawkers had molested the herds ahead of him. *Ibid.* 129: Lawless gangs, jayhawkers. **1934** S. Young *So Red the Rose* 382: They had…been infested with thieves, robbers, and jayhawkers. **1973** Seidman *Once in Saddle* 43: Even worse was the menace of armed ruffians whom the Texans called Jayhawkers. The Jayhawkers threatened to stampede the herds if they were not paid off.

c. *Union Army.* a forager.

1862–65 C. Barney *20th Ia.* 88: Great activity on the part of our indefatigable wide-awake "jayhawkers," to whose perserverance our tables bore unmistakable evidence. **1892** M.O. Frost *10th Mo.* 32: And you may rest assured that the "Jayhawkers" (as these two companies were afterward called) lived *fat* during their stay at Perreuque.

3. a Kansan. Now *colloq.*

1875 *Chambers's Journal* (Mar. 3) 171: Kansas is another Garden of the West, but, unlike its namesake Illinois, is occupied by Jayhawkers, which may be, however, only another name for Suckers. **1876** *Harper's* (July) 195: Dick Vose was a Jayhawker. The Kansas troops had accepted the appellation good-naturedly, though it had originally been given them by the Missourians as an intimation that they were only robbers of poultry-yards. **1863–82** W. Britton *Rebellion on Border* 110: The name Jayhawker was first given to an organization of Free State Men in Southern Kansas who…made military incursions into Missouri. The name is growing into a nickname for all Kansas people in the same sense as "Hoosier" is applied to Indianians. **1890** in *DA*: "Jay-hawker"…is the name that is applied to all citizens of Kansas. **1909** Ware *Passing Eng.* 159: *Jayhawkers* (American). People of Kansas. **1910** *Coll. Kans. State Hist. Soc.* XI 253: As time went on the name "Jayhawkers" lost its opprobrium.…Kansas [today] aspires to be called the "Jayhawker State." **1915–18** *Coll. Kans. State Hist. Soc.* XIV 207: To-day Kansas people are proud to be known as "Jayhawkers."

4. Esp. *Central Plains.* an ignorant rustic; CLODHOPPER.

1881 A.A. Hayes *New Colo.* 97: A—jayhawker as wouldn't give me no show to pass him on a narrer road. **1893** in Williams & Duffy *Chi. Wits* 150: At the Eiffel tower the "jayhawker" was laboring hard to defend himself. **1902** Bell *Worth of Words* 208: Hayseed, Reuben, *Jayhawker, Clodhopper* and so forth are impolite descriptive terms applied to rural cousins—they of a certain class. **1907** Siler *Pugilism* 39: Just to show the jayhawkers what I could do with him. **1910** in O. Johnson *Lawrenceville* 432: It's only the alcohol that counts, you jayhawkers. **1918** Ruggles *Navy Explained* 83: *Jayhawker.* Some new country boy who is continually star gazing at objects when he should be paying attention to his duty. **1958** (quot. at JAYHAWK, *n.*, 2).

jayhoo var. JEHU.

jazz *n.* [cf. JAZZ, *v.*, also JASM/JISM and JAZZBO, all of problematical origin and having various semantic relationships; authoritative discussions are D. Holbrook, which includes interviews with several journalists and musicians who used the word at a very early stage, and P. Tamony (for both see note at (**2**), below) and A.P. Merriam & F.H. Garner, "Jazz—The Word," *Ethnomusicology* XII (1968), pp. 373–96. Presumed West African origins (e.g., < Mandingo *jasi* 'to become abnormal or out of character' [D. Dalby]) are not convincing in the light of the available evidence; the 1917 *Sun* article cited at (**3**), below, which claims an African origin, was purely an invention of a press agent]

1.a. copulation; (*also*) an act of copulation.—usu. considered vulgar. Also **jass.** [Prob. the orig. sense; the 1924 and *a*1973 B. Kelly quots. may attest the verb.]

1918 Noyes MS. (unp.): [Navy slang:] *Hump=Jazz=Cunt.* **1918** in

Dos Passos *14th Chronicle* (Nov. 11) 229: Talk is mainly of seasickness and the possibility of French jazz. **1918–19** in Carey *Mlle. from Armentières* II (unp.): She'd give you a jazz like cats a-pissin'. **1924** *Etude* (Sept.), in *Storyville* L (Dec. 1973) 49: Thirty-five years ago, I played the trombone.…I made tours of the big mining centers when the West was really wild and woolly. I was piloted to dance resorts—honky tonks. The vulgar word Jazz was in general currency in those dance halls thirty years or more ago. The primitive music that went with the Jazz of those mining town dance halls is unquestionably the lineal descendant [*sic*] of much of the jazz music of today. **1927** (quot. at JAZZ, *v.*, 1). **1928** in Read *Lexical Evidence* 62: Take your girl out…in the bushes for a Jaz. *ca*1929 *Collection of Sea Songs* 11: I count each jazz and screw/And other things we'd do. **1930** Irwin *Tramp & Und. Slang* 109: *Jazz.*—Sexual intercourse. **1929–33** Farrell *Young Manhood* 286: You better come with me tonight and get yourself a fast and furious jazz. **1959** Bechet *Treat It Gentle* 3: Jazz…used to be spelled *Jass*, which *was* screwing. **1961** Anhalt & Miller *Young Savages* (film): My mother sells snow to the snowbirds,/My father sells barbershop gin,/My sister sells jazz for a living/And that's why the money rolls in. *a*1973 in *Storyville* L (Dec.) 49: The word Jazz was used as a colloquial term for coitus as early as 1898, at least [in New Orleans]. *a*1973 B. Kelly, early jazz musician, in *Storyville* L (Dec.) 48: The word jazz was first used as a sex word in California and was a common localism in San Francisco when I arrived there in 1899.…I shall be glad to swear an oath before a notary public that Jazz used as a sex word was not only used in San Francisco before the earthquake and first, but that it was of such common use that it was a localism.

b. semen.—usu. considered vulgar. Cf. syn. JIZM.

1932 in Read *Lexical Evidence* 62: Any-one/want to/swallow/a load/of Jazz/JACK-OFF/and eat your own.

2. spirit; vigor; energy; excitement. [See D. Holbrook, "Our Word Jazz," in *Storyville* L (Dec. 1973–Jan. 1974) 46–58 for facsimile reproductions of the columns from which the Mar. 3 and Apr. 5 1913 quots. are taken, and P. Tamony, "Jazz: The Word and Its Extension to Music," *JEMF Qly.* XVII (Spring 1981) 9–18, for a facsimile reproduction of the sports column from which the Mar. 6 1913 quots. are taken. Despite its juxtaposition with *ragtime*, the word *jazz* is not used there to denote music.]

1913 E.T. Gleeson, in *S.F. Bulletin* (Mar. 3): McCarl has been heralded all along the line as a "busher," but now it develops that this dope is very much to the "jazz." **1913** E.T. Gleeson, in *S.F. Bulletin* (Mar. 6) 16: Everybody has come back to the old town full of the old "jazz" and they [the S.F. Seals baseball team] promise to knock the fans off their feet with their playing. What is the "jazz"? Why, it's a little of that "old life," the "gin-i-ker," the pep.…the enthusiasalum. A grain of "jazz" and you feel like going out and eating your way through Twin Peaks. *Ibid.*: The team…comes pretty close to representing the pick of the army. Its members have trained on ragtime and "jazz." **1913** E.T. Gleeson, in *S.F. Bulletin* (Mar. 8): Spence the catcher zipped that old pill around the infield. He opened a can of "jazz" at the tap of the gong. Henley the pitcher put a little more of the old "jazz" on the pill. **1913** E.J. Hopkins, in *S.F. Bulletin* (Apr. 5): IN PRAISE OF "JAZZ," A FUTURIST WORD WHICH HAS JUST JOINED THE LANGUAGE.…"Jazz" can be defined, but it cannot be synonymized.…This remarkable and satisfactory-sounding word, however, means something like life, vigor, energy, effervescence of spirit, joy, pep, magnetism, verve, virility, ebulliency, courage, happiness—oh, what's the use?—JAZZ. Nothing else can express it. **1917** *Sun* (N.Y.C.) (Aug. 5) III 3: When a vaudeville act needs ginger the cry from the advisers in the wings is "put in jaz," meaning add low comedy, go to high speed and accelerate the comedy spark. **1917** *N.Y. Times* (Dec. 23) IV 6: "Nut acts"…deal in those brands of humor known as "jazz," "hokum," "jasbo," and "gravy." "Jazz" is fast comedy that speeds an act up. **1917** (quot. at JAZZ, *v.*, 3). **1918–19** Sinclair *Higgins* 186: Make the dirt fly! Put the jazz into it! That's the stuff! **1919** *12th Inf.* 289: Sergeants Peter Anderson and Mike Healy…went to Camp Funston, Kansas, to put some "jazz" in the Three Hundred and Fifty-third Infantry. **1919** in Bold *Selling West* 93: I quite realize there is a field for my Western junk as long as I have you to put the jazz in it. **1922** *DN* V 142: *Jazz*…animation, animal good spirits. **1926** Hormel *Co-Ed* 44: She had furnished much joyous "jazz." **1933** D.O. Stewart *Going Hollywood* (film): Come on, fellas! A big send-off! A lotta jazz, a lotta pep! **1938** E.T. Gleeson, in *Call-Bulletin* (S.F.)

(Sept. 3) 3 [ref. to 1913]: "Spike" had picked up the word in a crap game. Whenever one of the players rolled the dice he would shout, "Come on, the old jazz."...For the next week we gave "jazz" a great play in all our stories. **1955** *Pop. Science* (Nov.) 264: A Lincoln-built OHV engine has enough jazz to urge Mark II very nearly as fast as the fastest. **1984** Jackson & Lupica *Reggie* 5: I managed to put some jazz in [Yankee Stadium].

3. ensemble music of various styles (orig. ragtime played at rapid tempo and strongly influenced by the blues) that is characteristically complex, improvisatory, polyphonic, and freely experimental in rhythm, melody, tonality, etc., and that is especially associated with African-American culture. Now *S.E.* Also **jass.**

[The citation erroneously dated "1909" in *OED2* was not in fact recorded until 1919; see D. Shulman, "The Earliest Citation of *Jazz*," *Comments on Ety.* XVI (Dec. 1, 1986), pp. 2–6; the claim made in the 1938 quot. is given little credence by jazz historians.]

1916 in Brunn *Orig. Dixieland Jazz Band* 37: The shriek of women's laughter rivaled the blatant scream of the imported [Stein's] New Orleans Jass Band, which never seemed to stop playing. *Ibid.* 43: Fogarty's Dance Revue and Jass Band hit it off like a whirlwind. **1916** *Variety* (Oct. 27) 12: Chicago...has added another innovation to its list of discoveries in the so-called "Jazz Bands." **1916** *Variety* (Nov. 3) 20: *Variety*'s New Orleans correspondent [reports that]..."Jazz Bands" have been popular there for over two years. **1916** *Chicago Defender* (Nov. 4) 4: Florida Troubadours. Sentimental, Ragtime, Comedy and "Jaz" Singers. **1916** Tom York & L.J. Finks *The Jazz Rag* [musical composition] [N.Y.: Frank Laird Waller, 1916]. **1917** *N.Y. Times* (Jan. 15) 7: The First Sensational Amusement Novelty of 1917. "THE Jasz Band." Direct from its amazing success in Chicago....The JASZ BAND is the latest craze that is sweeping the nation like a musical thunderstorm. **1917** *N.Y. Times* (Feb. 2) 9: The First Eastern Appearance of the Famous Original Dixieland "JAZZ BAND." **1917** Victor Records Catalog (March 7) 1, in Brunn *Orig. Dixieland Band* (plate 5): Jass Band and Other Dance Selections. The Original Dixieland Jass Band. Spell it Jass, Jas, Jaz, or Jazz—nothing can spoil a Jass band. Some say the Jass band originated in Chicago. Chicago says it comes from San Francisco...across the continent. **1917** *Sun* (N.Y.C.) (Aug. 5) 3: Variously spelled Jas, Jass, Jaz, Jazz, Jasz and Jascz. The word is African in origin. It is common on the Gold Coast of Africa and in the hinterland of Cape Coast Castle....Jazz is based on the savage musician's wonderful gift for progressive retarding and acceleration, guided by his sense of "swing." **1917** *Variety* (Nov. 30) 2: No Ragtime Jazz. **1917** in Rust *Jazz Records* I 544: Frisco Jazz Band...Johnson "Jass" Blues [phonograph record]. **1917** W.B. Overstreet *The Jazz Dance: The Little Jazz Dance Ev'rybody's Crazy 'Bout* [song & fox trot] [Chicago: Will Rossiter, 1917]. **1917** W.J. Ruger *The Jass Rag* [musical composition] [Milwaukee, Wis.: W.J. Ruger, 1917]. **1918** *Times-Picayune* (N.O.) (June 20) 4: Why is the jass music, and therefore the jass band?...Indeed, one might...say that Jass music is the indecent story syncopated and counterpointed....In the matter of jass, New Orleans is particularly interested, since it has been widely suggested that this...musical vice had its birth in...our slums. **1919** *Literary Digest* (Apr. 26) 47: The phrase "jazz band" was first used by Bert Kelly in Chicago in the fall of 1915, and was unknown in New Orleans. *Ibid.* 48: Bert Kelly had about twenty orchestras known as Bert Kelly's Jazz Band [between 1915 and 1917]. **1922** *DN* V 142: *Jazz*...Present-day syncopated dance music. "Just listen to that jazz." **1922** Fitzgerald *Tales of the Jazz Age* [title]. [**1924** (quot. at (**1.a.**), above).] **1932** *AS* VII 241: Jazz is free; jazz is roughhouse; jazz may be sweet; jazz may be hot; but jazz is always throbbing with new life, with an exotic crude accent. **1938** Lomax *Mr. Jelly Roll* 62: I ["Jelly Roll" Morton] started using the word in 1902 to show people the difference between jazz and ragtime. **1955** A. Loyacano, in Shapiro & Hentoff *Hear Me Talkin'* 81: I was in Tom Brown's band, which was the first white band to ever go to Chicago and play jazz [in 1915]....That's when people started calling our music "jazz." The way the Northern people figured it out, our music was loud, clangy, boisterous, like you'd say, "Where did you get that jazzy suit?" meaning loud or fancy. Some people called it "jass." Later, when the name stuck, it was spelled..."jazz." **1955** in L. Patterson *Negro in Music* 108: The blues are the mother of jazz. **1958** *PADS* (No. 30) 41: There has always been a tendency in some circles to regard jazz as non-music. **1959**

Bechet *Treat It Gentle* 3: Jazz, that's a name the white people have given to the music. **1962** Charters & Kunstadt *Jazz* 14: In a 1903 minstrel recording, "The Cake Walk In Coon Town," the "dancing" is accompanied by a five-piece band—two clarinets, cornet, trombone, and piano, playing an unmistakable jazz style. **1967** M. Williams *Jazz Masters of N.O.* xvi: One encounters frustrations and contradictions in jazz research. **1973** Buerkle & Barker *Bourbon St. Black* 114: From this perspective, jazz is the black man's property. **1979** Gillespie & Fraser *To Be* 492: Jazz is an African word....As for what they call the "real jazz," there is no real jazz—there's only good and bad. **1988** Emery *Black Dance* 348: Cool jazz—and little dancing—were "in."

4. a short flight or ride.

1918 Guttersen *Granville* (Sept. 12) 60: I took a jazz in it this evening and tried to see if the thing was strong enough to stand some quick turns.

5.a. nonsense; nonsensical or meaningless talk.

1917 *Milwaukee Jour.* (Apr. 6) 16: You meet a young lady and tell her how extremely well she is looking....Then she responds: "Jazz, old fellow, pure jazz! Shut it off and talk regular." **1918** *DN* V 25: *Jazz*, n. Talk; "gas." College students. **1956** H. Ellison *Deadly Streets* 77: What was this jazz about me talkin' to Fairchild? **1955–57** Felder *Collegiate Slang* 3: (*All that*) *jazz*—equivalent to "all that stuff" or "all that chatter." **1958** H. Gardner *Piece of the Action* 228: I give you no jazz. **1958** Horan *Mob's Man* 64: None of the cons...ever kidded me about being a good thief or any jazz like that. **1961** in Cannon *Nobody Asked* 209: Don't you go writing Old Pork Chop's going to die. I never read such jazz in my life. **1963** E. Hunter *Ten Plus One* 1: A faithful husband, devoted father, all that jazz. **1965** N. Simon *Odd Couple* 462: Don't give me that analyst jazz. I happen to know I hate my guts. **1967** Kolb *Getting Straight* 14: But all I've heard is a lot of jazz about Units. Just what is a Unit? **1969** Moynahan *Pairing Off* 185: All that jazz at the beginning about how many cents he spent on nails and boards. **1973** M. Collins *Carrying the Fire* 72: Never mind all this theoretical jazz. **1987** S. Stark *Wrestling Season* 78: Will you can it with the new car jazz?

b. stuff; things.

[**1921** Wiley *Lady Luck* 70: Fingehs, lemme see kin you play de pickpocket jazz.] **1953** in *OED2*: What do you call that jazz, alpaca or something? **1953** in S. Allen *Bop Fables* 43: "What's in the basket?" "Oh, the same old jazz." **1959** Brosnan *Long Season* 48: You want to keep in step with modern medicine and all that jazz, Doc. **1959** De Roo *Young Wolves* 16: I'm through with that jazz. **1960** MacDonald *Slam the Big Door* 9: So that's why Connorly was bugging me about the duty of the citizen and all that jazz. **1964** Barthelme *Dr. Caligari* 142: Why did you write all that jazz on your sign, Carl? **1970** Baraka *Jello* 37: This is art for art's sake you're pulling, and nobody goes for that jazz anymore. **1972** *Business Week* (Feb. 19) 28: You still have to have all the jazz that people expect at a meeting....Some types come only to work, some only to play. **1981** *N.Y. Times Book Review* (Dec. 27) 7: Duden...would have given him 34 terms for an all-purpose medieval castle, plus 54 more on knights and all that jazz. **1981** *Daily Beacon* (Univ. Tenn.) (Nov. 2) 2: You know...this teachin' jazz ain't half as hard as I figured.

6. a cause for laughter; KICK.

1960 MacDonald *Slam the Big Door* 92: Safety belts for bar stools. Isn't that a jazz?

jazz *adj. Av.* (of a flight or flying) done recklessly or for excitement. [In 1919 and 1920 quots., *bus* ref. to an airplane.]

1919 *N.Y. Times Mag.* (Mar. 30) 4: "One day a strapping big kiwee climbed into my bus, just when I wanted to take a jazz ride by myself."..."A "jazz ride," in automobile parlance, is a "joy ride." **1920** *Amer. Leg. Wkly.* (Jan. 30) 17 [ref. to 1918]: I was taking a jazz ride in my bus one day—. **1946** Wead & Sheekman *Blaze of Noon* (film): No jazz flying. No circling low over dames taking sunbaths.

jazz *v.* [cf. *F & H* VI, pp. 23–24: "To possess carnally ... French synonyms ... *jaser* (also *jazer*)," a sense unrecorded in standard French dictionaries. Yet the French v. in its ordinary sense of 'to chatter or gossip' was indeed anglicized as *jazz* on at least one occasion: *1831 Lord Palmerston, in Ridley *Palmerston* 137: "I am writing in the Conference, Matuszevic copying out a note for our signature, old Talley[rand] jazzing and telling stories to Lieven and Esterhazy and Wessenberg." See also ety. note at JAZZ, *n.*]

1. to copulate with.—also used absol.—usu. considered vulgar. [Prob. the orig. sense; cf. 1924 and *a*1973 recollections at JAZZ, *n.*, 1.a., which may represent use of the v.]

    [*1896 J.S. Farmer *Vocab. Amatoria* 162: *Jaser* (or *Jazer*). To copulate; "to chuck a tread." *Tu as les genoux chauds, tu veux jaser.*—*La Comédie des proverbes.*] **1918** in M. Carey *Mlle. from Armentières* II (unp.): She jazzed a nigger, she jazzed a Jew. *Ibid.:* Oh, Mademoiselle from Armentières/Hasn't been jazzed for fifty years. **1920** in Inman *Diary* 167: He had had sexual relations with her (in his slang "had jazzed her"). **1924** C. Smith, in *Etude* (Sept.) 595: If the truth were known about the origin of the word "Jazz" it would never be mentioned in polite society....At fifteen and sixteen I had already made tours of Western towns including the big mining centres when the West was really wild and wooly....I naturally received information that was none too good for me and was piloted...to dance resorts....The vulgar word "Jazz" was in general currency in those dance halls thirty years...ago....The vulgar dances that accompany some of the modern jazz are sometimes far too suggestive of the ugly origin of the word. **1926** P. Whiteman & M. McBride *Jazz* 18 [ref. to *ca*1915]: Jazz...[He] undoubtedly knew the word as a slang phrase of the underworld with a meaning unmentionable in polite society. *Ibid.* 20: The origin of the word...probably has stirred up sentiment against the music. **1927** G.B. Johnson, in *Jour. Abnormal & Soc. Psych.* XXII 14: The word *jazz*....Used both as a verb and as a noun to denote the sex act, it has long been common vulgarity among Negroes in the South, and it is very likely from this usage that the term "jazz music" was derived.* It is almost unbelievable that such vulgarity could become so respectable, but it is true nevertheless....*Jazz music originated in Negro pleasure houses—"jazz houses," as they are sometimes called by Negroes. **1927** *Immortalia* 42: But when it came to jazzing, that gal could go. **1928** Levin *Reporter* 92: So this was the guy that jazzed Linda. **1929** Farrell *Guillotine Party* 302: She's cute. I jazzed her, too. **1930** *Lyra Ebriosa* 9: I'll tell you the story of old King Belshazzar:/The king loved a maid and he wanted to jazz her. **1930** Irwin *Tramp & Und. Slang* 109: *Jazz*...To have intercourse. **1931** Dos Passos *1919* 171: He'd been jazzing an Eyetalian girl only she'd gone to sleep and he'd gotten disgusted. **1931** in H. Miller *Letters to Emil* 85: She smoking while he jazzes her. **1932** in J. Goodman *Scottsboro* 195: Believe me i was jazed But those white Boys jazed me. **1946** Gresham *Nightmare Alley* 63: As if jazzing wasn't what they all want, the goddamned hypocrites. **1952** Bellow *Augie March* 196: When I heard they were married I had dreams about them jazzing. **1957** Herber *Tomorrow to Live* 60: He's been jazzing all those broads. **1963** McDavid *Amer. Lang.* 743: According to Raven I. McDavid, Sr., of Greeneville, S.C.,...*jazz* had never been heard in the Palmetto State [before 1919] except as a verb meaning to copulate. **1965** in Rosset *Evergreen Reader* 698: Yes, I was jazzing her...Jazzing her ON THE FLOOR. **1971** Horan *Blue Messiah* 287: How would you like to jazz a dame when her husband's snorin' next to you? **1973** *Zap Comix* (No. 6) (unp.): The pig is probably jazzin' someone else. **1967–80** Folb *Runnin' Lines* 243: *Jazz* engage in sexual intercourse. **1982** E. Leonard *Cat Chaser* 206: What's he gonna do to a guy he finds out's been jazzing his wife? *a*1973–87 F.M. Davis *Livin' the Blues* 36 [ref. to *ca*1920]: We all knew what it meant to "jazz a jane"...or "get a piece of tail."

2. to play or dance to jazz music.—also used trans. Now *S.E.* [The date of the *a*1926 quot. is possibly as early as 1914.]

    1917 M. Kollender *Jazzing Through Chinatown* [pop. song] [N.Y.: E.H. Kollender, 1917]. **1918** in Dolph *Sound Off!* 114: Oh, I'm going to a better land, they jazz there every night. **1919** F.S. Butler *Jazzin' Sam from Alabam'* [pop. song] [N.Y.: Butler Music Co., 1919]. **1919** *Lit. Digest* (Apr. 26) 28: While society once "ragged," they now "jazz." **1919** in Handy *Blues Treasury* 124: Soon you'll be sayin' "Hon jazz me 'round." **1922** *DN* V 142: Let's jazz a bit; the music's pretty good. *a*1926 in Handy *Blues Treasury* 74: If my blues don't get you my jazzing must.

3.a. to invigorate, enliven, inspirit, or accelerate; vitalize; (*hence*) to ornament or embellish.—usu. constr. with *up.* [The assertion made in the 1917 *Sun* quot.—frequently repeated—that the word appears in this or another sense in the works of Hearn (1850–1904) is without foundation.]

    1917 *Milwaukee Jour.* (Apr. 6) 16: Her hair dresser is consuming an unexpectedly long time in completing her coiffure. So she says, briskly, "O, jazz it up somehow! I gotto git a 5 o'clock furry." **1917** *Milwaukee Jour.* (June 20) 10: Any ordinary ragtime piece can be Jazzed. **1917** *Sun* (N.Y.C.) (Aug. 5) III 3: In his studies of the creole patois and idiom in New Orleans Lafcadio Hearn reported that the word "jaz," meaning to

speed things up, to make excitement, was common among the blacks of the South and had been adopted by the creoles as a term to be applied to music of a rudimentary syncopated type. In the old plantation days when the slaves were having one of their rare holidays and the fun languished some West Coast Africans would cry out, "Jaz her up," and this would be the cue for fast and furious fun. Curiously enough the phrase "Jaz her up" is a common one to-day in vaudeville and on the circus lot. **1917** J. Glogau & M. Helm *Jazz It Up: Novelty Fox Trot* [pop. song] [N.Y.: Al Piantadosi & Co., Inc., 1917]. **1917** in Charters & Kunstadt *Jazz* 61: [The Negro bands of N.O.] were the original jazz bands, and their expressions of "jazzing it" and "put a little jazz on it" are still very popular at their picturesque balls. **1919** S.M. Lewis, J. Young & T. Snyder *Jazzin' the Alphabet* [pop. song] [N.Y.: Waterson, Berlin & Snyder Co., 1919]. **1919** in *DA*: For ways that is dark and tricks which is vain, the daughters of Eve is peculiar, to jazz up a line of Bret Harte's. **1921** *Amer. Leg. Wkly.* (Mar. 18) 21: By way of jazzing up a recent meeting, the members...conducted a voting contest of their own. **1922** E. Pound, in Materer *Pound/Lewis* 132: Jazz 'em up a bit. **1922** *Variety* (Mar. 31) 3: Hicks has jazzed the principal role much as William Collier might have been expected to do. **1922** *Collier's* (Sept. 2) 5: What is these up-to-date nifties, anyway, but the old stuff jazzed up? **1924** P. Marks *Plastic Age* 172: A shot of gin might jazz me up a little. **1925** Faulkner *Soldier's Pay* 134: It might be jazzed a bit, you know....You might jazz your hair up a little, too. **1927** C.J. Daly *Snarl of Beast* 247: Is he dead?...Can't you jazz him up so's he'll talk, Doc? **1935** Algren *Boots* 168: We got my boots soled an' my tattooin' jazzed up. **1938** Bezzerides *Long Haul* 175: If you jazz it up, you'll make delivery by tomorrow morning. **1941** in C.R. Bond & T. Anderson *Flying T. Diary* 44: Paint...[would] jazz up the planes. **1947** Schulberg *Harder They Fall* 304: A jazzed-up Mercedes-Benz. **1958** *Time* (Feb. 17) 24: Permission to build twelve Jupiter-Cs—actually, almost the same jazzed-up Redstones with which he had proposed to put a small moon into orbit. **1966** Manus *Mott the Hoople* 30: I've been taking a new drug that jazzes up the thyroid. **1971** LeGuin *Lathe of Heaven* 96: It won't put you to sleep. Jazz you up a bit. **1975** Stanley *WWIII* 238: Putnam was...trying to jazz up some of the boys who were headed for the redoubts.

b. Esp. *Av.* to move (a throttle) rapidly back and forth; switch (an engine) rapidly on and off; (*also*) to cause (an engine) to accelerate.—occ. used absol.

    1919 *Power Plant Engineering* (Mar. 15): If the pilot finds himself with a suddenly stopt propeller or "dead stick," he will ordinarily first do a nose dive, "jazzing" the throttle meanwhile, to see if the tremendous blast of air on the propeller will start the motor. Frequently the attempt is successful. **1927** Faulkner *Mosquitoes* 302: Pete leaned out, jazzing his idling engine. **1944** Stiles *Big Bird* 15: Two P-51's came jazzing by, looking for game. **1944** H. Brown *A Walk in the Sun* 91: It came slowly for a motorcycle. The rider was obviously having trouble with the rutty road. He jazzed his motor, modulated it, then jazzed it again. **1946** Wead & Sheekman *Blaze of Noon* (film): Can you shake the ice free by jazzing the ship? **1951** Sheldon *Troubling of a Star* 70: "Jazz your engines back and forth," said Braith. "Get 'em out of synch." **1953** LeVier & Guenther *Pilot* 167: They would...dive through our formations and go jazzing back and forth like a yoyo. **1961** D.C. Smith *Seat of Pants* 71: He...jazzed the engine. **1962** Harvey *Strike Command* 6: Then they trundled back toward Operations, jazzing their engines in big sullen bursts. **1968** W. Anderson *Gooney Bird* 102: He jazzed [the throttle] a couple of times. **1980** W.C. Anderson *Bat-21* 89: He heard Birddog jazzing overhead. **1990** Berent *Steel Tiger* 387: "I'll jazz my engines for you."...Toby...moved his throttles back and forth a few times.

c. to thrill or excite. Cf. JAZZED, *adj.*, 1.

    1921 *Jazz Me Blues* [pop. song] [Victor phonograph record V-18772]. **1970** Grissim *White Man's Blues* 23: As for Chet Atkins, one of Nashville's thirty-nine Country millionaires, he only likes to produce artists who really jazz him.

4. to confuse, mess up, interfere with, ruin, or impair; botch; SCREW UP.—usu. constr. with *up*; in phr. **jazz up the detail** *Army.* (*obs.*) to make a botch; ruin things.

    1917 in Rossano *Price of Honor* 23: My orders were all jazzed up, but...they should be here in five or six days. *Ibid.* 40: I can't speak...French, and Rollie gets jazzed up once in a while himself. *Ibid.* 42: The Indians would have jazzed the party for sure if they'd been there. **1918** *Sat. Eve. Post* (Aug. 24) 9: Is that clown goin'? Then I don't!...He'll jazz up everything. **1919** *Literary Digest* (Apr. 26) 47:

But, says Joseph K. Gorham, "Daddy of the Jazz," the word,…frequent in the vocabulary of the Barbary coast and the southern darky for years, means…"to mess 'em up and slap it on thick." That's the verb "to jazz." The noun means just the same…except that the noun implies the process and the verb the action. **1920** Ade *Hand-Made Fables* 95: He got word that the Elysian Fields had been all jazzed up by War. **1932** Halyburton & Goll *Shoot & Be Damned* 206 [ref. to 1918]: That big tub of sour owl milk will jazz up the detail for all of us. **1943** Farrell *To Whom It May Concern* 17: So here I am, forty and 4F, and all jazzed up with an incipient civilian neurosis. **1961** H. Ellison *Memos* 110: That socking-around I'd gotten had jazzed my brains completely. **1972** R. Barrett *Lovomaniacs* 421: Sorry, kid, something jazzed up the phone at this end.

5. to lie to; deceive; (also) to tease; JIVE.

1927 in *AS* (Feb. 1928) 259: Today we "josh" him, "jazz" him, "razz" him, or "hand him the raspberry." **1959** "W. Williams" *Ada Dallas* 207: There would be a lot of feeling that we thought the people were easy to jazz, and then they would be hell-bent to show us they weren't. **1968** Myrer *Eagle* 477: You wouldn't jazz me, would you? **1969** Jessup *Sailor* 336: Don't jazz me, Mister Mate. I don't know the answers. **1972** N.Y.U. prof.: You still think I'm jazzing you? **1978** Cleaver *Soul on Fire* 84: And, over the years, I had refined my own technique of jazzing with the man, keeping him uptight. **1984** Sample *Racehoss* 228: Somebody…was always jazzing him about his looks. **1987** Univ. Tenn. instructor, age 35: There were five in there who were not aware I was jazzin' 'em. **1996** *Wash. Post* (July 30) E13: Then you're not jazzing me! You're really serious!

jazz around *v.* to fool around.

1917 E. Fuller *Jazzin' Around* [musical composition] [N.Y.: Earl Fuller, 1917]. **1918** *DN* V 25: *To jazz*…1. To talk to kill time. 2. To walk about to kill time. Rare. "I jazzed around all forenoon." **1919** Yarwood *Overseas Dreams* 103: We jazzed around for an hour and came down. **1920** in *DA*: The boys are "jazzing" around waiting for the proper word. **1922** *DN* V 142: College Slang…You mustn't expect to pass your quizzes if you keep jazzing around like this. **1929–33** Farrell *Young Manhood* 307: There would be no more jazzing around, drinking, can houses. **1942** Wilder *Flamingo Road* 42: "Sometimes we just jazz around in the car."…"Suppose you don't feel like—like jazzing around?"…"Most of the time I do."…"You mean with anybody?" **1961** H. Ellison *Gentleman Junkie* 150: You…went to the Heidelburg for beer and jazzed around at the fraternity house.

jazz baby *n.* a person, esp. an attractive young woman, who is a fan of jazz music.

1919 B. Merrill & M.K. Jerome *Jazz Baby* [pop. song] [N.Y.: Waterson, Berlin & Snyder Co., © Feb. 13, 1919]. **1919** *Variety* (Mar. 28) 29: "I'm a Jazz Baby." **1919** in Rust *Jazz Records* I 513: Lt. Jim Europe's 369th Infantry…Band…Jazz Baby [phonograph recording]. **1921** Hecht *Erik Dorn* 176: I'm a Jazz Baby. **1922** Fitzgerald *Beautiful & Damned* 29: You will be known during your fifteen years as a ragtime kid, a flapper, a jazz-baby, and a baby vamp. **1926** Hormel *Co-Ed* 200: Thank goodness we annexers are neither Puritans nor jazz-babies! **1929–33** Farrell *Young Manhood* 222: I fixes the lads with some flaming jazz-babies! **1944–45** in Campbell & Campbell *P-51* 50: Jazz Baby [name painted on nose of airplane]. **1974** Lahr *Trot* 86: I like to sing, George, but I'm no jazz baby. **1978** C. Crawford *Mommie* 19: The "jazz baby"…was finally becoming a lady.

jazzbo *n.* [orig. unkn., if not JAZZ + BO[1], 1] **1.** *Vaudeville.* **a.** low physical comedy; slapstick; vulgarity. Also **jasbo**.

[**1917** J.N. Klohr *Jasmo* [one-step dance tune] [Cincinnati, Ohio: John Church Co., 1917]. **1917** *Lit. Digest* (Sept. 25) 28: "Jasbo" is a form of the word common in the varieties, meaning the same as "hokum," or low comedy verging on vulgarity. **1917** *N.Y. Times* (Dec. 23) IV 6: "Jasbo" is actual vulgarity in desperation to force laughter. **1923** *N.Y. Times* (Sept. 9) VII 2: *Jazzbo*—Bladder and slapstick comedy. **1927** W. Winchell, in *Vanity Fair* (Nov.) 132: Jazz comes from the idea that a score is jazzed into an arrangement that is jasbo—a slang expression used many years ago by minstrels who resorted to cheap stuff for laugh material. Jazz…is musical hokum entertainment. "Hokum"…is low-down stuff. Actors who redden their noses, and wear ill-fitting apparel, and take falls to get laughs, are "hokum comics."

b. (see 1926 quot.).

1926 Whiteman & McBride *Jazz* 122: Sousa…says jazz slid into our vocabulary by way of the vaudeville stage, where at the end of a performance all the acts came back on the stage to give a rousing,

boisterous *finale* called a "jazzbo." **1947** Runyon *Poems for Men* 74 [ref. to 1917]: And your heart is aching/When you hear that sweet jazboe.

2. a black person, esp. a man.—used derisively. Also jasbo.

1918 *N.Y. Times* (Nov. 3): Yankee "Jazz Boes," as American coloured troops are called in France, constructing a railway behind the front lines. **1918** Woollcott *Command Is Forward* 23: French lancers, French of many a uniform, Jasbos and doughboys, doughboys, doughboys. **1919** G. Swan *Jazzing in Jazzbo Town* [pop. song] [N.Y.: George Swan, 1919]. **1919** Jacobsen *Blue & Gray* 113: What are you doing, Private Jasbo? **1942** *ATS* 573: *Jazz-bo, jazzbo*, a negro performer, esp. in a minstrel show. **1964** *PADS* (No. 42) 35: *Spook, spade,* and *jazzbo* were…elicited only from Negroes in this survey, but these three, especially the first two, are common [also] in the speech of Caucasian Chicagoans. **1968** Cuomo *Thieves* 288: Let him teach some of those jazzbos…how to hold a goddam wrench then, because let's face it, Mel hadn't yet met a nigger that knew which end went in your hand.

3. a man who is a jazz enthusiast; jazz musician. [The intended sense of the 1918 quot. is not at all clear.]

[**1918** P. Bradford *The Bullfrog Hop* (pop. song): First you commence to wiggle from side to side,/Get way back and do the Jazzbo Glide.] **1921** in Charter & Kunstadt *Jazz* 99: Lillyn Brown and her JazzBo Syncopators. **1940** *New Yorker* (Sept. 14) 18: Jazz Beau. **1950** *Time* (Dec. 11) 45: Like many another jazzbo, Muggsy drifted out of jazz into the bigger money. **1960** *New Yorker* (Nov. 5) 130: The good old jazzbo look of the twenties. **1962** *Time* (Feb. 2) 49: Progressive jazzbo (Bobby Darin) goes commercial; loses art, loses heart, loses girl. **1982** Sculatti *Catalog of Cool* 122: The new wave of beatniks, jazzbos, potheads and proto-punks.

4. BOZO.

1923 Witwer *Fighting Blood* 272: The old jazzbo shuts me off kind of angrily. *Ibid.* 302: Bootlicking jazzbos…worship the ground he walks on. **1930** Bodenheim *Roller Skates* 45: Want some gas, jazzbo? **1926–35** Watters & Hopkins *Burlesque* 49: Say, Bonn, when are you goin' to marry this jazzbo you wrote about? **1939** C.R. Cooper *Scarlet* 79: She meets some jazzbo who asks her why she should work for pretzels, pounding the streets and turning over everything she makes to me. **1957** Kohner *Gidget* 44: Listen, Jazz-bo…I know your mom a lot better than you do. **1974** Eble *Campus Slang* (Mar.) 3: *Jazzbo*—a fool or idiot. **1988** Chi. woman, age *ca*40: She's doing much better with the new doctor now that we got that jazzbo off the case.

jazzed *adj.* **1.** excited or enthusiastic.—also constr. with *up*.

1918 in Braynard *Greatest Ship* I 202: As a lady-killer, Mackintosh…gets the [girls] all jazzed up before they can get their second wind. **1943** in Eichelberger *Dear Miss Em* 73: At first, I was all jazzed up. **1947–48** J.H. Burns *Lucifer* 63: We couldn't get the results we do Around Here if we weren't all jazzed up. **1957** Kohner *Gidget* 24: I felt so jazzed up about this ride I could have yelled. *a*1961 Boroff *Campus U.S.A.* 46: "Jazzed" means feeling good, while "unjazzed" means depressed. **1966** Kenney *Caste* 53: What gives with old "Dean" Kaplan that he's so jazzed up about? **1968** Kirk & Heanle *Surfer's Hndbk.* 141: *Jazzed*: excited, keyed up, stoked. **1970** Grissim *Country Music* 228: I was just excited. Lord, I was so jazzed I think I wrote fourteen songs in the first week I was there. **1979** Hiler *Monkey Mt.* 303: Ah, Jesus, it's beautiful. Work eight to four, then take off and go wherever the hell you want to! I couldn't believe it. I was so fuckin' jazzed. **1986** Gilmour *Pretty in Pink* 143: Any girl that did that to me, I wouldn't be too jazzed to hold onto. **1988** *Day by Day* (NBC-TV): Man, I'm really jazzed about my trip to the Ice Age! **1989** *Roseanne* (ABC-TV): Sometimes I get jazzed about stuff that isn't even going to happen. **1992** *Stand By Your Man* (Fox-TV): Everybody was pretty jazzed.

2. intoxicated by liquor or drugs; HIGH.—usu. constr. with *up*.

1919 Wiley *Wildcat* 194: When I aims to git jazzed up I aims to git jazzed up. **1927** (quot. at POTTED). **1963** J. Ross *Dead Are Mine* 262 [ref. to 1944]: All jazzed up like this I'd drive right through the goddamn lines and end up right with the Krauts.

jazzer *n.* a catch; hidden difficulty.

1918 Guttersen *Granville* (Aug. 18) 47: There is absolutely no cause for worry, as all the possible "jazzers" can be discovered if the ship is properly inspected, and ours always is.

jazz garden *n.* an establishment where jazz dancing takes place.

1922 in *DN* V 148: *Jazz garden*—a cafe where dancing is permitted.

jazzhound *n.* **1.** an enthusiast or performer of jazz music.

1920 in Rust *Jazz Records* II 1460: Mamie Smith…Acc. by her Jazz

Hounds. **1928** Dahlberg *Bottom Dogs* 274: The L.A. jazzhounds shook a wicked hoof. **1929** Zombaugh *Gold Coast* 106: The prostitute, the dopey, the jazz hound, the gold digger.

2. a sexually promiscuous person.

1928 Dahlberg *Bottom Dogs* 263: Jack Gray…was a jazzhound in more than one way before his several operations.

jazz house *n.* a brothel.

1927 (quot. at JAZZ, *v.*, 1). **1928** R. Fisher *Jericho* 181: This burg has walls around it so thick that the gals could have their jazz-houses on top—not a bad idea at all; if a tight Oscar held out on 'em, they could jes' let him out on the wrong side o' the wall.

jazz up *v.* see JAZZ, *v.*, 3.a.

jazzy *adj.* **1.** exciting; lively; snappy.

1917 *Variety* (Nov. 30) 19: It is a dance number of the jazzy syncopated type. **1918** in Brunn *Orig. Jazz Band* 61: There's a jazzy band that's got me dippy. *Ibid.* 62: Ask that leader to play/That jazzy every day. **1922** *DN* V 142: College Slang…*jazzy*…animated, full of life. "She's the jazziest girl in Pem East." *a***1927** in *Jour. Abnormal & Soc. Psych.* XXII (1927) 15: I want a jazzy kiss. **1938** R. Chandler *Big Sleep* ch. xx: She'd make a jazzy week-end, but she'd be wearing for a steady diet. **1956** E. Hunter *Second Ending* 314: There was a real monkey on his back, and, gee, ain't that a jazzy way of saying it, real gone. **1957** in Elliot *Among the Dangs* 178: It wasn't the jazziest newreel I ever saw, but it was a popular success all right. **1966** Susann *Valley of Dolls* 22: Boy, it sure sounds jazzy working in that office. **1976** *Sat. Review* (Sept. 18) 12: The jazzy layout…made a textbook look like a sales brochure.

2. fancy; flashy; SNAZZY.

1923 M. Cowley, in Jay *Burke-Cowley Corres.* 147: I wrote a jazz poem in jazzy prose. **1937** in *AS* (1938) 46: *Jazzy*…showy, ostentatious. **1957** E. Lacy *Room to Swing* 124: What's wrong with that jazzy car you had?…You crash it? **1960** D. Hamilton *Death of a Citizen* 72: Some kind of a jazzy Plymouth with fins like a shark. **1962** Mahurin *Honest John* 29: These were jazzy red affairs with the insignia of each squadron brocaded in the middle. **1990** *Nation* (Aug. 13) 179: These film-makers love the old American B movies, but they express their admiration in a far less jazzy style. **1991** D. Anderson *In Corner* 71: People drove up in jazzy cars.

J.B. *n.* **1.** a hat made by the J.B. Stetson Company.

1930 "D. Stiff" *Milk & Honey* 138: The favorite adornment for the hobo head is a high-crowned and narrow-brimmed Stetson felt, which he calls a "J.B."

2. *Black E.* (see 1946 quot.).

1946 Mezzrow & Wolfe *Really Blues* 307: *J.B.*: jet black, a very dark Negro. **1994** in *Comments on Ety.* (Mar. 1995) 36: It might have been a reference to the Southern term *jay-bee* (for J.B., meaning a black person).

J-bird *n. Poker.* (see 1951 quot.).

1951 *AS* (May) 99: *J-bird.* A jack or knave. **1978** (cited in T.L. Clark *Dict. Gamb. & Gaming*).

J City *n. Local.* Jefferson City, Mo.

1957 H. Simmons *Corner Boy* 88: Who you know in J City?

J.C.L. *n.* JOHNNY-COME-LATELY; novice.

1942 *AS* XVII 91: Pitchmen's Cant…I guess that makes me a J.C.L. **1942–49** Goldin et al. *DAUL* 110: *J.C.L.* (Carnival…) A tyro; an inexperienced operator. *a***1962** Maurer & Vogel *Narc. Add.* 308: *J.C.L.*…A beginning addict. **1970** A. Lewis *Carnival* 26: Sam's the patch and only a J.C.L. but a fast learner. **1972** in J. Flaherty *Chez Joey* 216: A j-c-l [said] that if it weren't for the young holding up [their] end, not an ounce of grain would be shoveled out of a ship.

J.C. maneuver *n.* [*J.C.* (abbr. *Jesus Christ!*) + *maneuver*] *Av.* any of various desperate maneuvers taken to guide an aircraft out of an emergency. *Joc.*

1972–79 T. Wolfe *Right Stuff* 170 [ref. to *ca*1960]: In the J.C. maneuver you take your hands off the controls and put the mother in the lap of a su-per-na-tu-ral power. **1993** T. Taylor *Lightning in Storm* 171 [ref. to 1991]: The Apaches react instinctively, tense for a "JC maneuver" (Jesus Christ, here comes a SAM!)—a climb for the sun, the ultimate source toward which heat-seeking SAM's can be deflected.

JD *n.* **1.** *Orig. Police.* a juvenile delinquent; (*also*) juvenile delinquency.

1956 P. Moore *Chocolates for Breakfast* 97: I felt like a J.D. or something. **1959** N.Y.C. schoolboy: The kid's a JD. **1961** H. Ellison *Purgatory* 37: I *was* a hard rock j.d. from that moment on. **1965** Yurick *War-*

riors 88: An indignant voice said, "God-damned J.D.s." **1966** Young & Hixson *LSD* 6: Whatever happened to…Juvenile Delinquency?…The diethylamide of lysergic acid is what happened to JD. **1969** Moynahan *Pairing Off* 139: A hot-rod full of leather-jacketed J.D.'s went roaring past with a skull-and-crossbones pennon streaming from the radio aerial. **1973** Browne *Body Shop* 144: In high school I started being a JD. I stole cars, robbed houses, got caught on drug charges. **1978** Fisher & Rubin *Special Teachers* 27: I thought there was nothing but black JDs at that place. **1983** Marum & Parise *Follies* 95: All the national magazines [in the mid-1950's] were full of talk of juvenile delinquency (or "JD," as nearly everyone called it). **1981–85** S. King *It* 225: With Henry and his j.d. friends maybe still wandering around out there. **1988** *Miami Vice* (NBC-TV): How did four JD's with rap sheets like this ever get on the force?

2. *Police.* JOHN DOE.

1977 B. Davidson *Collura* 69: In short, there were four J.D.'s whom only Collura could find, and he was sent out to find them.

3. Jack Daniel's brand of sour-mash whiskey.

1981 (cited in Spears *Drugs & Drink* 287). **1984** Glick *Winters Coming* 296: Scotch water, JD rocks. **1985** N. Kazan *At Close Range* (film): We just wanted a bottle of JD. *a***1989** Berent *Rolling Thunder* 377: Gimme a double JD, straight. **1989** Leib *Fire Dream* 374: Now I owe…two cases of JD. **1990** *Mystery Sci. Theater* (Comedy Central TV): Here, suck on a little JD, buddy. **1993** Mowry *Six Out Seven* 51: How much it cost you…for this here J.D.?

jeans *n.pl.* ¶ In phrases:

¶ **cream (one's) jeans** see s.v. CREAM, *v.*

¶ **in (one's) jeans** in (one's) trouser pockets.

[**1895** Townsend *Fadden* 67: I taut de mug would slug me an' drag me jeans fer de boodle.] **1902** Townsend *Fadden & Mr. Paul* 82: Dat's pretty good woik for a loidy what's always making a holler dat she hasn't a penny in her jeans. **1904** Hobart *Jim Hickey* 35: Wouldn't we be a nice pair of turtles to stand around with coin in our jeans and see a nice girl like Amy getting the ice? **1907** J. London *Road* 13 [ref. to 1892]: I hadn't the price of the railroad fare in my jeans. **1910** Raine *O'Connor* 24: Dig up, Mr. Pullman. Go way down into your jeans. **1917–19** J. Boyle *Boston Blackie* 68: With the stranger's dough in his jeans. **1919** T. Kelly *What Outfit?* 76: I had a bar or two of chocolate in my jeans. **1922** *Variety* (June 30) 6: When they get one with his duke in somebody's jeans they throw the key away on him. **1927** H. Miller *Moloch* 147: I left…with seventy-five bucks in my jeans. **1942** *Yank* (July 1) 14: I got 57 fish in my jeans. **1954–60** *DAS* x: To be…without a *hog* in one's *jeans* is…more vivid and forceful than being penniless. **1963** *Twilight Zone* (CBS-TV): Career shot. Roughly eight dollars in your jeans. **1968** Smart *Long Watch* 160: My take came to about six hundred dollars, and I hadn't had that much money in my jeans for years.

jeasley, jeasly vars. JEEZLY.

Jebby *n.* a Jesuit.

1947 Sylvester *Moon Gaffney* 60: The Jebbies will give you space in their basement. **1965** Gallery *Eight Bells* 27 [ref. to *ca*1917]: The Latin, Greek, and ancient history that the Jesuits taught were of no use on those exams. The Jebbies didn't bear down too hard on Math, and the Navy did. **1971** Horan *Blue Messiah* 28: There's a great old Jebbie down at Xavier. **1977** Dunne *Confessions* 43: The jebbies wanted the Cardinal's approval on that new dormitory.

jeebies *n.pl.* HEEBIE-JEEBIES.

1938 "R. Hallas" *You Play the Black* 169: I began to get the jeebies.

jeeby *adj.* afflicted with HEEBIE-JEEBIES.

1989 P. Benchley *Rummies* 323: Y'okay, boss?…Lookin' jeeby.

jeep *n.* [fr. Eugene the *Jeep*, a small "fourth-dimensional" animal of comical appearance and amazing powers introduced by cartoonist E.C. Segar in his syndicated comic strip "Thimble Theater," March 3, 1936, and featured prominently thereafter; as the creature uttered no sound but *jeep! jeep!*, the word may well have occurred to Segar as an alter. of *cheep!*, a freq. representation in cartoons of the cry of small birds]

1. the cartoon character introduced by Segar.—also used fig.

1936 in Sagendorf *Popeye* 88: Eugene the "Jeep."…"Aw, it's some sort of a pet, I guess." "I never heard of a jeep." **1938** in *Great Music of D. Ellington* 132: The Jeep Is Jumping. **1953** LeVier & Guenther *Pilot*

86 [ref. to 1938]: Art Chester was flying the *Jeep*...and Steve Wittman was on hand with...*Bonzo* and...*Chief Oshkosh*.

2. [infl. by *JP*] a justice of the peace.

    1936 in Weinberg *Tough Guys* 6: You had to hock the engagement ring with the jeep for his fee and twenty dollars.

3. a foolish, inexperienced, or offensive individual; (*Mil.*) a recruit or basic trainee.

    1938 *Sat. Eve. Post* (July 16) 16: The Jeep [title]...He's been all over the country, popping sodas here and there, but with all that practice he's still a jeep. He'll never have the speed and accuracy of a fast worker. *ca***1939** in Fitzgerald *Notebooks* 297: Slang (collegiate). A Jeep....Orchid Consumer. **1941** in Cannon *Nobody Asked* 312: The chow line stretched from the processing building to the mess hall, where the jeeps eat their first meal in the army. They were [still] in civilian clothes. **1941** Kendall *Army & Navy Sl.* 8: In some camps a jeep is a rookie. **1942** *Sat. Eve. Post* (May 30) 67: He's an apprentice, a recruit, a rookie, a jeep. **1942** *Leatherneck* (June) 59: He's got the Lifebuoy habit, you jeep. **1943** *Yank* (May 7) 14: The Jeep felt glad as he saw the flag. **1970** *Current Slang V* (Summer) 16: *Jeep, n.* An inexperienced Air Force enlisted man or officer.—"He just got out of basic—he's a *jeep*."..."A jeep lieutenant." *a***1989** in Kisseloff *Must Remember This* 64 [ref. to *ca*1940]: My other brother, who was never in a hurry, they called him Jeep.

4.a. Esp. *Mil.* any of various relatively small motor vehicles, esp. (now solely, and capitalized as a trademark) the versatile, low-silhouette four-wheel drive reconnaissance car produced orig. for U.S. Army use by Willys-Overland Motors (a predecessor of Jeep Corporation, now owned by Chrysler). [In the specific sense, now S.E. A putative origin as an alter. of *GP* for 'general purpose' appears to be unfounded.]

    1940 (cited in *W10*). **1941** *Washington* (D.C.) *Daily News* (Feb. 20) 12: The first Jeep to conquer the cliffs of Rock Creek Park charged up and down brambled precipices yesterday....Technically, the baby brute is called the "¼–4x4," and Jeep is a pet name....At present the Army only owns 70. **1941** *N.Y. Times* (Feb. 22) 8: Army's "Jeep" Car Balks at City Hall....Officially termed a reconnaissance car and dubbed "jeep," "quad," or "bug" by Army men, the small open vehicle was one of two test cars built by Willys-Overland...which expects to begin production in four or five weeks on 1,500 such cars ordered by the Army. Like orders are held by Ford and Bantam in addition to seventy Bantams the Army now has. **1941** *Nat. Geo.* (July) 25: This midget car—a "Jeep" in army slang—rushes into field maneuvers. **1941** *Infantry Journal* (July) 68: By comparing the lists I have seen in various newspapers and magazines I find that a "jeep" is a bantam car...and an artillery primemover....I thought it was one of those little wheeled tractors they use in factories to pull mill trucks. **1941** *Army Ordnance* (July) 79: *Jeep*...Command car....Bantam car. **1941** *AS* (Oct.) 166: *Jeep*. A term applied to bantam cars, and occasionally to other motor vehicles; in the Air Corps, the Link trainer; in the Armored Force, the 1½ ton command car. **1942** Kahn *Army Life* 136: Soldiers are not even agreed on precisely what vehicle should be called a jeep. In some camps, it is a larger, less bouncy machine, and the midget car is known as a "peep." **1943** R.G. McCloskey, in *Amer. N & Q* (Dec.) 136: From the days of the early [1939–40] experiments at the Infantry and Cavalry schools it was variously referred to as a "puddle jumper," "blitz buggy," "jeep," and "peep"—regardless of whether it was a ¼-ton or ½-ton truck....In April, 1940...I [founder of *Army Motors* magazine] laid down an editorial ukase that the ¼-ton truck thereafter was to be the "jeep," and the ½-ton the "peep"—and since our circulation ran into the hundreds of thousands the names stuck. **1944** *Amer. N & Q* (Jan.) 156: In November, 1940, our firm, Willys-Overland Motors, Inc., delivered a pilot model of a ¼-ton combat car....Army employees [at Camp Holabird, Md.] nicknamed the Willys vehicle the jeep. *Ibid.* (May) 26: Earle Palmer Halliburton,...of Oklahoma and California, turned out, in 1937, a commercial vehicle—half truck and half tractor—which he himself named the "Jeep." **1944** *N.Y. Times Mag.* (July 2) 38: The soldier's affection for the jeep is based on something much more than simple sentiment. **1950** Boehm *Union Station* (film): I always wanted one of these jeeps [*sc.* a trolley having rimmed wheels for use in subway maintenance]. **1954** *AS* XXIX 260 [ref. to WWII]: We [in the 8th Armored Division] always made a point of referring to the ¼-ton truck as a *peep,* using *jeep* for the ½-ton car, but I follow here the present common use of *jeep* for the ¼-ton truck. **1962** *AS* XXXVII 77: The old command and reconnaissance car...was a large, very powerful,

five-seated touring car, developed, I believe, about 1939, to enable officers to move over any kind of terrain in comfort....Those of us in uniform and on maneuvers during the summer and fall of 1941 referred to that car as a *jeep*. **1989** Berent *Rolling Thunder* 63: Take my jeep. **1992** *Smithsonian* (Nov.) 63: The nickname "jeep" caught on quickly though its derivation is obscure. Some attribute it to Ford's Model GP. Others cite...Eugene the Jeep.

    b. *Mil.* (see quot.).

    1942–47 *ATS* (Supp.) 32: *Jeep,* a tiny observation plane.

5. *Mil.* any small object or device; gadget.

    1942 *Yank* (Nov. 11) 4: Navy [slang]...*Jeep*—Not a recruit or a four-wheeled vehicle, but a gadget used in gunfire. **1942** E.J. Kahn *Army Life* 136: "Jeep"...[is] now being applied to all small military objects. **1945** *AS* XX 261: In the Army *jeep* means a certain type of vehicle or a recruit, and has a host of other meanings at individual posts. **1942–47** *ATS* (Supp.) 20: *Jeep,* an all-inclusive nickname for anything insignificant or small.

6. *Mil. Av.* a Link Radio, Instrument, and Navigation Trainer.

    1941 (*AS* quot. at (4), above). **1942** *Randolph Field* 77: The Link Trainer—which aviation cadets call "The Jeep"—has made ground instruction possible.

7. *Navy.* an escort carrier. Now *hist.* In full, **jeep carrier.** [Quots. ref. to WWII.]

    1944 in Loosbrock & Skinner *Wild Blue* 269: Three "jeep" carriers were being shelled. **1945** Hamann *Air Words* 32: *Jeep.* A small aircraft carrier; baby flat-top. **1950** *Life* (July 24) 32: A crew of men swarmed aboard the U.S.S. *Cape Esperance*...a 10,000-ton "jeep" carrier. **1951** [VMF-323] *Old Ballads* 40: On a jeep carrier far out at sea/That's where you'll find ol' 323. **1956** Lockwood *Zoomies* 9: CVE's (escort aircraft carriers, better known as "jeep" carriers). **1956** Morison *Naval Ops. in WWII* X 41: *Casablanca,* first of these "jeep carriers" or "baby flattops," was not actually commissioned until July 1943. **1989** T. Blackburn *Jolly Rogers* 87: The jeep carrier *Prince William*..."Pee Willie" as she was universally called. **1991** Linnekin *80 Knots* 96: Smaller carriers, specifically the "Jeeps." **1995** Gingrich & Forstchen *1945* 379: Just the jeeps and the lame-duck carriers.

8. *Av.* (see quot.). Now *hist.*

    1991 Honey *Wing Must Fly* (Discovery Channel TV): The [Northrop] N-1M [in 1940] was known as "The Jeep."

jeep cap *n. Army.* (see quot.). Now *hist.*

    1990 Katcher *Amer. Soldier* 130 [ref. to WWII]: OD M1941 wool knit "jeep" caps...had a small stiff bill and knit ear flaps.

jeeped up *adj.* excited.

    1979 *Film Comment* XV (No. 4) 69: Occasionally, one turns on the set to get jeeped up (a big boxing match, an angry segment on *Sixty Minutes*).

jeepers *interj.* [var. Hiberno-E *japers!,* euphem. for *Jesus!*] (used as a mild oath).

    1928 Edmonds *Rome Haul* 16 [ref. to 19th C.]: Gentleman Joe. Jeepers! *Ibid.* 33: By Jeepers, George,...there ain't no ways out of it now! **1930** *AS* VI 98: *Jeepers*—an expression of astonishment. "By Jeepers!" **1936** Gaddis *Courtesan* 41: Well, jumpin' jeepers, if it ain't Dave's gal friend. **1942–43** C. Jackson *Lost Weekend* 69: Jeepers, Sam, you're certainly taking your time. **1945** D. Nichols *Scarlet St.* (film): Jeepers, I love you, Johnny! **1958** Hailey & Castle *Runway* 14: Jeepers, that's a likely story. **1965** Hersey *Too Far to Walk* 214: And then, jeepers, I really flipped. **1965** Spillane *Killer Mine* 28: Jeepers. She put her coffee down and walked away. **1974** *New Times* (Sept. 20) 38: "Jeepers," says Verdehan. **1976** Haseltine & Yaw *Woman Doctor* 55: "Jeepers." Dick's reaction was laconic. **1986** L. Johnson *Waves* 138: Jeepers! I'm already almost twenty-one years old. **1992** G. Wolff *Day at the Beach* 4: Jeepers!...I still don't know half the stuff in here. **1993** *New Yorker* (Oct. 6) 184: "Jeepers, it's cold...in here."..."She was always very conscientious about changing the exclamation "Jesus" to "Jeepers."

jeepers creepers *interj.* [euphem. for *Jesus Christ!,* elaborated from JEEPERS] (used as a mild or joc. oath). Also (*obs.*) **Jeepers Cripus.**

    1928 Edmonds *Rome Haul* 24 [ref. to 19th C.]: Spinning swore...Jeepers Cripus! **1937** in Grayson *New Stories* 148: Jeepers Creepers! **1938** Mercer & Warren (pop. song): Jeepers Creepers! [title]...Jeepers creepers! Where'd you get those peepers? **1944** in Bechet *Treat It Gentle* 227: Jeepers creepers. **1980** Conroy *Lords of Discipline* 94: Jeepers-creepers, you must be something very special. ***1992** *Absolutely Fabulous* (BBC-TV): Jeepers creepers!

jeepy *adj.* [JEEP, *n.*, 3 + -*y*] silly, crazy, or obnoxious.
    1941 Kendall *Army & Navy Sl.* 8: He's jeepy....not quite all there.

jeeter *n.* an ignorant countryman.
    [**1941** *AS* (Oct.) 166: *Jeeter.* A lieutenant.] **1954–60** *DAS: Jeeter*...A slovenly, ill-mannered person. From the character Jeeter Lester in E. Caldwell's novel *Tobacco Road.* **1968** "R. Hooker" *M*A*S*H* 100 [ref. to 1951]: I thought I lived with the two biggest rubes in Korea until this jeeter came along.

Jeez *interj.* [short for *Jesus!*] (used as a mild or euphem. oath). Also vars.
    *ca*1830 in Harlow *Old Bowery* 151: Tougher than a b'iled owl, b'Jes'! **1920** S. Lewis *Main Street,* in *DARE:* Jeeze, you'd 'a' died laughing. **1927–28** in R. Nelson *Dishonorable* 111: Jeez, you would! **1928** in E. Ferber *One Basket* 323: Sweet jeez, lookit. **1931** Rouverol *Dance, Fools, Dance* (film): For Jeez' sake, give us a break! **1932** Brody *Nobody Starves* 5: Geeze, we looked for you everywhere. **1933** Waters & White *B.E.F.* 100: Jeeze, you guys are a nice pair of "Reds." **1926–35** Watters & Hopkins *Burlesque* 11: Jees, Bonny, I don't wanna go. **1936** Monks & Finklehoffe *Brother Rat* 197: Leapin' geez! **1953** Manchester *City of Anger* 14: Jees, he thought bleakly....They never ever let a guy alone. **1966** Susann *Valley of Dolls* 21: Geez, you mean nobody told you about it? **1978** B. Johnson *What's Happenin'* 152: Jeez, these guys have good contacts back home. **1980** J. Carroll *Land of Laughs* 49: Jeez, I couldn't say what my favorite scene is. **1977–81** S. King *Cujo* 63: "Jeez, Mom, I don't know—" "Don't say jeez. It's just the same as swearing." **1987** B. Breathed *Bloom Co.* (synd. comic strip) (May 27): Jeez! I got 23 genetically pure, tube-grown kids I need advice! **1989** Hiaasen *Skin Tight* 2: Geez, you're right! **1996** *Time* (Apr. 8) 13: Ah, jeez, do you have to be a transplanted Midwesterner to appreciate the brothers Coen?

jeezer *n. N.E.* **1.** a fellow; JOKER.
    1972 in J. Gould *Maine Lingo* 146: The poor *jeezer* hardly got a word in edgewise. **1978** in *DARE* [ref. to Maine, *ca*1910]: A young jeezer with a tendency to spread himself around [hanging May baskets] would get an awful lot of popcorn and cocoa.

    2. something, as a storm, that is violent or remarkable.
    1981–85 S. King *It* 432: A proper old jeezer is starting to crank up outside. **1987** S. King *Misery* 11: It's going to be a proper jeezer and nobody is prepared.

Jeezle *interj.* [JEEZ + -*le* (perh. infl. by JEEZLY)] JEEZ. Also **jee-zle-peezle.**
    [**1942** in *AS* XVIII (1943) 154: *Jeezy Peezy.* An expression denoting surprise or disgust.] **1972** Carpentier *Flt. One* 204: "Jeezle-peezle!" said the young man...."Jeezle!" **1995** *Jerry Springer Show* (synd. TV series): Jeezle! I wanna go home.

jeezly *adj.* [reduction of *Jesusly*] **1.** darned; damned. Also **Jesusly** (*obs.*), **jeasley, jeasly.**
    1885 in Lummis *Letters* 228: "What a jesusly time" he had killing off...Navajos. **1930** S. Holbrook, in *Amer. Mercury* (Oct.) 236: Tell him...that here is his jeasley ol' pie and biscuit irons. **1938** S. Holbrook *Mackinaw* 187: Are you the bouncer in every jeasley saloon in this town? **1975** J. Gould *Maine Lingo* 146: Don't be so *jeezly* hard to get along with!...I never saw such *jeezly* poor fishing! **1980** in *N.E. Folklore* XXVIII (1988) 41: And, Jesus, it'd cut your jeasly head...right off. **1981–85** S. King *It* 358: A horse stall was his first thought, but who kept horses in the jeezly cellar?

    2. inferior; unsatisfactory.
    1992 *UTSQ:* What a jeezly party/dress/speech!

Jeff *n. Black E.* JEFF DAVIS; (*hence*) a stupid or inconsequential fellow; (*rarely*) a white man. [The 1917 quot. is a nonce reference to the popular comic strip "Mutt and Jeff" by Bud Fisher and does not illustrate the present sense of the word.]
    [**1917** in Cummings *Letters* 26: I escaped repairing with the bums, mutts and Jeffs.] **1938** Calloway *Hi De Ho* 16: *Jeff*—A pest, bore, icky. **1944** Burley *Hndbk. Jive* 141: *Jeff*—Someone who is not interesting, a pest. **1946** (quot. at JEFF DAVIS). **1961** R. Russell *Sound* 144: Them Jeffs is workin' together! **1964** R.S. Gold *Jazz Talk: Jeff*...A white person, but esp. one who is hostile to blacks. **1967** in *PADS* (No. 51) (Apr. 1969) 29: *Names* [for a black man who is subservient toward whites] used exclusively by Negroes...*jeff,...jeff davis, jeff artist, renegade shuffler, uncle tom.* **1970** Major *Afro-Amer. Slang* 70: *Jeff* (1930's)...a dull person; a horrible square.

Jeff *adj.* **1.** JEFF DAVIS.

    1863 H.Y. Thompson *In Civil War* 109: They had not seen coffee for a long time, but drank what they called "Jeff Coffee" being wheat or barley roasted and ground as if it were coffee.

    2. *Black E.* being or characteristic of a JEFF.
    1972 Andrews & Dickens *Big House* 22: He figured if he could work the Jeff Game right, he might be able to pick up enough for a meal. **1973** *Black World* (Apr.) 57: He wears a jeff hat and a light raincoat; his face shows the good-natured smile that earned him his street-name, "Sugar-Mouth."

jeff¹ *v.* [orig. unkn.] (among printers) (see *a*1889 quot.). [Moxon, whose book is still a standard text, describes the game in detail but never uses the term *jeff.*]
    [***1683–84** J. Moxon *Mechanick Exercises on the Whole Art of Printing* 324: They take five or seven or more m Quadrats (generally of the English body) and holding their hand below the surface of the correcting stone, shake them in their hand, and toss them up upon the stone, and then count how many nicks upwards each man throws in three times, or any other number of times agreed on: and he that throws most wins the bett [*sic*] of all the rest.] **1837** in Thornton *Amer. Gloss.:* We now that the printers of the U.S. divide of stone, halves, and "jeff" to see which shall go to digging ditches or picking stone coal for a living. **1868–71** C.G. Leland *Breitman's Ballads* 235: Jours.../ Who vouldt nefer Jeff no more. ***1888** Jacobi *Printers' Vocab.* 68: *Jeff.*—To throw or gamble with quadrats as with dice. **1888** in *F & H* IV 43: He...would smouch all the poetry, and leave the rest to jeff for the solid takes. *a*1889 *Century Dict.: Jeff.*...Among printers, to play a game of chance by throwing quadrats from the hand in the manner of dice, count being kept by the number of nicked sides turned up. **1891** Maitland *Slang Dict.* 153: *Jeff,* in printer's slang, to gamble by throwing "quads." Printers will "jeff" for anything—for the choice of the first "take" on the hook or for the beer, or their week's wages. **1932** in *Amer. N & Q* (May 1948) 31 [ref. to Calif., 1890's]: They would jeff quads...to determine who would be stuck for a pail of suds. **1944** in *Amer. N & Q* (Jan. 1945) 150: Jeffing...was once popular in printing offices. Apparently, em quads only were used, with the nick side representing *one* and the other sides *nought.*...a toss was called a "mary" or "mollie" if none of the nicks appeared uppermost in the throw. **1967** in *OED2: Jeffing*...is a very old custom, but now almost entirely out of practice. **1996** N.Y.C. typographer (coll. J. Sheidlower): I think it's safe to say that no one jeffs anymore, since it's pretty hard to even find two people setting type by hand in the same room.

jeff² *v.* [shift of JEFF, *n.*] *Black E.* (of a black person) to behave obsequiously toward whites, as by being an informer, UNCLE TOM, etc.; attempt to ingratiate oneself (with anyone) through obsequious or subservient behavior; humiliate oneself. Hence **jeffer.**
    1960 C. Cooper *Scene* 38: Alice looked guilty, then said, false-smiling, jeffing, "He sold it to me." *Ibid.* 308: *Jeff:* to ingratiate oneself shamelessly. *a*1962 Maurer & Vogel *Narc. Add.* (ed. 2) 308: *Jeff.* To be obsequious, esp. Negroes in relation to whites. **1967** in *PADS* (No. 42) (Apr. 1969) 29: *Jeffer,...uncle tom.* **1968** I. Reed *Yellow Back Radio* 93: He was nothing but a jeffing coon. **1969** C. Major *All-Night Visitors* 27: A slightly low way of *jeffing.* **1970** Cain *Blueschild Baby* 37: Only brothers they going to tell you about is those good jeffin' niggers. **1970** Major *Afro-Amer. Slang* 70: *Jeff*...to inform on someone. **1970** E. Knight *Black Voices* 80: You old Uncle Tom, stop jeffing so much. **1976** in *DARE* s.v. *boojum:* If you try to become friendly with the "boojums," you are accused of "jeffing." **1978** Sopher & McGregor *Up from Walking Dead* 20: I had never seen so much jeffin' in one room.

Jeff City *n. Local.* Jefferson City, Mo.
    1899 A.H. Lewis *Sandburrs* 26: D' cat-o'-nine-tails, which dey has at Jeff City, ain't a marker to d' dark hole. **1994** Weather Channel (Aug. 1): Possibly even in Jeff City.

Jeff Davis *n. Black E.* a black man from the rural South, esp. if obsequious to whites.—also used attrib.
    1946 Mezzrow & Wolfe *Really Blues* 187 [ref. to 1930's]: He's a Jeff Davis...and ain't been up here a hot minute. *Ibid.* 307: *Jeff Davis:* an unenlightened person, a hick from down south, sometimes shortened to *jeff.* **1967** (quot. at JEFF). **1972** A. Kemp *Savior* 9: Jeff Davis bastard!

Jeff Davis *adj.* [pop. nickname of *Jefferson Davis,* president of the Confederate States of America] of the Confederate States of America; Southern. Now *hist.*
    1885 (quot. at LINCOLN, *adj.*). **1941** in *DA:* My folks parched wheat

and we called it "Jef Davis Coffee."…Jef Davis money…was the confederate money.

Jeff Davis box *n. Confed. Army.* (see quot.).
   1871 Schele de Vere *Amer.* 283: The *Musical Box* of the Confederates was also known as *Jeff Davis' Box:* it was the humorous name given by the men to the lumbering, ill-built army-wagons, which were apt to creak horribly for want of greasing.

Jeff Davis necktie *n. Union Army.* an iron rail severed from a Southern railroad track, heated till pliable, and twisted about a tree trunk to prevent its reuse.
   1864 in J.W. Haley *Rebel Yell* 226: The rails were heated and bent into fantastic shapes around the trees. We facetiously call these "Jeff Davis's neckties." *ca*1885 A.C. Stearns *Co. K* 230: When red hot, take the rails by the ends and twist them around a telegraph pole. These were called Jeff Davis necktie[s].

Jeff's boys *n.pl. Union Army.* Confederate soldiers.
   1863 [Fitch] *Annals of Army* 639: Two of "Jeff's boys"…were neatly ensconced in the cupboard.

Jehosaphat *interj.* [var. of *Jehoshaphat*, King of Judah, in 2 Chron. 17–21, used as a euphem. for *Jehovah* or *Jesus*] (used as a mild or joc. oath). [The reason for "Bumstead" in 1857 quot. is unclear.]
   [**1857** in C.A. Abbey *Before the Mast* 108: Aint it a blowing "*Jehosaphat Bumstead*" & cold.] **1857, 1866** in *DARE.* **1873** Bailey *Almanac* (unp.): "Pickled Jehosophat!" said he. **1924** *DN* V 271: Holy jumping Jehosaphat! **1950** Hartmann & O'Brien *Fancy Pants* (film): Jumpin' Jehosophat! **1965** Matthiessen *Fields of Lord* 23: "Jumping Jehosophat!" Hazel cried. **1977* T. Jones *Incredible Voyage* 305: If he thinks this is a good track, what in the name of Jumping Jehoshaphat was the old trail like? **1978** J. Reynolds *Geniuses* 13: Jee-hosophat!

jehu *n.* [app. a sense development of joc. S.E. *jehu* 'a coachman or driver', usu. used disparagingly] a stupid or provincial fellow; yokel. Also **jayhoo.**
   1837 *Crockett Almanac*, in *DA:* A coat of strong blue cloth of the Jehu cut, with white bone buttons of the Jehu size…served…to hide the neckcloth. **1906** *DN* III 120: [Dialect of Southern Indiana:] *Jehu*, n. A greenhorn; country fellow. "That Jehu's silly." **1947** Overholser *Buckaroo's Code* 46: You mean Sandra Taney hired you two jayhoos?

jell or **jel** *n. Stu.* JELLO BRAIN.
   1982 Pond *Valley Girl's Gde.* 59: *Jel*—OK, like a Jello-brain,…a total geek. **1982** S. Black *Totally Awesome Val Guide* 21: *Jel*—Someone with a brain made of gelatin. An airhead, but with definite nerd tendencies. **1980–84** in P. Eckert *Jocks & Burnouts* 70: You got the Jocks and the Jells. *Ibid.* 96: Then…you hit, like, high school and, Jells like kind of, back off, you know. *a*1989 Spears *NTC Dict.* 201: The guy's a jel. Forget him.

jell or **gel** *v. Stu.* to idle, daydream, etc.; VEG. Cf. JELLY, *v.,* 1.
   1934 Weseen *Dict. Amer. Slang* 187: [College slang:] *Jell*—To loaf in a lunch room. **1983** in P. Munro *U.C.L.A. Slang* 42: *Gel*…participate in activities of little value. **1990** P. Dickson *Slang!* 218: *Gel.* To relax. **1993** *Village Voice* (N.Y.C.) (June 22) 32: The verb "to gel" [was] synonymous [in the early 1980's] with "veg" and "mold."

jellied out *adj. Stu.* fancily dressed.
   1935 E. Anderson *Hungry Men* 50: I'd like to be jellied out and staking Lundgren and run into boats.

jello brain *n.* [*Jell-O*, trademark for a flavored gelatin dessert + *brain*] *Stu.* a foolish, eccentric, or scatterbrained person.
   1982 (Pond quot. at JELL, *n.*). **1980–84** in P. Eckert *Jocks & Burnouts* 3: Jello Brains. **1984** Algeo *Stud Buds:* A rather stupid person…*jello brain.*

jelly *n.* [**1.** sperm; seminal fluid.—usu. considered vulgar. Orig. *S.E.* [Not attested in U.S., but perh. ult. the orig. of following senses.]
   **ca*1600 J. Donne, in *OED:* A female fishes sandie Roe / With the males ielly newly lev'ned was. **1605* in *OED:* The ielly or sperme of frogges. **1622* J. Fletcher, in *F & H* IV 143: Give her cold jelly / To take up her belly. **1661* in J. Farmer *Merry Songs* 24: The most heroick Jelly. **ca*1775 *Frisky Songster* 20: No one in my storehouse shall jelly drops spend. **a*1890–96 *F & H* IV 80: *To give juice for jelly*=to achieve the sexual spasm.]

   2.a. an attractive young woman; girlfriend; (*rarely*) a sweetheart of either sex; JELLY ROLL.

*1889 Barrère & Leland *Dict. Slang* I 496: *Jelly,* or *All Jelly,* a buxom, good-looking girl. **1925** Faulkner *New Orleans Sketches* 96: So we told them jellies we couldn't be out late account of something fixed at the track tomorrow. **1927** in Oliver *Meaning of Blues* 147: I got a sweet jelly, a lovin' sweet jelly roll. **1931** Faulkner *Sanctuary* 23: He's got a jelly there. He takes her to the dances. **1936** "Leadbelly," in Lomax & Lomax *Cowboy Songs* 41: If yo' house catch afire, an' dey ain' no water roun', / Throw yo' jelly out de window, let de doggone shack burn down. **1935–38** *AS* XIV (1939) 28: *Jelly*…A [Citadel] cadet in love. *Archaic.* **1968** in *DARE: Jelly*…Boyfriend. **1992** *Martin* (Fox-TV): This has *got* to be *jelly!* 'Cause jam don't shake like *that!*

   b. *Black E.* a close friend.
   1973 Duckett *Raps* 51: My godson, seventeen, / …refers to Mr. Nixon as/ "the cat who has no jellies."

3. Now *Black E.* the penis or vagina; copulation; JELLY ROLL.—usu. considered vulgar.
   [**ca*1775 *Frisky Songster* 32: My c—t is all in a jelly.] *a*1926 in Odum & Johnson *Negro Workaday Songs* 112: Why I like Roberta so, / She rolls her jelly / Like she do her dough. **1927** in Oliver *Meaning of Blues* 147: If you taste my jelly, it'll satisfy your worried soul. **1928** in Oliver *Blues Tradition* 208: Jelly, oh jelly look what you have done done, / You caused your grandmother to marry her youngest son. **1929** in Leadbitter & Slaven *Blues Records* 527: Good Jelly Blues. **1935** in Oliver *Meaning of Blues* 153: I will roll your jelly and also grind you deep. **1936** in Oliver *Blues Tradition* 188: And you have taken my lovin' and your jelly to your other man. **1936** in Leadbitter & Slaven *Blues Records* 46: Whippin' That Jelly. **1942** *Amer. Mercury* (July) 94: *Jelly*—sex. **1947** in Randolph & Legman *Blow Candle Out* 600: Polecat grease and 'possum belly, / All you gals come taste my jelly. **1963** in Charters *Poetry of Blues* 134: It takes her jelly to satisfy my soul. *Ibid.* 135: I got good jelly.…My sweet woman likes to have it every day. **1970** in Van Peebles *Sweetback* 115: Clean on down to the bone.…You got it, Sweetback.…Jelly, jelly, jelly.

4. *Mil.* gelignite; (*also*) napalm. Cf. HELL-JELLY.
   1939 Howsley *Argot* 11: *Can o' Jelly*—a container of nitro or gelatine explosive. **1941* (cited in *OED2*). **1953** Dodson *Away All Boats* 407 [ref. to WWII]: This stuff here will burn as good as jelly bombs. **1968** C. Victor *Sky Burned* 24: Dynamite, jelly, nitro, you name it. **1970** *Playboy* (Apr.) 214: Planes came in low and dropped napalm, the jelly canisters falling like fat cigars into the treetops. **1974** Former L/Cpl. USMC [ref. to 1968]: Napalm was *jelly.*

jelly *v.* **1.** *Stu.* to spend time in flirtatious conversation or the like, esp. at a soda fountain or café; (*broadly*) to waste time; JELL.
   1931 *AS* VI 205: *Jelly:* loiter for idle conversation in university buildings, or join friends to pass the time of day at a café or drugstore near the campus. **1937** *Life* (June 7) 34: To "jelly" is to…sip 10¢ "cokes" or sweet milks during an hour of talk. **1937** *AS* (Oct.) 241: At Columbia, Missouri, the home of the state university, "We'll *jelly* at such and such a café" is equivalent to the older "We'll cake." **1968** Baker, Ladd & Robb *CUSS* 144: *Jelly.* Waste time, not study.

2. to dance; BOOGIE, 1; JITTERBUG. Also (*vulgar*) **jelly-ass.**
   1935–38 in *AS* XIV (1939) 28: *Jelly,* to dance eccentrically. **1967** Salas *Tattoo* 127 [ref. to *ca*1950]: The back of a hand on…[his] hip,…he jelly-assed…in a mincing, knock-kneed gait…and called out: "Boogie, baby, boogie!"

3. *Black E.* to copulate.—usu. considered vulgar. [Perh. the orig. sense; cf. JELLY-ROLL.]
   1959 (quot. at JELLYBEAN, *n.,* 1.a.).

4. to pound with the fists; beat up.
   1978–89 in Jankowski *Islands in Streets* 163: We kicked ass, and I went in…and jellied a number of the [rival gang members].

jellyball *n.* a weak-willed person; jellyfish.
   1971–73 Sheehy *Hustling* 57: These Johns are jellyballs or they wouldn't be sniffing around chippies in the first place.

jellybean *n.* **1.a.** a sweetheart.
   1918 Ruggles *Navy Explained* 82: The best girl is the…jelly bean, fair one, or wench. **1959** Oliver *Meaning of Blues* 147: So a lover admires his "jelly bean" and the way she can "jelly."

   b. a sharply dressed young man who attempts to win young women through style and flattery; CAKE-EATER. Now *hist.*

1921 in *DARE*: [Cartoon:] Those jelly beans give me a pain. [*DARE* note: The jelly bean here is portrayed as an overdressed, supercilious young man.]. **1928–29** Faulkner *Sound & Fury* 229: Are you hiding out in the woods with one of them damn slick-headed jellybeans? **1932** in M. Taft *Blues Concordance* 1326: Down on Franklin Avenue: jellybeans standing to and fro./Well you hear one jellybean ask…which way did the good girl go? **1929–33** Farrell *Young Manhood* 366: A lot of these goddamn two-bit jellybeans [are] around the place. **1934** Peters & Sklar *Stevedore* 29: Keep yo' hands off, jelly-bean. **1936** Levin *Old Bunch* 23: It made them all feel glowingly united, not just flappers and jellybeans, but a new young generation capable of facing the serious things of life. **1936** in Armitage *J. Held, Jr.* 36: Supremely the artist of youth in the Jazz Age…was John Held, Jr., [with his]…sardonic sketches of "Flappers," Jelly Beans, and Drugstore Cowboys. **1937** E. Anderson *Thieves Like Us* 18: I want to go bare-headed anyway. Like these jelly beans. **a1973–87** F.M. Davis *Livin' the Blues* 49 [ref. to 1920's]: The jazz model suit was the unofficial uniform of the sheik, the "lounge lizard," "cake eater," "jelly bean," or "drugstore cowboy."

2. a foolish, weak-willed, or worthless person. Usu. *joc.*

1919 *DN* V 65: *Jelly-bean.* An indifferent individual. "Mary is such a *jelly-bean* that she never gets her lessons." New Mexico. **1920** in Fitzgerald *Stories* I 198: "Jelly-bean" is the name throughout the undissolved Confederacy for one who spends his life conjugating the verb to idle in the first person singular—I am idling, I have idled, I will idle. **1923** *Chi. Daily Trib.* (Feb. 26) 18: Why did I ever think of getting that jelly bean brother of hers in [to the fraternity]. **1930** Farrell *Calico Shoes* 151: Daown home, now, they was a jellybean who was a bashful guy, and he couldn't…find himself a piece of honey. **1951** *Western Folk.* X 171: *Jelly bean.* A person who doesn't tip. **1947–53** Guthrie *Seeds* 332: My, my, where have you jellybeans hidden your lantern? **a1957** McLiam *Pat Muldoon* 10: His mama's pride and beauty…they call him jellybean. **1958–59** in Abrahams *Deep Down in Jungle* 43: What you mean, jellybean?/What I said, cabbagehead. **1959** N.Y.C. schoolboy: Know what I mean, jellybean? **a1961** Longman *Power of Black* 298: Hello, you jelly bean. **1971** J. Brown & A. Groff *Monkey* 112: That long-winded, young jelly bean preached a solid hour. **1975** *Kojak* (ABC-TV): See the other jellybean? **1978** S. King *Stand* 90: I know what you mean, jellybean.

3. *Narc.* **a colored capsule containing a depressant or stimulant drug.**

1964 Harris *Junkie Priest* 47: Junkie talk for barbiturates floated through his mind: *goofballs, nembies, yellow jackets, redbirds, blue heavens, jelly beans.* **1977** (cited in Spears *Drugs & Drink*).

jelly-belly *n.* **1. a person having a fat belly.**

***a1890–96** F & H* IV 44: *Jelly-belly*…a fat man or woman. **1913** J. London *Valley of Moon* 196: Old Jelly Belly's got three bullet holes in him. **1953** Manchester *City of Anger* 123: Who you pointin' at, Jelly-belly? **1964** in Gover *Trilogy* 216: I hear the jelly belly jabberin of at me on somethin. **1976** Whelton *CB Baby* 27: You just give the Jelly Belly…a shout. **1993** *Wkly. World News* (July 13) 23: They call me jelly belly, lardbutt, blob.

2. a coward. Also as quasi-adj.

1972 A. Kemp *Savior* 90: There were…black sympathizers, a jelly-belly or two who had secretly admired Nicholas in private while he had damned him in public. **1974** Millard *Thunderbolt* 100: You gettin' jelly-belly over the deal you promoted your own self? **1981** N.C. woman, age 33: These people are such jelly-bellies they won't even stand up for their own interests.

jellyfish *n.* **a spineless person;** JELLYBEAN, 2; JELLY-BELLY, 2.

1932–33 Nicholson & Robinson *Sailor, Beware!* 212: Quitter!… Jelly fish.

jelly-pot *n.* *Black E.* **(one's) darling.**

1858 E.A. Pollard *Black Diamonds* 23: Her favorite is little Nina, whom she calls…"her *jelly-pot.*"

jelly roll *n.* [perh. fr. earlier JELLY] *Black E.* **copulation;** (*occ.*) **the penis or vagina;** (*also*) **one's lover.—usu. considered vulgar.**

[***a1890–96** F & H* IV 43: *Jelly-bag*…The *scrotum.…*The female *pudendum.*] **1914** in Handy *Treasury of Blues* 72: Cause I'm most wile 'bout ma Jelly Roll.…He'd make a cross-eyed 'oman go stone blind. **1905–15** in A. Lomax *Mr. Jelly Roll* 292: The Jelly Roll Blues. **1915** H.W. Lantley & P. Wendling *Jelly Roll* [fox trot] [N.Y.: Waterson, Berlin & Snyder Co., 1915]. **1916** in Blesh & Janis *Played Ragtime* 163: You can talk about your jelly rolls,/But none of them com-

pare/With my baby, pretty baby. **1917** in Peat *Legion Airs* 77: Goin' to dance out both my shoes,/When they play the "Jelly Roll Blues." **1920** in F.S. Fitzgerald *Stories* I 202: Her Jelly Roll can twist your soul. **1916–22** Cary *Sexual Vocab.* IV s.v. *penis*: Jelly roll. **1923** in Leadbitter & Slaven *Blues Records* 498: Nobody In Town Can Bake A Sweet Jelly Roll Like Mine. **a1926** in N. Cohen *Long Steel Rail* 427: Some old rounder stole my jelly roll. **1926** in Oliver *Meaning of Blues* 137: My man says sissy's got good jelly roll. **1926** Odum & Johnson *Negro Workaday Songs* 31: "Sweet mama," "Sweet papa," "daddy," "jelly roll," and a few other expressions have been thoroughly popularized among certain classes, white and Negro, by the blues songs. **1927** *Jour. Abnormal & Social Psych.* (Apr.) 13: *Jelly roll*…stands for the vagina, or for the female genitalia in general, and sometimes for sexual intercourse. **1927** in P. Oliver *Blues Tradition* 66: Just wanna teach you how to save your good jelly roll. **1928** in P. Oliver *Blues Tradition* 178: His jelly roll sure is nice and hot. **1932** in P. Oliver *Blues Tradition* 51: But now he preaches just to buy jelly roll. **1936** in Lomax & Lomax *Our Singing Country* 330: But all I wanted was Betty's jelly roll. **1940** *Tale of a Twist* 17: "Your jelly roll is going to be stale," she said…"if you don't put it to work pretty damn soon." **1943** J. Mitchell *McSorley's* 230: Old Uncle Bud…is the jelly-roll king. Got a hump on his back from shaking that thing. **1951** Willingham *Gates of Hell* 182: He'd recently been getting some sweet jelly roll from this fat little whore. **1955** McGovern *Fräulein* 199: Nobody gonna get none uh my jelly roll. **1959** in A. Lomax *Where Blues Began* 272: Well, it's Georgia women, baby,/Got the sweet jelly roll. **1960** Kirkwood *Pony* 220: Pearl, you ain't given jelly roll to nobody 'til I get me my slice. **1965** in B. Jackson *Swim Like Me* 139: Say, now, if you don't believe my jellyroll is fine,/Ask Good-Cock Lulu, that's a bitch a mine. **1974** Angelou *Gather Together* 151: Jelly Roll killed my pappy, and ran my mammy stone blind. **1984** Sample *Racehoss* 172: The women in dat Houston town got sum sweet jelly roll. **1985** Swados & Trudeau *RapMaster Ronnie* 5: Give me your sweet jelly roll! **a1973–87** F.M. Davis *Livin' the Blues* 36 [ref. to ca1920]: We all knew what it meant to…"whip that jellyroll to a fare-thee-well," or "get a piece of tail" or ass.

jelly-roll *v. Black E.* **to copulate.—usu. considered vulgar.**

1927 in Oliver *Meaning of Blues* 147: I'm a jelly-rollin' fool. **1933** in Oliver *Blues Tradition* 196: Who's gonna do your sweet jelly rollin'…when I'm gone. **1966** "Petronius" *N.Y. Unexp.* 38: Everything, and lots of looking, but shopping exceeds jelly-rollin'.

jelly-roller *n. Black E.* **a seducer of women;** COCKSMAN.—usu. considered vulgar.

1961 C. Cooper *Weed* 89: That…bastard. That jelly-roller.

jelly-snatchers *n.pl. Black E.* **hands.**

1972 Andrews & Dickens *Big House* 25: He got his jelly-snatchers on some ancient manuscripts.

jelly-tight *adj. Black E.* **splendid.—usu. constr. with** JAM-UP. **Also as adv.**

1962–68 B. Jackson *In the Life* 130: How was the Tennessee joint? It was jam-up. Jelly-tight.…'Cause you did your time there and nobody wasn't constantly riding shotgun on you. **1973** Andrews & Owens *Black Lang.* 75: Ah, everything is jam up and jelly tight. **1976–77** Kernochan *Dry Hustle* 83: She knew how to run the joint straight up and jelly tight. **1991** Hasburgh *NYPD Mounted* (film): We got it jam-up and jelly-tight.

Jemima *n.* [sugg. by Aunt *Jemima*, a trademark of General Foods, Inc.] *Black E.* **a black woman who is subservient to whites; a female** UNCLE TOM. Also as v. See also AUNT JEMIMA, 2.

1955 Childress *Trouble in Mind* 153: If I'm a "Tom," you a "Jemima." **1967** Colebrook *Cross of Lassitude* 333: Don't think that just because you Jemima'd up to him like that, that I went for that shit.

Jemmy Ducks var. JIMMY DUCKS.

Jemmy Legs var. JIMMY LEGS.

jemson *n. Ozarks.* **the penis.—usu. considered vulgar.**

1939 in Randolph *Pissing in Snow* 91: Then he out with his old jemson, and it sure was a dandy. **1953** Randolph & Wilson *Down in Holler* 100: In several parts of the Ozark region I have heard a term for penis, which sounds like *jemson* or *jemmison.*

jen *n.* **a young woman;** JANE, 1. Cf. earlier JENNY.

1917 T.A. Dorgan, in Zwilling *TAD Lexicon* 111: Watching the city editor…show off as a couple of jens step in to see how a newspaper office works.

Jenny *n.* **1.a.** *Av.* a Curtiss JN training biplane. Now *hist.*

1924 *Adventure* (Dec. 10) 23: Sell those — Jennies, go East, marry my girl and settle down. **1925** Faulkner *Soldier's Pay* 46: He was briefly in a Jenny again, conscious of lubricating oil. **1926** *Writer's Monthly* (Nov.) 395: *Jenny*—A training plane of the "JN" type. **1927** Lindbergh *We* 39 [ref. to 1923]: The Government had auctioned off a large number of "Jennies," as we called certain wartime training planes. **1928** Hall & Niles *One Man's War* 184 [ref. to 1918]: It was a Curtiss JN-4—a Jenny. **1943** Scott *God Is My Co-pilot* 2: In 1921 I read of an auction sale of war-time Jennys in Americus, Georgia. **1956** In Loosbrock & Skinner *Wild Blue* 99: Surplus warplanes, mostly tired old Jennies and DH-4s. **1958** Camerer *Damned Wear Wings* 71: One was killed tryin' to snap-roll a Jenny. **1963** E.M. Miller *Exile* 23: The state had gotten its first JN-3 Jennies in 1924. **1968** Hudson *Hostile Skies* 21: In May, 1917, the Aircraft Production Board recommended the construction of 1,500 of these planes—popularly called "Jennies." **1983** *N.Y. Times* (Jan. 9) Travel 3: Lindy sold his Jenny when he began formal flight training with the Army Air Corps. **1993** D. Rich *Queen Bess* 33: The Curtiss JN-4, or "Jenny," was a favorite learner's plane in the United States [*ca*1921].

b. an early biplane of any type. Now *hist.*

1956 *Private Secretary* (ABC-TV): First they called them "Jennies," then "crates," and now "honeys." **1981** K.E. Olson *Music & Musket* 67: The leather helmets, long silk scarfs, goggles, and jennies [of WWI aviators].

2. (*l.c.*) a generator.

1942 *ATS* 599: *Jenny*, a generator. **1971** Lavallee *Event 1000* 49: Ritter wants us to trouble shoot on the oh-two jenny. **1994** *X-Files* (Fox-TV): Fuel that'll keep this jenny powered tonight.

jenny *n. Stu.* a young woman. Cf. JEN.

1877–78 *Cornelian* 86: *Jenny.* A female distinction; *vide* Fem.

Jenny Lind steak *n.* [alluding to *Jenny Lind* (1820–87), Swedish soprano, toured U.S. 1850–52) (see quot.). *Joc.*

1891 Bourke *On the Border* 66 [ref. to *ca*1870]: A Jenny Lin' steak, mee son, 's a steak cut from off a hoss's upper lip.

jep *n. TV.* jeopardy.

1992 *TV Guide* (Mar. 14) 22: Like the "bodice-ripper" novels of print, "women in jep" rape-dramas, as insiders call them, evolve…with a cookie-cutter sameness. **1992** *New Yorker* (July 13) 68: "Unlawful Entry" is short on observation and long on jeopardy. It's what TV executives call "a Jep movie"—except that in TV movies the victimized woman avenges herself. **1993** *TV Guide* (Apr. 10) 43: Over and over—in the so-called "women in jep" movies—we've watched the lives of decent women shattered by what seems the innate indecency of men. **1995** *TV Guide* (Apr. 22) 53: *TV Guide* invited readers to make a pitch for their favorite programs in jep.

jerk[1] *n. R.R.* a railroad branch line. Also **jerk road.**

1897 in J. London *Reports* 320: *Jerk*, a branch road, or one little traveled. **1907** J. London *Road* [ref. to 1892]: I had missed the main line and come over a small "jerk" with only two locals a day on it. **1927** *DN* V 451: *Jerk road*…A small, branch railway. **1950, 1965–70** in *DARE.*

¶ In phrase:

¶ **get a jerk on** *Army.* to get moving; get a move on.

1919 McKenna *Battery A* 19: I learned to "get a jerk on," and I learned "to make 'em click."

jerk[2] *n.* [cf. JERK-OFF, *n.*, 2 and JERKY, *adj.*; infl. by JERK TOWN] **1.a.** a contemptible fool; dolt; (*broadly*) an offensive or worthless person.

1919 Ashton *F,63* 40: The night of the St. Mihiel drive "Jerk" Manley rushed in with the words "Say, did you hear about the ork eenikin' on the jazbo?" **1935** *Amer. Mercury* (June) 229: *Jerk*: eccentric fellow; fool. **1935** Pollock *Und. Speaks*: *Jerk*, a boob; chump; a sucker. **1936** Kingsley *Dead End* 694: Fawty-two hundred bucks is pretty big dough fer a joik like yew. **1937** Weidman *Wholesale* 45: "Kill the goddam scabs," they kept yelling, "kill the lousy jerks." **1938** O'Hara *Hope of Heaven* 58: It's easy enough to go around being a jerk if your father happens to be President of the United States. **1939** Fearing *Hospital* 74: It had to be a jerk like Cleary. **1941** Lardner & Kanin *Woman of the Year* (film): You're a pretty silly lookin' jerk. **1941** Brackett & Wilder *Ball of Fire* (film): Oh, that's that professor jerk. **1942** Seaton *Magnifi-*

cent Dope (film): If I may use the jargon of the street, I would say Mr. Page is a jerk. **1943** Snell & Marks *In Brooklyn* (film): The fact is they're just a couple of *jerks!* **1946** Dadswell *Hey There, Sucker!* 96: *Jerk*…a no-good person. **1946** *Printers' Ink* (Mar. 1) 24: For an advertiser, agency or publisher to attempt to deal with the public as anything but a jerk would in many cases be disastrous. **1949** in Hemingway *Sel. Letters* 658: A jerk can get away with a lot and a little jerk can get away with it longer. **1950** *Western Folk.* IX 118: *Jerk.* A very young or inefficient logger. **1952** W. Brown *Sox* 202: They let me know I was a jerk. **1953–55** Fine *Delinquents* 201: Her need to prove to the other girls she was not a "jerk" (inadequate or inferior). **1957** Mayfield *The Hit* 204: You're a number one, first-class jerk. *a***1960** Federoff *Side of Angels* 167: She thought Madame Bovary was a jerk. **1962** G. Olson *Roaring Road* 107: Some jerk blocked me off with his Caddy. **1963** Boyle *Yanks Don't Cry* 242: Some jerk from a camp across the lake got hopped up on sake and split the old man's skull open with an empty bottle. **1972–75** W. Allen *Feathers* 99: All right, then don't talk like a jerk. **1984** J. McCorkle *Cheer Leader* 124: Yeah but she's a jerk. **1994** *TV Guide* (June 25) 14: We've done 73 shows and he's never become a jerk. **1994** *Friends* (NBC-TV): The jerk missed his flight.

b. a male masturbator.—usu. considered vulgar. [Perh. the orig. sense.]

1938 "Justinian" *Amer. Sexualis* 26: *Jerk*…*n.* Same as *Jagoff.* **1943** *AS* XVIII 150: *Jerk*…one who hangs about burlesque or strip-tease shows for erotic stimulation (1930 or earlier). **1947** *Tomorrow* (Aug.) 30: *Jerk*, from a derogatory name first applied by burlesque performers to members of their audience, has become acceptable even to the movie censors. **1942–49** Goldin et al. *DAUL* 110: *Jerk*…the original definition,…a chronic masturbator, is still current in underworld usage.

2. SODAJERK.

1942 *ATS* 766: Soda fountain clerk…*jerk.* **1945** *Calif. Folk. Qly.* IV 54: This ordinarily instructs the "jerk" or cook to cancel the order.

3. *Soda Fountain.* (see quots.).

1967 *AS* XLII 63: *Jerk*, *n.* (1940 or earlier [in Lawrence, Kans.]) An ice cream soda. **1983** Mariani *Dict. Food & Drink* 239: *Jerk.* An ice cream soda, referring to the jerking motion of a seltzer spigot.

jerk *adj.* stupid; ridiculous.—only used attrib.

1964 Thompson & Rice *Every Diamond* 3: I guess those are home runs in that jerk league you guys just came out of. **1983** Eilert *Self & Country* 57: It reminded me of all those jerk signs in football locker rooms and even in boot camp. **1990** Univ. Tenn. instructor: Another one of her jerk ideas.

jerk *v.* **1.a.** to draw (a hand weapon).

1847 W.H. Richardson *Jour.* 82: And what was my surprise when I found that I had jerked my old knife from my pocket and was cutting my meat…in my usual fashion. **1866** in Rosa *Wild Bill* 84: I saw John Orr jerk his pistol and put it up against the man. **1877** *Puck* (June) 5: Gunpowder McCluskey jerks his iron and blows top of Natick's head off. **1881** in A.E. Turner *Earps Talk* 47: Jerk your gun and use it. **1905–07** Hough *Story of Outlaw* 10: I…jerked my gun and covered him. **1930** Sage *Last Rustler* 45: Smoky had jerked his six-shooter. **1931** Lake *Earp* 112: If you're so good with your guns, why don't you jerk 'em? **1943** in *Calif. Folk. Qly.* III (1944) 79: Just as he fell I jerked my 30-30 rifle and turned. **1956** Neider *Hendry Jones* 199: He jerked his fortyfive and shot him. **1991** Brown & Angus *A.K.A. Narc* 25: He jerked a gun.

b. to draw or dispense (beer, soda, etc.) from a tap. Now *colloq.*

1873 in *DA* s.v. *beer*: You will have the beer jerker at a disadvantage. **1883** Peck *Bad Boy* 126: Well, I must go down to the sweetened wind factory and jerk soda! **1884** in *DA*: They…went on jerking beer behind the counter. **1929** Asch *Pay Day* 94: The runt took a glass, filled with soda water, jerked syrup into it. **1935** *Amer. Mercury* (May) 102: They had spent their tender years jerking sodas. ***1949** in *OEDS*: I also jerked sodas. **1985** B. Ebsen, on *American Focus* (WKGN radio) (June 9): I could jerk soda. So…I got a job jerking soda.

c. *Narc.* to inject.

1918 Swan *My Company* 65: The kid's clever all right. Does he snuff that stuff or jerk it in his arm?

2. to filch; snatch.

1862 in *Tenn. Hist. Qly.* XXXV (1976) 298: We all thought that here was a chance to get what we wanted.…[But] so well did they treat us that we could not find it in our hearts to jerk anything. **1865** in *S.C.*

Hist. Mag. LIX (1958) 81: When we were trying to escape I jerked a gun from an Irishman.

3. to write or utter.—also constr. with *out*.

1862 C.F. Browne *A. Ward* 99: I can Jerk a Poim ekal to any of them Atlantic Munthly fellers. *Ibid.* 157: This play was jerkt by a admirer of Old Ossywattermy. **1866** in *Iowa Jour. of Hist.* LVII (1959) 202: She accordingly "jerked" out the following. **1871** "M. Twain" *Roughing It* 249: The thing I'm on now is to roust out somebody to jerk a little chin music for us and waltz him through handsome. **1873** B. Harte *Skaggs's Husbands* 155: Can jerk a rhyme as easy as turnin' a jack. *a1890–96 F & H* IV 47: To *jerk a poem, article* or *book*=to write.

4. to masturbate; JERK OFF, 1.a.—usu. considered vulgar.

1888 *Stag Party* 95: Common, old fashioned f—k $1.00....Pudding jerking $2.00. **1889** Barrère & Leland *Dict. Slang* I 497: *Jerking* (low), masturbation. [*a1890–96 F & H* IV 47: To *jerk one's juice* or *jelly*...to masturbate.] **1927** [Fliesler] *Anecdota* 137: I've been screwed, sucked, jerked, everything. **1968** P. Roth *Portnoy* 230: Jerk your precious little dum-dum ad infinitum! **1973–74** (quot. at PLANK, *v.*).

5.a. to remove or disqualify (a person, esp. an athlete from a sporting event).

1912 *N.Y. Tribune* (Apr. 21) 10: Quinn...was jerked out of the box and Jim Vaughn entered. **1928** in Paxton *Sport* 127: I don't believe in jerking out your best men....Let 'em stay in and run up a score. **1943** in Rea *Wings of Gold* 106: Twenty foot underwater swim—passed. Two hundred yard stroke test—got jerked on breast stroke. **1944** in Tapert *Lines of Battle* 193: I'll jerk him off the line and use him to carry chow. **1971** *Playboy* (Dec.) 114: You brazened out an episode during the filming of *Macbeth* when the English insurance company was ready to jerk you for being so slow. **1982** WKGN radio news (July 23): When he was due up in the ninth, he was jerked for a pinch hitter. **1990** Knoxville, Tenn., man, age *ca*30: If he's a full-time employee we just call up and say—pfft! jerk him!

b. to take back, reclaim, withdraw, revoke, etc.

1930 *AS* VI 127: To *pull* is to remove the furniture from the home of a customer who has failed to pay for it, or refuses to pay for it. To *jerk* means the same thing. **1933** Duff & Sutherland *I've Got Yr. Number* (film): I'm going to jerk those phony attachments. **1942–49** Goldin et al. *DAUL* 110: The mouthpiece...wants...that hooker (pending warrant) jerked. **1953** H. Carter *Main Street* 163: They asked us...to jerk those two pages and replace them. **1953** G. Webber *Far Shore* 60 [ref. to WWII]: They're jerkin' his license for six months after this trip. **1957** Bannon *Odd Girl* 152: You mean you'd jerk my [sorority] pin?...You'd *blackball* me? **1961** L.E. Young *Virgin Fleet* 73 [ref. to 1941]: I'll jerk your liberty cards. **1977–81** S. King *Cujo* 66: Needless to say, the...ads had been jerked from the tube. **1987** J. Thompson *Gumshoe* 255: My...license would be jerked and my reputation ruined. **1988** *Larry King Show* (Mutual Radio Network) (June 20): If I ever trespassed where I wasn't supposed to be, or tampered with evidence, my livelihood and my license would be jerked.

c. (see quot.).

1935–38 in *AS* XIV (1939) 28: *Jerk*...To enter a delinquency report against...(a West Point term).

6. *Baseball.* to hit (a pitched ball) with great force, esp. for a home run.

1961 Brosnan *Pennant Race* 56: One of these days I'll jerk one out of here during a game, too.

7.a. to cheat.

1984 S. Hager *Hip Hop* 109: He jerked me out of twenty dollars. **1995** *N.Y. Times* (Mar. 1) B1: We was talking to him about the counterfeit money. Stanley told him that he jerked us. **1996** *New Yorker* (June 3) 31: These girls geesed—that's old-school for when you get jerked—his Moët.

b. to interfere or fool; mistreat; JERK AROUND, 1.a.

1993 *World News Tonight* (ABC-TV) (Aug. 18): She's jerkin' with my six-year-old son's head and I *don't* like it!

8. to assault with violence; hurt.

*a***1992** in Ratner *Crack Pipe* 125: Don't do that kind of nonsense on the street because one day you're gonna get jerked.

9. JERK AROUND, 2.

1995 S. Moore *In the Cut* 6: The boys jerking restlessly on the streets outside the bars.

¶ In phrases:

¶ **jerk (someone's) chain** to *pull (someone's) chain*, 1, s.v. CHAIN, *n.*

¶ **jerk it into (someone)** to treat (someone) severely; let (someone) have it.

1832 [M. St.C. Clarke] *Sks. of Crockett* 58: I jerked it into him. I told him...that he didn't know who he was fooling with.

¶ **jerk (one's) jaw** [or *jaws*] to *jack (one's) jaw* [or *jaws*] s.v. JACK[1], *v.*

1988 Poyer *The Med* 504: They love to jerk their jaws.

¶ **jerk to Jesus** to execute by hanging.

1879 *Nat. Police Gaz.* (Mar. 8) 14: The Chicago *Times*...headed its article..."Jerked to Jesus." *a1890–96 F & H* IV 47: *Jerked to Jesus* (American)=hanged. **1923** *DN* V 227: Many readers may remember when the pages of the daily papers headlined a hanging as "Jerked to Jesus."

jerk around *v.* **1.a.** to treat roughly, unfairly, or with contempt; mistreat. [The 1884 quot. is clearly literal S.E.]

[**1884** Huftalen *Diary* 79: Pa is mad I should judge by the way he jerks the horses around.] **1932** D. Runyon, in *Collier's* (June 11) 7: Coppers are always heaving her into the old can when they find her jerking citizens around and cutting up other didoes. **1966** H.S. Thompson *Hell's Angels* 124: The only outlaws who didn't get jerked around by the law were those who made the rally. **1970** *Nat. Lampoon* (Apr.) 54: Has the big ouija board in the sky been jerking you around? **1973** Maas *Serpico* 166: You keep jerking me around, telling me you'll be there, and you're never there. **1974** in H.S. Thompson *Shark Hunt* 361: This is all crazy bullshit....We're just being jerked around. He's not going to do anything serious today. **1978** Schrader *Hardcore* 66: Now why would you wanna jerk me around?...I've always been straight with you, Andy. **1987** WINS radio news (June 20): A growing number of law-makers believe that North is jerking them around and intends never to testify. **1995** *Dr. Katz* (Comedy Central TV): So you're just jerking me around. You really don't know what you're talking about.

b. to tease or hoax.

[**1966** in IUFA *Folk Speech*: *Jerk*—this means to make fun of someone.] **1977** Bredes *Hard Feelings* 87: I knew he was jerking me around, but craziness in people is a thing you learn to tolerate.

2. to fool around.

1968 Baker, Ladd & Robb *CUSS* 145: *Jerk Around*. Waste time, not study. **1977** Torres *Q & A* 50: I got no time to be jerkin' around. **1979** in Fierstein *Torch Song* 177: It means it's time for me to stop jerkin' around. **1982** *Fury of Firestorm* (Jan. 1983) 8: No more jerking around...I'm gonna teach that worm a *lesson*. **1988** *Supercarrier* (ABC-TV): Quit jerkin' around and let's show this jackass the exit. **1989** S. Lee *Do the Right Thing* (film): Make sure Mookie don't jerk around. **1992** *Seinfeld* (NBC-TV): Let's stop jerkin' around.

jerk-ass *n.* JERK[2], 1.a.—also used attrib.—usu. considered vulgar.

1964–70 J. Carroll, in *Paris Rev.* (No. 50) 101: I was just another jerk-ass freshman....This jerk-ass went to some strict Catholic school. **1980** M. Baker *Nam* 128: You're a jerk-ass. *a***1987** Bunch & Cole *Reckoning for Kings* 419: Jerkass Limeys with stiff upper lips.

jerked *adj.* extremely stupid.—constr. with *up* or *off*.

1953 Paley *Rumble* 159: I ain't that jerked up! **1977** in L. Bangs *Psychotic Reactions* 230: It's nauseating and moronic, and I don't mean good moronic, I mean jerked off.

jerker *n.* **1.** *Horse Racing.* a spirited horse.

1840 *Spirit of Times* (Oct. 10) 379: Black Boy...is a *jerker*, no matter who "tackles" him—and ... will make one of our best Four-milers next year.

2. SODA-JERKER.

1926 Finerty *Criminalese* 31: *Jerker*—Fountain man.

3. a masturbator, esp. one who frequents burlesque shows or the like.—usu. considered vulgar.

1941 "G.R. Lee" *G-String* 64: Soon as the jerkers think we're cleaning up the show, business takes a dive.

jerkface *n.* a foolish-looking person; dolt.

1977 Univ. Tenn. student: He's such a jerkface. **1978** Eble *Campus Slang* (Apr.) 3: *Jerk-face*—a foolish, dull person: She doesn't want to date that jerk-face anymore. **1985** Briskin *Too Much* 34: Hello, Mr. Jerkface, how are you today Mr. Jerkface. **1986** E. Weiner *Howard the*

Duck 19: That's a turkey, jerk-face. **1987** Univ. Tenn. law student: He was a complete total jerkface. **1990** *Kid 'n' Play* (NBC-TV): You doofus! You jerkface! Why don't you look where—. **1991** *Night Court* (NBC-TV): Get used to it, jerkface.

jerk fiend *n.* a chronic masturbator.—usu. considered vulgar.

    1952 Mandel *Angry Strangers* 256: You big jerk fiend, you want to school me like you school kids and idiots?

jerkhead *n.* JERKFACE.

    1984 *Newsweek* (May 21): Reagan's aides…were heaping the well-respected economist with such epithets as "jerkhead" and "dummy." **1995** *Houston Post* (Feb. 5) (Nexis): It's really unfortunate that the jerkheads that were there set it back. **1995** *Boston Globe* (Sept. 1) (Nexis): These are real people, not jerkheads living on the moon having no relationships with anyone. **1996** Senate FBI Files Hearing (CNN-TV) (June 28): I want the FBI file on old Joe Jerkhead.

jerkneck *adv. West.* (see quot.).

    1927 C. Russell *Trails Plowed Under* 43: We're drivin' these vehicles jerkneck; that is, the trail pony's tied to the lead cart so one man can handle both.

jerko *n.* [JERK + -O] JERK², 1.a.

    1948 Kingsley *Detective Story* 321: Then the jerko took a bus. **1958** Appel *Raw Edge* 115: The jerkos….A pack of dummies. **1967** G. Green *To Brooklyn* 207: What a sucker….Jerko. **1970** Gattzden *Black Vendetta* 117: What…correspondence school did that jerko judge go to? **1984** Hindle *Dragon Fall* 92: [You] Jerko. **1978** Carpenter & Hill *Halloween* (film): Jerko got caught. **1987** S. Stark *Wrestling Season* 130: Shut up, jerko.

jerk-off *n.* **1.** an act of masturbation.—usu. considered vulgar. Also as quasi-adj.

    1928 in Read *Lexical Evidence* 63: Try a jerk off. **1940** Farrell *Father & Son* 475: You're nothing but the dribblings of a Chinese jerk off against a lamppost. That's all you are! **1961** Forbes *Goodbye to Some* 66: He's not all wrapped up in…jerk-off literature. **1970** Southern *Blue Movie* 89: I had fantasies, wet dreams, a million jerk-offs. **1997** *Details* (Feb.) 114: You want to buy a jerk-off magazine.

    2. a chronic masturbator (*rare* in literal sense); (*hence,* generally) a dolt; a lazy or worthless fellow.—usu. considered vulgar. Also as quasi-adj. [Bracketed quot. undoubtedly euphemizes this term.]

    [**1935** in K. White *First Sex. Revolution* 89: [His street nickname of] "Joe the Chronic Masturbator."] **1937** Di Donato *Christ in Concrete* 127: He was the diapered one,…he was the half-pint jerk-off. **1944–46** in *AS* XXII 55: *Jerk-off.* A goof, rookie. **1942–49** Goldin et al. *DAUL* 110: *Jerk-off*…a chronic masturbator. **1949** in Hemingway *Sel. Letters* 680: I hope you will not get into the high jerk-off notch about that portable or potable Hemingway book. **1961** J. Jones *Thin Red Line* 19: He's a jerkoff. *ca*1969 Rabe *Hummel* 26: That ain't what I said, Jerkoff! **1970** Thackrey *Thief* 8: And…even then, the jerkoffs would probably be looking at the train stations or the bus stations or the airport. **1976** Whelton *CB Baby* 149: The jerkoff who made that remark is a pimple on this town's ass. **1978** Strieber *Wolfen* 43: It makes the men look like a bunch of jerkoffs. **1983** P. Dexter *God's Pocket* 99: Everybody…thinks we're a bunch of jerk-offs down here. **1985–87** Bogosian *Talk Radio* 66: You're a jerk-off and a loser.

    3. an imposition or fraud.—usu. considered vulgar.

    1975 Sepe & Telano *Cop Team* 161: Wadda ya say we go up and find out if this whole story is a jerk-off. **1979** C. Higgins *Silver Streak* (film): The Chevvy? That's a jerkoff. This [sports car] is pure pussy. **1993** Adams & Stadiem *Madam* 213: All show and no go, a giant jerk-off.

jerk-off *adj.* doltish; stupid; worthless.—usu. considered vulgar.

    1937 in Perelman *Don't Tread on Me* 11: Working away on that jerk-off musical and hating it more and more. **1972** Hannah *Geronimo Rex* 250: That was a hell of a fine moral, but it was a stupid jerk-off story. **1977** Schrader *Blue Collar* 21: Except for the jerk-off elections, he was damn near the same as those educated guys with a guaranteed salary. **1987** *Campus Voice* (Winter) 29: It was a jerk-off program that our manager made us do. **1995** *X-Files* (Fox-TV): Is this another jerk-off assignment where I do the dirty work?

jerk off *v.* [JERK, 4 + *off*] **1.a.** to masturbate; to masturbate (someone).—usu. considered vulgar.

    a*1890–96 *F & H* IV 47: To *jerk off*=to masturbate. **1916 Cary *Ven-*

ery I 155: *To jerk off*—To masturbate. *a*1925 in Fauset *Folklore from N.S.* 133: She went upstairs for a drink of cider,/And there stood a dirty buggar jerkin' off a spider./She went upstairs for a drink of gin,/And there was the dirty buggar jerkin' off again. *a*1927 in P. Smith *Letters from Father* 47: She jerked me off. **1934** H. Roth *Call It Sleep* 418: Runnin' hee! hee! hee! Across the lots hee! hee! jerkin' off. **1940** *Tale of a Twist* 80: She stuck her fingers into herself and began to jerk off. **1942** H. Miller *Roofs of Paris* 199: Jerking off, to be frank. **1948** M. Cowley, in Jay *Burke-Cowley Corres.* 282: Probably he didn't jerk off more than anyone else. **1955** Caprio *Sexual Behavior* 14: Once I jerked off five times in one day. **1961** Hemingway *Islands* 402: What the hell you think I'm going to do? Go in there and jerk off? **1965** in Di Donato *Naked as Author* 54 [ref. to *ca*1930]: Kid, if you shake it more'n three times yuh're jerkin' off. **1968** P. Roth *Portnoy* 175: The tycoon…jerked his dong off. **1969** Jessup *Sailor* 99: You old enough to stop jerking off?…Are you man enough to leave it alone? **1970** Sorrentino *Steelwork* 46: If you jerk off you get hairy palms. **1977** in Cheever *Letters* 334: I shaved, jerked-off, [etc.]. *ca*1989 in Ratner *Crack Pipe* 52: He wanted…to…jerk off. **1992** in *Harper's* (Jan. 1993) 83: Elisabeth jerked me off into a glass bottle.

    b. to handle or touch nervously or repeatedly.—usu. considered vulgar.

    1969 N.Y.C. editor, age *ca*40: Are you just going to sit there jerking off that pencil? **1976** Price *Bloodbrothers* 19: He'll fuck aroun' down there four years, then get a job jerkin' off a pencil for eight grand? **1985** Siefert *Coyote Ugly* 25: *Red.*…What was they doing to my Buick? *Scarlet.* Jerking it off. *Red.* I don't want you talking that way about the family car.

    c. to assuage or assure in an insincere manner.—usu. considered vulgar.

    1984 Caunitz *Police Plaza* 30: The burglaries and robberies get a fast phone call to jerk off the complainant and then they're filed.

    2.a. to fool around.—usu. considered vulgar.

    1955 Graziano & Barber *Somebody Up There* 242 [ref. to 1942]: What's up?…What you guys all jerking off about? **1968** Baker, Ladd & Robb *CUSS* 145: *Jerk Off.* Waste time, not study. **1976** Price *Bloodbrothers* 199: So, if we wanna jerk off an extra hour? **1982** Hayano *Poker Faces* 37: You're jerking off and telling jokes and holding up the game. **1984** D. Jenkins *Life Its Ownself* 38: You got a season to jerk off; why not? **1987** Estes *Field of Innocence* 201: He been in the hooch, jerkin' off with the PF's radio.

    b. to interfere maliciously.—usu. considered vulgar.

    *a*1972 W. Mackey in W. King & R. Milner *Black Drama Antho.* 342: The Beast is jerking off again. Piss-assing around with every goddamn body.

    3. to get out; go away.—used imper.—usu. considered vulgar.

    [**1941** Macaulay & Wald *Manpower* (film): G'wan an' jerk yourself a soda.] **1966** Bogner *Seventh Ave.* 315: Shush, he's listening. Levy, why don't you jerk off?

    4. to cheat; impose upon; lie to; fool; harass; treat with contempt.—usu. considered vulgar.

    1968 Baker et al. *CUSS* 145: *Jerked off* Treated unfairly on an exam. *Jerk off* Tease or annoy someone. **1970–71** Higgins *Coyle* 84: I think Coyle was jerking you off. **1974** Charyn *Blue Eyes* 57: A schmuck by the name of Pimloe. He's been jerking me off the last few days. **1975** Sepe & Telano *Cop Team* 11: You've jerked my guys off for more than an hour. Now…either book him or we take him out of here. **1966–80** McAleer & Dickson *Unit Pride* 393: Do you really think it'll do any good or are you just jerkin' me off? **1982** Hayano *Poker Faces* 58: Another kind of ethically marginal ploy that some players use to humiliate or "jerk off" opponents is the *slow-roll*. **1983** Ehrhart *VN-Perkasie* 257: Don't jerk me off. When'd I tell you that? **1988** T. Harris *Silence of Lambs* 272: Think Lecter was jerking her off too? **1992** Launer *My Cousin Vinny* (film): I didn't come down here just to be jerked off.

    5. to infuriate.—usu. considered vulgar.

    1974 Terkel *Working* 581: Bullshit! That jerked me off.

jerk over *v.* to interfere with or botch; SCREW OVER.

    1987 Stroud *Close Pursuit* 84: Well, you know, just generally jerking it over. **1989** Munro *U.C.L.A. Slang* 52: My professor jerked me over when he refused to accept my paper two days late.

jerks *n.pl.* (see quot.).

    1889 Barrère & Leland *Dict. Slang* I 497: *Jerks* (American), got the *jerks*, has the delirium tremens, is nervous, or under religious excitement at a camp-meeting.

jerk-simple *adj.* stupid or feeble-minded, supposedly from chronic masturbation.—usu. considered vulgar. Also **jerk-silly.**

    1935–62 Ragen & Finston *Toughest Pris.* 805: *Jerk-silly*—Applied to an inmate who chronically masturbates. **1963** J. Ross *Dead Are Mine* 269 [ref. to WWII]: Christ! I must be jerk simple to want to go back to action. *a*1967 Maurer & Vogel *Narc. & Narc. Add.* (ed. 3) 367: *Jerk simple.* Mentally disturbed as a result of masturbation.

jerk town *n.* a remote provincial town; JERKWATER, 2.

    1900 Willard & Hodler *Powers That Prey* 61: They nearly lynched Jerry Simpson and the Michigan Kid in a jerk town in Georgia las' winter. **1902** "J. Flynt" *Little Bro.* 103: One night we was put off a freight at a jerktown. **1939–40** O'Hara *Pal Joey* 25: The only fine decent thing that has happened to me since coming to this jerk town. **1956** M. Wolff *Big Nick.* 38: She was the liveliest kid in that whole jerk town.

jerk up *v.* **1.** to take into police custody; arrest; HAUL UP. Also **jerk in.**

    1843 *Spirit of Times* (July 22) 241: The Commissioners "made no bones" about jerking us up. **1901** in *DA:* He'll probably try to make out a case of criminal carelessness against me, and get me jerked up. **1903** McClallen *He Demons* 298: They jerk you up and put you in the penitentiary for stealing money. **1910** in *DA:* The cops…jerk up a circus man on the slightest excuse. **1912** Field *Watch Yourself* 219: The *Clipper* says you were all jerked up and slid out between two days. **1949** W.R. Burnett *Asphalt Jungle* 138: I hate to jerk him in, Cobby.

    2. to reprimand sharply; JACK UP, 2.a.

    1908 in "O. Henry" *Works* 817: You want to jerk Bradshaw up about them last hams he sent us. **1918** H.E. Townsend *War Diary* 85: Two Colonels have been severely jerked up for denying us privileges.

    3. to impose upon; JERK AROUND, 1.a.

    1991 Brown & Angus *A.K.A. Narc* 198: [Don't] try to jerk them up and make them wait to be paid.

jerkwad *n.* [JERK[2] + *wad*] JERK[2], 1.b.—usu. considered vulgar.

    1990 Thorne *Dict. Contemp. Slang* 274: *Jerkwad*…American. a term of abuse meaning literally a (male) masturbator.

jerkwater *n.* **1.** a railroad train, stagecoach, etc., serving a remote provincial area. Cf. JERKWATER, *adj.*, 1.

    1878 Hart *Sazerac* 16: I wish I may be runned over by a two-horse jerk-water if there was a sage-hen in sight. **1905** *DN* III 84: *Jerkwater (train),* n. Train on a branch railway. "Has the *jerkwater* come in yet?"

    2. a remote station with a water tank for the use of a railroad or stagecoach line; (*hence*) a small or remote provincial town.

    1927 (quot. at FILLING STATION). **1942** *ATS* 729: Small station or town:…*jerkwater, jerkwater town,* [etc.]. **1945** in Mencken *Amer. Lang. Supp. II* 716: In June, 1870, the New York Central made, at Montrose, N.Y., the first installation that permitted locomotives to pick up water on the fly. The term *jerkwater* came into the language to designate localities whose importance consisted almost solely of the water pans between the tracks there. **1948** J. Stevens *Jim Turner* 168: The freight train stopped at a jerkwater siding just over the county line. **1969** Eastlake *Bamboo Bed* 155: "What did you say the name of your jerkwater was?"…"Amityville." **1974** Millard *Thunderbolt* 59: Why *here* in this God-forsaken jerkwater? **1982** Least Heat Moon *Blue Hwys.* 6: Podunk and Toonerville…the burgs, backwaters, jerkwaters, the widespots-in-the-road, the don't-blink-or-you'll-miss-it-towns.

    3. an incompetent; JERK[2], 1.a.

    1958 Talsman *Gaudy Image* 172: This guy is…fat like that jerkwater at the club.

jerkwater *adj.* **1.** (of a stagecoach, railroad train, rail line, etc.) serving a remote or rural area.

    1869 *Overland Mo.* (Mar.) 273: "Jerkwater" stages, which had been three or four days making the trip of one hundred and ten miles. **1909** *Sat. Eve. Post* (May 15) 9: The more disgusted he became with the prospect of living on jerk-water trains. **1915** Bronson-Howard *God's Man* 56: Provincial trolley lines, "jerkwater" railroads. **1916** C.C. Davis *Olden Times* 82: This little "jerk-water" road was reaping its golden harvest. **1916** L. Stillwell *Common Soldier* 269: At a way-station on some "jerk-water" railroad, waiting for a belated train. **1917** in Bernheim *Passed* 111: The French railroad system compares to our little jerk-water roads. **1922** in Hemingway *Sel. Letters* 75: The railroad there is a little

jerkwater and doesn't sell tickets outside of the country. **1925** I. Cobb *Many Laughs* 25: Down in Arkansas in the old days there was a jerkwater railroad with a reputation. **1950** A.L. Brooks *So. Lawyer* 88: Attaching a boxcar to the rear of the jerkwater passenger train.

    2. of or characteristic of a small provincial town; provincial; (*broadly*) insignificant.

    1897 *Chi. Tribune* (July 25) 15: The Kansas Dialect…*Jerkwater*—Insignificant—"John J. Ingalls regards the Swiss mission as a jerkwater job, and would not take it if it were offered to him." **1918** in "M. Brand" *Coll. Stories* 20: A jerk-water shanty village like Three Rivers. **1927** Tully *Circus Parade* 96: Some little jerk-water place.…The Missouri Pacific crosses here. **1927** Faulkner *Mosquitoes* 150: Gus? Belong to one of those jerkwater clubs? I guess not. He's a Yale man. **1934** Kromer *Waiting* 95: We pull to a stop in front of this jerkwater station. **1936** D. Runyon, in *Collier's* (Nov. 21) 8: I go across France…to a little jerkwater town just over the border from Spain. **1936** in Pyle *Ernie's Amer.* 4: Back roads…jerkwater hotels. **1938–39** Dos Passos *Young Man* 84: Any little snotnosed punk from a jerkwater cowcollege. **1939** I. Shaw *Sailor off Bremen* 99: This little jerkwater school. **1953** in Burroughs & Ginsberg *Yage* 39: No one will admit anything is wrong with his jerk water country. **1958** D. Stanford *Ski Town* 7: This stupid little jerkwater, backwoods ghost town in the Rockies. **1968** "R. Hooker" *M*A*S*H* 126: He went to some jerkwater colored college. **1974** Millard *Thunderbolt* 19: It'll be dark soon and that jerkwater street'll be lined with cars. **1976** Whelton *CB Baby* 2: They'd rather stay in some jerkwater burg at half the salary and be safe. **1982** R.M. Brown *So. Discomfort* 94: For that jerkwater town in eastern Alabama? **1983** Flaherty *Tin Wife* 322: Any little jerkwater paper out in the boroughs. **1988** H. Gould *Double Bang* 79: They could have been buried in some jerkwater [police] squad out in Queens.

    3. stupid; JERKY.

    1984 Ehrhart *Marking Time* 213: Some jerkwater fiasco like Vietnam. **1984** "W.T. Tyler" *Shadow Cabinet* 9: This jerkwater staff aide says he doesn't remember anything.

jerkweed *n.* a stupid or obnoxious person; JERK[2], 1.a. Cf. DICKWEED.

    1990 in *Harper's* (Jan. 1991) 20: Jerkweed…Pinhead…Slimeball …Scuzzbucket.

jerky *n. West.* a stagecoach.

    1902 Wister *Virginian* ch. xiv: Six legs inside this jerky to-night? *Ibid.:* Shorty shot from the jerky.

jerky *adj.* [cf. JERK[2], *n.,* 1.a.] imbecilic; stupid or silly.

    1932 in Eells & Musgrove *Mae West* 331: Jerky…[played by] Harry Wallace. **1942** in Marx *Groucho Letters* 52: This must sound exceedingly jerky. **1944** Guthrie *Born to Win* 222: I don't sing any silly or any jerky songs. **1944** in *Combat* 147: We're gonna look jerky enough when we go down there. **1951** Spillane *Lovely Night* 41: Don't be jerky! **1953** *Mr. & Mrs. North* (CBS-TV): That jerky dame. **1957** E. Lacy *Room to Swing* 29: At least she was jerky in a friendly way. **1960** *Twilight Zone* (CBS-TV): Have you ever seen such jerky-looking creatures? **1963** Blechman *Camp Omongo* 16: Jerky little bungalows. **1966** Susann *Valley of Dolls* 47: Some jerky little insurance guy. **1971** Cameron *First Blood* 56: I guess I did act sort of jerky back there…didn't I? **1972** B. Harrison *Hospital* 347: I bet it's because of that jerky friend of hers. **1994** *The Jerky Boys* [title of film about prank telephone calls].

jerries *n.pl.* [orig. unkn.] JIMJAMS.

    1910 in McCay *Little Nemo* 241: "Part angle worm and part squash.… I wish the captain was here." "If he was, he'd have the jerries sure!"

Jerry[1] *n. R.R.* a section worker, orig. one who is Irish.

    *ca*1867 in Mayer & Vose *Makin' Tracks* 79: There have been times when the "Jerries" and the "Dagos" have got mixed, when the boss and his assistants have been obliged to face the rioters…with a…display of firearms. **1888** in N. Cohen *Long Steel Rail* 200: There was many a joke among the "Jerrys"…on the Hand-Car that never returned. **1906** *McClure's Mag.* (Nov.) 20: What air we? Jerries, tarriers, hobos, bums. **1922** N. Anderson *Hobo* 93: If he works on the Section he may be called a "snipe" or a "jerry." **1926** *AS* I (Jan.) 250: A track laborer, "jerry" or "snipe." **1931** "D. Stiff" *Milk & Honey* 208: *Jerries*—Men who work on the section gang. They do maintenance work while *gandy-dancers* do contract jobs. **1945** Hubbard *R.R. Ave.* 349: *Jerry*—Section worker; sometimes applied to other laborers.

Jerry[2] *n.* [prob. sugg. by *German*] *Mil.* **1.** a German, esp. a member of the German armed forces; (*hence*) a German aircraft or naval vessel; (*also*) the German armed forces collectively. Now *hist.*

1915 in Roy *Pvt. Fraser* 67: Jerry had several shots at me and missed. **1918** O'Brien *Wine, Women & War* 38: When it reaches the rough-and-tumble, there'll be some startled Jerries. **1918** in *St. Lawrence Univ. in the War* 20: There isn't much excitement except when Jerry comes over to serenade. **1918** in Straub *Diary* 138: The Jerries started to drop 77s all around us. **1919** S. Prentice *Padre* 232: Every little while the "Jerries" drop a shell along this stretch. **1919** Hamilton & Corbin *Echoes from Over There* 28: We had the Jerries on the run. **a*1925 Fraser & Gibbons *Soldier & Sailor Wds.* 131 [ref. to WWI]: *Jerry up,* a warning call on the approach of a German airplane. **1929** Springs *Bright Blue Sky* 272: It won't take long to chase Jerry back to the Rhine. **1941* in *AS* XIX (1944) 11: *Jerry...*is the term which remains in use in the present war. **1942** *Harper's Mag.* (July) 210: There's a Jerry [German submarine] on our tail. **1943** G. Biddle *Artist at War* 23: The Jerries dug in. **1944** in *Combat* 42: His patrol was surprised by the Jerries. **1944** Pyle *Brave Men* 186: They said Jerry didn't scare as easily as all that. **1948** Lay & Bartlett *12 O'Clock High* 27: Our crews give us pretty good reports on how the Jerries react. **1971–72** in M.P. Motley *Invisible Soldier* 51: That very same night Jerry came over in waves. **1975** *Black World* (May) 56: The Jerries got enough of this war same as us.

2. a German heavy artillery shell. Now *hist.*

1919 C.W. Johnson *321st Inf.* 96: With Fritzie a few feet away,/With Jerries and Minnies a-whistling around. **1919** C. Emmett *Give 'Way* 198: A big "Jerry" whined out of the skies and crashed into the cemetery.

Jerry *adj. Mil.* of or characteristic of German armed forces; German. Now *hist.*

1926 Nason *Chevrons* 85 [ref. to 1918]: And sour jerry bread we found in a ration dump in Voisard. **1937** Parsons *Lafayette Esc.* 98 [ref. to 1918]: The jerry pilot fired a few more shots. **1942** *Yank* (Dec. 30) 6: A wrecked Jerry tank. **1943* in *OED2:* The well known Jerry boat. **1944** Liebling *Back to Paris* 8: It's those Jerry eighty-eights. **1944** in *Combat* 46: I saw a Jerry soldier walk past. **1945** in Litoff et al. *Miss You* 257: The only souvenir left was a Jerry knife and two coins. **1972* in *OED2:* Give us a Jerry paper, love.

jerry[1] *adj.* [orig. unkn.] **1.** Esp. *Und.* aware; cognizant; in the know; WISE.—usu. constr. with *to;* in phr. **be jerry** to know or understand.

1902 T.A. Dorgan, in Zwilling *TAD Lexicon* 50: He pulled off a ball in New York a little while ago and oney [*sic*] the big guys dere was "jerry" to it. **1904** Hobart *Jim Hickey* 16: I'll put you jerry to it right now before it gets cold. **1905** T.A. Dorgan, in Zwilling *TAD Lexicon* 50: Instead of trying to get jerry to the clever game, he hires a bunch of giants to box who are slower than a cop. **1908** McGaffey *Show Girl* 200: She accepted the attentions of the comedian, which his wife was not supposed to be jerry to. *Ibid.* 211: I got jerry. **1908** in H.C. Fisher *A. Mutt* 157: "I'll give you a chance to grab some dough....But don't breathe it." "I'm jerry. I wouldn't tell my own mother." **1908** Beach *Barrier* 107: Never mind who put us Jerry. We're here, ain't we? **1910** T.A. Dorgan, in *N.Y. Eve. Jour.* (Jan. 21) 16: Guess that...diplomat is not Jerry to the fact that Colma helps to pay his salary. **1915** Bronson-Howard *God's Man* 132: See? I'm jerry. **1915–16** Lait *Beef, Iron & Wine* 167: "Get jerry," said the Canada Kid. "I sees the wrinkle in a flash." **1916** E.R. Burroughs *Return of Mucker* 41: Who put youse jerry to all dat? **1919** *Bookman* (Apr.) 209: X gets jerry too late to be able to initiate...action. **1921** Casey & Casey *Gay-Cat* 155: I'm wise, kid; I'm jerry. *a*1923 Stringer *Diamond Thieves* 156: My Gawd, man, aren't you jerry to what's happened? **1925** *Sat. Eve. Post* (Jan. 3) 15: It don't take me no more'n five minutes to get jerry to the facts. **1932** D. Runyon, in *Collier's* (Jan. 31) 8: She is jerry to the stuff Doc is telling her when she is five years old.

2. (see 1933 quot.).

1904 T.A. Dorgan, in Zwilling *TAD Lexicon* 50: (Britt–Corbett Fight Will Be A Red-Hot Affair...) Oh, maybe that won't be a jerry little scrap. **1933** Ersine *Pris. Slang* 47: *Jerry,* adj. Happy, okay, good. "Everything is jerry now."

jerry[2] *adj. Med.* geriatric.

1968 "J. Hudson" *Case of Need* 12: They said Conway avoided jerry cases*...**Geriatrics.

jerry can *n.* [JERRY[2] + *can;* supposedly copied by the British from a German prototype] *Mil.* a narrow, flat-sided, usu. five-gallon container for fluids. Now *S.E.*

1945 in *Combat* 187: He went over to the Jerry can and drank. **1964** Peacock *Drill & Die* 107: Yes, sir! And a five-gallon jerri-can of water. **1978** Groom *Better Times* 205: The water point was a collection of dozens of fifteen-gallon jerry cans. **1980** Manchester *Darkness* 168: Water and gasoline were kept in almost identical...five-gallon "jerry-cans." **1982** D.J. Williams *Hit Hard* 141 [ref. to WWII]: Damn frog got him a jerry can.

Jersey *n.* a glass of milk.

1947 Schulberg *Harder They Fall* 183: Tell Room Service to send up one Jersey.

Jersey lightning *n.* Esp. *N.J.* illicitly distilled whiskey or applejack.

1852 Hazen *Five Years* 23: I saw three of them empty a pint bottle of apple jack, Jersey lightning, or some other equally nauseous distillation. **1860–61** (quot. at LEG-STRETCHER). **1863** in Horrocks *Dear Parents* 29: A great many of them sell whiskey of their own make which has got the name of "Jersey Lightning." **1867** in W. Goldstein *Playing for Keeps* 80: Numerous draughts of "Jersey lightning." **1891** Maitland *Slang Dict.* 167: Jersey lightning is a variety of alleged whiskey, which kills at forty rods. **1891** Bourke *Border* 10: Its juice could be formulated into an alcoholic drink very acceptable to the palate, even if it threw into the shade the best record ever made by "Jersey lightning" as a stimulant. **1908** Sullivan *Crim. Slang* 13: *Jersey lightning*—Bad whiskey. **1929** Bowen *Sea Slang* 75: *Jersey Lightning.* An American sailor's term for intoxicating liquor of a particularly potent description. **1935** Harris *Flying Trapeze* (film): Jersey lightning! **1945, 1966** in *DARE.*

Jerusalem cricket *n. & interj.* **1.** (used in mild or joc. oaths).—also constr. in pl.

1849 [G. Thompson] *City Crimes* 173: Or by de big Jerusalem cricket I'm bound to dump yer all off de stools! **1890** *Puck* (Feb. 26) 4: Jerusalem cricket! **1903** *DN* II 298: *Jerusalem crickets,* isn't it cold! ... Cape Cod Dialect. **1905** *DN* III 62: *Jerusalem crickets,* interj. ... Nebraska.

2. *Naut.* a louse or flea. *Joc.*

1870 [W.D. Phelps] *Fore & Aft* 161: It seemed as if...we had got to return to Cochrane, cockroaches, and Jerusalem crickets.

Jerusalem pony *n.* [in allusion to Jesus' arrival in Jerusalem on an ass, Matthew 21] an ass; donkey. *Joc.*

*1806 in *OED2:* The Jerusalem ponies have been in high requisition all the morning. **1842* in *F & H* IV 50: We saw a Jerusalem pony in Clare market yesterday. **1876* in *F & H:* The proper thing is to have a real *Jerusalem pony,* i.e. donkey. **1882** Miller & Harlow *9'51"* 266: Six policemen mounted on Jerusalem ponies.

Jerusalem Slim *n.* (among radical syndicalists, hoboes, etc.) (see 1931 quot.).

1921 in Bruns *Kts. of Road* 23: You call me Christ Jesus...But I was a rebel called Jerusalem Slim. **1931** Adamic *Laughing* 208: They...derived satisfaction from referring to Jesus as "Jerusalem Slim" and describing religion as "cheap perfume for the halitosis of the soul." *Ibid.* 221: The Man on the Cross, to Whom the atheists referred as "Jerusalem Slim." **1976** Braly *False Starts* 254: I thought this the greatest injustice since they nailed up Jerusalem Slim. *a*1979 Toelken *Dyn. of Folklore* 65: Some of the guys even had names for Jesus Christ, like Nazareth Blacky or Jerusalem Slim.

jerve *n.* [perh. var. of JARVEY] **1.** *Und.* a vest or vest pocket; (*hence*) a watch pocket.

1851 [G. Thompson] *Jack Harold* 60: I got...a gallus jerve*....*Jerve,* a vest. **1871** Banka *Prison Life* 492: Vest....*Jerve.* **1897** *Pop. Sci. Mo.* (Apr.) 832: Such expressions are...*to spiel,* to make a speech; *jerve,* a waistcoat pocket; [etc.]. *a*1909 Tillotson *Detective* 92: *Jerve*—A vest pocket. **1914** Jackson & Hellyer *Vocab.* 49: Go after the left jerve for a bundle of scratch. **1930** Lait *On Spot* 206: *Jerv* [*sic*]...Vest pocket. **1955** D.W. Maurer, in *PADS* (No. 24) 125: The watch pocket...is a *fob, jerve,* or *britch jerve* (often pronounced *jarve*).

2. *Und.* JERVER.

1914 Jackson & Hellyer *Vocab.* 49: The jerve was nailed bang to rights coming through the tip.

jerver *n.* [JERVE, 1 + *-er*] *Und.* a pickpocket; WIRE. Also **jarber.**

1903 *Enquirer* (Cincinnati) (May 9) 13: *Jarber*—A pickpocket. *a*1909 Tillotson *Detective* 92: *Jerver*—A pickpocket. **1924** in Partridge *Dict. Und.* 363: The pickpocket, or "jerver."

jesse *n.* [perh. a punning ref. to Isaiah 11:1, "And there shall come forth a rod out of the stem of *Jesse*"] **1.** punishment, esp. in the form of a severe beating or scolding, or a vigorous attack.—usu. constr. with *give*, *get*, or *catch*.

1839 *Spirit of Times* (Oct. 19) 396: I'd give him jessy with my butcher knife. **1840** *Spirit of Times* (Mar. 7) 7: "Old Whitenose"…gave Omega "jessy" a second time. **1840** in *DA*: If any of you ever come to Saco, I kalkilate you'll get *jesse*. **1842** *Spirit of Times* (Mar. 19) 30: She would give them Jesse. **1844** W. Porter *Big Bear of Arkansas* 133: Sol cooked the liver jest to the right pint, and we giv it Jessy. **1844** in Thornton *Amer. Gloss.*: Lo, the Saints, the Mormons, bless ye!/Felt thy glory most severely,/When Missouri gave them jesse. **1846** *Spirit of Times* (July 4) 223: One of the combatants "caught Jessie." **1846** in *DAE*: Our boys did give them "*most particular Jesse.*" **1847** Robb *Squatter Life* 33: That's the way to give him jessy. **1848** Judson *Mysteries of N.Y.* 504: That's the feller I gived jessy to. **1858** Vielé *Following Drum* 172: General Harney…had come down…to administer "jesse" generally to all delinquents. **1860–61** R.F. Burton *City of Saints* 78: Here, in 1855, the doughty General Harney, with 700 to 800 men, "gave Jessie" to a large war-party of Brulé Sioux,…killing 150…with but seven or eight casualties in his own force. **1863** in Thornton *Amer. Gloss.*: We are sure to catch jesse on our sore arm. **1863** in Boyer *Naval Surgeon* I 82: The speech…in which he gives the Copperheads particular jessie, or hell. **1888** *Jour. Amer. Folk-Lore* I 78: When two American boys are fighting…and a crowd is watching…, a spectator will often encourage one…by crying, "Give him jessy!" *a*1889 *Century Dict.*: To give one *Jesse* (sometimes, *to give one particular Jesse*), to give one a good scolding or dressing; punish one severely. (Slang, U.S.). **1930, 1939** in *DARE*. **1946** *AS* (Apr.) 153: *Give him Jesse.*…In February, 1946, I heard the expression used in a game of bridge by a player from Sidney, Nebraska. **1991** Least Heat Moon, in *DARE*: Not long ago I received a letter from a stranger who gave me jessie for several failures in my writing.

2. a commotion.—constr. with *raise*.

1845 in Robb *Squatter Life* 59: The affar raised jessy in Nettle Bottom.

3. *Und.* a bluff or threat. Occ. as v.

1914 Jackson & Hellyer *Vocab.* 49: *Jessie*…A bluff; a threat. Example: "He rang in a jessie and got away with it." **1930** Irwin *Tramp & Und. Sl.* 109: *Jessie.*—A bluff or threat. **1936** in Partridge *Dict. Und.* 364: I knew…that they would try to toss a Jessie (bluff) into me before resorting to guns or knives….I pretended that I had been thoroughly jessied (bluffed) by the ultimatum.

4. see s.v. *go jesse*, below.

¶ In phrase:

¶ **go jesse** to be energetic or skillful.—often as misconstrued n. phr. **[a] going jesse** an energetic or skillful person or thing.

*ca*1950 in *DARE*: He's a goin' Jessie. **1968** in *DARE*: Going jessie … term for an automobile that runs well … "Boy, she's a going jessie, ain't she?" **1967–70** in *DARE*: A very skilled or expert person … He's a … [g]oin' jessie. **1970** in *DARE*: He married a 60-year-old lady … he's eighty years old, never had a sick day in his life, he's really goin' jesse.

Jesus *n.* BEJESUS, 1; DAYLIGHTS, 1.b.—constr. with *the (living)*.

1948 McHenry & Myers *Home Is Sailor* 92: The company can kick the Jesus out of the crew. **1962** S. Smith *Escape from Hell* 98: Captain, we … kicked the living Jesus out of 'em tonight.

Jesus *adj.* perfervidly Christian or evangelical.—usu. used disparagingly.

1927 *DN* V 451: *Jesus stiff*, n. A neuropathic tramp whose particular insanity is to disseminate the gospel. **1930** Irwin *Tramp & Und. Sl.* 109: *Jesus Stiff.*—A tramp who travels about the country painting exhortations on boulders and fences along the way: "Jesus saves, come to Jesus," and the like. **1931** "D. Stiff" *Milk & Honey* 208: *Jesus guy*—A mission stiff. **1959** Morrill *Dark Sea* 118 [ref. to WWII]: The Old Man was quite a Jesus-boy about stuff like that. **1971* in *OED2*: The Jesus people. **1971** Grier & Cobbs *Jesus Bag* 3: Thus…the strictures of religion which have haunted blacks from slavery to this day, we call *The Jesus Bag*. **1979** *Army Times* (June 4) 7: A soldier who sits on his bunk reading religious tracts is apt to be labeled a "Jesus boy." **1991** D. Gaines *Teenage Wasteland* 68: He thought the Jesus girl was nice.

Jesus boots *n.pl.* imaginary footwear that enables one to walk on water; (*hence*) boots; (now *usu.*) sandals. *Joc.* Also **Jesus shoes, Jesus slippers.**

1942 *AS* (Dec.) 280: *Jesus Slippers.* Boots. **1961** L.E. Young *Virgin*

Fleet 162 [ref. to 1941]: "How did you get off the ship that night?" … "You lousy bastard, I had on my Jesus shoes and walked." **1961** Carse *Moonrakers* 65: Tales of mates he had outsmarted, the bosun who had webs between his toes and could walk on the sea "just like he had on them Jesus shoes." **1961** in *AS* XXXIX (1964) 235: Student Slang … a type of sandal … *Jesus boots*. **1966* Shaw & Spiegl *Scouse* 37: *I wanna purra Jesus-boots.* I require a pair of sandals. **1971** Dahlskog *Dict.* 34: *Jesus boots, Jesus shoes, n.* Men's sandals. **1973** *TULIPQ* (coll. B.K. Dumas): *Jesus boots* (flip-flops). **1983** S. King *Christine* 67: In his gross purple Bermudas and his Jesus-shoes. **a*1984 in Partridge *DSUE* (ed. 8) 617: *Jesus boots.* Used in reference to any requirement to cross water barriers: e.g. "You'll need Jesus boots for that." … RAF: WW2.

Jesus freak *n.* a fervent or self-righteous Christian.—usu. used contemptuously.

1966 Braly *On Yard* 174: The…little Jesus freak…moved into Red's cell with a Bible and a plastic crucifix. **1970** *Seattle Times* (July 5) E1: Jesus Freaks was a term first applied in derision to young people who had been "turned on by Jesus" in a pentecostal experience. Now the term is accepted gladly. **1971** *Ramparts* (Aug.) 20: Ah, a Jesus freak. **1971** in H.S. Thompson *Shark Hunt* 203: Rabid *Jesus Freaks* attempting to get things like "Today's Prayer Message," etc., into our editorial columns. **1973** in L. Bangs *Psychotic Reactions* 119: *Jesus Freaks*—longhaired hippie youngsters claiming conversion to Christianity. **1973** O'Neill & O'Neill *Shifting Gears* 20: Or you can take your choice among Billy Graham, the Jesus Freaks, or the latest guru from India. **1980** M. Harris *Why Nothing Works* 142: The Children of God, one of the first Jesus freak movements, appeared in California in 1968. **1980** J. Carroll *Land of Laughs* 165: For a moment I was afraid that she was a…Jesus freak or something. **1983** Nelkin & Brown *Workers* 139: They got this Jesus freak for a doctor who is a…quack and a half. **1983** *Daily Beacon* (Univ. Tenn.) (May 11) 2: I would just like to say that I am now, though I have not always been, one of those Christian zealots, or "Jesus Freaks," [and] am proud and happy about it. **1984** D. Smith *Steely Blue* 106: The money he gives to the Jesus freaks. **1989** "Capt. X" & Dodson *Unfriendly Skies* 45: The pilot community contains a subcult of Jesus freaks. **1991** McCarthy & Mallowe *Vice Cop* 110: That woman happens to be an upstanding Jesus freak today.

Jesus H. Christ *n. & interj.* [the *H.* is prob. fr. Gk epigram for Jesus, *IHS* or *IHC*, with the *H* (the Gk letter eta) reinterpreted as the E letter *H*; see Roger Smith, "The *H* of *Jesus H. Christ*," *AS* 69:3 (Fall 1994), pp. 331–35] (used as a profane oath). Also **Jesus H.**

1892 in A. Lomax *Folk Songs of N. Amer.* 116: Jesus H. Christ, will you lay there all day? *a*1910 "M. Twain" *Autobiog.*, in *DARE* [ref. to *ca*1850]: In that day the common sweareres of the region had a way of their own of *emphasizing* the Saviour's name when they were using it profanely.…He enlarged the offending J.C. into Jesus H. Christ. **1924** *DN* V 271: [Exclamations in American English:] *Jesus: —*, oh — Christ, — H. Christ, holy jumping — Christ. **1927** Faulkner *Mosquitoes* 202: Jesus H., if I ever get out of this alive. **1931** Farrell *McGinty* 149: I wouldn't let him in, even if he was Jesus H. Christ. **1938** Steinbeck *Grapes of Wrath* 10: This guy had words in it that Jesus H. Christ wouldn't know what they meant. **1951** Styron *Lie in Darkness* 49: Jesus H. Christ, it was awful. **1971** *N.Y. Times Mag.* (Sept. 5) 11: "Jesus H., he was a terror," a colleague remembers. **1982** Del Vecchio *13th Valley* 111: Jesus H., what happened to you? **1986** Thacker *Pawn* 32: Jesus H.,…when was the last time you changed your socks? **1990** M. Blake *Dances with Wolves* (film): Jesus H. Christ! What are you, crazy, boy?

Jesusly var. JEEZLY.

Jesus nut *n. Av.* a fastener securing the rotor assembly of a helicopter to its mast. *Joc.*

1966 Shepard *Doom Pussy* 3: He pointed out the large retaining nut which holds the rotors to the mast. "This," he said, "allows the thing to fly. If it comes off we lose the main rotors.…We call it the Jesus nut." **1979* in Partridge *DSUE* (ed. 8) 618: The "Jesus nut"…keeps the main [rotor] blades on. **1983** T. Page *Nam* 17 [ref. to Vietnam War]: The clackety-thud of blades straining at their Jesus nuts gets everyone running hot and cold at peak pitch. **1983** R.C. Mason *Chickenhawk* 97: We carefully inspected the Jesus nut at the top of the mast, which held the whole works in the air. **1988–89** in Safire *Quoth the Maven* 67: The final fastener holding everything together atop a helicopter's…rotor mast is called the Jesus nut. **1990** P. Dickson *Slang!* 240: *Jesus nut.* The bolt that holds the rotor blade to a helicopter.

jet *n.* ¶ In phrase: **cool (one's) jets** to be patient or relaxed; take it easy.

  1973 *TULIPQ* (coll. B.K. Dumas): Cool your jets! **1983** Goldman & Fuller *Charlie Co.* 43: He's telling me just keep your jets cool, Kit thought. **1984** J. McCorkle *Cheer Leader* 135: All right, baby. Cool your jets. **1984** McInerny *Bright Lights* 154: Cool your jets. It's Saturday. **1986** *Daily Beacon* (Univ. Tenn.) (Dec. 3) 4: Is the radical left gettin' a little hot? Well, cool your jets. **1990** Knoxville, Tenn., attorney, age 37: She better cool her jets awhile. **1995** *Talk Back Live* (CNN-TV) (June 6): The judge should have called him in and said in a judge's way, "Cool your jets."

jet *v.* Esp. *Stu.* to leave; go, esp. hurriedly.

  1968 Baker, Ladd & Robb *CUSS* 145: *Jet.* Leave a place. **1987** Univ. Tenn. student theme: The tallest student said, "I'm gonna jet." He was not flying anywhere; he was simply leaving. **1989** Munro *U.C.L.A. Slang* 53: *Jet*...to leave quickly. **1990** "Special Ed" *I'm the Magnificent* (rap song): One before the show and one when I jet. **1992** *Jerry Springer Show* (synd. TV series): He said he was going to help me, so I jetted off with him. **1993** *N.Y. Times* (Apr. 13) A1: They sentenced me to 18 months, but I jetted after four.

jet fuel *n.* (see quots.).

  *a*1983 Baugh *Black Street Speech* 49: A homemade brew consisting of a mixture of a hearty wine and a stout malt liquor....."I ain't gon drink no jet fuel." **1994** Knoxville, Tenn., graphic artist: *Jet fuel* is any very strong drink, especially if it's mixed at random, like whiskey and gin or something. It was used in my college days (*ca*1977).

jet jockey *n. Av.* a pilot of a usu. one- or two-seat jet aircraft.

  1950 *Nat. Geographic* (Sept.) 281: Now I knew what a jet jockey meant when he said, "It's like riding in a 1950 Cadillac after a Model T." **1955** R.L. Scott *Look of Eagle* 19: Pilots were an ungrateful bunch of morons but especially these jet jockeys. **1959** in *AS* XXXV (1960) 159: Those jet jockeys from the carrier. **1983** Van Devanter & Morgan *Before Morning* 133: A jet jockey overshot his target.

jew *v.* to bargain sharply with; cheat; beat down in price; haggle.—usu. constr. with *down*, occ. with *out.*—also (*obs.*) used absol.—usu. considered offensive.

  1818 in Glanz *Jew in Folklore* 6: A Yankee can Jew a Jew directly. **1825** in *OED2*: We hope...that neither the legislature nor the people, will Jew the items of expence. *a*1834 in *DAE*: If they will *Jew* people, they cannot flourish among Yankees, who are said to "*out-jew*" them in trading. **1848** in Eliason *Tarheel Talk* 279: I Jewed old Galloway down to 1.50 for ploughs. **1849** P. Decker *Diaries* 54: I jewed him down to 10 cts. **1859** Bartlett *Amer.* (ed. 2) 220: To *Jew.* To cheat. To *Jew* a person, is considered, in Western parlance, a shade worse than to "Yankee" him. **1863** in G. Whitman *Letters* 88: Walt you see I aint got my furlough yet....I dont know but they will jew me out of my chance after all. *a*1870 in *DAE*: To *Jew*...This word is used all over the U.S. In N[ew] E[ng]. Jews themselves use it in the same way. *a*1871 in Schele de Vere *Amer.* 495: Don't you think the old hunks wanted to jew me down to three thousand dollars? **1872** in *DAE*: If he jews, he will get it for comparatively little. **1873** *Slang & Vulgar Forms* 14: To speak of "Jewing down" in connection with trying to get a seller to reduce the price of his goods, is to speak very offensively. *ca*1880 in *Century Dict.*: It has become a saying that a person swindled in any manner was simply *Jewed.* **1882** "M. Twain" *Life on Miss.* 249: There's one thing in this world which a person don't ever try to jew you down on. That's a coffin. *a*1889 *Century Dict.*: *Jew*...To overreach; cheat; beat unfairly at a bargain: as, to *jew* one out of a dollar....To *jew down*, to beat down the price of; persuade the seller to take a lower price for....(This verb, in these uses, is well established in colloquial speech. Though now commonly employed without direct reference to the Jews as a race, it is regarded by them as offensive and opprobrious.) **1891** Maitland *Slang Dict.* 153: *Jew*, to beat down in a bargain; a habit of the Israelite trader. **1931** in H. Miller *Letters to Emil* 85: Arguing..., trying to jew her down to ten francs. **1973** "J. Godey" *Pelham* 182: The city is trying to jew them down to half a million each. **1976** Mamet *Amer. Buffalo* 6: Like when he jewed Ruthie out that pig iron. **1983** S. King *Christine* 99: But he "jewed 'em down," as he put it, to $2100 with the trade-in. **1982–84** Safire *Take My Word* 86: When *jew* or *jew down* is...used as a verb meaning "haggle," the intent is usually bigoted, and Jews as well as others take offense. **1987** *Daily News* (N.Y.) (July 2) 70: I want this bicycle, and I want to know whether I should go steal it or Jew him down. **1993** Mowry *Six Out Seven* 443: "How much?" "Depend. Y'all gonna try an jew me down?" **1994** N.

Karlen *Babes in Toyland* 145: One could catch bands talking of being "Jewed down" by a record-company executive. **1994** *Parade* (Sept. 4) 18: I'm Jewish....There weren't enough napkins, and I said, "Oh, they Jewed us out on the napkins." I was kidding around. **1995** M. Jackson *They Don't Care About Us* (pop. song): Jew me, sue me, everybody do me/Kick me, kike me, don't you black or white me.

Jewboy *n.* a Jewish boy or man.—now usu. used contemptuously.—usu. considered offensive. [In early use, S.E. when referring to boys only.]

  *1796 in *OED2*: Jew Boys...go out every morning. **1817* in *OED2*: Mowbray easily engaged me to join him against the Jew boy. **1866** Dallas *Grinder Papers* 77: Just then a wretch of a Jew boy thrust himself before us. **1880–81** in Glanz *Jew in Folklore* 57: Curley-headed Jew-boy, Jew! **1887** DeVol *Gambler* 264: I forgot all about being sleepy while I was working up the Jew boys. **1892* in Ware *Pass. English* 48: I've given the Jew another brief. I hope he'll pay me this time. **1904* Kipling *Traffics* 334: Pij, were you scuppered by Jewboys? **1909** F. Harris *Bomb* 10: Another acquaintance I made on the steamer was a Jew boy from Lemburg, Isaac Glueckstein, who had no money and knew but little English. **1929–31** J.T. Farrell *Young Lonigan* 138: And this for you, Jewboy. **1939** I. Shaw *Sailor off Bremen* 241: I'm damaging the poor little Jewboy's ear. Isn't that too bad? **1947** Schulberg *Harder They Fall* 268: Since when could a Mick ever beat a Jewboy at pinochle? **1953** Wicker *Kingpin* 17: The Yankees an the Jewboys an the niggers is a-marchin down on us. **1958** Appel *Raw Edge* 18: Wops or jewboys or black bastids. **1970** Boatright & Owens *Derrick Floor* 64: The first outfit that come in there was a couple of Jew boys. **1979** in R. Carson *Waterfront* 55: Now, we don't want to damage those Jewboys' precious violins. **1991** R. Rubin *Never Forget* (film): This is America, Jewboy! **1995** *Donahue* (NBC-TV): Somebody who's using words like "Jewboy" and all the other epithets.

Jew buggy *n.* JEW CANOE.—usu. considered offensive. *Joc.*

  1960 IUFA *Folk Speech: Jew buggy*: another word for Cadillac.

Jew canoe *n.* a luxury automobile.—usu. considered offensive. *Joc.* Also **Jewish submarine.**

  1973 N.Y.C. man, age 25: A Cadillac is a *Jew canoe.* **1974** *West. Folk.* XXXIII 309: White Christians, blacks, and Jews, all...call the Cadillac a "Jew canoe." **1976** Conroy *Santini* 198: Why don't you ride shotgun up there in the Jewish submarine? *Ibid.* 397: Dad, let me have the big Jew canoe tonight. **1977** Dunne *Confessions* 223: I thought a Jew would want a Cadillac at least....A Jew canoe, that's what they call a Cadillac, you know. **1994** N.Y.C. couple, ages 26 and 27 (both Jewish) (coll. J. Sheidlower): "What, your dad got another Jew canoe?" "What's that?" "A fancy car."

jewel *n.* **1.** *pl.* the male genitals; (*specif.*) the testicles.—usu. considered vulgar. See also FAMILY JEWELS.

  a*1796 in Legman *Horn Book* 140: For out he drew, before my view/The Jewels of a Mason. *ca*1888 *Stag Party* 117: A beautiful babe, its parents' joy,/With its *tiny jewels*—it was a boy. **1962 Quirk *Red Ribbons* 70: Mung, you got the kick of a mule. I'm glad your aim was good and you didn't get me in the jewels. **1965** Gary *Ski Bum* 133: Listen, Lenny, now it's not only my ass, my jewels are getting frozen, too.—What can a priest need his jewels for?—Energy. That's where energy is stored. **1967** Mailer *Vietnam* 174: Man, hold your hairy jewels, cause a shock is coming up. **1968** Mares *Marine Machine* 116: I don't care if he's white, purple, Chinese, French, Russian or Hindu, he wants to protect those jewels and that's your opportunity to strike him in another vital spot. **1971** *Nude, Blued & Tattooed* 30: The dog laid down and started washing his jewels. **1973** Overgard *Hero* 38: Hero turned the pain up one notch and said quietly, "Just relax, friend, and you won't lose your jewels." **1973** *Atlantic* (Sept.) 72: We stripped him and threw pebbles at him. He protected his jewels. **1977** Bredes *Hard Feelings* 123: I used to hate having my jewels crammed in [underpants]. **1987** *Lame Monkey* (Univ. Tenn.) (Sept. 21) 12: I slid round...and kicked Nin-jar in the jewels. **1993** P. Munro *U.C.L.A. Slang II*: Oh, man, that soccer ball hit me right in the jewels!

  2. *Irish-Amer.* (used in ironic direct address); fellow.

  [**1808** J.N. Barker *Indian Princess* I ii: "But arrah, take something for remembrenace," said they; and then I dug up this neat jewel [*shows a potato.*].] **1824** in R. Glanz *Jew in Early Humor* 85: When a clever Irishman wishes to have a fight...with a countryman, he says, "my *jewel!*" and knocks him down. **1845** Corcoran *Pickings* 14: Recorder, jewel,...is me life goin' to be sworn away by a vagabone haythin'? **1861** in W.H.

Russell *My Diary* 115: Sarjent, jewel, wud yes ayse the shtrap of me baynit? **1927** Kyne *They Also Serve* 143: Up wit' you, me jewel.

jewelblock *n. Naut.* a testicle; the scrotum.—usu. considered vulgar.

> *a***1900** in Niles et al. *Songs Mother Never Taught* 155: For 'twas there I had me mainyard sprung and me jewel block stove through.

jewelry *n.* **1.** handcuffs; fetters; shackles. Cf. earlier BRACELETS.

> **1843–45** T.J. Green *Tex. Exped.* 245: Colonel Fisher and myself being first ironed, we laughed at the "jewelry," as the boys called the chains. **1862** in Bensill *Yamhill* 51: All the prisoners turned out with "jewelry" on. **1865** H.M. Davidson *14 Mos.* 198: The "jewelry" was continued, upon the men for three or four weeks. **1865** in H. Johnson *Talking Wire* 293: That is the kind of jewelry culprits wear in the Laramie prison. **1885** "Lykkejaeger" *Dane* 42: All the consolation offered me was the jeering of my shipmates and sarcastic inquiries as to how I liked Uncle Sam's jewelry. **1927** (cited in Partridge *Dict. Und.* 364). **1927** *DN* V 451: *Jewelry*...Handcuffs. Also *bracelets*.

2. *Constr.* chains, steel bands, padlocks, etc.

> **1942** in *Dict. Canadianisms: Jewelry*—rigging, hooks, knobs, etc. **1944** Huie *Can Do!* 117: The magic "jewelry"—the self-tightening, interlocking bolts and straps which connected the boxes—weighed another 100 pounds per pontoon. **1950** *Western Folk.* IX 118: *Jewelry.* The blocks, lines, hardware, and other material used in logging. **1953** Dodson *Away All Boats* 220 [ref. to WWII]: Well, my outfit was boltin' on jewelry—that's the steel straps that holds sections of a pontoon together. **1963** in *Dict. Canadianisms:* He climbs out and puts on the "jewelry"—the tire chains.

Jewish Alps *n.pl.* [because the site of popular resort hotels patronized by Jewish New Yorkers] the Catskill Mountains, a resort area of southeastern New York. *Joc.*

> **1966** Manus *Mott the Hoople* 20: I hustled for five months, beginning at Monticello in the Jewish Alps. **1978** Univ. Tenn. grad. student, age 34: Ace wants me to go work with him in the Catskill Mountains this summer—the Jewish Alps. **1984** D. Smith *Steely Blue* 158: The Concord Hotel, high up in the part of the Catskill Mountains he called the Jewish Alps. **1991** Marcinko & Weisberg *Rogue Warrior* 30: Summer vacations in the Catskill Mountains—the Jewish Alps. **1995** N.Y. man, age 64 (coll. J. Sheidlower): I used to hear *Jewish Alps* for the Catskills around 1950. I worked there when I was in college.

Jewish-American princess var. JEWISH PRINCESS.

Jewish cavalry *n. Army.* the quartermaster corps. *Joc.*

> **1918** in *AS* V (June 1930) 384: *Jewish cavalry*—Quartermaster's force.

Jewish flag *n.* a currency note; dollar bill.—usu. considered offensive. *Joc.* Also **Jew flag.**

> **1915** "High Jinks, Jr." *Choice Slang* 51: *Jewish flags*—Five dollar bills. **1920** Weaver *In American* 37: Four Jewish flags I blow, four lovely bucks. **1923** McKnight *Eng. Words* 225: *Shinplaster,* or *Jewish flag,* for paper money. **1929** *AS* IV (June) 341: *Jewish flag*—A one dollar bill. **1930** Graham & Graham *Queer People* 197: I won't let 'em stay fooled—not without a great many Jewish flags—right on the line. **1932** in *DARE* I 553: A silver dollar is a *caser,* a dollar bill is a *Jew flag.* **1941** *AS* (Feb.) 23: *Jew flag.* A dollar bill. **1967–70** in *DARE.*

Jewish penicillin *n.* chicken soup. *Joc.*

> **1968** in *DARE:* Jewish penicillin (chicken soup). **1972** R. Barrett *Lovomaniacs* 238: He grinned crookedly at me. "Jewish penicillin....My old lady used to make it up by the gallon." **1972** *CBS Eve. News* (CBS-TV) (Dec. 6): Chicken soup is good for anything. Take any medicine you want to name, the Jewish penicillin is the best. **1975** *N.Y. Times Book Rev.* (Aug. 24) 4: Chicken soup, because of its universal curative power, is sometimes known as "Jewish penicillin." **1983** Groen & Groen *Huey* 171: I'm just not too wild about Jewish penicillin. **1984** *Mayo Clinic Health Letter* (Oct.) 5: Chicken soup has been confidently administered by Jewish mothers to family members with head colds from time immemorial and is sometimes referred to in jest as "Jewish penicillin." **1990** *N.Y. Times Mag.* (Feb. 4) 45: Historians are divided as to exactly which Catskill comedian first uttered the words "Jewish penicillin."

Jewish piano *n.* a cash register.—usu. considered offensive. *Joc.*

> **1935** Pollock *Und. Speaks: Jewish piano,* a cash register. **1951** *Western Folk.* X 171: *Jewish piano:* A cash register. [New Mexico]. **1975** *N.Y. Post* (June 13) 37: Most of these men are anti-Semitic. They

sometimes refer to the cash register as a "Jewish piano." **1986** Merkin *Zombie Jamboree* 213: I thought all you guys did was play the Jewish piano....In Hough that's what we call a fuckin' cash register, man. **1989** Chafets *Devil's Night* 197: I can play that Jewish piano, you know, the cash register.

Jewish prince *n.* [modeled on JEWISH PRINCESS] a young, usu. middle-class Jewish man who is spoiled, conceited, etc.—usu. used disparagingly.—usu. considered offensive.

> **1982** M. Lerner, in *N.Y. Post* (Aug. 28) 13: He is the New York Jewish prince, burdened with a willful, possessive mother. **1983** Ephron *Heartburn* 28: Jewish princes are made, not born....You know what a Jewish prince is, don't you? **1996** *N.Y. Times* (Nov. 23) 19: A half-hour of hilarious comedy about Jews without a Jewish mother, Jewish-American princess or shiksa-chasing Jewish prince in sight.

Jewish princess *n.* a young, usu. middle-class Jewish woman who is conceited, pampered, etc.—usu. used disparagingly.—usu. considered offensive. Also **Jewish-American princess.** Cf. JAP.

> **1972** (quot. at JAP). **1973** N. Mailer, in *Atlantic* (Aug.) 33: Jewish Princess [title of article]. **1976** Rosen *Above Rim* 152: A ball-nagging, tight-lipped, coffin-twatted Jewish Princess from Long Island's North Shore. **1977** (quot. at JAP). **1983** Ephron *Heartburn* 30: I was not raised as a Jewish princess. **1984** H. Searls *Blood Song* 33: Now, I don't want you to be a heavy-duty Jewish-American Princess—. **1988** D. Reskin & G. Clark *Skinheads* (film): Maybe they're a couple of Jewish princesses. **1990** *Newsweek* (Mar. 5) 62: The Lady Macbeth, the Wounded Bird and the Jewish Princess. **1991** *Santa-Barbara* (Calif.) *News-Press* (Jan. 12) B10: A judge says he meant nothing demeaning when he referred to a woman in a divorce case as a "Jewish-American princess." **1996** (quot. at JEWISH PRINCE).

Jewish submarine var. JEW CANOE.

Jew's abomination *n. West.* (see quot.). *Joc.*

> **1853** Delano *Life on Plains* 109: We regaled ourselves on antelope steak and Jew's abomination (bacon).

Jew York *n.* New York City.—usu. used disparagingly.—usu. considered offensive.

> **1931** E. Pound, in Ahearn *Pound/Zukofsky* 104: Dere orter be a decent publishinkg house in Jew York. **1939** Farrell *To Whom* 190: "Down with the Jews of Jew York!" Tommy boomed. **1939** in R. Hughes *Dewey* 334: Jew York Democracy in Action. **1939** *N & Q* (Sept. 2) 178: "Jew York"...Moses Jacob Brix of Bucharest (1866–1930), better known as Maurice Brix, the blind antiquary of Philadelphia, used the above expression to me...about 1920. **1947** Mailer *Naked & Dead* 56: And for two weeks he had heard Conn talk about the...depravity of the Negro, and the...fact that Jew York was in the hands of foreigners. **1990** Vachss *Blossom* 237: Maybe it ain't as bad as Jew York yet. **1995** *CBS This Morning* (CBS-TV) (Nov. 1): On one of the shows somebody said "Jew York."

J-factor *n.* [*J* for *Jesus*] *Navy.* the possibility of divine intervention.

> **1956** Lockwood & Adamson *Zoomies, Subs & Zeroes* 89 [ref. to WWII]: At that point, only the J-factor could save him. The J-factor, it should be mentioned, was a very real thing to our submariners and reverently spoken of. It recognized...that some situations can be resolved only by the divine intervention of Jesus.

jib *n.* [app. abstracted from *cut of (one's) jib,* below; but cf. **1860, *1889 quots. at (2), below, indicating the confluence of two unrelated etyma] **1.** Now esp. *Black E.* one's lip (now usu. *pl.*); the mouth (also in form *jibs*); (*pl.*) the teeth.

> **a***1825** in *OED: Jib,* the under-lip. Of a whimpering child it is said "he hangs his jib." *****1865** *OED:* Cock up thy jib, an' let's have another smeawtch [kiss]. **1932** V. Fisher *In Tragic Life* 309 [ref. to *ca*1908]: I'll smack your jib in a minute. *Ibid.* 329: Shut your jib. **1938** in *DARE:* If Pa put his jib in I would tell him to stay out of my love affair. **1953** Kramer & Karr *Teen-Age Gangs* 24: Maybe I shoot off my jib too much. **1958–59** in Abrahams *Deep Down in Jungle* 262: *Jibs*—Teeth. **1970** Major *Afro-Amer. Slang* 71: *Jib:* mouth. **1970** Landy *Underground Dict.* 88: *Gibbs* [sic]...Mouth—eg. He hides his drugs in his gibbs. **1970** A. Young *Snakes* 34: You probly saved the cat from a awful beatin splittin him in his jibs right quick like that. **1971** S. Stevens *Way Uptown* 292: Don't come up here jacking off your jib about how you is a black man. **1971–72** in Abernethy *Bounty of Texas*

205: *Gibbs*, n.—a person's lips. **1972** Claerbaut *Black Jargon* 70: *Jibs*...lips: It hit him in the jibs. **1972** Andrews & Dickens *Big House* 23: Then don't sit there running off at the jibs. *Ibid.* 35: Now, as for putting your paws in my reverend jibs—don't! **1967–80** Folb *Runnin' Lines* 243: *Jibs, jaw at the/run off at the* 1. Talk too much. 2. Engage in foolish or irrelevant talk. **1983** Wambaugh *Delta Star* 18: Slap that dog upside the jibbs.

2. Orig. *Und.* speech; language; talk, esp. impudent chatter; in phr. **slide (one's) jib** (*rare*) to talk to no purpose.
    ***1860** Hotten *Slang Dict.* (ed. 2): *Jibb*, the tongue.—*Gipsy* and *Hindoo*. (Tramps' term.) Thence extended to mean language. ***a1889** Barrère & Leland *Dict. Slang* I 499: *Jib*...(Gypsy), language, speech. (Hindu *tschib*). Also used in canting. "Dré savo *jib* rakdé o mush?"—in what language did the man talk? **1903** *Pedagog. Sem.* X 371: Enough of your jib. **1929** Hotstetter & Beesley *Racket* 229: *Jib*...frivolous conversation. **1956** Hargrove *Girl He Left* 81: He's just sliding his jib again...I can't get tuned in on him. **1964** in B. Jackson *Swim Like Me* 108: Just a minute, old broad, now you knife your jib whilst I'll crack my whip.

3. *pl. Black E.* **a.** the buttocks; ASS, 1.a.
    1958 I.H. Freeman *Out of Burning* 137 [ref. to *ca*1950]: Ahm gonna blow their chibbs off. *Ibid.* 153: I...foot Gus one in the chibbs. **1972** Claerbaut *Black Jargon* 70: *Jibs*...buttocks. **1983** *Reader's Digest Success with Words* 86: Black English...*jibs* = (1) "lips" (2) "buttocks."

b. a woman's breasts.
    1986 *Playboy* (Apr.) 20: Breasts...Boobs,...Hooters,...Jibs, [etc.].

¶ In phrases:

¶ **bowse up the jib, 1.** *Naut.* to drink heavily; get drunk.
    1841 [Mercier] *Man-of-War* 46: Godfrey went below, perhaps to *freshen the nip*, for he appeared to be bousing his jib pretty taught ever since the accident. *Ibid.* 168: Those...had been *bowsing their jibs up* during the morning. **1883** C. Russell *Sailors' Lang.* 19: *Bowse up the jib.*—Said of a man who drinks in order to get drunk. **1886** P.D. Haywood *Cruise* 20: I left the service, sir....bowsed up my jib too often.

2. *Naut.* to speak foolishly or in excess.
    1946 Gordon *Years Ago* 93: Don't be bousin' your jib....Money's a damn lovin' friend, too!

¶ **cut of (one's) jib** Orig. *Naut.* (one's) features, bearing, or appearance. Now *colloq.* [This phr. is already entered in CUT OF (ONE'S) JIB in *HDAS* I; the following citations provide additional evidence. The first citation is repeated for the sake of completeness.]
    1796 in Whiting *Early Amer. Prov.* 91: By the cut of your jib. ***1831** Trelawny *Adv. Younger Son* ch. xxxv: I can't say I like the cut of his jib. **1833** A. Greene *Nullifiers* 100: I know you're a Yankee by the cut of your jib. **1834** Caruthers *Kentuckian in N.Y.* 190: They don't look at the cut of a feller's coat, but at the cut of his jib. **1844** J.F. Cooper *Afloat & Ashore* 43: He...understood "by the cut of his jib," that Rupert was not likely to make a weather-earing man. **1875** A. Pinkerton *C. Melnotte* 198: From the "cut of his jib," as the sailors say, I took him to be a gambler. **1899** Stratemeyer *Cuban Waters* 256: You're true blue—I can see that by the cut of your jib. **1924** Anderson & Stallings *What Price Glory?* 111: I like the cut of your jib. **1945** Colcord *Sea Lang.* 108: A phrase in common use ashore is "the cut of one's jib," i.e. one's general appearance and get-up. **1955** C.D. Funk *Heavens to Betsy!* 79: *To dislike...the cut of one's jib.* To dislike, or be chary of, the appearance of a person, or his character....Certain characteristic shapes of [a vessel's jib] served, among sailors, to identify the nationality..., and, therefore, whether the vessel might be friendly or hostile. **1972** Meade & Rutledge *Belle* 43: I like the cut of your jib.

¶ **fly off (one's) jib** *Naut.* to become infirm.
    1848 in *AS* X (1935) 40: *Hanks flying off his jib.* Getting old, or in poor health.

¶ **pay off with the jib-downhaul** *Naut.* to desert one's ship. Now *hist.*
    1904 J.H. Williams, in *Independent* (Mar. 24) 656: I guess he was one of the old packet rats, who paid himself off with the jib downhaul at each port. *a*1966 Hugill *Sailortown* 263: It didn't take much of this to make John want to pay off with the jib-downhaul.

¶ **torque (one's) jibs** [sugg. by syn. *tighten (one's) jaws* s.v. JAW, n.] *Mil.* to cause (one) to grind or grit (one's) teeth in anger.
    1989 D. Sherman *There I Was* 247 [ref. to Vietnam War]: One thing...torques my jibs every time I...think about it.

¶ **up jib** *Naut.* to be off; depart.
    1848 in *AS* X (1935) 40: *Up jib.* Be off. **1871** Schele de Vere *Amer.* 349: "Let's *up jib*, and say no more," is a phrase often heard on the Eastern coasts....the hoisting of the jib is a signal of departure, and hence the sailor's phrase has become synonymous with, "let us be gone." **1877** Bartlett *Americanisms* (ed. 4) 728: *To up Jib.* To be off. A sailor's phrase, much used in familiar language in Nantucket, Salem, and other localities in Massachusetts. **1945** Colcord *Sea Lang.* 108: "Up jib!" is a piece of humorous advice to one who seems to be getting into difficulties.

jib *v.* to talk excessively or nonsensically.
    1967–80 E. Folb *Runnin' Lines* 44: Jibbin' too damn much!...Talkin' 'bout nuthin. *Ibid.* 118: Frontin' off like a pimp—be jibbin' 'bout his 'hos.

jiblets var. JIGLETS.

jib boom *n. Naut.* the penis.—usu. considered vulgar.
    *a*1900 in Cray *Erotic Muse* 188: And into her parlor I run my jib boom. *ca*1929 *Collection of Sea Songs* 15: So I took a reef in my shirt tail/And rammed the jibbon [*sic*] up her ass. *Ibid.* 21: He could tell by the feel of his rap a tap tap/His flying jibboom was sprung.

jiboney *n.* [orig. uncert.; prob. ult. < an It word, perh. Milanese *giambone* 'ham', as calque of U.S. slang HAM; also cf. JAMBONE] Esp. *Ital.-Amer.* a stupid, foolish, or offensive person; (*also*) a hired thug; hoodlum; (*broadly*) a man; fellow. Also **jaboney, shaboney,** etc.
    1921 J. Conway, in *Variety* (May 4) 9: This giboney comes back with, "Sorry, this is a five-story buildin' and we ain't got no sixth floor." **1921** J. Conway, in *Variety* (May 20): I take this giboney and get him more publicity than he ever got in his life. **1921** *Variety* (Dec. 30) 4: Them giboneys wouldn't know a good act if it jumped up and bit them. **1922** *Variety* (Aug. 4) 5: Some of these giboneys that own this club will take turns croakin' each other. **1931** *AS* VI 439: *Jaboney*...A greenhorn; a newly-arrived foreigner. **1952** *Esquire* (June) 84: He had a couple of his jiboneys with him. **1952** H. Grey *Hoods* 176: A couple of shabonies, you know, the demolition squad from Mulberry Street, to blow the joint apart. **1954** Matheson *Born of Man & Woman* 127: And that jiboney across the hall. He makes life worse than it is. **1970** Gattzden *Black Vendetta* 143: Those jabonies are the ones that should be balling. **1974** Nyack, N.Y., man, age 29: A *jiboney* is a real idiot, a guy you don't like. **1976** R. Price *Bloodbrothers* 6: Stony....Fuckin' jibone. *Ibid.* 196: Vinny, you're a real jibone, you know that? **1977** Torres *Q & A* 152: You, you fucking jadroney. **1993** in *Vanity Fair* (Jan. 1994) 130: Koppel can see each jaboney on a monitor, but they can only hear him.

jib rat *n.* [JIB (fr. Joint Information Bureau) + RAT] *Mil. & Journ.* (see quots.). Now *hist.*
    1991 Dunnigan & Bay *From Shield to Storm* 361: Kuwait War Slang...*Jib Rat*—See REMF. **1993** P. Dickson *War Slang* 314: *Jib rat*...A reporter who watched the war on television, from a hotel room,...almost exclusively...the Dharan International Hotel's JIB.

jiff *n.* an instant; jiffy. Now *colloq.*
    ***1797** in *OED2*: 'Twould raise a mutiny in a jiff. **1881** C.M. Chase *Editor's Run* 88: The deer...was out of sight in a jiff. ***1892** in *F & H* IV 53: Put me at 'ome in a Jiff. **1935** Lorimer & Lorimer *Heart Specialist* 8: Promised to unpack in a jiff. ***1939** in B.J. Whiting *Mod. Provs.* 343: I'll be along in half a jiff. **1951** in Kerouac *Letters* 299: In a jiff I was in. **1976** Hayden *Voyage* 412: He'll be back in a jiff. **1976** Rosten *To Anywhere* 27: Seeya in a jiff. **1981** G. Wolf *Roger Rabbit* 78: Lunch will be ready in a jiff.

jiffy mart *n.* [sugg. by *Jiffy Mart*, a trademark for a chain of convenience stores] *Mil.* (see quot.).
    1991 LaBarge *Desert Voices* 29: A jiffy mart was what they called it. A resupply point.

jig[1] *n.* [perh. sugg. by the obs. S.E. sense (1592–1735 in *OED*), 'a trick'] ¶ In phrase: **the jig is up** [or (*obs.*) **over** or **out**] the trickery, plotting, wrongdoing, etc., is over.
    1777 in Thornton *Amer. Glossary*: Mr. John Miller came in and said, "The jig is over with us." **1778** in Whiting *Early Amer. Prov.* 239: The Gig is up with us. **1787** in Whiting *Early Amer. Prov.*: I think this Man's Jigg is up. **1800** in Thornton *Amer. Glossary*: The Jigg's up, Paddy. **1821** Waln *Hermit* 25: The *jig's* up. **1832** in [S. Smith] *Letters of Downing* 82: I'm afraid my jig would be up. **1845** Hooper *Simon Suggs* 121: And then I concluded the jig was up. **1848** in *F & H* IV 54: I know'd the jig was up. **1883** Larison *Silvia Dubois* 67: The jig was

out. I knew I must go. **1891** Maitland *Slang Dict.* 155: *Jig* (Am.). "The jig's up," it is all over. **1893** W.K. Post *Harvard* 238: The jig is up with poor Jack Rat. **1935** C.J. Daly *Murder* 263: The full realization that the jig's up. **1937** Odets *Golden Boy* 261: Sweetheart, the jig is up! **1958** in H. Rawson *Wicked Words* 221: The Jig is Up for Adam Clayton Powell Jr. **1966** in I. Reed *Conjure* 9: Refusing to believe the jig is up. **1973** in *Submiss. Rec. Pres. Convers.* 434: The jig is up.

jig[2] *n.* [see 1950 quot. and cf. JIGWALK, JIGABOO] a black person.—usu. used contemptuously.—usu. considered offensive.

    1922 Colton & Randolph *Rain* 79: What's that the old jig does? **1925** Van Vechten *Nigger Heaven* 50: Rather, they are inclined to ignore it, until some jig or other annoys them, and then they lynch him or start a riot or something. *Ibid.* 286: *Jig-chaser.*—a white person who seeks the company of Negroes. **1927** Nicholson *Barker* 88: Nat Brody's here, and a crew of jigs. **1928** R. Fisher *Jericho* 8: One jig in danger is ev'y jig in danger. **1911–29** in *PADS* (No. 11) 7: *Jig*, n. A Negro. Low colloquial. **1933** *Fortune* (Aug.) 47: A couple of jigs got on the bus. **1934** L. Hughes *Ways of White Folks* 60: Mr. Lloyd, jealous of a jig! **1935** *Amer. Mercury* (June) 229: *Jig Show:* minstrel show. **1938** in *AS* (Dec.) 310: All West Indians are [called] *Jigs.* **1940** O'Hara *Pal Joey* 165: They are primative and not very close to civilization like jigs. **1947** Willingham *End as a Man* 23: You're as cute as the pecker on a baby jigg. **1947** Spillane *I, the Jury* 47: I grabbed the two jigs by their collars and yanked them out the door. **1950** Blesh *All Played Ragtime* 23: [Clarinetist] Tom Ireland recalls that up to [1897] ragtime piano was called "jig piano" [in St. Louis], and the syncopating bands, like Joplin's, were called "jig bands." This term, taken from jig dances, even came a little later to be a designation for the Negro himself. **1957** Gutwillig *Long Silence* 89: That Jackie Robinson's a hell of a ball player for a jig. **1959** E. Hunter *Matter of Conviction* 189: Man, did you see me hit that jig? **1963** *Time* (Aug. 2) 14: *Jig,…member,…soul brother.* Fellow Negro. **1970** Sorrentino *Steelwork* 15: A lot of crazy jigs in the desert throwing spears at Italian planes. **1974** Pi74 *A Short Eyes* 115: *Jig* Derogatory term for a black man. **1988** S. Lee *School Daze* (film): Jigaboo!…Jig!

jigaboo *n.* [orig. unkn.; cf. JIG[2], *n.* and ZIGABOO] a black person.—used contemptuously.—usu. considered offensive. [The relationship, if any, of bracketed examples is problematical.]

    [**1909** Weston, Barnes & Scott *I've Got Rings on My Fingers* 2 (sheet music)*:* "I've Got Rings on My Fingers;" or, Mumbo Jumbo Jijjiboo J. O'Shea.…Jim O'Shea.…The natives…called him Jijjiboo Jhai [sic].] [**1912** H. Chalmers-Rego *Jingaboo; march-song and two-step* [title] [Akron, Ohio: Akron Music Co., 1912]. **1926** Finerty *Criminalese* 32: *Jiggaboo*—A negro or yellow race chauffeur. **1928** R. Fisher *Jericho* 148: That jigaboo's jes' jivin'. **1928** in Grayson *New Stories* 212: He called them jigaboos. **1929** E. Sullivan *Look at Chicago* 3 [ref. to 1919]: The paper's been giving the jigaboos all the best of it. **1930** *Amer. Mercury* (Dec.) 456: *Jiggabo, n.:* A Negro. "Me broad's squawkin' the jiggabo hop tries to make her." **1931** L. Hughes *Mulatto* 18: 'Bout a dozen colored guys standing around, too, and not one of 'em would help me—the dumb jiggaboos! **1935** O'Hara *Butterfield 8* 110: There's a jiggaboom [sic] had this job before me is working down the street now. **1937** Reitman *Box-Car Bertha* 172: They both live with Earl Walker, a "jigaboo" pimp from the south side. **1948** Cozzens *Guard of Honor* 32: He's an Engineer Corps jigaboo. **1959** in Griffin *Black Like Me* [entry for Nov. 14]: He does not become calloused to these things…—hearing himself referred to a nigger, coon, jigaboo. **1965** Conot *Rivers of Blood* 182: What you want,…jigaboo? **1988** S. Lee *School Daze* (film): You a jigaboo! **1990** *New Yorker* (Dec. 10) 50: Jigaboos don't. **1990** "Public Enemy" *Burn Hollywood Burn* (rap song): I figure you to play some jigaboo/On the plantation, what else can a nigger do? **1996** Alson *Ivy League Bookie* 138: You fuckin' asshole motherfuckin' niggers, jigaboo spear-chucking pieces of shit.

jigadier brindle *n.* [intentional spoonerism] *Army.* brigadier general. *Joc.*

    1862 in C.H. Moulton *Ft. Lyon* 56: Honored with the epithet of "Jigadier Brindle." **1887** Hinman *Si Klegg* 581 [ref. to Civil War]: A brigade commander was a "jigadier brindle." **1887** Peck *Pvt. Peck* 209 [ref. to Civil War]: I'll shall love you if you get to be a Jigadier Brindle. **1893** Frye *Field & Staff* 87: He…held 'most every title in the milishy 'ceptin' jigadier-brindle—which is what the boys useter call the brigadier gen'ral. **1920** *Amer. Legion Wkly.* (Dec. 17) 11: "You're a fine old reprobate…," declared the jigadier brindle. **1924** T. Boyd *Pts. of Honor* 41: You'll look like a Jigadier Brindle. **1963** E.M. Miller *Exile* 133: One of the best-type gigidier brindles going.

jig-a-jig *n.* copulation. usu. considered vulgar. Also **jiggy-jig, jig-jig.** Also as v. [Chiefly in mil. pidgin.]

    *a***1890–96** *F & H* IV 54: *Jig-a-jig*…(American).—To copulate. **1918** in M. Carey *Mlle. from Armentières* (unp.): Mademoiselle from St. Nazaire,/She'd jig-a-jig-jig for a pomme de terre. *****1930** Brophy & Partridge *Songs & Slang* 132: *Jig-a-jig.*—Copulation.…United States in origin. *****1932** in *OED2:* This was…the red-lamp district.…The women stopped.…"Jig-a-jig, Johnny? Very nice!" they said. **1935** Pollock *Und. Speaks:* *Jig-jig*, a lewd act. *****1936** Partridge *DSUE* 438: Popularised in and by the [Great War], when used by French touts in form *jig-a-jig très bon.* **1951** W. Williams *Enemy* 168: Who knows words besides *coucher* and jigajig? **1952** Bellow *Augie March* 184: You got plenty of jig-jig ahead of you before you settle down. **1964** Mirvish *There You Are* 48: Get anything you want. Only no jiggy-jig. All off limits. *****1973** in Partridge *DSUE* (ed. 8) 619: *Jiggy-jig*…spread throughout the Brit. Army; whence to Egypt, where I first heard it [1915]. **1978** *Atlantic* (Apr.) 95: "Dated her.…You mean a little boom-boom?" "Jig-jig," he said. "But it comes to the same thing."

jigamaree *n.* [fanciful formation] a thingamajig, esp. a foolish or novel contrivance. Also vars.

    1824 in Thornton *Amer. Gloss.:* O the wonderation, what a nation sight of jiggermarees! **1850** in Blair & McDavid *Mirth* 102: One of them-ere all-fired Yankee peddlers come along with a outlandish kind of a jigamaree to make the women's coat sorta stick out in the t'other end. *a***1889** *Century Dict.:* *Jigamaree*…Something new, strange, or unknown; a jiggumbob or thingumbob. (Prov. or slang). **1908** *DN* III 324: *Jigamaree*…A gewgaw, a thingumabob. [East Ala.]. **1918** in Kornbluh *Rebel Voices* 269: Paul…came back with a jiggermaroo that dumped 800 of the crew down the skid road onto the bread line. **1929** Bowen *Sea Slang* 75: *Jiggamaree.* An attempt to substitute a new fangled idea for established sea custom. **1974, 1979** in *DARE.*

jigged *adj.* *jiggered* s.v. JIGGER[1], *v.,* 1.

    1908 in McCay *Little Nemo* 129: He's made that blind girl see! I'll be jigged! **1950** in *DARE.*

jigger *n.* [the first sense may represent a different word] **1.a.** *Und.* a door. *Rare* in U.S.

    *****1567** Harman *Caveat* 27: *A gygger,* a doore.…*Dup the gygger*…open the doore. *****1610** [Rowlands] *Martin Mark-All: Gilkes for the gigger,* false keyes for the doore or picklockes. *****1698–99** "B.E." *Dict. Canting Crew: Dub the Gigger*…open the Door with the Pick-lock that we may go in and Rob the House. *****1718** in Partridge *Dict. Und.* 286: *Jigger* [door]. **1807** Tufts *Autobiog.* 292 [ref. to 1794]: *Jigger*…a door. *****1812** Vaux *Vocab.: Jigger:* a door. *****1851** H. Mayhew *London Labour* I 314: Such men are always left outside the jigger (door) of the houses. **1859** Matsell *Vocab.* 46: *Jigger.* A door. "Dub the jigger," open the door. *****1864** in *Comments on Ety.* (Dec. 1, 1987) 25: Joe had managed to reach our "jigger" and walked in. *****1865** in *Comments on Ety.* (Oct. 1, 1987) 40: I'll have the "jigger" ready "unslewed" for you.

    b. *Army.* a guardhouse or lockup.

    *a***1890–96** *F & H* IV 55: *Jigger*…(military).—A guard-room. **1906** M'Govern *Sarjint Larry* (gloss.): *Jigger:*—Guard-house. **1909** M'Govern *Krag Is Laid Away* 122: Land him in the jigger before he gets real violent! **1918** Griffin *Ballads of Regt.* 58: He finished each "jag" in the "jigger."

    2.a. a thingamajig.

    [*****1825** in *OED:* For forming saucers, and other small circular articles, there has been recently introduced a small vertical shaft, called a *jigger* [etc.].] **1861** E.S. Ellis *N. Todd* 66: I can't see how them jiggers [letters] can speak, but I s'pose they does. *****1873** Hotten *Slang Dict.* (ed. 4): Jigger has many meanings, the word being applied to any small mechanical contrivance. **1890** *DN* I 74: *Jigger:* thing (very vague), "thingemajig." **1914** *DN* IV 158: *Jigger*…Thing. **1926** *AS* I 628: In America, jigger is often used as an indefinite name, not too dignified, of the same order as thingumbob. **1968, 1982** in *DARE.*

    b. *Esp. West.* an inconsequential or foolish person.

    *****1825** in *OED: Jigger,* an airy, swaggering person. "A comical jigger." *****1880** *Jamieson's Scot. Dict.: Jigger*…a term of reproach or disrespect. **1895** in J. London *Tramp Diary* 61: I'm onto meself for a jigger w'en it comes to dem people. **1922** in E. Ferber *One Basket* 175: Aren't you getting pretty thick with this jigger? **1925** in Hammett *Big Knockover* 229: Did I do right, shooting that jigger? **1947** Overholser *Buckaroo's Code* 10: This towheaded jigger with the fancy drinking ideas don't have to ride very far to get trouble if that's what he's looking for. *a***1956** Almirall *College to Cow Country* 63: Lemme straighten this jigger out. *a*1960 Federoff *Side of Angels* 97: Bunch of dumb jiggers. **1961** R.E. Pike *Spiked Boots* 76: He was a funny old jigger. **1962** W. Robinson *Barbara* 310: I told you this little jigger had the hots for her. **1965** Foreman *Mustang* 23: I've got to take along some jigger who knows the country down there. **1971** Heckelmann *Durango* 23: Maeve, what are you tellin' all that to this jigger for? **1986** *Mama's Family* (NBC-TV): Does the bigger jigger carry hospitalization?

c. about 1-½ ounces of whiskey or other liquor, now usu. as a cocktail ingredient; (*hence*) a small liquor glass. Now *S.E.*

1836 in *OED2*: These canal labourers have a boy to supply them with Whiskey, called a *Jiggar boss*, who goes on the canal and carries a half gill…of Whiskey to every man sixteen times a day! **1839** Crockett's *Comic Alm.* (unp.): Twelve dollars a month, and fourteen jiggars a day, arrah! **1879** in *OED2*: A jigger … is a conical metal cup in which to mix fancy drinks. **1891** Maitland *Slang Dict.* 155: *Jigger* (Am.), a small measure used by barkeepers. **1916** L. Stillwell *Common Soldier* 75 [ref. to Civil War]: I drank my first "jigger," as it was called, and then quit. **1927** E. Stockwell *Pvt. Stockwell* 35 [ref. to Civil War]: Whiskey … was dealt out … by the orderly sergeant, about a gill to a dose, called a jigger. **1964** Thompson & Rice *Every Diamond* 60: A jigger for medicinal purposes. **1975** R.P. Davis *Pilot* 139: You'll have to buy a jigger, a four-ouncer.

d. *Billiards.* a supporting rest for the cue; bridge.

*1847 in *OED*: The long cue and the "jigger." **1891** Maitland *Slang Dict.* 155: *Jigger* (Am.), the bridge or rest used in billiards.

e. the vulva or vagina.—usu. considered vulgar.

a*1890–96 *F & H* IV 55: *Jigger*…The female *pudendum*. **1935 in Legman *Limerick* 193: Out of her jigger/Jumped a cast-iron nigger.

f. (among beggars) a usu. bogus sore, bandage, or the like displayed to elicit sympathy.

1894 "J. Flynt," in *Century* (Mar.) 713: He usually carries a "jigger,"—in other words, an artificially made sore, placed usually on an arm or leg. **1894** "J. Flynt," in *Atlantic* (Sept.) 321: The "jiggers" were…bandages wound around the legs and arms to excite the sympathy of credulous and charitable people. **1912** Berkman *Prison* 165 [ref. to 1893]: I had him put a jigger on me; kept it up for four years. **1914** Jackson & Hellyer *Vocab.* 49: *Jigger*…A fake wound, burn, scald or other crippled condition. Example: "They're all jigger bums." **1922** N. Anderson *Hobo* 44: In Hobohemia a pretended affliction is called "jiggers" or "bugs." **1927** *DN* V 451: *Jigger*…An artificial sore, so called because it is sometimes made by applying a jigger. [**1927** E. Stockwell *Pvt. Stockwell* 101 [ref. to Civil War]: A good many of the boys were getting what the doctor called "jiggers," the forerunner of scurvy.]

g. a tattoo.

1902 "J. Flynt" *Little Bro.* 195: A wanderer from the South had offered to tattoo a ship on Benny's arm.…A "jigger" was "damn foolishness"….."They'll find you out if you have ships and things jiggered into your skin."

h. *N.J.* a scoop of ice cream; (*also*) an ice-cream scooper.

1909 in O. Johnson *Lawrenceville* 7 [ref. to 1890's]: Give me a coffee jigger, with chocolate syrup and a dash of whipped cream—stick a meringue in it. *Ibid.* 21: A jigger is unlike any other ice cream. It is dipped from the creamy tin by a cone-shaped scoop [also] called a jigger.…A double jigger fills a large soda glass.

3. [fr. JIGGERS] *Und. & Pris.* one who acts as a lookout during the commission of a crime.

1925 in Partridge *Dict. Und.* 364: *Jigger* [a lookout man]. **1942** *ATS* 419: *Jigger man*…a criminal lookout.…*jigger moll*, a female criminal lookout. **1971** in Abernethy *Bounty of Texas* 208: *Jigger*, n.—a lookout to warn others by relay.

4. *R.R.* (see quots.).

1927 *DN* V 451: *Jigger*…A very slow freight. **1931** *Writer's Digest* (May) 42: *Jigger*—A full tonnage train of dead freight.

jigger¹ *v.* [orig. unkn.] **1.** to confound; darn.

*1837 in *OED2*: I'm jiggered if he don't tell a lie. ***1861** Dickens *Great Expectations* ch. xvii: Well, then,…I'm jiggered if I don't see you home. **1886** Burnett *Little Lord Fauntleroy*, in *DARE*: Well…I be—jiggered! *ca*1900 *Buffalo Bill* 65: "Better give me that [gun]." "I'll see you jiggered first," cried the cowboy. **1901** Evans *Sailor's Log* 170 [ref. to 1873]: I declared I would "be jiggered" if I would. **1907** J.C. Lincoln *Cape Cod* 77: He said cod be jiggered. **1936** "E. Queen" *Halfway House* 158: I'll be jiggered if I see that. **1945** T. Williams *Menagerie* 37: I'll be jiggered! I didn't know that. **1978** Gann *Hostage* 479: Wal I'll be

jiggered.…I didn't really think y'all was real. **1992** *Simpsons* (Fox-TV): Well, I'll be jiggered!

2.a. to fatigue; exhaust. [The 1899 quot. may belong to this sense, but the citation is ambiguous.]

*1862 in *OED2*: Av tramp'd a matter o' forty mile to-daay, an' am fair jigger'd up. ******a*1865 Smyth *Sailor's Wd.-Bk.* 412: *Jiggered-up.*—Done up; tired out. ***1885, *1896** in *EDD* s.v. *jiggered*. [**1899** Willard *Tramping* 394: *Jiggered*: "done," beaten.] **1934** McCarthy *Mosshorn*: *Jiggered*, adj. An overrun horse or cow [*sic*].

b. to spoil; ruin; break.

1894 "J. Flynt," in *Century* (Feb.) 520: And these are the kind of fellows, too, who jigger our riding on this railroad. **1911–12** J. London *Smoke Bellew* 37: It's a good-lookin' boat, but it's jiggered the other bunch. **1914** Jackson & Hellyer *Vocab.* 49: You've jiggered the lock. ***1923** in *OED2*: I've "jiggered" up my Rolls-Royce. ***1949, *1969** in *OED2*.

3. to fool or cheat.

1894 "J. Flynt," in *Century* (Feb.) 518: No, my young bloke; you can't jigger the old boy. **1913** J. London *Valley of Moon* 100: Three dollars…I'm jiggered out of on the room I'm rentin'. **1916** in J. London *Short Stories* 703: Fifty quid I'd jiggered him out of in a deal in Fiji. **1931** in D.O. Smith *Cradle* 216: But the O.C. was jiggered. We didn't do it.

4. to tattoo.

1902 (quot. at JIGGER, *n.*, 2.g.).

jigger² *v.* [fr. JIGGERS; cf. JIGGER, *n.*, 4] *Und. & Pris.* to act as a lookout.

1962–68 B. Jackson *In the Life* 112: He sat with the police car radio and jiggered (acted as lookout) while I made joints.

jigger *interj.* var. JIGGERS.

jigger boss *n. West.* a foreman.

1985 H. Cannon *Cowboy Poetry* 138: *Jigger boss* a Nevada term for cowboy boss.

jiggered *adj.* **1.** see s.v. JIGGER¹, *v.*

2. drunk; tipsy.

1923 in Partridge *Slang* 313: [Intoxicated:] *loaded,…jiggered, corned.*

jigger man *n. Und. & Pris.* a man who acts as lookout during the commission of a crime. Also **jiggers guy.**

1924 Henderson *Keys to Crookdom* 409: *Jiggerman.* Lookout. **1926** *N.Y. Times* (Oct. 10) VIII 20: The "jigger man" acts as lookout while the lay is being looted. **1945** in *DAS*: Michael…acted only as "the two-block jiggers guy." **1978–80** in Cardozo-Freeman *Joint* 509: *Jigger man.* One who acts as a lookout and gives a signal when the bulls are coming.

jiggeroo *v.* JIGGER¹, *v.*, 1.

1913 J. London *Valley of Moon* 108: I'll be ever-lastingly jiggerooed if I put up for a wigwam I can't be boss of. *Ibid.* 173: We're jiggerooed. We're hornswoggled.

jiggeroo *interj. Und.* JIGGERS, 2.

1912 Berkman *Prison* 179 [ref. to 1893]: Now, jiggaroo,* screw's comin'.…*Look out. **1919** *DN* V 41: *Jiggeroo, interj.* = *cheese it:* a warning to be careful or escape. **1927** *DN* V 452: *Jiggeroo, interj.* A warning that the police are coming.

jiggers *interj.* [perh. orig. euphem. for *Jesus!*] **1.** (used to express astonishment).

1898 Stevenson *Cape Horn* 55: Holy jiggers … there's the "Flyin' Dutchman." **1924** *DN* V 271: Jigger, holy jigger, by jiggers, oh jiggers. **1968** in *DARE*: Well, by jiggers, they sure are in nice flesh. **1969** in *DARE*.

2. *Juve. & Und.* (used to warn of the approach of a police officer, person in authority, witness, etc.); in phrs. **give jiggers** to give warning or act as lookout; **keep jiggers** to act as lookout. Also **jigger.** [Defs. in bracketed quots. may be erroneous.]

[******a*1890–96 *F & H* IV 55: *Jigger*…In Hants. = a policeman] [**1903** *Enquirer* (Cincinnati) (May 9) 13: *Jiggers*—A copper or policeman.] **1911** *DN* III 545: Jigger, kids, the teacher's coming. **1914** Jackson & Hellyer *Vocab.* 49: Jigger! The bull's coming. **1915** "High Jinks, Jr." *Choice Slang* 51: *Jigger the bull*—Universally used by small boys as a warning…that a policeman is approaching. **1916** Thompson *Round Levee* 45: "Keeping jiggers" means watching while some one commits a crime. **1924** Henderson *Keys to Crookdom* 409: *Jiggers*—Warning. *Giving jiggers*—on lookout. **1928** Bodenheim *Georgie May* 30: Jiggahs, jiggahs, theah's a dick down t' other end. **1930** C. Shaw *Jack-Roller* 11:

I always stayed outside and gave jiggers. **1929–31** Farrell *Young Lonigan* 137: Benny Taite suddenly gave jiggers. **1932** Harvey *Me and Bad Eye* 211 [ref. to 1918]: He said he would give us jiggers at the last minute. **1934** W. Smith *B. Cotter* 132: I'll give you jiggers when they come. *a***1940** in Lanning & Lanning *Texas Cowboys* 173: He'd...keep jiggers on danger. **1952** Chase *McThing* 48: Jiggers, boys—it's the boss. **1956** Ross *Hustlers* 79: You want us to give jiggers?

jiggle *n.* **1.** *S.W.* a ride on horseback. Also as *v.*

1934 Weseen *Dict. Slang* 100: *Jiggle*—the ordinary gait of about five miles an hour; to ride at this gait. *a***1940** in Lanning & Lanning *Texas Cowboys* 64: They would jiggle back to the camp and take up routine work. *Ibid.* 145: The new ramrod took a jiggle over the range.

2. *TV.* images of actresses in sexually titillating clothing; in phr. **jiggle show** a show exploiting such images.—often used attrib.

1978 (cited in *BDNE2*). **1979** *TV Guide* (Aug. 11) 35: Meanwhile, the television critics are currently preoccupied with what they call "the jiggle factor," of which *Charlie's Angels* is considered the mother. But "jiggle" has always been around. **1979** *People* (Sept. 24) 67: Suddenly ABC's *Charlie's Angels* is threatening to junk the "jiggle." True, the series opened the season last week with bounteous Cheryl Ladd stuffed into a bikini. **1984** *Nat. Lampoon* (Dec.) 40: Enraged by injustice or jiggle shows. **1984** in "J.B. Briggs" *Drive-In* 238: We get a lot of jiggle action. **1986** *World News Tonight* (ABC-TV) (June 3): There's a lot of gore, glop, and jiggle in summer movies. **1986** Merkin *Zombie Jamboree* 35: A live jiggle show would have destroyed the spell. **1991** *Day Watch* (CNN-TV) (Oct. 30): *Charlie's Angels*: critics...called it and considered it a "jiggle show." **1992** *N.Y. Times Bk. Rev.* (Oct. 27) 36: NBC put a jiggle show on television about student nurses...but it was killed by the outrage from nurses. **1993** *New Yorker* (Mar. 15) 80: "Baywatch" can't really be derided as "jiggle TV"...The most jiggle is the sight of Hasselhoff running in slow motion to flag down a snow cone.

jiggly *n. TV.* a filmed sequence that features JIGGLE, 2.

1978 *N.Y. Post* (Nov. 1) 7: A jiggly scene is a trade term for undue emphasis on female anatomy. **1980** Pearl *Pop. Slang* 80: *Jigglies n.* (Broadcasting) television scenes showing actresses moving their bodies in sexually suggestive ways. **1982** Sculatti *Catalog of Cool* 50: Jayne Mansfield...does lots of horseback riding in what is obviously the first "jiggly."

jiggy *adj.* crazy; (hence) jittery; fidgety.

1933 *Amer. Mercury* (Mar.) 343: They've got him up in the Blue Room (the observation ward). He's gone completely jiggy. **1983** Stapleton *30 Yrs.* 26: By midnight he was getting a little jiggy. The phone rang and he almost jumped out of his boots. **1989** Radford & Crowley *Drug Agent* 6: If I was too jiggy to hold the syringe, he'd shoot me up. *Ibid.* 53: Murphy got double jiggy when Gander jumped in the seat behind him.

jiggy-jig, jig-jig vars. JIG-A-JIG.

jig-juice *n.* JIG WATER.

1897 A.H. Lewis *Wolfville* 70: A heap habit, same as tobacco an' jig-juice. **1908** McGaffey *Show Girl* 67: The captain sold us about two quarts of jig-juice—the kind that makes a jackrabbit spit in a bulldog's eye. **1931–33**, **1968** in *DARE*.

jiglets *n.* [orig. unkn.] *N.E.* NIBS.—used disparagingly. Also **jiblets.**

1888 in *F & H* IV 56: Ain't his jiglets pretty near ready to see de rat, Jimmy. **1903** Merriman *Letters* 88: I came an old-time Soldier's Field tackle on his jiglets. **1911** A.H. Lewis *Apaches of N.Y.* 106: His jiblets wit' th' cleaver chops off their youthful beans.

jigs *interj.* Esp. *Chi.* JIGGERS.

1927 Thrasher *Gang* 58: "Jigs, de bulls!" someone would shout, and they would scatter. **1929–31** Farrell *Young Lonigan* 137: O'Brien hung outside in the alley to give jiggs. **1942** Algren *Morning* 69: All they'll do is holler jigs for me in case the cops show.

jigwalk *n.* [orig. unkn.] *Black E.* a black person. Also **jigwalker.**

1922 in Charters & Kunstadt *Jazz* 95: Jig-walk your middle name is Jazz! **1928** R. Fisher *Jericho* 301: Jig, Jigaboo, Jigwalker. See *boogy.* **1929** T. Gordon *Born to Be* 236: *Jigwalk, Spade,...Jigaboo, Dinge*...Nicknames for Ethiopians. **1930** G. Schuyler *Black No More* 214: "Well," said Bunny, grinning, "it sure is good to be able to admit that you're a jigwalk once more." **1941** Handy *Father of Blues* 105 [ref. to 1890's]: What do de jigwalk do wen de preacher make 'em happy, eh? *Ibid.* 117 [ref. to N.O., *ca*1910]: A white person was always "ofay," a Negro "jigwawk" [*sic*]. **1969** Kimbrough *Defender of Angels* 141 [ref.

to *ca*1920]: A jig-walk detective is supposed to know every other jig-walk in town. Our ofay superiors lump everything black together.

jig water *n.* liquor, esp. whiskey.

1888 in *F & H* IV 56: A...countryman had just tottered away from the counter over which jig-water is dispensed. **1890** Crook *Autobiog.* 100: Col. Hugh Ewing became full of "jig water" and ventilated himself on Gen. Cox, abusing him for being a coward and an imbecile. **1895** C.C. King *Fort Frayne* 231: There isn't one in that gang could tell a 'Rappahoe from a raw recruit with six fingers av Bunco John's jig wather in him. *ca***1895** McCloskey *Across Continent* 107: Melican woman like jig water. Me likee, too. [**1901** *DN* II 142: *Jig-water, n.* A drink made from a mixture of alcohol, sugar, water and wintergreen.] **1968** in *DARE.*

jill *n.* [generic use of *Jill*, female given name] a young woman. Cf. JANE.

1934 Smith & Cohn *Harold Teen* (film): You're not the jack for this jill. **1942** Davis & Wolsey *Call House Madam* 161: The college jill...chased him like a rabbit after a hound. **1945** Himes *If He Hollers* 73: I heard the manager say to the Arky Jill, "You've got to out with them." **a***1961** Partridge *DSUE* (ed. 6) 1150: *Jill*...A girl: since *ca*1945; not very common. **1991** Nelson & Gonzales *Bring Noise* 134: It is a successful outing for this new jill on the block. **1993** *Mystery Sci. Theater* (Comedy Central TV): Three jerks and a jill.

jillion *n.* [alter. *million;* cf. ZILLION] an indeterminate, extremely large number. Also as *adj.* Hence **jillionth,** *adj.*

1939 in D. Runyon *More Guys* 294: War Admiral must be worth a jillion. **1942** in Loosbrock & Skinner *Wild Blue* 320: There's a jillion of them! **1951** Pryor *The Big Play* 44: I'm gonna make me a jillion dollars! **1947–53** Guthrie *Seeds* 392: Blue jillions of 'em. **1956** G. Green *Last Angry Man* 46: Any outfit that can *give away* so much stuff must make jillions on what they sell. **1961** Forbes *Goodbye to Some* 204: Leeches! By the gillion! **1967** J. Kramer *Instant Replay* 140: I've got a jillion things to do. **1968** *Harper's* (Feb.) 31: Repeated for maybe the jillionth time what virtually nobody believes: that he really doesn't want to be President of the United States. **1978** Abernethy *Paisanos* 18: I've been all over that country a jillion times. **1985** J. Dillinger *Adrenaline* 103: There's always just jillions...around. **1988** J. Gay *Inherit the Wind* (NBC-TV): A jillion years ago. **1995** *Calif. v. Simpson* (Court TV) (Feb. 21): It could be a jillion things.

jillionaire *n.* a person of vast wealth.

1935 *Amer. Mercury* (June) 230: *Jillionaire:* person possessing illusions of great wealth. **1973** Ellington *Music Is My Mistress* 180: Telling the jillionaire what he thought should be done. **1992** *New Republic* (Aug. 3) 17: Perot, a self-made jillionaire and action man. **1996** *TV Guide* (Dec. 21) 44: Cast as jillionaire John Jacob Astor.

jill off *v.* [modeled on JACK OFF, *v.*] Esp. *Homosex.* (of a woman) to masturbate.—usu. used attrib.

1989 *Playboy* (Apr.) 64 (Nexis): The most imaginative safe-sex invention we came across was undoubtedly The World's First Jack-and-Jill-Off Party held, of course, in San Francisco in November 1987. **1990** S. Bright *S. Sexpert's Lesbian Sex World* 138: The only question I had when I was invited to my first Jill-Off party was: "Where are the outlets?" ******1990** T. Thorne *Dict. Contemp. Slang: Jill off*...(of a woman) to masturbate. A term coined by women in the 1970s. **1992** in *Utne Reader* (Mar./Apr. 1993) 134: There are also "Jill-off" clubs, as well as Jack-and-Jill-off clubs that cater to both sexes. **1992** *Esquire* (Dec.) 89: After Karen does her last dolly for the "jill off" (that is to say, the group ejaculation, a truly glorious video scene with Debi and her glass dildo leading the ladies like Octavian at the battle of Actium), some of the women...relax in the makeup room. **1993** *Utne Reader* (July/Aug.) 58: Jack and Jill Off Parties.

jilt *n.* a prostitute, esp. one whose confederate robs her customers; in phr. **jilt shop** a brothel that employs jilts; PANEL HOUSE. Now *hist.*

******1674** in Duffett *Burlesque Plays* 8: Then hungry Jilt that rails at Play,/'Cause Cully will not bite to day/...[is] eager grown for want of prey. ******1681** in Otway *Works* II 92: But your true Jilt...can extract Bawdy out of the chastest sence. ******1698–99** "B.E." *Dict. Canting Crew: Jilt,* a Tricking Whore. ******1703** E. Ward *London Spy* 72: A parcel of Women, some looking like Jilts who wanted Cullies. ******1698–1706** in D'Urfey *Pills* IV 319: The Theatre Jilts/Would S—ve for a Crown. ******1708** *Modern World Disrob'd* 93: An expert Jilt...[may] impose a crack'd Virginity, for a whole One, on some Leacher of Quality. ******1749** in J. Atkins *Sex in Lit.* IV 91: A *Jilt* is a *Procurer, Bawd,* and *Whore*

compounded together. **1776** in Commager *Spirit of '76* 420: These bitchfoxly jades, jilts, haggs, strums, prostitutes. **1859** Matsell *Vocab.* 46: *Jilt*. A prostitute who hugs and kisses a countryman while her accomplice robs him. **1902** R.A. Woods *Amer. in Process* 192 [ref. to *ca*1860]: "Jilt shops"—those...brothels into which the sailor was enticed merely for robbery—were strewn thickly along Ann Street, now North Street [Boston]. **1902* *EDD*: *Jilt*...a prostitute. **1983** Duis *Saloon* 252 [ref. to *ca*1900]: Revelations that prostitutes had moved into dance halls as places of assignation revived the old image of "sailors' jilt shops" of the mid-nineteenth century.

jilter *n.* *Und.* a sneak thief.
    1859 Matsell *Vocab.* 46: *Jilter*. A sneak-thief. **1863* in Partridge *Dict. Und.* 365: "Jilters," or "hotel lurkers."

Jim *n.* Esp. *Black E.* (used in direct address to a man); BUD, 1; MAN; (*rarely*, not in direct address) a man; fellow. Cf. JACK[1], 1.b., c.; JOE, 5.b.
    1899 Cullen *Tales* 27: Is there anything ailing you, Jim? **1941** in Oliver *Meaning of Blues* 150: It's gonna be too bad, Jim. **1945** Fay *Be Poor* 163: Don't be cheap and bourgeois, Jim! **1959–60** R. Reisner *Jazz Titans* 159: *Jim:* a form of unfriendly address, cold, as in, "Jim, don't bug me." *ca*1962 in A. Lomax *Where Blues Began* 292 [ref. to 1940's]: This time the jim tapped me on the shoulder. *Ibid.* 297: Is the jims and janes still knockin' theirself out? **1965** Yurick *Warriors* 188: Jim, you been playing soldier. When will you learn? **1964–66** R. Stone *Hall of Mirrors* 270: Jim, you conned yourself right out of your head. **1967** Riessman & Dawkins *Play It Cool* 64: *Jim n.* a person, usually male: Some jim on the subway was trying to sell us a magazine. *ca*1969 Rabe *Hummel* 47: He one baffled motherfucker, Jim. **1971** *Black Scholar* (Sept.) 30: Ain't I done told you to leave my people alone, Jimmmmm? **1971** *N.Y. Times Mag.* (Nov. 28) 91: You wanna talk hate, I'll tell you somethin' about hate, Jim. **1978** W. Zevon *Werewolves of London* (pop. song): He'll rip your lungs out, Jim. **1986** Merkin *Zombie Jamboree* 16: "What the hell is your name, anyway?" "Richard." "Okay, Jim,...you got to look sharp."

jim *v.* **1.** to injure, spoil, or ruin; (*also*) to botch or bungle; bring into confusion.—often constr. with *up*. [Prob. the orig. sense.]
    1907 *McClure's Mag.* (Feb.) 384: I've seen crowds suddenly jimmed up in my time. **1912** Lowrie *Prison* 139: Men sometimes "jim" themselves intentionally; that is, deliberately place a finger in the cog wheels in order to "beat" a loom. **1914** Jackson & Hellyer *Vocab.* 49: Lay off! You'll jim the whole works. **1914** in Truman *Dear Bess* 168: Also, I know how to jim the thing so it won't go at all and then suddenly fix it. **1918** in R. Casey *Cannoneers* 183: About three divisions are all jimmed up on the Front and nobody knows where the hell he's going. **1918** in *AS* (Oct. 1933) 28: *Jim a deal.* To bungle a criminal plot. **1927** J. Stevens *Mattock* 187 [ref. to 1918]: Such rotten officers they would even jim up service records. **1930** Lait *On the Spot* 80: You know how to jim up that signal system. **1931** Gallegher *Bolts & Nuts* 102: One Lieutenant tried to "jim" the works one day on the bolt situation. **1932–33** P. Cain *Fast One* 296: We ain't got time to jim it up. **1935** J. Conroy *World to Win* 168: Bettah not jim me up. Bettah not mess me up. **1939** Ruskin & Goldbeck *Calling Dr. Kildare* (film): Don't give me any more ideas on how to handle Kildare or you're going to jim up the entire business! **1954, 1967** in *DARE*.

2. to fool around.
    1903 A.H. Lewis *Boss* 315: He's jimmin' along th' edge of th' wharf, an' no one noticin' in particular. **1912** *DN* III 579: *Jim*...to potter, to trifle. **1939** *AS* XIV 156: "To gin (or jim) around"...means "just to dabble around, to fool around." **1971** *Amer. N & Q*, in *DARE*: To wander around looking for amusement....go "Jimming."

jimbrowski *n.* [joc. elab. of JIMMY, *n.*, 6] *Rap music.* the penis.
    1988 "Boogie Down Prods." *Jimmy* (rap song): Keepin' in mind about Jimbrowski. **1991** in *Rap Masters* (Jan. 1992) 60: "Jimbrowski," by the Jungle Brothers. **1993** *Source* (July) 46: The album...left his reality holding its jimbrowski.

jim-cracker *n.* a remarkable person or thing. Also **jim-crack.**
    1834 in *DARE*: Billy had been a great man in his day....He was a thorough bred jim-crack. **1937** *AS* (Oct.) 239: Mrs. A.H. Rulkoetler reports that "He's a *jimcracker!*" is frequent in Minnesota to indicate that the person commented upon has exceptional skill. **1961** Serling *More Stories* 36: It's a handy-dandy, jim-cracker; A-one piece of merchandise.

Jim Crow *n.* [popularized and perhaps coined by Thomas Dartmouth Rice (1808–60), "father of the minstrel show,"

as the title of his earliest and best-known song (1828), which became first a national, then a transatlantic hit 1832–35; but cf. dial. E *Jemmy Rook* 'a rook' in **1811 quot. at JIMMY, *n.*, 1] **1.** a black man; a black or (*rarely*) Asian person.—used derisively, esp. as a nickname.
    1827–28 T.D. Rice, in Damon *Old Amer. Songs* (No. 14): Jim Crow is courting a white gall,/And yaller folks call her Sue. [**1835** *Knickerbocker* (Jan.) 47: Slaves...singing some Jim Crow song.] **1838** in *DA*: Don't be standing there like the wooden Jim Crow at the blacking maker's store. **1841** in *DA*: Hundreds of nigger-porters, or Jim Crows, who swarm at the many landing-places to *help* passengers. **1852** Stowe *Uncle Tom's Cabin* ch. xx: She was rather a funny specimen in the Jim Crow line. **1952** G. Aiken *Uncle Tom's Cabin* I ii: Hulloa! Jim Crow!...Pick that up now. **1878** Willis *Our Cruise* 110: His family name was Wing-Kang-Loo,/ But the sailor men called him "Jim Crow."

2. anti-black racism, esp. in the form of segregationist legislative policies. Now *S.E.*
    1919–21 Chi. Comm. Race Rel. *Negro in Chi.* 302: There's no lynching or Jim Crow. **1933** Heyward *Emperor Jones* (film): There ain't no chain gangs or Jim Crow. **1940** Zinberg *Walk Hard* 18: There's places you can forget about jim-crow, but you need money—real money. **1944** *New Republic* (Mar. 13) 339: Jim Crow in the Army. **1946** *Amer. Sociol. Rev.* XI 713: To the Negro any joke is particularly humorous if it shows Jim-Crow "backfiring" on a Southerner. **1953** Manchester *City of Anger* 109: Get the delegation talking Jim Crow. **1957** Rowan *Go South* 3: The Southland...braced for the decisive battle that both whites and non-whites had termed "Jim Crow's last stand." **1988** *Channel 2 News at Five* (WCBS-TV) (June 29): Jim Crow is alive and well in New York. **1992** *Sonya Live* (CNN-TV) (Sept. 1): A friend of mine was very active in the anti–Jim Crow movement, before the '60s.

3. a railroad car or section of a bus segregated for the use of blacks. Cf. JIM CROW, *adj.*, 1.a.
    1947–52 Ellison *Invisible Man* 139: You riding back here in the Jim Crow just like me.

4. *R.R.* a tamping bar.
    *a*1889 *Century Dict.*: *Jim-crow*...A tool for bending or straightening iron rails or bars. **1951–59** F. Ramsey *Been Here* 86: The "caller" transmits the "cap'n's" orders, telling the men where to set down their "Jim Crow bars" and when to leave. *Ibid.* 91: "O, make...the Jim Crow talk."

¶ In phrase:

¶ **jump Jim Crow** [alluding to the chorus of T.D. Rice's minstrel song, which describes a dance step introduced in Rice's performance: "Ebery time I wheel about I jump Jim Crow"] Esp. *Pol.* to do a dexterous turnabout in one's principles.
    1836 in *OED2*: A Mr. Collier of Virginia has "jumped Jim Crow." **1840** in *DA*: Fo he's the man to jump Jim Crow,/And prove that black is white. **1842** in *DA*: The Kentucky delegation jump Jim Crow to perfection. They found the people would not sustain them in their former course. **1844** in *DA*: If they were *honest* in going for Harrison *and* a Bank in 1840, then never did any set of politicians jump Jim Crow more expeditiously.

Jim Crow *adj.* **1.a.** for or of blacks only; (*usu.*, now *solely*) set apart by whites for the enforced exclusive use of blacks. Now *hist.* [Prob. the orig. sense.]
    1842 in *DA*: It is this spirit alone that compels the colored man to set in the "negro pew," and ride the "Jim-Crow car." **1843** Strong *Diary* 217: Just think of a Jim Crow Society for the republication of the *African Minstrelsy of the Nineteenth Century*—patronized by H.R.H. the Prince of Pottowattomy. **1853** W.W. Brown *Clotel* 172: The "Jim Crow" carriage is the one in which the blacks have to ride. **1861** in *DA*: I was now put into a "Jim Crow car," on our way to Rockaway. *a*1889 *Century Dict.*: *Jim Crow car*, a railroad-car set apart for the use of negroes: said to have been so called originally in Massachusetts about 1841. **1899** *Colored American* (Nov. 25) 3: Put your foot down and stamp [out] this jim crow business. *Ibid.* 4: We do not think the...Washington courts will "stand for" a "Jim Crow" theater. *Ibid.*: Its "Jim Crow" tactics. **1910** W. Archer *Afro-Amer.* 70: The Jim Crow car is defended by many Southerners as a means of keeping the peace. **1915** *New Republic* (Nov. 27) 88: The very phrase "Jim Crow car" seems to have been first used in 1841 with reference to a railroad car in Massachusetts set apart for the use of Negroes. **1916** *Chi. Defender*

(July 22) 5: In the "Jim Crow" section of the street cars. **1919–21** Chi. Comm. Race Rel. *Negro in Chi.* 34: They refused to use the "Jim Crow" sleeping quarters in a police station. **1934** Cunningham *Triggernometry* 82: Take a negro out of the "Jim Crow" section and try to put him among the whites and the only question will be how *large* the riot. **1938** Ward *Fog* 285: Teach school!...It's Jim Crow...even if you ever do get an appointment. **1939** *Pittsburgh Courier* (July 15) 7: Women Win Jim-Crow Restaurant Suit Under Ohio Civil Rights Law. **1949** Allport *Individ. & Religion* xii: One travels through America and notes its Jim Crow churches. **1954** Himes *Third Generation* 97: Snores and stink and smoke, fatigue and pain and discomfort filled the Jim-Crow car. **1954** Killens *Youngblood* 17: And the men kept coming towards the jim crow coach. **1958** R. Wright *Long Dream* 35: Don't you ride Jim Crow trains?...Don't you go to Jim Crow restaurants? Jim Crow schools?...Ain't your...graveyards Jim Crow? **1990** M. Cliff, in C. Major *Calling Wind* 575: De black gal ride in de Jim Crow car.

b. segregationist; (*also*) racially prejudiced against blacks. Now *S.E.*

1904 *Nation* (Mar. 17) 202: The "Jim Crow" bills now before the Maryland Legislature. **1919–21** Chi. Comm. Race Rel. *Negro in Chi.* 63: They might use it to overthrow "Jim Crow" laws in certain states. **1943** in P. McGuire *Jim Crow Army* 171: Plenty of down dixie Boys...enforce Jim Crow laws. **1946** Halsey *Color Blind* 78: But there are Jim Crow laws in South Carolina and no Jim Crow laws in New York. **1962** T. Berger *Reinhart* 25: Everybody who believed that was perforce Jim Crow. **1975** T. Berger *Sneaky People* 89: That Buddy's business was Jim Crow was all Clarence knew or cared to know. **1979** in Terkel *Amer. Dreams* 355: The army was strictly Jim Crow at the time. **1992** in *Reader's Digest* (May 1994) 145: Along the Mississippi in the era of lynchings and Jim Crow laws. **1989–93** K. Grover *Make a Way* 123: That was rich, rich people, but they was so Jim Crow. **1994** Bak *Turkey Stearnes* 105: Local Jim Crow customs and ordinances.

2. Esp. *West.* contemptible; worthless; second-rate.

1838 in *DA*: Gov. Marcy's message, Mr. Secretary Woodbury's Letter [etc.]...are Jim Crow performances. **1880** Martin *Sam Bass* 142: What kind of a Jim Crow story did you tell those folks up there? **1885** Siringo *Texas Cowboy* 30: I got a little "Jim Crow" barlow the first throw. **1890** in *DA*: These jim-crow physicians. **1897** *Cosmopolitan* (Mar.) 567: Why, I went into a little jim-crow town wunst where I warn't acquainted any and I got 'rested by the city marshal for a tramp! **1897** A.H. Lewis *Wolfville* 193: Turnin' little jim-crow tricks for the express company. **1902** A.H. Lewis *Wolfville Nights* 67: A stiff hat with a little jim crow rim. **1903** A. Adams *Log* 203: I wasn't responsible if their Jim Crow outfit lost the cattle. **1903** Ade *Society* 64: Once there lived in a Jim Crow Town a glowing Intellect who was Posted on all the Issues of the Day. **1927** Finger *Frontier Ballads* 66: But the dad-gummed, jim-crow laws, they don't care about a man's good heartedness. **1928** Santee *Cowboy* 73: It's always been our luck to work for some Jim Crow outfit instead of the bigger spreads. **1958** McCulloch *Woods Words* 99: *Jim Crow load*—A lone log load. **1962** in *Dict. Canadianisms*: "Snide," "jim-crow," [etc.] are applied to anything worthless on the Eastern slope of the Rockies.

Jim Crow *adv. Black E.* under segregationist restrictions, esp. in transportation; in racially segregated facilities. Now *hist.*

1937 R. Wright, in A. Chapman *Black Voices* 288: The Ethics of Living Jim Crow. **1944** C.B. Davis *Leo McGuire* 174: So I browned my hands and face and went Jim Crow in a day coach to Denver. **1956** Childress *Like One of Family* 14: I get annoyed ridin' Jim Crow because you see...more than just *separate seatin'*. **1962** in W. King *Black Anthol.* 152: I ain't going Jim Crow. I'm going first class, Booker. **1982** Downey *Losing the War* 10 [ref. to 1940's]: Ridin' ol Jim Crow, us black folks gotta bring all our own stuff.

Jim-Crow *v.* Esp. *Black E.* to subject to anti-black discrimination, esp. by law. Now *hist.*

1918 *N.Y. Age* (Apr. 27) 1: Pupils Strike at Musicale When Negroes Are "Jim-Crowed." **1918** *Scribner's* (Aug.) 176: They was looked down at an' Jim-Crowed an' teetotally put on the wrong side of th' fence. **1919–21** Chi. Comm. Race Rel. *Negro in Chi.* 301: Few white people realized how uncertain the southern Negro felt about making use of his new privilege of sitting anywhere in the car, instead of being "Jim Crowed." **1922** W. White *Fire in the Flint* 116: No wonder the South lynched, disfranchised, Jim-Crowed the Negro. **1925** Van Vechten *Nigger Heaven* 45: Why, in one or two places, they've actually tried to do a little jim-crowing! **1928** Bradford *Ol' Man Adam* 68: Can't you

Jim Crow 'em? **1929** T. Gordon *Born to Be* 182: Would you believe it, there are places right here in beloved Harlem, run by white men, where negroes can't go unless they are jimcrowed? **1940** Zinberg *Walk Hard* 187: There isn't a colored man in the country that doesn't know he's been jim-crowed. **1945** A.C. Powell *Marching Blacks* 4: They could not fly in the air corps or fight in the marine corps and were Jim-Crowed in the army. **1945** in P. McGuire *Jim Crow Army* 179: Negroes have been jim-crowed at this theater ever since I came here in 1942. **1956** Childress *Like One of Family* 46: Folks hatin' and Jim Crowin'. **1966** *New Yorker* (Sept. 3) 82: Negroes could be described, in the words of the late Kelly Miller, as "anybody who'd be Jim-Crowed in Virginia." **1971** N.Y.U. professor: When I heard that, I knew I'd been Jim-Crowed again! **1978** A. Rose *Eubie Blake* 66: They used to Jim Crow the [phonograph] records in those days....They called 'em race records. *a*1973–87 F.M. Davis *Livin' the Blues* 5: Negroes [in Kansas] were not jim crowed on transportation. **1989–93** K. Grover *Make a Way* 123: We was Jim Crowed a lot. **1996** *Harper's* (Apr.) 56: We were perceived as a separate people—enslaved, Jim Crowed, and segregated.

jim-dandy *n.* an extraordinary or excellent example of a person or thing. Also (*obs.*) **jim hickey.** Cf. JACK-DANDY, JOE-DANDY.

1887 in *DAE*: Let me say you are a "Jim Dandy." **1891** *Outing* (July) 316: He's a dandy second-base, a Jim dandy. **1894** S. Crane *Red Badge* 51: Well, he was reg'lar jim-dandy fer nerve, wa'n't he?...A reg'lar jim-dandy. *Ibid.* 98: That's Flemin', an' he's a jimhickey. **1894** in F. Remington *Sel. Letters* 208: You're a jim-dandy. **1907* Masefield *Tarp. Muster* 131: Them topsails had a good look along the yard...or there was a jim hickey of a stink raised. **1960** *Many Loves of D. Gillis* (CBS-TV): As for breaking dishes—boy, you are a jim-dandy. **1972** R. Barrett *Lovomaniacs* 112: That is a little jim-dandy of a bod. **1977** Coover *Public Burning* 521: And that word "integer" was a jimdandy, too! **1984** Groening *Love is Hell* (unp.): "Mr. Right"...Also known as: Mr. Perfect, Jim Dandy, answer to a woman's prayers.

jim-dandy *adj.* first-rate; excellent; stylish. Also as *adv.*

1887 in P. Dickson *Baseball Dict.* 227: Whereas on Wednesday night they were proclaimed "Jim Dandy" players, they were on Thursday proclaimed to be "no good." **1888** in Farmer *Amer.*: Arrayed in a jim-dandy suit of clothes. **1906** *Independent* (Nov. 29) 1259: That was a jim-dandy run of Sam's! **1923** *DN* V 212: That was a jim dandy meal. **1931** Lubbock *Bully Hayes* 16: [We] made a jimdandy race of it. **1931** Z. Grey *Sunset Pass* 49: I want a jim-dandy outfit, you bet. **1950** Jacoby & Brady *Champagne* (film): That'll do it jim-dandy, lickety-split. **1950** M. Shulman *Sleep Till Noon* 77: He doesn't know there's anything wrong with the world. He thinks it's jim-dandy, and he loves everybody. **1958** C. Beaumont *Best* 70: Everything went jimdandy. **1959** G. Wells *Gazebo* (film): "How's the pulse?" "Bully. Jim-dandy." **1965** Horan *Seat of Power* 37: Just a Jim-dandy fellow. **1968** Blackford *Tarp. Sailor* 11: A jim-dandy sailor made his liberties in over sixty dollars' worth of clothing.

jiminy crickets *interj.* [elab. of earlier *jiminy*, var. of *Gemini*] (used to express surprise).

1848 in *AS* X (1935) 40: By *Jiminy Cricket*, an exclamation of surprise. **1909** in O. Johnson *Lawrenceville* 69: Jiminy crickets, what a waste. **1937** *Walt Disney's Snow White* (film): Jiminy crickets! The door's open! **1942** in Litoff et al. *Miss You* 78: Jimminy cricket!...everything that happens to me! **1954** Matheson *Born of Man & Woman* 137: Holy Mackerel! Jiminy crickets!

jimjams *n.pl.* **1.** delirium tremens; (*also*) an alcoholic hangover; (*occ., obs.*) a strong craving for alcohol.

1865 in *Prospects* XVI (1991) 263: I ain't had a drink for two days....I've got the "jim-jams." **1871** Rickey *Bad Whiskey* 5: Faith, I think he has the jim-jams; I'll try and make him leave off the drink. **1871** Willis *Forecastle Echoes* 25: He saw, while crazy with "jim-jams,"/Rats! **1873** in J. Chisholm *So. Pass* 105: Holbrook...had Jim-jams. **1877** Burdette *Mustache* 291: For the cure of...jim-jams, katzen-jammer, [etc.]. **1877** Bartlett *Amer.* (ed. 4) 323: *Jim-Jams.* Delirium tremens. Kentucky. *ca*1880 Bellard *Gone for a Soldier* 15: One of our men who had imbibed rather too freely, was taken with the Jim Jams (Dilirum [*sic*] Tremens). **1882** Peck *Peck's Sunshine* 97: Pulled to the nearest saloon...as is the man who has the jim jams. **1884** *Accidentally Overheard* 19: The jimjams, the tremenses. **1886** Nye *Remarks* 35: How could you describe the jimjams so graphically. **1886** F. Whittaker *Pop Hicks* 27: Got what? The jim-jams? **1889** Barrère & Leland *Dict. Slang* I 500: *Jimjams, the* (society), delirium tremens. **1889** Trumble

Mott Street 41: Him dlinka Melican man dlinks. Him getta jlim jlams. **1891** McCann & Jarrold *Odds & Ends* 36: After awhile he got the jim-jams….Used to sit over there in the corner and play with the little white elephants he'd see running up his pants leg. **1891** Maitland *Slang Dict.* 155: *Jim-Jams*, delerium tremens. **1942** in *Combat* 133: Suffering from the Jim Jams after a hard night in a local juke joint. **1943** *Yank* (Nov. 26) 19: Get ridder dese jim-jams. **1969** in *DARE.*

2. a feeling of fear or strong apprehension; JITTERS, 1.

[**1888** in *F & H* IV 57: We are glad to see *Harper's Weekly* suffering the jim-jams of distortion on the envenomed pencil of an extraordinary artist.] **1896** "M. Twain," in *Harper's Mo.* (Sept.) 537: They gave me the jimjams and the fantods and caked up what brains I have. *ca*1903 in Dolph *Sound Off!* 196: We've the dhobee-itch and the hamstring hitch,/The jimjams and the fever. **1911** *DN* III 545: *Jim-jams*…A violently upset or disturbed feeling. "Her talking so long gave me the jimjams." **1925** Dos Passos *Manhattan Transfer* 134: Wow, Ruth that place gives me the infernal jimjams. **1939** Fearing *Hospital* 84: That fellow gives me the jim-jams. **1940** W.R. Burnett *High Sierra* 125: This place gives me the jim-jams. **1980** Garrison *Snakedoctor* 12: That guy gives me the jim-jams. **1993** *Sci. American* (July) 5: A coffeemaker may produce brew that gives imbibers the jimjams.

jimmy *n.* **1.** [cf. JIM CROW] *Orig. Und.* a crowbar, as used by burglars. Now *S.E.* Earlier **jemmy.**

1811 Lexicon Balatron.: *Jemmy.* A crow. This instrument is much used by house-breakers. Sometimes called *Jemmy Rook.* *1837 in *F & H* IV 44: They call for crowbars—*jemmies* is the modern name they bear. **1848** Judson *Mysteries* 36: I'm agoin' to open it with a jimmy and a dark lantern. **1848** Thompson *House Breaker* 8: Small iron crow-bars (*London jimmies*). **1866** *Night Side of N.Y.* 106: He removes them softly with a "jimmy," or short iron bar. **1867** *Galaxy* (Aug.) 426: The gang will…with a short crowbar, called a "jimmy," pry open a shutter and thus obtain an entrance. **1872** McCabe *N.Y. Life* 527: Their favorite instrument is a "jimmy," or short iron bar with a sharp end. **1873** Lening *N.Y. Life* 149: They prefer the crowbar or "jimmy." **1882** Pinkerton *Bank-Robbers* 89: The door [had been] forced open with a "jimmy," or small crow-bar. **1901** *Chi. Tribune* (July 28) 38: An ax or a jimmy would be of no avail in this case. **1902** in "O. Henry" *Works* 974: The short but powerful "jimmy,"…the blued drills and punches. **1903** *Enquirer* (Cincinnati.) (May 9) 13: *Jimmie*—A small crowbar. **1914** Ellis *Billy Sunday* 277: A burglar couldn't get in with a jimmy. **1974** Radano *Cop Stories* 100: They play their lights on the front door of the store and see jimmy marks in the wood and fresh shavings laying on the ground. A burglary in progress!

2. *pl.* **a.** JIMJAMS, 1.

1900 J.C. Harris *On Wing* 42: Take 'im to the hospital, Tim; 'tis the only way to clear the jimmies from his head. *Ibid.* 77: I believe he's got the jimmies. **1905** *DN* III 84: *Jimmies*, n. Delirium tremens; blue. *1921 in *OED2:* You drank too much Scotch last night; be careful that you don't get the Jimmies and jump overboard. **1938** in A. Banks *First-Person* 81: Most assayers were drunkards and had the jimmies so bad that they didn't know what they were doing.

b. JIMJAMS, 2.

1918 *Stars & Stripes* (Aug. 16) 6: One who is skittish will sure get the jimmies. **1927–28** in R. Nelson *Dishonorable* 206: Well, with the jimmies you old women're in it's a wonder you didn't phone McQuigg. **1928** *New Yorker* (Dec. 22) 18: Well, frankly, it gives me the jimmies. **1931** Wilstach *Under Cover Man* 28: His room…gave him the jimmies, sometimes. **1949** W.R. Burnett *Asphalt Jungle* 83: It gives you the jimmies sometimes looking at it like this. *1961 in *OED2:* The grey light…gave her the jimmies.

3. a wide-brimmed straw hat.

1903 *Independent* (Aug. 13) 1911: With…an old straw "Jimmy," its brim torn and hanging, crowning his grizzled head, he stood knee deep in the waters of Panther Creek.

4. *pl.* **candy sprinkles added to ice cream or other desserts.**

*ca*1947 (cited in *W10*). **1963** in *DARE*: A generous ice cream cone, dipped in chocolate "jimmies." **1966** Fariña *Down So Long* 61: He chops peyote buds into the froth with chocolate jimmies. **1972** N.Y.U. student: Upstate they call those candy sprinkles you put on ice-cream cones *jimmies*. **1984** C. Francis *Who's Sorry?* 12 [ref. to 1940's]: Hey Luigi, what happened? You forgot my jimmies? Please,

Luigi, put some chocolate jimmies on top. **1986** Ciardi *Good Words* 161: The word was in common use in Boston in the 1920s and beyond, when every soda fountain kept a supply of jimmies to sprinkle on ice-cream cones….I knew the term intimately from… 1922 or 1923.

5. (*cap.*) **an engine or motor vehicle manufactured by General Motors Corporation (GMC).**

1951–53 in *AS* (May 1954) 99: *Jimmie, n.* A GMC engine; a car with a GMC engine. **1962** Tregaskis *Vietnam Diary* 63: A Chevvy with a '48 Jimmie (GMC) mill in it. **1971** *AS* XLIV 204: *Jimmie* GMC (trade name) truck. **1971** E. Sanders *Family* 193: Sunshine Pierce went back down to the GMC, the "jimmy" as it is known in trucker circles. **1974** E. Thompson *Tattoo* 398: A dump truck….A Jimmy, I think. Yeah, a Jimmy. Blue cab. **1978–86** J.L. Burke *Lost Get-Back Boogie* 168: I did a song about gyppo loggers…("the jimmy roaring, the big wheels rolling, the dirt and bark a-flying"). **1989** R. Miller *Profane Men* 197: Kenilworths and Jimmies…roared down the interstate.

6. *Rap Music & Black E.* **a.** **the penis.**—usu. considered vulgar. Cf. JIMMY, *v.*, 1.b.

1988 "Boogie Down Prods." *Jimmy* (rap song): Protect your jimmy and keep it fresh. **1989** "Beastie Boys" *Three-Minute Rule* (rap song): Never sleep alone because jimmy's the magnet. **1991** Univ. Tenn. student: *Jimmy* is rap music language for the male organ. **1993** *Source* (July) 71: My Jimmy Weighs A Ton. **1993** Mowry *Six Out Seven* 147: The dude seemed to have a real thing about getting his jimmy sucked-off.

b. **a condom;** JIMMY HAT. [This sense is considered erroneous by rap aficionados; see, e.g., *Village Voice* (N.Y.C.) (Dec. 4, 1990), p. 69. The later examples may have been adopted from exposure to song in first cite, by a performer considered inauthentic.]

1990 "Vanilla Ice" *Ice Cold* (rap song): I wore a jimmy that I slapped on. **1990** Eble *Campus Slang* 5: *Jimmy*—condom. **1993** P. Munro *U.C.L.A. Slang II: Jimmy hat/jimmy* n. condom.

7. item; object.

1991 *True Colors* (Fox-TV): One of these babies here and one of these jimmies, and I'm outa here.

jimmy *adj.* [var. of syn. E dial. *gim*] stylish; fashionable; spruce; neat; fit. Earlier **jemmy.** Also as adv.

*1750 in *OED*: His great ambition was to be deemed a "jemmy fellow." *1754 in *F & H* IV 45: The jemmy attorney's clerk—the prim curate. *a1825 in *OED*: *Gimmy*, spruce, neat, smart. *1825 in *F & H*: *Jemmy*, spruce. A low word. **1836** *Naval Mag.* (Nov.) 559: I sweeps right Jemmy, sir. **1889** Barrère & Leland *Dict. Slang* I 500: *Jimmy* was in use fifty years ago in America, meaning exactly, fit, suitable. **1889** Howells *Hazard* 217: He's made the thing awfully *chic*; it's jimmy; there's lots of dog about it. **1898** Green *Va. Folk Speech* 204: *Jimmy, adj.* Spruce; neat; smart; handy; dextrous. **1899** Ade *Fables* 60: The Kind that Wears a…jimmy little Tuxedo at Night. **1922** S. Lewis *Babbitt* 120: It's P.A. that jams such joy in jimmy pipes.

jimmy *v.* **1.a.** to pry open or break into with or as if with a JIMMY, Now *S.E.*

1854 in J.K. Williams *Vogues in Villainy* 41: [A] bag of jimmy tools. **1890** Roe *Police* 296: Shorton…"jimmied" the front door. **1893** J. Hawthorne *Conf. of Convict* 49: We took the safe…and…jimmied it open in no time. **1927** [W.H. Wright] *"Canary" Murder Case* 127: It came out of that jimmied jewel case—or I'm Ben Hur. *Ibid.* ch. xx: That box wasn't jimmied open—it was unlocked with a key. **1960** Bluestone *Cully* 73: Someone'd jimmied the side window of his car. **1973** *Sat. Review/Society* (May) 42: Any attempt to jimmy the doors, hood, or trunk will cause the horn to begin sounding. **1991** C. Fletcher *Pure Cop* 149: When they jimmy a door open…they leave…marks.

b. to copulate with (a woman).—usu. considered vulgar.

1918 in Carey *Mlle. from Armentières* I (unp.): The little Marine he grew he grew,/And he learned to jimmy the women, too. **1961** Gover *$100 Misunderstanding* 74: Hey, Jimmy the Burgler, you figgerin on jimmyin somethin wiff that?

c. to cajole or cheat; CHISEL, 1.a.

1921 in E. O'Neill *Letters* 160: I thought…I might jimmy some definite info. out of him. **1927** in Hemingway *Sel. Letters* 253: I feel that I let you in for a lot more expense than you figured on and then Jimmyed you out of more.

2.a. to meddle or interfere.—constr. with *with;* (hence) to arrange unfairly.—constr. with *up.*

1892 in *Kans. Univ. Qly.* (Jan. 1893) 139: To jimmy with [something]. **1927** Coe *Me—Gangster* 173: The system is jimmied up to help them.

b. *Esp. Und.* to injure, wound, spoil, ruin, etc.

1919 *Bookman* (Apr.) 209: Estimate the chances of X jimmying a bull and getting settled for a fiver in consequence. **1926** Finerty *Criminalese* 33: *Jimmying a bull*—To shoot an officer. **1928** Callahan *Man's Grim Justice* 64: I'm going to jimmy (cripple) myself, Jack....I'm tired of being sapped for not doing the task. **1933** Ersine *Pris. Slang* 47: *Jimmy, v.*...To spoil. **1944** in C. Gould *Snowflake* (unp.): Why, that dirty temperamental ham—he's jimmied our plans!

Jimmy Ducks *n. Navy.* a sailor or boy put in charge of a ship's poultry or other livestock. Also **Jemmy Ducks.**

1841 [Mercier] *Man-of-War* 83: He...asked Jemmy Ducks... whether that was the *big* rooster or not. "No!" returned Ducks. **1848** Melville *Redburn* ch. ix: He...laughed...and called me a "Jimmy Dux." **1849** Melville *White Jacket* 23: These fellows are all Jimmy Duxes— sorry chaps, who...are consigned to the congenial superintendence of the chicken-coops, pig-pens, and potato-lockers. **1870** [W.D. Phelps] *Fore & Aft* 323: Four boys, cook, steward, and "Jemmy Ducks." **1887** Davis *Sea-Wanderer* 290: When a cow, pigs, sheep, chickens, and other livestock were carried, the sailor who took care of them was called "Jimmy Ducks." **1889** *United Service* (Sept.) 276: Jimmy Legs is the master-at-arms, and "Jemmy Ducks" the poulterer. **1890** Erskine *Twenty Years* 304: I can't get promoted even to a Jimmy Duck's berth. **1929* Bowen *Sea Slang* 75: *Jimmy Ducks.* Butcher's assistant. Galley boy....In the old Navy he was the rating in charge of the ship's poultry. **1938* in *OED2.*

jimmy hat *n. Black E.* a condom. *Joc.* Also **jimmy cap, jim hat.**

1988 "Boogie Down Prods." *Jimmy* (rap song): Get your jimmy hats. **1990** *Mystery Science Theater* (Comedy Central TV): Are you wearing your jimmy hat? **1990** *Village Voice* (N.Y.C.) (Dec. 4) 69: "Jimmy hat," a condom. **1990** "Tribe Called Quest" *I Left My Wallet* (rap song): It was a brown wallet....Had my jimmy hats. **1991** *Houston Chronicle* (Nov. 13) 5D: *Jimmy hat, jim hat:* Condom. **1991** Nelson & Gonzales *Bring Noise* 55: De La sing the praises of wearing "your jimmy caps." **1992** Eble *Campus Slang* (Fall) 4: If you sleep with her, you better wear a jim hat. **1994** O'Leary *Univ. Delaware Sl.* 19: I need to get some Jimmy Hat's [*sic*] for tonight.

Jimmy Hicks *n.* [rhyming slang] *Craps & Poker.* a six. Also **Hicks.**

1919 Wilkins *Co. Fund* 45 [ref. to 1917]: Hicks [a 6 in craps]. **1921** Benet *Beginning of Wisdom* 262: The dice showed three and three. "Jimmy Hicks!" **1932** *AS* VII (June) 331: 6—Captain Jimmy Hicks of the Horse marines. **1951** *AS* (May) 99: *Jimmy Hicks.* Any six-spot. This name was probably borrowed from the vocabulary of dice.

Jimmy Hope *n.* [rhyming slang] *Pris.* soap.

1912 Lowrie *Prison* 52: The "Jimmy Hope" soap furnished is such as is ordinarily used for scrubbing floors. **1978–80** in Cardozo-Freeman *Joint* 509: *Jimmy Hope.* Soap.

Jimmy Legs *n. Navy.* a master-at-arms; (hence) *U.S. Nav. Acad.* a yard watchman. Now *hist.* Also (*obs.*) **Jemmy Legs, Jimmy Bowlegs.**

1839 McNally *Evils & Abuses* 89: There was an individual on board...whose name was Sterritt; but he was better known in the navy, by the cognomen of "Jemmy Leggs." He had been on board the frigate Constitution, as a master-at-arms. **1847** Downey *Portsmouth* 22: Jimmy Legs...is required by law to be the most inveterate enemy to liquor in a Ship. **1875** Sheppard *Love Afloat* 43: "Yes, sir," says Jimmy Legs. **1884** Blanding *Sailor Boy* 34: "Jimmy Legs"...proved to be the master-at-arms. **1894** *Lucky Bag* (No. 1) (U.S. Nav. Acad.) 4: A "lucky bag" is the receptacle into which "Jimmy Legs" gathers the odds and ends left adrift about the decks. **1904** in Connolly *Navy Men* 77: I've smothered Jimmy Bowlegs and the Old Man and the Cook. **1905** *Nat. Police Gaz.* (Sept. 23) 6: The Jimmy Legs is likely to be hovering around somewhere. **1917** *Lit. Digest* (Apr. 14) 1114: Every man-of-war carries a policeman on board...the master-at-arms, or "Jimmy Legs," as he is usually called. **1919** *Our Navy* (May) 36: The desk officer had the "jimmy legs" arrest him for direct disobedience of orders. **1925** *Sat. Eve. Post* (Dec. 19) 38 [ref. to 1890's]: He had been Jimmy Legs, so called from the insignia on the arm of a master-at-arms. **1936**

Mulholland *Splinter Fleet* 200: "Can't have him," retorted the *Jimmy Legs.* **1941** *Guide to the U.S. Nav. Acad.* 151: *Jimmylegs*—A yard watchman. **1982** T.C. Mason *Battleship* 81 [ref. to 1941]: He reported to the Jimmy legs and was immediately placed under house arrest.

jimmy protector *n. Rap Music & Black E.* a condom; JIMMY HAT.

1989 "Beastie Boys" *Sound of Science* (rap song): Had to get up to get the jimmy protector. **1990** *Village Voice* (N.Y.C.) (Dec. 4) 69: Probably he meant "jimmy protector"...a condom.

jims *n.pl.* JIMJAMS, 1.

*1894 in *Austral. Nat. Dict.:* Cure him of D.T.s and "jims." **1899–1900** Cullen *Tales* 193: Another went off on a toot...and landed in the bug ward of a free hospital with the jims. **1902** in *DAS:* I ain't dead anxious ter get next de Jims. **1906* in *Austral. Nat. Dict.:* Only a touch o' the jims. **1929** Milburn *Hobo's Hornbook* 114: I've blowed another winter's stake,/And got the jims instead.

jim-swinger *n. So.* a long-tailed or Prince Albert coat.

1893 in *DARE: Jim-swinger*...The common negro name for a *Prince Albert coat.* **1895** *DN* I 389: *Jim-swinger,* long-tailed coat, especially a "Prince Albert." **1902** Corrothers *Black Cat* 30: He still wore the conventional ministerial garb—plug hat, Prince Albert coat or "Jim Swinger" as he called it. *a1907* J.C. McNeill *Cotton Land* 125: My coat's a jim-swinger en my ves' is tan. **1924** W. White *Fire in the Flint* 49: He always wore coats which resembled morning coats, known in local parlance as "Jim-swingers." **1948** McIlwaine *Memphis* 228 [ref. to ca1880]: His battered, long, black coat; "a jim-swinger," he called it. **1972, 1984** in *DARE.*

jing *n.* JINGLE, 3.

1973 Eble *Campus Slang* (Mar.) 2: *Jing*—money: I can't buy a new stereo because I'm low on jing. **1973** Huggett *Body Count* 318: Nobody getting my jingbao, not my R 'n' R ging. **1976** C.R. Anderson *Grunts* [ref. to 1969]: "Got any jing?" "I told you. They fucked up my pay record in Nam." **1991** Jenkins *Gotta Play Hurt* 67: "Lot of jing in this house." "Some of them only look like they're rich."

jing-bang *n.* [orig. unkn.; cf. similar use of SHEBANG] ¶ In phrase: **the whole jing-bang** the entire lot. *Rare in U.S.*

*1866 in *OED: Jingbang,* the whole number. **1877** Burdette *Mustache* 242: The whole jing-bang ov thim. **1886* R.L. Stevenson *Kidnapped* ch. vii: The chief mate...was..."the only seaman of the whole jing-bang." **1890* in *OED.*

jing-bao juice *n.* [< Mandarin; lit. 'air raid' + *juice*] (*Mil. Av. in China.*) rice or plum wine. Now *hist.* [Quots. ref. to WWII.]

1943 *Yank* (Aug. 27) 7: Citizens of a Chinese province give...300 bottles of "jingbao (air raid) juice" to the Fourteenth's U.S. Air Force. **1945** *Yank* (Mar. 23) 7: Rice wine...tastes like wood alcohol and is called *jing-bao* or air-raid juice. **1945** Hamann *Air Words: Jing bow juice.* Rice liquor. **1957** E. Brown *Locust Fire* 21: All this rice and buffalo beef and *jing bao* juice. **1959** R.L. Scott *Flying Tiger* 83: The potent alcoholic liquor which the Chinese distilled from fermented rice mash and which the AVG called "jing-bow juice." **1982** W.R. Dunn *Fighter Pilot* 165: The Chinese...produced a rice wine, which we called "ging-bao juice." The term means "air raid" in Chinese. **1990** in M. Chennault *Up Sun!* 24: Plum wine....I took another slug of that jing bao juice.

jing-jang *n.* [cf. YING-YANG] (see quots.).—usu. considered vulgar.

1954–60 *DAS: Jing-jang*...1. The penis. 2. The vagina. 3. Sexual intercourse. **1964** in *Fact* (Jan. 1965) 26: Homosexual Slang...*jing-jang n.* The penis. **1972** R. Wilson *Forbidden Words* 151: *Jing-jang,* in parts of the South, is the vagina.

jingle *n.* **1.** liveliness; spirit.

1852 in J. Levy *Saw the Elephant* 50: [The trip] has taken the jingle out of him. **1864** J.R. Browne *Apache Country* 182: These Mexicans were dead-alive sort of cusses. The men had no grit and the women no jingle.

2.a. a drink of liquor.

1878 [P.S. Warne] *Hard Crowd* 5: Come up an' le's have a jingle all roun'! **1920** Ade *Hand-Made Fables* 12: The parched Pilgrims [were] rounded up for the twilight Jingle and trying to kid themselves into believing that they didn't care whether they got it or not.

b. a state of drunkenness.

1913 J. London *J. Barleycorn* 7: He sat with me...in my pleasant, philanthropic jingle.

3. cash, esp. coins.

*1906 in *Austral. Nat. Dict.:* Ther Elder dug in 'n' brought up er

'andful iv jingle. **1933–34** Lorimer & Lorimer *Stag Line* 135: "Got any jingle?" "Two bucks." **1945** Fay *Be Poor* 151: In other rhetoric, if "jingle" is in the "right hands," they do the bossing. **1948** Manone & Vandervoort *Trumpet* 156: At night the filthy rich mingled with the celebrity big shots, and I mingled with the jingle, too. **1965** *Elementary Eng.* (Nov.) 783: Coins…jingle,…dust. **1966** Braly *Cold* 67: But every time I rack up a little jingle I race myself to the store. **1973** *TULIPQ* (coll. B.K. Dumas): Cash, bills,…jack, bread, jingle. **1982** WINS radio news (Aug. 13): So plan ahead now, and you'll have a lot more jingle in your pocket when the holidays roll around.

4. a telephone call.

1949 in *DAS*: We never hear from you, not even a jingle. **1987** *N.Y. Times* (July 7) A12: He is always "giving people a jingle" and "scooting right over." *a***1989** Spears *NTC Dict.* 202: Give me a jingle when you get into town.

5. JITTERS.

*a***1977** T. Barnett *Golf Is Madness* 112: No more jingles, jangles, [or] heebie jeebies.

jingle *v. West.* to wrangle (horses).

1928 Santee *Cowboy* 159: George…was to jingle the ponies that fall.

jingleberry *n.* a testicle. [Bracketed quot. in sense 'a wealthy man' (based on JINGLE, *n.*, 3) is app. a nonce usage.]

[**1932** Hecht & Fowler *Great Magoo* 167: Some jingleberries she married is backing her.] **1952** Randolph & Wilson *Holler* 103: Jingleberry is another backwoods word for testicle: there is an old song about a boy and a girl who "set right down to *jingle-berry tea.*"

jingle-brained *adj.* scatterbrained.

[***1698–99** "B.E." *Dict. Canting Crew: Jingle-brains*, a Maggot-pated Fellow.] [***1796** Grose *Vulgar Tongue* (ed. 3): *Jingle Brains.* A wild, thoughtless, rattling fellow.] **1927** in Hammett *Big Knockover* 284: He was jingle-brained, of course, and needed holding, but I would rather work with him than with a lot of old-timers I knew.

jingled *adj.* intoxicated; elated by drink.—also constr. with *up.*

1908 in *DA*: So plausible a pretext for getting comfortably jingled. **1913** J. London *J. Barleycorn* 180: Some of us got magnificently jingled. **1927** Shay *Pious Friends* xi [ref. to 1890]: Our first impulse when pleasantly jingled was to burst into mellifluous song. **1927** (quot. at SQUIFFY). **1952** Sandburg *Strangers* 326 [ref. to *ca*1890]: He didn't get drunk, only "liked to get a little jingled." **1955** Post *Little War* 18 [ref. to 1898]: A little jingled up, maybe.

jingler *n.* **1.a.** Esp. *Und.* a tricky or dishonest horse dealer.

***1608** in Pendry *T. Dekker* 238: These horse-coursers are called "Jinglers." ***1698–99** "B.E." *Dict. Canting Crew: Jinglers*, Horse-Coursers frequenting Country Fairs. ***1788** Grose *Vulgar Tongue* (ed. 2) 205: *Jinglers.* Horse cosers, frequenting country fairs. *Cant.* **1847** *Nat. Police Gaz.* (June 26) 332: The resident "knucks" and "ginglers" of this city have…been…most active.

b. *West.* a horse wrangler.

1936 McCarthy *Mosshorn* (unp.): *Wrangler*, n. Sometimes called a jingler, wrang or wrangatang. **1941** *WPA Gde. to Wyoming,* in *DARE.* **1985** in H. Cannon *Cowboy Poetry* 137: The Jingler fogged 'em in.

2. usu. *pl.* a coin or piece of money; (*also*) a dollar.

1917 Cahan *D. Levinsky* 181 [ref. to *ca*1890]: Of what use is a good heart unless he has some jinglers* to go with it?…*Coin, money. **1925** *Sat. Eve. Post* (Jan. 3) 14: For thirty thousand jinglers.

jink *n.* Orig. *Mil. Av.* a sudden JINKING movement.

*a***1989** R. Herman, Jr. *Warbirds* 256: The…F-4s were doing jinks back and forth and hoped the…missiles could not match their turns. **1990** Rukuza *West Coast Turnaround* 27: Eddie…leaned all his weight into a left jink.

jink *v.* [Scots dial. *jink* 'to dodge'] **1.** *Mil. Av.* (of an aircraft) to make sudden, sharp evasive maneuvers in flight so as to avoid enemy fire.—also used trans.

***1917** in Lee *No Parachute* 139: From underneath, before the pilot could jink, I got in a long burst along the underbelly. **1941** *Sat. Review* (Oct. 4) 11: *Jinking.* Dodging anti-aircraft fire. **1943** Mears *Carrier* 85: I sideslipped, I chopped the throttle, I turned and twisted and jinked. **1945** O'Sheel & Cook *Semper Fidelis* 132: I wobble my wings like mad and jink up and down. **1946** G.C. Hall, Jr. *1000 Destroyed* 314: Blakeslee…jinked his craft to clear himself and tore down. **1948** Wolfert *Act of Love* 134: The PBY…came in low over the beach, jinking good-by. **1951** Sheldon *Troubling of a Star* 248: Then Ronsdale

wondered if the Colonel had seen him jink fearfully when that hidden battery had opened up. **1956** Heflin *USAF Dict.* 282: *Jink,* v. tr. To jerk an *aircraft* about in evasive action. **1960** Caidin *Black Thursday* 159: "Jinking" is all we can possibly do—moving suddenly a few feet up or down. **1961** Forbes *Goodbye to Some* 181 [ref. to WWII]: We used to practice…jinking and corkscrewing. **1964** Newhafer *Last Tallyho* 374: Dusane was jinking now, swerving his plane from side to side in an effort to throw the Jap gunners off. **1965** in J.C. Pratt *Vietnam Voices* 215: "Jinking smartly" to avoid any radar tracking or gunfire. **1975** in Higham & Siddall *Combat Aircraft* 85: I started a jinking pull-out. *a***1989** R. Herman, Jr. *Warbirds* 302: He jinked the Phantom hard as he escaped. **1989** Navy pilot, on *Prime News* (CNN-TV) (Jan. 5): The bogies appear to be coming, jinking to the right now.

2. to duck the head, as in boxing; dodge.

1990 G. Lee *China Boy* 177: Don't jink. Don't feint. *Parry* so's ya can counterpunch.

jinny *n.* [prob. resp. of *ginnie,* fr. GIN MILL] GIN MILL.

1930 *Amer. Mercury* (Dec.) 456: *Jinny,* n.: A blind pig. "From here out this jinny takes ten half barrels a week, see?" **1943** in *Amer. N & Q* (Oct. 1944) 111: That jinny takes three cases a day.

jinx *n.* [< L *jynx* 'the wryneck' (a bird used in witchcraft), hence 'a magic charm or spell'; app. reintroduced as sports slang *ca*1905 from its occurrence in T. Urquhart's translation (1693) of Rabelais—the sole E quot. given by the *OED*] Orig. *Sports Journ.* a spell or period of bad luck; (*also*) a bringer of bad luck; HOODOO. Now *colloq.* or *S.E.*

1908 in H.C. Fisher *A. Mutt* 25: There's a jinx on me. Here's where I quit. *Ibid.* 28: That hedge always was a jinx to me. **1911** in *DA*: Dave Shean and "Peaches" Graham…have not escaped the jinx that has been following the champions. **1913** *Chi. Daily Trib.* (May 1) 15: Edward Cicotte's jinx worked overtime today but failed to beat him because the White Sox made too many runs for it. **1915** in W.C. Fields *By Himself* 62: You have put the jinx on anything I wanted to do for him. **1928** in *DA*: The jinx had been broken. **1934** Appel *Brain Guy* 7: It'd been a jinx all day. None of his horses'd come in. The numbers'd been n. g. And pay-day was a mile off. *a***1937** Dollard *Southern Town* 263: An informant said that a jinx is when you have a run of bad luck. **1942** *New Yorker* (Oct. 17) 19: I'm the original jinx boy.…I'm the dog evveybody is talkin' it shouldn't happen to! **1945** in Litoff et al. *Miss You* 259: Friday the 13th…has been really full of the so-called jinx, too. **1955** G.D. Adams *3 Bad Sisters* (film): Lady, with all this publicity I'm a jinx. **1969–71** Kahn *Boys of Summer* 166: That sophomore jinx. I'm not gonna let that bother me. **1988** von Hassel & Crossley *Warriors* 58: Talking about death in combat situations is a jinx, like pilots talking about crashes.

jinx *v.* Esp. *Sports.* to bring bad luck to; HOODOO. Now *colloq.* or *S.E.*

1912 Mathewson *Pitching* 244: He outjinxed our champion jinx killer. **1914** *Lit. Digest* (May 9): Most of them think a change in hotels would surely "jinx" or hoodoo them. **1917** in *DA*: You jinxed my ball club. **1929–33** Farrell *Manhood of Lonigan* 205: Them damn things is jinxed! **1940** E. O'Neill *Iceman Cometh* 147: I's an ole gamblin' man.…But it's white man's bad luck. He can't jinx me. ***1950** in *West. Folklore* X (1951) 83: The girl…thought she had "jinxed" the two men. **1956** Neider *Hendry Jones* 105: You aiming to jinx me Bob? **1962** T. Berger *Reinhart in Love* 156: If it ain't my old car, then it's you who jinxed me. **1966** Kenney *Caste* 66: What you trying to do—jinx me? **1991** *CBS This Morning* (CBS-TV) (Oct. 28): I didn't want to tell anybody because I didn't want to jinx anything.

jip *n.* [prob. identical with *gyp:* "U.S.…a bitch" (1878–95 in *OED2*)] (used as a vulgar term of abuse applied to a woman).—used contemptuously.

1845 F. Douglass *Narrative* 61: Move faster, you black *gip!* **1855** F. Douglass *Bondage & Freedom* 149 [ref. to *ca*1830]: Move faster, you black jip!…take that, you black jip!

jip var. GYP, *v.*

jism *n.* [orig. unkn.; cf. *EDD chissom* n. & v. "A shoot, budding out," "To sprout, bud, germinate," fr. 1757; also cf. JASM] Also **gism, gyzm, jizzum, chism,** etc.

1. spirit; energy; spunk; in phr. **bit of gism** (*rare*) a pert young woman.

1842 *Spirit of Times* (Oct. 29) 409: His horse was knocked up—"the gism" and the starch was effectually taken out of him. **1866** [H.W. Shaw] *J. Billings* 232: But none...had the jism she had. **1877** Bartlett *Amer.* (ed. 4) 245: *Gism.* Spirit. "I knocked all the *gism* out of him." **1889** Farmer *Amer.*: *Gism.*—A synonym for energy, spirit. **1937** Weidman *Wholesale* ch. xxxii: Put a little jism into it, will you? **1937** L. Zukofsky, in Ahearn *Pound/Zukofsky* 190: In fact, his Viola Concerto, has more gism. **1951** Styron *Lie Down in Darkness* 140: She say ever since dat time you was fallin by de wayside yo'self and not seekin Jesus and all de gizzum run clean on out of you someways. **1953** Dibner *Deep Six* 16: I was only a kid, but I had plenty jism. **1960** Barber *Minsky's* 238: Depends when you de-nut 'em. You have to wait six months, otherwise they still got the old jism. **1965** Longstreet *Sporting House* 116: He'd take his favorite bit of gism upstairs. **1984** Wilder *You All* 96: To "put a little jism to it" means apply extra effort.

2.a. semen; sperm; (in 1854 quot.) the spray of a polecat.—usu. considered vulgar. [Perh. the orig. sense.]

1854 Doten *Journals* I 171: [The] big polecat...couldn't throw his "jesum" well against the wind. *ca***1888** *Stag Party* 192: His ponderous cods, a sight for Gods! were both surcharged with gism. **1899** Green *Va. Folk-Speech* 85: *Chism, chissum.*—seminal fluid. **1916** Cary *Venery* I 119: *Gysum*—The semen. **1917** E. Pound, in Materer *Pound/Lewis* 81: If the discharge be perfectly clean and white and of jismatic appearance. **1934** "J.M. Hall" *Anecdota* 106: G stands for gism,/The grandest of goos. **1938** "Justinian" *Amer. Sexualis* 26: *Jizzem.* n. The *semen virile.* U.S., 1920—, used chiefly by boys of grammar school and high school age. **1942** McAtee *Supp. to Grant Co. Dial.* [ref. to 1890's]: *Gism,* n., a semen [sic]....[also spelled] *jism.* **1942** H. Miller *Roofs of Paris* 51: I scatter jism like spray. **1944** Campbell & Robinson *Skeleton Key to Finnegans Wake* 29: Patrick is HCE...fructifying Mother Ireland with the gyzm of life eternal. **1945** PADS (No. 3) 10: *Gism*...Common among boys in Conn. [in 1890's]. **1966** "T. Pendleton" *Iron Orchard* 7: Six months o' that an' you'll never git you no boy-babies. Strains the boy-baby jizzum right outa you. **1968** P. Roth *Portnoy* 148: You've got to...walk around downtown Newark dripping gissum down your forehead. **1970** Cain *Blueschild Baby* 123: Got my pants down and jissom shooting everywhere. **1970** Wakefield *Going All the Way* 150: There was a little...mat that...probably wouldn't show the jizm too badly. **1971** *Playboy* (July) 183: The gizzum flew. **1974** Price *Wanderers* 91: You get gizzem on my bed I'm gonna make you eat it with a spoon. **1987** Univ. Tenn. prof.: In Albany, N.Y., [*ca*1930] the pronunciation was always *chism.* **1990** Steward *Bad Boys* 83: I had a buddy once who took a tattoo off with shark gyzm.

b. gravy or cream sauce.—usu. considered vulgar.

1935 in *DARE.* **1942** McAtee *Supp. to Grant Co. Dial.* 5: In various parts of the South *gism* has the meaning "gravy" or "cream sauce." **1942** ATS 808: Gravy...*gism.*

jit[1] *n.* [short for JITNEY] a nickel; five cents.

1913 in OED2: We went to the second jit show. **1915** *Variety* (June 4) 5: There's an Oriental Midway at three jits for the gate. **1915–16** Lait *Beef, Iron & Wine* 35: That bed and them brekfests was worth every jit of it. **1925–26** Black *You Can't Win* 318: A "jit," as the Southern negro affectionately calls his nickel. **1927** *Amer. Leg. Mo.* (Feb.) 66: A few jits every day, a little playing ball with the pay check. **1929** Milburn *Hobo's Hornbook* 233: And a lawyer comes and shakes you down for the last jit of your kale. **1930** Bodenheim *Roller Skates* 173: Anything that nosy Greek ever missed was worth less than a jit'! **1934** H. Roth *Call It Sleep* 306: I buys a couple o' franks on a roll fer a jit. **1935** *Amer. Mercury* (June) 230: *Jit:* five cents. **1939** "E. Queen" *Dragon's Teeth* 26: "Nothing for Monica, eh?" "Not a jit." **1942** "D. Ormsbee" *Sound of American* 269: Someone put a jit in the music box. **1944** PADS (No. 2) 34: *Jit:* n. A nickel. (W[estern] N.C.). **1973** Longstreet *Chicago* 368: With a mooched jit for beer.

jit[2] *n.* [perh. alter. of JIG[2] or JIP] (see quot.). [Later cites, as in OED2, Mencken *Amer. Lang.* (ed. 4), et al. appear to be drawn solely fr. Irwin.]

1930 Irwin *Tramp & Und. Slang* 110: *Jit*...A negro, or, more usually, a negress, and seemingly a term of derision.

jit[3] *n.* [orig. unkn.] JISM, 2.a.—usu. considered vulgar.

1974 Eble *Campus Slang* (Mar.) 4: *Jit or git*—semen. **1978** Wharton *Birdy* 33: My jockey shorts are slimy with jit.

jits *n.pl.* JITTERS.

1935 Lorimer & Lorimer *Heart Specialist* 47: In as complete a state of jits as I was. **1942** ATS 277: Nervousness...*jits.*

jitney *n.* [orig. unkn.] **1.** a nickel; five cents.

1903 *Enquirer* (Cincinnati) (May 2) 11: A "gitney" is a nickel. **1914** Jackson & Hellyer *Vocab.* 50: He hasn't got a jitney. **1914** in Handy *Blues Treasury* 78: The smoke was broke, no joke, not a jitney on him. **1915** *N.Y. Eve. Jour.* (Aug. 11) 10: He slipped the...chauffeur just a jitney for the fare. **1915** Bronson-Howard *God's Man* 138: A trey for a jitney—less than two cents per smoke. **1916** E.R. Burroughs *Return of Mucker* 116: I won't get a jitney of it. **1918** *Radiator* (Aug. 22) 2: To find you I would mooch/A jitney from a passing friend/John Barleycorn, my hooch. **1929** Milburn *Hobo's Hornbook* 50: And he spent every dime and jitney that little Nell could make. **1930** Pasley *Al Capone* 58: If the dinner cost a jitney, it cost $25,000. **1942** *Pittsburgh Courier* (Jan. 17) 13: It's your turn to put a jitney in the pic. **1952** Bellow *Augie March* 506: Half a buck, a quarter, a dime, a jitney, and a penny. **1975** McKennon *Horse Dung* 500: *Jitney:* Five cents.

2.a. a motor vehicle used as a bus to carry passengers over a usu. short regular route for a fixed fare, orig. five cents; (*broadly*) a bus. In full, **jitney bus.**

1914 in *Nation* (Jan. 14, 1915) 50: This autumn automobiles, mostly of the Ford variety, have begun to run in competition with the street cars in [Los Angeles]. The newspapers call them "Jitney 'buses." **1915** "High Jinks, Jr." *Choice Slang* 51: *Jitney buss*—An auto which runs on a regular route and competes with street cars. **1915** *N.Y. Times* (May 7) 5: Gov. Whitman Hears Fight Over Jitneys....Ex-Senator W.W. Armstrong, representing the Rochester Jitney Association of 600 members, opened the argument for the opposition....The jitney he described as the poor man's taxi and said that if the fare were fixed at 10 cents there would be no opposition. The 'buses, he went on, should be regulated by the various cities. **1917** McCann *With Nat. Guard* 133: As soon as we had gotten him onto the "jitney" another...asked if he couldn't also ride. **1918** McNutt *Yanks Are Coming!* 125: An electric road, several bus lines, and innumerable jitneys connect the camp with Des Moines. **1925** in *AS* II (1926) 214: For the purposes of this act a *jitney* is defined as any motor vehicle advertised or regularly used for carrying passengers for hire. **1955** Robbins *79 Park Ave* 259: The jitney dropped her at the house. **1956** M. Wolff *Big Nick* 10: Hey, there goes the jitney. **1972** N.Y.U. student: My grandfather [in Jersey City] calls any bus "the jitney bus." **1979** in Terkel *Amer. Dreams* 89: I used to see black women [in Chicago] get off the bus at night and off jitneys as late as two in the morning and walk three blocks home on a summer night. **1985** E. Leonard *Glitz* 106: Say you want to go a few blocks on Pacific you hop a jitney, six bits. **1989** *Nat. Lampoon* (June) 38: A jitney ticket back to the city. **1992** G. Wolff *Day at the Beach* 39: These jitneys, big old...DeSotos and Hudsons.

b. a small or inexpensive automobile; jalopy.

[**1915** H.L. Mencken, in Riggio *Dreiser-Mencken Letters* I 208: My new jitney bus makes at least 12 miles an hour on level roads.] **1917** in *DARE.* **1919** *Fifth Div. Diamond, S.O.L. Edition* (July 4): We're up in old Esch where you never have the blues,/Where the bandits steal the jitneys and the M.P.'s steal the booze. **1930** *AS* VI 85: He dubs his car a *flivver,...a jitney,...a Lizzie.* **1933** *Amer. Mercury* (June) 179: A young high-school student trying to crank a Ford jitney. **1931–34** Adamic *Dynamite* 271: The license number...was the number of Weinberg's jitney. **1964** in Chipman *Hardening Rock* 28: They bought a souped-up jitney, 'twas a cherry-red fifty-nine. **1967** Talbot *Chatty Jones* 102: This is my night to roar, and the old jitney is waiting outside.

c. (applied to various small utility vehicles).

1916 in R.C. Brown *Hard Rock Miners* 170: There's the trammer with his jitney that is sometimes off the track. **1940** *R.R. Mag.* (Apr.): *Jitney*—Four-wheel electric truck that carries baggage around inside a [railroad] terminal. **1950** *West. Folk.* IX 121: *Jitney.* A motor vehicle that straddles a load of lumber and picks up the load by means of flanges which slide under the ends of the blocks.

jitney *adj.* costing or charging five cents; (*hence*) cheap; second-rate; TWO-BIT.—not used predicatively.

1914 (quot. at JITNEY, n., 2.a.). **1916** H.L. Wilson *Somewhere in Red Gap* 59: He...sells these jitney pianos and phonographs and truck like that. **1916** P.A. Lewis & B.G. Clements *The Jitney Ball* [pop. song] [San Antonio, Tex.: Lewis & Clements, 1916]. **1920** Fitzgerald *This Side of Paradise* 110: Here's the old jitney waiter. **1921** Benet *Beginning of Wisdom* 115 [ref. to 1915]: Playing footie with the jitney *demi-vierges* of New Haven was a Freshman sport. **1925** *AS* I 152: That bastard word "jitney" is still used in outlying places, where a "jitney dance" means a nickel dance. **1933** Milburn *No More Trumpets* 163: I fallen for a little "dame" in a jitney dance hall. **1935** *Amer. Mercury* (Aug.) 472: The prolificity of these jitney St. Georges…has been…amazing. **1936** in *AS* (Feb. 1937) 4: Jitney Marxes.

jitney *v.* to go or convey in a JITNEY or other small motor vehicle.

    1915 in *DA*: An omnibus in which seventeen men were jitneying to Salem, New Jersey. **1942** *ATS* 719: Travel by bus or taxi…*jitney (it)*. **1955** Goethals *Chains of Command* 116: It chilled him to think that Miles was going to jitney about the countryside in an open jeep. **1956, 1969** in *DARE*.

jitney girl *n.* (see quot.).

    1965–67 Herndon *Way It Spozed to Be* 54: "Where are the whores? Where are the goddam jitney girls?"…Jitney girls drove up and down the streets of the South Side in Chicago in oversized cars, picking up men who flagged them down for a quick one.

jitney wrestle *n.* (see quot.).

    1940 Simonsen *Soldier Bill* 46 [ref. to 1917]: The old penny dance hall progressed into the nickel dance hall—or the jitney wrestle. Whoever named these dance halls jitney wrestles had done a good job.

jitterbug *n.* [JITTER(S) + BUG, app. coined by Cab Calloway (1907–94), U.S. band leader] **1.a.** a JITTERY or nervous person.

    1934 C. Calloway, I. Mills & E. Swayzee *Jitter Bug* (pop. song) (N.Y.: Mills Music, Inc.) 2: They're four little jitter bugs. **1935** C. Calloway, in *Call of Jitterbug* (film): A jitterbug party. It's where everybody gets the *jitters* and goes *bugs*!…Become a jitterbug. *1939 in OEDS*: Information which would largely dispel the apprehensions of the "Jitter-bugs," who…are vocal and often influential. [**1939** Spence et al. *Flying Deuces* (film): I feel as fidgety as a jitterbug.] *1940 in AS* XIX (1944) 11: People in Britain who were inclined to panic last September were called *jitterbugs* by Mr. Neville Chamberlain. **1941** Huston & Burnett *High Sierra* (film): I ain't worried about you. It's those jitterbugs you got with you.

    b. a person, usu. a teenager, who dances energetically, often acrobatically, to boogie-woogie or swing music.

    1937 *Down Beat* (Feb.) 9: Jives of the Jitterbugs. **1937** *AS* (Oct.) 183: *Jitter Bugs*. The same as *cats*, only more so. **1938** *Sat. Review* (July 23) 22: I have become an absolute jitterbug recently. Did you go to the swing carnival at Randall's Island? **1938** *Life* (Aug. 8) 56: Jitterbugs are the extreme swing addicts who get so excited…that they…must prance around in wild exhibitionist dances…or yell and scream. **1939** P. Tamony, in Mencken *Amer. Lang. Supp. II* 710: *Jitterbug* [a fan] whose reaction to swing is always physical [came into currency] late in 1935. **1939** *Pittsburgh Courier* (July 15) 21: "Jitterbugs" On Way Out, Says Lunceford. **1939** in L. Patterson *Negro in Music* 53: Neither are "jitterbugs" insincere. **1943** *N.Y. Times* (May 9) II 5: I'm a jivin' jitter-bug. **1943** in Himes *Black on Black* 193: A big dance was held for the young jitterbugs. **1950** *Metronome* (Dec.) 20: It's too bad the jitterbugs are gone. In those days jazz was the thing. **1951** E. Paul *Springtime* 218: Jitterbugs and Lindy hoppers.

    c. a teenager or other young person who is foolish, ignorant, or immature.

    1944 W. Duff *Marine Raiders* (film): I can't spend time nursing a lot of jitterbugs when there's a war going on. **1951** M. Shulman *Dobie Gillis* 88: Look at Petey—a knothead, a jitterbug, a guy who'll never know where his next meal is coming from. **1962** Crump *Killer* 352: "Look, *officer*," the blue-clad jitterbug corrected. **1964–70** in *Paris Rev.* (No. 50) 96: Just like those jitterbugs down in Acapulco got to time their jumps so they hit the water just as the wave is beginning its break. **1970** A. Young *Snakes* 75: That just aint where it's at, as the jitterbugs say. *Ibid.* 86: These old so-called hip niggers, these little jitterbugs. And that's all they are is jitterbugs. **1967–74** in R. Rosenthal et al. *Different Strokes* 24: A lot of jitterbugs will come over there, with their parent's car…and pick up a bunch of girls and stay around half the night, with them record players…out in front. **1975** Wambaugh *Choirboys* 107: Most a these young jitterbug social workers don't look like they got all their shit in one bag anyhow. **1980** McDowell *Our Honor* 16: You jitterbugs who don't have rear pockets, you can carry it wherever it's convenient for the time being, but Christ help you if you lose it. **1993** A. Lomax *Where Blues Began* 348: "Jitterbug"…seems to refer to a little bug or a small child.

    d. Esp. *Black E.* a rowdy youth, esp. a member of a street gang; juvenile delinquent.

    1967 in T.C. Bambara *Gorilla* 71: Realer type people…get right out

there in the street with all the jitterbugs and take your side against the landlords and the cops. **1965–68** in D. Glasgow *Black Underclass* 49: These little jitterbugs threaten you, and still the parents protect them. **1964–69** in Calt *Rather Be Devil* 335: These "jitterbugs" (young criminals) get 'em. **1970–71** Rubinstein *City Police* 232: You think I'm gonna walk around here without some protection? You know what them fuckin' jitterbugs do to you for no reason at all? **1971** Woodley *Dealer* 106: I was born in and raised in New York. I was a jitterbug, you know, a gangfighter. **1975** S.P. Smith *Amer. Boys* 47: Got so high that even the jittybugs he was with thought he was crazy. **1976** G. Kirkham *Signal Zero* 49: Jitterbugs was all the time breaking in. Robbing the place. **1979** D. Milne *Second Chance* 47 [ref. to 1950's]: Well…you don't look like you're a jitterbug, anyway. **1986** Heinemann *Paco's Story* 80: And right out of nowhere this jitterbug…whipped out this little .22 pistola. **1969–87** D. Rose *Black Street Life* 58: He had a whole trunkful of knives he had taken off *jitterbugs*.

2. a fast, vigorous dance for couples, done usu. to boogie-woogie or swing music, and consisting of a few standardized steps augmented by twirls, splits, etc. Now *S.E.*

    1941 in M. Taft *Blues Concordance* 1328: Oh she do that new dance you call jitterbug. **1943** in *OEDS*: The wildest Jitterbug yet is danced by Dorothy Lamour. **1970** Major *Afro-Amer. Slang* 71: *Jitterbug*…a dance done to swing music; the Lindy hop. **1978** De Christoforo *Grease* 157: We broke…into a jitterbug.

3. (applied to various small utility vehicles).

    1941 Kendall *Army & Navy Sl.* 8: *Jeep.…*reconnaissance truck, also known as a jitterbug. **1974** N.Y.C. man, age 27: A jitterbug is a conveyance to haul lumber or similar stuff. They use it in Maine. **1977** Bartlett *Finest Kind* 103: One jitterbug races out the main door of the warehouse with a skid piled high with empty boxes.…"Up yours," one of the jitterbug jockeys hollers back.

jitterbug *v.* **1.** to dance the JITTERBUG, **2.** Now *S.E.*

    1938 in *OED2*: Jitterbugging is just a phase.…It isn't music. **1939** in *OED2*: Susy Shag…begins thinking seriously of marrying the guy she's been jitterbugging with. **1943** in Himes *Black on Black* 193: There'll be no jitterbugging in heaven as long as I'm a god. **1946–51** Salinger *Catcher in the Rye* ch. x: She started jitterbugging with me. **1952** J.O. Killens, in Chambers & Moon *Right On!* 94: I guess Mr. Charlie wants us to jitterbug onto his pretty white boat. **1958** Salisbury *Shook-Up Generation* 29: The argot [of the street gang] seems to derive from the world of bebop, jitterbugging and jazz. **1960** in T.C. Bambara *Gorilla* 54: You knew she'd been jitterbugging since kindergarten. **1973** in *OED2*. **1978–86** J.L. Burke *Lost Get-Back Boogie* 38: They jitterbugged and did the dirty boogie.

    2.a. to hop or move about rapidly, esp. in evasion or hesitation; (*broadly*) to fool around.

    1942 Algren *Morning* 261: Quit the jitterbuggin' 'n give us a fight! **1963** Williamson *Hustler!* 146: You're just jitter-buggin'* down there with them three bricks.…*To jitter-bug—to fool around. *a*1972 A. Shepp, in W. King & R. Milner *Black Drama Anthol.* 63: Youth is wasted/Once it's tasted/Jitterbuggin' ain't forever. **1974** Blount *3 Bricks Shy* 277: But the kind of dancing Preston was criticizing was jitterbugging, or pussy-footing, when you're a running back charged to hit a certain hole. **1984–88** Hackworth & Sherman *About Face* 654 [ref. to 1969]: We also "jitterbugged" (a series of predesignated helicopter insertions made one by one until contact was made).

    b. *Black E.* to saunter or swagger; DIDDLYBOP.

    1974 Matthews & Amdur *Race Be Won* 46: You bumped into me and you just go jitterbuggin' on, and you ain't even gonna say you're sorry. **1975** *Black World* (June) 74: Butchie [was] jitterbuggin up to us. **1979** D. Milne *Second Chance* 16 [ref. to 1950's]: Dominating the sidewalk, we jitterbugged down St. Edward Street.

    3. to engage in gang fighting. Now *hist.*

    1958 Salisbury *Shook-Up Generation* 57: He himself never jitterbugged until he…was drafted by the Cobra Juniors. **1959** E. Hunter *Matter of Conviction* 198: Danny…never punked out of nothing, either. Whenever we jitterbugged, he was there with us. He never let us down. **1965** *Esquire* (July) 45: The Gallo gang got wasted bad when they *jitterbugged* with the Mafia. **1967** in T.C. Bambara *Gorilla* 71: But it turned out to be a cool summer. Hot in all the usual ways, but no jitterbugging. **1979** D. Milne *Second Chance* 60 [ref. to 1950's]: A born troublemaker. A real jitterbugger.

    4. to shudder or vibrate rapidly.

1984 Trotti *Phantom* X: Like maintaining formation on a jitterbugging wingtip at night in a thunderstorm.

jitter joint *n.* a cheap nightclub or similar establishment where JITTERBUG dancing is done. Now *hist.*

> **1947** *ATS* (Supp.) 8: Dance hall...*jitter joint*,...juke joint. **1955** Shapiro *Sixth of June* 236 [ref. to 1944]: How 'bout that jitter joint on Wardour Street?

jitters *n.pl.* [orig. unkn.] **1.** uncontrolled fidgeting, apprehensiveness, or fright; nervous anxiety; shakes. Now *S.E.*

> **1929** Sturges *Dishonorable* II: *Isabelle.* Willie's got the jitters—. *Judge.* Jitters? *Isabelle.* You know, he makes faces all the time. **1931** in *AS* VIII (Feb. 1933) 74: Swift moving elevators and roller coasters also give her the jitters. **1932** in *AS VIII* (Feb. 1933): *Jitters.* This is a good slang word. **1932** Cromack & Ornitz *Thirteen Women* (film): She gives me the jitters. **1932** Hecht & Fowler *Great Magoo* 156: Nothing's the matter....It's the wedding-bells jitters. **1932** E. Wilson *The American Jitters* [title]. **1933** *AS* VIII (Oct.) 77: In such expressions as *to have,* or *get, the jitters,* and *good for the jitters,* it denotes nervousness, distraction, great excitability, a condition of unease, fidgeting, sometimes trembling and starting. **1934** Kromer *Waiting* 19: I jumped in and out of so many doorways I got the jitters. **1940** Ellis & Logan *Star Dust* (film): I get the jitters, I shake, I bite my fingernails. **1941** *New Yorker* (July 26) 15: I got a double dose of jitters today. **1945** in *DA*: A nation with the reconversion jitters. **1949** in *DA*: His scream enhanced the drama, gave the crowd the jitters. **1951** in J.P. Cannon *Notebook* 260: The jitters have yielded to the sedative of time. **1991** *Newsweek* (Jan. 21) 19: War jitters swept college campuses.

2. a feeling of unsteadiness, as caused by intoxication; (*also*) delirium tremens or an alcoholic hangover.

> **1931** *Harper's Mag.* (Mar.) 420: How much do you have to drink to get "jitters?" **1934** Weseen *Dict. Slang* 357: *Jitters*—A dizzy feeling. **1942–43** (quot. at KATZENJAMMER). **1945** in *DAS*: "Jitters"...is from a Spoonerism ["bin and jitters" for "gin and bitters"]...and originally referred to one under the influence of gin and bitters.

jittery *adj.* afflicted with JITTERS. Now *S.E.*

> **1931** in H. Crane *Letters* 369: I'm too jittery to write a straight sentence. **1931** in *DA*: The editors will go home all jittery unless the Junior League girls...quit parading around the mezzanine. **1933** *AS* VIII (Oct.) 78: The adjective *jittery* means *on edge,* jerky, jumpy, overexcited. *a***1938** Adamic *My America* 514: This one...was a little drunk 'n' jittery. **1957** E. Lacy *Room to Swing* 79: I was jittery riding down the elevator.

jive *n.* [perh. dial. var. of *gibe, jibe*] Orig. *Black E.* **1.a.** deceptive flattery; lies; boasting; insincerity; humbug.

> **1928** R. Fisher *Jericho* 95: Pat comes up and puts on his jive....But you lap it up. **1929** T. Gordon *Born to Be* 236: *Jive:* A misleading remark. **1929** in Oliver *Meaning of Blues* 223: Don't come back with that line of jive. **1929** in M. Taft *Blues Concordance* III 1329: My baby...tried to cop a jive/I got something to tell you: going to make you mad. **1931** in Oliver *Blues Tradition* 191: She needn't a-come with that line of jive, says she knows she's lyin'. **1932** in M. Taft *Blues Concordance* III 1328: Tell you men I don't mean no jive. **1932** in *AS* (Feb. 1934) 26: *Gieve.* n. Conversation; misleading talk. **1938** Ward *Fog* 282: You don't see any of our really big people falling for Marcus Garvey's jive, do you? **1945** Himes *If He Hollers* 70: Don't hand me this hockey....That is the saddest jive; that is pitiful. **1946** H.A. Smith *Rhubarb* 70: Go peddle that jive someplace else, and get the hell out of here. **1950** Bissell *Stretch on the River* 133: You got quite a line of jive, ain't you? **1955** McGovern *Fräulein* 195: When I tell you that America is the most...that's not jive. **1957** Myrer *Big War* 103: I couldn't go around giving a lot of war workers a big line of jive about get-in-there-and-pitch and gung-ho and all that. **1961** J. Baldwin *Another Country* 345: Would you believe it? I fell for that jive. **1964** Brewer *Worser Days* 173: He come back in the poolroom talkin' his jive,/He say, "Who wanna try the baddest guy alive?" **1973** *Harper's* (Sept.) 10: I could see this white New England lawyer take one look at this black kid and figure that some sort of jive was going on. **1995** S. Moore *In the Cut* 160: You and me don't never talk. It's always just jive.

b. Esp. *Jazz.* banter or talk, esp. a flippant, self-assured, or bantering style of diction prob. arising from the DOZENS and associated with urban black youths, some jazz and swing musicians, disc jockeys, etc., that makes use of much slang and other wordplay and sometimes of rhythm or rhyme; (*also*) (*broadly*) Esp. *Journ.* slang, esp. the slang and jargon of swing musicians and fans. Also **jive talk.** [See esp. D. Burley, *Original Handbook of Harlem Jive* (1944).]

> **1928** Cow-Cow [Charles] Davenport *State Street Jive* [pop. song]. [Chicago: State Street Music Pub. Co., Inc., 1928] **1938** Calloway *Hi De Ho* 16: *Jive*...Harlemese speech or lingo. **1941** *Chi. Daily News* (July 5) 4: Jive Talk Flourishes at Camp Beauregard. **1942** *Pittsburgh Courier* (Dec. 19) 6: It is very difficult to say just what it is that makes people use slang, the language we now call "jive." **1944** Burley *Hndbk. Jive* 79: Jive Phrases...Fine as wine, Mellow as a cello, Like the bear, nowhere. *Ibid.* 80: The language of Jive presents an unusual opportunity for experimentation in rhymes....""I'm a solid dreamer, you're a low-down schemer," [etc.]. **1947** *ATS* (Supp.) 7: *Jive*...the slang of the "hepcats." **1948** Manone & Vandervoort *Trumpet* 26: He's laying the wrong kind of jive on that gal. She don't go for it, atall. **1948** *Look* (Jan. 6) 26: Prison Jargon...*Jive*—Small talk. **1950–52** Ulanov *Hist. of Jazz* 352: *Jive:* comic speech, usually larded with ambiguous jazz terms. **1953** in Cannon *Like 'Em Tough* 54: Son, if you don't like this brand of jive, you know where you can go. **1971** in Cannon *Nobody Asked* 182: The language Frazier talks is musicians' jive, and Ali speaks in a sort of street poetry traced with religious cant. **1972** Claerbaut *Black Jargon* 70: *Jive*...informal language; popular jargon; slang. **1973** H. Foster *Ribbin'* 26: In jive talk, the Man is the white man. **1978** B. Johnson *What's Happenin'* 92: He was feeling loose, full of jive. **1981** *Nat. Lampoon* (Mar.) 70: Hip Jive: Later, Gator! **1985** J.M.G. Brown *Rice Paddy Grunt* 140: Telling stories and talking his cool, low street jive. **1986** J.J. Maloney *Chain* 75: But I forgot to listen to my own jive. **1988** *Time* (July 11) 59: I spoke in caló, street jive from the streets of East L.A.—a mix of Spanish, English and Gypsy. **1990** *Newsweek* (July 2) 52: But some blacks find this defense degrading, as if all black culture were street-corner jive. **1992** "Fab 5 Freddy" *Fresh Fly Flavor* 36: *Jive*...Slang. **1993** *Sally Jessy Raphaël* (synd. TV series): She likes to talk jive—or at least what we used to call jive.

2. *Black E.* an act of sexual intercourse; copulation; (*hence*) a person regarded as a sex partner.

> **1928** R. Fisher *Jericho* 54: Figgerin' on a jive already—the doggone dicky hound. Why the hell dickties can't stick to their own women 'thout messin' around honest workin' girls. **1958–59** in Abrahams *Deep Down in the Jungle* 262: *Jive*...Originally and still used in the sense of "fuck" and "jazz," i.e., the sexual act. **1954–60** *DAS: Jive*...sex; sexual intercourse. **1965** Trimble *Sex Words* 114: *Jive*...n. A person as a sex object.

3.a. (*loosely*) stuff; things; goings-on; way or ways of doing things; (in 1988 quot.) situation.

> **1938** *AS* XIII 317: Hip me to the jive!..."put me wise." **1938** in R.S. Gold *Jazz Talk* 148: *Jive:* stuff and things. **1942** Breslow *Blondie Goes to College* (film): Relax, honey. You'll get the jive in no time. **1944** in Himes *Black on Black* 201: Well look at that jive!...What's that stuff, man? **1946** Mezzrow & Wolfe *Really Blues* 307: *Jive that makes it drip:* clouds that produce rain. **1953** W. Fisher *Waiters* 112: All you gotta do is stop by an' drop the jive. **1954** L. Armstrong *Satchmo* 193: I bought a lot of cheap jive at the five and ten cents store. *Ibid.* 214: She boiled this jive down to a gravy. **1954** W.G. Smith *South St.* 98: I went overseas and got hep to all the culture jive. **1956** Ross *Hustlers* 58: They wanted to know...who killed him, who we been having trouble with. Jive like that. **1964** in B. Jackson *Swim Like Me* 98: We can soon have all this jive in my moving van. **1970** A. Young *Snakes* 59: You wanna get your ears opened up so you can hear some of this jive the way it's supposed to be heard. **1974** Matthews & Amdur *Race Be Won* 41: You can do this jive. **1980** L. Fleischer & C. Gore *Fame* 149: I ain't into that stuff....It ain't my jive. **1982** D.J. Williams *Hit Hard* 176 [ref. to WWII]: We got big trouble....You better come on over yourself. Bad jive! **1982** Goff, Sanders & Smith *Bros.* 50: Wasn't that much food on it. I gobbled that little jive up in a hurry. **1988** R. Robertson & J. Wynorski *Earth* (film): What's the jive? **1990** in Wimmer *Schoolyard Game* 101: I don't know any of that jive about fingertips and watching the rim.

b. *Narc.* illicit drugs, esp. marijuana or heroin; a marijuana cigarette.

> **1936** "A. Kirk and the Twelve Clouds of Joy" *All the Jive Is Gone* [blues record]. **1939** in Botkin *Sidewalks* 575: "Knock me a jive there, Gates." That means, "Give me a marijuana cigarette." **1946** (quot. at GASSER). **1948** Schwartz *Blowtop* 146: I made a new connection. This is the stuff! Real African jive! **1952** E. Brown *Trespass* 118: Here, man...pick up on some of this jive. **1952** Mandel *Angry Strangers* 58: Lots of jive and goofballs, maybe a couple caps of Horse. **1956** E.

Hunter *Second Ending* 24: They were getting all the jive they wanted free....And it was certainly a hell of a lot better than...that methadone. **1958** Gilbert *Vice Trap* 40: The place smelled of jive. **1960** *Esquire* (Mar.) 87: Tea, jive, pot, hay, hemp, Maryjane. **1963** Williamson *Hustler!* 149: He was a dope fiend...and needed some jive.*...*Jive—narcotics. **1970** E. Knight *Black Voices from Prison* 79: Can that crap, Gino, and give me 2,000 mgs of acid—quick!...You faggot, give me that jive 'fo I cut your fucking throat. **1973** Goines *Players* 131: I had some bomb stuff, man. Some sure 'nuff good jive. **1976** "N. Ross" *Policeman* 71: You got jive and reefer in the car? **1988** T. Logan *Harder They Fall* 193: Let me get a half spoon of mixed jive until later?

4. swing music (now *S.E.*); (*broadly*) jazz, rock and roll, rhythm and blues, etc.

1937 *New Yorker* (Apr. 17) 27: The music of hot bands...is referred to as *swing* or *jive*. **1943** G. Biddle *Artist at War* 21: A Negro "jive" company...performed for the wounded. **1944** Burley *Hndbk. Jive* 71: Since 1930 Jive has been accepted as the trade-name for "swing" music. **1948** Manone & Vandervoort *Trumpet* 16: I took my trumpet and let out a blast that upset the class for half an hour....The teacher...didn't dig my jive. **1948** Lait & Mortimer *New York* 93: Eating is an art at Luchow's, undisturbed by raucous talk or jive. [**1950–52** Ulanov *Hist. of Jazz* 352: Jive...[is] *never* a kind of jazz, as it has sometimes been thought to signify.] **1960** *Down Beat* (June 9) 115: Jive...is...an obsolete slang term for jazz. **1971** in L. Bangs *Psychotic Reactions* 8: There was so much good jive wailing out. *a*1981 in McKee & Chisenhall *Beale* 172: They slap a jazz [record] on there [and] go to playing jive.

5. *Black E.* JIVE-ASS, 1.

1969 C. Brown *Mr. Jiveass* 31: I mean Byron was just like me, man, he was a jive too. **1971** H.E. Roberts *Third Ear: Jive*, n....an unreliable person...one who is not in the know. **1978–89** in Jankowski *Islands in Street* 222: So...we go out and work...for the jive's candidate.

6. (see quot.).

1991 *CBS This Morning* (CBS-TV) (Dec. 6): An expert at trick turns [in wind surfing] or "jives."

¶ In phrase:

¶ **hep** [or **hip** or **hipped**] **to the jive** see s.v. HEP, *adj.* and *hipped to the jive* s.v. HIPPED³, *adj.*, 2.b.

jive *adj.* Orig. *Black E.* **1.** engaged in false posturing; pretentious; conceited; (*hence*) false; fake; worthless; contemptible; stupid. Also (*vulgar*) **jive-ass.**

1946 J.H. Burns *Gallery* 5: His cap was set on his head, not at the jive angle that young parachutists love but strategically. **1952** Ellson *Golden Spike* 165: Why don't you leave that jive bitch alone? *Ibid.* 166: You're jive, you try to be slick. **1955** in *Tenn. Folk. Soc. Bull.* XXII 23: "That was a jive tip"—Unreliable information. **1958–59** in Abrahams *Deep Down in the Jungle* 142: I was standing before some jive-ass judge. **1959** in R.S. Gold *Jazz Talk* 148: *Jive*...used to describe an unscrupulous person. **1960** I. Freeman *Out of Burning* 194 [ref. to *ca*1950]: You jive-ass punk. **1964** R.S. Gold *Jazz Lexicon* 169: Jive-ass mother-fucker. **1965** C. Brown *Manchild* 142: He had been blamed for shooting somebody....It was a jive tip. *Ibid.* 144: You could tell that these cats were jive by the way they went around saying, "Yeah, man, do you shoot stuff?" and all this sort of nonsense as though they were bragging about it. **1966** Manus *Mott the Hoople* 38: It's worth a hundred bucks just to shut your jive mouth up. **1966** *Down Beat* (June 16) 24: Hippies were...jive punks. **1968** Bullins *In Wine Time* 390: You, you jive-ass sucker! **1968** in A. Chapman *New Black Voices* 149: How you expect me to get into anything on a jive horn? **1968** I. Reed *Yellow Back Radio* 11: That jive fur trapper who's always handing you subpoenas. **1967–69** von Hoffman *Parents Warned Us* 110: Ain't that a bitch! Jive-ass po-lice comin' in here las' night an' wrecking the place. **1971** G. Davis *Coming Home* 38: Of course she gon' pretend that she doesn't want to talk to me either, but she's jive. **1973** Wambaugh *Onion Field* 90: Stealin' from a partner is jiveass bullshit. **1973** Childress *Hero* 13: Dig it, *maintenance man* ain't nothin but a jive-ass name for a janitor. **1974** Univ. Tenn. student: That buncha jive turkeys can't do anything right. **1980** Gould *Ft. Apache* 47: All of a sudden you ain't makin' no jive-ass remarks. **1989** S. Robinson & D. Ritz *Smokey* 73: A real manager wouldn't book us into no jive-ass joint like that.

2. trivial or foolish. Also (*vulgar*) **jive-ass.**

1965 C. Brown *Manchild* 184: I knew...I was going to get busted for something jive...like smoking reefers. **1970** A. Young *Snakes* 94: She

was kinda, you know—jive....She...went for all this hippy-dippy shit. *Ibid.* 98: I was so jive and petrified that...I got smaller and smaller. **1974** Gober *Black Cop* 53: He didn't feel like fuckin' around with crazy white folks and their jive games. **1972–79** C. Major *Emergency Exit* 69: That little old jiveass poverty program job. **1988–93** Wilcock & Guy *Damn Right* 61: He didn't bring me to hear 'em where they worked their jive gigs. *a*1994 N. McCall *Wanna Holler* 57: If we couldn't take a jive beating now and then, we'd never survive the serious thumpings.

3. glib or spirited; JIVEY, 1.

1988 *Time* (July 11) 54: His jive, cajoling pep talk has begun to win the men over.

jive *v.* Orig. *Black E.* **1.a.** to flatter deceptively; trick; lie to; hoax; kid; bluff; etc.; attempt to mislead.—occ. constr. with *up.*—also used intrans. Hence **jiver**, *n.*

1928 R. Fisher *Jericho* 78: He would stride in...proclaiming his own excellence in this or that particular....Accordingly his fellows declared him to be a "jiver from way back." *Ibid.* 144: [He's] jivin' a dicty gal now. *Ibid.* 148: That jigaboo's jes' jivin'. *Ibid.* 149: When two folks gits to jivin' each other, first thing y' know sump'm happens. **1929** in M. Taft *Blues Concordance* III 1328: You can jive me baby: but I don't believe a thing you say. **1932** in *AS* (Feb. 1934) 26: *Gieve. v.* To mislead with words; to take into one's confidence....*Jive.* See *Gieve.* **1935** L. Hughes *Little Ham* 95: That little jiver don't own nothing. **1938** Ward *Fog* 282: They've got too much sense to let a monkey-chasing mountebank...jive them out of their cold cash! **1938** in A. Lomax *Mr. Jelly Roll* 172: I...jived the expressman to haul my trunks...by telling him my money was uptown. **1942** *Pittsburgh Courier* (Aug. 22) 7: *Jiver*—(one who flatters). **1945** Himes *If He Hollers* 164: He'd figure I was trying to jive him. **1945** Drake & Cayton *Black Metropolis* 571: He had met her at Streeter's Tavern, bought her a few beers, and "jived" her. **1952** E. Brown *Trespass* 12: You scared? Who you trying to jive, man? **1958** *Life* (Apr. 14) 128: It did not make much difference if Gus were jiving us up about an attack by the Robins. *Ibid.* 131: Don't jive me up. **1959** L. Hughes *Simply Heavenly* 134: I was trying to jive that girl, you know. **1967** Lit *Dictionary* 24: *Jived*—Duped, fooled, falsely promoted. **1970** A. Young *Snakes* 121: Now, as far as talkin and rappin in Spanish is concerned, I cant hardly say "how do you do," but I can jive. Jivin' is what's happenin! Same in chem. **1971–72** in M.P. Motley *Invisible Soldier* 109: I knew my way around the navy and I knew how to "shuck" and "jive." **1976** Haseltine & Yaw *Woman Doctor* 116: Why, Momma, I ain't jivin' you.

b. to make fun of; tease.—also used intrans.; in phr. **jive around** to fool around.

1938 *AS* XIII 317: *To jive around*..."to fool around." **1939** in Dundes *Mother Wit* 281: Willy kept "jiving" him until Jimmy finally left. **1944** Burley *Hndbk. Jive* 71: Jive is a distortion of..."jibe."...In the sense in which it came into use among Negroes in Chicago about...1921, it meant to taunt, to scoff, to sneer—an expression of sarcastic comment. **1952** Himes *Stone* 223: I knew I was being jived lightly but I was flattered anyway. **1959–60** R. Reisner *Jazz Titans* 159: *Jivin'*: fooling, jesting or teasing. **1970** Whitmore *Memphis-Nam-Sweden* 16: The Saints didn't jive around with their religion. **1971** Wells & Dance *Night People* 1: I was jiving around with him, backing under the axe and jumping away. **1994** *Smithsonian* (Nov.) 23: I don't go for all this jiving around in the end zone after a score.

c. to concoct falsely; fabricate.—constr. with *up.*

1948 Manone & Vandervoort *Trumpet* 9: And that stuff about me cutting my teeth on a cornet is jived up too. **1972** Ponicsan *Cinderella Liberty* 174: You don't have to jive up an alibi with me.

d. to talk JIVE, *n.*, 1.b.

1954–60 *DAS: Jive*...To talk...in a jazzy rhythm and up-to-date slang.

2. *Black E.* to copulate; JAZZ, 1. Also used trans.—usu. considered vulgar.

1928 in Oliver *Meaning of Blues* 100: Now when a man starts jivin' I'm tighter than a pair of shoes,/I'm a mean tight mama, with my mean tight mama blues. **1929** in Leadbitter & Slaven *Blues Records* 93: Sweet Jivin' Mama. **1952** E. Brown *Trespass* 125: Why didn't you jive that old Viola tonight? **1966** in B. Jackson *Swim Like Me* 136: You pull off every stitch—/You starts to slow jivin', Mike.

3.a. Esp. *Jazz.* to get going vigorously or enthusiastically; (*also*) to have a good time.

*ca*1938 in *OED2:* "Jiving," meaning to improvise [swing music]. *ca*1959 N.Y.C. high school student: This is number five/And we both began to jive/Roll me over, lay me down, and do it again. **1965** Conot

Rivers of Blood 230: Man!...When we gonna start jiving? **1970–72** in *AS* L (1975) 62: *Jive*...Go out on the town, have a good time. **1981–86** R. Parker & R. Rashke *Capitol Hill* 17: Then black Washington began jiving in clubs like Gracie's and Linsey's.

b. to dance, as to boogie-woogie or swing music; (*also*) to move one's body to music, snap one's fingers, etc., while seated.

    1938 M. Brooks et al. *Radio City Revels* (film): Everybody swing!...Everybody jive! **1939** in *OED2:* If you should dance to the rhythms of either gentleman you will be jiving. **1943** *N.Y. Times* (May 9) II 5: You feel like getting up and jiving to that fine music that comes out of the magic trumpet of Harry James. **1957** *Sing Out!* (Spring) 28: You can jive to it; I have seen a roomful of people jiving through a talking blues. **1974** E. Thompson *Tattoo* 60: He started shaking from the shoulders down, letting his feet go, his dusty cowboy boots slapping the boards, coming down on his heels, sliding around on his toes, jigging, jiving. **1981** Wambaugh *Glitter Dome* 257: Griswold...was...jiving to Pink Floyd. **1984** Univ. Tenn. instructor: When you hit a certain age, you jive to the beat of a different drummer.

c. to saunter, swagger, walk rhythmically, etc.; (*also*) to dodge; JUKE.

    1967 J. Kramer *Instant Replay* 177: He kept jiving up and down the aisle, showing off his rug and shades. **1972** Jenkins *Semi-Tough* 189: And old Billy Clyde go jivin' for six [points]....He run so har-rud. **1978** J. Webb *Fields of Fire* 315: Cannonball...jived across the dust clearing. **1982** Castoire & Posner *Gold Shield* 30: The bigger of the two boys bumped Don and jived past.

4. to use or operate in a vigorous or skillful manner.

    1943 in *Best from Yank* 215: I...have yet to learn how to load an M1 and jive it.

5. to be in accord; make sense; jibe. Now *colloq.*

    1943 *AS* XVIII 153: *Doesn't jive*, doesn't make sense. **1950, 1965–70** in *DARE.* **1980** *Daily News* (N.Y.) (Sept. 6) 6: Can you take seriously as a writer anyone who refers to the "the welfare roles of this country" and reports that everything a character said "had jived with the facts"? Such a person may be taken seriously only as a symptom of decay in our language.

jive-ass *n.* **1.** *Black E.* an untrustworthy, conceited, pretentious, or contemptible person.—*usu. considered vulgar.*

    1967 L. Jones, in C. Major *Calling Wind* 266: Who told you to try to steal it, jive ass. **1969** C. Brown *Mr. Jiveass* 8: He became a hustler, a jiveass,...a well-read hanger-on. **1975** S.P. Smith *Amer. Boys* 172: If he didn't get it together he'd be just one more jive ass when he got home.

2. JIVE, 1.a.—*usu. considered vulgar.*

    1970 T. Wolfe *Radical Chic* 102: It's part of his psychological jiveass.

jive-ass *adj.* see s.v. JIVE, *adj.*

jive-ass *v. Black E.* to JIVE, *v.*, 3.b., c.—*usu. considered vulgar.*

    1983 Flaherty *Tin Wife* 200: Puerto Rican thugs were being led to arraignment, jive-assing it for the cameras. **1989** R. Miller *Profane Men* 190: He watches two colored men jive-ass back and forth...saying hello in their endlessly complex handshake.

jive stick *n. Narc.* a marijuana cigarette.

    1955 in *OED2:* "Sticks," "reefers," jive sticks. **1967** J.B. Williams *Narc. & Halluc.* 113: *Jive sticks*—Marijuana cigarettes.

jivetime *adj. Black E.* worthless; deceitful; stupid.

    1962 H. Simmons *On Eggshells* 162: A jive-time [army] base in Virginia. **1965** in D. Glasgow *Black Underclass* 45: Jive-time brothers...running games about what they're trying to do. **1965** *Esquire* (July) 45: A Harlem youth quietly stated, "He's jive time." **1968** in Giallombardo *Impris. Girls* 147: Jive time butch...jive time fem. **1968** Bullins *In Wine Time* 391: They only got to look my god in the face once and forget about you, you jive-time sucker. **1970** Ifetayo *Black Woman* 14: That/pale face jive time man. **1971** *Black Scholar* (Feb.) 10: A brother (jokingly, thank goodness!) called me a "Jive Time Nigger." **1972** Claerbaut *Black Jargon* 70: A jivetime dude. **1973** *Black World* (Apr.) 57: Since when do you have to get all pretty for ol' jive-time me? **1983** *Reader's Digest Success with Words* 86: Black English...*jivetime* = (1) "insincere, not serious" (2) "dishonest, deceptive" (3) "stupid, ignorant."

jive-time *v. Black E.* to deceive.

    1969 Gordone *No Place to Be Somebody* 435: Oh, no? You ain't jive timin' me, you just like Gloria.

jive up *v.* see s.v. JIVE, *v.*

jivey *adj.* **1.** jazzy; lively; spirited.

    1947 *ATS* (Supp.) 5: Alive with jive...hep with helium, jivey. **1973** Flaherty *Fogarty* 97: Everything he had done was quirky, jivey, and jazzy. **1975** Hinton *Rumble Fish* 69: I couldn't explain how I felt. Jivey, juiced up, just alive. **1987** S. King *Misery* 110: He felt jivey, happy, almost drunk.

2. full of nonsense or JIVE, *n.* 1.a.

    1967 Baraka *Tales* 89: O.K., be intellectual, go write some more of them jivey books. **1972** in *OED2:* That sort of a jivey explanation.

jiving *adj.* exciting; wonderful.

    1994 Breckman & Leeson *I.Q.* (film): Jivin'!

jizz *n.* [short for JISM] semen.—*usu. considered vulgar.*

    1941 in Legman *Limerick* 161: He loved to eat jizz. **1959** *ISR Graffiti MS:* Hard, hairy, and full of jiz. [*1967 S. Beckett, in *OED2:* A week in spring, that puts the jizz in you.] **1968** Updike *Couples* 311: Said his jizz ran down her leg. **1974** E. Thompson *Tattoo* 18: Barney's cock...[was] flecking great raindrops of jiss as he...rammed the thing into the cartoon women. **1975** S.P. Smith *Amer. Boys* 415: I'd like to have a dollar for every bucket of jizz that's been dropped here today. **1981** in Safire *Good Word* 270: "Jizz"...or "gism" (seminal fluid). **1982** Del Vecchio *13th Valley* 505: I got so much jizz stored up. **1983** Wambaugh *Delta Star* 19: When Leery saw the jizz he lost his temper. **1990** Westcott *Half a Klick* 250: Old donkey jizz, that what you is. **1993** "Pansy Division" *Beercan Boy* (pop. song): I want to...feel his silky jizz. **1995** *N.Y. Press* (May 31) 17: It's all subtext and hushed porn lingo: the jizz-sucking, schlong-stabbing, [etc.].

jizz *v.* to ejaculate semen.—*usu. considered vulgar.*

    1983 Wambaugh *Delta Star* 19: Please don't jizz on Leery's table! **1985** J.A. Friedman *Times Sq.* 107: He...jizzed on her ass. **1989** P. Munro *U.C.L.A. Slang* 53: *Jis* to ejaculate...—rhymes with "fizz."

jizzbucket *n.* SCUZZBUCKET.—*usu. considered vulgar.*

    1987 Aykroyd et al. *Dragnet* (film): You...jizzbucket!

jizzum var. JISM.

j.o. *v.* [J(ERK) O(FF); J(ACK) O(FF)] to masturbate.—*usu. considered vulgar.*

    1958–59 Southern & Hoffenburg *Candy* 216: Kept wanting to "jay-o" too. **1985** "Blowdryer" *Mod. Eng.* 73: *J/O*...Jack off.

j.o. *n.* an act of masturbation; (*also*) a dolt; JERK-OFF, 2.—*usu. considered vulgar.*

    1972 N.Y.U. student: He's a real j.o. **1986** Univ. Tenn. men's room graffito: Gay guy wants to form j.o. club with gay or bi guys. **1989** Chapple & Talbot *Burning Desires* 303: At J/O parties.

jo *v.* **1.** to spoil; (*also*) to exhaust.

    *ca*1800 in Dolph *Sound Off!* 503: As to Saratog' he came, thinking how to jo the game. **1932** *AS* VII (June) 333: *Joed*—tired; exhausted.

2. *Gamb.* (see quot.).

    1988 Gryczan *Carnival Secrets* 203: *Joing*—rigging a game so it cannot be won.

joan *v.* [orig. unkn.] *Black E.* to engage in stylized, usu. obscene insults in the manner of the DOZENS; (*also*) to bait or taunt. Now usu. **jone.**

    1939 in Dundes *Mother Wit* 286: In this city there is another name for the Dozens, "joaning." *Ibid.* 287: Keep on joanin'/You'll make me mad. **1969** Hannerz *Soulside* 129 [ref. to 1966]: This is the phenomenon which has become most known as "the dozens," but it is also known as "sounding" and under some other local names. The term most often used in Washington, D.C., is "joning," which we will therefore use here. **1971** "H.E. Roberts" *Third Ear: Joning* See *signifying*. *a*1990 P. Dickson *Slang!* 220: *Joanin'.* To insult publicly, as in "They were joanin' me about my car." **1991** Eble *Campus Slang* (Fall) 4: Stop joaning me. **1993** *Wash. Post* (Nov. 9) B1: Today...it's called "joning"....In Gary, Ind., we called it "playing the dozens" or "jiving." *Ibid.:* All kinds of kids jone. *Ibid.:* My kids use joning as a stress-busting way to insult each other. [*Ibid.* B8: Mothers have been the favorite target of jone-meisters since biblical times.] *a*1994 N. McCall *Wanna Holler* 23: Good jonin' required a brutal wit, a sharp tongue, and a thick skin....Guys built reps if they could jone hard....They were jonin' me about my pants.

Job *n.* ¶ In phrase: **as poor as Job's turkey** very poor. Also vars. [An elab. of earlier S.E. provs. *as poor as Job* or *as patient as Job.*]

   1810 in E. Fletcher *Letters* 11: I was as poor as Job's Cats. **1817** in Whiting *Early Amer. Prov.* 240: To be as poor as Job's turkey, has passed into a proverb. **1824** in Thornton *Amer. Gloss.*: We have seen fit to say "the patience of Job's turkey," instead of the common phrase, "as patient as Job." **1830** in *DA*: I am…Poor as Job's turkey, or a starv'd church mouse. **1838** [Haliburton] *Clockmaker* (Ser. 2) 26: Captain Jack does look as poor as Job's turkey. **1845** *So. Lit. Messenger* XI 668: He don't own nothing: he's poor as Job's turkey, and he ain't got chick nor child. **1854** in *OED2*: I should rather be as poor as Job's cat all the days of my life. **1891** Garland *Main-Travelled Roads* 63: We were poor as Job's off-ox. **1955** Broonzy & Bruynoghe *Big Bill Blues* 55: As poor as Job's turkey, and he was so poor that he had to lean up against a fence to gobble. **1962** Crump *Killer* 387: Bullshit. You were as poor as Job's turkey, which was so weak with poverty he had to lean against a fence to gobble. **1968** Swarthout *Loveland* 52: Even the hitchhiking that year was slower than Job's goat. **1968** R. Martin *GI War* 402: Poor as Job's turkey.

job *n.* **1.** Orig. *Und.* a robbery or other criminal act done esp. for profit.

   *ca***1690** in Ebsworth *Roxburghe Ballads* (Ser. 2) VIII (1895) ix: She rode about seven miles further, and then a Stage Coach she did rob;/The passengers all cry'd out "Murther!": but this was a Fifty-pound Jobb. *1722 Defoe *Moll Flanders*, in *OED*: It was always reckoned a safe job when we heard of a new shop [to rob]. *1739 (cited in Partridge *Dict. Und.* 366). *1811 *Lexicon Balatron.*: *Job.* Any robbery. *To do a job*; to commit some kind of robbery. *1812 Vaux *Vocab.*: *Job*: any concerted robbery, which is to be executed at a certain time, is spoken of by the parties as *the job*, or having *a job* to do at such a place. **1846** *Lives of Felons* 37: He bore his share in several "jobs" (robberies). **1856** "H. Hazel" *Jack Waid* 38: I give a month's airnin's to know the coves what did that clever job. **1865** *Rogues & Rogueries of N.Y.* 36: Highwaymen…while preferring the dark and unfrequented streets,…are still not averse to "a job" even in gas-lit Broadway. **1873** Lening *N.Y. Life* 149: Safe-bursters…do not undertake any "job" which they are not confident will pay them well. **1879** Dacus *Frank & Jesse* 201: The James boys were there, and "bossed the job." **1887** Francis *Saddle & Moccasin* 172: And if they catch you *altering* a brand—hell! that's a penitentiary job. **1887** Walling *N.Y. Chief of Police* 539: I…was pretty well posted concerning some of the many "jobs" in which he was engaged. **1889** Barrère & Leland *Dict. Slang* I 502: *Job*…(Thieves), a thieving affair, a murder. **1892** L. Moore *Own Story* 160: Carr…and…"Foxy Vos" had a good bank job near New York City. **1908** in "O. Henry" *Works* 317: The police are calling it an inside job. **1914** Z. Grey *West. Stars* 132: The Don's got you figgered fer thet little job at El Cajon last fall. **1920** in Hemingway *By-Line* 15: Anybody can do a job. It's the getaway that counts. **1927** "S.S. Van Dine" *"Canary" Murder Case* ch. xix: I know a professional job when I see it. **1929** Hotstetter & Beesley *Racket* 230: *Job*—Any criminal or illegal act, such as robbery, arson, bombing, slugging, etc. **1929** "E. Queen" *Roman Hat* 85: How about the lowdown on tonight's job [homicide], Inspector? **1939** "E. Queen" *Dragon's Teeth* 153: You think I bumped off Margo and then framed Kerrie for the job, do you? **1952** Chase *McThing* 46: How did it go—the bank job? **1960** Roeburt *Mobster* 21: Yaeger's a torpedo for hire. He's already done jobs for…[one] mob. **1972** Kopp *Buddha* 216: The dream began with my assembling a crew with whom to pull off a bank job. **1972** P. Thomas *Savior* 74: Like the long walk…to pull a job. **1979** R. Foster *Concrete Cowboys* (film): You gonna pull jobs together? **1981** Patchett et al. *Great Muppet Caper* (film): It's probably the same gang that pulled that first job. **1983** *Batman* (Apr.) 6: Don't know how you found out about that supermarket job, Batman, but it ain't my fault that dame got caught in the crossfire. **1978–89** in Jankowski *Islands in Street* 41: When I did a job, I didn't want to share it with the whole group. **1994** *X-Files* (Fox-TV): Barnett was doing armed jobs all over D.C.

2.a. an example of a specified or contextually evident type, orig. and usu. of something that has been constructed or manufactured, esp. an aircraft or motor vehicle; device or contrivance; (*broadly*) a one.—usu. constr. with prec. adj.

   1896 Hamblen *Many Seas* 415: He pointed…to a splendid mansion. …He had built it himself. "None o' your contract jobs fer me," said he. "I want a house that will carry me safe through all weathers." **1926** *Writer's Mo.* (Nov.) 395: *Job*—A term used to refer to any particular design of aircraft. **1928** *New Yorker* (Dec. 15) 56: You run it out with

dealers' plates and you've got as pretty a job as you want. **1930** *Liberty* (July 19) 24: We have to cruise through four or five towns until we locate the right job parked on the street. **1932** Hawks *Crowd Roars* (film): I sure liked this old job [*sc.* an automobile].…She sure is a sweet job. **1933** Mahin & Furthman *Bombshell* (film): I've a neat little sports job outside. **1933** Saunders & Hanemann *Ace of Aces* (film): Scouts, bombers, balloons, observation jobs. **1934** O'Hara *Appt. in Samarra* ch. ii: That was a sport job. A LaSalle. **1937** E. Anderson *Thieves Like Us* 67: The cars were Ford V-8's. One [was] a black job with a trunk. **1938** Steinbeck *Grapes of Wrath* 172: Big car…cream-color, special job. **1941** Brecher & Kurnitz *Shadow of Thin Man* (film): When you go eighty miles an hour in this job you don't even feel it. **1942** in Gould *Prune Face* (unp.): This furnace doesn't burn coal. It's a gas job. **1942** Epstein & Epstein *Male Animal* (film): He just drove up to the Beta house in a big open job. **1942** Wylie *Vipers* 107: Cowboy hats, Stetson, ten-gallon jobs, are especially strong medicine. **1943** Wakeman *Shore Leave* 177: A big 4-engine job, a PB2Y, roared out of the bay below the airplane tower. **1945** in *Combat* 55: A good pilot in an orthodox ship can outmaneuver and turn inside a jet job. **1945** in T. Williams *Letters* 165: I am back … in a race-track suit!—loud black & white check job I bought in Saint Louis. **1952** Holmes *Go* 122: We were … stealing cars the whole way. We'd pick up some slick job, drive it a hundred miles or so, sell it and grab another one. **1954** E. Hunter *Runaway Black* 4: He looked up to the big apartment buildings … and he wondered how it felt to live in one of those jobs. **1956** M. Wolff *Big Nick*. 55: Driving a special job and everything! **1956** in Loosbrock & Skinner *Wild Blue* 203: Those two-seater jobs came in crawling. **1958** P. O'Connor *At Le Mans* 30: The Black Tiger was an opposed six, rear-engine job of three and a half liters. **1966** Susann *Valley of Dolls* 93: And please, a fur jacket. That camel-hair job has to go! **1967** Sankey *Golden Screw* 66: Why don't you get a new suit? Maybe one of those Carnaby Street jobs. **1973** Overgard *Hero* 18: He ate two of our suckling pig jobs, TWO! **1974** in Mamet *Sexual Perversity* 11: I'm working on a stack of those raisin and nut jobs. **1975** Mostert *Supership* 133: The old Cunard cargo liner *Andria*. … She was a two-funneled job. **1976** C.R. Anderson *Grunts* 37 [ref. to 1969]: Make sure your troops run aggressive patrols now, not just them regular SOP jobs—Ha! **1980** Lorenz *Guys Like Us* 83: He removed his hat, a glossy black job with a gray band. **1986** Merkin *Zombie Jamboree* 122: The house was an old brick job. **1994** Headline News Network (Aug. 3): A two-run job [*sc.* a home run] for his seventeenth this season.

b. a man or woman, esp. in regard to toughness or sexual attractiveness.

   1927 in Hammett *Knockover* 327: She's a tough little job who was probably fired for dropping her chewing gum in the soup the last place she worked. **1932** *AS* VII (June) 336: *Sex job*—a woman who is easily possessed. **1941** M. Caniff, in *Chi. Sunday Trib.* (July 20) (Comics) (unp.): She's talking to the blonde job now. **1941** Kendall *Army & Navy Sl.* 8: *She's a neat job.* … a comely female. **1942** S.J. Perelman, in *New Yorker* (Nov. 21) 17: I was in the hut with this tall job from Papeete. **1943** in P. Jordan *Tunis Diary* 170: I heard another American-ism for a woman to-day: "a job." **1948** I. Shulman *Cry Tough!* 145: So she's a good-looking job. So's lots of other babes. **1949** Gordon & Kanin *Adam's Rib* 67: I followed him up and caught him muzzlin' that tall job. **1952** Uris *Battle Cry* 396: It was mostly the fourteen- to sixteen-year-old jobs that caused the greatest commotion. **1954** L. Crockett *Magnificent Bastards* 105: Who's the blond job? **1957** H. Ellison *Web of the City* 104: The mousey one was not as hot a job as the fat slob. **1962** Mandel *Wax Boom* 76: I don't even understand that beard-job's status in this outfit. **1971** W. Allen *Getting Even* 106: She's that peroxide job with the bazooms from Radcliffe. **1979** in Terkel *Amer. Dreams* 54 [ref. to *ca*1950]: I wanted to be one of those [sexy] girls. … I wanted to be one of those blond jobs. That's what they used to call them—jobs. A tall job. A slim job. Somebody you could work on.

3.a. a procedure, process, or action, or its result; something done; (*often*) a surgical operation.—constr. with prec. adj. See also BOOB JOB, BUZZ JOB, NOSE JOB.

   1943 D. Hertz *Pilot #5* (film): "You passed." "A skin-of-the-teeth job, eh?" **1943** (quot. at BUZZ JOB). **1953** R. Chandler *Long Goodbye* 3: Looks like this one had a plastic job [plastic surgery] one time. **1959** E. Hunter *Killer's Wedge* 61: The ash blond hair was a bleach job. **1984** W. Gibson *Neuromancer* 4: Nerve-splicing. Give me the mainland for a nerve job any day. **1995** *Seinfeld* (NBC-TV): I'm getting an eye job.

b. a masturbatory or (*usu.* oral) copulatory act.—usu. as comb. form. Often *joc.* See also BLOW JOB.

1942 (quot. at BLOW JOB). **1952** Lait & Mortimer *USA* 169: For those in a hurry jobs are performed in the men's rooms and telephone booths. **1965** Linakis *In Spring* 332: Take the dark one. You're sure of a job with her. **1970** Zindel *Your Mind* 34: Chinese basket job—TQ9 1212. **1973** N.Y.U. student: Did the ancient Egyptians give pyramid jobs? **1974** Price *Wanderers* 101: H.J.—Handjob…B.J.—Blowjob…F.J.—Foot Job. **1987** Norst & Black *Lethal Weapon* 201: "Ever had a Korean sponge bath?" "No, a basket job in Hong Kong once."

4. *Police.* police work as a profession.—constr. with *the*.

    1975 Sepe & Telano *Cop Team* 27: Hey, man.…I'm on the job. I have my shield in my left pocket. **1987** R. Miller *Slob* 28: In a city where the way of life on The Job is the "pad" or "arm," a kind of acceptable blue-suit payola. *Ibid.* 30: A healthy ego is mandatory in The Job. **1990** Murano & Hoffer *Cop Hunter* 239: All I wanna know is the guy ain't on the job. **1995** *N.Y. Times* (May 9) B1: The officers…asked him whether he was carrying a weapon and whether he was "on the job," police talk for, "Are you a cop, too?"

¶ In phrases:

¶ **do a job** to move one's bowels.

    *1936 Partridge *DSUE: Job for oneself, do a.* To defecate: late C.19–20…coll. **1942** in Randolph & Legman *Roll Me in Your Arms* 66 (song learned *ca*1892): Old woman got up to do a little job. **1942** (quot. at *do (one's) business s.v.* BUSINESS). **1970–72** in *AS* L (1975) 62: He did a job in his pants.

¶ **do a job on** to wreck, injure, spoil, etc.; victimize; (*hence*) to kill.

    1943 W. Simmons *Joe Foss* 113: Casey and Danny "did a job" on the absentees' tent. **1947** Bowers & Millhouser *Web* (film): Two weeks ago he does a job on his uncle with a meat cleaver. **1942–49** *DAUL* 111: "To do a job on"—to beat severely. **1952** Lait & Mortimer *USA* 235: Word got out…that we were in Kansas City to do a job on Harry's town. **1956** Ross *Hustlers* 122: His eyes boiled up. China'd do a job on me, too. **1963** J.A. Williams *Sissie* 137: Man, he thought, those goddam Methodists do a *job* on a cat. **1969** *Playboy* (Dec.) 112: When those guys are coming at you, they're going to do a *job* on you. **1971** N.Y.U. professor: You really got to do a job on it to fail this course. **1971** N.Y.U. student: Don't let him do a job on you. **1973** R. Roth *Sand in Wind* 378: Somebody did a job on a platoon commander for three hundred dollars. **1973** Toma & Brett *Toma* 104: After the threats on the phone there was the possibility that someone had chosen him to do a job on me.

¶ **do the job** to engage in copulation; *do the deed s.v.* DEED.

    1961 L.E. Young *Virgin Fleet* 122 [ref. to 1941]: Think what it would be like if I tried to do the job.

¶ **get a job!** Esp. *Stu.* go away and stop bothering me! get out!

    1958 J. Davis *College Vocab.* 3: "Get a job"—I'm not doing any personal favors, mind your own business. **1969** Salerno & Tompkins *Crime Confed.* 203: Most men of organized crime really *believe* that the whole world is crooked ("Only saps work").…A favorite insult…is: "You oughta get a job." **1982** Eble *Campus Slang* (Nov.) 3: *Get a job*—to stop bothering someone: Would you go *get a job* for awhile because I'm sort of busy. **1984** *Miami Vice* (NBC-TV): "So which one of you two guys can write?" "*Get a job!*"

¶ **put [up] a job** to prepare or employ trickery, treachery, or deceit.—usu. constr. with *on*.

    1872 Crapsey *Nether Side of N.Y.* 122: In police parlance, they "put up a job on her," Captain Thorne was secreted in a closet…the next time she called. **1877** Burdette *Mustache* 113: This incredulous young angel "put up a job on him." **1878** Bardeen *Hume* 238: I say, fellows,…let's put up a job on Riker. **1881** Small *Farming* 54: Budd put up a job on the tender susceptibilities of his wife. **1882** Campbell *Poor* 18: The devil…goes round puttin' up all sorts of jobs on sinners. **1888** *Stag Party* 20: Some medical students put up a job on a Dutch saloon-keeper. **1889** Meriwether *Tramp at Home* 92: "Mebbe we have got the wrong man."…"No; he's a-puttin' a job on us." **1912** Siringo *Cowboy Detective* 42: Schofield put up a slick…job on me, but it failed to work. **1967** W. Crawford *Gresham's War* 172: He puts a job on her, lots of snow.

job *v.* **1.a.** to cheat or deal treacherously with, esp. to contrive evidence against; FRAME, 1.a.

    1889 in S. White *Colored Base Ball* 137: The…players…endeavor to "job him" out of the business.…An effort is always made to have an error scored against him. **1903** A.H. Lewis *Boss* 100: A jury, despite his

protestations that he was "being jobbed," instantly declared him guilty. **1904** *Life in Sing Sing* 250: Jobbed.—Convicted by perjured testimony; persecuted. **1905** *Nat. Police Gaz.* (July 1) 10: In plain words, too, Fitz says he was to be "jobbed." **1913–15** Van Loan *Taking the Count* 167: I been framed.…They jobbed me! **1924** Henderson *Keys to Crookdom* 409: To job a man—To railroad him. **1925–26** Black *Can't Win* 366: I know you got "jobbed." I'll take your case for nothing. **1931–34** in Clemmer *Pris. Community* 333: Jobbed.…To be convicted on a false charge. **1981** P. Sann *Trial* 227: You got jobbed, pal. I never seen a dirty deal like this. **1995** *Today* (NBC-TV) (Oct. 3): Do the majority of African-Americans in this city think O.J. Simpson got a fair trial, or was he jobbed?

b. *Specif.*, to prearrange (a contest) illicitly; FIX, 2.

    1896 in A.E. Turner *Earps Talk* 175: Police Commissioner Gunst is satisfied that the fight was "jobbed."

c. *Black E.* to boast or lie.

    1958–59 in Abrahams *Deep Down in Jungle* 154: You was up there all jobbing and jiving and swinging your arms.

d. to steal.

    1962 Kesey *Cuckoo's Nest* 88: Pinched. Jobbed. Swiped. Stole.…You know, man, like somebody boosted my threads.

2. *Jazz.* to be employed as a jazz musician for short or irregular periods; GIG², 1.

    1931 Goodman & Kolodin *Swing* 35: I jobbed around with "Murph" quite a bit after that, playing whatever dates there were.

jobber *n.* a job; position of employment; (*also*) a hard chore.

    1929–30 Farrell *Young Lonigan* 41: Maybe I'll get myself a jobber. **1943** Farrell *Days of Anger* 124: I'm getting a swell jobber. Soft hours, big pay. **1970** Landy *Underground Dict.* 113: *Jobber*…Difficult undertaking—eg. *That's a real jobber.*

jobbie *n.* **1.** JOB, 2.b.

    1902 T.A. Dorgan, in *S.F. Bulletin Mag.* (Jan. 5) 12: And the jobbie who yells fake after every fight. **1918** T.A. Dorgan, in *N.Y. Eve. Jour.* (Aug. 13) 12: *I'm* the jobbie she's engaged to. **1920** Witwer *Kid Scanlan* 105: If he could only breeze past the jobbie on the door. **1927** in Hammett *Knockover* 336: The jobbie who's tailing you…is a barber named Arlie. **1938** in D. Runyon *More Guys* 176: And no smarter jobbie ever breathes than Haystack.

2. JOB, 2.a.; item.

    1960 Bluestone *Cully* 74: It's one of these new three-blade jobbies. **1974** M.J. Smith *When I Say No* 161: Bob, go get that little red jobbie in the back lot and bring it out front. **1976** J.W. Thomas *Heavy Number* 35: Unless you want a plastic jobbie from a Hollywood magic shop. **1987** S. Stark *Wrestling Season* 240: "Silk-screened these jobbies myself," she said.

job description *n.* (one's) personal responsibility.—used in negative contexts.

    1990 Univ. Tenn. instructor, age 43: That's not my job description. **1991** McCarthy & Mallowe *Vice Cop* 53: I don't buy cigarettes for anybody…that's not my job description.

job shark *n. Labor.* an employment agent.

    1938 Holbrook *Mackinaw* 181: A *job shark* is an employment agent. **1942** *AS* (Dec.) 222: Job Shark. An employment agent.

Jo-burg *n. Foreign Service.* Johannesburg, Republic of South Africa.

    *1909 Ware *Passing Eng.* 160: *Joburg* (Military, 1900 on). Johannesburg. **1982** "W.T. Tyler" *Rogue's March* 71: They've got a couple of C-141 MAC flights holding in Jo-burg.

Jock *n.* [Scots form of Jack; cf. JACK] *Naut. & Mil.* a Scottish soldier or sailor; Scotsman. Now *rare* in U.S.

    *1788 Grose *Vulgar Tongue* (ed. 2): *Jock*…a jeering appellation for a north-country seaman, particularly a collier. *a1865 Smyth *Sailor's Word-Book* 413: *Jocks.* Scotch seamen. **1915** in Roy *Pvt. Fraser* 56: I came across a Jock who was one of the sappers there. **1917** in Burton *Letters* 256: I there saw the same Jock just finishing chopping up the same log. **1917** Empey *Over the Top* 62: The "Jocks" suffered a lot of casualties. **1918** *Lit. Digest* (Oct. 5) 61: And the Jocks—I doubt if the Jocks have superiors [as fighters]. **1918** *Stars & Stripes* (May 3) 8: I was out here in the road when a regiment of Jocks went by. **1919** *With 114th MG Bn.* 133: A.E.F. Glossary…*Jock.*—Scotch soldier. **1923** Henderson *14th Engrs.* 62: "Jocks" in Rest. **1943** *Yank* (June 18) 9: The Jock…won't leave your side after you declaim "Scots wha hae wi'

Wallace bled." **1977** Berry *Kaiser* 61: The 15th Scottish Division. They marched those jocks right into the lines to the tune of bagpipes. **1946–92** Westheimer *Sitting It Out* 54: We called all Scots [in the POW camp] "Jock."

jock¹ *n.* [fr. earlier thieves' cant *jockam, jockum,* of unkn. orig. though perh. an alter. of *Jock,* Scots form of *Jack;* cf. syn. JOCKEY] **1.** the penis.—usu. considered vulgar.

[*1566 Harman *Caveat* 29: He tooke his Iockam in his famble, and a wapping he went.] [*1610 [Rowlands] *Martin Mark-All:* Iockam, a man's Yard.] *a1790 in *OED2:* Jock, private parts of a man or woman. *1791 in Barke & Smith *Merry Muses* 141: And if Jock thief he should slip out,/I'll ding him wi' my heel, jo. *ca1835–40 in Speaight *Bawdy Songs of Music Hall* 32: A jock, so strong as Billy's was,/The blowen's heart would cheer. *1846 in *OED2:* Jock, man's privates. *1879 *Pearl* (July) 29: They gazed on their privates with mutual delight,/And she soon found a hole to put jock out of sight! *1882 *Boudoir* 114: Whilst I my jock employ. *1889 Barrère & Leland *Dict. Slang* I 502: Jock (popular), the male organ of generation. **1918** in Carey *Mlle. from Armentières* II (unp.): She's got no jock, but that's no sin,/For she's got a nice place to put one in. **1924** Wilstach *Anecdota Erotica* 18: Man invited to join the Jock Club. "I am going to be President of this Club, cause mine is 13 inches long." **1927** [Fliesler] *Anecdota* 15: A certain tragedian, noted for the size of his jock, was invited by a flapper to her home. **1939** M. Levin *Citizens* 20: Mike Sisto had a cannon as big as an elephant's jock. **1956** (quot. at DINGDONG, 3.b.). **1965–68** E.R. Johnson *Silver St.* 25: With your jock out...like you were taking a leak. **1968** R. Beck *Trick Baby* 218: French ticklers...and jock collars. **1971** Dahlskog *Dict.* 34: Jock....the penis. **1984** in Randolph & Legman *Blow Candle Out* 612: Did you ever see a nigger with a foot-long jock?

2. JOCKSTRAP, 1. Now *colloq.*

1922 (cited in *W10*). **1940** Zinberg *Walk Hard* 23: Don't use the shoes unless they fit you. And that goes for the jock too! **1945** Monks *Ribbon & Star* 57: Like I'd been kicked in a football game and hadn't worn a jock. **1951** Robbins *Danny Fisher* 64: I'd make sure muh jock is on good an' tight before she got here. **1956** H. Ellison *Deadly Streets* 181: He'll split ya from your jock to your top! **1958** F. Davis *Spearhead* 77 [ref. to WWII]: We may get our jocks shot off, but at least we'll be moving when it happens. **1959** Morrill *Dark Sea* 67: Put on your asbestos jock—you're painting the stack today. **1961** Terry *Old Liberty* 8: It smelled kind of...like a jock that's been left hanging in a locker room for two or three years. **1963** Blechman *Camp Omongo* 21: He peeled off the clammy bathing suit, pulling out the wet jock. **1968** P. Roth *Portnoy* 55: I want a bathing suit with a built-in athletic supporter....I want a jock. **1970–71** G.V. Higgins *Coyle* 57: I'll be beating the bushes with snow to my jock until Washington's Birthday. *a1981 "K. Rollins" *Fighter Pilots* 215: If the jock fits, wear it. **1986** Cosby *Fatherhood* 71: A training bra....I never had a training *jock*. **1986–89** Norse *Memoirs* 91 [ref. to 1940's]: "Did he move in?"..."Lock, cock, and jock," said George coolly. **1990** *CBS This Morning* (CBS-TV) (Aug. 21): He said the White Sox weren't good enough to carry his jock.

3. *Und. & Pris.* JOCKER, 1.

1942 *ATS* 421: Jock, jocker...an older tramp who takes a boy under his care, usually for a perverted reason. **1978–80** in Cardozo-Freeman *Joint* 509: Jock, Jocker. A homosexual who plays the male role in prison.

4.a. [short for JOCKSTRAP, 2] Esp. *Stu.* an athlete or athletic person. [Orig. applied only to men.]

1958 *Harvard Crimson* (Feb. 21), in G. Lawless *Harvard Crimson Anthol.* 295: [Princeton] athletes tend to turn up, according to their inmost natures, either in Tiger Inn, the lair of "the gentlemen jocks," or in Cannon, home of "the sweaty ones." **1958** T. Capote *Breakfast at Tiffany's* 30: I find out she's some jock's regular. **1958** J. Davis *College Vocab.* 5: Jock—H.P.E.R. [Health, Physical Education, and Recreation] major. **1959** Farris *Harrison High* 15: Nothing but the best for us Harrison jocks. **1960** Swarthout *Where the Boys Are* 153: A jock is a college athlete. **1961** Sullivan *Shortest, Gladdest Years* 15: The jocks played touch. **1963** Doulis *Path* 333: I want two jocks to volunteer for the PT. **1963** A. Morgan *Six-Eleven* 119: Bud, stop being a big jock. Who the hell cares...whether his team ever won a football game. **1964** in *AS* XL (1965) 194: Jock...has become a common [campus] word for "athlete," and *jock talk* is the language of athletes....In the vocabulary of some of the girls, a *jock* was someone desirable on a date because of his masculinity, but either boys or girls may also refer to a *jock* derogatorily as a brawny but dumb male student. **1963–64** Kesey *Great Notion* 273: Just who's a dumbass jock an' who ain't. **1966** Goldstein *1*

in 7 65: The athletic or "jock" students can usually be found at Winthrop Hall. **1969** (quot. at PREPPY). **1970** *Nat. Lampoon* (Apr.) 73: [Ad for *Jock* magazine:] Who had the poor taste to name a magazine Jock? **1975** Lichtenstein *Long Way* 86: Chris [Evert], teenage girl first, jock second. **1976** Eble *Campus Slang* (Nov.) 3: Jock—n an athlete, either male or female, often derogatory. **1977** Univ. Tenn. student: She's such a jock. She's always playing tennis and doing that kind of jock stuff. **1979** *N.Y. Post* (June 29) 20: They have this 13-year-old daughter named Tracy who's a real jock. **1979** Savage *Cowboy Hero* 131: It was...encouraging to hear rodeo performers refer to themselves as "jocks." **1995** Rochester, N.Y. woman, on Usenet newsgroup alt.usage.english: I agree...about "at least the 1950s" in the case of "jocks"; we called them that at Syracuse Univ. as early as 1948, so the term must have spread from Harvard even before the 1950s.

b. *Stu.* a politically conservative, athletic, convivial, often glib and imperceptive, usu. white middle-class young man.—used disparagingly.

1968 *N.Y. Times* (May 12) IV 13: Some students and faculty members...smear all anti-strike students with the blanket label of "jocks." **1969** Rapoport & Kirshbaum *Is the Library Burning?* 9 [ref. to ca1965]: The "jock" fraternity houses kept up their files of old exams as faithfully as they polished their trophies. **1973** in *Playboy* (Jan. 1974) 48: Through my job, I have been approached by many attractive, well-off straight [*i.e.*, conservative] guys who'd like to date me....Is it possible to ball meaningfully with jocks? **1987** *Magical World of Disney* (NBC-TV): Those jocks sure have great taste in cars. **1988** Terkel *Great Divide* 418: I was the only one in school with long hair, and the jocks—I wish I had a better word—hated me. **1989** P. Eckert *Jocks & Burnouts* 3: In common [student] usage the term *Jock* has extended beyond athletes to all students who make...[traditional school social] activities run,...someone whose life-style embraces a broader [middle-class conformism]...associated in American culture with sports.

c. Esp. *Computers.* an unimaginative or obtuse technician; an uninspired fellow.

1983 Naiman *Computer Dict.* 80: Jock...A programmer whose programs tend to achieve their results by means of brute force rather than elegance. **1984** Algeo *Stud Buds* 3: A rather stupid person...*jerk,...jock,...lunkhead* [etc.]. **1989** *TV Guide* (Mar. 4) 43: War and Peace... [let's] hope...that no trigger-happy jock pushes the button.

5. Orig. *Stu.* an enthusiast or expert, esp. a devoted student of a particular academic subject.—usu. used in combs.

1961 Kohner *Gidget Goes Hawaiian* 22: Just another surfing jock. **1968** Baker, Ladd & Robb *CUSS* 145: Jock. A person who does well academically. **1967–69** *Current Slang I & II* 56: Jock, n. A devoted student in any subject, as "Math jock," "English jock," etc....Minnesota. **1972** Nilsen *Slang at UNI:* Jock: Athlete. There are also art jocks, music jocks, drama jocks, science jocks, etc. **1975** U.C.L.A. student: So you're the English jock. **1988** *Highwayman* (NBC-TV): You're the technical jock. I just move this rig, remember? **1988** P. Hoffman *Archimedes' Revenge* 10: Stuyvesant High School, a Manhattan enclave for math and science jocks. **1990** T. Fahey *Joys of Jargon* 34: You need to talk to the computer jocks about a resource allocation report. **1995** *Business Week* (Dec. 4) 13: Netscape Communications Corp., the startup run by former University of Illinois computer jock.

¶ In phrases:

¶ **hang [up] (one's) jock** [or **jockstrap**] *Sports.* to quit; retire; (*also*) *Mil.* to be killed.—occ. used fig.

1958 Whitcomb *Corregidor* 276 [ref. to WWII]: They would simply say, "Smitty hung up his jock today." **1958** Frede *Entry E* 20: If one brandy's gonna cut down on your efficiency, you might as well hang up the jock. **1959** Brosnan *Long Season* 88: One close shave like this...and I hang up my jock. **1963** Dwiggins *S.O. Bees* 192: I've got to hang up my jock....I can't go through that again. **1978** J. Webb *Fields of Fire* 204: The day I gotta count on you I'm hanging up my jock, Senator. **1978** Druck *Final Mission* 29 [ref. to WWII]: And if it's that pilot's turn to hang his jock, you get it too. *Ibid.* 68: Fate...hasn't a damn thing to do with whether you hang your jock. **1984** in N. George *Buppies, B-Boys* 197: If he wanted to hang up his rock 'n' roll jockstrap he'd still be drinking Dom Perignon.

¶ **knock** [or **beat**] **(someone's) jock off** to overcome or defeat violently or decisively; overwhelm.

1958 Camerer *Damned Wear Wings* 104: He beat my jock off. I never took any beating like that. **1973** Flaherty *Fogarty* 125:

Pow!...That...cat just knocked your jock off. **1973** Droge *Patrolman* 164: If you want to bust your ass knockin' the jock off these niggers, go right ahead. **1975** Durocher & Linn *Nice Guys* 23: [The pitcher] kept getting his jock knocked off. **1966–80** McAleer & Dickson *Unit Pride* 41: Shut your...face before I knock your jock right off.

¶ **lose (one's) jock** (see quot.).

1969 *Current Slang I & II* 59: Lose...jock, v. To be fooled—normally used in sports.—Air Force Academy cadets.

¶ **on (someone's) jock** *Rap Music.* constantly pursuing or annoying (someone). Cf. JOCK, *v.*, 4.

1984 Toop *Rap Attack* 158: She's been on my jock all week. **1986** "T La Rock" *Breakin' Bells* (rap song): I possess an element to start you on my jock,...then I'll laugh in your face. **1987** "Public Enemy" *M.P.E.* (rap song): Girls on my jock like ants on candy. **1989** P. Munro *U.C.L.A. Slang* 19: *Be on my jock* to be persistently pursuing me (especially sexually; used by a male speaker). That chick calls me every night. She's always on my jock. **1989** "EPMD" *So What Ya Sayin'* (rap song): Girlies on my jock for my dope [i.e., skillful] control/...Brothers on my jock 'cause the way I hold a piece of steel.

¶ **out of (one's) jock** Esp. *Basketball.* into confusion or defeat.—usu. constr. with *fake.* Cf. *out of (one's) jockstrap* s.v. JOCKSTRAP.

1973 W. Crawford *Stryker* 26: Any day I can't fake that phony out of his jock, I'll hang up my own. **1978** Shem *House of God* 115: The slick move that would fake your best friend out of his jock. **1986** Univ. Tenn. instructor: He can fake you out of your jock on the court. **1995** Cormier et al. *Wildcats* 198: You've scared that poor Russian out of his jock.

¶ **toss in the jock** [sugg. by syn. *throw in the towel* s.v. TOWEL] to give up; quit.

1967 Flood *More Lives* 37 [ref. to 1950]: Maybe pretty soon the gooks...really toss in the jock, and we can use trucks and go up maybe fifteen, twenty miles a day.

jock² *n.* **1.** *Horse Racing.* a jockey; (see also 1880 quot.).

***1826** in *OED2*: A neat horseman, and quite at the top of the tree amongst Northern jocks. **1839** *Spirit of Times* (June 8) 159: 'Tis my opinion if her Jock had received a good flogging before mounting, with a promise of a second for bad riding, another set of lungs would have cried "hurra for victory." **1840** *Spirit of Times* (Dec. 5) 474: The jocks discovered it was a false start. **1844** *Spirit of Times* (Mar. 30): The "jocks" [were] comfortably seated in the "pigskin." **1880** *N.Y. Clipper Almanac* 44: *Jock.*—Jockey, driver, or horsedealer. **1891** Maitland *Slang Dict.* 156: *Jock,* a jockey. **1899** A.H. Lewis *Sandburrs* 127: Then he lavished $15 on a "jock" to ride him. **1900** Cullen *Tales* 366: This weazen-faced ex-jock. **1911** D. Runyon *Tents of Trouble* 37: Me, as is king o' the lightweight jocks. **1925** Hemingway *In Our Time* 159: If a jock's riding for somebody too, he can't go boozing around. **1925** W. Faulkner *New Orleans Sketches* 66: Now, this little jock I'm telling you about, he's my cousin, see? **1931** in Woods *Horse-Racing* 66: Ain't you Les Armstrong, the jock? **1946** H.A. Smith *Rhubarb* 41: The average jock doesn't actually work more than five or six minutes a day. **1964** *Sat. Eve. Post* (Sept. 26) 44: In the middle of a win streak a jock puts two grand on another dog in the same race. **1973** Haney *Jock* 144: It's a big problem to get the right jock on the right horse. **1983** *N.Y. Post* (Sept. 2) 63: Terry Lipham, a former quarterhorse jock. **1986** *Hardcastle & McCormick* (ABC-TV): I've talked to the top jocks.

2. DISC JOCKEY; (*later*) video jockey.

1947 *Tomorrow* (Aug.) 27: "A list of jocks and record reviewers"—*jocks* being disc-jockeys, or conductors of record-playing programs on the radio. **1959** *Life* (Nov. 23) 48: If the jock goes to another station he'll get $1500 a week. **1959** in Russell *Permanent Playboy* 248: Tad's unkind friends, song pluggers, rival jocks, ex-wives, used to claim that his youth was preserved by alcohol. **1961** Ellison *Gentleman Junkie* 113: The Conlan gets the big shove from *this* jock. **1968** Lockridge *Hartspring* 156: I've got the best patter of any jock between the two oceans. **1968** Johnson & Johnson *Count Me Gone* 102: They don't spin these disks, the jocks don't, not over the...airways. **1980** *Pearl Dict. Slang* 2: *All-night jock*...the radio broadcaster who works on an all-night show, often the newest or least experienced member of the staff. **1981** in N. George *Buppies, B-Boys* 46: Rapping...will become a prerequisite for all black club jocks (and many whites). **1983** S. King *Christine* 343: "If you don't want to be spending Christmas Day in the breakdown lane of I-76 somewhere between Bedford and Carlisle, I'd leave early or not at all," the FM-104 jock advised his listening audience.

3. *Mil. Av.* a pilot.—usu. used in combs.

1959 *41st Ftr. Sq. Songbk.* 21: There are no bomber jocks in our club. **1962** Harvey *Strike Command* 12: He was the only guy aloft who could keep a pair of desperate fighter jocks from going into the water at night. **1963** E.M. Miller *Exile* 28: Both of us can imagine this young fighter jock twisting and turning and rolling trying to get a good look up at these guys who are diving on him. **1966** E. Shepard *Doom Pussy* 15: Helicopter jock. *Ibid.* 26: Chopper jocks. *Ibid.* 52: Marty was now one of the sharpest jocks in the 13th. **1972** *Airman* (Oct.) 22: Within a few weeks, the *Phantom* jocks had given *Paveway I* an unofficial nickname—"White Lightning." **1973** *N.Y. Times Mag.* (June 10) 16: From the beginning, he was a "hot jock," a fighter pilot, one of a special breed. **1974** Stevens *More There I Was* 46: Here's one jock what ain't gonna be no target for Charlie. **1972–79** T. Wolfe *Right Stuff* 23: The "fighter jocks," as they called each other with self-satisfied irony. *Ibid.* 24: Some eager jock. **1985** Heywood *Taxi Dancer* 6: Mostly they were flown by NVA jocks. **1985** Boyne & Thompson *Wild Blue* 295: You are just a goddamn jock; nobody told you to volunteer any opinions. **1989** Berent *Rolling Thunder* 225: Carrier landings as taught by a real Navy jock. **1991** *Toxic Avenger* (Dec.) (unp.): I ain't no [flying] saucer jock.

4. a driver or operator; worker; JOCKEY², 4.—used in combs.

1974 A. Bergman *Big Kiss-Off* 139: You shouldn't be an elevator jock. **1974** G.V. Higgins *Cogan's Trade* 59: Just a big hole. All the construction jocks, that's all there is. **1978** J. Webb *Fields of Fire* 207: Gonna be a Motor-T jock, huh? **1983** *Business Week* (Apr. 25) 53: Even the computer jock is no longer immune [to job-security worries].

jock *adj.* of, for, being, or characteristic of an athlete or athletes.

1973 *Seattle Times Mag.* (July 22) 14: A panel of "jock" authors— Wilt Chamberlain, Roosevelt (Rosie) Grier, [etc.]. **1974** *Business Week* (Aug. 10) 26: She invades the "jock sisterhood" of the likes of Billie Jean King, Chris Evert, [etc.]. *a***1977** T. Barnett *Golf Is Madness* 102: Lacey was very Ivy League, very jock. **1977** (quot. at JOCK¹, *n.* 4.a.).

jock *v.* [shift of JOCK¹, *n.*] **1.** Esp. *Und.* to copulate or copulate with (a woman); (*hence*) to pedicate.—usu. considered vulgar.

***1698–99** "B.E." *Dict. Canting Crew: Jock* or *Jockumcloy*...to copulate with a Woman. **1889** Barrère & Leland *Dict. Slang: Jock*...(American thieves) *"jocking* it with a high-flyer," taking pleasure with a fancy woman. **1969** Jessup *Sailor* 108: If you try to jock him again, I'll do a job on you myself. **1989** P. Munro *U.C.L.A. Slang* 53: *Jock.* 1. to have sex. 2. to have sex with.

2. *Sports.* to engage in athletics.—also constr. with *it* and *up*.

1968 *Seattle* (Apr.) 27: Paul was a pretty good student and a good athlete...but he just didn't have time to jock it up. **1975** Lichtenstein *Long Way* 31: Could the Old Lady hang tough? Could any woman jock?

3. *Communications.* to work as a DISC JOCKEY.

1978 De Christoforo *Grease* 36: 'Cause when I'm jockin' there ain't no stoppin'.

4. *Rap Music.* to pay adulatory, usu. unwanted attention to (a person of the opposite sex, usu. a man); (*hence*) to flatter; BROWN-NOSE.—also used absol. Cf. *on (someone's) jock* s.v. JOCK¹, *n.*

1986 "Beastie Boys" *Girls* (rap song): I seen her just the other day/Jockin' Mike D. to my dismay. **1988** "N.W.A." *Dope Man* (rap song): Strawberry, Strawberry, jockin' me so early. **1989** "Tone Lōc" *Funky Cold Medina* (rap song): The girls I saw jockin' at...the bar,/Havin' drink with some no-name chump. **1990–91** *Street Talk!* 4: *"That girl jockin' me."* "That girl likes me too much." **1991** Nelson & Gonzales *Bring Noise* 130: "Back up off me...," he demands of a woman jocking him blindly. **1992** *Real World* (MTV): These girls...they're jockin' L.L. **1992** "Fab 5 Freddy" *Fresh Fly Flavor* 38: This very wack guy at school is jockin' me real hard and I hate it. **1993** *Source* (July) 62: But Oakland is not like a real big groupie type of city, as far as wantin' to jock somebody or all that. *Ibid.:* There's this guy on the block that all the girls is jockin'. **1996** *Dangerous Minds* (ABC-TV): You mean jock him....Kiss his ass.

jocker *n.* [JOCK, *v.*, 1 + -*er*] **1.** *Und. & Pris.* a tramp who is accompanied by a boy who begs or steals for him or acts as his catamite; (*also*) an aggressive homosexual pedicator, esp. the protector of a catamite in prison.

1893 *Century* (Nov.) 107: For years he has been subject to the whims and passions of various "jockers," or protectors, and...when released from his bondage...is only too likely to wreak his pent-up feelings on the nearest victim. **1895** in *Atlantic* (Jan. 1896) 68: He is forced to do what his "jocker" commands, and disobedience, willful or innocent, brings down upon him a most cruel wrath. **1903** *Charities Survey* XI 432: Jockers and the Schools They Keep. **1916** Livingston *Snare* 20: Boys and cripples…were held in servile leash by heartless "jockers." **1918** in *AS* (Oct. 1933) 28: *Jocker*. A sweet daddy [in prison]. **1922** N. Anderson *Hobo* 103: A jocker is a man who exploits boys;…he either exploits their sex or he has them steal or beg for him or both. **1927** Rosanoff *Manual of Psych.* (ed. 6) 208: *Turk, wolf,* or *jocker,* an active sodomist. *a***1929** Milburn *Hobo's Hornbook* 62: The punk rolled up his big blue eyes,/And he said to the jocker, "Sandy." **1930** "D. Stiff" *Milk & Honey* 34: The punk serves the jocker, begs food for him, builds his fire, washes his shirt and runs errands. **1933** Ersine *Pris. Slang* 47: *Jocker*…A homosexual man. **1941** G. Legman, in Henry *Sex Vars.* II 1169: *Jocker*. A pedicator…(Tramp Slang). **1935–62** Ragen & Finston *Toughest Pris.* 805: *Jocker*—An active homosexual. **1966** Elli *Riot* 228: The jockers are as freakish as the queens. **1972** Wambaugh *Blue Knight* 54: Roxie hustles the guys who want a queen, and the kid goes after the ones who want a jocker. **1972** Bunker *No Beast* 89: They say all jockers are punks lookin' for revenge. **1978–80** (quot. at JOCK[1], 3).

2. *Und.* a lecher.

1969 Jessup *Sailor* 265: That big boob? Him? With no girl for thirty days? Mister Cadiz, that jocker is straight to Pearl's. **1970** Thackrey *Thief* 44: He'd be mad as hell if he…found out I was too damn dumb even to cop a feel from any of those other girls I told him I was laying. Old jocker.

jocker *v. Und.* (of a tramp) to act as a JOCKER, 1, toward (a boy).

1895 *Harper's* (Oct.) 782: There was no need to "jocker" the boy any longer. His welfare depended upon his mother.

jockey[1] *n.* [see note at JOCK[1], 1] the penis.

1612** in Pendry *T. Dekker* 298: This "Great Bull" [a libertine] by report had in one year three and twenty *doxies,* his *jockey* was so lusty. *Ibid.* 299: Oftentimes there is *glimmer* [burning] in the *jockey.* ***1665** R. Head *English Rogue* ch. v: *Jocky,* A flail, or man's Privities. ***1688** in Partridge *DSUE* (ed. 8) 623: *Jocky,* A Man's Yard. *ca1925** in Logsdon *Whorehouse Bells* 68: Took my old jockey to the watering trough,/Washed him and I scrubbed him till his head fell off.

jockey[2] *n.* **1.** a person, orig. a boy, who works as an assistant or accomplice; *(specif.)* (see 1945 quot.). Orig. *colloq.*

1846** Dickens *Dombey & Son* 77: "You're Dombey's jockey, an't you?" said the first man. "I'm in Dombey's House, Mr. Clark," returned the boy. ***1911** O'Brien & Stephens *Austral. Slang* 26: *Brewer's jockey* (Melbourne) a man who rides about with the driver of a brewer's waggon helping him load and unload on the chance of a share of the drinks which fall to the lot of a brewer's man. **1928** in E. Ferber *One Basket* 323: No, I only got just this one hack. No, I wouldn't want no jockey. I drive it alone. **1935** in Mencken *Amer. Lang.* (ed. 4) 587: An assistant cameraman is a *jockey.* [*a1940** in Mencken *Amer. Lang. Supp.* II 720: *Jockey.* A passenger or friend who rides in front when the [taxi] driver.] ***1945** S.J. Baker *Austral. Lang.* 140: A *jockey* is a taxi-driver's accomplice who pretends to be a passenger in order to encourage legitimate travellers to pay extortionate fares to secure the taxi.

2. [sugg. by PONY] *Stu.* (see quot.).

1900 *DN* II 43: *Jockey, n.* One who uses a translation habitually.

3. *Und.* a professional horse thief. Cf. obs. S.E. sense 'a horse-dealer, esp. if dishonest'.

1904 *Life in Sing Sing* 249: *Jockey.*—Horse thief. **1935** D.W. Maurer, in *AS* (Feb.) 17: *Jockey.* One who steals valuable horses, especially race horses. (Obs.).

4.a. an operator, handler, or worker; hand.—usu. used in combs. See also more freq. colloc. listed as main entries.

1908 W.G. Davenport *Butte & Montana* 8: We have to pay our lino-type jockeys double price. **1922** T.A. Dorgan, in Zwilling *TAD Lexicon* 113: What would you say his dodge is? I say he's a ledger jockey—He's there with the book keeper's back. **1937** (quot. at BEAN JOCKEY). **1939** *AS* (Oct.) 240: *Jockey.* Elevator operator. **1941** (quot. at SOUP JOCKEY). **1941** Kendall *Army & Navy Slang* 1: A barrow jockey.…pushes a wheelbarrow. **1943** *Yank* (July 26) 11: Good news to typewriter jockeys. **1951** *West. Folklore* X 170: *Beer jockey.* Barmaid; waitress. **1954** Freeman *Francis Joins WACs* (film): Just because you think women are fit only to be typewriter jockeys and secretaries. **1956** Heinlein *Door* 21: We hired her as a typewriter jockey and bookkeeper. **1958** in *AS* XXXV (1960) 159: Some elevator jockeys…take their tolls.…He was a mop jockey in the air force! **1958** McCulloch *Woods Words* 139: Power

saw jockey—A gas engine mechanic. **1959** Himes *Crazy Kill* 16: I ain't interested in that whiskey jockey [bartender]. **1959–60** Bloch *Dead Beat* 76: Since when are you an elevator jockey? **1966** Cassiday *Angels Ten* 58: One of the base ordnance jockeys. **1971** Horan *Blue Messiah* 315: The Hi-Lo jockey watched us approach. **1972** R. Barrett *Lovomaniacs* 266: And that overgrown hoist jockey back there's Willie Wojinski. **1974** A. Bergman *Big Kiss-Off* 7: The elevator jockey…vanished into the gray mist. **1983** *Newsweek on Campus* (May) 32: When the newspaper gave out passwords for our video terminals, the computer jockey gave me "shj." **1987** Henzel *Doggerel* 23: She's a clipboard jockey, riding herd on data. **1988** *TV Guide* (Mar. 19) 14: Commercials are tough to avoid, even for VCR jockeys. **1988** Cogan & Ferguson *Presidio* 167: He told the maintenance jockey. **1991** Brown & Angus *A.K.A. Narc* 135: This jockey work for you long? **1994** *N.Y. Times* (Sept. 20) C3: The director of the National Center for Human Genome Research…and a certified gene jockey.

b. a driver (or, in 1915 quot., conductor) of an automobile, truck, or other motor vehicle; *(rarely)* an assistant, such as a parking lot attendant, employed to drive and park motor vehicles.—usu. used in combs. [The 1912 quot. given by *OED2* is a journalist's metaphor rather than a slang sense in free use.]

1915 T.A. Dorgan, in Zwilling *TAD Lexicon* 111: He's a conductor on a jitney bus. A jitney jockey. **1919** Day *Camion Cartoons* 104: We got a ride on a truck, the driver of which would be a wonder as a tank jockey. *Ibid.* 110: We went out to the corner to wait for the return of the jitney jockeys. **1929–31** Runyon *Guys & Dolls* 77: Her papa is a taxi jockey by the name of Skush O'Brien. *Ibid.* 103: Dave is jerking me into the cab and telling the jockey to go to the Penn Station. **1940** Wexley *City for Conquest* (film): You guessed it, jockey. **1941** *Amer. Mercury* (Apr.) 462: This does not exhaust the idiomatic esoterica of the highway jockeys [truck drivers]. **1949** Bezzerides *Thieves' Highway* (film): You're a truck jockey now. You know what you're gonna be when you grow up? A truck jockey. **1957** E. Brown *Locust Fire* 95 [ref. to 1944]: Burma Road jockeys, all riding high on the Nanping Gai. **1962** G. Olson *Roaring Rd.* 135: Many callow sportscar jockeys. **1968** J.P. Miller *Race for Home* 314: Your average truck jockey ain't got the reflections to handle a situation like that. **1972** in Terkel *Working* 219: They call 'em car hikers, they call 'em jockeys. **1982** T.C. Mason *Battleship* 56: A battered Yellow Cab and an equally battered car jockey.

c. (used in other, freq. nonce, combs.) one who rides or is habituated to (something specified in the initial element).

1919 (quot. at COT JOCKEY). **1930** Lait *On the Spot* 215: *Wild-wave jockey*…A rum-runner who transports stuff by water. **1971** Curtis *Banjo* 125: She could borrow on his strength to turn away the buzzard-eyed pushers and hop-jockeys [drug addicts]. **1978** T. Sanchez *Zoot-Suit* 220: To keep her public from knowing she was a Horse jockey [heroin addict]. **1980** *Mutual Radio Theater* (WHEL radio) (May 13): A red-hot time jockey [operator of a time machine] with a heavy hand on the temporal drive.

d. *Av.* a pilot.—usu. used in combs.

1944 Olds *Helldiver Squadron* 70: "Bogie high to port. Closing fast," he shouted to his "jockey," and opened fire with his thirties. ***1945** S.J. Baker *Australian Lang.* 160: *Jockey.* A pilot. **1951** in *DAS*: The jockey is in the panic rack and ready to go. **1951** *Air Cadet* (film): We're fire-can jockeys, jet pilots. **1955** Blair *Beyond Courage* 53: A year later, a hot-shot fighter "jockey," he was sent to Japan. **1955** R.L. Scott *Look of Eagle* 191: The bomber jockeys walk into the club. **1955** in Loosbrock & Skinner *Wild Blue* 495: He…had gained quite a reputation as a post-bellum Rocky Mountain helicopter jockey. **1958** Mayes *Hunters* (film): I got to keep up with the jet jockeys. **1959** in *AS* XXXV (1960) 159: You crazy chopper jockeys. **1961** Joswick & Keating *Combat Cameraman* 12: These bomber jockeys did not want me around. **1962** S. Smith *Escape from Hell* 143: He climbed out of the jockey's seat. **1962** Mahurin *Honest John* 87: If our pilots had not been good sports, that Mig jockey would never have reached the ground in one piece. **1963** D. Tracy *Brass Ring* 319: I was a B-17 jockey. **1965** Beech *Make War in Madness* 116: You're a [B-]26-jockey, aren't you, Price? **1966–67** W. Stevens *Gunner* 56: You can't keep formation one week without some recruit jockey slicing your tail off. **1969** Searls *Hero Ship* 19: They flew carrier qualifications for two weeks and almost lost a fighter jockey on a cold-cat shot off the bow. **1970** *Adam-12* (NBC-TV): What really bugs me is the way that chopper-jockey rubbed it in. **1971** Cole *Rook* 346: Pilots, MATS jockeys, DAC's.

5. *Baseball.* BENCH JOCKEY.

   1927 *N.Y. Sun* (July 18): A [baseball] player who "rides" the opposing players…is known as a "jockey." **1941** *Sat. Eve. Post* (May 17) 18: Jimmy Dykes…is celebrated as the most vociferous, vehement and vituperative jockey in baseball. A baseball jockey is a fellow who yells coarse, crude remarks at…the opposition. **1946** *N.Y. Times Mag.* (July 14) 18: *Jockey:* one who "rides" opposition.

6. disc jockey.

   1959 *Life* (Nov. 23) 46: Other jockeys around the country see these listings. **1961** Ellison *Gentleman Junkie* 113: Every other jockey's fallen in line to give it the big play.

jockey *v.* **1.a.** to drive (a truck) or pilot (an aircraft).—occ. used absol. [Prob. the orig. sense.]

   1948 in Galewitz *Great Comics* 280: Your job was jockeying airplanes. **1950** in F. Brown *Honeymoon* 24: The plane…that took him back—with Granham jockeying it—…cracked the sonic barrier. **1952** H. Grey *Hoods* 48: Once in awhile he jockies one of his brothers cabs. **1956** Heflin *USAF Dict.* 282: *Jockey*…To fly or pilot an *airplane*; to manipulate an *airplane* along an intricate flight path…."the copilot jockeyed while I rested." **1963–64** Kesey *Great Notion* 358: Just so's he could jockey a truck.

   b. to carry or handle (merchandise or the like).

   1937 Weidman *Wholesale* 88: Why should I be jockeying their bundles?

2. *Baseball.* to act as a BENCH JOCKEY; taunt (a member of an opposing team).

   1936 in Dickson *Baseball Dict.*: It was bitterly fought and there was much jockeying between the benches. **1950** P. Cummings *Dict. of Baseball* 8: *Bench jockey*….A player who "jockeys" (taunts) the opponents from the bench, notably one with marked talent for such jockeying. **1950** Cleveland *Great Mgrs.* 23: Today "jockeying" from the bench to rattle the opponents is an accepted part of the game. **1952** Malamud *Natural* 73: The crowd assisted the boys by working on the nerves of the visiting team with whammy words, catcalls, wise-cracks, the kind of sustained jockeying that exhausted the rival pitchers and sometimes drove them out of the game.

jockey soldier *n. Army.* a cavalryman.

   1869 Fobes *Trooper's Diary* 35 [ref. to Civil War]: Here comes these jockey-soldiers, ridin' over us; soft thing they have of it!

jock itch *n.* a skin infection of the genital area. Now *colloq.* or *S.E.* Also **jockey itch.**

   1950 (cited in *W10*). **1959** *41st Ftr. Sq. Songbk.* 20: He had the crabs and jocky itch. **1961** Coon *Meanwhile at the Front* 308: I've got jock itch, colonel. *a***1968** in Haines & Taggart *Ft. Lauderdale* 123: I didn't want no jock itch. **1969** Searls *Hero Ship* 41 [ref. to WWII]: He had jock itch…and a headache. **1970** Ad on N.Y.C. bus: Medicated Spray-On Powder for Jock Itch (Tinea Cruris). **1975** Schott *No Left Turns* 68: Cure that jock itch.

jock major *n. Stu.* a physical education major.

   1961–62 in *AS* XLII (1967) 229: *Jock major*…Any male student majoring in physical education.

jocko *n.* **1.** a man or boy who is a dolt; blockhead.—often used as a contemptuous form of address.

   1926 MacIsaac *Tin Hats* 80 [ref. to 1918]: Ain't got a nose ring?…I'll give you a nose ring, Jocko. **1958** Frede *Entry E* 86: Just one moment, jocko mio. **1961** Granat *Important Thing* 10: The jockos, not a single thought in their collective skulls. **1966** Samuels *People vs. Baby* 35: Fuck off, Jocko. **1968** Tauber *Sunshine Soldiers* 194: I catch any of you jockos pulling a wise-ass one like that, I'll have you in the Guard House. **1976** Conroy *Santini* 132: It still counts two points, does it not, jocko? **1984** W. Wharton *Scumbler* 74: These two jockos never come down while I'm painting.

2. JOCK¹, 4.a.

   1969 Bouton *Ball Four* 83: He was just another jocko, but he was an ace because he was always out with Mickey Mantle and the boys. **1972** *N.Y. Post* (Sept. 30) 37: Jenkins, a senior editor at *Sports Illustrated*, knows his jockos. **1988** *Outside* (Mar.) 33: Most of us mistakenly assume we are simply one morph or another—fatso, jocko, or bones.

jock-piece *n.* the penis.

   1921 in Dreiser *Diaries* 377: Each had to do a stunt and he who failed had to produce his jock-piece.

jock rot *n.* JOCK ITCH.

   1982 Del Vecchio *13th Valley* 419 [ref. to Vietnam War]: I…got some cuts en some jock rot. **1984–87** Ferrandino *Firefight* 50 [ref. to

Vietnam War]: The Chu Lai Jockrot Club. **1989** Cassell *S.S.N. Skate* 342: They all got jockrot from the damp.

jock-sniffer *n. Sports.* an offensively forward person who attempts to fraternize with notable athletes.

   1971 Meggyesey *Out of Their League* 87 [ref. to 1960's]: The players called guys like this "jock-sniffers." They were wealthy Syracusians who would contribute to the under-the-table fund for the privilege of rubbing shoulders with big-name football players. [*a***1972** B. Rodgers *Queens' Vernacular* 118: *Jock-sniffer* towel boy; attendant in a gym.] **1978** B. Johnson *What's Happenin'* 176: This is the reporter as jock-sniffer. **1985** *USA Today* (Sept. 12) 2A: His attorney calls him "a pitiful little jock-sniffer" who enjoyed fraternizing with baseball stars.

jockstrap *n.* **1.** a men's undergarment consisting of an elasticized belt with a pouch for supporting or protecting the genitals, worn esp. while participating in athletics; athletic supporter. Now *S.E.* Also vars.

   [**1845** Corcoran *Pickings* 183: The dilapidated hat of Jacques Strop.] **1886** (cited in *W10*). [**1896** in *OED2*: Suspensories, Jockey Straps.] **1897** in *OED2*: Combined jock-strap and suspensory. **1919** in E.E. Cummings *Letters* 61: But many thanks for the jock-strap offer. **1927** [Fliesler] *Anecdota* 56: A jockstrap, Mr. Gallegher? **1931** Farrell *McGinty* 107: McGinty…wearing a jock strap. **1934** Wylie *Finnley Wren* 9: He went back to his locker, donned a moldered jock strap. **1937** Weidman *Can Get It Wholesale* 324: A fur-lined jockstrap I'd get him. **1938–39** Dos Passos *Young Man* 36: Paul stepped out with nothing on but a jockstrap. **1956** W. Brinkley *Don't Go Near Water* 27: There isn't a jockstrap on the whole island. **1962** N.Y.C. high school students: Jockstrap. Jockstrop. Jackstrap. **1963** W.C. Anderson *Penelope* 41: I've seen some miserable slobs in my day, but you win the fur-lined jockstrap. **1972** Bunker *No Beast* 93: Put yourself in my jock strap. **1976** Atlee *Domino* 36: Kimchi….unkind foreigners have been known to liken its aroma to a ripening of wrestler's jock straps. **1980** Manchester *Darkness* 302 [ref. to WWII]: You…wakened…with your head fuzzy and a terrible taste in your mouth, resembling, Rip once said, "a Greek wrestler's jockstrap." **1981** *Hill St. Blues* (NBC-TV): You know I'll support you tighter than a brown jockstrap. **1992** *Mystery Sci. Theater* (Comedy Central TV): They're wearing jackstraps on their heads! **1993** G. Lee *Honor & Duty* 4: Photographed in a jockstrap. **1994** N.Y.C. book reviewer, age *ca*70: From my GI days…1942–43…I had a barracks mate from the Boston region, an Irishman and a heavy drinker, he had an expression to describe how dry his throat was the morning after: "My throat feels like an Arab's jockstrap after a hard day on the desert."

2. *Esp. Mil.* an athlete, esp. a boxer, wrestler, or football player.—in early use, often used attrib.—usu. used derisively.

   1944 Kendall *Service Slang* 36: *Jock strap Marine*…athlete. **1948** I. Shaw *Young Lions* 271: The Regular at Fort Dix…had been in the Army thirteen years, playing on Army baseball and football teams in time of peace. Jock-strap soldiers, they called them. **1946–51** J. Jones *From Here to Eternity* ch. iv [ref. to 1941]: Unless…you happen to be a jockstrap. Any kind of a jockstrap…but preferably a punchie. **1956** Boatner *Military Customs & Trads.* 120: *Jockstrap outfit* A unit which places much emphasis on athletic achievement. **1956** *AS* XXXI (Oct.) 192: A healthy, athletic young man addicted to sports may wince under the pointed *jockstrap marine*. **1959** in J. Blake *Joint* 244: Evergreen, okay, but that Hefner jazz is for retarded jockstraps. **1962** in *AS* (Oct. 1963) 169: A college athlete…*jock…jockstrap*. **1963** Doulis *Path* 332: A couple of the jockstraps are gonna lead us in calisthenics. **1963** Coon *Short End* 7: Jesus Christ Almighty, what this company needs most is another jockstrap. **1966** Derrig *Pride of Green Berets* 94: Me, I had nothing but the jock-strap scholarship. **1966** Braly *On Yard* 268: The…team was closely controlled by a…clique of jockstraps. **1967** in J. Flaherty *Chez Joey* 45: The rest of the ringside seats were populated by Village poets and jockstrap intellectuals. **1984** Algeo *Stud Buds*: A college athlete…*jock strap*. **1987** Eyre *What Price Victory* (film): 50 K! That oughta buy us some jockstraps!

3. *Juve.* a stupid or obnoxious fellow.

   1963 N.Y.C. high school student: Don't be such a jockstrap. **1965** in Waldman *World Anthol.* 14: Bobby…[is] a real jockstrap. **1968** Brasselle *Cannibals* 278: What a jockstrap. The jerk was really beyond help. *a***1972** B. Rodgers *Queens' Vernacular* 118: *Jock-strap*…a slow-witted person; a dumbbell.

¶ In phrases:

¶ **can't carry (someone's) jockstrap** *Sports.* lacks (someone's) ability; is no equal of (someone).

1978 in Lyle & Golenbock *Bronx Zoo* 242: He can't carry Paul Blair's jockstrap, and not only that, [he] isn't going to hit. **1985** in P. Heller *Bad Intentions* 187: Marciano couldn't carry my jock strap. **1990** *Married with Children* (Fox-TV): A man whose jockstrap none of you are fit to carry. **1991** D. Anderson *In Corner* 143: To be technical, Rocky...couldn't carry my jockstrap.

¶ **hang [up] (one's) jockstrap** See s.v. *hang [up] (one's) jock* [or *jockstrap*] s.v. JOCK[1].

¶ **out of (one's) jockstrap** utterly (frightened or confused). Cf. *out of (one's) jock* s.v. JOCK.

1975 Larsen *Runner* 89: He's scared out of his jock strap.

jockstrap *v. Mil. & Sports.* to compete in athletics, esp. boxing. Rarely **jackstrop.**

1946 in Leadbitter & Slaven *Blues Records* 136: Jackstropper Blues (The Jackstropper). **1946–51** J. Jones *From Here to Eternity* 15 [ref. to 1941]: There's nothin in the ARs says a man has got to jockstrap when he doesn't want to. **1980** Cragg *Lex. Militaris* 252: *Jockstrapper.* A soldier who earns his Army pay in the sports program.

J.O. Country *Navy.* junior officers' quarters on shipboard.

1956 (quot. at COUNTRY, 2).

jo-darter *n. So.* a hard or stinging blow; (*hence*) anything extraordinary.

1851 Burke *Polly Peablossom* 151: I got close...so as I could hit him a jo-darter. **1857** in Walser *Tar Heel Laughter* 57: I dealt him a double-distilled jo-darter that spread him...as flat as a pancake. **1859** "Skitt" *Fisher's R.* 106 [ref. to 1820's]: Dick turned upon him with a "jodarter." **1880** J.C. Harris *Uncle Remus* 240: She hit de ole nigger a joe-darter. **1882** *Harper's Mo.* (Oct.) 806: He's a joedahter! **1893** in Mencken *Amer. Lang. Supp.* II 172: *Jodarter,* anything superior. **1905** *DN* III 84: It's a *Joe Darter* of an elephant. **1908** *DN* III 325: He's a *joe darter* when it comes to trading. **1965–67** in *DARE* [in both senses].

jo-darting *adj. So.* extraordinary; HUMDINGING.

1903 in "O. Henry" *Works* 165: The Jo-dartin'est hustler.

Jody *n.* [var. of JOE THE GRINDER; see esp. D.W. Maurer & A. Futtrell, "Jody's Chinese Relations," *AS* LVII (1982), pp. 304–07] *Mil.* **1.** JOE THE GRINDER. [Notably in marching chants; cf. JODY CALL.]

1944 in A. Lyon *Unknown Station* 28: Ain't no use in going home/Joady's got your girl and gone....Gonna get a three-day pass/Just to kick old Joady's ass. **1945** Beecher *All Brave Sailors* 113: "Some guys worry about their wives...going out with Jody." (Jody is the mythical character who takes care of seamen's wives and girl friends while they're away). **1949** Pirosh *Battleground* (film): Jody's got something you ain't got./It's been so long I almost forgot. **1952** in Yates *Loneliness* 48: Jody was your faithless friend, the soft civilian to whom the dice-throw of chance had given everything you held dear. **1960** Bluestone *Cully* 68: He told her all about Jody, the Army's legendary stud, who serviced all the girls the soldiers left behind. **1961** in *JAF* LXXVIII (1965) 58: Ain't no need in turnin' back/Jody's got your Cadillac. **1968** Tauber *Sunshine Soldiers* 120: "Jody" is an Army invention, used to keep the troops fired up. At this writing Jody is sleeping with every trainee's wife, mother or sister...drinking his liquor, watching his TV, driving his car, spending his money. **1975** S.P. Smith *American Boys* 377: You know Jody got that hometown pussy all sewed up anyway. **1982** Downey *Losing the War* 25 [ref. to WWII]: "Jodie"...was a shortening of "Joe-the-Grinder," a mythical character...grinding away on top of all the women back home while...us less-fortunates were in the service. **1984–87** Ferrandino *Firefight* 194: That's what Jodie be doin' to your ol' lady. **1989** C. Bianchi *Dancing with Charlie* 68: What's the matter, Corp? Jody got your gal? **1990** G. Lee *China Boy* 105: Jody got somethin dat you ain't got. **1991** J.T. Ward *Dear Mom* 179 [ref. to Vietnam War]: There I lay, and a "Jody" was back home taking care of my girl. **1996** *Donahue* (NBC-TV): Like in the military, that guy Jody is waiting around the corner for when you go off.

2.a. a male civilian, usu. of draftable age.—used disparagingly or contemptuously. Also as adj.

1944 Burley *Hndbk. Jive* 108: But still the Jodies—Buy the chicks "sodies"...as soldier boys frown. **1942–45** Caniff *Male Call* (unp.): Why ain't that Joadie in uniform? He looks healthy enough. **1945**

Himes *If He Hollers* 75: The servicemen were always hostile toward a Jodie, especially a black Jodie in his fine Jodie clothes. **1964** Rhodes *Chosen Few* 211: Most of 'em are jodies but a few jarheads go up when they feel in a mood t'lock asses with some jodies. **1965** Linakis *In Spring* 164 [ref. to WWII]: What're you talking to him for? He's a puking jody. *Ibid.* 170: Jody shoes. **1982** Downey *Losing the War* 25 [ref. to WWII]: All servicemen envied the Jodies....As far as the older Marines were concerned, Missip and I were a couple of former Jodies. **1982** Del Vecchio *13th Valley* 239: So your gal's off with some Jody. **1984** Glick *Winters Coming* 208: Typical jody windbags. **1986** Clayton & Elliott *Jazz World* 117 [ref. to WWII]: "Jody! Jody! Jody!" they would yell at us as if we were the newcomers and they were the experienced soldiers, hard and tough.

b. (see quot.).

1944 Kendall *Service Slang* 43: [Among women in the U.S. Coast Guard] a jody [is] a girl in civilian life.

3. *pl.* men's civilian clothes. In full, **Jody clothes.**

1945 (quot. at **(2.a.)**, above). **1950** L. Brown *Iron City* 216: Man, I was in the army while you were still wearing Jodie clothes and worrying bout your draft board. **1964** Rhodes *Chosen Few* 159: All we gotta do is wear jody clothes. **1965** Linakis *In Spring* 62 [ref. to WWII]: A kraut came toward us in jodies but wearing his old Afrika Korps campaign cap with the long peak. **1981** Former E-4, U.S. Army [ref. to 1972–79]: A few old-time top sergeants still refer to civilian clothes as *jodies.*

4. JODY CALL.

1993 G. Lee *Honor & Duty* 381 [ref. to 1960's]: Singing West Point jodies ("Left my baby in New Orleans/Twenty-four babies and a can of beans./Sound off"). **1994** *New Yorker* (Sept. 5) 72: Many of the chants are the usual military "jodies," well known for their misogynistic lyrics.

Jody call *n. Mil.* an antiphonal marching song or chant, often concerning JODY, 1, used in close-order drill. Also **Jody song, Jody rhyme.**

1963 P. Cameron *Jody Calls* 1: He learned these jody calls while in the Naval Reserve and attending summer camp in...1962. **1963** Doulis *Path* 78: Damianos ignored her, chanting a Jody rhyme that was suspiciously off key. **1982** *AS* LVII 304: Examples of...cadence chants, often referred to as *Jody songs* or *Jody calls.* **1981–89** R. Atkinson *Long Gray Line* 521: As in a jody call used to count cadence while marching. **1995** Former infantryman, U.S. Army, age *ca*60 (coll. J. Sheidlower): We sang Jody calls (and called them that) in high school ROTC in the mid-1950's....In Sacramento, in 1954–57.

Jody drill *n. Mil.* close-order drill, usu. to the accompaniment of JODY CALLS.

1965 Linakis *In Spring* 44 [ref. to WWII]: We did jody drill in the yard.

Jody sign *n.* [orig. unkn.; the early date of occurrence, as well as the sense, makes it unlikely to be related to JODY] *Sports.* a defeat; INDIAN SIGN.—constr. with *the.*

1911 G. Herriman, in *N.Y. Eve. Jour.* (Jan. 9) 11: Tear right in and slip the Jody sign on 'em proper.

Joe *n.* **1.** the double Johannes, a Portuguese gold coin. [The coin was current in the U.S. in the colonial and early national period.]

1765 in Thornton *Amer. Gloss.*: Into the L...rs hands (full) many a Jo/We've slily put. **1772** in *OED*: Let Mr. Ripley have a guinea, half a jo, and 9 coppers. **1776** in *Maryland Hist. Mag.* LXXII (1967) 242: The Army was mostly paid in *Joes, Half-Joes,* & Dollars. **1782** in *DAE*: I received the two Joes you was so good as to send for interest. **1807** J.R. Shaw *Autobiog.* 45 [ref. to *ca*1780]: The guard...agreed for three half joes to conduct us to New York. **1823** J.F. Cooper *Pioneers* 14: I...rattled three buck-shot into his naked hide, so close, that you might have laid a broad joe upon them all. **1825** J.C. Neal *Bro. Jonathan* I 160: I shows him a handful of the royal gold....I do lay one of 'em out—jest a joe. **1833 Marryat *Peter Simple* ch. xxxi: I think they were half a joe, or eight dollars each.

2.a. a privy.

1847 in *Amer. N & Q* VI (1946) 61: Feeling quite lively after my return, disguised myself, and...nailed up all the South College joe-doors [at Amherst]! **1856** B. Hall *College Wds.* (ed. 2) 271: *Joe.* A name given at several American colleges to a privy. **1866–71** Bagg *Yale* 45: *Joe,* the college privy. **1900** *DN* II 43: College Words...*joe, n.* Water-closet [at seven N.E. colleges]....*joe-trots, n.* Diarrhœa....*joe-wad,* n. Toilet-paper.

b. *Army.* an imaginary person supposed to be the source of latrine rumors; rumor. Now *hist.* In full, **Joe Latrine** or **Joe Latrinsky.** [Quots. ref. to WWI; cf. JO-JO.]

1918 Swan *My Co.* 35: "Joe" said we were soon to go to the Front.…"Joe Latrinsky" (sometimes spelled differently), the father of Dame Rumor. Everyone from commanding generals to buck privates…spoke of "Joe Latrinsky," or plain "Joe," and what he was saying. **1918** in *Story of E Co. 101st Engrs.* 112: "Joe" busy. *Ibid.* 116: "Joe" now busy with rumor of 26th going home. *Ibid.* 118: "Joe Latrine" … failed to materialize. **1919** W. Duffy *GPF* 245: Only arrived, but Joe is on deck. **1928** Havlin *Co. A* 8: "Joe L'trine" was especially active with rumors of all sorts. **1976** Berry *Kaiser* 196: According to Joe Latrinsky, we were going everywhere but the North Pole for a rest.

3. *Navy.* JOE-PAN.

1854 McCauley *With Perry* 120: Their sole amusement since our arrival in Joe. has been the keeping of a journal in newspaper style.

4. JOE MILLER.—constr. with *old.*

1871 O. Wood *Scrapbook* 288: All the pointed stories have been repeated so often, that to try to renew them now would be much like writing as original the "Old Joes" of Harper's Magazine.

5.a. a foolish, inept, or offensive fellow.—also used attrib. Now *rare* in U.S.

*1906 in *OEDS:* Why, man, it's meat 'n' beer t' them Joes what go in fer bringin' ther wanderers 'ome. **1909** T.A. Dorgan, in Zwilling *TAD Lexicon* 112: It's a pipe that he works for a joe editor. **1910** *N.Y. Eve. Jour.* (Mar. 8) 14: Abe did so, and finding the fellow was a terrible "Joe," let him…outbox him as he pleased. **1910** *N.Y. Eve. Jour.* (Mar. 10) 16: Bill Squires is about as big a "Joe" at the referee game as he was in the box-fighting line. **1910** T.A. Dorgan, in *N.Y. Eve. Jour.* (May 5) 14: What a lot of Joe fighters there must be in Australia, eh? **1918** *Stars & Stripes* (May 10) 4: I'm not a simp; I'm not a joe./I'm on when cream is full of flies. **1948** Mencken *Amer. Lang. Supp. II* 738: *Joe.* A customer who does not tip. **1974** (quot. at JOE McGEE). **1978* in Partridge *DSUE* (ed. 8) 623: *Joe.* Weak person, easily imposed on.

b. an ordinary fellow; man.—often used in direct address; a likable person of either sex.—(usu. constr. with *good*). [The 1846 quot. given by *OED2* does not correspond to this sense; 1911 quot. below may belong to **(a)**, above.]

[**1849** *Spirit of Times* (Feb. 3) 595: He tried right hard to catch this child,/But he could not come it Joe.] **1911** T.A. Dorgan, in *N.Y. Eve. Jour.* (Jan. 16) 12: "Look at that Joe." "Oh it's a pipe that I can skate if he can." **1932** *AS* VII (June) 333: *Joe*—term used to designate anyone whose real name is unknown. **1934** H. Miller *Tropic of Cancer* 93: I call him Joe because he calls me Joe. When Carl is with us he is Joe too. Everybody is Joe because it's easier that way. **1936** (quot. at KILL, *v.*). **1938** Sherman & Sherman *Crime School* (film): Cop a gander, Joe.…You ain't goin' nowhere, Joe! **1938** in Gelman *Photoplay* 209: A great gang around this lot.…Regular Jo's. **1940** J. Ross *Don't Dance* 42: He always wore clothes to make him look like a College Joe. **1943** *AS* XVIII 154: *Sorry Joe.* A dumb person. **1944** *Slanguage Dict.* 60: Hiya, Joe, what do you know? **1944** Wakeman *Shore Leave* 12: But he must've been some Joe in his time. **1946** K. Archibald *Shipyard* 182: Just plain Joes like any of us here. **1949** *The Set-Up* (film): I never seen a college Joe yet could take a belt on the kisser without phoning his mother. **1949** R. MacDonald *Moving Target* 41: I was a good Joe after all. **1953** Peterson *Take a Giant Step* 50: You're a real good Joe. **1955** Robbins *79 Park Ave.* 314: Is that all I am to you? Just another Joe? **1957** Murtagh & Harris *First Stone* 186: I guess I feel that every time I do something one of those Joes wants, I'm getting even for something another Joe did to me. **1958** Ferlinghetti *Coney Island* 72: I am a good Joe. **1968** Lockridge *Hartspring* 70: You've always seemed like such a good Joe, one of the boys. **1969** in S. Lee *Son of Origins* 145: Those Joes out there deserve the best. **1982** Least Heat Moon *Blue Hwys.* 211: Hey, Joe, what's your name? **1987** Univ. Tenn. student theme: I believe that the average Joe may ask one of these questions if she is made to take an English course which studies language. **1995** *Pub. Mod. Lang. Assoc.* (May) 378: Nick…is an ordinary joe…who must work for a living.

c. *Mil.* an ordinary enlisted man in U.S. military service; GI JOE.

1943 *Yank* (Jan. 20) 5: The Joes in the company were taking it pretty hard. **1944** H. Brown *Walk in the Sun* 127: But to get back to the traveling salesman, how many of those Joes do you think would of become traveling salesmen if they'd had to walk everywhere? **1945** in

Mencken *Amer. Lang. Supp. II* 780: The *GI* doesn't mind being called a *GI* or a *Joe* by other soldiers. **1945** in Litoff et al. *Miss You* 261: Ernie Pyle…told…everybody…in the States the things "Joe" saw, did, and felt. **1965** Linakis *In Spring* 284 [ref. to WWII]: Command should not concern itself with menial tasks. "Sure, that's for the joes," I said.

6. (used freely before a n. or adj. to create nonce expressions denoting a man who personifies or represents the specified quality, identity, or association). Cf. earlier similar use of JOHN; also cf. JOE HEP. See also more freq. colloc. listed as main entries.

1912 Siringo *Cowboy Detective* 176: Billy S. had to pull Joe Buttinsky out from under the table. **1923** in J. O'Hara *Sel. Letters* 9: The man who … [says that] is either old Joe Athlete who is sure of his letters and gold footballs or he's Joe's brother. **1925** *Lit. Digest* (Mar. 14) 65: If a [college] man is called "Joe Brooks" he is the acme of perfection in dress. This comes from the popularity of a well-known sartorial authority [Brooks Bros., Inc.]. … "Old Joe Brooks himself, aren't you?" **1932** *AS* VII (June) 333: When used with a place or profession "Joe" indicates a perfect example of the type connected with that place or profession. Thus "Joe College" is a perfect specimen of the college man. … "Joe Artist himself." **1936** in *AS* XII (1937) 46: *Joe Union.* A union official or any union influence. "If you cut scale, *Joe Union* will be on you." **1937** Weidman *Wholesale* 50: I [gave] him the old toothpaste grin. Joe Personality. **1941** *Washington* (D.C.) *Daily News* (Feb. 19) 9: Joe Public will soon get his chance to help. **1941** "G.R. Lee" *G-String* 278: The Sergeant was playing "Joe Generous." **1958** Schwitzgebel *Streetcorner Research* 46: The ordinary Joe, Joe Truckdriver, Joe Factory-worker, Joe Worker,…Joe Nobody. **1959** Morrill *Dark Sea* 87: How'd you like to see the Joe Tough of this bucket sing like a sick dog? **1959** De Roo *Young Wolves* 160: Ya been a good chum. A real Joe-pal with me. *ca*1960 in Schwendinger & Schwendinger *Adolescent Subculture* 83: Some of the guys are rich and they are regular guys, but they go out of their way to act tough.…We call them Jo-Bads. **1964** Faust *Steagle* 121: I tellya, Mend, they love it when you're Joe Prick. **1970** N.Y.U. students: "Can I borrow a nickel?" "Don't look at me. I'm Joe Poor." **1965–71** in *Qly. Jour. Stud. on Alcohol* XXXII (1971) 732: *Joe Bum.* A bum. **1971** N.Y.U. students: "Have you got a dime?" "Don't ask me. I'm Joe Broke." **1971** Sheehan *Arnheiter* 112: I was Joe Naive…wet behind the ears. **1986** J.J. Maloney *Chain* 49: The next day you're Joe Nobody. **1987** E. Spencer *Macho Man* 101: What really gets me are the sunglasses they wear. Joe Skier! **1989** P. Munro *U.C.L.A. Sl.* 53: Joe Friendly…Joe Hopeless…Joe Potential. **1992** *Crier & Co.* (CNN-TV) (Mar. 4): What is it that interests Joe Voter?

7. *Narc.* a fit caused by withdrawal sickness. Cf. Austral. slang *Joes* 'a fit of depression or revulsion' (1910 in *Austral. Nat. Dict.*) and *Joe Blakes* 'snakes', as in bracketed quot.

[**1905* in *Austral. Nat. Dict.*: I saw a lot of *Joe Blakes*, but don't know if they were dinkum or just the after effects of the grog.] **1925** in Hammett *Big Knockover* 231: He's going to throw a joe on you, chief, if you don't give him a pill.

8. [perh. as sugg. in 1980 quot.; the Foster song was extremely popular] (usu. *l.c.*) Esp. *Navy.* Coffee.

1930 Irwin *Tramp & Und. Sl.* 110: *Joe.*—Coffee. **1931** Erdman *Reserve Officer's Manual* 441: *Jamoke, Java, Joe.* Coffee. Derived from the words Java and Mocha, where originally the best coffee came from.…*Jilpot.* Coffee pot. A corruption of "joe-pot." **1933** *Leatherneck* (Mar.) 27: He observed that more is learned in a "jo" party than in any class instruction, so "coffee and" rank marksmanship problems after all. **1939** O'Brien *One-Way Ticket* 78 [ref. to late 1920's]: Here, take a shot of jo. **1941** Brackett & Wilder *Ball of Fire* (film): Just Joe—no cow. **1943** Bayler & Carnes *Wake I.* 51: Coffee is the marine's best friend and the Corps might well adopt the good old "joe-pot" for its emblem. **1951** "W. Williams" *Enemy* 32: This joe will make your hair curly. **1953** Eyster *Customary Skies* 172: You'll still never get a pot of jo from the I.C. room. **1954** Schulberg *Waterfront* 90: "Le's go down get some more joe," Jimmy said. "My eyeballs are draggin' on the floor." **1958** Gilbert *Vice Trap* 136: I was getting loaded on that black joe. **1965** in H. Ellison *Sex Misspelled* 342: Without joe I'd be dead. **1967** Dibner *Admiral* 123 [ref. to WWII]: For twenty-two years he had drunk Navy coffee round the world—black gang coffee, gunner's brew, shaft alley juice, old black joe. **1980** Mack & Connell *Naval Trads.* (ed. 5) 260: Some sailors call coffee "joe," which some say is a derivative of [Stephen] Foster's song, "Old Black Joe." **1990** *Twin Peaks* (ABC-TV): Can I offer you gentlemen a cup of joe? **1992** *Early*

Prime (CNN-TV) (Feb. 11): Is a cup or two of joe anything to get steamed about? Coffee and cholesterol. **1993** *Living in '90's* (CNN-TV) (Nov. 22): Coffee, java, joe. **1995** *Entertainment Tonight* (synd. TV series) (May 29): A steamin' cuppa joe.

9. *Mil. in Korea.* Communist Chinese or North Korean armed forces. Now *hist.*

1951 [VMF-323] *Old Ballads* 41: Joe may have politicians/That will linger on and on. **1961** Barbeau *Ikon* 194: Joe could wipe out...division headquarters...if he wanted to. **1963** *Sat. Eve. Post* (July 27) 25: Joseph Stalin is dead, but the enemy is still called "Joe," the name he acquired right after the armistice when the command started discouraging the use of "gook" and "gooney." *Ibid.* 30: Now, remember, if we make contact with one of Joe's patrols, we'll move to the south side. We'll stand there and let him pass. **1970** Former sgt., U.S. Army [ref. to 1967]: *Joe* is the North Koreans. They used to tell us, "When Joe jumps, you're all expendable." **1971** Sloan *War Games* 16: "Joe hasn't jumped. Everybody cool." Joe being the yellow man on the target silhouettes. *a*1993 Rishell *Black Platoon* 61 [ref. to 1950]: So that we would not draw fire from "Jo," the name we gave the North Koreans.

¶ In phrases:

¶ **by Joe** (used as a mild oath). Cf. S.E. *by Jove.*

1846 in *Utah Hist. Qly.* V (1932) 100: By Joe, it is rich. **1862** in *Manuscripts* XXX (1978) 17: There by joe said the yankey. **1865** in Hilleary *Webfoot* 55: They did, by Joe. **1899** F.E. Daniel *Rebel Surgeon* 234: Aneurism, by Jo! Man's dead. *ca*1943 (quot. at PRO).

¶ **not for Joe** [or **Joseph**] not for me; no.

*1844 in *F & H* IV 76: Not for Joseph! You asked me to tea. **ca*1867 in *F & H*: Not for Joe....Not for Joseph. **1869** in "M. Twain" *Stories* 21: "Help me out, please." "Not for Joe." **1870** *Comic Songster* 12: "Not for Joe," "Not for Joe." **1871** Crofutt *Tourist's Guide* 93: I don't want any of that mine; no, thank you, none for Joe. **1876** J. Miller *First Fam'lies* 6: The Camp silently but firmly shook its head, and said, "Not for Joseph." **1877** *Puck* (Apr.) 7: No, I 'pine not....Not for Joe. **1928* J. Galsworthy, in *OEDS*: Not if he knew it—not for Joe.

Joe *adj.* **1.** aware; in the know; HEP, 1. Also **Joseph.** Cf. JOE HEP.

1903 *Enquirer* (Cincinnati) (May 9) 13: *Joe* or *Joseph*—To get next. **1908** in Fleming *Unforgettable Season* 136: The various officials... always bar the way to those who are not Joseph to their elaborate system of graft. *a*1909 (quot. at JOE HEP). **1914** Jackson & Hellyer *Vocab.* 50: *Joe*...General currency. Wise; sophisticated. See "*hep*," of which "*Joe*" and "*Jake*" are subdivisions.

2. inconsequential; foolish; tedious. Cf. JOE, *n.*, 5.a.

1992 M. Myers et al. *Wayne's World* (film): I've had plenty of Joe jobs. Nothing you'd call a career.

Joe Average *n.* an average man.

1936 Grayson *Stories for Men* 111: The trials and tribulations of Joe Average, alias the Man in the Street. **1948** Maresca *My Flag* 42: I used to believe that I was Joe Average. **1972** Friday *Secret Garden* 5: The sidewalk figure of Joe Average eyeing the passing luscious blonde. **1990** *CBS This Morning* (CBS-TV) (Apr. 30): Which will be the more common for Joe Average? **1992** *Donahue* (NBC-TV): They're looking for Prince Charming instead of giving Joe Average a chance. **1992–95** J. Mack *Abduction* 51: He experiences himself as a "Joe average" person.

Joe Balls *n.* Esp. *Mil.* a man who makes a show of toughness.—usu. considered vulgar.

1945 in *AS* (Oct. 1946) 238: *Joe Balls.* Degenerate form of G.I. *Joe* (Army) or *Joe Blow* (Marines). **1966–67** W. Stevens *Gunner* 83 [ref. to WWII]: He's from some lousy bomber squadron, another Joe Balls type like Bradeway. *Ibid.* 183: The dude who thought that his Joe Balls costume made him a soldier. **1970** N.Y.U. student: What is this, the Joe Balls Society?

Joe Blow *n.* an ordinary, unsophisticated fellow; the average working or (*Mil.*) enlisted man; an anonymous or nondescript person; in phr. **Joe Blow story** *Journ.* (see 1984 quot.). [It is perhaps coincidental that *Blow* is an actual albeit uncommon U.S. family name; braggadocio is probably implied in the bracketed 1867 quot., which appears to be unrelated to current usage.]

[**1867** in McConnell *Five Years a Cavalryman* 133: I'm Private Blow of the U.S.A./At first Bull Run I ran away,/If I'd been killed that fatal day,/I wouldn't be now in the Army.] **1924** *Our Navy* (Mar. 15) 30: Joe Blow...lets you look at this one. **1941** Kendall *Army & Navy Sl.* 8: *Joe*

Blow....means any soldier. **1944** in Hodes & Hansen *Sel. from Gutter* 4: They didn't merely want to know where Joe Blow is playing now. **1945** J. Bryan *Carrier* 81: Just so some Joe Blow can see his picture in his home-town paper. **1947** Devereux *Wake I.* 114: Pfc Joe Blow knew enough history to know what happened at the Alamo. **1956** Holiday & Dufty *Lady Sings the Blues* 86: But just let me walk out of the club one night with a young white boy of my age, whether it was John Roosevelt...or Joe Blow. **1962** G. Olson *Roaring Road* 119: I don't think it would sink in so fast with just any Joe Blow. **1965** Herndon *Sex & Racism* 158: If you mean, am I like the "average Joe Blow" in the streets—the answer is no. **1977** in C.G. Fuller *UFO Cong.* 344: Once...a professional academician steps outside the narrow field in which he was trained, he's no better than Joe Blow on the street. **1983** *Agronsky and Co.* (WKGN radio) (June 19): If we're confused, what about Joe Blow out there? **1984** in Terkel *Good War* 365 [ref. to WWII]: There were the Joe Blow stories. That's what they were called. Marine private so-and-so, somewhere in the Pacific....They were mostly the little human-interest stories. They'd appear in home-town papers. **1988** Rancour-Laferriere *Mind of Stalin* 16: Joe Blow's delusions of grandeur can never be quite the same as Joe Stalin's feelings about his *real* grandeur. **1988** Fussell *Wartime* 155: Pyle specialized in what his profession called "Joe Blow stories"—charming or odd vignettes of home-town boys designed for home-town consumption. *Ibid.* 158: It seemed that the correspondents sending back Joe Blow stories were all in Europe. **1991** C. Fletcher *Pure Cop* 202: Joe Blow...is cancelling his contract. **1994** D. Levin *From Battlefield* 13: We were the bards recruited to sing the deeds of the Joe Blows.

Joe Chink *n.* **1.** *Army in Korea.* Chinese Communist military forces. Now *hist.*

1950 in Fehrenbach *This Kind of War* 324: The Second Division sat on the hill/Watchin' Old Joe Chink get set for the kill. **1953** *Combat Forces Journal* (Feb.) 8: They don't have to worry too much about Joe Chink slipping up on them while they are on a listening outpost. **1953** IUFA *GI: Army Songs* 29: Old Joe Chink comin' down the pass/Playin' the burp-gun boogie on the C.O.'s ass. **1961** Barbeau *Ikon* 59: Joe Chink's on the other side of the hill. **1961** Crane *Born of Battle* 55 [ref. to 1950]: It'll keep me from freezin' before Joe Chink gets here. **1971** Cole *Rook* 214: There was nearly the equivalent volume of fire coming this away from Joe Chink too. **1982** Cox & Frazier *Buck* 40: Listen, sir, do you think we've stopped Joe Chink? **1984–88** Hackworth & Sherman *About Face* 97: We were set for Joe Chink.

2. *Narc.* a heroin addiction.

1973 "A.C. Clark" *Crime Partners* 8: A drug addict has to have that shit at certain times. It ain't like a drunk, when Joe Chink says it's time to fix it's time to fix, with no shit about it.

Joe Citizen *n.* a man who is a typical U.S. citizen.

1986 *Campus Voice* (Sept.) 62: Most police officers go through more adrenalin pumps in a shift than Joe Citizen does in a lifetime. *a*1990 C. Fletcher *What Cops Know* 23: And every Joe Citizen in the world has to flash their lights at you and tell you your lights are off. **1990** Ruggero *38 N. Yankee* 276: Start pulling Joe Citizen out of the workplace and America would sit up and take notice.

Joe College *n.* a typical college man.—often used derisively.

1932 (quot. at JOE, *n.*, 6). **1929–33** Farrell *Young Manhood* 342: You're all dressed up like Joe College. **1937** *Life* (June 7) 24: The successor to Joe College has yet to be glorified in fiction or made easily recognizable to the general public. **1939** Wald et al. *Roaring Twenties* (film): You know, all that Joe College stuff. **1942** in Kerouac *Letters* 27: With its orgiastic Joe Colleges. **1951** Lampell & Buchman *Saturday's Hero* (film): You wanna be Joe College. You want to...make believe you're a rich little snob like the rest of them. **1960** Bannon *Journey* 154: You look so—Joe College. **1962** Dougherty *Commissioner* 142: "You look like Joe College," she said. **1973** Lucas, Katz & Huyck *Amer. Graffiti* 44: Joe College strikes out. **1974** Fair *New Nonsense* 87: The Joe Colleges out drinking bootleg booze. **1978** S. King *Stand* 19: Now, you, Jess, you're joe college all the way. **1986** *Ampersand* (Fall) 11: At first glance the kid is Joe College. **1992** M. Gelman *Crime Scene* 96: I...looked too much like Joe College for them to trust me. *a*1994 in C. Long *Love Awaits* 103: I can get Joe College anywhere.

Joe Cool *n.* a man who is extremely COOL or HIP.—often used ironically. [The "Joe Cool" in 1949 quot. is a fictional character whose name is not explained.]

[**1949** W.R. Burnett *Asphalt Jungle* 20: Thank God for Joe Cool!] **1971** N.Y.U. student: They call me Joe Cool. **1975** Silliphant *Dr.*

Durant (film): Don't expect me to play Joe Cool the swinging resident with the nurses. **1978** J. Webb *Fields of Fire* 132: The angle is to put *Kersey* on the spot, and let the Colonel play Joe Cool and save us. **1980** L. Fleischer & C. Gore *Fame* 110: Michael…kept his offhand manner, Joe Cool. **1983** M.S. Peck *People of Lie* 26: Having resumed his Joe Cool manner, he rather facilely talked about these realities. **1984** Ehrhart *Marking Time* 89: I was perfectly happy to have them think I was Joe Cool.

Joe-dandy *n. West.* JIM-DANDY.

    1887 Francis *Saddle & Moccasin* 312: Can I make a *duck stew!*….Well, you may talk about your chickabiddies and your chick-aweewees, and your Smart-Alicks and your Joe-dandies, and daisies, but when it comes to making a duck stew I'm a darling! **1890** in *DA*: Ben is what is termed a "Joe dandy," and undoubtedly knows how to build grades in a rapid and workmanlike manner. **1913** J. London *Valley of Moon* 352: An' the horses are Joe-dandies. **1926** Branch *Cowboy* 57: Mounted on a "cutting pony" that was a "Joe-dandy," he made a figure…to admire. **1940** in Welsch *Got Yourself a Horse* 49: I do have one that's a "Jo Dandy."

Joe Doakes *n.* an average or unsophisticated man.

    1926 Norwood *Other Side of Circus* 77: We call him Joe Doaks—you know, sort of a rube. [**1935** Pollock *Und. Speaks: Doak,* a boob; sucker or chump.] **1940** *Time* (Mar. 25) 48: Ostensibly written by John Doe and Joe Doaques. **1941** Riskin *Meet John Doe* (film): He's Joe Doakes, the world's greatest stooge. **1943** *AS* XVIII 109: *Joe Doakes,* generic term for all ball players. **1945** *Nation* (Apr. 28) 480: John Doe and Joe Doakes, along with the Cabots and the Lowells. **1954** N. Johnson *Night People* (film): This is not Joe Doakes' son this time. **1958** Drury *Advise & Consent* 48: Take a letter to whom it may concern—Joe Doaks, Susie Soaks, and all the folks. **1963** D. Tracy *Brass Ring* 374: He'd forget he was Kelly Brinkman…and be Joe Doakes. **1967** K. Hepburn, in *Look* (July 11) 32: It may be perfectly logical to Joe Doakes for me to look my age, but it will NEVER be logical to me.

Joe Gish *n. Navy.* an ordinary or nondescript fellow; JOE BLOW.

    1928 *AS* III (Aug.) 453: *Joe Gish*—Midshipman John Doe. **1935** Lorimer & Lorimer *Heart Specialist* 182: You can only see "Joe Gish's Room"—a sample Midshipman's room. **1943** Wakeman *Shore Leave* 189: One cool rosy-fingered morning at dawn, Ensign Joe Gish was busily engaged in delivering a fish to a battleship of the Haruna class. **1945** in *Calif. Folk. Qly.* V (1946) 385: Any drafted or enlisted sailor is *Joe Gish,* while the civilian youth is *Joe Blow.*

Joe Goss *n.* [rhyming slang; prob. ref. to Joe Goss (*fl.* 1880), U.S. prizefighter] *Und.* a boss; person in charge.

    1923 T.A. Dorgan, in Zwilling *TAD Lexicon* 50: Joe Goss (that's the boss.). **1934** (cited in Partridge *Dict. Und.* 368). **1935** Pollock *Und. Speaks: Joe Goss,* the boss. **1941** in D.W. Maurer *Lang. Und.* 128: Right in front of the female Joe Goss. **1963** Westlake *Getaway Face* 11: They killed a Joe Goss that time….It would of been a good strike up to then. **1970** Thackrey *Thief* 242: You haven't touched bases with the head Joe Goss who runs the action there. *Ibid.* 287: I went to see the number-two Joe Goss, the one who had set it up, and sort of talked it over with him. *Ibid.* 350: That means he was the head Joe Goss. **1978–80** in Cardozo-Freeman *Joint* 510: *Joe Goss.* Boss.

Joe Hep *adj.* [cf. JOE, *adj.* and HEP; the eponymous orig. asserted by D.W. Maurer (*Lang. of Und.,* p. 64) cannot now be substantiated] *Und.* aware; clever; HEP. Also **Joe Hip, Joe Hept.** Also as *n.*

    1902 (quot. at HIP, *adj.,* 1). **1906** H. Green *Actors' Boarding House* 316: Was it my fault the old geezer can't get Joe Hep to which shell the pea's under? *a*1909 Tillotson *Detective* 86: One thief may say to his pal, "Are you hept?" or "Are you Joseph?" or "Are you jo hept?" His pal will say, "I'm wise." **1944** Burley *Hndbk. Jive* 15: "Pops, I'm tops," replied Joe Hipp. **1987** Mamet *House of Games* (film): What are you, Joe Hep? I didn't ask what you think.

joe-house *n.* JOE, 2.a.

    1922 E. Pound, in V. Eliot *Letters* 505: An inscription…in the…city hall jo-house at Charleston, S.C.

Joe Latrine, Joe Latrinsky see s.v. JOE, *n.,* 2.b.

Joe Lunchpail *n.* an ordinary working man. Also **Joe Lunchbox, Joe Lunchbucket.**

    1965–66 in Maurer & Vogel *Narc. & Narc. Add.* 353: Square apple, Joe lunch pail, lame. **1981** *Chicago Trib.* (Sept. 15): Some of them are even being sent to school to learn how to talk to "Joe Lunch Pail," as

one PR executive puts it. **1983** *Wash.* (D.C.) *Monthly* (May) 34: Joe Lunchbucket gets docked out of every paycheck. **1988** *CBS This Morning* (CBS-TV) (Aug. 17): So that's the Joe Lunchbox category people have been talking about. **1990** Univ. Tenn. instructor: But does it appeal to Joe Lunchbucket? **1992** *Time* (Aug. 24) 52: Like many a Joe Lunchpail, he wants to move to the suburbs.

Joe McGee *n. & adj.* (see quots.).

    1927 Kyne *They Also Serve* 14: Horses…who had made up their minds to go A.W.O.L. and quit being Joe McGees. **1935** Pollock *Und. Sp.: Joe McGee,* counterfeit; phoney; unreal. [**1938** in Partridge *Dict. Und.* 166: *Crow McGee*—not real, no good, a double crosser.] **1974** Cherry *High Steel* 139: "I don't want to…take any Joe McGees they send out."…A "Joe McGee" is a dumb, goof-off, careless ironworker. He is celebrated in the couplet: You can tell the Joes/By their fingers and toes. Nobody seems to know who the original Joe McGee was.…His name has labelled every klutz for the last thirty or forty years.

Joe Miller *n.* [earlier, S.E. for a joke book of the type of *Joe Miller's Jests* (1739), by John Mottley, named for the English actor and comedian Joseph Miller (1684–1738)] a usu. stale joke.

    *1816 Sir W. Scott, in *OED:* A fool and his money are soon parted, nephew: there is a Joe Miller for your Joe Manton. **1823** [J. Neal] *Errata* II 173: "It was like pulling the old fellow by the tooth, all round a barber's shop, and only charging sixpence." "*Joe Millar,*" he replied. **1841** *Spirit of Times* (Dec. 18) 499: She was as stale as the Joe Millers revamped for the New Orleans "Sap Tub." *1850 in *F & H* 67: Well, of all the vile puns I ever heard, that, which I believe to be an old Joe Miller, is the worst. *1870 in *OED:* Many of the anecdotes are mere Joe Millers. **1918–19** MacArthur *Bug's-Eye View* 73: A lot of Joe Millers were resurrected in this fictitious cheer. **1923** Ornitz *Haunch, Paunch & Jowl* 74: I pulls…a couple of good old Joe Millers…out. **1923** *N.Y. Times* VIII (Sept. 9) 2: *Joe Miller:* An old joke.

Joe-pan *n. Navy.* Japan.

    1854 McCauley *With Perry* 120: To my huge gratification I may say that the Joe-Pan Expedition or cruise is over.

Joe Roke *n.* [rhyming slang] smoke. Also **Joe Hoke.**

    1928 Sharpe *Chicago May* 288 [ref. to 1890's]: *Joe Roke*—smoke. **1978–80** in Cardozo-Freeman *Joint* 510: *Joe Hoke.* Smoke. Rhyming slang.

Joe Sad *n. Black E.* (see quots.).

    1929–32 in *AS* (Dec. 1934) 288: *Joe Sad.* Name applied to anyone unpopular or undesirable. **1983** *Reader's Digest Success with Words* 86: Black English…*Joe Sad* = "person without friends, unpopular person."

Joe Schmo *n.* [JOE, 5 + SCHMO] a nondescript, foolish, or unsuccessful fellow; a nobody. [For 1993 quot., cf. quots. with *ragman* at JOE SHIT.]

    1950 Jacoby & Brady *Champagne* (film): Do you think I enjoy being Joe Schmo from Kokomo every week? **1982** W. Safire, in *N.Y. Times Mag.* (Dec. 19) 19: *Joe Schmo* is best portrayed by Woody Allen. **1985** M. Baker *Cops* 289: They're just another Joe Schmoe out there looking for a job. **1992** D. Burke *Street Talk* I 207: Every Joe Schmoe thinks he can be president! **1993** G. Lee *Honor & Duty* 330: It's really Joe Schmoe the ragman.

Joe Shit *n.* the personification of a slovenly, stupid, or worthless fellow; a nobody. Also **Joe Shit the Rag Man, Joe Crap,** etc. [The 1838 quot. either euphemizes or adumbrates this expression; cf. JOE ZILCH and 1993 quot. at JOE SCHMO.]

    [**1838** *Crockett Almanac 1839* 28: My name's Joe Dowdle the rag-man. In Kentuck, they call me roaring and scattering Davy Crockett; but on the levee a rale Bengal tiger.] **1942** in Mailer *Ad. for Myself* 40: Listen, bud, you ain't talkin' to Joe Crap, see,—you watch what you say with me. **1949** in Hemingway *Sel. Letters* 680: They could not lick Joe Shit let alone Mr. Tolstoi. **1971** Former USAF airman: [In Libya in 1962] there was a guy they nicknamed Joe Shit the Ragman. **1966–80** McAleer & Dickson *Unit Pride* 25 [ref. to 1950's]: Jackie was just a plain-looking average Joe Shit the Ragpicker. **1983** Beckwith & Knox *Delta Force* 260: Both [Iranian generals] were intelligent and well educated and neither was "Joe Shit, the Rag Man." **1993** J. Watson & K. Dockery *Point Man* 296: They looked like Joe Shit the ragman. They needed shaves and haircuts and their uniforms were terrible.

Joe Six-pack *n.* the ordinary beer-drinking working man.

    1977 *L.A. Times* (Nov. 8) I 5: By that time Billy had become a sort of Joe Sixpack folk hero. **1981** *Time* (Dec. 21) 73: The learned historical reference is what distinguishes this talk from that heard from any Joe Sixpack in a neighborhood bar. **1982** W. Safire, in *N.Y. Times Mag.* (Dec. 19) 18: "How do you expect Joe Sixpack should react?"..."I don't think Joe Sixpack should be concerned in the least." **1987** V. Pozner, on *Larry King Live* (CNN-TV) (Dec. 7): I'd say that the average Russian lives very much like Joe Six-pack. **1990** *Evans & Novak* (CNN-TV) (Sept. 15): Joe Six-pack might say, "Why don't we do something about government waste?" **1990** *NBC News at Sunrise* (Oct. 25): Well, for Joe Six-pack you've got an increase in...taxes.

Joe Tentpeg *n. Army.* an ordinary enlisted soldier.
   1993 Carhart *Iron Soldiers* 103: Some acts...can't be explained away to Joe Tentpeg, the common junior enlisted man who carries a rifle [etc.].

Joe the Grinder *n.* [see GRIND, *v.*] Orig. *Black E.* a mythical figure presumed to seduce and usu. live off the wives and sweethearts of prisoners and military servicemen. Also **Joe De Grinder, Joe D. Grinder, Jody [the] Grinder.** Cf. JODY.
   1939 in Leadbitter & Slaven *Blues Records* 458: Joe De Grinder. **1943** in Viereck *Men into Beasts* 89: Joe D. Grinder, Henry explained to me with a smirk, is the guy who takes the inmate's place in bed with his wife or sweetheart while he is in jail. **1958–59** in Abrahams *Deep Down in Jungle* 170: Jody the Grinder, meet G.I. Joe. **1962** Killens *Heard Thunder* 9 [ref. to WWII]: Old Saunders Solomon standing up there daydreaming about his old lady and Jody Grinder already....I'll give a 4-F a break all right. I'll break Jody's mother-loving neck. *ca*1962 in A. Lomax *Where Blues Began* 293 [ref. to 1940's]: She's out with Joe the Grinder, if she's like the other gals. **1967** deCoy *Nigger Bible* 32: "Jody" is a contraction of "Joe-the-Grinder." ("Sweet spot finder"), whose balls weighed forty-four pounds [etc.]. **1973** D. Maurer, in McDavid & Duckert *Lexicog. in Eng.* 183: Chinese Joe the Grinder. **1978–80** in Cardozo-Freeman *Joint* 510: *Joe the Grinder.* A cad who moves in when the husband or boyfriend is in prison.

Joey *n.* **1.** a banjo.
   1884 Rowbotham *Prairie-Land* 146: An occasional performance on the "Joey," as the banjo is familiarly termed.

   2. [for *Joseph* Grimaldi (1779–1837), English clown] *Circus.* a circus clown.
   *****1889** Barrère & Leland *Dict. Slang* I 502: *Joey*...a popular synonym for clown, derivable from *Joey* Grimaldi, the great pantomimist. *****a*1890–96** F & H IV 67: *Joey*...(theatrical).—A clown. (From *Joey* Grimaldi). *****1896** G.B. Shaw, in *OEDS*: Common Joeys with red-hot poker and sausages. **1925** in *AS* (Feb. 1926) 283: I'm through with bein' a joey. Gettin' too old. **1931** *Amer. Mercury* (Nov.) 353: *Joey*, n. A clown. **1939** *Sat. Eve. Post* (Mar. 25) 18: Circus slang for clown is "Joey," in memory of the great Joseph Grimaldi. **1939** in A. Banks *First-Person* 202 [ref. to *ca*1890]: The Joeys used lard for taking off their make-up.

   3. a dolt.
   *****1990** Andersson & Trudgill *Bad Language* 88: "Stupid Person"...diphead,...goof,...Joey,...zombie. **1993** *Real World* (MTV): What a bunch of Joeys!

Joey *interj.* JIGGERS, 2.
   1993 N.Y.C. police detective, on *CBS This Morning* (CBS-TV) (July 1): You'll be driving down the street [in a squad car] and you'll hear the cry go up, "Joeyyy!" *Joey* means the police.

Joe Zilch *n.* [JOE, 5 + *zilch* (orig. unkn.; cf. ZILCH)] an ordinary or nondescript man; a nobody.
   1925 *Lit. Digest* (Mar. 14) 65: "Joe Zilsch" corresponds to "John Doe" in the college world, and is used indiscriminately to designate any one, usually with a humorous intention...."Zilsch" seems to have been coined at first as an imaginary instrument in an orchestra vaguely resembling the big bass horn. **1943** *Time* (July 19) 16: Joe Zilch guesses he doesn't have to put so much of his pay check into war bonds. **1962** Houk & Dexter *Ballplayers* 63: This here Joe Zilch of ours ought to win twenty next year with that Yankee infield behind him. *Ibid.* 138: They made Larry look like Joe Zilch up from the minors for his first trial.

jo-fired *adj. & adv.* ALL-FIRED.
   1824 in Thornton *Amer. Gloss.:* Whate'er joe fir'd racket they kept up. **1833** A. Greene *Among Nullifiers* 29: He's a jo-fired smart horse for all that. **1835** D.P. Thompson *T. Peacock* 168: I have lately found out a most Jo-fired discovery. **1845** Durivage & Burnham *Stray Subjects* 50: Always know'd Badger was a jo-fired fool. **1851** in *DA:* I don't

write my name as handsome as some, but it's Joe-fired plain. **1853** "P. Paxton" *Yankee in Texas* 219: The jo-fired mean whelp wouldn't stake me. **1858** [S. Hammett] *Piney Woods* 40: That jofired Stray Yankee went and put me down in the book. *Ibid.* 42: I was too jofired smart for that. **1861** in *DAE:* A Jofired Wagon-trade. **1977** C. Johnson, in C. Major *Calling the Wind* 388: Teach you everything I know, son, which ain't so joe-fired much.

John *n.* **1.** (used freely before a *n.* or *adj.* to create nonce expressions denoting a man who personifies or represents the specified quality, identity, or association). [Now far less common than JOE, 6; 1778 quot. sugg. a literary orig. For 1930, 1932, and 1935 quots., see SCISSORBILL, ROSCOE, and FINK.]
   1778 J. Adams, in *DAE:* I never was however much of John Bull. I was John Yankee and such I shall live and die. *****1826, 1834** (quots. at JOHN CHINAMAN). *****1831** B. Hall *Voyages* II 238: His feet...would very soon be snapped off by John Shark [a shark]. **1854** Sleeper *Salt Water Bubbles* 83: John Shark was at last compelled to give in. **1865** in H. Johnson *Talking Wire* 237: You must blame "John 'rappaho [Arapahoe]" for that. **1904** *Life in Sing Sing* 250: *John Yeg.* Safe blower who travels in the guise of a tramp. **1918** *Stars & Stripes* (July 19) 7: Old John Itch don't care who he picks on. *****1924** in *OED2:* John Citizen's Job. **1926** *AS* I (Dec.) 651: *John Hollow Legs:* a hungry man. **1930** "D. Stiff" *Milk & Honey* 106: I might pick cotton, but I don't think I will;/I'll leave it to be picked by some John Scissorbill. **1931** D. MacLean *Caught Plastered* (film): It's just a question of...giving old John J. Customer what he wants. **1931** D. Runyon, in *Collier's* (Sept. 26) 8: I put the old convincer on him by letting him peek down the snozzle of my John Roscoe. **1932** D. Runyon, in *Collier's* (June 11) 8: My friend outs with a large John Roscoe. **1935** E. Levinson *Strikes* 91: Outwardly they bore none of the distinguishing characteristics of John Fink. **1943** Farrell *Days of Anger* 326: He's John Dub, the dumb Americano. **1948** McHenry & Myers *Home Is Sailor* 207: We can't fight John Shipowner. **1965–71** *Qly. Jour. Stud. on Alcohol* XXXII (1971) 732: *Joe Bum.* A bum. Also *John Bum. John Alcoholic.* An alcoholic. Also *John Drunk.* **1973** Eble *Campus Slang* (Mar.) 2: *John Stud*—a male who *thinks* he is knowledgeable about styles and women. **1986** E. Weiner *Howard the Duck* 106: John Nobody, who you don't even have to return his damn phone calls.

   2. a male servant. Cf. *OED2* def. 1.b., and *****1633 quot. at **(5),** below.
   1807 W. Irving *Salmagundi* 9: The whole corps [of actors] from the manager...to honest *John* in his green coat and black breeches. *****1848** in *OED:* It was pitiable to see the other poor Johns slink off at this arrival! **1853** G. Thompson *Gay Girls* 15: "Make haste, Barney."..."All right, Mr. Wallingford," said the sagacious and well-pleased John. *****1906** in Partridge *DSUE* (ed. 8) 624: All men-servants are "Johns" at Shrewsbury. **1906** Cornell *Kenelm's Desire* 3: Father didn't bring up his girls to work, and ma'd have thought it a disgrace. She's always had a "John" of some description in her kitchen. I never saw ma do a day's work in the kitchen in my life.

   3. JOHN BULL.
   *****1814** in Wetherell *Adventures* 263: We are not franks but true blooded Johns! **1835** in Paulding *Bulls & Jons.* 47: Without being insulted or having some of their rowers taken away by John's boats. **1856** *Harper's Mag.* (Dec.) 125: Jonathan has not been as anxious as John to build monuments.

   4.a. (used, esp. in pidgin, in direct address to a man whose true name is unknown). Cf. CHARLIE, 2.a.
   *****1818** in *OED2:* This [Chinese] interpreter is called "John" by all the parties. *ca*1855 in R.W. Paul *Mining Frontiers* (opp. 108): Strings of Chinamen pass, and greet you in broken English with "how do you do, John?" **1868** in W.C. Davis *Orphan Brig.* 104: Hey, John!—what brigade do you belong to now? **1876** W. Wright *Big Bonanza* 385: How much-ee, John? **1919** *DN* V 37: *John*, n. Proper first name, applied to any male Indian by the whites. **1917–20** in J.M. Hunter *Trail Drivers* I 273: Indians saluted all white men by, "How, John!" **1923** Wheeler *Buffalo Days* 140: After a while, Anzi called out, "Oh, John." (It was customary for Indians to call all white men "John.") **1926** in Thomason *Stories* 244: All pelicans are amazingly dignified and answer to the name of "John."

   b. Esp. *West.* a Chinese man; (*also*) the Chinese collectively.—used derisively or patronizingly, esp. in direct address. Now *hist.* Cf. JOHN CHINAMAN.

[*1818 (quot. at (4.a.), above).] **1853** in *DA:* The May Adams brought 118 "Johns" from the terrestrial kingdom of heaven. **1850–54** F. Marryat *Mountains & Molehills* 300: A gorgeously dressed "John" emerged. **1854** Soulé, Gihon & Nisbet *Annals of S.F.* 384: Huge, gaudy standards...delight the saffron-colored Johns. **1858** in *Dict. Canadianisms:* The Johns had a high time, drinking brandy and eating fried hog. **1869** *Overland Mo.* (Sept.) 256: The first imperative necessity for us, having to deal with these people, is to understand them. This we shall not do until we stop calling them, indiscriminately, JOHN. *ca*1870 in Foner *Labor Songs* 110: Now Coolie labor is the cry,/"Pat" must give way to pagan "John." **1871** Crofutt *Tourist's Gde.* 204: The following bill will *settle* "John." **1873** Beadle *Undevel. West* 771: The melancholy "Johns," with glazed caps and black pig-tails. **1880** Sala *America Revisited* II 258: The newly arrived "John" gathers up his scanty effects. **1885** in Caughey *Mob* 101: There was a running to and fro and gathering of bundles that showed John was preparing to move out. **1894** in Dreiser *Jour.* I 240: As fast as one sporty John "goes broke" at...fan-tan another takes his place. **1898** Markey *Iowa to Philippines* 130: Some had pajamas that were made in the Celestial Kingdom and would look well on the almond-eyed "John" for whom they were intended. **1915** C. Peters *Autobiog.* 43: A Mongolian John and a Mexican Don. **1922** Rollins *Cowboy* 165 [ref. to 1890's]: If...the cook were a Chinaman [he was called] "John." **1923** H.L. Foster *Beachcomber* 376: In Mexico...the peons hate old John, and...the slaying of a "Chino" is considered diversion rather than murder. **1928** A. Young *On My Way* 87: "Where are you going, John?"..."Gettee out," said the Chinaman. **1932** Ford *Worst Taste* 184: When those Jap's were through, "John's" guns were as silent as Cal Coolidge!

c. *West.* an American Indian man; (*also*) American Indians collectively.—used derisively or patronizingly. Now *hist.*

1870 Duval *Big-Foot* 92 [ref. to 1840's]: We had outwitted "Mr. John" completely. *Ibid.* 94: This satisfied me at once that "Mr. John" had paid us a sociable visit during the night. **1891** in Davidson *Old West* 131: Then to John they'll say,/"You had better stop your fooling or we'll bring our guns to play." *Ibid.* 132: They only ask and pray to God to make John hold his base. **1977** T. McCoy *Remembers* 45 [ref. to *ca*1910]: To a cowboy...in search of stray cattle...every Indian he encountered was "John." The first thing cowboys...said when they hailed an Indian on the open range was, "Hello, John, how the hell are you?"

5. a gendarme; (*hence*) a police officer. Now *rare* in U.S. [Though accepted by *OED2,* the *1633 quot. is unlikely to represent this sense.]

[*1633 B. Jonson *Comp. Plays* 64: All constables are truly John's for the king,/What e'er their names are; be they Tony, or Roger.] [1858 [S. Hammett] *Piney Woods Tavern* 63: He larnt...to let the John Darmes hunt their own varmint.] **1888** Spear *Sailor's Story* 33 [ref. to *ca*1830]: Let us have some fun with the "Johny arms."...Here come the "gends" [*sic*] upon the double-quick. *1898 in *Austral. Nat. Dict.:* There was not a sign when the "Johns," as the police are called in that neighborhood, passed along. *1909 in Wilkes *Dict. Austral. Colloq.* 190: He had er John in tow...ther policeman was fer me. **1927** Shoup *Marines in China* 16: Now a little explanation to the one of the suave "Johns"...and you are on your way. *Ibid.* 146: The "Johns" are Moroccans....The Chink is very meek in the presence of these cops. **1938** Chandler *Big Sleep* 80: The local johns drop in every morning and watch me open it [*sc.* the safe]. I have an arrangement with them. **1940** Chandler *Farewell My Lovely* 216: The johns tied me to it. **1944** *Papers Mich. Acad.* XXX 599: Prison Jargon...johns, the police. **1966** R.E. Alter *Carny Kill* 54: He...winked and showed me a pair of handcuffs. "Off that john?...Why, for godsake?" *Ibid.* 94: Take that john's gun for a minute. *1975 in Wilkes *Dict. Austral. Colloq.* 190: Brumby Toohey...had the Provosts after him, instead of the Johns as of old.

6. *Union Army.* a Confederate soldier; JOHNNY, 3.c. Now *hist.*

1864 in *PADS* (No. 70) 39: We had a smart skirmish with the Johns who held a strong position. **1864** in Redkey *Grand Army* 116: But the Johns did not succeed in breaking through our lines. **1864** in J.W. Haley *Rebel Yell* 212: During the day it was quiet, but in the evening the Johns made up for any excess of inactivity. **1865** in W. Wilkinson *Mother* 334: The Victory is *ours,* and the "Johns" paid very dear for their "Attempt." **1896** in *War Papers* II 38: "How are you, John?" and "How are you, Yank?" rang pleasantly along the line.

7. *Naut.* a merchant seaman. Now *hist.* [The sense in *1726

quot., otherwise unexplained, appears to be 'a member of a pirate crew'; its relevance to the present usage is uncertain.]

[*1726 G. Roberts *4 Yrs. Voyages* 39: All the rest of the Johns, that were standing by, in a seeming friendly manner, told me, that it would be much better for me, to make a full and true discovery of every thing...which...they sought after.] *1888 R.L. Stevenson *Black Arrow,* in *OED* s.v. tarry-John: Long-headed tarry-Johns, that fear not fire nor water. **1890** Erskine *Twenty Years* 269: When a sailor was flush they called him "Jack" and treated him like a king; when his money was gone they called him "John" and turned him out. **1906** *Yachting Mo.* (Oct.) 452: The term is not heard now, but years ago a merchant seaman was never a "Jack" tar, as his naval brother, but a "John." A crew of men was spoken of as "the Johns," particularly in Liverpool.

8.a. a man; fellow. See also HONEST JOHN. [No continuity of usage can be shown between 1772 and 1884 quots.; indeed the precise nuance intended in 1772 quot. is somewhat obscure.]

1772 in Whiting *Early Amer. Provs.* 241: Mr. A. Z....would give us to understand that he is one Big John, of great consequence in the world. **1884** Hartranft *Sidesplitter* 148: Never did Paddy utter a better bull than did an honest John, who, being asked by a friend, "Has your sister got a son or a daughter?" answered, "Positively I do not yet know whether I am an *uncle* or an *aunt.*" **1896** S. Crane *George's Mother* 172: Some udder john'll git yer smoke. Come ahn! **1906** H. Green *Actors' Boarding House* 125: Want to be careful of those Johns on the other side [*i.e.,* in Europe]. They're not like we are. **1918** Streeter *That's Me* 69: Am going around with a new swell John and he writ this fer me. Itll make the fellos think Im a swell dame when you show it to them. **1923** McKnight *English Words* 62: The girls' list of names for members of the other sex is nearly as rich. Noncommittal in general are *dude, goof, john, jake, raspberry, yap, guy, kid.* **1925** *Sat. Eve. Post* (Oct. 3) 20: I'm a solid John in the community. **1927** in Brookhouser *Our Years* 172: You know there are some of these fancy Johns who look like they were the class....One of the Johns I met...steered me to it. **1937** in *AS* (Oct.) 232: Me and Melvina got a date with a couple of johns. **1943** *Yank* (Nov. 26) 18: Any John over here...can...wear the Asiatic-Pacific ribbons. **1944** Burley *Hndbk. Jive* 59: Hitler and his Johns are kicking the gong around in the layout across the drink. **1949** Bezzerides *Thieves' Highway* (film): Every John in the business'll know about apples by tomorrow morning. **1951** Sheldon *Troubling of a Star* 22: I've watched you johns on forward control. Okay, some of you have guts. **1957** E. Lacy *Room to Swing* 41: You haven't been seeing any other john. **1959** O'Connor *They Talked to a Stranger* 46: And some of these quiet Johns are just as dangerous as the ones that do all the talking. **1971** *Playboy* (Apr.) 149: The straight Johns were here because Zubin Mehta was going to conduct the Los Angeles Philharmonic....The denim...crowd...was here because Frank Zappa was going to play. **1980** in L. Bangs *Psychotic Reactions* 332: If I blasted whoever this john is it'd be no special treat. **1984** W. Gibson *Neuromancer* 51: Besides, you're a clever john.

b. *Army.* a recruit; (*hence*) an inexperienced soldier.

[*1883 in *OED:* My ignorance of the manners and customs of Sandhurst cadets prevented my knowing that "John" was a generic title applied to all first-termers.] **1917** *Editor* (Jan. 13) 33: Army Vernacular..."Rookey" or "John"—Recruit. **1918** *Baltimore News* (Oct. 24): You know they call a man who has seen no service a "John." Well, I am not a "John" any more. **1922** *Amer. Leg. Wkly.* (May 26) 14: "I got 'em all right," answered the john. **1926** *Sat. Eve. Post* (Sept. 25) 12: Why I'm outta C Company, yuh big John! **1926** Nason *Chevrons* 162: There's a John for you....He should have steered that messenger somewhere else. **1930** Barkley *No Hard Feelings!* 22 [ref. to 1917]: There were a lot of sunburned old soldiers fresh from service on the border, and others from the 15th Infantry, recently transferred from China. We liked them, all right, but we weren't so sure we liked having them call us "Johns." **1934** *Our Army* (Dec.) 25: Get under cover, you big Johns. **1941** *AS* (Oct.) 163: *Big John.* Recruit. **1955** *Tenn. Folklore Soc. Bull.* XXI 101: In the old Army [1916–17]...officers said, "Recruit," but soldiers called a new comrade "John." **1957** Willingham *Strange One* (film): Now stop acting like a dumb John!

c. *Army, USAF & USMC.* a lieutenant.—usu. specified as *first* or *second.*

1944 Ciardi *Saipan* 12: A circle of saucer-eyed GI's and Johns were inching toward the 29's. **1945** *AS* (Dec.) 261: A *second John* is a second lieutenant, usually a new one. **1942–49** F.A. Johnson *One More Hill* 4:

Three other second johns. **1952** Mauldin *In Korea* 108: What the hell is it to you if a captain wants to break in a new second john the hard way. **1955** R.L. Scott *Look of Eagle* 67: The second and first Johns—the lieutenants. **1956** *AS* XXXI (Oct.) 227: A Second Balloon, or Second John, a second lieutenant. **1962** Mandel *Wax Boom* 8 [ref. to WWII]: Did you see the new lieutenant?...Did you see the new John that just arrived? **1963** Doulis *Path* 41: If you men hear of any First John who's about to become captain, just let me know. **1964** Rhodes *Chosen Few* 18: First John, huh. **1966** Newhafer *No More Bugles* 160: I wonder what ass-backward second john got the idea to set up a perimeter way the hell down near Saigon. **1971** Cameron *First Blood* 26: A worried looking Second John. **1974** Former SAC navigator, age 33: *First john* or *second john* is a first or second lieutenant. *a*1987 Bunch & Cole *Reckoning for Kings* 300: Second johns come and go.

9. (among tramps) a skillful professional tramp; (*also*) YEGG, 1.

   1900 (cited in Partridge *Dict. Und.* (ed. 2) 836). *ca*1920 *Hobo Songs* (unp.): The John got busy and took a risk. **1926** *Amer. Mercury* (July) 335: The hobo...sometimes works for his living; the john, or tramp...begs for it; the highway yegg...robs for it. **1927** (*AS* quot. at CAT, *n.*, 4). **1927** *DN* V 452: *John family...*Yeggs. **1928** Callahan *Man's Grim Justice* 132: The well-dressed boys were the Johns and the plingers, the professional tramps....The poorly dressed boys were the dynamiters, shovel stiffs, Gay Cats, Ring Tails, Ding Bats, the men who couldn't beg successfully, who are not recognized by the Johns and who are detested because they work now and then. **1948** J. Stevens *Jim Turner* 158 [ref. to *ca*1910]: We aim no trouble for any man who is good work stock and no john. **1980** Bruns *Kts. of Road* 92: But for years afterward yeggs paid homage to their fallen martyr—the best of the "Johns."

10.a. *Theat.* any man unconnected with the theater who attempts to fraternize with actresses or showgirls; JOHNNY, 1.c.; (*hence*) a man who patronizes burlesque shows.

   1908 McGaffey *Show Girl* 167: You'll go out and mace a good fellow for a big feed just as if he was a John. **1910** *Variety* (Aug. 13) 14: The chorus misses...love to have the "Johns" chase them. **1915–16** Lait *Beef, Iron & Wine* 197: Many a chorus girl preferred him to some flimsy John. **1921** *Variety* (Jan. 14) 10: He was [refused permission to interview a chorus girl], the manager intimating he believed Schuster to be a Syracuse "John" attempting to make a date with the girl. **1922–24** McIntyre *White Light* 29: Stage door Johns with patent leather hair, buck teeth and adenoidal smiles. **1941** "G.R. Lee" *G-String* 68: Gypsy's got a new John. **1960** Barber *Minsky's* 138: I now get notes in my box every day from three Johns who never made a play for anybody before except Mae Harris. **1971** in Boydell et al. *Deviant Behaviour* 539: [Many strippers have] a contemptuous feeling for...the "johns" and "marks" in the audience.

b. *Und. & Theat.* a gullible wealthy man who keeps or seeks a mistress, esp. a showgirl or prostitute (now *rare* except in homosexual use); (*also*) (*Prost.*) (now the usu. sense) a male customer of a prostitute.

   1906 *Nat. Police Gaz.* (July 28) 3: Why, I had a John in here and he was trying to buy me a new dress, and I thought he was wanting to know where I lived. **1904–11** D.G. Phillips *Susan Lenox* II 154: It's no fun having a John....A John's a sucker—a fellow that keeps a girl. Well, it'd be no fun to have a John unless you fooled him—would it? **1914** Jackson & Hellyer *Vocab.* 50: *John...*General currency amongst the demi-monde....a "sucker"; an amorous fool with money and free love proclivities...."She's got a John keeping her." **1921** *Variety* (Sept. 16) 9: The existence of a "John" is a travail and trouble if he dallies with Muriel DeForrest of "The Midnight Rounders."...Eimer became a John when seeing and knowing Muriel in Atlantic City....Muriel accepted everything that came her way from the New Yorker. **1927** McIntyre *Slag* 59: These dames always have a john around, some place. **1928** Sharpe *Chicago May* 58 [ref. to 1890's]: He [a prostitute's customer] was a degenerate....In the old days, almost all Johns, including the natural ones, were treated with scant courtesy by the minions of the law. **1937** Reitman *Box-Car Bertha* 174: When a "John," or customer, came in he was ushered into the parlor where half a dozen girls sat around. **1938** in A. Lomax *Mr. Jelly Roll* 127 [ref. to N.O., *ca*1905]: This is a highclass place. We don't want no poor johns in here. **1941** G. Legman, in G. Henry *Sex Variants* II 1169: *John* The regular lover...of a male homosexual prostitute. **1946** Mezzrow & Wolfe *Really Blues* 29: The girls sat there while the johns (customers) moped around and gave them the once-over. **1948** in Himes *Black on Black*

269: One of the prostitutes was dancing with a John. **1949** *Gay Girl's Guide* 11: *John*—NYC term for an *auntie* with financial potentialities. **1954** L. Armstrong *Satchmo* 95 [ref. to N.O., *ca*1915]: Our hustlers sat on their steps and called to the "Johns" as they passed by. **1959** Trocchi *Cain's Book* 35: Past forty, and with her blue look, Fay finds it difficult to interest a John. **1966** S. Harris *Hellhole* 89: This prostitute, Louise...says to me, "I make $150 a day lying on my back. There's a lot of Johns around, a lot of tricks." **1972** Kopp *Buddha* 106: Hookers...made it clear to me that the Johns...were suckers. **1972** *Anthro. Ling.* (Mar.) 104: *John...*A customer in a homosexual relationship who pays for sexual services, either by means of gifts or money, usually an older man. **1977** WINS radio news (Aug. 18): The people say they want the streets safe. They want the Johns to go home. **1978** Fisher & Rubin *Special Teachers* 3: Jim could hardly remember what he and his Times Square John had done together. **1984** J. McNamara *First Directive* 73: The prostitution scene: hookers, Johns, pimps, and assorted onlookers. **1988** Kienzle *Marked for Murder* 5: Who could depend on a john? **1995** *Jerry Springer Show* (synd. TV series): If a john is gonna treat me better than a pimp, then why not?

c. *Und.* a male victim of a swindle or other crime; (*also, derisively*) any law-abiding male citizen; SUCKER.

   1914 Jackson & Hellyer *Vocab.* 50: *John...*a man in a contemptuous sense...."Ask this John what time the train starts." **1922** *Variety* (Oct. 13) 7: Once inside, the racket began. Each girl grabbed a "John," dragging him to the money exchange desk, and from there to a roulette wheel. **1928** Sharpe *Chicago May* 35 [ref. to 1890's]: Sometimes the Johns (suckers) would...put up a holler. *Ibid.* 388: *Johns, suckers*—Men who are lured by crooks, mostly women. **1928** Callahan *Man's Grim Justice* 38: I've got an old John nibbling over here on my right. **1929** Hotstetter & Beesley *Racket* 230: *John*—Anyone who is an easy victim. **1940** *Current Hist. & Forum* (Nov. 7) 22: [Prison slang:] a *John* (a decent, law-abiding citizen). **1944** C.B. Davis *Leo McGuire* 128: He'll start leaving notes after each job trying to kid the john or the law. **1946** Gresham *Nightmare Alley* 152: One live John and we're set. **1954** Chessman *Cell 2455* 199: A square, a John, with its effete, futile, burlesque connotations. **1971** Cameron *First Blood* 86: That's the trouble with you workin' johns.

d. Esp. *Black E.* a gullible or unsophisticated fellow, esp. as in 1944 quot.; fool.

   [**1930** Irwin *Tramp & Und. Slang* 111: *John.*—A free spender, probably from John D. Rockefeller.] **1944** Burley *Hndbk. of Jive* 141: *John*—A square, jaded, white male seeking thrills in colored communities. **1947–52** R. Ellison *Invisible Man* 427: Get away from me, you dumb John. **1958** Hughes & Bontemps *Negro Folklore* 485: *John.* A dupe, a stooge, a sucker. **1961** Himes *Pinktoes* 51: In Harlem idiom a square is a lain, a doe, a John, a mark—in other parlance a fool, a chump, a sucker, a simpleton.

e. (among female homosexuals) a man who habitually associates with lesbians.

   1960 Bannon *Journey* 106: Who are they?...Johns?...Do they hang around gay girls all the time? *Ibid.* 178: He was no damn "John."...He was the detective. **1972** B. Rodgers *Queens' Vernacular* 71: Lecherous man who pesters [lesbian] women in gay bars...*john.*

11. money. Cf. syn. JACK.

   1871 (quot. at JOHN DAVIS).

12. [punning on the male given name *Jack*, a hypocoristic form of *John*] *Poker.* a jack.

   1906 *DN* III 143: *John...*Facetious name of the knave or jack in a pack of cards. **1928** Hecht & MacArthur *Front Page* 445: Two Johns. **1938** Baldwin & Schrank *Case of Murder* (film): Full house. Kings and Johns. **1951** *AS* (May) 99: *Johns.* A pair of jacks.

13.a. a toilet commode. Cf. earlier syn. CUZ JOHN. Cf. JOHNNY, 5.b. [The bracketed quot. appears in satirical verses addressed to Confederate Col. John Harralson [*sic*], who suggested in 1862 that urine might provide an inexpensive source of nitrates for the manufacture of gunpowder.]

   [*a*1866 *Lay of John Haroldson* [dedication]: To John [illus. of two chamberpots] This Work is Most Appropriately Dedicated.] **1942** in Mailer *Ad. for Myself* 48: I gotta put in fifteen johns on the third floor of the apartment house we're planning. **1951** Mailer *Barbary Shore* 111: I'm peeking through the keyhole to see fat papa on the john. **1953** Wicker *Kingpin* 60: Can you imagine Stalin sitting on the john? *ca*1953 Hughes *Lodge* 143: There were four beds in it and a john and a sink. **1960** D. Hamilton *Citizen* 47: The john flushed. **1967** Spillane *Delta* 112: She perched on the edge of the tub and I sat on the lip of the john and explained it to her. **1968** Stahl *Hokey* 7: Sitting on the john in his bathroom. **1978** Truscott *Dress Gray* 157: Johns were flushing, showers started and stopped. **1995** *New Yorker* (May 8) 75: And a case of toilet paper standing beside the john.

b. a lavatory; (*Mil.*) a latrine. Cf. JOHNNY, 5.a. [The assertion in R. Spears *Slang & Euphemism* (1981) that a sense 'privy' has existed "since the 1600s" appears to be groundless.]

   1932 *AS* VII 233: *John, Johnny*—a lavatory. **1935** H. McCoy *They Shoot Horses* 24: I was so weak I used to have to crawl to the john on my hands and knees. **1949** Bezzerides *Thieves' Market* 199: She hides in the john and won't come out. **1949** Robbins *Dream Merchants* 8: How did you ever guess that the one thing I wanted was a private john? **1950** M. Shulman *Sleep Till Noon* 113: She went to the john. **1953** Peterson *Giant Step* 48: In the john—the can, Gram. The Men's Room. **1958** T. Capote *Breakfast at Tiffany's* 25: Any gent with the slightest chic will give you fifty for the girl's john. **1968** Bogdanovich *Targets* (film): He just went to the john. **1980** L. Fleischer & C. Gore *Fame* 116: The girls' john. **1985** N. Black *Mischief* (film): I gotta go to the john. **1988** M. Felsen *Anti-Warrior* 7: Out back were crude, two-holer johns. **1994** *Frasier* (NBC-TV): Can you still get through the night without having to get up to go to the john?

14. the penis.—usu. considered vulgar. Cf. JOHN THOMAS. [Though not improbable, Thorne's 1990 assertion of 19th-C. currency lacks documentary foundation.]

   1918 in *Lyra Ebriosa* 10: Each man began to seek a place/To sink his festive John. **1927** [Fliesler] *Anecdota* 18: Now let's see how big your john really is. **1936** J.T. Farrell *World I Never Made* 376: He would be hot for Lizz, and his old john would stand up for her, and he'd go at her. **1938** "Justinian" *Amer. Sexualis* 26: *John. n.* One of the more popular U.S. euphemisms for the penis. **1941** in Legman *Limerick* 36: There was a young fellow of Harrow/Whose john was the size of a marrow. **1947–53** Guthrie *Seeds* 104: I wished for my hips to be just as pretty as you say your long john is. **1973** *AS* XLVI 82: Penis:…Peter…Dick…long John, John. ***1990** Thorne *Dict. Contemp. Sl.* 281: *John* is…a 19th-century personification of the penis.

15. the menses.

   1972 Hannah *Geronimo Rex* 36: When "John was home" the first time, that is, when she had her first menstrual period, she missed a day of school.…She…would say, "I was with John."

16. JOHN HANCOCK.

   1984 Knoxville, Tenn., woman, age *ca*45 (to another woman): Just put your John on the dotted line.

¶ In phrases:

¶ **for John's sake** (a euphem. for) for God's sake.

   1928–29 Nason *White Slicker* 270: How's he gonna walk, for John's sake?

¶ **goodbye, John** the end of everything; GOOD NIGHT.

   1885 *Puck* (June 17) 251: If…that crowd got hold of us, it was good-by, John. **1886** Nye *Remarks* 192: A man may lose all his wealth…but, when he loses his immortal soul it is good-bye John. **1914** D.W. Roberts *Rangers* 71: To lose a horse, right then, was "goodbye John" to the rider.

¶ **honest to John** honestly, truly. Also as adj.

   [**1933** quot. at *honest-to-God* s.v. HONEST.] **1953–57** Ruark *Old Man & Boy* 157: Now, honest to John, what is a feller going to say to this question? *a***1972** A. Shepp, in W. King & R. Milner *Black Drama Antho.* 50: A real live honest-to-john hard-on.

John B. *n. S.W.* a hat manufactured by the John B. Stetson Company.

   1933 *AS* (Feb.) 31: *John B.* A hat. No hat was worthy of the name unless it was a Stetson. **1933** J.V. Allen *Cowboy Lore* 6: The hat is known as a "John B" and ranges in price from $16.50 to $35.00. **1980** in *DARE*: The cowboy's most distinguishable feature was his wide-brimmed Stetson, sometimes called his "John B."

John Bates see s.v. BATES.

John-Brown *adj. & adv. So.* damned. Also **John-Browned.** See also *be John-Browned* s.v. JOHN-BROWN, *v.*

   1954 Killens *Youngblood* 160: He seems to be a John-Brown good teacher. **1987** Stage magician, Knoxville, Tenn., age *ca*65: I still can't work the john-browned thing.

John-Brown *v.* [ref. to the hanging of John Brown, U.S. abolitionist (1800–59)] Esp. *So.* to execute by hanging (*obs.*); in phr. **be John-Browned** to be "hanged" or damned.

   1869 *Overland Mo.* (Aug.) 130: You need apprehend nothing dreadful, for boobies seldom "John Brown" each other. **1870** *Overland Mo.* (May) 477: No White Man as respects hisself is ever gwine to do it. He'll be John-Browned fust. **1905** *DN* III 84: I'll be John(ny) Browned. **1924** in Clarke *Amer. Negro Stories* 27: if there's a monkey-chaser in Harlem can gyp him if I know it. **1928** R. Fisher *Jericho* 230: Well, I'll be john-browned. *ca*1965 IUFA *Folk Speech* [111]: I'll be John Brown if I'll do it. **1966, 1975, 1978** in *DARE* [all for *John Browned* 'damned'].

John Bull *n.* [after *John Bull*, a character in John Arbuthnot's *The History of John Bull* (1712)] Esp. *Naut.* an English or British sailor; an Englishman; a British vessel; the English or British collectively; Great Britain. Also **Johnny Bull.** Also as adj.

   1778 (quot. at JOHN, *n.*, 1). ***1803** in J. Ashton *Eng. Satires on Napoleon* 177: Johnny Bull Giving Boney a Pull. *ca*1809 in N.E. Cunningham *Pop. Images Presidency* 183: I've placed myself beyond the reach of John Bull & Boney. **1812** W. Dunlap *Yankee Chronology* 7: Johnny Bull now…lays her main top-sail to the mast. **1813** in Howay *New Hazard* 157: Got waist cloths for a review when we shall see John Bull. **1815** in Nevins & Weitenkampf *Cartoons* 29: Johnny Bull and the Alexandrians. ***1815** in J. Ashton *Eng. Satires on Napoleon* 399: Hell broke loose or the John Bulls made Jack Asses. **1815** Breckenridge *Mod. Chivalry* 613: Nothing offends…an Englishman [so much] as to be called a John Bull.—The nation is called John Bull; but that is a generic term; but when applied to the individual, [it] is not so well taken. *Ibid.* 671: Scalp a few Johnny Bulls. **1819** Noah *She Would Be a Soldier* II iii: At the battle of Queenstown, crossing to fight Johnny Bull. **1823** J.F. Cooper *Pilot* 278: Don't you see that Congress want us to cut up Johnny Bull's coasters. **1833** A. Greene *Travels* 203: He did lick the John Bulls, that's true. **1836** *Spirit of Times* (Feb. 20) 3: There's a John Bull for you. **1839–40** Cobb *Green Hand* I 89: Down here, you Johnny Bull, and learn manners from your betters. **1843** Field *Pokerville* 138: It takes an Ole not a *Johnny* Bull to find music in…the "American Bottom." **1845** in Thornton *Amer. Gloss.* II 327: John Bulls, Paddies, Pukes, Wolverines…Hoosiers, [etc.]. **1846** J.H. Ingraham *P. Fenning* 19: You don't see no such land-lubber work aboard John Bull. **1849** in Eliason *Tarheel Talk* 279: His round-tailed coat is altogether *John Bull.* **1853** Kelley *Disappointed Love* 11: No! you miserable John Bull! **1856** in C.A. Abbey *Before the Mast* 46: She proved to be another crack John Bull. **1859** in C.A. Abbey *Before the Mast* 218: To windward I discovered a Johnny Bull…ploughing along. **1860** Sleeper *In Forecastle* 88: We had fallen in with one of John Bull's cruisers. **1865** Williams *Joaquin* 41: Good thing for the John Bulls. **1868** Williams *Black-Eyed Beauty* 36: Oh! you peppered the big Johny Bull of a moll! **1869** in Boyer *Naval Surgeon* II 137: Saw a game of baseball played between some American and English officers. The Yankees had the best of the Johnnie Bulls. **1870** [W.D. Phelps] *Fore & Aft* 212: Here was a chance to…get ahead of Johnny Bull. **1871** in Botkin *New York Folklore* 45: What's that John Bull a-saying? **1906** H. Green *Boarding House* 82: Them Johnny Bulls are daffy over it. **1907** Cook *Border & Buffalo* 327: Say, my dear Johnny Bull, you are chock-full of sand. **1925** Robinson *Wagon Show* 111: This was too much for the Johnny Bull. **1977** Coover *Public Burning* 8: So whar's that Johnny Bull to stomp his hoof…at *my* Proklymation?

John Chinaman *n.* **1.** a Chinese man; the Chinese collectively.—used contemptuously or derisively. Also **John Chinee.**

   ***1826** in *OED2*: The seamen…not caring whether John Chinaman, as they called him, understood them or not. **1834** in *OED2*: They are required to…ascertain the height of John Chinaman in a breath. **1865** *Harper's Mag.* (May) 685: John Chinamen, with long tails rolled up on the backs of their heads. **1866** in B. Harte *Harte's Calif.* 27: As an individual, John Chinaman is generally honest. **1891** Campbell, Knox & Byrnes *Darkness & Daylight* 136: Dat ere kid…ain't got no more sand'n a John Chinee. **1903** *Independent* (Nov. 26) 2795: I surely don't envy John Chinaman his happiness in the Kingdom Come.

2. *West.* (see quots.).

   1936 R. Adams *Cowboy Lingo* 149: "John Chinaman" was boiled rice with raisins. **1939** Rollins *Gone Haywire* 137 [ref. to 1880's]: The only feasible menu … seemed … to be beans, "sow belly," … "saddle blankets" (griddle cakes), and "john chinaman" (boiled rice with raisins). **1950** in *DARE*.

John Crapeau see s.v. CRAPEAU.

John Davis *n.* money.—constr. with *the*.
   1871 Schele de Vere *Americanisms* 296: Among the less generally known terms [for money] are *John Davis* or the *Ready John*, sometimes simply *John* or *Ready, spondulics, dooteroomus*, often shortened into *doot; tow, wad…hardstuff* or *hard, dirt, shinplasters*, or simply *plasters; wherewith, shadscales*, or *scales…dyestuffs, charms*, and also the more modern designation of *stamps*. **1886** Nye *Remarks* 299: Eastern capital was furnishing the ready John Davis, if you will allow me that low term.

John Donkey *n.* a jackass.
   1859 in Walser *Tar Heel Laughter* 60: Sampson…with the jawbone of a John Donkey.

John Doughboy *n.* [JOHN, 1 + DOUGHBOY, 2] *Army.* the typical American infantryman of World War I. Now *hist.* Also **Johnny Doughboy.**
   1918 F. Gibbons *They Thought We Wouldn't Fight* 245: "Whoa, Johnny Doughboy, don't you get frightened,"…said one…gunner. **1921** *Amer. Legion Wkly.* (Oct. 14) 7: John Doughboy was always a cussin' citizen. **1934** Forrest *Behind Front Page* 180: Calico on the blond German frauleins looked like silk to John Doughboy. **1942** A. Goodhart & K. Twomey *Johnny Doughboy Found a Rose in Ireland* [pop. song] [N.Y.: Larry Spier, Inc.]. **1971** Faust *Willy* 15: The Floradoras were marrying too well to worry about Johnny Doughboy.

John Elbow *n.* [JOHN, 1 + ELBOW, 1] *Und.* a detective.
   1928 Sharpe *Chicago May* 286: Bulls, Dicks, Harness Bulls, John Elbows, or John Laws—police officers, depending on the kind.

John Farmer *n.* (esp. among itinerants) a typical farmer or farmers.—usu. used derisively.
   1927 (quot. at PLOW JOCKEY). **1929** Milburn *Hobo's Hornbook* 102: John Farmer needs a lot of men/To work beneath the Kansas dew. **1938** Holbrook *Mackinaw* 147: So that John Farmer, as lumberjacks somewhat disdainfully termed husbandmen, could get on with his work. **1948** Chaplin *Wobbly* 87 [ref. to ca1908]: Sometimes we would walk into town to look for a job; sometimes "John Farmer" would hire us in the "jungles," where we cooked our meals, usually near a bridge or water tank. **1970** Boatright & Owens *Derrick* 160: Well, by golly, John Farmer's sand has produced lots of oil.

John Hall *n.* [JOHN, 1 + HALL] (among tramps) alcoholic liquor.
   1927 (quot. at HALL).

John Hancock *n.* [alluding to the boldness and legibility of John Hancock's signature on the Declaration of Independence] (one's) signature; (rarely) (one's) name.
   [**1846** in *DARE*: Avoiding…the pretentious boldness of John Hancock…I subscribe myself Yours very truly.] **1887** [C.C. Post] *10 Yrs. Cowboy* 338: Would you mind tellin' me if this is your "John Hancock"? **1902** Cullen *More Tales* 66: I'll be…at the Harrison street station, with "false pretences" opposite my John Hancock on the blotter. **1902–03** Ade *People You Know* 150: He got through filling the Blank Spaces with his John Hancock. **1903** McClallen *He Demons* 95: This grand "Sneezer" beholds the "John Hancock" of some one of our "forty cent" aristocrats attached to the letter of introduction. **1914** Jackson & Hellyer *Vocab.* 50: *John Hancock*…A signature. **1915** Bronson-Howard *God's Man* 261: Put your neat little John Hancock along with March's. **1936** Steel *College* 326: He'd tear up the ten grand worth of IOU's he held with your John Hancock on 'em. **1987** *Miami Vice* (NBC-TV): Is this your John Hancock, Trudi? **1991** *Bill & Ted's Excellent Adv.* (Fox-TV): I need a John Hancock on line 6. **1993** *CBS This Morning* (CBS-TV) (Nov. 5): I'm going to put my John Hancock right here. **1994** *TV Guide* (July 16) 1: His collection includes the John Hancocks of…Washington…[and] Lincoln.

John Hancock *v.* to sign one's name to.
   1967 Colebrook *Cross of Lassitude* 105: Baby, you're going back to Wentworth jus' as soon as that judge can John Hancock the papers. **1984** MacRauch *Buckaroo Banzai* (film): Just John Hancock this, sir.

John Harvard *n.* a male student at Harvard University.
   1979 Charyn *7th Babe* 33: They were from South Boston, where all the "John Harvards" were afraid to go at night.

John Haultaut var. JOHNNY HAULTAUT.

John Henry *n.* **1.** the penis.—usu. considered vulgar.

*ca***1888** *Stag Party* 217: "John Henry" is hard as a bone. *ca***1915** in Logsdon *Whorehouse Bells* 54: He pulled John Henry out of her, and put it in his pants. **1916** Cary *Venery* I 159: *John Henry*—The penis. **1944** *PADS* (No. 2) 34: *John Henry*…In S. Va. and upper S.C.: the penis. **1963–64** R.P. Warren *Flood* 32: "Poor little John Henry," she murmured. **1973** Gent *N. Dallas* 152: John Henry was achin'. **1994** "G. Indiana" *Rent Boy* 73: He starts rubbing his ass lips against the head of my john henry.

2. JOHN HANCOCK.
   1914 *DN* IV 109: *John Henry* or *John Hancock.* Autograph. **1917** in Truman *Dear Bess* 227: I…asked Captain Jobes if he would lend me three thousand dollars on my John Henry to start one. **1933** *AS* (Feb.) 31: *John Henry.* Signature. A cowboy never signed a document; he put his John Henry on it. **1940** Jones & Houser *Dark Command* (film): If you're lookin' for excitement, put your old John Henry down on the paper. **1943** Wray & Geraghty *Falcon & Co-Eds* (film): OK, sister, what's your John Henry? **1959** Lederer *Never Steal Anything Small* (film): When you get your John Henry on these, I've got a new job for you. **1976** W. Johnston *Sweathog Trail* 36: If you'll just put your John Henry here…and here…and here. **1966–80** McAleer & Dickson *Unit Pride* 449: Put your John Henrys right here.

John Indian *n. Army.* American Indians collectively.
   1857 in Stacey & Beale *Uncle Sam's Camels* 111: We returned to camp, and tonight there will be no guard set over old "John Indian" and if he wants to go he may. *ca***1875** Bemrose *Seminole War* 46: We watched through the night…hoping not to see John Indian.

John Law *n. Orig. Und.* a law officer; (now *usu.*) the police or forces of the law collectively. Also **Johnny Law.**
   1906 J. London *Moon-Face* 44: We go mooching along the drag, with a sharp lamp out for John Law. **1907** J. London *The Road* 107 [ref. to ca1893]: John Law would never find me there. **1912** Livingston *Curse* 17: Every policeman—called in the vernacular of the road "John Law"—had become my deadly enemy. *Ibid.* 32: It was a "John Law." **1922** Tully *E. Lawler* 190: A fellow can't beat John Law. **1925** *Collier's* (Sept. 19) 7: I…turned down Barbara's offer to make me a John Law. **1926** Norwood *Other Side of Circus* 268: This here John Law insisted that he'd have to attach something belonging to the show. **1926** *AS* I (Dec.) 651: *Johnny Law.* detective. **1929–30** Farrell *Young Lonigan* 78: He was proud of the way he had given Johnny Law the slip. **1930** "D. Stiff" *Milk & Honey* 43: The Bible Belt John Laws like…to raid a hobo jungle and…chase the hobos through the cane brakes. **1936** Duncan *Over the Wall* 42: Forces of John Law were literally brushing my heels. **1942** L.R. Foster *Mayor of 44th St.* (film): A guy named John Law came in and asked him some questions he couldn't answer. **1955–57** Felder *Collegiate Slang* 3: *John Law*—the police, mainly those who checked I.D.'s. **1968** Gover *JC* 62: With the johnlaws up one side an the pimps down the other. **1973–74** M. Smith *Death of Detective* 224: Fuck you, John Law! **1975** S.P. Smith *Amer. Boys* 100: Bip! he hit Johnny Law right in the neck. **1980** *AS* (Fall) 197: Heat,…hog,…Johnny Law. **1995** *Leeza* (synd. TV series): Him and his little brother tried to play Johnny Law that time.

John L's *n.pl.* long woolen underwear; LONG JOHNS.
   a*1940** in Hugill *Shanties from Seven Seas* 405: So I had to pop me suit, me John L's an' me boots/Down in Park Lane pawn shop Number Nine. **1940** *AS* (Apr.) 212: *John L's* is the sobriquet applied to the trunks of our heavy winter underwear. **1941** Kendall *Army & Navy Sl.* 8: *John L's.*…woolen underwear.

Johnny *n.* **1.a.** a young fellow; (*Naut.*) a fellow seaman; a ship's crewman.
   *****1724–27** in *F & H* IV 71: Where she that is bonny/May catch her a johnny,/And never lead apes below. *****1803** in *OED:* The Johnnys rubbed their hands. *****1831** B. Hall *Voyages* III 316: By witchcraft,…in the opinion of the Johnnies. *****1832** B. Hall *Voyages* (Ser. 2) I 233: If the captain be influenced by any petty motives…the Johnnies will see through it all. *****1832** B. Hall *Voyages* (Ser. 2) III 282: The words Marine and Mariner differ by one small letter only; but no two races…differ from one another more completely than the "Jollies" and the "Johnnies." **1839–40** Cobb *Green Hand* I 158: Crack away, my Johnny, you can make killing no murder, but you can't easily mend the shot-holes in your best bower cable. *****1889** in *F & H* IV 69: A straight line is the way you Johnnies will go…when I've done with you. **1908** Paine *Stroke Oar* 177: You are a bully good lot of Johnnies. **1912** *N.Y. Tribune* (Apr. 21) (Mag. Section) 14: Ugh! Pleasant johnny, I must say! **1914** Knibbs *Outlands* 56: Not a Johnnie in the reg'ment says a word

about the flag. **1918** King *Bk. of Chanties* 19: Heave away, my Johnnies, heave away! **1923** Platt *Mr. Archer* 325: The hardest-hittin' Johnnies in the land. **1927** "S.S. Van Dine" *"Canary" Murder Case* ch. xvi: "Who are they thinking of arresting?"..."A johnny named Skeel." **1943** G. Biddle *Artist at War* 35: A little stumpy, muscle-bound, bow-legged English Johnny...was crossing the square. **1968** W.C. Anderson *Gooney Bird* 76: The FAC johnny reconfirms the target area he's marked with the grunts. **1994** Calt *Rather Be Devil* 109: World War One veterans, whom he termed "Johnnies off the front."

b. a jaunty but shallow or soft fellow; a vacuous young man about town.

*1883 in *F & H* IV 69: Ah! who is more brave than your Johnny of note,/With his showy shirt-front and his dainty dust-coat. *1889 in *F & H:* He...did not intend to leave her, as many a Johnny would have done. **1895** in *DA* s.v. *kill*, v.: A picturesque young "Johnny," dressed to kill. **1899** Boyd *Shellback* 13: One of them, jerking his head toward me, remarked that "he s'posed I was the Johnny as owned the leather bag." **1902** in "O. Henry" *Works* 97: He's tryin' to do de Johnny act. **1906** (quot. at TINHORN). **1916** in Roy *Pvt. Fraser* 81: He remarked...in a very effeminate manner...that he must have his tea. We thought him a regular Johnnie. **1942** "D. Ormsbee" *Sound of American* 14: Modern Johnnies couldn't teach their grandmothers to suck eggs.

c. *Theat.* (see 1915 quot.); JOHN, 10.a.; usu. in phr. **stage-door Johnny.**

1904 *Life in Sing Sing* 250: *Johnny*—A person who enjoys himself in the company of ballet girls. **1906** H. Green *Actors' Boarding House* 149: Johnnies is better kep' off. **1915** [Swartwood] *Choice Slang* 51: *Johnnies* (stage-door)—Young men who frequent the stage door of theaters for the purpose of meeting and enjoying the companionship of actresses and chorus girls. **1923** Toomer *Cane* 94: Stage-door johnny; chorus girl. **1925** Dos Passos *Manhattan Transfer* 27: I guess the Johnnies wont let her get by the stage door. **1927** [Fliesler] *Anecdota* 143: Two old Johnnies were discussing a proposed trip abroad. **1987–90** M.H. Kingston *Tripmaster Monkey* 15: He was a Stagedoor Johnny, then a backstage electrician, then emcee on stage. **1990** Citino *House of Memory* 45: Like platinum chorines and stage-door Johnnys.

d. [infl. by JOHNNY RAW and JOHNNY-COME-LATELY, but cf. (a), above] *Naut.* (obs.) *& Fire Dept.* a new man, esp. if inept.

1900 Hammond *Whaler* 388: The *bill*, yeh darned mummy of a *Johnny*, yeh!...You're a *Johnny*, and that's all yeh be—jest a Johnny. **1903** *Naval Apprentice* (June) 34: In a milder sense *Jackie* is expressive of derision. So with *Johnnie*, a word...for a novice, a raw hand, or a "greeny." **1944** *Amer. N & Q* (Apr.) 5: *Johnny*. A recently appointed fireman with little experience in fire-fighting. **1971** D. Smith *Engine Co.* 41: One of the younger guys, or "johnnies," will go to the store. **1984–89** Micheels *Braving Flames* 18: I was a new fireman, what they call a Johnny.

2. JOHN, 1.

1817 (quot. at JOHNNY CONGRESS). **1862** (quot. at JOHNNY REB). **1862** Duganne *King's Man* 50: Dis yer soljer-chile knows de bark ob Johnny Bull-dog [cannon; see BULLDOG, 1.c.]. **1863** in C.E. Stedman *Sketchbk.* 160: It was too much for Johnny Secesh. **1863** in *DA:* Stirring up Johnny Navajo. **1864** in J.W. Haley *Rebel Yell* 219: A Reb who thought himself *smart*...Johnny Smart hunted his hole. **1867** Clark *Sailor's Life* 38: Pilot Fish and Johnny Shark. **1918** (quot. at JOHN DOUGHBOY). **1924** Henderson *Keys to Crookdom* 409: *Johnny Yegg*—Safe-blower. **1996** *New Yorker* (Sept. 23) 82: Now, how did it work?...The scam....How much did you take in before Johnny Fuzz?

3.a. (used in direct address to a man whose true name is unknown).

*1842 in *OED2:* Addressing us as "Johnny," [they] were very officious in offering their services. "Johnny" is, in this part of the country, the national appellation of an Englishman by the lower orders of Spaniards. **1869** "G. Ellington" *Women of N.Y.* 302: [The prostitutes] are bold and openly solicit you, calling every one Johnny. **1889** B. Harte *Dedlow Marsh* 190: Well, Johnny, what's your name? **1898** Brooks *Strong Hearts* 104: Say, Johnny, wasn't that President Grant? **1938–39** Dos Passos *Young Man* 57: "What's your hurry, Johnny," came a low hoarse voice. **1943** G. Biddle *Artist at War* 190: Hello, Johnny....Wanna glass wine? **1952** Brossard *Darkness* 135: What's on your mind, Johnny? **1956–60** J.A. Williams *Angry Ones* ch. xxi: "Look, Johnny...I'm trying to help out." "Thanks. The name's Mr. Hill, not Johnny." **1977** Coover *Public Burning* 116: This ain't just another ballgame, johnny.

b. a Chinese man; JOHN, 3.b.

1857 in *DA: He* knows. He's seed the *Johnnies* goin' into that there doorway next block. *a1870* in *DAE: Johnny*...A Chinaman.—Recent use in Cal., &c.

c. *Union Army.* a Confederate soldier; JOHNNY REB, 1; Confederate troops collectively. Now *hist.*

1862 in *Jour. Ill. Hist. Soc.* XVIII (1926) 833: The Johnnies halted. **1862** Galwey *Valiant Hours* 63: Captain Butterfield...assured them that the "Johnnies" could not successively put three shells in the same place. **1863** Connolly *Army of the Cumberland* 49: Some "Johnnie" in the cedars who was a tolerably good shot sent a bullet through my overcoat collar and down I went. **1863** in Swinfen *Ruggles' Regt.* 99: The heavy long rifles...are our advantage, and Johnny knows it. **1864** in *Civil War Hist.* XXVIII (1982) 335: Johnny assaulted our rifle pits in force last Thursday. **1865** Andrus *Letters* 132: *Our Div* (the 3d) remains at this place to see that the *Johnnies dont eat each other up.* **1879** in R. Cowden *Brief Sketch* 113: The Johnnies brought up...the old stars and stripes and trailed it in the dust. **1887** Hinman *Si Klegg* 249: I've hearn 'em call the Johnnies, graybacks, but I didn't know there was any other kind. **1887** J.H. Wilson *Life Gen. Alexander* 127: He replied that there were "too many Johnnies" on the road for him. **1892** Frye *From Headquarters* 57: Oh, yis, th' Johnnies practised on me a little. **1917** Kuykendall *Frontier Days* 74: As though he were...about to engage an army of "Johnnies." **1927** E. Stockwell *Pvt. Stockwell* 86: He found the boys having a talk with the Johnnies, as we called them.

4. JOHN, 5.

[*1838 Glascock *Land Sharks* II 168: D'ye think as these here thundrin' Johnny Darmeries knows the true bearin' o' the place?] *1851 H. Mayhew *London Labour* II 154: If you was known to touch the traps, you'd git hauled up afore the beak....The "Johnnys" on the water are always on the look out, and if they sees...us, we has to cut our lucky. *1886 in *OED2:* Constables used to be known as "Johnny Darbies," said to be a corruption of the French *gensdarmes*, and they are still occasionally called "Johnnies." **1933** Ersine *Pris. Slang* 47: *Johnny*, n. a uniformed patrolman.

5.a. a privy or lavatory; JOHN, 13.b.

*1850 Halliwell *Dict. Archaic & Prov. Wds.* (ed. 2): *Johnny*...A jakes. These terms are clearly connected with each other. Also called Mrs. Jones by country people. **1932** (quot. at JOHN, 13.b.). **1934** O'Hara *Samarra* ch. iv: "No, not exactly. Kitty Hofman came in the johnny while I—" "God, you women, going to the can together!" **1940** Zinberg *Walk Hard* 95: The poor bastard is taxed on everything from the cat to the lousy outdoor johnny. **1941** in W. Burnett *Best* 609: And in the "johnny" Tod de Tocqueville's murals. **1941–42** Gach *In Army Now* 27: In the train's lady's johnny. **1954** Collans & Sterling *House Detect.* 143: The johnny stalls...were about an inch and a half narrower than those in modern establishments. **1956** M. Wolff *Big Nick* 117: Jamie and I introduced ourselves while you were in the johnny. **1960** Albee *Amer. Dream* 7: Try to get the leak in the johnny fixed. **1974** Shaara *Killer Angels* 24: The whole...mess...aint fit to lead a johnny detail.

b. a toilet commode; JOHN, 13.a.

1943 in P. Smith *Letters from Father* 229: On the johnnie. **1943** in Kochendoerfer *Woman's War* 11: Cleaning johnnies or scrubbing floors. **1953** Wicker *Kingpin* 23: I haven't had so much fun since Grandma fell through the johnny-seat. **1961** Terry *Old Liberty* 8: The hinges were mostly undone on the johnny seats. **1965** Gallery *Eight Bells* 136: My johnny was warmed by the fannies of many Very Important People. **1970** *Nat. Lampoon* (May) I 2, 8: I marched right into the bathroom and flushed the pot drug...right down the johnny! **1987** C.M. Carver *Amer. Reg. Dials.* 114: A *johnny* and a *commode* are toilets [in the South]. **1987** *Wkly. World News* (Sept. 8) 43: The prehistoric johnny was discovered in a Swedish peat bog.

6. the penis; JOHN, 14.—usu. considered vulgar.

[*ca*1930 G. Legman, in *F & H* I (rev.) (1966 ed.) lxx: One thrust his Johnnie Long into her Shorts.] **1942** H. Miller *Roofs of Paris* 28: It doesn't make any difference to Johnny what color she is. **1947–53** Guthrie *Seeds* 290: My Little Johnny's gonna be lots madder...if you don't let him come in. **1957** IUFA *College Songs: Bawdy Parodies:* I laid fifty cents in the palm of her hand/and she tickled my belly till my johnie did stand. **1986** *UTSQ:* Penis...*Johnny.*

7. *Poker.* a jack; JOHN, 12.

1936 Kingsley *Dead End* 704: Angel. (Reveals a pair of Jacks.) A pair of Johnnies.

8. *Hosp.* a hospital gown.

1958 *AS* XXXIII (Feb.) 75: [Common in Boston area hospitals from *ca*1900, but apparently unknown elsewhere.] **1985** Frede *Nurses* 73: I still can't get any johnnies from the laundry. *Ibid.* 90: You haven't got enough linen and johnnies.

9. a condom. *Rare* in U.S.; labeled as exclusively British in *ODMS*.

*1965 (cited in *ODMS*). *1970 in *ODMS*: Full intercourse without a johnny. **1973** *TULIPQ* (coll. B.K. Dumas): Prophylactic: a *johnny*.

Johnny *adj. Union Army.* Confederate. Now *hist.*

1863 in Mohr *Cormany Diaries* 390: Geese, Turkeys, [etc.]...somewhat reluctantly given to the Boys at times by Johnie Farmers. **1864** in O.J. Hopkins *Under the Flag* 235: We resembled a company of Johnny cavalry. **1864** in C.W. Wills *Army Life* 294: Six Johnnie lines of battle debouched from the woods. *ca*1885 A.C. Stearns *Co. K* 298: The next morning the Johnnie pickets would apologize for the shots being fired. **1934–41** in Mellon *Bullwhip Days* 216 [ref. to Civil War]: All the Johnny money is in there.

Johnny Arm *n.* [pun on *gendarme*] *Naut.* a gendarme.

1888 Spear *Old Sailor* 33 [ref. to N.O., *ca*1830]: We bade adieu to the French gendarmes, or police....I said to the crew, let us...have some fun with the "Johny arms."

Johnny-at-the-rat-hole *n.* JOHNNY-ON-THE-SPOT.

1906 H. Green *Actors' Boarding House* 19: I'm Johnny at the rathole to-night for some white meat. **1908** W.G. Davenport *Butte & Montana* 151: The X-Ray [a newspaper] will be Johnny-at-the-rat-hole. **1937** in D. Runyon *More Guys* 118: As a rule, Harley is Johnny-at-the-rat-hole when it comes time to scoff.

johnny bar *n.* [var. JOHNSON BAR] *Trucking.* (see quot.).

1990 Rukuza *West Coast Turnaround* 26: Eddie dropped the johnny bar..., locking the trailer brakes while leaving the tractor tires rolling free.

Johnny-be-damned *n.* a gendarme.

1847 in Blair & Meine *Half Horse* 119: De Jonny be dams was a comin'!

Johnny Bull var. JOHN BULL.

Johnny Butternut *n.* [JOHNNY, 2 + BUTTERNUT] *Union Army.* Confederate troops. Now *hist.*

1863 in Swinfen *Ruggles' Regt.* 23: Johnny Butternut is not very good natured.

johnnycake *n.* a New Englander, esp. a rustic.

1834–40 Dana *2 Yrs. Before Mast* ch. viii: I've been through the mill...and come out a regular-built down-east johnny-cake. **1842** Dickens *Amer. Notes* 58: Down Easters and Johnny Cakes can follow....I an't a Johnny Cake....I am from the brown forests of the Mississippi. *a*1850 in *N.E. Folklore* I (1955) 56: The ladies from the windows cried, "There goes a johnny cake."

Johnny-come-lately *n.* a naive young fellow; a raw or unqualified newcomer. Now *colloq.* or *S.E.*

1839 Briggs *H. Franco* I 249: "But it's Johnny Comelately, ain't it, you?" said a young mizzen topman. **1855** *Harper's Mag.* (Dec.) 37: The yaller fever....It don't take the acclimated...but let it catch hold of a crowd of "Johnny come latelys," and it plants them at once. **1859** in *New Eng. Qly.* LXIII (1990) 542: Johnny Come Lately...is the comedy of my forecastle life. **1893** in F. Remington *Sel. Letters* 163: Johnnie come-lately. **1926** Norwood *Other Side of Circus* 112: A First-of-May....Sometimes they're called Johnny-come-latelys, especially if they are clowns just starting in the business. **1929** *Sat. Eve. Post* (Oct. 12) 29: *Johnny-Come-Lately:* A novice pitchman. **1975** Dillard *All-American English* 33: It is likely that...*Johnny-come-lately* [is] Pidgin. **1995** *Talk Soup* (E! TV) (May 28): *They* won an Emmy. You're just a Johnny-come-lately.

Johnny Congress *n.* the U.S. Congress.

1817 in *DA*: What roaring cheer/Was spent by Johnny Congress O! **1827** in *DA*: In the rural, but significant speech of the swains, this body is called Johnny congress.

Johnny Crapeau see s.v. CRAPEAU.

Johnny Gow *n.* [orig. unkn.] *U.S. Nav. Acad.* the study of mechanics.

1922 Taylor *Song Book of Nav. Acad.* 27: We have studied Navigation, Seamanship and Higher Math, English, Spanish, French and Johnny Gow. **1928** *AS* III (Aug.) 453: *Johnny Gow.* The subject of Mechanism.

Johnny Grab *n. Pris.* (see quot.).

1848 *Ladies' Repository* VIII (Oct.) 315: *Johnny Grab,* An executioner; hangman.

Johnny Grayback *n.* [JOHNNY, 2 + GRAYBACK, 3] *Union Army.* JOHNNY REB. Now *hist.*

1864 in *Civil War Hist.* XXVIII (1982) 335: On Saturday night Johnny Grayback attempted a big thing by moonlight.

Johnny Green *n.* **1.** GREENHORN; JOHNNY RAW.

1870 Duval *Big-Foot* 267: "Come along, Johnny Green, I want to introduce you to some particular friends of mine."..."My name ain't Johnny Green."..."Oh! never mind that."

2. *Naut.* (see quot.).

1925 Farmer *Shellback* 56 [ref. to 1890's]: The *Kremlin*...[carried] a skys'l yard and stuns'l...and, in fine weather, any other bits of rag familiarly known as "Johnie Greens" which could be attached to her person.

Johnny Haultaut *n. Naut.* a naval seaman. Also *vars.*

1859 in C.A. Abbey *Before the Mast* 171: Envious looks of the English "Johnny Haultaughters" from the *Calipso*. **1883** Russell *Sailors' Lang.* xiii: Merchantmen...will speak of a Navy sailor as "Johnny Haultaut," in reference to the well braced yards, the taut running rigging and the snug bunts of the man-of-war. **1885** *United Service* (Jan.) 33: John Haultaut, Esq. **1903** *Bluejacket* (May) 8: The "Johnny-Haul-Taut," the youthful sailor who talks shop ashore and afloat, is much in evidence in the Navy, and does what he can to keep alive the dying vernacular of the sea. **1929** Bowen *Sea Slang* 76: *Johnny Haultaut.* A term of derision used by American seamen in referring to men-of-war's men who are under severe discipline.

Johnny Law var. JOHN LAW.

Johnny Newcome *n.* a man or boy who is a newcomer or novice. Also **Johnny Newcomer.**

*1815 in *OED2*: The military adventures of Johnny Newcome. *1833 in *OED2*: A Johnny Newcome (as all strangers are there called). *a*1845 N. Willis *Dashes* 107: The sober eye of a Johnny Newcome. *1853 Chesterton *Peace, War & Adv.* I 17 [ref. to 1812]: My companions agreed in designating me a "Johnny Newcome;" and I was the good-humoured object of their raillery. **1853** "P. Paxton" *In Texas* 93: Being almost as much of a Johnny Newcome as myself. **1865** in Thornton *Amer. Gloss.* I 499: The Johnny Newcomes had to...deposit 75c. for the bit of blue paste-board. **1885** in *DAE*: His Hawaiian Majesty,—a king with more alien Johnny Newcomes and coolies than subjects. **1923** *N.Y. Times* (Sept. 9) VIII 2: *Johnny Newcomer*—An amateur. **1946** *Railroad Mag.* (Feb.) 89: Unless you're a Johnnie Newcomer you know this as well as I do. *1950 Granville *Sea Slang* 134: *Johnny Newcome.* A green hand; a newcomer. (Merchant Navy).

Johnny-on-the-spot *n.* an unusually alert fellow who is capable of decisive action, seizing an opportunity, etc. Also (*obs.*) **Johnny-on-the-job.**

1896 Ade *Artie* 19: She was settin' over in the corner, and...a Johnny-on-the-spot, with a big badge, marked "Committee," was tryin' to keep cases on her. *Ibid.* 63: I'll be Johnny-on-the-spot to see that everything's on the level. **1905** in "O. Henry" *Works* 1675: I'll be...Johnny-on-the-spot. **1906** in McCay *Little Nemo* 65: You can't fool me that easy! No sir! I'm Johnny on the spot! **1911** Spalding *Base Ball* 266: The umpire...must be "Johnny on the spot." **1911** H.B. Wright *Barbara Worth* 107: Bill, you're [sic] comin' is some opportune. You're sure Johnny-on-the-spot. **1912** *Adventure* (July) 502: That's how she came to be so Johnny-on-the-job when the hold up got through with me. *ca*1915 in Bruns *Kts. of Road* 116: When some nice lady wants the snow shoveled...we're Johnny on the job. **1916** in Botkin *Sidewalks* 27: They're "Johnny on the spot." **1975** McCaig *Danger Trail* 26: He's always Johnny-on-the-spot with his Circle C outfit.

Johnny Raw *n.* a GREENHORN; an inexperienced youth; novice or raw recruit.

*1813 in *OED2*: A grand attack was made on the Johnny raws of Blandford. *1819 [T. Moore] *Tom Crib* 50: Poor Johnny Raw!...So *rum* a *flat*. *1821 Stewart *Man-of-War's-Man* I 20: Oho! you're one of the Johnie Raw's, are you! **1823** J.F. Cooper *Pioneers* 170: If-so-be he is thinking of putting any Johnny Raw over my head, why I shall resign. *Ibid.* 176: Stop my grog, if you don't find all the Johnny Raws laughing at him! **1834** A. Greene *Pearl St.* 53: The opposite bidder is probably some novice from the country—some honest Johnny Raw. **1836** *Spirit of Times* (Oct. 1) 257: We were much amused at the advice one Johnny Raw gave another. **1840** *Crockett Almanac 1841* 12: A

Jonny Raw from Squantum, applied to a noted Surgeon. **1841** [Mercier] *Man o' War* 109: There was a soft-pated "Johnny Raw," a steady cook on the berth-deck. **1851** W. Kelly *Ex. to Calif.* II 173: Johnny Raws...are always to be found. **1890** Finerty *War-Path* 261: The Cheyennes and Crows were grinning on the banks at the awkwardness of the "Johnny Raws." ***1891** R. Kipling *His Private Honour*: It's me, you Johnnie Raws—you Johnny *bloomin'* Raws!

Johnny Reb *n.* **1.** *Union Army.* a Confederate soldier; a Southern Confederate; Confederate forces collectively. Now *hist.*

1862 in *Manuscripts* XXX (1978) 271: "Johnny Reb"...and one of our 4th O.V.I. picket boys. **1862** in R.G. Carter *4 Bros.* 96: Could "Johnny Reb" have struck us just then, "John Gilpin's race" would have been as nothing compared with the "skedaddle" on that fearful night. **1863** in *Civil War Times Illus.* (Nov. 1965) 46: Everyone [was] acting as if Johnnie Reb wasn't within miles of us. **1863** in A.M. Stewart *Camp, March* 320: A general shout, cheer, scream or yell, went up from the rebel ranks. This strange, curious, unearthly sound, seems peculiar to Johnny Reb. The nearest transfer into print may be by "Ki-*yi*-ki-*yi*-*yi*," with a vigorous screech on the "*yi*." **1864** in *Civil War Hist.* XXVIII (1982) 328: Up all night looking for Johnny Reb. **1864** in J.W. Haley *Rebel Yell* 166: Johnny Reb [is] all around us. **1864** Brobst *Letters* 80: We had two visitors day before yesterday. They were Johnny Rebs. **1865** in D. Chisholm *Civil War Notebk.* 75: Poor old Johnnie Rebs. **1865** Blake *Army of the Potomac* 203: How are you, Johnny Reb! **1866** in Eppes *Eventful Yrs.* 315: You Johnnie Rebs keep your tempers pretty well. **ca1885** A.C. Stearns *Co. K* 61: We expected and hoped to find some Johnie Rebs. **1910** in McIlvaine *Chi. in Civil War* 11: Ten thousand..."Johnny Rebs" [were] corralled at Forts Henry and Donelson, and Island No. 10. **1967** L'Amour *Matagorda* 24: Some renegades that would have strung me up...for bein' a Johnny Reb.

2. a man who is a Southerner.

1884 "Craddock" *Where Battle Was Fought* 21: I hope ye don't take no grudge at bein' called like a Johnny Reb. **1908** in "O. Henry" *Works* 757: And the Johnny Rebs answered the call [in 1898]. **1940** F. Hunt *Trail from Tex.* 15 [ref. to 1870's]: He ain't at all like what you'd think Johnny Rebs was. **1980** Bruns *Kts. of Road* 17: Slim, a malarial, crusty Johnny Reb, hated Yankees. **1981** C. Nelson *Picked Bullets Up* 306: She plays guard on the Johnny Reb football team, center on the basketball team, and first base during softball games....Johnny Rebs 23, Yanks 0.

Johnny Tinplate *n.* (among tramps) a constable.

1917 *Editor* (Feb. 24) 153: *Get your orders*—To be met by a Johnny Tinplate, or constable, and be told to leave town by a specified time. **1921** Casey & Casey *Gay-Cat* 40: Every Johnny Tinplate has made us beat it out o' them towns without us even moochin' a measly handout.

Johnny War *n.* *Naut.* a warship.

1835 *Knickerbocker* (Jan.) 16: "You have a regular man-of-war brig here." "Yes...She's a Johnny War."

Johnny Wise *n.* a clever fellow.

1901 Ade *Modern Fables* 67: That is why he will be a Mark for a cool-headed Johnny Wise. **1908** W.G. Davenport *Butte & Montana* 261: He played Johnny Wise and proceeded to use his head for something beside a hatrack.

John O *n.* JOHN O'BRIEN, 1.

1914 Jackson & Hellyer *Vocab.* 51: You can tell by his clothes that he has been riding John O's.

John O'Brien *n.* **1.** (among tramps) a railroad boxcar; (*also*) a freight train. Also **Johnny O'Brien.**

*a*1909 Tillotson *Detective* 92: *John O'Brien*—A freight train; a box car. **1914** Jackson & Hellyer *Vocab.* 51: *John O'Brien*...A freight train, used in contradistinction to a "rattler," a passenger train. **1922** *Variety* (June 30) 6: They climbed into a John O'Brien and hugged the rods until the next town loomed up. **1926** *AS* I (Jan.) 251: *Johnny O'Brien*—A box car. **1927** *DN* V 452: *John O'Brien*, n. A slow freight.

2. (see quot.).

1914 Jackson & Hellyer *Vocab.* 51: *John O'Brien*...Amongst "yeggs" it signifies also a moneyless safe.

John Q. Public *n.* *Journ. & Pol.* the general public; a man who is typical of the general public. Also **John Q. Citizen, John Q.,** etc. Cf. JANE Q. PUBLIC. Now *colloq.*

1937 *N & Q* (Mar. 6) 177: John Q. Public. **1937** in *N.Y. Times Mag.*

(Dec. 19, 1982) 19: We are all the children of John Q. Public. **1939** "E. Queen" *Dragon's Teeth* 22: Look at it this way, Master-Mind,...because this is the way it's going to be looked at by John Q. Public. **1941** *Pittsburgh Courier* (Nov. 1) 7: Presently Old John Q. gets his number. **1947** in *DA*: Plain John Q. Citizens. **1960** *Twilight Zone* (CBS-TV): You're John Q. Citizen. You're Tom, Dick and Harry. **1970** R. Vasquez *Chicano* 290: No one ever before brought items of culture to the front door of Mr. and Mrs. John Q. **1973** Schiano & Burton *Solo* 120: You protect yourself as well as John Q. Citizen. **1973–76** J. Allen *Assault* 105: Say John Q, Average American, played 000 every day. **1977** Butler & Shryack *Gauntlet* 12: The average John Q Public....What the hell could you talk to a John Q about? **1980** Brands Mart ad (WINS radio) (Aug. 30): And we're open to the public. That means you, John Q. **1984** "W.T. Tyler" *Shadow Cabinet* 184: So I'm trying to live up to the John Q. Public image. **1994** Ft. Worth, Tex., policeman, on *Cops* (Fox-TV): The hell with John Q. If they're gonna fight with the police I don't care if they're a man or a woman. **1995** *New Yorker* (May 15) 33: At the expense of Mr. and Mrs. John Q. Public.

john-rabbit *n.* *West.* a jackrabbit. *Joc.*

1884 in Lummis *Letters* 106: Shadow spied one of the John rabbits scurrying through the brush.

Johnson *n.* **1.a.** Now esp. *Black E.* the penis.—usu. considered vulgar.

***1863** Cheadle *Journal* 107: Bitterly cold; neck frozen. Face ditto; thighs ditto; Johnson ditto; & sphincter vesicae partially paralysed so that I had great difficulty to retain. [*a*1890–91 *F & H* II 329: *Dr. Johnson*...(old).—The *penis*.] **1970** *Current Slang* V (Fall) 9: *Johnson*, n. The penis. **1971** Simon *Sign of Fool* 43: My johnson was well on its way to becoming mincemeat. **1973** I. Reed *La. Red* 82: Old Sam whips out his "Johnson," as they say. **1977** Dillard *Lexicon of Black Eng.* 33: Other Black terms for the penis include...*Jones*...and *Johnson*. The last achieved a very wide dispersion through the film *Putney Swope*. **1986** J.A. Friedman *Times Sq.* 94: One of the...guys was...demanding a warm-up, some contrivance to stiffen his johnson before the main event. **1989** *Spin* (Aug.) 12: Is his Johnson...an interesting topic over 16 songs? **1989** *Dream Street* (NBC-TV): All work and no play make your Johnson get small. **1993** *Beavis and Butt-head* (MTV): You think he has a long Johnson? **1994** *Time* (Feb. 14) 58: Let one-third of his instrument of crime be removed....The rapist's johnson.

b. *Pros.* a dildo.

1975 Harrell & Bishop *Orderly House* 48: The girl would shove the Johnson up his ass.

c. *pl.* breasts.

1978 *Nat. Lampoon* (Aug.) 44: See, a set of Johnsons.

d. a thingamajig.

1981 Univ. Tenn. grad. student: What are all these little Johnsons?...I've used that expression since high school [1970, in Nashville]. **1985** Spears *Drugs & Drink* 290: *Johnson*...An underworld term meaning thing.

e. the buttocks.

1986 in Thorne *Dict. Contemp. Sl.* 281: He can kiss my Johnson.

2. *Und.* an itinerant, esp. a burglar or safecracker; YEGG. Hence **Johnson boys, Johnson brothers, Johnson man;** in phr. **one of the Johnson family** a fellow itinerant or professional criminal, or a protector of criminals.

1925–26 J. Black *You Can't Win* 104 [ref. to 1890's]: This party...is one of the "Johnson family." (The bums called themselves "Johnsons" probably because they were so numerous.) *Ibid.* 190: We enlisted two other "Johnsons." **1927** *AS* (June) 385: Yeggs...were called the *Johnson Boys*, from the "Johnson-bar," the reverse lever of the locomotive of those days; yeggs used a tool somewhat similar to it. **1928** Hammett *Red Harvest* 96: A pair of Johnson-brothers named Blackie Whalen and Put Collings that only got out on bail around five yesterday. **1928** T.A. Dorgan, in Zwilling *TAD Lexicon* 50: [Two tramps talking:] Putting the chill on the country's prosperity as you chat with another "Johnson." **1933** *Amer. Mercury* (Apr.) 392: The original yeggs were called Johnson men...because, before explosives began to be used, they opened safes with Johnson bars. **1944** C.B. Davis *Leo McGuire* 48: A good crook neither lies to nor steals from a member of the Johnson family....If you're a right guy....you're a member of the Johnson family.

3. *Black E.* a fellow.

1973 Wideman *Lynchers* 39: If they find the Johnson out he goes....Find that Johnson and out his ass would go.

Johnson bar *n.* **1.** JOHNSON, 1.a., b.

   1923 *Poems, Ballads & Parodies* 39: Then with his nine-inch Johnson bar/He broke my maidenhead. **1967** W. Crawford *Gresham's War* 173: I had taken her back to my old bedroom workbench and put a Johnson Bar job on her. **1975** Harrell & Bishop *Orderly House* 48: A Johnson bar is...a dildo.

2. any of various long, heavy bars or levers for use by hand, esp. a tamping bar or a heavy lever operating the reverse drive of a railway locomotive.

   1930 *Railroad Man's Mag.* II 471: *Johnson bar*—reverse lever on a locomotive. **1933** *Amer. Mercury* (Apr.) 392: A Johnson bar was a steel crow-bar with a claw on the end...used by railroad section laborers to pull up spikes. The Johnson men used it to pry open the doors of the old-time safes. **1938** Beebe *High Iron* 222: *Johnson bar:* The hand-operated reverse lever of a locomotive. **1938–41** in *AS* (Apr. 1941) 104: *Johnson Bar.* Emergency brake lever [of a heavy truck]. **1953** Botkin & Harlow *R.R. Folklore* 163: Twisted sideways on his seat, hurling a heavy Johnson bar back and forth. **1976** *Urban Life* V 231: This was also true aboard ship, except when older "Johnson-bar" steam winches were being used. *ca***1978** in A. Lomax *Where Blues Began* 246 [ref. to 1930's]: It's got a long handle on it, called the Johnson bar. When the pan get full, then the wheeler loader, he pull down on the Johnson bar....When that...loader unbuckle the Johnson bar, the...[mule] team stops. **1989** P.H.C. Mason *Recovering* 50: Take a Johnson bar and drive the pins in to hold the [runway sections] together.

Johnson rod *n.* an imaginary rod blamed for the malfunctioning of an engine, as in a motor vehicle. *Joc.*

   1951–53 in *AS* (May 1954) 99: *Johnson rod,* n. A nonexistent part of a car. Hot rodders sometimes yell "Your Johnson rod's draggin'!" to a party of girls or others who look gullible. **1960** T. McPherson *Dragging & Driving* 139: *Johnson rod:* There is no such rod. When you can't figure out what's ailing your engine, you blame it on the Johnson rod. **1983** *Tenn. Folk. Soc. Bull.* XLIX 76 [ref. to 1940's]: But when Sam presented the man with the bill, there were a few additional items such as "tuning the fiberator" and "a new Johnson rod." **1995** *Seinfeld* (NBC-TV): He said it's the Johnson rod.

John Thomas *n.* the penis.—usu. considered vulgar.

   *ca**1866** *Romance of Lust* 228: My own John Thomas was in all the pride and panoply of prickdom. ***1867**, ***1874** (cited in Partridge *DSUE* (ed. 7) 1227). ***1884** *Randiana* 68: I...let my John Thomas approach his lair. *a**1890–96** *F & H* IV 71: *John Thomas*...The penis. **1927** [Fliesler] *Anecdota* 187: *The Contented Wife* [by] John Thomas Everhard. **1966** Manus *Mott the Hoople* 73: "Where's John Thomas?" "He's all tuckered out." **1977** Coover *Public Burning* 411: And that ain't just another name for your old John Thomas! **1985** *Nat. Lampoon* (Sept.) 86: Give me some of that teenage John Thomas. **1993** *Beavis and Butt-head* (MTV): Dick, Peter, Rod, Johnson, even old John Thomas.

John Tuck *n. Naut.* a customs official of the Chinese government. Now *hist.*

   1813 in Howay *New Hazard* 125: John Tuck was on board to measure the ship this forenoon. ***1929** Bowen *Sea Slang* 76: *John Tuck.* The seaman's name for the Chinese mandarins with whom the traders had any dealings.

John Wayne *n. Mil.* [the professional name of Marion M. Morrison (1907–79), U.S. film star famous for his portrayals of heroic cowboys and military men] **1.a.** a man who takes daring or reckless, often self-consciously heroic, action.—usu. used derisively. Also as adj.

   1960 Bluestone *Cully* 48 [ref. to *ca*1955]: All right, John Wayne, just knock it off. **1971** in J.C. Pratt *Vietnam Voices* 475: Our gung-ho John-Wayne-type commander. **1979** Former USAF enlisted man: A *John Wayne* in Vietnam was the nut who stands up in the middle of something and starts shooting. Or you could *pull a John Wayne.* **1984** J. McNamara *First Directive* 244: You did your usual John Wayne bit, covering her so completely that when the chandelier got shot away, it crashed down on your head.

   b. a reckless, usu. showy, act, esp. an attempt at heroism; (*broadly*) heroics or bravado.

   1978 Hasford *Short-Timers* 107 [ref. to Vietnam War]: Craze did a John Wayne. **1978** Diehl *Sharky's Machine* 139: Take out the old pistol and spin it on your finger, do a couple of John Waynes for her. **1979** (quot. at **(a)**, above). **1982** W.E.B. Griffin *Lieuts.* 44: What...was I

supposed to do? Do a John Wayne? Charge with a...bayonet in my hand? **1983** Ehrhart *VN-Perkasie* 161: No heroics, no tank rides, no John Wayne. **1984** H. Searls *Blood Song* 290: He tried to grab this gun....Too much John Wayne. **1997** *L.A. Times Bk. Rev.* (Mar. 2) 3 [ref. to Vietnam War]: Don't Pull a *John Wayne*...don't, that is, try any stupid heroics and endanger the lives of your fellow soldiers.

2. a military-issue (P-38) can opener.

   1973 Kingry *Monk & Marines* 112: I opened a can...with my John Wayne can opener. **1976** Former U.S. marine (served 1971–74): Your *John Wayne* is your little metal can opener. It's just a piece of sharpened metal that you use to open your C-ration cans. It's called a *John Wayne* because it takes the strength of ten to use it. That's a Marine Corps–wide expression. **1987** R. Miller *Slob* 262: Wire-cutter pliers, det cord, fuses,...John Wayne (opener), utensils, [etc.]. **1990** G.R. Clark *Wds. of Viet. War* 388: The Marines called their P-38s John-Waynes.

John Wayne *adj.* suggesting or reminiscent of the heroic film characters played by John Wayne.

   1961 Barbeau *Ikon* 55 [ref. to Korean War]: Look at Hollywood with the John Wayne gun. **1970** W.C. Woods *Killing Zone* 156: It's a real John Wayne ride. **1972** Haldeman *War Year* 4: No John Wayne stuff, right? You'll get your chance. **1974** Radano *Cop Stories* 132: Johnson...pulled out his cannon and made a John Wayne entrance. **1982** *N.Y. Times* (Jan. 3) IV E19: Scrape the mold off World War II battle gear and head for North Africa with a John Wayne glint in still-proud eyes. **1985** *Newsweek* (Apr. 22) 24: Several pilots...were transferred for not being "John Wayne enough." a**1987** Bunch & Cole *Reckoning for Kings* 197: This John Wayne shit be gettin' wearisome.

John-Wayne *v.* to attack, overcome, deal with, etc. with great force and little deliberation; (*also*) to take decisive, often self-consciously heroic action.—also constr. with dummy-obj. *it.*

   1972 Wambaugh *Blue Knight* 161: Nothing I like better than John Wayne-ing a goddamn door. **1975** Wambaugh *Choirboys* 235: He John Wayned the door, kicking it right next to the lock and sending it crashing across the bathroom. a**1982** Medved *Hospital* 26: I'm supposed to go around John Wayne-ing it all the time. a**1986** K.W. Nolan *Into Laos* 202: He and Keg had been given...the Silver Star for John Wayneing the NVA bunker. **1987** Estes *Field of Innocence* 103 [ref. to 1968]: I had had my share of crawling and John Wayneing it.

John Wayne bar *n. Army.* a field-ration candy bar. [Quots. ref. to Vietnam War.]

   1986 Thacker *Pawn* 36: I'll trade you...for...a John Wayne bar. **1990** G.R. Clark *Words of Viet. War* 289: The candy bars [included in LRRP rations] were nicknamed "John Wayne Bars" by the GIs. **1991–93** W.T. Grant *Wings of Eagle* 46: A John Wayne bar was the round, chocolate-and-rice crunch bar that came in the C rations.

John Wayne cookie *n. USMC.* a field-ration biscuit. Also **John Wayne cracker.** [Quots. ref. to Vietnam War.]

   1978 Hasford *Short-Timers* 157: A B-3 unit, a little can containing John Wayne cookies, cocoa, and pineapple jam. **1990** Helms *Proud Bastards* 182: Peanut butter...on a John Wayne cracker. **1993** P. Dickson *War Slang* 278: *John Wayne cookies.* The nearly inedible biscuits in every C-ration box.

John Wayne course *n. USMC.* an infantry-combat simulation course.

   1990 Helms *Proud Bastards* 160 [ref. to Vietnam War]: The John Wayne course back at Camp Geiger with all those pop-up targets.

John Wayne hat *n. Mil.* a bush hat.

   1987 D. Sherman *Main Force* 92 [ref. to Vietnam War]: "Why are you wearing that John Wayne hat?" "It's what I was wearing when I was med-evaced, sir. And it's not a John Wayne hat."

John Wayne High School *n. Army.* (see quot.).

   1991 Reinberg *In Field* 117 [ref. to Vietnam War]: *John Wayne High School*...the Special Warfare Training School at Fort Bragg, North Carolina.

John Wayne rifle *n. Mil.* (see quot.). *Joc.*

   1968 in P. Dickson *War Slang* 278: A .45 caliber service pistol—which almost nobody can shoot accurately—is called a "John Wayne rifle" in Vietnam because in the movies the Duke could knock down a running man at 300 yards with one. **1991** *Village Voice* (N.Y.C.) (Aug. 27) 50: The unwieldy .45-caliber service pistols were known as "John Wayne rifles" [in Vietnam].

join *v.* to join in wedlock; marry.

1847 in Oehlschlaeger *Reveille* 186: "I hear you've been jined, old hoss; here's luck to you." "Jined to what?"…"Jined to Suze Sloper."

join out *v.* **1.** Esp. *Circus & Und.* to join as an employee or associate.—often used intrans., constr. with *with*.

1895 Coup *Sawdust* 48: The Dahomey [giant] "joined out" with a side show. **1911** A.H. Lewis *Apaches of N.Y.* 39: Spanish…had joined out with a mob of [pickpockets]. **1914** *Amer. Mag.* (June) 34: I "joined out" with a mob and we prospered financially. **1914** Jackson & Hellyer *Vocab.* 32: No one can join out unless he puts up five centuries for fall dough. *Ibid.* 36: There'll be no hop heads joining out with this mob for they can't stand the gaff. **1921** *Variety* (Mar. 11) 7: The other night I joined out some boys on the bill and one guy said he knew a spot. **1921** Casey & Casey *Gay-Cat* 62: I'd joined out with a feller name o' Blondy. **1922** J. Conway, in *Variety* (Jan. 6) 7: I'll…let you know if we join out the burlesque troupe. **1925** Cohan *Broadway* 101: It was the first time any of the Union Square crowd had voluntarily "joined out" with me. **1927** Kyne *They Also Serve* 18: Rory had j'ined out with the bhoys afther the Easter Rebellion. **1949** Houston *Gun Smugglers* (film): Aimin' to jine out with the cavalry?

2. *Carnival.* (see quot.).

*ca*1950 in *AS* XXVIII (1953) 117: Carnie Talk … *Join* (someone) *out* … To take along. "We joined Dan out and made a couple of nautch joints."

¶ In phrase:

¶ **join out the odds** *Und.* to become a pimp.

*a*1955 in D.W. Maurer *Lang. Und.* 244: *Join out the odds*…To have one's girlfriend work as a prostitute during hard times. **1956** H. Gold *Not With It* 17: I used to join out the odds, had myself a stable of clappers for the gash-hounds too dumb to do their own howling.

joint *n.* [semantic development uncertain; an Anglo-Irish quot. of 1821 adduced by *OED2* (quoted more fully in Partridge *Dict. Und.*) is of uncertain meaning and not obviously related to the present senses] **1.a.** *Und.* a place set up temporarily for the purpose of swindling; (*also*) a small outdoor table, stand, etc., set up by a bookmaker or pitchman.

*1877 in Partridge *Dict. Und.* 370: The *joints*, the offices where the swindle was carried on…a cant word. **1885** *Puck* (June 24) 259: Bunko Joint. **1889** Barrère & Leland *Dict. Slang* I 505: *Joint, working the* (thieves), swindling in the streets with a lottery table. **1899* in *OED*: It was positively ridiculous to see police knocking down bookmakers' "joints" every time the inspector came round. **1902** in *McClure's Mag.* (Jan. 1903) 1: An account kept by a swindler of the dealings of his "Joint" with City Officials. **1930** *Variety* (Jan. 8) 123: I took my joint, my drop-case and a super…and lammed to grab a rattler. **1936** Fellows & Freeman *Big Show* 116: Active partner in the big joint…and manager of a mob which included grafters, card sharks, [etc.].

b. *Carnival.* a carnival booth or concession.

1894 F.P. Dunne, in Schaaf *Dooley* 183: Hinnissy…was runnin' th' knock-th'-baby-down-an'-get-a-nice-seegar joint. **1928** *AS* III (June) 414: *Joint.* A carnival concession is known as a joint or a store. A joint is said to be strong when grift can be worked in connection with it. **1935** *Amer. Mercury* (June) 230: *Joint:* concession; a place of business. **1951** Mannix *Sword-Swallower* 63: If the marks do win, the joints can pay them off in slum.

2. (among burglars) a place to be robbed; (*broadly*, now the usu. slang sense) any establishment, business, or residence that is small, shabby, disreputable, or the like, often a small eating place; (*ironically* or *disparagingly*) house, apartment, premises, esp. one's domicile; (*broadly*) town, place, locale.

*1880 in Partridge *Dict. Und.* 370: They soon found him a "joint" to do….Doing a "joint" means effecting a burglarious entry. **1885** *Puck* (Mar. 11) 22: He says chicken-pie is the only temperance pie….thousands of young journalists…are now traveling…the steep road to ruin which leads through the pie-joints of our large cities. **1886** *Lantern* (N.O.) (Nov. 10) 4: A tough joint. **1887** [C. Mackenzie] *Jack Pots* 53: The Sheriff had learned of the little private [gambling] joint and had come to pull the place. **1887** in *DAE*: The student, upon reaching his "joint," as the club is called, hurriedly bolts a few mouthfuls of breakfast. *a*1889 *Century Dict.*: *Joint*…A place of meeting or resort for persons engaged in evil or secret practices of any kind: as, a tramp's *joint*. **1894** in S. Crane *Stories* 142: You show me th' joint—that's all you've got t'do. **1895** Townsend *Fadden* 180: He has de long green t'burn a wet dog wid, and a joint in de country and

a yacht and more horses dan a circus. **1895** Wood *Yale Yarns* 63: We were mortal hungry, and nothing was open, for we'd tried several joints on the way up and they were closed tight as drums. **1896** Ade *Artie* 102: I'll have to give up my job here and move Mr. Trunk up to the Carroll joint. **1899** *Nat. Police Gaz.* (Mar. 18) 3: He took me down to a cheap joint on Sixth avenue, where they had tough steaks and bad beer. **1899** Cullen *Tales* 105: Then we all went to a clothing joint and rigged out in…ready-made suits. **1899** Norris *McTeague* 1: McTeague took his dinner…at the car conductors' coffee-joint on Polk Street. **1901** Irwin *Sonnets* (unp.): Steering for Grunsky's ice-cream joint. **1901** McGonnigle *Went West* 68: The town…was about as "hot" a "joint" as could be found in the West. **1903** Ade *Society* 126: "You have a charming Joint here," said the Financier. **1904** in "O. Henry" *Works* 912: Movin'-picture joints. **1906** *Nat. Police Gaz.* (Dec. 22) 3: She's on her way to the home joint. **1906** in W.C. Fields *By Himself* 36: Why didn't you get a first class place to stop at? What's the idea of sticking at that *joint*? **1908** in H.C. Fisher *A. Mutt* 29: There's a pool room at this address. Go up and pinch the joint. *Ibid.* 77: Judge Crawler has just been kicked out of a chop suey joint. *Ibid.* 121: He'll give his wife the rush act and tear out of the joint on a dead run. **1911** Bronson-Howard *Enemy to Society* 257: Here, git away from this joint. **1914** S.H. Adams *Clarion* 35: Let's take a turn around the joint. **1914** Ellis *Billy Sunday* 292: The Church has degenerated into a third-rate amusement joint, with religion left out. **1916** Lardner *Gullible's Travels* 110: Who owns this joint? **1916** in Truman *Dear Bess* 202: You'll probably get a phone call from Grandview tomorrow….If you don't get one you'll know I was not able to leave this unwholesome joint. **1918** Witwer *Baseball* 25: No doubt I have got the wrong joint. **1918–19** MacArthur *Bug's-Eye View* 103: Brouch [Luxemburg]—what an awful joint! **1920–21** Witwer *Leather Pushers* 19: I'll leave him flat in this Sandusky joint if he don't come through on the bit! **1924** P. Marks *Plastic Age* 9: We're going to have a swell joint here. **1927** C. McKay *Harlem* 11: From the pool-room they went to Aunt Hattie's chitterling joint in One Hundred and Thirty-second Street. **1929** "M. Brand" *Beacon Creek* 9: Even into a joint like this town! **1930** C. Shaw *Jack-Roller* 73: There is a joint (meaning a place to rob) I'm going to make soon. **1934** Appel *Brain Guy* 81: He couldn' be all over the joint. **1936** N. West *Cool Million* 233: He has loused the continent up good. But is he trying to de-louse it? No, all his efforts go to keep on lousing up the joint. **1947** Beloin & Rose *Favorite Brunette* (film): Then I got a load of the mansion. What a beautiful joint! **1948** Sheldon et al. *Easter Parade* (film): This isn't an all-night joint. **1954** Matheson *Born of Man & Woman* 43: "This joint is haunted," he concluded with a vague shake of his head. **1956** M. Wolff *Big Nick*. 177: Boy, they sure make good milk shakes in this joint. **1957** E. Lacy *Room to Swing* 31: "I'm hungry." "Nothing but joints around here." **1935–62** Ragen & Finston *Toughest Pris.* 805: *Joint*—A prospective place of burglary or robbery. **1963** E. Hunter *Ten Plus One* 45: Oklahoma, Iowa, I don't know. One of those hick joints. **1966** W. Wilson *LBJ Brigade* 20: Charlie hit a village. He's gone but we gotta secure the joint. **1970** A. Young *Snakes* 59: We moved past the shrimp shacks, rib joints, record shops, bars and crowds. **1972** Jenkins *Semi-Tough* 77: Is it near the caviar joint? **1977** Harnack *Under Wings* 41: We ate supper at a steak joint on the lake road. **1991** D.W. Louie, in J. Hagedorn *Chan Is Dead* 270: A sushi joint. **1991** C. Fletcher *Pure Cop* 268: Nice joint. **1993** *Garfield & Friends* (CBS-TV): I better scram to another locale. I got all the money I can from this joint.

3. (in specif. senses now often subsumed under (2), above):
a. a gambling den or casino.

1878 *Nat. Police Gaz.* (Apr. 27) 6: When a man is "steered against the joint" in Chicago, and gets beaten,…he hunts up…a special [officer]….When the squealer comes up and makes his complaint, the "joint" is interviewed by the [police]. **1879** A. Pinkerton *Crim. Remin.*: He secured an understanding with the police, and at once [opened]…four "joints," or playing places. **1890** Quinn *Fools of Fortune* 491: With a solitary exception, the gambling rooms…are located in…the business blocks. The exception…is a Chinese "joint," operated in connection with a Mongolian laundry in a basement. **1898** L.J. Beck *Chinatown* 97: The "joint," or place where the game is to be conducted, is secured and fitted up. **1905** in E. O'Neill *Letters* 14: One of the most fashionable (and notorious) gambling joints in the world. **1912** Quinn *Gambling* 283: A gambler who knows every ramification of the "protection" business said that there were in the greater city more than 2,000 illegal "joints" which pay for non-molestation.

b. a saloon, esp. if disreputable; (in early use) a place where liquor is sold illicitly; (*later, disparagingly*) a cabaret, nightclub, etc.

1877 in Miller & Snell *Why West Was Wild* 20: A Bloody Prizefight in Dodge City....The sport took place in front of the Saratoga [saloon], at...4:30 a.m....Promptly at the appointed time the two...[brawlers] were at the joint. *a***1889** in Barrère & Leland *Dict. Slang* I 505: Carew said...his saloon was a "tough joint." **1889** Reynolds *Kansas Hell* 51: There are no "joints" in the Pen. No Assistant Attorney Generals are necessary to enforce prohibition there. **1889** Field *Western Verse* 1: The camp wuz all astir,/With the joints all throwed wide open 'nd no sheriff to demur! **1890** in *Mo. Hist. Rev.* XLIII (1949) 311: The worst beer joint that ever infested Salem is in full blast. **1893** *Harper's Mag.* (Apr.) 708: Club drinking and "joints" are not unknown, but the saloon has vanished. **1893** in S. Crane *Stories* 112: Say, young feller...where th'ell is Billie Carcart's joint round here? **1895** Townsend *Fadden* 178: He was just putting up a front dat he didn't know dat on the Bow'ry de right name for a joint is a drum. **1896** Ade *Artie* 46: The minute I meets him he steers me into a joint, makes me heave in a couple and then says: "Come on; I've got a good thing for you." **1905** *Nat. Police Gaz.* (Nov. 11) 3: Elinore was dug up out of just such a joint as this. **1908** in Rose *Storyville* 65: The most notorious "joints" in the city where women of questionable repute habitually congregate have been converted into "restaurants." **1913** in J. Reed *Young Man* 27: Sure, I went to all the joints. Montmarter is just like New York. **1915** Bronson-Howard *God's Man* 190: You see him in the joints every night—in Cleary's and The Kid's, sporting girls at his table and all. **1926** C.M. Russell *Trails* 33: When he steps in this joint, he walks to the bar and asks them all up. **1937** *AS* (Oct.) 184: *Joint*. Small nightclub where the pay is poor. **1963** in Cannon *Nobody Asked* 110: They padded their checks in the joints. **1984** W. Allen *Broadway Danny Rose* (film): All I know, he's a big talent and he's been playing joints.

c. an opium den. Now *hist.*

1881 H.H. Kane *Opium* vii: Ah Sing, keeper of a "joint" in Mott Street. **1883** in Smith & Smith *Police Gaz.* 40: A number of the [opium] joints were "pulled" last week. **1883** A.S. Williams *The Demon of the Orient and His Satellite Fiends of the Joints* [title]. **1883** *Harper's Mag.* (Nov.) 944: I...have smoked opium in every *joint* in America, but never saw anything so curious as this. **1884** Costello *Police Protectors* 517: Captain McCullagh...and Detective Gerow, have...made an important "raid" in one of these "joints" where opium is smoked and arrested a number of the denizens..."hitting the pipe." **1886** T. Byrnes *Prof. Crim. Amer.* 385: I have seen men and women come in the joints under the influence of liquor. **1887** "Zor" *Breaking Chains* 48: The Chinaman...won the day for the "opium joint." **1893** in T.C. Cox *Blacks in Topeka* 106: Joints, bar rooms, and drug stores [are] running wide open. **1902** Crothers *Morphinism* 72: [The opium smoker] goes to a "joint," or a room which persons of a similar desire frequent. **1904** *Life in Sing Sing* 261: Well, I'm off to the joint to smoke up. **1953** Anslinger & Tompkins *Traf. in Narc.* 311: *Joint*...an opium den.

d. a brothel. [The precise sense intended in the 1877 quot. is unclear.]

[**1877** in Miller & Snell *Why West Was Wild* 277: The Joint [headline]. A Battle of the Beauties.] **1894** Gardner *Dr. & Devil* 61: In Hattie Adams's "Joint" she had given me a fifty-cent counterfeit silver piece. **1909** Chrysler *White Slavery* 20: She...goes down to "Bunkville" to..."locate a joint." **1916** Cary *Venery* I 160: *Joint*—A brothel. **1918** in Carey *Mlle. from Armentières* I (unp.): She went to church and said her prayers/While her daughter ran the joint upstairs. **1923** Ornitz *Haunch, Paunch & Jowl* 41: Pimps on the street pulled at us....The Elizabeth Street joints were crude and dirty places. **1930** Waldron *Old Sergeant* 25: When you go to a regular joint you know that every woman you meet there has one or more of the venereal diseases. **1952** Uris *Battle Cry* 135: The first time I went to a joint, Marion, I was just about your age and just about as innocent. **1956** Chamales *Never So Few* 243: You find her a spot and put her in a joint....She discovers that society frowns on whores. **1953–57** Giovannitti *Combine D* 148: We were asking this bartender if he could tell us a joint. We needed it bad. **1963** Coon *Short End* 114: I thought Nick wanted to go into one of the joints, but he didn't. **1962–68** B. Jackson *In the Life* 196: I've never had a joint. I am a nickel-and-dime pimp.

e. Orig. *Pris.* a prison.—usu. constr. with *the*.—often used attrib.

1933 Ersine *Pris. Slang* 48: *Joint Wise*. Knowing in the ways of

prison. **1933–35** D. Lamson *About to Die* 197: Sure...I'm in Quentin now. But this is the first time...that I ever made a big joint. **1935** Pollock *Und. Speaks: Joint*, a prison. **1936** Duncan *Over the Wall* 156: I never hit the booze till Murray got grabbed and went to the joint. **1939** *AS* (Oct.) 240: *To make the joint*...to go to jail. **1948** Lipman *Alias a Gentleman* (film): Two years over there at the joint. **1949** in W.S. Burroughs *Letters* 47: Trying to send me to the State joint at Angola. **1951** Kerouac *Visions of Cody* 56: He...had stolen several other cars to try his skill since his time in the "joint." **1956** Holiday & Dufty *Lady Sings Blues* 134: During my months in the joint they told me I was receiving packs of mail every day. **1958** Gilbert *Vice Trap* 40: The parole board saw things John's way. The joint's no good for John, hombre. **1963** in L. Bruce *Essential Lenny* 17: Then he told me about his old lady being pregnant, getting thrown in the joint, and his getting in jail. **1966** Bullins *Goin' a Buffalo* 162: Now the Muslims were in a hassle at the joint with the guards. **1968** M.H. Albert & J. Guss *Lady in Cement* (film): I just wrapped up two years in the joint on account of she ratted on me. **1969** Whittemore *Cop!* 198: "How much were you in the joint for?" asked Ernie. "Six years....Armed robbery." **1972** Wambaugh *Blue Knight* 69: Who does time? You ever see a book do joint time? **1972** T.C. Bambara *Gorilla* 174: Ain't my man in the joint doing five to seven? **1984** D. Jenkins *Life Its Ownself* 28: Sentenced to fifteen years in a Florida joint.

f. a detoxification facility.

1989 P. Benchley *Rummies* 46: Every been in a joint before?...Gotta beat jail, though.

4.a. *Und.* the particular decisive action or the precise moment on which the accomplishment of one's purpose turns, as the actual taking of the victim's money during a swindle or confidence game; crux.—constr. with *the*; in phrs. **get** [or **go**] **to the joint** (*obs.*) to effect one's purpose, as by determined action; **turn the joint** (among pitchmen) to solicit customers or make sales. Cf. 1889 quot. at (**1.a.**), above.

1877 in R.M. Wright *Dodge City* 167: The gang got to the joint in good shape....Suppose Hayes and Morton should get on a bender and put their jewelry in soak for booze, then it would be appropriate to say they "got to the joint" by this means. **1877** in Miller & Snell *Why West Was Wild* 276: Joe is a quiet young man...but will not fail to "go to the joint" in case of a row. He will make a good officer. **1909** Irwin *Con Man* 58: We got ready for the joint ("the joint" is a term used by confidence men to describe the actual operation by which the victim's money is taken away). *Ibid.* 140: At last I approach the "joint," which is our term for the actual operation of separating the good thing from his money. **1930** Irwin *Tramp & Und. Slang* 192: *Turn the Joint.*—To solicit business or to make sales to the crowd attracted by the "ballyhoo" at a pitch.

b. Orig. *Und. & Carnival.* (more or less indefinitely, with specific nonce applications) thing, item, undertaking, etc. [The following established senses presumably arose as specialized instances.]

1935 *Amer. Mercury* (June) 230: *Joint*:...also used interchangeably with *thing*. **1942–49** Goldin et al. *DAUL* 111: *Joint*...A newspaper, magazine, or any periodical....(Very rare; Negro) A package of cigarettes. **1969** *New York* (Sept. 22): I saw you wheeling that fine joint [automobile] Saturday....A black man's got as much right to own a Cadillac as a whitey. **1981** in Spears *Drugs & Drink* 290: *Joint*...a capsule of heroin. **1990** *Houston Post* (May 24) A3: *Joint*...a fight.

c. the penis; in phr. **cop a joint** Esp. *Pris.* to perform fellatio.—usu. considered vulgar.

1931–34 in Clemmer *Pris. Community* 333: *Joint*...3. Also the penis. **1943** in Legman *Limerick* 36: There was a young fellow named Harry,/Had a joint that was long, huge and scary. **1942–49** Goldin et al. *DAUL* 49: *Cop a joint*...To serve as a male oral degenerate. **1958** Cooley *Run for Home* 47: You can take your joint outta that bag tonight. The medicine killed everything by now. **1958–59** Lipton *Barbarians* 156: "Joint"...can also mean the penis or a stick of marijuana. **1958–59** Southern & Hoffenberg *Candy* 215: I dug his joint. **1935–62** Ragen & Finston *Toughest Pris.* 795: *Cop a joint*—Sex pervert expression. **1957–62** Higginbotham *Folklore of USMC* 4: *A joint*—the penis. **1965** Herlihy *Midnight Cowboy* 32: You been kissing Anastasia, you better go swallow a drugstore and I ain't kidding. She's copped every joint in Albuquerque. **1966** Longstreet & Godoff *Wm. Kite* 324: No joint-copping in the contessa's gondola. **1974** Mamet *Sexual Perversity* 42: Reaches over...and grabs *me* by the joint.

d. the vulva or vagina.—usu. considered vulgar.

1971 *Nude, Blued & Tattooed* 15: Hear about the drunk midget who walked into the home for girls and kissed everybody in the joint?

e. *Narc.* a usu. makeshift hypodermic syringe; (*also*) (see 1936 quots.).

1935 Pollock *Und. Speaks: Joint*, a complete hypodermic outfit consisting of syringe and needles. **1936** Dai *Opium Addiction* 172: The paraphernalia of a drug addict…consist of a hypodermic needle, an eye dropper, a spoon in which to make a solution of the drug, and, in the case of a "vein shooter," an old necktie to be used as a tourniquet. The whole outfit is called a "plant" or "joint." **1936** Benton & Ballou *Where Do I Go?* 212 [ref. to 1920's]: The "junkies" had…to keep their "joints" or "setups"…out of the way. *a***1965** B. Jackson, in *JAF* LXXVIII (1965) 326: In Texas,…*joint* means…paraphernalia for injecting narcotics. **1967** [Beck] *Pimp* 133: When I jack this joint off the "horse" kicks my ass groovy. **1980** in Courtwright et al. *Addicts Who Survived* 87 [ref. to 1930's]: If…you've broken your pipe, you had to learn how to make one, what you call a homemade joint.

f. Orig. *Narc.* a marijuana cigarette; (*also*, now *joc.*) a tobacco cigarette.

1942 *ATS* 443: Tramp and criminal [Slang]…*butt, fag, joint,*…a cigarette. **1951** in *AS* XXVII (1952) 27: I first got joints, then got wise and got in bulk. **1952** "R. Marsten" *So Nude* 16: That was when he'd smoked his first joint. **1952** Mandel *Angry Strangers* 164: You got a couple of joints to take along?…Take some pod, Dinch. **1953** W. Brown *Monkey on My Back* 31: Vesta got out some marijuana cigarettes and offered Dave a "joint." **1956** Ginsberg *Howl* 32: My national resource consists of two joints of marijuana. **1958** Meltzer & Blees *H.S. Confidential* (film): Give me a joint, please? **1959** A. Anderson *Lover Man* 160: He…lit up a stick, or "a joint." **1962** Kesey *Cuckoo's Nest* 251: I don't get too high, not on a little middlin' joint like that one. **1963** Rubin *Sweet Daddy* 86: They find one stick, one lousy little joint and they rap me. **1967** *Time* (July 7) 21: The finest variety is "Acapulco Gold"…selling for $1 a joint. **1968** Baker, Ladd & Robb *CUSS* 146: *Joint.* Cigarette. **1973** Haring *Stranger* 149: Eat early. Smoke a joint tonight, O.K.? **1981** in N. George *Buppies, B-Boys* 191: Pass the joint. *a***1983** in Jackson & Jackson *Doing Drugs* 19: At eight-thirty in the morning…they'd be smoking a joint. **1985** Flowers *Mojo Blues* 15: A group [was] smoking a joint. *****1990** in Thorne *Dict. Contemp. Sl.* 281: Several large joints passed along the room. **1994** (quot. at J, 2). **1995** *Newsweek* (Sept. 25) 84: They had smoked grass (three joints) on one occasion.

g. *Und.* a pistol.

1953 W. Brown *Monkey on My Back* 68: Sure, the f— stud almost s— his pants when I pulled a joint (gun). **1953–55** Fine *Delinquents* 93: I bought a nice pistol from one of the older guys and…I decided to keep me a joint (gun) for myself. *Ibid.* 94: I got my Joint and hoofed it back. *****a***1981** *Macquarie Dict.: Joint*…a concealable firearm. **1994** Smitherman *Black Talk* 147: *Joint*…a gun.

h. *Horse Racing.* an illegal device used by a jockey to goad a horse into running faster during a race.

1973 Haney *Jock* 19: The guys would think nothing of carrying chains, or even joints, to make these cripples go….A "joint" or "buzzer" is an electrical device that shocks a horse into running faster.

i. *Black E.* something excellent, exciting, desirable, etc.—constr. with *the*; in phr. **the serious joint** the real thing.

1973 in S. Hager *Hip Hop* 47: It's the joint. **1977** *Watch Your Mouth* (WNET-TV): The real deal! The serious joint! **1979** "Sugar Hill Gang," in L. A. Stanley *Rap* 321: We're a treacherous trio, we're the serious joint. **1983** in G. Tate *Flyboy* 58: What we on this side of the color line call the joint, the bomb. **1984** Mason & Rheingold *Slanguage* (unp.): *Joint*…An expression meaning excellent. **1988** "De La Soul" *Say No Go* (rap song): It's the joint.

j. *Black E.* a film, song, or other production.

1988 S. Lee *School Daze* (film): A Spike Lee Joint. **1991** Nelson & Gonzales *Bring Noise* 145: Pairing "joints that haven't been sampled yet" with recorded breaks and live music. **1991** *Source* (Oct.) 57: Singing that old hippie joint, "American Woman." **1993** *Source* (July) 36: His newest joint, *Looks Like a Job For*…was in my tape deck.

jojo *n.* [alluding to *Jo-Jo*, the Dog-Faced Boy, exhibited by P.T. Barnum] **1.** a homely or peculiar fellow; character.

1903 Hobart *Out for the Coin* 16: I'm wise to that old jojo. **1964** *Sat. Eve. Post* (Sept. 26) 48: That finky cop….You know that jojoe directs traffic Saturday mornings on Warren and California?

2. the penis.

1967 in Wepman et al. *The Life* 135: He had to play with Jojo 'cause he didn't have a dime. **1976** in Wepman et al. *The Life* 183: *Jojo n* Personification of the penis.

joker *n.* **1.** an ordinary, odd, or foolish fellow; character.

*****1810** in *Austral. Nat. Dict.*: Six jokers on horseback were standing stock still/Like as many dragoons that were learning to drill. **1839–40** Cobb *Green Hand* II 37: Depend upon it, my joker. **1852** Hazen *Five Years* 37: So unexpected a resistance made the old joker desperate. **1851–54** in Mead *Shanties* 587: Although quite demure he was a stiff joker/You'd have sworn his back bone was made out of a poker. **1856** Wilkins *Young N.Y.* 15: Jupiter! if a joker wanted to make love to her, now, she'd go into a philosophical disquisition on the origin and progress of the divine passion. *Ibid.* 16: A joker got into the Tombs for indulging in that luxury, the other day. **1878** Willis *Our Cruise* 10: The three old jokers got tangled together so savage that it took a whole watch of foretopmen to separate them. *****1897** in S.J. Baker *Australian Lang.* (ed. 2) 122: And a bosom friend's a *cobber*, And a horse a *prad* or *moke*, While a casual acquaintance Is a *joker* or a *bloke*. *****1897** J. Conrad *Nigger of Narcissus* ch. ii: Yon's an uncanny joker. I dinna ken what's wrang wi' him, but there's something verra wrang, verra wrang. *****1900** in Wilkes *Dict. Austral. Colloq.* 191: Where's the old joker hanging out at all? *****1908** in Wilkes *Dict. Austral. Colloq.*: So yer didn't get that joker? **1918** in *AS* (Oct. 1933) 28: I don't like dat joker dey give me fer a bunky. **1923** in D. Hammett *Continental Op* 34: Who do you think this joker is? **1927–28** Tasker *Grimhaven* 42: Once or twice some joker has stayed under cover for a couple of days. **1935** L. Hughes *Little Ham* 50: That joker can't keep time. Ham can't do nothin' but truck and love. **1936** Kingsley *Dead End* 695: Dee old joker said ee didn't know. **1950** Felsen *Hot Rod* 22: You jokers still here? **1969** Joseph *Me Nobody Knows* 91: I handed the swan a banana peel and that joker pulled me in. **1971** Woodin *Circle of Sun* 64: Hope the commotion dies quietly without sucking in the rest of these jokers. **1972–75** W. Allen *Feathers* 33: I figured there must be a lot of jokers in his position. **1995** *Strange Luck* (Fox-TV): Now some other joker's got his phone. **1996** *Jerry Springer Show* (synd. TV series): This joker got out of jail…ain't got no job, on probation.

2.a. any small object or contrivance, esp. one that causes or allays annoyance or difficulty; (*hence*) an advantage.—usu. constr. with *little*; (*often*) an unlawful or cheating device; (*later*) an item or device.

1847 in Oehlschlaeger *Reveille* 207: The Major discovered the little joker [*sc.*, a coin he was seeking] in his pocket. **1854** in Nevins & Weitenkampf *Cartoons* 73: This six barrel'd joker [pistol]. **1870** "M. Twain," in A.L. Scott *Twain's Poetry* 79: I'd have a little joker. **1885** *Harper's Mo.* (Sept.) 648: You're trying to cheat me half of the time,/With a "little joker." **1905** in RH files: The "Little Joker" won for [us] the contents of the vault of New Windsor Bank of Westminster, Carroll County, Maryland….All of the combinations were mastered in five nightly sittings. **1969** in Cornish & Dixon *Chicory* 38: If somethin' go wrong with a typewriter who/gonna take the cover off that joker.

b. *Gamb.* the pea or other marker used in a thimble or three-shell game.—constr. with *little*.

1856 Thomson *Plur-i-bus-tah* 176: The game of thimbles…. Thimbles three and "little joker." **1858** O.W. Holmes *Autocrat* 30: Something to bet upon, as much as the thimble-rigger's "little joker." **1859** Greeley *Overland Journey* 143: Robbing the miners…through the instrumentality of cards, roulette, and the "little joker." **1908** in "O. Henry" *Works* 282: Watch the little ball….Guess where the little joker is.

c. a drawback, esp. if hidden; catch; difficulty.

1869 "M. Twain," in A.L. Scott *Twain's Poetry* 67: This is the pint that seems "a joker." **1914** S.H. Adams *Clarion* 241: Even her simple mind grasped the "joker" in the contract. **1944** in Hassler *Diary* 35: An "option to serve sentence," a little joker turned over to men on appeal. **1952** Lait & Mortimer *USA* 192: The joker in the income tax…allows oil speculators to take 27½ per cent off the top…for depletion. **1955** Graziano & Barber *Somebody Up There* 216: I…was trying to find the joker in this deal. **1956** in Loosbrock & Skinner *Wild Blue* 101: The joker was the mountains.

jolly *n.* **1.** *Naut.* **a.** a marine.

*****1825** (cited in Partridge *DSUE* (ed. 8) 627). *****1829** Marryat F. *Mildmay* 143 [ref. to 1809]: And the jollies fired tolerably well, did they? *1832 B. Hall *Voyages* (Ser. 2) III 284: Jack wears a blue jacket, and the Jolly wears a red one. *1833 Marryat *P. Simple* 427: We're all to flog one another, and then pay off the *jollies*.*...*Marines. 1844 *Spirit of Times* (Mar. 2) 3 [ref. to 1801]: Lay yourself all along like a dead jolly. 1847 Downey *Portsmouth* 141: Our Jollies had their skins well saturated the major part of the time while their valorous Commander had never less than 15 or 16 inches of raw Brandy imprisoned under his Jacket.

b. a naval seaman.

1899 Robbins *Gam* 149: The blue-jacket—or, as some would say, the jolly—was proud of his former service in the navy.

2.a. *Und.* an excuse or pretense.

1859 Matsell *Vocab.* 47: *Jolly*...an excuse; a pretence. *1879 *Macmillan's Mag.* XL 504: I see a reeler giving me a roasting (watching me), so I begin to count my pieces for a jolly (pretence).

b. a taunting, teasing, or bantering remark; (*also*) light or cajoling talk.—also constr. with *the.*

1894 in S. Crane *Stories* 164: I taut they was jest givin' me er jolly. 1895 Townsend *Fadden* 158: Say, I taut he was giving me de jolly, and so I says to him, says I: "What t'ell, Mr. Paul?" 1899 A.H. Lewis *Sandburrs* 9: Billy chases up to Mary an' goes in to give her d' jolly of her life. 1900 *DN* II 43: *Jolly*, n....Light, flippant conversation. 1906 Ford *Shorty McCabe* 310: They was all pattin' me on the back, and givin' me the grand jolly. 1908 McGaffey *Show Girl* 58: You...ought to have heard the line of jolly some of those boys tried to hand out to me. 1915 [Swartwood] *Choice Slang* 74: Umpire Bait, and Jollys for Pitchers and Batters....He couldn't hit a bunch of bananas with a base fiddle [etc.]. 1966 Cassiday *Angels Ten* 22: Come on, Rand!...This is no time for jollies....Now get off the phone.

c. a deception; hoax; jest.

1895 *Billboard* (May 1) 7: This is no "jolly." It is reality. 1895 *Harper's Mag.* (May) 917: No, t'at ain't no jolly; t'at's straight. 1898 in S. Crane *Stories* 421: Well, you can laugh all you like, but—no jolly, now, boys—I tell you I'm a winner. 1899 Ade *Fables* 3: A good Jolly is worth Whatever you Pay for it. 1900 in Duis *Saloon* 47: Oh boys, it was a fierce jolly those brewery people threw into me when I handed over the forty bucks. They predicted...I would make all kinds of money. 1900 *DN* II 43: *Jolly*, n....A story trumped up to deceive. 1917 Crowley *Moonchild* 232: And that's no jolly.

3.a. usu. *pl.* enjoyment, esp. perverse pleasure.—usu. constr. with *get (one's).*

[1955 *AS* XXX 303: *Jolly*...Something good...."It's a jolly."] 1956 Hargrove *Girl He Left* 100: Different people...have different ways of getting their jollies. 1958 Gardner *Piece of Action* 209: Sign the damned contract and get some jollies from it now. 1956–60 J.A. Williams *Angry Ones* ch. xii: I suspected Rollie was really getting his jollies. 1963 Boyle *Yanks Don't Cry* 63: It was pretty obvious that he got his jollies from making us squirm. 1963 Coon *Short End* 171: Nobody could, unless he got his jollies out of torture. 1965 Bonham *Durango St.* 71: Crime is the way these guys get their jollies. 1966 "Petronius" *N.Y. Unexp.* 117: Now the dirty D.O.M. will get his jollies, mind you. 1967 P. Welles *Babyhip* 15: These people were not actually murderers or violently destructive, not at all; they just achieved their jollys in other ways. 1971 Curtis *Banjo* 108: There's people stayin' in this hotel shoot people for nothing, they get a big jolly off it. 1972 *Sanford & Son* (NBC-TV): I'm talkin' about you sittin' around here all day gettin' your jollies with that piano. 1983 K. Rowell *Outsiders* (film): Go ahead, get your jollies. 1984 Riggan *Free Fire* 150: When you were a kid, you would have gotten your jollies if someone had done this for you. 1988 *N.Y. Post* (June 22) 64: Lyin' around in the sand for two weeks isn't my idea of major jollies. 1995 *Donahue* (NBC-TV): We seem to be immature sexually and get our jollies off of naughty TV.

b. *pl.* an orgasm.—usu. constr. with *get (one's).*

1962 Kesey *Cuckoo's Nest* 253: I'd be scared...that just about the time I was gettin' my jollies she'd reach around behind me with a thermometer and take my temperature! 1964 H. Rhodes *Chosen Few* 127: Did you ever make her get her jollies? 1966 H.S. Thompson *Hell's Angels* 192: A lot of women can't make it with one guy at a time, they can't get their jollies. 1982 Castoire & Posner *Gold Shield* 127: Can't get your jollies that way, can you...? 1987 *Nat. Lampoon* (Dec.) 37: The woman...rotates her gizzard until the man attains his jollies.

4. see JOLLY GREEN GIANT.

jolly *v.* **1.** to taunt, abuse, or ridicule; (*also*) to tease; chaff; KID. Hence **jollier**, *n.*

1859 Matsell *Vocab.* 127: *Jollying.* Low expressions used by one combatant [prizefighter] to the other during the fight, for the purpose of irritating him and diverting his attention. *1873 Hotten *Slang Dict.* (ed. 4): *Jolly*, to abuse or vituperate. *1874 in *N & Q* (May 24, 1879) 406: Jolleying...hooting, hissing, and making demonstrations of violence. *1879 *N & Q* (May 24) 406: "Jolleying" is a common term among workmen in London, and it is used to express nearly every description of ridicule and abuse...."Well, it's hardly the Cheshire to jolly a bloke after he's snuffed it." *1879 *N & Q* (June 7) 454: "Chaff" or badinage, is known amongst workmen as "jolleying," and, in some instances, hoaxing a man is described by the term "jolleying." *1889 Barrère & Leland *Dict. Slang* I 506: To *jolly* a person is to "chaff" or "get at" him, or to hold him in ridicule. 1895 *DN* I 419: *Jolly*...To tease, poke fun at. N.Y. 1895 Townsend *Fadden Explains* 241: The work was nearly as much to "jolly" the eleven as anything else. 1896 Ade *Artie* 46: He's one of the biggest jolliers that ever came over the hills. 1900 *DN* II 43: *Jolly*, v.t.....3: To tease a person, good-naturedly or otherwise. 1900 in W.A. White *Letters* 30: Kansas towns like to "jolly" each other. 1904 in "O. Henry" *Works* 636: Wonder if old Patterson is trying to jolly me! 1911 in Truman *Dear Bess* 61: We all jollied Luella...about not being able to get dinner by herself. 1915 [Swartwood] *Choice Slang* 51: *Jolly* (to)—To joke. "To kid." *a*1928 in Shay *More Pious Friends* 142: Ye monkey-face divil, I'll jolly ye through! *a*1994 H. Roth *Mercy of Rude Stream* 137: The shop teacher...jollied Ira about the incident. 1996 *Good Morning America* (Mar. 8) (ABC-TV): Can you jolly her out of it?

2. to humor or make good-natured, esp. by flattery; speak ingratiatingly to; attempt to win the favor of.—also constr. with *up.*

*1865 in *Comments on Ety.* (Jan. 1995) 19: So much have they "jollied" the girl that...she has promised to become his wife. 1890 in *DA*: I jollied him along as strong as I could. 1891 Maitland *Slang Dict.* 157: *Jolly*, to speak well of a friend is to "jolly" him. 1892 Gunter *Miss Dividends* 232: You've left her alone all day—you ain't been near to jolly her up. 1893 F.P. Dunne, in Schaaf *Dooley* 191: They cud jolly a man f'r givin' big an' roast him f'r givin' a little. 1894 Bangs *In Politics* 65: We want a man who'll go about and jolly the voters. 1895 *DN* I 419: *Jolly*...To flatter. N.Y., O....To do a favor with the idea of a possible return, or in order to get on good terms. 1896 Ade *Artie* 20: I put up the tall talk, jollied her along. 1897 Ade *Pink* 143: Call 'em misteh so-and-so. 'At's someping 'ey don't of'en get an' it jollies 'em. 1908 H.C. Fisher *A. Mutt* 126: I'll go into the smoker and jolly up the boys. 1929 E. Wilson *Thought of Daisy* ch. iv: I thought that I'd jolly him along a little.

3. to impose upon; trick.

*1889 Barrère & Leland *Dict. Slang* I 506: *Jolly*, *to* (thieves), to impose upon. 1893 Frye *Field & Staff* 173: I'd jollied de boys out'n a pocketful.

jolly-bag *n.* a condom.

1988 *Nat. Lampoon* (Apr.) 28: Condom Corner...Put [on] a jolly-bag. *a*1990 P. Dickson *Slang!* 197: *Jolly bag.* Condom.

Jolly Green Giant *n.* [joc. allusion to the *Jolly Green Giant*, a trademark of Green Giant Foods, Inc., notably featured in animated television commercials in the early 1960s] *Mil. Av.* any of several large Sikorsky or Boeing-Vertol rescue or cargo helicopters. Also **Jolly, Jolly Green.**

1965 in J.C. Pratt *Viet. Voices* 215: They ejected and were picked up by a "Jolly Green Giant" helicopter. 1968 *Airman* (Feb.) 11: The Jolly Green HH-3E rescue helicopters. *Ibid.* 12: He can call on the two Sandys who escort the Jolly Greens. *Ibid.* 41: I kept looking and listening for the Jollys. 1968 in Tuso *Vietnam Blues* 96: The Air Force cried for Jollys. 1970 Flood *War of Innocents* 125: The second Jolly Green Giant...had also been driven off by gunfire and was limping home. 1971 *N.Y. Times* (Mar. 7) 2: CH 53 Sea Knight: The Marine Corps' 67-foot-long "Super Jolly Green Giant" is a heavy cargo carrier. Cost: $2.5-million. 1976 Lavalle *Airpower* 50: The third Jolly, piloted by Capt. John R. Weimer, came out with 50 people. 1979 D.K. Schneider *AF Heroes* 34: The Jolly was equipped with armor plating and self-sealing fuel tanks. 1982 F. Hailey *Soldier Talk* 35: *Jolley* [sic] green giants. CH-47 Chinook...helicopters. 1983 Elton, Cragg & Deal *Dict. of Soldier Talk* 171: *Jolly* (Vietnam and later)...The HH-53 air rescue helicopter. 1990 Berent *Steel Tiger* 373: A second Jolly orbited in the distance. **1991** Reinberg *In Field* 118: *Jolly Green Giant*...the CH-54...and...CH-3. *a***1992** T. Wilson *Termite Hill* 99: The Jolly Greens don't like going past the Black [River].

jolly pills *n.pl.* pills or capsules containing a strong stimulant. Also **jolly beans.**

> **1962** Shepard *Press Passes* 6: There was Kaopectate, Seconal, jolly pills, nose drops...pellets to drop in drinking water, even death certificates. **1968** *Med. Science* XIX 35 [ref. to 1967]: "Speed" was so great that a few gave up the "acid" to concentrate their drug-taking careers on meth. They ate the "jolly beans" by the handful. **1970** *Sat. Review* (Nov. 14) 21: *Jolly beans.* Pep pills.

jolt *n.* **1.a.** a stiff drink of liquor.

> **1904** *McClure's Mag.* (Mar.) 560: I...had...a big jolt of whiskey. **1907** in H.C. Fisher *A. Mutt* 3: I...must get a jolt of booze on this. **1908** in H.C. Fisher *A. Mutt* 109: What's your rush, Ima? Let's have a jolt. **1908** J. London *M. Eden* 312: Wait till they get a few jolts in them and they'll warm up. **1912** Siringo *Cowboy Detective* 196 [ref. to 1890's]: Here I put a "jolt of the critter"—good old red "licker"—under Irish's belt. **1913** J. London *Valley of Moon* 227: I ain't drunk....I've only had two or three jolts. **1920** Fitzgerald *Paradise* 243: We'll...give you a wee jolt of Bourbon. **1925** I. Cobb *Many Laughs* 198: He...called for a jolt of sloe gin. **1925** S. Lewis *Arrowsmith* 695: Think you could stand a little jolt of first-class Kentucky bourbon? **1942** Horman & Corley *Capts. of Clouds* (film): Give him a jolt of whiskey. **1956** Hume *Forbidden Planet* (film): There's just about one jolt left. **1969** Turner *Mayberly* 131: One good jolt of good whisky. **1987** *Beauty & Beast* (CBS-TV): Have a little jolt. It'll help.

b. *Narc.* a dose of opium, morphine, or other drug; an injection; FIX, 3.a.; (*also, rarely*) (see 1975 quot.).

> **1907** in H.C. Fisher *A. Mutt* 16: I wonder if I can bull this pill roller into selling me a jolt. **1916** (cited in *ODMS*). **1922** Murphy *Black Candle* 294: It was requisite that he take a "jolt" of cocaine. **1925–26** J. Black *You Can't Win* 162 [ref. to 1890's]: He wouldn't give us a jolt if we had the horrors. **1929** Tully *Shadows of Men* 213: He would seek other addicts and tell them marvelous tales until they would give him a "jolt." **1957** Murtagh & Harris *First Stone* 56: My muscles began to hurt and I started to burn up. I told him I was liable to die right in his kitchen if I didn't get a jolt. **1966–67** P. Thomas *Mean Streets* 118: I let a little jolt of H fall on my thumbnail. **1975** V.B. Miller *Trade-Off* 38: He'd gotten a jolt—a hotshot—an intentional overdose designed to end his complaining.

c. a thrill of pleasure, as from liquor or drugs; KICK.

> **1923** Fishman & Perlman *Crucibles* 121: They will use any substance which will give them a "kick" or a "jolt." These drugs include cocaine, heroin,...opium,...and in fact anything they can obtain. **1927** Faulkner *Mosquitoes* 247: Mostly words...a sort of cocktail of words. I imagine you get quite a jolt from it, if your taste is educated to cocktails. **1951** in *AS* (Feb. 1952) 27: *Jolts*...The effect of use of [a] drug. **1968** Johnson & Johnson *Count Me Gone* 128: And if you don't get a jolt, *some* kind of a blast, what good is it?

2. *Und.* a prison sentence.

> **1912** Lowrie *Prison* 17: A six-year "jolt." *Ibid.* 280: We'll boost to get you off with a light jolt. **1914** Jackson & Hellyer *Vocab.* 51: He did a jolt once before in Joliet. **1917–19** J. Boyle *Boston Blackie* 237: Gladrags...got...a life jolt. **1925** Mullin *Scholar Tramp* 218: I won't take you into custody, being as y'all have just served a jolt. **1928** in J.P. Cannon *Notebook* 65: Billings did a short "jolt" before. **1930** F. Marion *Big House* (film): You'll stand up and take your jolt like a man. **1953** Roman *Vice Squad* (film): You'll be keeping an innocent man from taking a jolt. **1959** Duffy & Lane *Warden's Wife* 267: What he did fear was a stiff jolt at Folsom. **1961** *Sat. Eve. Post* (Aug. 26) 40: A many-time loser who was doing a jolt for robbery. **1978–86** J.L. Burke *Lost Get-Back Boogie* 49: Is this your first jolt?

jolt *v.* **1.** *Und.* to inflict a prison sentence upon.

> **1912** Lowrie *Prison* 128: Once in a while an old-timer gets jolted, but more oftener he knows enough not t' fight th' case...an' gets off light. **1915–16** Lait *Beef, Iron & Wine* 161: He jolts me the limit. **1926** (quot. at LAG).

2. *Narc.* to take heroin, morphine, etc., by injection.

> **1953** W. Brown *Monkey on My Back* 122: But he declared that he was "off the stuff," that he would never "jolt again." **1994** *Street Terms: Drugs* (Internet): *Jolt*—to inject a drug.

jomoke var. JAMOKE.

Jonah *n.* [ref. to the Old Testament prophet cast overboard during a tempest at sea caused by his impiety] **1.a.** Orig. *Naut.* a person or thing whose presence brings ill luck or disaster; JINX.

> **1849** Melville *White Jacket* 315 [ref. to 1843]: Damn you, you Jonah. **1849** in Chittick *Roarers* 209: He was a Jonah, cuss hem. **1862** Sill *Journal* 37: Capt. "never knew such wind in this latitude," talks disgustedly of "Joners." **1886** in *AS* XXV (1950) 34: Does it mean that Billy was a Jonah? **1894** Henerson *Sea Yarns* 104: A Jonah are what a sailor-man calls any person wot he thinks makes bad luck fur the ship. **1897** Kipling *Capts. Courageous* 119: A Jonah's anything that spoils the luck. Sometimes it's a man—sometimes it's a boy—sometimes it's a bucket. **1903** *Enquirer* (Cincinnati) (May 9) 13: Modern Slang Glossary...*Jonah*—A hoodoo. ****1909** Ware *Passing Eng.* 160: *Jonah* (Theatrical, 1883). An actor who brings bad luck to a theatre. ****1929** Bowen *Sea Slang* 77: *Jonah, A.* Anybody who is supposed to bring bad luck to the ship. **1934** Weseen *Dict. Slang* 144: *Jonah*—An actor who exerts an unfavorable influence on others. *Ibid.* 258: Sports...*Joner*...that which brings bad luck. **1938** "E. Queen" *4 Hearts* 22: You hooked me to a Jonah! **1943** G. Biddle *Artist at War* 196: I hope I am not a Jonah. **1942–49** Goldin et al. *DAUL* 111: *Jonah*...Any person or thing superstitiously believed to attract bad luck. **1962** *Car 54* (NBC-TV): He's a jinx! A Jonah!

b. an evil spell.

> **1911** Roe *Prodigal Daughter* 71: The landlady was furious, declaring that we were "putting a Jonah" on the house.

2. a person who chronically suffers misfortune.

> **a***1885** in *OED*: You must be very lucky in love...for you are a regular Jonah at cards. **1896** Ade *Artie* 22: When the balls stopped rolling they were scattered all over the table, but not one of them had gone into a pocket. "A dead rank Jonah," muttered Artie, as he backed away from the table. **1896** in A. Charters *Ragtime Songbk.* 59: I...had no luck, was a Jonah. **1949** G. Coffin *Winning Poker* 180: *Jonah*—A player in bad luck. Anyone who brings bad luck. **1965** L. Mitchell, in W. King & R. Milner *Black Drama Anthol.* 602: I'm a Jonah man, I'm a Jonah man/And no matter how much right I do/It always comes out wrong.

¶ In phrase:

¶ **heave** [or **throw**] **up Jonah** to vomit copiously, as from seasickness.

> **1863** in C. Mattocks *Unspoiled Heart* 65: Many of the men have been "throwing up Jonah" today, as it has been quite rough. **1865** in J. Crawford *Dear Lizzie* 369: Oh! You should have seen the Boys *throwing up Jonah.* It was [a] most awful rough sea. **1865** in Glatthaar *March to Sea* 117: The Sea was very ruff & so we hove up Jonah a good deal. **1899** Skinner *4th Illinois* 31: Even the chaplain..."heaved up Jonah," keeping in his state room. **1917** *DN* IV 393: *Heave up Jonah....*To vomit violently. **1943**, **1965–70** in *DARE.*

Jonah *v.* **1.** to bring ill luck to; JINX.

> *****1887** in *OED*: I seem to Jonah everything I touch. **1897** Kipling *Capts. Courageous* 97: I've known a splittin' knife Jonah two trips till we was on to her. **1942** *ATS* 245: Bring bad luck [to]...jinx, Jonah. **1975** McKennon *Horse Dung* 500: *Jonahed*: A show [*i.e.,* circus] suffering a long run of hard luck.

2. *Black E.* to trick or swindle.

> **1967** Colebrook *Cross of Lassitude* 329: She'd been through all those experiences endemic to the life, been "Jonah'ed," played-on, "Georgia'd."

Jonathan *n.* a New Englander; (*Naut.*) a New England vessel.

> **1780** in *DA*: [The loyalists] also took and destroyed a piece of cannon, which the Jonathans in vain endeavored to defend. **1812** in *DAE*: "*Jonathan*" was ready for *John Bull* in any way. **1839** *Spirit of Times* (Aug. 31) 310: What's the meaning of them words [*sic*] that Eagle's got in his mouth, said a John Bull to a Jonathan. **1849** in Borden *Dear Sarah* 162: We can fall in with a "Johnathon" bound out to the West Indies with a load of lumber.

jone var. JOAN.

jones *n.* [fr. *Jones*, common family name; semantic devel. unkn.] Orig. *Black E.* **1.** *Narc.* **a.** a drug addiction, esp. to heroin.

> *a***1962** Maurer & Vogel *Narc. Add.* (ed. 2) 308: *Jones.* A drug habit. **1965** C. Brown *Manchild* 272 [ref. to N.Y.C., 1950's]: Yeah, baby, that's the way it is. I've got a jones. **1965** in Sanchez *Word Sorcerers* 192: I mean, I don't have a long jones. **1967** Gonzales *Paid My Dues* 100:

Carmen explained she had a jones. **1969** Joseph *Me Nobody Knows* 72: Many of the dope addicts in the street are strung out. (Up in Harlem we use the expression he's got a Jones.) **1970** D. Long *Nia* 8: He got a jones/she a dike. **1973–76** J. Allen *Assault* 162: I started off with a snorting jones. **1974–77** A. Hoffman *Property Of* 248: You are one edgy dude for a man who's kicked his jones. **1980** in Courtwright et al. *Addicts Who Survived* 115 [ref. to Phila., *ca*1940]: Then you'll find out if you've got a Jones or not. **1981** in Courtwright et al. *Addicts Who Survived* 58 [ref. to N.Y.C., 1950's]: What? Damn, he got a Jones? **1987** S. King *Misery* 151: No bad habits (except for his codeine jones).

b. symptoms of heroin withdrawal.—also constr. in pl.

1965 C. Brown *Manchild* 272 [ref. to N.Y.C., 1950's]: My jones is on me...something terrible. I feel so sick. **1970** *Evergreen Review* (Apr.) 78: When the Joneses comes on [the sickness of withdrawal] there's nothin they can do but yell their guts out. All the guards do is tell em to shut up. **1970** Cortina *Slain Warrior* 34: I woke up with a Jones...you know, I felt achy and my stomach was upset, my nose was running and my eyes...I thought I'd caught a cold. My friend said: "Sal, that ain't a cold. Honey, you got a Jones." **1970** in Thigpen *Streets* 18: My jones is really down. **1971** *CBS News* (CBS-TV) (June 15): A Jones is the feelin' you get when you need to get skag. Like with some guys their Jones is a nervous feeling, or cold chills. When I don't get skag my back hurts. That's *my* Jones. **1971** *N.Y. Times Mag.* (Dec. 5) 112: Soon after, he came to know the family of symptoms known as "the Joneses." **1974** V.E. Smith *Jones Men* 144: His jones comes on him so bad he starts to lose his cool. **1978–86** E.M. Miller *Street Woman* 110: To keep...from getting "a Jones" (withdrawal symptoms). **1989** P. Benchley *Rummies* 107: I'm on a *bad* fuckin' jones.

c. a heroin addict.—usu. used in joc. direct address; (*hence*) one who is psychologically addicted, as to gambling.

1965–66 in Maurer & Vogel *Narc. Add.* (ed. 3): *Jones*...A variable term used widely by [black drug addicts] as a greeting. **1970** Horman & Fox *Drug Awareness* 468: *Jones*—the habit, an addict. **1973** (cited in T. Clark *Dict. Gambling* 111).

d. heroin.

1968–70 in Agar *Ripping & Running* 161: *Jones*...1. Heroin habit. 2. Heroin. **1971** *Newsweek* (July 5) 27: All those guys sitting there with a gun trained at your head while you stand in line to get the Jones. **1968–73** Agar *Ripping & Running* 51: The *junkie* finds his heroin, or *stuff* (*smack,...jones, boy*) packed differently from region to region. **1974** V.E. Smith *Jones Men* 12: All I wanta do from now on is sell coke....No more jones, see?

e. a feeling of drug-induced euphoria.—constr. with *on*.

1972 N.Y.U. student: Man, has he got a Jones on!

2. any sort of habit, habitual craving, or fixation, usu. regarded as perverse or consuming; YEN.

1970 Major *Afro-Amer. Slang* 71: *Jones:* a fixation;...compulsive attachment. **1970** *Current Slang V* (Fall) 9: *Jones,* n. A great need for stimulus—drugs, coffee, tobacco. **1971** in T.C. Bambara *Gorilla* 3: Blind people got a hummin jones if you notice. **1972** Burkhart *Women in Pris.* 448: *Jones.* A strong desire for something or someone; also, a habit. **1972** *Tuesday Mag.* (May) 17: This young man's parents didn't know that they were subsidizing their son's card-playing "jones" (habit), but for all we know they might be heavy card players, too. **1973** I. Reed *La. Red* 95: She knows that La Bas has a "twenties" jones. **1974** *Black World* (Nov.) 61: With a jones for jockey straps. **1978** W. Brown *Tragic Magic* 13: It's a well-known fact that we have a heavy jones for highly seasoned foods and fine threads. **1981** *N.Y. Post* (Dec. 15) 58: There's a far greater chance of curing herpes than The Phantom's Basketball Jones. **1982** Sculatti *Catalog of Cool* 151: Potato Chips of the Gods: The Ultimate Junk Food Jones. **1987** E. Spencer *Macho Man* 95: In Nam I have a real bad jones—an addiction—to food. **1987** Cher, in *Newsweek* (Nov. 30) 69: When I feel stress, I get this chocolate jones. **1988** H. Gould *Double Bang* 163: That's what the junkie needs for his sugar jones. **1992** G. Wolff *Day at Beach* 154: I've got a *bad* root beer...jones. **1993** *Lompoc* (Calif.) *Record* (USA Weekend) (June 25–27) 8: He gets the jones for rich, cholesterol-straight-to-the-heart Mexican tripe soup. **1994** *CBS This Morning* (CBS-TV) (July 25): So I've got a carbohydrate jones. What do I do about it?

3.a. Esp. *Black E.* the penis; in phr. **get (one's) jones off** (of a man) to experience an orgasm.—usu. considered vulgar. [Prob. the orig. sense.]

1966 in IUFA *Folk Speech*: Folk Speech, Negro: *Jones* The male's sex

organ. **1969** Beck *Black Widow* 292: A...freak queen kept rubbing... against my Jones. **1972** T.C. Bambara *Gorilla* 164: As if he weren't in my bed trying to get his jones off without quite letting himself know it, just in case Inez ask if he been messin around with me. **1972** R. Wilson *Forbidden Words* 153: She was hot for his Jones. **1977** (quot. at JOHNSON, 1.a.). **1990** Thorne *Dict. Contemp. Sl.* 282: *Jones*...penis. Now...used by black speakers and their imitators.

b. *Black E.* copulation.

1965 in Baraka *Tales* 10: "Oooooo, that was some good box."..."Yeh? You mean you got a little Jones, huh?"

4. *Black E.* a black person.

1971 in E. Lewis *Who Took Weight?* 83: Revolution—/is jones taking jeff's [*sc.*, Jeffrey Hunter's] place in the [film] king of kings. *a*1979 E. Blake, in A. Rose *Eubie Blake* 130: I don't think that *ever* happens to the Joneses. White people got so much to lose...*they* can get scared, but a Jones ain't got nothin' to lose. Nothin' can scare him.

5. a thing; JOHNSON, 1.d.

1986 Spears *Drugs & Drink* 292: *Jones*...a term meaning thing.

jones *v.* **1.** *Narc.* to experience drug withdrawal symptoms; (*hence*) to feel a strong craving; yearn.—often constr. with *out*.

1974 K.C. street musician, age 23: He's *jonesing out* means he's getting paranoid about needing more drugs. **1975** in Spears *Drugs & Drink* 292: Jonesing. **1981** in *West. Folklore* XLIV (1985) 7: Say if...you ask me for a cigarette...and if I just say "no" to you, you gonna jones until the next campus shop open. **1989** P. Munro *U.C.L.A. Slang* 53: She's jonesing for those diamond earrings. **1992** *UTSQ: Jonesin'*—really wanting something, craving. **1992** *Amer. Detective* (ABC-TV): You are strung. You'll be jonesin' like a big dog. **1992** J. Nichols *Elegy for September* 18: Boy, have I ever been jonesing for you. **1995** N.Y.C. artist, age 30: They said, "Can't you tell he's jonesing?" And I'm like, "What is *jonesing?*" And they go, "He's a junkie. He needs heroin."

2. to idle; kill time.

1984–88 Safire *Language Maven* 23: *Jonesin'*—Doin' nothin'.

joneser *n.* *Narc.* a heroin user.

1989 P. Munro *U.C.L.A. Slang* 53: He's become a joneser since he started going out with that girl who deals.

Jones hat *n.* *Army.* a jungle hat.

1987 in Katcher *Amer. Soldier* 178 [ref. to 1968]: Headgear is an ARVN camouflaged "Jones hat" with brim removed.

jones man *n.* *Black E.* a man or boy who sells heroin. Also **jones boy.**

1972 *Newsweek* (Feb. 28) 18: Today he is a heroin pusher, a "Jones man" (from the city's street word for the drug). **1973** Weisman & Boyer *Heroin Triple Cross* 111: Ole Mr. Gloves is tied in with the jones boys. **1974** V. Smith *Jones Men* 34: Everybody wanta be the jones man. *a*1977 in S. King *Bachman* 132: As if I were one of the original Placerville jones men. *a*1987 Bunch & Cole *Reckoning for Kings* 416: Money...was in being the Jones Man.

Jones's *n.* [fr. DAVY JONES'S LOCKER] *Naut.* the bottom of the sea.

1847 Neal *Charcoal Sketches* (Ser. 2) 37: Somebody else has gone to Joneses [*sic*].

joog var. JUKE[1], *n.*, JUKE[2], *v.*, JUKE[3], *v.*

joogie *n.* [cf. syns. BOOGIE, WOOGIE] *Black E.* (see quot.).—sometimes used derisively.

*ca*1974 in J.L. Gwaltney *Drylongso* xvi: *Joogies*—black people, a term which may or may not be derogatory, depending on who uses it and how. *Ibid.* 16: A whole passel of joogies!

jook var. JUKE[1], *n.*, JUKE[2], *v.*, JUKE[3], *v.*

josan *n.* [< Japn] *Mil. in Far East.* an Asian girl or young woman.—also used fig. Also **jo-jo-san.**

1956 Lasly *Turn Tigers Loose* 131 [ref. to Korean War]: Wait'll those 'Merican Jo-sans get a load of the Vitamin D I've been saving! **1964** Peacock *Drill & Die* 186: Then seven days to yourself with a carefully picked Jo-san, in a secluded room in a secluded hotel in Kyoto. **1982** Cox & Frazier *Buck* 39 [ref. to 1951]: A dogface Jo-Jo-San is not at all like a Dogface Soldier. *a*1989 C.S. Crawford *Four Deuces* 28: The josans were calling out and waving good-bye to the soldiers as they went up the gangplank.

José *n.* [fr. *José,* regarded as a stereotypical Hispanic male given name] a Puerto Rican, esp. a man.—often used disparagingly.

1976 in Mack *Real Life* (unp.): We employ 500 Josés who can't do anything else.

¶ In phrase:

¶ **no way, José** see s.v. NO WAY.

Joseph var. JOE, *adj.*

Josh *n.* [app. fr. hypocoristic form of male given name *Joshua*, regarded as a typically rustic name; cf. ALVIN, ELMER, HICK, RUBE, etc.; cf. earlier syn. JOSKIN] a countryman, esp. regarded as foolish or lazy; (*specif.*) (*obs.*) an Arkansan.

    1863 in Heartsill *1491 Days* 140: We were "gobbled up" and taken to the Arkansas Battalion H'd Q'rs...Luther says that the only thing he regrets in the affair is to be arrested by "Joshes." **1864** in S.L. Foster *Cleburne's Command* 80: The Arkansas troops...are nicknamed "Josh'es" and when ever a Texan meets an Ark. soldier, he says, how are you Josh. Or where are you going Josh &c. It is all the time Josh. **1869** *Overland Mo.* (Aug.) 129: The cant designation in the Rebel army for a man of Arkansas was "Josh." **1877** in J.M. Carroll *Camp Talk* 90: Never mind what "Joshes" say about the carpet—get it. **1878** in M. Lewis *Mining Frontier* 124: Ye think I'm jokin', do ye—ye take me for a josh, eh? **1889** Barrère & Leland *Dict. Slang* I 507: For some unknown reason a *josh* is supposed...to be always a sleepy person. **1904** *Life in Sing Sing* 249: *Josh.*—A countryman.

josh *n.* [orig. unkn.] **1.** (used as a shout of encouragement).

    1842 *Spirit of Times* (May 28) 145: His health is drank...in Bimbo daily, with all the honors, including a "Volcanic Josh!"...Go it, sonny, while you're young! Hip! hip! hip! *J-o-s-h!!!* **1845** (quot. at JOSH, *v.*, 1). **1870** in Bartlett *Amer.* (ed. 4) 325: A member [of the N.Y. Stock Exchange] falls asleep....*"Josh," "Josh," "Josh,"* comes roaring from a dozen...lungs, and the broker lifts his head...startled from slumber by the traditional rallying cry.

    2. a usu. good-natured hoax; (*hence*) a jest; piece of badinage. Now *colloq.* or *S.E.*

    1878 F. Hart *Sazerac* 57: Ain't it only one of them "joshes" they gits up in the *Reveille* sometimes? **1896** Ade *Artie* 21: That ain't no josh, neither. **1897** Norris *Vandover* 328: Geary made a "Josh" that was a masterpiece. **1898** in S. Crane *Stories* 422: We'll back you, and work a josh on Freddie. **1900** O. Wister, in *Harper's* (May) 899: What did he say to Trampas after...Trampas put the josh on him? **1906** Ford *Shorty McCabe* 37: It was a josh, all right, that he was handin' out. **1907** in C.M. Russell *Paper Talk* 63: This sounds like a josh but its on the square. **1910** T. Dreiser, in Riggio *Dreiser-Mencken Letters* I 46: Just a slight undertone of josh. **1913** J. London *Valley of Moon* 100: Can't you take a josh?

josh *v.* [orig. unkn.] **1.** to give a cheer or shout. Cf. JOSH, *n.*, 1.

    1845 in *DA*: Look out in future, and if you must *Josh*, why, give a *private* one.

    2. to hoax or tease, esp. good-naturedly; bait; joke; fool; KID. Now *colloq.* or *S.E.* Also (*obs.*) **joss.**

    1852 in *OED*: The...chap's been jossin' ye. **1864** in *Ohio Arch. & Hist. Qly.* LII (1943) 175: The Bay was rough...and the boys began to get sick. One called, "Steady there," another, "I want a piece of fat pork with a string to it." **1876** in *No. Dak. Hist.* XVII (1950) 173: "Boys" Joshing "Capt Michailes." **1878** F. Hart *Sazerac* 144: You're only joshing me, I know. **1889** Barrère & Leland *Dict. Slang* I 506: *Josh, to* (American), to chaff, to make fun of, to quiz. **1889** Field *Western Verse* 70: Go on, if joshin' gratifies ye. **1894** in Ade *Chicago Stories* 33: He always got sore when any of the gang joshed him. **1899** Norris *McTeague* 50: What a josher was this Marcus! **1903** *Enquirer* (Cincinnati) (May 9) 13: Modern Slang Glossary...*Josh*—To make fun of; to tease. **1911** Spalding *Base Ball* 75: Bob...kept up his nerve...by "joshing" the National players as they came to bat with his witticisms. **1914** Z. Grey *West. Stars* 11: The fellows were joshing me. **1915** H. Young *Hard Knocks* 109: Don't show your ignorance...as they will josh you. **1925** in Partridge *Dict. Und.* 372: *Josh. v.,* to fool. **1926** C.M. Russell *Trails* 84: As I said before, the bill ain't joshing. **1927** Rollins *Jinglebob* 136: You serious? Ain't joshin'? **1928** W.C. Williams *Pagany* 247: He joshed her.—I came out here...before sailing for Vinland. **1948** E.J. Melton *Towboat Pilot* 30: Let's stop an' josh the ole codger. **1978** De Christoforo *Grease* 179: I'm just joshin' ya, man. **1985** J. Dillinger *Adrenaline* 77: I was only joshing. **1990** *Daybreak Saturday* (CNN-TV) (Aug. 18): Her joshing, jazzy manner won fans over.

joskin *n.* [prob. of E dial. orig.] a country bumpkin; (*hence*) *Naut.* a raw recruit; GREENHORN. Now *hist.*

    ***1811** *Lex. Balatron.*: *Joskin.* A countryman. *The dropcove maced the Joskin of twenty quid;* The ring dropper cheated the countryman of twenty guineas. ***1819** C. Lamb, in *F & H* IV 76: I hate the *joskins,* a name for Hertfordshire bumpkins. ***1828** in *F & H*: The very sight of a countryman, either yokel or joskin. **1859** Matsell *Vocab.*: *Joskin.* A countryman; a silly fellow. **1866** *Nat. Police Gaz.* (Dec. 8) 2: He was convicted of "snatching a lushy joskin's dummy." **1889** Barrère & Leland *Dict. Slang* I 507: *Joskin*...a dull rustic or greenhorn. **1899** Hamblen *Bucko Mate* 42: In glaring contrast to these well-seasoned mariners were the poor greenhorns, or raynecks, and joskins, as they were called. **1901** King *Dog-Watches* 249: We tossed and plunged...causing the seasick "joskins" to be unutterably miserable. **1906** A.H. Lewis *Confessions* 206: These joskins gets leery at the noise of the gun. **1928** Harlow *Sailor* 22 [ref. to 1876]: All hands, including the cook, were taking me to be a "Joskin." ***1929** Bowen *Sea Slang* 77: *Joskin.* A green hand under sail. **1937** D. Runyon *More Guys* 113: A very old joskin with a chin whisker and rheumatism and a mean look. *a*1961 R.H. Dillon *Shanghaiing Days* 180: The four other men—all raynecks or joskins (hicks, landlubbers)...had been shanghaied in San Francisco.

joss-man *n.* [pidgin < Pg *Deos* 'God' + *man*] *Naut. in Far East.* a clergyman or missionary; (*Navy*) a chaplain.

    *a*1889 in Barrère & Leland *Dict. Slang* 508: Joss-man he smilee. **1889** *United Service* (Sept.) 276: The chaplain is often called the "joss man." ***1913** in *OED2*: A missionary is known as a European "joss-man." ***1964** in *ODMS*: I was watch aboard and tried to get a sub, but no joy. I asked the Jossman if I could go ashore, and he told me to go.

jostle *v.* **1.** *Und.* to engage in petty confidence games.

    [**a*1890–96 *F & H* IV 77: *Jostle*...(Old Cant.)—To cheat.] **1965** C. Brown *Manchild* 160: He was always looking for cats who were down there jostling.

    2. *Und. & Police.* to pick pockets. Cf. earlier JOSTLER, 1.

    1969 Smith & Gay *Don't Try It* 113: Jostling (picking pockets). **1973** *N.Y. Times Mag.* (Mar. 18) 39: One female addict...[gave] details on a junkie vocation known as "jostling," a sophisticated form of pickpocketing....At the end of the meal, she returned the researcher's wallet.

jostler *n.* **1.** *Und. & Police.* the member of a pickpocketing team who jostles and distracts the victim.

    1929, 1934 (cited in Partridge *Dict. Und.* 372). **1956** Resko *Reprieve* 182 [ref. to 1940's]: The jostler's task was distracting the victim's attention while the hook...extracted the wallet. **1957** Murtagh & Harris *Cast First Stone* 305: *Jostler* A pickpocket.

    2. *Und.* a petty swindler.

    1965 C. Brown *Manchild* 161: After a while, you got to know all the jostlers down there.

jots *n.* [orig. unkn.] bread.

    1935 (cited in Partridge *Dict. Und.* 372). **1961** A.J. Roth *Shame of Wounds* 12: I got first take at the jots.

jour *n.* *Labor.* a journeyman. Also **jur.**

    1835 in *DA*: The *jours* are in the habit of *spouting* their work from one week to another. **1844** in Foner *Labor Songs* 64: O, the shoe jours, they are rising....you will see the jours a-coming. **1849** [G. Thompson] *City Crimes* 175: An indignant "jour" once told him. **1857** *Harper's Mo.* (May) 749: I traveled round when I was a "jour." **1859** Bartlett *Amer.* 222: *Jour,* or *Jur.*...journeyman. The boss quarrelled with the *jurs,*" i.e. the master quarrelled with his journeymen. **1860** (quot. at SNOB). **1863** in C.H. Moulton *Ft. Lyon* 128: We will then be...efficient "jours" at this peculiar trade. **1868–71** Leland *Breitmann's Ballads* 235: Dere vas Yankee jours extincted/Who lay upon de vloors. **1898** in *DAE*: Hundreds of old "jours"...in the palmy days of typesetting.

joy *n.* *Mil. Av.* success, esp. in locating a target on radar.— usu. used in negative constrs. [In Air Force radiocommunications, now an official term.]

    ***1945** in *OEDS*: There's even less joy in sending us the money. ***1945** in *OEDS*: "Johnnie took the new kite up this morning—had bags of joy," or "no joy at all." ***1946** Brickhill & Norton *Escape to Danger* 294: The workers [British airmen in a German prison camp] had been down nearly forty minutes and still "no joy." **1956** *Amer. Mercury* (Mar.) 21: A message rasps earthward: "Toe Joe, this is Pocket Fuzz Red. Tally-ho. I have joy."..."I have joy" indicated the pilots had the target on their own radar. "Tally-ho" meant they were closing in for identification. **1957** *Sat. Eve. Post* (Aug. 10) 41: No joy yet, Gay

Girl. **1984** *Call to Glory* (NBC-TV): Rodge. No joy. **1986** Merkin *Zombie Jamboree* 42: He'd...[asked] two lieutenant colonels and one full colonel with no joy by the time he left Benning. **1989** T. Blackburn *Jolly Rogers* 93: There was no joy there so I decided to proceed to Guadalcanal.

joy berry *n.* a coin.
   1918 (quot. at JACK). **1923** *Our Navy* (Apr. 15) 20: Me with thirty good bucks and him without one joy berry.

joy-bone *n.* the penis.—usu. considered vulgar.
   1985 *Nat. Lampoon* (Sept.) 36: Belshazzar's own joy-bone...turned the otherwise savvy sultan into a sap.

joybox *n.* **1.** *Jazz.* a piano or radio.
   1942 *Pittsburgh Courier* (Aug. 22) 7: Joy box—(radio). **1946** Mezzrow & Wolfe *Really Blues* 47: One of the greatest blues piano players that ever pounded a joybox.

   2. the vagina.—usu. considered vulgar.
   1974 Heard *Cold Fire* 113: Her joy-box...surrounded the essence of me.

joyboy *n.* an offensively clowning fellow; (*hence, ironically*) a sour-tempered or offensively gloomy fellow.
   [**1923** McAlmon *Village* 223: Whatcha throwing off on us for?...My girl's across the lake with Tennessee; I'm no joybird tonight myself.] **1925** (cited in Partridge *Dict. Und.* 372). **1940** Hartney *Up & At 'Em* 84 [ref. to 1918]: Joy-boy's dead! **1942** "D. Ormsbee" *Sound of American* 45: Joyboy...and Ox. **1960** MacCuish *Do Not Go Gentle* 115: Hop to, Buzz....The joy boys'll be back in a jiff. **1961** Kanter & Tugend *Pocketful of Miracles* (film): Hey, joyboy, looks like the lucky apple is workin' already. **1966** Cassiday *Angels Ten* 113: Dawson wasn't a joy boy. He was serious about eberything he did. **1968** Baker et al. *CUSS* 146: Joyboy A person who always fools around. **1972** B. Harrison *Hospital* 26: Nick didn't favor the waste of time any more than he favored joyboys, and so throughout David's internship Nick gave him more attention than was usual. **1989** *Eyewitness News* (WATE-TV) (June 29): This guy must be the last of the original joyboys. **1994** *Seinfeld* (NBC-TV): I got a flash for you, joyboy. Party time is over.

joy button *n.* the clitoris.—usu. considered vulgar.
   1972 A.K. Shulman *Ex-Prom Queen* 46: There was no joy button in the hygiene book. **1996** *Big Sister is Horny*, pornographic story on Usenet newsgroup alt.sex.stories: Eddie's glistening tongue was lashing...over Joan's incredibly-aroused little joy button.

joy cart *n.* a wagon; vehicle.
   1928 Havlin *Co. A* 32 [ref. to 1917]: The red wagon, or "joy cart"...was to be used in place of the Ford truck.

joy cubes *n.pl. Gamb.* dice.
   1920 in Hemingway *Dateline: Toronto* 35: Its dalliance with the joy cubes has plenty of precedence.

joy dust, joy flakes vars. JOY POWDER.

joyful *n.* liquor.—constr. with *the*.
   1835 *Mil. & Nav. Mag. of U.S.* (Mar.) 32: We have a little jug of the joyful back in the bushes. **1893** Hampton *Maj. in Washington* 213: He limbered up himself with a little bit of the joyful.

joy girl *n.* [< F *fille de joie*] a prostitute.
   1931 Stevenson *St. Luke's* 318 [ref. to ca1914]: Keeps joy-girls—'partment in town. **1953** Chandler *Goodbye* 82: Fifty-dollar joy-girls. **1961** Barbeau *Ikon* 30: Lookit the joy girls. **1961** Granat *Important Thing* 96: What was Paris to the forty-year-old "joy girls" themselves.

joy hole *n.* the vagina. Also (*Naut.*) **joy-hatch.**
   ca**1939** in Barkley *Sex Cartoons* 109: Take it easy big boy. After all I want to use this joy hole again some time. **1973** U.S. Navy seaman, Taiwan, age ca20 (coll. J. Ball): Boy, I'd like to get down in that joy-hatch! a**1990** P. Dickson *Slang!* 197: Joy hole. Female genitalia.

joy house *n.* [< F *maison de joie*] a brothel.
   1916–22 Cary *Sexual Vocab.* IV s.v. *prostitution*: Joy house. **1927** *DN* V 452: Joy house, n. A brothel. **1940** Chandler *Farewell, My Lovely* 16: I ain't been in a joy house in twenty years. **1965** N. Daniels *Moments of Glory* 28: Never walk into a joy house with a lot of money. **1973** Ward *Sting* (film): Gotta check all the joy houses till I find 'em. **1974** Wilder & Diamond *Front Page* (film): Can I mention his half interest in that Chinese joy house?

joy jelly *n.* (see a1972 quot.). Also **joy jell.**
   a**1972** B. Rodgers *Queens' Vernacular* 118: Joy jelly fruit-flavored body salve [or] lubricant jelly. **1985–87** Bogosian *Talk Radio* 30: These three bimbos baste this guy with joy jell.

joy joint *n.* a saloon. Also **joy parlor.**
   1899–1900 Cullen *Tales* 222: If you walk into a Portland joy-joint just to get out of the wet...you're dead liable to get vagged. **1926** C.M. Russell *Trails* 147: We leave this joy parlor arm-in-arm and visit a friend of mine who owns a livery stable. **1966** R. Anderson *Sand Pebbles* (film): I'm sure you all got your own joy joints to go to.

joy juice *n.* **1.** an alcoholic beverage, esp. whiskey.
   1913 T.A. Dorgan, in Zwilling *TAD Lexicon* 51: Up to the rail he waddled and asked for some joy juice. **1946** Boulware *Jive & Slang* 5: Joy Juice...Whiskey. **1955** McGovern *Fräulein* 184: You really must have been hittin' the joy juice to walk across the street like that. **1958** Frankel *Band of Bros.* 45: First he says no dice, then he hands us all this joy juice. **1962** Blake *Heartbreak* 127: Barkeep....pour a little joy juice. **1968** Swarthout *Loveland* 126 [ref. to 1930's]: People danced and had another go at the joy juice. **1971** Cole *Rook* 153: Cord used to go with him to dinge joints over in Ohio—smuggled him a pint of jigaboo joy juice. **1970–72** *AS* L (1975) 62: Joy juice...Beer. **1979** *Playboy* (Aug.) 52: My brain [was] half-dazed from too much joy juice. **1983** *Reader's Digest Success with Words* 86: Black English...joy juice = "wine, whiskey." **1987** D. Sherman *Main Force* 188: No, that was your joy juice.

   2. *Esp. Hosp.* a sedative or narcotic in solution. *Joc.*
   1954 Wertham *Innocent* 25: One needleful of joy-juice and you...forget your obligations! **1969** Lingeman *Drugs A to Z* 118: Joy juice. Chloral hydrate. **1971** Guggenheimer *Narc. & Drug Abuse* 28: Joy juice. chloral hydrate. **1987** Surgical nurse, Knoxville, Tenn., age ca60: With some of this joy juice we use, you won't have a worry in the world.

   3. semen.—usu. considered vulgar.
   1980 Ciardi *Browser's Dict.* 214: Joy-juice...2. A sexual emission. **1987** G. Matthews *Red Rooster* 28: A dog that humps the ground and licks up its own joy juice. **1996** *Jail*, pornographic story on Usenet newsgroup alt.sex.stories: Jet after jet of thick...joy juice squirted onto the floor.

joy knob *n.* **1.** JOYSTICK, 2.—usu. considered vulgar.
   1954–60 *DAS:* Joy knob...the penis. **1996** *Rig Man*, pornographic story on Usenet newsgroup alt.sex.stories: "Touch my cock, Mac"...He was pounding my joy knob.

   2. a movable knob attached to a steering wheel to allow one-handed steering.
   1974 E. Thompson *Tattoo* 196: Glenn took his right hand from the wheel and put it around her shoulders, steering with the death's-head joy knob.

joy pop *n. Narc.* a usu. subcutaneous injection of narcotics taken by a nonaddict. Also **joy shot.**
   1922 Murphy *Black Candle* 128: The..."joy shots" are among the most vicious elements in the [morphine] plague. **1939** in *OED2:* If you should happen to hear anyone speaking of a...joy-pop...bring him right here. **1951** *Time* (Feb. 26) 24: An injection [of heroin] under the skin [is] a "joy pop." **1968** "H. King" *Box-Man* 9 [ref. to ca1920]: Dick...would take what they called joy pops.

joy-pop *v. Narc.* to inject narcotics without becoming addicted; CHIPPY, 1. Hence **joy-popper,** *n.*
   1936 *AS* (Apr.) 123: Joy-popper. A person, not a confirmed addict, who indulges in an occasional shot of dope. However, joy-popping is usually the beginning of a permanent addiction. **1951** in *AS* (Feb. 1952) 27: When the youngsters first start on drugs, they are called "joy-poppers." **1956** H. Gold *Not With It* 27: No joypopping, hear? **1958** A. King *Mine Enemy* 33: I'm gonna joy-pop, just on weekends. **1964** Anslinger & Gregory *Protectors* 229: Joy-pop to take drugs not out of habit but occasionally for pleasure.

joy powder *n. Narc.* heroin, morphine, or cocaine in crystalline form. Also **joy dust, joy flakes.**
   1922 *DN* V 182: Morphine...Joy Powder. **1928** in Starks *Cocaine Fiends* 43: A bunch of "Snow Birds" with their "happy dust" or "joy powder" [cocaine]. **1938** in Partridge *Dict. Und.* 372: Joy dust [cocaine]. **1939** Howsley *Argot* 28: Joy Dust—Heroin. **1947** *Look* (Jan. 6, 1948) 26: Joy powder—Morphine. **1953** Anslinger & Tompkins *Traff. in Narc.* 311: Joy dust. Drugs, especially cocaine. joy flakes, joy powder. Morphine, cocaine, or heroin. **1971** *Inter. Jour. Add.* VI 360: Joy powder heroin. **1973** D. Smith & D. Wesson *Uppers* 147: Joydust—Vietnamese heroin.

joy prong *n.* the penis.—usu. considered vulgar.

> **1916** Cary *Venery* I 161: *Joy Prong*—The penis. **1930** *Lyra Ebriosa* 17: There came to town one Joy-Prong Pete. **1949** Monteleone *Crim. Slang* 135: *Joy prong*…The male pudendum. **1960–69** Runkel *Law* 29: How lucky she's been…having first divvies on such a big joy prong!

joy-rider *n.* **1.** (among tramps) (see 1927 quot.).

> **1927** *DN* V 452: *Joy rider, n.* A legless beggar who rides about on a board mounted on roller skates, propelling himself by pushing on blocks held in the hands. Also *skater* or *skooter.* **1939** *New Yorker* (Mar. 11) 38: Blind men and "joyriders," as the legless who push themselves around on little wheeled platforms are known, are stubborn about giving up their trade.…Police even found one joyrider who hung around in a Broadway bar.

2. *Narc.* an occasional user of narcotics who is not yet addicted.

> **1932** Nelson *Prison Days & Nights* 178: So that the average criminal is far more likely to become merely a "joy-rider" (a man who takes a "shot" or two to tide him over dreary weekends in the cell…), and not a genuine drug addict. **1954–60** *DAS:* *Joy rider* A nonaddict who sometimes takes a narcotic drug.

joy smoke *n. Narc.* marijuana.

> [**1908** J. London *M. Eden* 373: The "Smoke of Joy"…was a shock to bourgeois morality and prejudice.] **1938** (cited in Spears *Drugs & Drink* 293). **1954–60** *DAS* 297: *Joy smoke* Marijuana.

joystick *n.* **1.** Orig. *Av.* a control stick. [The sense 'lever used to control motion of graphical element on computer' is S.E.]

> ***1910** in *OED2:* In order that he shall not blunder inadvertently in the air, the central lever—otherwise the *cloche,* or joy-stick is tied well forward. ***1917** in Lee *No Parachute* 21: The Pup is so sensitive on the controls that any abrupt movement of the joystick or rudder makes her jump like a startled cat. **1918** in Grider *War Birds* 139: Map case, throttle, joystick and rudder bar. **1919** Yarwood *Overseas Dreams* 40: Great little manipulator of the "joy-stick." **1927** Saunders *Wings* 91: His hands knew little except the trigger and the throttle and the joystick. **1934** Brewer *Riders of the Sky* 93: More sensitive to the joy-stick than a Nieuport;/The slightest touch would turn her. ***1974** P. Wright *Lang. Brit. Industry* 5: In the R.A.F.…*control column* is a technical term but *joy-stick* its slang equivalent. **1975** in Higham & Siddall *Combat Aircraft* 68: He…placed the joystick in the full back position against the seat. **1980** T. Jones *Adrift* 150: He pushed his joy-stick down and down he goes…straight into the North Atlantic. **1989** Cassell *S.S.N. Skate* 44: The "joystick" controlled the huge diving planes rigged forward in the bows. **1993** T. Taylor *Lightning in Storm* 25: They bend the joy stick, "yank and bank."

2. the penis.

> **1916** Cary *Venery* I 161: *Joy Stick*—The penis. ***ca1929** *Adventures of Grace & Anna* 87: She seized hold of his joy-stick and gave it a wicked tweak. **1931** Farrell *McGinty* 156: Slip ur…de…joy stick. **1941** *Chippie Wagon* 38: I haven't seen a joystick on a guy that size before in my life. **1957** E. Brown *Locust Fire* 29: The lady luck is tired of my joy stick. **1966** Harris & Freeman *Lords of Hell* 93: Help me get my joystick up so I don't go crazy. **1974** Lahr *Trot* 57: Duragrip zippers…were murder on the old joystick when humping. **1986** R. Walker *AF Wives* 256: He's also into women—and I do mean *into* them. You know, a real joystick man. **1992** N. Cohn *Heart of World* 236: These…cocks…looked just ludicrous. These dicks, pricks, joysticks.

3. *Narc.* **a.** an opium pipe.

> **1936** D.W. Maurer, in *AS* (Apr.) 123: *Joy Stick.* An opium pipe.

b. a marijuana cigarette.

> **1962** H. Simmons *On Eggshells* 166: Passing her the…joy-stick. **1966** S. Stevens *Go Down Dead* 121: It make me sad thinking about my mother like that I don't know why. Maybe it just the joy stick and the beer and getting ready for Tigers. **1970** Landy *Underground Dict.* 114: *Joy stick*…Marijuana cigarette. **1990** Vachss *Blossom* 190: As thin as a chiba joystick.

joy water *n.* liquor; JOY JUICE, 1.

> **1907** *Army & Navy Life* (July) 810: There wasn't scarcely any chance whatever for the man that got gay with joy water. **1909** T.A. Dorgan, in Zwilling *TAD Lexicon* 51: Dear Bunk Come up to 63 Chop St tonight one flight up—Big time Lots of skirts and joy water. **1912–14** in E. O'Neill *Lost Plays* 185: Are you soused too? Where have you hidden the joy-water? **1918** F. Gibbons *Thought We Wouldn't Fight* 267: Rum or alcohol has never been part of the United States

army ration. In the memory of the oldest old-timers…"joy water" had never been issued. **1919** Wilkins *Company Fund* 39: He was told to "Lay off" the "Joy Water." **1929** (quot. at THIRD RAIL).

joy weed *n. Narc.* marijuana.

> **1937** in Starks *Cocaine Fiends* 103: This bunch sure uses up the joy weed, don't they? **1940** (cited in Partridge *Dict. Und.* 372).

JP *n. Mil.* Japan.

> **1988** DeLillo *Libra* 83: Welcome to JP—land of sliding doors and slant-eyed whores. **1990** D. Sherman *Squad* 64 [ref. to Vietnam War]: He spent a couple months in JP. *Ibid.* 212: Maybe I'll get married to…a geisha in JP.

J school *n. Stu.* a school of journalism. Cf. B SCHOOL.

> *ca*1968 W. Branch, in W. King & R. Milner *Black Drama Anthol.* 454 [ref. to 1950's]: You young J-school Pulitzer Prizes give me a pain in the ass. **1978** E. Thompson *Devil to Pay* 37 [ref. to 1950's]: The J-School's daily tried to ignore the weekly's existence. **1981** Eble *Campus Slang* (Oct.) 4: *J school*—Journalism School. **1986** *N.Y. Post* (Mar. 26) 13: J-school dean quits Columbia. **1988** *Newsday* (N.Y.) (June 28) 19: A full 85 percent of entry-level newspaper journalists are hired out of those places known as "J Schools." **1989** *Larry King Live* (CNN-TV) (June 27): We didn't even have to go to J school. **1996** *N.Y. Observer* (Aug. 5) 17: His interviewer (who was rejected from that same J-school).

J.S.T. *n. Jewish E.* "Jewish Standard Time."—used *joc.* by Jews, otherwise offensive. Cf. much earlier C.P.T.

> [**1952** in *DARE* s.v. *Jewish time:* Do you mean regular or Jewish time?] **1991** in *DARE* s.v. *Jewish time* [ref. to 1960's]: You'd say, "Meet you at 9:30 J.S.T." and that meant people could show up 15 minutes to half an hour late. **1994** N.Y.C. man, age 26 [Jewish] (coll. J. Sheidlower): 8:00, is that J.S.T., or do I have to be on time?

J.T.O. *n.* JAILHOUSE TURNOUT.

> **1965** Ward & Kassebaum *Women's Pris.* 121: Seventy-five percent of the girls are J.T.O.'s. *a*1972 B. Rodgers *Queens' Vernacular* 117: Jailhouse turnout (JTO).

J-town *n. S.W.* Juarez, Mexico. Also **J-city.**

> **1968–70** *Current Slang III & IV* 74: *J-city,* n. Juarez, Mexico.—New Mexico State. *Ibid.* 76: *J-town,* n. Juarez, Mexico.

judge *n.* (used in familiar address to a man whose name is not known); CAP, 1; GOVERNOR, 2.

> **1845** in Oehlschlaeger *Reveille* 226: Yes, Judge, that's the talk, I believe! **1878–81** W.G. Marshall *Through Amer.* 239: To be called "boss," "captain," [or] "judge"…by the people you meet when you are travelling is all very well.

Judge Colt *n. West.* a Colt revolver regarded as a settler of disputes.

> **1903** A. Adams *Log* 208: I referred the matter to Judge Colt.

Judge Lynch *n.* lynch law. Now *hist.*

> **1835** in *DA:* These tumults are an eastern branch of Judge Lynch's western courts. **1844** in *DAE:* The…creditor…committed him at once to the care of "Judge Lynch" for trial. **1851** in Strong *Diary* II 60: What was the *Vehmgericht* more than a medieval Judge Lynch…? **1944** Micheaux *Mrs. Wingate* 367: "Georgia is the home of Judge Lynch." "Judge Lynch?…who is he?" **1948** in *DA:* One of the Mexicans robbed a sluice and Judge Lynch stepped in. **1948** McIlwaine *Memphis* 74: A flatboat robber was offered the choice of a jail sentence or "Judge Lynch." Preferring the latter, he was…stripped naked and given a hundred lashes.

Judy *n.* **1.** [generic use of the female given name; cf. JANE] a woman.

> ***1812** Vaux *Vocab.*: *Judy:* a *blowen;* but sometimes used when speaking familiarly of any woman. **1853** Ballantine *Autobiography* 20: Do yiz iver see me duck me head like a gandher going under a gate or bent two double like some old Judy going to a wake. **1918** Ruggles *Navy Explained* 82: The best girl is the Jane,…broad, judy, dame, [etc.]. ***1929** Bowen *Sea Slang* 77: *Judies.* The old sailing ship man's usual name for women. **1936** in D. Runyon *More Guys* 156: A very beautiful young Judy…speaks to me in…Spanish. **1943** Hersey *G.I. Laughs* 47: He starts spinning me a story about a classy judy from South of the Border. ***a1961** Hugill *Shanties from Seven Seas* 401 [song learned *ca*1925]: Them Liverpool judies have got us in tow!

2. a fool.

> **1842** *Spirit of Times* (Feb. 19) 598: Hackett is making a Judy of him-

self. [**1845** Corcoran *Pickings* 21: Don't be makin' a Judy Fitzimmons of yerself.] **1846** Neal *Ploddy* 145: It can't be the punch that makes me such a Judy. **1855** in Meserve & Reardon *Satiric Comedies* 151: Don't make a *Judy* of yourself! **1858** [S. Hammett] *Piney Woods* 68: They…made pretickelar Judies of theyselves ginerally. *a*1859 in Bartlett *Amer.* (ed. 2): It is thought that a set of men never did make greater *Judies* of themselves.

Jug *n.* [sugg. by earlier spelling *Jugoslavia*] *Mil.* a native or inhabitant of Yugoslavia.—also used attrib.

  1944 Inks *Eight Bailed Out* 25: I'm learning Jug talk. **1948** *New Yorker* (Apr. 3) 66: "Trieste's one hell of a place," a Fifth Army veteran told me. "A lot of crooks on one side and a lot of Jugs on the other." **1951** Hunt *Judas Hour* 124: I'd do it if he were a Rumanian or a Hungarian or a Jug. **1961** Garrett *Which Ones Are the Enemy* 19: Guarding the Jug border. **1963** Hayden *Wanderer* 302 [ref. to 1944]: We were down at the Jug headquarters in the ravine. **1966** Eddy *Best by Far* 136: How about that old *Jug* who could talk English? *Ibid.* 141: You could see all these *Jug* farmers down looking over their strips. *Ibid.* 142: I couldn't speak *Jug.* **1982** *Nat. Lampoon* (Sept.) 34: A Yugoslav bouzouki player gives a way rendition of "The Old Rugged Cross." **1984–88** Hackworth & Sherman *About Face* 36 [ref. to 1947]: The Yugoslavs (or "Jugs," as we called them).

jug[1] *n.* **1.a.** a jail or prison; lockup; (*Mil.*) a guardhouse.—usu. constr. with *the.*

  1815–16 in *DAE:* A full grown villain, who with an accomplice, were…safely lodged in the jug. **1848** *Life in Rochester* 87: "Money or the jug: cash, or the Blue Eagle," them's her terms. **1847–49** Bonney *Banditti* 110: If John had been timid…Bundy would now be in jug. **1851** [G. Thompson] *Jack Harold* 58: I took his keys, and let myself out of the infernal jug. **1861** in J.R. Lowell *Poetical Works* 224: So arter this they sentenced me…to ten years in the Jug. **1861** Guerin *Mountain Charley* 24: I can just introduce her to your amiable self in your true character of a police officer, and give her the choice between the jug and—and—you know! **1863** "E. Kirke" *So. Friends* 91: If I hadn't a ben in the cussed jug, I'd a killed him. **1865** in *PADS* (No. 70) 39: I had a Negro arrested and put in the jug. **1883** G.H. Holliday *On Plains* 23 [ref. to 1865]: The boys had been marched off to the "jug." **1886** E.L. Wheeler *N.Y. Nell* 8: Shall we bundle him off to the "jug"? ***1897** in S.J. Baker *Australian Lang.* 117: A gaol is called a "jug." **1898** Bellamy *Blindman* 287: I'll put ye in jug overnight, sure's taxes. **1906** M'Govern *Sarjint Larry* (gloss.): *Jug:*—Same as "mill" [guardhouse]. **1908** in H.C. Fisher *A. Mutt* 36: Detective Tobasco…declared that he would land Mutt in the jug. **1919** T. Kelly *What Outfit?* 54: I'll never forget my first night in France. I got put in the jug. **1926** Maines & Grant *Wise-Crack Dict.* 9: *Hand him the jug*—Put him in jail. **1947** Motley *Any Door* 182: I just got out of the jug. Can I take a bath here. **1947** Bowers & Millhouser *Web* (film): One was in the jug. Another'd gone straight. **1968** P. DeAnda, in W. King & R. Milner *Black Drama Anthol.* 480: The joint, Lana. The jug, jail, the slammers.

  b. *Pris.* solitary confinement cells.—constr. with *the.*

  1928, ***1932** (cited in Partridge *Dict. Und.* 373). **1931–34** Clemmer *Pris. Community* 333: *Jug*…The "hole" in prison. **1935–62** Ragen & Finston *Toughest Pris.* 805: *Jug*—Solitary. **1977** Bunker *Animal Factory* 85: "He wasn't in the jug."…"He can do a week in the hole."

  c. *Stu.* after-school disciplinary detention.

  1970 N.Y.U. student: If you came in late or did anything wrong, you got jug.

2. *Und.* **a.** a bank.

  1845 *Nat. Police Gaz.* (Nov. 15) 3: Jim Morgan…disdained no branch of business, from "cracking a jug" (entering a bank) to picking a pocket. **1859** Matsell *Vocab.* 47: *Jug.* A bank. **1889** Bailey *Ups & Downs* 19: "Give me the stuff." "What stuff?" "Why, the boodle of course, that you just got in the jug." I stopped and looked at him saying, "I am not giving the dust up to you." **1904** *Life in Sing Sing* 249: *Jug.*—A lockup; a bank. **1919** *Amer. Leg. Wkly.* (Sept. 12) 8: I'll put the cleaner on every "jug" in the state before I'll see you working, Laura. **1920** Murphy *Gray Walls* 25: I soon fell for a jug (bank). I pulled a long jolt in a California stir. **1925** *Variety* (Dec. 29) 5: The [pickpocket] buzzes glibly about…"right britch," [etc.]. **1930** Sutherland *Pro. Thief* 47: Some cannons prefer the jug touch, which is picking pockets of suckers who are in or are coming out of banks with money which they have just secured. **1933** *Amer. Mercury* (Apr.) 393: To a yegg, a bank was a *jug,* and a *keister* was the inside box of a safe, where the money was kept. **1936** Duncan *Over the Wall* 146:

After Murray's incarceration in prison for heisting the Fort Louden jug. **1944** *Collier's* (Feb. 12) 12: All my potatoes are planted in a jug in England. **1950** *Sat. Eve. Post* (Aug. 19) 130: I…knocked off a jug—bank—for $23,000. **1958** *N.Y. Times Mag.* (Mar. 16) 88: *Jug*—A bank. **1972** Bunker *No Beast* 199: I've got tear off another score.…Whether it's that jewel sting or another jug. **1977** Caron *Go-Boy* 177: Blackie and Marcel got out of the car and walked swiftly towards the jug.

  b. a safe.

  1925 in Partridge *Dict. Und.* 373: This is a seven-plate jug.…I'll shoot her from the outside. **1926** Clark & Eubank *Lockstep* 174 [ref. to *a*1900]: *Jug*…a safe in a country bank. **1935–62** Ragen & Finston *Toughest Pris.* 805: *Jug*—A safe.

3. a top hat.

  1868 Macy *There She Blows!* 54: "Here, Cooper, take my hat."…"No, no…I don't want your old jug."

4. *Esp. So.* a bottle of whiskey or wine (regardless of shape).

  1925 in Mencken *New Ltrs.* 188: Subscribers…began to show up with jugs under their coats. **1933** Ersine *Pris. Slang* 48: *Jug*…A booze bottle. **1959–60** R. Reisner *Jazz Titans* 159: *Jug:* a bottle of liquor. **1961** L.E. Young *Virgin Fleet* 61: Married to a man with the jug habit. **1963** D. Tracy *Brass Ring* 353: Then he had walked out, back to his ward and the smuggled jug. **1973** Flaherty *Fogarty* 247: Besides, you're holding the jug. **1982** W.R. Dunn *Fighter Pilot* 51: We proceeded to kill Doc's jug then and there. **1979–83** W. Kennedy *Ironweed* 7: We can get a couple of jugs and a flop tonight.

5. a dilapidated motor vehicle.

  1938 Steinbeck *Grapes of Wrath* 129: 'F we can on'y get to California…before this here ol' jug blows up.

6. a carburetor.

  1942 *ATS* 84: Carburetor…*jug.* **1952** *Sat. Eve. Post* (Mar. 8) 122: Looks like a jug change. It was rough on the check comin in, remember? **1951–53** in *AS* (May 1954) 99: *Jug,* n. A carburetor. **1953** Felsen *Street Rod* 47: "I imagine my carburetor needs work," Ricky said, looking at the dark smoke. "Get new jugs," Sherm said. "Don't fool with that old one." **1961** Forbes *Goodbye to Some* 126: He's losing a jug, poor guy. **1985** Boyne & Thompson *Wild Blue* 492: Here he was…changing jugs, troubleshooting, swapping engines.

7. (usu. *cap.*) *Mil. Av.* a Republic P-47 Thunderbolt fighter airplane. Now *hist.*

  1944 in Loosbrock & Skinner *Wild Blue* 345: They're Jugs.…P-47s. **1951** *Sat. Eve. Post* (Apr. 21) 154: If we had had some jugs over there in Korea for close support, we'd have shown them something. **1956** Lasly *Turn Tiger Loose* 47: He claims he picked it up from a Jug jockey—somebody who lived through a hundred Thunderbolt missions in World War Two. **1958** Johnson & Caidin *Thunderbolt* 142 [ref. to WWII]: I want to look over the jug. **1961** Forbes *Goodbye to Some* 243 [ref. to WWII]: "What are you flying?" "Jugs. They got us skip-bombing whorehouses up in Baguio." **1965** LeMay & Kantor *Mission with LeMay* 293: Not one damn Jug (P-47) or one damn Spit did I see. **1968** Broughton *Thud Ridge* 28: The P-47, nicknamed the Jug, with its big radial engine out in front, did its job in World War II and the first time I strapped a Jug to me I thought it was the biggest thing I had ever seen. **1991** B.O. Davis, Jr. *Davis* 122: The P-47 [was] affectionately known as the "Jug."

8. usu. *pl.* a woman's breast.

  1957 Kohner *Gidget* 54: Some jugs! **1958** Camerer *Damned Wear Wings* 63: Jugs on her like cantaloupes. **1959** Farris *Harrison High* 386: Turn just a little this way and stick those jugs out at me. **1966** Brunner *Face of Night* 20: "And you oughta see the jugs on her," the man said. **1968** Lockridge *Hartspring* 13: Exposing one of her firm, small jugs. **1970** Gaffney *World of Good* 220: "What a set of jugs," said Donelli, amazed. "That dame could sell titty by the pound." **1977** T. Berger *Villanova* 122: What's her name, huh, Tumulty, one with the big jugs? **1972–79** T. Wolfe *Right Stuff* 139: Young juicy girls with stand-up jugs. **1985–90** R. Kane *Veteran's Day* 50: Watch those jugs jiggle. *a*1994 A. Radakovich *Wild Girls Club* 136: I hope I don't get big jugs like yours.

9. *Narc.* (see quots.).

  1970 Landy *Underground* 114: *Jug*…Bottle containing a liquid drug, such as Methedrine. **1971** Guggenheimer *Narc. & Drug Abuse* 28: *Jugs.* injectable methamphetamines.

10. *Rock Climbing.* JUGHANDLE, 2.

  1974 *Atlantic* (June) 51: If he uses the left foot, there is a fine jug (a projection that gives an unshakable handhold) within reach of his right hand. **1994** Rock climber in N.Y. park (coll. J. Sheidlower): There's a great jug just past the overhang, if you can make it.

11. *Baseball.* a sharply breaking curve ball; JUGHANDLE, 1.

> **1983** Whiteford *How to Talk Baseball* 106: *Jughandle*...a curve...sometimes called a jug.

¶ In phrases:

¶ **in a jug** caught and under control.

> **1894** *Confed. War Jour.* (Mar.) 192: Sigel's Dutch soldiers passed...crying, "Shackson in a shug!" (jug.) "Shackson in a shug!"

¶ **knock into a jug** to defeat; thrash.

> **1885** in Lummis *Letters* 239: But being thus knocked into a jug...I have no particular use to tarry.

jug² *n.* [abbr. JUGGINS] a simpleton. *Rare* in U.S.

> *****1889** Barrère & Leland *Dict. Slang* I 509: *Jug*...(Common), a simpleton. **1956** H. Gold *Not with It* 96: It was nice to find the born jug of the continent.

jug *v.* **1.** to place in jail or prison; lock (someone) up.—also (*obs.*) constr. with *up.*

> **1836–41** Catlin *N. Amer. Ind.* II ch. xxxv: The poor fellow was soon "jugged up"; where he could...dream of...the free and cooling breezes. **1848** Judson *Mysteries* 34: One of them got jugged and found a temporary home in the State-prison. **1849** [G. Thompson] *Venus in Boston* 37: I came...to be *jugged*...for manslaughter. **1850** in A. Pratt *Journals* 69: He would like to take a parting glass...before he was jugged up. **1856** in Dwyer & Lingenfelter *Songs of Gold Rush* 171: And never a judge or attorney/Shall catch me and jug me at home. **1853–60** Olmsted *Texas* 314: Nigger-hunting; poor business....Yes; it's more trouble to get the money, after you've jugged 'em, than it's worth. **1862** Gilbert *Confed. Letters* 9: Those without wealth are "jugged" in a jail. **1863** [Fitch] *Annals of Army* 488: It is very strange that he should be jugged. **1867** *Nat. Police Gaz.* (Jan. 5) 3: The "jugging" of Hendrick was the only protection. **1876** "M. Twain" *Tom Sawyer* 179: He was the justice of the peace that jugged me for a vagrant. **1882** Watkins *Co. Aytch* 201: Well, after "jugging" Stoneman, we go back to Atlanta and occupy our same old place near the concrete house. **1892** Gunter *Miss Dividends* 66: Buck Powers told me I'd be jugged if I shot at 'em. **1893** Hill *Rhetoric & Composition* 280: The *dummer wired his lady* that he had been *jugged.* **1898** Dunne *Peace & War* 11: He sets there in his office in Havana, smokin' a good seegar, an' a boy comes in an' tells him they've jugged an American citizen. **1908** McGaffey *Show Girl* 98: They threatened to jug me, so I slid. **1914** Paine *Wall Between* 183: No. Pinched—jugged—arrested—under guard. **1944** C.B. Davis *Leo McGuire* 196: It showed I hadn't been jugged for the Denver caper at all. **1947–52** R. Ellison *Invisible Man* 238: By God, I'll jug you. **1955** in Perelman *Don't Tread on Me* 179: He's about to be jugged by the FBI. **1970** A. Lewis *Carnival* 115: I'm a third-generation carny, on my mother's side, and I guess I'm proud of never bein' jugged. **1980** Hogan *Lawman's Choice* 73: With a little proof I could jug the lot of them.

2. *Stu.* to place in disciplinary confinement or detention.

> **1895** Wood *Yale Yarns* 6: My chum was jugged and rusticated last June, just before Commencement. **1965** Gallery *Eight Bells* 27 [ref. to *ca*1917]: The Prefect of Discipline's classroom was known as the Jug. If you got "jugged" for some infraction, you had to go there after school, memorize a half a page of Caesar in Latin and recite it perfectly. **1970** N.Y.C. prep. school student: Did you get jugged?

jug³ var. JUKE², *v.*

jug-fuck *n. Mil.* **1.** a drinking bout.—usu. considered vulgar.

> **1980** D. Cragg (letter to J.E.L., Aug. 10) 4: I first ran across this in a list of Pro Signs given to me after April, 1977. "Let's go have us a jug fuck!"

2. a confused or frustrating situation; mess; CLUSTERFUCK, 2.—usu. considered vulgar.

> *a***1987** Coyle *Team Yankee* 116: Not until, and only if, we get this jug fuck unscrewed. **1988** Dye *Outrage* 10: Until we get out of this Ethiopian jug-fuck, I don't want to see you any more than six feet away from...your squad.

jugful *n.* ¶ In phrase: **not by a jugful** not at all; not in the least; by no means.

> **1831** in *DA*: Vote on your side!...Not by a jug full! **1833** J. Neal *Down-Easters* I 126: Not by a jug-full. **1833** A. Greene *Duckworth* I 179: That's not it by a jug full. **1837** Strong *Diary* I 79: But those exhibitions

went off...better than this, by a jugfull. **1840** in Haliburton *Sam Slick* 138: Won't be long enough by a jug full. **1858** [S. Hammett] *Piney Woods* 31: That don't come up to my ideas of smartness, by a jug full. **1859** Bartlett *Amer.* (ed. 2) 222: "Not by a *jugfull*," is a phrase commonly used to mean, not by a great deal, by no means. **1899** Lounsberry *West Point* 156: Not by a jugful, Mr. Conrad. **1927–30** Rollins *Jinglebob* 38 [ref. to 1880's]: Do I want to go back? Not by a jugful. **1949** Houston *Gun Smugglers* (film): I ain't dead. Not by a jugful I ain't.

jugged *adj.* drunk.—also constr. with *up.*

> **1923** in Partridge *Slang* 313: [Intoxicated:] *jugged, soused, ... jagged.* **1965–71** in *Qly. Jour. Stud. Alcohol* XXXII (1971) 733: *Jugged up* Intoxicated.

jugger *n.* **1.** *Und.* a bank burglar.

> **1925** (cited in Partridge *Dict. Und.* 373). **1949** Monteleone *Crim. Slang* 135: *Jugger*...A bank robber. **1965** "R. Stark" *Jugger* 43: Joe Sheer was an old-time jugger who'd cracked his first safe the other side of the First World War.

2. *Und.* a banker.

> **1933** *Amer. Mercury* (Apr.) 395: The unregistered Liberty Bonds were purchased at a discount by crooked bankers, who were known [to safecrackers] as *juggers.* **1935** Pollock *Und. Speaks: Jugger*, a banker.

3. [fr. JUG¹, *n.,* 4] (see quot.).

> **1965–71** in *Qly. Jour. Stud. Alcohol* XXXII (1971) 733: *Jugger* An alcoholic.

juggins *n.* [orig. unkn.; perh. obscurely from *Juggins*, E family name] a simpleton; dolt. *Rare* in U.S.

> *****1882** in *OED2*: Why a telephone of course, you Juggins! **1889** Barrère & Leland *Dict. Slang* I 510: *Juggins*...This term is also used in America. *****1893** in *F & H* IV 80: He was a juggins though he could write songs. *****1899** Whiteing *John St.* 203: One juggins called me "madmyzel" t'other d'y.

juggle *v.* **1.** to handle or move about (esp. large or heavy objects).

> **1898** *Amer. Soldier* (Manila) (Nov. 19) 8: Frank Leonard, the world renowned cocktail juggler. **1917** in Bowerman *Compensations* 1: Juggle *new* garbage cans; help build barracks. **1926** in Eckstorm & Smyth *Minstrelsy of Me.* 163: We juggled birch at Grindstone/For the A.T. Company. **1929** (quot. at GAT, 2.a.). **1930** Sage *Last Rustler* 127: I seen more freight cars juggled in one week than I ever imagined was on the globe.

2. *Narc.* to sell heroin or other drugs to addicts, esp. to support one's own addiction. Hence **juggler**, *n.*

> **1969** Smith & Gay *Don't Try It* 106: The next distributor is known as a *juggler,* who is the seller from whom the average street addict buys. **1975** V. Miller *Trade-Off* 6: That means that by the time the "juggler," or pusher, puts his hands on the goodies the actual amount of heroin he's serving up is somewhere around 3.3 percent pure. **1976** Chinn *Dig Nigger Up* 158: Addicts that I grew up with, hustled with, juggled with and jailed with.

jug-grafter *n.* [JUG, *n.,* 2.a. + GRAFT, *v.,* 1.b. + *-er*] *Und. & Police.* a bank robber.

> **1866** *Nat. Police Gaz.* (Nov. 3) 3: This "jug" grafter"...was "copped" in Philadelphia on the "vag" about a "moon" ago.

jughandle *n.* **1.** *Baseball.* a sharply breaking curve ball.

> **1921, 1932, 1937** (cited in Nichols *Baseball Term.*). **1953** M. Harris *Southpaw* 205: I...threw him a jughandle curve that he went for like a fool. **1970** N.Y.U. student: A *jughandle curve* breaks real sharply over the plate. **1983** Whiteford *How to Talk Baseball* 106: *Jughandle*...a curve. Its path follows that of a jughandle.

2. *Rock Climbing.* a protuberance or crack in a rock face big enough to be grasped firmly as a handhold.

> **1976** *Webster's Sports Dict.* 237.

3. projecting ears. *Joc.*

> **1992** *Wkly. World News* (Aug. 11) 13: Professor...Hartenbach...has studied 30,000 pairs of jug-handles.

jughandle *adj.* one-sided. *Joc.* Also **jughandled.**

> **1856** [Burwell] *White Acre* 138: They said the compromise was like the handle of a jug, "all on one side." So it was known as the jug handle compromise. **1881** in *DARE*: English reciprocity in pleasure travel...is comparatively jug-handled. **1893** Frye *Staff & Field* 93: So far it had been a jug-handled discussion—meaning that all the talkin' had bin on one side. **1904** in *DA.* **1914** *DN* IV 109: *Jug-handle....*One-sided.

jughead *n.* **1.** a fool; dolt.

1899 Gatewood *Yankees* 214: He too has been victimized and made a "Jug Head" of by those who sent him. 1925 W. James *Drifting Cowboy* 50: Nothing much, you jughead. 1926 Nason *Chevrons* 86: Hear that, you jugheads? 1928 Panzram *Killer* 157: *Jug head*—dumbhead. 1933–34 Lorimer & Lorimer *Stag Line* 167: They're jug-heads. 1942 Lindsay & Crouse *Strip for Action* 222: What am I kicking about? Those jugheads out there getting all the laughs. That's what I'm kicking about. 1946 Brackett & Thery *To Each His Own* (film): Blow, ya jugheads! 1960 Archibald *Jet Flier* 136: Shut up, jughead. 1972 *Banyon* (NBC-TV): You jughead! 1995 *Jerry Springer Show* (synd. TV series): I just want to say to jughead—.

2.a. a mule; (*also*) a stupid horse.

1918 Griffin *Ballads of the Reg't.* 52: The bell mare...gave "Jug Head" a kick. 1919 Wiley *Wildcat* 34: The old jug head is lonesome for his kind, so I guess I'll get him some mules. 1926 Branch *Cowboy* 40: The "jug-head" seemed never to remember his hazing of the day before. 1926 Nason *Chevrons* 151 [ref. to 1918]: Sergeant, if you knew how much you sounded like a jughead brayin' way up that chimney you wouldn't laugh so hard. 1938 Noble *Jugheads Behind the Lines* 137 [ref. to 1918]: What makes me mad is that they take my horse, and leave me a team of jugheads! 1960 *Disneyland* (ABC-TV): Whoa, you jughead! 1965 W. Crawford *Bronc Rider* 45: I'm tellin' you, one of the jugheads breaks in two, you ride him if you have to pull leather with both hands. 1966 Olsen *Hard Men* 142: Hannah brought the sluggish jughead to a halt. 1967 Gries *Will Penny* (film): You jughead bastard [*sc.*, a horse]. 1969 Kimbrough *Defender of Angels* 9: I could crack the narrow end of a bridle line on a mule's ass, and make him...pull like hell....I dared the jughead to twitch his tail and ease up.

b. *Army.* a member of a machine-gun company. [Quots. ref. to WWI.]

1926 Nason *Chevrons* 231: The jughead gunners had it off the tripod and were tappin' heads with it. 1929 *Our Army* (Feb.) 34: We had bets down not only with the jugheads of H and M—how those machine-gunners do stick together!—but with every other outfit on the reservation.

3. a U.S. marine; JARHEAD.

1970 Former sgt., U.S. Army: A *jughead* or a *jarhead* is a Marine. 1973 Former U.S. Army helicopter mech. [ref. to 1968]: Marines were called *jugheads.* 1981 Former U.S. Navy yeoman, Knoxville, Tenn. [ref. to 1970]: *Jarheads* and *jugheads* were Marines. 1983 Eilert *Self & Country* 26 [ref. to Vietnam War]: And here these dumb jugheads sit getting rained on all night long without any sleep.

4. [fr. JUG[1], *n.*, 4] an alcoholic.

1973 *AS* 46: 77.

5. [fr. JUG[1], *n.*, 7] *Mil. Av.* a P-47 pilot. *Joc.* Now *hist.*

1981 "K. Rollins" *Fighter Pilots* 26 [ref. to 1940's]: There is a spattering of applause from all the ex-Jugheads, of course.

jugheaded *adj.* Esp. *West.* blockheaded; doltish.

1939 "L. Short" *Rimrock* 19: Why don't these jugheaded big ranchers get together? 1942 *ATS* 176: Stupid...*jugheaded.* 1948 Hayward *Blood on Moon* (film): A bunch of poor, jugheaded homesteaders.

jughouse *n.* a jail.

1932 *Our Army* (May) 33: I bin in sweller jug-houses 'n' this post's. 1954–60 *DAS* 631: *Jug-house*—jail. *1961 Hugill *Shanties* 593: *Hoosegow.* Prison, from the Spanish word "juzgo" [*sic*], hence "jug" or "jughouse."

juice *n.* **1.a.** wine or whiskey; alcoholic liquor.

*1699 E. Ward *London Spy* 117: By this time we had Tippled off our Salubrious Juice. 1708 in W.H. Kenney *Laughter in Wilderness* 106: A few whose Heads...could better bear the potent Juice. 1847 Downey *Portsmouth* 220: Nor were the men alone in this spree, the Officers had all imbibed their juice and save only the Old General and the Commodore. 1863 "E. Kirke" *So. Friends* 49: Stranger, I never keeps none but th' clar juice, th' raal, genuwine critter. a1867 in G.W. Harris *Lovingood* 188: The sperrits...sot his bristils 'bout es stiff es eight ove the uther doggery juice wud. 1883 *Life* (June 14) 281: "The wust av it is the Juice." "Indeed! Is the whiskey so bad down here?" 1885 in Lummis *Letters* 242: In many the juice-dispensary is the only building beside the section house. 1905 in Paxton *Sport USA* 24: By George, we certainly did punish the juice! Good fellow, you know; best ever, but drink has got him and he won't last long. 1905 *Nat. Police Gaz.* (Dec. 16) 3: On...Broadway...a bottle of wine [costs]...$5...a quart, while on the other side of town [it costs]...80 cents. Of course it's a different kind of juice. 1908

DN III 325: East Alabama...juice, n. whisky. 1920 Ade *Hand-Made Fables* 269: A Lush went to the Bad because of a low-down craving for the old Juice. 1920 in O'Brien *Best Stories of 1920* 199: There was more kick in a glass of the stuff that cost sixty cents today than there was in a barrel of the old juice. *1921 *N & Q* (Oct. 29) 346 [ref. to WWI]: *Juice.* Rum ration issued by British. 1931 Hughes *Mulatto* 11: Taste bettr'n this old mountain juice we get around here. 1941 in Botkin *Treas. Amer. Folk.* 125: He was sure he could pull off some kind of conjuration to get his morning's juice. 1946 in Himes *Black on Black* 259: I saw the old hag sitting at the bar guzzling juice. ca1953 Hughes *Fantastic Lodge* 34: After a couple of bottles of juice we'd just turn out the lights. 1954 L. Armstrong *Satchmo* 117: Liquor...was much stronger than the present-day juice. 1959–60 R. Reisner *Jazz Titans* 159: *Juice:* any form of liquor.

b. *Narc.* a drug in liquid solution; (*hence*) heroin or methadone. [The 1957 quot. in *OED2* illustrates **(a)**, above.]

1971 H. Roberts *Third Ear*: *Juice*...content of intravenous drug injection. 1971 Dahlskog *Dict.* 35: *Juice*...a narcotic injected intravenously. 1973 Droge *Patrolman* 143: Usually, heroin addicts offered little resistance—the opium content of the "juice" they shot into their veins sapping their strength. 1975 *Kojak* (CBS-TV): No time to flush the juice down the tubes, baby? 1981 *New Yorker* (Nov. 23) 159: Don't...resort to street slang..."I've got to pick up my juice" (methadone).

2.a. vitality or vigor; energy; (*often*) sexual energy.

*1698–1706 in D'Urfey *Pills* III 133: No Grape...so soft as She,/Nor half so full of Juice. 1869 Stowe *Oldtown* 180: An old gal like her ain't nobody to bring up a child. It takes a woman that's got juice in her to do that. 1922 in O'Brien *Best Stories of 1922* 18: He hasn't got the old juice in him. 1928 in Hemingway *Sel. Letters* 283: Got to stop—all the juice has to go in the book—Isn't much juice today. 1951 Leveridge *Walk on Water* 11: You were fresh out of juice twenty years before we were thought of. 1959 W. Miller *Cool World* 19: She a woman with a lot of juice. 1965 Carmichael & Longstreet *Sometimes I Wonder* 32: It was a...world...with a flavor and a juice of its own. 1966 "T. Pendleton" *Iron Orchard* 69: It seems to me...that a young man with any juice in him would be in town on a Saturday night pleasurin' the girls instead of sitting out here counting his money. 1966 Harris & Freeman *Lords of Hell* 15: She a woman with a whole lot of juice and that what I got to show in my picture. 1970 Landy *Underground Dict.* 114: *Juice*...Strength; guts; stamina. 1974 Lahr *Trot* 18: They probably think of me during their kinky capers to give their couplings a little juice. 1977 Hamill *Flesh & Blood* 74: You gotta get some new *lines*, man. Some *words.* Some *juice.* 1977 Bredes *Hard Feelings* 7: I'm not sure if he's more of a man because he's got so much juice or whether I am because I control it better. 1981 Wambaugh *Glitter Dome* 187: The Nigel St. Claire case had given Marty some fresh juice. 1988 W. Frazier & N. Offen *W. Frazier* 5: I would...store up my juice for the game.

b. effort.

1913–14 London *Elsinore* 368: "More juice, Davis!"...And Davis...visibly increased his efforts. 1988 McDowell & Skaaren *Beetle Juice* (film): Now—let's turn on the juice and see what shakes loose!

c. copulation.

1989 in *Jour. Negro Hist.* LXXIX (1994) 89: Just a little bit of juice keeps him in line.

3.a. semen or vaginal fluid.

*a1720 in D'Urfey *Pills* II 237: Oh! how I would squeese my Juice in thee. *1884 *Randiana* 44: She was by no means wanting in juice. *a1890–96 *F & H* IV 80: *Juice*...(venery).—Spendings...*To give juice for jelly* = to achieve the sexual spasm. a1927 in P. Smith *Letters from Father* 78: She always swallowed my juice. 1938 "Justinian" *Amer. Sexualis* 26: *Juice.* n. Male sexual fluid. 1962 Gilbert *Jody Calls* 7: She jumped like a goose when I shot her the juice. 1970 Peters *Sex Newspapers* 4: It was...gleaming wetly with juice. 1974 Loken *Come Monday Morning* 177: Makin' sure the hole was there where his juice came out.

b. blood.

1938 Bellem *Blue Murder* 43: He would have been red from head to foot, the way her juice had spewed out. 1939 M. Levin *Citizens* 72: Mitch brought the donor over to him...."He's going to lend you a little juice." 1940 in Goodstone *Pulps* 115: I don't like corpses strewn around my living room; especially when they leak lots of juice. 1942 *ATS* 151: Blood...*Claret*, juice, [etc.]. 1980 *AS* (Summer) 145: The blood that flows from open cuts [during a wrestling match] is called *juice.* 1983–90 L. Heath *CW2* 210: I think about him slipping around in the dark, letting the juice out of some...slope. **1992** Jernigan *Tin Can Man* 139: I had seen a lot of juice fly all over the Solomons.

4.a. electric current; power; (*hence*) *U.S. Nav. & Mil. Acad.* a course in electrical engineering; *Theat.* (as a nickname) a stage electrician.

1896 in *DA*: Now we know what a blessing the trolley is—when the juice isn't turned off. **1900** Willard & Hodler *Powers* 3: The conductor...requested the motorman in polite reference to the electric fluid to..."turn on the juice." **1906** M'Govern *Bolo & Krag* 263: Our signal corps had stretched a line of temporary telegraph and one day the "juice" refused to work. **1910** *N.Y. Eve. Jour.* (Feb. 3) 14: Mr. Buckley...tipped off the switchman to turn on the juice again. **1915** Braley *Songs of Workaday World* 21: Where the modern priests of the "Juice" hold sway;/where the lights are born and the lightnings made/To serve the needs of the world of trade. **1919** Murrin *With the 112th* 395: Even enough "juice" was obtained from the electric line into Travernon to furnish the electricity for two lamps. **1928** *AS* (Oct.) 67: American Stage-Hand Language...the electrician [is nicknamed] *Juice.* **1931** Ellsberg *Pigboats* 83: That's all the juice we got, captain. **1934** Cain *Postman Rings Twice* 11: It was all in red, white and blue neon letters, and I waited until dark to turn on the juice. **1938** Smitter *Detroit* 39: He'd throw on the juice and see how it worked. **1941** *Guide to U.S. Naval Acad.* (gloss.): *Juice.* Electrical Engineering. **1961** L.G. Richards *TAC* 123: Colonel Tara...cut off all the juice to number two engine. **1967** Lockwood *Down to the Sea in Subs* 31: "Juice" from a 60-cell storage battery...drove this motor to propel the sub when submerged. **1973** Gwaltney *Destiny's Chickens* 11: That was one candy-apple that could stand on its tail when a man throwed the juice to'er. **1981–89** R. Atkinson *Long Gray Line* 114: I'm dumb as dirt in juice. **1990** Crow Dog & Erdoes *Lakota Woman* 132: Bob Free, our first chief of engineers, kept the juice going. **1993** G. Lee *Honor & Duty* 107: While cursing the heritage, progeny, and anatomy of Juice. **1995** *Newsweek* (July 17) 41: At the annual electric-car rally, a vehicle running on Ovonic's juice went 238 miles without a recharge.

b. *Esp. Av.* gasoline; liquid fuel.

*1909 in *OED2*: We are not faced with a threepenny tax on each gallon of "juice." **1918** Roberts *Flying Fighter* 28: The tank was nearly empty. That meant that I would have to go in search of "juice." **1920** Loomis *304th Ammo. Train* 75: Perhaps water's in the juice. **1949** in *DAS*: If you have a light supply of juice you climb at about 200 m.p.h. **1955** R.L. Scott *Look of Eagle* 43: Duck Butt Five to Early Bird Flight. Have juice for you and will orbit. **1961** Foster *Hell in the Heavens* 190 [ref. to WWII]: Some of the fighters had to pancake for juice at Torokina. **1962** S. Smith *Escape from Hell* 121: "How're you fixed for juice?"..."Enough." **1972** *Playboy* (Sept.) 209: I need gas. Landed at the field over there. About out of juice. **1990** Yarborough *Da Nang Diary* 251: I was burning up the juice at a wicked rate.

c. nitroglycerine.

1924 Tully *Beggars of Life* 270: I'll show you how to pour the juice and blow a safe so's it won't wake a baby. **1928** *Amer. Mercury* (Aug.) 487: The juice was no good....The nitro-glycerine. ***1941** in Partridge *Dict. Und.* 373: *Soup, juice.* Nitroglycerine. **1954** Gordon & Wood *Jail Bait* (film): That safe's gonna be opened whether you open it or I use a little juice on it.

d. *Gamb.* the rigging of gambling equipment by electrical means.

1952 Lait & Mortimer *USA* 376: There have been rumors of "juice" before...that's [Honolulu] slang for a rigged or thrown game. **1969** King *Gamb. & Org. Crime* 232: *Juice*...any game gaffed by electromagnets.

5.a. money.

1934 Weseen *Dict. Slang* 296: *Juice*—Money in general. **1966** Neugeboren *Big Man* 176: You mind if Frankie over there holds the juice? **1972** P. Thomas *Savior* 38: They were doing piece work and that's like if you don't produce, you get no juice. **1984** S. Hager *Hip Hop* 109: *Juice*...money. **1988** W. Safire, in *N.Y. Times Mag.* (Feb. 7) 13: *Juice*....In current usage, the word has taken on the added meaning of "money."

b. *Und. & Police.* money used for or obtained through corrupt practices, as extortion, bribery, kickbacks, or usury; (*hence*) usurious interest charged by a loanshark; VIGORISH; (*broadly*) loansharking. [No continuity of usage is apparent between *1698 and 20th-C. quots.]

*1698 E. Ward, in Partridge *Slang* 69: He has good Friends at *Newgate*, who give him now and then a Squeeze when he is full of Juice. **1935** Pollock *Und. Speaks: Juice*, corrupt influence (shake-down) for protection to operate unlawfully. **1950** R. Chandler, in Partridge *Dict. Und.* 837: The juice (the pay-off money from the gambling interests). **1951** Kefauver *Crime in Amer.* 186: "Juice"...is the California gambling profession's euphemism (in Florida the term is "ice") for "protection" money. **1954** Chessman *Cell 2455* 131 [ref. to ca1940]: "Juice" is money paid to the police for protection. **1956** in Woods *Horse-Racing* 51: But Jonas gets the commission, the 5 per cent juice from bookmakers on losers. **1961** *Chi. Daily Trib.* (Aug. 12) 2: The recent slayings...were tied to [the] syndicate juice racket by police....Under the terms of the juice racket a borrower must pay 20 per cent a week on his loan. **1965** in *BDNE* 238: One proposal...would grant the feds jurisdiction over "juice"...by which sharks and syndicates have milked and bankrupted laboring men and businesses. **1965** Horan *Seat of Power* 124: Can you imagine those thieves if their juice was cut off? **1966** Bullins *Goin' a Buffalo* 170: If he can't get the bail for her or the juice to pay off somebody downtown like Shaky done you to have your time cut to one third. **1969** King *Gambling* 232: *Juice*—Formerly, bribe money; now generally...usorious and extortionate lending operations. **1971** *Black Scholar* (Sept.) 29: White gangsters...the bad juice boys, the hit men, etc. **1982** Hayano *Poker Faces* 99: If a gambler borrows $1,000 [from a loan shark] on a 5 percent weekly loan, he must pay, in addition to the principal, $50 per week in "juice" (interest). **1983** R. Thomas *Missionary* 38: Dates, time of day, and how much the juice was down to the dime. **1989** Radford & Crowley *Drug Agent* 42: The clinics *must* be in on the juice. **1992** McCaffrey *Textures* 43: They murdered, were in the juice rackets, sold numbers [etc.].

c. *Gamb.* the percentage of a wager retained by a bookmaker for facilitating a bet.

1956 "T. Betts" *Across Board* 317: The bookmakers still have 10 percent and more going for them...the juice...the commission. **1975** Mahl *Beating Bookie* 54: You are bucking his...vigorish, and your handicapping history must show a greater percentage advantage to overcome this juice. **1981** Jenkins *Baja Okla.* 32: The church had only wanted $1000, but Foster [gave $1100 because he] thought the church ought to get the juice just like the bookmaker. *a***1989** in Safire *Coming to Terms* 277: "Juice" is...the ten percent penalty a losing bettor pays his bookie. **1996** Alson *Ivy League Bookie* 16: The juice, or the vigorish or the vig...was the ten percent commission that bookies collected on all losing bets.

6. flattering talk.

1936 Cain *Double Indemnity* 366: If I had used that juice trying to keep out, that might have got me somewhere. **1962** Perry *Portrait of a Young Man* 101: But it disgusts me the way she melts all over the floor when he turns on the juice.

7.a. personal or political power or influence, often of a corrupt nature. Cf. 1935 quot. at **(5.b.),** above.

1957 Fenton & Haines *Wings of Eagles* (film): "How'd you do it?" "Same as you. Drag. Pull. Juice." **1961** in L. Bruce *Essential L. Bruce* 77: Cause it's juice, man. That's it. The only rights you got are knowing the right guy. **1963** Breen *PT 109* (film): You got the juice in Washington...Juice, muscle, glycerine. Don't they teach you any practical talk at Harvard? **1963** Braly *Shake Him* 144: Dino must be out of his gourd...unless he's got giant juice. **1966** Elli *Riot* 211: He had some juice. His uncle owns one of the biggest hotels in this state. **1966** *N.Y. Times* (Dec. 4) II 13: The important thing now is I got juice as an actor. **1972** *Banyon* (NBC-TV): I got enough juice in this town to shock you right out of business. **1974** *Police Story* (NBC-TV): You got juice. **1977** Bunker *Animal Factory* 184: I've got long juice with this dude. **1978** *N.Y. Times Mag.* (July 23) 23: *Clout* has been replaced by *juice*, and *the System* is now *the process.* **1978** Nolan & Mann *Jericho Mile* (film): Now I know yo' man's got the juice. **1984** J. McNamara *First Directive* 5: No-balls Foley, in the face of that kind of political juice, had quickly put three homocide dicks on the case. **1984** S. Hager *Hip Hop* 13: The toughest guy...had the juice to do what he wanted.

b. *Rap Music.* recognition or publicity; respect.

1984 Toop *Rap Attack* 136: We started really getting juice, which is people knowing us. **1984** S. Hager *Hip Hop* 55: Spoonie had an ego...'cause he had the most juice from his record. **1985** Swados & Trudeau *RapMaster Ronnie* 4: He's the man,/Who's got more juice than Jesse J. **1988** "R. Shanté" *Have a Nice Day* (rap song): That's why I'm queen of the crew with the juice. **1992** *Daily Beacon* (Univ. Tenn.)

(Feb. 14) 4: Juice…Respect. How far will you go to get it? **1991** Nelson & Gonzales *Bring Noise* 76: Rhymes that should've garnered Fresh and the Crew juice as well as sales. **1992** *60 Minutes* (CBS-TV) (Apr. 5): Those kinds of things give you juice, and pretty soon I had credibility. **1993** P. Munro *U.C.L.A. Slang II*: Some kids gangbang to get juice, others do it out of fear.

8. daylights; PEE.

   1971 Ark. man, age *ca*20 (coll. J. Ball): Man, that really scared the juice out of me. **1977** Bredes *Hard Feelings* 252: I thought we're goin' to scare the juice out of Helen. **1986** *Heart of the City* (ABC-TV): Where do you think he is now—beatin' the juice out of some kid.

9. titillating or inside information; (*also*) juicy gossip.

   1982 *N.Y. Post* (Sept. 3) 48: I asked my colleagues.…Here's the juice. **1989** Chapple & Talbot *Burning Desires* 174: That guy was not my lover. Bob…needed a little juice to sell his book. **1991** *Geraldo* (synd. TV series): They're not here to hear about Poland, they're here to hear all this juice.

10. *Meteorology.* moisture; precipitation.

   1990 *CBS This Morning* (CBS-TV) (Dec. 28): The brighter clouds [on the weather map] are holding all the juice.

juice *v.* **1.a.** to drink liquor, esp. to excess; get drunk.—also constr. with *[it] up* or (*rarely*) *down*.

   1893 Putnam *Blue Uniform* 165: So, on the first pay-day…they proceeded with the usual process of juicing down and getting all the drunkenness they could out of their pay. **1953** W. Fisher *Waiters* 203: Everybody's juicing. **1956** in W.S. Burroughs *Letters* 335: I don't juice and I don't mainline. **1962** in L. Bruce *Essential L. Bruce* 148: The guy who juiced will suffer some absence syndromes. **1969** J. Joplin, in *N.Y. Times* (Feb. 23): So I juice up real good…it's a damn sight better than being bored. **1970** Corrington *Bombardier* 18: For Christ's sake, Al, have you been juicing? **1970** *Playboy* (Aug.) 174: Janis rushes down to Max's Kansas City to celebrate and "juice." **1972** Smith & Gay *Don't Try It* 61: One outfit will juice it up the night before patrol and all go out with hangovers. *a*1979 Pepper & Pepper *Straight Life* 184: I was still juicing and everything felt fine. **1978–86** J.L. Burke *Lost Get-Back Boogie* 105: You were juicing in the saloon at Lolo.

b. to make drunk.

   1958–59 Southern & Hoffenberg *Candy* 117: It'll juice you to the gills.

2. to milk (a cow).

   1915 *DN* III 227: West Texas…*juice*, v.t. To milk. Formerly very common, this verb is now chiefly used facetiously. **1928** *AS* (Dec.) 131: Nebraska…To "juice a cow"…is to milk one. **1951** in *DAS*: As nonchalantly as a farmer juices a gentle Jersey cow. **1965–70** in *DARE* [very many informants].

3.a. to electrocute; kill or torture with electricity.

   1929 M.A. Gill *Und. Slang* (unp.): *Juiced*—Electrocuted. **1935** Pollock *Und. Speaks*: *Juice him*, to get information by torture. **1951** C. Lederer *Thing* (film): When that thing [an alien creature] gets in the right spot, juice it! **1958** Heinz *Professional* 176: He killed some poor slob run a candy store. They shoulda juiced him, but they give him twenty to life. **1982** "J. Cain" *Commandos* 153: Juiced him for fifty minutes. **1988** *Married with Children* (Fox-TV): Juice me till I'm ash. **1993** *Danger Theater* (Fox-TV): He sits in this chair and gets juiced.

b. *Mil.* to expose to nuclear radiation; kill by means of nuclear radiation.

   1961 *Newsweek* (July 10) 39: [A neutron bomb would leave] tanks and terrain untouched, but all the troops and living things struck down (or "juiced" in the latest nuclear jargon) by a burst of cell-destroying radiation.

c. *Mil.* to kill or destroy, as by automatic-weapons fire.

   1972 in W. King *Black Anthol.* 142: He…is known for juicin' people just 'cause they smoke the wrong cigarettes! **1983** S. Wright *Meditations* 176 [ref. to Vietnam War]: Juice 'em!…Give 'em the fucking juice! **1990** Ruggero *38 N. Yankee* 353: Cobras must have juiced him.

4.a. (see 1942 quot.).—constr. with *up*.

   1942 *ATS* 57: *Hop up, juice up, soup up*, to speed up or intensify, as the action of a motor. **1995** Gingrich & Forstchen *1945* 377: Two hundred juiced-up Bearcats.

b. *Av.* to fuel.—constr. with *up*.

   1961 R.L. Scott *Boring Holes* 164 [ref. to WWII]: There's a flight…getting juiced up.

c. Esp. *Baseball.* to hit or throw (a ball) with great force.

   1961 Brosnan *Pennant Race* 87: Juice two or three off Spahn quick. **1969** Bouton *Ball Four* 271: Any pitch like that is bound to be *juiced*, with some kind of power. **1983** Whiteford *How to Talk Baseball* 106: *Juice*…to hit the ball a long way, usually for a home run.…A player "juices one" or "juices one out." **1996** McCumber *Playing off Rail* 94: Relying on getting the correct angle rather than having to juice the cue ball. **1996** *World Series* (Oct. 20) (Fox-TV): And did he ever juice this one!

d. to excite or enliven; lend vitality to.—also constr. with *up*.

   1964 *Time* (Oct. 23) 61: "A thing like that can really juice you up," said Long, who promptly set an Olympic record. **1988** Frazier & Offen *W. Frazier* 156: The cheers and the screaming juiced me. **1990** in N. George *Buppies, B-Boys* 120: The clothes…juice old-school slickness with youngblood freshness. **1990** in A. Sexton *Rap on Rap* 70: I juice the party like jumper cables. *a*1994 A. Radakovich *Wild Girls Club* 203: It's juiced up by the music. **1995** *Newsweek* (June 5) 61: A new book might juice ratings.

5. to pay protection or bribe money to; GREASE, 1.a.

   1953 R. Chandler *Goodbye* 63: I got to make lots of dough to juice the guys I got to juice in order to make lots of dough to juice the guys I got to juice.

6. *Gamb.* to tamper with (a deck of cards).

   1965 Lardner & Southern *Cincinnati Kid* (film): You know there was a guy there who accused *me* of juicin' the deck?

7. *Black E.* to copulate with (a woman).—also used intrans. usu. considered vulgar.

   1971 S. Stevens *Way Uptown* 173: 'Stead of juicing the fox, you could drink it up or shoot it up or smoke it up. **1978** (quot. at KEISTER, 2.a.). **1977–81** Holm & Shilling *Dict. Bahamian Eng.* 116: They bin juicing away, boy, and we just was hiding and watching. **1989** P. Munro *U.C.L.A. Slang* 53: Did you juice her?

8. *Baseball.* (of a pitcher) to moisten (a baseball) illicitly.—also constr. with *up*.

   1974 Perry & Sudyk *Me & Spitter* 124: Absolved me from any suspicion of juicing up a baseball. **1975** *Urban Life* IV 239: The pitcher was "juicing" the ball.

9. *Sports.* to take metabolic steroids.

   1989 *Geraldo* (synd. TV series): Usin' steroids…juicin'.

juice ball *n. Baseball.* a spitball.

   1975 *Urban Life* IV 238: The pitcher's performance is regulated by rules intended to prevent the "juice ball."

juice bill *n. Pol.* (see quot.).

   1988 W. Safire, in *N.Y. Times Mag.* (Feb. 7) 13: A legislative bill that causes lobbyists…to loosen the purse strings is known as a *juice bill*—"so named…for the hundreds of thousands of dollars that could be squeezed from it."

juice box *n.* an electric battery. Also **juice can.**

   1941 in *AS* XVI 240: *Juice Box*. Battery [for an automobile]. **1966** Young & Hixson *LSD* 97: Yeah, the juice cans for the Panasonic.

juiced *adj.* **1.a.** drunk; (*hence*) *Narc.* intoxicated by drugs; HIGH.—also constr. with *up* or (since *ca*1968) *out*.

   1941 *Pittsburgh Courier* (Mar. 22) 23: "Juiced" Hep Cat Bashes Detective In Eye. **1946** Mezzrow & Wolfe *Really Blues* 182: Other cats…[are] juiced to the gills. **1946** in Himes *Black on Black* 260: She was an old wino used to come there every night and get juiced up. *a*1950 R. Spence *Gorilla* 59: Boy! Has *he* been juiced-up! *ca*1953 Hughes *Fantastic Lodge* 46: They would go out nights and get juiced together. **1956** Holiday & Dufty *Lady Sings the Blues* 20: But he was too juiced even for that. **1958** Frede *Entry E* 116: She'd do it anyway even if she weren't juiced up. **1961** Kohner *Gidget Goes Hawaiian* 50: He too had just been juiced up at the Moana and what I had interpreted as a love light had merely been a gasser on the blink. **1966** Manus *Mott the Hoople* 135: Some shanty Irish…get juiced up and brawl all night long. **1970** *Playboy* (Dec.) 118: Get thoroughly and quietly juiced. **1972** Pearce *Pier Head Jump* 22: I was all juiced up and I figured the ship needed a good laugh. **1975** Univ. Tenn. student: I was down in Miami getting juiced out. **1989** P. Benchley *Rummies* 236: He…was juiced on decongestants. **1995** *Jerry Springer Show* (synd. TV series): You were usually too juiced up.

b. [pun on LOADED; cf. DRUNK] *Baseball.* (of bases) loaded. *Joc.*

   1990 *Daybreak Saturday* (CNN-TV) (Sept. 1): And the bases are juiced. **1992** *CNN Sports Close-up* (CNN-TV) (Apr. 20): With the bases juiced.

2.a. excited or enthusiastic; worked up; (*also*) (*vulgar*) (of a woman) sexually aroused.—usu. constr. with *up*.

1978 *N.Y. Post* (July 28) 65: He hit well....I imagine he was just a little more juiced up today. **1979** *High Society* (Aug.) 76: He felt how juiced up I was and told me to lay across one of the beds. **1984** *All Things Considered* (Nat. Pub. Radio) (July 27): The American team is really juiced up for this. **1984** (quot. at SNAKE OIL). **1988** *China Beach* (ABC-TV): You don't sound too juiced. **1990** *CBS This Morning* (CBS-TV) (July 16): He was juiced-up—excited. **1991** Lott & Lieber *Total Impact* 157: He was so juiced I found him in tears on the sideline.

b. nervous; keyed-up.

1989 Sorkin *Few Good Men* 102: I'm just psyched, brother. I'm juiced...wired. **1992** Strawberry & Rust *Darryl* 198: I was...juiced up on tension. **1994** *CBS This Morning* (CBS-TV) (Feb. 24): "I'm not nervous enough."...So she ran out into the corridor to get herself a little juiced up.

juice freak *n.* JUICEHEAD, esp. as contrasted with a person who uses other drugs.

1971 *Current Slang VI* (Winter) 7: *Juice freak*, n. An alcoholic (who does not use drugs). **1970–72** *AS* L (1975) 62: *Juice freak*...Person who regularly drinks liquor, presumably instead of taking drugs or smoking marijuana. **1973** Karlin, Paquet & Rottmann *Free Fire Zone* 80: Lederer went...banging on the lockers and waking up the juice freaks while he moved his stuff out.

juicehead *n.* [JUICE, 1.a. + HEAD] a drunkard.

1954 Schulberg *Waterfront* 25: At least if the juice-head got to sing let him sing Galway Bay or something. **1959** H. Ellison *Gentleman Junkie* 210: I sent word round to him by a juicehead. **1963** Coon *Short End* 233: We all were out in the open air beer hall along with some other juiceheads, flatfooting half pints of apple brandy. **1964–66** R. Stone *Hall of Mirrors* 67: Say, I didn't know you were such a juicehead, baby. **1966** Elli *Riot* 11: The juiceheads...should be straining off their weekly ten-gallon batch of raisinjack. **1969** Hannerz *Soulside* 19: Wild Irish Rose is the drink of the winos, "wineheads" or "juiceheads" in ghetto parlance. **1969** Pharr *Numbers* 362 [ref. to 1930's]: And Kelly's smile was so damn superior that Dave wondered how anybody could call her a juicehead. **1971** N.Y.U. student: There were a couple of juiceheads in my outfit. **1996** *New Yorker* (June 24) 113: I'm a juice-head. I'm a boozer.

juicehound *n.* JUICEHEAD.

1940 D. Ellington, in *OED2*: Everybody in our band at that time was a juice-hound.

juice joint *n.* **1.** *Circus & Carnival.* a soft-drink concession.

1922 *Variety* (Aug. 4) 8: "Grab-joints," "juice-joints," cookhouses and refreshment stands. **1924** H.L. Wilson *Professor* 241: Word was given by Stanley to dismantle our juice joint. **1927** Nicholson *Barker* 54: The thermometer over t' th' juice joint sez ninety-four in the shade. **1928** *AS* III (June) 414: *Juice joint.* A lemonade or other soft drink concession. **1946** Gresham *Nightmare Alley* 6: Get me a bottle of lemon soda from the juice joint.

2.a. a place where liquor is sold and consumed; (*specif.*) a speakeasy.

1932 in *AS* (Feb. 1934) 27: *Juice-Joint.* A speakeasy. **1939** in Leadbitter & Slaven *Blues Records* 455: Juice Joint Blues. **1943** *Yank* (Jan. 13) 20: Near a juice joint (tavern). **1964** R.S. Gold *Jazz Lexicon* 171: *Juice joint.* A cabaret, a night club...current since *c*1935. **1968** Klein *Police* 225 [ref. to 1940's]: The establishments where such liquor could be purchased...were known as "juice joints." **1973** Droge *Patrolman* 111: "Juice joints"—usually apartments, where one could buy a bottle of booze on Sunday or whenever the liquor stores were closed. **1974** Radano *Cop Stories* 41: When we'd walk into a poolroom or a juice-joint where things looked a little tight, he'd push aside his coat and whip out the sawed-off shotgun.

b. a liquor store.

1962 Crump *Killer* 296: Hey, there's a juice joint over there....let us cop righteous on the grog.

3. *Gamb.* a crooked gambling establishment that operates electrically controlled games.

1945–50 in D.W. Maurer *Lang. of Und.* 187: *Juice-joint.* A gambling house where electric dice are used. **1961** Scarne *Comp. Gambling Gde.* 378: The croupier in a *juice joint* (gambling house which has an electromagnetic [roulette] wheel) can successfully operate the gaff only when the wheel is spinning very slowly. **1981** D.E. Miller *Jargon* 295.

juice line *n.* *R.R.* (see quot.).

1945 Hubbard *R.R. Ave.* (gloss.): Electric railways (*juice lines*).

juice man *n.* **1.** an electrician.

1923 *N.Y. Times* VIII (Oct. 7) 4: *Juiceman:* Electrician in a vaudeville theatre. **1951** Mannix *Sword-Swallower* 196: The juice men ran a cut-in line under the midway light.

2. *Und.* a loan shark or underworld loan collector.

1961 *Chi. Daily Trib.* (Aug. 12) 1: The body of...a "juice man" (loan collector) for syndicate hoodlum bosses, was found...in the trunk. **1967** in *BDNE* 239: A professional criminal...often must make a loan from a "juice man"...which may involve an interest rate of 20 per cent per week. *a*1976 Roebuck & Frese *Rendezvous* 183: "Juice men" (loan sharks). **1982** Hayano *Poker Faces* 98: The loan shark, also called a "shylock" or "juiceman."

3. *Pris.* a convict who wields influence.

1977 Bunker *Animal Factory* 27: You can do it....You're the juice man around this camp.

juice mill *n.* GIN MILL.

1906 *Nat. Police Gaz.* (Sept. 22) 6: A great many fellows will ask to stop off at some juice mill...for a last drink.

juiceoline *n.* [JUICE, 4.b. + *gasoline*] gasoline. *Joc.*

1976 *N.Y. Folklore* II 238: Gasoline may be either *go juice* or *juiceoline*.

juicer *n.* **1.** *Naut.* LIMEJUICER, 1, 2.

1867 Clark *Sailor's Life* 124: The "Charger" Underway—Life on Board a "Juicer." **1896** Hamblen *Many Seas* 131: I've earned my money mighty hard aboard of this old "juicer," and I'm going to have it. *Ibid.* 306: So I chose the society of "juicers," who were good fellows. **1922** *Marine Corps Gaz.* (June) 214 [ref. to 1906]: There was one of the lieuts who sure was a peach, and he could give any Juicer cards and spades when it came to putting on the high grade "Me Lord the Duke has arrived" stuff.

2.a. Esp. *Theat.* an electrician.

1928 *N.Y. Times* (Mar. 11) VIII 6: *Juicers*—Electricians. **1928** *AS* III (June) 365: "Operators" (cameramen) and "juicers" (electricians). **1941** in Botkin *Sidewalks* 491: *Juicers* are [film] electricians. **1957** in *DAS*: He treated the grips and the juicers the way he had always treated them, as employees.

b. *Radio.* DISC JOCKEY.

1976 Bibb et al. *CB Bible* 64: His...radio role has inspired a host of other juicers around the country....Bob is a fast-talking, on-target juicer.

3. a heavy drinker, esp. as distinguished from a marijuana smoker.

1960 C. Cooper *Scene* 69: Reefer-smokers and juicers. **1967** (cited in *ODMS*). **1970** R.N. Williams *New Exiles* 136: Either they were juicers—or they were shooting horse—or they were smoking Js. **1970** *Look* (June 16) 72: We found a split between the younger soldiers, who were "potheads" and the older sergeants and officers who might be "juicers" or alcoholics. **1972** *Playboy* (Apr.) 98: Avoid the juicers and avoid the heads. **1979** T. Baum *Carny* 121: He's a juicer himself. **1989** P. Benchley *Rummies* 36: You're a juicer.

juicery *n.* *So.* a barroom; saloon.

1853 J.G. Baldwin *Flush Times of Ala.* 241 [ref. to 1838]: A place of departed spirits,—...we mean an evacuated doggery, grocery or juicery, as, in the elegant nomenclature of the natives, it was variously called. **1892** in *DA*: I stepped up to one of the crowd collected around this "juicery" and enquired if anything unusual had happened.

juice shop *n.* a liquor store.

1970 Conaway *Big Easy* 89: Some spook juice shop.

juice truck *n.* **1.** a truck that carries an electric generator.

1951 Mannix *Sword-Swallower* 75: The carnival didn't carry its own generator and the juice truck had to plug into the main city line.

2. a truck that transports gasoline.

1985 Univ. Tenn. instructor, age 36: Truck drivers call gasoline trucks *juice trucks*.

juicy *adj.* **1.** drunk.

1737 *Pennsylvania Gaz.* (Jan. 6) 1: He's Intoxicated, Jolly, Jagg'd,...Juicy.

2. *Fire Dept.* (of a fire) smoky.

1983 Stapleton *30 Yrs.* 16: A coupla windows just blew out too, so it's not too juicy. *Ibid.* 53: It was a little juicy, so I kept holding my facepiece on my face and taking breaths as I went along.

juju *n.* a marijuana cigarette.

> **1940** R. Chandler *Farewell* ch. ix: I knew a guy once who smoked jujus....Three sticks of tea and it took a pipe wrench to get him off the chandelier.

juke¹ *n.* [prob. short for Gullah *jook* (or *joog*) *house* 'a disorderly house, a house of ill-repute' (L.D. Turner *Africanisms in the Gullah Dialect* (1949) p. 195); cf. Bambara *jugu* 'wicked; violent'; cf. also JUKE², *v.*] **1.** Orig. *Black E.* (Fla. & So. Ga.) a usu. lower-class establishment, as a roadhouse or tavern, providing liquor, food, music, dancing, etc. Also **jook, jouk.**

> **1933** Heyward *Emperor Jones* (film): Joe's Juke. **1934** Z.N. Hurston, in *DARE: Jook*, the pleasure houses near industrial work. A combination of bawdy, gaming, and dance hall. **1935** Z.N. Hurston *Mules & Men* 82: Jook*...*A fun house. Where they sing, dance, gamble, love, and compose "blues" songs incidentally. **1936** *Scribner's Mag.* (Dec. 27) 2: Jim's daddy owned the General Store and a nigger jook. **1938** W. McGuire, in *Fla. Review* (Spring) 28: *Jook* as a noun means a rather ordinary road-house outside the city limits...where beer is for sale, and where there is a coin phonograph, or nickelodeon, and space for dancing. **1939** C.R. Cooper *Scarlet* 77: There are the hordes of jitterbugs, "pig-joint" or barbecue girls, "jook-girls" from Southern points, entertainers, working their way by car or bus from one tavern to another. **1936–40** McDonogh *Fla. Negro* 48: He knows his "jook" music well. *Ibid.* 57: Nightly "jooks," the popular term for any place of amusement. **1941** *AS* XVI 319: [In 1936] *jouk* was in good standing among high school students who applied it to resorts of respectable character. **1942** Z.N. Hurston *Dust Tracks* 182: Polk County in the jooks. Dancing the...belly-rub. Knocking the right hat off the wrong head, and backing it up with a switch-blade. **1959** W. Williams *Ada Dallas* 67: I even picked up pocket money playing at the jukes. **1988** Emery *Black Dance* 221: These dances made the rounds of the Southern jooks.

2. JUKEBOX.

> **1941** *Pittsburgh Courier* (Nov. 8) 21: Basie On...Juke. **1942** Algren *Morning* 31: The big bass jukes played only Polish songs. **1942** in Litoff et al. *Miss You* 42: We played the "juke" and danced. **1943** P. Harkins *Coast Guard* 74: We can have a few tunes on the juke. **1953** Manchester *City of Anger* 124: Guess I'll have to get new stuff for the juke. **1996** D. McCumber *Playing off Rail* 251: A well-known poolroom...with juke and bar and a lot of smoke and chatter.

juke² *n. Sports.* an act of faking an opposing player out of position.

> **1980** Wielgus & Wolff *Basketball* 49: *Juke* (*n* or *v*) A sudden move used by either an offensive or a defensive player, usually as a decoy. **1983** *N.Y. Post* (Sept. 2) 71: Tackle...Butch Woolfolk still pussyfoots too much on his jukes.

juke¹ *v.* [of Scots dial. orig. *a*1510; see *OED2*] **1.a.** Esp. *Sports & Mil. Av.* to duck, dodge, or take similar evasive action.— also used trans. Also (now *rare*) **jouk.**

> ***1513** in *OED*: And jowkit in vnder the speyr has he. ***1535** in *OED*: It is oure lait to juke quhen that the heid/Is fra the hals. **1834** in *DARE*: They say *three hundred thousand dollars* was drawn from the Nashvil Bank tu aid your election, that there is positive proof of this, and that there isn't any way tu jouk it. **1864** in *Del. Hist.* XXI (1984) 108: We can walk about...without having to "juke" our heads in order to avoid being hit by a Minnie. **1891** *DN* I 74: *Jook*...to avoid a blow by dodging. [Eastern Pennsylvania]. **1896** *DN* I 419: *Juke*...(v.t.) To dodge, as in tag. Can[adian]. **1942–45** in Campbell & Campbell *War Paint* 207: Jukin' Judy [name given to a combat aircraft]. **1953** *AS* XXVIII 250: *Jouk*...To duck, to dodge. Popular speech [in Bedford Co., Pa.]. **1958** *Newsweek* (Dec. 22) 79: *Juke*: Make a false move to confuse the offense. *Ibid.* 80: Then he outlined specific Cleveland plays, instructing the defense when to key and when to juke. **1978** De Christoforo *Grease* 106: Danny was dazzling, jukin' to one side, fakin' with his hips to the other, and finally making his break for the net. **1979** Gram *Foxes* 101: He juked instantly to his right, pounded around the corner toward the near front door. **1982** Least Heat Moon *Blue Hwys.* 102: Walker was alone, juking and shooting [baskets]. **1984** Jackson & Lupica *Reggie* 32: No blocking. No faking by me. No juking. **1986** Zeybel *First Ace* 149: Juke the same SAMs, eat the same flak. **1988** M. Maloney *Thunder Alley* 74: The F-5 pilot jinked when he should have juked. **1991** *N.Y. Times* (Nat. Ed.) (Jan. 23) 1: Technology for pilots...[enables] them to...juke to avoid ack-ack.

b. *Sports.* to FAKE OUT (an opposing player).

> **1975** R. Hill *O.J. Simpson* 13: My game is to juke (fake out) the tough guys. **1976** *6000 Words* 104: Sometimes I juke him right out of his shoes. **1980** *Mork & Mindy* (ABC-TV): Did you ever see Oral Roberts juke a linebacker out of his socks?

2. to trick or victimize.

> **1833** S. Smith *President's Tour* 32: Then tu that tarnal Dutchman would git to be President, and I should be juked out of it as slick as goose grease. **1980–81** in T.K. Pratt *Prince Ed. I. Dict.* 84: For example, "juked them in a land deal" means to trick or cheat someone. **1982** in T.K. Pratt *Prince Ed. I. Dict.*: I jouked that fellow. **1984** Mason & Rheingold *Slanguage* (unp.): Looks like I juked you all with my royal flush. **1984** Eble *Campus Slang* (Sept.) 5: *Juke*—to trick: "You know you didn't rub that snake, so stop juking me." **1988** *Wkly. World News* (Apr. 5) 32: But best of all, you can juke the tax man by putting...[your wife] on your payroll at some outlandishly high salary. **1989** P. Munro *U.C.L.A. Slang* 53: I got juked by the system. **1993** in P. Munro *U.C.L.A. Slang II* 54: He juked me out of fifty cents.

juke² *v.* [prob. of Afro-Caribbean dial. orig.; cf. JUKE¹, *n.*; but also cf. *SND joog*..."to prick, pierce with a sharp instrument"] Orig. *Black E.* Also **jook, joog, jug, jugg.**

1. to punch; stick; stab; jab.

> **1877** in Cassidy *Dict. Jamaican Eng.* 253: Wen me see him so wid de begnet...me ting say de man da go jook me wid it. **1884** in *DARE: Joog* which means...'to punch'. **1893** in *DARE: Joog*...used by negroes and illiterate whites to mean *to punch* or poke. **1932** in P. Oliver *Songsters & Saints* 122: Took his knife and juked him. **1968** I. Reed *Yellow Back Radio* 55: This one black cowboy took a Bowie and jugged the woman in the chest. **1968** P. DeAnda, in W. King & R. Milner *Black Drama Anthol.* 482: When she jugged you with that stick I coulda swore...it come out the other side. **1970** Wambaugh *New Centurions* 58 [ref. to 1960]: Well, she atoned for it by juking Cornelius Arps. **1972** Wambaugh *Blue Knight* 34: I turned the guy that juked that taxi dancer in the alley. The one that almost cut her tit off, remember? **1973** Wideman *Lynchers* 250: Some needle to jug 'em halfway up the ass. **1992** E. McBain *Kiss* 210: He certainly hadn't been "juked," no one had stabbed him.

2. to copulate with.—also used absol.—usu. considered vulgar.

> **1943, 1958** in Cassidy *Dict. Jamaican Eng.* **1965** C. Brown *Manchild* 115: There were few women...that Johnny wanted to jugg and didn't jugg. *Ibid.* 119: She'd started jugging everybody. *Ibid.* 120: Maybe we just jugged because good friends were supposed to do that sort of thing. **1966–67** Braly *On the Yard* 27: Ask him did he want to juge a colored girl. *a*1972 B. Rodgers *Queens' Vernacular* 88: Fuck...*joog, jook, jug* (hustler sl. mid '60s). **1973** Wideman *Lynchers* 37: I said to myself she jugging herself with that thing. **1974** in J.L. Gwaltney *Drylongso* 161: You can't just go around here jooging everything you see. **1989** P. Munro *U.C.L.A. Slang* 53: *Juke*...to have sex. **1991** *UTSQ*: "To juke"...also means to fu—.

3. to fool, meddle, or fool with; tease; JIVE; MESS.

> **1967** Colebrook *Cross of Lassitude* 94: Oh Frankie, they juggin' with me....they put my bond too high. *Ibid.* 236: What you doin'...? Juggin'? **1968** Heard *Howard St.* 30: Aw, Franchot, who you think you juggin', tryin' to be so hard? **1969** in D. Rose *Black Street Life* 63: You can't talk to me unless you *jug* me. **1971** in Sanchez *Word Sorcerers* 110: They won't jug around with the money; dig? **1971** Guggenheimer *Narc. & Drug Abuse* 28: *Jugging*. teasing. **1971** *Who Took Weight?* 183: He keeps juggin' 'round, she gone have him right back in lock-up again. **1972** A. Kemp *Savior* 199: That Clyde...gone be doubly rough if he catch you juggin' with his stuff.

juke³ *v.* [perh. a creolized form of Wolof *dzug* 'to misbehave, lead a disorderly life'; cf. JUKE¹, *n.*] Orig. *Black E.* (Fla. & So. Ga.) Also (*obs.*) **jook, jouk.**

1.a. to play music in a style, such as boogie-woogie or bottleneck, popular in JUKES.—usu. constr. with *it*.

> **1933** in *OEDS*: Jook it Jook it. **1935** in Leadbitter & Slaven *Blues Records* 190: Jooking. **1941** *AS* XVI 319: Jouk it boy. **1942** *Amer. Mercury* (July) 94: *Jooking*—playing the piano, guitar, or any musical instrument in the manner of the Jooks.

b. to dance or move one's body to usu. blues or rock music.—also constr. with *it.*

1937 in *OEDS:* In the "jukin' joints" there is, of course, the prime requisite of liquor. **1941** *AS* XVI 319: *Jouk* is defined by a South Georgia high school girl as "dancing to *boogie-woogie* or *jive* rhythm." **1942** Z.N. Hurston, in *Amer. Mercury* (July) 94: *Jooking*...Dancing and "scronching." **1942** *ATS* 345: Dance...*juke...strut, swing* [etc.]. **1961** in Oster *Country Blues* 121: They...go off to another place an' drink and jook. **1970–72** in *AS* L (1975) 62: *Juke* vi...Dance. **1974** Blount *3 Bricks Shy* 199: Frank tauntingly juked back and forth. **1978** De Christoforo *Grease* 72: We were snapping our fingers in rhythm to Kenick's jukin'. *Ibid.* 144: Me and Danny were jukin' around my room in our shorts, gettin' loose. **1979** L. Heinemann, in *TriQuarterly* 181: Jonesy danced this way and that—shucking and jiving, juking and high-stepping, rolling his eyes and snapping his fingers in time. **1980** Eble *Campus Slang* (Oct.) 4: *Jukin'*—Dance, most often in a place or situation which enables only the moving of the upper part of the body to the music.

2. *So.* to visit jukes, dance halls, or taverns; (see also 1977 quot.).

1939 in *DARE:* Now to go "jooking" means to attend any night club. **1941** *AS* XVI 319: "Let's go joukin'" is a request for a date. **1942** Wylie *Vipers* 243: Virtue: A Field Course in Juking. **1942** in Botkin *Sidewalks* 389: There's something about jooking that gets in your blood. **1952** Clayton *Angels* 39: Makin' a dollar or two now to go jookin' with. **1957** T. Williams *Orpheus* 32: I'd like to go out jooking with you tonight....That's when you get in a car and drink a little and drive a little and stop and dance a little to a juke box and [repeat the entire process several times]. **1977** Univ. Tenn. student theme: One of the first weekends he was there, she stayed out all night juking. That is, at a hotel or motel, partying, drinking, smoking dope, etc. **1984** in "J.B. Briggs" *Drive-In* 268: A couple brain-damaged jukers.

jukebox *n.* [JUKE[1], *n.* + *box*] a coin-operated phonograph that automatically plays any of a number of recordings selected by the customer. Now *S.E.* Also (*obs.*) **jook box.**

1939 *Time* (Sept. 4) 36: The "juke box"...retailed melody in small barrooms, lunch counters and dance joints at 5¢ a shot....With an estimated consumption rate of more than 30,000,000 discs annually, the 300,000 juke boxes in the U.S. are today the record industry's largest customer. **1939** *Time* (Dec. 25) 3: Where did you get the name "juke box" for nickel phonographs...? In Michigan, Indiana and Ohio, everyone calls them "Groan Boxes" and the expression, "Flip a nickel on the groan," is generally understood. **1941** H.A. Smith *Low Man* 125: Juke boxes in saloons were in large measure responsible. **1942** *New Yorker* (May 2) 15: Juke boxes are the curse of the world. **1943** *Newsweek* (Oct. 25) 46: Winston Churchill once danced to juke-box tunes with local belles. **1944** E. Caldwell *Tragic Ground* 50: The juke box music started again, and he was glad he could no longer see the girls or hear their laughter. **1944** M. Chase *Harvey* 599: Harvey and I sit in the bars and we have a drink or two and play the jukebox. **1945** Peeples *Swing Low* 222: He didn't notice who was in the place or what the juke box was playing. **1948** Vidal *City & Pillar* 11: The jukebox stopped playing. **1952** Clayton *Angels* 37: The jook box was playing one of those dreamy pieces. **1975** *Black World* (June) 68: This crummy juke box in this two-bit bar.

juked *adj. So.* intoxicated.

1981 [Reported as common in Ga. by Univ. Tenn. student]. **1981** Univ. Tenn. student: He's juked. **1982** Least Heat Moon *Blue Hwys.* 123: But too many of them are juked on drugs.

juke joint *n.* [JUKE[1], *n.* + JOINT] JUKE[1], *n.*, 1; (*hence*) any establishment where patrons can dance to the music of a jukebox. Also (now *rare*) **jook joint, jouk joint.**

1937 in S. Kennedy *Palmetto Country* 186: Justice Rivers Buford, who spent his boyhood in the Apalachicola timberlands...explained: "Before white folks started using the word, there were negro jookjoints as far back as I can remember." **1939** C.R. Cooper *Scarlet* 12: I had seen many thousands like him in the sprawl of youngsters which nightly crowds the "jook joints," the "massage parlors" or taxi dance halls, the Dine and Dance dumps, [etc.]. *Ibid.* 94: Did you ever go to a jook joint [in Pensacola]? Well, it's just like a tavern, only they call it a jook joint. **1941** *Amer. Mercury* (Nov.) 661: Honky-tonks and "juke joints" where the [prostitutes] are ostensibly waitresses. **1941** *AS* XVI 319: What jouk-joint do you want to go to? **1942** Wilder *Flamingo Road* 197 [ref. to *ca*1929]: Picked her up at a juke joint. **1944** Wakeman *Shore Leave* 29: But, say, did you notice any stuff around here you'd like? Or would you rather shop around the juke joints first? **1945** in Mencken *Amer. Lang. Supp. II* 710: The roadside houses gen-

erally referred to as *jouk-joints* have become a menace to society and the welfare of the people [of Tift Co., Ga.]. [**1949** L. Turner *Africanisms* 195: *Juke house,* "a disorderly house, a house of ill-repute."] **1951–52** P. Frank *Hold Back Night* 31: San Diego and Norfolk dance halls and juke joints. **1953** in T. Sturgeon *Unicorn* 48: And while she was listening to it, someone in the juke-joint recognized her and called her by name. **1957** in Chipman *Hardening Rock* 35: Right up to the juke joint, you go in./Drop the coin right into the slot. **1958** J. Jones *Pistol* 64 [ref. to 1941]: Sure wish they hadn't of closed the jookjoint, don't you? **1959** W. Williams *Ada Dallas* 67: Then we picked up a couple other [musicians], and the first thing we knew we were making a living playing at juke joints and on hillbilly radio shows. **1960** in Oster *Country Blues* 93: I gotta go out there to that ole jook joint tonight. **1970** Winick & Kinsie *Lively Commerce* 155: The thirties saw the advent on a fairly large scale of the "juke joint," a roadhouse in which prostitutes were available. **1972–79** C. Major *Emergency Exit* 52: Cindy is in a juke joint. **1985** *Campus Voice* (Apr.) 44: There are still juke joints where you can hear first-generation black blues [played live]. **1993** *Wilson Qly.* (Summer) 12: Lowlife rowdies raising hell in a Memphis juke joint. **1995** *N.Y. Times* (Jan. 22) II 30: I was in the yard of his juke joint looking at the full moon in the clear Mississippi night.

juke organ *n.* Esp. *Fla. & Ga.* JUKEBOX.

1937 in *Fla. Review* (Spring 1938) 25: The screeching of the "jook" organ. **1939** *Time* (Dec. 25) 3: To the Florida man, such an instrument is a jook organ. **1941** *AS* XVI 319: Feed the jouk-organ (nickelodeon). **1942** in Botkin *Sidewalks* 389: The whine of boogie-woogie from the resplendent jook organ.

jum *n. Narc.* (see quots.). Also **jumbo.**

1988 *Spin* (Oct.) 58: Making $2000 to $5000 a day selling "jums" (or "jumbos," the big pieces of crack). *a*1992 in Ratner *Crack Pipe* 125: I dropped the *jums* (vials of crack) on the floor and I kept walking.

jumble-fuck *n.* CLUSTERFUCK, 1.—usu. considered vulgar.

1938 "Justinian" *Amer. Sexualis* 27: *Jumble-Fuck.* n. U.S., low coll., *ca* 20 for *Daisy-Chain.*

jumbo *n. Entertainment Industry.* a prominent entertainer, writer, etc.

1966 Susann *Valley of Dolls* 11: "But I thought actors and writers had managers and agents." "They do....But the 'jumbos,' the kind I handle, they also need me to advise them." *Ibid.* 399: We have to get a few jumbos, sell them on TV and tie up the package.

jump *n.* **1.** the very beginning.—constr. with *the.*

[**1831** in *DA:* I'll give you a history of Henry Clay, from the *first jump* of him.] **1848** in Bartlett *Amer.* (ed. 2) 223: A whole string of Democrats...had been going the whole hog for Cass from the jump. **1852** in Eliason *Tarheel Talk* 280: I will give time, but Interest from the Jump. **1865** Dennett *South as It Is* 258: He wasn't much of a rebel at the jump, but when the war got a-going it sort o' inspired him. **1913** J. London *Valley of Moon* 201: She got Martha's goat from the jump. **1957** in W.S. Burroughs *Letters* 361: Like I thought from the jump. **1964** K. Clark *Dark Ghetto* 93: I feel that if they had given me some kind of break from the jump...then I might have done something for myself. **1973** H. Foster *Ribbin'* 32: Always having to act tough and crazy and to be willing to fight *from the jump.* **1987** Mamet *House of Games* (film): So you had her made from the jump. *a*1994 N. McCall *Wanna Holler* 120: Liz had no problem connecting from the jump.

2. liveliness.

1871 *From Ocean to Ocean* 5: The "City of Washington" coming up astern *put more jump* into our too-careful engineer. **1918** *Stars & Stripes* (Apr. 5) 4: Your paper has the real American jump. Good luck!

3. *pl.* delirium tremens (*obs.*); (*also*) extreme nervousness.—constr. with *the.*

*1879 in *F & H* IV 81: I thought he had been drinking, and in fact was on the verge of the jumps. **1889* in *F & H:* Only suffering from an attack of the jumps. **1954–60** *DAS: Jumps, the* = jitters, the. **1967** Michaels *Berets* 17: "I'd like you to leave me alone if you don't mind."..."Got the screaming jumps?"

4. Esp. *Circus.* a journey, esp. by rail.

1916 *Variety* (Nov. 3) 6: He made an estimate of his railroad jumps, his hotel bills, [etc.]. **1922** N. Anderson *Hobo* 83: He likes to tell of making "big jumps" on passenger trains as from the Coast to Chicago in five days. **1925** Robinson *Wagon Show* 30: In the old wagon show days, owing to the impossibility of making long "jumps," performances were made in practically every town along the route. **1928** Guerin *Crime* 40:

I took a long jump to New York. **1938** Adamic *My America* 64: He…had worked at these trades between "jumps," which often were long and far between jobs. **1975** McKennon *Horse Dung Trail* 41: Lots of the towns we have to play to "break the jumps" just don't…pay the expense.…We gonna have it all on trains for every jump next season.

5.a. an act of sexual intercourse.—usu. considered vulgar.

1931 Farrell *McGinty* 135: Catch me, if you want a good jump, big man. **1934** O'Hara *Samarra* ch. vii: And then you get cockeyed and take her out for a quick jump and ruin the whole works. **1938** O'Hara *Hope of Heaven* 33: I'd give her a jump in the car. **1938** "Justinian" *Amer. Sexualis* 27: *Jump*…n. An act of coitus, usually with a temporal connotation. **1946** Gresham *Nightmare Alley* 11: Maybe I could give her one jump and then blow the show. Jesus, it would be worth it, to get into that. **1956** Chamales *Never So Few* 242: When I take her home I am going to try and give her a jump. **1960–61** Steinbeck *Discontent* 194: You've never had a quick jump in the hay in your life. **1972** G. Walton *Capt. Madam* 131: When those [pimps] learn how much a jump their girls are making. **1989** *Married with Children* (Fox-TV): We're married. You deserve a jump now and then.

b. a sexually promiscuous young woman.

1935 Pollock *Und. Speaks: Jump*, a woman of easy virtue. **1942** Algren *Morning* 41: You should see the jump I picked me up once there. The dew was still on it. *Ibid.* 56: How's that new jump of yours, Left'? You got her with ya?

6.a. Esp. *Black E.* a dance party; HOP.

1954 Yablonsky *Violent Gang* 51: Now you guys gonna let us throw a jump there. **1954–60** *DAS: Jump*…any dance or other social event.…*general teenage use by c1955.* **1962** (quot. at **(b)**, below). **1966–67** P. Thomas *Mean Streets* 66: You meet your boys and make it to a jump, where you can break night dancing. **1983** *Reader's Digest Success with Words* 86: Black English..*jump* = (1) "a dance" (2) "a fight."

b. a fight, esp. between street gangs; RUMBLE.

1954–60 *DAS: Jump*…n….= rumble. *Teenage street-gang use since c1955.* **1962** in Ricks & Marsh *Patterns in English* 48: [Among N.Y.C. gangs] a *jump* is a dance or a fight. **1983** (quot. at **(a)**, above).

¶ In phrases:

¶ **give the jump** to evade or escape (someone).

1930 Sage *Last Rustler* 9: If he's done that, he sure gave Joe Rush the jump.

¶ **[go] take a jump!** *go jump [in the lake]!* s.v. JUMP, *v.*

1901 Irwin *Sonnets* (unp.): Go take a running jump and chase yourself! **1937** M. Mooney *You Can't Buy Luck* (film): Aah, go take a jump! **1988** *N.Y. Post* (June 21) 14: He slammed down a bottle of his salad dressing and told the lawyer to "take a jump."

¶ **on the jump** on the run; (*hence*) right away.

1859 in *DA:* I run down stream, and I meets Bill on the jump. **1876** in S.L. Smith *Sagebrush Soldier* 49: So him and me started out a hed on the jump. **1889** "M. Twain" *Conn. Yankee* 479: Send five hundred picked knights with Launcelot in the lead; and send them on the jump. **1894** in Remington *Wister* 47: I want to make some pictures of the ponies going over the hell-roaring mal-pai after a steer on the jump. **1896** Ade *Artie* 91: I don't want to get too gay on the jump. **1933** Ersine *Pris. Slang* 48: *Jump*, n. Living in fear of capture, the *lam*. "Don is on the jump."

jump v. **1.a.** Orig. *West.* to take possession of (another's property, mining claim, etc.) unlawfully. Now *S.E.*

1836 in *DA:* The quarter (near Plainfield, Ill.) that I claimed originally myself has been "jumped" by a person with whom reasoning is of no avail. **1850** P. Decker *Diaries* 216: River claims are…being "jumped." **1855** in *F & H* IV 82: If a man jumped my claim,…I appealed to the crowd. **1858** in *Calif. Folk. Qly.* I (1942) 277: Any miner then may jump my claim. **1859** Greeley *Overland Journey* 163: "O, I've jumped a cabin."…finding an uninhabited cabin that suited him, he had quietly entered and [stayed]. **1860** in L. Barney *Letters* 59: Making abortive attempts to "jump claims." **1863** [Fitch] *Annals of Army* 518: They "jumped" a claim and went to mining. **1867** in B. Harte *Harte's Calif.* 147: Attempts have been made to "squat" and "jump" lots. **1880** in Earp & Boyer *Wyatt* 94: Shooting and rows of various kinds. [Town] Lots being jumped. **1881** in A.E. Turner *Earps Talk* 74: As soon as I heard of him robbing the stage I…jumped his ranch. **1897** Hayne *Klondyke* 128: They did their level best to "jump" the legal claims of men who had got in in proper time. *a*1916 D.E. Conner *In Gold Fields* 76 [ref. to 1860's]: A body of tramps would unite

and "jump" the whole district, drive out the original owners and pass new laws, and work until they would be served the same way.

b. *West.* to rob (someone) of a claim, as to a mine, land, livestock, etc. [The sense of the *1789 quot. is 'to swindle or cheat'.]

[*1789 in *F & H* IV 82: They…pick him up and take him to the above alehouse to jump him, or do him upon the broads, which means cards.] **1870** in Schele de Vere *Amer.* 170: Gold is sure to come out 'er that theer claim, but the old proprietor…was green, and let the boys about here jump him. **1963** R.W. Paul *Mining Frontiers* 23 [ref. to 1850's]: Rules and procedures for protecting individual claimants to land or livestock from being "jumped."

c. *Mil.* to secure (a military bounty) unlawfully by enlisting and then deserting.

1863 in *Manuscripts* XXX (1978) 276: "Substitutes" and "bounty jumpers"…deserted. **1863** in J.W. Haley *Rebel Yell* 120: Doubtless they have enlisted several times and jumped a bounty on each occasion. **1864** in Morgan & Michalson *For Our Beloved Country* 169: After jumping several bounties, he deserted to the enemy. *ca*1865 in Bartlett *Amer.* (ed. 4) 62: So the thought struck him that he would go and *jump the bountie.* **1871** Schele de Vere *Amer.* 283: Men would receive in one State a bounty,…enlist…and run away after a few days; they went into another State, enlisted once more, [etc.].…They obtained the title of *bounty-jumpers.* **1884** in *DA:* The man…"who broke his leg attempting to jump the bounty." **1886** F. Wilkeson *Recoll.* 2: How many times have you jumped the bounty?

d. Esp. *Und.* to snatch or steal (an object).

*1871 in Partridge *DSUE* 447: Five thousand bricks were jumped the other night from…[a] brickyard at Klipdrift. *1879 in *OED2:* Some fellows…prowl around…with a single eye to "jumping" anything conveniently portable. *1889 Barrère & Leland *Dict. Slang* I 512: (Cape settlers), to *jump*, to steal. An English officer camping out was told to take care they did not *jump* his candlestick. **1899** (quot. at GUMP[1], *n.*, 2). **1984** J. McNamara *First Directive* 229: He just came up to us about ten minutes before we jumped the purse.

2.a. to spring upon or attack, esp. from concealment; assault, esp. suddenly. Now *S.E.* (as applied to persons).

*1859 Hotten *Slang Dict.: Jump*…"To *jump* a man," to pounce upon him, and either rob or maltreat him. **1867** A.D. Richardson *Beyond Miss.* 239 [ref. to El Paso, 1859]: To "jump a man" was to attack or kill him. **1874** in *Calif. Folk. Qly.* I (1942) 277: Jumped the hunter, I reckon, to scalp him. **1879** J.B. Fry *Army Sac.* 199: Captain Jackson's troop, …using that officer's words, *"jumped the camp of Captain Jack's Modoc Indians soon after daylight."* **1882** Triplett *Jesse James* 165: The Kansas bully…"jumped" a quiet stranger in a small saloon. **1884** in Lummis *Letters* 87: Fourteen of the most desperate cases employed in the…quarries "jumped" their walking boss. **1885** Bourke *Campaign* 92: They had "jumped" "Bonito's" and "Chato's" *rancherias*, killing nine and capturing five. **1886** L. Wood *Geronimo* 35: They had jumped an Indian camp during the day, getting a number of saddles. **1887** Zogbaum *Horse, Foot & Dragoons* 160: Some of them are suspected of being members of the band that "jumped" the paymaster some weeks ago. **1892** F. Harris *Conklin* 154: I guess he wanted to jump me. **1895** Townsend *Fadden* 195: If youse jump me, de cop will see yer wood legs is fakes, and run you off de beat. *ca*1900 *Buffalo Bill* 67: He was "jumped" by a band of Indians. **1922** in Ruhm *Detective* 32: One of the richest gem beds in Asia—a bed that was hidden by the *Mran-ma* when the British jumped the country. **1927** in Hammett *Knockover* 308: Red was jumped. They got him. **1987** Chinnery *Life on Line* 218: When the Cobras jumped the bad guys they started to receive 50-caliber fire. *a*1990 E. Currie *Dope & Trouble* 6: That's all we *do* is jump people, man. **1995** Donahue (NBC-TV): I got jumped.… They proceeded to beat me and take my wallet.

b. to rebuke angrily.—occ. constr. with *up*. Cf. colloq. *jump on.*

1880 in Roe *Army Letters* 268: Faye says that the men were…simply trying to keep their rifles from being marred and scratched, for if they did get so they would be "jumped" at the first inspection. **1887** Francis *Saddle & Moccasin* 146: Doc Gilpen and the Marshal jumped him.*…*Took him to task. **1894** C.C. King *Cadet Days* 241: Do you remember how the colonel jumped him that morning for some error in the guard list? **1898** *Munsey's Mag.* (June) 398: He proceeded to jump us at the very first parade he attended. **1905** *DN* III 84: *Jump up,* *v. tr.* To censure. "He got *jumped up* for that." **1906** in J. London *Letters* 211: You ought to have jumped Vance…before you jumped me. **1907** Moss *Officers' Manual* 243: *Jump*—to admonish. **1908** in H.C. Fisher *A. Mutt* 154: I cannot jump you for telling the truth. **1918** Griffin *Reg't.* 34: He would "climb" a slouchy rookey till he straightened out his back;/Then he'd "crawl" him from his shoe-strings to the rifle in the rack;/Next he'd stand out there "forninst" him and he'd "jump" him once "agin,"/Whilst he asked him why they 'listed brats instead of full-grown "min." **1918** in Rossano *Price of Honor* 159: I got unmercifully jumped for it. **1932** Harvey *Me and Bad Eye* 89: I jumped Bad Eye about it afterwards. **1933** Tuchock & Schubert *No Other Woman* (film): Oh, so that's why you jumped me! **1954** (quot. at *cut under* s.v. CUT, *v.*). **1958** S.H. Adams *Tenderloin* 76: All I ask is that…you jump me when I go wrong. **1971** *Black World* (Apr.) 59: Why you got to jump me about it?

c. *Police.* to raid (an illicit establishment).

1889 Barrère & Leland *Dict. Slang* I 512: *Jump the game, to* (American). In gambling or poker slang to raid a gambling den by the police. **1966** Brunner *Face of Night* 153: He kept jumping Annabelle's place; he couldn't think of anything else to do.

3. *Law.* to forfeit (one's bail or bond) by absconding.—also used absol. Now *S.E.*

1859 Matsell *Vocab.* 47: *Jumped His Bail.* Run away from his bail. **1877** Bartlett *Amer.* (ed. 4) 227: "Boss Tweed *jumped his bail;*" *i.e.*, he ran away. **1891** Maitland *Slang Dict.* 157: *Jumping bail* (Am.), absconding while under bail. **1911** Vance *Cynthia* 177: He's jumped bail on a bigamy indictment. **1976** C. Keane *Hunter* 225: Jumped three months ago. Ten thousand forfeiture. **1985** D. Killerman *Hellrider* 13: You jumped bail back in L.A.

4.a. to escape, flee, or abscond from; (now *rare*) to SKIP; (*specif.*) to desert (one's ship, military unit, team, or the like); (*obs.*) *Stu.* to absent oneself from (class).—also used absol.

1865 Williams *Joaquin* 4: Your term out, Ned? or did you jump Sing Sing? **1867** *Nat. Police Gaz.* (Jan. 12) 3: She…"jumped the town." **1874** in A.E. Turner *Earps Talk* 17: The Higgenbottom outfit…attempted to jump the county…to Wichita. **1878** Hart *Sazerac* 60: Hopin' one day to git a horse and jump the country. **1885** Clark *Boy Life in USN* 133: As for the boys I spoke of, they would have "jumped" any way. **1892** L. Moore *Own Story* 370: He got the "tip" that the officers were looking for him. Without stopping to pack his trunk, he "jumped" to Montreal. **1898** *Munsey's* (June) 398: Cochise had "jumped" the San Carlos reservation with his band of Chiricahuas. **1899–1900** Cullen *Tales* 326: Say, has McGinley jumped? **1900** *DN* II 44: *Jump*, v.t. To absent one's self from a lecture. **1900** Willard & Hodler *Powers That Prey* 61: It won't cost us over ten days to take it in, an' then we can jump West. **a1904** in *DA*: The men, discouraged, would begin to "jump," would ask for their "time." **1908** *Hampton's Mag.* (Dec.) 770: Sing small, work hard, and jump at Hongkong. The skipper'll give you every chance to jump. **1908** H. Green *Maison de Shine* 87: We'll jump this burg to-morrow. **1914** *Collier's* (Aug. 1) 5: But, I tell you, I wouldn't have jumped the team anyhow! **1918** Riesenberg *Under Sail* 40: He had "jumped" a schooner, leaving everything behind. **1921** *Variety* (Aug. 26) 7: He jumped the club after the opening game and hasn't been heard from since. **1922** Rollins *Cowboy* 110: The Crow Indians had "jumped" their reservation and were on the war-path. *1929 Bowen *Sea Slang* 77: *Jump a Ship, To.* To desert. **1951** Breen & Duff *Appt. with Danger* (film): Sohnequist jumped the [police] tail. **1958** Frankel *Band of Bros.* 242 [ref. to 1950]: Why you figure he jumped hospital? **a1961** R.H. Dillon *Shanghaiing Days* 209: Their shipmates…had "jumped" the *Drumlanrig*…after a…hard passage from Cardiff. **1970** Benteen *Apache Raiders* 50: Apparently, Fallon…had received no official word about that many bucks having jumped the Reservation. **1971** "L. Short" *Man from Desert* 122: Well, that damned Hanaway…has jumped the country, looks like. Leastways, he's not around. **1973** Weisman & Boyer *Heroin Triple Cross* 28: That boy jumped from the Marine Corps six months ago. **1975** in Eastman et al. *Norton Reader* (ed. 4) 23: He told me that for jumping the club I was suspended without salary from Eau Claire. **1977** Langone *Life at Bottom* 179: I wouldn't go back to Nam, I'd jump ship first. **1980** Manchester *Darkness* 22: I left my cot, jumped hospital, hitchhiked to the front. **1982** *All Things Considered* (Nat. Pub. Radio) (June 9): If that meant he had to jump the team he was playing for and run off and play for another one, he'd do it. **1992** N. Russell *Suicide Charlie* 38: [One] day I jumped training and hid out in the woods.

b. to quit or leave (a task or activity).

1876 J. Miller *First Fam'lies* 94: Even the head man of the company…jumped a first-class poker game…to come in and weigh out dust. **1908** Whittles *Lumberjack* 13: Snowed so blank hard that half the gang jumped the job.

c. to avoid payment of (a debt, bill, fare, or the like).

1879 in *DA*: The circus springboard vaulter never gets arrested for "jumping his board." **1888** in Farmer *Amer.*: He arose at early dawn and jumped his bill. **1908** J. London *M. Eden* 141: "And I'm broke—when I pay my board." "Jump it," Joe advised. "Can't. Owe it to my sister." *ca*1910–18 Hoyt *Buckskin Joe* 72: We had to jump hotel bills as we beat our way from town to town. **1942** *Calif. Folk. Qly.* I 327: The little old lady had "jumped" her fare. **1959** Duffy & Lane *Warden's Wife* 191: In most states…it is only a misdemeanor to "jump" a hotel bill. **1980** *N.Y. Daily News* (Tonight ed.) (Aug. 20) 9: The clerk said that he also recognized the youth as a fare jumper.

d. to break (a contract or formal agreement).

1884 in *DAE*: Agents have been working for them on the quiet to jump their contracts. **1911–12** J. London *Smoke Bellew* 27: It's an idea…and you can jump the deal as soon as I tell you it. Are you game? *Ibid.* 36: The Indians jumped the contract and took off their straps. **1950** Roeder *J. Robinson* 82: Many players have "jumped" their contracts in mid-season and nothing has ever been done about it. **1984** Bak *Turkey Stearnes* 67: Players who jumped their contracts to sign with another team.

5. to steal a ride on (a railroad train). Now *S.E.*

1885 "Lykkejaeger" *Dane* 44: I proceeded to try "jumping" the freight trains. **1891** in *DA*: I jumped a freight here. **1902** "J. Flynt" *Little Bro.* 46: And you'll know how to jump trains, too.

6. [perh. orig. of livestock, as in 1974 quot.] (of a man) to copulate with.—usu. considered vulgar.

1918 in Carey *Mlle. from Armentières* I (unp.): The English Tommies stayed behind,/Jumping the W.A.A.C.'s behind the lines. **1929–33** Farrell *Manhood of Lonigan* 178: A big tough guy should only want to jump a girl, and think that…love was crap. **1948** I. Shulman *Cry Tough!* 77: I sure woulda liked to jump her. **1954** Schulberg *Waterfront* 12: He kept an apartment, but he only went there to sleep or jump a broad. **1959** W. Miller *Cool World* 32: Now it gonna cost evry time you jump her. **1974** Loken *Come Monday Morning* 23: A stallion. Nothin' to do but stand around…an' jump mares. **1980** *Oui* (Aug.) 90: He was known for jumping the girls. **1981** *Time* (Nov. 30) 88: You men, ever eager to jump the secretary for an hour's sport. **1985** J. Ferrell & M. Lichter *Vixens* (film): Your father's been jumping his students.

7.a. Orig. *Jazz.* to be filled with activity, liveliness, or excitement.

1938 Calloway *Hi De Ho* 16: *Joint is jumping:* the place is lively, the club is leaping with fun. **1939** Goodman & Kolodin *Swing* 135: A good rhythm section that would kick out, or jump, or rock, or swing. **1946** Mezzrow & Wolfe *Really Blues* 14: When I get on my horn the joint still jumps. **1953** W. Fisher *Waiters* 50: The place "jumped like a revival meeting," to quote the bar-flies. **1957** Mayfield *Hit* 43: Drink up, girls. I know a jumping joint on Hundred-twenty-third street. **1968** Heard *Howard St.* 22: The joint was jumping tonight. **1981** *Rod Serling's Mag.* (Sept.) 16: Philly was wide open in them days, this joint was jumpin'. **1994** *CBS This Morning* (CBS-TV) (Feb. 25): Can you hear Michael Jackson in the background? This place is jumpin'!

b. *Black E.* to dance and have fun; celebrate.

1941 *Pittsburgh Courier* (May 10) 7: They…go to Petersburg every night. That is where they do most of their "jumping." **1944** Burley *Hndbk. Jive* 141: *Jump*—Frolic, have fun, dance.

8. Orig. *Black E.* to behave (in a specified manner) suddenly; turn; in phrs. **jump salty** [or **bad** or **stink**] to become angry, belligerent, or dangerous; **jump Western** to become violent; **jump smooth** to begin acting intelligently.

1938 *AS* (Dec.) 314: *Jump salty*…become suddenly angry. **1939** in Leadbitter & Slaven *Blues Records* 179: My Man Jumped Salty On Me. **1946** Mezzrow & Wolfe *Really Blues* 116: The whole town jumped stink on us. **1947–52** R. Ellison *Invisible Man* 427: All right, daddy, you don't have to jump evil on me. **1952** E. Brown *Trespass* 93: Don't you jump salty, now. **1953** Peterson *Take a Giant Step* 57: Listen, Frank, don't you be jumping salty with me. **1956** Childress *Like One of Family* 23: Please don't jump so salty. **1958** *Life* (Apr. 14) 141 [ref. to ca1950]:

We decided unanimously to jump independent. *Ibid.* (Apr. 28) 84: The Deacons nearly flipped when I told them I had jumped smooth. **1959** Murtagh & Harris *Who Live in Shadow* 55: They went hincty on me, too. Those cats jumped stink on their own boy. They was better than brothers to me in the old days and now they jumped stink. They clammed tight. Talk about a bringdown. **1961** O. Davis *Purlie Victorious* 316: No more shouting hallelujah! every time you sneeze, nor jumping jackass every time you whistle "Dixie"! **1962** Killens *Heard the Thunder* 96: Don't get mad with me, good kid....don't jump salty with me. **1966–67** P. Thomas *Mean Streets* 59: Macho, their president, jumped stink. **1968** Bullins *Wine Time* 403: I'm tired of your little ass jumpin' bad around here. **1970** A. Young *Snakes* 49: I dont want you to go jumpin all jiggedy just cause I tell you this. *a*1972 C. Gordon, in W. King & R. Milner *Black Drama Anthol.* 409: But you need to relax, man, you jump salty too quick....Now don't jump serious. *a*1972 *Urban Life & Culture* I 86: Wanted to jump sharp…and be mellow. **1972** *N.Y. Times Mag.* (Sept. 24) 94: We want to walk the streets without the burden of having jumped paranoic. **1973** Wideman *Lynchers* 49: How come little dudes always the first to jump bad and call the dozens? **1974** V. Smith *Jones Men* 13: The dude jumped smart and Joe cracked him. **1976** Price *Bloodbrothers* 147: Shit, anybody even *thinks* a jumpin' bad he'll get eighty-sixed so fast he ain't gonna even *know* about it until it's in the papers. **1976** Braly *False Starts* 227: Otherwise he wouldn't have jumped so salty. **1978** Kopp *Innocence* 107 [ref. to 1940's]: One of them was jumping Western about some cat from my neighborhood. **1978** *Penthouse* (Apr.) 128: I'm jumpin' crazy doin' this article. **1978** W. Brown *Tragic Magic* 27: I'm gonna see how bad you jump when you ain't got a audience. *a*1987 Bunch & Cole *Reckoning for Kings* 285: So maybe you oughta start listenin' to people who've been here a while before you start jumping airborne ranger. **1996** "Sapphire" *Push* 47: Jermaine give Rhonda a piss on you look. Rhonda cut her eyes at Jermain like jump bad if you want to.

9. *Black E.* to take place; occur or begin to occur, esp. suddenly.—usu. constr. with *off.*

1946 Mezzrow & Wolfe *Really Blues* 26: The First World War was jumping then. **1964–69** in Calt *Rather Be Devil* 96: Anything was liable to jump off. **1970** (quot. at TASTE, *n.*). **1974** R.H. Carter *16th Round* 56: Then we'll see what's jumping off. **1974** "A.C. Clark" *Death List* 19: If I hadn't given the party for them, none of this would have jumped off. **1984** S. Hager *Hip Hop* 38: If you weren't on the dance floor when that shit was jumping off, you missed out. *Ibid.* 47: Anything could jump off. **1989** S. Lee *Do the Right Thing* (film): No rawness is jumpin' off tonight. **1990** Vachss *Blossom* 284: It jumps off, one of the boys'll radio for help. **1991** B. Adler *Rap!* 15: There was an excitement in the air, like anything could jump off. *a*1994 N. McCall *Wanna Holler* 372: In case something ugly jumped off.

10. *Mil.* to launch an attack; jump off.

*a*1950 P. Wolff *Friend* 10: At H [-hour]…we jump.

11. to drive through (a stop sign or signal) unlawfully.

[**1938** in *OED2*: *Jump*, v.t., to anticipate (the *go* signal of a traffic director).] **1947** G. Homes *Out of the Past* (film): I jumped a [red traffic] signal. **1950** G. Homes *Lawless* (film): How 'bout it—did you jump the stop sign? **1961** *Car 54* (NBC-TV): "He jumped the stop sign!"…"When you jump a stop sign you endanger pedestrians and motorists alike."

¶ **In phrases:**

¶ **go jump [in the lake]!** go away! *get lost* S.V. GET.

1912 (quot. at FADE, *v.*, 2.a.). **1914** Elliott *Animated Slang* 5: I requested, entreated and implored him to go JUMP IN THE LAKE. **1914** Lardner *You Know Me Al* 84: She says Yes and I suppose I can go and jump in the lake. **1926** Donahue *What Price Glory?* (film): Aw, go jump in the creek. **1933** Hammett *Thin Man* 313: The D.A. will tell you to go jump in the lake, and he'll refuse to prosecute. **1943** M. Shulman *Barefoot Boy* 197: Aw, go jump in the lake. **1948** A. Murphy *Hell & Back* 35: Aw, go jump in a lake and pull the water up over you. **1951** J. Reach *My Friend Irma* 60: Go jump in the lake! **1972** [V.M. Grosvenor] *Thursdays* 36: So you,…your hippie daughter, and your junkie son can all jump. **1973** O'Neill & O'Neill *Shifting Gears* 150: There are times when it may even be necessary to tell the rest of the world to go jump in the lake. **1983** *Good Morning America* (ABC-TV) (Apr. 20): Here's a memo…from the front office. It says, "Go jump in the lake." **1990** *News-Sentinel* (Knoxville, Tenn.) (Oct. 2) B1: If Hollywood…offered me a part in a movie, I probably wouldn't tell them to go jump. **1991** *Sally Jessy Raphaël* (synd. TV series): "Why don't you

butt out?" "Aw, go jump in the lake!" *a*1995 M. Kelly *Proudly* 118: You could tell them to go jump in the lake or something.

¶ **jump back!** go away! get out!

1965 James Brown *Papa's Got a Brand New Bag* (Lois Pub. Co.): Jump back, Jack,/See you later alligator. **1975** Wambaugh *Choirboys* 103: Hey, jump back, Jack! I made my decision. **1978** Tenn. high school teacher, age 25: He'll walk in for that [job] interview, and they'll say, "Jump back, Jack!" **1985** Bodey *F.N.G.* 103: "What'm I going to do…? Wait until then?" "Jump back, for chrissakes." **1987** S. Hasenecz *Sorority Babes* (film): Jump back—prom queens on the loose! **1989** *Open House* (Fox-TV): Stay away from me with the forms! Jump *back*, lady!

¶ **jump cases** (see quot.).

1909 in *Iowa Jour. of Hist.* LVII (1959) 76 [ref. to 1870's]: Many a compositor on the Register "jumped cases"—that is, quit.

¶ **jump down (someone's) throat** see s.v. THROAT.

¶ **jump in** to initiate or be initiated into a street gang, usu. by a beating. Also trans.

1990 L. Bing *Do or Die* 24: Jumped in…initiated (by being beaten up by other gang members). **1993** *Geraldo* (synd. TV series): I was little so I just got jumped in by three people….I hit back, though. You supposed to hit back. **1993** K. Scott *Monster* 9: I had heard about being "courted in"…or "jumped in," but somehow…I had envisioned it to be a noble gathering, paperwork and arguments about my worth. **1994** *Details* (June) 101: Like most of his crew, Ram"…or "jumped in," but somehow…I had envisioned it to be **1996** *Leeza* (synd. TV series): A girl gets jumped in just like a guy does. **1996** *Leeza* (synd. TV series): When people jump in a gang. **1996** *Dangerous Minds* (ABC-TV): We jumped in together. We always looked out for each other.

¶ **jump in** [or **into** or **on**] **(someone's) shit** Esp. *Mil.* to attack, rebuke, haze, harass, etc.—usu. considered vulgar.

1968 Tauber *Sunshine Soldier* 117: Unless you get your shit straight, I'm gonna jump in your shit. **1970** Whitmore *Memphis-Nam-Sweden* 42: Occasionally he would jump in a brother's shit and kick his ass around the barracks. *Ibid.* 43: He was really jumping in their shit. *Ibid.* 52: So we jumped in his shit whenever we could. **1978** Truscott *Dress Gray* 260: They were always jumping in his shit, coming down on him like…jackhammers. **1983** Univ. Tenn. student, age 25: I didn't mean to jump on your shit like that. **1983** Van Devanter & Morgan *Before Morning* 227: By the time she finished jumping in my shit, I felt like I had a new asshole of my own. **1983** Eilert *Self & Country* 152: Al jumped square in her shit. **1985** Bodey *F.N.G.* 142: I didn't expect him to jump into my shit and it hurt my feelings. *a*1987 Coyle *Team Yankee* 19: I am going to come down and jump in your shit.

¶ **jump on (someone's) program** *Mil.* to haze or punish.

1978 Hasford *Short-Timers* 60: Sergeant, you *will* be wearing chevrons…or I will definitely jump on your program.

¶ **jump out** see JUMP OUT.

¶ **jump ship** [fig. application of freq. colloc. of **(4.c.)**, above] to quit membership in a company, organization, etc.; go back on one's associates; leave others in the lurch.

1933 Seff & Seymour *Footlight Parade* (film): You jumped ship. What's your game? **1977** *Dallas Times Herald* (May 29) 8B: Enough members are frustrated enough with the Clayton regime to jump ship. **1979** *Business Week* (Dec. 17) 42: There was a feeling that compensation policies were making it too easy to jump ship. **1983** *Business Week* (Nov.) 124: The heads of marketing, sales, quality control, and research engineering, as well as several key salespersons, have jumped ship. **1984** *L.A. Times* (Nov. 27) VI 18: Though KPRZ-AM (1150) is not supposed to shut down…for another month, its deejays are already jumping ship. **1985** *Working Woman* (Feb.) 4: In the period of uncertainty that followed, key staff members jumped ship. **1994** *Morning Edition* (Nat. Pub. Radio) (Dec. 21): [White House press secretary] Myers insists she is neither jumping ship nor being shoved off.

¶ **jump [on] (someone's) bones** see s.v. BONE[1], *n.*

¶ **jump (someone's) case** to rebuke or upbraid (someone) angrily.

1989 P.H.C. Mason *Recovering* 82: He'd done jumped our case, and he'd leave.

¶ **jump (someone's) hand** *Rap Music.* to threaten or attempt to victimize (someone).

1980 "Grandmaster Flash & Furious Five," in L.A. Stanley *Rap* 147: It takes a sucker's man to try to jump my hand.

¶ **jump the broom[stick]** [orig. ref. to a literal jumping over a broomstick as part of a folk wedding, as in bracketed quots. below; extended metaphorically to ref. to any wedding ceremony] to get married; to marry.

[**1856** in *DARE*: Let's make up a wedding party—*let's jump the broomstick!*] [**1899** Green *Va. Folk-Speech.* 247: *Jump over the broom*....Phrase for an irregular marriage.] **1918** *DN* V 20: *Jump the broom*, to get married (facetious). **1941** in *DARE*. **1953** Randolph & Wilson *Down in Holler* 257: *Jump the broomstick*....To marry....to propose marriage. **1965–70** in *DARE*. **1996** *Living Single* (Fox-TV): A lot of neighbor couples jumpin' the broom.

¶ **jump up (someone's) butt** to punish, rebuke, or act decisively against.

1974 *Nat. Lampoon* (Oct.) 84: My old man's been jumping up my butt ever since I racked up the Pinto. **1979–82** Gwin *Overboard* 201: They woulda got me to a doctor or I woulda jumped up their butt.

jump-butt *n.* (among teamsters) a whip.

1936–37 Kroll *Share-Cropper* 241: The bull-drivers would...lift their long whips—"jump-butts," these whips were called.

jump city *n.* ¶ In phrase: **from jump city** from the start; *from jump street* s.v. JUMP STREET. Cf. CITY.

1987 Knoxville, Tenn., attorney: He's been a crazed son of a bitch from jump *city!* **1993** G. Lee *Honor & Duty* 18: The yards were Jump City for flight out.

jumped-up *adj.* JUMPING, 1.

1922 Kyne *Pride of Palomar* 48: Great jumped-up Jehoshaphat! ***1932** Hanley *Stoker Haslett* 32: You're a liar, a dirty jumped-up liar.

jumper *n.* **1.** one who jumps a claim.

***1854** in *Austral. Nat. Dict.*: The Commissioner...decided in favour of the jumpers. **1859** Bartlett *Amer.* (ed. 2) 223: *Jumper*...One who takes a squatter's claim. **1860** in L. Barney *Letters* 59: There was much menacing on the part of the "jumpers," and a few shots fired. ***1871** *Austral. Nat. Dict.*: This claim is not yet lawfully blocked off, but an enterprising party of jumpers have blocked it off. **1880** in *DAE*: There were no courts convenient to settle disputes, and a class of miners called "Jumpers"...became very numerous. **1888** Gunter *Miss Nobody* 96: His bravery in fighting off jumpers.

2. (see quot.).

1862 in *Manuscripts* XXX (1978) 93: Some old box cars the boys cald them jumpers instead of cars....we went on board of a nother train of jumpers for Baltimore.

3. *Army.* a paratrooper.

1942 *Yank* (June 6) 4: These jumpers...volunteered for duty. **1964** R. Moore *Green Berets* 240: Well, even if I never did get to be a jumper, I'm not a leg at heart. **1966** J. Lucas *Dateline* 342: Mike's a qualified jumper. **1979** J. Morris *War Story* 30: One of the [Montagnard] jumpers went inside.

4. one who has jumped bail or bond; absconder.

1942 *ATS* 428: *Jumper*, an absconder. **1985** D. Killerman *Hellrider* 43: No more hunting down jumpers in *this* city.

5. *Police.* a person who threatens, attempts, or carries out suicide by leaping from a great height.

1964 Walsh & Da Gradi *Mary Poppins* (film): There's a nice spot by the bridge, popular with jumpers. **1975** Wambaugh *Choirboys* 50: Seven-A-Eighty-five...A possible jumper, Wilshire and Mariposa. **1980** Gould *Ft. Apache* 102: Murphy wracked his memory to see if he and Corelli had ever handled a jumper. **1984** J. McNamara *First Directive* 32: Did rigor mortis set in that quickly in jumper cases? **1985** M. Baker *Cops* 88: We got a call one day, a jumper....He's hanging from the fire escape. **1989** *Married with Children* (Fox-TV): I had a few doughnuts this morning waiting for a jumper to make up his mind.

6. *Nuclear Engineering.* (see quot.).

1987 *Atlantic* (May) 100: *Jumper*...is shoptalk for a temporary nuclear worker who hops into a plant's radioactive area and repairs what he can before exceeding his exposure limit to radiation.

jumping *adj.* **1.a.** (used in various oaths).

1815 in M. Mathews *Beginnings of Amer. Eng.* 59: *Jumping jings, jingoes*, expletives indicative of confirmation. **1827** in *JAF* LXXVI (1963) 294: By the jumpin jingo. **1849** "N. Buntline" *B'hoys of N.Y.* 77: When he was mad, jumpin' Caesar! **1861** M.A. Denison *Ruth Margerie* 81: By the jumping Jupiter! this is worse nor being in the Indys a eating *ghee.* **1864** Hill *Our Boys* 354: Jumping Joseph! if that isn't a place for a

fellow to sleep! **1868** G.W. Harris *High Times* 102: BRAKEMAN by the jumpin' geminy. **1882** Triplett *Jesse James* 40: By the jumping J---- C----- they'll do it. **1886** F. Whittaker *Pop Hicks* 19: And we a-paying you seventy-five dollars a week, by the jumping Jerushy Crambo Crap!!! ***a1890–93** *F & H* III 335: Holy jumping mother of Moses! **1893** Frye *Field & Staff* 69: Jumpin' Jonah! won't it do 'em up? **1901** *DN* II 142: By the *jumping Judas.* **1913** J. London *Valley of Moon* 156: Holy jumping Jehosaphat! **1924** *DN* V 264: Holy jumping Jesus Christ. **1924** Anderson & Stallings *What Price Glory?* II: In the name of the holy sweet Jumping, are you gentlemen bound for a masked ball? **1926** Norwood *Other Side of Circus* 2: Jumping buckshot! Where does the time go to, anyhow! **1928** Wharton *Squad* 24 [ref. to 1918]: Holy jumpin' Jesus! ***1931** J. Hanley *Boy* 196: Oh Holy jumpin' Jesus! **1938** in Rawick *Amer. Slave* III (Pt. 3) 11: Oh, great jumpin mercy! **1945** Slesinger & Davis *Tree Grows in Bklyn.* (film): Sweet jumpin' Christopher! **1955** L. Shapiro *Sixth of June* 160: Holy jumpin' Jerusalem—I must be outa my mind! **1957** Hecht *Charlie* 93: Holy jumping Judas, I'm on fire! **1961** Himes *Pinktoes* 70: Good jumping Jesus! **1968** E.M. Parsons *Fargo* 10: Good jumpin' goddam, Virg, these hides won't last till noon. **1980** in *N.E. Folklore* XXVIII (1988) 65: Jumping Jehovah! **1983–90** Heath *CW2* 344: Holy jumping Jesus Christ. *a*1994 H. Roth *Mercy of Rude Stream* 258: Jumpin' Jesus. **1994** *Simpsons' Comics* (No. 2) (back cover): Holy jumpin' Moses! Selma's new lover is...Homer Simpson!

b. damned.

1934 Lomax *Amer. Ballads & Folk Songs* 58: Ninety-nine years so jumpin' long,/To be here rollin' an' cain' go home.

2. *Jazz.* GROOVY; SWINGING. Cf. JUMP, *v.*, 7.a.

1952 Mandel *Angry Strangers* 165: The General, he's a jumpin cat.

3. crowded.—constr. with *with.*

1953 Hackett & Goodrich *Give Girl a Break* (film): This town is *jumping* with talented kids. **1966–67** (quot. at SLIP-TIME).

jumping bean *n.* a fidgety or nervously active person.

1982 R. Sutton *Don't Get Taken* 9: These folks are jumping beans, nervous customers.

jumping-off place *n.* the edge of the earth; (*also*) the farthest limit of civilization. *Joc.*

1826 T. Flint *Recoll.* 366: Being, as they phrase it, the "jumping off place," it is necessarily the resort of desperate, wicked, and strange creatures who wish to fly away from poverty, infamy, and the laws. **1863** in Cumming *Kate* 142: I cannot see how we are to move farther south, for, as the saying is, we are almost at the "jumping-off place." **1865** H.M. Davidson *14 Mos.* 258: We thought for a moment we had reached the far-famed "jumping off" place, and had jumped. **1870** Keim *Troopers* 224: Religious superstition also teaches that the earth is a great plain, and that there is a jumping off place. *a*1942 Alderson & Smith *Bride Goes West* 46: I can just see Mother out here [in Montana]. She thinks Montana's the jumping-off place.

jump joint *n.* Esp. *Black E.* JUKE JOINT.

1939 in A. Banks *First-Person* 242: Jump joints....where they dance and drink and smoke the marijuana weed. **1940** Ottley & Weatherby *Negro in N.Y.* 247: Ed Small's...Sugar Cane Club...was Harlem's main "jump joint" [in the late 1920's]. **1942** *Pittsburgh Courier* (Mar. 28) 7: They visited a Deep Wylie "jump joint." **1958** W. Burroughs *Naked Lunch* 119: So they drive to this plush jump joint, and the father say,..."When the woman come give her the twenty dollars and tell her you want a piece of ass."

jump off see JUMP, *v.*, 9.

jump out *v.* **1.** *Und.* to engage in a crime or crimes.

1902 Hapgood *Thief* 39 [ref. to *ca*1880]: He is greatly handicapped and can not "jump out" (steal) with any boldness.

2. *Black E.* to be unfaithful.

1986 *Miami Vice* (NBC-TV): You been jumpin' out on me!

3. *Und.* to expel (from a street gang) as by administering a beating. Cf. *jump in* s.v. JUMP, *v.*

1996 *Leeza* (synd. TV series): I'd take him to the neighborhood and jump him out....I would have his homeboys jump him out of the neighborhood. **1996** *Dangerous Minds* (ABC-TV): "You jump out? Is it bad?"..."If I hadn't left that gang I'd be dead now or doin' hard time." **1996** *Dangerous Minds* (ABC-TV): If he tried walkin' away from that gang without bein' jumped out, they would have killed him.

jump sack *n. Mil. & Av.* a parachute.

*1942 in *OED2:* A parachute is called a *brolly* or a *jumpsack.* **1943** Twist *Bombardier* (film): You're pretty handy with that jump sack. So take off and show them how easy it is. **1955** Archibald *Av. Cadet* 155: *Jump sack:* parachute. **1955** *AS* XXX (May) 118: *Jump Sack; Laundry Bag; Nylon, n.* Parachute. **1961** Forbes *Goodbye to Some* 54 [ref. to WWII]: My old jump sack....I wonder who's got her now. *ca***1969** in Tuso *Vietnam Blues* 128: That's all, brother, hit the jumpsack. **1972** R. Barrett *Lovomaniacs* 217: Jumpsacks are to be used in emergencies only. **1974** Stevens *More There I Was* 74: That's all brother, hit the jumpsack.

jump-steady *n. Black E.* alcoholic liquor.
  [**1923** in Kimball & Balcolm *Sissle & Blake* 175: How much is Jump Steady [a racehorse] quoted at?] **1935** in Dixon & Godrich *Blues & Gospel* 101: Jump steady Daddy. **1946** Gresham *Nightmare Alley* 273: No more jumpsteady for me, honey, let's "make a baby"—I got to get back. **1942–49** Goldin et al. *DAUL* 112: *Jump-steady.* (Borrowed from Negro jargon) Gin. **1967–80** Folb *Runnin' Lines* 244: *Jump steady* Liquor. **1993** Rebennack & Rummel *Under Hoodoo Moon* 4: Jump Sturdy [*sic*] was a home-brewed liquor popular in New Orleans.

jump street *n.* ¶ In phrase: **from jump street** *Black E.* from the start.
  1972 T.C. Bambara *Gorilla* 175: Why didn't he...say to her from jump street, "Look, baby, three years is a long haul." **1980** D. Hamill *Stomping Ground* 252: You better get that clear from jumpstreet, man. **1982** in G. Tate *Flyboy* 42: A...groove routine going against it from jump-street. **1989** D. Sherman *There I Was* 217: So he made me strong, right from jump street. **1989** R. Miller *Profane Men* 114: You busted from jump street, boy. **1991** *Sally Jessy Raphaël* (synd. TV series): A lot of it was rock-bottom right from Jump Street. *a***1994** N. McCall *Wanna Holler* 237: It let me know from jump-street that those preachers were messing up black folks' heads.

June *n.* In phrase: ¶ **from June to Jericho** (see quot.).
  1856 *Spirit of Times* (Feb. 16) 1: He can "beat you any race from June to Jericho."

june *n. Stu.* a junior, esp. at Yale College.
  1846 *Yale Banger* (Nov. 10): Rowdy Sophs, magnificent Juns, and lazy Senes. **1853** Root & Lombard *Songs of Yale* 36: I once to Yale a Fresh did come / But now [am] a jolly June.

jungle *n.* **1.** *pl.* rough back country; (*hence*) hinterlands; "sticks."
  1893 in G. Shirley *W. of Hell's Fringe* 136: Think of a gentlemanly moralist running into a tough out in the jungles and...declaring: "My deah suh,...be ouh prisoner." **1925** *AS* I 151: The traveling salesman, who cannot resist a snappy word, speaks of the suburbs as the "jungles."

  2.a. *Pris.* a prison or other corrections facility.
  1904 *Life in Sing Sing* 258: Jungle. Prison. *Ibid.* 260: *Crushing the jungle.* Escaping from prison....I've got to be sprung on paper or go to the jungle. **1926** Finerty *Criminalese* 33: *Jungle*—A prison. **1978** Sopher & McGregor *Up from Walking Dead* 10: Some juvenile jungle.
  b. Esp. *Police.* a dangerously crime-ridden area.
  1926 Finerty *Criminalese* 33: *Jungle*...tough district. **1928** Sharpe *Chicago May* 288: Jungle—crooks' territory. **1960** C.L. Cooper *Scene* 207: And you can start looking out there, in the jungle, not here among decent kids playing volleyball and basketball. **1962** Crump *Killer* 54: Tell those apes over in the jungle that they're barred from 111th street, cop? **1973** Droge *Patrolman* 80: "Where the fuck is the Eight-O [precinct]?"..."Sounds like the jungle, though."...Sure enough, the Eight-O was in...Bedford-Stuyvesant. **1992** *Melrose Place* (Fox-TV): Down where, Billy? The "jungle"? Where "those people" live? **1992** S. Straight *Been in Sorrow's Kitchen* 275: My hood called the Jungle.

  3. *Hobo.* a makeshift camp frequented by itinerants.
  1908 in Kornbluh *Rebel Voices* 40: We will congregate around the camp fire in the "jungles." **1908** W.G. Davenport *Butte & Montana* 127: I'se brought back a combination to de jungles. **1909** in *JAF* LXXIII (1960) 208: Meet Me in the Jungles, Louis. **1911** *JAF* (July) 272: If you don't find me there, come to ole Birmingham, / Ain't goin' to be in jungles long. **1914** *Sat. Eve. Post* (Apr. 4) 11: Frisco Red slouched into the jungle. **1916** Scott *17 Yrs.* 79: The yegg is a rough worker and dresses in the jungles (outside the city) to suit his calling. *Ibid.* 109: We lay the following evening in the "jungles" (outside the city) waiting to continue our journey. **1918** Livingston *Mother Delcassee* 82: Their fellows had vacated the jungle. **1922** N. Anderson *Hobo* 11: Behind the Field Museum, on the section of the park that is still being used as a dump for rubbish, the hobos have established a series of camps or "jungles." **1933** *Amer. Mercury* (Apr.) 393: The

news...traveled swiftly to the jungles of the nation. **1938** in Oliver *Meaning of Blues* 89: It's the railroad for my pillow, this jungle for my happy home. **1971** Galarza *Barrio Boy* 203: The shanties and lean-to's of the migrants who squatted in the "jungles" along the levees of the Sacramento and American rivers. **1982** D.A. Harper *Good Company* 15: Figured I'd...take a bath in that cattle watering tank by that jungle. **1985** J.M.G. Brown *Rice Paddy Grunt* 31: I rode freights with old hobos...lived in "jungles," [etc.]. **1988** M. Felsen *Anti-Warrior* 28: We left our railroad-siding "jungles" to beg for food.

jungle *v. Hobo.* to make camp in a JUNGLE, 3.—usu. constr. with *up.*
  1911 *Adventure* (Mar.) 904: We had jungled up—camped—in a little cottonwood grove. **1921** Casey & Casey *Gay-Cat* 95: The two gay-cats were allowed to jungle up in The Willows. **1922** Tully *Emmett Lawler* 267: In the rear of the saloon was a yard in which the men "jungled up." **1929** in Hammett *Knockover* 56: I knew him, but didn't know where he jungled up. **1936** in Pyle *Ernie's Amer.* 148: We ain't pioneering; we're jungling. **1939** in A. Banks *First-Person* 88: We just kind of jungled up...wherever we could. **1949** Emrich *Wild West* 165: They jungled up together. **1970** Terkel *Hard Times* 13: We jungled up there for a little while, and then we bummed the town. **1973** Mathers *Ridin' the Rails* 14: Plenty of space to "jungle up." **1982** D.A. Harper *Good Company* 59: And nobody'll jungle with old Blackie no more. **1989** *Harper's* (June) 52: The depot where Slim's supposed to be jungled up.

jungle bird *n. Hobo.* JUNGLE STIFF.
  1919 U.S. Inf. *Twelfth Inf.* 81: If that cook isn't a jungle bird I'd like to know who is!

jungle blaster *n.* GHETTO BLASTER.
  1991 *N.Y. Times* (Sept. 8) E19: Two "Columbians" wearing thick gold chains drink beer as a jungle blaster plays loud salsa and chicha music.

jungle bunny *n.* **1.** a black person.—used contemptuously.—usu. considered offensive.
  1959 Maier *College Terms* 2: *Jungle Bunnies*—colored people. **1959** Farris *Harrison High* 240: Watch it, jungle bunny. **1959** F.L. Brown *Trumbull Pk.* 42: "Nigger!" "Jungle bunny!" "Eight balls!" **1964** Rhodes *Chosen Few* 211 [ref. to *ca*1950]: Unless it's really closed an' all them jungle bunnies...there are my imagination. **1967** Mailer *Vietnam* 65: He talks like a cannibal in a jungle bunny movie. **1968** Cameron *Dragon's Spine* 112: "Jungle bunnies," that was one of the things chuck called soul brothers. **1968** Vidal *Breckinridge* 83: The dozen or so jungle bunnies I have trafficked with. **1969** Searls *Hero Ship* 62: She might be a goddamn jungle bunny...on a island a million miles from nowhere. **1971** *All in the Family* (CBS-TV): There's one thing Archie Bunker will never do, and that's break bread with a bunch of jungle bunnies. **1974** Univ. Tenn. student, age 23: I heard *jungle bunny* in the eighth grade in 1964 in Alcoa, Tennessee. **1979** Coleman Young, Mayor of Detroit, in Terkel *Amer. Dreams* 365: The police paper constantly referred to blacks as jungle bunnies. **1980** Whalen *Takes a Man* 88: Some jungle bunny down on Dean Street just threw a *hammer* at us. **1992** *Harper's* (Dec.) 70: We got a hunting season on jungle bunnies.

  2. *Mil.* a military serviceman, esp. a U.S. marine, in or from a jungle area of operations. [The sense reported in bracketed 1982 quot. appears to be unique.]
  1961 Peacock *Valhalla* 31 [ref. to 1953]: At least you Jungle Bunnies don't have to chip paint. **1967** W. Crawford *Gresham's War* 161 [ref. to 1953]: Better listen to Gomez, junglebunny. **1977** Carabatsos *Heroes* 14: The guys knew that blank jungle-bunny stare and didn't mess with him. ***1981** in Partridge *DSUE* (ed. 8) 632: Camouflaged combat kit, known officially [in the RAF] as disruptive-pattern clothing and unofficially as jungle-bunny outfits. [**1982** F. Hailey *Soldier Talk* 35: *Jungle bunnies.* How our GIs referred to the Japanese...on Guadalcanal and other heavily jungled islands in the Pacific during WW-II.] **1985** Westin *Love & Glory* 277 [ref. to 1944]: Swell! So MacArthur himself wants me to be a jungle bunny. **1986** F. Walton *Once Were Eagles* 145: We're gonna be the grunts, gravel crunchers, or jungle bunnies. We're gonna get a rifle and be on our way.

jungle buzzard *n. Hobo.* one who begs, scavenges, or steals from tramps or hobos in a JUNGLE, 3.—used contemptuously.
  1912 Livingston *Curse of Tramp Life* 85: "Jungle Buzzards," the lowest class of tramps. **1918** Livingston *Mother Delcassee* 115: A mob of intoxicated jungle buzzards. **1920** in *JAF* LXXIII (1960) 213: If he tends to live further on the charity of the newcomers he is styled a "jungle buzzard" and cast forth. **1929** Tully *Shadows of Men* 102: Even

jungle buzzards were treated as equals. These men, who were too far down in the scale to beg or steal, and who ate the crumbs from more ambitious hoboes' tables, were now drink warmed and well fed. **1929** *AS* IV (June) 341: *Jungle buzzard.* One who lives, for the most part, off the enterprise of his fellow hobos. **1933** *Amer. Mercury* (Apr.) 395: None…ever became a jungle buzzard, the scavenger among hoboes.

jungle fever *n.* [in ref. to Spike Lee's 1991 film] romantic interest between a black person and a white person.
   1990 *Ebony* (Sept.) 76: Pre-production work on his fifth film, *Jungle Fever,* a story about a Black architect who has a relationship with an Italian-American secretary. **1991** S. Lee *Jungle Fever* [film title]. **1991** in *Harper's* (Jan. 1992) 66: Nor do I think that it was any strain of "jungle fever" that caused us to marry who we did. **1995** *Newsweek* (Feb. 13) 16: Denise expressed concern that I might be coming down with a "fever."…As it turns out, she was referring to "jungle fever," the condition where a black man or woman is attracted to someone of the opposite race. **1995** Black woman, age *ca*20, on *Jerry Springer Show* (synd. TV series): She got jungle fever [*i.e.,* became interested in a white man]!

jungle-happy *n. Mil.* crazy or eccentric from overlong jungle service.
   1944 *Yank* (June 9) 5: The marauders and the Japs they fought each had at least one jungle-happy poet laureate among them. **1945** *Reader's Digest* (June) 49: But some of the boys really are a bit eccentric…jungle-happy. **1944–46** in *AS* XXII 55: *Jungle happy.* A state of mind ascribed to any GI who has been in the jungle too long. **1946** *AS* (Oct.) 209: Boys who served in Burma tell me that *jungle happy* was often used in that campaign. **1983** E. Dodge *Dau* 131 [ref. to Vietnam War]: He's smiling and winking like he's gone jungle happy.

jungle hound *n. Hobo.* JUNGLE STIFF.
   1929 Milburn *Hobo's Hornbook* 114: And it's "blanket-stiff" and "jungle-hound,"/And "Pitch him out the door."/But it's, "Howdy, Jack, old-timers,"/when you've got the price for more.

jungle juice *n.* **1.** *Mil.* an alcoholic beverage made illicitly and from ingredients at hand in the tropics, usu. by servicemen.
   *1942 in *Austral. Nat. Dict.*: It was started by a liquid with the name of Jungle Juice. **1945** *Yank* (Apr. 20) 6: "Jungle Juice" [is] the lethal New Guinea drink made by letting the water of a coconut stand and ferment. **1945* S.J. Baker *Austral. Lang.* 157: *Jungle juice.* Any alcoholic beverage concocted by servicemen in the tropics. **1944–46** in *AS* XXII 55: [Army:] *Jungle juice.* Any variety of homemade drinks, fermented from raisins, apricots, potatoes, coconut, or what have you. **1946** Heggen *Mr. Roberts* 31: At any given time there were apt to be brewing on the ship fifteen different batches of jungle juice. **1955** S. Wilson *Gray Flannel Suit* 145: Well, this is better than that old jungle juice we used to drink in New Guinea. **1956** *AS* XXXI (Oct.) 193: *Jungle juice.* An alcoholic beverage concocted in the field. **1958** Frankel *Band of Bros.* 219: The men drank jungle juice—an underfermented three-day old mixture of raisins, prunes, white rice, yeast and sickbay alcohol. **1957–61** Ruark *Boy Grows Older* 268: I survived…Australian whisky, [and] South Sea jungle juice. **1961** L.E. Young *Virgin Fleet* 140: "What in the hell is jungle juice?" "Native whiskey." **1962** Killens *Heard Thunder* 259: You must be drinking jungle juice. **1966** Marks *Letters* 167: What a headache I now have—never drink too much "jungle juice." *a*1990 Poyer *Gulf* 50: Bring your glasses over. I got some jungle juice in my flight bag.
   2. men's cologne presumed to arouse the sexual interest of women.
   1976 Conroy *Santini* 294: You gonna let me use some of that English Leather jungle juice?

jungle rat *n.* **1.** *Army.* a soldier accustomed to jungle operations.
   1925 *Infantry Jour.* (Apr.) 411: The other two companies as usual are relying on the good old mule, aided by the boats, and are sure that they are the only original "jungle rats" and are always inquiring when the two companies supplied by truck are really going to the jungle.
   2. a hobo.
   1939 I. Baird *Waste Heritage* 279: A bunch of jungle rats, gettin' smacked off freight cars.

jungle rot *n. Mil.* any of various tropical fungal infections. Now *colloq.*
   1945 Huie *Omaha to Okinawa* 21: Scratching my jungle rot. **1944–46** in *AS* XXII 55: *Jungle rot.* Any tropical skin infection, but specifically a wet skin rot. **1947** Blankfort *Big Yankee* 300: Dengue

fever, dysentery, malaria, ringworm and other illnesses which the docs and corpsmen call jungle rot. **1978** Hasford *Short-Timers* 88: No immersion foot. No jungle rot. **1992** Jernigan *Tin Can Man* 125: I was having a bad time with jungle rot all over my crotch and backside. **1994** J. Shay *Achilles in Viet.* xviii: My skin is all black in my groin from the jungle rot and Agent Orange.

jungle stiff *n. Hobo.* one who camps in a JUNGLE, 3.
   *ca*1920 in Bruns *Kts. of Road* 80: A good jungle stiff can make anything from a frying pan to a bath tub out of them. **1930** G. Irwin *Tramp & Und. Slang: Jungle Stiff*…A bum who lives in jungles instead of in a town.

jungle telegraph *n.* GRAPEVINE TELEGRAPH.
   1984 *Working Woman* (June) 42: Many employment experts call it the pyramiding technique; others refer to it as the jungle telegraph. You talk to your friends, relatives, religious leader, neighbors, doctor, dentist—all the people in your address book. **1989** Joss *Strike* 58: The gouge went out quickly to…pilots and crew via the usual jungle telegraph.

junior *n.* boy.—used disparagingly in direct address.
   1953 in Cannon *Like 'Em Tough* 50: What's your name, junior? **1958** Cooley *Run for Home* 44: Look, Junior, I don't want to know your life story. **1960** Bonham *Burma Rifles* 12: What's he going to say about that, junior?

Junior Birdman *n. Mil.* an aircrewman; (*specif.*) a fighter pilot.—used jocularly or derisively.
   1944 *AAF* 369: *Junior Birdman.* recipient of air medal. **1948** A. Murphy *To Hell & Back* 131: Drink up to the Junior Birdman. **1961** Plantz *Sweeney Squadron* 17: "Let's have some respect, Junior Birdman," Greg said. **1962** Harvey *Strike Command* 92: Here is one place…where the junior birdman gets his big chance. **1963** Dwiggins *S.O. Bees* 34: Where're all your junior birdmen? **1965** *Air Officer's Guide, 1965–1966* 437: *Junior Birdman:* inexperienced pilot. **1989** Care *Viet. Spook Show* 121: Up in the air, junior birdman. **1995** Cormier et al. *Wildcats* 100: I sold my…Ford to another junior birdman.

juniper *n.* [cf. JUNIPER JUICE] **1.** whiskey.
   1840 *Crockett's Comic Alm.* (unp.): Them copper worms has the juniper running down their throats all the time.
   2. Esp. *West.* a yokel.
   1894 O. Wister, in Remington *Wister* 90: The same knack of imagery that upon our Eastern slope gave visitors from the country the brief, sure name of hayseed, calls their Western equivalents *junipers.* **1895** *Harper's* (Nov.) 840: He ain't the unexperienced juniper he looks. **1899–1900** Cullen *Tales* 200: There's been about forty or fifty of the junipers that shipped in Mare Island as landsmen and coalheavers jumped her down here—couldn't stand the gaff. **1906** in A. Adams *Chisholm Trail* 244: So Bill and some juniper of a pardner thought they would make a call on him. **1944** *Slanguage Dict.* 52: *Junipers*—raw recruits.

juniper juice *n.* gin. Also **juniper berry juice.**
   1929 V. Randolph, in *AS* IV (June) 386: *Gin* does not seem to be much in favor here, but I take it that *Gordon water* and *juniper juice* are names for this beverage. **1979** in Raban *Old Glory* 204: Best gin you'll ever drink.…They used to put juniper in there.…That's why it's called juniper juice. **1985** Dye *Between Raindrops* 21: Your Goddamn juniper-berry juice is a poor…substitute for my…R & R. *a*1992 T. Wilson *Termite Hill* 184: You didn't stop imbibing juniper juice when you gave up on women, did you?

junk[1] *n. Naut.* a ship (of any sort).
   *1821–26 Stewart *Man-of-War's Man* II 157: If there doesn't go a piece of the haughtiest old junk I ever set eyes on. **1867** Clark *Sailor's Life* 254: How are you, old junk; want to ship any landsmen?

junk[2] *n.* **1.** poor or indigestible food.
   *1831 B. Hall *Voyages* III 148: He washes down His Majesty's junk, as he roughly but good-humouredly styles the…beef. **1898** Kountz *Baxter's Letters* 24: It…will cleanse the system of all the indigestible junk with which it has been overtaxed.
   2.a. belongings; possessions.
   1899 Fiala *Troop "C"* 15: Many an embryonic trooper had secret misgivings as to his ability to take care of all his "junk," as our equipment was facetiously termed. **1918** Straub *Diary* (July 1): I had just finished shaving when the order came down to pack junk and get ready to leave. **1924** P. Marks *Plastic Age* 182: Keep my junk…and sell anything you want to. **1962** L'Engle *Wrinkle in Time* 42: As a matter of fact I have some junk of mine to finish up.

b. stuff (in the broadest sense); in phr. **and junk** and so forth.

1929 *AS* IV (June) 342: *Junk.* loot. **1939** M. Levin *Citizens* 196: You just cover their lectures and rallies and junk. **1949** Gordon & Kanin *Adam's Rib* 54: Give me the junk for the salad. **1957** E. Lacy *Room to Swing* 50: "Not bad," I said, taking another sip of the junk in my cup. **1983** Nelkin & Brown *Workers* 5: It can cause sores, ulcers, and all this junk. **1996** Boam *Phantom* (film): There's a lot of valuable junk here.

c. (see quot.).

1992 Eble *Campus Slang* (Fall) 4: *The junk*—great; the best. "I'm really happy you got early acceptance to med school—yo, that's the junk." "Man, those shoes are the junk."

3. *Und.* jewelry.

1904 *Life in Sing Sing* 249: *Junk.*—Plated jewelry. **1915–17** Lait *Gus* 53: I stole a lot o' junk—a lot o' jewlery. **1922** *N.Y. Times* (June 4) VI 7: For years, jewelry was "junk" to a burglar or pickpocket.

4. (see quot.).

1910 Hapgood *Types from City Streets* 36: But dere are some good gals wat a bloke's a junk (bad man) if he don't treat right....When a bloke wat ain't got a nickel asks a junk for a nickel, the junk wat ain't a gent, calls him a bum. You can always tell a junk that way.

5.a. nonsense; rubbish.

1910 *N.Y. Eve. Jour.* (Mar. 15) 12: Junk, all junk....Steve isn't side-stepping anybody. **1914** in R. Lardner *Round Up* 342: Girls always writes the same junk. ***1923** G.B. Shaw, in Partridge *Slang* 125: Our huge national stock of junk and bilge. **1925** *Sat. Eve. Post* (Oct. 31) 8: And all that bunk and junk. **1928** Bodenheim *Georgie May* 109: To hell with this lo-ove-you junk. **1931** in Leadbitter & Slaven *Blues Records* 511: I Don't Want That Junk Outa You. **1935** in W.C. Fields *By Himself* 152: It makes me laugh when I read of some of the "junk" written about my dear friend, Bill Rogers. **1940** Ellis & Logan *Tin Pan Alley* (film): If I was you I'd get out of this publishing junk. Honest! **1944** Kapelner *Lonely Boy Blues* 40: So don't gimme that junk. **1950** Vorhaus *So Young, So Bad* (film): Liar! Dirty liar! Handing us a line of junk just so you can come here and snoop on us! **1950** Spillane *Vengeance* 102: Clyde isn't one to take any junk from a guy like Anton. **1971** Freeman *Catcher* (film): It was junk....It wasn't true. **1974** Matthews & Amdur *Race Be Won* 24: I don't want to hear that junk, I want the glove. *a***1976** Roebuck & Frese *Rendezvous* 101: You get chummy, but with others you talk junk. **1994** in C. Long *Love Awaits* 201: We talk all this junk.

b. boastful or disparaging statements.—constr. with *talk.* Cf. TRASH TALK; *talk trash* s.v. TRASH.

1974 Matthews & Amdur *My Race* 91: They depend on building up their own confidence to help them in a race, and "talkin' junk," as the term goes, is the sprinter's trade, like gunfighters arguing over who was the fastest draw.

6. *Narc.* narcotic drugs, esp. opiates; (specif., now *esp.*) heroin.

1918 in *AS* (Oct. 1933) 28: *Junk.* Drugs. **1921** *Variety* (Oct. 21) 7: He was a pipefiend....He would get a skin full of junk and tell everybody he met to [hit him hard]. **1922** *N.Y. Times* (June 4) VI 7: Cocaine, heroin, and other drugs became [known as] "junk." **1929** Booth *Stealing Through Life* 267 [ref. to 1918]: But a few drinks, a shot of junk, or a few hours with the bunch—aw, you know how it is. **1930** Sutherland *Prof. Thief* 29: The boss then got into the junk (narcotic drug) racket. **1933** Ersine *Prison Slang* 48: *Junk Peddler.* One who sells dope illegally and in small quantities. **1936** *AS* (Apr.) 123: *Junk.* 1. Narcotics in general....2. Often used to refer specifically to morphine. **1941** in Garon *Blues* 95: That using junk, pardner, was gonna be the death of you. **1944** Liebling *Back to Paris* 231: They forget that newspapermen as a class have a yearning for truth as involuntary as a hophead's craving for junk. **1952** Grey *Hoods* 26: I'll bet he's back handling "junk."...Why do people smoke opium? **1955** Q. Reynolds *HQ* 266: I can take a drink or leave it alone—I thought it would be the same with junk. **1958** in Loosbrock & Skinner *Wild Blue* 234: Doc shot me full of junk and tucked me into bed. **1959** W. Burroughs *Naked Lunch* xxxvii: I mean an addict to junk (generic term for opium and/or derivatives including all synthetics from demerol to palfium). **1972** B. Harrison *Hospital* 151: How many times do we see people come in here and know they're on junk even before we run tests? **1974** Radano *Cop Stories* 119: When I first got into the Narcotics Squad junk was a rich man's vice. **1973–76** J. Allen *Assault* 1: You want some junk, then I would take you to the dude who handles drugs. **1980** Schruers *Blondie* 15: She was "really mixed up bad and into junk." **1984** Glick *Winters Coming* 290: I can smell a big junk deal. **1987** "10,000 Maniacs" *Hey*

Jack Kerouac (pop. song): Cool junk-booting madmen, street-minded girls in Harlem howling at night.

b. medicine.

1918 in Bowerman *Compensations* 112: I...am now waiting for Hub to ransack the medicine chest to see what new kind of medicine he can discover. I imagine I will be OK in a day or so if I take his junk & go to bed.

7.a. *Baseball.* knuckle balls, forkballs, or deceptive off-speed pitches.—also used attrib.

1949 in P. Dickson *Baseball Dict.* 231: Haefner, noted for his knuckle ball, said he didn't use much "junk." **1952** in *DAS:* Ed Lopat, another "junk ball pitcher." **1954–60** *DAS: Junk-ball n.* In baseball, a pitch that is unorthodox, tricky, or anything but a straight fast ball. **1973** Flaherty *Fogarty* 95: A southpaw, a junk pitcher of some repute. **1977** in G.A. Fine *With the Boys* 98: "Junk" is a baseball term referring to off-speed pitches such as the curve, slider and knuckleball. **1978** Alibrandi *Killshot* 160: Can he handle your lefthanded junk? **1978** Bill White, on N.Y. Yankees vs. Texas Rangers (WPIX-TV) (July 6): The older you get, the cuter you get. You get 'em out with junk. **1980** F. Healey, on N.Y. Yankees Baseball (WINS radio) (Aug. 18): Palmer's the kind of guy that if he doesn't have the overpowering fastball, he'll throw the junk.

b. *Sports.* any unusual, soft, or deceptive shot.—often used attrib., as **junk shot.**

1976 *AS* LI 294: *Junk shot.* Any type of soft spinning shot. **1978** *Atlantic* (Dec.) 77: A couple of black guys were out there throwing up junk shots, making the white guys look like clods. **1980** Wielgus & Wolff *Basketball* 49: *Junk (n)* An awkward or unusual shot not normally in the shooter's repertoire; may be outmoded set shots, spin shots, or even *garbage.* **1982** *Psychology Today* (Mar.) 86: What do a junk shot in tennis and *Guernica* have in common? **1988** Schwed *How to Talk Tennis* 44: *Junk*...shots that have no velocity....A good junk player is infuriatingly steady.

¶ In phrases:

¶ **junk in (one's)** [or **the**] **trunk** the buttocks, esp. if large. *Joc.*

1995 *Jerry Springer Show* (synd. TV series): I've got too much junk in my trunk [woman shakes very large buttocks]. **1995** *Young & Restless* (CBS-TV) (Oct. 4): That girl's got some junk in the trunk. **1996** *Young & Restless* (CBS-TV): Turn around. Fellas want to see that junk in the trunk. **1996** *Martin* (Fox-TV): My wife's got some junk in her trunk, too!

¶ **junk on the bunk** *Mil.* a complete inspection of an enlisted marine's equipment in barracks by a commissioned officer.

1978 Hasford *Short-Timers* [ref. to Vietnam War] 15: Inspection. Junk on the bunk. *a***1982** in Berry *Semper Fi* 338 [ref. to WWII]: My "junk on the bunk," you know, the 782 gear, was always perfect. **1983** Elton, Cragg & Deal *Dict. Soldier Talk* 173: *Junk on the bunk* (Modern)...showdown inspection.

junk *v.* **1.** to give (a person) a dose of JUNK², 6.a.—also constr. with *up.* See also JUNKED [UP].

1930 *Liberty* (July 5) 23: He takes a needle out of a drawer, junks himself in the arm. **1987** *21 Jump St.* (Fox-TV): He junked my mother up again. She almost had it beat!

2. (see quot.).

1953 Manchester *City of Anger* 21: A supervisor had found him junking—salvaging tin cans for sale outside.

3. to wreck (a motor vehicle).

1984 "W.T. Tyler" *Shadow Cabinet* 27: That cop car...nearly junked me, coming up like that.

junk bond *n. Finance.* a corporate bond that offers a potentially high yield at high risk. Now *S.E.*

1976 (cited in *W10*). **1986** *Money Line* (CNN-TV) (Sept. 30): So-called "junk bonds," high-yield, high-risk bonds. **1987** Lipper *Wall St.* 12: He was promised a partnership...for building the junk bond department. **1988** *Day Watch* (CNN-TV) (June 8): Drexel's made a lot in junk bonds—that is, below-investment-level bonds.

junk box *n.* a rickety or dilapidated motor vehicle; JALOPY.

1955 Graziano & Barber *Somebody Up There* 100: To run his junk box, he siphoned gas out of somebody else's car. **1961** C. Francis *Red Zone Cuba* (film): Check that junk box and see if she'll run.

junk buzzard *n.* (see quot.).

　　1976 Lieberman & Rhodes *CB* 131: *Junk Buzzard*—Bum of bums; dregs of bum society.

junked [up] *adj.* intoxicated by JUNK², *n.*, 6.a. Cf. JUNK, *v.*, 1.

　　1930 Lait *On the Spot* 206: *Junk…*Cocaine. (An addict is a "junky," or is "junked up.") **1930** *Liberty* (July 5) 24: He was so junked up he walked right into the law. **1958** Chandler *Playback* 62: The night man was junked to the eyes. *a***1972** I.A. Baraka, in W. King & R. Milner *Black Drama Anthol.* 20: you got a way to get the militants junked up? **1976** Chinn *Dig Nigger Up* 110: Hey, this guy is all junked up! **1985** Bodey *F.N.G.* 230: Forget it, man….He's junked up.

junker *n.* **1.** *Und.* JUNKIE², 1.a., b.

　　1922 Murphy *Black Candle* 270: An addict or "junker" is found in illegal possession of drugs. **1925** *Writer's Mo.* (June) 487: *Junker*—One who uses dope. **1927–28** Tasker *Grimhaven* 159: There was a genuine wave of dismay among the junkers. **1930** Shaw *Jack-Roller* 157: He seemed to delight in razzing the negroes and "junkers." **1932** Burns *I Am a Fugitive* 73: I also began to realize that my affable friend was a "junker." **1932** *Writer's Digest* (Aug.) 48: *Junker*, peddler of narcotics. **1934** L. Berg *Prison Nurse* 27: Now we have a new set of "prison junkers" on our hands. **1936** Duncan *Over the Wall* 144: The only thing is, she's a junker. **1936** Dai *Opium Addiction* 141: They would not be "junkers" for long. **1941** in Garon *Blues* 95: They call me a junker 'cause I'm loaded all the time.

2. a broken-down motor vehicle, aircraft, or vessel that ought to be or has been junked. Now *colloq.*

　　1948 *Amer. N & Q* VIII 120: "Junker" (car so decrepit that it cannot be economically repaired). **1951** *Sat. Eve. Post* (July 7) 34: A motorist…asked the garageman to explain the differences between a jalopy, a heap, a junker and an antique automobile…."A junker is a heap it won't even move; maybe it's got wheels." **1953** Gresham *Midway* 212: For no two old cars, called "junkers," are ever alike. **1953** Felsen *Street Rod* 45: Boy, wouldn't they stare when what they thought was a worn-out junker suddenly racked them all up. **1973** W. Crawford *Gunship Cmndr.* 80: Marston can have that junker of yours flying again. **1972–79** T. Wolfe *Right Stuff* 158: Two F-102s…absolute junkers in the eyes of the seven pilots. **1978–86** J.L. Burke *Lost Get-Back Boogie* 42: The broken streets of the town were lined with…junker cars.

junk hawk *n. Narc.* JUNKIE², 1.a.

　　1972 Grogan *Ringolevio* 42: Kenny Wisdom was becoming what is known as a junk hawk, that is to say, all he ever did…pertained to junk, as his tolerance for the stuff grew even beyond his greed for it.

junkhead *n.* JUNKIE², 1.a.

　　1963 Gann *Good & Evil* 64: A dealer or a junkhead, a seller or a buyer. **1972** *Nat. Lampoon* (Oct.) 61: JUNKHEAD.

junk hustler *n.* (see quot.).

　　1944 Boatright & Day *Hell to Breakfast* 142: A Tool Pusher is in charge of one or more drilling rigs. The name originated in the days when his main job was to keep the rig supplied with drill bits or tools and the day driller was king of the rig. Now the bits are handled by a truck driver known as the "junk hustler," and the Tool Pusher has authority over all drilling crews.

junkie¹ *n.* a person who operates a small boat, esp. (in 1909 quot.) for the purpose of transporting stolen merchandise.

　　1909 *Sat. Eve. Post* (July 3) 14: In that lay the promise of a cover which might let the fleeing "junkie" get well away around the Battery to Red Hook or Gowanus. **1970** Flood *War of Innocents* 325: These boats were converted, motorized junks, and these Vietnamese were the men of the Coastal Force, better known as the Junk Fleet, with the sailors being known as "junkies."

junkie² *n.* **1.a.** Orig. *Und.* a person addicted to JUNK², 6.a., esp. heroin or morphine.

　　1922 N. Anderson *Hobo* 102: One type of dope fiend is the Junkie. He uses a "gun" or needle to inject morphine or heroin. **1931** *AS* VI (Aug.) 439: *Junkie*. A drug addict. **1933** Hammett *Thin Man* 246: "What's a junkie?"…"Hop-head." **1933** Ersine *Prison Slang* 48: *Junkie*, *n.* A dope addict. **1934** L. Berg *Prison Nurse* 28: Once a junkie, always a dope, is my opinion. **1936** Benton & Ballou *Where Do I Go?* 212: There was a constant war of wits…between the guards and the "junkies." **1943** J. Mitchell *McSorley's* 28: I knew this babe was a junky. **1959–60** R. Reisner *Jazz Titans* 159: *Junkie:* a drug addict. **1972** Kopp *Buddha* 203: Some of them are now dead junkies. **1981** in

Courtwright et al. *Addicts Who Survived* 222: I'd find the junkies hanging out. **1990** C. Fletcher *What Cops Know* 241: Pops lived with her, her husband, and her junkie son. **1992** N. Cohn *Heart of World* 16: Clara was a junkie who hooked to support her habit.

b. a dealer of JUNK², 6.a.

　　1955 Q. Reynolds *HQ* 31: A dope peddler [was called] a "junkie." **1971** *Current Slang* V (Spring) 15: *Junky*, *n.* A person who sells drugs.

2. a person who deals in junk (in the S.E. sense).

　　1939 Howsley *Argot* 28: *Junkey*—One who gathers rags, paper, iron and other waste. **1971** E. Sanders *Family* 125: Scrap iron junkies have long since hauled away the cable and metal for the hopper. **1982** Courtwright *Dk. Paradise* 113 [ref. to *a*1920]: Junkie, in its original sense, literally meant *junkman*. *a***1989** in Kisseloff *Must Remember This* 57 [ref. to *ca*1910]: The junkies (junkmen) they bought all the stuff you stole.

3. a habitué; one who is devotedly attached to a specified interest, sport, etc.—used with attrib. *n.*

　　1962 Crump *Killer* 193: I didn't come here to amuse you or these bottle junkies. **1969** Gustaitis *Turning On* 29: I had become a self junkie. **1972** in H.S. Thompson *Shark Hunt* 122: Nixon is…a serious *politics junkie.* He's totally hooked. **1972** Jenkins *Semi-Tough* 34: Barbara Jane once called her an eye-shadow junkie. **1977** Sayles *Union Dues* 278: Liberal preppie folk-junkie. **1978** *N.Y. Post* (June 6) 1: We run the risk of turning New York City into a "guarantee junkie" coming back and back every four years. **1979** Charyn *7th Babe* 250: You're a baseball junkie is what you are. **1980** *Mork & Mindy* (ABC-TV): I'm a people junkie. I need a conversation fix. **1981** D. Burns *Feeling Good* 251: You are a "love junkie." You see love as a "need" without which you cannot survive. **1981** W. Safire, in *N.Y. Times Mag.* (June 27) 7: Baseball's third strike has impoverished the daily reading of the nation's national-pastime junkies. **1984** Ad on *CNN News* (CNN-TV) (May 22): *Baseball America…*is the baseball junkie's newspaper. **1984** *Eternal Alternative* (WUTK radio) (July 22): I'm not a Bible junkie…I'm a Jesus junkie. I'm hooked. On the real thing. **1985** Boyne & Thompson *Wild Blue* 171: Father Borman was an airplane junkie. **1987** Santiago *Undercover* 118: You're a love junkie, hooked on love. **1990** G.R. Clark *Words of Vietnam War* 8: *Adrenaline Junkie…*Slang name for…a sort of slave to the excitement caused by combat, the nearness of death [etc.]. **1994** *Morning News* (CNN-TV) (Feb. 25): It's pure magic for all you tool junkies out there. **1995** *Newsweek* (Mar. 6) 40: He's a news junkie, a believer in the value and virtue of broadcast journalism.

junkman *n.* **1.** *Police & Und.* a seller of narcotics; JUNKIE², 1.b.

　　1959 Miller *Cool World* 21: Put some money in Bloods hands he aint goin to no supermarket he goin to the junkman for a fix. **1978** Diehl *Sharky's Machine* 49: I just retired a junkman.

2. *Baseball.* a pitcher who throws JUNK², 7.a.

　　1959 Brosnan *Long Season* 234: People…refer to Stu Miller as a junkman, or a magician. **1960** Meany *Yankee Story* 216: Ed Lopat…[was] known as the junkman because of the variety of soft stuff he threw. **1992** Strawberry & Rust *Darryl* 196: "Junkman," Bob Krepper, who threw pitches that were so cheap, rummies on the Bowery would have walked by them without taking a poke.

junko *n.* JUNKIE², 1.a. Also attrib.

　　1971 Cameron *First Blood* 85: I know a junko when I see one….He's either on horse or snow. **1993** Rebennack & Rummel *Under Hoodoo Moon* 31: I had a lot of junko partners….Shank…turned me on to drugs.

junk shot see s.v. JUNK², *n.*, 7.b.

junk squad *n. Police.* a narcotics squad.

　　1952 Lait & Mortimer *USA* 159: So the city police are burdened with maintaining one of the largest junk squads in the country.

junk surf *n. Surfing.* (see quots.).

　　1967 *Holiday* (Sept.) 64: If the waves are poor and uneven—real junk surf—he will paddle faster. **1968** Kirk & Hanle *Surfer's Hndbk.* 141: *Junk surf:* small, choppy waves—rideable, but not pleasant.

junk tank *n.* [modeled on S.E. *drunk tank*] *Police.* a place in a prison where JUNK addicts are forced to give up drugs cold-turkey.

　　1966 Harris *Hellhole* 95: Listen, most of the girls in the junk tank at the House of D. are prostitutes, right?

junkwagon *n.* a small or low-powered motorcycle.

　　1966 Thompson *Hell's Angels* 90: And those silly goddamn junkwagon bikes?

junky *adj.* extremely inferior; rotten.

1943 J. Mitchell *McSorley's* 224: I'm sick of the junky grub in those cafeterias.

junkyard dog *n.* **1.** [sugg. by cliché *meaner than a junkyard dog*] *Pol.* a person in a position of authority who is notably vigorous about investigating graft.

1983 *U.S. News & W.R.* (July 25) 50: Leading the charge are the inspectors general—or "junkyard dogs," as the White House has labelled them—that he appointed early in his term to ferret out waste. [**1989** *N.Y. Times* (July 30) (Week in Rev.) 22: Nothing would be more in...the Administration's interest than to pursue the political abuses in H.U.D. like a junkyard dog.] **1990** *Wash. Post* (May 22) A23: A self-described "junkyard dog," Robinson as the controversial sheriff...showed an uncanny talent for gaining media attention. **1992** *Wash. Post* (June 3) 7: Kusserow is a "shake-the-boat, junkyard-dog kind of IG [Inspector General]....He knows where to look." **1993** *Wash. Post* (Jan. 2) A19: Portions of that transcript had been read into the Congressional Record by that junkyard dog, Rep. Robert K. Dornan (R-Calif.).

2. *So.* a worthless person.

1990 *Tenn. Ling.* X (Winter) 39: [Insults:] "S.O.B." ... "Whore" ... "Junkyard dog."

Jupe *n.* [abbr. L *Jupiter Pluvius* 'Jupiter the god of rain'] *Sports Journ.* the rain god. *Joc.*

1908 in Fleming *Unforgettable Season* 62: "Old Jupe" and the grouchy weather man combined and made an enemy of every fan in Manhattan. **1961** Brosnan *Pennant Race* 161: The rain started. "Come on, Jupe," we implored, in the bullpen. "We could use a break and win a shortie."

jur var. JOUR.

juve *n.* a juvenile.—also used attrib.

1936 *Esquire* (Sept.) 159: The kiddies (juve trade) favor these esoteric forms of [show business] *divertissement.* **1942** *ATS* 383: Child...*juve*, kid, [etc.]. **1952** Lait & Mortimer *USA* 37: They frequent places the radio oracles plug, which is done deliberately to hook juves. **1954** Schulberg *Waterfront* 40: Foley knew them. They were marked tough juves who bore watching.

juvie *n.* **1.** *Police.* a juvenile, esp. a juvenile offender.—also used attrib.

1941 Smiley *Hash House Lingo* 34, in *OED2*: *Juvie*, child. **1956** H. Ellison *Deadly Streets* 190: They just didn't look like juvies. **1960** Stadley *Barbarians* 111: This kid's a juvie. **1966** in *BDNE* 240: First, Los Angeles County police went after the "juvies" (minors under 18). **1968** Camp *Night Beat* 18: Missing juvie...Seven-year-old female. **1972** Carr *Bad* 56: Only a few cops around to watch the juvies. *a*1974 in J. Jacobs *Deviance* 60: He busted out of juvy hall. **1979–82** Gwin *Overboard* 190: Juvey hall tattoos on his...forearms. **1983** W. Walker *Dime to Dance* 48: He was arrested more than once when he was a juvie. **1986** *Miami Vice* (NBC-TV): These juvies almost never roll over 'cause the courts can't hit 'em hard enough. **1987** *21 Jump St.* (Fox-TV): He was a three-time loser as a juvie. Now he's...eighteen. **1990** *TV Guide* (May 12) 48: Bobby [is] a mean juvie. **1992** L. Johnson *My Posse* 22: Bad kids are in jail, in juvi hall.

2. a juvenile court; (*also*) a detention home for juvenile offenders.

1965–67 Herndon *Way It Spozed to Be* 36: Teacher, Maurice just got back from Juvi! **1967** in *BDNE* 240: But the teacher at juvey said, "You have to finish it." **1972** Burkhart *Women in Pris.* 57: The first time I was in juvie, I was twelve. *Ibid.* 447: *Juvie.* Juvenile hall; reform school. **1975** in *West. Folklore* XXXV (1976) 279: They're getting ready to haul us off to Juvy (Juvenile Hall). **1978** T. Sanchez *Zoot-Suit* 62: You'd all be cooling your heels downtown in Juvie right now. **1988** M. Schiffer *Colors* (film): I did my time, finally made it up to juvie. **1995** *House of Buggin'* (Fox-TV): You're lucky I don't run you down to juvie.

3. *Police.* **a.** a member of a police juvenile division.

1970 Landy *Underground Dict.* 114: *Juvie*...Juvenile officer. **1972** Wambaugh *Blue Knight* 304: Those juvies said you was really some kind of cop.

b. a police juvenile division.

1986 *Miami Vice* (NBC-TV): I been workin' juvie for sixteen months.

J-ville *n. Local.* Jacksonville (Florida, Oregon, etc.).

1948 in Applegate & O'Donnell *Talking on Paper* 143: Do the present J'ville kids do that sort of thing wiith you? **1964** Rhodes *Chosen Few* 62: Scoutmaster for a troop in J-ville.

K¹ *n.* ["The symbol used by scorers to indicate a strikeout. Originated in the 1860s by *New York Herald* sportswriter M.J. Kelly, who chose the last letter of 'struck' (out) to differentiate between a strikeout and a sacrifice, indicated by the symbol 'S'"—T. Considine *Lang. Sport* (1982); P. Dickson *Baseball Dict.* (1989) attributes the scoring system to Henry Chadwick, 1861. Neither source offers documentation.] *Baseball.* a strikeout.

[**1942** *ATS* 655: *K*, score card indication for a strike-out, e.g. K1, K2 &c., the first, second &c. strike-out.] **1946** in P. Dickson *Baseball Dict.* 232: Feller Setting "K" Record. **1964** *Time* (Oct. 23) 62: The Yankees got nothing from...Bob Gibson but Ks (12) and goose eggs (8). **1982** T. Considine *Lang. Sport* 28: K...a strikeout. **1984** *N.Y. Post* (Aug. 3) 72: Nine hits, four runs, four K's, no walks.

K² *n.* [clipping of *kilo*-] **1.** one thousand dollars.

1965 Lurie *Nowhere City* 54: "Is it expensive?" "In the neighborhood of nine or ten K...And of course it costs another K or so a year to operate." **1970–71** G.V. Higgins *Coyle* 56: Four bastards no smarter'n you and me got ninety-seven K out of some little bank in the woods this morning. **1972** in *Playboy* (Jan. 1973) 238: Fifty-four K, appraised value....Fifty-four thousand. **1980** in *Nat. Lampoon* (Jan. 1981) 83: My tab at Elaine's has cracked five K. **1980** Gould *Ft. Apache* 89: Me, I'm sittin' with my twenty-three K over here, waitin' for the fuckin' P.B.A. to get me thirty-cents every two years. **1982** E. Leonard *Cat Chaser* 165: Use clean new hunner-dollar bills, George, a hunner K's. [**1992** W. Nash *Jargon* 163: K The *yuppie* word for one thousand pounds.] **1996** McCumber *Playing off Rail* 24: You'd won more than twenty K.

2. *Narc.* a kilogram, esp. of illicit drugs; KEY¹.

1975 De Mille *Smack Man* 22: You the dude that's looking to score a K, man? **1982** (cited in Spears *Drugs & Drink* 299).

K *v.* (see 1977 quot.).

1977 *Webster's Sports Dict.*: *K baseball* 1 *of a pitcher* To strike out a batter. 2 *of a batter* To strike out. **1978** *N.Y. Post* (Aug. 3) 62: Jackson K'd four times last night. **1984** *N.Y. Post* (Aug. 23) 74: Dwight Ks nine Padres to reach 200 plateau.

K var. KAY, *interj.*

kabeezer *n.* [< Sp *cabeza*; cf. BEEZER; CABEZA] the head.

1966 Gordon & Gordon *Prowls Again* 194: Five minutes later you want to toss him out on his kabeezer.

kabillion *n.* [*ka*- (emphatic prefix, as in KERFLOOEY, CABOODLE, etc.) + *billion*] an uncountable number; ZILLION. Also **kazillion** (cf. ZILLION), **kajillion** (cf. JILLION).

1987 in G. Tate *Flyboy* 97: Never mind how many of those kerzillion LPs we bought. **1991** *Darkwing Duck* (ABC-TV): Ninety kazillion dollars. **1992** Sprint, Inc., TV ad: Sprint didn't go down and leave a kabillion people stranded. **1994** *Mystery Sci. Theater* (Comedy Central TV): A million, billion, kajillion pieces!

kabitz, kabitzer vars. KIBITZ, KIBITZER.

kablooey var. KERFLOOEY.

kaboodle see under CABOODLE.

kabosh var. KIBOSH.

kack¹ *n.* [orig. unkn.; perh. cf. *kyack* 'a form of packsack ... swung on either side of a packsaddle'—*DA* (1907)] *West.* a western saddle, as used in herding livestock.

*a***1928** in Dobie *Drinkin' Gou'd* 179: And slap your old kack well fast upon his back. **1931** Rynning *Gun Notches* 21: In those early days [*ca*1882] some of the punchers called a saddle a caque (pronounced kak), but, wherever it came from, that name never got to be used...much. **1936** R. Adams *Cowboy Lingo* 47: The saddle also inherited many slang names, such as...*kack*. **1942** *ATS* 825: Saddle...*cack*...*kack*. *a***1956** Almirall *College to Cow Country* 30 [ref. to *a*1918]: Saddles had different names sych as "hulls," "kacks," or "trees."

kack² *n.* [orig. unkn.] *Black E.* a snob.

1928 R. Fisher *Jericho* 155: Meantime the kacks is closin' in and you can't make a quick getaway. *Ibid.* 302: *Kack* Extreme sarcasm for *dickty*. **1932** in *AS* (Feb. 1934) 27: *Kack.* A refined or nice person. *a***1934** R. Fisher, in A. Chapman *Black Voices* 81: A kack like that never means a woman no good.

kadody var. KAJODY.

kady var. CADY.

kaflooey var. KERFLOOEY.

kahuna *n.* [< Hawaiian 'priest or wise man'] **1.a.** *Surfing.* an expert surfer.—often constr. with *big*.

1957 Kohner *Gidget* 12: Gone was the Quonset hut of the Great Kahoona. [**1961** Kohner *Gidget Goes Hawaiian* 11: A Kahoona in Hawaiian is a big medicine man.] **1984** Glick *Winters Coming* 161: This is my Big Kahuna shirt. **1989** *Newsweek* (Aug. 28) 8: These would-be *kahunas* show up with all the newest and most expensive [surfing] gear. **1992** Cornum & Copeland *She Went* 37: Eric had on a pair of wild, baggy work-out pants from...Hawaii. Of course we called him the "Big Kahuna." **1995** *N.Y. Observer* (Sept. 18) 21: The Big Kahuna himself, Duke Kanahamoku, Hawaii's surfing progenitor, surfed here in 1912.

b. *Orig. Hawaii.* an expert of any sort.

1983 *Reader's Digest Success with Words* 312: Hawaiian English...*kahuna*...expert in any profession.

2. a large or important thing or person.—often constr. with *big*.

1987 E. Spencer *Macho Man* 177: I am a witness for those big Kahunas, the B-52's. **1991** *N.Y. Newsday* (Feb. 7) ("City Living") 83: To this big *kahuna*, all things tiki really are quite chic-y. **1993** *Frasier* (NBC-TV): This is for *television!* The big kahuna! **1996** *L.A. Times* (Nov. 4) A12: To surrender their critical thinking and personal autonomy to the will of the big kahuna.

kaieye var. KI-YI.

kaintuck var. KENTUCK.

kajillion var. KABILLION.

kajody *n.* [orig. unkn.] (see quots.). Also **kadody.** [The two citations may represent different words.]

1938 *AS* (Apr.) 156: *Kajody.* A term for an indefinite object. **1960** in H. Ellison *Sex Misspelled* 296: The manager...called the tourists and perverts who shopped for "different" books in our shop *kadodies.*

kale *n.* money. Also (*obs.*) **kale seed.** Cf. CABBAGE, 4; LETTUCE.

1902 C. Munn *Rockhaven* 4: "Wal," he says, pullin' out a roll o' bills....."Here's the kale seed." **1906** *DN* III 143: *Kale-seed, n.* money. "I'd go, if I had the *kale-seed.*" **1908** *Sat. Eve. Post* (Dec. 5) 16: He just naturally hones and hones and hones to hand us this nice little bundle of kale. **1911** G. Ade, in *Chi. Daily News* (Sept. 16) 28: He was out for the Kale, if you know what I mean. **1912** *DN* III 580: *Kale* or *kale seed*...Money. **1914** in Cummings *Letters* 9: Mr. C. offered me an equal amt. of kale (mazuma, $). **1914** Elliott *Animated Slang* 5: He spent some time in trying to induce me to part with my kale. **1917** in Kornbluh *Rebel Voices* 332: We will not fight unless we get a portion of the kale. **1927** *AS* II (May) 358: *Kale Seed.* Money. "He has put all his kale seed in the bank." **1929–31** Farrell *Young Lonigan* 114: A ritzy neighborhood where everybody had the kale. **1960–61** Steinbeck *Discontent* 191: The woman went out, dangling the bale of kale. **1961** Gover *$100 Misunderstanding* 18: Ain you got no skins, no kale? No bread? **1970** Barney's (N.Y.C.) radio ad (WINS): Come to Barney's summer sale/Where you'll save a bale of kale. **1973** Gwaltney *Destiny's Chickens* 70: I ain't got the kale to lay it out. **1992** *Batman* (Fox-TV): You never pay us our piece of kale for letting you work that corner.

kami *n. Mil. in Pacific.* a kamikaze. Now *hist.*

1961 Forbes *Goodbye to Some* 143 [ref. to 1945]: There is no longer doubt about the victory. The Kamis have dispelled it.

kamikaze cab *n.* a Tokyo taxicab. *Joc.*

1964 in *OEDS:* The Ginza was crowded....The kamikaze cabs did not seem to be affected...by the condition of the streets. **1973** Huggett *Body Count* 317: Small Toyopet cabs were buzzing into position, revving their motors. They were called Kamikaze cabs because all the drivers were said to be Kamikaze pilots who didn't make their big trip during the war.

kangaroo *n.* **1.** an Australian.—used derisively. Also as adj.

    1842 *Spirit of Times* (May 28) 153: If...the aforesaid penny-a-liner will favor him with his company, he will no doubt treat him to a little *kangaroo* sauce. **1888** Gunter *Mr. Potter* 126: Calling him..."Kangaroo, Esq.," and other jovial expressions of malice! *1888 in OED:* The "kangaroos"—as our colonial friends are sometimes dubbed. [**1906** *Nat. Police Gaz.* (Nov. 17) 7: George Gunther, the lanky boxer, known as the Australian Kangaroo.] **1922** *Sat. Eve. Post* (Aug. 26) 6: He had knocked 'em all cuckoo in Europe...and was going to show the Kangaroos what's what. **1933** in S. Smith *Gumps* 75: I'll show that kangaroo! *Ibid.* 82: She'll be plenty proud...when I've finished trimming the big kangaroo. **1981** P. Sann *Trial* 55: Peddled it to some kangaroo named Rupert Murdoch.

    2. (among itinerants) KANGAROO COURT.—also used attrib.

    1902 "J. Flynt" *Little Bro.* 124: Both he and Blackie were summoned by one of the prisoners to appear before the "Kangaroo." ...It don't pay, pris'ners, to buck against the Kang'roo. *Ibid.* 128: An' the Kang'roo is adjourned. **1935** Algren *Boots* 168: This is about all what's left o' my kangaroo money.

    3. *pl.* big feet. *Joc.*

    1908 in Fleming *Unforgettable Season* 178: Devlin had his foot between the bag and Lobert's "kangaroos."

    4. (see quot.).

    1989 Leib *Fire Dream* 300 [ref. to Vietnam War]: The rest of his gear was in a small pouch the marines called a kangaroo, originally designed to carry battle dressings.

kangaroo *v.* Orig. *Pris.* to convict by means of a prisoners' KANGAROO COURT; *(hence)* to convict unjustly in an actual court.

    1907 *Reader* (Sept.) 344: The bunch used to kangaroo me something fierce and make me boil myself and my clothes about nine times a week. *a*1909 Tillotson *Detective* 92: *Kangarooed*—Given a false trial. **1912** *Hampton's Mag.* (Jan.) 848: No guy was ever kangarooed like Portsmouth Fat in that Los Angeles stir. **1921** U. Sinclair *K. Coal* 210: His circulars had been confiscated, his posters torn down, his supporters "kangarooed." **1923** in Kornbluh *Rebel Voices* 91: Kangarooed again, by God! **1934** Kromer *Waiting* 28: [The judge] is kangarooing them. They haven't got a chance. **1935** Algren *Boots* 145: I guess I must of kangarooed twelve Mexes in that jailhouse. **1935** Pollock *Und. Speaks: Kangarooed*, sentenced to prison when innocent. **1983** Goldman & Fuller *Charlie Co.* 312: "They kangarooed me"—found him guilty and sentenced him to six months' hard time in the stockade.

kangaroo court *n.* [the orig. allusion, presumably to Australia, is now obscure; cf. 1862 quot., perh. sugg. that the kangaroo's appearance seems to defy laws of nature]

an unauthorized or irregularly conducted court; (in 1853 quot.) such a court created on the frontier before the establishment of territorial law; *(also) Pris.* a mock court set up by prisoners to initiate and extort money from new inmates; *(now usu.)* a flagrantly unfair court or similar proceeding. Now *colloq.* or *S.E.*

    1853 "P. Paxton" *In Texas* 205: Judge G....was elected to the bench, and the "Mestang" or "Kangaroo Court" regularly organized. [**1862** in A.P. Hudson *Humor of Old So.* 376: As in the case of the Kangaroo, the law was altogether inoperative against this dangerous class of man.] **1890** in *DAE:* Organizing "kangaroo courts" for the slightest offense, were some of their daily amusements. **1895** "J. Flynt," in *Harper's Mag.* (Apr.) 718: The "Kangaroo Court"...is found almost entirely in county jails....The "Kangaroo Court"...consists of all the prisoners. **1902** "J. Flynt" *Little Bro.* 124: There were thirty inmates all told, and...one...notified the fresh arrivals that they were in the presence of the local "Kang'roo Court," and that they were under indictment of having money in their pockets. **1917–20** in J.M. Hunter *Trail Drivers* I 68: We organized a kangaroo court and tried the engineer...for disturbing the peace of passengers. **1930** Irwin *Tramp & Und. Slang* 115: *Kangaroo Court*....the prisoners waiting for trial...try each newly received prisoner...on a charge of "breaking into jail." **1951** C. Palmer *Sellout* (film): A prisoners' court. Kangaroo court....Some new fish for

you, Little Jake. **1981** Gilliland *Rosinante* 162: This is a kangaroo court...and I will file an immediate appeal. **1982** L'Amour *Shadow Riders* 3: They're fixin' to hang him. Kangaroo court.

kangaroo straight *n. Poker.* a worthless hand resembling a straight but having gaps or "jumps" between consecutive cards. *Joc.*

    1953 *Abbott & Costello Show* (WPIX-TV): That's a kangaroo straight. **1978** De Christoforo *Grease* 34: He'd fold like he was holding a kangaroo straight in a poker game.

kangaroo ticket *n.* [perh. as in 1984 quot.] *Pol.* a political ticket, as for the offices of president and vice president, where the primary candidate is less appealing to voters than the running mate.

    1971 *N.Y. Times* (Oct. 23), in Safire *Pol. Dict.* (1978 ed.): [John Connally would run for vice president if asked by President Nixon, but] he would insist that the Nixon-Connally partnership be advertised as a "kangaroo ticket." **1977** Coover *Public Burning* 384: It was virtually a kangaroo ticket after that, old war hero at the top or no. **1980** in Safire *Good Word* 138: A couple of kangaroo tickets will lead to a big clothespin vote. **1984** *N.Y. Post* (Sept. 3) 11: "It's a kangaroo ticket," sighed one disappointed Texas politician after FDR's nomination [in 1932]. "Stronger in the hindquarters than in the front."

kanoodle *v.* to cajole; CANOODLE.

    1887 Peck *Pvt. Peck* 156: Do not let her kanoodle you with soft words and looks of love, because she is full of 'em.

kaput *adj.* [< G *kaputt* < F *(etre) capot* 'without tricks (in the card game of piquet)'] done for; destroyed; dead; broken; tired out; etc. [The *1895 quot. app. represents a use of the German word in English.]

    [*1895 in *OED2:* The thing would then go *wie's Donnerwetter* and the man would be *kaput* at once.] **1919** *Fifth Div. Diamond* (Apr. 23) 2: I am unable to take her out due to the fact that my francs are usually "kaput." **1919** in Cornebise *Amaroc News* 27: Everything looks rather "caput" at the present time. **1924** *Adventure* (June 20) 172: The sergeant observed the German. No doubt of his being *kaput.* **1928** in Dos Passos *14th Chronicle* 386: They...say that the theatre is capoot. **1928–29** Nason *White Slicker* 75 [ref. to WWI]: It's lucky we didn't send your friend there over to that dressing station. They'll be kapoot after dark. *Ibid.* 118: "And how about the crowd that was out in front last night?" "I guess they're kapoot." *Ibid.* 153: That outfit is kapoot! **1929** "E. Queen" *Roman Hat* ch. vi 72: Well, gentlemen, the great search is finished, over, *kaput.* **1959** Pohl *Star of Stars* 78: Dead. Destroyed. Kaputt. **1962** Crump *Killer* 57: We're through. Quits; done; kaput. Dig? **1965** Linakis *In Spring* 62: She's kaput....There were five other guys there before we got here and she's kaput. **1967** in Rowan & MacDonald *Friendship* 29: The [muscles] I used to use are kaput. **1973** C. Cussler *Mediterranean Caper* 101: Thanks to you our ghost from World War I is kaput. **1973** Overgard *Hero* 150: You all ready done it, Top, he's kaput, zapped—bought the farm. **1983** R. Thomas *Missionary* 33: If something goes kaput, call a carpenter or a plumber or an electrician. **1984** R. Baker, in *N.Y. Times* (Dec. 19) A27: Santa Claus will be through. Washed up. Kaput. **1983–89** K. Dunn *Geek Love* 56: Fed up with the kaput generator that kept the show closed.

kaput *v. Mil.* to destroy.

    1961 Granat *Important Thing* 162 [ref. to WWII]: The French general's got a big mansion in town and he don't want it kaputed. **1991** *Darkwing Duck* (ABC-TV): You have kaputted the entire craft!

karma *n.* (orig. among hippies) feelings; emotional atmosphere; whatever is evaluated as pleasant or unpleasant; VIBES; *(also)* luck.—usu. constr. with *good* or *bad.* [Usages cited here appear to have little or no direct ref. to Hindu or Buddhist belief.]

    1969 Mitchell *Thumb Tripping* 178: You aren't smoking, are you? You're putting us on, you're not—no wonder you're giving off this bad karma. *Ibid.* 189: Look for the good karma, not the bad. The good vibes. **1971** *Rolling Stone* (June 24) 32: John Sebastian's recording career has been plagued with...bad karma. **1978** Rascoe & Stone *Who'll Stop Rain?* (film): It's [*sc.,* smuggling heroin] bad karma, man! **1983** *N.Y. Post* (Sept. 2) 71: Bad karma follows the Giants like O.J. followed the Electric Company. **1989** R. Miller *Profane Men* 74: Operation Toledo Blade is...radiating poisoned karma and fear. **1994** *My So-Called Life* (ABC-TV): "The karma in this house is really low."..."I bet the karma in Rae Anne's house is through the roof!" **1995** Poker players in N.Y.C. (coll. J. Sheidlower): You're messing with the karma [by dealing cards in an unorthodox manner]!

Katy[1] *n.* (see 1929 quot.).

    1890 in Dobie *Rainbow* 160: But they cotcht me on the Katy, an' he brings me back. **1904** in "O. Henry" *Works* 839: The Katy Flyer showed up. **1925** Mullin *Scholar Tramp* 274 [ref. to *ca*1912]: I had known perfectly well I was riding the Katy out of Fort Scott. **1929** Ferber *Cimarron* 130: The Missouri, Kansas & Texas Railroad, familiarly known throughout the Territory, by a natural process of elision, as the Katy. **1961** McMurtry *Horseman* 6: The railroad was just the other side of the highway, and about sundown the Katy freight chugged by.

¶ In phrase:

¶ **Katy, bar the door** [or **gate**]! watch out! (used to suggest finality or impending disaster). Also **it's Katy bar the door** the end; disaster.

    1902 Hobart *Up to You* 30: It was "Katie, bar the door" with her. **1926–28** in A.P. Hudson *Folksongs of Miss.* 44 [title of fiddle tune]: Katie, Bar the Door. **1952** Haines & Krims *One Minute to Zero* (film): Katie, bar the door! **1956** "T. Betts" *Across the Board* 165: There's a switch in riders and it's Katy bar the door. **1963** D. Tracy *Brass Ring* 309: Either he put Noble in on top or it would be Katie-bar-the-door. **1968** J.P. Miller *Race for Home* 285 [ref. to 1930's]: Luther said, "Hoooeeee! Katy bar the gate!" **1970** L.D. Johnson *Devil's Front Porch* 65: If he happened to slip as he jumped, it was "Katy bar the door." It was all over for them both. **1982** *N.Y. Times Mag.* (Aug. 29) 66: After that, it's Katie-bar-the-door. **1983** Van Riper *Glenn* 94: Anytime John gets his sights set on something, it's Katy-bar-the-door. **1994** *20/20* (ABC-TV) (Apr. 15): And once that happens, it's Katy bar the door.

Katy[2] var. CADY.

katydid *n.* **1.** individual; person.

    1873 G. Small *Knights of Pythias* 3: If there's a riot, I'm yer kittydid.

    2. *Logging.* (see quots.).

    1905 in *DA*: Logging wheels...Syn.: big wheels, katydid, timber wheels. **1909** *WNID*: Katydid...A pair of logging wheels. **1958** McCulloch *Woods Wds.* 101: Katydid—an old name for a set of big wheels in the pine country. **1967** in *DARE*.

katzenjammer *n.* [< G, lit. 'cats' discomfort'] **1.** an alcoholic hangover; (*broadly*, as in 1904 quot.) great nervousness; WILLIES.—often constr. in pl.

    1846 in *Ill. Hist. Soc. Jour.* XXVI (1934) 363: I have nothing to show but a case of "Katzenjammer" which I took back...with me. **1849** in *DARE*: Some of Mr. Hale's men had kept up a drunken frolic all night—general kakenjammer [*sic*], therefore, all day. **1877** Burdette *Mustache* 291: Has...no equal for the cure of...katzenjammer. **1877–78** *Cornelian* 86: Katzenjammer. The depression following a spree. **1904** in "O. Henry" *Works* 1323: But the katzenjammer I've got don't spell violets. It spells your own name. **1913** J. London *J. Barleycorn* 186: Intellectual intoxication, too, has its katzenjammer. **1919** in Mencken *New Ltrs.* 106: He left...with...katzenjammer from a couple of milk punches I made for him last night. **1942–43** C. Jackson *Lost Weekend* 165: The jitters,...the katzenjammers,...the moaning after. **1965** in *DARE*.

    2. noisy quarreling or confusion.

    1929 Perelman *Ginsbergh* 188: I've seen enough katzenjammer around this place in my time to give even a divorce judge a thrill.

kay *interj.* O.K. Also **K.**

    1959 in *AS* XXXIX 2 (May 1964) 95: She greeted the news with "'K." Not "O.K." just "'K." ***1959** in *OED2*: "How about a quick half-hour *now*?" I said. "Kay." **1968, 1972** in *OED2*. **1992** Mowry *Way Past Cool* 243: Kay, man. I there'n less'n five. **1993** P. Munro *U.C.L.A. Slang II* s.v. *K.O.*: We're leaving now, K? **1994** A. Heckerling *Clueless* 38: Is our regular table available?...Well, there'll be an extra joining us...K. [ellipses in orig.].

kaydet *n. Mil.* a cadet. *Joc.*

    1882 Miller & Harlow *9'51"* 217: Sir, that's a K-det. **1925** (quot. at KIWI, 2). **1930** in D.O. Smith *Cradle of Valor* 9: The first "kaydet" I saw was in a full white uniform. **1985** Boyne & Thompson *Wild Blue* 21: A Kaydet, back in the days when they flew DH-4s.

kayo var. K.O.

kazillion var. KABILLION.

kazip *n.* [orig. unkn.] ¶ In phrase: **off (one's) kazip** crazy.

    1904 in "O. Henry" *Works* 257: "You're off your kazip," declared another of the gang. **1906** *Univ. Tenn. Vol.* (unp.): If you didn't like Tip,/You were "off your cazip." **1908** *DN* III 290: You're *off'n* your *kerzip* if you think I'd do that. **1932** D. Runyon, in *Collier's* (Jan. 30) 8: Israel...goes right off his ka-zip about her.

Kazoo *n. Local.* Kalamazoo, Mich.

    1917 in Morgan & Michalson *For Our Beloved Country* 269: I returned to Kazoo and finished my school. **1954–60** *DAS: Kazoo n.* Kalamazoo. *Obs.*

kazoo *n.* [orig. unkn.] **1.** the anus; (*occ.*) the vagina or penis; in phr. **up** [or **out**] **the kazoo** in abundance or to excess. Also **gazoo.**

    1965 Pollini *Glover* 95: [Britons] up the goddamn gazoo and out, man. **1968** Spooner *War in General* 18: Taxpayers, right up your kazoooo! **1969** Tynan et al. *Oh! Calcutta!* 155: Now we're all laughing and they're standing down there looking up my kazoo. **1970** N.Y.C. man, age 30: He can stick it up his gazoo. **1971** Sonzski *Punch Goes Judy* 171: Punch had a spare ignition key up the kazoo. Punch was the liberated woman. **1972** Pendleton *Boston Blitz* 149: People down there have empaneled a special grand jury, and they're handing out indictments up the kazoo. **1973** Flaherty *Chez Joey* xiii [ref. to *ca*1950]: And our swearing [in Brooklyn] would baffle them....I'm sure nobody in Ohio said "Up your kazoo!" (quot. at GAZOOKUS, 3). **1972–79** T. Wolfe *Right Stuff* 62: A lab rabbit...with...a wire up the kazoo. **1980** *Bosom Buddies* (ABC-TV): The one thing I really love is sensitivity. And you've got it up the *kazoo*! **1983** R. Thomas *Missionary* 114: She's got credit cards coming out the kazoo. **1985** Frede *Nurses* 47: These people are ghettoed here. Economically and politically, right up the kazoo. **1990** *Sydney* (CBS-TV): I haven't exactly had clients up the kazoo here. **1991** McCarthy & Mallowe *Vice Cop* 168: Liquor code violations coming out the kazoo. **1992** J. Feiffer, in *New Yorker* (Nov. 2) 55: They want vision? Vision up the kazoo! **1993** W. Styron *Tidewater* 36 [ref. to 1940's]: And then he got his hand down there—you know where...and suddenly he felt...this big, stiff...gazoo!

    2. important element or factor.—constr. with *the.*

    1957 M. Shulman *Rally* 181: I think the kazoo here is product identification.

kazootie *n.* KAZOO, 1.

    1979 Shem *House of God* 227: I'm just a fed-up Catholic whose had it up the kazootie with the nuns.

k-ball *v.* [by alter. & syncope] *Mil. Av.* to cannibalize for spare parts.

    1985 Heywood *Taxi Dancer* 119 [ref. to 1967]: If they lost all three, they'd be down to forty-nine birds and even with fifty-two they were already scrounging and k-balling everything they could get their hands on. *Ibid.* 174: So they could get to the wreckage and k-ball it. **1986** *NDAS: K-balling*...Air Force The cannibalizing of one aircraft to repair another.

K-boy *n.* [perh. *king* + (COW)BOY, 3, despite the slightly later attestation of the latter term; otherwise fr. *king* + *boy* in familiar use] *Cards.* a king.

    1943 *Newsweek* (Feb. 22) 4: I tried to sweat out that third K-boy but it wouldn't drop. **1949** G.S. Coffin *Winning Poker* 180: K-boy, or Cowboy—Any king. **1957** McGivern *Against Tomorrow* 70: "And here come the K-boys," Ingram said, tossing out the kings.

K.C. *n.* Kansas City, Mo. Now *colloq.*

    1895 *Harper's* (Oct.) 778: I was sittin' in Sal's place in K.C.*....*Kansas City. **1899** Kountz *Baxter's Letters* 70: He was from K.C., Mizzoo. **1914** in Handy *Blues Treasury* 88: I'll count each pole and water hole/To K.C., M.O.

keaster var. KEISTER.

keck *n.* pocket; KICK, 3.b.

    1899 A.H. Lewis *Sandburrs* 156: I won't do a t'ing but make it a t'ousand dollars in d' kecks of the ducks who's doin that now. **1906** A.H. Lewis *Confessions* 17: Half of 'em's got...chloroform bottles in their kecks right now. **1911** A.H. Lewis *Apaches of N.Y.* 76: Then they pinches a fiver out of me keck.

kee var. KEY[1], *n.*

keed *n.* KID, 1.c.—used in direct address. *Joc.*

    1920 Fitzgerald *This Side of Paradise* 208: Couldn't say, old keed. **1923** in J. O'Hara *Sel. Letters* 6: Keep it up Fish, old keed. **1947** in Kerouac *Letters* 125: So long keeds. **1947–51** Motley *We Fished* 134:

Hello, keed! **1954** Collans & Sterling *House Detect.* 77: We ain't the kind to get excited over a dame's pants, are we, keed? **1956–60** J.A. Williams *Angry Ones* ch. x: Whaddaya say, keed? **1970** C. Harrison *No Score* 54: Aren't they, keed? **1972** R. Barrett *Lovomaniacs* 336: Whatcha say, keed? That fair? **1978** S. King *Stand* 564: You're not responsible for Harold Lauder's actions, keed. *a***1993** in Wimmer *Schoolyard Game* 25: Atta way, big man. Atta way, *keed.*

keel *v.* **1.** to fall or turn on one's back; fall over; (*often*) to faint; (*hence*) (now *rare*) to become ill or incapacitated, or to die.—usu. constr. with *up* (*obs.*) or *over* (now *colloq.*).

   1832 in S. Smith *Letters of Downing* 98: The poor fellow keeled up and couldn't go another step. **1837** Neal *Charc. Sks.* 124: He must keel up in an hexcruciating manner, flip-flopping it about on the stage as he defuncts, like a new-caught sturgeon. **1844** "J. Slick" *High Life in N.Y.* 112: Over went the captin...and keeled up a'most under the table. *Ibid.* 126: [She] would a keeled over [in a faint] if I hadn't a ketched her. **1849** Melville *White Jacket* 314: I shouldn't wonder if I myself was the next man to keel up. **1850** in Blair & McDavid *Mirth* 103: She kinda keeled up like a possum. **1853** "P. Paxton" *In Texas* 228: Then down he drapped, gin a beller, and keeled up. **1857** Willcox *Faca* 39: On either side of the wheel, seamen lay "keeled up" with sleep. **1857** in *DA:* The bear keeled over onto his back with a jerk. *a***1859** Bartlett *Amer.* (ed. 2) 225: *Keel over* they must, and a gradual *career* would be much better than a sudden *capsize.* **1861** in *DA:* I only keeled for the shake of a tail. **1880** J.C. Harris *Uncle Remus* 12: Brer Possum fetch a grin fum year to year, en keel over like he was dead. **1888** G. King *Time & Place* 226: She'll just keel over when she sees me a-lyin' here all tied up. **1894** Henderson *Sea-Yarns* 65: Hiram keeled over sun-struck. **1903** *Enquirer* (Cincinnati) (May 9) 13: Keeled—Died. **1915** [Swartwood] *Choice Slang* 52: *Keel over*...To faint or collapse. **1915** O'Brien *Best Stories of 1915* 96: I—I'm going to keel. **1935** Kromer *Waiting* 209: People just don't go around on the streets keeling over from starvation. **1936** Riskin *Mr. Deeds* (film): I suggest you break it to him gently. He's likely to keel over from the shock. **1938** "R. Hallas" *You Play the Black* 24: I couldn't have run any more or I'd have keeled over. **1942** in Kernan *Crossing Line* 48: I ran until I was ready to keel. **1970** R. Vasquez *Chicano* 99: One day he just keeled over dead. *a***1987** Bunch & Cole *Reckoning for Kings* 142: The kid would keel over from the heat. *a***1994** A. Radakovich *Wild Girls Club* 106: Who supposedly lived 256 years and was still fertile when he keeled. **1995** *Newsweek* (Dec. 25) 125: Strom Thurmond, now 93, will run for the Senate until he keels.

2. to knock down or over; (*hence*) to incapacitate or kill.—usu. constr. with *over* or *up.*

   1844 Carleton *Logbooks* 43: Strike him!—knock him down!—keel him over! **1844** "J. Slick" *High Life in N.Y.* 118: I wish...the old shote had got up and keeled me over with both fists...insted of blamin hisself. **1850** Garrard *Wah-to-yah* 163: I grabs my knife, "keels" one, an' made for timber. **1852** Stowe *Uncle Tom's Cabin* 70: More'n all, I've got free papers for 'em all recorded, in case I gets keeled up any o' these times. **1864** in R.G. Carter *4 Bros.* 478: I have been keeled up; my left thigh in front has been swelled to twice its natural size, from the effect of ivy poison. **1872** Eggleston *End of World* 239: S'posin' they was a woodpecker on that air stump, wouldn't I a keeled him over? **1874** Alger *Julius* 42: He blazed away, and keeled him over on his back. **1897** Kipling *Capts. Courageous* 8: It would take more'n this to keel me over. **1900** Willard & Hodler *Powers That Prey* 170: There's a push o' guns in this town that thinks flatties don't count, that there won't be much of a kick when one of 'em's keeled over.

keeler *n.* *Und.* MICKEY.

   1917–19 J. Boyle *Boston Blackie* 54: The keys [and] the "keeler" for the guards in the tower, were in their hands.

keelhaul *v.* to defeat or ruin.

   1821 Waln *Hermit in Phila.* 25: "Now you're keel-hauled"—"Come, knock under."

keen *n.* *Stu.* a joke or jest.

   1878 Flipper *Colored Cadet* 53: "A keen."—See "Gag."

keen *adj.* Esp. *Stu.* exciting; attractive; splendid; fine; O.K. Also as *adv.* [Esp. common *ca*1920–50; 1863 quot., transcribed from handwriting, is unique in its era and should be regarded with caution. Date and wording of 1915 quot. are given inaccurately in *OED2.*]

   [**1863** in Mead *Shanties* 480: Now I don't know what you was

after/All dressed up so keen.] **1915** [Swartwood] *Choice Slang* 52: *Keen*—Fine. (Examples:) "A keen day. "A keen time." [*sic* punctuation]. **1917** in Bowerman *Compensations* 1: Up at 6....Keen ball game but we lose. **1918** in Grider *War Birds* 159: She sure was keen. I'm going back to see her if I ever break my monastic vows. **1923** in Kornbluh *Rebel Voices* 90: This system of ramblin' around sure is keen. **1926** Hormel *Co-Ed* 6: We've got a keen bunch of fellows in the chapter this year. **1928** Dahlberg *Bottom Dogs* 175: A keen-looking skirt...threw him off his resolution. **1928** in E. Wilson *Twenties* 474: Oh, that's keen! **1929** T. Gordon *Born to Be* 186: A bewitching creature five feet six, exquisite figure, dark eyes, fascinating face with a head full of jet black hair and keen feet! **1930** in Johnson & Williamson *Whatta-Gal* 73: All the rest of the teams get payed keen and lots more than any of us do. **1930** Sage *Last Rustler* 97: He sure had a keen string of saddle horses—ten head by now. **1932** Cormack & Ornitz *13 Women* (film): That's keen! Come in! **1932** *AS* VII (June) 333: *Keen*—excellent; likable; attractive. **1933** J. Conroy *Disinherited* 172: "Gee! That's keen!" she whispered softly, ceasing to chew gum. **1933** in Galewitz *Great Comics* 37: I'm happy you quit wearing shorts at the games. 'At's keen. **1935** A.G. Kennedy *Current Eng.* 29: When the favorite word of approval was *keen*, it might be applied to anything from a cake to an especially lovely sunset. **1935** Marion, Hanemann & Loos *Riffraff* (film): You got somethin' special there, boss. It's keen....Boy, that's keen. **1938** in Hammerstein *Kern Song Bk.* 189: You couldn't be cuter, you couldn't be keener. **1940** Burnett *High Sierra* 25: On his trip west he'd seen hundreds of dames; some of them pretty keen, too. **1944** Busch *Dream of Home* 132: They have keen records. **1948** M. Shulman *Dobie Gillis* 50: I think she's a keen kid. **1951** Pryor *The Big Play* 176: Tom! It's keen to see you. **1954** Bissell *High Water* 23: Gee, Pop,...this house...burnt clear to the ground. Boy was it ever a keen fire. Me and Charlie Schroeder saw the whole thing. **1963** *Dick Van Dyke Show* (CBS-TV): We all get along...keen. **1963** D. Tracy *Brass Ring* 6: Looks like a keen place, Kelly. Real keen. **1987** *Night Court* (NBC-TV): Come on, Roz—it'll be keen! **1993** P. Munro *U.C.L.A. Slang II* 54: *Keen*...exceptionally good. *That was a keen movie.*

keener *n.* a keen, sharp, or wide-awake individual. Also **keenie.**

   1839 in *DA:* The filly is a keener, but looked out of fix. **1859** Bartlett *Amer.* (ed. 2) 225: *Keener.* A very shrewd person, one sharp at a bargain, what in England would be called a "keen hand." Western. **1871** Schele de Vere *Amer.* 496: I tell you he is a keener, you can't get on his blind side. **1900** J.C. Harris *On the Wing* 42: He'll be nabbed be thim keenies at the dure.

keeno *adj.* [KEEN + -o, perh. infl. in early use by KENO] KEEN.

   1918 in *AS* (Oct. 1933) 28: *Keeno.* Preferred form of keen, meaning fine, excellent, beautiful, all right, etc. **1960** Swarthout *Where Boys Are* 112: He...was a keeno dancer. **1961** Kohner *Gidget Goes Hawaiian* 18: Keeno sports like surfboard riding or skiing. *Ibid.* 69: So I had this real keeno idea.

keep *n.* ¶ In phrase: **for keeps, 1.** (of a game) for permanent possession of the loser's marbles or the like. Now *S.E.*

   1861 in *DA:* He and I played "for keeps," and I was the best player and won all his. **1886** in Farmer *Amer.:* We...promise not to play marbles for keeps, nor...gamble in any way. **1907** T.A. Dorgan, in Zwilling *TAD Lexicon* 114: When it comes to playing for "keeps" he refuses to start. **1957** N.Y.C. schoolboy: We only flip [baseball cards] for keeps.

2. permanently. Now *colloq.*

   1864 in H. Johnson *Talking Wire* 129: A great many are leaving Salt Lake for "keeps." **1912** Siringo *Cowboy Detective* 58: He said...I could be hung for "keeps." **1917–19** J. Boyle *Boston Blackie* 119: I'm done for keeps. **1928** Guerin *Crime* 112: It didn't follow that they had me for keeps. **1940** (quot. at DUST OFF, 5.a.). **1955** M. Jessup *Case for UFO* 144: Cody and Adams just disappeared—for keeps.

3. with serious intent or purpose; thoroughly. Now *colloq.*

   1866 Shanks *Personal Recollections* 174: "Fighting for keeps" is army slang, and signifies fighting in deadly earnest. **1871** in *OED2:* Winter has at last set in "for keeps." **1889** in *DA:* Joe Kappel is hitting the ball for keeps. **1897** Siler & Houseman *Fight of Century* 20: He began with four hard rounds with Billy Woods, in which the latter was instructed to "come at me for keeps." **1915** T.A. Dorgan, in *N.Y. Eve. Jour.* (Aug. 2) 11: They belted one another for keeps. **1931** Dos Passos *1919* 400:

The town was full of rumors that on that day the hall would be raided for keeps.

keester var. KIESTER.

keg *n.* **1.** collection; CABOODLE, 1.

1864 in C.H. Moulton *Ft. Lyon* 204: The "whole keg of us" "played in" again.

2. the stomach; one's capacity for food or drink; esp. in phr. **fill (one's) keg** to get drunk; in phr. **beer keg** a beer belly.

1877 W. Wright *Big Bonanza* 366: His "keg" was evidently "full" to overflowing, yet he was still athirst. 1882 Peck *Peck's Sunshine* 263: He can never see a person with his keg full of bug juice without giving him a talking to. 1882 F. Triplett *Jesse James* 119: He felt that he must "fill his keg"—in plain English must get drunk. 1887 Francis *Saddle & Moccasin* 270: We'd been having a time and my keg was pretty full too. *a*1888 Addy *Sheffield Gloss.* 122: *Keg*....the belly. "He filled his *keg*." 1966–69 in *DARE*: An oversize stomach that results from drinking...*beer keg*.

¶ In phrase:

¶ **keg of nails** a keg of alcoholic drink, esp. beer; in phrs. **have a keg [of nails] aboard** to be drunk; **open [up] a keg of nails** to celebrate (with or without alcohol).

1881 Nye *Forty Liars* 88: I have...prepared the wedding dinner, and opened a keg of nails, and all things are ready for the blow-out. 1887 in *AS* XXV (1950) 35: Judging from the way Frank and his friend walked, they must have had a keg aboard. 1895 (quot. at ABOARD, 1). 1901 Ade *Modern Fables* 93: Come with me to the Club and I will open a Keg of Nails. [1941 H.A. Smith *Low Man* 17: The stuff available at two dollars a pint resembled the liquid poured off a keg of nails rather than whisky. It was nose-holding liquor.] 1952 Sandburg *Strangers* 170 [ref. to *ca*1895]: They meant they were going to drink and have fun when they said, "stick around, we're going to open a keg of nails." 1952 Mandel *Angry Strangers* 27: Won't you stay? We're about to open a keg of nails. 1971 *Mary Tyler Moore Show* (CBS-TV): We'll open up a keg of nails!

keg *v.* **1.** to abstain from alcohol.

1789 in *DAE*: "I'll *keg* myself for six months, directly I get home." The word *keg*...is a cant word that the soldiers have among them, when they wish to refrain from liquors. 1832 in *DAE*: From the cheapness of rum, the labouring people...acquire habits of excessive drinking, which they have only resolution to resist by swearing....that they will not taste rum, or spirits of any kind. This act is called Kegging, extending to one or more years, and often for life. 1838 [Haliburton] *Clockmaker* (Ser. 2) 122: I kag'd for a month, (that is, he had taken an oath to abstain from drawing liquor from the keg—they calls it kaggin'). 1855 Barnum *Life* 36: Once in a while he would "keg," as he called it; that is, he would abjure strong drink for a certain length of time.

2. *Stu.* to picnic.

1965 Reagan & Hubler *Rest of Me* 42 [ref. to *ca*1929]: There was the custom of "kegging." Eureka was the only place...where you could walk down a street with your girl on one arm and a blanket on the other without starting a scandal.

kegger *n. Stu.* a party at which beer is available from a keg.

[1915 [Swartwood] *Choice Slang* 52: *Keg bust*...A beer party.] 1968 Baker et al. *CUSS* 147: *Kegger*. A drinking party. 1974 *Everett* (Wash.) *Herald* (July 1) 8C: We had been to a kegger earlier that night, but that got busted so we left. 1979 W. Cross *Kids & Booze* 16: You can have a "kegger" and make everybody pay a couple of bucks. 1981 Crowe *Fast Times* 91: They were heading for the Laguna kegger. 1989 P. Munro *U.C.L.A. Slang* 54: You should go to the kegger at Bill's on Friday night. 1993 *Rolling Stone* (Jan. 7) 30: The Vikings never practice on Sundays, so there was a kegger at Bubba's place. 1995 *Critic* (Fox-TV): There's gonna be a real bitchin' kegger...tonight.

keg toss *n.* KEGGER.

1995 *New Yorker* (May 8) 77: A Norwegian party at the Rotary Club...and a keg toss...at a horse stable.

keister *n.* [< G *Kiste* 'box, case, chest' also (slang) 'rump'] Also **kiester, keaster, keester, keyster.**

1.a. a traveling bag or satchel; suitcase; valise; (*often*) a pitchman's sample case.

1881 Trumble *Man Traps* 14: Prominent among the small army of confidence operators in [New York City] are "Grand Central Pete,"..."Boston Charlie,"..."Kiester Bob," "The Kid," "Hungry

Joe." 1882 Peck *Peck's Sunshine* 227: The boy took the Knight's keister and went to the elevator. 1908 Sullivan *Crim. Slang* 15: *Keister*—A grip or bag. 1913 *Sat. Eve. Post* (Mar. 15) 10: Say, lady,...won't yer let me carry de keester? 1918 in *AS* (Oct. 1933) 29: *Keester.* Suitcase. 1925 *Atlantic Monthly* (Dec.) 755: The master cracksman and his two assistants appear outside the door with the "keister" or satchel holding the money and stamps. 1926 Norwood *Other Side of Circus* 272: A suitcase or bag—a keester. 1928 O'Connor *B'way Racketeers* 70: The bad ones went to the bottom of the keyster. 1932–33 P. Cain *Fast One* 211: Three big pigskin keesters. 1935 J. Conroy *World to Win* 59: "Hey, you gonna leave yer keister?"...Dude was a pitchman, and he had one of the small satchels which street merchants set upon legs to serve as a display stand. 1935 in Botkin *Sidewalks* 292 [ref. to 1880's]: Before him, on a low tripod, was an open sample case of liberal dimensions, the typical "tripe" and "keister" of the street hawker. *ca*1940 in Botkin *Treas. Amer. Folk.* 550: Now he feels like locking up his keister and throwing away the key. 1944 C.B. Davis *Leo McGuire* 85: Your well-meaning Buffalo friends gave you a keister with L. McG. stamped on it. 1946 Gresham *Nightmare Alley* 230: I've got the keyster parked uptown in a check room. 1948 *Ga. Review* II 164: I get the keyster...and dress by moonlight. 1958 J. Thompson *Getaway* 99: It might just be there was nothing in this keister. 1962 in Cannon *Nobody Asked* 240: The joint is operated as if the owners were going to pack their keisters and take the next train out of town.

b. *Und.* a strongbox or safe; (*also*) a locked compartment built into a safe.

1913 Stringer *Shadow* 36: He made a mental record of...yeggs and till-tappers and keister-crackers. 1917 *Editor* (Feb. 24) 153: *Keester*—the strong box of a safe. 1921 Casey & Casey *Gay-Cat* 147: They...breaks inter the keester o' the bank safes, an' gits away with all the stored-up jack of all them reubens round about. 1928 Callahan *Man's Grim Justice* 74: We got the "kiester" (burglar-proof chest in the bottom of the safe where the money is stacked). 1930 *Liberty* (Aug. 2) 40: The keester...is a compartment that's built into most safes. 1931–34 in Clemmer *Pris. Community* 333: *Keyster*...A steel safe, usually enclosed in a vault. 1968 "H. King" *Box-Man* 35: A keister. It's a small safe inside of a big one. 1971–72 in Abernethy *Bounty of Texas* 208: *Kiester*...the name of a circular-type safe.

c. *Und.* a jail; lockup.—constr. with *the.*

1942–49 Goldin et al. *DAUL* 114: *Keister*...A local jail. 1966 Bogner *Seventh Avenue* 422: While I'm in the *keister*: Raymond Street, or the Tombs.

2.a. the posteriors; BUTT, 1.a.; (*also*) the anus or rectum.—also used in fig. senses. Also **keisters.**

1931 *AS* VI (Aug.) 439 [ref. to *ca*1925]: *Keister, n.* A satchel; also what one sits on. 1938 "Justinian" *Amer. Sex.* 27: *Keyster.* n. Posterior; buttocks. Becoming a euphemism, 1925—. 1942 *ATS* 148: Anus...*keester, keister, keyster* (esp. as a place to conceal valuables). 1945 Kanin *Born Yesterday* 188: I bought a kid out with a swift kick in the keister. 1953 in Wepman et al. *The Life* 119: You can shove that...up your kiester. 1963 D. Tracy *Brass Ring* 299: They must have given it to him right up the keister and then broken it off. 1970 *Adam-12* (NBC-TV): He nails me with a left and I fall down on my keister. 1971 Sorrentino *Up from Never* 117: Kee-rist what a keesta. 1971 Dahlskog *Dict.* 35: *Keester, keister, kiester*...vulgar, the anus. 1974 Terkel *Working* 229: I told him, "Stick it in your keester." 1978 C. Miller *Animal House* 58: Oh, God, thought Bluto, I'd like to juice *her* keisters. 1983 *ABC World News* (ABC-TV) (Jan. 10): A newspaper quoted...President [Reagan] as saying, "I've had it up to my keister with these [news] leaks."

b. copulation with a woman or (*Pris.*) anal copulation, as with a catamite.—usu. considered vulgar.

*ca*1935 in Holt *Dirty Comics* 51: I'd like to buy a little of your kiester if we could get it over with before my wife gets back from the store. 1942–49 Goldin et al. *DAUL* 114: *Keister bandit* 1. An active homosexual...2... A seducer or rapist. 1968 Gover *JC* 88: I better troll the bottom, put some keyster in his way, see can I stir up what he's freaky for.

c. one's body; self. Cf. syn. ASS.

1968 Brasselle *Cannibals* 166: Get your cute little kiester *in* here. 1974 Wilder & Diamond *Front Page* (film): Get your keister outta here. 1981 *Hill St. Blues* (NBC-TV): He'll eighty-six your keister. 1985 C. Busch *Times Sq. Angel* 69: Milton! Georgie! Get your keysters in here! **1991** *Murphy Brown* (CBS-TV): You get your little keister right over here.

keister *v.* Esp. *Pris.* to hide in the rectum; SLAM.

[**1942** *ATS* 478: *Keyster plant,* narcotics concealed in the rectum.] **1987** E. McBain *Poison* 168: With the money, Marilyn bought clothing, blankets, and a mattress, and was able to keester the remainder for the purchase of food. It was Belita who taught her to put the money inside a condom…and slide it up into her rectum. **1993** K. Scott *Monster* 324: "Man, where you get that [*sc.* a knife]?" "I keistered it and brought it from L.A. County Jail."

kelly *n.* [prob. sugg. by *derby* 'hat' with ref. to Eng. rhyming slang *Derby Kelly* 'belly'] a man's hat, usu. a derby or straw hat; usu. in phr. **iron** or **tin kelly** *Mil.* a steel helmet.

1908 T.A. Dorgan, in Zwilling *TAD Lexicon* 51: Hey, douse the kelly. I can't see third [base] at all. **1909** T.A. Dorgan, in *N.Y. Eve. Jour.* (Jan. 19) 14: Every one of them is…looking at the man in the funny kelly. **1910** T.A. Dorgan, in *N.Y. Eve. Jour.* (Jan. 10) 12: Monocle, English kelly, fur coat, and a lot of junk. **1918** Witwer *Baseball to Boches* 78: All them birds takes off their Kellys. **1919** Murrin *With the 112th* 54: Each aspiring youngster got his "tin kelly," or steel helmet. **1920** in Hemingway *Dateline: Toronto* 14: The old kelly will have to do another season. **1923** *Nashville* (Tenn.) *Banner* (Jan. 13) 10: Cap' Huston's old iron kelly is back in the…ring. **1928** Havlin *Co. A* 33: The "steel kellys" proved…useful. **1929** L. Thomas *Woodfill* 246: We certainly doffed our tin kellys to the Heinies for their thoroughness. **1935** Pollock *Und. Speaks*: Kelly, a derby. **1942** *Leatherneck* (Nov.) 147: *Iron Kelly*—steel helmet…Also [called] *tin derby.* **1951** Algren *Chicago* 114: Rolling the summer's last straw kelly across second into center. **1953** Paul *Wayland* 61: The homburg he brushed gently…and said, "Now there's a proper Kelly." **1958–59** Lipton *Barbarians* 275: I had to…invest a buck fifty in a straw kelly. **1972** *Playboy* (Feb.) 76: I supervised a super Sinclair Station wearing a J.B. Stetson hat. Never a yellow kelly.

Kelsey *n.* [fr. *Kelsey*, Eng. family name; perh. orig. alluding (with pun on slang NUT 'testicle') to the permanence of welded nuts and bolts on wheels manufactured by the Kelsey Wheel Co., prominent in the U.S. automotive industry in the 1920's; see P. Tamony, "Like Kelsey's Nuts…," *Forum Anglicum* XIV (1985), pp. 120–23] ¶ In phrase: **Kelsey's nuts** (used in vulgar similes).

[**1933** in *Forum Anglicum* XIV (1985) 121: So the town is deader'n Kelseys so far as sportin' is concerned.] [**1947** in *Forum Anglicum* XIV (1985) 121: Colder than the late Mr. Kelsey's knuckles.] *a*1955 in D. Maurer *Lang. Underworld* 251: *Safe as Kelsey…*Euphemism for "safe as Kelsey's nuts." **1954–60** *DAS*: *Tight as Kelsey's nuts…*Very stingy or parsimonious. **1961** Brosnan *Pennant Race* 91: "We don't have any more life than Hogan's goat."…"We're deader than Kelsey's nuts." **1965** Di Donato *Naked and Dead* 98: Left side paralyzed.…arm and leg dead as Kelsey's nuts. **1966** IUFA *Folk Speech* (Apr. 7): As dead as Kelsie's nuts. **1967** G. Green *To Brooklyn* 104 [ref. to 1930's]: Your colleagues…will shortly be pronounced…deader than Kelsey's nuts. **1970** Thackray *Thief* 286: If I ever saw either one of them again—anywhere, anytime—they had my bound promise to kill them deader than Kelsey's nuts! **1979** McGivern *Soldiers* 169 [ref. to WWII]: "What about the radio?" "They got one all right, but it's dead as Kelsey's nuts." **1980** Gould *Ft. Apache* 211: Advancement in the department can't be it, because, Sonny, you're about as dead as Kelsey's nuts, as far as that goes. **1980** S. Fuller *Big Red* 77: Other GIs have tried and are now deader than Kelsey's nuts. **1980** J. Ciardi *Browser's Dict.* 218: *Dead (cold) as Kelsey's nuts…*very dead (cold) indeed. **1981** Ehrlichman *Witness to Power* 19: As [Richard Nixon] was fond of saying, politically he was "as dead as Kelsey's nuts." *a*1982 in Berry *Semper Fi* 191 [ref. to WWII]: For instance, who was Mr. Kelsey and why were his nuts any colder (or deader) than those of any other person? **1982** in *Forum Anglicum* XIV (1985) 120: Like Kelsey's nuts, they're always together. Tight as Kelsey's nuts. Deader than Kelsey's nuts.

kelsey¹ *n.* [orig. unkn.] *Carnival.* a prostitute.

1935 *Amer. Mercury* (June) 230: *Kelsy:* a broad on a cash basis.

kelsey² *n.* [app. var. of KELT] **1.** see KELT.

2. *Black E.* (see quot.).

1976 Wepman et al. *The Life* 184: *Kelsey n* straight hair style formerly popular among black prostitutes.

kelt *n.* [orig. unkn.; often confused (app. by proofreaders) with *Celt,* but relation to *Celt* is unlikely on var. phonetic grounds] *Black E.* a white person, esp. a woman; in phr. **half-** [or **three-quarter**] **kelt** a very light-skinned black person, esp. a woman. Also **kelch, keltz, kelsey.**

1912 in *OED2*: That kelch! **1928** C. McKay *Banjo* 107: But I'm different from you. I haven't any appreciation at all for the kelts. *Ibid.* 217: "Kelt" I picked up in Marseilles.…I don't know if it has anything to do with "keltic." **1929** in *AS* (Dec. 1930) 158: *Kelt* means a white person. **1932** in *AS* (Feb. 1934) 27: *Three-quarter kelt.* A light-skinned Negro. **1938** *AS* (Apr.) 151: *Celt* [*sic*]. Nordic woman, blond or brunette, but never one whose skin is swarthy. Lincoln Univ. only. *Three-quarters Celt.* Technically a quadroon, a very near-white negro. **1938** in Himes *Black on Black* 173: And then he met a high-yellah gal, a three-quarter keltz, from down Harlem way, and she sent him to the dogs. **1942** *ATS* 358: White person…*kelt, kelth.* **1964** in B. Jackson *Swim Like Me* 146: Now there was Light-Haired Nell, French Estelle,/they was both three-quarter Kelsey to the bone. **1970** Major *Dict. Afro-Amer. Sl.* 73: *Kelt, keltch:* white person; Negro passing for white. *a*1971 in *West. Folk.* XXXIII (1974) 292: Now this bitch was three-quarter Kelsey. **1994** Calt *Rather Be Devil* 69: She was the product of a mixed marriage, or what James [in 1964–69] termed "half-Celt [*sic*]," and was considered attractive by virtue of her light complexion and acqualine [*sic*] nose.

kemo sabe *n.* [introduced on *The Lone Ranger,* the radio and television series created by George Trendle (radio premiere Jan. 30, 1933 in Schenectady, N.Y.) as a term from the Native American language supposedly spoken by Tonto, the Lone Ranger's "faithful Indian companion"] friend.—used in direct address. Usu. *joc.* Also vars.

1933 G. Trendle, in J. Dunning *Tune in Yesterday* 368: "Your name is Tonto."…"You remember." "Years ago you called me 'kemo sabe.'" "That right. And you still kemo sabe. It mean 'faithful friend.'" **1949** *Lone Ranger* (ABC-TV): You kemo sabe.…That mean "trusty scout." **1949** *Lone Ranger* (ABC-TV): Me wait, kemo sabe. **1954** *Lone Ranger* (ABC-TV): Kemo sabe, if you join gang, how we keep in touch? **1955** *Lone Ranger* (synd. TV series): Yes, kemo sabe. **1958** Frede *Entry E* 14: Sure thing, old Red, old hombre, old keemosabe. **1980** Grizzard *Billy Bob Bailey* 97: It's no big thing, *Kemo Sabe.* **1976–83** Glimm *Flatlanders* 128: Kimosavy. **1983** R.C. Mason *Chickenhawk* 408: That's it, kimo sabe. **1987** Weiser & Stone *Wall St.* (film): So what's on your mind, kemo sabe? **1988** *Teenage Mutant Ninja Turtles* (TV): Au contraire, kemo sabe! *a*1989 in Safire *Coming to Terms* 334: Tonto referred to him as "kemo sabe." **1993** *Mystery Sci. Theater* (Comedy Central TV): You're starting to catch on, kemo sabe. **1995** *Critic* (Fox TV): Bad news, kemo sabe. **1995** *Reader's Digest* (Aug.) 113: No More Kemo Sabe.

kemp *n.* [orig. unkn.] Esp. *West Coast.* an automobile. Also **kimp.**

1951–53 in *AS* XXIX (1954) 99: Let's take your kemp to the beach. **1958** Meltzer & Blees *H.S. Confidential* (film): I'll give you a ride in a real kemp. **1959** Zugsmith *Beat Generation* 63: Hop in my kemp and let's take off for the casbah. **1971–72** in Abernethy *Bounty of Texas* 208: *Kimp, n.*—a car (1950s).

ken *n.* [orig. unkn.] *Und.* a house or business establishment. *Rare* in U.S. Often in combs. See also BOOZING KEN.

*1567 in *OED*: A ken, a house. *Ibid.:* Yander is the kene. **1673* [R. Head] *Canting Academy* 40: Ken An house. **1725 New Canting Dict.:* Burnt the Ken, when Strollers leave the Ale-house without paying their Quarters. **1789* G. Parker *Life's Painter* 136: Till from this *ken* we go. *Ibid.* 158: Ken. Is a house. **1812* Vaux *Vocab.:* Ken: a house; often joined to other descriptive terms, as, a *flash-ken,* a *bawdy-ken,* &c. **1851* H. Mayhew *London Labour* I 217: After some altercation with the "mot" of the "ken." *Ibid.* 351: Up she goes to any likely ken…and commences begging. **1859** Matsell *Vocab.* 48: Ken. A house. *Ibid.* 99: I kidded a swell in a snoozing-ken. **1872** Burnham *Secret Service* vi: Ken.—a house, or booth, or small hotel for criminals. **1875* in Ribton-Turner *Vagrants* 644: A quack who was lodging at the same "ken" with me. **1936* in Partridge *Dict. Und.* 379: Rolling up to his mort's ken with a bunch of violets. **1961* in P. Kennedy *Folksongs of Britain & Ireland* 770: Far frae my mither's ken.…Far from my mother's house.

kennel *n. Army.* a PUP TENT; DOG KENNEL.

1864 in *Kans. Hist. Qly.* VII (1938) 7: Build fire before our "kennel."

keno *interj.* [orig. uttered in the game of *keno* to announce a winning row of numbers; cf. BINGO] (used to express enthusiasm, excitement, or success).

1839–40 Cobb *Green Hand* II 153 [ref. to 1815]: If a rush was made…or a quick gathering for whatever purpose…their watch word "keno!" was sung out by some one near by, "keno!" was taken up by the next, "keno!" was answered from afar. [**1868** in *DA:* When they thus got three beans in a row they were to call out "Keno!" and rake in the pot.] **1889** in Davidson *Old West* 81: Shake yer spurs and make 'em rattle!/Keno! Promenade to seats. **1890** in *DARE* [ref. to *ca*1845]: In the death scene, just as *Richard* expired, a voice, signifying that the game was over, shouted "Keno!" **1905** Hobart *Get Next!* 64: Keno!…Right again! **1913–15** Van Loan *Taking the Count* 192: "Keno!" cried Joe. **1936** Adams *Cowboy* 230: The conquering of a horse, the throwing of a steer, anything might evoke "keno!" **1958** S.H. Adams *Tenderloin* 94 [ref. to 1890's]: Keno! I getcha!

Kentuck *n.* a Kentuckian. Now *hist.* Also **Kaintuck.**

1824 in Nevins & Weitenkampf *Cartoons* 33: Your old Kentuck's come to a standstill. **1826** T. Flint *Recoll.* 15: You learn the received opinion, that a "Kentuck" is the best man at a pole. **1852** in *DAE:* "And you waded in like a raal Kaintuck," rejoined Nine-Eyes. **1856** in *DA:* Them heathenish Kentucks & niggers. **1864** in O.J. Hopkins *Under the Flag* 25: One Kentuck stumbled upon a whiskey-still in full blast. **1942** in Wentworth *Amer. Dial. Dict.* 338: The Kaintucks were spared a feud with the N.Y.C. police. **1946** in *DARE:* The Creoles called them Kaintocks on the assumption that they were all from Kentucky.

Kentucky bite *n.* a tearing bite on the ear or nose while fighting.

1849 Melville *White Jacket* 108: *Kentucky bites* were given.

Kentucky breakfast *n.* (see quots.). *Joc.*

1882 *Century Mag.* (Apr.) 884: A simple Kentucky breakfast—"three cocktails and a chaw of terbacker." **1907** S.E. White *Ariz. Nights* 82: [The bartender] staked me to a Kentucky breakfast. What's a Kentucky breakfast?…a three-pound steak, a bottle of whisky, and a setter dog. What's the dog for? Why, to eat the steak. **1934** *Louisville & Nashville* (Dec.) 28: Bring me a Kentucky breakfast….A bull dog, a sirloin steak and a quart of bourbon whiskey, [the dog to eat the steak]. **1968** in *DARE:* A "Kentucky Breakfast," the ingredients of which are a bottle of bourbon, a beefsteak, and a dog. The dog, of course, is to eat the beefsteak.

Kentucky mule see s.v. MULE.

Kentucky pill *n. Hunting.* a bullet. *Joc.*

1861 in Thornton *Amer. Gloss.* I 511: Phillips gave him a Kentucky pill, and brought the wasps about our ears. **1932** in *DARE:* It is rather common in the southern part of West Virginia to hear mention of "Kentucky pills."

Kentucky sunshine *n.* strong liquor, esp. bourbon. *Joc.*

1930 Nason *Corporal* 132: Well, here's a lil Kentucky sunshine.

Kentucky windage *n.* **1.** *Shooting.* allowance made for the effects of wind or other conditions upon the accuracy of a shot, orig. with a rifle.—also used fig.

1945 *AS* (Oct.) 238: "Kentucky windage," in rifle parlance, means aiming to one side of what is shot at, to allow for the wind or an inaccurate rifle. Real "windage," of course, refers to an adjustment of the rear sight. **1957** A.K. Moore *Frontier Mind* 83: A term familiar to U.S. Army parlance, *Kentucky windage,* acknowledges even yet the uncanny ability of these backwoodsmen to make offhand allowance for cross winds. **1961** *Twilight Zone* (CBS-TV): Is this a scientific analysis…or just some Kentucky windage? **1977** R.S. Parker *Effective Decision* 5: The experienced marksman…compensates for this by taking "Kentucky windage," or changing the sights on his rifle to correspond to realistic conditions. **1987** E. Spencer *Macho Man* 73: *Kentucky windage* refers to flintlock rifles, which had…non-adjustable sights. When a cross-wind was blowing, you allowed for it with an inspired guess. **1987** Averill *Mustang* 16: How to apply leads—Kentucky windage they used to call it. **1987** D. da Cruz *Boot* 301: *Kentucky windage* adjusting (rifle) aiming point by intuition. *a***1989** C.S. Crawford *Four Deuces* 121: Then I added some "Kentucky windage." **1990** Ruggero *38 N. Yankee* 172: The sight must be off. I'll use some Kentucky windage. **1991** Linnekin *80 Knots* 87: Using some variant of…"Kentucky windage."

2. KENTUCKY SUNSHINE.

1986 Dye & Stone *Platoon* 87: How about a gust of Kentucky Windage, El-tee?

keptie *n.* a kept woman; mistress.

1931–34 in Clemmer *Pris. Community* 333: *Keptee,* n. A kept woman. **1948** Lait & Mortimer *New York* 51: Park Avenue…has taken up where Riverside Drive left off, as the place to hole up your "keptie." **1966** "Petronius" *N.Y. Unexpurgated* 22: Girls include kepties and divorcées.

kerflooey *interj.* [*ker-* (emphatic prefix; see *DARE*) + FLOOEY] (used to indicate the sound of an explosion); in phr. **go kerflooey** to break down completely; go utterly amiss; become chaotic. Also **kaflooey, kablooey.** Also as adj.

1918 in Rossano *Price of Honor* 160: Voilà! The chance to be a hero gone caflooey! **1924** in Clarke *Amer. Negro Stories* 29: Then the whole scheme would go gaflooey. **1926** (quot. at FADE-OUT, 1.). **1927** H. Miller *Moloch* 22: The whole place went kerflooey. **1939** Farrell *To Whom It May Concern* 178: He had a hat store out in Flushing and he was doing good, and then with bad times it went kerflooie, and he's out on his ear now. **1977–81** S. King *Cujo* 133: Guess it's still kerflooey. **1985** *Newsweek* (Apr. 22) 83: So here it comes and, kerflooey, the newspaper critics gag, retch, and guffaw. *a***1986** in *NDAS:* Will I make it…without the air conditioner in the car going kablooey. **1986** Thacker *Pawn* 81: Mines. Kablooey! **1990** N.Y.C. woman, age *ca*50: Before everything goes kaflooey. **1994** *Time Trax* (synd. TV series) I'll *never* forget that explosion! Kablooey! **1995** *Hercules* (synd. TV series): Hercules unleashes his mighty right hand! Kablooey!

kerflummix *adv.* [*ker-* (emphatic prefix) + *flummix,* var. FLUMMOX] with a thump or crash. Also vars.

*ca***1849** in *DAE:* Down you come ker-flummox. **1855** *Spirit of Times* (Sept. 29) 387: Down he comes kerflumix. *****1890** in *EDD:* He come down curflummox. **1908** in *DN* III 326: He fell *kerflummux* off the bench.

kerflummix *v.* **1.** to confound, flabbergast, bewilder, discomfit, etc.; FLUMMOX. Also vars.

1867 in *Iowa Jour. of Hist.* LVII (1959) 227: Teetotally "kerflumixed" with emotion. **1883** Peck *Bad Boy* 119: It kerflummixed Ma when I went into the dining-room the first night that I got home from the store, and broke Pa all up. **1884** Beard *Bristling* 10: "Captured!" … "Keflumexed!" "Wallopped!" "Took! Burned!" **1888** Nye & Riley *Railway Guide* 4: You've got him clean kaflummixed, and you want to hold him there! **1900** Hammond *Whaler* 44: Ye-ah, an' git kerflummoxt all over the deck fer 'is pains. **1905** *DN* III 62: *Kerflummux, v.* Bewilder, daze.

2. to fall heavily or noisily; drop. Also vars.

1877 Wheeler *Deadwood Dick, Prince of the Road* 81: When a feller kerflummuxes rite down onter a payin' streek I opine he's goin' ter roost thar till he gits reddy to vamoose. **1887** J. Nichols *Hear My Horn* 152: He fell down kerflumix. **1897** in *DAE:* I went a kerflummuxin' daown yunder through the bushes. **1906** in *DN* III 143: He *kerflummuxed* on the ice.

keskydee var. KISKEEDEE.

ketchup *n.* blood. *Joc.*

1942–49 Goldin et al. *DAUL* 114: *Ketchup-hounds.* Bloodhounds. **1976** C.R. Anderson *Grunts* 64 [ref. to 1969]: The redder they get the redder the ketchup flows and then they don't say ouch any more.

kettle *n.* **1.a.** a steam engine or boiler.

1828 in N. Cohen *Long Steel Rail* 39: And while the kettle boils/We will ride three hundred miles. **1866** in *Nebr. Hist.* XLVI (1965) 308: Our captain…intends to "keep the 'inside-track' if the kettles…hold together." **1897** Hamblen *General Mgr.* 181: He had been right with me ever since we left Chicago, the day before, shovelling fine feed into the old kettle. **1958** McCulloch *Woods Wds.* 101: Kettle—Most any steam equipment, a donkey or locie or other engine, especially if it leaked steam.

b. *Naut.* a steamship; (*also*) an iron or ironclad vessel. Now *hist.*

1863 in Gibbons *Tales That Were Told* 77: It surely must arouse their mettle/To view this tame inglorious work—/Bombarding Sumter from a kettle! *****a***1889** in Barrère & Leland *Dict. Slang* I 517: The…ludicrous plan of applying "poultices" to their *kettles* is now being tested. *a***1961** R.H. Dillon *Shanghaiing Days* 27: All the world hailed the seagoing "kettles."

c. *R.R.* a steam locomotive.

> **1934** in Fenner *Throttle* 81: And the old kettle…couldn't put the hat off your head. **1945** Hubbard *R.R. Ave.* 124: I used to pull the throttle on that old kettle.

2. *pl. Army.* artillery shells.

> **1863** in O.J. Hopkins *Under the Flag* 65: Artillery … came into position … to throw "pots and kettles" into their works. [**1864** in Hicken *Ill. in Civil War* 270: [The Confederate shells at night resemble] camp Kettles.]

3. Esp. *Und.* a pocket watch.

> *a***1889** in Barrère & Leland *Dict. Slang* I 517: Two *red kettles* a week will bring in about four pounds. ***1889** *Ibid.* 516: *Kettle* (thieves), a watch; *red kettle*, gold watch. **1902** Townsend *Fadden & Mr. Paul* 98: Hully chee!…De copper tinks I swiped de kettle. **1904** *Life in Sing Sing* 250: *Kettle.* A watch. **1906** H. Green *Boarding House* 86: I ain't got no use fur a dame what can't even stall while a guy gits off a kettle. **1916** *Literary Digest* (Aug. 19) 53: A watch…may be called…a "turnip," or a "kettle." **1919** I. Cobb *Life of Party* 21: "Say, where've you got yore leather and your kittle hid?"…"I'm—I'm—not carrying a watch or a purse to-night."

¶ In phrase:

¶ **too hot for (one's) kettle** too frightening or dangerous to put up with.

> **1982** "W.T. Tyler" *Rogue's March* 142: And when it got too hot for your kettle [you'd] come crawling back for…a good lawyer.

kettle *v.* (esp. of a horse) to become or cause to become frightened or unnerved; RATTLE.

> **1925** Nason *Sgt. of Cavalry* 39 [ref. to 1918]: "Now," muttered Nell to himself, "if we don't get kettled we ought to be able to get out of this place." **1926** W. James *Smoky* 40: Maybe a rider had been spotted that morning which had kettled 'em into a run. *Ibid.* 65: He…kettled 'em into a stampede. *Ibid.* 142: Whenever he felt like "kettling" the most, Clint's hand and voice was there to quiet him down. **1933** Nason *Among the Trumpets* 127 [ref. to 1918]: Keep your head! Don't get kettled! Compree? Follow me!

kettlebelly *n.* a fat-bellied person. Hence **kettle-bellied**, *adj.*

> **1878** Hart *Sazerac* 87: Kettle-belly Brown. **1895** Townsend *Fadden Explains* 231: "Kettlebelly," we called him. **1928** Bodenheim *Georgie May* 4: These kettle-bellied, rancidly kind owners of the earth.

kettle jockey *n. Naut.* a cook. *Joc.*

> **1969** Hardy *Ship Called Fat Lady* 85 [ref. to 1941]: Look, you're the number one kettle jockey on this old bucket.

kettle of fish *n.* an awkward or complicated state of affairs. Now *colloq.*

> ***1742** Fielding, in *OED2*: Here's a pretty kettle of fish. ***1749** Fielding, in *OED2*: Fine doings at my hose! A rare kettle of fish I have discovered at last. **1807** W. Irving *Salmagundi* 170: O, what a fine kettle of fish. ***1811** *Lexicon Balatron.*: When a person has perplexed his affairs in general, or any particular business, he is said to have made a fine kettle of fish of it. **1837** J.C. Neal *Charc. Sks.* 29: A whole "kettle of fish" was in preparation. **1838** [Haliburton] *Clockmaker* (Ser. 2) 45: A pretty kettle of fish he's made of it. **1862** in McClellan *Civil War Papers* 358: This was a pretty kettle of fish! **1895** *Harper's* (June) 152: What a kettle of fish this is, to be sure! **1940** in T. Williams *Letters* 13: Wouldn't it be a beautiful kettle of fish if they had abruptly decided to…leave me stranded down here. **1981** D. Burns *Feeling Good* 164: Well! That's a fine kettle of fish! **1982** Eldredge *Monkey Business* 96: The *other* meaning of uniformitarianism, however, is another kettle of fish entirely. **1994** *CNN & Co.* (CNN-TV) (Sept. 13): That's a whole other kettle of fish.

Kettles *n. Naut.* (a nickname for) the engineer of a steamboat.

> **1855** [S. Hammett] *Capt. Priest* 87: You must be a nice fellow to trust Mr. "Kettles," to get drunk before sunrise. *Ibid.* 88: Look here, old "Kettles," hold on a bit.

key[1] *n.* [fr. < *ki*logram] Orig. *Narc.* a kilogram, esp. of illicit drugs. Also **ki, kee.**

> **1966** (cited in Spears *Drugs & Drink* 299). **1968** *Rolling Stone* (Oct. 18) 5: Two "keys" of grass. **1968** Carey *College Drug Scene* 87: Her big thing was that the person who brought the five Ki's to her said, "you're out of your mind—you'll never get rid of it." **1970** Cortina *Slain Warrior* 8: Why don't you take these five keys and get rid of them for me and I'll cut you a nice piece of bread. **1975** V.B. Miller

Trade-Off 6: Maybe you ought to know that kilo, or "kee," is short for kilogram. **1983** T. Page *Nam* 17: After the endless plod humping 20 keys of gear. **1983** O. Stone *Scarface* (film): Here's the stuff—two keys. **1994** *Walker: Texas Ranger* (CBS-TV): Three keys of smack. **1995** Slavsky, Mozeson & Mozeson *A 2 Z* 59: I was riding around with ten *keys* in my trunk.

key[2] *n. Basketball.* KEYHOLE.

> **1977** *Webster's Sports Dict.* **1979** *Texas Monthly* (Sept.) 150: Any player from either team grabs a ball, walks to the top of the key, and fires a shot. **1987** *Time* (July 6) 13: I favor a jump shot from the top of the key. **1994** *N.Y. Times Mag.* (Apr. 17) 33: Suddenly, he hits a three-pointer from the left corner; another from the right corner; a third from the top of the key.

key *adj.* [development of S.E. (orig. prenominal) sense 'absolutely essential'] Orig. *Stu.* superlative.—used predicatively.

> [**1980** Birnbach et al. *Preppy Handbk.* 220: *Key*…Crucial, especially to being Prep.…"Webbed belts are key."] **1984** Mason & Rheingold *Slanguage*: *Key* adj. Anything excellent.…"That brand new Porsche is key." **1989** P. Munro *U.C.L.A. Slang* 54: *Key*…good. **1991** B.E. Ellis *Amer. Psycho* 387: Oh that's bloody marvelous. Really key.

keyhole *n. Basketball.* the area at either end of the court consisting of the free-throw lane and the restraining circle.

> **1949** Cummings *Dict. Sports* 236. **1977** *Webster's Sports Dict.* **1982** Considine *Lang. Sport* 68.

keyster var. KEISTER.

keystone *n.* [alluding to the *Keystone Kops*, motion-picture comedy ensemble created by "Mack Sennett" [1884–1960; pseud. of Michael Sinnott] of Keystone Studios in 1912] a foolish or incompetent local police officer. In full, **keystone cop** [or **kop**].

> **1929** *Sat. Eve. Post* (Apr. 13) 54: A detective is…a *keystone* or…the law. **1935** Pollock *Und. Speaks* 66: *Keystone*, a special, uniformed police officer. **1942–49** Goldin et al. *DAUL* 114: *Keystone cop.* A small-town or curiously uniformed private policeman. **1956** "T. Betts" *Across the Board* 156: O'Grady…led task forces of keystone kops, taking movies in the clubhouse. **1968** Radano *Walking the Beat* 173: We got to wait until the Keystones leave. **1984** Knoxville, Tenn., attorney, age *ca*30: So the keystones show up and block off just one exit and the guy escapes.

key-winder *n.* (see quot.). *Joc.*

> **1916** Cary *Venery* I 165: *Key Winder*—A girl…*Stem Winder*—A boy.

KG *n.* Orig. *Police.* a known gambler.

> **1972** J. Mills *Report* 14: *KG* known gambler, files on whom are maintained at the precinct level. **1984** Caunitz *Police Plaza* 209: A KG—Known Gambler—wanted to buy them a drink.

khaki *n. Navy.* a commissioned officer or chief petty officer. —also used collect. Also **khak.**

> *a***1990** Poyer *The Med* 369: The fucking khaki can't see us down here. **1995** Former U.S. Navy submariner, Knoxville, Tenn. [ref. to early 1980's]: *Khakis* or *khaks*: officers or CPOs; *khak attack*: group of the above approaching.

khaki-wacky *adj.* (of a young woman) enamored of military servicemen. *Joc.* Now *hist.* [Quots. ref. to WWII.]

> **1944** *Slanguage Dict.* 60: *Khaki-wacky*—crazy for the Oliver Drabs; in other words, uniform nuts. **1984** J. Dailey *Silver Wings* 164: Khaki-wacky, they call it.…Some of these young [girls] go crazy over anyone in uniform. **1985** Westin *Love & Glory* 27: Less than one day in this women's army and already you're khaki-wacky and man-starved.

ki var. KEY[1], *n.*

KIA Travel Bureau *n.* [fr. *K*illed *I*n *A*ction, standard mil. initialism] *Mil.* units responsible for the transport of corpses for burial. *Joc.* [Quots. ref. to Vietnam War.]

> **1968–77** Herr *Dispatches* 23: The real substance of the ceremony was being bagged and tagged and shipped back home through what they called the KIA Travel Bureau. **1981–89** R. Atkinson *Long Gray Line* 252: The living sometimes sat on body bags in the crowded Chinook bays, joking bleakly about…"the KIA Travel Bureau."

kibbets *v.* [< Yid. *kibeyts* 'to gather'] (see quot.).

> **1922** *N.Y. Times* (June 4) 6: If the merchant has not the ready money he will say, "I'll kibbets it." This means that he will form a syndicate of small capitalists who will jointly furnish the money needed.

kibitz *n.* **1.** unwanted talk or advice; remark. Also **kabitz.**

    1930 *Amer. Mercury* (Dec. 12) 456: *Kabitz,* n.: Unwanted advice. "Ixnay on the kabitz, get me?" **1935** Odets *Paradise Lost* 200: Don't gimme no kibitz. **1959** Maier *College Terms* 2: *Kabitz*—talk. **1968** Brasselle *Cannibals* 145: I winked at Winant, who by now was on to my *kibitzes.*

2. a gossipy chat.

    1970 Feinsilver *Taste of Yiddish* 320: It's sometimes heard as a noun, as in "a good kibitz."

kibitz *v.* [either back formation fr. KIBITZER or directly < Yid *kibitser* (G *Kiebitzer*), agential form of *kibetsn* (G *kiebitzen*); see KIBITZER] **1.a.** *Intrans.* to look on at a game of cards, chess, etc., and make critical or distracting comments or offer unwanted advice; (*hence*) to give unwanted advice in a meddlesome way. Now *colloq.*

    1927 in *AS* IV (1928) 159: Kibitzing. **1930** Benchley *Chips* 52: By "watching" is not meant "kibitzing." **1932** *AS* VII (June) 333: *Kibitz*—v.—to give unwanted advice. **1933** Odets *Awake & Sing* 51: For Chris' sake, don't kibitz so much! **1932–34** Minehan *Boy & Girl Tramps* 13: Four play rummy…while another four kibitz. **1935** Lorimer & Lorimer *Heart Specialist* 73: Boyd had appointed himself head cook and Sylvia, Marge and Elsie were having a fine time kibitzing. **1935** Kreymborg *Queen's Gambit* 11: Your talk was always a treat—…Providing you didn't kibitz. Dietz. What is a kibitzer for? **1947** T. Williams *Streetcar Named Desire* 63: Poker is so fascinating. Could I kibitz? **1951** Morris *China Station* 171: The Chief and I, we got an acey-deucy game. You're welcome to kibitz. **1977** Lieb *Baseball* 101: I wasn't in the [poker] game, just kibitzing in back of them. **1991** *True Colors* (Fox-TV): Can I just kibitz?

b. *Trans.* to watch or examine (a game, a participant, etc.) and give unwanted advice or make distracting or critical comments; criticize.

    1941 in C.R. Bond & T. Anderson *Flying T. Diary* 49: Bob Prescott and John J. "Five-Star" Hennessy took it upon themselves to kibitz Pappy's antics in the great delight…of the gathering crowd of natives. **1942** *Word Study* (Feb.): A Devoted Reader Kibitzes the lexicographers. **1944** D. Runyon, in *Collier's* (Feb. 12) 70: Schultz kibitzes the captain on one hand and me on the next. **1946** J. Adams *Gags* 50: I "kibitzed" the card games. **1950** J. Wechsberg, in *New Yorker* (July 15) 32: Discussing Kafka and Rilke and kibitzing the *taroky* players. **1950** *Sat. Eve. Post* (Dec. 2) 131: Engineers from several air lines had kibitzed the airplane's design. **1961** *N.Y. Times* (Dec. 17) V 25: Stopping to join a conversation here, kibitz a card game there. **1974** E. Thompson *Tattoo* 41: They silently kibitzed the old men's domino games at the White Way Pool Hall. **1978** *Pop. Sci.* (Dec.) 80: Chess with an electronic adversary that's programmed to kibitz your wrong moves.

2. to chat or gossip.

    1930 G. Kahn & W. Donaldson *My Baby Just Cares for Me* (sheet music) (N.Y.: Bregman, Vocco & Conn, Inc.) 3: She don't like a voice like Lawrence Tibbett's,/She'd rather have me around to kibitz. **1939** Bessie *Men in Battle* 185: So we kibitzed the time away, had political arguments and sang. **1939** I. Baird *Waste Heritage* 182: Coming over to kibitz casually. **1952** *N.Y. Times* (May 18) VI 59: You've seen me standing out on the bally kibitzing with the customers. **1969** *Harper's* (Aug.) 51: I'd like to have Wilkinson in the room with Nixon before the show to kibitz around, get Nixon loose. **1970** in P. Heller *In This Corner* 68: We used to stay out around the stable at night…we used to sit down and talk, kibitz, you know. **1968–71** Cole & Black *Checking* 77: The store owner and the kids kibitz like a bunch of old Lower East Side Jews. **1978** R. Price *Ladies' Man* 140: I could greet him like a long-lost friend, kibitz, laugh, slip him his money and get down to work. **1987** B. Ford & C. Chase *Awakening* 123: She will spend hours in the coffee lounge kibitzing with patients. **1989** Horwitt *Call Me Rebel* 37: Alinsky would kibitz with them about mutual friends. **1996** *TV Guide* (Feb. 24) 14: Back on the sofa kibitzing with Bryant.

3.a. to annoy with unwanted talk or questions.

    1934 Appel *Brain Guy* 127: It's a detective 'n he wants to kibitz you boys. Sam and Joe first. Then Murray. **1971** I. Faust *Willy Remembers* 88: Through all our first night in Cuba, we were kibitzed by…Tracy Beecy…[of] the *Brooklyn Eagle.*

b. to cajole; speak in a cajoling or wheedling way.

    1943 Farrell *My Days of Anger* 386: "Well, watch your step if you want to stay in school. I'm not going to tell you again." "You don't

want to throw me out of school, now, Bobby." "Don't kibitz with me." **1957** Thornton *Teenage Werewolf* (film): Right now he challenges me. I tried to kibitz him out of it. **1965** *N.Y. Times* (Dec. 26) V 125: We're not trying to kibitz the Yankees from 52d Street.

4. to eavesdrop.

    1936 Cain *Double Indemnity* 401: Believe me, it's an awful thing to kibitz on a man and his wife, and hear what they really talk about.

kibitzer *n.* [< Yid *kibetser* (G *Kiebitzer*) < *kibetsn* < G (colloq. or slang) *kiebitzen* 'to be an onlooker at a game' < *Kiebitz* 'a plover or lapwing', in G slang usage (*a*1896) 'a meddlesome or annoying onlooker at a game'] **1.** a meddlesome onlooker, as at a game of cards, chess, etc.; one who intrudes with unwanted advice or annoying comments. Now *S.E.* Also, **kabitzer.** [Bracketed quots. are titles of Yiddish-language periodicals.]

    [**1908** *Kibezser* (N.Y.C.).] [**1919** *Kibetser* (Chicago).] **1922** T.A. Dorgan, in Zwilling *TAD Lexicon* 51: Trying to play pinochle with a flock of kibitzers standing behind your chair. **1925** (cited in *W10*). **1926** Dunning & Abbott *Broadway* 216: Ruby. How can we get it right if Miss Billie Moore don't take the trouble to come to rehearsals? *Roy.…*Hey, don't be a kibitzer. **1927** in *AS* IV (1928) 159: Kibitzers are out in full force at the [lighting] fixture shows.…Whether one gains a pleasant laugh, a worthwhile bit of information, or a grouch depends upon the kibitzer. **1927** *Vanity Fair* (Nov.) 134: A "kibitzer" is some one who watches card players and offers suggestions. **1928** R. Fisher *Jericho* 263: There would have been…less gentle hints about the value of fresh air to kibitzers. **1929** Bodenheim *60 Secs.* 231: Professional yes-men, embryo-eyed kibitzers, perverts trying not to reveal their spirits. **1929** in Perelman *Old Gang* 70: Hands Off! Mr. Kibetzer Warned the Circassian Mamma in Angry Tones. **1930** Irwin *Tramp & Und. Slang* 115: *Kabitzer.*—One who volunteers advice and who endeavours to conduct another's affairs. **1930** Benchley *Chips* 52: A kibitzer gets very close to whatever he is watching, usually a game of cards. **1934** Appel *Brain Guy* 174: Three young men were playing pinochle. Duffy watched as if he were happy to be official kibitzer. **1939** Appel *Power-House* 252: The players and half-dozen kibitzers laughed. **1942** Johnston *Queen of Flat-tops* 22: A kibitzer, of course, is one who peers over the shoulder of an active player in any game and contributes unhelpful suggestions.…A nibitzer is the lowest form of kibitzer. **1955** Post *Little War* 51: Once I saw a trooper reach for his knife, and a half-dozen kibitzers swarmed over him till he calmed down. *a*1973 E.G. Robinson & L. Spigelglass *All My Yesterdays* 97: The Summer of 1927 I was…doing a play in Atlantic City called *The Kibitzer*…by…Jo Swerling.

2. a person who meddles or clowns in order to attract attention; one who will not mind his or her own business.

    1947 Helseth *Martin Rome* 39: You'd think some kibitzer would have turned her in before now. **1942–49** Goldin et al. *DAUL* 115: *Kibitzer*…A convict who makes a nuisance of himself by playing pranks, or by being jovial at the expense of others. **1984** C. Francis *Who's Sorry?* 66 [ref. to 1950's]: Heh, heh, he's some kibbitzer, Miss Francis.…Some sense of humor, huh?

kibo var. KYBO.

kibosh *n.* /ˈkaɪbɑʃ/ or /kəˈbɑʃ/ [orig. unkn.; the sugg. that it derives fr. Yid or Heb is without foundation] **1.** an effectual stop or finishing action; usu. in phr. **put the kibosh on** to put a stop to; deliver a finishing stroke against; do for; quash, etc. Also **kybosh.** [The *-sk* sp. in the **a*1836 quot. is meant to repr. Cockney pron.]

    a*1836 in Dickens *Sketches* 70: "Hooroar," ejaculates a pot-boy in parenthesis, "put the kye-bosk [*sic*] on her, Mary!" ***1846 in *OEDS*: *Kybosh on, to put the,* to turn the tables on any person, to put out of countenance. **1881 Nye *Forty Liars* 130: The…imperial pie-biters of the realm…congregate on a special date and put the kibosh on the new czar. **1896** Wister *Red Men* 213: Put the kybosh on 'em. **1899** A.H. Lewis *Sandburrs* 284: Dinky Pete puts d' kybosh on d' notion. **1907** London *Road* 39: And all that time I was praying that the kid wouldn't wake up, come down out of the cab, and put the "kibosh" on me. **1908** McGaffey *Show Girl* 195: Them Senators…put the kibosh on that racetrack bill. **1922** *Variety* (Aug. 4) 8: Article 41 about puts the kibosh on every concession on the midway. **1927** in Sandburg *Good Morning* 16: Send 'em to the cleaners. Put the/kibosh on 'em so they'll never

come back. **1928** R.A. Bartlett *Log* 248: Don't you realize that this Polar game is all off? Cook put the ky-bosh on it. **1929** "C. Woolrich" *Times Sq.* 166: When are you going to put the kibosh on her?...Are you waiting for her to fold up and die of old age, or what? **1942** Garcia *Tough Trip* 436: This would put the kibosh on us good and plenty. **1942** Boucher *Werewolf* 36: All I'm trained for is academic work, and this scandal has put the kibosh on that forever. **1956** E. Hunter *Second Ending* 218: Well, the time machine had certainly put the old kibosh on the Milton exam. **1980** (N.Y.) *Daily News* (Dec. 20) 40: Ron Guidry's agent may have put the final kibosh on any Yankee deal involving his client for Fred Lynn. **1984** *N.Y. Post* (Aug. 3) 6: ICM president Jeffrey Berg has put the kibosh on [the] agreement. **1988** *It's Garry Shandling's Show* (Fox-TV): People all over the world are talking about how Sara gave you the kibosh on that romance. **1995** *World News Tonight* (ABC-TV) (Apr. 24): He believes he's gonna put the kibosh on [insufferable] talkers. **1996** *New Republic* (Feb. 26) 7: Why would anyone put the kibosh on such cuddly, popular legislation?

2. nonsense; humbug; BOSH; usu. in phr. **put the kibosh on** to fool or hoodwink.

1873 Hotten *Slang Dict.* (ed. 4): *Kibosh*, nonsense, stuff, humbug; "it's all *kibosh*," i.e. palaver or nonsense. *a1889* in Barrère & Leland *Dict. Slang* I 517: This is *kibosh* purtending to pass for a joke. **1891** Maitland *Slang Dict.* 158: To *put the kibosh on* one is to deceive him. [**1903** Ade *Society* 34: He was proud to be the Husband of the Lady Ki-Bosh of the Local Knickerbockers.] **1906** *DN* III 152: *Put the kibosh over*...To haze, play a joke on. "They *put the kibosh over* that poor fellow, all right." **1909** *WNID*: *Kibosh*...Nonsense; stuff. **1917–20** J.M. Hunter *Trail Drivers* I 40: I do not think there ever was a cow trail in Texas called the McCoy Trail....I think they are trying to put the "kibosh" on us.

3. fashion; style; mode.—constr. with *the*.

1880 *Puck* (Jan. 14) 728: Quite the Correct Ki-Bosh in Its Way. *a1889* *Century Dict.*: *Kibosh* (ki-bosh´)...Also *kybosh*...The form, manner, style, or fashion of something; the thing: as, that is the proper *kibosh*; full dress is the correct *kibosh* for the opera....[Slang.].

¶ In phrase:

¶ **on the kibosh** in a bad way, impaired, ruined, etc.

1873 Hotten *Slang Dict.* (ed. 4): To "put on the *kibosh*," to run down, slander, degrade, &c. **1919** in Cornebise *Amaroc News* 23: The A.E.F....put the Hun on the kibosh. **1929–33** Farrell *Young Manhood* 442: His heart is on the kibosh from that bum gin he'd been guzzling. **1952** Malamud *Natural* 105: A whole apparatus of physical and mental pleasures was on the kibosh.

kibosh *v.* to put a stop to; suppress; (in 1972 quot.) to hit squarely; CLOBBER. Also **kabosh.**

1884 in *OED2*: An' handed the pill that wid kibosh the fun. **1889** in Somers *Sports in N.O.* 173: Kilrain Kiboshed....Batter Blows that Bedizened the Brave Baltimore Boy. *1892* in *F & H* IV 95: A dig in the ribs.../Seemed to kibosh the Frenchman completely. **1952** *Sat. Eve. Post* (Sept. 27) 24: He wired Selznick in New York that Hudson warranted a screen test. Selznick irritably kiboshed it. **1972** M. Casey *Obscenities* 17: Yesterday they kaboshed him on the head.

kick *n.* **1.a.** fashion; style; mode; (*hence*) a novelty.—usu. constr. with *the*. Cf. **(6.f.),** below; perh. orig. short for *kick-shaw*. [Current use stems from **(6),** below.]

1698–99 "B.E." *Dict. Canting Crew: A high Kick*, the top of the Fashion; also singularity therein. *1715* in E. FitzGerald *Medley* 90: French Fashions reprobated, a Farewell to French Kicks [By a Doctor Harris]. *1785* Grose *Vulgar Tongue: Kick....It is all the kick*; it is the present mode. *1787* in *OED2*: I...twirled my stick....The girls all cry'd "He's quite the kick." *1804* in *OED2*: This [headdress] obtained the name of Nancy Dawson's new kick. *a1828* Jamieson *Scot. Dict.* III 25: *Kick*...A novelty; or something discovering vanity or singularity. *A new kick* is often used in this sense. **1833** J. Neal *Down-Easters* I 64: What do ye pay for sech a pair o' boots as them in Europ? Newest fashion there—all the kick I spose, hey? **1838** J.C. Beckell *Old Rosin the Beau* (sheet music) (Phila.: Osbourn's Music Saloon) 2: Some youngsters were panting for fashions/Some new kick seemed now all the go. *1869* E. FitzGerald *Medley* 90: Kick—"All the Kick," all the "Go," the Fashion. *1894* in *OED2*: Mrs. West naturally wanted "the last new kick." **1898** Green *Va. Folk Speech* 208: *Kick*, n. Fashion; novelty; thing in vogue: as "The latest *kick*." **1995** Boston teenager, on *CBS This Morning* (CBS-TV) (June 7): Marijuana was the kick last year.

b. the proper method or thing.—constr. with *the*. [Current use prob. stems from **(6),** below.]

1871 Banka *Pris. Life* 78: There, that's the kick, think you can do that? **1954** W.G. Smith *South Street* 286: That ain't the kick. You ought to try the real stuff. The needle.

2. a sixpence. *Rare* in U.S.

ca1700 in *OED2*: *Kick*, Sixpence. *1725* *New Canting Dict.*: *Kick, Six-pence: Two, Three, Four,* &c. *and a Kick; Two, Three, Four,* &c. *Shillings and Six-pence.* *1812* Vaux *Vocab.*: *Kick*, a sixpence, when speaking of compound sums only, as three and a kick, is three and six-pence. **1837** J.C. Neal *Charcoal Sks.* 173: I knows old Grimsings—he lent me a kick and a levy t'other day, and...I mean to stick up for him. *1851* H. Mayhew *London Labour* I 52: A bob and a kick. *1871* in *F & H* IV 96: Two-and-a-kick means half-a-crown.

3.a. *pl. Und.* breeches (*obs.*); trousers.

1698–99 "B.E." *Dict. Canting Crew: Tip us your Kicks, we'll have them as well as your Loure*...pull off your Breeches, for we must have them as well as your Money. *1819* [T. Moore] *Tom Crib* 13: Old Georgy's bang-up togs and kicks. **1848** *Ladies' Repository* VIII (Oct.) 315: *Kicks*, Pantaloons. **1851** [G. Thompson] *Jack Harold* 60: I got a pair of flash kicks....*Kicks*, pantaloons. **1871** Banka *Pris. Life* 492: *Pants...kicks.* **1965–71** in *Qly. Jour. Stud. Alcohol* XXXII (1971) 733: *Kicks...*Trousers.

b. *Orig. Und.* a trouser pocket where money is kept; a pocket in one's clothing; (*hence*) (*fig.*, now *usu.*) a supply of cash.

1846 *Lives of the Felons* 94: "Is that man a *gonnauf*, Charley?" "Yes, and one of the best at the *kick* (pantaloons pocket) in Paris!" *1851* H. Mayhew *London Labour* I 52: I having some ready in my kick, grabbed the chance, and stepped home with my swag, and am now safe landed at my crib. **1859** Matsell *Vocab.* 48: *Kick*. A pocket. "The Moll stubbled her skin in her kick," the woman held her purse in her pocket. *1864* in *Comments on Ety.* (Dec. 1993) 39: Taking the flask from my "kick," I took a pull at it. **1866** *Nat. Police Gaz.* (Nov. 3) 2: While the clerk is listening to her misfortune...she is "planting" some of his stock in her capacious "kick." **1891** DeVere *Tramp Poems* 78: Your overcoat "hocked," not a cent in your "kick." **1891** in F. Remington *Sel. Letters* 115: It will bring in dollars to your "kick." **1896** Ade *Artie* 64: He's gone right down into his kick and dug up the long green. **1902** Cullen *More Tales* 38: He had in every kick a bundle that 'ud trip a white wings. **1904** Hobart *Jim Hickey* 24: You say there's eighty cents in the kick? **1907** in H.C. Fisher *A. Mutt* 19: Mutt added 100 round bucks to the wad, making $503 in the kick. **1908** in H.C. Fisher *A. Mutt* 35: I should worry with a thousand in my kick. **1910** T.A. Dorgan, in *N.Y. Eve. Jour.* (May 4) 14: The roll is "in the kick." **1911–12** Ade *Knocking the Neighbors* 203: A Handy Boy...goes out and trims a Boob for everything in his Kick. **1914** in R. Lardner *Round Up* 256: He'd been in the World Serious and had plenty o' dough in his kick. **1915–16** Lait *Beef, Iron & Wine* 115: I got 40 cents jinglin' in my kick. **1926** Norwood *Other Side of Circus* 104: Got a route card in your kick? **1929–30** Farrell *Young Lonigan* 20: He had rented a buggy, even though it cut a terrible hole in his kick. **1935** O'Hara *Butterfield 8* 233: He had $23 and some change, he didn't know how much, in his kick right now. **1950** Blackburn *Raton Pass* 7: And there's a little money left in the kick. **1952** Bankhead *Tallulah* 200: I had $200,000 in my kick. **1955** Graziano & Barber *Somebody Up There* 276: When I retire from the ring with several Gs in my kick. **1983–89** K. Dunn *Geek Love* 98: The bastards got my kick, too.

c. *Und.* the practice of picking pockets.—constr. with *the*.

1846 *Nat. Police Gaz.* (Jan. 10) 162: Ah!...all you Philadelphy "mob" say you good at de "kick" eh!...If you want to know any ting about de "kick," you must go to France, sar!

d. usu. *pl.* a shoe.

1897 *Pop. Sci. Mo.* (Apr.) 832: A pair of shoes [are] a *pair of kicks.* **1899** Cullen *Tales* 105: Patent leather kicks, five dollar lids. **1902** "J. Flynt" *Little Bro.* 115: "A pair of shoes an' three dollars," Benny proudly replied, pointing with one hand to the new "kicks" on his feet. **1908** in H.C. Fisher *A. Mutt* 56: On his kicks were a pair of radiant spats. **1919** Amerine *Alabama's Own* 286: The shoes were...dry, so we'd empty out the ashes, put our "kicks" on and "fall in." **1927** Perelman *Old Gang* 27: Beige lizard kicks are being worn a good deal this season. **1929** Barr *Let Tomorrow Come* 267: *Kicks*—Shoes. **1969** Bouton *Ball Four* 272: Shoes are *kicks* and clothes are *vines.* **1970** *Playboy* (Mar.) 72: All I want is a pair of kicks that don't hurt my feet. **1975** Sepe & Telano *Cop Team* 169: Hey man, beautiful pair of kicks you got there. **1984** *USA Today* (Mar. 13) D1: Here at the Roxy Roller Rink, sneakers are called "kicks." **1993** P. Munro *U.C.L.A. Slang II: Kicks* n. athletic shoes. *Those are sweet kicks you got on.* **1993** "Us3" *I Got It Going On* (rap song): Sport the dope threads and the $100 kicks.

4. a protest, complaint, or objection; in phr. **have no kick [coming]** to have no justifiable cause for complaint. [The sense intended in the 1839 quot. is problematical.]

   1839 in Thornton *Amer. Gloss.* I 515: My spirit now is languid, and funny is my snore,/So take the hint without a kick, and shut the open door. **1863** in *DA*: As the coat belonged to him, I had no kick coming. **1887** *Courier-Journal* (Louisville, Ky.) (Jan. 5) 6: Kicks Sent to Congress. **1887** Francis *Saddle & Moccasin* 308: I haven't got any kick against Don Juan. *a***1889** *Century Dict.*: Kick...A sudden and strong objection; unexpected resistance. (Slang.) **1889** Bailey *Ups & Downs of a "Crook's" Life* 14: I noticed that "Yaller" Davis looked like a wilted sun-flower and made no more kick. **1893** in F. Remington *Sel. Letters* 161: I hear the same kick from other young men. **1897** F.P. Dunne, in Schaaf *Dooley* 214: I've no kick comin' again th' r-rich man that thrust their hands down in their pockets an' dhraw out f'r th' poor. **1904** in "O. Henry" *Works* 329: His talk would make the conversation of a siren sound like a cab driver's kick. **1904** "B.M. Bower" *Chip of Flying U* 93: But she couldn't find no kick about *my* cake. **1910** Mulford *Hopalong Cassidy* 57: We ain't got no kick, have we? **1912** Mathewson *Pitching* 56: There is a kick against these tactics from the other bench. **1913** Jocknick *Early Days* 39: Instead of making a "kick" right off, I deferred it. **1919** *Fifth Division Diamond* (Apr. 16): The only kick that has been registered so far comes from a few of the Privates who do not like...the extra guard duty. **1922** in Cornebise *Amaroc News* 59: We hear lots of kicks about the high salaries paid movie actors. **1928** in Goodstone *Pulps* 43: It's not our fault you didn't know. You ain't got a kick. **1935** H. McCoy *They Shoot Horses* 35: Anybody got any kicks about anything? **1936** M. Watkins et al. *Libeled Lady* (film): You've got no kick. **1948** Lay & Bartlett *Twelve O'Clock High* 107: "The air inspector has no kick coming," said Savage, "as long as the group as a whole has no overages in grade." **1956** Neider *Hendry Jones* 66: I don't reckon you got any kick coming. **1958** Talsman *Gaudy Image* 26: Well, remember the rules, 'cause I ain't repeatin' them, and if you break the littlest one, out you go with no kick back, understand? **1984** J.R. Reeves *Mekong* 14: We asked for it....so we got no kick comin', do we?

5.a. dismissal, jilting, or discharge.—constr. with *the*.

   ****1844** in *EDD*: She was soon to get the kick. ****1885** in *EDD*: Should a brither be sick,/They'll no gie him the kick. **1937** Reitman *Box-Car Bertha* 159: He'll give them the kick, and then we'll get married.

b. *Mil.* a dishonorable discharge; (*hence*) a bad-conduct discharge.

   1906 Beyer *Battleship* 85: "Straight kick"—dishonorably discharged. **1918** Ruggles *Navy Explained* 139: Six months and a kick—six months in prison and a dishonorable discharge. **1927** *Amer. Leg. Mo.* (Sept.) 87: The sentence of the court was a dishonorable discharge and loss of citizenship. This verdict is known in the service as The Kick. **1941** *AS* (Oct.) 166: *Kick.* A dishonorable discharge. **1953** *ATS* (ed. 2) 810: *Three and a kick,* three months' confinement and a dishonorable discharge. **1961** Peacock *Valhalla* 332 [ref. to *ca*1953]: With what's on your record since you been in Japan you'll get the load: six six and a kick—a Bad Conduct Discharge or a Dishonorable. *Ibid.* 374: They's [*sic*] still a chance they'll remit the kick. **1966** Little *Bold & Lonely* 20: You tell 'em he appreciates the promotion and the open arms but he also hasn't forgotten the straight kick when the chips were down. **1987** E. Spencer *Macho Man* 16: All my deserters got 6, 6 and a kick—6 months in a brig at hard labor, 6 months loss of pay, loss of rank and a bad-conduct discharge. **1988** Dye *Outrage* 147: He did me right...even if it means six, six and a kick.

6.a. a highly stimulating or intoxicating effect, as afforded by liquor or drugs; (*hence*) power or effectiveness.

   ****1844** in *OED2*: I then demanded a common cocktail. "With the kick in it?" said he....It was...somewhat strong; but then that was my fault, for having ordered it "with the kick in it." **1903** in *DA*: With cayenne and mustard (to give their food the missing "kick" [of alcohol]). **1913** J. London *J. Barleycorn* 4: Alcohol...I drank it only for its "kick." **1914** *Sat. Eve. Post* (Apr. 4) 12: Gee, that stuff had a kick to it! **1915–16** Lait *Beef, Iron & Wine* 263: He packs a kick in his right what'd jar a buildin'. **1916** S. Lewis *Job* 62: The editor...wanted "short, snappy stuff with a kick in it." **1918** Grider *War Birds* 71: A bottle of...whisky that had the kick of Brown's mule. **1918** E. O'Neill

Moon of Caribees 37: Rum wid a kick in it loike a mule's hoinde leg. **1920** in Hemingway *By-Line* 4: The present scheme has been for each of the young women to have two pictures and after their kick—to use a slang phrase—has worn off...to trade with her nearest fellow member of the gallery. **1921** A. Jennings *Through Shadows* 244: It must have a wonderful kick in it. **1925** *Sat. Eve. Post* (Oct. 31) 21: It'll have that gin kick. **1934** Faulkner *Pylon* 114: During the last couple months I have got to where a whole cigarette aint got any kick to it. **1976** Dillard *Amer. Talk* 85: Rough tough miners wanted kick...in their liquor. **1979–81** C. Buckley *To Bamboula* 134: Balancing beer (for bulk) with whiskey (for kick). **1989** P. Benchley *Rummies* 62: Lady, I don't know what you're on, but it's got some kick to it. **1995** *World News Tonight* (ABC-TV) (Oct. 18): A bigger kick of nicotine to the brain.

b. the sudden euphoria or stimulation afforded by the consumption of liquor or drugs; BUZZ, 2.a.; HIGH; RUSH.

   1912 Lowrie *Prison* 44: I have seen the Count drink an entire bottle of patent medicine...in the hope that he might get a "kick" from it....at first the doctor thought he had taken the stuff with suicidal intent, but...the victim admitted he had done so to get a "kick." **1922** N. Anderson *Hobo* 38: One can still get a "kick" out of stuff...sold across the bar. **1934** (quot. at **(c),** below). **1952** Kerouac *Cody* 160: Man, I'm sure gettin a goofy kick this time. *ca***1953** Hughes *Fantastic Lodge* 64: Some cats turned us on for the first time....Lil...had a hard time getting the kick, you know, but not me. ****1967** Glatt et al. *Drug Scene* 39: He no longer got a "kick" or "flash" from taking drugs....His body had developed...a tolerance for narcotics. **1970** R. Vasquez *Chicano* 215: They give you about a five-minute kick like you never had before....Your heart takes off.

c. a surge of excitement or pleasure; thrill; (*hence*) enjoyment, amusement, etc., in any degree.—usu. *get a kick out of.* [Though accepted by *OED2*, the bracketed **1899 quot. is better explained as an instance of the British phr. *to have the kick,* defined by Barrère & Leland (1889) as "(sporting), to have luck. From a football phrase."]

   [****1899** Whiteing *John St.* 202: My Gawd! won't them chaps from the collynies 'ave the kick!...Eat an' drink as much as yer like, an' never mind the bill.] **1917** C.E. Van Loan, in Woods *Horse-Racing* 291: I used to like this game for the excitement in it—for the kick. ****1917** in Lee *No Parachute* 39: It gave me quite a "kick" to say hello! in this way, for they'd been jolly good to me. **1918** Witwer *Baseball* 123: He can look at a dame...and get the same kick they is in gin. **1922** Hisey *Sea Grist* 83: To him it is keen enjoyment, his big kick from life. **1922** N. Anderson *Hobo* 160: I get a lot of "kick" out of riding trains...when I know the "dicks" are trying to keep me off. **1927** in Spectorsky *College Years* 391: All the kick lay in..."student activities." **1927** Thrasher *Gang* 276: [Gang members] get a great "kick" out of feeling how diabolical they are. ****1928** in *OED2*: I was told I should get a kick out of that journey—and I certainly did. **1928** Burnett *Little Caesar* 127: You'd've got all the kick you're looking for if you'd heard that dame yell. **1928** Santee *Cowboy* 126: But when he said he was breakin' horses for the Turtles now, I got a great big kick. **1934** C. Porter *I Get a Kick Out of You* (pop. song) (N.Y.: Harms Music, Inc.) 2: I get no kick from champagne....But I get a kick out of you. **1939** *Bedside Esquire* 73: He gets an enormous kick out of the idea. **1948** in *DA*: We used to get a kick out of the stuff we read...about Sande. **1951** in *DAS*: He was having a real kick. **1969** in *Rolling Stone Interviews* 290: He even gets a kick out of it. **1993** Atlanta, Ga., teenager, on *World News* (CNN-TV) (Dec. 9): Mortal Kombat [a video game] is really gruesome, and people get a kick out of that. **1993** K. Scott *Monster* 108: We joked a bit about me shouting at Dr. Blakewell—which she got a tremendous kick out of.

d. an exciting or intensely enjoyable experience; (*hence*) a source of or cause for excitement, enjoyment, amusement, or pleasure.

   1922 Murphy *Black Candle* 322: Running with sports and rounders, seeking a new "kick" or sensation from life....His conceit in his ability makes him try a new "kick" just to prove his superiority over the numskulls who have let cocaine put them in the gutter. **1929** Booth *Stealing* 303: What a kick!...That fat broad that keeled over when you captured the first guy! **1929** McEvoy *Hollywood Girl* 49: I'm in Hollywood....What a kick! **1930** *Liberty* (July 19) 22: It's a kick to hunt them up next day and hear them tell what happened. **1930** Mae West *Babe Gordon* 17: If it promised anything different—a new kick—

she'd go out for him. **1934** in *DAS:* That's a kick....Ridin' a guy down Wilshire in daylight. **1934** Jevne & Purcell *Joe Palooka* (film): This is the kick of a lifetime! **1938** Steinbeck *Grapes of Wrath* 110: She's a kick. *Ibid.* 170: They's a ol' war horse in here that's a kick. **1939** Goodman & Kolodin *Swing* 77: Being the youngest member of a band like Pollack's was a kick. **1942** B. Morgan & B. Orkow *Wings for Eagle* (film): Isn't it a kick building planes? **1942** Davis & Wolsey *Call House Madam* 164: A naked woman in furs is a big kick to some men. **1949** E.S. Gardner *Negligent Nymph* 121: The two girls with the older guys are a kick. **1959** W. Williams *Ada Dallas* 57: That was a kick. That was funny. **1959** A. Anderson *Lover Man* 153: Bird, Miles Davis, Dizzie, Bud Powell...strictly the kick. **1966–67** P. Thomas *Mean Streets* 24: But summer is really the kick. **1988** J. Thomas *Heavy Number* 1: It was a kick for a while. **1988** *21 Jump St.* (Fox-TV): Look at that floor. That's the original tile! Isn't it a kick? **1994** *Young & Restless* (CBS-TV): This was really a kick. **1994** *Sunday Morning* (CBS-TV) (July 17): It's always a kick to watch...astronomers go ballistic.

e. *pl.* intense enjoyment; fun; diversion; in phrs. **get (one's) kicks [off]** to enjoy (oneself), often sexually; **bust (one's) kicks** to have an orgasm (*rare*).

    1928 Callahan *Man's Grim Justice* 40: "Come up and see us and we'll cook y' a few pills, Jimmy." "No....I never smoke nothing but honest long cut; that gives me all the kicks that I need in my bizness." **1930** Mae West *Babe Gordon* 15: She got too many kicks out of life in other ways. **1936** in *Comments on Ety.* (Dec. 1994) 4: I kept rubbin', the clock struck six,/She said you got time to get your kicks. **1939** Goodman & Kolodin *Swing* 32: We got our kicks...out of playing. **1942** "D. Ormsbee" *Sound of Amer.* 305: Hollywood people...want kicks. **1944** in Himes *Black on Black* 202: Fifty flags [dollars] a day would be solid kicks, please believe me. **1946** Mezzrow & Wolfe *Really Blues* 159: Just for kicks. **1946** *New Directions* 233: Sexually undernourished middle western school teachers thirsting for vicarious kicks writing writing. **1946** J. Adams *Gags* 293: *Kicks.* Show business vernacular for having fun. **1947** in Kerouac *Letters* 115: Unless you *really* want to come out here for kicks. **1947** *Tomorrow* (Aug.) 27: Get your kicks on Route 66. **1948** Manone & Vandervoort *Trumpet* 113: Fats Waller used to come in to dig the band and get his kicks. **1952** Viereck *Men into Beasts* 49: They were a pornographic set with lewd pictures on the back. "Getting your kicks?" asked Joey with a knowing smile. **1952** Brossard *Darkness* 5: Porter finally went to an analyst...for kicks. **1955** G. Adams *3 Bad Sisters* (film): "I only get kicks out of a man when I know I'm stealing him from another woman."..."That wasn't just for kicks." **1957** *Social Problems* V 8: The "cat" recounted his search for "kicks." **1957** J.D. MacDonald *Death Trap* 79: You got a new way to get your kicks, chief? Go feel a woolly sweater. I know a guy goes for shoes. **1958** in J. O'Hara *Sel. Letters* 271: "For kicks"...is strictly rock-and-roll switchblade talk. **1959** Zugsmith *Beat Generation* 84: He looked like real gone kicks. **1962** D. Hamilton *Murderers' Row* 91: Erotic stimulation. That's fancy for kicks. **1965** Bryan *P.S. Wilkinson* 231: Is this how he gets his kicks? **1962–68** B. Jackson *In the Life* 97: If I didn't have my habit I swear to God I'd bust my kicks (have an orgasm) right here. **1968** Heard *Howard St.* 15: Probably up there getting her kicks along with that john....She'd always been partial to big guys, anyway. **1971** Goines *Dopefiend* 124: Maybe then the son of a bitch will see enough to get his kicks off. **1973** Ellington *Music Is My Mistress* 73: I was getting my kicks writing and recording. **1981** in L. Bangs *Psychotic Reactions* 357: Show me some kicks. **1985** *World News Tonight* (ABC-TV) (Feb. 4): Just to get their kicks off, they'll torment and torment. **1989** *Newsweek* (Nov. 6) 45: The gang started as a pack of adolescents who robbed for kicks. **1990** Alexander & Karaszewski *Problem Child* (film): Let's have some *kicks!* **1993** *New Yorker* (Feb. 8) 104: This kamikaze quest for kicks. **1994** Chicago high school student, on *Oprah* (synd. TV series): They just did it for kicks, not that they meant anything by it.

f. a strong usu. temporary interest or enthusiasm; (*hence*) a way of thinking or behaving, usu. regarded as shallow, insincere, inappropriate, annoying, etc.; in phrs. **on a ——— kick** passionately enthusiastic for ———; **be (one's) kick** to be (one's) special preference. Cf. (**1.a.**), above.

    1946 Mezzrow & Wolfe *Really Blues* 40: I wasn't on any health kick. **1946** in R.S. Gold *Jazz Talk* 154: The whole jazz world was on a Hawkins kick. **1948** *Neurotica* (Summer) 42: On the bitterness kick, eh? **1949** in T. Williams *Letters* 238: Frankie's passion is clothes, and this week we have been on a haberdashery kick. **1951** Styron *Lie Down*

in Darkness 95: Get off this gloom kick, will you? **1952** E. Brown *Trespass* 28: Let's not get back on that old kick again. **1952** Brossard *Darkness* 21: I think you ought to come off that kick, Harry. *ca*1953 Hughes *Fantastic Lodge* 70: Well, I'm sorry, he certainly wasn't my kick. **1955** Reifer *New Words* 116: He's on a new kick. **1955** Yates & Smith *It Came from Beneath the Sea* (film): Let's get off this Hawaiian kick. **1956** Resko *Reprieve* 234: That overtime pimp kick ain't nowhere. **1956** E. Hunter *Second Ending* 129: I didn't steal the bag, so get off that kick. **1953–58** J.C. Holmes *Horn* 26: Fats (Pichon, Waller, Navarro, or Domino, depending on your kick). **1959** *Twilight Zone* (CBS-TV): Snap out of this kick! **1968** Van Dyke *Strawberries* 173: What's your kick? **1970** A. Young *Snakes* 55: Claude stayed on that kick the whole summer. **1979** in Terkel *Amer. Dreams* 315: They were on the cultural kick. **1982** M. Mann *Elvis* 74: This time Elvis was on a peach yogurt kick. **1983–88** J.T. McLeod *Crew Chief* 329: Get off your self-righteous kick. **1992** *Donahue* (NBC-TV): Doctors do *not* give people AIDS. We've got to get *off* that kick! **1993** *Mystery Sci. Theater* (Comedy Central TV): Are you still on that kick?

g. *Broadly* (*Narc.*) any form of psychotropic drug.

    1950 in W.S. Burroughs *Letters* 61: Anti-gun, anti-sex, anti-kick laws. **1951** in W.S. Burroughs *Letters* 77: I have a quantity of Cocteau's kick.... $40 per pound. **1994** *Street Terms: Drugs* (unp.): *Kick* ... inhalant.

h. a fit; JAG.

    1952 in Kerouac *Letters* 370: Bill got on a talking kick. **1966–67** P. Thomas *Mean Streets* 132: We...fell all over the room on a laughin' kick.

i. *Black E.* (trivially) a thing, idea, or situation.

    1956 E. Hunter *Second Ending* 342: Dizzy Gillespie...wears a little beard here under his lip, a sort of a goatee, a little triangular thing. We call it a "Dizzy kick" in the trade....Those are his trademarks—the kick and the beret. **1966–67** P. Thomas *Mean Streets* 109: My boys were the important kick, and for good reasons. **1978** Price *Ladies' Man* 240: At that moment I became hip to the kick.

j. a spree.

    1958 Frankel *Band of Bros.* 56: I'd won two thousand bucks in craps....So I went on a kick.

k. *Rock.* rhythm; beat.

    1995 Slavsky, Mozeson, & Mozeson *A 2 Z* 60: Those rugged *kicks* will hypnotize you. **1995** *N.Y. Press* (May 31) 26: There are lots of jangly guitars and cymbals, and no bass and kick at the bottom.

7. a more or less elusive quality or effect; (*also*) an unexpected twist or source of irony.

    1913–15 Van Loan *Taking the Count* 117: Kid...there was a queer kick to that little show of ours the other night—a few things I haven't been able to figure out. **1924** P. Marks *Plastic Age* 101: "La Belle Dame sans Merci"...It's one of those bedtime stories with a kick. **1946** Mezzrow & Wolfe *Really Blues* 101: He kept parodying the slurs and the colloquial kicks in my speech. **1960** Swarthout *Where Boys Are* 21: But, and here's the kick, they don't want brains [in young women].

8. a damn.

    1965–70 in *DARE:* Go ahead—I don't give a...kick.

¶ In phrases:

¶ **better than a kick in the ass** better than nothing.— usu. considered vulgar. Also vars.

    1933–34 "M. Brand" *Mt. Riders* 47: Money is better than a kick in the face. **1938** T. Wolfe *Web & Rock* 404: Well, as Daddy used to say...it's better than a kick in the eye, isn't it? **1966** E. Shepard *Doom Pussy* 173: Sounds better than a kick in the ass with a frozen mukluk. **1970** Ponicsan *Last Detail* 134: It's better than a kick in the head with a icy galosh. **1974** Millard *Thunderbolt* 64: Twenty-five bucks...is a helluva lot better than a kick in the ass.

¶ **kick in the ass** [or (*euphem.*) **pants**] **1.** Esp. *Horse Racing.* a certainty; CINCH.—usu. considered vulgar.

    1925 T.A. Dorgan, in Zwilling *TAD Lexicon* 52: (Kidding the guy at the track who always has a bet on the winner) I guess you got your taxi fare on that one eh Phil—That was a kick in the pants. **1927** in Hammett *Big Knockover* 283: I'm telling you this [robbery] is the fastest picking ever rigged, a kick in the pants to get through—air-tight. **1932** in Runyon *Blue Plate* 365: Here I am...with a race that is a kick in the pants for my horse at fifty to one, and me without a quarter to bet. *a*1951 D.W. Maurer, in *PADS* (No. 16) 39: *Kick in, kick in the ass, kick in the pants*...A horse which is heavily touted to win a race easily. Also *shoo-in*.

2.a. a strong reproof; (*also*) an unexpected reversal; injurious surprise; shock.—usu. considered vulgar. Also vars.

1929 McEvoy *Hollywood Girl* 19: He'll get a good journalistic kick in the pants from me. **1929** in E. O'Neill *Letters* 330: They never reflect that a kick in the pants…is a grand stimulant. **1939** Goodman & Kolodin *Swing* 148: That was another kick in the pants, which looked like a real tragedy at the time. **1940** Hartney *Up & at 'Em* 135: It was the final "kick in the pants" for the conservative element of the field personnel. **1963** D. Tracy *Brass Ring* 303: Haven't you ever heard of a man gettin' drunk when he got a kick in the balls he wasn't expectin'? **1965** Borowik *Lions* 56: Ain't that a kick in the head? **1968** Coppel *Order of Battle* 163: Just when it looks like they've had it, they come up with a kick in the balls like this. **1968** Brasselle *Cannibals* 27: That's a nice kick in the ass. **1969** Whittemore *Cop!* 49: He skimps and scrapes to send his kids to college, only to find out the kid is using junk! What a kick in the ass! **1974** N.Y.U. student: What a swift kick in the ass that was. **1978** Maggin *Superman* 30: Maybe he's the President in disguise. Wouldn't that be a kick in the head? **1978** Selby *Requiem* 87: The kick in the ass came when they found out they wouldn't get paid that night. **1985** Dye *Between Raindrops* 230: Ain't *dis* a kick in the ass. **1985** E. Leonard *Glitz* 23: This day had been a kick in the ass. **1991** Coen & Coen *Barton Fink* (film): Well, ain't that a kick in the head!

b. a cause for amusement or source of enjoyment; KICK, 6.d.—usu. considered vulgar. Also vars.

1962 J. Clifford *Carnival of Souls* (film): Oh, *that* must have been a kick in the head. **1970** Conaway *Big Easy* 122: She wants to join the club. Ain't that a kick in the ass? **1973** Overgard *Hero* 90: He renamed her the *Revuelta*, that's supposed to mean return in Spanish. Ain't that a kick in the head! The only thing that clown will return is a six-pack of empties. **1978** J. Webb *Fields of Fire* 167: Well, don't think it hasn't been a kick in the ass. Even if it hasn't. **1978** Univ. Tenn. instructor, age *ca*35: She's so funny. She's such a kick in the pants. **1985** Frede *Nurses* 109: Well, Lady Macbeth there…sure is a kick in the ass. **1989** S. Robinson & D. Ritz *Smokey* 136: And it was a particular kick in the ass to know that the artists doing it were friends. **1995** Norwegian Cruise Lines TV ad: Cruising is a kick in the pants!

c. an addition of energy, vitality, encouragement, etc.—usu. considered vulgar.

1953 W.C. Williams, in Norse *Memoirs* 231: Somehow the book as a whole needs a good kick in the ass to make it stand up by itself. **1955** in Kerouac *Letters* 502: A foreword by you is better than anything, it would really give it…class and a…kick in the ass. **1974** in Asimov, Greenberg & Olander *Sci. Fi. Short Shorts* 19: I've given the field its biggest kick in the pants since Lopez. **1988** M. Maloney *Thunder Alley* 65: Giving the ship an extra powerful "after-burning" kick in the ass. **1988** Beck & Massman *Rich Men, Single Women* 65: Travis needed a good kick in the pants.…He may *never* have taken the initiative.

¶ **kick in the balls** [or **head**] see s.v. *kick in the ass*, above.

kick *adj. Narc.* pertaining to the eradication of a drug habit.—used attrib. only.

1958–59 Lipton *Barbarians* 22: Dolophenes are kick pills to alleviate the discomfort of being without heroin when you're sick. **1972** Wambaugh *Blue Knight* 35: I went to a kick pad over on the east side and asked them to sign me in. **1972–74** Hawes & Asher *Raise Up* 118 [ref. to 1950's]: After the physical I was taken straight to the kick ward. *a*1979 Pepper & Pepper *Straight Life* 139 [ref. to 1953]: In the county jail…they had a kick tank.

kick *v.* **1.a.** to go, walk, amble, wander, etc.; (*also*) to dance.—usu. constr. with following adv. or dummy-obj. *it.*

1725 New Canting Dict.: *Kick'd*, gone, fled, departed; as, *The Rum Cull kick'd away*, i.e. The Rogue made his Escape. *1829* Marryat *Frank Mildmay* 247: Tired of kicking about at sea, he should take all his *duds* with him, and bring himself to an anchor on shore. **1839** in *DA*: We heard that he was better, and would be able to "kick around" pretty soon. *ca*1840 in Holloway & Black *Broadside Ballads* II 312: Dusty Tom…dancing now teaches—he knows how to kick it. **1846** in *Amer. Heritage* (June 1966) 93: I have been kicking about with scarcely leisure enough to take my meals. **1863** A. Tourgée, in *Ohio Hist.* LXXIV (1965) 114: Morgan [the Raider] is still kicking around in Ind. and Ohio. He will be "nabbed" yet. **1866** Locke *Round the Cirkle* 38: Our men uv character commenst leavin us. Silas Write kicked out, and wood hev gone over agin us. **1908** McGaffey *Show Girl* 47: The other evening I kicked down to a show I once worked in. **1928** J.V. Weaver

Poems 200: I had enough of kickin 'round the world. **1957** Laurents & Sondheim *West Side Story* 157: Let's get the chicks and kick it. **1984** Algeo *Stud Buds* 4: To leave a place, go away…*head out,…kick,…split.* **1992** *Fresh Prince* (NBC-TV): Let's kick it over to Roscoe's.

b. to *kick the street*, below.

1966 S. Harris *Hellhole* 95: I would have to start kicking because I wasn't a good call girl any more.

2. to utter a protest or complaint; in phr. **kick like a steer** to protest vigorously. [A narrowing of (now rare) S.E. sense 'to rebel or resist', exemplified by bracketed quots.; to the extent that the older usage still occurs in AmE, it is largely inseparable from the present sense.]

[**1799** in Thornton *Amer. Gloss.* I 515: Davis complained, and Grove *kicked*, but 'twas all to no purpose.] [**1842** in Thornton *Amer. Gloss.*: [Members of Congress] kicked against receiving any more petitions.] [**1848** *High Private* 23: They *kicked*, refused to do duty, and swore to return unless they were honorably dealt by.] **1857** in Thornton *Amer. Gloss.* I 515: I have to live under their laws, and when they take a notion to swear away my character, I mustn't kick. **1877–78** *Cornelian* 86: *Kick.* To object. **1879** *Nat. Police Gaz.* (Aug. 2) 11: He has no wish to see a "kicking sucker" about his place. **1882** Peck *Peck's Sunshine* 114: I kicked about it to the landlord. **1883** Hay *Bread-Winners* 163: That's the game, and I'm a-kickin'!…I'm a-kickin' like a Texas steer. **1884** in Leitner *Diamond in Rough* 134: It made the Providence team mad,/And so they kicked like mules. **1884** in *Mo. Hist. Rev.* XLIII (1948) 94: But blanked if we ain't disposed to kick. **1885** Siringo *Texas Cowboy* 21: The old fat fellow kicked like a bay steer. **1886** Lummis *Ft. Bowie* 73: Would steal…coppers…and then kick because they weren't half-dollars. **1887** Hinman *Si Klegg* 10: Tain't 'cause I wants ter back out, fer I don't, but ye see I'm 'feard pap'll kick. *a*1889 *Century Dict.*: *Kick*…To manifest opposition or strong objection; offer resistance. (Now chiefly slang.). **1890** *Vices of a Big City* 12: He protested, but she laughingly told him that he should not "kick" about a little thing like that. **1909** in O. Johnson *Lawrenceville* 18: I say, we ought to kick. **1910** W. Archer *Afro-Amer.* 14: They knew that I would "kick" less than any other chief of department. **1917** in Truman *Dear Bess* 233: We had things in fine shape inside but he kicked like a bay steer because the Puritan distributor hadn't return for his empty bottles. **1927** Rollins *Jinglebob* 119 [ref. to 1880's]: Jus' only kickin' never got nobody nowheres, 'less he was a mule! **1931** J.T. Adams *Epic of Amer.* 217: There grew up naturally another American trait, that of "boosting" and of objecting to criticism as "kicking." **1931–34** in Clemmer *Pris. Community* 333: *Kick*…To object. **1935** *Chi. Tribune* (Oct. 4) 7: He gave me only $2. I kicked about it because I generally charge $5. **1938** Smitter *Detroit* 194: And I'm the guy who used to kick like a steer about the food we ate in the camps. **1942** *New Yorker* (Nov. 28) 16: The boss of this saloon on Third Avenue was kicking out loud to himself…about how things were going. **1942** Lindsay & Crouse *Strip for Action* 222: What am I kicking about? Those jugheads out there getting all the laughs. **1971** O'Neal *Damn Foreigners* 118 [ref. to 1914]: He'd kick…if he was hung with a brand new rope.

3. to ask (someone).

1809 in Partridge *Dict. Und.* 381: *Kick*…to ask a favour. **1890** *Overland Mo.* (Nov.) 502: He put on a bold face,…asked for the boss, and "kicked" him for a job.

4.a. to dismiss or discharge; reject (a suitor); rid oneself of or abandon.

1809 in *DA*: A lady whom I met…affirmed that poor Ashby had been kicked by you. **1845** in Eliason *Tarheel Talk* 280: [If] I would be fool enough to make a speech to [a girl]…I would get kicked so far I would hardly get back in a coons age. **1864** in Geer *Diary* 176: Captain King relieves Lt. Edmeston.…Tom Jennyson is kicked by Gen. Leggett. **1865** Byrn *Fudge Fumble* 59: This love affair is what proved too much for his constitution.…He never knew the difference till he got "*kicked*." **1871** Schele de Vere *Amer.* 319: An unfortunate lover, who is simply "jilted" at the North, is more violently *kicked* at the South. **1882** *Harper's* (June) 47: Why, Sarann kicked me three times han' runnin'. **1884** in *AS* XLVIII (1973) 93: His first love kicks him and begins to run with another fellow. **1908** *DN* III 326: *Kick*…To jilt, reject as a suitor. **1941, 1950** in *DARE*. **1965** Bonham *Durango St.* 14: Why don't I run away? Kick this town for good? **1986** in *DARE*.

b. Orig. *Narc.* to break oneself of (an addiction or habit); end one's dependence upon or give up (a drug or the like).—often used absol. or constr. with *it;*—occ. also constr. with *out.*

1927–28 Tasker *Grimhaven* 163: The sick user who is "kicking a habit" will do practically anything for dope. **1932** Berg *Prison Doctor* 62: Whitey, like all the other "junkies," "kicked it out" in a cell for three days, and in a few weeks only his scarred body testified to his habit. **1934** Weseen *Dict. Slang* 23: *Kick the habit*—To try to break the drug habit. **1937** Johnston *Prison Life* 108: When I began my work as warden at Folsom it was the practice to "let the hopheads kick it out."…He was put in a cell and left to wrestle with his craving until he got over it. **1949** in W.S. Burroughs *Letters* 34: It is hard to kick here. **1952** Mandel *Angry Strangers* 280: I don't think I can kick Horse. *Ibid.* 291: But she'd kick, she'd kick! **1953** Paley *Rumble* 133: He'd heard of guys kicking the habit. **1953** W. Brown *Monkey on My Back* 8: I'm a junkie but I'm trying to kick it. **1961** *Social Problems* IX 135: I was very sick but after a couple of days I kicked. **1965** C. Brown *Manchild* 221: He'd already been down to Kentucky about seven times, and he hadn't kicked. **1978** Hamill *Dirty Laundry* 2: I had finally kicked Anne Fletcher, the way some people kick cigarettes, and others kick smack. **1980** Schruers *Blondie* 16: A "semireligious experience" enabled her to kick. **1984** H. Gould *Cocktail* 19: Kick the booze and cigarettes. **1989** Courtwright et al. *Addicts Who Survived* 380: *Kick it out:* to endure withdrawal symptoms in order to quit using narcotics. **1990** *True Colors* (Fox-TV): The longer you keep playing mah-jongg with those old ladies, the harder it's gonna be to kick. **1995** *Getting Healthy* (TV Food Network) (Apr. 10): I kicked nicotine seven years ago.

c. *Pris.* to serve (a prison term).

1953 T. Runyon *In for Life* 105: You ought to get yourself a hobby, Tom.…It's a good way to kick your time. *Ibid.* 129: I only have to kick this fifteen years for writing that check.

d. *Police.* to release (a suspect) from custody.

1994 *L.A. Times* (Dec. 19) B1: One officer said he planned to "kick" a suspect when he got back to the station. **1994** *Cops* (Fox-TV): We're just gonna go and kick her. There's no…arrest.

5.a. [short for *kick the bucket,* below] to die.—also constr. with dummy-obj. *it.*

*1857–58 Trollope *Dr. Thorne* II 216: I say, doctor, you don't really think I'm going to die?…fellows have done ten times worse than I, and they are not going to kick. *1889 Barrère & Leland *Dict. Slang* I 518: *Kick, to* (Australian popular), an abbreviation for "kick the bucket." *1892 in *F & H* IV 99: Four on [sic] them sickened…and…kicked it. *a*1890–96 *F & H* IV 98: *Kick*…(American).—To die. **1898** Riis *Mulberry St.* 88: Never mind, Schultz.…I guess I won't kick; so long! **1911–12** J. London *Smoke Bellew* 145: He's all starved.…He'll kick at any moment. *a*1946 in Halsey *Color Blind* 65: He "kicked it" for America—the good, the bad, and the indifferent. **1958** Talsman *Gaudy Image* 201: When did she kick? **1960** Barber *Minsky's* 346: It's a blessing Billy Minsky kicked before them broads took over uppen downa street. **1971** N.Y.U. student: It's better than sitting around waiting for the old man to kick. **1984** N. Stephenson *Big U.* 47: If you breathe it pure you'll kick in no time, because you got to have oxygen. **1986** Holland *One Crazy Summer* (film): So old man Eldridge finally kicked. **1989** *ALF* (NBC-TV): And if Kate kicks, I'll get you another redhead. **1990** J. Elroy, in Pronzini & Adrian *Hard-Boiled* 491: The girl, a diabetic,…went into sugar shock and kicked.

b. *Und.* to kill. Cf. KICK OFF.

1993 Mowry *Six Out Seven* 85: His gang had finally kicked someone. *Ibid.* 483: My dudes comin to kick you. Get your ass out this hood.

6.a. *Jazz.* to perform with great intensity and energy; SWING.—also constr. with dummy-obj. *it.*

1937 in *AS* 46: *Go, kick it,* v. To improvise rhythmically and expertly on a given melody. "He really goes on that tune; listen to him kick it." **1938** in R.S. Gold *Jazz Talk:* The band is kicking like mad in this one. **1973** Broven *Walking to N.O.* 6: 'Fess was playing and kicking on the piano.

b. *Narc.* to BOOT, *v.,* 7.

1952 Ellson *Golden Spike* 32: He kicked four times, drawing his blood up into the syringe and mixing it with the drug.

c. to delight or please greatly.—also constr. with *off* or *down;* (later) (intrans.) to be exciting; *kick ass,* 2.c., below.

1956 Childress *Like One of Family* 12: What kicks some people just bugs me and vice is versa! **1962** Crump *Killer* 49: If it kicks you off to go around warring with other people, it's all right with Treetop. **1984** J. Mason & D. Rheingold *Slanguage:* That song kicks; it's bitchin.

1996 *Jerry Springer Show* (synd. TV series): I kick you down sexually, what more do you need?

d. Esp. *Entertainment Industry.* to do very well on; manage handily; in phr. **kick live** to perform well before a live audience.

1969 *Current Slang Cum. I & II:* Kickin' hard…Doing well at something.—College males, South Dakota. **1992** "Fab 5 Freddy" *Fresh Fly Flavor* 38: *Kick it live*—To do it well. **1995** *Newsday* (N.Y.) (Apr. 9): Students who *kick the final* [pass] the course.

e. to happen; go on; GO DOWN, 3.—constr. with *down.*

1983–85 in Safire *Look It Up* 147: Hey, man, what's kickin' down?

f. [infl. by *kick it around,* 2, below] Esp. *Black E.* to gossip or chat; (*hence*) to relax; hang out.—usu. constr. with dummy-obj. *it.*

1983–86 Zausner *Streets* 50: He was my friend's brother. We started kicking it.* …**Talking.* **1987** (cited in P. Munro *Slang U.*). **1989** *Life* (July) 27: She wants someone she can just *kick it* with. **1989** in N. George *Buppies, B-Boys* 259: Awaiting Public Enemy, I kick it with a bunch of other [people]. **1990** P. Munro *Slang U.: Kick it* to relax, sit down; to hang out. **1991** *Source* (Oct.) 31: We chilled for a while in the back of the studio and kicked it. **1992** *L.A. Times* (Mar. 22) E8: One of the few respected famous white rappers…was discovered kickin' it (lounging) in a dark corner of the club. **1992** *L.A. Times* (Aug. 18) E5: *Kick it:* To relax. **1993** K. Scott *Monster* 14: We formally introduced ourselves and I asked him if he wanted to kick it with us. *Ibid.* 119: "Please come in the house." "Awright, but just let me kick it a minute out here."

g. to enjoy oneself intensely; have fun.—usu. constr. with dummy-obj. *it.*

1988 *Harper's* (Aug.) 28: All my homeboys is just kickin' it.…We just be kickin' and having fun. *a*1990 E. Currie *Dope & Trouble* 8: Fifteen-year olds havin' *millions.*…Kickin!…havin' money. **1990** Univ. Tenn. instructor, age *ca*35: We're gonna kick it hard. **1993** *Jerry Springer Show* (synd. TV series): You was out kickin' it with your friends. **1993** *Young & Restless* (CBS-TV): And we'll have a little band in case we feel like kickin' it.

h. to get on well (with someone).—constr. with dummy-obj. *it.*

1993 *Jerry Springer Show* (synd. TV series): I just can't kick it with you no more. **1993** in Stavsky, Mozeson & Mozeson *A 2 Z* 60: I *kick it* with everyone. **1995** *Jerry Springer Show* (synd. TV series): "Me and him was kicking it." "Meaning doing well." "Yeah."

7.a. *Poker.* to raise the bet of (someone).

1949 (cited in T.L. Clark *Dict. Gambling & Gaming* 112). **1976** Mamet *Amer. Buffalo* 81: He takes two on your standing pat, you kicked him thirty bucks?

b. *Rap Music.* to raise; boost; increase.

1989 "LL Cool J" *Big Ole Butt* (rap song): I kicked the bass like an NFL punter. **1991** Nelson & Gonzales *Bring Noise* 137: I kick my volume way past ten.

8.a. Esp. *Rap Music.* to convey (an idea or utterance); create (something artistic); put across; promote; express.—occ. constr. with *up.*

1989 *CBS This Morning* (CBS-TV) (Aug. 30): *Kickin' flavor* is explainin' somethin'. **1991** "Vanilla Ice" *Ice by Ice* 36: Walkin' down the hall, kickin' up the lyrics hard. **1991** *Source* (Oct.) 48: You've been kickin' a world (human) mindset rather than a racial thing. *Ibid.* 58: Base Poet kicks simple ballistics [*i.e.,* vivid rap music] about a subject you probably might think sounds corny. **1991** in *Rap Masters* (Jan. 1992) 58: Groups who are into kickin' street knowledge for the masses. **1991** in *RapPages* (Feb. 1992) 48: Kick the facts, don't just put up a front. **1992** *In Living Color* (Fox-TV): He couldn't kick that sorry line that she was just a friend. **1993** "Wu-Tang Klan" *Method Man* (rap song): Let's get lifted as I kick ballistics. **1993** "Snoop Doggy Dogg" *Every Single Day* (rap song): It's my duty to…kick phat mad styles. **1994** in Slavsky, Mozeson & Mozeson *A 2 Z* 60: Most MC's start out…just *kicking* regular rhymes. *Ibid.:* We wanted to *kick* the real. What we're talking about [in our music] is everyday life. **1995** *Jerry Springer Show* (synd. TV series): I'm gonna kick a rhyme about the plays here.

b. *Rap Music.* to display; exhibit.

1991 *Source* (Oct.) 59: A smooth [recording] that kicks a soulful organ bassline riff.

c. to discuss; KICK OVER, 3.

1993 *Martin* (Fox-TV): We gotta chitchat and kick the actual factual.

¶ In phrases:

¶ **kick a foot** to dance.

1878 B. Harte *Drift* 46: There's to be a dance down at the hall at Eureka, and I haven't kicked a fut since last spring.

¶ **kick ass** [or (*euphem.*) **butt** or **tail**] **1.** Esp. *Mil.* to enforce one's authority or otherwise assert oneself mercilessly or pugnaciously; (*also*) (prob. the orig. sense) to subdue others by beatings; (*hence*) to play the bully; in phr. **kick ass and take names** to do so with great determination or success.—also used fig.—usu. considered vulgar.

1962 (quot. at (2), below). **1968** Mares *Marine Machine* 29: The juniors take the role of bad guys, "kicking ass and taking names," in DI parlance. **1969** *Playboy* (Oct.) 130: The dispatcher gave him two rummies....Oswald had to kick ass every half hour. Then he started drinking with them. **1972** Wambaugh *Blue Knight* 88: All they respect is force. You just gotta kick ass and collect names. **1975** S.P. Smith *Amer. Boys* 22: Sometimes going down to the hillbilly bars on High Street with the other jocks to kick ass on the stupid farmers. **1976** Mamet *Amer. Buffalo* 74: It's kick ass or kiss ass, Don, and I'd be lying if I told you any different. **1978** W. Brown *Tragic Magic* 29: I had failed to kick ass and take names. And that's the calling card for getting over anywhere and the foundation for all credit. **1980** Gould *Ft. Apache* 69: "What's your name, Sergeant?" The sergeant put down his pencil, and gave Connolly a slow, mocking salute. "Kicking ass and takin' names, huh, Captain?" *a***1982** Medved *Hospital* 38: It's a good way for everybody to kick ass. Even the nurses get on him. **1982** R. Sutton *Don't Get Taken* 27: But why did he have to keep kicking ass to make people work? **1985** Briskin *Too Much* 172: You're saying that when things went sour at the office, your father kicked ass at home? **1988** M. Bartlett *Trooper Down!* 9: The classic, hard-nosed, aggressive [state] trooper who "kicks ass and takes names." **1988** in Terkel *Great Divide* 423: J.R. Ewing...kicks butts. I like to do it in sports....I'm known as an intimidator. **1989** *Rage* (Knoxville, Tenn.) (Feb.) 15: Let's kick some tail in the second half of this...SEC season. **1991** Lott & Lieber *Total Impact* 218: They kicked ass and took names every single [football] play. **1991** "Vanilla Ice" *Ice by Ice* 44: Everybody started making fun of [my hair style] so I started kicking butt. **1994** Bak *Turkey Stearnes* 137: He was hired for just one reason: to kick ass. **1995** *CBS This Morning* (CBS-TV) (May 2): The last movie kicked some serious television butt.

2.a. to inflict punishment or defeat (in general).—usu. considered vulgar.

1962 Killens *Heard the Thunder* 44 [ref. to WWII]: Them Japs are kicking asses and taking names [in the Pacific]. **1967** Ford *Muc Wa* 30: The major ached to be out in the field...kicking ass. **1968** Gover *JC* 36: It sure do grieve my heart how the downpeoples kick ass on each others. **1968** in B. Edelman *Dear Amer.* 178: My division...kicked ass but pretty well got wiped out doing it. **1971** *N.Y. Times Mag.* (Nov. 28) 94: If you over 16 [the courts] come down on you like you was King Kong....Then they kick ass. *a***1989** C.S. Crawford *Four Deuces* 180: They hit us last night and kicked ass on the other side of this hill. **1989** *Tracey Ullman Show* (Fox-TV): We're gonna kick butt [in a race].

b. Esp. *Stu.* to celebrate or enjoy oneself riotously.—usu. considered vulgar. [The unusual form of the expression in the 1970–72 quot. presumably reflects a nominalization of this phr.]

1970–72 in *AS* L (1975) 62: *Kicking ass*...Wild time "We went to the Rink and had a kicking ass." **1990** *Club MTV* (MTV) (Mar. 17): We're gettin' ready to kick butt down here at Daytona Beach!

c. Esp. *Stu.* to be extraordinarily vigorous, daunting, effective, energetic, exciting, etc.—usu. considered vulgar.

1981 Eble *Campus Slang* (Oct.) 4: *Kick ass*—work hard: I'm going to have to kick ass to do well in this course. **1982** S. Black *Totally Awesome Val Guide* 21: *Cranking*—Something that kicks butt. **1982** Eble *Campus Slang* (Nov.) 4: That Chem 21 test kicked ass. **1982** in G. Tate *Flyboy* 20: The Brains kick too much ass to be denied for the form. **1984** Algeo *Stud Buds* 2: To do well on a test:...kick ass,...kick some ass. **1985** Eble *Campus Slang* (Apr.) 5: *Kick butt*—to succeed: "I kicked butt on that exam." **1985** *Amazing Stories* (NBC-TV): Good catch! Now you're kickin' butt, Elvis. *a***1986** in *NDAS*: Country [music] that kicks ass and entertains. **1988** in N. George *Buppies, B-Boys* 85: That Brown

and Riley kick ass isn't surprising. *a***1989** P. Munro *U.C.L.A Slang* 54: I kicked ass on my midterm....Even though Joe thought our midterm was really difficult, I thought I kicked butt. **1986–91** Hamper *Rivethead* 52: This [poetry] really kicks ass. **1993** *Beavis and Butt-head* (MTV): Guar [a rock group] kicks ass! **1995** *CBS This Morning* (CBS-TV) (May 18): He kicks butt [in a film role]. He's good.

¶ **kick back** see KICK BACK.

¶ **kick chorus** *Theat.* to dance in a chorus line.

1981 O'Day & Eells *High Times* [photo caption]: I'd begun to bloom enough to get a job kicking chorus in a tavern...by the time I was 17 years old.

¶ **kick gravel** to run.

1962 Crump *Killer* 239: In another hour, you'll be kicking gravel.

¶ **kick it around, 1.** [sugg. by *kick* [or *boot*] *the gong* [*around*], 2, s.v. GONG¹] to carouse.

1935 Wead *Ceiling Zero* (film): You gotta learn to kick it around. Look at Dizzy—he's having a great time. **1941** Ryan & Granet *Girl, Guy, & Gob* (film): We'll take ya out some Saturday night and kick it around.

2. [sugg. by colloq. *kick around* 'to discuss (something)'] to chat.

1962–68 (quot. at *chop it up* s.v. CHOP UP). *a***1976** Roebuck & Frese *Rendezvous* 100: You kick it around with several people during your stay.

¶ **kick it to (someone)** *Rap Music.* to give to (someone); let (someone) have it; *sock it to (someone)* s.v. SOCK, *v.*

1991 in *RapPages* (Feb. 1992) 33: Yo...kick it to 'em. **1994** in C. Long *Love Awaits* 31: Now the girls are kick'n it to you. Now what is a nigga from Bed-Sty gonna do?

¶ **kick mud** *Pros.* to work as a streetwalker. Cf. MUDKICKER.

1963 in Wepman *et al. The Life* 85: There ain't a bitch in the Game with your kind of name / For kicking the mud you kick.

¶ **kick (someone's) ass** [or **butt**] **1.** to inflict a beating upon (someone); (*hence*) to defeat soundly; thrash.—usu. considered vulgar. [The bracketed *1749 quot. is presumably literal.]

[*1749 Fielding *Tom Jones* VI ch. ix: The Wit...lies in desiring another to kiss your A— for having just before threatened to kick his.] **1959** F.L. Brown *Trumbull Pk.* 94: We'll kick their asses. **1981** Romero *Knightriders* (film): I kicked his round ass square. **1987** Covin *Brown Sky* 240: They dragged me out o' there and kicked my ass, kicked my ass somethin' terrible. **1989** Dorsett & Frommer *Running Tough* 40: We kicked the Bulldogs' butt 27–3. **1989** S. Robinson & D. Ritz *Smokey* 69: He'd play us at pool with one hand and kick our ass. **1990** *Bill & Ted's Adventure* (CBS-TV): We'd like to stick around and kick some Tory butt.

2.a. to overcome the mental, emotional, or physical resources of (someone); to exhaust, dispirit, or discourage.—usu. considered vulgar.

1965 C. Brown *Manchild* 179: Geometry and algebra were kicking my ass. **1968** in B. Edelman *Dear Amer.* 82: After they had taken him away, it almost "kicked my ass," as the saying goes. I almost cracked. But...I snapped myself out. **1971** H. Roberts *3d Ear*: That test sure kicked my butt. **1972** Former sgt., U.S. Army [ref. to 1967–68]: Carrying too much gear in that heat would kick your ass in about no time at all. **1972** Pelfrey *Big V* 30: It's kickin his ass, sir. He'll be all right. *Ibid.* 48: The ravines and ridges...had kicked my ass the first day. **1976** C.R. Anderson *Grunts* 59: This crap is kicking my ass. **1990** L. Nieman *Boomer* 35: This kind of existence would kick a Marine's ass. **1990** Helms *Proud Bastards* 88: Goddamn can of gun ammo is just about to kick my ass.

b. to amaze or astonish.—usu. considered vulgar.

1971 H. Roberts *3d Ear*: That house is so fine it will kick your butt.

¶ **kick the bucket** [despite much speculation, the orig. remains uncert.] to die. Now *colloq.*

*1785 Grose *Vulgar Tongue: To kick the bucket*; to die. **1789** in Whiting *Early Amer. Proverbs* 47: And ev'ry mother's son soon *kick the bucket*. *1821–26 Stewart *Man-of-War's Man* II 127: He thought you'd have kicked the bucket. **1830** N. Ames *Sketches* 54: All the diseases above mentioned may as well be called death at once, for to be taken sick and to "kick the bucket" are synonymous terms in Calcutta. **1840** *Crockett's Comic Alm.* (unp.): Do you know that our particular friend, J—, kick'd the bucket last night? **1850** Doten *Journals* I 74: I shook pretty much all the flesh off my bones, and would probably have "kicked the bucket," as Shakespeare says. **1857** *Tricks & Traps of N.Y.C.* 27: The gentleman…was in…a hurry to get to New Haven and see his respected uncle kick the bucket. **1859** in C.A. Abbey *Before the Mast* 212: Two of our 3 kittens have *"kicked the bucket."* **1862** Duganne *King's Man* 50: And take care of that grog, even though you kick the bucket. **1863** in Boyer *Naval Surgeon* I 223: One of the porkers has "kicked the bucket," or, as some have it, "pegged out." **1872** G. Gleason *Specter Riders* 69: Are you ready to kick the bucket? **1901** H. Robertson *Inlander* 187: Folks kickin' the bucket around here, are they? **1912** in Truman *Dear Bess* 97: Of course they had a perfect right to kick the bucket. **1929** Tully *Shadows* 49: Everybody kicks the bucket sooner or later. **1939** Ruskin & Goldbeck *Calling Dr. Kildare* (film): Just when you were going along so swell he had to kick the bucket. **1945** A.C. Powell *Marching Blacks* 98: Old man Mose had kicked the bucket. **1951** Kerouac *Cody* 52: Anybody I know kick the bucket? **1974** Terkel *Working* 480: I love to work with 99s, emergencies, when patients are kicking the bucket. *1977** T. Jones *Ice* 58: He kicked the bucket last August. **1983** Helprin *Winter's Tale* 360: Maybe the Spanish ambassador kicked the bucket. **1992** *Young & Restless* (CBS-TV): Since then he's been hovering around me like a vulture hoping that I'll kick the bucket.

¶ **kick** [or **boot**] **the gong** [**around**] see s.v. GONG¹, *n.*

¶ **kick the street** *Pros.* to work as a streetwalker; *kick mud*, above.

1966 S. Harris *Hellhole* 92: I stopped being a call girl and begun kicking the street. *Ibid.* 95: To kick the street like any dirty whore.

¶ **kick to the curb, 1.** to reject or dismiss callously.

1991 *USA Today* (Mar. 19) 3C (Nexis): He [*sc.* Michael Spinks] basically shuns the boxing establishment, rarely attends big fights and keeps to himself. "When you're out of it for a while, they just kick you to the curb," he says. *a***1994** Smitherman *Black Talk* 150: *Kick to the curb*…To reject someone…[or to] end an established relationship with someone. **1994** J. O'Leary *Univ. Del. Sl.* 19: *Kicked to da Curb* To blow someone off…That girl has kicked me to da curb, she was supposed [*sic*] to go to the movies with me tonight. **1995** *Donahue* (NBC-TV): Don't kick me to the curb. **1995** *Talk Soup* (E!-TV): She's sick of the lies, and she's ready to kick him to the curb. **1995** *Jerry Springer Show* (synd. TV series): You ought to kick your wife to the curb. Get a new wife who'll be faithful to you.

2. to quit with finality.

1995 Stavsky, Mozeson, & Mozeson *A 2 Z* 60: Charlene's got a man, so you can kick that to the curb.

kickapoo juice *n.* [coined in 1941 by Al Capp, U.S. cartoonist, in the comic strip *L'il Abner;* inspired by the names of patent medicines as in *a*1900 quots. and KICK, *n.;* ult. an application of the *Kickapoo,* an Algonquian Indian nation of the Midwest] strong liquor, esp. if homemade. In full, **kickapoo joy juice.** Also **kickapoo.**

[**1858** in M. Simmons *Santa Fe Trail* 54: The "Kickapoo Rangers" [a band of Kansas-Missouri border ruffians].] [*a*1900 in *Amer. West* (Feb. 1967) 35: Kickapoo Indian Oil. Kickapoo Indian Worm Killer. Kickapoo Indian Salve. *Ibid.* 37: The Kickapoo Medicine Company.] **1952** Uris *Battle Cry* 321 [ref. to WWII]: The joyjuice was a jolter.…The kikipoo hit me fast. **1955** N.Y.C. man, age *ca*40: What's in that bottle? Kickapoo juice? **1944–57** Atwell *Private* 513: We bring along some GI alcohol and lemon powder, an'…make a great big batch of kickapoo juice. **1972** Pearce *Pier Head Jump* 173: What do you say we make up a batch of Kickapoo Joy Juice? **1980** Ciardi *Browser's Dict.* 219: *Kickapoo joy-juice* WWII slang, Pacific Theater…Any improvised form of alcoholic drink, as fermented fruit juice drunk green and raw, with whatever additives of paregoric, lemon extract, or worse could be stolen from supply. *a*1981 "K. Rollins" *Fighter Pilots* 102: Charles gives him our secret formula for kickapoo. **1986** Clayton & Elliott *Jazz World* 100: Ed was from Indian extraction like I was and sometimes he and I would drink "kikapoo juice" and go out on some pretty…drunk excursions.

kick-ass *adj.* **1.a.** given to violence; pugnacious.—also used fig.—usu. considered vulgar. [The 1970 quot., which is unavailable for examination, is defined as "strikingly tough, aggressive, or uncompromising"; it is not possible based on this to place the quot. accurately in the current arrangement of senses.]

1970 (cited in *W10*). **1984** W.M. Henderson *Elvis* 36: Another personality, a kick-ass, scary hillbilly. **1987** *New Yorker* (Apr. 13) 20: Sgt.

Barnes is a kickass boozer—a psycho. **1989** R. Miller *Profane Men* 86: About to walk into the next kick-ass ambush.

b. powerful; (*also*) vigorous; forceful.—usu. considered vulgar.

1988 M. Maloney *Thunder Alley* 84: The sheer joy of flying a $40 million kick-ass jet fighter. **1992** Strawberry & Rust *Darryl* 190: You play kick-ass baseball until you're the only one still standing on the field. **1993** *Village Voice* (N.Y.C.) (June 22) 6: You know what it means to see a girl be so kickass with her mind and her guitar.

2. intensely exciting or enjoyable; (*hence,* with weakened force) splendid; DYNAMITE, 2.—usu. considered vulgar. Also (*euphem.*) **kick-butt.**

1980 Conroy *Lords of Discipline* 377: We had a great night. A fabulous, kick-ass night that we'll tell our children about. **1984** Algeo *Stud Buds* 4: A particularly rough and noisy party…*good time,…great party,…kick-ass party,…wild bash.* **1985** *Campus Voice* (Aug.) 25: Mount Holyoke [College] is a kick-ass place—if you're a guy that is. **1988** *Lame Monkey* (Univ. Tenn.) (Jan. 4) 8: This is not a class; this is an emotional experience. Really into material, gives kick-ass lectures. **1989** *21 Jump St.* (Fox-TV): He's in this kick-ass band that plays down at The Lizard. **1989** Chapple & Talbot *Burning Desires* 236: The kick-ass, radical prole Detroit band MC5. **1992** *Rolling Stone* (June 11) 59: The Rolling Stones played kick-ass rock & roll in tiny little trade-union halls. **1992** *Middle Ages* (CBS-TV): That was considered a kick-ass career move. **1993** *Entertainment Tonight* (synd. TV series): I like hanging out with Heidi. She's kick-ass! **1993** *TV Guide* (Feb. 20) 44: On Saturday night, I want to watch some good old "kick-butt" television. **1994** *New York* (Mar. 21) 33: In love with the kick-ass lingo of tabloid life. **1994** *Simpsons* (Fox-TV): I got us some kick-ass seats! **1996** *Melrose Place* (Fox-TV): You want a kick-butt campaign? You got to bring your product into the '90's.

kickback *n.* **1.** an unpleasant repercussion or response; consequences.

1914 S.H. Adams *Clarion* 52: Never…advertise an unwilling testimonial because that kind always has a kick-back. **1924** in D. Hammett *Continental Op* 44: So that he will have an alibi in case there is a kick-back. **1930** Lait *On the Spot* 206: Kickback…also unexpected and unfavorable result. **1936** Twist *We About to Die* (film): You keep on hammerin', you'll get a real kickback one of these days. **1940** R. Chandler *Farewell, My Lovely* ch. xxxiii: And no kickback. No chance for a doctor to back up a complaint if I made one. **1944** *Yank* (Mar. 10) 16: The nurses would be glad to go out with us if only they weren't so afraid of official kick-backs. **1956** M. Wolff *Big Nick.* 147: You know, there's more to getting a divorce than I thought there'd be. There's more kickback to it. **1957** Miller & Childs *Collector's Quest* 106: Aren't you afraid of kick-backs? **1962** Fraley & Robsky *Last Untouchables* 183: Maybe it won't be strictly legal.…But there will be no kickbacks. **1964** *Newsweek* (Aug. 17) 27: F-102s at Saigon Airport: Part of the force that was poised for a kickback. **1966** R.E. Alter *Carny Kill* 95: I can turn in one of two reports and there will be no kickback.

2. *Orig. Und.* a return under coercion or duress of a portion of money or stolen goods; (*also*) (now *S.E.*) a usu. illicit or coerced payment, gift, or return of wages to the facilitator of a transaction or appointment.

1930 Lait *On the Spot* 206: Kickback…Payment pro rata of loot. **1933** Ersine *Prison Slang* 49: They had to make a kickback when the marks beefed. **1934** *Atlantic* (Aug.) 139: The kick-back operates in the following manner. **1940** Riesenberg *Golden Gate* 308: Longshoremen were finding it tougher than ever to get jobs, even through kickbacks of pay, bottles of liquor, and cigars. **1941** *Amer. Mercury* (Oct.) 581: Kickback—any form of secret rebate. **1954** Arnow *Dollmaker* 426: They git kickbacks in money er favors frum th people they give a good…contract to. **1956** "T. Betts" *Across the Board* 317: Professional bettors…receive a kickback of 5 percent from bookmakers on losing bets. **1964** Deutsch *Unsinkable Molly Brown* (film): Guess he deserves a little kickback. **1989** L. Roberts *Full Cleveland* 79: It was like taking kickbacks.

kickback *adj.* relaxing; for relaxation; low-key.

1984–85 in Schneider & Schneider *Sound Off!* 134: I was looking forward to…shore duty in some kickback place. **1990** Bing *Do or Die* 16: Our treehouse, our kickback place.

kick back *v.* **1.** *Orig. Und.* to repay or return (money or stolen goods), usu. (now solely) illicitly or under duress.—also used intrans.

1915–16 Lait *Beef, Iron & Wine* 178: I jus' wants about a twenny....I'll kick it back soon. **1922** *Variety* (Sept. 22) 7: When they saw a chump was getting real hostile they would make themselves solid by "kicking back the dough" (returning the money). **1925** *Collier's* (Aug. 8) 30: Stolen goods returned to the rightful owner are "kicked back." **1926** Maines & Grant *Wise-Crack Dict.* 10: *Kick-back*—Have to return a sucker's money. **1930** *Amer. Mercury* (Dec.) 456: *Kick back, v.:* To return to the victim that of which he has been robbed. "Kick back with that hooch or we give you the works." **1942** L. Foster *Mayor of 44th Street* (film): Somebody was kickin' back to somebody else. **1953** W. Brown *Monkey on My Back* 49: They go on relief, then kick back to the politicians. **1955** Graziano & Barber *Somebody Up There* 140: I didn't realize the other guys are kicking back to the foreman. **1962** in B. Jackson *Swim Like Me* 120: Things is so tight,/I had to kick back a pocketbook from last Saturday night. **1974** "A.C. Clark" *Revenge* 14: I'd rather kick back your money and keep your friendship. **1978** C. Crawford *Mommie* 12: If they didn't kick back, they didn't work that studio the next time a picture was casting. **1980** in McCauley *Dark Forces* 138: See, I put the hours down on Dom's pay so it comes out right with the taxes, but he has to kick it back.

2. to lie back to rest; relax; in phr. **kicked back** relaxing or relaxed.

1972 N.Y.U. student: Just kick back and mellow out. **1972** Carr *Bad* 54: We're kicked back in the next room grinning at Esther's act. **1980** Santoli *Everything* 215: There weren't very many Americans there, so the VC would come into the area to kick back. **1980** in *Penthouse* (Jan. 1981) 26: I was kicked back, enjoying the best head I'd ever had. **1983** *PM Magazine* (ABC-TV) (Apr. 21): Time to come in here, kick back, and relax for a while. **1989** P. Benchley *Rummies* 41: Kick back and let it happen. **1990** P. Dickson *Slang!* 221: *Kick back.* To relax. **1990** Ramada Inns TV ad: It's good to see them kick back and relax. **1994** *Nation* (Aug. 22) 191: The gangsta rapper...is kicking back with smooth, laconic beats. **1995** *Jerry Springer Show* (synd. TV series): We sat around and talked a bit. Kickin' back.

3. to drink; KNOCK BACK.

1989 *21 Jump St.* (Fox-TV): Aaron's kickin' back ... a couple of cool ones.

¶ In phrase:

¶ **kick it back** *CB.* to reply to a CB transmission.

1976 Whelton *CB Baby* 34: We going west to that Ayla town, kick it back. **1977** Dills *CB Slanguage* (ed. 4) 60: *Kick it back:* answer back.

kick-butt var. KICK-ASS.

kicker *n.* **1.** usu. *pl.* **a.** a leg or foot.

1837 *Davy Crockett's Almanack* I (No. 4) 13: Set your kickers on land, and I'll give you a severe licking. **1887** Call *Josh Hayseed* 32: Frog's kickers. **a*1890–96 *F & H* IV 100: *Kicker*...in pl. (common).—The feet. **1977** Coover *Public Burning* 9: A Freeman...can outrun...any...thing in the shape of human that's ever set his unfortunate kickers on Yankee soil!

b. a shoe.

1942 *Yank* (Dec. 9) 5: Arab bootblacks...keeping...G.I. kickers shining. **1942** *ATS* 87: Shoes...*kickers, kicks.* **1958** *AS* XXXIII 224: The *cat*...dons his...*threads*, his *skypiece*, and his *kickers*. **1970–72** in *AS* L (1975) 62: *Kickers*...shoes, especially canvas shoes with rubber soles.

2. a complainer or grumbler.

1876 in *DA:* One "kicker" in a nine will spoil the other eight. **1877** *Puck* (Mar.) 5: Tom is a chronic "kicker," always ready to grumble about something. **1888** Pierson *Slave of Circumstances* 81: You're a regular old kicker; s'pose you dry up? **1888** in *F & H* IV 100: The chronic kicker is always on hand when any improvement is proposed. **1892** Cox *5 Yrs. in Army* 167: Don't degenerate into a chronic grumbler or "kicker." **1921** U. Sinclair *K. Coal* 107: There's sure to be kickers in every coal-camp. **1931** J.T. Adams *Epic of Amer.* 218: The man who criticized or went back East was considered...a "kicker."

3. [perh. fr. phr. *in the kick* (KICK, *n.*, 3.b.)] *Poker.* a card of high rank retained with a pair or three of a kind as a bluff or in hopes of improving one's hand.

1892 in *OEDS:* To keep two small cards and an ace is called holding up "a kicker." **1925** in Grayson *Stories for Men* 20: You're holding that ace for a kicker. **1948** J. Stevens *Jim Turner* 122: He probably thought I was drawing to two pair, or at most to a low set of threes and a kicker. **1949** G.S. Coffin *Winning Poker* 180: *Kicker*...an idle card held up with a pair or triplets in the draw, often for deception. **1995** Poker players in N.Y.C. (coll. J. Sheidlower): "Whaddaya got?" "Nines with an ace kicker."

4. *Naut.* an auxiliary or outboard motor; (*hence*) a boat equipped with an outboard motor.

1909 *Sat. Eve. Post* (July 3) 14: With her "kicker" eating white water and a smell of gasoline streaming half across the Hudson. **1911** *Hampton's Mag.* (Oct.) 434: Get me a tub with a kicker in, and two or three tools. *Ibid.* 436: We row into that slip...with the kicker shut off. **1920** Carter *Devil Dog* 19: Sixty men at a time were loaded in "kickers" (liberty party boats) and carried back to their ships, all happy...and swapping experiences with shipmates. **1929** Bowen *Sea Slang* 78: *Kicker.* An auxiliary motor fitted into a Canadian or American sailing ship. **1949** Cummings *Dict. Sports* 237. **1966–68, 1986** in *DARE.* **1989** Singerman *Amer. Hero* 221: It came with...another five-horse Buccaneer kicker for trolling.

5. a thrill of enjoyment; KICK, 6.c.

1941–42 Gach *In Army Now* 179: What a kicker we get out of receiving a package! **1984** Algeo *Stud Buds* 5: Something that is very good...*awesome...the real kicker.* **1991** R. Carew, on *DayWatch* (CNN-TV) (Jan. 9): I always thought the World Series would be the big kicker, but this [induction into the Baseball Hall of Fame] is the big kicker.

6. a hidden complication or surprising twist; (*hence*) a punch line or striking conclusion.

1941 Riskin *Meet John Doe* (film): And here's the kicker for you—we were in the same outfit. **1945** *Best from Yank* 228: That's where the kicker is, in that "decolletage" jive. **1959** Morrill *Dark Sea Running* 69 [ref. to WWII]: I figured this was a new kicker—spanking the Bosun and putting him to bed. **1959** W. Williams *Ada Dallas* 137: That was the kicker, all right. **1962** in H. Ellison *Sex Misspelled* 92: We sat and listened...and we waited for the kicker. **1968** Bouton *Ball Four* 9: The real kicker came the following year. **1972** *N.Y. Times Book Review* (Mar. 21) 3: The kicker in the social contract is that the private citizen reasonably expects that his agreement to the rules of society will get him something in return. **1976** *N.Y. Post* (Dec. 10) 24: Then he gave me the kicker. **1978** B. Johnson *What's Happenin'* 168: They didn't have room to get the kicker of my McAdoo story in the paper. **1982** in *Nat. Lampoon* (Feb. 1983) 22: And the *final* kicker?...We *feed* the fire this time! **1991** Jenkins *Gotta Play Hurt* 33: Kill the kicker line [of a news story] and be rid of it. **1996** *New Yorker* (June 17) 78: The ideologies of modernity have a kicker, which is that they permit no exit.

7. *Army.* TOPKICKER.

1946–51 J. Jones *Eternity* 34 [ref. to 1940]: All I know, he's the best kicker in the Regimnt....You don't see many Firsts like him no more.

8. *Naut.* a mate on a sailing vessel. Now *hist.*

1958–70 Mjelde *Glory of Seas* [ref. to 1875]: His mate...had quit...so another chief "kicker" had to be shipped.

9. Esp. *S.W.* a countryman; SHITKICKER.

1976 *Nat. Lampoon* (July) 76: Pickers 'N' Kickers. **1980** *AS* (Fall) 200. **1981** *N.Y. Post* (Dec. 14) 25: "Kicker Culture"—all about drinkin' and dancin', Texas music and mechanical bulls. **1986** in *DARE: Kicker*—runs around in cowboy hat, pickup truck.

10. *CB.* (see quot.).

1976 Bibb *CB Bible* 100: *Kicker*...Linear amplifier.

11. *Journ.* (see quot.).

1989 *N.Y. Times* (Dec. 31) IV 8: The tagline (called a "kicker") in the upper left corner labels the story a Review.

12. a chaser.

1990 Berent *Steel Tiger* 252: Marijuana cigarettes with a hash kicker.

¶ In phrase:

¶ **for a** [or **the**] **kicker** extra; for good measure.—often used ironically. Also **for kickers.**

1966 Braly *Cold* 132: The trap was damaged, the man warned and now humiliated for a kicker. **1972** Pendleton *Boston Blitz* 171: He clipped on a couple of grenades, just for kickers, then got into the topcoat. **1981** *Penthouse* (Apr.) 32: For a pledge of just $1,000 you'd get a really nice wood carving. Of course, salvation was thrown in for the kicker.

kick in *v.* **1.a.** to put up, pay, or hand over (what is expected); contribute.—also constr. with *with.*

1906 T.A. Dorgan, in Zwilling *TAD Lexicon* 51: Come on kick in. **1907** in H.C. Fisher *A. Mutt* 7: Say! If you don't kick in with that ice bill by Saturday night, I'll separate you from your breath, see? **1907** *McClure's Mag.* (Feb.) 381: I failed to hear any one kick in with their right name. **1908** H. Green *Maison de Shine* 111: All yuh got to do is

kick in. 1908 McGaffey *Show Girl* 210: A few more will kick in this week. **1909** Chrysler *White Slavery* 20: She…goes down to…"kick in a few dimes with the saloon keepers." **1910** *Variety* (Aug. 20) 13: The twenty members…were all satisfied to kick in the three bucks each. **1911–12** J. London *Smoke Bellew* 13: I'll kick in twice as hard when I get back. **1915–16** Lait *Beef, Iron & Wine* 121: A fat hog what's got dough in every bank kicks in eight a week to you. **1921** *Pirate Piece* (May) 1: Kick in with Fifty Cents or a Buck. **1930** Conwell *Professional Thief* 10: This mob had plenty of money and would kick in $1,200 rather than fight it. **1937** Schary & Butler *Big City* (film): I'll meet you right here. The boys'll kick in. **1947** Motley *Knock on Any Door* 41: Guys who don't kick in get all their stuff taken away from them.…Understand? **1970** Boatright & Owens *Derrick* 143: Nearly everybody would kick in a little money, you know.

b. to take part; *(hence)* (of conditions, machines, etc.) to set in, take effect, begin operation, etc.
   1908 in H.C. Fisher *A. Mutt* 112: There's a…poker game up in Jones' room. Let's kick in. **1908** McGaffey *Show Girl* 30: Now that the first of the year has kicked in. **1913** J. London *Valley of Moon* 58: Come on, kid, an' kick in. **1915** in E. O'Neill *Letters* 48: The English actor in our class is to play a part and wants me to kick in also. **1972** WINS radio news (July 19): The generator kicks in when the power goes out. **1978** J. Webb *Fields of Fire* 208: Before the draft kicked in, when we had what they called "true volunteers." **1981** *Rod Serling's TZ Mag.* (June) 82: A pair of kid truckers [were] hovering over cups of coffee in one of the booths while waiting for their uppers [stimulant pills] to kick in. **1987** *'Teen Mag.* (Jan. 1988) 82: When the ice-cold weather kicks in, my lips suffer.

c. to speak up.
   1930 Rosener *Doorway to Hell* (film): Come on. Come clean. Kick in. **1942** in F. Brown *Angels & Spaceships* 56: What's it about? Kick in. **1974** Beacham & Garrett *Intro 5* 67: Now she kicks in, schemin' on that bit about the money, too young to realize the difference.

d. to do what is demanded or expected; COME ACROSS; *(trans.)* to demonstrate or impart.
   1990 Bing *Do or Die* 18: They'll just rape a girl…if she…don't wanna kick in. **1993** in Stavsky, Mozeson & Mozeson *A 2 Z* 60: We wanted to kick in the funky, mellow side of us instead of the hardcore.

2. to die.
   1908 in H.C. Fisher *A. Mutt* 155: A lady just fell off the Howard Street wharf and is about to kick in. **1912** Lowrie *Prison* 247: He just hangs there swingin' until his heart stops beatin' and the croakers announce that he has kicked in. **1918** in D. York *Mud & Stars* 109: Here, take this overcoat,/Cover that wounded bloke,/Pull it around his throat—/He's kickin' in! **1920** S. Lewis *Main Street* 132: Not that I care a whoop what they say, after I've kicked in and can't hear 'em. **1926** Mazzanovich *Trail of Geronimo* 195: The dead man was too slow on the draw, so had "kicked in" with his boots on. **1930** C. Shaw *Jack-Roller* 160: The lad is very low. He will kick in (die) before the end of the month. **1943** in Truman *Dear Bess* 497: The insurance will keep you when I kick in. **1965–70** in DARE. **1992** in DARE: Kick in—die, kick the bucket.

3. *Und. & Police.* **a.** to break into and rob (a place); burglarize.
   1912 Lowrie *Prison* 280: If I was you I'd cough up about kicking in the P.O. and take your chance with the U.S. people. **1926** J. Black *Can't Win* 78 [ref. to 1890's]: I'll kick in the first private house that looks good. **1930** *Liberty* (July 5) 24: We see a freight depot that looks good. We kick it in about midnight. *Ibid.* (July 19) 22: We're kicking-in barber shops, groceries, and clothing stores. **1944** C.B. Davis *Leo McGuire* 59: Suppose there's a small-town bauble shop that's been practically advertising for a burglar and it gets kicked in. **1973** J.E. Martin *95 File* 83: You knew Highsmith was going to kick in someplace. It's the only thing he does after dark. **1986** J.J. Maloney *Chain* 119: Caught me kicking in a tavern.

b. to raid (an illicit establishment).
   1955 Q. Reynolds *HQ* 10: If you had to kick in a place filled with a lot of hoods with guns, it was good to have Frank Phillips with you.

kicking *adj.* exciting; thrilling; terrific.
   1988 Univ. Tenn. student theme: I made a pass at this broad who had a kickin' bod. **1989** *Dream Street* (NBC-TV): I was just in the middle of a kickin' dream. **1989** *CBS This Morning* (CBS-TV) (Aug. 30): Somethin's hot, somethin's cool, somethin's kickin'. **1989** Univ.

Tenn. student: Knoxville used to be a pretty kickin' town. **1990** in N. George *Buppies, B-Boys* 177: One of several kickin' jams on Prince's *Graffiti Bridge*. **1992** "Sir Mix-a-Lot" *Baby Got Back* (rap song): Cuz your waist is small and your curves are kickin'. **1993** P. Munro *U.C.L.A. Slang II*: That pizza we ate last night was kickin'. **1994** N. Karlen *Babes in Toyland* 134: The song pounded out and Carr smiled.…"That sounds tight, it's kicking!" **1995** *House of Buggin'* (Fox-TV): We got a slammin', kickin' show! **1996** N.Y.C. man, age *ca*30, on *World Today* (CNN-TV) (Apr. 2): That's a pretty kickin' hat!

kick off *v.* **1.** to die.
   [**1905** Belasco *Girl of Golden West* 324: After all, gents, what's death? A kick and you're off.] **1908** in H.C. Fisher *A. Mutt* 131: Well, I'll kick off in good spirits—hic—anyway. **1912** T.A. Dorgan, in Zwilling *TAD Lexicon* 52: He told a friend that his sweetheart had kicked off and he was in mourning. **1915** T.A. Dorgan, in *N.Y. Eve. Jour.* (Aug. 7) 6: He's liable to kick off at any moment. **1920** O'Brien *Best Stories of 1920* 353: I thought you'd kick off, sure. **1927** J. Stevens *Mattock* 185: But I guess I won't kick off and it's me for the States. **1935** in Sagendorf *Popeye* 114: I yam positiff he's kicked off, Doc. **1941** Schulberg *What Makes Sammy Run?* 9: All I know is that my old man kicked off because his brains were muscle-bound. **1953** Roman *Vice Squad* (film): Yeah, he kicked off this mornin'. **1971** *Playboy* (Aug.) 196: You look like you're going to kick off.

2. to kill; KNOCK OFF, 5.a.
   1928 Wharton *Squad* 140 [ref. to 1918]: An' the few that got underground got kicked off by machine-guns when they came out later.

kickout *n.* a dismissal or discharge; *(Mil.)* a dishonorable discharge.
   *****1895** in Partridge *Slang To-Day & Yesterday* 98: I told him all about my having the kick-out from home. **1918** in Truman *Letters Home* 38: If I get a kickout for incompetence then I'll know I've tried anyway. **1948** Webb *Four Steps* 46: You know they can talk swell and flop you and talk tough and give you a kick-out. **1949** Houston *Gun Smugglers* (film): I got myself a fine kick-out. **1967** Spradley *Owe Yourself a Drunk* 13: The good judge gave me a kickout—two days suspended—since this was my first appearance in his court. **1971** Hilaire *Thanatos* 163: I don't want to blow a kick-out over a plan that might blow up.

kick out *v.* **1.** to die.
   *****1898** in *OED:* Here comes the parson…he thinks I'm going to kick out, but I'm not. *****a1898–1902** EDD III: *Kick…out* or *up:* to die. **1926** Wood & Goddard *American Slang* 27: *Kick out.* To die. **1968** I. Reed *Yellow Back Radio* 12: Doc John kicked out. **1986** in *DARE.*

2.a. *Black E.* to hand over; pay up.
   1973 "A.C. Clark" *Crime Partners* 172: If I find what I'm lookin' for, you guys are going to kick out the twenty dollars, ain't you?

b. to produce; create.
   1990 *Guys Next Door* (NBC-TV): The '70's kicked out some stupid stuff.

3. to come to naught; fall through.
   1983 Mamet *Glengarry Glen Ross* 17: A deal kicks out…I [still] got to *eat.*

kick over *v.* **1.** to murder; KNOCK OVER, 1.
   1927 C.J. Daly *Snarl of Beast* 246: The girl—she knew too much—had to be kicked over.

2. *Und. & Police.* KICK IN, 2.a., b.
   1929 Hotstetter & Beesley *Racket* 230: *Kick over*…to raid and demolish an illegal or suspected establishment; *e.g.* "They kicked over his joint yesterday." **1930** *Amer. Mercury* (Dec.) 456: *Kick over,* v.: To rob. "We kick over the spot for five yards."

3. to discuss; chat about.
   1981 Sann *Trial* 165: You must have had fun kicking over old times with Ed.

kick-shins *n.* an annoying or offensive person.
   1867 Clark *Sailor's Life* 95: Yes, old kick-shins, what will you give, to save your neck from the bow-string.

kicksies *n.pl.* [app. var. of KICK, 3.a.] *Und.* breeches; trousers. Also vars.
   *****1708** in Partridge *Dict. Und.* 382: *Kicksey* [*sic*], Breeches. *****1753** in Partridge *Dict. Und.*: *Nap his Tuggs and Kixes;* take his Cloaths and Breeches. **1807** Tufts *Autobiog.* 291 [ref. to 1794]: *Kickses*…breeches. *****1812** Vaux *Vocab.: Kickseys:* breeches.…To *turn out* a man's *kickseys*

means to pick the pockets of them. **1846** in H.L. Gates, Jr. *Sig. Monkey* 93: "Kicksies"...inexpressibles. ***1851** H. Mayhew *London Labour* I 52: A pair of Kerseymere Kicksies, any colour, built very slap up. **1852** *Harper's Mo.* (Dec.) 90: The sooner you peels off them cloth kicksies the better.

kick-stick *n. Narc.* a marijuana cigarette.
 1966–67 P. Thomas *Mean Streets* 66: The steady hiss of cats blasting away on kick-sticks.

kick through *v.* to provide or pay up; come across.—often constr. with *with.*
 1915–17 Lait *Gus* 93: Kick t'rough with eighty-five cen's. **1925** in Grayson *Stories for Men* 17: We work for anybody who kicks through with the kale. **1937** in Goodstone *Pulps* 18: I'm broke. Come on—kick through. **1938** Steinbeck *Grapes of Wrath* 69: It'll surprise you how many'll kick through with the rest. **1941** Mahin & Grant *Johnny Eager* (film): You didn't send it in, Luce. You're not kickin' through. **1942** Boucher *Werewolf* 238: Will you kindly kick through with your half of the bargain? **1942** E.S. Gardner *Drowning Duck* 70: He's threatening to go to you with the facts, unless she kicks through with some dough to buy his silence. **1995** *NADS* (May) 11: *Kick through*—to pay up. From seven [*DARE*] informants: California, Oregon, Washington. Clearly a northwest phrase.

kick-up *n.* **1.** a frolic; party.
 1778 in *Md. Hist. Mag.* III (1908) 116: Tuesday Decr 1 we Collected the Girls in the neighbourhood and had a kick up in the Evening. ***1796** Grose *Vulgar Tongue* (ed. 3) s.v. *kicks: A kick-up*; a disturbance, also a hop or dance. **1804** in *DAE*: See what lasses we can pick up/For our famous village kick up. **1852** B.R. Hall *Freeman's Barber Shop* 104: The darkies were to have a special "kick-up" to themselves. ***1899** Whiteing *John St.* 100: There's a little bit of a kick-up to-night with a few of us—sort of sing-song. ***1910** in *OED2*.

 2. a disturbance or dispute; row; commotion.
 a1793** in *OED2*: I knew nothing of this kick-up, and I ought to have been informed of it beforehand. ***1796** (quot. at **(1)**, above). ***1812** in *OED2*: No chance of a kick-up, or row being plann'd. **1840** Crockett *Almanac 1841* 14: When we had the last kick up with John Bull. **1848** *Rough & Ready Songster* 87: There's a kick-up just coming with him and John Bull. **1851** *Harper's Mo.* (Sept.) 469: What's the kick-up? *a1889** *Century Dict.: Kickup*...A disturbance. (Slang.). **1931** Lubbock *Bully Hayes* 26: And weren't there a kick-up...when they found the *Otranto* had sailed in the night!

 3. a novelty; KICK, 1.a.
 1818 in Royall *Letters from Ala.* 125: I am opposed to all these new kick-ups. Whenever I see a gal so very coy and prudish...it gives me a bad opinion of her.

 4. (see quot.).
 *a***1889** *Century Dict.: Kickup*...A steamboat with paddle-wheel astern. (Mississippi river.).

kicky *adj.* delightful; diverting; exciting.
 1942 *Pittsburgh Courier* (Mar. 28) 7: The "cats" were purring and the music was "kicky." **1966** (cited in *W10*). **1967** R. Kent *Hot Rods to Hell* (film): Those pajamas—the real kicky ones with the lace. **1967** Taggart *Reunion of 108th* 206: I guess that part of it was pretty kicky. **1969** *Rowan & Martin's Laugh-In* (NBC-TV): Time for a tricky, kicky quickie! **1970** Corrington *Bombardier* 32: It won't be kicky, no. **1972** in J. Flaherty *Chez Joey* 25: No revolutionary berets present, no kicky ethnic costumes. **1983** *Mother Jones* (May) 58: McCourt gets a kicky turn of phrase into nearly every sentence. **1990** Bing *Do or Die* vii: A fashion editor...decided it would be "kicky." **1994** *New York* (Nov. 28) 45: The willowy six-foot-four (in heels) Oriana, resplendent in a kicky black wig, a black PVC jumpsuit, and five-inch spikes.

kid[1] *n.* **1.**[**a.** *Scots.* (used as an endearment).
 ***ca1508** in Dunbar *Poems* 41: Quod he, My kid, my capircalyeane,/My bony bab...Ye brek my hairt, my bony ane.]

 b. a child; (*also*) an inexperienced youth or youngster. Now *colloq.* or *S.E.* [With contemptuous force in ***1618** quot. (incorrectly dated "1599" in *OED2*). In 20th C., often used attrib., leading to KID, *adj.*]
 ***1618** Middleton & Rowley *Old Law* III ii: I'm old, you say? Yes, parlous old, kids, and you mark me well; This beard cannot get chil-

dren, you lank suck-eggs,...you lecherous dog-bolts. ***1690** T. D'Urfey, in *F & H* IV 101: And at her back a Kid that cry'd/Still as she pinch'd it, fast was ty'd. ***1694** in J. Dryden *Dramatic Wks.* VI 476: And not to be too Coming before Marriage:/For fear of my Misfortune in the Play,/A Kid brought home upon the Wedding day. ***1698–99** "B.E." *Dict. Canting Crew: Kid*...a Child; also the first Year of a Roe, and a young Goat. ***1719–20** D'Urfey *Pills* II 193: *She*....Yet but do take the Child, all I'll forgive thee. *He*. Send your *Kid* home to me, I will take care on't. *Ibid.* V 109: For if you should chance to get me with Kid. ***1748** in *F & H* IV 101: *Kid*...a nickname for a child or young person. ***1789** G. Parker *Life's Painter* 135: Scamp the ballad-singing kid,/Call'd me his darling frow. *Ibid.* 139: Seedy brims and kids. *Ibid.* 173: *Kid*...a young boy. ***1812** Vaux *Vocab.*: *Kid*: a child of either sex, but particularly applied to a boy who commences thief at an early age; and when by his dexterity he has become famous, he is called by his acquaintances *the kid* so and so, mentioning his surname. **1851** [G. Thompson] *Jack Harold* 78: But what became of the young *blowen*—the *kid*? **1859** Matsell *Vocab.* 48: *Kid.* A child; a youth; a young one. ***1862** Cheadle *Journal* 99: Arrival of Kinamontayoo, wife, kid. **1868** Aldrich *Bad Boy* 57: By the way, Bailey, you were a good kid not to let on to Grimshaw about the candy....Phil Adams and Jack Harris were considerably our seniors, and though they always treated us "kids" very kindly, they generally went with another set. **1869** *Overland Mo.* (Aug.) 116: Never picked a pocket since I was a *kid*. **1872** "M. Twain" *Life on Miss.* 295: I...picked up seven kids (*little boys*) & got them to come in. **1872** Crapsey *Nether Side* 40: "Kids"...not more than ten years of age. **1875** Daly *Pique* 315: I think I ought to have the kid for safe keeping. **1875** in F. Remington *Sel. Letters* 11: There was a durned "country kidd" came here some time ago and the fellows...call him "Golic." **1882** Peck *Peck's Sunshine* 181: I want you kids to go through your studies like a tramp through a boiled dinner. **1883** *Life* (Mar. 8) 118: She's going to talk about my Highly Intelligent Kids, and say "Father, dear Father, come home with me now." **1889** Alger *Snobden's Office Boy* 122: Get out of the way, kid, or you'll get hurt. **1893** W.K. Post *Harvard* 30: I'll look after all your indigent kids for you. **1894** Bridges *Arcady* 32: No dead kids in my literature, please. **1896** F.P. Dunne, in Schaaf *Dooley* 260: I wint down to th' Polish school hall las' Wins'dah f'r to see th' young kid [William Jennings] Bryan. **1905** in Opper *H. Hooligan* 68: Somebody left dis kid on your doorstep. **1904–11** D.G. Phillips *Susan Lenox* I 107: What a nerve for a kid—and a lady, too! *a***1940** in Lanning & Lanning *Texas Cowboys* 18: I was just a happy-go-lucky kid. **1945** Horman & Grant *Here Come the Co-Eds* (film): I know all the kids'll chip in. **1960** *Dinosaurus!* (film): Get the kid out of the way. **1965** Hersey *Too Far to Walk* 21: He had...had a Shakespeare seminar of only six kids. **1970** Boatright & Owens *Derrick Floor* 74: Well, I started hanging around the livery stable when I was a pretty small kid. **1975** Burchard & Burchard *O.J. Simpson* 87: It's something to tell my kids about. **1979** Kiev *Courage to Live* 18: I'm worrying about my kid making it to college. **1985** P. Donahue *Human Animal* 26: Like a lot of creative kids, Charles [Darwin] didn't make a very good student. **1989** Guare *Six Degrees* 52: We called our kids.

 c. a person (orig. a young man) who is active, clever, or companionable; young fellow; sport; (*hence*) (in direct address) fellow or friend (now usu. *pl.*, to a number of adult friends, usu. of both sexes); in phr. **this** [or **the**] **kid** I or me (usu. *joc.*); **the —— kid** a person notable for ——.
 ***1811** *Lexicon Balatron: Kid.* A little dapper fellow. ***1821** in Partridge *Slang* 81: Cyprians fine,/Kids full of wine [etc.]. ***1834** Ainsworth *Rookwood* 258: Two *milling coves*, each vide awake,...Both *kids* agreed to *play a cross*. **1877** Wheeler *Deadwood Dick, Prince of the Road* 81: Ye ar' a right peart-lookin' kid, stranger. **1890** in F. Remington *Sel. Letters* 105: The 1st cavalry...good kids. *Ibid.* 106: You 10th Cavalry Kids. **1894** C.C. King *Under Fire* 86: It's just when you can't see one that a valley's most apt to be full of 'em, kid. **1896** S. Crane *George's Mother* 154: Yez can't [fool] that kid! **1905** S.E. Griggs *Hindered* 38: I got Indian blood in me and if they pester this kid they are goin' to hear sump'in' drap. **1905** *DN* III 85: *Kid n.* [College] Student, fellow-student. "I worked that problem with another *kid*." "Come on, *kids*" (used by students of both sexes). **1907** in H.C. Fisher *A. Mutt* 7: Ain't I the hard luck kid? Only $12 left. **1910** *N.Y. Eve. Jour.* (Feb. 4) 20: Jones is a smart kid. **1911** *N.Y. Eve. Jour.* (Feb. 11) 8: Hello,

Schmalz, old kid. **1911** Van Loan *Big League* 68: I'm the heart-breaking kid. That's the best thing I do. Leave it to me. **1926** Tully *Jarnegan* 238: I want to take a long ride, kids. **1926** Nason *Chevrons* 81: Here's Eadie. Good kid! **1933** R. Fisher, in C. Major *Calling Wind* 65: Go to it, kids. **1941** Rossen *Blues in Night* (film): Hang on to your lids, kids....Hello, kids. **1947–51** Motley *We Fished* 9: Okay, kids, let's clear out. **1953** in Wepman et al. *The Life* 120: I said..."Don't let them burn the kid." **1961** *Dick Van Dyke Show* (CBS-TV): Kids, can we get to work please? **1970** N.Y.U. student: Things were looking bad for the kid, but I managed to get through it. **1982** in G. Tate *Flyboy* 20: Because in the beginning, the kid couldn't hang. **1983** Stapleton *30 Yrs.* 32: Keep it movin', Jack, old kid, that's the boy, back and forth. **1988** S. Lee *School Daze* (film): "Who's comin' with me...?" "Not the kid." **1993** *Garfield & Friends* (CBS-TV): The kid tried everything.

d. a young woman.—usu. used patronizingly or affectionately. Now *rare* except in affectionate direct address; in phr. **O, you kid** (addressed jocularly to an attractive young woman, often preceded by "I love my wife, but").

[*1851 in D.R. Cox *Sex. & Vict. Lit.* 138: Mother Willit...calls [the whores who work for her] her *darters,* her *chickens,* and *kids.*] [**1905** (*DN* quot. at **(c)**).] **1908** W.G. Davenport *Butte & Montana* 13: Oh, gee, be sweet to me, kid. **1911** Van Loan *Big League* 72: An awfully nice little kid!...I'll bet that big slob has been annoying her almost to death. **1914** Kreymborg *Edna* 15: Cause there ain't no soft lights and soft music there, kid. **1917** in Dreiser *Diaries* 237: Then we go up to Madeleine Sullivan's....Madeleine [is] a sweet dirty kid. **1918** Grider *War Birds* 116: She's a cute little kid and a good dancer. She's been living with one of the boys for a couple of months. **1918** Mencken *Amer. Lang.* 303: I love my wife, but O you kid. **1935** in Fortune *Fugitives* 140: Are you all right, honey?...Can you make the river, kid? **1937** Steinbeck *Mice & Men* 56: "Seen the new kid yet?"..."What kid?"..."Why, Curley's new wife." **1939–40** O'Hara *Pal Joey* 16: The local Winchell links my name constantly with the name of a very sweet kid that I go to the club and play golf with. **1946** I. Shulman *Amboy Dukes* 21: Frank winked at some trim-looking kids who passed the restaurant. **1951** Spillane *Lonely Night* 10: The way the kid's body stiffened with the shock of seeing him was enough. **1954** Johnson *Black Widow* (film): I took a kid I met there out to dinner. **1972** Dorson *Folklore & Folklife* 154: Such expressions as "Twenty-three skidoo" and "Oh, you kid" are meaningless to anyone born after the first World War. **1993** *Simpsons* (Fox-TV): Hubba hubba! O you kid!

e. *Pris.* a catamite.

1893 (quot. at PRUSHUN). **1912** Berkman *Prison* 169 [ref. to 1893]: You're over twenty-two and don't know what a kid is! Well, if it don't beat raw eggs, I don't know what does. **1934** Fishman *Sex in Prison* 103: It wasn't that I wanted a "kid." **1969** Hopper *Sex in Prison* 94: If a young prisoner is forced into a homosexual relationship, he may be known as a "gal-boy," "kid," "punk kid," or simply "boy." *a*1979 Pepper & Pepper *Straight Life* 284: A few people decided this cat was my kid, my punk, my girl friend.

2. *Journ.* a kidnapper.

1862 *N.Y. Tribune* (Apr. 9) 6: He was informed by one of the kidnappers that they were going to take him to his master, as he was a runaway slave....The sentinel...ordered...the "kids" to get out of the carriage...The "kids" were taken before Col. Childs.

kid² *n.* a teasing or joking statement; jest; (*usu.*) in phr. **no kid** no kidding; (this is) the truth.

*1873 Hotten *Slang Dict.*: "No kid, now?" is a question often asked by a man who thinks he is being hoaxed. *a*1889 *Century Dict.*: *Kid*...A hoax; humbug.—*No kid,* without fooling or chaffing. (Slang, U.S. and Australia.). **1896** Ade *Artie* 7: That ain't no kid. **1899** in Ade *Chicago Stories* 248: I thought it was a kid, on the level. **1906** *Independent* (July 5) 142: Youse made a hit wit me, an' that's no kid. **1906** H. Green *Actors' Boarding House* 186: That goes fur the whole bunch, an' it ain't no kid! **1912** Ade *Babel* 177: Then just for a kid I told her. **1913–15** Van Loan *Taking the Count* 183: You think it's a kid? All right...stick around and see! **1917** W.R. Burroughs *Oakdale Affair* 15: Can't yuh take a kid?...I knew youse all along. **1919** *Variety* (Apr. 4) 23: This is no kid. **1927–28** in R. Nelson *Dishonorable* 110: Sullivan: I ain't used to nothin' ever happenin' any more'n you. *Miller:* No kid? **1950** Medford & Weidman *Damned Don't Cry* (film): No kid!...As simple as that, huh? **1964** in *OED2.*

kid *adj.* **1.** (of a sibling or other relative) younger; (*also*) youthful and inexperienced.—used prenominally. Now *colloq.*

1895 J.L. Williams *Princeton* 143: Guying his kid brother Dick. **1896** Ade *Artie* 85: There was a kid cousin o' mine. **1912** Spalding *Base Ball* 75: Their kid pitcher would surely become rattled and go to pieces. **1919** in Hemingway *Sel. Letters* 22: One of the kid sisters just brought up a plate of lobster salad sandwiches. **1929–30** Dos Passos *42d Parallel* 345: He's my kid brother, Fred. **1954** Chayefsky *Marty* (film): My kid brother Nicky got married last week. **1961** Dillon *Judi* 9: Is this really Jan's kid sister?

2. fit only for children.—used prenominally; in phrs. **kid stuff** things fit only for children or for the immature; childish nonsense (in early use infl. by KID², *n.*); **greasy kid stuff** any thick hair dressing for men (*joc.,* coined in ads for Vitalis and its "nongreasy formula"). Now *colloq.*

1911 Bronson-Howard *Enemy to Society* 30: I'm getting old enough to have something else beside "kid" books. **1912** *Adventure* (June) 241: Cut out the kid-stuff. **1915–16** Lait *Beef, Iron & Wine* 9: Kids are kid-stuff, anyhow. **1918** *N.Y. Sun* (Aug. 25) V 7: All that stuff I wrote you...was just kid stuff and I know you caught it Gertie. **1929** Brooks *Psych. of Adolescence* 605: The little fellow looked at the book a minute, leaned back in the seat, and in a very caustic, critical manner sneered, "Kid stuff." **1934** Weseen *Dict. Slang* 360: *Kid stuff*—Immature thought or speech; childish conduct. **1943** Crowley & Sachs *Follow the Leader* (film): That's all kid stuff...I've outgrown that. **1956** TV safety message (CBS-TV): Kid stuff! Kid stuff! Careless driving is kid stuff! **1958** D. Stanford *Ski Town* 60: It was silly kid stuff to be susceptible to the sight of...[a] pretty girl. **1959** Campbell *Cry for Happy* 4: Go on! That's kid stuff—just a trick. **1966** Vitalis TV ad (ABC-TV): Still using that greasy kid stuff?...So get rid of that greasy kid stuff [etc.]. **1966** *Time* (June 24) 33: Today's sports hero...loses glamour when seen combing greasy kid stuff out of his hair. **1975** Wambaugh *Choirboys* 263: Harold...parted his...hair and combed it back. "Help if you had some greasy kid stuff," said Scuz. **1981** *Daily News* (N.Y.) (July 30) 37: And Clark, give me a break with that greasy kid stuff! **1993** *Are You Afraid of Dark?* (Nickelodeon TV): he can't scare me with that kid stuff.

kid *v.* [orig. unkn.] **1.** to joke with; (*hence*) to tease or make fun of; (*intrans.*) to joke, tease, or pretend. Now *colloq.*

*1811 *Lexicon Balatron.:* Kid...To amuse a man or divert his attention while another robs him. *The sneaksman kidded the cove of the ken, while his pall frisked the panney;* the thief amused the master of the house, while his companion robbed the house. *1867 in *Amer. Mercury* (Mar. 1929) 334: Coburn [a prizefighter] *kidded* McCoole, as the English say. *1873 Hotten *Slang Dict.* (ed. 4): *Kid,* to joke. *1888 in *OED2*: The champion kidder. *1889 Barrère & Leland *Dict. Slang* I 520: *Kid, to* (popular), to impose in any way, pretend. **1892** L. Moore *Own Story* 464: He was made to say he was only "kidding" the Boston officers when he told them it was a Chicago "mob"...who had done the job. **1895** Sinclair *Alabama* 141: To those who saw this stalwart giant under the "kidding" of his messmates, the memory will always bring a smile. **1896** Ade *Artie* 71: Oh-h-h, but you t'ink you're a kidder. *Ibid.* 85: A lot o' the hands used to come over and kid me. **1896** in S. Crane *N.Y.C. Sks.* 165: I was only kiddin', Johnnie. **1900** *DN* II 44: *Kid,* v.t....To make sport of. **1904** *Life in Sing Sing* 250: *Kid*...to joke. **1905** in "O. Henry" *Works* 1256: Quit yer kiddin'. **1912** Field *Watch Yourself* 369: But like all so-called kidders, they could not stand the gaff. **1914** S. Lewis *Mr. Wrenn* 229: Males should be jocular and show their appreciation of the ladies by "kidding them." **1920** F.S. Fitzgerald *Paradise* 82: Kerry was only kidding. **1920** Hurst *Humoresque* 64: That's right—kid me to death. **1920–21** Witwer *Leather Pushers* 95: Oh, a kidder, hey? **1938** J. Vogel *Man's Courage* 177: Look here, Wolak, what's the use of kidding yourself? **1951** in Kerouac *Letters* 296: I was the youngest, was known to be a former college boy, and so was kidded. **1955** Yates & Smith *It Came from Beneath the Sea* (film): Are you kidding me? **1959** *Alfred Hitchcock Presents* (CBS-TV): What a great kidder you are! **1994** Gabor *Speaking Your Mind* 11: She protests, "I was just kidding."

2. to cajole or persuade, esp. by humor or flattery.

*1811 *Lexicon Balatron:* Kid. To coax or wheedle. *1839 Brandon *Poverty* (gloss.): *Kidding on*—to entice one on. *1865 in *Comments on Ety.* (Nov. 1, 1987) 22: So thee "kid" Jess tu let ur 'ave ennuf tu goa tu t' butchers in. **1928** Guerin *Crime* 247: She...successfully "kidded" him that she had water on the knee. **1929–30** Dos Passos *42d Parallel*

53: Ike kidded her into bringing them each another cup of coffee without extra charge.

3. to fool, trick, or deceive.—also used intrans.

*1811 *Lexicon Balatron.*: Kid...To inveigle. *1812 *Vaux Vocab.*: To kid a person out of anything, is to obtain it from him by means of false pretence. 1859 Matsell *Vocab.* 48: Kidded...humbugged. *1872 in *F & H* IV 103: Kidding...throwing dust in a fellow mortal's eyes....[They] were themselves kidding with the greatest activity. *1879 *Macmillan's Mag.* (Oct.) 505: I thought they was only kidding (deceiving) at first. *1883 Russell *Sailors' Lang.* 77: Kid or cod.—To joke. To deceive by joking misrepresentations. 1892 L. Moore *Own Story* 124 [ref. to 1860's]: He is the biggest "kidder" (meaning deceiver) I ever saw. *a1890–96 *F & H* IV 103: To kid oneself...(common).—To be conceited. 1896 in Robinson *Comics* 161: Now they are kidding me. They say I am a populist but you can't kid a billy goat. 1902 Hobart *Back to Woods* 103: Quit your kidding! 1908 in McCay *Little Nemo* 146: Who do you think you are kiddin'? 1911 in O. Johnson *Lawrenceville* 447: It's a con game—he's kidding us. 1912 Mathewson *Pitching* 77: What are you trying to do—kid me? 1915 [Swartwood] *Choice Slang* 52: Kid yourself...To deceive yourself. 1920 in De Beck *Google* 84: No kiddin Tim—There's a dollar o' mine in this box. 1928 R. Fisher *Jericho* 185: There is no better advice, I think, than that of the ruffian on the street, whose motto is "Don't kid yourself." 1929–30 Dos Passos *42d Parallel* 53: You don't think you can kid me, do you? 1938 T. Wolfe *Web & Rock* 480: It's your fault I ever kidded myself into thinking I was a writer. 1977 R.S. Parker *Effective Decisions* 5: Are you aware how many decisions you make? If you think there are only a few you are kidding yourself.

¶ In phrases:

¶ **I kid you not** I promise you this is true. Cf. *I shit you not* s.v. SHIT, *v.*

1956 E. Hunter *Second Ending* 277: I kid you not. 1958 Camerer *Damned Wear Wings* 51 [ref. to WWII]: I kid you not when I say he's going to have a rough time. 1961 Kohner *Gidget Goes Hawaiian* 25: I kid you not. 1964 Howe *Valley of Fire* 57: I kid thee not one pound. 1971 N.Y.U. student: His exams are murder. I kid you not. 1989 *Donahue* (NBC-TV): I kid you not—...the most interesting mold you ever saw in your life. 1990 *Sally Jessy Raphaël* (synd. TV series): And I kid you not—wealth corrodes you.

¶ **kid on the square** [or **level**] to banter with underlying serious intent.

1907 *McClure's Mag.* (Feb.) 379: I'm kiddin' on the square....I was an out-and-out snoljer [*sic*] with the milish...in Colorado. 1913–15 Van Loan *Taking the Count* 340: "Quit your kidding!" "But I might be kidding on the square!" 1930 Graham & Graham *Queer People* 116: It was supposed to be kidding, but it was kidding on the level. 1937 *Esquire* (Feb.) 63: And that's kidding on the square, baby. 1944 E.S. Gardner *Crooked Candle* 108: *I'm* kidding on the square....You're stringing me along. 1956 H. Gold *Not with It* 28: Fact I'm kidding on the square, Grack. 1991 *CBS This Morning* (CBS-TV) (Dec. 18): He's kidding on the square.

kiddo *n.* [KID[1], *n.* + -o] **1.** KID[1], *n.*, 1.c., d.—usu. used in direct address.

[*1896 in *OED2*: Josh was up almost before Kiddo Cook reached him.] 1905 *DN* III 85: Kiddo, *n.* (in the vocative case only.) Used by students to each other in familiar address. "Say, *kiddo*, what are you going to do this evening?" 1906 H. Green *Boarding House* 20: And that's no dream, kiddo. 1908 in H.C. Fisher *A. Mutt* 60: I want to tell you something, kiddo. 1918 E. O'Neill *Moon* 37: Oh, you kiddo! 1926 W. White *Flight* 217: Don't worry, kiddo. You'll make 'em. 1928 Guerin *Crime* 21 [ref. to a1880]: "Cheer up, kiddo," they all said to me, "it won't be long before you're used to it." 1928 MacArthur *War Bugs* 244: The prevalent joke was to misunderstand all the new kiddos' orders. 1929 Bodenheim *60 Secs.* 231: He was a nice kiddo. 1937 Di Donato *Christ in Concrete* 39: Well, what is it, kiddo? 1958 Johnson *Henry Orient* 90: Well, kiddo...how's tricks? 1967 S.E. Hinton *Outsiders* 18: Listen, kiddo...he don't mean nothin'. *Ibid.* 118: This kiddo can use his head. 1976 Haseltine & Yaw *Woman Doctor* 42: None of your switching tactics, kiddo. 1983 in Waller et al. *Lexington Intro. to Lit.* 84: You're one in a zillion, kiddo. 1978–86 J.L. Burke *Lost Get-Back Boogie* 118: What do you think, kiddo? 1989 *Roseanne* (ABC-TV): You're an amazing woman, kiddo.

2. KID[1], 1.b.

1942 *ATS* 357: Child...*kidlet, kiddo.* 1987–89 M.H. Kingston *Tripmaster Monkey* 84: In front of the customers and their kiddos. 1990 *Morning News* (CNN-TV) (Nov. 27): When I was a kiddo in elementary school. 1994 *Reader's Digest* (Apr.) 210: Iney...called Roger and me "the kiddos."

kiddy *n.* **1.** Orig. *Und.* a flashy young man who is usu. a rake or a thief.

1778 in G.G. Carey *Song Bag* 88: This girl she married a railing [*sic*; prob. for *rolling*] Kidday,/One of the Bully's of the Town. *1781 in Partridge *Dict. Und.* 383: My time, O ye kiddies, was happily spent. *1789 G. Parker *Life's Painter* 136: Like *natty* shinning [*sic*] *kiddies.* 1805 *Port Folio* (Aug. 24) 261: No kiddy cuts a better dash. *1796 Grose *Vulgar Tongue* (ed. 3): *Kiddeys*, young thieves. *1812 Vaux *Vocab.*: *Kiddy:* a thief of the lower order, who...dresses in the extreme of vulgar gentility, and affects a knowingness in his air and conversation, which renders him in reality an object of ridicule....*My kiddy* is a familiar term used by these gentry in addressing each other. 1821 Waln *Hermit in Phila.* 23: I felt some curiosity to observe the manners of the company, which—he took care to inform me—consisted entirely of "*regular built kiddies.*" Tom is one of the fraternity, a little addicted to the bottle, more to the slang, and, according to his vocabulary, "*up to any thing.*" *1823 in Byron *Works* 920: Poor Tom was once a kiddy upon town,/A thorough varmint, and a *real* swell. *1863 in *OED.* *1864 in *Comments on Ety.* (Dec. 1993) 39: This old "kiddy"...[won't] turn white at any "graft" on the board.

2.a. Now *Black E.* a young fellow; chap.

*1816, *1818 (cited in Partridge *DSUE* (ed. 8) 1236). 1840 *Spirit of Times* (June 27) 193: Well, my kiddy,...here you are. *1860 in *F & H* IV 107: Hollo, my kiddy, stir your stumps. *1873 Hotten *Slang Dict.* (ed. 4): *Kiddy*, a man or boy. Formerly a low thief. 1912 Berkman *Prison Memoirs* 143 [ref. to 1892]: Bes' thing for the blues, kiddie. 1928 MacArthur *War Bugs* 205: One kiddie named Ludwig, a hungrylooking Bavarian with a handlebar moustache, paused in his rush to the rear. 1942 *Yank* (Aug. 5) 9: Honey, you shouldn't come on that way with a...kiddie like me. 1962 H. Simmons *On Eggshells* 114: Answer the kiddy's question. 1965 *Esquire* (July) 45: *Down kiddies*...spend their lives trying to *waste* each other.

b. a child.—now usu. constr. in pl.

*1858 A. Mayhew *Paved with Gold* 102: An old woman and a child....A doll and a kiddy!" shout two of the lads in one voice. *1889 in *OED:* Ever since they was little kiddies. 1905 J. London, in Paxton *Sport U.S.A.* 29: A wife and two kiddies that must be fed. 1910 *Variety* (June 11) 16: For kiddies' matinees the act ought to get away splendidly. 1914 S. Lewis *Mr. Wrenn* 107: The penalty for my having been a naïve kiddy, hungry for friendship, once. 1916 in R. Lardner *Round Up* 126: Them and his wife and kiddies.

c. a young person, esp. a young woman.

1904–11 D.G. Phillips *Susan Lenox* I 255: Let the kiddie enjoy herself. 1937 Kober *Wonderful Time* 119: Make it snappy, kiddies. I got a heavy date. 1952 E. Brown *Trespass* 118: My gals is okay....They straight kiddies, you know that.

kiddy court *n.* *Police.* juvenile court.

1975 Sepe & Telano *Cop Team* 9: His destination would be Children's Court or, as police call it, "Kiddie Court."

kiddy cruise *n.* *Navy.* a period of enlistment beginning at age seventeen and requiring written parental consent.

1966 in IUFA *Folk Speech: Kiddie cruise* Navy expression for cruise [enlistment] by young sailors. 1992 Jernigan *Tin-Can Man* 15 [ref. to 1941]: "We'll be starting the new kiddie cruises sometime in December."...(A kiddy cruise meant you were in the Navy from age 17 to 21; then you were discharged.).

kiddy joint *n.* *Police.* a juvenile corrections facility. Also **kiddie camp.**

1970 J. Howard *Please Touch* 83: You're eighteen and you did two years in some kiddie joint and you come on like Al Capone. 1990 Vachss *Blossom* 108: Every joint's got one, especially the kiddie camps.

kiddy porn *n.* representations, as photographs or stories, depicting children in lewd poses or engaged in sexual acts.

1979 in *Barnhart Dict. Comp.* I (1982) 63: Kiddie porn. 1981 Wambaugh *Glitter Dome* 136: What? Porn?...Kiddy porn? 1995 *CNN & Co.* (CNN-TV) (Aug. 30): They smacked too much of kiddy porn.

1995 *Newsweek* (Sept. 11) 60: America's best-known designer drops his controversial "kiddie porn" ads under pressure.

kiddy-vid var. KIDVID.

kidlet *n.* a small child. *Joc.* Also **kidlets** (used as an affectionate term of address for a young woman).
    *1889 Barrère & Leland *Dict. Slang* I 519: *Kidlet*, a boy or girl. **1899** "J. Flynt" *Tramping* 31: The other "kidlets," as they were nicknamed, were as deformed morally as was the adopted girl physically. **1903** J. Dewey, in R.B. Perry *W. James* II 521: We won't attempt to father you with all the weak kidlets...crying...to be born. **1912** Siringo *Cowboy Detective* 10 [caption]: The Kidlet Author After he Became a Cowboy. **1916** *DN* IV 276: *Kidlet*, n. Diminutive of *kid*, child. ([Nebr.] Also Pa., Kan.). **1929** *Variety* (Oct. 30) 1: She shussshed the Winchell kidlets. **1936** Gaddis *Courtesan* 110: Stay where you are, kidlets—I'll see who it is. *a***1942** M. Wolff *Night Shift* 447: Hey, you kidlets, I've got something for you. *1959 in *OEDS*: A lot of kidlets helping him to do so. *1989 T. Thorne *Dict. Contemp. Sl.* 292: *Kidlet* n *British* a small child. A middle-class term.

kidnapper *n.* [KID[1] *n.* + NAP + -*er*] Orig. *Und.* one who steals or entices (a person) away (orig. for indentured servitude or slavery, now usu. for ransom). Now *S.E.* Hence, by back formation, **kidnap**, *v.* [Well established as S.E. in early 19th C.]
    *1666 in Partridge *Dict. Und.* 384: Kid-napper. *1669 *New Acad. of Complements* 193: A Kid-napper,/Spirits young men. *1673 [R. Head] *Canting Acad.* 40: *Kidnapper* A fellow that walketh the streets, and takes all advantages to pick up the younger sort of people, whom with lies and many fair promises he inticeth on board a ship and transports them to foreign plantations. *1676–77 E. Coles *Dict.*: *Kidnapper*, c[ant]. a stealer or enticer away of Children, etc. *1682 in Dryden *Dramatic Works* IV 474: Mr John Wilmore having kidnapped a boy of 13 years of age to Jamaica. *1698–99 "B.E." *Dict. Canting Crew*: *Kidnapper*, one that Decoys or Spirits...Children away and Sells them for the Plantations. *1699 E. Ward *London-Spy* 55: *Kidnappers*...walk...the Town. in order to seduce people...and Young Fools...to go beyond the sea, getting so great a Head of Masters of Ships, and Merchants who go over, for every Wretch they Trapan into this Misery. Those...*Tatterdemalions*...are drawn by their Fair Promises to Sell themselves into *Slavery*, and the *Kidnappers* are the Rogues that run away with the Money. *1785 Grose *Vulgar Tongue*: *Kidnapper*. Originally one who stole...children or apprentices from their parents or masters, to send them to the colonies...but now used for all recruiting crimps for the king's troops, or those of the East India company, and agents for indenting servants for the plantations, &c. **1792** Brackenridge *Mod. Chivalry* 145: Have him kidnaped and taken away. **1807** W. Irving *Salamagundi* 195: Kidnapping...an Emperor of Morocco. **1836** Hildreth *Slave* 29: The business of kidnapping is one of the native fruits of...American...slavery. **1843** [W.T. Thompson] *Scenes in Ga.* 30: Thieves! burglary and kidnapping! *1859 Hotten *Slang Dict.*: *Kidnapper*...[is now] applied without reference to the age...of those stolen. **1902** in "O. Henry" *Works* 197: Collier was kidnapped. **1923** in W.F. Nolan *Black Mask Boys* 60: Boro...kidnaps him and tortures him. **1929** McEvoy *Hollywood Girl* 234: He kidnapped the steward. **1936** in Weinberg *Tough Guys* 10: Kidnapers! **1936–40** McDonogh *Fla. Negro* 47: Kidnapper Blues. **1960** *Alfred Hitchcock Presents* (CBS-TV): Those are the men who kidnaped you. **1984** J. McNamara *First Directive* 10: His special kidnap team couldn't catch the flu.

kidney *n.* ¶ In phrase: **tap** [or **tilt**] **a kidney** to urinate.
    1975 Washington, D.C., woman, age *ca*22: *Tap a kidney* means urinate. I heard that in Washington about 1960. **1975** N.Y.C. man, age *ca*35: Gotta go tap a kidney. **1984–87** Ferrandino *Firefight* 45: I gotta tap a kidney. *a***1989** C.S. Crawford *Four Deuces* 16: I took my time and even tapped my kidneys. **1989** Strieber *Majestic* 97: I had to tilt a kidney.

kidney-buster *n.* **1.** see KIDNEY-WIPER.
    2. a truck or other vehicle that gives an exceptionally jolting ride.
    1938 in *AS* (Apr. 1942) 104: *Kidney buster*. Hard-riding truck. **1945** *Sat. Rev. of Lit.* (Nov. 3) 7: In Kidney Buster you have a succinct comment on the riding qualities of a particular vehicle.
    3. *Navy.* a hammock. Now *hist.*
    1961 L. Young *Virgin Fleet* 99 [ref. to 1941]: We call them kidney

busters, 'cause you can't straighten up in the morning. *Ibid.* 116: You pass out as soon as you climb into your kidney buster.

kidney-foot *n.* a person having flat feet. *Joc.*
    1839 Olmstead *Whaling Voyage* 46: Our cook with his various appelations of "Spot," "Jumbo," "Congo," "Skillet," "Kidney foot," &c. **1932** Miller & Burnett *Scarface* (film): "Who wants to see me?" "The chief [of police]." "That kidney-foot?" *Ibid.*: [To a detective:] Come on, kidney-foot.

kidney pad *n. West.* an English saddle.—used derisively. *Joc.*
    1922 Rollins *Cowboy* 120: The flat English saddle the cowboy termed a..."kidney pad."

kidney-wiper *n.* a large penis.—usu. considered vulgar. *Joc.* Also vars.
    1888 *Stag Party* 95: Liberal allowance made for button-hole pricks, commonly called cunt robbers, hair curlers, liver disturbers, kidney wipers, belly ticklers, bowel starters, etc. **1916–22** Cary *Sexual Vocab.* IV s.v. *penis*: Kidney wiper. **1927** *Immortalia* 92: Oh, his long, long dillywacker,/overgrown kidney-cracker. *ca***1935** in Holt *Dirty Comics* 124: You could play vit dot dingbusted kidney-buster of mine. **1969** Cray *Erotic Muse* 9: The tinker's attraction is explicitly based upon the size of his kidney-wiper. **1969** *Playboy* (Dec.) 157: Kidney prodder, stump,...bowsprit.

kid show *n. Circus.* a sideshow.
    *1873 T. Frost *Circus Life* 221: The "kid" show, as the side show is called, shuts up and does not open again until about five minutes before the big show is out. **1921** Casey & Casey *Gay-Cat* 175: I'm ticket-butcher for this bloomin' kid-show.

kid stuff see s.v. KID, *adj.*, 2.

kidvid *n.* [KID[1] + *video*] *TV.* television programs for children. Also **kiddy-vid**.
    1955 (cited in *ODMS*). **1971** (cited in *BDNE3*). **1972** *Science* (Feb. 11) 611: Saturday morning fare, which is known among nonfans as "kidvid ghetto." **1975** *L.A. Times* (Oct. 6) IV 18: I'm almost willing to overlook certain imperfections in the programs themselves. But will kidvid viewers be as lenient? **1977–81** S. King *Cujo* 26: A sea of animated kiddie-vid ads. **1981** D.E. Miller *Jargon* 101: *Kidvid*: children's television. **1984** *Nat. Lampoon* (Dec.) 84: Cable kidvid tallies down. **1985** *Newsweek* (Dec. 23) 60: A cartoon series about Rambo...is in production for the Saturday-morning kidvid hour. *a***1988** C. Adams *More Straight Dope* 15: The contrast...was bizarre even by the relaxed standards of kidvid. **1989** *TV Guide* (Feb. 18) 13: The networks occasionally offer quality kidvid during the week. **1994** *Newsweek* (Jan. 31) 8: Where we leave our 5-year-old, the television is blasting kidvid.

kielbasa *n.* the penis; SAUSAGE.—usu. considered vulgar.
    1978 N.Y.C. man, age *ca*30: Those guys [in erotic films] always have giant kielbasas. *a***1994** Radakovich *Wild Girls Club* 141: His nickname at school was Kielbasa Man.

kiester var. KEISTER.

kife *n.* [orig. unkn.] copulation with a woman; women as objects of sexual gratification.—usu. considered vulgar. *Rare* in U.S. Also vars.
    *1882 *Boudoir* 88: We are so often bilked by mean fellows, who can't afford a proper bit of kyfer. **a***1890–96** *F & H* IV 91: *Keifer*...(venery).—Generic for [copulation]. **1942–49** Goldin et al. *DAUL* 117: *Kife*, n....Prostitutes; loose women. *1975 C. Allen *Plain Tales* 235 [ref. to India, *a*1947]: *Khyfer*—skirt, thus "a bit of khyfer."

kife *v.* [cf. KIFE, *n.*] **1.** to copulate with.—also used intrans.—usu. considered vulgar.
    *ca***1889** E. Field *Bangin' on Rhine* st. 3: O, many a widow had he kifed, when Harry Smith and he/Were on the turf together in the country of the free. *Ibid.* st. 6: How could she tell that stripling that she really did not kife,/When she had rogered up and down that river all her life.
    2. to swindle or cheat; treat unfairly.
    1931 *Amer. Mercury* (Nov.) 353: Circus Words...*Kife*, v.—To swindle the suckers. **1942–49** Goldin et al. *DAUL* 117: What a kifing my shyster...gave me!
    3. to steal. Cf. KIPE.
    1982 in S. King *Bachman* 790: I kifed that battery myself.

kike [orig. uncert.; perh. alter. of *Ike*, hypocoristic form of male given name *Isaac;* cf. 1926 quot., esp. in connection with bracketed 1888 quot.; for discussion see esp. Mencken *Amer. Lang. Supp. I* (1945), 613–16; also L. Rosten *Hooray for Yiddish!* (1982), 179–81, and I. Allen *Lang. of Ethnic Conflict* (1982) 121–23]

an uncouth Jewish immigrant from Russia or Eastern Europe (*obs.*); (*hence*) a Jewish person; (*also*) (*obs.*) a usu. Jewish peddler or old-clothes merchant.—all used contemptuously.—usu. considered offensive. Also **kyke.** [Regarded as the most virulent anti-Semitic epithet.]

    [**1888** in Selzer *"Kike!"* 101: Look carefully before taking any risks offered by men whose names end in *-ein, -ky,* or *-kie.*] **1904** McCardell *Show Girl & Friends* 16: The customer...had a fit-'em-quick hand-me-down some kike had unloaded on him. *Ibid.* 49: He had the impudence to tell me that Louie Zinsheimer was a kike. **1904–05** in R. Glanz *Jew in Folklore* 205: The Bavarian grandee would mention the "kike" as an object of ridicule and loathing....No longer is it limited to the Russian Jew. Noble Bavarian hurls the epithet at equally noble Prussian and Swabian...and we have heard of "kike" goyim too. **1905** in "O. Henry" *Works* 1449: Judas....I always thought that Kike's squeal on his boss was about the lowest-down play that ever happened. **1904–11** D.G. Phillips *Susan Lenox* II 407: A kike shot him. **1911** Bronson-Howard *Enemy to Society* 290: You keep yer tongue for them as needs it, you kike! **1914** Graham *Poor Immigrants* 126: I should say for the benefit of English readers that illiterate Russians and Russian Jews are called "Kikes," illiterate Italians are "Wops," Hungarians are "Hunkies." These are rather terms of contempt. **1916** K. Burke, in Jay *Burke-Cowley Corres.* 32: You resemble my idea of what a Harvard kike ought to be. **1917** Cahan *D. Levinsky* 407: And now go for him, young ladies! You know who Mr. Levinsky is, don't you? It isn't some kike. It's David Levinsky, the cloak-manufacturer. **1917** in Dreiser *Diaries* 232: Former kikes all, raised to ridiculous heights by wealth! **1923** Ornitz *Haunch, Paunch & Jowl* 155: Kikes, Micks, and Heinies. **1926** J.H.A. Lacher, in *AS* I 322: Since the names of so many...eastern European Jews ended in "ki" or "ky," German-American Jewish traveling men designated them contemptuously as "kikis."...When I heard the word "kikis" for the first time at Winona, Minnesota, about [1886], it was a Jewish salesman of German descent who used it and explained it to me; but in the course of a few years it disappeared, "kike" being used instead. **1924–27** Nason *Three Lights* 216: I ain't a kike. Kikes come only from Russia. **1927** Hemingway *Men Without Women* 213: George is a kike just like all the rest of them. **1928** Carr *Rampant Age* 129: There also is too many kikes and niggers here. **1931** Dos Passos *1919* 383: He's a kike, hit him again for me. **1935** S. Lewis *Can't Happen Here* 204: Why don't you kikes take a tumble to yourselves and get out, beat it...and start a real Zion, say in South America? **1947** Motley *Knock on Any Door* 26: Tony didn't like Jews and called them kikes. **1960** Ashmore *Other Side of Jordan* 150: Cultivated Jews...put as much distance as they could between themselves and the noisy and grasping co-religionists they agreed deserved the epithet, "kike." **1968** N.Y.C. woman, age 79: *Kike* and *sheeny* were insulting names for Jews used by schoolchildren in the late 1890's [on the E. Side of Manhattan]. **1968** Rosten *Joys of Yiddish* 180: *Kike* was born on Ellis Island, when Jewish immigrants who...could not use Roman-English letters, when asked to sign the entry-forms with the customary "X," refused—and instead made a circle. The Yiddish word for "circle" is *kikel* (pronounced ky-*kel*). **1979** C. Freeman *Portraits* 133: The kids said that they don't like Kikes or Catholics. **1982** R.M. Brown *So. Discomfort* 133: That filthy kike. He started it. **1982** Rosten *Hooray for Yiddish!* 179: *Kike*...(As used by Jews) A cheap, unpleasant, ill-mannered, greedy, conniving, deceitful or money-grubbing Jew. **1991** B.E. Ellis *Amer. Psycho* 152: You retarded cocksucking kike. **1993** Ai *Greed* 29: The kind who calls you kike. **1995** *New Republic* (Apr. 24) 46: Almost everybody he meets that day calls him a yid or a kike.

kike *adj.* Jewish; concerning or characteristic of Jewish persons.—used contemptuously.—usu. considered offensive.

    1904 McCardell *Show Girl & Friends* 16: Them kike clothes. **1918** in Truman *Dear Bess* 254: If I could only have stayed these two days in Kansas City instead of this—Kike town. **1929–31** Farrell *Young Lonigan* 110: He'd break his kike neck. **1959** Morrill *Dark Sea* 66: All my troubles began when I signed on a stinking tanker under that Kyke

Bosun, Hymie Gunzinger. **1989** P. Benchley *Rummies* 18: Her father had launched into one of his litanies of kike jokes...and Preston had called him a troglodyte asshole.

kikey *adj.* Jewish.—used contemptuously.—usu. considered offensive.

    1936 E. Pound, in Materer *Pound/Lewis* 183: Ever since kikey Leon [Blum] got into office. **1977** Torres *Q & A* 43: The guy was...Kikey, he thought. **1981** *Nat. Lampoon* (May) 43: You're money-grubbing, greedy kikey Jews!

kiki *n.* [orig. unkn.] **1.** (sense uncertain; see quot.).

    1899 in J. Katz *Gay/Lesbian Almanac* 297: I wanted to show you a little advertisement that I had from the Manilla Hall [a homosexual resort] to go down there and see the rag-time, and the ki-ki.

2. *Homosex.* **a.** (used as an opprobrious or derisive term for a homosexual man). Also as adj.

    1935 Pollock *Und. Speaks.: Kiki,* a sexual pervert who has an affair with a member of his clique, and is therefore in very bad repute. **1941** G. Legman, in G. Henry *Sex Vars.* II 1169: *Ki-ki*....A homosexual male who is sexually attracted only to other homosexuals, or who engages in an affair with another homosexual for want of the money or personal attraction necessary for contact with heterosexuals....As an adjective in *ki-ki queen*...*To go ki-ki.*

b. a homosexual woman who plays the active as well as the passive role in lesbian copulation.

    1947 in J. Katz *Gay/Lesbian Almanac* 626: In New York, so I am told, the expression is "ki-ki," but no one elsewhere seems to be familiar with this peculiar term [for a role-reversing lesbian]. **1961** R.E.L. Masters *Forbidden* 167: [Lesbians] who overtly and freely move from one role to the other are known by the term *ki-ki* (high-high), which is one of disapproval. **1963** Stearn *Grapevine* 12: "Kiki" (pronounced *ky-ky*) was a fundamental reversal in the femme-butch role.

c. (see quot.).

    1954 in Krich *Homosexuals* 93: Kikis are male homosexuals who indulge in the oral and genital homosexual method at the same time.

kiki *adj. Homosex.* (see quots.).

    1941 (quot. at KIKI, *n.,* 2). **1949** *Gay Girl's Guide* 11: Kai-Kai—NYC...term. As an adjective, anally-minded. As a verb, to have sex with someone. **1970** *AS* XLV 57: *Kiki*...adj. 1: Bisexual. 2: Ambivalent in the active or passive roles of a homosexual relationship. **1983** Neaman & Silver *Kind Words* 247: A bisexual...is also called *ki-ki* (1970's).

kiki *v. Homosex.* (see quot.).

    1949 (quot. at KIKI, *adj.*).

kill[1] *n.* **1.** Esp. *Journ.* a killing; murder. [Orig. rare, but popularized in pulp crime fiction.]

    1865 *Harper's Mag.* (May) 687: "Do many people get killed on this route?"..."Nary kill that I know of." **1932–33** P. Cain *Fast One* 125: I don't think Rose would have come along if it was a kill. **1934** in Ruhm *Detective* 116: Would you like the low-down on the Penfields kill? **1935** C.J. Daly *Murder* 8: Putting me wise to an attempted kill. **1938** "E. Queen" *4 Hearts* 92: But it doesn't smell like a gang kill. **1954** E. Hunter *Runaway Black* 8: Taking the rap for Luis' kill was just as nuts. **1957** Collins & Powell *My Gun Is Quick* (film): If this is a kill it belongs in my department.

2. *Black E.* KILLER, 1.a.

    1942 *Yank* (Aug. 5) 9: She's a kill. **1956** H. Ellison *Deadly Streets* 184: I heard all the cats say, "Yeah, yeah, it's a real kill."

3. *Narc.* strong marijuana; KILLER, 1.b.

    1989 in Costello & Wallace *Sig. Rappers* 2: Smoke Some Kill.

kill[2] *n.* a kilometer.

    1921 Dos Passos *Three Soldiers* 326 [ref. to 1918]: How many kills is there to Paris, Yank?

kill *adj. Stu.* KILLER, 1.

    1982 Corey & Westermark *Fer Shurr!* (unp.): I got these *kill* Guess jeans with a split at the ankle. **1982** S. Black *Totally Awesome* 22: I just saw this *kill* movie. **1984** Algeo *Stud Buds* 5: Something that is very good...*killer, real kill.* **1985** *Daily Beacon* (Univ. Tenn.) (Apr. 15) 5: *Kill*—really good, as in "That's so kill." **1990** P. Dickson *Slang!* 221: *Kill.* Really good. **1993** P. Munro *U.C.L.A. Slang* II: They got some kill buds for tonight.

kill *v.* **1.** to consume (food or, usu., drink) completely; drink the contents of completely.

1832 [M.St.C. Clarke] *Sks. of Crockett* 145: I can kill more lickur…than any man…in…Kentucky. **1887** *Lantern* (N.O.) (Aug. 20) 2: The lady had killed a dozen [oysters]. **1918–19** MacArthur *Bug's-Eye View* 40: He killed half a dozen bottles of liquid rebellion. **1928** Bodenheim *Georgie May* 93: Ah felt too sleepy to kill it las' night—jus' took one good swig. **1929** Williamson *Hunky* 29: Krusack seized the bottle by the neck. "Let us kill it." **1931** Farrell *McGinty* 224: They killed the moon they had. **1940** Longstreet *Decade* 27: Here, kill this bottle. **1955** Broonzy & Bruynoghe *Big Bill Blues* 61: Every time I had killed a drink he would break the glass I used. **1961** L.G. Richards *TAC* 22: We…had killed a bottle of excellent Bourbon. **1962** S. Smith *Escape* 121: He killed the coffee, then snapped on the intercom. **1980** McAleer & Dickson *Unit Pride* 101: Dewey…had just killed my drink.

2.a. Esp. *Theat.* to dazzle or delight (the public, an audience, etc.).—rarely absol. or constr. *it.* Cf. *OED2* def. 6.a.

1844 in Barnum *Letters* 30: His carriage, ponies, & servants in livery will *kill the public dead.* **1895** Townsend *Fadden Explains* 106: I killed 'em dead. **1896** Ade *Artie* 92: W'y, she kills 'em dead in her street clothes. **1899** *Colored American* (Nov. 25) 3: [The performers] expected to "kill it" here in their own bailiwick. **1899** Ade *Fables* 38: They killed 'em in Decatur and had 'em hollerin' in Lowell, Mass. **1925** Cohan *Broadway* 62: You paralyzed 'em, kid, you killed 'em. They're all dead out there. **1928** McEvoy *Show Girl* 4: Boy, that will kill them here in Indiana. **1936** L. Raymond, W. Bishop & C. Williams *Swing Brother Swing* (pop. song): Come on! Kill me, Joe! Swing it, brother, swing! **1954** *TV Guide* (Dec. 4) 5: George Gobel "kills the people" with offbeat quips, deadpan look and a disappearing bowling ball. **1956** Lennart *Meet Me in Las Vegas* (film): You dance like that on opening night and I guarantee you'll *kill* the people. **1959–60** R. Reisner *Jazz Titans* 160: *Kill:* delight. **1991** "Vanilla Ice" *Ice by Ice* 41: I got stuff to kill 'em on the beat-box. **1997** *Larry Sanders* (HBO): Those jokes killed!

b. to amuse greatly.—now usu. used sarcastically; (*hence*) to infuriate.

1934 Duff & Sauber *20 Million Sweethearts* (film): That guy kills me. He's always kiddin'. **1935** Bartley *Tales of World War* 27 [ref. to 1918]: Then he handed me a picture of his mother in overalls. He said, "Wouldn't that kill you?" **1936** *N.Y. Times* (Aug. 21) 20: That Frisch! He kills me. **1937** Schary & Butler *Big City* (film): It don't kill me. **1952** *Sat. Eve. Post* (May 10) 20: [That] makes Ski really boil….That kills Ski. **1990** Univ. Tenn. instructor: You know, you really kill me. **1995** *Dr. Katz* (Comedy Central TV): Oh, Dr. Katz! You kill me!…Who says you're a big square nerd with no sense of humor?

3.a. Orig. *Printing.* to cancel or delete (written matter, news, etc.). Now *S.E.*

1865 in *DA*: Two galleys of equal length, one being marked "Must," the other "Kill this." **1887** in *DAE*: Please kill the deer story sent by Associated Press this morning. **1893** M. Philips *Newspaper* 8: Market reports as seem to be of a conclusive character, and not likely to be "killed" by later despatches. **1914** S.H. Adams *Clarion* 14: You wouldn't hardly expect me to kill the story. **1936** Milburn *Catalogue* 14: What am I supposed to kill on the front page? **1943** (quot. at PICKLE BARREL). **1995** N.Y.C. editor, age 26: They killed the story.

b. to stop (talking or making noise).—usu. used imper.—usu. constr. with *it* or *that.*

1912–14 in E. O'Neill *Lost Plays* 184: Kill it, kill it, you bone! **1918** in Cornebise *Doughboy Doggerel* 116: Tom, Tom, in the next door billet,/Sings all night till we holler "Kill it!" **1944** H. Brown *Walk in Sun* 27: "All I know is, in 1958 we're going to fight the Battle of Tibet. I got the facts." "Kill that," Porter said. **1952** Wilder & Blum *Stalag 17* (film): Kill it, Duke. It's got us all spinnin'. **1962** Carr & Cassavetes *Too Late Blues* (film): Kill it! Knock it off! **1995** Stavsky, Mozeson, & Mozeson *A 2 Z* 60: Yo, man, kill the noise!

c. Esp. *Theat.* to turn off (lights or other electric equipment); in phr. **kill the house** to extinguish the house lights.

1928 *N.Y. Times* (Mar. 11) VIII 6: *Kill 'Em*—Lights out. **1935** S.I. Miller *"G" Men* (film): Kill the lights! **1936** Kenyon & Daves *Petrified Forest* (film): Kill that radio, Ruby. **1965** Linakis *In Spring* 91: Kill those lights. **1980** Teichmann *Fonda* 17 [ref. to 1948]: "Kill the house." Even the lamps on the sides of the auditorium went out. **1984** W.M. Henderson *Elvis* 87: Let's kill the jukebox, please. **1995** *JAG* (NBC-TV): You want to kill that damn horn?

d. to eliminate; get rid of (as an item of fashion); LOSE.

1993 A. Adams & W. Stadiem *Madam* 139: Kill the [eye]glasses, go with the hair. **1995** N.Y.C. writer, age 25 (coll. J. Sheidlower): Kill the tie, it doesn't work at all. **1996** *Good Morning America* (Mar. 11) (ABC-TV): I'd kill the soup and instead go with a salad.

4. *Sports.* to hit (a ball) with great force.

1896 (cited in Nichols *Baseball Termin.*). **1908** in Fleming *Unforgettable Season* 228: Hit the ball! Kill it! **1911** Van Loan *Big League* 97: The Big Chief was first at bat in the last of the ninth…."Kill it, Chief!" they yelled. **1914** Patten *Lefty o' the Bush* 81: Kill it, Bingo, if he puts one across! **1935** Lorimer & Lorimer *Heart Specialist* 25: Kill it, nut, kill it! **1989** P. Dickson *Baseball Dict.* 234: One of the commonest bits of advice given to youngsters learning the game is: "Don't try to kill the ball."

5.a. *Stu.* to earn a high grade on or pass easily; (*also*) to master.

1900 *DN* II 44: *Kill,* v.t. 1. To do easily. 2. To recite perfectly. 3. To do perfectly. **1905** in Burton *Letters* 41: As George Wagstaff said, when he killed his hour exam, "You can't keep a good man down." **1906** *DN* III 143: I *killed* math. **1915** [Swartwood] *Choice Slang* 52: *Kill it…*To decisively master. **1965** C.D.B. Bryan *Wilkinson* 418: "You gonna kill the exam?" "I hope so." **1971** *Current Slang V* (Spring) 15: *Kill,* v. To do exceptionally well on an exam. **1985** Eble *Campus Slang* (Oct.) 6: *Kill*—to master or overcome something. "I killed that exam."

b. to fail (a test) badly.

1972 N.Y.U. student: I think I killed that test. **1989** P. Benchley *Rummies* 45: And I fail the breath test—*fail* it! I think I *killed* it!

killbear *n. West.* a heavy-caliber hunting musket.

1860–61 R.F. Burton *City of Saints* 212: His battery of "killb'ars" was heavy and in good order.

kill-crazy *adj.* Esp. *Journ.* psychotically intent upon killing or murdering. Also (*obs.*) **kill-simple**.

1936 R. Chandler, in Ruhm *Detective* 144: Kill-simple….I've met lots of them. **1937** J.E. Hoover *Persons in Hiding* 51: Karpis, however, remained remorseless, coldly kill-crazy. **1945** in Tapert *Lines of Battle* 233: There will be some [veterans who are] kill-crazy and unsettled. **1952** Himes *Stone* 153: He was a sadistic little gray-haired kill-crazy man. **1988** Clodfelter *Mad Minutes* 93: Kill-crazy imperialist running dogs.

kill-devil *n.* **1.a.** strong rum. [The first Josselyn quot. refs. to 1639 and appears to be drawn from Josselyn's journal of that year, hence the discrepancy in dating between *DAE* (1639) and Whiting *Early Amer. Prov.* (1674), both of which render the text somewhat inaccurately.]

1651 in Earle *Old New England* 174: The chief fudling they make in this island is Rumbullion, alias Kill Divil—a hot hellish and terrible liquor. **1654** in *DAE*: Berbados Liquors, commonly called Rum, Kill Devill, or the like. **1661** in *Century Dict.* s.v. *rum*: Rum is…called Kill-Devil in New England! **1639–74** Josselyn *Two Voyages* 26: Among the rest, Captain *Thomas Wannerton*…drank to me a pint of kill-devil *alias* Rhum at a draught. *Ibid.* 139: The *French* and *English* traded with that cursed liquor called *Rum* [*sic*], *Rum-bullion,* or *kill-Devil* [*sic*], which is stronger than spirit of Wine, and is drawn from the drouth of Sugar and Sugar Canes. **1698–99* "B.E." *Dict. Canting Crew: Kill-Devil,* Rum. **1699** E. Ward, in Winship *Boston* 52: *Rum,* alias *Kill Devil,* is as much ador'd by the *American English,* as a dram of *Brandy* is by an old *Billingsgate.* **1728** in Whiting *Early Amer. Proverbs* 244: Most of the Rum they get…is so bad and unwholesome, that it is not improperly call'd "Kill-Devil." **1773* in Stedman *Narr.* 96: Distils the kildevil there….Kildevil is a Species of rum which is distilled from the Scum and dregs of Sugar chaldrons. **1785* Grose *Vulgar Tongue: Kill Devil.* New still-burnt rum. **1885** in *DAE*: Rum, or "kill-devil," as it was everywhere called, was rendered plentiful by the trade with the West Indies and by the New England stills. **1889** Barrère & Leland *Dict. Slang* I 520: *Kill-devil* (American), new rum….an appalling beverage. **1893** Earle *Old New England* 175: New England distilleries…found a more lucrative way of disposing of their "kill-devil."

b. any strong alcoholic liquor, esp. whiskey.

a1867 G.W. Harris *Lovingood* 138: I kin chamber more cork-screw, kill-devil whisky, an' stay on aind, than anything. *Ibid.* 164: See the orful consekenses ove drinkin kill-devil by the gallun. **1913** *Century Dict.* (Supp.): *Kill-devil…*Among sailors, etc., alcoholic spirits of bad quality; a strong raw liquor. **1953** Randolph & Wilson *Down in Holler* 258: *Kill-devil….*High-proof whiskey of poor quality. "*Kill-devil* don't do a feller's stummick no good." *ca***1960** in *DARE: Kill-devil*—bad, strong whiskey.

2. a musket.

    1703** (cited in Partridge *DSUE* 455). **1838** *Crockett Almanac 1839* 6: I creeps toward him…tralein killdevil arter me. *ca1845** in Botkin *Treas. Amer. Folk.* 24: I hung kill-devil up and begun to thrash my hands when a wolf cum along. **1889** O'Reilly & Nelson *Fifty Years* 83: I know where to take aim through the sights of my old Kill Devil, which never misses a mark.

killed *adj.* heavily intoxicated.

    1981 (cited in Spears *Drugs & Drink* 303). **1988** H. Gould *Double Bang* 72: Vinnie got killed on vodka and Seven-Up.

killer *n.* **1.a.** a formidable or impressive person or thing; (*hence*) one that is especially good, delightful, amusing, or exciting. [Bracketed quots. illus. the earlier colloq. sense 'a finishing blow, argument, etc.'.]

    [***1835** in *EDD:* This tirade was a perfect killer to Auld Cocky Fenton. He said not a word more.] [**1852** in *Ark. Hist. Qly.* XVIII (1959) 6: The "Maine Liquor Law" is a killer to the Rumseller.] **1900** *DN* II 44: [College slang:] *Killer*…1. One who does things easily. 2. One who recites perfectly. **1909** in F. Remington *Sel. Letters* 445: If this [sculpture] isn't a killer I'll quit clay. **1912** in Truman *Dear Bess* 82: Did you read the article on "Getting Up Pinafore" in *Everybody's?* It's a killer. **1937** in R.S. Gold *Jazz Talk* 156: That Zutie drummer-man is really a killer! **1939** Goodman & Kolodin *Swing* 212: "House Hop" brought the expression "killer" into the musician's language. **1940** Zinberg *Walk Hard* 15: Hey, ain't that a hot one!…That's a killer. **1941** Schulberg *Sammy* 258: "Well, Sweetheart," he said, "it's a killer. Even tops *Deadline* for my dough." **1947** in Kerouac *Sel. Letters* 109: I would like to see this fall's Texas-Rice game, which is always a killer (among us football characters). **1949** *Merrie Melodies* (animation): A mouse as big as me! Ah ha ha ha ha ha! That's a killer! **1955** *AS* XXX 303: *Killer, n.* Strict instructor. **1956** M. Wolff *Big Nick.* 152: Girls are sure killers with that stuff.…I bet girls eat a ton of that junk…in a year's time. **1958** Hughes & Bontemps *Negro Folklore* 485: *Killer.* A great thing, something or somebody wonderful. Harlem is a killer, man! **1971** Wells & Dance *Night People* 38: "Man, that's a killer, isn't it?" he said. "Yes," I said, "it sounds good." **1981** Wambaugh *Glitter Dome* 63: I got a killer of an idea!

    b. *Narc.* (see quots.).

    1943 *Time* (July 19) 54: Cigarets made from [marijuana] are killers…or reefers. **1953** Anslinger & Tompkins *Traffic in Narc.* 311: *Killer.* A marihuana cigarette.

    c. LADY-KILLER.

    1941 in Ellington *Music Is My Mistress* 179: *Killer*…dandy. ***1965** in Partridge *DSUE* (ed. 7) 1236: He was a killer with the sheilas. **1981** Graziano & Corsel *Somebody Down Here* 36: This guy Raft was one of the biggest Hollywood killers of all time. **1984** Algeo *Stud Buds* 5: A man who is known for his aggressive efforts at sexual behavior: … casanova,…killer. **1986** R. Walker *AF Wives* 261: He's a real killer with the girls.

2. something that is extremely difficult to execute or deal with.

    1940 in R.S. Gold *Jazz Talk* 156: "Farewell Blues" is another of those very fast killers. **1965** N.Y.C. high school student: That exam was a killer.

killer *adj.* **1.** supremely effective; exciting; superlative; DYNAMITE, 2. Also as adv. [The very early 1951 cite is unfortunately unavailable for examination, but seems to be genuine. Adjectival use in this sense became common only in the early 1970's, esp. among students and hippies.]

    1951 (cited in *W10*). **1971** in L. Bangs *Psychotic Reactions* 8: A group called the Leaves had a killer hit with "Hey Joe." **1972** Smith & Gay *Don't Try It* 203: *Killer.* Really good. ***1979** in *OED2*: The band were going to deliver a killer set. **1983** Helprin *Winter's Tale* 240: She probably had some killer recipes for blueberry muffins. **1982–84** in Safire *Take My Word* 241: Your dad bought you a Porsche? Killer! **1987** Yoplait yogurt ad (USA-TV) (July 4): "This ice cream is really decadent!" "Killer!" **1987** *Show Biz Today* (CNN-TV) (Nov. 24): And if they did and they sounded killer, then they'd be killer. **1988** *New Yorker* (Jan. 11) 26: I make a chicken once in a while.…And one guy makes killer stews. **1989** Univ. Tenn. student theme: *Killer*—awesome. "I did killer on that zoology exam." **1989** S. Robinson & D. Ritz *Smokey* 115: We'd have killer Ping-Pong tournaments, killer chess

tournaments, killer poker games. **1992** *Knoxville* (Tenn.) *News-Sentinel* ("Detours") (Aug. 14) 8: The label is selling killer. **1988–93** Wilcock & Guy *Damn Right* 62: Man, he was killer. **1994** *New Yorker* (Jan. 31) 44: "So how was your show?" "Killer.…They loved it."

2. supremely trying or demanding; exceedingly frustrating; very difficult. Also as adv. Cf. S.E. sense 'severe or powerful'.

    1988 Frazier & Offen *W. Frazier* 20: Red had his killer drills to whip us into shape. **1992** D. Burke *Street Talk* I 128: It wasn't such a *killer* class.…It wasn't such a *difficult* class. **1994** *Mystery Sci. Theater* (Comedy Central TV): Another killer day at the office. **1994** *N.Y. Times* (Aug. 9) D18: Outdoor [advertising] is not killer expensive.

Killer Bee *n. USAF.* a General Dynamics F-16 Fighting Falcon operating as a bomber.

    1991 Dunnigan & Bay *Shield to Storm* 203: F-16 (Falcon or "Killer Bee," when operating as a bomber).

killer-diller *n.* Orig. *Jazz.* KILLER, 1.—occ. used attrib.

    1938 *New Yorker* (Jan. 8) 34: The…quartet of musicians…steams out "killer-dillers." **1938** *Life* (Aug. 8) 56: He hears Benny Goodman announce his next radio number as a "killer-diller." **1939** "E. Queen" *Dragon's Teeth* 219: You heard that statement, Sampson? That's the killer-diller. That's a demonstrable lie! **1940** Zinberg *Walk Hard* 82: Yeah, I'll be a killer-diller. **1940** in R.S. Gold *Jazz Talk* 156: The Krupa band…is not all the killer-diller affair that a lot of people anticipated. **1941** Brackett & Wilder *Ball of Fire* (film): The cat's a killer-diller. **1942** A.C. Johnston *Courtship of A. Hardy* (film): "It's a diller-killer of a day for football." "Killer-diller." **1943** Ottley *New World* 188: He's a killer-diller! **1944** Busch *Dream of Home* 6: Oh, you killer-diller.…Can't take it, huh? **1946** Boulware *Jive & Slang* 5: *Killer Diller*…Ladies man. **1953** R. Wright *Outsider* 4: When Cross first came to work in the Post Office, he was a nonstop riot, a real killer-diller. **1953** W. Fisher *Waiters* 78: Good evening, Mrs. Faulks. You sure are a killer-diller this evening. **1956** Bellow *Seize the Day* ch. iv: Oh, Tamkin, you really are a killer-diller! **1969** Beckham *Main Mother* 33: Uncle…was sort of a killer-diller when it came to getting vined up. *a***1987** Bunch & Cole *Reckoning for Kings* 312: Had me a killler-diller car.

killer weed *n. Narc.* marijuana; (*also*) marijuana laced with another drug, esp. phencyclidine. Now *joc.* [Orig. a non-slang epithet applied to marijuana to discourage its use; see also KILLER, *n.,* 1.b. and WEED.]

    1967 *Newsweek,* in Abel *Marihuana Dict.* 60: But so many myths about marihuana as the "killer weed" have been spread. **1971** *Ramparts* (Aug.) 23: All high on the Killer Weed. **1973** Gent *N. Dallas* 10: Now where's dat killer weed? **1978** Petersen & Stillman *Phencyclidine Abuse* 1: Some of the street names for phencyclidine include angel dust,…killer weed, [etc.]. **1979** H.W. Feldman et al. *Angel Dust* 73: In Philadelphia since at least the late 1960s…small groups of aficionados smoked…"killer weed". (PCP-treated marihuana). **1985** D. Killerman *Hellrider* 51: You think I really care if your brain rots from killer weed?

killing *n.* an extraordinary financial success. Now *S.E.*

    1888 in *OED2:* Many…would like to know something relative to the man who was fortunate enough to "make a killing." **1899** A.H. Lewis *Sandburrs* 244: I stan's to make a killin'—stan's to win a t'ousand plunks, see! **1902** K. Harriman *Ann Arbor Tales* 229: Ain't I got as big an interest in th' killin' as you have…? **1908** McGaffey *Show Girl* 196: He said he was hep to a few killings and…he would give them to me. **1909** W. Irwin *Con Man* 44: The news of my killing got around that night. **1920** Sandburg *Smoke & Steel* 214: [They] make a killing in steel. **1922** *Sat. Eve. Post* (Mar. 4) 12: A group of financiers had just scored a killing in Wall Street. **1922** "M. Brand" *Garden* 141: First he outlined his plans for raising the cash for the big "killing." **1953** in D. McKay *Wild Wheels* 118: His dad made a sudden killing in oil. **1988** Terkel *Great Divide* 304: I'm sick of being pushed around by real estate people out to make a killing.

killing *adj.* **1.** [weakening of the earlier S.E. sense (illus. by bracketed quots.) 'captivating; of bewitching loveliness'] stylish or fashionable in appearance; attractive.

    [**ca***1622** in Beaumont & Fletcher *Works* VI 291: Younger:/As killing eyes as yours: a wit as poynant.] [***1634** in *OED:* Those who are suddenly taken with a killing beautie.] ***1765** O. Goldsmith, in *F & H* IV 106: Your modern Briton cuts his hair on the crown, and plasters it with hog's lard and flour; and this to make him look killing. ***1768–74** in *OED:* The maid…tiffing out her mistress in a killing attire. **1796** in St. G. Tucker *Poems* 60: This muslin's so lovely—This feather's quite killing. **1832** [M. St.C. Clarke] *Sks. of Crockett* 38: Expressed in fancy, they looked "very killing." **1843** "J. Slick" *High Life in N.Y.* 25: They do look tarnal killing in their furbeloes. **1848** Baker *Glance at N.Y.* 29: I tell you—how killin' he looks! **1883** *Life* (Aug. 16) 76: He did look too *killing* in his knickerbockers. *a***1903** in R. Stiles *4 Years* 289: The dress ain't no great shakes; it's the woman in it that makes it so killing!

2. excruciatingly funny. Now *colloq.* and *rare* in U.S.

****1874** in Troubridge *Life Amongst Troubridges* 83: She was in her dressing gown and looked too killing, exactly like those fat chinamen...on Amy's...screen. **1887** in *DAE*: Frank's rendering, to a tune of his own, and playing his accompaniment with one finger, was killing. **1889** "M. Twain" *Conn. Yankee* 112: The killingest jokes. **1895** *DN* I 419: *Killing*...Ridiculous. "Her dress was perfectly *killing*." ****1984** J. Green *Dict. Contemp. Slang* 160: *Killing*...(U.K. "society" use) very funny.

3. remarkably good, enjoyable, or interesting; wonderful; extraordinary.

1895 *Harper's* (May) 917: I'll teach you the varsovienna, that everybody's dancing. It's too killing for anything. **1895** *DN* I 419: *Killing*...wonderful, fascinating, interesting. "That child is just too *killing* for anything." **1903** *Pedagog. Sem.* X 374: It is simply fierce....It's too killing. **1911** in Truman *Dear Bess* 31: I do think that Mr. Micawber is the killingest person I have run across in any book anywhere. He is exactly true to life. **1934** Weseen *Dict. Slang* 360: *Killing*—Highly entertaining...or enjoyable. **1985** "Blowdryer" *Mod. Eng.* 64: *Killing*...Great.

kill-me-quick *n.* whiskey.

1861 Newell *Orpheus C. Kerr* I 236: [He] was...a standin' in the door, and sippin' kill-me-quick. **1885** Siringo *Texas Cowboy* 91: I...had a gay old time drinking kill-me-quick whisky and swinging the pretty indian maidens. **1903** J.H. Williams, in *Independent* (Dec. 31) 3104: Spike called out for "kill me quick," while I sung out for mixed ale. **1908** W.G. Davenport *Butte & Montana* 167: Good old Dublin Gulch Killmequick.

killout *n. Black E.* (see quot.).

1983 *Reader's Digest Success with Words* 86: Black English...*killout* = "a fascinating person or an extremely exciting situation or thing."

killpecker *n.* (among cowboys) a night shift guarding a cattle herd. Now *hist.*

1936 R. Adams *Cowboy Lingo* 114: "Killpecker" was the guard from sundown until eight o'clock.

kill-preacher *n.* whiskey.

[****1785** Grose *Vulgar Tongue: Kill Priest.* Port wine.] [****1846** in *EDD*: Kill-priest [port wine].] **1890** in *DAE*: He spread through all that section yet another name for whisky—"Kill Preacher."

kill-simple var. KILL-CRAZY.

kilo *n.* [abbr. mil. comm. alphabet *Kilo India Alfa* for *KIA* 'killed in action'] *Mil.* a person, esp. a U.S. soldier, killed in action. [Quots. ref. to Vietnam War.]

1973 Browne *Body Shop* 124: I saw a Chinook coming in with seventeen kilos (corpses). **1986** Thacker *Finally the Pawn* 9: It was better with wounded....Kilos just aren't much of a priority.

kiltie *n.* a kilted Scots Highlander, esp. a soldier. *Rare* in U.S.

****1842** in *OED*: In double quick time did the kilties career. ****1902** in *OED*: The "kilties" are devils to fight. **1925** *Sat. Eve. Post* (Oct. 3) 54: Remember that band of kilties?

kimchi *n.* [joc. euphem. for *in deep shit* s.v. SHIT, alluding to Korean *kimchi* 'dish of pickled cabbage'] ¶ In phrase: **in deep kimchi** Orig. *Mil. in Korea.* in deep trouble.

1979 Hiler *Monkey Mt.* 88 [ref. to Vietnam, 1969]: If something happens before we can get backups flown in, then we're in deep *kimchi*. **1980** D. Cragg, letter to J.E.L. (Aug. 10) 3: I've heard this expression in the Army since...1959, used then by Korean War veterans. "We are in deep kimchi now!" **1983** LaBarge & Holt *Sweetwater Gunslinger* 52: We're in deep kimsche. **1984** Trotti *Phantom* 49 [ref. to Vietnam War]: Luckily the North Vietnamese didn't have anything of that caliber or we'd have been in deep kimchee. **1988** Poyer *The Med* 295: I've been in deeper kimchee than you can imagine and come up smelling like a rose. *a***1989** R. Herman, Jr. *Warbirds* 202: We'll be in deep *kimshi*...if we lose another bird. **1989** Berent *Rolling Thunder* 38

[ref. to Vietnam War]: They would be in deep kimchi for negative thinking. **1991** *Crossfire* (CNN-TV) (Feb. 12): We're gonna be in deep kimchi if that happens. **1996** *New Yorker* (May 13) 102: I won't pussyfoot around:...you, my friend, are knee-deep in kimchi.

kimono see s.v. WOODEN KIMONO.

kimp var. KEMP.

kin *n.* [orig. unkn.] *Und.* (see quot.).

1807 Tufts *Autobiog.* 293 [ref. to 1794]: *Kin*...a stone.

kinch *n.* [abbr. of KINCHEN] Orig. *Und.* a child.

1848 *Ladies' Repository* VIII (Oct.) 315: *Kinch*, or *kinchen*, A child in general. **1874** in W.H. Jackson *Diaries* 292: With Bob, Steve, & the two *Kinches*.

kinchen *n.* [prob. < G *Kindchen* 'a little child'] *Und.* a small child, esp. a boy.—also (esp. in early use) used attrib.

****1561** in *OED2*: A kitchin [*sic*] Co is called an ydle runagate Boy. ****1567** in *OED2*: A Kynching Morte is a lytle Gyrle. ****1673** [R. Head] *Canting Acad.* 40: *Kinchin* A little child. **1807** Tufts *Autobiog.* 291 [ref. to 1794]: *Kinchen*...a child. ****1812** Vaux *Vocab.*: *Kinchen*: a young lad. **1826** in J. Katz *Gay Amer. Hist.* 28: Sodomy...is said to be constantly practised among [penitentiary inmates]....Boys are said to be kept and rewarded...*Kinshon*...is the name given to a boy thus prostituted. ****1838** C. Dickens *Oliver Twist* ch. xlii: The kinchins...is the young children. **1848** *Ladies' Repository* VIII (Oct.) 315: *Kinchen cove*, or *prig*, a young thief. **1849** [G. Thompson] *City Crimes* 28: A lether that a *kinchen* stales from a lady's work bag. **1851** [G. Thompson] *Jack Harold* 15: Who the devil is that little *kinchen* you've brought with you? ****1897** in *OED2*.

kind *n.* ¶ In phrases:

¶ **all kinds of, 1.** a great deal or amount of; a perfect example of.

1899 Cullen *Tales* 109: I...had all kinds of a shave and a shine when I went out to hunt for work. **1898–1900** Cullen *Chances* 46: There'll be all kinds of a price on him. **1908** in H.C. Fisher *A. Mutt* 22: She's got all kinds of dough. **1912** Siringo *Cowboy Detective* 277: Allowed us to spend "all kinds" of money for drinks and high-living. **1932–33** Nicholson & Robinson *Sailor, Beware!* 175: I'm all kinds of a heel— lettin' you and the gang down.

2. extremely; *some kind of,* below.

1987 Estes *Field of Innocence* 18: We all got drunk....I mean all kinds of fucked up. *Ibid.* 141: I was about six kinds of crazy.

¶ **some kind of** extremely.

1972 in Bernstein & Woodward *President's Men* 237: John Sirica is some kind of pissed at you fellas. **1968–90** Linderer *Eyes of Eagle* 27: It was some kinda hot. **1993** *Low-Cholesterol Gourmet* (Discovery Channel TV): It is some kind of good! **1994** Berendt *Midnight in Garden* 110: That abortion was some kind good.

¶ **the worst kind** very badly.

1839 in *OED*: He loves Sal, the worst kind. **1859** Bartlett *Amer.* (ed. 2): "I licked him the *worst kind*," i.e. in the worst manner possible, most severely. **1904** in *OED*: "So you want to go to Cuba, do you?"..."I do, worst kind."

king *n. Naut.* a steward, petty officer, or ship's officer responsible for a named material or substance.—used in combs.

****1929** Bowen *Sea Slang* 79: *King.* The steward in charge of any kind of material in the saloon of a modern liner—the Linen King, Crockery King, or Silver King. **1945** Dos Passos *Tour* 112: We had trouble running down the ammunition king, Captain Palmer, because he was busy with the British. **1966** Noel & Bush *Naval Terms* 160: *Fresh water king*: Enlisted man in charge of the ship's evaporators. *Ibid.* 244: *Oil king*: Petty officer who keeps fuel oil records. **1993–95** M.P. Kelly *Proudly We Served* 17: The first steps that led him to join the Black Gang and to become the "oil king."

king *adj. Stu.* first-class; superlative; preeminent. [In earliest (Australian) use, solely in *king hit* 'a sudden, damaging blow; a knock-out punch', etc. (*Austral. Nat. Dict.*). U.S. usage appears to be an independent development; cf. KING BEE. Cf. other related fig. senses in *OED2*, fr. which the slang uses are often only contextually distinguishable.]

[****1917** in *Austral. Nat. Dict.* 292: K is the King-hit we'll give to the guy.] **1983** Univ. Tenn. instructor, age *ca*30: In Chicago, *king* means great. Like *keen.* **1993** Eble *Campus Slang* (Fall) 4: *King*—excellent:

"That new dress of yours is king." **1994** Johnson et al. *Ensucklopedia* (unp.): You're like the king symbol of wuss. **1994** in C. Long *Love Awaits* 67: He must be black Black. It's like black Black is king dick. You can't get no better. **1996** G. Vidal, in *Nation* (Mar. 11) 10: You want me to die because then Edmund White will be King Fag!

king bee *n.* the most important or celebrated fellow of a group.

     1868 in G.W. Harris *High Times* 102: He had been the king-bee at all the neighborhood frolics…and at the…fighting ground, and now he felt that he was a king-bee on railroads. **1870** "M. Twain," in A.L. Scott *Twain's Poetry* 72: I'm king bee wid the dimmy crats. **1877** Pinkerton *Maguires* 26: Mr. Pinkerton is after sending me to England…to look after the King Bee of all the forgers. **1897** Fox *Hell fer-Sartain* 44: Abe tells Polly Ann the king bee air comin'. **1903** in "O. Henry" *Cabbages & Kings* 105: In slid the king bee, the governor of the district. **1904** Ade *True Bills* 76: The one who came in last of all was sure to be the King Bee. **1912** Siringo *Cowboy Detective* 414: He…was considered a king-bee among the "moonshiners." **1963** Rifkin *K. Fisher's Rd.* 24: Think you're the king bee, doncha? **1965–70, 1986** in *DARE*.

kingfish *n. Pol.* a powerful political organizer or boss. [Now familiar as the nickname of Huey P. Long (1893–1935), governor of Louisiana.]

     1926 Finerty *Crim.* 33: *Kingfish*—an organizer or backer. **1933** H.P. Long *Every Man* 277: We from time to time termed various of our political enemies the "Kingfish," most prominent of which was…a certain corporation lawyer. **1982** Braun *Judas Tree* 135: He's no king-fish or power behind the throne. **1993** Spot promo (AMC-TV): There he was—the big cheese, the kingfish, the top dog.

king-hell *adj.* formidable in impact, violence, or size.

     1960 N. Mailer, in *Playboy* (Jan. 1969) 178: And then bang, as the ball was passed back, you'd get a bony king-hell knee in the crotch. **1966** H.S. Thompson *Hell's Angels* 139: The scene had all the makings of a king-hell brawl. **1969** in H.S. Thompson *Shark Hunt* 206: The Inauguration weekend was a king-hell bummer in almost every way. **1971** in H.S. Thompson *Shark Hunt* 185: A king-hell gold-mine with no end in sight. **1979–82** Gwin *Overboard* 170: The mate huffed far behind us, wrestling with that kinghell hose. *Ibid.* 276: Calling up a kinghell kick of adrenaline. **1984** W. Gibson *Neuromancer* 167: That's king hell ice, Case,…slick as glass. **1985** Dye *Between Raindrops* 3: A King-Hell balls-to-the-wall war story. *Ibid.* 273: Swearing king-hell vengeance. [***1988** Fussell *Wartime* 92 [ref. to WWII]: "How are things up ahead, mate?" "kin 'ell."]

King Kong *n.* [fr. the eponymous apelike monster in the motion picture *King Kong* (1933)] **1.** *Black E.* cheap, powerful wine or whiskey.

     1940 Ottley & Weatherby *Negro in N.Y.* 250: A drink…of "King Kong" (home-made corn whiskey). **1942** *Pittsburgh Courier* (Jan. 17) 13: It was King Kong….a shot of it was like a right cross. **1942** *Yank* (Dec. 23) 18: King Kong and sweet reefers were all the cats had. **1943** Wolfert *Tucker's People* 65: It was nickel-a-drink whiskey, the kind the Negroes called King Kong. **1943** Schrank *Cabin in Sky* (film): You may give me a double King Kong. **1952** E. Brown *Trespass* 22: We brung along plenty King Kong. **1956** Longstreet *Real Jazz* 102: It was a scuffle and had its salty moments and you buried your blues in King Kong, the cheapest whisky there was. **1965** C. Brown *Manchild* 29: Ain't no six-year-old child got no business drinking that King Kong. **1968** Klein *Police* 224: Years ago in Harlem, the name given to illicitly made whiskey was King Kong.

     2. *Narc.* a very strong addiction to an opiate; GORILLA, 3.

     1970 R. Vasquez *Chicano* 226: You want to keep popping steady? You got a King Kong and you know it. You either do it my way or I cut you off.

kingpin *n.* a person having the greatest importance, ability, prominence, or authority among a particular number (now *rare*); (now *S.E.*) the chief of a criminal syndicate.

     1867 in *DA*: His best position was as a batter. He was a "King-pin" there. **1887** Walling *Chief of Police* 585: He was undoubtedly the "king pin" of the great army of those who gain their living by…their wits. **1891** Maitland *Slang Dict.* 160: *King-pin* (Am.), the tallest pin at skittles or ten-pins. Used by analogy to signify the chief or superior. *ca*1900 *Buffalo Bill* 94: The "kingpin of the outfit," the boss. **1914** *Amer. Lumberman* (Apr. 25) 33: Paul Bunyan…He was the king pin of 'em all. **1914** S.H. Adams *Clarion* 23: Today we come pretty near to

being king-pins in this town. ***1915** in *OED2*: But 'struth! 'E is king-pin! The 'ead serang! **1928** Callahan *Man's Grim Justice* 26: I always wanted to be the boss, the king pin, the director. **1931** *Writer's Digest* (May) 40: *Kingpin*…Conductor [aboard a passenger train]. **1934** Weseen *Dict. Slang* 81: *King pin*—A boss. **1936** *New Directions* 67: The kingpin had a great weakness for lemonade, said the warden with an indulgent smile. **1965** D.G. Moore *20th C. Cowboy* 50: From what I heard later, he was the "king pin" of the gang. **1968** Brasselle *Cannibals* 93: I know you're the kingpin, but do you have some dissidents. **1973** Michelson *Very Simple Game* 18: She was really the kingpin of the girls. **1989** Radford & Crowley *Drug Agent* 202: Drug kingpins are scum. **1990** *NBC News at Sunrise* (NBC-TV) (Dec. 13): A reputed mob kingpin is arraigned on murder charges.

king's elevator *n.* [pun on *royal shaft* s.v. SHAFT] complete victimization.—constr. with *the. Joc.*

     1969 *Esquire* (Aug.) 71 [ref. to 1950's]: The Royal Screw, hence The Royal Shaft, hence The King's Elevator. Up the creek without a paddle. **1984** *Daily Beacon* (Univ. Tenn.) (July 31) 4: The King's Elevator…Roth got the royal shaft.

King Shit *n.* a man who has sole authority, preeminent influence, etc.—used ironically or sarcastically.—usu. considered vulgar. Also (*euphem.*) **King Spit**. [The *a*1950 quot. is a euphem.]

     ***1944** in *So. Folklore Qly.* XL (1976) 74: His guest, Richard the Turd, King Shit. **1945** in Shibutani *Co. K* 241: Just becaus' he get four stripes he t'eenk he king sheet. [*a*1950 P. Wolff *Friend* 102: They thought I was king shoot.] **1953–57** Giovannitti *Combine D* 54 [ref. to WWII]: That son-of-a-bitch, he thinks he's king shit. **1957** Myrer *Big War* 147 [ref. to WWII]: A big-ass hero. Thinks he's King Spit. Thinks he pisses Coca-Cola. **1961** Granat *Important Thing* 181 [ref. to WWII]: Tough guys, think they're King Shit. **1967** Sankey *Golden Screw* 73: I walked around all day…and I felt like king shit. **1968** in B. Edelman *Dear Amer.* 95: I got a company of own now, and I'm King Shit. **1971** Horan *Blue Messiah* 97: You may think he's king shit, Tom. **1971** Selby *Room* 148: Probably…driving around like king shit. **1972** Sapir & Murphy *Death Therapy* 103: He walks like King Shit. Well, he's not. *a*1987 Bunch & Cole *Reckoning for Kings* 417: He was treated like king shit. **1991** *New Yorker* (June 17) 74: Years ago, you were King Shit if you imported two hundred pounds of heroin.

king snipe *n.* [king + SNIPE] **1.** *R.R.* the foreman of a section gang.

     1916 *Editor* XLIII (Mar. 25) 343: King snipe. **1918** in *AS* (Oct. 1933) 29: *Kingsnipe*. Boss of a section gang. **1927** *AS* II (Sept.) 506: "Kingsnipe," I am inclined to think should be accorded place as a compound. It is spoken as one word in designation of the section foreman. **1931** "D. Stiff" *Milk & Honey* 214: A section boss is a *king snipe*. **1933** *Amer. Mercury* (Apr.) 393: The section boss of a railroad was a *king snipe*. **1942** *AS* (Dec.) 222: *King Snipe*. The boss of a crew of track layers. **1979** Edson *Gentle Giant* 85: There was, the king snipe concluded, only one way to deal with the intrusion.

     2. *Navy.* (see quot.).

     1918 Ruggles *Navy Explained* 139: In a gang of snipes below there is generally one dude who is known as the "king snipe." He is considered the leading snipe of the watch.

King Tut's revenge *n.* diarrhea contracted by a traveler in Egypt. Cf. MONTEZUMA'S REVENGE.

     1977 Letter to J.E.L. from Cairo: Since I have been drinking the water I am waiting to see if Montezuma's revenge (here called King Tut's revenge) will strike. **1980** Univ. Tenn. student theme: At an Egyptian dinner party, the cocktail hour lasts for three or four hours, and they don't serve you dinner until two in the morning. That's when you really get King Tut's Revenge.

kink *n.* **1.a.** a quirky or whimsical notion; crotchet; idiosyncracy; (*hence*) a touch of eccentricity or madness.

     1803 T. Jefferson, in *DAE*: Should the judges take a kink in their heads. **1805** Brackenridge *Mod. Chivalry* 508: He has got some kink in his intellect that gars him conceit strange things. **1812** T. Jefferson, in Thornton *Amer. Gloss.* I 517: Adair had his kink. He believed all the Indians of America to be descended from Jews. **1843** in Thornton *Amer. Gloss.*: He has taken a kink into his head that he will not go. **1848** *Spirit of Times* (Dec. 16) 507: I know a kink worth two of it. **1894** *DN* I 332: *Kink*…used in N.J.…=idiosyncrasy. **1898** Green *Va. Folk-Speech* 209: *Kink, n.* An unreasonable or obstinate notion; a crotchet; a whim. **1912** *Adventure* (June) 242: The guy seems to have a kink in the coco. **1927** Sandburg *Good Morning, America* 200: There was a screw loose somewhere in /him, he had a kink and he was a crank, he was nuts and be-/longed in a booby hatch. **1929** in Hammett *Knockover* 32: She grew out of childhood with a kink that made her dislike the polished side of life, like the rough.

b. a development or aspect, esp. if surprising, clever, or tricky; wrinkle; (*also*) a tricky way of doing something.

1825 J. Neal *Bro. Jonathan* III 291: There he goes, now!…that's a new kink! **1830** in [S. Smith] *Letters of Downing* 38: You always want to find out all the kinks about politics. **1846** [C.W. Webber] *Jack Long* 9: I'll show you a kink or two, Captain Hinch, about the clear thing in shootin'. **1846** in Thornton *Amer. Gloss.* I 517: This new boat is coming out with several new "kinks" about her, as the river men say. **1860** Olmsted *Back Country* 150: That was "a new kink" to our jolly host and troubled him as much as a new "ism" would an old fogy. **1863** in Thornton *Amer. Gloss.* I 517: [Powdering the hair] is a capital kink for red-haired, mouse-colored, and greyish-haired girls to take advantage of. **1863** in Applegate & O'Donnell *Talking on Paper* 172: I'll tell you how I came to learn the new "kink." **1882** Campbell *Poor* 170: It's them d— riverthieves…with a new kink, — 'em! **1887** in *DAE*: See the latest kink in Full Dress Shirts. *a***1889** in Barrère & Leland *Dict. Slang* I 521: The very newest kink, I take it, is a revival of the Louis XVI fashion. **1908** A.J. Eddy *Ganton & Co.* 72: This idea of letting Borlan's men go out two weeks in advance…is a new kink. **1910** *Sat. Eve. Post* (Sept. 24) 64: Learn this little kink and your collar troubles are over. **1949** in Botkin & Harlow *R.R. Folklore* 165: They…were continually picking up new kinks.

c. usu. *pl.* a refractory nature or tendency.—now used solely of horses or other livestock. Now *colloq.*

1862 in J.W. Haley *Rebel Yell* 49: He ought to have…been put on extra duty long enough to take some of the kink out of him and teach him a little decency. **1884** Baldwin *Yankee School Teacher* 167: Ef yer was a high-strung nigger yer was toler'ble sure t' be sended down dar t' hab de kinks taken outen ye. **1925** W. James *Drifting Cowboy* 62: They hadn't been rode since I left and they sure looked it, all fat as butter and full of kinks.

d. a perverse desire or inclination; (*specif.*) a fetishistic or otherwise unconventional sexual preference; (*hence*) an unconventional or abnormal form of copulation or sexuality.

1959** *Encounter* (May) 22: Hates kissing. Undertakes most kinks if she's feeling like it, but no buggery. *Ibid.* 23: When the "normal citizen" reads…kink stories…he is tempted to consider them as myths. ***1965** in *OED2*: The sexual hallucinations of a young girl…played for flat-out kink. **1967** Talbot *Chatty Jones* 137: These were women willing to satisfy the strange yens of their clientele, kinks that men often concealed from their wives. **1972** R. Barrett *Lovomaniacs* 289: That Golden Shower routine…it's kind of a kink, and who does it hurt? **1973** Hunter & Dahinden *Sasquatch* 42: He does not sound like someone with a kink for playing hoaxes. **1977** Univ. Tenn. student: They call him the King of Kink. **1981** *N.Y. Post* (Dec. 14) 20: Sizzling sex scenes and just the right amount of kink! *a1984** in E. Goode *Deviant Behavior* 169: All they ever talk about is kink. **1986** *Miami Vice* (NBC-TV): This guy's kink was he liked old men. **1989** Chapple & Talbot *Burning Desires* 253: Her…picante autobiography, *Beyond Kink*. **1994** *Newsweek* (Oct. 17) 85: The stiletto heels…and glimpses of gartered stockings lent the models a sinister air—including Isabella Rossellini, 38 and no stranger to kink.

e. a person having bizarre tastes or ideas, esp. one habituated to unconventional sexual practices; WEIRDO.

1964 in *Harper's Bazaar* (Jan. 1965) 54: His phone is…[unlisted] because of all the kinks who used to phone at 2 a.m. **1967** Hamma *Motorcycle Mommas* 77: There was something really funny about that kink. I would have done anything for him he might have asked. **1970** Thackrey *Thief* 204: That old Sol! A kink, but a smart kink, you know? **1970** Peters *Sex Newspapers* 5: The men…are either slobs or kinks…[with] peculiar sexual tastes. **1970** Conaway *Big Easy* 166: High time…for law and order. We're cracking down on the kooks, queers, kinks, and Commies—the deadwood and the deadwood sympathizers. **1972** R. Wilson *Forbidden Words* 155: *Kink* A sexual deviate. *a***1988** C. Adams *More Straight Dope* 376: And you guys think *I'm* a kink. *a***1991** C. Fletcher *Pure Cop* 96: And generally…the guy's…not a kink.

2. *So.* a black person; KINKYHEAD.—used contemptuously.

1865 J.H. Browne *Secessia* 288: "Running a kink"…[or] "Coming the kink" was to steal a negro from the country, and dispose of him in

town.…Those fellows would steal the Ethiop and sell him again [and again]. **1944** *AS* XIX 173: *Kink* shows an obvious allusion to the Negro's hair.

3. *Und.* (see quots.).

1914 Jackson & Hellyer *Vocab.* 52: *Kink*…A crook; a larcenous criminal.…Also used by yeggs to designate a non-criminal tramp, or one who is not initiated into the particular craft of the speaker. **1942–49** Goldin et al. *DAUL* 117: *Kink*…A thief, especially an expert in stealing automobiles.

4. *Naut.* a usu. short sleep; nap.

1929 Bowen *Sea Slang* 79: *Kink, to have a.* In American ships to have a short sleep. **1955** in *Dict. Canadianisms* 406: The "hard guy that kiled (coiled) down on the locker for a kink (sleep)." **1976** Hayden *Voyage* 549: Lie your ass down and take a little kink and build up some strength.

¶ In phrases:

¶ **let out the kinks** *West.* to go at top speed.

1870 Duval *BigFoot Wallace* 27: I could run like a scared wolf when I let out the kinks. *Ibid.* 67: It took a pretty fast Spanish pony to beat me a quarter when I "let out the kinks."

¶ **throw a kink into** *West.* to create a difficulty for; thwart.

1930 Sage *Last Rustler* 108: This throwed a kink into Jim and Nick. They curled up and quit.

kink-chaser *n. Fire Dept.* (see quots.).

1944 *Amer. N & Q* (Apr.) 5: *Kink Chaser.* Fireman delegated to straighten out the kinks or bends, in hose line. **1945** *New Yorker* (Mar. 31) 75: "Kink Chasers"…are the men who straighten bends in fire hose. **1984–89** Micheels *Braving Flames* 191: He wasn't aggressive;… he was always out on the street. He was…a kink chaser: "I'll stay in the street and straighten the hose out." He had no physical strength either.

kinked *adj.* KINKY, 3.a.

1993 *Entertainment Tonight* (synd. TV series) (Mar. 2): Playing characters who are straight-looking but slightly kinked.

kinker *n. Circus.* a circus performer.

1909 W. Irwin *Con Man* 82: A circus is always divided into two camps, the performers—we call them "kinkers"—and the gamblers. **1925** Robinson *Wagon Show* 30 [ref. to 1870's]: The circus life had a singular attraction for them, no less than for the "bosses" and the "kinkers," as the performers were called. **1926** *AS* I (Feb.) 282: *Kinker.* A performer or acrobat. **1927** Tully *Circus Parade* 22: The performers…were known as "kinkers" to us. We looked upon them with mingled disdain and awe. **1931** *N.Y. Eve. Post* (Apr. 10) 22: I was…glomming the kinkers. **1945** Coplan & Kelley *Pink Lemonade* (unp.): Al Powell, aerial contortionist, epitomizes the big-top "kinker" (performer). **1952** F. Frank et al. *Greatest Show* (film): I've scraped too many of you kinkers up off the sawdust. **1961** Clausen *Season's Over* 145: Aw, who wants to be like those dumb kinkers? **1963** J. Rose *Papa's Delicate Condition* (film): We want to break the news to the kinkers in our own way.

kinkhead var. KINKYHEAD.

kinko *n.* a person who is KINKY; WEIRDO.

1967 Hamma *Motorcycle Mommas* 57: The dikes…the "kinkos,"…you name 'em! *a***1991** C. Fletcher *Pure Cop* 87: Others stare hard at us, perhaps thinking they've got two kinkos cruising from…the 'burbs.

kinky *n.* **1.** *So.* KINKYHEAD.—used contemptuously.

1926 in Dobie *Rainbow in Morning* 154: The Fayette County and other South Texas "kinkies" whose songs I have been noting for nearly forty years. **1942** *ATS.*

2. *Und.* a stolen car.

1927 *Collier's* (July 23) 14: A kinky—Any stolen car. **1929** in *AS* V (1930) 236: *Kinky*, noun—a stolen car. **1930** *Liberty* (July 19) 24: One fence leads to another, so before long I have five of them all begging for kinkies. **1941** *Amer. Mercury* (Mar.) 347: First stop for a kinky (hot car) is a well-equipped drop.

3. [**a.** *Pros.* a person, esp. a prostitute's customer, who prefers an abnormal or unconventional kind of sexuality or copulation. [Though no U.S. quots. are known, this is prob. due to a gap in the evidence.]

***1959** *Encounter* (May) 23: A staple of conversation among prostitutes is the kinkies.]

b. *Entertainment Industry.* low-budget film devoted mainly to the depiction of cruelty combined with graphic, esp. unconventional, sexual acts.

1967 A. Knight & H. Alpert, in *Playboy* (June) 187: *Kinkies*…a sick genre of fetichistic, sadomasochistic, sexploitation films in which the woman appears…as a wanton, wilfull destroyer of men. **1974** Turan & Zito *Sinema* 23: A few years later, the team of Anna Riva and Julian Marsh produced, wrote, and directed the Kinkies called *The Touch of Her Flesh* and *The Curse of Her Flesh.*

kinky *adj.* **1.** Esp. *So.* markedly fanciful or eccentric.

1847 in Schele de Vere *Amer.* 497: It is said…that all the members of the Randolph family have been more or less kinky. **1859** Bartlett *Amer.* (ed. 2): *Kinky.* Queer; eccentric; crotchety. **1898** Green *Va. Folk-Speech* 209: *Kinky, adj.* Crotchety; eccentric. "His head is always full of *kinky* notions." **1920** Acker *Thru the War* 63: Their hair is just as kinky as their minds. **1969** Gordone *No Place to Be Somebody* 428: You mus' be plumb kinky.

2.a. high-spirited (*obs.*); (of livestock) hard to manage; spirited.

1902 in *AS* XXXVII (1962) 253: He ain't over and above kinky, though. **1913** *DN* IV 4: [Maine:] You seem to be feeling pretty *kinky* to-day. **1925** W. James *Drifting Cowboy* 209: He'd got on a fat, kinky, raw bronc. **1926** W. James *Smoky* 82: He'd climbed on one after another of these wild, kinky ponies. **1930** Sage *Last Rustler* 140: Those…ponies…was all kinky in the morning. I'd uncork them…by riding them two or three hundred yards. *ca***1930** in Fife & Fife *Ballads of West* 158: Them dogies are kinky, and try for to scatter. **1958** in *DARE*: As kinky as a bobcat.

b. given to loose or immoral behavior.

***1889** in *F & H* IV 111: The kinky ones…are made to partake of the toke of contrition and the skilly of repentance. **1929** E. Booth *Stealing Through Life* 64 [ref. to *ca*1915]: If a girl was respectable and conducted herself according to the prescribed standards, she was worthy of respect, and she was "square." Otherwise she was "kinky." I've forgotten where I first acquired those definitions, but they have remained with me for years.

c. *Und.* dishonest; crooked.

1903 *Enquirer* (Cincinnati) (May 9) 13: *Kinkey*—Crooked. **1930** Irwin *Tramp & Und. Slang* 117: *Kinky.*—Criminal; crooked…said of…an individual known to be without the law. **1933–34** Lorimer & Lorimer *Stag Line* 168: All morals and no horse sense.…Drop into anything maybe a little bit kinky, and he's just fifty cards in the deck. **1935** Pollock *Underworld Speaks: Kinky,* dishonest; crooked; unreliable; unprincipled. **1940** D.W. Maurer, in *AS* (Apr.) 117: A kinky kay-ducer will always cop the short. **1942** Pegler *Spelvin* 133: You are kinky yourself and so is your old lady.…You are the one that is yellow. **1970** Perl & Davis *Cotton Comes to Harlem* (film): If they find something kinky in Reverend O'Malley, I've got to respect it. **1976** "N. Ross" *Policeman* 121: He comes and sees me, because he knows I'm a little kinky.…As good and honest as he is, he wants to beat the rap.

d. *Und.* stolen; BENT, 3.b.

1927 *Collier's* (July 23) 15: Those…cars were kinky. **1929** in *AS* V (1930) 236: *Kinky, adj.*—stolen. **1930** Irwin *Tramp & Und. Slang* 117: *Kinky.*—Criminal; crooked…Said of stolen goods [etc.].

3. Orig. *Pros.* sexually unconventional or perverse. [Now the usual sense.]

1942 "D. Ormsbee" *Sound of American* 71: She smelled of kinky lusts and…phallic wonders. ***1959** *Encounter* (May) 21: Also "kinky" (perverse) and lesbian [photographs] and trios for twenty…shillings. ***1964** in *BDNE* 244: References to a man sleeping with two women at once and other kinky behavior. **1965** G. Legman, in *F & H* I (rev.) (1966 ed.) ixxix: Compare the British slang *kinky,* sexually perverted. **1965** Lurie *Nowhere City* 273: He might jump you when he had you on the table, or something kinky. **1968** P. Roth *Portnoy* 151: Every kinky weirdo thing you want to do. **1969** in *Playboy* (Jan. 1970) 78: But women are rapidly changing their ideas [about sex] and becoming much kinkier. **1970** Winick & Kinsie *Lively Commerce* 53: There are lots of guys who are kinky for young girls. **1980** *N.Y. Post* (July 9) 19: Capitol Hill is riddled with homosexuality and kinky sex. Members and aids romp together. **1980** J. Carroll *Land of Laughs* 152: Not that she was into any kind of bondage or kinky stuff. **1982** M. Mann *Elvis* 102: Kinky sex disgusts me. **1982** in Thom *Letters to Ms.* 14: Sometimes I want to be kinky…, sometimes I want to make love on the supermarket floor. **1986** Heinemann *Paco's Story* 80: *Kinky* is when

you use a feather, see, and *perverted* is when you use the whole chicken! **1988** J. Brown & C. Coffey *Earth Girls* (film): I'm really not into kinky scenes. **1990** C.P. McDonald *Blue Truth* 37: We're talking about sex and…kinky ladies.

4. very odd or unusual; arousing suspicion.

1948 Kingsley *Detective Story* 338: There's something kinky about this. **1971** Torres *Sting Like a Bee* 172: The Commission…felt there was something "kinky" about the fight. **1974** M. Brooks *Blazing Saddles* (film): "Stampeding cattle…through the Vatican." "Kinky."

5. angry.

1978 Pici *Tennis Hustler* 197: When I put her off, she got kinky as hell.

kinkyhead *n.* a black person.—used contemptuously. Also **kinkhead.**

1860 in *Ala. Hist. Qly.* XLIV (1982) 95: We found…plenty of kinky heads out picking cotton. **1916** in J. London *Short Stories* 703: I ran in cargoes of kinky-heads from Malaita. **1936–38** in Yetman *Voices from Slavery* 71: Kink head, wherefore you skeered? **1944** *AS* XIX 173: In 1936, Cab Calloway, the Negro musician, used *kinky-head* in a broadcast. **1966–68, 1970, 1986** in *DARE.*

kinny *v. TV.* to show by or record on a kinescope. Now *hist.*

1952 in Conklin *Sci. Fi. Omnibus* 187: The deluge of fan mail caused that first showing to be kinnied all over the country. **1954** *New Yorker* (May 1) 24: C.B.S. is contributing to the pool but is only kinnying the hearings.

kioodle var. KIYOODLE.

kip[1] *n.* [cf. Dan *kippe* 'a low tavern'] **1.** a brothel.

***1766** O. Goldsmith, in *OED:* To assist at tattering a kip, as the phrase was, when we had a mind for a frolic.…[Note by S. Baldwin:] *Tattering a kip:* we have never heard this expression in England, but are told that it is frequent among the young men in Ireland. It signifies, beating up the quarters of women of ill fame. ***1915–22** J. Joyce *Ulysses* 541: Kipkeeper! Pox and gleet vendor! **1927** *DN* V 453: Scotch "kip" = "brothel."

2. Esp. *Und.* bed.—constr. with *the.*

1859 Matsell *Vocab.* 48: *Kip.* A bed. ***1889** Barrère & Leland *Dict. Slang* I 521: *Kip* (popular and thieves), a bed. **1914** Jackson & Hellyer *Vocab.* 52: *Kip*…A bed; a place to sleep. **1915–16** Lait *Beef, Iron & Wine* 111: A dime for a flop on de kip. ***1918** *Bodleian Qly. Rec.* II 125: *Kip,* bed. **1938** *AS* (Apr.) 156: *Kip.* A berth in a sleeper plane. **1940** O'Hara *Pal Joey* 189: Mike…and his…bride were in the kip and did not want to be interrupted. **1953** Dodson *Away All Boats* 14: I'm ready for the kip after this screwball day. **1961** B. Wolfe *Magic of Their Singing* 77: I'll rest my wearies here on the kip. **1963** A. Morgan *Six-Eleven* 242: We may be back in the kip ten minutes from now. **1966** Susann *Valley of Dolls* 97: He may be lousy in the kip. **1968** *Playboy* (Apr.) 122: In any effort to aim her for the downy kip, it's an ingenious way to curry her favor. **1970** C. Harrison *No Score* 76: You can afford half an hour in the kip. **1976** J. Simon *Murder by Death* (film): I don't know what them society dames are like in the kip. **1977** Dunne *Confessions* 51: I tell you this is a bad guy to be in the kip with.

3. (esp. among itinerants) a lodging house; lodgings, esp. a hotel room or apartment.

***1883** in *OED:* The common lodging-house, or "kip." ***1903** J. London *Abyss* 104: Nor do they think of lookin' for a kip (place to sleep), till nine or ten o'clock at night. **1908** Sullivan *Crim. Slang* 14: *Kipp*—A lodging house. **1921** J. Conway, in *Variety* (Mar. 18) 5: He takes his room key and blows to the kip. **1970** *Playboy* (Dec.) 226: I'd get Kip up to my kip, out of her pants and in bed.

4. sleep, rest; a nap; in phr. **do a kip** to sleep.

***1893** in *OED2:* "I only came here for a *kip.*"…*Kip* means sleep, I believe. ***1903** J. London *Abyss* 112: An' another night's kip won't 'urt me none. **1918** *Chi. Sun. Trib.* (June 30) V (unp.): He had come to almost yearn for the night hours before "kip," which is the yegg's word for sleep. **1918** E. O'Neill *Lost Plays* 22: What good kin I do watchin' her do a kip? **1934** W. Smith *Bessie Cotter* 189: I was taking a kip. **1940** E. O'Neill *Iceman Cometh* 119 [ref. to 1912]: A couple of hours good kip will fix me. **1967** Talbot *Chatty Jones* 32: It's been a rough day. I need some kip. **1975** *M*A*S*H* (CBS-TV): Let's get some kip. **1986** R. Campbell *In La-La Land* 111: He's on his cot having a kip right this minute.

5. *Und.* (see quots.).

1924 G. Henderson *Crookdom* 75: A "kip" is some one who sleeps in a store or immediately overhead who is likely to hear the noise.

1926 *N.Y. Times* (Oct. 10) VIII 20: The place chosen for the deed may have a watchman. If so, the joint is "kipped." A "kip" is generally a man sleeping on the premises and likely to be awakened by the yeggs.

kip[2] *n.* [orig. unkn.] (see quot.).
  1859 Matsell *Vocab.* 48: *Kip*…half a fool.

kip *adj.* KIPPY, 1.
  1931 Stevenson *St. Luke's* 190 [ref. to *ca*1910]: Cheese and I have some pretty kip idears.

kip *v.* **1.** to sleep or lodge.
  1889 Barrère & Leland *Dict. Slang* I 522: *Kip, to* (popular and thieves), to sleep or lodge. **1897 *Pop. Sci. Mo.* (Apr.) 832: Such expressions are *to kip*, meaning to sleep, [etc.]. **1903** J. London *Abyss* 128: There was one American tramp royal whom I found particularly enjoyable.…Where was I hanging out? he asked. And did I manage for "kipping"?—which means sleeping. *a*1909 Tillotson *Detective* 92: *Kip*—To sleep. **1915** Bronson-Howard *God's Man* 204: Swell kipping at cut rates in the shed she owns. **1925** Mullin *Scholar Tramp* 40: I persuaded them after much argument to go back to the lumber-yard, which seemed to be a safe place to kip (sleep) for the night. **1926** Norwood *Other Side of Circus* 151: This is where they kip through the day. **1929** Milburn *Hobo's Hornbook* 152: I've napped in Ritzy Hotels. **1933–35** D. Lamson *About to Die* 165: I ain't goin' to take no chances…while I'm kippin'! **1944** in W.C. Fields *By Himself* 491: I am sorry you did not get a place to kip during your visit to New York. **1946** Mezzrow & Wolfe *Really Blues* 38: It would have been more restful kipping on a pile of hardtack. **1981** O'Day & Eells *High Times* 36: Kip is a yiddish [*sic*] term for sleep or sack out.
  2. (see quot.).
  1914 Healy *Delinquent* 548: "First time I was here [*i.e.*, reform school] for kipping." (This is a term used in the youthful underworld for sleeping out at night.) "We slept in a milk wagon."

kipe *v.* to pilfer; steal. Also **kype.** Cf. KIFE, 3.
  1932–34 Minehan *Boy & Girl Tramps* 199: Three long butts I kipped [*sic*] right in front of the entrance. **1938** *AS* (Apr.) 151: *Chip.* To steal, kipe. **1953** in L. Davis *MiG Alley* 66: Kiped. **1969** Spetz *Rat Pack Six* 192: "Wonder where they kyped this tent?" mused The Bat. **1970–72** in *AS* L (1975) 62: They kiped that car last night. **1974** Univ. Wisc. student: That dumbshit kyped my ruler. **1985** "J. Blowdryer" *Mod. Eng.* 25: I kiped this nice pair of neon green sunglasses from Woolworths. **1989** *Village Voice* (N.Y.C.) (Oct. 17) 6: It was on her desk and someone kyped it. **1996** *Mystery Sci. Theater* (Comedy Central TV): They kiped that banner from the Catholic Church.

kipped *adj.* *Und.* occupied by a night watchman. Cf. KIP, *n.*, 5.
  1914 Jackson & Hellyer *Vocab.* 67: The dump was kipped, but we muffled the puff. **1924** G. Henderson *Crookdom* 410: *Kipped*—Place protected by person sleeping within. **1933** Ersine *Prison Slang* 49: If it's a kipped joint, you better leave it alone.

kipper *n.* *Naut.* a torpedo.
  1943 in J. Gunther *D Day* 87: The big ship that he was on "caught a kipper" [but] managed to limp back to port. **1950 Granville *Sea Slang* 140: *Kipper.* A torpedo. (Submariner's term.). **1953, *1959 in *OED2*.

kippered *adj.* drunk.
  1903 Hobart *Out for the Coin* 52: He gets good and kippered with the souse thing.

kippings *n.pl.* (among itinerants) lodging; KIP[1], 3.
  1916 L. Livingston *Snare* 85: I was getting ready to brace the ex-bo who makes his kippings here for a chance to tell of the doings of the bums.

kippy *adj.* [orig. unkn.] **1.** attractive; neat; NIFTY.
  1910 T.A. Dorgan, in Zwilling *TAD Lexicon* 52: Al Kaufman…passed out a rather kippy interview in Frisco the other day. **1911** *DN* III 545: *Kippy, adj.* Striking, or prepossessing; term of approbation. "That's a kippy hat." "She's a kippy-looking girl." **1923** *Amer. Legion Wkly.* (June 1) 14: Hot dog! That's kippy! **1927** *AS* II (Mar.) 277: *Kippy*: neat. **1931** Stevenson *St. Luke's* 9 [ref. to *ca*1910]: Oh, that's kippy! **1980–81** in T.K. Pratt *Dict. P.E.I. Eng.* 86: She's quite the lady, she's quite kippy.
  2. chipper; bright.
  1935 Lorimer & Lorimer *Heart Specialist* 46: Everybody in the cast was simply kippy with enthusiasm.

kishkes *n.pl.* [< Yid *kischkes*] a person's guts; belly. Also vars.
  1902 T.A. Dorgan, in Zwilling *TAD Lexicon* 52: (Johnny Wise Had

A Dream At A Fight Where Sam Pruitt Was Winning "Hands Down") In his kishkus. **1908** in H.C. Fisher *A. Mutt* 120: I'll slam him on the kishkuss. Call me a zob, huh? **1923** Ornitz *Haunch, Paunch & Jowl* 5: Butt him in the *kischkes* (guts). **1938** in Gelman *Photoplay* 236: Sock him in the kish-kish, Abie. **1941** Schulberg *Sammy* 228: "Kill the dirty sheeny," they were yelling. "Hit him in the *kishkes*." **1973** *N.Y. Times* (Mar. 25) 1: Fat ladies who can find no resting place for the sharp steel point of their umbrellas but in your *kishkes*. **1974** A. Bergman *Big Kiss-Off* 78: A familiar pang would shiver through my kishkas. **1984** C. Francis *Who's Sorry?* 239: I was eating my *kishkas* out.

kiskeedee *n.* [< F *qu'est-ce qu'il dit?* 'what is he saying?'] a French-speaking person; a French, French-Canadian, or Creole person. Also **keskydee.**
  1857 Borthwick *Gold Hunters* 233: The Frenchman, in his impatience, was constantly asking…"*Qu'est ce qu'il dit?*" "*Qu'est ce qu'il dit?*" This caught the ear of the Americans…and [in California 1851–54] a "Keskydee" came…to be a synonym for a "Parleyvoo." **1945** in *DARE*: Creole children…refused even to speak French because the others taunted them with the appellation of "Kis-kee-dee!" when they did so. **1956** H. Gold *Not With It* 255: They call us Frenchies Kiskeedees because it's *qu'est-ce qu'il dit, qu'est-ce qu'il dit* all the time. **1971** in *DARE* [ref. to 1850's]: The French were disliked because they kept to themselves, and became known as "Keskydees" because they kept asking "Qu'est-ce qu'il dit?"

KISS *interj.* Orig. *Mil.* keep it simple, stupid! *Joc.*
  1971 Rowe *Five Years to Freedom* 120 [ref. to 1963]: The old "KISS" formula, "Keep it simple, stupid," served as my guide as I built the biography. **1975** Univ. Tenn. student: *KISS*—Keep It Simple, Stupid! I learned that in the army [*a*1970]. **1977** Langone *Life at Bottom* 203: Used to have what we called the KISS System. Which means, Keep It Simple, Stupid. **1980** *Time* (May 12) 33: The complex mission violated an old Army rule called KISS, meaning "Keep it simple, stupid." **1983** *TalkNet* (NBC radio network) (Oct. 28): Use the KISS method—right?—Keep It Simple, Stupid. **1986** Zeybel *First Ace* 230: Our planning is based upon the KISS principle: Keep It Simple, Stupid. **1989** CNN news (CNN-TV) (Nov. 4): K-I-S-S—"keep it simple, stupid"—a popular saying in the [drug-abuse] recovery community. **1990** *Wings* (Discovery Channel TV): The KISS principle: "Keep It Simple and Stupid."

kiss *n.* **1.** a drink (from a bottle). Cf. *kiss the baby* s.v. BABY, *n.*, 2.
  1925 Mullin *Scholar Tramp* 287 [ref. to *ca*1912]: An' all we had was a little kiss apiece off'n it [a bottle].
  2. *Juve.* a blow. *Joc.*
  1928 in Galewitz *Great Comics* 143: Ya-a-a-h! There's a kiss for yuh, monkey-face. **1991** *Get a Life* (Fox-TV): Daddy's got a little *kiss* for ya!

kiss *v.* **1.** to flatter. Cf. KISS UP.
  1904–11 D.G. Phillips *Susan Lenox* II 159: A dirty bilker! Tryin' to kiss his way out!
  2. to strike (esp. a baseball) hard; wallop; hit.
  1912 (cited in Nichols *Baseball Term.*) **1914** in R. Lardner *Round Up* 339: He kisses the first thing they hands him for three bases. **1921** in R. Lardner *Round Up* 421: Kiss him on the brow with a meat ax. **1936** Twist *We About to Die* (film): I hate to see…you get kissed by a blackjack. **1984** Jackson & Lupica *Reggie* 6: I mean, it was *kissed.* **1990** Rukuza *West Coast Turnaround* 3: That worthy kissed the sheet metal, pitching over backward.
  ¶ In phrases:
  ¶ **kiss ass** see *kiss* [or *suck*] *my ass* and *kiss* [or *lick* or *suck*] *(someone's) ass* s.v. ASS, *n.*
  ¶ **kiss goodbye** to resign oneself to the loss of.—occ. used absol.—usu. used sarcastically.
  1906 *Nat. Police Gaz.* (May 5) 3: "I'll kiss mine goodbye," said Nell as she dropped her pasteboards in the discard. **1911** Van Loan *Big League* 151: You've been gettin' away with a lot…but here's where you can kiss yourself good-by! **1924** Nason *3 Lights* 73: Uncle Sam…kiss good-by to ten thousand dollars. **1970** Novelty poster, N.Y.C.: In Case of Nuclear Attack, Place Your Head Between Your Legs—And Kiss Your Ass Goodbye! **1994** *Nation* (Sept. 5) 220: The rest of us can kiss goodbye any idea of stabilization of the region (which is particularly bad news for the poor folk of Macedonia).
  ¶ **kiss the baby** see s.v. BABY, *n.*, 2.
  ¶ **kiss the dog** (among pickpockets) to face a victim while picking his or her pocket.

1933 Ersine *Prison Slang* 49: Ed kissed the dog and lifted his block.

¶ **kiss the rosin** [or **canvas**] *Boxing.* to be knocked down by a blow. Cf. CANVAS-KISSER.

1919 T.A. Dorgan, in Zwilling *TAD Lexicon* 52: Just slant at the casualty list of champs who kissed the canvas before the end of their scheduled bouts. **1920–21** Witwer *Leather Pushers* 5: That is if you can keep from kissin' the rosin for a coupla rounds. **1934** Weseen *Dict. Slang.* **1992** N. Cohn *Heart of World* 66: But I never did kiss canvas.

¶ **kiss the wooden lady** *Navy.* (see quot.). Now *hist.*

1980 Valle *Rocks & Shoals* 328 [ref. to a1860]: Kiss the wooden lady. Slang. To be forced to stand facing the bole of a mast with arms encircling it and wrists lashed as a minor punishment. Shipmates were encouraged to kick the offender in the buttocks while passing by.

kiss-ass *n.* a sycophant.—usu. considered vulgar.

1973 *TULIPQ* (coll. B.K. Dumas): He's a kiss-ass. **1993** P. Munro *U.C.L.A. Slang II: Kiss-ass*...person who uses flattery to improve his position: brown-nose, kiss-up. **1996** *L.A. Times* (Mar. 19) F3: I...prayed to God Almighty that I would not become a kiss-ass. **1996** *Politically Incorrect* (Comedy Central TV) (Aug. 15) Eddie Haskell was a kiss-ass.

kiss-ass *adj.* sycophantic.—usu. considered vulgar.

1918 in E. Wilson *Prelude* 274: A kiss-ass attitude. **1970** Vance *Courageous & Proud* 17: Everyone thought he was a kiss-ass soldier because he had made Specialist Fourth Class before the line soldiers. **1977** Schrader *Blue Collar* 57: Get off your butts, you kiss-ass monkeys! **1985** J. Dillinger *Adrenaline* 65: Some fifty-year old kiss-ass Hollywood nonentity. **1992** N. Russell *Suicide Charlie* 125: Major is the most kiss-ass rank in the army.

kiss-ass *v.* to be subservient or sycophantic (to).—usu. considered vulgar. See also *kiss* [or *suck*] *my ass* and *kiss* [or *lick* or *suck*] *(someone's) ass* s.v. ASS.

1936 M. Levin *Old Bunch* 517: He'd be disbarred before he'd kiss-ass to that two-faced mutt. **1945** in Shibutani *Co. K* 234: They want to kiss-ass them guys. **1959** Morrill *Dark Sea* 131 [ref. to WWII]: You're a yellow-belly....You kiss-ass the Mate.

kisser *n.* **1.a.** Orig. *Boxing.* the mouth.

*1860 in *F & H* IV 113: His mouth is his "potatoe trap"...or "kisser." **1867** in Somers *Sport in N.O.* 161: [Turner] planted a stinging lefthander on the kisser, which rattled Tom's ivorys. **1867** in A.K. McClure *Rocky Mtns.* 370: Hit him in the eye, Jimmy...Peg him on the kisser! **1870** *Putnam's Mag.* (Mar.) 301: The combatants struck each other...upon...the mouth, the kisser, the whistler, the oration-trap. **1889** Barrère & Leland *Dict. Slang* I 522: *Kisser* (popular), the mouth. **1891** Maitland *Slang Dict.* 160: *Kisser*...the mouth. **1910** T.A. Dorgan, in *N.Y. Eve. Jour.* (Apr. 7) 16: Then he uppercuts me on the kisser and knocks out two tusks. *1904–14** Joyce *Portrait of the Artist* ch. iv: Eh, give it over, Dwyer, I'm telling you or I'll give you a stuff in the kisser for yourself. **1916** Cary *Venery* I 167: *Kisser*—The mouth. *1917** *Living Age* (Nov. 10) 378: Others...refer to the mouth as the "kisser," the "chirper," and the "box of dominoes." **1924** *Amer. Mercury* (Feb.) 132: Want a bunch o' fives in yer kisser? **1936** *Mr. Deeds* (film): Every time you opened your kisser you gave her another story. **1946** Kober *That Man Is Here Again* 8: Insteada keepin' his kisser closed. **1950** *New Yorker* (Feb. 18) 39: Then he hit me in the kisser. **1963** D. Tracy *Brass Ring* 5: That didn't mean he wouldn't get it right in the kisser if he tried it. *a1973–87** F.M. Davis *Livin' the Blues* 33: She'd...clip Sister White on the kisser. **1990** *Maclean's* (May 7) 58: Glenn caught a rising bullet [sc., a hockey puck] just below his nose that knocked him out. When he came to a doctor was working on his beseiged kisser with a needle and thread.

b. the face.

1904 *Life in Sing Sing* 250: Kisser. The mouth; the face. **1913** *Sat. Eve. Post* (Mar. 15) 10: Peepers maroon. Hair black. Kisser smooth. **1925** Mullin *Scholar Tramp* 285: Dis guy's nose was broke, 'is kisser wuz cut to hell, an' one ear hangin' jes by a piece o' gristle. **1930** Conwell *Pro. Thief* 32: In rackets where one must show his kisser (face), experience and intelligence are necessary. **1937–40** in Whyte *Street Corner Society* 39: I'll tell you to your kisser—you're lazy. **1941** Lees et al. *Hold That Ghost!* (film): Out falls a body, right on its kisser. **1942** Liebling *Telephone* 11: She would land right on her kisser on a mattress. **1950** Medford & Weidman *Damned Don't Cry* (film): Stop planting your kisser on the front pages with every thrill-happy dame that comes along. **1950** *Time* (Dec. 11) 39: That Greta's wonderful.

When you see her up close, she's really got a beautiful kisser. Real sharp chiseled features. **1955** Q. Reynolds *HQ* 80: Nobody uptown knows your kisser. **1966** Elli *Riot* 87: If my kisser got splashed over nationwide TV, they'd have heart attacks. **1968** Huss & Silverstein *Film Experience* 1: The film is a Saturday afternoon entertainment during which James Cagney shoves grapefruit into Mae Clarke's "kisser." **1988** Cassell *S.S.N. Skate* 145: Now get that expression off your kisser and tell me how we're doing. **1992** in *Harper's* (Jan. 1993) 34: There was a time when all animals shared...the bug-eyed, jittery kisser of the marsupial shrew. **1995** *Knoxville* (Tenn.) *News-Sentinel* (Aug. 10) 1: Yep, that's my kisser!

2. ASS-KISSER.

1951 Leveridge *Walk on Water* 180 [ref. to WWII]: They were the "Kissers." Conversation with an officer gave them a sense of prestige. **1985** *Cheers* (NBC-TV): You think I'm a kisser, don't you?

kiss-off *n.* a rude or abrupt dismissal or rejection, esp. if final.

1926 Finerty *Criminalese* 34: *Kiss-off*—Dismissal, farewell. **1942** Horman & Corley *Capts. of Clouds* (film): This is the kiss-off, isn't it? **1945** Gerraghty & Frank *Whiplash* (film): What am I doin' here, waitin' for the kiss-off? **1952** J.D. MacDonald *Damned* 33: The kiss-off punch lifted the bullfighter's feet from the floor. **1970** *N.Y. Times Mag.* (July 5) 24: At the end of a telephone conversation they have literally told me—on several occasions—"I'll call you; don't you call me." The old kiss-off. **1981** G. Wolf *Roger Rabbit* 43: What a considerate guy I am, even in the face of the big kiss-off. **1983** *Rolling Stone* (Feb. 3) 45: David Bowie's kiss-off to his Thin White Duke persona.

kiss off *v.* [prob. of billiards orig.; see 1904 quot.] **1.a.** to reject, spurn, dismiss, or abandon, esp. rudely, abruptly, or permanently; *(ironically)* to bid farewell to.

1904 Ade *True Bills* 86: Fate kissed him off and he lay froze against the Cushion. **1935** Pollock *Und. Speaks: Kissed off*, defrauded of share of loot or plunder. **1941** Ryan & Granet *Girl, Guy, & Gob* (film): So you're kissin' off the fleet, are ya? *Ibid.* I guess it means she's kissin' you off! **1946** Kober *That Man Is Here Again* 63: He's gonna kiss off the [film] industry fa good. **1947** Schulberg *Harder They Fall* 86: Any more crap out of him and we take him down to the boat and kiss him off. **1949** Bezzerides *Thieves' Highway* (film): How do ya like that? We get kissed off before we even have a chance to pick it up. **1951** Lampell & Buchman *Saturday's Hero* (film): You can kiss off your chances for All-American. **1952** Felton & Essex *Las Vegas Story* (film): She kissed me off. So get out of town. **1953** Brackett, Reisch, & Breen *Niagara* (film): We're gonna kiss off this place right now. **1979** G. Wolff *Duke of Deception* 206: "We" kissed off the pushers, strivers, tweedbags,...jocks,...lounge lizards [etc.]. **1981** C. Nelson *Picked Bullets Up* 131: You can kiss off easy duty.

b. to murder.

1943 Perrin & Mahoney *Whistling in Brooklyn* (film): After the Inspector is kissed off, we deliver Benton's body to headquarters. **1946** "J. Evans" *Halo in Blood* 134: I'm a private eye and I have a customer who wants to know who kissed off Marlin.

c. to casually dispose of, slight, disregard, or ignore; give up on.

1948 "J. Evans" *Halo for Satan* 83: [He] had kissed off all raps except...the one...for income tax evasion. **1952** in Botkin *Sidewalks* 379: An ability to kiss off any situation with an apt...remark. **1960** Stefano *Psycho* (film): I ain't about to kiss off $40,000. **1969** Whittemore *Cop!* 256: They just kiss it off, disregard it. **1976** *Bob Newhart Show* (NBC-TV): About this Christmas present nonsense—let's just kiss it off. **1986** *Hunter* (NBC-TV): Let's kiss this off. **1986** Gilmour *Pretty in Pink* 105: Maybe we should just kiss it off.

2. to go away and stop giving annoyance; depart.—usu. used imper.; *(rarely)* to die.

1911 T.A. Dorgan, in Zwilling *TAD Lexicon* 52: The person doc said his temperature was 227 and that he would kiss off at any moment. **1945** in *OED2: Kiss off*, to die. **1961** Rossen & Carroll *The Hustler* (film): Kiss off! **1971** Faust *Willy Remembers* 80: "Kiss off," I said. **1977** Univ. Tenn. student: Flunk prelims and they tell you to kiss off. **1985** *Diff'rent Strokes* (ABC-TV): Kiss off, turkeys! **1988** *Miami Vice* (NBC-TV): Kiss off, Crockett. **1991** McCarthy & Mallowe *Vice Cop* 25: He's gonna kiss off...and go out and do whatever [he wants to do]. **1995** Gingrich & Forstchen *1945* 50: "Just a couple more questions, Mel." "Kiss off."

kiss out *v.* KISS OFF, 1.a.

1925 in *DAS:* When a member of a mob is deprived of his share he is "kissed out." **1925** S. Lewis *Arrowsmith* 749 [ref. to 1914]: We'll kiss out all these glittering generalities and get messages from men as kin talk.

kiss-up *n.* a sycophant; SUCK-UP.

1967 in Purnell *Adolesc. in Amer. High School* 21: "Kiss-ups"…try to get good grades through flattery. **1992** *Mystery Sci. Theater* (Comedy Central TV): What a little kiss-up! **1993** P. Munro *U.C.L.A. Slang II: Kiss-up* n. person who kisses up to a teacher in an effort to improve his grade: brown-nose, kiss-ass.

kiss up *v.* to curry favor; ingratiate oneself. Cf. KISS, *v.*, 1.

1965 Linakis *In Spring* 326 [ref. to WWII]: The ass-kissers…'d go kissing up to Randy or Blake. *ca***1965** in Schwendinger & Schwendinger *Adolescent Subcult.* 211: A member of our fraternity…shouldn't kiss-up. **1987** *ALF* (NBC-TV): Alf—don't kiss up. **1990** *Open House* (Fox-TV): I have never kissed up in my life. **1995** Court TV (Aug. 15): Kissing up to Bob.

kissy-face *n. Stu.* affectionate kissing; necking.—often constr. with *play.*

1958 J. Davis *College Vocab.* 14: *Play kissy face*—Neck. **1961** Sullivan *Shortest, Gladdest Years* 123: Oh, I admit to a bit of kissy-face now and then. **1964** (quot. at HUGGY-BEAR). **1969** Cassill *Intro #2* 129: You've been going out for what, four years now? You couldn't be holding hands and playing kissy-face still. **1978** *Just Friends* (CBS-TV): No, mom, we didn't play kissy-face! **1983** Breathed *Bloom Co.* 123: Come out and give me some kissy-face! **1989** *Night Court* (NBC-TV): Others run down to the Records Room to play kissy-face. **1989** P. Bench-ley *Rummies* 84: About as convincing as social kissy-face in the Grill Room at The Four Seasons. **1994** *Mystery Sci. Theater* (Comedy Central TV): Watch him and his wife make kissy-face. **1994** "Born Loser," synd. cartoon strip, in *Wash. Post* (July 6) F10: Why don't we play a little kissy-face, like old times?

kissy-kissy *n.* sycophantic behavior.

1981 Peyser & Peyser *Sarah McDavid* (film): A little kissy-kissy and you'll be…[promoted] in a minute. **1984** *L.A. Times* (Dec. 20) V 1: The eating, schmoozing, chatting, wheeling, dealing, kissy-kissy and critiquing following the film.

kitchen *n.* **1.** the stomach.

*****a***1890–96** F & H IV 115: *Kitchen*…The stomach. **1927** *DN* V 453: *Kitchen,* n. The stomach. **1942** (quot. at BASKET, 1). **1944** Kendall *Service Slang* 50: *Kitchen*….stomach. **1986** *UTSQ:* Stomach…*kitchen.*

2. *R.R.* the engineer's cab of a steam locomotive.

1940 *Railroad Mag.* (Apr.) 47: *Kitchen*…engine cab.

3. *Baseball.* (see 1989 quot.).

1989 P. Dickson *Baseball Dict.: Kitchen*…The area of a batter's torso inside or at the edge of the high and inside portion of the strike zone…."Gettin' in his kitchen."…The term is also used in more elaborate metaphors: "He got in his kitchen and broke a few dishes." **1996** *World Series* (Fox-TV) (Oct. 22): *Severely* in Tino Martinez's kitchen with that fastball.

¶ In phrases:

¶ **clean** [or **sweep**] **up the kitchen!** *Restaurant.* an order of hash.

1931 D. MacLean *Caught Plastered* (film): Hash? Clean up the kitchen for one! **1981** in Safire *Good Word* 111 [ref. to 1910–13].

¶ **clean up** [or **scrub**] **the kitchen** *Pros.* to perform cunnilingus or anilingus.

[*****a***1890–96** F & H IV 115: *Kitchen*…The female *pudendum.*] **1931** Farrell *McGinty* 77: Harry, wouldn't you like Mr. McGinty to scrub your kitchen?…I'd just adore it, the apparition lisped. **1941** G. Leg-man, in Henry *Sex Variants* II 1161: *Clean up the kitchen* to practice cunnilinctus. **1972** *Anthro. Ling.* (Mar.) 104: *Kitchen cleaner*…an individual who performs [homosexual] anilingus.

¶ **clear the kitchen!** [introduced or popularized by the minstrel song of this name; see *a*1850 quot.] run away! watch out!

1845 in Oehlschlaeger *Reveille* 59: [At] a given signal,…every man drops his cat—and then, "*clar de kitchen!*" *a***1850** T. Rice *Clar de Kitchen* (minstrel song): Clar de kitchen, ol' folks, young folks!/Ol' Virginny neber tire!

¶ **everything but the kitchen sink** everything available

or imaginable.—also (as in 1981, 1982 *N.Y. Times* quots.) used allusively.

*ca***1944** *Screwy Squirrel* (MGM animated cartoon): He hit me with everything but the kitchen sink! *****1948** Partridge et al. *Forces' Slang* 106 [ref. to WWII]: They chucked everything they'd got at us except, or including, the kitchen sink. **1958** *Wall St. Jour.*, in *OED2:* We are such perfectionists that we want everything but the kitchen sink in a weapon. **1977** *Business Week* (May 2) 57: We justified it with econometric modeling…but to get to the minimum threshold, we had to throw in every favorable assumption but the kitchen sink. **1981** P. Sann *Trial* 125: I'd just been hit with the kitchen sink. **1982** W.R. Dunn *Fighter Pilot* 70: They fired everything they had at me, including the kitchen sink. **1982** *N.Y. Times* (July 7) C17: Rzewski's "The Silence of Infinite Spaces" was a kitchen-sink piece, mysticism, cosmology, politics, motoric minimalism, cantata scope and tape all in one rather unfocused mélange. **1989** Joss *Strike* 11: Everything but the kitchen sink.

kitchen mechanic *n.* a cook or dishwasher, esp. a woman.

1877–78 (quot. at K.M.). **1887** *Lantern* (N.O.) (July 23) 2: A dirty looking kitchen mechanic called Maggie Howard. **1900** *DN* II 44: *Kitchen mechanic,* n.…A hired girl. **1901** *Chicago Tribune* (Aug. 25) 8: "Servant girl," she is only a "kitchen mechanic," that's what many people say. **1919** Duffy *G.P.F. Book* 267: One of Battery "F's" classy kitchen mechanics. **1922** in Leadbitter & Slaven *Blues Records* 229: Kitchen Mechanic Blues. **1925** in Oliver *Meaning of Blues* 148: I'm just a…poor workin' gal, "kitchen mechanic" is what they say. **1926** Tully *Jarnegan* 148: They're all a bunch of cheap kitchen mechanics anyhow. **1936** Reddan *Other Men's Lives* 201: "Kitchen Mechanics." Mess Sergeant and Cooks of Company B. **1940** Ottley & Weatherby *Negro in N.Y.* 249: Mostly employed as "pot rasslers," "kitchen mechanics," [etc.]. **1958** Hughes & Bontemps *Negro Folklore* 485: *Kitchen Mechanic:* A domestic servant. **1958** McCulloch *Woods Wds.* 102: *Kitchen mechanic*—Used in some places to mean cook, but more often means…a dishwasher. **1980** D. Cragg (letter to J.E.L., Aug. 10) 3: I first heard this…in Saigon around early 1969. "He's got as much leadership potential as a double-slotted kitchen mechanic."

kite *n.* **1.** a contemptible or despicable person; (*often*) a sexually promiscuous woman.

*****a***1553** N. Udall *Roister Doister* V v: Roister Doister, that doughty kite….Fie! I can scarce abide ye should his name recite. *****1599** Shakespeare *Henry V,* in *OED:* The Lazar Kite of Cressids kinde, Doll Teare-sheete. *****1606** Shakespeare *Antony & Cleopatra* III xiii: What art thou, fellow?…Ah, you kite! *****1608** Shakespeare *King Lear* I iv: Detested kite, thou liest. *****ca***1614** J. Fletcher, in *OED:* Maintaining hospitals for kites and curs. **1895** Wood *Yale Yarns* 87: Bounce de kite! **1908** Sullivan *Criminal Slang* 14: *Kite*—An immoral woman. **1925** in Partridge *Dict. Und.* 388: *Kite*—a low, mean and dirty fellow. *****1931** J. Hanley *Boy* 69: Get down to the bloody engine room you pair of kites. **1942–49** Goldin et al. *DAUL* 118: *Kite*…A prostitute.

2. *Commercial & Und.* (see *a*1889 quot.); (*hence*) a negotiable instrument such as a bank check or securities certificate that is worthless, has been fraudulently altered, etc.—usu. (in early use, solely) constr. with *fly.* [The 1859 def. is prob. incomplete.]

*****1805** in *OED:* Flying a kite in Ireland is a metaphorical phrase for raising money on accommodation bills. **1837** Neal *Charcoal Sks.* 116: Franklin Fipps, if in the mercantile line, is pretty sure to be a great flier of kites, and a speculator in vapors. **1856** Wilkins *Young N.Y.* 2: A retired Merchant, addicted to note-shaving, kite-flying. **1859** Matsell *Vocab.* 49: *Kite*…fancy stocks. **1870** Medbery *Wall St.* 136: *Kite-Flying.* Expanding one's credit beyond wholesome limits. **1885** *Harper's Mo.* (Nov.) 841: A broker or operator…"flies kites" when he expands his credit beyond judicious bounds. *a***1889** *Century Dict.: Kite*…An accommodation bill; a negotiable instrument made without consideration;…in the plural, mere paper credit not based on commercial transactions. (Commercial slang.). **1926** Finerty *Criminalese* 34: *Kite flyer*—Check raiser. **1927** *DN* V 446: *Fly a kite*…to pass a bad cheque….to sell worthless stocks and bonds. **1933** Ersine *Prison Slang* 49: *Kite*…A check written without sufficient funds in the bank. *****1969** in *OEDS:* He's in for what they call "kites," dud cheques, you know.

3.a. *Pris.* a note or letter, as sent between prisoners or smuggled out of prison; (*broadly*) a letter.

1859 Matsell *Vocab.* 49: *Kite.* A letter. **1867** *Nat. Police Gaz.* (Oct.

26) 4: He might send a "kite" and let his friends know. **1918** in *AS* (Oct. 1933) 29: *Kite.* Outgoing underground letter. **1927–28** Tasker *Grimhaven* 224: Do me a favor and write me a kite when you get out. **1930** *Liberty* (Aug. 2) 38: But in October he sends me a kite saying business conditions are very good in Muncie, Indiana. **1931** *AS* VI (Aug.) 439: *Kite, n.* A note or letter. "If I hear anything I'll fly you a kite." **1942** *Life* (May 4) 32: For weeks warden Frank D. Henderson had been receiving "kites" (notes) from prisoners, asking for Army service. **1959** Duffy & Lane *Warden's Wife* 116: Still each week, "kites"—messages from one prisoner to another—would wind up in the Women's Department. **1970** E. Knight *Black Voices from Prison* 169: I "flew a kite" informing the men. **1974** A. Davis *Autobiog.* 61: Any written communication between prisoners is illegal; these notes are called "kites" because of the shape they are folded in for easy concealment. **1979** *Easyriders* (Dec.) 8: If you'd quit blabbin' and say something, maybe we'd print your kites. **1986** *Morning Call* (Allentown, Pa.) (Aug. 18) D3: *Kite:* Letter from prison.

b. *Police.* a notice or memorandum.

1974 Charyn *Blue Eyes* 14: But a "kite" came down from the District Attorney's office; a Chinese gentleman in one of Chino's games was wanted for murder in Port Jervis, New York.

4. *Av.* an airplane. Now *rare.* [Earlier quots. in *OED2* are metaphorical S.E.]

*1917 in *OED2*: He…managed to fly his kite back with great difficulty. **1918** in Hart *135th Aero Squadron* 170: I looked at the schedule/And shivered with fright,/For I'm going to Conflans/In a camera kite. **1940** Hartney *Up & At 'Em* 44 [ref. to 1918]: This is madness, sending us over here to fly in old untried kites. **1946** G.C. Hall, Jr. *1000 Destroyed* 64: This is my new kite and I just took it out to test-fire the guns. **1953** Michener *Sayonara* 71: For Christ sake, tell junior to land that kite. **1953** LeVier & Guenther *Pilot* 22: There was no government control of aircraft at that time, and people could fly any kind of kite. **1955** Klaas *Maybe I'm Dead* 86: A kite flew over and they thought it was a strafing. **1966** J. Lewis *Tell It to Marines* 17: I was twenty miles back of the enemy lines in a war surplus kite before I realized some bastard was shooting at me. **1982** W.R. Dunn *Fighter Pilot* 82: Most of the Hun kites [were] Me.109Es. **a1986** Muirhead *Those Who Fall* 40: If you notice anything wrong with these kites, write it up.

¶ In phrase:

¶ **go fly a kite!** (used as a sarcastic retort); go away! get lost!

1942 Chandler *High Window* 335: Tell him to go fly a kite! **1964** Walsh & DaGradi *Mary Poppins* (film): That's what I said, sir: "Go fly a kite." **1970** Hatch *Cedarhurst* 159: He told me to go fly a kite. **1991** Univ. Tenn. student: I'd tell her to go fly a kite.

kite *v.* **1.a.** *Commercial.* to sustain one's credit by means of an accommodation paper; (*also*) to write or pass (a fraudulent or temporarily unsupported check), or sell (bogus securities); (*hence*) *Und.* to fraudulently raise the amount of (a check).—in early use, also constr. with dummy-obj. *it.* Now *colloq.*

1839 Briggs *H. Franco* II 35: He stuffed half a dozen blank checks into his hat, and said he must go out and kite it to save his credit. **1864** in *OED2*: *Kite, v.i.* (Literally, to fly a *kite.*) To raise money, or sustain one's credit, by the use of mercantile paper which is fictitious. **a1889** *Century Dict.*: *Kite*…To fly commercial "kites"; raise money or gain the temporary use of money by means of accommodation bills, or by borrowed, illegally certified, or worthless checks. (Commercial slang.) **1898–1900** Cullen *Chances* 7: A two-months' campaign of highly successful check-kiting. **1905** *N.Y. Times* (May 28) III 4: Safe in jail…for check-kiting in San Francisco. **1908** Sullivan *Criminal Slang* 5: *Check kiting*—Dating a check ahead and expecting to have money to meet it when due. **1918** Stringer *House of Intrigue* 48: He'd rather be a check-kiter any day. **1933** Ersine *Prison Slang* 49: *Kite, v.*…To write a check larger than one's bank balance. **1939** *AS* (Oct.) 240: *To kite paper.* To pass bad checks. **1958** *N.Y. Times Mag.* (Mar. 16) 88: *Kite*—To raise the amount of a check. **1959** Duffy & Lane *Warden's Wife* 187: A [forged] check artist who…gave kiting a brand new twist. **1975** V.B. Miller *Trade-Off* 86: You were the best check-kiter in Manhattan, Faxy. In your hand, a ball-point pen was a Stradivarius. **1981** G. Wolf *Roger Rabbit* 72: I had enough checks kited.

b. to increase or exaggerate the value or amount of.

1968 Cuomo *Thieves* 129: That really got him, that goddamn owner kiting up his take from the insurance.

2. *Pris.* to send (a note or letter) illicitly.

1924 in *Flynn's Mag.* (Jan. 3, 1925) 665: *Kite*…to send a message. **1932** Lawes *20,000 Years in Sing Sing* 185: The penalties attached to "kiting" letters out of the prison through irregular channels are explained in detail. **1950** Duffy *S. Quentin* 161: The practice of sending or receiving secret messages is called "kiting." **1951** in J. Blake *Joint* 14: Incoming mail is not opened at all, and it's easy to kite a letter out, as I'm doing this. **1952** Viereck *Men into Beasts* 24: One or two will kite out letters for you. **1956** Resko *Reprieve* 240: The threatening notes were kited out—smuggled out of prison and mailed by a corrupt employee. **1971–72** in Abernethy *Bounty of Texas* 208: *Kite*…to send out a letter illegally.

kitten *n.* **1.** *pl.* a cat-o'-nine-tails. *Joc.* Cf. CAT, 2.

1843 in Leyda *Melville Log I* 171: 6 lashes with the kittens for fighting & abuse.

2. a bottle of liquor.

1890 *United Service* (Nov.) 444: "The men seem to be quite hilarious to-night….Have they been fondling the kitten?" "Oh, no; the boys never drink anything in camp."

3. the fellow for a particular purpose. Cf. CAT, 3.a.

1894 in S. Crane *Complete Stories* 209: I scrap wid a man jest as soon as he ses scrap, an' if yeh wanta scrap, I'm yer kitten.

4. a young woman. [In earlier use, a colloq. endearment for a little girl; see *OED2*.]

1923 in D. Hammett *Continental Op* 18: A sleek kitten—that dame! *Ibid.* 22: That Dexter kitten didn't do it. **1941** in Ellington *Music Is My Mistress* 179: *Kitten*…girl. **1944** Breslow & Purcell *Follow the Boys* (film): I'm a kitten with my mittens laced. **1949** "J. Evans" *Halo in Brass* 41: What's that flat-chested kitten been up to? **1958** Meltzer & Blees *H.S. Confidential* (film): I dig pretty kittens. **1971** Jacobs & Casey *Grease* 41: So, okay, cats, throw your mittens around your kittens.

¶ In phrase:

¶ **have kittens** to become very upset, nervous, or angry.

1900 *DN* II 44: [College slang:] "Get kittens," "have kittens." 1. To get angry. 2. To be in great anxiety, or to be afraid. **1931** *AS* VI 206: *To have kittens:* to be angry. ***1940** Hunt & Pringle *Service Slang* 38: "The Colonel is having kittens"—the Colonel is upset, and…angry. **1955** N.Y.C. woman, age 40: Your grandmother will have kittens when she finds out. **1959** Farris *Harrison High* 363: Mother is going to have kittens. **1960** Barber *Minsky's* 141: If…Mr. Buzby knew that I got the idea for the Garden of Eden number from the Pilgrim's Progress he gave me, he would simply have kittens! **1965** Friedman *Totempole* 278: Well, we better go now before the colonel has kittens. **1971** Faust *Willy Remembers* 86: For what did we do, we waited. Hurry up, Yost would have had kittens. **1984** C. Francis *Who's Sorry?* 35: My father will have kittens, Mr. Godfrey! **1985** Sawislak *Dwarf* 100: He said Morgan would have a kitten if we spent that kind of money.

kitty[1] *n.* [perh. fr. *kidcote* 'a prison' (obs. S.E. *a*1515–1886, *OED*)] a prison or other place of confinement.—constr. with *the.*

*1825 in *OED*: *Kitty,* the house of correction. Newcastle. ***1827** in Ribton-Turner *Vagrants* 637: He would put him in the Kitty "for an *imposteror.*" ***1864** in *OED*: If ane gangs t' the kitty, we'll a' gang. **a1889** *Century Dict.*: *Kitty*…A prison or jail….(Prov. Eng. or slang). **1942–49** Goldin et al. *DAUL* 118: *Kitty, the*…A prison; a jail; a reformatory.

kitty[2] *n.* **1.** Orig. *Poker.* (see 1887 quot.); (*hence*) a cash fund raised for a particular use; the sum of available funds; (*also*) the sum of money at stake in a poker game.

1887 in *OED2*: *Widow,* or *Kitty*—A percentage taken out of the pool to defray the expenses of the [poker] game or the cost of refreshments. **a1889** *Century Dict.*: *Kitty*…A pool into which each player in a card-game puts a certain amount of his winnings, to be used in meeting expenses, as for room-rent, refreshments, etc. **1901** in "O. Henry" *Cabbages & Kings* 14: His Nibs skedaddled…with all the coin in the kitty. **1909** W. Irwin *Con Man* 42: You know the "kitty" in a poker table—the square hole or slit at the center into which you slip the house percentage? **1910** *Variety* (Aug. 20) 13: I fingered the kitty and dug for the paper. **1928** *Amer. Mercury* (Aug.) 398: This is done if a guest comes up for water more than once and refuses to contribute to the kitty. **1931** Harlow *Old Bowery* 512: To install him as kitty keeper in the poker game. **1950** *Sat. Eve. Post* (Apr. 1) 75: Groups were advised to keep the kitty low. **1952** McCoy & Dortort *Lusty Men* (film): Sweeten up the kitty. **1957** T. Williams *Orpheus* 31: Whenever paper money was dropped in the kitty you blew a whistle. **a1961** R.H.

Dillon *Shanghaiing Days* 188: With the kitty thus obtained, they financed a one-man pursuit of Jim. **1961** Peacock *Valhalla* 63: Cold beer from the payday kitty. **1965** N.Y.C. high school student: If you want to play, feed the kitty. **1971** J. Brown & A. Groff *Monkey* 74: My kitty was getting fatter and I could soon put my lawyer back to work. **1977** Coover *Public Burning* 565: America's greatest asset: her bottomless kitty. **1978** Alibrandi *Killshot* 107: Every dime of the proceeds goes into our kitty. **1994** J. Eliason *Oldest Confed. Widow* (TV show): Like he ain't had his fist in the town kitty.

2. a young woman.
   1936 R. Adams *Cowboy Lingo* 190: Shake yo' feet an' ketch yo' kitty. **1942** *Yank* (Sept. 23) 14: He thought he could trick this small-town kitty. **1956** Holiday & Dufty *Lady Sings the Blues* 21: I was only thirteen, but I was a hip kitty. **1971** in L. Bangs *Psychotic Reactions* 63: Red Guard kats an' kitties would bop down in droves. **1977** Torres *Q&A* 130: Do you think a barrio kitty like Nancy Bosch can't see through this dude's silk underwear? **1992** *Roc* (Fox-TV): A little kitty in a Caddy, eh?

3. a Cadillac automobile. Cf. CADDY.
   1945 Himes *If He Hollers* 41: Of course if I had my way I'd take a kitty. **1959** in S. King *Christine* 343: She took the keys to my Cadillac car,/Jumped in my Kitty and drove her far. **1967** [R. Beck] *Pimp* 130: Take the key to the "kitty" and get there fast.

4. *Jazz.* a young man; CAT, 3.b.
   1952 Ellson *Golden Spike* 23: Some kitty. I don't know his name. *Ibid.* 39: I don't know that kitty at all. **1966** I. Reed *Pall-Bearers* 110: How To Be A Hip Kitty And A Cool Cool Daddy O.

kitty whomper *n.* a tractor-trailer.
   1976 (quot. at CACTUS PATCH).

kiwash *n.* [perh. alter. of *cash*] money.
   1978 Diehl *Sharky's Machine* 101: All those assholes are interested in is their own chunk of the kiwash.

kiwi *n.* **1.** Esp. *Mil.* a New Zealander. Often *cap.*
   1918 in *OEDS*: The "Kiwis" gave a performance to a crowded hall. **1943 *Yank* (June 18) 10: Tommies, Jocks, Aussies, Kiwis. **1944** in *Best from Yank* 58: I found myself…in the company of a Kiwi who wasn't wearing a helmet. **1946** J.H. Burns *Gallery* 10: There was a small Kiwi listening now at the back of the bar. **1952** Uris *Battle Cry* 180: The Kiwis gave a happy sigh. **1954** Crockett *Magnificent Bastards* 99: Lemme tell you how your sonny boy snowed them Kiwi gals in Auckland. **1980** Leland *Kiwi-Yank. Dict.* 13: A Kiwi sees the world differently from an American. **1986** G. Woods *9B* (film): We got all sorts here—an Aussie, a Kiwi, a couple of Brits. **1987** Chinnery *Life on Line* 36: We worked with the Aussies and Kiwis for several weeks. **1995** *All Things Considered* (Nat. Pub. Radio) (May 12): Americans are just as pleased to see the kiwis do well [in America's Cup preparations] as anyone.

2. [in ref. to the flightlessness of the bird] *Mil. Av.* an air force administrative officer having no flying experience; *(hence) (occ.)* an aircrewman who dislikes flying; *(rarely)* an aviation cadet who has yet to solo.
   1918 *Wadsworth Gas Attack* (Jan. 26) 26: An officer in the flying service without flying status is called a "kiwi," after an Australian bird. **1918** in Blodgett *Letters* 140: We have what are called "kiwis" here, or the boys who have lost their nerve. It comes from the Australian bird of that name, that spends its time sitting on the ground, flapping its wings and making a lot of noise. **1918** in H. Berry *Kaiser* 394: We don't have to fly over Germany,/We are the kiwi birds. **1919** *Law Second Army Air Service Book* (unp.): A Day in the Life of a Kiwi. *Ibid.*: We'll get Old Pete to give us wings/And back to earth we'll fly,/And haunt those gol-darned Kiwis/Until the day they die. **1925** Faulkner *Soldiers' Pay* 18: Who can't date a single girl/Long as kee-wees run the world?/Kay-det! **1928** *Writer's Mo.* (Feb.) 122: A kiwi…is anyone connected with a flying organization who is himself not a flyer. **1928** *Pop. Science Mo.* (May) 72: A "kiwi" is a "groundhog" or pilot who does not like to fly. **1933** *Leatherneck* (Sept.) 6: Try to forget that you are a kiwi for once and try to act like a rational pilot. **1938** *AS* (Apr.) 156: *Kiwi.*…A person with no practical flying experience; often used as a term of disparagement. **1944** *AAF* 369: *Kiwi.* A non-flying officer. **1956** Heflin *USAF Dict.*: *Kiwi.* A student who has not flown solo. *a*1962 in Morris & Morris *Dict. Wd. & Phr. Orig.* 207: Many times [during WWI] I stood in military formations which were in charge of a *kiwi* and heard the subdued cry of "Kiwi, kiwi!" from…the rear ranks

where the callers could not be definitely located. **1965** Reagan & Hubler *Rest of Me* 254: Everyone flew but me (the Kiwi).

ki-yi *n.* [orig. used to represent the yelp of a dog or coyote; see *DA*] **1.a.** a noisy little dog, esp. a mongrel; (in 1905 quot.) a worthless racehorse.
   1895 *Harper's* (Nov.) 962: The ki-yi gun…it shoots dogs.…My dear boy,…I'm not really a ki-yi. **1904** in Opper *H. Hooligan* 35: Get out of the way, you worthless ki-yi. **1904** in *DA*: Doubtless the Brussells kiyis yelped for joy. **1905** *Nat. Police Gaz.* (Nov. 18) 3: Never take a chance on a kiyi like that. **1913** J. London *Valley of Moon*: Mangy ki-yis. **1914** E.R. Burroughs *Mucker* 49: De ol' woman an' de ki-yi.

   b. a low or contemptible fellow; cur.
   1898 B. Harte *Light & Shadow* 182: He called himself a man, skunkin' in the open and afraid to show himself except with a crowd of other "Ki-yi's" around a house of women and children. **1906** Mulford *Bar-20* 190: Yore th' snortingest ki-yi that ever stuck its tail between its laigs. **1942** Pegler *Spelvin* 132: So you are yellow. A ki-yi, hey? And a bum, too.

2. *Navy.* a small, stiff-bristled scrub brush. Also as *v.*
   1898 Doubleday *Gunner* 219: Scrubbed the deck with stiff "kiyi" brushes. **1917** *Collier's* (Nov. 3) 13: The ki-yi is a scrubbing brush…with stiff fiber bristles. It is the washing machine of the navy. **1918** Ruggles *Navy Explained* 84: *Ki-yi.* A small brush with very stiff bristles. **1920** *Amer. Leg. Wkly.* (Apr. 9) 11: [The admiral] never had been down on his hands and knees manipulating a ki-yi brush. **1944** E.H. Hunt *Limit* 27: Then he began scrubbing a pair of khaki shorts with the ki-yi. **1988** Poyer *Med* 80: Dump it on the deckplates with some scouring powder and get Blaney to kaieye it before he secures.

kiyoodle *n.* [orig. unkn.; perh. infl. by *coyote*] **1.** a small noisy dog. Also **kyoodle.** Also vars.
   1893 Thomas *Mizzoura* 477: Ain't you got some soup-meat or sumpthin' you kin spare that little ki-yoodle? **1906** *Nat. Police Gaz.* (Nov. 10) 3: Nearly everyone in this town has a kiyoodle of some kind. **1906** Kildare *Bailiwick* 136: Say, kid, so you was going to have me arrested for finishing that kyoodle o' your'n? **1918** Livingston *Delcassee* 57: There were the "fivers," the aristocrats of the kiyoodles. *Ibid.* 77: But sold the kiyoodle to the Chink at his own figure, men. **1923** Revell *Off the Chest* 131: A yellow creature of the type commonly referred to as "pup," "kiyoodle," or "cur." **1925** in W.A. Graham *Custer Myth* 81: Like a scared kioodles yipping. **1930** in Blackbeard & Williams *Smithsonian Comics* 125: Sure he's a kioodle! **1985** in Safire *Look It Up* 164: New Orleans has its own dialect.…Some words such as *cayoodle* for a little dog are found in other parts of the country. (*Cayoodle* turned up in New England.).

2. a worthless person; an oaf. Also vars.
   1902–03 Ade *People You Know* 109: A bunch of Kioodles who wore No. 6 Hats and talked…Piffle. **1903** *Pedagog. Sem.* X 373: You crazy kioodle. **1936** Miller *Battling Bellhop* (film): You got nothin' to worry about. He's a kiyoodle. **1945** Gerraghty & Frank *Whiplash* (film): Duke Carney's a set-up! He's a kiyoodle who should be pickin' daisies in a field. **1967** G. Green *To Brooklyn* 266: It's better than kiying like a kiyoodle with your tail between your legs.

kiyudle *v.* [of fanciful orig.; cf. KIYOODLE] to discharge from employment.
   1916 S. Lewis *Job* 264 [ref. to *ca*1910]: I've been fired!…Canned… Bounced. Kiyudeled.

KJ *n.* [allegedly fr. *k*rystal (for CRYSTAL) *j*oint 'a marijuana cigarette laced with phencyclidine'] *Narc.* phencyclidine.
   1977 (cited in Spears *Drugs & Drink* 305). **1978** Petersen & Stillman *Phencyclidine Abuse* 120: Such names include Hog, Angel Dust, Dust,…Crystal Joints, CJ, KJ, [etc.]. *a*1990 E. Currie *Dope & Trouble* 244: Joints and KJ.…KJ? That's PCP. **1994** *Street Terms* (Oct.): *KJ*—PCP.

klem *v.* [orig. unkn.; perh. related to CLEM] *Und.* (see quot.).
   1859 Matsell *Vocab.* 49: *Klem.* To strike. "Klem the bloke," hit the man.

klep *n.* a kleptomaniac. *Rare* in U.S. Also **klepper.**
   1889 Barrère & Leland *Dict. Slang* I 523: *Klep* (popular), a thief; to *klep*, to steal. From *kleptomania.* **1920 in Hemingway *Dateline: Toronto* 13: There are no such people as kleptomaniacs.…At least, we have never run into a genuine klep. **1949 in *OED2*. **1972** *All in the Family* (CBS-TV): I ain't no klepper!

klepto *n.* a kleptomaniac.

1953 *ATS* (ed. 2) 377: Dipso, klepto, nympho. **1956** Algren *Wild Side* 87 [ref. to 1931]: There were creepers and kleptoes and zanies and dipsoes. **1969** in Cheever *Letters* 268: An Indiana klepto and a socialist millionaire. **1976** R. Daley *To Kill* 21: The kid's a klepto, Chief. **1979** Gutcheon *New Girls* 144: Do you think Cindy could be the klepto? **1980** *N.Y. Post* (July 2) 36: Neighbor is a real klepto. **1987** *Wkly. World News* (Sept. 8) 28: Krazed Klepto, Washington, D.C. **1989** Radford & Crowley *Drug Agent* 193: He was also a klepto.

klick, klik vars. CLICK³, *n.*

kloof *n.* [orig. unkn.] an oaf; GOOF, 1.
    1924 H.L. Wilson *Ruggles* 254: He watches this poor kloof wave his flag at us.

kluck *n.* CLUCK, 2.
    1937 Weidman *Can Get It Wholesale* 122: A kluck like Meyer Babushkin.

kludge /kluʤ/ *n.* [coined in 1962 by J.W. Granholm, ironically sugg. by G *Klug* 'clever'] **1.** *Computers.* an inferior or unreliable computer system put together from mismatched components; (*hence*) an ill-conceived patchwork, mishmash, etc.; an improvised solution to a problem in electronics, engineering, etc.
    1962 J.W. Granholm, in *OED2*: The building of a Kludge…is not work for amateurs. **1969** in B. Stevens *25 Years* 66: Airmen's Unabridged Dictionary…*Clooge*…(espec. among missile men) Any improvised or makeshift repair, using old tin cans, chewing gum, etc., to simulate first-class work in Tech Order compliance. **1969** Jordain & Breslau *Condensed Comp. Encycl.* 271: *Kludge* A…term denoting a poorly designed system composed of ill-fitting, mismatched components…."This kludge shouldn't work but, somehow, it does." **1981** D. Miller *Jargon* 186: When a kluge fails, however, everyone says, "Well, what did you expect?" **1982** Trudeau *Dressed for Failure* (unp.): So you want a kludge that's built for civilians, huh? **1983** Naiman *Computer Dict.* 83: This whole program is one big kluge. *a*1984 T. Clancy *Red Oct.* 63: "Skipper, SAPS works…most of the time, but sometimes it's a real *kludge.*" Jones' epithet was the most pejorative curse of electronics people. **1986** *Crossfire* (CNN-TV) (Aug. 7): Do you know why there was such a kluge of different services all coming together [unsuccessfully] at that time?
2. KLUTZ.
    1984 D. Barthelme, in *New Yorker* (Sept. 24) 45: Well, this knee looks like the soldier was just doing what he thought he was supposed to do. The poor kludge.
3. a difficulty; snarl.
    *a*1990 R. Herman, Jr. *Force of Eagles* 90: I've got a problem I can't handle….A real kludge….Kludge means bottleneck.

kludge *v. Computers.* to compose or repair (a computer system, program, etc.) by makeshift means.—also constr. with *up.* Also **kluge.**
    1969 M. Simon *Marooned* (film): I'm in Hunstville kludgin' up a simulator of the XRV. **1983** Naiman *Computer Dict.* 83: I didn't have time to fix it right so I just kluged it. **1983** *Verbatim* (Winter) 17: *To kludge* means to put together some hardware (or write a program) by combining parts of existing computers or their programs.

kludgey *n.* (see 1990 quot.). Also **klugy.**
    1983 Naiman *Computer Dict.* 83: *Kluge*….The adjective is *klugy.* **1990** T. Fahey *Joys of Jargon* 99: Software can be *elegant*…or *kludgey* (ugly, clumsy product [*sic*]).

klunk var. CLUNK, *n. & v.*

klunk out *v.* to break down; CONK OUT, 1.
    1979 in Terkel *Amer. Dreams* 162: The machine klunks out, an' it's *us* that are fixin' it.

klutz *n.* [< Yid *klutz*, var. *klots*] a clumsy person; oaf.
    [**1918** *Jester* (Columbia Univ.) (Feb.) 3: [On a statue:] HEZEKIAL KLUTZ who fought in the trenches of Flanders from 1914–1918 and didn't write a book about it.] [**1925** in Partridge *Dict. Und.* 389: Klotz.] [**1936** Levin *Old Bunch* 147: He's a *klutz*. He can't do no repairs. He got wooden fingers.] **1956** G. Green *Last Angry Man* 411: He sits there with his stupid wife, and the big klutz of a son. **1960** Barber *Minsky's* 254: Some dumb klutz sat on my musketeer hat. **1971** *Aerial Phenomena Research Organization Bulletin* (Sept.) 3: And sometimes we feel like klutzes beyond hope, stupid, lost, hurting, the eternal fire banked by pounds of clay. **1977** R.S. Parker *Effective Decisions* 7: You felt like the worst klutz in the world. **1983** *Good Morning Amer-*

ica (ABC-TV) (May 9): Is the child a klutz who doesn't have the athletic coordination of his peers? **1986** Wilson & Maddock *Short Circuit* (film): You klutz! See what you did! **1994** *N.Y. Daily News* (Feb. 24) 1: A Total Klutz. **1994** *The Nanny* (CBS-TV): A bit of a klutz, eh? **1995** *Guiding Light* (CBS-TV): That means you're a klutz.

klutz *v.* to bungle; botch.—usu. constr. with *up.*
    1977 Butler & Shryack *Gauntlet* 168: In case I klutz this up and break my neck or something. **1978** Pici *Tennis Hustler* 94: That Romeo…klutzed it and spilled his drink all over me. **1996** *L.A. Times Bk. Rev.* (Aug. 25) 5: He knows what's been klutzing up the system.

klutzy *adj.* clumsy; oafish. Also **clutzy, clutsy.** Hence **klutziness,** *n.*
    1965 in *DARE*: The dancers look good and the artists look a little *klutzy*. **1967** Coppola *You're a Big Boy Now* (film): You're a little klutzy, aren't you? **1974** V.B. Miller *Girl in River* 106: This clutzy-looking piece of rock. **1980** *N.Y. Daily News* (Sept. 6) 16: She was the tall, clutsy dancer who Roy Scheider told, "I can make you a good dancer but not a great dancer." **1980** Schruers *Blondie* 16: Often described as "klutzy" (usually with a modifier like "endearingly"). **1981** C. Nelson *Picked Bullets Up* 60: I become self-conscious and "Klutzy." **1981** *Film Comment* (May) 4: The charms of her klutziness are limited. **1995** *US* (Sept.) 46: He wanted to encourage that side of the character—that the character be a little bit klutzy.

K.M. *n.* KITCHEN MECHANIC.
    1877–78 *Cornelian* 86: K.M. Kitchen mechanic; servant girls. **1895** Gore *Stu. Slang* 7: *K.M.* n. Kitchen mechanic. **1900** *DN* II 44: *K.m.,* i.e. *kitchen mechanic,* a servant girl. **1913** *DN* IV 11: She is a K.M. **1915** *DN* IV 246: *K.m.* Kitchen mechanic. **1928** R. Fisher *Jericho* 71: The K.M.'s seldom turn up their noses at the school teachers. **1929–31** Farrell *Young Lonigan* ch. iv: Screwy…bragged that he had put the blocks to nearly every K.M. in the neighborhood. **1941** in Ellington *Music Is My Mistress* 179: *K.M.*…kitchen mechanic.

k.m.a. *interj.* kiss [or *suck*] *my ass* s.v. ASS.—usu. considered vulgar. Also vars.
    1889 in *Kans. Hist. Qly.* XIII (1944) 128: Murphy, k.m.a. **1914–22* Joyce *Ulysses* 146: K.M.A.—Will you tell him he can kiss my arse?…Tell that straight from the stable. *Ibid.* 147: K.M.R.I.A.—He can kiss my royal Irish arse. **1996** *New Yorker* (July 8) 62 [ref. to *ca*1900]: Saint-Gaudens and Stanford [White] habitually…signed off with "K.M.A.," meaning "Kiss My Ass"—Saint-Gaudens would sometimes spell it out.

knacker var. KNOCKER, 2.a.

knappy *n. Army.* knapsack.
    1864 in *PADS* (No. 70) 39: We took off our knappies, and laid them at our feet.

knapsack drill *n. Army.* an unauthorized absence; absence without leave. *Joc.*
    1865 in D. Chisholm *Civil War Notebk.* 95: Bolen and Yauger came back, been to the city on a (Bolen pass) *knapsack drill.*

kneecap *v.* to deliberately cripple by shattering the kneecaps of, usu. as an act of vengeance or terrorism.—also used fig.
    1974 (cited in *W10*). **1976* C.C. O'Brien, in *Harper's* (Dec.) 37: Their murders of civilians in their houses; their knee-cappings and tarrings and featherings. **1978** *N.Y. Times Mag.* (July 23) 23: In terrorism, shooting at victims' legs has been called *kneecapping.* **1982** E. Leonard *Cat Chaser* 158: My good name, being seen with a kneecapper. **1984** J.R. Reeves *Mekong* 110: I'll kneecap your ass and leave you for 'em! **1988** *thirtysomething* (ABC-TV): We could pay some guy to kneecap him at halftime. **1989** P.H.C. Mason *Recovering* 150: We had a boy kneecapped….Shot in the legs. **1990** *New Yorker* (July 2) 65: In March House Majority Leader Dick Gephardt got kneecapped by the White House for suggesting [economic aid to Russia]. **1994** *Harper's* (Feb.) 49: Execution for drug dealers and violent freelance criminals, beatings and kneecappings for juvenile delinquents and auto thieves.

knee-high *adj.* ¶ In phrase: **knee-high to a grasshopper** being a very small child. Also vars.
    1814 in *DA*: About knee-high to a toad. **1838** [Haliburton] *Clockmaker* (Ser. 2) 126: A boy about knee-high to a goose. **1858** [S. Hammett] *Piney Woods* 30: When my father was about knee-high to an injin puddin? **1877** Pinkerton *Maguires* 108: Haven't I known him since he was knee-high to a rabbit? *a*1881 G.C. Harding *Misc. Writings* 157: Sence she was knee high to a duck. **1905** *DN* II 12: *Knee-high to a*

grasshopper, adj. phr. Short in stature. **1906** M'Govern *Sarjint Larry* 95: I was a shirt-tail kid not knee-high to a lame duck. **1906** in A. Adams *Chisholm Trail* 205: I've known you since you weren't knee-high to a grasshopper. **1907** in "O. Henry" *Works* 188: She told me how you adopted me when I was knee-high to a puddle duck. **1909** Corwin *Ethel Wright* 59: I have handled one ever since I was knee-high to a grasshopper. **1926** Hormel *Co-Ed* 13: Mere matter of being on his own since he was knee-high to a cricket. **1928** York *Sgt. York* 36: Since I was knee-high to a duck I've heard tell of these men. **1934** Weseen *Dict. Amer. Sl.* 360: *Knee-high to a grasshopper*—Very small. **1940** F. Hunt *Trail from Tex.* 172: I've knowed that old hoss thief since I was knee-high to a duck. **1946** J. Adams *Gags* 25: Ever since I was knee-high to a grasshopper, I've had an ambition to live at the Waldorf-Astoria. **1960** I. Freeman *Out of Burning* 89: Let's wait until you grow knee-high to a louse anyway. **1964** J.M. Brewer *Worser Days* 35: Den one of de members what been knowin' de boy from time he was knee-high to a duck riz up. **1988** Terkel *Great Divide* 295: I remember from the time I was knee-high to a duck. **1988** B.E. Wheeler *Outhouse Humor* 60: When I was knee-high to a grasshopper.

knee-knocker *n.* **1.** *pl.* knickerbockers; (*also*) knee-length shorts.—also used attrib. [Prob. the orig. sense.]
   1968 Cuomo *Thieves* 383: Those co-eds *were* rather cute in their knee-knocker outfits. *a*1982 Story et al. *Dict. Newf. Eng.* 287: *Knee knockers*: men's trousers gathered at the knees; knickerbockers.

2. *Navy.* any low shipboard structure over which an inattentive person may stumble, esp. a hatchway coaming in a vertical bulkhead.
   1966 F. Elkins *Heart of Man* 45: In the rush…a chief petty officer…was pushed into a knee-knocker and trampled. **1988** Poyer *The Med* 13: They tripped over knee-knockers. **1988** Coonts *Final Flight* 21: At this point the openings in the frames that supported the flight deck were oval in shape and only wide enough for people to pass through in single file. "Knee-knockers," Tarkington called them. **1991** K. Douglass *Viper Strike* 67: The passageways…were interrupted by a cross frame with an oval-shaped door called a "knee-knocker." **1991** K. Douglass *Carrier* 45: He stepped through the knee-knocker partitions where bulkheads crossed the passageway. **1991** J. Weber *Rules of Engagement* 188 [ref. to Vietnam War]: Sonuvabitchin' knee knockers.

knee machine *n. Surfing.* a very short surfboard.
   1977 Filosa *Surf. Almanac* 189: Knee machine. A *paipo* board. A kneeboard.

knees *n.pl.* BEE'S KNEES.
   1942 Davis & Wolsey *Call House Madam* 92: Princes Road was the knees plus ultra!

kneesies *n.* playfully amorous knee-to-knee contact, as while seated at a small table. Often constr. with *play*. Also **kneesie.** Cf. FOOTSIE.
   1950 Spillane *Vengeance* 38: That left me playing kneesies with his mistress. **1956** *Social Problems* III 258: Playing kneesies under the table all night long. **1958** T. Capote *Breakfast at Tiffany's* 57: I let him play kneesie under the table. **1963** Stearn *Grapevine* 172: "Oh, kneesies," Ann said with a little laugh. **1964** Faust *Steagle* 36: Snowing Maguire and playing kneesie. **1970** G. Walker *Cruising* 57: Sidewalk glances, subway jostlings, movie kneesies. **1972** Pearce *Pier Head Jump* 105: We're holdin' hands and we're playin' footsies and kneesies. **1981** G. Wolf *Roger Rabbit* 19: We…laughed and played kneesies under the table.

knee-slapper *n.* an amusing joke.—usu. used ironically.
   1966 *New Yorker* (Nov. 5) 128: "How's the World Treating You," an English comedy at the Music Box, is full of knee-slappers like that one. **1970** Grissim *White Man's Blue* 63: Embry uses his plastic prop to crack a couple of pretty good knee-slappers. **1980** J. Carroll *Land of Laughs* 55: I looked over my shoulder…to see how these knee-slappers were going down. **1983** S. King *Christine* 267: It was a funny thought…wotta knee-slapper. **1985** in Groening *Work Is Hell* (unp.): Ha ha what a kneeslapper. **1996** *Good Morning America* (Oct. 7) (ABC-TV): That was a big knee-slapper.

knee-walking *adj. So. & West.* so drunk as to be unable to stand. In full, **knee-walking drunk.**
   1973 W. Crawford *Stryker* 158: Get falling-down, knee-walking drunk. **1974** Univ. Tenn. students: "Let's go out an' get knee-walkin'."…"He was knee-walkin' drunk." **1974–75** Powledge *Mud Show* 16: Falling-down, knee-walking drunk. **1979** Eble *Campus Slang* (Mar.) 5: *Knee-walking*—drunk: My roommate was knee-walking the

other night. **1987** Zeybel *Gunship* 53 [ref. to 1960's]: They remembered who was who…even when they were knee-walking. **1995** Cormier et al. *Wildcats* 198: Some sailors can get knee-walking drunk on two cans.

knickers *n.pl.* ¶ In phrase: **get (one's) knickers in a twist** [or **knot**] to become excited or agitated.
   *1980 Economist (Feb. 23) 3: When a bicyclist has momentum, he glides forward with admirable grace…when he tries to reverse, on a machine with no built-in facility for doing so, he can crash with his knickers in fearful twist. **1986** *Financial Times* (Jan. 8) 19: For a moderately complicated device, the problem can translate into devising 10,000 different interconnections. "You can easily get your knickers in a twist," observes Dr Andy Hopper, a director of Qudos. **1986** *L.A. Times* (Feb. 10) V 2: Other Views: Enough to Get One's Knickers in a Twist. **1987** R.M. Brown *Starting* 158: I can bear all of the above, but…this one really gets my knickers in a twist. **1990** *Major Dad* (CBS-TV): Now don't get your knickers in a twist. We've still got that Eagle to sell. **1995** *L.A. Times* (Dec. 19) E4: Hey, sarge. Got a civilian here with his knickers in a knot.

knickknacker *n.* NUT. Also **knicknack.**
   1966 Reynolds & McClure *Freewheelin Frank* 136: Many of us…have no driver's license, because of the knickknackers in white shirts in the…Department of Motor Vehicles. **1971** *Black Scholar* (Sept.) 35: I thought you was some kind of knicknack.

knickknacking *adj.* eccentric.
   1966 Braly *On the Yard* 175: It was bad enough trying to cell with someone halfway regular, let alone some knickknacking nut.

knife *n.* rejection or dismissal; AX, 1.—constr. with *the*.
   1911 Runyon *Tents of Trouble* 39: An' me money had gone in a sucker way before they slipped me the knife. **1926** *Variety* (Dec. 29) 7: It would have been given the official knife.

knife *v.* Orig. *Pol.* to strike at treacherously; betray. Now *colloq.*
   1888 in *DA*: The strongest men in the party cannot be nominated, because they are hateful to the Blaine faction, and are certain to be knifed in the Convention in case Blaine does not get the nomination. *a*1889 *Century Dict.: Knife*…To endeavor to defeat in a secret or underhand way in an election, as a candidate of one's own party. (Political slang, U.S.). **1891** Maitland *Slang Dict.* 161: *Knife* (Am.), to knife a person is to do him harm, to stab him in character, if not in person. **1911** Harrison *Queed* 323: What chance'd there be of namin' to lead the party in the city the man who had knifed the party in the State? **1918** E.E. Rose *Cappy Ricks* 70: Why, that old rascal would knife his mother in a business deal! **1922** in Hemingway *Sel. Letters* 64: Its [*sic*] hell when a male knifes you—especially when you still love him. **1927–28** in R. Nelson *Dishonorable* 157: If I don't put this over with you, they'll knife me, next election. **1929** McEvoy *Hollywood Girl* 79: Test turned out swell but that Chiquita knifed me. **1932** Farrell *Guillotine Party* 187: This fraternity cannot afford to have members who knife their…fraternity brothers. **1948** in *DA*. **1964** D. Berg *Looks at U.S.A.* (unp.): I wonder how many guys he *knifed* in order to get that job?

knife fight *n. Mil. Av.* an intense aerial dogfight, usu. between two fighter planes.
   1983 M. Skinner *USAFE* 51: *Knife Fight:* An aerial engagement where both aircraft are committed to a duel to the death. **1989** Joss *Strike* 90: ACM furballs and knife fights. **1995** *JAG* (CBS-TV): I wanted to see if you had the guts for a knife fight. **1995** *Space: Above & Beyond* (Fox-TV): I'm here because I've been in a knife fight with them.

knife-thrower *n. Pol.* (see quot.).
   1982 W. Safire, in *N.Y. Times Mag.* (Jan. 2, 1983) 6: *Knife-thrower*—a "lobbyist who knows who the decision maker is three or four rungs down the ladder and knows how to get to him."

knob *n.* **1.** the head; in phr. **off (one's) knob** crazy. Also **nob.**
   *1673 [R. Head] *Canting Academy* 42: Nab [*sic*] An Head. *Nab-cheat* An Hat. **1698–99* "B.E." *Dict. Cant. Crew:* Nob, a Head. **1725 New Canting Dict.: Knob.* The Head or Skull. **1733* in *F & H* V 53: To do pop up your nob again,/And egad I'll crack your crown. **1751** in Breslaw *Tues. Club* 295: Boldly exposing his brave Nob to the fire of the enemy [*sic*]. **1785* Grose *Vulgar Tongue: Knob.* The head. **1819** in *OED*: A tremendous lunging blow on his nob. **1835* in *EDD*: His nob was all a melancholy blankness. **1837* Dickens *Pickwick Papers* ch. xliii: Dick put a couple of balls in his nob. **1837** *Davy Crockett's Almanack* I (No. 4) 13: I hit him a crack over his knob with my big steering oar. **1853** McCauley *Perry* 36: He has been threatened with "fracturing a hard

tack (i.e. Biscuit) o'er the nob." **1866** (quot. at FROG AND TOE). **1870** *Overland Mo.* (Jan.) 32: "A couple of balls in his nob," was Mr. Turpin's persuasive method. *__1889__ Barrère & Leland *Dict. Slang* I 524: One on the *knob*, a blow on the head. **1895** Foote *Coeur D'Alene* 9: The mountains is crackin' their ould nobs together. *__1899__ Whiteing *John St.* 263: They…"ketch it in the knob," in the form of a bilious headache. **1904** *Life in Sing Sing* 250: *Knob.* The head. **1907** in H.C. Fisher *A. Mutt* 20: A. Mutt almost got the gas pipe right on the nob. **1910** T.A. Dorgan, in *N.Y. Eve. Jour.* (Feb. 5) 14: Put yer head down. Duck the knob. **1921** *Variety* (July 8) 5: We carried him off the field with a lump on his knob that you could do a handstand on. **1928** Dahlberg *Bottom Dogs* 264: Sticking his knob out of the fresh-air window for all he was worth. **1942** Algren *Morning* 19: All a guy does is get his knob shaved by the barber. **1962** Mandel *Wax Boom* 124: He's off his knob, Sal. **1970** E. Thompson *Garden of Sand* 310: I'll throb his dang knob. **1981–89** R. Atkinson *Long Gray Line* 30: Right now, hang your nob out!

2. the penis; in phr. **polish** [or (*rarely*) **slob**] **a knob** to perform masturbation or (now *usu.*) fellatio.—usu. considered vulgar. [Prob. a deriv. of **(1)**, above, despite the dates.]
*__1660–63__ in R. Thompson *Unfit for Modest Ears* 68: [Prostitutes] tickling the knobs [of their customers] till they burst out with laughing. *__1922__ in T.E. Lawrence *Mint* 135: Bugger off, lad. There's more fucking cheese on your knob than hair on my block. **1941** in Legman *Limerick* 51: This knob out in front/Attracted foul cunt. **1947** *Ballad of Dead-Eye Dick* (unp.): And to finish the job he polished his knob/With a Cayenne pepper pot! **1964** H. Rhodes *Chosen Few* 202 [ref. to *ca*1950]: How much woul'ja charge t'polish a knob real quick, without bitin'? **1972** McGregor *Bawdy Ballads* 44: When men grow old and their balls get cold and the tips of their knobs turn blue. **1978** Alibrandi *Killshot* 253: He's been polishing my knob. **1989** *Nat. Lampoon* (June) 38: Courtney had my knob screamin' "Pull me!" **1989** "3rd Bass" *Steppin' to the A.M.* (rap song): Slobbin' a knob. **1968–90** Linderer *Eyes of Eagle* 66: Missy Li's…that's where you go to get your nob polished.

3. usu. *pl.* a woman's breast or nipple. Also **knobby.**
1934 "J.M. Hall" *Anecdota* 108: K stands for Knobbies,/Like pumpkins they grow. **1963** Rubin *Sweet Daddy* 139: One dame getting her tits sucked in a corner, not one guy but one on each knob. **1971** N.Y.U. student: The one with the big knobs. I never look at the faces. **1967–80** Folb *Runnin' Lines* 244: Knobs breasts. **1987** *Nat. Lampoon* (Dec.) 91: Mom's knobs awoke in me an altruistic sense.

4.a. a freshman at a military academy, esp. the Military College of South Carolina (The Citadel).
1980 Conroy *Lords of Discipline* 51 [ref. to 1966]: Sir, Alexander and I had a fight when we were knobs. **1987** *Chrons. Higher Educ.* (Feb. 4) 25: The Fourth Class system at the Citadel may seem almost barbaric. Freshmen, called "knobs," are forced to wake up before 6 a.m. and…are constantly [harassed] by upperclassmen…."He wasn't the sharpest knob." **1991** *DayWatch* (CNN-TV) (Nov. 4): The knobs—so called from heads shaved clean as doorknobs—keep coming. **1993** G. Lee *Honor & Duty* 10 [ref. to 1960's]: You sorry…grossed-out knob! **1994** *N.Y. Times* (Jan. 21) A12: The lowly status and shaved heads of freshmen, known as "knobs." **1995** Spokesman for Mil. College of S.C., on *News Hour* (CNN-TV) (Aug. 18): They have other cadets—other "knobs," as we call them—to undergo training.

b. a blockhead; JERK. [Perh. the earlier sense, if **(a)**, above is a specialization, but no early cites are available.]
*__1990__ Andersson & Trudgill *Bad Language* 88: "Stupid person"…*knob end…knob.* **1993** P. Munro *U.C.L.A. Slang II*: *Knob*…idiot: dork. *The knob went surfing with his sandals on.* **1996** *Mystery Sci. Theater* (Comedy Central TV): What a knob!

5. (see quot.).
1982 Downey *Losing the War* 24 [ref. to 1940's]: Shoes included the faddish orange-red "knobs" worn by hip-cats.

¶ In phrase:

¶ **with knobs on** (used for emphasis); *with bells* [*on*] s.v. BELL. *Rare in U.S.*
*__1922__ in T.E. Lawrence *Mint* 193: A bit of the real life-with-knobs-on. *__1930__ in *OED2*: "I'm waiting for the Marchese…." "With knobs on," agreed Gemma airily. **1931** in Butterfield *Post Treasury* 305: Same to you, wi' knobs on it, you old gafoozeler. **1954–60** *DAS* 584: I'll be there with knobs on.

knob *v.* [fr. KNOB, *n.,* 2] to copulate.—usu. considered vulgar.

1991 *Houston Chronicle* (Nov. 13) 5D: *Shag, knob, or bonk:* Have sex.

knobber *n.* **1.** *Police.* a male transvestite prostitute.
1972 *New York* (Nov. 13) 57: Knobbers are female impersonators who do a brisk business as prostitutes in the hallways along Ninth and Tenth. **1971–73** Sheehy *Hustling* 9: Knobbers are men dressed as female hookers who…charge the same price but offer only stand-up service, pleading monthly indisposition. **1975** De Mille *Smack Man* 19: Knobbers, or young boys with hormone-inflated breasts, sold oral sex to unsuspecting men in a hurry. **1975** *N.Y. Times* (Sept. 8) 33: It is where the knobbers, or transvestites, hang out, and often their real sex is never discovered by the john. **1980** W. Sherman *Times Square* 14: Brucie was…a "knobber" who snared drunken johns and knelt to suck "knob jobs" for five dollars. He was harmless…unlike some of the other transvestites.

2.a. KNOB JOB.—usu. considered vulgar.
1989 P. Munro *U.C.L.A. Slang* 54: *Knobber* blow job. **1995** Former U.S. Navy submariner, Knoxville, Tenn. [ref. to early 1980's]: *Knobber* fellatio (not related to my own submarine experiences).

b. a stupid or obnoxious person. [Despite the ambiguous context, the 1991 quot. belongs here and not at **(1)**, above.]
1990 *UTSQ: Knobber* Retard. "You knobber!" **1991** *Vancouver Sun* (Dec. 12) D8: I won't look like a knobber crusing this.

knobby var. NOBBY.

knobhead *n.* KNOTHEAD. Also **knobknot.**
1926 *AS* I (Dec.) 652: *Knobhead.* Mule. **1928–29** Faulkner *Sound & Fury* 42: You're a knobnot. **1930** Irwin *Tramp & Und. Slang* 118: *Knob Head*…a stupid individual. **1979** Edson *Gentle Giant* 69: A knobhead like you.

knob job *n.* an act of fellatio.—usu. considered vulgar.
1968 *Zap Comix No. 3* 12: I've been getting a superb knob job. *a*__1972__ B. Rodgers *Queens' Vernacular* 34: *Knob job* ([heard during] early '60s). **1972** R. Barrett *Lovomaniacs* 63: She had just given him a knob job after balling him all night. **1974** Univ. Tenn. student: A *knob job* is a blow job. They used to say it in Nam in 1971. **1980** D. Hamill *Stomping Ground* 309: That and an odd knob job. *a*__1987__ Bunch & Cole *Reckoning for Kings* 68: A…city…that had a lot more Baptist churches than knob jobs.

knob-knocker *n.* *Hobo.* a railroad policeman.
1984 Sample *Racehoss* 105 [ref. to 1940's]: The "knob-knockers" were already walking down the tracks inspecting the long string of cars while the train waited.

knob-thatcher *n.* a wig maker.
*__1823__ in *OED*: Some of our…nob-thatchers in Burlington Arcade. **1859** Matsell *Vocab.* 49: *Knob-Thatcher.* A wig-maker.

knock *n.* **1.a.** *Gamb.* a financial loss, esp. in betting.—usu. in phr. **take the knock;** (*hence*) a setback.
*__1889__ Barrère & Leland *Dict. Slang* I 524: "To take the *knock,*" is to lose more money to the book-makers than one can pay, and thus to be incapacitated from approaching the ring. *__1890__ in *OED2*: A broken backer of horses, who has taken, what is known in the language of the turf, as the knock. **1928** Guerin *Crime* 268: Instead of paying me the barber took the "knock" and disappeared. **1929** D. Runyon, in *OED2*: It will be a knock to his reputation. **1937** in D. Runyon *More Guys* 101: She claims it is a knock to her socially. **1996** McCumber *Playing off Rail* 171: The Southwest [a pool cue] *was* a bit of a knock. It was fifteen hundred bucks' worth of cue, minimum, and people did tend to notice.

b. an adverse criticism, judgment, or remark; disparagement; (*broadly*) an insult; in phr. **put the knock on** to disparage or criticize. Now *colloq.*
1895 F.P. Dunne, in Schaaf *Dooley* 282: They're goin' to get up a new Bible f'r women. A woman's Bible, d'ye mind, with anything in th' ol' Bible that's considered be th' female bicycle club to be a knock f'r women cut out. **1897** Siler & Houseman *Fight of Century* 53: Nary a "knock" did I hear. **1905** *N.Y. Times* (May 29) 9: If anybody has any knocks to register against the "Kid" they want to get them in before Sept. 1. **1905** "H. McHugh" *Search Me* 50: A knock from any one of them is [really] a boost. **1905** in Paxton *Sport USA* 24: He heard about the "knock"; it was…printed the next day in many newspapers. **1924** Galewitz *Great Comics* 138: But you lay off the Annie knock—she's an orphan. **1940** in J. O'Hara *Sel. Letters* 157: I would hear some of his fellow members of the Racquet Club putting the knock on him. **1947** Schulberg *Harder They Fall* 104: George never put the knock on any-

one. **1951** O'Hara *Farmers Hotel* 67: Who wants money if that's what it does to you?…It puts the knock on the capitalistic system. **1956** "T. Betts" *Across the Board* 51: There was a clocker's knock against the horse. *a***1961** Boroff *Campus U.S.A.* 29: The fraternities "got the big knock" as a result of a riotous water fight. **1967** in Rowan & MacDonald *Friendship* 18: Ruark…put the gratuitous knock upon Hemingway. **1973** in J. Flaherty *Chez Joey* xviii: They dared put the knock on Mike Hammer! **1981** Sann *Trial* 50: I had never put the knock on her thing with the Reverend. **1987** *Larry King Live* (CNN-TV) (May 5): Nobody puts that kind of knock on Gary Hart.…There are certain knocks that are put on a candidate that are very hard to shake. **1989** Dorsett & Frommer *Running Tough* 17: That's not to take knocks at the coaches who were there before. **1990** *AARP Bulletin* (Apr.) 1: Everyone's doing it—so why are we putting the knock on "aging"? **1992** *Sports Close-up* (CNN-TV) (June 30): [He] doesn't want to put the knock on the Nordiques.

c. *Pris.* an accusation or criminal charge; (*hence*) a prison sentence.

1908 Kelley *Oregon Pen.* 16: The warden puts in the knock which results in the punishment. **1912** Lowrie *Prison* 282: I thought it was all a bluff about the judge being hard and their going to him with a knock. **1918** in *AS* (Oct. 1933) 29: *Knock.* Prison sentence. "'Sthis yer first trick?" "Naw, I took a knock for a year at Joliet."

d. *pl.* a beating.

1931 Bontemps *Sends Sunday* 64: From now on I'm gonna be de one to give you yo' knocks when you needs 'em.

2. a charge for services.

1969 L. Sanders *Anderson Tapes* 98: By the way, I'm picking up the knock.

3. a shot of whiskey; SLUG.

1972 R. Barrett *Lovomaniacs* 149: I poured a double knock into my glass.

4. usu. *pl.* a woman's breasts; KNOCKERS.

1964–78 J. Carroll *Basketball Diaries* 48: I…got a…peek at those perky knocks. **1986** *UTSQ*: Breasts…*knockers, knocks, lungs,* [etc.].

knock *v.* **1.** to copulate or copulate with.—usu. considered vulgar. See also *knock boots,* below. Cf. KNOCK OFF, 4.e.

*****1598** J. Florio, in *OED: Cunnuta,* a woman nocked. *****1663** in R. Thompson *Unfit for Modest Ears* 60: Now the privat whores have got the knack on't to knock in corners. *****1775** in *F & H* V 58: *Nock,* to perform the act of generation on a female. *****1785** Grose *Vulgar Tongue: Knock, to knock a woman,* to have carnal knowledge of her. *a***1936** in Lomax & Lomax *Singing Country* 89: When I was a young man, in my prime…I knock those young gals, two at a time.

2.a. to bewilder or astound; flabbergast; stun.—also constr. with *flat.* Orig. *colloq.*

1715 in Sewall *Diary* II 784: I said Let us write and all subscribe. Mr. Winthrop was so knockt that he said it could not be done, if the Secretary declin'd. **1850** *Spirit of Times* (June 8) 183: The last fact…knocked Dodge *flat!* **1889** Barrère & Leland *Dict. Slang* I 526: "That *knocks* me," that is too much for me. **1896** Ade *Artie* 102: What knocks me is to think this mamma's boy got on to me. **1913** Z. Grey *Desert Gold* 140: "What knocks me is Rojas holding Thorne prisoner."…"Shore. It'd knock anybody." **1919** in Dreiser *Diaries* 291: Her beauty just knocks me. It is unbelievable. **1931** Z. Grey *Sunset Pass* 50: And if they don't knock the punchers on this range, I'll eat them. **1954** *AS* XXIX 228: Telling me of bad news she had heard, she said, "That knocked me." *****1961** C.S. Lewis *Exp. in Criticism* 92: At a first reading of some great work they are "knocked flat." Criticise it? No, by God, but read it again. **1972** J. Mills *Report* 105: He almost went into shock. Just the idea, the suggestion, knocked him.

b. to excel; outdo; surpass.

1847 *Nat. Police Gaz.* (Feb. 20) 186: Here's the cretur that "*knocks*" the field. **1853** in Thornton *Amer. Gloss.* I 521: He "knocked" all the adjacent male population…in the matter of looks. **1859** in Doten *Journals* I 475: Thought we could *knock* that last survey—easily. **1890** Quinn *Fools of Fortune* 411: I've got something that knocks 7-30's clean out of the ropes. **1891** W. DeVere *Tramp Poems* 79: And we wound up the show with a "Ghost in the Pawn Shop."/It knocks the new-fangled ones, you bet your life. **1891** Garland *Main-Travelled Roads* 135: I tell yeh, boys, this knocks the swamps of Loueesiana into kingdom come.

c. to dazzle or delight (usu. an audience).—later (now solely) constr. with emphatic *dead.*

1862 C.F. Browne *Artemus Ward* 44: Thay was rehersin Dixey's

Land & expected it would knock the peple. **1863** in Lyman *Meade's HQ* 26: I certainly knocked the crowd by having a pair of cotton gloves. **1865** G. Derby *Squibob Papers* 197: He told Miss Stebbins/That she "just completely knocked him." *****1883** in *F & H* IV 123: "It's Never too Late to Mend," with J.H. Clynds as Tom Robinson, is knocking 'em at the Pavilion. **1889** "M. Twain" *Conn. Yankee* 409: A good blacksmith, who came near knocking him dead with kindness. *****1892** in J.S. Farmer *Musa Pedestris* 190: Laugh! I thought I should 'ave died,/Knock'd 'em in the Old Kent Road! **1900** Dreiser *Sister Carrie* 134: You did that about a thousand per cent better than you did the other scene. Now go on and fire up. You can do it. Knock 'em. **1908** in W.C. Fields *By Himself* 36: W.C. Fields…is "knocking 'em out of their seats" at the Orpheum this week. **1915–16** Lait *Beef, Iron & Wine* 199: You knocked 'em out o' their seats with that soprano. **1918** in Truman *Letters Home* 50: A strut that knocks 'em dead. **1917–20** Dreiser *Newspaper Days* 588 [ref. to 1890's]: Each conveying to the other…how he "knocked 'em" here, there or somewhere else. **1923** Ornitz *Haunch, Paunch & Jowl* 73: I got a new step.…It's gonna knock 'em dead. **1929** in Gelman *Photoplay* 125: Ruth Chatterton is knocking 'em dead in the talkies. **1930** Cozzens *S.S. San Pedro* 22: Going to knock them dead, Bradell? **1963** E. Hunter *Ten Plus One* 113: I've written a gag that'll knock him dead. **1980** L. Fleischer & C. Gore *Fame* 60: Be good, kid, and knock 'em dead. **1989** Guare *Six Degrees* 110: Wear your best clothes and knock 'em dead. **1995** *Simpsons* (Fox-TV): Baby, you're gonna knock 'em dead.

d. to overcome or defeat; ruin; do for; put an end to (an affliction).

1864 Armstrong *Generals* 40: I prosper occasionally in small things, but totals knock me. **1874** in Chesnutt *Journals* 42: There was no money for that school. That knocked my school "higher than a kite." *Ibid.* 48: This knocks…my chance…"higher than a kite." **1875** Daly *Pique* 291: I could sit down and cry. All our little game knocked. **1875** *John Kelly…Against…Wallis* 2: That such a writ not being served aright,/Should be knocked higher than a kite. **1877** Burdette *Mustache* 19: [He] has a formula…[that] will cause warts to disappear…or, to use his own expression, will "knock warts." **1898** Stratemeyer *Volunteer* 267: Up, boys, up. We're to knock the Dons tomorrow! **1906** *Nat. Police Gaz.* (July 28) 3: That guy up there has me deaf with that flute he's playing.…That knocks this place. **1927–28** in R. Nelson *Dishonorable* 180: It's me that'll knock them, with this case I got. **1928** Dobie *Vaquero* 8 [ref. to ca1870]: About this time we learned that kerosene would "knock ticks." **1929** McEvoy *Hollywood Girl* 100: That's what knocked her. Celebrating. **1937** Hemingway *To Have & Have Not* 238: But he can knock the worry if he takes a Scotch and soda. **1962** W. Robinson *Barbara* 96: I gave you enough [morphine] to knock the pain. If you can stand it, you can keep going. *ca***1962** in A. Lomax *Where Blues Began* 297 [ref. to 1940's]: I'm down here wrestling with a long stretch and it's knockin me.

e. *U.S. Mil. & Nav. Acads.* to earn (a high academic grade); (*hence*) to pass (a course) easily. [Perh. cf. *have it knocked,* below.]

1877 Lee *Fag-Ends* 48: Make it "5T," and to prevent "two fives" being "knocked"/Let your examination be the worst you can concoct. **1897** *Lucky Bag* (U.S. Nav. Acad.) 108: *Knock.* To do well or succeed in, as to knock Math; also to obtain a good mark, as to knock 3.5 in Skinny. **1906** *Army & Navy Life* (Nov.): To *knock* a thing is to do it well.

3. *Und.* to break into and rob (a safe).

[*****1767** in *OED2*: I heard him say that he got twelve shillings once by *knocking the lobb* [*i.e.*, till].…What that?…That is breaking open a place.] **1924** G.C. Henderson *Crookdom* 397: Blowing a safe open with explosives…[is] called knocking a peter. **1962–68** B. Jackson *In the Life* 70: Nobody knew how to knock a safe at that time. *Ibid.* 86: We was knocking safes from everywhere. **1970** Rudensky & Riley *Gonif* 82: I knocked a couple of safes for them, hit a jewelry store for a smaller North Side mob.

4. to hit with a bullet; (*hence*) to shoot dead; KNOCK OUT, 2.a., KNOCK OFF, 5.a.

1805 Brackenridge *Mod. Chivalry* 569: We get our provisions for nothing,/Just knock down a wolf or a bear. **1864** in D. Chisholm *Civil War Notebk.* 135: You ought to see me knock 2 sand bags off the Rebel Works. I can knock a Johnny every clip at 4 or 5 Hundred yards with my rifle. **1898** Stratemeyer *Volunteer* 177: "We've knocked him!"…The sharpshooter had been caught at his own game and his body came crashing down among the bushes. *1920 in *Austral. Nat. Dict.* 352: Eat, drink, and be merry...for to-morrow we may get knocked. **1924** in Goodstone *Pulp* 97: He was about three quarters across Clay when he was knocked. *1937, *1939 (cited in Partridge *DSUE* (ed. 7) 1240). *1967 in *Austral. Nat. Dict.* 352: *Knocked*, to be murdered. Shortened from the American to be knocked off. **1978–80** in Cardozo-Freeman & Delorme *Joint* 512: *Knock yourself.* To commit suicide.

5.a. to find fault with; criticize harshly; disparage.—also used intrans. Now *colloq.*

1865–67 DeForest *Miss Ravenel* 363: The War Department...admit[s] your faithfulness, ability, and services. It is the Senate that knocks you. *1892 in Wilkes *Dict. Austral. Colloq.* 198: It's the only paper that dares knock things. **1896** Ade *Artie* 63: They're knockin' him all they can. *Ibid.* 79: You ain't goin' to begin knockin' the first thing. **1901** "H. McHugh" *John Henry* 54: I'm not knocking....I'm only saying what I think. **1905** *Variety* (Dec. 16) 9: Say, don't tell I was knocking. **1906** in "O. Henry" *Works* 15: Originally from Mattawamkeag, Maine, he said...and he wouldn't stand for no knockin' the place. **1914** Ellis *Billy Sunday* 250: They began to knock and said, "Who is this Moses anyway?" **1916** Miner *Slavery of Prostitution* 2: I admit I'm a prostitute, yer Honor, but I didn't speak to no cop. He's just tryin' to knock me. **1919** Hedges *Iron City* 22: To mention problems was to "knock," and knocking was the cardinal sin. **1922** S. Lewis *Babbitt* 141: I don't want to knock—I believe in boosting wherever you can—but say, of all the rotten dumps that pass 'emselves off as first-class hotels, that's the worst. **1936** in H. Gray *Arf* (unp.): But he's knockin' you to ever'body in town. *1945 S.J. Baker *Austral. Lang.* 121: He...*knocks* him, criticizes him. **1951** Longstreet *Pedlocks* 107: Don't knock. Some of my best friends are madams. **1957** in Cannon *Nobody Asked* 113: He pretends he was close to Grantland Rice, Damon Runyon, and Hype Igoe. The new punks, he says, knock too much. **1961** Griffith *Little Shop of Horrors* (film): Look—don't knock it till you've tried it. **1968** "J. Hudson" *Case of Need* 20: Maybe he goes overboard, but I can't really knock him. **1973** M. Harris *Hatter Fox* 163: Just don't knock Rhinehart. She's done everything in her power to help you. **1981** D. Burns *Feeling Good* 350: Don't knock happiness until you've tried it. **1981** in B. Williams *John Henry* 165: But you still can't knock it, because he believed in hisself. **1989** Radford & Crowley *Drug Agent* 16: The same addicts...who knock Botenkranz say good things about Zalt. **1990** *CBS This Morning* (CBS-TV) (Jan. 18): I don't see anything to knock *or* to support.

b. *Und.* to inform or complain.

1896 Ade *Artie* 64: He's got to make good with 'em to keep 'em from knockin'. **1897** Ade *Pink* 174: He tol' huh ev'ything he knows 'bout me. Yes, seh, he's been knockin' good an' plenty. **1900** "Flynt" & Walton *Powers* 120: I ain't goin' to knock against you; nobody'll ever find out from me. **1906** A.H. Lewis *Confessions* 41: Certainly the neighbors know, but they're not going to knock. **1908** Sullivan *Criminal Slang* 14: *Knock*—Also means to squeal. **1930** Irwin *Amer. Tramp & Und. Sl.* 118: *Knock.*—To inform. **1946** (cited in Partridge *Dict. Und.* 390).

6.a. *Jazz.* to drink copiously from (a bottle of liquor); (*hence*) to consume (food or drink). Cf. KNOCK BACK.

1931 in Leadbitter & Slaven *Blues Records* 143: Papa Wants To Knock A Jug. **1941** in Ellington *Music Is My Mistress* 179: *Knock a scarf*...eat a good meal. **1948** Manone & Vandervoort *Trumpet* 170: At lunchtime we...kept on talking horses while knocking our groceries. **1953** W. Fisher *Waiters* 232: Come on, everybody....Let's knock one. **1954** *Tenn. Folk. Soc. Bull.* XX 80: *Hit the jug* obviously meant to drink heavily from the jug, but so did *knock the jug.*

b. *Black E.* to obtain for oneself; in phr. **knock a nod** to take a nap.

1929–32 in *AS* (Dec. 1934) 289: *Knock a nod.* To take a nap. **1944** in Himes *Black on Black* 202: I could knock me that Clipper and live on Central Avenue.

c. to earn.

1944 in Himes *Black on Black* 198: Knock seven or eight hundred then jump down. **1970** in B. Jackson *Swim Like Me* 110: Now you were all right down home with the few nickels you knocked.

7. to embezzle; KNOCK DOWN, 1.a.

1942 Liebling *Telephone* 125: Better a kid who takes ten in tips and knocks a buck...than a dummy who gets half the tips and turns in all she gets.

8. to give or impart to.

1944 *Slanguage Dict.* 60: *Knock me a kiss*...Give me a kiss. **1967** Baraka *Tales* 9: Baby, knock me a kiss. **1994** A. Heckerling *Clueless* 93: Knock me a kiss.

9. *Und.* to apprehend or place under arrest; (see also 1971–72 quot.).

1942–49 Goldin et al. *DAUL* 118: *Knock*...To arrest; to prosecute; to sentence or commit to prison. **1971–72** in Abernethy *Bounty of Texas* 209: *Knocked*, v.—arrested; written up for disciplinary action by [a prison] official. **1986** Stroud *Close Pursuit* 101: He knock you so fast. *Ibid.* 333: *Knocked* Slang for getting arrested.

10. to discharge from employment.

1975 R.P. Davis *Pilot* 6: They could knock you for drinkin' on the job.

¶ In phrases:

¶ **have it knocked** Esp. *Mil.* to have something successfully under control or accomplished; (*broadly*) to be in an easeful or desirable situation.—rarely constr. with *up* [*tight*].

1953 Michener *Toko-ri* 26: When I looked up and saw that [helicopter pilot] I knew I had it knocked. **1957** H. Ellison *Web of City* 12: He had it knocked now. **1959** Brosnan *Long Season* 18: He said that you and he got it knocked up down here. Train on your own, and all that. **1960** Hoagland *Circle Home* 15: A fighter had it knocked. Loaf around, take a few punches, work a couple of hours a day. **1962** in J.A. Williams *Beyond Angry Black* 152: Why in hell you join the army? We used to have it knocked, you know? **1963** in E. Knight *Black Voices* 148: The inmate-drivers who travel throughout the state delivering the products of the prison industries...are sometimes gone for two and three days. They got it knocked up. **1969** *Esquire* (Sept.) 120: Man, when I go home I'll have it knocked. **1970** Sorrentino *Steelwork* 84: You guys had it knocked. The Good Army life. You bet. **1978** Nolan & Mann *Jericho Mile* (film): I got it knocked, baby. **1985** J. MacDonough *Platoon Leader* 64: I got it knocked....I just carry the radio. **1987** Averill *Mustang* 12: We had it knocked up tight and we knew it.

¶ **how are you knocking them?** (used as a form of greeting).

1873 Such *Book for an Hour* 8: "Well, how goes it?"..."So-so. How are you knocking them?"

¶ **knock a glim** to strike a light.

1834 *Mil. & Naval Mag. of U.S.* (Sept.) 41: "Why don't you knock a glim, Sal?" The woman then brought a wax candle.

¶ **knock boots** [prob. infl. by BOOTY] *Stu.* to copulate. Cf. earlier *put* [or *throw*] *the boots to*, 3, s.v. BOOT, *n.*

1986 "Salt-N-Pepa" *Tramp* (rap song): You ain't gettin' paid,/You ain't knockin' boots,/You ain't treatin' me like no prostitute. **1989** P. Munro *U.C.L.A. Slang* 54: He knocked boots with her. **1991** *UTSQ*: *Knock boots*—To have sex. **1992** *Martin* (Fox-TV): I want to knock her boots, man! **1992** *Fresh Prince* (NBC-TV): Last I heard, it was called "knocking boots." **1995** *Jerry Springer Show* (synd. TV series): We're talkin' 'bout straight knockin' boots. **1995** Stavsky, Mozeson, & Mozeson *A 2 Z* 60: You been knockin' the boots with anyone on campus? **1995** S. Moore *In the Cut* 98: *To knock boots*, phr., to have sexual intercourse.

¶ **knock cold, 1.** to KNOCK, 2.a.

1859 in K.C. Phillipps *Lang. & Class* 115: Mary struck the old lady dumb—"knocked her cold," our American cousins would say. **1913** *Sat. Eve. Post* (Jan. 4) 12: How the Sam Hill did you git her anyhow?...That's what knocks me cold. **1925** McAlmon *Stockings* 62: My god, Mary, I was knocked cold.

2. to KNOCK, 2.b.

1899 F.H. Smith *Other Fellow* 69: As for palaces! Why, the State House at Al-ba-ny knocks 'em cold. **1922–24** McIntyre *White Light Nights* 200: Watch me build a theater and knock 'em cold!

3. to KNOCK, 2.c.

1896 Ade *Artie* 91: Here's a funny thing about that. Here's somethin' that'll knock you cold. **1908** (quot. at DIPPY). **1922** Fitzgerald *Beautiful & Damned* 151: Believe me, in my next book I'm going to do a wedding scene that'll knock 'em cold! **1925** Cohan *Broadway* 16: I...told him how sure I was of "knocking 'em cold."

¶ **knock dead** see s.v. (**2.c.**), above.

¶ **knock for a loop** see s.v. LOOP, *n.*

¶ **knock for a row** Esp. *Mil.* to knock sprawling; *knock silly*, below.

1918 Sherwood *Diary* 159: If you had guts enough to take them stripes off I'd knock you for a row of Latrines. **1919** Hubbell *Company C* 190: I'll knock you for a row of pup tents. **1920–21** Witwer *Leather Pushers* 199: You knock the champ for a row of milk cans. **1922** in Hemingway *Sel. Letters* 65: Some day I will get careless and he will knock me for a row of latrines. **1924** T. Boyd *Points of Honor* 172: I'd knock him for the longest row you ever seen. **1924** Stalling *Plumes* 101 [ref. to 1918]: If you don't sit down, I'll damn well knock you for a row of G.I. cans. **1924** Nason *Three Lights* 73: I'll knock you for a row of brick gools! **1927** Stevens *Mattock* 122 [ref. to 1918]: Didn't that dozen-egg omelet knock us for a row? **1928** Nason *Sgt. Eadie* 252 [ref. to 1918]: I could knock you for enough brick kitchens to supply a division. **1928** Bodenheim *Georgie May* 78: You come 'long now or I'll knock you for a row uh ghouls. [*i.e.*, goals]. **1930** Farrell *Calico Shoes* 41: Wouldn't that...knock the boys for a row or two! **1936** in Thomason *Stories* 383: A reception afterward that would knock all hands for a row of Inner Mongolian yurts. **1936** Green *Johnny Johnson* 164: That knocks me for a row of stumps—it does!

¶ **knock into a cocked hat** to knock flat; thrash; ruin or do for; (*hence*) to spoil.
1833 in Thornton *Amer. Gloss.*: I told Tom I'd knock him into a cocked hat if he said another word. **1835** A. Longstreet *Georgia Scenes* 43: Billy wanted only one lick at him to knock his heart, liver, and lights out of him; and if he got two at him, he'd knock him into a cocked hat. **1837** Neal *Charcoal Sks.* 66: There's a young Timpkins smashed and spoilt!—knocked into a cocked hat! **1844** Porter *Big Bear* 116: Now conollogy tells us that witchcraft has been nocked into a cock'd Hat ever sense the time of old King Joemes of Ingland, and Krumwill. **1847** in J.R. Lowell *Poetical Works* 204: Formaly to knock a man into a cocked hat wus to use him up, but now it only gives him a chance fur the chief madgustracy. *a*1859 in Bartlett *Amer.* (ed. 2) 233: It was enough to knock the spirit of the meeting into a "cocked hat." **1862** in *Manuscripts* XXXIII (1981) 118: We knocked their batery [*sic*] into a cocked hat. **1960** N.Y.C. woman, age *ca*60: So all her plans were knocked into a cocked hat.

¶ **knock loose** to thrash; manhandle or injure.
1928 in Tuthill *Bungle Family* 65: Give the Browns justice or be knocked loose. Yours for quick results.

¶ **knock seven bells out of** see s.v. BELL, *n.*

¶ **knock silly** to knock senseless or nearly senseless with blows; (*hence*) to strike with awe or amazement; thrill, delight, amuse, etc.
1867 Williams *Brierly* 9: He...had beaten in the face of a "swell," and knocked silly the last man he fought in the P.R. **1884** in Lummis *Letters* 166: He knocked them all silly in a few rounds. **1885** *Puck* (Apr. 22) 115: We knocked them silly in the first round. Their cavalry charged us. **1886** Lummis *Ft. Bowie* 69: Clad in flaming colors that would have knocked Solomon silly. **1886** Nye *Remarks* 469: He is a little rattled, and temporarily knocked silly by the pomp and pageant. **1889** Pierson *Vagabond's Honor* 89: The poor man got hit wid a fallin' timber that knocked him silly, so's he cudn't remember his own name nor nothin' at all, at all. **1894** Bangs *Water Ghost* 70: I suppose, though, if you were the shade of a duchess, you could simply knock Bangletop silly? **1894** Henderson *Sea Yarns* 63: Blow me fur pickels ef I warn't knocked clean silly to here that Esquimau talk United States.

¶ **knock (someone's) block off** see s.v. BLOCK, *n.*, 1.

¶ **knock (someone's) eye out** to be stunningly impressive or attractive to the sight of.
1926 Nason *Chevrons* 270 [ref. to 1918]: There's some mamselles I know in that town would knock your eye out. **1991** Univ. Tenn. student: Her [engagement] ring would knock your eye out.

¶ **knock stiff** to knock unconscious, as with a blow; (*hence*) to astound or impress greatly; (*rarely*) (*obs.*) to shoot (someone).
1859 (quot. at KNOCK-'EM-STIFF). **1872** "W. Dexter" *Young Mustanger* 17: Quick as a wink, I up with ole Knock-'em-stiff and sent a bullet squar' through his for'ead. **1885** "Lykkejaeger" *Dane* 122: It "knocked me stiff." **1887** DeVol *40 Yrs. a Gambler* 29: I knocked him stiff, and the gun dropped on the floor. **1908** in H.C. Fisher *A. Mutt* 88: I bet this Marshall Field sky piece knocks 'em stiff when I breeze up Van Ness. **1904–11** D.G. Phillips *Susan Lenox* I 250: We'll ring in some hymns....That'll knock 'em stiff. **1915–16** Lait *Beef, Iron & Wine* 198: Say, I remember when you first turned out in "The Toy Hussar."...You knocked 'em stiff at the Stuyvesant. **1928** T.A. Dorgan, in Zwilling *TAD Lexicon* 52: Taking a few city snaps to send back to the home folks who will be knocked stiff with jealousy.

¶ **knock the [or (one's)] socks off [of]** see s.v. SOCK, *n.*

¶ **knock [the] spots out of** [or **off**] to thrash, smash, or trounce; (*also*) to surpass greatly.—also used absol.
1856 in *DA* s.v. *spot*: Addison County leads the van (or "knocks the spots off," as we say here) in Vermont, and is celebrated over the world for its fine horses. **1861** in Thornton *Amer. Gloss.* I 521: I'd...knock spots out of Secession. **1863** in C.H. Moulton *Ft. Lyon* 95: It "knocks spots" out...of...your little country villages. **1865–67** De Forest *Miss Ravenel* 297: They ain't going to attack the Fort, be they?...We can knock spots out of 'em. **1868** Williams *Black-Eyed Beauty* 13: Knocks spots out of Green and Mercer. **1869** *Putnam's Mag.* (Sept.) 321: The never-ceasing encouragements of the officers, generally taking the form of "Give 'em —, boys!" or "Knock spots out of them, boys!" or "Rake — out of 'em, boys!" **1887** Francis *Saddle & Moccasin* 152: She can knock the spots out of these boys at that game. **1889** Barrère & Leland *Dict. Slang* I 526: *Knock the spots off, to*...This was current in America as long ago as 1850. It means to surpass, confound,...beat. **1889** in S. Hale *Letters* 209: The money...was made by the reaping-machine that "knocked spots out of McCormick." **1913** in Butterfield *Post Treasury* 159: Should there be a war Franklin Roosevelt will simply resign as assistant secretary of the navy, simply organize a regiment, simply take command, and simply knock the spots off the invading foe. **1926** Mac Isaac *Tin Hats* 44: It would enable him to knock the spots out of mutinous morons who had put on the uniforms.

knockaround *n.* a drinking spree.
1837 Neal *Charcoal Sketches* 175: The protegé...longed to indulge himself in that which he classically termed a "knock-around."

knockaround *adj.* having had much rough worldly or criminal experience.—used prenominally.
1942–49 Goldin et al. *DAUL* 118: *Knock-around.* Sophisticated, as a result of long underworld experience. **1952** H. Grey *Hoods* 51: It was puzzling to me, a knock-around guy, acting like a schoolboy. **1963** Cameron *Black Camp* 127: I've seen a lot of knockaround guys. **1970** La Motta, Carter & Savage *Raging Bull* 89: Look, Pete,...you're a knock-around guy, you know the score, I can level with you. **1977** Torres *Q & A* 30: Here's the list. Mostly knock-around guys. **1980** in Courtwright *Addicts Who Survived* 142: These were just knock-around guys, you know, guys that didn't want to work.

knock around *v.* to travel or loiter aimlessly. Now *S.E.*
1848 [W.T. Thompson] *Maj. Jones's Sks.* 8: I'm gwine...to...spend the summer nockin round in them big cities. **1861** in W.R. Howell *Westward* 78: Write home. "Knock round" generally. **1864** J.R. Browne *Apache Country* 182: It was so jolly to be knockin' around among the Apaches! **1880** Martin *Sam Bass* 144: We knocked around town and finally dropped into the best store in town. *Ibid.* 147: We were knocking around. **1950** *N.Y. Times* (Sept. 10) VII 1: The new novel is Hemingway's thirteenth book in what appears to be twenty-seven years of writing and knocking around.

knock back *v.* to eat or, usu., to drink, esp. rapidly or heartily. Cf. KNOCK, 6.a.
***1931** Brophy & Partridge *Songs & Slang* (ed. 3) 326 [ref. to 1915–18]: *Knock it back.*—To eat; sometimes, to drink. **1952** Wildman *Zorba* 85: We knocked back a good many bottles of vodka. **1955** Shapiro *Sixth of June* 117: He poured himself a cup of coffee, and knocked it back in one huge swallow. **1958** Hailey & Castle *Runway* 16: Four of them have been knocking back rye pretty steadily. **1971** Dahlskog *Dict.* 36: *Knock back, v.* To eat, as: to *knock back* an order of fries. **1982** in *Nat. Lampoon* (Feb. 1983) 33: He "knocks back a few frosty ones." **1989** P. Benchley *Rummies* 30: He would have...knocked back six ounces of...Smirnoff's. **1993** *New Yorker* (May 17) 106: He'd rather be knocking back a few Buds.

knockdown *n.* **1.** a fistfight; brawl. See also KNOCK-DOWN [AND] DRAG-OUT.
1834 Caruthers *Kentuckian in N.Y.* 94: What a rascally appetite I've got now for a knock down. **1848** Judson *Mysteries* 191: What shall it be?...a genteel knock down, or a knock down and drag out? **1860** in Swisshelm *Crusader* 103: A knock-down took place between two Frenchmen.

2. a social introduction.
1865 Byrn *Fudge Fumble* 61: I asked...if he would...give me a

"knock down" to the family, and Miss Kate, more especially. **1886** E.L. Wheeler *N.Y. Nell* 3: But, come, boy, ye hain't given me a knock-down tew the lady, heer. **1887** *Lantern* (N.O.) (Aug. 20) 3: An' got a knock-down to all the officers. **1895** Townsend *Fadden* 122: Den he gave dem bote a knockdown t' me by dere names. **1889–96** in J.W. Crawford *Plays* 152: I wanter give you a knock down to some friends. **1896** Ade *Artie* 19: Gi' me a knock-down to the queen in the corner. **1942** Freeman & Gilbert *Larceny, Inc.* (film): You think you might give me a formal knockdown to that manicurist. **1943** *Yank* (May 7) 19: The...hostess arranges a knock-down. **1947** Motley *Knock on Any Door* 218: Come on, give me a knockdown to her. **1948** Ives *Stranger* 191: Go downstairs and arrange a knockdown to that gal before some smooth character nabs her. **1952** *Sat. Eve. Post* (Apr. 26) 23: I got to meet her....How about giving me a knock-down to her at the dance tonight? **1965* S.J. Baker *Australian Lang.* (ed. 2) 170: *Get a knock-down to*, to be introduced to. **1967** Dibner *Admiral* 241: I'll take you home and give you a knockdown to my mother-in-law.

3. information; LOWDOWN.

  1930 Irwin *Amer. Tramp & Und. Slang* 118: *Knock Down*...Information. **1962** Perry *Young Man Drowning* 111: The Bug will give us the knockdown. *Ibid.* 138: The Bug has been giving me the knockdown.

4. *Business.* a discount.

  1942 *ATS* 530: Price Reduction; discount...*knock-down.* **1962** T. Berger *Reinhart in Love* 146: The cost...was actually fifty-two fifty, because he always gets a ten to fifteen knockdown there. **1978** *Houston Chronicle* (Mar. 19) ("Zest") 19: It can be repaired, but if you buy it, ask for a knockdown.

5. *Fire Dept.* the extinguishing of a fire. Cf. KNOCK DOWN, v., 6.

  *a*1988 D. Smith *Firefighters* 64: Pull the hose line...and make the initial knockdown.

knock down *v.* **1.a.** to embezzle or pilfer (fares, tips, or other small sums), usu. habitually.—also used intrans.

  1853 G. Thompson *Gay Girls* 101: You tend the door, Louis, and take the change; but no *knocking down.* **1854** St. Clair *Metropolis* 10: Drivers...look after every sixpence and "knock down" all they can..."Knocking down" is a phrase demonstrating the act of appropriating their employer's money to their own...purposes. **1859** in Cazden et al. *Folk Songs of Catskills* 550: And he never was known to knock down a cent. **1860** Holland *Miss Gilbert* 220: Now tell a feller: is there any chance to knock down? **1867** *Galaxy* (Nov.) 793: A driver on the Knickerbocker line—a young man highly respected and who was never known to "knock down" a cent. **1872** McCabe *N.Y. Life* 214: The conductors "knock down"...about thirty-five or fifty cents a day. *Ibid.* 216: I tell ye a man ought to have leave to knock down lively to stand all this. **1881** Nye *Forty Liars* 89: I am a conductor on thy line, and I have reformed and have ceased to "knock down." **1889** "M. Twain" *Conn. Yankee* 513: They would "knock down" fares—I mean rob the company. **1891** Maitland *Slang Dict.* 161: *Knock-down* (Am.), to embezzle. **1906** *DN* III 144: W'y, he'd *knock down on* his own daddy. **1921** Conklin & Root *Circus* 221: Mr. Bailey, Rose is knocking down on the kid money. **1923** *Nashville* (Tenn.) *Banner* (Jan. 13) 7: I took in so little I can't "knock down" a dime. **1923** Witwer *Fighting Blood* 191: The only thing you [a prizefighter] ever knocked down...is nickels when you was a street-car conductor. **1937** E. Anderson *Thieves Like Us* 23: Him knocking down in that Commissary every day so they would have a stake. **1942** A.J. Liebling *Telephone* 117: If a member is caught by her employer "knocking down" a tip, her union card is suspended. **1951** C. Palmer *Sellout* (film): You wouldn't be knockin' down on your own wife, would you? **1953** Brossard *Bold Saboteurs* 185: I learned how to knock down (steal)....I invariably increased the rates ten or fifteen cents per message.

b. to obtain (money, usu. wages) handily.

  1929 in *OED2*: Authors who knocked down $3000 for a short story of 5000 words. **1942** in Stilwell *Papers* 128: The top gang must be knocking down a lot of jack. **1949** *New Yorker* (Nov. 5) 86: And you wanna know how much that animal knocks down a week? **1961** Heller *Catch-22* 51: Fifty grand a year I was knocking down. **1967** Wolf *Love Generation* 254: Washed dishes, uh, used to wash the tables in the pool halls in the Student Union, used to knock down about five dollars a night out there. **1970** A. Young *Snakes* 122: I'm startin' to knock down a few coins. **1992** G. Wolff *Day at Beach* 66: A demure trade in hashish knocked me down about a hundred a month.

2. to sell at auction. Cf. KNOCK OFF, v., 2. Now *S.E.*

  1865 C. Barney *Field Service* 235: He was finally "knocked down" at that price. **1866** in B. Harte *Harte's Calif.* 19: One [was] knocked down to Moses Ellis, Esq. **1917–20** Dreiser *Newspaper Days* 92: I saw tin-gilt jewelry..."knocked down" to unsuspecting yokels. **1940** J.W. Coleman *Slavery Times in Ky.* 139: The girl was "knocked down" to [a] Lexington slave-trading firm. **1961** R.L. Scott *Boring Holes* 19: Before the auctioneer "knocked down" one to me.

3. to introduce (someone).

  *a*1889 in Barrère & Leland *Dict. Slang* I 525: "*Knock me down* to that daisy," *i.e.,* "Introduce me to that fine girl." **1908** *DN* III 327: *Knock-down*....To introduce. "I'll knock you down to that girl." **1954** Chessman *Cell 2455* 95: Playboy would knock him down (introduce him) to those worth knowing. **1965–70** in *DARE*. **1986** in *DARE*: *Knock you down*—introduce you, strictly slang.

4. to request (money) of.—constr. with *for.*

  1942 *ATS* 348: Beg; request a loan or gift...*hit (up),...knock one down for.* **1952** H. Ellson *Golden Spike* 101: Last night you were going to knock her down for money.

5. KNOCK BACK.

  1952 in *DAS*: I have knocked down one quart of Scotch whisky every day for the last 24 years. **1985** Former SP5, U.S. Army: *Knocking down* beers was a common expression in the military [in the 1970's].

6. *Fire Dept.* to bring under control or extinguish (a fire).

  1983 Stapleton *30 Yrs.* 183: It knocked down a great deal of the fire. **1985** WINS radio news (Aug. 28): Fire officials say that three of the four fires have now been knocked down....The main body of the fire has been knocked down. There are still some residual flames. **1992** N.Y.C. firefighter, age *ca*35, on *Daywatch* (CNN-TV) (Mar. 23): We knocked down the fire....We were knockin' it down.

7. *Pris.* to serve (time in prison).

  *a*1994 N. McCall *Wanna Holler* 203: I'd knocked down more than two years in the joint and had less than one to go.

knock-down [and] drag-out *n.* a brawl; (*broadly*) a prolonged acrimonious dispute.

  1827 J.F. Cooper *Prairie*: Making it a real knock-down and drag-out! **1834** Caruthers *Kentuckian in N.Y.* I 61: I never saw a prettier knock down and drag out in all the days of my life, even in old Kentuck. **1848** Baker *Glance at N.Y.* 17: Den for a knock-down and a drag-out—den I retires like a gentleman. **1886** Nye *Remarks* 381: Then there is a row or social knock-down-and-drag out which goes along with the church debt. **1915** "High Jinks, Jr." *Choice Slang* 52: *Knock down and drag out*...A fight or squabble carried to extremes. **1954** Collans & Sterling *House Detect.* 98: Only once did I get into a real knockdown and dragout. **1958** P. Connor *At Le Mans* 13: I think you and Mary Jane are going to be all right—when you've had a couple of knock-down-and-drag-out fights. *a*1979 Pepper & Pepper *Straight Life* 20: Daddy and Millie fought all the time. They'd have regular knockdown-drag-outs nearly every day. **1986** *Daily Beacon* (Univ. Tenn.) (Oct. 28) 7: I think it's a ceremony known as a "knock-down-drag out." **1993** *TV Guide* (Nov. 27) 17: We used to have knockdown dragouts.

knockdown money *n.* small sums received as gratuities.

  1838 in N. Hawthorne *Amer. Notebooks* 96: The hostlers, at taverns, call the money given them "Pergusus"—corrupted from perquisites. Otherwise, "knock-down money." **1980** in Courtwright et al. *Addicts Who Survived* 168: That was knockdown money too....Tips...you wouldn't turn in.

knocked out *adj.* **1.a.** see KNOCK OUT, 3.b.

b. heavily intoxicated.

  1942 *ATS* 124: Dead drunk...*knocked out.* **1962–68** B. Jackson *In the Life* 79: I had to be so knocked out and goofed up...to [engage in acts of prostitution].

2. (see quot.).

  1891 Maitland *Slang Dict.* 161: A bankrupt is said to be "knocked out."

3. Esp. *Jazz.* extremely stylish, attractive, or exciting; great.

  1944 Stiles *Big Bird* 85: I could see her in saddle shoes and a knocked-out sweater and skirt. **1947** *Tomorrow* (Aug.) 28: That's a knocked-out number. **1952** Brossard *Darkness* 275: You should dig that surf. It is really something. Knocked out. **1956** Bellow *Seize the Day* ch. i: That's a real knocked-out shirt you got on. **1956** Chamales *Never So Few* 243: If you ain't got a knocked out pad you take her to a motel. **1964** Gold *Jazz Lexicon* 180: *Knocked-out*. Excellent, thrilling, superb....current *c*1938–*c*1946, rare since.

knock-'em-stiff *n. So.* strong whiskey.

  1859 "Skitt" *Fisher's River* 18 [ref. to 1820's]: A rifle, shot-pouch, butcher-knife, and an article they dubbed "knock-'em-stiff" were of vastly more importance than "larnin'." *a*1860 Hundley *So. States* 268: Died, poor fellow, of mean whisky,/...Knock-'em-stiff and flaming red-eye. **1864** "E. Kirke" *Down in Tenn.* 87: I'll prime the guard with knock-em-stiff. **1905** in *DA:* Ah jedge thez plenty a knockem stiff fer the crowd.

knocker *n.* **1.** *Boxing.* a prizefighter; BUFFER[2].

  1870 *Putnam's Mag.* (Mar.) 301: Knocking the unfortunate knocker off his pins, his pegs, his stumps.

2.a. *pl.* testicles.—usu. considered vulgar. Also (*obs.*) **knacker.**

  1889 Barrère & Leland *Dict. Slang* I 523: *Knackers*...the testicles, also "knuckers." **1898 Green *Va. Folk-Speech* 210: *Knackers*, n.pl. Testicles. Knockers. **1916** Cary *Venery* I 168: *Knockers*—The testes. *a*1944 Binns *Timber Beast* 324: It looks as if Martin has by the knockers, all right. **1947** Heggen & Logan *Mr. Roberts* 423: Won't that frost the Old Man's knockers? **1953** in Randolph *Pissing in Snow* 36: She carried a little sharp knife, and would whack a man's knockers off every time she got a chance. **1961** Boyd *Lighter Than Air* 3: This is gonna stop so fast it'll shrivel your knockers, understand. **1974** Cull & Hardy *Drug Abusers* 194: *Knockers*—The testicles. **1976** Berry *Kaiser* 199 [ref. to 1918]: "Adams...you're all right; I don't have to take your KNOCKERS off!" Now, I promise you that was exactly what he said.

b. usu. *pl.* a woman's breasts.—usu. considered vulgar. [Occ. with joc. pronun. as in 1951, 1975 quots.]

  1934 H. Roth *Call It Sleep* 414: A sweet pair o' knockers. **1938** "Justinian" *Amer. Sexualis* 27: *Knockers*. n.pl. The breasts; mammae. **1946** I. Shulman *Amboy Dukes* 160: Her breasts were tremendous....If a fellow were hit across the head with one of Rosie's knockers he'd be driven into the sidewalk up to his ankles. **1947** Mailer *Naked & Dead* 377: Look at the knockers on her. **1948** Wolfert *Act of Love* 507: The knockers on the chest is hard...to see. **1950** Calmer *Strange Land* 176: That girl used to make my mouth water....All knockers and tail. **1951** Leveridge *Walk on Water* 203: And you should have seen her g'knockers. **1952** in Yates *Loneliness* 30: Ooh, Eddie—what a paira *knockers!* **1956** H. Gold *Not With It* 168: There were them as admired my knockers. **1960** Wohl *Cold Wind* 182: What a pair of knockers. **1969** Marshe & Lifton *Centerfold* 61: What a pair of knockers! **1970** Southern *Blue Movie* 111: All the bare knocker you want. **1975** Univ. Tenn. student: Has she got giant /ˈknɑkərz/? **1982** "J.R. Roberts" *One-Handed Gun* 69: Nice knockers, huh? **1988** De Lillo *Libra* 263: You got the knockers, Brenda. **1995** *Esquire* (Dec.) 55: Lingerie....The sight of a real-life woman with her own knockers smacking her in the chin and her lower torso sheathed...in what appeared to be battered piano wires.

3. that which is stunning or impressive.

  1888 in Thornton *Amer. Gloss.* I 521: Neat, clean-cut, effective, and trim, her figure was a knocker.

4.a. a carping critic; habitual complainer; faultfinder; disparager.

  1898 "B. Baxter" *Baxter's Letters* 20: I've heard knockers in my time, but Estelle is the original leader of the anvil chorus. **1898** in *DAS:* That pack of knockers and snapping curs. **1900** in *DA: Knocker*—n. One who "knocks." A discontented actor who generally receives less than $40 a week. **1904** *Life in Sing Sing* 250: *Knocker.*—One who speaks ill of another. **1905** J. London *Game* 26: A dub, and a softy, and a knocker. **1915** H.L. Wilson *Ruggles* 299: Just to spite Jackson and his band of lady knockers. **1917–20** Dreiser *Newspaper Days* 248 [ref. to *ca*1893]: I did not wish to appear to be "a knocker," as the phrase went,...a complainer. **1929** Perelman *Ginsbergh* 37: Well this same bunch of cheap knockers and Bolsheviks has come forward again. **1939** Appel *People Talk* 79: I'm a knocker! I see something wrong, I squawk.

b. *Und.* an informer, accuser, or complainant.

  1908 Kelley *Oregon Pen.* 74: Now for the "knockers."...After hearing the knock, the guards will conclude that the knocker is a pretty good fellow, and the poor convict that was lied about...[gets] the worst of it. **1942–49** Goldin et al. *DAUL* 119: *Knocker*...A complaining witness in criminal proceedings. **1935–62** in Ragen & Finston *Toughest Pris.* 806: *Knocker*—One who informs....The principal witness or complainant.

5. *R.R.* CAR-KNOCKER.

  1958 McCulloch *Woods Wds.* 102: *Knocker*—A car repairman on a logging railroad.

6. a large drink; HOOKER.

  1983 Helprin *Winter's Tale* 109: To drink, I'll have a knocker of buttered rum.

¶ In phrase:

¶ **up to the knocker** perfect or perfectly; thoroughly; very well. *Rare* in U.S.

  1844 in *F & H* IV 128: *Jack*. How do you feel? *Ned*. Not quite up to the knocker. **1864 in *F&H*: It's a splendid turn out. Right up to the knocker, as they say. **1899 Boyd *Shellback* 24: He must know his duty "up to the knocker," as they say.

knocking shop *n.* [fr. KNOCK, *v.*, 1] a brothel. Also **knocking house.**

  1860 Hotten *Slang Dict.* (ed. 2): *Knocking-shop*, a brothel, or disreputable house frequented by prostitutes. **1889 Barrère & Leland *Dict. Slang* I 525: *Knocking-shop* (English and American), a house of ill-fame. **1898 in *EDD: Knocking house* [a brothel]. **1938** "Justinian" *Amer. Sexualis* 27: *Knocking-House*. n. A brothel....Obsolescent.

knock-nutty *adj. Boxing.* punch-drunk; SLUG-NUTTY. *Joc.*

  1942 Algren *Morning* 4: You got ever'thin', Casey,...if just you wasn't knock-nutty.

knock-off *n.* **1.** *Labor.* quitting time; (*also*) a rest from work.

  1899 Cullen *Tales* 178: Ten days...was to be the period of his knock-off after nine solid months on the range. **1904** *Independent* (Mar. 24) 656: If we happened to finish up at one port just at knock off time we would spend half the night making preparations and getting under way for the next port, for no time was to be lost. **1905** *Nat. Police Gaz.* (Sept. 23) 6: Bouts after knock-off in the afternoon. **1931 J. Hanley *Boy* 89: The whistle for knock-off sounded.

2. Esp. *Police & Und.* an underworld killing; RUBOUT.

  1928 in Inman *Diary* 386: I'll fix him....I know all the big knock-off men here an' in New York. Just say the word. **1929** Hammett *Dain Curse* 231: Anyway, nobody's tried to kill her. It's her friends who get the knock-off. **1930** Lait *On Spot* 45: What did she know about...the Edgewater Kid's knock-off? **1945** Fay *Be Poor* 36: When the "knock-off" of "Slasey"...came about. **1954** Schulberg *Waterfront* 37: Maybe if he had known it was to be his pitch to call Joey out for the knock-off. **1971–75** J. Mills *On Edge* 69: It's not even a clean knock-off. It's, I don't know, savages.

3. *Business.* a discount.

  1942 *ATS* 530: Price reduction; discount...*knock-off*.

4.a. *Und.* a police raid.

  1953 Manchester *City of Anger* 208: You had a knockoff or something?...We can fix it. **1959** Horan *Mob's Man* 78: We were set up for a knock-off by a pusher.

b. a robbery.

  1969 in *ODMS:* The really profitable knock-off, like the Train Robbery. **1985 *Miami Vice* (NBC-TV): I noticed...this first knock-off.

c. *Police.* an undercover purchase of illicit goods, to be followed immediately by the arrest of the seller.

  1986 Philbin *Under Cover* 51: When you made a knockoff, or bust buy, you could come upon more money...than you would make for the rest of your life.

5. Orig. *Fashion Industry.* the practice of manufacturing a less expensive copy of a designer fashion; (*also*) such a copy; (*hence*) a usu. inferior imitation; parody or spoof. Now *colloq.*

  1963 *Sat. Eve. Post* (Sept. 21) 34: "The very, very few people who set the fashions in this country are the only ones concerned about piracy."...The industry doesn't want the knock-off outlawed. **1966** in *BDNE* 44: Copying designs to sell for less has a name in the industry. It is called the "knockoff." **1971** *Time* (Jan. 25) 38: Private customers paid $700 for the original; buyers, intent on knockoffs, paid close to $1500. **1973** *N.Y. Times Mag.* (Apr. 1) 45: Then came the knock-offs, as they're called in the trade. The fake blinds that looked like Levelor. **1972–79** T. Wolfe *Right Stuff* 196: Feed him the lines for his José Jiminez knock-off. **1981** *N.Y. Times Bk. Review* (Dec. 27) 7: As for the claim that this is an "entirely new...system of visual classification," no. It isn't. It's a knock-off...from a German series of reference books known...as Duden. **1984** WINS radio news (Dec. 21): Police have confiscated a batch of knock-off Cabbage Patch dolls. **1987** *Star Trek: Next Gen.* (synd. TV series): He's only a facsimile—a knock-off—a cheap imitation. **1990** *TV Guide* (Apr. 14) 49: This shameless knockoff of the "Alien" movies has a pretty fair cast. **1991** *TV Guide* (June 22) 129: A zany "Little Shop of Horrors" knockoff. **1994** *Married with Children* (Fox-TV): These knock-offs look just like the originals!

knock off *v.* **1.a.** to desist, leave off, cease; esp. (now *usu.*) to stop work, as at the end of the day or for a respite; (in early use *esp.*) to give up one's occupation or business; retire.—also used trans.

　*1649 G. Daniel, in *OED2*: The Sun...knock's of/And can noe more. *1662 in *F & H* IV 124: In noting of their nativities, I have wholly observed the instructions of Pitœus, where I knock off with his death, my light ending with his life. *1688 J. Bunyan, in *OED2*: If thou do not...knock off from following any farther. *1689 Shadwell *Bury-Fair* III: At Dinner time...I knock off. *1698–99 "B.E." *Dict. Canting Crew*: *Knock off*, to give over Trading; also to Abandon or Quit one's Post or Pretensions. *1708 E. Ward *Mod. World Disrob'd* 109: She at Length...makes him knock off his good hospitable House-keeping, to take fine Lodgings in...*St. James's.* *1725 *New Canting Dict.*: *Knock Off.* To give over Thieving. *1767 in *OED*: As for McSnip, he intends to knock off business, home to England and purchase a title. *1804 in Wetherell *Adventures* 105: Knock off pumping and get topmasts over the side. **1813** in Howay *New Hazard* 135: They had knocked off work. *1821–26 Stewart *Man-of-War's Man* I 140: He had certainly finished the black fellow at once...if, by the interference of his mates...he hadn't been forced to knock off. **1826** in *Del. Hist.* XXII (1986) 193: Comm Jones disapproving of keeping a regular log journal—knocked off accordingly. **1832** Wines *2½ Yrs. in Navy* I 192 [ref. to 1829]: After they had continued this operation awhile, they "knocked off" and fell to cracking our joints most lustily. **1835** *Knickerbocker* (Feb.) 110: Knock off firing! Hold on, every body! **1844** Ingraham *Coachman* 37: Riches don't come of hard work...so [I] have knocked off, this eight months. **1846** Codman *Sailors' Life* 39: Now knock off plaguing the boy, will you? **1849** Melville *White Jacket* 316: I would take it as a particular favour if you would *knock off* blasting him. **1850** in Windeler *Gold Rush Diary* 98: Turned in, in spite of rain. Shortly after it knocked off raining. **1851** W. Kelly *Ex. to Calif.* II 39: The miners knocked-off working, as they term it. **1854** St. Clair *Metropolis* 49: At ten or eleven o'clock the little fellow "knocks off" from his work. **1854** G.G. Foster *15 Mins.* 87: They knock off work punctually at 3 o'clock. **1854** "Youngster" *Swell Life* 36: Knock off firing! Hold on, everybody! **1855–56** in Valle *Rocks & Shoals* 219: Knock off quarreling. **1862** in G. Whitman *Letters* 61: It is now about time for dress parade so I must knock off and get ready. **1863** in Mead *Shanties* 479: But instead of knocking off/He kept on at the same rate. **1867** in W.H. Jackson *Diaries* 137: Hard work. Knocked off early. **1878** Willis *Our Cruise* 79: Boys, just knock off skylarking for a minute and pay attention to business. **1882** Peck *Peck's Sunshine* 275: We might as well knock off work Friday and Saturday. **1882** Campbell *Poor* 55: Chew and smoke, smoke and chew, an' then spit!...I tried to stop. *Couldn't* stop. Knocked off, an' then begun agin. *1888 Jacobi *Printers' Vocab.* 71: *Knock off.*—A somewhat slangy term used by printers occasionally to express leaving off work for meals or for the day. **1890** Howells *Hazard* 463: Do you generally knock off here in the middle of the afternoon? **1891** Maitland *Slang Dict.* 161: *Knock off*, to quit work. **1894** J. Slocum *Liberdade* 50: Knock off...and put away your tools. **1897** Siler & Houseman *Fight of the Century* 26: They "knocked off" work for the day in honor of the hero. **1897** *Lucky Bag* (U.S. Nav. Acad.) (No. 4) 137: Knock off that jaw and let's get to work. **1899** Dunne *Hearts of Countrymen* 10: Th' throuble was he didn't know whin to knock off. **1914** T.S. Eliot, in V. Eliot *Letters* 44: I enclose...some of the themes for the "Descent from the Cross."...I am disappointed in them and wonder whether I should knock it off for a while. **1917** in Dreiser *Diaries* 165: Bert wants me to knock off this afternoon and go to a movie, but...I can't. **1922** Hisey *Sea Grist* 52: This was Saturday, and the First told us to "knock off" at noon for the day. **1924** Anderson & Stallings *Glory* 72 [ref. to 1918]: Knock off that chat. **1939** Appel *Power-House* 107: "You know you can't behave small-time anymore." "Oh, gee!" she exclaimed hopelessly. "I'll knock off." *ca*1937 in Rawick *Amer. Slave* II (Pt. 1) 333: Dey al'ays knock offen early on uh Saturday evenin'. **1934–41** in Mellon *Bulkwhip Days* 47: So le's knock off and git dinner. **1946** Heggen *Mr. Roberts* 27: If he doesn't knock it off, that new ensign is going to wake up some day with a marlinspike through his skull. **1955–57** A. Miller *View from*

Bridge 8: I was just knockin' off work. **1965** N.Y.C. high school student: Knockin' off early? **1967** *U.S. News & W.R.* (Jan. 1, 1968) 10: They can end this war any time they want to. All they have to do is "knock it off." **1990** Univ. Tenn. instructor: Let's knock it off for awhile. **1994** *Mystery Sci. Theater* (Comedy Central TV): You wanna just knock off and get some coffee?

b. to die.

　*a*1704 in *OED2*: Perverse people...that would not knock off in any reasonable time, but liv'd long, on purpose to spite their relations. **1938** in Partridge *Dict. Und.* 391: They knocked off without a whisper. **1944** Burley *Hndbk. Jive* 142: *Knock off*—To die. **1944** in *DAS*: There...waiting for me to knock off, was Maloney! *a*1982 Medved *Hospital* 6: You collect quite a stable of sick friends. Then they start knocking off. **1994** N.Y.C. editor, age 60: He's so old, won't he knock off soon?

c. to abstain from; give up (a habit, practice, etc.).

　1872 in "M. Twain" *Life on Miss.* 292: I nocked off swearing 5 months before my time was up. *1877 in *EDD*: Oor parson allus knocks off his bacca e' Lent. *1883 Clark-Russell *Sailors' Lang.* 77: *Knock off!*...also to give up, as "To knock off the sea." **1884** Symondson *Abaft the Mast* 102: Our steward also left us, being determined, as he said, "to knock off the sea." **1898** Green *Va. Folk-Speech* 211: *Knock off*...To discontinue some ordinary practice: as, "He *knocks off* drinking." **1899** Thomas *Arizona* 79: I tried to knock off whisky once, and it was a deuce of a pull. **1902** Hapgood *Thief* 207: Jim, before you try to knock off the hop, you had better wait till you reach the next world. **1974** Hejinian *Extreme Remedies* 256: Ever consider knocking off the booze?

d. in phrase: **knock [it] off!** Orig. *Naut. & Mil.* stop it! (*often*) shut up! [The shorter form has become increasingly obs. since *ca*1950.]

　*1883 Clark-Russell *Sailors' Lang.* 77: *Knock off!*—Desist, stop. *1900 in *EDD*: Knak aff, Sibbie, or dan be G— A'll set dee i' da say head foremist. *1902 in *OED2*: Knock it off, boys. **1926** J. Thomason *Red Pants* 90: "Aw—knock it off!" growled the hard-headed lieutenant of Marines. **1927** J. Thomason *Marines & Others* 126: Here, you—knock it off. Love and business don't mix. **1941** Kendall *Army & Navy Sl.* 8: *Knock off*—please refrain from talking. **1942** *Leatherneck* (Nov.) 147: *Knock It Off!*—Quit whatever you're doing. Right now! **1945** Kanin *Born Yesterday* 226: Who asked you? Knock off! **1946** Michener *So. Pacific* 141: His listeners started to laugh. "Knock it off! Knock it off!" he shouted. **1949** Rodgers & Hammerstein *S. Pacific* 361: Aw, knock it off, man. **1960** J.A. Williams *Angry Ones* 171: Knock it off, man. **1961** J. Jones *Thin Red Line* 434 [ref. to WWII]: Knock off, First Sarn't....I'm a patient here like you. **1979** Kiev *Courage to Live* 11: It's almost equivalent to demanding of a cancer patient that he or she "knock it off" and get back to work. **1988** P. Beck & P. Massman *Rich Men, Single Women* 27: Mom, Daddy—please knock it off. **1993** *New Yorker* (June 14) 77: "Knock it off," Dad says.

e. Esp. *Naut.* to relieve (a worker or workers) of duty, as at the end of a shift or at the completion of a task.

　1922 Hisey *Sea Grist* 73: The First knocked Bill off after chow. **1933** in Clarke *Amer. Negro Stories* 69: The foreman knocked off the crew and let the steam die down. **1968** Maule *Rub-A-Dub* 37: Boats knock off the deck gang early? **1977** in Curry *River's in My Blood* 22: I finally took a shower when they knocked me off. **1979** Hurling *Boomers* 227: I'm going to knock the crew off early today. *a*1990 Poyer *Gulf* 411: "Knock off everybody you can to get topside." "Okay, XO, but most of us snipes are gonna have to stay on station."

2. to assign to a bidder at auction, as by a blow of the gavel.

　1747 in *DA*: He being the highest bidder, the same was knocked off to him. **1843** "J. Slick" *High Life in N.Y.* 74: Going to knock her off. **1852** Stowe *Uncle Tom's Cabin* ch. xxx: Adolph...was knocked off, at a good sum, to the young gentleman. **1858** J.C. Reid *Tramp* 78: The [auction]...closed after twenty-five pairs of mules, a half dozen wagons, &c. &c. were *knocked off.* **1865** in S. Hirshson *Lion* 120: [He should] offer her at auction and knock her off for a pot of beer or a shilling, and marry another. **1876** McKay *Hosp. & Camp* 217: Knocked off to the highest bidder. **1883** in *DA*: A quick "Sold!" as...he knocked off this lot or that. **1887** J.W. Nichols *Hear My Horn* 38: He was knocked off...for 451 dollars.

3. to impress very favorably; dazzle.

　*ca*1780 in Silber *Songs of Independence* 75: For brother Jo is come to town,/He's gone to knock them all off,/He plays upon a swamping fiddle/As big as father's hog trough.

4.a. to complete, perform, accomplish, make, or otherwise dispose of quickly or easily; in phr. **knock it off** (*obs.*) to do anything with great enjoyment or animation.

*1817 T.L. Peacock, in *OED2*: He had...to dispose of...a christening, a marriage, and a funeral; but he would knock them off as fast as he could. 1829 J. Hall *Winter Eves.* 8: [I] knock off all my small jobs first, and keep the heavy ones to the last. 1832 [M. St.C. Clarke] *Sks. of Crockett* 39: Soon the whole house was up, knocking it off—while old Ben thrummed his banjo. *1838 Glascock *Land Sharks* II 39: "Nancy Dawson," "Morgan Rattler," or any other rattler which "Black Pompey"...was able to "scrape-up, or knock-off," in the way of a rattling reel. 1847 Henry *Campaign Sks.* 172: We knocked it off at three miles an hour in glorious style. 1886 in *AS* XXV (1950) 35: When he knocked off a few stanzas of poetry. 1919 *Our Navy* (Oct.) 36: As to speed, we can knock off about thirteen knots with a cargo of three million gallons of fuel oil. 1933 Duff & Sutherland *I've Got Your Number* (film): I'll knock this off. 1934 Jevne & Purcell *Palooka* (film): Watch me knock off dis cadenza. 1939–40 O'Hara *Pal Joey* 9: Well at last I am getting around to knocking off a line or two. 1941 Hargrove *Pvt. Hargrove* 118: Painted by a friend of mine up in Columbus. Guy knocks them off like that in about twenty minutes. 1945 O'Sheel & Cook *Semper Fidelis* 140: You'll be knocking off those babes like nothing. 1947 Schulberg *Harder They Fall* 77: I'll bet Ruby knocks off three books a week. 1960 Hoagland *Circle Home* 63: On a table he knocked off a few push-ups and other exercises. 1974–75 Powledge *Mud Show* 86: Jeff...knocked off a little Brandenburg Concerto on his sousaphone. 1987 Rugoff & Gottlieb *Mannequin* (film): You're supposed to knock off three or four of these a day! 1991 Lott & Lieber *Total Impact* 142: I knock off 200 half sit-ups.

b. *Specif.*, to drain (a glass or bottle) by drinking; consume (food or drink) rapidly. [The long gap between 1805 and 1927 quots. is curious.]

1805 *Port Folio* (Aug. 24) 261: I'm Brick-dust Ben, as queer a blade/As e'er knock'd off a glass, sir. 1927 Coe *Me—Gangster* 165: We might as well knock off the bottle. 1931 in J. O'Hara *Sel. Letters* 46: At night we sometimes knock off a bottle of ale and a bottle of porter. 1936 Cain *Double Indemnity* 424: I knocked off a quart of cognac, but it didn't have any effect. 1937 in Mencken *New Letters* 403: I put in an evening knocking off malt liquor. 1937 in D. Runyon *More Guys* 113: Nicely-Nicely keeps expecting someone to come in and knock off these victuals. 1946 Kober *Man Is Here Again* 98: His steak, which he knocks off in no time flat. 1949 A.J. Liebling, in *New Yorker* (Jan. 22) 33: I said "Skoal," and we knocked off the whiskey. 1953 W. Fisher *Waiters* 14: Go on, knock your drink off, man. 1955 Q. Reynolds *HQ* 215: So all truck drivers get into the habit of knocking off a cup of coffee like other men knock off a shot of Bourbon. 1970 A. Young *Snakes* 41: I'll...maybe smoke me some charge or knock off a little pluck or drop a coupla goofballs. 1974 A. Bergman *Big Kiss-Off* 46: Knock off some Blatz and a salami sandwich. 1977 *Texas Monthly* (June) 89: He had knocked off a bottle of vodka daily at one time.

c. to obtain (usu. money) for oneself, esp. casually or with little effort.

1923 (quot. at SODA JERK). 1932 L. Berg *Prison Doctor* 217: I suppose I could knock off twenty-five bucks a week, banging a typewriter. 1934 Appel *Brain Guy* 49: Game guys can knock off some real dough. 1941 Attaway *Blood on the Forge* 71: Think I knock off a few winks right now. 1943 J. Mitchell *McSorley's* 36: To hear them tell it...all the bums on the Bowery were knocking off millions down in Wall Street when they were young. 1943 Steinbeck *Once There Was a War* (Sept. 1): Let's go up on the beach and knock off a little sleep. 1946 Gresham *Nightmare Alley* 28: Any gal who could knock herself off a gambling man was doing something. 1946 Rivkin *Till End of Time* (film): Knocked off over six thousand dollars shootin' craps in Paris.

d. in phrase: **knock off a piece** to engage in copulation.—usu. considered vulgar. Also vars.

1921 in Randolph & Legman *Roll Me in Your Arms* 133 (song learned *ca*1900): I throwed her on the floor an' knocked off some. *ca*1937 in Barkley *Sex Cartoons* 80: I thought you wuz anxious to knock off a chunk! 1946 in Shibutani *Co. K* 405: We don't give a shit if you wanna go out and knock off a piece now and then. 1948 Cozzens *Guard of Honor* 262: What does your wife do if she thinks you're

knocking a little off, every now and then? 1953 R. Wright *Outsider* 97: I just came in here to knock off a piece of tail 'fore going to work. 1958 T. Berger *Crazy in Berlin* 17: Then take your broad to the couch, knock off a piece and then wash up. 1971 S. Stevens *Way Uptown* 130: They'd just go in the bedroom and knock off a piece. 1976 C.R. Anderson *Grunts* 90: I'd smile—real big, like I'd just knocked off a piece, you know. 1987 Estes *Field of Innocence* 244: I still get a hard-on and have to knock off a piece once in a while.

e. to copulate with.—usu. considered vulgar. Cf. KNOCK, 1.

1934 Appel *Brain Guy* 13: A coupla plainclothes rats knock the dame off, then pull the marked two bucks outa her sock and they got a pinch. 1937 Weidman *Can Get It Wholesale* 151: If I had to knock off a dame to prove I didn't like her, there was something wrong. 1945 Bellah *Ward 20* 42: I wonder has he knocked off Mahon yet? 1946 I. Shulman *Amboy Dukes* 136: He knew he could knock her off whenever he wanted to. *a*1949 D. Levin *Mask of Glory* 8: I wanted to be a Marine. Knock off the women. Save the country. 1959 W. Williams *Ada Dallas* 117: And I would think how easy it would be to knock off a few of them, how I could really knock off one or two because their husbands had too much on their minds to pay them any attention. 1963 Rubin *Sweet Daddy* 9: We were knocking off this here ugly skinny board of a broad. 1965 C. Brown *Manchild* 109: While the cat was sleeping after she'd knocked him off—she'd steal his keys and give them to Johnny. 1969 Hannerz *Soulside* 56: You don't go around knocking off young broads like that. 1970 S.J. Perelman, in *New Yorker* (Oct. 17) 40: It was worth a detour to knock off such an exotic cooz. *1981 N.F. Blake *Non-standard Lang.* 189: *Knocked off* "had intercourse with." *a*1984 in Terry *Bloods* 26: A guy would...take the broad...to the bunker, knock her off, and take her back outside the wire.

5.a. Esp. *Mil. & Und.* to kill (a person); BUMP OFF., 1.a.—used esp. in passive.

1879 *Nat. Police Gaz.* (Apr. 12) 13: Knox Knocked Off....Between twelve and fifteen thousand spectators witnessed the execution of Knox Martin [in Nashville] this afternoon. 1918 R.J. Casey *Cannoneers* 151: I couldn't but think how happy it might have made him had I been knocked off. 1918 Bellamy *Diary* (June 10): Everyone dug holes in the ground to fit his body, but even in our P.C. men were knocked off. 1919 T. Kelly *What Outfit?* 181: Guess they had regular funerals and church services for the guys that got knocked off. 1919 Streeter *Same Old Bill* 28: If I get knocked off you will have something to amuse you in case you go into a convent. 1919 *Variety* (May 9) 9: Heart disease. Not the kind that knocks off most guys. 1923 T. Boyd *Through the Wheat* 150: Did he get knocked off, too? 1927 Niles *Singing Soldiers* 118 [ref. to 1918]: Loco'd been knocked off a few days past—they hadn't rolled his stuff up yet. 1927 Baker *Argonne Days* 82: If I were to get knocked off the last day, why, I'd never get over it. 1927 C.J. Daly *Snarl of Beast* 142: No wonder so many of the cops get knocked off. 1931 Lake *Earp* 97: We'll ask Ben if he wants us to knock this fellow off. 1932 C. McKay *Gingertown* 29: Teresa's own husband done knocked Rascoe off. 1938 "R. Hallas" *You Play the Black* 37: All I could think about was this Mex going to be knocked off maybe for murder. 1947 Rackin *Riffraff* (film): Might get a little messy lookin' around for somebody who knocked off one of your men. 1955 in Loosbrock & Skinner *Wild Blue* 42: Capt. René Fonck knocked off eleven Germans in his experimental Spad 13. 1959 Horan *Mob's Man* 37: They would probably have us knocked off. 1973 Longstreet *Chicago* 426: Walter the Runt was knocked off by the son of Paddy the Bear. 1977 Bredes *Hard Feelings* 81: Hitch-hikers...get knocked off every day of the week. 1979 L. Carter *Eubie Blake* 74: Becker probably had him knocked off. 1994 *New York* (Oct. 10) 31: He's trying to have all the witnesses against him knocked off. 1995 *New Yorker* (May 15) 29: The children knock off any townspeople who threaten their plans for world domination.

b. *Mil.* to put out of action. [No longer used of persons as in 1918 quot.]

1918 R.J. Casey *Cannoneers* 324: Tomlin has just been knocked off—no telling whether it's permanent or not. A fragment got him through both legs. 1944 E.H. Hunt *Limit* 103: He might have knocked off our cruisers. 1944 H. Brown *Walk in the Sun* 111: Once they knocked off the armored car they'd have to make time—good time. 1945 Beecher *All Brave Sailors* 128: One time, almost the entire convoy was knocked off.

c. Esp. *Sports.* to defeat.

1927 in Partridge *Slang* 345: He *can't* knock you off....The referee owes me ninety bucks. **1928** in Goodstone *Pulps* 40: If you went out there expecting a waltz, and got knocked off, you'd never forgive me. **1931** in J. O'Hara *Sel. Letters* 55: I now pick Cornell to knock her off this week, and Cornell to knock off that big Green team the following week. **1943** *New Yorker* (Apr. 17) 19: I kinda figgered there'd be somebody on the train I could knock off in gin rummy. **1944** Stiles *Serenade* 6: We were going out to knock off the Germans. **1950** Cleveland *Great Mgrs.* 190: The Yankees promptly knocked them off four straight. **1958** Traver *Anatomy of a Murder* 16: I was pretty bitter about being beaten by a young legal fledgling who hadn't even tried a...fender case when he knocked me off. **1960** Serling *Stories from Twilight Zone* 12: All I can think about is knocking off the Giants. **1978** B. Johnson *What's Happenin'* 133: If Tommy comes to play, I think we can knock off these guys. **1994** *TV Guide* (Mar. 5) 37: Massachusetts was first to knock off the top team.

d. *Law.* to discredit (a witness).

   1989 Hynes & Drury *Howard Beach* 270: There was no way that anyone could "knock off" this witness.

6.a. *Und.* to burglarize; enter and rob.

   1917 *Editor* (Feb. 24) 153: *Knocking off a peter*—breaking the door of a safe. **1923** in Partridge *Dict. Und.* 391: I knew where there was a bank...that could be "knocked off." **1928** Callahan *Man's Grim Justice* 9: To-night...we'll knock off Martin's home. **1928** Coe *Swag* 141: Imagine that, knockin' off a whole truck right in broad daylight. **1930** *Liberty* (Aug. 23) 31: Take that bank we knocked off in a town just outside Cincinnati. **1938** Baldwin & Schrank *Murder* (film): Those are the guys that knocked off the bookies' truck. **1940** in W.C. Fields *By Himself* 381: Crooks..."knock off" a bank. **1964** Maibaum & Dehn *Goldfinger* (film): Knock off Fort Knox? Ha ha ha ha ha ha! **1983** Mamet *Glengarry* 38: Someone should rob the office...knock it off. **1996** *Dangerous Minds* (ABC-TV): Let's knock off a *bank!*

b. to steal.

   *1919 *Athenæum* (Aug. 8) 729: "Someone knocked it off" for "Someone pinched...it." **1927** Coe *Me—Gangster* 211: Suppose we knock off fifty grand, where would I sit then? **1928** *New Yorker* (Dec. 8) 60: This was after I knocked that Dodge off. **1932** Berg *Prison Doctor* 259: Find out where they hid that load of furs they knocked off last week. **1962–68** B. Jackson *In the Life* 178: You said you knocked off $18,000? **1984–88** Hackworth & Sherman *About Face* 179: My watch...[had] been knocked off in the hospital. *a*1989 in Kisseloff *Must Remember This* 583: I went to reform school for knockin' off junk in George M. Cohan's warehouse.

7. *Police & Und.* to raid (an establishment); (*also*) to catch or place (a suspect) under arrest; (*hence*) to seize (contraband).

   1925 in Hammett *Knockover* 79: "Myra Banbrock just went into the joint through a cellar window....Let's knock it off."..."We ought to have papers even at that." **1926** in *OED2:* "Willie of Detroit is...knocking everybody off." (Meaning, arresting them.). **1927** Coe *Me—Gangster* 216: An' in case you should git knocked off...we'll spring you outa the can. **1928** Guerin *Crime* 108: They didn't bother to "knock off" Frank then and there. **1929** Sullivan *Look at Chicago* 185: An Assistant Chief of Police...knocked off eight of Tennes' best places. **1930** *Amer. Mercury* (Dec.) 456: *Knock off, v.:* To raid; to arrest. "The feds knocked off the Scatter." **1932** L. Berg *Prison Doctor* 63: Afraid if I was knocked off by the bulls I'd spill my guts for a shot. **1933** C. Wilson & J. Cluett *What—No Beer?* (film): Then if the cops knock off this brewery—you take the rap. **1934** (quot. at PUSH). **1942–69** Goldin et al. *DAUL* 119: *Knock off...*To seize...contraband or stolen stores. **1963** Rubin *Sweet Daddy* 58: Sure some babe sets up two three hookers—papers holler about cops knocking off a house. **1966** Herbert *Fortune & Men's Eyes* 78: Did you get a chance to keep any of the stuff you got knocked off for? **1962–68** B. Jackson *In the Life* 304: He...starts laying this paper....They knock him off, thirty miles from the joint. **1970** Terkel *Hard Times* 37: They used to get knocked off every so often, but not too often. Because the police captain was [bribed]. **1977** P. Wood *Salt Bk.* 157 [ref. to *ca*1930]: When the [bootleg liquor] reached its destination, we knocked the cars and drivers off and picked up Boyer. *a*1994 Smitherman *Black Talk* 151: *Knocked off* Arrested; busted for a crime.

8. *Orig. Fashion Industry.* to manufacture copies of (an established or higher-priced item); (*hence*) to make a counterfeit of. Now *colloq.*

   1963 *Sat. Eve. Post* (Sept. 21) 30: "Knocking-off" is trade slang for copying a competitor's dress, cutting corners to sell it for a lower

price, then marketing it to harvest dollars that might otherwise go to the dress's creator. **1975** *L.A. Times* (Dec. 28) VIII 4: We decided they'd be knocked off so we would do it first and offer both. **1978** *Houston Chronicle* (Jan. 22) X 4: Soon huge textile mills in Japan, Hong Kong and Taiwan were "knocking off" cheap imitations. **1986** *N.Y. Times Mag.* (June 22) 55: Many successful products are being "knocked off" to the detriment of consumers ....Beware of *similar looking* imitations. **1992** in *Harper's* (Jan. 1993) 69: Artful forgery, rigged document, a knocked-off passport of the soul.

knockout *n.* **1.** a brawl.

   1891 *United Service* (Dec.) 633: Pawnee and Sioux had their knockouts so near to the ranch, we could see/The hair fly.

2.a. a person or thing that is stunningly impressive, attractive, amusing, exciting, or successful.

   *1892 in *F & H* IV 130: Oh! 'e's a little champion, Do me proud, well 'e's a knock out. **1901** Hobart *Down the Line* 43: It was a knockout. **1906** H. Green *Boarding House* 123: I got some new stuff that'll be a knockout. **1908** *Hampton's* (Oct.) 456: You want to get in on the latest knock-out, "Oh, you, kiddo, she then Did Say to Me!" It's a peach. **1909** *Sat. Eve. Post* (June 5) 17: A knockout....Pronounced success. **1913** *Sat. Eve. Post* (July 5) 5: We'll make a circus picture and it'll be a knockout! **1914** in E. O'Neill *Letters* 27: This epistle is going to be a screaming comedy knock-out. **1917** in Fitzgerald *Corres.* 21: The whole thing is a knock-out. **1918** Witwer *Baseball* 22: The livin' is elegant, the clothes is knockouts. **1921** McArdle *Collier's* 224: I might not be much of an actor, but as a smiler I was a knockout. **1928** Coe *Swag* 6: You must know some people that are just naturally knock-outs for laughs. **1929** *Sat. Eve. Post* (Oct. 5) 21: He was a knock-out for looks. **1935** in Galewitz *Great Comics* 21: Boy! That [photo] should be a knockout! **1936** Connell & Adler *Our Relations* (film): Why, it's a knockout! **1956–60** J.A. Williams *Angry Ones* ch. ix: You look very cute in that outfit....It's a knockout. **1983** *Time* (July 18) 60: By any standards the summer is a knockout. **1990** *Cosmopolitan* (Nov.) 60: *GoodFellas* [movie review]...Martin Scorsese's study of male bonding, Mafiastyle, is a knockout.

b. *Specif.*, a stunningly attractive member of the opposite sex.

   *1894 in *F & H* IV 130: Some of the lads...preferred to describe her with fervour as "A fair knock-out." **1906** H. Green *Boarding House* 282: The kid in the back row...was a knockout. **1918** Grider *War Birds* 132: But one of them, oh, la, la, what a knockout! Her name is Billy Carlton. **1928** *AS* III (Feb.) 220: *Knockout.* An extremely pretty and attractive girl. **1929** Bodenheim *60 Secs.* 230: The men...were knock-outs and knew it....it was hard not to fall for [them]—a girl was only human. **1929** Hammett *Falcon* 3: You'll want to see her anyway: she's a knockout. **1944** Kapelner *Lonely Boy Blues* 55: A guy in a yellow raincoat was on the make for a knockout under a blue umbrella. **1950** *Sat. Eve. Post* (Aug. 19) 126: I saw that she was a knockout, and she acted as if she liked me, but I was cagey. **1980** Lorenz *Guys Like Us* 41: Hard-to-get knockouts melted under his charm.

knockout *adj.* **1.** being or consisting of a stupefying drug, esp. one surreptitiously administered by criminals to render a victim unconscious.—used prenominally. usu. with *drops*. Now *colloq.*

   1895 Townsend *Fadden Explains* 12: If Mr. Burton wasn't good t' Miss Fannie I'd put a knock-out pill in his cocktail. **1895** J.S. Wood *Yale Yarns* 152: Our dandy team played a logy, tired sort of game, as if each man had been given knock-out drops. **1896** Ade *Artie* 64: You wouldn't have to feed him no knockout drops to make him take the coin, I guess. **1897** in Hoppenstand *Dime Novel Detective* 74: Hydrate of chloral...knockout-drops. **1899** A.H. Lewis *Sandburrs* 88: "I'll smoke a glass on d'stiff," said Jack softly. "It's better than a knockout drop." **1901** Dunne *Mr. Dooley's Opinions* 50: They give us th' products iv th' sile an' we give thim cottage organs an' knock-out dhrops, an' they think they've broke even. **1901** Irwin *Sonnets* (unp.): The steerer feeds me knock-out dope. **1902** Clurman *Nick Carter* 284: I took knock-out drops. *1904 in *OEDS:* What is known as "knock-out" drops is chloral hydrate. **1923** McKnight *Eng. Words* 45: The drug store contributes: *knock-out drops* for carbolic acid. **1922–24** McIntyre *White Light* 17: The scrofulous...bazaars that specialized in "knock-out drops." **1925–26** J. Black *Can't Win* 152: The...shanghaier with his knockout drops. **1975** Betuel *Dogfighter* 38: I just put some knock-out drops inna meat.

2. very exciting, attractive, impressive, etc.; wonderful.—no longer used predicatively.

    1920 Fitzgerald *Paradise* 84: It's a good finish, it's knock-out. *Ibid.* 162: We'll have really knock-out rooms. **1927** Mayer *Just Between Us Girls* 233: It was simply knockout to be talking to somebody like that. **1928** Levin *Reporter* 226: He approached his knock-out climax. **1932** in Dos Passos *14th Chronicle* 402: All the accounts of individual fighters towns etc, are knockout. **1949** *N.Y. Times* (Nov. 4) 3 (adv.): A knock-out black five-to-midnight outfit. **1989** *Cosmopolitan* (Jan. 1990) 172: It Takes More than Knockout Looks to Make a Model. **1990** Niemann *Boomer* 132: Knockout business women in pumps and heels. **1996** *All Things Considered* (Nat. Pub. Radio) (Sept. 18): The [CD] collection's knockout track.

knock out *v.* **1.** to obtain for oneself; (*hence*) to earn.

    *1873 in *OEDS:* Two industrious young men who worked very hard for a bare living—"just knocking out tucker," as the phrase went. **1919** T. Kelly *What Outfit?* 192: We'll both crawl in and knock out some sleep. **1920** *Sat. Eve. Post* (Mar. 27) 3: I was knocking out about eighteen hundred dollars per annum. **1953** W. Fisher *Waiters* 47: But look at the money you knock out here.

2.a. to kill (a person).

    [**1877** Wheeler *Deadwood Dick, Prince of the Road* 79: Abel got knocked out o' time by his cuzzin Cain.] **1885** *Puck* (July 29) 347: Here I used to nick my rifle / When I knocked out any white man. **1891** Riis *Other Half* 167: His name…is proudly borne by the gang of which, up till the night when he "knocked out his man," he was an obscure though aspiring member. **1914** Paine *Wall Between* 252: If I am knocked out, you will find the memorandum among my papers. **1917–18* in W. Owen *Coll. Poems* 71: Ye get knocked out; else wounded—bad or cushy.

b. *Mil.* to destroy or put out of commission.

    *1917 in Lee *No Parachute* 176: The tanks might have pulled off a far bigger success, and even reached Cambrai, but for a hold-up at Flesquieres, where a single battery knocked out about a dozen of them. **1925** J. Thomason *Fix Bayonets!* 188: Hell that our machine-guns got knocked out so quick, wasn't it? **1950** *Time* (Nov. 27) 24: The Soviet aim is to make each of these regions as self-sufficient as possible, so that if one is knocked out in a war, the others can fight on.

c. *Und.* to apprehend (a criminal).

    1935 Pollock *Und. Speaks: Knocked out,* arrested. **1942–49** Goldin et al. *DAUL* 119: *Knock out…*To arrest.

d. *Und.* to enter and rob.

    1974 Kurtzman *Bobby* 119: Okay now, let's go knock out a gas station.

3.a. to surprise or stun; (*also*) to overcome or defeat. Now *colloq.*

    1887 Peck *Pvt. Peck* 165: That letter knocked me out in one round. **1889** Reynolds *Twin Hells* 266: I passed through all the fiery ordeal of trial…but…in the penitentiary…I was "knocked out." Then I felt keenly the sting of disgrace. **1894* in *OED:* Aston Villa [football club] knocked out Sunderland. **1906** *Independent* (Nov. 29) 1258: The sister:…There was a game, all right; only our side was knocked clean out. The mother (anxiously): Knocked out? I hope none of them were permanently injured?

b. to tire to exhaustion.—used esp. as p.ppl.

    *1889 Barrère & Leland *Dict. Slang* I 525: *Knocked out* (pugilistic), exhausted. **1896** Ade *Artie* 50: "How do I look?" "You looked knocked out." "Well, I feel the part." **1897** Hamblen *General Mgr.* 76: In other words, it is no trouble at all to the engineer to "knock out" the best fireman that ever handled a shovel. **1898** *Sat. Eve. Post* (July 30) 74: Greenhorns. We had three of them knocked out before you joined us at Hampton Roads. We left them in the hospital. It's the heat that does it. **1904** London *Faith* 33: We'd had a hard time together and were badly knocked out when we plumped upon Tattarat. **1918** O'Neill *Straw* 76: After their Sunday visits…you're utterly knocked out. It's a shame! **1954** Chayefsky *Marty* (film): I'm all knocked out. I may just hang around the house. **1970** N.Y.U. student: You look kind of knocked out.

c. Esp. *Black E.* to dazzle or delight; impress strongly and favorably; thrill.

    1890 Howells *Hazard* 313: The combination of your picturesque past and your aesthetic present is something that will knock out the sympathies of the American public the first round, I feel. **1912** in

Mencken *New Letters* 38: That next volume.…You will knock them out with it. **1944** L. Armstrong, in Hodes & Hansen *Sel. from Gutter* 79: There's one blues there, oh, it jus' knocks me out. **1944** Stiles *Big Bird* 6: What I wanted to do tomorrow was ski down Baldy at Sun Valley, or wade out into the surf at Santa Monica, and get all knocked out in the waves. **1945** Himes *If He Hollers* 10: I could knock myself out just walking along the street with her. **1946** Mezzrow & Wolfe *Really Blues* 20: When he played the blues he really knocked us out. **1952** Brossard *Darkness* 5: His fiction did not knock me out, but it was not bad. **1956** Holiday & Dufty *Lady Sings the Blues* 70: The chicken knocked Artie out. **1965** Elder *Dark Old Men* 97: Don't get knocked out—it ain't no real job. **1967** Colebrook *Cross of Lassitude* 131: I still dig him because he knocks me out. **1970** in *Rolling Stone Interviews* 421: I would be so knocked out to…do any kind of music with that dude. **1995** Headline News Network (Apr. 29): A movie about Mike Tyson might knock out some viewers.

4. to deprive.

    1887 DeVol *Gambler* 56: They knocked me out of $400 in one deal. *Ibid.* 77: You have knocked me out of many a good dollar. *ca*1952 in Oliver *Blues Tradition* 146: You're knockin' the poor people outa whole lotta dough.

5. *Black E.* to engage in copulation.—also constr. with dummy-object *it.*—usu. considered vulgar.

    1967–69 Foster & Stoddard *Pops* 46: If you picked up a chick there.…You'd take her upstairs, knock out, and then go on home. **1967–80** Folb *Runnin' Lines* 244: *Knock it out* Engage in sexual intercourse.

¶ In phrases:

¶ **knock out of the box** see s.v. BOX, *n.*

¶ **knock yourself out!** go ahead! enjoy yourself! do as you please!

    1942 Z.N. Hurston, in *Amer. Mercury* (July) 27: Knock yourself out—Have a good time. **1986** Thacker *Finally the Pawn* 89: "Say, I think I'll read my letter now."…"Knock yourself out." **1987** Tristan & Hancock *Weeds* (film): Go ahead, go ahead. Knock yourself out.

knockover *n.* **1.a.** *Und.* a police raid.

    1926 Finerty *Criminalese* 34: Knockover—Police raid.

b. *Police.* an armed robbery or burglary.

    1927 in Hammett *Big Knockover* 275: The Big Knockover. **1928** Hammett *Red Harvest* 48: He was in on the Keystone Trust knockover in Philly two years ago, when Scissors Haggerty's mob croaked two messengers. **1940** W.R. Burnett *High Sierra* 13: They've never had a knock-over in Tropico Springs. **1975** *Kojak* (CBS-TV): Another knock-over.

2. an easy task; WALKOVER.

    1977 Schrader *Blue Collar* 50: "Is it a knockover or not?" "It's a knockover, all right. Baby food."

knock over *v.* **1.** to shoot and kill (game); (*hence*) to kill (a person). Cf. syn. KNOCK OFF, 5.a.

    [**1770** in W.L. Katz *Eyewitness* 56: This stout man [Crispus Attucks] held the bayonet with his left hand and twitched it and cried kill the dogs, knock them over.] **1823** J.F. Cooper *Pioneers* 251: It's wicked to be shooting into flocks in this wasty manner; and none do it, who know how to knock over a single bird. **1839** in Blair & Meine *Half Horse* 65: The rest of the time he spent in nocking over bar and turkeys, and bouncing deer, and sometimes drawing a lead on an injun. **1847** Buhoup *Narrative* 26: Weel, do you think it would be any harm to sort of *skeer* him out of it, provided you could do so without knocking the old chap over?—for you see, that would be wasting ammunition. **1847** Robb *Squatter Life* 13: Poor fellows,…how soon old time will knock them over. **1848** in Appel *People Talk* 118: Our boys now and then knock over a deer. **1862** in H.L. Abbott *Fallen Leaves* 112: His…position as leader of the regiment would have ensured his being knocked over in a general engagement. **1863** in Hay *Lincoln* 54: If I should get knocked over, Gus will come down and take care of matters. **1863** in Brett *Civil War Letters* 41: I do not want the rebs to get much if they should knock me over. **1863** in *Del. Hist.* XXI (1984) 98: Our enterprising "nigs" knocked over a couple of chickens and stole half a peck of corn meal. **1873** Ballantyne *Black Ivory* 156: It wos invented by the great Nelson…just before he got knocked over at the glorious battle of Trafalgar. **1875** Sheppard *Love Afloat* 434: He has been so much cut up worrying over the risks his sweetheart ran, it would be hard for him to get knocked over now. **1881** in Rosa & Koop *Rowdy Joe* 49: After the second or third you don't mind knocking over one of these gunfighters any more than you would a sheep. **1883** Keane *Blue-Water* 149: They meant to get that gun into a good position, and they did, though we knocked a good many of 'em over. **1891** Kirkland *Capt. of Co. K* 114: I was just telling the boys how I knocked over two of the Johnnies. **1917** Depew *Gunner Depew* 50: They took great pride in the number of Germans they knocked over. **1924** in Goodstone *Pulps* 101: They couldn't, afoot, safely knock him over within a block or two of the Hall of Justice. **1929** Segar *Thimble Theater* 72: But if you interfere with my plans, I'll knock you over like rats! **1931–34** Adamic *Dynamite* 371: You've heard of bombings and killings. Now and then the boys just can't help knockin' some guy over. Too bad. **1935** C.J. Daly *Murder* 5: I'm willing to pay you to knock over a guy. **1940** in Weinberg et al. *Tough Guys* 184: So maybe you didn't knock Craig over? **1942** Garcia *Tough Trip* 80: The elk were close, and he could knock them over easily. **1948** A. Murphy *Hell & Back* 123: I knocked over a kraut after you left me. **1975** McCaig *Danger Trail* 67: And if you spot a fat young buck…knock it over and we'll have fresh meat for supper.

2. to drink readily or completely.

1832 *Spirit of Times* (Apr. 4) 3: They can "put out a squirrel's eye" or "knock over a pint of whisky" with any "Mike Fink" of Kentucky or Mississippi. **1913** T.A. Dorgan, in Zwilling *TAD Lexicon* 52: Sit down Judge and knock a couple over. **1921** *Pirate Piece* (May) 3: Again we gather round the festive board to knock 'em over and fill 'em up. **1932** Riesenberg *Log* 113: He was knocking over his sixth rickey. **1958** Camerer *Damned Wear Wings* 97: Been knockin' over a quart of corn every day since I can remember.

3.a. to overcome or dispose of by forceful or violent action.

1862 in R.S. West *Lincoln's Navy* 167: Another fort knocked over by the Navy is my reward. **1976** Humez & Humez *Latin* 13: One morning, Caesar looked into his mirror and said to himself, "You know, you should knock over Gaul." **1977** Dunne *True Confessions* 155: I knocked over [*i.e.*, raped] an old broad on Western and Romaine last night.

b. *Und. & Police.* to raid (an establishment); (*also*) to catch and arrest (a criminal) or (*Pris.*) to catch and punish (a prisoner) for an infraction.

1924 Henderson *Keys to Crookdom* 410: *Knock over.* To arrest. **1929** *AS* IV (June) 342: *Knocked over*—Raided or arrested by the police. **1933–35** D. Lamson *About to Die* 114: And for him to go and get knocked over for a childish little con trick like that. *Ibid.* 197: The big shot,…sooner or later he's a cinch to get knocked over. **1935** S. Miller *G Men* (film): The G-men and cops are knockin' over every place in town. **1940** in H. Gray *Arf!* (unp.): Why *not* knock over Elpaso's joint?…I'll get the squad together. **1942** J. Larkin *Secret Agent of Japan* (film): Don't make a reputation for yourself by knocking me over. **1949** in W.S. Burroughs *Letters* 34: A pusher is knocked over…daily. **1950** Maddow & Huston *Asphalt Jungle* 26: Gus told me the Club Royal got knocked over.…The cops have all gone crazy. **1970** (quot. at SPEAK). **1991** McCarthy & Mallowe *Vice Cop* 60: Go knock over Harry's gambling operation.

c. *Und. & Police* to enter and rob (a place); (*hence*) to rob (a person).

1925 *Collier's* (Aug. 8) 30: They "knock over," or rob, a store or house. **1925** in Hammett *Knockover* 88: Maybe we suspected him of being tied up with the mob that knocked over the St. Louis Bank last month. **1939** Wald et al. *Roaring Twenties* (film): You like it well enough to knock over this boat for $100,000 dollars worth of it. **1956** Kubrick & Thompson *Killing* (film): You mean he seriously told you that he and a mob are going to knock over the race-track? **1970** Wambaugh *New Centurions* 142: But that place has been knocked over two or three times and it's usually early in the morning. Last time the bandit fired a shot at a clerk. **1971** B.J. Friedman, in *Playboy* (Dec.) 130: His 70-year-old father…is grateful that his apartment has been knocked over only twice. **1975** T. Berger *Sneaky People* 43: Did anybody ever knock over this bank? **1982** Castoire & Posner *Gold Shield* 127: You figured you'd knock her over, huh? **1991** McCarthy & Mallowe *Vice Cop* 201: I told Brody I had knocked over some dealer to get it. **1995** *Smithsonian* (Sept.) 94: Williams knocked over banks throughout the United States.

4. to seduce or copulate with (a woman).

1945 in Marx *Groucho Letters* 229: This is usually the opening line used in attempting to knock over a dame. **1960** Sire *Deathmakers* 175: I…promised my old lady I wouldn't knock over any other snatch.

knock-up *adj.* excellent; BANG-UP, 1.b.

1983 K. Miller *Lurp Dog* 61: Determined to do a knock-up, top-notch job of it.

knock up *v.* **1.** to injure or make infirm; impair; incapacitate; (*hence*) to tire out; make exhausted. [Now superseded by (2), below.]

*1737 in *OED:* Where the Horse is young,…it would splint him, or knock him up (as we say) if the Rider were to make his Flourishes upon his Back like a Rope-Dancer. **1770* in *OED:* Here is a lady who is not at all tired,…and here am I knocked up. **1796** in Eliason *Tarheel Talk* 187: I feel now almost knocked up…my hand shakes…my spirits dull. **1807** W. Irving *Salmagundi* 122: [Weather changes] have completely knocked up my friend Langstaff, whose…spirits sink and rise with the mercury. **1830** J. Neal *Authorship* 63: We are most knocked up now, Sir. **1834** Hoffman *Winter in West* II 178: We care not for anything but shelter and food for our horses, which are nearly knocked up. **1837** Strong *Diary* I 75: Harry Ward has gone to Europe. His pedestrian tour knocked him up. **1838** *Crockett Almanac 1839* 2: I was knocked up with one game leg. **1841** in Bleser *Secret & Sacred* 58: I cannot be a man of intellect for an hour's reading knocks me up completely. **1854** "Youngster" *Swell Life* 415: You must be thoroughly knocked up. **1855** W.G. Simms *Forayers* 207: Our beasts are pretty well knocked up, Willie. **1862** in Wightman *To Ft. Fisher* 44: The weather…has knocked us up. **1863** in H.L. Abbott *Fallen Leaves* 188: Our artillery…[was] so knocked up that only one or two shots were fired. **1865–67** De Forest *Miss Ravenel* 219: I have to make my staff officers ride day and night and knock up their horses. **1879** *Puck* (Dec. 3) 635: Fact is he felt a trifle knocked up. **1901** J. London *God of His Fathers* 159: Here I am…knocked up and stiff and sore.

2. to make pregnant, now usu. out of wedlock. [Euphemistic in early use, but now often considered vulgar.]

1813 in McPhee *Pine Barrens* 32: William Mick's widow arrived here in pursuit of J. Mick, who she says has knocked her up. **1860** *Hotten Slang Dict.* (ed. 2): *Knocked-up*…In the United States, amongst females, the phrase is equivalent to being *enceinte*. **1860–61** R.F. Burton *City of Saints* 548: "Knocked up"—a phrase which I should advise the Englishman to eschew in the society of the fair Columbian. **1861** Berkeley *Sportsman* 160: "She's knocked up" replied the matter-of-fact guest. "What! *dear me, again in that interesting situation?*" **1863** Andrus *Letters* 69: But it seems as though she might stand it without being knocked up for 9 mos longer. **1867** Doten *Journals* II 952: [In cipher:] She had…all the other usual symptoms of a woman knocked up. **1871** Schele de Vere *Amer.* 321: Characteristic of the false prudery of the people,…*knocked up*…[is] used in speaking of ladies…in interesting condition. **1888** *Stag Party* (unp.): They say it is dangerous, but what do I care,/ If I am knocked up on the Delaware. **1916** Cary *Slang of Venery* I 168: *Knocked Up*—Pregnant. **1925** Hemingway *In Our Time* 144: Hell, no girls get married around here till they're knocked up. **1927** in E. Wilson *Twenties* 364: He had knocked up a girl, wanted an abortion. **1928** Dahlberg *Bottom Dogs* 257: What was that I hear about your knockin' her up? **1930** Dos Passos *42d Parallel* 94: [She] carried on and bawled an' made out he'd knocked her up. **1933** J. Conroy *Disinherited* 62: He had knocked up Mattie Perkins. **1938** T. Wolfe *Web & Rock* 121: I got to watch her all the time now to keep some son-of-a-bitch from knockin' her up an' ruinin' her. **1941** Cain *Mildred Pierce* 308: If you mean why you got yourself knocked up, I suppose you did it for the same reason I did—for the money. **1952** Sandburg *Strangers* 326 [ref. to *ca*1890]: It's about a preacher who knocked up a woman and a baby came and there was hell to pay. **1956–60** J.A. Williams *Angry Ones* 177: Woman trouble? Knock somebody up? **1966** Bogner *7th Ave.* 58: You're pregnant. He's knocked you up, the bastard. **1972** *N.Y. Times Mag.* (Nov. 26) 102: He knocked this one girl up. **1978** Maupin *Tales* 246: Go get somebody else to knock you up. **1987** B. Raskin *Hot Flashes* 239: I was scared I'd get knocked up. **1988** *Cheers* (NBC-TV): I knocked up Annie good! **1995** *Martin* (Fox-TV): You shoulda thought about that before you was knockin' me up! **1995** *Jenny Jones Show* (synd. TV series): I was told he has a woman named Liza knocked up.

knockwurst *n.* the penis; SAUSAGE.—usu. considered vulgar. *Joc.*

1972 Wambaugh *Blue Knight* 287: The old boy [was] throwing the knockwurst to his girlfriend. **1974** Sann *Dead Heat* 38: Maybe he's slipping the knockwurst to a rich widow in the Towers.

knot *n.* the head; KNOB, 1.

    [**1950** in *DARE*: A person's head...*muscle knot.*] **1954** in Wepman et al. *The Life* 40: I'm going for your knot and gut. **1954** in *DARE*: *Knot*...head. **1965–70** in *DARE*. **1978** Sopher & McGregor *Up from Walking Dead* 267: "I don't go around looking for heads to pound on." "Wow, blood, you really would go to my knot if it came to that."

    ¶ In phrases:

    ¶ **jerk a knot in** to strike (someone); punish.

    1942 McAtee *Supp. Grant Co. Dial.* in '90's 6: *Jerk a knot in one's tail,* v. phr., threat of condign punishment for doing, or failing to do, the thing in view. **1967** Ford *Muc Wa* 176: I'm gonna tie a knot in old Charlie's tail, tonight. **1979** Crews *Blood & Grits* 39: I told you enough, Mayhugh,...I'm gone jerk a knot in you about cussing.

    ¶ **make knots** Esp. *Navy.* to make speed; hurry.

    1906 Beyer *Battleship* 84: "Making knots"—hurrying. **1918** Ruggles *Navy Explained* 99. **1925** Thomason *Fix Bayonets!* 65 [ref. to 1918]: But comin' out—boy. We make knots! **1928** in Thomason *Stories* 471: And you can make knots outa here. **1941** *AS* (Feb.) 23: *Makin' knots.* Traveling at high speed. **1949** Daves *Task Force* (film): I'm gonna make knots back to the gal who ties 'em. **1988** Poyer *The Med* 446: Every Russki sub and destroyer in the Med is making knots for us right now.

    ¶ **tie the knot** to get married.

    1906 Ford *McCabe* 215: He's got his trunk packed for England, where the knot-tyin' is to take place. **1981** Wolf *Roger Rabbit* 19: We flew to Reno and tied the knot. **1981** P. Sann *Trial* 160: Not that he didn't tie the knot again. **1994** *Real News for Kids* (CNN-TV) (Aug. 6): Yep, they tied the knot.

knot *v.* [sugg. by *tie*] *Baseball Journ.* to even (a count on a batter); tie (a score or a game). Hence **knotter**, *n.* a tying run.

    1915 (cited in P. Dickson *Baseball Dict.* 236). **1934** Weseen *Dict. Amer. Slang* 213: Baseball...*Knot the count*—to even the score. **1942** *ATS* 634: Tie...*knot the score.* **1961** *Daily News* (N.Y.C.) (Oct. 13) 57: With one across and the knotter on base, Shantz was replaced by Jim Coates. **1988** *N.Y. Post* (June 7) 61: Steve Hosey's...single knotted the game in the bottom of the evening.

knot-bumper *n.* *Logging.* (see quot.).

    1956 Sorden & Ebert *Logger's* 20 [ref. to *a*1925]: *Knot-bumper,* A man who works on the landing and unhooks chokers, and chops off limbs missed by the buckers.

knothead *n.* **1.** a stubborn or unintelligent animal, esp. a horse or mule.

    *ca*1910 in T. McCoy *Remembers* 33: My other knot-head broncs. **1920** *DN* V 82: *Knot head.* A bucking horse. **1936** R. Adams *Cowboy Lingo* 26: If he could not "ketch" on" to the work required of him, he was a "knothead." **1940** *AS* XV 447: *Knot head.* Low intelligence. **1940** F. Hunt *Trail from Tex.* 15 [ref. to 19th C.]: Be sure to watch that big brown jinny...that knot head right there. **1957** Bean *Fancher* 28: They gelded the knot-heads and kept the good mares and studs. **1975** Kennedy *Train Robbers* (film): Do you suppose they'll let Cal have that knothead back? **1977** Garrity *Canal* 22: We won't be bothered by that knothead anymore.

    2. a dolt.

    1929 *AS* V 57: If these prospective "he-men" never attain skill in their riding and work, they are "knotheads." **1932** Binyon & Bolton *If I Had a Million* (film): Big knothead. **1942** *Leatherneck* (Nov.) 147: *Knot-Head*—A not very clever character, slow on the uptake. **1948** M. Shulman *Dobis Gillis* 61: Look at Petey—a knothead, a jitterbug, a guy who'll never know where his next meal is coming from. **1950** M. Shulman *Sleep Till Noon* 79: This knothead will absolutely *massacre* people. **1953** M. Shulman *Affairs of Dobie Gillis* (film): You're gonna think I'm an awful knothead. **1957** *Father Knows Best* (CBS-TV): Come on, sit down, knothead. **1959** Wurthman & Brackett *Rio Bravo* (film): Found yourself another knothead who don't know when he's well off? *1961** Loring & Hyatt *Gorgo* (film): You little knothead! **1967** Mailer *Vietnam* 87: The f.p.s. (foot per second, knothead!). **1972–76** Lynde *Rick O'Shay* (unp.): Give that knot-head a haircut. **1990** *Twin Peaks* (ABC-TV): My knothead husband might peek in the ledger.

knotty-headed *adj.* stupid. Also **knot-headed.**

    1919 *Twelfth U.S. Inf.* 80: Well, I'm a knotty-headed hound!...You sure are a prize package as a K.P.! **1934** L. Hughes *Way of White Folks*

219: Let old knotty-headed Willie go on being a white-folks' nigger if he wants to, I won't! **1937** Schary & Butler *Big City* (film): You...knot-headed apes!

know *v.* ¶ In phrases:

    ¶ **know beans** see *not know* [or *care*] *beans* s.v. BEAN, *n.*, 2 and *know beans* s.v. BEAN, *n.*

    ¶ **know from** see s.v. *not know from nothing,* below.

    ¶ **know (one's) onions** [or **oats** or **oil** or **apples**, etc.] to be astute or have thorough knowledge, esp. from personal experience; be very knowledgeable. [For *hockey* in the 1929–32 quot., cf. HOCKEY.]

    1922 *Harper's* (Mar.) 530: Mr. Roberts knows his onions, all right. **1925** *Writer's Mo.* (Jun.) 487: *Oil*—My stuff; as, I know my oil. **1925** Stallings *Big Parade* (film) [ref. to WWI]: My boy, you certainly know your onions! **1926** Dunning & Abbott *Broadway* 247: He's a smart cop, that fella; he knows his oats. **1928** Ruth *Baseball* 43: Shawkey wasn't talking through his hat at all. He just knew his onions, that's all. **1928** T.A. Dorgan, in Zwilling *TAD Lexicon* 53: Smart manager that—he knows his sweet potatoes. **1928** Levin *Reporter* 33: They know their oats....they have to come. **1928** MacArthur *War Bugs* 168: He knew his oats, that boy. *Ibid.* 265: The Greek knew his groceries by this time. **1928** in Tuthill *Bungle Family* 65: Take warning from a Brown who knows his eggs. **1929** *AS* IV (June) 343: *Knowing your oil*—capable, qualified. **1929** in Hemingway *Sel. Letters* 297: The man who wrote Sergeant Grischa...knows his eggs also. **1929** Bodenheim *60 Secs.* 226: I guess you know your onions, Jack....What's your drift? **1929** in E. O'Neill *Letters* 328: I ought to know my onions and my critics better than that! **1930** Schuyler *Black No More* 19: Doc, you sho' knows yo' onions. **1929–32** in *AS* (Dec. 1934) 288: [Lincoln Univ.:] *Hockey.* A name applied to one's specialty, or the field of knowledge over which one has the greatest command, as in Prof. Smith certainly knows his hockey! **1932** *AS* VII (June) 334: *To know one's onions* (*fruit, stuff,* etc.)—to be familiar with a subject. **1929–33** Farrell *Manhood of Lonigan* 182: He'd bet she knew her onions, and could teach him plenty that he ought to know. **1937** Parsons *Lafayette Escadrille* 64: Naturally, believing my boy pal knew his onions, I didn't trouble to put any chocks under the wheel. **1945** E. Moran *Eve Knew Her Apples* [film title]. **1946** Gresham *Nightmare Alley* 158: Whoever figured out dames' clothes knew his onions. **1947–53** Guthrie *Seeds* 45: This clamper gave me a good chance to bluff my way along and to sound like I really knew my okra on the handle of my guitar. **1966** Bogner *7th Avenue* 37: But from Solomon Bell, the man who knows his onions. **1973** *Oui* (Feb.) 113: But Loren knows his oats pretty good and he knows the absurdity of Western popular science. **1976** *N.Y. Times Bk. Rev.* (July 11) 38: I'm glad Mr. Vogel knows his own onions. **1984** Glick *Winters Coming* 114: He'd have to know his shit...to stay alive that long. **1992** G. Wolff *Day at the Beach* 134: She knew her apples.

    ¶ **know what it's all about** to have mature or sophisticated knowledge of life in general; know the score.

    1929 Hammett *Maltese Falcon* 159: Jesus! you don't know what it's all about either.

    ¶ **[not] know from nothing** [< Yid *tsu visn fun gornisht* 'to be ignorant'; lit., 'to know from nothing'] to know absolutely nothing. Hence **know from** to know about.

    1934 L. Berg *Prison Nurse* 49: We get it. You didn't know from nothing. You was innocent, pal, wasn't you? **1934** De Leon & Jones *You're Telling Me* (film): He don't know from nothin'. **1935** Algren *Boots* 224: "I don't know from nothin'," Herman said. **1935** Odets *Waiting for Lefty:* He don't know from nothing, that dumb basket ball player! **1937** Kober *Wonderful Time* 157: These college boys, they know fomm nothing. **1937** in *DAS*: If they ask you any questions, you don't know from nothing. **1941** Schulberg *Sammy* 84: I know from nothing about what I'm supposed to be doing. **1943** *AS* (Feb.) 48: Dat jerk don' know f'om nuttin'. **1945** in Mencken *Amer. Lang. Supp. II* 695: A *square* doesn't know from nothin' and a *creep* is worse'n a *jerk.* **1945** in *DAS*: A dizzy blonde...who knows from nothing, but is got everything. **1956** Ross *Hustlers* 5: The baby was sleeping...not knowing from nothing. **1958** H. Gardner *Piece of the Action* 9: He's flanked...by Saint Nick and the Easter Bunny. He doesn't know from people. **1977** Natkin & Furie *Boys in Co. C* (film): He knows from baseball like I know from polo. **1977** Butler & Shryack *Gauntlet* 41: Look, buddy, I don't know shit from horses. **1992** *New Yorker* (Mar.

30) 4: Mr. Perloff knows from bar-mitzvah parties....He has played at over a thousand bar mitzvahs. **1994** *N.Y. Times* (Feb. 20) ("Arts & Leisure") H26: You don't know from life. You must live, and suffer, and have joys.

¶ **not know (one's) ass from ——** see s.v. ASS, *n.*

¶ **you know it!** yes, indeed! I agree completely!
    1896 Ade *Artie* 55: "Aha! The best man, I believe?" ... "You know it.... You know it." **1899** Ade *Fables* 68: "Do they Pay to get in?" "You know it." **1961** Barbeau *Ikon* 41: "You better know it!" he added with a bite.

knowledge box *n.* **1.** the head; mind; BRAIN BOX, 1.
    *__1785__ Grose *Vulgar Tongue: Knowledge Box.* The head. *__1798__ in *F & H* IV: Coal-black is my knowledge-box. **1821** Waln *Hermit in Phila.* 27: "Knowledge-box very small."—"*Idea-pot* cursed empty." **1830** Ames *Sketches* 65: Laying hold of my head with both hands...as though the "knowledge box" which he handled so unceremoniously, had been mounted on a ball and socket. **1832** *Spirit of Times* (Mar. 3) 3: Which...rather confuted his *knowledge box* for some moments. **1839–40** Cobb *Green Hand* I 147: The marine...will bring upon your knowledge box, some of the threatenings the old commodore so lavishly dealt out. **1848** [W.T. Thompson] *Jones's Sks.* 53: I ain't much of a frenologist myself, or I'd give you a full description of Uncle Sam's knowledge-box. **1859** "Skitt" *Fisher's River* 134 [ref. to 1820's]: Wavin'...thar tommyhocks over my knowledge-box. **1870** *Putnam's Mag.* (Mar.) 301: The combatants struck each other...upon the head, the nut...the knowledge-box. **1880** Nye *Boomerang* 34: He will emerge...with a knowledge-box loaded up to the muzzle with...useful information. **1903** *Enquirer* (Cincinnati) (May 9) 13: *Knowledge box*...the head. **1946** Mezzrow & Wolfe *Really Blues* 13: What they piled into this knowledge box of mine hasn't brought me down any. **1968** Heard *Howard St.* 74: You ain't right in the knowledge-box. **1969** C. Major, in Girodias *New Olympia Reader* 379: As a matter of fact, the best head I've had came from the knowledge box of a beautiful, down, black chick, long-standing.

    2. Esp. *Hobo.* a schoolhouse or college building.
    1903 *Enquirer* (Cincinnati) (May 9) 13: *Knowledge box*—A schoolhouse. *a*__1909__ Tillotson *Detective* 92: *Knowledge box*—A college. **1910** in Wilstach *Stage Slang* 46: They call a college a "knowledge box"...and an insane asylum is referred to as being a "nut college." **1926** *AS* I (Dec.) 652: *Knowledge-box.* School house. **1927** *AS* II (June) 390: A country schoolhouse, a rather good place to flop in the summer-time, is a *knowledge-box*. **1927** *DN* V 453: *Knowledge box*, n. A country school house. **1928** Callahan *Man's Grim Justice* 98: The sheriff organized a posse and came back to the knowledge box (schoolhouse) and glomed (arrested) us. **1929** Milburn *Hornbook* 152: I've flopped out...in a hoosier knowledge box. **1945** *AS* (Oct.) 234: [Univ. Minn.:] *Knowledge Box, Foundry.* University. **1952** Sandburg *Young Strangers* 393 [ref. to *ca*1895]: One fellow saying, "I had a good snooze in a knowledge box last night," meant he had slept in a country schoolhouse. **1978–80** in Cardozo-Freeman & Delorme *Joint* 512: *Knowledge Box.* A school house.

    3. *Labor.* an administrative shed or office; BRAIN BOX, 3.
    1926 *AS* I (Jan.) 250: *Knowledge-box*...Yardmaster's office. **1966** "T. Pendleton" *Iron Orchard* 75: Wakely...sketched out the situation on paper at the rough stand-up desk called the "knowledge box." **1945** Hubbard *R.R. Ave.* 350: *Knowledge Box*—Yardmaster's office; [? also that of the] president of the road.

    4. *Petroleum Industry.* (see quot.).
    1942 *ATS* 516: *Knowledge-box*, a box in which drillers' orders and reports are kept.

knowledge factory *n.* a school, college, or university. Cf. ANGEL FACTORY.
    1905 Hobart *Get Next!* 99: Go to Oxford and become the squeegee professor in the Knowledge Factory. **1928** Lawes *Life & Death* 61: Next day we visited the knowledge factory, and...the head teacher asked if I had ever been sent to school. **1969** J.R. Froines, in Hoffman et al. *Conspiracy* 82: Clearly a university is a "knowledge" factory in any society and must do more than prepare another generation of academics.

knowledge pot *n.* KNOWLEDGE BOX, 1; IDEA POT.
    1919 *Our Navy* (May) 54: Zowie!...Eighteen boxes of canned peaches drop on your old knowledge pot.

knowledge works *n.* a school.

1902 Hobart *Up to You* 59: Darcey could beat a banjo longer...than any man in the Knowledge Works. **1902–03** Ade *People You Know* 26: The Corporate Interests got many a Whack here at the Knowledge Works.

knuck *n.* **1.** *pl.* **a.** knuckles.
    1858 in G.W. Harris *High Times* 140: Two ove my 'nucks went inter each ove his red eyes. **1908** *DN* III 327: *Knucks*...The knuckles. "He hit me on the knucks." **1957** *Sat. Eve. Post*, in *DARE*. **1973** in *DARE*.
    b. brass knuckles.
    1878 Shippen *30 Yrs.* 164: I hope you've got your brass "knucks," for you'll want 'em with this crowd. *ca*__1880__ in P.G. Brewster *Ballads of Indiana* 332: And in one pocket is a pair of knucks/And in the other a gun. **1897** in *OED2*: Knucks, heavy nickel plated and polished. $0.30 per pair. **1913** in *DA*: The fat fist armed with a set of...heavy knucks. **1921** J. Conway, in *Variety* (Nov. 18) 29: The brass knucks have been workin like a pair of charms. **1928** Tilton *Cap'n George Fred* 151: That was the lad who used the "knucks." **1928** Springs *Above Bright Blue Sky* 7: I'm not afraid of a pistol, a rifle, a knife or brass knucks. **1931** Harlow *Old Bowery* 497: A nice assortment of pistols, knucks, stilettos, etc. **1932–33** Nicholson & Robinson *Sailor, Beware!* 59: You'll wear a pair of knucks when you go out social. **1954** Arnow *Dollmaker* 458: Knucks, lead pipe, and truck tire chains, I'd say. **1971** Cole *Rook* 34: Remember...no knives or knucks in this. **1973** J. Reese *Weapon Heavy* 107: You could kill a man with these knucks. **1984** J. McNamara *First Directive* 228: I unlocked the weapon locker and held up the brass knucks. **1989** *TV Guide* (Feb. 18) 27: Brass knucks...may help.

    2. *Und.* a pickpocket.
    *__1812__ Vaux *Vocab.: Knuck, knuckler,* or *knuckling cove,* a pickpocket. **1845** *Nat. Police Gaz.* (Nov. 15) 97: Charley gave a handsome entertainment to a select few of his friends among [t]he "knucks." **1847** *Nat. Police Gaz.* (June 26) 333: The old police...could have ferreted out the "knucks" without much difficulty. **1848** Judson *Mysteries* 527: "*Knuck.*"...a pickpocket. **1848** (quot. at CROSSMAN). **1859** Matsell *Vocab.* 49: *Knuck.* A pickpocket. **1865** (quot. at LIPPY). **1866** *Night Side of N.Y.* 78: The houses were...well patronized by "knucks" and "cracksmen." **1889** Bailey *Ups & Downs* 32 [ref. to 1871]: Among them was Hughy Kelly, better known as "Blinkey," a notorious "Knuck." *Ibid.* 40: And, sure enough, while we were talking, in came this gang of "knucks," but neither Primrose nor I knew any of them. **1902** Hapgood *Thief* 68 [ref. to 1885]: A mob of "knucks"...had been "tearing open" the Third Avenue cars outside of the Post Office.

    3. *Baseball.* a knuckle ball.
    1969 (quot. at PIZZAZ).

    4. *Black E.* a fistfight.
    1969 in Cornish & Dixon *Chicory* 20: Got me in a knuck today (like put up your dukes).

knuck *v.* to pick a pocket.
    1845 (implied by quot. at KNUCKSMAN). **1848** *Ladies' Repository* (Oct.) 315: *Knuck,* To pick pockets. **1848** Judson *Mysteries* 13: You might have larnt 'em some lessons in the knucking line. *Ibid.* 36: It's enough to break my heart to see a man of your talent and standing forced to pry prancers, knuck tickers, and go on the low sneaks! **1866** *Nat. Police Gaz.* (Dec. 8) 2: He "knucked" a woman in a stage. **1867** *Nat. Police Gaz.* (Oct. 26) 2: Unless the Dutchman she "knucked" is "croaked." **1889** Bailey *Ups & Downs* 78 [ref. to *ca*1871]: Look here, "Mouthy,"...you can't fool me with any $40; I saw at least $100 in it before you "knucked" it off the old gentleman.

knuckle *v.* to give in.
    1872 Burnham *Secret Service* 99: Then the Colonel proceeded to an interview with his prisoner, who at once "knuckled" to the Chief, whose men had run him "to [*sic*] close." Dow caved! **1950** Duffy *S. Quentin* 31: If it wouldn't look as though I were knuckling to the cons.

knucklebrain *n.* KNUCKLEHEAD.
    1946 Michener *Tales of So. Pacific* 362: But this knuckle-brain Hendricks.

knuckleburger *n.* KNUCKLE SANDWICH. *Joc.*
    1973 Roberts *Last American Hero* (film): How'd you like a knuckleburger? **1978** Wheeker & Kerby *Steel Cowboy* (film): Sport, I'm about to feed you a knuckleburger.

knuckle-buster *n.* **1.** a crescent wrench.
    1941 *Army Ordnance* (July) 79: *Knuckle buster*....Crescent wrench. **1961** McKenna *Sons of Martha* 76 [ref. to 1930's]: Now ordinarily we despise monkey wrenches....Unless you get 'em real tight on a nut,

they slip off and bang your hand and that's why we call 'em "knuckle-busters." **1965** O'Neill *High Steel* 272: Knuckle buster. a wrench.

2. a mechanic.

1972 *Airman* (Aug.) 22: The Lady Knuckle-Buster of Korat.

knuckle drill *n. Mil.* fighting with fists; fisticuffs.

1978 W. Brown *Tragic Magic* 151: During the term of your incarceration you will be trained in the fine art of close-order knuckle-drill. **1984–88** Hackworth & Sherman *About Face* 312: And I knew the kid needed a little knuckle drill.

knuckle-duster *n.* **1.** a set of brass knuckles. Now *colloq.*

1858 in *OED2*: Knuckle-duster...a formidable American instrument, made of brass, which slips easily on to the four fingers of the hand...is calculated...to inflict serious injury on the person against whom it is directed. **1862, *1872, *1883* in *F & H* IV. **1891** Maitland *Slang Dict.* 161: *Knuckle dusters*, iron or brass instruments worn on the hands and used as a means of offence. **1903** A.H. Lewis *Boss* 14: He struck me with a knuckle duster. **1912** R.C. Murphy *Logbook for Grace* 22: He looped over a belaying pin in the rail a pair of iron knuckle dusters, which had four knobs on the business side. **1929** in R.E. Howard *Book* 62: They claimed that the old man had a knuckle-duster on his right. **1930** in R.E. Howard *Iron Man* 10: It was a heavy iron affair, resembling brass knuckles, and known in the parlance of the ring as a knuckle-duster. **1963* K. Roberts *Capt. of Push* 4: They fought with boots, bottles and knuckle-dusters. **1978** *Gamblers* 142: A sterling-silver knuckle-duster. **1984** Tiburzi *Takeoff!* 69: A fashion model with rings like knuckle dusters on my fingers.

2. a large ring.

*a1896 *F & H* IV 134: *Knuckle-duster*...(common). A large, heavy, or over-gaudy ring. **1935** Pollock *Und. Speaks* 5: *Knuckle duster*, a large finger ring. [**1984** (quot. at **(1)**, above).]

3. a boxer; KNUCKLE-PUSHER.

1906 *Nat. Police Gaz.* (Apr. 21) 3: The aspiring young knuckle-duster, as soon as he wins a prominent battle, will at once...blow himself in a chunk of the purse for a new silk hat.

knucklehead *n.* a blockhead; BONEHEAD, 1. Now *colloq.*

1942 *Life* (May 25) 9: Knucklehead gets his name from an aviation slang word meaning thick-skulled. **1943** Binyon *No Time for Love* (film): C'mon, you knucklehead. **1944** Sturges *Conquering Hero* (film): Listen, knucklehead, you take one more crack at your mother and I'll—. **1945** in *Calif. Folk. Qly.* V (1946) 384. **1945** Hamann *Air Words*: *Knucklehead*: An awkward, irresponsible airplane mechanic. **1946** Nason *Contact Mercury* 6 [ref. to WWII]: My estimate is that the knuckleheads were retiring anyway, under cover of the fog. **1951** *New Amer. Mercury* (Apr.): Hit the deck, you bird-brained knuckleheads! **1951** *Reader's Digest* (Nov.) 39: Papa's Not a Knucklehead. **1954** F. Coen *Johnny Dark* (film): If one of those knuckleheads wrecks the car, I'll—. **1957** Bradbury *Dandelion Wine* 101: Okay, Douglas....Be a knucklehead. **1958** Frankel *Band of Bros.* 5: You stupid knuckleheads. **1959** Trocchi *Cain's Book* 106: Where's your stash, knucklehead? **1963** Boyle *Yanks Don't Cry* 91: Christ! Do I have to draw you knuckleheads a picture? **1967** in G. Jackson *Soledad Bro.* 105: He will...be looked upon as a fool, knucklehead, buffoon. **1989** *Village Voice* (N.Y.C.) (May 9) 32: She too was a knucklehead, always getting into trouble. **1990** *Yo! MTV Raps* (MTV): Then this knucklehead joined. **1993** in C. Barkley *Sir Charles* 37: Some knucklehead teaches you to be racist. **1996** *Good Morning America* (ABC-TV) (Oct. 4): One to three percent of these kids are knuckleheads....You're guaranteed to get a handful of knuckleheads.

knuckleheaded *adj.* BONEHEADED.

1939 Stegner *Darkling* 107: And you're just a knuckle-headed farmer girl. **1948** Lay & Bartlett *Twelve O'Clock High!* 62: That knuckle-headed Kraut navigator sure bitched us up today. **1951** Pryor *The Big Play* 334: [He] began to castigate himself for fifteen varieties of a knuckleheaded fool.

knuckleknob *n.* KNUCKLEHEAD.

1950 Jacoby & Brady *Champagne* (film): What are you telling me this for, ya knuckleknob? **1990** *Mystery Sci. Theater* (Comedy Central TV): You two knuckleknobs. **1993** *Mystery Sci. Theater* (Comedy Central TV): What is this, knuckleknob?

knuckle poultice *n.* a punch in the face. *Joc.*

1873 in R.H. Dillon *Shanghaiing Days* 170: A knuckle poultice.

knuckle-pusher *n. Boxing.* a prizefighter.

1904 T.A. Dorgan, in Zwilling *TAD Lexicon* 113: Hints To The Star

Knucklepushers For Winter Jobs. **1910** *Variety* (Aug. 20) 13: We had a knuckle pusher on duty to keep the crowd quiet. His name was Kid Murray. **1921** J. Conway, in *Variety* (June 24) 7: I can just hear Mead tellin' that flock of knuckle pushers how he sneaked in a ringer on me.

knuckler *n.* KNUCKLE-PUSHER.

1922 *Variety* (Mar. 31) 8: You know how it is when the sun hits these knucklers. They like to loaf as much as anybody.

knuckle sandwich *n.* a punch in the mouth. *Joc.*

[**1941** Macaulay & Wald *Manpower* (film): Stop poppin' off to me, brother, or I'll give you a mouthful of knuckles.] **1960** MacCuish *Do Not Go Gentle* 357 [ref. to WWII]: You dealin' in for a knuckle sandwich, too? **1961** *Many Loves of Dobie Gillis* (CBS-TV): I consider you are looking for a knuckle sandwich, Chauncey. **1963** Doulis *Path* 74: Shut up, candy-ass. Are you looking for a knuckle sandwich? **1968** "R. Hooker" *M*A*S*H* 45: Therefore Trapper John administered a knuckle sandwich. **1970** *Nat. Lampoon* (Nov.) 36: Wanna knuckle sandwich? **1973** Lucas, Katz & Huyck *Amer. Graffiti* 70: Look, creep, you want a knuckle sandwich? **1974** Millard *Thunderbolt* 11: And unless you're suckin' around for a knuckle sandwich, don't ask me the usual "Are you part Indian?" **1976** C.R. Anderson *Grunts* 38: "Seek out, close with and destroy the enemy by all available means,"...means anything from a Phantom jet to a knuckle sandwich. **1980** in *Penthouse* (Jan. 1981) 130: I...told Snyder I wasn't getting paid enough and he said maybe a knuckle sandwich would do the trick. **1982** *GI Joe* (Dec.) (unp.): You're gonna be more annoyed when I plant this knuckle sandwich in yer flappin' yap. **1983** G. Larson *Beyond Far Side* (unp.): Why, yes, thank you, I would like a knuckle sandwich. **1995** *N.Y. Times* (Oct. 17) B15: Domi sucker-punched him with a solid left hook to the jaw....Samuelsson will surely not sue Domi for Saturday night's knuckle sandwich.

knuckle soup *n.* a punch in the mouth.

1842 C. Mathews *Puffer Hopkins* 223: "Joe Marsh's distributing knuckle soup...and he wants you to take a sup."..."Knockin' down time'll come afore to-morrow daylight!"

knuckle up *v.* to punch; fight with the fists.

1968 Cuomo *Thieves* 289: They were the kind that got a big charge out of knuckling guys up. **1995** *Three Ninjas Knuckle Up* (film title).

knucksman *n.* a pickpocket.

1845 *Nat. Police Gaz.* (Dec. 6) 121/2: Jim Webb and Bill Thompson, two brilliant "*knucksmen*." **1848** *Ladies' Repository* (Oct.) 315: *Knucksman, or Knucker*, A pickpocket.

K.O. *n.* **1.** [initialism for the facetious *Kommanding Officer*] *Army.* commanding officer, esp. a company commander; C.O.

1889 King *Faith* 247: Did you hear the K.O.W.'s* speech about her? **Army* argot for commanding officer's wife. **1891** *United Service* (Jan.) 73: The commanding officer...the K.O. **1893** King *Croesus* 178: You'll be K.O. here tomorrow. **1893** King *Waring's Peril* 8: Let me in. The K.O.'s orderly is after me. **1898** Parker *Gatling Gun* 179: They were...as punctilious about saluting as a K.O. on "official relations." **1906** M'Govern *Sarjint Larry* 42: It was one dat would have been completely contint to go roight back dere an' then ta camp an' make me report to de K.O. **1906** Moss *Officer's Manual* 243: K.O. the commanding officer. **1906** Stewart *N'th Foot* 133 [ref. to 1898]: "Take your companies into the trenches," said the K.O. **1918** *Sat. Eve. Post* (July 13) 90: We've got a hot one on the Old Man—the K.O., I mean. **1919** Amerine *Alabama's Own* 240: The Colonel says it's damn lucky the regiment leaves for home before we get our third service stripes, as the sleeve of the K.O. of the 37 mm platoon is getting pretty crowded. **1919** Bates *Fighting* 201: "Come on, I'll take you to the K.O.," offered the sergeant. **1919** Lovejoy *Story of 38th* 134: That regiment is the Thirty-Eighth and that K.O. is Colonel Adams. **1920** *Inf. Jour.* (Nov.) 460: They had hard heads, did those ancient K.O.s. **1921** *15th Inf. Sentinel* (Feb. 4) 8: It was all off just as soon as the new K.O. blowed in. **1933** Clifford *Boats* 111: Well, I'm off to call on the K.O. **1936** *Our Army* (May) 37: The K.O. had different ideas on the subject. **1947** *AS* (Apr.) 109 [ref. to WWII]: *C.O.* continued in use for "commanding officer," though the novel *K.O.* rapidly achieved wide circulation.

2. *Boxing.* a knockout. Also vars. Now *colloq.*

1911 T.A. Dorgan, in Zwilling *TAD Lexicon* 53: Mickey Finnegan who took a fine lacing for a round then put the k.o. on his man. **1916** E.R. Burroughs *Return of Mucker* 40: The athletic figure of Byrne would have discouraged any attempt to roll him without first handing him the "k.o.," as the two would have naively out it. **1917** E.R. Burroughs *Oakdale Affair* 128: Two of us can tackle this Bridge and hand him the k.o. quick. **1924** Hemingway *Sel. Letters* 142: Kitty's hat is a K.O. on Hadley. **1930** Pasley *Al Capone* 297: Al figured on taking a rap and he took a kayo.

K.O. or **kayo** *v.* **1.** Orig. *Boxing.* to knock out; (*hence*) to knock unconscious. Now *colloq.*

1921 *Variety* (Mar. 25) 4: Jones…was lucky enough to K.O. a local boy in the first round. **1921** T.A. Dorgan, in Zwilling *TAD Lexicon* 51: Champion Has Two Sets To Kayo. **1928** in Goodstone *Pulps* 39: The quicker he's K.O.'ed, the better. **1929** Burnett *Iron Man* 22: He couldn't K.O. a good flyweight. **1930** Buck & Anthony *Bring 'Em Back* 128: The orang, landing flat on his back, slept the sleep of the kayoed. **1935** Mackenzie *Been Places* 24: The crowd was yelling for me to K.O. him. **1971** Torres *Sting Like a Bee* 133: But I'm gonna make the referee's job easy by kayoing Cooper. **1995** Foreman & Engel *By George* 52: He'd K.O.'d all comers.

2. *Baseball.* to score many hits against (a pitcher).

1961 Brosnan *Pennant Race* 137: Pinson's three-run homer kayoed Koufax in the fourth. **1962** Houk & Dexter *Ballplayers* 105: The crowd was big and noisy as the Angels kayoed Terry, chased Sheldon and McDevitt.

3. to kill.

1978 Diehl *Sharky's Machine* 263: Mr. Grimm says this stiff got kayoed around the end of October sometime.

4. Esp. *Sports.* to defeat; (*hence*) to take precedence over; preempt.

1983 *N.Y. Post* (Sept. 5) 40: Gator & Goose Combine to KO Mariners, 4–3. **1995** *TV Guide* (Knoxville-Chattanooga ed.) (Apr. 18) 47: The CBS *Schoolbreak Special*…was KO'd by O.J. coverage in January.

K.O. or **kayo** *adj. & interj.* O.K. [The sense of the 1916 quot. is unclear; it may simply be a typographical error.]

[**1916** *Milwaukee Jour.* (Nov. 3) 18: "Ko. O! [*sic*] "All right!"] **1918** *Stars & Stripes* (Paris) (July 12) 7: If everything is all K.O., he can't say much to the M.P. **1919** in De Beck *Google* 42: This is K.O.—I'll take it. **1922** *Sat. Eve. Post* (Aug. 26) 78: But outside of that they were K.O. **1926** Dunning & Abbott *Broadway* 240: Any friends of Steve's is K.O. with me. **1928** McEvoy *Show Girl* 89: That's K.O. with me. **1930** Franklyn *Take-Off!* 48: You'll be one hundred per cent. kayo! **1930** Bodenheim *Roller Skates* 60: She's k.o. now, Mr. Barberlit. **1936** Levin *Old Bunch* 113: Kayo, if I come back. **1942** Davis & Wolsey *Call House Madam* 255: "Let's sit down, Lou." "Kayo, Bee." **1980** *Mork & Mindy* (ABC-TV): "I'll be back by, say, two o'clock tomorrow." "K.O." **1993** P. Munro *U.C.L.A. Slang II*: Meet me in half an hour, K.O.?

K.O.'ed *adj.* heavily intoxicated by alcohol or drugs. Cf. earlier KNOCKED OUT, 1.b.

1968 Baker et al. *CUSS* 146: KO'ed Drunk and passed out. **1974** Price *Wanderers* 52: Stinger…was K.O.'ed on Nembutals.

koko var. COCO.

Kong *n.* Black E. KING KONG.

1970 Major *Dict. Afro-Amer. Slang* 74: Kong: home-made whisky. **1983** *Reader's Digest Success with Words* 86: Black English…kong = "homemade whiskey."

koniacker *n.* *Und.* a counterfeiter. [The following quots. provide additional evidence for this spelling of the term, the main entry for which is s.v. CONIACKER. An antedating for that spelling may be found in G.A. Thompson, "Counterfeiter's Jargon of the 1820s." *AS* 71 3 (Fall 1996) pp. 334–35].

1839 in *AS* 71 3 (Fall 1996) 335: The trial of Smith Davis, the noted "King of the Koniackers." **1851** [G. Thompson] *Bristol Bill* 36: Kate…was an apt creature for a koneyacker. **1859** Matsell *Vocab.* 49: Koniacker. A counterfeiter. **1872** Burnham *Secret Service* vii: Koniacker, a counterfeiter, or coney man. *Ibid.* 46: This notorious and accomplished koniacker…led the tribe of counterfeiters in the great northwest.

konk var. CONK.

kooch *n.* hootchy-kootch dancing. Also **kootch.** Hence **kootcher,** *n.*

1946 Gresham *Nightmare Alley* 7: There was a Hawaiian dance show—what they called a kooch show. **1970** A. Lewis *Carnival* 223: But it sure isn't stripping. It's plain, ordinary kootch and that's all. *Ibid.*: I mean the kootchers get the marks so excited they don't know what the hell they're doin'.

kook /kuk/ *n.* [resp. of *cuck*, clipping of CUCKOO; cf.

KOOKABOO] **1.** an insane person; (*hence*) one who is amusingly eccentric; a zany. Also **kuke.** [Common only after *ca*1958; see note at KOOKY.]

1922 *Amer. Leg. Wkly.* (June 16) 27: But the cuck (cuckoo) who lost the official deck, be he corporal or first-class private, got a balling out. **1956** Algren *Wild Side* 78: Wingies, dingies, zanies, and lop-sided kukes; cokies and queers and threadbare whores. **1959** Serling *Twilight Zone* (CBS-TV): I'm not some sort of kook. I've never had this kind of trouble before—I mean trouble with my mind. **1959** in Cannon *Nobody Asked* 160: Often, on that corner, as the kooks and flips took over Broadway, Tony would show me how he would fight Ray Robinson. **1959** G. Wells *Gazebo* (film): Kooks! Why do I always get kooks? **1959** on *Golden Age of TV* (A&E-TV, 1988): She's a kook! She's bugged! **1959** H. Ellison *Gentleman Junkie* 206: I set up that kook against the building wall and belted him again. **1960** R. Reisner *Jazz Titans* 160: Kook: a crazy person. **1960** *Many Loves of Dobie Gillis* (CBS-TV): I'm gonna miss that kook. Life's not gonna be the same. **1960 in *OEDS*: A kook, Daddy-o, is a screwball who is "gone" farther than most. **1960** *Twilight Zone* (CBS-TV): Some kook who's left the world behind. **1961** Brosnan *Pennant Race* 20: Some baseball fans go batty. One kook, not even lovably harmless, sends a mimeographed letter to visiting major league clubs. **1962** *Car 54* (NBC-TV): [He's] a complete kook about horses. **1962** Carr & Cassavetes *Too Late Blues* (film): How'd you get involved with this kook? **1962** Algren *Notes from a Sea Diary* 168: She was brooding about her American engineer. Whoever he was, he was a kuke; he had bewildered this girl. **1966** Susann *Valley of Dolls* 393: The male kooks get all caked up. **1973** Haney *Jock* 92: The people looked at me like I was some sort of kook. **1978** Strieber *Wolfen* 207: We'll come across as a couple of kooks. **1984** *Alfred Hitchcock Presents* (NBC-TV): It's just part of being a psychologist. Kooks get your number sometimes. **1988** R. Dizazzo *Hollow Gate* (film): Happy Hallowe'en, kook! **1989** P. Heller *Bad Intentions* 38: A crook he is not; a kook he may be. **1992** *CBS This Morning* (CBS-TV) (Apr. 6): Is he a visionary or a kook? **1995** *Omni* (Fall) 96: He…feared being branded a kook.

2. *Surfing.* an unskilled or novice surfer; a nonsurfer.

1961 *Life* (Sept. 1) 48: A new vocabulary has sprung up, with such words as "kook" (a beginner)…."If you're not a surfer,…you're not 'in.'" **1961** Kohner *Gidget Goes Hawaiian* 27: Wally and Judge…were surrounded by a bunch of screaming kooks, all of the surfing fraternity. **1967** W. Murray *Sweet Ride* 11: It had been a sweet ride, maybe the best of the morning, probably the last now that the kooks were all out. **1968** Kirk & Hanle *Surfer's Hndbk.* 141: Kook: beginner; novice; unskilled or non-surfer. **1973** *Urban Life & Culture* II 148: Consequently, from 1958 on,…newcomers [to surfing]…were labeled "kooks," connoting lack of skill, stupidity and complete repulsiveness. **1977** Filosa *Surf. Almanac* 189: Kook.…A raw beginner just starting to surf.

kookaboo *n.* [poss. alter. *kookaburra* 'Australian bird whose call resembles human laughter', infl. by CUCKOO] a crazy person.

[**1935** Pollock *Und. Speaks*: Kickerboo, a person with money; live one; sucker.] **1955** Stern *Rebel Without a Cause* (film): Got a kookaboo inside with a gun. **1956** H. Ellison *Deadly Streets* 45: The kid was just a *natural-born* cuckaboo! **1959** H. Ellison *Gentleman Junkie* 196: The weirdest part…was the cuckaboo with the hood. **1986** Knoxville, Tenn., lab technician, age 32: Verlaine's mother had had four or five miscarriages, and she kept them preserved in jars on a shelf in the closet. One night Verlaine came home drunk and smashed them one by one on the kitchen floor. They were a couple of kookaboos!

kook up *v.* to make KOOKY.

1959 *Time* (Oct. 26) 60: Weiner…handled the business details and helped kook up the campaigns. **1965** S. Alinsky, in *Harper's* (June) 44: In this kooked-up irrational world, you really have to have a sense of humor to survive.

kooky *adj.* crazy; (*also*) zany; eccentric; odd. Hence **kookieness,** *n.* [Actor Edd Byrnes became a teen idol following his creation of the jive-talking character Gerald Lloyd Kookson III ("Kookie") on the ABC-TV detective series *77 Sunset Strip* (premiered Oct. 10, 1958).]

1959 on *Golden Age of TV* (A&E-TV, 1988): It's that kooky dame. **1959** in *OEDS*: The kookiest cat in town—Edd Byrnes. **1959** G. Wells *Gazebo* (film): Something pretty kooky happened here last night. **1959** Tony Curtis, in *Sat. Eve. Post* (July 25) 26: "I wake up one day and I'm the master of an estate. Man, it's kookie." (Meaning "crazy," here used in the slang sense of "weird but wonderful."). **1960** *Twilight*

Zone (CBS-TV): It's a kooky camera, that's all. **1960** *New Yorker* (May 7) 35: They have the wonderful sustained kookieness of youth. **1961** Kohner *Gidget Goes Hawaiian* 49: The female contingent…went kookie over him. **1962** Tregaskis *Vietnam Diary* 61: They say it's because Frickie and I are kookie. **1962** Reiter *Night in Sodom* 118: Kookie place. **1965** S.J. Perelman, in *New Yorker* (Aug. 28) 29: Of course, he has to pick a real kookie locale like the Mayflower Donut Shop at 2:30 in the morning. **1965** Lurie *Nowhere City* 276: She's all charged up and talking kind of kooky. **1978** Sopher & McGregor *Up from Walking Dead* 164: Dixon wore gloves all year round.…He was kooky. **1987** Pedneau *A.P.B.* 229: He takes stuff to build up his muscles. He's kooky. **1992** *Harper's* (Jan.) 32: The kooky, pleasantly mal-adjusted oddball. **1995** *Space Ghost* (TV Cartoon Network): A little zany, a little wacky, a little kooky!

kooky house *n.* a mental hospital; CRAZY HOUSE.
 1959 *Life* (Nov. 23) 45: If a disk jockey had to listen to all these records, he'd go to the kookie house.

koosh var. CUSH, 1.

kootch var. KOOCH.

kopeck *n.* [fr. S.E. sense 'monetary unit of Russia'] a dollar; (*rarely*) a cent; (*pl.*) money.
 1880 Nye *Boomerang* 22: This statement I am prepared to back up with the necessary kopecks. **1886** Nye *Remarks* 307: It prevented his pursuit of kopecks and happiness. **1896** Ade *Artie* 13: I stands pat on the draw, and then the first crack out o' the box I whoops it a half-fifty kopecks. **1896** (quot. at WHOOP). **1900** *DN* II: Copeck. n. Silver dollar. **1904** Ade *True Bills* 3: The chips were two Kopecks per Stack. **1904** in "O. Henry" *Works* 1493: You can't touch me for a kopeck less than two-fifty per. **1907** *McClure's Mag.* (Jan.) 332: I'd be called on for sixteen hundred an' ninety kopecks, V.D.Q. **1908** in H.C. Fisher *A. Mutt* 35: Slip me the thousand kopecks. **1911** *N.Y. Eve. Jour.* (Jan. 14) 8: Put every copek I had on the red and lost. **1918** Ruggles *Navy Explained* 102: Kopex. **1920** *Variety* (Dec. 24) 5: So I ought to get some kopecks with him. **1920–21** Witwer *Leather Pushers* 91: Them big hands…was to make him a mint full of kopecks. **1934** Halper *Foundry* 147: See if I can't win a few kopecks from the boys. **1938** in W.C. Fields *By Himself* 449: I…have since garnered a few elusive kopecks. **1972** Cleaves *Sea Fever* 67 [ref. to 1920's]: American… kopecks. **1974** Radano *Cop Stories* 57: Did you ever in your life pay me as much as a kopeck?

kosher *adj.* **1.** genuine; correct; legitimate; honest; innocent.
 a*1890–96** F & H IV 135: Kosh (or Kosher)…Adj. (common).—Fair; square. **1898** Cahan *Imported Bridegroom* 8: Show a *treif* gendarme a *kosher* coin, and he will be shivering with ague. Long live the Ameri-can dollar! **1901** (quot. at BUNCO ARTIST). **1***911** O'Brien & Stephens *Australian Sl.* 43: Cosher or Kosher /slang/ good, all right. Jewish /kosher/ meat killed according to Jewish custom is known as kosher meat. **1918** in Mencken *New Letters* 81: I have an open mind. Let me hear the kosher version. **1924** in *DA*: It don't sound kosher to *me!* **1927** Simon *Bronx Ballads* 40: But it all sounds kosher to me. **1929** "C. Woolrich" *Times Sq.* 185: He would give the case to the best detective agency in town and let them find out if everything was "kosher" in the matter, which is a word he got from Mr. O'Leary, the assistant-manager of the Company. **1930** *Amer. Mercury* (Dec.) 456: Kosher, adj.: Not guilty of; above reproach; clean. "Listen, shamus, you got me wrong. I'm strictly kosher." **1930** *Collier's* (Sept. 13) 7: Every-thing is very kosher.…You need not be afraid of anything whatever. **1935** Sherwood *Idiot's Delight* 118: So we must crave your indulgence and beg you to give us a break if the rhythm isn't all kosher. **1935** Pol-lock *Und. Speaks*: Kosher, not guilty; clean; reliable. **1936** Monks & Finklehoffe *Brother Rat* 132: Isn't strictly kosher. But it's got to be done. **1937** *Esquire* (Feb.) 63: There was something wrong, it wasn't kosher. **1938** Baldwin & Schrank *Murder* (film): Stay kosher. Keep your nose clean. **1943** Crowley & Sachs *Follow the Leader* (film): That don't look kosher to me. **1947** Schulberg *Harder They Fall* 10: All right, all right, so it happened a little different.…I suppose you never write stuff it ain't a hunnert percent kosher! **1951** *Halls of Montezuma* (film): Sir, to me it don't look kosher. **1976** "N. Ross" *Policeman* 68: This guy gets his money somewhere, and nine times out of ten he's not too kosher. **1990** *New Republic* (Mar. 19) 22: When bringing home the pork, keep it kosher. Standards are inevitably murkier when it comes to everyday contract hustling and grantsmanship.
 2. Jewish.—used contemptuously.

1972 A. Kemp *Savior* 68: He called her many filthy names: "dirty whore" and "kosher douche bag" and the like.

K-pot *n.* [Kevlar + (STEEL) POT] *Mil.* a Kevlar helmet.
 *a***1990** R. Herman, Jr. *Force of Eagles* 155: They're…wearing K-Pots.

KP pusher *n. Army.* a soldier in charge of a kitchen police detail.
 1943 *Yank* (June 18) 4: The CO…is a old KP pusher. **1943** in P. McGuire *Jim Crow Army* 67: It is true that K.P. pushers (Head K.P.) are made Cpl. and Sgt. but the K.P.'s themselves are a miserable group. **1983** Elton, Cragg & Deal *Dict. Soldier Talk* 178: An Old Army cook did not need a KP pusher.

Kraut *n.* [colloq. form of sauer*kraut*] **1.** a German.—also as adj.—usu. used contemptuously.
 1841 [Mercier] *Man-of-War* 15: One of them hit old Crout, the Dutchman,…*bim* in the eye. **1864** in C.W. Wills *Army Life* 309: Some puppy finally cried out "kraut," and another echoed it with "kraut by the barrel." [General Osterhaus] wheeled his horse and rode up to us, his face white with passion. "Vat regiment ish dis?" No one answered.…Yelping "sauer kraut" at a German is a poor way to gain his favor. **1918** Casey *Cannoneers* (entry for Aug. 26): "Dead Krauts and dead Yanks all over the place," the lieutenant replied petulantly. *Ibid.* (entry for Sept. 28): "The Krauts have a perfect range on that road," he said. **1918** Griffin *Ballads of the Reg't.* 34: But he always loved a soldier, be he "Chummy," "Krout" [*sic*] or "Mick." **1918–19** MacArthur *Bug's-Eye View* 19: George Daugherty…was the only member of the battery who didn't split a wishbone with a Kraut. **1919** Hoyt *Heroes of Argonne* 41: The Frogs and Krauts got it fixed up between 'em to spend their vacations where there ain't nothin' to bother 'em but the scenery. **1926** Nason *Chevrons* 139 [ref. to 1918]: I ain't had much to do with Krauts in France, but I've had some truck with 'em in Wisconsin an' they're bad Indians. *Ibid.* 229: Get that big Kraut! Get him! **1928** Scanlon *God Have Mercy* 321 [ref. to 1918]: Four Krauts came in over the rear wall and there is a machine gun just below that rise. **1930** Fredenburgh *Soldiers March!* 151 [ref. to 1918]: We can't blow our nose but some Kraut makes a note of it up on this hill. **1930** *Our Army* (Feb.) 10 [ref. to 1918]: A big Kraut charges around the corner of the trench and throws a potato masher grenade. **1932** Halyburton & Goll *Shoot & Be Damned* 62 [ref. to 1918]: I ducked around a corner of a trench and right into a Kraut. **1936** Mul-holland *Splinter Fleet* 200 [ref. to 1918]: It looks as if Captain Nelson has become tired of letting those Kraut submarines carry the fight to us. **1937** Parsons *Escadrille* 322: He was immediately surrounded by a crowd of curious Krauts. **1938** Johnson & Platt *Lost Bn.* 17 [ref. to 1918]: There were "kraut" machine guns barking at them in the dark. **1940** Raine & Niblor *Fighting 69th* (film) [ref. to 1918]: I'll show them Krauts! **1944** H. Brown *Walk in the Sun* 132: That farmhouse is sure a hell full of Krauts. **1950** Seaton *Big Lift* (film): You Krauts…try to give the world a hotfoot every twenty-five years. **1955** F.K. Franklin *Combat Nurse* 13: Are they kraut? **1963** J. Ross *Dead Are Mine* 34 [ref. to 1944]: There's about two squads of Kraut up there, this side of the junction. **1965** Linakis *In Spring* 22 [ref. to WWII]: She held onto a big towel…humming a marching song that sounded kraut. **1968** M. Brooks *Producers* (film): Oh, the Kraut. He's on the top floor, number 23. **1972** Childress *Wedding Band* 24: Somebody wrote cross the side of our house…"Krauts…Germans live here!" **1984** Glick *Winters Coming* 29: You krauts think you have a monopoly on sausage. **1986–91** Hamper *Rivethead* 189: You fat kraut.
 2. the German language.—usu. used contemptuously.
 1944–48 A. Lyon *Unknown Station* 222: She talks Kraut when she talks to the men. **1955** McGovern *Fräulein* 120: It's pretty tough when you don't speak Kraut. **1955** in Hemingway *Sel. Letters* 850: I can…command a platoon in Kraut. **1962** T. Berger *Reinhart* 30: Wearing a fake mustache and speaking Kraut like a native. **1965** Linakis *In Spring* 232: You could hear those bastards talking their kraut and chopping wood. **1965** Eastlake *Castle Keep* 141: He kept making light remarks in kraut. **1970–72** in *AS* L 62: Kraut…German language…Course in German.

kraut-eater *n.* a German.—usu. used contemptuously.
 1839 Briggs *Harry Franco* II 12: There was my milkman, old poppy Van Krouteater. **1919** *Ambulance Co. 139* 29: For those dirty kraut-eaters had torn my playhouse down. **1932** Halyburton & Goll *Shoot & Be Damned* 349 [ref. to 1918]: That kraut-eating farmer worked all of us from before daylight until late at night. **1936** *Our Army* (Feb.) 14: I hap-

pened to have met him over there in France where we and the Kraut-eaters were mixing it up to make the world safe for bigger better wars.

krautface *n. Mil.* a German.—used contemptuously.

> **1948** I. Shaw *Young Lions* 398: I'll tell you what, Kraut-face. **1955** McGovern *Fräulein* 106: *Mach schnell*, kraut faces. **1975** Stanley *W W III* 285: Over there with krautface and young Hemingway.

krauthead *n.* a German.—used contemptuously.

> [A popular story that Ty Cobb, standing on first base in the 1909 World Series, shouted at shortstop Honus Wagner, "Hey, Krauthead, I'm coming down on the next pitch!" cannot be verified; it is not attested until much later.] **1928** Scanlon *God Have Mercy* 4 [ref. to 1918]: What gives me a pain in the neck is all the time we wasted up at Verdun in the old trenches when we might have been killing Krautheads. **1932** C. MacArthur *Rasputin & Empress* (film): Get out, you krauthead! **1935** Archibald *Heaven High Hell Deep* 216: They'll run you out of here, old Krauthead. **1943** Tregaskis *Invasion Diary* (Sept. 16) 106: Once we get on to it, it's gonna be hard for the kraut-heads to stay in Altaville. **1945** T. Williams *Glass Menagerie* 31: LAURA....How is—Emily Meisenbach getting along? JIM. Oh, that kraut-head! **1947** R. Carter *Devils in Baggy Pants* 52: The Krautheads began counterattacking. **1951** Longstreet *Pedlocks* 103: That kraut-head! **1958** Berger *Crazy in Berlin* 135: Go on, you goddam Kraut-head. **1960** Sire *Deathmakers* 24: You want us to get the rest of the Krautheads? **1966** Keefe *Investigating Officer* 61 [ref. to WWII]: You bumped off them two Krautheads, didn't you? **1968** J.P. Miller *Race for Home* 151 [ref. to ca1930's]: "Leave it to a krauthead to know that," Caroline said. **1971** Curtis *Banjo* 160: We could play ball with this dumb Krauthead. **1970** Rudensky & Riley *Gonif* 86: I doubt if the Krautheads could have handled this bunch of hoods.

Krautland *n.* Germany.—used contemptuously.

> **1955** F.K. Franklin *Combat Nurse* 200 [ref. to WWII]: If I ever make it to krautland I'm gonna show them squareheads something! *1966 G.M. Williams *Camp* 81: Before they were posted to krautland. **1975** *Argosy War Annual* 12: We'd received a lot of orders and taken a lot of cities in Krautland. **1978** Truscott *Dress Gray* 32: A lot of GIs got it in the back in Krautland, General.

kriegie *n.* [< G *Krieg*sgefangener 'prisoner of war' + *-ie*] *USAF.* an Allied prisoner of war in Germany during World War II. Now *hist.* [All quots. ref. to WWII.]

> **1944** *Amer. N & Q* (June) 39: Kriegies: "old" American prisoners of war in German camps. *ca*1944 in Kaplan & Smith *One Last Look* 83: Kriegie. **1945** *N.Y. Times Mag.* (Nov. 4) 12: The richest contribution to the...language...is being made by the men who were held in German prison camps—the "Kriegies," as they unvaryingly called them-selves. **1946** G.C. Hall, Jr. *1000 Destroyed* 382: As prisoners, they called themselves *Krieges* [*sic*], and settled down to the suffocating monotony of life in a prison camp. **1946** J.H. Burns *Gallery* 367: The two remaining Kriegies trudged by themselves. **1945–49** F.A. Johnson *One More Hill* 160: It houses 700-odd Allied soldiers who call them-selves "Kriegies." **1955** Klaas *Maybe I'm Dead* 19: That's something every new Kriegie should know about. **1953–57** Giovannitti *Combine D* 44: The new kriegie is a Negro. **1968** Westheimer *Young Sentry* 225: Kriegie brew. A concoction distilled from fermented dried fruit. Kriegie was the name the prisoners had given themselves from the German word for prisoner of war, *Kriegsgefangener*. **1985** *Santa Barbara* (Calif.) *News-Press* (May 3) B1: Friendships have endured for hundreds of former "kriegies" who have gathered to commemorate the end of World War II and their own liberation. **1989** *Verbatim* XVI:2 (Autumn) 5: Conversations with these old "kriegies" (P.W.s) from almost everywhere in the world where the King's and everyone else's English and American were spoken.

krud var. CRUD.

kuke var. KOOK.

kumquat *n.* a young woman. *Joc.*

> **1984** N. Bell *Raw Youth* 24: Like a kumquat of schoolgirl age. **1988** Cherbak *Broken Angel* (film): The jerk left me for this twenty-year-old kumquat.

kvell *v.* [< Yid *kveln* 'to be delighted'] to be bursting with pride; boast; gloat.

> **1967** in *OED2: The New York Spy*...conscientiously *kvelling* through "the city's pleasures." **1968** Rosten *Joys of Yiddish* 199: Your children...[make] you *kvell*. **1970** Feinsilver *Taste of Yiddish* 364: Is he kvelling? **1977** J. Lahr, in *Harper's* (May) 97: Fuller positively *kvells* when he reveals that her first name is Regina. **1994** A. Heckerling *Clueless* 47: My heart is totally bursting. DIONNE (just as happy) I know. I'm kvelling. **1995** N.Y.C. woman, age 58 (coll. J. Sheidlower): Give us a chance to kvell over you.

kvetch *n.* a chronic complainer; (*fig.*, as in 1972 quot.) a complaint.

> **1964** S. Bellow *Herzog* 61: She's got a...*kvetch* of a mother. **1968** L. Rosten *Joys of Yiddish* 200: He's such a kvetch. **1972** *Atlantic* (Nov.) 53: Womanhouse [an art project] was a total environmental feminist kvetch, redeemed by humor and rage. *a*1978 Cooley *Dancer* 18: He called her a "kvetch." **1981** WINS radio news (Aug. 7): Actress Sandy Dennis has absolutely perfected the frumpy, neurotic kvetch. **1982** WINS radio news (Aug. 22): In case you haven't heard the word before, a *kvetch* is a chronic complainer. **1983** *Portfolio* (WKGN radio) (Mar. 13): The woman who runs the Rent-a-Kvetch service....She, as the head kvetch, decides which complaints are legitimate. **1991** *L.A. Times* (Aug. 25) 3: We don't need fiction to make the acquaintance of *kvetches*.

kvetch *v.* [< Yid *kvetshn* 'to squeeze'] to complain; GRIPE, 2.

> **1950** in *DARE: Kvetch*—Meaning: To complain....Reports *kvetching* as very common in New York. *ca*1952 (cited in *W10*). **1953** Russ *Last Parallel* 145: And I hate to start kvetching again, but there is a definite strain involved in keeping these shambicular notes. **1965** in *OEDS*: A wave of *kvetching*. **1967** Crowley *Boys in the Band* 811: I don't want to have to listen to him kvetch about how nobody does anything for any-body but themselves. **1978** *N.Y. Times* (Feb. 10) C2: For years my wife has been saying, "Stop kvetching about the work available and instead go ahead and make work available for other actors." **1987** *N.Y. Times Bk. Rev.* (June 28) 36: So busy "kvetching" in his "shrill" review of my novel. **1993** *Donahue* (NBC-TV): Stop kvetching! **1995** *New Yorker* (May 15) 102: One Yiddish word that all New Yorkers are familiar with is "kvetch"—which actually means "to complain." You often hear them say to each other, "quit kvetching"—to no apparent effect.

kvetchy *adj.* cranky, whining.

> **1981** in *Nat. Lampoon* (Jan. 1982) 44: What's wrong, Stewie?...You've been kvetchy all day.

K-whopper *n. Trucking.* (a nickname for) a motor vehicle, esp. a truck tractor, built by Kenilworth Corporation.

> **1976** Lieberman & Rhodes *CB* 131: K-Whoppers—Kenworth. **1976** Bibb et al. *CB Bible* 28: The old 1958 K-Whopper in his driveway has logged over two million miles. **1976** Whelton *CB Baby* 29: Now he leased a big 18-wheel K-whopper. **1979** J.H. Thomas *Long Haul* 125: Drivers of the so-called "K-Whoppers" are the most envied.

KY *n. Narc.* the Federal Narcotics Hospital at Lexington, Ky.

> **1962** Larner & Tefferteller *Addict in the Street* 236: Roy had kicked at K-Y. **1964** Harris *Junkie Priest* 91: Father Egan had paid a visit to..."K-Y." **1966** J. Mills *Needle Park* 74 [ref. to 1964]: So after a while I got really strung out again and I went to KY. **1968–73** Agar *Ripping & Running* 161: KY...Hospital [*sic*]. **1989** Courtwright et al. *Addicts Who Survived* 380: K.Y.:...U.S. Public Health Service Narcotic Hospi-tal at Lexington, Kentucky.

kybo *n.* [orig. unkn.; perh. as in 1971 quot.] a lavatory or toi-let commode, esp. at a campground. Also **kibo**.

> **1971** Dahlskog *Dict.* 36: *Kybo*, n. Keep your *b*owels *o*pen, an expres-sion used in children's summer camps; hence, a john at a camp or campground; an outhouse. **1975** T. Berger *Sneaky People* 133: What happened to Horse? He flush himself down the kibo?

kyke var. **kike**.

kyoodle var. KIYOODLE.

kype var. KIPE.

L *n.* **1.** [for the Roman numeral *L* 'fifty', formerly printed on such notes] a fifty-dollar currency note.
    1839 *Spirit of Times* (Apr. 13) 66: I had no idea of betting more than an "L," or a "C." **1845** in *DA:* "You are as lucky as a jailor," I remarked, as my friend began to smooth down the V's, X's, L's and C's.

2. [orig. unkn.] *Rap Music.* a marijuana cigarette; (*also*) marijuana. Cf. LA.
    1993 in Stavsky, Mozeson, & Mozeson *A 2 Z:* If you smoke L, you'll enjoy listening to it more. **1994** "Notorious B.I.G." *Big Poppa* (rap song): Watch a movie in the Jacuzzi, smoke Ls while you do me. **1994** *Totally Unofficial Rap Dict.:* L...Another name for *blunt.* **1995** Message on Usenet newsgroup rec.music.hip-hop: After puffing blunts of L's, I ascend straight to the heavens. **1995** N.Y.C. woman, age 27 (coll. J. Sheidlower): *L* is one of the words for pot. It's in a lot of rap songs, but only this year or so; it's not an old one.

L.A. *n.* Orig. *Calif.* Los Angeles, Calif. Now *S.E.*
    1901 in J. London *Letters* I 249: Will be unable to foregather with you in L.A. **1910** in W.C. Fields *By Himself* 191: Where shall I address you [in] L.A.? **1925** in Hammett *Knockover* 159: I got a hunch your men have gone down to L.A. **1930** *Bookman* (Dec.) 397: If you can't develop a personality or mental power in L.A. (*Variety* for Los Angeles) it's not the fault of swamis, [etc.]. **1938** Bezzerides *Long Haul* 33: I couldn't find work in Frisco...so I thought I'd try L.A. **1939** Appel *People Talk* 356: You never saw an auto town like L.A.

la *n.* Esp. *Black E.* marijuana; *L,* 2.
    1994 *N.Y. Times* (Sept. 4) (City) 13: Some people are smoking "lahs" (weed). **1996** *Village Voice* (N.Y.C.) (Sept. 24) 28: They both liked to spend money and crack jokes and sip cognac and smoke la and fuck girls. **1996** N.Y.C. man, age *ca*30 (coll. J. Sheidlower): The 1 train is the most civilized—no radios, no one smoking la on the train, [etc.].

lab *n. Stu.* a chemistry student.
    1866–71 Bagg *Yale* 45: *Lab* (abbreviated from laboratory), a word formerly used to indicate a student in chemistry.

label *n.* a person's name.
    1928 in Galewitz *Great Comics* 98: Say, Babe, the poor kid wants your label on a ball. **1942** *ATS* 203: Personal Name. *Handle, label,* [etc.].

labes *n.pl.* the genital labia.—usu. considered vulgar.
    1983 K. Miller *Lurp Dog* 166: Cunts and clits and labes.

lab hound *n.* **1.** *Police.* a forensic scientist.
    1958 J. Thompson *Getaway* 118: Then some eager beaver of a lab hound had managed to raise a latent print on the man's corpse.

2. a person who enjoys being the subject of psychology experiments.
    1970 J. Howard *Please Touch* 33: Such zealots are known to group leaders, a little ruefully, as "lab hounds," "group freaks" or "sensitivity heads."

labonza *n.* [prob. < It *la pancia* 'the paunch'] **1.** the pit of the stomach.
    1934 Jevne & Purcell *Joe Palooka* (film): "Labonza! Labonza!" "I hit him right in the labonza!" **1943** Wolfert *Tucker's People* 121: It was Murray reporting the day's losses. $39,374!..."Quite a kick in the labonza." **1961** R. Davis *Marine at War* 76 [ref. to 1944]: He nudged me in the ribs. "Pasquale gives it to 'em—right in the old La Bonza!" **1971** *N.Y. Times* (Oct. 10) 30: You want the truth? Right from the labonza? **1971** Sorrentino *Up from Nowhere* 57: Give ya *labonza* a little woikout. **1986** (quot. at SPARE TIRE).

2. the buttocks. Cf. 1943 quot. at **(1),** above.
    1954–60 *DAS: Labonza*...the posterior.

labor faker *n. Labor.* **1.** a worker who loafs on the job; malingerer; (*hence*) a corrupt union leader.
    1907 in R.L. Tyler *Rebels* 55: Liar...labor faker. **1915** in Kornbluh *Rebel Voices* 54 (caption): Labor-Fakir. **1936** Dos Passos *Big Money* 130: We're just labor fakers.

2. a political agitator among workers.

1938 Steinbeck *Grapes of Wrath* 209: You sure you ain't one of these here troublemakers? You sure you ain't a labor faker? **1938–39** Dos Passos *Young Man* 257: No, Mr. Connolly wasn't a crook or a social-fascist labor faker any more, he was a noble progressive fellow traveller. **1946** *Amer. Mercury* (Apr.) 462: Learn the truth about the labor fakers, get into the One Big Union.

labor skate *n.* [*labor* + SKATE] *Labor.* a corrupt or ineffective labor-union official; LABOR FAKER, 1.
    1930 *Amer. Mercury* (Dec.) 456: So I says to the labor-skate, "Screw, monkey!" *ca*1935 in F.P. Dunne *Dooley Remembers* 31: Some labor leader—labor skate we used to call him. **1948** J. Stevens *Jim Turner* 166 [ref. to *ca*1910]: An overalls brigade vowed to drive the labor skates, the politicians, and the socialist drivelers out of the One Big Union. **1951** in J.P. Cannon *Notebook* 294: The patriotic labor skates have all the advantages....They enjoy the solid backing of the government. **1964** Tamony *Americanisms* (No. 2) 2: Ostensibly for the benefit of those who moil and toil, the Norris-La Guardia Act now cornerstones the Union *pie-card, pork-chopper* and *labor-skate.* **1990** *Capital Gang* (CNN–TV) (Aug. 11): He's joining labor skates and left-wing Congressmen.

labrick *n.* [orig. unkn.] a naive or foolish person; LUMMOX. Also **laverick.**
    1889 "M. Twain" *Conn. Yankee* 382: As a rule, a knight is a lummux, and sometimes even a labrick, and hence open to pretty poor arguments. **1893** "M. Twain" *Puddin'head Wilson* ch. i: He's...a Simon-pure labrick if there ever was one. **1895** *DN* I 390: *Laverick:* slightly contemptuous name for a man, usually a stranger. [Used in the] West. **1966** in *DARE:* A dull and stupid person....*Laverick.*

lab wretch *n.* a performer of distasteful laboratory tasks.
    1988 T. Harris *Silence of Lambs* 74: The position is called "lab wretch," or some prefer "Igor"—that's what's printed on the rubber apron they give you.

Lac *n. Rap Music.* a Cadillac automobile.
    1990 "C.P.O." *Ballad of a Menace* (rap song): I roll cold in my Lac. **1993** "Big Mello" (unidentified rap song): Macks drive Lacs.

lace *v.* **1.a.** to set upon with a whip or a lash (*obs.*); (*hence*) to thrash; drub. Now usu. **lacing,** *n.* a beating. [The sense of the 1599 quot. is ambiguous; see *OED.*]
    [*1599 in *OED:* I goe to lace a rascal.] *1615 in *OED:* If I meet thee I will lace thee roundly. *1618 J. Fletcher, in *OED:* He was whipt like a top; I never saw a whore so lac'd. *1750 *Exmoor Scolding* 6: "Chell lace tha." "Thee lace ma?" *1785 Grose *Vulgar Tongue: Lacing.* Beating. I'll lace your jacket handsomely. **1835** in *F & H* IV 137: An ever-lastin' lacin' with the cowskin. *a1867 Smyth *Sailor's Word-Book: Lace,* to beat or punish with a rattan or rope's end. *a1889–90 Barrère & Leland *Dict. Slang* II 1: *Lacing* (popular), a beating. **1911** *N.Y. Eve. Jour.* (Jan. 11) 12: Bat received the lacing of his life. **1921–25** J. Gleason & R. Taber *Is Zat So?* 11: And what a lacin' he give that bum. **1930** Irwin *Tramp & Und. Sl.* 118: Lace.—To punch, beat or manhandle. **1932** *Sweet Loops* (film): I'll give you a lacing you'll never forge. **1966–70** in *DARE.*

b. *Baseball.* to hit (a ball) hard.
    1891 *Chi. Herald* (June 12) (cited in Nichols *Baseball Term*). **1908** in Fleming *Unforgettable Season* 233: The tenth inning saw Pittsburgh lace pitcher Crandall all over the farm.

c. to swindle.
    *a1971 J. Brown & A. Groff *Monkey* 74: I'd laced me one joker for eleven hundred dollars.

d. to shoot (with an automatic weapon); STITCH.
    1981 Ballenger *Terror* 54: I thought sure they'd lace us after they got the photos.

2. to add alcohol to (a drink). Now *S.E.* Hence, usu., **laced,** *ppl.*
    *1677 W. Wycherley *Plain Dealer,* in *OED2:* Let's go drink a dish of laced coffee, and talk of the times. *1815 W. Scott, in *OED2:* He had

his pipe and his tea-cup, the latter being laced with a little spirits. **1885** *Uncle Daniel's Story* 43: "What is the matter with that coffee?" "Nothing; it is only laced a little." "Laced? What's that?" "Why, I put a little brandy in it. That's all." **1950** F. Brown *Space* 30: "Let's have coffee."..."Want it laced?"...Within moments he came back with two cups of steaming *cafe royale*.

lace-curtain Irish *n.* successful, middle-class Irish-Americans.—sometimes used derisively. Cf. SHANTY IRISH.
   1929–34 J.T. Farrell *Young Manhood of Lonigan* 366: Hell, it was all artificial. They were all trying to put on the dog, show that they were lace-curtain Irish, and lived in steam-heat. **1947** in *DAS*: Those who have done rather better and become lace-curtain Irish...moved across the tracks. **1964** N.Y.C. man, age 21: *Lace-curtain Irish* means middle-class or rich Irish people in the United States. **1964** *PADS* (No. 42) 35: Lace-curtain Irish move into lower middleclass communities and work hard to approximate the ideals of vulgar respectability. **1985** Boyne & Thompson *Wild Blue* 17: We're Irish....But not lace-curtain Irish, not even shanty Irish. We're aluminum-window Irish. **1994** N.Y.C. woman, age *ca*60: *Lace-curtain Irish* means Irish-Americans who have become respectable and middle-class. I heard it in Brooklyn in the mid forties. **1994** Wagner & Miller *Out of Ireland* (PBS-TV): Large numbers of Irish worked themselves up from "shanty Irish" to "lace-curtain Irish."

lace curtains **1.** *n.pl.* a beard. *Joc.*
   1919 Darling *Jargon Book* 20: Lace Curtains—Whiskers. **1930** Irwin *Amer. Tramp & Und. Sl.* 118: Lace Curtains.—Whiskers, especially when full and verdant.

   2. usu. *pl. Homosex.* the foreskin. *Joc.* [The def. in the 1970 *AS* quot. appears to be simply a poor definition.]
   *1966 Partridge *DSUE* (ed. 6) 1218: *Lace curtain.* Foreskin: raffish; homosexual: C. 20. **1970** Major *Afro-Amer. Slang* 75: *Lace curtains*: the prepuce (homosexual term). **1970** *AS* XLV (Nos. 1–2) 57: *Lace curtains*...Genitalia of an uncircumcised male. **1972** *Anthro. Linguistics* (Mar.) 104: *Lace curtains* (n.): The prepuce (foreskin) of an uncircumcised male. *a*1989 in Goodwin *More Man* 92: *Lace curtains* is a gay term for the foreskin.

laced *adj.* **1.** see s.v. LACE, 2.
   2. [extended fr. ppl. of LACE, 2] intoxicated by alcohol or drugs.
   1988 Lewin & Lewin *Thes. Slang: Drunk*...knockered, laced [etc.]. **1994** A. Heckerling *Clueless* 42: It's one thing to spark up a doobie and get laced at parties.

laced jacket *n.* (see quot.).
   1824 in *DAE*: [Settlers] cut a few good hiccories [*sic*], and gave them what was called in those days a 'laced jacket,' that is a sound whipping.

lachie *n.* [< Sp *leche*] *Navy.* milk.
   1918 Ruggles *Navy Explained* 22: Milk is "lachie" (Spanish).

lacing see s.v. LACE.

lackanooky var. LAKANUKI.

lacy *adj.* effeminate.
   1941 Kendall *Army & Navy Sl.* 8: He's a bit lacy...girlish.

lacy-pants *n.* FANCY-PANTS.
   1940 in Galewitz *Great Comics* 46: If I haft'a run around in a monkey suit and act like a lacy pants—I hope they ain't gonna be no wedding! [**1988** von Hassel & Crossley *Warriors* 29: Graduates of Parris Island might refer to their counterparts from San Diego as "Lace Pants Marines" or "Hollywood Marines."]

ladder *n. Navy & USMC.* a stairway (of any sort). Cf. BULKHEAD.
   1986 L. Johnson *Waves* 33: In the Navy they are always pretending buildings are ships, calling the walls "bulkheads" and the stairs "ladders" and stuff. **1988** von Hassel & Crossley *Warriors* 164: Marines refer to...stairs as "ladders"...aboard ship or on shore.
¶ In phrases:
¶ **pull in the ladder** *Navy.* (see quots.). Also **pull the ladder up.**
   *1945 in Partridge *DSUE* (ed. 3) 1143: "Pull the ladder up, Jack, I'm all right"...had long been current [in the Royal Navy before 1942]. **1961** G. Forbes *Goodbye to Some* 156 [ref. to WWII]: Even Ainsworth is animated. He slaps people on the back and says over and over, "Well, I'm up. Pull in the ladder."

¶ **up Ladder Lane and down Hemp Street** *Naut.* up to a yardarm or gallows to be hanged. *Joc.*

1830 Ames *Mariner's Sketches* 228: As for hanging...sailors call it, "taking a walk up Ladder Lane, and down Hemp Street." **1849** Melville *Redburn* 80: When a man is hung at sea, which is always done from one of the lower yard-arms, they say he "*takes a walk up Ladder-Lane, and down Hemp-street.*"

la-di-da *n.* language or behavior characterized by affectation, pretension, or preciosity; (*hence*) a person notable for such behavior. Also vars. [Farmer & Henley, perh. erroneously, date the **ca*1883 quot. below as "1871."]
   1874 (quot. at LAVENDER, *adj.*). **1882** in L. Levy *Flashes of Merriment* 280: Oh, your [*sic*] a lally cooler, Pete, a reg'lar la-di-da. **ca*1883 in *OED2*: The young 'un goes to music-halls/And does the la-di-da. **1893* in *OED2*: That French brother of his, Frank, the Parisian la-de-da. **a*1890–96 *F & H* IV 155: La-di-da = a swell or fop. **1928** MacArthur *War Bugs* 198: There's that ten page la-de-da from Ruth. All sunshine, she is. **1935** F.H. Lea *Anchor Man* 15: He's no mincing la-de-dah. **1982** *Psychology Today* (Aug.) 60: I learned the vocabulary of la-di-da so I could hide behind words when I had to. *a*1982 Flexner *Listening to Amer.* 481: *La(h)-de-da(h)*...as the years go by the connotation is shifting from timid or unmanly boy to effeminate youth.

la-di-da *adj.* [shortening of earlier BrE *lardy-dardy*, perh. imit. of affected speech] affected; pretentious; precious in expression or manner. Also vars. Also as interj.
   [**1861* in *F & H* IV 156: With your *lardy-dardy* ways and your cold-blooded words.] [**1873* in Weekley *Etym. Dict. Mod. Eng.* 816: With our lardy-dardy garments we were really "on the spot."] *a*1889–90 in Barrère & Leland *Dict. Slang* II 7: A group...composed of *lah-de-dah* youths (now known as imitation dudes). **1895* in *OED2*: We are all homely girls. We don't want any la-di-da members. **1921* Weekley *Etym. Dict. Mod. Eng.* 816: *La-di-da*...Dates from the Sixties, but its great vogue was due to a music-hall song of 1880—He wears a penny flower in his coat, La-di-da! **1922–24** McIntyre *White Lights* 4: A la-de-dah soda fountain on Fifth Avenue that charges forty cents for a glass of soda water. **1935** Lorimer & Lorimer *Heart Specialist* 27: Those la-de-da Englishmen. **1952** *New Yorker* (Apr. 5) 37: She addressed to Emily cutting remarks couched in stilted language, and assumed a la-di-da manner. **1962** *N.Y. Times* (Oct. 21) VI 42: Most of his speech is today conventionally, but not consistently, la-di-da. **1976** in *Harper's* (Jan. 1977) 27: No liberal la-de-da lawyer was going to make him say anything more than he goddamn well pleased. **1985** Westin *Love & Glory* 379: You'd think they was a pack of la-de-da virgins. *a*1989 C.S. Crawford *Four Deuces* 10: Raised eyebrows and la-di-da smirks. **1993* J. Green *Slang Down Ages* 231: To act effeminately is to...*swish*...; effeminate is *la-di-dah*. **1994** *N.Y. Times Mag.* (July 17) 36: We come by bus—"motorcoach," if you want to get la-di-da about it.
¶ In phrase:
¶ **la-di-da land** LA-LA LAND, 2.
   1987 in K. Marshall *Combat Zone* 171: Going over we were all still in la-di-da land. We probably said, "Isn't it great that we're going to Vietnam!" We hadn't the foggiest idea of what we were doing or what we were getting ourselves into.

Ladies from Hell *n.pl.* [in joc. reference to the kilts] *Army.* a kilted Scottish Highland regiment. *Joc.* Now *hist.* Also vars.
   1918 in *Wisc. Mag. of History* LXII 235: The Ladies from hell, about to "go over the top." **1918** *Camp Pike Carry-On* (Dec. 19) 6: "Ladies of Hell," as they called the Scotch highlanders. **1982* W.R. Dunn *Fighter Pilot* 18 [ref. to 1940]: The "Imperial Seaforths" of the British Army—"The Ladies from Hades." **1988** *Daily News* (N.Y.) (June 21) 8: It was brave lads like these who came to be called "The Ladies From Hell" during World War I.

lady *n.* [cf. OLD LADY] **1.a.** one's girlfriend. [Common only from late 1960's.]
   1893 Hill *Rhet. & Comp.* 280: The *drummer* wired his *lady* that he had been *jugged.* *a*1890–96 *F & H* IV 141: *Lady*...(American).—A sweetheart. **1962** T. Berger *Reinhart in Love* 189: I don't want to embarrass your lady. **1966** in *Trans-action* IV (Apr. 1967) 7: If I have a good lady and she's on County [Welfare], there is always some money to get. **1969** in *Playboy* (Jan. 1970) 77: And his lady is afraid as hell that she can't fulfill her fantasy role as an erotic amazon. **1974** *Police Woman* (NBC-TV): Just because she parked her butt on my bike a couple of times don't mean she's my lady. **1982** P. Michaels *Grail* 146: Asked him if he wanted his lady to be found like that. **1982** *World's*

Finest Comics (Sept.) (unp.): Like I told your lady—I only play by my *own* rules.

b. *Pris.* one's effeminate homosexual partner.

1932 L. Berg *Prison Doctor* 119: I'm going to cut your heart out and feed it to the dogs. I'll teach you to leave my "lady" alone!

c. *Prost.* a prostitute, usu. as associated with a particular pimp.

1972 *Urban Life & Culture* I 417: They accept the idea that they are not a "qualified ho" until they are so-and-so's lady. **1975** (cited in J. Green *Dict. Contemp. Slang* 164). *a***1984** Sereny *Invisible Children* 43: At fourteen she became a runaway and the "main lady" of Lucky, a twenty-nine-year-old player. *Ibid.* 44: Big Daddy…had all those ladies, nine then. **1985** *Children of the Night* (TV movie): I used to be Spanish's main lady!

2. *Cards.* a queen in a deck of cards.

1900 *DN* II 44: *Lady,* n. Queen at cards. **1928** Hecht & MacArthur *Front Page* 445: Two Johns. Ladies. **1928** Guerin *Crime* 31: The three-card trick…and all those…variants of "finding the lady." **1939** de Leon et al. *Union Pacific* (film): You'll die with your boots on. And your four ladies won't be walkin' behind you. **1963** *Sat. Eve. Post* (Mar. 23) 35: Eight, Lady…Twin cowboys. Ah can't play no more. **1964** *Fugitive* (ABC-TV): "What have you got?" "Pair of ladies." **1970** Hatch *Cedarhurst* 175: Two pair of queens…Four Ladies. **1981** Ballenger *Terror* 117: Anybody beat these three ladies?

3. Esp. *USMC.* a recruit in basic training.—used contemptuously. [A term used by drill instructors.]

1965 in *Nat. Observer* (May 3, 1975) D: The DI…just calls his platoon *ladies* habitually, *girls* when they have disappointed him as a group and *sweetheart* when the old DI would have employed stupid. (He used to use these terms [in WWII] only for emphasis; what is new is their frequency.). **1978** Hasford *Short-Timers* 4: If you ladies leave my island, if you survive recruit training, you will be a weapon. **1980** M. Baker *Nam* 39: All right, ladies. You look like shit, so we're going to do a little PT now. **1983** Ehrhart *VN–Perkasie* 31 : You scuzzy shitbirds are *mine,* ladies. **1988** C. Roberts & C. Sasser *Walking Dead* 17: Saddle up, ladies. First four over the side. Second four, stand by. **1989** Care *Viet. Spook Show* 53: I would suggest that you ladies buddy up.

4. [sugg. by WHITE LADY] *Narc.* cocaine.

[**1969** Lingeman *Drugs A to Z* 122: *Lady snow* cocaine.] **1974** Weisman & Boyer *Heroin Triple Cross* 79: I'll give 'em a taste of smack. And I'll give you a snort of lady. **1978** Diehl *Sharkey's Machine* 44: Take a little taste o' the lady here and you won't give a shit how cold it is. **1979** *N.Y. Times Mag.* (Nov. 14) 20: Names for cocaine ("nose candy," "toots," "lady," "pearl"). **1985** K. O'Connell *End of Line* 54: Names for cocaine…toot, blow, lady, and snow.

5. (*cap.*) *N.Y.C.* the Statue of Liberty.

1986 WINS radio news (June 26): The Lady's isn't the only grand opening in New York next weekend.

ladyfinger *n.* a weak or effeminate fellow.

1942 *ATS* 372: Weakling; coward…*lady-finger.* **1976** Hayden *Voyage* 470: This is something you ladyfingers don't never take into account.

lady five-fingers var. WIDOW FIVE-FINGERS.

lady-killer *n.* a man who is or who fancies himself to be irresistible to women. Now *colloq.*

1825** "Blackmantle" *English Spy* I 170: Captain P—r—y, a perfect lady-killer. ***1839** C. Lever, in *F & H* IV 142: I believe your regular *lady-killer*…becomes a very quiet animal for being occasionally jilted. **a1848** Thackeray *Vanity Fair* ch. xiii: I don't set up to be a lady-killer. **1849** [G. Thompson] *Countess* 11: Young gentlemen who styled themselves…"lady-killers." **1860** Victor *Alice Sylde* 55: Some other…lady-killer like the one that's given her the mitten. **1874** Pinkerton *Expressman* 97: He was…remarkably good looking…and in Philadelphia he was known as a perfect "lady-killer." **1909** in O. Johnson *Lawrenceville Stories* 115: You lady-killers! **1917** in R. Peyton *At Track* 151: This here lady-killer…thinks he can pick 'em. **1939** Appel *People Talk* 351: He was quite a lady-killer. He had a deep dramatic voice and a theatric manner. **1958** J. Thompson *Getaway* 3: Didn't figure I'd know you were the town lady-killer. **1971** Michelson *Very Simple Game* 81: No, I wasn't a lady-killer. **1978** De Christoforo *Grease* 89: He's such a lady-killer. **1990** in N. George *Buppies, B-Boys* 176: The zoot-suited lady-killer. **1995** *TV Guide* (Knoxville-Chattanooga ed.) (Mar. 18) 42: The lady-killer of UPN's *Pig Sty.*

Lady Lex *n.* *Navy.* the aircraft carrier U.S.S. *Lexington.*

[There have been two aircraft carriers with this name in service in the U.S. Navy.]

1948 S.E. Morison *Naval Ops.* III 235 [ref. to WWII]: It had to be "Sara" rather than "Lady Lex" or the "Big E." **1993** Ebbert & Hall *Crossed Currents* 249: In 1980…7 women officers and 130 enlisted women…reported to "Lady Lex."

lady-love *v.* [back formation from LADY-LOVER] to engage in lesbian activity.

1934 Burns *Female Convict* 77: They've been lady-loving—and they don't want the bull to catch them at it!

lady-lover *n.* a woman who is homosexual; lesbian.—usu. used contemptuously.

1921 in J. Katz *Gay/Lesbian Almanac* 401: The "fairy" and the lady lover. *a***1927** in P. Smith *Letter from Father* 83: She stoutly contended that Dorothea…was not a lady-lover. **1934** Burns *Female Convict* 160: It's the dope addicts and lady-lovers running back to their own cells before morning inspection. **1937** Reitman *Box-Car Bertha* 94: Keep away from them, too. They're lady lovers. **1952** Lait & Mortimer *USA* 43: The lady-lovers are now…firmly entrenched. **1954** Caprio *Female Homosexuality* 310: *Lady Lover.* A slang term for a lesbian. **1967** Colebrook *Cross of Lassitude* 155: Beppo is a "bull-dagger," a "low dyke," a "lady-lover."

lag *n.* **1.** *Pris.* a convicted felon, esp. one long imprisoned; (*occ.*) an ex-convict. Now *rare* in U.S. [In earliest Brit. use, usu. a convict transported for penal servitude.]

***1811** *Lex. Balatron.*: *Lag*…a man transported. ***1828** in *F & H* IV 142: A few are returned *lags.* **1856** "H. Hazel" *Jack Waid* 10: I 'ired myself out…to a rich lag. **1859** Matsell *Vocab.* 49: *Lag.* A convicted felon. **1868** Macy *There She Blows!* 290: I'm an escaped convict…or, as I should say, a runaway lag. ***1881–84** Davitt *Pris. Diary* I 161: *Broadmoor* for all laggs as go off their chump. **1886** P.D. Haywood *Cruise* 5 [ref. to Civil War]: The fellow was told…we didn't want any "Limehouse lags" in our society. **1888** in *Amer. Heritage* (Oct. 1979) 21: I've had conversazioné with the learned "lags" and tony [at Sing Sing]. **1899** Cullen *Tales* 164: I t'ought by your looks you might ha' b'en a lag…and w'en you answered th' signal I knowed it. **1906** *Nat. Police Gaz.* (Sept. 22) 6: I'd rather…hook up with an old lag for the ride to the pen than the new ones bound over the road for their first bit.…When a lag's getting back to a pen where he's put in time before. **1931** D. Runyon, in *Colliers'* (May 16) 12: They are both trained…to track down…lags who escape from the county pokey. **1954** McGraw *Prison Riots* 269: Young men are thrown together in crowded conditions with old lags.… *Lag:* A jailbird, usually of long-standing. ***1993** J. Green *Slang Down Ages* 330: *Lag*…now means no more than a prisoner.

2. *Und.* (see quots.).

1914 Jackson & Hellyer *Crim. Slang* 53: *Lag.* Noun. Current amongst statutory criminals. A prison sentence of one year; sometimes used to signify an indefinite term of years in prison.…Also used as a verb as the equivalent of "railroading" a criminal to prison. **1930** Irwin *Tramp & Und. Sl.* 118: *Lag.*—A prison sentence, usually of a year or more.

lag *v.* *Und.* **1.** to convict or sentence; send to prison. [In earliest Brit. use, usu. to transport for penal servitude.]

***1797** in Partridge *Dict. Und.* 394: *Lagged,* transported. ***1811** [T. Moore] *Tom Crib* 78: A relative of poor Crockey, who was *lagged* some time since. ***1811** *Lex. Balatron.*: *The cove was lagged for a drag.* The man was transported for stealing something out of a waggon. ***1865** in *Comments on Ety.* (Jan. 1995) 26: May I be "lag'd" if I ain't in love! ***1873** Hotten *Slang Dict.* (ed. 4): *Lagged,* imprisoned, apprehended, or transported for a crime. ***1881–84** Davitt *Prison Diary* I 152: *I did a snatch near St. Paul's, was collared, lagged, and got this bit of seven stretch*.…I attempted to steal a watch near St. Paul's, but was taken again, convicted, and sentenced to seven years' penal servitude. ***1889–90** Barrère & Leland *Dict. Slang.* II 3: *Lag, to*…to send…to prison. **1914** (quot. at LAG, *n.*, 2). **1926** Nichols & Tully *Twenty Below* 56: She's the one got me lagged last time I was jolted. **1933** in D. Runyon *More Guys* 10: The G-guys finally lag me for not paying the government its share of wrong money.

2. to place under arrest; apprehend.—also used fig., as in 1878 quot. Now *rare* in U.S.

***1835** Marryat *Midshipman Easy* 163: HI'll hamend and lead a good life—a drop of water—oh! *lagged* at last! ***1838** Glascock *Land Sharks* I

197: I had the misfortun' to be lagged one day, and was sent across the water, where I reg'larly sarved my seven years' 'prenticeship. **1867** *Nat. Police Gaz.* (Apr. 20) 2: If you like to take that you can have it; if you don't then "lag" me. I haven't a b—y cent left. ***1870** in Davitt *Prison Diary* I 151: I was in quod, doin 14 days when I heerd you was lagged. **1878** Willis *Our Cruise* 119: De master-at-legs my coat did lag/And put it into de lucky bag. ***1881–84** Davitt *Prison Diary* I 23: They declare this to be the way in which they are "lagged" (arrested) when not taken in the performance of a "job." **1899** A.H. Lewis *Sandburrs* 10: She says he's got to got to woik; he'll get lagged if he don't. **1899** Gunter *Bradford* 41: Dalton swore he'd never be lagged alive. **1902** F.P. Dunne *Observations* 15: Maybe he does an' maybe he don't; but annyhow that's what he's lagged f'r. **1903** A.H. Lewis *Boss* 17: I want her lagged too. **1911** A.H. Lewis *Apaches of N.Y.* 49: The Dropper having been lagged for robbery, and safely caged. **1927** "M. Brand" *Pleasant Jim* 17: A lot of hard-boiled gents with a U.S. marshal at their head may try to lag you. **1935** Pollock *Und. Speaks*: Lagged, arrested. **1955** in D.W. Maurer *Lang. of Und.* 245: *Lag.* v.t. To arrest.

3. to execute by hanging.

    1848 *Ladies' Repository* VIII (Oct.) 315: *Lagg*, To hang. *Lagged*, hung.

lagging *n.* *Und.* a prison term. Now *rare* in U.S. [In earliest Brit. use, a sentence of transportation for penal servitude, as in bracketed quots. below.]

    [***1812**, ***1818**, ***1823**, ***1827**, etc., cited in Partridge *Dict. Und.* 395.] **1888** Bidwell *Forging His Chains* 64: They run us in and by the time the "lagging" is done we are…ready for another splurge. **1935** Pollock *Underworld Speaks* 50: *Lagging*, a prison sentence. ***1942** in Partridge *Und. Dict.*

Lah *n.* Los Angeles, Calif. *Joc.* Cf. LA-LA LAND.

    1978 Maupin *Tales of City* 262: "Good ol' Lah." "Huh?" "Lah. L.A.…L.A. is Lah. S.F. is Sif."

lah var. LA.

laid *adj.* *Black E.* **1.** LAID-BACK, 2.

    1962 H. Simmons *On Eggshells* 174: He stayed laid all the time. **1972** Claerbaut *Black Jargon* 71: *Laid to the bone*…drunk. *a***1994** Smitherman *Black Talk* 151: *Laid*…High on liquor or drugs.

2. well-furnished or well-dressed.

    1972 Claerbaut *Black Jargon* 71: *Laid crib*…a nice house; attractive residence. **1974** V.E. Smith *Jones Men* 134: You really got it laid in here. **1978** *UTSQ*: Well-dressed…*laid*. *a***1994** Smitherman *Black Talk* 151: *Laid*…Stylishly dressed.

laid-back *adj.* **1.** relaxed or easygoing; unconcerned; casual; unhurried; (also, esp. of popular music) soothing. Now *colloq.*

    1969 *Harper's* (July) 60: The argot of rock.…The instrument is your "axe."…Something serious is "heavy," something relaxed "laid back." **1970** Landy *Underground Dict.* 118: She is a laid-back chick. **1972** Wurlitzer *Quake* 14: You just lie there thinking you're some kind of laid-back local star. **1972** N.Y.U. student: Nobody's *that* laid-back. ***1973** in *OEDS*: This hit-writer…came out with a highly contemporary style which fitted the fashionable term "laid-back." **1974** in R.S. Gold *Jazz Talk* 159: It's a simple, tasteful, laid-back session. **1977** N.Y.C. man, age 29: Leisure suits are supposed to give you that kind of laid-back look. **1980** J. Carroll *Land of Laughs* 52: She's a hip lady. Very laid-back. **1980** in *Penthouse* (Jan. 1981) 130: We were both totally mellow and laid back and happy. **1984** J. Green *Dict. Contemp. Sl.* 164: *Laid back*…soothing, peaceful, passive, calm: used both of people and music. **1985–88** in Terkel *Great Divide* 72: I run a real laid-back insurance business. *a***1988** D. Smith *Firefighters* 32: I like the job real well. On the midnight shift, it's pretty laid back. **1991–93** W.T. Grant *Wings of Eagle* 169 His energy complemented the laid-back Sugar Bear. **1994** *Inside Politics* (CNN-TV) (Dec. 2): Is Robert Dole too laid-back to be Majority Leader? **1995** *New Yorker* (May 8) 94: Sexy and involving, scrappy and laid-back, "Burnt by the Sun" is a wonderful [film].

2. stupefied by drugs or alcohol. [Perh. the orig. sense; cf. LAID, 1 and LAID OUT, 1.]

    1973 Univ. Mich. student: When you're very drunk or very stoned you're *laid back*. **1975, 1981** (cited in Spears *Drugs & Drink*).

laid out *adj.* **1.** stupefied by alcohol.

    1928 *AS* IV 102. **1931** *AS* VII 81ff. **1934** Weseen *Dict. Slang*. **1978** *UTSQ*: [Drunk]…*laid out, bombed, happy.*

2. *Black E.* attractive or well-dressed.

    1968–70 *Current Slang Cum.* III 78: *Laid out*, adj. Handsome or

attractive.—College students, both sexes, Negro, Ohio. **1989** Spears *NTC Dict. Slang* 219: Look at those silks! Man, are you laid out!

lain var. LANE.

lakanuki *n.* [respelling, in joc. imit. of a Polynesian word, of *lack of* + NOOKY] Esp. *Mil.* lack of sexual activity, facetiously regarded as an illness. *Joc.* Also vars.

    *ca***1944** in Valant *Aircraft Nose Art* 295: Lakanuki. **1944** Barracks sign, 7th Weather Squadron, USAAF, Canton I., (photo in coll. of W. Miller): Hotel Lakanooki. **1945** in Campbell & Campbell *P-51* 11: Lacka Nookie. **1952** H. Grey *Hoods* 103: And you look like you're suffering from that rare Hawaiian disease…Lack a nooky. **1956** Waldhorn *Concise Amer. Dict.* 115: *Nooky*. Slang. Sexual intercourse; vulva. In WWII, a common joke was that soldiers in the Pacific theater died of a tropical disease called *lackanookie*. **1962** W. Crawford *Give Me Tomorrow!* 188: That rare Hawaiian disease lack-a-nookie. **1966** Cassiday *Angels Ten* 63: That old Hawaiian disease, laka-nuki. **1966** Brunner *Face of Night* 99: "I know what it is, it's that Hawaiian disease," Larry grinned. "Lackanookie." **1967** Dibner *Admiral* 18: I won't bother you with the details of…human failures due to gunfire, wet pants, and that incurable Oriental illness called lakanuki. *a***1989** C.S. Crawford *Four Deuces* 268: Like that other rare Oriental disease "lacka-nooky."

La-La *n.* LA-LA LAND, 1.

    1996 *All Things Considered* (Nat. Pub. Radio) (July 2): La-La, New York, and Washington.

lala *n.* **1.** var. LOLLA.

2. the buttocks.

    1974 in Mamet *Sexual Perversity* 52: Do you want me walking around with a naked la-la?

La-La Land *n.* **1.** Los Angeles, Calif. Cf. LOTUSLAND. *Joc.*

    1984 Blumenthal *Hollywood* 163: Nicknames for "The Coast"…*La-La Land*…*Tinseltown*. **1986** R. Campbell *In La-La Land* 13: That's the way things happen on a rainy night in La-La Land. **1987** Trudeau *My G-G-Generation* (unp.): I do deals out in La-La Land. *a***1988** C. Adams *More Straight Dope* 149: Building a gigantic sand castle in La-La Land is sure to make the world aggressors think twice. **1988** *CBS This Morning* (CBS-TV) (Dec. 30): In sports, the Dodgers and Lakers brought glory to La-La Land. **1991** *Morning Report* (CNN-TV) (June 21): Last night in La-La Land the Dodgers ran their win streak to five. **1994** *Details* (July) 74: We leave La-La-land and fly to Australia. **1995** *Talk Back Live* (CNN-TV) (June 6): With little impact being felt beyond La-La Land.

2. (*l.c.*) a state of being out of touch with reality; dreamland; (*also*) a state of drunkenness.—usu. constr. with *in*.

    1985 *Night Court* (NBC-TV): He's in la-la land, sir. **1989** Ganz & Mandel *Parenthood* (film): Come back from la-la land—because it *ain't* gonna happen! **1989** *Donahue* (NBC-TV): You're living in la-la land because that has nothing [to do with reality]. **1990** *Inside Edition* (synd. TV series): And they go off into la-la land. **1992** *Donahue* (NBC-TV): I think this columnist is kind of in la-la land. It's all unreal. **1993** *N.Y. Times* (Jan. 10) 4A 21: Stanford is a multicultural la-la land.…It's not the real world. **1993** *L.A. Times* (Oct. 27) E3: We all do it—we daydream, we drift into la-la land. **1994** *Morning News* (CBS-TV) (Oct. 18): I must have been in la-la land.

lalapalooza var. LOLLAPALOOZA.

lallycooler var. LOLLYCOOLER.

lallygag var. LOLLYGAG.

lam *n.* [perh. a development of LAM, *v.*, with which certain senses are associated here for convenience] **1.** *Pris.* an act of running or flight, esp. a dash to escape from custody; escape.—constr. with a word such as *make* or *do*.

    1897 *Pop. Sci. Mo.* (Apr.) 832: *To do a lam*, meaning to run. **1914** Jackson & Hellyer *Crim. Slang* 53: *Lam*…A hasty get-away; a running escape. "He heeled to the door and made a lam." **1928** Panzram *Killer* 158: *To make a lam*—to crush out of the hoosegow. **1929** Barr *Let Tomorrow Come* 209: Some vic made a lam. I hope he makes it stick. *ca***1935** in R.E. Howard *Iron Man* 129: Dutchy…took a lam with the gate receipts. **1936** Benton & Ballou *Where Do I Go?* 123: Jim…had made the sensational "lam"…two years before. *Ibid.* 132: An abortive "lam." **1943** Farrell *Days of Anger* 275: I stuck up a joint recently, and I had to take a lam. **1970** Rudensky & Riley *Gonif* 93: I was being hounded by the Feds for the lams.

2. a punch; blow. Cf. LAM, *v.*, 1.a.

1934 H. Roth *Call It Sleep* 292 [ref. to ca1915]: Wanna ged a lam onnuh eye?

¶ **In phrases:**

¶ **hit the lam** to *take it on the lam,* below.
1986–91 Hamper *Rivethead* 190: Free to flee….hittin' the lam.

¶ **on the lam, 1.** on the run; running; at top speed.—also used fig., as in 1948 quot.
1911 Bronson-Howard *Enemy to Society* 315: Take a taxicab….Go on the lamm, boys! **1922** J. Conway, in *Variety* (Jan. 13) 7: So I sent Merlin on the lam to our dressin' room for the old sneezin' powder. **1927** *DN* V 457: *On the lam,* adj. At top speed. **1948** Manone & Vandervoort *Trumpet* 65: I was on the lam again, winging around and finally winding up down in good old New Orleans 'cuz I decided to make a visit to the home folks. *a*1956 Almirall *College to Cow Country* 247: Now we had them [cattle] on the lam, as the saying went [in Colorado, *ca*1916].

2. *Orig. Und.* in flight or in hiding from authorities.—also used fig., as in 1992 quot. Cf. *take it on the lam,* below.
1928 *Amer. Mercury* XVI 475: On the Lam[,] by David Purroy….I had seen dozens of men framed…because they had records….So I…went—on the lam….Red…[was] on the lam from Buffalo. **1931** *AS* VI (Aug.) 439: *Lam, to be on the.* To be a fugitive from justice. **1940** Lawes *Meet the Murderer!* 187: This car's hot, and I'm on the lam. **1951** Bowers *Mob* (film): He's on the lam from New Orleans. **1955** Graziano & Barber *Somebody Up There* 27: Him and his brother is on the lam for armed holdup. **1962** Riccio & Slocum *All the Way Down* 37: She figures you're on the lam again. **1980** *N.Y. Post* (July 9) 5: Also on the lam is "Yippie" Abbie Hoffman, 43. He jumped bail in 1974 after being indicted in a $36,000 cocaine sale to a New York undercover cop. **1982** *Flash* (Dec.) 7: I never thought I'd be on the lam from Goldface and his whole syndicate. **1992** G. Wolff *Day at the Beach* 87: Middle class hoboes on the lam from the burbs. **1993** *Sally Jessy Raphäel* (synd. TV series): He went on the lam and changed his name. **1994** *Donahue* (NBC-TV): This guy is on the lam for how long?

¶ **take it on the lam** *Orig. Und.* to run away; flee, esp. from authorities; escape.
1904 *Life in Sing Sing* 263: He plugged the main guy and I took it on a lam for mine. **1921** J. Conway, in *Variety* (Mar. 11) 7: I…expect to get word any day now to…take it on the lam. **1922** *Variety* (June 30) 6: Two of the touts had to take it on the lam and were lucky to get out of town. **1926** Maines & Grant *Wise-Crack Dict.* 15: *Take it on the Lamm*—Run away. **1927** *Vanity Fair* (Nov.) 132: "Take it on the lam" is making a quick getaway or hurried disappearance. **1927–28** Tasker *Grimhaven* 40: Did you ever think about taking it on the lam? **1930** *Collier's* (Jan. 20) 12: Louie…takes it on the lam through an areaway. **1932** Mankiewicz & Myer *Million Dollar Legs* (film): Come my dear, we must take it on the lam. **1942** Millhauser *Big Shot* (film): I ain't going to do anything. Except take it on the lam. **1958–59** Lipton *Barbarians* 112: I'll take it on the lam. Hide out in Mexico. **1981** G. Wolf *Roger Rabbit* 171: We'd better take it on the lam before he gets back.

lam *v.* [orig. dial., perh. ult. of Scand. origin] **1.a.** to beat, pound, or strike (usu. a person).
*1595 in *N & Q* CCXXVII (1982) 401: His wife sore lamming him. *1596 in *OED: Defusto,* to lamme or bumbast with strokes. *1611 Cotgrave *Dict.: Gaulée*…a cudgelling, basting, thwacking, lamming. *1636 in *OED:* They will not sticke to strip and lamme them soundly. *1710 in *F & H* IV 146: A fellow whom he lambed most horribly. *1748 in *F & H* IV 146: *Lamb*…to thresh or beat severely. *1783 in *OED:* Lammed, *Verberatus.* **1848** Baker *Glance at N.Y.* 19: When them fellers come mussin' round 'im, I'll lam 'em. **1849** in *Calif. Hist. Qly.* LXIII (1984) 316: I'll lam yer…if you git in over my berth. **1850** "N. Buntline" *G'hals of N.Y.* 16: Why, *lam* 'em! I'd 'a done it! *a*1852 in *F & H* IV 146: He seed er fellow he thought he could lamm without no danger. **1855** in S. Clemens *Twain's Letters* I 48: Will serve to enlighten you as to his reason for "lamming" the lady. *a*1860 Hundley *So. States* 194: Stout enough to give them a *lamming* in a regular fisticuffs fights. **1863** in Stanard *Letters* 2: I am…ready to give that [scamp] "Avril" a *laming* [sic]. **1862–64** Noel *Campaign* 73: In peace he was a lamb./In war a *lammer.* **1865** "M. Twain," in A.L. Scott *Twain's Poetry* 50: And "lam" like all creation / This infernal Tom Maguire! **1867** A.K. McClure *Rocky Mtns.* 424: He will lam the "chick" certain, you *bet.* **1882** *Judge* (Oct. 28) 7: We went for him sudden, an lammed him black and bloo. **1883–84** Whittaker *L. Locke* 156: I'd lam him. **1895** Gore *Stu. Slang* 21: *Lam it to him*…Lay on the blows well. **1913**

J. London *Valley of Moon* 221: An old woman…lammed the chief of police full in the face with a dead cat. **1916** S. Lewis *Job* 73: You don't believe any such ting. Or else you'd lam me. **1921–25** J. Gleason & R. Taber *Is Zat So?* 13: He shoulda lammed [him] once. **1931** Harlow *Old Bowery* 208: Lam hell out of 'em! **1926–35** Watters & Hopkins *Burlesque* 16: I've just been waitin' for a chance to lam her one. **1936** J.T. Farrell *World I Never Made* 123: I'll lam the shit out of you! **1941** Hargrove *Pvt. Hargrove* 44: Salt pork, which you rarely see in the Army, is called *lamb chop.* "They lam it against the wall to get the salt out of it and then they chop it up into the beans." **1942** Z.N. Hurston *Dust Tracks* 43: Lam hell out of 'em with the first lick and keep on lamming.

b. to defeat decisively, esp. in a fistfight; drub.
1848 Bartlett *Amer.: To Lam*….To beat soundly; to drub. **1860** Hundley *So. States* 224: Yankees fight! Blamnation, man, we'd lam 'em afore they could say Jack Robinson! **1861** in F. Moore *Rebel. Rec.* I 137: The sovereign State of Alabama/Will try her hand before they lam her. **1871** "M. Twain" *Roughing It:* He could lam any galoot of his inches in America.

c. *Specif.,* (*Sports.*) to strike (a ball) hard.
*a*1890 in Barrère & Leland *Dict. Slang* II 5: To lamm the ball to a certain and distant part of the ground. **1908** in Fleming *Unforgettable Season* 257: Herr Beecher lammed out another three-bagger. **1914** in R. Lardner *Round Up* 268: Doyle…lams it up against the fence.

2.a. *Esp. Und. & Police.* to abscond; make an escape (from); flee; (*hence*) (now *rare*) to run.—sometimes constr. with *out*; rarely with *it.*
1886 A. Pinkerton *30 Yrs. Detective* 41: After he has secured the [victim's] wallet, he will utter the word "lam!" This means…to get out of the way as soon as possible. **1893** F.P. Dunne, in Schaaf *Dooley* 54: Mack,…lam over with me to the A-art Institoot. **1902** Cullen *More Tales* 40: I couldn't lam away from him. **1904** *Life in Sing Sing* 250: *Lam*—To run. **1906** Green *Boarding House* 327: Has he lammed with the bankroll? **1908** Hopper & Bechdolt *9009* 109: Thought you'd lam out, eh? *a*1909 Tillotson *Detective* 93: *Lam*—To run. **1911** A.H. Lewis *Apaches of N.Y.* 130: For my end of it I'm goin to lamm. **1914** Jackson & Hellyer *Vocab.* 53: *Lam,* verb…to run; to flee. Most frequently employed in the imperative mood. **1918** in *AS* (Oct. 1933) 29: *Lamb.* To escape. **1919** *DN* V 41: *Lam* v.i. To run. **1930** Conwell *Pro. Thief* 95: Sometimes it is necessary to lam (leave the jurisdiction) and forfeit the bond. **1931** Rynning *Gun Notches* 12: We turned southeast and kept lamming beside the North Fork of the Canadian. **1932** in *AS* (Feb. 1934) 27: *Lam the joint.* To escape from prison. **1933** Mahin & Furthman *Bombshell* (film): You better lam out to her house right now. **1933** Creelman & Rose *King Kong* (film): You gotta lam back and get some more bombs. **1932–34** Minehan *Boy & Girl Tramps* 42: Then he bangs me with a chair, and I lams it. **1936** Kenyon & Daves *Petrified Forest* (film): Boss, let's lam out of here. **1939** *AS* (Oct.) 240: *To lam.* To leave without paying. **1940** Zinberg *Walk Hard* 14: Some of these cops are a little nuts. You'd better lam. **1942** Liebling *Telephone* 24: When trouble comes he lams and leaves me with the grief. **1943** M. Shulman *Barefoot Boy* 122: Mind your business or lam out of here. **1955** Q. Reynolds *HQ* 74: Malone comes back and says they've lammed. **1958** J. Thompson *Getaway* 35: Might even lam out on us. **1960** Barber *Minsky's* 261: One-Eye,…less lam outta here. **1965** Himes *Imabelle* 130: We're lamming, ain't we? **1970** Terkel *Hard Times* 33: We lam out of there, too. We grab the midnight freight and get off at Phoenix. **1974** L.D. Miller *Valiant* 126: Maybe they lammed out too. **1980** D. Hamill *Stomping Ground* 160: Kids whose father lammed and whose mother was fourteen. **1990** A. Baraka, in T. McMillan *Breaking Ice* 53: We'll…lam outa here. **1993** A. Lomax *Where Blues Began* 7: Let's lam outa this town.

b. *Und.* to chase.
1934 in Horwitt *Call Me Rebel* 28: To illustrate, if the question, "Have you ever been chased by the police while you were in a stolen car and have the police shoot at you" is phrased "Have you ever been in a hot short and got lammed by the heat and have them toss slugs at you," a warmer and more responsive answer usually results.

lamb *n.* **1.** a victim of criminals; SUCKER; (*Stock Market*) a gullible investor.
*1666–68 in *F & H* IV 145: They call him a *lamb*; then a rook (who is properly the wolf) follows him close and…gets all his money, and then they smile and say, "The lamb *is bitten.*" **1886** in *OED:* A recent estimate…puts the amount of which the "lambs" in this New York stock market alone at eight hundred million dollars a year. *a*1889–90 Barrère & Leland *Dict. Slang* II 4: *Lamb*…name formerly given to a

dupe, now a "pigeon," [etc.]. **1890** Quinn *Fools of Fortune* 186: Even "suckers" are known [in the stock exchanges], but they are termed "lambs." **1925** *Collier's* (Aug. 8) 30: The lamb (victim) has...beefed. **1966** R.E. Alter *Carny Kill* 109: I sure hate to give a lamb a fleecing. *a***1990** P. Dickson *Slang!* 62: *Lamb.* Inexperienced investor.

2. Esp. *Pris.* a catamite.

1922 N. Anderson *Hobo* 148: The investigator during his study of this phase of the tramp problem made two unsuccessful attempts to step between men and their boys, or "lambs." **1927** (quot. at PUNK). **1932–34** Minehan *Boy & Girl Tramps* 143: I have seen wolves and their little "lambs" or "fairies." **1954** Gaddis *Birdman* 91: He had seen the wolves and the lambs, the pathetic and fantastic "marriages" between prisoners.

lambchop *n.* an attractive girl.

1985 in "J.B. Briggs" *Drive-In* 302: The fifteen-year-old lambchop who goes to high school in the daytime and then goes down to Hollywood Boulevard.

lamby *n. Naut.* a heavy woolen overcoat. Also **lammy**. [Prob. erroneously, Farmer & Henley date the *1886 quot. to 1866.]

[*1886 in *OED*: The look-out, who, wrapped in his lammy suit, was stationed in the bows.] **1894** J. Slocum *Liberdade* 16: With the same old "lamby" on. *a***1890–96** *F & H* IV 149: *Lammy*...(nautical).—A blanket: originally a thick quilted frock, or jumper made of flannel or blanket cloth, worn by sailors as an outside garment in cold weather. *a***1950** W. Granville *Sea Slang* 141: *Lammy.* A duffel coat. A cowled overcoat made of lamb's wool and worn by men in severe weather.

lame *n.* [cf. LANE] **1.a.** Orig. *Black E.* a person who is LAME; fool; idiot. Occ. **lamer**.

1958 Motley *Epitaph* 209: They're nothing, they're nobody. In other words, they're lames. **1959–60** R. Reisner *Jazz Titans* 160: *Lame, a:* One who doesn't know what's happening, unsophisticated. **1961** Peacock *Valhalla* 365 [ref. to 1953]: They were all positive...that he was not a *pogue*, or a *lamer*, but was, in fact, one of them. **1964** R.S. Gold *Jazz Lexicon* 181: *Lame*...an unsophisticated, unaware person...currency since c. 1950. **1965** C. Brown *Manchild* 164: I couldn't let this bitch get into the cocaine while I just sat there like a lame. **1966** Reynolds & McClure *Freewheelin Frank* 149: I can very quickly put the lames who believe in the Bible down in their ignorant place. **1970** Thackrey *Thief* 195: What kind of a lame did they think they were talking to, anyway? Crazy stuff! Weird! **1970** Cain *Blueschild Baby* 25: This is how a sucker gets taken off. Those sick "junkies hanging round down there laying for a lame copping dope." **1970** A. Young *Snakes* 19: There's this little local lame that's tryna make it with Cyrano's cousin Roxanne. **1978** Selby *Requiem* 15: The lames and squares all make it home from the 9 to 5 and sit down to a dinner with the wife and kids. **1985** Flowers *Mojo Blues* 107: She and this lame...sat across from him. **1994** N. McCall *Wanna Holler* 25: If a guy wore...cheap, off-brand shit...he was dismissed as a lame.

b. *Und.* a noncriminal; SQUARE; (*hence*) one who may be taken advantage of; victim.

1968 Heard *Howard St.* 176: She was a whore...in love with a lame. **1968–70** in Agar *Ripping & Running* 161: *Lame*...[among addicts] Non-drug user. **1973** *N.Y. Post* (Apr. 24) 33: We spotted the "lame" (prison word for victim) and decided to take him off....Almost all my "lames" were white men—that's where all the money was. **1977** *Urban Life* VI 134: Some [muggers] will see women or old people as ideal "lames." *a***1985** Schwendinger & Schwendinger *Adolescent Subcult.* 171: They are called Lames because they cannot defend themselves against violence.

2. *Narc.* a tobacco cigarette (as opposed to a marijuana cigarette).

1967 Kolb *Getting Straight* 88: Jake...got out a pack of regular cigarettes. "Want a lame?"

lame *adj.* **1.** [sugg. by LAME DUCK, 1.a.] bankrupted by speculation or gambling.

1854 G.G. Foster *15 Mins.* 15: Wall Street and The Merchants' Exchange...who is "short," who is "lame," who has been "cornered." *a***1961** Scarne *Comp. Guide to Gambling* 683: *Lame, (To come up)* to be unable to pay off lost wagers with a bookmaker. "Jake came up lame and took a powder."

2. Esp. *Black E.* socially unsophisticated; naive; SQUARE; (*hence*) easily imposed upon; stupid; inept; ineffectual. Also as adv.

1935 C. Calloway, in *Call of Jitterbug* (film): Don't be among the lame ones,/Keep up with the up-to-date ones! **1942** *ATS* 458: *Easy to take, lame,...strictly lame,* easily victimized. **1957** H. Simmons *Corner Boy* 90: She's going to college, so she wouldn't be lame. **1964** R.S. Gold *Jazz Lexicon* 181: *Lame*...unaware, unsophisticated, inexperienced. **1964** H. Rhodes *Chosen Few* 93: "Ain't that about th' most freakish thing you ever heard of?" "Not quite, but it's kinda lame." **1964** Smith & Hoefer *Music* 4: A good many modern jazz pianists play lame. **1965** C. Brown *Manchild* 165: It would have been real lame to say anything about that to him, because this must have been something he did most every night. **1965** Conot *Rivers of Blood* 68: It was considered real lame if you didn't get high. **1970** A. Young *Snakes* 19: He let her old lame boyfriend move on into the picture an cop. **1972–73** in M.J. Bell *Brown's Lounge* 11: He's not lame. I'd trust him to take my back. **1983** *Reader's Digest Success with Words* 86: Black English...*lame*...(2) (adjective) "not fashionable, dull or boring" (3) (adjective) "stupid, ignorant." **1989** *Dream Street* (NBC-TV): Sometimes you are so lame!

3. Esp. *Black E.* of no interest or value; (*also*) contemptible; offensive; execrable.

1955 *AS* (Dec.) 303: *Lame* is the opposite of *solid.* **1959** F.L. Brown *Trumbull Pk.* 153: Arthur, man, what caused you to come to this lame joint? **1972** Claerbaut *Black Jargon* 71: *Lame*...uninteresting; dull; boring. **1976** C. Keane *Hunter* 65: A sick combination of insanity and meanness....Yup, the guy is lame....The cream of the crap. **1978** J. Webb *Fields of Fire* 76: But he was pulling some lame shit, man. Really bugging me. **1984** Mason & Rheingold *Slanguage*: Food at school is lame. **1985** *Hill St. Blues* (NBC-TV): This is *lame*, man! You didn't have to rat us out! **1992** L. Johnson *My Posse* 154: We got these lame candy bars for good answers [in class]. **1992** *Mystery Sci. Theater* (Comedy Central TV): That is so *lame!* He's rifling the mummy for change!

lamebrain *n.* a dolt; blockhead. Also as adj. Hence **lamebrained**, *adj.*

1919 Piesbergen *Overseas with Aero Squadron* 70: It was really too severe to call John by the awful cognomen of "Lame-brain." **1922** J. Conway, in *Variety* (Mar. 31) 8: He has a lame brained idea. **1932** Lorimer & Lorimer *Streetcars* 172: Hey, lame-brain! **1945** in *Calif. Folk. Qly.* V (1946) 388: Careless, unalert fellow...*meathead, knuckle-head,...twerp, lamebrain,* etc. *a***1946** in Logsdon *Whorehouse Bells* 115: Take the lame-brain from cold Colorado. **1948** Cozzens *Guard of Honor* 327: So this lame-brain opens it good and wide without a drop of oil in it and freezes both engines solid. **1968** *New Yorker* (Sept. 14) 58: None of your lame-brain philosophers ever cut any ice with me. *1972 in *OEDS*: Disaffected lamebrains. **1989** P. Benchley *Rummies* 46: The Emerald City spa for the rich and lamebrained. **1994** *Mystery Sci. Theater* (Comedy Central TV): Some lamebrain gets it into his head he can't make it on his own. **1995** *N.Y. Press* (Sept. 27) 9: His moronic so-called poems, and his left-wing lame-brain laments.

lame duck *n.* **1.a.** Orig. *Stock Market.* a person bankrupted by stockjobbing or financial speculation.

*1761 H. Walpole, in *OED*: Do you know what a Bull, and a Bear, and a Lame Duck are? *1766 in *F & H* IV 148: I shall perhaps be obliged to make use of your money, that in case of the worst I may not be a *lame duck*. *1771 D. Garrick, in *F & H* IV 148: The gaming fools are doves, the knaves are rooks, Change-alley bankrupts waddle out lame ducks. *1847 Thackeray *Vanity Fair* ch. xiii: Unless I see Amelia's ten thousand down you don't marry her. I'll have no lame duck's daughter in my family. **1851** W. Kelly *Ex. to Calif.* II 122: A miniature...of the Bull and Bear system was got into operation, which hatched its small clutch of lame ducks. **1855** [S. Hammett] *Capt. Priest* 246: The "Board"...pronounces...even on those unhappy wretches the "lame ducks," until they have satisfied their creditors. **1865** *Harper's Mag.* (Apr.) 616: "Lame ducks" [are speculators who] owe money which they can not pay. **1870** Medbery *Wall St.* 135: The "Lame Duck" is a broker who has failed to meet his engagements; and a "Dead Duck" is one who is absolutely bankrupt past all recovery. **1885** *Harper's Mag.* (Nov.) 842: [A broker caught by worthless securities] runs the risk of classification as a "gosling," or a "lame duck," who cannot meet his engagements, or a "dead duck," who is absolutely bankrupt. *1890 in *F & H* IV 148: We learn that it is actionable to call a stockbroker a *lame duck*, because on the Exchange "the word has acquired a particular meaning."

b. one not able to pay his way or to meet debts; DEADBEAT, 3.

1875 in Huckaby & Simpson *Tulip* 277: I sent him out into the country...looking after the "lame ducks"...but accomplished little.

Don't think him a good collector. **1905** U. Sinclair *Jungle* 295: "What's the matter with him?" "Just crazy drunk," said the [bartender]. "A lame duck, too....Youse had better call the wagon." **1919** *DN* V 65: Dialect Speech of High School Pupils... *lame-duck*, one who cannot pay his debts. "They had to sue that lame-duck over there for his board bill." New Mexico. **1928** C.T. Harris *Mem. Manhattan* 50: When I was on top of the heap I was "Commodore" Stockwell. When I was a heavy loser I was "Mister" Stockwell. When I was dead broke and a sure lame duck I was "that old red-headed cuss Stockwell."

2.a. a lame or incapacitated person, or one who is old, weak, or ineffective; invalid; (*hence*) someone or something of no use or value. [See note at **(b)**, below.]
    *1814 in Wetherell *Adventures* 249: We had...Waggons...in the rear to pick up [the] lame ducks [on the march]! **1863** in H.L. Abbott *Fallen Leaves* 168: Give my love to him & the other lame ducks. **1863** in *DAE*: In no event...could it [the Federal Court of Claims] be justly obnoxious to the charge of being a receptacle of "lame ducks" or broken down politicians. **1885** in S. Hale *Letters* 150: Family generally of ten persons. Chiefly hungry boys. Three very "lame ducks" in the kitchen. **1893** Wawn *So. Sea Islanders* 347: My right eye...had been a "lame duck" since 1859, when it was injured at Bombay. **1907** Corbin *Cave Man* 56: Andrews, he explained, was a chronically lame duck, who had disappointed every hope of reformation. **1915** *DN* IV 211: *Lame duck*... incompetent. "They...called him a *lame duck* because he was almost blind and couldn't steer straight." **1924** Le Fevre *Stockbroker* 244: They get rid of the good [investment] and keep the lame ducks. **1928** *AS* IV 123: *Lame duck*—"An inefficient person." **1956** M. Wolff *Big Nick.* 147: How do you really fit in with these frustrated lame ducks of yours? **1984** McInerny *Bright Lights* 46: The lame-duck husband. **1984** Mason & Rheingold *Slanguage*: Lame duck...annoying person.

b. *Specif.*, *(Pol.)* an elected official or legislative body whose term of office is nearing an end, esp. a legislator still in office after losing an election or a U.S. president not running for reelection.—often used attrib. Now *S.E.* [Though appearing in a political context and accepted by earlier dictionaries as the earliest ex. of this specif. sense, the 1863 *DAE* quot. at **(a)**, above, is more prudently placed there: "broken down politicians" are likely to be already out of office.]
    1910 in *DAE*: The Congress which assembled Monday for its last session is full of what they call "lame ducks," or representatives who failed of re-election and senators who will fail when the legislatures meet. **1922** *N.Y. Times* (Dec. 6) 18: Senator Norris is all for the plan "to have the convening of Congress moved up to avoid lame-duck Congresses." **1924** in *DAE*: A "lame duck" Congress is not likely to be very competent. **1934** Weseen *Dict. Slang* 361: *Lame duck*—A politician in office who has been defeated for re-election. **1948** *Amer. College Dict.*: *Lame duck*...a Congressman who has failed of re-election and is serving at the last session of his term. **1975** Boatner et al. *Dict. Amer. Idioms* 195: In the last year of their second terms, American presidents are lame ducks. **1982** Flexner *Listening to Amer.* 539: In 1932 the *Lame Duck Amendment*, the Twentieth Amendment to the Constitution, was passed, calling for Congress and each new Presidential administration to take office in January instead of March and eliminating the *lame duck session* of Congress. **1989** S. Robinson & D. Ritz *Smokey* 183: I knew what it meant to be a lame-duck President. **1994** Univ. Tenn. prof., age 50: You know [a senator serving the remainder of another's term but not running for reelection] is a lame duck. **1994** *World Today* (CNN-TV) (Nov. 29): The first lame-duck session of Congress since 1982....The last hurrah for the lame ducks on Capitol Hill.

3. *Naut. & Av.* a severely damaged or defenseless vessel or aircraft.
    *1876 in *OEDS*: A lame duck on the sea means a ship which has been more or less damaged while crossing the perilous ocean. **1928** F. Harlow *Making of Sailor* 273: The [damaged] ship, a proper "lame duck," wallowed in the sea throughout the night. *1933 in *OEDS*: Our old "lame duck" had not done so badly after all. **1941** *Sat. Review* (Oct. 4) 9: *Lame duck*. Damaged plane. **1943** Mears *Carrier* 112: Harry March told of shooting down a "lame duck," a float plane which was just taking off. **1958** Cope & Dyer *Petty Officer's Guide* (ed. 2) 353: *Lame Duck*. (slang). Damaged aircraft. **1961** L.G. Richards *TAC* 123: So he held that lame duck of his at 230 knots. **1985** Heywood *Taxi Dancer* 31: Powder Room, Powder Room. Dusty six is a lame duck, proceeding home direct.

4. *Mil.* a military discharge button; RUPTURED DUCK. Now *hist.*
    1945 in Shibutani *Co. K* 319: Lame duck [lapel pin].

lamehead *n.* LAMEBRAIN.
    1978 T. Wolfe, in *Harper's* (Mar.) 117: The next one of you peckerwoods who...refers to me as "you mollyfoggin' lamehead" is gonna get a new hole in his nose.

lame-o *n.* *Stu.* LAME.—often used attrib.
    1977 *NBC's Saturday Night* (NBC-TV): I met this pathetic lame-o. **1980** Univ. Tenn. student: A *lame-o* is a Massachusetts word for a real fool. It comes from *lame*. **1986** *Head of the Class* (ABC-TV): They are lame-o's, man. **1987** *Nat. Lampoon* (Oct.) 38: Those backup singers, those lame-o Jordanaires. **1987** Des Barres *I'm with the Band* 64: Get lost with this lame-o situation...how disgusting...forget this shit.

lamer var. LAME, *n.*

lamester *n.* [LAME + *-ster*] a foolish or contemptible person; LAME.
    1978 Truscott *Dress Gray* 110: Lamester politicians running around saying a lot of sorry-ass shit.

lammie *n.* LAMSTER.
    1933 D. Runyon, in *Collier's* (Dec. 23) 8: The Dutchman is generally a lammie from some place.

lammister var. LAMSTER.

lammister *v.* to abscond; *take it on the lam* s.v. LAM.
    1921 Marquis *Carter* 90: He lammistered, and I ain't seen him since.

lammy var. LAMBY.

lamous *adj.* (among tramps) (see 1914 quot.). [The etymology proposed by Jackson & Hellyer remains unconfirmed.]
    1914 Jackson & Hellyer *Vocab.* 54: *Lamos*...General currency. Gold-plated; flimsy; unsubstantial. Derived from the name of a firm of Chicago jewelers who supplied the cheap jewelry trade with "PHONIES," or fake jewelry. Example: "You can't hock it for two bits; it's lamos." Also used to signify inferior personal qualities. **1916** L. Livingston *Snare* 95: A professional tramp who was considered to be a most "lamous" (harmless) chap.

lamp *n.* **1.a.** usu. *pl.* an eye; in phr. **keep a lamp lit** to keep an eye open; keep alert. [In Shakespeare as a poetic term; cf. also Matthew 5:22.]
    [*1592–93 Shakespeare *Comedy of Errors* V i: My wasting lampes some fading glimmer left.] *1811 *Lex. Balatron.*: Lamp. An eye. *The cove has a queer lamp.* The man has a blind or squinting eye. *1812 Vaux *Vocab.*: Lamps. The eyes; to have *queer lamps*, is to have sore or weak eyes. **1859** Matsell *Vocab.* 127: Lamps. The eyes. **1867** *Nat. Police Gaz.* (Apr. 6) 217: The "fly-cops"...keep their "lamps" open. **1874** Carter *Rollingpin* 221: Got his lamps on the White House—the President's char [*sic*]. **1875** *Minstrel Gags* 14: "I tried to sleep, but sleep has deserted dese lamps—" "Eyes, you mean?" "Yes; I couldn't sleep." **1889** Bailey *Ups & Downs* 18: However, I kept my "lamps" pretty well peeled on both of them, and followed Billy up through Mott Street to the saloon down in the basement. **1889–90** Barrère & Leland *Dict. Slang* II 4: *Lamps* (thieves and others), the eyes. **1898** Bullen *Cachalot* 9 [ref. to 1875]: Captain Slocum, he said, was "de debbil hisself, so jess yew keep yer lamps trim" fer him, sonny, taint helthy ter rile him. **1899** Kountz *Baxter's Letters* 34: Talk about lavish eyes...but this dame was there with the swell lamps. **1902** Cullen *More Tales* 41: My crooning friend with the blue-gray lamps and grayish curly hemp. **1902–03** Ade *People You Know* 56: That is how I happened to get this Bum Lamp. **1903** in "O. Henry" *Works* 1279: Bowled over by those pretty lamps of yours. **1904** Hobart *Missouri* 45: I worked eighteen hours a day every day and I slept with one lamp lit. **1906** J. London *Moon-Face* 44: We go mooching along the drag with a sharp lamp out for John Law. **1908** *New Broadway* (Aug.) 142: I'll keep my lamps on you lads from Sicily hereafter. a1909 Tillotson *Detective* 93: *Lamps*—Eyes. **1910** *N.Y. Evening Jour.* (Apr. 7) 17: His lamps were as bright and clear as a bell. **1912** Berkman *Prison* 111 [ref. to 1892]: Lay low and keep your lamps lit at night, watch the screws and the stools, they is worse than bulls. **1914** E.R. Burroughs *Mucker* 140: Keep yer lamps peeled. **1934** O'Brien *Best Stories of 1935* 199: But if any of the rest of you guys want to pop off at me about this lamp, make sure it's *me* you're kidding. ca1965 in IUFA *Folk Speech*: *Lamps*=Eyes. **1977** Stallone *Paradise Alley* 20: What blue lamps she had! **1980** Lorenz *Guys Like Us* 20: "Shut your lamps."...Buddy closed his eyes.

b. *pl.* spectacles; (*sing.*) (*rare*) a monocle. Cf. GIG-LAMP, 1.
    1907 T.A. Dorgan, in Zwilling *TAD Lexicon* 113: A thin, wise looking

coot with lamps, white spats and a fifty-cent cane. **1936** Steel *College* 151: A bird't looked like a broken down pug wit' a busted beak anna lamp on one glim sent me over from Avenoo A wit' a message. **1971** Rodgers *Queens' Vernacular* 117: Sunglasses…*bad* [*i.e.*, stylish] *lamps* (dated).

2. a look; glance; (*hence*) an inspection.—constr. with *give* or *take*.

　　1926 Dunning & Abbott *Broadway* 250: Let's take a lamp at him. I want to see what he looks like married. **1942** Davis & Wolsey *Call House Madam* 88: I was looking my girls over, as I do, giving their get-ups the full lamp.

lamp *v.* **1.** to look; see.—occ. constr. with *over*.

　　1907 *Lippincott's Mag* (Oct.) 503: I lamps on top to see what was going on. **1911** A.H. Lewis *Apaches of N.Y.* 105: I lamps a yacht once w'at's called *Atalanta*. **1913** *Sat. Eve. Post* (Mar. 15) 6: My gracious, to get the entire place lampin' us like this! I got no desire for notoriety. **1912–14** in E. O'Neill *Lost Plays* 174: You ought to have seen the bear I lamped this afternoon. Some queen, take it from me. **1914** in E. O'Neill *Letters* 23: As I lamp over your last epistle. **1924** H.L. Wilson *Professor* 169: Turn around slow and let me lamp…you once again. **1924** Marks *Plastic Age* 127: Carl handed him the cards. "Lamp those," he said. **1924** Tully *Beggars of Life* 12: A guy's only in the world once. He may as well lamp it over while he's at it. **1924** *Amer. Leg. Wkly.* (July 11) 15: Lamp that, will ya? **1926** Maines & Grant *Wise-Crack Dict.* 10: *Lamp it*—Look it over. **1927** in Dundes *Mother Wit* 204: I know 'em if I lamp 'em a mile off. **1929** Farrell *Calico Shoes* 223: I'll get you the swellest red catgut dress you ever lamped. **1936** in Himes *Black on Black* 129: Big Mama May…lamped the lain when he drew up. **1959–60** Bloch *Dead Beat* 2: He lamped the flashy redhead and the character with the long sideburns. **1965** in B. Jackson *Swim Like Me* 101: She lamped my roll, fell heart and soul. **1971–72** in Abernethy *Bounty of Texas* 209: *Lamp*…to look over; to examine. **1994** *Simpsons* (Fox-TV): Lamp those gams!

2. [prob. as in *a*1994 quot.] *Rap Music.* to loaf or relax.

　　[**1959** in *DARE*: *Lamppost*….To talk. Rare.] **1988** in G. Tate *Flyboy* 131: Ice-T and Big Daddy Kane are lamping by a limo. **1988** "Public Enemy" *Nation of Millions* (rap album). **1989** *Rolling Stone* (Oct. 19) 49: Flavor is…the "cold lamper" singing "live lyrics from da bank of reality." **1990** P. Dickson *Slang!* 221: *Lampin'.* Hanging out, as one does when standing around a lamppost. **1991** *Houston Chronicle* (Oct. 8) 2D: *Lampin'*…Relaxing. *a*1994 Smitherman *Black Talk* 152: *Lamp*…To hang out. Possibly from the idea of hanging out under street lamps on urban corners. **1995** N.Y.C. man, age 25 (coll. J. Sheidlower): I'm just lampin' all afternoon [at home].

lampblack *n. R.R.* coal.

　　1897 Hamblen *General Mgr.* 90: when the extra man started I began as usual to "ladle in the lampblack" until we were about five miles out.

lampers *n.pl.* (sense uncertain; see quot.).

　　1891 H. Garland *Main-Travelled Roads* 134 [ref. to Civil War]: I've chawed [hardtack] when my lampers was down, and when they wasn't.

lamp oil *n.* whiskey.

　　1944 Adams *West. Words: Lamp oil*—A slang name for whisky. **1950** W. Faulkner, in *DARE*: "Where does yawl keep dat…lamp oil whut yawl drinks[?]"…"Oh….You mean corn."

lamppost *n. Army.* a large artillery shell. [Quots. ref. to Civil War.]

　　1862 in Berkeley *Confed. Arty.* 15: The boys call these big shells "lamp posts," from their resemblance to the butt end of city gas lamp posts. *Ibid.* 85: A lamp post (i.e. a nine-inch shell) whizzing from the Maryland Heights, "busted" about three yards rear of John's mule's tail. **1884** Hedley *Marching Through Ga.* 115: An elongated shot—a "lamp post," as that sort of projectile was called—struck the root of a tree. **1885** in *DAE*: The Yankees throwed them lamp-posts about too careless like. *ca*1895 G.B. Sanford *Rebels & Redskins* 237: Our gunboats took us for Rebel cavalry and commenced pitching their enormous shells, which the men called "Lamp posts," at us.

lamster *n.* [sugg. by *on the lam* s.v. LAM + *-ster*] *Und. & Pris.* a fugitive; absconder. Also vars.

　　1904 *Life in Sing Sing* 250: *Lamaster*—A fugitive from justice; one who forfeits bail bonds. *Ibid.* 258: *A lamaster from Boston.* A fugitive from Boston. *a*1909 Tillotson *Detective* 93: *Lamaster*—A fugitive from justice. **1911** A.H. Lewis *Apaches of N.Y.* 130: Do we stand pat, or do we do a lammister? **1930** *Collier's* (Jan. 20) 13: It seems Louie is a lammister out of Detroit. **1931** *AS* VI (Aug.) 439: *Lamster, n.* One who is

hiding out. **1932** in *AS* (Feb. 1934) 27: *Lamster.* One who is dodging the law. **1935** Pollock *Underworld Speaks: Lamster,* a person who jumps bail and runs away; flees from the law. **1936** Mackenzie *Living Rough* 121: There were drifters there, lamsters, honest working stiffs. **1936** Benton & Ballou *Where Do I Go?* 121: The merciless floggings with which all returned "lamsters" are greeted. **1944** C.B. Davis *Leo McGuire* 207: There are two lamisters and that's about all. **1946** Gresham *Nightmare Alley* 274: The hair was dirty black….Dyed. A lammister. **1949** *Harper's* (Aug.) 15: Lamisters and hallroom boys. **1955** Q. Reynolds *HQ* 31: A fugitive was a "lammister." **1962** Riccio & Slocum *All the Way Down* 79: And that meant jail. Or the life of a lamister. **1970** Thackrey *Thief* 292: I told him who I was and what I was—a lamster from California. **1971** P. Hamill, in *N.Y. Post* (Apr. 14) 47: I thought the man must have been one of those New Yorkers who had given up, sold the furniture, and lammed out of town….The lamsters make a neat, glib case against New York.

lance *n.* **1.** the penis; in phr. **get (one's) lance waxed** (of a man) to engage in copulation.—usu. considered vulgar. *Joc.* Cf. LANCE, *v.*, 2.

　　*1622 in *F & H:* And when I charge, my lance in rest, I triumph in delight. *1675 in *F & H:* And Mankind must in darkness languish Whilst he his bawdy launce does brandish. **1988** Univ. Chicago student, age 20 (coll. J. Sheidlower): *To get your lance waxed* means to get laid.

2. *Narc.* a hypodermic needle.

　　1952 Mandel *Angry Strangers* 359: I got your lance up here.

lance *v.* **1.** to swindle.

　　1908 McGaffey *Show Girl* 183: He's inside lancing the management for a…free lunch.

2. [fr. LANCE, *n.*, 1] (of a man) to copulate with.—usu. considered vulgar. [Perh. the earlier sense.]

　　1960–69 Runkel *Law* 151: I went over to her and started to bend down to get between her legs for the lancing.

lance-jack *n.* [*lance* + JACK, prob. in sense 'fellow'; see JACK and *jack* in *OED*] *Army.* a lance-corporal; (*hence*) an acting corporal.

　　*1912 in *OED2*: A junior corporal is a "lance-jack." **1916** in Roy *Pvt. Fraser* 179: The much abused position of "Lance Jack." **1919** U.S. Army 114th M.G. Bn. *With the 114th* 133: "*Lance Jack.*"—1st Class Pvt. acting Corporal. *1919 Downing *Digger Dialects* 31: *Lance Jack* Lance-corporal. **1925** *15th Inf. Sentinel* (Jan. 9) 9: We wonder why Lieutenant Honnen bawled out Acting Corporal Bunosk: and Miller. It's hell to be a lance jack, isn't it boys? **1926** R. Carter *Old Sgt.'s Story* 67 [ref. to *ca*1873]: We were both appointed "Lance Jacks." **1930** *Our Army* (Mar.) 26: This guy was goofy as a Lance-Jack. **1942** *Yank* (Nov. 25) 6: One of the lance jacks in the 99th [Infantry Batallion].

land *n.* ¶ In phrase: **under the land** at a disadvantage.

　　1821 Waln *Hermit* 24: "Always *under the land*, by Saint Patrick"—"Look out for your applecart;"—"Up a slim pine, by Jupiter"—"Up a gumtree, by Jove."

land bird *n. Naut.* a landlubber.

　　1827 J.F. Cooper *Rover* 280: Besides, you shall never say to your friends…that we leave you without the means of reaching the land, if you are indeed a land-bird at all.

land crab *n. Naut.* a landlubber.

　　1861 in *DAE*: We "Old Whales"…are not supposed by some "land-crabs" to have much of a taste for the feathery tribe done up brown. **1959** Morrill *Dark Sea* 91 [ref. to WWII]: This kid is a land crab. First blow we have he'll bury his head in a bucket.

landing gear *n. Av.* the legs. *Joc.*

　　1941 Kendall *Army & Navy Slang* 9: Shall we exercise the landing gear?…take a walk? **1945** Hamann *Air Words: Landing gear.* Legs.

L and L *n.* ["*l*iquor *and l*ove"] rest and recreation leave; R & R. *Joc.* Cf. A AND A, B AND B, I AND I.

　　1969 (quot. at I AND I).

landlady *n. Prost.* the proprietress of a brothel; madam. Hence **the landlady's** a brothel.

　　1879 *Snares of N.Y.:* The "street" or…"the landlady's." **1939** Ramsey & Smith *Jazzmen* 52: Those girls of various shapes, sizes and colors to whom she was "landlady." **1974** *Socio. Symposium* XI 62: She began working in a joint under a madam ("landlady").

land marine *n. Naut.* a policeman.

    1853 "Tally Rhand" *Guttle* 16: I see that ere land marine…standin' by the coach. **1875** Daly *Pique* 308: Policemen! Land marines, as you call them!

Land of the Round Doorknob *n. Mil. Overseas.* the United States. *Joc.* Cf. *Land of the Big PX* s.v. BIG PX.

    1970 *Current Slang V* (Summer) 16: *Land of the Round Doorknob*, n. United States. **1984–88** Hackworth & Sherman *About Face* 213: And the blushing bride got her coveted passport back to the Land of the Round Doorknob.

land on *v.* to rebuke or take decisive action against.

    1940 Goodrich *Delilah* 59 [ref. to 1916]: First he lands on me for leaving the engines too much to Stengle; now, when they really need attention, he wants me to go scratching around in the jungle ashore. **1942** *ATS* 298: Scold; reprimand.…bawl hell out of,…land on. **1960** N.Y.C. man, age *ca*75: Somebody should land on him with both feet. **1995** *Frasier* (NBC-TV): One day you're going to misquote someone and I'm going to land on you like a sumo wrestler! **1996** J. Logan *Tornado* (film): If one person gets injured because of your incompetence, I am gonna land on you like a ton of bricks.

land pike *n.* LAND SHARK, 2. *Joc.*

    1841 in *DAE*: I am anxious that he should soon get rid of his land-pikes and alligators at such prices as will enable him to buy a better breed. **1890** in *DAE*: I think the term *land-pike* more frequently designates a thin, lank, half-wild swine.

landprop *n.* [prob. *land*lord, *land*lady + *prop*ietor] *Black E.* a landlady or landlord. [Quots. ref. to a person in charge of a brothel.]

    1936 in Himes *Black on Black* 129: Big Mama May, the landprop…lamped the lain when he drew up. **1961** Himes *Pinktoes* 17: Although Mama Meow, the madame, or landprop as they say in that part of the world, conducts a cathouse in a land of black cats, she is not at all opposed to serving white cats.

land shark *n.* **1.** *Naut.* a person, esp. a lawyer, who preys avariciously upon seamen ashore. Now *hist.*

    *1769 in OED: Let all beware of these land-sharks. **1821 Real Life in Ireland* 14: There he was boarded by a *land-shark*, a sort of *May*-day lawyer, who contrived to cheat him. **1836** *Naval Mag.* (May) 222: Sometimes we see an old tar, who has been many a time cheated by these scoundrels, steering clear, as he imagines, of the "land sharks." **1838* in *F & H* IV 152: Landsharks and Seagulls. **1839–40** Cobb *Green Hand* I 43: The land sharks on board…rob the honest and unsuspecting. **1847** in Garner *Letters* 197: What is the most needful for the speedy progress of California is a large body of immigrants, with some capitalists, and no lawyers. Only keep that destructive race of men called *land shark* from California, and it will…become a great and prosperous country. **1858** S. Barry *Dutchman* 6: The scoundrel! the landshark! to rob me of my dear…Arabella. **1860** Shipley *Reefer* 75: A lawyer!—a land shark!—you a lawyer! **1866** "M. Twain" *Letters from Hawaii* (Apr.): There's more land sharks (lawyers) in 'Frisco than there's fiddlers in hell, I tell you; and you'll get "pulled" before your anchor's down. **1884** *United Service* (Mar.) 237: Some had…been robbed of their three years pay by the landsharks. **1889** *United Service* (Sept.) 277: An argumentative sailor is a "sea-lawyer," the brown shark is a "sea-attorney," and a lawyer is a "land shark." **1889–90** Barrère & Leland *Dict. Slang* II 5: *Landsharks* (nautical), crimps, pettifogging attorneys, shop-mongers, and the *canaille* infesting the slums of seaport towns. *a1900* in Colcord *Roll & Go* 103: They send you to New Bedford, that famous whaling port,/And give you to some land-sharks to board and fit you out.

    2. a free-running or half-wild hog. *Joc.*

    1840 in *DAE*: That vile race of animals which infest the country, and which, before the discovery of the name of "land sharks," used to be known by the name of hogs. **1849** in *DAE*: They looked too well to be even distant relations of the *Land Sharks*, as the gaunt races [of swine] were called. **1860** in *DAE*: Hogs…land sharks.

land-tacks *n.pl. Naut. & N.E.* ¶ In phrase: **take aboard (one's) land-tacks** to go ashore.—also used allusively. Also vars.

    1776 in *DAE*: Maj'r Meigs & I agree'd to take our Land Tacks on board and quit the boat. **1813** in *DAE*: The farms of Nantucket men were formerly upon the ocean, but Madison's war has bliged them to take land tacks on board, and pass the mountains. **1823** J.F. Cooper *Pilot* 57: Mr. Griffith, I find you are willing to haul your land-tacks aboard. Well, it's natural for youth to love the earth. *Ibid.* 191: I was once left by the craft I belonged to, in Boston, to find my way to Plymouth, which is a matter of fifteen leagues, or thereaway; and so, finding nothing was bound up the bay, after laying-by for a week, I concluded to haul aboard my land-tacks. **1838** *Crockett Almanac* (1839) 2: I kepp my land tacks aboard till I had sounded the old feller pretty well. **1883** Russell *Sailors' Lang.* 78: *Land-tacks*—"take to his land-tacks" said of a sailor when he goes ashore for a frisk.

lane or **lain** *n.* [poss. as representing a Black E pronun. of LAME with strongly nasalized vowel and consequent obscuration of following consonant, but attested prior to corresponding sense of LAME] Esp. *Black E & Und.* a person easily imposed upon or cheated; victim; SUCKER; (*also*) (now *usu.*) one who is foolish or socially unsophisticated; SQUARE.

    1933 Ersine *Prison Slang* 50: *Lain*, n. A sucker. **1936** in Himes *Black on Black* 129: This little white lain pulled up out front in a big Lincoln. **1940** *Current Hist. & Forum* (Nov. 7) 21: *A lane from Spokane* or *a lane from Spain*. *Ibid.* 22: The inmate…will be careful not to be marked a *lane* (fool). **1941** *Pittsburgh Courier* (Apr. 19) 24: *Lane*—A potential sucker. **1942** *Yank* (Dec. 23) 18: Never…give a square lane a break. **1944** in Himes *Black on Black* 203: I couldn't wait to get back to L.A. to tell her what a lain she was. **1945** Himes *If He Hollers* 43: I got a lain hooked down here and all he needs is digging. **1946** Mezzrow & Wolfe *Really the Blues* 307: *Laine*: hick, innocent, sucker. **1958** Hughes & Bontemps *Folklore* 485: *Lane*: a simpleton, an unhip person. **1961** Himes *Pinktoes* 51: (Author's note:) In Harlem idiom a square is a lain, a doe, a John, a mark—in other parlance a fool, a chump, a sucker, a simpleton. **1962** in Wepman, Newman & Binderman *The Life* 105: He didn't do business with lanes. **1964** Gold *Jazz Lexicon* 182: *Lane.* One who is inexperienced or unsophisticated.…some currency c. 1930–c. 1945, very rare since. **1967** Fiddle *Shooting Gallery* 318: I would say, oh, the hell with you now, talkin' this lane outta this money.

lank *n.* a lanky person.

    *1881 in *OED*: You are not such a peaky lank as you were. **1977** Appel *Hell's Kitchen* 35: They…[saw] a long, redheaded lank watching them.

lank *adj.* hungry.

    1883 Sowell *Rangers & Pioneers* 253 [ref. to 1871]: "Say, old pard, don't you begin to feel kinder lank?" was his cheery greeting. **1977** in *DARE*. **1982** in *DARE* [ref. to 1930's].

lap *n.* liquor.

    *1725 New Canting Dict.: 'Tis rum Lap…strong Drink of any Sort. **1725* in Partridge *Dict. Und.* 398: There's more *Lap* in the Cellar. **1874* Hotten *Slang Dict.* (ed. 4): *Lap*, liquor, drink. *Lap* is the term invariably used in the ballet-girls' dressing-room for gin. *a1889–90* Barrère & Leland *Dict. Slang* II 6: *Lap*…(American)…a term for gin. **1931** *AS* VI 159: *Lap* is liquor. **1929–32** in *AS* (Dec. 1934) 288: *Lap* (also *Juice*). General name for alcoholic liquor [at Lincoln University].

lap [up] *v.* **1. a.** to drink (liquor) greedily; guzzle.

    a1889–90 Barrère & Leland *Dict. Slang* II 6: *Lap, to* (common), to drink. (American). **1908** McGaffey *Show Girl* 39: I had been down to the bar lapping up a few drinks. **1914** Lardner *You Know Me Al* 181: You was out lapping up beer. **1929** Brecht *Downfall* 140: You were lapping it up. **1929* Manning *Fortune* 152: The Greyhound…was chock-a-block wi' chaps lappin' it up as fast as they could. **1936** West *Klondike Annie* (film): All I've been thinkin' about is lappin' up liquor. **1942** *Yank* (Sept. 23) 14: A G.I.…was lapping Saki. **1977** Olsen *Fire Five* 29: I didn't do anything except lap up vodka.

    b. to take in eagerly; revel in; enjoy.

    1926 (quot. at HOUND). **1934** O'Brien *Best Stories of 1935* 193: "And he puts up with it?" "Laps it up." **1992** Strawberry & Rust *Darryl* 144: The press lapped it up because they liked conflict.

    2. to perform active oral copulation, esp. cunnilingus, upon.—usu. considered vulgar. Hence **lapper,** *n.*

    1934 (quot. at DICKY-LICKER). **1949** Monteleone *Crim. Slang* 141: *Lapper*…A sodomite. **1971** Rader *Govt. Inspected* 62: I stood with legs spread…being lapped by a john. **1972** B. Rodgers *Queens' Vernacular* 139: Cunnilinctrice…*lapper*. **1975** S.P. Smith *Amer. Boys* 183: Chambers is a gook lapper.

lap-ear *n. Stu.* (see quot.).

    1851 B. Hall *College Wds.* 176: At Washington College Penn., students of a religious character are called *lap-ears* or *donkeys*.

lapper, *n.* **1.** the tongue.
  1851 M. Reid *Scalp-Hunters* 90: At that very spring the Injun'll cool thur lappers.
  2. see s.v. LAP [UP], 2.

larceny *n.* Esp. *Und.* an inclination toward theft; cupidity for illicit gain; dishonest acquisitiveness or cunning.
  1927 *Vanity Fair* (Nov.) 134: An act that is "full of larceny" is an act that has stolen its material from many others. **1931** Wilstach *Under Cover Man* 131: I have so much larceny in my soul...I don't even trust myself. **1933** *Amer. Mercury* (Apr.) 392: Many a yegg has remarked [of William A. Pinkerton]...to me, "he had plenty of larceny in him." It was a compliment; they wanted a man they admired to be like themselves. **1933–35** D. Lamson *About to Die* 196: It's the larceny in his heart that makes him a sucker. **1935** in R. Nelson *Dishonorable* 273: Say, that guy's as full of larceny as Dannemora. **1942** *Pittsburgh Courier* (Jan. 10) 7: His heart was polluted with larceny. **1945** in Kober *That Man Is Here Again* 229: Now, some other [theatrical] agent who got larceny in their heart, he'da give the guy a fast shuffle. **1949** *New Yorker* (Nov. 5) 82: A character who's simply got one thing in his heart, namely, larceny. **1949** W.R. Burnett *Asphalt Jungle* 79: Brannom was full of larceny and knew all the angles. **1958** in D. McKay *Wild Wheels* 164: I call it the kind of thing that happens to a man with larceny in his heart. **1970** in P. Heller *In This Corner* 94: He had too much larceny, because he had a fighter with ability and instead of taking advantage of it he didn't. **1991** *N.Y. Times* (Nat. Ed.) (Feb. 5) 1: Some "Larceny in Your Heart" required to get war supplies.

larceny *v.* *Und.* to attempt to cajole with insincere flattery.
  1960 C.L. Cooper *Scene* 9: "I like your style."..."You don't have to larceny me—I won't flip on you."

lard *n.* **1.** human fat; esp. in phr. **tub** [or **pail**] **of lard** a grossly fat individual.—usu. used derisively.
  1928 Hecht & MacArthur *Front Page* 460: Listen, you big pail of lard! **1942** *ATS* 150: Posteriors...*lard.* **1943** W. Guthrie *Glory* 16: Who'n the hell are you? Tubba lard! **1956** W. Taylor *Roll Back Sky* 51: You know that big tub of lard. **1961** Boyd *Lighter Than Air* 146: Hey, you big tub of lard, wake up! **1963** D. Tracy *Brass Ring* 370: I've been tryin' to lose some lard, toughen up. **1966** Elli *Riot* 39: He's faking....Ain't nothin' wrong with the tub-a lard. **1971** *Black World* (Apr.) 56: Ole four-flushin' tub-a-lard. **1977** J. Olsen *Fire Five* 8: D'Arcy. You gotta get rid of that lard.
  2. butter or margarine. *Joc.*
  1942 *ATS* 98: Butter...*lard.* **1956** Sorden & Ebert *Logger's* 21 [ref. to *a*1925]: *Lard.* Butter or oleo.

lard-ass *n.* **1.** a person with fat buttocks; a grossly fat person.—used derisively.—usu. considered vulgar. Hence **lard-assed,** *adj.* Also in euphem. vars. and (in 1918 quot.) as v.
  1918 in Hecht *From Bohemia* 190: She's gone, let her go, God bless her,/For she never belonged to me./She can lard ass her way through the A.E.F.,/But she'll never find a sucker like me. **1928** Hammett *Red Harvest* 35: Go talk to the lard-can that sent you. [**1931** J. Gleason *Beyond Victory* (film) [ref. to 1918]: "Get in, lug." "Come on, lard."] **1935** J. Conroy *World to Win* 212: Hey, lardass, don't let that popgun go off in ya hand! **1939** N. West *Locust* 376: Get over, lard-ass. **1946** Heggen *Mr. Roberts* xv: He is bow-legged and broad-beamed (for which the crew would substitute "lard-assed."). **1966** "T. Pendleton" *Iron Orchard* 107: Come on, lard-ass, hit them tongs! **1967** Dibner *Admiral* 205: Lard-assed shore-based bureaucrats. **1971** Vaughan & Lynch *Brandywine's War* 105: You lard-assed...son of a bitch. **1971** Horan *Blue Messiah* 224: You mean lard ass with the big mouth? **1980** McDowell *Our Honor* 3: You better get on your feet, lard ass, or you're gonna wish you had. **1982** R.M. Brown *So. Discomfort* 80: Shut up, Lardass. **1990** *Night Court* (NBC-TV): She is a lard-ass! **1994** *Mystery Sci. Theater* (Comedy Central TV): Out of the way, lard-ass! **1994** Lackey et al. *Trashcan* (unp.): Wrong move, lardass!
  2. a slow-moving vehicle.
  1963 A. Morgan *Six-Eleven* 13: We were stopped twelve minutes waiting outside Runsted before that lard ass showed up.

lard belly *n.* a grossly fat person.—used derisively.
  1930 Botkin *Folk-Say* 110: There was a big lard belly pusher there. **1944** C.B. Davis *Leo Mcguire* 12: Nuts to you, Lard Belly!

lard blossom *n.* LARD-ASS.—used derisively.
  1976 Woodley *Bears* 87: You know what the Yankees call me? Lard-blossom.

lard bucket *n.* LARD-ASS.—used derisively.
  1958 Frankel *Band of Bros.* 204 [ref. to Korean War]: What's with you, Lardbucket? **1966, 1966, 1967** in *DARE* I 416. **1973** W. Crawford *Stryker* 122: How...does a lard bucket like you stand this heat? **1982** Trudeau *Dressed for Failure* (unp.): Who wants to be seen in public with a lard bucket?

lard-butt *n.* LARD-ASS.—used derisively.
  1968 W.C. Anderson *Gooney Bird* 24: First we'll render a few pounds from the lard butts among us by indulging in some calesthenics and other fun and games. **1972** Jenkins *Semi-Tough* 191: Especially them lard butts who have to play down in that trench where the men are. **1973** Overgard *Hero* 23: Get the big lard-butt outta here. **1982** *Diff'rent Strokes* (ABC-TV): That's what you get for messing with Arnold Jackson, lard-butt! **1985** *Daily Beacon* (Univ. Tenn.) 10: So go on a diet, lardbutt. **1990** *Mystery Sci. Theater* (Comedy Central TV): Get into the little crawl space, ya lard-butt. **1993** (quot. at JELLY-BELLY).

lardhead *n.* FATHEAD.—used derisively.
  1936 J.T. Farrell *World I Never Made* 453: Fisher and Mostil are lard-heads. You can't tell them a damn thing, not even for their own good. **1945** F. O'Rourke *E Co.* 37: He can make these lard-heads understand maps. **1946** H.A. Smith *Rhubarb* 50: That motley crew of louts and lard-heads who were nosed out yesterday by St. Louis. **1962** Hecht *Gaily, Gaily* 19 [ref. to *ca*1920]: You lard head, I'm speaking about after you're hanged. **1975** Boatner et al. *Dict. Amer. Idioms* 195: You'll never convince Donald; he's a lardhead.

lardo *n.* FATSO.—used derisively.
  1987 *Wkly. World News* (Sept. 1) 32: Dear Fat and Happy: Bully for you, Lardo! **1989** *Heathcliff* (Nickelodeon TV): Come back here, Lardo! **1990** P. Dickson *Slang!* 221: *Lardo.* Fat person. **1992** D. Burke *Street Talk* 133: You're gonna turn into a lardo. **1996** Graham & Hubbell *Night of Twisters* (film): Don't be so defensive, lardo.

lard sack *n.* the belly of a fat individual.
  1966 Elli *Riot* 221: And keep your snitchin' mouth shut, or I'll sink a couple in that lard sack of yours.

lard stand *n.* a fat individual.—used derisively.
  1867 G.W. Harris *Lovingood* 224: He flung the skin ove ole lard stand's hed away.

large *n.* Orig. *Gamb.* a thousand dollars; GRAND, 1.—constr. with prec. numeral. Cf. LARGE ONE.
  1972 Jenkins *Semi-Tough* 230: Somebody will...bet four or five large on it. **1973** W. Crawford *Stryker* 11: It went down OK, better than thirty-six large. **1977** Torres *Q & A* 110: For ten large. **1979** V. Patrick *Pope* 9: He's got to wind up with fifty large, no? **1981** Sann *Trial* 19: You're talkin' about the two large you left with the tailor. **1984** Caunitz *Police Plaza* 262: And, a legal fight could cost you twenty-five large. **1985** *Kids' World Almanac* 148: $1000—grand, G, a large. **1986** *Miami Vice* (NBC-TV): "What's the price tag on that conversation?" "Say, thirty large." **1987** *21 Jump Street* (Fox-TV): I borrowed two large from Hoff's account. **1987** Mamet *House of Games* (film): You say Billy Hahn lost 25 large to me. **1990** Vachss *Blossom* 38: A hundred large. Minimum. **1994** *Mystery Sci. Theater* (Comedy Central TV): I owe Big Lenny forty-two large. **1996** McCumber *Playing Off Rail* 363: You're giving away the store, and you want me to put up *two large*?

large *adj.* **1.** (of an activity or period of time) fine; very enjoyable; exciting. Also (*obs.*) **large-sized.**
  1874 in Chesnutt *Journals* 46: I suppose they had a "large-sized" time. **1895** *DN* I 420: *Large.* "A large evening," a fine evening. **1895** Gore *Stu. Slang* 21: *Large*...Fine, pleasant. "It is a large day." **1920** S. Lewis *Main Street* 299: We're going to have a large wide time, and everything'll be different when we come back. **1930** *AS* V (Feb.) 239: *Large:* very active. "That was a large evening." **1937** Rossen & Finkel *Marked Woman* (film): Here's to a large evening. **1945** in *DAS*: The good doctor has had himself a large evening. **1970** Major *Dict. Afro-Amer. Sl.* 75: *Large:* (1930's–40's)...thrilling. **1986** in *DARE*: [It's] a nice, large day.
  2. impressive, esp. in amount or degree. Also as adv. [Current use is founded chiefly upon *live large*, below.]
  1883 *Life* (Feb. 8) 80: He had four ten Speck-ers all the time, and guessed they were tol-er-ab-ly Large. **1895** *DN* I 390: *Large:* much. "He has *large* money." Cincinnati, O. **1896** Ade *Artie* 7: He was...puttin' up the large, juicy con talk. **1940** R. Chandler *Farewell, My Lovely* ch. xi: I stood up and took my wallet out. The five twenties were still in it. "High-class boys....They only took the large money."

1968 Brasselle *Cannibals* 105: We're going to win large. **1969** Cray *Erotic Muse* 135 [song learned 1943–45]: The admiral rides in a barge./It don't go a fucking bit faster,/But it makes the old bastard feel large. **1992** *Martin* (Fox-TV): Try these [sunglasses]. They'll think we look *large*. **1995** Eble *Campus Slang* (Apr.) 6: "That play you made was large." "That's a large guitar player."

3. *Entertainment Industry.* popular; successful. Also as adv. See also *live large*, below.

1957 Blumgarten *Mr. Rock and Roll* (film): It's bound to be very large among bakery people coast-to-coast. **1954–60** *DAS: Large*…popular; successful.—Orig. theater and jazz use c1945. **1970** Major *Dict. Afro-Amer. Sl.* 75: *Large* (1930's–40's) successful. **1991** Nelson & Gonzales *Bring Noise* 206: You gotta do a story on them…they're gonna be large! *Ibid.* 235: Ricky was hanging large with his crew at New York's trendy China Club. **1991** in *Rap Masters* (Jan. 1992) 20: Rap is *definitely* large and rock is *definitely* large. **1992** *Newsweek* (May 4) 64: People [give you respect] when they think you have the flavor and you're gonna do something fly….But my life's not *about* bein' large, ya know? **1994** *Martin* (Fox-TV): I used to be large. I had the number-one radio show in the world. **1996** Joseph & Schepps *Encino Woman* (film): Busin' moves and gettin' *large*!

4. enthusiastic.—constr. with *for*. Also as adv.

1967 Sann *Fads, Follies* 141: Dr. Hyslop…was very large for trance mediums. *a***1968** in Haines & Taggart *Ft. Lauderdale* 34: I never have gone in too large for that skiing stuff. **1986** *NDAS:* This week they're large for Renato Zero; next week, who knows.

¶ In phrases:

¶ **live large** Esp. *Rap Music.* to be extremely, esp. ostentatiously, successful, popular, wealthy, etc. Cf. **(3)**, above. [Orig. a motto of The Executioner, crime-fighting hero of a popular action-adventure series by Don Pendleton, published 1969–.]

1975 D. Pendleton *St. Louis Showdown* 32: If that's what you call living large, Sergeant Bolan, then it's been nothing but *small* for me. **1976** in D. Pendleton *Executioner's War Book* vii: Live large and stay hard! **1979** D. Pendleton *Terrible Tuesday* 29: Live large, big fella. **1988** *L.A. Times* (Aug. 29) VI 1: [Rap music glossary:] *Living large*—doing well. **1989** *CBS This Morning* (CBS-TV) (Aug. 30): Chillin' and livin' large. **1989** Ramsey Lewis *Urban Renewal* (pop/jazz album): Livin' Large [song title]. **1989** S. Lee *Do the Right Thing* (film): Livin' large, bro! **1990** *New Yorker* (Sept. 10) 66: I was livin' large…new clothes and gold…all *kinds* of girls. **1990** *In Living Color* (Fox-TV): Just 'cause you're livin' large…don't give you the right to dis! **1991** *Houston Chronicle* (Nov. 13) 5D: *Living large:* Doing well financially. **1992** S. Straight *Been in Sorrow's Kitchen* 274: Oh, man, we livin' large. We can *choose* the ride, the crib. **1992** *Roc* (Fox-TV): Now I'm livin' large like a rock star. **1994** N. McCall *Wanna Holler* 7: We were broke as hell, but it felt like we were livin' large.

¶ **talk large** to boast; talk big.

1833 S. Smith *Maj. Downing* 149: Other folks may talk larger and bluster more. **1859** in C.A. Abbey *Before the Mast* 168: The passengers talk "large" about things they "no savee." **1872** in *DAE:* He had talked large about the Ku-Klux.

¶ **what's the large idea?** what's the big idea? what do you mean by this action?

1927 Liggett *AEF* 279: "Who the hell is he?"…"What's the large idea?"

large one *n.* one thousand dollars. Cf. LARGE.

1981 Yates *Cannonball Run* (film): You've got a bet! Twenty big large ones.

lark *n.* **1.** (a instance of) diverting merriment or excitement; prank; (*hence*) a merry spree or excursion; in phr. **on the lark** playing about; on a spree (*obs.*). Now *S.E.*

****1802** (cited in Partridge *DSUE* (ed. 7) 1246). ****1811** *Lex. Balatron.: Lark.* A piece of merriment. People playing together jocosely. ****1812** Vaux *Vocab.: Lark*, fun or sport of any kind, to create which is termed *knocking up a lark.* ****1815** Byron, in *F & H* IV 157: If so, you and I (*without* our wives) will take a lark to Edinburgh. ****1819** [T. Moore] *Tom Crib* 37: Is any spark/Among you ready for a *lark?* ****1820–21** P. Egan *Life in London* 37: He was fond of…"*kicking up a lark.*" *Ibid.* 68: Poll…mentions the *lark* to a Coster-monger. *Ibid.* 255: No one…created more *fun*, [or] showed more *lark.* ****1836–37** C. Dickens *Pickwick*

ch. ii: "Here's a lark!" shouted half a dozen hackney coachmen. **1838** [Haliburton] *Clockmaker* (Ser. 2) 20: Many's the lark you and I have had together in Slickville. **1841** [Mercier] *Man-of-War* 3: A sailor's characteristic for enjoying a *lark* upon any occasion. **1844** *Spirit of Times* (Mar. 2) 3: The jockey was…ready for…a lark, on the very shortest notice. **1850** [Lippard] *Killers* 5: In a lark…we attempted to abduct the daughter of one of the Professors. **1862** in *Manuscripts* XXX (1978) 15: A yankey [*sic*] from down east who is constantly on the lark. **1863** in H.L. Abbot *Fallen Leaves* 165: He is on a regular lark now. **1869** "G. Ellington" *Women of N.Y.* 323: He is happy in the thought of the "lark" he is helping to carry out. **1886** *Lantern* (N.O.) (Oct. 6) 3: Out on a lark, spending his money like a thoroughbred. *a***1909** Tillotson *Detective* 93: *Lark*—A picnic. **1958** T. Capote *Breakfast at Tiffany's* 99: It was a light-headed lark compared to the journey to Joe Bell's bar. **1995** Gingrich & Forstchen *1945* 193: "This was a lark," Skorzeny replied.

2. a fellow; person; BIRD, 3. Also **larky**.

1833 in *DARE:* I say, my larkie….I say, my honey, a'n't you a doctor? **1835** A. Longstreet *Ga. Scenes* 15: Fetch up your nag, my old cock. You's jist the lark I wanted to get hold of. **1839–40** W.G. Simms *Border Beagles* 266: You ought t' have done all that before, my lark. **1840** in *DAE:* The other lark told Betsy a different story. **1850** J. Greene *Tombs* 118: So, merely to make the game more interesting, my larkey, I will try you with two thousand dollars. **1859** in *DAE:* Old Wolverton's…was a moughty hard place for the gal, whatever kind of a lark she mought be. **1861** in Walser *Tar Heel Laughter* 62: I…descried a…box-ankled, bandy-shanked lark. **1873** in Miller & Snell *Why West Was Wild* 581: They overtook the property and the "larkies" at Eureka, Greenwood county [*sic*]. **1876** in Walser *Tar Heel Laughter* 62: A dozen…relatives gathered around the lark. *a***1890** in Barrère & Leland *Dict. Slang* II 7: "Boy, why don't your father take a newspaper," said a man to a small lark.

lark *v.* to fool about; seek amusement.—occ. constr. with dummy-obj. *it.* Now *S.E.* Cf. SKYLARK.

****1813** in *OED:* Much as larking was in force, there had been no spree to top this. ****1821** *Real Life in London* II 247: Where they'd wish for a morning to "*lark it.*" ****1826** in *OED:* He has been a bit of a larker in his time. **1840** *Spirit of Times* (Mar. 7) 8: Here goes my larkin'. **1845** Corcoran *Pickings* 113: I didn't mean vot I said. I vas but larkin'. **1845** C. Mathews *Big Abel* 3: Where are you larking to? **1871** Banka *Prison Life* 501: He slept by day and "larked" at night. ****1888** in *F & H* IV 157: Plenty of chatter and *larking* when the taskmaster was out of sight.

larkey *n.* MALARKEY.

1970 Hannah *Geronimo Rex* 233: "That's some larkey." She was teased.

larrikin *n.* [orig. Brit. dial., 'a mischievous or frolicsome youngster'] a hooligan; rowdy. *Rare* in U.S.

****1868** in *Dict. Austral. Eng.:* One of the most accomplished swindlers ever imported into the colonies….Why, you infernal old larrikin! **1913–14** J. London *Elsinore* 99: He'll be consorting with those other three larrakins I gave a piece of my mind to. **1954–60** *DAS: Larrikin*…A hoodlum. *From Austral. sl.*

larry *n.* [perh. ult. a dial. var. of LEERY] **1.** *Und.* cunning or deception; (*also*) a deceptive remark.

1859 Matsell *Vocab.* 58: *Larrey.* Cunning. **1902** Hapgood *Thief* 180 [ref. to ca1890]: To get him to talk, I was forced to throw a few "Larrys" into him, such as: "Well, old man, only for your few mistakes of the past you might be leader of Tammany Hall." **1906** T.A. Dorgan, in *N.Y. Eve. Jour.* (Feb. 5) 8: Tom fell for the larry, shook the navy blue scenery, hired a typewriter and became a fighter. *Ibid.* (July 13) 8: That's a fact; there's no larry in that.

2. (among pitchmen) a defective or worthless article offered for sale; (*broadly*) anything unsatisfactory.

1934 Weseen *Dict. Slang* 160: *Larry*—A broken novelty; a punctured toy balloon. **1935** *Amer. Mercury* (June) 230: *Larry:* a broken or worthless article. **1959–66** in *AS* XLI (1966) 279: *Larry*, n. An unprofitable spot [for business]. **1974** *Socio. Symposium* XI 33: Another factor that may reduce the [peddlers'] gain is if they get too many "larrys," i.e. defective merchandise. Many larrys will reduce the profit.

larry *adj.* [fr. the n.] (among pitchmen) of unsatisfactory quality; poor.

1939 *Life* (July 31) 24: In [pitchman's] argot, the World of Tomorrow is *larry*, meaning business is bad. **1943** *Sat. Eve. Post* (Sept. 25) 13: "Now the average rad worker is pushing larry merchandise." By larry...he meant phony. **1949–53** in *AS* XXVII (1953) 117: Carnie Talk...*larry*, adj. Faulty, bad. "Larry" merchandise is below standard, flawed.

lash *n. Und.* a sword.

　1791 [W. Smith] *Confess. T. Mount* 19: A sword, *a lash. Ibid.* 20: With pops [pistols]...and lashes.

lashings *n.pl.* plenty; lots. Now *rare* in U.S. Also **lashins.**

　1848 Baker *Glance at N.Y.* 17: Up with no work, up with no watch-house!...Up with lashings of grog and insiders! **1877** Pinkerton *Maguires* 381: There's *lashins* of better men for such a thing. **1878** in Miller & Snell *Why West Was Wild* 366: Amid "lashins" of free whisky the following officers were elected. **1894** *DN* I 332: Lashins o' money. **1940** Raine & Niblo *Fighting 69th* (film): What I couldn' do to a grilled steak with lashin's of mashed potatoes. **1984** Wilder *You All* 71: *Lashin's an' lavin's*: An abundance; plenty and some to spare.

lashup *n.* **1.** Orig. *Naut. & USMC.* **a.** something set up, as by lashing or tying elements together, esp. as a makeshift; a jury-rigged contrivance; (*broadly*) apparatus. [The 1954–60 *DAS* def. appears to be overly specific.]

　*1898 in *OED2*: Such a godforsaken lash-up of a bridge I never clapped eyes on! **1924* in *OED2*: A "lash-up"...was erected at the Marconi Works. **1954–60** *DAS*: *Lash-up*...a house, barracks, a tent. WWII Army use. *Not common.* **1961** F.H. Burgess *Dict. Sailing* 130: *Lash-up.* Anything untidily put together or insecurely lashed. **1991** Linnekin *80 Knots* 39: You can imagine the booby-trap aspects of such a lash-up.

　b. state of affairs or undertaking, esp. if difficult or unpleasant; situation; setup.

　*1902 Masefield *Salt-Water Ballads* 7: "'N' many a queer lash-up have I seen," says he. **1944** Kendall *Service Slang* 25: *What's the lash-up?*....set-up or organization. **1948** McHenry & Myers *Home Is Sailor* 23: She looked as weary of the whole lashup as Billy felt. **1953** G. Webber *Far Shore* 27: D'ya think he knows any more about this lashup than Sedwick? **1956** *AS* (Oct.) 193: *Lash-up.* Organization or project. **1956** G. Green *Last Angry Man* 472: Dec is...finalizing the lash-up. **1958** Camerer *Damned Wear Wings* 61: I figure [he's]...just crazy enough to wiggle out of this lashup too. *Ibid.* 86: Why, since the big lashup, half the crews in our squadron been drunk! **1960** MacCuish *Do Not Go Gentle* 226: Well, after this lash-up's over I'm gonna start all over again—that is, after being carefully psychoanalyzed. **1972** Sapir & Murphy *Death Therapy* 23: The next operation I get returns me to something like what I looked like before I got suckered into this lashup. **1976** Hayden *Voyage* 209: Life was a funny damn lash-up. **1979** Silliphant *Pearl* (ABC-TV): I don't know what our lash-up is yet. It all depends on what the Japs do.

　2. *Naut. & USMC.* a collection of things or persons, esp. a naval or military unit; outfit.

　*1907 J. Masefield, in *OED2*: And down they all go...Jimmy and the whole lash-up. **1939** O'Brien *One-Way Ticket* 38 [ref. to ca1925]: I ain't been in this lash-up as long as I have for nothin'! *Ibid.* 51: Time was when men in this lash-up talked ten languages. **1944** (quot. at (1), above). **1947** Devereux *Wake I.* 108: What you beatin' your gums for? Nobody asked you to join this lash-up. **1952** Uris *Battle Cry* 101: I had never quite met a guy like him in four hitches in this lash-up. **1957** Myrer *Big War* 146: Shoot your mouth off in *this* lash-up and you've got trouble. **1958** Frankel *Band of Bros.* 58: They picked a man's lash-up to do a man's job. **1961** R. Davis *Marine* 110: They're all gone, boy. Done, the whole lash-up. **1964** H. Rhodes *Chosen Few* 120: You're suppose' t' shave each and every day in this lash-up! **1968** E.M. Parsons *Fargo* 78: And if you're the he-mule in this here lash-up, why'd I'd be obliged if you'd send someone to care for my animals. **1984** D. Jenkins *Life Its Ownself* 78: Twelve games left in the regular season....These darn lashups [football teams] are getting more and more expensive. **1984–88** Hackworth & Sherman *About Face* 657: Your lash-up's beginning to act like a parachute battalion.

lash up *v. Esp. USMC & Navy.* to come into close association (with); join up.—often used in passive.

　1952 Uris *Battle Cry* 63 [ref. to 1942]: I'm sure lucky I got lashed up with you and L.Q. *a*1961 Peacock *Valhalla* 126: Let me know...or I['ll] probably lash up with someone else. **1965** Bonham *Durango St.* 16: There are over three hundred "clubs" in the city, now, so you won't have any trouble getting lashed up with one. *Ibid.* 50: If anything happens before I lash up with the Moors, he thought.

lat *n. Naut.* latitude.

1856 in C.A. Abbey *Before Mast* 34: Now we are out of the rainy "Lats." **1981** Ballenger *Terror* 25: Tell them we're twelve north lat, one-thirty-five east long.

latch *n. Und.* a buckle or pin.

　1791 [W. Smith] *Confess. T. Mount* 18: Buckles, *latches.* **1848** *Ladies' Repository* VIII (Oct.) 315: *Latch,* A breast-pin.

latch *v. Stu.* to embrace.

　1959 Farris *Harrison High* 104: Bart and Cootie started latching and he and Ruthie necked too.

latch on *v.* Orig. *Jazz.* to become aware; grasp; catch on; understand.—often constr. with *to.*

　1938 Calloway *Hi De Ho* 16: *Latch on*...get wise to. **1946** Mezzrow & Wolfe *Really the Blues* 77: It's probably tough...to latch on to its real meaning. **1958** L. Hughes & A. Bontemps *Book of Negro Folklore* 485: *Latch on*...Become aware, understand, learn. **1960** Carpenter *Youngest Harlot* 33: Mom would probably climb all over her if she ever "latched" on to the truth. **1971** Wells & Dance *Night People* 51: When I was a kid, my mind might have been going along with Mama and Papa saying Grace, with no idea the other four minds were on the nearest platter, but by and by I latched on. **1973** Childress *Hero* 17: Neither do I latch on to all this civil-rights-struggle jive. **1978** Selby *Requiem* 178: He couldn't really latch on to what it was or why. **1983** Eble *Campus Slang* (Mar.) 4: *Latch on*—comprehend, understand: I hope I can latch on to my physics before I'm in big trouble.

late *interj. Stu.* LATER, 1.

　1990 P. Munro *Slang U.* 121: *Late!* goodbye, see you later. **1996** Lyday-Lee *Elon College Coll.* (Spring) 4: *Late* All right man, *late!* (interjection) I'll see you later on.

later *interj.* [elliptical for *see you later (on)* or *see* [or *dig*] *you later, alligator* s.v. ALLIGATOR] **1.** Orig. *Jazz.* good-bye! so long! I'll be seeing you!—occ. constr. with *on.* Also **laters.**

　[**1922** F.L. Packard *Doors of Night* 182: "See youse later"...[is] a common and slang expression of adieu.] [**1941** Brecher & Kurnitz *Shadow of Thin Man* (film): "Just stick around downstairs. We'll see ya later." "Yeah. *Later,* Whitey."] **1954** *Time* (Nov. 8) 70: *Later*...Catchall word for "I'll be seeing you." **1957** Simmons *Cornerboy* 16: "Later on." "Later," they said. **1953–58** J.C. Holmes *Horn* 34: Well, I'll cut out then....Later, pops. **1958** Mayes *Hunters* (film): Later. **1958–59** Lipton *Barbarians* 317: When you're ready to leave the pad you cut out and say, "Later." **1959** *AS* (May) 154: Farewells like *later, gator.* **1959** *Swinging Syllables: Later*—standard word of departure, used in place of "Goodby." **1964** *Outer Limits* (ABC-TV): I'm going to get my gear and go out to the scarp. Later! **1965** Hentoff *Jazz Country* 145: But don't be too cool. Later. **1967** Flicker *President's Analyst* (film): Later. Keep the faith, baby. **1970** Quammen *Walk the Line* 210: Later on, brother. **1982** Pond *Valley Girls' Gde.* 59: Instead of "goodbye," you go, "Later," cool, huh? **1989** *Married with Children* (Fox-TV): Later, gators. **1991** B.E. Ellis *Amer. Psycho* 42: "Later," Price is saying. "Later, fellas." **1994** *Mystery Sci. Theater* (Comedy Central TV): Later on, guys! **1994** *New Yorker* (Dec. 26) 148: So, later, guys. **1996** *Dangerous Minds* (ABC-TV): "Laters, OK?" "O.K. Laters."

　2. Esp. *Black E.* (used to dismiss someone or something); forget it!; to hell with (something).—usu. constr. with *for.*

　1946 Steinbeck *Wayward Bus* 168: No, later for that. **1953** in R.S. Gold *Jazz Talk* 120: Later for the happenings, baby. **1955** *Science Digest* (Aug.) 33: His scorn can be indicated by saying "that doesn't quite make it" or "Later..." to anyone who has made a suggestion too unsatisfactory to consider. **1958** Gilbert *Vice Trap* 129: Later on that talk. **1956–60** J.A. Williams *Angry Ones* ch. ix: After all you've told me about that place, well...*later* [ellipsis in orig.]. **1959–60** R. Reisner *Jazz Titans* 160: *Later:* means nothing doing. **1966–67** P. Thomas *Mean Streets* 234: I couldn't make like a *loco.* Later for that! **1969** B. Beckham *Main Mother* 51: Later for this stuff. **1969** *Black Panther* (Oakland, Calif.) (Nov. 19): We say down with the American fascist society. Later for Richard Milhous Nixon....Later for all the pigs of the power structure. Later for all the people out here who don't want to hear me curse. **1970** Eckels *Business* 24: "Later, square!"/you screamed. **1973** Childress *Hero* 10: I'm a man and if I can't take it, well, later! **1975** *N.Y. Post* (July 22) 71: Come on. Later for this fool. **1976** Selby *Demon* 33: Later for that shit....Forget it!

lather *v.* Orig. *Boxing.* to thrash; defeat soundly.

　1788 S. Low *Politician Out-witted* III i: I'll lather you for less yet. **1797* in *OED*: He was so well lathered that he was near his end. **1835**

J.P. Kennedy, in *OEDS*: He shut that up…by giving Huger a most tremenjious lathering. ***1850** in *OED:* The uxorious cleric too…was lathered with a cane. **1866** G. Townsend *Non-Combatant* 262: We're lathered, that's the long and short of it….Boys, I guess we're beat. **1934** in Gardner & Chickering *Ballads So. Mich.* 373: If we'd kept her much longer, she'd lathered all hell. **1942** *ATS* 318: Beat; thrash….*lam,… lather,…shellac.*

latrine *n. Army.* LATRINE RUMOR.
   1918 Ross *With the 351st* 3: Others, with the "latest Latreen," had it that we were to sail from an "Atlantic port" in less than a week. *Ibid.* 24: Surely we are to follow, but there is no "Latreen" to that effect yet. **1929** Pottle *Stretchers* 15 [ref. to 1917]: A "latrine," we learned, was not only a building, but also the name for any particularly exciting but quite unfounded rumor emanating therefrom.

latrine dope *n. Army.* LATRINE RUMOR.
   1917 McCann *On Border* 203: What church people call gossip and the soldiers call "latrine dope." **1919** U.S. Army 114th M.G. Bn. *With 114th* 133: "*Latrine Dope*"—Another name for "Bull."

latrine lawyer *n. Army.* GUARDHOUSE LAWYER; SHITHOUSE LAWYER.
   1943 *Yank* (Feb. 26) 22: Latrine orderlies sometimes graduate to latrine lawyers, frequently known under another name. **1945** in *AS* (Oct. 1946) 238: The latrine lawyer [is a soldier] who talks too much. **1958** Swarthout *Cordura* 105: By disposition a griper, a plotter, a latrine lawyer, he would lick an officer's boots and profane him when his back was turned. **1963** Doulis *Path* 317: Peculiar guy….Just an old latrine lawyer. **1963** Coon *Short End* 259: "You can't give me that kind of an order, sir." He focused his eyes on me. "Latrine lawyer, Hawkins?" **1975** Larsen *Runner* 62: Now he spoke more like the well-known latrine lawyer. **1984** "W.T. Tyler" *Shadow Cabinet* 299: Too flashy, too much talk—a goddamned latrine lawyer.

latrineogram *n. Army.* LATRINE RUMOR. *Joc.*
   1941 *Amer. N & Q* I (Sept. 4) 94: *Latrineogram*—baseless rumor. **1941** Kendall *Army & Navy Sl.* 9: *Latrinegram*….a wild rumor. **1943** *Yank* (Aug. 6) 22: Latrinograms. **1946** in *OEDS* s.v. bush telegraph: We had heard too many "latrinograms." **1956** I. Shulman *Good Deeds* 57: That, friend,…is a latrinogram. More crap than truth. **1982** F. Hailey *Soldier Talk* 38: *Latrine-O-gram.* A rumor which is spread during idle barracks talk.

latrine queen *n. Mil.* a latrine orderly. *Joc.*
   1971 N.Y.C. draftsman [ref. to WWII]: The guy supposed to police the latrine was called the *latrine queen.* **1981** Former USAF broadcaster [ref. to 1975–80]: The *latrine queen* was the latrine orderly.

latrine rumor *n. Mil.* an unsubstantiated rumor. Now *S.E.* Also vars.
   1918 *U.S. Army Ambulance Co. La Trine Rumor* [title of unofficial newspaper]. **1921** Dos Passos *Three Soldiers* 168: That's the latest edition of the latrine news. **1928** Harrison *Generals Die in Bed* 76: Aw, latrine rumors! **1930** *Our Army* (Feb.) 44. **1937** Parsons *Lafayette Escadrille* 31: When, by the usual latrine telegraph, the news filtered through that the French had consented to the formation of an all-American squadron of volunteers, a dozen other aspiring young eaglets hurried to transfer or enlist in the aviation. **1939** *AS* XIV (Feb.) 28: *Latrine Rumor*, n. Rumor, generally accurate [*sic*], of unknown origin. *Latrine Wireless*, n. Rumor (grapevine telegraphy, militarized). **1961** Plantz *Sweeney Squadron* 237: It sounds a lot like a latrine rumor, but if it's true, thank God. **1962** Killens *Heard the Thunder* 200: A latrine rumor got started that they were being readied to be shipped overseas and directly to the front.

latrine sergeant *n. Army.* **1.** a latrine orderly.
   1928 McCartney *Additions* 305 [ref. to WWI]: *Latrine sergeant,* a private whose duty it was to keep the latrines in order, clean the floors, keep the fires going, etc.

   2. LATRINE LAWYER. Also **latrine lieutenant.**
   1941 Kendall *Army & Navy Sl.* 9: *Latrine sergeant*….an enlisted man who takes it upon himself to issue orders. **1942** Lindsay & Crouse *Strip for Action* 7: "Is he one of your officers?" "Yeah. He's a Latrine Lieutenant." "Well, if he ain't an officer and he ordered us to put this stuff in…he can go to the guardhouse."

lats *n.pl. Bodybuilding.* the latissimus dorsi muscles.
   1977 *Texas Monthly* (July) 12: Are you ready for an evening of viewing lats, traps, pects, and delts?…It's the 1977 Mr. Texas contest. **1981** D.E. Miller *Jargon* 231: Highly developed lats look like wings added onto the back. *a***1984** in *AS* LIX (1984) 200: *Lats n* Latissimus dorsi muscles. **1994** "G. Indiana" *Rent Boy* 38: Three hours at the gym, pumping lats and abs and pecs.

laugh *n.* (in *pl*). fun; diversion. Now *colloq.* or *S.E.*
   1931 Hellinger *Moon* 34: We'll have loads of laughs and things. **1940** Hartman & Butler *Rd. to Singapore* (film): Sell the other seventy-nine, sail around and have some laughs. **1959** N.Y.C. schoolboy: I'm not doin' this just for laughs. **1959** *Many Loves of Dobie Gillis* (CBS-TV): So, like, what do you do for laughs? **a***1970** Partridge *DSUE* (ed. 7) 1247: *Laughs, for.* As a joke; for the fun of it: coll.: since ca. 1950. **1977** (quot. at JACK). **1984** N.Y.C. man, age 37: Come on. It'll be laughs.

   ¶ In phrase:
   ¶ **give the laugh** to laugh at in a ridiculing fashion; (*hence*) to scorn; jeer; deride.
   1892 L. Moore *Own Story* 371: When these officials returned, they were told by Caldawood what I had said, and they were "given the laugh." **1893** Frye *Field & Staff* 174: Dey give 'm de gran' laff. **1894** F.P. Dunne, in Schaaf *Dooley* 323: I made him go down on his knees…an' declare on his oath he was between fifty-five an' sixty. Thin I give him th' laugh an' he had to go to Canada f'r to escape the dhraft. **1895** Townsend *Fadden* 20: 'E gives me de laugh….Gives me de laugh, an' says I'm a ig'rant wagabone. **1896** Ade *Artie* 88: A lot of fresh kids stood around and give me the laugh. **1898** Kountz *Baxter's Letters* 8: [The deer] gave me the laugh and cut into the woods. **1932** "M. Brand" *Jackson Trail* 9: We all give him the laugh, but he was right.

laugh *v.* ¶ In phrases:
   ¶ **it is to laugh** it's bitterly ironic.
   1897 in Outcault *Yellow Kid* [p. 80]: It is to laff. **1909** in Sampson *Ghost Walks* 487: It is to laugh, and you do laugh. **1961** *Twilight Zone* (CBS-TV): It is to laugh.

   ¶ **laugh** *that* **off!** you can't make light of that.—used sarcastically.
   1918 Grider *War Birds* (Feb. 5) 77: That's what I call tact. Try and laugh that off! **1923** Witwer *Fighting Blood* 15: "Laugh that off!" I says to Rags. **1926** Maines & Grant *Wise-Crack Dict.* 11: Laugh that off. **1965** N.Y.C. high school student: Just say, "Laugh *that* off, asshole!"

laugher *n.* **1.** *Sports.* (see 1976 quot.).
   1961 Brosnan *Pennant Race* 88: I think we got a laugher goin'….How can you walk anyone with an eight-run lead? **1976** *Webster's Sports Dict.*: *Laugher* A game that a team wins by a wide margin; an easy win. **1978** Bill White, *N.Y. Yankees vs. Tex. Rangers* (WPIX-TV) (Aug. 1): Yankees lead 7-0. They're working on a laugher. **1978** P. Rizzuto, *N.Y. Yankees vs. Boston Red Sox* (WPIX-TV) (Aug. 2): The Yankees scored five runs in the second inning and it looked like a laugher. **1990** P. Dickson *Slang!* 206: *Laugher.* (Basic jock talk) Lopsided victory.

   2. something ridiculous or amusing.
   1974 Sann *Dead Heat* 107: It's a laugher to me.

laughing academy *n.* an insane asylum. Also vars.
   1947 Schulberg *Harder They Fall* 11: Coombs was ready for the laughing academy. **1955** Bezzerides *Kiss Me Deadly* (film): So you're a fugitive from the laughing house. **1958–59** Lipton *Barbarians* 82: Hadn't Allen Ginsberg been to the laughing academy? **1963** Coon *Short End* 111: You don't have that treated and…you'll end up in a laughing academy. **1966** S. Stevens *Go Down Dead* 32: Dancer say you ready for the laughing school you keep thinking about them things. **1967** Wolf *Love Generation* 48: I'd been to prison, I'd been to the laughing academy, I'd been using heroin. **1970** Sorrentino *Steelwork* 75: Hey, Joe said, hey, Ziggy, you better go back to the laughin farm. **1970** Thackrey *Thief* 265: A month later, they took him off to the funny farm. You know, outer space? The laughing academy. **1972** Pearce *Pier Head Jump* 36: This ship will be a floatin' laughin' academy. **1975** *Nat. Lampoon* (Feb.) 59: The undergraduates…have turned their universities into laughing academies. **1985** Sawislak *Dwarf* 123: Mellaril….Used in the best laughing academies.

laughing boy *n.* [ironic use, perh. alluding to "A Laughing Boy But Yesterday," song fr. the Gilbert & Sullivan operetta *The Yeomen of the Guard* (1888)] a morose or unpleasant fellow.—used ironically.
   1940 Meehan & Tugend *Seven Sinners* (film): Laughing boy is here again. **1941** Brecher & Kurnitz *Shadow of Thin Man* (film): Here's laughing boy. **1941** Macaulay & Wald *Manpower* (film): I can handle that, laughing boy. **1945** MacDougall *Mildred Pierce* (film): Laughing

boy seems slightly burned at the edges. **1947** Bowers & Millhouser *Web* (film): Well, laughing boy, I thought I told you not to leave town. **1983** Breathed *Bloom Co.* 14: Put it in gear down there, laughing boy!

laughing grass *n.* [perh. sugg. by *laughing gas* infl. by GRASS; cf. LAUGHING WEED] marijuana. *Joc.*
    1954 Maurer & Vogel *Narc. & Add.* (gloss.): *Laughing grass.* Marijuana. **1977** (cited in Spears *Drugs & Drink* 309). **1978** UTSQ: [Marijuana]...pot, weed, green stuff, joints, laughing grass.

laughing farm *n.* FUNNY FARM.
    1965 Carmichael & Longstreet *Sometimes I Wonder* 157: It's crazy as a laughing farm.

laughing soup *n.* Champagne; (*also*) any liquor. *Joc.* Also **laughing water.**
    1908 in H.C. Fisher *A. Mutt* 154: And fill the bath with laughing soup. **1930** Lait *On the Spot* 206: *Laughing Soup*...champagne. (Var.: "Giggle water."). **1930** *Variety* (Jan. 8) 106: Whatever stimulating kick one can get out of the laughing soup. **1931** (quot. at GIGGLE-WATER). **1933** Ersine *Pris. Slang* 50: *Laughing Water*—Alcohol. **1939** Wald et al. *Roaring '20's* (film): [You're going to jail] for handling this laughing soup. **1941** *Slanguage Dict.* 24: *Laughing water*....intoxicating liquor. **1966–72** Winchell *Exclusive* 282: Desi was busy sampling some 100-proof Laughing Soup.

laughing weed *n.* marijuana. *Joc.* Cf. LAUGHING GRASS.
    1925 *Writer's Mo.* (June) 487: *Laughing-Weed, Mary Ann*—A Mexican "dope" rag-weed.

launder *v. Mil. Av.* to eliminate from flight training; WASH OUT.
    1944 in Rea *Wings of Gold* 198: If caught, a gouger is usually laundered.

laundry *n.* **1.** clothing that is being worn (regardless of its condition).—esp. constr. with *drop* or *lose.*
    1953 Chandler *Goodbye* 7: Is the gentleman in the soiled laundry a real close friend of yours? **1966** Reynolds & McClure *Freewheelin Frank* 117: She asked if she could turn the light off and I bellered out, "NO! DROP YOUR LAUNDRY!" (Ie, take off your clothes). **1975** in *Tenn. Folklore Soc. Bull.* XLIV 139: *Drop your laundry*, to undress. **1983** Leeson *Survivors* (film): Get out of that laundry. **1995** Knoxville, Tenn., attorney, age 43: The real question is, will she [a film star] lose her laundry [in a film]?
    2. women.
    1977 J. Olsen *Fire Five* 81: Once a month we all go out and chase laundry. *Ibid.* 232: That you been chasing laundry? What's new about that?
    ¶ In phrases:
    ¶ **dump (one's) laundry** *Av.* to crash.
    1983 S. Wright *Meditations* 48: A guy, thirty years a pilot...suddenly dumps his laundry at the end of a runway on a routine takeoff in clean weather.
    ¶ **get (one's) laundry in a bundle** to get upset.
    1969 *Current Slang Comp. I & II* 39: *Get...laundry in a bundle*, v. Get upset.—College students, both sexes, Minnesota.
    ¶ **go to the laundry** *Baseball.* (of a player) to be removed or ejected from a game.
    1962 Houk & Dexter *Ballplayers* 151: Ten of 'em went to bat in the fifth. Mossi went to the laundry.
    ¶ **hang out the laundry** Orig. *USAF.* to drop paratroopers from an airplane; (*hence*) to open a parachute, as behind a drag racer. *Joc.*
    1944 *AAF* 368: *Laundry, hang out the.* dropping [sic] paratroops. **1976** *Webster's Sports Dict.* 204: *Hang out the laundry. drag racing* To release the parachute when crossing the finish line.

laundry bag *n. Mil. Av.* a parachute. *Joc.*
    1955 *AS* XXX (May) 118: *Jump sack; Laundry bag; Nylon, n.* Parachute. **1956** Heflin *USAF Dict.* 294: *Laundry bag.* A parachute. *Slang.*

laundryman *n.* a Chinese man; (*broadly*) an Asian man.—used contemptuously.
    1884 *Life* (Sept. 4) 136: A large army of Chinese laundrymen...is garrisoned at Too-Lung. **1885** *Puck* (Apr. 22) 116: I have been systematically styled a "pig-tailed renegade," a "moon-eyed leper," a "demon of the Orient," a "gangrened laundryman," a "rat-eating Mongol," etc. [**1907** *World To-Day* (Feb.) 115: There is not one American in a hundred thousand who can think of the Chinese as other than curiosities or laundrymen.] **1960** Leckie *March to Glory* 158 [ref. to Korean War]: Blast the balls off those goddam laundrymen! **1976** Simon *Murder by Death* (film): You're one clever laundryman, Inspector Wang.

1984–88 in Berry *Where Ya Been?* 71 [ref. to 1950]: You know what [General] Amond said? "You Marines aren't going to let a few laundrymen stop you, are you?"

laundry queen *n.* a laundress.
    1897 Ade *Horne* 171: If there's anything makes me sore it's to have one o' them laundry queens try to sew buttons on me. **1945** Huie *Omaha to Okinawa* 116: Few of these "Laundry Queens" had any teeth.

laundry spike *n. Mil.* a laundress. Now *hist.*
    1905 *Howitzer* (U.S. Mil. Acad.) (No. 6) 294: *Laundry Spike*—A femme employed in the laundry. **1934** Wohlforth *Tin Soldiers* 126: You can't let a decent girl mix with the factory hands and laundry spikes and the cheap tarts that come here. **1937** Nye *Carbine & Lance* 281 [ref to ca1875]: There are cases on record during the good old days when the officer of the day had to be sent to Sudsville to break up arguments among the laundry "spikes" which surpassed the cigarette-factory scene from Carmen.

lav *n.* a lavatory.
    *1913 in OEDS. **1942** "D. Ormsbee" *Sound of American* 126: We pushed into the...lav. **1975** R.P. Davis *Pilot* 33: Give the passengers a chance to go to the lavs. **1980** Kotzwinkle *Jack* 96: Miss...Legge snuck by the boys' lav and smelled him smoking a stogie. **1989** "Capt. X" & Dodson *Unfriendly Skies* 123: Pot [marijuana] in the lavs.

lavender *adj.* effeminate; (*hence*) (esp. of men) homosexual; (*hence*) of or pertaining to homosexuality or homosexual interests. Occ. as *n.* [The color lavender is popularly thought to appeal chiefly to women and girls.]
    [**1874** in R.W. Synder *Voice of City* 19: Yea, you may talk about your Broadway belles, your Fifth Avenue swells, your exquisitely dressed creatures, with their lavender kids, and their la-de-das.] **1929** Goulding & Masson *Broadway Melody* (film): Your hats would look better in *lavender!* [Said to a markedly effeminate costume designer.]. **1940** *Time* (Mar. 25) 48: NBC revealed that 147 songs are on its blacklist. Because their titles are suggestive 137 may not even be played instrumentally. Among them: *Lavender Cowboy*, [etc.]. **1953** in Bérubé *Coming Out* 116: The swish jargon of its many lavender customers. **1956** Fleming *Diamonds* 107: Coupla lavender boys. You know, pansies. **1965–66** Pynchon *Crying* 110: You're going to the members of the third sex, the lavender crowd this city by the Bay is so justly famous for. **1972** *Anthro. Linguistics* (Mar.): [Among homosexuals:] *Lavender* (adj): Homosexual, commonly used by heterosexuals as in "the lavender set." **1972** R. Barrett *Lovomaniacs* 365: She's never seen with any guy who doesn't have a lavender rep. *a*1979 in S. King *Bachman Bks.* 397: Maybe a little bit queer in the bargain? Touch of the lavender? **1991** *Village Voice* (N.Y.C.) (Aug. 13) 11: Duane has been involved in lavender activism for 17 years. **1993** B. Ehrenreich, in *Time* (June 21) 78: He dropped the gays like a flaming potato, suggesting they might serve in special lavender units. **1995** *CNN & Co* (CNN-TV) (Aug. 30): Bob Dole is not a secret member of the lavender Bund!

lavender *interj.* (used to intensify exclamations).
    1930 *AS* V (Jun.) 391: *Lavendar* [sic] *Jesus*...a choice bit of profanity, probably a variation of "blue Jesus." **1957** in *DARE*: An angry man...swore like "lavender Jeasus [sic]."

lavender gizzard *n.* the Purple Heart. *Joc.*
    1945 Bowman *Beach Red* 76: He'll get the lavender gizzard for this and maybe the DSC.

laverick var. LABRICK.

law *n.* Esp. *Und.* a law officer; policeman.—also used collect. [The 1835 quot. is best considered a literary usage.]
    [**1835** in *DA*: The law opens the house and the belligerent couple are extracted like an oyster from its shell.] **1893** W.K. Post *Harvard* 118: The colonel had got the law pretty well zigged, too. **1918** in *AS* (Oct. 1933) 29: [Ft. Leavenworth:] *Law (the).* Any officer of the law, such as the Executive Officer, a sentry, or a policeman. Always singular in form and in meaning. **1922** *Variety* (Aug. 11) 8: It was Kelly the Fixer, and all of the Law....The Laws were still tight so I hopped in. **1927** *AS* (June) 387: An officer of the law is called *The Law*, sometimes *John Law.* **1929** *Amer. Mercury* (Sept.) 50: So law come up to me an' says I better watch my step. **1929** in Calt *Rather Be Devil* 37: The laws talked so fast [I] didn't have time to say not nary a word. **1930** Pasley *Capone* 242: He learned to talk the argot....A policeman was The Law. **1930** in Fortune *Fugitives* 66: Those laws are all so nice, sugar. They aren't like those Denton laws. **1931** *AS* (June) 333: [Carnival:] *Law, n.* Any local officers such as policemen, sheriff, or constable. **1935** *Esq. Bedroom Companion* 198: Maybe we done wrong

by lettin' the Laws take him. **1937** Anderson *Thieves Like Us* 13: No Laws jumping us here. **1939** "E. Queen" *Dragon's Teeth* 118: Wow, look at those laws pour in! *a*1940 in Lanning & Lanning *Texas Cowboys* 56: When Pat became a law, he sent for Billy the Kid. **1945** *AS* (Apr.) 83: Three of them laws tried to take me to jail an' I flat-out tol' 'em they wasn't to run me in! **1947** J. Lomax *Ballad Hunter* 154: I left him in the car gloomy and uneasy because so many "Laws" were close by. **1950** L. Brown *Iron City* 54: Wont till the laws come. **1956** Algren *Wild Side* 245: I got a pivot tooth now in place of one some ham-handed law cracked out. **1964** in H. Ellison *Sex Misspelled* 255: He said hello to some chick on the street and followed her till she called the laws. **1962–68** B. Jackson *In the Life* 66: So the laws heard the shots. **1970** Thackrey *Thief* 333: And I knew the quickest way to wind up with a houseful of law is to work with a hype. **1993** in Stavsky, Mozeson & Mozeson *A 2 Z* 63: The law shot Rudy....He shot my homie.

law *v.* **1.** *Und.* to arrest.
  1935 Algren *Boots* 53: Law that guy!
  2. to be a law officer.
  1936–75 Earp & Boyer *Wyatt* 47: Wyatt...later told me, "I had my belly full of lawing."

law dog *n.* Esp. *West.* a law officer. Occ. **law hound.**
  1889 "M. Twain" *Conn. Yankee* 482: A sort of raiment which was a surer protection from meddling law-dogs in Britain than any amount of mere innocence and purity of character. *ca*1895 Mason *Sci. Prospecting* 62: Never suspected us, has them law hounds! **1926** "M. Brand" *Iron Trail* 7: Sheriff Cliff Matthew...was an antitype of the true "lawhound." **1927** "M. Brand" *Pleasant Jim* 201: I want all the law-dogs called off and the farm give back to me. **1967** in Sonnichsen *Hopalong to Hud* 26: Know why I like you, old lawdog? **1970** Benteen *Sharpshooters* 42: Okay, you damned lawdog. **1971** G. Wilson *Lawman* (film): Beat the hell out of that law dog. **1982** Braun *Judas Tree* 93: You talk like he's some tough lawdog! **1986** *Outlaws* (CBS-TV): And there's only one law dog to stop us!

law ghost *n.* *Law.* (see quot.).
  1908 Sullivan *Criminal Slang* 15: *Law ghost*—a lawyer who seldom appears in court, but makes a specialty of preparing cases for trial, looking up law, etc.

lawn dart *n.* [sugg. by *Lawn Darts,* trademark for an outdoor game played with plastic-winged darts] *USAF.* (see quot.). *Joc.*
  1992 Cornum & Copeland *She Went to War* 8: Air force [fliers]...call the...little F-16s "lawn darts," partly because of how they look but also because of how they crash.

lawn mower *n.* **1.** *Baseball.* a hard-hit ground ball; GRASS-CUTTER, 1.
  1891 *Chi. Herald* (May 7).
  2. *Mil.* a razor. *Joc.*
  1921 *15th Inf. Sentinel* (Jan. 7) 8: Herbert ought to get a Chinese lawn mower and cut some of that underbrush from his upper lip. **1941** Kendall *Army & Navy Sl.* 9: *Lawnmower*...a razor.
  3. *Und.* a machine gun.
  1930 Lait *On the Spot* 214: *Typewriter*...machine gun. (var.: Lawnmower). **1933** Ersine *Prison Slang* 50: *Lawnmower, n.* A sub-machine gun.
  4. (see quot.).
  1956 Heflin *USAF Dict.* 294: *Lawnmower: Electronics.* 1. A kind of preamplifier used with a radar receiver to cut down the "grass" interference on a radar screen. *Slang* 2. A machine used to cut chaff into various lengths. *Slang.*

law sharp *n.* Esp. *West.* a lawyer.
  1899 A.H. Lewis *Sandburrs* 155: A dip named Jim Butts comes an' touts this law sharp away. **1912** Stringer *Shadow* 145: I'd have the best law sharps money could get. **1935** Coburn *Law Rides Range* 45: I'll stand trial with Joe fer my law sharp.

lawyer *n.* **1.** *Naut.* SEA LAWYER.
  1821–26 Stewart *Man-of-War's Man* II 220: A pretty fellow, indeed, to have the cheek to call honest Jack Morris a lawyer,—a man, so help me, mate, who has more brains in his great toe, than Allen has in all his carcass.
  2. a catfish. *Joc.* Cf. senses in *DAE.*
  1833 Paulding *Lion* 24: Yes, I was chuckle head enough to go down the Mississippi fishing for lawyers one day...I call catfish lawyers—'case you see they're all head, and they're all mouth.

¶ In phrase:
¶ **saltwater lawyer** a shark. *Joc.*
  1830 Ames *Sketches* 21: Shortly afterwards a pig on board an English ship near us...walked out of the gangway overboard, and immediately supplied a great number of "salt water lawyers" with a very loquacious client.

lay *n.* **1.a.** a promiscuous woman; (*also*) a person, esp. a woman, considered as a sexual partner.—usu. considered vulgar.
  [Not always easily distinguishable from **(b)**, below. The early appearance in Shirley's play of *1635 is remarkable but apparently beyond question; the other terms ('tumbler', 'device', and '*bona roba*') were all 17th-C. euphemisms for prostitutes. No other quots. are known before this century.]
  *1635 J. Shirley *Lady of Pleasure* V ii: My blood is rampant, too; I must court somebody. As good my aunt [*i.e.*, a proprietress of a brothel] as any other body....[We have been] At the bridge, at the Bear's Foot....We could not get a lay, a tumbler, a device, a *bona roba* for any money. **1930–31** Farrell *Grandeur* 142: The two girls looked like swell lays with perfectly grand toilets on them. **1932** Hecht & Fowler *Great Magoo* 25: She ain't a lay—she's a man-killer. **1929–34** Farrell *Judgment Day* 464: He could have left a sweet little lay behind him in every town. **1934** H. Miller *Tropic of Cancer* 122: Bessie...couldn't...regard herself as a lay. **1935** Pollock *Und. Speaks: Lay,* a woman of easy virtue. **1936** Levin *Old Bunch* 121: The dump is full of farmers and dollar lays. **1940** W.R. Burnett *High Sierra* 119: If you stick with me, you're just a lay. That's all. **1942** P. Wylie *Vipers* 63: Madam, are you a good lay? **1951** in Kerouac *Letters* 298: Bob...said the blonde was a well-known lay. **1956** P. Moore *Chocolates* 116: What an easy lay she is. **1956** I. Shulman *Good Deeds* 93: Well, well....The lay of the land's returned. **1959** Zugsmith *Beat Generation* 11: She, or her lay,...thought of that. **1960** Wohl *Cold Wind* 203: I'm a good juicy lay for you, aren't I? **1965** Gary *Ski Bum* 210: You're the best lay I ever had. **1966** Little *Bold & Lonely* 152: "Anyway, I was a good lay," she said bitterly. **1970** Ebert *Beyond Valley of Dolls* (film): She said I'm a lousy lay too. **1979** in Terkel *Amer. Dreams* 250: I was a lousy lay. My heart wasn't in it. **1981** Gilliland *Rosinante* 109: Was she a good lay, boss? **1990** L.B. Rubin *Erotic Wars* 68: They were always talking about it, whether this girl or that one was a good lay.
  b. an act of copulation.—often constr. with an evaluative adj.—usu. considered vulgar. [See note at **(a)**, above.]
  1928 Levin *Reporter* 134: Maybe I'll get a coupla good lays out of it but what the hell. **1931** in H. Miller *Letters to Emil* 82: Did you give her a good lay last night?...She promised to give me a lay. **1931** Farrell *McGinty* 217: One lay with that and I'd say, Devil here's my soul. **1934** H. Miller *Tropic of Cancer* 93: She hadn't had a lay for six months. **1935** McCoy *They Shoot Horses* 94: Why don't you old dames go out and buy a lay once in a while? **1936** Dos Passos *Big Money* 232: There's never been a girl got a spoken word by givin' that fourflusher a lay. **1938** "Justinian" *Americana Sexualis* 28: *Lay*...n. An act of coitus. Also, a woman. U.S. coll., c[entury] 19–20. **1939** C.R. Cooper *Scarlet* 301: If one of them looks extra good, I'll hand her a lay. *a*1941 Schulberg *Sammy* 81: Of course, all he's out for is a good lay. *Ibid.* 215: Slip 'em a lay, I could hear him saying. **1948** Cozzens *Guard of Honor* 263: I think...quite a number of women...don't give the ice man a lay every morning as soon as their husbands go the office. **1953** Hughes *Fantastic Lodge* 13: He would...tell her what a lousy lay she was. **1960** Matheson *Beardless Warriors* 13: "Where'd you get your last lay?" asked Wendt. **1960** Krueger *St. Patrick's Bn.* 17: Yeah. He wouldn't know much about the country but he'd sure get the lay of the land. **1961** T.I. Rubin *In the Life* 59: Anyway, she called it a mass lay, you know. **1961** R. Considine *Ripley* 177: It means..."I wish you one thousand lays." **1963** T.I. Rubin *Sweet Daddy* 60: They break their balls working and get paid off by the old lady with a nothing lay. **1969** *Harper's* (Nov.) 93: He could have a quick lay whenever he felt like it without having to worry about the girl. **1990** N.Y.C. man, age 39: I wonder if he ever got a lay out of what's-her-name.
  2.a. an enterprise; an undertaking (of any kind).
  *1706 in *F & H* IV 163: After having reconnoitred it, I would have given something to be off of the lay, having found it quite another sort of a place than what it was represented to me to be. *1707 Farquhar *Beaux Stratagem* III iii, in *OED*: Cou'd I bring her to a Bastard, I shou'd have her all to my self; but I dare not put it upon that Lay, for fear of being sent as a Soldier. *1725 *New Canting Dict.*: *Lay,* an Enterprize, or

Attempt. *To be sick of the Lay,* To be tir'd in waiting for an opportunity to effect their Purposes. *1779 in *F & H* IV 163: We would be fain to know what lay we are to be upon. **1850** "N. Buntline" *G'hals of N.Y.* 15: But *we* ain't on that lay...no how. *Ibid.* 17: I'm on another lay now. *1865 in *F & H* IV 163: Captain Corbett said the vessel was going upon the same lay the Alabama had gone. **1870** *Overland Mo.* (Sept.) 201: Mayor, there is the biggest kind of a lay going on down below....they are digging a tunnel across the yard. **1873** in Bunner *Letters* (July 4) 16: You are in more sympathy with me on that "lay" than any one else. **1878** B. Harte *Drift* 98: Just now your lay is to turn in. **1884** Carleton *Poker Club* 16: De soffes' lay I ever hear. **1891** Clurman *Nick Carter* 16: Ye've struck the wrong party, boss. I ain't on that kind of a lay. **1896** in J.M. Carroll *Benteen-Goldin Letters* 300: I have intimated...that he ought to be choked off that lay. **1898** Norris *Moran* 46: Os-tensiblee we are after shark-liver oil...but also we are on any lay that turns up; ready for any game, from wrecking to barratry. **1940** R. Chandler *Farewell, My Lovely* ch. iv: "Cop?" "Private—on a confidential lay."

b. pursuit; occupation; business.

*1713 in *F & H* IV 163: He an' the Treasurer have been at much pains to break steele [*sic*] off the lay he is upon. *1721 C. Cibber, in *OED:* The Puppy will play, tho' he knows no more of the Lay than a Milkwoman. *1819 [T. Moore] *Tom Crib* 36: We, who're of the *Fancy-lay* [*i.e.,* pugilism],/As dead hands at a *mill* as they. *1852 C. Dickens *Bleak House* ch. xxii: He's not to be found on his old lay. **1859** Matsell *Vocab.* 50: *Lay.* A particular kind of...trade or profession. **1862** C.F. Browne *Artemus Ward* 65: You air full of sentiments. That's your lay, while I'm an exhibiter of startlin curiosities. **1884** "M. Twain" *Huck. Finn* 123: Jour printer by trade....Oh, I do lots of things. What's your lay? **1891** Maitland *Slang Dict.* 165: *Lay*...a pursuit or practice.

c. a scheme or plan.

*1715 in *OED:* To distinguish myself from the refusers on a Jacobite lay. *1838 C. Dickens *Oliver Twist* ch. xliii: The lay is just to take that money away. **1848** (quot. at (**3.d.**), below). **1866–71** Bagg *Yale* 45: *Lay,* a trick of policy, a little game. *a1890 in Barrère & Leland *Slang Dict.* II 9: The victim of a heartless lay. **1891** Maitland *Slang Dict.* 165: *Lay,* a dodge...."What lay are you on?" What scheme...have you on hand? **1928** in Galewitz *Great Comics* 149: Now you've got the lay, see? All you birds have gotta do is what I tell yuh—get me? **1932** L. Berg *Prison Doctor* 84: Now listen. Here is the lay.

d. one's hidden intention; one's game.

1877 E. Wheeler *Deadwood Dick, Prince of the Road* 79: What mought yer lay be ag'in me? [*i.e.,* what do you want with me?]. **1891** Clurman *Nick Carter* 21: You're a fly cop....And we want to know your lay. **1895** Townsend *Fadden* 6: "Wot's yer lay now?" says 'is whiskers, or somet'in like dat. **1902** Cullen *More Tales* 46: I doped it that when he wanted to tip me off as to his lay he'd do it. **1903** in "O. Henry" *Works* 156: He ain't no farmer...and he ain't no con man, for sure. W'at's his lay? **1906** A.H. Lewis *Confessions* 214: Oh, that's your lay! **1913** *Sat. Eve. Post* (Mar. 15) 10: What's his lay, I wonder. **1915–16** Lait *Beef, Iron & Wine* 42: What's your lay? **1916** E.R. Burroughs *Return of Mucker* 68: Put me wise to the gink's lay. **1923** in W.F. Nolan *Black Mask Boys* 43: They don't get my lay at all. **1936** R. Chandler, in Ruhm *Detective* 154: Haven't seen a dick in a year. To talk to. What's your lay? **1949** R. Chandler *Little Sister* 30: "What's the lay?" "I have to find this Orrin P. Quest."

e. a (proper) course of action; one's preference or style of behavior.

1870 *Overland Mo.* (Jan.) 88: I may meet Canvas in heaven, if I keep my word, which the preacher says is the right lay. **1873** Small *Grangers* 6: "That thar's our lay, that is," was the verdict, and about a dozen of the "boys" trotted up and took adult drinks without a wince. **1902** Remington *John Ermine* 134: I do not go to war for fifty dollars,/You can bet your boots that is not me lay. **1903** A.H. Lewis *Boss* 70: What you're out for now is the respectable young workin'-man racket; that's the lay. **1914** Atherton *Perch* 196: Respectful devotion...and pained self-control. That's your lay. *Ibid.* 207: The severely practical is my lay.

3. *Und.* **a.** kind of crime; criminal specialty; RACKET; (*hence*) a specific theft, swindle, or other crime.

*1708 in Partridge *Dict. Und.* 122: *Cheiving layers.* Such [rogues] as cut the Leathers which bears up Coaches behind, [etc.]. *Ibid.* 229: *Fam Layers.* Such [rogues] as go into Goldsmith's Shops, with pretence to buy a Ring, [etc.]. *Ibid.* 440: *Mill Layers.* Such [rogues] as break into Houses, [etc.]. *Ibid.* 528: *Prad Layers.* Such as cut Bags from behind

Horses as People ride along in the Dark. *1714 in Partridge *Dict. Und.* 399: And other Sharpers upon that cheating Lay. *1726 A. Smith *Mems. of J. Wild* 3: The Gentlemen of the *Wipe-Lay,* the *Kid-Lay, File-Lay, Lob-Lay,* together with the *Locks* and *Fences.* *1740 in P. Rawlings *Drunks, Whores* 128: *Jenny* and her *Quondam Spouse* were obliged to turn out by themselves upon the *Slang mort Lay,* described in the following adventures. *1768 in Partridge *Dict. Und.* 399: [We] found it necessary to change the *lay.* **1845** *Nat. Police Gaz.* (Oct. 16) 54: Ex-officers who followed the panel "lay."...Hence the few arrests of the rogues of this "lay." **1848** *Ladies' Repository* VIII (Oct.) 315: *Crib Lay,* An expedition from stealing out of houses. *Ibid.: Lay,* An expedition for any dishonest purpose. **1866** *Night Side of N.Y.* 110: At night the river thief, when not upon his "lay," takes his amusement in the low dance-houses and groggeries. **1872** Burnham *Secret Service* 190: The man was known as "Doctor Blake," and his assumption of the "pious lay," in the course of his travels he found to be the most...advantageous dodge—during his long career of crime. **1872** Crapsey *Nether Side* 18: They worked what was called the "eatable lay," and for a time quite a profitable "lay" it was. *a1890 in Barrère & Leland *Slang Dict.* II 9: But the man in blue responded, "It's a very common lay." **1899** A.H. Lewis *Sandburrs* 108: Yes, d' Rat's a crook all right....He always woiks alone, an' his lay is diamonds. **1899** in "O. Henry" *Works* 522: We five are on a lay....The boss of this plantation thinks he's going to pay this wealth to the hands. He's got it down wrong; he's going to pay it to us. **1903** J. London *Abyss* 94: The country was too overrun by poor devils on that "lay." **1932** "M. Brand" *Jackson Trail* 47: "If I went crooked, what was my lay?"..."You were almost always the outside man." **1968** in *Jour. Pop. Culture* VI (1973) 600: You could always find some of the old-time grifters to help you with a good *lay.* The best ones I ever put down were [at Coney Island].

b. the life or practice of crime.—constr. with *the;* in phr. **on the lay** engaged in crime.

*1781 in W.H. Logan *Pedlar's Pack* 159: Ye Scamps, ye Pads, ye Divers, and all upon the lay. **1791** [W. Smith] *Confess. T. Mount* 21: Ye'll rue the day,/That e'er you scampt upon the lay. *1821 *Real Life in London* I 149: *Upon the lay*...*Upon the lookout for opportunities for the exercise of their [criminal] profession. *ca1824 in J. Farmer *Musa Pedestris* 91: His flaming mot was on the lay. **1851** [G. Thompson] *Jack Harold* 60: The jovial times we had when we went upon the lay*....*Lay,* the pursuit of robbery. **1866** G.A. Townsend *Non-Combatant* 244: General Crawford...orders these boys to be locked up in the jail. They...belong to a gang of young varmints that follers the "lay." **1883** Needham *Arabs* 458: Other boys were after him to "go on the lay," as they called it—that is to break open stores...instead of working hard every day. **1891** Maitland *Slang Dict.* 195: *On the lay* (crooked implied), on any scheme for swindling. *1895 in *F & H* IV 163: He...was very useful, both to us on the lay and to the traps.

c. a quantity of stolen merchandise; loot.

1807 Tufts *Autobiog.* 293 [ref. to 1794]: *To scrag a lay*...to take clothes from the hedges. *1821 in Partridge *Dict. Und.* 400: Flash kanes, where I might fence my snib'd lays.

d. a place to be robbed.

1848 Judson *Mysteries* 36: 'Ave you found a bang-up lay? *Ibid.* 528: "*Lay.*" A place or plan, where and how a theft can be committed. **1931–34** in Clemmer *Pris. Comm.* 333: *Lay*...A prospect for a robbery: "he got the lay while still in prison." **1936** Duncan *Over Wall* 75: In the good old days...our...jobs were always prefaced by a thorough casing of the lay beforehand by our "gay cat." *Ibid.* 158: I can case a lay without suspicion. **1942–49** Goldin et al. *DAUL* 122: Case...the lay and spot...the sleeper (watchman). **1956** Margulies *Punks* 140: We use that for recasing the lay and checking the escape route again.

4. situation; state of affairs.

1864–77 Bartlett *Amer.* (ed. 4) 346: *Lay*...Situation; condition; relative aspect. **1898** Norris *Moran* 189: Here's the lay. Your men can fight—you can fight yourself. **1904** *Life in Sing Sing* 260: The conny fell to the graft and tipped the sucker to the lay. *Ibid.* 263: The stiffs tipped me to the lay. **1915–16** Lait *Beef, Iron & Wine* 166: I takes one look an' I tumbles to the lay. **1921** "M. Brand" *Black Jack* 105: That was a rotten lay, all right. **1922** in Ruhm *Detective* 3: Get the game? I guess I'm just one of the few that see how soft the lay is. **1925** in Hammett *Knockover* 90: I'll give you the lay, and you can name it. **1931** Grant *Gangdom's Doom* 83: You've figured the lay, I guess, Hymie. **1932** L. Berg *Prison Doctor* 249: Get the lay now, don't you? **1936** Duncan *Over the Wall* 126: Now, here's the lay. I've got twelve hundred slugs…planted outside and I want you to get it. **1938** Bellem *Blue Murder* 18: I'm beginning to get the lay now. **1958–59** Southern & Hoffenberg *Candy* 215: Natch I was hip to the lay.

5.a. a bed or bunk; place to lie down.

1919 (quot. at DOG, 11.a.). **1936** *AS* (Apr.) 123: *Lay*…a place to lie down and smoke opium. **1936** R. Adams *Cowboy Lingo* 13: The word "lay" had a rather broad application. Not only might it refer to the general environment of a ranch as a "good lay" or a "tough lay," but…one cowboy might, in the way of asking [another] to share his bed, say, "There's the lay, turn in."

b. *Narc.* the act of reclining so as to smoke opium.

1925–30 in B. Buckley *Frankie* 42: While Frankie goes to work on the Barbary Coast,/ Johnny takes his lay on the hip. **1936** *AS* (Apr.) 123: *Lay*….the act of smoking [opium].

lay *v.* **1.a.** (of either sex) to copulate with.—often used in passive, constr. with *get*.—usu. considered vulgar.

[The earliest quot. prob. reflects a literal euphem. rather than slang usage, but this is less certain of the following two quots.; the existence of the *1635 quot. at LAY, *n.*, 1, sugg. that the verb arose still earlier.]

[*1677 in D'Urfey *Two Comedies* 230: And he took her by the middle small,/And laid her on the plain;/With a hey down derry down, come diddle.] [*ca1786* in S. Rodman *Amer. Poems* 45: Whores will be whores, on the floors/ Where many have been laid.] [*ca1800* in Child *Eng. & Scot. Pop. Ballads* II 471: Is this your tricks abroad, Richard,/Is this your tricks abroad,/Wheneer ye meet a bonny may/To lay her on the road?] **1852** Doten *Journal* I 125: After a while I…took her into my tent and…was about to lay her altogether but the damned old bitch of a squaw came in. **1918** in Carey *Mlle. from Armentières* II (unp.): The Artillery men are doing fine,/Laying the women and drinking wine. **1928** Dahlberg *Bottom Dogs* 136: Burlesk whores….He's been layin' too many of them. **1929** in J. O'Hara *Sel. Letters* 40: She's probably going out with a guy whom she likes and whom she doesn't lay but whom she want to lay because he's been so nice to her. **1930** Van Vechten *Parties* 244: Bliss's ribald witticism: Why is Norma like a valuable hen? Because she lays a new good egg every day. **1930–31** J.T. Farrell *Grandeur* 149: Jack…suggested that they go down to Twenty-second Street and get laid. **1932** Hecht & Fowler *Great Magoo* 16: I'm the only cutie on this whole island that boy ain't laid and forgotten. **1933** Hemingway *Winner* 37: You never layed Steve Ketchel in your life and you know it. **1934** H. Miller *Tropic of Cancer* 93: They all come over here to get laid. **1934** Faulkner *Pylon* 289: Do you suppose…they were both laying her? **1935** Odets *Waiting for Lefty* 12: He's probably been coming here every morning and laying you while I hacked my guts out! **1936** Levin *Old Bunch* 508: It was just laying that big bitch Celia that had done the trick. **1936** Dos Passos *Big Money* 278: Maybe I could lay Elsie Finnegan. **1937** Weidman *Wholesale* 140: If I wanted to get laid, I knew where to go. **1939** C.R. Cooper *Scarlet* 100: A girl blamed me for being the guy when she was laying half the fellows in town. **1937–40** in Whyte *Street Corner Society* 31: If you lay one of them girls, you'll marry her. **1940** R. Wright *Native Son* 185: Did Jan lay the girl? **1934–41** in Mellon *Bullwhip Days* 122 [ref. to a1865]: I can tell you that a white man laid a nigger gal whenever he wanted her. **1941** Schulberg *Sammy* 243 [ref. to ca1925]: Every time a guy gets laid around here it's dough in his pocket. **1941** H.A. Smith *Low Man* 172: I ain't tryin' to lay you, Polly. **1943** in Inman *Diary*: I laid her right there. **1944** R. Brooks *Brick Foxhole* 28: And that's the trouble with you. You want to get laid. **1945** Himes *If He Hollers* 9: Ellie Maye laying me because I wasn't married. **1946** Petry *Street* 263: Suppose I want to lay her myself. **1948** Vidal *City & Pillar* 44: Only they're not really so damned nice, they're just afraid of getting laid. **1951–52** P. Frank *Hold Back Night* 49: Well, he tried to lay her. **1956** Levin *Compulsion* 178: Artie was willing to bet a ten-spot he could lay Ruth on his first date. **1958** Talsman *Gaudy Image* 59: He hadn't laid that many queers. **1958** J. Steinbeck *Acts of K. Arthur* 389: Igraine has been laid by someone she thought was her husband. **1958** Cooley *Run for Home* 38: At least we get laid. **1965** Cassavetes *Faces* 121: Yes, I also had an analyst. I layed him. **1966** Susann *Valley of Dolls* 89: She'll lay anything in pants. **1970** *Atlantic* (Feb.) 76: Things can be sexy when you get laid without a great deal of feeling. *a*1974 R. Fitzgerald *Iliad* 43: I say we pull away for home, and/leave him here on the beach to lay his captive girls! **1990** *CBS This Morning* (CBS-TV) (June 25): "Ten years before that?" "I'd want to get laid." "Don't you still?" "Sure!" **1991** *Donahue* (NBC-TV) (Apr. 4): You are accused of wanting to get laid with *everybody*! **1995**

Jerry Springer Show (synd. TV series): I and a friend of mine bet each other who could lay her first.

b. to engage in copulation.—usu. considered vulgar.

[**1864** in R. Mitchell *Vacant Chair* 71: Some of them looked good enough to *lay* with.] **1918** in M. Carey *Mlle. from Armentières* II (unp.): You never could beat their lowest price,/And the way they'd lay was seldom nice. **1926** Tully *Jarnegan* 182: Too charitably inclined, the kid was—accommodating little pullet—laid to help the roosters out. He smiled grimly. **1928** Bodenheim *Georgie May* 10: Weah all boozing, and stealing, and laying, and getting it as easy as we can. **1930** Mae West *Babe Gordon* 300: Da's all duh lazin' he kin do now. **1929–33** J.T. Farrell *Manhood of Lonigan* 209: Listen, she lays for every punk in the neighborhood. **1933** Odets *Awake & Sing!* 57: Not like other dames—shove 'em and they lay. **1938** "Justinian" *Amer. Sexualis* 28: *Lay. v.* To copulate. **1947** Willingham *End as a Man* 160: I never heard of women who won't lay. **1951** Robbins *Danny Fisher* 60: Does she lay, Danny? **1959** E. Hunter *Killer's Wedge* 50: Okay, you're not a hooker, okay? You lay for money, okay? That's different. **1962** T. Berger *Reinhart* 367: Hey, you getting much? Them college broads lay for yuh?

2. to knock unconscious; LAY OUT, 2.—usu. used in var. similes. Also constr. with *out*.

1836 *Spirit of Times* (July 9) 162: You'll lay him cold as a waggon tire. **1841** (quot. at LAY OUT, *v.*, 2). **1921–25** J. Gleason & R. Taber *Is Zat So?* 8: If you pull that…yarn again, I'll lay you like a rug. **1925** *Colliers'* (Sept. 19) 48: To-day Tierney would lay you like a carpet. **1929** in R.E. Howard *Book* 79: I'll lay this bird like a rug in the next round! **1932** L. Berg *Prison Doctor* 135: You can lay that dinge like a carpet. **1933–34** Lorimer *Stag Line* 75: Pipe down or I'll lay you like—like the egg you are. **1939** I. Shaw, in *New Yorker* (Mar. 11) 23: Dempsey would lay Louis out like a carpet.

3. *Und.* to pass (counterfeit money, forged checks or securities, etc.); *lay paper* s.v. PAPER.—usu. constr. with *paper* (see s.v. PAPER); also with *down*.

1886 in Partridge *DSUE* (s.v. *lay down*). **1889** Bailey *Ups & Downs* 15 [ref. to 1871]: He said I was going to lay down a paper at the jug, and pull off a good big trick. *Ibid.* 22: One of the members of the gang was then told what bank to take the check to, and he was expected to return with the money. This branch of the business was called laying down, and was the most dangerous work of all. **1906** *Nat. Police Gaz.* (Apr. 14) 3: If I lay this…we're on the sunny side of Easy street.

4. *Gamb.* to wager with.

1919 Witwer *Alex the Great* 115: Did you come all the way up here to-night to lay me on a horse race?

5. *Black E.* to idle; loaf.

1971 *Who Took Weight?* 193: Wha's happenin'?…Jus' layin', y'know.

¶ In phrases:

¶ **laid, relaid, and parlayed** frequently or vigorously copulated with.—usu. considered vulgar. *Joc.* Also vars. [The second sense in 1954–60 *DAS* quot. has never been independently attested; thus it seems unlikely that it represents "the most common use." Perh. the frequency labels for the definitions were erroneously switched.]

1953–57 Giovannitti *Combine D* 478 [ref. to WWII]: "They must have got laid last night." "And relayed and parlayed!" **1954–60** *DAS*: *Laid, relaid, and parlayed*…to dispense with all, esp. sexual, restrictions and enjoy oneself thoroughly. *Not common*…2. Completely deceived, cheated or taken advantage of. *The most common use.* **1961** T.I. Rubin *In the Life* 7: Well, let me tell you: I've been laid a million times—no ten million. I've been laid, relaid, and parlayed; screwed, blewed, and tattooed. **1970** C. Harrison *No Score* 110: What she wants is to get laid and relaid and parlayed. **1972** Pearce *Pier Head Jump* 10: I could just see myself over there. Drinkin' up on all that vino. Gettin' laid, relayed and marmalade. **1987** Zeybel *Gunship* 97: Laid for sure….Plus waylaid, parlayed, relayed, delayed, and inlaid.

¶ **lay a batch** [or **patch**] (see quots.). Cf. earlier *lay 'em down*, 2, s.v. LAY DOWN.

1969 *Current Slang I & II* 58: *Lay a batch*, v. Leave black tire marks during acceleration.—High school students…California. **1971** Dahlskog *Dict.* 37: *Lay a patch*, to accelerate rapidly in an automobile or motorcycle, leaving skid marks and making a screeching noise.

¶ **lay [back] in the cut** *Black E.* to rest, take it easy; wait.

1962 in Wepman, Newman & Binderman *The Life* 48: I lay in the cut on Carmen's big butt. **1971** *Essence* (Aug.) 47: Ours is mostly for layin' back in the cut clee-e-an, watchin' them fine mamas swivelin' by. *a*1994 Smitherman *Black Talk* 152: When they tell you yo cancer in remission, all that mean is that bad boy layin in the cut waitin for yo ass!

¶ **lay iron** see s.v. IRON, *n*.

¶ **lay it** *Jazz.* to perform skillfully or energetically.

    1939 in A. Banks *First Person* 225: I was singing for that man. I was really laying it, Jack, just like Marian Anderson. **1942** *ATS* 566: Play "hot jazz"; "swing":...*lay it, lay it in the groove. Ibid.* 567: Send me, gate!...kill me!...lay it! *Ibid.* 568: *Lay it,* to sing well.

¶ **lay it on the line, 1.** see *lay* [or *put*] *it on the line* s.v. LINE, *n*. **2.** to LAY, *v.*, 1.b.

    1946 Gresham *Nightmare Alley* 251: You can't blame no gal for laying it on the line for money.

¶ **lay it on the wood** to *lay* [or *put*] *it on the line,* 2 s.v. LINE. [Despite the ref. to cards, this is not in a gambling context.]

    1927 in Dundes *Mother Wit* 203: They got to come across for once and lay it on the wood for black men according to Hoyle. They got to put the cards on the table.

¶ **lay like a rug** [or **carpet** or **roll of linoleum**], **1.** see **(2)**, above. **2.** *Theat.* to impress or delight (an audience).

    1929 Goulding & Mason *Broadway Melody* (film): We'll lay that dame like a roll of linoleum!

¶ **lay paper** see s.v. PAPER.

¶ **lay pipe, 1.** *Pol.* to engage in any of various forms of political intrigue.

    1848 in Bartlett *Amer.* 251: The result of the Pennsylvania election would be in the least doubtful, if we could be sure of fair play and no *pipe-laying.* **1848** J.R. Bartlett in *Ibid.*: To lay pipe means to bring up voters not legally qualified....The term...arose from an accusation brought against the Whig party of...New York...some years ago, of a gigantic scheme to bring on voters from Philadelphia....As if for the purpose of concealment,...the number of men hired to visit New York and vote, being spoken of as so many yards of pipe—the work of laying down pipe for the Croton water being at that time in full activity....The accused were acquitted. The term *"pipe-laying,"* however, was at once adopted as a synonym for negotiations to procure fraudulent votes. **1856** in Bartlett *Amer.* (ed. 2) 323: There is a magnificent scheme of *pipe-laying* and log-rolling going on in Pennsylvania. **1862** in *DAE*: To charge him, in the technical language of his party, with "pulling wires," and "laying pipes" for the Presidency. **1877** Bartlett *Amer.* (ed. 4) 468: *Pipe-Layer...*A [?political] trickster.—*N.Y. Tribune.* **1888** in *F & H* IV 212: There are not a few who are *pipe-laying* and martialling forces for the fray. **1891** Maitland *Slang Dict.* 165: *Laying pipe,* making arrangements to ensure the passage or defeat of some measure before a legislative body. **1893** in *DA*: The Irish...who began by laying our water-pipes...now lay a different kind of pipe, and make our city government. *a*1890–96 *F & H* IV 212: *Pipe-layer...*(American).—A political intriguer. **1942** *ATS* 794: *Pipelaying,* political intriguing, securing illegal votes.

2. to engage in copulation.—usu. considered vulgar. Also **lay bricks.**

    1931 J.T. Farrell *McGinty* 266: Before Adam laid bricks with Eve, you was. **1931–39** Dos Passos *Young Man* 85: He could lay a little pipe himself when they were through. Ben's girl broke out in a giggle. **1969** Cray *Erotic Muse* 235 [song learned *ca*1940]: But wouldn't we have a helluva time laying pipe together? **1972** *Anthro. Linguistics* (May) 104: *Lay pipe* (v.): [Among homosexual men] To perform anal intercourse. **1978** Schrader *Hardcore* 107: You trying to lay some pipe, right?...You wanna get laid, right? **1979** in R. Carson *Waterfront* 67: Payday, ain't it?...Reckon I'll lay me some pipe t'night. **1994** S. Johnson et al. *Ensucklopedia* (unp.): These guys...heh heh, lay pipe.

¶ **lay the leg** see s.v. LEG.

¶ **lay the note** *Und.* to engage in shortchanging or various other elementary swindles.

    1928 M. Sharpe *Chicago May* 286: *Laying the note*—crooked advertising. **1946** Dadswell *Hey, Sucker* 159: Back in those days the bosses went around laying-the-note. Glitter gals worked the hotels. **1966** Braly *Cold* 73: Bunco. He was trying to lay the note. He picked a cashier whose boyfriend was the beat cop....That's a burnt-out hustle.

Laying the note went out with gold bricks. **1968–70** in Agar *Ripping & Running* 161: *Lay the note...*Short change.

¶ **lay away, 1.** to knock unconscious; PUT AWAY.

    1897 Ade *Pink* 163: 'Ey's one ol' boy 'at can jus' fold 'em up an' lay 'em away as fast as you hand 'em to him. **1995** *Jerry Springer Show* (synd. TV series): If I had ever talked like that to *my* father, he'da laid me away like *that.* And if I threatened to call the cops, he'da laid me away again.

2. to eat or consume; PUT AWAY.

    1909 "Clivette" *Café Cackle* 71: The way he laid away that steak was a caution.

laydown *n.* **1.** a rest or a sleep; a place to rest or sleep.

    1863 Massett *Troubadour* 25: A bath and a lay down. ***1909** in Partridge *Dict. Und.* 400: In tramp language, it was at least a decent "lay down"—*i.e.,* bed. ***1936** (cited in Partridge *Dict. Und.* 400).

2. the act of collapsing.

    1899 Cullen *Tales* 20: When they finally told me...that my first trip was to be to St. Louis, I was ready to do a lay-down.

3. something easily done; PUSHOVER.

    1935 Pollock *Und. Speaks: Lay down,* virtually a certainty; a cinch. **1989** *Newsweek* (Aug. 28) 8: *Lay down.* An extremely easy sell....That customer was a real lay down.

lay down *v.* **1.a.** to fall from a strong blow.

    1848 Judson *Mysteries* 193: At each blow he gave, a darkie laid down.

b. *Sports,* esp. *Boxing.* to throw a bout or contest; *take* [or *do*] *a dive* s.v. DIVE.—also used fig.

    [**1907** T.A. Dorgan, in Zwilling *TAD Lexicon* 53: I know for a fact he was going to "lay" to Nelson.] **1909** Irwin *Con Man* 41: The fight comes off, and his man lays down. **1909** T.A. Dorgan, in Zwilling *TAD Lexicon* 53: Would he have so much fear of Johnson that...he would pay the colored champion to lay down? **1911** in J. London *Short Stories* 521: Lay down, kid,...and I'll help you to the championship. **1912** *Adventure* (July) 504: I...punched him out aftah Web told me to lay down. **1913–15** Van Loan *Taking the Count* 162: You laid down...for one measly little poke on the jaw...you're going to fight on the square, to-night, understand? **1916** in R. Lardner *Round Up* 114: Me lay down for fifty bucks? Not me! *a*1917 J. London, in M.H. Greenberg *In Ring* 283: You gotta lay down, Rivera....I'll let you lick Danny next time. **1925–26** J. Black *You Can't Win* 193: James Hamilton Lewis...an ambitious fighting young lawyer who never laid down on a client. **1931** (quot. at SQUEAL). **1931** J.T. Farrell *McGinty* 12: The White Sox laid down to the Cincy Reds in the World Series last year. That's my opinion! **1934** Jevne & Purcell *Joe Palooka* (film): They were all set-ups. Hand-picked. I paid every one of them guys to lay down. **1949** A. Cohn *Set-Up* (film): They wanted me to lay down. I was takin' that kid.

2. to cease talking; shut up.—used in imper. only.

    1922 T.A. Dorgan, in Zwilling *TAD Lexicon* 53: (Talking about your boys progress in school now that the world's series is coming on) Aw lay down Sisler will lead both leagues. **1933** Ersine *Pris. Slang* 50: *Lay down...*Be quiet, still; stop. (The term is generally used as a command). Lay down, you yap.

3.a. Esp. *Black E & Jazz.* to perform; present; perpetrate; (*hence*) to say, speak; tell. Cf. *lay it* s.v. LAY, *v.*

    1943 *Time* (July 19) 54: Are ya laying down the hustle? **1950** Blesh & Janis *Played Ragtime* 194: He laid down a terrific stomp [rhythm]. **1947–52** R. Ellison *Invisible Man* 470: Listen to old Du lay it down—he's a bitch, ain't he? **1958** in R.S. Gold *Jazz Talk* 162: Gene must have really laid down some shuck to Barton about your playing. **1959** H. Ellison *Gentleman Junkie* 210: I picked up what the kid was laying down. **1964** R.S. Gold *Jazz Lexicon* 184: *Lay down.* To present, perform, or contribute (something)...current since c. 1935. **1966** Fariña *Down So Long* 285: You know what I'm laying down. **1966** Neugeboren *Big Man* 29: Lay it down, babe. **1966** *New Yorker* (Dec. 31) 28: He's a bit of a masochist, and I pick up what he lays down. **1967** in Wepman, Newman & Binderman *The Life* 114: I had taken a trip to Liverpool just to lay the larceny down. **1970** (quot. at RAP). **1972** N.Y.U. student: Then he starts laying down his existentialism rap. **1978** J. Carroll *Basketball Diaries* 5: The stuff she laid down about Mary was the worst. **1978** *Muppet Show* (CBS-TV): Man, you lay down some fine percussion. **1982** D.J. Williams *Hit Hard* 140: Them others inside with the old lady trying to lay down some French shit.

b. *Entertainment Industry.* to record phonographically.

1983 *Rolling Stone* (Feb. 3) 35: She laid down a total of 180 [recordings].

¶ In phrase:

¶ **lay 'em down, 1.** to die.

[*1859 Hotten *Slang Dict.*: Lay down the knife and fork, to die.] **1933** J.V. Allen *Cowboy Lore* 21: His favorite songs are always melancholy—about home and mother or the cowboy who laid 'em down far away from his friend. **1942** *ATS* 133: Die…*lay 'em down.*

2. to go very fast.

1942 *ATS* 56: Run…*cut dirt*…*lay 'em down.* **1976** Whelton *CB Baby* 21: I turned northbound [in a vehicle]…and began to really lay 'em down.

lay-down joint *n. Narc.* an opium den.

1936 Dai *Opium Add.* 201: *Lay down joint.* A place where one can go and smoke opium. These places supply one with everything needed for a price. **1980** in Courtwright *Addicts Who Survived* 167: I used to go to a lay-down joint. *Ibid.* 380: *Lay-down joint:* a place where opium is smoked, often a specially equipped hotel room.

layer *n.* a currency note; (*hence*) money.

1933 Ersine *Prison Slang* 50: *Layer,* a piece of currency. **1944** in Himes *Black on Black* 198: Cat's say they's goin' east—slip up there and make them layers. *Ibid.* 201: I don't care who knows I'm slavin' long as I get my proper layers. **1954** Himes *Third Generation* 265: I'm going to get some layers, man…He [returned with] thirty-two dollars.

layer-down *n. Und.* a gang member who cashes a forged check. Cf. LAY, *v.*, 2.

1889 Baily *Ups & Downs* 22 [ref. to 1871]: Everything depended, in a very large degree, upon the layer-down, and he must be sure to be a man of cool nerve, who could approach the cashier of any bank with a business-like air, and meet any questions on the spur of the moment in such a manner as to inspire confidence and disarm any suspicion.

lay it *v Black E.* (see quot.).

1929–32 in *AS* (Dec 1934) 289: [Lincoln Univ.:] *Lay it* (also *lay it away*) To do something extremely well. [Used most often in the imperative.] There are many expressions of a similar nature in "Lincolnese" such as knock it out; ramp down; stroke; take out; take the man out; turn it out.

layoff *n.* a respite, as from work. Now *S.E.*

1889 in *DA*: Fred Diamond is taking a lay-off. **1913** Jocknick *Early Days*: Scotty took a short "Lay off" about this time…to visit his girl. **1949** in *DA*: He resumes work after a layoff. **1985** N.Y.C. man, age 36: It's tough to get back to jogging after a two-week layoff.

lay off *v.* [cf. *OED* s.v. *lay* def. 54f] **1.a.** to refrain or rest from work or activity; (*often*) to loaf.

1839 *Spirit of Times* (June 22) 181: A— is anxious to know whether he is "hanging out" at Washington or "laying off" at Aldie? **1850** "N. Buntline" *G'hals of N.Y.* 17: Do you want me ter lay off…while we're all a starvin'? **1856** in *Calif. Hist. Soc. Qly.* IX (1930) 51: Layed off feeling very sick. **1863** in E. Marchand *News from N.M.* 66: If you miss a call without a good excuse you go to the Guard house. But still I have plenty of time to lay off through the day. **1865** Dennett *South as It Is* 40: They'll work a day, and then they want to lay off a day. **1876** in L. Hearn *Amer. Misc.* I 168: These will work two or three months and then "lay off" until all their money has found its way to whisky-shops and brothels. **1881** Nye *Forty Liars* 28: I…grubstaked myself for the winter, and allowed I'd lay off till the snow left the range in the spring. **1895** Coup *Sawdust* 59: As a rule, all shows "lay off" during the winter. **1897** W.D. Howells, in *OED*: When the husbands come up Saturday nights, they don't want to go on a tramp Sundays. They want to lay off and rest. **1898–1900** Cullen *Chances* 24: I got a couple of fingers crushed between two salt fish boxes…and I had to lay off from work. **1910** *Variety* (Aug. 20) 5: Asking her to take the open place instead of "laying off" this week on her way to Grand Rapids. **1920** in E. O'Neill *Letters* 107: I still feel pretty bum and I'm not sorry to lay off. **1922** *In the Clutch of Circumstance* 161: The thought that a good hand might give me a chance to "lay off" decided me.

b. to cease, esp. one's meddling or interference.—often used imper.

1911 Van Loan *Big League* 53: He's just battin' us to death this season. If he don't lay off pretty soon, I'm going to take down the sign! **1915** *N.Y. Eve. Jour.* (Aug. 16) 8: Ah, lay off—this is important stuff. **1915–16** Lait *Beef, Iron & Wine* 264: He gets a hunch sent his way to

lay off. **1916** D. Runyon, in Paxton *Sport* 91: Say lissen, do you think I'mah nut? Whadduh I wanna go in for? To see 'at football stuff? To see 'at crowd? Say, lay off! Lay off! **1917** *Variety* (Nov. 30) 5: Paid For "Laying Off." **1918** *Stars & Stripes* (Feb. 8) 3: Aw, lay off! Don't blame him! **1919–21** Chi. Comm. Race Rel. *Negro in Chi.* 12: The coppers…were all fixed and told to lay off on club members. **1923** in J. O'Hara *Sel. Letters* 5: Now that you're bored to tears I'd better lay off for a time. **1923** Ornitz *Haunch, Paunch & Jowl* 51: Lay off, I'm taking care of this for Black Reilly. **1925** Asch *Office* 62: Come on, lay off. **1927** Wylie *Heavy Laden* 84: Lay off, brother.…Cut it! **1931** Uhler *Cane Juice* 42: Lay off!…Leave him alone. **1934** in Ruhm *Detective* 95: Tell him to lay off. **1933–35** D. Lamson *About to Die* 154: And somebody's going to catch himself a mouthful of fist if he don't lay off! **1937–40** in Whyte *Street Corner Soc.* 121: Whadda you mean trying to shake down Billy Whyte? You better lay off. **1982** Rucker *57th Kafka* 62: Lay off, Harry. I'm not interested. *1984 J. Green *Dict. Contemp. Slang* 166: *Lay off!* a warning:…stop doing a given action.

2.a. to stop forcibly.

1895 T.L. Williams *Princeton* 22: Your services will not be required unless Billy is laid off before he reaches the foot of the entry stairs.

b. to keep away from (usu. a person or place); (*esp.*) to stop annoying, abusing, or interfering with (someone). Also **lay off of.**

1908 McGaffey *Show Girl* 172: For he saw no show of being able to lay off work. **1911** *Hampton's Mag.* (Feb.) 194: Anyway, lay off of me. **1912** C. Mathewson *Pitching* 69: Lay off that Mathewson kid. Leave him alone. **1918** *Wadsworth Gas Attack* 14: He wants to know why the kleptomaniac has to "lay off" the officers' showers and pick on him. **1918** Casey *Cannoneers* 230: "Lay off of it," I suggested. "It's a punk place." **1920** Witwer *Kid Scanlan* 27: Dick tells a gunman by the name of MacDuff to lay off him or he'll knock him for a goal. **1920** Hurst *Humoresque* 119: Lay off my territory. I seen him first. **1922** Colton & Randolph *Rain* 72: Lay off me or I'll show you what it means when I start to get mad. **1927–28** in R. Nelson *Dishonorable* 132: It's your business to lay off Scarsi now! **1928** F.R. Kent *Pol. Behavior* 123: They forgive him for robbing the rich so long as he "lays off" the poor. **1928** Callahan *Man's Grim Justice* 30: He's a bad hombre, Jackie, so lay off his broad. **1928** Carr *Rampant Age* 3: Lay offa the kid a little. **1926–35** Watlers & Hopkins *Burlesque* 9: Hey lay off a me. **1935** D. H. Clarke *Regards to Broadway* 77: You lay off Sarah. She's my skirt. See? **1936** Kenyon & Daves *Petrified Forest* (film): Lay off him, Boze. **1936** Dos Passos *Big Money* 246: You lay off him, do you hear? **1944** W. Duff *Marine Raiders* (film): Aah, will ya lay off me? **1955** J. Epstein *Tender Trap* (film): Why don't you lay off me? **1963** Blechman *Omongo* 114: Lay off him. **1968** L.J. Davis *Whence All Had Fled* 31: "You said I should lay off Goldfarb," Probish said. **1971** Flicker *Nichols* (NBC-TV): Get your kid here to lay off Feeney. **1986** D. Wellington *Zombie Nightmare* (film): Lay off me!

c. *Specif.,* to cease (annoying speech or behavior).

1918 *Sat. Eve. Post* (Jan. 19) 66: So you lay off that stuff. **1918** in D. York *Mud & Stars* 126: Lay off that stuff! You got us wrong. **1918** in *St. Lawrence Univ. in War* 39: Lay off those hero rumors about me. **1925** McAlmon *Silk Stockings* 44: Lay off the chatter, Foster, for the love of Mike. **1927** C.J. Daly *Snarl of Beast* 17: Lay off that stuff.…back, you! **1933** Creelman & Rose *King Kong* (film): Say, lay off the shovin', will ya? **1936** Monks & Finklehoffe *Bro. Rat* 154: "Gee, that's a pretty moon!"…"Lay off the moon." **1955** Q. Reynolds *HQ* 142: Will you lay off that Mister Mayor business.…Call me Jim. **1958** T. Capote *Breakfast at Tiffany's* 32: "What's David O. Selznick's phone number, O.J.?" "Lay off."

d. to abstain from the use or consumption of (something). Also **lay off of.**

1927 P.A. Rollins *Jinglebob* 144: I laid off all liquor an' mosies cold sober…to Fort Collins. **1931** F. Marion *Champ* (film): I'm gonna lay off the booze. Word of honor! **1954** Bruce & Henley *Rocket Man* (film): You'd better lay off the fried stuff. You know what the doctor said. **1981** Ehrlichman *Witness* 22: If he wanted me to work with him he would lay off the booze.

lay on *v.* Orig. *Black E.* to tell or give (to someone); impart (to someone). [The 1929 quot. may exemplify S.E. sense 'hold accountable for (blameworthy activity)'.]

[**1929** in Leadbitter & Slaven *Blues Records* 114: Stop Laying That

Stuff On Me.] **1936** in P. Oliver *Meaning of Blues* 143: Lay it on me, boy, it's bad! **1936** in Leadbitter & Slaven *Blues Records* 246: Mama Let Me Lay It On You. **1942** Z.N. Hurston, in *Amer. Mercury* (July) 86: Lay de skin on me [*i.e.,* shake hands], pal! **1944** Burley *Harlem Jive*: I'm gonna lay a little spiel on you about a chippie I once knew. **1946** Mezzrow & Wolfe *Really Blues* 186 [ref. to 1930's]: Lay some of that [stuff]…on me. **1953** W. Fisher *Waiters* 239: Man, I'm tellin' you. Ah! Lay it on me, papa. **1954** Krasna, Panama & Frank *White Christmas* (film): "I'll tell you." "Well, then lay it on me." **1956** E. Hunter *Second Ending* 226: Rog never laid a bad bindle on me ever. **1958** Meltzer & Blees *H.S. Confid.* (film): I'm gonna lay a little history on you. **1959** A. Anderson *Lover Man* 127: Don't be laying that jive on me. **1959** Murtagh & Harris *Who Live in Shadow* 41: "Man," he says today, "she kept laying the same old story on me all the time." **1961** J.A. Williams *Night Song* 26: Hey, you cats, lay some bread on me and I'll play your sides. **1962** T. Berger *Reinhart in Love* 199: Now don't lay no communism on me. **1970** T. Southern *Blue Movie* 201: "Lay it on me Tone."…"Then dig…*Nicky Sanchez*." **1972** Claerbaut *Black Jargon* 71: Lay it on me, man.…Tell it like it is. **1978** Selby *Requiem* 17: Hahahaha, lay it on me, and they gave each other five [*i.e.,* slapped palms in congratulation]. **1989** *Night Court* (NBC-TV): OK, Art. Lay it on me. What's the problem? **1994** *Marriage Counselor* (Lifetime TV): They didn't like lay any huge guilt-trip on me or anything.

layout *n.* **1.a.** *Gamb.* cards or numbers laid out or represented on a gaming table for players to wager on. Now *S.E.*
   1851 in *DAE*: As the fellers say at monte, he was a lay out I didn't want to bet on. **1859** Matsell *Vocab.* 113: The "lay-out" is comprised of all the cards in a suit…posted upon a piece of velvet, which can be spread upon the table whenever the dealer chooses to open the game. **1864** in *DAE*: This is called the "lay-out" and upon these cards the players place their bets. **1868** in T.L. Clark *Dict. Gamb. & Gaming* 116: Upon the centre of the table is a suit of cards arranged in order, upon which the players place their money or stakes, and which is called the lay-out. **1887** [C. Mackenzie] *Jack Pots* 119: I chalked out a lay-out on my cell floor…and dealt faro for him. **1987** in T.L. Clark *Dict. Gamb. & Gaming* 117: A crap layout on a large craps table is frequently the same at each end of the table.

b. an outfit of equipment, clothing, etc. Now *colloq.*
   1867 in A.K. McClure *Rocky Mtns.* 219: They get up a most expensive "layout" for him. **1890** in *DA:* Mr. Armour's daughters must have struck their pa for a new layout of spring clothes and somebody had to be squeezed.

c. *Narc.* equipment for smoking opium.
   1881 H.H. Kane *Opium* 11: All…who can afford it now have their own lay-outs for smoking in their sleeping rooms. **1883** A.S. Williams *Demon of Orient* 60: Nearly every [Chinese laundry] has its lay-out. **1892** (quot. at HABIT). **1898** L.J. Beck *Chinatown* 147: The paraphernalia or "lay out" for smoking is brought to the bunk on order. *ca*1905 in Spaeth *Read 'Em & Weep* 104: Round the lay-out a couple of hopfiends. **1906** Wooldridge *Hands Up* 215: A layout can be purchased for any amount up to $5. **1915** Howard *God's Man* 194: A hypodermic syringe in their hip pockets, or a lay-out in the basement. **1922** Murphy *Black Candle* 43: The users of the pipe borrow the lay-out belonging to the Chinese cook. **1988** Courtwright et al. *Addicts* 380: Layout: outfit for smoking opium.

d. a contraption.
   1903 Townsend *Sure* 14: And you straddles dat layout!

e. *Und.* (among pickpockets) (see quots.).
   1925 *Writer's Mo.* (June) 487: Layout—watch and chain. **1942–49** Goldin et al. *DAUL* 122: Layout…(Pickpocket jargon) A watch and chain.

2. a party, group, or collection of people; outfit, bunch; (*Mil.*) (*obs.*) a military unit.
   1862 in Jackman *Diary* 35: I am in a room…occupied by "Morgan's men," the boys I came with, belonging to that "lay-out." **1863** in Heartsill *1491 Days* 175: We would have fared finally, had they believed us to be deserters, for this "layout" are no doubt Unionists. **1867** B. Duke *Morgan's Cav.* 508: By this time our small "lay out" found the fighting rather interesting. **1869** *Overland Mo.* (Aug.) 128: Several persons in our lay-out (*i.e.,* our company) in New Mexico swapped good American horses for mustangs. **1873** G. Custer *Life on Plains* 107: It would be astonishin' ef that lootenint and his lay-out gits into the fort without a scrimmage. **1882** S. Watkins *Co. Aytch* 198: That Georgia militia, every man of them, charged forward, and in a

few moments we ran into a small squad of Yankees, and captured the whole "lay out." **1891** B. Duke *Remin.* 20: I belong to Colonel Censer's "lay-out," but don't know wher [*sic*] it is. **1904** in *DAE:* I hain't never seed nothin' good in him nur his layout [family]. **1907** *McClure's Mag.* (Feb.) 379: Take us all together, and there wasn't forty cents Mex in the layout. **1914** Giles *Rags & Hope* 58: The corporal marched the layout off. **1922** *Sat. Eve. Post* (June 3) 10: I could get together a team of players…and in six months run away from the best layout in the country. **1966** in *DARE*.

3.a. a plan.
   1867 in A.K. McClure *Rocky Mtns.* 211: A "Lay-out" is any proposed enterprise, from organizing a State to digging out a prairie dog. **1892** Bierce *Beetles* 260: A scheme that is the boss lay-out. **1949** in *Harper's* (Feb. 1950) 74: The better the mob, the more thorough the layout.

b. a situation; state of affairs; setup.
   1873 Beadle *Undevel. West* 103: Apostle Sammy Richards truly had, as our companion expressed it, "the softest layout in the business." **1886** in *AS* XXV (1950) 35: Who may never have seen such a lay-out. **1895** in J.I. White *Get Along Dogies* 66: That verse is the apple dumpling of the whole lay out. **1912** R. Beach *Net* 138: Here's the layout; the Rukertons have an operative who knew Sabella in New York. **1915** Howard *God's Man* 264: I'm wise to the layout now. **1931** Rynning *Gun Notches* 11: That was the layout ahead of us. **1944** C.B. Davis *Leo McGuire* 162: But it's a tough layout, boy. *Ibid.* 177: I says, "Oh, yes," begining to get the layout. **1954** G. Kersh, in Pohl *Star of Stars* 21: I'm not giving you anything you can make anything of, see? This is the layout, see? **1954** Lerner & Lowe *Brigadoon* (film): What a loony layout this is! **1964** Westheimer *Von Ryan* 21: Brief me on the layout before we go inside.

4. a place, as of residence or business. Now *colloq.* [The def. in 1933 quot. is perh. overly specific.]
   1883 Hay *Bread-Winners* 128: What a lay-out this is, anyhow: and his small eyes darted rapidly around the room. **1892** Frye *From Hq.* 166: I axed youse de damage on de whole layout! **1893** F.P. Dunne, in Schaaf *Dooley* 194: Th' booths was something iligant.…Next to hers was th' ice crame layout. **1905** in "O. Henry" *Works* 1273: Are there any peaches in this layout? **1933** Ersine *Pris. Sl.:* Lay-out…A place robbed or to be robbed. **1947** in *DA:* It's a good-looking layout. Nice furniture. Nice suite of offices. **1958** S.H. Adams *Tenderloin* 66: The old stone church on the next block, that's Hellfire Farr's layout, ain't it?

lay out *v.* **1.** to cause the defeat, death, or humiliation of. *Specif.:* **a.** to defeat decisively.
   1829 in *DAE:* I want to lay out [this candidate] as cold as a wedge. **1867** *Harper's Mag.* (Feb.) 276: They…tried ter get up a scrimmage, and then they thought they could lay him out. **1864–77** in Bartlett *Dict. Amer.* (ed. 4) 347: A Detroit man who failed to get a bill through Congress, alluding to that body, says, "Well, they *laid me out,* but I'll be even with them yet." **1893** Hampton *Maj. in Washington* 45: I was happy, too, over the layin' out we gave that red fox, Mr. Iceman Turner. **1894** in *OED:* Never…were so many demagogues laid out in one day as in the elections a fortnight ago. **1919** S. Anderson, in Woods *Horse Racing* 34: A new colt named Strident…will lay them all out.

b. to kill. [Undoubtedly the orig. sense.]
   1834 *Mil. & Naval Mag. of U.S.* (June) 248: They came mighty near laying us out as cold as a wagon-tire. **1853** Lippard *New York* 236: We laid yer man out, we did. Dat cool hundred, ef yer please. **1864** "E. Kirke" *Down in Tenn.* 51: Thet little chunk uv a feller thar…laid three on 'em. **1871** Crofutt *Tourist's Guide* 34: One of their numerous victims turned on them and laid them out. **1878** Shipper *30 Yrs.* 348: One of them was flourishing a revolver, threatening to lay out a few Yanks with it. **1882** "M. Twain" *Life on Miss.* 162: As fast as one generation was laid out, their son took up the feud and kept it a-going. **1883–84** Whittaker *L. Locke* 310: "And what do you mean by laying them out stiff?" "Why, killin' them, of course, boss." **1884** "M. Twain" *Huck. Finn.* 112: But he didn't git much chance to enjoy his luck, for inside of a week our folks laid *him* out. **a*1890 in Barrère & Leland *Dict. Slang* II 9: "I've laid one out."…Witness also saw the knife, and there was blood on it. **1922** Farrar *Jack* 20: There isn't a guy in the town I wouldn't lay out cold like that [*Snaps his fingers.*] if he quit me on a job. **1942** Garcia *Tough Trip* 351: The only thing that is bothering me now was whether I could lay him out for good the first shot.

c. to surpass.
   1847 Field *Pokerville* 93: It is "bound" to lay every thing in the way

of architecture... "out cold," and no mistake. **1890** Janvier *Aztec Treasure House* 147: But this just lays that little horror out cold.

d. to rebuke forcefully.

1908 Beach *Barrier* 5: I had to give him a talking to when we came back. Oh, but I laid him out! **1923** McAlmon *Companion Volume* 42: Did you hear about the way the chief laid out Allison for what he said about his wife the other night? **1925** Cohan *Broadway* 48: I gave Keith and Albee a laying out such as they never heard in all their days. *ca*1960 in *DARE: Lay out....*Scold severely. **1967** in *DARE*: I laid that fellow out about his plumbers....I told him off, let him know they didn't do satisfactory work.

e. to amaze or astound.

[**1942** *ATS* 283: Please Highly....*knock dead,...lay one out,...slay.*] **1967** in S.O. Barker *Rawhide Rhymes* 9: Well, it kinder laid me out/To realize such ignorance was still a runnin' rife. **1968** in Knight *Black Voices* 178: You know, you lay me out. **1971** in Sanchez *Word Sorcerers* 112: But dig; this is the part that really laid me out man. **1972** Kellogg *Lion's Tooth* 107: Man, I got a project that will lay you out.

2. to knock down or unconscious.

1836 *Davy Crockett's Alm.* 1837 26: The old brown had laid him out straight as a fishhook. **1841** in Damon *Old Amer. Songs* (No. 29) (sheet music): I laid him flat with a large big brick...I laid him right out on the stone. **1885** Siringo *Texas Cowboy* 46: He laid me out with his open hand for trying to carve one of the boys up with a butcher knife. *a*1890 in Barrère & Leland *Dict. Slang* II 3: Mr. M— is horizontally laid out. **1889** "M. Twain" *Conn. Yankee* 441: The mason was big, but I laid him out like nothing. **1891** Clurman *Nick Carter* 19: Did you lay him out, John?...As stiff as a door, cap. **1944** Kendall *Service Slang* 10: *Laid out for inspection....*unconscious for any reason.

3. to try vigorously to turn the talents or capabilities of (someone or something) to advantage.

1899–1900 Cullen *Tales* 215: I certainly did just dazzle that old clergyman. I laid myself out. **1968** Gover *$100 Misunderstanding* 10: I really laid her [an automobile] out on the Seashore Expressway.

¶ In phrase:

¶ **lay out like a carpet** see s.v. LAY, *v.*, 2.

lay over *v.* to surpass.

1853 in *AS* XLIII (1968) 99: The Chinese...lay over the genuine Yankee even in buying and selling. **1855** Doten *Journal* I 233: They acknowledged themselves beaten and agreed that we laid over them heavy. **1858** in Rosa *Wild Bill* 26: He is turning out an awfull [*sic*] mustache and goatee but I think my mustache and goatee lays over hisen considerable. **1863** Patrick *Rebel* 128: Thompson's Colt was noted for being extraordinarily foolish, but in my humble opinion, I do not think he could lay over my horse. **1886** B. Harte *Tasajara* 90: I'm goin' to have a town along the *embarcadero* that'll lay over any town in Contra Costa. **1888** in F. Remington *Sel. Letters* 46: Running jacks lays over any sport going. **1889** "M. Twain" *Conn. Yankee* 227: I have seen a good many kinds of women in my time, but she laid over them all for variety. **1894** *Harper's* (Jan.) 223: I've allus heerd that for shows New York could lay over everything in syht. **1896** Ade *Artie* 55: I gave Mame a wad o' roses that laid over anything the bride could flash. **1902–03** Ade *People You Know* 146: He wore a chapeau...which rather laid over anything that Napoleon ever wore. **1923** in *DAE*: In Luther's language, she laid over the whole bunch.

¶ In phrase:

¶ **lay it over, 1.** to fool; deceive.

1878 Bardeen *Hume* 202: A man that takes me in at billiards...must stand high in the profession. Own up now, haven't you been laying it over me a little?

2. *West.* to surpass.

1903 A. Adams *Log of Cowboy* 163 [ref. to 1880's]: The old South Canadian...can lay it over them both. **1911** in *DA*: He let on as how anybody...could lay it all over you.

lay up *v.* **1.** to die.

1883 "M. Twain" *Life on Miss.* 29: It's all on account of the water the people drink before they laid up.

2. to copulate.—usu. constr. with *with*.

1924 Hecht & Bodenheim *Cutie* 46: We will stop first at my little love nest and lay up for a few repairs. **1930** Waldron *Old Sgt.* 25: No woman may lay up with a number of men without contracting a venereal disease. **1933** Odets *Awake & Sing!* 50: Sure, every big general

laying up in a Paris hotel with a half dozen broads pinned to his mustache. **1934** W. Smith *Bessie Cotter* 74: The Pony don't lay up with every dame he meets. **1936** Duncan *Over the Wall* 143: They know I'm your gal, that we've been laying up together for over a year. **1962** Killens *Heard the Thunder* 11: Jody Grinder is a civilian—any lucky four-goddamn-F that's laying up with your old lady and grinding her all night long while you away in the service. **1970** A.Young *Snakes* 90: Shakes is probably laid up with one of his mythical lovelies, doing that thing. **1971** Curtis *Banjo* 94: You want to lay up with her, all right.

LBFM *n.* [see 1971 quot.] *Mil.* a Southeast Asian woman who is sexually promiscuous, esp. a bar girl or prostitute.—used derisively. [Quots. ref. to Vietnam War.]

1971 *Playboy* (Aug.) 203: LBFM's never come. What's an LBFM? A little brown fucking machine. **1974** J. Pratt *Laotian Fragments* 12: *Remember:* The Golden Palace LBFMs in their spangled padded bras saying "Melly Clistmas, GI." **1985** Heywood *Taxi Dancer* 61: The...Thais—what the airmen called Little Brown Fucking Machines, LBFMs for short. *Ibid.* 225: Where's my LBFM?...Colonel loves LBFMs. **1991** Marcinko & Weisman *Rogue Warrior* 165: No LBFM's today. *a*1992 T. Wilson *Termite Hill* 377: Swede probably thought she was just another LBFM.

LBJ *n.* [*Long Binh Jail*, partially punning *LBJ*, journalists' nickname for Pres. Lyndon B. Johnson] *Mil. in Vietnam.* the military prison at Long Binh army depot, South Vietnam; (*also*) Long Binh Junction. Now *hist.*

1967 *Time* (May 26) 16: The white inmates of L.B.J., as the Long Binh Jail is unfondly known. **1968** *Playboy* (May) 61: Reports claim that pot parties are going on even in such a high security area as "the L.B.J." (Long Binh Jail)—the Army's own prison in Vietnam. **1969** Spetz *Rat Pack Six* 7: After [Vietnamese National Highway 13] departs from its historic landmark, the junction with National Highway 1 at Long Binh—known affectionately to American troops as "LBJ" (Long Binh Junction)—the highway barrels north. **1969** Briley *Traitors* 18: The Long Binh Jail got dubbed LBJ as a joke, but there was no joke about being in it. **1970** *Playboy* (Feb.) 217: The infamous Long Binh Jail (dubbed L.B.J. by Vietnam veterans) seems to have had a riot at just about every turn of the moon. **1971** T. Mayer *Weary Falcon* 158: But they might catch him, and then he wouldn't deros, wouldn't ride the freedom bird, they would put him in LBJ, the Long Binh Jail. **1972–76** Durden *No Bugles* 183: Three months in LBJ. **1982** Del Vecchio *13th Valley* 82: He...was sent to L.B.J., Long Binh Jail. **1991–93** W.T. Grant *Wings of Eagle* 109: If I wrote this up, he would wind up in LBJ.

L.D. *n.* **1.** [abbrev. L(ATRINE) D(OPE)] *Army.* LATRINE RUMOR.

1919 Ellington *Co. A* 113 [ref. to 1918]: L.D.—Latrine Dope...Latrine Drop—Gossip. **1919** Haterius *137th Inf.* 181 [ref. to 1918]: A messenger had arrived with the first news [of the Armistice], and for a long time we did not place very much faith in the rumor, as we had heard so much "L.D." (meaning Latin Dictum).

2. *Black E.* EL D.

1970 *Current Slang* V (Fall) 9: *L.D.,* n. An Eldorado Cadillac. **1972** R.L. Williams *BITCH* 4. **1972** Claerbaut *Black Jargon* 71: *L.D....*a Cadillac Eldorado.

lead *n.* bullets; gunfire; in phr. **piece of lead** a bullet; often in phr. of the sort **pump full of** [or **fill with**] **lead** to shoot, esp. repeatedly. Orig. *S.E.*

1839 in R. Moody *Astor Pl. Riot* 157: Would not have been there if I had thought they had been going to use lead. **1865** in C. Mattocks *Unspoiled Heart* 266: Leaping upon a horse and running off under a heavy shower of lead. **1868** G. Chisholm *So. Pass* 108: Applying to the [buffalo] bull a quieting dose of lead. **1879** in Miller & Snell *Why West Was Wild* 392: Another one of the party told his chum to "throw lead." **1882** D.J. Cook *Hands Up* 117: "Stop there, d—n you, or we will fill you full of lead," one of them shouted to him. **1884** in Lummis *Letters* 110: I'll pump enough lead into you to patch a mile of hell! **1884** Beard *Bristling with Thorns* 145: Dat niggah ain't nebbah sass'fite 'less some one feedin' him wid lead. **1887** Frances *Saddle & Moccasin* 131: They'll pump him so full of lead that if a prospector happens to find the corpse, he'll "denounce" it for a mining claim. **1889** in Miller & Snell *Why West Was Wild* 624: They...were "pumping" lead into them thick and fast. **1891** in J.I. White *Get Along Dogies* 102: With Colt's forty-five protectors/With lead their bodies cram. **1896** in A.E. Turner *Earps Talk* 11: One of the cowboys...was trying to pump some lead into me with a Winchester. **1903** Benton *Cowboy Life in Sidetrack*

159: He promptly filled his rivals' anatomy full of lead. **1906** Buffum *Bear City* 34: I'll fill [him] so full of lead there will be nothing left of him but solder. **1909** Harris *Bomb* 263: Again and again they had called upon Bonfield and his helpers to "use lead" against us. **1912** Ade *Babel* 250: A Johnny Reb…pumpin' lead into you till you get too heavy to run. **1918** in Loosbrock & Skinner *Wild Blue* 58: Their best flyers…come up behind the leader and pump lead into him. **1926** in Thompson *Youth's Companion* 39: Either you eat enough to keep up, or I'll fill you so full of lead you can't travel. **1928** W.R. Burnett *Little Caesar* 180: Rico rushed him, pumping lead. **1930** Sage *Last Rustler* 215: They'll stop lead if I ever catch up with them. **1938** T. Wolfe *Web & Rock* 148: We sure did fill him full of lead. **1975** V.B. Miller *Deadly Game* 84: Blue's dead. He caught three pieces of lead yesterday. **1976** *Kojak* (CBS-TV): Two cockroaches file out pitching lead. **1985** T. Wells *444 Days* 10: The windows were blown out and lead was flying in. *Ibid.* 11: General Stone wanted to start spitting lead back at these guys who were shooting in at us.

¶ In phrases:

¶ **eat lead** to be shot to death, esp. in a gun battle. Cf. 16th-C. *eat iron* 'to be stabbed', in *OED* s.v. *eat.*

   1927 in Paxton *Sport* 120: Someday she hoped to make [him] eat lead. **1929** in Segar *Thimble Theater* 75: One false move and you'll eat lead. **1969** Whiting *St.-Vith* 183: Now turn your platoon around or you'll eat lead!

¶ **get the lead out [of (one's) pants** [or (*vulgar*)] **ass]** to become active; get moving; hurry.—also used allusively Also vars. [Most of the pre-1933 quots. ref. to WWI.]

   1919 Kauffman *Lost Squadron* 5: Come on, move! Git de lead out of it! Don' stand theah like a flock of dam' sheep! **1926** *Sat. Eve. Post* (Oct. 23) 134: Take the lead out of your shoes! A little speed! **1926** Donahue *What Price Glory?* (film): Get th' lead out of your pants! **1927** *AS* II (Mar.) 278: Shake out the lead. **1927** Shay *Pious Friends* 1: Only with such assistance are we able to get the lead out of our feet. **1928** J.M. March *Set-Up* 38: Take the lead out of your tail! **1930** Creelman & Herbert *Danger Lights* (film): Aah, get the lead out of your [*pause*] feet! **1932** Harvey *Me & Bad Eye* 237: Get the lead out, soldier, you're not in the army now, you bum. **1932** Halyburton & Goll *Shoot & Be Damned* 16: Get the lead out of your pants and get out. **1933** J.T. Farrell *Whom It May Concern* 102: I hope it took some of the lead out of your feet! **1934** in Fenner *Throttle* 60: Get the lead outta your pants!….Get that engine outta the way! **1934** Halper *Foundry* 428: Step on it, kid, get the lead outta your can! *ca***1936** in Holt *Dirty Comics* 140: Shake th' lead out of your ass you ol' fart and rassle me up a shot. **1937** Hellman *Dead End* (film): Will ya get de lead outta ya pants? **1937** Weidman *Wholesale* 41: So just shake the lead out of your ass for a change and pass the word around that you want them to stop all scabs with force. **1939** Bessie *Men in Battle* 110: Pick up your feet; get the lead outta your ass. **1939–40** Tunis *Kid from Tomkinsville* 12: A hustling ball club, no lead in their tails. **1943** Horan & Frank *Boondocks* 4: A lot of lead is kicked out, and that's a fact. **1948** Cozzens *Guard of Honor* 271: Why don't you shake the lead out of your pants? **1948** Lay & Bartlett *12 O'Clock High!* 101: "Shake the lead out of your butt," said Baxter. "Breakfast in fifteen minutes." **1948** A. Murphy *Hell & Back* 190: Tell those joes to shake the lead out. **1949** *Harper's* (June) 94: "Double time and jerk the lead," he shouted. **1953** A. Petry *Narrows* 276: Quit brawling in the street, stop hanging out on the corner, get the lead out. **1957** R. Marcus *Chi. Confidential* (film): Get the lead out! **1962** C. Ryan *Longest Day* (film): Shake the lead! **1963** Boyle *Yanks Don't Cry* 235: Get the lead out of your ass! **1966** "T. Pendleton" *Iron Orchard* 36: If you come to work, then git the lead outa your ass and *commence* to makin' up some pipe. **1984** *Prairie Home Companion* (Nat. Pub. Radio) (Nov. 10): Get on the stick and get the lead out of your pants. **1991** *Simpsons* (Fox-TV): Come on, Homer! Get the lead out!

¶ **have lead in (one's) pencil** (of a man) be sexually potent; to have an erection of the penis. [In 1925 and 1946 quots., as joc. toast.]

   1925 Dos Passos *Manhattan Transfer* 76: Here's lead in yer pencil, George. **1927** [Fliesler] *Anecdota* 119: I want to put some lead in my pencil. **1929** Brecht *Downfall* 149: Take a puff on that kid….It'll put lead in your lead-pencil. **1938** "Justinian" *Americana Sexualis* 34: He is impotent.…*He's got no lead in his pencil.* **1938** in V. Randolph *Pissing in Snow* 86: This Hot Springs water will put lead in your pencil. ***1945** S.J. Baker *Australian Lang.* 172: Indigenous toasts are…here's lead in

your pencil! [etc.]. **1946** Gresham *Nightmare Alley* 160: Okay, sport. Here's lead in your pencil. **1962** Perry *Young Man Drowning* 75: "First, you got to get some lead in your pencil." She uses her hands on me. **1962** Killens *Heard the Thunder* 420: I used to eat those delicious things for breakfast with condensed milk. Put lead in your pencil. **1967** Dubus *Lieut.* 174: "No lead in his pencil," Hahn said. ***1972** in *OEDS*: The couscous is supposed put lead in your pencil.…an aphrodisiac. **1977** T. Berger *Villanova* 234: "I still got lead in the pencil, though." He [pointed]…crotchwards.

¶ **swap lead** to exchange gunfire.

   1908 Raine *Wyoming* 109: We're not going to get out without swapping lead. **1954** Overholser *Violent Land* 107: They had to swap lead with a gent who wanted to kill 'em.

¶ **swing the lead** *Mil.* to loaf or avoid work. *Rare* in U.S. [Discussed in Partridge *DSUE* (ed. 1) 473.]

   ***1917** in *OED2*: It is evident that he had "swung the lead" (using Army phrase) until he got his discharge. **1917** in Grider *War Birds* 51: There were a lot of young English kids that had been there some time swinging the lead. **1935** *AS* (Feb.) 79: *To swing the lead.* To loaf, to avoid work.

lead *v.* [fr. LEAD, *n.*] to shoot (someone).

   1865 Williams *Joaquin* 86: Somebody's "leaded" him for thumbing a jack?

lead balloon *n.* [extracted fr. *go over like a lead balloon*, below] a failure; FLOP, 3.a.—also used attrib.

   1954–60 *DAS: Lead balloon*…a failure; a plan, joke, action or the like that elicits no favorable response.…*That…was a lead balloon.* ***1970** in *OED2*: *What the Dickens?* was a lead balloon literary quiz wherein the experts showed only how little they knew.

¶ In phrase:

¶ **go over like a lead balloon** to be an utter failure; FLOP, 3.b.

   1950 *Best Army Short Stories* 87: As far as the gorgeous Miss Carney is concerned it goes over like a lead balloon. **1954** Ellson *Owen Harding* 50: That went over like a lead balloon. **1960** Swarthout *Where Boys Are* 182: This went over like a lead balloon. **1960** Kirkwood *Pony* 201: That would have gone over like a lead balloon. **1966–80** McAleer & Dickson *Unit Pride* 293: This east surprise went over like a lead balloon. **1983** *L.A. Times* (Aug. 27) V 3: Malcolm Arnold's "Grand, Grand Overture" for vacuum cleaners went over like, ah, a lead balloon.

leaden tonic *n. West.* LEAD POISONING. *Joc.*

   1882 *Frank James on the Trail* 35: "Come on," retorted Frank, "I'll give a leaden tonic to the one who first comes."

leadfoot *n.* **1.** a motor vehicle driver who habitually drives fast. Hence **lead-footed,** *adj.* given to speeding. Hence **leadfoot,** *v.* to drive fast.

   1938 in *AS* (Apr. 1942) 104: Lead Foot stepping on the gas. *ca***1950** in D. McKay *Wild Wheels* 60: "Leadfoot" Murphy…his foot "heavy" on the accelerator. **1954** in D. McKay *Wild Wheels* 93: The cops could spot a leadfoot in the hot rod through a block of brick buldings. **1970** Wambaugh *Centurions* 46 [ref. to 1960]: Sometimes I'm a leadfoot. I can't help stomping down [on the accelerator] on a four-five-nine call. **1974** Scalzo *Stand on Gas* 154: Imploring the leadfoots among them to take it easy, that this wasn't Ascot. **1975** *Atlantic* (May) 43: I can outhaul…any leadfoot this side of truckers' heaven. **1986** *Daily Beacon* (Univ. Tenn.) (Nov. 20) 5: Drivers here also are speed demons and leadfoots for the most part. **1990** J. Elroy, in Pronzini & Adrian *Hard-Boiled* 500: I leadfooted it to Wax's office. **1991** *DayWatch* (CNN-TV) (Dec. 20): Efforts to crack down on lead-footed police.

   2. a clumsy person. Hence **lead-footed,** *adj.* clumsy or slow.

   1955–57 Felder *Collegiate Slang* 3: *Leadfoot*—a male dancing partner who stepped on feet. **1957** *Life* (Sept. 9) 59: The bungling, leadfooted fellow who is so stupid that he cannot escape. **1958** McCulloch *Woods Wds.* 105: *Leadfoot*—A slow or clumsy logger.

leadhead *n.* a blockhead; idiot.

   1952 Mandel *Angry Strangers* 365: He's a leadhead cat I used to know. **1990** *Captain Planet* (ABC-TV): Hey, leadhead!

lead pill *n.* a bullet. *Joc.*

   1850 J. Greene *Tombs* 91 [ref. to 1833]: I went on board on purpose to give Sumpter a lead pill (meaning a bullet). **1878** Bellew *Tramp* 23: It would…have been better to regulate things a little, rather than to have them left to regulate themselves with lampposts and lead pills.

1887 Peck *Pvt. Peck* 139 [ref. to Civil War]: I told him to halt or I would fill his lungs full of lead pills. **1951** Twist *Fort Worth* (film): I got a lead pill all labeled for you.

lead-pipe *n*. ¶ In phrase: **lead-pipe cinch.**

1. a firm grip. Cf. *have a cinch on* s.v. CINCH.

1891 Maitland *Slang Dict.* 155: *Cinch* (Am.), "to have a cinch on" anything is to have "a dead pull." The word comes from the "cinch," or saddle-girth that properly manipulated, holds the saddle or load in place. A "leadpipe" or "grapevine" cinch are superlatives. **1899** Bowe *13th Minn.* 176: Everybody who did not have a lead pipe cinch on a post or who was not anchored to something solid went with the roll.

2. an absolute certainty; (*hence*) someone or something certain to succeed. Cf. CINCH, 1.

1894 Bridges *Arcady* 39: A regular lead-pipe cinch. It does not matter what he writes, the people are bound to buy it. **1899** A.H. Lewis *Sandburrs* 64: It's a lead-pipe cinch then, we goes back. **1901** Wister *Mother* 54: They are a lead-pipe cinch. **1903** in "O. Henry" *Works* 217: An engagement ain't always a lead-pipe cinch. **1948** Schwartz *Blowtop* 157: We can prove it's your gun. That's a lead-pipe cinch. **1949** in Thompson & Rice *Every Diamond* 112: But one thing is a lead pipe cinch...the Dodgers will always be interesting. **1960** *N.Y. Times* (Sept. 11) V 52: He unquestionably was the world's fastest human and seemed a lead pipe cinch to win...perhaps three gold medals at Melbourne. **1970** *Business Week* (Mar. 28) 45: [It is] possible to draw up a list of the activists' potential targets. One lead-pipe cinch is General Motors Corp. **1988** Kienzle *Marked for Murder* 90: Possible...but certainly not a lead-pipe cinch.

3. an easy task; CINCH, 2.a.

1918 in Catlin *With Help of God*: Fritz came at us with blood in his eye. I estimated them at about 500 and they were in fairly compact masses. We waited until they got close, oh, very close. In fact, we let them think they were going to have a lead-pipe cinch. **1946** Kober *That Man Is Here Again* 57: It ain't gonna be no lead-pipe cinch placin' somebody in your category. **1952** *Sat. Eve. Post* (July 19) 70: It would have been "a lead-pipe cinch for the commie leaders...to get out of the country on a Panamanian ship." **1961** R.L. Scott *Boring Holes* 79: It was a lead-pipe cinch. **1961** L.G. Richards *TAC* 134: And that wasn't the lead pipe cinch it might seem.

lead-pipe *adj*. being a certainty. [Discussed in Safire *I Stand Corrected* 223–26.]

1898–1900 Cullen *Chance* 4: The ticket writers have instructions never to turn any man's money down, no matter how big the sum or how lead-pipey the cinch he appears to have. **1903** Ade *Society* 110: Inasmuch as all of the real Tessies were more or less crazy about Wilbur, it seemed a lead-pipe certainty that he would land an Heiress who would take him to Palm Beach on a wedding tour. **1908** in Fleming *Unforgettable Season* 183: The game looked lead-pipe to a certainty. **1951** *Sat. Eve. Post* (Aug. 25) 27: One Finnish newspaper has already written off the 1952 Olympics as a lead-pipe travesty.

lead plum *n. West*. a bullet. *Joc*. Cf. LEAD PILL.

1922 Rollins *Cowboy* 77 [ref. to *a*1900]: A "lead plum" was a bullet.

lead poisoning *n*. a serious, esp. fatal, bullet wound. *Joc*.

1883 in J.R. Ware *Passing Eng.* 166: A disease which he euphemistically termed "lead-poisoning," the result of being shot through part of the lungs by a desperado. **1893** Hampton *Maj. in Washington* 128: There is just a little bit of danger that Sanders will die of lead poisoning. **1908** Raine *Wyoming* 89: Miss Messiter don't want to be responsible for y'u getting lead poisoning. *ca*1921 in Edwards & Kelley *Coffeehouse Sngbk.* 39: But a big Mauser bullet got stuck in his craw/And he died of lead poisoning in Erin go Braugh. **1931** Grant *Gangdom's Doom* 79: They don't find it healthy here in Chicago. A lot of them die from lead poisoning. **1935** C.J. Daly *Murder* 7: If Phil...should die of lead poisoning, there's a thousand dollars in it for you. **1944** C.B. Davis *Leo McGuire* 94: Maybe someday they'll pass a national Sullivan law so a guy isn't running the risk of lead poisoning on the job. **1945** in *Calif. Folk. Qly.* V (1946) 378: This same grimness is apparent in their describing death through bullet wounds as *lead poisoning*. **1952** Overholser *Fab. Gunman* 50: Most...has cashed in their chips from lead poisoning. *a*1973 E.G. Robinson & L. Spigelglass *All My Yesterdays* 239: Or there's going to be an epidemic of lead poisoning. **1989** Zumbro & Walker *Jungletracks* 182: He got...[a] bad case of lead poisoning.

lead-pusher *n. West*. a pistol.

1922 Rollins *Cowboy* 148 [ref. to *a*1900]: The affronted citizen..."dug for" his own "lead pusher."

lead sandwich *n*. a bullet; LEAD PLUM. *Joc*.

1978 S. King *Stand* 83: Have a lead sandwich, ya lousy copper.

Lead Sled *n*. **1.** *Mil. Av.*, *esp. USAF*. any of various aircraft considered to be slow or unmaneuverable, as the Republic F-100 Super Sabre fighter-bomber, the B-58 Hustler, or the F-105 Thunderchief; (*also*) a very stable or reliable aircraft.

1961 L.G. Richards *TAC* 187: The F-100 "Lead Sled" wasn't designed for dogfighting. [*a*1967 K.F. Cook *Other Capri* 107: "Suppose it would fly on *one* engine?" "Like a lead sled."] **1967** D. Robinson *B-58* 26: Flying The Lead Sled [B-58 Hustler]. **1968** *Airman* (May) 2: The aircraft gracing this month's cover [*sc.*, the F-105] bears little resemblance to a "lead sled." Yet this and other more graphic descriptions were applied to it in the earlier days of its career. *Ibid.* 4: "Lead sled," they called it, referring to its limited gliding ability and its heavy weight. **1979** D.K. Schneider *AF Heroes* 23: Called the "lead sled" by some pilots because of her size and weight, the Thunderchief was aerodynamically clean. **1982** W.R. Dunn *Fighter Pilot* 211: The F-105 Thunderchief—the "Thud," the "Lead Sled." **1984** Trotti *Phantom* 244: F-100 Super Sabre (Lead Sled). **1989** Halberstadt *Army Av.* 118: The Black Hawk [helicopter] is a "lead sled"!...You can...stack people in there until it's full—and still fly!...When you move the controls, the airplane moves—now!

2. (*l.c.*) a slow motor vehicle. [Perh. the orig. sense, if it is indeed a 1950's term.]

1993 *Smithsonian* (July) 54: Hot-rodders tended to dismiss these looks-over-speed custom cars as "lead sleds." **1996** Dalzell *Flappers 2 Rappers* 78 [ref. to 1950's]: *Lead sled* A slow car.

lead-spitter *n*. a firearm.

1927 *DN* V 453: *Lead-spitter, n*. A revolver. **1976** Hayden *Voyage* 521: Bring that lead spitter aft an' point it the other way.

lead squirt *n. Navy*. a light-caliber shipboard gun. Now *hist*.

1970 Dierks *Leap to Arms* 74 [ref. to 1898]: The only defense would be the searchlights of the warships, which it was hoped would illuminate the attacking enemy for the crews manning the 1-, 3-, and 6-pounder "lead squirts" which would, it was also hoped, drive them off.

lead towel *n*. a length of lead pipe used as a bludgeon; (*also*) (see 1823 quot.). *Joc*. Cf. OAKEN TOWEL.

1807 *Port Folio* (June 6) 357: Wipe his pate with a pair of lead towels. **1823* "J. Bee" *Slang*: Lead towel.—A pistol.

leaf *n*. **1.a.** a dollar bill; dollar. Cf. CABBAGE, *n.*, 4; LETTUCE, *n.*, 1.

1929 Bodenheim *60 Secs.* 237: You can bet your last leaf. **1947** J.C. Higgins *Railroaded* (film): You get fifty bucks....Fifty leaves. **1959** (cited in Partridge *Concise Sl. Dict.* 261). **1961** in Himes *Black on Black* 103: Nine leaves in the circle. You got him, back man?

b. a one-hundred-dollar bill; one hundred dollars.

1929 E. Sullivan *Look at Chicago* 110: Tim Murphy...it was who first called hundred dollar bills "leaves." **1929** Gill *Und. Slang*: *Leaves*—One hundred dollars. **1935** Pollock *Underworld Speaks*: Leaves, hundred dollar bills.

2. *Narc*. **a.** cocaine. [The sense 'coca leaf' is a nonslang technical term.]

1942 *ATS* 473. **1959** (cited in Spears *Drugs & Drink*). **1970** Landy *Underground Dict.*: *Leaf, the....*Cocaine. **1971** Curtis *Banjo* 113: "So I take a little leaf," she said. **1981** *Time* (July 6) 56: Otherwise known as cocaine, coke, C, snow,...leaf, flake, [etc.].

b. marijuana. Cf. GRASS, *n.*, 3.

1961 Russell *Sound* 17: It's a cryin' shame they outlawed the leaf. **1978** *UTSQ* (Nov. 29): Marijuana...*pot, mary jane, hash, reefer, stuff, leaf*. **1990* T. Thorne *Dict. Contemp. Sl.*: *Leaf*...marihuana.

leaf colonel *n*. [fr. the silver-leaf insigne] *Army*. a lieutenant colonel.

1944–46 in *AS* XXII 55: *Leaf colonel*. A lieutenant colonel. **1958** Camerer *Damned Wear Wings* 146 [ref. to WWII]: The black-haired leaf colonel was in full cry.

leaf-peeper *n. Esp. N.E.* a person who travels to rural areas to see the autumn foliage.

*ca*1965 in *DARE*: *Leaf peepers*—Tourists who come to Vermont to view the colored leaves. **1978** in *DARE*: Leaf-peepers are very nice, appreciative people. **1983** *Chi. Sun-Times* (Sept. 11) 1: Autumn...—a season of harvest and plenty, and a season of great beauty, especially for dedicated leaf peepers. Leaf peepers are those people who drive down a winding, narrow country road to look at leaves. **1987** *CBS*

News Sunday Morning (CBS-TV) (Oct. 11): But the leaf-peepers, as the locals call them, are a hardy breed….They get bumper-to-bumper leaf-peepers who jump out of their cars with cameras and easels. **1987** *Newswatch* (CNN-TV) (Oct. 4): The [U.S.] Weather Service has leaf-peepers all over the country who keep us up to date on the condition of the foliage. **1995** Vt. innkeeper, age *ca*65 (coll. J. Sheidlower): Our busiest season is the early fall. That's when the leaf-peepers come up….It's a humorous term, not disparaging.

leak *n.* **1.** an act of urination; usu. in phr. **take** [or occ. **spring**] **a leak** to urinate.—usu. considered vulgar.

   1918 in Carey *Mlle. from Armentières* I (unp.): The proper place to take a leak/Is right on the corner of the main street. **1930** in Randolph *Pissing in Snow* 7: A salesman…went back there to take a leak. **1931** Farrell *Guillotine Party* 101: I'm only taking a leak. **1934** H. Miller *Tropic of Cancer* 102: He has been dying to take a leak. **1935** Read *Lexical Evidence* 63: The popular *to take a leak*, meaning "to urinate," is in good colloquial usage. **1936** Dos Passos *Big Money* 188: I got to take a leak. **1936** Levin *Old Bunch* 622: Can I take a leak? **1939** M. Levin *Citizens* 238: If he had to take a leak, he could always hop off and do so. **1943** Wolfert *Tucker's People* 143: I need a leak. **1944** Kapelner *Lonely Boy Blues* 100: Sue me, but I couldn't spring a leak. **1945** in Shibutani *Co. K* 234: I just step outside and take a leak. **1947** Mailer *Naked & Dead* 144: If you have to take a leak, Robert,…go outside. **1947** Motley *Knock on Any Door* 180: It was there you took a leak, standing like a horse. **1952** Larson *Barnyard Folklore* 84: Urinate…*spring a leak.* **1956** Levin *Compulsion* 20: They thought maybe the kid got locked in taking a leak. **1962** Perry *Young Man Drowning* 211: I got to take a leak bad. **1963** Boyle *Yanks Don't Cry* 146: She wouldn't take a leak anywhere but in a corner of the shack, and every time she did it the damned place stunk a little bit more. *1968 in *OED2*: I thought he'd got out for a leak. **1968** L.J. Davis *Whence All Had Fled* 152: I have just got to take a leak in the worst possible way. **1970** Gattzden *Black Vendetta* 163: Max went down the hall…to take a leak. **1972** Madden *Bros.* 129: He took a leak in the john. **1976** Whelton *CB Baby* 76: "I gotta take a leak," CB Baby whispered. **1976** G. Kirkham *Signal Zero* 167: Like you were…taking a leak. **1979** Hurling *Boomers* 18: Hey! You goin' for another leak? **1983** Moranis et al. *Strange Brew* (film): I got to take a leak so bad I can taste it. **1989** P. Benchley *Rummies* 103: He took a leak. **1992** *Likely Suspects* (Fox-TV): I gotta take a leak. **1994** *Early Prime* (CNN-TV) (June 8): They'll be taking a leak over here or breaking into the shed over there.

2. *Pol.* **a.** a disclosure of secret, esp. official, information. Now *S.E.*

   [**1933** Ersine *Prison Slang* 76: The cops took him into the bullring and he turned on the leaks.] **1939** in Brookhouser *Our Years* 456: The presence of two New York police cruisers…startled Hoover as well as Lepke. The G-man later admitted he feared "a leak." **1949** *N.Y. Times* (Sept. 26) 3: So vital a bit of information should not be the subject of a "leak" but should be released with…solemnity. **1960** *Time* (Feb. 15) 46: Because of his partisanship…he was fed the first official "leaks." **1964** *Atlantic Monthly* (June) 8: Minor leaks to the press about his plans infuriate him. **1974** *N.Y. Times* (June 29) 13: "The leak is the safety valve of democracy," and without it the country would get only Government-controlled news. *Ibid.:* By Washington's definition, a leak is an unauthorized disclosure of confidential official information, usually by an unidentified "source."

b. the source of such a disclosure. Now *S.E.*

   1954–60 *DAS: Leak*…The person who "leaks" news or secret information.

¶ In phrases:

¶ **spring a leak, 1.** s.v. see **(1)**, above.

2. (see quot.).

   1933 Ersine *Prison Slang* 70: *Spring [a] Leak*….To become insane. "A lifer sprung a leak this noon."

3. (see quot.). Cf. LEAK, *v.*, 2.

   1933 Ersine *Prison Slang* 70: *Spring [a] leak* 1. To rat.

¶ **take a leak** see s.v. **(1)**, above.

leak *v.* **1.** to urinate.—usu. considered vulgar.

   *1596 Shakespeare *1 Henry IV* II i 22: We leake in your Chimney. *a1661, 1673, *1731 in *OED2*. *1796 Grose *Dict. Vulgar Tongue* (ed. 3): *To leak.* To make water. **1854** in G.W. Harris *Lovingood* 34: "Yus leakin now; see thar?" Ha! ha! from the crowd, and "Still-tub" went into the doggery. **1935** Algren *Boots* 129: Drank too much cerveza in

Juarez one night an' leaked on the street-car all the way comin' home. **1939** Appel *People Talk* 15: He was a bull terrier….He'd tear up everything in sight and leak all over the place. **1954** E. Hunter *Blackboard Jungle* 47: You goan to watch me leak, man? **1957** E. Lacy *Room to Swing* 55: Second a woman gets anyplace she has to leak. **1959** Cochrell *Barren Beaches* 115: Come in before five thousand other guys remember they can do more than leak through it.

2. to divulge (a secret); SQUEAL; RAT.—also used intrans. Now *S.E.* Cf. earlier colloq. sense '(of a secret) to be revealed in spite of efforts at concealment'.

   1859 Matsell *Vocab.* 50: *Leak.* To impart a secret. **1933** Ersine *Prison Slang* 50: *Leak, v.* To squeal, rat. **1949** *New Yorker* (Nov. 5) 64: Johnson, however, who likes to talk, leaked his news to the press before Calder had decided whether to take the job or not. **1952** *Sat. Eve. Post* (Mar. 22) 37: The congressmen had leaked news of the executive session to the press. **1958** *Time* (July 14) 38: Colonel John Nickerson, court-martialed for leaking Army rocket secrets to newsmen. **1960–61** Steinbeck *Discontent* 224: You won't leak, Ethan? **1966** *Harper's* (Mar.) 42: In the totalitarian countries, of course, there is no "leaking" of information at all, except on pain of death. **1974** *N.Y. Times* (June 29) 13: Isn't it illegal to leak official information or accept it? **1975** V.B. Miller *Deadly Game* 11: I don't like to…worry about how they'll be leaked off. **1982** *U.S. News & W.R.* (Dec. 20) 38: It isn't that difficult to find out who's leaking. When you see some really sensitive stuff oozing out, fire somebody.

3. to weep.

   1883 Peck *Bad Boy* 61: When his eyes began to leak, Pa put his hand in his tail pocket for his handkerchief. **1896** Ade *Artie* 57: As soon as she said it she commenced to leak again. **1903** Ade *Society* 22: As the Train pulled away from Pewee Junction Wilbur began to Leak. The Salt Tears trickled down through the Archipelago of Freckles. **1963** Morgan *Six-Eleven* 212: I've been leaking like an old woman for the past couple of days. I'm sorry to burden you with it, Leo.

leaky *adj.* **1.** unable to keep a secret. Now *colloq.* Cf. LEAK, *v.*, 2.

   *1692 in *OED2*: Women are generally so leaky, that…I have hardly met with one of the Sex that could not hold her Breath longer than she should keep a secret. *1703, *1740 in *OED2*. *1796 Grose *Vulgar Tongue* (ed. 3): *Leaky.* Apt to blab. **1847–49** Bonney *Banditti* 83: He is leaky as an old boat, always telling everything. **1859** Matsell *Vocab.* 50: *Leaky.* Not trustworthy. **1979** *Toronto Star* (Dec. 22) ("Weekend") 16: No one wants to talk about spooks, or why Ottawa has always had the reputation for being "leaky." **1980** *Macleans* (Apr. 28) 56: He had a reputation as being the leakiest minister.

2. [fr. LEAK, *v.*, 3] given to tears; *(also)* characterized by weeping.

   1905 in *OED2*: "I ain't the leaky sort," she added fiercely, still gasping. **1962** Shepard *Press Passes* 173: It was a very leaky afternoon—I was pretty much of a red-eyed wreck myself.

lean *adj.* ¶ In phrase: **lean and mean, 1.** Orig. *USMC.* (of service personnel) robust and pugnacious; *(hence,* with weakened force) (of other persons) fit and confident. Also **lean, mean.**

   1974 Former l/cpl., USMC [ref. to 1971]: At Parris Island they promised they'd make us into "lean, mean, killin' machines." **1986** *Mama's Family* (NBC-TV): Feeling lean and mean tonight? **1984–88** Hackworth & Sherman *About Face* 33: Lean, mean combat-ready troops. **1988** Schneider & Schneider *Sound Off!* 24: The Corps structures boot camp to teach them to be "lean, mean, and green [*i.e.*, loyal to the USMC]." **1989** Spears *NTC's Dict.* 222: Ron got himself lean and mean and is ready to play in Saturday's game. **1991** *Donahue* (NBC-TV): We like thin girls, too—lean and mean. **1995** *Simpsons* (Fox-TV): I am not a lean, mean machine.

2.a. unencumbered in design; direct and uncomplicated; efficient.

   1974 Lahr *Hot to Trot* 6: The MG is my style: lean and mean. **1995** *Talk Back Live* (CNN-TV) (Jan. 19): A lean and mean case…[based] upon DNA evidence.

b. Orig. *Business.* (esp. of companies) economical and aggressive; *(specif.)* having relatively few employees; *(broadly)* energetic; intense.

   1983 *L.A. Times* (Oct. 15) I 1: Regardless of how lean and mean your organization is, you're going to be in trouble if you suddenly lose that much income. **1984** *Business Week* (May 7) 76: "Then the temptation gets pretty strong to start spending money"—though so far, he adds, "we're still lean and mean." **1989** *Daily Beacon* (Univ. Tenn.) (Oct. 27) 4: An era of [business] takeovers and lean, mean strategies. **1989** Kanter & Mirvis *Cynical Amer.* 60: He vowed to make the organization "lean and mean." **1990** *Nation* (Dec. 17) 756: If workers had to be laid off, or R&D budgets cut, those were the unfortunate side effects of getting lean and mean.

lean and fat *n.* [rhyming slang] a hat. Also **leaning fat.**
   1857 "Ducange Anglicus" *Vulgar Tongue* 11: Lean-and-fat…Hat, used by marine store-shop keepers &c. **1928** Sharpe *Chicago May* 287: *Leaning fat*—Hat. **1938** *AS* (Apr.) 156: *Lean and fat.* A hat. [Calif.]. **1960** Franklyn *Dict. Rhyming Sl.: Lean and fat* A hat….It is seldom heard in England, but had currency in America.

lean and linger *n.* [rhyming slang] a finger.
   1929 (quot. at SIMPLE SIMON). **1943** Holmes & Scott *Mr. Lucky* (film): Put the Simple Simon on your lean and linger. **1960** Franklyn *Dict. Rhyming Sl.: Lean and linger* Finger. American…Employed by Damon Runyon, 1930–40.

leaner *n. Sports.* a hanger-on who gives unwanted advice or makes obnoxious comments.
   1981 D.E. Miller *Jargon* 245: The leaner never misses an opportunity to groan at your faults. **1984** *Hardcastle & McCormick* (ABC-TV): He's got this leaner with him, asking a lot of stupid questions…."What's a leaner?"…"A leaner is what the guys on Pit Row call a guy who just leans up against something and gives advice….At least a gofer goes for things."

lean on *v.* **1.** to strike (a blow).
   1911 T.A. Dorgan, in Zwilling *TAD Lexicon* 113: I have a mind to go up and lean one on his chin. **1912, 1914** in Zwilling *TAD Lexicon.*
   2.a. to coerce by threats or violence; (*hence*) to pressure.
   1929–31 J.T. Farrell *Young Lonigan* 144: But if anybody ever leaned on Kenny, the whole gang would…send him to the hospital. **1954–60** *DAS: Lean on*…to threaten to beat up someone or a member of one's family in order to get information. **1963** Braly *Shake Him* 49: He lean on you? **1964** in S. Lee *Son of Origins* 130: He looks like trouble….Want we should lean on 'im a little? **1969** L. Sanders *Anderson Tapes* 79: I just don't like to get leaned on. **1973** *Harper's* (July) 38: You bend a little because nobody wins if you got to lean on him. **1977** *U.S. News & W.R.* (Sept. 26) 21: Black leaders are leaning hard on the White House to spend more money to create jobs. **1982** P. Michaels *Grail* 252: In turn, the Feds would lean on the Commissioner.
   b. to assault; beat up.
   1954–60 *DAS: Lean on*…To beat up someone. **1983** *Reader's Digest Success with Words* 86: Black English…*lean on* = "to hit, beat up."
   c. *Black E.* (see quot.).
   1967–80 Folb *Runnin' Lines* 245: *Lean on (one)* Disparage or ridicule.

lean up against *v.* to consume; eat and drink.
   1918 F. Gibbons *And They Thought We Wouldn't Fight* 118: The rest of us "leaned up against" steak, hot biscuits, syrup, and coffee.

leap *n.* an act of copulation.—usu. considered vulgar. Cf. earlier S.E. *leap, v.* '(of a male animal) to mount and copulate with (a female animal)', in *OED2*.
   *a*1896 E. Field, in *Immortalia* 15: How dear to my heart was the oldfashioned harlot/ Whose regular price was five dollars a leap.

leaper *n. Narc.* an amphetamine; (*specif.*) an amphetamine-soaked ball of cotton from a nasal inhaler. Cf. earlier LEAPING.
   1966 Braly *On the Yard* 77: The wads of charged cotton were known as leapers. ***1968** (cited in Partridge *Concise Dict. Sl.* 260). **1972** Smith & Gay *Don't Try It* 204: *Leapers.* Stimulants, especially amphetamines. **1979** D. Marsh, in *Rolling Stone* (Oct. 19) 11: I've seen him take twenty-five leapers [amphetamines] and then drink a bottle of brandy many times. [Brackets in orig.].

leaping *adj. Narc.* intoxicated by drugs or alcohol; HIGH.
   1925 *Writer's Mo.* (June) 487: *Leaping*—under the influence of dope. **1935** Pollock *Underworld Speaks: Leaping*, overdosed with dope. **1953** W. Fisher *Waiters* 122: Man, I'm leapin', he said to himself.

leaping dominoes *n.pl. Gamb.* the game of craps; (*also*) dice. *Joc.*
   1921 Schauble *First Bttn.* 114: "African golf," "leaping dominoes," or just plain "craps" was the favorite indoor sport of the AEF. **1925** T.A. Dorgan, in Zwilling *TAD Lexicon* 113: Watching the slaves of the wheel as they dally with the leaping dominoes at the local garage.

Leaping Lena *n.* a small car; FLIVVER, 1.a.
   1936 Levin *Old Bunch* 165: Sam heard a terrific honk…and barely jumped aside in time to escape a Leaping Lena. **1954–60** *DAS: Leaping Lena*…An automobile. *c*1915; *obs.*

leaping lizards! *interj.* [coined or pop. in Harold Gray's syndicated comic strip, "L'il Orphan Annie"] (used to express surprise).
   1924 in Galewitz *Great Comics* 139: Leapin lizards! This is no place for me. **1979** *Newsweek* (Aug. 13) 41: Leapin' Lizards!…The largest land animal ever to lumber across the face of the earth.

leaps *n.pl.* a state of nervousness; JITTERS; (*broadly*) *Narc.* severe withdrawal sickness.
   1922 Murphy *Black Candle* 51: When on the verge of suicide for need of the drug, they are said to have "the cocaine leaps." **1965** Capote *Cold Blood* 108: No wonder you got leaps.

leary var. LEERY.

lease hound *n. Petroleum Industry.* a person who speculates in real estate that may contain oil deposits.
   1924 *Adventure* (Dec. 10) 5: We might take a stab at being lease-hounds, but we don't know enough. **1951** Pryor *The Big Play* 255: At that time Tulsa probably sheltered more oil companies, both major and minor, more independent operators, more wildcatters, lease-hounds, oil scouts, oil refiners, and rock hounds than any other city in the world. *a*1961 Longman *Power of Black* 195: Or letting some lease hound hambone you into signing away your mineral rights. **1970** Boatright & Owens *Derrick* 161: The fellow that got out and bought leases and traded in them was a lease hound. **1985** in H. Cannon *Cowboy Poetry* 187: The Lease Hound.

least *n.* [coined as the antonym to MOST] *Jazz & Black E.* very unsatisfactory; dull; tedious.—constr. with *the.*—used predicatively only.
   1953 in S. Allen *Bop Fables* 36: Honey, your grandma is feeling the least. **1958** *PADS* (No. 30) 46: *Least, the*…Opposite of *the most.* Occ[asionally used]. **1959** *Swinging Syllables: Least*—Bad scene or situation. **1964** R.S. Gold *Jazz Lexicon* 186: *Least*…some currency since c. 1952. **1983** *Reader's Digest Success with Words* 86: Black English… *least* = "dull person or situation." **1990** T. Thorne *Dict. Contemp. Sl.: The least*…something very bad…"Boy, that movie was the least."

leather *n.* **1.a.** the human skin or flesh; hide. Orig. *S.E.* Rare in U.S.
   *1303, etc., in *OED.* ***1725** J. Swift, in *OED:* Returning sound in Limb and Wind, Except some Leather lost behind. ***1796** Grose *Vulgar Tongue* (ed. 3): *To lose leather;* to be galled with riding on horseback. **ca*1800 in Holloway & Black *Broadside Ballads* 59: Having lain full six days till his Leather was shrunk,/She cram'd the poor Cobler into an old Trunk. **1841** in Lofaro *Davy Crockett* 74: Thar war no kritter but a Yankee that wood hav been so particklar about his leather. ***1872** Hotten *Slang Dict.* (ed. 4): The skin…is often called *leather.* ***1901** *OED: Leather*…Skin. Now only *slang.*
   b. the vulva or vagina; (*hence*) a promiscuous woman; (*hence*) an act of copulation.—usu. considered vulgar.
   *1540 Sir D. Lyndsay, in *F & H* IV 170: It is half ane yeir almaist, Sen ever that loun laborde my ledder. ***1691** in Adlard *Forbidden Tree* 34: My mistress is a shittlecock….Each battledore…bumps her on the leather. ***1720** D'Urfey *Pills* VI 92: In dressing of the Leather;/I straightway whip my needle out. **a*1890–93 *F & H* III 206: To go…*leather-stretching,…quim-sticking* [etc.]. **1935** Pollock *Und. Speaks: Leather,* a woman of easy virtue. **1936** Partridge *DSUE* 475: *Nothing like leather,* nothing like a good ****, C.19–20.
   c. *Prost. & Homosex.* the anus (in sexual contexts).—usu. considered vulgar.
   1941 G. Legman, in Henry *Sex Variants* II 1141: *Leather* The anus. The verb form meaning to pedicate is prostitutes' slang, as the verbal noun, *leathering,* for pedication. **1962** D.W. Maurer, in McDavid *Amer. Lang.* 727: [Among pimps and prostitutes, a] woman's anus is a *leather.* *a*1972 Rodgers *Queens' Vernacular* 19: A-hole…*leather* (*obs* '30s).
   2. any of various leather items. *Specif.:*
   a. *Und.* a leather pocketbook, wallet, billfold, etc.; (*hence*) a purse or the like made from any material.
   *1753 in Partridge *Dict. Und.* 402: Come, let us pike to glee for a Pitter or Leather. **1845** in Robb *Squatter Life* 114: He handed his wallet to the express messenger. "To the d—l with your old *leather,* give

me a *message paper!*" shouted the *express*. **1859** Matsell *Vocab.* 51: *Leather.* A pocket-book; portmonnaie. "The bloke lost his leather," the man lost his pocketbook. **1866** *Nat. Police Gaz.* (Nov. 24) 3: He found the missing "leather" under Annie's feet. **1871** Banka *Prison Life* 492: Pocket Book, *Leather* or *Dummy*. **1872** (quot. at PULL OFF). **1879** *Snares of N.Y.* 35: The stranger must flash his leather and soothe "Mollie's" wounded senses with the balm of greenbacks. **1891** McCann & Jarrold *Odds & Ends* 83: Here's the leather and here's the bones. **1897** *Pop. Sci. Mo.* (Apr.) 832: A purse is a *leather.* **1906** *Nat. Police Gaz.* (July 28) 3: Billy's just been pinched....For swiping a bloke's leather. *a*1909 Tillotson *Detective* 93: *Leather*—A pocketbook. **1910** Hapgood *City Streets* 316: Women kept their leathers on a big open pocket in the back of their dresses, and any door-mat thief could get all he wanted. **1921** Conklin & Root *Circus* 168 [ref. to *ca*1880]: The "dips" began making "touches," and frequently by the time it was over had quite a collection of "leathers." **1926** *AS* I (Dec.) 652: *Leather.* pocket-book. **1929** *AS* IV (June) 342: *Leather.* A purse or pocket-book. **1931–34** in Clemmer *Pris. Comm.* 333: *Leather*...A pocketbook or wallet. **1931–35** D. Runyon *Money* 185: Other dolls...remember leaving their leathers lying around upstairs. **1936** Fellows & Freeman *Big Show* 113: "Lifting the leathers" was a simple operation. **1940** R. Chandler *Farewell* ch. xxxvi: Once in a while he will lift a leather. **1955** in D.W. Maurer *Lang. Und.* 245: *Leather*...A wallet, even one that is not made of leather.

b. Esp. *Sports Journ.* a leather-covered ball.—usu. constr. with *the*.—also used collectively.

*1868 in *OED*: They can see no delight in the way of getting in the way of "leather." *1882 in *OED*: Spofforth resigned the leather to Boyle. **1883** *Chi. Inter Ocean* (June 6) (cited in Nichols *Baseball Term.* 36). **1888** *N.Y. Press* (Apr. 7) (cited in Nichols *Baseball Term.*) **1939** Nichols *Baseball Term.* 36: *Leather.* The ball....*Hunt leather.* To attempt to hit pitched balls. **1942** *ATS* 649: Baseball...*leather. Ibid.* 660: Basketball...*leather. Ibid.* 662: Football...*leather.* **1954–60** *DAS* 315: *Leather*...A football.

c. a whip; smart strokes with a whip.—usu. constr. with *the*.

1914 Hawthorne *Brotherhood* 188: Still he favored whipping for them; he said the use of the "leather" was really more humane than the dungeon. **1927–30** Rollins *Jinglebob* 24 [ref. to 1880's]: Owens...began to ply his long-lashed whip—began to "pour on the leather," as old-time Western teamsters called it. **1934** Cunningham *Triggernometry* 303: She "poured the leather" to the team.

d. *Boxing.* boxing gloves; esp. in phrs. **push leather** to box; be a pugilist; **throw leather** to deliver punches; box.

1920–21 Witwer *Leather Pushers* 115: You have took to pushin' leather like Theda Bara to a camera. **1936** Tully *Bruiser* 110: Come on, stumble bum...I'se goin' to push leather down the glory road. **1938** Lennon et al. *Crowd Roars* (film): He crowds McCoy, throwing leather from all angles! **1939** O'Brien *One-Way Ticket* 30: I...work my points for this leather-throwin' cowboy. **1947** *Looney Tunes* (animation): That's mixin' it, boy. Now let's really throw some leather. **1954** G. Kersh, in Pohl *Star of Stars* 24: But what about a baseball player or a boxer?...What would they do?...swing bats or throw leather! **1955** Graziano & Barber *Somebody Up There* 3: He backpedals and I roar after him,...throwing leather by the ton. **1954–60** *DAS* 315: *Leather*...boxing gloves. **1971** Torres *Sting Like Bee* 21: I saw Quarry throwing a lot of leather. **1977** Caron *Go-Boy* 149: C'mon, man, put the leather to him.

e. a holster; in phrs. of the type **slap leather** to draw a gun from its holster.

1921 "M. Brand" *Seventh* 158: I never seen none do it the way you did—with your gun in the leather at the start. **1934** E. Cunningham *Triggernometry* 3: Gunfighters who could match speed at "leather slapping" and deadly accuracy...with [anyone]. *Ibid.* 8: I come to see him try slappin' leather with *me!* **1937** Haycox *Sundown Jim* 149: He went quickly into the leather. **1949** J. Schaefer *Shane* 110: Do I have to crowd you into pushing leather? **1955** "W. Henry" *Who* 10: You see me again you'd better scratch leather without waiting for any invitations. **1964** in B. Jackson *Swim Like Me* 65: Light as a feather they both slapped leather. **1969** D. Pendleton *Death Squad* 96: The sarge pulled leather on me tonight. **1975** Stanley *WWIII* 268: "Hit the deck," I yelled, for I could see that Higoshita had cleared leather.

f. Esp. *Und.* shoes or boots used to kick or stamp on an opponent in a fight; brutal kicks.—constr. with *the*. Cf. earlier S.E. sense 'leather boots or shoes', in *OED*.

1931 in Partridge *Dict. Und.* 403: Once, having downed him, they...gave him "the leather." **1931** D. Runyon, in *Collier's* (Nov. 14) 9: Furthermore, they are using the old leather, kicking guys in the stomach when they are not able to hit them on the chin. *1936 in *OED2:* Old boys never could stand the leather. **1946** D. Runyon, in *DAS* 315: He would give his fallen foe what we called "the leather," meaning a few boots abaft the ears.

g. (see quot.).

1967–80 Folb *Runnin' Lines* 245: *Leather*...leather or leatherlike jacket.

h. *Baseball.* a baseball glove; (*hence*) fielding ability; fielding plays.

1983 Whiteford *Talk Baseball* 109: *Leather*...a glove or an all-purpose word for fielding. A good fielder is one with "a lot of leather." **1986** in P. Dickson *Baseball Dict.* 243: We told Teufel, "Way to get leather on it....He just got the wrong leather." **1989** P. Dickson *Baseball Dict.* 243: *Leather*...Fielding. A game containing a number of stellar defensive plays is said to be "full of leather."

3. Esp. *Mil. & Pris.* meat; in phr. **leather and wood** *Naut.* meat and bread. *Joc.*

1912 R. Murphy *Logbook* 79: The Old Man and the mate soak their bread in coffee and water, swallow "leather and wood" without chewing, and then squirm with the mulligrubs. **1923** McKnight *Eng. Words* 56 [ref. to 1918]: *Leather* for "meat." **1934** *Jour. Abn. & Soc. Psych.* XXX 359: *Leather*—beef.

4. *Und.* a pickpocket.

1936 N. West *Cool Million* 161: "Some smart leather must have gotten it." "Leather?" queried our hero, not understanding the argot of the underworld with which the train boy was familiar. "Yes, leather—pickpocket."

¶ In phrases:

¶ **fork leather** *West.* to ride a horse.

1931 Rynning *Gun Notches* 2: I've...forked leather wherever there's been a West." *Ibid.:* In those days you couldn't make a living forking leather without always fighting Indians and Mexicans.

¶ **hit leather** *West.* to ride away.

1947 Overholser *Buckaroo's Code* 28: He was ready to hit leather. There was nothing...that made him his staying longer worth while.

¶ **pull** [or **hunt**] **leather** *West.* to reach for a hand-hold on the saddle horn while riding a bucking horse.

1893 in Wister *Out West* 198: *To hunt leather* to hold on by the horn of the saddle, or any strap or string. **1908** Raine *Wyoming* 223: To save himself he caught at the saddle horn. "He's hunting leather," shouted a hundred voices. **1910** in C.M. Russell *Paper Talk* 77: No Jimmy aint no frade strap man/he aint pulled leather yet. **1914** in C.M. Russell *Paper Talk* 104: Iv rode buck bords an stage coaches with drunken drivers an cyuses that made me pull leather. **1916** Knibbs *Riders of Stars* 282: I was ridin' broncs and didn't have to pull no leather. **1917–20** in J.M. Hunter *Trail Drivers* I 48 [ref. to *ca*1890]: I managed to mount him, but after I got up there I had to "choke the horn and claw leather," but to no avail. **1922** P.A. Rollins *Cowboy* 290 [ref. to 1890's]: Less accomplished men in large numbers might be willing to "hunt leather"...[or] "pull leather"...as a hand hold upon any part of the saddle, its accoutrements or the horse was interchangeably known. **1923** J.L. Hill *Cattle Trail* 56: A cowboy hates to have to grab the saddle horn to stay on, but often has to do so, and help of that sort is called "Pulling Leather." **1928** Santee *Cowboy* 63: I was pullin' leather by the time we went into the fence, an' the old bronc hit that fence on high. **1933** *AS* (Feb.) 28: *Pull leather.* To grab the saddle horn—the unforgivable sin. *a*1940 in Lanning & Lanning *Texas Cowboys* 12: We sure would have to pull leather to stay on. **1934–43** F. Collinson *Life in Saddle* 16 [ref. to 1870's]: "You're pulling leather," she'd shout. **1948** J. Stevens *Jim Turner* 42 [ref. to *ca*1910]: Don't pull leather! Let her buck! *a*1956 Almirall *College to Cow Country* 380: Among the things which disqualified a rider were "chokin' the horn" or "pullin' leather"...catching hold of the saddle horn. **1958** Bard & Spring *Horse Wrangler* 177: He had me pullin' leather with both hands. **1976** Wren *Bury Me Not* 61: Never once "pulling leather" so much as touching the saddlehorn.

¶ **stand on (one's) own leather** to stand up for (oneself).

1877 Wheeler *Deadwood Dick, Prince of the Road* 83: Dassen't stand on his own leather fer fear of gettin' salted fer all he's worth!

¶ **stomp leather** to stamp one's feet, as while dancing.

1916 in Davidson *Old West* 81: Keep a stompin' leather while you got one eye.

leather *adj.* Esp. *Homosex.* (usu. of men) of or characterized by a preference for leather fetishism, usu. as connected with sadomasochistic, esp. homosexual, sexual acts. Now *colloq.* or *S.E.* See also earlier LEATHER BAR, LEATHER BOY.

1967 *DAS* (Supp.): *Leather*...Of or pertaining to sadists and masochists, whether heterosexual or homosexual; affecting leather jackets, boots, chain bracelets, etc. **1971** Dahlskog *Dict.* 37: *Leather*....*a.* Reveling in perverted punishment of oneself or others; sadistic and homosexual. **1975–76** T. McNally *Ritz* 44: Don't howdy me you big leather sissy. **1977** S. Gaines *Discotheque* 29: Greenwich Village waterfront hangouts with...leather and bondage freaks toting whips and chains. **1984–88** in Safire *Lang. Maven* 295: Gay men who practice sadomasochistic, or "leather" sex. **1990** Steward *Bad Boys* 63: Harry...was... involved in the early "leather" movement. **1995** B.G. Henderson *Waiting* 233: I was the only straight guy....I noticed that there were all these Leathermen around.

leather *v. Prost. & Homosex.* to pedicate.—usu. considered vulgar. Cf. LEATHER, *n.*, 1.c.

1935 Pollock *Underworld Speaks: Leathering*, sodomy; buggery. **1941** (quot. at LEATHER, *n.*, 1.c.).

leather-ass *n. West.* a tough, stubborn or aggressive individual; (see also 1977 quot.).—usu. considered vulgar. Hence **leather-assed**, *adj.*

[**1913** Mulford *Coming* 368: Who is your leather-pants friend who don't like mutton?] **1970** L.D. Johnson *Devil's Front Porch* 29 [ref. to 1925]: This is a penitentiary, and you'll find out damn quick that you ain't tough. We tame leather-asses here, and you ain't no exception. **1977** T. McCoy *Remembers* 128 [ref. to 1917]: The doughboys...[called] the cavalry "leather-assed sonsofbitches."

leather bar *n.* Esp. *Homosex.* a bar that is a gathering place for leather fetishists, esp. practitioners of sadomasochistic, esp. homosexual, sexual acts.

*a***1963** Rechy *City of Night* 179: Leather bars. **1966** *Time* (Jan. 21) 40: "Leather" bars for the tough-guy with their fondness for chains and belts. **1966–71** Karlen *Sex. & Homosex.* 160: I used to drive to the leather bars down on Christopher Street. **1973** *Oui* (July) 75: Hanging out at the leather bars that day, I was made conscious of the mile-wide gap between S/M games and the real thing....New York's leather-bar scene, unlike California's, is primarily homosexual. **1971–74** in *West. Folk.* XXXIII (1974) 207: Leather bars where the bikers and sadomasochists gather. **1985** J. Dillinger *Adrenaline* 70: The Backfire was...[a] Hollywood leather bar. **1985** D.K. Weisberg *Children of Night* 29: Here, bathhouses, "leather bars," and sex parlors cater to those gay men who affect a rough style. **1981–89** J. Goodwin *More Man* 13: A bar frequented by men who dress in black leather, who often ride motorcycles, and who are generally presumed to prefer sadomasochistic [homo]sexual acts is called...a *leather bar. a***1991** C. Fletcher *Pure Cop* 107: In a leather bar on North Clark Street.

leather boy *n. Homosex.* a male leather fetishist.

*****1963** G. Freeman *Leather Boys* [title of film about homosexual motorcyclist]. *****1969** M. Jagger *Memo from Turner* (pop. song): A faggy little leather boy with a smaller piece of stick. **1978** (quot. at DRAG QUEEN). **1984** Hindle *Dragon Fall* 32: He turned to see a leather boy. His hair was bleached orange and his face was snow white, given color only by the cosmetics he wore.

leather-face *n.* an emotionless face; deadpan.—also used attrib.

1842 in *AS* XVIII (Apr. 1943) 126: He had the impassable leather-face of the pilgrims of Plymouth. **1884** "M. Twain" *Huck. Finn:* You ain't one of these leather-face people.

leather freak *n.* Orig. *Prost. & Homosex.* a leather fetishist.

1969 *Playboy* (Dec.) 157: Bull-dyke leather freak. **1970** *Nat. Lampoon* (Aug.) 47: Attention Leather Freaks! **1966–71** Karlen *Sex. & Homosex.* 157: Harvey is a leather freak. **1972** Wambaugh *Blue Knight* 163: He's a leather freak and likes to savage a broad. **1980** W. Sherman *Times Square* 31: Four men had been killed by the leather freaks who patronized the bars. **1983** *Newsweek on Campus* (May) 32: Complimenting a friend's leather jacket led to accusations of fetishism, so I got into the act playing the leather freak. *a***1988** C. Adams *More Straight Dope* 198: I have seen my share of leather freaks, transvestites, and lesbian couples.

leather-glommer *n. Und.* a pickpocket's confederate who escapes with the stolen goods.

1956 Resko *Reprieve* 182 [ref. to 1940's]: The wallet...would be immediately passed on to the leather glommer.

leatherhead *n.* **1.** a dull-witted person; idiot; dolt. Hence **leather-headed,** *adj.*

*****1614** B. Jonson *Bartholomew Fair* III i: Let's inquire of Master Leatherhead, or Joan Trash here. *****1698–99** "B.E." *Dict. Canting Crew: Leather-head*, a Thick-skull'd, Heavy-headed Fellow. *****1796** Grose *Vulgar Tongue* (ed. 3): *Leather-headed;* stupid. **1839** *Spirit of Times* (Dec. 21) 498: S[t]op, you d—d leather-head! **1873** "M. Twain," in *DARE:* You leather-head, if I talk in Boston both afternoon and evening March 5, I'll have to go to Boston the 4th. **1879** "M. Twain" *Tramp Abroad* 41: As many leather-headed opinions about it as an average crowd. **1884** Blanding *Sailor Boy* 315 [ref. to Civil War]: Say the word, Steve, and we will bounce the old leather-head over the side. **1899** Robbins *Gam* 84: Open it yourself, then, you leatherhead! **1907** "O. Henry" *Heart of West* 266: You leather-headed, rip-roarin', low-down son of a locoed cyclone. **1907** *DN* III 246: Don't know that, do you, leather-head? **1915** in E. O'Neill *Letters* 53: Why...do the leather heads who select the plays always pick out such hard ones? **1919** *DN* V 61: "Come on, you old *leather-head*, if you do not hurry we will be late." New Mexico. **1925** Nason *Three Lights* 150: No, I ain't crippled, leatherhead. **1928** Nason *Sgt. Eadie* 13: Any leatherhead can swear, but it takes a man to lay off it. **1959** McKenna *Sons of Martha* 68: When I find leatherheads sitting on two cents' worth of knowledge like it was the great Inca treasure I like to take whoever they think is the dumbest man aboard and teach him a nickel's worth. **1981** *Prairie Home Companion* (Nat. Pub. Radio): Get your face on the floor, leatherhead!

2. (*cap.*) an inhabitant or native of Pennsylvania.

1845 in *DAE:* The inhabitants of...Pennsylvania [are called] Leatherheads. **1886** in *DA:* Pennsylvania...its people are Leatherheads for some unknown reason.

3. [see 1868, 1884 quots.] a watchman or police officer. Now *hist.*

1845 Corcoran *Pickings* 22: You be d—d, old leather head. **1846** in *DA: Watchman.*—He said as how I was a leather-sconced corporate reality, and that we leatherheads were the only real offering of chartered rights. **1868** in *DA:* The guardians of this city were watchmen...and were known as leather-heads, from the leather cap they wore. **1884** Costello *Police Protectors* 72 [ref. to *ca*1830, N.Y.C.]: Watchmen wore a fireman's old-fashioned leathern hat, bereft of its upright front plate. This hat was varnished twice a year, and soon became as hard as iron. From this they came to be called "Leather-heads." They were also dubbed "Old Charlies." They had no other badge of office than this hat, and a thirty-three inch club. **1887** G. Davis *Sea-Wanderer* 174. **1947** in *DA:* The town called these watchmen "leatherheads" because of the heavy helmets they wore on duty. **1983** Helprin *Winter's Tale* 61 [ref. to *ca*1910]: Leave your sword...or the leatherheads will take after you.

4. a louse.

1926 *AS* I (Dec.) 652: *Leatherheads.* Certain lice. **1927** *DN* V 453: *Leather head,* n. A louse.

5. a U.S. marine; LEATHERNECK. *Joc.*

1968 Crawford *Gresham's War* 8 [ref. to Korean War]: "Hello, Chancre-mechanic." "How's it go, Leatherhead?"

leather-lips *n.* (used as an abusive epithet).

1844 [C.F. Briggs] *Working a Passage* 97 [ref. to 1832]: He used to call Derrick leather-lips, instead of carpenter, which vexed the soul of the old man the more because his habit of duty would not allow him to make any reply.

leather-lung *n.* a person who shouts. *Joc.*

1975 Durocher & Linn *Nice Guys* 369: This leather-lung yells, "Durocher, you dummy, are you trying to cripple that man?"

leather medal *n.* an imaginary reward for laziness, ineptitude, etc. *Joc.*

1831 in *OED2:* He must be a cute chap and deserves to have a leather medal. **1837** in Thornton *Amer. Gloss.* II: A leather medal his reward should be. **1851** B. Hall *College Wds.* 183: At Harvard College, the Leather Medal was formerly bestowed upon the laziest man in College. *****1890** B. Stoker, in R.W. Dent *Colloq. Lang. in Ulysses* 268: I'm afeerd it's only a leather medal ye'd get as yit. **1892** Bierce *Beetles* 252: The Peace Society bestowed on me/Its leather medal. *****1914–22**

J. Joyce *Ulysses* 750: He ought to get a leather medal with a putty rim for all the plans he invents. **ca*1900–25 in *Northwest Folklore* III (Winter 1968) 19: He wore a leather medal that/He'd won in the Crimean War. **1948** Morison *Naval Ops. in WWII* III 291: The "leather medal" goes to the Japanese admiral who led his combat ships out to sea just when the transports needed his protection.

leatherneck *n.* [after the leather-lined collar formerly a part of the USMC uniform (abandoned in 1875); U.S. use not attested before 1907, but cf. 1823 quot.] **1.** *Mil.*, orig. *Navy.* a marine; (now usu.) a U.S. marine. Now *colloq.* [In 19th-C. use, *soldier* (as in 1889–90 quot.) freq. also connoted 'marine'.]

  [**1823** Cooper *Pilot* 158: Let the riptyles clew up the corners of their mouths to their eyebrows now; when they come to hear the raal Yankee truth of the matter, they [Royal Marines] will sheet them down to their leather neckcloths!] ***1889–90** Barrère & Leland *Dict. Slang* II 11: *Leather-necks* (naval), a term for soldiers; from their leather stock, which, to a sailor, with his neck free from any hindrance, must appear such an uncomfortable appliance. ***1903** in Kipling *Traffics & Discoveries* 56: The lower deck wasn't pleased to see a leather-neck [marine] interpretin' a strictly maritime part. **1907** *Army & Navy Life* (Dec.) 744: "Yah, yah, twelve eighty and a horse blanket; yah, yah, leather neck!" "Sergeant, who the devil is that?" "An ex-flat-foot [sailor] who is driving a truck, sir; he passes every morning and devils the man on watch at the door." [**1913** Meyer *10 Yrs.* 9 [ref. to 1854]: The most objectionable part of the whole uniform was the leather stock or "dog collar," as we called it, intended to serve as a cravat and keep the [army] soldier's chin elevated.] **1914** Paine *Wall Between* 99: Dear me, 'tis a gr-rand man ye are wid your soft berth ashore an' rid of cruisin' among us leathernecks. *Ibid.* 146: "Stow the gab," snapped the ensign, who cherished the traditional dislike of his calling for all "leathernecks" of marines. *Ibid.* 257: Blow the charge, you leathernecked brat! **1918** Ruggles *Navy Explained* 89: *Leatherneck*...marine. **1919** *Marine Corps Gazette* (Sept.) 265: The fame of the black leather stock [worn in 1799] lives today in the epithet "leatherneck." **1919** Peixotto *Amer. Front* 44: Superb fellows they were, these "leather-necks." **1919** *Lit. Digest* (Jan. 11) 45: I wasn't gonna let them Leathernecks have nothin' on a dough-boy. **1922** Paul *Impromptu* 177: Regulars and leathernecks with the bronze of many suns. **1927** *Marine Corps Gazette* (Mar.) 34: The fact that early Marines wore a black leather stock has given rise to a name which has been current for several generations. Yet the first sailor who called a Marine a "leatherneck" was unaware of the fact that thereby he started a tradition. **1928** Scanlon *God Have Mercy* 72 [ref. to 1918]: Oh, the infantry, the cavalry, the dirty engineers,/They couldn't lick a leather-neck/In a hundred thousand years. ***1929** Bowen *Sea Slang* 82: *Leatherneck.* A Royal Marine. **1937** Thompson *Take Her Down* 57: "Hey, you big leatherneck, who's the little guy?" a deck hand inquired of the marine. **a*1950 Granville *Sea Slang* 143: *Leather-necks.* Royal Marines. They're tough. **1950** *Nat. Geographic* (Nov.) 649: That nickname, "Leathernecks," came from a black leather stock, part of early Marine uniforms, worn to keep a man from getting his throat slit by the whistling sweep of a "snickersnee." **1958** Cooley *Run for Home* 152: Pretty soon we'll have leathernecks all over the world—protecting the new American empire! **1962** Morris & Morris *Dict. Word & Phr. Origins* 212: Sailors...coined *leatherneck wash* and *Marine wash* to describe a method of washing one's face without taking one's shirt off. **1967** Dubus *Lieut.* 75: Let's go, Leatherneck. You're disturbing my colleagues. **1971** Sonzski *Punch Goes Judy* 207: He was a "career Leatherneck." **1973** Layne *Murphy* (unp.): And the old leatherneck preferred [to be called] Pop. **1978** Hasford *Short-Timers* 105: Hey, hit the deck, leatherneck, we're moving. **1980** Manchester *Darkness* 31: He was proud to have been a leatherneck himself. **1982** E. Leonard *Cat Chaser* 183: He's a fighting leatherneck. **1983** Beckwith & Knox *Delta Force* 228: These leathernecks were being asked to do something extraordinary. **1991** *Newsweek* (Jan. 21) 27: The leatherneck grunts are leaning forward in their foxholes.

  2. a tough or uncouth fellow; ROUGHNECK; (*also*) a lout. Cf. LEATHER-ASS.

  ***1897** in *Austral. Nat. Dict.*: The "rouseabout"...he sneeringly terms "loppy" and a "leatherneck." **1918** F. Gibbons *Thought We Wouldn't Fight* 245: Gwan, you leatherneck....You smell like a livery stable. **1919** *DN* V 62: *Leather-neck*, an uncouth person. "See that boy, what a *leather-neck* he is!" New Mexico. **1926** Tully *Jarnegan* 252: You keep away from me...you ol' leather neck. **1923** *Chi. Sun. Trib.* (Oct. 14) ("Comics") (unp.): Well! I give the old leathernecks a thrill. **1942**

ATS 627: Strong, husky player...*leatherneck.* **1942** in P. McGuire *Jim Crow Army* 109: He...is a rough dried leather neck Negro hating cracker from Louisiana. **1966** in *DARE: Leatherneck*...a real roughened cowboy.

leather-pounder *n.* a horseman; (*Mil.*) a cavalry soldier. Hence **leather-pounding**, *adj.*
  1932 *Leatherneck* (May) 23: This time he offers eight rollicking yarns about the leather-pounding cavalry. **1936** Adams *Cowboy* 22: The cowboy was known, too, by such slang names as..."leather pounder." **1938** Burt *Powder River* 223: Leather Pounders.

leather-pusher *n. Boxing.* a boxer. Hence **leather-pushing,** *n.* Also **leather-puncher, leather-slinger.**
  1920–21 Witwer *Leather Pushers* 41: The fair Irene heard he was a leather pusher. **1924** *Inf. Jour.* (Apr.) 452: About once a month a smoker is given between the local "leather punchers" and those of the navy. **1929** in R.E. Howard *Book* 67: Slade...was the shiftiest, trickiest leather-slinger in the whole merchant marine. **1934** Jevne & Purcell *Joe Palooka* (film): I could make a great leather-pusher outta you! **1935** Mackenzie *Been Places* 78: I guess before Firpo started leather-pushing very few people down here knew what it was all about. **1942** *Pittsburgh Courier* (Aug. 29) 7: Ten leather-pushers...were lined up as barriers. **1950** Bissell *Stretch on the River* 6: I could see myself as a...leather pusher with several coeds cheering from the ringside.

leather queen *n. Homosex.* a male homosexual leather fetishist.
  1965–72 E. Newton *Mother Camp* 33: "Leather queens" do not look like straight men. **1977** A. Patrick *Beyond Law* 116: He was now "Kiki," an apparently dumb but sweet leather queen. **1985** J. Dillinger *Adrenaline* 70: The leather queen was leaning against a tree, black leather chaps over faded Levi's, black leather vest open....His ears and tits were pierced and studded. **1986** Calif. man, age *ca*32, on *Story of English* (PBS-TV series): There are...feather queens and leather queens.

leatherskin *n.* an American Indian. Used derisively.—usu. considered offensive. Hence **leather-skinned,** *adj.*
  1834 Caruthers *Kentuckian in N.Y. I* 22: This Pete Ironsides that I'm ridin' on, has more of a Christian soul in him than any leatherskin between Missouri and Red River. **1898** Brooks *Strong Hearts* 42: I'll brain you like a mad-dog, you leather-skinned yelper.

leather-strap *n. Naut.* molasses.
  1887 Davis *Sea Wanderer* 290: Molasses [is called] leather-strap or black-strap.

leather-worker *n.* [fr. LEATHER, *n.,* 2] a pickpocket or purse-snatcher.
  1901 *Our Naval Apprentice* (Oct.) 12: The only thing for mine was to conclude that I'd been buzzed for the roll by some San Francisco leather-worker.

leave *v.* ¶ **left** left behind or at a disadvantage; stymied; defeated; outwitted.—used predicatively.—usu. constr. with *get.*
  1877 Burdette *Mustache* 178: When I got on into the heavy business, I was left. **1880** Nye *Boomerang* 102: A disappointed bronco who has high aspirations for being a circus horse, and has "got left." *Ibid.* 176: He...kicketh against buck beer and getteth left. **1882** E. Field *Tribune Verse* 211: For of all words from a heart bereft,/The saddest are these, "You bet I'm left." **1883** *Life* (Jan. 11) 22: Lots of men would like to...not work Sundays, but if any one does it, all of 'em in that line must, or they get left. **1885** "Lykkejaeger" *Dane* 5: I hear individuals of the present time, who are inclined to slang, say, "It is a cold day when I get left." **1889** "M. Twain" *Conn. Yankee* 160: The Jack Cade or the Wat Tyler who tries such a thing without first educating his materials up to revolution-grade is almost absolutely certain to get left. **1897** *Harper's Wkly.* (Jan. 23) 86: Usually the brakeman "gets left." **1914** Atherton *Perch* 174: They tried to corral your mine for delinquent taxes but got left.

Leb *n.* a Lebanese.—also used attrib.
  1983 *Daily News* (N.Y.) (Aug. 31) 2: Marines in third day of Leb battle. **1988** Dye *Outrage* 4: Until the Lebs can take over.

lech var. LETCH, *n. & v.*

leery or **leary** *n.* (see quots.). Cf. LARRY. [Despite form of defs., an *adj.* sense may be intended.]
  1929 *Sat. Eve. Post* (Oct. 12) 29: *Leary.* Damaged merchandise. **1930** Irwin *Tramp & Und. Sl.: Leary.*—Damaged goods or inferior merchandise; especially that which is peddled by pitchmen.

leery or **leary** *adj.* **1.a.** Orig. *Und.* (of persons) wary; distrustful; (hence) (*obs.*) fearful; afraid. Now *colloq.* or *S.E.*

   *1718 in Partridge *Dict. Und.* 402: The Cull is leery, *alias* the Man is shy. *1796 Grose *Vulgar Tongue* (ed. 3): *Leery.* On one's guard. *1812 Vaux *Vocab.*: *Fly:* vigilant; suspicious…*Leary:* synonymous with *fly.* *ca1835 in Holloway & Black *Broadsides* II 61: The mot she seemed leary and gave me a frown,/I muched [*sic*] her over, and flash'd half a crown. **1848** *Ladies' Repository* (Oct.) 315: *Leary,* shy; suspicious; doubtful. **1859** Matsell *Vocab.* 51: *Leary.* On guard; look out; wide awake. **1890** *DN* I 62: *Leery,* adj.…suspicious. "He was leery of me." **1891** Maitland *Slang Dict.* 166: *Leery* or *Leary,* doubtful, uncertain. **1895** in J. London *Tramp Diary* 62: Den jes' take it easy, an' don't get leary and grab me like dat again. **1896** Ade *Artie* 21: The old lady's a little leary of me, but I can win her all right. **1897** in Hoppenstand *Dime Novel Detective* 72: I'm…leery of such coves. **1902** Hapgood *Autobiog. of a Thief* 38: So we got "leary" (suspicious) and quit. **1903** A.H. Lewis *Boss* 135: An' it's th' judge in partic'lar, I'm leary of. **1904** *Life in Sing Sing* 250: *Leery.* Afraid. **1904** A.H. Lewis *President* 423: You've nothin' to be leary of in me. **1909** "Clivette" *Café Cackle* 120: He was "leary" of the outcome…as some of the "boys" were pretty "tough." **1911** A.H. Lewis *Apaches of N.Y.* 28: It's the Dropper he's leary of; an' now th' Dropper's in hock he's chased back. **1913** *Sat. Eve. Post* (July 5) 39: Jack's really leary. **1913** J. London *Valley of Moon* 196: He never was leary of anything on two feet. **1921** Casey & Casey *Gay-Cat* 116: I'm leary, I'm scared stiff! **1927** "S.S. Van Dine" *"Canary" Murder* ch. xxii: He may have got leery, and tipped off some pal. **1934** H. Roth *Call It Sleep* 347: Awri', don' git leary! **1952** Mandel *Angry Strangers* 255: If you're so goddam leery, what're you doing here? **1975** Ebon *Bermuda Triangle* 102: It scared the hell out of me, but it didn't make me leary about going back down in that Bermuda Triangle again.

b. careful.

   1911 in *OED2:* But be leery that we don't get stuck for non-performance.

2. Esp. *Und.* on the alert; cunning; clever; knowing. *Rare* in U.S.

   1791 [W. Smith] *Confess. T. Mount* 19: Oliver's leary. *ca1811 in J. Farmer *Musa Pedestris* 77: A Leary Mot. Rum Old Mog was a leary flash mot. *1812 Vaux *Vocab.*: *Fly:*…cunning; not easily robbed or duped; a shopkeeper or person of this description, is called a *fly cove,* or a *leary cove.* *1839 Brandon *Poverty, Mendicity & Crime* (gloss.): *Leary*—Cunning. *1841 in *F & H* IV 169: The dashy, splashy, leary little stringer. **1859** Matsell *Vocab.* 127: [Boxing slang:] *Leary.* Active; smart. *1888 in *F & H* IV 169: The…gipsy smiled in leary fashion.

3. drunk or groggy.

   1891 Maitland *Slang Dict.* 166: *Leery* or *Leary….*Also, drunk. **1911** *DN* III 545: *Leary,* adj.…to be [*sic*] dazed or bewildered….To be [*sic*] foolish, half-imbecile, etc.

4. tending to arouse suspicion; suspect.

   1903 in Partridge *Dict. Und.* 402: He…kept signallin' that things looked leary. **1966** "Petronius" *N.Y. Unexp.* 181: Don't have your purchase shipped…prepaid if the store looks leery. They'll send you damaged goods.

leeward *n.* ¶ In phrase: **to leeward** *Naut.* at a disadvantage; toward defeat or ruin.

   *1826 in *OED:* His friend…ought not…to be suffered to drop to leeward in the conversation. *1834 (cited in Partridge *DSUE* (ed. 7) 1249). **1841** [Mercier] *Man-of-War* 49: Taking part in every row…and very seldom going to *leeward,* for the fellow that could *whip* him…had to work sharp. **1878** G. Willis *Our Cruise* 7: Its [*sic*] as plain as the noses on your faces that all creation is drifting to leeward mighty fast. **1903** *DN* II 294: I've had so many doctor's bills that I've run *to luard* this year. *1929 Bowen *Sea Slang* 82: *Leeward of, To get to.* To fall foul of a man. *a1950 W. Granville *Sea Slang of 20th C.* 144: *Leeward, to go to.* To place oneself in a disadvantageous position.

left *n.* In phrase: ¶ **over the left** not at all.—used postpositively or as a retort. Now *hist.* [Abbr. of earlier *S.E. over the (left) shoulder;* see *OED* s.v. shoulder.]

   [**1705** in *F & H* IV 173: The said Waters, as he departed from the table, said, "God bless you *over the left shoulder.*" The court ordered a record thereof to be made forthwith.] *1837 C. Dickens *Pickwick Papers* ch. xlii: "*Can* I live anywhere else? I thought I could not."…And then each gentleman pointed with his right thumb over his left shoulder. This action [is] imperfectly described in words by the very feeble

term of "over the left"…; its expression is one of light and playful sarcasm. *1841 in *F & H* IV 173: I am thine, and thine only. *Thine!*—over the left. *1843 in *F & H* IV 173: I think she will come. *Ned.* Yes, over the left—ha, ha, ha! **1848** *Life in Rochester* 67: Yes, I did, *over the left.* **1848** Baker *Glance at N.Y.* 13: *Mike.* You brought the change back, of course? *Jake.* Oh, yes, I did, over the left. **1853** Delano *Life on Plains* 31: I had made sixteen miles, "*over the left,*" and learned a lesson to keep near the train. **1854** G.G. Foster *15 Mins.* 94: Private houses "over the way," where servants attend them "over the left." **1854** St. Clair *Metropolis* 6: "I have been here a week in succession, looking for you. Over the left," he added in a lower tone. **1855** in Dwyer & Lingenfelter *Songs of Gold Rush* 21: California Over the Left. **1863** in Geer *Diary* 113: Rations getting so scanty as to cause much satisfaction (over the left) among the boys. **1867** "M. Twain," in A.L. Scott *Twain's Poetry* 57: She proved it—o'er the left. **1873** De Witt *Dundreary* 21: "We've taken off from the price." "Over the left; it's three pence too high now." **1882** (quot. at *in a [hog's] horn* s.v. HORN). **1907** *DN* III 215: Word-List from Northwestern Arkansas…*Over the left.*…An expression giving the words it accompanies a meaning opposite to that which they would otherwise have. **1947** in Botkin *Sidewalks* 240: "Over the left" implied the reverse, as "He's a fine fellow—over the left." ca1960 in *DARE:* Used in sayings to indicate the exact opposite of what is said: "That's a fact, over the left."

left *ppl.a.* see s.v. LEAVE, *v.*

Left Coast *n.* Esp. *Pol.* the West Coast of the U.S., esp. Los Angeles and Southern California; (hence) (*l.c.*) any west coast.

   1988 Lewin & Lewin *Thes. of Slang* 422: West Coast…*left coast, the Coast.* **1993** Univ. Tenn. student: Conservatives call California *the Left Coast.* **1995** *CNN & Co.* (CNN-TV): On the West Coast—or is it "the Left Coast"? [*Laughter from panelists*]. **1995** Gingrich & Forstchen *1945* 371: On the left coast of England.

left field *n.* [of baseball origin; semantic development obscure; perh. sugg. by the fact that, owing to the distance involved, a putout throw from left field to first base is extremely difficult; see discussion in W. Safire *I Stand Corrected* 232–35]

¶ In phrases:

¶ **from** [or **out of**] **left field, 1.** as if from nowhere; from out of the blue; (hence) without warning; most unexpectedly.

   1947 Bowers & Millhauser *Web* (film): I really solved this one from left field. **1952** *The Hunter* (CBS-TV): Where are these putouts [murders] coming from, left field? **1960** *Sat. Eve. Post* (Aug. 13) 74: You see a little wiggle that suddenly comes out of left field. She is absolutely unexpected. **1961** *Time* (Jan. 20) 25: Canadian businessmen last week were playing host to two more trade missions out of far left field. **1966** N.Y.C. high school student: That one [*sc.,* an exam question] came right out of left field. **1969** *Seattle Times* (Jan. 5) 76: A conglomerate can come in from left field…and set a whole industry on fire. **1969** Ad in *Business Week* (May 10) 101: The need in one field is answered by an insight coming in from "left field." **1978** *Rolling Stone* (Sept. 23) 18: The songs…"come from left field." **1981** G. Wolf *Roger Rabbit* 193: They had come out of left field in the business world. **1989** L. Ganz et al. *Parenthood* (film): This is *really* coming out of left field. **1990** *Donahue* (NBC-TV): She must have come from left field with this. *1992 W. Nash *Jargon* 165: *Field, out of left* Familiar in American English, this expression, meaning "quite unpredictable," "coming from an unexpected quarter," or even "preposterous," is relatively recent in British usage. **1995** *Pyramids & Sphinx* (Learning Channel TV): Here comes somebody way out of left field with a coherent, beautifully written [theory].

2. *out* [or *off*] *in left field,* below.

   1949 KFRC radio (S.F.) (July 24) (Tamony Coll.): Maybe I was a little dreamy and from left field. **1958** Lindsay & Crouse *Tall Story* 30: He's strictly from left field.

¶ **out** [or **off**] **in left field, 1.** (of persons) eccentric; (hence, broadly) absurd; nonsensical; unreasonable; entirely wrong; far from the mark. Also as quasi-*adv.*

   1937 *S.F. Chronicle* (Apr. 19) 2H (Tamony Coll.): Lefty Gomez [New York Yankees pitcher noted for his eccentric humor] is "way out in left field without a glove" in baseball jargon. In other words he is as proficient at whipping over a smart crack as a sizzling strike. **1945** Rossen *Walk in the Sun* (film): There's the right way, the wrong way and the Army way. The Army way is strictly out in left field! **1947** *Time* (Sept. 29) 72 (Tamony Coll.): Out in Left Field [headline of story about comedian Jack Paar]. *Ibid.* 73: Way out in left field, that's where my humor really lies. **1957** J.D. MacDonald *Death Trap* 157: You are way, way out in left field. **1957** M. Shulman *Rally* 182: It's so far out in left field, I'm not sure I ought to bring it up. **1959** *Time* (July 27) 54: The virus theory of cancer causation long seemed to be far out in leftfield. **1959** *Sat. Eve. Post* (Nov. 28) 97: Teen-agers will buy *anything* for themselves...and the farther out in left field...the better they like it. **1961** *Harper's* (Feb.) 6: Indicting American "big dough" because the nineteenth-century robber barons were less than altruistic seems far out in left field. **1961** *Sat. Eve. Post* (Feb. 11) 78: His thoughts are way out in left field. **1978** Rodale *Syn. Finder* 336: Eccentric...*off one's rocker, off the wall, out in left field.* **1979** in Terkel *Amer. Dreams* 311: He's very right-wing....He'd be so far out in left field, you couldn't talk to him. **1985** MacLaine *Dancing* 209: I choked on the word. It was from so far out in left field that it stopped my crying. *a***1989** Spears *NTC's Dict.* 268: That guy is out in left field—a real nut.

2. distracted; unconscious.

1958 G. Abbott *Damn Yankees* (film): It's just that your mental state is off in left field somewhere. **1964** "Doctor X" *Intern* 134: Goodfellow had agreed to use "twilight sleep," which simply means giving enough Demerol and Scopolamine and Seconal that the patient is out in left field through the whole affair.

3. very far away; (*hence*) out of touch; in obscurity; in a difficult position; at a disadvantage; at a loss.

1945 Rossen *Walk in the Sun* (film): Why do they always stick you [a machine-gunner] out in left field? **1960** *N.Y. Times* (Sept. 18) I 68: He intends to hold a meeting with labor leaders, [but] no such talks have been held...."We've been left out in left field." **1962** *Sat. Eve. Post* (Sept. 15) 40: I talked to him long enough to find out that his hobbies are growing begonias and collecting stamps. So where did that leave me? Out in left field. **1963** *Wash. Post* (Oct. 6) E6: When he started to interpret, using Kierkegaard and Hollywood symbols, he left the reader way out in far left field. **1970** *Business Week* (Sept. 19) 32: Let Detroit know that we're out in left field pricewise with this car. **1970** *Seattle Times* (June 14) B1: You feel like you're kind of out in left field—sort of cut off from all of society.

left-field *adj.* unorthodox; unconventional; unexpected.

1967 Dubus *Lieut.* 77: What's this left field crap, Hahn? If you want me to interrogate like I did this morning then I'll by God do it but you're pissing me off. **1977** *L.A. Times* (Sept. 18) I 26: This separate business retains some of the left-field bohemian tradition from which it sprang. **1982** *L.A. Times* (July 18) ("Calendar") 82: This record may be the biggest left-field hit of all. **1985** W. Gray *Homer to Joyce* xvi: Such left-field interpretations cause students to...challenge their own ideas.

left-handed *adj.* **1.** unsanctioned by law; illicit. Orig. *S.E.* Cf. *S.E. left-handed compliment.*

***1889–90** Barrère & Leland *Dict. Slang* II 11: *Left-handed wife* (common), a mistress. **1930** Lait *On the Spot* 206: *Left-handed Wife*...kept woman. **1946** in *DAS:* Left-handed honeymoons with somebody else's husband.

2. homosexual.

1929 Tully *Shadows* 266: He became attached to Nitro Dugan. That brigand was in his own words "a woman hound." But Dugan had no prejudice against such boys. "I'm just not left-handed," he used to say. **1931** J.T. Farrell *McGinty* 304: I ain't got no use for a left-handed male. **1972** *N.Y. Post* (June 5) 21: *Left Handed* For mature adults: a feature length homosexual love story.

3. clumsy; no good; (*also*) strange; sinister. Orig. *S.E.* Cf. earlier *S.E.* sense 'ill-omened, inauspicious, sinister' in *OED2.*

1930 Lait *On the Spot* 171: Shut up, you left-handed bohunk. **1935** in Pyle *Ernie's Amer.* 61: That sounds a little left-handed somehow, thinking that finding a body would make people happy. **1944** *AS* XIX 109: A ship [undesirable for serving in] is...*wrong* or *left-handed.*

left-handed monkey wrench *n.* a nonexistent tool that inexperienced workers are sent to find as a hazing prank. Also vars. [About seventy-five similarly nonexistent objects are listed by O.F. Emerson, "Beguiling Words," *DN* V 93–96; many of these are repeated in *ATS* 288. Despite the context of "searching," *a*1653 quot. (earliest for *left-handed* 'adapted for the left hand') is prob. not apposite here.]

[*a*1653 in *OED:* Rather than want a Target, Perkins Tents are Search't vp, for Left-handed Implements.] **1921** *DN* V 94: Left-handed monkey wrench...Left-handed screw driver...Left-handed saw. **1933** J. Conroy *Disinherited* 74 [ref. to *ca*1918]: Left-hand monkey-wrench. *ca*1963 N.Y.C. high school student: You gotta use the left-handed monkey-wrench. **1995** N.Y.C. editor, age 27 (coll. J. Sheidlower): In the novelization of *Star Trek II: The Wrath of Khan* (but not in the movie), I remember a young ensign is sent to find a left-handed spanner. I didn't understand it at the time.

left-hander *n.* (see 1976 quot.). Also **left-footer.**

*a*1948 Mencken *Amer. Lang. Supp. II* 745: *Southpaw,* or *left-footer* (Catholics). A Protestant. **1950** in *DARE:* Left-handers (Lutherans). **1976** Univ. of Notre Dame graduate, age 29: Catholics call non-Catholics *left-handers* because they cross themselves with the wrong hand. A Catholic is a *right-hander,* but only among Catholics. You'd hear, "He got the job because he's an old right-hander."

left out *n.* [pun on *left out* 'omitted', sugg. by *left [out]field*] *Juve.* a nonexistent fielding position in a baseball or softball (or, *rarely,* football) game. *Joc.*

1958 N.Y.C. grade school pupils: "So what am I playing?" "Left out!" [*Laughter*]. **1996** N.Y.C. man, age 27 (coll. J. Sheidlower): "Myron's so terrible, we'll put him in left out." Yeah, it's a joke. **1996** *New Yorker* (June 24) 155: When [he]...asks his brothers if he can play football, they tell him to play Left Out.

leftover *n.* a has-been.

1926 Nichols & Tully *Twenty Below* 17: You bunch of left-overs. You ain't worth it.

lefty *n.* **1.** [sugg. by pronunciation (*obs.* in U.S.) /lɛfˈtɛnənt/] *Mil.* a lieutenant.

1840 *Spirit of Times* (May 9) 109: I say, Lefty, you put your foot in it again.

2. a left-handed person. Now *colloq.* Also as adj. or adv.

1886 *Sporting Life* (Apr. 7) 2, in *OED2:* In last Wednesday's game Nashville presented her left-handed battery,...to offset our "lefty" battery. **1902** *Sporting Life* 11 (July 12). **1930** Irwin *Tramp & Und. Sl.: Lefty....*A left-handed person. **1950** in *DAS:* Ted Gray, a young lefty, is ready to resume pitching. **1980** Lorenz *Guys Like Us* 54: I'll...play lefty.

3. *Pol.* a leftist. Also as adj.

1935 C. Odets *Waiting for Lefty* [title of play]. ***1937** in Partridge *Concise Dict. Sl.* 261: Counterblast to Lefties. **1948** *Sat. Eve. Post,* in *DAS:* Truman's Central Error: Fear of Libero-Lefties. **1977** Coover *Public Burning* 416: Our decision to burn them two lefties. **1977** Sayles *Union Dues* 75: So it was some lefty hotshot from *Rolling Stone.* **1978** Hamill *Dirty Laundry* 35: The Communists were in the hills, the government was full of Lefties. **1979** in Terkel *Amer. Dreams* 233: I know Seeger's a leftie, but I like his music. **1983** *Newsweek* (Feb. 28) 50: They're a bunch of lefties, aren't they? ***1984** T. Jones *Heart of Oak* 160: All the Lefties on board were in a state of high excitement. **1992** *Crier & Co.* (CNN-TV) (Sept. 30): That's a typical lefty response. **1994** *New Yorker* (Sept. 5) 110: An unreconstructed lefty. **1996** *New Yorker* (May 13) 38: A brilliant Strangelovian "modest proposal" hatched by a bunch of New York lefties.

4. *Entertainment Industry.* a left-handed compliment; innuendo.

1968 Brasselle *Cannibals* 204: Drink your drink, and save your "lefties" for someone else, you rascal. *Ibid.* 266: "They praised your talent." "Any lefties?" "Bryan said in his catty way that he'd...be making you a millionaire."

leg *n.* **1.** a swindler; BLACKLEG, 1; (*broadly*) a gambler.

***1815** in *OED2:* The Goose that laid the Golden Egg should be a lesson to the legs on the turf. ***1821** *Real Life in London* I 172: He is a well known *leg*,...present...to bet on the...races. ***1825** "Blackmantle" *Eng. Spy* I 213: Not so low as to turn *confederate* to a leg. **1839** *Spirit of Times* (June 22) 181: But the turfmen and the jockeys are vulgarly made to answer for all the sins of the betting men—the London *Legs.* These men...often attempt to insure their speculations by the foulest practices. **1859** Matsell *Vocab.* 51: *Leg.* A gambler. ***1872** Hotten *Slang Dict.* (ed. 4): *Leg,* or *blackleg,* a disreputable sporting character and racecourse *habitué*; that is, one who is disreputable among sporting men.

2. *pl.* (used as a nickname for a person having long legs).

1847 Downey *Portsmouth* 113: Legs and the Corporal of the Guard were ordered to convey him to the Brig. **1847** G.W. Harris *High Times* 68: "Legs" said, "I be durned." **1889–90** Barrère & Leland *Dict. Slang* II 11: *Legs* (American cadet [slang]), a nickname given to a tall lanky man.

3. *pl.* **a.** *Naut.* (of a ship) the capability of making good speed.

*1929 Bowen *Sea Slang* 82: Legs, To have. To sail fast. **1941** Kendall *Army & Navy Sl.* 20: Have legs....speed it. **1961** Burgess *Dict. Sailing* 133: A fast ship is said to have legs.

b. effective range.

1976 Whelton *CB Baby* 39: A legal CB set...hardly has the legs to reach out fifteen miles. **1981** "K. Rollins" *Fighter Pilots* 23: We had nothing [in the way of aircraft] with legs that could fight. **1986** Zeybel *First Ace* 22: Today the F-4s had short legs,...no six-hundred gallon centerline tanks. **1989** G. Hall *Air Guard* 46: The A-7D's...incredible "legs," or range.

4. copulation; (*hence*) women regarded as sexual objects.—sometimes constr. with *piece of.*—usu. considered vulgar. See also *lay the leg*, below.

[**1938** H. Miller *Tropic of Capricorn* 267: "Get a look at that," he'd say, pointing to a girl strolling along the sidewalk. "Jesus, what a leg!"] **1966** H.S. Thompson *Hell's Angels* 16: Hell, those broads didn't come out there for any singsong....They were loaded and they wanted to get off some leg, but it just got to be too many guys. **1967** in Kochman *Black & White Styles* 76: I want some leg, baby. *a*1968 in Haines & Taggart *Ft. Lauderdale* 60: When it comes to pulling leg, I get my share, you know. **1969** D.L. Lee *Don't Cry* 57: When u ask for a piece/of leg/it's not for/yr/self/but for yr/people. **1969** Hannerz *Soulside* 126: There is the concern with sex; already boys less than ten years old talk in the group context about "getting some pussy" (or "some leg" as boys in Washington started saying about 1967). **1968–70** *Current Slang III & IV* 78: Leg, n. A girl.—New Mexico State. **1970** D. Long *Nia* 14: The alphas approaching/everything philosophically/even a piece of leg. **1970** Wertheim & Gonzalez *Talkin' About Us* 13: Jivers figure the leg they're going to get. **1968–71** Cole & Black *Checking* 320: He's been trying to get some leg all trip but everywhere we've gone the broads have turned him down. **1971** Sonzski *Punch Goes Judy* 95: All the Georges...are pissed off in their middle age because Georgias did not give enough leg. **1973** Andrews & Owens *Black Lang.* 26: Big Sam...was always trying to get a piece of leg from Lucy. **1974** Gober *Black Cop* 96: Them cats wearing theyselves out on some broad that couldn't do nuthin' but give up a little leg is crazy. **1975** in *Tenn. Folklore Soc. Bull.* XLIV 139: Sexual intercourse: "get some leg," "have some leg."...Form used...at Fort Jackson, South Carolina, in 1970 was "a shot of leg." **1982** "J. Cain" *Commandos* 366: She's the most beeeeyoutiful piece of leg in this land! 441: Just a lot of hot leg in here. **1983** *Reader's Digest Success with Words* 86: Black English...*leg* = "female." **1990** Rukuza *West Coast Turnaround* 45: He could stand a shot of leg, but...he'd have to wash his dick in gasoline afterward!

5. the attractive legs of young women.—used collectively.

1961–64 Barthelme *Dr. Caligari* 132: Look at all that "leg" glittering there! **1966** "Petronius" *N.Y. Unexp.* 146: Going down the Vanderbilt Ramp...you can see much leg.

6.a. [fr. STRAIGHT-LEG] *Army*, esp. *Av.* a member of the armed forces who is not qualified as a parachutist or (*hence*) is not a member of an airmobile unit; (*specif.*) an infantry soldier.—also used attrib.

1964 R. Moore *Green Berets* 150: If the legs had their way they'd get Special Forces out of Vietnam entirely. **1965** J. Lucas *Dateline* 232: The legs (ground troops) have run into Viet Cong out there. **1966** *N.Y. Times Mag.* (Oct. 30) 102: An infantryman is a "grunt" and, unless he is also a paratrooper, a "leg." **1967** *Time* (May 26) 18: Any paratrooper can whup five "legs." **1968** Schell *Military Half* 107: The men of the 1st Brigade of the 101st Airborne, who were extremely proud of their paratrooper training, referred contemptuously to all infantrymen as "legs." **1969** Moskos *Enlisted Man* 154: Likewise, paratroopers express disdain for "legs" (as non-airborne soldiers are called). **1969** Maitland *Only War We've Got* 89: It means the Airborne against the Legs, that's what it means. **1970** R.N. Williams *New Exiles* 276: I was into being a foot soldier, a leg, really gung ho. **1971** Former SP5, U.S. Army, age 29 [ref. to 1961]: A *leg* was a nonairborne guy. **1973** Herbert & Wooten *Soldier* 90: What the hell are you doing in a leg outfit? **1979** J. Morris *War Story* 225: Not some leg general. **1981** Rogan *Mixed Co.* 250: The airborne name for the rest of the Army is "legs," synonymous with all that is vile, verminous, and groveling. **1983** T. Page *Nam* 32: Legs, officers, corpsmen, ARVN, ROKs. **1983** Goldman & Fuller *Charlie Co.* 149 [ref. to 1969]: The jet pilots were putting on a show for the legs, their haughty term for infantrymen.

1992 L. Chambers *Recondo* 121: I hate the leg air force! **1993** Watson & Dockery *Point Man* 104 [ref. to 1962]: We really didn't get along with... the "legs" (non-Airborne soldiers).

b. one who runs errands or does legwork.

1976 *L.A. Times* (July 19) II 1: The swarms of teenaged boys and girls (called "legs," not "gofers" at JPL) who run errands.

7. *Pris.* (see quot.).

1969 Hopper *Sex in Prison* 114: Half-trusties are usually called "legs." They are not guarded during the day but are locked up...at night. "Legs" wear blue denim trousers with a white strip running halfway down each leg.

8. *pl. Entertainment Industry*, esp. *Film.* popularity; success; (*specif.*) staying power.

1978 *N.Y. Times Mag.* (July 23) 22: Hype...sells books that used to be called *page-turners* but are now referred to as books *with legs*, presumably because they seem to walk off the shelves. **1981** *L.A. Times* (Jan. 9) VI 1: This is a film that has legs (staying power), and we should have the opportunity to make money from it. **1981** *Film Comment* (May) 2: Coppola...relied on a Seattle run to demonstrate to an antsy United Artists that the film did indeed "have legs" in the general market. **1981** J. Valenti, on *Larry King Show* (Mutual Radio Network) (Nov. 2): *Raiders of the Lost Ark* has what we call in the industry "legs"—staying power....when you get a movie that has legs, that keeps on going for five or six months, that's very unusual. **1982** *N.Y. Times* (July 7) C15: In the long run, what counts is what Hollywood calls "legs"—the ability to attract audiences week after week. **1985** *Time* (Feb. 4) 85: Sometimes...movies can elude their death warrants and flourish into cult objects through doggedness and word of mouth. They acquire "legs." **1986** G. Trudeau, in *Daily Beacon* (Univ. Tenn.) 4: In a fickle market, this is one chocolate chip cookie with legs. **1990** *Show Biz Today* (CNN-TV) (Dec. 26): In the parlance of the [film] industry, they have no "legs"—their runs are short. **1990** *Nation* (Sept. 10) 224: Bush's new war may not have legs. **1991** *CBS This Morning* (CBS-TV) (Oct. 7): I do have legs in this [movie] business. **1992** *Rolling Stone* (Jan. 23) 9: Michael Jackson's album does have legs.

¶ In phrases:

¶ **best part of you ran down your mother's leg** *Mil.* (used as a contemptuous insult).

1966–80 McAleer & Dickson *Unit Pride* 180: Because they know that the best part of you ran down your mother's leg. **1987** *Full Metal Jacket* (film): The best part of you ran down your mother's leg and wound up as a stain on the mattress!

¶ **break a leg, 1.** *Und.* (see *a*1935 quot.). Cf. FALL.

1908 Sullivan *Criminal Slang* 8: *Broke a leg*—Got arrested. *a*1935 in D.W. Maurer *Lang. Und.* 72: To *break a leg.* To be arrested or convicted of a crime. (Obs.)

2. (see 1942 quot.).

1915 *N.Y. Eve. Jour.* (Aug. 5) 15: Tear up to 1492 Columbus and slip this wire to Mr. P. J. Flanigan—and break a leg getting back—remember fast, faster, fastest. **1942** *ATS* 55: *Break a leg*...to hasten or go in a breakneck fashion.

3. *Theat.* (used to wish a performer good luck, esp. in a debut appearance).

1964 E. Wilson *Wilson's N.Y.* 26: *Break a leg*—Show Biz expression for "Good luck, knock 'em dead." **1964** N.Y.C. high school drama coach [ref. to 1930's]: We used to say "Break a leg!" instead of "Good luck!" to avoid jinxing the performance. **1974** Angelou *Gather Together* 112 [ref. to 1940's]: Okay, Rita, break a leg. **1975** in Partridge *Dict. Catch Phrs.* (ed. 2) 37: *Break a leg!*...The phrase was more popular in the 30's and 40's. It was used among actors just before one of them [was due to go] before an audience for the first time. **1979** Gutcheon *New Girls* 263: "Wish me luck."..."Break a leg." **1985** *Fame* (syndic. TV series): "Go break a leg." "I'll break two." **1987** Tristan & Hancock *Weeds* (film): Break a leg!

¶ **give (someone) leg** to tease someone; *pull (someone's) leg*, 2, below.

1970–71 Higgins *Coyle* 69: Remember last time I saw you, you're giving me a little leg about there's nothing going on?

¶ **lay the leg** (of a woman) to engage in copulation.

[*1669 *New Acad. of Complements* 257: Bonny Kate,...lay thy leg o're [*sic*] me.] **1918** in *AS* (Oct. 1933) 29: *Lay the Leg.* Have sexual intercourse. **1927** *Immortalia* 77: I tried my best to get 'er to lay the leg. **1942–49** *DAUL* 123: *Lay the leg.* To engage in an act of sexual intercourse. **1975** in Partridge *Concise Sl. Dict.* 259: She could not very well have her admirers know that she was laying the leg with Old Horny.

¶ **pull (someone's) leg, 1.** to deceive (someone), esp. playfully; hoax. Now *S.E.*

1821 Gallatin *Diary* 184: I really think father, in a covert way, pulls his leg. I know he thinks little of his talents and less of his manners. ***1888** in *F & H* 318: Then I shall be able to pull the leg of that chap Mike. He is always trying to do me. **1892** S. Crane *Maggie* ch. xiv: She was pulling m'leg. **1893** in F. Remington *Sel. Letters* 169: A page of "leg pulling" dedicated to you. **1894** in L. Levy *Flashes of Merriment* 151: I have no leg to pull. ***1897** in S.J. Baker *Australian Lang.* 117: And the jester "pulls your leg." ***1907** *N & Q* (Mar. 2) 164: "*Pull one's leg.*"—…in England…is generally used to express an intention to deceive or hold up to ridicule. ***1914–22** Joyce *Ulysses* 140: A.E. has been telling some yankee interviewer that you came to him…to ask him about planes of consciousness. Magennis thinks you must have been pulling A.E.'s leg. *Ibid.* 510: I won't have my leg pulled. **1925** F.S. Fitzgerald *Great Gatsby*: I suspected that he was pulling my leg, but a glance at him convinced me otherwise. **1935** Lorimer & Lorimer *Heart Specialist* 12: Are you pulling my leg? **1936** G. Fort *Dracula's Daughter.* **1961** L.G. Richards *TAC* 21: Whose leg are you trying to pull? ***1965** S. Cooper *Over Sea* 134: He might have been pulling our legs all the while. **1979–82** Gwin *Overboard* 109: He couldn't resist doing what he called "pulling their legs off" by "acting unnatural." **1983** Ad for Nike shoes (WINS radio) (Dec. 21): There's no such thing as an average runner. And whoever tells you otherwise is not only pulling your leg. He's totally ignoring your foot. **1995** *Calif. v. Simpson* (Court TV) (Sept. 5): As if he were pulling your leg with these outrageous remarks. **1995** Gingrich & Forstchen *1945* 261: I'll bet it's those Lowrie boys again, pulling your leg.

2. to ask (a person), esp. for money.

1886 *Lantern* (N.O.) (Oct. 20) 3: Some days ago she bumped his head for stuff [*i.e.*, money], and a few nights ago pulled his leg for more.…Some blokes can never see when they are being played for suckers. **1894** Bangs *Three Weeks in Politics* 24: "They thought his leg would pan out well"…In politics…the verb "to-pull-his-leg" means to extract from his pocket all the lucre it will yield.…The candidate who says "I will win that office if it costs a leg" means "I'll spend all I've got to win." In short, "leg" is a contraction for "bank account," derived, I presume, from the word "legacy." *Ibid.* 25: These people gain no personal advantage from this leg-pulling exercise. **1895** Townsend *Fadden* 103: 'E was meanin' de times de Duchess pulled me leg fer de boodle wot I touched mugs fer. **1897** in Outcault *Yellow Kid* (pl. 64): Liz pulled me leg fer a [theatrical] boks fer her mudder. **1903** Jarrold *Bowery* 19: What'll I give y' fifty cents fer. Youse rags make me tired. You're always pullin' me leg. **1908** in H.C. Fisher *A. Mutt* 69: He pulled Pickels' leg 'Till his victim did beg But…he needed the money. *Ibid.* 100: I want to give your leg another pull. **1916** Flipper *Negro Frontiersmen* 37: If you will pardon the slang, he "pulled my leg" and nothing more.…He got two or three hundred dollars out of me this way. **1977** Monaghan *Schoolboy, Cowboy* 43 [ref. to 1908]: Never let a girl think yer stingy, but never let her pull yer leg neither.

3. *Stu.* (see quot.). Cf. LEG-PULLER, 1.

1895 Gore *Stu. Slang* 18: *Pull one's leg.* To curry favor with.

¶ **right as my** [or **this**] **leg** as right as may be; absolutely right.

***1719** in *F & H* IV 177: Jolly Ralph was in with Peg,…And she as right as is my leg. ***1762** in *F & H* IV 177: Fear nothing. All's well, and as right as my leg. ***1767** in *F & H* IV 177: A whore, she's as right as my leg. **1849** Melville *White Jacket* 189 [ref. to 1843]: "You are right," said Jack. "Right as this leg."

¶ **show a leg** Esp. *Naut.* to get out of bed; (*hence*) to hurry up; get busy.—usu. used imper.

1833 N. Ames *Old Sailor's Yarns* 282: Rouse out there, starbowlines—show a leg or an arm! **1838** *Crockett Almanac 1839* 2: I showed a leg all I knew to get 'em rigged out…in time. **1924** Colcord *Roll & Go* 114: Show a leg! Show a leg! **1953** Dodson *Away All Boats* 9: Come on, boys, rise and shine! Show the Navy a leg.

leg *v.* **1.** to run; (*rarely*, as in 1892, *1986 quots.) to walk.—constr. with *it*. Now *colloq.*

***1601** in *OED*: Let vs legge it a little. ***1790** in *OED*: The wives leg

hame and trim their fires. **1838** [Haliburton] *Clockmaker* (Ser. 2) 160: We ran up stairs as fast as we could leg it. **1840** *Spirit of Times* (Nov. 21) 446: As fast as I could leg it. **1859** Matsell *Vocab.* 51: *Leg It.* Run away. Clear out. **1865** Derby *Squibob Papers* 150: Leg it! the cars are off. ***1873** Hotten *Slang Dict.* (ed. 4): *Leg it,* to run. **1892** Bierce *Beetles* 105: He legged it into space. **1929–30** Farrell *Young Lonigan* 76: They legged it to O'Brien's basement. **1950** Raine *Six* 19: He's legging it for safety by this time. **1958** "W. Henry" *Reckoning* 98: The two of them came legging it back. **1985** Grave *Fla. Burn* 151: Legging it for the twisted wreck edged sideways in the alley. ***1986** Bowles *G'Day* 9: They have to leg it home.

2. to run errands or do legwork.

1844 in *DA*: There are a number of men here "legging" for the Colonel. **1902** Harben *Abner Daniel* 74: Durin' election…he was leggin' fer a friend o' his'n.

3. *Und.* to shoplift by concealing between the legs.

1962–68 B. Jackson *In the Life* 99: Stuff I legged (boosted by hiding it between her legs under her skirt). *You legged a power saw? Ibid.* 128: I'll be a lot better off if I can learn a little boosting, how to leg and so forth.

4. *Black E.* to copulate with (a woman).—usu. considered vulgar.

1970 Whitmore *Memphis-Nam-Sweden* 164: No sooner was he out the door than Joe was in the sack legging his broad.

5. to manufacture or distribute liquor illicitly; BOOTLEG, *v.*, 2. See also LEGGER.

1972 in *DARE* [ref. to 1956]: *Lag.* Short for bootleg. "I didnt 'lag myself. My business was farmin'." **1991** in *DARE*: The enormous appeal "leggin" enjoyed…it was so deliciously outside the law.

legal *n.* [short for *legal tender*] money.—constr. with *the*.

1878 Bellew *Tramp* 12: You ain't got henny of the legal about you, 'ave you? I'm dead broke.

legal *adj.* of legal age to be involved in a given activity

*a***1990** Westcott *Half a Klick* 172: Don't worry, I'm legal [*i.e.*, old enough to drink].

legal beagle *n.* an attorney, esp. one who is notably skillful or zealous. Usu. *joc.*

1949 Gordon & Kanin *Adam's Rib* 31: Why do you stay married to a legal beagle with ten thumbs? **1956** "T. Betts" *Across the Board* 42: A venerable legal beagle from Brooklyn. **1957** Ness & Fraley *Untouchables* 10: Well, well, Joe Reilly, the legal beagle. **1959** Serling *Twilight Zone* (CBS-TV): Well, Cooper, the legal beagle. How are you? **1961** Bosworth *Crows* 40: Legal officers…are always known, irreverently, as "legal beagles." **1968** N. Nye *Lost Mine* 56: In restraint of her old man's legal beagle. **1969** Gallery *Cap'n Fatso* 47: Some of their legal beagles say they gotta discharge him and some claim he still owes them two years. **1970** Gattzden *Black Vendetta* 46: Legal beagles Howley and Eurilicar. **1972** *N.Y. Post* (Nov. 17) 86: The CBS legal beagles apparently insisted on the damn legal beagle. **1988** Poyer *The Med* 351: It sounded like some goddamn legal beagle had written it.

legal eagle *n.* an attorney, esp. one who is notably skillful or zealous. Usu. *joc.*

1939 Brecher *At the Circus* (film): J. Cheever Loophole, Legal Eagle…with the legal eagle on your case, the money is practically in your pocket. **1943** W. Simmons *Joe Foss* 21: He had studied at the Harvard Law School…, he was known as the "Legal Eagle." **1981** *Daily News* (N.Y.) (July 6) 35: We know that legal eagles and other nitpickers will protest that cops can't really operate on a bounty system. **1986** Cash & Epps *Legal Eagles* [film title]. ***1986** Bowles *G'Day* 25: A legal eagle is someone you go to if you cop a bluey.

leg-bags *n.pl.* stockings; (also) trousers.

1791 [W. Smith] *Confess. T. Mount* 18: Stockings, leg-bags. **1807** Tufts *Autobiog.* 291: *Leg-bags*…Stockings. **a***1890–96** *F & H* IV 176: *Leg-Bags*…(common).—1. Stockings; and (2) trousers.

leg bail *n.* an escape; desertion; act of fleeing; FRENCH LEAVE.—usu. in phr. **to take** [or **give**] **leg bail** to run away, esp. from a debt or a responsibility.

***1759** in Fowke et al. *Canada's Story* 46: Pay your debts at the tavern by giving leg-bail. ***1774** in *F & H* IV 177: They took leg-bail and ran awa'. **1774** in Whiting *Early Amer. Proverbs* 258: Pay your debts at the tavern by giving leg-bail. ***1775** in *F & H*: I had concluded to…give them leg-bail…by…making for a deep swamp. ***1796** Grose

Vulgar Tongue (ed. 3): *To give leg-bail and land security; to run away.* ***ca1819** in J. Farmer *Musa Pedestris* 83: I tip him leg-bail. ***1821** *Real Life in London* I 89: *Giving leg-bail*—making the best use of legs to escape detection. **1828** Bird *Looking Glass* 88: Come, leg-bail's the word, and damn all penitentiaries. **1835** in Paulding *Bulls & Jons.* 107: He gave leg-bail, and ran away like a brave fellow. **1843** Leech *30 Yrs. from Home* 102 [ref. to 1812]: A multitude of the crew were ready to give "leg-bail," as they termed it. **1854** Sleeper *Salt Water Bubbles* 79: The whale...took leg-bail and started off with a rush. **1856** in Dwyer & Lingenfelter *Songs of Gold Rush* 76: The poor honest miner may take his leg-bail,/What else can he do when the good diggings fail. **1861** in C. Brewster *Cruel War* 61: We...told him he was a fool not to take 'leg bail.' **1863** in D.M. Holt *Surgeon's Civil War* 69: Last night, nineteen enlisted men and noncommissioned officers took leg bail and have not been heard from since. **1864** in H. Johnson *Talking Wire* 89: One of the prisoners...took leg-bail last night about six o'clock. **1865** in Glatthaar *March to Sea* 161: Skedaddle [or take] leg bail. **1872** Burnham *Secret Service* vi: *Take Leg-Bail*, to escape, or run away from court or prison. **1881** C.M. Chase *Editor's Run* 209: One minister...has been shot...while others have been compelled to take leg bail for parts unknown. **1888** Bidwell *Forging His Chains* 90: Thought you were too old a head to accept leg bail. ***1889–90** Barrère & Leland *Dict. Slang* II 12: *Leg-bail, to give* (common), to run away, or decamp from liability. **1903** *Independent* (Dec. 31) 3104: We ran out into God's night and took leg-bail, followed by a volley of curses and saloon furnishings. **1922** *DN* V 189: Negro Lingo...*Leg bail to give*...to run away. ***1929** Bowen *Sea Slang* 82: *Leg Bail, To give.* To desert. *a***1931** in Kephart et al. *Smoky Mtn. Voices* 103: He give 'em leg-bail an' lit out fer home.

leg-breaker *n. Und. & Journ.* a hired strong-arm thug; ENFORCER.
   1975 *Atlantic* (May) 43: Wunt he a leg-breaker for the Teamsters? **1987** *Miami Vice* (NBC-TV): Keep an eye out for the couple of leg-breakers that just visited Izzy. **1987** *Beauty & Beast* (CBS-TV): I just found out Mundy's leg-breakers are back on the street. **1991** McCarthy & Mallowe *Vice Cop* 156: He moonlighted as a legbreaker for McKinney.

leg business *n.* **1.** *Theat.* (see 1869 quot.).
   1867 *Galaxy* (Aug.) 440: The "leg business," as known to managers, players, and dramatists, is the same thing that is known to the outer world as the "naked drama." **1869** Logan *Foot Lights* 583: I will explain that the "leg business" is a term in common use among theatrical people, and means the displaying in public, by women, of their persons, clad in close-fitting flesh-colored silk "tights," and as little else as the law will permit.
   2. copulation.—usu. considered vulgar. Cf. LEG, 3.
   ***a1890–96** *F & H* IV 178: *Leg-business*...Copulation. **1938** "Justinian" *Americana Sexualis* 28: *Leg-Business.* n. Sexual intercourse. Low coll., C. 19–20, obsolescent in U.S.

legger *n.* BOOTLEGGER, 1.
   [***1788** Grose *Vulgar Tongue* (ed. 2): *Sham leggers;* cheats who pretend to sell smuggled goods.] **1926** in *OED2*: I sashayed for a legger. **1927** *Variety* (Jan. 5) 34: The 'legger's phone number is 234,789. **1929** *AS* IV (June) 342: *Legger.* A boot-legger. **1935** Algren *Boots* 131: They brang a Mex 'legger in here one afternoon way last fall. **1938** Chandler *Big Sleep* 27: Oh, you mean the ex-legger the eldest girl picked up and went and married. **1946** Faulkner et al. *Big Sleep* (film): You mean that Irish ex-legger? **1951** Pryor *The Big Play* 252: The 'leggers back home kept their stuff buried in their orchards. **1969** L. Sanders *Anderson Tapes* 147: I was driving for a legger.

leggins *n. Pris. & Homosex.* copulation in which the penis is rubbed between the legs of the receptive partner.—usu. considered vulgar.
   1931–34 in Clemmer *Pris. Comm.* 333: *Leggins*...a simulation of coitus between two males. **1971** in *Urban Life* V (1977) 420: "Leggins" (interfemoral intercourse). *a***1972** Rodgers *Queens' Vernacular* 156: *Leggins* consists of reaching ejaculation by...getting someone right between the thighs.

leg hitter *n. Baseball.* a batter who frequently beats out infield hits. Hence **leg hit,** *n.*
   1937 (cited in P. Dickson *Baseball Dict.* 244). **1942** *ATS* 646: *Leg hitter*, a fast runner who beats out infield hits. **1953** in P. Dickson *Baseball Dict.* 244: It brought no joy to leg hitters. **1964** Thompson & Rice *Every Diamond* 141: *Leg-Hitter:* Batter with no power who beats out

infield hits. **1977** *Webster's Sports Dict.: Leg hit*...A ground ball that is beat out for a single. **1989** P. Dickson *Baseball Dict.* 244: He accomplished this with a number of leg hits.

legit *n.* **1.** *Theat.* **a.** an actor in legitimate theater; a dramatic actor (as contrasted with a vaudevillian).
   1897 *Nat. Police Gaz.* (May 26) 6, in *OED2*: Bob is envious of Corbett's success as a "legit." **1899** Ade *Fables* 40: When a Legit loses his Voice he goes into Vodeville. **1903** Ade *Society* 201: The Stage-Manager employed by the bold Amateurs was an Ex-Legit who had lost his Voice asking for Salary. **1906** *Variety* (Mar. 24) 8: We just had in one of those actor boys, the "legits." **1906** H. Green *Boarding House* 53: Although a "legit," she had the desire of all females to rustle pleasantly through life. **1923** *N.Y. Times* (Sept. 9) VIII 2: *Legit:* An old-time actor who played with Booth and Barrett. *ca***1945** in Marx *Groucho Letters* 187: A legit who played with Booth and Barrett.
   b. legitimate theater.
   1897 *Nat. Police Gaz.* (May 26) 6, in *OED2*: Bob now wants to go into the "legit." **1906** H. Green *Actors' Boarding House* 50: I'm in vodeville...an' no two false alarms from the legit kin stick up their noses at me. **1926** *Variety* (Mar. 24) 23: Only Two Legits Now in Balto. **1929** McEvoy *Hollywood Girl* 15: I was off the legit for a while. **1936** in E. O'Neill *Letters* 454: The so-called Legit. rewarded your work so miserably and thanklessly.
   2.a. a person engaged in a legitimate business.
   1928 Sharpe *Chicago May* 94: He was a legit, but he did like to show off that he was such a rounder.
   b. *Und.* legitimate business.—constr. with *the*.
   1933 in D. Runyon *More Guys* 11: I got smart. I went in for the legit.
   ¶ In phrase:
   ¶ **on the legit** legitimately; legally. Also as adj.
   1930 Pasley *Capone* 312: They talk about me not being on the legitimate. Nobody's on the legit. **1930** Julia *Liberty* 26: Now the car is on the legit. **1936** Duncan *Over the Wall* 165: We're going to try to spring him on the legit. **1943** Darling *Dancing Masters* (film): From now on we're strictly on the legit. **1946** Mezzrow & Wolfe *Really Blues* 28: Once Sid got a shipment of a hundred cases of booze on the legit. **1965** Karp *Doobie Doo* 29: Why, lady, nobody's on the legit when it comes down to cases.

legit *adj.* [clipping of *legitimate*] legitimate (in any sense); authentic; genuine; (*hence*) lawful; legal; law-abiding; honest. Also as adv.
   1909** J.R. Ware *Passing Eng.* 167: *Legit.* (Theatrical). Shortening of legitimate, in its turn the curtailing of the legitimate drama. **1924** (quot. at HOLLER). **1928** M. Sharpe *Chicago May* 47: There were others, perfectly legit. **1940** Lawes *Meet the Murderer!* 98: Legit guys get legit ways of doing business. **1942** Liebling *Telephone Booth* 6: He is a legit guy, a businessman. **1950** Maddow & Huston *Asphalt Jungle* 14: You better be legit, pal. **1959** E. Hunter *Killer's Wedge* 51: "The guy whose throat you slit is Kassim."..."Is this legit?" **1963** W.C. Anderson *Penelope* 24: This is entirely legit. **1963** T.I. Rubin *Sweet Daddy* 43: You think legit broads got it so rosy? **1970** in I. Reed *Conjure* 75: Gangster Goes Legit. **1976** (quot. at WARM). **1963–78** J. Carroll *Basketball Diaries* 14: Old coachie thought I was in there legit. *a1979** A. Rose *Eubie Blake* 40: Our people got *some* parts in legit plays. **1983** *Good Morning America* (ABC-TV) (June 24): Are you thinking, as they say, of "going legit"—legitimate theater? **1990** in Stavsky, Mozeson & Mozeson *A 2 Z* 63: They think if they use the word "homeboy" or "G.", they can be legit or down. **1993** E. Richards *Cocaine True* 114: If I'm gonna be a criminal, then be a criminal in a legit way—sell some drugs. **1995** Gingrich & Forstchen *1945* 173: If the letter's legit, they know. **1996** *Variety* (Aug. 26) 36: DAVID WARREN [¶] LEGIT DIRECTOR....rapidly turning into one of Off Broadway's hottest young directors. He has helmed legit works for nearly every major house.

legman *n.* **1.** a person who uses his legs. *Specif.:*
   a. *Journ.* a reporter or researcher who gathers news firsthand.
   1923 *Nation* (Oct. 24) 454, in *DA:* Newsboys and "legmen" and a foreign news service keep the streets of Mecca aware of all that goes on. **1949** *Harper's* (May) 55: At the New York Public Library,...*Time's* legman could have found the...map. **1951** *Time* (Aug. 6) 5: At the rewrite desk he took calls from 48 legmen who blanketed the city. **1958** *Sat. Eve. Post* (Feb. 1) 40: I'm a leg man, Frank. I don't write. **1958** *New Yorker* (Oct. 18) 192: The *Times*, which had bought exclusive rights from the expedition...couldn't...keep enterprising leg men off the

mountainside. **1981** *Times-Picayune* (N.O.) (Apr. 6) V 1: A leg man is not someone who watches calves and thighs—he's the guy the editor sends out to get quick, accurate information or a breaking story—when the heat is on. **1997** *N.Y. Times* (Apr. 30) B9: He dedicated a book of his newspaper columns…to his "legmen," or research assistants.

b. a person employed as an assistant.

1949 *Sat. Eve. Post* (May 14) 43: The Japanese worked through a network…of dummy chiefs…who carried out the orders of the Japanese executives. Parallel to these legmen there was an in-between class. **1950** *N.Y. Times* (July 30) VII 11: His leg-man Joe Spinder, who takes part in various beatings and shootings. **1951** *Sat. Eve. Post* (Sept. 15) 201: For the next two years [he] performed duties which he describes as "leg man" for the Under Secretary of State. **1957** *Time* (Mar. 18) 23: Pearson's legman took Pearson's copy of the Nickerson memorandum to the Pentagon. **1963** *Time* (Mar. 15) 33: Daley honed his inborn political instincts [and] became a valued legman for Kelly and Arvey. **1975** V. Miller *Trade-Off* 8: Ralph is Laurie's leg man. *Ibid.* 12: A leg man will pick up the sample in Brooklyn and run it over here.

c. a runner.

1950 *Daily News* (N.Y.) (Oct. 1): Abrams…streaked around third.…Abrams is a better than average legman.

d. *Logging.* (see quot.).

1958 McCulloch *Woods Wds.* 105: *Leg man*—A field man for a timber outfit.

e. *Army.* a ground soldier; infantryman. Cf. LEG, 6.a.

1972 O'Brien *If I Die in a Combat Zone* 49: You're leg men now, and we don't need no infantry in Piccadilly or Southampton.

2. a man who is particularly aroused by a woman's legs. Cf. ASS MAN, TIT MAN.

1958 Elgart *Over Sexteen (No. 6)* 42: A group of men were exchanging their opinions about the opposite sex. They agreed there were "chest-men," "leg-men," etc. **1969** *Playboy* (Dec.) 108: I'm a leg man more than a chest man. **1971** *Essence* (July) 46: Or, maybe your guy is a "leg-man" who eyes a lot of other gal's thighs. **1974** Hejinian *Extreme Remedies* 127: I'm a leg man myself. **1983** Flaherty *Tin Wife* 46: Her father was a self-pronounced leg man. **1994** *Seinfeld* (NBC-TV): I thought you were a leg man.

lego *n.* [LEG, 6.a. + *-o*, infl. by *Lego*, trademark for interlocking toy building blocks] *Army.* (see quots.). [The 1971 quot. may be misdefined; no other evidence of this collective use is known.]

1971 Glasser *365 Days* 243: *Lego* Infantry unit. *a*1989 P. Dickson *Slang!* 241: *Legos/Legs.* Unit that is neither airborne nor mechanized; ground soldiers to airborne rangers.

leg pull *n.* a prank or hoax.

1895 J.L. Williams *Princeton* 160: Leg pull. All over. **1947** J. Thurber, in *New Yorker* (Dec. 6) 19: The wisecrack and the gag, the leg pull and the hotfoot. **1950** T.S. Eliot *Cocktail Party* III 148: You always did enjoy a leg pull.

leg-puller *n.* **1.** *Stu.* a student who behaves sycophantically toward professors; BROWN-NOSE. Hence, **leg-pulling,** *n.*

1877–78 *Cornellian* 86: *Leg Pulling.* Flattery. **1898** *Amherst College Portfolio* 48: For the biggest leg-puller, Bliss receives 34 votes. **1902** Fulbright *Baylor Round-Up* 127: Priv. Sec'y, Author and Gen. Leg-Puller. **1912** *Amherst College Four-Leaf Clover* (Feb.) 4: A Leg-Puller, a student who is afraid of the professors; synonym, a Boot-Licker.

2. *Und.* a blackmailer or extortionist. Hence, **leg-pulling,** *n.*

1927 *AS* II (Mar.) 281: *Leg pulling*—Blackmail. **1942–49** *DAUL* 124: *Leg-puller.* An extortionist. *Leg-pulling.* Extortion; blackmail.

leg show *n. Theat.* a show featuring chorus girls who expose their legs.

*1882 in *OED2:* Burlesque with its blonde attributes kept the country in a rage…and the minor musical attractions of the *quasi* legitimate stage have usurped its principal feature—the leg show. **1895** in *DA:* The entertainment was a sort of Zozo leg show. **1900** *Amer. Jour. Sociol.* VI 447, in *OED2:* Next follows a cinematograph reproduction of…a "leg show" of the most shameless character. **1919** *Variety* (Mar. 28) 33: It was the first time a "leg show" had been seen in Chicago. **1936** Fellows & Freeman *Big Show* 40: Burlesque, or leg shows, possessed a tremendous fascination for the…male population. **1947** Schulberg *Harder They Fall* 26: Like a young matron who would look more at home in Junior League musical than in a Broadway leg-show.

leg-spreaders *n.pl. Mil. Av.* (see quot.).

1967 *Northwest Folk.* II [ref. to 1950's]: It probably took as much courage for the flyer to turn in his wings (sometimes called "leg-spreaders" [for their presumed effect on women]) as it would have taken him to continue flying.

leg worker *n. Prost.* a streetwalker.

1930 Mae West *Babe Gordon* 29: It took energy to be a leg worker and they were wasted skeletons.

lemon *n.* **1.a.** a sour-tempered or disagreeable person. [Now subsumed into **(b),** below.]

1862 [P. Davis] *Young Parson* 222: Mrs. Trimble…had a great deal to say, and no little acrimony in her way of saying it. Indeed, she was what the knowing ones denominated "a lemon." [**1896** Ade *Artie* 92: The first one I ever see in bloomers was a lemon-faced fairy that ought o' been picked along about centennial year.] **1934** Weseen *Dict. Amer. Sl.* 362: *Lemon*—A disgreeable person. **1942** *ATS* 373: Gloomy or irritable person; pessimist…*grouch,…lemon*.

b. a person who is disappointing, foolish, untrustworthy, inept, or the like.

1906 Hobart *Skiddoo* 11: I'm a lemon if I didn't draw an upper berth in the sleeping car thing! **1906** *Nat. Police Gaz.* (June 23) 3: The Manicure Girl and the Lemon. **1908** McGaffey *Show Girl* 58: A crate of lemons got off to crab the act. **1910** T.A. Dorgan, in *N.Y. Eve. Jour.* (Feb. 23) 15: We cannot say that Wolgast is a lemon. The boy may have just hit his stride. Nelson was no bear himself when he started. **1911** Van Loan *Big League* 80: I always *did* say Kennedy was the greatest lemon picker in the country. **1912** Mathewson *Pitching* 35: "$11,000, or $22,500, for a lemon." That is the dread of all ball players. *Ibid.* 220: The papers were mentioning him as the "$11,000 lemon." **1915** [Swartwood] *Choice Slang* 53: *Lemon*…A pill. **1916** S. Lewis *Job* 260: She had…"been stuck with a lemon of a husband." **1930** J.T. Farrell *Calico Shoes* 190: He'd crush a lemon like Kid Tucker dry. **1932** Lorimer & Lorimer *Streetcars* 150: Act, lemon, act! **1935** Pollock *Und. Speaks* 70: *Lemon,* one who turns state's evidence. **1937** Weidman *Can Get It Wholesale* 135: That big lemon of yours, that Babushkin. **1940** M. Goodrich *Delilah* 20: You know…that new lemon from the Galveston they dumped on us last month at Cavite? **1944** Kapelner *Lonely Boy Blues* 35: Haven't I got enough troubles of my own without that big lemon starting one more batch? **1945** Mencken *Amer. Lang. Supp. I* 447: *Lemon,* in the sense of something unattractive, *e.g.,* a homely woman, is not listed by the DAE. **1958** Drury *Advise & Consent* 145: She was an absolute lemon. **1960** I. Freeman *Out of Burning* 102: Such jive talk was for lemons in the Y.M.C.A. **1962** Quirk *Red Ribbons* 15: It took Paul sixty seconds to conclude that he had a lemon on his hands. **1963** Braly *Shake Him* 164: She's built and her face is good, but she's a lemon. **1964** Barthelme *Dr. Caligari* 35: Father Beau was wrong, we get some lemons just like any other group. ***1990** Anderson & Trudgill *Bad Language* 88: Words For "Stupid Person"…*idiot,…lamebrain,…dunce,…lemon.*

c. *Und.* a swindler's victim; MARK; SUCKER.

1908 Sullivan *Criminal Slang* 21: *Sucker* or *lemon*—A victim of criminals and tramps. **1908** *Sat. Eve. Post* (Dec. 5) 18: They wear the lemon sign on their faces. **1981** in *West. Folklore* XLIV (1985) 10: A "lemon" or a "grapefruit" is someone who is being hustled for money (that is, being "squeezed").

2.a. a disappointment; (*hence*) anything considered as worthless, unworkable, fraudulent, defective, etc.; (*esp.*) a defective automobile; an unprofitable prospect.—in early use, usu. in phr. **hand (someone) a lemon** to cheat (someone). —occ. used attrib. Now *S.E.*

1906 *Nat. Police Gaz.* (June 2) 10: [Boxer] Marvin Hart is still…trying to square himself for the "lemon" he handed to the Madison Square Garden promoters when he met Mike Schreck. **1906** H. Green *Actors' Boarding House* 36: Him gettin' handed a lemon in that English act. **1906** T.A. Dorgan, in Zwilling *TAD Lexicon* 54: Lemon idea. **1907** in Fleming *Unforgettable Season* 9: Did Joe Kelley hand McGraw a lemon? **1909** *Sat. Eve. Post* (Feb. 20) 38: There is your prize—or your lemon. **1911** *Hampton's Mag.* (Oct.) 435: Well, you've picked a lemon.…There's nothin' doin', kiddo, nothin' doin'. **1915** [Swartwood] *Choice Slang* 53: *Lemon*…A disappointment. **1919** Darling *Jargon Book* 42: *Handing him a lemon*—Giving him the worst of a deal. **1924** G. Henderson *Keys to Crookdom* 190: There is a class of car dealer who sells "lemons." *Ibid.* 410: *Lemon.* Something worthless.

1934 Weseen *Dict. Amer. Sl.* 362: *Lemon*...a purchased article that turns out to be worthless or nearly so. **1936** *AS* (Apr.) 192: "When I bought that second-hand car I bought a lemon." "My new washing machine is a lemon." **1938** Steinbeck *Grapes of Wrath* 67: We got to move that lemon for thirty-five dollars. **1947** in *DA*: Lemon Sale...Not fruit but buyers [*sic*] mistakes. Join the throng and enjoy the fun for it's real fun buying these lemons. **1963** Pres. J.F. Kennedy (address): I don't think it's fair to say I handed Sarge a lemon [*i.e.*, the Peace Corps] from which he made lemonade. **1977–81** S. King *Cujo* 7: If life hands you lemons, make lemonade! **1991** Stone & Sklar *JFK* (film): And they sold this lemon [a false or ridiculous theory] to the American people. **1988–93** Wilcock & Guy *Damn Right* 60: Butter didn't bring me to hear no lemons [inferior songs].

b. *Narc.* LEMONADE, 2.

1952 Ellson *Golden Spike* 199: They resorted to selling "lemons," the drug so heavily mixed with milk sugar that it carried no kick. **1975** *DAS* (Supp.): *Lemon*...A weakened or diluted narcotic drug, or a non-narcotic powder substance sold as a narcotic drug.

3. *Gamb.* any of several gaming swindles, esp. one based on pool (see 1930, *a*1989 quots.).—constr. with *the.*—also used attrib. Also as v.

1908 Sullivan *Criminal Slang* 15: Lemon game.—Defrauding a sucker at a pool game. **1911** *Hampton's Mag.* (Oct.) 432: Unsavory cellars where lemon-steerers and slough-beaters foregathered. **1914** Jackson & Hellyer *Crim. Slang* 55: *Lemon*, Noun...A confidence game in which skill at pool is the bait. A *lemon joint* is a crooked pool and billiard room. **1930** Conwell *Pro. Thief* 68: The lemon is an agreement between the inside man, an expert pool player, and a prospect, by which the prospect will win bets on the pool games played by the expert. Through a supposed fluke the expert wins the game which the prospect had bet he would lose, and the prospect thereby loses his money. The foot race was similar to the lemon except that it involved foot-racing rather than pool. Both the lemon and the foot race are now ancient history. **1964** Smith & Hoefer *Music* 33: It was somewhere around 1913 that I first met Charles...Roberts who wandered into the Coast, passing himself off as a lemon pool player.*...*An expert pool player who pretends he is a novice at the game. **1967** Colebrook *Cross of Lassitude* 101: [Those criminals] who carry out the "lemon," the "tap," the "wire." **1969** R. Beck *Mama Black Widow* 158: It's possible in spots to pick up nice money playing the lemon, but it's a hard hustle. *a*1979 A. Rose *Eubie Blake* 149: I used to try to stop him from gettin' in those lemon pool games. *a*1989 Courtwright et al. *Addicts* 380: *Lemon hustler:* A con man who specializes in the *lemon game*, in which victims are enticed to meet beautiful women and, while waiting for them, are inveigled into a card, dice, or pool swindle. **1996** McCumber *Playing off Rail* 83: It's one thing to lemon around when you're playing a pretty good player who's trying to rob you. *Ibid.* 174: It was hard, playing on the lemon all night, purposely missing balls, trying to disguise your stroke.

4. *Black E.* the genitals; often in phr. **squeeze (one's) lemons** to copulate.—usu. considered vulgar.

1935 in Oliver *Blues Tradition* 233: Now you done squeeze my lemon, now you done broke and run./Now youse a dirty mother fuyer. **1935** in Leadbitter & Slaven *Blues Records* 151: Let Me Roll Your Lemon. **1937** R. Johnson "Traveling Riverside Blues," in *Complete Recordings*: You can squeeze my lemon till the juice run down my...till the juice run down my leg, baby, you know what I'm talkin' 'bout. *a*1963 in Charter *Poetry of Blues* 140: Well, you squeezed my lemon, baby, and you started my juice to run. *Ibid.*: But as it was sung by the Brownsville, Tennessee, singer Charlie Pickett, it was feminine. "Now let me squeeze your lemon, baby,/Until my love comes down." **1963** Charters *Poetry of Blues* 140: The "lemon" is also used in the same sense as the black snake and the sweet potato, but it is sometimes interpreted as either masculine or feminine.

5. *pl.* the breasts.—usu. considered vulgar.

1949 Mende *Spit & Stars* 114: But look at that pair of lemons bouncing in her sweater. **1962** Sagarin *Dirty Words* 79: From the language of fruit, one obtains *lemons* [for breasts]. ***1990** T. Thorne *Dict. Contemp. Sl.*: *Lemons*...The breasts.

¶ **In phrases:**

¶ **cut lemons** to *cut ice*, s.v. CUT, *v.*

1900 Ade *More Fables* 158: A Man...does not cut very many Lemons around his own House, where they are Onto him.

¶ **go** [or **pitch**] **in[,] lemons** (used as a cry of encouragement).

1848 Baker *Glance at N.Y.* 18: *Mose.* Go in, lemons! [*Mose upsets bench, and pitches into Jake.—General row, stove upset, etc.*]. **1854** St. Clair *Metropolis* 75: Go it while your [*sic*] young....Go in, lemons! **1856** (quot. at TWISTER). **1862** in G. Whitman *Letters* 77: Dont be afraid to use the money for there is plenty more where that came from, so go in lemons. **1862** in R.G. Carter *4 Bros.* 141: Down came the children...and they pitched in "lemons." **1866** [H.W. Shaw] *J. Billings* 23: Band plays "Go in Lemons!" **1885** Byrn *Greenhorn* 6: Go In Lemons. **1888** *Stag Party* (unp.): Now Lemons, go in.

¶ **squeeze the** [or **(one's)**] **lemon 1.** to urinate.

a*1890–96 F & H IV 179: *To squeeze the lemon*...(common). To urinate. **1952 Larson *Barnyard Folklore* 84: Urinate...*spring a leak, drain your tank, squeeze your lemon, shake your sprinkler, water your stud-horse, pick daisies (or flowers)*.

2. see **(4)**, above.

lemonade *n.* **1.** [prob. pun on *eliminate*] *Mil. Av.* elimination from flight training.—constr. with *get* [or *give*] *the*.

1941 Kendall *Army & Navy Sl.* 6: He is *getting the lemonade*....getting eliminated or dismissed. **1941** in Wiener *Flyers* 45: *Getting the lemonade.* Another term for washout. **1944** Wiener *Flyers* 64: Several flight instructors had concluded that the only thing they could do for the cadet was to "give him the lemonade."

2. *Narc.* crystalline heroin that has been cut excessively. Cf. slightly earlier LEMON, 2.b.

1957 H. Simmons *Corner Boy* 45: Son-of-a-bitch sold me some lemonade....Four cents for the plunge, and it's lemonade. **1966** Brunner *Face of Night* 233: Lemonade—weak drugs. **1970** *Sat. Rev.* (Nov.) 21: *Lemonade* poor heroin.

3. urine.

*a*1977 in S. King *Bachman Bks.* 14: I needed to whiz piss make lemonade whatever you wanted to call it.

lemonade *v.* [pun] to promenade. *Joc.*

1859 in C.A. Abbey *Before the Mast* 189: Capt Gardner has on two coats today, lemonading the quarter deck.

lemonader *n. Naut.* LIME-JUICER.

1896 Hamblen *Many Seas* 97 [ref. to 1870's]: On signing these shipping articles, I became what is regarded by American sailors as about the most despicable being afloat, that is, a "British tar," or, as Yankees say, a "lime-juicer," or "lemonader," or "lemon-pelter," or just simply a "pelter."

lemon-peeler *n. Naut.* LIME-JUICER. Also **lemon-squeezer.**

1903 Sonnichsen *Deep Sea Vagabonds* 38: British ships are known the world over as Limejuicers, and this name is even applied to British seamen by Americans when speaking of them with contempt, being then sometimes converted into "lemonsqueezers" or "Lemonpeelers."

lemon-pelter *n. Naut.* LIME-JUICER. Hence **lemon-pelting,** *adj.*

1896 Hamblen *Many Seas* 69: "You lemon-pelting son of a sea cook," said Jake, as he grabbed the Englishman by the throat. *Ibid.* 96: None of your lubberly canvas-pants lemon-pelters...but good smart New York Yankee boys. *Ibid.* 97: (quot. at LEMONADER). *Ibid.* 172: You great, big, dirty, lemon-pelting sucker. **1900** T.A. Dorgan, in Zwilling *TAD Lexicon* 54: (At Tim Murphy's Training Quarters) Many "lemon pelters" come out to see Timmie. **1968** in *DARE*.

lemon-sucker *n.* [prob. a ref. to pursed lips] a prissy or effeminate man or boy; (*also*) a sour-faced individual.

1922 S. Lewis *Babbitt* 99: Oh, there's a swell bunch of Lizzie boys and lemon-suckers and pie-faces and infidels and beer-bloated scribblers that love to fire off their filthy mouths and yip that Mike Monday is vulgar and full of mush. **1942** *ATS* 373: An effeminate man...*lemon-sucker.* **1961** *Twilight Zone* (CBS-TV): This lemon-sucker here is the worst of the bunch.

lens *v.* to film (a motion picture).

1982 in *Nat. Lampoon* (Feb. 1983) 16: The big-budget *John Glenn Story,* set for lensing early next fall. **1988** *ALF* (NBC-TV): Let me lens this flick, OK?

lens lizard *n.* LENS LOUSE; (*also*) a photographer or film maker.

1921 T.A. Dorgan, in Zwilling *TAD Lexicon* 114: Quite a flock of lens lizards are in town making films while the sun shines. **1977** *Oui* (Apr.) 128: Photographed by *Oui* lens lizards.

lens louse *n.* Esp. *Film & Journ.* an egotistical person who is eager to be filmed or photographed, esp. by photojournalists.

   1928 *AS* III (June) 367: Actors who strive for the most advantageous positions [before the camera] are also called "lens lice." **1929** McEvoy *Hollywood Girl* 57: Tomorrow I will start making faces at the camera. I will be what they call out here a lens louse. **1935** Lorimer & Lorimer *Heart Specialist* 36: A lens louse that spent all her time mugging for the camera. **1942** *Yank* (July 29) 17: I never saw a lens louse like a sailor. All they want to do is have their picture taken. **1950** Riesenberg *Reporter* 16: Don't…get friendly with every lens-louse that made the trip. **1976** Atlee *Domino* 122: General Douglas MacArthur…a lens louse and oversized ego.

les var. LEZ.

lesbo *n. & adj.* [a] lesbian.

   1927 in Hemingway *Sel. Letters* 268: Hearst's have offered him 182,000 bits for a serial about Lesbians who were wounded in the war.…Bumby is calling the thing lesbos Lesbos LESBOS. **1940** O'Hara *Pal Joey* 175: The Lesbos even come and watch the dress rehearsals. **1942** in T. Williams *Letters* 29: These two women are not sisters but out and out "Lesbos." **1949** "J. Evans" *Halo in Brass* 89: Turns out this Conrad babe was a Lesbo. Queer as a set of purple teeth. **1957** J. Jones *Some Came Running* 34: You mean she's a lesbo? **1965** Yurick *Warriors* 106: The Intervale Avenue Lesbos said they…had more manhood than any little-boy. **1970** *Nat. Lampoon* (Apr.) 81: After a few sessions with the same masseur, clients turn lesbo. **1980** in *Penthouse* (Jan. 1981) 166: She decided to be a lesbo. *a***1982** G. Naylor *Women of Brewster Place* 162: You need a good spankin' for taking up with a lesbo. *****1986** Bowles *G'Day* 10: *Lezzo* a lesbian…Also *lesbo*. **1987–89** M.H. Kingston *Tripmaster Monkey* 78: Lesbo…weirdo homo combos. **1992** N. Baker *Vox* 118: It didn't turn out to be a lesbo scene. *a***1994** A. Radakovich *Wild Girls Club* 50: We could turn lesbo.

let *v.* ¶ In phrase: **let one** [**go** or **fly** or **rip**] to break wind noisily.

   1970 Landy *Underground Dict.:* Let one…Emit gas through the anus. **1977** Bredes *Hard Feelings* 49: *Jesus*, Harlan. Harlan let fly. **1990** Munro *Slang U.:* Let one go to pass gas, fart.…let one rip.

letch or **lech** *n.* **1.** a strong or perverse craving or desire, esp. for sexual activity; (*also*) a variety of sexual activity; KINK.

   *****1796** Grose *Vulgar Tongue* (ed. 3): Letch. A whim of the amorous kind, out of the common way. *****1862** in *OED2:* The letch for blood which characterizes the savage. *****1910** in Partridge *Concise Sl. Dict.* 260: She has what is vulgarly known as a "lech" for *The Times* Peking correspondent. **1927–28** in R. Nelson *Dishonorable* 195: These politicians got such a lech' for jack! **1929** McEvoy *Hollywood Girl* 15: I had a big letch for the movies. *****1932** (cited in Partridge *DSUE* (ed. 7) 1249). **1940** S. Lewis, in *DAS:* Your letch for power. **1948** in T. Williams *Letters* 226: Sandy was very drunk and so cute I had a letch for him. **1957** M. Shulman *Rally* 99: He had…had an occasional letch for a woman other than his wife. **1967** Dibner *Admiral* 343: You bastard, I got a real letch for you.

   2. a lecher.

   1943 in *DAS:* If anybody noticed what I was doing, they'd think I was an old letch. **1957** Gutwillig *Long Silence* 38 [ref. to 1951]: The only way to get through Bennett's course is to be a girl. God, what a lech. **1958** H. Gardner *Piece of the Action* 137: You look like an absolute letch tonight. **1961** Kohner *Gidget Goes Hawaiian* 73: A tender young squab in the clutches of a middle-aged lech. **1962** J.P. Miller *Days of Wine & Roses* (film): That old letch likes to have you around to lean on when he gets drunk. **1969** *New Amer. Rev.* (No. 6) (Apr.) 34: You arrogant, elderly letch. **1980** Whalen *Takes a Man* 18: Sit down, you old lech. **1983** Eble *Campus Slang* (Nov.) 3: Lech—dirty old man. **1986** *Matlock* (NBC-TV): I realized what a drunken letch he was. **1993** *As World Turns* (CBS-TV): Roger is a letch.

letch or **lech** *v.* to lust; (*hence*) to behave in a lecherous manner toward.

   *****1911** J. Masefield, in *OED2:* And drunk and leched from day till morrow. **1940** in Pound *Letters* 334: Not that I am letching to. **1958** Kerouac *Subterraneans* 91: Frank's leching after Adam. **1968** Hudson *Case of Need* 25: I had a vision of her going to a smelly back room somewhere and meeting a leering little guy who would letch her and maybe even manage to kill her. **1969** *Current Slang* I & II 58: Lech, v. To lust after females or actively pursue the vice. **1979** C. Martin *Catullus* 33: That letching asshole!

letter *n.* ¶ In phrase: **letter in the post office** (used to indi-

cate that one has a hole in one's trousers or that one's fly is open). Also vars.

   1855 in *DARE.* **1894** *DN* I 341: *Letter in the post-office:* expression current among boys, denoting that the seat of the trousers is so out of repair that the shirt-tail is visible. **1907** *DN* III 192. **1912** *DN* III 568. **1954, 1960, 1965–70** in *DARE.*

lettuce *n.* **1.** paper money; money. Also **lettuce leaf.** Cf. CABBAGE, 4.

   1903 Harriman *Homebuilders* 37: All right, partner,…unroll that bunch of lettuce you got in your mit and count out thirty-five bucks. **1921** Wiley *Lady Luck* 24: "I mows de lettuce!" Honey Tone picked up his winnings. **1931** Dos Passos *Nineteen Nineteen* 49: He still had…quite a roll of lettuce. **1941** Hargrove *Pvt. Hargrove* 84: *Pocket lettuce*—paper money. **1942** Algren *Morning* 44: You mean what you'd do if you had the old lettuce, huh? **1946** H.A. Smith *Rhubarb* 14: Lettuce, Pop! I need lettuce! **1981** (quot. at BOFFO, *n.*, 1).

   2. *Mil.* campaign medals or ribbons. Cf. CABBAGE, 5.

   1956 Lockwood & Adamson *Zoomies, Subs & Zeroes* 56 [ref. to WWII]: With this trophy added to his "lettuce salad" Galvin returned to the *Bunker Hill.* **1990** Helms *Proud Bastards* 121 [ref. to Vietnam War]: More lettuce on his chest than a goddamn migrant farmworkers' convention. **1991** W. Chamberlain *View from Above* 142: Soldiers display campaign ribbons and medals…on their uniforms…"lettuce," as they call it.

levant *v.* [perh. < Sp *levantar* 'to lift'] Orig. *Gamb.* to make a wager with the intention of running away if it is lost; (*hence*) to decamp, esp. so as to escape one's creditors; SKIP.

   [*****1714** in *F & H* IV 184: He hath ventured to come the *levant* over gentlemen; that is, to play without any money at all in his pocket.] *****1781** G. Parker *View of Society* II 168: *Levanters.* These are of the order and number of *Blacklegs.* *****1797** in *OED:* She found that the sharps would dish me, and levanted without even bidding me farewell. *****1809** in *OED:* [He] must produce a certificate that he has never levanted at any race-course. *****1825** "Blackmantle" *Eng. Spy* I 330: Those who had *nothing to give,* but yet were too honourable to *levant.* **1842** *Spirit of Times* (Oct. 29) 410: To Bolt…to mizzle…to Levant. **1881** *N.Y. Clipper Almanac* 44: Levanted.—Applied to a word-of-mouth bettor who disappears as soon as he ascertains that he has lost. **1885** Ingraham *Buffalo Bill's Grip* 8: They had both levanted. *****1889** Barrère & Leland *Dict. Slang: Levant*…to run away from one's creditors, to abscond. *****1929** Bowen *Sea Slang* 82: *Levant, To.* To desert.

level *n.* truth.—constr. with *the.*

   1949 Taradash & Monks *Knock on Any Door* (film): That's the level, Nelly.

¶ In phrase:

¶ **on the level, 1.** (of persons) telling the truth; dealing fairly and honestly; sincere; honest; (*hence*) respectable; upright; law-abiding; (of activities, proposals, etc.) lawful; ethical. Now *colloq.* Also as *adv.*

   1872 Burnham *Secret Service* 413: I always like to meet a man on the level, and quit him on the square, Franc. **1896** S. Crane *George's Mother* 173: Yeh's can't have not'in on d' level wid youse damn' tanks! **1896** in S. Crane *Complete Stories* 315: I've lived at a pretty hot gait all my life, but I've always been on the level. Never did a crooked thing since I was born. **1896** in S. Crane *N.Y.C. Sketches* 169: She's on the level with him, though. **1898** Kountz *Baxter's Letters* 16: I wonder if this George is on the level. **1902** Cullen *More Tales* 102: I used to think you were on the level, but on-the-level people make good their markers. **1902** "J. Flynt" *Little Bro.* 100: They never convicted him on the level. **1905** in Paxton *Sport USA* 22: He will draw advance money although he does not need it, just to see if a [baseball] club is "on the level." **1908** in H.C. Fisher *A. Mutt* 25: I'm going to pass it up to show that I am on the level. **1910** Hapgood *City Streets* 49: The thief, if he is a good thief, is "on the level" with his pals. *Ibid.* 316: It's so bad that I am getting to adore a guy that's got a job, even if it's on the level. **1904–11** Phillips *Susan Lenox* II 122: Good livings can't be made on the ways that used to be called on the level—they're called damfool ways now. **1912–14** in E. O'Neill *Lost Plays* 44: Why don't yuh cut this [criminal] life and be on the level? **1915** in W.C. Fields *By Himself* (May 10) 58: You would have had a house long ago had you been on the level. **1923** Ornitz *Haunch, Paunch & Jowl* 96: Are you on the level, or are you just stringing me? **1932** L. Berg *Prison Doctor* 213: But I'm on the level. I'm going straight. **1937** Kalmar et al. *Life of*

Party (film): I'm through trying to make you see I'm on the level. **1953** Morheim & Treiberger *Beast from 20,000 Fathoms* (film): Are you on the level? You certainly sound serious. **1970** in P. Heller *In This Corner* 43: Now, that fight with Jess Willard, that was on the level. **1993** *Simpsons* (Fox-TV): "Were you sent here by the Devil?" "No, my friend, I'm on the level!"

2. (of statements) true. Also as adv.

   1892 Norr *China Town* 63: Say, Mame, this is on the dead level. I'm givin' it ter yer straight. **1894** *Harper's* (Dec.) 106: An' that's on the level. *Ibid.* On the level, doctor, what I want's a mother. **1896** Ade *Artie* 13: On the level, no kiddin', that's what he said. *Ibid.* 28: On the level, I'm surprised you ain't on to that. **1896** in S. Crane *Complete Stories* 319: Oh, that's on the level all right. **1899** Ade *Fables* 13: Take it in the Morning when she showed up on the Level. **1910** Hapgood *City Streets* 51: Don't jolly, but tell me on de level, where is he now? **1926** Dunning & Abbott *Broadway* 229: On the level. You used to be dancing—the Golden Bowl, didn't you? **1933** Block & Gibney *Massacre* (film): But, say, Joe. On the level—. **1940** O'Hara *Pal Joey* 97: Who knows I may be kidding on the level and that would be quite irony if it ever happened. **1948** L. Hayward *Blood on Moon* (film): On the level, Jim. What *are* you doing here? **1953** Paley *Rumble* 75: What Jimmy said was on the level. **1966** in T.C. Bambara *Gorilla* 40: "This on the level?" the big guy asked.

level *adj.* trustworthy; legitimate; honest; true; (*also*) frank, candid.

   1879 R. Wheeler *In Leadville* 3: This nig's all level. **1920–21** Witwer *Leather Pushers* 6: The second mêlée would be level, as Dummy figured the Bearcat was too much of a ham to be worth while savin' for any more. **1951** in *DAS* 317: There's never a place for guys like me....That's level. **1951** Twist *Ft. Worth* (film): Let's be level, Neal.

level *v.* to be frank and honest; behave honestly.

   1920–21 Witwer *Leather Pushers* 174: Are you levelin' with the kid in this one? **1932** D. Runyon, in *Collier's* (Dec. 10) 7: I am now convinced that the guy is leveling. **1934** L. Berg *Prison Nurse* 106: "Do you know what you're saying?"..."I'm leveling." **1938** in *DAS* 317: I want you to level with me and tell me if it is true. *a*1948 Mencken *Amer. Lang. Supp.* II 768: *Level*, v. To fight honestly in a framed bout. **1948** F. Brown, in *DAS*: You're going to level about that. **1957** R. Marcus *Chi. Confidential* (film): Why don't you level with yourself, Blaine? **1960** L'Amour *Sacketts* 94: We've got to level with him. **1976** Haseltine & Yaw *Woman Doctor* 65: To the only doctor who would level with me. **1977** Newman & Berkowitz *Take Charge* 57: Level with yourself. **1994** *Wild Oats* (Fox-TV): All right, I'm gonna level with you.

¶ In phrase:

¶ **level on** to aim a firearm, esp. a pistol, at (someone).

   1933 Boehm & Gelsey *Life of Jimmy Dolan* (film): Is he afraid somebody'll level on him? **1942** *ATS* 327: *Level on*...to aim a gun at.

lever-jerker *n. R.R.* (see quot.).

   1931 *Writer's Dig.* (May) 42: *Lever-Jerker*—Interlocker lever man.

Levinson *n.* [see quot.] *West.* a boxing glove.

   1925 T.A. Dorgan, in Zwilling *TAD Lexicon* 114: Sol Levinson, the boxing glove manufacturer, died in San Francisco last week. One could hardly look at a boxing glove without thinking of Sol Levinson. In fact, out West, they call the padded mitts Levinsons.

levy *n.* [fr. *eleven cents*, approx. equivalent] a Spanish real, formerly acceptable as currency in the U.S.; (*broadly*) a shilling; 12½ cents. Now *hist.*

   1829 in *AS* XVI 27. **1836** (quot. at FIP). **1865** *Harper's Mo.* XXX 605: *Levy*...was formerly used in Pennsylvania and Ohio for the old twelve-and-a-half-cent piece; the "long bit" of New Orleans. **1891** Maitland *Slang Dict.* 167: *Levy* (Am.), a shilling. **1928** in *DA*: The Secretary of the Treasury prescribed the rate at which the "Levy" and the "Bit"...should be received in exchange.

levy *v.* ¶ In phrase: **levy onto** to seize; take hold of.

   1858 in G.W. Harris *High Times* 152: I wer monsous hungry miself, so I levied ontu a chunk ove beef fried in cake taller.

lez *n. & adj.* [a] lesbian. Also **les.** Cf. LESBO.

   1929 M. Lief *Hangover* 235, in *OED2*: "Certainly," responded the Les. **1938** (quot. at LEZZIE). **1942** Davis & Wolsey *Madam* 19: Yammy Ashbell, the two hundred and sixty pound colored lezz. **1951** Kerouac *Cody* 90: It was a Les bar. **1952** Brossard *Darkness* 261: The les started up the stepladder of the platform. **1966** S. Harris *Hellhole* 214: Well, Miss

Madison wasn't a straight les, you know. She turned out to be one of those bisexual bitches. **1970** Southern *Blue Movie* 88: She's *lez*, Sid. **1977** Dunne *Confessions* 284: Are you going to say that on the air, she was lez?

lezzie *n.* a lesbian. Also attrib.

   1938 "Justinian" *Amer. Sexualis* 28: *Lezzie* (*Lez*). A Lesbian. Diminutive euphemism, C. 20. **1956** Holiday & Dufty *Lady Sings Blues* 87: But before long they got acting like lezzies because it's so easy. **1971** Rader *Govt. Inspected* 144: She beds other women...lezzies. **1986** *Daily Beacon* (Univ. Tenn.) (Nov. 20) 4: Shit, the bitch is probably a lezzie. **1993** *Jerry Springer Show* (synd. TV series): Faggots, dykes, lezzies. **1994** "G. Indiana" *Rent Boy* 20: Sandy's giving out a little lezzie action with his wife.

Lib *n. Mil. Av.* a Consolidated Vultee B-24 Liberator heavy bomber; (*Navy*) a PB4Y-2 Privateer patrol bomber. Now *hist.* [Quots. ref. to WWII.]

   *ca*1944 in Kaplan & Smith *One Last Look* 83: Lib. **1945** Dos Passos *Tour* 88: "I got an unidentified plane." "It's a Lib, it's a Lib." **1945** in Loosbrock & Skinner *Wild Blue* 254: There goes one Lib. *1945 (cited in Partridge *DSUE* (ed. 7) 1251). **1959** R.L. Scott *Flying Tiger* 220: The Libs of the 308th also did many things their designers had never intended them to do. **1961** Forbes *Goodbye to Some* 54: Not a Navy Lib in sight. **1970** Ziel *Steel Rails* 202: Another "Lib"...flew over the burning Kreinsen marshalling yards. **1946–92** Westheimer *Sitting It Out* 156: Three Macchi 200s...had attacked twelve Libs.

lib *n.* **1.** LIBBER. [As an abbr. of *liberation (movement)*, this term has always been colloq.]

   *1973 in *OED2*: Lillian Thomas is a member of the Suffrage Fellowship Movement...and is delighted with the Libs. **1981** Jenkins *Baja Okla.* 127: Libs ran in clusters, like motorcycle gangs.

2. *Pol.* a political liberal.

   1981 Ehrlichman *Witness* 102 [ref. to 1969]: President Nixon was under great political pressure to nominate a "lib." **1987** *Daily News* (N.Y.) (July 2) 5: Libs hone their hatchets.

3. *pl. Navy & USMC.* shore leave; liberty.

   1988 Poyer *The Med* 53: You goin' on libs, bro'?

libber *n.* a supporter of the women's liberation movement; feminist. [The form *women's libber* has always been colloq.]

   1972 *Village Voice* (N.Y.C.) (June 1) 26, in *OED2*: Now the star-maker has decided to calm the libbers with another token. **1972** Eble *Campus Slang* (Oct.) 4: *Libber*—one who believes in women's liberation. *a*1976 Roebuck & Frese *Rendezvous* 178: These screwy women libbers....If they lived in my world they wouldn't want to be libbers. **1978** S. King *Stand* 549: She got to be an even bigger libber than the roomie. **1978** Pici *Tennis Hustler* 83: And that's nothing to be ashamed of—even for a libber. **1981** Sann *Trial* 26: The libbers are very strong for pants suits. **1981** in Thom *Letters to Ms.* 175: What is your wife, one of those libbers? **1986** R. Walker *AF Wives* 434: Don't get one of those libber types. **1991** J. Lamar *Bourgeois Blues* 76: Let her be a libber!

libby *n.* LIBBER.

   1974 Millard *Thunderbolt* 87: You damn freak....I only wanted to make love to you like a gentleman. So what the hell are you, sister, a goddam libby?

libe *n. Esp. Stu.* library. Also as v., to study in a library.

   1915 *DN* IV 236: *Libe.* Library, n. and v. Meaning as verb "to study in the library." "I'm going to libe a little." **1921** *DN* V 111: *Libe*...library. **1954–60** *DAS*: *Lib[,] libe* n. A library. vt., v.i. To study in a library. *a*1961 Boroff *Campus U.S.A.* 138: Unflinching solitary labor in the Libe (Library). **1961** Sullivan *Shortest, Gladdest Years* 24: Leave Libe fifteen minutes before closing so as not to appear like a grind. **1978** C. Miller *Animal House* 57: Hoover was back from the libes. **1981** in Safire *Good Word* 86 [ref. to 1940's]: Hit the libe. **1981–85** S. King *It* 503: The libe closes at seven.

liberate *v.* Orig. *Army.* to obtain by theft; steal; (*broadly*) to pilfer; SCROUNGE, often as a military souvenir. *Joc.* [1944–58 quots. refer to WWII; in addition, since *ca*1968 the term has been used as left-wing jargon with antiestablishment overtones.]

   1944 in Litoff et al. *Miss You* 203: A liberated pig. *1944 in *OED2*: Excuse me, Canon, but I rather think you've liberated my matches. **1946** J.H. Burns *Gallery* 366: We loot—we call it liberating materials. **1951** *Amer. Jour. Socio.* XXXVII 416: Soldiers [in ETO] used "liberating" to mean any kind of appropriating and looting. **1955** Klaas *Maybe*

I'm Dead 455: I got to go back and liberate some food. **1958** F. Davis *Spearhead* 102: This isn't looting. This is liberating. **1969** H. Brown *Die Nigger Die* 53: I stole some stuff out of the White House. I liberated everything I could! **1970** Hammer *One Morning* 89: Hobscheid managed to "liberate" from somewhere tables, chairs and the equipment for a mess hall. **1971** E. Sanders *Family* 218: Malibu Brenda had liberated various furs from her mother's closet. **1972** [V.M. Grosvenor] *Thursdays* 40: So when I needed a dress...I "liberated" me a dress. **1978** S. King *Stand* 223: I liberated it. I don't think the Baptists will miss it. **1983** *Reader's Digest Success with Words* 87: Black English...*liberate* = "to steal." **1986** R. Zumbro *Tank Sgt.* 181 [ref. to 1967–68]: Yes sir, but I'll have to liberate some parts. **1988** *Sonny Spoon* (NBC-TV): I think she liberates 'em from the Fremont Hotel. **1990** Crow Dog & Erdoes *Lakota Woman* 58: Shoplifting, "liberating" a lot of stuff. **1992** L. Chambers *Recondo* 168: An NVA officer's belt buckle! And I had just liberated it! **1995** *Publisher Wkly.* (July 3) 45: Blumberg, who in 1990 was sentenced to six years in prison for "liberating" nearly $5 million worth of material from libraries.

liberty *n.* money. Also (in 1918 quot.) *Navy* **liberty bait.**

   1918 (quot. at JACK, *n.*, 7). **1929** Segar *Thimble Theater* 83: Just look at the bags of liberty our boy brought home! [**1946** Boulware *Jive & Slang* 5: Liberty...A quarter.]

liberty hound *n. Navy & USMC.* a sailor or marine who is eager to go on shore leave. Also **liberty hog.**

   1939 O'Brien *One-Way Ticket* 57: Go ahead ashore, you liberty hound! **1942** *Leatherneck* (Nov.) 147: *Liberty Hound*—This guy has gone when liberty call sounds and isn't heard from again until liberty is up; but he gripes because he doesn't get enough. **1944** Kendall *Service Slang* 25: Liberty hound....lad who tries to spend his enlistment ashore. **1968** Yglesias *Orderly Life* 104: Fuck off, fellas, we got enough liberty hounds already. **1982** T.C. Mason *Battleship* 94 [ref. to 1941]: The "liberty hounds" began returning with grandiose tales of adventures in Long Beach, Redondo Beach, Santa Monica, Los Angeles, and Hollywood. **1992** Jernigan *Tin Can Man* 49 [ref. to WWII]: I was always a regular "liberty hog."

libo *n.* [*liberty* + *-o*] *Navy & USMC.* shore leave; liberty.

   *a***1961** Peacock *Valhalla* 43 [ref. to 1953]: We got libo; but we're broke. *Ibid.* 56: Be ready for libo on Friday.

libs *n.pl.* see LIB, 3.

lick *n.* **1.a.** often *pl.* a smart blow; (*Baseball*) a batting or striking of a ball. Now *colloq.*, esp. *So. & West.*

   *****1678** in *OED*: [He] gave the fellow half a dozen good licks with his cane. *****a1701** in *F & H* IV 187: He gave me a lick across the face. *****1724** in *OED*: I'll give him a lick in the chops. *****1753** in *F & H* IV 187: I lent him a lick in his lanthorn-jaws. *****a1785** in *F & H* IV 187: He committed all these tricks, For which he well deserv'd his licks. *****1785,** *****1810** in *OED2*. *****1819** [T. Moore] *Tom Crib* 21: His *lick* is no *polisher.* *****1820** in *OED2*. *****1840** in *F & H* IV 187: I gave him a lick With a stick, And a kick. **1845** in Oehlschlaeger *Reveille* 87: [The boat] has only "struck a log;" a few "licks back" sets her free again. **1846** in Oehlschlaeger *Reveille* 130: He [was] shaking the panther, and putting in big licks...with his fists and feet. **1846** in H. Nathan *D. Emmett* 433: I gin her a lick dat tipped her over. **1860** in Longford *A. Lincoln* 82: It...[is] very singular that we three should strike "foul"...while old Abe made such a "good lick." *a***1881** G.C. Harding *Misc. Writings* 137: The way he put in the licks was truly astonishin'. **1889** in L. Levy *Flashes of Merriment* 354: He tightly grabbed his stick/And hit the driver a lick. **1908** in Fleming *Unforgettable Season* 43: His licks were for one, two and three [bases]. **1937** *So. Folk. Qly.* I 45: He taken a stick an' crep' clost enough to hit him a good solid lick. **1995** *X-Files* (Fox-TV): "How badly was he beaten?" "He took his licks."

   b. *Gamb.* an instance of good luck.

   1964 L'Amour *Hang* 20: I got into this dice game, and I was hitting a few hot licks.

   c. a blow of fate; unfortunate occurrence.

   1974 E. Thompson *Tattoo* 136: "That's a tough lick." "Ain't it though?" **1968–90** Linderer *Eyes of Eagle* 13: Hey, man, that's a lick. But that shit happens.

   d. a mark against (someone).

   1983 Beckwith & Knox *Delta Force* 284: I should have thought before I spoke. It's a lick on me.

   2.a. a vigorous attempt; try; chance; (now usu. *pl.*) a vigor-

ous effort; in phr. **last licks** a last try or chance in a competition. Now *colloq.*, esp. *So. & West.*

   *****1794** in *OED*: A Lick at the French Convention. *****1803** in *OED*: The tars are wishing for a lick, as they call it, at the Spanish galleons. **1832** in [S. Smith] *Letters of Downing* 99: Duff Green wants to have a lick at you, does he? **1835** in *DA*: When you come to put in the scientific licks, I squat. **1846** in G.W. Harris *High Times* 63: This was...given in "have-the-last-lick" spirit of mind. **1847** Robb *Squatter Life* 106: He was puttin' in the biggest kind a licks in the way of courtin'. **1847–49** Bonney *Banditti* 85: Jack preached several times in the neighborhood....Jack put in the big licks, till he made some of them look blue. **1851** in *DA*: I saw comin' my grey mule, puttin' in her best licks. **1861** in *OED*: At length I went to mining, put in my biggest licks. **1862** in C.W. Wills *Army Life* 67: Their gunboats...put in their best licks all day. **1863** in Theaker *Through One Man's Eyes* 39: Let him come, we will give him our best lick. **1864** in Morgan & Michalson *For Our Beloved Country* 189: Put in the big licks now....Here's where a double-distilled Reb lives. *a***1877** in Walke *Naval Scenes* 62: Jack [was] ever on the alert to put in the first licks. *****1882** in *F & H* IV 187: Till I'd done some *big licks* in the sporting line. *****1883** R.L. Stevenson *Treasure I.* ch. xviii: I wish I had had a lick at them with the gun first, I replied. **1903** *DN* II 299: "Put in the licks," work hard. **1906** Canfield *Forty-Niner* 77: We put in good licks all the week and took out thirty-eight ounces [of gold]. **1962** S. Smith *Escape from Hell* 24: Now we fight. Now we get our licks in! **1967** G. Green *To Brooklyn* 38 [ref. to 1930's]: Second picks, last licks. **1986** S. Becker *Tax Tips* (leaflet): In addition, 1986 is the "last lick" for nonitemizers to get a charitable deduction. **1987** *21 Jump Street* (Fox-TV): Good licks! Good licks, Hansen! **1995** Knoxville, Tenn., attorney, age 42: You just give it your best lick.

   b. a race, as between horses.

   1836 in Haliburton *Sam Slick* 50: That are colt beat him for a lick of a quarter of a mile easy. **1838** [Haliburton] *Clockmaker* (Ser. 2) 24: If you are for a lick of a quarter of a mile I don't feel much up to it.

   c. an act or action.

   1843 [W.T. Thompson] *Scenes in Ga.* 41: Cursing and swearing, and biting, and gouging, and such..."licks." *****1892** in *F & H* IV 187: Stage licks.

   d. pace, rate; in phr. **show a lick** (of a horse) to show speed.

   1847 in *F & H* IV 187: He went up the opposite bank at the same lick, and disappeared. **1864** "M. Twain," in *DARE*: He [*sc.* George Washington] kept up his lick for seven long years, and hazed the British from Harrisburg to Halifax. **1869** "M. Twain" *Innocents* 48: She [*sc.* a watch] is good on shore, but somehow she don't keep up her lick on the water. *****1898** Bullen *Cachalot* 215: Starting off at a great lick. **1905** *DN* III 86: Lick...Gait, rate of progress. "You'll have to hit a different *lick*, if you expect to accomplish anything." *****1934** Yeates *Winged Victory* 404: They would go...at an almighty lick. **1968** M.B. Scott *Racing Game* 20: He...does not show a lick (that is, he refuses to extend himself).

   e. a minor adjustment.

   1855 *Harper's Mag.* (Dec.) 39: Give the engine a lick back.

   f. *pl. Baseball.* (a player's) turn at bat.—also used fig.

   1883 *Sporting Life* (May 6) 1. **1913** T.A. Dorgan, in Zwilling *TAD Lexicon* 114 [Boys getting up a baseball game]: Who's got first licks? **1942** *ATS* 656: *Take one's lick,* to have one's turn at bat. **1988** Dye *Outrage* 97: Light bird is definitely gettin' his licks.

   g. *Und.* a robbery or other crime; JOB.

   1932–33 P. Cain *Fast One* 231: Your cut on this lick is ten grand. **1990** Bing *Do or Die* 33: I do jewelry licks. I go in jewelry stores, jack 'em up, go sell the jewelry. **1995** Stavsky, Mozeson & Mozeson *A 2 Z* 63: Where's the lick?

   h. one's preference.

   1972 *Urban Life & Culture* I 271: Well, honey, whatever your lick is.

   i. *Narc.* (see quot.).

   1988 Knoxville, Tenn., paralegal investigator, age *ca*45: [Among drug addicts] *to get your lick* or *to shoot up* [is] to inject intravenous drugs.

   3.a. *So. & Black E.* the correct thing to do; proper course of action.—constr. with *the.*

   1845 Hooper *Simon Suggs* 180: Trust in Providence—that's the lick! **1945** Trumbull *Silversides* 96: "Dat's de lick!" he yelled. "Dat's de lick!" **1947–52** R. Ellison *Invisible Man* 488: One of 'em started shooting. And *that* was the lick! Ole Ras didn't have time to get his gun. **1955** S. Allen *Bop Fables* 54: We've had it. So here's the lick. Take this beat-up bovine to market. **1965** Himes *Imabelle* 106: That ain't the lick either. What you got to do is steal your boss's hearse.

b. plan; idea.—*constr. with* the.

1955 S. Allen *Bop Fables* 54, in *OED2:* So here's the lick. Take this beat-up bovine to market. **1970** C. Major *Afro-Amer. Slang* 76: *Lick:* a plan, an idea, outline of a situation.

4. *West.* syrup or molasses.

1893 in *DARE: Lick*...syrup, molasses. **1909** in *DA:* The range boss...trifled with bits of biscuit and "lick" so that he might not be uncomfortable sitting alone. **1927** in *DA:* The chuck box also holds lick—sirup. *a***1940** in Lanning & Lanning *Texas Cowboys* 181: Syrup [was] called lick. **1934–43** F. Collinson *Life in Saddle* 34 [ref. to 1870's]: "Lick" (sorghum molasses) was the only dessert we had in the chuck wagon.

5. *Jazz.* a musical phrase, as by a soloist, esp. in improvisation. Now *S.E.*

1932** in *OED2:* They manage to steal a "lick" from an American record. **1933** *Fortune* (Aug.) 47: His *licks* (musical phrases) are original to the point of being *screwy* (fantastically exciting). **1936** *Harper's* (Apr.) 574: A few of the "licks"...were originally conceived in performance. **1937** *New Yorker* (Apr. 17) 27: The musical phrases which constitute a swing style are called *licks, riffs,* or *get-offs.* **1941** in *Great Music of D. Ellington* 80: I hope you'll understand this lick. **1950–52** Ulanov *Hist. Jazz* 352: *Lick:* see "break"; also used in early days of swing to designate any solo; sometimes called, in early days, "hot lick." **1983** Mandrell & Collins *Family Album* 126: She did some unreal "licks" [on the guitar]. *a1987** *World Bk. Dict.: Hot lick,* Slang. a special flourish or improvisation in jazz, generally upon a trumpet or clarinet.

¶ In phrase:

¶ **stick the lick into** to take advantage of.

1846 Codman *Sailors' Life* 95: Don't we stick the lick into them underwriters.

lick *v.* **1.a.** to assault physically; thrash; beat up; (with weakened force) to spank (a child). Now *colloq.* Cf. earlier sense 'to cut (off)', fr. 1535 in *OED.* [Now generally subsumed into **(b)**, below.]

***1567** Harman *Caveat* (gloss.): *Lycke,* to beat. ***1719** in *OED.* ***1726** A. Smith *Mems. of J. Wild* 82: So we severally lick'd the Coachman, as he did well deserve. **1770** Munford *Candidate* 33: I can lick you, by God! ***1796** Grose *Vulgar Tongue* (ed. 3): *To lick.* To beat....Jack...nastied his best clothes, for which his father stept up, and licked him neatly. **1824** in Paulding *Bulls & Jons.* 186: The naval officer threatened to "lick" me, as he called it, for my surly ill manners. **1862** [P. Davis] *Young Parson* 82: Now,...what makes you think I am going to lick him [a child]? **1878** R. Wheeler *On Deck* 12: I'll guarantee to lick the cuss as sez so. **1881** *Atlantic Mo.* XLIX 41, in *OED:* I've tried to lick the badness out of him....You can, out of some boys, you know. **1904** Bower *Lonesome* 173: It caused me to lick six kids a day, and to get licked by a dozen, when I went to school. **1965** "L. Short" *First* 112: My old man can lick your old man.

b. to defeat; ruin; overcome; overwhelm; (*hence*) to surpass; be superior to.—*occ.* (*obs.*) *constr. with* up. Now *colloq.*

***1800** in *OED:* By Dane, Saxon, or Pict We had never been lick'd Had we stuck to the king of the island. **1837** *Spirit of Times* (June 24) 149: I'll bet you two drinks she licks him! **1840** *Spirit of Times* (Oct. 10) 378: All the others [racehorses] would have been "licked up like salt" [by distemper]. **1843** Field *Pokerville* 116: I can lick that man, by thunder! **1846** N.J.T. Dana *Monterrey* 53: Unless they want to get licked badly. **1847** *Davy Crockett's Alm.* (unp.): Old hoss, I can lick you like a sack. **1861** in Walke *Naval Scenes* 41: We "licked them like h—l." **1862** in Cheadle *Journal* 18: Admits that our railroads & mutton chops lick the American. **1874** Alger *Julius* 79: Did he ever lick the boys? **1876** "M. Twain" *Tom Sawyer* 116: Tom Sawyer, he licked me once. **1916** in R. Lardner *Round Up* 115: I think we could lick him now. **1916** S. Lewis *Job* 266 [ref. to *ca*1910]: Their husbands came home clean-licked, like I am. **1930** Mulford *Eagle* 182: Me and Panhandle can lick any two fellers on earth. **1937** Haycox *Sundown Jim* 196: Hell, if we were ridin' together we'd lick the world.

c. to be victorious.—used intrans.

1861** in *OED2:* A gentleman will always lick in a fair fight. *ca1865** O.W. Holmes, Jr., in M.D. Howe *Shaping Yrs.* 104: Oh, troops were

crossing to the Virginia side, and we were going to lick. **1865** C.F. Browne *Ward: Travels* 92: It's rather necessary for somebody to lick in a good square, lively fite, and in this 'ere case it happens to be the United States of America. **1867** Clark *Sailor's Life* 259: I don't care which side licks, for I live in Jersey. **1876** in F. Remington *Sel. Letters* 12: I had a fight a day or so ago, I licked. **1893** in Dreiser *Jour.* I 117: The two clubs may...lay the much mooted question as to "which can lick" forever to rest. **1975** Univ. Tenn. student: I believe UT can lick [in a football game].

2. to run or ride at full speed—*usu. constr. with* dummy-obj. *it.*

1850 Garrard *Wah-to-yah* 21: Chad fired; the mad animal, directed by the rifle report, charged. How they did "lick it" over the ground! **1886** in *DAE:* He'd nothin' ter do but lick it like blazes. ***1889** in *OED.:* A horseman...rattled down the stony track as hard as he could lick. **1901** in *DARE:* Toot drove nipitytuck down the street...as fast as he could lick it.

¶ In phrases:

¶ **have it licked** to be in a successful or easeful position; have it made.

1957 Shulman *Rally* 134: They've got it licked. They've turned the goddam country into a goddam matriarchy.

¶ **lick me!** (used to express dismissal or contempt). Cf. BLOW, *v.,* 4, and related senses; cf. LOVE PUMP.

1974 Univ. Tenn. grad. student: Yeah. Lick me. **1990** Munro *Slang U.: Lick me!*...Shut up!...Kiss my ass! **1996** *Mystery Sci. Theater* (Comedy Central TV): You! Lick me!

¶ **lick up on** to beat up.

1931 Stevenson *St. Luke's* 32 [ref. to *ca*1910]: Oh I licked up on that red-head.

lickety-split *n.* [pun] cunnilingus.—*constr. with* go *or* come.—*usu. considered vulgar. Joc.*

1970 in *Playboy* (Jan. 1971) 74: Mae West jokes are in again (e.g., Mae on phone to Chinese laundry: "Where the hell is my laundry? Get it over here right away." Chinaman on arrival: "I come lickety-split, Mae West." Mae: "Never mind that. Just gimme the laundry."). **1971** *Blushes & Bellylaffs* 122: A fellow isn't necessarily running when he's going lickety-split. **1971** Dahlskog *Dict.* 37: *Lickety-split....vulgar.* cunnilingus. **1985** Boyne & Thompson *Wild Blue* 199: He met Roberts at the tail of their airplane, 0069. "Hello, Wash, looks like we got old lickety split today, eh?"

lickety-split *adv.* at great speed; headlong. Also vars. Now *colloq.* Also as adj. [For addit. vars., see *DARE.*]

1831 in *DARE:* He ran down the street licketty cut, and is probably at home by this time. **1847** Robb *Squatter Life* 116: They started, "lickety click," and arrived at the winning post within touching distance. **1848** in *AS* X 40: Lickoty split. **1892** *DN* I 236: *Lickity-split...*at full speed. **1905** *DN* III 86: *Lickety-split* adv. At a rapid gait. **1950** in Kerouac *Letters* 268: About the time of the lickety-split ride on the bikette. **1987** Norst & Black *Lethal Weapon* 126: A patrol unit was on the scene lickety-split. *a***1995** M. Kelly *Proudly* 98: Skinny and I got off the ship lickety-split.

lick log *n.* [fr. S.E. sense 'a salt lick for cattle'; though this use is not attested until 1851, this is presumably due to a gap in the evidence] **1.** a gathering place; point of contention or decision; in phr. **stand to (one's) lick-log, salt or no salt** to stand firm; act decisively; **come to the lick-log** to face facts; make a difficult decision; **down to the lick-log** down to business. [The above definition is paraphrased from *DARE,* from which most of this entry is taken; see *DARE* for additional evidence.]

1834 Crockett *Narrative,* in *DARE:* I was sure I would do a good business among them. At any rate, I was determined to stand up to my lick-log, salt or no salt. **1840** [Haliburton] *Clockmaker* (Ser. 3) 175: I like a man to be up to the notch, and stand to his lick-log; salt or no salt, say the word, or it's no offer. **1898** in *DARE:* When I got back to the old family lick log I found things powerful changed around. **1942** in *DARE:* To bring him to taw: to make him "come up to the lick log." **1975** in *DARE:* The term "lick-log" was sometimes applied to preaching places. **1982** in *DARE:* One of the men said, "we are at the lick log" (meaning we must now decide). **1992** in *DARE:* Texas Gov. Ann Richards...said Democrats were encouraged that Clinton had proved to be a fighter on the campaign trail. "When it really gets down to the licklog, we're going to have somebody in the Democratic Party who's going to get in there and slug it out with them." **1992** Launer *My Cousin Vinny* (film): Let's get down to the lick log.

2. a drinking saloon. *Joc.*

1867 G.W. Harris *Lovingood* 188: Wirt hed changed his grocery range, an' the sperrits at the new lick-log hed more scrimmage seed an' raise-devil intu hit than the old biled drink he wer used tu.

lickspittle *n.* a contemptible person; sycophant. Now *S.E.* Also **lickskillet**.

*1796 Grose *Vulgar Tongue* (ed. 3): *Lickspittle.* A parasite, or talebearer. *1825 in *OED2*: To hear his lickspittles speak you would think that a man of great and versatile talents was a miracle. **1846** in Bleser *Secret & Sacred* 164: He sent Torre, a lick-spittle of his. **1893** in *DARE*: *Lickskillet*…Used by illiterate whites to mean a *contemptible or detestable person*. **1906** Tomlin *H. Tomlin* 227: Old Eli Millston, a poor, old, pitiful, bowlegged, pigeon-toed lickskillet. **1955** O'Connor *Last Hurrah* 49: The little lickspittle is always pussyfooting around the ward.

licorice stick *n.* **1.** *Jazz.* a clarinet. Hence **licorice-sticker,** *n.*

1935 *Vanity Fair* (Nov.) 71: *Licorice stick* for clarinet. **1937** *New Yorker* (Apr. 17) 27: Some pet names for instruments are…*agony-pipe, wopstick,* or *licorice stick* for clarinet. **1945–51** Salinger *Catcher in Rye* 97: She called his clarinet a "licorice stick." Was she corny. **1955** V. Davies *Benny Goodman Story* (film): He's a mean man with that licorice stick. **1955** F. Morgan & N. Malkin *Hey, Mr. Banjo* (Mills Music, Inc.): Hey, Mr. Clarinet….Go man go with that licorice stick. **1956** I. Shulman *Good Deeds* 5: The clarinetist easing those high notes out of the licorice stick. **1964** Hill *One of the Casualties* 80: No telling how many touchdowns yon erstwhile ragtime licorice-sticker had caused with a few well-timed hot licks. **1966** I. Reed *Pall-Bearers* 9: Boy dat Sammy sure can blow the licoric [*sic*] stick and tickle da ivory. **1968** K. Hunter *Soul Bros.* 100: A clarinet for me!…A long, fine licorice stick. **1970** *Nat. Lampoon* (May) 21: Excuse me, sir, but doesn't the term "licorice stick" refer to the clarinet?

2. a billy club.

1954 L. Armstrong *Satchmo* 167: He was so angry he hit her cute little Creole head with his licorice stick, making her head bleed terribly.

lid *n.* **1.a.** a hat; (*hence*) a helmet.

1896 Ade *Artie* 4: Hang up your lid and come into the game. **1900** Ade *More Fables* 98: He was a Gentleman that wouldn't want to go anywhere with a Lady whose Lid was Tacky. **1901** Irwin *Sonnets* (unp.): I'll get…a straw lid. **1901** Archibald *Blue Shirt & Khaki* 201: A British soldier would admire the useful campaign hat of the American, who in return would declare what a good souvenir the "dinky lid" of the Britisher would make for his family at home. **1902** Townsend *Fadden & Mr. Paul* 98: Den he took off his lid to scratch his head. **1902** Cullen *More Tales* 75: That's when the lid went sailing. *a*1909 Tillotson *Detective* 93: *Lid*—A hat. **1914** Ellis *Billy Sunday* 55: He was dressed to kill with a silk lid and a big diamond and the latest cut Prince Albert. **1922** P.A. Rollins *Cowboy* 105: These other [cowboy] names [for a hat] included "lid," "war-bonnet," [etc.]. **1938** "E. Queen" *4 Hearts* 12: Get your lid. **1942** *ATS* 802: Steel helmet…*lid.* **1943** Crowley & Sachs *Follow the Leader* (film): That's a pretty nice lid. **1956** Holiday & Dufty *Lady Sings Blues* 15: These lids were the thing. **1960** R. Reisner *Jazz Titans* 160: *Lid:* hat. **1970** Wambaugh *New Centurions* 63: You don't have to wear your lid in the car, you know. **1972** Claerbaut *Black Jargon* 71: *Lid*…a hat. **1980** Lorenz *Guys Like Us* 80: Some skinny punks wearing shiny lids and black leather jackets. *a*1990 Poyer *Gulf* 85: He hated the issue lids.

b. the head; mind. See also *blow (one's) lid, flip (one's) lid,* below.

1899 Cullen *Tales* 78: With a scheme in my lid, I took a train for San Francisco. **1908** in H.C. Fisher *A. Mutt* 82: The lid inspector took one peep at Pickels' bean. **1968** Myrer *Eagle* 60: Just *supposing* all hell's broke loose…and the officer forgets the command, or he goes loose in the lid? **1970** Landy *Underground Dict.: Lid popper*…Amphetamine. Comes from lid, which means head.

c. *Prost.* fellatio.—usu. considered vulgar. Cf. DERBY, HEAD for semantic devel.

1963 Wepman et al. *The Life* 82: Why, you could cop her lid for the lowest bid. **1967** Beck *Pimp* 177: Carl, you test her lid and snatch.

2.a. good order; calm; customary, esp. officially imposed; propriety or restraint, esp. against vice.—constr. with *the* and *off* or *on.* Now *S.E.*

1904 in *DA:* He has taken frequent occasion to deny that the "lid" was off, to use the slang definition of a lax police administration. **1905** *Nat. Police Gaz.* (Nov. 18) 3 [ref. to *ca*1894]: "Now," remarked this minister, "New York will be hell with the lid off." And ever since then the city has had a figurative lid, which is off and on as a spasm of virtue makes itself felt.…If the lid was off New York altogether the red lights would spring up like mushrooms and the blondes would be in clover. **1905** in E. O'Neill *Letters* 14: I was in gay Saratoga where "the Lid" is off for good. **1908** in Fleming *Unforgettable Season* 156: The "lid" was clamped on the gambling end of metropolitan horse racing. **1912** Lowrie *Prison* 78: Everybody had money, an' th' place was wide open; th' lid was off. **1912** Quinn *Gambling* 214: This [slot] machine is said to be able to run in any town where "the lid is on," even in "Old Puritanical New England." **1915** [Swartwood] *Choice Slang* 53: To put the lid on a town means to close the saloons, gambling houses and all other resorts except summer resorts. **1918** *Chi. Daily Trib.* (Oct. 16) 9: Many "seers," believing the "lid" was off, had come to Chicago to share in the lucrative "graft." **1922** P.A. Rollins *Cowboy* 82: Few of the men were able long to "keep the lid on their can of cuss-words." **1926** C.M. Russell *Trails* 51: Somebody's kicked the lid off and I'm coming like a bat out of hell. **1927–30** P.A. Rollins *Jinglebob* 64 [ref. to 1880's]: Sorry the lid blowed off an' delayed our eatin'. **1930** J.T. Farrell *Can All This Grandeur Perish?* 201: Joe, the lid's off tonight, and the top of the sky's the limit. The old woman is away. **1932** Mahin *Red Dust* (film): Go down to Saigon and blow the lid off [*sc.*, celebrate wildly]. **1943** Wendt & Kogan *Bosses* 247: There is no lid on that burg. **1974** Blount *3 Bricks Shy* 14: James Parton, writing in 1868, called Pittsburgh "Hell with the lid taken off." **1979** Cassidy *Delta* 114: The Viet Cong were preparing to blow the lid off [*sc.*, launch an offensive]. He couldn't prove it, but he knew it.

b. Esp. *Gambl.* an upper monetary limit.

1910 Raine *O'Connor* 129: Playing with the lid off back there, ain't they? **1968** Brasselle *Cannibals* 327: "What's the tariff [*i.e.*, price]?" "What's your lid?" he countered. **1984** "W.T. Tyler" *Shadow Cabinet* 193: I don't wanna put a lid on it—the money I mean. Maybe it was more.

c. the protection of confidentiality; secrecy.—usu. constr. with *the.* Now *colloq.* or *S.E.*

1918 Stringer *House of Intrigue* 92: I guess I understand about keeping the lid on. *Ibid.* 212: I'm going to blow the lid off the whole bunch of you! **1928** in *DA.* **1936** Mulholland *Splinter Fleet* 32: Then the lid blew off. The *Utah* was six telephones short. **1943** Halper *Inch from Glory* 23: You blew the lid off. My troubles have been public property. **1982** Trudeau *Dressed for Failure* (unp.): But keep the lid on. No leaks until we make our move.

3. Esp. *Army.* a novice or incompetent telegrapher or radio operator.

1941 *Newsweek* (Mar. 10) 39: The Signal Corps maintains a big school…for Army "lids"—so called because they "talk through their hats"—at Fort Monmouth, N.J. **1941** *AS* (Oct.) 166: *Lid.* Apprentice operator. An incompetent operator. (Signal Corps). **1954–60** *DAS: Lid*…An unskillful telegrapher. **1977** *Amer. Dict. of CB Slang* 44: *Lid*— Name given to an inept CB radio operator.

4. *Narc.* an ounce of marijuana.

1964–66 R. Stone *Hall of Mirrors* 161: I'm just looking to score a lid. **1968** J. Carey *College Drug Scene* 35: The kilos of marihuana are broken down at the street-pushing stage into ounces called "lids" which are sold for $10–$15. **1969** Whittemore *Cop* III 289: The undercover man said, "Do you have any lids?" referring to marijuana. **1969** Bullock *Watts* 158: See, it costs about fifty cents a joint, a stick, and you can get a matchbox for $3.50; $7.50 for a can, $10 for a bag, people refer to it as a lid; a can for $15, and then you go into your half a pound. **1965–70** J. Carroll, in *Paris Rev.* (No. 50) 103: A lid of dynamite grass I was about to deal. **1977** Sayles *Union Dues* 287: He sold mediocre grass for ten dollars a lid, coke for fifty a gram…and a hit of windowpane acid for two bucks. **1980** Novak *High Culture* xxiii: A "lid" is a measurement of marijuana, either an ounce, or slightly less, depending on the year and the city. **1981** Wambaugh *Glitter Dome* 147: Probably Tuna Can Tommy smoked a couple of lids a week. **1986** Merkin *Zombie Jamboree* 130: He…hangs out in the student union buying and selling lids and tabs.

¶ In phrases:

¶ **blow (one's) lid** to *flip (one's) lid,* below. [These quots.

provide additional evidence for the term; the main entry, with variants, is found s.v. BLOW, *v.*]

    1935 (quot. at *blow (one's) lid* s.v. BLOW, *v.*). **1947** Carter *Devil's in Baggy Pants* 269: Arab, I hear ye've blown your lid. **1958** Hughes & Bontemps *Negro Folklore* 481: Don't let a woman make you blow your lid. **1962** Sarlat *War Cry* 84 [ref. to WWII]: We're just like Vesuvius up there, smoking and spitting so we don't blow our lids. **1963** Marshall *Battle at Best* 73: You all blew your lids.

¶ **flip (one's) lid** to lose (one's) mind or composure; go crazy. [These quots. provide additional evidence for the term; the main entry, with variants, is found s.v. FLIP, *v.*]

    1941 Horman *Buck Pvts.* (film): If boogie-woogie sent you like I think it did,/Four-to-the-bar will flip your lid! **1943** Guthrie *Bound for Glory* 113: Oil! Flipped 'er lid! Gusher! **1953** Hammerstein *Me & Juliet* 500: Every man is flipping his lid/Over that phenomenal kid. **1959** Cochrell *Barren Beaches* 92: "For god's sake," Willy said. "Don't flip your lid." **1963** Boyle *Yanks Don't Cry* 65: Without reason, he would flip his lid and begin swinging his bamboo cane around like a wild man, all the while screaming at the top of his lungs. **1969** Whittemore *Cop* I 78: "People are always flipping their lids around here," Minelli observed, almost as if he were conducting a guided tour.

¶ **put a lid on, 1.** to quit (an action or activity); abandon (a place).

    1918 Stringer *House of Intrigue* 50: He put the lid down on the marriage talk for the rest of the winter. **1969–71** Kahn *Boys of Summer* 313: But when this building gets through, it's in the barrel. I put the lid on this city.

    2. to cease, esp. talking, immediately.—usu. used imper.—usu. constr. with *it.*

    1971 Mishkin et al. *All in the Family* (CBS-TV): Put a lid on it, will ya? **1978** *Barney Miller* (NBC-TV): Say, would you guys put a lid on it? I'm typing up a report! **1979** Gutcheon *New Girls* 32: You can put a lid on that girl chat for just a minute, can't you? **1980** Lorenz *Guys Like Us* 158: Why don't you put a lid on that shit? **1982** in *Nat. Lampoon* (Feb. 1983) 67: Put a lid on it, Merchant! **1983** *Tales of Gold Monkey* (ABC-TV): Oh, put a lid on it, Jack! **1984** *Night Court* (NBC-TV): Put a lid on it! **1984** *Miami Vice* (NBC-TV): Put a lid on it! **1986** D. Tate *Bravo Burning* 137: Screw a lid on it, tiger! **1988** *Tour of Duty* (CBS-TV) [ref. to Vietnam War]: Sergeant, put a lid on it! **1995** *Space Ghost* (TV Cartoon Network): Put a lid on it, Zorak!

lid-lifter *n.* *Baseball Journ.* the opening game of a doubleheader.

    1948 L. Allen *Reds* 120: After dropping the lid-lifter, 2 to 1, to Jim Vaughn, Hod defeated Vic Aldridge, 6 to 2, in the six-inning nightcap halted by darkness. *a*1989 P. Dickson *Baseball Dict.* 245: *Lid-lifter...*First game of a doubleheader.

lie *v.* ¶ In phrase: **if I'm lying, I'm dying** [or **flying**] Esp. *Black E.* I assure you this is the truth.

    1973 Wideman *Lynchers* 38: If I'm lying, I'm flying and my feet sure ain't got no wings. **1977** "Wolfman Jack," in TV ad (WPIX-TV) (N.Y.C.) (July 5): When it comes to music, the Wolfman knows! And if I'm lyin', I'm dyin'. **1990** *Donahue* (NBC-TV): If I'm lyin', I'm dyin'!

lie box *n.* *Police.* a lie detector; (*hence*) a lie detector test.

    1955 Deutsch *Cops* 150: FBI Director J. Edgar Hoover...has often expressed strong dislike for the "lie box" and skepticism about its value. **1959** O'Connor *Stranger* 13: And you had better make a date with John Reid to put him on the lie box. **1976** Hoffman & Pecznick *Drop a Dime* 270: But the "lie box" found them out. **1976** "N. Ross" *Policeman* 156: He was ordered to submit to a lie-box test, which he promptly flunked with flying colors. *Ibid.* 180: Prove it! Prove that you never told me....Take a lie-box. **1992** Hosansky & Sparling *Working Vice* 190: You will take a lie box test.

lieu var. LOO.

lieut *n.* [a written abbr. later taken over into speech] *Army.* a lieutenant. Also **loot.**

    1759 in *AS* (Oct. 1940) 231: Lut. **1803* in Wetherell *Adventures* 57: Lieutenant Leftwidge our second lieut. was acting in his place. **1813** B. Palmer *Diary* (entry for Dec. 11): We were soon boarded by a Lieut. then it was in to the boats You dam Yankee Rascals and on board the Loire Frigat with You. **1833** *Mil. & Nav. Mag. of U.S.* (Oct.) 83: A *Lieut.* at 19 *will* certainly be a Captain at 30. **1839** McNally *Evils & Abuses* 115: The first lieut. replied in his usual tone. **1847** Downey

Cruise of Portsmouth 39: The boys were called on deck at 10 A.M. and...[received] a lecture from the 1st Lieut upon the necessity of coming on board in due time. **1862** Bear *Letters* 6: The Colonel give our Lieut fits today after drill. **1862** in L.J. Daniel *Soldiering* 150: The Lieut's brother was stabbed in the thigh. **1862** in C.H. Moulton *Ft. Lyon* 49: One shoulder displayed the rank of a captain, and the other of a 2nd lieut. **1863** in H. Johnson *Talking Wire* 58: The Lieut came...and asked me to come out next time at stable call. **1864** in W. Wilkinson *Mother* 184: *Watches* and other valuables were handed to one of our Lieuts who was not *going in* Lt. John H. Cook. **1864** in Mohr *Cormany Diaries* 437: One of my men...remarked "Lieut! That Johny has pretty close range of you." **1864** in O.J. Hopkins *Under the Flag* 191: Believe me your ever faithful "Lieut." **1864** in Bensell *Yamhill* 136: Grimsley says, "Bensell, Lieut wants you!" **1891** in F. Remington *Sel. Letters* 123: The Lieut has slighted the thing. **1898** Dunne *Peace & War* 11: R-run over an' wake up th' loot at th' station, an' let thim Americans out. **1899** Elderkin *Sketches* 76 [ref. to Mexican War]: The servant, finally recognizing the horse, said, "It is your horse, lieut." **1910** in Camp *Custer* 85 [ref. to 1876]: McVeigh said, "They are leaving the timber, Lieut." **1918** Grider *War Birds* 51: There was a U.S. Lieut here named Gaines and he forbade them to try it. **1918** in Paine *First Yale Unit* II 69: There I found the "Loot" and others who could talk nothing but Northern Bombing Group. **1930** Fredenburgh *Soldiers March!* 187 [ref. to 1918]: The Loot wants you. **1932** T.S. Eliot *Sweeney Agonistes* 17: The Loot has told us a lot about us. **1948** Cozzens *Guard* 331: Don't thank the loot! You'll spoil everything!

lieut-colonel *n.* *Army.* a lieutenant colonel. Also **loot-colonel.**

    1863 in Swinfen *Ruggles' Regt.* 76: The Lieut-Colonel rolled himself up in his...overcoat. **1864** Armstrong *Generals* 258: Our Colonel and Lieut.-Colonel, I know, feel outraged at the bare idea of being subjected to such an order. **1918** *Stars & Stripes* (Dec. 27): He's a loot-colonel now and a D.S.C.

lieut-comm *n.* *Navy.* a lieutenant commander. Also **loot-comm.**

    1961 G. Forbes *Goodbye to Some* 17 [ref. to WWII]: He and Ashton made loot comm...last October.

lieuy var. LOOIE.

life *n.* **1.** *Baseball.* an unexpected chance to score or steal a base. Cf. colloq. *alive* 'not put out; safe, esp. unexpectedly'.

    1868 in P. Dickson *Baseball Dict.* 245: Howe had a life given him by Schaffer muffing his fly in right field. **1914** Patten *Lefty o' the Bush* 80: A poor throw...presented the runner with "a life."

    2. any of various professions, activities, or behaviors as a way of life.—all constr. with *the*. Specif.:

    a. *Pros.* prostitution as a way of life.

    1909 Chrysler *White Slavery* 17: They did not enter the life of their own free will. *Ibid.* 27: The girl expressed her willingness to enter the life. **1916** Miner *Prostitution* 4: "All us girls hate the life."...She had become enslaved by cocaine, by the drink and by the "life." **1920** in W.I. Thomas *Unadjusted Girl* 144: He told me he could "help" me a lot in the life. **1936** Washburn *Parlor* 26 [ref. to *ca*1900]: The "life" grated against her fine nature and she didn't worry whether she earned her share of the big stakes or not. *Ibid.* 125: She was engaged to be married to the janitor of a church and "the life" was about to be banished when she stepped into the $2 parlor only to be met...by her future husband. **1940** Asbury *Gem of Prairie* 121 [ref. to 1890's]: Then they were broken in to what in red-light circles was known as "the life," a process which involved rape and almost unbelievable brutalization. **1942** Algren *Morning* 193: "I weighed a hundred thirty-four before I entered the Life," Chiney-Eye Helen recalled, using a phrase she had read in a magazine. **1957** Greenwald *Call Girl* 17: They [prostitutes] speak of them as being "in the racket," as being "in the life," as "a regular girl," or "one of the girls," with particular emphasis given to the word "girl." **1957** Murtagh & Harris *First Stone* 131: I been in the life thirty years and had one pimp or another every single day of it. **1960** R. Reisner *Jazz Titans* 160: Life, The: the world of prostitution. **1961** T. Rubin *In the Life* 9: What are you trying to do, try to get me out of the life? **1966** Samuels *People vs. Baby* 7: She had been "in the life," prostituting for years. **1968** *N.Y.P.D.* (ABC-TV): Someone said she quit the life. **1973** Toma & Brett *Toma* 163: Talking to [prostitutes], trying to convince them to get out of the "life" rarely worked.

1973 Schulz *Pimp* 7: Some of my ladies might even run away. But that happens outside the life too. **1974** Angelou *Gather Together* 29: Are you in the life?...The life. You turn tricks? **1977** T. Berger *Villanova* 91: All his sisters are in the life. **1983** Sturz *Widening Circles* 61: She dropped out to involve herself with a dude in "the life"—a...hustler who dealt in whatever was around, including female flesh. *a*1984 Sereny *Invisible Children* 14: Cleo was the name by which she was known in the "life."

b. *Und.* the criminal underworld as a way of life.

1916 MacBrayne & Ramsay *One More Chance* 94: But if it never did pay, why did you so often return to the life? **1972** Burkhart *Women in Pris.* 447: *Life, The.* Way of living on the streets that involves illegal moneymaking activities; a culture separate from mainstream society. *a*1976 Roebuck & Frese *Rendezvous* 83: Well-dressed customers who don't mind spending money. Important people in and out of the life. **1987** *Newsweek* (Mar. 23) 58: Honk...was thinking about retiring from The Life after 20 years. **1991** McCarthy & Mallowe *Vice Cop* 101: You can't have too many people from the Life who are willing to [cooperate with the police].

c. *Homosex.* homosexuality as a way of life.

1955 Lindner *Must You Conform?* 50: "The life" (as he calls the homosexual world). **1962** Perry *Young Man Drowning* 274: When I first saw you looking at me that way in the elevator, I knew right away you were "in the life." **1965** Trimble *Sex Words* 110: *In The Life*...Homosexual.

d. *Carnival.* the carnival as a way of life.

1956 Gold *Not With It* 28: Beat it. Get from the life.

e. *Narc.* drug addiction as a way of life.

1967 Fiddle *Portraits from a Shooting Gallery* 63: In fact, if one talks to more astute addicts, one learns that they are painfully aware of the contradiction between reason and their conduct. They themselves know how in their lives they had been perfectly aware of the high costs they pay for staying "in the life."

¶ **get a life** to start living a gregarious, secure, or rewarding life; improve one's lot.—usu. used broadly as an expression of impatience or disdain.—also used allusively, as in 1991, 1995 quots.

1985 Eble *Campus Slang* (Apr.) 4: *Get a life*—advice given to a geek. **1986** Univ. Tenn. student: *I gotta start getting a life* means "I've got to start having more fun and excitement." **1986** *ShowBiz Today* (CNN-TV) (Oct. 29): Shut up, Christie, and get a life for yourself! **1988** *Married with Children* (Fox-TV): "Kelly, it's so great!" "Ugh. Get a life, willya?" **1989** S. Lee *Do the Right Thing* (film): Why don't you get a fuckin' life! **1990** TV ad, Knoxville, Tenn.: Get real! Get it together! Get a life! **1990** *Designing Women* (CBS-TV): I just want to say...get a life! **1990** *21 Jump St.* (Fox-TV): "You're an addict." "Get a life!" **1991** Ganz & Mandel *City Slickers* (film): I have no life. We're all agreed on that. *a*1994 in C. Long *Love Awaits* 19: Fuck you....Sisters, get a life. **1995** *Jerry Springer Show* (synd. TV series): Just 'cause you don't have a friggin' life, don't take it out on me, boy!

¶ **it's a great life if you don't weaken** (used to comment on the difficulties of one's situation).—used ironically.

1917 F. Hunt *Draft* 60: Great life if you don't weaken. **1918** Kauffman *Navy at Work* 147: "It's a great life," said my observer..."If you don't weaken," added the pilot. *Ibid.*: "It's a merry life," said the observer. "And a short one," the pilot concluded. **1920** Skillman *A.E.F.* 173: Familiar Expressions of the A.E.F.: *It's a great life if you don't weaken.* **1921** Dos Passos *Three Soldiers* 74 [ref. to 1918]: "It's a great life if you don't weaken," murmured Fuselli automatically. **1927** C. McKay *Harlem* 47: Great life, boh, ef you don't weaken. **1971** N.Y.C. elevator operator, age *ca*35: It's a great life if you don't weaken.

¶ **it's nothing in my young life** it's of no consequence to me.

1919 *Amer. Leg. Wkly.* (July 11) 6: The armistice had been signed, but "that meant nothing in our young lives," as one of the privates said. **1923** *Iowa State College Bomb* 408: It's simply nothing in my young life. **1970** Thackrey *Thief* 194: So, don't go if you don't feel like it. It's nothing in my young life.

¶ **life of Riley** see s.v. RILEY.

¶ **that's life in the big city!** life is unfair and there's nothing one can do about it.

1974 M.J. Smith *When I Say No* 62: Sometimes one offends. That's

life in the big city! **1993** Knoxville, Tenn., attorney, age 40: Well, that's just life in the big city.

lifeboat *n. Pris.* a pardon, esp. of a death sentence.

1908 Sullivan *Crim. Slang* 15: *Life boat*—A pardon (Western slang). **1918** *Amer. Law Rev.* (Dec.). **1927** *DN* V 454: *Life boat*, n. A pardon, first for a capital offense, then by extension, for any offense. **1930** *Amer. Mercury* (Dec.) 456: *Lifeboat*, *n.*: A pardon or commutation of sentence. "He goes stool for a lifeboat." **1931** *AS* VI (Aug.) 440: *Lifeboat:* A commutation of a death sentence.

life preserver *n.* a doughnut. *Joc.*

1941 in *OED2: Life preservers*, doughnuts. **1945** Hubbard *R.R. Ave.* 326: Switch me a coupla life preservers.

lifer *n.* **1.** *Pris.* **a.** a convict serving a life sentence.

*1830 in OED2: Some were seven years' men, and others were what they call "lifers." **1831* in Partridge *Dict. Und.* **1883** Duffus-Hardy *Down South* 271: The leader...is a "lifer," in for arson, a very common crime among the negroes. **1891** Maitland *Slang Dict.* 167: *Lifer.* A convict sentenced for life. **1899** A.H. Lewis *Sandburrs* 133: "D" mug who chases in an' takes a trip for ten, he's a lifer. **1904** *Life in Sing Sing* 18: So the lifer stood at my door and told me that this wasn't a bad joint. **1914** J. London *Jacket* 21: Forty hard-bitten lifers waited for the guard Barnum to go to sleep on his shift. **1954** J. Hayes *Desperate Hrs.* 5: Another con, a lifer by the name of Robish. **1970** L.D. Johnson *Front Porch* 112: "Ace" was a lifer who was well liked by guards and cons alike. **1971** J. Brown & A. Groff *Monkey* 16: Give my outfit to some lifer. **1971–72** in Abernethy *Bounty of Texas* 209: *Lifer*...one who is serving a life sentence. **1977** M. Franklin *Last of Cowboys* 128: Beebo hung like a lifer on the bars. **1986** J.J. Maloney *Chain* 107: Lifers don't earn good time. **1995** *TV Guide* (Oct. 28) 219: The bond formed between an introverted inmate and a cynical lifer.

b. a life sentence.

*1832 in *OED2:* Is it not a shame to give me a lifer, and they only a month each? **1863* in T. Taylor *Plays* 168: If I'm nailed, it's a lifer. **1902** Cullen *More Tales* 90: Now he's doing his little lifer at a French penal settlement. **1928** Guerin *Crime* 205: Luigi...[was] serving a "lifer."

2. *Mil.* a person, esp. a senior noncommissioned officer, whose career is in military service.—often used derisively.

1962 in *Harper's* (Feb. 1964) 38: The lifers (professionals) were glad to be getting out of something. **1966** *N.Y. Times Mag.* (Oct. 30) 102: A "lifer" is the draftee's name for a career soldier. **1966** in IUFA *Folk Speech:* Military Slang for a career man in the service. *Lifer.* **1969** L. Hughes *Under a Flare* 32: Despite the fact he was a lifer, John and I became good drinking buddies. **1969** Crumley *One to Count* 26: You ain't no lifer, are you? **1970** Ponicsan *Last Detail* 32: To tell you the truth, Mule, better things were expected of me back there than to be a lifer in the navy. **1971** *Newsweek* (Jan. 11) 30: Draftees continually heap scorn upon the "lifers," as career soldiers are known. **1983** K. Miller *Lurp Dog* 2: They bring in a lifer E-6 and tell me he's gonna be our new team leader. **1984** T.K. Mason *Cactus Curtain* 32: Among the Navy's "lifers." **1986** L. Johnson *Waves* 60 [ref. to *ca*1971]: You're a lifer....And you know what that stands for—a "Lazy Ignorant Fucker Expecting Retirement." **1988** M. Maloney *Thunder Alley* 82: This guy is good...Probably a lifer. **1994** J.M. Boyle *Apache Sunrise* 40: Na, he's a lifer....Gonna make the army a career. **1995** *Donahue* (NBC-TV): His father's family are lifers in the Navy.

3.a. a person who intends to work at the same job until retirement; careerist.

1970 T. Wolfe *Radical Chic* 110: Whatever you're angry about,...he's there to catch the flak. He's a lifer. **1977** Schrader *Blue Collar* 2: The lifers came next, eager to rest their bones, lunch buckets dangling from their weary hands.

b. a person whose life style, attitudes, or behavior appears to be unchangeable or incorrigible.

1970 Landy *Underground Dict.* 120: *Lifer*...Person who takes drugs for...15 to 20 years. **1973** *TULIPQ* (coll. B.K. Dumas): What do you call a person that is taking drugs? *Lifer.* **1985** "Blowdryer" *Mod. Eng.* 25: *Lifers*...Is what I call people who aren't going to hang out and then outgrow it or find themselves.

lifer dog *n.* LIFER, 2.—often used derisively.

1989 P.H.C. Mason *Recovering* 32 [ref. to Vietnam War]: It was..."Us vs. Them," with them being the lifer dogs. **1991** Univ. Tenn. student paper: *Lifer dog* "He's a lifer dog"—one who lives, breathes, sleeps, thinks his career. Doesn't retire unless forced to. Not…a compliment. [U.S. Navy].

lifer juice *n.* [see 1974 quot.] *Mil.* coffee. *Joc.*

[**1974** Former l/cpl, USMC, N.Y.C., served 1967–69: This is "lifer's finger." [*Crooks finger as if holding coffee cup.*] Lifers get it after twenty years—once you make top kick you've got nothing to do but loaf with a cup of coffee in your hand.] **1987** Palfrey & Carabatsos *Hamburger Hill* 30 [ref. to Vietnam War]: He filled an empty discarded C-ration can from a pot that had *Lifer Juice* written on it.

lifesaver *n. Pris.* LIFEBOAT.

1935 *AS* (Feb.) 18 [ref. to 1910]: *Lifesaver* or *Lifeboat*. A reprieve, pardon, or stay of execution.

lifing *adj. Mil.* being a LIFER, 2.

1988 Dye *Outrage* 89: Prob'ly a result of spendin' too much time around that lifin'…Sergeant Barlow.

lift *n.* **1.a.** a theft or robbery. Cf. earlier quots. in *OED2*.

1845 *Nat. Police Gaz.* (Nov. 8) 92: They intend to make a "lift" either on the steamboat or in the cars. **1866** *Nat. Police Gaz.* (Apr. 21) 3: He [a fence] buys all that he's brought to him on the "lift," and can safely make his fifty "cases" a day, without any chance of being "copped." **1867** *Nat. Police Gaz.* (Oct. 26) 2: [He] had made a "lift" out of some unlucky wight. **1872** Burnham *Secret Service* 95: He succeeded in relieving the Concord Bank of some $300,000 in good money; and at another time he made a big "lift" at the Wolfboro', N.H., Bank. *1881–84 Davitt *Prison Diary* I 24: Recounting with an I-took-part-myself-in-it air such recent burglaries or clever "lifts" as may have excited unusual interest in the public press. **1905** White *Boniface* 224 [ref. to 1869]: As suggested by Taylor, the closing hour of business was selected in which to make the "lift."

b. Orig. *Und.* the practice of theft or, esp., shoplifting.— constr. with *the*. [Prob. a deriv. of (a), above.]

1791 [W. Smith] *Confess. T. Mount* 19: *Taking chattery upon the lift, taking goods in the day time.* *1851–61 H. Mayhew *London Labour* III 386: She went on the lift in London (shopping and stealing from the counter). **1961** B. Wolfe *Magic of Their Singing* 25: I don't want to go on the lift. Not today. Please.

2.a. a strong stimulant effect from alcohol or drugs; KICK, 6.

1942 *ATS* 113: Alcoholic content or reaction. (Especially a strongly stimulating effect.)…*buzz,…jolt, kick, lift*. **1957** in *DAS*: The girl had to rush back to the pusher and complain that it didn't give her "a lift."

b. *Narc.* a pill containing a stimulant; amphetamine. In full, **lift pill**.

1968 J. Hudson *Case of Need* 185: Bombs.…Speed. Lifts. Jets. Bennies. **1970** Landy *Underground Dict.*: *Lift pill*…Amphetamine; an upper.

3. *Carnival.* a loan.

1953 Gresham *Midway* 25: We started broke and we wound up broke, and I went to my friends again for a lift. You know, in the carny, it isn't a loan, it's a lift.

lift *v.* **1.a.** to steal; (*esp.*) to pilfer. [Orig. S.E., esp. as applied to the thieving of cattle. The related sense 'to plagiarize' has always been S.E.]

*1526 in *OED2*: Conuey it be crafte, lyft & lay aside. *1592, *1595, *1666 in *OED2*. *1722 in *OED2*: Thieves that came to lift their cattle. **1821** Martin & Waldo *Lightfoot* 26: I succeeded at last, in *lifting* something from the kitchen. **1848** Baker *Glance at N.Y.* 16: His watch ain't worth lifting. **1868** *Overland Mo.* (Aug.) 134: We do not organize raids to "lift" the cattle of a too prosperous neighbor. **1882** in "M. Twain" *Stories* 202: This property was not "lifted" by a novice. **1890** E. Custer *Guidon* 76 [ref. to 1868]: "'Tain't no kind…of use to try to lift* my plunder now."…*"Lift," a word meaning steal. **1905** Brainerd *Belinda* 75: See what swag she has beside the diamonds we saw her lift. **1929** "M. Brand" *Beacon Creek* 143: This here law…prizes murder more'n cattle-lifting. **1931–34** in Clemmer *Pris. Community* 333: *Lifted the jack* v. phr. To steal [*sic*] the money. **1942** Garcia *Tough Trip* 58: Many of those gentry promptly took up horse stealing and cattle lifting. **1944** C.B. Davis *Leo McGuire* 155: I might figure on lifting a car for the job. **1987** Ohara (ABC-TV): I lift wheels, man. I ain't no killer.

b. *Und.* to pick the pocket of (someone); rob.

1915–16 Lait *Beef, Iron & Wine* 186: I lift a boob for $106.60…yesterday. **1925** Robinson *Wagon Show* 108: They "lifted" me as they were

crowding me onto the car. **1965–70** J. Carroll, in *Paris Rev.* (No. 50) 103: Some prick lifted me for a lid of dynamite grass I was about to deal.

2.a. *Poker.* to raise the bet of (someone).

1859 (quot. at SCAD). **1884** Carleton *Poker Club* 21: I sees yo' dat, and I liff yo' a dollah mo'. **1887** [C. Mackenzie] *Jack Pots* 30: He came at me with a twenty, and I lifted him for a couple more.

b. to raise (a glass of liquor) to the lips and drink; HOIST.

[*1796 Grose *Vulgar Tongue* (ed. 3): *To lift one's hand to one's head*; to drink to excess, or to drink drams. *To lift or raise one's elbow*; the same.] **1954** N. Johnson *Night People* (film): My idea was that you and I would step out afterwards and lift a couple. **1971** N.Y.U. student: Sometimes he's kind of crazy after he's lifted a few. *1990 Thorne *Dict. Contemp. Sl.* 314: What say we go and lift a few? **1994** N.Y.C. man, age 25 (coll. J. Sheidlower): Let's go lift some cold ones.

3. to kill (someone).

1873 in Rosa *Wild Bill* 216: We have little sympathy for the worthless brute of an Indian, and still less for the white man who knows no higher amusement than to brag of the number of "Indians he has lifted."

4. *R.R.* to take up (a ticket).

1898 in *DAE:* The conductors put…[the tax stamps] on when the ticket is lifted. **1942** *Sat. Eve. Post* (June 13) 27: But don't think he would stoop to taking up your [railroad] ticket. "He lifts your transportation."

lifted *adj.* intoxicated by alcohol or drugs; HIGH.

1942 *ATS* 123: [Drunk:] *jagged (up),…likkered (up),…lifted.* **1993** "Wu-Tang Klan" *Method Man* (rap song): I got fat bags of skunk…and I'm about to go get lifted. *Ibid.:* Let's get lifted as I kick ballistics. **1994** *N.Y. Times* (Feb. 6) IV 18: Words on the Street:…*To get high* To get lifted, booted, red, [etc.].

lifter *n.* **1.** *Und.* a shoplifter. Cf. broader sense 'thief', in *OED2* fr. *a*1592.

*1781 G. Parker *View of Soc.* II 139: *Lifters.…A* genteel-looking woman goes into a large shop [to decoy the clerk while her confederates steal merchandise]. [*1796 Grose *Vulgar Tongue* (ed. 3): *Lift.* See *shoplifter.*] **1866** *Nat. Police Gaz.* (Apr. 21) 4: I am now able to inform them about the Dutch "lifters" that arrived here recently. *1889 Barrère & Leland *Dict. Slang*: A *lift* or *lifter* is an old word for a thief or shoplifter. **1904** *Life in Sing Sing* 250: *Lifter*—A shoplifter. **1929** Zorbaugh *Gold Coast* 138: "Boston" Nell…[was] a nationally known "lifter."

2. a drink of whiskey.

1875 Nowlin *Bark Covered House* 53 [ref. to 1836]: There I stopped again and took what I called "a good lifter."

light *n.* **1.** *pl.* Esp. *Black E.* the eyes. Cf. TOP-LIGHTS.

*1820 in *F & H* IV 193: She knew a smart blow, from a handsome giver Could darken lights. **1827** J.F. Cooper *Red Rover* 505: Who dare to cast a seaman into the brine, with the dying look standing in his lights, and his last words still in his messmate's ears. *1889–90 Barrère & Leland *Dict. Slang* II 17: *Lights* or *top-lights* (popular), the eyes. **1900** *Colored American* (Jan. 27) 8: Surely the treatment that Brother Benjamin has been taking for his eye-sight is not doing him much good, for his "lights" must be very dim if he does not perceive [etc.]. **1967** [R. Beck] *Pimp* 125: Preston might have made it if "Sweet" hadn't turned those lights on him. **1973** Andrews & Owens *Black Lang.* 106: *Lights*—Eyes.

2. *Boxing.* a lightweight.

1940 J.T. Farrell *Father & Son* 165: You lights can't cop anything this year.

3. *pl.* one's intelligence, coherence, etc.; usu. in phr. **the lights are on but nobody's home** (said of a person who is dazed, stupid, or unaware). Cf. earlier *put (someone's) lights out*, below. Cf. *nobody home* s.v. HOME, *n.*

1983 Eble *Campus Slang* (Nov.) 3: *The light's on but no one's home*— expression meaning that the person is unaware. **1983** Leeson *Survivors* (film): You're lookin' at me right now like the lights are on but nobody's home. **1984** A. Pincus *How to Talk Football* 14: *All the lights aren't on*…what one player says about another…who will never be confused with a rocket scientist. **1984** Heath *A-Team* 32: Maybe the senator's son talked. I never thought that kid had all his lights on. *a*1990 in *Maledicta* X 33: *Lights are on, but nobody's home* refers to a patient who…appears oriented but cannot carry on an appropriate conversation.

¶ In phrases:

¶ **in the light** (of coffee) served with cream.

1900 Ade *More Fables* 152: Feed me Everything, with One in the Light to come along.

¶ **put (someone's) lights out, 1.** to kill (someone). Also vars. Allusively, **lights out.** [Orig. poetic S.E., as in Shakespeare.]

[**1602* Shakespeare *Othello* V ii: Yet she must die, else she'll betray more men. Put out the light, and then—.] [*1619 Beaumont & Fletcher *Maid's Tragedy* IV i: 'Tis a justice, and a noble one, to put the light out of such base offenders.] **1825** in R. Tyler *Verse* 233: Othello … put out Desdemona's light. ***1884** in *F & H* IV 1944: So now, the malefactor does not murder, he "pops a man off," or *puts his light out.* **1885** Siringo *Texas Cowboy* 132: Come up and take your last drink on this earth, for I am going to blow your light out. **1898** in Remington *Own West* 184: By gar, dat weare freeze, too! Come dam near put my light out. Um-m-m! **1900** Willard & Hodler *Powers That Prey* 180: You put his light out all right.…They picked him up croaked. **1903** A.H. Lewis *Lion Inn* 75: Little Enright Peets would up an' blow his youthful light out. **1927** in Hammett *Knockover* 307: Everybody knows you bunk there, and if you go back, it's lights out for yours. **1936** Fellows & Freeman *Big Show* 96 [ref. to 1890's]: Keep your hands up or we'll blow your light out. **1969** R. Beck *Mama Black Widow* 221: I'm gonna' put her light out. **1971** E. Sanders *Family* 405: When interrogating officers suggested that De Carlo…may have been involved in the murder, De Carlo replied, "I got no balls to put anyone's lights out." **1974** Gober *Black Cop* 36: I feel it my duty to be the one that puts that cop's lights out for keeps. **1977** Bunker *Animal Factory* 107: But he knew he had to get off the yard or my partners would turn his lights out.

2. to knock (someone) unconscious. Also vars.

1866 "M. Twain" *Letters from Hawaii* (Dec. 25): And when nobody was looking, he harnessed the provisions and ate up nearly a quarter of a bar'l of bread before the old man caught him, and he had more than two notions to put his lights out. **1899** in Davidson *Old West* 150: Refuse to take a drink with him, and out would go your light. **1903** A.H. Lewis *Boss* 273: They naturally see to it that no one puts his lights out. **1966** R. Anderson *Sand Pebbles* (film): "You ever see a slopehead fight?" "He'd put out your light." **1966** Elli *Riot* 74: Don't talk parole to me. I'll punch your lights out. **1969** B. Beckham *Main Mother* 38: I can put your lights out. **1968–70** *Current Slang III & IV* 98: Punch…lights, v. To fight.—College males, Kansas. **1975** Mahl *Beating Bookie* 46: Our champ might carry his patsy for a few rounds just to get in a bunch of TV commercials before he turns out his light at will. **1975** Wambaugh *Choirboys* 325: I oughtta punch your lights out. **1981** *Penthouse* (Apr.) 200: I wanted to punch his fucking lights out. **1982** E. Leonard *Cat Chaser* 182: I told him it was me almost put out your lights with the one-oh-six. **1982** L. Fleischer *Annie* 138: Mr. Warbucks is gonna knock your lights out! Mr. Warbucks is gonna rearrange your teeth! **1983** in "J.B. Briggs" *Drive-In* 116: Ralphus…knocks out her lights, drags her back to the theater, [etc.]. **1988** Dietl & Gross *One Tough Cop* 16: And before they even knew what hit them, Bo would turn off their lights.

light *adj.* **1.** intoxicated, esp. by drugs; HIGH.

1737 B. Franklin, in *Penn. Gazette* (Jan. 6) 2: He's in Liquor,…Light, Lappy. **1933** Guest *Limey* 35: Get him "light" with a "shot" of morphine and he became a smooth and deadly ruffian. *Ibid.* 37: He was only half-light with a shot o' the junk (dope) he used. **1985** J.M.G. Brown *Rice Paddy Grunt* 180: He was stoned, he was light, he was cool, he was a pleasure to know.

2.a. Orig. *Black E.* short of cash; (*also*) with insufficient money.

1955 in Wepman et al. *The Life* 77: His pockets were light. **1954–60** *DAS*: Light…Lacking a specif. sum of money; owing a specif. sum of money. **1971** *Who Took Weight?* 187: I got two dollars and sixty-five cents, an' you *know* Chill Will ain't lettin' *nobody* cop light. **1972–73** in M.J. Bell *Brown's Lounge* 70: You're a little light and somebody buys you one. **1973** Schiano & Burton *Solo* 83: I'm light.…I've only got two bucks. **1974** E. Thompson *Tattoo* 107: You guys go on. I'm a dime light. **1984** *Miami Vice* (NBC-TV): "How much are you light?" "Six grand."

b. (of money) in small amounts.

1962 Wepman et al. *The Life* 48: I scored some light bread.

3. *Black E.* stupid.

1967 Baraka *Tales* 13: I told you not to take Organic…as light as you are. **1970** Landy *Underground Dict.* 120: Light…Not too smart.

¶ In phrase:

¶ **light in the loafers** [or **on (one's) feet**] (of men) effeminate or homosexual.

[**1967** *DAS* (Supp.): Lightfooted…Homosexual. *Fairly common since c1955.*] **1968–70** *Current Slang III & IV* 79: Light on…feet, adj. Pertaining to effeminacy in a fellow.—College students, both sexes, New Hampshire. **1989** "Capt. X" & Dodson *Unfriendly Skies* 158: "Light in the loafers" will be one slur you'll hear against them [male flight attendants]. **1989** Rock Hudson (ABC-TV): We'd say, "Is he musical?" Never *gay*.…Sometimes "light in the loafers." **1990** *Nat. Lampoon* (Apr.) 6: You're light in the loafers and…cruddy in the bung. **1992** *New Yorker* (July 6) 57: He launches into his light-in-the-loafers Herod [acting role]. **1993** *Mystery Sci. Theater* (Comedy Central TV): A little light in the loafers. **1996** *N.Y. Press* (Feb. 7) 13: The garment business is popularized by citizens who are "light in the loafers."

light *adv.* ¶ In phrase: **take it light** take it easy; calm down; (*hence*, in parting) so long!

1959 W. Bernstein *That Kind of Woman* (film): Take it light. **1974–77** Heinemann *Close Quarters* 35: It'll be right inna coupla minutes. Take it light. **1981** in Safire *Good Word* 83: Take it light. **1988** T. Logan *Harder They Fall* 218: Okay, okay, take it light.

light *v.* **1.** see s.v. LIGHT OUT.

2. see s.v. LIGHT UP, 3.

¶ In phrases:

¶ **light a rag** *So. & West.* LIGHT OUT.

1903 *DN* II 319: *Lit a rag, v. phr.* Humorous for "started suddenly." "He got skeered and *lit a rag* for home." **1919** (quot. at *light a shuck*, below). **1931** *PMLA* XLVI 1304: The dog tuk out after him, an' he lit a rag fer home. **1941** L. Short *Hard* 16: Light a rag then.…Get out.

¶ **light a shuck** *West.* LIGHT OUT.

1905 *DN* III 86: *Light a shuck, v. phr.* To go in a hurry, to move on, to keep away from danger. n.w. Ark. **1915** Raine *Steve Yeager* 72: We'd better light a shuck out of here. **1919** *DN* V 37: *Light a shuck, to, v.phr.* To strike out, in a hurry. "You ought to have seen that jack rabbit *light a shuck* out across the prairie." In Kentucky, "light a rag." **1917–20** J.M. Hunter *Trail Drivers* I 237 [ref. to 1877]: Mr. Withers gave him his time and told him to "light a shuck." **1934** Cunningham *Triggernometry* 25: Bill…"lit a shuck" for Comanche County. **1936** N. Nye *No-Gun Fighter* 176: Light a shuck outa here. **1939** "L. Short" *Bounty Guns* 11: How do you know I wouldn't light a shuck once I had your money. **1947** Overholser *Buckaroo's Code* 19: Time we lit a shuck out of here. **1956** Overholser *Desperate* 40: You'd better light a shuck out of the country. **1958** *Sat. Eve. Post* (Apr. 12) 94: What got into you to light a shuck the way you did? **1969** L'Amour *Conagher* 70: Kris, you pack up and light a shuck. I got no use for a traitor. **1970** Thackrey *Thief* 49: But I tell you I lit a shuck out of there before he could take his second shot. **1978** L'Amour *Proving Trail* 1: Was I you I'd git straddle of that bronc an' light a shuck.

light artillery see s.v. ARTILLERY, 2, 3.

light bird *n.* [LIGHT (COLONEL) + (full) BIRD, 6.b.] *Army.* LIGHT COLONEL.

1974 Former WO, U.S. Army [ref. to 1969]: A *light bird* was a lieutenant colonel. **1975** Former 1Lt., U.S. Army: A *light bird* is a lieutenant colonel. **1982** W.E.B. Griffin *Lieuts.* 119: They don't want twenty-six-year-old light birds, either. **1988** Dye *Outrage* 97: Light bird is definitely gettin' his licks. **1992** N. Russell *Suicide Charlie* 66 [ref. to 1968]: Our local "light bird" (slang for lieutenant colonel) swooped down for a gander.

light bob *n. Army.* a soldier of a regiment of light infantry.

1778 in F. Moore *Songs & Ballads of Revolution* 225: We light bobs are tough and hardy. ***1785** Grose *Vulgar Tongue*: Light Bob. A soldier of the light infantry company. ***1821**, ***1828** in *OED2*.

light colonel *n. Mil.* a lieutenant colonel.

1954 Davis & Lay *SAC* (film): Our aircraft commander'd be a major instead of a light colonel. **1956** Heflin *USAF Dict.* 299: Light colonel. A lieutenant colonel. *Colloq.* **1959** W. Williams *Ada Dallas* 374 [ref. to WWII]: I was a light colonel commanding an infantry battalion. **1961** Coon *Meanwhile at the Front* 180 [ref. to WWII]: I was a light colonel. **1961–63** Drought *Mover* 27: Some fifty-year old drunken light-colonel. **1965** LeMay & Kantor *Mission with LeMay* 136: They are thinking of an organization which puffed like a mushroom overnight, and oozed with majors or light-colonels who had been high school sophomores only a few years before. **1967** "M.T.

Knight" *Terrible Ten* 8: You probably would have been a light colonel by now. **1967** Taggart *Reunion* 140 [ref. to WWII]: A full colonel, a "light" colonel, a major…a captain, and two first lieutenants. **1970** Hersh *My Lai* 95: When we got off the operation, somebody—a colonel or light colonel—asked us if anything out of the ordinary had taken place. **1982** R.A. Anderson *Cooks & Bakers* 144: This place is full of majors and light colonels. **1993** T. Taylor *Lightning in Storm* 460: *LTC.* Lieutenant colonel. Colloquially, "light colonel."

lighten up *v.* to calm down; (*hence,* esp. *imper.*) to go easy; stop (one's interfering or annoying); be less serious or earnest; relax. Cf. earlier S.E. sense 'to remove a burden from, relieve (the heart or mind)', fr. *ca*1430 in *OED2.*

   1946 Rivkin *Till End of Time* (film): When she lightens up she can write me a long letter. **1970** C. Major *Dict. Afro-Amer. Slang* 77: *Lighten up:* a plea for compassion or restraint. **1970** Landy *Underground Dict.* 120: *Lighten up*…Command meaning get off my back, go easy on me. *a*1972 *Urban Life & Culture* I 84: The rowdy dudes who fail to "lighten up" join the ranks of "fuck-ups." **1974** *Police Woman* (NBC-TV): Lighten up, Bobo. That's his mission in life. **1972–76** Durden *No Bugles* 46: That muthaafuckah [*sic*] don't never lighten up.…He's always on somebody's ass. **1976–77** Kernochan *Dry Hustle* 208: Lighten up, now. I'm a skilled laborer like anyone else. **1977** Corder *Citizens Band* 60: Oh, lighten up. **1978** Selby *Requiem* 16: Hey man, lighten up. Whats with you? **1966–80** Folb *Runnin' Some Lines* 245: *Lighten up* 1. Stop. 2. Calm down. **1980** Gould *Ft. Apache* 247: "Hey, man, who you pushin'?"…"Lighten up, man." **1982** Trudeau *Dressed for Failure* (unp.): Hey, hey, lighten up, guy! *a*1988 C. Adams *More Straight Dope* 165: Lighten up, doc. *1995 *Absolutely Fabulous* (BBC-TV): Lighten up, sweetie! Lighten up!…You don't get things done just by being uptight.

light-finger *v.* to steal; pilfer; rob. Cf. earlier S.E. *light-fingered* 'thievish'.

   1956 *Time* (Feb. 13) 32: Juan Perón…anted up a $225 deposit (from the mountain of loot he light-fingered from Argentina's coffers). **1959** Sabre & Eiden *Glory Jumpers* 37: All right, which one of you beetle-headed jokers light-fingered my canteen? **1964** *N.Y. Times* (Dec. 27) VI 35: [He] deftly light-fingered more than $700,000 in diamonds from mansions in Westchester County. **1977** *L.A. Times* (Feb. 9) III 2: While the New Jersey Reds were playing…the Harlem Globetrotters in Mobile, Ala., there [*sic*] were being light-fingered by somebody else in the dressing room.

lighthouse *n.* **1.** *Und.* a lookout or contact man for tramps or criminals; (*specif.*) *Prost.* such a person who procures customers for a brothel.

   1899 Willard *Tramping* 386: "Lighthouse"…means a man who knows every detective of a town by sight, and can "tip them off" to visiting hoboes and criminals. **1912** in Rosen *Lost Sisterhood* 76: [A pimp is] a young man…who after having served a short apprenticeship as a "light house," secures a staff of girls and lives upon their earnings. **1913** Kneeland *Prostitution* 6: A "lighthouse" [is employed] to stand in the street for the purpose of procuring "trade" and to give warning. **1916** Miner *Slavery* 57: The eldest brother…was a "light house," which means that he solicited patronage for a disorderly house. **1921** Woolston *Prostitution* I 99: A regular "light-house," or lookout man,…steered visitors into the resorts and warned the inmates of the appearance of the police. **1927** *AS* (June) 385: A *lighthouse* was a vag who knew all the ropes in a particular territory and tipped off the visiting vag regarding rocks and shoals.

   2. *Naut.* a salt or pepper shaker, or small vinegar bottle, fancied to resemble a lighthouse in shape.

   *1909 Ware *Passing Eng.* 168: *Light-house* (Navy). Pepper-castor. **1918** Kauffman *Our Navy at Work* 6: "Put a fair wind behind the lighthouse"…means…"pass the salt-cellar." **1922** *Leatherneck* (Apr. 29) 5: *Light House*—Vinegar. From the shape of the regular vinegar bottle. **1941** Kendall *Army & Navy Sl.* 9: *Lighthouses*.…salt and pepper shakers. **1945** *Sat. Review* (Nov. 24) 14: *Lighthouses:* salt and pepper. **1965** E. Hall *Flotsam* 311 [ref. to 1910]: The salt and pepper shakers on the mess-room table were called lighthouses.

lightly *adv.* ¶ In phrase: **lightly and politely** (see 1964 quot.).

   1933 Martin *International House* (film): Now pat that thing slightly, lightly and politely. **1939** in Gold *Jazz Talk*: Louis Armstrong somewhere says, "lightly, and politely." **1961** in Gold *Jazz Lexicon*: "Lightly and po-lightly!" Red exclaimed. **1964** Gold *Jazz Lexicon: Lightly and

politely: (from rhyming slang vogue c. 1935–c. 1940, very rare since.) Neatly, "niftily," effortlessly, smoothly, satisfactorily (done).

lightning *n.* **1.a.** gin, corn whiskey, or other strong, esp. illicitly distilled, liquor; white lightning. Also **liquid lightning.** See also JERSEY LIGHTNING.

   *1789 G. Parker *Life's Painter* 137: We'll give you a *noggin* of *lightning. Ibid.* 140: *Noggin of lightning,* a quartern of gin. *Ibid.* 184: *Lightning* is gin. *1796 Grose *Vulgar Tongue* (ed. 3): *Lightning.* Gin. **1842** C. Mathews *Puffer Hopkins* 272: Decatur was struck in the pit of his stomach with a couple of quarts of lightning. **1844** *Davy Crockett's Almanac* (unp.): So I jist gin him a snifter o' liquid lightnin'. **1858** in *DA:* A few kegs of liquid lightning. **1863** in *DA:* A disproportionately large stock of "lightning whisky." **1873** Miller *Modocs* 164: All ranged themselves…before the bar, calling out "Cocktail," "Tom-and-Jerry," "Brandy-smash," "Gin-sling," "Lightning straight," "Forty rod," and so on. **1876** in Hearn *Amer. Misc.* I 189: Lightning whisky. **1877** in Asbury *Gem of Prairie* (opp. 136): Do you soak your feet in the old guy's barrel of lightning? **1936** in Himes *Black on Black* 129: Every other door opened into a cathouse or a lightning joint. **1941** Kendall *Army & Navy Sl.* 21: *Liquid lightning.*…Okulehau.…sugar cane and rice beverage made in Hawaii. Three drinks makes you wicky wacky better than a native. **1949** in *DA:* Believe I'll have a slight stroke of that Old Lightning. **1959** Horan *Mob's Man* 51: He gave me the secret of how to make a powerful drink called "Lightning." **1975** McCaig *Danger Trail* 29: They took also a few jugs of Benton lightning.

   b. *Narc.* (applied to strongly stimulating drugs).

   1977 (cited in Spears *Drugs & Drink*) [as 'amphetamines']. **1990** T. Thorne *Dict. Contemp. Sl.:* *Lightning*…another name for the drug *crack.*

   2.a. (*cap.*) a telegraph operator.—used as a nickname.

   1867 Duke *Morgan's Cavalry* 185 [ref. to Civil War]: Mr. Ellsworth (popularly known as "Lightning"), the telegraphic operator on Colonel Morgan's staff.

   b. a telegraph.—usu. in combinations, for which see LIGHTNING JERKER and following forms.

   1880 Pinkerton *Prof. Thieves & Detective* 193: Corrupt manipulators of the "lightning" grew rich upon the spoils.

   3. anything or any person that is formidable or extremely difficult; DYNAMITE, 1.—also constr. with *old.* Cf. the adj.

   1867 in McClure *Rocky Mtns.* 133: But never scare!…they're "lightnin'" when you scare! **1867** in W.H. Jackson *Diaries* 180: Creek not fordable.…Went down & up steep hills that were just "lightning." **1873** G. Custer *Life on Plains* 193: I hed a kind of sneaking notion then that he'd hurt somebody ef they ever turned him loose. Lord, but ain't he old lightnin'?

   4.a. electric current.

   1889 "M. Twain" *Conn. Yankee* 561: Why not take the lightning off the outer fences, and give them a chance?

   b. *USAF Acad.* the study of electrical engineering.

   1969 *Current Slang I & II* 59: *Lightning,* n. Electrical engineering.—Air Force Academy cadets.

¶ In phrases:

¶ **Jersey lightning** see JERSEY LIGHTNING.

¶ **ride the lightning** *Pris.* to be executed in the electric chair.

   1935 *Journ. Socio. & Abn. Psych.* XXX 364: *Ride the lightning*—to be electrocuted. **1964** in L. Bruce *Essent. Bruce* 273: *All Right Ruby, You's Gonna Ride the Lightning!* **1977** *Nat. Lampoon* (July) 21: Bobby gets ready to "ride the lightnin'" into the afterlife. **1995** *Jake Lassiter: Justice on Bayou* (TV movie): He's gonna ride the lightning.…We still use the electric chair in Louisiana.

lightning *adj.* **1.** extraordinary; exceptionally skilled. Also as adv.

   1867 in *DA:* Ball's "lightning" pitching…was something they were not posted in. **1875** "M. Twain" *Old Times* 57 [ref. to *ca*1860]: By the Shadow of Death, but he's a lightning pilot! **1880** Pilgrim *Old Nick's Camp Meetin'* 26: He's just lightning, he is. **1899** Hamblen *Bucko Mate* 26: I tole 'im w'at a lightnin' smart rooster you are. **1934** Cunningham *Triggernometry* 5: Man! but he's a lightning gunfighter! **1982** E. Abel *Maribuana Dict.* 63: *Lightning Hashish.* Potent hashish used by dealers for their own personal enjoyment. **1983** Curry *River's in My Blood* 77: Determined to make a "lightning clerk" out of young Fred Way.

   2. great fun; very enjoyable.

   1867 A.D. Richardson *Beyond Miss.* 484: We found the cold intolerable; but the cheery drivers merely remarked that this was "lightning."

lightning jerker *n.* a telegrapher.
  1891 Maitland *Slang Dict.* 167: *Lightning jerker,* a telegraph operator. **1907** *Army & Navy Life* (Dec.) 253: If I die he'll be stuck for a lightning jerker. **1919** Darling *Jargon Book* 21: *Lightning Jerker*—A telegraph operator. **1936** Mulholland *Splinter Fleet* 118 [ref. to 1918]: The radio operator on watch, sometimes called the "Lightning Jerker," quits fussing with the new inductance coil he's winding and tunes his receiver a little finer. *1945 S.J. Baker *Australian Lang.* 249: *Lightning jerker* or *lightning squirter,* a telegraph operator.

lightning rod *n.* **1.** *Mil.* a sword. *Joc.*
  1863 in C. Boyd *Diary* 119: "Provosts" came down to near where I was with their "lightning rods" up.
  2. *Army.* (see quot.).
  1917 *Editor* (Jan. 13) 33: "Doughboys"—Infantry. "Lightning rods"—Signal Corps. "Pill rollers"—Hospital Corps.
  3. (see quot.).
  1954–60 *DAS: Lightning rod* A jet fighter plane. *Some Air Force use.*

lightning shover *n.* *R.R.* a telegrapher. Later also **lightning slinger.**
  1871 Crofutt *Tourist's Guide* 141: Telegraph operators are called "lightning shovers." **1938** Beebe *High Iron* 222: *Lightning slinger:* Telegrapher. **1941** in Fenner *Throttle* 170: This is the tramp lightning slinger what caused our accident. **1945** Hubbard *R.R. Ave.* 281: R.L. Metcalfe...was a Santa Fe lightning slinger and agent at Skull Valley, Ariz.

lightning stock *n.* *West.* a rifle.
  1850 Garrard *Wah-to-Yah* 238: Ef you're here for b'ar, grab your lightnin'-stock (my rifle) and make "Pimo" tracks for yon butte.

lightning striker *n.* a formidable or impressive thing.
  1867 in W.H. Jackson *Diaries* 185: Took the steep hill...& a "lightning striker" it was too. **1885** Siringo *Texas Cowboy* 82: My intention was to...make a race horse out of him; he was only three years old and according to my views a "lightning striker."

lightning water *n.* strong whiskey; FIREWATER, 1.
  1845 in Leach *Texan* 22: I...can swoller a Lake Superior o' lightnin' water, meanin' whiskey, in a superior fashion. **1971** Wells & Dance *Night People* 96: One thing about Ol' Man Ignorant Oil, alias Bug Juice, alias John Barleycorn, alias Lightning Water, alias Red Eye, alias Fire Water—he sends you a lot of messages.

light out *v.* *So. & West.* to hurry off; clear out. Now *colloq.* Also **light.** [Early quots. ref. to Civil War.]
  1865 J. Pike *Scout & Ranger* 268: I "lit out" amid the...confusion. **1866** E.C. Downs *Scout & Spy* 321: I told the boys to "light out." **1870** Keim *Sheridan's Troopers* 65: We mounted and "lit out," as rapid locomotion is called in that locality. **1866–71** Bagg *Yale* 45: *Light out,* to hurry away, make one's self scarce. **1873** in *DAE:* The young man thereupon could not wait but lit out. **1877–78** *Cornelian* 86: *Light Out.* To exit. **1878** R. Wheeler *On Deck* 8: Ye had a pard...who stole a haul o' money and lit out for parts unknown. **1882** *Judge* (Oct. 28) 7: Then me an Muggsy Lit Out. **1882** *N & Q* (Ser. 6) V 65: Words and Phrases in Use in the Far West...*Light out,*...to leave secretly and hastily, as when pursued by an enemy. **1884** Beard *Bristling with Thorns* 23: "When'd he git?" "Dun'o. He's lit fo' sho'." **1884** "M. Twain" *Huck. Finn* ch. i [ref. to 1850's]: And so when I couldn't stand it no longer, I lit out. **1885** Ingraham *Buffalo Bill's Grip* 11: I'd hev gone ther same way ef I hadn't lit out. **1888** Gunter *Miss Nobody* 34: Light out as if hell was behind you! **1890** E. Custer *Guidon* 282: He will "light out" for civil life soon. **1890** in *F & H* IV 194: I wawnt to...light right out o' here and get back West again. **1908** Raine *Wyoming* 246: I...lit out kinder unceremonious. **1917–20** in J.M. Hunter *Trail* 231: We left the Lockhart pasture about the first of April, took the Chisholm Trail and "lit out." **1925** in *DA:* I lit out for camp as if all the animals in the forest were after me. **1928** Z. Grey *Stairs* 21: Take a canteen and some grub and light out. **1941** Haycox *Trail* 131: So I lit out. **1945** in Bradbury *Golden Apples* 84: Jimmy lit out for first base. **1954–60** *DAS: Light...*To depart, esp. rapidly. See *light out.* **1963** L'Amour *Sackett* 87: My advice is to light out. **1978** Evans *Longarm* 76: He's either lit out for good, or he wants us to think he's lit out for good.

light piece *n.* *Hobo.* a dime or quarter.
  1897 (quot. at FLY, *n.*). **1907** London *Road* 62 [ref. to *ca*1894]: You see, I was trying delicately to hit them for a "light piece." **1926** *AS* I (Dec.) 652: *Light pieces*—quarter of a dollar. **1927** *AS* (June) 385: A *light-piece*...was a piece of silver money; probably because of its color.

lights-out *adj.* dazzling.
  1981 D. Jenkins *Baja Okla.* 75: Her shape...was..."just fuckin' lights-out."

light up *v.* **1.** to light a cigarette. Now *colloq.*
  ***1861** in *OED2:* "I suppose I may light up," said Drysdayle...pulling out his cigar-case. **1933** Farrell *McGinty* 3: He and Komoroski...hastily lit up.
  b. *Narc.* to take cocaine; (*also*) to give drugs to.
  1922 Murphy *Black Candle* 228: A soldier-fellow whom I know boasts that he was in jail for a month and "lit up" every day....[On his person] he carries his supply against emergencies. *a*1990 E. Currie *Dope & Trouble* 250: We started lighting each other up...[sniffing] coke.
  c. to light and (by implication) smoke a marijuana cigarette, crack pipe, or the like.
  1938 Calloway *Hi De Ho* 16: *Light up:* to smoke a reefer or weed. **1946** Mezzrow & Wolfe *Really Blues* 53: He'd light up and get real high...groovy as a ten-cent movie. **1948** Schwartz *Blowtop* 18: As soon as Phil leaves, I light up. **1952** Kerouac *Cody* 123: So we go on over there, and we lit up. **1952** Mandel *Angry Strangers* 191: Come on, Buster, light up; let's get on. **1958–59** Lipton *Barbarians* 172: Before I light up I'm drug with...ten thousand things. **1964** Smith & Hoefer *Music* 200: You are bound to run up with sidemen who light up.*...*Smoke marijuana. **1994** Smitherman *Black Talk* 153: *Light up...*To light a marijuana cigarette or crack pipe.
  2.a. to fire a gun.
  1953–55 Fine *Delinquents* 93: I stole my first Pistol....I told the other three to move away from me because I was going to light up.
  b. Esp. *Mil.* to kill or destroy by gunfire; shoot at; bombard; riddle with bullets.
  1966–67 P. Thomas *Mean Streets* 25 [ref. to 1950's]: Light him up like Scarface in that gangster picture. *Ibid.* 223: Don't come any closer or you'll get lit up. **1971** Glasser *365 Days* 70: Any way you move they can light you up. *Ibid.* 131: Two Dust Offs got lit up trying to get into the LZ. **1975** S.P. Smith *Amer. Boys* 272: Okay, Four-two,...let's light up the back of the valley....You fire the rockets, Mr. Woolsey. **1972–76** Durden *No Bugles* 73: We should light up Hanoi with A-bombs. **1977** Natkin & Furie *Boys in Co. C* (film): That is a VC village and we're gonna light it up like the 4th of July. **1981** *Magnum, P.I.* (CBS-TV): The LZ was north of the paddy. That's where Froggy got lit up. **1983** E. Dodge *Dau* 132: Anyway, we make a lot of noise coming in to the perimeter so they won't light us up. **1984–87** Ferrandino *Firefight* 17: Those fuckers up there will light us up sure as shit. **1994** in C. Long *Love Awaits* 6: Whitey would have said fuck and lit the car up. **1996** *MI v. Younes* (Court TV) (Apr. 1): I'm gonna take my shotgun and light that house up!
  c. to strike or attack; thrash; ambush.—also used fig.
  1972 Claerbaut *Black Jargon* 71: *Light up...*to hit someone, strike: *I'll light up the cat.* **1973** "A.C. Clark" *Crime Partners* 31: I'm going to take your badge number and see to it that your fuckin' ass is lit up for this shit you tried to pull on me back there. **1974** R.H. Carter *16th Round* 328: The rest of the inmates vamped down on him and lit his stupid ass up. **1972–76** Durden *No Bugles* 72 [ref. to Vietnam War]: If we git lit up 'n' we need you, you goan be there? **1983** *Reader's Digest Success with Words* 87: Black English...*light up (someone)* = "to hit or strike." **1994** Smitherman *Black Talk* 155: Michael Jordan lit up the Knicks for 54.
  3. Orig. *Mil. Av.* to start (a jet or rocket engine); arm (a guided missile); (*broadly*) to start an engine of any sort.—also used absol. Also **light.**
  1956 Heflin *USAF Dict.: Light,...*To start a *jet engine. Slang.* **1955** R.L. Scott *Look of Eagle* 67: But we'll watch the fuel mighty close nevertheless. Let's light 'em up. **1988** M. Maloney *Thunder Alley* 358: Light our Sidewinders....Give me a reading on the lead jet. **1992** D. Burke *Street Talk* I 121: *Light it up...*(among car aficionados) to light the engine. **1995** Gingrich & Forstchen *1945* 371: Have the test pilots power down the Merlins before lighting up. **1996** *JAG* (NBC-TV): Light 'em up.
  4. to arouse sexually.
  1968 R. Beck *Trick Baby* 137: I got my money's worth after I lit her up.

lightweight *n.* an inconsequential, unsuccessful, unimpressive, or unintelligent person. Now *colloq.*
  1878 *Annals of the War* 508: They were both "light weights" in their profession [as spies]. ***1885** in *OED2:* I am not good at these high pas-

sions!…In everything I am a light weight. **1896** in J.M. Carroll *Benteen-Goldin Lets.* 298: Hughes didn't care to measure pens with such a lightweight. **1906–07** Ade *Slim Princess* 77: Then you'll see that you're not wasting your time on a light-weight. **1925** Van Vechten *Nigger Heaven* 266: Oh, you're good-looking enough, but just a light-weight, after all. **1929** in Hammett *Knockover* 37: Pop off, you lightweight, or I will. **1940** O'Hara *Pal Joey* 65: "What is he your cousin?" said one of the lightweights in the band. **1968–70** *Current Slang III & IV* 79: *Light-weight*, n. A person with low intelligence. **1966–80** Folb *Runnin' Some Lines* 245: *Lightweight* 1. One who lacks prominence or credibility. 2. One with little or no knowledge of the streets. **1982** P. Newman, in *Time* (Dec. 6) 71: He always thought of as pretty much of a lightweight. **1986** P. Markle *Youngblood* (film): "Lightweight!" "Learn to take a drink, man."

lightweight *adj.* minor; trivial; unimpressive; second-class. Also as quasi-adv. Now *S.E.*

*1809 in *OED2*: May we not see in them the handwriting on the wall,…the end of the government of light-weight princes? **1891** Maitland *Slang Dict.* 167: *Light-weight*, of little importance, weak. *a*1890–96 F & H IV 197: *Light-weight*…American.…Of little importance; weak. **1941** H. Gray *Arf* (Mar. 24) (unp.): Light-weight, two-for-a-nickel windbags…blowin' off their yaps. **1966** (quot. at SHUCK). **1966** (quot. at SKINS). **1970** A. Young *Snakes* 55: The mention of his name was enough to throw her into a lightweight bind. **1974** V. Smith *Jones Men* 11: Compared to Joe's, this thing ain't nothing. This lightweight. **1975** Wambaugh *Choirboys* 220: "You sick?"…"Lightweight, lightweight," the hype said, wiping his eyes and nose on his shoulder. **1976** Braly *False Starts* 355: "A violation." "That's lightweight. What're your charges?" **1990** *New Republic* (Oct. 8) 30: All Nichols needs is a lightweight script, and he can soar.

like *n.* ¶ In phrase: **in like** mildly attracted to someone in a romantic way but not in love with that person. Cf. *in lust* s.v. LUST.

1973 N.Y.U. student: We are very definitely in *like*. **1981** B. Schneider *Take This Job* (film): We are very definitely in like.

like *adv.* [extensively discussed in R. Underhill, "*Like* is, Like, Focus," *AS* LXIII (1988) 234–46] **1.** in a way; so to speak; more or less.—used postpositively. [Equivalent to *-like* (suff.) in OED defs. 2a, 2b.; orig. colloq., now often regarded as rhetorically indistinguishable from **(3)**, below.]

*1778 F. Burney, in *OED2*: Father grew quite uneasy, like, for fear of his Lordship's taking offense. *1801 Sir W. Scott, in *OED2*: Of a sudden like. **1829** J. Hall *Winter Eves.* 8: *Jist* give us a *small idee*, a bit of a *hint like*, where you are going. **1843** in *DARE* s.v. *like* G.a.: Turn to the left, but not quite—'cos the path goes to the rite [*sic*] like. **1867** in Rosa *Wild Bill* 61: So we went out onto a little island which was neutral ground like. **1867** "M. Twain," in *DARE* s.v. *-like suff.* 1.: She'd get excited and desperate-like. **1881** in A.E. Turner *Earps Talk* 63: Mr. Earp raised his left hand or fist-like, and run it into Tom McLowery's face. *1917–18 in W. Owen *Coll. Poems* 71: T' other was 'urt, like, losin' both 'is props. **1923** in W.F. Nolan *Black Mask Boys* 61: Then I lift my hand cautiously like and signal him. **1926** Furfey *Gang Age* 58: In reporting the dream he called it a "revolution, like." **1927** "S.S. Van Dine" *"Canary" Murder* ch. xxiv: Then it hit me sudden-like, and the whole case broke wide upon. **1931** *AS* (Oct.) 92: Ellen has got sich a friendly-like turn about her house that folks love to go there. *Ibid.* 93: Hit were a lonesome-like tune. **1952** Mandel *Angry Strangers* 87: I like to send Edna a little gift-like. Lemme surprise her-like; you know? *Ibid.* 118: I gotta get over somewhere-like. **1954** *Time* (Nov. 8) 70: *Like, interj.* Filler word for pauses of uncertainty, e.g., "You wanna hear some jazz, like?" **1955** *AS* XXX 304: A real gas, like. **1956** in *DAS* 319: When he dies, I'll be robbed like. I'll have no more father. **1986** *NDAS* 259: Like I was like groovin' like, you know? **1995** Univ. Tenn. prof., age 46: He was running around all crazy like.

2. just about; almost; approximately. [Orig. colloq., now partially subsumed into **(3)**, below.]

1942 *New Yorker* (Nov. 14) 22: You could hardly figure out who was right becoss like everybody in it said everybody got rights. **1962** N.Y.C. high school student: I got like fifteen minutes to get to class. **1970** C. Major *Dict. Afro-Amer. Sl.* 77: Man, I was out in Wyoming, like two years. *a*1975 *Doubleday Dict.* 416: We had like two weeks to get ready. **1988** *AS* LXIII 235: It's like six or seven at night. **1990** P. Munro *Slang U.* 122: My tie only cost like ten dollars. **1993** Knoxville, Tenn., woman, age *ca*40: It's only got like twenty thousand miles on it.

1994 *My So-Called Life* (ABC-TV): I've said like eight sentences to you in my entire *life!* **1995** TV ad for Dove Beauty Bar: I haven't seen my college girlfriends in like five years! **1995** *TV Guide* (Dec. 9) 22: My mom was standing like three feet away.

3. (used as an interjection chiefly to introduce or call attention to the following clause); (*also*) (used elsewhere in an utterance to express tentativeness or emphasis as suggested by tone of voice or context, or else as a nearly meaningless filler). [In orig. perh. merely indicating uncertainty in the middle of a thought; affected as slang only from the early 1950's, when popularly assoc. with jazz musicians, later with beatniks, hippies, and teenagers.]

1950 *Neurotica* (Autumn) 45: Like how much can you lay on me? **1952** Mandel *Angry Strangers* 29: Like—I'm diggin' a lot of Armstrong, 'cause he's the man. *Ibid.* 88: That's like a different kind of name. *Ibid.* 117: Like—why doncha wait for me, doll? Like—it's the way to smoke jive. **1954** in R.S. Gold *Jazz Talk* 167: He flipped, or as he put it later, he like flipped. **1955** *AS* XXX 304: Like, we was up in this freak's pad, man.…We told her, like, that it interfered with our introspection, man. **1953–58** J.C. Holmes *Horn* 189: Like, listen, can't you cats keep it down! **1958** in Hogan & German *Chronicle Reader* 48: Like WOW, man! Gone! **1958** *PADS* (No. 30) 42: *Like* is becoming the most commonly used word in some [jazz] men's speech, used as a sort of filler, instead of "uh," in sentences such as, "Like he blows real cute, like," or "Let's go and dig like some real music, you know?" ("You know" is a common filler too.). **1954–60** *DAS* 319: "It's like cold" = it is cold. *Used by jazz, beat, and cool groups, esp. in New York City.* **1965** S.J. Perelman, in *New Yorker* (Aug. 28) 29: She turns strong men to like stone. **1970** *Time* (Aug. 17) 32: Even "like"—as in "like you know how it is, man" is on the blacklist [as an obsolete expression]. **1972** Claerbaut *Black Jargon* 71: *Like man* used as a form of punctuation or as an exclamation: *Like man, it's out of sight.* **1973–76** J. Allen *Assault* 9: Man, like what happened? **1982** Pond *Valley Girls' Guide* 59: *Like*—What you say when you're like, um, attaching one word to another, in a, like, sentence. **1986** Univ. Tenn. student theme [ref. to 1984]: Every sentence began with "like" and ended with "awesome."—"Like that dude is totally awesome."…"Wow, like that food is good to the max." **1987** Univ. Tenn. student theme: I was sitting there and like this nerd he like sits next to me and like I thought I was going to die! **1989** Pini *Portrait of Love* (unp.): Father and Vincent want us to bring Catherine…like now! **1991** Landau & Ison *Don't Tell Mom* (film): Isn't your mom like leaving for like months? **1993** *New Yorker* (May 17) 108: Like, wow. **1993** P. Munro *U.C.L.A. Slang II* 56: Like what's the tape recorder for?…And like I have this paper to write by Monday, the day of my like Bio exam! **1994** *TV Guide* (July 23) 3: Rob Estes…is, like, Hunk City! **1995** *My So-Called Life* (ABC-TV): "Yeah, in some imaginary universe that exists like in my mind."…"I've been like really busy. I'm carrying like a triple minor."…"So you like asked her to the dance."

¶ In phrases:

¶ **be like** Esp. *Stu.* (in introducing direct or reported speech) to think or say. Now *colloq.* [Extensively discussed in Blyth et al., "I'm Like, 'Say What?!': A New Quotative in American Oral Narrative," *AS* LXV 3 (Fall 1990) 215–227; and in Ferrara & Bell, "Sociolinguistic Variation and Discourse Function of Constructed Dialogue Introducers: The Case of *be + like*," *AS* LXX 265–90.]

1982 F. Zappa *Valley Girl* (pop. song): She's like "*Oh my God*," like "*Bag those toenails*." **1982** S. Black *Totally Awesome Val Gde.* 18: I'd be like, "Oh m'God!…I can't handle this!" **1982** *AS* LVII 149: Many speakers who use narrative *go* also have a narrative use of *to be* (usually followed by *like*) where what is being quoted is an unuttered thought, as in *And he was like "Let me say something."* **1982** in Goodwin *More Man* 45: And she was like, "You mean you don't have to go home and fix dinner?" **1984** L.I., N.Y., high school student: I was like, "So what?" And then he was like, "What's the matter with *you*?" *1987 *Tracey Ullman Show* (Fox-TV): In England, they're sort of like, "For God's sake, get out of those things!" *a*1988 D. Smith *Firefighters* 159: When she…saw the commotion, she was like, uh-oh. **1988** R. Menlo & R. Rubin *Tougher Than Leather* (film): [She's] suckin' harder and harder—I'm like, *yeah!* **1992** in *AS* LXX 282: I was like, "Ahhggh." **1992** *Amer. Detective* (ABC-TV): We're like, "She went into the bathroom to take a bath." **1994** *N.Y. Times* (May 3) A16: We were in here talking, and she was like, "I'm not getting that mess in my arm." **1995** AT&T ad, in *AS* LXX 287: I'm like, "This is hard work!" **1996** *Harper's* (July) 31: Clare is like, "I'm sorry, Kelly."

¶ **how do you like them apples?** see s.v. APPLE. [The following citations provide additional evidence for the term.]

　1950 Shulman *Dobie Gillis* 177: How do you like them apples, kid? **1957** Herber *Tomorrow to Live* 263 [ref. to WWII]: "How do you like them apples?" he crowed. **1971** McDonald's ad (WNEW-TV): How about them apples, Captain?

Li'l Abners *n.pl.* [sugg. by the oversized brogans worn by *Li'l Abner*, a comic strip character introduced (1934) by cartoonist Al Capp] heavy work shoes; (*esp.*) (among WACs) army field shoes.—also used attrib.

　1943 Hersey *G.I. Laughs* 73: Fifty Bucks per and Lil' Abner Shoes. **1944** *N.Y. Times Mag.* (Sept. 17): *Li'l Abners*—Wac ankle-high field and hiking shoes. **1944** Kendall *Service Slang* 10: *Li'l Abners*...army shoes, also [called] groundhogs or bundockers. **1952** Englund *Never Wave at a WAC* (film): Wait a minute! You forgot your Li'l Abners. **1957** *Sat. Eve. Post* (July 6) 66: Gloves, stockings, one pair of heavy-duty shoes, known as "Li'l Abners," and two pairs of dress oxfords. **1959** *Time* (Nov. 30) 15: Heavy woolen socks, rubberized boots (called Li'l Abners), [etc.]. **1983** Sturz *Wid. Circles* 16: Lil Abner construction boots, French cut shirt. **1985** Westin *Love & Glory* 225 [ref. to WWII]: Up at 4:30, stumble into my fatigue dress and Li'l Abner boots. *Ibid.* 416: They'd have to make do with their Class-A service shoes when their Li'l Abners fell apart. *a***1990** Bérubé *Coming Out* 56 [ref. to WWII]: There were all these dykes...in fatigues with Li'l Abner boots.

lilacs *n.pl.* comparatively full side whiskers. Now *hist.*

　*ca***1919** Sandburg *Smoke and Steel* 20: They were calling certain styles of whiskers by the name of "lilacs." **1952** Sandburg *Strangers* 125 [ref. to *ca*1880]: You could tell he kept his sideburns thin because he didn't care for the side whiskers that stuck out and the boys called "lilacs."

lily *n.* **1.a.** a black person.

　1823 J.F. Cooper *Pilot* 278: Come, my lilies! let these two gentlemen look into your cabin-windows.

　b. *Black E.* a white person.

　1967 Ragni & Rado *Hair* 135: My Mother Calls 'Em Lilies. **1967–80** Folb *Runnin' Some Lines* 245: *Lily* White person.

2. an effeminate boy or homosexual man; PANSY; SISSY.—usu. used derisively. Also (*joc. & obs.*) **lily of the valley** [or **alley**].

　1898 F. Norris *Moran* 36: There's your fit-out, Mister Lillee of the Vallee. *****1921** in *OED2*: But in order once more to consider and console that lily, the Educational Expert, let us turn to "grind." **1927–28** in R. Nelson *Dishonorable* 216: Afraid o' two newspapers and the lilly vote? **1929** Springs *Carol Banks* 197: They weren't lilies of the alley. They didn't look around, and they were dressed quietly in very good taste. **1933** Ersine *Prison Slang* 51: *Lilly*...An effeminate man. **1935** *Amer. Mercury* (June) 230: *Lily:* homosexual. **1940** (quot. at NANCY). **1943** *School & Soc.* LVIII 169: *Lily:* someone who is afraid of things. **1943** Seaton *Coney Island* (film): What did you say about bricklayers? They're a "bunch of lilies," eh? **1965** *Time* (Mar. 5) 44: For them, a lily is a homosexual. **1968** Baker et al. *CUSS:* *Lilly.* An effeminate male. **1971** Merrick *One for Gods* 180: "Well, a couple of lilies," one of them said. *****1990** T. Thorne *Dict. Contemp. Sl.:* *Lily*...an effeminate male, sissy.

3. a fine specimen of a given kind; DANDY, 2; LULU. Also **lil.**

　1899 in Ade *Chicago Stories* 249: The head was a lily. **1923** in Eckstorm & Smyth *Minstrelsy of Me.* 149: He's a Lilly Picadilly, Sure t'ing! **1923** Revell *Off the Chest* 219: I gotta book here that'll knock you right off the Ostermoor. It's a *lil.* **1929–31** Runyon *Guys & Dolls* 108: Dolores is a lily for looks. **1934** W. Smith *B. Cotter* 44: Well, some of these customers are no lilies. **1938–40** W. Clark *Ox-Bow* 121: You've been a lily since this started, Croft. **1952** in *DAS* 319: I told my best joke...it's never missed, a real lily.

4. usu. *pl.* a (white person's) hand. Also **lily-presser** a handshaker. Cf. LILY-WHITE, 1.a.

　1917 (quot. at MITT-WOBBLER). **1927** *DN* V 454: *Lilies,* n. The hands. "I butchered wood all day and dug the splinters out of me *lilies* fer a week after." **1930** Irwin *Tramp & Und. Sl.:* *Lilies.*—The hands.

5. a livid bruise; (*also*) a brickbat. [Quots. ref. to 1918.]

　1925 Nason *Three Lights* 29: You're tired and all that, but don't blackguard this outfit or I'll hang a lily on your nose myself! **1928–29** Nason *White Slicker* 146: Let's fade before they throw a lily at us!

6.a. a virgin.

　1928 Dahlberg *Bottom Dogs* 264: Anyhow, he always said, she sure was one peach of a lily. **1932** Nicholson & Robinson *Sailor, Beware!* 49: BARNEY...They say she's a lilly. CHET (*Incredulously.*) A virgin! BARNEY. Yeah! Can y'imagine that?

　b. *Und.* a naive or innocent person.

　1929 Hostetter & Beesley *Racket!* 231: *Lily,* an easy victim, exceptionally gullible person.

7. *Gamb.* (see quot.).

　1935 Pollock *Underworld Speaks:* *Lilly* [*sic*], a queen (playing cards).

8. the penis.—usu. used in phr. ref. to urination or masturbation.—usu. considered vulgar.

　1942 in Legman *Limerick* 131: A hermit who lived on St. Roque/Had a lily perfected to poke. **1966** IUFA *Folk Speech:* I'm going to go drain my lily. **1970** in *Western Folklore* (Jan. 1971) 49: According to San Francisco police, overt masturbation by exhibitionists is termed "waving the lily." **1974** E. Thompson *Tattoo* 203: "Rise up a little, pud, you're bending my lily." Nina lifted herself up. **1990** P. Munro *Slang U.* s.v. *knock:* Knock the dew off the lily...to urinate (of a male). **1996** *Mystery Sci. Theater* (Comedy Central TV): Ow! Rope burns on the lily!

9. *Bowling.* a 5-7-10 split.

　1949 Cummings *Dict. Sports* 251. **1979** Cuddon *Dict. Sports & Games* 513.

Lily Law *n. Homosex.* a policeman; the police.—used derisively. Also **Lilly Law.**

　1949 *Gay Girl's Guide* 12: *Lily:*...a policeman. Often, *Lily Law* (especially in plural). **1960** Kirkwood *Pony* 220: "Not with Lilly Law lookin' on," she said, indicating the cops. **1967** Crowley *Boys in the Band* 833: Oh my God, it's Lily Law! Everybody three feet apart! **1972** *Anthro. Linguistics* (Mar.) 104: *Lily Law* (n.): The police.

lily-livered *adj.* cowardly; pusillanimous. [Hist. S.E. (sugg. by earlier *white-livered*), but long avoided in serious prose; as in *a*1974 quot., retains some standard currency in elevated poetic diction.]

　*****1605–06** Shakespeare *King Lear* (Quarto) sc. 7: A knaue; a rascall,...a lilly lyuer'd, action taking knaue, a whorson...rogue...and the sonne and heire of a mungrell bitch. **ca***1606** Shakespeare *Macbeth* V iii: Go pricke thy face, and ouer-red thy feare/Thou Lilly-liuer'd Boy. *****1857** A. Trollope, in *F & H* IV 197: You will not be so lily-livered as to fall into this trap which he has baited for you. **1942** *ATS* 303: Cowardly...gutless,...lily-livered. **1948** Beath *F. Feboldson* 122: Febold ain't no lily-livered cake-eater. **1958** W. Henry *Seven Men* 80: You know what old John said to those lily-livered stockholders? *a***1974** R. Fitzgerald *Iliad* 21: How lily-livered I should be called,/if I knuckled under to all you do or say! **1975** Julien *Cogburn* 30: Them lily-livered lawbookers ain't gonna risk their necks. **1981** Doss *Survival* 21: Bunch of weak-kneed, lily-livered pups. Haven't got the strength of your dear old granny. **1988** J. Heller *Picture This* 91: Cleon labeled him lily-livered,...a bleeding heart, and a knee-jerk liberal. **1989** *Mystery Sci. Theater* (Comedy Central TV): Why, you lily-livered, flea-bitten federal boys! **1996** *Good Morning America* (ABC-TV) (Mar. 27): It just plays into the image of lily-livered liberals. **1996** Juhl et al. *Muppet Treasure Island* (film): Mewling little lily-livered wuss of a crustacean!

lily white *n.* **1.a.** usu. *pl.* a hand (of a white person).

　1935 Pollock *Und. Speaks: Lilly white,* the hand. *ca***1940** in Botkin *Treas. Amer. Folk.* 532: Just lay your lily whites on some of them brick, slap 'em down on that there sand. **1978** Diehl *Sharky's Machine* 215: No powder burns on your lily whites, is there? *****1979** "J. Gash" *Grail Tree* 31: Right from the artist's lily-whites into your very own.

　b. the rump (of a white person).

　1944 Kendall *Service Slang* 57: *Dunk the lilywhite*....take a shower.

2. *pl. Black E.* bedsheets.

　[**1946** Boulware *Jive & Slang* 8: *White Lilies*...Sheets.] **1946** Mezzrow & Wolfe *Really the Blues* 92: To stash my frame between a deuce of lilywhites. **1953** in *Tenn. Folk. Soc. Bull.* XXII (1956) 24: He...stashed himself between the lily whites. **1959** Horan *Mob's Man* 102: "Lily Whites,"...referred to the clean sheets on the bed. **1954–60** *DAS:* Lily whites...Bed sheets. Usu. in *slip between the lily whites* = go to bed. *Negro use.* **1971** *Playboy* (Apr.) 43: I have slipped between the lily-whites with different guys five or six times in the past six months.

lily-white *adj.* bigoted or segregated against black persons.

　1903 *N.Y. Times,* in *OED2:* The report that the President was seeking reconciliation with the "lilywhite" faction, which eliminated the negro from the last State Convention. **1932** in *DA:* The "lily white" movement in the Southern Republican party was another indication of the South's opposition to Negro suffrage. **1943** Ottley *New World* 115 [ref. to 1933]: A store that did not employ Negro help in any capacity was labeled "lily-white." **1950** *N.Y. Times* (Oct. 15) I 51: Labor unions are doing away with "lily-white policies." **1956–60** J.A. Williams *Angry Ones* ch. xx: What is it you can't accept, Lois—that Negroes can think and feel and want revenge? Is that what your lily-white mind tells you? **1964** R. Kendall *Black School* 140: The Muslims are gonna have the lily-whites pickin' up their garbage! **1971** *Ramparts* (Nov.) 54: The Zephyr, a straight, lily-white restaurant. **1982** *L.A. Times* (Sept. 3) I 3: More blacks are moving into formerly lily-white arenas.

limber dick *n.* ¶ In phrase: **slip (someone) a limber dick** to betray or cheat after gaining (the victim's) trust.—usu. considered vulgar.

  1969 Pharr *Numbers* 220 [ref. to 1930's]: Somebody's gonna slip you a limber dick. *Ibid.* 270: Life slipped us a limber dick and all we got left to do is drink.

limber-dicked *adj.* impotent.—usu. considered vulgar.

  1984 Sample *Racehoss* 45: Tired uv screwin all them old limber-dicked, 'lapidated bastards.

limbo *n.* *Und.* a jail; (*Naut.*) shipboard cells.—constr. with *in*.

  *1590 Shakespeare *Comedy of Errors* IV ii 32: He's in Tartar limbo, worse than hell. **1649, *1687* in *OED2.* **1796* Grose *Vulgar Tongue* (ed. 3): *Limbo.* A prison, confinement. **1821–26* Stewart *Man-of-War's Man* I 184: He's only in limbo, that's all…as fast, my boy, as if the devil had him, or the ship's darbies can make him. **1851** [G. Thompson] *Jack Harold* 60: I've oft times been in limbo, but I'll go there no more. **1872** Burnham *Secret Service* vi: Limbo, a prison; "in limbo," confined to jail. **1878** Flipper *Colored Cadet* 55 [ref. to ca1875]: Limbo.—Confinement. **1889** Reynolds *Twin Hells* 161: We next find him in "limbo" in Indiana. **1889** Reynolds *Kansas Hell* 147: We next find him in "limbo" in Indiana. **1908** Sullivan *Criminal Slang* 13: *In limbo*—Doing time. **1935** *AS* (Feb.) 18 [ref. to 1910]: *Limbo.* Prison.

limb-skinner *n.* *West.* a cowboy who works in brush country; BRUSH-POPPER.

  1936 R. Adams *Cowboy Lingo* 23: The cowboy expert at running cattle in the brush country…was known as a…"brush popper"…or "limb skinner." **1968** I. Reed *Yellow Back Radio* 96: O.K. all you brush poppers, ranahans, limb skinners and saddle warmers.

Limburger *n.* [fr. *Limburger,* a type of cheese that actually comes from Belgium and the Netherlands] a German.—used derisively.

  1889 Barrère & Leland *Dict. Slang: Limburger*…anything actually or genuinely German. **1907** "O. Henry" *Heart of West* 256: The dad-blamed little Limburger he went for me, didn't he! **1918** *Radiator* (Oct. 17) 2: It now gives me great pleasure to tell you royal gang of limburgers to *go to hell.* **1954–60** *DAS: Limburger* [derog[atory].]…A German.…*Not common.*

lime juice *n.* **1.** LIME-JUICER, 1.

  *1886 in *F & H* IV 201: In these Colonies [Australia], where pretty nearly every one has made several sea voyages, that subject is strictly tabooed in all rational society. To dilate upon it is to betray a "new chum"—what they call in Australia a lime juice. **1887* in *F & H*: A young man newly arrived in the Colonies [Australia] from the old country is styled a new Chum of a lime juice. **1923** Riesenberg *Under Sail* 25: I won't have no "lime juice" sleeping on deck this voyage.

  2. the variety of English spoken in England; English idiom.

  1937 C.B. Davis *Anointed* 21: Nipper…is Limejuice for kid or punk.

lime-juice *adj.* *Naut.* English; British.

  ca1871 in R.H. Dillon *Shanghaiing Days* 205: You're not in bloody lime-juice country, now, but in God's country, where one man is as good as the next! **1881** *United Service* (Sept.) 448: How changed since one on the "lime-juice" plan. **1896** Hamblen *Many Seas* 69: His ship had been insulted by a "lime-juice sailor." **1898** Bullen *Cachalot* 51 [ref. to 1875]: Ef yew spects ter fool dis chile wiv any dem lime-juice yarns, 'bout lanterns 'n boats at night-time, yew's way off. **1899** *Century* (Sept.) 660: We'll show the lime-juice thief who's doin' this! **1904** *Independent* (Jan. 7) 21: The nine firemen in the neighboring forecastle were, like the common run of "lime juice" stokers, hard working, honest fellows, but rather quarrelsome and inordinately fond of grog. **1924** Isman *Weber & Fields* 43 [ref. to ca1880]: Ain't you ashamed of

yourself, you lime-juice humbug you? **1924** Colcord *Roll & Go* 3: But now I'm on a lime-juice ship, hauling on the braces. **1929** *Sat. Eve. Post* (Oct. 12) 29: You used to have a lime-juice accent in those days. **1939** Linscott *Folk Songs* 145: He joined a limejuice whaler. **1965** Schmitt *All Hands Aloft!* 53 [ref. to 1917]: Damn good riddance, the lime juice bastards both had the syph, anyway.

lime-juicer *n.* [fr. the use of lime juice as an antiscorbutic, mandated on British naval vessels from 1795 and in the British merchant marine from 1844] Esp. *Naut.* **1.** an Englishman or Britisher, esp. a sailor.—also used attrib. Now chiefly *hist.*

  1856 Nordhoff *Merchant Vessel* ch. x [ref. to ca1848]: "To growl like a *Lime-juicer*" has become a proverb among American sailors. [Note:] British sailors are called [lime-juicers] from the fact that, on board English vessels, the law requires that the crews be furnished with a weekly allowance of the extract of limes or lemons as a preventive of scurvy. **1857* in *Austral. Nat. Dict.*: The black gins kept calling out as I passed…"Ah! white fellow, limejuicer" (which is a term used in all the colonies to newly arrived emigrants). **1873** Scammon *Marine Mammals* 267: Shoot, and be d—d, you old lime-juicer! **1883** Russell *Sailors' Lang.* 82: *Lime-juicer.*—Nickname given by Americans to British ships and sailors on account of the lime-juice served out in our Mercantile Marine. **1893** *Our Navy* (Nov. 1) 8: A self-respecting American blue-jacket cannot afford to follow in the footsteps of a "Lime-juicer" Marine Sergeant. **1899** Boyd *Shellback* 49: Curse him for a lime-juicer. **1912** R.C. Murphy *Logbook* 143: What is the world coming to, when a peaceful whaler and sealer can't go about its business without being pestered and bled white by a gang of ——, ——, ——, limejuicers! **1913** *Review of Reviews* XLVIII 203: In Manila there are dozens of Englishmen (whom the soldiers long ago dubbed "lime-juicers"). **1914** *DN* 150: *Lime-juicer. n.* Britisher. **1918** Ruggles *Navy Explained* 89: *Lime-juicer.* An Englishman. **1923** T. Boyd *Through the Wheat* 128: I'd like to take a crack at them lime-juicers. **1930** Fredenburgh *Soldiers March!* 41 [ref. to 1918]: Chew on that, you yellow-bellied lime-juicers. **1951** *JAF* LXIV 441: We in America call the British "Lime Juicers." *a1961* R.H. Dillon *Shanghaiing Days* 102: The lime-juicer spilled his guts.

  2. an English or British vessel.

  1856 Nordhoff *Merchant Vessel* ch. xiii [ref. to ca1848]: Now, boy, you're on board a lime-juicer; look aft and see the red cross waving over your head. **1884** in *OED2*: They would not go on a "lime-juicer," they said, for anything. **1899** Robbins *Gam* 112: We…lowered away, and pulled to the merry lime-juicer. **1907** J. London, in *DA*: He had sailed always on French merchant vessels, with the one exception of a voyage on a "lime-juicer." **1917** Depew *Gunner* 18: There is a saying in the merchant service that the bucko mate of a Lime-juicer is the toughest guy in the world, but they do not think so in the navy. **1922** Hisey *Sea Grist* 173: They had shipped out…on a "Lime Juicer." **1926** Traven *Death Ship* ch. xlv: "Has any of you sailors seen that lime-juicer yonder there?…I mean the *Empress of Madagascar?*" I asked while we were eating. **1928** C.T. Harris *Mem. Manhattan* 68: It was very easy to distinguish a vessel hailing from the Baltic or North Sea, or a "lime-juicer" from a British port. **1976** Hayden *Voyage* 225: She may have th' looks of a Limejuicer, but she ain't a Limejuicer.

lime-juicer *adj.* English; British.

  1893 *Our Navy* (Nov. 1) 8: A self-respecting American blue-jacket cannot afford to follow in the footsteps of a "Lime-juicer" Marine Sergeant. **1930** Nason *Corporal* 129: One o' them lime-juicer M.P.'s like to skewer me with a bayonet! **1931** Dos Passos *1919* 37: There were four of 'em Americans in this lousy limejuicer town.

limejuicy *adj.* English; British.

  1929–30 Dos Passos *42d Parallel* 62: I want to get out of this lime-juicy hole an' get back to God's country.

Limerick *n.* [fr. *Limerick,* town and county in Ireland; the allusion is obscure; perh. cf. "Will You Come Down to Limerick," title of slip jig in F. O'Neill *The Dance Music of Ireland* (1907)] ¶ In phrase: **come to Limerick** (of a person) to behave properly; come to the point; make sense.

  1864 Northrop *Chronicles* 175: "Abe is after you another four years…." "Ho, Johnny, come to limerick." **1877** in J.M. Carroll *Camp Talk* 114: Don't go about it in a sneaking…way, but "come to Limerick!" at once with the question. **1887** Hinman *Si Klegg* 609 [ref. to

Civil War]: "I'll bring him to Limerick," said a burly Confederate as he placed the muzzle of his musket to Si's head.

limey *n.* [fr. LIME-JUICER] Orig. *Naut.* **1.** an Englishman or Britisher.

> **1917** Depew *Gunner Depew* 18: A little while ago I spoke of a British sailor as a "Limey." The old British ships used to carry large quantities of lime juice aboard because they thought it was a cure for the scurvy. So, all over the world, British ships are called "Lime-juicers" and their sailors "Limeys." **1918** O'Brien *Wine, Women & War* 210: Common remark: "When we get through with Jerry, we'll clean up the God damned limeys." **1918** Paine *Fighting Fleets* 87: [He] announced that he could whip any three "Limeys" that ever trod a British deck. **1919** Kauffman *Lost Squadron* 8: Paul Revere…saved the day…by mounting his roan mare and informing the countryside that the "limies" were coming. **1921** Casey & Casey *Gay-Cat* 175: From his aspirated and nasal accent, the boy knew him to be a "Limey" of some kind. **1923** McKnight *Eng. Words* 55: *Gobs* for men in the navy, *leathernecks*, for marines, *limeys* for English sailors, became firmly established [during 1917–18]. **1929** *AS* IV (June) 342: *Limey.* An Englishman. **1929** *AS* V 384 [ref. to 1917]: *Limey:* Any British soldier. **1922–37** Gleaves *Admiral* 16 [ref. to 1878]: The Englishmen…were known as "limeys" [in the U.S. Navy], and were not liked forward or aft. *1937 in *Austral. Nat. Dict.*: All you limeys are nutty. **1943** Hersey *Adano* 157: "What have the limeys done now?" he asked. *1953 in *Austral. Nat. Dict.*: Them Limeys sure fan the breeze. **1935–62** Ragen & Finston *Toughest Pris.* 807: *Limey*—An Englishman. **1972** Pearce *Pier Head Jump* 4: The Limeys wouldn't let nobody go ashore. **1973** in J. Flaherty *Chez Joey* xxi: The Irish I missed totally,…but I was a little better on the limeys. **1982** R.M. Brown *So. Discomfort* 44: Who cares if a bunch of Limeys, Krauts, and Frogs kill each other off? *a*1990 Poyer *Gulf* 162: Maybe we can get a drink from the Limeys.

2. an English or British vessel.

> **1918** McCartney *Texas Review* (Oct.) 86: In our fleet a British ship is regularly called a "limey" from the old lime-juicers. The British seaman is likewise a "limey." **1929–30** Dos Passos *42d Parallel* 149: I deserted in B.A., see, and shipped out on a limey, on an English boat. *a*1950 in Doerflinger *Shantymen* 121: I found myself aboard/A Limey bound to the islands. **1958** Cooley *Run for Home* 11: The Dutch and the squareheads were the cleanest [ships], the French and the Limeys were the dirtiest, with their Lascars and African crews. **1961** Burgess *Dict. of Sailing* 135: *Limey.* The American name for a British ship or seaman. **1976** Hayden *Voyage* 409: Lassiter gets the…binoculars…and stares at the stranger. "A Limey," he says to himself.

limey *adj.* English; British.

> *1888 in *Austral. Nat. Dict.*: They'd seen old stagers and limey new chums. **1922** J. Conway, in *Variety* (May 5) 12: Among the stokers there's a limey socialist and a Liverpool Irishman. **1934** in E. O'Neill *Letters* 431: Stupid Limey nonsense. **1945** in Truman *Dear Bess* 523: I've got to lunch with the Limey King when I get to Plymouth. **1950** Calmer *Strange Land* 87: I suppose our Limey friends are going to sit this one out? **1953** G. Webber *Far Shore* 41: Damned limey beer. **1955** F.K. Franklin *Combat Nurse* 10: They may be Limey…but they're better'n nothing! **1965** Linakis *In Spring* 233: I squeezed in the jeep among parked limey camions. **1966** H.S. Thompson *Hell's Angels* 97: It is not unusual for people who ride these limey bikes to…humiliate a cop on a Harley. *a*1989 R. Herman, Jr. *Warbirds* 131: Her attempt at a limey accent broke down in a laugh. **1989** L. Roberts *Full Cleveland* 65: A phony limey accent. **1991** *Village Voice* (N.Y.C.) (Aug. 27) 83: Not impressed by Limey rhyming skills.

Limey Land *n.* England.—used derisively.

> **1920** Norton *639th Aero Squadron* 88 [ref. to 1918]: A representative of "Limy Land." **1950** P. Wolff *Friend* 13: Didja ever stop in Limey Land? **1963** Cameron *Black Camp* 69: They've got screwball nights in Limey land. **1970** Gaffney *World of Good* 117: Pay up when we get back to Limey Land then. **1971** Faust *Willy Remembers* 115: Ben Lyon and Bebe Daniels made theirs in the U.S. of A., then took off for limeyland. **1966–73** W. Burroughs *Exterminator!* 111: To keep the royal family…in Limey Land.

limit *n.* someone or something that is the most notable of its kind; (*specif.*) a cause for delight or wonder.—constr. with *the*.

> **1899** Ade *Fables* 1: Conscientiousness, Hope, and Ideality—the Limit! **1900** in *DAS:* She's the limit. **1903** *Independent* (Apr. 2) 773: I've seen Mayors an' Controllers ridin' in five-cent cars. I thought that was the limit. **1906–07** Ade *Slim Princess* 55: "These are what you call beautiful women?" she asked. "These are about the limit." **1922** S. Lewis *Babbitt* 123: Honest, George, what do you think of that rag Louetta went and bought? Don't you think it's the limit? **1928** Rice *Street Scene* 573: Ain't men the limit? **1936** C. Porter "It's De-lovely," in Kimball *Complete Lyrics* 147: When I kiss you just say to me, "It's delightful, it's delicious,…it's delimit, it's deluxe, it's de-lovely."

¶ In phrases:

¶ **go the limit** to engage in coitus.

> **1922** *Variety* (Feb. 17) 1: [The police] have listed…a half dozen girls who have been in the habit of appearing at these [stag parties] and "going the limit" for collections, after they have performed the regular turn they were engaged for. **1924** P. Marks *Plastic Age* 53: "I've never gone the limit either," he confessed shyly. **1928** Bodenheim *Georgie May* 95: She'd fooled 'round with him 'thout going the limit. **1930** Farrell *Calico Shoes* 43: Often, he guessed, such girls would go the limit. **1932** *AS* VII (June) 332: *Go the limit*—copulate. **1929–33** Farrell *Young Manhood of Lonigan* 195: She'd go the limit, and what the hell if her breath was bad. **1933** J. Conroy *Disinherited* 93: Ed said she'd go the limit. **1950** C.W. Gordon *High School* 123: Boys who "went the limit" seemed to enjoy even higher status among boys, but were viewed as "too fast" among girls. **1955** O'Hara *Ten North Frederick* 295: Have you ever gone the limit? **1968** in *OED2:* She'd heard girls in school talk about going the limit, or all the way.

¶ **take the limit** *Boxing.* to remain down from a knockdown until the count of nine.

> **1927** Shay *Pious Friends* 98: He took the limit on one knee,/A chance to get his wind and see.

¶ **up to the limit, 1.** extraordinary; amazingly well.

> **1891** [quot. at SNOOZER]. **1895** Townsend *Fadden* 29: Say, mebbe ye tink she can't drive? Wy, she drives out er sight; up ter de limit, I'm tellin' ye. *Ibid.* 55: Say, I'm feelin' up ter de limit dis week. **1897** Townsend *Whole City Full* 134: Say, she liked that up to the limit.

2. stylish; high-toned.

> **1896** Ade *Artie* 95: Any of 'em that's got himself staked to a spring suit…thinks he's up to the limit.

Limo *n.* (see quot.).

> **1937** C.B. Davis *Anointed* 21: Seamen call all Englishmen either Limey or Limejuice or sometimes Limo.

limo *n.* a limousine. Now *colloq.*

> **1928–29** Nason *White Slicker* 187: The front seat of the general's limmo. **1968** *New Yorker,* in *OED2:* "You ride in the limo, dear," he said,…helping her out of the Daimler. **1971** *Harper's* (Oct.) 44: The band rushes into a black limousine…the limo streaks across the field. **1976** *Atlantic* (July) 22: His love of the perquisites of power, the television camera's attention, the long black limos, the special plane. **1980** *Mother Jones* (July) 4: The expensive renovation of [Young's] office and his high-priced limo. [Brackets in orig.].

limp dick *n.* Esp. *Mil.* a weakling or coward; wimp.—usu. considered vulgar.

> **1970** T. Taylor *Piece of This Country* 19: You gutless son of a bitch!…No one's shooting at you, you limp —. **1972–76** Durden *No Bugles* 23: He wanted to charge that hedgerow an' ninety percent of these limp dicks still had the safety on. **1981** in L. Bangs *Psychotic Reactions* 340: Limp dick wouldn't lift one eyelid for dolly parton herself. **1986** Zeybel *First Ace* 2: In civilian clothes he felt dull, like another taxpayer, a real limp dick. **1986** Stinson & Carabatsos *Heartbreak* 18: It's true I had some differences with some limp-dicks. **1987** Knoxville, Tenn. attorney, age 34: If he lets somethin' like this stop him, he's a bigger limp dick than I pegged him for. **1984–88** Hackworth & Sherman *About Face* 608: When the Chief of Staff…looks at [this unit], I want him to see studs.…I'm not bringing in any limp dicks.

limp-dick *adj.* weak or cowardly; lame.—usu. considered vulgar. Also **limp-dicked, limp-prick.**

> **1984** Glick *Winters Coming* 31: You limp-dicked Okie, you couldn't get a dozen hard-ons in a week. **1984** D. Jenkins *Life Its Ownself* 44: Don't come near me, you limp-prick motherfucker. **1986** Dye & Stone *Platoon* 47: A limp-dick civilian would ask him if he'd done his share for his country. **1984–88** Hackworth & Sherman *About Face* 231: After forty days in this limp-dick outfit I'm convinced you could not run a good Boy Scout troop.

limp line *n. Army.* the line of soldiers reporting for sick call. *Joc.*

1941 *AS* (Oct.) 167: *Limp Line.* Men reporting at Sick Call. **1941** *Amer. N & Q* (Dec.) 140: *On the limp-line:* on sick report.

limpster *n.* [app. var. of LAMSTER] *Circus.* (see quot.).

　　1978 Ponicsan *Ringmaster* 13: Everybody is a limpster, a thief. Everybody will swing with the soft.

limp wrist *n.* an effeminate fellow; homosexual; PANSY.—usu. used derisively. Also **limp-wrister.**

　　1954–60 *DAS: Limp wrist…*A homosexual or effeminate man. **1971** *All in the Family* (CBS-TV): "He said he wouldn't let no limp wrist into his mouth.…You know what he called that dentist?" "The tooth fairy." **1972** Jenkins *Semi-Tough* 242: I reminded her that Boke Kellum was a limp wrist. **1974** *Coq.* (Apr.) 44: We would've hung-up on this limp-wrister but pronto. **1978** R. Price *Ladies' Man* 51: A short, skinny limp wrist with a sinus cold. **1981** P. Sann *Trial* 164: Barbara…could only marry herself seven or eight limp wrists. **1983** Wambaugh *Delta Star* 130: He looked like a peroxided limpwrist from Santa Monica Boulevard. **1984** D. Jenkins *Life Its Ownself* 150: We recommended losing all references to "dykes" and "limp wrists." **1984** Glick *Winters Coming* 19: You limp wrist!

limp-wristed *adj.* (of men) effeminate; soft; weak; homosexual.—usu. used derisively.

　　1957 H. Danforth & J. Horan *D.A.'s Man* 315 [ref. to 1949]: I had enough of this reeking room and these limp-wristed men. **1954–60** *DAS: Limp wrist…*Homosexual; said of male homosexuals; effeminate. **1981** *Hill St. Blues* (NBC-TV): Grace, is there anything you find limp-wristed about me? **1984** N. Bell *Raw Youth* 28: The whole limp-wristed swan expiring. **1985** B.E. Ellis *Less Than Zero* 95: And I don't mean those limp-wristed Stray Cats. *a***1989** C.S. Crawford *Four Deuces* 11: Whenever I had to own up to the type of work I was doing…I always felt a little bit limp wristed.

Lincoln *n.* [fr. the portrait of Abraham *Lincoln* on the note] a five-dollar banknote; five dollars.

　　1960 (quot. at HAMILTON). **1970** Rudensky & Riley *Gonif* 22: Jack Johnson…'d say to me,…"When we get out of this cold shack we'll make a pile of Lincolns."

Lincoln *adj. Civil War.* of or from the federal government.—often in jocular nonce coinages. Now *hist.*

　　1864 in A.W. Petty *3d Mo. Cav.* 55: We were…anxious…to get some Lincoln coffee, as were getting very tired of our substitute. **1864** in Wightman *To Ft. Fisher* 220: We had some codfish, which the boys called "Lincoln trout," and a few rations of dried herring, which they have christened "Lincoln's sardines." **1862–65** C. Barney *20th Ia.* 64: The lady informed us that "Lincoln money" would not be received. **1866** Shanks *Personal Recollections* 272: He did, however, give Sherman his rations—of the plainest materials he could gather—"Lincoln platform" (hard bread) and rye coffee. **1867** in *DA:* Nectar in the likeness of Lincoln coffee—no bad substitute either to hungry and toil-worn soldiers. **1885** Cannon *Where Men Only* 171: "Lincoln coffee" and "Jeff. Davis coffee" [were] names for the real article or a substitute [in E. Tenn.].

Lincoln coffee *n.* **1.** see s.v. LINCOLN, *adj.*

　　2. *Civil War So.* ersatz coffee.

　　1864 in *Ark. Hist. Qly.* XLII (1983) 135: I must run and see if the "Lincoln coffee" was not forgotten. **1885** (quot. at LINCOLN, *adj.*).

line *n.* **1.** a piece of useful information, esp. obtained surreptitiously; confidential tip.

　　1896 Ade *Artie* 7: I think I'll give the bank a line on Percy. Any man that wears that kind of a necktie hadn't ought to handle money. **1899–1900** Cullen *Tales* 227: Get a line on what they've done for the great and glorious West. **1911–12** J. London *Smoke Bellew* 232: We've got to get a line on the situation. **1920** Ade *Hand-Made Fables* 45: He had a line on the performances of every Goat [*i.e.*, horse] from the cradle up. **1929** Hammett *Maltese Falcon* 33: I've got to have some sort of a line on Floyd. **1947** in *DA:* If we can find any one who saw her at a dance after 10:30 p.m. we may be able to get a line on whom she was dancing with. **1968** "Spirit" *I Got a Line on You* (pop. song title). **1984** *Miami Vice* (NBC-TV): We understand you have a line on this man.

　　2. an area where many houses of prostitution are located; red-light district. See also *go down the line* and *on the line,* below.

　　1897 Norris *Vandover* 359: I…held down the "line" on Kearney Street for an hour or two. **1909** Chrysler *White Slavery* 14: Every large city and many small ones have a vice district, a tenderloin, a levee, or a line, which are the polite names for a street, or a number of

streets, where the houses are located that are occupied by immoral women. **1921** Woolston *Prostitution* I 104: The district, or "line," may consist of a single block of *cribs.* **1928** Harrison *Generals* 3 [ref. to 1918]: Some of the recruits are beginning to dribble into the barrack bunk-room after a night's carousal down the line. **1929** T. Gordon *Born to Be* 20 [ref. to *ca*1905]: Her house was the Palace on the line.…Before Maude came, a round of drinks cost a dollar anywhere on the line. **1937** Reitman *Box-Car Bertha* 17: Aberdeen had "a line," a row of houses of prostitution just outside city limits. **1954** Gaddis *Birdman* 23: Kitty had continued as a denizen of the line, but Charlie's death and Stroud's long sentence put a mark on her. She left Alaska. **1961** *Sat. Eve. Post* (Feb. 11) 64: Terre Haute is one of perhaps a dozen communities of any size left in the country with "a line"—a well-defined red-light district. **1975** Swarthout *Shootist* 18: They had a "Line" on Utah Street with some of the fanciest parlor houses and flossiest girls in Christendom.

　　3.a. a usu. rehearsed insincere statement or style of conversation intended to impress or influence.—often constr. with *feed.* [The long form *line of talk*, orig. colloq., is now S.E.]

　　[**1897** Ade *Pink* 171: Misteh, you can't feed it to 'em f'eveh.] [**1903** "H. McHugh" *Out for Coin* 83: Are you handing me a line of bogus conversation?] [**1910** in *DA:* He developed a line of talk which was pronounced strictly paralyzing.] **1914** Elliott *Animated Slang* 4: At last I became interested and he FED ME A WONDERFUL LINE. **1928** Dahlberg *Bottom Dogs* 45: Mush Tate had a line when it came to talking himself up. **1933** Boehm & Gelsey *Life of Jimmy Dolan* (film): That's just a line for the suckers. **1934** P. Peters & G. Sklar *Stevedore* 13: And don't you go calling me up with this line of yours about something important to tell me, either. **1936** Levin *Old Bunch* 97: The boys at the garage were always pulling a big line about the swell bums they picked up in their hacks. **1941** Lees et al. *Hold That Ghost* (film): If this is a line, it's at least a new one. **1953** *Popeye the Sailor* (animated cartoon): Dat sap soitenly fell fa *dat* line! ***1958** in *OED2:* He gave me a terrific line about the hold-up. Said it was his partner's fault. **1965** C.D.B. Bryan *P.S. Wilkinson* 84 [ref. to *ca*1960]: Don't feed me that line, Wilkinson. You went all the way through that line of crap about international incidents and status of forces agreements. **1973** Lucas, Katz & Huyck *Amer. Graffiti* 58: I'm not just feeding you a line.

　　b. *Specif.,* such a line intended to impress or seduce a potential romantic partner, esp. a woman.

　　*ca***1915** in Fitzgerald *Corres.* 15: I hear you've got a "line"!…Don't be afraid of slang…but be careful to use the most modern and sportiest like "line," camafluage [*sic*], etc. **1919** Cober *Btry. D* 74: He certainly had a "line" that was powerful. We hesitate to figure out the number of "mademoiselles" and "frauleins" that are now mourning his absence. **1919** in Inman *Diary* 160: The welsher wrote her a letter slingin' a long line about his conscience,…promisin' to marry her. **1920** Fitzgerald *This Side of Paradise* 48: What line do you throw 'em? **1926** Hormel *Co-Ed* 12: "By golly, Miss Leigh, you must know you're a knock-out in that shade of blue."…A year later Lucia would have recognized this as the beginning of a "line." **1926–35** Watters & Hopkins *Burlesque* 17: One o' the girls heard your whole line. **1941** *Pittsburgh Courier* (Apr. 19) 24: Chicks always fall for a hep-cat's line. **1943** J.T. Farrell *Days of Anger* 307 [ref. to 1926]: You didn't pull a line on an intelligent girl. **1951** D. Wilson *My Six Convicts* 43: "I know, Connie, it sounds like a line," I admitted. **1955** Bram *Lang. & Society* 37: Our contemporary slangy expression "to hand a girl a line." **1962** E.A. Smith *Amer. Youth Culture* 113: In later dating activities, the use of the "line," a stylized conversation routine, is crucial. *Ibid.* 114: Members learn to "throw the line" and flirt. **1969** Marshe & Lifton *Centerfold* 29: I thought it was a line. "Don't you think we ought to get married first?" **1969** Mitchell *Thumb Tripping* 43: Gary tried to think when he'd last used a line to score ass. **1974** in Mamet *Sex. Perversity* 20: *Joan.*…I do not find you sexually attractive.…*Bernie.* What is that, some new kind of line? **1977** Rudolph *Welcome to L.A.* (film): Did that sound like a line? I didn't mean it to. Everything sounds like a line these days. **1994** "Notorious B.I.G." *Big Poppa* (rap song): Who they attractin' with that line, "What's your name and what's your sign?" **1995** *Jerry Springer Show* (synd. TV series): The guy is handing her a line.

　　4.a. *Orig. Und.* Now *Black E.* money.—now usu. constr. in *pl.*

　　1930 *Variety* (Jan. 8) 123: I couldn't let umpchay screw with all that line. **1935** Pollock *Und. Speaks:* Lots of line…an abundance of money. **1967** [Beck] *Pimp* 188: What kinda lines you got? *Ibid.* 315: *Lines…*money. **1968–72** Agar *Ripping & Running* 161: Line…Money.

1972 Claerbaut *Black Jargon* 71: *Line*, n. Money. See also *jack*, [etc.]. **1983** *Reader's Digest Success with Words* 87: Black English...*lines* = "money."

b. *Black E.* (see quots.).

1954–60 *DAS: Line*...The cost of an item, the purchase price of an item. *Mainly Negro use.* **1983** *Reader's Digest Success with Words* 87: Black English...*line* = "price of an item."

5. *Narc.* (see quots.).

1938 in D. Maurer *Lang. of Und.* 104: *Line.* The main-line or vein into which the addict injects narcotics. **1969** Lingeman *Drugs A to Z* 128: *Line*....the main vein in the arm; to "shoot in the *line*" is to inject heroin into this vein. **1970** Landy *Underground Dict.* 121: *Line*...Vein. a.k.a. mainline.

6. *Jazz.* a melodic phrase used in improvisation; RIFF; LICK.

1956 A. Shaw *West Coast Jazz* 127, in *DAS*: [West] Coasters talk of "lines," not licks, breaks, or riffs.

7. *Narc.* a thin line of powdered cocaine (or another drug) laid out for inhalation.—now often used without either antecedent or restrictive subsequent phr.

1973 *Drug Forum* II 424: A "line" of cocaine is inhaled into a nostril, often through a rolled, high denomination bill. **1974** *Oui* (May) 18: Two lines of coke...an amyl nitrite...and a tequila sunrise. **1976** *L.A. Times* (Oct. 5) IV 6: They'd sniff a "line" or two, then go off not really knowing what quality cocaine they had purchased. **1979** *N.Y. Times Mag.* (Oct. 7) 18: Cocaine...is laid out in a one-inch "line" and sniffed. **1984** McInerny *Bright Lights* 54: Elaine and Amanda are doing lines on Yasu Wade's desk. **1989** *48 Hours* (CBS-TV): We started doin' lines [of methamphetamine]. **1989** P. Benchley *Rummies* 125: Cut me a line. *a***1990** E. Currie *Dope & Trouble* 134: We were choppin' lines. **1995** *Leeza* (syndic. TV series): I'd smoke a joint and probably have another line. **1995** *Morning News* (CNN-TV) (Apr. 10): All three of us were there doin' lines.

¶ In phrases:

¶ **feed a line** see (3.a.), above.

¶ **get into line with** to provide oneself with.

1896 Ade *Artie* 40: Come right in here [a florist's shop] and get into line with a bunch o' violets. There's nothin' too good for the sunshine o' the North Side.

¶ **get (someone) in a line** (see quot.).

1891 Maitland *Slang Dict.* 168: *Line*, "to get one in a," to get some sport out of him.

¶ **go down the line** to go carousing in a red-light district.

1905 *Nat. Police Gaz.* (Dec. 9) 3: It may be that you...don't know what it means to go "down the line." **1908** W.G. Davenport *Butte & Montana* 263: He has evidently been up and down the line. **1910** Hapgood *City Streets* 59: He...treats all his friends as he goes "down the line." **1916** Cary *Venery* I 112: *Going Down the Line*—To go whore hopping. **1929** Milburn *Hornbook* 193 [ref. to *ca*1900]: I took a stroll along the "line"; "set up" for all the boys. **1948** Cozzens *Guard* 32: I want that jeep back right away, tell him. I may have to go down the line. **1952** Sandburg *Strangers* 237 [ref. to *ca*1892]: If I had his looks, Jesus wept, would I go down the line! **1965** Longstreet *Sportin' House* 17: "Going down the line" on a Saturday night to the sporting houses was often a ritual for the Southern male and his guests. **1970** Winick & Kinsie *Lively Commerce* 124: If he called "Taxi!" they would ask if he wished to go "down the line" to the red light district.

¶ **lay** [or **put**] **it on the line** [fr. the gambling sense 'to put money on the line [space on a craps table for placing chips]']
1. to put down or hand over money. Now *colloq.* or *S.E.*

1929 D. Runyon, in *OED2*: My rent is away overdue...and I have a hard-hearted landlady....She says she will give me the wind if I do not lay something on the line at once. **1932** L. Berg *Prison Doctor* 106: You wanted an easy job to pass the hours waiting for freedom? Simple. All you had to do was to lay it on the line with so-and-so. It passes from hand to hand. **1935** Sistrom *Hot Tip* (film): "Can you handle two hundred on Honey Girl?" "Sure. Lay it on the line. We can handle it." **1942** *ATS* 528: Pay...*lay* or *put on the line*. **1955** in D.W. Maurer *Lang. of Und.* 245: *Lay it on the line*...To spend money extravagantly.

2. to explain; speak one's mind firmly and directly. Now *colloq.*

1944 Butler & Cavett *Going My Way* (film): Like Tony says, I'm gonna lay it on the line. **1957** Collins & Powell *My Gun Is Quick* (film): Now look, Mike. Put it on the line. Tell me what you know. **1968** Brasselle *Cannibals* 162: Captain, let me lay it on the line for

you. *****1989** Partridge *Concise Slang Dict.* 259: *Lay it on the line*. To explain thoroughly, with the implication that the hearer must act accordingly.

3. see *lay it on the line*, 2 s.v. LAY, *v.*

¶ **on the line** engaged in prostitution, esp. in a red-light district.

1910 in Roe *Prodigal Daughter* 83: Oh, if everybody did know the awful shame and degradation of such a life there would surely be very few girls "on the line." **1942** Wilder *Flamingo Road* 113: I hear she's on the line now, down to Lute-Mae's. **1942** Algren *Morning* 172: Barber put me on the line long, long ago. **1967–69** Foster & Stoddard *Pops* 33: If you had more than one girl on the line you had to meet them at different times and be very careful. The cops would raid the District once in a while.

¶ **out of line** behaving unexpectedly or improperly. Now *colloq.*

*****1791** in *OED2*: I cannot help noticing that in one of his publications (stepping out of line) he betray'd extreme weakness and credulity. **1932** D. Runyon *Guys & Dolls* ii 37, in *OED2*: Reasonable safe for anyone who does not get too far out of line. **1938** D. Runyon, in *OED2*: He is out of line in giving Frankie the hot foot. **1940** *AS* (Oct.) 334: *Out of line.* Behaving abnormally. **1950** A. Lomax *Mr. Jelly Roll* 15, in *DAS*: You was considered out of line if your coat and pants matched. **1957** Trosper *Jailhouse Rock* (film): She wasn't out of line.

¶ **pull lines** to attempt to use one's influence; pull strings.

1960 C.L. Cooper *Scene* 263: Dig, baby, I don't think they got no case!...I think my man is pullin some lines. I think I'll get out some time.

¶ **run a line on** to LINE UP, 3; GANGBANG, 1.

1976–77 Kernochan *Dry Hustle* 188: We had a chick turned out on the pool table, we were runnin a line on her the whole day.

¶ **shoot a line** to utter a line ((3.a.), above); (esp.) to boast or exaggerate. [Common in BrE, esp. during WWII.]

*****1925** in Ward-Jackson *Airman's Song Book* 84: A budding line-shooter,.../ Who thinks first-termers worms. **1939** Appel *People Talk* 88: I was so bored listening to those boys shoot their line. *****1942** in Partridge *DSUE* (ed. 7) 1398: "Shooting a line," for boasting, probably the most characteristic of all R.A.F. phrases. *****1945** Partridge *RAF Slang* 62: *Shoot a*—or *the—line* To boast; to exaggerate; to talk excessively on a subject. **1963** M. Shulman *Victors* 58: Brooklyn?...You must be shooting me a line. That ain't in Texas. **1975** Higham & Siddall *Combat Aircraft* vii: We acknowledge also that an ingredient of flying life is the tendency to "shoot a line."

line *v.* **1.** to copulate with.—usu. considered vulgar. [S.E. in ref. to animals, esp. dogs; *OED2* has extensive citations fr. 1398.]

1942 McAtee *Supp. Grant Co. Dial. in '90's* 6: *Line*, *v.*, to fuck a female, used both of men and animals.

2. [clipping of MAINLINE, *v.*] *Narc.* (see quots.). [A citation of "1969" attributed in Spears *Drugs & Drink*, ref. to Lingeman *Drugs A to Z*, is app. erroneous; there is no verbal entry for *line* in that book.]

1970 Landy *Underground Dict.* 121: *Line v.*...Inject a drug directly into a vein. *****1990** T. Thorne *Dict. Contemp. Sl.: Line (up/out)*...to sniff *lines* of cocaine or amphetamine.

line dog or **doggie** *n. Army.* a frontline soldier. Also **line animal.** [Quots. ref. to Vietnam War.]

1967 (quot. at BOONIE RAT). **1969** in B. Edelman *Dear Amer.* 129: Yes, I was in Vietnam. Yes, I was a line dog. **1985** J.M.G. Brown *Rice Paddy Grunt* 192: If there's anything a line-dog in the infantry learns, it's how to get along on little. **1986** D. Tate *Bravo Burning* 47: The average line doggie...would be very leery to pull that trigger. *a***1987** Bunch & Cole *Reckoning for Kings* 64: The line animals always went armed when they went outside the wire. **1987** Gadd *Line Doggie* 4: Think of him as the "line doggie," a name he was proud to claim. **1968–90** Linderer *Eye of Eagle* 33: We were different than...line-doggies. **1992** L. Chambers *Recondo* 99: One of the Cav line doggies.

liner *n.* a man who frequents a LINE, *n.*, 2.

1970 Winick & Kinsie *Lively Commerce* 125: If I have two liners a week, that's a lot.

line-up *n.* **1.** an association or group of individuals that share some common characteristic. Now *colloq.*

1904 in *DA:* Thus we have a line-up of corporations against the people. **1913** in *DA:* It was a rigid line-up against the bosses. **1978** R. Price *Ladies' Man* 15: You ever see such a line-up of freaks?

2. an instance of several men having sexual intercourse with one woman in rapid succession; GANGBANG.

1913 Kneeland *Prostitution* 62: A "line up" is the ruin of a girl who flirts with men and accepts their…immoral suggestions. Finally she yields to an invitation to visit a furnished room and the word quickly passes among the "gang." One by one the boys and men…visit this room. **1929** M. Gold *Jews Without Money* 28 [ref. to *ca*1905]: Then the other men went in, one after the other….this was a "line-up." **1931** Cressey *Taxi-Dance Hall* 35 [ref. to 1925]: *Line-up, the.*—Immorality engaged in by several men and a girl. **1934** Appel *Brain Guy* 55: He remembered her story, the lineups in Brooklyn…and now whoring it regular. **1951** Elgart *Over Sixteen* 144: I just heard one of the girls ask the Sultan if she was in tomorrow's line-up. **1956** G. Green *Last Angry Man* 98: A *line-up!* Man, I don' mess wit dat stuff. **1957** Atwell *Private* 461: They're the ones the boys had a line-up on the day befoah yesterday. **1961** Rubin *In the Life* 59: Thought it'd be a quiet line-up, like the crap game, see. **1966** Bogner *7th Ave.* 349 [ref. to *ca*1940]: Seymour from Carrol Street says she likes line-ups, and he ought to know, 'cause they had a gang-bang in his clubroom and she was one of the girls. Her and another broad from St. John's Place. Fourteen guys screwed them. **1966** Samuels *People vs. Baby* 35: They got a line-up with a girl from 105th, she's all junked up and needs the dough.

line up *v.* **1.** to join; throw in one's lot with; be associated with.

1900 in *DA:* He made a serious social mistake when he "lined up" with the truck farmers. **1906** in *OED2:* The university president must refuse to be lined up by any clique or party. **1929–33** J.T. Farrell *Young Manhood* 309: I'm also lined up with a can house, and get my split on anybody I bring there. **1934** in J.P. Cannon *Notebook* 85: Then he lined up with the Dunnskovitskys and muscled into the union racket. **1960** Roeburt *Mobster* 79: I lined up with you. I bought you as the new boss.

2.a. to secure; make available; find; obtain; (*hence*) to arrange to one's advantage. Also (*obs.*) **line.**

1906 H. Green *Actors' Boarding House* 85: He was lining up a live one for the…wiretapping game. **1909** *Sat. Eve. Post* (July 3) 15: Say, youse tink youse got me lined, don't youse? Youse tink you've got me in a dead sure plant? **1909** Chrysler *White Slavery* 38: When they have ten or twelve girls "lined up" (interested) they leave…for Chicago. **1925** Dos Passos *Manhattan Transfer* 295: Got anything lined up yet? **1948** Wilder & Monroe *Song Is Born* (film): Got a justice of the peace all lined up. **1950** Shulman *Dobie Gillis* 182: I've got the books all lined up. **1958** Cooley *Run for Home* 335: We'll line up a dame and if he goes ashore tomorrow night we'll move in. **1968** Brasselle *Cannibals* 94: Believe me, this can be lined up. **1969** Smith *Buskin'* 85: Gotta get outa here before the bars close and line up a piece of ass.

b. *Und.* to rob.

1925–26 Black *You Can't Win* 181: We located a big poker game in a soft spot and decided to "line up" the players.

c. to make a profitable and esp. illicit arrangement with.

1933 (quot. at SQUARE). **1972** in *Playboy* (Jan. 1973) 242: He's still a businessman. He tried to line up the Bar Association….Some of those guys, you can really make out on them. They got good dough. **1976** "N. Ross" *Policeman* 9: I still lined up the parking lot for a sawbuck a week.

3. to engage in a LINE-UP, 2 with (a person, usu. a woman); gang-rape.

1913 Kneeland *Prostitution* 65: She was "lined up" about a year ago by a gang that "hangs out" in a cigar store on East 14th Street. **1928** Bodenheim *Georgie May* 113: The gang…lined up on her and raped her when she was fifteen. **1934** Appel *Brain Guy* 51: They were linin' me up two years ago. **1941** Attaway *Blood on the Forge* 118: Hey, guys, they linin' up on ol' Betty back in the weeds! **1946** Shulman *Amboy Dukes* 27: The Dukes were lining up one or two girls on the cots. **1962** Yablonsky *Violent Gang* 199: In the "gang bang" pattern a promiscuous female is "lined up," and often as many as fifteen or twenty boys will indulge themselves with her in some form of sexual act. **1962** Mandel *Wax Boom* 91: We gonna line up on them before Squadron gets them? **1962–68** B. Jackson *In the Life* 296: A boy was lined up on and eighteen or twenty men lined up and fucked him.

lingie *n. Navy.* a linguist.

1989 Care *Viet. Spook Show* 74 [ref. to 1969]: Only lingies were assigned to this shit.

lingo *n.* **1.** (*cap.*) *Naut.* an interpreter—used as a nickname.

1840 in *Essex Inst. Hist. Coll.* LXXXIV (1948) 307: Good Morning Mr. Lingo.

2. an untrustworthy utterance or utterances.

1918 in *AS* (Oct. 1933) 29: [Ft. Leavenworth:] Lingo. Rarely, a language or a dialect. Frequently, a yarn: So I give His Honor a swell *lingo* about wantin' t' serve de country, an' be damned if 'e didn't let me off 'n' tell de dick t' take me over t' de recruitin' office. **1927** M. Brand *Pleasant Jim* 79: Aw, say,…does he hand out that lingo?

Link *n. Army & USMC.* the Communist Chinese army; (*broadly*) the North Vietnamese army.—used derisively. In full, **Link the Chink.**

*a*1961 Peacock *Valhalla* 21 [ref. to Korean War]: Luke the Gook and Link the Chink. **1964** Peacock *Drill & Die* 15: Looks like Link's got his lantern up again. Now, who would have thought that. **1980** DiFusco et al. *Tracers* 15: Now, Luke the Gook, Link the Chink, and Charlie Cong like to hide in that tall green elephant grass.

link *n.* ¶ In phrase: **let out links** to extend one's lead, as in a race; gallop.

1839 *Spirit of Times* (Apr. 6) 54: Oscar began to let out a few additional links, and…won the heat handily. **1868** in *DA* s.v. *let:* Lancet…in the third heat, let out the links. **1880** in *DA:* [The buffaloes] let out a few more links, and ran much faster.

lintback *n. West.* (see quot.).

1928 Santee *Cowboy* 73: Me an' Tex is just a couple of lint-backs (cotton-pickers) that is doin' the best we can.

linthead *n.* **1.** *So.* a worker in a cotton mill; (*broadly*) a poor rural white person.

1933 E. Caldwell *God's Little Acre* 59: Gussie thinks she's too good to speak to us. She makes Jim Leslie call us lint-heads. **1934** in *DA:* Hill-billies and niggers, poor whites, and planters, Cajans [*sic*] and Lintheads are sometimes aware of the intangible net that encompasses them. **1939** McIlwaine *So. Poor-White* xxiv: The Southern poor-white in the cotton mills…is…a "lint-head," an industrial pawn. **1944** Inks *Eight Bailed Out* 25: You linthead….How're you doing? **1953** Wicker *Kingpin* 114: Good God! My daddy giving in to that lint head. **1953** *New Yorker* (Mar. 7) 40: You can almost see those lint-heads yodelling around the hills. **1966** Gilchrist *Observer* 12 [ref. to 1918]: Pale "lint heads" who had worked in cotton mills. **1970** Voigt *Amer. Baseball* II 57: A foul-mouthed, illiterate "linthead" from a southern mill town. **1983** R. McDavid, Jr., in *Amer. Studies* XXIV 123: Southern textile centers had a *de facto* tri-racial system, of whites and blacks and *lint-heads*, the last segregated from the other groups and hostile to both.

2. a foolish or ignorant person. Also **lintbrain.**

1960 MacDonald *Slam the Big Door* 38: He was glad he didn't have to deal with such lintheads any more. *a*1970 Longstreet *Nell Kimball* 31: He taught us lintheads to spell and cipher. **1990** T. Thorne *Dict. Contemp. Sl.:* Lintbrain, Lint-head…American a dim-witted or foolish person.

lion *n.* ¶ In phrase: **see the lions** to have worldly experience; see remarkable sights; *see the elephant,* 2.a., s.v. ELEPHANT.

*1590 in *OED2:* Francesco was no other but a meere nouice, and that so newly, that to vse the olde prouerbe, he had scarce seene the Lions. *1600, *1622, etc., in *OED2.* **1845** Cleveland *Forecastle* 334 [ref. to 1818]: A good night's rest was attended with refreshing effects; and with renovated energy I went forth, in the morning, "to see the lions." **1873** Lening *N.Y. Life* 114: Some acquaintances…had come from the country "to see the lions."

lip *n.* **1.** insolent or disrespectful talk; back talk.

*1803 in Wetherell *Adventures* 68: Stop his damnd lip. *1821 in *OED2:* I was at no loss in vindicating myself and giving him plenty of lip. **1835** in Meine & Owens *Crockett Alms.* 51: We did'nt [*sic*] mean to take any of his lip, for ary one of us could double up two such fellows any minute. **1841** [Mercier] *Man-of-War* 179: You wouldn't feel disposed to shove your lip in amongst white folks again. **1848** Baker *Glance at N.Y.* 21: None of your lip, old fellow. **1861** "Citizen" *So. Chivalry* 74: None of your saucy lip! **1861** in W.C. Davis *Orphan Brigade* 54: You've got too much lip yourself. **1864** in D. Chisholm *Civil War Notebook* 10: Charles Yauger was tied up for lip to the capt. **1866** Locke *Round the Cirkle* 130: I chastised wun who gave me lip.

1868 Williams *Black-Eyed Beauty* 43: I want none of your lip, Miss Howard. **1873** Sutton *N.Y. Tombs* 329: None of your lip; where were you born? **1877** Wheeler *Prince of the Road* 79: Who told *you* to mix in your lip, pilgrim? **1878** Hart *Sazerac* 156: If you expect to spar me out of a drink on that kind of lip. **1883–84** Whittaker *L. Locke* 216: I don't want none of your lip. **1889** Bailey *Ups & Downs* 30 [ref. to 1871]: If he gives you any more lip, pull out your gun on the quiet, and hold it behind him. **1891** Maitland *Slang Dict.* 168: *Lip*, impudence. **1893** W.K. Post *Harvard* 74: If this man gives you boys any lip,…see me. **1896** Hamblen *Many Seas* 63: To use Old Ned's favourite expression when alluding to me, he gave more lip than a right whale. **1898** Riis *Mulberry St.* 225: Sometimes one of the tenants would jostle them in the yard and "give lip," in the alley's vernacular. **1914** *Collier's* (Aug. 1) 6: I'll never take any more lip from that old stiff as long as I'm running this club. **1939** Cain et al. *Stand Up & Fight* (film): Don't pay no attention to his hifalutin lip. **1948** Cozzens *Guard* 131: If he gives me any lip, I'll doubletime him around Lake Armstrong. **1975** *Kojak* (CBS-TV): I don't want any more of your lip! **1976** Fleischer & C. Gore *Fame* 123: Less lip, Monroe. **1982** Del Vecchio *13th Valley* 90: Doan give him lip, Man.…He's drunk. **1983** in N. George *Buppies, B-Boys* 171: When somebody would give him some lip. **1988** Poyer *The Med* 385: You have given me one ration of lip too much.

2. *Jazz.* **a.** the strength of embouchure of a brass musician; (*hence*) musical ability. Cf. CHOPS, 2.a., b.

1889 *Century Dict.*: *Lip*…the power or facility of adjusting one's lips to the mouthpiece of a metal wind-instrument.…the term is used in a general sense to indicate his method and style. **1933** *Metronome*, in Gold *Jazz Lexicon*: He's got the ideas, but his lip's weak yet. **1937** *AS* (Feb.) 47: *Lip*…used in relation to the state of muscular strength of brass instrument players' lips and their resultant ability to play high notes accurately. **1953** in S. Allen *Bop Fables* 23: What condition is your lip in? **1973** Buerkle & Barker *Bourbon St. Black* 40: His lip is "down" and he never quite makes the good gigs again.

b. a person who plays a brass instrument.

1983 N. Proffitt *Gardens of Stone* 19: The boy who had played Kennedy's funeral—the best lip on post.

3. *Und.* an attorney; criminal lawyer; MOUTHPIECE.

1929 *Sat. Eve. Post* (Apr. 13) 54: A lawyer is a mouthpiece or a shyster or a lip. **1930** *Amer. Mercury* (Dec.) 456: Lip, *n.*: A lawyer. "So I says, 'Get a lip for a writ an' I'll lam.'" **1931** *AS* VI (Aug.) 440. **1932** *Writer's Digest* (Aug.) 48: If a criminal is apprehended he obtains the services of a "lip" (criminal lawyer) or a "shyster lip" (unscrupulous lawyer). **1942** *N.Y. Times Mag.* (Jan. 25) 30: *Lip*—A lawyer. **1944** C.B. Davis *Leo McGuire* 204: My lip was…named Ralph Wendell. **1949** Goldin et al. *DAUL*: *Lip.* A lawyer. **1967** [R. Beck] *Pimp* 46: Christ! I thought, a deep South Nigger "lip."…Most of them turned to jelly when defending a criminal case. **1972** Bunker *No Beast* 91: Abe wants to help you—get you a lip. **1983** *Reader's Digest Success with Words* 87: Black English…*lip* = "defense lawyer."

¶ In phrases:

¶ **beat (one's) lip** (see quot.).

1957 Murtagh & Harris *First Stone* 124: "You're not just beating your lip," Lorraine said. "Doggone right." *Ibid.* 303: *Beat the lip* To talk nonsense.

¶ **keep a stiff upper lip** to suppress the display of emotion. Now *S.E.*

1833 J. Neal *Down Easters* I ii 15, in *OED2*: What's the use o' boo-hooin'?…Keep a stiff upper lip. **1835** T. Haliburton, in *F & H* IV 207: He was well to do in the world once, carried a stiff upper lip, and keered for no one. **1849** in Eliason *Tarheel Talk* (Feb. 23) 297: Keep a "Stiff upper lip." **1861** in M. Lane *Dear Mother* 40: Keep a stout heart, or, as someone has elegantly expressed it, "keep a stiff upper lip."

¶ **lay a lip over, 1.** to taste. *Joc.*

1921 Marquis *Carter* 118: She could rustle up some of the best grub you ever threw your lip over. **1953** Petry *Narrows* 262: Here, Sonny,…lay your lip over this. **1979** Decker *Holdouts* 30: That was the roughest stuff I ever layed a lip over. *Ibid.* 94: Best stuff you ever laid a lip over. **1979** R. Foster *Concrete Cowboys* (film): I'm gonna lay a meal on you like you never laid a lip over.

2. to kiss (someone). *Joc.*

1942–45 Caniff *Male Call* (unp.): Come here and I'll lay a lip over you.

¶ **read** [or **watch**] **my lips** listen closely to my words; (*hence*) I assure you I speak the truth. [Popularized as a

political slogan by George Bush in the 1988 presidential campaign.]

1984 *Night Court* (NBC-TV): Read my lips, Dan. Does the State object to a fine and time served? **1985** *Miami Vice* (NBC-TV): Read my lips, Richard—nobody's buying! **1985–87** Bogosian *Talk Radio* 34: Am I speaking English? Read my lips. **1987** "J. Hawkins" *Tunnel Warriors* 144: Hey! Read my lips, dildo nose. **1988** *Evans & Novak* (CNN-TV) (Jan. 24): Daniel Ortega and his people promised those very same things nine years ago—watch my lips—*nine years* ago. **1988** TV ad for Eggo NutriGrain waffles: It's—read my lips—*nutritious!* **1988** G. Bush, acceptance speech, Republican National Convention (Aug. 18): The Congress will push me to raise taxes and I'll say no, and they'll push and I'll say no, and they'll push again. And all I can say to them is, "Read my lips. No new taxes." [**1988–89** in Safire *Quoth Maven* 241 [ref. to 1978]: I would say to him, "We got it that time," and he would say, "Read my lips—we didn't." That phrase arrested me. *Ibid.* 243: In my high school days in the late 60's…we would mouth [an expected] obscene answer after calling for the questioner to "read my lips."] **1989** P. Benchley *Rummies* 171: Hey! Read my fucking lips.

¶ **shoot from the lip** [sugg. by equivalent fig. usage of S.E. *shoot from the hip*] *Journ. & Pol.* to make incautious remarks. *Joc.*

1995 *TV Guide* (Nov. 18) 5: Shooting from the Lip. **1996** *Good Morning America* (ABC-TV) (June 13): He kind of "shoots from the lip," so to speak.

¶ **zip (one's)** [or **the**] **lip** to keep quiet; keep a secret. Hence **lip-zipping,** *n.*

1978 S. King *Stand* 580: Can we be sure he'll keep his lip zipped? **1984** *N.Y. Times* (June 1) A31: CBS News chose…to remain mum about the whole thing.…The lip-zipping at CBS News has been a mistake. **1988** Groening *Childhood* (unp.): Zip the lip.

lip *v.* **1.a.** to utter, as by singing or speaking; (*rarely*) to speak. Cf. *OED2.* [The 1946 quot. appears to reflect recoinage rather than survival.]

*1789 G. Parker *Life's Painter* 132: I'll lip ye a chaunt [song]—as *rum* a one as ye ever heard. **1799* in *OED*: Sir John lipt us the favourite chaunt of Jerry Abershaw's "Ye Scamps [etc.]." **1885* in *F & H* IV 207: Millions lipped my name. **1946** Boulware *Jive & Slang* 5: Let's Lip A While…Let's talk.

b. to speak insolently.—also used absol.

*1898 in *OED2*: He lipt mi rarely. **1902* in *EDD*: He's lipt mi as Ah was never lipt afoor. **1941* in *OED2*: Young Ernie was lippin' me just before you come in. **1943** in *DARE*: Rabbits is the sassiest critters in the woods. I near bust my sides listenin' to they sassy lippin'. **1961** H. Ellison *Memos* 170: They lipped the guard, or were just generally surly. **1965** Yurick *Warriors* 104: And in the meantime, the bitch kept lipping them, one and all. **1983** in N. George *Buppies, B-Boys* 171: They always used to fall out with Benny, probably because he used to lip a lot.

2. *Jazz.* to play (a brass instrument). Now *S.E.*

1956 in *DAS*: His teeth fell out and he couldn't lip anything proper any more. **1990** T. Thorne *Dict. Contemp. Sl.*: *Lip*…to play a wind instrument, blow.…"Lip that thing."…"Cool lipping."

lip fart *n.* *Juve.* a derisive sputtering sound made with the lips in imitation of flatulation.—usu. considered vulgar.

1930 Farrell *Grandeur* 207: The kid…gave him a lip-fart. **1964** Howe *Valley of Fire* 135: Someone made a lip-fart. **1979** Charyn *7th Babe* 208: Billy, did you tell him no more lip farts?

lip-fart *v.* *Juve.* to make a LIP FART.—usu. considered vulgar.

1929–33 Farrell *Young Manhood of Lonigan* 225: "B.S.," Young Rocky said, lip-farting. **1936** Farrell *World I Never Made* 133: "Artie Lenehan, who always makes trouble and does this all the time," Danny said, lip-farting to show his grandmother what Artie always did. **1958** Berger *Crazy in Berlin* 107: The Russian…lip-farted at his own image in the mirror. **1962** T. Berger *Reinhart* 312: C. Roy lip-farted and took his cap off.

lip in *v.* (see 1942–49 quot.).

1899 Markey *Iowa to Philippines* 265: It was seldom that a reader of the "Times" did not "lip in" and attempt to settle the matter by quoting from his authority. **1929** Tully *Shadows* 248: Don't let him kid you, Dippy, he's always lippin' in. **1942–49** Goldin et al. *DAUL*: *Lip in.* To break into a conversation rudely.

lip-lock *n.* **1.a.** a tight hold with the mouth. *Joc.*

    1975 Wambaugh *Choirboys* 324: Roscoe, this might just be the night I get you in a lip lock and shut you up for good. **1984** Sample *Raceboss* 186: He had gotten a double lip-lock on somebody's toe. **1985** Dye *Between Raindrops* 174: This is champagne. Wrap a liplock on *that* one time.

    b. an act of fellatio.—usu. considered vulgar.

    1976 *Nat. Lampoon* (July) 77: A liplock on the Chisholm Trail is better than a hired hand. **1983** K. Weaver *Texas Crude* 81: Put a lip-lock on my love-muscle. **1985** *Maledicta* VIII 243: Why don't you just take a triple lip-lock on my love muscle, motherfucker?

    2. a passionate kiss. Also as v.

    1979 *Penthouse* (Dec.) 46: Tammi was putting a lip-lock on me. **1987** *Night Court* (NBC-TV): OK! Commence lip-lock! **1989** *Roseanne* (ABC-TV): You had [him] in a lip-lock. **1994** *CBS This Morning* (CBS-TV) (July 19): How was the lip-lock? **1994** *Wild Oats* (Fox-TV): They're lip-lockin', that's what they're doin'! **1995** *TV Guide* (Feb. 4) 34: A sudden surprise lip-lock. **1997** *New York* (Feb. 17) 12: Sources spotted [her] recently at Jet Lounge engaged in a steamy lip-lock with another woman.

lip off *v.* to speak insolently; mouth off. Cf. earlier LIP, *v.*, 1.a.,b.

    1958 Gilbert *Vice Trap* 83: One of the girls was…lipping off to the heat about it being her birthday. **1959** Sabre & Eiden *Glory Jumpers* 29: A busted top-kick, and he's lipping off. **1964** in Gover *Trilogy* 369: I'm lippin off right back. **1965** *Sat. Eve. Post* (Nov. 20) 82: Danny Muldoon…had already sealed his doom by lipping off to Red Hankins even before the dismal performance on the field. **1971** Flanagan *Maggot* 210: Black boy always lippin' off. **1975** Wambaugh *Choirboys* 183: Ever hear of somebody lipping off to you? **1977** Dunne *True Confessions* 35: Lipping off is probably what she was doing. **1979** Shaber & Hil *Warriors* (film): No matter what he says, don't nobody lip off or get hot. **1980** W.C. Anderson *Bat-21* 81: It's not Air Force policy for a smart-assed captain to lip off to a superior officer! **1983** *Reader's Digest Success with Words* 87: Black English…*lip off* = "to talk back, verbally rebel."

lippy *adj.* impertinent; impudent.

    1865 Williams *Joaquin* 132: Ned, you are too cheeky altogether. You are as lippy as a Tombs' shyster who's fingered a knuck's fee. **a1893** W.K. Post *Harvard* 195: The lippy dude! **1900** Ade *More Fables* 134: He would slam the Boxes around and be Lippy and give them the Eye. **1907** London *Road* 30 [ref. to *ca*1893]: Orator Kid (who could tell how it happened), and Lippy Kid (who was insolent, depend upon it). **1902–03** Ade *People You Know* 100: There was the lippy Boy with the Williams and Walker Shirts. **1952** Himes *Stone* 13: He's a lippy son of a bitch. **1957** Herber *Tomorrow* 42: Sergeant Rogells says you're a pretty lippy guy. **1964** Brister *Renegade Brand* 55: I offered him a job riding for me, and he got lippy with me. **1965** Spillane *Killer Mine* 61: He always was a lippy guy with Hymie. **1967** Edson *Fast Gun* 56: I never could stand lippy help in a bar. **1972** D. Jenkins *Semi-Tough* 43: You're a lippy son of a bitch. **1986–91** Hamper *Rivethead* 176: What had possessed me to get lippy in print…?

lip salve *n.* insincere flattery.

    1882 Campbell *White Slave* 202: Tell de chilern…[to] put dere whole hearts in dem prayers.…De Lawd ain't gwine to pay no 'tention to lip salve.

lipstick *adj.* (of a lesbian) markedly feminine in appearance and behavior. Also as n.

    1987 *N.Y. Times* (Sept. 29) B2: "Lipsticks"—high-fashion "radical-chic lesbians." **1987** *Chi. Trib.* (Dec. 7) 3: He supported the successful aldermanic candidate [*sic*] of Janet Canarias, "a lipstick lesbian," against the wishes of his boss. **1990** T. Thorne *Dict. Contemp. Sl.*: Lipstick…a lesbian interested in high-fashion, a "feminine" lesbian. A Yale University term of the 1970s. **1992** *New York* (June 8) 40: Known as lipstick lesbians, they are pretty and dress sexy. **1994** *Nation* (Nov. 21) 612: I'd expected a little, unobtrusive lipstick lady from south of the border; Carmela turned out to be the butch from 10,000 fathoms. **1996** *Village Voice* (N.Y.C.) (Apr. 16) 122 (personal ad): WM CEO age 40 seeks two lipstick Lesbians for daytime fun. Can watch or join in.

Lipton's *n.* [fr. the trademark name of a type of tea, punning on TEA] *Narc.* poor-quality narcotics. Also **Lipton tea.**

    1964 R.S. Gold *Jazz Lexicon* 193: Lipton's…synonymous with all marijuana of poor quality.…Current since *c*1940…oral evidence only. **1970** Horman & Fox *Drug Awareness* 468: Lipton tea—poor quality narcotics. **1970** C. Major *Afro-Amer. Sl.* 77: Lipton's…fake or poor marijuana.

lip-wrestle *n.* to engage in romantic kissing. *Joc.*

    1992 *Simpsons* (Fox-TV): I'm tired of watching you guys lip-wrestle.

lip-zipping see *zip (one's)* [or *the*] *lip* s.v. LIP, *n.*

liquefied *adj.* drunk.

    *1939 (cited in *ODMS*). **1942** *ATS* 123: [Drunk:] *liquefied, liquored (up),…lit.* **1993** *Bold & Beautiful* (CBS-TV): So you went out and got liquefied, like an idiot!

liquidate *v.* **1.** to take a drink of liquor. *Joc.*

    1888 *Stag Party* 6: They all smoked. Crane liquidated.

    2. [sugg. by the euphemism used in Soviet pronouncements on imprisonments and executions carried out during Stalinist purges] to kill (someone). Now *S.E.*

    1937 Kober *Wonderful Time* 81: My God, you'd think he was going to be liquidated tomorrow! ***1943** C.S. Lewis, in *OED2*: Once we killed bad men: now we liquidate unsocial elements. **1955** Q. Reynolds *HQ* 9: Joe…removed a gun from the belt of a hoodlum…just as he was about to use it to liquidate Phillips. **1954–60** *DAS*: Liquidate…To kill a person. **1967** "M.T. Knight" *Terrible Ten* 99: If I didn't have to catch a plane…I swear I'd liquidate the brat. **1995** *New Republic* (Aug. 7) 13: Of those Bosnian fighters who had attempted to break free, Bosnian Serb radio said "most were liquidated" and the rest captured.

liquid courage *n.* DUTCH COURAGE.

    1942 *ATS* 111: Liquor (Generally.)…*Dutch courage…liquid courage.* **1979** *Maclean's* (July 23) 13: Hot-rodders, fuelled with liquid courage, turned the traffic circle on Main Street into a mechanized maypole. **1984** *Harper's* (Nov.) 57: This wife, her husband absent, guards his liquor—his little bottle of liquid courage. **1994** Indianapolis, Ind., policeman, on *Cops* (Fox-TV): He's got a midnight load of liquid courage.

liquid death *n.* cheap, powerful liquor. *Joc.* Also **liquid crime.**

    1862 "E. Kirke" *Among Pines* 228: "Mine host" and two assistants were dispensing "liquid death," at the rate of ten cents a glass. **1881** Nye *Forty Liars* 260: It was way billed over the Union Pacific as "Liquid Crime."

liquid fire *n.* strong liquor, esp. whiskey.—also used attrib.

    *1815 in *OED2*: It is in this way that the various kinds of cordial waters are prepared.…The term liquid-fire has not unaptly been given them. **1830** in *DA*: I have not taken cold since I stopt taking the *liquid fire.* [***1838** in *OED2*: Runjeet produced some of his wine, a sort of liquid fire.] **1889** O'Reilly & Nelson *Fifty Years on the Trail* 73: A bottle of "Minnie-wah-kah," or liquid-fire whiskey.

liquid horseshoes *n.* liquor, esp. whiskey, with an exceptional KICK, 6.a. *Joc.*

    1920 Simmons *20th Engrs.* (unp.): Bottled crime, third rail, T.N.T., liquid horseshoes go only part way in describing it.

liquid laugh *n.* an act of vomiting caused by drunkenness.

    *1986 Hudson & Pickering *Austral. Dict. Vulgarities*: Liquid laugh. Vomit. **1990** T. Thorne *Dict. Contemp. Sl.*: Liquid laugh…a bout of vomiting…part of the vocabulary of the influential late 1960s cartoon character Barry McKenzie, the Australian boor…[heard] especially on campus, in the USA.

liquid lunch *n.* liquor taken instead of an actual lunch. *Joc.*

    1963 A. Morgan *Six-Eleven* 274: I had a…liquid lunch…I'm loaded. ***1969** in *Austral. Nat. Dict.*: We used to go down to Jim Buckley's…for a liquid lunch. ***1970** in *OED2*: The caretaker, aroused from his post-liquid-lunch slumber. **1990** *Working Woman* (Mar.) 31: Today the exclusively intuitive approach to making decisions is as dated as the liquid lunch.

liquid sky see s.v. SKY.

liquor *v.* **1.** to drink liquor.—now usu. constr. with *up*. Cf. earlier S.E. sense 'to supply with liquor', in *OED2* from *ca*1560. See also LIQUORED UP.

    1831 in *DA*: Come, let's liquor again. ***1837** Marryat *Diary* 149: It's a bargain then (*rising up*), come let's liquor on it. **1838** J. Neal *Charcoal Sks.* i 36, in *F & H*: Come, boys, let's liquor—what'll you have? **1844** Porter *Big Bear* 43: "Now," said the boss, "suppose we licker again." **1846** in *Minn. Hist.* XXXVI (1958) 42: "Doctor Renfrew"…asked me if I would "liquor with him." **1848** *Life in Rochester* 94: Let's step over and *licker*. **1850** in *DAE*: Hast "liquored up" at Parker's? **1851** M. Reid *Scalp Hunters* 13: Just time to "licker." Come along! **1873** Small *Grangers* 10: Come boys,…let's licker some more. **1882** Sala *Amer.*

Revisited 59: Swearing fealty to the Republic by *"liquoring up."* **1904** in *DA:* "Let's liquor," he said. **1929** Sturges *Dishonorable* 627: They liked to make love, gamble and likker up. **1965** Yurick *Warriors* 22: The chosen seven had liquored up—two drinks a man—for spirit.

2. [back formation fr. LIQUORED UP] to make drunk.—constr. with *up.*

1967 Kolb *Getting Straight* 41: Buy case of booze to liquor up sports writers for golf tourney.

liquored up *adj.* drunk. Rarely **liquored.**

[*1870 in *F & H* IV 208: I'll die well liquored, and with my dinner in my belly.] **1924** P. Marks *Plastic Age* 150: I was all liquored up, and I guess she was too. **1928** Dahlberg *Bottom Dogs* 4: They were pretty well soused and lickered up. **1950** Bissell *Stretch on the River* 8: You had to be willing to kiss the old girls who got liquored up. **1954** Chessman *Cell 2455* 3: One night he got likkered up and grew broodingly belligerent. **1954–60** *DAS: Liquored...Drunk. Not common....Liquored up...common.* **1990** Yarborough *Da Nang Diary* 30: Periodically those dudes get all liquored up and try their hand at night target practice. **1991** "R. Brown" & R. Angus *A.K.A. Narc* 29: Some liquored-up trucker or cowboy.

liquorhead *n.* Esp. *So.* a drunkard.

1923 Toomer *Cane* 176: You take a man what drinks, th biggest licker-head around will come int th church an yell th loudest. **1928** Fisher *Jericho* 195: I don' think you ought t' have no licker-head for a boss. **1935** Wolfe *Time & River* 68: Where'd you be if Emmet Wade ever got the idea you're a liquor-head! **1940** McCullers *Golden Eye* 117: There were a few lady morphinists and any number of rich young liquor-heads. **1912–43** *Frank Brown Collection* I 560: *Liquor-head: n.* A drunkard.—West. **1944** *PADS* (No. 2) 35: *Liquorhead: n.* A habitual inebriate. N.C. Common. (Also Va., S.C., Tenn.) **1945** in Brougher *Bataan* 157: Perhaps three years as a PW has been a good "Kelly cure" for him and some other old "liquor heads" among us.

liquorize *v.* to drink liquor; (*also*) to supply with liquor.

1819 in *DA:* A Mister McBeth, who seemed to have been liquorising. **1833** in *DAE:* Here is the Bar, you must liquorise. **1836** in Cather *Voyage* 103: Major, we're about *liquorizing.* **1840** in *DAE:* Friends, you liquorize too freely—its a bad thing. **1895** in *DAE:* The proposition to invest saloons with a legal right to liquorize the community on Sundays.

liquor-up *n.* a drink.

1860–61 R.F. Burton *City of Saints* 356: After taking kindly leave and a last "liquor up." **1872** in *F & H* IV 209: He...accepted the general invitation given by De Castro to have a "shout," or, as the Americans would say, a liquor-up, at the hotel. **1889** Barrère & Leland *Dict. Slang: Liquor up...a drink....Of American origin.*

listen *v.* to strike one's ear as; sound.

1908 McGaffey *Show Girl* 78: That listened very well indeed. **1909** "O. Henry" *Strictly Business* 1511: B'gee...this listens like a spook shop. **1922** E. Rice *Adding Machine* 128: Say, that listens good to me. **1934** R. Chandler, in *DAS:* It don't listen. There's something screwy about it.

listener *n.* usu. *pl.* an ear.

1820–21 P. Egan *Life in London* 181: Put your *listeners* forward. *1821* in *OED2:* Sampson was floored from a tremendous wisty-castor, under the listener. **1832** *Spirit of Times* (Mar. 3) 3: O'Hegan made an attempt to close, but met Mc's *mawly* under the left listener. **1859** Matsell *Vocab.* 51: *Listeners.* Ears. **1913** *Sat. Eve. Post* (Jan. 4) 26: Y're going to glue yer listeners to the hole. **1917** *Everybody's* (June) 722: Dja see me hit 'im, though, right in the listener? **1918** *Stars & Stripes* (Sept. 13) 7: I...tucks 'em in me listeners. **1970** in *DARE: Listeners*—pigs ears. **1972** in *DARE.*

listening tackle *n. Naut.* an ear or ears. *Joc.*

1854 Sleeper *Salt Water Bubbles* 358: *Lend me your ears,* as the monkey said when he sliced off the cat's listening tackle with one of the captain's razors.

Lit *n.* a Lithuanian; Litvak.—also used attrib.—usu. used derisively. Also **Lith.**

1963 D. Tracy *Brass Ring* 7 [ref. to 1920's]: The public schools were already being overrun with sheeny, wop, polack, Litt, Uke and Slovak kids. **1964** *PADS* XLII 40: Lit. **1970** in *DARE: Lits*—Lithuanians. **1971** J. Sharkey, in P. Heller *In This Corner* 158 [ref. to 1920's]: They called me the "Lispin' Lith."...But it didn't bother me as long as I got the old paycheck. **1995** in *DARE: Lit* is a fairly common term for a

Lithuanian in the Chicago area. It's neutral when used by people of Lithuanian descent, but mildly derogatory when used by outsiders.

lit see LIT UP.

little boys' room *n.* a men's lavatory. *Joc.*

1935 (quot. at WASH-MY-HANDS). **1942** *Leatherneck* (Nov.) 146: Latrine. In civil life, "the little boys' room." **1946** Burns *Gallery* 168: I take a notion to relieve myself in the little boys' room. **1953** in Cannon *Like 'Em Tough* 9: A little to the right of the bar was a door with a sign that cutely said, *Little Boys.* **1968** L.J. Davis *Whence All Had Fled* 151: Washroom? John? Head? Little boys' room? Toilet? **1989** *Moonlighting* (ABC-TV), in T. Thorne *Dict. Contemp. Sl.:* I need a cup of joe, a trip to the little boys' room, a glance at the sports pages. Then we'll talk.

little breeches or **britches** *n.* **1.** (see quots.).

1785 Grose *Vulgar Tongue: Little Breeches.* A familiar appellation used to a small boy. **1856** in *DARE:* We boys didn't like him no how,...because his pride made it imperiously necessary that some of the "little breeches" should do small chores. **1903** *DN* II 299: *Little breeches...*[New England] epithet of a small boy. **1967** in *DARE:* Little Britches Rodeo, for children 15 years of age and under.

2. (*cap.*) *Craps.* the point three.

1984 Sample *Raceboss* 32: It settled on three. She won *big* that night and became famous for making "Little Britches."

little casino *n.* **1.** a small or inconsequential person.

1904 in "O. Henry" *Works* 110: We march between little casino and the North Grand Custodian of the Royal Hall Bedchamber. **1908** in H.C. Fisher *A. Mutt* 131: Howdy, little casino. Lonesome? **1958** McCulloch *Woods Wds.* 107: *Little casino*—a. A hanger-on. b. A small-bore helper.

2. gonorrhea (in contrast to syphilis).

1968 (quot. at BIG CASINO). **1977** Platt *Pretty Baby* (film): Are you afraid you'll catch little casino?...The clap?

little friend *Mil. Av.* a friendly fighter plane, as when flying as a bomber escort. Now *hist.* Cf. BIG FRIEND.

1944 Stiles *Big Bird* 13: Every direction...there were airplanes, big birds and little friends. **1945** in *AS* (Dec. 1946) 310: *Little Friend.* A fighter plane. See *big friend,* above. **1951** Sheldon *Troubling Star* 16: Little friend, little friend....Four Fox eighties. **1977** J. Wylie *Homestead Grays* 276: Be seeing you, little friends. **1984** J. Dailey *Silver Wings* 278: The...P-47 Thunderbolt...was earning the name "Little Friend" to the Flying Fortresses. **1994** M. Bowman & P. Bunce *Thunder in Heavens* 60: I called for help with, "Little Friend, Little Friend, this is Big Friend."

little girls' room *n.* a women's lavatory. *Joc.*

1949 in *OED2:* "Where are you going?" "To the little girls' room." **1951** Styron *Lie Down in Darkness* 54: "She means the little girls' room," he said with an explanatory wink. *1959, *1975* in *OED2.* **1988** *L.A. Law* (NBC-TV).

Little Joe *n. Craps.* a throw of four on the dice. Also **Little Joe from Kokomo**; occ. in other vars.

1890 (quot. at BIG DICK). **1894** Ade *Chicago Stories* 98: He confided stories about "passin' de bones," "Little Joe" and "gettin' ole eight." **1897** Ade *Pink* 219: I had 'em comin' good, but little Joe use me bad, an' somebody get in hosses. **1912** (quot. at LITTLE PHOEBE). **1943** *Am. N & Q* (Oct.) 112: "Little Joe picked the cotton"...appears to be a [more] commonly accepted form [than]..."Little Joe from Kokomo." **1945** Himes *If He Hollers* 33: Liddle Joe frum Kokomo. **1954** Ruby *Making Sense* 35: Or the player may commune mysteriously with "Little Joe" or "Big Dick." *a1961* Peacock *Valhalla* 9 [ref. to 1953]: Little Joe from Yong-dong-po! **1962** Killens *Heard the Thunder* 290: Little Joe from Chicago. Be four when you stop, good dice. **1968** J.P. Miller *Race for Home* 57: "Come on, th'ow! You ain't gonna make no fo'!" "Little Joe! Little Joe from Kokomo!" **1969** in *Playboy* (Jan. 1970) 297: Yeah! Little Joe from Kokomo, you ain't let Daddy down!

little joker see JOKER.

little men *n.pl. Mil.* Japanese or Vietnamese, esp. enemy soldiers.—usu. used derisively. Now *hist.* Also **little people, little guys.**

1950 Calmer *Strange Land* 172 [ref. to WWII]: We have the little men so scared around here now they are completely on the defensive. *Ibid.* 174: There's an awful lot of the little men...but...they can't last forever. *a1970* Partridge *DSUE* (ed. 7) 1255: *Little (Yellow) Men.* Japanese: coll., mostly in Army. 1942+. *a1973* in B. Edelman *Dear*

Amer. 141: The little men struck again last night. **1976** C. R. Anderson *Grunts* 51: We ain't calling in no medevac bird to tell the little guys and the world where we are, you got it? **1980** Cragg *Lex. Militaris* 278: *Little Men.* The Viet Cong or North Vietnamese Army soldiers. **1983** C. Rich *Advisors* 228: Do not risk that bird to save your little people line twos. *Ibid.* 444: *Little people*—slang for Vietnamese people. **1987** Pelfrey & Carabatsos *Hamburger Hill* 5 [ref. to Vietnam War]: Little Bear, Three, I got little people to my front, over. **1993** G. Lee *Honor & Duty* 295: You kill the gook little people and they keep comin'.

little people *n.pl.* **1.** *Theat.* bit players. Cf. modern colloq. sense 'people of no importance; common people'.

    1854 G.G. Foster *15 Mins.* 63: The actors and actresses—the "little people" and "general utilities"—drop along, one by one, from trapdoors and wings.

    2. see LITTLE MEN.

Little Phoebe *n. Craps.* a throw of five on the dice.

    1908 W.G. Davenport *Butte & Montana* 65: "Come on Big Dick."..."Little Phoebe from the south." **1912** J.W. Johnson *Ex-Coloured Man* 94: "Come, dice."..."Little Phoebe," "Little Joe," "Way down yonder in the cornfield." **1942** *ATS* 705: *Little Phoebe*, a throw of five. **1982** D.J. Williams *Hit Hard* 182: You mean they too damn dumb to know little Phoebe is five?

little school *n. Und.* a reformatory (as contrasted with a prison). Cf. BIG SCHOOL.

    1926 *AS* I (Dec.) 652: *Little School.* Reformatory of [*sic*] House of Correction. **1927** *DN* V 454: *Little school*, n. The reformatory. The penitentiary is the *big school.*

little shot *n.* [coined antonymously to BIG SHOT] a person of relatively small importance.

    1931 in *DA:* The millenium [*sic*] of Prohibition has passed for the Little Shots. **1949** in *DA:* Maragon "continued to live like a little shot in a lower-middlebrow home." **1980** *Daily News* (N.Y.) ("Tonight" ed.) (Aug. 23) 3: Big time for little shot. Billy Carter: classic study in failure.

lit up *adj.* **1.** intoxicated by liquor or (*later*) drugs; HIGH. Also **lit.**

    1899 Kountz *Baxter's Letters* 42: Every time the general gets lit up, he places his arm around your shoulder. **1902** Ade *Girl Proposition* 62: He came back a trifle Squiffy. He was all Lit Up. *ca*1903 in L. Levy *Flashes of Merriment* 292: I went home very late and pretty well lit up. **1906** *Nat. Police Gaz.* (Aug. 11) 6: The old restaurant man was...pretty well lit up. **1908** H. Green *Maison* 267: Trippet's a devil when he gits lit up. **1910** T.A. Dorgan, in *N.Y. Eve. Jour.* (Jan. 24) 10: Sig got all lit up last night. **1913** J. London *J. Barleycorn* 2: I was not drunk....I was lighted up. **1915** Lardner *Travels* 104: He was all lit up like the Municipal Pier. **1917** in Grider *War Birds* 43: Kelly and Bird were all lit up and had a bottle of whiskey which they had brought to springs. **1918** Kelland *Highflyers* 1: "Bad enough drivin' a car when you're lit up," I says. **1918** in Grider *War Birds* 82: We all got lit and had a hell of a time. **1919** Ellington *Co. A* 112: He was lit up like a Polish weddin'. **1922** E. Murphy *Black Candle* 300: She can absorb much whiskey even when "lit up" with cocaine. **1921–25** J. Gleason & R. Taber *Is Zat So?* 10: You're lit like Broadway. **1927** *New Republic* (Mar. 9) 72: Lit up like the sky...the commonwealth...a Christmas tree...a store window...a church. **1928** Santee *Cowboy* 85: He was lit for fair. **1952** Randolph & Wilson *Holler* 184: He was "lit up *like a church-house*, so drunk he didn't know which from t'other." **1962** Quirk *Ribbons* 120: I feel lit up like a Christmas tree. Now I see what people see in drinking. **1970** Horman & Fox *Drug Awareness* 468: *Lit up*—under the influence of drugs. **1976** Schroeder *Shaking It* 111: Greg lit the joint, passing it around. For the next five minutes nobody spoke; sounds only of deep inhaling and exhaling...."Anybody lit yet?" **1986** Univ. Tenn. student theme: New slang words referring to being drunk are "toasted" and "lit." **1993** *Bold & Beautiful* (CBS-TV): She's lit, man....She's high as a kite. **1996** McCumber *Playing Off Rail* 267: He didn't play at his best...if he was too lit up.

    2. showily dressed.

    1928 W.R. Burnett *Little Caesar* 91: All lit up, ain't you, Rico? **1929** in Grayson *Stories for Men* 59: Them sure are swell ties, Blue....Won't we be lit up, though?

live *adj.* **1.** exceptionally wide-awake or energetic; acute; ardent; full of life.

    1853 in Harlow *Making of Sailor* 92: *Live Yankee* [extreme clipper ship built at Rockland, Me.]. **1857** in *DAE:* A neighboring bathhouse, kept by a live Yankee of the name of Martin. **1861** in *DAE:*

Our County Society...numbers among its members most of the *"live farmers"* in the county. **1866** in Rapoport & Kirshbaum *Is Library Burning?* 20: Oshkosh is a live town; I've just been up there having a little fun with the boys. **1875** in *DAE:* The politics, or rather religion of his paper, was changed, and it became a "red-hot," "live" Gentile sheet. **1877* in *OED2:* I shall only get live people to write for me. **1888** in *OED2:* An enterprising man...created a new type of "live" newspaper. **1889–90** Barrère & Leland *Dict. Slang: Live...*In the Western newspapers "a *live* man" seems to generally signify one who is vigorous and intelligent but uneducated. **1893** in *DAE:* Good chance [for employment] for a live man. **1896** in J.M. Carroll *Benteen-Goldin Lets.* 273: He was what is known as a "live" man, and they were disirous [*sic*] of shirking their duties. **1932* in *OED2:* A varied, learned and very live and amusing book would be the result. **1934** *Scouting* (June) 31: The "live" Scoutmaster will start now to talk his Troop into Shorts [for summer wear] as soon as possible. **1960** Garagiola *Funny Game* 4: We would go to...watch our "live guys," the Hawks, beat the North St. Louis champs.

    2. [sugg. by LIVE ONE, 3] *Und.* (of a prospective victim) gullible; easily fooled.

    1908 (quot. at LIVE ONE). **1912** Lowrie *Prison* 193: He was playing me for the livest sucker he'd ever patted on the back.

    3. *Horse Racing.* (of a racehorse) demonstrating reasonable or overwhelming likelihood to win a given race. Cf. LIVE ONE, 1.

    1942 *ATS* 687: *Live horse*, a horse on which betting action is reported. **1984** W. Murray *Dead Crab* 145: It's hard enough to find one live horse.

    4. [sugg. by the show business sense 'broadcast or appearing at the time of performance; not recorded'] thrilling; exciting; wonderful; COOL, 3.a.

    1978–80 in Cardozo-Freeman *Joint* 513: Hey, Don, I hear the movie tonight is really live; want to hit it? **1982** Pond *Valley Girls' Guide* 59: *Live*—O.K., you go, "She's live," that means she's great. **1987** Townsend & Wayans *Hollywood Shuffle* (film): That was live!...That was live! **1986** *NDAS: Live...esp teenagers* Lively; exciting: *a very live party/a live dude.* **1989** P. Munro *U.C.L.A. Slang* 56: *Live...cool...*The decor in that apartment is live, I love it. **1993** P. Munro *U.C.L.A. Slang II* 57: *Live...*fun; great; excellent; hype; jumping. *a*1994 Smitherman *Black Talk* 46: "My boy was all the way live at that concert!" Also *live* (newer form). **1994** in C. Long *Love Awaits* 13: I was bugg'n. I was like, "Oh, this is live."...I have girlfriends who have told me how live it is.

live *v.* ¶ In phrases:

    ¶ **live large** see S.V. LARGE.

    ¶ **where (one) lives, 1.** (one's) vital or vulnerable spot. Now *colloq.*

    1860 in *DA:* When that little wife of mine says, "Tom, you're a good feller, God bless you," it goes right in where I live. **1861** Guerin *Mountain Charley* 25: There's where you hit me right where I live! **1886** in *DA:* If I could only have reached him where he lives, as our slang says! **1900** Willard & Hodler *Powers That Prey* 122: "Hit him where he lives!" "Kick him out o' the street!"

    2. (one's) area of special expertise; strong point.

    1907 S.E. White *Arizona Nights* 82: "I want you to buy hosses for me!"..."You bet you. Why, hosses is where I live!"

live lumber *n. Naut.* shipboard passengers. *Joc.*

    *1785 Grose *Vulgar Tongue: Live Lumber.* A term used by sailors, to signify all landsmen on board their ships. **1841** [Mercier] *Man-of-War* 2 [ref. to 1839]: We experienced uncommonly rough weather on the passage round, and the captain of the barque found that his freight of *live lumber* was anything but dis-agreeable [*sic*] when the wind began to freshen.

live one *n.* something or someone that is especially deserving of interest or attention; *Specif.:*

    1. *Horse Racing.* a fast horse. [F & H incorrectly dates the 1840 quot. as "1838."]

    1840 [Haliburton] *Clockmaker* 18: He is all sorts of a hoss, and the best live one that ever cut dirt this side of the big pond. **1898–1900** Cullen *Chances* 107: Say, it's a wonder you don't dig up a live one 'casionally. **1907** in H.C. Fisher *A. Mutt* 8: If I could only grab a couple of live ones to-day....Sevenfull and Glorio, huh? Cinch, huh?...Lead me to it!

    2.a. a person who is LIVE, 1; (*hence*) one worthy of attention or favorable regard because of intelligence, skill, friendliness, or the like.

1896 Ade *Artie* 60: I'm a good mixer and I've kind o' got next to the live ones. **1899** Ade *Fables* 77: The Unknown was a Scrapper who had been fairly Successful at one Time, but had ceased to be a Live One several Years before. **1906** *Nat. Police Gaz.* (Oct. 20) 10: The other live ones are at present in this country trying to make a little coin. **1912** T.A. Dorgan, in Zwilling *TAD Lexicon* 54: Oh judge we were just wishing that we would meet a live one—we want to go out rowing—you'll come won't you. **1913** (quot. at DEAD ONE, 3.a.). **1914** E.R. Burroughs *Mucker* 18: Byrne had…been…sparring with live ones. **1914** Jackson & Hellyer *Crim. Slang* 55: *Live One*, General currency. An informed individual…an ambitious or keenly alert person. **1919** S. Lewis *Free Air* 204: Like to chat to live ones from the big burg. **1934** Weseen *Dict. Amer. Sl.* 188: *Live one*—an attractive girl; a popular girl. **1956–60** J.A. Williams *Angry Ones* ch. xiii: All the slumbering drunks darted to their feet…as if a live one had walked in. **1964** Faust *Steagle* 63: You're a live one, Hal. Usually you get stiffs on the three o'clock planes. **1971** *Playboy* (Dec.) 338: Hand them a bill for four dollars and they call the police. My business is stiffs and phonies, maybe four live ones in a whole building. **1971** *Qly. Jour. Stud. Alcohol* XXXII 733: *Live one* A person who is willing to share his good fortune with those less fortunate. Also *live wire*.

b. something that is lively and interesting.

1909 T. Dreiser, in Riggio *Dreiser-Mencken Letters* I 26: I secured control of The Bohemian [magazine].…I am going to make it a live one.

3. *Und.* a prospective victim of a swindle, esp. a wealthy, gullible person; one who can be easily taken in or exploited, esp. for money; SUCKER.

1908 McGaffey *Show Girl* 116: The only time they don't catch a live one is when their hands are tied. **1910** *N.Y. Eve. Jour.* (Feb. 3) 16: Huh? Investor? Can this be a live one? **1910** *Variety* (Aug. 13) 14: His song, "I've Got a Live One," [is] technical to the chorus misses who love to have the "Johns" chase them. **1912** *Adventure* (May) 26: If he's a live one I'll land him in an hour. **1914** Jackson & Hellyer *Crim. Slang* 55: *Live One*, Noun General currency…a prospectively profitable victim. **1920** Ade *Hand-Made Fables* 48: Maw suddenly sat up and exchanged Glances and fell to the Fact that they were harbouring a Live One. **1920** *Variety* (Dec. 31) 26: Crowds of flashily dressed Janes sitting at tables and waiting for live ones. **1922** S. Lewis *Babbitt* 117. **1922–24** McIntyre *White Light* 3: The capricious cuties who live by their ability to find the "live one" do not angle for visiting Babbitts. **1941** G. Legman, in G. Henry *Sex Variants* II 1170: *Live one* A male prostitute's homosexual client who is generous with money and valuable gifts. **1942** Sonnichsen *Billy King* 99: The town was full of "live ones" with money. **1951** Algren *Chicago* 121: Hey Maw! Hey Paw! Two Bums Waitin' Fer A Live One! **1954** in Botkin *Sidewalks* 490: The "live one" is a client with a fat wallet. **1957** *Social Problems* V 312: "Live ones" (workers or others who have money [that may be obtained through begging]). **1962** T. Berger *Reinhart* 95: They roared toward a couple of "live ones," which was to say, clients, people in the market for a house. *a***1967** Bombeck *Wit's End* 153: Here comes a couple of live ones. **1982** Hayano *Poker Faces* 48: The result is a consistent loser, a *turkey, pigeon, live one,* or *juicy* player. **1987** J. Thompson *Gumshoe* 216: The only "live one" in this story was the journalist [who naively wrote it]. **1995** *Donahue* (NBC-TV): "We would keep the live ones in the joint [in Las Vegas]." "Big spenders?" "High rollers."

liver-chops *n.* a person having very thick and dark lips; (*specif.*) a black person.—used derisively.

1839–40 Cobb *Green Hand* II 141: Why, they would…make a man turn inside out, to avoid being recognized in the same latitude where such liver-chops sail.

liver-disturber *n.* an exceptionally large penis; KIDNEY-WIPER.—usu. considered vulgar. Also **liver-lifter.**

*ca***1888** *Stag Party* (quot. at KIDNEY-WIPER). *Ibid.* 195: He has a liver-lifter, child,/ With which he ripped their wombs.

liver-lips *n.pl.* Esp. *Black E.* (esp. of a black person) very thick and dark lips; (*hence*) (occ. *sing.*) a person having such lips.—used derisively. Also **liver-lipped,** *adj.* Cf. earlier LIVER-CHOPS.

1911 *JAF* (Oct.) 377: She had liver lips an' kidney feet. **1919** Wiley *Wildcat* 156: Liver Lip…slammed a pair of sinful cubes. **1928** C. McKay *Banjo* 72: If it was in Dixie, you wouldn't be sitting there now,

blowing a whole lot a nonsense off'n you' liver lips. **1929** Connelly *Green Pastures* 204: Hello, Liver Lips. **1931** *Collier's* (Nov. 14) 8: She takes old Liverlips by the arm. **1935** T. Wolfe *Time & River* 409: Git dat ugly ole livah-lipped face o' yo'n out o' my way! **1938** T. Wolfe *Web & Rock* 69: Outa my way, ole Liver Lips! **1950** Taylor & Mann *Jackie Robinson Story* (film): Hey, liver lips! **1952** Himes *Stone* 148: A liver-lipped colored convict. **1954** F.I. Gwaltney *Heaven & Hell* 22: His lips were thick and amazingly dark, for which a slang term existed, "liver lips." **1964** J. Thompson *Pop. 1280* 23: Answer me, you goddanged liver-lipped idjit! **1965–67** J. Herndon *Spozed to Be* 69: All the abusive nicknames, …liver-lips, burr-heads, [etc.]. **1969** in Girodias *New Olympia Reader* 729: Keep your goddamn liver lips off'n me! **1994** *Mystery Sci. Theater* (Comedy Central TV): Hey, Liver-lips!

liver pad *n.* **1.** a person; HAIRPIN. *Joc.*

1882 in Sweet *Texas* 31: When it comes to fightin' Indians, I'm just the sort of a liver-pad you want.

2. *pl.* (see quots.). *Joc.*

1942 *ATS* 97: Griddle cakes.…flapjacks…liver pads. **1950** in *DARE*. **1958** McCulloch *Woods Wds.* 107: Liver pads—Flapjacks.

Liverpool button *n. Naut.* (see quots.).

a*1890–96** *F & H* IV 212: *Liverpool-button*…A kind of toggle used by sailors when they lose a button. **1925** Farmer *Shellback* 158: When buttons were scarce, a useful substitute was found in the "Liverpool button" consisting of a piece of wood attached with a ropeyarn.

Liverpool kiss *n.* Esp. *Naut.* a blow to the face or chin.

1944 *AS* XIX 107: A *Liverpool kiss* is a kick in the chin. **1954–60** *DAS: Liverpool kiss* A hit on the mouth. **1967** *Lit Dict.* 50: *Liverpool Kiss*—A hit in the mouth. **1990** Rukuza *West Coast Turnaround* 176: Eddie butted the suit's chin with his forehead in the "Liverpool Kiss."

Liverpool pennant *n. Naut.* a piece of line or yarn used to replace a missing button, as on a jacket or pair of trousers.

*1933 J. Masefield, in *OED2: Liverpool pennants,* rope yarns used instead of buttons. **1961** Burgess *Dict. Sailing* 135: *Liverpool pennants.* Small line or spunyarn substituted for buttons.

liver rounds *n.pl. Hosp.* cocktails or other alcoholic drinks; a drinking party. *Joc.*

1988–89 in Safire *Quoth Maven* 198: You need liver rounds (cocktails)! **1990** P. Dickson *Slang!* 145: *Liver rounds.* A staff party, so called because of liver-damaging alcohol.

livestock *n.* **1.** verminous insects.

*1785 Grose *Vulgar Tongue: Live stock.* Lice or fleas. **1863** in C.H. Moulton *Ft. Lyon* 127: The "live stock"…are imperishable. **1908** W.G. Davenport *Butte & Montana* 345: How much time should be allotted a crummy Montana lumberjack to pick the live stock off of himself with a pair of boxing gloves? **1931* Partridge *Grose's Dict.* 221: *Live stock.* Lice or fleas. (So too in 1914-18.). **a1970* Partridge *DSUE* (ed. 7) 1255: *Live stock*…House bugs: domestic: C.20. Orig., and still mainly, euphemistic.

2.a. *Slave Trade.* slaves.—now usu. considered offensive.

1842 in *DA:* Negro slaves which sold formerly at 1,000 dollars, now sell for 500 dollars. There was not so much depreciation in the value of the "live stock," as these are called, as in the land. **1852** Stowe *Uncle Tom* xii, in *DA:* The trader waked up bright and early, and came out to see his livestock. **1860** in Fornell *Galveston Era* 247: Into this pocket a slaver could run at any hour of the night…[to unload his] live stock.

b. women, esp. prostitutes, as objects of sexual attention.

1927 *DN* V 454: *Live stock*, n. Prostitutes in a crowded house. **1955** Doud *To Hell and Back* (film): These boys got a corner on all the livestock?

liveware *n.* [sugg. by *hardware* and *software*; cf. WETWARE] *Computers.* human beings, esp. computer operators. *Joc.*

*1966 in *OED2:* The three elements which comprise a working computer system are hardware, the equipment itself; software, the vital programming aids; and the "liveware," or personnel. **1974* P. Wright *Lang. Brit. Industry* 25: *Liveware,* the computer operators. **1979** Homer *Jargon* 146: *Liveware* is a tongue-in-cheek reference to computer scientists. **1982** Trudeau *Dressed for Failure* (unp.): "Do you have any user-friendly sales reps?" "You mean, consumer-compatible liveware?"

live wire *n.* a person who is exceptionally energetic, animated, alert, intelligent, or the like; LIVE ONE, 2.a.—also used attrib. Now *colloq.*

1899 Kountz *Baxter's Letters* 50: It is only a matter of time until they will stumble over a live wire, and then it will be pay-day on the

Wabash. **1909** in *DA:* He was probably known to many people as an aggressive "comer" of the live-wire kind. **1904–11** D.G. Phillips *Susan Lenox* II 110: I sized you up as a live wire the minute I saw you. **1913** *Sat. Eve. Post* (July 12) 7: Tib Tinker was a live wire in a dead town. **1915** Raine *Highgrader* 126: You're a live wire. **1918** in Rossano *Price of Honor* 217: He is a live wire, he is the life of the board. **1919** *Variety* (Mar. 28) 10: Irene Meara, a diminutive live wire, is the soubret. **1922** Colton & Randolph *Rain* 60: You sure are a live wire, Sadie. **1924** P. Marks *Plastic Age* 197: Cripes, I felt most of the time he was talking only to me. I'm sore all over....Jimmie's a live wire, all right. **1926** *AS* I (Dec.) 652: *Live Wire.* One free with his money. **1927** "S.S. Van Dine" *"Canary" Murder* ch. ix: She didn't run around with many men—limited herself to a few live wires. **1928** Bodenheim *Georgie May* 20: Now ah had a real live wire las' night, ah did. He's a big, big pol'tician, and he handed me 'n extra twenty 'foah he left. **1929** *AS* IV (June) 342: *Live Wire.* A free spender. **1934** Weseen *Dict. Amer. Slang* 364: *Live wire.* An active and aggressive person. **1936** H. Gray *Arf* (unp.): "She's a live wire, ain't she?" "Live wire! That kid carries a million volts." **1974** Radano *Cop Stories* 57: The men in his squad were all live wires, hustlers. **1978** Severin *Brendan* 96: Soon to develop into *Brendan's* jester and resident live wire.

living large see s.v. LARGE.

liz *n.* **1.** TIN LIZZIE. Now *hist.*
    *****1936** Partridge *DSUE* 488: *Lizzie*...A (cheap) motor-car, orig. and mainly a "Ford."...Occ., from ca. 1924, *Liz.* **1942** *ATS* 81: Small, cheap automobile...*jalopy...Liz...liz...tin can.* **1953–57** Ruark *Old Man & Boy* 19 [ref. to 1920's]: Let's go crank up the Liz.
2. LEZ.
    1957 in W.S. Burroughs *Letters* 353: The liz fuck [*sic*] this boy with a joke prick. **1958** W.S. Burroughs *Naked Lunch* 91: When I was a transvestite Liz in Chi [I] used to work as an exterminator. Make advances to pretty boys for the thrill of being beaten as a man.

lizard *n.* **1.** an Alabaman.
    1845 in *DA:* The inhabitants of...Alabama [are called] Lizards. **1948** in *DA:* The residents of Alabama have been called "lizards."
2. (see quots.). [See *DARE* for addit. evidence.]
    1870 in *DA:* One end was placed on a sled called a "lizard," to which the horse was hitched. **1906** in *AS* VI 465: Down in Texas a sledge or jumper is evidently called a lizzard. **1948** in *DA:* A type of sled used in Missouri before the era of the wagon was known as a lizard. It was made of a V-shaped forked tree and furnished with a bed or brush to haul a load. **1956** Sorden & Ebert *Logger's* 21 [ref. to *a*1925]: *Lizard,* see dray.
3.a. a worthless animal, esp. a racehorse.
    1907 S.E. White *Arizona Nights* 84: You have to leave town for a couple of days, and you want back that lizard you sold me. Well, wait. **1932** in D. Runyon *Blue Plate* 358: Generally it is some broken-down lizard that he buys. **1954–60** *DAS: Lizard*...A racehorse, esp. an inferior one.
b. a despicable person.
    1927 P.A. Rollins *Jinglebob* 185 [ref. to 1880's]: No, them lizards didn't look a-tall like ordinary, standard-bred nephews. **1964** in *Time* (Jan. 1, 1965). **1973** Eble *Campus Slang* (Mar.) 2: *Lizard*—a loser; a law student at UNC. **1987** R.M. Brown *Starting* 167: The Internal Revenue Service. I wish I could figure out a way to starve the flaming lizards. **1987** Norst & Black *Lethal Weapon* 179: It still pays to be the nastiest lizard in the swamp. **1989** *Murphy Brown* (CBS-TV): The guy is a lizard. **1992** *CNN World News* (CNN-TV) (Mar. 11): I'm sure the lizard didn't deserve it. Ha ha ha.
4.a. LOUNGE LIZARD.
    1920 Ade *Hand-Made Fables* 16: A certain Lizard was on hand wearing a Blue Tie. **1935** in Pound *Letters* 269: As you are writing English, you can't call *them there bloody* gallants, "cake-eaters" or "lizards." **1990** Niemann *Boomer* 134: I found a seedy afternoon bar,...a few no-veins lizards on the stools.
b. [abstracted fr. LOUNGE LIZARD] a frequenter of (a specified place); (*hence*) one who is excessively interested in or enthusiastic about (something specified).—used in combs. See also LOUNGE LIZARD.
    1923 McKnight *Eng. Wds.* 61: [Student slang:] Library lizard, poor prune, hambone. **1954–60** *DAS: —— Lizard* A hound for something, a hog....A *"chow lizard"* is known for eating a lot, a *"couch lizard"* is known for necking on a couch with his girl. **1987** *U.S. News & W.R.* (Dec. 14) 74: Q. What are the most common kinds of problem employes?

[A.] People who...cheat on their time—the time wasters, the bathroom hiders, the lunch lizards. **1991** "R. Brown" & R. Angus *A.K.A. Narc* 61: A chronic bar lizard.

5. Esp. *So.* the penis; in phrs. **bleed** [or **leak**] **(one's) lizard** (of a male) to urinate; **drain (one's) lizard** (of a male) to urinate or (*rarely*) to ejaculate; **stroke** [or **whip**] **the lizard** (of a male) to masturbate.—usu. considered vulgar. *Joc.*
    [**1942** Hurston *Dust Tracks* 63: Or some woman would come switching past the store porch and some man would call to her, "Hey, Sugar! What's on de rail for de lizard?"] **1962** Ravenden, Ark., man (coll. J. Ball): Gotta go inside and drain my lizard. **1969** in Girodias *New Olympia Reader* 794: It was almost as if I were adding a new coat of cadmium hue to Larry's lovely lizard with each new thrust. **1970** Landy *Underground Dict.* 178: *Stroke the lizard, v.* Masturbate. **1970** *Current Slang V* (Summer) 6: *Drain the lizard, v.* Urinate.—Wait while I *drain the lizard.* **1971** *Nat. Lampoon* (Dec.) 37: You know, whipping your lizard. **1973** *TULIPQ* (coll. B.K. Dumas): Urination...*bleed your lizard.* **1975** C.W. Smith *Country Music* 54: Where's Rabbit? Rabbit?...Bleeding his lizard, I guess. **1975** in *West. Folk.* XXXVI (1977) 359: Whip my lizard. **1978** *NBC's Saturday Night* (NBC-TV): A man shouldn't care about the woman's pleasure as long as he drains the lizard. **1979** *NBC's Saturday Night* (NBC-TV): There are hundreds of women...waiting for the Garvin lizard. **1984** J.R. Reeves *Mekong* 185 [ref. to 1970]: Go use the latrine; don't bleed your lizard here in public. **1985** Heywood *Taxi Dancer* 20 [ref. to Vietnam War]: The best piece of ass you ever had....the one that drained your lizard for a week. **1986** McLoughlin *Jason Lives* (film): He's in the can draining his lizard. **1994** N.Y.C. book review editor, age *ca*70: A euphemism for the act of urination that I can remember from my GI days—I'm thinking of 1942–43—was "I gotta go bleed a lizard."...It may have originated as a Southern expression. **1994** *Harper's* (May) 42: I whipped out my lizard and whizzed all over. **1994** *X-Files* (Fox-TV): I've gotta drain the lizard.

6. *Mil.* (see quot.).
    1989 Leib *Fire Dream* 301 [ref. to Vietnam War]: He dropped to the ground silently, and began to move in what the infiltration instructors called the lizard. Moving first an arm, then the opposite leg, then the other arm, then the other leg....He crawled...using the lizard.

7. *Rap Music.* a young woman.
    1989 "Too Short" *Freaky Tales* (rap song): Gave me a lizard, said her name was Laverne. **1996** N.Y.C. woman, age 27 (coll. J. Sheidlower): Yeah, I've heard *lizard* for "woman" in a lot of rap songs. There's tons of ways they refer to us [women].

lizzie *n.* **1.a.** an effeminate man or boy; sissy.—often *cap.*— usu. used derisively. Also **lizzie boy.**
    1899 Kountz *Baxter's Letters* 36: Now will you kindly tell me why it is that a girl will throw a good fellow down every time for one of those Lizzie boys? **1902** Townsend *Fadden & Mr. Paul* 255: I'm no airy, fairy Lizzy, and de bull-dog was walking on de edge of his foot like he'd die wit joy if any old kind of a fight came his way. **1905** *DN* III 87: *Lizzie (boy), n.* An effeminate young man. "He's a regular *Lizzie* (*boy*); he parts his hair in the middle, and wears red socks and toothpick shoes." **1904** in "O. Henry" *Works* 32: Demps Donovan picked a scrap with your Lizzie-boy, and they've waltzed out to the slaughter room with him. **1917** E.R. Burroughs *Oakdale Affair* 72: We'll get you, you colledge Lizzy. **1922** S. Lewis *Babbitt* 99: Oh, there's a swell bunch of Lizzie boys and lemon-suckers and pie-faces and infidels and beer-bloated scribblers that love to fire off their filthy mouths and yip that Mike Monday is vulgar and full of mush. **1928** Hecht & MacArthur *Front Page* 454: I hear all the reporters in New York are lizzies. **1938** "R. Hallas" *You Play the Black* 41: Get an old lizzie,...and then drive right up to a tree. **1939** A. Johnson et al. *Hardys Ride High* (film): With some...lizzie [like him].
b. *Stu.* a young woman.
    1902–03 Ade *People You Know* 206: Now and then a man may have a Passing Fancy for a Lizzie who talks Piffle. **1914** E.R. Burroughs *Mucker* 118: If I gets de lizzie outen de jug...youse'll be here. **1925** Paine *First Yale* I 118 [ref. to 1917]: Charlie and Henry are coming along with a couple of Lizzies.
c. a lesbian; LEZZIE. Also as *adj.*
    *****1949** in *OED2:* I wish you wouldn't talk to those Lizzies. **1954** Collans & Sterling *House Detect.* 145: Where the aggressive Lizzie was a guest in the hotel and invited her passive partner up to her room, we

would merely notify the desk. **1954** in W.S. Burroughs *Letters* 245: His dungaree-wearing Lizzie wife. **1963** Horwitz *Candlelight* 199 [ref. to WWII]: This has become a town for lizzies and self-assured faggots. ***1966** J.B. Priestly, in *OED2*: She has a Lizzie crush on me. **1977** J. Olsen *Fire Five* 128: One or two of your lizzies is bound to creep in. **1996** M. Kearney *Southeastern La. Univ. Coll.* (May): Lizzy— a homosexual (female).

2.a. a Ford automobile; TIN LIZZIE; (*broadly*) a car.

1913 in *OED2*: When you get tired of rolling around in your Lady Lizzie...hie yourself to the nearest news dealer. **1915** in Truman *Dear Bess* 180: Old Lizzie was as warm as a church. **1919** *DN* V 65: *Lizzie*, a Ford automobile. **1923** in Kornbluh *Rebel Voices* 88: I spies the lizzie pickin' up my gladhanders. **1942** "E. Queen" *Calamity Town* 128: I'm not the spoiled brat you used to neck in the back of your lizzie. **1946** Mezzrow & Wolfe *Really Blues* 118: This Lizzie may not look good, but she'll run...like a mountain goat. **1953** Paley *Rumble* 295: Get somebody to put in a call for patrol lizzies.

b. an airplane.

1918 Cushing *Surgeon's Jour.* 310: French hydro-aeroplanes are circling around, and a big yellow "Lizzie" has just gone over—low enough to see her pilot's head.

3. the Cunard White Star liner *Queen Elizabeth.*—constr. with *the.*

***1916** (cited in Partridge *DSUE* (ed. 7) 1255). **1917** Depew *Gunner Depew* 140: Yet the old Lizzie just sailed right along, with her band up on the maindeck playing "Everybody's Doing It."

lizzie *v.* **1.** to drive in a LIZZIE, 2.a.

1919 in Baldwin *Canteening* 192: Yesterday at 8 AM we "lizzied" out to the carnival grounds.

2. to pedicate; punk; queer.—constr. with *up.*

1934 Appel *Brain Guy* 219: On the second floor, in the flat with the beds, a bunch got steamed up and were going to lizzy up one of the younger kids who had a girl's complexion. They'da fixed his wagon.

Lo *n.* [joc. fr. "Lo, the poor Indian! whose untutor'd mind/Sees God in clouds," in Pope *Essay on Man* I 99 (1733–34)] *West.* an American Indian; American Indians collectively. Also **Mr.** [or **Mrs.**] **Lo.** *Joc.* Now *hist.*

1866 in Hilleary *Webfoot* 159: "Lo" had departed hence. **1867** in A.K. McClure *Rocky Mtns.* 329: "Lo" and his dusky bride visited me. **1870** Ludlow *Heart of Cont.* 193: In Denver...Indians...are always called "the Lo Family." "How are you, Lo (or Mr. Lo)?" is the familiar address of a copper-colored warrior. **1871** Crofutt *Tourist's Guide* 72: The Colonel rushed out and was immediately dispatched by the Mr. "Lo's." **1873** E. Custer *Plains* 44: I wonder if we will catch Mr. Lo? **1873** *Custer's Yellowstone Exped.* 17: The forests showed...that "Mr. Lo," as the soldiers familiarly call him, had been here very recently. **1873** Beadle *Undeveloped West* 367: Mr. Lo, "the poor Indian." **1874** Ewert *Diary* 57: Hunting grounds for "poor Lo." **1874** McCoy *Cattle Trade* 139: This arises from a desire existing in the breasts of the contractors to feed full-blood Los instead of half-breeds and mongrels. **1881** A.A. Hayes *New Colo.* 36: The "Lo family" (as the noble red man—"Lo, the poor Indian"—is called on the plains). **1882** Triplett *Jesse James* 110: Amusing little amenities of Lo. **1885** E. Custer *Boots & Saddles* 175: Mrs. "Lo" is the Venus who prepares Mars for war. **1893** Lockwood *Drummer-Boy* 189: The commandant...cracked a shell into the ravine, making the "poor Los skedaddle." **1923** J.L. Hill *Cattle Trail* 18: At times poor Lo suffered grievous wrongs at their hands. **1925** Z. Grey *Vanishing Amer.* 16: Have you met Lo?...He's the Indian crack. **1931** R.G. Carter *On Border* 58: The advent of this new Colonel...sent rifles and shot-guns to the rear...until that larger and more troublesome game, "Lo, the poor Indian," should be sought and conquered. *Ibid.* 343: The proverbial "Mr. Lo, the poor Indian," was beautifully scalped. **1990** Crow Dog & Erdoes *Lakota Woman* 113: A government lawyer decided to do something for "Lo, the poor Indian."...Poor benighted Mr. Lo was to have the blessings of democracy bestowed upon him.

loach *n.* [pron. of official abbr. *LOH*] *Mil.* a light observation helicopter. [Quots. ref. to Vietnam War.]

1986 "J. Hawkins" *Tunnel Warriors* 333: *Loach* Small spotter/scout chopper. **1984–88** Hackworth & Sherman *About Face* 664: I want you to take my loach. **1990** Yarborough *Da Nang Diary* 185: An OH-6 Loach contacted me. **1991** Reinberg *In Field* 130: *LOH* (pronounced loach).

load *n.* **1.a.** a state of drunkenness.—often constr. with *on.*

***1678** in *OED*: Proverbial Periphrases of one drunk....He has a jagg or load. ***1767** in *F & H* IV 212: He has a jag or load, drunk. **1864** Armstrong *Generals* 276: The Commissary [whiskey] was too much for their empty stomachs....I saw at once that Division Headquarters had a good load on. **1877** Wheeler *Deadwood Dick* 79: Nightly the...miners come in from such claims as are within...six to ten miles, and seldom is it that they go away without their "load." **1891** Maitland *Slang Dict.* 169: "He has a load," he is drunk. **1893** in B. Matthews *Parts of Speech* 202: Intoxication...*to carry a load.* **1898** in S. Crane *Complete Stories* 413: Where did they get their loads? **1904** in "O. Henry" *Works* 69: It was plain that Jerry had usurped the function of his cab, and was carrying a "load." **1939–40** O'Hara *Pal Joey* 24: Some guy is going to get his load on...and take a poke at you. **1942** "E. Queen" *Calamity Town* 59: He's carrying a real load. **1943** J. Mitchell *McSorley's* 34: When a bum is sleeping off his load, you could saw off his leg and he wouldn't notice nothing. **1948** Ives *Stranger* 148: In such wise I went from one joint to another; usually I'd end up with a few bucks and a load on. **1949** W.R. Burnett *Asphalt Jungle* 65: Maybe I had a slight load on. **1952** Uris *Battle Cry* 76: Easy, Marine, you've got a full load on. **1954** Ellson *Owen Harding* 31: He really had a load on by the end of the meal. **1955** Q. Reynolds *HQ* 304: Now the kids have their loads on....Now they're wanting to show off, maybe. **1961** Plantz *Sweeney Squadron* 33: That boy can sure tie a load on. **1966** Braly *Cold* 33: Hugo made his load and threw Gloria out of the house bare-ass naked....After Hugo passed out, she crawled in through the kitchen window. **1968** O.H. Hampton *Young Runaways* (film): He always does that when he's got a load on. **1990** Crow Dog & Erdoes *Lakota Woman* 48: One of those winos was out in his car getting a load on.

b. a state of drug intoxication.

1898 L.J. Beck *Chinatown* 173: How's a man to keep his load on with all that caterwauling going on?

2. *Und. & Gamb.* all the valuables or money on one's person; (*also*) the proceeds of a crime.

***1754** in Partridge *Dict. Und.* 412: The other ordered her to leave me alone, for that she had got my *load*; by which I suppose she meant my watch and chain. **1836** *Spirit of Times* (July 9) 1621: If a man goes in for betting, I say let him go his load. **1847–49** Bonney *Banditti* 85: A good load, that of Jacks! wasn't it?

3.a. feces; a bowel movement; usu. in phr. **drop (one's) load** to defecate.—usu. considered vulgar.

*a*1865 in Rable *Civil Wars* 162: Pulled down his pants and emptied his bowels of [a] stinking load. **1927** [Fliesler] *Anecdota* 166: I guess I'd better lay my load on the floor in the corner, and clean it up in the morning. **1937** Weidman *Wholesale* 42: You sound like you dropped a load in your pants. **1968** Westheimer *Young Sentry* 217: He [a horse] dropped a load. We're gonna have a good garden next summer. **1968** Baker et al. *CUSS* 152: *Load, Get A—Off Your Mind* Defecate. **1966–71** Karlen *Sex. & Homosex.* 492: A truly Living Theater would not just strip bare and display their genitals but bend over, spread their buttocks and drop a load. **1977** Sayles *Union Dues* 19: Got to drop a load. **1986** Pietsch *Cab Driver's Joke Book* 47: A steaming load that a cow had just dropped. **1993** *Donahue* (NBC-TV): Parading around with his pants down like he's got a load in them.

b. an ejaculation of semen; (*rarely*, of either sex) an orgasm.—usu. in phr. of the sort **shoot** [or **drop,** etc.] **(one's) load** to ejaculate.—usu. considered vulgar.

1927 [Fliesler] *Anecdota* 90: Dropped one load. Got my hard on. She has it closed so I can't put it in! **1927** *Immortalia* 79: She threw the load into my face/And said, "Child, go kiss your pa!" **1928** Read *Lexical Evidence* 42: The prize cock...when shooting a load. ***ca*1929** *Adventures of Grace & Anna* 98: My goodness, what a load you shoot! **1938** "Justinian" *Amer. Sexualis* 13: He blew his load. **1942** in Legman *No Laughing Matter* 407: Just when you're gonna shoot your load, see, you kick out the brick! **1952** in Legman *Limerick* 49: But while shooting his load/It cracked like old Spode. **1962** T. Berger *Reinhart* 411: If you'd care to take a minute and drop your load....I mean take Billie Jo over behind the tent and put it to her. **1964** *AS* (May) 117: *To lose a load* or *to lose one's marbles* "to experience an orgasm." **1966** Bogner *7th Ave.* 151: What do you plan for me? A little two-room apartment...[where you] can visit me, drop your load, then go home and have dinner with your wife? *a*1968 in Haines & Taggart *Ft. Lauderdale* 108: I could have popped my load in ten seconds. **1968** P. Roth *Portnoy* 18: I was in the frenzy of dropping my load. **1969** in Girodias

New Olympia Reader 52: And resting to keep from shooting his load that very minute, so very close to climax was he. **1970** Sorrentino *Steelwork* 49: Girls shoot a load like men when they come. **1970** Woods *Killing Zone* 66: It would probably make Cox shoot his load. **1971** Contini *Beast Within* 160: Can't I just jerk you off, Joe?...You can shoot your load right onto the block. **1972** Wells *Come Fly with Us* 165: I thought I would drop my load right then and there. **1975** Harrell & Bishop *Orderly House* 8: The Load freak insists that the other man's semen be retained in the vagina so he can lap it all into his own mouth. **1976** Weldon *Sapphic Scene* 98: When I do blast a load, I want it in your pussy! **1981** *Penthouse* (Apr.) 26: I could no longer resist fucking her....I lost my load within seconds. *a***1994** A. Radakovich *Wild Girls Club* 115: Sex for him has always been a matter of "releasing a load." **1994** *20/20* (ABC-TV) (Apr. 15): Now a man can drop a load anywhere he wants to.

c. absolute nonsense; CROCK OF SHIT, 1.

1932 *AS* (Feb. 1933) 31: [W. Tex.:] *Load.* To deceive by yarns or windies. Also, a prevarication, a prevaricator. ***1945** Partridge *RAF Slang* 43: *Load bummer* an obsolescent variant of *line shooter.* The load is that in...*load of guff.* **1972** J. Pearl *Cops* 39: "That's a load."..."It's true." **1968–77** Herr *Dispatches* 20: All that's just a *load*, man. We're here to kill gooks. Period. **1987** *21 Jump St.* (Fox-TV): That's a load, man. It's a lie and you know it. **1989** *Cops* (Fox-TV): Boy, was *that* a load. **1990** *Parker Lewis* (Fox-TV): High school elections. What a load.

4. *Stu.* a prank.

1866–71 Bagg *Yale* 45: *Load*, a practical joke, a sell.

5. (among commercial drivers) a passenger or passengers.

1929 Hammett *Maltese Falcon* 105: "Where's the...driver that was here at noon?" "Got a load," one of the chauffeurs said.

6. a venereal infection.

***1936** Partridge *DSUE* (ed. 1) 488: *Load*...a venereal infection: Australia: late C.19-20: low. Hence *get a load.* **1942** Hollingshead *Elmtown's Youth* 421: "Trouble" involves two things, "knocking a girl up" (impregnation) or "getting a load" or a "dose" (venereal disease). ***1965** in *OED2*: They displayed their rubber goods, and...were doubly protected against finding themselves landed with either biological consequences or a load.

7.a. a very fat person.

1946 Kober *That Man Is Here Again* 95: "You mean Fitch is that...fat?"..."Boy, what a load!" **1979** Gutcheon *New Girls* 87: "Oh, *look* at that," Muffin pointed at the mirror. "I'm a load."

b. a person who is obnoxious, stupid, clumsy, or ridiculous.

[**1932** quot. at **(3.c.)**, above.] **1942–49** Goldin et al. *DAUL: Load*...clumsy and inept thief. "Chill...that load. He's stirwacky."...A clumsy or awkward fellow. **1958** in Reuss & Legman *Songs Mother Never Taught Me* (unp.): We must eliminate all loads and seeds. **1963** Reuss & Legman *Songs Mother Never Taught Me* (unp.): *Load* = an "all out loser," n.g. **1966** IUFA *Folk Speech: Load*—this is a word which describes a person who is not in with the crowd or does not know the latest happenings. **1968** Maule *Rub-A-Dub* 61 [ref. to WWII]: You a load....You're too much, Stringbeans. Any man get his kicks oiling on a Liberty [ship]. **1969** *Current Slang I & II* 59: *Load*, n. A dull companion, especially a dull escort.—College females, South Dakota. **1968–70** *Current Slang III & IV* 79: *Load*, n. An unattractive male.—College males, South Dakota. **1972** Eble *Campus Slang* (Oct.) 4: *Load*—a pest; That guy's a real load. **1980** Conroy *Lords of Discipline* 11: McLean, you load. **1988** H. Stern, on KROC radio (Nov. 2): That Dr. Joyce. She's a load, isn't she? **1988** Lewin & Lewin *Thesaurus of Sl.* 366: Stupid [person]...*dipstick, deadneck, dildo, load,* [etc.]. **1993** *Mystery Sci. Theater* (Comedy Central TV): Well, try harder, ya load!

8. an automobile or other motor vehicle; HEAP.

1937 (cited in Partridge *Dict. Und.* 412). **1946** I. Shulman *Amboy Dukes* 38: Boy, with a load like that, would I have me a time. **1942–49** Goldin et al. *DAUL* 127: *Load*...A stolen car. **1952** Mandel *Angry Strangers* 184: This load handles like a pair of shoes. **1953** Gresham *Midway* 62: In fact, the road riders with their heavily decorated "jobs" would refer to it [a motorcycle] disrespectfully as a "beat-up old load." **1961** *New Directions* (No. 17) 216: Ya shoulda seen this load. Chartreuse with white walls. **1972** D. Jenkins *Semi-Tough* 187: Movin' faster than I'm drivin' this old load. **1989** *Houston Chronicle* (Apr. 9): *Load*—A car.

9. *Narc.* a small portion of drugs; pac.

1969 Lingeman *Drugs A to Z: Load.* twenty-five to thirty *decks*

(packets) of *heroin* stacked and fastened together with a rubber band for delivery. **1970** Landy *Underground Dict.: Load*...Drugs—eg. *He has a load.* **1971** *Go Ask Alice* 102: Big Ass makes me do it before he gives me the load. **1989** Radford & Crowley *Drug Agent* 83: Pacs...[are also] known as..."loads."

¶ In phrases:

¶ **drop (one's) load, 1.** see **(3.a.),** above.

2. *Black E.* to be overcome with shock or surprise: "shit in (one's) pants."

1966 R.E. Alter *Carny Kill* 51: Man,...I nearly dropped my load when you jumped out like that. **1972** Carr *Bad* 115: When he told me he was working for my Aunt Harriet, I nearly dropped my load. **1975** Univ. Tenn. student: When I told her that she nearly dropped her load.

¶ **rusty load** (of men) a long abstinence from sexual intercourse; (*hence*) semen ejaculated after long abstinence.—usu. considered vulgar.

*ca***1937** in Holt *Dirty Comics* 163: Oh, it seems like I'll have to go thru with it and relieve you of your rusty load. **1951** in *Erotic Verse to 1955* 52: A shaky old prick, just in from the creek, with a rusty load in his poke. **1959** Burroughs *Naked Lunch* 174: Say, Archy boy, some night when you get caught short with a rusty load drop around. **1962** Crawford *Give Me Tomorrow* 37 [ref. to *ca*1952]: Yeah, man, my rusty load'll blow a hole through a gook gal's backside. **1967** Crawford *Gresham's War* 126: I got a load so rusty it'll turn solid iron when air hits it.

¶ **shoot (one's) load** to do or inflict all that (one) can; shoot (one's) bolt.—usu. used in past tenses.

1937 Weidman *Wholesale* 211: As far as I was concerned he'd shot his load. **1949** Robbins *Dream Merchants* 5: He was sick and tired and desperate and he knew he had shot his load. **1950** Stuart *Objector* 14: The old man shot his load....Tough for you, kid.

load *v.* **1.** Esp. *West.* to lie to or deceive; SNOW.

1883 "M. Twain" *Life on Miss.*, in *DARE*: He went on...reeling off his tranquil spool of lies...and proceeded to load me up in the good old-fashioned way. **1904** Bower *Lonesome Trail* 12: When he accused them openly of trying to "load" him, they were shocked and grieved. **1906** *DN* III 145: *Load*...To deceive or intimidate by a hint...."He just *loaded* them." **1912** Siringo *Cowboy Detective* 300: "Cunny" put in cycle time "loading" the "kid" with the bloody deeds of "Black Jack" and his gang. *Ibid.* 466: Mr. B. didn't "load" the newspaper reporters. He merely looked wise and they did the rest. **1926** W. Rogers, in C.M. Russell *Trails* xiii: Between you and me, in our own hearts we knew we were both trying to load each other. **1933** *AS* (Feb.) 31: *Load.* To deceive by yarns or windies. **1939** T. Abbott & H. Smith *Pointed Them North* 174 [ref. to 1880's]: I thought Pike was kind of loading me when he told me the story. **1946** N. Nye *Breed of Chaparral* 44: Somebody's been loading you.

2. *Baseball.* to moisten (a baseball), as with spit

1969–71 Kahn *Boys of Summer* 283: To "load one," Roe wiped his...hand across his brow and surreptitiously spat on the meaty part of the thumb.

loaded *adj.* **1.** intoxicated by liquor or drugs.—occ. constr. with *up.* Also with elaborations.

1879 Rooney *Quaint Conundrum* 29: A pistol is not half so dangerous when the owner is not loaded. **1881** Nye *Forty Liars* 74: He always spares the paleface who is loaded. **1886** Wilkins *Cruise* 67: I believe that fellow is loaded with St. Paul whiskey. **1889** Field *Western Verse* 143: Launcelot and all ye rest...sought their couches loaded. **1891** DeVere *Tramp Poems* 23: And every one on 'em got "loaded," and they had a great blow out and spree. **1892** S. Crane *Maggie* 58: Yer loaded an' yehs on'y makes a damn fool of yerself. **1893** in B. Matthews *Parts of Speech* 202: Intoxication...*to get loaded.* **1894** King *Capt. Close* 31: "You might as well pour whiskey in a knot-hole," said the sore-headed squad of youngsters that...had spent many hours and dollars one night in the attempt to get old Close "loaded." **1895** in Ade *Chicago Stories* 133: Bot' of us had been drinkin' some, but we w'an't loaded. **1899** A.H. Lewis *Sandburrs* 57: Then he'd chase home, an' bein' loaded, he'd wallop his family. *Ibid.* 134: Some mug comes wanderin' along, loaded to d' guards wit' booze. **1891–1900** in Hoyt *Five Plays* 126: Strong, in other room, is getting a bit loaded. **1902** Dunbar *Sport* 151: Drunk half the time and half drunk the rest. Well, you know what I told you the last time you got "loaded." **1908** J. London *M. Eden* 41: I was loaded right to the neck. *Ibid.* 328: I'm loaded to the guards now **1927** *New Republic* (Mar. 9) 72: Boiled as an owl, full as a tick, loaded for bear, loaded up to the muzzle, loaded up to the plimsoll-mark. **1927** Tully *Circus Parade* 266: When guys are loaded up on heroin it'll give 'em more nerve an' make 'em more desperate. **1936** Dai *Opium Addiction* 199: Filled with drugs. Also called *high…loaded*. **1939** Goodman & Kolodin *Swing* 238: Jazz musicians who get loaded on weed or high on liquor. **1942** in W.C. Fields *By Himself* 242: I'll bet he's loaded to the scuppers. **1947** R.P.T. Coffin *Yankee Coast* 74: Yes, Cap'n Harry was loaded to the gunnels tonight. **1952** Brossard *Darkness* 70: A real junkie. He was loaded with heroin on this record. **1955** Stern *Rebel* (film): He's just loaded, honey. **1956** Lennart *Meet Me in Las Vegas* (film): Could you be gettin' a little loaded—tight—drunk. **1957** Murtagh & Harris *First Stone* 39: "When a junkie's loaded," she explains, "she's not interested in sex." **1957** Simmons *Corner Boy* 20: I know you smoke pod….Last week when we came back from the dance you were loaded. **1960** Bannon *Journey* 55: He came in about five and he was loaded. **1961** *Twilight Zone* (CBS-TV): Look, Mom, Santa Claus is *loaded!* **1962** J.P. Miller *Days of Wine & Roses* (film): He gets himself loaded and cries on her shoulder. **1966** S. Harris *Hellhole* 94 [ref. to 1960's]: Now, the whole truth is that Nancy was also hooked, in fact, she was a bigger junkie than me. The girl couldn't even go with a trick unless she was loaded and she was on coke too, not just horse. **1966** Elli *Riot* 56: I'm loaded on Benny. **1975** Wambaugh *Choirboys* 186: They were loaded from sniffing paint and had felony records from when they were ten years old. **1979** Hiler *Monkey Mt.* 285: The lifers stay mostly drunk and the snuffies stay mostly loaded. It's a fact of life. **1983** *Hour Magazine* (ABC-TV) (May 6): I think I saw him loaded twice in my life. *a*1990 E. Currie *Dope & Trouble* 208: Took a hit [of marijuana], and I was…*loaded*. **1993** P. Munro *U.C.L.A. Slang II* 57: I was so loaded last night after four hits of L.S.D. **1994** *Instant Justice* (Court TV) (Sept. 24): If you go to the [drug] program loaded up, they're not going to take you….If you get loaded…, you'll blow it. **1994** *Reader's Digest* (Dec.) 91: I had always thought I could quit drinking by myself, but I'd always gone back to getting loaded.

2. extremely wealthy; having plenty of cash.

[**1839** Cobb *Green Hand* I 24: We should…return "loaded with distinction and dollars."] [**1895** *DN* I 420: *Loaded for bear*…Said of one who has a big supply of anything.] [**1910** in *OED2*: He's just loaded with the spondulix.] **1948** Vidal *City & Pillar* 73: She's probably explaining over the phone that we're just off a boat and really loaded. **1942–49** Goldin et al. *DAUL* 127: *Loaded*…Having a great sum of money on one's person or in one's possession. "…If he's loaded, we'll hustle (swindle) him." **1949** Taradash & Monks *Knock on Any Door* (film): This bookie is loaded. He's always loaded. **1949** in *DAS*: The boys were loaded after the [robbery]. **1950** Jacoby & Brady *Champagne* (film): It's frightening to have money…to be loaded. **1953** Wicker *Kingpin* 81: Hell, I'm loaded too. Want to see my checkbook? **1958** Arrowsmith *Satyricon* 46: He's so loaded he doesn't know how much he has. **1962** Perry *Young Man Drowning* 44: He went out last night stone broke and came back this morning loaded. **1967** *N.Y.P.D.* (ABC-TV): He must really be loaded. **1966–69** Woiwode *Going to Do* 84: If they're so loaded,…why don't they have servants, a maid and butler? **1969** C. Major *All-Night Visitors* 34: The motherfucker was drunk…*and loaded!*…He had about five hundred dollars in cash. **1980** L. Fleischer & C. Gore *Fame* 118: "She's loaded too." "Little Miss Moneybags." **1989** P. Benchley *Rummies* 159: We both know she's loaded. **1995** *Donahue* (NBC-TV): You're not walkin' around loaded, I mean independently wealthy.

3.a. *loaded for bear*, 1, below.

1889 "M. Twain" *Conn. Yankee* 153: As like as not, Sandy was loaded for a three-day stretch.

b. *loaded for bear*, 4, below.

1895 Gore *Stu. Slang* 14: *Loaded*…Prepared for. "He was loaded for the boys." **1957** H. Simmons *Corner Boy* 118: So each group will have three blades. That makes everybody loaded, don't it?

4. laced with drugs, poison, or (*usu.*) alcohol.

1921 Marquis *Carter* 213: I want to see which one is going to get that there loaded pill. **1923** in *OED2*: It was discovered that each of them [*sc.*, handkerchiefs] has a small ink mark in one of the corners…these handkerchiefs had been dipped in cocaine….The mark in the corner notified the "snowbird" that it was "loaded." **1939** R. Chandler *Big Sleep* 136, in *DAS*: We sipped our loaded coffee. **1971** Cole *Rook* 20: The young man talks and smokes and drinks loaded soda pop with a few friends.

¶ In phrase:

¶ **loaded for bear** [lit., '(of a firearm) loaded with heavy caliber ammunition suitable for bear-hunting'] **1.** heavily armed; (*hence*) ready for trouble; grimly or aggressively determined.

[**1875** in Bullen *Cachalot* 185: When yew fired thet ole gun, I guess it mus' have bin loaded fer bear, fer ye jest tumbled clar head over heels backward outen the boat.] **1883** Peck *Bad Boy* 101: I warned him that it was full of dangers, as the goat was loaded for bear. **1895** *DN* I 420: *Loaded for bear*. [1. Used of shot-shells which are so heavily loaded that the gun kicks when fired.] 4. Full of indignation which is likely to be vented upon its object. **1902** R. Service *Shooting of D. McGrew:* When in came a stranger, fresh from the creeks, dog-dirty and loaded for bear. **1919** Wiley *Wildcat* 244: "Always go loaded for bear, I suppose?" "Sho' do. I aims to pack a li'l equalizer all de time." **1927** *AS* II (May) 359: *Loaded for Bear*. Ready for any emergency. "We were loaded for bear before we started to the mountains. **1957** M. Shulman *Rally* 55: The O'Sheel woman is coming in loaded for bear this time. **1958** "R. Traver" *Anatomy of a Murder* 232: Surely a battered old ex-D.A. like you must be loaded for bear with all sorts of suave deviltry. **1962** L'Amour *Killoe* 48: It's quiet out there…too quiet. You better come loaded for bear. **1962** G. Olson *Roaring Road* 10: Cole's loaded for bear today. He'll overcook it on a curve [and] lose it in a spin. **1963** Boyle *Yanks Don't Cry* 14: The battleships were loaded for bear, and we always considered them the backbone of the U.S. Fleet. **1965** Himes *Imabelle* 115: You-all has sure come loaded for bear. **1970** *NBC News* (NBC-TV) (May 9): They left here loaded for bear, as the saying goes. **1978** in Lyle & Golenbock *Bronx Zoo* 218: I mean, we came into Boston loaded for bear. **1986** Clayton & Elliott *Jazz World* 193: Gee, son, you really came loaded for bear, didn't you? **1991** "R. Brown" & R. Angus *A.K.A. Narc* 21: The bad guys are coming and they're loaded for bear! **1992** *CBS This Morning* (CBS-TV) (Dec. 9): The Marines…hit the beach [in Somalia] loaded for bear. **1993** Tomedi *No Bugles* 133: We always walked around loaded for bear—hand grenades, pistols, knives. **1995** *World View* (CNN-TV) (Nov. 1): They're loaded for bear. They're ready for tough negotiations.

2. *Poker*: holding a strong hand.

1884 Carleton *Poker Club* 26: "We'se loaded fer bar over yar," retorted Mr. Smith. **1951** *AS* XXVI 2 (May) 100: *Loaded for bear*. To hold a strong hand.

3. highly intoxicated.

1889 Barrère & Leland *Dict. Slang*: *Loaded for bears* (American). This expression signifies that a man is slightly [*sic*] intoxicated. **1895** *DN* I 420: *Loaded for bear*….Very drunk. *a*1890–96 *F & H* IV 212: Drunk: also *loaded for bears*. **1927** (quot. at (**1**), above). **1967** in *DARE*: A person who is thoroughly drunk…Loaded for bear.

4. fully prepared or equipped.

1895 *DN* I 420: *Loaded for bear*….Said of one who has a big supply of anything. **1913** [W. Dixon] *"Billy" Dixon* 211: The buffalo hunters were "loaded for bear" by the time the Indians were within range. **1921** J. Conway, in *Variety* (Apr. 1) 7: Her maid…was totin' a suitcase. They sure had come loaded for bear. **1981–85** S. King *It* 280: "You got your ah-ah-aspirator, E-Eddie?" Eddie slapped his pocket. "I'm loaded for bear."

¶ **get a load of** to look at or hear; pay attention to; perceive. Also vars.

1922 J. Conway, in *Variety* (May 5) 12: Hop right over to the Plymouth [theater] and get a load of the "Hairy Ape." **1922** *Variety* (July 28) 5: Well get a load of this. **1927** T.A. Dorgan, in Zwilling *TAD Lexicon* 54: Get a load of that guy Phil. **1928** in Eells & Musgrove *Mae West* 85: Get a load of it and weep. **1929** E. Wilson *Twenties* 514: Get a load of this! **1930** Rogers & Adler *Chump* (film): Get a load of that puss! **1931** Hellinger *Moon* 161: Get a load of that dame over there. **1932** Berg *Prison Doctor* 122: This will get you plenty. Just wait until the warden gets a load of this. **1929–33** J. Lowell *Gal Reporter* 19: Yeah, and get a load of who it is. **1933** Creelman & Rose *King Kong* (film): C'mere and get a load of this! **1933** Benchley *Chips* 165: Just get a load of this! **1935** Lindsay *She Loves Me Not* 86: Grab a load of dis, baby. I come all the way from Philadelphia to see you. **1935** O'Hara *Butterfield 8* 233: He could even go to a movie now and then and get a load of Benny the Beetle. **1935** Sistrom *Hot Tip* (film): Do you want to hear it? Get a load of this! **1936** McCarty & Johnson *Great Guy* (film): Well, get a load of this—I'm not having any of those sudden accidents. **1937** Hellman *Dead End* (film): Get a load of that. **1939** Spence et al. *Flying Deuces* (film): Get a load of this diamond ring. **1941** Boardman, Perrin & Grant *Keep 'Em Flying* (film): Get a load of that guy. **1948** Cozzens *Guard of Honor* 14: "Get a load of Danny," he said, indicating Sergeant Pellerino. **1957** Mayfield *Hit* 177: Well, get a load of him, will you, fellas? **1992** N. Russell *Suicide Charlie* 4: Hey, catch a load of this dude.

¶ **pick a load into** *S.W.* to indulge in exaggerated talk with. Cf. **(3.c.)**, above.

 1926 W. Rogers, in C.M. Russell *Trails* xvii: Tie into that old Napoleon some time and pick a load into him, you ought to get something pretty good from him, if it aint nothing but about war, and women. **1932** in *AS* (Feb. 1933) 32: Pick A *Load* Into. To load. (q.v.).

¶ **take a load off [your feet]** have a seat and relax! Now *colloq.*

 1922 E. Rice *Adding Machine* 120: Well, sit down an' take a load off your feet. **1932** L. Berg *Prison Doctor* 75: Sit down, Gimpty, and take a load off your feet. **1934** O'Hara *Samarra* ch. viii: "Sit down and eat...." "I don't want to," said Froggy. "Well, then, sit down and take the load off." **1954–60** *DAS: Load off [one's] feet, take a* To sit down; to have a seat or chair. **1985** Briskin *Too Much* 36: Come on, get a load off. **1986** *L.A. Law* (NBC-TV): Sit down and take a load off. **1987** *ALF* (NBC-TV): Sit down! Take a load off! **1992** G. Wolff *Day at the Beach* 138: Take a load off....Enjoy a day of rest.

loadie *n. Stu.* a heavy drinker or habitual drug abuser.

 1979 Alibrandi *Custody* 61: He'll head back to his neighborhood. He's a loadie and he'll want to score. *a***1986** in *NDAS:* For every high school loadie you will find a National Merit Scholar. **1994** A. Heckerling *Clueless* 42: The loadies generally hang in the stairwell over there.

load-on *n.* [LOAD + *on*] sufficient liquor to cause intoxication; SKINFUL.

 1927 H. Miller *Moloch* 145: We had another drink....Boy, what a load-on!

load up *n.* to indulge in alcohol or drugs to the point of intoxication.

 1908 in Senechal *Race Riot* 19: Loading up [for a] big jag. **1969** in H.S. Thompson *Shark Hunt* 206: My first idea was to load up on LSD and cover the Inauguration that way. **1990** Munro *Slang U.:* John always loads up before he goes to fraternity parties. **1990** T. Thorne *Dict. Contemp. Sl.: Load up...American* to take illicit drugs.

loaf[1] *n.* **1.** LOAFER, 1.

 1846 Neal *Ploddy* 178: The very gals bump up agin him and say, "get out of the way, loaf!"

 2. an act of relaxing or being idle. Now *colloq.*

 1855 Whitman *Leaves of Grass* 39, in *OED2:* The farmer stops by the bars as he walks on a/First-day loafe and looks at the oats and rye. **1886** in *DAE:* A resolution...to enjoy a solid old-fashioned loaf this summer. **1897** in *DA:* A restful loaf is the principal object.

loaf[2] *n.* ¶ In phrase: **pinch a loaf** to defecate.

 1991 *In Living Color* (Fox-TV): Rudolph's pinching a loaf in the neighbor's yard. **1993** *Beavis and Butt-head* (MTV): "What's so funny, dude?" "The President of the United States pinching a loaf!" **1994** S. Johnson et al. *Ensucklopedia* (unp.): Birds...pinch loafs on people.

loaf *v.* **1.** to idle away time; lounge; relax. Now *S.E.* Cf. earlier LOAFER, 1.

 1835 in *DA* (Jan.): Loafing's dull at this season of the year. **1835** in *DA* (May): The propensity to loaf is confined to no rank in life. **1835** *Knickerbocker* (July) 66: His loafing's done. **1837** Neal *Charcoal Sketches* 13: Loafing on the stalls is jist as bad as rolling among the dishes. **1840** Strong *Diary* I 139: I have smoked, lounged, loafed, chessed, grumbled,...gaped, [etc.]. **1842** *Spirit of Times* (May 28) 145: I am the last man to "loaf" about bar-rooms and billiard-rooms. **1847** N.J.T. Dana *Monterrey* 202: I loafed about after we halted. **1848** in Peskin *Vols.* 251: Played alley ball and loafed. **1855** Whitman *Leaves of Grass* 25: I lean and loafe at my ease....observing a spear of summer grass. **1856** in *Calif. Hist. Soc. Qly.* IX (1930) 54: Loafed around. **1862** in Geer *Diary* 48: Had a good time loafing in town today. **1864** in O.J. Hopkins *Under the Flag* 195: An occupation fit only for...some worthless *loafing* man. **1871** Hay *Pike Co. Ballads* 16: A derned sight better business/Than loafing around The Throne. **1884** in Lummis *Letters* 70: You need not think I have been loafing.

 2. Esp. *Stu.* to steal.

 1851 B. Hall *College Words* 188, in *DAS.* **1889** Barrère & Leland *Dict. Slang* [ref. to 1835]: *Loafer...*was generally applied by boys to "pilfering." They would say in jest, "Where did you *loaf* that?" *Ibid.:*

Loaf, to...(American University), to borrow anything, generally without any intention of returning it.

loafer *n.* **1.** an idler or vagrant; no-account; bum. Hence (*Journ.*) **loaferess,** *n.fem.*

 1830 in *OED2:* Nor are they topers at taverns, or *benchers* at groceries, or loafers who "chase misfortune o'er the towpath." **1835** *Knickerbocker* (July) 63: The connivance of Susan and Samuel Smith, loafer and loafress of this burgh. *Ibid.* 64: Benjamin Smith...was a tall loafer, surmounted with a...well-entangled mat of hair. **1837** Strong *Diary* I 72: A couple of Indians, a squaw and a lot of little papooses, horrid little loafers in appearance. *Ibid.* 79: But the students are generally a poor-looking set of loafers. **1837** J. Greene *Glance at N.Y.* 27: He was a citizen loafer, and not a stranger. **1837** Neal *Charcoal Sketches* 162: Perhaps I'll be stuck up some day on a bench to ladle out law to the loafers. **1840** *Spirit of Times* (June 6) 158: An Irish Loafer...bawling "Vatermelings"—(watermelons, my love). **1845** Corcoran *Pickings* 31: You is Tom Trotter, the loafer, and no mistake. **1849** in *Western Folk.* VI (1947) 108: A loafer...stole a hen and invited four...miners to dine upon her. **1858** in *N. Dak. Hist.* XXXIII (1966) 282: The "loafers"...cleared out precipitately. **1861** in J.M. Williams *That Terrible Field* 12: I think that they are nothing but *loafers.* **1866** G.A. Townsend *Non-Combatant* 182: Wake up these——loafers. **1884** Hay *Bread-Winners* 117: Some high-steppin' snob whose daddy has left him the means to be a loafer all his days. **1885** in *DA:* The loafers and loaferesses...stared at her with unanimous admiration. **1886** F. Whittaker *Pop Hicks* 7: But I don't want my darter's name in every loafer's mouth, like a song-and-dance woman. **1891** Maitland *Slang Dict.* 169: *Loafer...*a lazy vagabond; an idle lounger. **1902** Naughton *Queensberry Realm* 203: "I hope Ryan will knock his head off."..."I'm with you....That big loafer deserves a licking." **1904** in Opper *Hooligan* 10: Loafer yet! Lobster alretty! **1906** in Robinson *Comics* 31: Loafer! **1934** Duff & Sauber *20 Million Sweethearts* (film): So now you're rough-and-tumblin' again, you loafer! **1937** Asch *The Road* 160: Don't let that loafer beat you.

 2. a ruffian. Hence **loafing,** *adj.*

 1834–40 Dana *Before the Mast* 234: He spent his own money...and went up to the presidio, where he lived the life of a degenerate "loafer" until some rascally deed sent him off...with men on horseback, dogs, and Indians in full cry. **1852** in Caughey *Mob* 40: Everybody thought as how Jim was considerable of a loafer. **1859** Matsell *Vocab.* 116: A loafer...is supported by a woman, but does not receive enough money to enable him to play faro. **1863** Strong *Diary* III 335: Every brute in the drove was pure Celtic—hod-carrier or loafer. **1866** *Nat. Police Gaz.* (Nov. 10) 2: A Raid on Thieves, Confidence Men, and Loafers. **1884** Costello *Police Protectors* 327: Now and then a newspaper affects to believe that...some..."gang" has the district in terror...but the Police, as in other precincts, have the loafing element under control. **1885** Siringo *Texas Cowboy* 36: They didn't want me to get into the habit of mixing with the street loafers. **1960** N.Y.C. woman, age *ca*70: They call them "juvenile delinquents" now. They used to call them "loafers."

 ¶ In phrase:

 ¶ **light in the loafers** see s.v. LIGHT.

loafer *adj.* false or disappointing.—used prenominally.

 1848 Baker *Glance at N.Y.* 24: It was a loafer fire, after all....Dere was none; it was only a false alarm.

Loafers' Hall *n.* prison.

 1861 in *DA:* He was compelled to retire for awhile from the gaities [*sic*] of society into the retirement of "Loafers' Hall."

loafer's loop *n. Navy.* an aiguillette. *Joc.*

 1947 Conarroe *Sea Chest* 282: *Loafer's Loop.* A kind of golden garter worn over the left shoulder and under the armpit of a staff officer playing toady to an admiral. **1966** Noel *Naval Terms: Loafer's Loops.* Slang for Aiguillettes.

loaner *n.* an item that has been given on loan, esp. to replace an item being repaired. Now *colloq.* or *S.E.*

 1926 (cited in *W10*). **1971** *U.S. News & W.R.* (Apr. 5) 37: He provided another unit while the broken one was in the shop. Two weeks later the repair job was finished—at a total cost of $80, including $15 for the use of the "loaner." **1971** *U.S. News & W.R.* (May 17) 21 (adv.): It would be great if our dealers could give every service customer a "loaner." **1974** *Business Week* (Feb. 23) (inside front cover) (adv.): If one of your cars is out of commission,...he'll get a "loaner" car with unlimited mileage. **1976** *Pop. Sci.* (June) 13: We'll even send you a loaner watch to use while your watch is being repaired. **1980** *L.A. Times* (Feb. 3) VIII 18: More than 36% of the visiting population drive loaner cars of friends and relatives. **1986** *Philip Morris Mag.* (Spring) 25: Her Jeep is a "loaner" and plastered with promotional logos. **1991** *NYNEX Information Resources* [i.e., N.Y.C. Yellow Pages] 1166: VCR-TV-Stereo Repairs...Free loaners available.

loan shark *n.* a usurer; (*specif.*) a usurer on a large scale who belongs to an organized crime syndicate. Now *colloq.*

   ***1905** in *OED2*. **1913** in *DA*: In New York the loan-sharks were doing a business of twenty-million dollars per annum. **1915** [Swartwood] *Choice Slang* 53: *Loan shark*...a money lender who charges an exorbitant rate of interest usually for short time loans. **1915–16** Lait *Beef, Iron & Wine* 241: Sickles was a loan shark. It isn't a pretty business. **1937** in D. Runyon *More Guys* 252: Jim...hocked his salary with a loan shark. **1945** Lindner *Stone Walls & Men* 50: "Fences," loan sharks, and unscrupulous businessmen. **1946** in *DA*: For years they've paid heavy interest to loan sharks.

loan sharking *n.* the practice of lending money at usurious rates; (*specif.*) this practice operated on a large scale by an organized crime syndicate. Now *colloq.*

   1914 (cited in *W10*). **1951** *N.Y. Times* (Jan. 27) IV 12E: It attributes kickbacks, loan-sharking, and other forms of extortion to this...system. **1952** *Harper's* (Apr.) 29: It is responsible for kickbacks, loansharking, and a large percentage of other crimes on the waterfront. **1961** *N.Y. Times* (Apr. 9) IV 2E: Narcotics traffic, prostitution, bootlegging, organized gambling, loan sharking, extortion and other rackets. **1963** *Wash. Post* (Oct. 23) A3: Other Senators were talking about gangster Joseph Valachi's loan sharking activities in Cosa Nostra. **1972** *U.S. News & W.R.* (June 5) 67: We try to find out not only who is doing the extortion or the loan-sharking or the gambling, but also who are their protectors, what officials they are corrupting. **1978** *L.A. Times* (May 3) I 1: They are moving for more and more control of gambling, loan-sharking and pornography. **1986** *Time* (Apr. 14) 82: An evil empire fed by murder, gambling and loan sharking.

lob[1] *n.* **1.a.** Esp. *Und.* a country bumpkin (*obs.*); lout; blockhead; oaf; no-account. In 1952 quot. as *v.* [Orig. S.E., described as "Now *dial.*" in *OED2*; 20th-C. U.S. use may be infl. by or have arisen directly fr. LOBSTER, 2. Senses grouped here are ult. linked by the notion of 'a lump' or 'lumpishness'.]

   ***1533, *1550** in *OED*. ***1577** in *F & H* VI 215: But as the drone the honey hive doth rob,/With woorthy books so deals this idle lob. ***1590** Shakespeare *Midsummer Night's Dream* II i: Farewell thou Lob of spirits. ***1603, *1609, *1658**, etc., in *OED*. ***1661** in *F & H* IV 215: This is the wonted way for quacks and cheats to gull the country lobs. **1830** (quot. at LOB-DOMINION). ***1854** in *OED*: We sometimes hear a heavy clumsy man called "a great lob of a felley." **1907** in H.C. Fisher *A. Mutt* 21: Take my tip and duck, you big lob. **1914** Jackson & Hellyer *Vocab.* 55: *Lob*...An awkward craftsman; a delinquent; an opprobrious character amongst thieves. Contracted from "lobster." **1915–17** Lait *Gus* 108: Of all the lobs, boneheads, rummies, numbskulls [etc.]. **1929–31** D. Runyon *Guys & Dolls* 91: The proud old Spanish nobleman does not wish his son to marry any lob. **1931** *AS* VI (Aug.) 439: *Lob*...A flunky, sucker, chump. **1936** Dai *Opium Addiction* 201: *Lobb*. A person who hangs around and runs errands. Also called *Lobby-gow*. **1936** in D. Runyon *More Guys* 138: He is generally figured as nothing but a lob as far as ever doing anything useful...is concerned. **1942** *Yank* (Nov. 11) 20: Just a yardbird, another lob. **1952** Mandel *Angry Strangers* 17: Mostly, I lob around the street looking at nothing. **1957** Gutwillig *Long Silence* 60 [ref. to 1951]: None of our friends was in class, for only the "lobs" (the dateless or the non-fraternity types) ventured up the hill on Houseparty Saturday. **1961** in Cannon *Nobody Asked* 141: No one got larceny in them except some lob of a fight manager who ain't got what to eat.

   b. *Horse Racing.* an inferior horse; (*also*) a good horse entered in a race that it is not intended to win.

   1935 Pollock *Underworld Speaks*: *Lob*, a racehorse not trying to win; of little value. **1949** Cummings *Dict. Sports* 432: "*Stiff*" Slang...A horse entered in a race without genuine intention (by the owner) of having it strive for a victory. It is usually a short-priced favorite....The intention is...to profit by longer odds on a subsequent race which the horse may win. Also called "cooler," "lob." **1951** in D.W. Maurer

Lang. Und. 218: *Lob*...A horse that never makes a very impressive showing....A horse that is not intended to win. **1968** Ainslie *Racing Guide* 470: *Lob*—A cooler or stiff.

   2. a fortune; PILE. [The *1863 sense is defined as 'a large lump' in *F & H*.]

   ***1812** Vaux *Vocab.*: To have *made a good lob*, is synonymous with making [a rich haul]. **1847** Downey *Cruise of the Portsmouth* 54: Mexico is the place where all the dollars do come from. If there's any war there, it's me is the child that will make a *lob* for Mrs. Troop and the children. ***1863** in *F & H* IV 215: He must have a regular lob of gold stowed away somewhere. ***1942** in Partridge *Dict. Und.* 413: *Lob*. A haul of money.

   3. an erection of the penis; the penis.—usu. considered vulgar.

   [***1785** Grose *Vulgar Tongue*: *Lobcock*. A large relaxed penis.] ***a1890–96** *F & H* IV 215: *Lob*...A partial erection: *e.g.*, a urinary *lob*. **1964** Selby *Last Exit to Bklyn.* 49: Whattsa matta Rosie? afraida my lob? *a*1972 B. Rodgers *Queens' Vernacular* 49: Cock...lob (dated). **1974** Sann *Dead Heat* 54: So the indictment is longer than your lob. **1981** Spears *Slang & Euphem.*: *Lob*...The penis, especially the erect penis....U.S. slang, mid-[20th C.] to present. ***a1989** P. Beale, in Partridge *Concise Dict. Slang* 260: *Lazy lob*. A semi-erection of the penis: low colloq.

lob[2] *n.* [orig. unkn.; earlier in Br criminal slang in sense 'box; trunk'; see Partridge *Dict. Und.*] *Und. & Police.* a till. Hence **lob sneak** a till-robber.

   ***1732** in Partridge *Dict. Und.* 412: We...stole a Baker's *Lobb*....a Money Drawer. Lobb is a general Name for any kind of Box. ***1811** *Lex. Balatron.*: *Lob*. A till in a tradesman's shop. To frisk a lob; to rob a till. ***1812** Vaux *Vocab.*: *Lob*: a till, or money drawer. ***1839** Brandon *Poverty, Mendicity & Crime* (gloss.): *Lobb*—a till. *To pinch a Lobb*—to rob a till. **1859** Matsell *Vocab.* 52: *Lob*. A money-drawer; the till. *Lobsneak*. A fellow that robs money-drawers. **1867** *Nat. Police Gaz.* (Mar. 23) 2: In the outset of his career...he was a "lob sneak." ***1868** in *OED*: "Lob" means the till.

lob[3] *n.* a lobster.

   1893 W.K. Post *Harvard* 97: Broiled lob. and musty.

lobby *n. Und.* LOBBYGOW, 1.

   1940 *Current Hist. & Forum* (Nov. 7) 22: The inmate...will be careful not to be marked a *lane* (fool) by acting as a *lobby* (running errands for other inmates without compensation). **1942–49** Goldin et al. *DAUL* 293: Person, slow-witted or inept...lob, lobby, lug.

lobby boy *n. Und.* LOBBYGOW, 1.

   1977 Torres *Q&A* 121: I don't know the other guy. Must be his lobby boy.

lobbygow *n.* [orig. unkn.] **1.** Esp. *Und. & Police.* **a.** a lackey; errand boy; (*hence*) a worthless fellow; no-account.

   [**1898** L.J. Beck *Chinatown* 119: [The prostitutes have] on hand messengers to do their bidding,...idle and worthless boys and young men, known...as Low Gui Gow. Low Gui means a common woman, and Gow a dog....Thus a Low Gui Gow is merely an attendant upon a common woman.] **1899** *Nat. Police Gaz.* (Mar. 25) 3: Shut that door, *lobby gow*. **1905** *Nat. Police Gaz.* (Nov. 4) 3: The lobbygows—by which I mean the errand men of the Chinese—the whites, who execute commissions for them, and do all sorts of services, both legitimate and illegitimate. **1909** C. Chrysler *White Slavery* 80: A "lobbygow"—a Chinaman who acts as stool pigeon and informer for the police—told two Mulberry street detectives. **1911** Bronson-Howard *Enemy to Society* 295: I ain't gunna have her think Stevey's tied up with a bunch of lobby-gows. **1923** Ornitz *Haunch, Paunch & Jowl* 102: Stay where you are, youse guzzlers and lobby-gows. **1928–30** Fiaschetti *Gotta Be Rough* 49: He was an errand boy, a "lobby gow,"...an understrapper anywhere. **1935** Pollock *Underworld Speaks*: *Lobby gow*, a hanger-on who runs errands. **1931** Wilstach *Under Cover Man* 24: Why, the cheap lobby gow. **1932** Lawes *Sing Sing* 318: When he was in the section where the other men were confined, he would be the "fall guy" or "lobby gob" [*sic*] for them, always pulling their own chestnuts out of the fire. **1950** *N.Y. Times* (Sept. 3) VII 4: A collection of bribe takers, time servers, hypocrites, lobbygows, pathological moralists, jelly-bellied back-room cynics, two-timing husbands [etc.]. **1950** *N.Y. Times* (Sept. 21) 20: Goldstein...is what gamblers call a "stiff"—a lobbygow who will submit to arrest in place of a boss gambler. **1956** "T. Betts" *Across Board* 177: He flung away fortunes in grubstakes to bums, heels and lobby-gows. **1964** Legman *Horn Book* 519: Quizzed by batteries of dirty-nailed lobbygows over…tapped telephones and processed "electronically" by white-coated business-machine tenders. **1976** *Harper's* (Aug.) 83: Chaps who want to be either a Vice-President or a Presidential lobbyglow [*sic*].

b. *N.Y.C.* a strong-arm robber, esp. of prostitutes.

*a***1904–11** D.G. Phillips *Susan Lenox* II 248: She was in the clutch of one of those terrors of tenement fast women, the lobbygows—men who live by lying in wait in the darkness to seize and rob the lonely, friendless fast woman.…"Those damn cops!…Ten to one the lobbygows divide with them."

2. *N.Y.C.* a person who guides tourists through Chinatown and the Bowery. Now *hist.*

1931 Harlow *Old Bowery* 430 [ref. to 1890's]: He became a "lobbygow," or tourists' guide, making Chinatown his specialty. *Ibid.* 432: It was a blow to the lobbygows when Steve Brodie died. **1954–60** *DAS: Lobby-gow*…A Chinatown tourists' guide. **1966** "Petronius" *N.Y. Unexp.* 192: Chuck Connors…became King of the Lobby Gows, Sage of Doyer Street, and the Bowery Philosopher.

lobby lizard *n.* LOBBY LOUSE.

1939 *AS* (Oct.) 240: *Lobby Lizards.* Loafers.

lobby louse *n.* a person (esp. a nonguest) who habitually lounges about a hotel lobby.

1939 *AS* (Oct.) 240: *Lobby-Lice.* Loafers. **1954** Collans & Sterling *House Detect.* 22: "Lobby lice"…were loungers, loafers and larrikins who hung around annoying, and sometimes swindling, desirable patrons.

lob-dominion *n. Naut.* inferior brewed tea or the like; thin or inferior stew.

1830 N. Ames *Mariner's Sketches* 125 [ref. to 1819]: The tea being almost uniformly damaged and unsaleable and the coffee made of rye, either of them forming a beverage which an English sailor on board very appropriately characterized as "*lobs*" dominion, two buckets of water and an old shoe. **1841** [Mercier] *Man o' War* 177: I thought I was pretty generally acquainted with all the several dishes that are held in repute by the Sons of Ocean, from a *dogs-body* to a *lob-dominion*. **1849** (quot. at SKILLAGALEE).

loblolly boy *n. Naut.* a boy who attends a ship's surgeon. Cf. earlier *loblolly* 'a lout', in *OED2*.

*1748 Smollett *Roderick Random* ch. xxvii: Among the sailors I was known as the Loblolly Boy. **1785* Grose *Vulgar Tongue: Loblolley Boy.* A nick name for the surgeon's servant on board a man of war, sometimes for the surgeon himself: from the water-gruel prescribed for the sick, which is called loblolley. *ca***1840** Hawthorne *Yankee Privateer* 146 [ref. to 1813]: [He] was good company for lieutenant or loblolly boy. **1849** Melville *White Jacket* 24: Messenger-boys, cot-boys, loblolly-boys, and numberless others. **1885* in *F & H* IV 216: Lor' bless ye, a loblolly boy can tell old hands how *not* to steer.

lobo *n.* [< Sp, lit. 'wolf'] **1.** *West.* a contemptible or villainous man, esp. a gunman. Now chiefly *hist.* Cf. earlier COYOTE, *n.*, 1.a.

[**1907** "O. Henry," in *OED2*: I'm not one of them lobo wolves…who are always blaming on women the calamities of life.] **1927** P.A. Rollins *Jinglebob* 183 [ref. to 1880's]: The two lobos told us…that they'd do the trailin'. **1927** Raine *Colorado* 243: He'd rather be a live coyote than a dead lion, that lobo. **1931** "M. Brand" *Ambush* 120: You worn-out old lobo. **1949** in *DAS*: "You crazy lobo!" "What's a lobo?" "A lobo's a gun, thug, hoodlum." **1963** L'Amour *Sackett* 98: I've read his sign and it reads pure lobo. **1973** F. Carter *Outlaw Wales* 170: They looked tame beside this 'un. A lobo. Tied-down .44's.

2. (see quot.). Cf. COYOTE, *n.*, 1.b.; COYOTE UGLY.

1946 Boulware *Jive & Slang* 5: *Lobo*…Ugly girl.

lobscouse *n. Naut.* a sailors' usu. improvised stew containing meat, potatoes, onions, hardtack, etc. Now *hist.* Also **lobscourse.**

*1706, *1751 in *OED2*. **1796* Grose *Vulgar Tongue* (ed. 3): *Lobscouse.* A dish much eaten at sea, composed of salt beef, biscuit, and onions, well peppered, and stewed together. **1845** Corcoran *Pickings* 161: The making of *lobscouse.* **1849** P. Decker *Diaries* 122: Made a soup called *Lobscouse* made of a little rice sliced meat fine dry bread, flour &c. **1862** in Wightman *To Ft. Fisher* 52: They make mixtures of meat, crackers, potatoes [etc.]…and call the conglomeration "lobscourse." **1909** in *Calif. Hist. Soc. Qly.* VI (1927) 267 [ref. to 1849]: We had "lob

scouse," a stew of meat and potatoes. **1987** J.I. Robertson *Blue & Gray* 69 [ref. to Civil War]: A soup made of salt pork, hardtack, and whatever else was available bore the general label "lobscourse."

lobscouser *n. Naut.* a seaman, esp. if old or superannuated.

*1884 in *F & H* VI 217: How many bunks does an old lobscouser like you want to sleep in? **1891* in *F & H* VI 217: He is superstitious, like most old lobscousers, no doubt. **1897** Kelley *Ship's Company* 150: In his Jack Bunshyan opinion the men who follow the sea in these degenerate days are, to say the least, lobscousers, canallers, mere stokers or baggage-smashers.

lobster *n.* **1.** a red-coated British soldier or marine.—often used attrib. Now esp. *hist.* Cf. earlier sense, ref. to Roundheads who wore armor, from *ca*1643 in *OED2*.

*1698–99 "B.E." *Dict. Canting Crew: Lobster,* a Red Coat Soldier. **1758** in *OED2*: This afternoon their [*sic*] was a Lobster Corperel married to a Road Island whore. **1770** in *AS* (Dec. 1934) 277: Come, you Rascals, you bloody Backs, you Lobster Scoundrels; fire if you dare, G-d damn you, fire and be damn'd. **1770** in W.L. Katz *Eyewitness* 55: The Sentinels were enraged and swearing at the boys: the boys called them lobsters, bloody backs, and hallooed who buys lobsters. **1776** in *DAE*: The Red Lobsters spied a little fire which a party of Centry made on a small hill. **1796* Grose *Vulgar Tongue* (ed. 3): *Lobster.* A nick name for a soldier: from the colour of his clothes. **1809* in Wheeler *Letters* 15: It was a fine treat for the blue jackets to see all the lobsters stuck fast to the decks. **1814** B. Palmer *Diary* [entry for May 15]: The next thing that attracted our attention was a Drunken Soldier comeing across the bridge, well guarded with some of his Brother Lobsters. **1821** Martin & Waldo *Lightfoot* 112: Mr. Lobster, get off directly. **1839–40** Cobb *Green Hand* I 148: As for the lobster soldier in the hatchway, no fear of him. **1840** *Crockett Almanac 1841* 24: The lobster sez…"let us go whar we can find gentlemen." **1864** in Tilney *My Life* 102: The next panel represents…a party of "boiled lobsters"…with an officer at their head. **1991–95** Sack *Co. C* 93: "The Brits are still saying, 'Don't take shit.'" "Go get 'em, lobsters," someone said.

2.a. a worthless, contemptible, or obnoxious individual. Cf. 17th-C. S.E. sense '(used as an opprobrious name for a red-faced man)', in *OED2*. [The *a*1868 quot. may properly belong to (1), above.]

1832 *Spirit of Times* (Feb. 4) 3: Yes, but show me three tails, you lobster. **1854** Sleeper *Salt Water Bubbles* 83: If I'm not revenged on *you*, old chap,…call me a *lobster,* that's all. *a***1868** N.H. Bishop *Across So. Amer.* 258: Here we have been loafing about like a set of lobster marines, doing nothing. **1885** *Puck* (Apr. 8) 90: Across the street from my place is an eating-den kept by a shock-haired, red-eyed Lobster, who…ought to be on the Island. **1896** Ade *Artie* 53: They say…he belongs with the real boys, but every time I see him he was a lobster. **1899–1900** Cullen *Tales* 223: Your horse would be backed 'way up for a lobster. **1901** *DN* II 143: *Lobster,* n. A generally uncomplimentary term applied to one who is awkward, unsociable, etc.; but not = chump. **1901** A.H. Lewis *Croker* 62: There'll be somethin' doin' that'll scare the hair off…every lobster that's got a million dollars. **1902–03** Ade *People You Know* 216: Link was whatever they called a Lobster in 1880. **1903** T.W. Jackson *Slow Train* 55: I called him a lobster, then he pinched me. **1903** *Pedagog. Sem.* X 374: You're a lobster. **1905** in Paxton *Sport USA* 24: That's baseball for you. Today you are a hero and tomorrow you are a lobster. **1906** Beyer *Battleship* 232: Go away, you lobster! **1906** "O. Henry" *Four Million* 47: What are you looking so sour about, you oakum trimmed lobster? She won't kiss you. **1906** *Nat. Police Gaz.* (Apr. 21) 3: "Just tell her Harry is here."…"What, that lobster? How did he get in?" **1907** in C.M. Russell *Paper Talk* 55: I received your long letter where you called me a lobster. **1914** Ellis *Billy Sunday* 86: The peanut-brained, weasel-eyed, hog-jowled, beetle-browed, bull-necked lobsters that owned the hogs. **1914** Paine *Wall Between* 166: I was loafin' on the dock when he went up the gangway, and a lobster from the barracks told me who he was. **1959** N.Y.C. woman, age 44: You lobster! **1973** I. Reed *La. Red* 26: I know a lot of you lobsters thought…I was through. **1986** J.A. Friedman *Times Sq.* 40: The forefathers of today's old lobsters watched this sexual exhibition with mute, unsmiling impassivity.

b. *Specif.,* a fool; dupe.

1894 in S. Crane *N.Y.C. Sks.* 9: Anybody could see that you, Thorpey, me boy, could make a lobster out of Holmes. **1897** Ade *Pink* 182: Ol' Hen'y land in heah 'ith a roll 'at made me an' Gawge Lippincott look like a couple o' dahk lobstehs. **1898** Kountz *Baxter's Letters* 8: I believe she saw me all the time, and knew I was a lobster. **1899** A.H. Lewis *Sandburrs* 94: As I sets there, I flashes me lamps along d' line, an' sort o' stacks up d' blokes, for to pick out d' fly guys from d' lobsters, see! **1899** Ade *Fables* 23: In Due Time he went to College, where he proved to be a Lobster. **1901** *Chi. Tribune* (July 28) 38: A soubrette can frequently get a pearl necklace out of the most unattractive lobster ever seen in Chicago. **1902** K. Harriman *Ann Arbor Tales* 242: And if it don't mean Morrison'll win,...I'm a lobster, good and plenty. **1903** in F. Remington *Sel. Letters* 342: You are such a lobster Louis—it's out of sight out of mind with your...nature. **1904** *Life in Sing Sing* 250: *Lobster.*—A dupe; slow person. *a***1909** Tillotson *Detective* 93: *Lobster*—A dead one. **1909** M'Govern *Krag Is Laid Away* 92: Lobsters like you don't know *black* ink is for writing just a man or your mother. **1911** *N.Y. Eve. Jour.* (Jan. 5) 22: "He's a lobster....We'll do him up." "He looks like a stiff." **1917** Cahan *D. Levinsky* 150: Don't be a lobster, Mr. Levinsky....Here a fellow must be no fool.

¶ In phrases:

¶ **catch a lobster** *Rowing.* to *catch a crab* s.v. CRAB, *n.*
  1836 in Haliburton *Sam Slick* 53: She is not the first hand that has caught a lobster by puttin' in her oar afore her turn.

¶ **upset (one's) lobster cart** to knock down; *upset (one's) applecart* s.v. APPLECART, 2.
  1824 in *F & H* IV 218: Ready up to take his part, I'd soon upset his lobster-cart; Make his bones ache, and blubber smart.

lobsterback *n.* **1.** a British soldier; redcoat. Now *hist.* Hence **lobsterbacked**, *adj.*
  *****1809** in W. Wheeler *Letters* 19: "Ugly Betty" kicked some of the men who were in his way, and called them "a —— set of lobsterbacked ——," adding "some of us would be in hell before tomorrow this time." **1840** *Crockett Almanac 1841* 24: Two British [naval] officers with a lobster back between 'em. **1870** [W.D. Phelps] *Fore & Aft* 108: One of the "lobster-back" gentlemen...hailed us with, "Captain, where are you from?" *a***1961** Longman *Power of Black* 8: The British lobster-backs burned our place at Greens Crossing. **1977** Coover *Public Burning* 606: Spectral Lobsterbacks and Coercive Acts.

2. a contemptible fellow.
  1899 Robbins *Gam* 39: Served him dead right, I swear! An' bless ye, boy, the old lobster-back [the Captain] can't swim a stroke!

lobster shift *n.* Esp. *Journ.* a late-night work shift typically extending from midnight to 8 A.M. Now *colloq.* Cf. LOBSTER TOUR, LOBSTER TRICK.
  1942 Liebling *Telephone* 153: Their press agent employed a lobster shift of assistants who went to work after midnight and [worked till dawn]. **1950** *N.Y. Times* (Aug. 20) I 51: An increase in differential pay for men working on night and "lobster" shifts. **1958** *N.Y. Times* (June 1) II 29: It was crowded at this hour, 5:30 A.M., with reporters, desk men and composing room men who had been working the lobster shift on a near-by daily. **1963** *New Yorker* (Nov. 2) 164: I was assigned the lobster shift, from midnight until eight in the morning. **1976** Price *Bloodbrothers* 54: He got the lobster shift. **1979** *Time* (Apr. 9) 8: Technicians on the lobster shift one night last week faced a tranquil, even boring watch. **1977–85** Carmen & Moody *Working Women* 161: Judges...in day court, night court, and the lobster shift. **1986** Ciardi *Good Words* 330: *Lobster shift*...A third work-shift on a big-city newspaper, commonly from 2:00–9:00 A.M. when little is happening and matters can be attended by a skeletal staff. **1995** *N.Y. Observer* (Sept. 18) 7: She got a job on the lobster shift at the *New York Post*.

lobster tour *n.* *Police.* LOBSTER SHIFT.
  1982 Castoire & Posner *Gold Shield* 251: She was on duty with her team from four in the afternoon until midnight. Then, alone, she was responsible for any...cases that came in until eight the following morning. Koala, sharing the lobster tour, was assigned to dispatch duty.

lobster trick *n.* Esp. *Journ.* LOBSTER SHIFT.
  1927 *AS* II (Feb.) 242: "Sunrise watch" and "lobster trick" are among the names applied on papers having both morning and afternoon editions to the force which occupies the office in the very early morning interval after the last regular morning edition has gone to press and before the staff of the afternoon edition has begun work. **1930** in *DA:* Munday was the "lobster trick" reporter at Police Headquarters for the Evening World. **1949** *Sat. Eve. Post* (Jan. 15) 133: He had the thankless lobster trick at the paper, making up the sport pages early in the morning. **1950** Riesenberg *Reporter* 15: Even during this early morning "lobster trick." **1969** H.A. Smith *Buskin'* 33: He found

out that a certain lobster-trick copy-reader, a man past sixty, was responsible. **1975** *L.A. Times* (Oct. 24) III 1: When the World Series becomes the lobster trick for a newspaper man, a lot of the bubbles go out of this racket. **1986** Ciardi *Good Words* 330.

loc /louk/ *n.* [fr. the adj.] *Rap Music.* a fellow gang member; (*hence*) friend; HOMIE.—used esp. in direct address between men.
  1991 "Ice Cube" *Colorblind* (rap song): Some say the little locs are gettin a little too loc. **1991** in P. Munro *U.C.L.A. Slang II:* Loc...[affectionate;...rhymes with *joke*]. What's up, loc? *ca***1992** "Easy-E" *Real Muthaphukkin G's* (rap song): You's a wanna-be loc. **1994** *Totally Unofficial Rap Dict.:* Loc...Term used for local person....Crazy one,...often used for friends or locals in a positive way. **1995** Stavsky et al. *A 2 Z* 64: Don't be playin' with guns. You might get smoked, loc.

loc /louk/ *adj.* Esp. *Rap Music.* LOCO; crazy. Cf. LOCS, LOC OUT.
  1991 ("Ice Cube" quot. at LOC.). **1992** "Fab Five Freddy" *Fresh Fly Flavor* 40: *Loc*—Loco, crazy. *a***1994** Smitherman *Black Talk* 155: *Lok* (pronounced *loke*) Messed up; loco; mentally unbalanced; fanatical. **1995** Stavsky et al. *A 2 Z* 64: She'll go loc if you leave her now.

local *n.* **1.** *Journ.* a local reporter or editor.
  1862 in *DA:* The "Local" departed for that city shortly before Christmas. **1866** in B. Harte *Harte's Calif.* 65: The "local" of the Reese River Reveille has been paying a visit to the county hospital. **1866** in *DA:* A good local must combine the loquacity of a magician with the impudence of the d—l. **1868** in *DAE:* We observe that Brier, local of the *News*, has on a new coat.

2. a neighborhood bar; one's local tavern.
  *****1934** in *OED2:* A modest beer or two at the "local." *****1937**, *****1943**, *****1957** in *OED2.* **1960** *Sat. Eve. Post* (Oct. 15) 115: We will stop at the local on the way back. **1965** N.Y.C. man, age *ca*30: Looks like I'll have to find myself a new local. **1969** *U.S. News & W.R.* (June 9) 61: Drinkers now go more to their "locals" rather than drive farther away. **1976** Rosten *To Anywhere* 56: Fellow denizens of their club or their "local" (pub). **1995** S. Moore *In the Cut* 53: You come here often? I mean, it's your neighborhood, right? Your local.

3. *Prost.* an act of masturbating a customer.
  1976 *Urban Life* V 277: I've just done hand jobs since the first day on the job....There's really nothing wrong with locals. **1976–77** Kernochan *Dry Hustle* 130: "You just 'command' them to jerk themselves off." "You don't even give them a local? For that kind of bread?"

local yokel *n.* an esp. ignorant or foolish country person or small-town dweller.
  1950 *Best Army Short Stories* 9: Okay, hot pilot, save your jive for the local yokels. **1956** I. Shulman *Good Deeds* 55: Don't...tell the local yokels how much bigger and better things are in New York. **1963** T.I. Rubin *Sweet Daddy* 15: She was real friendly with a few of the local yokels. **1972** Carpentier *Flt. One* 255: The goddamn local yokels. **1976** Lieberman & Rhodes *CB* 132: *Local Yokel*—Local police officer (usually in a small town). **1986** *NDAS: Local yokel*...A town or city police officer....A resident of a small town or rural area.

loced-out see s.v. LOC OUT.

locie var. LOKIE.

lock *n.* **1.** Orig. *Gamb.* an absolute certainty; CINCH, 1.a.; (*specif.*) a racehorse believed certain to win a particular race. Also **mortal lock.**
  1942 *ATS* 188: Certainty...cinch,...lock. Ibid. 687: Turf...Favorite...cinch,...lock,...sure bet. **1949** (cited in T.L. Clark *Dict. Gambling & Gaming*). **1951** E. Arcaro, in Woods *Horse-Racing* 38: The winter-spring racing season of 1937–38 saw the great Earl Sande moving eastward with what looked like an out and out lock to capture the Kentucky Derby. This was the colt Stagehand. **1951** in D.W. Maurer *Lang. Und.* 218: *Lock* or *mortal lock*...a race to be won easily by a certain horse....A "sure thing" bet....By implication, a fixed race. **1951** *AS* XXVI 2 (May) 100: *Cinch.* When a player...see[s] that it is impossible for any of his opponents to beat him, he has a cinch....*Lock.* See *cinch.* **1958** in *DAS:* This guy looks like a lock now. Not because he's won eight already, but because of the way he's pitching. **1961** *Chi. Sunday Trib.* (Aug. 13) II 6: Mortal Lock [a racehorse] Repeats in Fair Stake. **1961** Braly *Felony Tank* 183: We've got a lock on it. **1966** Braly *On the Yard* 26: "Well, we ain't gunna have no such worry for a while anyway." "That's a lock." **1966** *True* (Oct.) 104: I'd say he's a lock to earn a million. **1968** Ainslie *Thoroughbred* 470: *Lock*—A sure thing.

1969 in J. Flaherty *Chez Joey* 64: She had "a lock in the eighth." **1981** *N.Y. Post* (Dec. 23) 51: Poincelet had been engaged to ride a colt named Thunderhead in the English classic, the Two Thousand Guineas, and in Poincelet's view, he was a lock. **1983** P. Dexter *God's Pocket* 112: That horse...is a lock. **1984** W. Murray *Dead Crab* 79: It's what we used to call a mortal lock....An animal that cannot lose the race....Of which there ain't any such animals. **1984** D. Jenkins *Life Its Ownself* 179: They're a mortal lock to lose twelve games. **1989** *CBS This Morning* (CBS-TV) (Aug. 3): He was a lock for the job. **1993** *Class of '96* (Fox-TV): You are a virtual lock to win the Nobel Prize. **1995** *TV Guide* (June 24) 14: I...predict that you...will go see this picture. It's a lock. **1995** *N.Y. Times* (Aug. 9) B11: Johnson Seems a Lock To Win at 400 Meters.

2. complete control (over something); CINCH. Now *S.E.*

[**1928** R. Fisher *Jericho* 304: *Put (Get, Have) the Locks On* To handcuff. Hence to render helpless. Most frequently heard in reference to some form of gambling, such as card games and love affairs.] **1966** *Sat. Review* (Nov. 12) 104: Almost all the two-paper cities have but one publisher, who has a lock on the market. **1966** Braly *On the Yard* 273: They got a lock here. **1967** Lit *Dict.* 40: *(He Owns) The Lock*—The main man taking his stand; he has the power and complete control; Mess less if you got your smarts. **1970** Della Femina *Wonderful Folks* 89: Another guy had a lock on an enormous piece of cigarette business. **1973** in J. Flaherty *Chez Joey* xiv: Every woman contributed her own specialty....My mother had the lock on the Irish soda bread. **1981** P. Sann *Trial* 127: Her own boss had the lock on her.

¶ In phrase:

¶ **lock, stock, and barrel** completely; thoroughly. Now *colloq.* or *S.E.*

1842 in *OED2*: All moved, lock, stock, and barrel. **1855** S. Hammett *Capt. Priest* 76: He sold off his feathered stock, "lock, stock, and barrel." **1885** Siringo *Texas Cowboy* 19: He...persuaded mother to sell out lock, stock, and barrel and go with him. **1960–61** Steinbeck *Discontent* 79: Maybe you just hate Allen, lock, stock, and bobtail.

lock *v.* **1.** *Pris.* to occupy a cell or the like in a correctional facility.

1931 *AS* VI (Aug.) 439: *Lock.* To occupy a cell. "There's a gee who locks under me." **1980** Algren *Dev. Stocking* 17: When he was sixteen Red Haloways came in, on a mugging conviction, and they locked in the same cottage.

2. *Police.* to incarcerate; lock up.—also constr. with *down*. Cf. S.E. sense 'to shut up or confine with a lock; to put under lock and key', in *OED2* since *a*1300.

1970–71 J. Rubinstein *City Police* 399: How many pinches has he got for numbers? Five or six. I locked him myself once. **1980** Algren *Dev. Stocking* 121: By that time she's *anxious* to get locked. **1981** *Easyriders* (Oct.) 91: If you've ever been locked down—and who of us hasn't at one time or another—you know how hard it is to lose a celly. **1995** *Donahue* (NBC-TV): They'll lock you down forever!

¶ In phrases:

¶ **have it locked** to have something assured or under control.—also constr. with *in*.

1963 *Wash. Post* (Sept. 28) 1: I thought I had it locked....I was real wrong. **1963** Breen *PT 109* (film): Really, I had it all locked in.

¶ **lock and load** [fr. the order to chamber a round for firing, orig. *load and lock!*, as in 1941–42 quot., but altered as in 1982 quot.] *Mil.* to ready oneself for imminent action, confrontation, or the like.—used imperatively. [Early quots. ref. to WWII.]

[**1941–42** Gach *In Army Now* 231: One round, ball ammunition, load and lock!] **1949** Brown & Grant *Sands of Iwo Jima* (film): Lock and load, boy, lock and load. **1957** Myrer *Big War* 6: I'm going to get all the lucky babes and crowd 'em all into one small room...and...tell 'em: "All right, kids, this is it. I haven't got all the time in the world. Lock and load, that's all, lock and load." **1965** Linakis *In Spring* 18: "Lock and load"...I said to the big trooper. "That means she's yours." **1976** Atlee *Domino* 100: Okay, Joe....Time to lock and load, kid. **1982** F. Hailey *Soldier Talk* 39: *Lock and load.* A firing range command for soldiers to place safety levers of weapons in the "safe" position and load ammunition. Soldiers frequently used this expression when in a group and a brawl or confrontation was imminent. **1989** USMC veteran, age 41, Knoxville, Tenn.: Yeah. Lock and load. **1993** *New Yorker*

(Mar. 29) 65: We've been watching the revolution in Kashmir, the internal problems in India, and we look at the Pakistani pre-positioning. These guys have done everything that will lead you to believe that they are locked and loaded. **1995** *Time* (May 8) 64: The incursion is inevitable, he argues, and the only choice is "to lock and load." **1996** *Melrose Place* (Fox-TV): Time to lock and load!

¶ **lock horns** to tangle in a fight; argue. Now *S.E.*

1836 in *DA:* They are enemies, and let them lock horns. **1845** in G.W. Harris *High Times* (July 16) 52: *I know'd what it meant*, so we locked horns without a word. **1882** Sweet *Sketches* 42: I didn't want you and Jay to lock horns. **1901** in *OED2*: We should hardly feel warranted in locking horns with Tammany Hall. **1904** in *DAE*: It was largely the advice of Cockran that induced Murphy to lock horns with David B. Hill for the control of the State Committee. **1940** Faulkner *Hamlet* 30: You mean he locked horns with Pat Stamper and even had the bridle left to take back home? **1966** H.S. Thompson *Hell's Angels* 12: The idea...is...not to lock horns with hayseed cops along the way.

¶ **lock into** to obtain for oneself.

1979 *Army Times* (June 18) 12: On a good night the soldiers will "lock into" a few items to make the drive enjoyable—a few cases of beer and some high-quality "smoking dope."

locker *n.* *Naut.* **1.** a pocket.

1836 *Spirit of Times* (Feb. 20) 7: He...dallied about the shop, waiting to see if she'd come up, taking a long time in forking out the blunt, and another longer time in counting it, and passing the change into his starboard locker. **1837** *Spirit of Times* (June 24) 146/2: Not a friend from his *locker* would lend us a *shot*. **1872** Thomes *Slaver* 27: The men went, looking as contented as though about to be discharged with several hundred dollars in their lockers for a general blow-out. **1944** (quot. at SMUKE).

2. the belly.

1855 Wise *Tales* 224: Let's get a bite of breakfast into our lockers. **1985** M. Baker *Cops* 63: [The killer] put three [*sc.*, bullets] right in the fucking locker on this guy from about a foot away.

¶ In phrase:

¶ **shot in (one's) locker, 1.** a piece of money in (one's) possession.

1835 *Spirit of Times* (Dec. 12) 1: He complained of the expense of the article and talked of the "shot in his locker being low." ***1848** Thackeray, in *OED2*: As long as there's a shot in the locker, she shall want for nothing. **1883** Russell *Sailors' Lang.* 127: *Shot in the locker.*— Money possessed by a seaman. "There is still a shot left in the locker," or "the locker is low."

2. a final resource.

1894 J. Slocum *Liberdade* 77: With still a "shot in the locker"...we set to work with tools saved from the wreck.

lockup *n.* **1.** a jail. Now *S.E.*

[***1785** Grose *Vulgar Tongue*, in *F & H: Lock up house*...a public-house kept by sheriff's officers, to which they convey the persons they have arrested.] **1839** in *DAE*: He was seized, and carried to the "lock up." **1853** P.H. Skinner *Ragged Ten Thousand* 64: We staid in the lock-up, ma'am. **1865** in Hilleary *Webfoot* 40: The Indians in the "lock-up" gave us some amusement.

2. exclusive hold or possession; LOCK, 2.

1965 J. Smith & D. Stanford *Monster A-Go-Go* (film): I thought this was gonna be a lock-up. Just legwork. **1970** Terkel *Hard Times* 72: There's nobody with a lock-up on soul.

lock up *v.* to assure attainment of or victory in; claim securely; have complete control over; gain and keep.

1911 Van Loan *Big League* 64: "Here's where we lock it up in the valise!" howled Merry, pirouetting off third base. **1939** Calloway *Swingformation Bureau*: That chick is locked up in this direction, so just cut out while your conk is all in one portion. **1964** H. Rhodes *Chosen Few* 33: Who is she?...Anybody got it locked up yet? **1971** Dahlskog *Dict.* 38: *Lock up (something)*, to be assured of success, as: to *lock up* a test. **1984** J. McNamara *First Directive* 284: They been bragging for years how they going to lock up the California action.

Loco *n.* a Locofoco, a member of a radical faction of the N.Y. Democratic Party. Now *hist.*

1838 in *DA:* I thus claim to be a true Loco and Nullifier. **1840** in Eliason *Tarheel Talk* 282: The democrats or locos. **1841** H. Clay, in *OED2*: The Locos are...opposed to the scheme. **1847** E. Dickinson, in *OED2*: To say nothing of its falling into the merciless hands of a loco! **1848** in *DA*. **1860** in R.B. Browne *Lincoln-Lore* 337: How the frightened Locos run/From Uncle Abe the honest. **1947** in *DA*.

loco[1] *n. R.R.* a locomotive. Now *colloq.*

> **1833** in *DARE*: With the *loco*...he may start from one city in the morning and return again in the evening from a visit to the other. ***1869**, ***1898**, etc., in *OED2*. **1950** *Popular Science* (Dec.) 135: FRENCH LOCO HITS 100 M.P.H....This fast new electric locomotive will soon be speeding passengers and freight over French railways.

loco[2] *n.* [< Sp] **1.** a deranged or dangerously unpredictable person.

> **1852** in *DARE*: Your friend has been trying to injure you his best giving out on all sides that you are a *loco*. **1918** in *DARE*: We are the lads who'll smoke him out./On the trail of Loco Billy [*sc.* Wilhelm II]. **1937** Johnston *Prison Life* 35: Maybe if I...run around like that loco they call Squirrel maybe they might send me to Stockton. **1976** *L.A. Times* (Sept. 19) II 1: He also knows...which youths are "locos"—crazy enough to be altogether unpredictable.

2. marijuana; LOCOWEED.

> **1969** Lingeman *Drugs A to Z: Loco.* marijuana.

loco *adj.* [< Sp] Orig. *West.* crazy; deranged; (*hence*) wildly eager; infatuated.

> **1887** F. Francis *Saddle & Moccasin* 77: They said we were "loco" or mad. **1887** in *OED2*: You won't be able to do nuthin' with 'em, sir; they'll go plumb loco. **1896** in F. Remington *Sel. Letters* 281: I am going to go loco for 2 mo. **1898** Norris *Moran* 68: Clean loco from the gas. **1902** in Remington *Own West* 40: "The old man is loco," said a soldier. **1906** Mulford *Bar-20* 13: Johnny was shore loco about her. **1912** *Cosmopolitan* (May) 761: That shows how loco *he* was. **1913** Mulford *Coming of Cassidy* 212: So he drifts on, gettin' a li'l loco by now. **1918** in *AS* (Oct. 1933) 29: *Loco.* Insane. **1921** Casey & Casey *Gay-Cat* 103: Thet guy must be plumb loco 'bout dorgs. **1936** Gaddis *Courtesan* 86: There was one guy who was sure completely loco in the coco about you. **1940** F. Hunt *Trail fr. Tex.* 68: Not 'less he's done gone plumb loco. **1950** *Sat. Eve. Post* (May 13) 184: That single light winking across the strait drove Weston a little loco. **1956** Overholser *Desperate* 47: We'd be loco to take one poison to get rid of another! **1960** L'Amour *Sacketts* 191: That man's gone loco. **1973** Wagenheim *Clemente!* 68: You must be *loco* to pull a boner like that. **1972–75** W. Allen *Feathers* 90: He's crazy. Loco in the head. **1984** Mason & Rheingold *Slanguage: Loco.*...Crazy. Used to describe students who aren't actually crazy but enjoy acting crazy. **1989** Vidal *Billy the Kid* (film) I think Pat's gone loco.

locoed *adj. West.* confused; excited; crazed; wildly eager; infatuated. [Now generally supplanted by LOCO.]

> **1885** Siringo *Texas Cowboy* 57: I was too badly "locoed" to tell a good horse from a bad one. **1887** in *DAE*: Cattle showing signs of madness are said to be "locoed," and so finally the word extended to human beings. *a***1891** *Galveston News*, in *DN* I 249: Two Mexican families,—who all have the appearance of being *locoed*. **1899** Garland *Eagle's Heart* 158: Fo' fo'ty yeahs I have handled these locoed hosses. **1902** in "O. Henry" *Works* 435: They're plum locoed about Piggy. **1903** A.H. Lewis *Black Lion* 295: It looks like this Doc Chepp is locoed to collect wild anamiles [*sic*] that way. **1903** A. Adams *Log of a Cowboy* 235 [ref. to 1882]: My relations...all seemed to be rapidly getting locoed. **1903** Hobart *Out for Coin* 64: He's...locoed. **1905** W.J. Kelly *Lariats* 142: I thought she was "locoed" or somethin'. **1907** *Lippincott's Mag.* (May) 675: They got a girl locoed before she can...defend herself. **1917–20** in J.M. Hunter *Trail* 347: The roundup boss would let no one ride through the herd and "chouse," or unnecessarily disturb them: these fellows found guilty of such misconduct were called "loco'ed." **1926** C.M. Russell *Trails* 124: An' the bucks are just as locoed in their way. **1927** P.A. Rollins *Jinglebob* 64: He's locoed, an' ain't responsible. **1930** C. Mulford *Eagle* 112: Half a dozen locoed desert rats got th' idear there was gold in the crick.

locomote *v.* to travel; walk around. [Now only as a technical term in biology.]

> **1834** in *DAE*: Who but our author would represent him [*sc.*, a bard], "locomoting" on a long, dog-trot over the bogs of his neighborhood? **1845** in G.W. Harris *High Times* (July 16) 46: He throws...in...a bed too in the hay, if you git too hot to locomote. **1860** in *DA*: [Their] attention was attracted to the parson by his peculiar style of locomoting (being partially paralysed).

loc out *v. Rap Music.* to make insane; FREAK [OUT], 1; (*also*) to make CRAZY; make exciting. Often as ppl.a. Cf. LOC, *adj.*

> **1989** *21 Jump St.* (Fox-TV): I'm gonna get wid de fool dat loc'd you out. *Ibid.*: This is loc'd out! **1993** "Dr. Dre" *Nuttin' But a "G" Thang* (rap song): Two loced-out niggas so we're craaazy! **1994** A. Heckerling *Clueless* 4: Did I show you the loqued out jeep daddy bought me?

locoweed *n.* marijuana.

> **1930** G. Irwin *Tramp & Und. Slang: Loco*...The "loco weed" is a variety of the marajuana [*sic*] which is much used as a drug. **1933** in *Amer. Jour. Psychiatry* XCI (1934) 329: Loco Weed, Breeder of Madness and Crime. **1935** Pollock *Underworld Speaks: Loco weed,* mariahuana [*sic*]; hemp; hashish. **1936** in Lipton *Barbarians* 181: Marihuana is frequently called "locoweed." **1943** (quot. at MARY JANE). **1960** *Esquire* (Mar.) 87: After all, it's called loco weed, isn't it? **1960** in Rosset *Evergreen Reader* 273: You think my Dad don't know *Mex'can loco-weed* when he sees it? *a***1986** D. Tate *Bravo Burning*: Still on that damn locoweed?

locs /louks/ *n.pl.* [fr. LOC, *adj.*] Esp. *Rap Music.* sunglasses.

> **1990** "Above the Law" *Livin Like Hustlers* (rap song): We wear black on black with the locs and the romeos. **1993** K. Scott *Monster* 43: Dark shades, also called Locs or Locos. **1993** P. Munro *U.C.L.A. Slang II: Looks/locs* n. sunglasses....*locs*...rhymes with *jokes*. **1994** *Totally Unofficial Rap Dictionary:* Ice Cube's *Kill at Will* album...advertizes locs as sunglasses on the inside cover.

locust *n.* **1.** [because freq. made of *locust* wood] *Police.* a nightstick or billy club.

> *ca***1863** in Dannett *Civil War Humor* 39: Guess, Judge, I'll resign my locust. **1863** in *OED2*: Go in they did forthwith, and, where moral suasion had failed, the locusts succeeded. **1866** *Night Side of N.Y.* 38: The roundsman gives a certain number of raps with his "locust" upon the sidewalk flags. **1882** in *F & H*: "Give them the locusts, men," came in sharp ringing tones from the captain. **1891** Maitland *Slang Dict.* 169: *Locust,* a policeman's club, also known as a "hickory," from the nature of the wood. **1904** in *DA*: The policemen did not carry their "locusts." **1926** *AS* I (Dec.) 652: *Locust.* police club. **1930** Lavine *Third Degree* 78: A detective picked out the largest and heaviest locust in the group. **1938** Bellem *Blue Murder* 145: I saw...a harness bull patrolling his beat and swinging his locust.

2. a police officer.

> **1865** Sala *Diary* II 211: The New York policeman wears a handsome uniform....At his side hangs a club...made of "locust wood"...and by rowdies the policeman is often generically called (with the addition of a frightful expletive) a "locust."

lodge *n.* [fig. use of *lodge* 'a Native American dwelling'] *West.* the house or home of a trapper or western pioneer.

> **1847** Ruxton *Life in Far West* 17: This child's getting old, and feels like wanting a woman's face about his lodge for the balance of his days. **1850** Garrard *Wah-to-yah* 161: Sometimes he thinks of makin' tracks for white settlement, but when he gits to Bent's big lodge, on the Arkansa, and sees the bugheways, an' the fellers from the States, how they roll thar eyes at an Injun yell...he leaves for the Bayou Salade. **1866** Marcy *Army Life* 39: You'd fed and treated him to the best fixins in your lodge.

log *n.* **1.** a blockhead.

> **1895** F.M. Crawford *Johnstone's Son* 77: They used to call me Log. That was short for logarithm, you know, because I was such a log at arithmetic.

2. *Narc.* **a.** an opium pipe.

> **1935** Pollock *Underworld Speaks: Log,* an opium pipe. **1936** Dai *Opium Addiction* 199: *Gonger.* Pipe for smoking opium. Also called *the stick* or *log.* **1938** D.W. Maurer, in *AS* XIII 3 (Oct.) 187: *Log.* An opium pipe.

b. a marijuana cigarette. Cf. STICK.

> **1977** (cited in Spears *Drugs & Drink*). **1982** E. Abel *Marihuana Dict.* 63: *Log.* Marihuana cigarette.

3. a bar in a drinking establishment; MAHOGANY.

> **1967** (quot. at TWISTED). **1967** [R. Beck] *Pimp* 82: His...pinkie scooted the saw buck back to me across the log.

4. *Surfing.* (see quots.).

> **1967** in *OED2: Log,* a very heavy surfboard. **1968** Kirk & Hanle *Surfer's Hndbk.* 141: *Log:* heavy, difficult board.

5. a piece of excrement; in phr. **drop** [or **lay**] **a log** to defecate.—usu. considered vulgar.

1973 Univ. Michigan woman (Dec. 31): To take a shit is to *lay a log.* **1974** Newark, N.J., man (Jan. 7): You mean *drop a log.* **1978** in Lyle & Golenbock *Bronx Zoo* 48: Ron…took a shit on one of those cakes…on top of it was a big, brand-new shiny brown log. ***1989** P. Beale, in Partridge *Concise Dict. Slang: Logs.* Turds: teenagers': early 1980s.

6. the penis—esp. in phr. **flog the log** to masturbate.—usu. considered vulgar.

1974 Univ. Tenn. student: To *flog a log* means to jerk off. **1976** Rubels *One-Woman Show* 180: Jake started…banging his log into her. **1985** Dye *Between Raindrops* 195: How can a guy flog his…log with enemy soldiers in the area?

log *v.* **1.** *Naut.* to make note of; notice; commit to memory.

1828 Bird *Looking Glass* 113: "Wasn't it you that knocked me down in the street t'other night?" "I never logged it." **1887** Davis *Sea-Wanderer* 83 [ref. to 1831]: Now, youngster, you just log down what I say. **1993** J. Watson & K. Dockery *Point Man* 56: I put my annoyance away and logged it for later consideration.

2. *Av.* to spend (time); get (sleep).

1944 Stiles *Big Bird* 68: Sam probably logged more sack-time in his stretch in the ETO than any other squadron of men. **1945** Hamann *Air Words*: Log sack time, to. To sleep. **1955** Klaas *Maybe I'm Dead* 156: Gonna log a little pasture-time with that barmaid at the Baron of Beef. **1968** W.C. Anderson *Gooney Bird* 28: Log a little cockpit time if you like. **1980** W.C. Anderson *Bat-21* 189: I'll go log some shuteye. **1994** M. Bowman & P. Bunce *Thunder in Heavens* 18: Air crews…tried to log a little sack time.

log bird *n.* [*logistical* + BIRD, 7.e.] *Mil.* a logistical resupply helicopter. [Quots. ref. to Vietnam War.]

1982 Del Vecchio *13th Valley* 322: The third log bird came in with clothes from the company fund and sundry materials. **1983** Elting, Cragg & Deal *Dict. Soldier Talk* 188: Log bird…A helicopter that flew resupply missions to a unit's forward elements. **1983** C. Rich *Advisors* 445: *Log Bird*—Logistical resupply helicopter.

loggerhead *n.* a Pennsylvanian.

1888 W. Whitman, in *DAE*: Those [soldiers] from…Pennsylvania, [were called] Logher Heads [during the Civil War].

logger's smallpox *n. Logging.* puncture wounds from being stamped with spiked logging boots. *Joc.*

1938 Holbrook *Mackinaw* 111: Ears were chewed off.…"Logger's smallpox" was prevalent. **1939** (cited in Partridge *DSUE* (ed. 7) 1256). **1958** McCullough *Woods Words: Logger's smallpox*—This is the result of being stomped on by a man wearing calked shoes. **1967** *American Heritage* (Feb.) 67: The pockmarks Jigger got from his opponent's spiked boots, plus a good many others, he always referred to as "logger's smallpox." **1979** Decker *Holdouts* 24: Kick him! Stomp him! Give him the logger's smallpox.

logging berries *n. Logging.* prunes. *Joc.*

[**1928** in *DARE: Loganberries*—prunes.] **1941** in *DARE:* Cooks are still "stomick robbers"…prunes, "log berries." **1956** Sorden & Ebert *Logger's* 22 [ref. to a1925]: *Logging-berries,* Prunes. **1966** in *DARE:* They [*sc.* loggers] called a prune a loggin' berry.

log-leg *n.* a person having a wooden leg.

1837 R.M. Bird *Nick of Woods* I 58: I'm for any man that insults me! log-leg or leather-breeches.

logroll *v.* Esp. *Pol.* to practice favoritism or cronyism; (*specif.*) to use political influence or connections; accomplish or obtain (something) through such influence. Now *colloq.* Hence **logroller,** *n.*

1812 (cited in *W10*). **1823** in *OED2*: That sort of "management," now rather more fashionable, and known by the dignified appellation of "log-rolling"—that is, a buying and selling of votes. **1835** in *OED2*: My people don't like me to log-roll in their business, and vote away pre-emption rights to fellows in other states, that never kindle a fire on their lands. **1845** Corcoran *Pickings* 75: I calls that downright logrollin'. **1864** in *OED2*: A professional politician…lobbyer and logroller generally. **1899** Thomas *Arizona* 17: I log-rolled a transfer down here in the desert, where she can't possibly escape. **1929** E. Haycox *Chaffee* 152: There was something of the glorified log roller about him. **1949** *N.Y. Times* (Sept. 25) VI 2: It is a subtle conspiracy to logroll appointments through the Senate without opposition. **1950**

Time (Mar. 27) 32: Most of the world's gastronomic jargon was created in the 18th and 19th Centuries by log-rolling cooks to commemorate their masters' favorite dishes. **1950** *N.Y. Times* (Dec. 26) 22: The logrollers, the social-economic doctrinaires and the wasters are able…to discredit the effort. **1963** *Time* (Nov. 1) 50: Delegates lobbied and logrolled to gather votes.

loid *n. Police.* a celluloid strip used by a burglar to push back the bolt of a spring lock.—often used attrib.

[**1938** R. Chandler *Big Sleep* ch. xxvi: I reached my wallet out and slipped the thick hard window of celluloid from over my driver's license.…I pushed the celluloid plate into the wide crack and felt for the slope of the spring lock. There was a dry click.] ***1958** in *OED2*: You said you could use a loid. Let's see you open that door. **1967** *Harper's* (Feb.) 51: A "loid" expert wiggles a celluloid…in a door crack to open a spring lock. ***1968, *1968** in *OED2*. **1980** *Next* (July–Aug.) 66: "'Loid' burglars who insert a credit card or other celluloid strip against a spring latch to force it.

loid *v. Police.* to open (a door) by means of a LOID, usu. for the purpose of burglary.—also used intrans.

*1963 in Partridge *Dict. Und.* (ed. 2) 842: I "loided" the lock on a door at the rear of the premises. **1964** *N.Y. Times* (Dec. 27) VI 9: Madsen could only pass doors he could "loid" (open by forcing a celluloid…slip against the snap lock). **1967** *Harper's* (Feb.) 51: A door shaker…may learn from another addict how to loid a door or use a jimmy. **1968** *U.S. News & W.R.* (Sept. 9) 96: This type of lock must be forced or picked and cannot be "loided"—opened with a piece of celluloid. **1972** *Pop. Sci.* (Aug.) 95: A quality key-in-the-knob lock is more difficult to break and has a dead-locking latch that prevents "loiding." ***1990** T. Thorne *Dict. Contemp. Sl.: Loid*…to open a door by moving a strip of celluloid…up and down in the gap between the door and its frame.…in use since before World War II.

lokie *n. R.R.* a locomotive. Also vars.

1934 Weseen *Dict. Amer. Sl.: Lokey man*—A man who works on a locomotive that pulls logs from the woods to the mills. **1938** in *DARE: Lokie:* Diminutive for locomotive. **1950** *West. Folk.* IX 118: *Loci.* Steam logging locomotive. **1942** *ATS* 727: Locomotive.…*loco, lokey.* ***1947** in *OED2*: Sometimes she heard a lokey puffing. **1958** McCulloch *Woods Words* 108: *Locie* (or *lokie,* or *lockie,* or *loky*)—A logging locomotive. **1977** in *DARE* [ref. to *ca*1918].

lolla *n.* LOLLAPALOOZA. Also vars., esp. **lala.** Also as adj.

1886 *Lantern* (N.O.) (Sept. 8) 3: [A racehorse that is] a regular la-la boy. *Ibid.* (Sept. 22) 4: Gave him a quarter to find their la-la's, Messrs. Tim Davis and his friend Wertenberger. **1888** *Stag Party* 50: I'm a lolla, a whooper, I am! **1888** in F. Remington *Sel. Letters* 46: I would be a "lolly" [of a savage]—but why harrow ourselves with such vain regrets. **1889–90** Barrère & Leland *Dict. Slang: Loller* (American), usually applied to a lively, sportive damsel, or "bit of muslin." **1890** in F. Remington *Sel. Letters* 100: I have made some "lolla" water colors of U.S. soldiers. **1895** in F. Remington *Wister* 71: You ought to see the "great model" I am making. Its a "lolle." **1895** Gore *Stu. Slang* 3: *La la*…A delightful, charming person. Often used ironically. *a*1890–96 F & H IV 145: *Lala*…(American).—A swell. **1896** in Outcault *Yellow Kid* 140: Anudder box…o' dem lolla perfecktoes [*sc.* cigars]. **1897** *Chi. Tribune* (July 25) 15: The Kansas dialect…*Lala*—a lulu—"Eugene Ware, the poet, is a lala." **1899** Cullen *Tales* 134: He must ha' been a la-la. **1900** in F. Remington *Wister* 287: I want a lala too no d— newspaper puff. **1901** Ade *Modern Fables* 66: He must be a Lah-Lah if he can hold to that gait. **1913** *DN* IV 17: *La-la.* A swell, stylish person. Frequent in Nebraska.…"That lady is a la-la." "He's quite a la-la." **1915–16** Lait *Beef, Iron & Wine* 32: "It's nice?" she asked. "It's a lal-lah," said the Wolf. **1939** O'Brien *Best Stories of 1939* 425: It still is a lala of a battle.

lollapalooza *n.* [orig. unkn.; cf. LOLLA] **1.** something that is an extraordinary example of its kind; LULU. Also vars., esp. **lallapalooza.**

1896 Ade *Artie* 8: "But the girls—wow!" "Beauties, eh?" "Lollypaloozers!" **1898** *Sporting News* (Nov. 12) 6 (coll. B. Popik): "He is saying his team next season will contain a whole lot of lalapaloosas—" "What is a lalapaloosa?" "A lalapaloosa, my son, is a crackerjack." **1904** [Hobart] *From Missouri* 89: Our final parade with the fireworks finish…was a lallapalootza! **1907** *Army & Navy Life* (Sept.) 316: Mrs. Eddy, the chief lallapaloozer in the church. **1908** in Fleming *Unforgettable Season* 232: Which is being agitated almost as much these days as the...proper pronunciation of the word "lallapaloosa." **1911** *DN* III 545: *Lallapaloosa*...Something fine or grand...."You have a lallapaloosa of a hat." **1912** *DN* III 582: Isn't John's new buggy a lolly-paloozer? **1913** *DN* IV 17: *Lallapaloosa.* A stylish person. Something pleasing. In general use in Nebraska....*Lallapalooser.* Something pleasing, splendid, fine...Used in Nebraska, Wyoming and elsewhere. **1918** *DN* V 26: *Lollapalouser*, n. 1. Anything of excellence in its own way. 2. A great lie. General. **1919** Wilkins *Co. Fund* 13: That sure was a lolapalooser! **1922** Tully *Emmett Lawler* 295: That girl's a lalapolusa. **1929** Ferber *Cimarron* 130: "Ain't she," he demanded, "a lalapaloosa!" **1930** Sage *Last Rustler* 103: Them sure is some lollapoluzzers you found! **1934** Weseen *Dict. Slang* 364: Lollypaloozer. **1936** Tully *Bruiser* 189: But the boys out Minneapolis way tell me this gal's a lolapalooza. **1938** C. Wilbur *Swingtime in Movies* (film): A college lalapalooza. **1943** Wendt & Gogan *Bosses* 280: It's great! It's a lallapalooza! **1944** Huie *Can Do!* 45: Because the Japs can't pronounce L, our passwords are always shibboleths containing a lot of L's—Lollapalooza, lovely Lulu, etc. At night our sentries are ordered to shoot...anyone who fumbles the pronunciation. **1944** Ruskin et al. *Andy Hardy's Blonde Trouble* (film): A young woman...preferably a lalapalooza. **1944** W. Blair *Tall Tale Amer.* 64: So they had a shooting match that was a lolapaloosa. **1950** *Sat. Eve. Post* (Oct. 28) 144: Robinson has a lollapaloosa of a[n]... idea for the 1951 show. **1953** *I Love Lucy* (CBS-TV): I look for this well to be a real lollapalooza. **1961** *Sat. Eve. Post* (Nov. 4) 81: The ensuing preprimary campaign was, to put it mildly, a lollapalooza. **1971** in L. Bangs *Psychotic Reactions* 58: She grew up to be a wollapalooza of a...fashion model. **1971** Torres *Sting Like a Bee* 137: A lollapalooza of a fight. **1984** C. Francis *Who's Sorry?* 206: One lollapalooza of a migraine. **1995** *AS* LXX 326: Whoopee, this book is a lollapalooza!

2. *Poker.* any of various eccentric hands arbitrarily allowed to win the pot, usu. to deceive a newcomer. Cf. LULU, 1.d.

    1934 in *DARE:* The old lallapaloosa game in which the rules are changed to fit the occasion. **1939** in *DARE:* But I got a lalapalooza. Out here we call a deuce, four, six, eight and ten a lalapalooza and that beats everything, even a royal flush. Ain't that right, boys? **1949** (cited in T.L. Clark *Dict. Gambling & Gaming*). **1976** in *DARE.*

lollipop *n.* **1.a.** a woman, esp. an attractive young woman.

    1860 J.G. Holland *Miss Gilbert* 220: "Who is that fat old lollypop in the door yonder?" "That is Mrs. Ruggles." **1945** Scott & Friedman *Letter for Evie* (film): You know—tomatoes, lollipops, mice!

b. a sweetheart (of either sex).

    1913 T.A. Dorgan, in Zwilling *TAD Lexicon* 115: I just called up the old lady and told her that I wouldn't be home until quite late and she was nice as pie. Just said allright my lollypop and hung up. **1941–42** Gach *In Army Now* 177: He's your brother and I'm your lollypop. **1942** in *DARE* [ref. too1900–19]: *Lollipop*...sweetheart. **1956** in *DARE:* Grace Kelly, who vies with Gina Lollabrigida as the world's reigning lollipop. **a1970* Partridge *DSUE* (ed. 7) 1257: *Lollipop*...One's girl friend: R.A.F.: 1939–45.

c. an effeminate male, esp. a homosexual.

    1927 in Hammett *Knockover* 306: These bimbos were a couple of lollipops for fair. There wouldn't have been an ounce of fight in a ton of them. **1967** P. Roth *When She Was Good* 69: Since when did you become a lollipop, Roy? Is that what you were doing up there at the North Pole, turning pansy on the tax-payers' money?

2. (see 1965 quot.).—usu. considered vulgar.

    *1890–96 F & H: *Lollipop*...The penis. **1965** Trimble *Sex Words* 123: *Lollipop*...The Vagina or Penis as an object of Oral Intercourse.

3. *Und.* a very gullible person; SUCKER.

    [**1935** Pollock *Underworld Speaks*: *Lolly*, a person easily deceived.] **1942** *ATS* 365: Gullible person; dupe....*lollypop* (a "sucker"). **1982** *L.A. Times* (Dec. 5) I 3: The dummy—also called "lollipop" because he is such a sucker or "strawberry" because he is so easily plucked—is caught in the middle. **1983** (cited in J. Green *Dict. Contemp. Sl.*).

4. *Baseball.* a weakly thrown ball.

    1959 Brosnan *Long Season* 271: *Lollypop.* Any ball thrown with less than average speed or energy by any player on the field. **1963** in P. Dickson *Baseball Dict.* 248: No...he hasn't got the fast ball anymore...he throws lollypops.

5. a rotating red beacon atop an emergency vehicle.

    1977 A. Patrick *Beyond Law* 12: His way [was] blocked by a squad car, its lollipop flashing.

6. *Business.* a clever and attractive inducement.

    1990 T. Fahey *Joys of Jargon* 10: A *lollipop* is a premium held out to stockholders to interest them in selling their stocks back to a company.

lollipop *v.* **1.** to soft-soap; SUCKER.

    1953 Paley *Rumble* 135: "You're a real pal!" He slapped Jimmy on the back. Jimmy shook it off and his face got red with anger. He knew they were trying to lollipop him. **1961** *Sat. Eve. Post* (Mar. 11) 67: Don't try to lollipop me, Burton. I'm too old to be taken in by a line like that.

2. *Baseball.* to throw or hit the ball weakly.

    1959 Brosnan *Long Season* 19: Three men to a game, one hits, the other two field. And hit the ball! No lollypopping. That don't do you no good.

lollipop factory *n.* an insane asylum.

    1979 *Rockford Files* (May 25): He'll cop a plea of insanity and win a free trip to the lollipop factory.

lolly[1] var. LOLLA.

lolly[2] *n.* [orig. unkn.] the anus.—usu. considered vulgar.

    1964 Howe *Valley of Fire* 59: Up your lolly with a rusty meat hook.

lollycooler *n.* [orig. unkn.] LOLLAPALOOZA. Also **lallycooler.**

    1882 in L. Levy *Flashes of Merriment* 280: Oh, your [*sic*] a lally cooler, Pete, a reg'lar la-di-da. **1891** Maitland *Slang Dict.* 163: *Lallycooler*, one who is pre-eminently succesful in his line; a "daisy," a "dandy," a "darling," a "lulu." **1897** Ade *Pink Marsh* 126: Vussitle gen'us—'at's [a] lolly-cooleh. **1972** *N.Y. Times Book Review* (Nov. 12) 40: A lollycooler! Concho Bliss is a dead shot and he nailed me right through the heart but the only thing I spilled was laughter.

lollygag or **lallygag** *n.* [orig. unkn.] foolishness; nonsense; foolish or idle talk.

    1862 *Harper's Mo.* (Aug.) 324: [In N.Y.C.:] "Ain't got no money," said Mr. Biggs, still fingering the morsels. "Oh, come now, none o' that ere lallygag....Go in, bossy!" **1880** in *OED2*: I kin get lots o' jobs, if I'd take my pay in friendship an' all sech lollygag. **1949–50** *PADS* (No. 14) 43: South Carolina...*lallygag*...n. Chatter, idle talk.

lollygag or **lallygag** *v.* **1.** to court, flirt, or engage in romantic kissing or cuddling, esp. in public; SPOON. [Though recognized by *DAS*, 1944–46 sense 'intercourse' is uncorroborated elsewhere.]

    1868 in *AS* III (1928) 198: The lascivious lolly-gagging lumps of licentiousness who disgrace the common decencies of life by their love-sick fawning at our public dances. **1869** Carleton *Kaleidoscope* 18: I thought Tom was lallygagging round Laura Bodley. **1875** *Minstrel Gags* 103: I...was proceedin' to kiss her and paw her all over...."Stop dat lally gaggin' dere." **1883** Peck *Bad Boy* 72: I told Ma it was a shame for so many people to be sitting around lally-gagging right before folks. **1884** Peck *Boss Book* 30: They lallygag on the grass and talk...love. **1890** *JAF* III 311: *Lallygag*—To "spoon," make love. Maine. **1900** Doughty *Bradys & Girl Smuggler* 17: They'll be so busy spooning and lally-gagging that he won't have any time to attend to this smuggling game. **1904** Hughie Cannon *Little Gertie Murphy* (NY: Howley-Dresser Co., 1904) (sheet music): She just goes around wid her Mickey/And don't lalagagg wid de goils. **1906** *DN* III 120: *Lollygog*...Used [in So. Indiana] with disgust for expression of affection in a public way, especially of kissing. "They *lollygog* around before people like two fools." **1907** *DN* III 246: *Lalligag*...To make love in a silly and demonstrative manner. "It's getting down to business when a couple begin to lalligag." **1911** *DN* IV 545: She's a regular lollygagger. **1922** in *DN* V 148: *Lollygagger*—a young man addicted to attempts at hallway spooning. **1927** in D. Runyon *Trials* 112: When your correspondent was a "necker" of no mean standing in the dim and misty past, they called it "lally-gagging." Times have changed. **1931** *AS* VII (Oct.) 22: *Lollygagging*—necking. **1934** Weseen *Dict. Amer. Slang* 188: *Lollygagging*—Necking; hugging and kissing. **1940** De Leon *Annie Sails Again* (film): So you want to have Eddie to yourself, lollygaggin' in the moonlight? **1941** *AS* (Feb.) 23: [Indiana:] *Lollygagging.* Kissing, "necking." **1944–46** in *AS* XXII (1947) 55: Pacific War Language...*Lollygagging.* Necking or intercourse. **1948** J. Stevens *Jim Turner* 59 [ref. to *ca*1910]: I caught Gabe and Isabel Crumley grinning and whispering to each other...smirking and lallygagging around, the old fools, like a pair of young ones. **1949** *JAF* 63: "Lally-gaggin'" was Grandmother's word for love-making. **1956** J. Brown *Kings Go Forth* 90: Have you and Monique been lollygagging? **1991** Randolph & Legman *Roll Me in Yr. Arms* 16: While the...folklorists "specialist" lollygags gracefully with his or her more attractive students out in the hall.

2.a. to dally, dawdle, spend time idly; loaf; (now *esp.*) to move along sluggishly. Now *colloq.*

 1869 in *AS* III (1928) 198: Present appearances indicate that winter will "lollygag" in the lap of spring. **1891** McCann & Jarrold *Odds & Ends* 10: Hello, Mag, me jim-dandy crow, what're ye doin' here lallygaggin' agin de wall? **1910** *Sat. Eve. Post* (July 30) 19: Frank lallygagged through the first term and came back for the second. **1919** S. Lewis *Free Air* 338: You old lemon-pie-faced, lollygagging, flap-footed, crab-nosed son of misery, gee, but it's good to see you, Milt! **1931** Lorimer & Lorimer *Streetcars* 59: Haven't I watched 'em lollygogging by the hour? **1935** F.H. Lea *Anchor Man* 276: The blathering nincompoops!...The damned lally-gagging popinjays! **1945** Rodgers & Hammerstein *Carousel* 172: Still lallygaggin'. You'd think a woman with nine children'd hev more sense. **1946** Michener *So. Pacific* 95: An hour later, however, we saw thirty new F4U's lolly-gagging through the sky Rendova way. **1950** Schnee *Next Voice You Hear* (film): Now will you stop lollygagging around and get to work! **1951** *New Yorker* (Aug. 4) 20: That left most of the summer free for play, swimming, berry picking, and general lallygagging. **1951** Pryor *The Big Play* 138: Imagine how it'd be if you was to have Brock around the place every second...lollygaggin' around. **1957** R. O'Connor *Co. Q* 67: Don't let me catch you lallygagging again or it will go hard with you. **1967** Morris & Morris *Dict. Wd. & Phr. Origs.* II 153: Especially in the first fine days of spring, it was a great temptation to *lallygag* on the way from school. **1972** *WCBS-TV News* (CBS-TV) (Feb. 10): Meanwhile, this high pressure area is now lollygagging along toward the east coast. **1982** Least Heat Moon *Blue Hwys.* 98: Can I get me a Tom and Collins or is lollygaggin' all that gets done in here? **1985** Dye *Between Raindrops* 193: Couldn't afford to lollygag down the streets. **1987** Santiago *Undercover* 48: The sound of laughter and lollygagging. *a***1992** T. Wilson *Termite Hill* 503: He...complained...only when they were lollygagging around the sky, or practicing. **1995** *Simpsons* (Fox-TV): Lollygagger!

b. to conduct oneself in a foolish or negligent manner; (*also*) to talk foolishly or idly.—also constr. with *around*. Cf. LOLLYGAG, *n.*

 1866–71 Bagg *Yale* 45: *Lalligag*, to fool about. **1893** in *DAE*: He bin kip 'wake o' nights a-lissenin' at de gigglin' an' lallygaggin' (humbugging, chaff). **1926** *DN* V 387: Maine...*lallygag around*...To act foolishly. Obsol. **1949–50** *PADS* (No. 14) 43: South Carolina...*lallygag, lollygag*, v.i. To chatter, talk idly. **1958** Cope & Dyer *Petty Officer's Guide* (ed. 2) 355: *Lollygoggin.* Unmilitary behavior, posture, or excessive public familiarity with opposite sex.

3. *N.E.* to engage in or be suggestive of hoaxing.

 1866–71 Bagg *Yale* 45: *Lalligag*, to...get the better of, "come it over," a man. **1946** R. Gordon *Years Ago* 88: And don't give me no lallygaggin' favors. Pay me what the damn bonus would amount to if it was a weekly pay increase.

lone duck *n.* a person who works or remains alone; (*specif.*) (see *1890–96 quot.). Also *lone dove*.

 1889–90 Barrère & Leland *Dict. Slang: Lone ducks, lone doves*...Women who hire their apartments, where they receive gentlemen visitors....This class of women has increased incredibly...in all the larger American cities. ***1890–96** F & H: *Lone-duck* (or *-dove*)...A woman out of keeping; also a prostitute, who works away from home by means of houses of accommodation. **1942** Hollingshead *Elmtown's Youth* 218: Joe's "lone duck." His only friend is a "bush ape" from east of town.

lone hand *n.* [abstracted fr. *play a lone hand* s.v. HAND] *Und.* a criminal who works alone; LONE WOLF.

 [***1886** in *OED2*: *Lone Hand*, a hand so strong in trumps alone...that it will probably win five tricks if its holder plays alone.] **1926** Clark & Eubank *Lockstep* 174: *Lone hand*—A thief who works by himself. **1932** *Collier's* (Dec. 3) 9: Dancing Dan is one of the best lone-hand git-'em-up guys in the world. **1936** in D. Runyon *More Guys* 162: George is strictly a lone hand at his work.

lone wolf *n. Police & Und.* a criminal who works alone. [Hence S.E. sense 'a solitary person'.]

 *a***1909** Tillotson *Detective* 130: Occasionally the police run across Panhandlers known as "lone wolves"—that is they do not mix with others of their class. **1927** *DN* V 454: *Lone wolf*, n. A bandit or house breaker who works without confederates. **1930** Sage *Last Rustler* 152: I'm a lone wolf. **1929–31** J.T. Farrell *Young Lonigan* 99: Something

daring and famous like an aviator, a lone wolf bandit, an Asiatic pirate. **1932** V. Nelson *Prison Days & Nights* 81: He became a surly "lone wolf" in his criminal activity. **1932** L. Berg *Prison Doctor* 216: So I looked around to see where I could pull a good touch. I thought I'd be smart and do a "lone wolf." You know, keep all the sugar myself. ***1959** in *OED2*: He's no lone wolf from Leeds or anywhere else.

lone-wolf *v.* to live or act alone; (*also*) (*trans.*) to act on (something) alone.—also constr. with dummy-obj. *it.*

 1938 in *OED2*: Lone-wolf, v. **1939** I. Baird *Waste Heritage* 89: Before this it was always lone-wolfin'. **1944** R. Adams *Western Words* 93: *Lone-wolfing* Living alone, avoiding the companionship of others. **1951** *Sat. Eve. Post* (Sept. 8) 98: "You're pizen mean these days."..."You get that way, lone-wolfing." **1958** *N.Y. Times* (Jan. 12) VI 14: They come from all economic classes and neighborhoods, sometimes lone-wolfing it, but mostly with their pals. **1961** *N.Y. Times* (Mar. 26) VII 28: Is he lone-wolfing a top secret investigation in Italy?

long *n.* **1.** *Naut.* longitude.

 1981 (quot. at LAT).

2. *Black E.* money. Cf. LONG, *adj.*, 1.a.

 1993 Mowry *Six Out Seven* 433: Sebastian had often wondered where Hobbes stashed what had to be some major-time long.

long *adj.* **1.** *Black E.* **a.** (of money) in large quantity. See also earlier LONG GREEN, 2.

 [***1796** Grose *Vulgar Tongue* (ed. 3): *Long*. Great. *A long price*; a great price.] [***1809** in *OED2*: Great Britain the nation of the longest purse in Europe.] [**1849** in *DA*: A man...is also said to be "long" when he holds a good deal [of stock].] [**1871** in *OED2*: For longer purses there are hard woods in all combinations.] **1947** *AS* XXII 168: *Long dough*. A considerable amount of money. **1962** in Wepman et al. *The Life* 145: My long money banned them. **1963** in Clarke *Amer. Negro Stories* 297: My chance to make enough long bread to put her down. **1966** Braly *On the Yard* 199: His money grew long. **1967** in T.C. Bambara *Gorilla* 73: And there was a whole lotta long bread coming into our area. **1967** [R. Beck] *Pimp* 116: That's where the long scratch is. **1971** Woodley *Dealer* 65: That's true, unless you got long dough. **1974** V.E. Smith *Jones Men* 123: You can make anybody listen to you if your money long enough. **1976** "N. Ross" *Policeman* 102: I made some long cash while working on gambling. **1978** Sopher & McGregor *Up from Walking Dead* 11: Plenty of long cash. **1979** D. Glasgow *Black Underclass* 96: Able to provide "long bread," good money. **1983** *Reader's Digest Success with Words* 87: Black English...*long green* or *bread* = "a great deal of money." **1987** R. Miller *Slob* 215: I had to pay some fucking long coin of my own. **1992** Majors & Billson *Cool Pose* 48: I knew I was going to make me some long bread.

b. great in degree.

 1977 Bunker *Animal Factory* 184: I've got long juice [*sc.*, influence] with this dude.

2. having a large amount of; abundantly supplied with.—constr. with *on*.

 ***1913** Kipling, in *OED2*: He was long on Kings. And Continental crises. **1929** Burnett *Little Caesar*, in *OED2*: You're long on regard yourself, ain't you Rico? **1967** in *OED2*: The battered Dodge may not have been long on looks, but it started first time. **1970** Landy *Underground Dict.*: Long *adj*. Having an abundance of something, usually narcotics—eg. *He's long on heroin.*

3. *Narc.* (of a drug addiction) severe.

 1964 in Wepman et al. *The Life* 90: Soon her habit was longer than mine. **1965** C. Brown *Manchild* 158 [ref. to 1950's]: They were junkies all the way. They had long habits. *Ibid.* 333: He's...made cats who were strung out with long habits respectable people again. **1965** in Sanchez *Word Sorcerers* 192: I don't have a long jones. **1978** Selby *Requiem* 33: That mutha fucka got a habit thats so long even mule piss wouldnt get him high.

long ball *n. Baseball.* a home run.—often used attrib.—also used fig.

 1952 in Dickson *Baseball Dict.* 249: The fact that he [*sc.* boxer Rocky Marciano] is a long-ball hitter gives him extraordinary and exciting appeal. **1964** Thompson & Rice *Every Diamond* 178: Recently everyone just wants to play "long ball." **1986** *N.Y. Times Mag.* (Mar. 30) 83: When Babe Ruth proved what home runs could do, a whole baseball generation converted itself to long-ball thinking. **1991** *N.Y. Times* (Dec. 8) ("Arts & Leisure") 24: I knew immediately that she was a long-ball hitter, emotionally, intellectually and artistically.

long bit *n.* [*long* + BIT, 2] the sum of twelve and a half or fifteen cents (as distinguished from a dime (a SHORT BIT)); (*hence*) *Gamb.* fifteen dollars. Now *hist.* [This expression is already entered s.v. BIT, *n.*, 2.c.; the following citations considerably expand the evidence.]

1852 in *DARE:* How many liquors can I get for two long bits? **1857** in *DA* s.v. *bit:* We will receive nuffin but long bits for brackin of boots. **1859** in Thornton *Amer. Gloss.:* I'd give a long bit myself to see 'em pull hair. **1877** W. Wright *Big Bonanza* 354: The smallest coin in use [in Western mining districts] is the bit, ten-cent piece,—sometimes spoken of as a "short bit," as not being twelve and one-half cents, the "long bit." *a***1890–96** *F & H: Long-bit…*American…A defaced 20 cent piece (Matsell); also 15 cents in Western U.S. (*Century*). **1933** Ersine *Pris Slang: Long bit.* Fifteen cents or dollars. **1944** *ADD* 59: In the West…a dime was accepted in payment for anything priced at one bit. A *long bit* was the equiv. of 15¢, being the priced paid when a dime was returned as change from a quarter tendered for a purchase priced at one bit. **1957** in *DARE.*

long drink of water see s.v. DRINK OF WATER.

long ear *n.* **1.** *Stu.* (see quots.).

1856 B. Hall *College Wds.* (ed. 2) 298: At Jefferson College, Pennsylvania, a student of a sober or religious character is denominated a *long ear.* The opposite is *short-ear.* **1889–90** Barrère & Leland *Dict. Slang: Long ear* (American University), a sober, religiously-minded student.

2. a mule or donkey.

1886 Lummis *Ft. Bowie* 69: The ambulance and its sextette of long-ears. **a***1890–96** *F & H: Long-ear.…in pl.* (common).—A donkey. **1944, 1950, 1965–70** in *DARE.*

3. a tendency to eavesdrop; an eavesdropper.

1935 in *DARE* III 413: He talks everything out and she has long ears. **1942** *ATS* 145: *Long ears,* eavesdropping ears. *Ibid.* 597: Sound Technician.…*long ears.* **1955** H. Robbins *79 Park Ave.* 220: We can talk without them longears hearin' us.

long-eye *n. Naut.* a spyglass.

1885 S. Hall *Gold Buttons* 17: They had stood gazing through a "long-eye" at her.

long-geared *adj. Naut.* lanky.

1891 in *DA:* One of the most successful bronco riders…was a long-geared, lank Texas lad. **1904** *Independent* (June 23) 1428: He was a long-geared cadaverous looking individual, with a slight stoop and a resonant nasal twang.…The Yanks dubbed him "Razorback." **1906** *Independent* (Apr. 19) 909: Miss Hickory, a long geared, angular, scrawny looking dame,…wore goggles, and had evidently been on earth some time. **1906** Ford *Shorty McCabe* 93: In comes a long-geared old gent. *ca***1911** in T. McCoy *Remembers* 41: A long-geared 'Rapaho. **1940** F. Hunt *Trail fr. Tex.* 91: A long-geared, dun-colored critter.

long green *n.* **1.** a kind of cheap whiskey.

1837 in *DA:* The disturber, known by the name of "long green" and "blue ruin," in Pennsylvania,…was happily beyond their reach.

2.a. paper money; money, esp. in large amounts. Cf. LONG, *adj.*, 1.

1887 in P. Levine *Spalding* 41: Just hear those bank notes rustle.…Spalding's got the lengthy green. **1893** F.P. Dunne, in Schaaf *Dooley* 59: There did a long green shtickin' out iv vest pockets an' men'd drink nawthin' but champagny. **1894** Bangs *Three Weeks in Politics* 28: That fellow cornered me last night and wanted what he called the "long green." **1895** Townsend *Fadden* 180: He has de long green t' burn a wet dog wid. **1896** Ade *Artie* 46: He can always make a flash o' the long green. **1896** in Rose *Storyville* 129: Alma is green, but so green as not to have her eye on the long green. **1901** in "O. Henry" *Cabbages & Kings* 274: The long green! Is there nothing it will not buy, Captain? **1901** Oliver *Roughing It* 64: The paymaster was ready to distribute the "Long Green." **1906** A.H. Lewis *Confessions* 12: You'd have to come up with the long green. **1912** Siringo *Cowboy Detective* 371: A good supply of the "long green." **1920** O'Neill *Emperor Jones* 12: De long green, dat's me every time! **1928** Sharpe *Chicago May* 54: The long-green helps with the underlings. **1944** C.B. Davis *Leo McGuire* 93: The old son-of-a-bitch left us a stack of new long green. **1953** *Time* (Jan. 12) 65: Giving up the short green grass of amateur play for the long green of professional tennis: a whopping $100,000 guarantee from Pro Promotor Jack Kramer. **1961** *Sat. Eve. Post* (Apr. 22) 49: He's openhanded with the long green. **1966** Liebow *Tally's Corner* 70 [ref. to *ca*1962]: Leroy was trying to decide how best to go about get-

ting his hands on some "long green" (a lot of money), and his girl friend cautioned him about trouble. **1966** Neugeboren *Big Man* 74: Some other long green would be coming my way if I scored my load. **1967** Spillane *Delta* 73: You picked up more than a few bucks, then. That doll only goes after the long green. **1968** Spradley *Drunk* 58: At Pasco two colored gents give me long-green ($) to run for two pints of scotch and two pints of Walker Delux. **1983** *N.Y. Post* (Sept. 2) 50: L.I. Savings Bank goes for the L.I. long green.

b. a banknote; dollar bill.

1891 McCann & Jarrold *Odds & Ends* 87: I've got a hundred o' them long greens with Uncle Sam's name on 'em. **1895** Townsend *Fadden Explains* 36: Dere was fifty plunks. Dat's right. Fifty good long greens. **1956** Sorden & Ebert *Logger's* 22 [ref. to *a*1925]: *Long-greens,* Bills in the pay envelopes.

c. (see quot.).

1891 Maitland *Slang Dict.* 169: *Long Green* (Amer.), counterfeit bills of large denominations. **1954–60** *DAS: Long green…*Genuine money in [slang]., counterfeit money in argot.

2. *Narc.* a type of marijuana. Cf. GREEN, *n.*, 3. Cf. earliest U.S. sense, 'a variety of tobacco', in *DA* fr. 1788.

1961 Russell *Sound* 17: That crazy Mexican stuff, the real long green, I say this shit simply can't be beat!

long-gutted *adj. West.* having a huge appetite.

1940 F. Hunt *Trail fr. Tex.* 39 [ref. to 1870's]: I've done my best with them long-gutted cow hombres of this cockeyed outfit.

longhair *n.* [fr. the stereotypical notion that such people have long hair] **1.** an intellectual or artist.

1920 S. Lewis *Main Street* 210: Carol, honey, I'm surprised to find you talking like a New York Russian Jew, or one of these long-hairs! **1930** Conwell *Pro. Thief* 15: More specifically, the ex-thief or ex-prisoner who writes books is razzed. The other thieves think he has gone long-hair or something. **1933** C. Wilson & J. Cluett *What—No Beer?* (film): My business depends on these longhairs. **1945** D. Nichols *Scarlet St.* (film): The Village longhairs are selling these [paintings] for the price of the canvas. **1947** in Roethke *Sel. Letters* 132: If some of these long-hairs take the time to read it. **1949** *Sat. Eve. Post* (Dec. 31) 12: Few politicians like intellectuals—the President, who regards them with special suspicion, speaks of them as "longhairs." **1950** *Western Folklore* (May) 160: *Long hairs.* Scientists. **1950** *Time* (Nov. 27) 66: Norbert Wiener, professor of mathematics at M.I.T., was a "longhair" who had coined the word "cybernetics." **1952** *Time* (Feb. 11) 70: Steinberg has also made strides as an artistic longhair. **1955** P. Wylie *Generation of Vipers* (ed. 2) xi: Formal criticism…is regarded as an exercise of "longhairs" or "eggheads." **1966** *Star Trek* (NBC-TV): I'm getting a chance to read some of that longhair stuff you like.

2.a. a performer or aficionado of classical music.—also used attrib.

1936 *Amer. Mercury* XXXVIII x: *Long hair,* a symphony man. **1937** XII *AS* 46: [Jazz:] *Longhairs.* Symphony musicians. "Ft. Worth *Longhairs* play with Mister P.W.'s Band." Headline in *Downbeat.* **1943** *Billboard* (June 26) 5: Longhairs Kiss Coin from One-Nighters Goodbye; Eyeing Nitery, Vaude, Radio Jack. **1946** Kober *That Man Is Here Again* 101: Your longhair friend ain't the delicate type like you keep beatin' your gums he is. **1949** in Gold *Jazz Lexicon: Long-hair:* one who plays, appreciates, composes, or writes about concert music. **1949** *Time* (Oct. 17) 46: I still like pop tunes but I'm getting to be a longhair too. **1951** W. Herman, in *Sat. Eve. Post* (Jan. 6) 21: Only trouble with this bebop is that the longhairs get too gone on it. **1950–52** Ulanov *Hist. Jazz* 352: *Longhair:* a classical musician or partisan of traditional music (not much used by musicians). **1954–60** *DAS: Longhair…*Jazz musicians seldom use the word. **1971** H.S. Thompson *Las Vegas* 174: The two guys right behind me were longhairs. Arid people.

b. classical music.—often used attrib.

1951 *Sat. Eve. Post* (Jan. 27) 123: The Library of Congress, where some of the loftiest long-hair music in America is played. **1952** *N.Y. Times* (Mar. 9) II 31: Classical music, too, is gaining in the field.…M.G.M.…reports that 10 per cent of its business is "long hair." *Ibid.* (Nov. 23) II 1: A heated discussion of bebop, long-hair, politics or sex. **1955** *Phil Silvers Show* (CBS-TV): This is nothing but long-hair music! **1956** Longstreet *Real Jazz* 16, in *DAS:* What is sometimes called Western music, sometimes European music, and sometimes just longhair. *ca***1961** *Flintstones* (ABC-TV): It's OK if you like that long-hair stuff. **1962** *Harper's* (Oct.) 145: Carol was in the living-room and had the hi-fi going with something very longhair, which I did not expect as she is an Elvis Presley fan.

3. a person, esp. a hippie, wearing long hair; (*hence*, in 1994 quot.) a political liberal.

1969 *Rolling Stone*, in *OED2*: Would hippies and long-hairs sit on the youth commisssion. **1973** in *DAS* (ed. 3): He went along to the bank with another longhair, a member of our commune. **1974** V.B. Miller *Girl in River* 113: How many longhairs you get? **1980** *Texas Monthly* (July) 124: An off-duty Houston policeman fired his handgun at a van full of longhairs who allegedly tried to run him off the road. **1981** Romero *Knightriders* (film): You take in every damn longhair that can make a pair of sandals. **1985** J.M.G. Brown *Rice Paddy Grunt* 242: I had my first ugly incident with "long hairs," student radicals. **1985** D.K. Weisberg *Children of Night* 23: Although the Tenderloin continues to attract "long hairs," they tend to be more aggressive, less attractive, and more likely to be on drugs than the former hippie prostitutes. **1990** C.P. McDonald *Blue Truth* 182: They counted on the long-hair to have the money. **1994** *Newsweek* (May 2) 31: The late political scientist Hans J. Morgenthau, no longhair, wrote that the invocation of "national security" as justification for any government action was one of several practices of "a distinctly Fascist character."

longhaired *adj.* **1.a.** artistic; intellectual.

[**1871** H. James *Watch & Ward* ch. 11: A long-haired gentleman of foreign and artistic aspect, giving the finishing touches to a portrait.] [*1872 G. Eliot *Middlemarch*, in *OED2*: Romanticism...was fermenting still...in certain long-haired German artists at Rome.] [*1881 W.S. Gilbert, in *OED2*: The peripatetics/Of long haired aesthetics/Are very much more to their taste.] [**1909** C. Chrysler *White Slavery* 7: I am not a long-haired individual with a soft shirt and flowing bow tie, turning out a "pot boiler," but a man of the world who has gone out looking for trouble and information.] **1912** O. Johnson *Stover at Yale* 88, in *DAS*: Brockhurst...trying for the *Lit*. Clever chap, they say, but a little long-haired. **1916** S. Lewis *Job* 196: Motifs and symphony poems and all that long-haired stuff. **1922** S. Lewis *Babbitt* ch. xiv, in *OED2*: The long-haired gentry who call themselves "liberals"...and "intelligentsia." **1949** *New Yorker* (Oct. 22) 96: The idle dream of a long-haired theorist. **1951** *N.Y. Times* (May 22) I 26: An irresponsible brain trust of long-haired boys in ivory towers at Ottawa. **1952** *New Yorker* (Mar. 29) 38: The long-haired critics were too preoccupied with Kafka and Henry James. **1955** Deutsch *Cops* 228: Those long-haired theorists can't teach us nothing. **1962** *Time* (Oct. 12) 46: For a flyer this was long-haired stuff, and fine for Schirra's desire to emphasize the engineering side of aeronautics. **1969** *Business Week* (June 28) 150: Data processing was going to be more scientific than commercial. But IBM's attitude was: "Who cares about the long-haired stuff?"

b. *Jazz.* connected with classical music.

1935 *Vanity Fair* (Nov.) 71: Straight or commercial musicians are often derisively called *salon-men* or *long-haired boys*. **1937** *New Yorker* (Apr. 17) 27: Those who can't improvise but can just read the spots are known as...*long-haired boys*. **1943** in R.S. Gold *Jazz Lexicon*: It ain't a song. It's a composition. Long-haired. **1949** *New Yorker* (Apr. 30) 26: It amuses Mr. Sklar to be referred to as a long-haired musician. "I've slapped basses in hotels, dives, burlesque joints, and movie houses." **1950** *Time* (Dec. 4) 94: Benny has also become a patron of long-haired composers....He gave the first performance of the new *Concerto for Clarinet and Orchestra* that he commissioned from Aaron Copland. **1951** *N.Y. Times* (June 24) VI 12: The hardiest Lewisohn Stadium concertgoer these days is the long-haired, or serious, music lover. **1953** in *DAS*: American music (long-haired, not pop). **1956** "T. Betts" *Across the Board* 120: He loved music and his son...became a composer of long-haired pieces. *1963 in *OED2*: It [*sc.*, jazz] has begun an unwise flirtation with "long-haired music."

2. (of a person normally assumed to be male) female. *Joc.*

*1889–90 Barrère & Leland *Dict. Slang*: Long-haired chum (tailors), a young woman, a young lady friend. *1915 in *OED2*: Goin' to have a "long-haired chum," are we. **1928** *Our Army* (Dec.) 9 [ref. to 1918]: Gosh, think of having a long-haired bunkie. **1930** Fredenburgh *Soldiers March!* 272 [ref. to 1918]: What you need is a few drinks and a long-haired buddy to chase your blues away. **1934** *Our Army* (Nov.) 22 [ref. to 1918]: The Top Kick is in the habit of sleeping with a long-haired bunkie. And I'm not!

longhandles *n.pl.* long underwear. Now *S.E.* Earlier **long-handled,** *adj.*

1882 in *Mo. Hist. Rev.* XLIII (1948) 95: Found—A pair of long-handled hose [or] Grandmother socks. **1943** *Yank* (June 18) 6: One piece of shrapnel took out the seat of his G.I. long-handles. **1950** *N.Y. Times* (Dec. 20) 12: What few long-handled underwear we had for residents to sent north as Christmas presents were grabbed up in a hurry. **1960** in *Tenn. Folk. Soc. Bull.* XXVII 35: I had already shed my long handles and was nearly froze to death. **1961** E.S. Gardner, in *Sat. Eve. Post* (Aug. 5) 61: "Got my long handles on."..."Well, pull on your pants over your long handles." **1963** Boyle *Yanks Don't Cry* 117: This long-handled underwear kick was supposed to have been a pre-war fad. **1964** J. Thompson *Pop. 1280* 32: But I ain't got no clothes on....Nothin' but my long-handled drawers. **1988** B.E. Wheeler *Outhouse Humor* 56: He didn't...button up the back flap of his long-handles. **1993** *CBS This Morning* (CBS-TV) (Dec. 10): Thanks for the red long-handles.

long hooding *n.* (see quot.).

1986 Ciardi *Good Words* 176: *Long hooding*....In answer to the radio dispatcher's announcement of a fare waiting at a certain address, the act of a cabbie who reports himself closer than he really is to the waiting fare....First heard...in 1985 in a Virginia suburb of D.C. and then...in San Francisco.

longhorn *n. West.* **1.** a Texan.

1896 in A.E. Turner *Earps Talk* [ref. to 1877]: In the vernacular of the feud the...[Texans] were "longhorns," and the Northerners "shorthorns." **1910** *Univ. Tenn. Volunteer* 263: Sparks is a thoroughbred "long horn." **1911** (quot. at SHORTHORN). **1928** L.C. Roberts *Reminiscences* 47: The "Long Horns"...couldn't imagine anything worse than a Yankee. **1932** Harvey *Me and Bad Eye* 69: These Longhorns ought to of been put in the field artillery where there's horses and mules. **1932–33** Nicholson & Robinson *Sailor, Beware!* 35: TEXAS PATTON enters. He is a lanky longhorn, from the State that gives him his nickname. **1935** (quot. at RAZORBACK). **1945** in P. McGuire *Jim Crow Army* 163: We often laughed at how the longhorn used to pray when they heard they were going overseas. **1951** Twist *Fort Worth* (film): Why, you rampaging old longhorn! Biggest thing out since Sam Houston!

2. an experienced cowboy.

1903 A. Adams *Log of a Cowboy* 195 [ref. to 1882]: Those old long horns, McNulta and Lovell, got us in with the crowd. **1905** in *DAE*: There was a big chief on the range, an old longhorn called Abraham. **1906** in A. Adams *Chisholm Trail* 249: The result was, these old longhorns got owly, laid their heads together, and made a little medicine. **1913** C. Mulford *Coming of Cassidy* 83: Longhorn'd a' shot you quick. **1915** H.L. Wilson *Ruggles* 47: Jeff Tuttle, you...old long-horn!

longhorned underwear *n.* long underwear.

1950 Hemingway *Across River* 11: I don't have to get up before first light and wear long-horned underwear.

longies *n.pl.* **1.** long underwear.

1941 Hargrove *Pvt. Hargrove* 73: Some of the other less fortunate citizen-soldiers were issued simple, unglamorous longies in a color that could best be described as lemon custard. **1950** *N.Y. Times* (Jan. 15) I 36 (adv.): Knit Longies, warm but weightless! **1953** *Portland Oregonian Mag.* (May 24) 16: The writer was forced to buy a suit of long underwear....An extremely polite clerk sold the longies. **1957** *Sat. Eve. Post* (Nov. 2) 96: I had put on some winter woolen longies. **1969** *Seattle Times* (Apr. 6) ("T.V.") 26: You climb into the same set of longies every time out.

2. *Juve.* long trousers.

1954–60 *DAS*: Longies...long pants. **1977** Appel *Hell's Kitchen* 7 [ref. to ca1917]: A fellow only put on long pants—"longies"—when he graduated from public school.

long john *n.* **1.** a kind of potato.

*a1849 in C. Hill *Scenes* 179: Ten bushels of...potatoes..."blue noses;" no, they warn't,...they was "long Johns."

2. *Army.* (see quot.).

1937 *AS* (Feb.) 75: *Long John*—increased pay for length of service.

3. *pl.* long underwear. Now *S.E.*

1943 in *OED2*: Some odd garments affectionately known as "longjohns." **1951** *Time* (Jan. 15) 22: Their swirling Korean skirts revealing singularly unattractive expanses of olive-drab G.I. long johns. **1951** *Pop. Science* (Oct. 51) 177: Come winter when Grandpa was a boy, he'd haul out the long johns and woolen shirts. **1959** Searls *Big X* 21: Mitch hung his soaking long-johns on a hanger in the locker. **1954–60** *DAS: Long Johns* Long woolen underwear. **1961** *Time* (Dec. 29) 42: Swathed in long johns, mufflers and assorted ski clothing. **1964** T. Berger *Little Big Man* xvi: One could see gray long johns making a junction with black stockings. **1969** in Cannon *Nobody Asked* 18: They were usually their fathers' cut-down long johns. **1974** Radano *Cop Stories* 91: He tries to close the fly of his long-johns. **1978** Wharton *Birdy* 8: It began with an old pair of long johns he dyed dark blue. **1980** Lorenz *Guys Like Us* 88: Eyeballing long johns and fancy cakes. **1991** LaBarge *Desert Voices* 28: They shipped some…long johns. **1992** G. Wolff *Day at the Beach* 168: I felt preposterous in my long johns.

longlick *n. Naut.* molasses. Cf. LONG SWEETENING.
    1888 Spear *Old Sailor's Story* 8 [ref. to 1821]: We had…hardbread and coffee sweetened with "Long lick," (molasses). **1898** Bullen *Cachalot* 5 [ref. to 1875]: A bit of salt junk and a piece of bread…with a pot of something sweetened with "longlick" (molasses), made an apology for a meal. **1924** *DN* V 286: "Porty Reek long lick"…Porto Rico molasses.

longneck *n.* Esp. *S.W.* a bottle of beer having a relatively long neck.
    [**1907** *DN* II 246: *Long-necker, n.* Round quart whiskey-bottle.] [**1914** *DN* IV 76: *Long-necker, n.* A bottle of hard liquor.] [**1969** in *DARE: Long neck*—A bottle of whisky.] **1980** S.B. Flexner, handwritten note in RH files: *Longneck*…very, very common Texas use—in all Texas bars, etc.…It seem [*sic*] to have spread a little to Oklahoma & New Mex. **1981** D. Jenkins *Baja Okla.* 195: He wore a longneck in his hand and he hardly ever grinned. **1984** *Memphis* (special ed.) 95: Always clean and orderly, it's a great place to sip a long-neck Stag. **1990** *Village Voice* (N.Y.C.) (July 24): The pitchers sit in silence before their lockers, numbly sipping from long-necks. **1995** *Utne Reader* (Sept./Oct.) 41: A lesson on such topics as Mardi Gras beads, jazz funerals, oysters, and Dixie Longnecks.

long nine *n.* a cigar.
    1830 in *DA:* Some tugged at the bottle, some smoked long-nines. **1830** N. Dana, in *OED2:* The fourfold row of long-nine-smoking beaux. **1835** *Harvardiana*, in Thornton, in *OED2:* He unfolded the wrapper; it contained two long-nine segars. **1843** "J. Slick" *High Life in N.Y.* 1: John would a turned up his nose at a long nine, as if it had been pison. **1851** in Dorson *Long Bow* 74: He…purchased a "long nine." **1879** in *DA:* Boys smoke "long nines" while they still wear jackets.

long one *n.* a paper dollar; dollar.
    1970 Thackrey *Thief* 306: She got me drunk and took off with five hundred long ones from my poke.

long-range *n.* cheap potent whiskey. Cf. FORTY-ROD.
    1865 in McKee *Throb of Drums* 237: Drinking a great deal of lone [*sic*] range whiskey. **1875** in *DA:* They [hogs] were fed on slops from a distillery where they manufactured "Long Range."

long-rats *n.* [*long-range* + *rats* (comb. form of *rations*); cf. C-RAT] *Army.* special freeze-dried rations for use on long-range infantry patrols. [Quots. ref. to Vietnam War.]
    1973 R. Roth *Sand in Wind* 167: Gook long-rats.…Food, man. You just add water and heat them up. They're better than the crap they feed us. **1978** Hasford *Short-Timers* 89: Long-rats. Outstanding! **1987** R. Miller *Slob* 59: He carried a backbreaking storehouse…in which would be packed…every life-sustaining necessity from det cord to his precious freeze-dried "long rats," the goodies that let him have the slack to run free.

longshoe *n. Und.* a cunning or sophisticated fellow, esp. a pimp or confidence swindler.
    1955 in Wepman et al. *The Life* 154: I am the Master of the Long-Shoe Game. **1974** Piñero *Short Eyes* 125: *Longshoe* Someone who's hip, slick, and "has his act together." **1980** Pearl *Pop. Slang* 93: *Longshoe n.* A self-confident, urbane person.

long-sparred *adj. Naut.* tall; lanky.
    1925 Thomason *Fix Bayonets!* 87: Look at that long-sparred horse soldier yonder—seven feet if he's an inch.

long suit *n.* that in which a person excells; one's forte. Now *S.E.*
    1893 F.P. Dunne, in Schaaf *Dooley* 56: Pothry ain't my long suit savin' an' exciptin' Donnelly an' Cooper or Brinnin on the Moor. **1895** W.C. Gore *Stu. Slang* 14: *Long suit*…Something one is familiar with or expert in; as, "History is his long suit." **1904** Ade *True Bills* 9: His Long Suit was to know everybody and call him by his front Name. **a1904–11** D.G. Phillips *Susan Lenox:* bk. iv ch. xviii: Truth—espe-

cially disagreeable truth—is your long suit. **1920** Ade *Hand-Made Fables* 38: Her Long Suit was Home Atmosphere.

long sweetening *n. Naut.* molasses; (*also*) syrup. Now *hist.* [For other regional terms, see *DARE*.]
    1714 in *DAE:* Let who will go unpaid, Rum long sweet'n alias Mollasses, glystr. Sugar must be had. **1869** in *DAE:* The writer won his glory and victual by making the "long-sweetening," i.e. white sugar melted into a permanent syrup. **1886** in *DAE:* Home-made sorghum molasses, which they call "long sweetening." **1899** Munroe *Shine Terrill* 46: Black coffee with "long sweet'ning." **1966** Borden *Dear Sarah* 64: Sometimes "long sweetening," or molasses, was added.

long-timer *n. Pris.* a prisoner serving a relatively long sentence, usu. five years or more.
    [**1871** Banka *Prison Life* 67: Men who come on long sentences, or "long-time" men, as they are called, are usually given some work at which they can be steadily employed. Any thing over *three* years is considered a long time.] **1907** London *Road* 122 [ref. to ca1894]: Only the "long-timers" knew what it was to have enough to eat.

2. *Mil.* a person with a relatively long time remaining in his tour of duty.
    1918 O'Reilly *Roving & Fighting* 168 [ref. to 1901]: As time-expired men who had been discharged, we rather lorded it over the long-timers. **1921** *15th Inf. Sentinel* (Jan. 7) 7: But we're short timers, aren't we. Why worry. Cheer up, long timers, while you are swimming with the jelly fish next July, just picture…on some nice beach around Los Angeles. **1963** *Sat. Eve. Post* (July 27) 25: Everything…hinges on whether he is a "long-timer" (with his Korean future before him) or a "short-timer" (soon to leave).

long tog *n.* usu. *pl. Naut.* a long coat; (*also*) a man's civilian clothes, esp. dress clothes, as distinct from work clothing.
    1807 Tufts *Autobiog.* 291 [ref. to 1794]: Long tog…a coat. **1824** Cooper *Pilot* 16: I have seen a straggling rover in long-togs as much like my cousin—. **1834** F. Marryat, in *F & H:* I had fitted on what are called at sea, and on the river, long togs; *i.e.*, I was dressed as most people are on shore. **1839–40** Cobb *Green Hand* I 37: You, with the long togs,…I take it, are not much used to this way of taking your grub. **ca1840** Hawthorne *Yankee Privateer* 45 [ref. to 1813]: I have often seen him come up on deck in his "long togs," (i.e. long coat and pantaloons). **1841** [Mercier] *Man o' War* 182: When I get my long togs bent, I'm *there.* **1845** Durivage & Burnham *Stray Subjects* 48: "Mr. Badger must be a werry deef 'un," said a mariner on liberty, looking very awkward and ferocious in "long-togs." **1856** Sleeper *Tales* 14: Why have not I, and these good fellows here, a right to rig ourselves out in long togs? **1899** Robbins *Gam* 192: She had been down below, preparing our "long togs" to go ashore. **1913** R.C. Murphy *Logbook* 274: They clad their shipmate in his "long togs" (meaning a store suit as opposed to dungarees) and bound his head in a spotless white scarf…before he was stitched into sailcloth.

Long Tom *n.* **1.a.** *Navy.* a long, swivel-mounted deck gun. Now *hist.*
    1814 in Durand *Able Seaman* 116: The Americans, now finding their principal gun (Long Tom) and several others dismounted, deemed it folly to think of saving the privateer. **1823** Cooper *Pilot* 66: It has got the name which you perceive it carries—that of "Long Tom." **ca1840** Hawthorne *Yankee Privateer* 65 [ref. to 1813]: We lightened our schooner by throwing overboard all our guns, most of our provisions and water, all our small arms, irons, caboose, &c., except "Long Tom." **1848** "Corporal of the Guard" *High Private* 53: We should have been in a pretty "muss," if [the ship] had fired her "Long Tom" into three hundred brave soldiers who could not return the compliment. **1858** in Battey *70,000 Miles* 9 [ref. to 1814]: Captain Reid gave them another round of grape and cannister from "Long Tom," the ship's 48-pounder. **1864** *Harper's Mag.* 597 [ref. to 1814]: The pilot-boats usually carried a single long gun, mounted on a swivel in the center, and was called a "Long Tom." **1886** Abbot *Blue Jackets* 33: A puff of smoke from the "Long Tom" amidships was followed by a solid shot ricochetting along the water. **1895** W.N. Wood *Big I* 2 [ref. to Civil War]: Then was heard the roar of the enemy's "Long Tom," and a cannon-ball whistled over our heads.

    b. a long hunting rifle.—usu. as a nickname. Now *hist.*
    1849 in *DA:* How to begin to describe our gun, puzzles us. There is no use in calling it a "long tom," for that would convey no idea at all. **1851** Webber *Hunter-Naturalist* 142: He never went anywhere to land

without "Long Tom," which proved indeed to be a wonderful gun. **1864** Armstrong *Generals* 52: By the time the detail was ready, he had his bullets run, his powder horn and fixin's on, and long Tom, as he called his Kentucky rifle, slung across his shoulder. **1865** *Atlantic Mo.* (Feb.) 203: Your Long Tom will *reach* one gunshot. **1876** *Frank Leslie's Illustrated* (Aug. 12) 373: The infantry answered volley for volley with their "long Toms." **1880** C.C. King *Campaigning* 120: And now, filing over the ridge, comes the long column of infantry; and when they get to work with their "long toms" the Indians will have to skip in earnest. **1885** Bigelow *Trail of Geronimo* 93: At length…they came before the impatient spectators with their "Long Toms," and gave them a wardance. **1888** C.C. King *Deserter* 17: Their "long Toms" have sent many a stalwart warrior to the mythical hunting-grounds. **1888** McConnell *Cavalryman* 216 [ref. to 1868]: It took our people a long time to find out that a dozen infantryman with "long toms," riding in a six-mule government wagon, were more dreaded by the Indian than a whole squadron of cavalry or rangers. **1898** Parker *Gatling Gun* 146: The members of this crew practiced with "long Toms" upon the Spanish soldiers. **1906** Buffum *Bear City* 217: I laid my "long tom" on the outside of my bed. **1917–20** in J.M. Hunter *Trail Drivers* I 341: We used a long…cap and ball rifle, familiarly known as "Long Tom." **1923** Henderson *14th Engrs.* 111: The antiquated "Long Toms" were turned in and modern British Enfields issued. **1929** L. Thomas *Woodfill* 14: It was one of them old frontier muzzle-loaders called a "Long Tom," with an octagon-shaped barrel and bullets that ran thirty to the ground. That old Long Tom with its forty-two inch barrel was more'n a foot longer than I was. **1933** Vaughn *With Cook* 32 [ref. to 1876]: Our [cavalry] form of the rifle was known as a "carbine," theirs [*i.e.,* the infantry] was known as the "Long Tom."

c. a long-barreled pistol.

1854 in WPA *S.F. Songster* 44: You have heard of the steel he wore round him /….'Twas a long-tom iron to protect him in his crimes.

d. *Army.* a long-range artillery piece; (*specif.*) (during and since WWI) a rifled artillery piece of 155 caliber or greater; (*also*) a shell fired by such a weapon.

1861 in E.A. Pollard *First Yr. of War* 123: The remainder of Sherman's battery, including the thirty-two pound rifle-gun known as "Long Tom." **1862** in M. Lane *Dear Mother* 158: In front of "Old Long Tom," as we called it an ironclad battery which was built on the railroad and propelled by a large engine. **1864** *Battle-Fields of So.* 49: One of the enemy's heavy pieces, a thirty-two pounder, called "Long Tom." **1919** McKenna *Btry. A* 50: The Battery pulled onto the road and joined the column at midnight with the American "Long Toms" roaring a point-blank farewell. **1919** Duffy *G.P.F. Book* 60: Nevertheless our big long Toms were ready for business the next day. **1922** Jordan *Btry. B* 72: "Long toms," seventy-fives, one fifty-five shorts, railroad rifles and howitzers were cleverly concealed throughout the entire region. **1943** *Newsweek* (Oct. 25) 25: First, hundreds of Allied guns, including American 155-millimeter Long Toms, opened up from the Volturno's south bank. **1944** Pyle *Brave Men* 244: I had lunch with one of our artillery batteries which manned the big Long Toms. **1947** Carter *Devils in Baggy Pants* 106: Dozens of 105 howitzers and 155 long toms and other breeds of howitzers were all around us. ***1964** Whitehouse *Fledgling* 18 [ref. to WWI]: Cashiered…for allowing a Long Tom cannon to run away down a hill and wreck a French village. **1973** Huggett *Body Count* 229: The long Toms of the Army's heavy artillery began firing in volleys. **1980** Manchester *Darkness* 22 [ref. to WWII]: I could hear the Long Toms in the distance. **1983** Ehrhart *VN-Perkasie* 278 [ref. to 1967]: The sound of 175-millimeter artillery shells, "Long Toms."

e. a long cigar.

*a***1870** in *DAE: Long Tom*…A long cigar—usually of a quality inversely proportional.

f. the penis.—usu. considered vulgar.

1870 in Steinbach *Long March* 52: Nellie Smith don't know what she escaped. She would have been killed at one nab [*sic*] of our old long tom. **1916–22** Cary *Sexual Vocab.* IV s.v. *penis:* Long Tom.

2. *Mining.* a kind of trough for the washing of gold-bearing earth. Now *hist.* [Quot. dated "1850" by *DAE* is correctly dated "1906"; see note at LUNKHEAD.]

1839 in *DA:* The Long Tom…consists merely of a trough. **1880** in *DA:* The "Long Tom"…is placed at an incline and a stream of water introduced into the upper end. **1906** in *DAE:* He says there is a new

way of taking out gold by a machine called a Long Tom. **1963** R.W. Paul *Mining Frontiers* 20: "Long toms"…were similar to cradles except that they were stationary and elongated and were designed to handle a larger volume of auriferous "dirt."

3. *R.R.* (see quot.).

1992 J. Garry *This Ol' Drought* 33: The Union Pacific had a type of engine…they called a Long Tom….Its fire box was twenty-one feet long.

long underwear *n. Jazz.* **1.** commercial dance-band type music (as opposed to "hot" jazz); (*also*) a jazz musician who cannot improvise.—often used attrib.

1933 in Gold *Jazz Lexicon:* And *corny* music is what generally happens when a *sweet* band, or *long-underwear gang,* tries to play *hot.* **1936** in Gold *Jazz Lexicon: Long underwear gang:* musicians who can play only "as written." **1937** in Gold *Jazz Lexicon: Long underwear gang:* a band that plays straight [*i.e.,* unimprovised] music. **1937** *AS* (Oct.) 184: [Jazz:] *Long Underwear.* Synonymous with Long Hair; played sweet, not hot. **1954–60** *DAS: Long underwear*…Jazz music played in a sweet, popular, or corny way.…A poor jazz musician, esp. one who cannot improvise. **1965** Carmichael & Longstreet *Sometimes I Wonder* 95: A local long-underwear band in gold lamé jackets with an electric light in their banjo.

2. classical music.

1944 in *DAS:* Kay thought Howard was out of this world till she found out he was a long-underwear platterbug. **1956** in Gold *Jazz Lexicon: Long underwear:* concert stuff.

long yell *n.* a loud objection or complaint; scream.—used in var. phr.

1899–1900 Cullen *Tales* 354: Then I did set up the long yell for fair. **1903** Adams *Log of a Cowboy* 197: The audience raised the long yell and poured out through the windows and doors. **1908** McGaffey *Show Girl* 239: If he catches them…he will turn loose the long Rebel yell.

loo[1] *n.* [orig. unkn.] a lavatory. [Comparatively rare in U.S. and often regarded as an affected Briticism.]

1940** N. Mitford, in *OED2.* ***1943** C. Beaton, in *OED2.* ***1944** W.H. Auden, in *OED2.* **1961** *N.Y. Times* (Sept. 10) 10 1: A shower that spattered all over the bathroom floor and a "loo" across the patio. **1967** Crowley *Boys in the Band* 842: Is this the loo? **1972** in H. Ellison *Sex Misspelled* 112: She went to the loo. **1972** *N.Y. Post* (Oct. 20) 44: We do not write "Susie is a dope" on the white tiled walls of the loo. *a1978** Cooley *Dancer* 58: For a while the photographer thought he'd have to shoot the whole date in the loo. **1982** R.M. Brown *So. Discomfort* 158: Into the ladies' loo. **1982** *L.A. Times* (Jan. 24) VI 3: His executive washroom contains a loo that gives him a floor-to-ceiling view of Century City. **1986** S. Bauer *Amazing Stories* 178: Which way…to the loo?

loo[2] *n. Esp. Police.* a lieutenant. Also **lieu, lou.**

1968 Radano *Walking the Beat* 87: "You're too easy, Loo," the Sergeant answered him. **1974** Radano *Cop Stories* 26: Why did you do that, Loo? **1975** V.B. Miller *Trade-Off* 30: Loo, there's a guy here waiting for you. **1978** Strieber *Wolfen* 136: The Loo won't overhear us. **1980** Whalen *Takes a Man* 40: Blanchard's got it, Lieu. **1982** 'J. Cain' *Commandos* 257: He made lou. **1983** Stapleton *30 Yrs.* 239: Fire Lieutenant…Usually called "Loo" or "Luft." **1984** Caunitz *Police Plaza* 4: He addressed him as Lou, the diminutive of lieutenant that was routinely used in the NYPD.

looey[1] var. LOOIE.

looey[2] var. LOUIE, 5.

loogin[1] *n.* **1.** a clumsy or stupid person; oaf; LUG; (*hence*) esp. *Und.* a newcomer. Also **lugan.**

1919 *Blackhawk Howitzer* 50: Whose —— —— legs are these? Gettem off my chest, you squareheaded lugan. **1927** Thrasher *Gang* 27: At the corner of Blue Island and Forquer we found a lively game of ball between the "Reveres" and the "loogins" (second team) of the "Red Oaks." *Ibid.* 267: *Loogins, yannigens*—newcomers, second team, bumpkins. **1929** in Runyon *Guys & Dolls* 72: The poor loogin she is marrying will never have enough dough to buy her such a rock. **1929–30** J.T. Farrell *Young Lonigan* 39: He's nuts anyway. I know I wouldn't take what that loogin takes. **1930** G. Irwin *Tramp & Und. Sl.: Loogins.*—Recruits; amateurs or newcomers to a gang or tramp group.

2. a habitual fighter or brawler; ruffian; petty criminal; thug. Also **loogan.** [Def. in 1934 quot. appears to be overly specific.]

1932 in Partridge *Dict. Und.* 416: Better look out, kid, there's some tough Loogins over there. **1932–33** P. Cain *Fast One* 200: There's Rose, with his syndicate…and all the loogans he's imported from back East. **1934** Weseen *Dict. Amer. Sl.* 237: Boxing and Prizefighting…*Loogan*—A prizefighter. **1938** Chandler *Big Sleep* 89: "You think he sent that loogan after you?" "What's a loogan?" "A guy with a gun.…But strictly speaking a loogan is on the wrong side of the fence." **1939** in Partridge *Dict. Und.* 416: Loogans and crooks and shysters and hot shots used to tip their hats when I met them.

loogin² var. LUGAN.

loogie *n.* [perh. alter. of syn. LOUIE, 5] an expectorated bit of phlegm. [Pronun. intended by 1988 sp. is unclear.]

    1988 *Time* (Nov. 14) 62: I had a student [in Los Angeles] in last year who used to call his spit "luggies" [*sic*]. **1990** *In Living Color* (Fox-TV): See Roseanne as she hawks a loogie. **1992** M. Myers et al. *Wayne's World* (film): From this height you could really hock a loogie on someone! **1994** *Simpsons* (Fox-TV): Spittle County…Birthplace of the Loogie. **1994** *Details* (July) 56: Spitting a huge loogie on the floor.

looie or **looey** *n. Army.* a lieutenant. Also (*obs.*) **Lieuy, Louis,** etc.

    1916 *Rio Grande Rattler* (Oct. 11) 5: The "Looey" gaily saunters from his tent. **1918** Casey *Cannoneers* 61: I know a couple of looies in that outfit. **1919** Dos Passos *Initiation* 128: Well, our louie's name's Duval, but he spells it with a small "d" and a big "V." **1919** Hawke *E Btry.* 7: The red-headed Lieuy, you all know his name. **1919** T. Kelly *Outfit* 102: All the *soldats* believed it and a hell of a lot of second looeys. **1919** Lincoln *Co. C* 64: Heads up, fellows, here comes the "looie." **1920** *Amer. Leg. Wkly.* (Mar. 12) 15: I eased the buck along to the first looie who was commanding headquarters company. **1920** Baldwin *Canteening* 131: He said some "Second Louis" would give us information. **1926** Upson *Me & Henry* 120: So then the looeys started hollering to the sergeants. **1930** *AS* V (June) 384 [ref. to 1917]: *Looie.* Erroneously restricted to "second lieutenant." **1930** Fredenburgh *Soldiers March!* 269: I went on a reconnaissance with some Looey from A Battery. **1941** Hargrove *Pvt. Hargrove* 124: How would you like a second looey's commission in the Morale Branch? **1949** *Sat. Eve. Post* (Dec. 3) 53: Our hot, eager little second looie shot off his face to his sister. **1952** Uris *Battle Cry* 44: He's a private and she's a looey. **1965** Linakis *In Spring* 27: The nurse [was] a second looie. **1955** Shapiro *Sixth of June* 27: About a million first louies around the country. **1969** Twitchell *Drums of Eck* 20: The Looy's comin'. Knock it off! **1973** Huggett *Body Count* 139: What's that motherfuckin' green Looie want now? *ca***1933–74** Mackin *Didn't Want to Die* 37: A tall first Louis. *a***1987** Cole & Bunch *Reckoning for Kings* 26: He made first looey. **1987** Estes *Field of Innocence* 104: The Luey from the second platoon was blown away. **1995** Cormier et al. *Wildcats to Tomcats* 91: Dad…was commissioned a first louie.

look *v.* ¶ In phrase: **here's looking at you** (used as a toast).

    1884 in Lummis *Letters* 24: Illinois, here's looking at you. May your shadow never grow less. **1897** in Outcault *Yellow Kid* (pl. 68): Vicky [*sc.* Queen Victoria], ole goil, I sed, here's lookin' at ye. **1902** Brenton *Uncle Jed* 14: Here's lookin' at yer. **1904** in "O. Henry" *Works* 933: "Here's looking at you,"…said the reporter. **1928** J.M. March *Set-Up* 22: Well—…Here's lookin' at you! **1943** H. Koch *Casablanca* (film): Here's looking at you, kid.

looker *n.* **1.** an attractive woman; (*rarely*) an attractive man. Now *colloq.*

    1892 S. Crane *Maggie* 17: Dat Johnson goil is a putty good looker. **1898** Kountz *Baxter's Letters* 4: His second wife…was…not a bad looker at that. **1907** McDermott-Stevenson *Lariat Letters* 40: She ain't such a looker that every chuck-line riding cow-puncher in the country will want to hang around the old man's ranch till he's fired. **1922** S. Lewis *Babbitt* 172: The Calroza sisters are sure some lookers and will give you a run for your gelt. **1926** Dunning & Abbott *Broadway* 217: Why, that kid is one of the best lookers and neatest workers you got. **1943** R. Chandler *High Window* 390: The wop says she was a looker. **1949** O. Atkinson *Big Eyes* 67: He's a looker all right. **1950** *Sat. Eve. Post* (Mar. 25) 37: She's good looking herself, so you'd think she'd maybe pick out a looker to take along on a double date. **1951** Sheldon *Troubling of a Star* 74: Sachiko was really a looker. **1990** *Cosmopolitan* (Nov.) 152: She was a looker, all right. **1990** *UTSQ*: *Looker*—A good looking girl. "Boy, she is a looker." **1990** in *Texas Mo.* (Jan. 1991) 158: Looker, the sorority word for "good-looking guy." **1993** K. Scott *Monster* 42: Tamu was a looker, tall and graceful with a smile that shouted for attention. **1995** *JAG* (NBC-TV): A female! And a looker, too!

2. usu. *pl.* an eye; PEEPER.

    1913 *DN* IV 4: *Lookers*…eyes. *ca***1938** in Rawick *Amer. Slave* II (Pt. 1) 34: I ain't forgot de fust time I put dese lookers on you, in '76. **1978** Alibrandi *Killshot* 93: The ball exploded the right looker like a grape. **1987** in *Readers Digest* (Feb. 1994) 135: [The skunk] squirted Eddie right between the lookers.

lookie-loo *n. Calif.* a prospective buyer, esp. of real estate, who has no serious intention of buying; (*broadly*) an annoying sightseer; nosy person. Also **looky-; -lou.** Also as *v.*

    1978 *L.A. Times* (Aug. 27) VII 1: The first couple arrive. They are…"lookie-loos." I learn later that they have *almost* made an offer on every house in the neighborhood. **1980** *Santa Maria* (Calif.) *Times* (Nov. 18) 1: The restriction will discourage "looky-Lou's." **1981** *L.A. Times* (Nov. 20) ("Fashion '81") 2: Gucci is a Rodeo Drive shop in which most lookie-loos can't even afford the price of a key chain. **1982** *Lompoc Valley* (Calif.) *News* (Apr. 21) 11: "Looky-Loos" (folks who traverse neighborhoods inspecting For-Sale homes for the fun of it). **1982** *Calif. Business* (May) 56: To preclude "looky loos"…it's common for a business owner to require that his asking price be put into escrow before he will open his books. **1984** *L.A. Times* (Mar. 18) VIII 19: We decided to spend a couple of Sundays being what a national realtor once called "looky-loos." The more notorious looky-loos are the people who live next door to the house being offered and simply want to find out what they can get for their *own* domicile. **1985** *Santa Barbara* (Calif.) *News-Press* (Mar. 27) B4: Additional traffic from lookie-lous going to eyeball space shuttle shots. **1989** Headline News network (May 21): Then it was time to separate the "looky-loos" from the real bidders. **1990** Munro *Slang U.: Lookie-lou* nosy person. **1993** *L.A. Times* (Oct. 24) K1: A few cross over the line—looky-looing every weekend for years. **1994** *N.Y. Times* (July 3) 14: Police had cordoned off streets in the neighborhood to keep out sightseers, or "looky loos," as they are known in Los Angeles. **1995** *New York* (Sept. 25) 60: Most of the weekenders are hip Looky Loos more interested in the action on the stage than in the lounge.

look-in *n.* **1.** Orig. *Sports.* a slight chance of success.—usu. used in negative contexts.

    1870** in *F & H*: If Fawcett imagines he has got a look-in, young Mullins will fight him for all the money he can get together. ***1883** in *F & H*: Neither of them had a look-in as regarded the prizes. ***1884** in *F & H*: Easter fought with great gameness, but he never had a look-in from the commencement. **1905** in *OED2*: A team which never had a look-in for anything better than cellar championship. **1914** in M. Gardner *Casey* 69: For Mudville veterans didn't have a look-in from the start. **1920** Ade *Hand-Made Fables* 25: Her Dad may own a Check-Book, but she will never have a Look-In as a real Competitor. **1939** *New Directions* 147: Jordan Tim hasn't got a look-in to live the year out. **1948** J. Stevens *Jim Turner* 182: For some reason, Jack Hard had been given a look-in. **1958** S.H. Adams *Tenderloin* 95 [ref. to 1890's]: He ought to be a side-show automaton. I never had a look-in. **1962** *Sat. Eve. Post* (July 28) 30: [He] never had a look-in at the majors before. *a1973** in Bontemps *Old South* 187: Hound-dog, you ain't got a look-in.…You is messin' with Big Boy Blue now. ***1980** Leland *Kiwi-Yank. Dict.* 50: The election was a farce. Bazzer gave such a good speech Sam didn't have a look in. **1992** N. Cohn *Heart of World* 262: Legit businessmen,…we don't got a look-in.

2. concern; business.

    1933 H. Stephenson *Glass* 70: [As] if 'twere her look-in.

lookout *n.* **1.** one's responsibility, concern, business. Now *S.E.*

    1749 in Whiting *Early Amer. Provs.*: That is your Look-Out. **1813–18** Weems *Drunken Looking Glass* 94: "That's none of your look out," replied Collier, very roughly. **1844** Dickens *Chuzzlewit* ch. xxvii, in *OED2*: If he took it into his head that I was coming here for such or such a purpose, why, that's his look-out. **1868** in Trachtenberg *Vistas* 155: I *can't* say what they does. It ain't my look-out. ***1884** in *OED2*: The result would be that a less price would be got, but that is the vendor's look out. **1929** Mack & Boasberg *It's a Great Life* (film): What's it her lookout?

2. *Gamb.* (in faro) a croupier; (*hence*) an attendant at a gaming table who oversees the game.

    1845 J. Greene *Exposure* 119: The dealer has from one to four assistants, who are called "croupiers," or "look-out," whose business it is to assist the dealer by looking out for his interests all through the game. **1888** in *DAE*: The look-outs were held in 700 dols. bail each for examination to-morrow. **1893** in *DAE:* By each dealer's side sits the "lookout,"...lazily looking on in the interests of such fair play as is consistent with professional gambling. *a***1918** in *DAE:* Arnett was dealing and Germagin was "look-out" for him.

look over *v.* ¶ In phrase: **look them over** to investigate in a general way; (*also*) to idle on a street corner or elsewhere so as to watch passing young women.—used without antecedent.

    1909 Chrysler *White Slavery* 20: She or he...goes down to "Bunkville" to "look them over,"...."feel out the chief of police," "locate a joint," [etc.]. **1916** *Variety* (Nov. 3) 20: Fox Trots..."Looking Them Over." *ca***1929** *Collection of Sea Songs* 10: You can see the Johnny Horners/Standing on the corners/Looking them over.

look-see *n.* **1.** a quick visual inspection; look. Now *colloq.*

    1854 McCauley *With Perry* (May 17) 117: Went ashore to "make lookysee" as John Chinaman says. **1883** in *OED2:* I 'spec she just come here to makee look see how de people get on. **1904** in J. London *Reports* 73: Each day the men trickle back...to have a "look-see." **1911–12** J. London *Smoke Bellew* 14: He...intended to peep over the top of the pass for a "look see" and then return. **1931** in *DAS:* Let's have a look-see at our friend. **1940** R. Chandler *Farewell, My Lovely* ch. ix: Sit tight. I'm going down there and have a look-see. **1949** *N.Y. Times* (Aug. 3) 18 (adv.): It sure is time to drop in for a look-see at the biggest De Soto-Plymouth sales and service place in the East. **1951** Robbins *Danny Fisher* 310: I want yuh to run down there an' have a look-see. **1951** *Sat. Eve. Post* (Nov. 3) 12: One of them is asked by a journalist for a look-see into confidential top-secret State Department papers. **1963** *Wash. Post* (Dec. 22) G1: I love to sit in a hotel with a drink around 6 in the evening, and have a look-see and watch what's going on. **1968** Cuomo *Thieves* 355: We'll be heading up to the garage for a final look-see before I turn in.

    2. (see quots.).

    1929 *Sat. Eve. Post* (Oct. 12) 76: The [quack's] medical license is a "look-see," from the frequent demands made upon him by the authorities to produce it. **1954–60** *DAS:* Look-see...A medical license, as carried by a traveling medical-show doctor....Any license or pass which one may have to show to authorities.

    3. a lookout.

    1979 D. Thoreau *City at Bay* 149: Many of the boys were used by the tongs...as looksies for the gambling establishments and whore-houses.

look see *v.* to look quickly; have a LOOK-SEE.

    1868 in Boyer *Naval Surgeon* II 59: I took a walk up Curio Street "to look see" (as the Japs say). **1938** R. Chandler *Big Sleep* ch. ix: I'm dropping down to look see. **1940** W. Faulkner, in *DARE:* I reckon I'll go on a day or two and look-see them Northern towns. **1966** in *DARE.*

looky-loo var. LOOKIE-LOO.

looloo var. LULU.

loon *n.* [ult. of M.E. orig., prob. infl. by *lunatic*; see *OED*] a crazy person; lunatic. Also (*rare*) **loonhead.** Cf. earlier S.E. senses 'rogue; boor' and others. [Etymologically separate fr. the name of the aquatic bird, known for its wailing cry.]

    1823 J.F. Cooper *Pilot* 108: But nothing, you loon; a sentinel should always carry his keys about him like a jailer. **1845** in *DAE:* Why, you're both as crazy as loons! **1847** Downey *Portsmouth* 69: Oh by the Lord said one quite moody/We recognized, at once, as that Loon, B—y. **1849** Melville *White Jacket* 122: We thought him a loon; he thought us fools. **1862** in Upson *With Sherman* 18: After we had gone those crazy loons got it into their heads that we were spies or something like that. **1867** *Nat. Police Gaz.* (Jan. 12) 4: I wonder how "Slippery" likes the "loons"? **1898** in S. Crane *Complete Stories* 489: Why, this is the wildest loon I ever see. **1936** Levin *Old Bunch* 43: Just listen to that loon! **1957** Hall *Cloak & Dagger* 137: Sweet Saint Sebastian, what loonhead dreamed that one up? **1968** W.C. Anderson *Gooney Bird* 152: Oh, you loon! You had me worried. **1978** Wharton *Birdy* 3: Maybe he is a loon. **1981** *N.Y. Times* (Nov. 13) A35: Only a loon would make a statement such as this. **1990** P. Munro *Slang U.:* Loon weird person....Karen doesn't like ice cream. What a loon!

looney tune *n.* [fr. *Looney Tunes,* series title of Warner Bros. theatrical cartoon shorts produced 1930–69; since 1950's freq. rerun on children's television shows] an insane or

irrational person; lunatic. Also (*rare*) **looney tunes.** [Criticism of the cartoon series is provided, e.g., by S. Schneider, *That's All Folks!: The Art of Warner Bros. Animation* (N.Y.: Holt, 1988). The 1980 quot. may belong at the adj.]

    1966–67 W. Stevens *Gunner* 94: Any new looney tunes? **1973** *Oui* (Mar.) 45: New York is full of looneytunes, and surely the Seventh Avenue subway gets its share. **1976** N.Y.C. editor, age 25: God, you are a looney tune. **1980** L. Fleischer & C. Gore *Fame* 199: Are all the people here looney tunes? **1984** Heath *A-Team* 54: See, they think I'm a looney tunes. **1988** C. Dillon, J. Peace & J. De Bello *Return of Killer Tomatoes* (film): Y' tell me that old Looney-Tune's got a girlfriend?

looney-tunes *adj.* [see ety. and note at LOONEY TUNE, *n.*] insane; irrational. Also **looney-tune.**

    1971 E. Sanders *Family* 69: A looney-tune magical cult specializing in blood-drinking sado-sado sex magic and hatred of blacks. **1971** in L. Bangs *Psychotic Reactions* 12: A...looney-tune joker. **1977** Schrader *Blue Collar* 17: Smokey thought he was Looney Tunes. *Ibid.* 44: Fucker was Looney Tunes, but he sure was the main man. **1981** Univ. Tenn. student: That guy is going looney-tunes. **1983** N. Proffitt *Gardens of Stone* 253: This should convince them...that you're looney tunes. **1984** in "J.B. Briggs" *Drive-In* 223: The bimbo reporter for the media thinks they're Looney-Tunes. **1986** Ganz & Mandel *Gung Ho* (film): This is looney-tunes! **1988–92** R. Mains *Dear Mom* 242: This fucking place is fucking looney tunes. **1992** *N.Y. Observer* (July 13) 6: We just thought that was loony tunes. **1994** *New Republic* (Apr. 4) 14: The dustup involves nothing but a typical loony tunes S & L deal from the 1980s. **1996** *As World Turns* (CBS-TV): I'm not looney-tunes.

looney tuney *adj.* [see ety. and note at LOONEY TUNE; both quots. appear in Warner Bros. theatrical cartoons] crazy.

    1938 (quot. at RINGYDINGY). **1939** *Merrie Melodies* (animated cartoon): I'm so goony, looney tuney, tetched in the head.

loony or **looney** *n.* a lunatic.

    1883 *Life* (Aug. 30) 99: Looney!...don't you know nothing? **1889** B. Harte *Dedlow Marsh* 34: The hounds...said you was a heathen and a looney because you didn't go to school or church along with their trash. **1897** Kipling *Capts. Courageous* 32: Dad sez loonies can't...[tell] a straight yarn. **1914** Giles *Rags & Hope* 107 [ref. to Civil War]: Get out of the Wilderness with General Lee, you old looney! **1920** E. O'Neill *Emperor Jones* 57: I'll bet yer it ain't 'im they shot at all, yer bleedin' looney! **1925** in Faulkner *N.O. Sketches* 113: I ain't scared, but there ain't no luck in making a delivery with a loony alone. **1948** Maresca *My Flag* 82: You'd mark him up as a loony. **1950** *N.Y. Times* (Sept. 16) 12: Kicking up his heel and acting like an infantile looney. **1955** in C. Beaumont *Best* 31: Here he comes again, that loony! **1959** Hecht *Sensualists* 129: Well, Frank found me bawling like a loony. **1961** T. Williams *Iguana* 150: They look like a pair of loonies. **1965** Yurick *Warriors* 101: A bus passed them packed full of track-loonies from the train. **1972** Kopp *Buddha* 94: It was clear that he was a loony. **1972** Pearce *Pier Head Jump* 41: A ship loaded with loonies. **1979** Moore & Berlitz *Phila. Exper.* 21: Who's going to believe a certified looney? **1984** Holland *Let Soldier* 144: Just grinning like a loony.

loony or **looney** *adj.* lunatic; demented; insane; crazy. Also **luny.**

    1841 [Mercier] *Man of War* 21 [ref. to 1839]: "He's a little *luny* ain't he, Garnet?" enquired one of the crowd. "Well, I believe he is somewhat touched that way." **1853** Melville *Bartleby:* I think, sir, he's a little *luny.* **1863** in O. Norton *Letters* 191: I am half "luny" with delight. **1864** Ransom *Diary* [entry for July 8]: Getting loony, I guess, same as all the rest. **1867** *Galaxy* (Nov.) 833: That chap has lived alone with his paints so long that he's gittin' luny. **1877** *Puck* (Mar.) 13: She bein' sort o' looney in the head and they a goin' to shut her up in a loon-attic asylum. **1878** B. Harte *Drift* 33: You're that looney sort o' chap that lives alone over on the spit yonder, ain't ye? **1888** in *AS* XXXVII (1962) 76: You must be looney. **1899** Ade *Fables.* **1950** M. Gellhorn, in *Sat. Eve. Post* (Apr. 15) 168: The sort of passing whim that a rich, loony American—all Americans are rich and somewhat loony—might have. **1956** Algren *Wild Side* 123: What's so looney about that? **1956** Metalious *Peyton Place* 75: You never can tell what a loony person will do. **1958** Schwitzgebel *Research* 30: That guy was luny. Crazy as a bat! **1962** Dougherty *Commissioner* 21: For Christ's sake, Barney. This is looney. **1986** S. Bauer *Amazing Stories* 102: Brad edged away from the man, who seemed a little loony. **1988** R. Dizazzo *Hollow Gate* (film): That kid's just too damn looney. *a***1991** C. Fletcher *Pure Cop* 229:

Nobody ever listens to them because they're loony. **1994** *My So-Called Life* (ABC-TV): She *is* sort of loony.

loony bin *n.* a hospital for the insane. Now *colloq.*

> *1919 P.G. Wodehouse, in *OED2:* You're absolutely off your rocker, but don't find it convenient to be scooped into a luny-bin. *1921 P.G. Wodehouse, in *OED2:* Views on Art which would have admitted them to any loony-bin. **1943** J. Mitchell *McSorley's* 68: Some are in the grave, some are in the loony bin, and some are in the advertising business. **1944** Bellow *Dangling Man* 85: It's the world's greatest loony-bin. **1950** *N.Y. Times* (Dec. 22) 19: The boozer's family, reduced to despair by his behavior, try to clap him into the looney-bin. **1954** Sherdeman *Them* (film): This is no hospital. This is a loony bin, a nuthouse. **1957** Myrer *Big War* 73: This place is getting to be a loony-bin. **1958** in R. Russell *Permanent Playboy* 360: A few of the Americans have performed spectacularly—mostly in the loonybin. **1961** Rosten *Capt. Newman, M.D.* 47: My God, Doc,...you gonna put me in a loony bin? **1961** Sullivan *Shortest, Gladdest Years* 127: Poor old dear is rumored to have ended her days in a looney bin. **1965** Friedman *Totem-pole* 213: My father's youngest brother's in the loonybin...he just sits there like a corpse. **1967** P. Welles *Babyhip* 49: It's a wonder I'm not in the looney bin. **1988** De Lillo *Libra* 55: Here is a general who...is put in the looney bin. **1989** P. Benchley *Rummies* 26: A loony bin?...Forget it.

loony bird *n.* a crazy or irrational person.

> **1969** Eastlake *Bamboo Bed* 76: Do we look like loonybirds who can't keep our pants zipped. **1978** Diehl *Sharky's Machine* 272: I'm not saying he's a goddamn loony bird.

loony farm *n.* FUNNY FARM.

> **1977** Caron *Go-Boy* 4: Hey, buddy, you sure this ain't the loony farm? **1978** Univ. Tenn. student theme: He's about ready for the *looney farm.* **1984** J.R. Reeves *Mekong* 307: Looking at me like I'd just escaped from a loony farm.

loony house *n.* LOONY BIN.

> **1958–59** Lipton *Barbarians* 35: That's how they met. It was in this loony house. **1961** A. Roth *Shame of Wounds* 53: Maybe he's in a loony house.

loony pen *n.* LOONY BIN.

> **1984** Caunitz *Police Plaza* 201: Sounds like an escapee from a fucking loony pen.

loon platoon *n.* Orig. *Mil.* a group of people who are foolish, reckless, or the like. Cf. GOON PLATOON.

> **1977** Langone *Life at Bottom* 12: They are members of an elite corps looked upon as "the loon platoon" by those who have wintered over [in Little America] and hated it. **1995** *Simpsons* (Fox-TV): I'm *outta* this loon platoon!

Loonyville *n. Army.* Lunéville, France. *Joc.*

> **1928** MacArthur *War Bugs* 30: By the same strange process which made Meurcy Ferme "Murphy's Farm," the Ourcq River "O'Rourke,"...Lunéville became "Looneyville" ten minutes after our arrival.

loop *n.* ¶ In phrase: **knock** [or **throw**] **for a loop** to overcome; defeat; (*also*) to bewilder or stun; dazzle.

> **1923** Witwer *Fighting Blood* 359: You're always predicting I'm going to get knocked for a loop. **1925** Dos Passos *Manhattan Transfer* 177: I'll say that this cocktail sure does knock you for a loop. **1934** Cain *Postman Rings Twice* 9: Swell. That'll knock 'em for a loop. **1936** Kingsley *Dead End* 684: Boy, ahl knock yuh fer a loop! **1938** "E. Queen" *4 Hearts* 46: This marriage knocks the feud for a loop. **1938** Mast *Bringing Up Baby* 39: *David:*...I'll wow him. I'll knock him for a loop! *Alice:* David, no slang! Remember who and what you are! **1941** in Litoff et al. *Miss You* 18: We had such a good time and I've never been so knocked for a loop. **1965** *Time* (July 23) 36: The dust's effect on the sensor...really threw us for a loop. **1970** in P. Heller *In This Corner* 27: They were knocked for a loop because they thought I'd...sign some cockeyed contract. **1972** Wells *Come Fly with Us* 34: I wonder what would happen if she did remarry. I think it would probably throw Steve for a loop. **1974** *Business Week* (May 4) 14: Maybe business is going along as usual, when things like seasonal peaks, special projects [etc.]...throw you for a loop. **1980** Freudenberger & Richelson *Burn Out* 181: Sometimes I get spasms that knock me for a loop. **1982** *L.A. Times* (May 30) V 2: It is the surprises that always seem to knock the brokerage industry for a loop. **1985** Briskin *Too Much* 204: She really knocked me for a loop....It's the greatest thing

that ever happened to me. **1986** *New York* (Dec. 15) 56: It really threw her for a loop. **1993** N. Russell *Suicide Charlie* 172: That threw the bureaucracy for a loop.

loop *v.* ¶ **go looping** to visit bars in order to get drunk.

> **1929** E. Wilson *Thought of Daisy* 67: So there was nothing to do but go looping again—I was plastered for a week. [**1954–60** *DAS: Loop*...v.i. To go on a drinking spree.]

looped *adj.* **1.** drunk.

> **1934** Weseen *Dict. Amer. Slang.* 279: *Looped*—Intoxicated. **1936** S.I. Miller *Battling Bellhop* (film): You can't help it if he was looped enough to slug Chuck. **1952** "R. Marsten" *So Nude* 70: Drunks....They were really looped. **1954** L. Crockett *Magnificent Bastards* 325: She wasn't nut, she wasn't sick, *she was looped.* **1958** Gardner *Piece of the Action* 25: They were all looped...walking...with the glide of drunken whimsy. **1959** Cochrell *Barren Beaches* 329: But I think I'm getting looped. **1966** Brunner *Face of Night* 99: Anyway, at least I'm gonna get looped. I'll tell you that much. **1969** Gordone *No Place* 430: She's never been much of a drinker but one night she got too looped to drive.

> **2.** demented or infatuated.

> **1978** *Texas Monthly* (June) 12: If you're really looped on fruit, don't miss the nectarines at Pioneer Orchards. **1982** *L.A. Times* (Aug. 14) V 1: A wry, slightly looped personality.

loop-legged *adj.* unsteady on one's legs as a result of intoxication.

> **1944** in *DARE:* Them Welshmen drinkin' theirselves looplegged every night. **1957** (cited in Spears *Drugs & Drink*). **1954–60** *DAS: Loop-legged*...Drunk. **1969** N.Y.C. man, age *ca*25: Getting loop-legged drunk. *1979 in T. Thorne *Dict. Contemp. Sl.:* I'm often lit up by elevenses, loop-legged by luncheon and totally schnockered by 6. **1984** J.R. Reeves *Mekong* 14: They were all loop-legged as hell.

loop-o *adj.* LOOPED, 1.

> **1957** Myrer *Big War* 116 [ref. to WWII]: I'm getting loop-o.

loop-the-loop *n.* **1.** [rhyming sl.] a finger ring.

> **1929** Sharpe *Chicago May* 288: *Loop the loop*—hoop, or ring.

> **2.** *Prost.* (see quots.).

> **1970** Landy *Underground Dict.* 121: *Loop-de-loop n....*Simultaneous oral-genital copulation between two people. *a*1972 B. Rodgers *Queens' Vernacular* 182: Sixty-nine...*loop-de-loop* (late '60s).

loopy *adj.* stupid, silly, or eccentric; demented; (*hence*) drunk.

> *1925 Fraser & Gibbons *Soldier & Sailor Wds.* 147 [ref. to WWI]: *Loopy:* Silly, daft. *1930 Brophy & Partridge *Songs & Slang* 137 [ref. to WWI]: *Loopy* (or *Looby*).—Silly; slightly insane; unwise; eccentric. *1934 Yeates *Winged Victory* 63 [ref. to WWI]: Wing [headquarters] must be loopy. *Ibid.* 402: The Huns were just loopy,...irresponsible, irrational. **1942** R. Chandler *High Window* 374: That loopy guy whose handkerchief you cry into. **1966** *Sat. Eve. Post* (July 2) 22: Within recent months, great numbers of adults in this country have gone loopy over rock 'n' roll. **1976** *L.A. Times* (May 12) IV 1: Bridges, loopy on moonshine, does a wonderful jig. **1978** *Rolling Stone* (Nov. 16) 47: Scher...gives in to a slightly loopy grin. **1983** *Time* (June 27) 68: The Whitney show...will undoubtedly create even loopier bids for the few works...that are not already in museums. **1989** Care *Spook Show* 62: Two beers and I already feel loopy. **1995** *TV Guide* (Feb. 11) 6: Grodin...comes up with the loopiest talk on the dial. **1996** A. Wells *Truth About Cats & Dogs* (film): Donna's got this loopy story to tell you. And it's funny!

loose *adj. & adv.* unperturbed; indifferent to pressure; calm; in good spirits.—often constr. with *stay* or *hang*, for which see *hang loose* s.v. HANG, *v.* Also as *quasi-n.*

> **1952** Sperling & Sherdeman *Retreat, Hell!* (film): Stay loose, kid. Take it easy. **1953** Eyster *Customary Skies* 167 [ref. to WWII]: Stay loose, buster. **1954** Styron *Long March* [ref. to WWII]: Stay loose. **1956** Rose *Crime in Streets* (film): I feel loose. I've never felt this loose before. **1957** Yordan *Men in War* (film): Don't panic. Stay loose. **1958** J. Davis *College Vocab.* 3: Stay loose—Don't let anything worry you. **1961** L.G. Richards *TAC* 45: "Stay loose" is another Air Force aphorism. **1961** Terry *Old Liberty* 58: Well, so long. Stay loose. **1966–67** W. Stevens *Gunner* 75 [ref. to WWII]: Man, you got to get yourself loose. Get wound too tight and you'll never make it. **1968** M. Albert & J. Guss *Lady in Cement* (film): Stay loose, pal. **1970** Segal *Love Story* 38: "It's all under control," I replied. "Stay loose." **1983** S. King *Christine* 110: I'm just telling you to stay loose, that's all. **1988** F. Robinson & B. Stainback *Extra Innings* 62: As I said, big Moe kept us loose [with his pranks].

¶ In phrases:

¶ **loose as a goose** extremely loose (in any sense). [This phr. is already entered under GOOSE; the following quots. provide add. evidence.]

1954–60 *DAS*: *Loose as a goose* = loose, cool use. **1971** Coffin *Old Ball Game* 49: Originally, the phrase was "loose as a goose and twice as shifty," referring to a clumsy ballplayer.—As it was shortened to its present form, it began to be used to describe indifference to pressure. **1979** *L.A. Times* (Apr. 7) III 1: Philadelphia Phillies' manager Danny Ozark is loose as a goose despite intense pressure to win. **1991** *New Yorker* (Feb. 18): She's as loose as a goose off the stand.

¶ **on the loose, 1.** unconstrained by obligations or responsibilities; (*hence*) available for an action or activity, employment, or the like. Cf. obs. S.E. *loose* 'state or condition of looseness, laxity, or unrestraint; hence, free indulgence, unrestrained action of feeling' in *OED2* since 1593; see also bracketed note at *on the loose*, 3, below.

***1749** J. Cleland, in *OED2*: The giddy, wildness of young girls once got upon the loose. **1848** Ruxton *Life in Far West* 93: The victorious mountaineers…quickly disposed of their peltries, and were once more on "the loose." **1933** Ersine *Pris. Slang* 51: Ted is *on the loose*. **1934** Garrett & Mankiewicz *Manhattan Melody* (film): You're not on the loose. Are you, Blackie? **1942** *ATS* 263: Unemployed.…*on the loose*. **1961** H. Ellison *Gentleman Junkie* 57: The word's been goin' around you need a horn. I was on the loose, so I figured I'd come over. ***1970** in *OED2*: So your friend King Alfy is on the loose.

2. seeking unrestrained amusement; carousing.

***1849** in *OED2*: They were at Gibraltar, on the look-out for amusement—in modern parlance, "on the loose." ***1859** in *OED2*: Though he goes on the loose, or the Cut, or the Spree. ***1871** in *F & H* IV 234: He is not out on the rampage, the loose, or the spree, as the vernacular of the place may have it. **1891** Maitland *Slang Dict.* 170: *Loose*, "on the," on the spree. **1947** *ATS* (Supp.) 24: *A.W.O.L.*, a wolf or Wac on the loose.

3. engaged in prostitution; (*also*) engaged in usu. petty crime. [*OED2* places ***1749** Cleland quot. at *on the loose*, 1, above, with this sense, perh. incorrectly.]

***1859** Hotten *Slang Dict.*: *On the loose*, obtaining a living by prostitution, in reality, on the streets. The term is applied to females only. ***1872** (cited in Partridge *Dict. Und.*). **1891** Maitland *Slang Dict.* 195: *On the loose*, dissipated; picking up a living on the streets. **1935** Pollock *Und. Speaks*: *On the loose*, engaged in crime or a racket. **1952** Sandburg *Strangers* 326 [ref. to ca1895]: He knew by name most of the women "on the loose" in Galesburg and many of them in Monmouth and Peoria—they knew him.

¶ **turn** [or **cut**] **every way but loose** Esp. *So.* to assault and overcome violently; punish severely; (*hence*) (*turn* form only) to reduce to exhaustion.

1926 Van Vechten *Nigger Heaven* 247: Ah'll cut you every way but loose. **1941** in Botkin *Treas. Amer. Folk.* 124: Jesse…turned old Stack every way but *loose*. **1958** Motley *Epitaph* 118: I'm going to turn you every way but loose if you don't stop messing in my business! **1968** W.C. Anderson *Gooney Bird* 138: Just get one in bed.…They'll turn you every way but loose. Those slant-eyes really know how to make love. **1969** in Girodias *New Olympia Reader* 377: I want to turn her ass every way but loose!

¶ **turn loose** to deliver (a blow) with great force.—also used fig.

1896 Brown *Parson* 140: Gad, yer a preacher!…Well, b' Gad, turn her loose. Let's have a sermon so's we can write home that we's been to church. **1918** E. O'Neill *Moon of Caribbees* 47: I was goin' to turn one loose on the jaw of any guy'd cop my dame.

loose cannon *n.* Esp. *Pol. & Journ.* an uncontrollable and usu. dangerous person or thing.

[**1946** W.A. White *Autobiog.* 339 [ref. to 1901]: [Theodore Roosevelt] was worried about what he would do after he left the White House.…He said: "I don't want to be the old cannon loose on the deck in the storm."] [**1973** R.M. Nixon, diary entry for Apr. 14, in *RN: The Memoirs of Richard Nixon* (1979) II 351: I have a note here saying, "the loose cannon has finally gone off," that's probably what could be said because that's what Magruder did when he went in and talked to the U.S. Attorney.] [**1976** *Business Week* (Nov. 15) (Nexis):

"That money," says Arnold Packer, a senior Senate Budget Committee economist who is helping Carter draw up his shadow budget, "is like a loose cannon rolling around the deck" because a sudden reappearance of the funds could be inflationary.] **1977** *Wash. Post* (Mar. 13): New political sobriquets are heaped upon [Andrew] Young…almost as fast as he breaks into the headlines: the Moynihan of the Left, the loose cannon, the wayward missile of the Carter administration, the "Andy Young Problem." **1977** (cited in *BDNE3*). **1981** *Washington Wk. in Review* (PBS-TV) (Feb. 6): Is [he] a loose cannon? **1982** *News & Observer* (Raleigh, N.C.) A5: After all, Young had been something of a loose cannon on the deck of the Carter administration as ambassador to the United Nations, a black who seemed quick to find racism all around him. **1983** R. Thomas *Missionary* 261: You know, Morgan, sitting here listening to you just now, one phrase kept popping into my mind: loose cannon. **1985** Boyne & Thompson *Wild Blue* 451: But he was a loose cannon on the flight line. a**1986** D. Tate *Bravo Burning* 33: The lovable loose cannon…of military megalomania. **1986** *CBS Evening News* (CBS-TV) (Dec. 24): It could help answer the question of whether he was a loose cannon operating on his own—or a loyal soldier following the instructions of superiors. **1988** Headline News network (Aug. 14): He has a reputation as a loose cannon. **1990** *Time* (Nov. 5) 42: Saddam is a loose cannon with terrible weapons that must be eliminated. **1993** Namus *Shattered Dreams* (film): You're a loose cannon, Shari. You don't know how to control yourself.

loose deuce *n. Mil. Av.* a type of paired fighter formation.

1983 La Barge & Holt *Sweetwater Gunslinger* 115: Get into your loose deuce. **1986** M. Skinner *USN* xii: *Loose Deuce*—A Navy tactical fighter formation.

loose goose *n.* a person or thing that is loose (in any sense). Cf. *loose as a goose* s.v. GOOSE.

1958 Frankel *Band of Bros.* 8 [ref. to 1950]: "All mornin' he's been fidgety.…" "You wasn't no loose goose when you first come here." **1969** Pendleton *Death Squad* 109: Internal security is a loose goose, though. **1983** Goldman & Fuller *Charlie Co.* 206: A wide streak of the roustabout—the rabble-rousin' loose goose.

loosejaw *n.* whiskey; BUSTHEAD.

1967 W. Crawford *Gresham's War* 140: I'm trying some of the loosejaw.

looseners *n.* prunes. *Joc.*

1925 *AS* I (Dec.) 137: *Looseners*.…a dish of "looseners." **1935** in *AS* (Feb. 1936) 44: [Soda fountain, N.Y.C.:] *Looseners*. Prunes.

loosen up *n.* **1.** to loosen one's hold, esp. on money; pay.

1903 *Enquirer* (Cincinnati) (May 9) 13: *Loosen up*—To spend money. **1908** McGaffey *Show Girl* 125: Loosen-up.…You've got to donate for a couple of tickets to the annual benefit. **1921** in *DA*: Someone will have to loosen up to pay for the damage. **1922** C. Sandburg, in *OED2*: Come across, kick in, loosen up. **1928** in Galewitz *Great Comics* 147: Th' way those guys loosened up for me to-day yuh'd think they were millionaires. **1951** Bowers *Mob* (film): Loosen up tonight. Let's take a cab.

2. *Baseball.* (see 1969 quot.).

1937 (cited in P. Dickson *Baseball Dict.*). **1969** Bouton *Ball Four* 271: *Loosen him up*, meaning that if enough baseballs are thrown close to a hitter, he'll fall down easily.

loose wig see s.v. WIG.

loosey-goosey *adj. loose as a goose* s.v. GOOSE.

1967 *Time* (Aug. 4) 44: This…is as loosey-goosey as any team I've ever seen. **1971** Coffin *Old Ball Game* 50: From [*loose as a goose*] has come the conventionalized phrase "loosey goosey" as used by Willie Mays to describe the San Francisco Giants in the last of the ninth as they were defeating the Dodgers in the final game of the 1962 playoff: "We was all loosey-goosey out there!" **1972** *N.Y. Times Mag.* (Apr. 9) 39: His teammates are horsing and whooping around as only the loosey-goosey world champion Pirates can. **1972** Sapir & Murphy *Death Therapy* 20: A loosey-goosey, the world's going to end, top maximum priority. **1976** Rosen *Above Rim* 20: Silky laughed. He was feeling loosey-goosey. **1981** G. Wolf *Roger Rabbit* 216: In a loosey-goosey motion. a**1986** D. Tate *Bravo Burning* 10: One didn't…want to go waltzing off to war too loosey-goosey in the head. **1986** Heinemann *Paco's Story* 157: With his knees all loosy-goosy, like he's surfing. **1988** *N.Y. Post* (June 6) 52: Hearns was…[as] loosey-goosey as I've ever seen him 48 hours before a fight. **1997** *L.A. Times* (Mar. 7) E1: His jazzy vocals lent a loosey-goosey mood to the event that a standard canned rock soundtrack could never have achieved.

loosie *n.* a single cigarette, esp. one sold individually.

    1992 *L.A. Times* (Sept. 6) A1: Buying 20 "singles" or "loosies" is more expensive in the end than purchasing a 20-cigarette pack. **1995** Stavsky, Mozeson & Mozeson *A 2 Z: Lucy* or *loosie*…a cigarette. **1996** in *Utne Reader* (Feb. 1997) 36: Try to buy a 25-cent loosie—loose cigarette—at local bodega.

loot[1] var. LIEUT.

loot[2] *n.* money. [Esp. common *ca*1950–60.]

    [**1928** Sharpe *Chicago May* 43: That's what you want from me—after we spend the loot.] *ca*1929 *Collection of Sea Songs* 35: A prostitute of ill repute/But she collected lots of loot. **1943 Hunt & Pringle *Service Slang* 44, in *OED2*: *Loot*, Scottish slang for money received on pay day. **1944** in Himes *Black on Black* 199: I'da cut out right then and there but the loot had me. **1945** Fay *Be Poor* 159: And at the same time, you loosen that loot! **1946** J. Adams *Gag* 53: When they found out a girl had plenty of loot, they would immediately go on the make. **1948** Manone & Vandervoort *Trumpet* 138: I want to play, not stand around betting somebody else's loot. **1951** M. Shulman *Dobie Gillis* 40: "How much loot you got?" asked the man. **1953** M. Shulman *Affairs of Gillis* (film): How much loot ya got? **1954** L. Armstrong *Satchmo* 100: Several times I went to the pawnshop and picked up some loot on my horn. **1960–61** Steinbeck *Discontent* 77: I'd sure like to cut in on some of that loot. **1962** G. Olson *Roaring Rd.* 120: Would they pay that kind of loot? **1963** Hayden *Wanderer* 14: He needs the loot. **1964** Gold *Jazz Lexicon* 195: *Loot*. Money….Current among jazzmen *c*1930–*c*1945, when it was largely replaced by *bread*. **1967** Gonzales *Paid My Dues* 60: I…was "out of loot." **1970** F.D. Gilroy *Private* 6: I'll be coining loot back here. **1973** Buerkle & Barker *Bourbon St. Black* 119: I coulda made a lot more loot too, with the white bands. *a*1973–87 F.M. Davis *Livin' the Blues* 48: Separating suckers from their loose loot. **1993** in Stavsky, Mozeson & Mozeson *A 2 Z*: We all about making *loot*.

loot-comm var. see LIEUT-COMM.

lop *n.* **1.** (see quot.).

    1890 *DN* I 62: *Lop*, both *n.* and *v.*, trans. and intrans. Common among students at Jefferson College, Pennsylvania. As a noun, one who curries favor with the faculty; as a verb, to curry favor.

    2. a worthless or obnoxious fellow. Cf. LOB[1], 1.

    1977 Bunker *Animal Factory* 139: "Who is it?" "Some lop fuckin' with Ron." *a*1990 P. Dickson *Slang!* 221: *Lop*. A nerd or dork.

lope *v.* to run, esp. to run away. [Orig. S.E.; see *OED2*.]

    1698–99 "B.E." *Dict. Canting Crew: Let's buy a Brush* or *Let's Lope*,…let us scour off, and make what shift we can to secure our selves from being apprehended. **1785 Grose *Vulgar Tongue: Loap*. To run away; *he loaped down the dancers*, he ran down stairs. **1846 Codman *Sailors' Life* 97: I don't see no other way then, but for her to cut and run.…Yes, 'lope. **1884** Beard *Bristling with Thorns* 131: Some people think a regiment of contrabands would lope like a deer before a Southern man with a whip in his hand. **1928** *Amer. Mercury* (Aug.) 478: Lope, you yellow-bellied skunk! **1968** Spradley *Owe Yourself a Drunk* 44: Just then a cop on bike pulls up. I start to lope.

¶ In phrase:

¶ **lope (one's) mule** see S.V. MULE.

lop-ear *n.* an Oregonian. *Joc.*

    1862 in Bensil *Quiet on Yamhill* 58: The nickname for Oregonians, in most common use, is "Web-foot," but some insist that "Lop-ear," others that "Flop-ear" is the proper designation.

lop-eared *adj.* very stupid; exceptionally gullible; (often used as a generalized term of abuse).

    1863 in S. Clemens *Twain's Letters* I 248: These rotten, lop-eared, whopper-jawed, jack-legged [Californians]. **1876** W. Wright *Big Bonanza* 378: So this is the lop-eared cur of Calaveras who comes here to set up as a fighter? **1881** Nye *Forty Liars* 138: A preparatory institute for lop-eared idiots. **1915–16** Lait *Beef, Iron & Wine* 95: Or do I have to let a lop-eared chicken chaser like this run me all over town and get away with it? **1926** Nichols & Tully *Twenty Below* 16: Look at yourselves, you lop-eared mongrels! **a*1950 W. Granville *Sea Slang* 148: *Lop-eared*. A term of abuse on the lower-deck. "Get out of the way, you lop-eared ullage!"; "Of all the lop-eared, lubberly sons of sin, you're the perishing limit." **1968** L. Cameron *Warriors* 50: You lop-eared sonuvabitch! **1968** [R. Beck] *Trick Baby* 41: You're talking like a lop-eared mark.

loper *n.* a runaway.

    1855 in Mencken *Amer. Lang. Supp. I* 315: The term *loper* [is] applied to deserters from South Sea whalers. **1871** *Overland Mo.* (Sept.) 272: Now, you lazy lopers…get…to work.

loqued-out see S.V. LOC OUT.

Lord Harry *n.* ¶ In phrase: **by the Lord Harry** see S.V. HARRY.

Los *n.* *West.* Los Angeles, California.

    1913 Light *Hobo* 58: Did you get stuck in "Los"? **1924** in C.M. Russell *Paper Talk* 195: Its about forty miles from Los. **1925** *Writer's Mo.* (June) 487: *Los*—Los Angeles, California. **1930** G. Irwin *Tramp & Und. Sl.: Los.*—Los Angeles, Cal. **1948** J. Stevens *Jim Turner* 118 [ref. to *ca*1910]: Their talk was mainly lying brags on all the vile items of life in cities they called Chi, Cincy, K.C., Los and Frisco.

los *adv.* [< G *was ist los?* 'what's the matter?'] *Army.* happening; occurring.

    1975 S.P. Smith *Amer. Boys* 95: What's *los*, cool breeze? *Ibid.* 238: What the fuck is *los*? **1983** Elting, Cragg & Deal *Dict. Soldier Talk* 340: *What's los?* What's up? What's the matter?

lose *v.* **1.** to vomit.—used trans. with a specific or general food term, esp. **lose (one's) lunch.**—also constr. with dummy-obj. *it.*—also used fig.

    1852 Hazen *Five Years* 61: Part of my supper's lost, an I's come to lay in a fresh cargo. **1918** in E. Wilson *Prelude* 194: Jesus Christ! I loses my own lunch right in the cracked-ice pail. **1920** Haslett *Luck on the Wing* viii: I almost lost my breakfast at the thought of a ride in an airplane. **1928** J.M. March *Set-Up* 37: He…/Covered his mouth,/Ran…/For the door of the can./"Jeez!/The kid is losin' his lunch!" **1935** F.H. Lea *Anchor Man* 2: Regulations….I could lose my lunch at the sound of the word. **1949** Davies *Every Spring* (film): "What can you lose?" "My *lunch* is all." **1952** Rinehart *Swimming Pool*, in *OED2*: I'm going to lose my dinner. **1970** Landy *Underground Dict.: Lose your cookies*…Vomit. **1978** Strieber *Wolfen* 35: During the…autopsy Wilson had lost his lunch. **1982** Zicree *Twilight Zone Comp.* 201: When I saw the set I pretty near lost my lunch. **1985** Boyne & Thompson *Wild Blue* 40: Are you really losing your lunch in the air? **1990** P. Munro *Slang U.: Lose it*…to vomit. **1992** D. Burke *Street Talk* I 39: *Lose it*…to throw up.

    2. to kill.

    1871 Crofutt *Tourist's Guide* 98: A "Gentile" can *now* engage in business without fear of being "lost" by a "DANITE PILL," or being warned *out* of the territory, simply because he is *not* a Mormon. **1930** G. Irwin *Tramp & Und. Sl.: Lost.*—Murdered.

    3.a. to evade.

    1875 in F. Remington *Sel. Letters* 10: I received your letter to day and you can't lose me. **1886 in *OED2*: His great stride and iron legs would have enabled him, in the language of the turf, to lose his antagonist. **1914** *Sat. Eve. Post* (Apr. 4) 12: I told yuh to lose him, didn't I?

    b. to get rid of; discard; give up.

    1931 Wilstach *Under Cover Man* 7: I'll lose that [evidence] myself. **1949** Loos & Sales *Mother Is a Freshman* (film): I'd take those bobby pins and lose 'em. **1980** Di Fusco et al. *Tracers* 16: Lose the dark glasses, soul brother. **1988** Univ. Tenn. student: Lose the hat. **1996** *Good Morning America* (ABC-TV): Lose the gym and still lose weight!

    c. to turn off (lights, as on a film set); "kill."

    *a*1988 Price & Seaman *R. Rabbit* (film): Lose lights!

¶ In phrases:

¶ **get lost!** go away and stop bothering me!

    [**1908** Train *Crime Stories* 308: A few days later Bracken sent a gambler named Warner to Jesse, who offered the latter thirty-five hundred dollars to get "lost" long enough for the prisoner to slip over to Mexico.] **1942–47** *ATS* (Supp.) 10: ["Teen Talk and Jive Jargon":] "Beat it."…*Buzz off*,…*get lost*. **1952** McCoy & Dortort *Lusty Men* (film): Get lost. **1955** G.D. Adams *3 Bad Sisters* (film): No interviews, baby. Get lost. **1958** Frede *Entry E* 8: Get lost. **1954–60** *DAS: Lost, get* …"drop dead." **1965** I. Reiner *Wild, Wild Planet* (film): Get lost, huh? **1971 in Partridge *Catch Phrases* (ed. 2) 98: "I need your help, Betty."…"Get lost." **1977 in Partridge *Catch Phrases* (ed. 2) 98: *Get lost!* Oh run away and stop bothering me! Adopted from the US, *c.*1944 in Aus.…and *c.*1949 in UK. **1980** *Psychology Today* (Oct.) 37: He will dispense with his natural trustfulness and tell the college student to get lost. **1987** *Tracey Ullman Show* (Fox-TV): Get lost! **1992** Bleich *Dan-*

ger I. (film): "Come on, Brian. Let's be friends." "Get lost." ***1994** R. Doyle *Snapper* (film): Get lost!

¶ **lose it** to lose one's sanity, temper, composure, or abilities.

1974 Univ. Tenn. student: He'll really lose it when he hears about this! **1976** Schroeder *Shaking It* 147: [Sometimes] a prisoner "loses it" and begins to shout and pound on the door (it's pitch black in there) an attendant douses him with a burst of water. **1979** D. Thoreau *City at Bay* 271: Bryce told me you were losing it but he didn't say you were senile. **1982** *L.A. Times* (Jan. 11) I 3: I...was half way out into the chute when I lost it (slipped and fell). **1984** W.M. Henderson *Elvis* 64: Byron was starting to lose it. This wasn't his crowd. **1985** Bodey *F.N.G.* 5: They lifted us out, too many guys losing it, know what I mean? **1985** M. Baker *Cops* 78: What scares me is the mentally disturbed, the people that lose it. **1989** Dorsett & Frommer *Running Tough* 9: When Melvin died, I almost lost it. **1994** *Are You Afraid of Dark?* (Nickelodeon TV): Be cool. Don't lose it. **1994** J. Shay *Achilles* xiv: I lost it and they put me in the psych hospital. **1994** *X-Files* (Fox-TV): You saw him up there. He's losing it. **1995** *Time* (Apr. 24) 27: Thieu was really tough....But that day when Toan came in, Thieu lost it....His spirit was broken.

¶ **lose the ball** to *lose it*, above.

1979 W. Safire, in *N.Y. Times Mag.* (May 20) 10: An individual in any sort of difficulty is "losing the ball" or "coming undone."

loser *n.* **1.** Orig. *Und.* a person who has been convicted of a crime.—orig. and esp. used with *two-time, three-time,* etc.—also used fig. Often *joc.*

1912 Lowrie *Prison* 17: He...was already a "three-time loser." **1914** *American Mag.* (June) 31: To-day I am a convict serving my second penitentiary system—a "two-time loser" in the language of the underworld. **1914** Jackson & Hellyer *Crim. Slang* 56: *Loser,* Noun Current amongst prison habitues. An ex-convict....*"*Three time losers cop life in some states." **1915** *Thru the Mill* 5: Men in the jail with me...were one, two or three-time losers. **1921** Casey & Casey *Gay-Cat* 210: Devil take all these...sheriff posses...that are gone off'n their nuts 'cause a single lonely loser escaped from stir! **1926** Tully *Jarnegan* 236: Burglery [*sic*]...I was a two-time loser. **1927–28** Tasker *Grimhaven* 43: There was an older loser from here who told me about a tunnel. **1928** in J.P. Cannon *Notebook* 65: Men who have been convicted more than once—"the two-time losers." **1939** C.R. Cooper *Scarlet* 19: A four-time loser. Going back this time for murder. **1946** Gresham *Nightmare Alley* 241: "Your third wife?" "Yeah....Wait a minute. How'd you know I was a three-time loser?" **1950** Breen & Duff *Appt. with Danger* (film): I'm a loser. I've got to be careful. **1953** E. Wood, Jr. *Glen or Glenda?* (film): A four-time loser. **1961** *Sat. Eve. Post* (Aug. 26) 40: A many-time loser who was doing jolt for robbery. **1972–75** W. Allen *Feathers* 36: Once more and I'm a three-time loser. **1992** N. Cohn *Heart of World* 18: Already he was a three-time loser. **1994** *New Republic* (Mar. 21) 24: Another safety valve for three-time losers over the age of 60 who are sick or no longer dangerous. **1996** *New York* (Aug. 12) 25: He came to the aid of seven-time loser Steve Howe in 1991.

2.a. a markedly disappointing, unpleasant, or inferior thing or state of affairs.

*1936 in Partridge *DSUE*: It was a bit of a loser, getting bored before the trial had started. **1955** (quot. at **(2.b.)**, below). **1967** Briscoe *Short Timer* (Nov 28) 19: Movie tonight was a real loser. **1980** R. Salmaggi (WINS radio) (Aug. 6): This movie is a loser! *a***1987** Bunch & Cole *Reckoning for Kings* 133: Apricots. A serious loser. **1990** *Hull High* (NBC-TV): Nobody teaches. Not any more. The money's a loser. **1996** *World News Tonight* (ABC-TV) (Oct. 16): Is it a loser for him? A waste of time?

b. a person who is worthless, unappealing, chronically unsuccessful, etc.

1955 *AS* XXX (Dec.) 304: *Loser, n.* Something (or someone) hopeless. **1958** J. Davis *College Vocab.* 7: *Loser*—Boy or girl who is unattractive and has a bad personality. **1959** *AS* (May) 154: [Students] limited in ability or old-fashioned in dress or manners [are called] *losers. ca***1960** in *Worst from Mad, 5th Annual Ed.* 71: But Flynn blew one cool single, and the hipsters did a flip,/And Blake, who was a loser, gave the old ball quite a trip. **1961** in *AS* XXXIX (1964) 235: Student Slang...*Loser, n.* A non-appealing girl. **1965** "R. Stark" *Jugger* 24: It was too bad Tiftus was such a loser, so unreliable, such a mistake. *a***1967** Bombeck *Wit's End* 32: Heaven knows I try to bend to the dictates of fashion, but let's

face it, I'm a loser. **1967** W. Murray *Sweet Ride* 93: They're losers, baby, and they have it in for the whole crazy American scene. **1968** I. Reed *Yellow Back Radio* 93: Aren't you glad you came away with me from that loser you were with? **1970** Segal *Love Story* 5: Jenny, if you're so convinced I'm a loser, why did you bulldoze me into buying you coffee? *a***1977** M. French *Women's Room* 119: Hamp was a loser but...Daddy would never fire him. **1979** Kiev *Courage to Live* 21: He looked and acted like the proverbial "loser." **1982** Rucker *57th Kafka* 35: She was already wondering how to get rid of this obvious loser. **1983** *Batman* (Apr.) 14: You've got the downtown losers scared, man, but not us. **1986** *America: Nissan* (Spring) 26: He had assessed dozens of hikers, and he was able to spot the losers. **1987** *Beauty & Beast* (CBS-TV): She a lush. She was married to a lush. She's a complete loser. **1994** Danesi *Cool* 49: Eyeglasses....Only dorks and losers wear them. **1996** *Leeza* (synd. TV series): Yeah, you little *loser!*

loser *adj.* markedly inferior; worthless.—used prenominally.

1975 Univ. Tenn. student: This is a loser lunch. **1990** P. Munro *Slang U.*: I can't believe you get all these loser classes.

Lost Wages *n.* [intentional malapropism] Las Vegas, Nevada. *Joc.*

1961 L.G. Richards *TAC* 182: Millions flock to "Lost Wages" to lay millions on the gaming tables. **1976** Dills *CB Slanguage* (ed. 4) 65: *Lost Wages:* Las Vegas, Nevada. **1988** *Spin* (Oct.) 13: Cassandra became...the youngest showgirl to hit Lost Wages. **1994** *Garfield & Friends* (CBS-TV): Direct from an engagement in Lost Wages, Nevada!

lot *n.* ¶ In phrases:

¶ **all over the lot** everywhere in the vicinity; all over the place; (*hence*) (used as an intensive).

1910 in O. Johnson *Lawrenceville* 366: I'll kick myself all over the lot tomorrow. **1921** *Variety* (Feb. 11) 11: The Orpheum Circuit...[was] yelping all over the lot that it must have the Band. **1935** C.J. Daly *Murder* 69: A squawk that would be heard all over the lot.

¶ **a lot of** *Jazz & Black E.* superlative; extremely skilled. Cf. MESS, 4.

1946 in R.S. Gold *Jazz Lexicon*: Damn,...that's a lot of horn, that really is. **1956** in R.S. Gold *Jazz Lexicon*: He plays an awful lot of trumpet. **1960** D. Hamilton *Death of a Citizen* 120: It was a lot of car. **1961** in R.S. Gold *Jazz Lexicon*: I would rate it two stars for orchestral technique, for being able to handle an orchestra that size, even though it's not a lot of music.

lot lizard *n. Trucking.* a prostitute who works at truck stops.

1987 *Wash. Post* (Jan. 22) (Nexis): Sometimes, they said, they are awakened in the trucks by prostitutes seeking customers. The truckers call them "lot lizards." **1988** *Parade* (July 10) 5: At truck stops (where "lot lizards," or prostitutes, are plentiful at night). **1990** Rukuza *West Coast Turnaround* 28: Lot lizards don't give receipts,...only crabs. **1990** *Newsweek* (May 14) 8: *Lot lizards:* Prostitutes who frequent truck stops. **1991** *Sally Jessy Raphaël* (synd. TV series): A *lot lizard*...is a prostitute who works the truckstops. **1992** *L.A. Times* (Sept. 5) B2: I wonder what that lot lizard charges.

lot louse *n.* usu. *pl. Circus.* an annoying townsperson who wanders about a circus grounds.

1930 G. Irwin *Tramp & Und. Sl.: Lot Lice.*—Circus and carnival hangers-on who follow the show but are not part of the salaried staff. **1943** J. Mitchell *McSorley's* 92: "Lot lice"...in circuses, this term is applied to townspeople who do not buy tickets but stand around the lot, gaping at everything and getting in the way. **1961** (quot. at PIPE, *v.*). **1975** McKennon *Horse Dung Trail* 16: The "Lot Lice"...all crowded close to watch the battle. *Ibid.* 503: *Lot Lice:* Townspeople who spend nothing but time on the show grounds. Persons who stay on the "lot" all day and spend nothing.

Lot's wife *n.* Esp. *Naut.* a saltcellar; salt. *Joc.*

[**1867** [S.B. Putnam] *Richmond During War* 125: A fortunate speculator, having in store a vast quantity of salt...grew rich...and was afterwards facetiously styled "Lot's wife."] **1874** Rudge & Raven *I.O.G.B.* 51: Salt, from "Lot's wife." ***1921** *N & Q* (Nov. 26) 425 [ref. to WWI]: *Lot's wife.* Salt. ***1925** Fraser & Gibbons *Soldier & Sailor Wds.* 148 [ref. to WWI]: *Lot's Wife:* Salt (Navy). **1941** Hargrove *Pvt. Hargrove* 83: Salt is *sand* or *Lot's wife.* **1946** Bill *Beleaguered City* 127 [ref. to Richmond, Va., 1865]: Salt—"Lot's wife," in the slang of the day—had been scarce.

¶ In phrase:

¶ **salty as Lot's wife** very salty. [The form with *backbone* given in the *1950 quot. below euphemizes the vulgar form with *ass*.]

[**1865** in Dolph *Sound Off!* 310: They kives me peef, so ferry, ferry salt,/Like Sodom's wife, you know.] **1928** Tilton *Cap'n George Fred* 51: The beef was saltier than Lot's wife. ***1950** W. Granvile *Sea Slang* 149: Cf. the low civilian simile, *as salt as Lot's wife's backbone.* ***1969** Hugill *Shanties & Songs* 144 [song learned in 1920's]: An' the meat wuz as salt as Lot's wife's ass.

Lotusland *n.* Los Angeles, California. Cf. La-La Land.

1980 *Maclean's* (Jan. 21) 48: Alberta in winter…is quite something to see. A further jury of shrinks will have to be called in, but a softy from Lotusland insists there is a masochistic element to the industriousness. **1983** *Calif. Business* (Oct.) 31: A dilemma increasingly common to movie makers in Lotus Land: Should they film on location in Los Angeles? **1987** *Miami Vice* (NBC-TV): So how are things out in Lotusland? **1989** Radford & Crowley *Drug Agent* 37: Even in lotusland. **1992** *Melrose Place* (Fox-TV): Another beautiful day in Lotusland.

loud *adj. & adv.* (usu. of smells) powerful; offensive; strong. [Orig. literary.]

***1641** J. Milton, in *OED*: Their…mouths cannot open without the strong breath and loud stench of avarice. **1820** in C. Fanning *Exiles of Erin* 29: They smell very loud. **1842** C. Dickens *Amer. Notes* ch. xiv: Pretty loud smell of varnish, sir? **1845** Corcoran *Pickings* 142: You have some of the loudest kind of [rain] showers in these diggins. **1862** in J.W. Haley *Rebel Yell* 29: [It] smelled as loud as an old fish house. **1870** Duval *Big-Foot* 257: It…smells louder than an old brass candlestick. **1871** in *OED*: Carry…some drug that smells loud. **1899** in *OED2*: It is also said to make a very loud smell. **1940, ca1960, 1986, 1994** in *DARE*.

¶ In phrases:

¶ **loud and clear** [fig. use of radiocommunications jargon] *Av.* (of weather) clear and perfect for flying.

1960 Rankin *Rode Thunder* 41 [ref. to 1951]: The weather was, as we pilots say, "loud and clear." **1963** E.M. Miller *Exile* 91: One minute the place is socked in, the next moment loud and clear. *Ibid.* 144: The weatherman had said that the sky condition would be "loud and clear" all the way back to Capitola.

¶ **on the loud** mightily.

1844 in *DA* s.v. *go*: Millerism is again going it on the loud in Louisville, a large number of proslytes [*sic*] were recently added to their number.

¶ **out loud** to an intolerable degree. [Orig. of smells.]

1932 Hecht & Fowler *Great Magoo* 51: Our madrigal,…she assured us, reeked out loud. **1952** Holmes *Boots Malone* (film): That Cabbagehead smells out loud. And his agent with him! **1964** N.Y.C. high school student: This stinks out loud. **1976** *Nat. Lampoon* (July) 7: Her show sucks out loud. **1985** Eble *Campus Slang* (Oct.) 10: *Suck out loud*—be unfair or disgusting. "I studied for two weeks for that Chemistry test and only made a D. Does that not just suck out loud."

loud handle *n. Mil. Av.* a handle that operates an airplane's ejection seat.

1988 M. Maloney *Thunder Alley* 105: Bail out!…Hit the loud handle! **1990** Lightbody & Poyer *Complete Top Gun* 253: Loud handle: Ejection seat activator. **1991** J. Weber *Rules of Engagement* 332: I've got a grip on the loud handle. *Ibid.* 368: *Loud handle* Slang for the ejection-seat handle.

loudmouth *v. Black E.* to speak abusively or aggressively.—also used trans. [The *n.* has always been colloq.]

1938 in Leadbitter & Slaven *Blues Records* 187: Don't You Loud Mouth Me. **1950** A. Lomax *Mr. Jelly Roll* 237: The old whorehouse pianist…seemed to be trying to loud-mouth his way back to big time.

loud pedal *n. Mil. Av.* a pedal that operates an aircraft's afterburners.

1990 Lightbody & Poyer *Complete Top Gun* 253: Loud pedal: Slang for a jet aircraft's afterburners.

loudspeaker *n.* a braggart or loudmouth.

1934 Weseen *Dict. Slang* 188: *Loud speaker*—A person who is regarded as important or one who regards himself as important. **1938** Lennon et al. *Crowd Roars* (film): Ask that loudspeaker at the bar to come over and have a drink with it.

loudtalk *v. Black E.* to speak loudly and abusively to or to the detriment of; (*also*) to brag to.

1930 in *DARE*: Loud-talk: Argue in coarse strident tones. **1934** Z.N. Hurston, in *DARE*: Loud talk me, making your side appear right by making more noise than the others. **1935** Z.N. Hurston, in *DARE*: Look at her puttin' out her brags.…Loud-talkin' de place. **1942–49** Goldin et al. *DAUL*: Loud talk a ghee…To inform upon a fellow convict by indirection, as to utter such information while within earshot of guard or a known informer. **1954** L. Armstrong *Satchmo* 212: He did not take his eyes off me as I walked up, and he kept loudtalking me. "Come heah, you little sonofabitch." **1971** *Who Took Weight?* 188: She started loud-talkin' me, in front o' the kids. *a***1994** Smitherman *Black Talk* 156: *Loudtalk* To talk in such a way as to confront or embarrass someone publicly. *a***1994** N. McCall *Wanna Holler* 314: Williams…would loud-talk and browbeat you.

Louie *n.* [app. an arbitrary application of the given name; the 1988 quot. may reflect an independent coinage] **1.** a dollar; (*hence*) *pl.* money.

1901 Ade *Modern Fables* 189: It comes to Ten Louies. **1988** R. Menllo & R. Rubin *Tougher Than Leather* (film): It was my louies, my money that bought TV.

2. a native of Louisiana, esp. a migratory worker.—usu. used contemptuously. Cf. Arky, Okie.

1948 in *DAS*: Now [the fruit tramps]'re called Okies and Arkies and Louies.

3. var. Looie.

4. a left turn, esp. in an automobile.—constr. with *hang*. Cf. hang, *v.*, 7.

1967 in *OEDAS* II 140: If you're in your pig [*sc.*, car] and you "hang a Louie," you've just turned left. If you "hang a Ralph," it's a right turn. **1969** *Current Slang I & II* 47: Hang a Louis, v. To turn left.—College males, Michigan.—*Hang a Louis* at the next corner. **1972** N.Y.U. student: Hang a Louie means make a left. **1972** Eble *Campus Slang* (Oct.) 3: Hang a Louie—go left. **1972** *Seattle Times Mag.* (June 18) 14: Cut over to 140th, hang a louie at the first light, swing north a couple blocks…and there you are. **1985** Finkleman *Head Office* (film): I'm gonna hang a louie at the Prudential Building. **1989** *Dream St.* (NBC-TV): Hang a louie here.

5. a bit of expectorated phlegm; (*also*) solidified nasal mucus. Cf. loogie.

1970 *Current Slang V* (Winter) 8: *Hang a louie*, v. To spit on someone.—College students, both sexes, Minnesota. **1980** *Nat. Lampoon* (Aug.) 92 (adv.): Jimmy Picks! It's Real! Carter gets caught reaching for a Louie! "UN-ALTERED" photo. **1981–85** S. King *It* 887: She hocked a…looey onto…his head. **1990** G.R. Clark *Wds. of Viet. War* 288: Louies…GI slang for "spit,"…especially that less than clear variety.

6. *Juve.* (see quot.). Cf. noogie.

1972 N.Y.U. student: A *Louie* is a punch with your knuckles.

7. lulu, 1.b.

1995 N.C. man, age 26 (coll. J. Sheidlower): Hope you have a louie of a holiday, man.…Yeah, *looie* means "doozy."

¶ In phrases:

¶ **Ach, Louie** (used as a humorous interjection).

1914 Dale *Songs of Seventh* 87: Ach! Louie, Louie how we love our Lou! **1918** Dolph *Sound Off!* 169: Chorus (Ach, Louie) When you hear us raise the rebel yell, we'll/Grab our guns and "over the top" pell mell.

¶ **Louie the Louse** *Mil.* any of various Japanese scout planes making nightly runs over Guadalcanal. Now *hist.* Cf. Bedcheck Charlie.

1942 Tregaskis *Guadalcanal Diary* (entry for Sept. 12): The light spread into the glow of a flare, and then we heard the mosquito-like "double-hummer" tone of a Jap float plane. It was "Louie the Louse"—a generic name for any one of the Jap float planes which come to annoy us at night. **1952** Morison *Naval Ops. in WWII* V 139: The exasperated Americans listening to the peculiar *chug-chug* of their engines nicknamed these nocturnal pests "Washing Machine Charlie" and "Louie the Louse." **1961** Foster *Hell in the Heavens* 50 [ref. to 1942]: Jap night raiders are called Washing Machine Charlie after the original pest that harassed our boys on Guadalcanal. At various times he had been called Louie the Louse, Maytag Charlie, and other names less printable.

lounge lizard *n.* a foppish man who idles about the lounges of hotels, clubs, etc., usu. with or in search of women; (*specif.*) a gigolo; (*later*) any frequenter of nightclubs; (*also*) *Stu.* (*obs.*) (see 1923, 1971 quots.).

1918 *Stars & Stripes* (Apr. 19) 1: The city police will look after the lounge lizard and similar ornaments in particular. **1918** in K. Morse *Letters* 169: This is the Lounge Lizard's Roost. **1918** *Wadsworth Gas Attack* 7: I wasn't cut out for no lounge lizard. **1918** Mencken *Amer. Lang.* 163: Nothing could exceed the brilliancy of…lounge-lizard. **1921** in *DA:* The dead man looked to him like what was at one time expressively called a "lounge lizard." **1922** S. Lewis *Babbitt* 66: Zilla keeps rooting for a nice expensive vacation in New York and Atlantic City, with the bright lights and the boot-legged cocktails and a bunch of lounge-lizards to dance with. **1923** McKnight *Eng. Wds.* 62: The young man who does not take his girl about is a *chair-warmer*, a *lounge lizard.* **1925** in *DA:* Who will know a generation hence…that a…lounge lizard is one who suns himself eternally in good society. **1929** T. Gordon *Born to Be* 171: I played the part of lounge lizzard for men who couldn't find time to take their wives out. **1931** Uhler *Cane Juice* 64: They were he-men then—no lounge-lizards. **1940** *Encyc. Britannica* s.v. "Slang": *Lounge-lizard*, man who haunts tearooms for flirtation. **1950** Bissell *Stretch on the River* 6: I could…see myself as a…lounge lizard in dress suit. **1956** McPeek & Wright *Handbk. of Eng.* 67: Consider the chances [of survival] of the following: *all washed up,…blurb,…lounge-lizard,…B.M.O.C.* **1971** Morris & Morris *Dict. Wd. & Phr. Origs.* III 165: *Lounge lizard* In the 1920's this term was popular slang …[for] a chap who…operated a bit on the cheap side. His idea of a great evening was lounging in the quarters of his lady fair, the target of his evil designs. **1977** *American Way* (June) 28: Valentino worked there as a lounge lizzard [*sic*], and his job was to dance with the unescorted women. **1979** Levi jeans ad (WINS radio) (Dec. 20): *Not* the fancy styles you'd see on some lounge lizard. Just grown-up pants. **1981** *N.Y. Times* (Aug. 2) II 21: I pushed to get good roles…but the playboy image was too strong. Any time a character called for a good-looking suit and polished hair, they wanted me. I had a corner on the lounge-lizard market. **1984** *Cheers* (NBC-TV): The mating ritual of the…lounge lizard. **1985** "Blowdryer" *Mod. Eng.* 25: *Lounge lizards*…frequent the same clubs, night after night. **1991** Gergen *Saturated Self* xi: [The] lounge lizards will soon move on.

lour *n.* [orig. unkn.] *Und.* cash; money.

*****1566** Harman, in Partridge *Dict. Und.* 418: Lowre, monye….Why, hast thou any lowre in thy bonge to bouse? *****1673** [R. Head] *Canting Acad.* 40: *Lowr*, money. **1791** [W. Smith] *Confess. T. Mount* 18: Cash, *lowr. Ibid.* 20: To do them of their lowr,/It was our only care. **1807** Tufts *Autobiog.* 292 [ref. to 1794]: *Lour*…money. *****1812** Vaux *Vocab.*: *Lour*: money. *****1839** Brandon *Poverty, Mendicity, Crime* (gloss.): *Lowr*—coin.

louse *n.* **1.** a contemptible or despicable individual; lowlife; (*specif.*) (in 20th C.) one who is unfair, untrustworthy, or the like.—also used attrib.—pl. often constr. as *louses*. [Bracketed quots. seemingly show literary metaphors conveying the sense 'a parasitical person'; the present broader usage does not appear until the 19th C.]

[*****1633** in *OED:* Come away, fellow louse, thou art ever eating.] [*****1771** T. Smollett, in Rawson *Wicked Words* 241: He damns all other writers of the age….One is a blunderbuss…another a half-starved louse of literature.] **1864** Northrop *Chronicles* 28: Those who saw him hissed and cried "pimp, louse, fool" and other epithets. **1894** in F. Remington *Sel. Letters* 212: You may have to come out here and help us lick the lice from Central Europe. **1895** W.N. Wood *Big I* 115 [ref. to Civil War]: "Strange, you are a damned old louse." "Take that man to the guard house," was the reply. **1914** H.L. Mencken, in Riggio *Dreiser-Mencken Letters* I 141: The news that Kennerley is playing the louse brings no surprise. **1915** Bronson-Howard *God's Man* 362: Nobody has any sympathy for that kind of lice. **1916** S. Lewis *Job* 75: It was not too severe an indictment to refer to the advertising-manager as "S. Herbert Louse." **1918** in Niles, Moore & Wallgren *Songs* 48: Oh, it's grouse, grouse, grouse,/Our Colonel is a louse. **1922** in Butterfield *Post Treasury* 266: H-he's dad's cousin. He's a louse. **1926** C.M. Russell *Trails* 15: He don't need no gun to clean up that big louse. **1927** [Fliesler] *Anecdota* 74: Bastard!…Louse! **1927** *Amer. Leg. Mo.* (May) 25: You louse M.P. *****1927** R. Graves *Lars Porsena* 23: But the imputation of lousiness…carries serious implications with it; and…"You louse!" is ripe with hatred. **1929–30** Farrell *Young Lonigan* 66: Those guys were all louses. **1930** Fredenburgh *Soldiers March!* 15:

Bill, you louse! **1931** *AS* VI (Aug.) 439: *Louse.* A police informer; a convict who tells tales about other inmates. **1933** J.T. Farrell *To Whom It May Concern* 107: Yes, Tom felt like a louse. **1934** J.M. Cain *Postman* 75: That's what Sackett said when he put the spot on me, the louse. **1934** D. Maurer, in *AS* (Feb. 1935) 18 : *Louse….* A smalltime crook or petty thief. **1935** Odets *Lefty* 21: And the guy you're poking at? A real louse, just like you. **1936** Dai *Opium Addiction* 201: *Lice.* Informers. Also called *mice, rats, stool pigeons, stools,* etc. **1938** Bezzerides *Long Haul* 21: If I was a louse, I'd be in the can, wouldn't I? **1942** Rodgers & Hammerstein *Oklahoma!* 53: Don't treat him like a louse,/Make him welcome in yer house. **1948** A. Murphy *Hell & Back* 196: How you rear echelon lice feel now? **1949** *Sat. Eve. Post* (Oct. 8) 125: There was at least a strong likelihood that Scott Winship could not be a complete louse. **1968** M.B. Scott *Racing Game* 132: "Louse books" (the small, independent bookies). **1979** in Terkel *Amer. Dreams* 253: I may be a louse, but I want to be me. **1981** D. Burns *Feeling Good* 41: He's a goddam louse. **1982** M. Mann *Elvis* 48: I brushed those louses off but good. **1989** *Donahue* (NBC-TV) (May 12): I think this guy is a little bit of a louse for still associating with these women. **1990** G. Lee *China Boy* 158: Outta my cafe, you louse!

2. an idler or lounger; no-account.—used with qualifying *n.* See also LOBBY LOUSE.

[**1920** Bissell *63rd Inf.* 86: Some desk cootie discovered that the notary public had omitted the second "m" in the fourth word of the sixth line of the third page and he had the whole thing started all over again.] **1931** *AS* (June) 330: *Carnival-louse,* n. A hanger-on who follows a carnival, but who has no official connection with it. **1941** B. Schulberg *Sammy* 106: She had chased her share of brassy guys out of the office, ad-space salesmen and small-time agents and the usual studio lounge-lice. **1958** A. King *Mine Enemy* 70: Most of them were professional booze lice who crawled from one *vernissage* to another.

3. something of very poor quality.

1929 Goulding & Mason *Broadway Melody* (film): "The act is a louse." "It's not a louse."

louse *v.* to cheat (out of).

1958 Cooley *Run for Home* 316 [ref. to *a*1930]: We kind of loused you out of a place to sleep, didn't we?

louse around *v.* **1.** to loiter or fool about; trifle.

*ca*1920 in *DARE:* I don't see no use in jist louzin' around. **1923** *DN* V 214: *Louse around….*to loiter about aimlessly. **1932** *AS* VII (June) 334: *Louse around*—to loiter; to "kill time." **1934** Appel *Brain Guy* 75: Either be in the dough or get wiped. No use lousing around. *****1965** in D. Behan *Ireland Sings* 22: Oh, the boss is dead, the boss is dead….I'm going to louse around all day.

2. to mistreat; cheat.

1942–49 Goldin et al. *DAUL:* That creep loused me around for my broad…and my case dough.

louse cage *n.* **1.** a hat or cap. *Joc.*

1893 *DN* I 398: *Louse-cage:* n. common among school boys for "hat." Ill….Ia….N.E….N.Y. **1907** *DN* III 246: *Louse cage*…Hat or cap. Slang. **1925** *AS* I (Dec.) 137: In the bunkhouse they hang up their "louse cages"—hats—and "souse themselves."

2. a bunkhouse or railway caboose.

1925 *AS* I (Dec.) 138: They [I.W.W. lumbermen] took the term "louse cage (hat) and applied it to the whole bunkhouse. **1954–60** *DAS: Louse-cage…*A railroad caboose; a bunkhouse.

louse-catcher *n.* a fine-tooth comb used for removing lice.—also used fig.

1862 in C.H. Moulton *Ft. Lyon* 31: Handkerchiefs, needles, thread, "louse-catchers," etc. **1935** E. Levinson *Strikes* 67: Among the lordly nobles, finks are known also as "louse catchers."

louse house *n.* a verminous jail, lodging house, or the like.

*****1785** Grose *Vulgar Tongue: Louse house.* The round house, cage, or any other place of confinement. **1904** *Life in Sing Sing* 256: *Louse house.* Lodging house. **1928** C. MacArthur *War Bugs* 300: First-class soldiers who had the misfortune to embark from that louse-house port. **1931** *Amer. Mercury.* (Dec.) 413: He'd rather do six months in the louse-house. *Ibid.* 420: And they threw Hymie and poor Jack in the louse-house. **1935** in Partridge *Dict. Und.* 418: *Louse house…*A cheap hotel on the Bowery.

louse pasture *n.* a filthy individual.

*a*1868 G.W. Harris *Lovingood* 288: You dirty, drabbil-tail, slop eatin', ole louse pasture.

louser *n.* LOUSE.

    1934 H. Roth *Call It Sleep* 213 [ref. to *ca*1910]: He's a louser! He hits! **1935** Algren *Boots* 83: Awright, lousers, come awn out now. ***1960, *1966, *1968** in *OED2*.

louse trap *n.* [perh. sugg. by earlier BrE sense, 'a fine-tooth comb used for removing lice', as in "B.E." *Dict. Canting Crew* and Grose *Dict. Vulgar Tongue*] **1.** LOUSE CAGE, 1. *Joc.*

    1912 *DN* III 582: *Louse-trap, n.* A hat. The word is usually addressed to children. "Well, take off your *louse-trap* and stay awhile." **1941** *AS* (Feb.) 23: *Louse trap*. Hat or cap.

    2. LOUSE HOUSE; FLEABAG, 2.a.

    1946 Mezzrow & Wolfe *Really Blues* 45: It was like the Waldorf-Astoria compared to the louse-trap I'd been in first. **1942–49** Goldin et al. *DAUL: Louse trap.* A cheap lodging house; a verminous prison or jail.

louse-up *n.* a thing or situation that is problematic, botched, etc.; SCREW-UP.

    1971 *Pop. Sci.* (May) 26: Other louse-ups could be lack of good valve-stem seals, leaking in the manifold gasket, or improper crankcase venting. **1971** *Seattle Times* (June 13) H5: For me, that would just be a louse-up. **1977** *Pop. Sci.* (Apr.) 20: Give any assignment to a committee and the odds are in favor of a louse-up somewhere.

louse up *v.* **1.a.** to infest with lice. Hence **loused-up**, *adj.*

    1918 *Wadsworth Gas Attack* 12: That question being definitely decided upon we assume that we are right in our contention that the rest of the company evidently are loused up. **1931** in *OED2*: The last troupe loused up the beddin'. **1934** Kromer *Waiting* 97: I can't louse the jail up by locking you up. ***1968** in *OED2*: I was occasionally loused-up myself.

    b. *Pris.* to wash or delouse oneself.

    1929 Barr *Let Tomorrow Come* 4: G'wan in there and louse up. And if you slop up the floor, then clean it up again.

    2.a. *Trans.* to ruin; spoil; botch; thwart. Hence **loused up**, *adj.*

    1934 O'Hara *Appt. in Samarra* ch. ii: Lousing up your date. **1936** N. West *Cool Million* 233: He has loused the continent up good. **1938** *AS* (Oct.) 195: *Louse up* the show. **1939–40** O'Hara *Pal Joey* 25: 27: That is all loused up too. **1948** I. Shulman *Cry Tough!* 210: Everything's being loused up. If we paid people to make a mish-mash of everything they couldn't've done a better job. **1948** Lay & Bartlett *12 O'Clock High!* 22: Why can't we fight a war over here…without having the joint loused up with babes during working hours? **1950** Spillane *Vengeance* 8: Quit lousing me up, Mike. I want to find out what happened. **1951** D. Wilson *Six Convicts* 126: Jeez—ain't it a shame how a delicate mechanism can get all loused up. **1952** in Hemingway *Sel. Letters* 784: There is no reason I should louse-up your project that you worked so hard on. **1953** Peterson *Take Giant Step* 48: Well, I sure loused myself up proper this time. **1956** Resko *Reprieve* 115: So who the hell would want to louse me up? **1957** Leckie *Helmet for Pillow* 117: C'mon, don't go doing something stupid now, and louse yourself up. **1957** in Algren *Lonesome Monsters* 136: Really loused up, wasn't she? **1959** M. Harris *Wake Up* 214: Now you've gone and loused everything up. **1961** Clausen *Season's Over* 7: Get up there fast and quit lousin' up my act. **1961** in Cannon *Nobody Asked* 141: In my neighborhood you only wanted a lawyer when you got pinched. But fighters get them to louse up a manager. **1963** J. Ross *Dead Are Mine* 83: Something, I don't know why, always seems to louse me up. **1966** Bogner *7th Ave.* 427: I'm not gonna have a kid louse up the whole setup. **1968** Wojciechowska *Tuned Out* 19: I don't want to get my point of view loused up. **1969** Merrick *Lord Won't Mind* 208: Make sure you don't do anything that'll louse up your life. **1969** *Playboy* (Dec.) 118: The bread and all the fame hasn't loused me up. **1978** in Lyle & Golenbock *Bronx Zoo* 185: Loused up another one today. **1984** C. Francis *Who's Sorry?* 15: Sorry I loused up your big plans, Daddy!

    b. *Intrans.* to blunder; SCREW UP.

    1942–49 Goldin et al. *DAUL: Louse up*…To blunder and fail in a criminal enterprise. **1957** Myrer *Big War* 372 [ref. to WWII]: He'd louse up now for sure. **1958** J. Davis *College Vocab.* 15: *Louse up*—Make a mistake. **1944–61** D.K. Webster *Para. Inf.* 154: If they loused up once, they'll do it again. *a*1988 D. Smith *Firefighters* 202: I loused up. **1989** Martorano & Kildahl *Neg. Thinking* 15: Things are going down the tubes at work. I keep lousing up. **1996** *Good Morning America* (ABC-TV) (Oct. 30): You're gonna go out there and you're going to mess up, you're going to foul up, and you're going to louse up.

lousy *adj.* **1.** (orig. of persons and animals) despicable; contemptible; ignoble; base; vile; "dirty." Occ. as adv. Now *colloq.* [Orig. S.E.; in 20th C., subsumed by **(2)**, below.]

    ca*1386 Chaucer *Friar's Tale,* in *OED:* A lowsy Iogelour kan deceyue thee. ***1532** in *OED:* He loueth her with suche a lewde lowsye loue, as the lewde lousy louer in lechery loueth himself. ***1562** in *OED:* His base birth and lowsy lynage. ***1566** Harman *Caveat:* Here I set before the good reader the lewd, lousy language of these loitering lusks and lazy lorels. ***1599** Shakespeare *Henry V* IV viii: What an arrant, rascally, beggarly, lousy knave it is! ***1641** R. Brome, in R.G. Lawrence *Comedies* 225: Play this lousy game no further. ***1669** *New Acad. of Complements* 95: 'Tis not lousie Beer, boys,/But Wine that makes a Poet. ***1681** in Otway *Works* II 102: Fogh, ye Lowsy Red-coat rake hells. ***1708** in *OED:* Wicked Rhimes…sung to lowsey Tunes. ***1768** in *OED:* You can never after…be anything…but a lousy prebendary. **1776** J. Leacock *Fall of Brit. Tyranny* IV vii: A damn'd lousy, beggarly trade. ***1786** in *OED:* I might pick up the lousy guinea myself and be damned! ******ca*1798** in *Frisky Songster* 88: Our lousy landlord blamed me,/For doing of the deed. ***1804** in Wetherell *Adventures* 121: Them lousey Frenchmen. ***1821–26** Stewart *Man-of-War's-Man* I 49: "Mayhap, taking a small drop of grog, when one can touch it, may be both lubberly and lousy—" "Lousy! why, Jack, he didn't say lousy, man—he said beastly." *Ibid.* 50: You are a low, lubberly, lousy swab, Gibby! *Ibid.* II 216: I've been dragged forward in this lousy manner. **1839** in *DA:* True Friends of Freedom assailed with lousy lies. **1841** *Crockett Almanac* (unp.): This lousy, ignorant, unsuspicious heathen varmint. **1848** in Peskin *Vols.* 226: A lot of lousy Dutch and still more worthless natives. **1855** in Dwyer & Lingenfelter *Songs of Gold Rush* 33: Both tired and mad, without a cent, they damned the lousy hole [*sc.,* California]. *Ibid.* 42: Let's buy him out, the lousy son of a bitch. **1863** "E. Kirke" *So. Friends* 58: Har, you lousy sorrel-top…har, give us some mugs. **1864** Brobst *Letters* 34: Well, if that don't beat the lousy grayback rebs—. **1865** Andrus *Letters* 120: How I must pity the *Lousey Dog*. He certainly ought to have exemption from military duty on *acct.* of being a Damned Idiot. **1882** D.J. Cook *Hands Up* 178: You d—d lousy s-n of a b—— I won't pay it. **1885** in Lummis *Letters* 288: Reviled as "lousy horse thieves." ***1888** R. Kipling *The Big Drunk Draf':* Take ut off an' dance, ye lousy civilian! **1906** (quot. at BEAN, 1.a.). **1910** in Kornbluh *Rebel Voices* 74: That we might serve the master for the lousy dollar. **1913** J. London *Valley of Moon* 83: It's…an unfair, lousy world. **1915** H.L. Mencken, in Riggio *Dreiser-Mencken Letters* I 208: Who in hell is N.P.D.? Some lousy old maid? **1916** L. Stillwell *Common Soldier* 195 [ref. to Civil War]: Say, do you fellows suppose that we commanding officers…are going to give away to a lot of lousy privates a confidential communication from the Colonel? **1920** in Hemingway *Sel. Letters* 44: Did I send you one of the lousy magazines? **1929–30** Dos Passos *42d Parallel* 13: It's the system, John, it's the goddam lousy system. **1931** in *AS* VII 436 (Aug. 1932): A man drunk is "limp,"…"lousy drunk," "canned," [etc.]. **1933** R. Howard *Yellow Jack* 472: I was just a lousy lumberjack when he took me on! **1938** "R. Hallas" *You Play the Black* 2: Some place better than this lousy Oklahoma mining town. **1942** Liebling *Telephone* 65: There isn't a dime left in this lousy business. **1948** Maresca *My Flag* 142: You lousy cabdrivers are making hundreds of dollars a week these days. ***1966** Christopher *Little People* 179: Because you're so lousy jealous. **1995** N.Y.C. woman, age 60: *Now* I see what's wrong! I've got to enter the lousy *fucking* Zip Code of the *post-office* box!

    2. very poor in quality or ability; very bad (in any standard sense: extremely unpleasant; markedly inferior, unsatisfactory, or unskillful; ill or in low spirits; etc.). Also as adv. Now *colloq.* [The difficulty of separating the present, extended sense from **(1)**, above, partially accounts for the dearth of clear-cut, pre–20th-C. quots. Note that *DAS* and *OED2* accept an "1849" date for the material from Woodward dated *a*1944 below; yet its purported ms. source ("Andy Gordon's diary") is *prima facie* a pastiche innocently created for the purposes of historical fiction.]

    1807 J.R. Shaw *Autobiog.* 124: In as…miserable and lousy a situation as ever I remember to have been in. ***1821–26** Stewart *Man-of-War's-Man* II 70: We succeeded in taking an old lousy boat from a mob of your fishing chaps. **1928** *AS* III 345: "Lousy." How long will the vogue for this unpleasant adjective continue? It is applied indiscriminately and means nothing in particular except that it is always a term of disparagement….It is a comment on our period that it has lifted it into currency, tolerated it, and made no protest. **1928** Santee

Cowboy 120: Next to ridin' fence, wranglin' horses is the lousiest job in camp. **1929** in D. Parker *Portable D. Parker* 191: Crab, crab, crab, crab, that was all she ever did. What a lousy sport *she* was! **1929** J.M. Saunders *Single Lady* 25: "Did you graduate or anything?" "Magna cum lousy." **1930** in E. O'Neill *Letters* 371: It has been a lousy summer. **1933** N. West *Lonelyhearts* 46: I felt swell…and now I feel lousy. **1934** J.M. Cain, in *DAS:* "How are you?" "Lousy." **1936** *Amer. Mercury* (May) 93: The service here is getting lousy. **1937** I. Shaw *Sailor Off Bremen* 107: He's been pitching lousy. **1941** Foerster & Steadman *Writing & Thinking* 290: To confine one's critical adjectives to *swell* and *lousy* certainly does not indicate much critical ability. **1943** in Tapert *Lines* 72: Quinine…[makes] you feel weak and lousy. *a***1944** W.E. Woodward *Way Our People Lived* 268: "I wish I could never hear the word *lousy* again. I am willing to bet that Tommy Plunkett uses it fifty times a day, but he is no worse than the others. It is 'lousy' this and 'lousy' that. The rain is lousy, the trail is lousy, the bacon is lousy…and Gus Thorpe, losing in the card game, has just said that he has had a lousy deal."…[Ed. fn.:] The use of the word "lousy" as a slang term began during the 1849 gold rush. **1945** Peeples *Swing Low* 251: No, Willy Mack, it doesn't look right. It looks lousy. **1948** in *DA:* The book was lousy; the movie was slightly less so. **1948** in *DAS:* "How goes it?" "Lousy." *****1950** in *OED2:* She felt too lousy to come to work. **1951** in *DAS:* You make lousy witnesses. **1958** in Mjelde *Glory of Seas* 193: On the coast [a ship's] food was very good. On a long trip it's lousy. **1961** P. Marshall *Soul Clap Hands* 137: You did everything wrong. You were lousy. **1963** Blechman *Omongo* 139: What a lousy movie! **1964** Thompson & Rice *Every Diamond* 3: No matter how lousy we might play. **1965** Cassavetes *Faces* 127: I feel lousy. **1968** Johnson & Johnson *Count Me Gone* 144: Lousy luck. **1969** N.Y.C. woman, age 50: He treats you lousy. **1971** Patten *Track of Hunter* 20: The whole deal was rotten lousy. **1970–72** Densen-Gerber *Drugs, Sex, Parents* 77: This lousy cold. **1976** N.Y.C. man, age 28: You look lousy. Must be the flu. *a***1977** M. French *Women's Room* 245: I'll bet your husband is a lousy lover. **1978** in Lyle & Golenbock *Bronx Zoo* 248: He was lousy. He couldn't have caught a ground ball with a shovel. **1979** Kunstler *Wampanaki Tales* 2: Your table manners are simply lousy. **1981** D. Burns *Feeling Good* 42: I always do lousy on tests. **1989** Hiaasen *Skin Tight* 12: It went lousy. *a***1991** in *World Bk. Dictionary:* Bridge…is so hard that everybody's lousy at it. **1995** *Reader's Digest* (Mar.) 68: Who gave you that lousy haircut? **1996** *Kindred* (Fox-TV): You look lousy.

¶ In phrase:

¶ **lousy with** teeming or swarming with; well supplied with; abundant with. [Orig. S.E. The uniquely early use by Nashe is almost certainly fortuitous.]

*****1593–94** T. Nashe *Terrors of Night,* in *Works* I 349: The *Druides* that dwelt in the Ile of *Man,* which are famous for great coniurers, are reported to haue beene lousie with familiars. Had they but put their finger and their thumbe into their neck, they could haue pluckt out a whole neast of them. **1843** *Spirit of Times* (Mar. 4) 7: *He was lousy with money,* and dared any man to face him. **1850** in *DAE:* I struck a crevice in the bed-rock on the rim of the creek and it was lousy with gold. **1861** in E. West *Saloon* 6: Lousy with lawyers, pettifoggers and scrub doctors. **1868** J. Chisholm *So. Pass* 46: The vein…, to use a miner's phrase, is "lousy" with gold. **1870** "M. Twain," in A.L. Scott *Twain's Poetry* 79: My hand was frequent *lousy* with both bowers and the ace. **1915** C. Peters *Autobiog.* 186: The clay…was "lousy" with gold. **1917** in F. Lee *No Parachute* 187: At the salient the air was positively lousy with D-Vs at all levels. **1920** Riggs & Platt *Btry. F* 52: It made excellent concealment for guns and the bushes on the left of the road were "lousy" with big artillery. **1920–23** in J.M. Hunter *Trail Drivers* II 978: Stating that the country was "lousy" with Indians. **1926** C.M. Russell *Trails* 25: The country was lousy with meat but in open spaces it ain't easy to get when you're afoot. **1927** in Hammett *Big Knockover* 282: Everybody in on it will come home lousy with cash. *****1928** in *OED2:* The Totsuka Club was…"just lousy with liars." **1928** Dobie *Vaquero* 164: The average old time range man would not have known a "folk-tale" by name from Adam's off ox; just the same the open range was "lousy" with folk-tales. **1928** C. McKay *Banjo* 7: This heah burg is lousy with piformers. **1929** Brecht *Downfall* 302: The street's lousy with 'em new Fords. **1933** Odets *Awake & Sing!* 95: No, I see every house lousy with lies and hate. **1938** "R. Hallas" *You Play the Black* 120: The roads are lousy with hitchers. **1942** Garcia *Tough Trip* 96: It was a good all-around country to trap and hunt being just lousy with

beaver. **1951** Sheldon *Troubling of a Star* 134: Plenty. This place is lousy with troops down here. **1951** Haines & Burnett *Racket* (film): It's lousy with fingerprints. **1953** Wicker *Kingpin* 82: Whatever class is. You're lousy with it.

Lousy Anna n. Louisiana.—used disparagingly. *Joc.*
     1980 Bruns *Kts. of Road* 202: *Lousy Anna.* Less than affectionate title for Louisiana, a state less than hospitable to hoboes. **1982** F. Hailey *Soldier Talk* 39: *Lousyanna.* How soldiers referred to the State of Louisiana during army maneuvers there in 1941.

love n. ¶ In phrase: **for the love of Mike!** [orig. euphem. for *for the love of God*] (used to express exasperation, impatience, disappointment, etc.). Also vars., esp. **for the love of Pete.**
     1892 in S. Crane *Comp. Stories* 95: For the love of Mike, tell us, Billie. *ca***1892** in *Ibid.* 97: "For the love of Mike, madam, what ails you?" he spluttered. **1894** in S. Crane *N.Y.C. Sks.* 106: Well, for the love of Mike! **1906** S. Ford *Shorty McCabe* 303: Say, for the love of Pete, I couldn't tell what it was gave me a grouch. **1907** Corbin *Cave Man* 94: For the love of Mike, man, kill the cat! **1908** in H.C. Fisher *A. Mutt* 161: Oh! Pa, for the love of Mike speak to muh! **1910** in O. Johnson *Lawrenceville Stories* 197: And for the love of Mike, hustle 'em. **1910** T.A. Dorgan, in *N.Y. Eve. Jour.* (Apr. 18) 14: F'r the love o' Mike, please let me go. **1911** Howard *Enemy to Society* 234: For the love of Mike! **1912** *Pedagog. Sem.* (Mar.) 96: For the love of Mike…For Pat's sake. **1912** *Adventure* (June) 245: Go and get 'em, then, for the love o' Mike. **1912** Mathewson *Pitching* 47: Matty,…for the love of Mike, slip this fellow a base on balls and let me get my wind. **1914** Paine *Wall Between* 260: For the love of Mike, will somebody give me a drink? **1914** S. Lewis *Mr. Wrenn* 143: Say, for the love of Mike, don't let him know I told you. **1914** E.R. Burroughs *Mucker* 122: For de love o' Mike! Beat it! **1917** E.R. Burroughs *Oakdale Affair* 54: Fer the luv o' Mike have a heart! Don't leave us out here! **1918** in Rossano *Price of Honor* 217: For the love of Pete get me out of this. *****1914–22** J. Joyce *Ulysses* 778: For the love of Mike listen to him the winds that waft my sighs to thee. **1924** *DN* V 274: For the love of mud!…For the love of Pete! for Pete's sake! **1930** Dos Passos *42d Parallel* 112: Ben laughed. "Oh, for the love of Mike!" **1938** "E. Queen" *4 Hearts* 39: Not here, for the love of Mike. **1942** Breslow *Blondie Goes to College* (film): Bumstead! For the love of Joe! **1992** *Murphy Brown* (CBS-TV): Oh, for the love of Mike! **1994** *Mystery Sci. Theater* (Comedy Central TV): Oh, for the love of Pete! **1996** Boam *Phantom* (film): I was an altar boy, for the love of Pete! **1996** *Simpsons Comics* (No. 21) (unp.): Ach, for the love a' Pete!

love v. to fondle, caress, or engage in other sexual activity (with).—often constr. with *up.* See also LADY-LOVE, *v.*
     1876 in *DARE:* I was only a-lovin' you, cos you was good, and brought us candy. **1889** in *DARE:* Putting his arms round her neck, [he] "loved" her with his cheek against hers. **1914** *DN* IV 159: *Love*…to hug. **1920** O'Neill *Diff'rent* 231: No, all I'll say is, that to the boys who've knocked around over there [in France] the girls in town here are just rank amatoors. They don't know how to love and that's a fact. **1921** Dos Passos *Three Soldiers* 83: "You said you were goin' back and love up that goddam girl." "Did I?" said Fuselli, giggling. **1927** S. Lewis *Elmer Gantry* 16 [ref. to 1902]: Damn these co-eds here. The few that'll let you love 'em up, they hang around trying to catch you on the campus and make you propose to 'em. **1928** *DN* VI 62: If a hillman does admit that he loved a woman he means only that he caressed and embraced her—and he usually says that he *loved her up.* **1929–30** Dos Passos *42d Parallel* 95: She was saying in a little hotsweet voice, "Love me up, kid." **1932–34** Minehan *Boy & Girl Tramps* 143: In a mission older men give boys…candy…and take them into the toilet…and love them up. **1937** *Life* (June 7) 29: On isolated campuses romance is "smooching," "perching," "mugging," "loving up" or "flinging woo." **1970** *CeaCritic* (Feb.) 16: Dr. Joseph Whitt, more intuitive, loved him up and called him *le petit monstre.*

¶ In phrase:
¶ **love 'em and leave 'em** to seduce and abandon women.
     [*****1885** in *OED2: Love you and leave you,* a common saying [in Chester] when any visitor is going to take his departure. "Well, a' mun *love ye, an' leave ye.*"] **1923** J.V. Weaver *Finders* 28: Love 'em and Leave 'em—that's me, from now on. **1930** Dos Passos *42d Parallel* 95 [ref. to *ca*1910]: Love 'em and leave 'em, that's the only way for stiffs like us. **1945** Drake & Cayton *Black Metropolis* 584: The men, insecure in their economic power, tend to exalt their sexual prowess. They cultivate an attitude of "love 'em and leave 'em." *****1975** in *OED2.*

lovebirds *n.pl.* persons who are foolishly in love. Now *colloq.*

    1938 "E. Queen" *4 Hearts* 48: Suppose our friends the lovebirds refuse to be exploited? **1941** "G.R. Lee" *G-String Murders* 213: The two of them sailed out of the saloon arm in arm, two lovebirds on their way to…Forty-second Street. **1949** in *DAS:* Ma barged in on the love birds. **1972–75** W. Allen *Feathers* 136: Now we'll see what happens with you lovebirds. **1988** Cogan & Ferguson *Presidio* 10: Scared away a couple of lovebirds.

love boat *n.* **1.** an especially attractive member of the opposite sex; DREAMBOAT.

    1944 A. Scott et al. *Here Come WAVES* (film): You've always been my love boat!

2. a boat on which people engage in romantic or sexual activity. [Introduced by the ABC-TV series *The Love Boat* (premiered Sept. 17, 1977), about romantic escapades aboard a cruise ship.]

    1977 *The Love Boat* (ABC-TV). **1981** Raban *Old Glory* 296 [ref. to *ca*1920]: The "love boats" had come down from St. Louis: sternwheeled brothels with a girl in every cabin. **1983–86** G.C. Wilson *Supercarrier* 47: This is a capital warship, not a love boat. **1992** *New Yorker* (Jan. 13) 65: The S.D.U. sponsors lectures on how to date women, along with a variety of other activities, including evening cruises to nowhere that are dubbed "love boats." **1996** *New Yorker* (Sept. 16) 72: Ten per cent of these women had been evacuated because of pregnancy. The ship…became known as the Love Boat.

3. *Narc.* phencyclidine (PCP), esp. as mixed with marijuana; (*also*) a cigar or cigarette containing this. Cf. LOVELY.

    1987 R.M. Jackson, in *Black Amer. Lit. Forum* XXI 249: Pushing love boat, reefer/and smack. **1988** *West 57th* (CBS-TV): Some call it Angel Dust. Some call it Love Boat. It's PCP. **1989** *U.S. News & W.R.* (Apr. 10) 31: By 1985, they were also selling "Love Boat," or PCP. **1992** *Wash. Post* (Sept. 12) B1: He told me they were smoking loveboats—it's where they take a cigar and take the tobacco out and put in marijuana and PCP.

love bone *n.* the penis, esp. when erect.—usu. considered vulgar. *Joc.* Cf. BONE.

    1962 Crump *Killer* 386: Ya make me nervous…and my love bone goes down. *a*1994 Smitherman *Black Talk* 56: *Love bone* See Bone ["the penis"].

love box *n.* **1.** the heart. *Joc.*

    1865 (quot. at COOK, *v.*, 2.a.).

2. the vagina or vulva.—usu. considered vulgar. *Joc.* Cf. BOX, 1.a.

    1986 *UTSQ:* Vagina…*honey pot…love box.* **1988** Univ. Tenn. student theme: An offending but humorous name for a woman's reproductive organ is *love box.* **1989** *Maledicta* X 54: Vulva…*love-tunnel…love-box.* **1996** *Re: Fingering a Girl,* on Usenet newsgroup t-netz.sex.stories: Have her guide your head…over and around her love box.

lovebug *n.* a putative microbe responsible for people falling in love.

    1907 T.A. Dorgan, in Zwilling *TAD Lexicon* 55: (The Little Love Microbe That Does The Mischief) Oh I do wish at one o dem love bugs would spear him.

2. a frequently infatuated person.

    1981 O'Day & Eells *High Times* 54: Trilby was a lovebug, in and out of love every week.

love button *n.* the clitoris.—usu. considered vulgar. *Joc.* Cf. BUTTON, 3.a.

    *a*1994 A. Radakovich *Wild Girls Club* 131: Head right to the love button. **1995** *Fat Cock,* pornographic story on Usenet newsgroup alt.sex.stories: When his tongue pounced on my love button I almost passed out with ecstasy. **1995** *Story No. 5 for the Ladies—Caught!,* pornographic story on Usenet newsgroup alt.sex.stories: You felt your love button begin to stir.

love canal *n.* [punning on *Love Canal,* N.Y., site of a highly publicized ecological scandal in 1983] the vagina.—usu. considered vulgar. *Joc.*

    [**1983** N.Y.C. man, age *ca*35: "Love Canal." Can you believe that? What were those people *thinking*?] **1987** *UTSQ:* Vagina…*love canal.* *a*1988 Lewin & Lewin *Thes. Slang* 411: Vagina…*bearded clam,…love canal.*

love glove *n.* **1.** a condom. *Joc.* Cf. GLOVE.

    1987 *TV Guide* (Nov. 7) 6: But although their standards and prac-

tices permitted the words "prophylactic" and "contraceptive" [on a network TV program], and even a student who calls a condom a "love glove," the word "condom" was not allowed. **1991** *Boston Globe* (Nov. 13): A "glow in the dark love glove." **1994** *Men's Health* (July) (Nexis): CONDOMS. RUBBERS. Jimmy hats. Love gloves. Whatever you call them, they're not effective for contraception or protection unless you use them properly. **1995** *Interview* (June) (Nexis): Load up the car with everything you need for a picnic: lounges, boom box, hammock, baseball gloves, little white gloves, love gloves.

2. the vagina.—usu. considered vulgar.

    1989 *Playboy* (Feb.): The pet name for his yang (Enormous Heat-Seeking Moisture Missile, [etc].) and for her love glove (Alice, Gertrude and One Size Fits All).

love gun *n.* the penis.—usu. considered vulgar. *Joc.* Cf. GUN, 1.

    1978 in *Maledicta* VI (1982) 23: Penis…*love gun.* **1981** *Penthouse* (Apr.) 12: My love gun was aiming right at her face. **1997** *Movieline* (May) 58: He…whips out his jaw-dropping love gun.

love handle *n.* usu. *pl.* a bulge of fat at the side of the waist. *Joc.*

    1968–70 *Current Slang III & IV* 80: *Love handles,* n. The fat on one's sides.—New Mexico State. **1970** Landy *Underground Dict.: Love handle n.* The side and back part of the body at waist level where a bulge of fat may be….Flank fat. **1975** (cited in *W10*). **1984** *PM Magazine* (ABC-TV) (June 13): Now we're gonna get rid of those love handles. **1985** *L.A. Times* (Jan. 28) V 2: We begin to refer to our excess inches by endearing names like *love handles.* **1987** *Time* (Sept. 28) 58: Every middle-aged trauma from the onset of love handles around the midsection. **1987** *Rage* (Univ. Tenn.) (No. 3) 32: I hate…guys with acne…and love handles. **1989** "Mojo Nixon" *I'm a Wreck* (pop. song): Little love handles sticking out like fishing piers.

love hole *n.* **1.** the vagina.—usu. considered vulgar. *Joc.* Cf. HOLE.

    1986 *UTSQ:* Vagina…*box…love hole.* **1992** *Letters to Penthouse* III 193: I inserted my tongue into her love hole.

2. *Mil. Av.* an aircraft aperture used for refueling in flight. *Joc.*

    1988 M. Maloney *Thunder Alley* 96: The male organ-shaped nozzle would fit into the boom's "love hole" receptacle.

love housing var. LOVE MACHINE, 2.

love-in *n.* **1.** a public gathering for the expression of love; (*specif.*) an orgy. [Assoc. esp. with the hippies of the late 1960's.]

    1967 *L.A. Times* (Mar. 27) I 26: Bergman denied that the "love-in" was conceived and scheduled as an irritant to the Christian observance of Easter. **1967** in *OED2* (Mar. 28): The "love-in" in Elysian Park, Los Angeles, was equally odd but caused no more than a traffic jam. **1967** *L.A. Times* (May 22) I 3: A weekend "commercial love-in" ended quietly…Sunday after three carloads of Hell's Angels believed to be headed for the love-in were arrested by police. **1968** M.H. Albert & J. Guss *Lady in Cement* (film): I personally attended several love-ins. I need a rest. **1969** *Harper's* (May) 66: Maybe they're having a love-in down here. **1971** S. Stevens *Way Uptown* 86: It was parties I was pushing, very special parties called love-ins. **1988** *Newsweek* (June 27) 31: The U.S. Forest Service, familiar with past love-ins in other states, is seeking a permanent injunction against the group.

2. *Journ.* an event characterized by warm feelings or optimism.

    1967 *Seattle Times* (Dec. 3) 28: When the Synod of Bishops opened in Rome at the end of September, one observer called it an "ecclesiastical love-in." **1970** *Everett* (Wash.) *Herald* (Aug. 8) 9C: It began as a nationwide prayer revival…and it has grown to be a nationwide "love-in for God." **1981** *N.Y. Times* (Oct. 15) D2: An I.B.M.-sponsored "love-in."…The International Business Machines Corporation will play host to 100 representatives of independent software companies. **1982** *L.A. Times* (Nov. 29) IV 1: The two governments have been trying to foster a new era of good feelings. A participant has even described recent events as "a love-in." **1983** *Business Week* (Dec. 26) 42: MacDonald…has charmed Dome's 300 creditors but has not won them over. "I wouldn't suggest it's a love-in,…but it's certainly not antagonistic." **1991** *New Republic* (Sept. 16) 9: The forty-five minute love-in last month that passed for a confirmation hearing.

love juice *n.* the coital secretion of the vagina; (*also*) seminal fluid.—usu. considered vulgar.

    *1882 Boudoir 88: Every drop of…love juice. **a*1890–96 *F & H* IV

241: *Love-juice*…The sexual secretion. *a*1927 in P. Smith *Letter from Father* 135: In a minute or two her love juice came. **1962** Cory & LeRoy *Homosex. & Soc.* 265: *Love juice*…Semen. **1965** in *OED2:* The sheets smelt of linen instead of love-juice. ***1968** in *OED2:* "What is 'love-juice'?" "The liquid produced in the vagina of a woman when she is sexually excited." *a*1972 B. Rodgers *Queens' Vernacular* 52: Semen…*love juice*. **1972** in *OED2:* I could feel his lovejuice…trickling down into the start of my stomach. *a*1990 P. Dickson *Slang!* 192: *Love juice*. Semen.

lovely *n. Narc.* phencyclidine (PCP), usu. as mixed with marijuana; a cigarette containing this.
    1978 R. Peterson & R. Stillman *Phencyclidine Abuse* 120: [Synonyms for PCP:] Synthetic Marihuana,…Lovely, Lovely High, and Super Kools. **1986** *Special Assignment* (CNN-TV) (May 10): PCP is referred to on the street as "lovely," "angel dust," "killer weed" and "bolt." **1994** *L.A. Times* (Feb. 16) E3: Marijuana dipped in PCP…"lovelies." **1994** Lewin & Lewin *Thes. Slang* (ed. 2) s.v. *marijuana: Lovlies* [*sic*] (dipped in PCP).

love machine *n.* **1.** [coined or popularized in the title of J. Susann's best-selling novel (1969)] a passionate or insatiable lover, esp. a seducer of women; SEX MACHINE.
    1969 J. Susann *Love Machine* 1: Robin Stone was a handsome man. He could smile with his lips. He could think without emotion. He could make love to her with his body. Robin Stone was the Love Machine. **1985** Petit *Peacekeepers* 71: I ain't nothin' but a love machine.
    2. *Mil.* the male genital organs.—usu. considered vulgar. *Joc.* Also **love housing.**
    1982 in G. Dyer *War: Commentary* 121: You want to rip his eyeballs out, you want to tear apart his love machine, you want to destroy him, privates.…You want to send him home in a Glad Bag to his mommy! *a*1990 Westcott *Half a Klick* 112: Her knee struck hard between his legs…his "love housing."

love muffin *n.* a sexually attractive person.—also used fig. Cf. STUD MUFFIN.
    1987 *Sports Illustrated* (Sept. 28) (Nexis): Cornell players are a bunch of love muffins. **1993** *L.A. Times* (Feb. 14) (Nexis): We called a few video stores to see what L.A. romantics are reserving to watch with their love muffins tonight. **1995** *Denver Post* (Nexis): You say the love muffin of your desire doesn't know if you're alive? **1995** *TV Guide* (Feb. 18) 27: Paula…is the thinking man's love muffin.

love muscle *n.* the penis.—usu. considered vulgar. *Joc.*
    1958 Frankel *Band of Bros.* 242 [ref. to 1950]: I know'd this weather could dry up a feller's love muscle, but the cold's workin' on y'all's heads! **1975** T. Berger *Sneaky People* 204: That's my love muscle. **1978** in *Maledicta* VI (1982) 23: Penis…*love muscle*. **1981** Wambaugh *Glitter Dome* 168: The mirrored ceiling…reflected back…a lifeless love muscle. **1985** Petit *Peacekeepers* 105: Sure, if you think you can handle this huge love muscle. **1989** N.Y.C. man, age *ca*40: *Exercisin' your love muscle* means getting laid. *a*1994 A. Radakovich *Wild Girls Club* 228: I have a well-developed love muscle.

love nest *n.* **1.** [sugg. by sentimental cliché "a love nest for two," the home of a pair of loving newlyweds] Orig. *Journ.* a trysting place for usu. illicit lovers.
    1924 in Hemingway *Sel. Letters* 130: I got the clippings you sent me about Yenla and his love nest. **1930** Lavine *3d Degree* 141: They rode about town for several hours before going to their former "love nest." **1931** *Amer. Mercury* (Dec.) 418: A love nest, just like in the papers. **1934** Weseen *Dict. Amer. Slang* 145: *Love nest*—Usually, the apartment of a man and his mistress. **1955–57** Felder *Collegiate Slang* 3: *Lovenest*—a drive-in movie.
    2. the vagina.—usu. considered vulgar. *Joc.*
    *a*1994 A. Radakovich *Wild Girls Club* 131: Some women like a finger or two inserted into the love nest. **1995** *Heiress Mother,* on Usenet newsgroup alt.sex.stories: Burying myself in the warm embrace of her undulating love nest. **1995** *My Sexy Sister,* on Usenet newsgroup alt.sex.stories: My prick started slipping…into her moist love nest.

love pump *n.* the penis.—also used fig.—usu. considered vulgar. *Joc.* [Pop. by the satirical film *This Is Spinal Tap* (1984).]
    1984 C. Guest et al. *This Is Spinal Tap* (film): Lick my love pump. **1990** P. Munro *Slang U.* s.v. *lick: Lick my love pump!* Shut up! You make me sick! Get out of here! **1994** *Details* (July) 64: Lick my love pump, baby.

loverboy *n.* a male lover; Lothario. Usu. *joc.* or *ironic.*

1952 *ATS* (ed. 2) 355: *Lover-boy,* a masculine [film] idol. *Ibid.* 384: Beau.…*Boy-friend,*…*flame*…*lover-boy*. **1955** G.D. Adams *3 Bad Sisters* (film): Look, lover boy, I don't give a hoot what Nadine thinks. **1957** Collins & Powell *My Gun Is Quick* (film): Just back up and wait for her, lover boy. **1954–60** *DAS: Lover-boy*…A handsome man.…A woman-chaser. **1960** *Alfred Hitchcock Presents* (CBS-TV): Try that again, lover boy, and you'll be just a relic. **1980** "Loverboy" *Loverboy* [title of rock album]. **1984** *Wkly. World News* (Nov. 20) 42: Think what'll happen when one of hubby's friends spots you and your loverboy. **1989** *Current Affair* (synd. TV series): He's Hollywood's hottest loverboy! **1992** G. Wolff *Day at the Beach* 107: The would-be loverboy…composed himself with the lexicon of "lover's nuts" and "huge huggers."

lover's nuts *n.* testicular discomfort caused by sexual stimulation without ejaculation.—usu. considered vulgar. Also **love nuts, lover's balls, lover's knots.** Cf. BLUE BALLS, 2.
    *a*1961 Peacock *Valhalla* 36 [ref. to 1953]: I got lover's nuts. **1968** *Playboy* (May) 78: "Blue balls" or "lover's nuts," in which the male complains of severe pain in the testicles if he is stimulated without reaching orgasm. **1970** Landy *Underground Dict.: Love nuts n.* Pain in the testicles due to extreme sexual excitement without release through ejaculation. **1971** Cole *Rook* 85 [ref. to *ca*1948]: He was…already beginning to suffer from what the boys called Lover's Nuts, an acute ache in the groin, inside the bone, like neuralgia. **1972** *Nat. Lampoon* (Apr.) 35: *Lover's Balls:* Yes—No—. **1974** in Dundes & Pagter *Urban Folklore* 123: Have you ever…had "lover's knots" (passion cramps). **1979** G. Wolff *Duke of Deception* 180: I told her she had given me "blue balls, lover's nuts." This interested her. **1980** Manchester *Darkness* 189 [ref. to WWII]: I was too tired, and too sore with lover's nuts. **1992** (quot. at LOVERBOY).

lovesteak *n.* the penis.—usu. considered vulgar. *Joc.* Cf. TUBESTEAK.
    1990 P. Munro *Slang U.: Playgirl* always has men with big lovesteaks as their centerfolds. **1994** A. Heckerling *Clueless* 39: I don't see no lovesteak squeezed into your 501's so I can't call you "Man."

love stick *n.* the penis.—usu. considered vulgar. *Joc.* Cf. JOYSTICK.
    1924 Wilstach *Anecdota Erotica* 5: Negro came back from the war. Told his wife he brought back two love sticks, but that he gave one of them to Jim Johnson. **1986** *UTSQ:* Penis…*dork*…*love stick.* **1989** *Maledicta* X 54: Penis…*love-muscle*…*love-stick.*

love up see s.v. LOVE, *v.*

love weed *n. Narc.* marijuana. [Perh. a ghost term; attested solely in glossaries and synonymies and considered unfamiliar by marijuana aficionados.]
    1938 (cited in Spears *Drugs & Drink*). **1943** *Time* (July 19) 54: Marihuana may be called…love weed. **1952** *ATS* (ed. 2): *Marijuana*.…loco weed, love weed, Mary Jane, [etc.]. **1970** Landy *Underground Dict.: Love weed*…Marijuana. **1994** *Drugs & Crime Data Center & Clearinghouse Street Terms: Drugs & Drug Trade: Love weed*—marijuana.

lovey-dovey *n.* **1.** a lover; sweetheart.—often used in direct address.
    [**1819** in *OED2* s.v. *dovie:* My dearest love—lovey, dovey!] ***1841** in *F & H* IV 242: "The Prince's Title." Lovey-dovey has been spoken of; but it is not likely that His Royal Highness will assume the style and dignity of lovey-dovey for a considerable period. **1893** S.F. Batchelder *Hamlet* 36: Lovey-dovey, give me hope. ***1904** in *OED2:* We will…love one another as much as we can, lovey dovey. **1905** in Hammerstein *J. Kern Song Bk.* 9: How'd you like to be my lovey-dovey. **1945** in *DAS:* To help them with their foreign lovey-doveys—and, in some cases, with a small infant besides.
    2. love; (*also*) lovemaking.
    1946 H.L. Mencken, in *DAS:* A reign of peace, prosperity and lovey-dovey. **1992** G. Wolff *Day at the Beach* 34: Forest rangers sort of calmed them and this led to low-key lovey-dovey.

lovey-dovey *adj.* foolishly or embarrassingly affectionate or sentimental.
    [**1886** in *OED2:* I would wear gray, which mamma prefers, but which I think looks lovey-dovey.] **1900** in *OED2:* Just as lovey-dovey talk is important to her and nonsense to you. **1949** *Sat. Eve. Post* (Oct. 15) 3: They present a lovey-dovey scene of wedded bliss that's just too good to last. And it doesn't. **1952** *Time* (July 28) 74: When they are not being lovey-dovey on the air, dispensing commercials and "good,

clean, nauseating fun." **1960** *Father Knows Best* (CBS-TV): How can you two be so lovey-dovey after you've been married so long? **1966** *Life* (Sept. 16) 66: This lovey-dovey 1910 hit announced that under the Yum Yum Tree is "the yummiest place to be." *a***1979** Pepper & Pepper *Straight Life* 23: But she never was lovey-dovey, even with her own kids. *a***1982** Medved *Hospital* 31: The relationships aren't all lovey-dovey. **1983** *Nat. Lampoon* (Feb.) 16: Her favorite Halloween costume to don when feeling lovey-dovey?

loving *adj.* [prob. euphem. for FUCKING; cf. MOTHER-LOVING] damned.

    1944 H. Brown *Walk in the Sun:* To win the loving war. **1966** Halberstam *Very Hot Day* 51: You think we're going to see any lovin' Viet Congs today? **1974** *Kojak* (CBS-TV): Are you guys out of your loving trees? **1977** Langone *Life at Bottom* 76: "Eat and drink like a loving pig," he says, patting the bulge under his parka. **1991–95** Sack *Co. C* 150: At long lovin' last!

loving spoonful *n. Black E.* intoxicating liquor.

    1960 in T.C. Bambara *Gorilla* 57: And I gotta get a brand-new jug of Gallo....I don't never do no heavy traveling without my loving spoonful.

low *n. Narc.* (see quots.).

    1970 Landy *Underground Dict.: Low*...Bad reaction to any drug. **1975** *DAS* (ed. 3): *Low*...A bad reaction to a drug.

¶ In phrase:

¶ **take low** Now esp. *Black E.* to be humbled or humiliated; humble oneself.

    1881 Crofutt *Guide to Colo.* 63: The Spanish Peaks, too, took *low*. **1955** Childress *Trouble* 153: Sometimes I take low, yes, gotta take low. Man say somethin' to me, I say..."Yes, sure, certainly."...That ain't *tommin'*, that's common sense. **1958** Hughes & Bontemps *Negro Folklore* 488: *Take Low:* To be humiliated. Women love to see a man take low. *a***1994** Smitherman *Black Talk* 220: Take low and go.

lowball *n.* the practice of lowballing (LOWBALL, *v.,* 1).—also used attrib.

    1961 *Time* (Mar. 24) 54: The lowball: the salesman quotes a rock-bottom price for the new car to win the customer, later hikes up the price, declaring that a mistake has been made. **1967** *L.A. Times* (May 5) IV 13: Another effective low ball gimmick also involves a bargain priced "come on." **1980** *L.A. Times* (Aug. 11) IV 2: One company offered Norwalk...a basic subscription rate of $5.95. "Obviously these companies...are trying to do what I call low ball."

lowball *adj.* **1.** *Business.* operating at a low margin.

    1970 *Business Week* (Sept. 26) 45: Detroit, for instance, is a low-ball (low-margin) town. **1977** *Rolling Stone* (Nov. 17) 29: A brutal price war being waged between large "cutthroat," or "low-ball" retail chains selling new releases slightly over or...below cost.

2. *Business.* low or underestimated.

    1980 *Business Week* (Sept. 29) 85: We don't worry about lowball bids, because jobs are usually awarded on the basis of competence, not price. **1986** *L.A. Law* (NBC-TV): Then we come in with our lowball offer. **1988** M. Maloney *Thunder Alley* 161: That's the low-ball estimate. **1989** *Top of the Hill* (CBS-TV): We're not planning any lowball fares or price wars.

3. unethical; underhanded.

    1982 Sculatti *Catalog of Cool* 178: Low-ball cut-throats and cheats. **1983** *Maclean's* (Nov. 7) 54: An incongruous combination of high-level neurological research and lowball partisan politics. **1988** *Daily News* (N.Y.) (June 21) 6: He has never resorted to provocative, low-ball tactics like Alton.

lowball *v.* **1.** *Business.* **a.** to offer a customer a misleadingly low cost estimate.—also used trans., with the customer or the estimate as obj.

    1957 *Pop. Science* (May) 96: [Auto dealers' terms:] *Lowball*—either similar to "bushing" (mentioning an unbelievably low price) or giving a rube a very low trade-in. **1957** *N.Y. Times* (June 16) II 25: What the trade calls "low balling." In effect this is quoting a low price initially and then reneging or saddling a purchaser with extras when the time comes to consummate the deal. **1963** in H. Ellison *Sex Misspelled* 39: People...actually believe the lowballing of used car dealers. **1971** *Business Week* (Aug. 21) 86: "Lowballing." This is the practice of the booking agent deliberately, or as an honest mistake, under-estimating the cost of the move. **1975** *Business Week* (Sept. 22) 118: You were just disappointed by a dealer who

had "low-balled" you—quoted you one price, then upped that figure when you were about to close the deal. **1982** *U.S. News & W.R.* (Apr. 19) 51: Many CPA's who work independently or in small practices complain that larger firms are stealing clients by "lowballing"—charging fees that do not reflect the full costs of the audit. **1982** R. Sutton *Don't Get Taken* 62: You've just been low-balled, "put out" on a price they just know will bring you back tomorrow. **1988** *Money Week* (CNN-TV) (Oct. 8): They think you folks are lowballing the estimates. **1995** *N.Y. Times* (Dec. 3) ("Real Estate") 5: If one estimate's a lot lower, chances are they left something out, they're low-balling the estimate and will make up for it later.

    b. to make a deliberately low or inadequate offer to.

    1957 (*Pop. Science* quot. at **(1)**, above). **1986** *L.A. Law* (NBC-TV): They'd see it as a sign of weakness. They'd lowball us. **1992** Strawberry & Rust *Darryl* 33: If they wanted to lowball, we'd play along. **1994** A. Heckerling *Clueless* 15: Some teachers were trying to lowball me, daddy, and you always say "Never accept a first offer." I figure these grades are just a jumping off point to start negotiations.

2. *Journ.* to take a restrained approach (to); soft-pedal.

    1978 *L.A. Times* (June 8) I 14: This previously established name recognition enabled Younger to low-ball the primary campaign, take few risks, concentrate only on a few selected issues, [etc.]. **1986** *All Things Considered* (Nat. Pub. Radio) (Dec. 1): Senator Gore lowballs, as you can hear. He talks about restraint, caution, no crisis, [etc.]. **1990** B. Gumbel, on *NBC News Special* (NBC-TV) (May 31): They are generally trying to lowball it [a summit meeting] in the procedures. **1993** *World News Tonight* (ABC-TV) (Nov. 17): Isn't that [giving a very conservative estimate to avoid the appearance of overconfidence] what we in the media call "lowballing"?

lowboy *n.* a type of low trailer or tractor-trailer combination used to transport tracked vehicles or other heavy equipment. Now *colloq.* or *S.E.*

    1956 Lasly *Turn Tigers Loose* 103: Loring signaled the driver of the tractor with the long "low-boy" attached to back his trailer up to the tail of the aircraft. **1957** *Pop. Science* (Apr.) 246: It arrived on a giant lowboy trailer. **1968** in Morgan & Michalson *Beloved Country* 421: We took a jeep and a low boy (truck). **1970** *Business Week* (Mar. 14) 33: We have lowboys, flatbeds, vans, reefers and what-have-you. **1974** Terkel *Working* 24: I was putting the crane on a lowboy—the tractor that hauls it....The lowboy wasn't big enough...and the crane went over backward. **1986** R. Zumbro *Tank Sgt.* 150: This guy had been out on his own with a section of earthmovers, two front loaders on lowboys, and a pair of dump trucks. **1991** in Morgan & Michalson *Beloved Country* 473: Bringing hundreds of [Iraqi] prisoners in on "low boys."

low-bridge *v.* **1.** to disparage; LOW-RATE, 1.

    1954 in Botkin *Sidewalks* 489: One ad agency man [was] trying to talk down the ideas of another one. Snarled the second one..."Don't low bridge me."

2.a. *Baseball.* to force (a player) to duck or fall to the ground to avoid being hit by a thrown or batted ball.

    1964 Thompson & Rice *Every Diamond* 141: *Low Bridge the Hitter:* Brush hitter away from the plate. **1971** Coffin *Old Ball Game* 55: "Low bridge" (knock a batter down). **1977** R. Kiner, on *N.Y. Mets Baseball* (WOR-TV) (Aug. 20): And that's a base hit. Low-bridging [pitcher] Craig Swan on the first pitch.

    b. to knock unconscious; hit over the head.

    1965 Conot *Rivers of Blood* 52: I'm gonna lowbridge me one o' those motherfuckers!

lowbrow *n.* a crude, dull-witted person of coarse appearance; (*hence*) a person lacking cultivated tastes. Now *colloq.* Cf. HIGHBROW; MIDDLEBROW.

    1903 Ade *Society* 196: The Teamster was a Low-Brow with a 48-inch Chest and he did not know a thing about the Henry of Navarre Business. **1906** S. Ford *Shorty McCabe* 64: The spaghetti works was in full blast, with a lot of husky low brows goin' in and out...acting as if the referee had just declared a draw. **1909** Chrysler *White Slavery* 70: They leave that for the "rough necks" and the "low brows" to do. **1911** Van Loan *Big League* 57: What [can] any fine-looking gal like that...see in a low brow like Bohannon? *Ibid.* 42: "Biff" Bohannon was a "low brow" if ever there was one....The low, coarse instincts which go with that particular style of cranium became Biff very well when at the bat. **1929** "E. Queen" *Roman Hat* 17: The "low-brows"...had deserted the legitimate theatre for the more ingenuous delights of the motion picture palaces. **1934** Weseen *Dict. Amer. Slang* 365: *Lowbrow*—An unintelligent person; an uneducated person; a vulgar person. **1967** *Harper's* (Aug.) 19: To identify much of the folk culture...with lowbrowism. **1993** *Guiding Light* (CBS-TV): Lowbrow!

lowbrow *adj.* being, characteristic of, appealing to, or involving a LOWBROW; unintellectual; stupid. Now *S.E.* Also **lowbrowed**. Also as adv. Cf. HIGHBROW.
　　1902–03 Ade *People You Know* 23: All agreed that the Music which seemed to catch on with the low-browed Public was exceedingly Punk. **1908** McGaffey *Show Girl* 185: This is a low-browed dump, but any port in a storm. **1914** S. Lewis, in *OED2*: You ain't neither too highbrow or too lowbrow. **1919** in Cornebise *Amaroc News* 157: Those looking for "low brow stuff" will be disappointed. **1924** in *DAS*: What are you always pulling that lowbrow stuff for? **1936* in *OED2*: The simplicity of the lowbrowed. **1950** *New Yorker* (Apr. 29) 96: Written in a breezy, lowbrow style that does everything possible to make one suspicious of the author's fitness to deal with his subject.

low card *n.* an inconsequential individual.
　　1896 Ade *Artie* 30: I play no understudy to a low card.
　　¶ In phrase:
　　¶ **deal low cards** to put at a disadvantage.
　　1968 in Andrews & Dickens *Big House* 18: I took all the odds; you dealt all the low cards.

low cotton *n.* ¶ In phrase: **[in] low cotton** *So.* [in] a state of sickness or depression; unwell. Cf. HIGH COTTON.
　　1941 in *DARE*: I was in what Ford would call "low cotton." **1941–42** in *PADS* (No. 6) 20 [ref. to 1900–10]: I'm feeling sort o' low cotton today. **1965–68** in *DARE*. **1984** Wilder *You All* 206: *In low cotton:* In depression; morbid; in the dismals [*sic*]; low in spirit.

lowdown *n.* **1.** truth, esp. confidential or little-known truth. Now *colloq.* [The 1915 quot. is incorrectly transcribed in *OEDS*.]
　　1907 in Robinson *Comics* 44: The Lowdown Kid: I know a guy who knows a bloke who knows a friend of a fellow. **1908** in H.C. Fisher *A. Mutt* 34: I can give you the low down on A. Mutt. **1915** T.A. Dorgan, in Zwilling *TAD Lexicon* 55: Aw give us the low down on em Bill. **1916** Lait *Beef, Iron & Wine* 128: I got the low-down on the sichooation. **1918** in Hall & Niles *One Man's War* 292: He gave the low-down on the news side of the war. **1920** Witwer *Kid Scanlan* 236: I want the lowdown on this thing. **1921** Casey & Casey *Gay-Cat* 207: I got the hull low-down on thet kid! **1923** *Atlanta Constitution* (Feb. 1) 12: Slip us the low-down, princess. **1925** Nason *Three Lights* 7: There's more cook-house rumors afloat than I ever heard in my life, but let's get the low-down. **1926** Dunning & Abbott *Broadway* 225: You wait a couple of days and I'll give you the low-down on him. **1928** McKay *Banjo* 244: He had been of service to Ray in giving him the low-down on that interesting sailor town. **1931** Armour *Little Caesar* (film): Now listen, here's the lowdown. **1932–33** P. Cain *Fast One* 58: There's a gal...claims to have a million dollars' worth of lowdown on the administration. **1944** Duff & Milne *Step Lively* (film): We want the lowdown. **1949** in *DAS*: Eager to get the low-down on new aircraft. **1956** E.S. Gardner *Terrified Typist* 38: What is it, Della? Give me the low-down. **1968** Kirkwood *Good Times/Bad Times* 150: Give me the low-down, come on. **1972** Major *Dict. Afro-Amer. Sl.*: Lowdown... the inside information. **1977** Newman & Berkowitz *Take Charge* 72: And maybe you have good reason for not trusting others with the "low-down" about yourself. **1979** T.R. Kennedy *Gotta Deal* 56: I know the "low-down"...about almost everyone. *a***1994** Rudnick *Jeffrey* 29: Here's the lowdown on evil: it's the absence of love.
　　2. LOWLIFE. Cf. much earlier LOWDOWNER.
　　1987 B. Ford & C. Chase *Awakening* 82: You have to be a real lowdown not to respond to three loving kids.
　　¶ In phrase:
　　¶ **on the lowdown** truthfully, esp. confidentially.
　　1901 W. Irwin *Sonnets* (unp.): On the low down, dear Mame, my looty loo,/That's why I've cooked this batch of rhymes for you. **1902** T.A. Dorgan, in Zwilling *TAD Lexicon* 55: It is hinted on the low down that an entire new cast is in working order.

lowdowner *n.* LOWLIFE.
　　1868 in *DARE*: When...candidates refreshed their adherents by the barrelfull, the low-downer enjoyed his periodical benders without expense. **1871** De Vere *Amer.*, in *F & H*: So low a person....he appears as Conch or lowdowner in North Carolina. **1883** in *F & H*: They are at least known by a generic byword, as poor whites or low-downers.

lower Slobovia see s.v. SLOBOVIA.

low-five *n.* an act of slapping a person's outstretched palm held below shoulder height, usu. at waist level, as a form of congratulation. Also as v. Cf. HIGH-FIVE.
　　1982 *Time* (May 3) 80: Dodger Leftfielder Dusty Baker thought the San Diego hand-slapping (high fives, low fives) a little elaborate for April. **1992** Strawberry & Rust *Darryl* 213: Backslapping, high-fiving, low-fiving, giddy from the release of tension. *a***1994** Smitherman *Black Talk* 156: *Low Five* A *five* with the hands held low.

lowlife *n.* a contemptible person. Hence **lowlife[d]**, **lowlived**, *adj.*
　　[****1766** O. Goldsmith, in *F & H*: She shall choose better company than such low-lived fellows as he.] **1794** in *OED2*: Saint Crispin....The low-life Cobler's Tutelary Saint. [**1847** *Davy Crockett's Alm.* (unp.): The craven, low-lived, chicken-bred [fellow].] **1911** in *OED2*: I got better judgment as to let a low-life like him get into me. **1930** Sage *Last Rustler* 137: I can...whip any low-lifed-lyin'-son-of-a-curse that ever run it! **1932** in *OED2*: What do you expect from such a low life? **1933, 1955** in *OED2*. **1954–60** *DAS*: *Low-life n.* A vile person. **1972** (quot. at LOW-RENT, *adj.*). **1973** Sesar *Catullus* xii: It's as lowlife as you can get. **1985** (quot. at SLIMEBUCKET). **1991** McCarthy & Mallowe *Vice Cop* 55: They're...lowlifes. **1994** A. Heckerling *Clueless* 2: Don't tell me those brain-dead, low-lifes have been calling.

lowpo *n.* [prob. punning on HYPO] hypochondria; low spirits.
　　1801 in Turnbull & Turnbull *Season in N.Y.* 122: Miss Lydia...I am glad to hear keeps from the *lowpo*.

low-pressure hat *n.* a soft or low-crowned hat. Cf. HIGH-PRESSURE HAT.
　　1852 in *DA*: Flannel shirts, long boots..., belts, and low-pressure hats.

low pro *n.* *Black E.* a low profile.
　　1992 Mowry *Way Past Cool* 227: He keep a pretty low pro. **1992** "Fab Five Freddy" *Fresh Fly Flavor* 40: *Low pro*—low profile.

low-rate *v.* Esp. *So. & Black E.* **1.** to disparage; belittle.
　　1906 *DN* III 145: *Lowrate*...To depreciate, set a low estimate on. "That's *lowrating* him some." **1926* Walrond *Tropic Death* 120: Oi don't hav' to low-rate myself fi' suit any field han' neygah uman like yo'. **1931** Bontemps *Sends Sunday* 179: Damn if you's gonna low-rate me in ma own house. **1940** Zinberg *Walk Hard* 83: I never low-rate you. **1941** Hargrove *Pvt. Hargrove* 37: And then you low-rated the mess sergeant's recipe for creamed beef on toast and told him his chow was the worst in the Army. **1942** Hurston *Dust Tracks* 187: That is another way of saying play the dozens, which is also a way of saying low-rate your enemy's ancestors and him. **1945** Himes *If He Hollers* 100: She was lorating him. **1946** Mezzrow & Wolfe *Really Blues* 87: Lowrate him once and for all. *Ibid.* 308: *Lowrate:* ridicule, show up. **1952** Randolph & Wilson *Down in the Holler* 262: *Low-rate: v.t.* To criticize adversely. "That feller better quit *low-ratin'* my kinfolks!" **1959** Murtagh & Harris *Who Live in Shadow* 54: But we had a...screw who was always lowrating anybody went to see the bug doctor. **1961** O. Davis *Purlie* 305: Tease him—low-rate him—laugh at ol' Gitlow; he ain't nothing but a fool! **1964** J. Thompson *Pop. 1280* 51: It just don't seem quite fittin' to low-rate the dead with a lot of dirty names. **1966** Elli *Riot* 16: He'd...spend the nights...low-rating the prison officials. **1970** Perl & Davis *Cotton Comes to Harlem* (film): Goodbye to bein' kicked and low-rated.
　　2. to demean.
　　1968–73 Giallombardo *Impris. Girls* 209: To get caught breaking the institution rules is not only to "low-rate" oneself, but, by extension, it "low-rates" the entire family.

low rent *n.* *Stu.* one who is LOW-RENT.
　　1968–70 *Current Slang III & IV* 80: *Low rent*, n. A girl with low moral standards; an easy mark.—College males, South Dakota. **1978** *New West* (June 5) 29: Separations that govern social life at California high schools in 1978, where "stoners," "rahs," "four-wheel drivers," "low-rents," [etc.]...are not just names...but recognized tribes.

low-rent *adj.* cheap; inferior; contemptible; base.
　　1957 (cited in *W10*). **1969** *Current Slang I & II* 59: *Low rent*, adj. Base, gross, unacceptable, bad.—Air Force Academy cadets, college students...South Dakota. **1971** Dahlskog *Dict.* 38: *Low rent*, A. Base; unacceptable; cheap and vulgar, as: a girl who is strictly *low rent*. **1972** Jenkins *Semi-Tough* 236: Kick the pure zebra shit out of those rotten, low-life, low-rent, dog-ass motherfuckers. **1973** *Playboy* (July) 68: What do you

think of [science fiction] as a form? The standard critical appraisal is that it's low-rent. **1976** in H.S. Thompson *Shark Hunt* 535: I will leave the dreary task of chronicling this low-rent trip to Teddy White. **1972–79** T. Wolfe *Right Stuff* 40: But Pancho Barnes was anything but Low Rent. **1979** T. Baum *Carny* 34: "Low-rent assholes," Mickey muttered. **1981** in L. Bangs *Psychotic Reactions* 351: It was a bar where a lot of low-rent johns hung out. **1981** *N.Y. Times Mag.* (Jan. 4) 27: You'll probably lose some low-rent brand of traveler's checks in Tanzania next summer. **1985** *Miami Vice* (NBC-TV): Why the low-rent disguise? **1986** Merkin *Zombie Jamboree* 147: You are really low-rent....You bet against our side. *a***1988** C. Adams *More Straight Dope* 43: Diet Coke...trounced its low-rent competitor. **1995** *N.Y. Press* (July 26) 11: You're vulnerable, you're low-rent, you're just visiting, and the passersby say it to your face. **1995** *TV Guide* (Oct. 21) 4: I would advise him to make movies with Spielberg or Altman, rather than the low-rent guys he was dealing with.

lowrider *n.* **1.** *Black E.* (see 1982 quot.).

1931 in Leadbitter & Slaven *Blues Records* 490: Low Rider's Blues. **1982** A. Shaw *Dict. Pop/Rock* 115: *Easy rider.* Blues jargon for a pimp or inconstant peripatetic lover....Also *low rider.*

2.a. *Esp. So. Calif.* a person who drives a LOWRIDER ((**b**), below); (*hence*) a member of a street gang; (*broadly*) a contemptible person.

*ca***1963** in Schwendinger & Schwendinger *Adolescent Subcult.* 247: The Low-Riders are dressed better. **1965** Cleaver *Soul on Ice* 37: Low rider....A Los Angeles nickname for ghetto youth. Originally the term was coined to describe the youth who had lowered the bodies of their cars so that they rode low, close to the ground....when these youthful hipsters alighted from their vehicles, the term *low rider* stuck with them, evolving to the point where all black ghetto youth—but *never* the soft offspring of the black bourgeoisie—are referred to as low riders. **1970** Landy *Underground Dict.* 122: Low rider *n.*....2. Person who drives a lowered car. 3. Bastard. **1972** Carr *Bad* 36: An old low-rider named Billy...ran down the steps to save my ass. **1972** in *DAS* (ed. 3): There are what the blacks call low riders, these people who run around pushing their weight around, threatening the weak. **1973** Goines *Black Girl* 28: A young brother drove past slowly, his car broke down in the back, showing that he was a low rider. **1977** Bunker *Animal Factory* 11: Sure those lowriders stab each other, but if you mind your own business, nobody bothers you, except when a race war is happening. **1978** Schrader *Hardcore* 108: A stocky low-rider in a leather jacket. **1981** *California* (Dec.) 110: The curb was lined with low-riders, what Flo called "gang bangers." **1983** Goldman & Fuller *Charlie Co.* 41 [ref. to 1968]: Stagnaro was a low-rider, the possessor of a no-longer-recognizable ten-year-old Pontiac with a souped-up motor and a chassis dropped so rakishly low it nearly scraped the ground. **1993** Rebennack & Rummel *Under Hoodoo Moon* 37: Opium was viewed as low-class, strictly for low-riders. **1995** *L.A. Times* (Oct. 17) D1: Less committed enthusiasts—"weekend lowriders"—loaded the trunks of their cars with bags of cement.

b. a customized car having hydraulic jacks that permit the chassis to be lowered almost to the road. Now *S.E.*

1975 *DAS* (ed. 3): Low rider...A car with a lowered suspension. **1976** *L.A. Times* (Aug. 9) II 1: She used to cruise...at night with her boyfriends in their "low-rider" automobiles. **1979** *New West* (Oct. 22) 108: The toughest California *vato loco* in his lowrider. **1981** *L.A. Times* (Jan. 4) II 3: Two officers observed Graves driving a so-called "lowrider" west on Firestone Boulevard....The front of the car was so low it dragged the street. **1983** "B. Knott" *Tasteless Jokes II* 8: Why do Mexicans drive low-riders? So they can cruise and pick lettuce at the same time. **1988** *Parade* (Feb. 21) 5: A street gang took over the apartment building across from my house, and flowers and compact cars gave way to graffiti and low-riders. **1990** Rukuza *West Coast Turnaround* 78: A bright pink Buick lowrider blew the red light. **1995** *L.A. Times* (Oct. 17) D1: The first lowriders...were Chevrolets and Fords with severed front suspension springs and rears lowered so much that the bumpers rested just above the ground.

low-riding *n.* the hobby or culture of LOWRIDERS.—also used attrib.

*a***1972** *Urban Life & Culture* I 81: Rowdy life, the "low-riding bag" is impulsive and unrestrained. **1972** Grogan *Ringolevio* 494: Just another low-riding mug who...started knifing his brothers in the back when he got himself in a jam. **1979** *L.A. Times* (Sept. 14) I 26: Lowriding is becoming a big thing, and it's not a cheap hobby. **1980** *Santa Barbara* (Calif.) *News-Press* (July 25) B2: Lowriding goes back to the '30s. **1981** *N.Y. Times* (May 9): You could say low-riding is a life

style. **1984** *California* (Nov.) 151: Like customizing and low-riding, the goal of this unnamed subculture will not be high performance.

low tide *n.* the circumstance of being low on money.

*****1698–99** "B.E." *Dict. Canting Crew*, in *F & H*: Low-tide, when there's no Money in a Man's Pocket. **1859** Matsell *Vocab.* 52: *Low tide.* Very little money left. *****1863** in T. Taylor *Plays* 167: It's low tide here. (*pointing to his pocket*). **1867** Williams *Brierly* 20: "Well, I've taken a serious turn lately, I always do when it's low tide here." And he laid his hands on his pockets significantly.

lox *n.* a fool; LUMMOX.

1966 Susann *Valley of Dolls* 435: Bud Hoff is a lox....He sits around thinking he's God's gift to women. **1977** *New West* (July 18) 121: How she could remain obsessively in love with a lox like John Beck is never explained. [**1977** Butler & Shryack *Gauntlet* 113: With a lox-for-brains like you, I don't have a chance, *period!*] **1978** *New West* (Dec. 4) 41: The hero of the Hollywood novel is usually a young lox in from the East. **1984** C. Francis *Who's Sorry?* 183: Don't be a lox, Sheila! **1988** *ALF* (NBC-TV): Willie, you lox! *Ibid.:* Because he was a lox!

loxed out *adj. Hosp.* comatose.

1978 Shem *House of God* 45: She's a totally demented loxed out gomer. *Ibid.* 366: All but the most loxed-out gomers soon banished him from doing any procedure upon their bodies. **1981** in Safire *Good Word* 154: Patients in coma are "loxed out" perhaps referring to the flaccidity of a piece of lox.

lox jock *n.* a Jewish man.—used disparagingly. *Joc.*

1977 J.G. Dunne *True Confessions* 32: Jew....Ever notice the guys with the cushy jobs, they're all lox jocks.

L.P. *n.* [prob. fr. *lousy puss*] *Esp. U.S. Mil. Acad.* an unattractive or unpleasant young woman.

1900 *Howitzer* (U.S. Mil. Acad.) (No. 1): L.P.—A person who does not come up to one's expectations *Ibid.* 138: *Ell-pe*...A very dangerous person (see *Femme*). **1904** *Howitzer* (U.S. Mil. Acad.) (No. 5) 222: L.P.—A femme who is a poor dancer; or—not exactly charming. **1905** *Howitzer* (U.S. Mil. Acad.) (No. 6) 294: L.P., "One who steps on your toes at every hop and hops on your toes at every step." **1908** *Howitzer* (U.S. Mil. Acad.) (No. 9) 325: L.P., *n.*—A fem of questionable beauty and uncertain age. **1942** *ATS* 146: Sour or ugly face....L.P. ("*lousy puss*").

L.S. and M.S. *n.* (see quots.).

1930 Irwin *Tramp & Und. Sl.* 124: L.S. and M.S.—Less sleep and more speed. Originated along the line of the Lake Shore and Michigan Southern Railroad...over which it was possible to make speed if one gave up sleep and rest in order to watch for the railroad detective who thronged the line. **1942** *ATS* 260: L.S. and M.S., less sleep and more speed. *Ibid.* 448.

L-7 *n.* [prob. as in 1956, **1966 quots.] an overly conventional person; SQUARE. Also as adj.

1956 Shaw *W. Coast Jazz*, in *DAS*: L7...Hollywood's latest lingo for a square: form an L and a 7 with your fingers and that's what you get. **1958** Meltzer & Blees *H.S. Confidential* (film): You bug this joint like a real L seven. *****1966** S.J. Baker *Australian Language* 289: L7, "a square": apparently derived from the fact that L and the figure 7 when in conjunction make a rough square. **1972** N.Y.U. student: An *L-seven* is a "square," only worse. That's from the fifties. **1972** Claerbaut *Black Jargon* 71: L7, adj., *n.* completely out of style; not like the group. **1973** *Wash. Sq. Jour.* (Mar. 14) 2: Do you know what old "L-Seven" Edwards would say to these people? **1980** Eble *Campus Slang* (Oct.) 4: L7—Square (from the picture of joining the right angles of L and 7). **1988** "L7" L7 [name of rock group; self-titled album]. **1994** *Mystery Sci. Theater* (Comedy Central TV): L-7, man....There's an audible thud every time he tells a joke. **1995** N.Y.C. man, age 25 (coll. J. Sheidlower): That sounds pretty L-7....[Makes hand gesture as in 1956 quot.].

LST *n.* [facetious reinterpretation of offic. designation *Landing Ship, Tank*] *Navy.* ('a type of amphibious landing ship'; facetiously reinterpreted to mean) large, slow target. *Joc.* [Quots. ref. to WWII.]

1942 O'Sheel & Cook *Semper Fidelis* 27: Even at sea the LSTs are a relatively sluggish craft (whence the nickname: "Large Slow Target"). **1950** Morison *Naval Ops. in WWII* 141: They were literally what their crews nicknamed them, "Large Slow Targets." **1951** Thacher *Captain* 3: The Captain's ship was a Landing Ship for tanks, abbreviated officially as LST and labeled by the men who sailed her a Landing Ship for Targets, or, more succinctly, a Large Slow Target. **1968** Smart *Long*

Watch 1: After going to several camps and schools, I served on three different LSTs (Landing Ships Tank or "Large, Slow Targets").

lube var. LUBIE.

lube *v.* to lubricate. Now *colloq.* or *S.E.*

 1956 in *Pop. Science* (Jan. 1957) 208: I use it to pressure-lube the car. **1957** *Pop. Science* (Apr.) 86: The automatic-transmission fluid that lubes the supercharger. **1961** B. Malamud, in *OED2*: He had once lubed Levin's car. **1963** in H. Ellison *Sex Misspelled* 50: I got it lubed and checked out for the ride downtown. **1983** S. King *Christine* 109: Putting stuff away, lubing the lifts [etc.].

lubed see s.v. LUBRICATE.

lube job *n.* **1.** a lubrication, as of machinery. Now *S.E.*

 1950 *Pop. Science* (Nov.) 194: A car is on a hoist for a lube job. **1951** *Sat. Eve. Post* (Sept. 15) 189: A lube job starts anywhere from $2.50 and wanders on up. **1960** R. Serling *Stories from Twilight Zone* 60: How about an oil change and a lube job too? **1962** E. Stephens *Blow Negative* 58: And changed tires and did lube jobs. **1978** Truscott *Dress Gray* 112: His eyeballs felt like they'd gone 100,000 miles without a lube job. **1990** T. Thorne *Dict. Contemp. Slang: Lube*...A lube job (originally American) refers to a servicing of grease points.

 2. an act of coition or oral copulation.—usu. considered vulgar.

 1947–53 W. Guthrie *Seeds* 266: Oh ho, yes, what I need,/Ten bucka lube job,/That's what I need. **1988** Poyer *The Med* 268: Talk about lube jobs. We'd go into the head in the acey-deucy club. **1991** Marcinko & Weisman *Rogue Warrior* 300: Hey, baby, how about a lube job.

lubie *n.* a lubricated condom. Also **lube.**

 1971 *Current Slang V* (Spring) 16: *Lubie,* n. A lubricated condom. **1975** De Mille *Smack Man* 111: It was a big thing to have a Trojan lubie in your wallet. **1980** Gould *Ft. Apache* 234: A Trojan lube.

lubricate *v.* to take a drink of alcoholic liquor. Hence (*usu.*) **lubricated,** *adj.* drunk. Also (in recent use) **lubed,** *adj.*

 *a***1881** G.C. Harding *Misc. Writings* 131: I've lubricated with about forty drops o' instant death. **a***1890–96** F & H IV: *Lubricate*...To drink. **1911** in Herrin *Mencken* 12: Lubricated [intoxicated]. **1927** (quot. at SQUIFFY). **1931** Springs *Carol Banks* 85: He was well lubricated. **1954–60** *DAS: Lubricated adj.* Drunk. **1979** Univ. Tenn. student theme: *Drunk* wasted,...shitfaced, pie eyed,...lubed (or lubricated). [**1979–83** W. Kennedy *Ironweed* 209: Have a drink, pal. Lubricate your soul.] **1993** *CBS This Morning* (CBS-TV) (Jan. 1): The celebrants were a bit lubricated. *a***1994** A. Radakovich *Wild Girls Club* 74: Everyone was lubricated.

luck *n.* ¶ In phrases:

 ¶ **break luck** [Orig. a colloq. angling term, 'to make the first catch of the day'] *Prost.* (see 1975 quot.).

 1974 Angelou *Gather Together* 137 [ref. to *ca*1950]: It's already nine o'clock and I haven't even broke luck yet. **1975** *DAS* (ed. 3): *Break luck* To succeed in getting the first customer of the day (or night). *Prostitute* use. **1977–85** Carmen & Moody *Working Women* 69: But Mickey had not "broken luck" and was feeling desperate.

 ¶ **change (one's) luck, 1.** (of a white man) to copulate with a black woman.—usu. considered vulgar. [Cf. the superstition recorded in 1907 quot.]

 [**1907** in H.C. Fisher *A. Mutt* 17: I'll have to do something to change my luck. I've heard that to touch the head of a negro was sure to do it.] **1916** Cary *Venery* I 43: *Changing One's Luck*—To have carnal knowledge of a black woman. A superstition. **1925** (quot. at OFAY). **1927** [Fliesler] *Anecdota* 106: Eager to "change his luck" a white man approached a negress. **1934** W. Smith *Bessie Cotter* 46: Why'n't you let him change his luck? **1941** H.A. Smith *Low Man* 170: I walk up and say I wanna buy a red dress for a nigger lady. I suppose they all think I been out changin' my luck. **1943** in Himes *Black on Black* 223: A group of white servicemen look her over and wink or say, "Boy, Ah ought to change mah luck." **1948** Lait & Mortimer *New York* 116: The Harlem community accepts—though it despises—these Caucasians who cross the color line, or as it is known above 110th Street, "change their luck" or "deal in coal." **1958** Motley *Epitaph* 327: What are you trying to do—change your luck? **1965** Longstreet *Sportin' House* 136 [ref. to *ca*1890's]: White men of all classes had a firm belief that sleeping with a Negress brought about a "change of luck." **1973** Ace *Stand On It* 44: "So I thought I would eat me a whole mess of ribs and—" "And maybe change your luck?"

 2. (of a white woman) to copulate with a black (or in 1982 quot., Hispanic) man.—usu. considered vulgar.

 1964 D. Gregory *Nigger* 10: Hey, Flo, gonna take the little monkey home with you, change your luck. **1982** E. Leonard *Cat Chaser* 28: Change her luck and marry a spic, uh, with fifty million.

 3. (see quot.).—usu. considered vulgar.

 1965 Trimble *Sex Words* 40: *Change Your Luck*...To submit to a Homosexual act for the first time.

 ¶ **slip a little luck** to copulate with (a woman).—usu. considered vulgar.

 1929–31 J.T. Farrell *Young Lonigan* 111: "The first ting you know...why...I schlipt her a little luck." "Yeh?"..."Yeh. I schlipt her a little luck."

luck *v.* **1.** to rely upon luck for; manage or succeed in obtaining by luck. [Sense of *1530 S.E. quots. is 'to bring good luck to'.]

 [***1530** in *OED2*: I lucke one, I make hym luckye....He is a happy person, for he lucketh every place he commeth in.] **1935** H. McCoy *They Shoot Horses* 142: First come, first served. After that you luck it or hustle one on your own. **1942** in *WDEU*: Landing was the real job, in that fog. I was pretty sure about my navigation...and decided to luck it and set her down. **1966** Braly *On the Yard* 83: "I still don't see how you managed that." "I lucked it."

 2. to succeed in propelling or placing by luck alone.—used with complementary prep. or adv.

 *ca***1950** in M.H. Greenberg *In Ring* 71: I lucked one on his jaw and he went down. **1959** *Time* (June 29) 12: Mayer...lucked his smoking, limping Mercator back 300 nautical miles to a landing. **1963** *Time* (Aug. 9) 35: Occasionally he lucks one down the fairway. **1968** W.C. Anderson *Gooney Bird* 90: Hey, Spooky...you lucked one in. *a***1977** T. Barnett *Golf Is Madness* 16: I was afraid he might luck it in [*sc.,* a golf-ball into a cup].

luckboy var. LUCKY BOY.

lucked up *adj.* in very good luck.

 1944 Ind *Bataan* 36: Mindoro, maybe, if we're unlucky. Pany, if we're luckier. Mindanao, if we're all lucked up.

luck in *v.* **1.** *Intrans.* to meet with exceptional good luck; **luck into** to gain, come into, or come upon, through good fortune alone.

 1920 Barron *Deeds of Heroism* vii: Fame is a lottery with a few capital prizes. The winners show perhaps no more wisdom, no more courage, than all the other gamblers. In the baseball phrase they simply "luck in." **1959** in *OED2*: Loveless...lucked into booming revenues. **1962** *Bullwinkle Show* (NBC-TV): Well, Captain, you lucked in again! **1970** Grissim *Country Music* 206: But really most of the things he succeeded in he lucked into. **1972** D. Jenkins *Semi-Tough* 21: He lucked into the job as a compromise candidate. **1980** *U.S. News & W.R.* (July 14) 30: An ex-movie actor who lucked into the governorship of California. **1983** *L.A. Times* (June 28) IV 5: Those who luck into first-class. **1986** J. Maloney *Chain* 201: Let's hope she lucks into the right guy. **1992** (Port Authority official quot. at LUCK OUT, 1).

 2. *Trans.* see s.v. LUCK, 2.

luckout *n.* a stroke of good fortune. Cf. LUCK OUT *v.,* 1.

 1973–77 J. Jones *Whistle* 547: But this did not stop the cook from bragging about what a luckout and great night the two of them had had.

luck out *v.* **1.** to meet with exceptional good luck; win or succeed through luck alone.

 1945 in *Amer. Heritage* (Aug. 1985) 26: He..."lucked out" by the coming events. **1946** G.C. Hall, Jr. *1000 Destroyed* 254: He had lucked out. He would soon be a guest of the Swiss. **1949** G. Coffin *Winning Poker* 181: *Luck Out*—To outdraw and beat a good hand. **1951** *New Yorker,* in *WDEU*: Had been arrested by a plainclothesman, who, as they say in Harlem, had lucked out on him; that is, the officer had picked him up merely on suspicion, searched him in a hallway, and found his dope outfit. **1954** *AS* XXIX 303: I was startled in my freshman English class when one of the students...said, "He lucked out on the final examination." When I asked what he meant by "lucked out," the entire class was amazed and pleased that I did not know, and immediately proceeded to inform me. **1955–57** Felder *Collegiate Slang* 3: *Luck out*—to get off easily. **1962** in Wepman et al. *The Life* 33: You lucked out on me before I got a shot. **1969** *New Amer. Rev. #7* (Aug.) 82: We lucked out on our connections. **1972** *N.Y. Times* (May 14) 1:

This is a time to keep quiet and hope the President lucks out. **1986** D. Wellington *Zombie Nightmare* (film): I think we lucked out. **1990** *Sally Jessy Raphaël Show* (synd. TV series): Well, I lucked out—as the kids say. **1992** *Newsweek* (Dec. 14) 88: I totally lucked out....He's a devoted husband and father with an old-fashioned sense of morals.

2. to meet with misfortune; run out of luck; be unlucky.

1957 *Sat. Eve. Post* (Aug. 10) 43: Barney should have had the honor...but he'd lucked out. He'd given up a wife and a spot in God's country to die at sixty-four angels. **1958** in *WDEU*: Elementary school children get a day off Feb. 17....Junior and Senior High Schools are lucked out....Both will be in session. **1959** Maier *College Terms* 3: *Luck out*—To have bad luck. **1954–60** *DAS*: *Lucked out* To have met with ill fortune or disaster; specif. to be killed. *Some W.W.II use.* **1979** *Village Voice* (N.Y.C.) (Apr. 30) (Scott-Foresman Coll.) 52: As to lucking out, there was no way of predicting that each player's team would breeze through an undefeated season and then lose badly in the championship finals. **1986** in Partridge *Concise Sl. Dict.* 271: "Boy, you really lucked out that time!" (said sarcastically): to run *out* of luck. Since late 1970s [in Canada]. **1992** N.Y.C. Port Authority official, age *ca*50: In the fifties, to "luck out" *always* meant to have bad luck! To have good luck was to "luck in." **1992** N.Y.C. tech. editor, age *ca*60: I first began hearing *luck out* in the late 1950's, and it seemed to mean "to run out of luck." Then it began meaning the opposite. A little while later it switched back again. I'm still confused so I never use it.

luck-rider *n. Gamb.* (see quot.).

1964 Rule *Desert of Heart* 102: At the Club [casino] we have a name for people who bet with a man who's winning. We call them luck riders.

luck through *v.* to manage or succeed by good fortune alone.—also used trans.

1933 in Spectorsky *College Yrs.* 113: I'll try to remove the conditional grades, and maybe I can luck through on my finals. **1943** in *WDEU*: Just now I wouldn't give a nickel for the chances, but we may luck it through. **1954** in *Britannica Bk. of Yr. 1955* 814: *Luck through*...(by analogy with *muddle through*) To depend upon luck for getting through. **1966–67** W. Stevens *Gunner* 23: Peaches [a bombing plane] lucked them right through a Bucharest raid.

luck up *v.* Esp. *Black E.* to meet with good fortune. Cf. LUCKED UP.

1952 in *DARE: Luck up*...To have good luck in some venture. "I sure lucked up getting a good car."...Rare. **1954** L. Armstrong *Satchmo* 25: I lucked up. **1967–69** Foster & Stoddard *Pops* 98: They just lucked up on [*i.e.*, in] making some early records.

¶ In phrase:

¶ **luck up on** *Black E.* to come upon or obtain by luck. [Mod. use is app. independent of earlier S.E. syn. *luck upon*, in bracketed quots.]

[****1670** in *OED*: Whereas there be so many thousand words in the world, and that he should luck upon the right one.] [**a***1683** in *OED*: When such a lewd, incorrigible sot Lucks by meer chance upon some happy thought.] [*****1712** in *OED*: The most Renowned Thomas Gale...has luckt upon another Interpretation.] **1946** Mezzrow & Wolfe *Really Blues* 308: *Luck up on*: get by luck, come into possession of unexpectedly. **1953** W. Fisher *Waiters* 68: Now and again he managed to "luck up on a pound"—five dollars. **1961** *S.F. Chronicle* (Nov. 12) ("This World") 29: I don't have anything in mind when I sit down [to improvise at the piano]. I just stumble around until I luck up on something. **1973** *Black Panther*, in *DARE*: Riggs happened to luck up on a good hustle.

lucky *n. Und.* LOOT.

1848 Judson *Mysteries* 37: I've brought it over to put in the big bag, and draw our share of the lucky.

¶ In phrases:

¶ **cut (one's) lucky** to clear out; escape; abscond. [The main entry is found s.v. CUT; these additional quots. are the earliest known U.S. examples of the phrase.]

*a***1865** in *Confed. War Jour.* (Sept. 1894) 94: He'd...see that I didn't "cut my lucky." **1866** *Night Side of N.Y.* 77: The chaps who patronize the saloon have all "cut their lucky."

¶ **make (one's) lucky** to make (one's) (lucky) escape. Cf. syn. *cut (one's) lucky* s.v. CUT.

*****1837** Dickens *Pickwick* ch. x: Hold still, sir: wot's the use o' runnin' arter a man as has made his lucky, and got to t'other end of the Bor-

ough by this time. **1882** (cited in *F & H*). **1928** *New Yorker* (Dec. 8) 60: The guy makes his lucky with the Chrysler.

lucky *adj.* ¶ In phrase: **get lucky** to have one's requirements met; (*specif.*) to succeed in having sexual intercourse. [A narrowing of the S.E. sense, which freq. implies 'to have a specific requirement met by chance'.]

1982 *Hardcastle & McCormick* (ABC-TV): You didn't come home last night. What, did you get lucky? **1984** Univ. Tenn. student: Favorite Expressions:...Hey baby, ya wanna get lucky? Why don't you lay down? I'll give ya a pillow. **1989** Leib *Fire Dream* 105: Getting lucky with wholesome farm girls. **1992** *Mystery Sci. Theater* (Comedy Central TV): I bet they're getting totally lucky. **1994** *Frasier* (NBC-TV): Nobody refers to sex as "getting lucky" anymore. **1995** *Mystery Sci. Theater* (Comedy Central TV): Good place to get lucky under there.

lucky bag *n. Naut.* (see 1906 quot.). Cf. slightly earlier BrE carnival sense 'bag from which one draws a prize as game of chance'.

1832 Wines *2½ Yrs. in Navy* I 39 [ref. to 1829]: All property that falls in his way for which he cannot find an owner, is thrown into the "lucky bag," the contents of which, if not finally claimed, are sold at auction. **1840** in *DA*: Every man-of-war, you know, has her *lucky bag*, containing a little of everything, and something belonging to everybody. **1847** Downey *Portsmouth* 161: A Goose in the Lucky Bag! Was it dead or alive? **1884** (cited in *DAE*). **1906** Beyer *Battleship* 82: "Lucky bag"—a bag in which are placed all articles lost on the ship.

lucky boy *n.* a crooked professional gambler, esp. a three-card monte player; (*Carnival*) a carnival grifter. Also **luckboy**.

1922 *Variety* (Oct. 27) 8: At a well-fixed fair the "lucky boys" don't wait for the big day. **1925** Robinson *Wagon Show* [ref. to 19th C.] 108: I had messed around for many years and thought I knew all about all kinds of games played by the "lucky" boys. **1966** R.E. Alter *Carny Kill* 14: It was an old dodge. I grinned at the luckboy and held up my five dollar bill. *Ibid.* 17: Those luck boys were damn thorough. **1975** McKennon *Horse Dung Trail* 52: He received large payments from the "lucky boys" who were "following" the show with his blessing. *Ibid.* 112: The "Lucky Boys" were never given the "Go Ahead" by "the Patch" until "Local Fuzz" had been taken care of.

Lucky Pierre *n.* a man who has intercourse with two other people simultaneously.—also used fig. *Joc.*

1942 E.H. Hunt *East of Farewell* 216: That lucky bastard....Lucky Pierre, he though, always in the charthouse. **1953** Del Torto TS: Ever hear of "Lucky Pierre, always in the middle." **1957** Herber *Tomorrow to Live* 228 [ref. to WWII]: You're Lucky Pierre again tonight, Andreas. **1960** Kirkwood *Pony* 266: There was one [pornographic book] with three guys, called *Lucky Pierre*. **1973** N.Y.U. student: I've always had this dream of going to bed with two heterosexual chicks. I always wanted to be Lucky Pierre. **1982** *Nebr. History* LXIII 279: But, like the proverbial "Lucky Pierre," we attempt to shoot down the middle again.

Lucy *n.* [short for SWEET LUCY] alcoholic liquor, esp. muscatel.

1957 H. Ellison *Web of the City* 13: In the alley, slumped down with a ketchup bottle of Sweet Lucy, lay his father. **1961** H. Ellison *Memos* 99: "An' stay away from the Lucy and the shit."...And with that stern warning to avoid liquor and narcotics, Pooch closed the meeting. **1987** R. Miller *Slob* 248: I mean you'n May didn't get hold of no bad Lucy and trip out on some Phantom of the Opera thing?

lude *n.* [aph. fr. Quaa*lude*] a capsule or tablet of Quaalude, trademark for a brand of methaqualone; (*broadly*) any depressant drug. [A citation of 1969 in R. Spears *Slang and Jargon of Drugs and Drink*, ref. to Lingeman, *inf. cit.*, (ed. 1), is erroneous; the word is found only in ed. 2 of 1974. The only legal manufacturer of Quaaludes discontinued their production in 1983.]

1973 *N.Y. Times* (Aug. 5) II 13: "Ludes" (Quaaludes, or "downs") were the hot sellers. **1973** *Nat. Lampoon* (Sept.) 90: Got any 'ludes? **1974** Lingeman *Drugs A to Z* (ed. 2) s.v. *methaqualone*: Slang names: sopers, ludes. **1980** Whalen *Takes a Man* 75: The last ones were 'ludes, I think. **1980** T. Wolfe, in *Harper's* (May) 74: He's rich, he's good-looking, but all he can talk about is ludes, amies, vertical skiing. **1983** *Nat. Lampoon* (Feb.) 40: Wanna cop some ludes? **1984** *L.A. Times* (Aug. 19) I 17: We had more auto fatalities caused by people intoxicated with 'ludes than alcohol. **1985** B.E. Ellis *Less Than Zero* 21: You wanna lude, is that it? **1992** N. Cohn *Heart of World* 225: Smack, coke, booze, ludes. **1996** *New Yorker* (Aug. 26) 128: We tried to be really evil. We dropped 'ludes.

ludehead *n.* a habitual user of LUDES.

    1980 in *Nat. Lampoon* (Jan. 1981) 91: About a hundred 'ludehead chicks on Fire Island.

lude out *v.* to become intoxicated on LUDES.—usu. as **luded-out.**

    1973 *Jour. Amer. Medical Assoc.* 224: Methaqualone Abuse: Luding Out. **1974** Lingeman *Drugs A to Z: Luding out…using methaqualone.* **1979** Gram *Blvd. Nights* 70: The…receptionist stared with 'luded-out…eyes. **1980** in L. Bangs *Psychotic Reactions* 330: You don't have to be Elvis to stay luded-out all the time. **1981** *CBS Evening News* (CBS-TV) (Aug. 12): In the language of the streets, she's "luded out"—high on methaqualone or Quaaludes. **1981** *Nat. Lampoon* (Nov.) 60: It had the decorative touch of a 'luded-out bullfighter. **1984** N. Stephenson *Big U.* 115: She must be…luded out of her…head. **1995** Weisbard et al. *Spin Record Guide* 279: Singer Dexter Holland cheerfully bounces around the 'luded-out metal riffs.

luff[1] *n.* [perh. ult. fr. BrE pronunciation /lɛftənənt/ via pun on *luff-tackle* 'a purchase composed of a double and single block, variously employed on shipboard'] Esp. *Navy.* a lieutenant. Also (*obs.*) **luff-tackle.** [See phonological note in *OED2*; virtually obs. in U.S. Army after *ca*1900, but cf. LUFT.]

    ***1805** J. Davis *Post-Captain* 76: You had laid down the keel of a young luff [*i.e.*, fathered a lieutenant]. *Ibid.* 124: They called him Acting Dickey;…they asserted he was only half a luff-tackle. **1813** in W. Dunlap *Diary* 469: See! how the luf swims away with the bucket. ***1821** *Real Life in Ireland* 172: The jolly *first luff.* **1833** *Mil. & Nav. Mag. of U.S.* (Apr.) 122: We reported to the 1st Luff over night. ***1836** in *OED:* The Hon. Mr. B., our junior luff. **1847** Downey *Portsmouth* 17: Among other foolish and unnecessary things he proposed to the 1st Luff was to have all the combings of the hatches and the waterways scraped and kept bright. **1849** Melville *White Jacket* 24: The *First Luff,* otherwise known as the First Lieutenant. **1862** in C. Brewster *Cruel War* 162: A 2nd Luff likes to have command once in a while. *Ibid.* 206: A poor first Luff. **1862** in *JAF* LXV (1952) 297: With Lowry for our first luff. **1875** Sheppard *Love Afloat* 41: He was third luff in the Peacock. **1877** Lee *Fag-ends* 12: "There's thirty pounds to the square inch now," says the Luff. **1878** Willis *Our Cruise* 53: I asked the First Luff to let me go in one of the boats. **1891** Maitland *Slang Dict.* 111: *First Luff* (sea term), first lieutenant in the navy. **1896** Hamblen *Many Seas* 208: The quartermaster…notified the "first luff." **1899** Young *Reminiscences* 432: Lieutenants are "luffs" to the men. **1918** Griffin *Ballads of Reg't.* 34: He was human with his Captain, cold, official with the "Luffs." **1918** "Commander" *Clear Decks!* 222: I wonder if Striper is still there as first luff. **1919** Stokes *Songs of Services* 163: The First Luff thinks so too. **1941** Kendall *Army & Navy Slang: The Luff…*Lieutenant Junior Grade. **1954–60** *DAS: First luff* A first lieutenant in the Navy.…*still used in W.W.I and W.W.II.*

luff[2] *n.* ¶ In phrases:

    ¶ **hold** [or **keep** or **choke**] **(one's) luff** *Naut.* to keep or frustrate from talking; shut up. Now *hist.*

    ***1821** *Real Life in London* I 295: Poll, says I, hold your *luff*—give us no more *patter.* **1841** [Mercier] *Man o' War* 220: You better *choke the luff* of your *jaw-tackle;* you'll have the officer of the deck upon us in a moment. **1855** Wise *Tales* 165: Smash him, Tom. Stop his luff, sharp. **1875** Sheppard *Love Afloat* 154: "Avast heaving, bosun!" "Come down a snake!" "Heave and pawl!" "Take a turn!" "Choke his luff!" cried out the laughing youngsters. **1894** *U.S. Naval Acad. Lucky Bag No. 1* 66: *Choke a luff…*to hush up. **1899** Young *Reminiscences* 77: Choke your luff, will you,…that's the President of the United States. ***1961** Burgess *Dict. Sailing* 51: *Choke his luff.* Put someone in his place by silencing him, or stop him doing something for a while; frustrate. ***1961** Hugill *Shanties* 155 [ref. to 1920's]: Oh, I wisht Johnnie Slite would keep his luff,/The bastard thinks we've hauled enough.

    ¶ **spring (one's) luff** [sugg. by technical sense 'to bring (a ship's) head closer to the wind'] *Naut.* to move quickly or with agility; spring into action.

    ***1805** J. Davis *Post-Captain* 68: Pray, Flora, spring your luff. ***1838** Glascock *Land Sharks* II 92: Long had to "spring his luff, bolt from the bay, and pull foot for the fore-rigging." **1841** [Mercier] *Man-of-War* 144: But come, spring your luff, and [give me a shave]. *Ibid.* 266: Be quick and spring your luff. ***1870** in *OED:* I just want to know who "spring their luffs" most nimble up the rigging.

luft *n.* [LUFF[1] + excrescent *-t,* or clipping of BrE pron.] a lieutenant.

    1983 Stapleton *30 Yrs.* 81: Ya want to start movin' in too, Luft? *Ibid.* 239: *Fire lieutenant—*…Usually called "Loo" or "Luft" [in the Boston Fire Department].

L.U.G. *n. Stu.* (see quots.).

    1993 *N.Y. Times* (June 5) (Nexis): There is even a new term—"lugs," lesbians until graduation. **1993** *Newsweek* (June 21) (Nexis): The "LUG," or "lesbian until graduation" phenomenon, however, has alienated many people—not only straight alumni but lesbians. **1995** *N.Y. Observer* (June 19) 30: Seven Sisters graduates will…drink Samuel Adams—out of the bottle!—while reminiscing over their L.U.G. days. **1995** Female Yale graduate, age 28 (coll. J. Sheidlower): It was a big deal at Yale to be a "political lesbian"—you didn't *necessarily* have to sleep with women, just identify with feminism. People like this were called L.U.G.'s—Lesbians Until Graduation. **1995** N.Y.C. lesbian, age 28 (coll. J. Sheidlower): L.U.G.'s are girls like Sarah Lawrence students who spend a year awkwardly groping with their roommates, and then within a year of graduation their pictures are on the wedding page of the *N.Y. Times.* I first heard it when I was at Berkeley, before 1988 or 1989. **1995** *Town & Country* (Nov.) (Nexis): But while some women will be gay for life…others, sometimes called "LUGs" (lesbians until graduation), are experimenting. **1996** Indiana Univ. grad. student: L.U.G. was a term I heard frequently when I was in college [at Swarthmore College, mid- to late 1980's].

lug[1] *n.* [prob. of Scandinavian orig.] **1.** an ear. [Long established as the usu. colloq. form in Scotland, but of later and limited usage elsewhere; see *OED2*, which calls it "now *colloq.* or *joc.*"]

    ***1592** R. Greene, in *OED:* Then the gentlewoman let loose his eares, and let slip his head, and away went he home with those bloody lugges. ***1625** B. Jonson *Staple News* V i: A fine round head when those two lugs are off. ***1659** J. Shirley, in *OED:* If you have a mind to lose one of your lugs,…Talk on. **1691** in Whiting *Early Amer. Provs.* 272: I dare venture to give her my Lugs, if in ten years he comply with £20 of the purchase. ***1698–99** "B.E." *Dict. Canting Crew: Luggs,* Ears. ***1785** Grose *Vulgar Tongue: Lugs.* Ears. **1800** in Weems *Washington* xv: I've something to whisper in your lug. ***1819** [T. Moore] *Tom Crib* 7: Round *lugs* and *ogles* flew the [boxer's] frequent fist. **1891** Maitland *Slang Dict.* 170: *Lug,* the ear. **1897** F.P. Dunne, in Schaaf *Dooley* 139: "They took this lug, too," he says, puttin' his hand on his ear. **1902** Hapgood *Autobiog. of Thief* 219: Wherever thou goest, keep the portals of thy lugs open. **1903** *Enquirer* (Cincinnati) (May 9) 13: Modern Slang Glossary…*Lug—*A person's ear. **1916** *R.R. Man's Mag.* (Aug.) 702 (Tamony Coll.): He beats it so's he wouldn't have to get a lugful of th' bawlin'-out he should ought to have had comin' ta him. **1929** Barr *Let Tomorrow Come* 154: Get up, tinhorn, or I'll knock your lugs off. **1933** Hammett *Thin Man* 302: Pull in that lug—it's getting in our drinks. *Ibid.* 308: "What's a lug, Nicky?" "An ear." **1949** *Sat. Eve. Post* (Dec. 3) 99: He twisted one earphone off the headset [and] shoved it over against Bagramyan's good lug.

    2. *Prizefighting.* the face or jaw.

    1927 *AS* III 29: The fighter's chin…is "whiskers," "lugg," "chops," "mugg,"…"jaw." **1929** Hotstetter & Beasley *Racket* 231: *Lug—*Face; *esp.* a very fat face. **1935** Pollock *Und. Speaks* s.v. *the: The lug,* the chin. **1939** *S.F. News* (July 26) 15 (Tamony Coll.): Galento will stiffen Nova in three round [*sic*]. He stands up straight and he can't hit. Tony will pop him on the lug every time he throws his left. **1952** *S.F. Examiner* (May 28) 35 (Tamony Coll.): DeMarco Argument/How About His Lug?…An individual…said after the Gonsalves fight that DeMarco's lug wasn't too stout.

lug[2] *n.* [orig. unkn.] **1.** an affectation; air; unwarranted show of pride.—usu. constr. with *put on.*

    1878 Mulford *Fighting Indians* 13: The excursionists were up at the Fort…putting on "lugs" generally. **1883–84** Whittaker *L. Locke* 194: Why, I remember him jest a common 'prentice, and he puts on more lugs than a juke [duke] now. **1889** in *DA:* If you notice me…piling on any lugs…you just bump me down hard. **1890** *Century Dict.: Lug…pl.* Affected manners; "airs" : as, to put on *lugs.* (Slang). **a*1890–96 F & H VI 246: *To put on lugs* = to be conceited. **1900** Dreiser *Carrie* 350: They put on a lot of lugs here, don't they? **1901** A.H. Lewis *Croker* 60: The English…make me tired with the lugs they put on. **1903** Ade *Society* 114: Up to that time the Outfit had not tried to throw on any

Lugs. **1904** Ade *True Bills* 36: But Horace observed that those who never had been strong enough to throw on the Lugs while they were living at Home, were the very ones who put Crimps into the Bank Account before the Honeymoon played out. **1922** S. Lewis *Babbitt* 157: Makes me tired the way these doctors and profs and preachers put on lugs about being "professional men."

2. [perh. a diff. word] a demand, esp. for money; usu. in phr. **put** [or **drop**] **the lug on** to beg or borrow, often by means of intimidation.

    1929 *AS* IV (Dec.) 343: *Lug on, put the:* To beg from someone. **1930** Irwin *Tramp & Und. Sl.* 124: *Lug.*—A request, generally used as "dropping the lug." **1929–31** D. Runyon *Guys & Dolls* 79: Why do you not put the lug on him? You stand okay with him. **1931** D. Runyon, in *Collier's* (Nov. 14) 7: She will next be trying to put the lug on me for a ducket, or maybe for her railroad fare. **1935** Pollock *Und. Speaks*: *Put the lug on*, to borrow. **1936** Steel *College* 300: Put the lug on the Commissioner himself if you have to. **1936** L. Duncan *Over the Wall* 27: I learned how to…"mooch a meal" from restaurants…and how to "put the lug on a guy" in the streets. **1936** in *AS* XVII (Oct. 1942) 206: Indiana Uses the "Lug." **1940** in *AS* XVII (Oct. 1942) 206: Putting Lug on Newspaper. **1950** *New Yorker* (July 8) 63: I can't recall when a youngster of mine put the lug on me for a baseball or a bat. **1963** Wepman et al. *The Life* 86: I'm hip to the way you pimps try to play/And the lugs you drop on a frail. **1973** in *OED2*: My father [Pres. H. Truman] also knew…that the governor…was "putting the lug" (to use Missouri terminology) on state employees to contribute to his campaign fund.

¶ In phrases:

¶ **drop a lug on, 1.** see **(2),** above.

2. *Black E.* to insult; criticize haughtily.

    1973 Schulz *Pimp* 77: Someday some bitch is going to drop a lug on you, and you won't be able to talk no shit. *Ibid.* 123: One will drop a lug on the other at that point about some shit and they'll start to fighting. **1973** Goines *Player* 9: "I don't understand it, but every time you two get together, it always ends with both of you trying to drop lugs on each other."…"That's right. Instead of two pimps, you act like two bitches."

¶ **put the lug on, 1.** see **(2),** above.

2. to beat up; use force or violence against.

    1932 Hecht & Fowler *Great Magoo* 69: You take that back or I'll put the lug on you. **1935** Pollock *Und. Speaks*: *Put the lug on*, to beat up a racketeer…for muscling in on forbidden territory. **1936** Kenyon & Daves *Petrified Forest* (film): You'd better crawl, or I might have to put the lug on you. **1942–49** Goldin et al. *DAUL*: *Put the lug on*. To remove forcibly…an irate victim from the scene of the swindle, as at a carnival.

lug³ *n.* [prob. alter. LUNK] a lout; *(specif.)* a big or clumsy person. [Rarely used of women.]

    *a*1927 in P. Smith *Letter from Father* 83: I stopped seeing her—she was a mediocre lug. **1930** Thew & Starr *Show Girl in Hollywood* (film): I walked out on those dumb lugs. **1930** W. Smith *Silver Horde* (film): Why don't you learn to talk over a phone, you big lug! **1930** Lavine *3d Degree* 38: Wondering how Kid the Lug, after being accused of twelve killings and a thousand assaults, keeps out of jail. **1932** *AS* VII 334: *Lugg*—A fellow. **1932** Mahin *Red Dust* (film): [To a woman:] Come here, ya lug. **1934** L. Berg *Pris. Nurse* 95: A lot of these lugs have got plenty of scratch planted. **1935** Marion, Hanemann & Loos *Riffraff* (film): I gotta tell that big lug who saved his skin. **1935** J. O'Hara *Dr.'s Son* 20: And any lug of a lunkhead that don't stay in line will have me to answer to. **1936** Steel *College* 310: The lugs!…Yellow-bellied bastards. **1936** M. Levin *Old Bunch* 379: Those lugs downstairs should have sent him up last Monday. **1936** S.I. Miller *Battling Bellhop* (film): Why don't you lugs leave that poor kid alone? **1937** in H. Gray *Arf* (unp.): What's that lug…doin' to earn th' heavy sugar we're payin' him? **1938** Bezzerides *Long Haul* 166: Hey, you big lug, what's the idea? **1944** A. Scott et al. *Here Come WAVES* (film): Not…with you lugs [women] around. **1949** Maier *Pleasure I.* 35: A "lug" is—well, I don't know what you'd say: a louse, a disagreeable person. **1979** Gram *Foxes* 82: The other lugs picked up the cry. **1983** *Night Court* (NBC-TV): I'm crazy about the big lug. **1984** C. Francis *Who's Sorry?* 180: All those curse words you and the neighborhood guys like Louie the lug say all the time. **1989** *U.S. News & W.R.* (Apr. 10) 29: A big-boned lug. **1989** Hynes & Drury *Howard Beach* 42: That big, dopey lug.

1994 *TV Guide* (Mar. 5) 15: I find you an attractive lug. **1994** Auster *Smoke* (film): The poor lug. **1995** *N.Y. Times* (Sept. 26) C11: Aw, get outta here, ya big lug.

lug¹ *v.* to escort; bring or take along, esp. as a companion.

    *1881–84 Davitt *Prison Diary* I 152: I was lugged before the beak, who gave me six doss in the Steel. **1906** Ford *Shorty McCabe* 36: Sometimes he lugs me along and sometimes he don't. **1927** in Hammett *Knockover* 340: Then what do you want to lug him along for? **1930** Conwell *Pro. Thief* 123: It is almost uncanny the way some of these officers can pick out a thief who is lugging a sucker. *Ibid.* 239: *Lug, v.*—conduct, lead. **1944** Cosper *Your Language* 155: Who you luggin' to the prom? **1968** [R. Beck] *Trick Baby* 217: When I lug that sucker to you, I'm going to wink at the mark. **1979** T. Baum *Carny* 91: What about this jailbait you're lugging?

lug² *v.* [abstracted fr. *put* [or *drop*] *the lug on*, s.v. LUG², *n.*] **1.** *Und.* to beg or solicit from.

    1926 in *AS* LVII (1982) 262: *Lug. Beg. Lugger.* Beggar. **1942** *ATS* 348: Beg; request a lone or gift….*lug,*…put the lug on. **1945* (cited in Partridge *Dict. Und.* 419).

2. *Pris.* to pedicate; make into a catamite.

    1971 Hilaire *Thanatos* 159: You mean Leslie's going to be lugged by some creeps wanting his keister? **1977** Caron *Go-Boy* 107: In my case I was a super straight kid with a Puritan's outlook on sex and I wasn't giving anybody the opportunity to lug me.

3. *Und.* to beat up; drub. Cf. *put the lug on*, 2, s.v. LUG², *n.*

    1976 *L.A. Times* (Apr. 26) I 41: We want to see no more "luggings" (beatings).

lugan¹ *n.* [orig. unkn.] *Chicago.* a Lithuanian or person of Lithuanian descent.—used derisively. Also **lugie.** Also vars.

    1947 Motley *Knock on Any Door* 110: Inside, a bunch of the neighborhood men, polacks and lugans and a big Russian with an accordion got together week-ends. **1964** L.A. Pederson, in *PADS* (No. 42) 40: All ten instances of *lugen*…Lit, and *bohawk*…are in the speech of Chicagoans with social or business contacts in the Lithuanian communities of the South Side. *Lugen* is by far the most common…[but] its usage is quite specialized, even in Chicago. *Ibid.* 48: The etymology of *lugen* could not be explained by any of the informants who used it or by any of the Lithuanians or Balto-Slavicists I have since consulted. **1969** in *DARE* files: Lithuanians—*Lugies*. **1983** R.I. McDavid, handwritten note in RH files: *Lugun*…*esp. Chiago* [*sic*] a Lithuanian, or a person of Lithuanian descent. *a*1986 *NDAS*: *Lugan*…A Lithuanian or person of Lithuanian descent. **1995** Wisconsin history prof. of Lithuanian descent (coll. Joan Hall): Only people in Chicago knew the term *lugen*. And in Chicago, it seems to be restricted to southwestern Chicago, near what used to be known as "Little Lithuania" (near Marquette Park). **1995** Retired English prof., age *ca*70 (coll. J. Sheidlower): *Lugen*…It seems to me that I heard the term all through my childhood and early years on the south side of Chicago.

lugan² var. LOOGIN¹.

lugger *n. Gamb. & Und.* a person who escorts or transports a customer or victim to the scene of a usu. illicit enterprise.

    1931 in D.W. Maurer *Lang. of Und.* 32: *Lugger*…One who is paid to "lug in" customers to a certain [carnival] show or joint. **1945–50** in D.W. Maurer *Lang. of Und.* 189: *Lugger:* a steerer for a crooked gambling house or game. *ca*1950 (cited in Partridge *Dict. Und.* (ed. 2) 842). **1958** *N.Y. Times Mag.* (Mar. 16) 88: *Lugger*—Also *roper*. The first confidence man to approach a victim. **1961** Scarne *Comp. Guide to Gambling* 684: *Lugger* A person who transports players to the game. Not to be confused with a *Steerer*. **1969** King *Gambling & Org. Crime* 232: *Lugger*—Minion who brings players to an illegal game. **1980** W. Sherman *Times Square* 143: Helwig had worked years before as a "lugger," a man who chauffeurs players to and from high-action crap games.

lughead *n.* [perh. alter. of LUNKHEAD] a stupid person; blockhead.

    1958 Vittes *Married a Monster* (film): You big lughead. **1967** N.Y.C. man, age 20: A *lughead* is a dope. **1986** C. Horrall & C. Vincent *Wimps* (film): I don't know how you lugheads are doing it, but don't stop. **1995** *New Republic* (June 12) 50: [He] assailed the IQ of his fellow Yalies: "I've met lugheads there."

lugie var. LUGAN¹.

lugnut *n.* LUGHEAD.

    1992 *Herman's Head* (Fox-TV): Listen to me, lugnut!

Luke the Gook *n. Mil.* the Chinese, North Korean, or Vietnamese Communist armed forces; an individual member of such forces; (*broadly*) an Asian man.—used disparagingly. Also simply **Luke.**

1953 in *Hist. of Chaplain Corps U.S. Navy* VI 187: The enemy—Luke as we call him—3 years ago we called them "Gooks"—apparently did not always appreciate the services….The men holler "Chink on the way," and everyone ducks into a bunker….Luke had the entire area zeroed in. **1962** W.E. Blake *Heartbreak* 9: Hill 701, otherwise known as Luke the Gook's Castle. **1963** Fehrenbach *This Kind of War* 668: Old Joe Chink, Luke the Gook, the enemy….He would come again, even while they talked of peace at Panmunjom. **1966** J. Lewis *Tell It to Marines* 202 [ref. to Korean War]: They figgered I had personal hate for ole Luke, so they put me up here, where I kin shoot at him all day long. **1968** *Newsweek* (Mar. 18) 28: One North Vietnamese,…known to the marines as "Luke the Gook," has been ripping off his deadly bursts at low-flying aircraft. **1969** *Esquire* (Sept.) 156: Orrin was…looking out toward the hills and Luke the Gook. **1969** M. Lynch *Amer. Soldier* 140 [ref. to 1953]: We are not dealing with civilized people here, and life in one of Luke's P.O.W. camps is a brutal agonizing experience. **1971** Sorrentino *Up from Never* 243: Make believe you're Luke the Gook and you got a knife. **1971** Cole *Rook* 205 [ref. to 1953]: I have been out front eighteen times looking for Luke, and never even smelled garlic! **1978** J. Webb *Fields of Fire* 76 [ref. to Vietnam War]: Old Luke the Gook better be saying his damn Hail Marys. *Ibid.* 291: Finally Snake grabbed papasan by the nape of the neck…."Come on, Luke. We gonna take a look around your house." **1980** Di Fusco et al. *Tracers* 15: Now Luke the Gook, Link the Chink, and Charlie Cong like to hide in that tall green elephant grass. **1984** J. Fuller *Fragments* 48 [ref. to Vietnam War]: Luke the Gook set [the rockets]…crudely….Luke was long gone. **1985** J.M.G. Brown *Rice Paddy Grunt* 113: "I go tell MP you No. 10!"…"MP, my ass, Luke." *a*1989 C.S. Crawford *Four Deuces* 175 [ref. to 1951]: Luke-the-Gook's castle…was…a great outcropping of granite halfway up the slope of Hill 975.

lulu *n.* [orig. uncert.; perh. fr. *Lulu*, hypocoristic form of female given name *Louise*; yet *looly* is the earliest attested sp.; R.L. Chapman's sugg. (*NDAS*, p. 266) that it is ultimately fr. *loo* 'a kind of card game pop. esp. in the 18th C.', is not sustained by existing evidence] **1.a.** an attractive young woman; (*hence*) girlfriend. [Now subsumed into **(b)**, below.]

1857 in *DA*: She was then, in my eyes, the looliest *looly* of the loolies, she was. Her hair was a beautiful auburn,…fair complexion; and a figure—such a figure! **1893** in Dobie *Rainbow* 165: When I drink whiskey, my *luluh* drinks with me. **1894** *Harper's* (Oct.) 697: Look, gents, here comes Cordelia Mahoney. Ain't she a *loo-loo*? **1895** in Dobie *Rainbow* 161: My *luluh** said, "It's a shame…." *Luluh, sometimes a proper name, in the songs is generally a synonym for "honey," "woman," etc. **1895** in Levine *Black Culture* 409: If you don't quit monkeyin' with my *luluh*, tell you what I'll do:/I'll feel aroun' your heart with my razor, and I'll cut you half in two. **1929** Hotstetter & Beasley *Racket* 231: *Lulu*—Gangster's sweetheart. **1930** in J.T. Farrell *Grandeur* 206: That's what I call a lulu. **1931** (quot. at STAG, *n.*).

b. a notable or outstanding person or thing; something that is an extraordinary example of its kind; LOLLAPALOOZA. Also (*obs.*) as adj.

1886 *Lantern* (N.O.) (Nov. 11) 6: Farrell's two baser was a lu-lu. **1889** in *DAE*: Oh, that's lulu! It'll suit mamma right down to the ground. **1890** in F. Remington *Sel. Letters* 96: Bought a lulu mare from Kentucky….Never buy a horse again except in Kentucky. **1892** in Alter *Utah Jour.* 252: Have you seen this week's issue of the Index? She's a Lulu! **1893** *Life* (Feb. 2) 70: You may be lu-lus in de business, an' all dat. **1895** Townsend *Fadden Explains* 77: You're straight; it is a lulu. **1896** Ade *Artie* 45: Mebbe you think I ain't got a lulu of a head on me this morning. **1898** *Chi. Record's War Stories* 112: "That was a lulu," cried one soldier when a ball passed through his hat, "and lulus roost high." **1898** in McManus *Soldier Life* 90: Oh! Honolulu is, in fact, a veritable "lulu." **1899** Garland *Eagle's Heart* 320: You'd ought to see the Mississippi, she's a loo-loo. **1904** in "O. Henry" *Works* 1428: Give 'em another of them Yalu looloos and you'll be eatin' rice in St. Petersburg. **1905** Riordon *Plunkitt* 48: He's a lulu. He knows the Latin grammar backward. **1908** in Fleming *Unforgettable Season* 256: The National League race is now a lulu—the luluest kind of lulu what is. **1909** *DN* III 347: *Lulu*…A remarkable person. Sometimes [in east-

ern Alabama] *lulu-kapoodler.* **1915** H.L. Mencken, in Riggio *Dreiser-Mencken Letters* I 192: A Zeppelin raid…will be undertaken shortly, and it will be a lulu. **1930** Irwin *Tramp & Und. Sl.: Lu Lu.*—Anything unusually worthy or desirable. **1932** *AS* VII 334: *A lulu*—denotes perfection [at Johns Hopkins Univ.]; something out of the ordinary. **1950** *Sat. Eve. Post* (Dec. 3) 65: You're the funniest aide I have ever had. And I have had some lulus. **1952** *N.Y. Times* (July 13) I 50: Eisenhower's painting is good, but his wife can't find the right word to describe the first picture he made of her. Was it a lu-lu? She was asked today at her first press conference. **1953** S. Sheldon et al. *Dream Wife* (film): That fight with Effie must have been a lulu. **1956** E. Hunter *Second Ending* 324: I've got a lulu at nine. History of the English Language. You ever take that course? **1958** S.H. Adams *Tenderloin* 207: It's going to be a looloo of a story. **1961** Scarne *Comp. Gde. to Gamb.* 523: They take the rest of the chump's bankroll with a lulu of an angle that is customtailored to fit any sucker with even a little larceny in his heart. **1971** Le Guin *Lathe of Heaven* 13: And that last combination dose you took was a lulu. **1972** G. Walton *Capt. Madam* 59: He was not about to miss a fight, particularly…a scrap that was sure to be a "lulu." **1987** *Campus Voice* (Fall) 50: The first question…was a lulu.

c. an inept, demented, or offensive person. [Now interpreted as an ironic application of **(b)**, above.]

1888 (quot. at CAKE, 1.a.). **1896** *DN* I 420: Lulu…In [northern Ohio and southeastern Michigan] a term of disrespect. **1937** Steinbeck *Mice & Men* 56: Curley's new wife….Ain't she a looloo? **1948** Maresca *My Flag* 44: So I humor the lulu for a couple of blocks.

d. *Poker.* any of various eccentric hands arbitrarily allowed to win the pot, usu. to deceive a newcomer. [The humorous story narrated by J. Lillard in the 1896 quot., where "looloo" appears unexpectedly in the punch line, may have provided the basis for the practice reported by T. Clark in 1987.]

1896 J. Lillard *Poker Stories* 87: "A looloo?" he repeated. "What is a looloo, anyway?" "Three clubs and two diamonds," coolly replied the miner….He jerked his thumb toward a pasteboard sign which ornamented the wall of the saloon. It read: *A Looloo Beats Four Aces. Ibid.* 88: *The Looloo Can Be Played But Once a Night.* **1916** C.C. Davis *Olden Times* 322: A "lulu" beats a royal flush. **1938** Asbury *Sucker's Progress* 30: The most famous of all eccentric hands, the Looloo, is said to have been invented in Butte, Montana, during the 1870's, in a game between a stranger and a Butte miner. **1987** T.L. Clark *Dict. Gamb. & Gaming* 122: Looloo…In poker, an unusual or odd hand, such as a 2, 4, 6, 8, and 10 of various suits, which can be declared a winner the first time it occurs in a poker session, but only one time during a session.

2. [punning on LOO] a lavatory. *Rare* in U.S.

***1939** (N. Coward, cited in Partridge *DSUE* (ed. 7) 1261). **1959** W. Burroughs *Naked Lunch* 220: I am returning from The Lulu or Johnny or Little Boy's Room. ***1962** McDavid *Mencken's Amer. Lang.* 359: According to Nancy Mitford…*toilet* is now non-U; the current fad in England is *loo* or *lulu*.

3. [punning on *lieu*] **a.** *N.Y. State Pol.* a fixed allowance paid to a legislator in lieu of reimbursement for actual expenses.

1945 *Amer. N & Q* (Jan.) 149: Lu-Lu payments: "payments in lieu of something or nothing" (N.Y. *Herald Tribune*, December 9, 1944). **1957** *N.Y. Times*, in *DAS*: A "lulu" is an expense allowance that does not have to be accounted for. **1965** *N.Y. Times* (Jan. 17) I 46: Mr. McKeon had offered a bribe at the public expense" [punctuation *sic*]—a "double lulu," or tax-free expense fund, amounting to $10,000 a year. **1968** Safire *New Language* 242: *Lulu.* Payment made to legislators "in lieu of" expenses….New York State sets a fixed fee to be paid them in lieu of expenses; if they can skimp on the outlay, they can keep the extra money. **1969** *N.Y. Times* (Apr. 22): "Lulu"…[was] coined by the late Gov. Al Smith. **1995** *N.Y. Times* (Nov. 26) ("City") 12: Mr. Vallone awards himself a $35,000 lulu for serving as Speaker.

b. (see quot.).

1989 P. Benchley *Rummies* 53: He's like me, a lulu. He's here [in an alcohol treatment facility] in lieu of going to jail.

lumber *n.* **1.** a toothpick; toothpicks. *Joc.*

1936 *AS* (Feb.) 44: [Soda fountain, N.Y.C.]: *Lumber.* Toothpick. **1944** Kendall *Service Slang* 11: *Lumber*….toothpicks. **1967–69** in *DARE*.

2. *Baseball.* a baseball bat; (*fig.*) skillful hitters.

1958 in P. Dickson *Baseball Dict.*: [Photo caption:] Ready with their "lumber"…are the "big three" sluggers of the Pittsburgh Pirates. **1954–60** *DAS: Lumber*…A baseball bat. **1980** Lorenz *Guys Like Us* 140: There was no life in their lumber. **1983** Whiteford *Talk Baseball* 111: *Lumber*…good hitters….A team may boast "a lot of lumber." **1988** *Nat. Lampoon* (Feb.) 25: Watching the Royals' Jim Eisenreich swing that lumber.

3. *Gamb.* a nonplaying spectator at a gambling game.

    1961 Scarne *Comp. Guide to Gambling* 684: *Lumber* (1) Spectators in a gambling joint. (2) Broke players. "There's more lumber around here than players." *ca***1961** (cited in T.L. Clark *Dict. Gambling & Gaming*). **1969** King *Gambling & Org. Crime* 232: *Lumber*—kibitzers, small-time players, pikers.

4. the penis.—usu. considered vulgar.

    *a***1972** B. Rodgers *Queens' Vernacular* 211: Lumber à la mode. **1981** *Nat. Lampoon* (June) 54: When I finally slipped the lumber to her, we both began screaming. **1986** D. Tate *Bravo Burning* 161: She can have a load of my heavy lumber any ol' day. *Ibid.* 162: I'm gone lay the lumber on her. *a***1990** Westcott *Half a Klick* 122: Fucker…loafed his lumber to some woman.

5. *Narc.* stems or other unwanted debris in a quantity of marijuana. [A "1974" citation alleged in Spears *Drugs & Drink* for Lingeman *Drugs A to Z* (ed. 2) is apparently erroneous.]

    1974 in *Nat. Lampoon* (Jan. 1975) 43: It was ninety bucks a metric lid, but at least it doesn't have any "lumber." **1979** (Homer *Jargon*, cited in Spears *Drugs & Drink*). **1982** E. Abel *Marihuana Dict.* 64: *Lumber* Stems of the marihuana plant.

lumber[1] *v. Und.* **1.** to jail or arrest.—usu. used in passive. *Rare* in U.S.

    ***1812** Vaux *Vocab.*: A man apprehended, and sent to gaol, is said to be *lumbered*, to be *in lumber*, or to be *in Lombard-street*. ***1840** in *OED2*: Revelling in the reminiscences of the number of times they have been lumbered. ***1882** in *OED2*. **1936** in D. Runyon *More Guys* 149: He is finally lumbered in 1931 and sent to college. **1954–60** *DAS: Lumber*…To arrest. *Some underworld use c1935.* ***1961**, ***1970** in *OED2*.

2. to pawn. Hence **lumberer**, *n.* a pawnbroker.

    1812** Vaux *Vocab:* To *lumber* any property, is to deposit it at a pawnbroker's. **1891** Maitland *Slang Dict.* 170: *Lumber*, to put in pawn….*Lumbered*, pawned. *a1890–96** *F & H* IV 248: *Lumberer*… American thieves' [slang]…A pawnbroker.

lumber[2] *v.* to depart.

    1847 in Oehlschlaeger *Reveille* 208: We will jest take *anuther*…drink, and then lumber.

lumberjack strawberries see s.v. STRAWBERRIES.

lume *n. Army.* artificial tactical illumination; illuminating flares.

    1986 Thacker *Pawn* 102 [ref. to 1970]: Just get some 'lume out. *a***1990** P. Dickson *Slang!* 241: *Lum* [sic]. Illumination flares.

lummox *n.* [cf. BrE. dial. *lommocking* 'clumsy', of unkn. orig.] a clumsy or stupid person; oaf. Now *colloq.* Also (*rare*) **lummixer, lummy.**

    a*1825** in *OED2*: Look o' yin great lummox, lazing and lolloping about. **1839** Briggs *Harry Franco* I 34: Mr. Lummucks, I presume? **1841** *Spirit of Times* (Oct. 23) 408: Not he, the darned lummucks. **1854** in Thornton *Amer. Gloss.* II: Man in his original state is little more than a big lummux of a baby. **1858** J. Stone *Put's Golden Songster* 52: Good-by, you big lummox, I'm glad you backed out! **1867** in W.H. Jackson *Diaries* 109: A big lummox they call Jack. **1889** "M. Twain" *Conn. Yankee* 382: As a rule, a knight is a lummox. **1893** W.K. Post *Harvard* 186: A lazy lummox. **1895** F. Remington *Pony Tracks* 173: Who is the scoundrel, the lummux, humph? **1906** R. Casey *Parson's Boys* 218: I ain't afraid of no lummix like you. **1908** Kelley *Oregon Pen.* 15: I saw the big lummixer…stick his head out. **1930** L. Riggs *Lilacs* 148 [ref. to ca1905]: Don't set there, you lummy, answer when you're spoke to! **1957** J. Thompson, in T. Thorne *Dict. Contemp. Slang:* The awkward lummox of a kid who, though only ten years old, was almost as big as his fifth grade teacher.

lump *n.* **1.** a gold coin or nugget.

    1849 *Nat. Police Gaz.* (Sept. 29) 3: We mean to keep a bright lookout for the *lumps* and leave all other trash behind. **1859** *Spirit of Times* (Apr. 2) 88: All the "lumps" and "filthy lucre,"/All the "gelt."

2. seminal fluid; WAD.—usu. considered vulgar.

    *ca***1889** (quot. at *blow (one's) lump*, 1, below). **1916** (quot. at *blow*

(one's) lump, 1, below). **1927** *Immortalia* 121: He was always…ready to spill a lump.

3. *Hobo.* a handout of food, esp. a sandwich; a cold meal.

    1893 in *Independent* (Dec. 19, 1901) 3012: When a Bum goes to a house and gets a lunch they call it Hand out, Lump, Soup, Slop, etc. **1903** *Enquirer* (Cincinnati) (May 9) 13: Modern Slang Glossary…*Lump*—Something to eat. **1912** Lowrie *Prison* 105: I noticed he had a "lump" (lunch) with him. **1914** Jackson & Hellyer *Vocab.* 56: *Lump*…A donation of victuals intended for consumption outside the house. **1918** in *AS* (Oct. 1933) 29: *Lump.* Handout. So I starts out bummin' on de main drag till I gets me a *lump*. **1922** N. Anderson *Hobo* 17: For those who have no money, but enough courage to "bum lumps," it is well that the jungles be not too far from a town. **1925** Mullin *Scholar Tramp* 14: She may prepare a lunch and wrap it in an old newspaper or paper bag. Her parcel is known in Hoboland as a "lump," a "hand-out," a "poke-out," or a "dukee." "Lump" is in most common use. **1925–26** J. Black *You Can't Win* 67: Bring back a "lump" for us. **1929** *AS* IV (June) 342: *Lump.* Food handed out in a paper sack at back doors. **1930** Irwin *Tramp & Und. Sl.:* A "bald-headed lump" is one with nothing but bread and meat. **1935** J. Conroy *World to Win* 88: The punk…has mooched a lump….a bald-headed lump. **1935** Maltz *Black Pit* 32: Hallelujah give us a handout—/Hallelujah give us a lump. **1948** J. Stevens *Jim Turner* 163 [ref. to ca1910]: Stacks of what the hobos called lumps were on a table….The lumps were meat and cheese sandwiches. **1952** C. Sandburg *Young Strangers* 382 [ref. to ca1892]: He led me to where he had been eating bread and meat unwrapped from a newspaper. "I got three lumps last night," he said, and handed me a lump for myself. A lump was what they handed you if they wanted to give you something to eat at a house where you asked for it. **1968** Spradley *Drunk* 246: "Yeah, I got a lump"—which means a sandwich. **1975** McCaig *Danger Trail* 51: Sickles and…Wayne doled out the cold "lump" which would fuel the crew until the evening meal.

4. usu. *pl.* a beating; (*hence*) bruising punishment; reversals; criticism; blame; defeat.—usu. constr. with pronoun and with *give*, *take*, or *get*.—*occ.* constr. in sing.

    1930 E. Caldwell *Poor Fool* 189: That Blondy bastard is going to be…waiting for me to hand over some lumps to him. **1934** H. Roth *Call It Sleep* 250: C'mon, Pedey, let's give 'im 'is lumps. **1934** in North *New Masses* 267: With his gang of 17-year old savages, here the future critic boxed, wrestled and otherwise received his "lumps." **1936** Kingsley *Dead End* 727: Who fuh! I'll give yuh yuh lumps in a minute. **1949** *Sat. Eve. Post* (June 4) 55: I can turn myself in for him….I can take the lumps for him, I'll do that. **1955** Archibald *Aviation Cadet* 113: They all got their lumps….All except Nelz seemed to have soloed to Lieutenant Stuart's satisfaction. **1958** J. Ward *Buchanan* 6: The devil's taking his lumps in there. **1959** Lederer *Never Steal Anything Small* (film): Knock it off, sonny. You want some lumps? **1961** Braly *Felony Tank* 39: If you're old enough to sneak around…and bust into places, you're goddam well old enough to take your lumps. **1962** T. Berger *Reinhart* 37: Getting his lumps from a gantlet of furious natives. **1965** Spillane *Killer Mine* 39: He's lookin' for somebody to hand you lumps. **1965** *L.A. Times* (Feb. 25) II 5: He has taken many a lump in his time, and a good many of them…he had coming to him. **1966** Elli *Riot* 39: When the party was over, he'd take his lumps with the rest. **1967** G. Green *To Brooklyn* 172: Who's next? Who wants their lumps? **1971** *Business Week* (Nov. 20) 23: The EEOC came in for lumps of its own from one witness. **1972** *Business Week* (Mar. 11) 34: The corporate image had taken another lump. **1973** D. Morrow *Maurie* 12: Come and get your lumps, boy! **1981** Brenner & Nagler *Only the Ring* 17: Managers talked while their fighters took their lumps. **1981** A. Haig, in *U.S. News & W.R.* (May 18) 28: I know that some of our allies have been a little wary as a result of our rhetoric. I will take the lumps for that. **1995** Court TV (Mar. 2): You just have to sort of take your lumps and move ahead and get on with it.

5. (see quot.).

    1989 *Newsweek* (Aug. 7) 16: *Piece:* A piece of junk, used as a trade-in [automobile]. Also, a "lump."

6. usu. *pl.* a woman's breasts.—usu. considered vulgar.

    ***1990** T. Thorne *Dict. Contemp. Slang: Lumps*…breasts. **1996** N.Y.C. man, age 27 (coll. J. Sheidlower): She had some lumps like you wouldn't believe.

¶ In phrase:

¶ **blow (one's) lump, 1.** to ejaculate semen.—usu. considered vulgar.

*ca*1889 Field *Boastful Yak*: He blew his lump. **1916** Cary *Venery* I 19: *Blowing One's Lump*—To achieve emission.

2. *Narc.* to become high; enjoy oneself; GET OFF, *v.*, 8, 9.

1959 Murtagh & Harris *Who Live in Shadow* 52: After that first night, I smoked tea all the time. I blew my lump. I got sent.

lump *v.* **1.** to put up with against one's will.—usu. in phr. **like it or lump it.**

1791 in *DA*: As you like it, you may lump it. **1833** S. Smith *President's Tour* 57: If cousin Jack don't like it he may lump it, so there now. **1833** J. Neal *Down-Easters* I 104: Let 'em lump it if they don't like it. **1846** Durivage & Burnham *Subjects* 197: If you don't like it—you may lump it. **1862** "Barritt" *East & West* 6: "He ought to take what he can get, and be thankful!"…"If he don't like it, he can lump it." *1863 in T. Taylor *Plays* 168: It's like it or lump it. **1875** "M. Twain" *Old Times* 47: If he don't like it he'll have to lump it, I reckon. **1876** "M.Twain" *Tom Sawyer* 15: You can lump that hat if you don't like it. **1927** McKay *Home to Harlem* 52: If you no like it you can lump it! **1929–31** J.T. Farrell *Young Lonigan* 73: He thought up a brave story, about how he told the gumshoe to lump it. **1971** *All in the Family* (CBS-TV): If they don't like it, they can lump it, take it down the road and dump it. **1982** "W.T. Tyler" *Rogue's March* 146: Told you to lump it, did he? **1995** *Simpsons* (Fox-TV): I'm going to keep teaching your class—like it or lump it.

2. to drub; beat up.—often constr. with *up.*

1859 Matsell *Vocab.* 52: *Lump.* To beat. "*Lump the booby,*" flog the fool. **1931** Bontemps *Sends Sunday* 63: Occasionally they would turn and lump one another. **1934** Appel *Brain Guy* 86: I used to lick you…when we were kids, but I bet you could lump me with one fist. **1940** W.C. Fields *By Himself* (Jan. 25) 370: Badger comes over with his roughs and they take me out to lump me up. **1944** Bontemps & Cullen *St. Louis Woman* 6: Used to be you could take a lumping and know it's good for you. **1952** H. Grey *Hoods* 48: Once in awhile we get a contract from one of them bootleggers to lump somebody up. **1952** Mandel *Angry Strangers* 322: They lump me up a little. **1956** Rose *Crime in Streets* (film): The only time anybody pays any attention to ya is when they're lumpin' ya on the head. **1958** Talsman *Gaudy Image* 15: Lettum hear ya callum that. They'll lump ya up good. **1959** Morrill *Dark Sea* 91: The Old Man caught me lumping him up. **1960** H. Selby, Jr., in *Provincetown Rev.* III 74: One would hold him and the other(s) would lump him. **1966** Elli *Riot* 87: Show us the guys and we'll lump up their heads. *a*1989 in Kisseloff *Must Remember This* 533: Five or six goons with baseball bats would lump up a couple of guys.

3. to defecate.—usu. considered vulgar.

1977 Stallone *Paradise Alley* 29: I think El Suppa was so scared of dyin', he lumped in his pants!

lumper *n.* **1.** a longshoreman; (*broadly*) a person employed to load or unload any heavy cargo.

[*1781 G. Parker *View of Society* II 78: They then commence lumpers, which is skulking about ships, lighters, etc. hanging about quays, wharfs, etc. stealing old iron, fruit, sugar, or whatever comes to hand.] *1785 Grose *Vulgar Tongue*: *Lumpers.* Persons who contract to unload ships. *1796 in *F & H* IV 249: The prevailing practice of discharging and delivering the cargoes of ships by a class of aquatic labourers, known by the name of lumpers. *1840 F. Marryat, in *OED*: They go on board as lumpers to clear the ships. **1846** Codman *Sailors' Life* 30: He…took a fair survey of the lumpers and loafers about the wharf and the vessel. **1884** Symondson *Abaft the Mast* 86: The "lumpers" (men employed at the loading and unloading of ships) set to work. **1893** Barra *Two Oceans* 25: [The coal] was then trimmed by lumpers, and in two hours' time a two hundred tons' schooner would be ready to go down the river fully loaded. **1895** *DN* I 390: *Lumper:* common unskilled laborer. Boston, Mass.ˊ **1913** J. London *J. Barleycorn* 209: Work as…lumper [or] roustabout. **1928** Harlow *Sailor* 242: The "lumpers" were at work unloading our ballast. **1942** *ATS* 722: *Lumper,* a freight-shed laborer. **1952** *New Yorker* (June 28) 45: Little Joe that's a lumper on the pier. **1976** Hayden *Voyage* 655: A gang of lumpers were doing the heavy work. **1990** Rukuza *West Coast Turnaround* 2: Three or four of them had the overly muscle-bound look of lumpers. *Ibid.* 10: If those packing-plant lumpers 're as good as I think they are, the trailer'll be empty…by now.

2. an item of cheap merchandise to be sold in lots.

1937 *New Yorker* (Aug. 7) 21: These are "lumpers," worth, wholesale, sixty cents apiece.

3. a piece of excrement.—usu. considered vulgar.

1984 N. Bell *Raw Youth* 39: I used to wash the rank lumpers out of your didies.

lumphead *n.* LUNKHEAD.

1923 T. Boyd *Through Wheat* 60: You better get down, you lumphead.

lumtum [cf. LA-DI-DA] *n.* a person in fashionable society; SWELL.—used derisively.

1882 McCabe *New York* 221, in *F & H*: Altogether my first evening among the lumtums panned out well. **1882** *Judge* (Dec. 23) 5 (caption): Lumtum decides to try his new boots.

lunar *n.* ¶ In phrase: **take a lunar** [sugg. by technical sense 'take a lunar sighting with a sextant'] *Naut.* to thumb one's nose.

1893 Wawn *South Sea Islanders* 256: They poured out a torrent of chaff upon the French boatmen, accompanied by several expressive gestures, one of which was certainly an imported one, being what is commonly known among sailors as "taking a lunar."

lunch *n.* **1.** something easy or certain; CINCH.

1900 *DN* II 45: *Lunch,* n. Something easy. **1907** in H.C. Fisher *A. Mutt* 4: "Pajaroita" is a lunch in the first [race]. **1908** in H.C. Fisher *A. Mutt* 157: Don't tell a soul. Booger Red [a racehorse] is a lunch.

2. the stomach; (*hence*) the contents of the stomach (in contexts related to vomiting). [Additional quots. are at BLOW, *v.*, 11; *lose (one's) lunch* s.v. LOSE; *shoot (one's) lunch* s.v. SHOOT; in bracketed quot., the meaning is simply 'sounded the signal for my lunchtime'.]

1904 T.A. Dorgan, in Zwilling *TAD Lexicon* 116: A punch to the lunch lands them all. **1917** (quot. at SHOOT). [**1944** W.C. Williams, in Witemeyer *Williams-Laughlin* 104: The whistle has blown my lunch.] **1961** H. Ellison *Memos* 48: Oh boy, I thought, *here goes my lunch.*

3. *Stu.* a foolish or obnoxious person; JERK.—rarely used attrib. Also **lunchie.**

1963 *AS* (May) 159: [A] University of Buffalo…informant explained…that "a lunch guy might as well be out to lunch for all the good he's doing anyone where he is." **1971** Dahlskog *Dict.* 39: *Lunch, lunchie, lunchy,* n. One who is incompetent or who habitually goofs.…a dummy. **1973** Eble *Campus Slang* (Mar.) 2: *Lunch*—a person who is unaware, imperceptive, dull, i.e.…What a lunch—you just heard that album and you don't know what it is? **1979** Gutcheon *New Girls* 65: My date was some drip…she's a lunch. **1984** Algeo *Stud Buds* 7: An absent-minded or inattentive person…*lunch.* *a*1988 Lewin & Lewin *Thes. Slang* 260: Oaf…lamebrain,…lunchie.

4. one that is ruined or done for.

*1963 in Partridge *Concise Dict. Sl.* 272: *Lunch*…What you become after a [surfing] wipe out. **1983** S. King *Christine* 15: The engine block's cracked.…This car is lunch, my friend. It's just total lunch.

¶ In phrases:

¶ **catch (one's) lunch, 1.** to be vanquished.

1965 in *AS* XLV (1970) 301: This is the expression, currently fashionable in Chicago,…"he caught his lunch," translation, "he lost so badly he became nauseated." **1980** Lorenz *Guys Like Us* 141: The sticks were…catching their lunch from the Amalgamonsters.

2. *Mil.* to be killed. [Quots. ref. to Vietnam War.]

1983 Eilert *Self & Country* 148: He tripped the booby trap and an ambush. I caught the booby trap—he caught his lunch. **1986** Heinemann *Paco's Story* 128: I saw…the colonel himself catch his lunch. He got a direct hit with a mortar round.

¶ **eat (someone's) lunch** see s.v. EAT, *v.*

¶ **lose (one's) lunch** see s.v. LOSE.

¶ **out to lunch** Orig. *Stu.* inattentive; absent-minded; in a daze; stupid; naive; eccentric; insane; (of intellectual abilities) absent.

1955 *Science Digest* (Aug.) 33: "Out to lunch" refers to someone who, in other years, just wasn't "there"—and he is told immediately to "Get with it." **1958** (quot. at O.T.L.). **1959** *Time* (Aug. 31) 46: As a studio press agent describes it: "It's a drawing-room comedy, mostly outdoors." Or, as the teen-agers say, mostly out to lunch. **1954–60** *DAS*: Out to lunch…Unable to qualify socially.…Stupid. **1960** Swarthout *Where Boys Are* 39: If parents think their daughter can attain young womanhood in 1958 in a state of pristinity they are really out to lunch. *Ibid.* 217: I know it's out to lunch for a girl to be willing to wait five minutes these days but I am. **1966** in IUFA *Folk Speech: Out to lunch*—Not on the ball. **1968** D.L. Phillips *Small World* 131: I came to the conclusion that Australian city planning is "out to lunch." **1969** H. Wexler *Medium Cool* (film): You think you can change…all of the hate. You're probably out to lunch. **1971** *Nat. Lampoon* (Nov.) 26: You must be out to lunch. I need more time than that. **1977** Sayles *Union Dues* 49: He didn't seem to know much of anything. Permanently out-to-lunch, Darwin would say. **1978** W. Brown *Tragic Magic* 5: They said he…was not only out to lunch but should be fitted for the wraparound dinner jacket. **1978** Price *Ladies' Man* 32: They wanted back all the people who were either so out to lunch or so atrocious that they had to be seen again to be believed. **1979** Homer *Jargon* 94: This was an *out to lunch* campaign. **1983** Walford *Max. Life Span* 21: And many others whose judgments were out to lunch. **1990** *Sally Jessy Raphaël* (synd. TV series): My brains were out to lunch. **1992** *Bold & Beautiful* (CBS-TV): "Where is your *pride*, Karen?" "I guess it's out to lunch—with *your* self-esteem!" **1994** *Newsweek* (Oct. 3) 49: Clinton and his advisers have been almost comically out to lunch on the political dividends of "reinventing government." **1996** *Jerry Springer Show* (synd. TV series): Or have you found something that's saying they're out to lunch [in their psychic claims]?

¶ **take to lunch** to surpass or outdo; vanquish.

    1987 *This Week with D. Brinkley* (ABC-TV) (Dec. 13): Some people were saying that Raisa Gorbachev was going to take Nancy Reagan to lunch, in the colloquial sense.

lunch *v. Stu.* to damage extensively; ruin; (*also*) to fail (a course of study).

    1968 *Everett* (Wash.) *Herald* (Mar. 27) 5, paraphrase in RH files: *Lunch. Teenage Slang.* to ruin, as in "He really lunched his engine." **1969** *Current Slang I & II* 59: *Lunch*, v. to fail.—College males, Texas. *a*1990 P. Dickson in *Slang!* 31: He just lunched his second engine this month. **1996** Dalzell *Flappers 2 Rappers* 78 [ref. to 1950's]: *Lunch* To scatter parts around during an extreme engine failure.

lunchbag *n. Stu.* a dull, foolish, or obnoxious person. Also **lunchsack.** Cf. LUNCHBOX.

    1968 Baker et al. *CUSS* 154: *Lunch Bag.* An undesirable person. **1974** Lahr *Trot* 17: Sign on the bottom, lunchbag. **1977** M. Franklin *Last of Cowboys* 70: Don't call me Lunchbag. **1988** Eble *Campus Slang* (Fall): *Lunchsack*—dull, boring person. "My date was a total lunchsack."

lunch basket *n.* the belly. *Joc.* Also **lunch wagon.**

    1915 T.A. Dorgan, in *N.Y. Eve. Jour.* (Apr. 12) 15: A left to the lunch basket won the fight for Fitz from Jim Corbett. **1915** T.A. Dorgan, in Zwilling *TAD Lexicon* 116: James dropped his man with a belt in the lunch wagon. [*1990 T. Thorne *Dict. Contemp. Slang: Lunchbox*…the stomach, belly or abdomen.]

lunchbox *n. Stu.* LUNCHBAG. Also **lunchbucket.**

    1964 in *Time* (Jan. 1, 1965) 56: A *zilch* is a total loss, and so is a *wimp*…*gink*…*skag*…*lunchbucket.* **1968–70** *Current Slang III & IV* 80: *Lunchbox*, n. A simpleton.—University of Kentucky. **1970–72** in *AS* L (1976) 54: *Lunchbox* "simpleton." **1991** Rudnick *I Hate Hamlet* 40: What are you to be—artist, or lunchbox?

lunch-bucket *adj. Pol.* being or concerned with blue-collar issues. Cf. LUNCHPAIL, 2.

    1956 in Rowin *Go South* 151: In the audience was a liberal lunch-bucket representation. **1983** *L.A. Times* (Feb. 28) I 2: It's a lunch bucket issue. The dump would mean…100 jobs to an area where most people "are lucky to make $6,000 a year, if they have a job at all." **1987** Kent *Phr. Book* 154: Not exactly a lunch-bucket type of crowd. **1991** *New Republic* (Mar. 18) 43: Lunch-bucket liberal causes like labor and social welfare legislation.

lunched-out *adj.* out to lunch s.v. LUNCH, *n.*

    1978 *Rolling Stone* (Jan. 12) 5: Condemned buildings, winos and the "lunched out" dot this man's inquisitive past. **1987** Univ. Tenn. student: I'm making an F in there. I just sit there. Don't know what's goin' on. Lunched out, man!

lunch hook *n.* usu. *pl.* a finger or (usu.) hand; (*pl.*) clutches. Cf. GRUB HOOK. [The sense 'a tooth' given in 1900 quot. is perh. erroneous.]

    1896 Ade *Artie* 58: Florence and Tommy put their lunch-hooks together. **1900** *DN* II 45: *Lunch-hook*, n. Generally used in the plural. 1. The hands. 2. A finger. 3. A tooth. **1918** in *Wisc. Mag. of History* 62:230: Once they get their lunch hooks on this doroga it is going to

be a long, long time before they will let loose of it. **1931–34** in Clemmer *Pris. Community* 333: *Lunch hook*, n. The human hand. Get your lunch hook out of my kick. **1949** Algren *Man with Golden Arm* 16: Watch the lunch hooks now. **1968** W.C. Anderson *Gooney Bird* 201: Just keep your big lunch hooks off my girl. **1968** J.P. Miller *Race for Home* 368: She sure did hate to let a beautiful boy like him get away and ride off into the sunset for some other female to get her cotton-pickin lunch-hooks into. **1970** Ebert *Beyond Valley of Dolls* (film): The noble Porter Hall is trying to get his lunch hooks on *your* money. **1994** *CBS This Morning* (CBS-TV) (Apr. 20): The coyote…missed his opportunity to get his lunch hooks on a squirrel.

lunchie var. LUNCH, *n.,* 3.

lunchmeat *n.* **1.** Esp. *Stu.* a stupid, obnoxious, or inconsequential person; BALONEY, 1.

    1977 M. Franklin *Last of Cowboys* 117: Did it ever occur to any of you lunchmeats that we are about to get our asses busted so bad, we'll never sit again? **1979** G. Wolff *Duke of Deception* 212 [ref. to Princeton Univ., 1957]: "Lunchmeat," "banana," "wonk," "wombat," "turkey" [syns. for "obnoxious person"]. **1988–89** in Safire *Quoth Maven* 252: At Dartmouth…"feckless" souls…are referred to singularly or collectively as "lunchmeat." **1992** Minneapolis, Minn., man, age *ca*30: This guy is lunchmeat! **1992** *Batman* (Fox-TV): If this lunchmeat figured out where we are, Batman can't be far behind. **1994** *Jerry Springer Show* (synd. TV series): What am I, lunchmeat?

2. nonsense; BALONEY, 2.

    1987 *ALF* (NBC-TV): Aw, lunchmeat! **1992** *Jerry Springer Show* (synd. TV series): What? My points have been lunchmeat?

3. an easy victim or victims; GONER.

    1990 *Mystery Sci. Theater* (Comedy Central TV): I hope this works, or little Billy will be lunchmeat. **1994** *Sally Jessy Raphaël* (synd. TV series): People…like this are going to be lunchmeat.

lunchpail *n.* **1.** *Stu.* a stupid or obnoxious person; LUNCHMEAT, 1. Cf. LUNCHBAG.

    1968 Baker et al. *CUSS* 154: *Lunchpail.* An ugly person, male. An ugly person, female. **1979** Gutcheon *New Girls* 183: I don't see any reason to have a bunch of lunch pails standing onstage, do you? **1992** *Duck Tales* (CBS-TV): OK, lunchpail.

2. a blue-collar worker. Earlier **lunch-pailer.** Cf. LUNCH-BUCKET. See also JOE LUNCHPAIL.

    1958 *Time* (Nov. 3) 35: I don't need votes from lunch-pailers. *Ibid.*: For the "lunch-pailers" he plugged "free, autonomous trade unions." **1977** Sayles *Union Dues* 187: He was touching Inez then, softer than you'd expect from a lunchpail, more like one of those executive-suite smoothies just read the *Kama Sutra. Ibid.* 191: Over six hundred dollars. A lunchpail with that much. **1984** Vice-pres. W.F. Mondale, at Dem. Nat. Convention (July 19): Young and old, native and immigrant, male and female, yuppie and lunch-pail—we are all united here. **1992** *N.Y. Times Mag.* (Aug. 2) 50: Traditional lunch-pail liberals and progressive Democrats are beginning to question the vitality of their own programs.

lunchy *adj. Stu.* foolish; ridiculous; unfashionable.

    1964 *Sat. Eve. Post* (Feb. 22) 73: Having to share his new campus with a good number of lunchy undesirables. **1969** *Current Slang I & II* 59: *Lunchy*, adj. Performed in such a manner as to indicate that the performer was "out to lunch" when he did it. High school males, Kansas. **1970–72** *AS* L 52: *Lunchy* "dull, stupid." *Ibid.* 62: *Lunchy*…Absent-minded, "out to lunch"…Out of style "He looks so lunchy wearing that bow tie." **1974** Eble *Campus Slang* (Mar.) 4: *Lunchy*—strange, socially inept, lazy.

lung *n.* **1.** *R.R.* a railroad (car) coupling.

    1916 *Editor* XLIII (Mar. 25) 343: *Lung.* a coupling. **1923** McKnight *Eng. Words* 44: *Pulled a lung* for "pulled out coupling." **1929** *Bookman* (July) 524: Two minutes later we pull a lung out of a freezer and have to shove the bad order onto a passing track. **1930** in Botkin & Harlow *R.R. Folklore* 324: The engineer's jerked out a lung. **1954–60** *DAS: Lung*…A draw-bar connecting two railroad cars.

2. a cylinder; (*also*) an engine. See also ONE-LUNGER.

    1918 in Grider *War Birds* 101: We arrived in…a one lung taxi. **1944** (quot. at Maytag Messerschmitt).

3. usu. *pl.* a woman's breast. *Joc.*

    1951 H. Robbins *Danny Fisher* 274: She squirmed there for a moment, getting her seat right so that her lungs showed over the counter. **1956** I. Shulman *Good Deeds* 32: "Man, she's stacked like an acre." "So's the other one....With very nice lungs." **1959** W. Burroughs *Naked Lunch* 150: Women walk over this bridge with their lungs hanging out to arouse the desires of these dubious citizens. **1972** D. Jenkins *Semi-Tough* 20: She also has what obviously is a whole bunch of dandy lungs underneath a silk blouse. **1982** E. Leonard *Cat Chaser* 132: She's got a pair of lungs on her she could float across the sea on 'em. **1987** D. Fein & R.L. O'Keefe *Cheerleader Camp* (film): Willya look at the lungs on that girl?

lung-duster *n.* a cigarette. *Joc.* Also **lung-fogger.**

   1929 Gill *Und. Slang* : Lung-duster—Cigarette. **1940** *AS* (Oct.) 335: A cigarette is a *cig, fag, coffin-nail, smoke,* a *lung-duster.* **1943** G. Fowler *Sweet Prince* 55: Sweet Caporals, a brand of lung-foggers that had...in every package a colored picture of some famous athlete or actor. **1944** Burley *Hndbk. Jive* 143: Lung-duster—Cigarette.

lunger *n.* **1.** a person suffering from a lung ailment, esp. tuberculosis.

   1893 in *OED2*: The rainy season is hard for "lungers" and nervous invalids. **1907** *Lippincott's Mag.* (May) 625: Vesper's paw was a "lunger." **1907** Peele *N.C. to S. Calif.* 107: In the West Tucson is called the "lunger" town...from the large number of people who visit Tucson...for lung troubles. **1908** J. London *M. Eden* 281: Oh, I'm a lunger. **1911–12** J. London *Smoke Bellew* 180: It was filled to spilling with lungers. **1914** Callison *Bill Jones* 286: I noticed a great many Northern people there. They all had coughs, "lungers" they call them in Texas. **1914** in E. O'Neill *Letters* 24: This might interest you as a "lunger's" experience. **1925** in Hammett *Big Knockover* 221: "Lunger!" She tapped her chest. "A croaker told me I'd last longer out here." **1927** H. Miller *Moloch* 7: Penny arcade of lice, lungers, lifers, and hallucinations. **1928** Dahlberg *Bottom Dogs* 138: A lunger...had to take his family with him to L.A. to get into a warmer climate. **1930** Dos Passos *42d Parallel* 100: I'm through, that's all...I been a lunger all my life an' I guess it's got me now. **1934–43** F. Collinson *Life in Saddle* 204: A "lunger"...rode up to the house. **1949** Gresham *Limbo Tower* 64: I ain't fighting with no lungers. **1974** Hejinian *Extreme Remedies* 1: An intern over on the TB ward wanted me to check out one of his lungers. **1979** D. Halberstam, in *Atlantic* (Apr.) 55: He was a lunger, and was eventually taken in by a doctor who was also suffering from a serious lung disease. *a***1990** P. Dickson *Slang!* 145: *Lunger.* Patient with obvious lung disease.

   2. a cylinder. See also ONE-LUNGER.

   *a***1903** in *DA*: The gasoline cars, one or two "lungers," as they were called.

   3. an expectorated bit of phlegm. Also **lungie.**

   1946 Mezzrow & Wolfe *Really Blues* 44: Tell him to cough up a lunger. **1971** *Current Slang V* (Spring) 13: *Hang a lunger,* v. To spit. **1975** S.P. Smith *Amer. Boys* 313: Spit on him. Big lunger. Right in the face. **1979** V. Patrick *Pope* 216: I'll put a fucking lunger right into...his...cup. **1981–85** S. King *It* 458: He...spat a...lunger into the rainy air. *a***1989** in Kisseloff *Must Remember This* 416 [ref. to 1930's]: But when you spit on the shoes, you didn't give 'em a lunger, because...a lunger...has acid in it. **1996** *Jerry Springer Show* (synd. TV series): He's hackin' up a lungie!

lung hammock *n.* (see quot.). *Joc.* Cf. LUNG, 3.

   *a***1986** *NDAS*: Lung-hammock...A brassiere.

lung warts *n.pl.* a woman's breasts. *Joc.* Cf. LUNG, 3.

   1946 H.A. Smith *Rhubarb* 65: After seeing her on the stage...he...wrote: "Whatta pair of lung warts!" **1973** *TULIPQ* (coll. B.K. Dumas): Breasts: *lung warts, tits.* **1980** D. Hamill *Stomping Ground* 158: Hold onto them lung warts for dear life. **1983** Elting, Cragg & Deal *Dict. Soldier Talk* 190: *Lung warts* (1930s and later; all Services)...A woman's breasts.

lunk *n.* a blockhead; (also) a large, clumsy individual; oaf.

   1867 *Harper's Weekly,* in *DA* s.v. *lunkhead:* They're tigers, you thick-headed lunk. *****1907** in *OED2*: None but a red-headed runt'd have been such a lunk as to try it. **1935** Algren *Boots* 185: Don't tell me you got more, lunk. **1942** H. Miller *Roofs of Paris* 46: He tells Sid and me that we're a pair of lunks. **1947** Schulberg *Harder They Fall* 267: I want to beat Lennert. I just want to see if I can do it with this lunk. **1952** Clayton *Angels* 63: He was a big beefy lunk. **1963** in Bruce *Essential Bruce* 168: She's a lunk! **1965** Petrakis *Pericles* 2: They want some lunk for Congress. **1968** Young *Apollo* 144: You know a big lunk, name of Preston? **1983–89** K. Dunn *Geek Love* 249: One of the lunks...was loading the case. **1990** G. Lee *China Boy* 303: All youse

gotta do is lay fists onna lunk and youse done good. **1993** *New Yorker* (May 17) 106: Belushi [is] more of an action [film] lunk.

lunker *n.* **1.a.** *Angling.* a game fish that is unusually large for its kind; whopper. Now *S.E.*

   1867 Clark *Sailor's Life* 149: He is a lunker, and will give us a hard try. **1911** in *DARE*: Pewt knew where there were some bully perch, old lunkers. **1920** in *DA*: This old lunker of a rainbow gave me a bath. **1953** *Sat. Eve. Post* (May 3) 98: A spring salmon hit on a deep line, a lunker that set the pole creaking. **1956** *New Yorker* (Aug. 25) 26: I expect to catch some real honest-to-goodness lunkers. **1972** *Seattle Post-Intelligencer* (July 25) C1: 10 lunkers from 20 to 40 pounds. **1982** Least Heat Moon *Blue Hwys.* 47: Good fishin' along Sandy. Wasn't lunkers in it, but...the water moved. **1982** *N.Y. Times* (July 23) A11: You had so many hooks in and had landed so many lunkers. **1992** *Mystery Sci. Theater* (Comedy Central TV): I got a walleye, a northern. There are some *big* lunkers here.

   b. any large specimen. Now *S.E.*

   1912 *DN* III 582: *Lunker, n.* A large specimen. "Isn't that calf a *lunker*?" **1962** *Sat. Eve. Post* (Oct. 13) 36: Wherever possible, he pegs a lunker's wage to the grading system he devised many years ago. By running and rerunning game movies, Brown and his aides statistically score all of Cleveland players.

   2. an old or uneconomical motor vehicle.

   1973 *Seattle Times* (Dec. 2) E5: The development of small automobiles that make far more efficient use of gasoline than the lunkers we drive now. *a***1986** *N.Y. Times,* in *NDAS:* In old cars known as clunkers, lunkers, winter rats.

lunkhead *n.* a dull-witted individual; blockhead. Hence **lunkheaded,** *adj.* [The 1906 quot. is attrib. to the fictional "A.T. Jackson" and incorrectly dated "1852" by both *DAE* and *DA;* see *DA* biblio.]

   1868 H. Shaw *Billings on Ice* 31: Hambletonians and sum ov the kings ov England hav both sired lunkheads. **1866–71** Bagg *Yale* 45: *Lunkhead,* a stupid, slow-witted fellow. **1877** Bartlett *Amer.* (ed. 4) 375: *Lunk-Head.* A heavy, stupid fellow. **1883** in *DAE*: I want to get a naked-eye view of the crown-heads, to compare them with the lunk-heads at home. **1884** "M. Twain" *Huck. Finn* 150 [ref. to 1850's]: So the duke said these Arkansaw lunkheads couldn't come up to Shakespeare. **1884** in *DAE*: Her lunk-headed admirer. *a***1890** in Barrère & Leland *Dict. Slang* II: He calls our worthy Secretary of State...a "fossilised *lunkhead.*" The term *lunkhead* is usually applied by sporting men to a very sorry style of horse. **1893** Hoefler *Dr.'s Office* 9: No! you lunkhead, take that back. **1894** S. Crane *Red Badge* 76: B'jiminey, we're generaled by a lot 'a lunkheads. *a***1890–96** *F & H* IV 251: *Lunk-headed...*(American).—Senseless. **1906** C. Canfield *Forty-Niner* 136: Then Pard shut the book with a slam and said I was a lunkhead. **1912** in *DAE:* A complete lunkhead. **1932** Tasker & Baldwin *Dr. X* (film): Listen, ya lunkhead. I'm not clownin'. **1935** *Amer. Mercury* (June) 230: *Lunk head:* fool. **1949** in *DA:* You're a lunk-headed moon-calf. **1950** *Sat. Eve. Post* (Aug. 5) 112: Why don't you step on it, you lunkhead? **1951** H. Robbins *Danny Fisher* 41: I don't know how you ever came to marry that lunkhead anyway. **1951** *New Yorker* (Mar. 24) 24: He was a bulky, duckfooted lunkhead. **1956** Neider *Hendry Jones* 57: He was sure one lunkhead, with his horseteeth and his self-satisfied grin. **1958** *N.Y. Times Mag.* (Mar. 30) 21: They...think more clearly than the dashing lunkheads of yore. **1990** *Maclean's* (Aug. 27) 9: Steinbrenner was a rare natural resource—a lunkhead extraordinaire, a usurper of tradition, a destroyer of self-esteem. **1993** *21st Cent. Dict. Sl.:* So this lunkhead finally decides where to sit and takes my chair!

lunky *adj.* stupid; *lunkheaded* s.v. LUNKHEAD.

   1942 *ATS* 176: Stupid...*lunkheaded, lunky.* *a***1986** *Time,* in *NDAS:* Conflict between paternal authority and lunky adolescent waywardness.

luny var. LOONY.

lurk *v. Electronics & Computers.* to observe an ongoing discussion without participating in it. Hence (*usu.*) **lurker,** *n.*

   1984 *Scientific Amer.* (Sept.) 83 (adv.): That'll fool the "lurkers," those CB "see it alls" who get their kicks by watching. **1985** *Memphis* (Feb.) 32: Scads of curious on-lookers (dubbed "lurkers" by the regulars) who watch the proceedings without joining in. *a***1986** *Toronto Life,* in *NDAS:* Ian had found a lurker in the system. **1991** E. Raymond *New Hacker's Dict.: Lurker...*One of the "silent majority" in a [*sic*] electronic forum; one who posts occasionally or not at all....This term is not pejorative and indeed is casually used reflexively: "Oh, I'm just lurking." **1992** *N.Y. Times* (Dec. 1) C14: An important writer or producer is "lurking": reading messages but not posting one himself. **1993** Lambert & Howe *Internet Basics* (gloss.): *Lurking* The term used to describe "listening in" on a mailing list, online forum, or newsgroup without participating. **1994** Wolff *NetGuide* (gloss.): *Lurkers* Regular readers of messages online who never post.

lurp *n. Army.* **1.** [representation of usu. pronun. of *LRRP,* offic. initialism] a member of a long-range reconnaissance patrol. Also **lerp, lurpie.** Rarely as v. [See 1991 quot.]

    1968 *Everett* (Wash.) *Herald* (July 3) 6C: The four were members of a U.S. Army Long-Range Reconnaissance Patrol (LRRP), the jaunty, jungle-suited scouts known as "Lurps" who serve as the eyes and ears of regular U.S. troops. **1970** *N.Y. Post* (July 1) 4: GI Lurps: The Real Guerrillas...Bob and Mister John are Lurps—that's what the GIs call the lunatic guys who go out on the long-range reconnaissance patrols. The lurps are a kind of elite—the U.S. Army's only real guerrillas in this real guerrilla war. They go out on foot in five or six man teams and they stay out for days or maybe weeks on end. **1982** Del Vecchio *13th Valley* 59: I spoke personally with several LRRPs (he pronounced it "lurps"). **1983** K. Miller *Lurp Dog* 116: Mopar was glad he wasn't a Russian Lurp. **1986** Zumbro *Tank Sgt.* 166: The "lurps" (LRRPs) spotted signs of jungle-camp activity. *a***1987** Bunch & Cole *Reckoning* 36: The Lurpies know what they're doing. **1987** "J. Hawkins" *Tunnel Warriors* 27: Killed another Charlie last night while Lurpin' thru sector seven. **1989** Zumbro & Walker *Jungletracks* 16: The little fellow's a Lurp. **1991** S. Stanton *Rangers at War* 14: On 15 July 1961 the Seventh Army activated the U.S. Army Long Range Reconnaissance Patrol Company (Airborne), Wildflecken, for V Corps. The provisional company had...no numerical designation but was known as the "Victory Lerps." The Victory stemmed from V for V Corps, and...later Lerp became indifferently spelled as Lurp....The U.S. Army Long Range Reconnaissance Patrol (Airborne), Nellingen, [activated the same day,]...was known as the "Jayhawk Lerps." **1992** L. Chambers *Recondo* 92: I'm thinking about lurping on down there.

    2. [pronun. of offic. initialism *LRPR* 'long-range patrol ration', infl. by **(1),** above] a freeze-dried combat ration for personnel on long-range reconnaissance patrols. [Quots. ref. to Vietnam War.]

    1983 Elting, Cragg & Deal *Dict. Soldier Talk* 190: *Lurps*...Long-Range Patrol Rations. **1983–90** L. Heath *CW2* 12: You eating lurps? *Ibid.* 115: ARVN lurps....Freeze-dried rice. **1990** G.L. Clark *Wds. of Viet. War* 288: *Lurp Rations*...Some Lurp meals also included an orange-flavored..."cornflake" bar. **1991** Reinberg *In Field* 131: Long-range patrol rations, also called lurps. [**1992** L. Chambers *Recondo* 274: *LRRP*...a dehydrated ration used by special-operations units.] **1993** P. Dickson *War Slang* 280: Freeze-dried foods very much like those in the lurp have begun to show up in...stores selling to campers and backpackers.

lush *n.* [orig. unkn.] **1.a.** intoxicating liquor.

    [**ca***1745** (see note at LUSHINGTON).] *****1790** in *OED: Lush,* drink. *****1796** Grose *Vulgar Tongue* (ed. 3): *Lush.* Strong beer. *****1812** Vaux *Vocab.: Lush,* beer or liquor of any kind. *****1838** Glascock *Land Sharks* I 150: Put a glim in the t'other ken, and let any chaps as comes for lush go there. **1840** *Spirit of Times* (May 2) 103: Prime havannahs, and tip-top lush. **1848** G. Thompson *House Breaker* 6: Let us have...some good *lush.* **1848** *Ladies' Repository* (Oct.) 315: *Lush,* Spiritous liquors. **1851** [G. Thompson] *Jack Harold* 17: Give the candidate a bumper of *lush.* **1899** A.H. Lewis *Sandburrs* 95: Oh! he was a dream! He's one of them t'ings a mark sees after he's been hittin' it up wit d'lush for a mont'. **1930** Irwin *Tramp & Und. Sl.* 125: *Lush*...Any of the made-up liquor to be found in tramp or carnival circles, such as essence of peppermint, Jamaica ginger, paregoric or "rubbing" alcohol. **1944** Burley *Hndbk. Jive* 143: *Lush*—Drink, strong liquor, whiskey, wine, beer. **1950** A. Lomax *Mr. Jelly Roll* 51: Just swilling all the lush in the world. *a***1953** in *Amer. Jour. Socio.* LIX 240: They've been high on lush (alcohol). *ca***1953** Hughes *Fantastic Lodge* 60: I was staying stoned on lush. **1954** L. Armstrong *Satchmo* 202: From the way I was holding up you would have sworn I was immune to the lush. **1958** *Frees Beatniks* (film): I know where we can get all the lush we want, man. **1958** Gilbert *Vice Trap* 14: We need something to chase this lush. **1958–59** Southern & Hoffenberg *Candy* 156: Being out only for cheap strong lush. **1963** in Becker *Marihuana:* I mean, they've been high on lush [alcohol]. **1963** D. Tracy *Brass Ring* 467: Suppose Brinkman goes on the lush the first time he gets his hands on any money? **1965** Cleaver *Soul on Ice* 18: I had been getting high for four or

five years and was convinced...that marijuana was superior to lush. **1966** Fariña *Down So Long* 40: Take a sip of lush, don't hurry things. **1975** McKennon *Horse Dung Trail* 222: Do you know where the hands are getting their "lush"?

    b. a drinking spree.

    *****1841** in *OED:* We ended the day with a lush at Véry's. **1879** *Nat. Police Gaz.* (Sept. 20) 15: He begins a "lush" that lasts a month. *****1896** in *OED:* On very special occasions...there would be a "lush," when every mess brewed its punch, or egg-flip. **1965–71** in *Jour. Studies on Alcohol* XXXII (1971) 733: *On a lush* = on an extended drinking bout.

    c. a drunkard; sot.

    1851 [G. Thompson] *Jack Harold* 60: The lushes had to suffer.... **Lushes,* intoxicated persons. **1891** DeVere *Tramp Poems* 33: Bud Jones, "the Lush" sat in the corner. **1891** Riis *Other Half* 167: The first long step in crime taken by the half-grown boy, fired with ambition to earn a standing in his gang, is usually to rob a "lush," *i.e.,* a drunken man who has strayed his way, likely enough is lying asleep in a hallway. **1892** Norr *China Town* 18: Yer red-nosed lush! **1897** Ade *Horne* 3: "It's not unlikely," said Doc', with a look of dry disdain at the lush. **1902** Mead *Word-Coinage* 165: "A lush" is one who drinks. **1906** H. Green *Boarding House* 86: The Swede, being a lush, was rather looked down upon. **1920** Ade *Hand-Made Fables* 14: He was denounced as a Lush. **1923** Ornitz *Haunch* 56: "Roll a lush" (rob a drunken man). **1931** *AS* VI (Aug.) 440: *Lush, n.* A drunk. **1939–40** O'Hara *Pal Joey* 40: She is still plastered the little lush. **1941** Schulberg *Sammy* 77: "A good-natured lush called Franklin Collier," she said. **1942–43** C. Jackson *Lost Weekend* 124. **1943** in J. Mitchell *McSorley's* 8: The father was by no means a lush, but the son carried temperance to an extreme. **1944** Kapelner *Blues* 9: Is this lush your old man? **1948** Erskine *All My Sons* (film): She's always drunk. She's a lush. **1949** Huggins *Lady Gambles* (film): At least a lush'll pass out every once in a while. **1959** Morrill *Dark Sea Running* 89: Drinking the compass is an old trick for a lush after he's run out of hair tonic and everything else alcoholic. **1970** Major *Dict. Afro-Amer. Slang* 78: *Lush*...a person who drinks a great deal. **1989** P. Munro *U.C.L.A. Slang* 57: Mary is such a lush.

    2. *Und.* money or booty; SWAG.

    1845 *Nat. Police Gaz.* (Oct. 11) 57: $3000, in gold, which he had...sunk in the raceway at the bottom of the creek...."They raked hell out of the race for the lush." **1851** [G. Thompson] *Bristol Bill* 36: Thousands of dollars in spurious "lush" thus found its way into the business world. *Ibid.* 44: "Flush with the lush," he lived like a prince. **1872** Crapsey *Nether Side* 22: The thief might steal cart-loads of costly silks and not be a dollar the richer, were there no fences to take the "lush" off his hands. **1954–60** *DAS: Lush*...Money; cash. *Not common.*

    3. one easily imposed upon; a fool.

    1942–49 Goldin et al. *DAUL* 130: *Lush*...One easily victimized; a gullible person; a stupid fellow. **1968** Sebold *Adolescence* 324: To be at the other end of the line would mean to be a "sucker," "easy mark," or a "lush" and invite merciless ridicule.

lush[1] *adj.* [connected with LUSH, *n. & v.*] Orig. *Und.* drunk.

    *****1812** Vaux *Vocab.: Lush,* or *Lushy,* drunk, intoxicated. **1848** *Ladies' Repository* VIII (Oct.) 315: *Lush Blowen,* A drunken woman. **1866** *Night Side of N.Y.* 77: They came in "lush," after having indulged in a fight with their lovers. **1867** *Nat. Police Gaz.* (Jan. 12) 3: One of her most foolish exploits was getting "lush" one night and getting married to a notorious "gun" named Kelly. **1879** *Puck* (Sept. 27) 451: Hell! I was fearful lush. *****1888** R. Kipling *Only a Subaltern:* They *do* say that the more lush—in-*he*-bri-ated—'e is, the more fish 'e catches. **1930** Irwin *Tramp & Und. Sl.* 125: *Lush.*—Hopelessly intoxicated. *ca***1953** Hughes *Fantastic Lodge* 65: Lil was lush and high already, too. **1985** Univ. Tenn. student: "He's *lush*" means he's real drunk. **1989** P. Munro *U.C.L.A. Slang* 57: *Lush*...drunk, intoxicated.

lush[2] *adj.* **1.** prosperous; wealthy.

    1935 *Amer. Mercury* (June) 230: *Lush:* prosperous. **1944** (quot. at SLAVE).

    2. (usu. of women) extremely attractive; voluptuous; (*also*) desirable; wonderful; (in 1943 quot.) in good graces. [Cf. recent S.E. sense 'characterized by luxuriousness or opulence' (*OED2:* ***1939), earlier 'luxuriant'. In some cases taken as a shortening of *luscious.*]

    [*****1889–90** Barrère & Leland *Dict. Slang* II 35: *Lush* (Eton), dainty....It is a provincial term for rich, succulent.] *****1942** in *OED2:* I'd like her to grow up a lush bint. **1943** in Ruhm *Detective* 363: "I see a first edition of his in a museum once," I say, to get lush with her, see, and it works. **1946** H.A. Smith *Rhubarb* 14: "Dig the Ancient One!…Ain't he lush?" "It's zoomy! It's groovy! It's beauteous! It's lush! It's eighteen bucks!" **1947** *ATS* (Supp.) 1: "Smooth" girl.…*lush thrush*. *Ibid.* 4: *Lush*, delicious. **1949** *Gay Girl's Guide* 12: *Lush*: NYC…[homosexual] term for a terribly attractive but incorrigibly heterosexual young man. **a***1950** W. Granville *Sea Slang* 150: *Lush*. Short for *luscious*. Infinitely desirable, a *lush thrush* being a very pretty girl. This adjective is, in the Navy, as popular as *smashing*, which took hold in the Services in 1939-45. **a***1959** in Tawney *Grey Funnel Lines* 75: I think you're bleeding lush. **1959** Horan *Mob's Man* 55: Lush jobs are nurse in the hospital, porter, ground keeper, steward in the warden's house. **1961–64** Barthelme *Caligari* 86: Dolores…is lush, Lorenesque, and double foreign. **a***1970** Partridge *DSUE* (ed. 7) 1261: *Lush*…(Of a girl) extremely attractive, esp. sexually: Services: since ca.1915. An early use: "a *lush bint*" (W.W. I). *****1989** in Thorne *Dict. Contemp. Sl.* 327: You'll look lush. **1990** P. Munro *Slang U.*: *Lush*…sexually attractive. **1993** A. Adams & W. Stadiem *Madam* 39: You're so lush. You're so beautiful.

lush *v.* [fr. LUSH, *n.*] **1.a.** Orig. *Und.* to drink, usu. liquor.—also used intrans. or constr. with dummy-obj. *it.* See also LUSH UP.
    *****1811** *Lex. Balatron.*: To *Lush*. To drink. *Ibid.*: How the blowen lushes jackey. *****1812** Vaux *Vocab.*: *Lush*, to drink. *****1820–21** P. Egan *Life in London* 177: I say, come *lush*, Jem. *****1838** Dickens *O. Twist*, in *OED*: Some of the richest sort you ever lushed. *****1838** Glascock *Land Sharks* I 197: I never lushes with no one, till I first shakes him by the fist. **1840** *New Yorker* (Mar. 21) 7: I'd been chaffing and lushing, not above half drest. **1848** G. Thompson *House Breaker* 44: I happened to be *lushing it* at Joe Scragg's *crib*. **1866** *Nat. Police Gaz.* (Apr. 21) 3: Strike me blind if I'll lush any more b—y Bourbon. *Ibid.*: Mary Ann Taylor was in town, from Philadelphia,…"lushing" at the "Ruins." **1871** Banka *Prison Life* 493: Drinking,…Lushing. **1879** *Nat. Police Gaz.* (Mar. 15) 11: The slick un's lushin' to-night. **1887** in Somers *Sports in N.O.* 136: More Lushing by the Home Team. **1899** A.H. Lewis *Sandburrs* 189: Durin' d' summer he gen'rally lushes more whiskey than he lays bricks, an' is more apt to hit d' bottle than a job. *Ibid.* 195: Uncle is lushing tonight, and he is unpleasant when he has been tanking up. **1902** Dunbar *Sport* 86: Well, you're doin' a great piece of work, Miss Hamilton, whenever you can keep old Bill from goin' out an' lushin' between acts. **1904** in "O. Henry" *Works* 1438: He just lushes till he remembers he's married, and then he makes for home and does me up. **1914** Lardner *Al* 180: I know where you have been and you have been out lushing beer. **1919** Stokes *Songs of Service* 21: An' arter it was over we kep' lushin' all the night. **1929** McEvoy *Hollywood Girl* 42: Like those lushing parties where the liquor runs out about ten o'clock. **1930** Lait *On the Spot* 23: He lushes his own stuff. **1942** *Yank* (Sept. 23) 14: They sat there, lushing and having a ball. **1950** in R.S. Gold *Jazz Lexicon*: I hate people who don't know when to stop lushing. **1956** Lay *Toward Unknown* (film): If it bothers you to see me lushing, I'll leave it alone. **1962** Perry *Young Man* 213: Jeez, I never knew he lushed. **1963** Braly *Shake Him* 118: I don't lush. **1963** J. Ross *Dead* 66: And when I got tired of lushing and going AWOL there was always the guard-house to recuperate in for a month or two.
    b. to make drunk; intoxicate.—constr. with *out*. Cf. earlier BrE sense 'to ply with liquor; provide liquor for', in *OED2*.
    1959 W. Burroughs *Naked Lunch* 11: The guests…lush themselves out.
    2. *Und.* to rob (an intoxicated or unconscious person).—also used absol.
    1937–40 in Whyte *Street Corner Society* 6 [ref. to 1920's]: We didn't lush (steal from a drunk) or get in crap games. **1960** H. Selby, Jr., in *Provincetown Rev.* III 73: The guys…lushed a drunk. Or pulled a small burglary. *Ibid.* 74: When he left they'd lush him.

Lush Betty *n. Und.* (see quot.). Cf. BLACK BETTY.
    1848 *Ladies' Repository* VIII (Oct.) 315: *Lush Betty*, whisky bottle.

lush bin *n.* [patterned after LOONY BIN] a facility for the rehabilitation of alcoholics.
    1989 P. Benchley *Rummies* 26: Banner! This is a lush bin!

lush crib *n. Und.* LUSH KEN. Now *hist.* Also **lushing crib**.
    *****1812** (quot. at LUSH KEN). *****1818** P. Egan, in Partridge *Dict. Und.* 424: [Scroggins's] *lushing crib* was numerously attended. *****1821** in Partridge *Dict. Und.* 423: Then blame me not kids, swells, or lads of the fancy, For opening a lush-crib in Chancery Lane. **1846** *Nat. Police Gaz.* (Feb. 14) 204: Mrs. Harriet Smith…keeps the dark shop or "lush

crib" in Duane street. **1848** *Ladies' Repository* VIII (Oct.) 315: *Lush Crib*, A liquor store; sometimes used for coffee-houses. *****1857** "Ducange Anglicus" *Vulgar Tongue* 12: *Lush-crib*…A public-house. **a***1890–96** *F & H* IV 256: *Lush-crib* (or *ken*).…common. **1974** A. Cook *Armies of Streets* 109: The detectives raided six of the most notorious "lushing cribs" in the city.

lush dip *n. Und.* a pickpocket who robs drunken men; LUSH-WORKER.
    1918 Stringer *House of Intrigue* 32: Bud nursed an open contempt for…lush-dips. **1922** Murphy *Black Candle* 312: These persons…are known colloquially as "lush dips"—that is to say they rob drunken men.

lush drum *n. Und.* LUSH CRIB.
    1866 *Nat. Police Gaz.* (Nov. 10) 3: The "lush drums" and "flash pannys" are crowded with "guns" at all hours. **1872** Burnham *Secret Service* 167: No. 16 East Houston Street, a noted "lush-drum" then kept by Ike Weber.…Tom Hale was installed as bar-keeper.

lushed *adj.* drunk; (*hence*) *Narc.* intoxicated by drugs. Also **lushed up**.
    1927 Nicholson *Barker* 85: And if I was you I'd go kinda easy on that. You'll get all lushed up first thing you know. **1935** *Amer. Mercury* (June) 230: *Lushed up*: drunk and prosperous; doped. **1953** Nickerson *Ringside Jezebel* 73: Why you lushed-up little slut—! **1954** L. Armstrong *Satchmo* 146: A middle-aged colored woman was sitting … by the railing of the boat, lushed to the gills. **1956** H. Gold *Not With It* 164: I won't kill you, Stan, because you're lushed. **1958–59** Lipton *Barbarians* 39: He had arrived lushed and had a fit of the d.t.'s. **1959** Trocchi *Cain's Book* 153: If you didn't get so damn lushed it wouldn't've happened. **1954–60** *DAS*: *Lushed up*…Under the influence of a narcotic. **1962** in Rosset *Evergreen Reader* 467: The Upper Classes Are Lushed Out Of Their Heads Down In Carmel. **1964** Gold *Jazz Lexicon* 197. **1984** Heath *A-Team* 17: He ends up lushed out of his gourd in Costa del Sol.

lusher *n.* **1.** a heavy drinker; LUSH, *n.*, 1.a. [The 1914 def. is prob. erroneous.]
    1848 *Ladies' Repository* VIII (Oct.) 315: *Lusher*. A drunkard. **1848** Judson *Mysteries* 263: He's death on trappin' lushers. **1911** Spalding *Base Ball* 116 [ref. to 1870's]: Almost every team had its "lushers." **1914** *DN* IV 110: *Lusher, n.* A ligh liver, a voluptuary. "Once all the politicians, nearly, were *lushers*." **1928** Sharpe *Chicago May* 288: *Lusher*—lone drinker. **1931** *Amer. Mercury* (Sept.) 26: City editors are roughnecks and urbane gentlemen, lushers and Puritans. **1936** in Paxton *Sport USA* 6 [ref. to 1880's]: Almost every [baseball] team had its "lushers." **1946** Dadswell *Hey There, Sucker!* 101: *Lusher*…habitual drunkard.
    2. LUSH-WORKER.
    1934 (cited in Partridge *Dict. Und.* 424). **1935** *AS* (Feb.) 18 [ref. to *a*1910]: *Lusher*. A prostitute who preys on drunken patrons. Modern roller or rolling hustler. **1978–80** in Cardozo-Freeman *Joint* 514: *Lusher*…One who robs or rolls drunks.

lushhead *n.* LUSH, 1.a.
    1938 in R.S. Gold *Jazz Lexicon*: The thousands of…lushheads and "tea" worms. **1939** in Leadbitter & Slaven *Blues Records* 59: Nix On Those Lush Heads. **1946** Mezzrow & Wolfe *Really Blues* 163: Weaving from side to side like a lushhead. **1960** MacCuish *Do Not Go Gentle* 16: Gonna give ya a drink, lushhead. Gonna give ya a big fat drink. **1967** P. Roth *When She Was Good* 40: You weak, washed-out lushhead!

lushhound *n.* LUSHHEAD.
    1935 (cited in Partridge *Dict. Und.* 423). **1942** *AS* XVII 2 (Apr.) 92: *Lush hound.* An habitual drinker. **1946** Mezzrow & Wolfe *Really Blues* 86: The lushhounds with their false courage.

lushie var. LUSHY.

Lushington *n.* [prob. fr. LUSH, *n.*, punning on the family name *Lushington*] (used allusively in joc. ref. to drinking liquor); (*hence*) a drunkard; LUSH, 1.a. [*OED2* cites a drinking society called the "City of Lushington," alleged to have met since *ca*1745, but no confirmation of this assertion is available.]
    *****1812** Vaux *Vocab.* 251: Speaking of a person who is drunk, they [*sc.*, English thieves] say, *Alderman Lushington is concerned.* *****1820–21** P. Egan *Life in London* 228: Mr. *Lushington* had got "the best of them." *****1821** P. Egan, in Partridge *Dict. Und.* 424: The *Lushingtons*, on tipping off the *blue ruin*, made *wry* faces at its watery effects. *****1823** "J. Bee" *Slang*: "Lushington" or "dealing with Lushington," taking too

much drink. *1826 in *OED*: Lushington is evidently his master. *1851 in *OED2*: If they have any…a little stale…they sell it at the public-houses to the "Lushingtons." 1859 Matsell *Vocab.* 53: Lushingtons. Drunken men. 1867 *Nat. Police Gaz.* (Jan. 12) 3: She overcharges "lushingtons" for the rotgut dealt out. 1871 Banka *Prison Life* 493: One who is drunk…*Lushington*. *1890 in *OED*: The best eddicated chaps are the worst lushington when they give way at all.

lush ken *n. Und.* an alehouse or saloon. Also **lushing ken.**
   *1790 in *OED*: *Lush ken*, an alehouse. *1812 Vaux *Vocab.*: *Lush-crib*, or *Lush-ken*, a public-house, or gin-shop. *ca1835 in Holloway & Black *Broadsides* II 61: But first to a lush ken together we went/To toss off a strummond it was our intent. 1866 *Nat. Police Gaz.* (Nov. 3) 2: Tommy Ryan…is…about starting an opposition "cross blokes'" "lushing ken" to Whitey Bob's "drum" on Prince street. 1867 *Galaxy* (Mar. 15) 637: Pickpockets have their drinking saloons, or "lushing kens," as they are denominated in the thieves' vernacular. 1871 Banka *Prison Life* 493: Saloon…*Drum* or *Lush-Ken*.

lush-roller *n.* LUSH-WORKER.
   1919 Darling *Jargon Book* 21: *Lush Roller*—One who robs drunken men. *1936 (cited in Partridge *Concise Slang Dict.*). 1938 A.J. Liebling, in *DAS*: A lush roller rolls lushes. 1966 S. Harris *Hellhole* 84: Jerry…was known, despite her youth, to be one of the best lushrollers in Harlem.

lush-toucher *n.* LUSH-WORKER.
   1904 *Life in Sing Sing* 256: *Lush-toucher.*—A scamp who robs intoxicated people. 1927 (cited in Partridge *Dict. Und.* 423).

lush up *v.* to drink (liquor); become intoxicated. See also *lushed up* s.v. LUSHED.
   1893 W.K. Post *Harvard* 290: Let's go lush up with the rest of the crowd. 1908 T.A. Dorgan, in Zwilling *TAD Lexicon* 55: I'm lushing up on water while the rest hit "private stock." 1918 in *AS* (Oct. 1933) 29: *Lush up.* To get drunk. 1926 Maines & Grant *Wise-Crack Dict.* 10: *Lush up*—To get drunk. 1927 Nicholson *Barker* 150: Get lushed up, become intoxicated. *1933, *1952, *1960 in *OED2*.

lushwell *n.* a heavy drinker; habitual drunkard.
   1960 MacCuish *Do Not Go Gentle* 235 [ref. to WWII]: He glanced at Norman and motioned to the bottle. "Go ahead, slop it up, Lushwell." 1981 Wambaugh *Glitter Dome* 17: He's such a lushwell his liver's probably big as his ass.

lush-worker *n. Und. & Police.* a thief who robs drunken or unconscious persons.
   1908 McGaffey *Show Girl* 80: I wouldn't be a lush worker. 1911 A.H. Lewis *Apaches of N.Y.* 15: The men were thieves of the cheap grade known as lush-workers. 1912 in Partridge *Dict. of Und.* 1926 *N.Y. Times* (Dec. 26) VIII 3: Tell me whether any lush workers go there. 1927 *DN* V 454: *Lush worker*, n. (1) Any one who robs drunken men. (2) A prostitute who extorts money from a man by trickery, blackmail, blandishments, or robs him when drunk. 1928 O'Connor *B'way Racketeers* ix: The coke-filled lush worker…plies his thieving business on helpless drunks. 1930 Lait *On the Spot* 206: Lush-worker…A low form of pickpocket specializing in robbing drunks. 1940 *New Yorker* (June 8) 16: "Well, what *is* your racket?"…"Lush worker…a guy who rolls drunks." 1949 *Harper's* (Aug.) 95: Mush-workers and lushworkers. 1951 Kerouac *Visions of Cody* 91: Where ferret-faced hipsters…are also lushworkers. 1963 *True* (May) 43: There are lush workers on 10th Avenue, dope peddlers on Sixth. 1965 Horan *Seat of Power* 18: The bum…admitted he was a lush worker from Detroit. 1991 J. Dwyer *Subway Lives* 14: This was a class of thief known in transit police…statistics as a "lush worker." Any sleeping person robbed on a train is deemed a lush who has been worked.

lushy *n.* a drunkard. Also **lushie.**
   1944 *New Yorker*, in *OED2*: All our horn blowers were lushies. 1944 Burley *Handbk. Jive* 143: *Lushie*—Drunkard. 1946 Mezzrow & Wolfe *Really Blues* 86: The lushies didn't even play good music.

lushy *adj.* drunk; drunken.

*1811 *Lex. Balatron.*: *Lushey.* Drunk. The rolling kiddeys had a spree and got bloody lushey. *1812 Vaux *Vocab.*: *Lushy-cove*, a drunken man. *1820–21 P. Egan *Life in London* 165: She's…got lushy.*…*Drunk. *1837 Dickens *Pickwick Papers* 265: I was so uncommon lushey, that I couldn't find the place where the latch-key went in. *1838 Glascock *Land Sharks* I 192: "Lushy Dick"…had…a nose so red and fiery as…to have produced his dismissal. 1840 *Spirit of Times* (Sept. 12) 331: That was the stuff old Jove used to get lushy on. *1846 (quot. at DOSS, *n.*). 1848 Judson *Mysteries* 12: Yes, I am Big Lize, you lushy swell! 1866 *Nat. Police Gaz.* (Nov. 3) 2: Johnny Reardon…was also "lushy." *1876 in *F & H* IV 258: A lushy cove. 1899 A.H. Lewis *Sandburrs* 58: I meself has t'run a quarter or two in Emmer's lap when I'm a bit lushy. 1906 A.H. Lewis *Confessions* 202: He was lushy—put me to bed with a shovel, but that sucker was lushy! 1944 C.B. Davis *Leo McGuire* 174: They'd never in the world connect a lushy goof…with me.

lust *n.* ¶ In phrase: **in lust** sexually attracted rather than truly in love. *Joc.* Cf. *in like* s.v. LIKE, *n.*
   1963 Ark. high school student (coll. J. Ball): God, I'm falling in lust! I'm getting a bone on. 1972 N.Y.U. student: I don't know if I've been in love, but I *have* been in lust. 1976 Univ. Tenn. grad. student: I think he's in lust. 1983 Eble *Campus Slang* (Nov.) 3: *In lust*—attracted to another's body. 1991 J. Weber *Rules of Engagement* 161: "Harry, I'm in love with Leigh Ann." "You mean in lust." 1992 *Time* (Mar. 23) 65: He…falls in lust with her. 1995 *Time* (Oct. 23) 94: Hester and the Rev fall in lust.

lying *v.* ¶ In phrase: **if I'm lying I'm dying** [or **flying**] see s.v. LIE, *v.*

lynch *v.* [fr. S.E. *lynch law*; see M.M. Mathews in *AS* XXXIV (1959) 127] to inflict bodily punishment upon; (*later*, now *usu.*) to kill by mob action, typically by hanging, without legal authority. Now *S.E.* [The bracketed *1835 quot. app. means 'to render infamous'.]
   1835 in *AS* XXXII (1948) 315: They were soundly flogged, or in other words, *Lynched*, and set on the opposite side of the river. [*1835 Disraeli, in *OED2*: I could not think of meeting them now. I consider and every one else that they are lynched.] 1836 in *DA*: Some personal friend of Mr. Broux…proceeded to the mansion of Judge Bermudez, with a view to Lynch him, or to inflict some severe punishment upon his person. 1836 in *DA*: The Lynching of these children. 1838 [Haliburton] *Clockmaker* (Ser. 2) 48: Spittin',—gougin',—lynchin',—burnin' alive. *Ibid.* 51: It bears strange fruit sometimes, as the man said of the pine tree the five gamblers were Lynched up to [at] Vixburg. *Ibid.* 59: They jist lynched 'em and stoned 'em to death. 1852 in Caughey *Mob* 40: He wasn't lynched for that, was he? 1842 Strong *Diary* I 191: He'd inevitably be lynched if he did. 1862 *Six Months Among Secessionists* 20: Lynch the d—d Yankees! Hang 'em! Shoot 'em down! 1862 in C.W. Wills *Army Life* 92: Confederate scrip goes among the people here freely. If a man refuses to take it they lynch him. 1869 in Rosa *Wild Bill* 151: In all probability Connors would be lynched. 1872 G. Gleason *Specter Riders* 26: Ef he shows hisself now, he'll be lynched, sure as shootin'. 1876 J.M. Reid *Old Settlers* 86: They wanted to lynch Sugar Lip and Skin Johnson. 1900 P. Dunbar *Gideon* 274: Excited crowds…cried "Lynch 'em, lynch 'em! Hang the niggers up to the first tree!" 1910 in O. Johnson *Lawrenceville Stories* 221: "He ought to be lynched!" "The booby!" 1916 W. Pickens *New Negro* 190: The individual lyncher should be treated as a lawbreaker and murderer. 1917–20 Dreiser *Newspaper Days* 399: I arrived in time to see him lynched. 1972 A. Kemp *Savior* 128: Anyway, the honkies lynched him along with a young brother and left them in a swamp.

lynching bee *n. West.* a lynching. Now *hist.*
   1900 in *DA*: They have sometimes had "lynching bees,"…they have sometimes lynched men for murder, for arson, for rape. 1904 in *DAE*: They told me frankly that they were on the way to have a lynching-bee. 1931 *Amer. Mercury* (Dec.) 408: Quilting bees, lynching bees. 1943 in *DA*.

M *n. Narc.* **1.** morphine.

 1914 Jackson & Hellyer *Vocab.* 60: *M* or *Morph*, Noun Used by morphine fiends. Sulphate of morphia. **1921** in E. Murphy *Black Candle* 212: I could not get enough "M" or "C." **1922** Murphy *Black Candle* 160: He may stand on a corner and exchange the "M" or "C" for cash. **1922** *DN* V 182: Morphine...*M.* Very common. **1925** in Moriarty *True Confessions* 28: I had three decks of M., which would not last me very long. **1929** *AS* (June) 342: *M & C*—A mixture of morphine and cocaine—usually about four parts "M" to one part "C." *ca*1953 Hughes *Fantastic Lodge* 53: They gave me a little M—morphine. **1954** in J. Blake *Joint* 58: Danny was...an M. addict. **1957** Greenwald *Call Girl* 101: What did you go for—"horse" or "M"...? **1959** W. Burroughs *Naked Lunch* 221, in Gold *Jazz Lexicon:* Your reporter bang thirty grains of M a day.

 2. marijuana.

 1955 E. Hunter *Jungle Kids* 103: We wouldn't so much as give him a stick of M. **1956** E. Hunter *Second Ending* 279: "Half the cats on this band are hip to M." "What the hell is M?"..."It's...marijuana." **1965** in H.S. Thompson *Hell's Angels* 9: "M"...stands for marijuana. **1970** Landy *Underground Dict.* 125: *M*...Marijuana.

Ma Bell *n.* American Telephone & Telegraph, Inc.

 [**1926** *AS* I 659: Beware of all "Maw Bell" (telephone) wires.] [**1942** *ATS* 754: *Telephone*...hellophone, Maw Bell.] **1947** *Sat. Eve. Post* (May 10) 16: [Bell] is apparently interested in their every waking and sleeping hour—a maternal solicitude which is largely responsible for the title of Ma Bell. **1954–60** *DAS: Maw Bell* The Bell Telephone Company. *Not common.* **1969** *Business Week* (Dec. 6) 192: Ma Bell's "next best thing to being there" will become far better than trying to get there. **1971** J. Simon *Sign of Fool* 36: Anything even remotely connected with "Ma Bell" was stamped "Bell System." **1973** W. Crawford *Stryker* 12: Our guy from Ma Bell left twenty minutes ago. **1977** T. Berger *Villanova* 5: I picked up Ma Bell's jet-black baby from its cradle. **1981** *Mother Jones* (Aug.) 42: Ma Bell squeezes its customers as well as its employees. **1990** *U.S. News & W.R.* (Dec. 17) 71 (headline): Ma Bell dukes it out: a pugnacious new AT&T takes on NCR, MCI.

Mac *n.* **1.** an Irishman or Scotsman. *Rare* in U.S.

 ***1617** in *OED:* I can not dissemble how confident I am to beate these Spanish Dons, as well as ever I did our Irish Macks and Oes. **1776** J. Leacock *Fall of Brit. Tyranny* (Dedication): And ye Macs, and ye Donalds upon Donalds, go on. **1827** J.F. Cooper *Red Rover* 417: "He is a Scot."..."Will he fight?" "For money—the honour of the Macs—and his religion." ***a*1929–65** in *SND* VI: *Mac*...in colloq. use applied in Eng. to anyone known or thought to be a Scotsman, in Scot. common as a fam. form of address to any stranger. ***1990–91** in F. MacDonald *Island Voices* 47: A lot of businesses on the island are owned by English people. Before very long there won't be a Mac left in these parts.

 2. var. MACK.

 3. (used in direct address, esp. to a man whose name is not known). [The 1909 quot., addressed to an Irish policeman, is probably a nickname.]

 [**1909** Chrysler *White Slavery* 30: Oh, a girl and her fellow had a fight, Mack; have a good cigar.] **1918** Wallgren *AEF in Cartoon* (unp.): Ooh, Look'ut that poor boob without a mask....Hey, Mack!—Gas Gas!!! **1919** Wilkins *Co. Fund* 26: Well, Mac, whaddye do? **1923** in Hemingway *Dateline* 401: I'm sorry, Mac. We can't handle it. **1929** Brecht *Downfall* 155: I'm gonna meet a fellah. Thanks, mack. **1930** Mae West *Babe Gordon* 36: Hey, Mac, let me out [of your taxi] here. **1935** T. Wolfe *Death to Morning* 146: Podden me, Mac...I hope yuh don't mind my astin' yuh a question. **1935** O'Hara *Dr.'s Son* 100: I'm sorry, Mac, but you really got the wrong party. **1936** Mackenzie *Living Rough* 93: Say, Mac, have you got the price of a square meal? **1937** Schary & Butler *Big City* (film): Don't let yourself in for a lot of trouble, Mac. There's nothing you can do about it. **1942** Tugend *Star-Spangled Rhythm* (film): Ever been to Brooklyn, Mac? **1943** J. Mitchell *McSorley's* 16: Hey, Mac, if you want to see some real art, go look at the naked lady in the back room. **1944** E. Caldwell *Tragic Ground* 47:

"Well, take it easy, mac," he warned Spence. **1946** Petry *Street* 166: Don't know that I blame you for being late, Mack. **1949** N. Johnson *Everybody Does It* (film): You like music, Mac? **1950** Felton & Adams *Armored Car Robbery* (film): Got the time, Mac? **1959** E. Hunter *Matter of Conviction* 68: "Help you, Mac?" he said to Hank. **1963–64** R.P. Warren *Flood* 14: Thanks, Mac. ***a*1929–65** (quot. at **(1)**, above). **1973** Jackson *Fall Out* 344 [ref. to 1918]: He probably said Mack, a name loosely applied by a total stranger to anyone in the A.E.F. **1980** T. Jones *Adrift* 175: Hey, Mac, gotta cigarette? **1982** Kinsella *Shoeless Joe* 46: I'm a little short for a meal, Mac. Can you help me out?

mac *n.* macaroni.

 1966 Braly *Cold* 41: JD couldn't help contrasting it to the mac-and-cheese served every Thursday night on the main line. **1983** *Working Woman* (Feb.) 54: Mac 'n Cheddar Burger....Add...hot water, macaroni, [etc.]. **1986** Univ. Tenn. student: Give me some of that mac salad over there.

mac var. MACK.

mac *interj.* ¶ In phrase: **holy mac!** [short for *holy mackerel* s.v. MACKEREL] (used to express surprise or the like).

 1931 Adamic *Laughing* 253: "Holy mac!" said Harry Link. *a*1938 Adamic *My America* 489: Holy mac!

macaroni *n.* **1.** an Italian.—used contemptuously. [The *1711 quot. does not reflect English-language usage.]

 [***1711** J. Addison, in *F & H* IV 260: There is a Set of merry Drolls whom the Common People of all Countries admire...: I mean those circumforaneous Wits whom every nation calls by the Name of that Dish of Meat which it loves best. In Holland they are termed Pickled Herrings; in France Jean Pottages; in Italy Maccaronies.] ***1845** in *OEDS:* Surely I shall always be able, go where I will, among frogs or maccaronis, to procure *sucre noir,* or *inchiostro nero.* **1864** in H.L. Abbott *Fallen Leaves* 237: The "Garibaldi Guard," a beastly set of Dutch boors, Maccaronis, & Frogeaters. **1882** *Puck* (Nov. 15) 170: "How you vas, Maggaroni?" Mr. Schlammerstein [says]. **1883** *United Service* (Sept.) 272: Fire, you damned macaroni! **1887** Francis *Saddle & Moccasin* 102: "Mac" (an abbreviation...of "Macaroni")...was an Italian by birth. **1896** F.H. Smith *Tom Grogan* 7: Hold on, ye walleyed macaroni! **1907** J.C. Lincoln *Cape Cod* 44: My friend, Mr. Macaroni. **1919** Cortelyou *Ariz. to Huns* 108: One day Private Gregorio, a little macaroni lad about four feet tall, was selected for this important duty. ***1950** *Sat. Eve. Post* (May 6) 140: [Quoting a British smuggler:] We bought them in Tangier legally and delivered them at sea. That way the macaronis took the risk. **1966** Herbert *Fortune* 47: Queenie:...That wop's gonna get you good. *Rocky:* No Macaroni scares me, sister. **1972** Cleaves *Sea Fever* 38 [ref. to 1920's] 140: Here's the Macaroni. **1985** E. Leonard *Glitz* 108: The macaronis are shooting each other and it's hard to tell who's on whose side.

 2. nonsense; BALONEY, 2.

 ***1924** in *Austral. Nat. Dict.*: Yes. Jam, macaroni, cockadoodle. We're plain people out here-aways. Not mantle ornaments. **1939** Appel *Power-House* 328: "You're good, Sid," she cried. "Macaroni!" ***1965** in *ODMS:* What is flashed from the projector overhead will be the same old macaroni.

 3. *Logging.* (see 1958 quot.).

 1938 in *DARE.* **1942** *AS* (Dec.) 222: *Macaroni.* Sawdust. **1956** Sorden & Ebert *Logger's* 23 [ref. to *a*1925]: *Macaroni,* sawdust. **1958** McCulloch *Woods Wds.* 115: *Macaroni*—Long curls of sawdust cut by a well-filed crosscut saw.

 4. *Und.* a pimp; MACK, 1.a.

 1973 Pace College student: A *macaroni* is the same as a *mack* or a pimp. **1983** (cited in J. Green *Dict. Contemp. Slang*).

macaroni bar *n. Army.* (see quot.).

 1921 Lettau *In Italy* 55: About the first of December [1918] we received a red, white and green service stripe from the Italian government which denoted four months service on the Italian front. This was immediately christened the "Macaroni bar."

macaroon *n.* a ridiculous or doltish person; MAROON.

1942 (quot. at CLUCK, 2). **1974** Strasburger *Rounding Third* 2: What a macaroon this guy must be.

mace *n. Und.* **1.** a swindle usu. involving fraudulent offers of credit. Also as adj.

   1742** in Partridge *Dict. Und.* 425: He proposed to go upon the *Mace....*The *Mace* is perform'd by Confederacy, one or two persons take a House, and then get what quantity of Goods they can upon Credit, and then go off with them. ***1776** in Partridge *Dict. Und.* 425: I had them on the *mace...*upon credit in...the swindling way. ***1781** G. Parker *View of Soc.* II 32: A Dining-room elegantly furnished upon *the Mace* receives you. ***1826** "Blackmantle" *Eng. Spy* II 201: The *sharps...*have *tried on the grand mace* with him. **1859** Matsell *Vocab.* 53: "On the mace," to live by swindling. *ca1900** (cited in Partridge *Dict. Und.* 425). **1933** in Partridge *Dict. Und.* 425: Like th' *mace* joints that open up...leavin' a lot o' guys with bum notes. ***1937** in Partridge *Concise Dict. Sl.* 273: Getting stuff on the mace.

   2. a polished practitioner of the MACE, 1; confidence trickster.

   ***1781** G. Parker *View of Soc.* II 34: The *Mace...*goes to any capital tradesman...in an elegant vis-à-vis, with two or three servants behind it [in order to swindle and rob him]. **1859** Matsell *Vocab.: Mace.* A false pretense man; a swindler.

mace *v.* **1.** *Und.* to swindle; (now usu.) to obtain (an automobile) by swindling.

   ***1790** in *OED: Mace,* to cheat. **1896** Ade *Artie* 46: I think he'd mace a sucker if he got half a chance, but after he got the dough he'd spend it freely. **1919** *Bookman* (Apr.) 209: A certain hook...maces A and B for a split. **1941** *Amer. Mercury* (Mar.) 344: The...Uticans had been taken in by one of the [stolen-car] industry's pet production methods—"macing."...Bryan...maced his way up and down the country. **1950** *New Yorker* (Feb. 25) 43: It taught him the shell-and-pea game and other methods of skinning and macing suckers and getting ahead in the world. ***1975** (cited in Partridge *Concise Dict. Slang.* 273). **1978** Univ. Tenn. instructor, age ca30: "*Macing* a car" is an expression I've come across. It means obtaining it fraudulently through some kind of credit scam.

   2. to beg or demand money from.

   1906 *Nat. Police Gaz.* (Jan. 27) 6: Mace him, and see how quick you fall down. **1907** *McClure's Mag.* (Feb.) 379: We'd maced about everyone we could think of. **1908** McGaffey *Show Girl* 138: Wilbur...told me to mace every John I came across...for as many as he would stand for. *a***1909** Tillotson *Detective* 93: *Maced*—Asked. **1935** Pollock *Und. Speaks: Macer,* a person who constantly borrows small sums of money with no intention of repaying. **1956** *Harper's* (Aug.) 59: Macing, or forcing campaign contributions from payrollers, is a common practice of both parties. **1959** *Sat. Eve. Post* (Mar. 14) 79: Accused Lawrence of bribery and of macing state workers for campaign funds.

MacGuffin *n.* [fr. *MacGuffin,* family name; semantic devel. unkn.; coined by and assoc. with film director Alfred Hitchcock] Esp. *Film.* a plot device that though seemingly important serves only to set the plot in motion; gimmick; hook. Also **McGuffin.** [Permission could not be secured by press time to reprint the 1939 citation, from a previously unpublished manuscript. In the lecture, Hitchcock refers to the MacGuffin as the "mechanical element" in a story, and expresses his desire to be original, and not simply have the MacGuffin be a necklace in a crime story or government papers in a spy story.]

   1939 A. Hitchcock, lecture at Columbia Univ. (Mar. 30) [transcript in Film Studies Center, Museum of Modern Art, N.Y.]. **1950** A. Hitchcock, in *N.Y. Times* (June 4) II 4: There may have been a "MacGuffin" in my film appearance [in *Stagefright*] but not a ham....The "MacGuffin"—my own term for the key element of any suspense story—has obviously got to change. It can no longer be the idea of preventing the foreign agent from stealing the papers. **1962** in Truffault & Scott *Hitchcock* 137: *A.H.* That secret clause [in a film] was our "MacGuffin." I must tell you what that means. *F.T.* Isn't the MacGuffin the pretext for the plot? *A.H.* Well, it's the device, the gimmick, if you will, or the papers the spies are after....The theft of secret documents [in a Kipling story] was the original MacGuffin.... So the "MacGuffin" is the term we use to cover all that sort of thing: to steal plans or documents, or discover a secret, it doesn't matter what it is. And the logicians are wrong in trying to figure out the truth of a MacGuffin, since it's beside the point. **1977** W.P. Kinsella *Dance*

Me Outside: It about Alfred Hitchcock the movie man and how he have something in every picture he make called a McGuffin. Mr. Hitchcock say a McGuffin is the thing everybody get all hot and bothered about, like a diamond that been stolen or some secret papers that been lost. **1988** *Time* (Mar. 14) 84: It is she, vaporishly bearing *Frantic*'s MacGuffin, who mixes up her bag with the Walkers' luggage at the airport, thus starting off all their troubles. **1989** *TV Guide* (Feb. 4) 20: "The sex tapes are just the MacGuffin"—a Hitchcockian term for the plot device that gets the action started. **1992** *N.Y. Times Bk. Rev.* (July 12) 34: Napoleon's penis became the MacGuffin for a narrative that attracted a hodgepodge of other stories and themes. **1993** *New Yorker* (May 17) 105: The MacGuffin that will determine the outcome is a piece of software called the Go chip. **1995** *New Yorker* (Aug. 14) 86: Everything about this movie is a MacGuffin. There are stolen emeralds that don't matter, drugs that can't be found, a villain who's either an alibi or a myth.

macher *n.* [< Yiddish < G, lit. 'doer; maker'] Esp. *Pol. Journ.* an extremely influential person.

   1930 *AS* VI 2 (Dec.) 126: The "wise guy" of popular slang becomes...a *Macher.*...It is used derisively, referring to a braggart. **1973** *Harper's* (Sept.) 75: Candidates begin to run for Congress...without ever having to be *machers* in the Republican or Democratic party. **1978** *Business Week* (Apr. 24) 53: Chancellor Helmut Schmidt, a *macher* (doer) with a razor-sharp mind and a tongue to match. **1984** *N.Y. Times* (Apr. 8) H6: I have become a big *macher* in the senior citizen's group. **1986** in *N.Y. Times* (Jan. 4, 1987) ("Educ. Life") 15: [Parodic photograph:] B.G. Macher/Ass't to the Ass't to the Ass't Vice President. **1989** *New York* (Oct. 16) 32: Jake's grandfather, Seventh Avenue *macher* Abe Schrader. **1990** *New Republic* (Apr. 30) 26: Chief political *macher* for the White House. **1995** *Donahue* (NBC-TV): A hostess for the machers that come over from the Republican party. **1996** *Nation* (Feb. 19) 26: Colson has become a major evangelical *macher* since pleading guilty to his Watergate crimes.

machine *n.* **1.** the penis.—usu. considered vulgar. [The *1749 quot. is probably best regarded as literary S.E.]

   ***1749** J. Cleland, in *OEDS:* Coming out with that formidable machine of his, he lets the fury loose. **1960–69** Runkel *Law* 279: We was in bed—stark naked, with her working my machine like it was the lever handle on a one-arm bandit. **1978** in *Maledicta* VI (1982) 23: Penis...*machine, meat,...member.*

   2. a tireless or adept practitioner.—usu. constr. with prec. noun.

   [**1897** Kipling *Capts. Courageous* 7: "I haven't been sick one little bit. No sir!"..."Oh, you're a high-grade machine...," the Philadelphian yawned.] **1932** DeLeon & Perelman *Hold 'Em Jail* (film): The greatest football machine that ever thundered down the field! **1972** P. Fenty *Superfly* (film): Ain't I a clean, bad machine...Superfly. **1979** L. Blum et al. *Meatballs* (film): He's a sex machine. **1990** *Inside Edition* (synd. TV series): He is a lean, mean writing machine. **1993** *N.Y. Times* (May 5) C1: The Chicago Bulls' Michael Jordan, the ultimate basketball machine. **1996** McCumber *Playing off Rail* 213: "You played damned well against Parica." "Fat fuckin lot of good it did me. That little fucker's a *machine.*"

   3. an automobile. [The *1901 quot. is S.E.]

   [***1901** in *OEDS:* His assistant crouching at his feet out of range of the swift-flying currents of air produced by the mad flight of the machine.] **1908** in H.C. Fisher *A. Mutt* 121: He'll spring for a machine so as to not miss anything. **1908** McGaffey *Show Girl* 67: We decided to ride down there in the machine. **1911** in Truman *Dear Bess* 35: If I land that machine I'll *try and use it right.* **1908–13** J. London *Strength* 143: Is your machine running? **1914** *Amer. Mag.* (June) 33: I would 'phone to some public garage for a machine to be here at noon. **1920** in De Beck *Google* 100: I'll get some guy in a machine to gimme a lift. **1929** Hammett *Maltese Falcon* 13: A machine turning threw headlights up here. **1960** T. MacPherson *Dragging & Driving* 140: *Machine.* A hot rod. Any automobile. **1972** Claerbaut *Back Jargon* 71: *Machine...*a car; automobile. **1979** D. Thoreau *City at Bay* 210: I want you to keep an eye on my machine. **1983** S. King *Christine* 156: I was looking over your mean machine.

   4. a sexually attractive young woman.

   1929–31 J.T. Farrell *Young Lonigan* 149: They don't make machines any better than Iris. **1991** Univ. Tenn. student: Boy, is she a machine or what?

5. *Narc.* a hypodermic syringe; (*broadly*) all equipment necessary for the injection of narcotics. Usu. **machinery.**

1937 (cited in Spears *Drugs & Drink*). **1938** in D.W. Maurer *Lang. of Underworld* 99: *The biz.*...An outfit for taking drugs hypodermically; it consists of a hypodermic needle or some homemade substitute, a medicine-dropper, a cooking-spoon, and a piece of cotton for filtering purposes. Also...*machinery.* **1942** *ATS* 475: *Hypodermic syringe.*...machinery, nail, needle, spike, [etc.]. **1970** Landy *Underground Dict.*: *Machine*...Syringe used for injecting a drug. *Machinery*...Equipment for preparing and injecting drugs.

6. *Mil.* Green Machine.

1976 C.R. Anderson *Grunts* 48 [ref. to 1969]: Gunny was not "short in the Nam" but he was definitely "short in the machine," having only nineteen more months to go before his twenty-year career as a marine was completed. *a*1990 Westcott *Half a Klick* 256: Me? Miss the Machine?

mack *n.* [prob. < F *maquerrelle*] **1.a.** *Und.* a usu. flashy or successful pimp. [It is tempting to see in this term a shortened version of ME and early ModE *mackerel* 'bawd, pander, pimp' (*OED* *1426–**a*1700), but the gap of centuries makes this unlikely: the *mackerel* form in 1933 quot. is unique in modern times and is presumably a playful elab. of *mack.*]

1903 *Enquirer* (Cincinnati) (May 9) 13: *Mack*—A man of leisure. **1908** Sullivan *Criminal Slang* 16: *Mack*—A [prostitute's] lover. **1909** C. Chrysler *White Slavery* 180: All the...Slavers, cadets, pimps, maques [*sic*] and vermin of the vice district. **1912** Lowrie *Prison* 77: I ain't never been a mack. **1914** Jackson & Hellyer *Crim. Slang* 56: *Mac*, Noun General currency. A pimp; a lover of lewd women. A man who lives upon the earnings of a prostitute. Derived from the French term "Macquereau." **1921** in Cray *Erotic Muse* 195: Bring on your rubber-tired hearses,/Fill 'em up plumb full of maques. **1927** *Immortalia* 36: After that came a procession /Of about ten thousand macks. **1927** *Variety* (Jan. 19) 32: Playing a "mack" in a cabaret scene. **1929** Booth *Stealing* 69 [ref. to *ca*1916]: Never make a flashy appearance....No one but a cheap gambler or a "mack" does that. **1930** Huston *Frankie & Johnny* 91: The ten macks dance in, single file. **1931** Bontemps *Sends Sunday* 24: Compared with the macks and sports he met, Augie was nothing to blind the eyes. **1933** Ersine *Pris. Slang* 52: *Mack, Mackerel, n.* A pimp. **1934** W. Smith *Bessie Cotter* 192: Getting acquainted with all those macks and guns around that dump. **1944** Cullen & Bontemps *St. Louis Woman* 4 [ref. to 1890's]: The "Macks," as in all primitive society, are even more brilliantly attired than the women. **1946** Mezzrow & Wolfe *Really Blues* 29: The pimps, or macs,...kept wandering around downstairs. **1973** Goines *Players* 100: I ain't heard her doing nothing about the macks behind the whores. *a*1984 Sereny *Invisible Children* 12: "Did you see any macks?" (a term used for pimps).

b. *Black E.* a very ingratiating or deceptive talker.

1962 in Wepman et al. *The Life* 45: She [*sc.*, a prostitute]'s a cold-blooded mack from a long way back. **1990** "Ice Cube" *Who's the Mack?* [rap song title]. *a*1994 Smitherman *Black Talk* 157: *Mack*...A man who can sweet-talk women. **1995** Stavsky, Mozeson & Mozeson *A 2 Z* 66: *Mack*...any smooth operator or b.s. artist.

c. *Rap Music.* a clever, proficient, or influential person, usu. a man. [The 1990 quot. is a fig. use of **(b)**, above.]

1990 "Ice Cube" *Who's the Mack?* (rap song): I'm a/Mack in my own right/When it come to rhyme and rap,/'Cause all I do is kick facts. **1993** *21st C. Dict. Sl.* 166: Who's the mack in this gang? **1995** Stavsky, Mozeson & Mozeson *A 2 Z* 67: *Mack*...the best in one's field.

d. *Rap Music.* a ladies' man; playboy.

1991 "Tribe Called Quest" *Butter* (rap song): "We love you, Phife...Where you goin', where you at?" These girls don't know me from jack, yet I feel like the mack. **1992** *Knoxville* (Tenn.) *News-Sentinel* ("Detours") 16: *Mack*...Playboy. *a*1994 Smitherman *Black Talk* 157: *Mack*...A man who has lots of women. **1994** *Totally Unofficial Rap Dict.*: *Mack*...Ladies' Man. **1994** in C. Long *Love Awaits* 32: We don't like a man who thinks he's Mr. Casanova-get-over. He's the Mack, has everything and knows everything. **1996** *Martin* (Fox-TV): Bein' the true mack that I am, I put my hand on her knee, see?

2. *Und.* the business of pimping.—constr. with *the.*

1955 in Wepman et al. *The Life* 155: When you tell me about the mack,/You've got to run it down fact by fact. **1967** in Wepman et al. *The Life* 114: I...taught Honky-Tonk Bud the mack. **1973** R. Poole *Mack* (film): I'm talkin' 'bout the mack.

3. Orig. *Prost.* ingratiating or flattering talk, orig. of a kind intended to seduce women.—often constr. with *the.*

1968–72 Milner & Milner *Black Players* 31: The initial line a pimp uses in recruiting a girl is often referred to as *Mack* or *Mack talk.* **1974** Univ. Tenn. student theme: They had some out of sight damn good mack....Those girls [*sic*] conversation was so good until a young man would wonder could this be a girl talking like this. **1967–80** Folb *Runnin' Down Lines* 245: *Mack, the* Seductive, manipulative talk aimed at wining favor with a member of the opposite sex. **1989** P. Munro *U.C.L.A. Slang* 57: *Make mac with* to flirt with, to *come on to.* **1995** Weisbard *Spin Record Guide* 348: Dissing U.T.F.O.'s hapless mack with her own smart mouth.

4. *Black E.* French kiss.

1978 W. Brown *Tragic Magic* 48: Gone, Melvin, make that mack melt in her mouth.

mack *adj.* *Black E.* extremely masculine in appearance or behavior.

1967 Colebrook *Cross of Lassitude* 264: I want a man to be *mac* and aggressive, and not just a yard dog like they all are.

mack¹ *v.* **1.a.** *Und.* to be or work as a pimp.

***1887** W.E. Henley, in *F & H* IV 263: [To] Fiddle, or fence, or mace, or mack. **1964** in Wepman et al. *The Life* 165: Your broad...starts signifying about your not having a license to mack. **1970** Landy *Underground Dict.*: *Mack*...Procure clients for a prostitute. **1970** Major *Afro-Amer. Slang* 79: *Macking:* pimping. **1971** *Who Took Weight?* 160: I was sho'nuff macking. I had nine...whores. **1973** R. Poole *Mack* (film): You don't know nothin' about mackin'. **1991** Nelson & Gonzales *Bring Noise* 3: Lots of sexist, violent references to pimping and macking.

b. Orig. *Pros.* (of a pimp) to talk (to a woman) in a fluently ingratiating way; (*hence*) (usu. of a man) to speak flirtatiously or make a sexual advance (to); (*broadly*) to flirt (with).

1968 in *Trans-action* VI (Feb. 1969) 27: The pimp...by his lively and persuasive rapping ("macking" is also used in this context) has acquired a stable of girls. **1970** T. Wolfe *Radical Chic* 101: I don't want you women to be macking with the brothers if they ain't tending to business. *Ibid.*: If he ain't man enough to be out on the street working for the people, then he ain't man enough for you to be macking around with. **1972** Claerbaut *Black Jargon* 72: *Macking* v. to engage in conversation used by pimps to solicit women to work for them. **1974** Univ. Tenn. student theme: Those chicks could have mack you to death until a man was on cloud nine. The young ladies had some real good conversation. **1967–80** Folb *Runnin' Down Lines* 145: *Mack on/to*...Make verbal advances to a member of the opposite sex. **1989** "Too Short" *Freaky Tales* (rap song): Mack on, baby, like an ice-cold vet,/Everything she had is what I get. **1991** *UTSQ*: *Mack*—to try to talk someone into going out with you. "You macked on him first." To "hit on." **1991** Nelson & Gonzales *Bring Noise* 128: His macked-up modus operandi. **1993** "Snoop Doggy Dogg" *Gin & Juice* (rap song): I...get to mackin' to this bitch named Sadie. **1993** Eble *Campus Slang* (Fall) 4: *Mack*—flirt. "Why do you want to mack with me?" **1993** P. Munro *U.C.L.A. Slang II*: *Mac*...to start a relationship with; put the moves on. *He's trying to mac her.* *a*1994 Smitherman *Black Talk* 157: *Mackin* Refers to a man tring to *hit on*...a woman to make her his. **1994** "Notorious B.I.G." *Big Poppa* (rap song): Most of these niggers think they be mackin' but they actin'/Who they attractin' with that line? **1994** *Living Single* (Fox-TV): You [a woman] macked a *monk*? **1991–95** in A. Sexton *Rap on Rap* 34: "To mack" meant to seduce a woman with talk.

c. Orig. *Pros.* to lie or exaggerate so as to impress or influence others; convince or persuade in a deceptive way.—also used trans.

1975 *Seattle Post-Intell.* (Feb. 16) ("Northwest") 8: The junior pimps listen to the senior pimps when they're macking (telling lies, bragging) about beating up their women. **1990** "Ice Cube" *Who's the Mack?* (rap song): He starts mackin' and mackin'...."I'm down on my luck."...Mackin' is the game and everybody's playin'/As long as you believe what they're sayin'. **1995** Stavsky, Mozeson & Mozeson *A 2 Z* 67: Don't let that G be *mackin'* you into droppin' outta school.

d. *Esp. Black E.* (of a man) to be conspicuously successful, esp. through the use of flattery or deceiving talk; use one's cunning to advantage.

1991 in P. Munro *U.C.L.A. Slang II*: Mack 'to be successful, esp. with having sex with women.' **1992** "Fab 5 Freddy" *Fresh Fly Flavor* 40: *Mackin'*...Being in control of a situation with your wit as the chief tool.

e. Esp. *Black E.* to use to one's advantage; exploit; (*broadly*) to overcome.

1993 G. Tate, in A. Sexton *Rap on Rap* 18: Hip-hop is the plunder from down under, mackin' all others for pleasure. **1993** *21st C. Dict. Sl.* 165: *Mack*...to overcome someone. *Johnny just macked that guy in the last lap of the race.* a**1994** Smitherman *Black Talk* 157: *Mack*...To hustle or exploit someone.

2.a. *Black E.* to walk or amble rhythmically; PIMP; (*hence*) to swagger.

1963 in Clarke *Amer. Negro Stories* 305: With no music till Lynn finishes "macking"...across the stage. **1969** C. Major *All-Night Visitors* 27: The macking presence of New York's finest. **1970** A. Young *Snakes* 55: In he comes, doing that rhythmic walk, *macking* they called it; one arm stiff at his side, the fingers curled up....He macks into my room.

b. *Homosex.* (among lesbians) to comport oneself in a strongly masculine or aggressive manner.—usu. constr. with *it*.

1966 S. Harris *Hellhole* 233: "Bulldykes" or "stud broads"...when they are outside the institution, often "mac" it, or dress in men's clothes. **1967** Colebrook *Cross of Lassitude* 296: I'm macking tough when I'm pregnant! a**1972** B. Rodgers *Queens' Vernacular* 132: *Masquerade*...said of lesbian who dresses up as a man. Syn: *mack it* (les sl[ang], late 60s).

3. *Black E.* to FRENCH-KISS; kiss passionately.

1978 W. Brown *Tragic Magic* 48: "You know how to mack, don't you?" "Yeah....You just hold your mouth a certain way, that's all." "Aw, man, I bet you ain't never macked with a girl." a**1993** P. Munro *U.C.L.A. Slang II: Mac*...to kiss (each other)....*mac on* v....to kiss...*mac with* v. to kiss.

mack² *v.* [fr. *McDonald's* or *Big Mac*, trademarks of McDonald's, Inc.] *Stu.* to eat (or, *rare*, drink) heartily.—also constr. with *down* or *out*. Also **mac.**

1971 in L. Bangs *Psychotic Reactions* 7: "Mack down!"...meant the act of eating, of course. **1989** P. Munro *U.C.L.A. Slang* 57: *Mac, mac out* to eat something, have some food (usually, a lot): Let's go mac. He really macked out last night....We'll mac on hamburgers and fries tonight. **1991** *Virginian-Pilot* (Norfolk) Aug. 23 (Nexis): HOW TO SOUND RAD AT THIS WEEKEND'S SURFING COMPETITION...I shined on the rest of the afternoon, jumped in my stay-wag and jetted to the nearest food hut, where I macked out with a couple of lowies. **1991** *Houston Chronicle* (Nov. 13) 5D: *Mack, mack out:* Eat heartily. a**1993** P. Munro *U.C.L.A. Sl. II:* I macked some fries.

mackadocious *adj. Rap Music.* extremely stylish or fashionable.

1991 "311" *Slinky* (rap song): Mackadocious she's sweet and precocious. **1992** *Billboard* (Feb. 15) (Nexis): Through the efforts of "13 or 14" part-time promotion people, the "mackadocious" track began picking up airplay. **1993** in Smitherman *Black Talk* 190: We Use Words Like "Mackadocious." **1994** *Trincoll Journal* (World Wide Web) (Trinity College) (Dec. 1): The influential 60's, funkadelic, mackadocious, rock band *Sly and the Family Stone*. **1995** Stavsky, Mozeson & Mozeson *A 2 Z* 66: Those kicks are mackadocious! **1996** Message from "The Deth Veggie," on Usenet newsgroup alt.religion.kibology: [Message signature:] Deth "Daddy Mackadocious" Veggie.

mack daddy *n.* [prob. MACK + DADDY] **1.** *Und. & Rap Music.* a man who is successful as a pimp or (*later*) violent criminal. Occ. also as v. ["The Great MacDaddy" is the protagonist of an anonymous African-American rhymed recitation, perh. of 1950's orig., as in early quots. below.]

1958–59 in Abrahams *Deep Down in Jungle* 162: Now Dillinger, Slick Willie Sutton, all them fellows is gone,/Left you, the Great MacDaddy, to carry on. **1973** J.A. McPherson, in C. Major *Calling Wind* 360: He was a strong talker, a easy walker,...a *woman* stalker! the last *true* son of the Great McDaddy. **1989** "3rd Bass" *Product of the Environment* (rap song): Back in the days when kids were mack daddies....He almost caught a bad one when he tried to enter. **1990** "Above the Law" *Livin' Like Hustlers* (rap song): I take too many names, I kick too much ass; K.M.G., the number-one mack daddy. **1990** in N. George *Buppies, B-Boys* 149: Sporting a big brimmed, old school, mack daddy hat. **1990** "Shazzy" *Giggaboe* (rap song): Tryin' to call yourself a man? Mack-daddyin' on the corner. **1991** in P. Munro *U.C.L.A. Slang II:* Mackdaddy 'pimp.'

2. *Rap Music.* **a.** MACK, 1.d; (*also*) a very good-looking young man.

1991 "Prince" *Jughead* (rap song): Well, Mack daddy in the house over there/What you doin' dog? **1992** *Knoxville* (Tenn.) *News-Sentinel* ("Detours") 16: *Mack Daddy*—Playboy. **1992** Eble *Campus Slang* (Fall) 5: *Macdaddy*—handsome, sexy male. African-American. a**1993** P. Munro *U.C.L.A. Slang II:* Al gets all the girls. He's a true mac daddy. **1993** *Source* (July) 62: Banks joins his mack daddy partners. a**1994** Smitherman *Black Talk* 157: *Mack Daddy* A man who has a lot of women and *plays* them; a *player.*

b. MACK, 1.c. Also as adj. and fig.

1993 *Beavis and Butt-head* (MTV): Kris is the mack daddy. **1995** Eble *Campus Slang* (Apr.) 7: Jordan is the macdaddy when it comes to basketball. **1995** Stavsky, Mozeson & Mozeson *A 2 Z* 67: Barkley is the mack daddy of hoop. **1995** Eble *Campus Slang* (Dec.) 4: *Mack-Daddy*—expert, the best: "Jane Austen is the mack-daddy of English literature."..."I am the MacDaddy." **1996** M. Kearney *Southeastern La. Univ. Coll.* (May): *Mac daddy*—top of the line. The tour bus was mac daddy.

macked out *adj.* Orig. *Und.* (of a man) flashily dressed; (*hence*) stylish; attractive; flashy.

1933 Ersine *Prison Slang* 52: *Macked Out.* Well dressed. "Ted just pulled a good job and he's all macked out." **1994** *St. Petersburg* (Fla.) *Times* (July 17) (Nexis): Several skateboarders say they have moved on to new jargon like "fat," "tweaked," "fresh," "stylish" and "macked out." **1993** *Source* (July) 76: The album's...themes...complement the macked-out vibe of the project. **1995** *Orlando* (Fla.) *Sentinel* (June 2) (Nexis): Then I take the groceries out to their macked-out Caddie and get offered a $2 tip. **1995** *Village Voice* (N.Y.C.) (Sept. 12): Lynch, moreover, took the stage macked out in a feathered fedora.

macker *n. Und.* MACK, 1.a.

1956 Algren *Wild Side* 187 [ref. to 1930's]: Let's see what them damn mackers are up to, "hustlers would suggest to each other on afternoons off." **1959** in Russell *Perm. Playboy* 420: I think I make as sorry a whore as you make a macker. **1968** Algren *Chicago* 138: And the mackers have given up for the night.

mackerel *n.* **1.** a worthless or foolish fellow.

1863 in Johns *49th Mass.* 95: There is a company here belonging to the Third New York Merchants' Brigade. We call them "mackerels." They are a disgrace to the merchants of the metropolis, for they seem to be the refuse of Five Points. Many of them are not fifteen years old. **1902–03** Ade *People You Know* 84: Well, you're on [*i.e.,* occupying yourself with] a couple of Mackerels. **1920** Ade *Hand-Made Fables* 51: So Intellectual and Artistic that her Husband looked like a Mackerel alongside of her. **1921** Sandburg *Slabs of Sunburnt West* 6: You poor fish, you mackerel,/You ain't got the sense God/Gave an oyster. **1924** Hecht & Bodenheim *Cutie* 24: She was a daughter of Eve, but her father was a mackerel.

2. MACKEREL-SNAPPER.—used contemptuously.

1948 McIlwaine *Memphis* 27 [ref. to 1920's]: Heimie! Take in da goo-uds! Da mackerels iss comin'!

3. see MACK, 1.a.

¶ In phrase:

¶ **holy mackerel!** (used to express surprise, annoyance, or the like).

1885 in S. Crane *Complete Stories* 51: Holy Mackerel! I have gone and done it! **1894** Crane *N.Y.C. Sketches* 55: "Hully mack'rel," said Billie. **1902** Hobart *Woods* 78: Suffering mackerel! **1919** Hinman *Ranging in France* 39: Holy mackerel, Buddy...we damned near got into Germany before we knew it. **1927** Nicholson *Barker* 53: Holy mackerel, I'm dry! **1928** Nason *Sgt. Eadie* 331: "Holy mackerel!" cried the doughboys. "It was loaded!" **1935** D.H. Clarke *Broadway* 108: But, Holy Mackerel, Arthur. You promised. **1936** Mulholland *Splinter Fleet* 39 [ref. to 1918]: Holy Mackerel, you guys are in it up to your necks now! ca**1955** *Sgt. Preston of Yukon* (Mutual Radio Network): Holy *mackerel!* How'd you find that out? **1958** E. Wood *Plan 9* (film): Holy mackerel!...That's nothing from *this* world! **1979** in Terkel *Amer. Dreams* 3: "When you shake hands with a man, you always shake hands ring up."...I thought: Holy mackerel! **1989** "Capt. X" & Dodson *Unfriendly Skies* 113: "Holy mackerel," he'll mutter. **1993** *Sally Jessy Raphaël* (synd. TV series): I thought, "Holy mackerel!" **1995** *Wings* (USA-TV): Holy mackerel! What happened to your head?

mackerel-snapper *n.* a Roman Catholic.—used contemptuously. Earlier **mackerel-snatcher.**

1855 in *Calif. Hist. Soc. Qly.* IX (1930) 168: Mackerel-snatchers...Yankees...[and] abolitionists. **1954–60** DAS: Mackerel-snapper…A Roman Catholic. *Not common.* **1966** *Western Folk.* XXV 38: At [a football] game with St. Mary's College [*ca*1922–24] I…first heard the expression "mackerel snappers" applied to Roman Catholics. **1968** Hooker *M*A*S*H* 24: Duke was a foot-washing Baptist, and Trapper John was a former mackerel-snapper who had turned in his knee pads. **1971** *Reader's Digest* (Oct.) 196: Back in the mid-1950s, when I was a Naval aviation cadet at Pensacola Fla., Catholics were still required to abstain from eating meat on Fridays, and a common military slang expression for them was "mackerel snappers." **1972** R. Barrett *Lovomaniacs* 365: Because the way that mackerel-snapper brain of hers works, she's still married to *him.* **1973** Longstreet *Chicago* 422: In 1905 an Irish gang—"the wild micks, the mackerel-snappers"—led by the McGinnis boys, took on a Hunky Bohemian gang for a deadly warfare. **1974** Lahr *Hot to Trot* 49: Hear that, Vera? He's finally met a mackerel-snapper. **1977** Coover *Public Burning* 110: Ask that mackerel-snapper Joe McCarthy. **1993** *Daily Beacon* (Univ. Tenn.) (Apr. 23) 4: Kikes…Mackerel Snappers…Dagos.

mackinaw *n.* In phrase: ¶ **holy [old] mackinaw** (used as a mild oath).

   1907 in *DARE*: Th' Lord help Billy! Holy Mackinaw! **1924** *DN* V 273: Holy Mackinaw. **1925** J. Stevens *Paul Bunyan* 44: How in the name of the holy old mackinaw…do you figure you're wearing any shining crown of supreme authority in this man's camp? **1938** Smitter *Detroit* 67: Holy Mackinaw…I've got tickets, if that's what you want. **1959** in *DARE.* **1975** in *DARE*: "Holy Old Mackinaw!" became…a favorite mild, Maine-woods expletive.

mackman *n.* MACK, 1.a.

   1954 in Wepman et al. *The Life* 39: I thought you were a mackman, a master at the Game. **1960** C. Cooper *Scene* 74: Did those oldhead mackmen…think they were the only ones who could drive Hogs? **1968** in *Trans-action* VI (Feb. 1969) 27: The pimp or mack man. **1971** Thigpen *Streets* 9: The Mack Man. **1967–80** Folb *Runnin' Down Lines* 245: *Mack man* Equivalent to *pimp.*

mad *n.* a feeling of anger; fury; rage.—often constr. with *up,* now usu. with *on.*

   1834 in *DARE*: I will be damde [*sic*] if I can do anything with them and they all ways in the mads. **1847–49* in *OED*: Mad, madness, intoxication. *Glouc. a1867* G.W. Harris *Lovingood* 86: Thar wer a streak ove skeer in his mad. **1868** in W. Petersen *Steamboating* 379: Their "mad" has played out. **1871** Schele De Vere *Americanisms* 503: The word is even used as a noun, meaning anger: "The Squire's *mad* riz." **1884** in *OED*: His mad was getting up. **1897** in *OED*: Let the pony get his mad up. **1936** in Weinberg *Tough Guys* 6: Then I began to get a mad up. **1936** in Galewitz *Great Comics* 255: Let's go, before old pretzel-chest wakes up with a mad on. **1958** in *DARE*: Jim walked his mad off; and suddenly he burst out laughing. **1988** *Publishers Weekly* (July 15) 28: Get over your mad. If you don't bitterness and resentment will continue to haunt you. **1993** *CNN Sports* (CNN-TV) (July 6): Billy Hatcher with a mad on. **1995** *CBS This Morning* (CBS-TV) (July 27): Every character has a mad on.

mad *adj.* **1.** Esp. *Jazz.* CRAZY; notably appealing.

   1941 H.A. Smith *Low Man* 85: And then the best of all is the big, mad, red-hot, out-of-this-world date. **1944** Burley *Hndbk. Harlem Jive* 15: That's mad, ole man; so mad it's glad. *Ibid.* 143: *Mad*—Fine, capable, able, talented. **1949** *Gay Girl's Guide* 12: *Mad*: Extremely or excessively *gay.* Loosely used with many shades of meaning. **1961** Griffith *Little Shop of Horrors* (film): Gee, that sure is a mad plant. **1963** J.A. Williams *Sissie* 54: "That sounds *mad,*" Iris said. **1964** in B. Jackson *Swim Like Me* 90: I took her to my pad, my pad was mad, I always featured a pad as hard as this. **1991** "Tribe Called Quest" *Check the Rhime* (rap song): I kicks the mad style. **1991** *Source* (Oct.) 59: It has mad flavor. **1993** "Snoop Doggy Dogg" *Every Single Day* (rap song): It's my duty to…kick phat mad styles. **1993** *Source* (July) 36: Sportin' fly gear and the mad cameo cut. **1994** in C. Long *Love Awaits* 117: Madd orgasms are occurring.

2. Esp. *Black E.* many; much; plenty of.

   1991 Nelson & Gonzales *Bring Noise* xii: Made mad dough! **1992** "Fab 5 Freddy" *Fresh Fly Flavor* 40: *Mad*—Used to describe an abundance of something. **1994** "Notorious B.I.G." *Big Poppa* (rap song): I got mad friends with Benzes,/C-notes by the layers. **1994** *N.Y. Times Mag.* (Aug. 14) 49: She got mad publicity.

mad *adv.* Esp. *Black E.* extremely. Also **madd.** Earlier **madly.**

   *a*1972 B. Rodgers *Queens' Vernacular* 130: *Madly broke* very low on

funds. **1990–91** *Street Talk!* 8: *Mad* very…"We be mad-funny." "We were very funny." *a*1993 P. Munro *U.C.L.A. Slang II*: Mad…very. *That party was mad packed.* **1993** in Stavsky, Mozeson & Mozeson *A 2 Z* 67: My grandmother was mad cool. **1994** *New York* (Oct. 10) 37: When they first bring [*sic*] me [to prison], man I was mad scared. *Mad scared.* **1994** in C. Long *Love Awaits* 137: It's madd cool. **1996** *New Yorker* (Aug. 26) 88: I'm mad talented.

madball *n. Carnival.* a crystal ball as used by a fortuneteller.

   1948 in *DAS*: Made with the madball. **1966** R.E. Alter *Carny Kill* 75: Madame Esmeralda…made with the madball.

madball *adj.* crazy.

   1967 Mailer *Vietnam* 143: Grizzer's mad-ball charge is like a stroke across the strings of a nerve. **1977** *Dallas Times Herald* (Jan. 9) 4H: Marty Feldman and Michael York play identical twins…in "The Last Remake of Beau Geste," with madball Feldman making his directing debut.

Mad Dog *n.* [sugg. by initials for *Mogen David*] (a nickname for) Mogen David, trademark name of a brand of inexpensive red wine. Also **Mad Dog 20-20.** [In early BrE cant, coincidentally used for 'strong ale'.]

   1974 *N.Y. Times* (June 2) 46: I'll take Mogen David wine—"Mad Dog." It's 20 proof by volume and it knocks you out. **1974–75** Powledge *Mud Show* 15: A bottle of Mad Dog…or Thunderbird. **1976** *Nat. Lampoon* (July) 60: Mad Dog 20-20 Now in Handy Gallon Jugs. **1978** Eble *Campus Slang* (Apr.) 3: *Mad dog*—a cheap wine—MD 20 20. The MD originally stood for Mogen David. All the old winos drink Mad Dog and T-Bird. **1979** in J.L. Gwaltney *Drylongso* 232: Now, this Mad Dog is messin' up heaps of folks! **1981** in L. Bangs *Psychotic Reactions* 342: A whole bottle a madawg twenny twenny. **1986** Heinemann *Paco's Story* 205: That cheap booze—"Mad Dog 20/20," Unc called it. **1987** *Campus Voice* (Winter) 22: And then throwing up Mad Dog 20/20 all over the upholstery. **1993** *Martin* (Fox-TV): I can pull a Mad Dog out of my purse. Mad Dog 20-20. **1993** *Beavis and Butt-head* (MTV): "They give you a bottle of Mad Dog 20-20." "Hi-test!"…"Where's the Mad Dog?"

mad-dog *v.* to glare at with hostility.—also used attrib.

   1990 Bing *Do or Die* 5: Why the hell didn't he just say not to mad-dog somebody? *a*1993 P. Munro *U.C.L.A. Slang II*: "Don't mad-dog me," my friend said. **1993** *Santa Barbara News-Press* (Nov. 2) B2: Staring malevolently at somebody or "mad-dogging" is the latest excuse among touchy teenagers to start fights. **1993** K. Scott *Monster* 8: I practiced my "mad dog" stares on the occupants of the cars beside us. **1994** *L.A. Times* (Mar. 10) E1: They're even angrier when somebody looks at them the wrong way, or as they put it, "mad-dogs" them. **1994** *N.Y. Times* (Mar. 18) A16: "He would look at me and mad-dog me and say names under his breath."…To "mad-dog" is to give a hard, cold look, and in the world of the streets, it is a challenge to a fight. **1997** *Dangerous Minds* (ABC-TV): He's just mad-dogging you. Like he's loco.

made see s.v. MAKE, *v.*

Ma Deuce *n.* [fr. *M-2*] *Army.* a Browning M-2 .50-caliber heavy machine gun. [Quots. ref. to Vietnam War.]

   *a*1982 Dunstan *Viet. Tracks* 96: A .50 cal. M2HB Browning atop the commander's cupola, and a second "Ma Deuce" forward of the turret rack. *a*1987 Coyle *Team Yankee* 104: Every tank and personnel carrier had one M2 caliber .50 machine gun, called a Ma Deuce. *a*1987 Bunch & Cole *Reckoning for Kings* 425: Blind Pig lifted the 125 pounds of Ma Deuce gun off the pintle.

madhouse *n.* any place characterized by traumatic conditions. *Specif.:* **1.** *Naut.* a poorly run ship on which sailors are overworked or harshly disciplined. [The broader sense, 'a disorderly, often noisy place', is fig. S.E. and in recent use has subsumed the present usage.]

   1905 *Nat. Police Gaz.* (Dec. 23) 7: The old practice ships were what sailors call "madhouses." It was drill all day and watch and watch all night. **1916** *Army & Navy Jour.* (Oct. 14) 223: But it must be a fearsome thing to sail in a "madhouse." **1918** (quot. at RED HOUSE). **1927** *Amer. Leg. Mo.* (Sept.) 86: D'ja ever get this Rollins started on the battle-wagons he's been on? Some of them must 'a' been mad-houses. **1930** Buranelli *Maggie* 44 [ref. to 1918]: "Madhouse"…means to a sailor a bad boat, a craft to keep away from. **1940** Goodrich *Delilah* 372 [ref. to 1916]: The other man would have been no less bewildered at knowing that he thought of Delilah as a "madhouse," a term applied to a disorganized ship in which a miserable crew is overworked. **1953** Dodson *Away All Boats* 18: You may make her a home, or if you so prefer, you may make her a madhouse and I will help you. **1988** Poyer *The Med* 105: Let's get off this madhouse.

2. *Pris.* a prison having brutal discipline.

1928 Callahan *Man's Grim Justice* 155: I had been in the New England "madhouse" now about eleven months.

3. *Av.* an air-traffic control tower.

1944 *AAF* 369: *Madhouse.* control tower.

mad minute *n. Mil.* one minute of rapid fire against enemy positions; (*broadly*) any short period of intense military bombardment.

1917 Empey *Over the Top* 84 [ref. to 1916]: Usually when an Irishman takes over a trench, just before "stand down" in the morning, he sticks his rifle over the top aimed in the direction of Berlin and engages in what is known as the "mad minute." This consists of firing fifteen shots in a minute. He is not aiming at anything in particular. *1925 Fraser & Gibbons *Soldier & Sailor Words* 149 [ref. to WWI]: *Mad Minute, the:* A newspaper coined expression of the autumn of 1914 in accounts of the Retreat from Mons, in allusion to the musketry *feu d'enfer* of our men in action. **1966** S.L.A. Marshall *Battles in Monsoon* 64: He circulated instruction that Bravo Company would stage a "*mad minute*" when first light broke....In this exercise by the defense, all hands fire weapons around the perimeter and keep the blast going for sixty seconds, the central idea being that if the enemy is preparing to charge as the darkest hour ends, the shock fire will turn him about. **1969** Eastlake *Bamboo Bed* 188: "Just before dawn, or maybe it was beginning dawn, that first Vietnamese yellow-red light, Clancy told everyone to have a mad minute." "Mad minute?" That's when the whole outfit fires everything they got at the VC. It makes you feel better. **1971** *Selling of Pentagon* (CBS-TV) (Feb. 23): The last part is known as the "mad minute." It would be hard to argue with that description. **1971** *Newsweek* (Jan. 11) 31: Suddenly a siren sounded; this was the signal for a "mad minute"—one minute of small-arms firing around the entire perimeter of the base in case enemy troops had infiltrated the area. **1968–77** Herr *Dispatches* 62: Just compulsive eruption, the Mad Minute for an hour. **1982** Del Vecchio *13th Valley* 232: Bring yer ammo. Mad minute.

mad Molly *n. Army.* the M-60 machine gun.

1982 "J. Cain" *Commandos* 288 [ref. to Vietnam War]: "I'm gonna...rock their socks off with mad Molly," he muttered, referring to the M-60s mounted in the rear of most MP [jeeps].

mad money *n.* **1.** money carried by a woman in case she wants to return home from a date without her escort.

1922 in *DN* V (Mar. 8) 148: *Mad money*—money a girl carries in case she has a row with her escort and wishes to go home alone. **1926** S. Young *Encaustics* 5: Mad money, he explained, quite seriously, is what they take with them to get home on in case they fall out with the fellow they've gone with. **1927** in E. Wilson *Twenties* 416: "Mad money" (if she had to walk home). *1936 Partridge *DSUE* 503: *Mad money.* A girl's return fare, carried lest her soldier friend got "mad," i.e. too amorous for her: New Zealand soldiers': 1916–18. Mostly a legend, and concerning only English girls. **1950** *Sat. Eve. Post* (Dec. 16) 113: I haven't any mad money. If you are the kind of man that—that makes a girl walk back from a ride, I would be disappointed in you. **1951** E. Wood *Violent Years* (film): Need some mad money? Or is he a gentleman?

2. money that may be used for unplanned or impetuous purchases; extra spending money.

1954–60 *DAS: Mad money*—Money saved by a woman against the time when she wishes to make an impetuous or impulsive purchase. **1961** *Sat. Eve. Post* (Aug. 26) 74: The five dollars in change I had permitted him as mad money. **1963** *Time* (Oct. 11) 44: Her professional TV debut, *Elizabeth Taylor in London*, earned its star a tidy $250,000 in mad money. **1963** E.M. Miller *Exile* 228: In the zip pocket under the pencil holder on his upper left arm he kept a ten dollar bill—"mad money." **1969** *Everett* (Wash.) *Herald* (Feb. 24) 2B: If you want to pick up a little mad money, don't forget that, as of today, the city started taking applications [etc.]. **1980** *St. Louis Post-Dispatch* (Feb. 3) 3C: County Executive Gene McNary has had millions of dollars in "mad money" to play around with when he prepares the county's annual budget.

Mad Town *n.* Madison, Wisconsin. *Joc.*

1982 UPI news report (Oct. 27) (Nexis): The Rev. Jerry Falwell won't forget Mad Town either. **1987** *Advertising Age* (Mar. 2) (Nexis): McPizza Hits Mad-town. **1990** *CBS This Morning* (CBS-TV) (Jan. 18): We go to Mad Town—Madison, Wisconsin. **1990** *CBS This*

Morning (CBS-TV) (Sept. 24): Madison, Wisconsin—Mad Town. **1993** *CBS This Morning* (CBS-TV) (Sept. 27): Mad Town—Madison, Wisconsin. **1995** Weather Channel TV (Feb. 3): Mad Town—Madison, Wisconsin. Minus twenty-nine degrees. A record low.

Mae West *n.* [after *Mae West* (1892?–1980), full-bosomed U.S. actress] **1.** Orig. *Mil. Av.* a kind of inflatable life jacket. Now *S.E.*

*1940 in *OEDS:* The aviators have adopted amusing novelties. For example...*Mae West* for a life jacket. **1941** *Sat. Review* (Oct. 4) 9: *Mae West.* An aviator's life belt or jacket. **1942** *Time* (Jan. 19) 23: Larry Allen was wearing a *Mae West* life-jacket; he cannot swim a stroke. **1942** S. Johnston *Queen of Flat-tops* 216: The new rubberized "Mae Wests"...can be inflated either with little compressed gas bottles...or blown up by lung power. **1943** *Life* (Nov. 29) 72: Heated gloves and boots in one hand, and Mae West in the other. **1943** Pyle *Brave Men* 18: I chose for my own life jacket one of the aviation, Mae West kind. **1944** in Loosbrock & Skinner *Wild Blue* 349: Travis heaved a Mae West at him. **1945** Dos Passos *Tour* 41: The passengers were sweating under their Mae Wests. **1948** Lay & Bartlett *12 O'Clock High!* 60: Davenport passed Jesse Bishop and Heinz Zimmermann, who were shedding their Mae Wests near the nose. **1951** Morris *China Station* 185: I pulled the stops on my Mae West, but the CO_2 bottles were out. **1955** Ruppelt *Report on UFOs* 8: We landed at the fighter base, checked in our parachutes, Mae Wests, and helmets. **1958** Camerer *Damned Wear Wings* 43: Each man wore his yellow Mae West over his flight jacket. **1961** L.G. Richards *TAC* 77: Now you don the new "Mae West" life-preservers. **1972** Ponicsan *Cinderella Liberty* 10: He...sits tenderly on a Mae West. *a*1990 Poyer *Gulf* 407: The guy...had his Mae West on...but it wasn't inflated.

2. *Army.* an M-3 battle tank. Now *hist.*

1941 *Nat. Geo.* (July) 11: That tank with twin turrets they call Mae West. **1962** W. Robinson *Barbara* 8: When the battalion received its first real armor—the old, high-turreted "Mae West" M-3s—Major Grant was Captain Grant.

3. *Parachuting.* a parachute malfunction in which a line becomes caught over the canopy, dividing it into two bulging halves.

1958 *AS* XXXIII (Oct.) 182: *Mae West.* An especially dangerous malfunction in which several line-overs cross the center of the [parachute] canopy, depressing the center and dividing the canopy into two parts. The name derives from the appearance, which suggests a brassiere. **1962** F. Harvey *Strike Command* 27: A Mae West is caused by a shroud line going over the top of the canopy during deployment, constricting it into two cup-like canopies which can (although not always) increase the rate of descent dangerously. **1981** Hathaway *World of Hurt* 48: You'll know if you got a Mae West when you look up to check your canopy. **1982** F. Hailey *Soldier Talk* 39: *Mae West*...partial inversion of [parachute] canopy. **1988** Clodfelter *Mad Minutes* 59: Several chutes popped open into...Mae Wests (a malfunction occurring when one or more panels of the parachute are blown inward through the suspension lines to pop open on the opposite side, thus creating two smaller canopies resembling a king-sized bra, and bringing an often bone-cracking descent).

4. *Naut.* (see quot.).

1961 Burgess *Dict. Sailing* 140: *Mae West.* A large spinnaker.

5. a kind of sweet roll.

1981 in Safire *Good Word* 95: "Coffee and a Mae West" was an endearing cry to us of the waterfront fraternity [in "the old days"].

mag[1] see s.v. MEG[1].

mag[2] *n.* **1.** a magazine (in any sense). [The *1801 quot. is erroneously dated by *F & H* as "1796."]

*1801 in *OED:* Who wrote in mags for hire. **1885** in S. Hale *Letters* 144: Some or any London mag. *1888 Jacobi *Printers' Vocab.* 80: *Mag.*—An abbreviation very generally used by printers for "magazine." **1906** in Bierce *Letters* 115: If his mag is going to hold fire. **1929** McEvoy *Hollywood Girl* 57: Who write...for the mags. **1938** W.C. Williams, in Witemeyer *Williams-Laughlin* 31: I am *not* joining the editorial board of his new mag. **1938** "E. Queen" *4 Hearts* 23: Sam...will start the ball rolling in the mags and papers. **1942** in J. Jones *Reach* 19: I don't know any mags that publish poetry. **1949** *N.Y. Times* (Aug. 28) I 23: You think you can't afford one of those "good dark dresses" fashion mags play up. **1959** in A. Sexton *Letters* 63: But I forget you never read the mags around. **1960** J. Mitford *Daughters*

212: There's a mag called the *Radio Times* which is his favorite thing. **1969** *Harper's* (Apr. 13) 62: Anyone's scorecard or fan mag. **1978** Wharton *Birdy* 56: Remember when we were selling the mags? **1980** *L.A. Times Bk. Rev.* (July 27) 2: A whole new look that seems appropriate for a fashion mag. **1984** H. Gould *Cocktail* 16: National mags. **1986** "J. Cain" *Suicide Squad* 156: Throw a bandolier of mags *over here!* **1968–90** Linderer *Eyes of Eagle* 180: I…fumbled to insert a fresh mag into my [rifle]. *a*1991 J. Phillips *You'll Never Eat Lunch* 46: She reads a lot of books and mags, she is very brilliant.

2. a maggot.
  1886 Lozier *Forty Rounds* 9: A strolling mag/Got in our meat.

3. a magneto.
  1918 in Grider *War Birds* 89: He wasn't hurt but the Spad was a write-off and Foggin got one mag [from the wreck]. **1931** Post & Gatty *Around World* 61: Both "mags" were turned on. **1938* A. Christie, in *DAS.* **1952** *Pop. Science* (Dec.) 187: In [drag] racing a mag is frequently used in place of battery ignition.

4. *Industry.* magnesium.
  1952 *Pop. Science* (June) 122: The Navy has high hopes for an F9F it has built with an all-mag wing. **1961** *N.Y. Times* (Oct. 15) III 1: Trade circles wondered if "mag" prices would come down also. Magnesium pig sells at 35.25 cents a pound. **1986** *NDAS*: *Mag*…A car wheel made of a magnesium alloy.

5. a magnum pistol.
  1970–71 Higgins *Coyle* 21: That fucking mag looks just like a cannon. **1978** S. King *Stand* 83: Also two .38s, three .45s, a .357 Mag. **1986** *Miami Vice* (NBC-TV): A $400 nickel-plated mag.

mag *v.* [perh. fr. *magpie*] **1.** to chatter; talk glibly or persuasively.
  *1820 in *OED*: Don't you think she magged away pretty sharply. That's the worst of the young ones—they will cackle so confoundedly. **1837** *Spirit of Times* (Feb. 18) 7: We would advise the Russian…to "stow magging" and not provoke persons…who are always ready to give him a chance. **1881–84* Davitt *Prison Diary* I 201: I say, pals, who is the new chum in No. 7…who won't mag? (talk). **1954–60** *DAS*: *Mag*…To talk a great deal…*Not common*.

2. *Und.* to cheat by flattery or insincere talk; swindle.
  1859 Matsell *Vocab.* 53: *Magging*. Getting money by cheating countrymen with balls, patent safes, etc., etc. **1869* in Partridge *Dict. Und.* 427: *Magging*…means…swindling a greenhorn out of his cash by the mere gift of the gab. **1881–84* Davitt *Prison Diary* I 58: The operation of "maggin' the gowk" out of his purse…[depends]…upon the acting and conversational "confidence-inspiring" powers of the gentleman into whose hands he has fallen.

magazine *n.* *Pris.* (see quots.).
  1926 Maines & Grant *Wise-Crack Dict.* 11: *Magazine*—Crook's term for six months to a year in jail. **1929** *AS* IV (June) 342: *Magazine.* Six months in jail.

Magellan *n.* [after Ferdinand *Magellan* (*ca*1480–1521), Portuguese navigator, commander of first ship to sail around the world] *Av.* an aircraft's navigator; (*hence*) an automated navigational system.—often used as a nickname.
  *ca*1952 in Gertz *Wild Blue Yonder* I G1: Magellan yelled…"There's flak all over the sky." **1961** *Twilight Zone* (CBS-TV): Magellan, try to get me a ground-speed check. **1966** Cassiday *Angels Ten* 134 [ref. to WWII]: The Magellan from Minnesota.…A good solid navigator. **1972** Carpentier *Flt. One* 201: "George" was the name…given long ago to autopilots. And "Magellan" was a nickname of unknown origin for the automatic navigation system, with its computer.

maggie *n.* **1.** a prostitute, esp. a streetwalker.
  *1603 in *F & H* IV 267: Ye trowit to get ane burd of blisse, To have ane of thir maggies. **1932** L. Berg *Prison Doctor* 215: Got so bad even a good crook couldn't make an honest living! Even the maggies complained that the amateurs were ruining the business!

2. *Mil.* MAGGIE'S DRAWERS.
  1942–45 Caniff *Male Call* (unp.): It's a Maggie. **1945** F. O'Rourke *E Company* 41: "I never saw so many Maggies in my life." Gleason meant Maggie's drawers, the red flag that comes up when a man misses the target completely. Yates had so many Maggies he could have started a store.

3. a magnetron.
  1979 Hiler *Monkey Mt.* 88: I was dead tired after wrestling with that fuckin' maggie all night.

Maggie's drawers *n.pl.* [alluding to the ribald song cited in 1942 *AS* quot.; a fragmentary stanza appears in bracketed 1938 quot. below, and an extended version is in H. Morgan *Rugby Songs* (1967), p. 93] *Mil.* a red flag or disc used on a firing range to indicate failure to hit the target; (*hence*) a complete miss on such a range. Also vars.
  1936 *Our Army* (July) 37: Home, home on the range, where all of the bolos roam,/Where seldom is heard, "Bull's Eye" as a word,/And Maggie's drawers wave all the day. [**1938** Steinbeck *Grapes of Wrath* 304: Oh, the night that Maggie died, she called me to her side, an' give to me them old red flannel drawers that Maggie wore. They was baggy at the knees—.] **1942** Gach *In Army Now* 234: If it is a complete miss, the targeteer waves a red flag, and then everyone says, "You got in Maggie's britches." *Ibid.* 235: We do love to wave Maggie's pants at them. **1942** *Leatherneck* (Nov.) 148: *Maggie's Drawers*—Red flag used on rifle range to indicate a miss on the target. **1942** *AS* XVII 68: *Maggie's drawers*…common army slang; taken from an obscene song, "Those Old Red Flannel Drawers that Maggie Wore,"…dating from 1921 or earlier—probably the First World War. **1950** *Nat. Geographic* (Nov.) 661: When one unhappy lad missed the whole target, they waved a red flag.…At the sight of it the whole line yelled "Maggie's drawers!" **1952** Uris *Battle Cry* 59: In the pits there was also a red flag, the nemesis of a rifleman. "Maggie's Drawers," it was called—the signal for a complete miss. **1971** Flanagan *Maggot* 132 [ref. to *ca*1959]: He waited for the round markers to appear; white for bull's eye, red for a four and on down to "maggie's drawers," a red flag waved for a clean miss. **1980** McDowell *Our Honor* 199: A shot that missed the target completely received the ultimate ignominy: "Maggie's Drawers," signaled by waving a red flag from the butts. **1987** D. da Cruz *Boot* 302: *Maggie's drawers* red disk (formerly red flag) drawn across rifle target, denoting clear miss. **1988** DeLillo *Libra* 400: He'd missed with the third shot.…Missed everything. Maggie's drawers.

maggot *n.* **1.a.** a loathsome or despicable person; lowlife. [Defs. **(b)** and **(c)**, below, represent specific applications of this sense but have become fully lexicalized through recent frequent use.]
  *1680 Shadwell *Woman-Captain* V: How now Sirrah!…a Maggot as thou art. **1899** in J. London *Letters* 49: The maggots!—small wonder they have the nerve to call themselves gods!…Go ahead!…you maggots. **1930** Mae West *Babe Gordon* 188: The double-crossin' heel!…The garbage-can maggot! **1954** Rackin *Long John Silver* (film): You mutinous maggot! **1958** Constiner *Gunman* 30: Would you kindly…shoot all six of these maggots? **1994** J. Shay *Achilles* 4: They wanted to give us a fucking Unit Citation—them fucking maggots.

b. Orig. *USMC.* a court-martialed person confined to the brig; (*also*) a recruit, trainee, or newly arrived enlisted person; (*hence*) (in recent general use) a mere novice.—used contemptuously.
  1964 Brown *Brig* 49: You better speak low, boy, when the lights are out in the compound. You want to wake up the other maggots? **1968** Mares *Marine Machine* 30: White means all you maggots passed the Phase I exam. **1970** Ponicsan *Last Detail* 34: The grunt would say, "Come, maggot," and the guy would race up the ladder, clattering like hell, and put his nose against the bulkhead. **1971** Flanagan *Maggot* 183 [ref. to *ca*1959]: A marine is tough, maggots. Tough. **1976** Conroy *Santini* 219: What do you think the sergeant had for dinner last night, fat maggot? **1978** Diehl *Sharky's Machine* 70: You're a third or second-grade detective, you're a maggot to them. **1980** DiFusco et al. *Tracers* 15: Now Luke the Gook…and Charlie Cong…*love* to kill maggots. **1982** Goff, Sanders & Smith *Bros.* 54: Welcome to the Nam.…You maggots coming in to take my place? **1983** Elton, Cragg & Deal *Dict. Soldier Talk* 362: *Maggot* (World War II; Marines) Form of address to a prisoner undergoing sentence. Originated at…the Naval Prison at Portsmouth, New Hampshire. **1986** G. Quintano *Police Acad. 3* (film): Let's go, maggots! **1987** *Rage* (Univ. Tenn.) I (No. 2) 13: *Maggot*—[fraternity] pledge. **1988** von Hassel & Crossley *Warriors* 29: The DI will spare no effort to instill that spirit in his "maggots," the recruits…whom he loves.

c. *Police.* a felon or habitual criminal.
  1985 M. Baker *Cops* 273: By the time you even get some of the maggots…in court,…they walk free. **1990** C.P. McDonald *Blue Truth* 44: And woe be unto the street maggot that messed with him. **1996** Philbin *Cop Speak* iv: Some maggot did a mule out by the airport.

(Some criminal murdered a drug courier.). *Ibid.* 146: *Maggot*…This a favorite term that cops use to describe someone who is despicable and parasitical, such as a drug dealer.

2. a cigarette butt.

1963 S. Hayden *Wanderer* 44: Red took a mighty drag…then snapped the maggot over the rail.

3. *Black E.* a white person.—used contemptuously.

1985 Detroit man, age 24: White folks talk about *niggers*, we talk about *maggots*.

¶ In phrase:

¶ **enough to gag a maggot, 1.** something that is thoroughly repulsive. Also vars.

1966 Elli *Riot* 57: Those goddamn buckets are enough to gag a maggot. **1972** Hannah *Geronimo Rex* 47: In my crowd, whatever gagged a maggot passed for humor. **1974** *Sanford & Son* (NBC-TV): This stuff can gag a maggot! **1974** Loken *Come Monday Mornin'* 45: It'd still gag a maggot off a gut truck. **1979** Decker *Holdouts* 5: You look like you think it would gag a maggot. **1966–80** McAleer & Dickson *Unit Pride* 318 [ref. to Korean War]: The smell was enough to gag a maggot. **1985** *Maledicta* VIII 239: That's so bad it would gag a maggot in a gut wagon. (Used in the 1940's). *a*1990 Helms *Proud Bastards* 156: Godawful [music] that was enough to gag a maggot and knock a flock of buzzards off a gutwagon.

2. (see quot.).

1968 Baker *CUSS* 112: *Enough to gag a maggot.* A great deal (of something).

maggot bait *n.* Esp. *Mil.* an exposed or buried corpse. Also **maggot meat.** Cf. BUZZARD-BAIT; SHARK BAIT.

1955 F. Franklin *Combat Nurse* 78 [ref. to WWII]: He saved us from being maggot bait that day. **1975** Wambaugh *Choirboys* 158: Stop, you motherfucker, or you're maggot meat! *a*1990 Helms *Proud Bastards* 52: Maybe he's…maggot-bait.

maggoty *adj.* very drunk.

1920–22 in *DN* V 336: *Maggoty*…Drunk. **1929–33** J.T. Farrell *Young Manhood of Lonigan* 225: Two weeks ago you were maggoty and got your dose. **1929–34** Farrell *Judgment Day* 468: I was maggotty drunk. **1941** in C.R. Bond & T. Anderson *Flying T. Diary* 47: Smith, equally maggoty, was with him and not helping the situation. **1979** *Easyriders* (Dec.) 27: Kid will be asleep when he rolls in /Maggoty, loaded.

magic *n.* high-technology electronics, esp. as used in advanced computer systems.

1981 Stiehm *Bring Men & Women* 50: *Magic:* electrical engineering and all related hand-waving activities. **1986** Cogan *Top Gun* 114: The AWG-9 radar and the "magic" weapons systems were two more reasons why the Tomcat could beat anything going.

magic dust *n.* the drug phencyclidine; PCP.

1984 (cited in Spears *Drugs & Drink*). **1990** T. Thorne *Dict. Contemp. Slang: Magic, magic dust…American.* The drug PCP.

magic mushroom *n. Narc.* any of various mushrooms having hallucinogenic properties, esp. of the genus *Psilocybe.*

1967–68 von Hoffman *Parents Warned Us* 36: The exotics, like woodrow nuts, magic mushrooms, and opium…are quite rare. **1969** Lingeman *Drugs A to Z* 139: *Magic mushrooms*….various species of fungi growing in the Western Hemisphere with hallucinogenic actions. **1970** Landy *Underground Dict.: Magic mushroom*… Mushroom that produces effects similar to LSD when eaten. **1977** *Rolling Stone* (Dec. 29) 35: Police reported finding 2500 pounds of "magic mushrooms" and estimated their street value at $2.5 million. **1978** *Harper's* (Mar.) 89: The impulse to ingest magic mushrooms and their psychedelic cognates. **1983** *Psych. Today* (July) 33: Psilocybin, a consciousness-altering substance in the "magic mushroom." **1990** *New Republic* (Mar. 5) 28: A hallucinogenic brew that acts on him like magic mushrooms.

magic show *n. USMC.* a religious service. [Quots. ref. to Vietnam War.]

1978 Hasford *Short-Timers* 19: *Magic show.* Religious services in the faith of your choice….After the "magic show" we eat chow. **1987** E. Spencer *Macho Man* 5: Priests…turned The Man into a wafer in a magic show every day at mass.

magnet ass *n. Mil. Av.* a pilot who seems to attract enemy fire frequently. *Joc.*

1962 *We Seven* 36 [ref. to Korean War]: The other pilots in the squadron began called [*sic*] me [John Glenn] "Ol' Magnet Tail" because I was hit by antiaircraft on seven occasions. **1966** E. Shepard

Doom Pussy 3: Last mission he flew, that boy's ship had twenty-seven holes in it. He has seven in his body. At his farewell party the platoon presented him with a plaque: "From the Razorbacks to their Magnet Ass." **1966–67** F. Harvey *Air War* 39: The pilots of these [defoliation] planes are said to be the most shot-at people in the war. They are known by the crude but descriptive name of "magnet-asses." **1982** Basel *Pak Six* 115: Jack Hart, old "Magnet Ass," was the deputy commander. **1987** Robbins *Ravens* 143: After a month they started calling him Magnet Ass. **1989** P.H.C. Mason *Recovering* 74: "Magnet ass" was the Army's explanation for why I got hit forty-five times in one week. **1989** Berent *Rolling Thunder* 45: Good luck….Don't be a magnet ass. **1992** J. Campbell & D. Campbell *Allied Aircraft Art* 56: Magnet Ass.

magnif *adj.* magnificent.

1863 in R.B. Hayes *Diary* II 384: Three or four…comrades are singing…."Magnif!" **1885** (quot. at WAY UP). **1948** in M. Shulman *Dobie Gillis* 53: "Magnif," she said.

magnolious *adj.* grand, splendid.

1865 (quot. at SPANGLORIOUS). **1865** Sala *My Diary* 114: But, for anything I knew to the contrary she might be the sheriff's daughter or the mayor's sister-in-law, and accustomed to go out on Sundays with a "magnolious" parasol and a "spanglorious" crinoline. **1919** S. Lewis *Free Air* 210: "There's a magnolious medico ahead here on the pass," Pinky Parrott interrupted.

magoo *n.* [orig. unkn.; perh. an elab. of GOO] **1.** *Theat.* a cream pie thrown in slapstick comedy.

1926 Finerty *Criminalese* 27: *Get the magoo*—receive a custard pie in the face; generally, bad luck. **1954–60** *DAS: Magoo*…A custard pie used by actors to throw at one another in comedy scenes.

2.a. an important person. [Popularized in the 1932 Broadway comedy by Hecht and Fowler.]

1932 Hecht & Fowler *The Great Magoo* [title]. [**1935** Pollock *Underworld Speaks: McGoogle,* the big boss.] **1946** *N.Y. Times Bk. Rev.* (Dec. 1) 9: Thinly veiled lampoons of Washington magoos, professional…liberals, and glib slogan makers. **1949** in *DAS:* Darryl Zanuck, chief magoo of the studio. **1959** O'Connor *Talked to a Stranger* 194: He thinks he's the "Great Magoo," a name I got for all the muttonheads who think they're big wheels.

b. a useless or foolish person. [Recent quots. are prob. infl. by Mr. *Magoo,* profoundly nearsighted cartoon character introduced by UPA Studios and freq. seen on children's television into 1970's.]

1932 Hecht & Fowler *The Great Magoo* 98: If I ever lay my hands on that frizzly little magoo, I'll maim her for life. **1943** *Gertie from Bizerte* (pop. song): There's a love-sick magoo in the army. **1984** Algeo *Stud Buds* 7: An absent-minded or inattentive person…*magoo.* **1990** P. Munro *Slang Usage: Magoo* person driving a car slowly. **1996** *Skeptical Inquirer* (Mar.) 15: Among his nicknames…are…Senator Magoo, and the Senator from Outer Space.

3. sex appeal; (*also*) stuff; thing; situation; the right stuff, etc.—used in a vague way to indicate the subject of conversation.—usu. constr. with *the.*

1935 Pollock *Underworld Speaks: McGoo,* sex appeal. **1942** *ATS* 341: Sex appeal…(the old) magoo. **1947** *ATS* (Supp.) 4: Excellent; "super." …dreamy,…the magoo. *Ibid.* 25: The magoo, an awaited mission or attack. **1950** *Collier's* (Dec. 9) 17: Get right, chum….I don't go for that magoo. **1982** *California* (Feb.) 86: Once you replace the dialog [in a movie soundtrack],…you have to put back some of the engine, the water lapping on the side of the boat, the whole magoo.

magpie *n. Shooting.* a black-and-white flag or disc displayed on a target range to announce a shot that has hit the number three (inner) ring of a target; (*hence*) such a shot.

*1884 in *F & H* IV 269: Running through the scoring gamut with an outer, a magpie, and a miss. **1884** in Mattes *Indians, Infants, Infantry* 249: He fired his last shot….had it been a "magpie" the citizens of Bidwell would have carried off the coveted prize. *ca*1915 in Ludlum *Shooting Stories* 142 [ref. to 1880]: The officer discovered the disk marking a three, called the "Magpie," bringing my total up to twelve points for the three shots. **1980** Cragg *Lex. Militaris* 287: *Magpie.* A shot in the target on a rifle range that hits the inner circle of a target and is signaled by a black and white flag.

magsman *n.* [MAG, *v.* + *-s-* + *-man*] *Und.* a confidence man.

*1838 in *OED: A magsman* must of necessity be a great actor and a

most studious observer of human nature. **1859** Matsell *Vocab.* 53: *Magsmen.* Fellows who are too cowardly to steal, but prefer to cheat confiding people by acting upon their cupidity. **1869** *Overland Mo.* (Aug.) 117: Bill Smith, a Liverpool magsman. ***1881–84** Davitt *Prison Diary* I 48: The order of magsmen will comprise card-sharpers, "confidence-trick" workers, begging-letter writers, bogus ministers of religion, professional noblemen, "helpless victims of the cruel world," medical quacks, and the various other clever rogues that figure from time to time in the newspaper records of crime. **1899** A.H. Lewis *Sandburrs* 164: His name is "Windy Joe, the Magsman." **1928** Guerin *Crime* 32 [ref. to *a*1880]: Hard on their trail would come all the magsmen.

mahogany *n.* **1.** *Naut.* salt beef.

[***1821–26** Stewart *Man-of-War's-Man* II 26: *Salt junk*, as hard as mahogany.] **1830** Ames *Sketches* 166: I could see no better "provant" …than a piece of salt beef of that description or quality known to sailors by the expressive name of "mahogany." **1856** Sleeper *Tales* 288: A morsel of the old mahogany junk. *a*1890–96 F & H: *Mahogany* …(nautical).—Salt beef. **1899** Hamblen *Bucko Mate* 132: It ain't half an hour ago that you would have been glad to tackle the hardest piece of mahogany salt-horse that ever came from St. Helena.

2. a bar counter. See also *decorate the mahogany* s.v. DECORATE, 1.

1896 F.P. Dunne, in Schaaf *Dooley* 129: "Well, I dinnaw," said Mr. Hinnissy, crossing his legs and laying his glass down slowly on the mahogany. **1905** *Independent* (Nov. 2) 1025: Three blithesome barmaids…graced the mahogany. **1911** T.A. Dorgan, in Zwilling *TAD Lexicon* 55: Notice the two rising young American mahogany polishers. **1914** in C.M. Russell *Paper Talk* 107: No gentelman would think of insulting the littel lady behind the mohogony [*sic*]. **1929** Hotstetter & Beesley *Racket* 231: *Mahogany*—The bar of a cafe or saloon. **1965** Spillane *Killer Mine* 26: When the wise guy suddenly and quietly tried to scream from the short hook to the Kidney and spilled his drink across the mahogany, the grins stopped. **1995** *Time Out N.Y.* (Nov. 22) 109: I bellied up to the mahogany and the bartender immediately said, "Hello."

mahoney *n.* **1.** nonsense; MAHULA; MALARKEY.

1941 in W.C. Fields *By Himself* 393: Baloney—Mahoney—Malarky.

2. [perh. fr. Jerry *Mahoney*, name of ventriloquist's dummy used by popular 1950's children's TV performer Danny O'Day] a blockhead.

1960 L. O'Brien *Great Imposter* (film): The world is full of mahoneys and finks. **1974** *Coq* (Apr.) 44: What a bunch of Mahoneys!

mahoska *n.* [perh. < Ir *mo thosca* 'my business'] *Und.* a thing of importance or interest, esp. a weapon or an item of contraband; stuff, esp. addictive drugs.—constr. with *the*. Also **mahosker.**

1943 (quot. at MARY JANE). **1942–49** Goldin et al. *DAUL* 132: *Mahoska.* 1. Habit-forming drugs. 2. A pistol or revolver. 3…A knife or similar weapon. 4. Anything illicit or necessarily secret…as stolen goods, combustibles, and counterfeit money. "Ditch…the mahoska, Squint." **1973** in Maurer *Lang. Und.* 319: *Mahoska*…Any kind of narcotics especially heroin (East Coast, particularly New York City). **1986** Breslin *Table Money*: The mahosker isn't here.…The checks. **1987** D. Mamet *Untouchables* (film) [ref. to 1930]: Okay, pal, why the mahoska? Why're you packin' the gun? **1987** *Atlantic* (Mar.) 100: Jimmy Breslin says that *mahosker* means essentially "anything heavy—power, money, even a badge—or anything conferring power."

mahula *n.* [see note at MAHULA, *adj.*] nonsense; MALARKEY. Also **mahaha.**

1929–30 Dos Passos *42d Parallel* 359: Doc said that was all mahoula. **1933** Duff & Sutherland *I've Got Your Number* (film): I still think it's a lot of mahula. **1934** in Dos Passos *14th Chronicle* 446: All that cinema talk is the purest and most mouldy mahoula. **1941** in *DAS*: The local Reds are already receiving their old-time mahoola about Red Russia being actually a democracy. **1947** *ATS* (Supp.) 7: *Mahaha*, silly talk.

mahula *adj.* [< Yid *mekhule* < Heb *mechula* 'spoiled; out of order; bankrupt'] ¶ In phrase: **go mahula** to go bankrupt or otherwise come to grief.

1928 *AS* III (June) 375: *Mahula*—To go broke. **1948** Mencken *Amer. Lang. Supp.* II 687: The late Dr. William Rosenau of Baltimore, a distinguished Hebrew scholar, told me that *mahula* should be spelled *mechuleh*. It is derived from the Hebrew verb *kala*, signifying to finish and is commonly used for to go bankrupt. **1987** *Hunter* (ABC-TV): Unless you play ball with me, McCall goes mahula.

maiden *n.* [fr. S.E. *maiden* 'a horse that has not yet won a race' (1760 in *OED*)] *Horse Racing.* ¶ In phrase: **break (one's) maiden** (of a horse or jockey) to win (one's) first race.

1951 in D.W. Maurer *Lang. Und.* 204: *Break a maiden* or *one's maiden*…of an apprentice jockey: to ride his first winner.…Of a horse: to win his first race. **1968** M.B. Scott *Racing Game* 17: A "maiden" is a horse that has never won a race. *Ibid.* 17: When a horse wins his first race, he is said to "break" his maiden. **1978** *New West* (Apr. 10) 78: He went to the post ten times before he finally broke his maiden. **1984** *L.A. Times* (Jan. 9) III 1: Since breaking his maiden last November, the California-bred colt has won the Norfolk by a nose.

mail *n.* *Army & USMC.* artillery fire; (*also, rarely*) bombs.—often constr. with *incoming* or *outgoing.*

1919 Ellington Co. *A* 11 (caption): Mail from Berlin. *Ibid.:* Hip Boots (for sprinting from mail). **1944** in *Best from Yank* 108: Let's give them some incoming mail. **1944–48** A. Lyon *Unknown Station* 54: "Outgoing mail," someone said. **1948** A. Murphy *Hell & Back* 90: The midnight mail. **1948** Wolfert *Act of Love* 416 [ref. to WWII]: But only American guns were shooting thus far. It was "outgoing mail," as the troops called it. *Ibid.* 417: "Incoming mail," a soldier alongside him said. **1950** *N.Y. Times Mag.* (Aug. 6) 45: Up at the front our artillery is known as "outgoing mail"; the enemy's is known as "incoming mail." **1962** Tregaskis *Vietnam Diary* 45: I could hear the rustle of "outgoing mail." **1962** W. Robinson *Barbara* 231 [ref. to WWII]: Inside the tank is the safest place to be when the mail comes in. **1965** Linakis *In Spring* 67 [ref. to WWII]: Somehow the feeling was like waiting for big kraut mail, or what you expected when their planes pulled out of a steep dive. **1966** Cassidy *Angels Ten* 7: She could deliver the mail and get back, no matter what her condition. **1968** W. Crawford *Gresham's War* 11 [ref. to Korean War]: The noise was exactly that of incoming mail, a 60 mm mortar. **1979** McGivern *Soldiers* 156 [ref. to WWII]: Goddamn it, Bull! *Look.* We got mail coming in! **1980** Manchester *Darkness* 305: American guns (outgoing mail) replied. **1984–88** in Berry *Where Ya Been?* 211: We might catch some incoming mail tonight.

¶ In phrase:

¶ **haul** [or **tote**] **the mail** to run or travel rapidly. See also *carry the mail*, 1, s.v. CARRY.

1908 *DN* III 383: *Tote the mail*…To run away from something very rapidly; "hit the grit"…"I made him fairly *tote the mail* out of my canepatch." **1935** Hurston *Mules & Men* 173: He hauled de fast mail back into de woods where de bear was laid up. **1937** *Daily News* (N.Y.) (Feb. 14). **1938** *AS* (Dec.) 308: When he covers a good many miles in exceptionally good time…he has been "haulin' the mail." **1990** *Cops* (Fox-TV): We were haulin' the mail all right.

mail *v.* ¶ In phrase: **mail (someone) home** *Mil.* to transport (a corpse) back to the U.S. for burial.

1926 MacIssac *Tin Hats* 88 [ref. to 1918]: Suppose one of them enemy planes drops a bomb on a traitor? Hey?…They can mail what's left of us home to the folks in an envelope. **1963** Breen *PT 109* (film) [ref. to WWII]: He's afraid they're gonna mail him home.

mail-order *adj.* ridiculously inadequate or inferior. [Early quots. ref. chiefly to WWI.]

1923 T. Boyd *Through the Wheat* (paperback ed.) 30: I wouldn't have no God-damned mail-order shavetails tellin' me what to do. **1924** T. Boyd, in *Points of Honor* 5: But he didn't care; he was just like the rest of these mail-order lieutenants: all he cared for was that Sam Browne belt…and that brass bar on his shoulder. **1925–26** J. Black *You Can't Win* 122: It was a mail-order jail—two steel cells on a concrete foundation. **1926** Branch *Cowboy* 17: The range came to expect and recognize the "mail-order cowboy," who arrived already fitted in cowboy-wear as he knew it. **1928** MacArthur *War Bugs* 243: "Take that rubber out of your neck!" was yelled at so many mail-order officers that they…complained. **1931** Tomlinson *Best Stories* 361: The French are probably just as proud of him as we are of some of the mail order wonders we got. **1933** Clifford *Boats* 27: Some…mail-order shavetail had married her out of hand as soon as they had handed him a commission. **1936** R. Adams *Cowboy Lingo* 26: A tenderfoot in "custom-made" cowboy regalia and devoid of range experience was a "mail-order cowboy." **1957** Herber *Tomorrow to Live* 16: You're a damn mail-order stud with a pen for a penis.

main *n.* **1.** *R.R.* a main railroad line.

1932–34 Minehan *Boy & Girl Tramps* 55: You can't name a main I haven't hit or a road I didn't ride.

2. *Narc.* MAIN LINE.

    1952 H. Ellson *Golden Spike* 14: He shot it in the main. **1973** Goines *Players* 130: She continued to try desperately to hit a main.

main *adj.* **1.** (of persons) most important; in charge; chief; commanding.—used in miscellaneous rare slang collocations.—constr. with *the.*

    1896 Ade *Artie* 21: You could see that Mamie was the main screw o' the house and run things to suit herself. **1900** Ade *More Fables* 163: The Main Works of a Wholesale House was Jacking Up the Private Secretary. **1903** Hobart *Out for Coin* 75: Pass my name up to de Main Squash, will 'e? **1904** *Life in Sing Sing* 256: *Main bull.* Chief of detectives. **1911–12** Ade *Knocking the Neighbors* 179: The Main Swivel over at the Hall. **1923** in Kornbluh *Rebel Voices* 90: Who is the main push up there anyway? **1936** L. Duncan *Over the Wall* 121: The main cheese of the Department contended…that I should be compelled to pay for my first crime in California.

2. Esp. *Black E.* **a.** (of persons) favorite; closest, most intimate, or most loyal. [In this as in the following sense, *main man* has been by far the most freq. collocation, esp. as 'best (male) friend'; see also MAIN MAN.]

    1942 *ATS* 398: Steady Sweetheart.…*main dish.* **1944** *Slanguage Dict.* 60: *Main queen*—the present "heart throb." **1944** Burley *Hndbk. Jive* 143: *Main-queen*—Girl-friend, wife. **1953** in Wepman et al. *The Life* 118: I heard she was going with my main man Moose. **1955** in Wepman et al. *The Life* 74: Wheeler's main man Joe was an old wino. **1962** in Wepman et al. *The Life* 140: You remember your main man Red? *Ibid.* 145: Al will go back to his main girl Pearl. **1967** Baraka *Tales* 19: You talkin' about Ray's main man. **1967** *Lit Dict.* 1: Your *ace* number one friend is your *main man.* **1967–80** Folb *Runnin' Down Lines* 246: *Main bitch/ 'ho/ stuff* 1. Male's favorite or most frequent sexual partner. 2. Male's mate, lover, girlfriend. **1969** B. Beckham *Main Mother* 103: One of my main boys. **1970** T. Wolfe *Radical Chic* 102: Chaser had his two main men, James Jones and Louis Downs. **1971** *Current Slang VI* (Winter) 8: *Main man*, n. A favorite boyfriend. **1973** Andrews & Owens *Black Lang.* 30: The Lord is my main man; I can't dig wanting. **1974** Piñero *Short Eyes* 43: You'll always be my main nigger. **1975** B. Silverstein & R. Krate *Dark Ghetto* 149: "He's my main nigger" means he is my best [black] friend. **1975** Sepe & Telano *Cop Team* 140: This is my main man, Lou. **1974–77** A. Hoffman *Property Of* 152: How come you're here without your main man? **1978** Kopp *Innocence* 108: You're my main man, my mainest man. **1980** W. Sherman *Times Square* 60: His main lady and another pimp held her down. **1979–82** Gwin *Overboard* 285: They made a big mistake by firin' my main man. **1983** Van Riper *Glenn* 254 [ref. to 1974]: "John Glenn! My main astronaut!" a black girl exulted in Steubenville. **1985** B.E. Ellis *Less Than Zero* 180: Hey, Finn, my main man, how've you been? **1985** *L.A. Times* (Feb. 13) V 10: Before meeting her main man, Kroll remembers an endless shuffle of dating around. **1987** *N.Y. Times* (July 7) A12: "Mary," he coos, "it's your main man, the Macker. Got any wild dates this weekend?" **1989** S. Robinson & D. Ritz *Smokey* 25: I was Mama's main man.

b. held in one's great or highest regard, as for reputation or accomplishments.

    1970 C. Major *Dict. Afro-Amer. Sl.* 79: *Main man*…one's hero. **1973** in J. Flaherty *Chez Joey* xxi: [F. Scott] Fitzgerald…was my main man. **1979** E. Genovese, in *New Republic* (Apr. 17, 1995) 43: ["He has been the strongest influence on my own work as a historian, and in 1979 I dedicated a book…to"] Eric Hobsbawm: Our Main Man. **1983** *Reader's Digest Success with Words* 87: Black English…*main man*…"one's hero." **1984** *Atlantic* (Oct.) 55: A fondness for quoting the philosophers he used to teach ("My main man is still Hegel"). **1990** *N.Y. Times* (Feb. 4) ("Arts & Leisure") 27: The Reagan years is over, man, and I miss 'em. Ronnie, he was my main man. **1995** *Esquire* (June) 147: [Thelonious] Monk has always been my main man; it's his weird pause and attack that plays most naturally inside my head.

main *v. Narc.* MAINLINE, 1.

    1952 H. Ellson *Golden Spike* 52: She was the first one to show him how to main. **1956** E. Hunter *Second Ending* 247: I'd be maining it like a madman. **1970** *Time* (Mar. 16) 17: All my friends were on heroin. I snorted a couple of times…and after that I mained it. **1973** W. Burroughs, Jr. *Ky. Ham* 75: Bob was not one for skinny steel in the main. **1981** *Penthouse* (Mar.) 141: "Well, if you're gonna put a needle in, you might as well mainline it." I was scared to main, but I gave in.

main brace *n.* ¶ In phrase: **splice the main brace** *Naut.* to serve out grog or whiskey, esp. in double rations or for the purpose of celebration; (*hence*) to offer or partake of liquor.

    ***1805** in *OED*: Now splice the main brace. ***1815** in Wetherell *Adventures* 362: I ordered the Steward to Splice the Main brace. ***1833** Marryat *Peter Simple* ch. xv: Mr. Falcon, splice the main-brace, and call the watch. **1835** *Knickerbocker* (Jan.) 23: He ordered the boatswain to call "all hands to splice the main-brace." **1845** in Colton *Deck & Port* 73: Our sailors were allowed to splice the main-brace as a substitute. **1857** in Perkins *Letters of Capt. Perkins* 16: At meridian we fired a salute and *spliced the main braces,* that is, gave the men two drinks of whiskey. **1940** *AS* (Dec.) 451: When a sailor is asked to have a drink with his superior officer, he is invited *to splice the main brace.* **1993** J. Watson & K. Dockery *Point Man* 123: Besides, "splicing the main brace" helps warm you up after a cold swim.

main drag see s.v. DRAG, *n.*, 2.a.

main finger *n.* a man in charge; head man.—constr. with *the.*

    1894 F.P. Dunne, in Schaaf *Dooley* 158: He was th' main finger iv th' team iv Nothre Dame. **1902** in "O. Henry" *Works* 436: You know what I'd do if I was main finger of dis bunch? **1913–15** Van Loan *Taking the Count* 118: Logan's the main finger of the bunch—the boss. The others are cappers and steerers. **1921** A. Jennings *Through Shadows* 116 [ref. to 1899]: There's a new main finger. *Ibid.* 117: The new "main finger" meant a new warden. **1925** (cited in Partridge *Dict. Und.* 428).

main guy *n.* [MAIN + GUY, 2.a.] a man of importance, prominence, or authority; boss.—constr. with *the.*

    1882 (quot. at GUY, *n.*, 2.a.). **1891** De Vere *Tramp Poems* 87: The "main guy" winked and softly said,/"Hey Rube!" **1892** Norr *China Town* 75: Their "holt on the main guy," as they term it. **1902** Townsend *Fadden & Mr. Paul* 38: He is de main guy, and dat's why I'm putting you wise on him. **1903** McClallen *He Demons* 53: I concluded to go to one of the "Main Guys" for this information. **1906** J. London *Moon-Face* 51: The *main guy* is the leader. **1910** Hapgood *City Streets* 311: When a good gang o' hobos is on the road we always know where the main guy's joint is in any town we turn up in. **1925** Robinson *Wagon Show* 62 [ref. to *a*1900]: To a circus man the owner or manager of the enterprise is the "main guy." All others are merely guys. **1926** *AS* I 283: *Main Guy.* The leader or one upon whom many weighty matters are dependent. This is taken from the circus, for on the main guy line holds up the big top. **1929** E. Booth *Stealing* 281: The main guy with the screws to the vault gets there about eight-thirty. **1930** Irwin *Tramp & Und. Sl.* 126: *Main Guy.*—The boss; one with authority; God. **1933** Mizner & Holmes *20,000 Years in Sing Sing* (film): Who's the main guy here?

main hatch *n. Naut.* the mouth; (*also, vulgar*) the vulva or vagina. *Joc.* [The second quot. appears in a sea shanty ("A-Roving") of 19th-C. orig.]

    1846 J.R. Browne *Whaling Crews* [ref. to 1842]: Keep your main hatch closed and hold on! *a*1927 in *Immortalia* 114: Says she, "Young man that's my main hatch."

Mainiac *n.* [pun on *maniac*] a native or resident of Maine. *Joc.*

    1837 in Hawthorne *Amer. Notebooks* 45: The British have lately imprisoned a man who was sent to take the census, and the Maniacs are much excited on the subject. **1852** in *DA:* There is to be a great *Fast* throughout the State of Maine. The Mainiacs are to be *Fastmen.* **1856** in *DARE.* **1942** *ATS* 361: *Mainiac,*…a Mainite. **1974** N.Y.C. man, age 28: A Mainiac is one who hails from Maine. **1989** G. Hall *Air Guard* 114: Three planes from the 101st AREFW, the Bangor Maineiacs [*sic*].

main kazoo *n.* MAIN MAN. Also (*later*) **main kazaam.**

    1903 Ade *Society* 46: Also he had been prominent in the Sunday-Closing Movement and the Main Kazoo in the Citizens' Reform League. **1915** [Swartwood] *Choice Slang* 54: *Main kazoo (the)*—The important personage. **1974** R. Carter *16th Round* viii: To Richard Solomon—my main kazoo. *Ibid.* 221: Cassius Clay…had three days earlier defeated my main kazam [*sic*], Sonny Liston.

main line *n. Narc.* a large vein, usu. the median vein of the arm or thigh; (*hence*) an injection of a narcotic drug into such a vein.

    1931 *AS* (Aug.) 440: *Main line*…A vein in the arm just above the elbow; the median vein. **1933** Ersine *Pris. Slang* 52: Taking a bang in the mainline is very dangerous. **1936** *AS* (Apr.) 123: *Main Line.* The vein, usually in the forearm near the elbow, or in the instep, into which the *gutter* fires the dope. **1936** L. Duncan *Over the Wall* 21 [ref. to 1918]: The more advanced narcotic users…shot unbelievable doses of powerful heroin in the main line—the vein of their arms. **1954** in W.S. Burroughs

Letters 201: When you shoot C in main-line. **1957** Aarons *Stella Marni* 108: I was hooked.…Like a hophead on the main line. **1973** Childress *Hero* 70: I thought it would be a groove to…do my second or third mainline. *a***1979** Pepper & Pepper *Straight Life* 95: The mainline, the vein inside the crook of your arm. **1990** Steward *Bad Boys* 124: He had taken his fixes in the "main line" of the arm at the elbow bend.

¶ In phrase:

¶ **ride the main line** *Narc.* to take drugs intravenously.

1957 H. Simmons *Corner Boy* 10: Dammit, Scar, I told you about riding the mainline.

mainline *adv. Narc.* into a large or median vein.

1952 Mandel *Angry Strangers* 360: I want a blast, I want it quick.…I want it mainline for one blast. **1973** W. Burroughs, Jr. *Ky. Ham* 3: Fire the result mainline.

mainline *v.* **1.** *Narc.* to inject drugs, esp. heroin, into a vein, esp. the median vein of the arm or thigh.—also used trans.—also used fig.

[**1936** (quot. at MAINLINER).] **1938** *AS* XIII: *To main-line.* To inject narcotics into the vein. **1951** *New Yorker* (Nov. 10) 48: They'd been main-lining—you know, injecting the drug directly into a vein. **1953** E. Hunter *Jungle Kids* 26: He'd been main-lining it for a long time now. **1962** *Sat. Eve. Post* (Sept. 8) 68: He finally succumbed to the extent of sniffing a little heroin. Pabon soon taught him how to mainline it. **1963** *Sat. Eve. Post* (June 29) 39: The late-night marijuana set with clean collars, some mainlining musicians—you know. **1970** *Everett (Wash.) Herald* (Feb. 24) 5A: Students and faculty members who rolled up their sleeves to "mainline" for the college blood bank. **1974** Lahr *Hot to Trot* 168: Pregnant women who take LSD or mainline can do permanent brain damage to their child. **1976** Haseltine & Yaw *Woman Doctor* 115: I will not let you mainline here. **1981** *Texas Monthly* (Dec.) 264: He liked to mainline speed. **1982** M. Mann *Elvis* 173: Nor did I ever mainline or anything like that. **1985** B.E. Ellis *Less Than Zero* 156: Ever mainline? *a***1995** *Encyc. of Drugs & Alc.* III 986: *Mainline…v.* to inject morphine, heroin, or cocaine into any vein. **1995** *Newsweek* (Oct. 16) 86: Virtual reality has become a digital drug, mainlined straight to your brain through…a kind of electronic hairnet. **1996** *This Week with D. Brinkley* (ABC-TV) (Mar. 24): Inhaling gets it to your brain faster than mainlining.

2. *Journ.* to use or consume frequently or voraciously, as though addicted.—also used intrans.

1977 *Billings (Mont.) Gazette* (Aug. 9) 9A: You can always tell when a kid is mainlining the machines. Pale, glassy-eyed, calluses on his hands, pawing for a fix in the coin return shot, freaking out when he wins a free game. **1978** *L.A. Times* (Aug. 31) IV 24: The young audiences that mainline on movie houses. **1978** *Rolling Stone* (Sept. 7) 10: A persona not unlike Captain Bligh mainlining pure caffeine. **1995** *N.Y. Times Bk. Rev.* (Mar. 26) 24: Los Angeles and the San Joaquin Valley, a gigantic irrigated desert, mainlined northern California water and couldn't wait for the next fix. **1995** *Newsweek* (Jan. 16) 62: Technoids snarf pizza and mainline Coca-Cola in between customers.

mainliner *n. Narc.* a person, esp. an addict, who mainlines narcotics.

1934 (cited in Partridge *Dict. of Und.*). **1936** Dai *Opium Addiction* 201: *Main-liners.*…Addicts who inject drugs intravenously. Also called *vein-shooters,* and *main-line shooters.* **1936** *AS* (Apr.) 123: *Main-liner.* An addict who shoots narcotics into his veins. **1951** *New Yorker* (Nov. 10) 52: As a main-liner, Charlie used three capsules of heavily cut heroin a day. **1952** "R. Marsten" *So Nude* 97: You're a mainliner, aren't you, junkie? **1953** W. Brown *Monkey on My Back* 82: Mainliners [are] users who take heroin intravenously. **1954** Wertham *Innocent* 25: I am a mainliner. I want to get rid of the habit.…I have been hitting the mainline. **1955** Q. Reynolds *HQ* 221: He's a mainliner.…And this junk in the needle is heroin. **1958** Motley *Epitaph* 158: They are all mainliners except Nellie and Fran. **1964** in A. Chapman *New Black Voices* 72: Y'see?…She's a mainliner. **1965** in H.S. Thompson *Shark Hunt* 466: Jazz musicians, shoplifters, mainliners, screaming poets and sex addicts of every description. **1966–67** P. Thomas *Mean Streets* 195: I…now was a full-grown careless mainliner. **1978** Buchanan *Shining Season* 107: I've got kids in class who are mainliners!

main man *n.* **1.** an eminent or important man; MAIN GUY.—constr. with *the.*

[**1942** *ATS* 617: Circus manager.…*main guy, main-most man.*] **1977** B. Davidson *Collura* 62: Chuck was frequently referred to as the "main

man" on the street who supplied the other [drug] dealers. **1981** in *California* (Jan. 1982) 120: I was the main man in the state, dealing all the way from San Diego to Eureka. **1984** *Miami Vice* (NBC-TV): We haven't even met the main man yet. **1985** Boyne & Thompson *Wild Blue* 458: As the main man say, if you ain't part of the solution, you part of the problem. **1990** *New Republic* (Jan. 8) 13: Sununu…is the conservative movement's main man in the White House. **1996** *Young & Restless* (CBS-TV): Get in back of that desk. You look like the main man.

2. see MAIN, *adj.*

main pin *n. R.R.* a railway official.

1930 *Railroad Man's Mag.* II 471: Main Pin—An official. **1938** Beebe *High Iron* 222: *Main pin*—Executive.

mainsail collar *n.* a man's high wing collar.

1866 *Night Side of N.Y.* 26: A portrait of Sherman, unshaved, eating the corner of a main-sail collar.

mainside *n. Navy & USMC.* the main area of a shore base or the like.

1945 in Rea *Wings of Gold* 271: We…were instructed to proceed to…Mainside—Jax. **1957–62** Higginbotham *Folklore of USMC* 5: *Mainside*—the main section of the base or town or country. **1971** Flanagan *Maggot* 267: A driver from mainside will pick you up after noon chow. **1971** Jeffers & Levitan *See Parris* 2: Platoon 262 fell in for the march back to the barracks for the packing of gear and the return to "main-side" in the morning. **1984** Trotti *Phantom* 121: Ten miles down the road from "Mainside" Pensacola is Saufley Field. **1984** T.K. Mason *Cactus Curtain* 39: "Mainside," as the Windward sector is called on most bases. **1987** da Cruz *Boot* 302: *Mainside* main base. **1988** Hynes *Flights of Passage* 57 [ref. to WWII]: I reported to the old Main Station, "Main Side." **1991** Linnekin *80 Knots* 36 [ref. to WWII]: "Mainside"…was Naval Air Station Corpus Christi.

main squeeze *n.* **1.a.** a person having principal authority or influence; boss.

1896 Ade *Artie* 39: I went in and asked the main squeeze o' the works how much the sacque meant to him. *Ibid.* 60: He's the main squeeze in our ward, or any way he used to be. He's one o' the aldermen. **1897** Siler & Houseman *Fight of the Century* 19: The "main squeeze" of the Sagehen State then and there compounded a moral felony by "setting 'em up" as the price of silence. **1899** A.H. Lewis *Sandburrs* 111: He's d' main squeeze, this p'lice dub dey're waitin' for. **1903** Ade *Society* 31: He was for the Toiler as against the Main Squeeze. **1908** Sullivan *Criminal Slang* 15: Main squeeze—A head fellow. **1915** [Swartwood] *Choice Slang* 54: *Main squeeze (the)*—The important personage. **1927** in Hammett *Big Knockover* 282: Of those who weren't caught, Bluepoint Vance seems to be the main squeeze. He was in the car that directed operations. **1936** Washburn *Parlor* 88: Keeley secretly cherished the idea that some day he would be the "main squeeze." **1938** *AS* (Feb.) 71: *Main Squeeze.* Foreman. **1958** McCulloch *Woods Wds.* 115: *Main squeeze*—The boss. **1976** "N. Ross" *Policeman* 73: Until you find the main squeeze—the big connect with all the cash.

b. a group of such persons.

1903 A.H. Lewis *Boss* 158: I've invited three members of the main squeeze to see me.

2. one's boyfriend, girlfriend, or spouse.

1926 Maines & Grant *Wise-Crack Dict.* 11: *Main squeeze*—Best girl. *ca***1968** (cited in *W10*). **1970** Landy *Underground. Dict.* 125: *Main squeeze*, n. 1. Wife. 2. Girl friend, on a very intimate level. **1970** *Current Slang V* (Fall) 10: *Main squeeze*, n. A boy or girl friend. **1976** *Nat. Lampoon* (July) 59: D.D.'s my main squeeze. **1976** Price *Bloodbrothers* 155: She ain't gonna be my main squeeze, if that's what you mean. **1983** Breathed *Bloom Co.* 121: Be my main squeeze! **1984** Mason & Rheingold *Slanguage*: *Main squeeze*…Number one girlfriend or boyfriend. **1987** *Chicago Tribune* (Sept. 1) I 14: Sylvester Stallone's new main squeeze is Kathy Lynn Davis, a Paris-based American model. **1993** *Mystery Sci. Theater* (Comedy Central TV): He's my main squeeze.

main squirt *n.* a boss.

1910 in Kornbluh *Rebel Voices* 259: The "main squirt," or [lumber] superintendent, occasionally visits the camp and eats with his men.

main stem *n.* **1.a.** a celebrated person; person in charge.

1899 Ade *Fables* 18: I was just Thinking what chance have I got to grow up and be the Main Stem, like Mr. Jeffries. **1904** *Life in Sing Sing* 256: *Main stem.* Head person. **1935** D.W. Maurer, in *AS* (Feb.) 18: *Main stem*…The head of any organization.

b. one's close friend.

  1972 Kemp *Savior* 194: Yaquii Laster, my main stem!

2. see s.v. STEM, *n.*

3.a. the main street of a town; MAIN DRAG.

  1900 in Partridge *Dict. Und.* 429: Investigations that have been begun in "the main stem." **1903 *Independent* (July 23) 1720: The "main stem" of a town is its main street. **1904** *Life in Sing Sing* 256: *Main stem…*principal street. **1907** J. London, in *DAS* [ref. to 1894]: The kids began "battering" the "main stem." **1908** W.G. Davenport *Butte & Montana* 127: I went up de main stem. **1918** in *AS* (Oct. 1933) 29: *Main drag, main stem.* Principal street of town. **1922** Anderson *Hobo* 3: The hobos, themselves, do not think of Madison Street as the Rialto; they call it "The Main Stem," a term borrowed from tramp jargon, and meaning the main street of the town. **1935** Coburn *Law Rides Range* 68: She comes down the main stem on her high heels, in her silk and fur. **1973** in J. Flaherty *Chez Joey* xvii: We had seen every movie playing on the main stem.

b. *Specif.*, (*cap.*) the theater district of Broadway, a principal thoroughfare in New York City.

  1927 W. Winchell, in *Bookman* (Dec.) 378: To the lonely and aspiring hoofer, the fannie-falling comedian, Broadway is the Big Apple, the Main Stem, the goal of all ambition. **1929** *Variety* (Oct. 30) 65: Broadway…the Main Stem begins to take on the appearance of a new Chinatown district.

maintopsail *n.* ¶ In phrase: **back (one's) maintopsail** *Naut.* (of a person) to slow down in walking; come to a halt.

  1856 *Ballou's Dollar Mo. Mag.* (Nov.) 423: So backing my maintopsail at the first public house, I asked for a room. **ca*1925 in Hugill *Shanties from Seven Seas* 203: She backed her maintawps'l an' for me hove to.

main vein see *drain the [main] vein* s.v. DRAIN, *v.*

maje *n. Army.* a major.

  1847 R.L. Wilson *Ravelings* 35: But the "Maje" stopped not. **1862** in C.H. Moulton *Ft. Lyon* 70: He couldn't shake it like Old Maj. *a*1865 in *Confed. War Jour.* (Sept. 1894) 94: Haven't you got a Fed'ral maje/Now resting in some Dixie cage. **1911** A.W. Smith *Army Nurse* 87: I say, Maj., you know me. *a*1910 Veil *Memoirs* 164: "Old Maje," as he called him. **1921** Gillett *6 Yrs.* 122 [ref. to 1870's]: Was always known as "Major" or "Mage" Reynolds. **1984** Trotti *Phantom* 169 [ref. to 1960's]: Up to 25 degrees, Maj. *a*1990 Westcott *Half a Klick* 122: With the maj back, Screamin' Don's gonna have other things ta do.

major *adj.* **1.** absolute; thoroughgoing; utter; conspicuously worthy of the name. [The S.E. uses traditionally imply comparison with similar but lesser referents, "a major motion picture," for example, being supposedly larger in scope, more costly, important, etc., than most others; the slang senses already becoming colloq., ref. to absolute rather than comparative qualities.]

  [**1961** Ageton *Hit Beach* 26: A major miracle.] **1975** W. Allen *Love & Death* (film): You are a major loon! **1982** A. Lane & W. Crawford *Valley Girl* (film): I kissed Tommy off in a major way. **1989** *Dream Street* (NBC-TV): He's a major jerk. **1990** G. Trudeau *Doonesbury* (synd. comic strip) (Sept. 27): But you gotta figure he'll bring along some *major* babes. **1990** P. Munro *Slang U.* 126: My roommate's boyfriend is a major nerd, complete with polyester pants, a plastic pocket protector, and slicked-back hair. **1991** Eble *Campus Sl.* (Spring) 6: She's beautiful—one *major* babe. **1993** *Sally Jessy Raphaël* (synd. TV series): She is a *major* person.

2. highly impressive, as in number, amount, extent, or degree; splendid.

  *a*1972 B. Rodgers *Queens' Vernacular* 47: Wonderful…Syn.: *major* (…S[an] F[rancisco], '70). **1984** N. Bell *Raw Youth* 15: Nada….No major sweat. **1984** J. Hughes *16 Candles* (film): I just thought that turning sixteen would be so major that I'd wake up with an improved mental state that would show on my face. *Ibid.*: Sounds major. **1986** N.Y. State Lottery ad, WINS radio (Mar. 20): I'm talkin' major mazuma! **1988** *Daily News* (N.Y.) (June 18) 29: The place…gives you major gas. **1988** TV ad for Sega video game: This is major fun and games! **1990** *CBS This Morning* (CBS-TV) (Aug. 3): Any problems there? Like major bug bites? **1990** Univ. Tenn. student: Heading back to the crib for some major food. **1990** *Garfield and Friends* (CBS-TV): Jon is paying them major bucks to work as a ranch hand so he can

meet women. **1990** *Wings* (CBS-TV): Whoa! *Major* hooters [breasts]! **1995** *N.Y. Times Mag.* (Apr. 30) 53: Nicole Kidman and Sarah Jessica Parker possess major—and highly emotional—hair.

major *adv.* very; extremely.

  1982 Pond *Valley Girl's Gde.* 59: Major cool is clearly the best. **1985** *Miami Vice* (NBC-TV): That was uncool, lady. That was major uncool. **1990** *Hull High* (NBC-TV): Last time I did that I got busted major. **1990** *Saved by the Bell* (NBC-TV): This guy is *major* weird. **1991** *CBS This Morning* (CBS-TV) (Apr. 13): We are major pumped up for that. *Ibid.* (Apr. 16): Drinking and smoking and taking drugs while you're carrying a baby is known as major stupid. **1992** R. Perot, on paid political broadcast (CBS-TV) (Oct. 6): They have to really assume we are major dumb.

major-league *adj.* impressive; formidable; significant; BIG-LEAGUE; (*hence*) a notable degree or amount of.

  1941 Rose *Ball of Fire* (film): That's a major-league [engagement] ring! **1951** H.W. Wind, in *New Yorker* (Nov. 17) 71: Four pages of orchestration an hour…is considered major-league speed. **1960** *Sat. Eve. Post* (Oct. 15) 91: Edward (Big Jupiter) Fargo, a major-league hoodlum and reigning prince of profitable crime. **1972** Jenkins *Semi-Tough* 216: Joints…won't make you any kind of major league A-dict like the state of Texas says. **1975** *Business Week* (Oct. 13) 73: The highest return on investment of any major-league industrial company. **1984** Hindle *Dragon Fall* 86: There's gonna be some major-league trouble comin' your way. **1986** *CBS Evening News* (CBS-TV) (Aug. 10): We're gonna have some major-league fun right now. **1989** P. Munro *U.C.L.A. Slang* 57: There's major-league potato chips here. **1993** G. Lee *Honor & Duty* 11: You *are* in major-league, *very big* trouble. **1996** *New Yorker* (Feb. 26) 184: She was a major-league worrier—and for an editor to be a major-league worrier is a wonderful thing.

major-league *adv.* very; extremely; to a great extent.

  1990 *TV Guide* (Mar. 31) 32: A woman friend informed me that Cole is major-league attractive. **1991** *New Yorker* (Aug. 19) 23: We've been major-league screwed.…I just found out the trains are stopped.

majorly *adv. Stu.* **1.** extremely; thoroughly; to a great extent.

  1983 *Wash. Post* (June 27) (Nexis): "I'm never like that," she [Canadian teenage tennis player Carling Bassett] said. "I never feel like crying. It's never anything majorly serious." **1989** P. Munro *U.C.L.A. Slang* 57: My mechanical engineering class is majorly hard. *a*1990 E. Currie *Dope & Trouble* 111: I used to be like *majorly* skinny. **1990** Eble *Campus Sl.* (Fall) 3: I am majorly in the weeds. **1994** *Newsweek* (Jan. 10) 49: Their grades have suffered, though Shawn admits he also "slacked off majorly this quarter."

2. mostly; primarily. [The sense defined as "primarily" and dated to 1956 in *W10* does not represent slang usage.]

  1995 *Real World* (MTV): I've majorly been hanging out with Mike. **1996** *New Yorker* (Jan. 15) 27: Majorly, why I got it [*sc.*, a cellular telephone] is if a party gets busted,…you gotta get outta there.

major malfunction *n. Mil.* a ludicrous or irritating source of difficulty, esp. a problem attributable to stupidity or incompetence.

  1987 "J. Hawkins" *Tunnel Warriors* 118 [ref. to Vietnam War]: Well then just what the hell *is* your major malfunction, *pal?* **1987** Estes *Field of Innocence* 26 [ref. to 1968]: Today was a major malfunction. **1989** *Roseanne* (ABC-TV): What is your major malfunction…Private Conner? **1994** Knoxville, Tenn., graphic artist, age 40: My father used to talk about people's "major malfunctions" at Fort Campbell, Kentucky, about 1961–62. He also referred to his commanding officer as "Major Malfunction." **1994** Knoxville, Tenn., teenager: He said, "What's your major malfunction?" I said, "I don't see no stripes on you, dickhead." **1995** *Simpsons* (Fox-TV): What is your major malfunction, Sideshow Bob?

make *n.* **1.** *Und.* the proceeds of theft; loot.

  1918 Stringer *House of Intrigue* 27: I got so I could face a tight fade without a quaver, and do my gay-cat part in sloughing our make as easy as rolling off a log. **1914** Jackson & Hellyer *Crim. Slang* 78: The make was split three ways. **1911** Bronson-Howard *Enemy to Society* 331: If we're going to "slough" our "make," we've gotta keep our eyes open. **1942–49** in Goldin et al. *DAUL* 133: That was a nice make, eight bills…for my end. **1954–60** *DAS: Make*…The loot taken in a robbery.

2. *Esp. Police.* a description or identification, as of a suspect; in phr. **run a make** to seek an identification through the use of police records.

  1950 in *DAS*: We got a make on his prints. **1951** Haines & Burnett

Racket (film): That was a nice make, Johnson. Good work. **1955** Essex & Buffum *Teenage Crime Wave* (film): Call it in. Get a make on it. **1959** *Sat. Eve. Post* (Apr. 4) 125: "I'm trying for a make on this," said Matt, placing the snapshot…on the table. **1960** Stadley *Barbarians* 69: "Any make on him?" "Mac is running an R and I, but I don't think he'll find anything." **1961** *Bullwinkle* (NBC-TV): You got a make on a guy named Winkle? **1966** Cassiday *Angels Ten* 22 [ref. to WWII]: When you get a make on that village, let me know in the proper manner. **1967** Hamma *Motorcycle Mommas* 22: We were really highballing it along 99…when the fuzz put the make on us. **1968** Gover *JC* 94: Put through a call on his radio-phone for them to run a make on me. **1970** Dugan *Adam-12* (NBC-TV): We have a positive make on a possible kidnap-rape victim. **1974** R. Novak *Concrete Cage* 35: We got makes on seven of the…[victims] already. **1974** V. Smith *Jones Men* 60: We might get lucky with a make like that. **1977** *L.A. Times* (July 2) II 1: He radioed to headquarters for a make on the license. **1980** *Pearl Pop. Slang* 96: *Make n.* (police) a description. **1986** *Stingray* (NBC-TV): She's seen us. She can put a make on us! **1988** Cogan & Ferguson *Presidio* 94: I ran a make on Peale. **1988** T. Logan *Harder They Fall* 25: We got a make on the [license] plate.

3. a session of romantic kissing or petting; (*hence*) an attempted seduction; sexual aggression. Cf. *easy make*, *on the make*, 2, and *put the make on*, below.

1968 Baker et al. *CUSS* 155: *Make, Have a* To neck. **1968–70** *Current Slang III & IV* 78: *Lay the make*, to become sexually aggressive.—College students, both sexes, New Hampshire. **1971** *Dear Abby* (synd. column), in *Everett* (Wash.) *Herald* (June 12) 2C: With some guys, sweet lies bubble to their lips faster than a girl can hear them. Why? Because they are out for a make. **1974** M.J. Smith *When I Say No* 262: Dana was able to cope with John's "make" without telling him to go to hell.

4. *Narc.* a dose of a drug. Cf. MAKE, *v.*, 8.

1970 Landy *Underground Dict.*: *Make*…An injection of a narcotic. **1979** Homer *Jargon.*

¶ In phrases:

¶ **easy make** a woman who can be easily seduced.

1942 *ATS* 395: Woman of easy morals…*easy make*…*loose woman* [etc.]. **1952** Brossard *Darkness* 95: A girl who was a notoriously easy make. **1967** *DAS* (Supp.): *Make*…A woman considered only as a sexual object.…*Generally in the phrase "an easy make."* **1983** WINS radio news (Dec. 12): Set aside the argument that the myth of the liberated woman has merely reinforced the myth of the easy make. [***1990** T. Thorne *Dict. Contemp. Slang*: *Make*…a sex partner.]

¶ **on the make, 1.a.** strongly intent upon profit or advancement, often in a ruthless or unscrupulous manner. Also (*obs.*) **on (one's) make.**

1863 in Boyer *Naval Surgeon* I 158: The man who took Mr. Childs to Wood's Hole in his small boat had the audacity to charge him $5. It only being about 3 miles, I don't think he acted very friendly but have an idea that he is on the "make." Hope he won't have many more such chances to take in men. **1868** J.R. Browne *Apache Country* 507 [ref. to Nevada, 1865]: "Oh you're on the make, are you?" suggested my shrewd friend rather indignantly—as if he thought there was a large amount of moral turpitude in my being "on the make" while he, an honest miner, had no predelection at all in that way. "Why, yes, to be candid, I'd like to make fifty thousand or so." **1872** Burnham *Secret Service* vii: On the make, anxious, or intent on gain, no matter *how*. *Ibid.* 54: *They* were on their make, continually. They put up jobs on me, and cheated me with promises. *Ibid.* 129: A "smart old cuss," some of the knowing ones called him. And he was continually "on his make." **1873** Sutton *N.Y. Tombs* 213: Mr. P.T. Barnum…asked for a private interview with the prisoner.…"Oh," said Hicks, "Barnum's on the make; but if he can pay for it he can have it." **1877** W. Hoffman *Camp Court & Siege* 113: The character of these men "left much to be desired," as the Frenchman politely puts it. They were "on the make." **1884** in Lummis *Letters* 112: They rather discount the whites, who are all on the make. **1891** Maitland *Slang Dict.* 173: *Make, "on the"* (Am.), looking out for what one can get. **1891** Bourke *Border* 226: When he meets an agent who is "on the make," that agent's influence goes below zero at once. **1901** Oliver *Roughing It* 80: Now see here pal, you're on the make, aren't you? ***1917** C. Sharp *Folk Songs* xxiv: Here no one is "on the make"; commercial competition and social rivalries are unknown. **1918** Dodge *Yellow Dog* 60: It's those dollar-a-year boys down in Washington. They're mixed up with McAdoo. They're all on the make.

1928 in J. O'Hara *Sel. Letters* 36: I am on the make for a newspaper job and expect to have one between now and the first of the year. **1931** Wilstach *Under Cover Man* 45: Broads.…They're bad business for guys on the make. **1932** in *AS* (Feb. 1934) 27: *On the Make.* Open to any proposition. **1944** (quot. at KNOCKOUT). **1946** Gresham *Nightmare Alley* 168: I'm on the make. Nothing matters in this goddamned lunatic asylum of a world but dough. **1947** Boyer *Dark Ship* 241: I was strictly on the make. I was out for number one. Let number two stay number two. **1973** *Ms.* (Spring): Everybody was on the make for recognition.

b. improving one's status or situation; rising in position or influence; succeeding in one's business or vocation. Now *colloq.* or *S.E.* [The 1864 quot. puns an implied nonce sense, 'making (something)'.]

1864 in *Mil. Essays & Recoll.* I 201: And the guns he makes are striking./Keep him always "on the make." **1898** Bellamy *Blindman's World* 265: I tell you he's on the make, and don't you forget it. Some fellers allers has luck. ***1955** in *OED2*: I think we are on the make and that, on balance, the tide is running in our favour. **1961** *New Yorker* (Apr. 1) 80: Dallas—"a place that's on the make." **1935–62** Ragen & Finston *Toughest Pris.* 810: *On the make*—Doing well; making money; successful. **1968** *William & Mary Qly.* XXV 374: If the [typical colonial] seaman was a clean young farm-boy on the make—and likely to succeed—why was Josiah Franklin so apprehensive lest young Benjamin "break loose and go to sea"? **1969** in Dundes *Interp. Folklore* 81: Up to thirty, one is a comer, a good prospect, someone on the make. **1980** Birnbach et al. *Preppy Hbk.* 162 (caption): Investment banker.…Babson grad. On the make.

c. *Und.* engaged in theft or swindling.

1868 Williams *Black-Eyed Beauty* 9: Miss Howard?…Why, the worst bit of calico that ever an engine runner knew would be an angel to that woman! Bless your green spectacles, she's been on the make ever since there was a Spring street, and I don't remember them times! **1873** Beadle *Undeveloped West* 402: There won't anybody but a scamp or a rough take such an office as Deputy Marshal in this country. They're all on the make, and in with these roughs. **1921** (quot. at PINCHER). **1922** *Variety* (June 30) 6: I met a couple of the old mob up here travellin' aroun' on the make. **1928** O'Connor *B'way Racketeers* 253: On the Make—Working at a racket. **1934** L. Berg *Prison Nurse* 49: You don't look like you was ever "on the make." **1960** L. Jones, in *Blues People*: So of course with these cloak-and-dagger ideas and amidst all the backslapping, happy crowds…I got extremely paranoid. I felt immediately sure that the make was on. **1980** *Maclean's* (Sept. 29) 34: Weinberg has spent the better part of 55 years on the make. As a kid he used to throw stones through neighborhood windows so his father—a glazier—would get new business.…A few years ago he set up a dummy firm.

2. seeking amorous or sexual activity.

1929 McEvoy *Hollywood Girl* 16: He's one of those guys who's on the make for every dame on the lot. *Ibid.* 42: Of course he's on the make, all men are. **1930** Lait *On Spot* 75: He was on the make though he didn' have to be—every broad what ever saw him did a flop for him. But he didn' play the field. He was throwin' 'em over his shoulder. **1932** *AS* VII (June) 334: *To be on the make*—to be open to advances from one of the opposite sex. **1933** Hammett *Thin Man* 267: Nunheim…was on the make for her, but he didn't get nowhere that I could see. **1934** Appel *Brain Guy* 131: Women in their thirties on the make for young actors. **1937** Reitman *Box-Car Bertha* 174: Bad eye was the only man working there who did not have a girl of his own, but was constantly, "on the make." **1941** Halliday *Tickets* 10: There's younger and prettier girls than me on the make. **1942** Wylie *Vipers* 62: We are a sexy folk…frequently on the make in bush and juke joint. **1945** Himes *If He Hollers* 79: We must look like dames on the make. **1945** Hartman & Shavelson *Princess & Pirate* (film): Most of them go right on the make with a girl. **1946** G.W. Henderson *Jule* 110: Jake figures I'm on the make. He figures I'm looking for pig meat. **1948** Lait & Mortimer *New York* 65: Homosexuals…all on the make for strangers. **1950** Gordon & Gordon *FBI Story* 33: "Did she ever complain about any guy on the make?"…"They were all on the make—and she liked it." **1952** "R. Marsten" *So Nude* 70: I led them on, made them think I was on the make. **1953** W. Fisher *Waiters* 26: Jesus! He's really on the make. **1953** Wicker *Kingpin* 110: If Katherine had been just a pair of hot pants on the make. **1958** J.B. West *Eye* 9: Under most conditions a guy like me would have figured this dame was on the make.

¶ **put the make on** to attempt to seduce; make sexual advances toward.

1956 P. Moore *Chocolates* 130: Here was this practically a *seduction*, she was really throwing the make on him. **1962** Mandel *Mainside* 124: Well, one thing my years in the North had taught me was that if you want to put the make on a man, get him drunk. **1974** C.W. Smith *Country Music* 258: Then I put the make on this girl. **1974** M.J. Smith *When I Say No* 227: Just suppose that your roommate is gay and you only learn of it after he (or she) puts the make on you. **1976** *L.A. Times* (Dec. 1) I 2: I thought he was just another cop trying to put the make on me. **1980** J. Carroll *Land of Laughs* 57: He spent the whole time...trying to put the make on this girl. **1989** "Capt. X" & Dodson *Unfriendly Skies* 130: He has a lascivious leer spread all over his kisser, and he's trying to put the make on one of the sixteen-year-old tuba players! **1991** Nelson & Gonzales *Bring Noise* 242: Ed is putting the make on a cutie. **1995** J. Updike, in *New Yorker* (Oct. 9) 78: Or else it was his way of putting the make on her.

make *v.* **1.** *Und.* **a.** to steal.

*1698–99 "B.E." *Dict. Canting Crew: Made...Stolen. I Made this Knife at a heat...I Stole it cleverly.* **1859** Matsell *Vocab.* 53: *Made.* Stolen. "The copper asked me where I made the benjamin. I told him I didn't make it, but got it on the square," the officer asked me where I stole the coat, and I told him that I did not steal it, but got it honestly. **1866** *Nat. Police Gaz.* (Nov. 3) 3: Why, there's a "moll" across the street who has "made" a century. **1889–90* Barrère & Leland *Dict. Slang* II 40: To *make* clocks, to steal watches.

b. to rob; swindle.—often constr. with *for.*—occ. used intrans.

[**1889–90* Barrère & Leland *Dict. Slang* II 40: A *make* is a successful swindle.] **1926** in Partridge *Dict. Und.* 429: At twenty-five I was an expert house burglar...carefully choosing only the best homes...I "made" them in the small hours..., always under arms. **1927** Thrasher *Gang* 268: To make stores or "drunks"—to rob them. **1929** Booth *Stealing* 81 [ref. to *ca*1916]: The best way...is to make those places in the daytime. **1931** D.W. Maurer, in *AS* (June) 333: *Make...To rob.* "We just made that dude for his roll." **1939** *AS* (Oct.) 240: *To make the joint.* To defraud a hotel. **1946** Mezzrow & Wolfe *Really Blues* 119: Outlaws...fixing to make the local bank. **1953** W. Brown *Monkey on My Back* 39: They had done some making (stealing from parked cars). **1966** Brunner *Face of Night* 201: I don't know why I tried to make that doctor's office, Mr. Ramsey. I'm the worst burglar in the world. **1962–68** B. Jackson *In the Life* 113: I might make the safe and there wouldn't be anything in it. *Ibid.* 114: I quit making drugstores because they kept drugstores staked out for me. **1976** "N. Ross" *Policeman* 23: I once had a guy crumple up two single dollars. I thought it was two tens. He made me for eighteen, but it never happened again.

c. to succeed in obtaining (something) from.—constr. with *for.*

1936 D.W. Maurer, in *AS* (Apr.) 123: *Make...always transitive....For an addict to purchase dope from a peddler....To obtain drugs from a physician. To make a croaker for a reader.* To persuade a physician...to write a prescription for narcotics. **1970** S. Ross *Fortune Machine* 163: You make us for twenty-four grand [in gambling], then you want protection? **1978** Selby *Requiem* 139: Youre makin a croaker for speed, aint ya?

2. to promote; make successful; (*also*) to initiate, as into a secret society.

*1833 Marryat *Peter Simple* 337: Well, then, I expect that I'm right, and that Mr. O'Brien is made, and commands this craft. **1878** Flipper *Colored Cadet* 53: "Made."—Given an appointment, given chevrons as an officer in the battalion organization. **1889–90** Barrère & Leland *Dict. Slang* II 40: *Make...*(Freemasons), to initiate. **1928** in F.S. Fitzgerald *Stories* I 401: It had given him a tremendous pleasure, like the things that had happened to him during his first big success, before he was so "made" that there was scarcely anything better ahead. **1958** *N.Y. Times Mag.* (Mar. 16) 88: *Made—*To get a promotion. **1954–60** *DAS: Make...*To appoint a person to a job; to increase his rank or status; to attain success.

3.a. *Police & Und.* to recognize on sight; (*hence*) to identify.—often constr. with *for.* [Bracketed quots. illustrate S.E. sense 'to descry or discern (usu. land or a sailing vessel) from a distance' (*ca*1565–1890 in *OED*).]

[**ca*1565 in *OED:* Wee had sight of an Island, which we made to be Jamaica.] [**1726* G. Roberts *4 Yrs. Voyage* 36: They made me [and] the middlemost of the three [ships] stood right in for me....I made her

with my glass to be a scooner.] **1906** in *OEDS:* You wouldn't have come within a block of him. In the language of the guild, Sorg, he would have "made you" and got away. **1908** Sullivan *Criminal Slang* 16: *Make one—*Identify a person. **1912** Beach *Net* 117: "Have you 'made' him?" Donnelly inquired under his breath. **1914** Jackson & Hellyer *Vocab.* 57: *Make*, Verb General Currency. To recognize; to discern; to solve...."You had better ring up (disguise) so he won't make you." **1916** *Milwaukee Jour.* (Nov. 3) 18: I'll lay you a cuter to a meg he made you. **1918** *Stars & Stripes* (May 10) 4: I'm jerry to the fashions, bo,/I make the clerics by their ties. **1917–19** J. Boyle *Boston Blackie* 39: He called himself Jimmy Grimes, and the coppers never made him. They don't know who he is yet. **1920** Murphy *Gray Walls* 25: They made me (learned of his past record) at this prison through the finger print system before I was here three months. *Ibid.:* Every town I would light in some fly cop (detective) would make me (identify) before I was there an hour. **1927** Coe *Me—Gangster* 51: "Did somebody make us?" Gat asks, meaning did somebody know who we were. **1927–28** in R. Nelson *Dishonorable* 147: Say, I made that "Camino" for Nick's brother the minute I came in. **1939** in J. O'Hara *Sel. Letters* 145: Detectives are always saying "I made him the minute I sore him," meaning "I recognized him...". **1942** Liebling *Telephone* 258: During the Fiopian War I made him for a Fiopian. **1955** Q. Reynolds *HQ* 73: I needed someone the mob didn't know to do some tailing for me....someone that every hood in the city wouldn't make as soon as he saw him. **1958** Gilbert *Vice Trap* 7: Then I made the heavyset guy waiting behind the wheel. **1959** O'Connor *Talked to a Stranger* 59: Somebody "made me"...you know, spotted me, and gave my identification to the police. **1962** Dougherty *Commissioner* 178: The bartender, having "made" them as cops, began to walk toward the front with an uncertain smile on his face. **1966** J. Mills *Needle Park* 154: Department cars are too easy to make—to spot—and sometimes it's more convenient to use your own anyway. **1966–67** W. Stevens *Gunner* 32: I didn't make Klagenfurt yet. Are we [*sc.*, a WWII bomber crew] by it? **1969** in Hirsch *Treasury* 70: They can "make" a horse just as easily as the average person recognizes his friends. **1974** G.V. Higgins, in *Atlantic* (Apr.) 91: The rest...get no consideration for their tractability unless they can make somebody new—that is, turn a suspect into a defendant. **1979** *L.A. Times* (Nov. 18) II 5: Several street people "make" Bentley and his colleagues as cops almost immediately. **1994** *New York* (Dec. 12) 55: He thought their undercover patrol car...had been "made." **1996** McCumber *Playing off Rail* 185: "He made you." "Fuck, we're done, we may not get out of here."

b. *Police & Und.* to see or get a good look at, usu. in an act of wrongdoing; observe.

1906 A.H. Lewis *Confessions* 206: When I hears these sneaks scrambling at the fence to get away, I thought some bull had made us. **1910** *Variety* (Aug. 20) 13: Every time I'd make his map, I thought he was bleeding. **1915–17** Lait *Gus* 65: I'd like to make you, all harnessed up like a plush horse....I bet you'd be nifty. **1927** in Hammett *Knockover* 336: Made him....Thirty or thirty-two. Five, six. Hundred, thirty. Sandy hair, complexion. Blue eyes. **1929** Barr *Let Tomorrow Come* 40: I try to glom a brace o' spuds. He makes me doin' it an' I...duck. **1932** L. Berg *Pris. Doctor* 80: One or two "cons" were "made" hanging around the place all the time. **1975** Sepe & Telano *Cop Team* 63: Did you make his wrists, John?

c. to regard or estimate as.

1844 Ingraham *Midshipman* 62: "Sail ho!"..."What do you make her?" "A brig." **1931–35** Runyon *Money* 236: I make Your John a stand-out in the first. **1940** Chandler *Farewell, My Lovely* 214: I make the joint clean. I don't make no cops outside. **1961** Ellison *Purgatory* 33: He stared at me, sizing me, the way they say it "making me," as I advanced steadily on him. **1976** Whelton *CB Baby* 24: I make you to be twenty-four. Maybe twenty-five. **1981** Sann *Trial* 17: Golf....I always made that a sissy's game. **1983** A. Alvarez *Biggest Game* 122: I made you about eight-to-five dog [*i.e.*, an 8 to 5 underdog in a bet]. **1986** R. Campbell *In La-La Land* 96: I make that a question. So you owe me twenty-five bucks.

4.a. to strike up an acquaintance with (a person of the opposite sex) for the purpose of romantic or sexual involvement; (*also*) to make a date with (a person of the opposite sex).

1910 T.A. Dorgan, in *N.Y. Eve. Jour.* (Aug. 12) 8: Say the swellest broiler just passed here. Let's go over...and make her. **1918** in *OEDS:* Look at that big stiff tryin' to make the dame! **1924** in Hammett *Con-*

tinental Op 107: Elvira would then *make* this lad, get him all fussed up over her,…and then lead him…around to running away with her. **1924** in Lardner *Haircut* 176: N.Y. has got some mighty pretty girlies and I guess it would not be hard to get acquainted with them and I been here but I always figure that a girl must be something wrong with her if she tries to make a man that she don't know nothing about. **1927** in Perelman *Old Gang* 25: The best place to start making a sugar papa is at ringside at any good night-club about twelve-thirty. **1931** Cressey *Taxi-Dance Hall* 25: *Make*, "*to make*."—To secure a date with. **1932** *AS* VII (June) 334: *To make a person*—to have one's attentions accepted by a person of the opposite sex. **1948** Vidal *City & Pillar* 280: He watched an old man try to make a sailor who in turn was trying to make a soldier. **1956–60** J.A. Williams *Angry Ones* ch. III: Obie made the girls all right, and managed to avoid the politics.

b. to seduce; (*also*) to copulate with.
1923 (quot. at FLAT HAT, 2). **1924** Anderson & Stallings *What Price Glory?* 57 [ref. to 1918]: I guess even Lippy could make a kid if she slept on the other side of a paper wall. **1925** in W. Faulkner *N.O. Sketches* 95: I ain't one of them birds goes around trying to make janes all the time. **1926** Wood & Goddard *Amer. Slang* 32: *Make*. To seduce; as, a woman says, "He tried to make me." **1928** C. McKay *Banjo* 10: "And none a you fellahs can't make her?" cried Banjo. **1929–30** Dos Passos *42d Parallel* 347: Well, did you make her, kid? **1930** Mae West *Babe Gordon* 26: Joe Malone…had once made Babe and…occasionally smoked hop with Jenny. **1930** J.T. Farrell *Calico Shoes* 32: Hey, Caroline!…Didn't you make Wayne yet? **1932** L. Berg *Prison Doctor* 102: They hate us and call us "queer." But they all try to "make" us. **1932–34** Minehan *Boy & Girl Tramps* 195: I goes in [the shack], and four guys try to make me. **1940** R. Chandler *Farewell, My Lovely* 197: Them rich dames are easier to make than paper dolls. **1942** P. Wylie *Vipers* 46: Better, says our society, go out and make the guy. **1945** Lindner *Stone Walls & Men* 171: Half the football team were *making* her. **1951** Elgart *Over Sixteen* 168: "Okay, Baby, are you going to give me a kiss?" "Make me!" "All I want is a kiss!" **1960** Wohl *Cold Wind* 10: He thought she was going to let him make her. **1961** J.A. Williams *Night Song* 98: But them broads is hard to make, man. **1966–67** P. Thomas *Mean Streets* 185: The broad was still on the bed, wondering if I was going to make her again. *a***1972** B. Rodgers *Queens' Vernacular* 88: Fuck…lay…make…screw. **1978** Sopher & McGregor *Up from Walking Dead* 22: By the time we got [there], six Buccaneers had already made the chick. **1992** "The Odds" *Heterosexual Man* (rock song): I wanna make every woman I see.

5.a. to comprehend; understand.
1911 T.A. Dorgan, in Zwilling *TAD Lexicon* 55: Come again I don't make you. **1912–14** E. O'Neill *Lost Plays* 176: She doesn't make me at all—oh hell! **1920** Witwer *Kid Scanlan* 37: I didn't quite make that stuff, but I felt that somethin' was wrong somewheres. **1922** *Sat. Eve. Post* (June 3) 137: "That clear?" "I make you." **1928** Coe *Swag* 235: I don't make your end of this. **1957** MacDonald *Death Trap* 86: He says she's a sex pot. That I can't make. To me all she needs is a broom and a pumpkin.

b. to empathize with; DIG, 5.e.
1959 Sabre & Eiden *Glory Jumpers* 18: It's just the blood and glory bit I don't make. Not my scene, man. **1959** A. Anderson *Lover Man* 157: I dig [West Indian music]…but I can't make that time.

6. to meet; pay a visit to.
1913 Light *Hobo* 43: We'll divide up and "make" the surrounding farmers, then meet here for a mulligan pot. **1920** *Variety* (Dec. 31) 8: The three make Callahan's next, just a few steps around the corner. **1953–58** J.C. Holmes *Horn* 56: But I want to cut out, and make KayCee for a while. **1964** *Sat. Eve. Post* (Sept. 26) 48: "I'll make you later," he told me. **1965** Carmichael & Longstreet *Sometimes I Wonder* 304: Hoagy, there's a beat place you ought to make. **1968** Simoun *Madigan* (film): You just be sure you get me a nice funeral in case he makes me before you make him. **1979** *Texas Monthly* (Nov.) 185: He made a few bars before setting out and at two o'clock in the morning his car flipped over in the desert. **1980** in Courtwright et al. *Addicts Who Survived* 108: I got the Dilaudid by making doctors.

7. *Sports.* to match (a boxer or other athlete against another).
1951 A.J. Liebling, in *New Yorker* (Nov. 17) 102: Louis, who was thirty-seven, had been "made" with a new heavyweight, Rocky Marciano. **1981** Brenner & Nagler *Only the Ring* 117: We made Ellis with shavers, and it turned out to be a one-round fight.

8. *Narc.* **a.** to use (a drug).

*ca***1953** Hughes *Fantastic Lodge* 67: After you first make pot, there's this sort of…Cheshire-cat feeling. *Ibid.* 86: A cat who's making heroin.

b. to purchase drugs from.
1970 Landy *Underground Dict.*: Make…Buy drugs—eg. *I made him for some pot.*

9. to endure.
1959 in Cox *Delinquent, Hipster, Square* (Jan. 18) 35: I made those want ads for a week, man, lookin' for the most useless occupation in this whole gone world. **1961** Russell *Sound* 8: I can't make lush at all, baby. **1970** Whitmore *Memphis-Nam-Sweden* 15: Sunday school by itself was hard enough to make.

¶ In phrases:

¶ **have it made [in the shade]** to be in circumstances of assured ease or success.
[**1896** in Botkin *Treas. Amer. Folk.* 789: At picnics you will sometimes hear the children say:—Lemonade,/Made in the shade,/Stirred with a spade,/By an old maid.] [**1921** Conklin & Root *Circus* 229 [ref. to late 19th C.]: Here's your ice cold lemonade/Made in the shade.] [**1942** *AS* (Dec.) 221: *Got Her Made.* Expression used when quitting the job. The *boomer* has made *stake* enough to move on.] **1944** Boatright & Day *Hell to Breakfast* 139: The reply may be, "I was looking for a job when I got this one," or "I've got my sack full anyhow," or "I've got it made." The last two expressions mean he is independent, doesn't need a job. **1944** Inks *Eight Bailed Out* 46: For a couple of days we had it made. **1944–48** Lyon *Unknown Station* 27: You got it made, brother, you got it made! **1954** J.W. Ellison *Owen Harding* 179: We've got it made in the shade with this one. **1957** McGivern *Against Tomorrow* 5: How do you figure you're doing? Got it made yet? **1957** Kohner *Gidget* 119: He's got it made in the shade with *her*. **1960** Bluestone *Cully* 153: "You have it made." "Yeah, made in the shade." **1960** in Oster *Country Blues* 93: Boy, they walk like this all day, I got it made, ain't I? **1966** Guerin et al. *Hndbk. Crit. Appr. to Lit.* 39: In Calvinism, nobody "had it made." Introspection was mandatory. **1973** Haring *Stranger* 7: A happy life.…She's got it made. **1974** *Happy Days* (ABC-TV): Babysitting with Mary Lou Milligan! Man, you got it made in the shade! **1993** *Donahue* (NBC-TV): Oh, man! You've got it made in the shade! **1995** Maybelline TV ad: You've got it made in the shade!

¶ **make ass** to get going; *make it*, 2. below.—usu. considered vulgar.
1987–89 M.H. Kingston *Tripmaster Monkey* 51: Get your ass in gear.…Make ass.

¶ **make babies** to engage in copulation. [The literal sense, 'to produce children', has become conspicuous in adult speech only since the 1960's.]
*a***1972** B. Rodgers *Queens' Vernacular* 88: Fuck…*make babies*…(early 60s). **1983** N.Y. high school student (coll. J. Sheidlower): Wanna make babies? ****1990** T. Thorne *Dict. Contemp. Slang*: Make babies…to have sex, make love. A coy or jocular euphemism used by adults.

¶ **make book [on]** see s.v. BOOK, *n.*

¶ **make it, 1.a.** to get along; do.—used esp. in greetings.
*****1861** in *OEDS*: They were artisans and farm-labourers who couldn't make it out in the old country. **1863** [Fitch] *Annals of Army* 630: Confederate.—"Halloo, boys! how do you make it?" *Federal.*—"Oh, bully! bully!" **1887** M. Roberts *W. Avernus* 290: He asked me how I was "making it," or getting along, and I told him just how it was with me. **1899** Cullen *Tales* 58: "Hello there, pal!"…"How're you making it this morning, chum?" **1913** Light *Hobo* 73: "How are you, pal?" "How are you making it?" **1935** E. Anderson *Hungry Men* 203: Well, how are you making it? **1952** Mandel *Angry Strangers* 422: How're you makin it, boy? **1956–60** J.A. Williams *Angry Ones* ch. vi: How are you making it? **1961** Terry *Old Liberty* 123: How you making it, Red Hog? **1966** H.S. Thompson *Hell's Angels* 242: How you makin it? **1994** "G. Indiana" *Rent Boy* 10: I slouched against the wall, waiting for an invitation. He says: "How you makin' it?"

b. to succeed. Now *colloq.*
1872 Burnham *Secret Service* vi: *Make it*, to appropriate; to gain a desired point. **1906** (quot. at HAM). **1928** McKay *Banjo* 148: But how they make it [as panhandlers], all dressed up fine and dandy like that? **1958** Ferlinghetti *Coney Island* 11: As if he is the king cat/who's got to blow/or they can't quite make it. **1959–60** R. Reisner *Jazz Titans* 160: *Make It, To:* success in any venture, big or small. **1964** Harris *Junkie Priest* 25: I just never been able to make it any other way. **1965** Spillane *Killer Mine* 30: René making it big here? **1970** *Business Week*

(Apr. 4) 8: To most Americans,…"making it" means simply getting a decent job, a clean place to live, [etc.].

c. to be satisfying or acceptable.

1955 O'Connor *Last Hurrah* 58: Reet!…Mister Mayor-man, you are but definitely with it! I mean, you make it! **1958–59** Lipton *Barbarians* 317: To "make it" may be said of anything that succeeds, whether a dental appointment or a crazy chick. **1960** *Mad* (Sept.): Like finish the beer yourself, Man! It just don't make it when it's warm! **1965** B. Dylan interview, in *DAS* (Supp.): "I had to quit [playing rock] when I was 16 or 17 because I just couldn't make it that way."…"By 'making it,' do you mean making commercial success?"…"No.…It's being able to be nice and not hurt anybody." **1969** Mitchell *Tripping* 15: Oldtimer beakniks…and hippies…making it with the straights, showing them how to groove. **1994** Knoxville, Tenn., attorney, age 41: This just isn't makin' it.

2. Esp. *Black E.* **to go away; travel.**

[**1913** Light *Hobo* 42: While mounting the train at Spokane, I noticed four other young fellows "making it."] **ca1953** Hughes *Fantastic Lodge* 71: Go, make it. **1958–59** Lipton *Barbarians* 110: He used to make it up to Hoffman's at the Red Barn, and sleep on the stairs. **1956–60** J.A. Williams *Angry Ones* 16: Where you making it to? **1961** J.A. Williams *Night Song* 14: I got to make it. **1965** Yurick *Warriors* 69: It is always cooler up in the North, so we made it north. **1967** Salas *Tattoo* 116: "Let's make it," Dominic said, and Aaron hesitated. **1968** I. Reed *Yellow Back Radio* 85: What you say we pick up our gear and make it? **1972** Wambaugh *Blue Knight* 40: Okay, Wimpy, you can make it now. **1974** Gober *Black Cop* 142: Say what you got to say and then make it. **1975** J. Jones *Dolemite* (film): Come on, girls, let's make it.

3.a. to copulate; (*also*) **to accomplish a seduction.** [Infl. by recent S.E. euphem. *make love*.]

1952 "R. Marsten" *So Nude* 128: Her husband seems to think you were making it together. **1952** Mandel *Angry Strangers* 53: Pictures of fun—smoking jive, choosing men to make it with. *Ibid.* 266: Make it wit me, Diane, make it. **1954** Ellison *Owen Harding* 184: Did you really make it with her or didn't you? **1956** P. Moore *Chocolates* 89: Then I met this guy…and I figured what the hell, and we made it. **1958** Ginsberg *Kaddish* 53: He really understood me when we made it in Ignaz/Wisdom's bathroom. **1958** Kerouac *Subterraneans* 14: Man you gonna make it with her tonight? **1962** Algren *Sea Diary* 120: We were in the sack, making it. **1962** Wright *Messenger* 121: I can't make it with Laura, I can't make it with anyone, because I think it's dirty! **1965** *Time* (July 9) 98: Mysteriously endowed with the knack of "making it" with the opposite sex. **1970** Segal *Love Story* 37: I mean, Christ, Barrett, are you making it or not? **1977** *Rolling Stone* (Sept. 8) 36: Two people were making it in my back bedroom once. **1982** M. Mann *Elvis* 48: No man I'd tried to make it with had ever refused me. **1986** Pietsch *Cab Driver's Joke Book* 50: I sort of have the hots for you. So what I'd really like to is make it with you. **1994** "G. Indiana" *Rent Boy* 18: He wouldn't admit making it with me.

b. to experience an orgasm.

1956 in Algren *Lonesome Monsters* 204: And I've never been able to make it any other way since. **1963** Braly *Shake Him* 92: I was going to make it. Do you hear that? I was going to make it. **1970** E. Thompson *Garden of Sand* 295: "You make it?" he growled. "Um-hmmm," she murmured. **1982** S.P. Smith *Officer & Gentleman* 81: Did you make it too, sweetheart?

4. *Narc.* **to take narcotics, esp. opiates.**

1954 in *Social Problems* III (1955) 40: It was finally about 1948 that I really began to make it strong. **1966** Neugeboren *Big Man* 104: Oh yeah. These kids making it. Someday they all be strung out good. **1970** Landy *Underground Dict.*: Make it…Be on drugs; be using drugs.

¶ **make like, 1. to behave as though or like; pretend or make out that;** (*hence*) **to imitate.** [Orig. dial.; rare in general speech before *ca*1940.]

1870 in *DARE*: Then he…made like he neither had seen nor heerd [*sic*]. **1884** in *DARE*: *To make like* = to pretend. **1912** Green *Va. Folk-Sp.* 273: Make like.…To act in a certain way.…To pretend to do a thing. **1941** Schulberg *Sammy* 72: Let's go over to the Back Lot and make like crazy. **1941** "G.R. Lee" *G-String* 290: So you made like we were singing baby shoes. **1943** Wakeman *Shore Leave* 195: Nickie, don't make like a sorehead. **1945** F. Baldwin *Ariz. Star* 78: Do I make like a wolf? **1949** H. Robbins *Dream Merchants* 247: Farber's on the lot already, making like a big shot. **1950** Felton & Adams *Armored Car*

Robbery (film): You want me to make like I'm Mapes? **1951–52** Frank *Hold Back Night* 29: Think you can make like a Red Indian? **1951–53** *Front Page Detective* (synd. TV series): Next he'll start making like a Boy Scout, which he is at heart. **1953** Paley *Rumble* 224: I see two fellers in some parted reeds makin' like fags. **1955** Klaas *Maybe I'm Dead* 20: Well, he made like he didn't notice the colonel. **1971** Cameron *First Blood* 13: Palmer's making like Victor MacLaglan again. **1972** Wambaugh *Blue Knight*. 80: I hear you don't make like the other cops we've run into in these demonstrations. **1990** *Garfield & Friends* (CBS-TV): I say we all make like Robin Hood and steal from the rich guy to give to the poor. **1993** G. Lee *Honor & Duty* 9: Cluck! Make like a chicken!

2. (used in var. joc. similes indicating departure). [The 1985 quot. is lampooning the speaker, who is bungling the expression as used in the 1968 quot.]

1958 Meltzer & Blees *H.S. Confidential* (film): Why don't you make like bubblegum and blow? **1968** Baker et al. *CUSS* 155: *Make Like a Tree and Leave* Leave a place. **1968–70** *Current Slang III & IV* 80: *Make like a tree and leave*, v. To go away (command).—University of Kentucky. **1976** Conroy *Santini* 199 [ref. to 1962]: Let's make like horseshit and hit the trail. **1982** in Bronner *Children's Folk*. 41: Make like a drum and beat it. Make like a banana and split. Make like a tree and leave. **1983** S. King *Christine* 297: Make like a tree and leave, Jimmy, okay? **1985** Zemeckis & Gale *Back to Future* (film): Make like a tree—and get out of here. **1990** *UTSQ*: Phrases for Leaving: 1. Let's make like horse shit and hit the dusty trail. 2. Let's make like a tree and leave. 3. Let's make like a rubber and roll on. 4. Let's make like a baby and head out.

¶ **make nice** [imit. of baby talk] **to behave nicely or affably.**

1957 Laurents & Sondheim *West Side Story* 139: You're gonna make nice with the PRs from now on. **1957** in *DARE*: Make nice on the kitty—pet gently. **1979** L. Block *Burglar Quote Kipling* 155: Go make nice to the Blinns,…and I'll catch you later. **1979** *Harper's* (Dec.) 89: A column exhorting the United States, in its own self-interest, to make nice to Nicaragua. **1984** *N.Y. Times Bk. Rev.* (Dec. 16) 21: Both parties unite in making nice because one wants publicity and the other wants a story. **1986** Merkin *Zombie Jamboree* 16: Now go over and make nice to the subhumans. **1989** *Studio 5B* (ABC-TV): They sit in the circle, they talk to the doctor, and they all make nice. **1990** Alexander & Karaszewski *Problem Child* (film): Make nice with kitty. **1995** *Time* (Aug. 28) 75: His job is to make nice with investors. **1995** *N.Y. Times Bk. Rev.* (Sept. 17) 43: He didn't know how to make nice, was without tact. **1995** *Leeza* (synd. TV series): I'm so conditioned to make nice.

¶ **make the scene** see s.v. SCENE.

¶ **make with** [trans. of Yiddish *makhn mit*] **1. to use for a particular purpose;** (*also*) **to bring forward; produce.**

1940 O'Hara *Pal Joey* 131: The poor man's Bing Crosby is still making with the throat here in Chi. **1941** "G.R. Lee" *G-String* 233: Who's the old guy, whom you make with the fancy service for? **1941** H.A. Smith *Low Man* 128: When we get to the end, you make with the hand, like this. **1941** Rossen *Blues in Night* (film): Come on, make with the moola. **1942** S.J. Perelman, in *New Yorker* (Nov. 21) 17: Poi is one thing I have never refused anybody yet,…so…I made with the poi. **1947** M. Hart *Gentleman's Agreement* (film): Don't force me to make with the big words. **1949** *New Yorker* (Nov. 5) 86: Again he makes with the choppers. **1949** R. Chandler *Little Sister* 81: On your way, dreamboat. Make with the feet. **1950** Sheekman *Mr. Music* (film): Your secretary…says you start making with the music at nine. **1953** R. Chandler *Goodbye* 6: Straighten up and walk.…make with the feet. **1954** *Looney Tunes* (animation): All right, you comic-book Rembrandt. Make with the eraser! **1963** T.I. Rubin *Sweet Daddy* 134: They all like make with the hats.…That's right they tip their hats. **1967** in Partridge *Concise Dict. Sl* 276: Make with the beer! **1990** *In Living Color* (Fox-TV): Can we make with the Kleenex here? **1994** *Mystery Sci. Theater* (Comedy Central TV): Make with the chow, broads!

2. to endure; put up with.

1960 Lawless *Folksingers* 124: Burl…"couldn't make with the academic stuff," dropped out [and] played professional football.

makee-learn *n.* [fr. pidgin or a mock pidgin] *Navy.* **an apprentice. Also makee-learnee.**

1931 Ellsberg *Pigboats* 5 [ref. to 1918]: Ensign Blake, his "makee-learn" second, a mighty nice boy. **1954** Ellsberg *Mid Watch* 99 [ref. to 1908]: A makee-learnee engineer with less than a year's experience below. **1958** Grider *War Fish* 61 [ref. to WWII]: Lieutenant Commander Dudley W. Morton, five years my senior, was assigned to the *Wahoo* as prospective commanding officer, or makey-learn. His job was simply to take a ride with us on a war patrol and observe everything he could so that he would be qualified to command. **1962** Lockwood & Adamson *Hell at 50 Fathoms* 27 [ref. to 1915]: They, as old hands, commanded the sincere respect of a *makee-learn* such as I. *a***1990** E.B. Potter *Adm. Burke* 183 [ref. to WWII]: He took charge of Jocko Clark's Task Group 38.1 as a makee-learn.*…*Makee-learn: Navy lingo for apprentice or apprenticeship.

make-out *n. Stu.* **1.** a person adept at seduction; (*also*) a person willing to MAKE OUT, 2.
　　1962 in *Mad* (Jan. 1963) 31: The one sitting in the front on the right (who is usually the best "make-out") becomes the "Window Man." He leans out as they pass females, and shouts clever, daring pick-up phrases. **1972** *Nat. Lampoon* (Apr.) 32: If a chick goes out with me, I know she's a make-out on account of my rep. **1972** Hannah *Geronimo Rex* 111 [ref. to *ca*1955]: She told me she was a make-out in Holly Springs and had been the cause of a lot of breaking up among couples.
　　2. an act or session of romantic necking and petting; (*also*) a sex act.—often used attrib.
　　1971 *Harper's* (Aug.) 25: A Task Force on Acne and one on Make-out Technique. **1974–75** Powledge *Mud Show* 102: There have been three makeouts so far on this lot that I know about. **1978** De Christoforo *Grease* 182: We went into a heavy, juicy make-out. **1984** *Time* (July 16) 67: Michael makes mostly good-time make-out music. **1996** *Simpsons* (Fox-TV): Such films as *Make-out King of Montana* and *Electric Gigolo*.

make out *v.* **1.a.** to get along; manage; fare. See also *like a bandit* s.v. BANDIT. Now *colloq.* or *S.E.*
　　1776 in *DARE*: Amidst these interruptions, how shall I make it out to write a letter? **1839** in *DARE*: Mrs. Whitman…refused to let me have a bottle to feed him [*sc.*, a baby] with cow milk but I made out to find one & so fed him. **1861** in Heller & Heller *Confed.* 47: I like to hear from Benjamin and James how [they] are a maken out and how [they] like a [soldier's] life. **1862** in *Manuscripts* XXX (1978) 19: The other day I made out to get stamps…but they are all gone. **1914** in Lardner *Round-up* 331: Try it, and see how you make out. **1918** Roberts *Flying Fighter* 93: Well, Mike, how did you make out? **1920** in F.S. Fitzgerald *Stories* I 204: He had been there half an hour, totally uncheered by Clark's jovial visits, which were each one accompanied by a "Hello, old boy, how you making out?" and a slap at his knee. **1929** Connelly *Green Pastures* 209: See how dey makin' out inside, son. **1939** I. Baird *Waste Heritage* 99: His face took on an expression of complete innocence. "How should I know? Oh, say, how'd you make out with Hazel?" Matt avoided his eyes. "Okay," he said evenly. "I made out okay." **1946** D. Brennan *One of Our Bombers* 25: How'd you make out, fella? **1995** in *Nation* (Jan. 1, 1996) 19: Transnationals taking advantage of the accord and the devalued peso can make out like bandits.
　　b. to be of acceptable quality; serve; "do."
　　1931 B. Morgan *Five-Star Final* (film): "How's your June bride contest coming along, Ziggie?" "It'll make out." **1977** N.Y.C. woman, age 22: The cherry pie just doesn't make out.
　　c. to be very successful; make the grade.
　　1958 H. Gardner *Piece of the Action* 16: I always wanted to make out in Manhattan. **1964** Howe *Valley of Fire* 267: Guys like Greaves and Reynolds make out like burglars and good guys have it rough. **1962–65** Cavan *Liquor License* 84: Patrons may come to be labeled "the guy who always makes out with the chicks," "the big spender," [etc.]. **1967** Spillane *Delta* 105: Well…hope you make out.
　　2.a. to seduce a woman successfully; engage in sexual intercourse. [A specialization of (**1.a.**), above, app. arising fr. the question, "Did you make out?"; cf. 1962–65 quot. at (**1.c.**) Although several sources cited below reliably assign the term to the period *ca*1940 or earlier, the Canadian 1939 quot. adduced by *OED2* plainly belongs with (**1.a.**), above; context shows it to be no more than an evasive euphem.]
　　1951 W. Williams *Enemy* 8 [ref. to WWII]: "You got to have a wife here like the exec to have anything in this port." "Can't you guys make out here?"…"Not here." **1953** Eyster *Customary Skies* 217 [ref. to WWII]: What was there for a guy to do now? Go to dances. Try to make out. **1956** P. Moore *Chocolates* 17: "But have you ever really made out?" "When you say 'really' I never know what you mean. I've

slept with boys when neither of us had any clothes on, if that's what you mean." **1959** De Roo *Young Wolves* 77: She begged to make out with you. **1960** Swarthout *Where Boys Are* 57: I had made out; that is, made out in toto; with only one other boy besides TV Thompson. **1961** *AS* XXXVI 151: To *make out* in the thirties and forties…meant plainly to persuade a woman to "come across" with full sexual intimacy. **1962** *AS* XXXVII 39 [ref. to 1940's]: When I was young, if one "made out," his accomplishment was a good deal more total than was implied by either *to neck* or *to pet*, or both. **1963** Blechman *Omongo* 57: The rumor's all over camp you made out with the Big Chief's wife. **1963** Boyle *Yanks Don't Cry* 14 [ref. to 1941]: I knew how hard it was to make out in Honolulu—even under the most ideal conditions. **1970** in Nachbar *Focus on Western* 79: That slow fadeout on a frenzied embrace…in movies means: they make out. **1972** P. Thomas *Savior* 155: I dug a couple of dogs making out in the middle of the street. **1974** C.W. Smith *Country Music* 258: I'm testing the cushion in the back…and wondering what a good make-out mattress it would be. **1984–88** Alistair Cooke, in Safire *Language Maven* 25: In my years (1932–34) at…Yale [and] Harvard…"making out" was the operative [phrase]…in a "sub rosa" sense. The rough translation of "sub rosa" was "between the sheets."
　　b. to engage in amorous kissing or caressing; NECK. [Now the dominant sense.]
　　1949 (implied by MAKE-OUT ARTIST). **1952** Uris *Battle Cry* 203 [ref. to 1942]: I tried making out with her but she cut me down. **1956** P. Moore *Chocolates* 8: His roommate and Janet could "make out" in the back seat. **1957** Kohner *Gidget* 76: Making out in drive-in movies.…I guess you still call it necking. **1957** Shulman *Rally* 170: "Making out" was…what used to be called necking or petting. This activity, as older readers will recall, covered a good deal of territory, but always stopped short of fulfillment. **1960** *Chaparral* (Stanford U.) (June) 18: Let's go to my…clubhouse and make out! *a***1961** Boroff *Campus U.S.A.* 90: Coney Island is their littoral "make-out" center. **1961** *AS* XXXVI 151: To *make out*…As used now [by teenagers] it seems to imply achieving only the conventional romantic reward of kissing. **1971** Dibner *Trouble with Heroes* 126: She admired Daphne's casual views on premarital sex but could not bring herself, during the first months of freshman dating, to venture past "making out" to "making it." **1978** Wharton *Birdy* 59: I'm sitting out in the parking lot at school in Higg's car, making out with Lucy. **1987** *Village Voice* (N.Y.C.) (July 14) 18: A couple is clinging, shadowboxing and making out. **1989** *Roseanne* (ABC-TV): Everybody was making out. **1992** *Fresh Prince* (NBC-TV): When they weren't [clowning] they were making out! **1992** Straight *In Sorrow's Kitchen* 331: A city park.…Freeman can watch people…make out all over the grass. **1994** *Friends* (NBC-TV): I want to stay here and make out with my girlfriend. **1995** *GQ* (Mar.) 93: George…was tucked in the corner of the dark bar, actually making out with a girl from my high school.

make-out artist *n.* an individual adept at seduction or love-making.
　　1949 *N.Y. Times*, in *DAS*. **1966** Brunner *Face of Night* 99: "Relax," Larry said. "You're in the company of a makeout artist. I never miss." **1966** "Petronius" *N.Y. Unexp.* 6: Even the most successful out-of-town make-out artist is usually put off at first. **1970** Wakefield *Going All the Way* 241: He was a regular make-out artist. **1971** Rhinehart *Dice Man* 65: Shy girl assigned to date make-out artist. **1979** Gutcheon *New Girls* 107: "A make-out artist?" asked Sally. **1980** Gould *Ft. Apache* 142: She was a real make-out artist. She knew exactly how to maneuver.

make-up *n.* one's appearance; (*hence*) a costume; disguise.
　　****1870** in *F & H* 274: An elderly gentleman—who is seventy if he is a day, but wishes to pass himself off for—let us be charitable and say—half his real age. Certainly his make-up is wonderfully good. **1875** A. Pinkerton *C. Melnotte* 132: Mr. Beaver…[purchased] a complete suit of court costume for himself, and his "make-up" was really gorgeous. **1899** Cullen *Tales* 140: Upon getting a good look at my make-up he had concluded that he could use me in his business. **1901** Irwin *Sonnets* (unp.): As follows is the make-up I shall buy/Next week, when from the boss I pull my pay:—. **1906** A.H. Lewis *Confessions* 4: Red Bob expressed disdain for my make-up, calling me a dude. **1909** Irwin *Con Man* 98: Put a clown make-up on him and take him into the ring with you. **1912** Ade *Babel* 177: Gee, she had a swell make-up that night. Mr. Branford was dead stuck on her from the start. **1918** Livingston *Delcassee* 22: From a collection of "make-ups" kept in stock for the use of the detective force,

each selected a set of disguises. **1919** De Beck *Google* (Nov. 12) 36: That make-up he's got certainly hypnotizes the wimmen. **1942–49** in Goldin et al. *DAUL* 135: How come the make-up?

makings *n.pl.* tobacco and cigarette papers.—usu. constr. with *the.*

    1905 in *OEDS:* He took out his "makings" and rolled a cigarette. [**1907** *Lippincott's Mag.* (Oct.) 499: Private Hanks…[was] fishing what he called the "makings" of a cigarette from his blouse pocket.] **1908** W.G. Davenport *Butte & Montana* 249: Booze on the sideboard and plenty of the "makin's." **1910** Service *Trail of '98* 15: "Got the makings?" "No, I'm sorry. I don't smoke." **1912** *Adventure* (May) 116: *Vaqueros* from Durango exchanged cigarette papers and the "makings" with hardy American adventurers from beyond the border. **1915** H.L. Wilson *Ruggles* 98: He asked if she had "the makings."…They both fashioned cigarettes. **1918** *Sat. Eve. Post* (Mar. 23) 14: Oh! a bag o' makin's! **1922** P.A. Rollins *Cowboy* 109: "Makings"…cigarette papers and a bag of "Bull Durham" tobacco. **1933** in Fife & Fife *Ballads of West* 91: He rolls the "makin's." **1951** *Sat. Eve. Post* (Feb. 23) 83: Fuller grunted and dug the makings from his shirt pocket. *ca***1933–74** E. Mackin *Didn't Want to Die* 241: They break out "makings"…papers and little cotton sacks of…tobacco.

malarkey or **malarky** *n.* [perh. obscurely fr. the family name; semantic devel. unkn.] **1.** nonsense; BUNK, 1.a. [The 1924, 1929 variants *malachy, malaky* indicate an *r*-less pronoun.]

    [**1922** T.A. Dorgan, in Zwilling *TAD Lexicon* 57: Yes, Milarkey 609 J.] **1924** T.A. Dorgan, in Zwilling *TAD Lexicon* 57: *Malachy* [*sic*]—you said it. **1929** McEvoy *Hollywood Girl* 102: It's a wonder you notice me, I told him. That's a lot of malaky [*sic*], says he. **1930** *Variety* (Oct. 29): The song is ended but the Malarkey lingers on. **1933** Ersine *Pris. Slang* 52: It's the *old malarky.* **1934** W. Smith *Bessie Cotter* 171: That's a lot of mallarkey. **1943** Hubbard *Gung Ho* (film): That was all malarkey about Kathleen and me. *a***1944** Earp *Wyatt Earp* 5: It's high time all that malarkey got a firsthand going-over. **1946** Rossen *Martha Ivers* (film): That's enough of that malarkey. **1946** Michener *South Pacific* 181: "It's just good, clean malarkey," a newcomer observed. **1953** W. Brown *Monkey on My Back* 150: Any story you'd give me would be pure mullarkey. **1955** S. Wilson *Man in Gray Flannel Suit* 123: He's a professional real estate man—that's a lot of malarky he gave us about wanting to buy the place for his own use. **1964** "Doctor X" *Intern* 298: He started giving me this malarkey about how he'd come here because everyone said the nursing care was so good. **1970** Cortina *Slain Warrior* 4: That's malarky. **1972** Pearce *Pier Head Jump* 127: Why do I have to go through that kind of malarky? **1977** *Oui* (Apr.) 129: It was easier for the Air Force to say that UFOs were a lot of malarkey. **1985** *N.Y. Times* (Dec. 29) IV 15: The tests are just so much malarkey. **1989** Berent *Rolling Thunder* 95: He thought the attitude stuff a lot of malarkey. **1992** *CBS This Morning* (CBS-TV) (June 10): This is the kind of malarkey one would expect from [the tobacco] industry. **1994** Okla. man, on *CBS Evening News* (CBS-TV) (Nov. 1): That's malarkey.

2. a dolt.

    1946 Dadswell *Hey, Sucker* 197: My front attracted everyone. We had big decorative blow-ups of beautiful girls. Those melarkeys thought my outfit was the girl show. **1948** Hargrove *Got to Give* 31: You're a malarkey.

Malfunction Junction *n.* (a name applied to) an area characterized by exasperating and confused activity; (*specif.*) a bewildering or heavily congested highway intersection.

    1975 Univ. Tenn. student: That's Malfunction Junction [in Knoxville, Tenn.]. **1977** Dills *CB Slanguage* (ed. 3) 66: *Malfunction Junction:* traffic jam. **1982** F. Hailey *Soldier Talk* 39: *Malfunction junction.* Ordnance or motor pool repair shop. **1983** Elting, Cragg & Deal *Dict. Soldier Talk* 193: *Malfunction Junction* (1940s and 1950s) The receiving barracks…of the Parachute School at Fort Benning, Georgia. *a***1984** in Safire *Stand Corrected* 381: In Detroit, the most jammable interchange is called the *Malfunction Junction.* **1994** Knoxville, Tenn., graphic artist, age 40: The first time I remember hearing *Malfunction Junction* was here in Knoxville in 1971 or 1972. It meant the old intersection of I-40 and I-75 near downtown.

mallethead *n.* MULLETHEAD.

    1954–60 *DAS: Mallet-head*…A stupid person. *Not common.* **1987** *Miami Vice* (NBC-TV): Listen, mallethead, I'm tryin' to *help* here! **1991** *Frankenstein: College Years* (Fox-TV): Where's Frankenstein, you mallethead?

mallie *n.* MALL RAT.

    1985 C.M. Schulz *Peanuts* (synd. comic strip), in *L.A. Times* (Aug. 5) I 4: [We're going] over to the shopping mall. We're "mallies"…we like to hang around with the other mallies. *Ibid.* (Aug. 6): "Mallies" don't buy things, Marcie. "Mallies" just hang around the shopping mall acting cool. **1990** Thorne *Dict. Contemp. Slang* 331: *Mallie, mall rat…American* a (usually female) teenager who hangs around shopping malls to meet friends…or otherwise have a "good time."

mall rat *n.* a person, esp. a teenager, who hangs around a public shopping mall.

    1982 *Chi. Sun-Times* ("Parade") (Oct. 31) 6: It had been an aimless world of disconnected people, teenage Mall Rats hanging around arcades. **1988** *AS* (Winter 1990): For the area's youthful "mall rats," however, the majestic vistas can't compete with the climate-controlled, neon-lit enticements inside. **1990** Pynchon *Vineland* 68: One more teenage girl, no different from any of the mall rats she saw at work every day. **1990** *Wash. Post* (July 14): He looked like any other teenage mall-rat in a T-shirt. **1992** *Newsweek* (Apr. 6) 53: Thousands of pubescent mall rats are affecting Brenda's sultry bangs and Dylan's killer squint. **1993** *Source* (July) 11: A mall rat sporting a Raiders cap with a Garth Brooks T-shirt. **1995** *N.Y. Times Bk. Rev.* (May 7) 13: The story of a 14-year-old mall rat who flees from the Adirondacks to the Caribbean.

maloney *n.* BALONEY, 2; MALARKEY.

    1979 in Terkel *Amer. Dreams* 194: The young ones today, you tell 'em that, they say "maloney," ain't nothin' to it. *Ibid.* 199: One of the biggest bunches of maloney that ever was.

mama or **mamma** *n.* **1.a.** Orig. *Black E.* a young woman; woman; (*hence,* esp. in direct address) a girlfriend.

    1917 in *AS* VII (1932) 243: I'm a Real Kind Mamma, Lookin' for a Lovin' Man. **1920** in *DARE:* 'Twill even drive your "itty bitty" Mama mad. **1922** in Leadbitter & Slaven *Blues Records* 315: Beale St. Mama. **1923** Bodenheim *Sardonic Arm* iii: Swee-et Mama, well your papa's done gone mad! **1924** Hecht & Bodenheim *Cutie* 7: Cutie was a shapely Mamma of twenty-one summers. **1924** T.A. Dorgan, in Zwilling *TAD Lexicon* 56: Ya gotta see mama every night or you can't see mama at all. **1925** in Thomason *Stories* 483: Farewell and adieu to you, Panama mammas—Farewell and adieu to you, Balboa janes—. **1926** Dunning & Abbott *Broadway* 222: He says it was lifted off one of the classiest mammas in this town. **1926** in Handy *Treasury of Blues* 51: See pretty papa, pretty papa what you done done,/You made your mamma love you now your woman's come. **1930** M. West *Babe Gordon* 118: They're not good-time mammas like this dame. **1931** Cressey *Taxi-Dance Hall* 39: When I did, one evening, a tough-looking Polish girl yelled out at me, "Big Blond Mamma thinks she's stuck up, don't she?" **1940** *Accent* (Autumn) 34: Hey, sourpuss, gimme a ten spot. I got a new mama tonight. **1944** *Pistol-Packin' Mama* (pop. song): Lay that pistol down, babe,/Lay that pistol down!/Pistol-packin' mama, lay that pistol down! **1969** B. Beckham *Main Mother* 61: Cool mamas and slick daddies! **1975** Sepe & Telano *Cop Team* 68: Telano was still trying to free himself from the clutches of "big mama." **1978** De Christoforo *Grease* 118: How's…Sonny…and his swinging momma Marsha? **1985** *Lady Blue* (ABC-TV): Come on in, little mama. **1985** B. Breathed, in *Daily Beacon* (Univ. Tenn.) 7: That crazy mama Maced me right in the face. **1986** *Kate & Allie* (CBS-TV): Wow, Allie! You're one tough mama. **1990** Crow Dog & Erdoes *Lakota Woman* 131: We had two or three pistol-packing mamas swaggering around with six-shooters. **1994** in C. Long *Love Awaits* 172: Hey, sexy mama. **1995** *Living Single* (Fox-TV): The way you ripped my clothes off, mama, I knew it was 'bout the right time.

b. a woman who belongs to a motorcycle club without being the wife or girlfriend of any individual cyclist.

    1965 in *DAS* (ed. 2): If a girl wants to be a mama and "pull a train," which means make herself available to everyone, then she'll be welcome at any Angel party. **1966** H.S. Thompson *Hell's Angels* 170: Nearly all were "old ladies"—not to be confused, except at serious risk, with "mamas."…A mama is common property. **1967** W. Murray *Sweet Ride* 97: Naw, Big Jane here, she ain't nobody's Old Lady. She's a Mama. **1971** J. Simon *Sign of Fool* 48: A mamma is a chick who bestows her services upon any club member who so desires. **1982–84** Chapple *Outlaws in Babylon* 190: Motorcycle mamas.

2. an object, task, or event, esp. if very large or challenging; MOTHER.

    1970 in *Black Scholar* (Jan. 1971) 41: Man, this Cadillac had…power windows, power brakes, power steering, power's mamma! **1971** N.Y.U. student: That big fat mama [*sc.*, an examination] blew my mind! **1974** Eble *Campus Slang* (Mar.) 4: *Mama*—anything unusually large or difficult. **1976** Lieberman & Rhodes *CB* 139: *Twin Mamas*—Dual 9-foot antennas. **1980** Knoxville, Tenn., man, age 35: That album's a mama! **1984** Kagan & Summers *Mute Evidence* 81: The UFO…was so commonly sighted that the population had given it a nickname: Big Mama. **1986** *NDAS: Momma*…Any specified object, esp a large, admirable, or effective one.

3. an effeminate male homosexual.

[**1942–49** Goldin et al. *DAUL: Momma.*…Any convict who assumes mother-like protection over youthful or less self-reliant inmates.…There is no implication of effeminacy or perversion in the use of this term.] **1974** R. Carter *16th Round* 171: The good-doing "mommas" would lay back and dig it all.

¶ In phrases:

¶ **[Oh,] mama!** (used as an exclamation of wonder).

1891 Townsend *Negro Minstrels* 47: Oh mamma! Why you poor fool niggar, I kin tie yo' inter a bow knot an' stuff yo' inter a rat hole. **1896** in Outcault *Yellow Kid* 137: O mommer! **1896** Ade *Artie* 64: And the talk he gives you. Mamma! **1896** Wister *Red Men* 223: Oh, momma! Why, he's king round here. **1918** *Sat. Eve. Post* (Sept. 14) 54: Oh, mamma, but he's a good range-finder. **1919** Darling *Jargon Book* 24: *Oh, Mama*—An exclamation of mock surprise. **1921–25** J. Gleason & R. Taber *Is Zat So?* 7: And whose fault was that, huh?…Oh, mamma! **1922–26** Scoggins *Red Gods* 13: "Oh, mamma!" he murmured. "Jerry, Jerry, pinch me quick!" **1944** R. Brooks *Brick Foxhole* 3: "Red meet any of them actresses?" "Sure thing." "Oh, Mama." **1944** Kapelner *Lonely Boy* 110: The way she stands, Harry! Oh, Mamma. **1945** Wolfert *Amer. Guerrilla* 10: Oh, momma, I told myself. **1950** Bissell *Stretch on the River* 63: Oh pretty mama.…That's what we need, a deckhand in the hospital! **1952** Mandel *Angry Strangers* 158: When that Shylock sees no more worldly goods—oh, mama! **1958** S.H. Adams *Tenderloin* 106: Oh, momma!…I guess that's art! **1960** Barber *Minsky's* 130: The Winter Garden! Oh, Mama! **1968** MacKenzie *Bastogne* 40: Joe said, "Oh, Mama!" **1995** *CBS This Morning* (CBS-TV) (July 28): Oh, mama!

¶ **red-hot mama** a sexually attractive woman. Cf. RED-HOT. [Associated with singer Sophie Tucker (1884–1966), known as "the last of the red-hot mamas" (first thus billed in 1928 at the Palace Theatre, New York).]

1925 Dos Passos *Manhattan Transfer* 307: My you're a redhot mommer in that dress. **1926** *Life* (Oct. 21) (cover): Red Hot Mama. **1940** O. Nash, in *OED2*: Affection…leads to breach of promise/If you go round lavishing it on red-hot momise. **1941** Cain *Mildred Pierce* 126: The morals they give you credit for, you'd be surprised. To him, you were a red-hot mamma the second he found out about you. **1968** in *Rolling Stone Interviews* 60: She's sexy, she's a red-hot mama.

¶ **your mama!** Esp. *Black E.* (used alone, postpositively, or allusively as a derisive or contemptuous phr.). Cf. *your mammy!* s.v. MAMMY; *your mother!* s.v. MOTHER. [Association with the DOZENS and with MOTHERFUCKER, etc., freq. lends enormous provocative force to this expression; cf. 1916 quot.]

[**1916** Thompson *Round Levee* 45: The greatest insult that can be given to another is "to talk about his people," and the worst thing that can be said is, "I'll get your mamma." This last phrase will always bring a fight.] **1973** Whited *Chiodo* 31: "Hey, that motherfucker's gonna lock me up." She turned and screamed, "Hey, go home and lock up your mamma!" [**1974** A. Murray *Train Whistle Guitar* 83: Up your mama's ass, motherfucker.] **1981** Crowe *Fast Times* 52: "It's definitely her." "It's definitely your *mama*." **1984** *Folklore Forum* XVII 148: I use to get beat up for saying "ya mama." **1981–85** S. King *It* 497: Yo mamma!…Nobody ever told me that. **1989** T. Clancy *Clear & Present Danger* 500: "Give me my fuckin' soap back, motherfucker!" "Yo' *momma*," the other replied casually. He'd thought about his line. **1995** Soloflex TV ad: I've decided to become a trash-talking small forward: Your *mama!* **1996** M. Kearney *Southeastern La. Univ. Coll.* (May): *Ya momma!* This is a slang of last recourse used in our teen years. It means virtually nothing but except [*sic*] a cheap shot.

mamacita *n.* [< Sp (nonstandard)] Orig. *Hispanic E.* an attractive young woman.

1973 N.Y.U. student: The only time I was ever bothered was once I was walking down Christopher Street late in the evening and a drunk yelled at me, "Hey, mamacita! Where you goin'?" **1981** Stiehm *Bring*

Men & Women 257: One male cadet…mistakenly hallooed a woman officer as a "fucking mamacita." **1986** *Miami Vice* (NBC-TV): Hey, mamacita!

mama-huncher *n.* (a partial euphem. for) MOTHERFUCKER. Also vars.

1962 Killens *Heard the Thunder* 11 [ref. to 1942]: Who let that mama-huncher loose? *Ibid.* 32: Now ain't that a mama-jabber? *Ibid.* 195: You fat-ass mother-huncher. *Ibid.* 266: We gonna step higher than a mama-jabber. **1974** W. Carolina State student: You mama-sticker.

mama-jabbing var. MAMMY-JAMMING.

mama-san *n.* [*mama* + *-san*, Japn honorific; cf. BABY-SAN, BOY-SAN, GIRL-SAN] *Mil. in Far East.* **1.** an elderly or middle-aged East Asian woman (often applied to such a woman who manages a brothel).

1946 in *AS* XXII 55: *Mama-san.* The GI term for the madam of a [Japanese] joro house [pidgin form of "whorehouse"]. **1957** Campbell *Cry for Happy* 10: "How many babes in the place?" "A mama san and five girls." **1965** C.D.B. Bryan *P.S. Wilkinson* 19 [ref. to 1960]: P.S. knew some of the girls up there and knew the Mama-san. **1971** *Seattle Times* (Jan. 17) 48: The girls giggle and the watching mamasans shake their heads. **1971** Vaughan & Lynch *Brandywine's War* 6: Twittering little Vietnamese women, called mamasans by the GI whether they were mothers or not. **1982** "J. Cain" *Saigon Commandos* 13: He bought a thin roll of…bread from a passing *mama-san.* **1982** Del Vecchio *13th Valley* 275: Little kids dee-dee. Mama-sans run. **1983** Goldman & Fuller *Charlie Co.* 300: He negotiated a price with the local mama-san to hire her away for the week, then did his own deal with the girl. **1990** Ruggero *38 N. Yankee* 91: Looks like mama-san's here. *a***1995** Gallantin *Sub. Admiral* 44 [ref. to ca1937]: The…Pioneer Hotel…[in] Lahaina…was operated by a quiet, smiling Japanese couple known to submarine sailors only as "Papa-san" and "Mama-san."

2. an East Asian woman who is a prostitute or the lover of a U.S. serviceman.

1982 S.P. Smith *Officer & Gentleman* 11: Byron…kissed his two mama-sans goodbye, and strode out of the bar. **1983** Goldman & Fuller *Charlie Co.* 116 [ref. to 1968]: Rupert…walked into his mama-san's hooch…and surprised her with another boyfriend.

mammy *n. Black E.* (used with a possessive to emphasize amount, degree, etc.).

1942 *Amer. Mercury*, in *DARE*: I got money's mammy and Grandma change. **1953** W. Fisher *Waiters* 124: I'm gonna make money's mammy. **1965–70** T. Morrison *Bluest Eye* 40: "You rich, Miss Marie?" "Puddin', I got money's mammy." **1971** H. Roberts *Third Ear*: A wealthy person is said to have money's *mammy*. There is confusion's *mammy* in that room. **1993** in *DARE:* You got so much milk, you got milk's mammy.

¶ In phrase:

¶ **your mammy!** *your mama* s.v. MAMA.

1948 Webb *Four Steps* 134: "Hello, Trigger. Who let you sit up?" "Your mammy." "Cut out the routine and pass out some tailormades." **1950** L. Brown *Iron City* 28: "Catch you again tomorrow." "Catch your *mammy!*" *a***1995** M. Kelly *Proudly* 31 [ref. to WWII]: "I smell shit." "Smell yo' mammy," I said.

mammy-dodger *n. Black E.* (a partial euphem. for) MOTHERFUCKER. Cf. GRANNY-DODGER. Hence **mammy-dodging,** *adj.*

1939 in A. Banks *First-Person* 256: Hell yes, mammydodger. **1970** in *DARE* [ref. to 1920's]: Why that mammy-dodging potlicker didn't even know what shoes was till he was twenty-nine.

mammy-jammer *n.* Orig. *Black E.* (a partial euphem. for) MOTHERFUCKER.—often considered vulgar.—(in very recent use) also used *joc.* Also vars. Cf. POPPA-STOPPA.

[**1944–45** in Campbell & Campbell *P-51* 68: Alabama Rammer Jammer [name painted on nose of fighter plane].] **1948** Webb *Four Steps* 100: I sure nuff show ol' white boy mammy-dugger how's feel. **1956** Resko *Reprieve* 48 [ref. to 1940's]: The mammy-jammer…puts the rope aroun mah neck. **1963** L. Cameron *Black Camp* 12: Grab your socks, mammyjammers. **1963** Braly *Shake Him* 97: You know what that dirty mammy-jammer did to me? **1967** Baraka *Tales* 18: You talking about a lightweight mammy-tapper, boy. *Ibid.* 20: Yeh, mammy-rammer. **1969** H.R. Brown *Die Nigger* 109: I'd bought a rifle, which…was a sweet mama-jammer, too. **1969** Gordone *No Place* 413: I rassle with light'nin', put a cap on thunder. Set every mammy-jammer in the graveyard on a wonder. **1970** Major *Dict. Afro-Amer. Sl.:* Mammyjammer, mammysucker, mammyfucker, mammyhugger. **1971** Keith *Long Line Rider* 75: Hey, Max, this mammyjammer don't like my cookin'. Y'all oughta have his butt busted. **1972** (quot. at MOFO). **1972** R. Wilson *Playboy's Forbidden Words* 165: *Mammy-Sucker* In black slang, an insult that is felt to be even more offensive than motherfucker. **1966–80** McAleer & Dickson *Unit Pride* 31: You...dirty Yankee mammie-jammer. **1982** Downey *Losing the War* 59 [ref. to WWII]: What the fuck do we do with three of these mammy-jabbers? **1985** Dye *Between Raindrops* 279: I'd been outa this mammy-jammer like a fuckin' shot. *Ibid.* 291: We...a lucky bunch of mammy-jammers. **1987** J. Waters *Hairspray* (film): Just to see me, the big mammy-jammer. **1989** in G. Tate *Flyboy* 100: Mother Tate...advised her son to come cover the mammy-jammy. **1991** *In Living Color* (Fox-TV): This is one bad mammy-jammer. **1992** *Jerry Springer Show* (synd. TV series): I'm a bad mammy-jammer...I'm Wonder Woman! **1992** *Mystery Sci. Theater* (Comedy Central TV): You are one lucky mammajamma. **1995** MTV (Feb. 18): It's a mean mamma-jamma!

mammy-jamming *adj. Black E.* (a partial euphem. for) MOTHERFUCKING.—often considered vulgar. Also vars. [In 1956 quot., fig. 'very earthy'.]

   1946 Mezzrow & Wolfe *Really Blues* 105: Those Jim Crow mammyjamming whites. *Ibid.* 308: *Mammy-jamming:* incestuous obscenity. **1943** Killens *Heard the Thunder* 31 [ref. to WWII]: I just don't like the goddamn mama-jabbing Army, that's all. **1956** Longstreet *Real Jazz* 32: The music industry intuitively grasps the heroic loneliness of a people....From mammy-jamming to concert jazz, no matter how sleek, some form of this appears. **1958** Talsman *Gaudy Image* 30: Yeah, some real mammy-lovin' goddamn cheap tinhorn place. **1969** Jessup *Sailor* 268: Who! The mammy-rammy *law!* That's who! **1974** R. Carter *16th Round* 55: You must be out of your mammy-jammy mind! **1974** A. Murray *Train Whistle Guitar* 117: That ain't no goddamn mammy-hunching patent leather walk. **1977** Bunker *Animal Factory* 59: I ain' no mammy-fuckin' *dawg!* **1977** Langone *Life at Bottom* 76: Pour the stuff in the trench and it packs hard as a mammy-jammin' cement load. **1990** S. Lee *Mo' Better Blues* (film): Blame it on your mammy-jamming mother!

man *n.* **1.**[**a.** (used emphatically in direct address to a grown man to variously convey authority, impatience, encouragement, sympathy, remonstration, excitement, disdain, or the like). [Now rare in U.S. except as a reflection of older literary use; the long-established vocative *man,* used for centuries by all classes of speakers, cannot be considered "slang," but it provides a linguistic foundation for **(b),** below. *MED* offers numerous vocative quots., mostly undifferentiated as to nuance, some dating to the 12th C. or earlier; written medieval quots. cited here are difficult to distinguish from current slang usage as described in bracketed note below. *EDD* provides many additional quots., variously nuanced, most from the 19th C.]

   ca*1385 G. Chaucer, in *MED:* What saistow, man? Where arte? **a*1400 in *MED:* Why makyste pou suche mornynge, man? **ca*1380–1400 *Gawain & Green Kt.*, in *MED:* A! mon, how may pou slepe? **ca*1420 in *DOST:* And he, as burdened, sayd smethely, "Man, will thow have me off ʒustyng?" ***1530 in *OED2:* Plucke up thy herte, man, for Goddes sake. ***1589** in *OED2:* Here be non but frends man. **ca*1593 Shakespeare *Richard III* I i: We speak no treason, man. ***1599** Shakespeare *Julius Caesar* I ii: Why, man, he doth bestride the narrow world/Like a Colossus. ***1600** King James VI, in *DOST:* As tuicheing ʒour fatheris deid man I was bot ane minor. ***1600** in *DOST:* "I had nather God nor the devill, man, before my eyes," said the King. ***1680** Shadwell *Woman-Captain* IV: At it Man! ***1773** O. Goldsmith, in *OED2:* Why, that's it, man. **1822** in *AS* XXXVI (1961) 136: How do you do, Jack; what ails you[,] man? ***1826** B. Disraeli, in *OED2:* Here read it, read it, man. **1833** A. Pike *Prose Sks.* 139: Get up, man—get up—if you wish to see sport, and dress yourself. **1833** in *AS* XXXVI (1961) 137: Don't waste your powder[,] man, I want to shoot him just under the off ear....Be striking a fire[,] man. ***1846** in *AS* XXXVI (1961) 137: Tut, man,...its only talking ye are now. **a*1889 M. Oliphant, in *Century Dict.:* "You will think me—I don't know what you will think me—" "Get it out, man. I can't tell till I know." **1925** Faulkner *Soldiers' Pay* 10: Hell, man, I can't drink it. **1988** Knoxville, Tenn., physician, age *ca*50: Of course it's significant, man. You're increasing our knowledge of language. **1996** *Simpsons* (Fox-TV): Pull yourself together, man!]

b. (used in direct address, usu. without emphasis, appended to or inserted parenthetically into any kind of utterance, often conveying a sense of shared social status or background but just as often as a meaningless expletive; orig. applied to grown men only, later occ. extended to include women, children, and animals).

[In recent U.S. use, often with lengthened vowel. Perception of vocative *man* as "American slang" stems fr. its association with the speech of jazz and swing musicians, and entered general or middle-class use, notably among rock and roll enthusiasts, only during the 1950's; it has since been characterized also as "beatnik slang," "hippie slang," "street slang," etc. Yet this semantically weakened offshoot of **(a),** above is evident in Scots E as early as the 16th C.; cf. also pre-1530 quots. at **(a),** above, some of which are not conclusively distinguishable fr. present usage. In casual direct address, particularly at the end of a sentence, *man* has long been common in Scotland, Ireland, and parts of England and Wales, as well as in the West Indies and in other areas of Anglo-Celtic colonization. The usage has been notable in working-class U.S. Black E for over a century. The subtleties of intonation, emotive association, cultural context, etc., that distinguish modern "slang" usage from older dialectal and "prestige" uses of vocative *man* clearly illustrate how social rather than historical considerations determine speakers' recognition of a usage as "slang."]

   ca*1500–12 W. Dunbar, in *DOST:* "Wo is me," quod scho, "quhair will ye, man?" ***1535 Sir D. Lyndsay *Thrie Estaites* (unp.): Richt weel devisit, man, by Saint Blaise....Allace, man, thy cais, man,...I lament. **1714** in Meserve & Reardon *Satiric Comedies* 6: Don't mind me, Man, I sing for my own diversion. ***1806** in *SND:* Her answer, man, she winna gie't. ***1824** Sir W. Scott, in *SND:* That's something like it, man. Od, ye are a clever birkie! **a*1841 Lever *C. O'Malley* I 343 [Ireland]: "Well, Sparks, how goes it, man?"..."Are they really so pretty?" "Pretty! downright lovely, man." **1844** W.T. Porter *Big Bear* 172: Git up, man, git up! ***1851** in *EDD: Man*...Used [in Northamptonshire] in speaking to a female or even to a dog. **1880** J.C. Harris *Uncle Remus* 21: Hit was tech en go wid um, too, mon. *Ibid.* 157: En he kyo'd [*i.e.,* cured] 'im good, mon. *Ibid.* 160: I come up wid a Jacky-my-lantern, en she wuz bu'nin' wuss' a bunch er lightnin'-bugs, mon. *Ibid.* 236: Dey er gittin' on solid groun', mon. **1887** W. Watson *Life in Confed. Army* 185 [ref. to Civil War]: The darkness did not allow them to see the stumps...and their feet...often struck against them, causing...excruciating pain...made more vexatious by the laughing taunts of their comrades, such as, "Kick that stump again, man." ***1894** in *SND:* "Hey mon!" he called to Ralph. **1895** C.C. King *Capt. Dreams* 30: What a jag you've got on, man! **1895** Coup *Sawdust* 91: Whip up, man! The prairie's on fire! Move for the river straight ahead! **1899** Young *Reminiscences* 383: I'se guine tell yer, man. Don't argufy wid me. ***1903** *EDD: Man*...A familiar term of address to a person of either sex or of any age; often used at the end of a sentence to give it special emphasis, sometimes used as a meaningless expletive. ***1911** Warrack *Scots Dictionary: Man*...a familiar term of address. ***1913** in Partridge *DSUE* 507: *Man*...an exclamatory form of address in common use all over South Africa, employed often enough quite irrespective of either the age or the sex of the person addressed. ***1914** J. Joyce *Dubliners* 60 [Ireland]: One night, man,...I spotted a fine tart under Waterhouse's clock....Then next Sunday, man, I met her by appointment....It was fine, man. **1918** *Yank Talk* 6: Where'd you all get dat blighty, man? **1918** *Outlook* (Oct. 16) 253: Say, man, what's that? Sure, a New York one for mine. **1919** *Amer. Leg. Wkly.* (Aug. 22) 8: A dime, man! Yo' ain't talking to me. **1919** *JAF* XXXII 368: Get de spade, man! dig fo' um! **1922** in Mjelde *Glory of Seas* 88: As I came down the companionway he got me and say, man, you can tell 'um," I got as fine a rope's end as a kid ever got. ***1926** Walrond *Tropic Death* 42 [W. Indies]: Man, let me tell yo' something. *Ibid.* 60: What's the matter with you, mang, you mek too much noise, mang. **1927** [Fliesler] *Anecdota* 96: Man, ah knows you by now. **1929** A.C. Doyle *Maricot* ch. v: Shucks, man, how could we have someone expecting us? **1932** R. Fisher *Conjure-Man* 192: "I done seen number two." "Number two?" "Yea, man." *a*1934 in Lomax & Lomax *Amer. Ballads* 69: Drunk wine, man; drunk wine. **1944** Burley *Hndbk. Jive* 130: *First Cat:* Whatcha say,

man?…Whatcha know, man? *Second Cat:* I don't know, man.…*First Cat:* Solid! Man, solid! **1946** Mezzrow & Wolfe *Really the Blues* 187: Man, just look at him, dig that vine. **1950** *Commentary* X 62: Man, wut choo think you gonna do? **1952** E. Brown *Trespass* 118: Pick up, man. Come on. **1954** A. Becker *Go Man Go* [film title]. **1954* J. Masters *Bhowani Jct.*, in Dunkling *Dict. Epithets* 167 [India]: Mavis, what are you doing here, man? **1958** Smith & Douglas *Defiant Ones* (film): Look, man. Don't gimme that look. **1959** in R.S. Gold *Jazz Talk* 177: *Man:* omnibus salutation extended to men, women, domestic animals—saves cool cat hang-up of remembering names. **1954–60** *DAS:* *Man*…A term of direct address…usu. implying the person addressed is hip and the speaker is sincere.…*Common since c1935, esp. among jive and cool groups.* *a1961 F. Cassidy *Jamaica Talk* 397: The ubiquity of *man* (unstressed) appended to almost any kind of statement or question…is most common among the folk, but in familiar conversation it goes very far toward the other end of the scale. **1961** in *OED2:* "Cut that out, man," the beatnik said. **1964** R.S. Gold *Jazz Lexicon: Man*…current esp. among black jazzmen since c. 1920, among white jazzmen as well since c. 1940. **1966** *RHD: Man*…*Slang* a term of address to a man or a woman: *Hey, man, don't you dig that music?* **1970** Major *Dict. Afro-Amer. Sl.: Man:* a word brought into popular use by black males to counteract the degrading effects of being addressed by whites as "boy"; black males address each other as one man to another. **1971** *Go Ask Alice* 54: Daddy thinks I'm blowing his image as the College Dean. He even yelled at me at the table last night for saying "man." **1973** Burling *Eng. in Black & White* 87: In the late 1940s,…*man*, used as a calling word or term of address [was] already current in Harlem, but still virtually unknown in the white community. **1975* in Branford *Dict. So. Afr. Eng.:* You needn't screech like that, Myrtle, I'm not deaf, man. **1978** *Longman Dict. Contemp. Eng.: Man*…[vocative] *sl[ang], esp Am[erican] & Car[ibbean] E[nglish]* (used for addressing someone, esp. a fully-grown male): *The party's really great, man!* **1980** Peck & Young *Little Darlings* (film): This nature stuff's for the birds though, man [said to a teenage girl]. **a1982* Holm & Shilling *Dict. Bahamian Eng.: Man*…term of address to both sexes of all ages. *a1982* Naylor *Women of Brewster Pl.* 161: These [tough] young men…continually surnamed each other Man. **1985** Grave *Florida Burn* 72: Listen, man—I was thinking about what Rodriguez said. **1988** *Time* (July 11) 54: "I ain't smarter than anyone here, man," says Olmos, suddenly injecting street slang into his normally impeccable English. **1988** Univ. Tenn. student theme: Girls are sometimes called "man." **1989** Shyrack et al. *Turner & Hooch* (film): I'm sorry, man. I can't help it. **1990* Dunkling *Dict. Epithets* 167: A correspondent from Newcastle writes…"It is very common to address all and sundry (including women and children) as 'man.'" **1990** *It's Garry Shandling's Show* (Fox-TV): I gotta tell you something, man. The music business is nuts. **1996** N.Y.C. technical editor, age 62: I don't believe *man* was used in addressing specific people when I was in [public] high school [Queens, N.Y., 1948–52]. Kids would say, "Man! That was a hard test!" but I don't think they said, "That was a hard test, man." The two sound different to me. "That was a hard test, man," makes me think of beatniks and hippies. **1996** *Jerry Springer Show* (synd. TV series): Damn right, man. **1996** *Leeza* (synd. TV series): They're like, man, they're gone forever.

c. (used as an interj. to indicate amazement, excitement, anger, disappointment, frustration, etc.). Also **man alive!; [man,] oh man!** [Even with more extensive context, some quots. are difficult to distinguish fr. those belonging to **(b)**, above, with which this usage is now freq. associated.]

1823 [J. Neal] *Errata* 37: Man!—man!—I had a heart like a well—into it, every living creature might have dipped. **1829* in Partridge *DSUE* 507: Man alive! **1843** [W.T. Thompson] *Scenes in Ga.* 46: Man alive! can't you see? **1850** *Spirit of Times* (Jan. 19) 566: Man! I tell you, I was gettin to feel mad then! **1855** F. Douglass *Bondage & Freedom* 289 [ref. to 1830's]: I…said to him, "*Sandy, we are betrayed;* something has just told me so."…Sandy said, "Man, dat is strange; but I feel just as you do." **1876** "M. Twain" *Sawyer* 165 [ref. to *ca*1845]: Man, it's money! **1882** *Frank James on the Trail* 35: Man alive, I'm all on fire to know what you heard. **1885** B. Harte *Shore and Sedge* 38: Man! they'll kill *you*, the first thing. **1887** W. Watson *Life in Confed. Army* 188: Oh, man, don't hurt the pig, you might be a pig yourself one of those days. **1893** F.P. Dunne, in Schaaf *Dooley* 67: What ails ye, man alive? **1897** Ade *Pink* 139: Man, what could ol' Englan' do 'ith…'ese fo' million soljahs un an' a' comin'? **1903* in *EDD* [Ireland]: O man, isn't that great!…O man, O man, there's a grand house. **1903** A.H. Lewis *Boss*

58: In a game of ca-ards, which are ye loyal to, is it your hand or the game? Man, it's your hand av coorse! **1904** J. London *Faith* 19: O man, have I not told you I was mad?…Mad clean through. **1908** Hopper & Bechholt *9009* 169: Man,…what have you been doing! **1908** W.G. Davenport *Butte & Montana* 214: Why, man alive, you don't know old Nolan. **1910* P.W. Joyce *Eng. in Ireland* 14: "Oh man" is a common exclamation to render an assertion more emphatic, and sometimes to express surprise:—"Oh man, you never saw such a fine race as we had." In Ulster they duplicate it, with still the same application:—"Oh man-o-man that's great rain."…"I got £50 for my horse to-day at the fair." Reply, "Oh man, that's a fair price." **1914** *Amer. Mag.* (June) 33: Man!…Are you a mind reader? First you locate me here, then you tell me word for word the exact idea I had in mind. **1915** K. Burke, in Jay *Burke-Cowley Corres.* 10: Man alive, there are only three Universities in the United States. **1918** "M. Brand" *Harrigan* 7: But oh, man, I'm thinkin' it was swate while it lasted. **1918** R. Casey *Cannoneers* 237: Man, if they shell this road we'll be caught like rats in a trap. **1922** in H. Miller *Letters to Emil* 4: Man, I'll quote you so full of quotations you won't know plop from zowie. *Ibid.* 5: Man alive, I am on an intellectual bat. **1927** C.J. Daly *Snarl of Beast* 93: Cold? Man!…that Arctic wind. **1930** Schuyler *Black No More* 5: Man, I can tell a cracker a block away. **1933–35** D. Lamson *About to Die* 206: Man, man, that guy is full of larceny. **1956** M. Wolff *Big Nick.* 1: Man, that wind's sure whooping in tonight. **1958** Zinkoff & Williams *Harlem Globetrotters* 67: Man, you must *really* be dirty! **1962** J. Steinbeck, in Dunkling *Dict. Epithets* 167: Man, oh man, you going to see something. Man, oh man, you ain't never heard nothing like it when they get going. **1963** *Standard Coll. Dict.: Man…interj. Slang* An exclamation of surprise, pleasure, etc. *Man*, what a show! **1966** *RHD: Man…Slang.* (used as an interjection to express astonishment, enthusiasm, etc.): *Man! Listen to him blow that horn!* **1987** Mamet *House of Games* (film): Man, *you're* living in the dream. **1987** *Beauty & Beast* (CBS-TV): Man, where did he go? **1990** *It's Garry Shandling's Show* (Fox-TV): Oh, man! The *lambada?* This is the worst! **1995** N.Y.C. man, age *ca*50: Man, oh man! This stuff is gonna drive me nuts!

2. a dollar; IRON MAN.

1910 T.A. Dorgan, in Zwilling *TAD Lexicon* 56: Here's the salary with the three extra men for the night I worked. **1913** *Sat. Eve. Post* (Mar. 15) 10: Lend me one man, will yer? I'm hungry. **1920–21** Witwer *Leather Pushers* 174: I'll go to the cleaners for sixty thousand men if Kid Roberts don't [d]ash home in front. **1921** in Lardner *Round-up* 420: I'd take my seven hundred men and invest it. **1966–67** P. Thomas *Mean Streets* 109: Here's half a man.

3. (often *cap.*) an authoritative or controlling person or (*later*) group.—constr. with *the. Specif.*:

[Some of the following senses are more fully lexicalized than others; sense **(c)**, below, in its narrow sense is undoubtedly the parent of the remaining, more specialized, applications.]

a. *Naut. & Mil.* a commanding officer or officer in charge.

1918 in Battey *Sub. Destroyer* 302: Anybody in [naval] authority is "the man." **1939** *AS* XIV 28: *Man, The*, n. The Officer in Charge or the Officer of the Day, when making an inspection. **1946–51** J. Jones *Eternity* ch. xv: I heah the Man's sending him to the next NCO School, in April. **1952** Bissell *Monongahela* 209: It's a real pilothouse and you're The Man. **1960** Leckie *Marines!* [ref. to WWII]: An' you kin count yerselves lucky I'm not taking all of you to see the man! **1963** Coon *Short End* 246: The Man told you to talk Hey Yu into coming inside the compound. **1966** J. Lewis *Tell It to Marines* 40: Drink up, we'll grab a fast shave and go see The Man. **1981** Ballenger *Terror* 102: It was an order from the Man. **1984** *Call to Glory* (ABC-TV): I had orders from the Man. **1984** Riggan *Free Fire* 80: So he…gets the Red Cross to check it out and the Man to OK it. **1985** O'Neil *Lady Blue* (film): And if you think I chewed *you* out, you should see what I got from the Man. **1987** E. Spencer *Macho Man* 137: J.B. is The Man of 1st Battalion, 26th Marines.

b. *Pris.* the warden of a prison.

1918 in *AS* (Oct. 1933) 29: Another goddam word out o' you-all, an' Ah'll send ev'ry goddam one of ye up t' the Man. **1942–49** Goldin et al. *DAUL* 135: *Man*.…Prison keeper, warden, or other prison official. **1952** Himes *Stone* 209: Ah ain't got no hatred, lesson it be de man. **1963** Williamson *Hustler!* 46: Now I'm goin' a go in the room here, and see the man. **1970** Rudensky & Riley *Gonif* 34: Let me give this pitch to the Man. *Ibid.* 186: *Man*...the Warden or figure of authority.

c. *Orig. So. & Black E.* any man or group in a position of authority; authority as an abstract entity.

1928 R. Fisher *Jericho* 306: *The man:* designation of abstract authority. He who trespasses where a sign forbids is asked: "Say, biggy, can't you read *the man's* sign?" **1929–32** in *AS* (Dec. 1934) 288: [Lincoln U.:] *Man.* Anyone in authority. *When I rode in that exam I took the Man out!* means "When I cheated in that exam I put one over on the professor!" **1959–60** R. Reisner *Jazz Titans* 160: *Man, The*...Also anyone in a position of authority. **1968** *Business Week* (Nov. 23) 34: The Negroes are keeping their cool..., giving "the man" a chance....They show no vindictiveness toward the new Chief Executive. **1977** Sen. J. Abourezk (D.–S. Dak.), in Terkel *Amer. Dream* 340: You're not gonna get in trouble with The Man if you just let him do what he wants. The privileged can always manage to...legalize whatever...they want. **1995** *N.Y. Press* (May 17) 20: William Wallace, a low-born Scotsman who just wants to live in peace....But as usual, the Man (in this case, the occupying English) fucks it all up by killing [his wife].

d. *Orig. Und. & Black E.* a policeman, prison guard, or other law-enforcement officer.—also used collec.

1930 G. Irwin *Tramp & Und. Slang: Man.*—A prison guard. **1933–35** D. Lamson *About to Die* 201: No sir; if you're figurin' on startin' anything [illegal] at all, the first thing you do is...tell the Man all about it. Then everything will be all right, an' you don't have no trouble. **1935** L. Hughes *Little Ham* 63 [ref. to 1920's]: *Ham* Ssh-ssh! The man has been here, him and his brother....*Youth* What man? *Ham* Two bulls lookin' for numbers. **1944** *Papers Mich. Acad.* XXX 598: *Beat the man*, to deceive an official [of a prison]. **1952** Viereck *Men into Beasts* 16: "The Man is getting restless," he said. "The Man" was the guard. **1952** H. Ellson *Golden Spike* 74: "The man's on the scene"...meant the Law. **1959** A. Anderson *Lover Man* 158: The Man done put the finger on the kats and everybody's layin' low. **1959** Trocchi *Cain's Book* 74: You never know when the Man will bust in. **1962** H. Simmons *On Eggshells* 175: Here comes the man. **1962** *AS* XXXVII 270: *Man*...a policeman. A word used by teenaged drivers. "When I heard the siren, I knew it was the Man." **1962** T. Berger *Reinhart* 45: You sure you ain't The Man?...The Man,...the bulls, the po-lice. **1965** C. Brown *Manchild* 160: You just had to keep watching for the Man. **1967** Wolf *Love Generation* 222: You're always up against the Man*...*Police scrutiny. **1968** K. Hunter *Soul Bros.* 7: Run!...The Man is coming. **1968** Heard *Howard St.* 23: You wanna bring the man down on me or somethin'? **1969** B. Beckham *Main Mother* 135: The man could come and bust me. **1971** Contini *Beast Within* 43: The Man must know what's happening every Sunday. **1972** J. Mills *Report* 96: I heard you were the man. You're a cop. **1985** *Alfred Hitchcock Presents* (CBS-TV): You're calling the Man, aren't you? **1985** M. Baker *Cops* 146: They may open the door a crack and see you're the Man and—Blam!—they slam it. **1988** M. Bartlett *Trooper Down!* 190: I look forward to going to work because I know I'm "the man." **1990** *In Living Color* (Fox-TV): Bust a move, short shank, it's the Man! **1990** Vachss *Blossom* 129: Chill, Lloyd. The Man! **1995** *Simpsons* (Fox-TV): Marge, you being a cop makes you the *Man!*

e. *Narc.* a drug dealer.

1942 *ATS* 479: Narcotic trafficker....*hop merchant,...man,...peddler.* **1953** in *OEDS:* When I first hit New Orleans, the main pusher—or "the Man," as they say there—was a character called Yellow. **1956** E. Hunter *Second Ending* 242: I'll find the Man, and I'll roll into some pad where it's soft and quiet, and I'll boot that mother-loving White God until it comes out of my ears. **1967** "Velvet Underground" *I'm Waiting for the Man* [rock song title]. **1971** *Int. Jour. Addictions* VI 362: "The man" is usually the drug supplier. **1968–73** Agar *Ripping & Running* 44: *The man* can be glossed as "police" or "dealer," again depending on context. **1980** D. Hamill *Stomping Ground* 173: They were waiting for "the man" to come so they could cop their scag. **1993** E. Richards *Cocaine True* 53: You're always working for the man. **1995** Former heroin user, age 28 (coll. J. Sheidlower): *The Man* usually doesn't refer to a street dealer, but to a big supplier—the guy the dealers get their shit from. It's probably more common among blacks, too.

f. *Black E.* a man who is highly accomplished or respected; the best man in a given field or at a particular time.

1952 Mandel *Angry Strangers* 29: I'm diggin' a lot of Armstrong, 'cause he's the man. **1959** in R.S. Gold *Jazz Lexicon* s.v. *the man:* The *man*...Any cat who is deserving of great respect, musically or personally.

("Miles is the Man!"). *a***1979** A. Rose *Eubie Blake* 94: Here it is 1923....Eubie Blake is *the man* in colored show business. **1981** *Time* (Oct. 12) 10: I got a pair of $600 lizard shoes and I got silk shirts. I'm the Man, boy. I changes my clothes 15 times a day. **1992** *Martin* (Fox-TV): Say, I'm the man. I'm the *man!* **1993** Spectator at golf tournament (coll. J. Sheidlower): Way to go, Fuzzy! You the man! **1993** *Simpsons* (Fox-TV): "You're the *man*, Homer!" "Thanks, boy!" **1996** *N.Y. Times* (Sept. 8) ("Sports") 13: Everybody hypes Tyson as being the man....And if you fight the man, you'll be the man once you beat the man.

g. *Black E.* white people collectively regarded as oppressors of blacks; (hence, in radical politics) the white ruling class or U.S. government; (*rarely*) a white person.

1954 Killens *Youngblood* 22: How about going into the *man's* army? **1964** *Newsweek* (Aug. 3) 16: It is time to let the Man know that if he does something to us, we are going to do something back. **1965** *Time* (Aug. 27) 17: Told by Black Nationalists and civil rights demagogues that "The Man"—the white man—is responsible for his savage hopelessness. **1966** in *Trans-action* IV (Apr. 1967) 6: "The man" (...the man in power—the police, and by extension, the white man). **1967** *DAS* (Supp.): *Man, the*...A white man...white people, the white race; the white establishment, society, or culture. **1969** *U.S. News & W.R.* (May 19) 37: Avowed aim of the "Yippies" is to destroy "the Man"—their term for the present system of government. **1970** *Harper's* (June) 55: Now we've got the man where we need him and we can't take no promises. Black people are not gonna be pushed around anymore. **1977** Sayles *Union Dues* 190: Go up against the Man when he's got tanks and heelicopters and fighter jets and paratroops an all that? Forget it, sucker. **1979** *Easyriders* (Dec.) 110 (ad): California residents add 6% [sales tax] for The Man. *a***1981** D. Travis *Black Chi.* 113: How can you be happy when the man is constantly kicking your ass? **1981** N.Y.C. man, age 25: Numbers is better than state-run cause you don't gotta give nothin' to the Man [in taxes]. **1988** Poyer *The Med* 369: After Tet the Man was scared. *a***1994** N. McCall *Wanna Holler* 292: They talked white and thought white and even dressed goofy like the man.

h. a boss; employer.

1959 A. Anderson *Lover Man* 129: I...decided that this kat at the head of the table was The Man. **1966** R.E. Alter *Carny Kill* 7: Where do I find The Man? **1967** *DAS* (Supp.): *Man, the*...one's employer.

i. God.

1971 in Matthews & Amdur *My Race* 247: The Man made Adam and Eve. **1987** E. Spencer *Macho Man* 5: Priests were tight with The Man. **1984–88** Hackworth & Sherman *About Face* 30: To my mind I was really talking to God. I was talking to The Man.

4. the penis.—usu. considered vulgar.

1927 [Fliesler] *Anecdota* 107: He might be interested, but the man below was not. **1966** C. Cooper *Farm* 210: I could rest My Man on her thigh.

¶ In phrase:

¶ **my man 1.** Esp. *Black E.* (used in direct address between male friends or as a neutral form of address to another man). [Bracketed quots. illustrate S.E. usage, which—equivalent to "my good man"—has resembled that of **(1.a.),** above.]

[**1844** Ingraham *Coachman* 37: Ah, Donald, my man, glad to see you!] [**1884** "Craddock" *Where Battle Was Fought* 101: "Hello, my man, lend a hand here!" Estwicke called out fiercely.] [**1907** Corbin *Cave Man* 51: "Hello, my man!" some one called out, half good-naturedly and half in patronage.] **1947** Helseth *Martin Rome* 4: Don't play the fool, my man. You can't win. **1952** E. Brown *Trespass* 20: Crazy? My man, you know who you talking to? **1959** A. Anderson *Lover Man* 52: Did you hear what I said, my man? *Ibid.* 124: I'm with you all the way, my man. **1965** in W. King *Black Anthol.* 306: My man....You my man, jive nigguh. **1967** Baraka *Tales* 7: Where you off to, my man? **1968** Gover *JC* 98: Hey wait right here, ma-man, don't go way. **1967–80** Folb *Runnin' Down Lines* 247: *Man, my*...form of address between black males that connotes positive feelings between the two. **1987** Estes *Field of Innocence* 129: Jackson, my man! What it is! What it is! **1990** in N. George *Buppies, B-Boys* 146: Yo, my man, that book is slammin'. **1993** T. Davis et al. *Coneheads* (film): Beldar, my man, you tellin' me you don't have a Social Security number? **1994** Auster *Smoke* (film): Okay, my man. **1996** *Simpsons* (Fox-TV): Troy! My man! It's MacArthur Parker!

2. Orig. *Black E.* one's very good male friend; (*also*) a man that the speaker respects highly.

   1944 in Hodes & Hansen *Sel. from Gutter* 78: He was your idol, huh?…Yeah, he was my man. **1953** in R.S. Gold *Jazz Talk* 177: That was Frog—Ben Webster! My man! **1953–55** Fine *Delinquents* 94: I…told moms I'd forgot something…and hoofed it back to my man. **1959–60** R. Reisner *Jazz Titans* 161: *My Man:* friend. **1972** P. Fenty *Superfly* (film): Hey, I gotta talk to my man. **1973** D. Ellington *Music Is My Mistress* 251: "Francis, you know Al Hibbler." "Why, that's my man." **1973** Andrews & Owens *Black Lang.* 49: *My man* refers to someone you dig. **1973–74** in *Urban Life* VI (1977) 128: He's always coming to school every day with five or ten dollars. So me and my man watched him for a week. **1975** B. Silverstein & R. Krate *Dark Ghetto* 191: Quit messin' with Randolph, he's my man, Jim! **1983** P. Dexter *God's Pocket* 113: The reason I'm tellin' you…is you're my man, Mick. You helped me out.

manavalins *n.pl.* [of unkn., prob. dial., orig.; cf. *F & H* (1896) "*Manarvel*…(nautical).—To pilfer small stores.…*Menavelings*…(railway clerks).—Odd money in the daily accounts."] *Naut.* scraps of food; leftovers.

   1841 [Mercier] *Man o' War* 179: De way dey overhaul a range of every pan, dish, and kettle, to find de *manavalins*, is nobody's business. **1846** Codman *Sailors' Life* 150: "Hooking manavlins" was a favorite amusement with him: not so much for gratifying his appetite, as for exercising his dexterity. **1849** Melville *White Jacket* 134: Hence the various sea-rolls, made dishes, and Mediterranean pies, well known by man-of-war's men…all of which come under the general denomination of *Manavalins.* **1868** Macy *There She Blows!* 280: A very small sum…was sufficient to spread a table (or sea-chest…) with baker's loaves, fresh butter and cheese, new milk, eggs, and various other "manavelins," as Jack terms them. **1887** Davis *Sea-Wanderer* 290: Bread crumbs and other broken victuals from the cabin table are manavelins. **1906** *Independent* (Jan. 4) 28: Ye scoff all ther menavilins [*sic*] yerself. **1945, 1980** in *DARE.*

man-catcher *n.* Esp. *Logging.* a recruiter for an employment agency; HEAD HUNTER. Also vars.

   1922 N. Anderson *Hobo* 5: Here men in search of work bargain for jobs in distant places with the "man catchers" from the agencies. **1926** *AS* I 652: *Man-catcher.* employment agency [*sic*]. **1926** Tully *Jarnegan* 62: He then hurried toward the Labor Agency and turned it in, giving the "man hunter" a dollar and a half. **1927** *DN* V 454: *Man catcher,* n. A runner or agent for a hobo employment agency. Also *man hunter.* **1927** *AS* (June) 391: A *mancatcher* is either a foreman or an [employment] agent looking for men. **1936** Tully *Bruiser* 116: A "man-catcher" touched Shane's arm.…"You look like you could do a day's work. Go get a valise to show good faith." **1956** Sorden & Ebert *Logger's* 23 [ref. to a1925]: *Man-catcher,* A man employed by a lumber company to recruit lumberjacks. **1958** McCulloch *Woods Wds.* 116: *Man catcher*—a. An employment agent, hangs around pool halls trying to round up a crew. b. A foreman or other company man trying to hire a crew. *Ibid.*: *Man getter*—Same as man catcher. *Ibid.*: *Man grabber*—Same as man catcher. *Ibid.*: *Man shark*—An employment agent.

Manchu Law *n.* [sugg. by *Manchu,* last ruling dynasty of China] *Army.* (see 1983 quot.). Hence **Manchu,** *v.*

   1924 *Inf. Jour.* (Feb.) 185: Due to the operation of the "Manchu Law," 13 Colonels, 9 Lieutenant Colonels, and 3 Majors of Infantry will be relieved from detail on the General Staff in the near future. **1929** J. Moss *Officers' Manual* (ed. 7) 416: *Manchu.* Refers to a law requiring officers to return to troop duty after a four-year absence. **1982** F. Hailey *Soldier Talk* 40: *Manchued.* Sometimes referred to as the "Manchu law" [etc.]. **1983** Elting et al. *Dict. Soldier Talk* 194: *Manchu Law*…A law limiting line officers' tours of staff duty in Washington to four years out of six. Passed by Congress in 1912, the year in which the Manchu rulers of China were driven out by revolution, this…legislation broke up…comfortable personal empires…[informally established by staff officers].

man-eater *n.* **1.** a person who is ferocious, predatory, or the like.

   1884 (quot. at RUSTLER). ***1906** in *OEDS:* To Spats' Beanties she was always Porline or The Man Eater. **1983** "Hall & Oates" *Maneater* (rock song): Watch out, boys, she'll chew you up.…She's a maneater. *a***1985** J.D. Lawrence *Fighting Soldier* 34 [ref. to 1918]: One day he pointed out one of his man-eaters and said, "Lawrence, there's a fellow

that's going to give the Huns hell when he can get his hands on them." *Ibid.* 35: How are the other man-eaters?

2. a dangerous piece of machinery; FOOL-KILLER, 2.

   1897 Hamblen *General Mgr.* 101: D'ye think I want to stay down in that black hole an' ladle lampblack into these ole man-eater's all my life? [*sc.,* a locomotive]. **1983** La Barge & Holt *Sweetwater Gunslinger* 233: Sweetwater approached the front of a turning A-7 [aircraft], better known as a "man-eater" because its intake can suck a man up like a vacuum cleaner.

3. a fellator.—usu. considered vulgar.

   1971 Hilaire *Thanatos* 57: Get this man-eater off me.

mang *v.* [< Welsh Romani *mang* 'to ask alms, beseech'] *Und.* to talk; (*hence*) to boast. Hence **mangsman,** *n.* a lawyer.

   ***1812** Vaux *Vocab.*: *Mang:* To speak or talk. ***1821** in Partridge *Dict. Und.* 431: They said they had done nothing to mang about. **1848** *Ladies' Repository* VIII (Oct.) 315: *Mang,* To talk. *Mangsman,* A lawyer.

mango *n.* **1.** usu. *pl.* a woman's breast.

   *a***1986** in *NDAS:* There's the old mangoes. **1990** T. Thorne *Dict. Contemp. Slang: Mangoes…American* breasts.

2. [sugg. by the unusual shape of the fuselage] (*cap.*) *Av.* the Transavia PL-12 Skyfarmer agricultural aircraft.

   1990 *Wings* (Discovery Channel TV): Nicknamed *Mango,*…the Transavia PL-12.

mangy *adj.* contemptible; LOUSY.

   ***1896** in *OEDS:* I cannot see that it much benefits any man to tell him all these mangy quaverings. **1931** Uhler *Cane Juice* 109: L.S.U.'s a lousy school.…It's mangy. **1942–49** Goldin et al. *DAUL* 135: *Mangey…*Lacking in underworld principle and pride; dirty; mean.

¶ In phrase:

¶ **mangy with** having an abundance of; *lousy with* s.v. LOUSY.

   1927 *AS* II 6 (Mar.) 277: *Mangy with*—covered with. **1952** Holmes *Boots Malone* (film): How mangy with dough you think she is?

manhole *n.* the vagina.—usu. considered vulgar. *Joc.* See also MANHOLE COVER, 1.

   1916 Cary *Venery* I 196: *Manhole*—The vagina. **1928** in Read *Lexical Evidence* 20: Read the Covered man hole/by Kotex. **1978** in *Maledicta* VI (1982) 25: Vagina…*man hole.*

manhole cover *n.* **1.** a sanitary napkin.—usu. considered vulgar. *Joc.*

   *a***1948** in *Word* IV (1948) 185: Menstruation…*Manhole cover.* **1970** Byrne *Memories* 83 [ref. to 1940's]: The whole subject of menstruation and sanitary napkins ("manhole covers") was out-of-bounds. **1973** *AS* XLVI 82.

2. *Mil.* a pancake. *Joc.*

   1961 Forbes *Goodbye to Some* 30 [ref. to WWII]: Hot cakes…stove lids, manhole covers. **1967** *DAS* (Supp.): *Manhole cover* Any large, round, flat object, esp. a pancake. **1969** Garfield *Thousand-Mile War* 188 [ref. to WWII]: Our so-called pancakes were popularly referred to as manhole covers. **1977** *M*A*S*H* (CBS-TV): These manhole covers aren't bad.

man-hunter var. MAN-CATCHER.

maniac *n.* ¶ In phrase: **master maniac** *R.R.* a master mechanic. *Joc.*

   1930 *Rail Road Man's Mag.* II 471: *Master Maniac*—The master mechanic. **1945** Hubbard *RR Ave.* 351: *Master Maniac*—Master mechanic, often abbreviated M.M. Oil is called *master mechanic's blood.* **1958** McCulloch *Woods Wds.* 117: *Master maniac*—The master mechanic in charge of power on a logging railroad.

man in the boat *n.* the clitoris.—constr. with *the.*—usu. considered vulgar. Cf. BOY IN THE BOAT.

   *a***1890–96** *F & H* IV 278: *The little man in the boat…*(venery).—The clitoris. ***1959** *Encounter* (May) 21: The man in the boat's my mascot. **1969** *Zap Comix* (No. 4) (unp.): And so it was as it was told by the old "man in the boat!" **1969** C. Major *All-Night Visitors* 11: It is a small man-in-a-boat. **1984** Caunitz *Police Plaza* 96: Please observe that the glans clitoris resembles a man standing in a boat. Hence…the nickname, the man in the boat.

mano *n.* [< Sp *hermano* 'brother'; infl. by MAN] *Hispanic-Amer.* MAN.—used in direct address.

   1967 Rechy *Numbers* 33: "Oh, gee, *mano,*" using the hip Mexican appellation, "I knew you weren't the paying kind." *Ibid.*: "Hiyah,

mano!" he calls. **1970** Landy *Underground Dict.: Mano*…Brother. Form of address to close friends. **1988** Norst *Colors* 139: You're going to make it, *mano*.

mantee *adj.* [orig. unkn.] *Homosex.* (of a lesbian) very masculine in appearance or behavior; given to taking the active role in copulation. Also as *n.* Cf. MINTY, *n.* & *adj.*

    [**1935** Pollock *Und. Speaks.: Mantee*, a sexual pervert.] **1936** Dai *Opium Addiction* 167: Patient usually takes the active role in her relation with women—what is called "Mantee" in the lingo of homosexuals. **1941** G. Legman, in G. Henry *Sex Vars.* 1171: *Mantee* A female homosexual with very masculine characteristics. The etymology is obscure, although a French origin of an older form, *mintee*, seems probable. The very virile stride of such Lesbians is termed a *mantee walk*. *a***1972** B. Rodgers *Queens' Vernacular* 71: *Mantee* ('40s)…primarily in…*mantee voice* (a deep bass) and *mantee walk* (swagger).

Man Upstairs *n.* God.—constr. with *the.*

    1969 Angelou *Caged Bird* 271: The Man upstairs, he don't make mistakes. **1981** *Times-Picayune* (N.O.) (Apr. 6) V 1: The Man Upstairs has got to be amused and a little puzzled by the character we just sent Him. **1986** Wilson & Maddock *Short Circuit* (film): One thing we can't control is the weather. The Man Upstairs is still in charge of that department. **1995** *N.Y. Times* (Oct. 15) ("Metro") 35 (headline): A Room Upstairs to View the Man Upstairs: Worship Grows in Apartments. **1996** *N.Y. Times* (Jan. 14) ("Arts & Leisure") 27: In "God," from her second album…[she] took on the Man Upstairs.

manure *n.* **1.** [intentional malapropism] *Mil. in France.* monsieur. *Joc.* [Quots. ref. to WWI.]

    1919 in Acker *Thru the War* 165: In France I never got much beyond the "wee-wee manure" stage. **1922** Paul *Impromptu* 143: Oui, manure.

    2. rubbish; lies; nonsense; BULLSHIT, 1.a.

    1923 in Hemingway *Sel. Letters* 85: I suppose this sounds like all sorts of Merde from the good old manure spreader. **1927–28** in R. Nelson *Dishonorable* 181: That's a lot o' manure about "duty," too. **1962** Kesey *Cuckoo's Nest* 65: What about this democratic-ward manure that the doctor was giving me?

manure-spreader *n.* **1.** (see quot.). Cf. SHIT.

    1952 C. Sandburg *Young Strangers* 163 [ref. to *ca*1895]: Later a farm machine came along that sent manure flying and spread it even over the soil, and a man talking too big was called a "manure-spreader."

    2. *Army.* a cavalryman.—used derisively. Now *hist.*

    1953 E. Leonard *Bounty Hunters* 23: Those gray-coated, sorghum-eating manure spreaders are up there. **1964** Webb *Cheyenne Autumn* (film): Guess they must've skedaddled when they heard you manure-spreaders was comin'. **1970** Army veteran, N.Y.C., age *ca*55 [ref. to 1941]: Once I heard the cavalry referred to as "U.S. government manure-spreaders." Some old sergeant who'd served at Fort Riley, Kansas, before the war [said it]. I think it was him.

many *adj.* ¶ In phrase: **too** [or **so**] **many** beyond one's ability to manage or comprehend; too (or so) much; overwhelming.

    1862 C.F. Browne *Artemus Ward* 144: O life! life!—*you're too many for me!* **1869** "M. Twain" *Innocents* I 81: The old man's too many for 'em. **1871** "M. Twain" *Roughing It* 253: You're most too many for me. **1871** "U. Bet" *Pious Tchi-Neh* 28: He's too many for you. **1883** *Life* (Jan. 11) 14: It must be, the salmon on which I fed/Has been too many for me. **1896** Ade *Artie* 104: Maybe I ain't so many but I'm a purty good thing at that. **1923** O'Brien *Best Stories of 1923* 145: I guess you ain't so many.

map *n.* **1.** the face.

    [**1848** Judson *Mysteries* 18: He had one of those bland, ever-smiling faces…and features that would form quite a map of study for a physiognomist.] [**1855** *Harper's Mag.* (Dec.) 37: The wayfarer…was…"chawed up."…his hair gone, his eye closed, his lips swollen, and his face generally "mapped out."] **1899** A.H. Lewis *Sandburrs* 9: I sees d' map of a skirt—a goil, I means, on a drop curtain at a swell t'eatre onct, an' it says under it she's Cleopatra. *Ibid.* 59: He simply fetches one of d' young ones a back-handed swipe across d' map wit' his mit. **1902** Cullen *More Tales* 38: There was something familiar about his map. **1903** *Enquirer* (Cincinnati) (May 9) 13: *Map*—A person's face. **1904** Hobart *Jim Hickey* 23: I'll…spoil that man's map. **1908** in Fleming *Unforgettable Season* 107: With not a sign of a smile on his freckled map. **1908** in H.C. Fisher *A. Mutt* 73: Note look of anxiety on the old gent's map. **1908** McGaffey *Show Girl* 200: Wifey hangs one on Alla's map. **1910** *N.Y. Eve. Jour.*

(Mar. 16) 15: William Upham, the lad with the Gibson map,…started in the box for the regulars. **1914** in Lardner *Round-up* 251: I busted up a guy's map. **1918** Baldwin, in *Canteening* 92: One of them generously offered to "spread the map" of the other; which…means either complete or partial disfigurement to one and sometimes both parties concerned. **1936** McCarty & Johnson *Great Guy* (film): He hardly had enough time to get his map scraped and massaged. **1938** T. Wolfe *Web & Rock* 530: They'll be eatin' it up. We'll spread your map all over the front page, momma. **1967** [R. Beck] *Pimp* 162: Freeze your "map" and keep it that way. **1969** in *Playboy* (Jan. 1970) 294: And you, wipe that grin off yer map, Mack! **1971** Curtis *Banjo* 255: No mistaking that map.

    2.a. *Und.* a bank check, esp. if fraudulent.

    1926 (quot. at DROP, *v.*, 2.c.). **1928** J. O'Connor *B'way Racketeers* 29: The art of passing sheets or dropping maps, the alternative term employed in the jargon of the underworld. *Ibid.* 253: *Map Dropper*—One who cashes bad checks. **1956** "T. Betts" *Across the Board* 125: He gave me a contract to take care of a $10,000 map. *Ibid.* 317: *Map* A bank check; not necessarily bad, yet frequently heard in the sense, "He gave me a bum map." **1961** Scarne *Comp. Guide to Gambling* 684: *Map* a check.—"Don't take that guy's map; he's a paperhanger."

    b. a restaurant check.

    1952 *Park East* (Sept.) 20: A restaurant check is "the map."

    ¶ In phrase:

    ¶ **map of** —— facial features typical of natives of (the specified location).

    1902–03 (quot. at DIAL). **1928** Nason *Top Kick* [ref. to 1918]: I wish we had as fine a map of Munster in the war office as you've got on your face. **1935** Mackenzie *Been Place* 46: He was the phoniest-looking Irishman I had ever seen.…The map of Jerusalem was all over his face.…I'll bet…his real name is Levi or Cohen. **1940** E. O'Neill *Long Day's Journey* II ii: And keep your dirty tongue off Ireland! You're a fine one to sneer, with the map of it on your face!

maraca *n.* usu. *pl.* a woman's breast.

    1940 J. O'Hara *Pal Joey* 180: Gams and a pair of maracas that will haunt me in my dreams. **1961** T.I. Rubin *In the Life* 62: Knockers, maracas, boobies. Let's face it, Doc: I got a good shape. *Ibid.* 158: *Maracas.* Breasts. **1970** Thackrey *Thief* 68: It was her, all right.…The same build, the same walk, the same big maracas. **1978** T. Sanchez *Zoot-Suit* 195: A pair of maracas no bigger than pigeon's eggs! **1990** T. Thorne *Dict. Contemp. Slang: Maracas*…breasts. A mainly American usage.

marble *v.* [var. MARVEL] (see quots.).

    1873 *Slang & Vulgar Phrs.* 16: *Marble*, for move off; as, "If you do that again you must *marble*," *i.e.*. move quickly, be off immediately. **1889–90** Barrère & Leland *Dict. Slang* II 43: *Marble* (American)…To bound, bounce, or run along. From a boy's marble thrown along a sidewalk.

marble garden *n.* MARBLE ORCHARD.

    1962 Ark. teenager (coll. J. Ball): We don't have any Draculers in the marble gardens 'round here.

marblehead *n.* **1.** a dolt. Also **marble dome.**

    1919 *DN* V 62: *Marble-dome*, a dullard. There is no doubt about it, you are a *marble-dome*. New Mexico. **1951** Bowers *Mob* (film): All right, marbleheads, now shut up and listen to me.

    2. a bald man.—used derisively.

    1973 Lucas, Katz & Huyck *Amer. Graffiti* 66: I said go kiss a duck, marblehead.

marble heart *n.* an unfeeling rejection or refusal; cold shoulder.—constr. with *the.*

    [**1863** in Hay *Lincoln* 118: Spent evening at the theatre.…J. Wilkes Booth was doing the "Marble Heart."] **1896** in J.M. Carroll *Benteen-Goldin Letters* 271: "Custer's woman" gave him the marble heart in the finest of shapes. **1897** *Pop. Sci. Mo.* (Apr.) 833: To refuse a person's appeal is *to give him the marble heart.* **1897** Ade *Pink* 182: He sutny got 'e mahble h'aht f'om little Miss Lo'ena. **1897** in Outcault *Yellow Kid* [Pl. 75]: De marbil hart…dat goil guv me. **1902** Mead *Word-Coinage* 167: "A cold frost" and "frost crystals" and "he gave me the marble heart" mean to be treated coldly. **1904** in B. Buckley *Frankie* 238: He died with the marble heart. **1905** W.S. Kelly *Lariats* 237: Some goil has given yer de marble heart, has she? **1939** Howsley *Argot* 32: *Marble Heart*…a chilly reception.

marble orchard *n. Esp. West.* a cemetery.

    1925 T.A. Dorgan, in Zwilling *TAD Lexicon* 56: Listening to one of those ancestor pests as you stroll through an old marble orchard. **1929**

M. Gill *Und. Slang: Marble orchard*—Cemetery. **1935** Pollock *Und. Speaks: Marble orchard*, a cemetery. **1940** *AS* (Dec.) 447: *Marble Orchard.* Cemetery. "I don't like to pass through that marble orchard of a dark night." **1941** *AS* (Feb.) 23: *Marble orchard.* Cemetery. **1941** in *DAS:* You'll get your names in this marble orchard soon enough. **1944** Busch *Dream of Home* 147: It…[had] a notable nickname: "The Marble Orchard." **1959** *Swinging Syllables: Marble orchard*—Cemetery. **1977** *L.A. Times* (Nov. 14) II 1: Time never returns. I'll worry about time when I'm in the marble orchard. **1980** *L.A. Times* (Mar. 20) V 1: Nice old cemeteries of the kind called marble orchards.

marbles *n.pl.* **1.** possessions or interests; (*hence*) money, esp. stakes.

1864 Hotten *Slang Dict.* (ed. 3): "Money and *marbles*," cash and personal effects. *a*1890 in Barrère & Leland *Dict. Slang* II 43: It's rough, as he says;/No marbles, no lodging, no grub, and that sort o' thing for days! **1924** in Hammett *Continental Op* 62: I'm betting my marbles that the job was made in Tijuana. **1949** W.R. Burnett *Asphalt Jungle* 80: I've got no choice when you're playing for those kind of marbles. **1955** Mainwaring *Body-Snatchers* (film): Well, you win. Pick up the marbles. **1958** Frankel *Band of Bros.* 38: We're not in Korea to protect our own marbles. **1971** *Playboy* (June) 216: I enjoy the fact that we're playing for big marbles. **1972** B. Jackson *In the Life* 29: We have always defined out of the moral scheme those whose marbles we wanted: the Indians…were driven off. **1973** Walkup & Otis *Race* 25: It don't make bad sense, I mean, if you're not counting on picking up all the marbles. **1981** M. Frohman *All the Marbles* [film title]. **1995** *Time* (Sept. 18) 69: This is for all the marbles, you know. The presidency is riding on this one.

2. one's sanity or good sense; esp. in phr. **lose (one's) marbles.**

1902 Hobart *Up to You* 64: I see-sawed back and forth between Clara J. and the smoke-holder like a man who is shy some of his marbles. **1927** *AS* II 360: *Marbles, doesn't have all his*…mentally deficient. "There goes a man who doesn't have all his marbles." **1941** in Algren *Neon Wilderness* 65: 'N Hungry don't have all his marbles even. **1951** Hackett & Goodrich *Dividend* (film): What's the matter, Jack? You losin' your marbles? **1952** Mandel *Angry Strangers* 99: This guy got all his marbles, Robert? **1954** Gaddis *Birdman* 140: Stroud was a square con, always for his side. But he ain't got them marbles no more. **1957** Myrer *Big War* 182: "Where's his silver bells?" "In his head.…Instead of the marbles." **1959** Searls *Big X* 216: "What about his mental condition?" "Will he have all his marbles?" **1959** Cochrell *Barren Beaches* 257: I wondered if I was losing my marbles. **1959** Morrill *Dark Sea* 168 [ref. to WWII]: Sir, the Old Man's blown his marbles. He's spraying the Jap sub with gasoline. **1961** Brosnan *Pennant Race* 20: Presumably this guy lost a lot of his marbles betting against the Dodgers in the '59 World Series.…Particularly, he hates Duke Snider. **1962** *Twilight Zone* (CBS-TV): An old lady who had no marbles in her head! **1966** in T.C. Bambara *Gorilla* 42: He was in some kind of big house for people who lose their marbles. **1967** Dibner *Admiral* 287: He's lost his marbles, Nick. **1970** La Motta, Carter & Savage *Raging Bull* 174: He ended up in the loony bin, his marbles jarred loose. **1971** Freeman *Catcher* (film): Have you lost the last of your marbles? **1971** *Adam-12* (NBC-TV): I hope you're kidding, because if you're not I'm going to…trade you in for a partner with a full set of marbles. **1971** *N.Y. Times Bk. Rev.* (Mar. 21) 40: This up-to-date slant on an old subject actually enables Wallace to include women who have other things loose besides their morals—such as their marbles. **1972** *N.Y. Times Mag.* (Dec. 17) 62: Have you lost your marbles? **1972** W.C. Anderson *Hurricane* 146: I think your marble bag has a hole in it. **1972–73** A.J. Bell *Brown's Lounge:* He ain't got his marbles. **1973** *Odd Couple* (ABC-TV): That new book on psychiatry, *Find Your Marbles.* **1974** "A.C. Clark" *Revenge* 178: Do something about your brother! He's blowing his fuckin' marbles! **1976** Slate & Berry *Bigfoot* 90: So, I thought to myself, it's as plain as day, I'm losing my marbles! **1990** *Playwrights Theater* (A&E-TV): I think I might be losing my marbles. **1994** *Donahue* (NBC-TV): That guy has lost his marbles ninety-nine percent.…But that one marble saved everybody. **1996** Public service announcement (NBC-TV): Anybody who doesn't give teachers a big "Thanks!" has lost their marbles.

3. the testicles; in phr. **crack marbles** to induce orgasm (in a man).—usu. considered vulgar.—also used in fig. phrs.

1916 Cary *Venery* I 197: *Marbles*—The testes. **1952** Larson *Barnyard Folk* 78: Masturbation…*rolling your marbles.* **1953** Brossard *Bold*

Saboteurs 92: I will grab him by his marbles down there and threaten to change him into a girl. **1953–55** Kantor *Andersonville* 129: Ma'am, you got all the smart out of my marbles. **1957** E. Brown *Locust Fire* 175 [ref. to WWII]: Don't get your marbles in an uproar. **1964** McKenna *Sons of Martha* 145 [ref. to *ca*1935]: What you buy in Frisco is just the orgasm.…If they can crack a pair of marbles every two minutes, why, that's just the old Henry Ford spirit. **1973** Hirschfeld *Victors* 99: You know what, heaving them cans, you'll bust your marbles. **1978** in *Maledicta* VI (1982) 23: Testicles…*marbles.*

4. *Drag Racing.* pebbles or gravel lying on a racecourse.

1980 Pearl *Pop. Slang* 97: *Marbles* n. (Auto Racing) pebbles, gravel, dust, etc., making an area of a racing course slippery.

¶ In phrase:

¶ **pick up (one's) marbles** to quit or withdraw, usu. indignantly. Cf. **(1)**, above.

1928 C. MacArthur *War Bugs* 29: They implied that war wasn't any good and advised us to pick up our marbles and go home. **1950** Solt *Lonely Place* (film): You mean you picked up your little marbles, I hope.

marching order *n.* **1.** *pl.* a dismissal; walking papers.

1856 Doten *Journals* I 291: Today is the day on which those under *marching orders* from the V.C. have to leave. **1919** Darling *Jargon Book* 21: *Marching Orders*—Told to go away.

2. *Mil.* a pie crust.—constr. with *light* or *heavy.*

1918 (quot. at **slum**). **1918** Ruggles *Navy Explained* 127: If the stew is covered over with a crust, as is usually the case, they call it stew in heavy marching order. **1918** *Lit. Digest* (Oct. 19) 55: We can not help wondering if the party who wrote this Bose Pont letter can define "monkey meat," "gold fish," or "goulash in light marching order."

marching powder *n. Narc.* cocaine.—constr. with a So. American place name. *Joc.* Also **marching dust.**

1984 J. McInerney *Big City* 2: Your brain at this moment is composed of brigades of tiny Bolivian soldiers.…They need the Bolivian Marching Powder. **1987** *Miami Vice* (NBC-TV): Let me guess. It's some Medellín marching dust. **1988** Univ. Tenn. student theme: Cocaine…*blow, toot, snow, crack, freebase, Peruvian marching powder.* **1994** *Street Terms: Drugs* (Drugs & Crime Data Center) (Internet): *Bolivian marching powder*—cocaine.

mare *n.* a woman.—usu. used in sexual contexts. [The nuances posited in *1977 BrE quot. appear to be irrelevant to general AmE.]

*1303 in *OED:* And shame hyt ys euer to be called a prestes mare. *1590 in *OEDS:* The man shall have his mare again. *1708 in [J. Roberts] *Merry-Thought* I 24: But why the Devil should I care,/Since I can find another Mare? **1928** R.A. Bartlett *Log* 5: There was Inuaho on Peary's ship the *Roosevelt.*…Her name wasn't easy to say so we called her "The Black Mare" from the long ebony locks that hung over her shoulders. **1942** Algren *Morning* 174: The old mares holdin' theirselves up by the bar-rail at 4 A.M. cadgin' drinks…them's the ones been straight all their lives. **1942** Davis & Wolsey *Call House Madam* 302: I liked Sabina—but what a hot mare! [*1977 in Partridge *Concise Dict. Sl.:* "Bitch" connotes contrariness in addition to slight bad temper; "cow" the next degree of unpleasantness. "Mare" is easily the worst and most insulting.] **1987** "J. Hawkins" *Tunnel Warriors* 117: He likes to mount his mares from behind, baby. *a*1989 in Kisseloff *Must Remember This* 325: That's where all of the fast-track people would hang out to make contact with each other, the stallions, the mares, and the fillies. *1990 Thorne *Dict. Contemp. Sl.: Mare*…a woman. A derogatory working-class usage…Mare usually designates a drab, wearisome woman. **1990** Rukuza *West Coast Turnaround* 124: This mare is gonna need mounting.

mare's leg *n. So.* (see quot.). Cf. **hog-leg.**

1975 Camden, Ark., man, age *ca*23: A hog's leg is a big old-fashioned cap-and-ball pistol. A mare's leg is the same thing, or else a sawed-off Winchester like Steve McQueen used to carry [in the 1950's western series *The Bounty Hunter*] on TV.

marge *n.* [fr. *Marge*, hypocoristic form of female given name *Marjorie*; semantic devel. unkn.] *Homosex.* a lesbian who takes the passive role in copulation. Also as adj.

1956 Reinhardt *Sex Perversions* 48: *Marge*—noun. The very feminine passive dyke. Adjective—feminine. **1967** *DAS* (Supp.): *Marge*…A female homosexual who takes the passive, female role. **1982** R.I. McDavid, in RH files: *Marge*…*Slang* The passive partner in a Lesbian relationship. David Maurer—tapes. **1996** N.Y.C. lesbian, age 28 (coll. J. Sheidlower): I've heard *marge* for a passive lesbian, but not often. All the active/passive distinctions are becoming less common nowadays.

maricón *n.* [< Sp (vulgar slang)] *Hispanic-Amer.* a homosexual man; (often used as a general term of abuse).—used contemptuously.

    1967 *DAS* (Supp.): *Maricon...*A male homosexual....*often used as an interj. having a force equivalent to that of "bastard."* **1970** Landy *Underground Dict.* 105: Fag, faggot,...*maricón* **1983** *Harper's* (July) 56: If he is with her, that *maricón*) I will cut out his heart. *a***1986** in *NDAS:* "This is it, maricon," snarled the Puerto Rican. **1996** Philbin *Cop Speak* 148: *Maricon* A homosexual. This Spanish slang term is used by both Hispanic and non-Hispanic police.

marihoochie *n.* [*marijuana* + HOOCH[1], *n.*] *Stu.* marijuana. Also **marihooch.**

    1971 in L. Bangs *Psychotic Reactions* 81: North African marihooch. **1974** *TULIPQ* (coll. B.K. Dumas): Marijuana...*marihuchie.* *a***1990** P. Dickson *Slang!* 117: *Marahoochie.* Marijuana.

marine *n.* **1.** *Navy.* a drained liquor bottle; DEAD MARINE. *Rare* in U.S. [An anecdote fr. an 1864 jokebook crediting the usage to William IV is reprinted in *F & H* IV 282.]

    [*****1785** Grose *Vulgar Tongue: Marine officer.* An empty bottle: marine officers being held useless by the seamen. Sea wit.] *****1805** J. Davis *Post-Captain* 26: You, steward! don't you see the bottle is a marine! *****1831** Trelawny *Adv. Younger Son* 50: There's nothing but marines and bottoms on the table. **1883** Russell *Sailors' Lang.* 89: *Marine.*—An empty bottle. Sometimes called dead marine or marine officer. **1954–60** *DAS: Marine...*An empty whisky or beer bottle.

2. *Orig. Naut.* a landlubber or lubberly seaman; (*also*) a stupid or gullible person. Now chiefly *hist.* Cf. *tell it to the marines,* below.

    [*****1785** (quot. at **(1)**, above).] **1835** *Mil. & Nav. Mag. of U.S.* (May) 222: Tumble up, you lubbers, cooks, idlers, snobs, tailors and marines. **1835** [Ingraham] *South-West* I 15: A meddling, bustling passenger...is always a "lubberly green horn," or "clumsy marine." **1834–40** R.H. Dana, Jr. *2 Yrs. Before Mast* ch. xvii: "Marine" is the term applied more particularly to a man who is ignorant and clumsy about seaman's work—a greenhorn...a landlubber. **1851** [G.A. Worth] *Recoll.* 17: Their notion...might appear very plausible to the *marines,* but...[not to] him. **1889** "M. Twain" *Conn. Yankee* 44: Oh, call me pet names, dearest, call me a marine! In twice a thousand years shall the unholy invention of man labor at odds to beget the fellow to this majestic lie! **1902** M.W. Gibbs *Shadow and Light* 116: There may be some difference..."to the marines." **1934** W. White & T. Marquis *Custer* 17 [ref. to 1873]: He was the butt of many jokes. Some of the boys told him, "You have been promoted to the Marines."...The victim appeared fully convinced. **1942** Kline & MacKenzie *Boots On* (film): I've served four hitches in the U.S. Cavalry and I thought I've seen everything, but you can call me a marine if that isn't the——. **1959** Sterling *Wahoo* 37 [ref. to WWII]: I shouldered somebody aside and opened the hatch...saying, "Don't be a Marine all your life."

3. a tall tale; lie.

    1887 *Outing* (Dec.) 226: That there yarn, too, about the sailors bein' frightened is all a "marine." In the first place, if they was sailors they wouldn't be frightened.

¶ In phrase:

¶ **tell it to the marines** *Orig. Navy.* (used as an expression of disbelief). Also (*obs.*) vars., occ. elab. [Discussed by Col. A.F. Moe, "Tell It to the Marines," *AS* XXXVI (1961), pp. 243–57. In 20th-C. U.S. use, the notion of the "marine" as exceptionally credulous has been lost. Though the phr. did not orig. refer to the U.S. Marine Corps, writers have occ. tried to rationalize the presumptive [reference in var. unconvincing ways.]

    *****1805** J. Davis *Post-Captain* 25: "But the lady, sir, is English. Her husband at least said so." "He may tell that to the marines, but the sailors will not believe him." *Ibid.* 27: She may tell the marines that; but the sailors will not believe it. *Ibid.* 55: You may tell that to the marines, but I'll be d—d if the sailors will believe it. **1832** Wines *2½ Yrs.* 45: When a sailor hears a fish story, his only answer almost always is, "Tell that to a marine!" **1833** N. Ames *Yarns* 147: "She's the governor's niece," said Morton. "You may tell that to the marines," said Coffin. *Ibid.* 335: "Sed

non ego credulus illis," or, in plain English, "they may tell that to the marines, the sailors won't believe them." **1835** *Knickerbocker* (Jan.) 25: That will do for marines, Mr. Harris. **1843** [W.T. Thompson] *Scenes in Ga.* 138: Bah!...that'll do for the marines. **1849–50** in Glanz *Jew in Folklore* 181: Tell that to the marines...for you can't make us swallow that for duff. **1850** *Harper's Mag.* (Dec.) 33: Come, come, Jemmy, you should tell that dream to the marines; the sailors can't bolt it; it's rather too tough. **1851** Lynch *Naval Life* 11: One of my messmates...called out, "Tell that to the marines, you look too much as I do when I spin a yarn." **1855** Wise *Tales for Marines* 190: "Tell that to the marines!" exclaimed the useful matron standing before the fire. **1866** Shanks *Recollections* 28: The letter ends by advising Hood to tell his tale of oppression "to the marines" as he (Sherman) is not to be imposed upon. **1870** *Galaxy* (Aug.) 226: "We've heard that story before." "Tell that to the marines." **1871** Thomes *Whaleman* 17: "In two years ye'll all be so rich that you won't know what to do with your money." "That will do for the marines," grumbled one of the men. **1881** A.A. Hayes *New Colo.* 56: He made a remark common to naval men, about "telling that to the marines." *a***1881** G.C. Harding *Misc. Writings* 131: Don't drink? Tell that to marines. **1883** Sweet & Knox *Mustang* 45: Aw, now! tell that to the marines. **1887** W. Watson *Life in Confed. Army* 290: We have got them all penned up now, boys....Tell that to the marines. **1889** *United Service* (Apr.) 400: There are a great many stories told about marines which really do not pertain to the American marines, but come down to them from the English. "Tell it to the marines," is a big chesnut [*sic*], and as old as the hills. **1906** Beyer *Battleship* 82: "Tell it to a marine"—a remark used when one person does not believe a statement another is telling him. **1927** C. McKay *Harlem* 22: "I love you. I ain't got no man." "Gwan, tell that to the marines," he panted. *****1931** J. Hanley *Boy* 181: That's the truth, sir....You'd better tell that to the Marines. **1962** Morris & Morris *Dict. of Wd. & Phr. Orig.* 228: While it's true that the expression is sometimes heard as "Tell it to the horse marines," the simpler horseless version came first. **1966** J. Lewis *Tell It to the Marines* [title]. **1968** Spooner *War in General* 201: Tell it to the Marines. **1978** R. Price *Ladies' Man* 244: "But it's not as scary as it looks." "Oh, yeah? Tell it to the marines." **1996** N.Y.C. tech. editor, age *ca*60: *Tell it to the marines* is something you'd say to someone if you wanted to say, "That's incredible. I don't believe it."...It's said in a very sarcastic way....I don't think I've heard it since high school.

Marine Tiger *n.* (among Puerto Ricans in N.Y.C.) (see 1989 quot.).

    1952 H. Ellson *Golden Spike* (gloss.). **1959** E. Hunter *Killer's Wedge* 50: Look, you little slut, cut the Marine Tiger bit, will you? We know you didn't just get off the boat. **1989** Courtwright et al. *Addicts Who Survived* 214: The "Marine Tiger" was a Liberty ship that made several trips between San Juan and New York after World War II, carrying many thousand Puerto Rican immigrants. "Marine Tigers" became the derisive nickname for these newcomers, who were looked down upon by Puerto Ricans born or long settled in New York.

mark *n.* **1.** *Und.* an item to be stolen or a location to be robbed; (*hence*) (among tramps) a place where alms may be easily secured.

    *****1742** in Partridge *Dict. Und.* 432: I seeing there was a large Parcel of Plate, told my companions there was a *Mark,* and we agreed to have it. *****1753** in *OED:* He shew'd us all one particular Pack, and said that's your Mark. **1895** *Harper's Wkly.* (Aug. 10) 757: I asked one of the tramps...whether he knew of any "mark"* in the town....*A house where something is always given to beggars. *a***1909** Tillotson *Detective* 102: He proceeds to his "mark" at the most opportune time. *ca***1920** in Bruns *Kts. of Road* 93: The Safecracker...The Main Stem I prowl for a mark. **1930** "D. Stiff" *Milk & Honey* 210: A *mark* is a...place good for food, clothes or money. **1933** *Amer. Mercury* (Apr.) 393: A *mark* was a safe that could be blown, and *to kipp* was to sleep. **1931–34** in Clemmer *Pris. Comm.* 334: *Mark...*A safe which may be opened with an explosive. **1934** Weseen *Dict. Amer. Sl.* 25: *Mark*—A place selected for robbery. **1949** in *Harper's* (Feb. 1950) 70: A mark may be any considerable sum of money or the equivalent in readily convertible swag....Marks are either dug up or tipped off. **1968** "H. King" *Box-Man* 25: Every other joint...is a mark. **1984** *Time* (Aug. 27) 38: His home had been tossed by burglars, his stereo and video equipment stolen....It appeared that the welcoming signs of kindly neighbors had pointed out the mark.

2.a. *Und.* a victim or prospective victim of swindlers or other criminals; SUCKER.

*1749 in Partridge *Dict. Und.* 431: You are a full Mark; you can't well be missed. *1845 in *OEDS*: I heard it casually from the lips of apparently respectable settlers as they rode on the highway, "Such and such a one is a good mark!—simply a person who pays his men their wages, without delays or drawbacks; a man to whom you may sell anything safely. *1860 in Partridge *Dict. Und.* 432: "There's a mark!" exclaimed one to the other, looking towards the spot where Hatcher was standing. *1883 in *OEDS*: Publicans...are usually the unfortunate tradesmen fixed on as a mark. *1885 in *F & H* IV 283: The girl, a likely mark, was a simple country lass. 1886 (cited in Partridge *Dict. Und.* 432). *1889–90 Barrère & Leland *Dict. Slang* II 44: Mark (Swindlers), one marked by thieves or swindlers as easy to dupe or rob. 1890 Quinn *Fools of Fortune* 231: He has found a "soft mark," (which in the vernacular of the [gambling] profession means a particularly gullible dupe). 1896 Lillard *Poker Stories* 54: The dealer fixed the deck and dealt out a good poker hand to the mark. 1896 Ade *Artie* 96: When that kind of a mark comes in they get out the bottle o' knock-out drops and get ready to do business. 1902 K. Harriman *Ann Arbor Tales* 227: This town is jammed full of marks—soft, easy, mushy marks. 1914 Jackson & Hellyer *Vocab.* 57: Mark, Noun General currency. A man; a prospective victim. 1915 Wald *Henry St.* 222: The young lads...were often wholly unaware that they themselves were, to use their own diction, "easy marks." 1928 *Amer. Mercury* (May) 79: The *stall* is putting the *mark*...in the right position [for the picking of his pocket]. 1930 *Variety* (Jan. 8) 123: I'm working the gimmick on a mark who looks like a solid chump when the law grabs me....Every mark has larceny in his heart, and that makes it sweet for the pickers. 1944 *Papers Mich. Acad.* XXX 599: Prison Jargon...*Mark*, a victim. 1949 *N.Y. Times* (Aug. 28) I 63: His "marks"—as the gullible are called by pitchman [*sic*]. 1969 Angelou *Caged Bird* 214: They chose their victims (marks) from the wealthy bigoted whites. 1974 *Police Woman* (NBC-TV): Why did you pick Corbett as a mark? Wasn't that a little bit stupid? 1977 A. Patrick *Beyond Law* 24: This broad walks in—a real mark and coked up to the gills. 1978 *Gamblers* 20: One never gave the "mark," or sucker, an even break. 1982 Hayano *Poker Faces* 10: Anticipating a big score, the mark then places a big bet of his own. 1994 "G. Indiana" *Rent Boy* 67: It's this shanghai operation they've been planning....The mark's name is a Mr. Lindner.

b. Orig. *Und.* a naive or gullible person; one who may easily be imposed upon; (*obs.*) a fool.

   *1879 (cited in Partridge *Dict. Und.* 432). 1896 Ade *Artie* 29: I was a great big mark to ever go chasin' after her in the first place. *Ibid.* 49: I guess this girl Billy knew spotted us for a couple of easy marks, for she floated away somewhere and came back with a friend of hers. 1896 in *OEDS* s.v. *easy*: *Easy mark*, an easy prey to a joke. 1899 A.H. Lewis *Sandburrs* 11: You can see be d' little mark's mug he's got an awful scare t'run into him, t'inkin' he's out to boin in d' buildin'. 1899 Kountz *Baxter's Letters* 50: A lot of these handsome gazabes...have had a run of luck and landed in among a bunch of marks. 1900 Dreiser *Carrie* 29 [ref. to 1889]: You ought to have seen the tie he had on. Gee, but he was a mark. 1903 *Enquirer* (Cincinnati) (May 9) 13: *Mark*—An easy-going, unsuspicious person. 1905 *Variety* (Dec. 30) 8: Gee...New Yorkers are marks. 1917–20 Dreiser *Newspaper Days* 386 [ref. to 1893]: Don't you think I'm on? Don't be a mark. 1926 Siringo *Riata & Spurs* 63: I was an "easy mark" for the city people. 1938 *AS* (Apr.) 156: *Mark*. An exceptionally stupid beginner in the [Douglas Aircraft] factory. 1962 Crump *Killer* 298: Hey, you marks, pass me a bottle of that joy juice. 1983 Flaherty *Tin Wife* 205: You don't pity a willing mark.

c. *Sports.* an easily defeated opponent; pushover.

   1914 Patten *Lefty o' the Bush* 41: They're marks....Anybody with a straight ball...could have held 'em. 1913–15 Van Loan *Taking the Count* 14: He's lost it. And now he's a mark for a second-rater. 1920–21 Witwer *Leather Pushers* 127: He'd be a dazed mark for Capato then.

d. *Carnival.* a person other than a carnival worker, criminal, or police officer; carnival customer.

   1935 *Amer. Mercury* (June) 230: [Among carnival workers:] Mark: citizen; a word derived possibly from *mark*, meaning *target*. 1946 Gresham *Nightmare Alley* 4: The "marks" surged in—young fellows in straw hats. 1946 Dadswell *Hey, Sucker!* 96: *Mark*...town person, man or woman. 1952 *N.Y. Times* (May 18) VI 58: The marks get lost down the back end with all those girls and freaks. 1956 H. Gold *Not With It* 5: All he asked of them was to ease loose the marko's fist. 1958 A. King *Mine Enemy* 21:

The marks get a bang out of all that ice. 1962 T. Berger *Reinhart in Love* 124: And as to the audience, well how many marks you gonna draw on seven-eighty? 1972 *Playboy* (Feb.) 126: Fake fight or real, the holler 'n' uproar had been fair enough to fill the tent with marks. 1983 *Batman* (Apr.) 17: I wrestled alligators to entertain the marks.

e. *Pros.* a customer of a prostitute.

   1967 Spillane *Delta* 31: Cute little hooker...kept the room three years....She never brought her marks here with her. 1970 Major *Dict. Afro-Amer. Sl.*: *Mark*...a trick. 1978–79 in E.M. Miller *Street Woman* 165: I be thinkin' he was a good old mark.

mark *v. Und.* to identify (a target or victim).

   1942–49 Goldin et al. *DAUL* 135: *Mark*...to select, or *put the finger on*, as a prospective victim of murder or robbery. 1993 Stuart & Twohy *Fugitive* (film): I [just now] marked him. I got him now.

marker *n.* ¶ In phrase: **call in (one's) marker** to demand repayment of a favor.

   1983 N. Proffitt *Gardens of Stone* 59: You owe me, Gordy, and I'm calling in my marker. 1986 *T.J. Hooker* (CBS-TV): It's for favors previously rendered. I'm calling in your marker. *a*1990 R. Herman, Jr. *Force of Eagles* 156: General, why do I think you're calling in...what do your people say?...a marker?

Mark I *adj.* [sugg. by the custom of designating the orig. model of certain weapons *Mark I*, and succeeding models *Mark II, Mark III*, etc.; *Mod* for 'modification'] *Mil.* basic, unmodified, or unsurpassable; old-fashioned; in phr. **Mark I [, Mod O] eyeball** direct human vision as distinct from radar or a computer display.

   1926 Nason *Chevrons* 120 [ref. to 1918]: "No," said the captain, slowly, "this is going to be a real, old issue, Mark I scrap." 1967 W. Crawford *Gresham's War* 188 [ref. to Korean War]: He had...given that lash-up a Mark I Eyeball Inspection. *1981 in Partridge *Concise Dict. Sl.* 279: Mark-one eyeball. 1989 C. Bennett *Bitburg* 73: An unobstructed view for the "Mark One Eyeball." 1990 Berent *Steel Tiger* 194: We've got to get the Mark I, Mod O eyeball on the target. 1991 Dorr & Benson *TAC Fighters* 113: Difficult to see with your Mark One Eyeball. 1993 P. Dickson *War Slang* 354: *Mark one eyeball*. Human sight...This term came into play during the moon landings, which were helped considerably by the mark one eyeball.

Marlboro country *n.* [after the remote Western landscapes in advertisements for *Marlboro* cigarettes often with tag line "come to Marlboro country"] rough or remote country; wilderness.

   1968 Gover *JC* 73: Sure is marlboro country. Ain't a soul in sight. Nothin but sand and water. 1970 *Harper's* (Aug.) 39: One of the good things about Marlboro country and such, where men are men and pack something...to prove it. *a*1982 Dunstan *Viet. Tracks* 121: In the "Marlboro Country" west of An Khe. 1985 Real estate ad, in *RHD* files: Marlboro Country in California Pines. Your opportunity to own an acre hideaway north of Reno.

marlinespike *n.* [alluding to long, pointed tail feathers] a tropical bird; (*also*) a jaeger.

   1858 in C.A. Abbey *Before the Mast* 146: A number of "*marlin-spikes*" flying about & uttering their shrill cries. [*1867 in *OED*: Boatswain-bird, *Phaeton zitherens*...It is distinguished by two long feathers in the tail, called the marling-spike.] 1890 *Century Dict.*

¶ In phrase:

¶ **look marlinespikes** to glare; look daggers.

   *1805 J. Davis *Post-Captain* 27: Why, when I took his wife by the hand, he looked at me marlinespikes. 1833 Ames *Old Sailor's Yarns* 173: I took notice that he looked marline-spikes at Mr. Morton for paying so much attention to the girl. 1841 [Mercier] *Man O' War* 144: He looked marlin-spikes at you as he picked himself up.

maroon *n.* [joc. alter. of *moron*] an obnoxious or foolish person.

   1941 Horman *Buck Privates* (film): Go on, maroon, get a seat. 1945 Warner Bros. *Merrie Melodies* "Hare Conditioned" (animation): What a dope! What a maroon! 1947 Warner Bros. *Looney Tunes* (animation): What a maroon! What a ignoramus! 1947 *ATS* (Supp.): Unpopular person....maroon, a moronic "goon." 1978 *UTSQ*: What a *maroon!* 1990 *ALF* (NBC-TV): What a maroon! 1992 N. Cohn *Heart of World* 225: "What a maroon," she said.

marrowbone *n.* **1.** usu. *pl.* a knee.

   *1532 in *OED*: Down he fel vpon his maribones. *1667 in *OED*: Down on your marrowbones, and confess the truth. ***1791** in *OED:* Bring on his marrowbones th'apostate down. ***1814** in Wetherell *Adventures* 314: The old man [fell] down on his marrow bones. **1828** Bird *Looking Glass* 3: Mankind…/Went on their marrow-bones, and begged permission. **1843** "J. Slick" *High Life in N.Y.* 28: That would bring Jonathan Slick on his marrow bones. **1847** Downey *Portsmouth* 230: They dropped their muskets and off knap sacks, and down on their marrow bones they went and began to [drink]. **1855** W.G. Simms *Forayers* 141: I'll hev' you…on your marrow-bones before me. **1859** "Skitt" *Fisher's River* 38 [ref. to 1820's]: Rip shins and marrer bones! Wake snakes, the winter's broke! **1861** M.A. Denison *Ruth Margerie* 81: I'll double my marrow-bones t'ye, sir, if that'll do any good. **1866** Locke *Round the Cirkle* 24: Sed state…wuz the first to git down on her marrow bones, and beg for peace like a dorg. **1871** Hay *Pike Co. Ballads* 15: I jest flopped down on my marrow-bones…and prayed. **1881** Crofutt *Grip-Sack Guide* (preface): Expected to climb down on his marrow-bones and apologize for something. **1888** Pierson *Slave of Circumstances* 79: That'll bring the capitalists down on their marrows. **1891** McCann & Jarrold *Odds & Ends* 86: He kind o' got down on his marrer bones himself. **1902** "J. Flynt" *Little Bro.* 12: Her ability to bring certain well-grown pupils "down on their marrow-bones."

2. a knuckle; (*pl.*) the fists as used in fighting.
  *a1625 J. Fletcher, in *OED:* The great Band Of Maribones that people call the Switzers. ***1812** in *OED:* He was like a stranger to fear in the field of either bayonets or marrowbones. **1834** Caruthers *Kentuck. in N.Y.* I 62: I did the slight o' hand work, as you may see by the skin that's gone off these four marrowbones. *Ibid.* II 105: "I havn't told you half the good that comes of regulating the people by the five rules." "Five rules! What are they?" "These marrowbones!" (holding up his clenched fist.).

Mars *n.* ¶ In phrase: **from** [or **on**] **Mars** markedly eccentric; (*also*) very confused. Cf. MARTIAN.
  [**1949** D. Cooper & J. Davis *Duchess of Idaho* (film): That's just for people who live up on Mars!/Baby, come out of the clouds!] **1980** Lorenz *Guys Like Us* 44: You still look like the Chick from Mars. **1992** Strawberry & Rust *Darryl* 5: Your manager from Mars had glued your butt to a bench. **1991–95** Sack *Co. C* 23: I'm lost, I'm on Mars.

marshmallow *n.* **1.a.** a soft, weak, or sentimental person.—also used attrib.
  1965 Carmichael & Longstreet *Sometimes I Wonder* 104: They like marshmallow music. ***1966** in *OEDS:* The situations are witty, the songs as true, her eyes as mistily, romantically happy as I remembered. Perhaps it is just that I am more of a marshmallow than I was as a teenager. **1966–69** Woiwode *Going to Do* 70: You're a marshmallow, Grandpa….You're a marshmallow inside. **1974** Terkel *Working* 442: He's not struggling….He's a fuckin' marshmallow. **1979–81** C. Buckley *To Bamboola* 155: Harvey liked to put up a very bold front, but I knew inside he was a marshmallow. **1984** T. Wolfe, in *Rolling Stone* (Aug. 2) 22: You poor fatties! You marshmallows! Hens! Cows! **1986** *Newsweek* (May 26) 69: Hard-liners…portrayed Khrushchev as a marshmallow gulled by the warmonger Eisenhower.

b. a very fat person.
  1989 Hynes & Drury *Howard Beach* 49: See that big marshmallow walking through the door?

2. *Black E.* a white person.—used contemptuously.
  1969 in *DAS* (ed. 2): No Oreos, or, worse, an Oreo fronting for a "marshmallow" need apply.

3. *Baseball.* a weakly pitched, easily hit ball.
  1978 *N.Y. Post* (June 26) 62: Catfish Hunter is throwing marshmallows—when his arm stands still long enough to unload a baseball in it.

Martian *n.* an eccentric person.—also used attrib.
  1978 in Fierstein *Torch Song* 27: I feel like I'm a Martian or something. **1980** Lorenz *Guys Like Us* 22: Looking at him with her face surrounded by her Martian hair. **1986** Merkin *Zombie Jamboree* 172: You and your little Martian friend…started all this crap. **1987** R. Miller *Slob* 243: I'm gonna lose it any minute, he thought as he saw the green door open and a man with spiky Martian-green-and-pink hair come slithering in…."Hullo," the Martian said.

martooni *n.* [perh. orig. an intentional spoonerism, as in 1986 quot.] a martini. *Joc.*
  1954–60 *DAS:* Martooni…A martini cocktail. *Fairly common.* **1983** S. King *Christine* 356: She didn't like to think of her dad trying to drive home from the Stewarts' in this, half-soused from three or four martinis (except that he always called them martoonis, with typical adult kittenishness). **1986** E. Weiner *Howard the Duck* 78: Tee many

martoonies. **1995** *New Yorker* (June 5) 100: Precision Bartending Team…Eddie (Elbow) Flannigan and his Magnificent Martoonis. **1996** *N.Y. Observer* (July 22) 34: Pack up your picnic basket of martoonis and head your…Saab to Jersey.

maru *n.* [< Japn; used as a comb. form in names of merchant ships] *Navy.* a Japanese or (*joc.*) U.S. ship. Now *hist.* [Quots. ref. to WWII.]
  1942 R. Casey *Torpedo Junction* 10: In Navy slang any Japanese ship is now a *maru.*…Some U.S. ships are called *maru* by way of heavy humor—such as the *Swayback Maru. Ibid.* 216: There are said to be one large "maru" and four smaller "marus" in the lagoon at Wake. **1962** Bonham *War Beneath Sea* 34: Maybe this man had *maru* fever. Maybe when he saw a Jap *maru* steaming along, he'd…start throwing torpedoes like rocks. **1986** M. Skinner *USN* 105: [U.S.S.] *Coral Sea.*…The *Coral Maru* has recently undergone SLEP refit. *a*1995 Gallantin *Sub. Admiral* 85: About two thousand yards between us and the *maru.* **1995** Cormier et al. *Wildcats* 166: The *Ranger.*…During the "Ranger Maru" cruise we tested laser-guided bombs." *Ibid.* 180: *Midway*…had to be "Midway Maru."

marv *adj.* MARVY. Also as adv.
  1965–66 Pynchon *Crying* 138: "How's it going?"…"Just marv." **1967** *L.A. Times* (Feb. 15) V 1: Would you like to buy some cookies? They're marv! **1968** Swarthout *Loveland* 216 [ref. to 1930's]: Isn't it marv? *a*1970 Partridge *DSUE* (ed. 7) 1269: *Marv.* Marvellous: teenagers': since the late 1950's. **1994** *New York* (May 9) 5: At Sahara East, the moussaka's marv.

marvel *v.* [orig. unkn.] to go or depart, esp. quickly; travel.—occ. used trans.
  1841 [Mercier] *Man-of-War* 42: I had to *marvel* ashore on my own hook like *Mullins's dog. Ibid.* 190: You're stationed on the topsail-yard, So *marvle* [sic] up there now. **1842** in *New Eng. Qly.* LXIII (1990) 540: The…pig marvelled off…in double quick time….He was…marvelled forard with a kick in his a—e. **1848** *Ladies' Repository* VIII (Oct.) 315: *Marvel,* To shy off or walk away slowly. **1850** "N. Buntline" *G'hals of N.Y.* 8: Come, let's *marvel.* **1851** in Dorson *Long Bow* 129: I left seashore and salts, and *marvelled* at once into the interior of Connecticut. **1856** *Spirit of Times* (Feb. 16) 1: So he "marvles" down into Mexico and "wallops" the…Mexicans. **1889–90** Barrère & Leland *Dict Slang* II 43: *Marvel.* To bound, bounce, or run long. *a*1890–96 *F & H* IV 287: *Marvel*…(American).—To walk, to be off: e.g., "He marvelled for home."

Marvin *n.* [sugg. by *ARVN* 'Army of the Republic of Vietnam'] *Mil. in Vietnam.* a member of the military forces of South Vietnam; such forces collectively.—usu. in phr. **Marvin the ARVN.**
  1974 Former 1LT, 25th Inf. Div. [ref. to Vietnam, 1970–71]: Then there was *Luke the Gook,* which was the NVA and VC, and *Marvin the ARVN.* **1983** C. Rich *Advisors* 433: *ARVN*…Also called Marvin. **1983** N. Proffitt *Gardens of Stone* 337: Ol' Marvin the Arvin wasn't havin' none of it. **1987** Pelfrey & Carabatsos *Hamburger Hill* 65: Same-same Marvin the ARVN. **1991** Marcinko & Weisman *Rogue Warrior* 94: Marvin the ARVN's intelligence gophers would chatter about it. Marvin believed it to be a big VC R&R center. *Ibid.* 140: The Marvins generally liked to keep their heads down. **1991–94** W.T. Grant *Wings of Eagle* 339: *Marvin*—Nickname for Vietnamese soldier. Short for Marvin the ARVN.

Marvin Military *n. U.S. Mil. Acads.* an overly conscientious cadet.
  1969 *Current Slang I & II* 60: *Marvin military,* n. One who shines shoes, cleans his room, etc.—Air Force Academy cadets. **1990** Ruggero *38 N. Yankee* 22: The other cadets in the [Army] program called him "Marvin Military."

marvy *adj.* (esp. among teenage girls) marvelous. Also as adv.
  1931 Lorimer & Lorimer *Streetcars* 103: Welly and I had a perfectly marvy time. **1938** *Saturday Review* (July 23) 22: Crime School…was marvie! **1943** M. Shulman *Barefoot Boy* 88: I think your costume is simply marvy. **1946** M. Shulman *Dobie Gillis* 92: "Oo, marvy," said Sally. **1959** J. Lee *Career* (film): I just think it's a marvy idea. **1965** Lurie *Nowhere City* 320: Phoebe Demeray's having another kid?…That's marvy. **1965** Borowik *Lions* 162: Isn't it marvey? **1970** S.J. Perelman, in *New Yorker* (Oct. 17) 39: Marvy—now we can go on the trip together! **1971** B.B. Johnson *Blues for Sister* 113: Wasn't that just marvy! **1972** *Reggie's Wise Guy Jokes* 6: That was marvey, Reggie. **1976** Angelou *Singin' & Swingin'* 94: Didn't I say she's marvy? **1988**

Rage (Univ. Tenn.) (Dec.) 6: My house is super and the weather [has] been marvy. **1988** T. Landon *Slaughterhouse Rock* (film): We went out for burgers, and it was marvy. **1992** B. Watterson *Calvin & Hobbes* (synd. comic strip) (Sept. 1): "Two generations can be divided by the same language!"..."Marvy. Fab. Far out." **1993** *Beyond Reality* (USA-TV): He and his really marvy friend Zelda.

Mary *n.* **1.** Esp. *Homosex.* a homosexual man (usu. used in direct address).—used joc. or contemptuously.

  1925 McAlmon *Stockings* 51: I'm tellin' you, Mary, you shudda seen us when we stepped out of the stagedoor. **1948** J.H. Burns *Lucifer* 360: Those two fags...step lively...."Shut your hole, Mary!" **1953** Brossard *Bold Saboteurs* 117: Rough heterosexual trade, delicate homosexual Mary trade. **1954–60** *DAS*: *Mary*...A male homosexual who plays the female role....A female homosexual. **1971** Rader *Govt. Inspected* 162: Drunks and Miss Marys lingering furtively by the closed men's room door. **1965–72** E. Newton *Mother Camp* 58: "Look, Mary," I say to myself, "don't let this get you." **1981** Eells & Musgrove *Mae West* 85 [ref. to 1928]: Beat it, Mary, before Lizzie Law grabs you, too! **1985** C. Busch *Vampire Lesbians* 69: Fuck off, Mary.

2. the vulva or vagina.—usu. considered vulgar.

  [*a***1890–96** *F & H* IV 287: *Mary-Jane*...the female *pudendum.*] *a***1927** in P. Smith *Letter from Father* 76: For years I played with Lydia's "mary."...We diddled one another as we watched the picture.

3. *Narc.* **a.** marijuana; MARY JANE.

  1936 L. Duncan *Over the Wall* 102: Marijuana, pronounced "merry-hawána" [is] called "griefo" or "merry" by addicts that use it. **1952** *AS* XXVII (Feb.) 28: *Mary*...Marijuana. **1967** Hamma *Motorcycle Mammas* 86: "Mary"—pot—whatever you want to call it—that's another story. Like wild!

b. [arbitrary use of the given name to replace the letter M, q.v.] morphine.

  1949 Monteleone *Crim. Slang* 153: *Mary*...Morphine. **1952** *AS* XXVII (Feb.) 28: *Mary*....Morphine. **1970** Landy *Underground Dict.*: *Mary*...Morphine.

Mary Ann *n.* **1.a.** an effeminate or homosexual boy or man.—used contemptuously.

  *****1882** in Chester et al. *Cleve. St.* 51: Recollections of a Mary-Anne. *Ibid.* 52: The handsome youth...must indeed be one of the Mary-Annes of London. *****1889–90** Barrère & Leland *Dict. Slang* II 45: *Mary Ann* (popular), an effeminate youth or young man. *****1895** in *F & H* IV 286: I heard prostitutes jocosely apostrophizing the Mary-Anns who plied their beastly trade upon the pavement beside the women. *****a***1890–96** *F & H* IV 286: *Mary-Ann*...(common) a sodomite. *a***1972** B. Rodgers *Queens' Vernacular* 22: Stop eating your heart out over that military mary-anne.

b. *Und.* (see quot.).—constr. with *the.*

  1942–49 Goldin et al. *DAUL* 136: *Mary Ann, the.* The robbery of drunkards by combined pickpocketing and suave talk; frequently the thief pretends to be a sexual pervert to throw off suspicion that he is feeling for the victim's wallet.

2. a dressmaker's dummy.

  *a***1890–96** *F & H* IV 287: *Mary-Ann*....(dressmakers').—A dress stand. *a***1910** Bierce *Shapes of Clay* 78: Or just a gowned barbarian / With trousers on his Mary Ann?

3. *Boxing.* a powerful blow with the fist; HAYMAKER.

  1907 Siler *Pugilism* 192: "Mary Ann's [*sic*]"—See "Haymaker." **1922** T.A. Dorgan, in Zwilling *TAD Lexicon* 56: Now they tell us that Frank Moran, owner of the famous Mary Ann, is about to meet [Battling Siki]. **1925** T.A. Dorgan, in Zwilling *TAD Lexicon* 56: Now Buck, soon as de bell sings swing old Mary Ann right on dat palooka's button. **1942** *ATS* 669: *Mary Ann,* a right-hand "roundhouse swing."

3. (used as a mild oath).

  1908 "O. Henry" *Voice of City* 1355: "Oh, Mary Ann!" said they. "Must you always adorn every statement with your alledged humor?"

4. *Narc.* **a.** marijuana or a marijuana cigarette; MARY JANE.

  1925 (quot. at LAUGHING WEED). **1925** in Partridge *Dict. Und.* 433: *Mary Ann.* A Mexican drug—the "loco weed." **1939** (quot. at BOOJIE, *n.*).

b. morphine.

  1955 (cited in Partridge *Dict. Und.* 845). **1970** Landy *Underground Dict.* 129: *Mary ann*...Morphine.

5. *Logging.* a logging wagon.

  1930 *Amer. Merc.* (Oct.) 235: The elegant eight-horse team which hauled the Mary Ann wagon on the Connecticut river drive.

Mary Ellen var. MARY FIST.

Mary Fist *n.* the hand as used in male masturbation.—usu. used derisively. Also vars. Cf. FIVE-FINGERED MARY.

  1942–49 Goldin et al. *DAUL* 136: *Married to Mary Fist.*...addicted to the practice of masturbation. **1960** MacCuish *Do Not Go Gentle* 118 [ref. to WWII]: Bet those women of yours get real jealous of Mary Five-Fingers, eh? *Ibid.* 356: "He's gonna take out Mary Palm an' her five daughters." His fingers closing and the hand stroking the air. "The only piece you'll ever get, eh?" **1963** Coon *Short End* 178: For every time we laid a real broad, we laid Mother Five Fingers five hundred times. **1970** Sorrentino *Steelwork* 39: Jackie the Priest, who's got himself four good ole girlfriend, Mary Fist. OK? You get it? Mary Fist. A-ho, A-ha. **1971** S. Stevens *Way Uptown* 55: It was in the shape of Mary Fist and it had a glove on to make it soft. All you hadda do was slip your rig in the fist and start the arm goin'. **1971** Altman & McKay *McCabe & Mrs. Miller* (film): Go home and play with Mary Five-Fingers. **1972** *Nat. Lampoon* (July) 50: A special conference with Mary Palm and her five daughters. **1977** Carabatsos *Heroes* 11: "Put the old Mary Ellen on the ticker."...He...flexed his fingers. "Technical term. When you're lonely, Mary Ellen's your only friend." **1986** Stinson & Carabatsos *Heartbreak* 109: Don't be dreamin' of...Mary-five-fingers back in camp. **1986** R. Campbell *In La-La Land* 175: Some gazoony...having it off with Mary Fist. **1990** A. Baraka, in T. McMillan *Breaking Ice* 48: I know....You prefer Merry [*sic*] Fist.

Mary Five-Fingers var. MARY FIST.

Mary Jane *n.* [folk trans., as if *marijuana* were fr. *María* + *Juana,* Sp given names equiv. to *Mary* and *Jane*] *Narc.* marijuana; a marijuana cigarette.

  1928 in *OEDS*: What is Marijuana?...A deadly Mexican drug, more familiarly known as "Mary Jane," which produces wild hilarity when either smoked or eaten. **1939** Howsley *Argot* 32: *Mary Jane*—marijuana. **1943** *Time* (July 19) 54: Marijuana may be called muggles, mooter, Mary Warner, Mary Jane, Indian hay, loco weed, love weed, bambalacha, mohasky, mu, moocah, grass, tea, or blue sage. **1952** *ATS* (ed. 2) 462: Marihuana....*Mary Jane,*...pot [etc.]. **1958** Gilbert *Vice Trap* 11: Madrid took up with her...using plenty of maryjane. **1962** H. Simmons *On Eggshells* 177: I got busted...blowing some Mary Jane. **1963** Coon *Short End* 25: He says he used to push T. Mary Jane. You dig? **1963** Braly *Shake Him* 139: Too bad you can't stay happy with good old Mary-Jane here. **1966** Young & Hixson *LSD* 24: I had heard it as "Mary Janes" and "reefers." **1968** Hudson *Case of Need* 172: You're up for abortion but not maryjane, is that it? **1970** *Playboy* (Dec.) 287: They're out busting dope-fiend creeps like me who turn innocent teeners on to a stick of mary jane now and then. **1970** Gattzden *Black Vendetta* 109: Smoking Mary Janes. **1968–71** Cole & Black *Checking* 237: Stu, do you smoke Mary Jane? **1983** Ehrhart *VN-Perkasie* 304: How do you like Mary Jane. **1989** Radford & Crowley *Drug Agent* 176: She brought Mary Jane along. **1992** G. Wolff *Day at the Beach* 24: My father's prudish maledictions against reefer (which the flat-sharers called Mary Jane). **1996** *Mystery Sci. Theater* (Comedy Central TV): You do a lot of that Mary Jane?

Mary Palm var. MARY FIST.

Mary Warner *n.* [pun] *Narc.* a marijuana cigarette; marijuana.

  1933 *Newsweek* (Aug. 5) 26: Marihuana cigarettes, better known to users as "reefers," "muggles," or "Mary Warners." **1933** in *Amer. Jour. Psychiatry* XCI (1934) 304: Marihuana...*Mary Warner.* **1943** (quot. at MARY JANE). **1950** Riesenberg *Reporter* 171: I found out you used the Mary Warners. **1953** Anslinger & Tompkins *Traf. in Narc.* 312: *Mary Werner.* Marihuana. *Also* a marihuana cigarette. **1956** E. Hunter *Second Ending* 279: Tea, pot, weed, Rosa Maria, Mary Warner, take your choice. It's all marijuana.

mash *n.* **1.** an infatuation; an act of flirtation; crush; in phr. **on the mash** engaged in flirtation; courting.

  1877 *Puck* (May) 6: Do you remember your first professional mash? (That is what the stage people call it.). **1877–78** *Cornelian* 86: Mash. A deep but fleeting affection of the heart. **1878** *Nat. Police Gaz.* (May 11) 2: It was an unmitigated case of "mash" on his part. **1880** Sala *America Revisited* II 81: Mark Antony lying in a hopeless condition of "mash"—the "masher" is the superlative of a "spoon," and one of his most graceful attributes is to pour the maple syrup over the buckwheat cakes which Beauty eats at breakfast. **1881** Trumble *Man Traps* 27 (caption):

A "MASH" AND ITS CONSEQUENCES. **1882** *Puck* (Dec. 12) 234: "I would [like]…to know why those three old buffers are trailing me. Is it—" and her eyes grew more brightly tender: "is it a mash?" *1888 in *F & H* IV 287: An impecunious fellow who was always on the mash. **1889–90** Barrère & Leland *Dict. Sl.* II 45: To be on the *mash*, to be making love to; to go on the *mash*, to go about in search of amourettes. **1891** Maitland *Slang Dict.* 175: *Mash* (Am.), a school-girl's term for a street flirtation. **1895** *Harper's* (Sept.) 618: So kin you, Norah, unless you ain't got no respect fer yerself and yer out on de mash. **1954** L. Armstrong *Satchmo* 151: The lady has a mash on you. **1985** Univ. Tenn. student theme: Others get "crushes" or "mashes" on someone.

2.a. a sweetheart.

1879 *Nat. Police Gaz.* (Aug. 9) 15: He is her "mash." *1883 in *F & H* IV 287: He appears to be the *mash* (if it is permissible to quote the cant phrase of the day)…of Queen Anne, the Duchess of Marlborough, and his own legitimate sweetheart. **1886** F. Whittaker *Pop Hicks* 10: He's Zoe's mash, not mine.…She's dead game on him. **1895** Foote *Coeur D'Alene* 43: A young fellah turnin' his chin loose about his mash! **1896** Ade *Artie* 53: I've seen her two or three times, but she always had the mash along.…Oh, but they was gone on each other. **1899** *Nat. Police Gaz.* (Mar. 18) 3: "For me?" "Sure, you've got a mash. Open it and see what he says."

b. an attractive young woman.

1899 A.H. Lewis *Sandburrs* 287: It's be chanct I'm in Dinky Pete's meself d'time Jimmy is out to meet this blonde mash.

¶ In phrase:

¶ **make** [or **get**] **a mash, 1.** to strike up an acquaintance with a view to romantic intimacy; (*hence*) to flirt.—often constr. with *on*.

1879 Rooney *Quaint Conundrums* 67: When a fascinating young man has managed to make a vinegary old maid look upon him with favorable eyes, he is said to have made a sour mash. **1880** Sprague *Campus Melodies* 39: To the Little Brown Sem., we go with them/In hopes of making "mashes." **1883** Smith & Smith *Police Gaz.* 42: Wung Foo making a Mash. **1886** F. Whittaker *Pop Hicks* 2: The bold sport…resolved, in his own phrase, to "make a mash for all he was worth." **1889** in *AS* (1966) 106: *Mrs. M.* First I should like you to teach me—oh yes, the art to love.…*Meek.* [in hiding] Oh Lord! To think of my wife making a mash! **1892** Moore *Own Story* 306: When the rest of the fellows saw this one had made a "mash," they went away. **1899** A.H. Lewis *Sandburrs* 174: If any of them smooth marks try to make a mash, t'run 'em down an' t'run 'em hard. **1908** *New Broadway Mag.* (July) 124: Rose said…"I'm going to make a mash on Pete." **1928** Dahlberg *Bottom Dogs* 242: Dad had tried to get a mash on her after the second day he had eaten there.

2. to make a favorable romantic impression upon a person of the opposite sex.

1885 Siringo *Texas Cowboy* 164: Now was my time to make a "mash," so I assured her that I would bring in a dozen or two and lay them at her feet. **1899** in Boni *Gilded Age* 136: The ladies gather'd round me for I'd surely made a mash. **1904** in A. Adams *Chisholm Trail* 83: I mentioned to him that he had a made a mash on the little blonde milliner. **1905** W.S. Kelly *Lariats* 179: The girls would…all try to make a "mash" on you. **1958** S.H. Adams *Tenderloin* 119 [ref. to 1890's]: Dan—I've made a mash!

mash *v.* **1.** to assault; beat up; (*occ.*) to kill.

1872 Alger *Phil* 295: The little chap's showin' fight.…Look out, Tim; he'll mash you. **1884** in *DARE*: If you'll step out-doors I'll mash you! **1904** *Life in Sing Sing* 250: *Mashed.* Assaulted. **1935** *AS* (Feb.) 18 [ref. to *a*1910]: To *Mash*.…2. To beat up someone severely. **1961** C. Cooper *Weed* 144: Kill him!…Mash that little man! **1970** Whitmore *Memphis-Nam-Sweden* 31: When John Kennedy was mashed, we felt bad. **1993** P. Munro *U.C.L.A. Slang II*: I don't decide to mash someone unless he's a real pain in the ass.

2. to flirt with or make romantic advances toward; (*also*) (all *obs.*) to cause to be romantically smitten; succeed in romancing; seduce.—also (*obs.*) used intrans. or absol. [C. Leland's proposed ety. (1889–90 quot.) is not gen. accepted.]

1877 *Puck* (May) 3: Lester Wallack, Edwin Booth, and Montague [could] earn quite a respectable living…blacking the shoes of the young ladies they've succeeded in "mashing." **1882** *Judge* (Dec. 30) 7: Ah, Mary, you cannot mash me. I am married! **1882** *Puck* (Dec. 27) 261: Seven Drummers smiling—/Playing flirting-tricks/On a Maid beguil-

ing./One mashed! Only Six. *1883 in *F & H* IV 288: And looks so handsome that were he not so wicked he would be likely to *mash* all the ladies who see him. **1884** Peck *Boss Book* 27: He resolves…to take revenge on his girl by mashing other girls. **1886** E.L. Wheeler *N.Y. Nell* 10: Mebbe, too, he's on the romantic lay an' I can "mash" him. **1886** F. Whittaker *Pop Hicks* 9: He was mashing on your leading lady. *ca*1888 *Stag Party* 226: A girl will flirt and a girl will mash. *1888 R. Kipling *Only a Subaltern*: What's the yarn about your mashing a Miss Haverley up there? Not serious, I hope? **1889–90** Barrère & Leland *Dict. Slang* II 46: About the year 1860 *mash* was a word found only in theatrical parlance in the United States. When an actress or any girl on the stage smiled at or ogled a friend in the audience, she was said to *mash* him, and "mashing" was always punishable by a fine.…It occurred to the writer that it must have been derived from the gypsy *mash* (masher-ava), to allure, to entice. This was suggested to Mr. Palmer, a well-known impresario, who said that…the term had originated with the C—— family, who were all comic actors and actresses, of Romany stock, who spoke gypsy familiarly among themselves. *1892 in *F & H* IV 288: Successfully mash a girl by reciting poetry to her. **1892** S. Crane *Maggie* 34: Dere wasn't a feller come teh deh house but she'd try teh mash 'im. **1928** Dahlberg *Bottom Dogs* 36: She said he was only trying to mash and that he was a big josher. **1928** Bradford *Ol' Man Adam* 10: What you tryin' to do, Country Boy?…You tryin' to mash me? **1929** Connelly *Green Pastures* 201: You tryin' to mash me? **1935** *AS* (Feb.) 18 [ref. to *a*1910]: To *Mash* 1. To successfully storm a lady's virtue. **1986** E.M. Miller *Street Woman* 23: A group calling itself SMASH, Stop Mashing and Sexual Harassment, organized teams of irked neighborhood women [in Milwaukee in 1985].

3. *Black E.* to give; LAY ON.—also constr. with *on*.

1944 Burley *Handbk. Jive* 143: *Mash me*—Give me. **1944** Calloway *Hepster's Dict.*: *Mash me a fin* (command)—Give me $5. **1946** Mezzrow & Wolfe *Really Blues* 187 [ref. to 1930's]: Mash me a trey. **1962–68** B. Jackson *In the Life* 202: She mashed a little money on me. **1969** R. Beck *Mama Black Widow* 218: I'm gonna mash it on you next time you show. **1976** Calloway & Rollins *Moocher & Me* 182: Mash me a fin, gate, so I can cop me a fry. **1994** A. Heckerling *Clueless* 83: Can you mash me a fin? I'll pay you back.

4. *Stu.* to kiss and hug; MAKE OUT, 2.b.

[**1942** *ATS* 335: Court.…*mash (it).*] **1986** Univ. Tenn. student theme: "Mashing" and "grubbing" [are] the current synonyms for making out. **1989** *Beachin' Times* 7: How long can you mash with the Dude or Dudette of your choice? Find out in this mega-kissing contest. **1990** P. Munro *Slang Usage*: *Mash* to kiss, neck, make out. **1995** *N.Y. Press* (May 31) 5: A gratuitous and inarticulate chronicling of a regrettable "mashing" session. **1996** *Mystery Sci. Theater* (Comedy Central TV): Should we start mashin' now?

mashed *adj.* **1.** infatuated; smitten; STUCK.—usu. constr. with *on*.

1880 Nye *Boomerang* 192: I wot ye art the damsel who erst was mashed on Obejoyful. **1881** in Peck *Peck's Sunshine* 85: "Mashed" on some ethereal creature. **1881** Field *Tribune Verse* 183: Oh, I'm mashed on the belle of St. Joe. **1883** Peck *Bad Boy* 60: Ma came along afterwards with a deakin that is mashed on her, I guess. *1883 in *F & H* IV 288: There are nooks and passages which give sufficient cover for the smitten (or the *mashed*, as, alas! the current slang is) to exchange their confidences. **1885** in Lummis *Letters* 231: He was not the first that got mashed on [my meerschaum] this trip. **1885** "Lykkejaeger" *Dane* 119: I was dead gone, "mashed." **1887** Peck *Pvt. Peck* 88: I told him that I was not much mashed on war. **1888** *Stag Party* 11: I am mashed on you Billy, and wish that you knew. *1889–90 in Barrère & Leland *Dict. Sl.* II 46: He was *mashed*, so was she, they were married. **1904** in "O. Henry" *Works* 1265: I think I'd get mashed on him. **1952** *Sat. Eve. Post* (Apr. 19) 161: Deirdre doesn't want him, she's mashed on Prynn.

2. drunk.

1942 *ATS* 123: Drunk.…*mashed.* **1965** Summers *Flunkie* 31: He drank both six packs. He got mashed. **1979** Univ. Tenn. student theme: Drunk—*mashed, numb, messed-up.*

mashed-potato circuit *n. Pol.* a round of after-dinner speaking engagements. Cf. RUBBER-CHICKEN CIRCUIT.

1965 Reagan & Hubler *Rest of Me* 286: And the speaking I'd done in the industry's behalf along the "mashed potato circuit." **1988** *U.S. News & W.R.* (Nov. 21) 21: Gerald Ford, who rates $20,000 per talk, regularly performs for pay on what Reagan…fondly calls "the mashed-potato circuit." **1988** R. Reagan, on *ABC News* (ABC-TV)

(Dec. 22): I'm not going to retire. I'm going back out on the mashed-potato circuit.

masher *n.* **1.** a man who makes romantic or sexual advances to women, esp. in a public place; (now also, esp. *Police*) a frotteur or other individual who sexually harasses women.

1875 *Funny Fatherland* 56: The soldiers here are great "mashers" amongst the *dienst madchens.* **1877** *Puck* (Mar.) 5: Jed Baldwin is *the* "masher" of the club. He has broken up more homes, fallen in love with more women, rendered more men miserable for life than I have time to tell of. **1879** *Nat. Police Gaz.* (May 24) 15: The matinee "masher" is a peculiar individual. **1880** Sala *Amer. Revisited* II 81: What do you think of that conceited Phaon, most supercilious of Hellenic "mashers" ogling the unhappy Lesbian poetess, whose too sensitive heart he had won at a Connecticut church oyster stew? **1882** Peck *Peck's Sunshine* 130: "Mashers"…[are] young men who stand on the corners and [insult] women. **1882** Field *Tribune Verse* 120: He's a giddy, giddy masher,/And he's doing things up brown,/In a friskier way and rasher,/Since his wife is out of town. **1883** Peck *Bad Boy* 49: He is an old masher, that's what's the matter with him, and he was going to play himself for a bachelor. **1885** *Harper's Mo.* (July) 323: The word "masher," like many other…slang terms. **1904** in "O. Henry" *Works* 40: He made eyes at her,…smiled, smirked, and went brazenly through the impudent…litany of the "masher." **1904** *Life in Sing Sing* 250: *Masher.*—A loafer who annoys women by his attentions. **1909** C. Chrysler *White Slavery* 163: Even titled women of England have been ogled by "mashers." **1929–33** J.T. Farrell *Manhood of Lonigan* 218: There was a lot of damn mashers like that, and they all needed a sock in the puss. **1949** *New Yorker* (Oct. 15) 103: Seeing the girl shrink from him, as if afraid that he was a masher. **1952** Lait & Mortimer *USA* 19: Gumshoes are having a field day chasing mashers and shaking them down. **1960** *Twilight Zone* (CBS-TV): Look, lady, I ain't a masher. See, I know the girl who usually works here and—. **1963** *True* (May) 43: An arrest of a knife-wielding masher. **1965** Trimble *Sex Words* 129: *Masher*…One who commits Frottage in crowded areas.—*Mash,* v.t. **1977** S. Gaines *Discotheque* 72: Why won't you say hello? I'm not your regular masher type. **1979** *Playboy* (Aug.) 168: "How d'you do, Miss. Why don't we go up to your place and wrestle?" "Masher!" **1980** Freudenberger & Richelson *Burn Out* 180: Good Lord!…Do I look like a masher?

2. *Army.* POTATO-MASHER.

1926 Niles *Singing Soldiers* 105 [ref. to WWI]: When dat box o' mashers turned loose, it was Kingdom Come. **1955** F.K. Franklin *Combat Nurse* 185 [ref. to WWII]: Hey George, don't you drop one of them kraut mashers. **1982** W. Wharton *Midnight Clear* 77 [ref. to WWII]: 138: Dropping in a few mashers.

mash note *n.* a love note, as sent by a stranger or casual acquaintance.—also used fig. Also (*obs.*) **mash letter.**

1880 in *DA*: He had what is called a "mash letter" from a schoolgirl fourteen years old. **1890** in *DA*: He is greatly afflicted by that dreadful bane of fine-looking actors, yclept the "mash note" in the profession. **1900** T. Dreiser, in *DAS*: Letters were handed to her by the doorman.…*Mash notes* were old affairs. **1911** Van Loan *Big League* 58: Worryin' because some other lobster is writin' her mash notes? **1927** C.J. Daly *Snarl of Beast* 12: A movie star gets mash notes. **1950** *New Yorker* (Apr. 15) 68: The languid amusement a Park Avenue débutante might feel on reading a mash note from an impoverished and elderly farmer. **1950** *Sat. Eve. Post* (Nov. 25) 71: The administration doesn't worry too much if a few of the girls write mash notes to each other. **1988** *N.Y. Newsday* (July 7) II 21: My sons began receiving mash notes at 12 or 13. In every case the girls wrote explicitly about their willingness to do anything "to prove their love." **1988** *USA Today* (Feb. 12) 2D: He does not discuss these mash notes with his wife. **1991** *N.Y. Times Bk. Rev.* (Oct. 20) 11: Though Mr. Reston zinged the former President regularly, Mr. Reagan sent him a "mash note" when Mr. Reston retired in 1989. **1995** *Newsweek* (Sept. 25) 85: Mash Notes in the Newsroom.…They were plainly flirtatious—short, cryptic messages suggesting a crush that was getting harder and harder to handle. **1995** *Evans & Novak* (CNN-TV) (Dec. 23): He is still writing mash notes…to Mrs. Clinton.

mashook *adj.* MESHUGA.

1970 Gattzden *Black Vendetta* 95: Crazy jig.…You're mashook, man.

mask *n.* a hard facial expression.

[**1954–60** *DAS: Mask*…The face.] **1993** K. Scott *Monster* 90: I put on my mask (a mask is an extended version of a mad-dog stare; it's one's combat face).

maskee [pidgin; perh. < Mandarin] Esp. *Naut. in E. Asia & Pacific. interj.* **1.** never mind! let it be! Also *prep.,* in spite of.

*1864 Hotten Slang Dict. (ed. 3): *Maskee,* never mind, no consequence.—*Anglo-Chinese.* **1917** *Editor* (July 25) 121: A Pidgin English Vocabulary…*Maskee*—never mind, what is the use, let it be. **1918** O'Reilly *Roving & Fighting* 233 [ref. to 1901]: But "maskee his name," as they say on the China coast. **1922–24** McIntyre *White Light* 26: Maskee snow, maskee ice. **1929** *AS* V (Dec.) 149: Some of the [pidgin] terms from corrupted Chinese words are…"maskee" meaning "don't mind"; "chop-chop" meaning "quick! make haste!" **1950* W. Granville *Sea Slang* 153: *Maskee.* 'It doesn't matter', 'It is of no account'. **1975** J.L. Dillard *All-Amer. Eng.* 6: Portuguese…*mas que*…became *maskie,* "Never mind!"

2. satisfactory; good. Also as *adj.*

*1889–90 Barrère & Leland *Dict. Sl.* II 47: *Maskee*…the commonest interjection in [Anglo-Chinese and Anglo-Indian] pidgin, meaning all right,…"all good." **1942–45** Caniff *Male Call* (unp.): China-side job—very maskee. **1942–47** *ATS* (Supp.) 28: Good…*maskee, on the target* [etc.]. **1952** Cope & Dyer *Petty Officer's Guide* 447: *Maskee.* A navy expression of Asiatic origin which means "O.K." "all right." **1959** (quot. at DING-HOW).

massacree *n.* [orig. dial.] a massacre; (hence) *Sports.* (also **massacre**) a humiliating defeat. Cf. SLAUGHTER.

*1688 in *OED*: She went down into Egypt from Herods Bloody Massacry. **1803* in Wetherell *Adventures* 86: A dreadful Massacree. **1904* Kipling *Traffics* 280: It was a sanguinary massacree. **1921–25** J. Gleason & R. Taber *Is Zat So?* 53: Then it would turn into a massacree. **1932** H. Mankiewicz et al. *Girl Crazy* (film): Some massacre! Indians 11, Yankees nothing! **1991** W. Chamberlain *View from Above* 170: Color commentators say about a one-sided game, "It's a massacre" or "They were scalped."

massacree *v.* to massacre or murder; (hence, also **massacre**) to victimize; defeat, thrash, or humiliate thoroughly or cruelly. Cf. SLAUGHTER.

1727 in *OED*: Your Warriors…have Massacreed Men, Women, and Children. **1803* in Wetherell *Adventures* 50: They…take delight in massacreeing a white man. **1833** J. Neal *Down-Easters* I 65: They…massacree 'em most to death. **1909** in O. Johnson *Lawrenceville* 40: You jump in there now and cripple a few of those fellows or I'll massacre you! **1935** J. Conroy *World to Win* 197: He's massacring me! **1936** N. West *Cool Million* 224: I'll massacree the danged aboriginee. **1938** "E. Queen" *4 Hearts* 17: Alan Clark will massacre me. **1942** *ATS* 135: *Massacre,* to murder one person with cruelty; *massacree,*…to massacre.

massage *n.* a beating.

1927–28 in R. Nelson *Dishonorable* 213: Do you imagine I'm goin' to take a massage from dicks?

massage *v.* **1.** to strike or beat vigorously or repeatedly; assault or injure (someone); (hence, occ.) to kill (a person).

1926 Thomason *Red Pants* 111: One guy was all set to massage your dome wit' a table leg. **1930** Lavine *3d Degree* 109: The "Cry Baby Gangsters"…were foolish enough to complain of a mere *massaging.* **1932** *Baseball Mag.* (Oct.) 496. **1937** in *DAS*: The thugs have been caught and massaged with rubber hoses in the back room of some station house. **1972** Pendleton *Vegas Vendetta* 60: These two imaginary torpedoes cruise around wearing brass knuckles and massaging heads with blackjacks. **1980** Cragg *Lex. Militaris* 293: *Massaged.* Killed or wounded.

2.a. to attempt to improve through careful or detailed adjustment; (*specif.*) to manipulate (information) to produce a desired appearance or result. [Though not directly relevant, 1955 quot. exemplifies a freq. fig. use of the S.E. sense.]

[**1955** Q. Reynolds *HQ* 93: A couple of busboys were massaging dishes in the kitchen.] **1969** *Business Week* (May 10) 142: Buying…a record of the day's trading activity and having it massaged through their computer programs at night. **1972** W.C. Anderson *Hurricane* 146: We've been massaging your plan to rescue the sloop. **1973** *Business Week* (Sept. 15) 98: These young people have really helped us massage our future. **1973** *Pop. Science* (Dec.) 69: They simply persisted in massaging the weaknesses and drawbacks that showed up in the early prototypes until they perfected an engine. **1977** *Business Week* (Feb. 14) 37: Sitting in his office in Boston massaging financial statements. **1978** *Kansas City Star* (Jan. 22) 4G: Criticism that such reports are massaged and manipulated before publication. **1984** *Harper's* (Nov.) 60: [Computer hackers] talk of "playing" with the numbers, "massaging" the model.

b. to flatter or cajole. Cf. STROKE. [The phr. *massage (some-one's) ego* is recent S.E., perh. sugg. by *assuage the ego*.]

　　1973 *Business Week* (Mar. 3) 55: He is calling on Senators and Congressmen who need massaging. [**1975** *L.A. Times Bk. Rev.* (Nov. 16) 14: The wife's ego needs massaging too.] **1977** in *Los Angeles* (Jan. 1978) 210: Potential donors are cared for, massaged, given favored status, free services and, of course, recognition. **1979** *Atlantic* (June) 38: I'll go to a clothing store where I know the owner, where they massage me, instead of saving a hundred dollars a suit by shopping the manufacturers' factories. **1981** *L.A. Times* (Apr. 15) I 12: Reagan Seeks Action on Economic Plan/Will "Massage" Lawmakers, Urge Public to Put Pressure on Them. *a***1988** Lewin & Lewin *Thesaurus* 157: Flatter…*massage, massage one's ego.*

massive *adj. Stu.* striking; notable; IMMENSE.

　　[**1985** J. Schumacher & C. Kurlander *St. Elmo's Fire* (film): Get caught in a sex scandal. Retire in massive disgrace.] **1986** Knoxville, Tenn., junior high school student: Gee, Mom, you look massive!…That means you look great. **1987** Univ. Tenn. student theme: A good-looking male is [referred to as] *fine, hot,* or *massive.* **1991** *CBS Sunday Morning* (CBS-TV) (Mar. 24): "So you think he's a big star?" "Massive."

master blaster *n.* **1.** *Army.* a recipient of a Master Parachutist Badge.

　　1980 Cragg *Lex. Militaris* 293: *Master Blaster.* A soldier who is authorized to wear the Master Parachutist Badge. **1982** Goff, Sanders & Smith *Bros.* 40 [ref. to 1968]: He called himself a master blaster. He said he had more hook-ups than we got push-ups. **1983** K. Miller *Lurp Dog* 89 [ref. to *ca*1970]: Master Parachutist wings…masterblaster wings. **1984–87** Ferrandino *Firefight* 184: Master-blaster wings, and his combat infantryman's badge. **1984–88** Hackworth & Sherman *About Face* 449 [ref. to 1960's]: His master-blaster [wings] were on his hat.

2. a very effective person; master.

　　1989 *Beachin' Times* 12: I.M. Fletcher…the master blaster of multiple disguises.

master of the universe *n.* [coined by Tom Wolfe (see 1984–87 quot.), alluding to *Masters of the Universe,* trademark name for a series of superhero dolls] *Business.* a person who has achieved exceptional success.

　　1984–87 T. Wolfe *Bonfire of Vanities* ch. i: He had picked up the telephone and taken an order for zero-coupon bonds that had brought him a $50,000 commission, *just like that.*…On Wall Street he and a few others…had become precisely that[:] Masters of the Universe. *Ibid.* ch. iv: *I beat them both.* Never had there been such music in the ears of the Master of the Universe. Play on! Never stop! **1990** *U.S. News & W.R.* (Feb. 12) 19: Two masters of the universe step down.…The October, 1987, crash was a defining moment for two of Wall Street's biggest names. **1991** *N.Y. Times Book Rev.* (Oct. 13) 36: The triumphal progress to wealth and esteem of these Masters of the Universe. **1994** *N.Y. Times* (Apr. 3) ("Business") 1: Larry Kudlow seemed a master of the universe. Being a top Wall Street economist was not the half of it. Mr. Kudlow had been a prominent member of President Reagan's economic team [etc.]. **1994** *Wash. Post* (Aug. 14) H8: Inside, masters of the universe are buying large coffees and fighting over the last copy of the Financial Times of London or the Wall Street Journal. **1995** *New Yorker* (Aug. 14) 32: New Masters of the Universe will come and go, but for the moment Michael Eisner occupies center stage alone. **1995** *Vanity Fair* (Oct.) 273: David Geffen.…In his second decade as a master of the Hollywood universe.…A billionaire college dropout, [etc.].

master's stiff *n. Naut.* a ship's crewman who helps officers enforce discipline. Now *hist.*

　　1967 Raskin *True Course* 2: Harsh treatment would become harsher, laid on by officers and "master's stiffs" among the crewmen.

mat *n.* see s.v. MOT.

¶ **In phrases:**

¶ **go to the mat** [alluding to the sport of wrestling] to struggle; fight; (*also*) to refuse to compromise; go all out. Cf. *on the mat,* 1, below.

　　1908 W.G. Davenport *Butte & Montana* 273: Brown went to the mat with the grippe and failed to take the count. **1912** *Hampton's Mag.* (Jan.) 842: He done me dirt…and I ain't seen him since; but when I do, me and him goes to the mat. **1929** Barr *Let Tomorrow Come* 40: I nearly go to the mat with one cherry-picker. He cracks som'pin' about bums I don't like. **1956** in J. Jones *Reach* 247: I am prepared to go to the mat for it. **1977** *Kojak* (CBS-TV): He's indicted on seven counts of involuntary manslaughter during the commission of seven felonies. If he goes to the mat, that's twenty years each count. **1977** *U.S. News & W.R.* (Nov. 7) 23: Carter must carefully select the issues on which he is willing to go to the mat with Congress. **1980** *Atlantic* (Aug.) 73: I had gone to the mat with everyone at the company. And to what effect? **1983** in *Psychol. Today* (Jan. 1984) 48: Going to the mat with the boss is seldom conducive to a long career.

¶ **on the mat, 1.** [alluding to the sport of wrestling] near defeat.

　　1896 Ade *Artie* 101: Say, that boy kind o' had me down on the mat, didn't he?

2. Esp. *Mil.* called before a superior for admonition or punishment.

　　*****1898** in *OEDS:* The sergeant…shouts with military brevity: "On to the mat, John Smith." [*ante,* Close to the medical officer's desk is a thick padded carpet about a yard square.] [bracketed material in orig. quot.]. *****1917** Empey *Over the Top* (gloss.): *Mat, on the*—When Tommy is haled before his commanding officer. **1919** Darling *Jargon Book* 46: *On the Mat*—To be called before a superior for an explanation of some act or occurrence. **1937** *Our Army* (Jan.) 20: On the mat. **1954–60** *DAS: Mat, on the* = on the carpet. Some student use since *c*1930; some W.W.II USN use.

mate *n.* Esp. *Naut.* (used as a term of direct address between men, esp. seamen). [Quots. indicate that U.S. usage has been almost exclusively nautical; this has not been the case in Britain or Australia, and Americans often consider this form of address foreign to AmE.]

　　*****1450** in *OED.* **1841** [Mercier] *Man-of-War* 96: "You're wrong, there, mate!" another tar breaks forth. *****1863** in T. Taylor *Plays* 209: Thou'lt come back, mate? **1886** in Fife & Fife *Ballads of West* 188: Mates, you know as I ain't any Christian. **1916** *Variety* (Aug. 25): It's a sad story, mates. **1932** M. Anderson *Rain* (film): On your feet, mate. **1940** Meehan & Tugend *Seven Sinners* (film): Hey, mate! **1973** Norris & Springer *Men in Exile* 149: Mucho Gracias, Mate. **1974** E. Thompson *Tattoo* 30: OK, mate, let's see how smart you are. **1991** Marcinko & Weisberg *Rogue Warrior* 37: Mate, you ain't never gonna make it. *a***1995** M. Kelly *Proudly* 58: What ship are you from mate?

mater *n.* [< L] Orig. *Stu.* mother. *Joc. Rare* in U.S.

　　1859 Matsell *Vocab.* 54: *Mater.* Mother. *****1864** in *OED2.* **1887** [C. Mackenzie] *Jack Pots* 77: *Mater.*—But, Jeremiah, we must have something to wear. *****1888,** *****1897** in *OED2.* **1930** J.T. Farrell *Calico Shoes* 27: I'll bet her mater kicked her out again. **1979** G. Wolff *Duke of Deception* 181 [ref. to *ca*1955]: Had a great time with my mater in D.C. **1996** *Simpsons* (Fox-TV): Oh, hello, mater! Sorry to have pulled the plug on you.

matey *n. Naut.* MATE.

　　1841 [Mercier] *Man-of-War* 137: I don't think you'll smell gunpowder…this cruise matie. **1847** Downey *Cruise* 29: "Well, what is it Matie," said another of the occupants of the Cots. **1849** Melville *White Jacket* 366: Start my soul-bolts, maties, [if I ever go to sea again]. **1866** C.E. Hunt *Shenandoah* 31: I tell you what, Maty. *a***1868** N.H. Bishop *Across So. Amer.* 28: I wonder, mateys. **1884** Blanding *Sailor Boy* 258: Hurry up, matey, or I'm a goner. **1932** Hecht & Fowler *Great Magoo* 14: O.K., matey. **1941** Kendall *Army & Navy Slang* 21: A dime wouldn't break you, Matey.

matey *adj.* comradely; companionable. *Rare* in U.S.

　　*****1915** in *OED2.* **1919** Janis *Big Show* 84 [ref. to 1918]: I don't think it's very "matey" of you to laugh like that. **1952** *Sat. Eve. Post* (June 28) 90: Somebody got the matey idea that…the big bang should be posponed until…Bastille Day. **1957** *Time* (Sept. 30) 33: Presumably, all was matey once again.

matinee *n.* Orig. *Theat.* an act or instance of sexual intercourse during the afternoon; (*hence*) a person who engages in such intercourse.

　　1944 in P. Smith *Letter from Father* 429: When the husband was on the road, we would have matinees—she was a swell lay. **1957** Murtagh

& Harris *First Stone* 2: Some commuting businessmen, called *matinees*, reject the night hours altogether and come afternoons between two and four-thirty, so that they can be on the five-fifteen and five-thirty trains headed for Westchester and Connecticut. *Ibid.* 306: *Matinée.* A man who visits prostitutes in the afternoon and still gets home on time. **1959–60** R. Reisner *Jazz Titans* 161: *Matinee*: sexual intercourse in the afternoon. **1966** Fariña *Down So Long* 7: And doesn't your thigh-down tingle to think about it? Shame it's afternoon, never much on matinées. **1985** *N.Y. Times* (Aug. 5) A14: [Many teenage television viewers] heard Chris of "Cagney and Lacey" suggest a "quickie," and Julie of "Hotel" expounding on a "matinee." **1995** *N.Y. Times Bk. Rev.* (Dec. 24) 6: Paul…sends her into matinees with a good-looking lawyer who has a handy apartment.

matlow *n.* [< F *matelot*] *Naut.* a naval seaman.
   1847 Downey *Cruise of Portsmouth* 216: You was sure to meet lots of Matelo's wending their way to their various quarters. **1853** Downey *Filings* 142: They even rob a poor old matelot of his trade. **1866** *Nat. Police Gaz.* (Nov. 17) 3: He…has the rolling gait of the "matlow." **1903 in Kipling *Traffics & Discoveries* 50: "*Sub*scription, you pink-eyed matlow!" said the Marine. **1950 Granville *Sea Slang* 154: *Matelot.* The self-adopted nickname for all bluejackets….Pronounced *matlo.*

Mattel [toy] *n.* [after *Mattel*, U.S. manufacturer of children's toys, alluding to the plastic used for var. parts of the these weapons] *Mil.* an M-16 rifle or M-60 machine gun. Also **Matty Mattel** (after a figure in Mattel toy commercials). [Quots. ref. to Vietnam War.]
   [**1967** in B. Edelman *Dear Amer.* 179: I [had] an M-16. It's like that new one Mattel toy makers put out.] **1978** Hasford *Short-Timers* 106: "Where's my Mattel?" Cowboy hands me a grease gun. **1983** C. Rich *Advisors* 448: M-16…called "Matty Mattel"…so was the M-60 MG. **1985** Dye *Between Raindrops* 206: Mattie Mattel rifle shattered in your hands when the round hit it. **1986** R. Zumbro *Tank Sgt.* 127: I state categorically that the "Mattel toy rifle" is not fit for a grown man to fight a war with. *a***1987** Bunch & Cole *Reckoning for Kings* 157: The M-60….Due to the extensive use of nylon for the stock and forehand grip, it was dubbed the Mattel Toy by GIs. *a***1990** Helms *Proud Bastards* 188: Your Matty-Mattel M-16.

Mattel Messerschmitt *n. Army.* a small training helicopter. Cf. MAYTAG MESSERSCHMITT.
   1979 in Elting, Cragg & Deal *Dict. Soldier Talk* 195: The tiny choppers, painted bright orange, look so toylike that students call them "Mattel Messerschmitts." **1983–90** L. Heath *CW2* 199 [ref. to Vietnam War]: He was instructing in Matel [*sic*] Messerschmitts. *Ibid.* 368: *Matel* [*sic*] *Messerschmitt*—nickname for the Hughes TH-55 trainer.

matter *n.* ¶ In phrase: **that's what's the matter** that's the truth.—used for emphasis.—also constr. with *with.*
   1863 in A. Clark *Armies of Streets* 126: "We live in a happy day."…"Bully for you!" "Go on!" "That's what's the matter!" **1864** in McKee *Throb of Drums* 155: We gathered berries and had four of the gol durndest (kobblers) baked that you've ever seen…that's what's the matter. **1871** Hay *Pike Co. Ballads* 16: I want a chaw of terbacker,/And that's what's the matter of me. **1875** (quot. at PLAY). **1879** Rooney *Conundrums* 80: There are [vogue expressions] "That's what's the matter with Hannah,"/And "dead beats" on every side. **1890** *Aztec Treasure-House* (Jan.) 89: They're both of 'em lyin' like fiddlers; that's what's th' matter with *them.* **1896** T.H. Smith *Tom Grogan* 141: Oh, I'm onter yer. Ye set de stable afire. Dat's what's the matter.

mattress 1. *Baseball.* a chest protector. *Joc.*
   1908 *Baseball Mag.* (July) 393 (cited in Nichols *Baseball Termin.*).
   2.a. a beard. *Joc.*
   1926 Upson *Me & Henry* 17: Henry looked at the Frog's whiskers, and said, "What I can't figure is how you guys get them big mattresses inside them little bits of gas masks you got." **1929** Milburn *Hobo's Hornbook* 143: Take that mattress off yer face!
   b. pubic hair.—usu. considered vulgar.
   1938 "Justinian" *Amer. Sexualis* 28: *Mattress.* n. The pubic hair.
   3. a woman, esp. if promiscuous, considered as a sexual partner.—used contemptuously. Cf. MATTRESSBACK.
   [**1942–49** Goldin et al. *DAUL* 137: *Mat.* A prostitute or a very promiscuous woman.] **1963** Coon *Short End* 218: Bertha was just one great big warm mattress. **1968** Radano *Beat* 47: That's her. She was a good mattress. A very good mattress. **1974** Kingry *Monk & Marines*

166: The VC would just tell any poor puke on that hill who really tried to work with us just that he better remember he had a daughter or a wife in the ville that would be turned into a mattress for the troops or worse. **1988** *Golden Girls* (NBC-TV): You fifty-year-old mattress!
   ¶ In phrase:
   ¶ **go to** [or **hit**] **the mattresses** [prob. fr. the idea of mattresses being used as shields from gunfire] *Und.* (during a gang war) to arm oneself heavily and fortify a place or places as refuge from enemy gang members.
   1976 Hoffman & Pecznick *Drop a Dime* 254: The Campisis had completed all the preparations for "going to the mattresses"—holing up in a war against the remnants of Luciano's mob. **1979** *Nat. Lampoon* (Sept.) 19: But I'm prepared to go to the mattresses if I have to. **1980** Pearl *Pop. Slang* 71: *Hit the mattresses v.* (Crime) to go into hiding.

mattressback *n.* a sexually promiscuous woman, esp. a prostitute.—used contemptuously. Also vars. Cf., semantically, CANVASBACK.
   1960 Barth *Sot-Weed Factor* 466: Whore!…Trull!…Mattressback! **1963–64** Kesey *Great Notion* 193: She was the first of a long line of mattressback Montgomery girls. *a***1968** in Haines & Taggart *Ft. Lauderdale* 135: Real mattressbacks go there,…real nymphos. **1981** *Hill St. Blues* (NBC-TV): You nail some drugged-out, two-bit mattressbuster. **1987** *Night Court* (NBC-TV): [You] mattress mouseketeer!

mattress polo *n.* copulation. *Joc.*
   1931 J.T. Farrell *McGinty* 221: We're all professional mattress polo players, Casey replied; they leered and snickered. **1960** MacCuish *Do Not Go Gentle* 224 [ref. to WWII]: Liked the sack and mattress polo.

Maud *n.* **1.** a woman or an effeminate man. [The second quot. may refl. a var. of MOT.]
   1896 Ade *Artie* 98: You'd have to shake that Miss Maud business and comb your hair different. **1932** in *AS* (Feb. 1934) 27: [Md. prison:] *Maud.* A woman.
   2. *Petroleum Industry.* a heavy wrench, pair of tongs, or auxiliary engine.—often constr. with *old.*
   1925 Dobie *Hunting Ground* 65: "Old Maude"…is a big wrench used in screwing pipe together. **1928** Dobie *Drinkin' Gou'd* 51: "Maud," the heavy break-out tongs [used by petroleum workers]. **1944** Boatright & Day *Hell to Breakfast* 146: A very heavy set of chain tongs used only on hard-to-break drill collars is called "Old Maude" or the "Bull Tongs." **1956** in *DAS*: *Maud*—an engine. **1965** O'Neill *High Steel* 273: Old Maude. A large pipe wrench. **1972** Haslam *Oil Fields* 107: *Maud, n.* An engine.

maugh *n.* [orig. unkn.] *Und.* (see quot.).
   1846 J. Greene *Band of Brothers* 110: *Maugh*—a flash word, signifying Profession.

Maui Wowie *n.* a potent grade of marijuana grown on the island of Maui; potent Hawaiian marijuana.
   1977 (cited in Spears *Drugs & Drink*). **1978** Maupin *Tales* 252: There was a little Maui Wowie left. **1979** Alibrandi *Custody* 94: Colombian or Maui-wowie…marijuana. **1980** Ciardi *Browser's Dict.* 246: *Maui wowie*…A species of Hawaiian marijuana….In 1977…*Maui wowie* was going for $150 [an ounce]. **1980** Novak *High Culture* 181: Some…would be only too happy to toke…Hawaiian Mauie Wowie all night long. **1982–84** Chapple *Outlaws in Babylon* 219: Kona Gold, Maui Wowie. **1987** J. Thompson *Gumshoe* 61 [ref. to 1977]: His T-shirt had *Maui Wowie* emblazoned across the chest.

maul *v. Stu.* to engage in usu. passionate romantic embraces (with).—used with no sugg. of violence or clumsiness.
   1875 *Harper's Mo.* (Sept.) 618: She's de on'y girl a feller wants to maul, and she's de on'y one a feller can't. **1942** *ATS* 783: College [Slang:]…"Pet"; "Neck."…*go into a clinch*,…*maul a moll*,…*fling woo* [etc.]. [**1970** N.Y.U. student: I don't like getting mauled by some asshole.] **1990** P. Munro *Slang U.*: *Maul* to make out fervently….The ho at the party was mauling with every guy there.

mauler *n.* [prob. infl. by *maul, v.*] Orig. *Boxing.* **1.a.** MAULEY.
   1871 Banka *Prison Life* 149: *Third Round.* Offense…shies defense's "maulers." **1902** Jarrold *Mickey Finn* 79: His maulers is as big as me head. **1984 J. Green *Dict. Contemp. Sl.*: *Maulers*…hands. **1990 Thorne *Dict. Contemp. Sl.*: *Maulers*…hands. A mainly middle-class schoolchildren's usage, popular in the 1950s and early 1960s. "*Keep your maulers off my things, will you.*"

b. a heavy blow with the fist.

    1928 Dahlberg *Bottom Dogs* 271: For every one I get, you'll get ten maulers in the ribs.

2. a boxer.

    1920–21 Witwer *Leather Pushers* 44: What kind of a mauler *is* this guy Kelly? **1934** Weseen *Dict. Amer. Sl.* 239: *Mauler*—A prizefighter.

mauley *n.* [prob. fr. *maul* 'a massive hammer' + *-ey* dimin. suff., infl. by *maul, v.*] Esp. *Boxing.* a fist or hand. [An erroneous date of "1781" given in all eds. of Partridge's *DSUE* arose through a simple confusion of G. Parker's two books; *A View of Society*, published in 1781, does not contain this word. *F & H* oddly misdates this passage to "1800" and misspells "Slang" as "Sling."]

    ***1789** G. Parker *Life's Painter* 152: *Slang* [give] us your *mauly*. **1832** *Spirit of Times* (Mar. 3) 3: O'Hegan made an attempt to close but met Mc's *mawly* under the left *listener.* ***1836** *Spirit of Times* (Feb. 20) 7: Putting his *mauley* into the bag, out he brought a fine fresh egg. **1842** *Spirit of Times* (Sept. 3) 322: Sully planted his...mauley on Billy's snuff-box. **1848** *Ladies' Repository* (Oct.) 315: *Mauly*, A hand. **1848** Judson *Mysteries* 37: Ello, Charley, my kid! Tip us your *mawley.* **1870** (quot. at *bunch of fives* s.v. FIVE). **1873** B. Harte *Mrs. Skaggs's Husbands* 270: They fall easy victims to what he would call his "dexter *mawley.*" **1898** F.P. Dunne *Mr. Dooley in Peace & War* 166: Hurl yer *maulies* into his hoops. **1898–1900** Cullen *Chances* 140: He's pretty handy with his *maulies.* **1903** *Chi. Tribune* (Dec. 2) 8: His left "mawley" [was] sore and swollen. **1925** *Sat. Eve. Post* (Oct. 3) 21: A lad with the swiftest set of *mauleys* in this section. **1946** D. Runyon, in *DAS*: Now the guys grapple with each other...seldom using their *maulies.* **1950** *Sat. Eve. Post* (May 6) 146: She can hear...the crunching impact of leather-wrapped *maulies* on bone and flesh.

maven *n.* [< Yid *meyvn* < Heb] Orig. *Jewish-Amer.* a connoisseur; expert. *Joc.* Now *colloq.* [Pop. after 1964 as reported in 1984–88 quot. and further in the 1980's in W. Safire's weekly column "On Language" in the *New York Times Magazine.* Now usu. *Journ.*, with numerous 1980's nonce compounds listed by D.L. Gold in *Jewish Linguistic Studies* II (1990), pp. 134–58.]

    1952 *N.Y. Times Mag.* (Sept. 21) 58, in *DAS*: The most trying type [of customer] of all...is the "mayvin." The word is of Yiddish origin, has entered the language. **1965** Vita Herring TV ad: A word from the beloved herring maven. **1969** *Time*, in *BDNE* 279: Robert Gottlieb, then the editorial genie in residence at Simon & Schuster, now the mavin at Alfred Knopf. **1972** *Harper's* (Apr.) 96: The revolution "mavens" of academia and the higher journalism. **1973** in J. Flaherty *Chez Joey* xxv: Like most New Yorkers, I was a newspaper maven. **1974** *Oui* (Oct.) 34: Quoth the movie maven: nevermore. **1974** *Business Week* (Sept. 28) 77: A "hot money" scandal is giving a lot of tax haven mavens pause about stashing money in the Caribbean. **1983** *USA Today* (Aug. 2) 2D: Is Karen Black a pie maven? **1984** J. McNamara *First Directive* 68: My gadget maven....He's got the whole place wired like CBS. **1986** C. Freeman *Seasons of Heart* 267: After this morning, those tough birds will treat you like a born New York real-estate maven. **1984–88** M. Solow, in Safire *Language Maven* 41: The word "maven" began to creep into the language sometime late in 1964 when I launched a campaign for Vita Herring with the Beloved Herring Maven as spokesman. **1988** *TV Guide* (Mar. 19) 29: The paper's quirky-sweet murder maven, Edna Buchanan. **1989** "Capt. X" & Dodson *Unfriendly Skies* 21: If you're an airline maven,...you're probably aware how...United and Continental are practically shanghaiing passengers from each other. **1989** G. Hall *Air Guard* 33: TAC safety mavens yelled at them. **1991** D. Weinstein *Heavy Metal* 106: Hip culture mavens.

maw-dicker *n.* [*maw* 'mother' + DICK[2], *v.* + *-er*] *S.W.* (partial euphem. for) MOTHERFUCKER.—usu. considered vulgar. Hence **maw-dicking**, *adj.* Cf. MODICKER.

    1969–71 Kahn *Boys of Summer* 122: Dick Williams, who reasoned that he would be thrown off the bench for calling an umpire "motherfucker," cogitated and found a solution. "Hey," he'd shout. "Ump. You're a mawdicker." **1984** Sample *Raceboss* 145 [ref. to 1950's]: Why you Gotdam impudent shit-colored mawdicker. *Ibid.* 202 [ref. to *ca*1960]: I oughta throw yore mawdickin ass in the pisser.

max¹ *n.* [earlier *maxim* < L *maximus* 'best'] gin. *Rare* in U.S.

    [***1739** in Partridge *Dict. Und.* 435: A Glass of *Maxim*, (Geneva).] ***1800** in Partridge *Dict. Und.* 435: Tossed off...two noggins of max. ***1811** *Lexicon Balatron.: Max.* Gin. ***1819** Lord Byron, in *OED*: Oh! for a glass of max! ***1820–21** P. Egan *Life in London* 226: She loves a *drap* of max. ***1822** D. Carey *Life in Paris* I 76: No vulgar *max.* **1859** Matsell *Vocab.* 54: *Max.* Gin; intoxicating liquor.

max² *n.* **1.** Orig. *Stu.* the maximum academic grade; (*hence*) the maximum of anything; furthest limit. [In general use only since the 1960's.]

    1851 B. Hall *College Wds.* 197: *Max.* Abbreviated for *maximum*, greatest. At Union College, he who receives the highest possible number of marks, which is one hundred, in each study, for a term, is said to *take Max* (or maximum); to be a *Max scholar.* On the Merit Roll, all the *Maxs* are clustered at the top. **1854** in B. Hall *College Wds.* (ed. 2) 310: Probably not less than one third...confidently expect to "mark max," during their whole course. **1894** Maury *Recoll.* 26 [ref. to 1840's]: I got "max" on that...effort. **1900** *DN* II 45: *Max*, *n.* Maximum mark. **1942** *ATS* 24: *Max and min*, maximum and minimum. **1971** Woodley *Dealer* 94: See, that's the whole gimmick. You gotta be willing to take it to the max. **1982** Hayano *Poker Faces* 44: She doesn't know how to get the "max" out of her [cards]. **1983** Ad for Palisades Amusement Park, N.J. (WOR-TV) (Aug. 11): It's stupendous. The max! **1987** *Science News* (Sept. 5) 149: The disappearance...was abrupt, occurring in less than 850,000 years....That's an absolute max.

2. *Pris.* **a.** the maximum sentence for a crime.

    1942–49 Goldin et al. *DAUL* 137: *Max.*...The maximum limit of an indeterminate prison sentence; the maximum penalty, other than capital punishment, provided by law for any specific crime. **1966–67** P. Thomas *Mean Streets* 240: The rest of me was in Sing Sing, for a max of fifteen years. **1962–68** B. Jackson *In the Life* 122: She gave me the max, which was five years with no clemency. **1970** Gattzden *Black Vendetta* 43: A felony murder which carried the full max—the electric chair. **1974** Andrews & Dickens *Over the Wall* 29: His max would be up in six months.

b. a maximum security section of a prison; a maximum security prison.

    1961 *N.Y. Times* (July 23) VI 16: These girls in "max" (maximum security) must show improvement within three months, or they are referred back to court. **1977** *L.A. Times* (July 28) III 1: I was put in max (maximum security) for 50 days. **1983** *Maclean's* (June 6) 17: Life in the "maxes" is far grimmer than in Canada's minimum security institutions. [**1994** *N.Y. Times* (Oct. 17) A1: Adapted prisons to be "maxis."]

¶ In phrases:

¶ **bring** [or **give**] **the max** *Mil.* to exert maximum or lethal force. [Quots. ref. to Vietnam War.]

    1969 in Lanning *Only War* 198: Will bring the max on the man. **1972** Pelfrey *Big V* 13: That had happened to a guy in Delta company last month, brought the max to his young ass. *Ibid.* 15: That was eight-inch. They bring the max, shoot twenty-three miles. *Ibid.* 18: Wait till you see the Cobras work out. They bring the max. **1973** Karlin, Paquet & Rottmann *Free Fire Zone* 7 [ref. to 1969]: Better act like you're alive, Cruit. Fuckin dink could bring the max on you before you knew it. *Ibid.* 8: You know what bangalores are?...They bring the max. *Ibid.* 12: We brought the max....Fuckin dinks. **1975** S.P. Smith *Amer. Boys* 17: Jesus, Slagel....Why didn't you give this fool the max?

¶ **to the max** Esp. *Stu.* to the limit; utterly.

    1971 *Playboy* (Aug.) 207: We're lucky to have this captain....He's cool to the max. **1973** *TULIPQ* (coll. B.K. Dumas): *Drunk*...bombed; high to the max. **1973** Eble *Campus Slang* (Fall) 4: Some students hate this school to the max. **1974** Blount *3 Bricks Shy* 36: The man whom Gilliam "idolized to the max." **1978** *New West* (Aug. 14) 37: As the kids say—I'm pushing it to the max. **1979** Gram *Blvd. Nights* 43: Waxed to the max. **1981** *Penthouse* (Apr.) 200: Jeff had me turned on to the max. **1982** in *Nat. Lampoon* (Feb. 1983) (front cover): I disagree to the max! **1983** *L.A. Times* (June 23) II 6: I know "justice" will be done to the max when a police officer is killed. **1985** Yeager & Janos *Yeager* 146: In the sky and on the ground, we lived to the max. **1986** G. Trudeau, in *Daily Beacon* (Univ. Tenn.) (Apr. 3) 7: Is that awesome to the max or what? **1988** *Sonya Live in L.A.* (CNN-TV) (July 5): A lot of us...are stressed out to the max. **1992** *UTSQ*: That record was to the max. **1993** K. Scott *Monster* 330: I sat there in total darkness, in total silence, repressed to the max. **1994** *New Yorker* (Dec. 26) 148: Joy to the max, you splendid readers.

max *adj.* **1.** Esp. *Mil.* maximum.

    1951 Sheldon *Troubling of a Star* 214: I think we're probably going to make a max effort somewhere. **1956** in Harvey *Air Force* 62: They were at max altitude. **1958** *Sat. Eve. Post* (Oct. 11) 75: The idea was to reach top speed soon after the drop—coast to max altitude over the lake. **1959** *Sat. Eve. Post* (May 2) 70: He…heard the blessed explosive screech of max power from his right wing. **1964** R. Moore *Green Berets* 117: She cannot reach max performance without the help of the medic. **1966** F. Elkins *Heart of Man* 35: It's been nothing but max thrust since we arrived. **1969** in *Pop. Science* (Jan. 1970) 173: You got clean plugs, buddy, you got max power. *a***1989** R. Herman, Jr. *Warbirds* 274: I want max publicity.

    2. *Pris.* maximum security.

    1976 Braly *False Starts* 215: We were thrown into a max. tank. **1983** Glass & Glass *Touring Nevada* 183: Isn't this a fine isolated place for a "max" prison. **1995** *Nation* (Oct. 30) 504: Chilling, high-tech, super-max prisons driving their inmates to madness.

max *adv.* **1.** at the maximum; at most.

    1977 *Texas Monthly* (Feb.) 152: The first in a series of posters would be ready in "six weeks max." **1980** *Residence Hall Comp.* (Univ. Tenn.) 6: She borrows something maybe twice a month max. **1982** *California* (Jan.) 122: I'll be out in a year, year and a half max.

    2. extremely; as much as can be.

    1983 E. Dodge *Dau* 95: He and Ramirez the Greek were max tight, dig it. *Ibid.* 119: Selbig was my buddy. We were max tight.

max *v.* **1.a.** Orig. *U.S. Mil. Acad.* to perform perfectly on (a test or the like); (*hence*) to score the maximum number of hits on (a target).

    1871 Wood *Scrapbook* 339: *To max it*—to make a perfect recitation. *To make a cold max*—same as the above. **1878** Flipper *Colored Cadet* 238: In this particular subject, I "maxed it," made a thorough recitation. **1900** *U.S. Mil. Acad. Howitzer No. 1* 120: *Max.*—To accomplish or carry out something without a mistake. **1904** *U.S. Mil. Acad. Howitzer No. 5* 222: *Max*—To make a maximum mark; to do something perfectly. (obsolete). **1930** *Our Army* (Feb.) 43: *Max.* To secure the highest possible grade, or to do a thing perfectly. **1931** in D.O. Smith *Cradle* 197: I maxed it cold [got a perfect grade]. **1965** LeMay & Kantor *Mission* 66 [ref. to *ca*1930]: Boy, I said to myself, *I'm really going to max this*—(Slang: meant that I was going to do a hundred per cent.). **1973** Layne *Murphy* (unp.): No man's ever maxed that test, Murphy. **1982** in *Barnhart Dict. Comp.* III (1984) 40: Scott has just finished maxing the push-up test at 68. **1988** Schneider & Schneider *Sound Off!* 84: She could max (receive the highest score in) all her physical fitness tests. *a***1989** Care *Spook Show* 138 [ref. to Vietnam War]: Why don't we paint some big X's on the [airplanes] and see if they can max them?

    b. to extend to or exceed the limit. Cf. MAXED.

    1971 *Army Reporter* (Feb. 1) 5: "And your ears are maxed to the onions [very large]," comments the [Little Red Riding] Hood. **1978** *L.A. Times* (Jan. 3) III 2: Dallas…will tie Minnesota…by maxing a record Super Bowl appearance Jan. 15. **1985** Yeager & Janos *Yeager* 144: The pedal was to the floor and both cars were maxed. **1987** *21 Jump St.* (Fox-TV): All his credit cards were maxed…and the bank was getting ready to foreclose on his house.

    2. *Pris.* to serve a maximum prison sentence.

    *a***1979** Pepper & Pepper *Straight Life* 143: These guys were shipped out to max at the farm.

    3. *Rap Music.* to enjoy oneself thoroughly; relax completely.

    1987 "Public Enemy" *M.P.E.* (rap song): I'm gonna max and relax and chill. **1988** "EPMD" *Strictly Business* (rap song): When I am in action, there is no time for maxin' or relaxin'. **1990** *Fresh Prince of Bel Air* (NBC-TV): I was maxin' and relaxin'. **1990** *TV Guide* (Oct. 20) 19: *Maxin' and relaxin'*: laying lower than low, being cooler than cool. **1990** NBC-TV spot ad: Get ready for an hour of maxin' and relaxin' with Saturday Morning Videos on NBC! **1991** *Houston Chronicle* (Oct. 8) 2D: *Maxin'*…Relaxing. **1991** *Saturday Videos* (NBC-TV): We're chillin' like Bob Dylan and maxin' like Michael Jackson. **1991** *True Colors* (Fox-TV): I'm gonna be stone-cold maxin' at the Alpha jam. **1992** Mowry *Way Past Cool* 77: Partyin…and maxin.

maxed *adj.* highly intoxicated by drugs or alcohol. Also **maxed out.**

    1982 P. Dickson *Words!* (cited in Spears *Drugs & Drink*): Maxed out. **1986** *NDAS*: *Maxed*…Intoxicated with a narcotic.

maximax *adj. Business.* (of a decision) crucial and unalterable.

    1979 Homer *Jargon* 26: Said company has made a *maximax* decision (that is, it has put all its chips on one roll of the dice).

max out *v.* **1.** *Pris.* to serve out a maximum sentence without parole or be released at the end of a maximum sentence.

    1971 *Who Took Weight?* 196: I ain't on no parole, Ali. I maxxed [*sic*] out. **1972** Burkhart *Women in Pris.* 63: I…violated my CR and was sent to Alderson, to max it out. I was released in November, 1961. *Ibid.* 154: The pressure of possibly "maxing out." **1974** *Time* (June 17) 61: *Max out:* complete maximum [prison] sentence. **1974** Andrews & Dickens *Over the Wall* 28: They sent him to state prison; he would have to max out. **1976** Hoffman & Pecznick *Drop a Dime* 104: In prison argot, he "maxed out"—was released after serving his maximum sentence. **1979** Homer *Jargon* 76: A lifer who has died in prison has *maxed out.* **1995** *CBS This Morning* (CBS-TV) (Jan. 3): He maxed out. He served his term [and was released].

    2.a. to reach or cause to reach a maximum limit or capacity; (*hence*) to have had one's fill of something. [The *a*1986 quot. presumably ref. to reaching a state of exhaustion, but it may be an otherwise unrecorded subsense.]

    1978 *L.A. Times* (May 30) I 1: We were just maxed out.…Just scrambling to keep up. **1979** in *Barnhart Dict. Comp.* III (1984) 40: The policemen around the Mall call the overtime limit "the max."…There is a good deal of talk about "maxing out" and "having to work for free." **1981** Univ. Tenn. student: That's enough [Coca-Cola] for me. I've maxed out. **1982** *L.A. Times* (Feb. 12) V 29: Alvarado had "maxed out" at $38,000 a year working for Stevens. She wanted a new challenge. **1984** D. Jenkins *Life Its Ownself* 118: We can max out at…thirty thou a year. *Ibid.* 124: Mommie's Trust Fund was about to max out at a hundred guys. *a***1986** *NDAS*: *Max out*…v phr *college students* To go to sleep. **1986** Zeybel *First Ace* 186: The rain was enough to max out the humidity. **1989** *N.Y. Times* (Sept. 18) A18: Messinger…managed to "max out," collecting all of the $312,000 in matching funds available to her under the system. **1991** *N.Y. Times* (Aug. 26) A17: He's got a loan and a Pell Grant and he's maxed out his credit cards. **1992** *Knoxville* (Tenn.) *News-Sentinel Detours on Campus* (Apr. 2) 6: Moon Unit is, like, maxed out on Val-speak. **1994** N. Karlen *Babes in Toyland* 143: It had just a one-thousand-dollar limit, and it was already maxed out. **1995** IBM Corporation TV ad: "My hard drive's maxed out."…"Bummer." **1995** *As World Turns* (CBS-TV): You've maxed out my credit cards.

    b. to achieve complete success.

    1986 Univ. Tenn. student theme: A student who fails to max out [*i.e.*, get a perfect score on an examination]. **1989** Berent *Rolling Thunder* 81: The situation…was…Bates's one shot at the brass ring and he intended to max it out.

    c. to maximize.

    1995 Allstate Insurance TV ad: Max out your discounts!

    3. to relax; MAX, 3.

    1984 *N.Y. Times* (Sept. 24) D13: Some of the newest words and phrases.…"Max out!"—Take it easy. **1988** S. Lee *School Daze* (film): You need to max out, man.

maximum *adj. & adv.* extreme or extremely; maximally.

    1979 Homer *Jargon* 164: Being taken prisoner of war is *maximum bad.* **1982** Pond *Valley Girl's Gde.* 60: Maximum brilliant. **1985** *Teenage Mutant Ninja Turtles* (TV series): Maximum bummer, man!

maxy *adj.* [MAX[1] 'gin' + -*y*] intoxicated.

    1842 *Spirit of Times* (Sept. 3) 324: Hauled up for "cutting up shines" and getting "maxy" in New Orleans.

maybe *adv.* ¶ In phrases:

    ¶ **I don't mean maybe** certainly; definitely.—used for emphasis.

    1925 van Vechten *Nigger Heaven* 4: Her daddy done come home widout writin'…Ah doan mean mebbe. **1930–31** Farrell *Grandeur* 140: Then wouldn't life be the nuts, and I don't mean maybe. **1943** in M. Curtiss *Letters Home* 243: Truly it's hell and I don't mean maybe.

    ¶ **maybe not** emphatically so.

    1847 Downey *Cruise of Portsmouth* 60: By the Man of the Mast…that will carry us down to California and then maybe we won't kick up hell among the Mexicans. **1850** Garrard *Wah-to-yah* 163: *Maybe* thar wasn't coups counted, an' a big dance on hand, ef I was alone. **1883** Peck *Peck's Bad Boy* 218: As quick as she stopped against the hitching post she knew it was us boys, and she came down there, and maybe she didn't maul me. **1914** Lardner *You Know Me Al* 48: Looks like I got a regular girl now Al. We go up there the twenty-ninth and maybe I won't be glad to see her. **1925** Weaver *Collected Poems* 106: "Well, boys, how would you like to go to the circus?"/Say, maybe Ern and me didn't jump up!

mayo *n.* mayonnaise. Now *colloq.* or *S.E.*
    1954–60 *DAS: Mayo...Mayonnaise. Common lunchcounter use since c1930.* **1972** *Seattle Times* (Oct. 29) ("Pictorial") 7: Put the mayo in the tuna. **1975** *L.A. Times* (Oct. 19) I 3: Because of sanitary considerations the group was forced to "hold the mayo." **1978** *L.A. Times* (Feb. 16) VI 36: Add Garlic to Mayo for Fish Sauce. *1980 T. Jones *Adrift* 174: "Mayo?" "Yeah, mayonnaise." "Oh, of course...right."

maypop *n.* [punning on *maypop*, regional name for the passionflower (*Passiflora* sp.) or its edible fruit] *So.* a badly worn pneumatic tire. *Joc.*
    1980 Eble *Campus Slang* (Mar.) 4: Maypop tires—worn, slick tires which could burst at any time....(used by blacks. Stress on *may*). **1985** *New Yorker* (May 6) 107: Maypops, those are called. ("That tahr may pop any second").

Maytag *n.* **1.** see **MAYTAG MESSERSCHMITT.**
    2. *Pris.* a prisoner, usu. a catamite, compelled to do menial chores such as washing the clothes of an aggressive sodomist; **PUNK.**
    1971–72 in Abernethy *Bounty of Texas* 210: *Maytag, n.*—an inmate who is forced to hand-wash another inmate's clothes. **1982** "Grandmaster Flash & Furious Five" *The Message* (rap song): Got sent up for an eight-year bid/Now your man is took and you're a Maytag/Spend the next two years as an undercover fag. **1988** *Newsday* (N.Y.) (July 29) 38: "No one was gonna try to make him into a Maytag because he's so big."...A Maytag is a scared, small inmate who's made to wash the clothes of other more menacing inmates. **1990** P. Dickson *Slang!* 107: *Maytag.* Prison slang for a male inmate unable to protect himself from homosexual rape. **1995** *X-Files* (Fox-TV): [If] you talk, punk, I'm gonna make you my Maytag!

Maytag Charlie *n. Mil. Av.* a pilot of a small Japanese plane flying regular night reconnaissance and harassment missions over U.S. positions; **WASHING MACHINE CHARLIE.**
    1943 W. Simmons *Joe Foss* 61: "Maytag Charlie." That was the name we had for a Jap who flew over nearly every night in some kind of seaplane that sounded like a washing machine. **1944** *Amer. N & Q* (June) 39: Photo Joe and Maytag Charlie: German and Japanese aerial scouts respectively....N.Y. *Herald Tribune*, June 19, 1944.

Maytag Messerschmitt *n.* [fr. *Maytag*, U.S. manufacturer of home appliances + *Messerschmitt*, German aircraft manufacturer] *Mil.* a single-engine training aircraft or other light plane. *Joc. Occ.* **Maytag.** [Orig. as in 1942 quot., but cf. 1943 quot. at **MAYTAG CHARLIE;** quots. ref. to WWII.]
    1942 *Life* (Nov. 2) 10: The Army sometimes "washes out" (eliminates) cadets from flight training. At some time in every cadet's career, the possibility of becoming a washout stares him in the face. In fact, the planes we use have been dubbed "Maytag Messerschmitts" because of their "washing" characteristics. **1943** Trumbo *Guy Named Joe* (film): How many times have I got to tell you to quit slippin' this Maytag Messerschmitt when you're in a spin? **1943** in *Aviation Illustrated* (Feb. 1997) 29: We give the Axis fits in our Maytag Messerschmidts [*sic*] [*sc.* a Piper Cub]. **1944** Mellor *Sank Same* 41: One trip over the ocean and that one-lung Maytag will be ready to go back to country club flying. **1965** Newcomb *Iwo Jima*: The Grasshoppers (Stinson Sentinels), or "Maytag Messerschmitts,"...took off again. **1974** B. Stevens *More There I Was* 83: They leaped off in their "Maytag Messerschmitts (PT-22s)." **1978** Ardery *Bomber Pilot* 30: I continued to chafe at being relegated to flying "maytag messerschmitts."

Mazola party *n.* [fr. *Mazola*, trademark for a brand of corn oil] (see 1970 quot.).
    1968 Baker et al. *CUSS* 156: *Mazola Party* A wild party. **1970** Landy *Underground Dict.* 129: *Mazola party n.* Two or more people who get together to engage in sexual play and intercourse with their bodies covered with vegetable oil. This produces a unique sexual sensation. **1971** *Nat. Lampoon* (Oct.) 65: Hi! I'm giving a Mazola party and you're invited! **1983** *Newsweek on Campus* (May) 32: She had a lot of fun with the piece. She even mentioned "Mazola parties."

mazoo *n.* [abbr. of **MAZUMA**] **MAZUMA.**

1957 Myrer *Big War* 18 [ref. to WWII]: Kind of low on the mazoo? **1954–60** *DAS: Mazoo...Money. Not common.* **1963** Serling *Twilight Zone* (CBS-TV): He's got cash, lettuce, kale, the old mazoo.

mazoola *n.* [alter. of **MAZUMA;** cf. **MOOLA**] **MAZUMA.**
    1951 D.P. Wilson *Six Convicts* 125 [ref. to *ca*1933]: Anyway, he made it clear there wasn't no mazoola. **1959** H. Pugh *Navy Surgeon* 89 [ref. to 1917]: A sock was the orthodox container for the "mazula" of a real "blackjacker," who on payday went around looking for one blackjack game after another. **1954–60** *DAS: Mazoola* [or] *mazula...Money.* **1961** Gover *$100 Misunderstanding* 19: All that mazoola, he kin be jus's dum's dum kin be! **1963** Rubin *Sweet Daddy* 98: Like there's lots of mazoola in Canada.

mazoom *n.* **MAZUMA.** Also vars.
    1901 Ade *Modern Fables* 66: But they need the Vulgar Mazume, so they lighten him. **1902** Cullen *More Tales* 173: I got...a toss from my mazoom in Philadelphia. **1904** Hobart *I'm from Mo.* 12: All that mazoom! **1904** Hobart *Jim Hickey* 15: We're a sad bunch of ploughboys when we haven't a little mazume in the vest pocket. **1924** Wilstach *Stage Slang* 29: "Mazum," "mazuma," "cush," "denoya," "rocks," "spons," "spondulix," "long green," "yellowbacks," "dough," "mononny," "da mon." **1925** *Sat. Eve. Post* (Jan. 3) 14: How...would you like to use some of that loose mazum to elevate public morals?

mazuma *n.* [< Yid *mezumen* < Heb *mezūmān* 'set, fixed'] Orig. *Jewish-Amer.* **1.** money. [In 1898–1900 quot., a joc. nonce term for a cocktail; but the same author uses the current sense in 1902, below. Earlier dates cited in some recent dictionaries remain undocumented.]
    [**1898–1900** Cullen *Chances* 111: High-ball mazuma for the house, Red.] **1901** T.A. Dorgan, in Zwilling *TAD Lexicon* 56: Easy mazuma for us. **1902** Cullen *More Tales* 31: I was...wondering how I was going to annex the mazuma. **1903** Ade *Society* 88: The Man who is being gnawed by the Mazuma Bacillus thinks he is a Pauper unless he can count up Seven Figures. **1904** in "O. Henry" *Works* 1173: Married for the Mazuma. **1907** in H.C. Fisher *A. Mutt* 19: We get our bit out of that mazuma. **1907** "Clivette" *Red Flag* 4: The "mazuma" has reached the right end of a pocket. **1908** W.G. Davenport *Butte & Montana* 157: He may not hand her enough of the mazuma. **1910** (quot. at **HOOK**). **1911** H.L. Mencken, in *Manuscripts* XXXI (1979) 176: If the publisher comes down with the mazuma. **1914** Ellis *Billy Sunday* 208: Come across with the mazuma. **1920** Huneker *Painted Veils* 162: So, my sweet laddy-buck, plank down the mazuma. **1920** S. Lewis *Main Street* 149: He taught them...to wear Klassy Kollege Klothes, and to shout, "Oh, you baby doll, watch me gather in the mazuma." **1926** *AS* I 456: How many of those using the word *mazuma* know its meaning? As originally used by the Jewish people it is "m'zumon" and is a Chaldean word meaning in literal translation the "ready necessary." It is employed in the Talmud which is written in Chaldean and not Hebrew. **1942** *U.S. Naval Institute Proceedings* LXVIII 57 [ref. to 1898]: How much mazuma have you got in that bag? **1944** C.B. Davis *Leo McGuire* 184: Cliff...was scooping mazuma into his bag. **1945** H.L. Mencken *Amer. Lang. Supp. I* 433: Ganov..., kosher, mashuggah, mazuma, and tochos. I heard all of them used by German schoolmasters in Baltimore, *c*1888. [Mencken's own recollection] **1972** *All in the Family* (CBS-TV): They're walkin' 'cause they ain't got no mazuma. *1990 Thorne *Dict. Contemp. Sl.: Mazooma, mazuma...money. An American term...revived in British speech in the late 1980s. **1996** N.Y.C. tech. editor, age *ca*60: I haven't heard *mazuma* in ten years at least. For some reason I associate it with a young Frank Sinatra [*ca*1950].
    2. a dollar.
    1966 I. Reed *Pall-Bearers* 49: That'll be five mazumas. **1985** Ad (WINS radio) (Dec. 21): Couldn't you spring for a few extra mazumas and get me the *best*?

mazzard *n.* the face; (*hence*) the nose. Also vars.
    *1602 Shakespeare *Hamlet* V i: Knocked about the mazard with a sexton's spade. *1604–05 Shakespeare *Othello* II iii: I'll knock you o'er the mazard. *1819 [T. Moore] *Tom Crib* 14: One damaging touch [blow] in so dandy a *mazzard*. *1821 *Real Life in Ireland* 52: A *clink* on the *mazzard*. *1821 *Real Life in London* I 220: Told him to hide his d—d ugly masard. **1859** Matsell *Vocab.* 54: *Mazzard.* The face. **1870** *Putnam's Mag.* (Mar.) 301: The combatants struck each other...upon...the nose, the sneezer, the snorer, the snuffer,...the mazzard.

Mc- *prefix.* [fr. *McDonald's*, international chain of uniform fast-food restaurants] Orig. *Stu.* (used to emphasize the generic nature, mediocre quality, commercialization, or mass-market appeal of the following noun).—used derisively. *Joc.* See also McJob. [Discussed with extensive citations fr. 1986–88 in G. Lentine and R.W. Shuy, "*Mc-*: Meaning in the Marketplace," *AS* LXV (1990), pp. 349–66.]

1984 Mason & Rheingold *Slanguage*: Mcmoon ["moon"]. **1985** *Wash. Post* (Apr. 13) 12, in *Barnhart Dict. Comp.* IV.4 (Winter 1985) 138: "Surgicenters" and "quick care centers" that have sprung up in business districts and shopping centers. There are 2,500 such mini-clinics—sometimes dubbed "McDoctors"—today. **1986** in *AS* LXV (1990) 364: Three "McReads" just right for an airport layover. **1989** P. Munro *U.C.L.A. Sl.*: McPaper poor, hurriedly written paper done without much research or forethought. **1990** *New Republic* (May 21) 28: The homogenization of the non-profit stage. I called this process "McTheater." **1991** *N.Y. Newsday* (July 26) 51: A trend in print journalism toward…shorter stories, more soft journalism, more gossip, more celebrity news. Some have called it…McNews. **1991** *Village Voice* (N.Y.C.) (July 30) 43: Arnold [Schwarzenegger] should be referred to as McStar. **1992** *Atlantic* (June) 8: Transnational entities like the European Community (what he calls McWorld). *Ibid.* 10: There are several aspects of the McGlobalization phenomenon that are hardly democracy-neutral. **1992** *Nation* (June 15) 807: Next—McSchool.…Benno Schmidt Jr. is leaving Yale to plan the privatization of secondary and primary education. **1992** *L.A. Times* (June 26) F16: Existing, planned or contemplated Guggenheim outlets in Spain, Italy, Austria, and Massachusetts.…The creation of a "McGuggenheim" chain represents the loss for the special character of the venerable institution. **1992** *Utne Reader* (July/Aug.) 167: Dailies…have launched their own alternative weeklies, a phenomenon dubbed "McAlternatives" by critics sceptical that these papers can break free from the conventions of mainstream journalism. **1992** *N.Y. Review of Books* (Sept. 24) 67: Books & Bucks…Publishing: An Industrial Strength Symposium.…[cartoon:] McPublishers/Over 100 Billion Sold. **1993** *N.Y. Times* (Apr. 4) ("Business") 13: There is nothing intrinsically wrong with the "McFirm" model for building a global network of lawyers. **1995** *New Republic* (Jan. 1, 1996) 42: Popular music, [the] dreaded purveyor of "girl-poisoning" "McSex." **1997** *N.Y. Times* (Mar. 4) C16: Generic situation comedies with…"McWifes [*sic*] and McJobs."

McClellan pie *n.* [for Maj. Gen. George B. *McClellan* (1826–85), commander of the Army of the Potomac 1861–62] *Army.* a hardtack biscuit. *Joc.*

1864 F.C. Adams *Story of Trooper* 587: In fine, "McClellan pies," as the soldiers called their hard bread, came to be a luxury.

McCoy *n.* [fr. *McKay, Mackay, McKie, McCoy*, Scottish family names; semantic development obscure; see bracketed notes at **(1.a.)** and **(1.b.)**, below] **1.a.** genuine or unadulterated Scotch whisky or other liquor; good whiskey.—constr. with *the (real)*. Earlier BrE **McKay, Mackay**. ["*The real Mackay*…was adopted as an advertising slogan by Messrs. G. Mackay and Co., whisky distillers of Edinburgh, in 1870" (*SND*). Yet according to another source (*World Book Dictionary*, 1991), the whisky was "exported to the U.S. and Canada by A. and M. Mackay of Glasgow." Discussed by P. Tamony, "Names and Slang," *Forum Anglicum* XIV (1985), pp. 106–16.]

***1856** in *SND* X: A drappie o' the real McKay. ***1880** in *SND* VI: A thimblefu' o' the "rale Mackay" to mak' a' right. **1908** W.G. Davenport *Butte & Montana* 20: I took a good-sized snort out of that big bottle in the middle and I declare I thought I was going to throw up my guts during the first hymn. Have you none of the clear McCoy handy around the house? ***1911** O'Brien & Stephens *Australian Slang* 89: *Mackay, the real:* pronounced Muckeye: slang term to denote absolute genuineness or purity. A dram of really good spirits would be spoken of as "a drop of the real Mackay." The real thing itself, unadulterated and unsophisticated. **1923** Witwer *Fighting Blood* 253: 'At's the real McCoy [*sc.*, commercially distilled whisky] you got there, brother.…Comes right down from Canada! **1932** *Writer's Digest* (Aug.) 47: "Real mokoy" [*sic*]…means uncut liquor or any genuine goods. **1931–34** in Clemmer *Pris. Commun.* 334: *McCoy*…Genuine liquor. **1950** Girard & Sherdeman *Breakthrough* (film): Like some of the McCoy? **1960** Barber *Minsky's* 230: You smell something. It smells

like the McCoy. **1960** Aarons *Hell to Eternity* 102: A drink.…A belt of the old McCoy.

b. the genuine article; the real thing; that which is unadulterated, unaltered, or superior.—usu. constr. with *the (real)*. Earlier BrE **McKay, Mackay**. [Perh. the orig. sense. BrE quots. of *McCoy* in senses **(a)** or **(b)** are recent and uncommon. No reliable evidence exists to show that the Scottish phr. *the real McKay/Mackay* became *McCoy* in the U.S. through association with Amer. champion boxer "Kid McCoy" (Norman Selby) (1873–1940, *fl.* 1896–1916), who became national news again in 1924 when he was convicted of murder. It has been claimed that the headline, "Now You've Seen the Real McCoy!" appeared over the *San Francisco Examiner*'s May 25, 1899, coverage of a match between McCoy and Joe Choynski; but neither this alleged headline nor the phr. appears in the microfilm copy inspected by the editor. The prizefighter was probably the most publicized McCoy in the U.S. in the early 20th C.; but this fact does not by itself indicate that the Amer. expression orig. alluded to him. Nor does documentation support the more recent claim (repeated, e.g., by P. James, 1989, below) that general usage stems fr. the high quality of hydrostatic lubricators for machine applications patented 1872 and after by U.S. inventor Elijah McCoy (1843–1929); it is noteworthy, however, that the inventor had lived for a time in Scotland. In any case, the synonymy of the Scottish and U.S. forms militates strongly against independent and coincidental development. The slang term is discussed by E. Partridge, "The Real McCoy and the Real Mackay," in *From Sanskrit to Brazil*, pp. 44–53. See also T. Pyles in *AS* XXXIII (1958), pp. 297–98; the note in *SND* VI, s.v. *Mackay*; and that in R. Cantwell's biography of the boxer Selby, *The Real McCoy*, p. 164. An untraced "Irish ballad, *c.*1870, telling of a woman named *McCoy* [*sic*]," cited by Mencken, may be that quoted by Muir 1965 below, learned in Scotland in 1906; its precise date of orig. is uncertain.]

***1883** in R.L. Stevenson *RLS* 123: For society, there isnae sae muckle; but there's myself—the auld Jonstone [*sic*], ye ken—he's the real Mackay, whatever; and there's the wife,…an' there's Powel the druggist, a fine canty body. ***1886** in R.L. Stevenson *Letters* II 55: My dear Colvin, ever yours, THE REAL MACKAY. ***1893** in R.L. Stevenson *Letters* II 361: We had mixed you [James Payn] up with John Payne…[and] found ourselves…well prepared for examinations on the novels of the real Mackay. ***1903** in Partridge *DSUE* (ed. 7) 1263 [ref. to late 19th C.]: There was an indescribable something…which made us feel that [Australian sheep-]station aristocracy to be mere bourgeoisie, and ourselves the real Mackay. **1915** T.A. Dorgan, in *S.F. Call & Post* (Jan. 13) 14: Gee whiz, Dick—you look great—goin' to a blowout? I heard the boss say that you dolled up and looked like the real McCoy—well, a fellow with a nice shape like you couldn't help but look great. **1917** F. Hunt *Draft* 49: The infantry's real McCoy. **1918** *N.Y. Sun* (Aug. 25) 5: And Gertie all that stuff I wrote you about the girls over here in Franse being the real McCoys was just kid stuff and I know you caught it Gertie. **1921** Casey & Casey *Gay-Cat* 156: It's the real McCoy, thet idea. **1928** J. O'Connor *B'way Racketeers* 69: The kid saw me hand over what looked like the real McCoy, with a grand note on the outside. **1931** *AS* VI (Aug.) 441: *McCoy, the*…Genuine. "That ballad is the McCoy." **1931** *Sat. Review* (July 18) 978: *McCoy*—Genuine goods; a person dependable. **1931** D.W. Maurer, in *AS* (Dec.) 111: This bird has used McCoy [*sc.*, commercial nitroglycerine] on this job. ***1934** M. Allingham, in *OED2*: There's something very attractive about the real McKie when you meet it. **1934** Weseen *Dict. Amer. Sl.* 385: *Real McCoy*—A person who is much liked. **1935** Spewack *Boy Meets Girl* 339: Get a load of this. It's the real McCoy. **1942** P. Wylie *Vipers* 44: He repudiated the court phonies and set out to find the McCoy. **1944** Breslow & Purcell *Follow the Boys* (film): That uniform's the real McCoy, eh? **1948** Mencken *Amer. Lang. Supp. II* 671: Mr. G. Dundas Craig, of Berkeley, Calif., tells me that he heard *the rale McKay* "long before 1898." **1948** Maresca *My Flag* 145: He flashes a badge on her that is the

McCoy all right. **1949** Leahy *Notre Dame* 149: Then when the "real McCoy" is called, the left halfback will be doing exactly the same thing. **1958** J.B. West *Eye* 16: Maybe that letter was the McCoy, after all. **1962** Farago *10th Fleet* 13: The next alert you get is likely to be the McCoy. ***1965** W. Muir *Living with Ballads* 40 [song learned 1906]: Like a fool I married a wife,/My fortune for to try,/'Twas the cause of all my strife,/For she was the real Mackay. **1972** *N.Y. Times Bk. Rev.* (Mar. 12) 47: He has turned water into wine for me, parted seas, healed the lame and halt, etc., to the extent that I am convinced we have the McCoy. **1975** J. Jones *Dolemite* (film): That's the real McCoy all right. **1981** Hofstadter & Dennett *Mind's I* 74: Your argument (that a simulated McCoy isn't the real McCoy) is fallacious. **1988** in *N.Y. Times Bk. Rev.* (Jan. 1, 1989) 21: His animal friends look more like stuffed plush than the real McCoy. **1983–89** K. Dunn *Geek Love* 288: They always think the real thing is phony and that the tricks are the McCoy. **1989** P. James *Real McCoy* 73: McCoy's...standard of quality was so rigorous that the term "the real McCoy" came to be applied to his lubricators and to stand for the highest quality products available. **1992** G. Wolff *Day at the Beach* 133: I wanted a water fight...the real McCoy, not just splashing. **1994** Berendt *Midnight in Garden* 127: Always insist on the real McCoy when you can get it.

2. *Gamb.* money.—also constr. with *the.*
   1902 T.A. Dorgan, in Zwilling *TAD Lexicon* 68: Waitin fer "McCoy" from home. **1905** in T.A. Dorgan, in Zwilling *TAD Lexicon* 68: Plant your McCoy where it's bound to get bigger. **1935** Algren *Boots* 173: We want some place...where is lots of the ol' McCoy.

3. authentic information; truth.—constr. with *the.*
   [**1917** *Columbus* (Ohio) *Journal* (June 10): The real McCoy [in interview with Kid McCoy] *American Wkly.* 6/13/1907.] **1934** Duff & Sauber *20 Million Sweethearts* (film): I'm puttin' you on to somethin' good. This is the McCoy. **1935** C. Calloway, in *Call of Jitterbug* (film short): They really mean it. It's the real McCoy. **1936** Boothe *Women* 465: Sounds like the McCoy to me, Crystal. **1937** in H. Gray *Arf* (unp.): This is no fairy tale—this is th' real McCoy. **1945** Bryan *Carrier* 57: If this [rumor] turned out to be the McCoy, when would I get back to the *Yorktown*? **1965** Gallery *Eight Bells* 266: It looked like the cloak-and-dagger boys had given us the McCoy on this operation.

McCoy *adj.* [fr. the *n.*] genuine; unadulterated; superlative; true; honest; legitimate.
   1928 *New Yorker* (Dec. 15) 55: Everything looks McCoy, see? **1930** *Amer. Mercury* (Dec.) 456: *McCoy, adj.* Genuine liquor. "This is McCoy. You can't fake Quebec wrappers." **1930** Irwin *Tramp & Und. Sl.*: *McCoy.*—Neat; good-looking; unusually excellent or genuine. From the pugilist, "Kid" McCoy, who was for some time at the head of his class. **1931** D.W. Maurer, in *AS* VII (Dec.) 111: *McCoy, adj....*Pure, reliable, O.K. "This is McCoy." "He is McCoy." **1937** in *DAS*: Like every other McCoy biz [etc.]. **1942** R. Casey *Torpedo Junction* 120: The beating of gongs...certified it to be a McCoy alarm.

McGimp *n.* [app. an arbitrary rhyming coinage; cf. earlier MACK, 1.a.] *Und.* a pimp.
   1914 Jackson & Hellyer *Vocab.* 58: *M'Gimp, Megimp*, Noun. Current in western circles. A pimp: a lover in the vicious meaning. *ca*1927 in B. Buckley *Frankie* 34: Any how she was a sportin' woman and he was a McGimp. **1928** Panzram *Killer* 157: A pimp is a pimp and a McGimp is both or worse than either. **1930** Lait *On the Spot* 207: *McGimp...*White slaver. **1933** Ersine *Prison Slang* 52: *Magimp, n.* A pimp. **1949** W.R. Burnett *Asphalt Jungle* 59: One of the dance-hall bums...insisted Louis...was...a M'Gimp. **1962–68** B. Jackson *In the Life* 205: I've been running whores quite a long time, but a lot of the time I'm what they call a "would-be" or a "mo-gimp." That's a pimp without a whore.

McGuffin var. MACGUFFIN.

McJob *n.* [*Pop.* by Douglas Coupland in his novel *Generation X* (1991), in allusion to *McDonald's*, popular chain of fast-food restaurants; allegedly coined by McDonald's in 1983 to describe a jobs program.] an unstimulating, low-wage job with poor benefits, esp. in a service industry. Hence **McJobber.** Cf. Mc-.
   1991 D. Coupland *Generation X* 5: *McJob:* A low-pay, low-prestige, low-dignity, low-benefit, no-future job in the service sector. Frequently considered a satisfying career choice by people who have never held one. **1991** *Business Week* (Aug. 19) 83: The people who end up in these "McJobs"...wait longer to land full-time positions. **1992** *Atlantic* (Dec.) 75: Bicycle messengers, pizza drivers, yard workers, Wal-Mart shelf-stockers...McJobbers in the low-wage/low-benefit service economy.

1993 *N.Y. Times* (Jan. 20) C2: I'm a dropout poet with a McJob. **1993** *L.A. Times* (Apr. 28) 421: A string of McJobs that included janitorial duties at San Jose Hospital, order-taking at Taco Bell..., and loading tractor-trailer rigs. **1994** *Harper's* (July) 22: Young people regard themselves as hopeless...marking time...at McJobs. **1995** *Newsweek* (Sept. 18) 82: Two likable losers...toil at mailroom McJobs.

MCP *n.* [*m*ale *c*hauvinist *p*ig] a man who behaves in a sexist manner toward women.
   1972 (cited in *BDNE3*). **1974** *Atlantic* (Nov.) 106: We meet the MCP in his various forms—warrior, sexual bumbler, office autocrat, sports freak. **1975** *DAS* (ed. 2): *MCP...*male chauvinist pig. [**1975** *Seattle Post-Intell.* (Feb. 9) D3: Any self-respecting male ape that doesn't want aggressive females to criticize him as a sex-object-worshiping MCP: male chauvinist primate.] **1976** C. McFadden *Serial*, in T. Thorne *Dict. Contemp. Slang*: A waitress who was a real throwback, an MCP's delight. *a*1977 M. French *Women's Room* 8: That mcp Jason. **1980** *L.A. Times Bk. Rev.* (Apr. 27) 20: The stock MCP allusion to the, ugh, disgusting earthy realities of sex. **1990** *Nation* (Feb. 19) 250: Tim Curry...comes across as an abrasive, abusive MCP to whom artistic genius has been granted by pure accident.

M.D. *n. Army.* a mule driver. *Joc.*
   1889 *United Service* (May) 506: That's our M.D....He is a perfect gentleman...even if he is a mule-driver. **1890** Finerty *War-Path* 260 [ref. to 1879]: Despite the current, the "M.D." whacked his animals over.

M.D.U.S.A. *n.* "Medical Department, U.S. Army," facetiously reinterpreted as "many die, you shall also."
   1920 *Inf. Jour.* XVII (Dec.) 614 [ref. to WWI]: "What's that for?" he finally asked, pointing to the letters M.D.U.S.A. on his blanket. "Oh, that?" said the orderly carelessly. "That don't mean nothing much. It just means, 'Many die, you shall also.'" **1943** Tregaskis *Invasion Diary* 198: Those who could walk would eventually be given red corduroy robes, with the letters "M.D., U.S.A." sewn in white on the pocket. Typical of hospital humor was the grim interpretation we attached to those initials: "Many Die, You Shall Also." **1945** Bellah *Ward 20* 20: They had their...jumpers on over their pajamas with M.D.U.S.A. on the pocket. "Here comes many die you shall also," Daley said. **1966–80** McAleer & Dickson *Unit Pride* 231 [ref. to Korean War]: It was a hospital blanket and had "M.D.U.S.A." on it, which the medics said meant "Many Die. You Shall Also."

me *pron.* ¶ **me for** I am heading for; I want.
   1905 *Nat. Police Gaz.* (Nov. 11) 3: Me for the wine afterwards. **1908** J. London *M. Eden* 405: Me for...a good front, with big iron dollars clinkin' in my jeans. **1929** A.C. Doyle *Maricot* ch. iv: It's me for the water, for there is sure something worth our seeing. *Ibid.* ch. v: It's me for cutting loose and having a dash at it.

meadow muffin *n.* [sugg. by COW-PIE] a pile of cow droppings.—also used fig. *Joc.*
   1974 Miami Univ. student: Don't step on those meadow muffins. [Heard in early 1960's]. **1976** *Business Week* (July 12) 45: And even a modest plan to turn cow manure...into natural gas. Some people at DR refer to this last venture as "the meadow muffin project." **1977** Sen. L. Weiker (R.-Conn.), in *U.S. News & W.R.* (Apr. 25) 64: I intend to fight tooth and nail to block passage of this political meadow muffin. **1986** *Daily Beacon* (Univ. Tenn.) (May 28) 8: A metaphorical pile of meadow muffins. **1987** *Night Court* (NBC-TV): "It looks like you're—" "Chin-deep in meadow muffins?" **1992** *Mystery Sci. Theater* (Comedy Central TV): It looks like a meadow muffin. **1995** L. Rubin *Rubes* (synd. comic strip) (Dec. 23): ["A visit to the dung-beetle bakery":] One cowpie, a dozen meadow muffins, [etc.].

meal pennant *n. Navy.* HASH MARK.
   1918 Ruggles *Navy Explained* 75: This red mark is called a hash mark, assuming that the man re-enlisted for his hash. It is also called a meal pennant.

meal ticket *n.* a source, often a person of the opposite sex, exploited or relied upon for one's financial support or livelihood.
   [**1870** in *OEDS*: The rather scrubby party who occasionally purchases a "Meal Ticket", and thus gets entrance to the festive dining hall.] **1899** Willard *Tramping* 388: "Meal-ticket"...is a tramp term for a person who is "good" for a meal, and the carpenter did not care to have this reputation. **1902** G. Ade *Girl Proposition* 93: Tessie never came back for she had found her Meal-Ticket. **1906** *Nat. Police Gaz.* (Feb. 24) 3: As she dropped to the floor the "meal ticket" walked away. **1908**

in H.C. Fisher *A. Mutt* 106: When you have a little rough stuff with your meal ticket, don't go home to your mother. **1913** in J. London *Letters* 394: Am I merely your meal-ticket? **1914** Jackson & Hellyer *Vocab.* 57: *Meal Ticket*, Noun General currency. A female of the open market who supports a lover; any gratuitous source of subsistence. **1921** Casey & Casey *Gay-Cat* 102: She sure must be a good meal-ticket all right, Portugee. Setdowns, I s'pose. **1921** J. Conway, in *Variety* (Mar. 4) 9: If she didn't let my meal ticket alone and stop tryin' to put Winter Garden notions in his nut, I would smack her husband in the kisser. **1922** Rice *Adding Machine* 103: Yes, sir, they could look a long time before they'd find a steady meal-ticket like me. **1929** *AS* IV (June) 342: *Meal ticket.* One who carries the wherewithal of another's eats. **1938** in Inman *Diary* 884: Boy, dat girl was a gold mine…a meal ticket for the rest of my life. **1939** in Ade *Letters* 214: The play remained at the Garden…and next year it was being played by three companies. It turned out to be my meal ticket. **1943** *Yank* (Oct. 8) 23: *Meal Ticket.* Club's winningest pitcher. **1949** *N.Y. Times* (May 22) II ix: "Man and Superman"…is the title of Maurice Evans' current meal ticket. **1950** *N.Y. Times* (July 2) II x5: To him she is a termporary haven, a meal ticket. **1956** Evarts *Ambush Riders* 139: Usin' me for a meal ticket! You cheap two-timin' little ——. **1954–60** *DAS: Meal ticket*…Any skill, instrument, talent, part of the body, etc., which provides a living for its possessor. **1975** R. Hill *O.J. Simpson* 14: I keep telling the players, "He's your meal ticket; block for him!" *a***1982** Medved *Hospital* 83: I was his meal ticket. **1984** J. Kahn *Temple of Doom* 4: Lao Che…was currently her mealticket. **1994** Berendt *Midnight in Garden* 227: Danny was worried that he'd just lost his meal ticket.

mean *adj.* **1.** splendid; superlative, esp. in skill; WICKED; usu. in joc. phr. **to —— a mean ——** to do or use (something) skillfully and effectively.

1919 D. Parker, in *Vanity Fair* (July) 37: And there are the Drawing-Room Stars;/The Ones That Swing a Mean Tea-Cup. **1920** H. Witwer, in *OEDS:* Everything was jake until K.O. Krouse shook a mean dice and win [*sic*] $28 from Battlin' Lewis on the way to Toledo. **1920–21** H. Witwer *Leather Pushers* 87: Jim Coffey shook a mean controller on the front end of a New York City street car. **1921** Benet *Wisdom* 116 [ref. to 1915]: I like that baby, you know, she's got a mean eye. **1922** in Charters & Kunstadt *Jazz* 95: And for mean harmony, don't overlook Handy's orchestra. **1922** E. Rice *Adding Machine* 106: But, believe me, you're goin' to sling a mean dish-towel when the company goes tonight! **1926** S. Young *Encaustics* 4: To throw a mean bust…"To have a fine figure."…She's a mean kisser. **1928** Dahlberg *Bottom Dogs* 145: Mawx rolled out a mean wad of greenbacks, too. **1929–30** J.T. Farrell *Young Lonigan* 82: Corbett…could wiggle a mean lip. **1931** in R.S. Gold *Jazz Lexicon:* [Brief record review:] General remarks: Fairly mean. **1947** in R.S. Gold *Jazz Lexicon:* Plays a mean piano. **1955** H. Robbins 79 *Park Ave.* 229: I hope you like shrimp. Tom makes the meanest shrimp salad. **1959–60** R. Reisner *Jazz Titans* 161: Mean: the best, greatest. *ca***1960** in Partridge *DSUE* (ed. 7) 1270: He swings a mean bat! **1962** D. Hamilton *Murderer's Row* 12: He did fry a mean flapjack. **1964** (quot. at BRUTAL, 1). **1970** *Current Slang* V (Fall) 10: Mean, adj. Admirable. **1970** D. Long *Nia* 6: Cause Mary Sue had the meanest box in town. ****1973** in *OEDS:* Jack Palance smokes a mean cigar in *Oklahoma Crude.* **1987** *Cosby Show* (NBC-TV): "Was I mean?" "You were OK." **1992** *Fresh Prince of Bel Air* (NBC-TV): A woman known…for her mean sweet-potato pie. **1993** *Guiding Light* (CBS-TV): You make a mean waffle, Dylan.

2. Now esp. *Black E.* exceptionally attractive or stylish.

1934 Weseen *Dict. Amer. Sl.* 189: College [slang]…*Mean baby*—An attractive girl. **1971** H. Roberts *Third Ear* (unp.): *Mean*…fine, attractive. **1972** Claerbaut *Black Jargon* 72: *Mean*…fashionable; attractive; in vogue: *a mean hog, man.* **1973** *Black World* (Apr.) 63: But you was mean…still zoot-suitin'. **1977** TV ad: [Youngster combing hair in front of mirror:] You are one mean dude. **1983** Sturz *Widening Circles* 17: The tactics they'd both employed to obtain their "mean vines." **1991** M. Rich *Straight Out of Bklyn.* (film): Look at that fly car!…That's mean, man!

mean actor *n.* BAD ACTOR, 1.

1974 C.M. Rodgers *Ovah* 63: Yeah, he must have been some kind/of dude, I'm telling you/he must a been a real mean actor….Jesus was a militant dude.

meanie see BLUE MEANIE.

mean machine *n.* [MEAN + MACHINE, 3] a fashionable or powerful motor vehicle, esp. a sports car.

1981 Safire *Good Word* 80: While rolling in your *ride* or *mean machine.* **1984** N.Y.C. man, age *ca*25: Man, you got one mean machine!

measle map *n. Mil.* a tactical war map marked with colored pins. *Joc.*

1966 E. Shepard *Doom Pussy* 29: On the wall of Fatum's office was a "measle" map. The areas were marked with colored pins—blue for secured, diagonal lines for undergoing security, green for cleared, black for destroyed or abandoned, plain square box for contested, and pink for VC-controlled. [**1968** MacKenzie *Bastogne* 36 [ref. to 1944]: Ewell scanned the situation map while the Generals watched. They wanted to see his reaction to all those red blotches showing the enemy's advance…."It looks like it's got the measles," he drawled.]

measles *n. Naut.* salt pork.

1883 C. Russell *Sailors' Language* xi: "What's for dinner today, Bill?"…"Measles," was the answer, that being the man's name for the pork aboard his vessel.

measly *adj.* insignificant; contemptible. Now *colloq.* or *S.E.*

****1864** in *OEDS:* The audacity to offer a measly hundred pounds or so for the discovery of a great crime! **1895** Gore *Stu. Slang* 21: *Measly*…Disagreeable, mean, contemptible. **1896** Ade *Artie* ch. xiv: Except how to hold down his measly job. **1903** *Enquirer* (Cincinnati) (May 9) 13: Modern Slang Glossary…*Measley*—Small, mean. **1915** in Bader *Prohib. in Kans.* 182: Something that these measley cranks now so much in evidence…will never understand. **1939** I. Baird *Waste Heritage* 219: I'll stick up his measley little office.

measure *v.* [perh. fr. S.E. phr. *measure out blows*] *Und.* to deliberately strike and knock down.

1904 *Life in Sing Sing* 250: "Measured." Struck. **1942–49** in Goldin et al *DAUL:* The first dude…who beefs…, measure with the butt of your biscuit (gun).

meat *n.* **1.** the penis.—also constr. with *piece of.*—also used collectively.—usu. considered vulgar.

****1595** in *OEDS:* That you should coutch your meat in dish, And others feele, it is no fish. **ca***1775** *Frisky Songster* 92: Roast meat for the speaking mouth, and raw for the dumb./May the back never fail in the cause of the tail. **1925** McAlmon *Silk Stockings* 59: He would sit with his right hand in the left pocket of his policeman when they were in queer cafes, and would babble, "My god, Mary, I've got my hand on a real piece of meat at last, oh Mary." **1933** in Oliver *Blues Tradition* 196: Uh-uh, mister baby, you jus' a li'l too fas',/You'll not cram all that meat up my ——. **1934** "J.M. Hall" *Anecdota* 23: You have a very beautiful piece of meat. *ca***1937** in Atkinson *Dirty Comics* 95: His nibs…is socking that meat home. **1944** in Legman *Limerick* 89: There was a young girl, very sweet,/Who thought sailors' meat quite a treat. *ca***1944** in J. Costello *Love, Sex & War* 166: Always a good sign of a big piece of meat. **1956** H. Gold *Not With It* 295: Supplying that wife of his with fresh meat. **1959** Morrill *Dark Sea Running* 113 [ref. to WWII]: Let's play lion—you roar and I'll throw the meat atchoo. **1967** Humphreys *Tearoom Trade* 72: If a man has a very large piece of meat…I will not have somebody ram that thing down my throat. **1967** in W. King *Black Short Story Anthol.* 341: Teddy slipped the meat to her. **1970** N.Y.U. student: If they found somebody who'd buy Napoleon's meat they'll find somebody who'll buy Cromwell's head. **1971** Cole *Rook* 178: The angle of the dangle and the heat of the meat varies in direct ratio to the mass of the ass and the bore of the whore. **1981** *Penthouse* (Apr.) 30: I led her into the bedroom, my meat standing at attention. **1983** *Nat. Lampoon* (Feb.) 42: Ochs probably wants to slip the meat to her. **1990** A. Baraka, in T. McMillan *Breaking Ice* 43: Wow. First you don't even wanna leave the base and stop your meat pullin'. **1993** *Beavis and Butt-head* (MTV): The angle of the dangle is inversely proportional to the heat of the meat. **1993** *Source* (July) 40: Nobody's stickin' no meat in me or crazy homo stuff. **1994** "G. Indiana" *Rent Boy* 30: Ride that stiff meat.

2.a. a person, usu. a woman, as an object of sexual gratification; (*hence*) nonmasturbatory sexual gratification.—also constr. with *piece of.*—usu. considered vulgar.

a*1518** J. Skelton, in *OED* s.v. *mutton* (def. 4): And from thens to the halfe strete, To get vs there some fresh mete. ****1597–98** Shakespeare 2 *Henry IV* II ii: Away you mouldie Rogue, away; I am meat for your Master. ****1597–98** in *F & H* IV 297: I am no meat for his mowing. ****1664** in *F & H* IV 297: But is she man's meat? I have a tender appetite and can scarcely digest one in her teens. **1845** in Eliason *Tarheel Talk* 283: There is lots of good stuff floating up and down the streets every

night…the best sort of mulatto meat. *1851 in D. Cox *Sex. & Vict. Lit.* 137: She [a brothel owner] does not keep her meat too long on the hooks.…You may have your meat dressed to your own liking. *a1890–96 F & H IV 296: *A bit of meat* = the sexual favour. **1897** Norris *Vandover* 360: He looked after the girl a moment and muttered scornfully: "Cheap meat!" **1922** Tully *Emmett Lawler* 190: I had a girl in Cleveland…she was sweet meat. **1924** Anderson & Stallings *What Price Glory?* 75 [ref. to 1918]: I didn't know she was his meat when I first saw her. *ca*1929 *Collection of Sea Songs* 35: Looking for a piece of meat/From the harlots of Jerusalem. **1930** *Lyra Ebriosa* 17: Where everyone could get a seat/And see the half-breed get his meat. **1929–33** J.T. Farrell *Young Manhood* 351: She was easy meat. **1936** in Leadbitter & Slaven *Blues Records* 275: She Sells Good Meat. **1938** Bezzerides *Long Haul* 12: Here's a new customer for you, Mary. Nice, sweet meat for you to break in. **1942** Hollingshead *Elmtown's Youth* 399: No likely meat here. **1951** H. Robbins *Danny Fisher* 159: Take a good look at that, kid.…The sweetest meat in town. **1956** Resko *Reprieve* 118 [ref. to *ca*1940]: That's why my meat was always married. **1958** H. Gardner *Piece of the Action* 23: Always figured she was good meat. **1960** Sire *Deathmakers* 44: There's nothing like grabbing a big piece of raw meat…and feeling her bucking under you. **1965** C. Brown *Manchild* 160: He said to use slang words like…"piece-a meat" when talking about girls. **1967** W. Murray *Sweet Ride* 17: She was his piece of meat, Mr. Crawford, not mine. **1967** *DAS* (Supp.): *Meat*…A male considered as a sexual object; homosexual gratification. *Homosexual use.* **1970** Rudensky & Riley *Gonif* 21: He was a homo…and…wanted me as young meat. **1971** *Blushes & Bellylaffs* 99: Faithful Wife…one man's meat. **1977** A. Patrick *Beyond Law* 21: It was a hangout for male hustlers.…It was still early in the day, so there wasn't much meat on the rack. **1983** Univ. Tenn. student theme: He is a stupid, insensitive son-of-a-bitch, who…considers his wife as just another piece of meat. **1984** "W.T. Tyler" *Shadow Cabinet* 75: "Never get your meat where you get your potatoes," a nimble bachelor senator had told him. **1994** "G. Indiana" *Rent Boy* 29: Maybe they've been going in for a little [sexual] variety and hitting a lot of bad meat on the trail.

b. (as in **(a)**, above, but esp. applied to a person of another race).—constr. with adj. description of skin color.—usu. considered vulgar. See also DARK MEAT.

1888 (quot. at DARK MEAT). **1927** in P. Smith *Letter from Father* 170: He was getting used to fucking black meat. **1958** Motley *Epitaph* 337: That chick done caught herself…white meat. **1962** Reiter *Night in Sodom* 99: A white man's world and some did like black meat and some didn't. **1963–64** Kesey *Great Notion* 23: You reckon he's been slippin' off to Siskaloo for some of that red meat? **1969** Sidney *Love of Dying* 71: You ever had a piece of white meat? **1971** Rader *Govt. Inspected* 104: They want black meat.

c. the vulva or vagina.—usu. considered vulgar. [*OEDS* dates Killigrew quot. to 1664, the year of publication, but specialists accept that the play was written before the Puritans closed the theaters in 1642.]

*1611 in *OEDS*: Faith take a maide, and leaue the widdow, Maister. Of all meates I loue not a gaping oyster. *ca*1640–64 T. Killigrew *Parson's Wedding*, in *OEDS*: Your bed is big enough for two, and my meat will not cost you much. *ca*1850 in Pinto & Rodway *Common Muse* 419: The widow disposed of her meat/Often behind the bed curtain. *Ibid.* 420: Don't go smelling about after meat,/When strange it's not worth a button. *1882 *Boudoir* 115: Keep me out of my meat, then heaven's no treat. **1953–58** J.C. Holmes *Horn* 28: The ofay strippers threw their meat right over your head. **1954–60** *DAS*: *Meat*…The vagina. **1970** A. Young *Snakes* 99: I…fiddled with her meat.

3. Esp. *So.* a person's flesh, body, or HIDE, 1; tissue; *(hence)* one's self.

1834 Caruthers *Kentuk. in N.Y.* I 27: If I hadn't had so many inches, he'd have been into my meat. **1845** Hooper *Simon Suggs* 149: I tell you, it took raal nice judgment to keep the infernal hook outen my meat. **1845** in Robb *Squatter Life* 59: Old Tom Jones' yell…gives my meat a slight sprinklin' of ager whenever I think on it. *a1890–96 F & H IV 296: *To flash meat* = to expose the person. **1897** Ade *Pink* 174: If he eveh gets on 'e same street 'ith me…people be pickin' up dahk meat all oveh 'e South Side. **1935** Algren *Boots* 179: Well, he never got mah meat, an' ah reck'n he's learned some different now. **1948** Wolfert *Act of Love* 437: You put those brass knucks on a piece of meat, and the fellow whose meat it is ain't going to be particular was he hit by the blade or not. **1960** Leckie *Marines!* 21 [ref. to WWII]: Doan lemme see

nobody shootin' less he's got meat in his sight. Yaller [Japanese] meat. **1961** J. Jones *Thin Red Line* 16: If I'm gonna get blown-fucking-up…I dont wanta ged my guts and meat all mixed up with a bunch of strangers from another regiment. **1989** P. Dickson *Baseball Dict.* 258: To "take one on the meat" is to be hit by a pitched ball.

4.a. one's intended or actual victim.

1844 W.T. Porter *Big Bear* 123: It war about one hundred and twenty yards to him, but I kneed he were *my* meat without an accident. **1871** "M. Twain" *Roughing It* ch. vii 60: Looked up as much to say, "You are my meat, friend." **1878** [P.S. Warne] *Hard Crowd* 7: You dog-gauned whelp! I reckon your my meat! **1878** Pinkerton *Reminiscences* 205: And the Texan clown put his money down,/And said, "Thou art meat for me." **1887** J.W. Nichols *Hear My Horn* 169 [ref. to 1861]: The first man that crosses that fence is my meat. **1896** Gore *Stu. Slang* 19: *Easy meat.* One easily duped. **1897** A.H. Lewis *Wolfville* 19: The signs an' signal-smokes shorely p'ints to this yere Cherokee as our meat. **1901** Oliver *Roughing It* 221: Let me get at him.…He's my meat. **1912** Lowrie *Prison* 243: The hangman comes up the day before the bumpin' off is to take place and has a long talk with his meat. **1916** L. Stillwell *Common Soldier* 125 [ref. to Civil War]: Right here's our meat. **1918** Swan *My Co.* 109: The huns looked easy meat. **1925** in Grayson *Stories for Men* 4: He's my meat. I seen him first. **1927** in Hammett *Big Knockover* 286: He's your meat, Jack. **1929** W.R. Burnett *Iron Man* 203: He wouldn't last one round.…No; he's meat for me. **1931** Lubbock *Bully Hayes* 50: Jay was easy meat. **1989** Leib *Fire Dream* 277: "You meat to me *any* time!" he finished with a bark of laughter.

b. a person (*obs.*) or thing that is particularly suited to one's needs or abilities. [The general context of 1871 quot. sugg. that it illus. the present sense, but the quot. may well belong to **(a)**, above.]

1871 "M. Twain" *Roughing It* ch. i 322: Come along—you're my meat *now*, my lad, anyway. **1875** Sheppard *Love Afloat* 152: Take your time—you're my meat. **1892** in F. Remington *Sel. Letters* 130: Give me all particulars and I'm your meat. **1907** S.E. White *Ariz. Nights* 82: That's a large order. But I'm your meat. **1911–12** J. London *Smoke Bellew* 51: My pardner is the real meat with boats. **1917** in *OEDS*: I gleefully fell in with the scheme, and told Cassell I was his meat. **1921** E. O'Neill *Hairy Ape* 210: Dis was meat for me! It's my meat, get me! **1979** Jenison *Kingdom in Sage* 18: Tamin' broncs is my meat.

c. *Baseball.* (see quot.). Cf. syn. MEATBALL, 5.

1983 L. Frank *Hardball* 103: A pitch that a batter thought was easy to hit is also described as…"It was meat."

5.a. a corpse or corpses. Cf. COLD MEAT, 1.

1904 "O. Henry" *Heart of West* 164: A doctor that couldn't tell he was graveyard meat ought to be skinned with a cinch buckle. **1942** *ATS* 507: Corpse.…*meat.* **1948** A. Murphy *Hell & Back* 96: We been packing meat all night. This guy got his dog tags? **1960** Sire *Deathmakers* 30: The meat yards, the acres and acres of black frozen corpses with their dog tags around their necks, stretched out stiff in the snow by the burial companies. **1961** J. Jones *Thin Red Line* 330 [ref. to WWII]: Get the meat board and blankets and get him out of here. We need the fucking bed.

b. a person marked for retribution; DEAD MEAT, 1.a.; GONER.—used proleptically.

1987 E. Spencer *Macho Man* 39: A squad leader is either tight with his men or he is meat. **1992** Strawberry & Rust *Darryl* 177: I was swollen with power.…"Daley, you're meat!" I screamed to myself.

6. *Sports.* the thickest part or center of gravity of a baseball bat, a tennis racket, the head of a golf club, etc.

*1909 in *OEDS*: If you did not take the gutta-percha ball right in the middle of the club (right "on the meat", according to the modern abominable phrase) it declined to go at all. *1922 P.G. Wodehouse, in *OEDS*: She fails to slam the ball squarely on the meat. *1925 in Partridge *DSUE* 515: [*Meat*.] The thickest part of the blade of a [cricket] bat. **1989** P. Dickson *Baseball Dict.* 258: *Meat*…The thickest part of the bat.

7.a. Orig. *Baseball.* MEATHEAD (used in joc. direct address); *(hence)* an unintelligent or unskilled athlete.

1959 Brosnan *Long Season* 8: Put it in the car, Meat. *Ibid.* 271: *Meat.* A term of indiscriminate affection [among baseball players]. **1963** *Time* (Oct. 18) 51: [M.I.T. girls] scorn "meats" (inarticulate athletes), and go for "tools" (grinds) only if they can be "unlocked" (relaxed). **1978** in Lyle & Golenbock *Bronx Zoo* 192: Lemon calls everybody Meat. Before the game, he called me over. He said, "Hey, Meat, I'd like to talk with you." *a*1986 in *NDAS:* To see a bunch of meats play. **1989** P. Dickson *Baseball Dict.* 258: *Meat*…A ballplayer.

b. a living person, esp. an athlete, regarded impersonally as worthless, inconsequential, undeserving of respect, etc.—used collectively. Cf. *fresh meat,* 2, below. [Presumably the orig. sense; the 1942 quots. represent **(4.a.),** above.]

[**1942** *ATS* 365: Gullible person; dupe.…*meat. Ibid.* 636: Opponent…*meat.*] **1967** *DAS* (Supp.) 695: *Meat*…A strong but stupid person; one whose physical deeds overshadow his mental powers; esp. a professional or college athlete. **1969** *Current Slang I & II* 61: *Meat factory,* n. Athletic department.—College males, South Dakota. **1972** G. Shaw *Meat on the Hoof* [ref. to college football players] [title]. **1983** L. Frank *Hardball* 103: The common description of an ineffective pitcher is that he is "meat." **1984** R. Jackson & M. Lupica *Reggie* 1: But if you put the meat [*sc.,* spectators] in the seats and made the game count…then I wanted to play. **1986** *Condor* (ABC-TV): He was just hired meat. *a*1994 *21st Cent. Dict. Sl.: Meat wave.*…Surferspeak: vehicle full of surfers *We got a meat wave going to the barbecue tonight.* **1996** Univ. Tenn. instructor, age 43: If people have no souls or minds, like behaviorists say, then you're just meat walking around.

¶ In phrases:

¶ **beat (one's) meat, 1.** (of a man) to masturbate; (also used as a phr. of dismissal).—usu. considered vulgar. Also vars.

*ca*1936 in Logsdon *Whorehouse Bells* 107: And I was damn fed up with beatin' my meat. **1947** Mailer *Naked & Dead* 70: Go beat your meat! **1920–54** in Randolph & Legman *Blow Candle Out* 797: Masturbation, in the male…*pulling his pud, pounding his meat,* or *lathering a bar of soap.* **1958–59** Southern & Hoffenberg *Candy* 76: You know—onanism—"beating your meat." **1959** *41st Ftr. Sq. Songbk.* 28: Last night I stayed up late to beat my meat. **1960** Sire *Deathmakers* 117: Ah, you've been beatin' your meat too much, Reverend. **1962** Killens *Heard the Thunder* 293: Man, go on over to your bunk and beat your meat one more time. **1962** in Wepman et al. *The Life* 143: I got more kick out of beating my meat. **1969** Briley *Traitors* 200: I'll be beatin' my meat for a month just thinking about it. **1970** M. Thomas *Total Beast* 10: What are you doing in there old Barnes? Beating your meat? Hnnn? **1970** E. Thompson *Garden of Sand* 146: Go beat your meat, old man! **1971** Dahlskog *Dict.* 6: *Beat (pound) the meat*…To masturbate. **1967–72** Weesner *Car Thief* 67: Hey, who's beatin' his meat…? **1973** Gwaltney *Destiny's Chickens* 83: "Beat your meat," Minnie said. **1977** Langone *At Bottom* 200: I don't care if you beat your meat without missin' a beat, you're goin' to that friggin' ice. *a*1982 in Berry *Semper Fi* 19 [ref. to *ca*1930]: They had a big red pig sign hanging near the door [of the butcher shop]…"You can't beat Hempel's meat on Hatamen Street." The boys got a huge laugh out of that one. *a*1994 N. McCall *Wanna Holler* 47: He had to go in a corner and beat his meat!

2. to brag.—usu. considered vulgar.

1947 Mailer *Naked & Dead* 422: I was president of our junior class in high school. … I don't mean that that's anything to beat my meat about.

¶ **brown (one's) meat** (of a man) to engage in sexual intercourse.—usu. considered vulgar.

*a*1896 E. Field, in *Immortalia* 8: Behind the whore-house on the hill/Where all the boys could get a seat/And watch that half-breed brown his meat.

¶ **don't let your meat loaf** (used as a coarsely humorous form of encouragement). *Joc.*

1963 Fry TS. (Feb.): Don't let your meat loaf. *ca*1965 IUFA *Folk Speech:* Keep a cool tool and don't let your meat loaf. **1974** Newburgh, N.Y., man, age 24: Don't let your meat loaf. **1990** *UTSQ: Don't let your meat loaf.* [Don't be] a couch potato.

¶ **drop your meat and hit your feet** *Mil.* wake up!—usu. considered vulgar. Cf. *drop your cocks and grab your socks!* s.v. COCK, *n.*

1988 C. Roberts & C. Sasser *Walking Dead* 156 [ref. to *ca*1966]: Drop your meat and hit your feet.

¶ **fresh meat, 1.** a new sexual partner.—usu. considered vulgar.

a*1890–96 *F & H* IV 296: *Fresh meat* = a new *piece.* **1966 Liebow *Tally's Corner* 122 [ref. to 1962]: A "new" woman is, by common consent, more stimulating and satisfying sexually than one's own wife or girl friend. The man also sees himself performing better with "new meat" or "fresh meat" than with someone familiar to him sexually.

1975 Legman *No Laughing Matter* 87: Lifelong compulsive fellators, searching for "fresh meat" at all times.

2. *Mil. & Pris.* a newcomer, as a combat replacement or newly arrived new prisoner. Cf. NEW MEAT. [The 1925 and 1931 quots. ref. to WWI.]

1925 *Amer. Leg. Wkly.* (Aug. 28) 15: "New man," he inquired. "Yes, fresh meat for the wolves." **1931** Gallegher *Bolts & Nuts* 148: The Major joined our regiment in July, 1917, and as he came into the barracks on the first morning in civilian dress he was greeted with the well-known battle cry, "Fresh Meat." **1945** Laurents *Home of the Brave* 563: Maybe he only wants us. Fresh young meat for the grinder. **1948** A. Murphy *Hell & Back* 42: He flips his head toward the replacements and in a loud sardonic voice asks, "Has anyone ever seen a nicer pack of fresh meat?" **1959** Cochrell *Barren Beaches* 45: "Oh Jesus," he said. "The fresh meat they send out. It makes you puke to think what the sonsabitches want done with it." **1969** Ellis *Alcatraz* 22: We have some fresh meat for you. **1971** *Newsweek* (May 17) 99: "Here comes fresh meat," Day chortled. **1972** G. Shaw *Meat on Hoof* 37: We got some fresh meat here, some real high school stars. **1977** Sayles *Union Dues* 14: You'll get your turn, son, they'll be comin in under you soon enough. You go down the high school and look over the senior class, pick you out some fresh meat. **1985** M. Brennan *War* 6 [ref. to 1965]: He flashed a big grin, probably at the thought of riding with a bunch of "fresh meat" just in from the United States. **1987** Tristan & Hancock *Weeds* (film): Fresh meat! [convicts].

¶ **hang (one's) meat** (of a man) to urinate.—usu. considered vulgar.

1918 Noyes MS. (unp.): *To Hang one's Meat* = to empty this, to wring out one's swab.…"to relieve one's self."

¶ **make meat of** *West.* to kill (someone).

1847 Ruxton *Far West* 12: I takes the hair off the heads of the two we made meat of. **1850** Garrard *Wah-to-yah* 163: I takes t'other Injun by the har, an' "makes meat" of him *too.* **1868** "J.F. Henderson" *Two Trails* 25: If the red-skins knowed how bad off we are, they would soon make meat of us. **1893** Wawn *So. Sea Islanders* 43: At first they treated him well, but during the second night, he had overheard the headmen saying it was their intention to "make meat" of him. [**1973** Norris & Springer *Men in Exile* 45: I'm gonna blow your head off. I'm gonna make you meat.…I'm gonna kill you.]

¶ **step on (someone's) meat** to rebuke.—usu. considered vulgar.

1972 Wambaugh *Blue Knight* 71: Cruz smiled now that he was through stepping on my meat. *Ibid.* 105: Wall…used to jump on our meat every night at rollcall because we weren't catching enough burglars.

¶ **swing on meat** [alluding to fellatio; see SWING, *v.*] to be subservient to; *kiss* [or *lick* or *suck*] *(someone's) ass* s.v. ASS.—usu. considered vulgar.

1944 Kendall *Service Slang* 54: *Swinging on the meat.*…overanxious to please officers.

meat ass *n. Navy.* a master-at-arms.—usu. considered vulgar.

1961 L.E. Young *Virgin Fleet* 27 [ref. to 1941]: The M.A. Force…the meat asses. *Ibid.* 116: Listen, Meat Ass.

meat ax *n.* **1.** (used in var. slang similes).

1831 in M. Mathews *Begin. Amer. Eng.* 117: Clear meat-ax disposition. **1834** in *DA:* In Kentucky parlance, "is as savage as a meat-axe." **1838** in *DA:* As wicked as a meat-axe. **1843** in *F & H* VI 297: It would be a charity to give the pious brother some such feed as chicken fixins and doins, for he looks half-starved and as savage as a meat axe. **1855** in *OEDS:* I feel as mad as a meat-ax. **1856** in *DA:* Why you are as sharp as a meat axe. **1856** in A.P. Hudson *Humor of Old So.* 464: I went aboard as sassy as a meat-axe.

2. the penis.—usu. considered vulgar. *Joc.* Cf. MEAT LANCE.

1976 *Nat. Lampoon* (Mar.) 64: Well, I'm going to lay some pipe!…Beat her with the meat ax!

meat bag *n. West.* the belly; stomach. *Joc.*

1847 Ruxton *Far West* 4: Well, Dick was as full of arrows as a porkypine: one was sticking right through his cheek, one in his meat bag, and two more 'bout his hump ribs. **1850** Garrard *Wah-to-yah* 47: I bet I'll make you eat dog meat in the village, and you'll say it's good, and the best you ever hid in your "meat-bag" (stomach).

meatball *n.* **1.a.** *Navy.* a black ball on a field of solid color on various flags and pennants; (*hence*) a battle-efficiency pennant bearing a black ball on a red field, or any flag of comparable design, as used in signaling or hoisted to indicate excellent performance.

    1919 *Our Navy* (May) 22: The long minutes of waiting for the umpire's report and finally the joy of winning the pennant and hoisting the old "meat-ball." **1929** Bowen *Sea Slang* 90: *Meat Ball, The.* In the U.S. Navy, the battle efficiency pennant....It is the red "meal pennant" with a black ball in the centre. **1941** Kendall *Army & Navy Slang* 22: *Meat ball....* pennant flown to indicate excellence in some field. Often athletics. **1945** in *Calif. Folk. Qly.* V (1946) 382: *Meatball.* A U.S. Navy tactical signal flag bearing a black dot on a yellow field. **1953** Morison *Naval Ops. in WWII* 192: *PC-1452...* hoisted a No. 1 "meat-ball" pennant at each yardarm five minutes before H-hour. **1966** Noel & Bush *Naval Terms* 216: *Meatball:* (Battle Efficiency Pennant). **1967** Lockwood *Subs* 73 [ref. to 1916]: That meant we would have no chance to win the "Meatball," as the Engineering Trophy insignia was called. **1984** Trotti *Phantom* 126: Pass after pass is made against the jaunty [target] banner with a "meatball" adorning its middle.

    b. *Orig. Navy & USMC.* the rising-sun emblem of Japan as it appears on flags, aircraft, etc.; (*hence*) a Japanese aircraft. [Quots. ref. to WWII.]

    1944 Hubler & DeChant *Flying Leathernecks* 181 [ref. to 1942]: It took some squinting to detect the red "meatballs" of the Japanese on its sides. **1944** D. Trumbo *30 Secs. over Tokyo* (film): Pacific. To get us a few meatballs. **1948** Johnston *Follow Me!*: The enraged survivors hauled down the "meatball" and Pfc. Edward Cooke of Missouri fished a small American flag out of his pack. **1952** Morison *Naval Ops. in WWII* III 101: The plane turned up the main channel...and he saw the "meatball" insignia painted on its side. **1953** Dodson *Away All Boats* 310: It's a meat ball all right. Where's the Army Air Force? **1959** R.L. Scott *Flying Tiger* 118: With field glasses we would distinctly make out the red "meat ball" of the Jap. **1961** Foster *Hell in Heavens* 233: I saw a flash of red as from the meatballs of a Jap plane. **1961** G. Forbes *Goodbye to Some* 47: I can see the meatballs on both upper wing surfaces. **1963** Boyle *Yanks Don't Cry* 25: See that red meat ball in the center of those flags? Look at 'em. Those meat balls are the flaming grommets of the Jap Navy. **1963** D. Wiggins *S.O. Bees* 36: Some meatball gets on my tail and I got to sit there and let him shoot me down? **1964** Newhafer *Last Tallyho* 183: He could plainly make out the red meatball on its fuselage. **1980** Manchester *Darkness* 230: A Jap helmet, a sword, and a meatball banner.

    c. *Naval Av.* a reflected beam of light used to guide pilots in landings, as on aircraft carriers.

    1957 *Science Newsletter* (July 27) 60: The "meatball" is the key to the Navy's mirror landing system. ***1957** in *OEDS* (Aug. 31): The mirror reflects a bright light astern and upward into a beam which the pilot follows straight to a landing by keeping the "meatball" light precisely centered in the mirror. **1965** Harvey *Hudasky's Raiders* 39: The pilot used the new Landing Mirror system. He watched a bright orange light on the mirror, known as "the meatball," and tried to keep it squarely centered. **1966** Mulligan *No Place to Die* 189: Meatball. The two rows of green lights sandwiched between two rows of yellow lights on the big panel board just to the left of the [carrier] runway. **1969** Cagle *Naval Av. Guide* 396: *Meatball.* The spot of light which a pilot making a landing (carrier or field) keeps in the center of the landing system mirror, aligned with the datum bar. **1971** Gallery *Away Boarders* 34: The meatball is a spot of light from a gyro-stabilized projector on deck set to shine a narrow beam at the exact glide angle down which the plane must come. **1972–79** T. Wolfe *Right Stuff* 327: There was now a blob of light, known as the *meatball*, rising and falling on a dimly perceived [aircraft carrier]. **1984** Trotti *Phantom* 99: If you are on glide path, the meatball (the reflected source light) will appear in the center of the mirror. **1986** Coonts *Intruder* 15: The pilot could see the light, the "meatball," presented by the optical landing system...located on the port side of the landing area. **1991** K. Douglass *Viper Strike* 28: The Fresnel lens, or "meatball," an arrangement of lights which changed...positions as he changed his, showed him whether or not he was aligned properly with the carrier's deck.

    2. *Army.* the last partial day left to serve in an enlistment. Now *hist.*

    1930 *Our Army* (Feb.) 43: *Meatball.* The last day on an enlistment, when a soldier does no duty, is discharged at 11:00 am. and com-

mences his next day of service on the following morning. When he speaks of how much time he has to serve, he says he has "fifteen days and a meat ball." **1977** Monaghan *Schoolboy, Cowboy* 184 [ref. to 1913]: Now I have only two months, two days and a meat ball.

    3.a. a stupid or objectionable person; dolt.

    1939 Appel *Power House* 13: That for you, you big meatball! **1941** Wilder *Ball of Fire* (film): Drip...Meatball...Sad apple. **1943** Hersey *Bell for Adano* 68: Lieutenant Livingston was inclined to the opinion that it was too bad the army had sent such a meatball to be administrator of a town like Adano. **1944** *Yank* (Feb. 18) 22: Where you from, meatball? **1947** Schulberg *Harder They Fall* 257: Apparently he wasn't such a meatball that he couldn't find a way to get around Vince's reluctance. **1947** Mailer *Naked & Dead* 270: They shake rather self-consciously....What a meatball, Hearn thinks. **1948** J.H. Burns *Lucifer* 78: You *are* a meatball and a character. **1950** Bissell *Stretch on the River* 73: Hello, you meat ball....Merry Christmas, you silly bastard. **1953** M. Shulman *Affairs of Dobie Gillis* (film): Maybe you ain't such a meatball after all. **1955** *You'll Never Get Rich* (CBS-TV): Why those miserable meatballs! **1957** M. Shulman *Rally* 168: Grady...is one of the really big meatballs of our generation. **1957** Hall *Cloak & Dagger* 13: What do you think of the meatball we have for a chief instructor? **1959** E. Hunter *Matter of Conviction* 133: "You're a meatball," Frankie said. **1959** Morrill *Dark Sea Running* 26: I had to teach seamanship to guys with six thumbs—like that meatball, Joe Parker. **1971** N.Y.U. student: A *meatball* is about the same as a jerk. He's kind of a semi-jerk, but they get angrier if you call 'em that. It's a newer word, I'd say. Maybe from the '30's. **1972** *Playboy* (Dec.) 126: He's a *buffone*. A real meatball. **1973** P. Benchley *Jaws* 164: So why did he settle on a meatball for a second wife? **1978** T.H. White *In Search* 43 [ref. to ca1935]: I find some difficulty in describing what a "meatball" was. Meatballs...were at Harvard not to enjoy the games, the girls, the burlesque shows...[but] to get the Harvard badge, which...means a job somewhere in the future. **1979–81** C. Buckley *To Bamboola* 13: Rocco...said woe to those meatballs if he ever ran into them. **1996** *Everybody Loves Raymond* (CBS-TV): "Here we go: large meatball." "That's what we call him at home."

    b. *Pros.* a prostitute's customer.

    1956 J. Stern *Sisters* 5: From the hotels themselves, clerks, bellhops, and elevator operators were recruited to steer the customers—the "Johns" or "meatballs"—to the selected suites. **1970** Winick & Kinsie *Lively Commerce* 189: Prostitutes and their associates often call the client a "john." He may also be called a "sucker" or "meatball."

    c. a stupid or worthless thing.

    1980 *N.Y. Times* (Dec. 14) IIA 11: [Movie:] "Rollercoaster"...A mad-bomber meatball.

    4. *Esp. N.Y.C.* an Italian or person of Italian descent.—used contemptuously.

    1942–49 Goldin et al. *DAUL* 137: *Meat-ball....*An Italian. **1971** Contini *Beast Within* 82: You get tired of talking to meatballs. No pun intended, you guinea. **1981** Graziano & Corsel *Somebody Down Here* 173: I was used to being called names like wop, dago, guinea, meatball, greaseball...and...worse. *a***1989** in Kisseloff *Must Remember This* 577 [ref. to ca1930]: They used to call us guineas all the time, or wops or meatballs....We called them "Irish micks."

    5. *Baseball.* an easily hit pitch.

    1954–60 *DAS*: *Meatball...*In baseball, any pitched ball that can be hit readily by a given batter....*Not common.* **1978** Univ. Tenn. student: Is he throwing meatballs? **1978** in Lyle & Golenbock *Bronx Zoo* 63: It was a high meatball, and he swung and hit a nice high liner to Mickey Rivers in center field. **1980** *N.Y. Post* (June 21) 40: Jim Spencer...crunched a Steve McCaffy meatball for a two-run HR in the fifth.

    6. *Horse Racing.* a cathartic pill administered to a horse.

    1968 Ainslie *Racing Guide* 470: *Meat ball*—Cathartic pill.

    7. see MEATBALL, *adj.*

meatball *adj.* **1.** (of a criminal charge) trivial or false. Also as *n.*

    1944 in Hassler *Diary* 65: Nine years a square John...and now I'm in on a meatball rap! **1952** H. Ellson *Golden Spike* 240: Aw, that's a meatball rap, you'll get out tomorrow. **1959** W. Burroughs *Naked Lunch* 231: Lost back there with a meatball rape rap...statutory, brother. **1964** Harris *Junkie Priest* 83: The arrest was a frame, a meatball rap, but you took it in your stride. **1966** Braly *Cold* 153: That was a meatball beef. **1973** "A.C. Clarke" *Crime Partners* 103: You guys picked me up on a meatball. I ain't robbed nobody, so you ain't got no case on me. **1978** Sopher & McGregor *Up from Walking Dead* 269: That's sure a meatball rap, kid. **1980** D. Hamill *Stomping Ground* 168: A meatball charge like underage drinking. **1981** Sann *Trial* 12: A misdemeanor is…a meatball rap, which means the possible sentence is…trifling.

2. stupid; foolish.

   1965 Hardman *Chaplains* 7: In all of recorded United States Marine Corps history has there ever been such a meatball deal? **1966–67** W. Stevens *Gunner* 48: Those Krauts were in and out before any of those meatball fighter jockeys could get their fingers out of their asses.

meat box *n. Mil. Av.* a front gun turret or other cramped forward position in an aircraft.

   1941 Kendall *Army & Navy Sl.* 9: *Meat box.*…front gun turret on a bomber. **1942** *Life* (May 18) 77: The "meat box"…where the bombardier and instructor sit.

meatbrain *n.* MEATHEAD.

   1980 Conroy *Lords of Discipline* 393: Meatbrain over there talked me into it.

meat-eater *n. Police.* a corrupt police officer who engages aggressively and extensively in graft. Cf. GRASS-EATER. [Like GRASS-EATER, this term first came to public attention during the Knapp Commission hearings on police corruption, held in N.Y.C in 1972; some sources erroneously date these hearings to the 1960's.]

   1972 (quot. at GRASS-EATER). **1972** in *DAS* (ed. 2): Meat eaters, probably only a small percentage of the force, spend a good deal of their working hours aggressively seeking out situations they can exploit for financial gain. **1974** (quot. at GRASS-EATER). **1986** Philbin *Under Cover* 102: I know they accused you of grass-eating…As long as you aren't a meat-eater, that's fine. **1990** T. Fahey *Joys of Jargon* 185: *Meateater*…Cop who solicits bribes.

meat-flasher *n.* a sexual exhibitionist; FLASHER, 1.—usu. considered vulgar.

   1890–96 F & H IV 297: *Meat-flashing*…Exposure of the person. Hence, *meat-flasher* = a public offender in this line. **1916** Cary *Venery* I 201: *Meat Flasher*—One who exposes his or her person.

meat grinder *n.* **1.** a vehicle having a noisy engine.

   1942 A.C. Johnston *Courtship of A. Hardy* (film): I'm gonna change this old meat-grinder here into a tow-truck. **1954–60** *DAS: Meatgrinder*…An automobile.

2.a. *Mil.* fierce combat that results in many dead and wounded.—constr. with *the*; (hence) an area under devastating enemy ground fire; heavy enemy fire. Also **meat chopper.**

   1945 in Kennard *Letters* 100: Most infantry companies of our division have about twenty original men that landed on D-day.…This is the first time I have seen the "meat grinder" in process, as Frank calls it. **1959** Webb *Pork Chop Hill* (film): Welcome to the meat-grinder. **1960** Sire *Deathmakers* 87 [ref. to WWII]: Today you throw yourself into the meat chopper. **1967** Clarke *Over There* 26 [ref. to 1918]: The war itself was called *The Meat-Grinder.* **1967** Ragni & Rado *Hair* 114: Ship these Peaceniks to the Vietnam meatgrinder. **1968** Duay *Fruit Salad* 124: The lagoon was a meat grinder bastard! **1969** Linn & Pearl *Masque of Honor* 13: Three days ago his outfit was hit hard by the Commies, really put through the meat grinder. **1974** Kingry *Monk & Marines* 58: What I'd volunteered for wasn't anything but a god awful meat grinder. **1977** Natkin & Furie *Boys in Co. C.* (film): Khe Sanh. It's a meatgrinder. **1985** Dye *Between Raindrops* 87: Heavy return fire.…The Goddamn street is a meat grinder. **1984–87** Ferrandino *Firefight* 127: Nothing like the meatgrinder we walked into a while back. **1991** *Weekend Edition* (Nat. Pub. Radio) (May 25): Addis Ababa will be a meat grinder if the rebel advance continues.

b. a process that eliminates many competitors; a difficult or dangerous place or situation.

   1951 in *OEDS:* That man…whose school training wins him the privilege of getting at once into the technological meat grinder. **1964** in Marx *Groucho Letters* 280: I am…exhausted from five and a half days in the meat grinder. **1966** Thompson *Hell's Angels* 93: One little thing like that and you're into the meat grinder. The minute you hit the brakes you'll start losing it. **1984** A. Pincus *How to Talk Football* 48: *Meat grinder*…the area of an opponent's greatest resistance. **1991** Marcinko & Weisman *Rogue Warrior* 226: The training…it's gonna be a motherfucking meat-grinder.

meat hand *n. Baseball.* a fielder's hand unprotected by a glove. Hence **meat-handed,** *adv.* with the bare hand.

   1911 Van Loan *Big League* 17: It'll never be on the "meat-hand" side, either. **1912** *American Mag.* (June) 204: *Meat Hand*—The throwing hand of a player, the term resulting from the fact that the throwing hand is bare while the other is protected by a glove or mitt. **1936** C. Mack, in Paxton *Sport U.S.A.* 6: I remember that summer we chipped in and bought a [baseball] glove for two dollars.…Up to that time we had played with our "meat" hands. *Ibid.* 7: The fielders were still catching them meat-handed. **1962** Morris & Morris *Dict. Word & Phr. Orig.* 27: Most players are understandably loath to try catching hard-hit balls with their *meat hands.* **1983** Whiteford *How to Talk Baseball* 112: *Meat hand*…player's throwing hand.

meathead *n.* an oaf; stupid person; FATHEAD. Hence **meatheaded,** *adj.*

   1928 MacArthur *War Bugs* 140 [ref. to WWI]: We bawled them out for a lot of meatheads. **1942** L.R. Foster *Mayor of 44th St.* (film): OK, meathead. Start your slappin'. **1942** Lindsay & Crouse *Strip for Action:* Listen, meathead, don't you know you could go to Leavenworth for that? **1943** *Yank* (Oct. 22) 14: Take cover, you meat-heads! **1944** *Screwball Squirrel* (MGM animated cartoon): Don't worry, meathead. I'll save ya! **1944** *Papers Mich. Acad.* XXX 599: *Meathead,* a fool. **1944–49** Allardice *At War* 80: You're the one who calls Sergeant McVey "Meat-head." **1949** W.R. Burnett *Asphalt Jungle* 38: Look, meathead. **1949** in *DAS:* Some meat-headed tart. **1950** Seaton *Big Lift* (film): What do you want, meathead? **1951** Haines & Burnett *Racket* (film): This is McQuaig's district, you meathead. **1952** Chase *McThing* 65: You're a meat head, Mimi. **1955** *Phil Silvers Show* (CBS-TV): Now listen, you meatheads. **1957** Wilbur & Veiller *Monkey on My Back* (film): That stupid, stubborn meathead. **1958** McCulloch *Woods Wds.* 117: *Meat head*…a dimwit. **1971** *All in the Family* (CBS-TV): Wait a minute, meathead, *you* said dat! **1971** Wells & Dance *Night People* 12 [ref. to 1925]: Beside those I've mentioned before, we had "Hoagie" Walker, Johnny Williams and Harold McFarren on saxophones, "Meathead" or Mack Walker (Hoagie's brother) on bass, and Hubert Mann on banjo. **1981** *L.A. Times* (June 24) VI 8: Being cut off in the middle for a commercial by the meatheads at Channel 13. **1987** Konner & Rosenthal *Superman IV* (film): Move it, meathead!

meathook *n.* **1.** a tooth or fang.

   1844 W.T. Porter *Big Bear* 131: Look at them yaller eyes!—them ears laid back, and them meat hooks a shinin'! Ain't he stretchin' himself?

2. usu. *pl.* a hand or fist; (*rarely*) an arm or finger; (*pl.*) one's clutches.

   1919 Downing *Digger Dialects* 33: *Meat-hook*—arm. **1932** *AS* VII 334: *Meat hooks*—hands. **1942–49** Goldin et al. *DAUL* 137: *Meathooks.* The fingers; the hands. **1952** Uris *Battle Cry* 112: I'll tell you men, if I ever get my meathooks on that bastard, I'll rip him open from asshole to appetite. **1960** Barber *Minsky's* 188: Rudy…waggled a meat-hook of a finger at the drummer. **1963** Coon *Short End* 66: The big guy had his meathooks on his hips so his muscles could ripple better. **1965** Herlihy *Midnight Cowboy* 163: And keep your meathooks off my radio. **1973** Droge *Patrolman* 91: The meat hooks on a guy like that should be considered lethal weapons. **1974** Millard *Thunderbolt* 37: You must have got your meat-hooks in something really big. **1978** L'Amour *Proving Trail* 50: Wacker [was] rubbing his big meat-hooks on his pants. *a*1987 Bunch & Cole *Reckoning for Kings* 66: Not that this saved Taliaferro from being grabbed by one of Fritsche's meathooks.

3. the penis.—usu. considered vulgar.

   1978 in *Maledicta* VI (1982) 23: Penis…*meat, meat hook, member.*

meat hound *n.* **1.** CHOWHOUND.

   1918 Ruggles *Navy Explained* 102: Meat Hound. A man who thinks of nothing but eat, eat, and eat. He is generally kicking about the "chow," yet he is the biggest scoffer on the ship. **1918** in Matthews & Wecter *Our Soldiers Speak* (Oct. 17) 272: [U.S.Navy:] A bunch of meat hounds…gobbled up all the food before it got to my end.…The "pelicans" didn't have a word to say.

2. a lecher.—usu. considered vulgar.

   *a*1934 (quot. at WOLF, *n.*). **1942** *ATS* 394: Lascivious man.…*meat hound.* **1965** W. Crawford *Bronc Rider* 238: I'm a bull-rider. A wise God must judge me as one. Not as a man, not as a meathound, not even as a rodeo cowboy.

meat house *n.* **1.** a brothel; (*also*) a public lavatory used as a rendezvous for male homosexuals.—usu. considered vulgar. [The 1916 quot. may simply repeat *F & H*.]

    *a1890–96 *F & H* VI 296: *Meat-house* = a brothel. **1916** Cary *Venery* I 201: *Meat House*—A brothel. **1961** ISR Graffiti MS.: This is the Meat House.

2. *Police.* a morgue.

    1933 in D. Runyon *More Guys* 24: The meat house....That's the morgue.

¶ In phrase:

¶ **tear (someone's) meathouse down** *So. & West.* to thrash; do for.—also used allusively. Also vars.

    1903 in E.M. Rhodes *Rhodes Reader* 7: If you ain't right up to the scratch with that money you owe me, down goes your meathouse! **1923** Evarts *Tumble* 60: I forgot my timidity and pulled down his meat house. **1974** R. Carter *16th Round* 110: But now, you black bastard, you, I'm gonna tear your meathouse down!

meat injection *n.* an act of intromission of the penis.—usu. considered vulgar. *Joc.* Cf. *hot beef injection* s.v. BEEF, *n.*

    1983 K. Weaver *Texas Crude* 108: What's this, dear heart, your famous meat injection? **1988** Lewin & Lewin *Thesaurus* 338: Sexual Intercourse...*meat injection.* *1990 P. Beale, in Partridge *Concise Dict. Sl.*: *Meat-injection, give* (her) *a* To coit with a woman: Services': since late 1940s. *1993 I. Welsh *Trainspotting* 9: He pierces her flesh and injects a wee bit [of heroin] slowly....["]That beats any meat injection["].

meat lance *n.* the penis.—usu. considered vulgar. *Joc.* Also **meat spear, meat stick.**

    1974 Univ. Tenn. student: A *meat stick* is a dick. **1976** Atlee *Domino* 119: Any...man would want to bury his meat lance in them for five minutes, while he held his breath. **1990** in *AS* (Winter, 1992) 380: Meat spear.

meat market *n.* **1.a.** a place frequented by prostitutes seeking customers; (*also*) a brothel.

    *1871 (cited in Walkowitz *Prost. & Victorian Soc.* 202). *1890–96 *F & H* IV 296: *Meat-market*...any *rendezvous* of public women. **1916** Cary *Venery* I 201: *Meat Market*—A brothel. **1982** "J. Cain" *Commandos* 137: The girls...had been tricking at the meat market since day one.

b. any place or organized situation where people may be regarded as commodities.

    1971 Dahlskog *Dict.* 40: *Meat market, n.* A modeling agency. **1978** *Texas Monthly* (Mar.) 132: All of them were part of what academics refer to as the "meat market"—the convention. **1982** *Mother Jones* (Nov.) 44: Recruiting firms...are known as "meat markets" in the industry. **1995** *New Yorker* (Mar. 13) 7: The horrific meat market of the Nike summer camp for prime national hoop prospects.

2. a place where potential sexual partners may be met; MEAT RACK.

    [**1918** *DN* V 26: *Meet* [sic] *market, n.* A corner drugstore, or other convenient place for "meeting"; especially such places as the transfer points of car lines. Spokane, Washington, and vicinity. Common but ephemeral.] [**1942–49** Goldin et al. *DAUL* 136: *Market.* The rendezvous of male oral sodomists and pederasts...."Guess I'll nip the market and give the fruit (perverts) a play."]. *1957 in *OED2*: Every tart and pansy boy in the district are in that place....It's just a meat-market. **1966** C. Ross *N.Y.* 73: New York has become a public meat market...with prancing, walking and standing homosexuals everywhere in the city. **1971** in *Urban Life* IV (1976) 421: [Yale students refer to college mixers as] "body exchanges" and "meat markets." **1974** Cherry *High Steel* 205: A "swinging singles" neighborhood. In New York it's called "the meat market." **1980** *Daily News* (N.Y.) ("Manhattan") (Sept. 6) 9: Tired of making the scene at those meat-market singles bars or cruising the museums on Saturday afternoons? **1983** Eble *Campus Slang* (Mar.) 4: *Meat market*—place where members of the opposite sex are plentiful and available. **1995** *Wash. Post* (Mar. 8) B1: Gay bars...fill so many functions for so many men: part community center, part refuge, part meat market.

meat puppet *n.* a vacuous person easily directed or manipulated by others.

    1982 *Meat Puppets* [name of rock group; self-titled album]. **1984** W. Gibson *Neuromancer* 147: "Where's the meat puppet?" "There isn't any." **1989** *Newsweek* (June 12) 6: *Meat puppet:* Backstage lingo for

none-too-bright TV-news anchorman. Usage: "It's a good thing the meat puppet has a script." **1996** *Mystery Sci. Theater* (Comedy Central TV): Button it, meat puppet!

meat rack *n.* Orig. *Homosex.* an area where casual sex partners may easily be picked up; (*hence*) a singles bar; (*also*, in 1996 quot.) MEAT MARKET, 1.b.

    1962 Cory & LeRoy *Homsex. & His Soc.* 265: *Meat rack*...A gathering place of male homosexuals. **1966** C. Ross *N.Y.* 80: The longest meat rack in the world is on Central Park West. **1966** S. Harris *Hellhole* 222: Rusty came to the "meat rack" of Washington Square Park in Greenwich Village...the magnet for lonesome men and women homosexuals from all over. Everyone who's anyone in gay life descends on the "meat rack" sooner or later. **1966** "Petronius" *N.Y. Unexp.* 110: Fire Island...meat rack of the world. **1967** *Amer. Jour. Psychotherapy* XXI 170: The "Meat-Rack": A Study of the Male Homosexual Prostitute. **1965–72** E. Newton *Mother Camp* 95: Some areas are agreed-upon cruising places, "meat racks" where cruising is open. **1973** *New York* (Jan. 8) 54: I used to walk unnoticed down Christopher Street when it was called the Meat Rack. **1974** *Nat. Lampoon* (Oct.) 34: Those of you who look well in butch haircuts...need only "hang" at your local meat rack. **1974** Dubinsky & Standora *Decoy Cop* 104: That's the meat rack....It's where the fags hang out. **1978** Fisher & Rubin *Special Teachers* 153: There was nothing gay about the meat racks around Forty-deuce. **1979** Alibrandi *Custody* 9: Frequenting singles' parties or swingers' bars—both known as the meat rack—for some no-strings-attached sex. **1984** *N.Y. Post* (Aug. 14) 50: The big city singles bars so many readers say are "meat racks." **1985** Grave *Florida Burn* 106: The Key Biscayne Club was another in a long series of high priced meat-racks. **1990** Steward *Bad Boys* 54: A free and open meat rack atmosphere. **1996** *Time* (June 24) ("Digital") 40: The Plaza Hotel...is hardly a place where you would expect to find a meat rack. But in May the hotel was host to the second annual Venture Market...in which young CEOs...vie for the attentions—and seven-figure cash investments—of visiting high-tech venture capitalists.

meat show *n.* *Theat.* a performance that features nude or partially clothed young women.

    1943 in Ruhm *Detective* 361: You remember Daisy? That used to sing in the Empyrean meat show. **1951** in *DAS*: A divertissement known in the trade as a meat-show.

meat spear see s.v. MEAT LANCE.

meat stick see s.v. MEAT LANCE.

meat tool *n.* the penis; TOOL.—usu. considered vulgar. *Joc.*

    1965 L. Jones *Blues People*: But however she drew him to her, and he drew her, toward his thing, the mutilation characterizes the white man's insane fear of black creation. And the meattool of its physical manifestation is something to be destroyed. **1971** B. Malamud, in *OEDS*: What do you do...with your meat tool? You got no girl, who do you fuck other than your hand?

meat trap *n.* the mouth.

    1851 M. Reid *Scalp-Hunters* 82: Shet up yur meat-traps...an' I'll show 'ee. **1860** E.S. Ellis *Bill Biddon* 71: Shut up yer meat-trap; it's time we started. **1861** E.S. Ellis *N. Todd* 27: Jest put a stop on that meat-trap of yourn. *ca*1885 in Botkin *Sidewalks* 45: "Hush your meat trap!" said the countryman.

meat van *n.* *Police.* a patrol wagon; MEAT WAGON, 2.

    1975 De Mille *Smack Man* 107: You'll ride in the meat van and...spend some nights in the slammer.

meat wagon *n.* **1.a.** an ambulance.

    1925 Taber *168th Inf.* 189 [ref. to 1918]: By this time all of the old members of the regiment had experienced one tour of the trenches, and the initiated, who could now greet the whistle of a shell with shouts of "Be a dud" or "Gimme his hard-tack," and who cheerfully referred to the ambulance as the "meat wagon," hailed with glee any error or signs of nervousness among the replacements. **1937** Parsons *Lafayette Escadrille* 269 [ref. to WWI]: Not in the least shaky or upset by his incredible escape, he rode triumphantly back on the seat of the meat wagon which had been hastily dispatched to pick up his mangled remains. **1943** Trumbo *Guy Named Joe* (film): Nobody hurt....Get that meat wagon outta here. **1943** G. Biddle *Artist at War* 182: Wounded were coming down the road in jeeps and in the meat-wagons. **1949** *Sat. Eve. Post* (Dec. 3) 75: The crash truck was first, the meat wagon behind it. **1953** T.H. White *Down the Ridge* viii: If under stress he transposes everything into sturdy Anglo-Saxon, calling his ambulance a meat wagon or his abdominal trauma a gut shot, it is not that he wants to shock. **1954** Davis & Lay *S.A.C.* (film): Alert the fire truck and meat wagon. **1960** Stadley *Barbarians* 57: Ride this meat wagon and you'll see all kinds. **1962** *AS* XXXVII 270: *Meat wagon*...An ambulance [among traffic policemen]. **1978** Strieber *Wolfen* 166: Where's that friggin' meatwagon? **1978** in Higham & Williams *Combat Aircraft* 48: I could see the fire wagons and "meat" wagons lined up by the runway. **1980** D. Hamill *Stomping Ground* 210: Into the back of the Kings County meat wagon. **1981** Sann *Trial* 38: Them meat wagon drivers. **1983** *Judge Dredd* (comics) (Nov.) [10]: Judge Anderson took our meat wagon. **1983** Stapleton *30 Yrs.* 90: Rush right down the stairs and get him in the meat wagon. **1989** T. Blackburn *Jolly Rogers* 119: Crash trucks and meat wagons screeched to a halt.

b. a vehicle, as a hearse or police morgue wagon, in which corpses are transported.

1942 *ATS* 82: Hearse....*meat wagon.* **1943** R. Chandler *Lady in Lake,* in *DAS:* Murder-a-day Marlowe, they call him. They have the meat wagon following him around to follow up on the business he finds. **1949** Taradash & Monks *Knock on Any Door* (film): Up and down this street until the meat wagon comes and carts us all off. **1951** in Kerouac *Letters* 324: The smell of the morgue..., the presence of the meat-wagon...long, black, sleek Cadillac coffin car. **1956** Longstreet *Real Jazz* 7: The band would march out behind the meat-wagon, black plumes on the hearse horses, playing *Nearer My God to Thee.* **1963** J. Ross *Dead Are Mine* 110 [ref. to WWII]: Now let's take a look at the other meat wagon and see what's in it. **1963** A. Morgan *Six-Eleven* 209: I may beat you into the meat wagon yet. **1963** M. Shulman *Victors* 35: Hey, look, the meat wagon!...Bring out your dead! Where's the undertakers? **1966** "T. Pendleton" *Iron Orchard* 68: The Odessa undertaker's "meat wagon" had carted the bodies away. **1968** C. Victor *Sky Burned* 38: The meat wagon was waiting to pick up the bodies. **1971** *Night Gallery* (NBC-TV): Know what they call that oil-burner we brought him in? A meat wagon. **1971** Horan *Blue Messiah* 618: DOA. All of 'em. Leave 'em for the meat wagon. **a1977** in T.L. Blair *Retreat from Ghetto* 105: No black leaves Max Row walking. Either he leaves in the meat wagon or he leaves crawling. **1987** Taubman *Lady Cop* 25: They had already reported the death and...now it was just a matter of waiting for the meat wagon. *Ibid.* 269: *Meat wagon:* Vehicle used to take bodies to the morgue.

2. *Police.* a patrol wagon.

1944 in Weinberg et al. *Tough Guys* 549: You're bait for the meat wagon. I talked, boys. Oh yes, I talked. **1949** W.R. Burnett *Asphalt Jungle* 138: The coppers [are] knocking over all the joints ... mobs of 'em, meat wagons and all. **1959** Horan *Mob's Man* 36: We might land in the meatwagon. **1961** H. Ellison *Memos* 140: Charles Street station had been quiet the night before. I was the only passenger in the meat wagon. **1970–71** J. Rubinstein *City Police* 38: An assignment to work a patrol wagon (the "meatwagon" or, most commonly, the "wagon"). **1971** Keith *Long Line Rider* 73: Is this the new skinner Cap'n Reed brought in on the meat wagon? **1984** "W.T. Tyler" *Shadow Cabinet* 263: They dump us in this meat wagon...and take us out to the funny farm.

3. *Hosp.* a gurney.

1973–77 J. Jones *Whistle* 140 [ref. to WWII]: One or two or three stretcher cases might be rolled in in their surgeon's "meat wagons" and given precedence. **1983** Eilert *Self & Country* 54 [ref. to 1967]: With...a twist of his wrist Chief pointed the meat wagon down the gray corridor toward the ward. *Ibid.* 94: Wake up...meat wagon's here.

4. *Mil.* a hospital ship.

1973–77 J. Jones *Whistle* 28: Morning rounds...on this Godforsaken meat wagon were only a grotesque formality anyway.

5. (see quot.).

1980 M. Baker *Nam* 32: A first lieutenant...would...pick me up in his Oldsmobile convertible—a big, fat luxury car, a real meat wagon.

meatware *n. Computers.* a person; the human body. *Joc.* Cf. LIVEWARE; WETWARE.

1984 *Handling & Shipping Management* (Nov.) (Nexis): Computer systems have three components...The hardware, the software, and the meatware. **a1990** P. Dickson *Slang!* 77: *Meatware.* The human body ["Computerese"]. **1992** *CBS This Morning* (CBS-TV) (Aug. 3): Wetware [and] meatware. **a1994** *21st Cent. Dict. Sl.:* That all-nighter was hard on the meatware. **1996** "Re: Digital Tradition database gone?,"

message on Usenet newsgroup alt.music.filk: I think someone used communications meatware of the "expensive lawyer" variety.

meat whistle *n.* the penis as an object of fellatio.—usu. considered vulgar. *Joc.*

1965 Linakis *In Spring* 103 [ref. to WWII]: She didn't mind anything, and was quite a meat-whistle artist. *Ibid.* 121: How about the meat-whistle?...They all blow. **1966** Braly *On the Yard* 73: What are you going to do on the variety show?...Perform on the meat whistle? **1975** T. Berger *Sneaky People* 305: Soon's you play a little tune on my meat whistle. **1989** Univ. Tenn. student theme: Toot the meat whistle!

mech *n.* Esp. *Av.* a mechanic.

[**1895** Gore *Stu. Slang* 7: *Mech. lab....*Mechanical laboratory.] **1918** in Rossano *Price of Honor* 104: The C.O....sent an American mech out. **1931** Post & Gatty *Around World* 57: His "mech" was giving the Bellanca its last testing. **1932** Gates & Boylan *Hell Divers* (film): This man was my mech at Pearl Harbor last year. **1942** *Randolph Field* 100: Mechs we call them for slang, for short. **1943** W. Simmons *Joe Foss* 47: We watched "mechs" start the planes, check magnetos, props, engine, and tabs. **1943** Mear *Carrier* 105: The mechs told me that there was a stoppage in the carburetor. **1944** E.H. Hunt *Limit* 12: One of the mechs. **1950** *Pop. Science* (May) 142: Senior mech Harry Baker said, "Imagine a mechanic that's never on his back." **a1951* Partridge *DSUE* (ed. 4) 1107: *Mech...*Mechanic; esp. in the old *air mech* of the R.F.C. and the current *flight mech* of the Air Force: coll: since *ca*1912. **1962** S. Smith *Escape from Hell* 68: The motor mechs did a job on 'em.

mechanic *n.* **1.a.** *Gamb.* a gambler who can manipulate cards or dice deftly and unfairly; CARDSHARP. See also CARD MECHANIC.

1909 *Cent. Dict. Suppl.: Mechanic...*A professional card-shuffler usually employed to deal faro in a brace game. **1942** *ATS* 699: *Mechanic,* a dealer at faro adept at making the cards come as he pleases. **1944** *Collier's* (Feb. 12) 12: Are you a mechanic at gin? I mean if necessary? **1956** "T. Betts" *Across the Board* 121: No "mechanics" (sharps) were tolerated. **1961** Scarne *Comp. Guide to Gambling* 209: There was nearly always a *dice mechanic* (a cheat skilled at switching) around, ready to go into action if any big money showed. **1963** A. Morgan *Six-Eleven* 274: You got the idea I couldn't whip the ass off any of you mechanics without double shuffling or bottom dealing? **1966** S. Carroll *Big Hand for Lady* (film): He's a real expert mechanic. **1971** J. Brown & A. Groff *Monkey* 74: I...was what used to be called a "good mechanic."...I could go down to the seventh card of a deck to get what I wanted. **1982** Hayano *Poker Faces* 117: The experienced card manipulator, a *mechanic,* is able to shuffle, cut, and deal certain cards...to selected players, including himself.

b. *Und.* a pickpocket; (*also*) a safecracker.

1949 Monteleone *Crim. Slang: Mechanic...*The pickpocket who actually takes the purse; the one who does the actual work of opening a safe. **1973** *Reader's Digest* (Oct. 19) 202: "Mechanics"...work with a partner called a "stall" or "stick."

2. *Sports.* a mediocre player.

1975 Lichtenstein *Long Way* 88: I know I'm not a natural, but I don't think I'm a mechanic, either. I work at it!

mechanized dandruff *n. Mil.* lice or fleas. *Joc.* Also **mobile dandruff.** Cf. GALLOPING DANDRUFF.

1941 Kendall *Army & Navy Sl.* 9: Cooties...*mobile dandruff.* **1944** *Slanguage Dict.* 53: *Mechanized dandruff*—fleas. **1948** A. Murphy *Hell & Back* 11 [ref. to 1943]: I thought that dame in Palermo was perfectly okay until I woke up with the mechanized dandruff. **1950* W. Granville *Sea Slang* 155: *Mechanized dandruff.* Head lice. (Lower-deck.).

Med *n. Naut.* the Mediterranean Sea.—constr. with *the.*

*1943 (cited in Partridge *DSUE* (ed. 7) 1271). **1944** *Stars & Stripes* (Sicily) (Jan. 10): The "Med," as men of the Navy call her. **1951–52** Frank *Hold Back Night* 35: If the Russkies got Europe, then they'd have the Med too. **1959** Morrill *Dark Sea* 64: Everybody felt better when we sailed into the Med. **1964** in R. Marks *Letters* 29: The idea of seeing the Med. is nice, but who wants to be on a ship for 6–7 months? **1971** *CBS Reports* (CBS-TV) (Feb. 23): When did you last have three carriers in the Med? **1984** Hammel *Root* 10: The 1,800-man U.S. Marine amphibious units that regularly "cruise the Med."

med *n.* **1.** a medical student.

1851 B. Hall *College Wds.* 198: *Med, Medic.* A name sometimes given to a student in medicine. **1899** in *DA:* The Meds waited till the visitors were opposite them.

2. usu. *pl.* medicine; medication.

1930 G. Irwin *Tramp & Und. Slang: Med Man.*—In pitchman's argot and at a fair or carnival a "medicine man" or fake doctor. **1942** *ATS* 508: Medicine; drugs....*med.* **1943** *Sat. Eve. Post* (Sept. 25) 13: Pitchmen like myself...will not touch rad or med. **1974** Hejinian *Extreme Remedies* 85: Do you want an iv? Or any meds like Decadron? **1982** Gino *Nurse's Story* 339: I gave him all his meds. **1984** *Good Morning America* (ABC-TV) (July 18): Take your prescription meds with you. **1985** Frede *Nurses* 52: Put him on meds, Valium. **1989** P.H.C. Mason *Recovering* 180: I never saw a doctor, no meds.

medallion *n.* *N.Y.C.* a taxicab driver owning a taxi medallion. Cf. GYPSY, 2.

    1968 *N.Y. Times* (July 10) 36: If medallions want to start a fight, all right, but don't go looking for trouble.

meddie *n.* a medical student.

    1981 (quot. at TURF, *v.*).

medic *n.* **1.a.** a physician. Orig. *S.E.*

    *1659 in *OED:* The Medic heals the Body. **1661* in *OED: Medick*, a Physitian. **1885** in *DAE: Medic* is the legitimate paronym of *medicus*, but is commonly regarded as slang. **1901** in *DAE:* The medics, in common with other professions have furnished men who could be trusted to place a hand upon the helm of state. **1902* in *OEDS:* For ages medics have been laying down rules for the regimen of diseased people. **1951** Robbins *Danny Fisher* 315: But what could the guy do when his medic told him he had a bum ticker? **1965** Spillane *Killer Mine* 51: Two trips to the medic and I was okay. **1996** *TV Guide* (Apr. 13) 31: This malevolent medic.

    b. *Stu.* a medical student.

    1823 *Crayon* (Yale Univ.) 23: Who sent/The Medic to our aid. *Ibid.* 24: The Council are among ye, Yale!/Some roaring Medic cries. **1851** (quot. at MED, 1). **1866–71** Bagg *Yale* 45: *Medic*, a medical student. Rarely used. **1895** Gore *Stu. Slang* 7: *Medic*....A student in the medical department. **1900** *DN* II 46: *Medic*, n. Medical student. **1925** Lewis *Arrowsmith* 626 [ref. to *ca*1910]: "I'm sorry I hurt your feelings, but you did seem so young for a doctor." "I'm not. I'm a medic. I was showing off."

    2. *Mil.* a member of a medical corps; (*pl.*) a medical corps. Now *S.E.*

    1918 Campbell *Diary-Letters* (Apr. 15) 10: All the other men in the car were in branches of the service that don't or can't stand guard— "medics" and the like. **1918** Straub *Diary* 93: I also saw some Medics bring in a dead "doughboy." **1918** *Outlook* (Oct. 23) 294: I'll tell ye why I'm in the Medics. **1919** Law *Air Service* (unp.): The medics say they saved the line/with C.C. pills and iodine. **1919** Hubbell *Co. C* 100: Medics forward! **1920** *Amer. Leg. Wkly.* (Nov. 19) 17: The Overworked Medic of A—. **1921** *Pirate Piece* (July) 2: We tried to squeeze the Medics in here.

medic *v.* to be a MEDIC, 2.

    1986 Heinemann *Paco's Story* 29: I ain't gonna medic for you no more.

medicine *n.* **1.** *West.* **a.** a source of power or luck.—also used attrib. Cf. BAD MEDICINE.

    1825 in *OEDS:* Some of them have it that I am one of the "Masters of Life's Sons" sent to see "if their hearts were good" and others that I am his "War Chief" with bad medicine if their hearts were bad. **1844** Carleton *Logbooks* 81: That gun...was the "*biggest medicine*" they had seen yet. **1902** Remington *Ermine* 119: I'll keep the pony; he's medicine. **1922** Evarts *Settling* 64: Let's have a medicine chat. **1953** L'Amour *Hondo* 160: You whipped me....My medicine must have been bad.

    b. information.

    1911–12 J. London *Smoke Bellew* 75: My medicine's good. When I get a hunch, it's sure right. **1921** A. Jennings *Through Shadows* 45 [ref. to *ca*1890]: They sat under the wagon sheet, stowing in the biscuits and coolly doping out the "medicine." **1933** J.V. Allen *Cowboy Lore* 59: *Ain't got no medicine.* No information.

    2. whiskey; liquor. *Joc.*

    1847 in Oehlschlaeger *Reveille* 207: They...adjourned to the shanty, and called for the "medicine." **1874** (quot. at TANGLE-LEG). **1899** Thomas *Arizona* 9: Used to try to put a crimp in my medicine with the same scare. **1988–93** Wilcock & Guy *Damn Right* 22: A slug of "medicine" was a small price to pay.

¶ In phrase:

¶ **make medicine** *West.* to confer or make a plan.

    1904 in "O. Henry" *Works* 832: We rested our horses and "made medicine" as to how we should get about it. **1905** in *Chrons. of Okla.* XLVI (1969) 406: He spends three full months making medicine with his dirty little gang. **1906** in A. Adams *Chisholm Trail* 249: The result was, these old longhorns got owly, laid their heads together, and made a little medicine. **1956** Overholser *Desperate* 41: There was a man who was making big medicine a few years ago. **1958** McCulloch *Woods Wds.* 117: *Medicine maker*—A man thinking up trouble for somebody else.

medicine *adj.* persuasive.

    1873 *Overland Mo.* (Feb.) 113: So Smith had a medicine-talk with him, and tried to coax him, but the soft-soap dodge wouldn't work. **1907** S.E. White *Arizona Nights* 135: He had the medicine tongue! Ten days later him and me was occupyin' an old ranch fifty mile [sic] from anywhere.

medicine *v.* to take a drink of liquor.

    1844 *Spirit of Times* (Mar. 2) 12: Knock the bar-keeper up, and let's medicine.

medicine sharp *n.* a physician. *Joc.*

    1897 A.H. Lewis *Wolfville* 68: It takes seven months, an iron constitootian, an' three medicine-sharps. **1905** Hobart *Get Next!* 56: The medicine sharps tell us that the grip is caused by a little germ.

medico *n.* a physician; MEDIC, 1.a., 2.

    1853 in McCauley *With Perry* 54: I had the 1st Launch, with Bibbles and the doctor or Medico. **1883** C. Russell *Sailors' Lang.* 90: *Medico.*—Ship's doctor. **1894** C. King *Initial Experience* 110: Wait till we hev done with the mine, medico. **1918** O'Reilly *Roving & Fighting* 52 [ref. to 1899]: We filed by the "medicos" with our mouths gaping open for inspection of tongue and teeth. **1918** *Sat. Eve. Post* (Nov. 2) 24: The boches grabbed a couple of machine guns and captured a medico. **1918** Witwer *Baseball to Boches* 26: This medico had me right. **1927** Cushing *Doughboy Ditties* 25: I guess/I can last 'til a "Medico" reaches/Me here in the terrible mess. **1930** *Our Army* (Feb.) 43: *Medico.* Member of the medical corps. **1931** Grant *Gangdom's Doom* 9: This gangster that Prescott wounded is on his way to some crooked medico right now. **1934** Halper *Foundry* 198: The shop medico speaking. **1936** N. Johnson *Pris. of Shark I.* (film): Not very interesting to anyone but a medico. **1936** "E. Queen" *Halfway House* 64: That's all your medico reported. **1947** Overholser *Buckaroo's Code* 63: June pulled up in front of the medico's office. **1950** Miller & Childs *Collector's Quest* (Sept. 19) 50: I take it yours is a "psychosomatic" ailment— about 85% of all afflictions are, even the medicos admit that to-day.

med man *n.* a man who operates a medicine show. Now chiefly *hist.*

    1930 (quot. at MED, 2). **1942** *ATS* 422: *Med man*, a patent medicine seller. **1943** *Billboard* (June 26) 61: In England ... a med man is a crocus.

meemies *n.pl.* SCREAMING MEEMIES.

    1946 Mezzrow & Wolfe *Really the Blues* 270: The prison days,...the hophead oblivion, the jangled nerves, the reefer flights, the underworld meemies. **1948** in *DAS:* Knowing [that a chimpanzee] was on the loose gave him the meemies. **1953** W. Brown *Monkey on My Back* 150: If I don't get a shot soon, I'll have me the meemies. **1956** *N.Y. Times* (Apr. 8) I 64: Some Stevenson backers have exhibited what has been termed the "Minnesota meemies" whenever the Tennessean appears.

meet *n.* **1.a.** a meeting or appointment; (*specif.*, now usu.) *Und. & Police.* one made for an illicit purpose, such as the buying or selling of narcotics, the giving or receiving of a bribe, or the like; (*also*) the scene of such a meeting.

    *1865 in *Comments on Ety.* (Nov. 1, 1987) 23: They had decided upon holding their "meet" there, but in consequence of something dropped by a friendly "cop" the "meet" would be held at a public house. **1879* *Macmillan's Mag.* (Oct.) 503: At six I was at the meet (trysting-place), and...I piped the fence that bested me. **1889** "M. Twain," in *OEDS:* We'll manage a meet yet. **1892** L. Moore *Own Story* 109: The place of meet; time, 9 P.M. *Ibid.* 461: He made a "meet" for the following day with Bigelow. **1908** Sullivan *Crim. Slang* 17: *Meet*—An appointed place for thieves to see each other. **1916* in *OEDS:* I dunno 'ow I 'ad the nerve ter...make that meet wiv 'er fer Sundee week! **1922** E. Murphy *Black Candle* 229: It is clumsy to putter around with pockets and purses when you "make the meet"; the police might get you. **1933** *Amer. Mercury* (Apr.) 397: I have a meet with So-and-so on the next moon. **1936** *AS* (Apr.) 124: *Meet.* An appointment

arranged between an addict and peddler. **1936** Benton & Ballou *Where Do I Go?* 268: When you "make a meet" you are there on the dot. **1937** J.E. Hoover *Persons in Hiding* 108: He carried the word from gangster to gangster of the "meets," or congregating places. **1949** in *DAS:* She went out to make a "meet" to buy more bogus bills. **1949** in *Harper's* (Feb. 1950) 72: When he makes a meet, or engagement, he keeps it. *Ibid.* 75: In working a heist, the mob usually goes out from a meet, or appointment held a short time before the job is to go. **1955** in Abel *Marihuana Dict.* 68: I went on to the meet. **1958** in Partridge *Dict. Und.* (ed. 2) 845: *Meet*—A meeting, usually of gang chiefs. **1970–71** J. Rubinstein *City Police* 108: At least he should have called me for a meet. **1972** Barker & Lewin *Denver* 117: [The stolen money] was to be delivered in two "meets." **1974** R. Novak *Concrete Cage* 109: Howie Chase. He's coming down Halsey. It's apparently a meet. *a***1979** Pepper & Pepper *Straight Life* 285 [ref. to 1961]: He wants to make a meet with you. **1981** Graziano & Corsel *Somebody Down Here* 129: All we gotta do is make a meet and he's right on the minute. **1987** *Perfect Strangers* (ABC-TV): "We only deal with the top man." "I'll set up the meet."

b. *Orig. Journ.* a professional meeting or business conference.

1930 *AS* VI 118: Coast dental meet set for July 8–12. **1986** G. Trudeau *Doonesbury* (synd. comic strip) (Oct. 23): I got a big meet for you on a movie-of-the-week that Roger Ailes is doing at ABC. **1990** G. Trudeau *Doonesbury* (synd. comic strip) (Oct. 3): I got you a meet on a big new ad campaign.

c. *Jazz.* a jam session.

1957 *N.Y. Times* (Nov. 17) VII 48: What was known among hot musicians as a jam session has become in today's cool vernacular a "meet." **1959–60** R. Reisner *Jazz Titans* 161: *Meet:* a jam session.

2. an assembly for athletic or sports competition. Now *S.E.*

1908 W.G. Davenport *Butte & Montana* 272: At the thirty-days' racing meet we are having here in Butte. **1918** *Washington Post* (June 2) 15: Sailors Are One, Two in Big Meet. **1942** *ATS* 630: Hold a contest...*stage a meet.* *Ibid.* 644: Swimming meet...*swim meet.* **1954–60** *DAS: Meet*...A sporting contest, esp. a competition in track and field sports. **1972** N.Y.U. student: A swim meet. What else could you call it? There's no other word. You can't have a baseball meet or a football meet. That sounds crazy.

meg[1] *n.* [fr. earlier cant *make, meke* 'a halfpenny', of unkn. orig.] *Und.* a copper coin, as a halfpenny or penny; (*also*) a cent as a unit of value; (*broadly*) any coin of little value. Also (esp. in early use) **mag.**

[****1517** Copland *Hye Way:* Docked the del for a coper meke.] [****1566–67** Harman *Caveat: A make*, a halfpenny.] [****1673** R. Head *Canting Academy* 41: *Make* An half peny.] [****1688** Shadwell *Squire of Alsatia* (gloss.): *Megs.* Guineas. *Ibid.* II i: Here are more *Meggs*...you Rogue.] **ca***1775** (cited in Partridge *Dict. Und.* 427). *****1779** in Partridge *Dict. Und.* 427: D—n it, I have got a man in the room, and I will have his greatcoat and boots, and every meg he has. *****1789** G. Parker *Life's Painter* 132: Lay out a *mag* with poor *chirruping Joe.* *Ibid.* 150: *Mag*...a halfpenny. **1791** [W. Smith] *Confess. T. Mount* 18: Coppers, *maggs.* *****1797** in Partridge *Dict. Und.* 427: *Magg* or *megg,* a halfpenny, copper coin. *****1820–21** P. Egan *Life in London* 182: Dirty Suke can flash a *mag**...*Half-penny.* *****1829** in J. Farmer *Musa Pedestris* 107: Or we'll not shell out a mag. *****1830** in Barrère & Leland *Dict. Slang* II 37: You cares not a *mag* if our party should fall. *****1857** "Ducange Anglicus" *Vulgar Tongue* 12: *Mag*...Penny. "What did you get, a *mag?*" **1859** Matsell *Vocab.* 53: *Magg.* A half-cent. **1914** Jackson & Hellyer *Vocab.* 57: *Meig*...A nickel; a five-cent piece....*jitney.* Sometimes used to indicate the minimum basis of exchange medium, the cent, as a hundred meigs, fifty meigs, etc. **1915** *Wash. Post* (Mar. 28): The word comes from the slang of the street arab, who has a name for every coin. A "meg" is a cent, a "jit" or "jitney" is a nickel, a "dimmo" is a dime, and a "cute" is a quarter. **1916** *Milwaukee Jour.* (Nov. 3) 18: I'll lay you a cuter to a meg. **1917** Lardner *Gullible's Travels* 36: Some doll she was, too, in a fifty-meg evenin' dress marked down to thirty-seven. **1925** in Partridge *Dict. Und.* 427: *Meg*...One cent. **1926** Maines & Grant *Wise-Crack Dict.* 11: *Meg*—Any denomination of silver money between ten cents and a dollar; signified by fifteen megs, twenty megs, etc. **1930** G. Irwin *Amer. Tramp & Und. Sl.* 128: *Meig.*—A five cent piece; also one cent when found in the plural, as "fifty meigs" for fifty cents. *****1931** J. Hanley *Boy* 57: I've a meg here....Head or tail? **1942–49** Goldin et al. *DAUL: Meg*....A cent; a penny.

meg[2] *n.* **1.** *Mil.* a megaton.

1972 DeLillo *End Zone* 82: We wouldn't be the same strong industrial society after one thousand megs.

2. *Computers.* megabyte or megabytes. Now *S.E.*

1983 Naiman *Computer Dict.* 93: It comes with 128K but it's expandable up to a meg.

mega *adj. & comb. form.* [prob. abstracted fr. *megaton;* but cf. MEGABUCK] **1.a.** extraordinary; great in importance, size, or degree.

1969 in H.S. Thompson *Shark Hunt* 206: A scene that bad could only be compounded to the realm of mega-horrors by something as powerful as acid. **1975** *Harper's* (Aug.) 82: Much of the megafantasy had dropped away. **1977** S. Gaines *Discotheque* 198: The megastars of the disco world. **1978** *Bk. of Numbers* 408: Recognizing mega-madness for what it is. **1978** *Atlantic* (July) 24: Their fears...can be laid at the feet of modern megabusiness rather than of the media. **1980** *N.Y. Times Bk. Rev.* (Aug. 24) 3: Many titles are tough ordering choices, but others seem sure winners. A new Ken Follett novel, "The Key to Rebecca," and "Hollywood in a Suitcase" by Sammy Davis Jr. are, in Mr. Gilliland's phrase, the list's "megabooks" and step forth to speak their names. **1983** *Justice League of Amer.* (Apr.) 21: It was mega-star Brooke Shields. **1985** Univ. Tenn. student theme: If we are describing a good-looking male, we usually refer to him as a *hunk, mega man,* or *cool dude.* **1989** P. Munro *U.C.L.A. Sl.:* I have the mega headache. **1992** Mowry *Way Past Cool* 58: Mega trouble.

b. (as above but used predicatively).

1990 Eble *Campus Slang* (Spring) 6: The new Robin Williams movie is mega. **1990** T. Thorne *Dict. Contemp. Slang:* This band is going to be mega.

2. a large quantity of; much; many.

1968 Baker et al. *CUSS* 156: *Mega Load* A great deal (of something). **1980** Eble *Campus Slang* (Spring) 4: I'm going to eat mega calories. **1983** Eble *Campus Slang* (Spring) 4: I drank mega beers after the English 36 exam. **1990** P. Munro *Slang U.:* I have mega homework. **1991** Univ. Tenn. student: We ate mega ice cream.

mega *adv. & comb. form. Stu.* extremely; extraordinarily.

1966 *Sat. Eve. Post* (July 2) 22: "Wipe-out city"...is a mega-cool version of "hubba-hubba." **1969** *Current Slang I & II* 61: That girl is mega tough. **1980** Univ. Tenn. law student, age 26: There's a girl at the register who's mega beautiful. **1982** in *Nat. Lampoon* (Feb. 1983) (front cover): Like, the government's nuclear evacuation plans are...mega-stupid—I am *so* sure! **1986** *New Image Teens* (KPBS-TV): These guys try to pick up on me because I have mega-mondo breasts. **1990** P. Munro *Slang U.:* I'm mega tired.

megabuck *n.* one million dollars; (*pl.*) (*broadly*) a very large amount of money.

1946 in *OEDS:* Atomic research is so expensive that American scientists have ceased to use the dollar as their unit. They have laughingly coined the term "megabuck"—one megabuck equals a million dollars. **1952** *N.Y. Times* (Dec. 21) IV E7: The cosmotron cost about three and one-half "megabucks"—a megabuck being physicist's slang for $1,000,000. **1957** Lerner *America as Civ.* 811: Effective short cuts to meaning, like "megabuck" from the new science of atomic production. **1961** *Time* (Oct. 20) 24: "It costs megabucks," says Frank Jones of Chicago's Bell & Howell Co. **1967** *Business Week* (Dec. 30) 36: The "dreamy idea" for an airborne computer paid off in megabucks. **1969** Greenway *Folklore of Great West* 12: A failure of "megabuck" proportions. **1972** *Playboy* (Sept.) 14: The popularization of Soleri's views may stimulate the megabucks he needs. **1978** *N.Y. Times Mag.* (July 23) 22: "Biggies" make *big bucks,* sometimes *megabucks,* for turning on the *hype.* **1981** *N.Y. Post* (July 9) 49: We're looking for people with megabucks. **1983** *Newsweek on Campus* (May) 10: By the end of the summer, I plan to make the megabucks. **1984** *Scientific Amer.* (Sept.) 114: It took about a megabuck in research to put them where they are. **1990** *U.S. News & W.R.* (Nov. 5) 40: Her husband...has not been using the family name to make megabucks.

megaphone *n. Journ.* a film director. Also vars.

1936 *Esquire* (Sept.) 160: Cecil B. DeMille is a megger (director). **1942** *ATS* 605: Director...*meg, megaphoner, megger.* **1959** J. Lee *Career* (film): Maurice Novak, screen megaphone.

megillah *n.* [Yid < Heb *megillāh* 'a scroll'] **1.** a tediously complicated matter; situation or state of affairs; (*also*) a long explanation or story; usu. in phr. **whole megillah.**

1956 J. Rose & M. Shavelson *Beau James* (film): What's this megillah? **1957** in *OEDS: A gantse megillah* or "a whole *megillah*" has been thrown around by a number of TV personalities…presumably with little idea of the origin of the phrase. **1960** Kirkwood *Pony* 140: The papers like to make a big deal whenever a celebrity's mixed up in a magillah like this. **1962** Axelrod *Manchurian Candidate* (film): It would've started a whole big megillah. **1963** T.I. Rubin *Sweet Daddy* 126: Look, Doc—everything we make such a big migila. **1965** Borowik *Lions* 154: There's gonna be one hellafa m'gilla if anyone finds it. **1965** *N.Y. Times* (Nov. 14) VII 61: This is a big *megilla* of a novel. **1968** in Rowan & MacDonald *Friendship* 33: Unloading the whole megillah on you. **1970** Thackrey *Thief* 118: And that was it. The whole megillah. **1970** Gattzden *Black Vendetta* 165: The whole megilla was a trumped-up deal. **1979** in Terkel *Amer. Dreams* 218: We'd go through that megillah every six months. **1984** C. Francis *Who's Sorry?* 39: The whole *megillah*. **1996** *CNN & Co.* (CNN-TV) (Sept. 9): Maybe we all have some responsibility for this whole megillah.

2. the (whole) thing; all that might be expected; all that is necessary.—constr. with *the whole.*

1971 *Rowan & Martin's Laugh-In* (NBC-TV): We will find a way to pull the whole megillah out of shape. **1978** Selby *Requiem* 113: Houses, bridges, river, trees, cars, trucks,…the whole fuckin *megillah*. **1992** *Simpsons* (Fox-TV): Archery, wallet-making—the whole megillah. **1995** Wheaties TV ad: Wheaties….A whole mouthful of flavor! It's the whole megillah.

MEGO *n.* [*my eyes glaze over*] *Journ.* a boring topic or event.—also used attrib.

1977 *Texas Monthly* (Nov.) 190: Antitrust is one of those issues described by former Nixon speech writer William Safire as a MEGO issue. **1977** in *Barnhart Dict. Comp.* III (1984) 68: MEGO is a term coined during the Nixon years by White House staffers. It stands for My Eyes Glaze Over. It can be applied without discrimination to dull conversations, dreary sermons, federal and business memos, and even some newspaper articles. **1981** *N.Y. Times* (Feb. 18) D2: Brady has begun to worry about overkill. "We don't want to turn this into a MEGO." **1983** *Mother Jones* (Apr.) 23: The economy—which worked pretty well in this country—was a "MEGO" subject. **1983–85** in Safire *Look It Up* 58: The subject is a MEGO (My Eyes Glaze Over). **1988** *McLaughlin Group* (PBS-TV) (Jan. 10): "That budget—it looks like a MEGO issue that—" "*MEGO* meaning?" "MEGO meaning My Eyes Glaze Over." **1990** *L.A. Times* (Mar. 30) E4: Some activists quietly worry about what is known as the MEGO—"My Eyes Glaze Over"—phenomenon. **1993** Safire *New Polit. Dict.: MEGO*…was introduced to the author in 1969 by Mel Elfin, then Washington bureau chief of *Newsweek.*

meister *comb. form.* [prob. abstracted fr. SCHLOCKMEISTER, ult. < Yid *meyster* 'master'] **1.** Orig. *Journ.* a person expert in or prominent in connection with (something specified in the initial element). *Joc.* See also SCHLOCKMEISTER.

[**1942** in *AS* (Apr. 1943): Phil Baker, Quizmaster of the CBS program.] [**1943** in *AS* (Apr. 1943): The Nazi spymaster.] **1980** *L.A. Times* (Nov. 12) VI 1: That insufferably cheery cue-card banter that local TV newsmeisters pass off as spontaneous reactions. **1982** *L.A. Times* (Sept. 14) VI 1: Jean Marsh is "too good" to be slumming among the crass yockmeisters of American commercial TV. **1985** in G. Tate *Flyboy* 31: Swingmeister, bebopper, doo-wopper. *a*1986 in *NDAS* s.v. *Perkmeister:* Executive aide to "Perkmeister" John FW Rogers, who administers all agencies in the executive office of the president. **1988** *S.F. Chronicle* (Oct. 9) ("This Week") 16: The Pelican Inn…which had the requisite dark wood, smoky air, strong ales and crinkly, crotchety pubmeister. **1991** *Time* (Sept. 16): The motion pictures of American angst-meister Woody Allen. **1992** *Dr. Dean* (NBC-TV): We're not talking about hardcore tanmeister sun worshipers. **1992** *New Yorker* (May 4) 13: Hypemeisters searching for space and novelty. **1992** G. Wolff *Day at the Beach* 11: What jargonmeisters today call "the attack." **1994** *Wash. Post* (Feb. 23) C5: The trendmeisters in Southern California have moved on.

2. [pop. by "The Copy-Machine Man," sketch featuring Rob Schneider ("The Richmeister") on *Saturday Night Live* (NBC-TV) starting 1991; see 1991 quot.] *Stu.* (added

as a joc. suffix to a person's monasyllabic name or the first syllable of a polysyllabic name.).

1991 *Sat. Night Live* (NBC-TV): It's Steve…he's a copymaking man…the Stevemeister. **1992** Eble *Campus Slang* (Spring) 6: *-meister*—ending that can be added to any proper name…."The John-Meister." **1996** N.Y.C. girl, age *ca*7 (coll. J. Sheidlower): [To a dog:] Phoebe! The Phoebemeister! **1996** *N.Y. Times Bk. Rev.* (Jan. 5, 1997) 14: Sarah Ferguson….The Dutchess of York….The Fergmeister.

meller *n. Journ.* a melodrama.

[**1918** in Truman *Dear Bess* 258: It was good old mellerdramer.] [**1922** *Variety* (June 30) 3: Melo Ridiculed…"Spanish Lovers"…was roasted…as ridicula melodrama.] **1936** *Esquire* (Sept.) 64: The bucolic belt refuses to patronize mustang mellers….the society meller. **1985** Scheuer *Movies on TV* 120: *Cop Hater*…Mild meller about a cop killer.

mellow *n. Black E.* **1.** a homosexual. [Despite the dates, perh. merely a misapprehension of **(2)**, below.]

1959 P. Oliver *Meaning of Blues* 136: The homosexual is a "freak," a "mellow," a "sissy," or a "drag."

2. one's close friend; (*also*) one's lover.

1966 in Wepman et al. *The Life* 68: Tell my mellows I'll spring 'em. **1966** C. Cooper *Farm* 97: Now, there's never been a day in my life when I couldn't go to 1 of my main mellows and get some help. **1971** H. Roberts *Third Ear* (unp.): *Main mellow*…a man's closest woman friend. **1972** Claerbaut *Black Jargon* 72: What's happening, mellow? **1973** Goines *Players* 177: I'm glad you're lookin' out for me, mellow. **1974** *Black World* (Nov.) 60: Like I was your mellow. **1974** Piñero *Short Eyes* 42: This is me….Your main mellow man. *Ibid.* 125: *Mellow-man* Close friend. **1967–80** Folb *Runnin' Lines* 246: Mellow n. 1. Good friend. 2. Favorite lover, girl/boyfriend. **1994** "Beastie Boys" *Do It* (pop. song): Adam Yauch grab the mic 'cause you know you're my mellow.

3. the state of being MELLOW, 2.a.; relaxation; comfort.

1977 *New West* (Aug. 29) 38: No one can know what mellow is who hasn't traveled these highways. **1978** G. Trudeau *Doonesbury* (synd. comic strip), in *L.A. Times* (Aug. 27): I read today that "Winning through Mellow" is already this season's numero uno self-help manual. **1983** *L.A. Times* (Jan. 17) V 4: New Yorkers…still find gaps in Los Angeles' consummate Southern California mellow.

mellow *adj.* **1.** pleasantly intoxicated. Now *S.E.*

***1698–99** "B.E." *Dict. Cant. Crew: Mellow,* a'most Drunk. **1722** B. Franklin, in *AS* XV (Feb. 1940) 103: *Boozy, cogey, tipsey, fox'd, merry, mellow* [etc.]. **1884** "M. Twain" *Huck. Finn* 204: They both got powerful mellow, but I noticed the king didn't get mellow enough to forget to remember to not deny about hiding the moneybag again. **1928** Hammett *Harvest* 8: Bill Quint and I were both fairly mellow by the time we had got this far. **1931** Barry *Animal Kingdom* 343: Why shouldn't he have a right to get slightly mellow on his one day off? **1960** Sire *Deathmakers* 58: He was getting mellow again.

2.a. Esp. *Black E.* relaxed or comfortable; quiet; calm.

1938 in Bechet *Treat It Gentle* 224: Jack I'm Mellow. **1944** C.B. Davis *Leo McGuire* 173: If I'd dared I'd lammed it to Michigan because Jackson is mellow. **1959** H. Ellison *Gentleman Junkie* 209: He was good that night, really mellow like Jell-O. **1977** *L.A. Times* (Apr. 3) ("Calendar") 80: It was a mellow, laid-back time. Ambition waned. **1978** *Rolling Stone* (Oct. 5) 80: Differences in mood traceable to the coleaders: Rowles and Sims get mellow, while Rowles and Cohn bellow. **1990** P. Munro *Slang U.:* Tommy, you're so mellow tonight—is something bothering you?

b. Orig. *Black E & Jazz.* fine; acceptable; just right; (*also*) wonderful; perfect.

1938 Calloway *Hi De Ho* 16, in Gold *Jazz Lexicon: Mellow:* all right, fine. **1940** *Current Hist. & Forum* (Nov. 7) 22: *That's mellow* (that's good). **1942** *Pittsburgh Courier* (May 23) 7: One "mellow" night when the social jitterbugs were "jumping." **1943** *Yank* (July 2) 22: "You liked it?" "Colossal….Solid, on the beam, mellow." **1945** *Yank* (Mar. 2) 8: A boy whose mug and muscles appeal to the girls is a "mellow man." **1946** Boulware *Jive & Slang* 5: *Mellow*…Just right. **1946** (quot. at TALL). **1948** Manone & Vandervoort *Trumpet* 144: Anything that was solid, aw reet, etc., was "mellow as a cello." **1950** L. Brown *Iron City* 106: That's fine Man, that's really mellow. **1951** [VMF-323] *Old Ballads* 36: We're hep…your [*sic*] mellow. **1959** A. Anderson *Lover Man* 116: "How old is she?" "Twenty-four." "Mellow!" **1961** Russell *Sound* 12: Got to get a three-spot for that mellow chunk of wax, daddy-oh. **1967** Colebrook *Cross of Lassitude* 132: Oh that *Prophet* is so *mellow!*

1967 C. Cooper *Farm* 38: Well, man, it's mella, you just take my word for it. There ain't no other place in the hospital I'd rather be. **1968** Gover *JC* 19: Lissen heah, I might even fetch me my most mellowest trick an turn him out. **1969** Whittemore *Cop!* II 132: Everything's gonna be mellow, brother, don't worry about it. **1970** *Newsweek* (July 27) 24: "It's mellow in the woods," she says. "I had one acid trip and it straightened my head out. **1971** Goines *Dopefiend* 91: "When you go in, slide under the rail, and he won't even know you're in the fuckin' store."..."Mellow!" **1976** *U.S. News & W.R.* (Oct. 4) 60: I was living in a neat town and had a really mellow career going.

c. Esp. *Black E.* attractive; fashionable. [The hyphenated quots. with *-back* represent two words; see BACK, *adv.*]

  1943 Ottley *New World* 283: "Reet guys" and "mellow chicks." **1944** *Slanguage Dict.* 59: *A mellow mouse*—What a babe! **1954–60** *DAS: Mellow-back adj.* Smartly dressed. *Some Negro use.* **1967** *L.A. Times* (Apr. 27) I 30: Variations of the cool style are the "mellow person," who is most interested in parties and social life. **1970** C. Major *Dict. Afro-Amer Sl.: Mellow-back*...fashionably dressed. **1972** Claerbaut *Black Jargon* 72: *Mellow*...attractive; stylish.

3. *Black E & Jazz.* (of a friend) close; intimate.

  1941 in Leadbitter & Slaven *Blues Records* 108: My Mellow Man. **1948** Manone & Vandervoort *Trumpet* 185: He thought his mellow chick, Juliet, was dead. **1972** Claerbaut *Black Jargon* 72: *Mellow*...Intimate, close. *We're mellow.*

mellow out *v.* **1.** Orig. *Narc.* to become MELLOW; (*specif.*) to become more tranquil or relaxed, esp. under the infl. of a psychotropic drug; (usu. *imper.*) calm down.

  1974 U.C.L.A. student: I heard this in 1972. "Be cool, man. Just mellow out." **1974** in *DAS* (ed. 2): Critics...were saying he'd mellowed out..."drained the venom from his voice." **1978** *Harper's* (July) 29: Dope will be legal but automobiles will not, and everybody will have plenty of time to get mellowed out. **1978** Maupin *Tales* 39: Wanna mellow out?...Coke? **1980** "Dead Kennedys" *California Über Alles* (rock song): Mellow out or you will pay. **1981** *Penthouse* (Apr.) 196: We were sitting around at home, mellowing out on a couple of joints. **1984** Hindle *Dragon Fall* 33: Take it easy, m'man....C'mon, just mellow out. **1991** *Simpsons* (Fox-TV): Hey, mellow out, old dude! **1992** *Show Biz Today* (CNN-TV) (Feb. 3): My thing was to let the driver mellow out and take kind of a mind trip.

2. to make (a person or (*rare*) a thing) MELLOW.

  1977 *New West* (July 18) 56: We chose the Ortofon [phonograph cartridge] to mellow out the JBL sound. **1980** DiFusco et al. *Tracers* 48: It just mellows you out a little bit. **1985** *Psychol. Today* (Feb.) 14: You would expect intensive weeping to mellow out men and make them less aggressive. **1987** *Sun* (May 5) 2: By zapping [mental patients]...with a cattle prod to mellow them out. **1996** in *Reader's Digest* (Jan. 1997) 83: Take a drag....It'll mellow you out.

mellow yellow *n.* banana peel smoked for its supposedly hallucinogenic effect. [The 1966 quot., from an international hit song—still occ. heard on radio in the 1990's—is almost certainly the orig. of the phr. The 1968–70 quot. is presumably an error for an adj. form in *-ed.*]

  1966 "Donovan" *Mellow Yellow* (rock song): Electrical banana/Is gonna be a sudden craze/Electrical banana/Is bound to be the very next phase/They call it mellow yellow. **1967** Bronsteen *Hippy's Handbook* 34: *Mellow Yellow* (Banana). **1969** Fort *Pleasure Seekers* 187: [Mythical] bananadine, or as Donovan had called it, "Mellow Yellow." **1968–70** *Current Slang III & IV* 82–83: *Mellow yellow, v.* Intoxicated from smoking a banana peel.—Watts. **1972** *Drug Forum* I 228: The "Mellow Yellow" or Great Banana Hoax followed in short order the earlier hoaxes.

melon *n.* **1.** the head.

  1919 in De Beck *Google* 18: Say—hold your melon still for a minute. **1935** Pollock *Und. Speaks: Melon*, the head. **1945** *Yank* (Mar. 23) 14: He's going all off his melon. **1948** McHenry & Myers *Home Is Sailor* 94: What kind of nonsense goes on in that beautiful melon. **1965** Lardner & Southern *Cincinnati Kid* (film): One of these days you're gonna get your melon busted open. **1977** *S.F. Chronicle* (Dec. 31) 28: I...will...get smashed out of my melon. **1977** Caron *Go-Boy* 13: He looks just like my Uncle Bruno did when my pa hit him over the melon with the soapstone and Uncle Bruno was dead! **1979** *Easyriders* (Dec.) 51: One of the neatest methods of separatin' a dude from his melon was the guillotine. **1988** *Night Court* (NBC-TV): Just

plop the old melon down right here. **1991** *Beetlejuice* (ABC-TV): Glad you like the old melon. **1996** McCumber *Playing Off Rail* 89: I can hit somebody in the melon with one at ten feet.

2. [sugg. by *cut a melon,* below] an esp. unexpected profit; windfall; (*specif.*) *Finance.* an extra dividend.

  1934 Weseen *Dict. Slang* 367: *Melon*—A special dividend. [**1942** *ATS* 636: Sports...*Winnings; purse; prize*...Gold purse, gravy, melon, payoff [etc.].] **1949** *N.Y. Times* (July 24) I 1: The $2,800,000,000 "melon" is the result of an over-payment of premiums by the policyholders. **1950** *N.Y. Times* (Nov. 26) VI 44: Slices from the profit melon run as large now and then as $10 a worker. **1952** *Harper's* (July) 41: I won't sell jobs or promotions or cut myself in on any political melons....I won't take graft. **1959** *N.Y. Times* (Mar. 1) III 10F: The boss has always been very good about carving up a nice melon among his people. **1960** *N.Y. Times* (Dec. 4) XII 14xx: An estimated $100,000,000 in revenue for the steamship lines this year. The profitable melon will be divided among the regular cruise operators. **1979** Homer *Jargon* 26: Good news, stockholders. There'll be *melons* in your garden this year. **1986** *NDAS:* The stockholders have a meager melon to share this year.

3. usu. *pl.* a woman's breast.

  1953–57 Giovannitti *Combine D* 151: I'd get a good look at those melons. **1966** Lehman *Virginia Woolf* (film): I thought you'd come running at me, your melons bobbing. **1968** Baker et al. *CUSS* 156: *Melons.* The female breasts. **1978** Schrader *Hardcore* 85: You wanna squeeze the melons before you sucks the juice? **1982** "J. Cain" *Commandos* 164: Did you see those melons hanging out? **1986** R. Campbell *In La-La Land* 74: What the hell you doing...sittin' around with your melons hanging out like that?

4. *Baseball.* a ball that is easy to hit or catch on the fly.

  1980 Lorenz *Guys Like Us* 79: It was nothing but melons for Buddy in left.

¶ In phrases:

¶ **cut a melon, 1.** Esp. *Finance.* to share profits; (*specif.*) to announce an extra dividend.

  1908 in *OEDS:* The theory that any prospective melon-cutting will be postponed until next year. **1921** *Variety* (Apr. 22) 3: Melon of $24,600 Cut By C.A. & P. Soc. **1932** "M. Brand" *Jackson Trail* 187: "Then when he cuts the big melon, how much do you come in for?" "Oh, only about forty or fifty thousand apiece, I guess." **1935** Sistrom *Hot Tip* (film): There's a little melon cut every so often. **1936** M. Levin *Old Bunch* 396: General Electric was going to cut a melon pretty soon. **1943** Halliday *Mummer's Mask* 159: I've got to dicker with a couple of men about cutting a melon.

2. to offer generous hospitality.

  1920 Ade *Hand-Made Fables* 43: He is Rich and High-Toned...and we must cut a big melon when he comes.

¶ **know the right side of (one's) melon** to know what is best for (oneself).

  1870 *Overland Mo.* (Jan.) 84: It's curus a feller never knows the right side of his melon till it's too late.

melonhead *n.* a blockhead.

  1932 Mankiewicz & Myer *Million Dollar Legs* (film): Come on, get up, ya big melonhead. **1955** *Phil Silvers Show* (CBS-TV): They called me "melonhead." *a***1977** T. Barnett *Golf Is Madness* 103: "Melonhead" Cranshaw. **1981** *Nat. Lampoon* (Nov.) 12: My wife can sometimes be a real melonhead, but I love her dearly. **1984** *Night Court* (NBC-TV): You started it, melonhead! **1986** *New Leave It to Beaver* (TBS-TV): You are such a melonhead. *****1990** Andersson & Trudgill *Bad Language* 88: "Stupid person"...*melon head.* **1990** *Guys Next Door* (NBC-TV): You're safe from the NBC melonheads. **1994** *Simpsons* (Fox-TV): Quit your day-dreamin', melonhead!

melt *n.* one's self; HIDE.

  1844 W.T. Porter *Big Bear* 135: I raised my arm, trimblin' like a leaf, and says I, "Jem!—*I'll have your melt!*" **1858** in G.W. Harris *High Times* 134: Why, durn my melt ef the passon's sister didn't have his haslet outen him.

melt *v. Stu.* **1.** to strongly attract the romantic interest of; thrill. Cf. fig. S.E. quots. in *OED2.*

  1944 *Slanguage Dict.* 61: *You melt me*—I like you. **1947** *ATS* (Supp.) 4: *You melt me*...I'm thrilled. **1969** *Current Slang I & II* 61: *Melt, v.* To impress.—College males, New York.

2. to depart; leave.

[***1934** in *OED2*: David…melted from the room.] **1961** Kohner *Gidget Goes Hawaiian* 10: Melt means—*get lost!*

melvin *n.* [fr. male given name *Melvin*, regarded as foolish-sounding or old-fashioned] *Stu.* **1.** a person who is old-fashioned or unappealing; SQUARE. Also as adj.

1954–60 *DAS: Melvin*…A dull, uninformed, or obnoxious person; a profoundly objectionable person. **1982** Pond *Valley Girls' Gde.* 60: *Melvin*—Creepy, like out in space, like a weird person. **1992** *Simpsons* (Fox-TV): Some say to love your country is old-fashioned—uncool—melvin.

2. WEDGIE. Also as v.

1989 P. Munro *U.C.L.A. Slang* 43: *Give (someone) a melvin* to yank (someone's) underwear up abruptly or roughly. **1990** *AS* 65:3 (Fall) 239: *Wedgy*…Connie Eble reports the synonyms *melvin* and *murphy*. **1989–91** in *DARE* [numerous infs.]. **1993** P. Munro *U.C.L.A. Slang II* 58: *Melvin*…condition in which clothing is stuck between the buttocks….v. to give (someone) a melvin, generally by yanking up on the back of his pants or underpants:…*He melvined me.*

member *n.* **1.** a fellow; chap.—usu. constr. with qualifying adj.; esp. in phr. **hot member** a skillful, alert, or vivacious person. Cf. *OED2* def. 4.b. for early ModE quots. that correspond superficially to this usage. [Partridge *DSUE* dates the *ca*1875 quot. (from a song, "Keep It Dark") to "ca1895"; it is not established which date is more accurate.]

1863 in Wightman *To Ft. Fisher* 97: If an "old member" loses an overcoat or a blanket, he [steals] one from some [newcomer]. *Ibid.* 99: The abuse of recruits by "old members." [**1869** in T. Heffernan *Stove by Whale* 144: Another Member Gone [obituary].] *ca*1875 in *F & H* VII s.v. *warm:* Dr. Kenealy, that popular bloke, That extremely warm member, the member for Stoke. *1888 in *F & H* III 362: You're a red-hot member! *1891 in *F & H* IV 302: As warm a member as our hero was. **1896** Ade *Artie* 9: Oh, but they was hot members! One of 'em whenever he got better 'n jacks up, always lost his voice and could n't keep count o' the chips. **1902** Wister *Virginian* ch. xv: Is he the member who don't sing? **1903** McCardell *Chorus Girl* 28: He must be a purty hot member. *1914–22* J. Joyce *Ulysses* 304: Gob, he's a prudent member and no mistake.

2. *Black E.* a fellow black person, usu. as distinguished from a white. [*OEDS* dates 1963 quot. to "1964" and 1971 quot. to "1970."]

1962 *N.Y. Times Mag.* (May 20) 45, in Gold *Jazz Lexicon: Member:* a Negro. **1962** H. Simmons *On Eggshells* 227: I know you know what I mean if you're a member. **1963** in Clarke *Amer. Negro Stories* 301: Then three more, one of 'em a member, bolted out of the dressin' room. **1966** S. Stevens *Go Down Dead* 63: One cat near me he talking to this chick he saying to her "The word member means negro. You white are call grays or ofays." He say negro like it mean god too. Make me feel funny. **1967** Riessman & Dawkins *Play It Cool* 68: *Member*…a Negro. **1970** C. Major *Dict. Afro-Amer. Sl.* 81: *Member:* (1950's) one black person to another; club member; member of the race. **1970** Ponicsan *Last Detail* 124: I used to like white chicks best, but now the member chicks are changing. **1971** H. Roberts *Third Ear* (unp.): *Member* n. a fellow black person. SYN. *see* blood. **1987** Covin *Brown Sky* 91: Well, the shit has done got so bad, that the members just ain't gon' take it no more.

Memphis dominoes *n.pl. Gamb.* dice. *Joc.*

1942 *ATS* 704: Dice….*Memphis dominoes.* **1969** King *Gambling & Org. Crime* 233: *Memphis Dominoes*—Dice.

mensch *n.* [< Yid *mentsh* 'person'] Orig. *Jewish-Amer.* an admirable, often steadfast, decent person, usu. a man.

1953 Bellow *Augie March* 43: I want you to be a *mensch*. **1966** in *DAS* (Supp.): *Mensch*, a stand-up he-man. **1972** *Atlantic* (May) 81: Only once…did he seem to emerge as a leader, a *Mensch*. **1983** *N.Y. Times* (June 10) C2: He pays for all his tickets. He is a mensch. **1985** D. Steel *Secrets* 246: "He's a real mensch." Bill used the favorite L.A. term. But he was. A real man….A hero. **1986** E. Weiner *Howard the Duck* 218: Howard the Duck became a mensch. **1987** J. Thompson *Gumshoe* 224: I hear he's a real mensch. **1992** Strawberry & Rust *Darryl* 61: The highest praise a native New Yorker will give to someone who reacted well to a setback…is, "He was a *mensch* about it!" or even, "She was a *mensch* about it!" **1995** *Science News* (Apr. 15) 233: He or she fails to qualify as a "mensh," a Yiddish word for a person who

treats others with respect and dignity and who negotiates the social world with zest and compassion.

mental *n.* [fr. *mental* case] a crazy person.

*1913 in *OEDS*: Many a time I've asked him to have his bit of lunch with me and the other "mental"—O yes, she's a mental case, as I may have told you. **1977** *L.A. Times* (Aug. 4) I 22: The Nazis—whose numbers abound with what police intelligence officers call "the mentals." **1979** *St. Louis Post Dispatch* (Nov. 11) 5A: It's just scary. Any kind of guy. Mentals. Convicts. **1988** T. Logan *Harder They Fall* 95: What's your problem, jack. You some kind of mental? *a*1990 Westcott *Half a Klick* 88: He's a mental.

mental *adj.* (usu. of persons) crazy; insane.

*1927 in *OEDS*: I gather she was a little queer towards the end—a bit mental, I think you people [*sc.,* nurses] call it? **1951** *Sat. Eve. Post* (Oct. 6) 120: I decided that I was mental and I went right away. **1953** *New Yorker* (Jan. 24) 28: She won't eat, she probably doesn't sleep. I can't stand it if she's turning mental. **1954–60** *DAS: Mental job* One who is…a neurotic, psychotic, paranoid, manic depressive. **1966** Samuels *People vs. Baby* 47: She could never, it seemed, say no to any person. The girls said she was mental. **1968** Baker et al. *CUSS* 156: *Mental, go.* Go wild. **1973** *Atlantic* (Oct.) 63: As long as you don't get mental about it. **1978** R. Price *Ladies' Man* 175: Whata you goin' mental on me, Kenny? **1979** *Nat. Lampoon* (Sept.) 12: It's fuckin' *mental*. And sick. Know what I mean? **1985** M. Baker *Cops* 88: They put him in the nut house. He was mental. **1985** *Esquire* (Oct.) 216: This dude is mental. **1976–87** G.A. Fine *With the Boys* 119: Boys who regularly engage in physical aggression are derided as "mental" ("mentally ill"). **1987** J. Waters *Hairspray* (film): If I didn't know better, I'd swear she was mental. *a*1989 in Kisseloff *Must Remember This* 535: So that shows you how mental everybody was. **1992** *N.Y. Newsday* (Aug. 3) 5: Some teenagers thought he was mental and they used to pick on him. **1992** M. Myers et al. *Wayne's World* (film): I never seen you so mental over a girl before. **1995** A. Heckerling *Clueless* 87: I know it sounds mental, but sometimes I have more fun at home.

mental hernia *n.* an oaf; (*also*) a mental breakdown. *Joc.*

1970 Landy *Underground Dict.* 130: That guy is a real mental hernia. **1972** Hannah *Geronimo Rex* 26: The old man fell into his study for about two weeks of fake mental hernia.

mental midget *n.* a stupid person.

1966 N.Y.C. high school student: That mental midget. **1967** Spradley *One Drunk* 22: I confess that I must be a hedonistic masochistic mental midget or just a nut. **1974** Lahr *Hot to Trot* 17: The man's a mental midget. **1983** Goldaper & Pincus *How to Talk Basketball* 102: *Mental midget*…a player who makes dumb mistakes. **1984** Algeo *Stud Buds* 7: An absent-minded or inattentive person…*mental midget.* **1987** *Perfect Strangers* (ABC-TV): We're dealing with mental midgets.

meow *n.* (see quot.).

1995 S. Moore *In the Cut* 63: *Meow*, n., expedition, usually to make trouble or to shoplift (Brooklyn word).

Merc *n.* **1.** a Mercury automobile.

1961 Barbeau *Ikon* 99: It was a forty-eight Merc, a real beaut. **1962** E. Stephens *Blow Negative* 293: Tim's the guy who has the hot Merc that went 100.9 up at the lakes.

2. *Finance.* The Chicago Mercantile Exchange.—constr. with *the.*

1985 *N.Y. Times* (Aug. 16) D1: A Testing for Chicago's Merc….The Chicago Mercantile Exchange…was founded in 1898 as the Chicago Butter and Egg Board. **1987** Chicago student (coll. J. Sheidlower): I'm gonna be working at the Merc this summer.

merc *n.* a professional mercenary soldier. [The term came to public notice through reportage of events in Rhodesia (now Zimbabwe) precipitated by the secession act of November 1965.]

*1967 *Time* (Aug. 11) 28: Zambesi Club "mercs" are white Rhodesians and South Africans. *1974 (cited in Partridge *Concise Dict. Sl.*). **1979** in Terkel *Amer. Dreams* 390: We carry ads about…jobs as mercs….That's a slang term, more and more accepted. **1982** "W.T. Tyler" *Rogue's March* 101: We sold out…the army that had whipped the rebels and mercs. **1987** Norst & Black *Lethal Weapon* 44: How had the merc gotten close enough to Tyrone to clip him? **1987** R. Miller *Slob* 204: Killer of professional mercs. **1990** Vachss *Blossom* 167: Not a merc, either.

merchant *comb. form.* a person who employs or is associated with (something specified in the initial element); a pilot who flies (a specified type of aircraft). *Rare* in U.S. except in SPEED MERCHANT.

*1886 in *OEDS*: The success of "Indiana" mainly depends upon the extravagant humours of the chief low-comedy merchant. *1909 Ware *Passing Eng.* 175: The theatre coming to be called the "shop", actors dubbed themselves "merchants", qualified by their line. *1914 in *OEDS*: It may be that when the new road has been built the speed merchant and the road-hog...may pay their money and betake themselves to their favorite seaside haunt at any speed they like. *1917 in F. Lee *No Parachute* 7: I'm lucky to be a Pup merchant, and also to be clear of the Arras mess-up. 1919 Law *2nd Army Air Svc.* (unp.): A couple of the old S.E. "merchants" from the 141st and the 17th. *1925 Fraser & Gibbons *Soldier & Sailor Wds.* 154 [ref. to WWI]: *Merchant*; A fellow....Used with various applications, *e.g.* "A M.G. merchant"—a Machine gunner; "A paper merchant"—an officer given to worry people with unnecessary written communications. 1926 (quot. at CAMEL-DRIVER). *1934 Yeates *Winged Victory* 64: They dived right down on the Ak-W merchants just to learn 'em.

merchie *n. Navy.* a merchant vessel.
    1988 Poyer *The Med* 130: Oscar's the merchie off to starboard. *a*1990 Poyer *The Gulf* 156: The Pasdaran just rocketed a merchie.

mercy buckets *interj.* [intentional malapropism of F *merci beaucoup*] thank you very much. *Joc.* Also **messy bucket.**
    1954–60 *DAS*: *Messy bucket* = Merci beaucoup. *Some jocular W.W.II Army use.* *a*1967 in Partridge *DSUE* (ed. 6): *Mercy bucket*...Merci beaucoup!: Australian: C.20. 1968 Swarthout *Loveland* 40 [ref. to *ca*1935]: "Mercy buckets," he said. 1971 N.Y.U. student: Mercy buckets. *1979 T. Jones *Wayward Sailor* 72: Mercy buckets, M'sieur. *1983 in Partridge *Concise Dict. Sl.*: Mercy buckets. 1990 Eble *Campus Slang* (Spring) 6: *Mercy buckets*—thank-you. Mock pronunciation of French *merci beaucoup*.

mercy fuck *n.* an act of intercourse engaged in out of pity.—usu. considered vulgar. *Joc.* Also as *v.*
    1968 P. Newman, in Rawson *Wicked Words* 165: Mercy fucking...would be reserved for spinsters and librarians. 1978 Alibrandi *Killshot* 174: Consider your work here a mercy fuck. 1981 in *Nat. Lampoon* (Jan. 1982) 22: But let's not consider this a mercy fuck. There's no joy in that. 1989 R. Miller *Profane Men* 83: The first time had been what men sometimes call a mercy fuck. 1996 *Esquire* (Nov.) 89: Sleeping with Sally...felt desperate, like a mercy fuck.

merde *n.* [< F] (used as a euphemism, in var. senses and parts of speech, for) SHIT. [The "slang" nature of this term is problematic, since it is primarily used by educated persons in S.E. contexts.]
    1920 in E.E. Cummings *Letters* 74: I am *not* self-sufficient do I hear you say? Merde! 1923 (quot. at MANURE, 2). *1933 "G. Orwell," in *OED2*: "Merde!" he used to shout, "*you* here again?" 1958 T. Capote *Breakfast at Tiffany's* 19: Which is so much *merde*. 1968 *Harper's* (May) 70: Professor Lorenz was well-splattered with goose *merde*. 1970 *New Yorker* (Mar. 7) 36, in *OED2*: We cannot have that kind of pornographic *merde* in this majestic and high-minded sentence. 1990 *New Republic* (Mar. 5) 9: They can cease to fret. Merde!

merge *v.* ¶ In phrase: **the urge to merge** a desire to copulate. *Joc.*
    [1945 W. Winchell, in *DAS*: He confirmed that he would merge [*i.e.*, marry] next with [a] Mexican actress.] 1988 *St. Petersburg* (Fla.) *Times* (Sept. 18) (Nexis): Depriving Duke [a parakeet] of normal testosterone levels via neutering would definitely subdue the urge to merge and the often associated restlessness. 1989 Univ. Tenn. student: What's the definition of "horniness"? The urge to merge. 1994 *Esquire* (May) (Nexis): If you block DHT at other sites around the body, you'll lose your urge to merge and develop a vocal delivery that resembles Minnie Mouse's. 1995 N.Y.C. man, age 25 (coll. J. Sheidlower): I really had the urge to merge. 1995 *Sun-Sentinel* (Fort Lauderdale, Fla.) (Nov. 27) (Nexis): I still have the urge to merge, but high blood pressure medication has slowed me down a lot.

merit badge *n. Mil.* a decoration for military service.—used derisively.
    1962 Blake *Heartbreak Ridge* 26 [ref. to Korean War]: Bronze Stars....I guess the Army is awarding merit badges for prisoners this month. 1983 N. Proffitt *Gardens of Stone* 70 [ref. to Vietnam War]: They're...caught up in the stampede for merit badges, medals and

promotions. 1984 Riggan *Free Fire* 91 [ref. to Vietnam War]: "They give merit badges too?" "Purple Heart, Arcom, Silver Star."

merkin *n.* [prob. alt. of Early ModE *malkin* 'a mop'] **1.** a pubic wig, as worn by actors and prostitutes (now *S.E.*); (*hence, obs.* in U.S.) the vulva or vagina. [Farmer & Henley assign a date of "1620" to the *Percy Folio MS.*, but modern scholarship indicates a slightly later date, as reflected below.]
    *ca*1620–50 *Percy Folio MS.*, in *F & H* IV 302: A health to all Ladyes that neuer used merkin. *1656 in *OED*: Why dost thou reach thy Merkin now half dust? Why dost provoke the ashes of thy lust? *1671 in *OED*: Merkin, Pubes mulieris. *1680 in J. Thorpe *Rochester's Poems* 37: Dildoes and *Merkins*. 1682 *Letter fr. New Eng.* 9: Two chopping Girles with Merkins exposed. *1714 in *OED*: The hairy circle of her merkin. *1873 Hotten *Slang Dict.* (ed. 4): *Merkin*, a term usually applied to a woman's privities. Originally false hair for those parts. 1889 *Century Dict.*: *Merkin*...the female pudendum. 1958 Nabokov *Lolita* 27: I was looking merely for a soothing presence, a glorified *pot-au-feu*, an animated merkin. [1963 George, Kubrick & Southern *Dr. Strangelove* (film): Merkin Muffley [name of U.S. president].] 1967 in *OED2*: A...dildo-and-merkin combination. [*1969 *Can Hieronymus Merkin Ever Forget Mercy Humppe and Find True Happiness?* [film title].] *1972 in *OED2*: Making merkens [*sic*] and other "intimate wigs." 1973 Pynchon *Gravity's Rainbow* 95: He wears a false cunt and merkin of sable both handcrafted...by the notorious Mme. Ophir. 1992 *New Yorker* (June 15) 32: Its cover was an illustration, by Cassandre, depicting a pattern of feathers and what appeared to be floating merkins.

2. [pun on *American*] Esp. *Computers.* an American; (*also*) American English. *Joc.* Also as *adj.*
    1993 *Star Tribune* (Minneapolis) (Sept. 26) (Nexis): Computer software [in Portugal] is in "Merkin" (American English), and so are a lot of the courses at the Institute of Technology at the University of Lisboa, and so are the Mickey Mouse cartoons. 1994 *Morning Call* (Allentown, Pa.) (Aug. 21) (Nexis): Black related an anecdote about touring the South back in the 1960s when his group [*sc.*, Jay and the Americans] was referred to as "Jay and the Merkins." 1994 William Safire, in *N.Y. Times Mag.* (Sept. 11): Americans have seized on this Britishism, which has become the most important contribution of the mother country to the lingo we call Merkin since *not to worry* and *spot on.* 1996 FAQ file for Usenet newsgroup alt.usage.english (June 8, 1996 vers.): The word "merkin" is one of the perpetual bad puns of the Internet...."Merkin" was coined afresh to mean "an American."...Punning use of the word dates back to at least the early 1960s....On Usenet, "merkin" is only a few years old. 1996 Message on Usenet newsgroup alt.religion.scientology (June 28)]: Proud to be a Merkin [title]. 1996 Re: The Great Fishkill Controversy, message on Usenet newsgroup alt.folklore.urban (Sept. 9): The diphthong 'ui' has no equivalent in English nor Merkin. 1996 *R* Maybe *I* Magrat Garlic, message on Usenet newsgroup alt.fan.pratchett (Sept. 9): For those who haven't seen it "Scrooged" is a Merkin (which means more violent and less taste) version of the Dickens Christmas thingy.

mermaid's visiting card *n. Mil.* a personal identity tag; DOG-TAG. *Joc.*
    1918 Ruggles *Navy Explained* 98: Mermaid Visiting Card. 1925 Fraser & Gibbons *Soldier & Sailor Slang* [ref. to WWI]: *Mermaid's Visiting Card:* A U.S. Army term for the Identity Disc issued to U.S. Troops on embarkation to Europe, in allusion to possibilities of misadventure through German submarines in crossing the Atlantic.

merry *n.* ¶ In phrase: **all to the merry** splendid.
    1908 in Fleming *Unforgettable Season* 47: He was all to the merry at bat.

merry *adj.* (used in elaboration of various expressions). See additional quots. s.v. HA-HA, *n.*, 1.
    [*1821 (quot. at *raise hell* s.v. HELL).] 1879 in W.A. Graham *Custer Myth* 326: A recent letter in which...[we] catch, well, Merry H. 1883 Hay *Bread-Winners* 180: There is merry and particular bloom of h—— to pay. 1908 in W.G. Davenport *Butte & Montana* 49: He has sent the gang around to give us the merry ha-ha. 1904–11 (quot. at *raise hell* s.v. HELL). 1927 in Hammett *Knockover* 280: They bushwacked the police and made a merry wreck out of 'em. 1928 Hammett *Harvest* 142: They didn't fool the Old Man. He gave me merry hell. 1954–60 *DAS*: *Merry haha*...Ridicule; the laugh; usu. in expression "to give someone the merry haha." 1965 (quot. at *raise hell* s.v. HELL). 1990 Rukuza *West Coast Turnaround* 46: The potholes were playing merry hell with the suspension.

merry-go-round *n.* **1.** *Horse Racing.* a racetrack. *Joc.*

   1902–03 Ade *People You Know* 110: He might be out at the Merry-Go-Round showing the Ikeys how to take a Joke. **1935** Pollock *Und. Speaks: Merry go round,* a race track. **1954–60** *DAS.*

   2. RUNAROUND. Also (nonce) as v.

   1929 (quot. at RUNAROUND). **1942** in *ATS* 240: Evasion….*merry go-around.* **1963** *Time* (Apr. 5) 30: The Solidarity Congress organizers found themselves trapped, tricked, merry-go-rounded, bureacratized, buck-passed, blind-alleyed and discriminated against. **1976** *Atlantic* (Aug.) 31: The year of an extraordinary bureaucratic merry-go-round.

   3. *Carnival.* a gambling wheel.

   1942 in *ATS* 619: Merry-go-round, a gambling wheel. **1972** *Playboy* (Feb.) 185: Merry-go-round is a gambling wheel.

merry hand *n.* GLAD HAND, 1.

   1899 Cullen *Tales* 97: Got the merry hand from everybody.

merry-merry *n.* a chorus line.

   1908 McGaffey *Show Girl* 18: There is more than one of the merry-merrys putting her little sister through school. **1923** *N.Y. Times* VIII (Sept. 9) 2: *Merry-Merry:* The chorus. **1928** McEvoy *Show Girl* 1: Your little brown-eyed playmate has…gone into the merry-merry for better or worse.

merry widow *n.* [orig. a brand name] a condom.

   1928 Dahlberg *Bottom Dogs* 263: He took to carrying merry widows in his vest pocket. **1938** "Justinian" *Amer. Sexualis* 28: *Merry Widow.* n. A cundum. From trade-name of a popular brand of contraceptives.

mesc *n.* *Narc.* mescaline.

   1970 Landy *Underground Dict.: Mesc*…Mescaline. **1970** *Sat. Review* (Nov. 14) 21: Mesc. Mescalin, the alkaloid is peyote. **1976–77** C. McFadden *Serial* 48: Mesc made you realize that linear thinking was a total shuck. *a***1981** in S. King *Bachman* 639: How did you get the mesc? **1984** in *Rolling Stone* (June 11, 1992) 132: Jimmy…wanted me to buy mesc. *Ibid.:* Ricky had twenty-five hits of mesc.

Mese *adj.* *Mil.* Vietnamese.

   1981 Hathaway *World of Hurt* 238 [ref. to Vietnam War]: We run on Mese time here—two-hour lunch breaks.

meshuga *adj.* [< Yiddish < Heb] Orig. *Jewish-Amer.* crazy. Also in pron.-sp. vars. Also (by confusion with MESHUGGENER) **meshuggener.**

   *ca***1888** (quot. at MAZUMA). **1892** in *OED2:* She's *meshuggah*—quite mad! **1900** *Atlantic Monthly* LXXXVI 108, in *OED2:* "Meschugener," leered the banker. **1925** H.L. Mencken, in Riggio *Dreiser-Mencken Letters* II 543: Tom Smith is mashuggah. **1930** *Amer. Mercury.* (Dec.) 456: *Meshuga, adj.* Crazy. "He draws sol till he's meshuga." **1934** in Mencken *New Ltrs.* 310: I begin to believe that the whole world is mashuggah. **1935** Wald & Epstein *Stars over Broadway* (film): "Ha! Meshugga!" "Sure he's crazy!" **1936** Mencken *Amer. Language* (ed. 4) 580: They added two Yiddishisms to the common stock of all American rogues: *meshuggah* (crazy) and *goy* (a Christian). **1936** Levin *Old Bunch* 546: What is he, *meshuga?* **1940** *New Yorker* (Aug. 31) 13: "Meshugeh upstairs!" Jennie…tapped her forehead. **1949** H. Robbins *Dream Merchants* 89: Twenty-three thousand dollars for one picture!…A man's got to be *meshuggeh!* **1960** Kirkwood *Pony* 215: I also told myself I was—in Jay's language—"Mishoogena!" **1969** Salerno & Tompkins *Crime Confed.* 17: "How's the world today, Charlie?" … "Uhnnh … meshugah as per usual." **1972** in J. Flaherty *Chez Joey* 33: Was Fellini en route to shoot this meshuginer Satyricon? **1975** *L.A. Times* (Sept. 26) I 2: Berl Litman…is meshugga. **1977** in Mack *Real Life* (unp.): I'm tellin' ya this whole country has gone meshugah! **1982** M. Elias & R. Eustis *Young Doctors* (film): Dr. Phrang will not be performing the surgery today—he went meshugah. **1994** *Simpsons* (Fox-TV): Twenty simple questions to find out just how crazy or "meshuggeneh" a person is! **1995** L.A. assistant D.A., on *Calif. v. Simpson* (Court TV): I just said to myself these guys are meshuga. They don't know what they're up to. **1995** *Mystery Sci. Theater* (Comedy Central TV): Is he a beast or my meshuggeneh grandpa?

meshuggener *n.* Orig. *Jewish-Amer.* a crazy person. Also in pron.-sp. vars.

   [**1900** (quot. at MESHUGA).] **1946** I. Shulman *Amboy Dukes* 186: Do you know what that meshugener did? **1958** Frankel *Band of Bros.* 172: You *mischugunas!* Get back! **1968** M.B. Scott *Racing Game* 122: You think I'm a *mishugenah?* [**1968** I. Reed *Yellow Back Radio* 41: Entertaining the Great Meshuga.] **1972** in J. Flaherty *Chez Joey* 40: Meshugginers became messiahs. **1973** Flaherty *Fogarty* 93: Flowered shirts made them look like some meshuggeners from Delancey Street. **1982** *N.Y. Times* (Apr. 25) D29: She refers offhandedly to Idi Amin as a "meshugana." **1990** *Nation* (June 4) 768: As my grandmother might have said, that's one meshuggeneh Jew.

mess *n.* **1.** a great number; large amount.

   1826 in W. Morgan *Amer. Icon* 121: A mess of folks. **1827** in *JAF* LXXVI (1963) 292: Thare was a tarnal mess ov fokes frum Yawk. ***1832** B. Hall *Voyages* (Ser. 2) II 149: Try to get out of his pouch a whole mess of my stuff he has run off with. **1836** in C. Hill *Scenes* 130: [They] have such a "mess" of feelings for the dear people. **1843** "J. Slick" *High Life in N.Y.* 10: A mess of lingo that was enough to make a man larf. **1861** in *Ark. Hist. Qly.* XXXI (1972) 339: Think I will get a mess of Yankies ears before I come home. **1922** Rollins *Cowboy* 259 [ref. to 1890's]: He's up at the end of the big draw….Went over that high cut bank, him and a mess of cattle. **1930** Mae West *Babe Gordon* 103: You're walkin' right into a mess of dough. **1952** in R.S. Gold *Jazz Lexicon:* I've done a whole mess of 'em. *ca***1969** *Gunsmoke* (CBS-TV): You got a whole mess of sick folks to care of. **1973** Schiano & Burton *Solo* 40: There's a whole mess of cops in there.

   2. an odd, eccentric or contemptible person.

   1936 M. Mitchell, in *OEDS:* "Oh," thought Scarlett…"To have that mealy-mouthed little mess take up for me!" ***1938** *OEDS:* From what you say her mother was quite a mess. **1970** C. Major *Dict. Afro-Amer. Sl.* 81: To say to someone, "You're a mess," is to imply that he or she is remarkable or puzzling. **1991** D'Souza *Illiberal Ed.* 222: Abraham Lincoln was a racist.…He was a joke…a mess.

   3. *Black E.* (euphem. for SHIT in var. senses). [The sense 'excrement' is colloq.] *Specif.:*

   a. insolence; CRAP, 2.b.; *(hence)* nonsense; BULLSHIT, 1.a.

   1937 in *DARE:* Don't you let 'im beat you dat way anymo'. You fight 'im back.…You don' have ter take dat mess offen him. **1965** in *DARE:* I began spreading this "mess": "Well,…Mamie Smith has been booked for a vaudeville tour." **1966** in T.C. Bambara *Gorilla* 40: Manny don't take no mess from no cops. **1976** in L. Bangs *Psychotic Reactions* 186: Poppa don't take no mess. **1987** *TV Guide* (Nov. 28) 17: She'll play a cop…who "takes no mess from anyone." **1996** *Leeza* (synd. TV series): They take more mess from a man.

   b. stuff (in general).

   1956 R. Ellison, in W. King *Black Anthol.* 268: Those white boys don't play that mess. **1984** in G. Tate *Flyboy* 172: Which isn't to say hearing Baraka recite some of the mess couldn't make your ass snap to.

   c. *Narc.* narcotics; JUNK; STUFF.

   1974 Goines *Eldorado* 165: I don't cop my mess from him. His stuff changes too much for me.

   d. DAYLIGHTS, 1.b., "stuffing."

   1991 *Donahue* (NBC-TV): Then why did they beat the mess out of him? **1996** *Bold & Beautiful* (CBS-TV): A real friend would have beat the mess out of Nathan.

   e. the genitals.

   1996 *Mystery Sci. Theater* (Comedy Central TV): Ow! Right in the mess!

   4. *Jazz.* something exceptionally exciting or impressive; a lot of s.v. LOT.

   1938 Calloway *Hi De Ho* 16, in Gold *Jazz Lexicon: Mess:* something good. Example: "That last drink was a mess." **1954–60** *DAS: Mess*…Pleasure; excitement; anything pleasurable or exciting; a "ball." **1961** in R.S. Gold *Jazz Lexicon:* Lot of other cats blow a mess of trumpet, high notes, fast runs, and all, but Red always tells a story.

   5. *Naut.* a messboy.

   1972 Cleaves *Sea Fever* 37 [ref. to 1920's]: Well, mess,…what have we today?

mess *v.* **1.** [orig. back formation fr. MESS WITH] to interfere. Cf. MESS AROUND, 2.

   ***1873** Hotten *Slang Dict.* (ed. 4): Mess, to interfere unduly. Costermongers refer to police supervision as "messing." **1982** Least Heat Moon *Blue Hwys.* 138: Don't mess, Charley, or you'll be sorry. **1993** P. Munro *U.C.L.A. Slang II: Mess*…to get involved, disturb things.…*He's trying to mess.* **1993** *Are You Afraid of Dark?* (NICK-TV): Don't mess or I'll [hit you].

   2. [perh. alt. of MUSS] to fight.

   1935 *AS* (Feb.) [ref. to *a*1910]: To Mess. To fight. **1972** N.Y.U. student: You wanna mess? **1972–73** in M.J. Bell *Brown's Lounge* 76: She's ornery an' lookin' to mess.

3. to swindle.

   1962 Crump *Killer* 66: Nobody is gonna mess me out of that much money and get away with it.

mess around *v.* **1.** to engage in esp. promiscuous sexual activity; (*also*) to fool about or around; putter; kill time. Now *colloq.*

   a*1890–96** *F & H* IV 305: To *mess about*…(venery) to take liberties. [**1908** K. Graham, in *OEDS:* There is *nothing*—absolutely nothing—half so much worth doing as simply messing about in boats.] **1912** in P. Oliver *Songsters & Saints* 35: Messin' Around. **1918** D. Parker, in *Vanity Fair* (Oct.) 46: They are forever messing around with batik. **1920** Ade *Hand-Made Fables* 217: [He] had messed around a Small College until the first Call came. **1926** W. Rogers, in C.M. Russell *Trails* XIV: Every one of your old friends are too anxious to get into the book, to be messing around with any introduction anyway. **1926** in Emery *Black Dance* 223: The latest dance known as Messin' Around. **1931** (quot. at BLOKE, 1). **1932** *AS* VII (June) 334: *Mess around*—to "kill time"; to interfere; to meddle. **1932** Buffington *Haunted Gold* (film): The boss don't want none of you messin' around. **1965** C. Brown *Manchild* 58: Grace…messed around with all the boys on their block. **1968** J. Hendrix *Hey Joe* (pop. song): I caught her messin' 'round with another man. **1977** *Dallas Times Herald* (Apr. 24) D1: He came in full of cheap whiskey, accused me of messing around on him, and ordered me to get out of the house.

2. to handle unfairly or violently; mistreat; insult.

   [**a***1890–96** *F & H* IV 305: To *mess about*…To play fast and loose; to swindle; to put off.] [**1899** Whiteing *John St.* 187: This is what Radicals…are apt to forget when they begin to "mess the rich about." (I give this important scheme of thought as nearly as possible in the terms of the thinker.)]. **1946** Dadswell *Hey, Sucker* 198: Looky here, boss, we ain't going to mess you around none or tear down the joint, but just give us back our passes. **1954** L. Armstrong, in *DAS:* Nobody dared to mess around with Slipers. He was a good man with a pistol. **1962** H. Simmons *On Eggshells* 200: Jazz is the story of the black man being messed around…by the white man. **1985** Cook *Out of Darkness* (CBS-TV movie): They were also messing me around in the…reports.

messed up *adj.* **1.** ruined; emotionally or mentally impaired.

   [**1909** in *OEDS:* The house is all messed up.] **1919** in *OEDS:* I get my whole life messed up with people falling in love with me. **1924** P. Marks *Plastic Age* 156: Now, I'm all messed up about this sex business. **1932** Hawks *Crowd Roars* (film): You don't always get killed. You get crippled and messed up for life. **1968** in Cade *Black Woman* 46: Ain't no use getting messed behind somebody like that. **1970** Landy *Underground Dict.* 131: *Messed up*…Emotionally incompetent; unable to function. **1979** *Atlantic* (Apr.) 91: That is the message of religion. Unless you are able to make that distinction, you are an unhappy, messed-up person. *a***1986** D. Tate *Bravo Burning* 127: So's I won't get myself messed up. **1989** *ALF* (NBC-TV): The people you invited over seem really messed up.

2. Esp. *Narc.* intoxicated, esp. by drugs. Also (in recent use) **messed.**

   1963 Williamson *Hustler!* 74: All of us would be messed up.*…*High on dope. **1965** C. Brown *Manchild* 109: You could stay messed up all day long. All you did was nod. **1970** Landy *Underground Dict.* 131: *Messed up*…Extremely high on drugs. **1980** *L.A. Times* (Mar. 23) IX 14: Nice Ladies Get Messed Up Too.…Addiction to legally prescribed drugs…has become very much a women's issue. **1984** Univ. Tenn. student: *Messed up* means intoxicated. **1993** P. Munro *U.C.L.A. Slang II* 58: My roommate was so messed last night, she couldn't remember what room we live in. **1995** *Jerry Springer Show* (synd. TV series): Goin' out and partyin' and gettin' messed up all night.

messer *n.* *Und.* a strong-arm man.

   1935 *AS* (Feb.) 18: [Underworld, 1910:] *Messer.* A strong-arm man; a professional bully; a bouncer.

mess hound *n.* *Mil.* CHOWHOUND; (*also*) *Navy.* a mess steward. [Quots. ref. to WWI.]

   1919 J. Harris *Dizzed to a Million* 23: Our Mess Hounds. **1919** Jacobsen *Blue & Gray* 32: Mess Hounds' mess kits. **1919** T. Kelly *What Outfit?* 149: Guess Joyce's mess hound appetite did it. **1919** *110th Field Arty.* 86: Biggest Mess Hound. **1919** *Our Navy* (May) 48: Some very nutricious [*sic*] cabbage and cornwilliam was turned out by our artistic and efficient culinary cooks and served in delicate style by the mess hounds.

mess kid *n.* a mess steward; messboy.

   1942 *Yank* (Nov. 11) 4: Navy [Slang]…*Messkid*—A guy on KP.

mess kit *n.* *Mil.* ¶ In phrases:

   ¶ **go shit in your mess kit** [app. sugg. by *go shit in your hat,* var. of *in your hat!* s.v. HAT] (used as a dismissive retort).—usu. considered vulgar. Also vars.

   *a***1982** Berry *Semper Fi* 192 [ref. to WWII]: If you really wanted to give someone the business, you told him to go shit in his mess kit or his shelter half.

   ¶ **hope to spit** [or (*vulgar*) **shit**] **in** (someone's) **mess kit** [or (*Navy & USMC*)] **mess gear** beyond a doubt.—used as a joc. oath. [Early quots. ref. to WWI.]

   1924 *Adventure* (June 20) 168: I hope to spit in your messkit I can! **1926** Upson *Me & Henry* 11: I should hope to spit in my mess-kit if he didn't have a little trick oil stove that he lit up. **1927** Stevens *Mattock* 263: "I hope to spit in your mess-kit!" somebody in my rank sang back at them. **1928** Nason *Sgt. Eadie* 193: I hope to spit in your messkit there are! **1932** *Leatherneck* (Feb.) 13: Well, I should hope to spit in your messkit, I do! **1961** Peacock *Valhalla* 415 [ref. to 1954]: "You think they'll make his BCD stick?"…"I hope to shit in your mess gear." **1968** W.C. Anderson *Gooney Bird* 84: Ah hope to spit in yo' mess kit. They're wilder'n a Texas widow in heat. **1980** Cragg *Lex. Militaris* 356: Hope to shit in your messkit.

   ¶ **mess kit full** one's fill.

   1928 Hall *Balloon Buster* 82 [ref. to WWI]: He'll get a mess kit full of tough language from ol' man Grant.

   ¶ **shit in** (one's) **mess kit, 1.** to become furiously angry.—usu. considered vulgar.

   1988 Dye *Outrage* 80 [ref. to 1983]: Here it comes. The C.O.'s gonna shit in his mess kit.

   2. to blunder seriously; get oneself into trouble.—usu. considered vulgar. Also vars.

   1989 J. Weber *Defcon One* 44: Skipper, I think we've crapped in our messkit. **1968–90** Linderer *Eyes of Eagle* 42: Calm down, you idiot. You almost shit in your mess kit.

mess over *v.* Esp. *Black E.* to mistreat; victimize; (*hence*) to destroy; beat.

   1963 Williams *Sissie* 70: Iris, you're going to mess over me, you're going to shake me up. **1964** L. Jones, in *Blues People:* With black people all over the world dying the most horrible kinds of death imaginable some fools would still be walking around with their behinds in the air saying, "But I'm Cool." Well the word is No You're Not, not as long as one of your brothers and sisters is being messed over by "the man." **1965** C. Brown *Manchild* 320: I had just gone on and messed over her. **1965** in Cohen & Murphy *Burn* 109: We gon' mess over some devils. **1966** IUFA *Folk Speech* (Apr. 7): *Messed over.* To get a raw deal. **1968–70** in *DARE.* **1970** Eisen *Altamont* 128: When they started messing over our bikes they started it. **1985** in G. Tate *Flyboy* 37: So they were messing over you because you were getting your own business thing together? **1987** *USA Today* (Oct. 30) 11A: But what we're attempting is to deter the Iranians from messing over the area.

mess punk *n.* Esp. *Naut.* a mess steward; messboy.

   1935 E. Anderson *Hungry Men* 68: I can put you next to a mess punk's job. **1940** *AS* (Dec.) 451: *Mess Punk.* A waiter.

mess-up *n.* **1.** a blunder; botch; FOUL-UP, 1.

   1902 in *OED2:* I should say he feels this mess-up more than any of us. **1929** in *OED2:* I am afraid there has been a bit of a mess-up. **1978** *New West* (Nov. 20) 138: The $30 million mess-up on screen is one of the most disastrous film musicals of all time.

   2. a troublemaker or misfit; FOUL-UP, 2.

   1944 (quot. at FUCK-UP, 1). **1966** *Social Problems* XIII 218: Inmates sometimes referred to as "mess-ups," or "eightballs," etc. **1971** Klein *Street Gangs* 244: *Mess-ups:* These boys…have high offense records. *a***1972** in *Urban Life & Culture* I 80: Everybody was a mess-up, all the kids in West Oakland. *a***1974–78** J.W. Moore *Homeboys* 71: The square youth of the barrio considered them the biggest "mess-ups." **1994** *World News Sunday* (ABC-TV) (Aug. 28): I thought I was a mess-up.

mess up *v.* **1.** to beat up or handle roughly; injure; ROUGH UP.

   1914 London *Jacket* 28: We were caught dead to rights with our clothes on. Winwood crossed us and squealed. They're going to get us out one by one and mess us up.…And lyin's bound to be found out. **1917** in *Manuscripts* XL (1988) 108: We…lost a lot of horses but messed up about six times our own weight in Bosch. **1929** Asch *Pay Day* 83: If I did meet you, I'd mess you up, and you'd be sorry. **1934** Peters & Sklar *Stevedore* 85: Yo' face just made for messing up. **1946** *Amer. Mercury* (Apr.) 484: To use a knife on another boy is to "mess him up." **1955** S. Stern *Rebel without a Cause* (film): "Why'd you do it?" "Mess that kid up? He called me chicken." **1961** Odets *Wild in the Country* (film): Oh, we gonna have to mess him up, mess him up good. **1966** Brunner *Face of Night* 26: Open your mouth again, Brozek, and I'll mess you up. **1966–67** P. Thomas *Mean Streets* 38: I couldn't ask two or three *amigos* to break into Rocky's block and help me mess up his boys. **1984** (quot. at RENT-A-COP).

2. to botch; ruin; get into trouble; FUCK UP, 1, 2.a.

1918 in *AS* (Oct. 1933) 29: [Ft. Leavenworth:] *Mess Up.* Get into a scrape. Boy, I ain't a-goin' t' *mess up* no more from now on. I on'y got eighty-one more days 'n' a get-up. **1919** Emmett *Give 'Way to the Right* 268: Whenever things seem to be going best there is always somebody or something to "mess up the detail." **1928** Santee *Cowboy* 60: I'd finally got a chance at the thing I wanted all my life, an' I'd messed the whole thing up. **1942** *Pittsburgh Courier* (July 18) 7: Having messed up this Ned's play. **1947** *AS* (Apr.) 122: *Mess up.* (1) To get into trouble. (2) To cause trouble. **1955** T. Anderson *Own Beloved Sons* 55: He'll mess up for sure! **1965** C. Brown *Manchild* 294: These kids is goin' around here messin' up, killin' themselves. **1978** *Business Week* (Dec. 4) 56: Employees have "really got to mess up to get run off." **1983** Leeson *Survivors* (film): OK, I fell asleep. I'm sorry. I messed up. *a*1988 C. Adams *More Straight Dope* 13: William Holland hinted that perhaps O.C. Marsh had messed up and given the apatosaurus the wrong skull. **1988** M. Bartlett *Trooper Down!* 21: I thought everyone was watching me, waiting to see when I was gonna break under the pressure, when I was gonna mess up. **1995** *Donahue* (NBC-TV): When I first started messin' up, I started runnin' away [from home].

3. to fool around, often in a sexual manner; MESS AROUND, 1.

1979 *New West* (Jan. 29) 39: The times he messed up on her with other girls. **1995** Alicea & DeSena *Air Down Here* 33: So my math teacher lets us mess up—for a few minutes.

mess with *v.* to involve or associate oneself with; interfere with; harass. Now *colloq.*

1880 in Eliason *Tarheel Talk* 91: In this coast country [of N.C.] the peculiar word is "Mess."...A politician says "That fellow is 'messing' (associating) with the Radicals." A hunter says "You better not 'mess' with a wounded buck."...A lawyer says "What did you 'mess' (interfere) with the matter for?" **1931** Bontemps *Sends Sunday* 81: Any woman dat messes wid me gotta take de lumps. **1950** *Harper's* (Apr.) 89: When an eager undergraduate once demanded, "What is jazz, Mr. Waller?" the great pianist is said to have growled: "Man, if you don't know what it is, don't mess with it!" **1955** in R.S. Gold *Jazz Lexicon*: And what little lady is going to mess with you? **1965** C. Brown *Manchild* 46: I told her that she wasn't as pretty as Grace and not to mess with me any more. **1979–81** C. Buckley *To Bamboola* 13: This boy my *frien'*. So don't be messin' with 'im. **1984** R. Wilkinson *American Tough* 3: Everybody knows the modern tough guy...a man to joke with but not mess with. **1995** *Montel Williams Show* (synd. TV series): She shouldn't've messed with my boyfriend.

messy buckets var. MERCY BUCKETS.

metal-bender *n. Navy.* a machinist's mate.

1991 Linnekin *80 Knots* 274: VF-124's "metal benders" designed and constructed ladder extensions. **1995** Cormier et al. *Wildcats* 67: One of the genius metal-benders in the ship's machine shop.

metalhead *n.* a devotee of heavy metal music.

1982 "Blotto" *Metalhead* [title of rock song lampooning heavy metal]. **1984** *San Diego Union-Tribune* (May 24) (Nexis): And even though Carey once performed with the heavy-metal band Rainbow, he should in no way be considered a metal-head. **1987** *Campus Voice* (Spring) 10: Metalheads were boosting their power just to pick it up. **1989** *Spin* (Aug.) 27: Metalheads especially revere all things biker: the regalia, the machines, the life and, above all, the spirit. **1989** *Billboard* (July 15) 1: Metalheads Rock to Rap as Crossover Idiom Grows. **1990** in D. Weinstein *Heavy Metal* 259: The symbols and paraphernalia of hate movements, particularly Naziism, have been the staple diet of so-called metalheads for more than a decade. **1991** D. Gaines *Teenage Wasteland* 11: Two metalheads...blasting Metallica tunes off this huge boom box. **1992** *TV Guide* (Oct. 31) 5: My favorite scene was the one with all the metalheads...listening to the opera. **1995** Weisberg *Spin*

Record Guide 371: Its largest audience quickly began to consist of teenage metalheads.

metalmouth *n. Stu.* a person wearing orthodontic braces.

1978 *Daily Beacon* (Univ. Tenn.) (Nov. 10) 4: Painful kisses, baby food for dinner and nicknames like "metal mouth" and "tinsel teeth" are trials experienced by students who wear braces during college. **1986** *New Leave It to Beaver* (synd. TV series): They'll call you names like *tin grin, metalmouth, twinkle teeth, laser lips!* **1993** D. Lum, in Hagedorn *Chan Is Dead* 289: Hey, metal mout, you can staple my math papers wit your teet?

meth *n. Narc.* **1.** methamphetamine.

1966 (implied by METH HEAD). **1967** *Sat. Eve. Post* (Sept. 23) 27: He was on a Meth trip for three years in New York and Tangier before he found acid. **1967** Rosenthal *Sheeper* 83: Meth will make you go up to the angels. **1967–68** von Hoffman *Parents Warned Us* 155: Meth is a death drug. **1970** E. Landy *Underground Dict.: Meth.* Methedrine, an amphetamine. **1970** *Everett* (Wash.) *Herald* (Nov. 19) 7B: A nine-year user of methamphetamines—speed and meth—who is trying to kick the habit. **1985** E. Leonard *Glitz* 96: Try and sell him some meth. **1985** B.E. Ellis *Less Than Zero* 112: You have any meth? **1994** *Reader's Digest* (Feb.) 89: Meth is scarier than cocaine. **1996** *Montel Williams Show* (synd. TV series): You beat up both your parents one night on meth.

2. methadone.

1980 T. Jones *Adrift* 184: We're on methadone treatment at the meth center.

meth freak *n. Narc.* a habitual user of methamphetamine.

1967 Yablonsky *Hippie Trip* 33: Even some high priests and novices refer to the "new breed" as "Meth" or "speed" freaks. **1970** Landy *Underground Dict.* 131: *Meth freak...*Habitual user of Methedrine. **1971** *Nat. Lampoon* (Sept.) 36: Yvonne is a meth freak and a transvestite.

meth head *n. Narc.* a habitual user of methamphetamine.

1966 Dylan *Tarantula* 134: A meth-head but he's all beautiful. **1967** *Esquire* (Sept.) 193: A Meth-head is easy to spot. **1967** Kornbluth *New Underground* 111: After an overdose of these drugs the user undergoes excruciating depressions, when high "meth heads" may become compulsive talkers who stalk the streets in search of victims when experienced friends have bolted their doors. **1968** J. Carey *College Drug Scene* 40: Methedrine users, or "meth heads," are viewed as quite inconsistent. **1968** Louria *Drug Scene* 209: *Methheads* chronic and heavy users of Methedrine. **1969** *Fort Pleasure Seekers* 129: "Speed freaks" or "meth heads." **1972** Wambaugh *Blue Kt.* 73: She's a meth head and an ex-con and stir crazy as hell. **1981** Wambaugh *Glitter Dome* 142: Now he was a meth head, totally addicted to that drug. **1994** *Reader's Digest* (Feb.) 88: Let me guess. Another meth head.

meth monster *n. Narc.* METH HEAD; (*also*) METH, 1.

1967 Maurer & Vogel *Narc. & Narc. Add.* 156: Methedrine, which is widely used intravenously by addicts in the San Francisco area, causes such violent behavior that the term *methmonster* is used to describe it. **1968** *Look* (Mar. 5).

Mex *n. Esp. S.W. & West.* **1.** a Mexican.—usu. used contemptuously.

1847 Reid *McCulloch's Rangers* 204: Look here, boys, do you see those two *Mexes* on the corner of the house opposite me? **1867** in W.H. Jackson *Diaries* 152: The Mex. did most of the lassoing. **1878** Willis *Our Cruise* 56: Load up quick, for the Mex's will think we are going for the boats. **1882** Sweet *Sketches* 146: The latter calls for a policeman and has Mr. Mex. locked up. **1888** in F. Remington *Sel. Letters* 64: You can stand it if the Mex. can. **1902** in "O. Henry" *Works* 1642: I say now, Mex,...this here won't do. **1927** *Variety* (Jan. 5) 34: The Mex are treacherous. **1956** Algren *Wild Side* 33: City unions teach you that Chinamens are your brothers! Ayrabs! Mexes! **1969** Twitchell *Drums of Eck* 21: What direction are the Mexes? **1971** *Nat. Lampoon* (Sept.) 57: Nope, no Mexes.

2. the Spanish language as spoken in Mexico.—used contemptuously.

1858 Viele *Following the Drum* 158: Very little conversation took place between them, and that little in a language called "Mex," a kind of Spanish patois, differing widely from pure Castilian! **1933** Milburn *No More Trumpets* 205: She don't *sabe* anything except Mex anyway. **1939** Attaway *Breathe Thunder* 3: Ed, you know some Mex. What's it all about? **1946** in Himes *Black on Black* 256: Some pachuco kids were...talking in Mex and blowing weed. **1958** J. Ward *Buchanan* 44: "Your friend there don't have much to say, does she?" "Only in Mex."

1958 J. Thompson *Getaway* 13: El Rey—that means The King...in Mex. **1967–68** T. Wolfe *Kool-Aid* 296: She looks Mex and speaks Mex. **1979** Edson *Gentle Giant* 14: I can *habla* a might of Mex'.

3. Mexico; (in 1951 quot.) Mexico City.

1885 S.S. Hall *Gold Buttons* 2: I war tole yer follered some...clean inter Ole Mex'. **1913** Z. Grey *Desert Gold* 58: I'm regretful passin' the ribbon to the lady from Mex. **1951** in Kerouac *Letters* 319: I will dig Mex on lush this time and explore great Mexico. **1956** Neider *Hendry Jones* 26: We bought the finest boots and sombreros down in old Mex.

4. *Narc.* Mexican narcotics.

1979–82 Gwin *Overboard* 245: A certain guy with bags of good Mex for forty dollars.

Mex *adj.* **1.** Mexican.—usu. considered offensive. [The n. and adj. *Tex-Mex*, as applied esp. to cuisine, is colloq. or S.E. and as such is not usu. considered an offensive term.]

1854 in *OEDS*: I thought it proper to consult with one of the Quartermaster's agents...which resulted in my receiving the information that the "United States Hotel" upon the "Plaza" provided "chicken fixins and corn doins"—or, if a stranger wanted "Mex livin'," *frijoles* and *tortillas* to boot—in better style than any other establishment in Santa Fé. **1885** S.S. Hall *Gold Buttons* 2: Mex' style. **1934** J. Cain, in *DAS*: Ensenada is all Mex. **1950** in Kerouac *Letters* 245: Another Mex revolution. **1958** Swarthout *Cordura* 36: A private in C Troop who had served twenty years in the Army made up his mind to seek one of them if the Mex fire became too hot for comfort.

2.a. *Mil.* (of currency) foreign or devalued.—usu. considered offensive.

1898 *Amer. Soldier* (Nov. 12) 8: We will send a set of back copies of the American Soldier to any address in America for 25 cents (mex). **1899** Markey *Iowa to the Philippines* 164: The munificent sum of five dollars (Mex). **1905** Devins *Philippines* 50: Fifty cents, Mex. **1906** M'Govern *Sarjint Larry* 29: De prices range from 100 pesos, for a beauty of 18 or 20, to 50 cents, Mex fer an auld woman like Mrs. Datto Makar. *Ibid.* (gloss.): *Mex:*—One half value for or of anything. Also the name for the kind of bastard currency in use during the Days of the Empire, one dollar of American money being about equal to two dollars of the Mexican currency, which...was not really Mexican...about half of the time, but more frequently bitten Straits dollars, Japanese yens, or mostly any old piece of silver that resembled an American dollar in size, weight and superficial appearance. **1907** *Army & Navy Life* (June) 679: M stands for money, which is mostly in "Mex." **1913** *Review of Reviews* (Aug.) 203: Through [Manila] the silver from Mexico was spread through all the eastern countries and the word..."Mex" came into general use to describe a particular money standard. In Japan Anglo-Saxons speak of the Japanese coinage as "Mex." In Shanghai...the Chinese currency goes by the name of "Mex." **1924** *Our Navy* (July 15) 29: A boot who was worth about six cents Mex to the government. **1927** Shoup *Marines in China* 99: The cost was to be a mere twenty cents Mex. **1928** Tilton *Cap'n George Fred* 118 [ref. to Maui, *ca*1885]: They gave me the position...at a salary of two hundred and fifty dollars a month, "Mex," as they called the Spanish money. **1929–30** Dos Passos *42d Parallel* 276: He got a job...at the *Mexican Herald* at thirty mex dollars a week. **1936** in Thomason *Stories* 301: At the rate of fourteen dollars Mex. **1941** Cruse *Apache Days* 287 [ref. to *ca*1900]: The rent was $100 a month "Mex," which translated as $50 in gold. **1967** Lockwood *Subs* 142 [ref. to 1922]: "On the first day of each month every upper Yangtze skipper finds one hundred Mex dollars on his desk." ("Mex" is the pidgin English term for Chinese currency.) That's his pay for keeping his nose out of things that do not concern him—such as opium. **1967** Moorse *Duck* 8: Fifteen cents mex is paid out for every crate we fill with usable bottles.

b. a half quantity of anything.—usu. considered offensive.

1906 M'Govern *Sarjint Larry* 58: But it was not annie "Mex." foive mile we hoiked. *Ibid.* (gloss.): *Mex:*—One half value for or of anything. **1907** *Reader* (Sept.) 350: I make up my mind in about two seconds, Mex.

3. *Mil.* (of a military commission or rank) temporary or volunteer.—usu. considered offensive.

1901 Palmer *Ways of the Service* 156: Her husband's old Lieutenant...had a "Mex" commission as Major in the Sixty-third (volunteer commission). *Ibid.* 158: Why that young thing is putting on the airs of a general's wife over her Mex rank! **1920** *Inf. Jour.* (July) 140: With the single list in operation such preference can be secured only by legislation removing all officers of a certain branch from the single

list, or else by reviving the pernicious custom of giving "Mex." rank, abolished by the present act. **1941** Cruse *Apache Days* 288 [ref. to *ca*1900]: "Mex" this or that. *Ibid.* 297: But on June 1, 1901, all Volunteer commissions had expired; off had come my "Mex" oak leaves. **1942** Stilwell *Papers* 49: This is a lieutenant general writing. Just a Mex one. [**1952** Cope & Dyer *Petty Officer's Guide* 447: *Mexican rank* (Slang). Temporary appointment.]

Mexicali revenge *n.* MONTEZUMA'S REVENGE.

1973 *Atlantic* (July) 38: Nearly all of his guests developed classic cases of "Mexicali revenge" after being fed local produce.

Mexican athlete *n.* one who "throws the bull"; PHONY. *Joc.*

1912 T.A. Dorgan, in Zwilling *TAD Lexicon* 57: I'm tired of being the boob around town. I'm going to be a mexican athlete. Throw the bull about being a fighter and get away with it. **1918** *Camp Meade Herald* (Nov. 8) 1: He used to climb up on the throne and listen to a bull-throwing contest by the Mexican athletes. **1919** Law *2nd Army Air Service* (unp.): Every organization has its "Mexican Athlete," and these toreadors put out the "T" and exercise their prowess daily, much to the discomfort of their fellow squadron mates. **1920** Norton *639th Aero Squad.* 49: Daily the Mexican athletes had either sailing orders for the Squadron or some "straight" or "inside" dope that assured our departure by the end of January. **1923** *Iowa State College Bomb* 422: Bob Wright was engaged in Mexican athletics speaking of the queen he was with the night before. *Ibid.* 426: Contrary to the rumor that they have a few pseudo-athletes, I found the majority of them to be of the Mexican variety. **1929–32** in *AS* (Dec. 1934) 288: [Lincoln U.:] *Mexican athlete.* One who tries to gain a place on all the teams, but makes none.

Mexican bankroll *n. Gamb. & Und.* MICHIGAN ROLL; CHICAGO BANKROLL.

1941 "G.R. Lee" *G-String* 286: The bankroll...was no Mexican; the twenties went right through to the bottom. **1942–49** Goldin et al. *DAUL: Mexican bankroll.* See *Michigan bankroll.* **1970** Winick & Kinsie *Lively Commerce* 117: A pimp often has a "Mexican bankroll," a large bill on the outside covering a roll of singles.

Mexican breakfast *n. S.W.* a cigarette and a glass of water.—usu. considered offensive. *Joc.*

1954–60 *DAS: Mexican breakfast* A breakfast...which amounts to smoking a cigarette and drinking a glass of water. **1979** *N.Y. Times Mag.* (Dec. 2) 18: In Texas, a "Mexican breakfast" is a cigarette and a glass of water. **1990** T. Thorne *Dict. Contemp. Slang: Mexican breakfast* n. a cigarette and a glass of water.

Mexican brown *n. Narc.* Mexican heroin. Also **Mexican tar.**

1975 (cited in *BDNE*2). **1977** in *BDNE*2: The white Asian heroin...has begun reaching New York to compete with the more common Mexican brown. **1980** *New West* (July 14) SC17: California's heroin supply....The three varieties are usually called Mexican brown, China white and Persian. **1996** *Entertainment Weekly* (Aug. 9) 21: Mexican tar, the cheapest and most prevalent form of heroin in L.A., goes for as little as $10 a bag.

Mexican flush *n. Poker.* a poor hand as used to bluff other players.

1928 Dahlberg *Bottom Dogs* 259: Everytime he called, he put his foot into it, and when he didn't some one was holding a mexican flush.

Mexican lightning *n.* tequila. Cf. LIGHTNING; WHITE LIGHTNING.

1975 *Newsweek* (Jan. 13) 75: "Mexican Lightning" has become particularly popular among younger drinkers at singles bars and ski resorts.

Mexican mud *n. Narc.* Mexican heroin. Cf. MEXICAN BROWN.

1982 in RH files: *Mexican mud* Slang = heroin. **1986** *Time* (Apr. 7) 31: Black tar (also known as tootsie roll and Mexican mud) is most prevalent.

Mexican overdrive *n. Trucking.* (see 1976 quot.).—usu. considered offensive. *Joc.*

1955 *AS* XXX 94: *Mexican overdrive*...Coasting down hill with gears disengaged. **1975** *Nat. Lampoon* (Nov.) 51: Jest stick 'er in "Mexican Overdrive" 'n' coast. **1976** Lieberman & Rhodes *CB* 132: *Mexican Overdrive*—Neutral gear position used in going downhill.

Mexican seabag *n. Naut.* (see quot.).—usu. considered offensive.

1935 *AS* (Feb.) 79: *Mexican seabag.* A newspaper or paper bag in which the poor sailor carries his belongings.

Mexican standoff *n.* **1.** a deadlock resulting from the opposition of equally powerful adversaries; an impasse from which neither party dares to withdraw; stalemate.—now often considered offensive. Now *colloq.*

1891 in *DARE:* "Monk" Cline, who got a Mexican stand-off from Dave Rowe has signed with Louisville. **1929** J.M. Saunders *Single Lady* 241: It would be about a Mexican stand-off. **1935** Pollock *Und. Speaks: Mexican stand-off,* no chance to win. **1958** Cooley *Run for Home* 139: It's a Mexican standoff! No breeze southbound—and too much northbound! **1969** Whittemore *Cop!* III 291: They just built up, so to speak, and it looked like a Mexican stand-off. You know—a policeman on each corner and the crowd milling about, back and forth. **1970** Woods *Killing Zone* 50: "A Mexican standoff."...stalemate. **1971** N.Y.U. professor: By the end of the third century the Romans and the German tribes were face-to-face across the Rhine-Danube, but neither side was terribly anxious to start a full-scale war with the other. It was a Mexican standoff. **1971** Murphy & Gentry *2nd in Command* 85: With the Russians, Clark believed, we had reached something of a "Mexican stand-off." We had spy ships; they had spy ships....If they sank one of ours, they knew we could sink one of theirs. **1973** *Sub. of Pres. Convers.* 288: I really think these guys are concerned about this Mexican standoff. **1976** S.I. Hayakawa, in *L.A. Times* (Jan. 21) II 6: Detente, which is a diplomatic word for "Mexican standoff," is possible only when our armed strength is approximately equal to that of the Soviet Union. **1979** *N.Y. Times Mag.* (Dec. 2) 18: A "Mexican standoff" came to mean one of those impasses from which no good would come. **1985** MacLaine *Dancing* 243: He said fasting cured everything....I said it would kill me—a Mexican stand-off. **1993** J. Watson & K. Dockery *Point Man* 19: Chuck...laid the barrel up against the pilot's head! Then the copilot took his .45 and put it up to Chuck's head. We had a Mexican standoff right there in the cockpit of a Huey!

2. a partial victory or defeat; an unsatisfactory but roughly even outcome.—now often considered offensive.

1904 in *DARE:* Boys, as fur as the coin goes, we're out an' injured; we jest made a "Mexican stand-off"—lost our money, but saved our lives—and mighty lucky at that. **1921** T.A. Dorgan, in Tamony *Americanisms* (No. 19) 7: They got a "Mexican Standoff." That is to say, they lost their money but they saved their lives. **1926** C.M. Russell *Trails* 48: The way they start pilin' lead in our direction makes us hug the brush; we don't leave it till dark....It's a Mexican stand-off, which means gettin' away alive. **1932** Nelson *Prison Days & Nights* 13: It is a Mexican stand-off....Paddy is powerless to punish me. **1958** J. Ward *Buchanan* 110: Buchanan...would briefly mention the clash with Hallett & Co. as a Mexican stand-off—one in which everybody takes some amount of clobbering and no issue is decided. **1961** Scarne *Comp. Gde. to Gamb.* 685: *Mexican Stand-Off.* Act of quitting a gambling game when one is a very small winner or loser. "I played a Mexican stand-off." **1964** Faust *Steagle* 30: Which...once wrestled your underling to a Mexican stand-off. **1969** Pendleton *Death Squad* 89: This is no Mexican standoff, Bolan....I'm [a] police officer, and I'm ordering you to drop your weapon. **1976** *S.W.A.T.* (NBC-TV): Couldn't we call it a Mexican stand-off? **1983** *L.A. Times* (Nov. 18) VI 18: You could describe Bunuel's [*sic*] version as a Mexican standoff. His producer...allowed him to develop a script to his satisfaction only to force upon him a cast that [the producer] had hired for a musical.

3. execution by firing squad.

1929 Hotstetter & Beasley *It's a Racket* 231: *Mexican-standoff*—To kill in cold blood [*sic*]. **1934** O'Hara *Samarra* ch. vii: The men were the victims of the St. Valentine's Day massacre in Chicago, when seven men were given the Mexican stand-off against the inside wall of a gang garage.

Mexican tar var. MEXICAN BROWN.

Mexican two-step *n.* AZTEC TWO-STEP; MONTEZUMA'S REVENGE. Also vars.

1962 in *DARE:* The North American in Mexico has coined a number of names for the inevitable dysentary [*sic*] and diarrhea: "Mexican two-step," "Mexican fox-trot," "Mexican toothache." **1967–69** in *DARE:* Mexican disease...Mexican sickness...Mexican two-step.

Mexican strawberry see s.v. STRAWBERRY.

Mexie *n. S.W. & West.* a Mexican.—usu. considered offensive.

1899 "J. Flynt" *Tramping* 369: 'Member yer all 'Mericans, 'n' that yer fightin' Mexies. **1900** Willard & Hodler *Powers That Prey* 48: The push thinks I'm out at that crib in Mexico, rollin' the wheel....Tell 'em

I'm baskin' in the sun down among the Mexies. **1983** In RH files (Apr.): *Mexie* for a Mexican.

mezz[1] *n.* [fr. nickname of Milton "*Mezz*" Mezzrow (1899–1972), jazz clarinetist and drug dealer] *Jazz.* marijuana.—often constr. with *mighty.*

1937 in Partridge *Dict. Und.* 271: Marijuana. Commonly it is now being called "fu," "mezz," "mu," "moocah," "muggles," "weed," and "reefers"; but by any name at all, its ultimate effect is the same...insanity. **1938** *AS* XIII 188: *Mezz.* marijuana. **1946** Mezzrow & Wolfe *Really Blues* 185 [ref. to ca1936]: Overnight I was the most popular man in Harlem. New words came into being...: *the mezz* and *the mighty mezz,* referring...to me and to the tea [marijuana] both. **1956** in *DAS:* Dreamed about a reefer five foot long/The mighty mezz, but not too strong. **1967** Rosevear *Pot* 159: *Mezz:* An obsolete term for marihuana.

mezz[2] *n.* a mezzanine.

1954 Collans & Sterling *House Detect.* 46: The Security Office in that hotel was on the mezz.

mezzroll *n.* [MEZZ[1] + *roll*] a marijuana cigarette. Also vars.

1944 La Guardia Comm. *Marihuana* 9: The "panatella" cigarette, occasionally referred to as "meserole," is considered to be more potent and usually retails for approximately 25 cents each. **1946** Mezzrow & Wolfe *Really Blues* 215: *Mezzroll,* to describe the kind of fat, well-packed and clean cigarette I need to roll. **1961** Russell *Sound* 15: The very good ones were reputed to be regular customers of the reefer and mezziroll.

m.f. *n.* (a partial euphem. for) MOTHERFUCKER, in var. senses. Also **emm-eff.**

1959 in R.S. Gold *Jazz Lexicon* s.v. *mother:* You go and buy me a tenor saxophone and I'll play the m-f. **1964** Howe *Valley of Fire* 190 [ref. to Korean War]: Being able to call a gook an emm-eff in pig Latin and get away with it. **1965** Ward & Kassebaum *Women's Pris.* 158: And please let me touch you just once you M.F. **1965** Cleaver *Soul* 58: Why'n't they kill some of the Uncle-Tomming m.f.'s? **1965** in Sanchez *Word Sorcerers* 193: I'm a lucky M.F. to have found you. **1965** in W. King *Black Anthol.* 304: So I stole the m——f. [*sic*] **1966–67** P. Thomas *Mean Streets* 236: You poor m.f. **1969** Rodgers *Black Bird* 38: None of us can relax until the last m.f.'s/been done in. **1970** Terkel *Hard Times* 407: Today you get a guy in court, [he] don't like what the judge says, he calls him a *m f,* you know what I mean? **1970** Cain *Blueschild Baby* 77: A bunch of dirty white M.F.'s. **1971** in Matthews & Amdur *My Race* 246: There'd be a lot of dead "M.F.'s" around. **1971–73** Sheehy *Hustling* 89: Then in comes this m.f. from Midtown North, *our* precinct. **1974** Blount *3 Bricks Shy* 159: They say "m-f" worse than a colored person. **1976** G. Kirkham *Signal Zero* 63: *Adios,* MF! **1981** *L.A. Times* (Dec. 25) V 6: I had a kid call me an m.f. once. **1984** Univ. Tenn. student theme: *Hell, yeah, M.F.!* is an exclamation used when I'm very happy or very drunk. **1986** Clayton & Elliott *Jazz World* 101 [ref. to 1930's]: Billie [Holiday] called all of her close friends MF. **1987** *Newsweek* (Mar. 23) 61: He could stand out on the corner looking sharp as a MF in his Stacy-Adams wingtips and a $100 hat. **1992** *Donahue* (NBC-TV): I'm gonna take all you m.f.'s with me.

¶ In phrase:

¶ **MFWIC** Orig. *Mil.* motherfucker who's in charge.

1980 D. Cragg *Lex. Militaris* 285: *MFWIC. Motherfucker what's In Charge.* **1980** D. Cragg, letter to J.E.L. (Aug. 10) 5: *MFWIC.* This is certainly an old one, so much so that I can't remember when I first heard it used. "He is the *MFWIC* of this outfit." **1996** *Dr. Dobb's Journal* (Mar.) (Nexis): Frank Grossman, the MFWIC ("main fellow who's in charge") at Nu-Mega, was demonstrating BoundsChecker for Windows.

m.f. *adj.* (a partial euphem. for) MOTHERFUCKING. Also **emeffing,** etc.

1958 Motley *Epitaph* 120: Them emeffing guards is bringing it in in fountain pens. *Ibid.* 149: You emeffing right. *a*1972 in G.M. Simmons et al. *Black Culture* 219: That M-F-in' jive. **1973** Childress *Hero* 34: All over the emm-eff community. **1990** *New Yorker* (Apr. 2) 46: Graffiti...on the...training ship of the Maine Maritime Academy..."Only 13 more MFD's, Only 12 more MFD's, Only 11 more MFD's," and so on down a toilet stall. The "D" stood for "day." **1995** *CNN Saturday Morning* (CNN-TV) (June 17): A little two-year-old girl has said, "I want to be an m.f. gangster."

m.f. *v.* (a partial euphem. for) MOTHERFUCK, *v.*

1942 in W.N. Hess *B-17* 32: MFUTU [*i.e.,* "Motherfuck You Too";

inscribed on nose of B-17 bomber, accompanied by cartoon of General Tojo getting "the FINGER"].

MFL *n.* [sugg. by *NFL* 'National Football League'] *Baseball.* (see quot.).—usu. considered vulgar. *Joc.*

    1969 Bouton *Ball Four* (Aug. 9) 265: "Teddy Ballgame of the MFL." That's the Major Fucking Leagues.

mic var. MIKE[1], 1.

mice *n.* ¶ In phrase: **smell a mice** to become suspicious; detect a plot; smell a rat.

    1850 in Blair & McDavid *Mirth* 102: With that I smelt a mice and commenced laughin. **1859** in *N. Dak. Hist.* XXXIII (1966) 200: The men began to "smell a very large sized mice" & all hands burst into…laughter. **1862** in Swinfen *Ruggles' Regt.* 9: He began to smell a large-sized "mice." **1863** in Geer *Diary* 120: I smell a mice somewhere. **1863** in H. Johnson *Talking Wire* 27: I heard him order the cooks to prepare three days rations, the boys smell a mice when they heard that. **1864** in Redkey *Grand Army* 141: Our boys…began to "smell a mice." **1865** in Hilleary *Webfoot* 59: The little fellows seemed to smell a "mice" & skedaddled. **1871** in Miller & Snell *Why West Was Wild* 172: Before Gainsford arrived, Walker "smelled a mice," and commenced preparations to leave. **1872** Burnham *Secret Service* 182: But he had already smelt an enormous mice! **1872** Burnham *Secret Service* 171: Smelling a mice, perhaps, he concluded *not* to go too far. **1875** *Chi. Tribune* (Nov. 17) 3: The Collector begged so hard…that Trigg "smelt a mice." **1878** Pinkerton *Criminal Reminiscences* 142: By and by, I smelled a right smart-sized mice. **1884** Blanding *Sailor Boy* 54: We had begun to smell a large "mouse." **1894** *Confed. War Jour.* (Mar.) 192: Adjutant smells a mice. **1912** Siringo *Cowboy Detective* 268: The Anglo-Continental Mining Co. began to smell a "mice." **1912** Field *Watch Yourself* 219: I smelled a mice the minnit I seen yer face.

Michael *n.* **1.** a liquor flask.

    1914 Jackson & Hellyer *Crim. Slang* 58: *Michael*, Noun. Current amongst bottle drinkers. A flask of liquor. Example: "Have you got a michael on your hip?" **1930** G. Irwin *Tramp & Und. Slang: Michael.*— A bottle or flask carried on the hip.

    2. MICKEY FINN.

    1942 *ATS* 474: Opiate; "knockout drops."…*Michael, Michael Finn, mickey finn, Mickey Flynn.* **1945** (quot. at MICKEY, 4). **1951** G. Fowler *Schnozzola* 61 [ref. to 1920's]: The Mickey Finn.…"If a person acted any other thing but a gentleman, I had little Michael ready for him." *Ibid.* 62: I got the reputation as the best Michael giver in New York City. **1957* in *OED2*.

Michael Finn *n.* MICKEY FINN. Also **Mike Finn.**

    [**1915** T.A. Dorgan, in Zwilling *TAD Lexicon* 57: [Sign in saloon:] Try a Michael Finneka Cocktail.] **1924** T.A. Dorgan, in Zwilling *TAD Lexicon* 57: Why don't that big slob get on an excursion boat.…Wish I had a drink and a Mike Finn for him. **1940** [W.C. Fields] *Bank Dick* (film): "Has Michael Finn been in today?" "No, but he will be!" **1974** *Coq* (Apr.) 44: Joan,…introduce our friend over there to *Michael Finn.*

Michigan *n.* a criminal deception.—also used attrib.

    1914 Jackson & Hellyer *Crim. Slang* 58: *Michigan*, Noun. General currency. A spectacular ruse; a deceptive appearance, as a fake bank roll; a hoax staged with sinister intent. Example: "They started a michigan scrap and trimmed the sucker in the mix-up."

Michigan roll *n.* a phony bankroll, esp. one consisting of a high-denomination banknote wrapped around a large number of small-denomination banknotes; CHICAGO BANKROLL. Also **Michigan, Michigan bankroll, Michigan stake.**

    1914 (quot. at MICHIGAN). **1920** *Variety* (Sept. 3) 5: I'll tell him you are a Wall Street broker and just before you leave hand me a Michigan roll…Here's a $1000 bill for the wrapper. **1931** Wilstach *Under Cover Man* 122: That Michigan bank-roll I gave you. **1932** in *AS* (Feb. 1934) 27: [Md. prison:] *Michigan-roll.* A bankroll made up of stage money with a genuine banknote wrapped around the outside. **1942–49** Goldin et al. *DAUL: Michigan bankroll.…*A roll of paper [or single bills] with a bank note of large denomination wrapped around the outside. **1956** Sorden & Ebert *Logger's Lang.* 23 [ref. to a1925]: *Michigan stake*, A roll of dollar bills. **1979** L.T. Carter *Eubie Blake* 61: He would flash a "Michigan bankroll"—bills on the outside and toilet paper inside.

mick[1] *n.* [fr. *Mick[ey]*, hypocoristic form of *Michael*, common Irish male given name; reinforced by *Mc-*, common initial

element in Scots-Irish surnames] **1.a.** (often *cap.*) an Irish person or person of Irish descent.—used contemptuously.—usu. considered offensive. Occ. as adj.

    1850 in *Amer. Neptune* XLV (1985) 183: One of the "uncompressed micks"…exclaimed "there's no danger now for the priest is coming." *ca***1854** in R.L. Wright *Irish Emigrant Ballads* 509: In spite of all the micks you can raise to fight with sticks. *Ibid.* 510: The "Micks" provoked a fight. **1859** in C.A. Abbey *Before the Mast* 236: Whom the mate…has nicknamed the *Sintimintal* Mick. **1864** in R.L. Wright *Irish Emigrant Ballads* 517: A red-headed "mick." **1865** J.H. Browne *Secessia* 288: A Mick…an Irishman. **1865** in Hilleary *Webfoot* 59: A Mick said that it required the residence of a bishop to constitute a city. **1871** "M. Twain" *Roughing It* 253: The Micks got to throwing stones through the Methodis' Sunday School windows. **1885** *Puck* (Mar. 4) 11: You…called him a bog-trottin', pig-eatin' Mick. **1889** in Dolph *Sound Off!* 319: The German is fond of sauerkraut,/The Potato is loved by the Mick. **1891** Maitland *Slang Dict.* 176: *Micks*, Irishmen. **1892** S. Crane *Maggie* 3: "Naw," responded Jimmie with a valiant roar, "dese micks can't make me run." *ca***1895** in C.C. Davis *Olden Times* 321: The Mick replied, "I'll hunt a mine!" **1898** G.L. Giefer *Who Threw the Overalls in Mistress Murphy's Chowder?* [N.Y.: Mullen Music]: I can lick the mick that threw the overalls in Mistress Murphy's chowder. **1902** in R.W. Snyder *Voice of City* 113: There was a sudden transition from the Castle Garden greenhorn to the East Side "Mick." **1904** in Sampson *Ghost Walks* 317: The Irish…do not like the song "The Mick Who Threw the Brick." **1905** *Nat. Police Gaz.* (Dec. 23) 3: He ain't a Mick, he's a Dago, but he's all right just the same. **1908** *Atlantic* (Dec.) 753: The Irishman used to be characterized by the Americans as a "Mick," or "Paddy." **1910** *Everybody's* (May) 685: Look at that rusty-haired little Mick with the red tie. **1913** J. London *Valley of Moon* 27: You know what the Micks are for a rough house. **1918** E. O'Neill *Moon* 49: I'm wore out with you steppin' on my toes, you clumsy Mick. **1921** "M. Brand" *Black Jack* 120: And the first thing he does is try a joke on the Irish right in front of the Mick. **1923** Ornitz *Haunch* 28: Shimshin had bought a revolver and was determined to kill a few Micks. **1929** W.R. Burnett *Iron Man* 7: You bet on that nigger, you cheap shanty mick, and I'll give you the lacing of your life. **1930** in W.F. Nolan *Black Mask Boys* 162: Just a bullheaded mick, eh? **1933** Clifford *Boats* 22: They've got wops and micks and kikes from Russia over there fighting. **1942** Liebling *Telephone* 263: How do you like that, you mick? **1949** Bellah *Yellow Ribbon* (film): I'd love to throw that big mick in the cooler! **1955** Q. Reynolds *HQ* 189: But he was a tough mick when the chips were down. **1966** Susann *Valley of Dolls* 273: But underneath she's just a lousy little mick who's scared to death. **1981** *N.Y. Times Bk. Review* (Jan. 4) 4: For [Louise Bogan] was, in her word, a "Mick," and a Roman Catholic [who escaped] from the faith.

    b. (often *cap.*) a Roman Catholic. *Rare* in U.S.

    1924 P. Marks *Plastic Age* 201: You go chasing around with kikes and micks. **1948* in *OED2*: Mother is wrong to send a girl to a convent with a lot of micks. **1956* "N. Shute," in *OED2*: Stanley and Phyllis went to Church of England schools…but the rest of us are Micks. **1968** in *DARE*: Protestants used to call Catholics "micks." **1965–70** in *DARE*. **1971* in *OED2*: A Roman Catholic is never a Catho, but remains, in lower-level Protto usage, a Mick.

    2. *Pris.* a fellow prison inmate.

    1942–49 (quot. at MICKEY, 8).

mick[2] *n.* [short for MICKEY MOUSE *course*] *Stu.* an academic course that can be passed with a high grade for very little effort. Also as adj.

    1968 Baker et al. *CUSS* 157: *Mick.* An easy course. **1970** in *N.Y. Times Mag.* (Sept. 21, 1975) 15: This is Education 191D. There are two rumors about this course. One, it's a mick. Two, it's a trap for athletes. **1971** Dahlskog *Dict.* 40: *Mick, a.* Easy, as a test or college course. **1972** in Tamony *Americanisms* (No. 30) 9: It's a mick. **1978** Farkas et al. *Parasession* 303: If you hear a college student call an easy course a *mick*, you can assume that this usage is general for his classmates, though it may vary elsewhere. **1983** *Newsweek on Campus* (Dec.) 2: The course is [by no means] a "mick" (it is of significant intellectual content). **1993** P. Munro *U.C.L.A. Slang II: Mick n.* easy class.

mick[3] *n.* [alt. of MIKE[2], 2] *Mil.* a minute.

    1993 P. Dickson *War Slang* 316 [ref. to 1990–91]: Give me five micks. **1994** *21st Cent. Dict. Slang* 171: I'll need about ten micks to get my stuff together.

mick *adj.* (often *cap.*) **1.** Irish.—used contemptuously.—usu. considered offensive.

1894 in *DAE*: It's a Mick regiment. **1922** S. Lewis *Babbitt*, in *DAS*: This Mick agitator...De Valera. **1934** H. Roth *Call It Sleep* 303: It's a mick block. **1941** in Hemingway *Sel. Letters* 529: Barbara Stanwyck...is very nice with a good tough Mick intelligence. **1944** Brooks *Brick Foxhole* 223: You mick sonofabitch. **1964** N.Y.C. high school student: I know this stupid mick girl on Third Avenue. **1977** Dunne *True Confessions* 8: Boyle Heights was tough mick then, just like it's tough Mex now. **1973–78** D. Ford *Pappy* 3: They would remember a hundred childhood fights with the "Mick" gangs from across the tracks. **1983** Flaherty *Tin Wife* 11: It was so typically Mick. **1984** H. Gould *Cocktail* 2: Pretty fancy word for a mick lush, eh?

2. Roman Catholic. Cf. MICK[1] *n.*, 1.b.

1924 P. Marks *Plastic Age* 201: My one mick friend, although he isn't Irish.

mickey *n.* **1.** (often *cap.*) an Irish person; MICK[1], 1.—usu. used contemptuously.—usu. considered offensive.

[**1844** in B.C. Mitchell *Paddy Camps* 73: Mickey, my boy,...do you go to confession regularly?] *ca*1854 in R.L. Wright *Irish Emigrant Ballads* 509: Oh! the mickeys of New Orleans thought to carry the day. **1858** in *Amer. Neptune* XXI (1961) 112: D—d Irishman...d—d Mickeys. **1870** *Overland Mo.* (Dec.) 509: When this cruel war is over,/No Micky need apply. **1889–90** Barrère & Leland *Dict. Slang*: Mickey (American), a common word for an Irishman. **1915** Poole *Harbor* 8 [ref. to *ca*1890]: "Micks," Belle sometimes called them, and sometimes, "Finian Mickies." *Ibid.* 11: "Smash in his nut for him," piped the smallest Micky cheerfully. **1923** Wheeler *Buffalo Days* 131: He and my striker, O'Grady, a regular "Mickey," were great friends. **1939** Howsley *Argot* 56: Irish: Dinny, Mickey, Mick, Hibernian, Paddy, Mike, Pat, Mulligan. **1963–64** Aiken *Limericks* 5: There was an old micky named Cassidy/Who was famed for impromptu mendacity.

2. the penis.—usu. considered vulgar.

*1909 in Joyce *Sel. Letters* 185: Gently undo...the fly of my trousers and gently take out your lover's fat mickey. *1914–22 Joyce *Ulysses* 780: Let him have a good eyeful of that to make his micky stand for him. **1972** R. Wilson *Playboy's Forbidden Words* 168: *Mickey* The penis. **1973** "J. Godey" *Pelham* 176: She could no more not react in a professional way than she could grow a mickey between her legs. **1975** Legman *No Laughing Matter* 126: To someone smoking a cigar: EVERYbody's sucking mickeys! **1978** in *Maledicta* VI (1982) 23: Penis...*dong, dork*,...*mickey*. **1990** Murano & Hoffer *Cop Hunter* 210: I'm stewed to the Mickey....I am in-e-e-e-bri-at-ed.

3. a (now usu. small) bottle or a drink of liquor; MICHAEL, 1. [Now esp. common in Canad. E.]

1914 Jackson & Hellyer *Crim. Slang* 58: *Micky*, Noun. Current amongst bottle drinkers. A corruption of "Michael." **1925–26** J. Black *You Can't Win* 66 [ref. to *ca*1890]: A four-bit micky, a fifty-cent bottle of alcohol—Dr. Hall, white line. *Ibid.* 129: The "punks," young bums, were sent for "mickies," bottles of alcohol. **1933** Ersine *Prison Slang* 53: *Micky, n.* 1. A drink of hard liquor. 2. A bottle of booze. **1935** Pollock *Und. Speaks*: *Mickey*, half pint of boot leg whiskey. **1950, 1971** in *OED2*. **1973** *Atlantic* (July) 6: They spread a bedroll on the grass...and lay around on it, drinking little bottles of wine called "mickeys." **1967–80** Folb *Runnin' Down Lines* 247: *Mickey, a* Small bottle of wine.

4. MICKEY FINN, 1.

1936 Twist *We About to Die* (film): Say, did you put a mickey in this? **1936** Markey & Conselman *Private Number* (film): Nothing bothers me but a mickey. **1938** A.J. Liebling *Back Where I Came From* 88: Mickeys act so drastically that one may kill a drunk with a weak heart. **1939** Wald et al. *Roaring '20's* (film): And if anybody makes any noise, the waiters have been told to slip 'em a mickey. **1940** Zinberg *Walk Hard* 124: Andy was watching the bartender mix the drinks—still thinking of a mickey. **1942** B. Morgan & B. Orkow *Wings for Eagle* (film): We'll slip him a mickey right after the soup course. **1945** in Hodes & Hansen *Sel. from Gutter* 21: She was handed a Mickey—or Michael. Now, to you who don't know what a Michael is (and are there any who don't?) a mickey is a pill that works wonders with a stomach...for example, a horse's tummy. **1950** in F. Brown *Honeymoon* 68: I'm surprised he didn't give the guy a mickey before he phoned us. **1953** Caen *Don't Call it Frisco* 252: There are several recipes of concocting a Mickey. Sometimes it involves the use of Glauber's salts, a horse laxative. Sometimes it is made from chloral hydrate. But the true, historic Mickey is a preparation of antimony and potassium tar-

trate known as "tartar emetic." **1953** Manchester *City of Anger* 113: May-be duh doity ref give Wipe a Mickey before duh fight. Ya-ah! **1955** L. Shapiro *6th of June* 67: Wait a minute, fellas....He might put a mickey in our beer. **1957** Collins & Powell *My Gun Is Quick* (film): "I gave you a sedative [surreptitiously in a drink]." "A mickey, eh?" "No, just a mild sedative." **1959** "W. Williams" *Ada Dallas* 18: If he has more money than he can spend, she slips him a sedative known as a Mickey, and then certain other employees of the bar take him outside and relieve him of what is left. **1960** Himes *Gold Dream* 140: So I dropped a little mickey into her bottle of drinking water. **1962–65** Cavan *Liquor License* 175: They'll slip you a mickey and roll you. **1965** Spillane *Killer Mine* 97: You know the ingredients in a mickey? I nodded. "Sure. Generally chloral hydrate. For the knock-out kind, anyway." **1969** Hardy *Ship Called Fat Lady* 25: Somebody had slipped him a Mickey, probably some woman he had picked up in a bar. **1990** Niemann *Boomer* 140: Take care they don't slip you a mickey.

5. a potato, esp. a sweet potato, roasted outdoors.

1936 Kingsley *Dead End* 724: Hey, guys, I swiped two maw [*sic*] mickeys. Look! **1939** Appel *Power-House* 223: We used to buy sweet mickies from the sweet micky man. **1943** J. Mitchell *McSorley's* 18: Sometimes they roast mickies in the gutter fires. **1944** H. Brown *Walk in the Sun* 121: You ain't ever lived until you toasted a mickey over the coals. **1956** J. Rose & M. Shavelson *Beau James* (film): We roasted mickeys on Second Avenue. **1960** Barber *Minsky's* 2: A bunch of kids had built a fire to roast some mickies. **1965** C. Brown *Manchild* 308: We stole our first mickies together from Gordon's fruit stand. **1969** in Cannon *Nobody Asked* 13 [ref. to 1920's]: We stole sweet potatoes from the vegetable stores and roasted them in fires in oil drums or ashcans. We called them mickeys. Although they were charred and had an unpleasant taste, we cherished them as a great delicacy. **1988** De Lillo *Libra* 8: I know where to get some sweet mickeys off the truck. We go roast them in the lot near Belmont.

6. *Mil. Av.* a radar-equipped bombsight; (*hence*) (a nickname for) the operator of such a device. Now *hist.* [Quots. ref. to WWII.]

1944 *S.F. News* (Nov. 28), in *OED2*: "Mickey," a sensational radar device which "sees" through darkness, clouds and artificial smoke. **1944** Inks *Eight Bailed Out* 9: We've got a belly full of 500-pounders. I'd hate to have to press the mickey button and drop on other ships. **1945** *Yank* (Oct. 5) 17: Crews referred to the BTO [bombing-through-overcast radar]...widely and...fondly as "Mickey." First used by the British, Mickey was tried out by our Eighth Air Force in the raid on the Wilhelmshaven docks in November 1943. **1945** Hamann *Air Words*: Mickey. (1) Radar operator. (2) Radar bombsight. **1945** in *AS* (Dec. 1946) 310: *Mickey man.* The radar operator on a B-17 bomber. **1950** *Life* (July 17) 101: "You're going to have to drop the damn thing with your mickey." Mickey is what we called the radar. **1952** Landon *Angle of Attack* 187: "Navigator to Mickey," he called. **1956** Heflin *USAF Dict.* 324: *Mickey, n.* A popular name applied to various airborne radar sets, radar range finders, and switch boxes. In full, *Mickey Mouse.* Slang. *a*1983 Newby *Target Ploesti* 137: A new kind of bombsight, basically a Norden, but equipped with radar. It was officially called H2X. Unofficially it was called "Mickey." Planes equipped with H2X were called "Pathfinders." **1984** M.W. Bowman *Castles* 99: H2X, or "Mickey Mouse" (later shortened to just "Mickey"), was a recently developed American version of the British H2S bombing aid. **1994** W.N. Hess *B-17* 60: British H2S radars...allowed accurate blind bombing when the target was obscured....This set [was] called "Mickey" by the Eighth Air Force crew members.

7. *Jazz.* MICKEY MOUSE, 2.—often constr. with *band.*

1946 in Tamony *Americanisms* (No. 30) 5: At Liberty. Violins—Three-man section desires work....No tenor or mickey. **1947** in R.S. Gold *Jazz Talk*: *Mickey band*: a type of popular orchestra, which plays commercial, uninspired jazz and/or swing....The term "mickey," for some mysterious reason, is a shortened form of Mickey Mouse. **1949** in Tamony *Americanisms* (No. 30): Traditionally, one of the dreariest elements of the music business has been the typical hotel band. Over the years this particular category has been primarily shared by tenor bands and mickey bands. **1958** *AS* (Oct.) 225: A *Mickey* or *Mickey Mouse* band sounds as if it is playing background music for an animated cartoon. **1959** in R.S. Gold *Jazz Lexicon*: I like mickey bands better than that.

8. *Pris.* a fellow prison inmate; (*also*) a fellow.

1942–49 Goldin et al. *DAUL: Mick or micky....*An inmate of a penal institution. 2. A person. **1956** Resko *Reprieve* 99 [ref. to *ca*1940]: The new mickey…proves himself to be a right guy. **1966–67** P. Thomas *Mean Streets* 178: You must be new mickies 'cause you don't call a ship a boat. *Ibid.* 253: I watched him huddle in a corner of the yard with all the green mickies.

¶ In phrase:

¶ **take the mickey out of** [chiefly BrE; perh. sugg. by Irish] to tease or mock; (*also*) to break the spirit of.
   *1948 A. Baron *From the City* [ref. to WWII]. *1952 in *OED2*: She's a terror. I expect she'll try and take the mickey out of you all right. *1954, *1956, etc., in *OED2*. **1972** Grogan *Ringolevio* 190: Filthy McNasty was a kid with a lot of heart and everyone was trying to take the mickey out of him. **1979** *New West* (Sept. 24) SC27: My paranoia took the mickey out of me, and I was just not resilient enough to raise my chin and rise above it. **1995** *N.Y. Times* (Mar. 5) ("Arts & Leisure") 34: Can you find it in your heart to forgive Robert Stern for taking the mickey out of Peter Behrens?

mickey *adj.* Mickey Mouse, *adj.*, 1, 3.a. 4.
   1958 *PADS* (No. 30) 46: *Mickey*, adj. "Corny," "old-fashioned," "ricky-tick" music. Short for "Mickey Mouse music," but usually abbreviated. Originally referred to the pseudo-jazz that accompanied animated cartoons. **1975** U.C.L.A. student: He takes these mickey courses. **1980** *L.A. Times* (Feb. 22) I 28: Every department in every university has what they call "Mickey" courses. **1992** *Newsmaker Saturday* (CNN-TV) (Jan. 25): He doesn't have to answer these mickey questions.

mickey *v.* to add a Mickey Finn to (a person's drink, etc.); (*also*) to stupefy (a person) with a Mickey Finn.—also constr. with *up*.
   1946 *New Directions* 196: All they'd had to do was…mickey the bottle up real nice. **1967** W. Crawford *Gresham's War* 132: She's probably rich off the guys she's rolled and mickeyed in here. **1970** Gattzden *Black Vendetta* 109: I belt away some bourbons only someone's mickeyed them up. **1987** Norst & Black *Lethal Weapon* 49: The barbiturate capsules had been mickeyed with potassium cyanide. **1995** Foreman & Engel *By George* 115: I believed my water may have been mickeyed.

Mickey D's *n.* Orig. *Stu.* a McDonald's restaurant.
   1977 *Wash. Post* (Aug. 28) (Nexis): At midnight, McDonald's—fondly known as "Mickey D's" to those who follow the fast-food circuit—is jam-packed with black teenagers who have just left the roller-skating rink. **1983** *Daily News* (N.Y.) (Mar. 25): Teentalk glossary…*Mickey D's*—McDonald's. **1984** Mason & Rheingold *Slanguage*: *Micky d's* [sic]…McDonalds [sic]. **1986** *Daily Beacon* (Univ. Tenn.) 4: Walk down to Micky-Dee's for a scrumptious Egg McMuffin. **1987** Univ. Tenn. student theme: *Mickey D's* is McDonald's. **1988** Terkel *Great Divide* 73: Working for $3.50 an hour at Mickey D's. **1989** McDonald's TV ad (June 3): I need something to eat. Mickey D's? **1989** *Reporters* (Fox-TV): "The homeless kids—where do they hang out?" "Mickey D's!" **1990** *Newsday* (N.Y.) (May 24) 19: *Mickey D's*: McDonalds [sic]. **1991** D. Gaines *Teenage Wasteland* 48: Beyond White Castle, Micky D's (McDonald's) or Taco Bell. **1992** *In Living Color* (Fox-TV): Maybe Mickey D's is hiring.

Mickey Finn *n.* **1.** *Und.* a drink, as of liquor, to which has been added a purgative, emetic, or other drug to render the drinker helpless; (*also*) the drug so added; (in 1928 quot.) (*obs.*) a double drink intended to render someone helplessly drunk. Cf. earlier quots. at Michael Finn, later quots. at Mickey, 4, and D. Hammett's unique earlier use of *take a Mickey Finn*, below. [A circumstantial account in Asbury (1940), pp. 173–76, rests upon the incident summarized in bracketed 1903 quot. but remains unconfirmed in detail. Most significant is Asbury's assertion that patrons who innocently tried a so-called "Mickey Finn Special" were then made helpless, robbed, and disposed of; although the *Chicago Tribune* seems not to have reported this detail, it may well have appeared in the regulatory committee testimony that led to the closing of Finn's locally infamous saloon. An unsupported "legend" claiming that a San Francisco bartender named Michael Finn (allegedly *fl. ca*1870) was the eponymous inspiration of the term is recounted in Herb Caen, *Don't Call it Frisco* (1953), pp. 251–54.]
   [**1903** *Chicago Trib.* (Dec. 17) 1: "Micky" Finn's saloon at 527 State street [was] closed…following charges of robbery there.] **1928** M.

Sharpe *Chicago May* 99: I got a bottle of brandy.…I shot a few more Mickey Finns (double drinks) into him.…I slipped his little drops into the last drink. In a few minutes he was…dreaming. **1930** Lait *On the Spot* 207: *Mickey Finn*…Knockout drops. **1931** Wilstach *Under Cover Man* 225: That's for what we call a Mickey Finn. When a customer gets loud and boisterous we slip a little…in his drink. **1931** Harlow *Old Bowery* 410 [ref. to N.Y.C., ca1905]: Crooks learned to mix other drugs for the obliteration of consciousness, some…more dangerous even than chloral [hydrate]. There was one lethal dose called the Mickey Finn, which some old-timers still believe was the cause of Chuck Connors's death. **1931** *Amer. Mercury* (Dec.) 419: She used to make up the Mickey Finns for him and toss the sailors out in the gutter. **1933** Ersine *Prison Slang* 53: *Mickey Finn.* A drink spiked with knockout drops. **1934** O'Hara *Appt. in Samarra* 61: The cheap bastard.…I'd like to give him a Mickey Finn. **1935** Pollock *Und. Speaks*: *Mickey Finn*, a concoction given to offensive drunkards, which rapidly purges or causes vomiting, in order to sober or get rid of them. **1936** *AS* (Apr.) 124: *Mickey Flynn* or *Mickey Finn.* A knockout dose (often cigar ashes in a carbonated drink) administered to an addict or a sucker. **1937** in J.P. Cannon *Notebook* 115: It was a bad sign for the people who had slipped them the Mickey Finns. **1938** Bellem *Blue Murder* 111: The floor was rocking up and down. I knew Dixie had fed me a Mickey Finn. **1940** Asbury *Gem of Prairie* 176: [By 1904, Mickey Finn of Chicago] had sold the formula for his "Special" to half a dozen ambitious dive-keepers, and the potion was known throughout the underworld simply as a "mickey finn." The name was soon applied to knockout drinks of every description. **1941** Cady *Saint in Palm Springs* (film): He got a Mickey Finn that'll keep him quiet for two days. **1942** in Cheever *Letters* 74: They serve him a mickey finn [and] empty his pockets. **1944** D. Runyon, in *Collier's* (Jan. 15) 50: If you have any more Mickey Finns on your person, please take them yourself instead of dropping them in officers' drinks. **1945** Drake & Cayton *Black Metropolis* 107: A bartender in an Irish neighborhood contiguous to the Black Belt boasted to a white interviewer of the "Mickey Finns" that he prepared to discourage Negroes who came in and ordered drinks. **1949** in Hemingway *Sel. Letters* 660: I told the bartender that if he ever showed again to give him a Mickey Finn which he promised to do. **1951** Boehm *When Worlds Collide* (film): You gonna give the animals a Mickey Finn, Doc? **1958** in Roethke *Coll. Poems* 112: And nobody slipped me a Mickey Finn. **1960** Himes *Gold Dream* 140: And I has to have some kind of way to protect myself. So I just carries me a little Mickey Finn. **1964** Smith & Hoefer *Music* 148: A Mickey Finn…made it necessary to make frequent trips to the men's room. **1968** Longstreet *Wilder Shore* 117: The man who drank too little got the deadly *Mickey Finn*, which was a powerful cantharides or a bladder-destroying dust called *Spanish fly*. **1992** *People* (Aug. 10) 70: Chloral hydrate.…It would have worked like a Mickey Finn.

2. *Baseball.* (see quot.).
   1936 Nichols *Baseball Term.*: *Mickey Finn.* A printed schedule of league games for a season; named for a former news reporter who became the first expert modern schedule maker. *Sporting Life*, Mar. 10, 1906, p. 6.

¶ In phrase:

¶ **take a Mickey Finn** to abscond.
   1924 in D. Hammett *Continental Op* 92: There's a hundred thousand he's holding—a third of it's mine. You don't think I'm going to take a Mickey Finn on that, do you? **1925** in D. Hammett *Continental Op* 206: There's two of you to see I don't take a Mickey Finn on you.

Mickey Mouse *n.* [fr. *Mickey Mouse*, trademark for a popular animated cartoon character introduced by Walt Disney in *Steamboat Willie* (1928)] **1.a.** *Cinema.* a small spotlight.
   1937 in Tamony *Americanisms* (No. 30) 5: The smallest "spot" [light] used in the studio…is…known as a Mickey Mouse.

b. a small, timid, inconsequential, or foolish person.
   1941 in *OEDS*: George Graham, a timid, middle-aged mickey mouse who was afraid of crowds, people, anything. **1948** Manone & Vandervoort *Trumpet* 40: We used to go backstage when the Mickey Mice went out to get their cheese. We would put rugs in the piano, soap on the sax reeds, [etc.]. [**1967** Riessman & Dawkins *Play It Cool* 68: *Mickey mouse* n. (plural -es) a white person: *Just because he's a mickey mouse doesn't mean he's square.*] **1971** Dahlskog *Dict.* 40: *Mickey mouse*…a simpleton. **1974** *Business Week* (July 27) 4: There are many Mickey Mouses in office across the country, from both parties and at all levels of government.

2. *Jazz.* music that is MICKEY MOUSE, *adj.*, 1.

1940 in Tamony *Americanisms* (No. 30) 4: Coleman Hawkins Refuses To Play Mickey Mouse. **1942** *ATS* 561: Musical effects...*Mickey Mouse,* a dainty, high-pitched rendition. **1947** *ATS* (Supp.) 10: *Mickey Mouse*..."sweet" music, nonswing. **1954** in Tamony *Americanisms* (No. 30) 5: Glenn Miller's Music Was All Mickey Mouse. **1963** Braly *Shake Him* 22: He couldn't refuse a job that wasn't outright mickey-mouse. **1973** *Oui* (Feb.) 113: You can walk through an endless rice field...playing mickey mouse on your mandolin.

3. *Mil. Av.* an electric gun trigger or bomb-release mechanism.

***1941** in *OEDS:* This war is producing a new batch of army slang....An R.A.F. pilot calls his cockpit the "pulpit"....The instrument releasing the bombs, an electrical distributor, is called a "Mickey Mouse." **1942** S. Johnston *Queen of Flat-tops* 185: I squeezed the "Mickey Mouse" (the gun- and bomb-release trigger) a little too hard and my guns fired. **1945** Hamann *Air Words: Mickey Mouse.* The electric switch box of the bomb release.

4. *Mil.* an instructional film, esp. one concerned with the prevention of venereal disease. In full, **Mickey Mouse movie.**

1944 in *AS* XX 148: *Mickey Mouse Movies.* Personal hygiene movies. **1958** Cope & Dyer *Petty Officer's Guide* (ed. 2) 359: *Mickey Mouse.* (Slang). Any film used in instruction. **1954–60** *DAS: Mickey Mouse (movie)* A documentary or short movie vividly showing the means of prevention, the causes, development, and care of venereal diseases; a documentary or short movie vividly showing methods of hand-to-hand combat. **1966–67** W. Stevens *Gunner* 89 [ref. to WWII]: A two-minute Mickey Mouse would be added, a trailer of clinical shots showing diseased organs in full color.

5. MICKEY MOUSE MONEY, 1. Now *hist.*

1945 Dos Passos *Tour* 152: A small boy comes running up to me with a roll of Jap issue hundred-peso Filipino bills in his fist. "It's Mickey Mouse," he shouts....By Mickey Mouse he means Japanese issue. There's a story that somebody put a Mickey Mouse in the watermark. **1945** in Tamony *Americanisms* (No. 30) 7: The Jap money was called "Mickey Mouse" by all Filipinos.

6.a. foolish or tedious activity or routine; trivialities; *(specif., esp. Mil.)* petty regulations or enforcement of discipline. [The 1947 quot. almost certainly belongs to **(2)**, above.]

[**1947** *ATS* (Supp.) 5: Teen Talk and Jive Jargon...*Mickey Mouse, razzmatazz, ricky-tick, schmaltz*...anything "corny" or in poor taste.] **1958** J. Davis *College Vocab.* 13: *Mickey mouse*—An activity which has no purpose. **1962** Mandel *Mainside* 251 [ref. to ca1956]: Why go through all Mr. Ives' mickeymouse? **1963** in Tamony *Americanisms* (No. 30) 6: At Mission High (San Francisco), Mickey Mouse means "home work." **1965** C.D.B. Bryan *P.S. Wilkinson* 361 [ref. to ca1961]: Well, I think we'd probably be better off at the airstrip since there's bound to be less "Mickey Mouse" down there. **1970** *U.S. News & W.R.* (June 1) 24: Our kind of school....Irrelevant, outdated and filled largely with methodological "Mickey Mouse." **1970** *Just Military Men* 31: The entire system was at fault, the daily grading, the rigid classroom atmosphere, the Mickey Mouse...all the time. Shined shoes, Haircuts, Bracing. **1971** *N.Y. Times* (Apr. 18) 61: The Army is also seeking to make military life more attractive by eliminating regulations that are sometimes called "Mickey Mouse"—rules likely to cause more irritation than they are worth. **1972** *N.Y. Times Mag.* (Mar. 12) 113: My God, what Mickey Mouse! **1978** *Kansas City Star* (Jan. 8) 17A: "The big reason they don't have enough men [*i.e.,* police officers] on the highways is because they're doing too much other Mickey Mouse."...Tasks such as finger printing and questioning of witnesses should be left to local enforcement agencies. **1978** Groom *Better Times* 218: There was no saluting here or other Mickey Mouse. **1980** Cragg *Lex. Militaris* 300: *Mickey Mouse.* Anything that is unnecessary, stupid, confusing....I remember that it was current in the Army in 1958. **1983** Goldman & Fuller *Charlie Co.* 204: He...resented the KP and the guard details, the dress code and the war games, the chickenshit and the Mickey Mouse. **1983** Van Devanter & Morgan *Before Morning* 226: Too concerned with military Mickey Mouse.

b. a blunder.

1965 *Time,* in *DAS* (ed. 2): Logistically so far, the only big Mickey Mouse...was a brief shortage of...jungle boots.

c. *Business & Finance.* deceptive or improper practices or arrangements. Cf. MICKEY MOUSE, *adj.*, 5.

1975 *Business Week* (June 23) 74: There began to build up and grow a whole body of unregulated markets. The very fact that they were unregulated led, I think, to a public suspicion. I can't give you a specific example of "Mickey Mouse" that is occurring today.

d. foolish or nonsensical talk.

1980 Ciardi *Browser's Dict.* 249: *Mickey-Mouse*...Gibberish. Double-talk. *All I got from him was a lot of mickey-mouse.* **1987** S. Stark *Wrestling Season* 80: Lot of Mickey Mouse....It's clear as day what happened. **1993** *NewsHour* (CNN-TV) (Oct. 1): To the French that's just a load of Mickey Mouse.

7. *Cinema.* a kind of film editing apparatus. Also as *v.*

1957 in Tamony *Americanisms* (No. 30) 11: Film editors can recognize words being sounded backwards, as tape is run back, on the Mickey Mouse. *1957** in *OEDS:* "Mickey-Mousing" in film musical terminology...means the exact, calculated dove-tailing of music and action. *1973** in *OEDS:* What is known in the film-music trade as "Mickey-Mousing"—the action of the film gets a simultaneous musical parody. When Tarzan swings down on his rope, a harp plays a descending glissando.

8. [alluding to inexpensive children's watches with a representation of Mickey Mouse on the face, first marketed in the 1930's] a wristwatch.

1959 *Swinging Syllables: Mickey Mouse*—Watch. **1967** [R. Beck] *Pimp* 104: My "Mickey Mouse" read one-thirty A.M. [**1969** Spetz *Rat Pack Six* 66 [ref. to 1967]: Hartman glanced at his Army-issue Mickey Mouse watch, hung through a button hole in his shirt. The little plastic watch, mass-produced for Army use and disposable should it falter, indicated the time was almost 1900 hours.]

9. a black-and-white police squad car; *(hence)* a police officer.—also used attrib.

1970 Landy *Underground Dict.* 132: *Mickey mouse*...Policeman. **1971** Horan *Blue Messiah* 57: There's a Mickey Mouse outside and cops. **1971** S. Stevens *Way Uptown* 161: Two Mickey Mouse wagons are down the end of the block at Park Avenue, their blood-red eyes turning 'round and 'round. [**1975** Wambaugh *Choirboys* 171: "Mickey Mouse ears" on the roof of the police car, which is what students call the siren lights.] **1987** N.Y.C. housewife, age 53: When I was in high school [1946–50], a police car was called a *Mickey Mouse car.*

10. *Mil.* MICKEY MOUSE EARS.

1986 (quot. at MICKEY MOUSE EARS). **1989** Zumbro & Walker *Jungletracks* 108 [ref. to Vietnam War]: I'm using the Mickey Mouse radio, Jimbo.

11. *Finance.* shares in Walt Disney Corporation.

1987 Lipper *Wall St.* 8: We're looking for...100,000 Mickey Mouse.

Mickey Mouse *adj.* **1.** *Jazz.* (of music) reminiscent of music played as background to animated cartoons; performed in a trite or uninspired manner; (of a band) performing such music or playing in such a manner.

1938 in Tamony *Americanisms* (No. 30) 4: Introduces an original style combining the precise tempos and rhythms of mickey-mouse-moosic with the "anything-can-happen" type of swing and novelty numbers....A strictly "mickey-mouse"...band is still box office. **1943–47** in Hodes & Hansen *Sel. from Gutter* 35: He could have...featured mickey-mouse music or girlie acts. **1948** Manone & Vandervoort *Trumpet* 103: Jack was playing with a Mickey Mouse band then...making ninety dollars per week. **1950–52** Ulanov *Hist. Jazz* 352: *Mickey Mouse band:* an orchestra that plays "corn," usually identifiable by some non-musical noise, such as agonizing trombone glissandos or out-of-tune saxes. **1963** Braly *Shake Him* 46: He was through with mickey-mouse bands. **1981** O'Day & Eells *High Times* 92: Artistic fulfillment with an obscure jazz group was more important to me than singing with a Mickey Mouse band for a lot of bread. **1981** *Harper's* (June) 65: The younger jazz and club-date musicians scorned them as "mickey-mouse" or "ricky-tick" players.

2. *Orig. Journ.* of small size *(obs.); (hence)* inadequate. [The *1936 quot. means 'characteristic of an animated cartoon featuring Mickey Mouse', a standard usage; the 1941–42 quot. carries the related nuance 'depicted in a humorous cartoon form'.]

[*1936 in *OEDS:* You have moved too much away from the ordinary world into a sort of Mickey Mouse universe where things and people don't have to obey the rules of space and time.] **1940** *S.F. News* (Sept. 26) 22 (Tamony Coll.): The big, bad Bears [a football team], outweighing their Mickey Mouse rivals by some 20 pounds per man. [**1941–42** Kennerly & Berry *Eagles Roar* (plate 4): The aircraft wears a Mickey Mouse version of the Eagle [Squadron] insignia.] *a***1949** T. Roscoe *Pig Boats* 106 [ref. to 1942]: The three launches…comprised a tiny task force that won fame as "Uncle Sam's Mickey Mouse Battle Fleet." **1951** in Tamony *Americanisms* (No. 30) 10: Troops Lack Equipment. Woes of "Mickey Mouse Army." **1952** in Tamony *Americanisms* (No. 30) 6: Montana State…has won two or three in the "Mickey Mouse League" while losing eight against decent competition. **1962** S. Smith *Escape from Hell* 72 [ref. to WWII]: Bridget's Mickey Mouse Navy—40-foot liberty launches fitted out as miniature destroyers. **1963** Dwiggins *S.O. Bees* 12 [ref. to WWII]: We've only got a Mickey Mouse rig on this jeep, you know. The hayrake [antenna]. The best we can give you is a beam 30 degrees wide. **1963** in Tamony *Americanisms* (No. 30) 6: At Redwood High (Larkspur), Mickey Mouse means "not up to par." **1976** *L.A. Times* (Oct. 29) IV 6: If I couldn't get a job from January to now, how can I get one during this Mickey Mouse extension of two weeks?

3.a. ridiculous or puerile; inane; silly-looking; poorly planned, designed, etc.; (*also*) trivial; pointless; (*broadly*) worthless; contemptible. Cf. **(1)**, above, and MICKEY MOUSE MONEY, 1.

1957 H. Simmons *Corner Boy* 170: He didn't believe that heaven and hell crap, or that God looked out for what happened on earth and the rest of that Mickey Mouse junk. **1958** Gilbert *Vice Trap* 72: Hell, I'll take one of their Mickey Mouse buses, to Juarez. **1960** Swarthout *Where Boys Are* 63: TPF was very Mickey Mouse. About a hundred girls sat in a lecture section day after day listening to pep talks about the needs of the nation's children. *Ibid.* 237: I could depend upon him not to be Mickey Mouse. *a***1961** Boroff *Campus U.S.A.* 27: The word "Mickey Mouse," UW argot for trivial, is constantly in use. *Ibid.* 31: The sorority stuff…is even more Mickey Mouse than the Union. **1961** *Sports Illustrated* (Apr. 24) 72: But it is definitely "Mickey Mouse," hot roddese for bad taste, to fly a foxtail or use mud flaps. **1965** Bonham *Durango St.* 85: We ain't taking this garbage from no Mickey Mouse social worker! **1965** Eastlake *Castle Keep* 106: I'm willing to take this Mickey Mouse French money. **1966** W. Wilson *LBJ Brigade* 124: It is strictly a Mickey Mouse operation, none of them know what they are doing. **1966** Fariña *Down So Long* 161: It's not all as Mickey Mouse as you might think. **1966** E. Shepard *Doom Pussy* 128: These Mickey-Mouse double-breasted bloomers with the auxiliary pockets. **1966** in Tamony *Americanisms* (No. 30) 6: She had a "nine to five Mickey Mouse job" before becoming a model. **1967** Yablonsky *Hippie Trip* 280: It is infinitely multiplied over the little mickey-mouse high that I had in 1957. **1967** Spradley *Owe Yourself a Drunk* 13: Arrogance and Mickey Mouse vindictiveness irritates the hell out of me. **1972** Claerbaut *Black Jargon* 72: *Mickey Mouse*…adj. unimportant. **1973** *Seattle Times* (Mar. 11) A2: Marijuana is a "Mickey Mouse" problem, just as acceptable among young people as drinking is for veterans' groups or service clubs. **1979** in Terkel *Amer. Dreams* 189: We got a Mickey Mouse educational system that doesn't teach us…how the government works. **1983** Stapleton *30 Yrs.* 59: You almost fooled us with that mickey mouse suit you got on. **1984** *All Things Considered* (Nat. Pub. Radio) (June 18): The President remarked that the Soviets can "keep their mickey-mouse system if they want to." **1986** Zumbro *Tank Sgt.* 127: Another problem…that Mickey Mouse M16 rifle. **1988** Terkel *Great Divide* 32: Years ago, I stopped using the Mickey Mouse eighth-grade books. **1990** *CBS This Morning* (CBS-TV) (Feb. 14): Banning fur sales was a Mickey Mouse issue to some. **1993** *N.Y. Times* (July 22) B7: The state police don't have time to come here for Mickey-Mouse stuff. **1995** Headline News network (July 1): A Mickey Mouse idea.

b. *Specif.,* esp. *Mil.* characterized by or typifying petty discipline or rigid enforcement of rules or regulations; nitpicking; CHICKENSHIT, 1.c.

1961 Terry *Old Liberty* 41: Every Monday night was the Mickey Mouse time, when the fraternity had its meetings.…We all had to wear the gray suits and Liberty ties. **1965** Pruden *Vietnam: The War* 157: Epaulets, oversize pockets.…Very Mickey Mouse. **1973** *Everett* (Wash.) *Herald* (July 7) 6A: In the plaintiffs' eyes regulation Marine

haircuts are "Mickey Mouse." And the all-volunteer military services promised to do away with "Mickey Mouse" regulations. **1977** *U.S. News & W.R.* (June 20) 49: The end has come to "Mickey Mouse" regulations.…OSHA will focus on serious health hazards instead of nitpicking safety rules. **1977** *Dallas Times Herald* (June 26) I 1: Mickey Mouse rules that burdened employers without really protecting workers. **1992** Strawberry & Rust *Darryl* 139: That sounds a little Mickey Mouse, but when you're a rookie even Mickey Mouse is better than the silence of doubt. **1993** Univ. Tenn. professor, age 63: In 1954–56 I was stationed at the Walter Reed Army Institute for Research in Washington, D.C. And even though we were all scientists who constantly had to stand inspection for the commanding officer, who was interested mainly in whether we had been sure to polish our shoes with Kiwi tan polish. We used to call these inspections "Mickey Mouse inspections."

4. *Stu.* (of an assignment or course of study) vapid or uninteresting; (*also*) easily passed; (of an undertaking) easy.

1958 J. Davis *College Vocab.* 13: *Mickey mouse major*—Education major. **1958** *AS* XXXIII 226: At Michigan State…a "Mickey Mouse course" means a *snap* course. **1959** in Tamony *Americanisms* (No. 30) 8: Any assigned dull "busy" work that is routine and unintellectual is Mickey Mouse [at Univ. of Illinois–Champaign-Urbana]. **1962** in *AS* (Oct. 1963) 176: An assignment which is regarded as foolish and a waste of time is a *Mickey Mouse.* **1963** *Time* (Sept. 27) 55: Any course, including "Mickey Mouse" guts like driver education. **1964** *Nat. Observer* (Jan. 13) 11: Teacher Training Sharply Attacked…"Mickey Mouse" Courses, Stressing Methodology, Draw Critics' Attention. **1969** Rapoport & Kirshbaum *Is the Library Burning?* 73: The athletes…are encouraged to take specially-tailored mickey-mouse courses so as not to jeopardize their athletic standing. **1977** *N.Y. Times* (July 11) 25: A bright senior told me they were "Mickey Mouse" exams that cheated really good students. **1980** Fleischer & Gore *Fame* 64: This is no Mickey Mouse school…You're not getting off easy. **1981** Univ. Tenn. student: Algebra 1540 is called *Mickey Mouse Math.* **1983** *Time* (May 23) 54: Choose a major in one of the sciences and fill out the rest of the schedule with "Mickey Mouse" subjects. **1990** G.R. Clark *Wds. of Viet. War* 327: *Mickey Mouse Mission*…An easy or nonhazardous mission or task. **1991** *Atlantic* (Nov.) 74: Too much of their time in college and graduate school taking Mickey Mouse courses on how to construct a lesson plan. **1994** *Newsweek* (Oct. 24) 61: We threw out the Mickey Mouse curriculum and introduced…Regents-level courses.

5. Esp. *Business & Finance.* (of practices and arrangements) deceptive or of doubtful propriety; bogus.

1963 in Tamony *Americanisms* (No. 30) 6: Even before the California Young Republicans…angry charges of "stacked delegations," "Mickey Mouse politics," "power grabs" and "backroom deals" were rattling around. **1964** in Tamony *Americanisms* (No. 30) 8: "Mickey Mouse" loans [are loans] influenced by the establishment of fictitiously high selling prices, double escrows, over-appraisals, and other deceitful stunts intended to mislead all lenders. **1962–68** B. Jackson *In the Life* 35: It was a Chevy.…We had mickeymouse papers on it. They were false but…they appeared good. **1971** in Tamony *Americanisms* (No. 30) 8: Mickey Mouse Loan Described. **1973** *Business Week* (Apr. 21) 68: Leaving the insurance investigators to wend their way through a maze of Mickey Mouse accounting methods. **1974** *Pop. Science* (Apr.) 58: It's the only thing I know that would truly help you, short of some Mickey Mouse deal. **1974** *Business Week* (Nov. 30) 66: In one of its rare ventures into "Mickey Mouse" financing, the company issued 31.3-million warrants.…But…the warrants may be worthless when they expire. **1975** *L.A. Times* (Nov. 2) I 4: Walker accused Daley of "fiscal irresponsibility," "Mickey-Mouse financing" and "slippery budget procedures." **1981** *Santa Barbara News-Press* (May 10) F1: There is often a thin line between what is termed "a creatively structured transaction" and a gimmicky or mickey mouse transaction. **1981** in *California Business* (Jan. 1982) 15: Each deal "is a Mickey Mouse transaction…there are few rules and hardly any criteria."

Mickey Mouse *v.* to fudge; FINAGLE; (*also*) to fool around; behave foolishly.—often constr. with *around* or with dummy-obj. *it.*

1968 *Everett* (Wash.) *Herald* (Oct. 28) 10A: The whole project is being so Mickey-Moused back into production that it will be hard to match what went before. **1969** Cagle *Naval Av. Guide* 396: *Mickey Mouse.* To fly or perform aimlessly, haphazardly, or foolishly. **1972** in Tamony *Americanisms* (Nov. 30) 11: We'll show you how to Mickey

Mouse the front end of the deal....We'll show you how to skirt the loopholes from beginning to end—nothing really crooked—just a little Mickey-Mousing. **1973** *Pop. Science* (Nov.) 64: A smarter-than-average mechanic Mickey-Mouses it. **1973** in *DAS* (ed. 2): We can't Mickey Mouse around while faced with technological challenges from other countries. **1983** *Santa Barbara News-Press* (Apr. 23) B10: The Army had been "Mickey-Mousing around for nine years." **1984** *Calif. Business* (Sept.) 176: The legitimate ones who have solid track records and don't Mickey Mouse around...won't be hurt. **1989** *World News Saturday* (ABC-TV) (Aug. 5): The voters want to know where you stand—and no Mickey-Mousin' around about it. **1992** *NewsHour* (CNN-TV) (Feb. 28): When Elizabeth Taylor throws a party, she doesn't Mickey Mouse around.

Mickey Mouse boots *n.pl.* [because fancied to resemble the big shoes worn by Walt Disney's Mickey Mouse] Esp. *Army & USMC.* heavily insulated cold-weather boots.

1952 in Tamony *Americanisms* (No. 30) 10: "Mickey Mouse" Boots for All GIs. **1973** N.Y.U. student: When I was in the Army in '60–'63, we had thermal boots we called *Mickey Mouse boots.* They were good and warm, too. **1980** Millett *Semper Fidelis* 512 [ref. to Korean War]: The "Mickey Mouse" boots prevented frostbite. **1982** Cox & Frazier *Buck* 34: He wished he dared remove his snow-packed Mickey-Mouse boots. **1984–88** in Berry *Where Ya Been?* 223: In March [1952]...they issued...the shoepacs. We used to call them the Mickey Mouse boots. **1988** von Hassell & Crossley *Warriors* 130: The boots are white, made of heavy insulated rubber, and are commonly referred to as "Mickey Mouse boots." Rated to –65 degrees, they weigh five pounds each. **1990** Katcher *Amer. Soldier* 162: Known as "Mickey Mouse" or "VB" (vapor-barrier) boots, they are extremely warm. **1995** *Morning News* (CNN-TV) (Dec. 14): We call these "Mickey Mouse boots" simply because of the shape and design. They're very big.

Mickey Mouse cop *n.* a private security guard; RENT-A-COP.
1976 Price *Bloodbrothers* 274: Fucking spic Mickey Mouse cop.

Mickey Mouse ears *n.pl.* [because fancied to resemble the black, "mouse"-eared novelty caps worn by "The Mouseketeers," performers on *Walt Disney's Mickey Mouse Club,* a children's daily variety show (premiered 1956); the caps are also sold commercially]

Mil. a headset of any sort, esp. a noise-suppressing helmet worn by aircraft handlers or gun crews; MICKEY MOUSE HAT. Also vars.

1966 Adler *Vietnam Letters* 89: The sailors you see standing around are helping to launch the planes. They have on what is called "head sets," which we sailors call "Mickey Mouse" ears. **1984** Trotti *Phantom* 164: The sound becomes unbearable, even when you wear both ear plugs and Mickey Mouse (sound suppressor) ears. **1985** Heywood *Taxi Dancer* 264: The crew chief...[adjusted] his Mickey Mouse ears to reduce the assault on his hearing. **1986** Former SP4, U.S. Army, age 35 [ref. to 1972–76]: Gun crews wear these protective headsets to protect their hearing from the blasts of heavy guns. They were called *Mickey Mouse ears, Mickeys,* or *Mickey Mouses.* Radio headphones were sometimes called those things too. **1987** Nichols & Tillman *Yankee Sta.* 111: Still wearing the "Mickey Mouse" ear protectors and plastic goggles. **1988** Poyer *The Med* 210: The armorer...was hovering behind the firing line with his Mickey Mouse ears bulky atop a shaven head. *a*1989 R. Herman, Jr. *Warbirds* 185: A set of Mickey Mouse ear protectors. **1991** K. Douglass *Viper Strike* 7: The bulbous radio headgear known as Mickey Mouse ears. **1991** Linnekin *80 Knots* 182: Hence the "Mickey Mouse" ear protectors worn by today's carrier flight crews.

Mickey Mouse hat *n. Navy.* headgear worn to protect the ears from high noise levels on a carrier deck. Also **Mickey Mouse helmet.** Cf. MICKEY MOUSE EARS.

1965 *Life* (July 30) 29: Wearing the flopeared "Mickey Mouse" hats of aircraft carrier launch crewmen. **1965** F. Harvey *Hudasky's Raiders* 4: The...Mickey Mouse sound-suppressor helmets. **1969** Cagle *Naval Av. Guide* 396: *Mickey Mouse Hat.* A helmet worn by personnel on the flight deck of a carrier to reduce the high noise level. New models being tested also have built-in radios. **1972–79** T. Wolfe *Right Stuff* 21: Men...with black Mickey Mouse helmets over their ears skittered about on the [flight deck].

Mickey Mouse money *n.* **1.** *Mil.* in *Philippines.* paper curren-

cy printed by the Japanese government of occupation. Now *hist.*

1945 *Amer. N & Q* (May) 23: *Mickey Mouse Money:* Filipinos' nickname for Japanese paper occupation currency (dispatch of May 12, 1945, Manila). **1945** *Time* (July 16) 73: Inflation. Manila Market. The Mickey Mouse Era....The Japs flooded the Islands with their "Mickey Mouse" paper money. **1963** Keats *They Fought Alone* 72 [ref. to 1942]: The Chinese would not accept the new Japanese pesos, which they called Mickey Mouse money. **1967** in Tamony *Americanisms* (No. 30) 8: A Filipino organization has failed in its bid to get the United States to redeem with genuine currency millions of dollars worth of counterfeit [Japanese] "mickey mouse" money the U.S. issued in the Philippines in World War II.

2. *Mil.* U.S. military payment certificates; scrip. Now *hist.* [First issued in September 1946 and discontinued in March 1973 (Elting et al., *Dictionary of Soldier Talk,* p. 199).]

1952 in Russ *Last Parallel* 37: Our US currency has been substituted by a military script referred to as Mickey Mouse money. **1961** Bosworth *Crows* 88: No breeze came through it to flutter the thin "Mickey Mouse money," as it was irreverently described. **1966** J. Lewis *Tell It to the Marines* 80: First, we'll go over t' the Army Finance Office and change some Mickey Mouse money into *yen.*

Mickey Mouse movie see MICKEY MOUSE, *n.,* 4.

mid *n. Navy.* a midshipman. Cf. 1900, *1916 quots. at MIDDY, 1.

1797 in *OED:* He put on the uniform of a mid. *1812 in *F & H* IV 306: I have written to Bedford to learn what mids of the Victory fell in that action. **1821** Stewart *Man-of-War's Man* I 12: I was Mid. with him in the Teneraire. *1831 B. Hall *Voyages* I 9 [ref. to *ca*1805]: The mids had little real business to attend to. **1834** *Mil. & Naval Mag. of U.S.* (Mar.) 62: The steerage...was pronounced by one of my brother Mids..."a d—d elegant one." **1863** in M. Turner *Navy Gray* 84: [I tried to] silence the Mids of their swearing proclivities. **1875** Sheppard *Love Afloat* 93: I see the other mids crowdin' round. **1882** Miller & Harlow *9'-51"* 20: The Mid. that first he chose, he thin then thinner grows. **1984** U.S. Naval Acad. midshipman, in RH files: "Mid" is much preferred to the odious "middy" (which is in your dictionary) or "middie" used mostly by the press and people unfamiliar with the academy. **1988** Poyer *The Med* 36: The other girls...thought the "mids" handsome. **1994** U.S. Naval Acad. graduate, in *Newsweek* (July 4) 14: The mids who stole the exam and sold it should have been expelled.

middle *n.* ¶ In phrase: **into the middle of next week** (used as an intensifying phrase after verbs of physical violence, esp. *knock*). Also vars.

*1821 in *OED:* They knocked me into the middle of next week—besides tipping me this here black eye. **1832** *Spirit of Times* (Feb. 18) 1: I had ya hea I'd come up da and knock boff ya up into next forf o' July, ya young scoundrel. **1837** *Every Body's Album* II 124: I thought you was trying to go clean through the mud into the middle of next week. *1837 Marryat *Diary* 57: I've a great mind to knock you into *the middle of next week, or month.* **1848** in *AS* (10) (1935) 42: *Knock you into the middle of next week, or month.* To hit one severely. [Nantucket]. **1851** Burke *Polly Peablossom's Wedding* 147: Arch would fetch him er side-swipe on the head, and knock him into the middle o' next week! **1936** Kingsley *Dead End* 695: I'll knock 'im intuh da middle a next week! **1967** Hersey *Motel* 39: You try to talk to those people...and they'll knock you into the middle of next year. **1987** Rugoff & Gottlieb *Mannequin* (film): I'm gonna knock you into the middle of next week!

middlebrow *n.* a person of conventional tastes; a moderately cultivated person. Also as *adj.* Cf. HIGHBROW; LOWBROW.

*1925 in *OED2:* A new type, the "middlebrow." It consists of people who are hoping that some day they will get used to the stuff they ought to like. *1928 in *OED2:* The standard of "middle-brow" music and plays is always rather low. **1934** in *OED2:* Hindemith is the journalist of modern music, the supreme middlebrow of our times. **1949** *N.Y. Times* (Dec. 25) VII 8: I like the "middlebrow." I like the "lowbrow." I have always despised the literary snob. **1951** *New Yorker* (Jan. 27) 76: "National Velvet," an agreeable middle-brow comedy. **1952** *Time* (Apr. 21) 32: A middlebrow beer parlor on the Seine's Left Bank. **1953** *N.Y. Times* (Jan. 18) VII 3: Brief exercises in amateur sociology...without sweat and tears addressed to the Middle Brow. **1959** *Harper's* (Feb.) 117: Griffith is a discontented middle-brow with an unusual insight into his own dissatisfaction. **1967** *Harper's* (Aug.) 18: They consider it smarter to be hip than highbrow, just as a great many others...think it is smarter to be mod than middlebrow. *1972 in *OED2:* Geoffrey Ashe, writer of distinguished middle-brow books on the problems of the historical Arthur. **1990** *New Republic* (Oct. 8) 7: The exercises of our culture (not least the safe ones that the middle-brows love, *Our Town* in Fresno, "Hungarian Rhapsodies" in Syracuse, the Helga paintings in Omaha).

middle leg *n.* the penis.—usu. considered vulgar.
   *a1890–96 *F & H* IV 307: *Middle-finger* (or *Leg*)...The *penis*. *1914–22 Joyce *Ulysses* 450: How's your middle leg? **1938** "Justinian" *Amer. Sexualis* 29: *Middle Leg.* n. The penis. **1971** Rhinehart *Dice Man* 80: And she laughed coldly at my...still unbending middle leg. *1990 T. Thorne *Dict. Contemp. Slang: Middle leg*...the penis.

middle name *n.* something that one is renowned for or characterized by. Now *colloq.*
   1905 T.A. Dorgan, in Zwilling *TAD Lexicon* 57: (Corbett Again Sings Sad Good-Bye To Ring)...For retiring you're—well, that's your middle name. **1920** G. Ade *Hand-Made Fables* 92: I take it that Mixer is your middle name. **1926** A. Christie, in *OED2:* "Modesty is certainly not his middle name." "I wish you wouldn't be so horribly American, James." *a1961 in *WNID3:* Trouble is our middle name. **1989** *N.Y. Times Book Rev.* (Sept. 24) 28: Subtlety is not Arthur T. Vanderbilt 2d's middle name. **1994** *Nation* (Mar. 28) 423: We have, in American English, a jocular way of indicating a particular degree of identification with something—baseball, say—by boasting that "baseball is my middle name."

middle-piece *n.* **1.** the stomach or belly.
   [*1675 in *F & H* IV 307: I'll lodge a cudgel in your middle-storey.] **1859** Matsell *Vocab.* 54: *Middle-Piece.* The stomach. *a1890–96 *F & H* IV 307: *Middle-piece*...(common).—The stomach.
   2. a vest.
   1926 Norwood *Other Side of Circus* 272: A vest—a middle-piece.

middy *n. Navy.* **1.** a midshipman. Now *colloq.* Cf. MID.
   *1818 in *OEDS:* A middy rudely said, He'd sell them [*sc.,* prisoners] for five pounds a head. *1821 *Real Life in Ireland* 172: The middy...deems himself unworthy of death's notice. **1832** Wines *2½ Yrs.* I 25 [ref. to 1829]: The *middies* are not allowed to have trunks on board. **1841** in R.B. Hayes *Diary* I 75: The young "middies" laughed with scorn. **1841** [Mercier] *Man-of-War* 98: This is the *middies'* school. **1849** Melville *White Jacket* 19 [ref. to 1843]: The *middies* were busy raising loans to liquidate the demands of their laundress. **1855** Wise *Tales* 48: All them Yankee middies. **1863** in *Civil War Times Illus.* (Nov. 1974) 27: [Ran] into a fellow Middy & had a pleasant walk. *a1899 B.F. Sands *Reefer* 19: But Jim...had his favorites among the middies. **1900** Benjamin *Naval Acad.* 363: The modern cadet resents being termed a "middy." *1916 in Partridge *DSUE* (ed. 7) 1274: To call a present-day midshipman a "middy" to his face would make him squirm.
   2. a sailor's blouse, or a garment of similar design.
   *1911 in *OEDS:* [Ad:] Child's Middy Dress, in white duck. Square neck and short sleeves. **1943** P. Harkins *Coast Guard* 198: His middies and skivvies [came] back white and smooth for two dollars a month.

midnight *n.* **1.** *Craps.* the point 12.
   1919 Piesbergen *Overseas with an Aero Squadron* 56: Midnight! **1927** Sandburg *Good Morning, America* 14: Fate's crapshooters fading each other, big Dick or snake/eyes, midnights, and deuces [etc.]. **1948** A. Murphy *Hell & Back* 22: Snuffy rolls a twelve. "Hot damn. Midnight. A mighty hard point but I think I can make it."
   2. *Restaurant.* black coffee.
   1936 *AS* (Feb.) 44: [Soda fountain, N.Y.C.:] *Midnight.* Cup of coffee without cream. **1942** *ATS* 764: Midnight, one in the dark, powder, tar, *black coffee.* **1954–60** *DAS:* Midnight...A cup of black coffee.

midnight *adj.* (of persons) racially black.—now used contemptuously.—usu. considered offensive.
   1864 "E. Kirke" *Down in Tenn.* 112: Nigger kentries, Mr. Midnight. **1916** T.A. Dorgan, in Zwilling *TAD Lexicon* 117: [Caption of panel showing two black women:] Midnight Blondes. **1985** Univ. Tenn. student theme: They were called "spades," "jungle bunnies," "midnight mollies,"..."coons" and "darkies."

midnight overdrive *n. Trucking.* MEXICAN OVERDRIVE.
   1976 Lieberman & Rhodes *CB* 132: *Midnight Overdrive*—Same as "Mexican Overdrive."

midnight requisition *n. Mil.* an unauthorized taking of supplies by night, esp. by theft or trickery; thievery. *Joc.* Also as *v.*
   1946 S. Wilson *Voyage to Somewhere* 112 [ref. to WWII]: "A mid-

night requisition!" said Mr. Stuart. "By God, I'll have to do that myself!" **1960** Caidin *Black Thurs.* 73 [ref. to WWII]: And of course there was always the shortage of coal, and the "midnight requisitioning" by officers and enlisted men. **1961** L.G. Richards *TAC* 31: The ingenuity of the GI at "midnight requisitioning." **1982** T.C. Mason *Battleship Sailor* 29: At thirty-six dollars a month for a seaman second class, some found "midnight requisition" an irresistible temptation. **1983** *L.A. Times* (Jan. 3) I 2: "Midnight requisitioners"...have raised fruit thefts to "monumental" proportions. **1985** Roskey *Muffled Shots* 82: A group of drunken "bachelors" would make a "midnight requisition" of a truck. **1986** R. Zumbro *Tank Sgt.* 98: The voltage regulators, hydraulics, and other necessities were distributed long before dawn. This was the "midnight requisition" with a vengeance. **1983–88** J.T. McLeod *Crew Chief* 237: Something like a "midnight requisition."

midnight small stores *n.pl. Navy.* MIDNIGHT REQUISITION. [The verbal def. in 1944 quot. is presumably an error.]
   1944 Kendall *Service Slang* 26: *Midnight small stores.*...to borrow another's clothes from the line under cover of darkness. **1942–47** in *ATS* (Supp.) 37: *Midnight small stores,* articles stolen from the clothesline at night. **1952** Cope & Dyer *Petty Officer's Guide* 447: *Midnight Small Stores:* Clothing that is robbed off the clothesline or drying racks in the hours of darkness. **1969** Bosworth *Love Affair* 95 [ref. to ca1925]: If a petty officer said, "Smitty, lay down to the sail locker"...pilfer it if it were not [attended]. That sort of pilfering, in the battleships days, was called "midnight small stores." [**1980** Eble *Campus Slang* 5: *Midnight Supply (Company)* and *five-finger discount* are similar in meaning, "pilfering, stealing": "Where did you get that bike, man, *Midnight Supply?*"]

mid-rats *n.pl. Navy & USMC.* food available to sailors or marines before and after a middle watch (midnight to 4 A.M.).
   1973 Huggett *Body Count* 154: Oh, no, sir, those are the mid-rats for the officers on the night watch in the command bunker. **1983** Elting, Cragg & Deal *Dict. Soldier Talk* 363: *Midrats* (Modern; Navy)...Leftovers. Food such as soup, crackers, sandwiches, served to sailors before and after mid-watch. **1988** Poyer *The Med* 257: I'll rip his yellow guts out and eat them for midrats. *a1990 Westcott *Half a Klick* 95: Still time ta grab some mid-rats over to the messhall.

midshipman's nuts *n.pl. Naut.* pieces of broken hardtack.
   *1828 in *OEDS:* "You shall have a fistful of midshipman's nuts to crack for your supper."...He gave me some broken biscuits. **1849** Melville *White Jacket* 94 [ref. to 1843]: The American sailors mess on the deck, and peck up their broken biscuit, or *midshipmen's nuts,* like fowls in a barnyard. *a1890–96 *F & H* IV 307: *Midshipman's-nuts*...Broken biscuit, eaten by way of dessert.

midships *n. Naut.* the belly.
   1871 Banka *Prison Life* 149: Strikes him mid-ships, and over they go. **1936** Mackenzie *Living Rough* 56: Petersen then sank one into his midships.

mifky-pifky *n.* [orig. unkn.; cf. earlier MOOEY-MOOEY] foolishness or mischief, esp. of a romantic or sexual nature; sexual activity; HANKY-PANKY. *Joc.* Also **moofky-poofky** and other vars.
   1985 *Chicago Trib.* (Nov. 18) (Nexis): It is as though many in the [anti-abortion] movement are subconsciously saying, "There's all this mifky-pifky going on, but not for me, and I'm envious." **1993** *Chicago Trib.* (Dec. 28) I 13: Mifky-pifky in the bushes. *Ibid.:* Some of us...still have...enough energy for occasional mifky-pifky. *Ibid.:* Bill Clinton's alleged mifky-pifky. **1994** *Wash. Post* (May 29) F1: Your Aunt Evelyn getting drunk as a rat and accusing your Uncle Phil of "making moofky-poofky with the coat check girl at Sardi's two days after we were married." **1996** *Village Voice* (N.Y.C.) (Sept. 17) 47: The family's baby slang ("coral seas" for lips; "moofty-poofty" for fellatio). *Ibid.* 48: Two of the characters are self-employed as squeaky-clean hustlers (alas, no moofty-poofty to divert the reader). **1997** N.Y. Woman; age 60: (coll. J. Sheidlower): [To a couple necking in a hallway:] Hey! What's all this schmoofky-foofky going on here?

MiG Alley *n. Mil. Av.* a region of northwestern Korea generally between the Ch'ongch'on River and the Yalu, the site of intense aerial combat during the Korean War. Now *hist.*
   1951 in Loosbrock & Skinner *Wild Blue* 448: We fight a private little war up in MIG Alley. **1952** *N.Y. Times* (Apr. 13) I 2: An enemy attempt to dominate "Mig Alley." **1955** Blair *Beyond Courage* 13: The planes were to take off and proceed toward the Yalu River, the northern extremity of MIG alley. **1955** R.L. Scott *Look of Eagle* 25: What...could you...have done with a Sabre jet at better than Mach

One in MIG Alley? **1960** *History of Chaplain Corps USN* VI 118: The area from the Yalu River south to the North Korean capital at P'yongyang … was dubbed "MIG Alley" by UN aviators. **1963** E.M. Miller *Exile* 107: I flew MIG Alley—I was there! **1963** Fehrenbach *This Kind of War* 594: The Valley of the Yalu—the famous MIG Alley. **1969** *Playboy* (Mar.) 78: He had fought in the Korean War and had somehow survived the ravages of MIG Alley with credit and skill. **1980** *Air Classics: Air War Over Korea* 6: The area known as MiG Alley, stretching over 70 miles between Sinuiju and Sinanju along the Antung valley.

miggles *n.* [app. alt. of MUGGLES] *Narc.* marijuana. Also **miggle** a marijuana cigarette.

    1956 E. Hunter *Second Ending* 279: Mootah, muggles, miggles,…tea, pot, weed.…It's all marijuana. **1954–60** *DAS: Miggle*…A marijuana cigarette.

mighty mezz see s.v. MEZZ.

Mighty Mo *n. Navy.* the battleship U.S.S. *Missouri.* Cf. BIG Mo, Mo.

    1955 R.L. Scott *Look of Eagle* 84 [ref. to 1945]: They had circled the Mighty Mo in Tokyo Bay, while General MacArthur accepted the formal surrender of Japan. **1962** Morison *Naval Ops. in WWII* XIV 45 [ref. to 1945]: "Mighty Mo," the battleship *Missouri*, drew her first blood of the war. **1964** Hunt *Ship with Flat Tire* 7: Not the "Big E" or the "Mighty Mo." **1986** CNN news (CNN-TV) (May 6): The ship called the Mighty Mo is on her way to rejoin the United States Navy. **1984–88** in Berry *Where Ya Been?* 119 [ref. to 1950]: There she was, the USS *Missouri*, the Mighty Mo, my former ship. **1991** *CBS This Morning* (CBS-TV) (Dec. 6): The *Mighty Mo*…is the last battleship built by the United States. **1992** *DayWatch* (CNN-TV) (Mar. 31): *Mighty Mo* had helped take Iwo Jima.

mighty mouth *n.* [sugg. by *Mighty Mouse*, cartoon character] a person who boasts or talks excessively.—often used as a nickname.

    1974 Millard *Thunderbolt* 82: So what did you do about it, Mighty Mouth? **1987** Spot ad (WOR-TV): Batten down the hatches! It's Mighty Mouth—Morton Downey, Jr.

migrate *v.* to depart, esp. hurriedly.

    1871 in *Mo. Hist. Review* XXXVII (1942) 259: Colonel Jeffers…migrated, vamosed, cut stick, evaporated, left.

Mike *n.* an Irishman; MICK[1], 1.a.

    1891 Maitland *Slang Dict.* 176: Mike, a generic term for an Irish laborer. *a**1890–96** F & H IV 309: *Mike*…(common).…An Irishman. **1939** Howsley *Argot* 33: *Mike*—an Irishman. **1962, 1968** in *DARE*.

¶ In phrases:

¶ **for the love of Mike** see s.v. LOVE, *n.*

¶ **holy Mike** (used as a mild oath to express surprise, disappointment, etc.). Also **mother of Mike.**

    1910 in O. Johnson *Lawrenceville* 307: Holy Mike! **1915** Gilman *Herland* 17: Mother of Mike, boys—what gorgeous girls!

mike[1] *n.* [by clipping] **1.** a microphone. Now *S.E.* Also **mic.** [In transcription of rap music, usu. written *mic.*]

    1927 in *OEDS*: I think it is more that he plays too loudly than that he is too near the "mike." **1929** in Gelman *Photoplay* 124: This is a story of Terrible Mike, the capricious genie of Hollywood. *Ibid.* 126: Some…have so far survived the terror of the mike. **1935** T. Husing *Ten Years Before the Mike* [book title]. **1939** J. O'Hara *Pal Joey* 28, in *DAS:* I brought her up to the mike. **1950** *Sat. Eve. Post* (Nov. 25) 110: Also available are desk mikes, lapel mikes, and chest mikes, in various sizes. **1993** "Snoop Doggy Dogg" *Every Single Day* (rap song): Snoop be rockin' on the mic. **1993** "Wu-Tang Klan" *Method Man* (rap song): Zoom, I hit the mic like boom.

    2. a microscope.

    1933 (cited in Partridge *DSUE* 520). **1942** *ATS* 76: *Mike*, a microscope. **1949** in F. Brown *Honeymoon* 75: I've…had hairs under the mike and studied musculature. **1950** F. Brown *Space* 36: A blink-microscope.…He…looked into the blink-mike again. **1950** *N.Y. Times* (Sept. 17) I 52: Ultra-thin slices of plant and animal tissue…are viewed under the powerful "mike." **1954–60** *DAS: Mike*…A microscope.

    3. *R.R.* a Mikado locomotive.

    1942 in *ATS* 728: *Mike*, mudscow, a mikado-type locomotive. **1945** *New Yorker* (Apr. 7) 45: All railroaders call MacArthur locomotives "Mikes," because the type was originally designed for Hirohito's

grandfather and was called the Mikado. Hence "Mick," hence "Mike." **1954–60** *DAS: Mike*…A Mikado engine.

    4. *Narc.* a microgram, esp. of LSD; a microdot of LSD.

    1967 *Sat. Eve. Post* (Sept. 23) 88: A 17-year-old street dealer who…feeds her 3,000 mikes. **1967–68** von Hoffman *Parents Warned Us* 26: How many mikes? **1970** Landy *Underground Dict.* 132: *Mike*…Microgram. **1973** in *DAS* (ed. 3): I feel like I've been up on 300 mikes of acid. **1979** *New West* (Aug. 13) 17: It was 1,000 mikes, which is more than anyone should ever take. **1994** *Details* (July) 71: Here's a guy tripping on twenty-five mics of red dot from L.A.

mike[2] *n.* [fr. mil. communications alphabet *Mike* 'M'] *Mil.*

    1. a minute.

    1986 Dye & Stone *Platoon* 58 [ref. to Vietnam War]: Chopper'll be here in about two-zero mikes. **1968–90** Linderer *Eyes of Eagle* 37: A pair of gunships would be heading out in zero-five mikes. **1991** M. Dunn *Sidewinder* 334: *Mikes*—Minutes. **1995** *Space: Above & Beyond* (Fox-TV): That we do in thirty mikes. So suit up.

    2. a meter. See also MIKE-MIKE.

    1968–90 Linderer *Eyes of Eagle* 191: The…LZ was three-five-zero-zero mikes away.

Mike boat *n.* [mil. communications alphabet *Mike* 'M' (for LCM 'Landing craft, medium') + *boat*] *Navy.* (see quots.).

    1988 von Hassell & Crossley *Warriors* 63: Grunts…on a "Mike boat," Rio Chagres, Panama. *Ibid.* 112: Mike-boats, small landing craft that can carry about 20 Marines at a time. **1990** G.R. Clark *Words of Viet. War* 276: *LCM-8 (Mike Boat)* Standard landing craft used in Vietnam…73 feet long, 21 feet wide,…max speed…9 knots. **1991** Marcinko & Weisberg *Rogue Warrior* 40: LCMs, or 45-foot Landing Craft/Mediums—Mike boats.

Mike Finn var. MICHAEL FINN.

Mike force *n.* [mil. communications alphabet *Mike* 'M' for Mobile Strike *Force*] *Mil.* (see quot.).

    1969 *U.S. News & W.R.* (Sept. 1) 29: We also have Mike forces—Mobile Strike Forces. They are [indigenous] mercenaries who go anywhere.

Mike Juliet *n.* [mil. communications alphabet *Mike* 'M' + *Juliet* 'J' for MARY JANE or M.J.] *Mil.* marijuana.

    1974–77 Heinemann *Close Quarters* 26: Why, smoke is M.J. Mike Juliet. Ya know—grass. **1990** G.R. Clark *Words of Viet. War* 322: *Mike-Juliet*…Marijuana.

mike-mike *n. Mil.* millimeter; (*hence*) a weapon whose caliber is measured in millimeters.

    1969 *Esquire* (Oct.) 118: The C-47…carried 20 and .762 mm guns in their doors, Mike-Mikes that could fire out three hundred rounds per second, Gatling style. **1972** Beckham *Runner Mack* 135: We got plenty of gunbirds with mucho mike-mike. **1980** M. Baker *Nam* 89: We called in the 80 Mike-Mikes—mortars. **1983** Ehrhart *VN-Perkasie* 364: I got a buddy in the 60-mike-mike platoon. **1988** Clodfelter *Mad Minutes* 183: Two exploded 82 "Mike-Mike" (millimeter) mortar rounds. **1989** Joss *Strike* 59: Mark 82 leftovers, 20 Mike Mike casings. **1990** Yarborough *Da Nang Diary* 53: Everybody's got four Mark-117s and twenty mike-mike.

mikeside *adv.* [MIKE[1], 1 + *-side* (abstracted fr. top*side*)] *Radio & TV.* (of a person) occupying a position at a broadcast microphone.

    1977 *Newsweek* (Mar. 14) (Nexis): For these instances, he had his issues man, Stu Eizenstadt, at mike-side and point men standing by at every agency of government. **1982** *N.Y. Times* (June 13) (Nexis): And now it's sports time on the Bob and Ray show. This is Biff Burns emanating from mikeside here in the Biff Burns Sports Room. **1990** *Simpsons* (Fox-TV): This is Dan Howard mikeside. **1995** Univ. Alaska, Anchorage, sports dept. press release (Oct. 16): Friday's game will be broadcast live by KBYR Radio (700 AM) with Tom Miller and Ted Emery mikeside.

mil var. MILL[2], 1, *n.*

mile *n.* ¶ In phrase: **look like forty miles of bad road** (of the face or skin) to look ugly or rough.

    1968 *Mike Douglas Show* (WCBS-TV): He always told me that my face looked like forty miles of bad Irish country road! **1969** Spetz *Rat Pack Six* 162: Yeah, Sarge. His chest looks like forty miles of bad road.

mileage *n.* **1.** use; profit; advantage. Now *colloq.* or *S.E.*

1955 *Encyc. Brit. Book of Year.* **1960** *Harper's* (July) 42: Governor Rockefeller…foresaw the political mileage in health legislation last fall. **1962** *N.Y. Times* (Nov. 4) III 12F: The major problem was to get maximum mileage from a rather limited budget. **1972** *Business Week* (Aug. 19) 18: His company might get extra mileage from future spin-offs of these new businesses. **1973** *U.S. News & W.R.* (Apr. 2) 44: If you stick to one basic color theme you'll find that "mixing and matching" gets you a lot of mileage out of a relatively small amount of clothes. **1981** *L.A. Times* (Mar. 19) I 23: Legislative oversight is not a very sexy subject.…It does not get you the mileage of a rape bill. *a***1986** J. Heller, in *NDAS* 161: All of us down here can start getting mileage out of that one right away. **1986** *NDAS: Mileage*…Advantage; profit.

2. (of a person) evident signs of age from long, active experience.

    1961 L.E. Young *Virgin Fleet* 20: I show a lot of mileage, but I'm only thirty-four. **1967** [R. Beck] *Pimp* 167: Several of "Sweet's" whores came in.…All of them were fine with low mileage.

Mile High Club *n.* people who have had sex on an airplane in flight, facetiously considered to be members of a special organization. *Joc.*

    1972 J. Wells *Come Fly with Us* 41: Jokes about the Mile-High Club, about balling pilots in the cockpit or passengers in the toilet. **1973** W. Crawford *Gunship Cmndr.* 124: Joe started joking about initiating her into the Mile High Club. **1989** *TV Guide* (Aug. 5) 4: The "Mile-High Club," in which membership is limited to couples who have had sex on commercial airline flights. **1991** *Current Affair* (synd. TV series) (Sept. 12): She joined the Mile High Club aboard…[a] private jet. **1997** *Frasier* (NBC-TV): She leaned over and suggested we join the Mile High Club.

mileposter *n. Black E.* a person's leg.

    1955 Broonzy & Bruynoghe [*sic*] *Big Bill Blues* 6: I still like to see them beautiful mileposters, better known as legs.

milish *n.* a militia; (*also*) a militiaman.

    1862 in R.B. Hayes *Diary* II 192: Three thousand milish…are on or near Flat Top Mountain. **1865** in Jackman *Diary* 158: The brigade had a battle with the "Milish." **1888** Beers *Memories* 129: A tall specimen of "melish." **1914** W.H. Fink *Ludlow* 23: Four "gunmen-melish" were seen to go up to the tent colony.

military *adj. Mil.* difficult or uncomfortable.

    1944 Kendall *Service Slang* 37: *Military.*…a word to describe anything tough or uncomfortable. Military wind, military bunk. **1947** in *ATS* (Supp.) 29: *Military,* an adjective descriptive of anything displeasing, as "military" weather, task, bed, etc. **1958** Cope & Dyer *Petty Officer's Guide* (ed. 2) 357: *Military.* Marine Corps slang for anything tough or uncomfortable.

milk *n.* whiskey or beer. *Joc.*

    [*****1821** in *OEDS*: What, my lily! here take a drop of mother's milk. (Gives black child gin out of measure he has received from Landlord.).] **1862** in Whitman *Civil War* 68: "Western milk" i.e. whiskey (when put in your coffee). **1874** *History of Mulligan Guard* 11: Even the Captain was showing the effect of the "milk" he had taken, and was giving impossible orders. **1891** McCann & Jarrold *Odds & Ends* 34: Wait till I give these two chaps their milk. Fifteen cents, please; ten for the shandygaff and five for the pony. **1925** Mullin *Scholar Tramp* 117 [ref. to *ca*1912]: "Milk of the wild cow, boys!" he shouted. "Let's all have another kiss." **1937** *AS* (Apr.) 153: [Texas:] *Wild Mare's Milk.* Hard liquor. **1968–70** *Current Slang III & IV* 83: *Milk, n.* Beer.

¶ In phrases:

¶ **bring to (someone's) milk** to subdue (someone).

    1857 in *OEDS*: There ain't anything that'll bring you to your milk half so quick as a good double-and-twisted thrashin. **1870** Duval *Big-Foot* 169: I gave him twelve inches of solid shoe leather on the shins that brought him to his milk in short order. **1885** Siringo *Texas Cowboy* 49: That would bring them to their milk, as they couldn't see the timber.

¶ **give** [or **let**] **down (one's) milk** *So.* to finally reveal what (one) knows.

    1973 W. Crawford *Stryker* 25: You're thinning out my patience.…Give down your milk before you give me the ass. **1977** *Texas Monthly* (Sept.) 89: To betray one brother [*sc.*, a fellow police officer] is the ultimate sin.…The only time an officer will break that code—will, as they say, "let his milk down" [etc.]. **1984** Wilder *You All* 22: *Let the milk down*: Tell it all; don't hold back; wring it out.

¶ **milk in the coconut** the secret; the heart of the matter.

    *****1840** in *OEDS*: All of "vich"…fully accounts…for the milk in the cocoa-nut. **1895** *Harper's* (Nov.) 962: Aha! That's the milk in the cocoanut, eh?

¶ **strain (one's) milk** to strain (oneself) through overexertion.—occ. used trans.

    1909 in *JAF* XXVI (1913) 128: Bought a cow of Farmer Jones,/She wasn't nothing but skin and bones;/Kept her till she was as fine as silk,/Jumped the fence, and strained her milk. **1935** J. Conroy *World to Win* 71: Take it slow and easy.…Don't strain your milk. **1937** Weidman *Wholesale* 264: Tell Mr. Babuskin not to strain his milk. **1958** McCulloch *Woods Words* 182: *Strain your milk*—To lift hard. **1958** Camerer *Damned Wear Wings* 75: We strained her milk some. Pulled her wings maybe ten degrees. **1966** "T. Pendleton" *Iron Orchard* 115: Don't want you strainin' your milk, bud. **1967** G. Green *To Brooklyn* 259: Easy, Charlie.…Don't strain yer milk. **1982** Rucker *57th Kafka* 114: I strained my milk, and ended up wishing I'd got the android to help.

milk *v. Gamb.* (see quots.).

    1845 J. Greene *Exposure of Gambling* 122: The dealer will "milk" the cards; that is, draw at the very same time one card from the top and one from the bottom, bringing them both off together, and laying them into a heap. **1942** *ATS* 702: *Milk*…to shuffle cards by taking one from the top and one from the bottom simultaneously and allowing them to shower on the table face down.

milk and honey route *n. Hobo.* a railroad route along which handouts are plentiful, esp. one passing through Mormon areas of Utah.

    1917 L. Livingston *Coast to Coast* 121: Railroads passing through [Mormon country]…were nicknamed Milk & Honey Routes. [**1925** Mullin *Scholar Tramp* 137 [ref. to *ca*1912]: On the basis of the kind of food he gets in certain localities, the hobo names the railroads. There is the famous Milk Poultice Route between Salt Lake City and Ogden, Utah, where the hobo goes on a diet restricted to bread and milk.] **1931** "D. Stiff" *Milk & Honey Rte.* 24: Often…hobos speak of a railroad as a "milk and honey route." The original…was a railroad from Salt Lake City south through…Utah. In the early days, before the Latter Day Saints got disillusioned by the great influx of bums and yeggs,…this was the greatest feeding ground for hobos.

milk-and-molasses *adj. New Eng.* of mixed racial ancestry.

    1833 J. Neal *Downeasters,* in *F & H:* The people of this country are of two colours, black and white…or half-and-half sometimes at the south, where they are called milk-and-molasses.

milk factory *n. usu. pl.* a woman's breast. Also **milk bottle.**

    1942 *ATS* 145: Breasts…milk bottles. **1946** J.H. Burns *Gallery* 228: Nuttin but rear ends bouncin like Jello and milk factories under dere dresses. **1974** Univ. Vermont student: Look at those milk factories!

milk man *n. Vaudeville.* (see quot.).

    1926 J. Conway, in *Variety* (Dec. 29) 7: A "milk man" was a real hambo, who stole more bows than the applause warranted at the finish.

milk route *n.* **1.** a profitable circuit of visits.

    [**1874** in *DA:* The most economical method of managing the delivery of milk at the factory is by establishing milk routes.] **1930** Pasley *Capone* 121: By 1925…they were firmly established, their milk route, as gangland calls it, numbering some two hundred saloons. **1929–31** in Partridge *Dict. Und.* 438: *Milk route.* List of road-houses, speakeasies, etc., to which bootleg trucks deliver the "goods." **1942** *Time* (Jan. 5) 16: The "Milk Route" is the daily round of visits a businessman makes trying to get a defense order.

    2. *Av.* a short route flown regularly by a secondary airline.

    1931 *Writer's Digest* (May) 40: *Milk route*—short feeder airlines. **1933** Stewart *Airman Speech* 78: *Milk Route.* A short feeder line servicing one of the major airlines, looked upon with contempt by the big time pilots.

milk run *n.* **1.a.** *Av.* a routine supply flight; (*hence*) a regularly scheduled flight of any kind; (*later*) a shuttle flight. Now *S.E.*

    1943 *Yank* (Jan. 20) 6: The "Morning Milk Run." **1944** J. Gunther *D Day* 18: This plane was an express ship going straight through instead of making the "milk run" via Casablanca and Oran. **1944** *AAF* 369: *Milk run.* routine mission flown repeatedly. **1946** G.C. Hall, Jr. *1000 Destroyed* 264: He would look up at the red crayon line from Debden to Berlin and say,…"Oh, hell, the milk run again." **1950** *Sat. Eve. Post* (Aug. 26) 106: It had, indeed, been a milk run, a flight so uneventful that those who made it would not long remember it. **1959** R. Scott *Flying Tiger* 118: He had decided to fly the "milk run" with me to Lashio, Burma. **1964** R. Moore *Green Berets* 77: I arrived at the air strip via the milk run from Saigon. **1974** J. Rubin *Barking Deer* 142: They caught the milk run to Ban Me Thuot. **1985** Knoxville, Tenn., businessman, age *ca*50: I see him on the milk run to Washington sometimes. **1985** J.M.G. Brown *Rice Paddy Grunt* 51: It's just a milk run. **1983–88** J.T. McLeod *Crew Chief* 312: We called them ash and trash, or milk runs.

b. an uneventful routine journey.—also used fig.

    1946 S. Wilson *Voyage to Somewhere* 165 [ref. to WWII]: "Another milk run!" the men groaned. "They ought to use a horse and wagon!" **1953** *Sat. Eve. Post* (Mar. 14) 21: A new ship....Just to break her in for combat, the Navy command sent her over from Guam to Rota....It was a milk-run setup. **1976** Dills *CB Slanguage* 69: *Milk run:* easy trip. **1982** T.C. Mason *Battleship* 129 [ref. to WWII]: The *Marblehead?* It's nothin' but an overgrown...destroyer, makin' the milk run from Cavite to Shanghai. **1984** *California* (Feb.) 149: The milk-run route [up Everest] first climbed by Edmund Hillary and Tenzing Norgay in 1953—no great feat these days.

2. *Mil. Av.* an air combat mission during which little opposition is encountered and no casualties are sustained; an easy or uneventful flying mission.

    1944 (quot. at JOYRIDE). **1944** Ciardi *Saipan* 52: For us it was a milk run. **1944** Mellor *Sank Same* 118: The "milk run" was about to begin. **1944** in *Best from Yank* 86: If you get back it's a milk run. **1950** *N.Y. Times* (July 23) VI 11: If the delivery of the atom bomb against Russian targets might be only a "milk run" for our bombers, some of the same bombs might be delivered to our own doors. **1956** Heflin *USAF Dict.* 328: *Milk run.* A routine mission or flight flown repeatedly; also a mission involving little danger. Slang. **1956** W. Taylor *Roll Back Sky* 147: We had a milk run, too. I slept half the way home. [**1958** Camerer *Damned Wear Wings* 30 [ref. to WWII]: This one's pure milk. Dump those bombs and get on home.] **1959** *Sat. Eve. Post* (May 2) 26: They're all milk runs...if a man's used to scrambling jet fighters at night in blowing snow. **1960** Archibald *Jet Flier* 90: It had not been a "milk run" after all. Planes had crashed and men had been killed. **1966** E. Shepard *Doom Pussy* 251: Sorry about this milk run, sweetie. But I guess you can make a story of it. **1969** R. Turner *Big Friend* ch. iii [ref. to 1943]: Our second mission ended as another milkrun—a term we came to use describing missions with no claims, no losses, and no enemy action. **1972** W.C. Anderson *Hurricane* 37: "Was it a rough storm?" "A milk run." **1973** Overgard *Hero* 194: They preferred to believe what they wanted to—that it would be a milk run, a breeze. **1978** *Atlantic* (Apr.) 98: My wingman and I broke left and started sauntering along toward our "milk run" target: boxcars on a railroad siding...where the flak was light. **1983** E. Dodge *Dau* 40: You want me to schedule you for the milk runs, Morg? **1985** Boyne & Thompson *Wild Blue* 465: I'll get you on one milk run a month, just enough to cover your flight pay. **1991** *N.Y. Times* (nat. ed.) (Jan. 18) A8: Their missions were not quite cakewalks or milk runs.

milk shake *n.* usu. *pl.* a woman's breast.

    1916 Cary *Venery* I 205: *Milk Shake*—A woman's breasts. From an American drink. **1935** J. Conroy *World to Win* 192: Look at them milk shakes! **1952** Larson *Barnyard Folklore* 78: Breast...*tit, dairy, nipple, "grape-fruit," boopie, milk-shake.* **1975** C.W. Smith *Country Music* 229: His gaze [was] leveling on the girl's breasts. "I really like them...milk shakes."

mill[1] *n.* **1.** *Boxing.* a prizefight; *(hence)* a fistfight, brawl. Now *hist.* Also **milling.** Cf. earlier MILL, *v.,* 1. [The "1785" quot. fr. Grose adduced by Farmer & Henley is nonexistent.]

    1819 [T. Moore] Tom Crib xxii: Rather a wrestling-bout than a *mill.* *1825 in OED:* To cut a dash at races or a mill. **1842** *Spirit of Times* (May 28) 152: The Morning of the Mill. **1842** *Spirit of Times* (Sept. 3) 322: The long expected "mill" came off on Monday last. **1859** in *West. Pa. Hist. Mag.* LII (1969) 63: A ring was formed and the "mill" commenced. **1864** in W. Wilkinson *Mother* 197: We must keep...the Mill going and satisfy the public. **1866** *Night Side of N.Y.* 23: They parry, they thrust, they go at it coolly and scientifically, as if trying each other's strength or feeling for weak points, like their wicked exemplars in a "mill." *Ibid.* 82: On the walls there are many sporting prints of former "mills." **1867** in A.K. McClure *Rocky Mtns.* 369: Con Orem and Jim Dwyer were the heroes of the "mill." **1869** in Rosa *Wild Bill* 154: "Wild Bill"...is always ready for a "mill." **1870** Medbery *Wall St.* 146: Two irate brokers...commence their "mill" at the Board, and adjourn to...[a] committee-room, where the fight is

carried to the bitter end amid the cheers of...bystanders. **1870** F.M. Myers *Comanches* 297: Apparently interested in the view they had of the little "mill" going on around them. **1870** *Putnam's Mag.* (Mar.) 301: You last reached me on the day after the mill. **1874** Carter *Rollingpin* 187: There's a mill I'd like here to explain. **1896** Eugene Field "Lady Lil," in *Immortalia* 8: And so we 'ranged to have the mill/Behind the whore-house on the hill. **1896** Ade *Artie* 31: Well, Artie, have you seen any good mills lately? **1896** S. Crane *George's Mother* 151: Why, Zeusentell an' O'Connor had a great old mill. They were scrappin' all over th' place. **1899** Hamblen *Bucko Mate* 54: The captain and pilot...stood at the break of the poop watching the mill. *ca*1900 *Buffalo Bill* 203: I saw Bill's fight with "Yellow Hand," you bet it was a "mill." **1905** *Nat. Police Gaz.* (Oct. 7) 6: When I began fighting [in the 1870's] you couldn't go to a milling without being sandbagged and robbed of your valuables. **1909** *Sat. Eve. Post* (July 3) 15: And their swains, the last beer-keg emptied, have closed in one grand, annual, all-satisfying "mill." **1911** H.S. Harrison *Queed* 85: Trying to arrange a mill at the Mercury between Smithy of the Y.M.C.A. and Hank McGurk, the White Plains Cyclone. **1911** *N.Y. Eve. Jour.* (Jan. 6) 16: It was a slashing ten-span mill with Maloney the winner from start to finish. **1914** E.R. Burroughs *Mucker* 8: He accompanied him to many mills. **1921–25** J. Gleason & R. Taber *Is Zat So?* 12: A ten frame mill with some local wop in Newark. **1925** *Sat. Eve. Post* (Oct. 3) 20: Mills had to be sneaked off in barns. **1927** *Immortalia* 9: She gave Short Pete a lively mill. **1933** in R.E. Howard *Iron Man* 88: They'll send Reynolds back after the mill. **1972** Somers *Sports in N.O.* 54: But traveling so far to see a bareknuckle "mill" was unusual.

2. [sugg. by *treadmill* and *jutemill*, places of hard prison labor] **a.** *Und.* a prison.

    *1851 H. Mayhew *London Labour* I 352: A few weeks after I was grabbed for this, and got a month at the mill....When I came out of prison, I went to Epsom races. **1853* in *F & H* IV 315: The latter...gave a policeman such a licking the other night, that he was within an ace of getting a month at the mill. **1908** Hopper & Bechholt *9009* 6: Same old mill! *Ibid.* 7: Ye'll wish that more'n once before ye've croaked in this mill. **1918** in *AS* (Oct. 1933) 29: [Ft. Leavenworth:] *Mill.* A prison or jail. **1942–49** Goldin et al. *DAUL:* He's back in the mill.

b. *Specif. (Mil.)* a guardhouse; post stockade.

    1874 in *N. Dak. Hist.* XXXIII (1966) 341: G. Clark put in the mill and released. *ca*1885 in Dolph *Sound Off!* 9: They run us in the mill. **1888** McConnell *Cavalryman* 194 [ref. to 1866]: Very few, indeed, are they who during their term of service can say: "They never had *me* in the mill." **1896** Wister *Red Men* 91: They go to put me in the mill fer that. **1899** Cullen *Tales* 104: He had been running mate of mine in the mill...ever since his chevrons were cut off. **1906** M'Govern *Bolo* 28: At the last I was slung in the mill, charged with violating the 62d article of war. **1915** in Garrett *Army Ballads* 21: And they put me in "the mill." **1918** O'Reilly *Roving & Fighting* 23: I thought he was goin' to slam me in the mill for bein' a thief. **1919** Cortelyou *Arizona* 71: He's *always* in the mill. **1926** Nason *Chevrons* 329 [ref. to 1918]: It didn't make no difference that he was in the mill up there; he was gone a month an' that was enough. **1928** Nason *Sgt. Eadie* 78 [ref. to 1918]: Why, put 'em in the mill!

3. chatter.

    [**1690* in *F & H* IV 316: *Mill clapper,...*The tongue: specifically of women.] **1885** *Puck* (July 29) 343: Shut off your word-mill and take a tumble! **1889** "M. Twain" *Conn. Yankee* 147: I hadn't minded her mill that morning, on account of having that hornet's nest of other troubles.

4. GIN MILL.

    1902 Cullen *More Tales* 47: There were products of France all that day...at the mills 'way over on the South Side. **1950** Bissell *Stretch on River* 26: What say we shove outa this mill?

5.a. [< F *moulin* 'engine', lit., 'mill'] the engine of an aircraft *(obs.)* or automobile. [Early quots. ref. to WWI aviation.]

    1918 in *OEDS:* Motor is "moulin"—to start it, one "turns the mill." **1923** McKnight *Eng. Words* 56: *Tail* and *joystick* and *mill* (French *moulin*) were names for different parts of the airship. **1937** Parsons *Lafayette Escadrille* 63: He grunted and perspired, pulled the prop through twenty times, but couldn't get a single pop out of the old mill. **1953** Felsen *Street Rod* 30: "Listen to that mill," Sherm said. **1955** *Pop. Science* (Apr.) 169: The little mills then develop up to four hp. **1959** Kellogg & Simms *Giant Gila Monster* (film): He was talking about a new blower—and a mill. **1960** D. Hamilton *Death of a Citizen* 118: That's not a racing mill under the hood. **1973** Lucas, Katz & Huyck

Amer. Graffiti 59: It's got a 327 Chevy mill with six Strombergs. **1978** Diehl *Sharky's Machine* 108: Take them Jessies and blow them mills out good. **1990** C.P. McDonald *Blue Truth* 191: A...Firebird with...a big mill under the hood.

b. *R.R.* a locomotive.

1926 *AS* I (Jan.) 250: Locomotives are "mills" or "kettles." **1932** *R.R. Mag.*, in *DARE*. **1945** Hubbard *R.R. Ave.* 327: The pop of the old mill lets go. *Ibid.* 352: *Mill*—Steam locomotive, or typewriter. **1958** McCulloch *Woods Words*: *Mill*...A term for a beat-up old locie, wheels flat, wedges down, steam leaking at every joint, but still running.

c. an esp. dilapidated automobile; rattletrap.

1933 Witherspoon *Liverpool Jarge* (unp.): The feller that sold it drove the old mill up. **1954–60** *DAS*: *Mill*...An automobile, esp. a fast one. *Not common.*

6.a. *Printing.* a linotype machine.

1905 E.F. Langdon *Cripple Creek* 141: The "mills" kept "turning over."

b. *Journ. & Mil.* a typewriter.

1913 in *OEDS*: After I got a good idea I would hustle to my "mill" and pound out some copy. **1915** Braley *Songs of Workaday World* 30: And I'll start to say, "Jim, got a good cigarette?"/And turn to his battered old "mill,"/And then I'll remember that "30" is in/For him who once sat in that spot. **1919** in Hemingway *Sel. Lttrs.* 21: I...set it by my typewriter, slang for mill, battered key board, etc. **1920** *304th Field Signal Bn.* 113 [ref. to 1918]: Asked...if he had...any typewriter practice, he...replied...that he could "use a mill." **1941** *AS* (Oct.) 167: *Mill.* A typewriter (Signal Corps). **1943** Bayler & Carnes *Wake* I. 149: The [radio] operator began pounding his "mill." He was receiving something in code. **1969** Crumley *One to Count Cadence* 38: They provided us with schedules and frequencies of transmissions in certain areas, and we recorded the messages—Morse Code groups by typewriter (mill) and voice on tape. **1982** T.C. Mason *Battleship* 33: A set of earphones lay across each "mill."

7. *Army.* a machine gun.

[**1923** McKnight *Eng. Words* 58 [ref. to WWI]: *Moulin à café*, "coffee mill," for "machine gun."] **1928** Hammett *Red Harvest* 81 [ref. to WWI]: "Tell him to set up his mill and start grinding," Noonan ordered. **1930** Lait *On the Spot* 107: He had learned to operate the "mill" overseas in a machine gun unit.

mill[2] *n.* **1.** a million; (*specif.* and *usu.*) a million dollars. Also **mil.**

1942 *ATS* 17: *Mill*, one million [dollars]. *Ibid.* 330: Thank you....mil gracias,...thanks awfully, —loads, —a million. **1963** in Cannon *Nobody Asked* 110: Doc got rid of money as if no fight ever drew less than a mill. **1966** R.E. Alter *Carny Kill* 58: This place grossed thirty mill last year. **1967** Spillane *Delta* 31: When you gonna give me a slice of that forty mil, Morgan? **1969** L. Sanders *Anderson Tapes* 111: Minimum of a hundred thousand. Closer to a quarter of a mil. **1970–71** Higgins *Eddie Coyle* 170: They made...about a quarter of a mil in a month. **1971** B.B. Johnson *Blues for Sister* 167: At least two mil. **1975** *New Yorker* (Jan. 20) 29: Thanks a mil for your letter. **1976** *L.A. Times* (June 27) ("Calendar") 37: His gross is anywhere from 3 to 5 mil a year. **1979** *Atlantic* (June) 39: He didn't care about the quarter of a mil; he wanted his perk. **1980** Gould *Ft. Apache* 172: His bail stayed at half a mill. **1984** *Nat. Lampoon* (Dec.) 70: We can have 25 mill printed by tomorrow. **1984** *Time* (Mar. 5) 4: Never $800,000, never $1.2 million, but a flat, cool mil. *a***1991** J. Phillips *You'll Never Eat Lunch* vii: Our picture would grose maybe fifteen mil.

2. a millimeter.

1960 in *OEDS*: Sandy, I'll be getting pictures of you in that outfit, don't worry, as good as anyone can take—*Best Man*, What, on 35 mill? **1983** T. Page *Nam* 21: A micro mill mistake spelt body bags all round.

mill *v.* **1.** *Und. & Boxing.* to strike, esp. repeatedly; beat in, out, or up; fight or brawl; (*also*) (*rare* in U.S.) to kill. [An earlier sense, 'to rob or steal', well-documented in *OED* fr. the 16th C., has not been discovered in American usage.]

***1698–99** "B.E." *Dict. Canting Crew*: *Milling the Gig with a Betty*,...Breaking open the door with an Iron Crow. *Mill them*,...Kill them. *Miller*,...a Killer or Murderer....*Mill a grunter*,...To Kill a Pig. ***ca1700** in *OED*: *Mill*, to beat. ***1748** in *F & H* IV 315: *Mill*....in the *Canting Language*, means to beat, thresh [*sic*], maul, or kill a person. ***1796** Grose *Dict. Vulgar Tongue* (ed. 3) s.v. *mill*: *I'll mill your glaze*; I'll beat out your eye. ***1812** Vaux *Vocab.*: *Mill*: to fight. To *mill* a person is to beat him. ***1819** [T. Moore] *Tom Crib* x: The early exploit of [Epeus]... in *milling* his twin brother. ***1820–21** P. Egan *Life in Lon-*

don 137: To *mill* his way out of a *row*. ***1821** *Real Life in London* I 145: His principal accomplishments are...swaggering [and] *milling*. *Ibid.* 150: Or b— me if I don't *mill* you. ***1840** W.M. Thackeray, in *F & H*: He had *milled* a policeman. **1848** G. Thompson *House Breaker* 44: He ought to be *milled*....*Milled*—beaten. **1848** Judson *Mysteries* 261: I'd just give a mug o' yale to mill that one-eyed buffer. **1853** G. Thompson *Gay Girls* 13: Two dashing courtezans...are "milling" each other in the most approved style of the fistic sciences. ***1857** "Ducange Anglicus" *Vulgar Tongue* 13: *Mill*, v. To beat or fight, to be beaten. *Pugil[ism]*. **1859** Matsell *Vocab.* 127: *Milled*...Severely bruised or cut in the fight. **1927** F. Shay *Pious Friends* 98: The next round started, from the go/ The millin' we did wasn't slow.

2. (among cowboys) to herd cattle into a circle.

1874, 1888, 1897 in *DARE*. **1917–20** in J.M. Hunter *Trail* 160 [ref. to *a*1890]: I knew how to turn the crank of a coffee-mill, but when it was necessary to "mill" a bunch of outlaw steers I did not know where to look for the crank. **1933** *AS* VIII 130: *Mill.* To cause to drift in a circle. Milling cattle is the best method of checking a stampede.

3. to leave; depart.

[***1889–90** Barrère & Leland *Dict. Slang: Mill the quod, to*...to break away from jail.] [**1930** G. Irwin *Tramp & Und. Slang: Mill.*—To ramble aimlessly about. In this sense, from the West, where a herd of cattle "mills"...when disturbed and kept in easy motion by its herders.] **1971** Woodley *Dealer* 43: We got to mill soon, no shit. We got to get out of here before the weekend. We *got* to.

millie *n.* [app. fr. *Millie*, hypocoristic form of *Mildred*, female given name] a weak or weak-willed fellow; SISSY.

1986 Ganz & Mandel *Gung Ho* (film): "You're a real millie, you know that?" "I am not a millie!"

millihelen *n.* [alluding to *Helen* of Troy, possessor according to Christopher Marlowe's *Doctor Faustus* (1604), of "the face that launch'd a thousand ships, And burnt the topless towers of Ilium"] *Stu.* an imaginary unit of measure of female beauty. *Joc.* Also (*nonce*) **milliherm** (applied to men).

1969 *Current Slang I & II* 61: *Millihelen*, n. That amount of beauty needed to launch one ship.—Air Force Academy cadets. **1974** G. Davenport *Tatlin!* 17: The girl was deemed by a jury to be less than five hundred millihelens. *Ibid.* 172: His penis...was accorded the full complement of milliherms. **1977** *Verbatim* (Feb.) 12: The unit of female beauty is the milli-helen, which is defined as the amount of beauty required to launch one ship.

Millimeter Pete *n.* *USMC.* Japanese artillery.—used in personification. Now *hist.* Also **Millimeter Mike.** [Quots. ref. to WWII.]

1943 W. Simmons *Joe Foss* 62: "Millimeter Pete," the Jap artillery man who always shelled the field just when we had tucked our feet under the table. **1944** Hubler & De Chant *Flying Leathernecks* 58: By day, the Japanese snipers sometimes put their bullets into the planes. By day, too, Millimeter Mike, or Pistol Pete, the nicknames for the Japanese field guns that were hidden in the jungle and kept dropping large caliber shells into the runways of Henderson [Field] would fire.

million *n.* ¶ In phrase: **feel [or look] like a million [bucks or dollars]** to feel [or look] wonderful.

1911 Roe *Prodigal Daughter* 58: A good dinner looked like a million dollars to me right then. **1915** T.A. Dorgan, in Zwilling *TAD Lexicon* 54: Did you get that manager with the trick coat—looks like a million. **1918** in Hemingway *Sel. Letters* 6: Our uniforms are regular United States Army officers' and look like a million dollars. **1919** in Cornebise *Amaroc News* 181: American girls...look like a million dollar bill. **1934** L. Berg *Prison Nurse* 114: She would blow in here, looking like a million. **1935** Wald & Epstein *Stars over Broadway* (film): Gee, Nora, you look like a million. **1937** E. Anderson *Thieves Like Us* 111: I feel like a million bucks. **1951** Sheldon *Troubling Star* 98: She would look like a million bucks. **1978** De Christoforo *Grease* 145: I had to admit, we looked like a million bucks—in small bills.

million-dollar *adj.* of tremendous value or worth; superlative.—used prenominally.

1892 in *OEDS*: The General Assembly...passed this milliondollar bill. **1918** Gibbons *Wouldn't Fight* 265: That barrage cost us a million dollars. He's the million-dollar baby of the raid. **1930** Sage *Last Rustler* 133: I was strolling up the street in one of them million-dollar moods. **1930** Graham & Graham *Queer People* 209: Why ruin a million-dollar jag...with ten dollars' worth of food? **1932** *AS* VII (Apr.) 250: Bing

Crosby plaintively croons that he has "Found a Million Dollar Baby in the Five and Ten Cent Store." **1938** Bellem *Blue Murder* 13: She had a million-dollar shape with plenty of curves—all in the right places. **1984** W. Murray *Dead Crab* 94: That horse showed us a million-dollar move, sweetheart.

million-dollar wound *n. Mil.* a nonfatal wound that requires a soldier's removal from combat and return to the United States.
   1947 Mailer *Naked & Dead* 335: Aaah, there ain't a goddam place you can get a million-dollar wound that it don't hurt. **1948** A. Murphy *Hell & Back* 153: I just got that million-dollar wound. **1956** I. Shulman *Good Deeds* 26: The guys call that a million-dollar wound. **1960** Matheson *Beardless Warriors* 132: "What are you bitching about?" asked Cooley. "That's a million-dollar wound, buddy." **1962** Tregaskis *Vietnam Diary* 22: The surgeons...told him he had a Million Dollar Wound (one calling for a long convalescence at home before return to active duty). **1969** S.L.A. Marshall *Ambush* 124: I think I got one in the spine. Feels like it paralyzed me. That one ought to be the million-dollar wound. **1972** West *Village* 61: That's a million-dollar wound the old man has....Someone should shoot me like that so I can go home. **1966–80** McAleer & Dickson *Unit Pride* 160: We saw lots of men with the "million-dollar wound." Instead of being upset they were happy. **1983** Ehrhart *VN-Perkasie* 13: Unless he got a million-dollar wound or a bullet in the head first. **1985** J. McDonough *Platoon Leader* 176: Although the bullet ripped into him deeply, it didn't exit his body. An exit wound from a shot fired at that range would have been devastating. "I got me a million-dollar wound, Lieutenant Mac," Taylor gloated. **1985** J.M.G. Brown *Rice Paddy Grunt* 314: The surgeon...told me that I might have a "million-dollar wound." *a***1991** J.R. Wilson *Landing Zones* 189: I had my million-dollar wound, my ticket home. **1994** E. Roth *Forrest Gump* (film): They said it was a million-dollar wound, but the army must've kept that money.

mill rat *n. Labor.* a mill worker.
   1977 *Indiana Folklore* X 98: The thousands of steelworkers—"mill-rats"—of the Region surely had something to say to folklorists.

milquetoast *n.* [fr. Caspar *Milquetoast*, main character of *The Timid Soul*, comic strip begun 1924 by H.T. Webster (1885–1952)] a timid or shy person; weakling.—also used fig. Now *S.E.*
   1938 in *OEDS*: Don't be a milquetoast either, and be afraid to add it [*sc.*, the bill] up. **1947** in *DARE*: Representative Monroney...called the GOP measure "a Casper [*sic*] Milquetoast' sent out to fight inflation." **1949** *Pop. Science* (Feb.) 152: Why one person becomes a Milquetoast and another a bully. **1962** Houk & Dexter *Ballplayers* 136: Only a Milquetoast will lie down and take it when he's given a raw decision. **1963** *Time* (Apr. 19) 75: Cotton...is one of the milquetoasts of the plant world. **1980** *L.A. Times* (July 20) I 5: It is the fear of a traffic ticket that has changed them from maniacs into milquetoasts. **1989** Z.Z. Gabor, in Thorne *Dict. Contemp. Slang*: [I resisted arrest because] I'm a Hungarian woman...not a milquetoast.

Milwaukee goiter *n.* GERMAN GOITER. *Joc.*
   1941 Kendall *Army & Navy Sl.* 9: *Milwaukee goiter*—obesity at the waistline. **1942** *ATS* 144: *Drunkard's Paunch....German or Milwaukee goitre* [*sic*]. **1954–60** *DAS*: *Milwaukee goiter* A large midsection if attrib. to owner's propensity for beer-drinking. **1992** G. Wolff *Day at the Beach* 228: A fine full belly of the sort termed "Milwaukee goiter."

Mimi *n.* SCREAMING MIMI.
   1961 Granat *Important Thing* 163 [ref. to WWII]: He prob'ly cou'n't even hear the goddamn Mimis. **1962** Mandel *Wax Boom* 49: No Mimis any more...no mortar, no nothing.

mincemeat *n.* a mangled individual; in phr. **make mincemeat of** to mangle or obliterate. Now *colloq.*
   a*1663** in *OED2*: I'll hew thee into so many Morsels, that....Thou shalt be Mince-meat. *****1708** in *OED2*: If I should find a man in the house I'd make mincemeat of him. **1836** *Davy Crockett's Alm.* (1837) 32: I'll make mince meat of ye. **1839** Briggs *Harry Franco* I 230: They will make mince meat of us if we are caught here. **1849** *Nat. Police Gaz.* (Aug. 18) 1: Their father had beaten them, and threatened to cut them into mince-meat. **1853** in A.P. Hudson *Humor of Old So.* 496: He'll chop you into 'mince meat.' **1864** "E. Kirke" *Down in Tenn.* 151: All waitin' an' ready ter make mincemeat uv my carcass. **1864** Hill *Our Boys* 93: Goens seized a fierce-looking butcher-knife, and told Hare...he'd manufacture mince-meat of him. **1879** Grant *Tin*

Gods 5: I'll make mince-meat of him that stops me. *****1881–84** Davitt *Prison Diary* I 126: He...offers the person thus caught the alternative of being punched into mince-meat in no time, or the forking out of all the loose cash he may have upon his person. **1928–29** Nason *White Slicker* 49: I saw you take the dive into the ditch and thought you were all mincemeat.

mince pies *n.pl.* [rhyming slang] the eyes.
   *****1857** "Ducange Anglicus" *Vulgar Tongue* 13: *Mince pies*, n. Eyes. *****1892** in *F & H* IV 319: I smiled as I closed my two mince-pies. *****1894** in *F & H*: My mince-pies are waterin'. **1928** M. Sharpe *Chicago May* 288 [ref. to 1890's]: *Mince pies*—eyes. **1944** *Pap. Mich. Acad.* XXX 599: *Mince pies*, eyes.

minch *n.* a stupid, contemptible, or unpleasant person.
   1928 *AS* III (June) 375: *Minch*—An undesirable spectator. **1972** *Playboy* (Feb.) 183: It's how we move the minches 'n' give the rubes dry shaves.

mind *n.* ¶ In phrases:
   ¶ **blow (one's) mind** see s.v. BLOW, *v.*
   ¶ **take** [or **get**] **(someone's) mind** to manipulate (someone's) thoughts or emotions.
   1971 Dahlskog *Dict.* 40: *Mind, take (someone's)* To dominate someone's mind to the point that that person is completely obsessed; to disturb or upset one emotionally.

mind *v.* ¶ In phrase: **mind the store** to tend to business in someone's absence.
   1925 Cobb *Many Laughs* (punchline): Who's minding the store? **1958** Simonson & Philips *Blob* (film): Richie, you mind the store. **1986** *NDAS*: *Mind the store*...To attend to routine business; carry on.

mindbender *n.* a person, drug, or event that profoundly affects the mind; MINDBLOWER. Also **mindbend.**
   [**1946** Kober *That Man Is Here Again* 5: The poor guy's knockin' hisself out with a problem he's got bendin' his mind.] *****1963** in *OEDS*: Oonagh has said that there were instincts in man laid too deep for the most skillful mind-bender to probe. **1967** *Esquire* (Sept.) 192: I'm talking about every mind-bender we can get our hands on. **1970** Landy *Underground Dict.* 132: *Mind bender n.* 1. Drug that expands the mind. 2. Person or event that expands the mind or increases one's knowledge or understanding. **1982** *Mother Jones* (May) 14: Hallucinogenic drugs....Its researchers discovered BZ—a powerful mindbender. **1989** J. Connolly & D. Loucka *Dream Team* (film): That's a real mindbender for you, right? **1993** K. Scott *Monster* 104: Gang members who are combat soldiers are subject to the same mind-bend as are veterans of foreign wars.

mind-bending *adj.* mentally overwhelming; astonishing.
   *****1965** in *OEDS*: The Socialist Labour League, furious exegetes of the gospel according to Trotsky, with their mind-bending vocabulary full of "Pabloism" and that mythical entity the "rank-and-file." **1966** H.S. Thompson *Hell's Angels* 181: The contrast was mind-bending. **1970** *Business Week* (Oct. 17) 14: His clear writing style of a subject he calls "mind-bending" in complexity. **1974** *Harper's* (Jan.) 18: Almost 4 hours of mindbending, tongue-tickling vocabulary growth. **1978** *New Republic* (Aug. 26) 13: Mind-bending drugs have revolutionized mental heath care in the last 30 years. **1983** *U.S. News & W.R.* (Apr. 4) 43: The 75 organizations branded by angry parents' groups as "mind-bending youth cults."

mindblower *n.* something that astonishes, shocks, or mentally overwhelms. Also **mindblow**, *n.* & *v.*
   1968 in *OED2*: Two chemicals...can have very different psychedelic properties: one might be a real mind-blower. **1970** Gattzden *Black Vendetta* 82: It's the very latest mindblower, it's THC. **1970** in *OED2*: It can mind-blow a long-haired GI to know he'll have to live straighter. **1970** Landy *Underground Dict.* 133: *Mind blower*...Unusual experience; sudden shock. Can be while under the influence of drugs. **1971** Sonzski *Punch Goes Judy* 55: Here's the euphemism of the week: "low-profile policy." Really a mindblow. **1971** Meggyesy *Out of Their League* 163: The contradiction between where my head was at while I was experimenting with acid and the location of the collective head of one of the St. Louis neighborhood Lion's Club was a real mindblower. **1972** Burkhart *Women in Pris.* 447: *Mind blower.* A discovery; a surprise or realization that is shocking. **1975** Trischka *Melodic Banjo* 70: It was another staggering thing. He did it melodically and it was a mind-blower. **1981** *N.Y. Times* (Nov. 10) A2: The old man is a radical

thinker, a bit of a philospher…"their mind-blower, their symbol of opposition to the endless search here for order."

mind-blowing *adj.* astonishing; shocking; overwhelming.

    *1967 in *OEDS:* While the music lasted little of this was evident; the spectacular mind-blowing ferocity of it all simply carried the group through. **1968** *Seattle* (Mar.) 58: Records…the current mind-blowing favorites include Ravi Shankar on sitar, Kimio Eto on koto, John Cage's electronic works [etc.]. **1969** *Atlantic* (Mar.) 43: They thought it was very mystical and mind-blowing to be in the hospital. **1971** *Business Week* (Dec. 4) 50: Marijuana…a drug of abuse—in common with cocaine, heroin, and mind-blowing LSD. **1977** *L.A. Times* (Aug. 27) III 1: Ty Cobb…While his feats and unorthodox, swashbuckling style may be all but lost in antiquity, his mind-blowing numbers insure him a permanent place in the record book. **1978** *Rolling Stone* (Oct. 5) 68: I sat in a kind of mindblowing euphoria. **1985** Ferraro & Francke *Ferraro* 22: It was all pretty mind-blowing for them, having been dumped in the middle of this fantastic happening with no warning at all. **1995** *Leeza* (synd. TV series): This is mind-blowing to me.

mind candy *n.* light, diverting material. Cf. EAR CANDY, EYE CANDY.

    1978 *Newsweek* (Nov. 6) (Nexis): Painfully thin and unrelentingly intense, [television producer Aaron] Spelling toils like a fiend to turn out what he unashamedly calls "mind candy." **1991** *Newsday* (Dec. 22) (Nexis): For after-dinner mind candy, Nick at Nite serves "Christmas Night in TV Land," starting at 8:30. **1994** *Newsweek* (July 4) 76: What he calls "mind candy" and critics prefer to call "schlock."

mindfuck *n.* **1.** imaginary copulation as a substitute for actual intercourse.—usu. considered vulgar. *Joc.*

    1964 Faust *Steagle* 265: We could lie down side by side and think. Oh, a mind fuck? That's nowhere. **1968** *Zap Comix* (No. 3) (unp.): A mind-fuck. *a*1977 M. French *Women's Room* 574: They masturbate to it.…It's a mind-fuck. *a*1991 J. Phillips *You'll Never Eat Lunch* 163: He rarely gets a hard-on, but the mind-fuck is really irresistible.

    2. a sensational or overwhelming experience; MINDBLOWER.—usu. considered vulgar.

    1971 in L. Bangs *Psychotic Reactions* 7: That electro-distort stuff…a real earthquake mindfuck. **1972** R. Barrett *Lovomaniacs* 385: Dolly's eyes said she was *stoned.*…I…know when someone's full of the…original superfreak mindfuck. **1977** *Nat. Lampoon* (Aug.) 33: His Pressed Wang on Stained Glass is a religious mind-fuck. **1978** *Rolling Stone* (June 1) 51: The second stage was dangerous too, but more on a head level. It really was kind of a mindfuck. **1980** M. Baker *Nam* 40: When you weren't going through that, you had your recruit regs held up in front of your face memorizing your eleven general orders. It was a real mind fuck. **1980** *Mother Jones* (Dec.) 50: I told her it was her own personal mind fuck…I cannot be in control. **1993** K. Scott *Monster* 164: You simply prepared ahead of time for the mind-fuck of being a prisoner.

    3. deception, esp. if elaborate.—usu. considered vulgar.

    1974 Bernstein & Woodward *President's Men* 119: Somewhere, Bernstein had been told that the CIA did that kind of thing abroad. He had heard it called Mindfuck but the agency called it Black Operation. **1987** "J. Hawkins" *Tunnel Warriors* 37: Despite the obvious game of mindfuck. **1988–90** M. Hunter *Abused Boys* 279: The mind-fuck you did on me.

    4. a person who engages in MINDFUCKING.—usu. considered vulgar. Cf. MINDFUCK, *v.*

    1975 *DAS* (ed. 2): Mind-fuck…*n.* =…A person who manipulates others.

    5. a psychotic person.—usu. considered vulgar.

    1977 Sayles *Union Dues* 176: He was a certifiable mindfuck and you had to keep him on a tight leash. *Ibid.* 312: Comes back such a mindfuck he can't remember. Fuckin space cowboy.

mindfuck *v.* to confuse or outwit, esp. by playing on someone's emotions; manipulate; trick; bamboozle; *(also)* to confound the thinking of.—usu. considered vulgar. Hence **mindfucker.**

    1967 Wolf *Love Generation* 17: Their consciousness has been permanently altered. Forever altered. They've been mind-fucked. *Ibid.* 281: Mind-fucked. Profoundly influenced by something. **1970** J. Howard *Please Touch* 235: Some [encounter] groups dismiss all abstractions as "headshit" and "mindfucking." **1970** Landy *Underground Dict.:* Mind fucker…person who attempts to manipulate another's thinking without consideration for the other. **1971** S. Miller *Hot*

Springs 66: They have nothing to teach you—they mind-fucked you. **1972** Gover *Mr. Big* 11: She mindfucks me again. **1975** *DAS* (ed. 3): *Mind-fucker*…A person who manipulates others. **1976** J.W. Thomas *Heavy Number* 105: He's really mind-fucked you. **1980** *Nat. Lampoon* (Aug.) 67: You're some kind of mindfucker. You're a witch. **1987** R. Miller *Slob* 156: They both felt giddy, hysterical, a little confused, mindfucked, spent. **1991** Marcinko & Weisman *Rogue Warrior* 165: I was a veteran of mind-fucking the Vietnamese. **1994** J. Shay *Achilles* xiv: Or their supervisors pushing them, mind-fucking them, pushing them till they lost it, so they could get rid of them. **1994** in A. Sexton *Rap on Rap* 180: People are…mind-fucked by the myth. **1996** *New Yorker* (Feb. 26) 84: Sigmund Freud, figurehead for all professional mindfuckers.

mindfucker *n.* **1.** something that is baffling or astounding.—usu. considered vulgar.

    1969 *Woodstock* (film): This thing is a real mindfucker! **1972** Pelfrey *Big V* 24: Wow man, that's a mind-fucker.

    2. see s.v. MINDFUCK, *v.*

mind-fucking *adj.* baffling or astounding.—usu. considered vulgar. See also MINDFUCK, *v.*

    1971 Kopp *Guru* 145: Away from intellectual "mind-fucking" words. **1986** Atlanta, Ga., man, age *ca*30: [Hands Across America] was mind-fucking, man! Such a great thing!

mind game *n.* an example of psychological manipulation, trickery, or the like.—also used attrib.—often constr. in pl.

    1973 J. Lennon *Mind Games* [pop. song and album title]. **1977** *Wash. Post* (Oct. 11) (Nexis): "What da ya want on the first pitch?" Sutton yelled after him, one-two-three times. It was the old pitcher-vs-hitter mind game. **1981** Univ. Tenn. student: These women are just interested in the mind games they play with you. **1984** *N.Y. Times* (Dec. 29): Some coaches insist on playing mind games with the most successful kickers by importing alleged competitors into training camps as a reminder that nobody's job is safe. **1987** *L.A. Times* (Nov. 29) (Nexis): After eight years of being single, I'd just as soon spend all my time with my grandchildren, who give me unconditional love, really need me and don't play mind games. **1989** *L.A. Times* (Dec. 30) (Nexis): The introduction of Bush oratory over the blaring loudspeaker system is the newest ingredient in the mind games that American forces are using to harass both Noriega and the diplomats who are providing him refuge from his American pursuers. **1994** *Wash. Post* (June 28) D3: The feds, I'm pretty sure, are playing mind games, trying to spook the speculators. **1995** *Esquire* (June) 106: Playground one-on-one mind game macho domination while going to the basket. **1996** *Esquire* (Mar.) 106: We got into this mind game where I'd have to demand something of her, and she'd refuse, but then I'd have to make her do it.

mine *n.* [prob. alluding to the phr. as used in ordering mixed drinks] ¶ In phrase: **in mine** for me.

    1874 Carter *Rollingpin* 57: No more "Turkish" in mine. **1901** Hobart *John Henry* 34: Not any in mine! **1906** London *Moon-Face* 38: No bouncers in mine, understand! I'll go along.

mingle *n.* usu. *pl.* either member of an unrelated, usu. nonromantic couple who share a residence.

    1974 *N.Y. Post* (June 6) 36: The overall total of "mingles"—a word to describe those living with non-relatives in a single household—is still relatively small. **1981** *Time* (Nov. 30) 62: Realtors have labeled those willing to share ownership and living arrangements as the "mingles market." **1982** *U.S. News & W.R.* (Mar. 1) 19: The company is marketing 800 housing units designed for "mingles," or unrelated singles. **1983** *Santa Barbara News-Press* (Feb. 9) D1: Mingles. Government statisticians coined the word to describe singles living together as a household.…"They can be mingling for fun, economy or companionship, or any combination thereof." **1984** *L.A. Times* (Feb. 5) VIII 2: A second townhouse had two master bedrooms and is aimed at what Carole Eichen calls "mingles"—two unmarried people who can't afford to buy a home of their own but can pool their funds to buy one together.

mingo *n. Stu.* a chamber pot.

    1775 in *DA:* 5 Mingos and a Bed pan. **1795** in B. Hall *College Wds.* (ed. 2) 322: A bottle full of *white face Stingo*/Another, handy, called a *mingo*. **1851** B. Hall *College Wds.* 207: *Mingo.* Latin. At Harvard College, this word was formerly used to designate a chamber-pot.

mingo *v.* [< L *mingo* 'I urinate'] *Stu.* to urinate.

    1734 in B. Hall *College Words* (ed. 2) 216: No Freshman shall mingo against the College wall.

mingy *adj.* miserly; (*hence*) cheap; unimpressive. Now *S.E.*
> ***1911** in *OEDS:* "Mingee" for greedy. ***1929** H. Green *Living* 22: He was so mingy, not a penny coming from his pocket without his making a groan. **1946** (cited in *DAS*). **1958** Taradash *Bell Book & Candle* (film): I've got your present, but I'm afraid it's kind of mingy this year. I've never been so broke. **1962** Plath *Bell Jar* 9: The thought of dancing with that little runt in his orange suede elevator shoes and mingy T-shirt and droopy blue sports coat made me laugh. **1974** *N.Y. Times Mag.* (Mar. 10) 92: A mingy fellow like J. Paul Getty. **1987** *Time* (Sept. 7) 64: None of his failures were mingy. **1994** *New York* (Jan. 17) 55: Doubtless her reason for taking on the otherwise mingy role.

Minié rifle *n.* [lit., a rifle that fires a *Minié* (pop. *minnie*) ball, named for Claude Etienne *Minié* (1814–79), French inventor] a kind of cheap, powerful whiskey. In full, **Minié rifle whiskey.**
> **1858** in *DA:* May Minie Rifle Whisky be your drink. *a*1860 Hundley *So. States* 268: Strychnine whisky…Minié rifle—,/…flaming red-eye. **1865** J.H. Browne *In Secessia* 194: Imbibing Minié rifle whisky, and assassinating unarmed men.

mini-sergeant *n. USAF.* a sergeant E-4; BUCK SERGEANT. [E-4 is the lowest pay grade for the various ranks of sergeant. *Mini-* became a fashionable prefix in the U.S. *ca*1965, infl. esp. by *miniskirt.*]
> **1970** *Current Slang V* (Summer) 17: *Mini-sergeant,* n. An Air Force Sergeant (E-4). **1974** Former USAF navigator, age *ca*32 [ref. to Vietnam War]: A *mini-sergeant* meant an E-4. The exact opposite of a master sergeant.

minister's face *n.* a boiled pig's head. *Joc.* Also **minister's snout, minister's head.**
> **1852–55** C.G. Parsons *Inside View* 82: The upper part of a pig's head—"the minister's face"—was on the table. **1872** Thomes *Slaver* 155: I'll give up eating old hoss and minister's faces, and have a farm and lots of pigs and not turn out…to…reef…sails. **1899** Green *Va. Folk-Sp.* 283: Minister's face….The upper part of the head of a hog…Usually boiled. **1926** *AS* (Dec.) 652: *Minister's face:* Pigs head served in a cheap restaurant. **1927** *DN* V 455: *Minister's snout,* n. Boiled pig's head. Also *minister's face.* **1934, 1941, 1952** in *DARE.*

mink *n.* **1.** (at Virginia Military Institute) a new cadet.
> **1863** in Stanard *Letters* 9: Among a parcel of rats, minks, [etc.].

2. Esp. *Black E.* a girlfriend; attractive young woman; FOX, 2.a., 3.
> **1899** Green *Va. Folk-Sp.* 283: Mink…a pert girl; a huzzy. **1962** in Ricks & Marsh *Patterns in English* 47: A *mink* is the term for one's girl friend. **1967** Riessman & Dawkins *Play It Cool* 68: Mink…girl friend: *A sailor's got a mink in every port.* **1973** "J. Godey" *Pelham* 176: This was a real mink, this girl, all you had to do was throw a dirty thought at her and she was down on her back. **1983** *Reader's Digest Success with Words* 87: Black English…mink = (1) "attractive woman" (2) "girlfriend." **1992** Mowry *Way Past Cool* 33: Deek had…minks that would never have looked twice at Ty.

3. a scoundrel; (*also*) a lecher.
> **1900** Wister *Jimmyjohn* 61: You ornery old mink!…You keep to the jewelry business hereafter. **1949** in *DAS:* The…doctor was a regular mink. **1971** Dahlskog *Dict.* 40: *Mink,* n. A lecher.

Minnie[1] *n. Army & USMC.* the German *Minenwerfer,* a kind of trench mortar; (*hence*) its projectile. Now *hist.* [Quots. ref. to WWI.]
> **1917** Empey *Over the Top* 25: A German "Minnie" (trench mortar) had exploded in the next traverse. **1918** McBride *Emma Gees* 162: A good many people, even among the soldiers themselves, think that *Minenwerfer* or "Minnie" for short, is the name of the projectile or torpedo, while, as a matter of fact, it is the instrument which throws it; a literal translation being "mine-thrower." **1918** *Sat. Eve. Post* (Jan. 19) 62: The Boche…let fly with a Minnie and caught the whole party. **1919** Bliss *805th Pioneer Inf.* 212: The whine of Minnie shells. **1919** Murrin *With the 112th* 338: Within shell range of the German Berthas or Minnies. **1925** Nason *Three Lights* 47: Minnies an' machine guns. **1928** Harrison *Generals* 23: "Minnies," he shouts, and dashes on. **1936** Reilly *Americans All* 132: However, at the stroke of half past five a veritable flood of large calibre "minnies" struck the area simultaneously.

Minnie[2] *n.* Minneapolis, Minnesota.
> **1925** *Writer's Mo.* (June) 487: *Minnie*—Minneapolis, Minn. **1989**

Harper's (June) 54: Minneapolis: "Good *bye,* Minny! And bye to your goddamn twin sister, too!"

Minnie Five Fingers *n.* MARY FIVE FINGERS.
> *a*1973–87 F.M. Davis *Livin' the Blues* 41 [ref. to *ca*1920]: You ain't never had nothin' but ol' Minnie Five Fingers!

minnow-muncher *n.* a Roman Catholic. *Joc.* Cf. MACKEREL-SNAPPER; FISH-EATER, 1.—used derisively.
> **1966** IUFA *Folk Speech* (Mar. 11): *Minnow muncher*—A Catholic. **1974** Iowa/KC guitarist in N.Y.C., age *ca*22: A *minnow-muncher* is a Roman Catholic.

minor-league *adj.* unimpressive; mediocre; small-scale; modest; etc. Cf. MAJOR-LEAGUE.
> **1949** *Sat. Eve. Post* (Oct. 8) 32: Most of the killings could be shrugged off as minor-league stuff. **1951** *Time* (Oct. 1) 43: Nelli had sung only in minor-league opera in the U.S. **1953** *N.Y. Times* (June 21) II 9: The Alfven work is a charming example of minor-league nationalism. **1963** *Sat. Eve. Post* (Mar. 2) 69: It is more likely that a minor-league nuclear nation would use its bombs against smaller rivals. **1977** in *Los Angeles* (Jan. 1978) 95: The minor-league facility the county operated. **1982** *Business Week* (Dec. 13) 115: He has been hobbled by a minor-league campaign staff, lack of money [etc.].

mint *n. Homosex.* effeminacy. Cf. MINTY, *n., adj.* [The literal *S.E.* phr. "with a hint of mint" has been freq. in commercial advertisements for var. products from at least the early 1960's.]
> *a*1972 B. Rodgers *Queens' Vernacular* 107: *Hint of mint* ('50s) trace of homosexual tendencies. **1981** *Village Voice* (N.Y.C.) (Sept. 23) 61: A suavely villainous crook, played by the gifted Leonard Frey with a rather noticeable hint of mint.

mint drop *n.* usu. *pl.* [pun on *S.E.* sense 'mint-flavored candy' and *mint* 'place where money is produced'] a gold coin; (*broadly*) a piece of money.
> **1835** N. Hawthorne, in *DA:* The bar-keeper had one of Benton's mint drops for a bosom-brooch! **1836** in W. Morgan *Amer. Icon* 33: Uncle Sam, take some more of my mint drops. **1837** *Spirit of Times* (May 13) 101: *Fanny Wright's* assumption of *John Bascombe's* station, will make old *Bertrand* worth his weight in "mint drops." **1840** *Spirit of Times* (Nov. 14) 438: Bright dreams of sparkling "yellow boys," the only genuine "mint-drops." **1842** *Spirit of Times* (Sept. 3) 319: He has to take "tickets" instead of the Benton "mint-drops." **1846** Neal *Ploddy* 178: I'll take a widder, for my part, if she's got the mint drops. **1851** *Spirit of Times* (Aug. 2) 281: If you've got a ten dollar mint drop in your purse, I'm ready for a swap. **1857** (quot. at MOPUS). **1859** *Spirit of Times* (Apr. 2) 88: All the "mint-drops"…and "filthy lucre." **1871** Schele de Vere *Americanisms* 291: When the Hon. T.H. Benton, of Missouri, put his whole strength forward on the floor of Congress and through the press to introduce a gold currency, he accidentally called the latter mint-drops, with a slight attempt at a pun….For many years gold coins were largely known as *Benton's mint-drops.*

mint leaf *n.* usu. *pl.* [pun on *mint* 'place where money is produced', reinforced by green color of paper money] a banknote; paper dollar; (*broadly*) money.
> **1942** *ATS* 537: Dollar Bill….*mint leaf.* **1952** M. Colton *Big Fix* 37. **1954–60** *DAS: Mint leaves* Banknotes. **1986** N.Y. State Lottery ad (WINS radio) (Mar. 20): I'm talkin' mega mint leaves! I'm talkin' major mazuma!

minty *n.* [orig. unkn.] *Homosex.* a homosexual person, esp. a lesbian. Cf. MANTEE.
> **1941** G. Legman, in G. Henry *Sex. Variants* II 1171: A female homosexual with very masculine characteristics…*mintée.* **1956** Reinhardt *Sex Perversions* 48: *Mintie*—noun. The very masculine aggressive dyke. **1967** *DAS* (ed. 2): *Mintie*…A homosexual, esp. an aggressive or masculine lesbian. **1966–72** Winchell *Exclusive* 6: In Harlem in 1910—If you weren't a Sissy, Queer, Minty, Petunia, Pansy, or Flaming Fhagott, you dated girls. *a*1972 B. Rodgers *Queens' Vernacular* 73: Stereotype effeminate homosexual…*mintie* ('40s). **1973** *AS* XLVI 77: Female homosexual: *Lesbian,…minty.*

minty *adj. Homosex.* effeminate; homosexual.
> **1965** Lurie *Nowhere City* 229: With that fag?…That guy's so minty he gives me the creeps. **1967** *DAS* (Supp.): *Mintie*…Homosexual; exhibiting or affecting mannerisms of the opposite sex. **1968** Kirkwood *Good Times/Bad Times* 143: Again Jordan sounded a little minty

(swishy) and Mr. Hoyt was looking confused. **1971** Rader *Govt. Inspected* 62: I was not gay, for my mind—my *un*minty imagination—was scouting past the mouthworker to other things. **1986–89** Norse *Memoirs* 126: People inquired if he was "that way" or "minty."

mis *n. Law.* a misdemeanor.
  1986 *L.A. Law* (NBC-TV): He'll plead to a mis.

miscue *n.* an error. Now *S.E.*
  1882 Peck *Peck's Sunshine* 46: Whoever it was made a miscue. **1920** Ade *Hand-Made Fables* 26: It suggested that there had been a Miscue at the Christening.

misdeal *n.* a mistake.
  1882 Peck *Peck's Sunshine* 19: He had always tried to lead a different life…but…he might have made a misdeal some way. **1903** A.H. Lewis *Boss* 32 [ref. to *ca*1870]: Sheeny Joe there has made a misdeal, that's all.

misery *n.* bad coffee.
  [**a*1890–96 F & H IV 321: *Misery*…Gin.] **1932–34** Minehan *Boy & Girl Tramps* xii: A cup of what the men appropriately enough called "misery." **1935** Algren *Boots* 40: Gimme an extra lot o' beans an' two cups o' misery. *Ibid.* 94: His misery's the hottest stuff in cups. **1953–58** J.C. Holmes *Horn* 162: Wanta stand a poor boy to a cup of misery?

misery harp *n. Logging.* a crosscut saw. Also **misery whip.**
  1958 McCulloch *Woods Words* 118: *Misery harp*—a crosscut saw. **1979** Toelken *Dyn. of Folklore* 56: *Misery whip* a two-man cross-cut saw.

misplaced eyebrow *n.* a mustache. *Joc.*
  1918 *N.Y. Eve. Jour.* (Aug. 13) 13: He won't have to cut that misplaced eyebrow. **1919** Yarwood *Overseas Dreams* 91: Misplaced eyebrows. **1921** *15th Inf. Sentinel* (Feb. 11) 10: I think I'll remove my misplaced eyebrow before I leave. **1926** Maines & Grant *Wise-Crack Dict.* 11: *Misplaced eyebrow*—So-called mustache.

miss *n.* a miscarriage.
  1969 N.Y.C. woman, age *ca*35: So she had a miss. **1994** *Donahue* (NBC-TV): The two of you [each] had a miss?

miss *v.* to miscarry a pregnancy.
  1994 *Donahue* (NBC-TV): Which of you missed?

Miss Ann *n. Black E.* a white woman or white women regarded as being hostile to or patronizing of blacks.—used contemptuously. Also **Miss Annie.**
  1925 Van Vechten *Nigger Heaven* 280: Dat ain' Miss Annie, dat's kinkout. *Ibid.* 286: *Miss Annie:* a white girl. **1928** R. Fisher *Jericho* 303: *Miss Anne, Mr. Charlie* Non-specific designation of "swell" whites.…"His *mamma*'s got a fur coat just like *Miss Anne's.*" **1929** T. Gordon *Born to Be* 184: For many years I came in contact with lots of cultured people, better known to the American Ethiopian as Miss Ann and Mr. Eddie. *Ibid.* 230: Bob Chandler proves to me that he is a real Mister Eddie, when he puts on his parties. *Ibid.* 233: [Bigots] are held down by the folks behind the closed doors, better known to all colored people as Mister Eddie and Miss Ann. If it wasn't for these people, the Negro couldn't live in the South at all. **1942** *Amer. Mercury,* in *DARE:* I had to leave from down south 'cause Miss Anne used to worry me so bad.…*Miss Anne*—a white woman. **1954–60** *DAS: Miss Anne* Any white woman. **1961** Baldwin *Another Country* 14: "Well, Miss Anne," he said, "if we both got the same thing on our mind, let's make it to that party." **1963** *Time* (Aug. 2) 14: *Miss Ann.* A white woman. **1964** Rhodes *Chosen Few* 23: Yassuh, Mistah Chawlie, no ma'am, Miss Ann. **1968** Gover *JC* 77: Is he gonna grow up t' be a big bad see-eye-aye man an keep the world safe fo' Missy Ann's fur coat? [**1971** Wells & Dance *Night People* 117: *Ann,* n. White girl.] **1974** Sanchez *Blues Bk.* 12: It ain't/easy being a queen in this unrighteous world/full of miss annes and mr. annes. **1974** V. Smith *Jones Men* 17: He jerked the shotgun in the direction of the girl. "What about Miss Ann there?"

missing link *n.* a crude or doltish person. *Joc.*
  [***1862** in *OEDS:* I…said that if we could take the trouble to make a post mortem on the Irish roughs I intend to kill next Sunday in the Park, he might convince himself that the "missing link" had been found.] **1901** in "O. Henry" *Cabbages & Kings* 21: The faces of missing links on [tintypes]. **1931** Uhler *Cane Juice* 21: "Right here"—he pointed to Bernard—"we have the missing link." **1990** *Golden Girls* (NBC-TV): No date with the missing link tonight?

mission shark *n.* MISSION STIFF, 2.
  1906 Kildare *Old Bailiwick* 51: This puts a premium on testimonies, and this is noticed by those contemptible rascals, the "mission sharks," a kind of men possessed of a certain glibness and familiarity with Bible texts.

mission squawker *n. Hobo.* a street missionary.
  1922 N. Anderson *Hobo* 217: The soap-boxers may contend with each other concerning what is best for the down-and-out in the here and now, but they are unanimous in their opposition to the "sky pilots" and the "mission squawkers." **1927** *DN* V 455: *Mission squawker,* n. A mission evangelist.

mission stiff *n. Hobo.* **1.** (among tramps) a missionary worker.
  1904 *Life in Sing Sing* 256: *Mission stiff.*—Missionary; a convert. **1914** *Survey* (Mar. 21) 781: How to Tell a Hobo from a Mission Stiff. **1934** Kromer *Waiting* 38: It don't pay to talk back to a mission stiff. **1935** (quot. at (2), below). **1982** D.A. Harper *Good Company* 17: The mission stiff, no longer able to make it on the outside, is least respected.

2. a tramp who frequents a religious mission, esp. one who pretends conversion.
  1904 (quot. at (1), above). **1922** N. Anderson *Hobo* 98: Old, helpless, and unemployable, these are the most pitiable and the most repulsive types of the down-and-outs. From this class are recruited the so-called "mission stiffs" who are so unpopular among the Hobohemian population. **1926** *AS* (Dec.) 652: *Mission stiff.* A man whose profession is getting "saved" and thereby getting a mission "flop" or something to eat. **1930** "D. Stiff" *Milk & Honey* 58: You may hang on to the good life for a time, while your erstwhile companions in sin dub you a "mission stiff." *Ibid.* 210: *Mission stiff*—Man who gets "saved" for food and a *flop.* **1931** Harlow *Old Bowery* 523: There were "mission stiffs," bums who affected a deep interest in…salvation…in order to get…free food and lodging at the missions. **1935** *AS* (Feb.) 79: *Mission stiff.* 1. One who is connected, professionally, with mission work, especially in a seamen's mission. 2. A sailor who lives or begs at dockside missions. **1968** Spradley *Owe Yourself a Drunk* 42: *Mission stiffs*…at Bethel Mission, Duluth. *Ibid.* 75: Joe over there is a mission stiff—he hangs around the missions all the time. A mission stiff just goes from one mission to another.

Mississippi lawyer *n. Miss. Valley.* a catfish. *Joc.*
  1835 in Meine & Owens *Crockett Alms.* 45: A monstratious great Cat-Fish, better known by the name of a Mississippi Lawyer, came swimming…under the bows of my boat.

Mississippi marbles *n.pl.* dice; a game of dice, esp. craps. *Joc.*
  1920 in Hemingway *Dateline: Toronto* 33: Now Mississippi Marbles play the role of the great kale transferer.…Toronto society is shooting craps. **1921** *Amer. Leg. Wkly.* (Apr. 1) 7: A pair of Mississippi marbles saved one buck from crying. **1924** *Our Navy* (Mar. 1) 29: A game of Mississippi marbles. **1954–60** *DAS.*

Miss Molly var. MOLLY.

Miss Nancy *n.* an effeminate fellow, esp. a homosexual; sissy. Cf. NANCY, NANCE.
  ***1820** in *OED2:* A Miss-nancy, is an effeminate man. **1836** *Spirit of Times* (Feb. 20) 1: A Miss Nancy—who cannot drink for gluttony, and whose shattered nerves are daily prostrated by coffee; yet scouts "the glories of a cigar," and faints from the titillation of rapee. **1840** *Spirit of Times* (Mar. 14) 13: "Miss Nancys" of the masculine gender. **1848** [W.T. Thompson] *Jones's Sks.* 101: A Miss Nancy sort of a feller. *Ibid.* 172: A Miss-Nancy sort. **1864** "Spectator" *Snoblace Ball* 68: O! vain, deceptive flight of fancy;/That seiz'd the brain of this "Miss Nancy." **1871** "M. Twain" *Roughing It* 141: They…did not go jiggering up and down after the silly Miss Nancy fashion of the riding schools. **1883** in *F & H* IV 322: The milksops and Miss-Nancys among the young men. **1898** Green *Va. Folk-Speech* 241: *Miss Nancy,* n. An affectedly prim young person of either sex; an effeminate young man. **1914** Nisbet *4 Yrs. on Firing Line* 83: Neither one of us was a mollycoddle, a Miss Nancy, or soldier of the over-righteous sort. **1916** Cary *Venery* I 209: *Miss Nancy*—…In America the term is used to designate a male cocksucker. **1929** J.M. Saunders *Single Lady* 15: I think he's kind of a Miss Nancy.

Missouri *n.* ¶ In phrase: **I'm from Missouri** I'm skeptical by nature. Now *colloq.* [Popularized by Missouri Congressman Willard Vandiver *ca*1899. Discussed extensively by G. Cohen and B. Popik in *Comments on Etymology,* Jan. 1993, Oct. 1994, Jan. 1995, Oct. 1995.]
  1898 in *Comments on Ety.* (Jan. 1995) 5: I'm from MISSOURI,/And I guess you'll have to SHOW me. **1899** *N.Y. Clipper* (Mar. 18) 58, in *Comments on Ety.* (Oct. 1995) 13: ARE YOU FROM MISSOURI? Do you know a good thing when you see it? I can show you how to get absolutely free the FINEST and GREATEST VARIETY of special Lithographic printing, [etc.]. **1900** in *DA:* Ex-Lieut.-Gov. Chas. P. Johnson thinks he knows

the origin of the extensively-used expression: "I'm from Missouri; you'll have to show me"; at least he can recall its use twenty years ago in Colorado. **1903** *Enquirer* (Cincinnati) (May 9) 13: From Omaha came the now world-wide familiar slogan, "I'm from Missouri and you've 'got ter' show me." A thousand different stories have been circulated as to how that saying was put on the market. [**1904** Hobart *Jim Hickey* 16: Well, I'm from Texas, so you'll have to steer me.] **1908** in H.C. Fisher *A. Mutt* 26: I want to invest in some of your airship stock, but I'm from Missouri and must be shown. **1912** Mathewson *Pitching* 2: But if you've found a way to hit him, why, I'm from away out in Missouri, near the Ozark Mountains. **1914** Ellis *Billy Sunday* 429: Boss, I'm from Missouri. Come across with the dough. **1950** *Mo. Hist. Soc. Bull.* VII 93. **1964** *Twilight Zone* (CBS-TV): The scoffers amongst you, and you ladies and gentlemen from Missouri. **1985** WINS radio news (Aug. 21): But at the moment Wall Street is from Missouri.

Missouri bankroll *n.* MICHIGAN ROLL. [Discussed by G. Cohen, "From Labor Lore: *Missouri Bankroll*," in his *Studies in Slang* IV, pp. 74–75.]
     1992 in G. Cohen *Studies in Slang* IV 74 [ref. to *a*1930]: The Missouri bankroll was…a roll or wad of toilet paper cut to the width of dollar bills and surrounded by several genuine bills of large denomination.

Missouri hummingbird *n.* a mule. *Joc.* Also **Missouri nightingale.**
     1918 in *Pap. Mich. Acad.* (1928): *Missouri hummingbirds:* Missouri mules. **1918** *Stars & Stripes* (Aug. 30) 3: Each animal has tied securely to his tail…a tag on which appears…the number of the horse (or Missouri nightingale). **1926** Wood & Goddard *Amer. Slang* 34: *Missouri hummingbird.* The Mule.

Miss Thing *n. Homosex.* an effeminate homosexual man.—used. as a joc. or insulting form of address, often to heterosexual men.
     *a*1972 B. Rodgers *Queens' Vernacular* 135: *Miss Thing*…affectionately effeminate. **1985** C. Busch *Vampire Lesbians* 69: Sweetie, has Miss Thing invited you to her dungeon room? **1985** "Blowdryer" *Mod. Eng.* 28: *Miss Thing*…A dragqueen insult. **1987** E. White *Beautiful Room* 41: "Miss Thing," Tex hissed, indignant. **1988** R. Snow *Members of Committee* 7: *Miss Thing* is an extremely common title which is used by homosexuals much as non-gays might say "Buddy." *a*1989 Goodwin *More Man* 18: Another vocative that can be used to express affection is *Miss Thing.* **1989** *N.Y. Times* (May 14) II H31: What you trying to say, Miss Thing? **1991** Univ. Tenn. student: "Miss Thing" is slang for an uppity gay man. It's used by drag queens a lot. **1995** *CBS This Morning* (CBS-TV) (Mar. 2): Lies, Miss Thing! Lies! **1995** *Jerry Springer Show* (synd. TV series): Whatever, Miss Thing! Whatever!…We're here! We're queer! Get used to it!

Mr. Big *n.* an important man, esp. a criminal ringleader; BIG SHOT.
     1940 in Marx *Groucho Letters* 26: I may motor east…to see your "Mr. Big." **1941** F. Ryan & W. Hamilton *Call Out Marines* (film): Think Mr. Big'll pay it? **1942** Pegler *Spelvin* 76: You were the one who could turn in a better job than Mr. Big. **1943** M. Cowley, in Jay Burke-Cowley Corres. 258: A radio address that Mr. Big was to deliver by shortwave. **1946** G.C. Hall, Jr. *1000 Destroyed* 300: Wonder who's coming this time?…Must be Mr. Big. **1949** Robbins *Dream Merchants* 4: Gonna start a scrapbook now that you're Mr. Big, Johnny? **1949** in Conklin *Sci. Fi. Omnibus* 125: Members of the Screen Team were the "Mister Bigs" in this city now—and twenty hours ago nobody'd ever heard of the Screen Team. **1952** Lait & Mortimer *USA* 15: The man behind the man who is behind all the publicized "Mr. Bigs." **1952** Bruce & Essex *Kansas City Confidential* (film): What happens when Mr. Big sees you? **1959** F.L. Brown *Trumbull Pk.* 94: I was the trash and they were the Mister Bigs. **1962** T. Berger *Reinhart* 38: I been… tramping to the groshery to get…real rye for Mr. Big. **1971** Hilaire *Thanatos* 285: The jailhouse Mr. Big. **1987** *Perfect Strangers* (ABC-TV): The boss. Mr. Big. The top banana. **1996** *N.Y. Observer* (Feb. 5) 6: Mr. Hardman…is known…as "Mr. Big" because of the amount of money he has pumped into the magazine.

Mr. Charles *n. Mil.* Viet Cong forces. Now *hist.* Cf. CHARLIE, 6.a.
     1968–90 Linderer *Eyes of Eagle* 24: We keep Mr. Charles from feeling secure in his own backyard.

Mr. Charlie *n. Black E.* CHARLIE, 4.—used contemptuously.
     1928 (quot. at MISS ANN). **1942** in A. Lomax *Where Blues Began*

129: Now, Mister Cholly. **1960** in *OEDS: Mister Charlie,* a white man. **1966** *Look* (June 28) [ref. to Watts, neighborhood of Los Angeles]: Other samples [of slang]: "Skam" (what's happening?), and "The Man," "Mister Charlie," "Whitey"—all standard derogatory terms for whites. **1967** *L.A. Times* (May 28) ("West") 21: Stokely and the Black Powers play a fierce brand of soul music that is all too comprehensible to young Mister Charlie. **1970** Landy *Underground Dict.: Mister Charlie*…White man; boss.…White Establishment man. *a*1994 N. McCall *Wanna Holler* 100: Pretty soon it's gonna be all over for Mr. Charlie.

Mr. Clean *n.* [after the bald, muscular genie *Mr. Clean,* trademark for a liquid household cleaner first marketed in the late 1950's] a man obsessed with cleanliness; (hence) *Pol.* (see 1986 quot.).
     [**1971** Rowe *Five Years* 69: Bob was a stocky, muscular individual with a Yul Brynner pate, which earned him the nickname "Mr. Clean."] **1971** Dahlskog *Dict.* 41: *Mr. Clean, n.* An obnoxiously neat or prudish fellow. **1986** *NDAS: Mister Clean*…A man, esp a politician, unsullied by suspicion of corruption or bad character.

Mr. Eddie *n. Black E.* a white man; CHARLIE, 4.b.—used contemptuously.
     1925 Van Vechten *Nigger Heaven* 286: *Mr. Eddie:* a white man. **1929** (quot. at MISS ANN). **1959** P. Oliver *Meaning of Blues* 38: He secretly calls the White man Mister Tom, Mister Charlie or Mister Eddie.

Mr. Five by Five *n.* [pop. by the popular song in 1942 quot.] a very short, fat man.
     1942 D. Raye & G. de Paul *Mister Five by Five* [pop. song title; Leeds Music Corp.]. **1947** *ATS* (Supp.) 1: *Five-by-five, Mr. Five-by-Five,* an obese person. **1957** Leckie *Helmet for My Pillow* 122 [ref. to 1943]: Mr. Five-by-Five got his nickname from his build—a few inches over five feet in height and almost that much in breadth.

Mr. Grim *n.* death.—used as a personification.
     1785 Grose *Vulgar Tongue* s.v. *Grim: Old Mr. Grim;* death. **1942 *ATS* 117: Morgue…*Old Mr. Grim's House.* **1987** M. Groening, on *Tracy Ullman Show* (Fox-TV): Passed away…kicked the bucket, pulled the croak chain, had a meeting with Mr. Grim.

Mr. Happy *n.* the penis. *Joc.*
     1984 Mason & Rheingold *Slanguage: Mr. Happy.* n. Penis. **1985** Petit *Peacekeepers* 89: Just keep saying hello to Mr. Happy. **1986** *UTSQ:* Penis…*Mr. Happy.* **1990** *In Living Color* (Fox-TV): That might have hurt—if I hadn't shifted Mister Happy. **1991** *Murphy Brown* (CBS-TV): You should've thought of that before you let Mr. Happy make a visit. **1994** *Esquire* (Mar.) 122: Erections are good for Mr. Happy. Fully dilated, its network of arteries and vessels is nourished by oxygen-rich blood. **1994** *Donahue* (NBC-TV): Sometimes Mister Happy isn't so happy! **1995** *Esquire* (Dec.) 70: Is Mr. Happy taking longer to snap back to attention?

Mr. Hawkins see s.v. HAWK.

Mr. Moto *n.* [fr. *Mr. Moto,* fictional Japanese detective created by J.P. Marquand (1893–1960)] a Japanese man; Japanese armed forces; (broadly) an Asian man of any nationality.—used derisively. Also **Moto.**
     1938 Bezzerides *Long Haul* 90: Moto wants 'em, too. **1942** *Time* (Feb. 9) 24: The Jap, who is variously "Mr. Moto," "Tojo," "Charlie," or "the Japanzy" to U.S. troops, was beginning to show a heavy preference for night movement.…Hacking out jungle trails, they often encounter "Mr. Moto." **1959** Cochrell *Barren Beaches* 83: "Take five," Salty said. "Then we'll move Mr. Moto topside." **1975** *M*A*S*H* (CBS-TV): Get the message, Mr. Moto?

Mr. Nice Guy *n.* a man who is unusually pleasant or agreeable.—usu. used ironically.—usu. constr. with *no more.*
     1966 *Get Smart!* (NBC-TV): All right. That's it. From now on, no more Mr. Nice Guy. **1973** "Alice Cooper" *No More Mr. Nice Guy* [rock song title]. **1975** V.B. Miller *Trade-Off* 50: The weatherman has stopped playing Mr. Nice Guy. **1982** *Maclean's* (Feb. 15) 64: So, no more Mister Nice Guy. That part of the message is clear. **1991** L. McKenna *No Quarter Given* 162: The next minute you're playing Mister Nice Guy. **1994** *Time* (Jan. 31) 116: Russia's Foreign Minister delivered a shocking speech announcing a return to empire and cold war. No more Mr. Nice Guy for "Greater Russia." **1995** F. Lee Bailey, on Court-TV (Nov. 15): You know the joke was that when they found Hitler in South America he was planning the Fourth Reich. They said,

"The Fourth Reich? What will you do different this time?" He said, "No more Mr. Nice Guy."

Mister Whiskers *n.* [sugg. by the image of "Uncle Sam"] the U.S. government or one of its law-enforcement agencies.
   1933 (cited in Partridge *Dict. Und.* 767). **1953** T. Runyon *In for Life* 234: But toward the minions of Mr. Whiskers' justice machine I still had plenty of resentment. **1967** "M.T. Knight" *Terrible Ten* 81: Mr. Whiskers' snoopers [couldn't make you talk].

Mr. Zip-Zip *n.* [pop. by popular song in 1917 quot.] Esp. *Mil.* a barber. *Joc.*
   1917 in Dolph *Sound Off!* 97: Good morning, Mister Zip-Zip-Zip, with your hair cut just as short as mine. **1945** in *Calif. Folk. Qly.* V (1946) 383: *Mr. Zip-Zip.* Ship's barber.

mistofer *n.* mister. *Joc.*
   *a*1867 G.W. Harris *Lovingood* 177: Yu go tu *hell*, mistofer; yu bothers me. **1867** in G.W. Harris *High Times* 185: Hello thar mistopher.

misty *adj.* tearful. [Early quots. are literary S.E.]
   [*1859 Tennyson, in *OED2:* Not so misty were her meek blue eyes.] [*1897 in *OED2:* I never took my misty eyes off Trieste and our home.] **1957** M. Shulman *Rally* 44: I still get misty when I think about it. **1973** *Odd Couple* (ABC-TV): I'm not a sentimental guy. I don't get misty about a lot of things. **1976** *Bob Newhart Show* (NBC-TV): Every once in a while I think about him and get a little misty. **1981** Wambaugh *Glitter Dome* 57: The film colony got misty in his presence. **1986** *New Gidget* (synd. TV series): Hey, guys, don't get misty on me.

mitt *n.* **1.a.** usu. *pl.* a glove.
   *1812 Vaux *Vocab.: Mitts*, gloves. **1900** Ade *More Fables* 125: The Maiden with the Lace Mitts…was going to write about it for the Weekly. **1911–12** J. London *Smoke Bellew* 222: Those blamed Siwashes had ate my moccasins [and] my mitts. [**1942–49** Goldin et al. *DAUL: Mitted.*…Gloved, as protection against leaving fingerprints.]
   b. usu. *pl.* a boxing glove.
   1877 in F. Remington *Sel. Letters* 17: To put on the "mitts" with him. **1903** Kildare *Mamie Rose* 71: Any one…could always get from a dollar and a half to two dollars for "donning the mitts." **1930** in *DAS:* Will have the big mitts on.
   c. a baseball glove; (*specif.*) a catcher's or first baseman's glove. Now *S.E.*
   1902 in *OED2.* **1908** (cited in P. Dickson *Baseball Dict.*). **1911** Spalding *Base Ball* 312: The "pillow mitt" was a later innovation.
   2.a. a hand.
   1893 (quot. at DUKE, *n.*, 1.a.). **1894** in Ade *Chicago Stories* 50: See them my mits?…I got 'em that way playing ball for John P. Hopkins. **1896** Ade *Artie* 52: It comes to takin' her by the mit and doin' the straight talk. *1897 in Franklyn *Rhyming Slang* 186: With her mit/She'd annexed the forbidden fruit. **1897** Ade *Horne* 174: "I'll tell you, Gert," I says, takin' hold of her mit. **1899** A.H. Lewis *Sandburrs* 24: An' more'n onct, when I'm in d'hole, he's reached me his mit an' pulled me out. **1903** *Enquirer* (Cincinnati) (May 9) 13: *Mitt*—A person's hand. **1904** *Life in Sing Sing* 250: *Mitt*—Hand. **1910** *N.Y. Eve. Jour.* (Jan. 4) 12: He would grip him by the mitt and hail him like a long-lost brother. **1927** in Dundes *Mother Wit* 202: Now shove me your mit and slip me the pass word. **1929** *N.Y. Times* (June 2) IX 2: They refer to hands as "mitts." **1930** W. Smith *Silver Horde* (film): Brother, you got a pair of mitts! **1943** M. Shulman *Barefoot Boy* 58: I'll show you how to get your mitts on some real dough. **1946** Kober *That Man Is Here Again* 97: The phone is still hot in my mitt. **1960** Simak *Worlds* 16: Bill wouldn't be caught dead with a dustcloth in his mitt. **1966** *Batman* (ABC-TV): As they say in the movies, "Stick up your mitts!" **1993** G. Lee *Honor & Duty* 51: His big, nicotine-yellowed mitt.
   b. usu. *pl.* the fist as used in fighting.
   1908 in H.C. Fisher *A. Mutt* 46: I am a powerfully built young man and rather shifty with my mitts. **1918** Brand *Harrigan* 86: I can sling my mitts with the best of them. **1928** Dahlberg *Bottom Dogs* 50: He was a good ball player and knew how to use his mits. **1938** Steinbeck *Grapes of Wrath* 206: I'll go for you an' your deputy with my mitts—here, now or jump Jesus.
   3. *Gamb.* a hand of cards. Cf. DUKE, 1.b.
   1896 Lillard *Poker Stories* 197: Did you suppose all those big "mitts" dropped onto you like angels from the skies? **1896** Ade *Artie* 13: I had two, four, six, seven and nine, in three different colors, all in my mit. **1913** T.A. Dorgan, in Zwilling *TAD Lexicon* 57: Whaddyatink

of a boob bidden 200 on a mitt like that. **1914** Jackson & Hellyer *Crim. Slang* 58: *Mitt*, Noun. Current chiefly amongst gamblers when the sense is a hand of cards…in any square game. **1915** T.A. Dorgan, in *N.Y. Eve. Jour.* (Aug. 19) 10: Kin ye beat a mitt like that? **1942–49** Goldin et al. *DAUL: Mitt.* One's holding in a card game. **1961** Scarne *Comp. Guide to Gambling* 685: *Mitt.* A hand of cards.
   4. *Carnival.* a palm reader; MITT READER.
   1931 *AS* (June) 333: *Mitt*, n. A palmist. (Short for mitt-reader.). **1942** *ATS* 321: *Mitt, mitt reader*, a palmist.
   5. *Und.* (see quot.).
   1983 *N.Y. Times* (Aug. 29) B2: A "mitt" is a roll of money and being "strapped" or having a "tool" means to have a gun.

¶ In phrases:

¶ **give the mitt** to reject; jilt. Cf. MITTEN, 1.
   1923 in O'Brien *Best Stories of 1923* 73: You can't lay everything to your paw's goin' off and the girl givin' you the mitt. **1949** *Sat. Eve. Post* (Oct. 1) 74: Is this your own peculiar way…of giving me the mitt?

¶ **glad mitt** see s.v. GLAD HAND, 1.

¶ **grease the mitt** *Und.* to bribe an official. Also **fit the mitt.**
   1926 Finerty *Criminalese* 27: *Grease the mit*—or *palm*—Pay bribe money. **1935** Pollock *Und. Speaks: Greased mits*, public officials, underworld boss[es] or politicians who have been bribed for protection. **1940** *AS* (Apr.) 118: *To Fit the Mitt.* To bribe an official….*Fitted Mitt.* A bribed official.

¶ **hold up (one's) mitt** to enlist.
   1906 M'Govern *Bolo* 24: I had to hold up my mit before night to get trun into the Pacific. **1906** M'Govern *Sgt. Larry* [gloss.]: *Hold Up His Mit:*—To enlist.

¶ **icy mitt** cold shoulder.
   *1907 in *OEDS:* The erstwhile hospitable farmers met us with the icy mitt. **1919** S. Lewis *Free Air* 178: They would hearken not. Gee, those birds certainly did pull the frigid mitt! **1921** Brand *Black Jack* 159: He likes her, in spite of the frosty mitt she handed him. **1926** Wood & Goddard *Amer. Slang* 12: *Cold shoulder.* Same as icy mitt. **1927** S. Lewis *Elmer Gantry* 168: A man like me, he gives me the icy mitt, and then he goes to the other extreme and slops all over some old dame that's probably saved already.

¶ **read mitts** *Carnival.* to practice palmistry. Cf. MITTEN READER.
   1951 Mannix *Sword-Swallower* 169: I wonder how she ever ended up reading mitts in a Ten-in-One.

¶ **the big mitt** *Und.* a kind of crooked card game.
   [**1843** J. Greene *Exposure of Gambling* 186: There is another hand, called a *big hand*, that is sometimes played in this game [*sc.*, seven-up]. It is a trick….The good hand promises so fairly to make four, that you would be very likely to bet and take the good hand….I would advise all persons not to bet on it.] **1903** in *DA*. **1905** in *OED2:* The "big mitt" game…an ingenious method of swindling by means of a stacked hand. [**1914** Jackson & Hellyer *Vocab.* 58: The *Mitt* is a confidence game of the same nature as the *Lemon* or the *Match*, involving a double-cross.] **1930** Conwell *Pro. Thief* 68: Some years back the duke was called "the big mitt." It was played successfully on railroad trains and in ninety-nine cases out of a hundred the conductor was "in." This is now practically obsolete.

¶ **throw the mitt** *Und.* to pick pockets.
   1902 Hapgood *Thief* 63 [ref. to *ca*1885]: Jack then came off his perch and gave his patron a lesson in the art of throwing the mit (dipping).

¶ **tip (one's) mitt** to *tip (one's) hand* s.v. TIP, *v.*
   1907 in H.C. Fisher *A. Mutt* 19: It's very unclublike to tip the mitt of the wire tappers. **1908** H. Green *Maison de Shine* 204: He's liable to tip my mitt to Banana. **1908** in Fleming *Unforgettable Season* 267: The wily John T. Brush tipped his mitt to Bancroft by asking a number of questions about switching the game here. **1914** Jackson & Hellyer *Crim. Slang* 58: If he spiels long enough he'll tip his mitt. **1913–15** Van Loan *Taking Count* 124: He tipped his mitt de minute he took off his dicer. **1920** Ade *Hand-Made Fables* 298: Tell them to go as far as they can without tipping their Mitts. **1923** in Hammett *Knockover* 149: She couldn't have taken any from home without tipping her mitt. **1923** in D. Hammett *Continental Op* 33: Or he wouldn't have made that raw play—tipping my mitt to Smith right in front of me. **1937** Schary & Butler *Big City* (film): Tongues hangin' down to here waitin' for me to tip my mitt! **1938** "E. Queen" *4 Hearts* 136: How about tip-

ping your mitt for a change? **1945** in Kober *That Man Is Here Again* 228: He prolly figgered he tipped his mitt by showin' me how excited he his. **1950** Girard & Sherdeman *Breakthrough* (film): If they had, Eisenhower would have tipped his mitt. **1970** La Motta, Carter & Savage *Raging Bull* 151: You didn't tip your mitt to the cops, you kept your mouth shut. That's what I like. **1971** Dibner *Trouble with Heroes* 115: At the same time I try not to tip my own mitt.

¶ **work the mitt** *Carnival.* to read palms.
    1922 *Variety* (Sept. 22) 6: Gypsies penetrate to all parts of the town, working the "mitt" from house to house.

mitt *v.* **1.** to welcome or congratulate by shaking the hand of; shake hands with.
    1908 in H.C. Fisher *A. Mutt* 82: This...photograph...shows Mr. Mutt in the act of being mitted by the Czar. **1908** T.A. Dorgan, in Zwilling *TAD Lexicon* 58: Turning to mitt a pal of mine at the ringside. **1910** T.A. Dorgan, in *N.Y. Eve. Jour.* (Feb. 5) 6: Coffroth...mitted a few pals, kissed a few glasses, then...tossed off a bit of the blarney concerning fights and fighters. **1911** A.H. Lewis *Apaches of N.Y.* 205: Mitt me, Charley, mitt me. **1915** Howard *God's Man* 280: He mitts me and says he thanks Gawd he's got *one* pal. **1924** Henderson *Keys to Crookdom* 411: Mitt me—shake my hand. **1924** *Adventure* (Mar. 30) 166: Get off that *chevaux* and mitt me. You're welcomer than pay-day. **1926** Maines & Grant *Wise-Crack Dict.* 11: *Mitt me*—Shake my hand. **1928** Nason *Sgt. Eadie* 319 [ref. to 1918]: "Mitt me," said the M.P. "Mitt me," he said again, and extended his hand. Eadie mitted him. **1929** W.R. Burnett *Iron Man* 84: Don't be mitting everybody that way. **1932** *AS* VII (June) 334: *Mit me kid*—"congratulate me." **1933** Ersine *Prison Slang* 53: Mit me, brother, I just made a pardon. **1950** *Sat. Eve. Post* (Nov. 11) 73: She expressed herself as simply dyin' to mitt the mitt of a post-office inspector.

2. to give; press into someone's hand.
    1910 *N.Y. Eve. Jour.* (Mar. 22) 15: I'm goin' t' make that gink mitt me th' hundred in advance. *Ibid.* (Apr. 28) 16: He'll mitt us a flock of coin for this. **1911** Howard *Enemy to Society* 294: O'Shea..."mitts" him five century notes. **1926** Clark & Eubank *Lockstep* 174: Mitt—put hush-money into an officer's hand.

3.a. to punch.
    1910 *N.Y. Eve. Jour.* (Mar. 9) 16: Get out o' my way you little shrimp....I got a good notion t' mit you one. **1928** Dahlberg *Bottom Dogs* 116: Mugsy wanted to mitt him one.

b. to seize; arrest.
    1915 Howard *God's Man* 128: A big green harness-bull...mitts *me*, while I'm trying to help Joe with his game leg. **1954–60** *DAS*: *Mitt*...To put handcuffs on someone; to make an arrest.

4. *Boxing.* to hold (the gloved hands) over one's head as a gesture of confidence or victory.—usu. constr. with *them [up].*—also constr. with audience as obj.—also used fig.
    1930 Burnett *Iron Man*, in *DAS*: Prince Pearl was sitting in his corner and mitting the crowd. **1942** *ATS* 591: *Mit 'em*, to acknowledge applause by clasping the hands above the head. **1952** *Time* (Aug. 4) 16: She tramped to the speaker's stand splendidly corseted, and garbed in lacy black. She clasped her hands over her head and mitted the crowd. **1955** Graziano & Barber *Somebody Up There* 255: And I would mitt 'em up and give him a big smile and a wink.

mitt artist *n. Sports. Journ.* a boxer.
    1904 T.A. Dorgan, in Zwilling *TAD Lexicon* 117: (Joe Walcott, The Fighting Marvel) Joe has been the stumbling block for many a mitt artist. **1906** Ford *Shorty McCabe* 87: Some of these mitt artists is nice, decent boys. **1906** *Nat. Police Gaz.* (Aug. 25) 7: Bouts in the Ring By the Many Mitt Artists During the Week. *****1918** *Bodleian Qly. Rec.* II 153: *A mit artist*, a boxer.

mitt camp *n. Carnival.* a palm reader's tent; MITT JOINT, 2.
    1927 Nicholson *Barker* 9: She is the proprietress of the fortune-telling booth, or as it is known in carnival parlance, the Mitt Camp. **1935** *Amer. Mercury* (June) 230: *Mit camp:* gypsy fortune-telling joint. **1946** Gresham *Nightmare Alley* 29: I do a little tea-leaf reading and one winter I worked a mitt camp in Miami. **1948** F. Brown, in *DAS*. **1951** Mannix *Sword-Swallower* 22: I have a mitt camp here...that's palmistry, you know. **1953** Gresham *Midway* 17: A psychiatric social worker went "with it" reading palms in the "mitt camp" and made so much dough she never went back to her old life. **1956** H. Gold *Not With It* 12: Palmistry Pauline, the queen of our mittcamp. **1963** *Carnival* (NBC-TV documentary): The mitt camp.

mitted *adj. & adv. Und.* armed.
    1917 *Editor* (Feb. 24) 153: *Go mitted or heeled*—to go armed. **1921** (cited in Partridge *Dict. Und.* 442). **1942–49** Goldin et al. *DAUL: Mitted.* 1. (Rare) Armed with any weapon capable of being used with one hand.

mitten *n.* **1.** rejection; dismissal; jilting.—usu. constr. with *give* or *get.*
    1842 in *DARE*: I'm glad enough...that Candace has given that young scamp the mitten! **1843** in A.P. Hudson *Humor of Old So.* 520: Ought a young man to foller a gal, after she gives him the mitten[?]. **1846** J. Neal *Ploddy* 14: Young gentlemen that have got the mitten or young gentlemen who think they are going to get the mitten, always sigh. **1848** in *OED2*: Dana,...Who'll be going to write what'll never be written Till the Muse, ere he thinks of it, gives him the mitten. **1852** Doten *Journals* I 122: She about gave me the mitten. **1856** B. Hall *College Wds.* (ed. 2) 324: At the Collegiate Institute of Indiana, a student who is expelled is said to *get the mitten.* **1857** in Dyer *Songs & Ballads* 221: Jacob Gets the Mitten. **1862** in C.H. Moulton *Ft. Lyon* 71: The expected visitors had "given us the mitten" and failed to appear. **1866** in W.A. White *Autobiog.* 13: But she gave me the *mitten.* **1873** Hotten *Slang Dict.* (ed. 4): "To get the *mitten*" is, in Canadian slang, to be jilted. **1876** in Applegate & O'Donnell *Talking on Paper* 79: I wonder if Miss Elzora...has *dared* give my brother the mitten? **1880** Bellamy *Heidenhoff* 43: That would be taking a good deal of trouble to get a mitten. If you are so anxious for it, I will give it to you now. **1882** C.C. King *Col.'s Daughter* 126: He has received more recommendations for brevet [for "military engagements"] and more "mittens" [for "matrimonial engagements"] than any man in the regiment. *****1888** in *F & H* IV 324: *To get the mitten*...Without doubt the Latin *mitto* to send (about your business), to dismiss, is the *fons et origo* of this term. **1891** Maitland *Slang Dict.* 177: *Mitten, "to get the."* To be rejected by one's sweetheart. **1891** in F. Harris *Conklin* 4: He wanted me to go with him tonight, and I didn't give him the mitten, as I should if I thought you were goin' to ask me. **1941, 1946, 1965–70** in *DARE*. **1994** Omaha, Nebr., psychologist, age *ca*62: So she gave you the mitten.

2. usu. *pl. Boxing.* a boxing glove. Cf. MITT, 1.b.
    1859 Matsell *Vocab.* 127: *Mittens.* Boxing-gloves. *****1887** in *F & H* IV 323: I'll get him to put the mittens on...and have three rounds. *****1889–90** Barrère & Leland *Dict. Slang: Mittens*...boxing-gloves. **1891** Maitland *Slang Dict.* 177: *Mittens*, boxing gloves. **1894** C.C. King *Cadet Days* 241: And with that the two Westerners doffed their coats, donned the "mittens," and hammered away at each other. **1902** Naughton *Queensberry Realm* 84: Corbett was extraordinarily deft with the mittens. **1910** (quot. at BEARCAT). **1970** in P. Heller *In This Corner* 148 [ref. to 1930's]: Took my mittens and I hung 'em up. That was it.

mitten *v.* **1.** to seize; grab.—usu. constr. with *onto.*
    1841 [Mercier] *Man o' War* 179: Both Flukes and Bowser, *mittened* on to de article in question, wid de rapidity of greased lightning. **1887** *Outing* (Dec.) 229: I jumps into the forecastle for to mitten Tom's dunnage afore I called the watch, when I run foul of Jim Walker animated by the same feelin's. So we agreed for to divide. **1898** Green *Va. Folk-Speech* 241: *Mitten on, v.* To seize and hold fast. When you get near enough *mitten on* to him.

2. to reject; jilt. Cf. MITTEN, *n.*, 1.
    1873 in *DARE*: For me she mittened a lawyer. **1878, 1881, 1941, 1949** in *DARE*.

mittflop *v.* MITTGLOM. Hence **mitt-flopper**, *n.*
    1941 *AS* (Oct.) 167: *Mitt Flopper.* A soldier who does favors for his superiors, or salutes unnecessarily; a *yes man.* **1942** *Yank* (Dec. 16) 19: Actually the best way to get service is to do a little mitt flopping with a Restaurant Romeo.

mittful *n.* a handful.
    1917 E.R. Burroughs *Oakdale Affair* 17: Didn't you lamp...de mitful of rocks and kale?

mittglom *v.* [MITT + GLOM] Esp. *Mil.* to ingratiate oneself with persons in authority. [Early quots. ref. to WWI.]
    1919 Wilkins *Co. Fund* 47: Imagine: Joe Luco mittglomming. **1927** *Amer. Leg. Mo.* (June) 74: I ain't no handshaker! Mittglommin' never was in my line. **1933** Ersine *Pris. Slang* 53: The rat is up there mitglomming with the screw now.

mitt-glommer *n.* Esp. *Mil.* one who attempts to ingratiate himself or herself with persons in authority; HANDSHAKER.
    1918 in *AS* (Oct. 1933) 29: *Mitt-Glommer.* Handshaker, fin-flipper. **1922** in H. Miller *Letters to Emil* 5: To hell with the Western Union

that feeds my brat and all the other slinking mit-glaumers that help the W.U. to do it. **1931** *Our Army* (Jan.) 17: Mitt-glommer. **1931** *AS* VI (Aug.) 440: *Mitt-glommer*, n. A hand-shaker. **1933** Ersine *Pris. Slang* 53: *Mitglommer*, n. A handshaker. **1934** *Our Army* (Nov.) 11: That two-striper must be a good mittglommer. **1973** Krulewitch *Now That You Mention It* 37 [ref. to ca1918]: Why you mitglommer punk....Holding out on your pals.

mitt joint *n.* **1.** *Und.* a crooked gambling house.

   1914 Jackson & Hellyer *Vocab.* 59: *A Mitt Joint* is a gambling house where victims are "steered" for fleecing by means of deceptively "sure thing" hands. **1935** Pollock *Und. Speaks*: *Mitt joint*, crooked, cheating gambling house.

   2. *Carnival.* a palmist's concession; MITT CAMP.

   1921 (cited in Partridge *Dict. Und.* 442). **1922** *Variety* (Sept. 22) 6: There are many types of "mitt joints," ranging from the elaborately staged "Gypsy Camp" to the single reader...in one small tent. **1927** Nicholson *Barker* 102: Mitt joint—Fortune teller's tent. **1942** Liebling *Telephone* 7: You want to open a mitt joint in my concession! Get outa here! **1943** J. Mitchell *McSorley's* 49: She operates a mitt joint, or fortune-telling tent, for...a small Southern carnival.

mitt man *n.* *Und.* a confidence man.

   1967 [R. Beck] *Pimp* 163: He should be maybe a "Murphy" player or even a "mitt man." *Ibid.* 315: Mitt Man...a hustler who uses religion and prophecy to con his victims, usually the victims are women. **1968** I. Reed *Yellow Back Radio* 11: What a line that guy had. A mitt man from his soul.

mitt pusher *n.* a boxer.

   1906 *Nat. Police Gaz.* (Feb. 10) 7: These Are Busy Days...For The Mitt Pushers. **1918** T.A. Dorgan, in Zwilling *TAD Lexicon* 117: St. Clair is one of the mitt-pushers who fights...at the local clubs.

mitt reader *n.* *Carnival.* a palmist.

   1928 *AS* III (June) 414: *Mitt reader.* A palmist, or fortune teller. **1938** *AS* (Oct.) 235: In the carnival world a fortune teller is called a *mitt reader.* **1943** J. Mitchell *McSorley's* 93: Every confounded swami-woman and mitt-reader in the nation [took] to calling herself Madame So-and-So. **1961** Clausen *Season's Over* 152: I was married ten years to a mitt reader on the carnie.

mitt wobbler *n.* *Army.* MITT-GLOMMER. [Quots. ref. to WWI.]

   1917 R. Lord *Boyd's Battery* 24: Handshaker n.—See Lily Presser, Mitt Wobbler, Dog Robber. **1919** Wallgren *AEF* (unp.): Every "blankety blank" non-com in our outfit was a mitt wobbler. **1923** *Amer. Leg. Wkly.* (Apr. 6) 11: Movie of the Amateur Mitt Wobbler and Hard Boiled Top.

mix *n.* a fight; brawl.

   1864 in H. Johnson *Talking Wire* 166: We expected to have a little *mix*, but soon learned that they were friendly indians. **1930** M. West *Babe Gordon* 18: The mix was stopped before the round was over. **1966–67** W. Stevens *Gunner* 96: I could sell tickets to a mix like that.

mix *v.* to fight.

   1895 Ade *Chicago Stories* 134: "W'at yer mixin' fer?" says the barkip. **1947** P. Dawson *High Country* 23: Quit the dancin' and let's mix, boys. **1993** P. Munro *U.C.L.A. Slang II* 59: Let's mix.

   ¶ In phrase:

   ¶ **mix it [up]** to fight, usu. with the fists; (*hence*) to argue volubly.

   1899 A.H. Lewis *Sandburrs* 207: Me only idee at d' time is...to mix it up wit' d' drunken bum who's soaked Sal. **1904** *Munsey's Mag.* (Oct.) 90: It is low to speak of a fist-fight as a "mill," or to say that the combatants "mixed it up" or had a "mix-up." **1919** De Beck *Google* 3: I was gonna see Dempsey mix up with the Jamaica Kid at three o'clock. **1920** F.S. Fitzgerald *This Side of Paradise*, in *DAS*: A prize-fight where the principals refused to mix it up. **1929–30** Farrell *Young Lonigan* 13: Studs was a little leery about mixing it with Reilley. **1931** Rynning *Gun Notches* 4: Him and his cowboys from the Washita come rampsing in there on purpose to mix it. **1952** *New Yorker* (Apr. 26) 28: The armed forces have repeatedly challenged Joe Louis, Rocky Marciano...and other boxers and wrestlers to mix it up with him but they won't. **1978** *Atlantic* (June) 96: It was pleasing to see two women characters in a movie mixing it up over something other than the leading man. **1994** *Donahue* (NBC-TV): Come on, let's mix it up! **1995** *House of Buggin'* (Fox-TV): Let's mix it up! Let's mix it up!

mixmaster *n.* [fr. *Mixmaster*, trademark for a type of kitchen appliance] a helicopter; (*also*) the O-2 Super Skymaster observation aircraft.

   [**1946** in *OED2*: *Mixmaster*, army bomber propelled by two rear counter-revolving propellers.] **1951** in *OEDS*: In the business they refer jocularly to the helicopter by a number of descriptive names: "eggbeater," "windmill," and "mixmaster," to mention a few. **1972** W.C. Anderson *Hurricane* 192: Let's mush this Mixmaster over to Jones Beach. **1984** Trotti *Phantom* 248 [ref. to Vietnam War]: 0-2 Super Skymaster (...Mixmaster).

mix-up *n.* a fistfight; brawl. Now *S.E.*

   [*1841** in *OED2*: I had expected being conducted to London alone, and certainly was not prepared for a mix-up with these men.] **1894** Ade *Chicago Stories* 117: "Tubby" Bite, sewer inspector and a handy man in a "mix-up." **1899** Cullen *Tales* 48: The tall man, in emerging from a hot mix-up, shot out his left. **1904** *Life in Sing Sing* 256: *Mixup*—A fight. **1922–26** Scoggins *Red Gods* 59: I was with him in one mix-up in Honduras and he sure is one Foxy Grandpa in a scrap. **1929–30** Farrell *Young Lonigan* 20: He had almost gotten into a mixup with some soused mick.

mizzard *n.* [var. MAZZARD] the head; the mind; the mouth.

   1877 Bartlett *Amer.* (ed. 4) 895: Tease not your own gizzard; fret not your own mizzard. *1893** in *F & H* IV 325: If the beds ain't all made....and everything fat and lean in the kitchen, they open their mizzards and slam I can tell you.

mizzle *v.* to abscond; run away; clear out; (with weakened force) to go; walk.

   *1781** G. Parker *View of Society* II 176: *Rum Mizzlers.* Fellows who are clever in making their escape. *Ibid.* 231: He preferred *mizzling* off to France. *1789** G. Parker *Life's Painter* 134: Don't mizzle yet. *1812** Vaux *Vocab.*: *Mizzle*: to quit or go away from any place or company; to elope, or run away. *1820–21** P. Egan *Life in London* 25: As she *mizzled* through Temple-Bar. *1821** *Real Life in London* I 89: *Mizzled*—Ran away. **1840** (quot. at HAINES). **1842** *Spirit of Times* (Oct. 29) 410: To Bolt...to mizzle...to Levant. **1846** (quot. at VAMOOSE). **1846** Neal *Ploddy* 80: "Mizzle!" said he, in a hoarse, suppressed whisper. **1849** *Spirit of Times* (Nov. 10) 452: The varmint...mizzled. **1849** Doten *Journals* I 44: A large sword fish was seen under the stern, but when we all run aft to get a sight at him he "mizzled." **1851** M. Reid *Scalp-Hunters* 98: Thar a goin' to mizzle! **1854** Avery *Laughing Gas* 108: Jim mizzled. **1855** Wise *Tales* 15: I've written the Hon. Soketary of the Navy to send you off to sea; so mizzle. *1857** "Ducange Anglicus" *Vulgar Tongue* 13: *Mizzle*, v. To disappear. **1858** in G.W. Harris *High Times* 138: Jehosefat! how he mizzled t'uther way. **1859** Matsell *Vocab.* 55: Smasher...touched the swag, and mizzled like a bull....*Mizzle*. Go; run; be off. **1864** O.W. Holmes, Jr., in M.D. Howe *Shaping Yrs.* 163: Cavalry sent up the road, but got stampeded & mizzled. **1865** *Harper's Mo.* (June) 12: Just fork over four bits or mizzle! **1865** in Horrocks *Dear Parents* 147: I had...begun to believe they had "mizzled." *a1867** in G.W. Harris *Lovingood* 73: He jis' mizzel'd, skar'd. **1868** J.R. Browne *Apache Country* 368: Just fork over four bits or mizzle! **1857–71** Leland *Breitmann's Ballads* 22: Breitmann...down de Corso mizzled. *1881–84** Davitt *Prison Diary* I 153: Misle! Dog the copper!...Vanish! See the policeman! **1889** in Leitner *Diamond in Rough* 168: Half the spectators have "mizzled." *1896** *Gentleman's Mag.* (Oct.) 350: "Mizzle" (to go) represents the Shelta (miesli). *1970** in *OED2*.

Mizzoo *n.* Missouri; (*also*) the Missouri River.

   1899 (quot. at K.C.). **1914** in Handy *Blues Treasury* 88: I'll...wash my hands in the Old Mizzou' in K.C. **1936** in Pyle *Ernie's Amer.* 141: He came...from Missouri. That's why they call him Mizzoo. **1943** in Rea *Wings of Gold* 67: The river, "old Missou," is very high. *a1953** in B. Ives *Song Book* 154: The old Mizzoo, she's a mighty river.

M.J. *n.* *Narc.* marijuana.

   1966 Young & Hixson *LSD* 10: Marijuana, m.j., Mary Jane, grass, tea, boo, pot. **1974–77** Heinemann *Close Quarters* 26: Why, smoke is M.J. Mike Juliet. Ya know—grass. **1994** *Totally Unofficial Rap Dict.* (Internet): Marijuana...*Mary Jane (mj)* .

Mo *n.* *Navy.* the battleship U.S.S. *Missouri*. Cf. BIG MO, 1.a., MIGHTY MO.

   1956 Hess *Battle Hymn* 124: Recalling the "Mo's" recent mishap in Chesapeake Bay.

mo[1] *n.* **1.** a moment; second; usu. in phr. **half a mo.**

   *1896** in *OEDS*: In half a mo'—half a mo' your pluck and perseverance you can show. **1956** *Ernie Kovacs Show* (CBS-TV): We have but thirty moes to go. **1966** Cassiday *Angels Ten* 139: Bear with me, half a mo. **1971** LeGuin *Lathe of Heaven* 133: Half a mo. I think we'll have a session without hypnosis today.

2. a month.

1928 Wharton *Squad* 7 [ref. to 1918]: Ain't it a hell of a war, when a fellow makin' an honest $30 a mo's gotta fork out near half of it to support a goddam whore! **1952** Mandel *Angry Strangers* 87: "How long a trip?"…"Six moes."

mo² *n. Stu.* HOMO.—used derisively.

1968 Baker et al. *CUSS* 158: *Mo.* An effeminate male. A homosexual. **1976** in G.A. Fine *With Boys* 169: *Mo,* n. Homosexual. **1986** Eble *Campus Slang* (Oct.) 4: *Mo*—a homosexual or someone who acts like one:…"Yeah, he's a mo." Also *Bufu, Fag, Fruit, Queer.* **1987** *Nat. Lampoon* (Oct.) 10: Gay…insurance plan…MoLife Mutual. **1987** West Georgia College instructor: "He's not a nitwit but he is a mo." "A mo?" "A *homo.*" **1988** *Nat. Lampoon* (Apr.) 26: Homosexuals…Nellies, 'mo's. **1990** *Newsweek* (Feb. 5) 17: My nickname for homosexual is 'mo—you know, the 'mos. [**1993** P. Munro *U.C.L.A. Slang* II 59: *Moe* n. socially inept or awkward person. *Look at how he dresses—he's such a moe!*]

mo³ *n.* [shortened from BIG MO, 2] *Pol.* momentum, as of a political campaign.

1980 *Maclean's* (Oct. 27): The central figure in this quickening American presidential campaign is a character called Mo. Everyone wants Mo on his side, but Mo's loyalties are fickle. **1988** *McLaughlin Group* (synd. TV series) (Sept. 4): A week after Labor Day, who will have the big mo—Dukakis or Bush?….Four say that the mo will be with Bush. **1989** *Capital Gang* (CNN-TV) (Aug. 5): "Does the abortion lobby have the big mo now?" "Well, I think they have a little mo."

mo *v.* to touch someone in a way that could be perceived as a homosexual advance.

1980 Birnbach et al. *Preppy Hndbk.* 222: *Stop moing me…*Don't touch me. When boys inadvertently touch each other in elementary and secondary school; homophobic. (Also, mo, moing out, heavy mo action.). **1990** T. Thorne *Dict. Contemp. Slang: Mo…*(to behave like) a homosexual.

moat *n. Und.* a river.

1848 *Ladies' Repository* VIII (Oct.) 315: *Moat,* A river. *Ibid.: Moat Palace,* A steamboat.

mob *n.* **1.** a turbulent crowd or rout of people. (now *S.E.*); (with weakened force) a sizable group of persons; clique.

*****1688** Shadwell *Squire of Alsatia* IV i: Here honest Mob, course this Whore to some pupose. *****1699** E. Ward, in Winship *Boston* 47: Laugh'd as heartily at their Disapointment, as the *Mob* in the Fable at the *Mountain-mouse.* *****1702** in *F & H* VI 326: If so, you'll have both the mob and the law on your side. *****1708** in D'Urfey *Pills* I 79: How fast thy Mob Army could run. **1729** *Pa. Gazette* (Apr. 12) [3]: Two or three Citizens that withstood the Mob, were wounded. **1745** in *AS* (Oct. 1940) 231 [cited without quotation]. **1776** in East & Judd *Loyalist Amer.* 41: Our Departure…Shall not be a Spectacle to the mobbs thro which we shall pass. **1834** Caruthers *Kentuckian in N.Y.* I 222: And see that Feller that sets at the top of the mob [*sc.,* an orchestra]. **1836** (quot. at GOLDFINCH, 2). **1837** Strong *Diary* I 68: Virgil, and Plautus, and Terence and all the rest of that mob have weak points *ad infinitum.* **1895** *Harper's* (Sept.) 620: Don't monkey wid no tough mob of girls nor no crooked fellers. **1908** *New Broadway* (Aug.) 142: When we of the Italian Squad have to visit Giuseppi's Black Hand headquarters we go in mobs of five. **1939** Goodman & Kolodin *Swing* 41: The kids I had played [music] with at Harrison and Austin were called the "Wild West Side Mob," by the…professionals. **1963** in *Black Scholar* (Nov. 1971) 3: A "natural" to the fight mob connotes any fight which pits a white man against a Negro.

2. *Und. & Police.* a band or gang of criminals; (*hence*) a crime syndicate; in phr. **the mob** organized crime in general. Now *S.E.*

1791 [W. Smith] *Confess. T. Mount* 21: To head a mob Jack ne'er would fail. **1832** *Spirit of Times* (Mar. 31) 2: John Williams, alias Roberts, alias Hervy, alias twenty other names, who belongs to the respectable fraternity of thieves, vulgarly denominated the "Swell Mob," was charged with stealing a fowl. *****1843** in *F & H* VI 45: Rich Charities the Chapel throng, The swell mob they are there, The Bishop's sermon is not long, The fogle-hunter ware! **1866** *Nat. Police Gaz.* (Nov. 3) 2: The "mob" took a short cut through Myrtle avenue. **1872**

Crapsey *Nether Side* 17: They work in "mobs" of three or four persons. **1879** *Snares of N.Y.* 38: Thieves are…divided into associations of five, six, or seven persons, known in the expressive slang of the profession as "mobs." **1884** Costello *Police Protectors* 324: In 1877 Captain Allaire…broke up the "Dutch Mob" which was composed of Johnny Irving, Sheeney Mike, Dutch Chris, Billy Porter, and Little Freddie. **1887** Walling *N.Y. Chief of Police* 263: During the three years preceding the robbery several mobs were got up for the purpose of consummating the scheme. *****1889–90** Barrère & Leland *Dict. Slang* II 58: *Mob* (thieves), gang. **1891** Campbell, Knox & Byrnes *Darkness & Daylight* 707: A "mob" is always composed of not less than three men working in harmony. **1892** L. Moore *Own Story* 179: This "mob" had journeyed from Philadelphia bound for Olean to do this very job. **1904** *Life in Sing Sing* 250: *Mob.*—Three or more people who travel to steal. **1911** Bronson-Howard *Enemy to Society* 168: Send that mob of yours back where they came from. **1925** (quot. at KNOCK OVER). **1926** in Ruhm *Detective* 66: You've been waiting for your mob to come back and grab me. **1936** Benton & Ballou *Where Do I Go?* 204: He was boss of a "mob" of three or four who were hijacking liquor trucks for a living. **1941** M. Wolff *Whistle Stop* 120: There ain't been no mob around this town since repeal. **1949** in *Harper's* (Feb. 1950) 71: A heist mob may comprise from two to six or eight members. **1949** W.R. Burnett *Asphalt Jungle* 93: A fifty-grand haul had been a huge one, even for a mob of four. **1952** Chase *McThing* 85: I joined the mob. You can't get out of a mob. **1955** Q. Reynolds *HQ* 73: I needed someone the mob didn't know to do some tailing for me. **1961** Horan *Mob's Man* 32: We made elaborate plans for an expansion of our mob. **1961** Anslinger & Oursler *Murderers* 143: We have a setup in France with a mob over there. **1963** *Car-54* (NBC-TV): You were right, Bubbles. They are a mob, and I think they're planning a caper. **1965** Horan *Seat of Power* 94: A policy mob was in operation. **1962–68** B. Jackson *In the Life* 186: I work…with what they call a "bust-out" mob. Craps in conventions, picnics, things like that. There you work eight- or ten-handed. **1971** J. Blume *Then Again* 15: My father is in trouble with the Jersey City mob. **1974** R. Novak *Concrete Cage* 122: Howie Chase walks out a free man the moment the rest of your mob are picked up. **1977** L. Jordan *Hype* 104: You mean the Mob's gonna get me if I don't watch out? **1980** Hillstrom *Coal* 412: "The mob."…"You mean the Mafia?" **1989** Hiaasen *Skin Tight* 15: They think it's a mob hit! **1991** Jankowski *Islands in Street* 3: As time moved on…*mob* became the term used for organized crime groups, and *gang* gradually became associated with adolescent boys. **1992** *NewsHour* (CNN-TV) (Feb. 27): Was the murder…a hit by the Japanese mob?

3.a. *Naut.* a ship's crew.

1845 (cited in Partridge *DSUE* 1277). **1941** Wald et al. *Navy Blues* (film): That *Topeka* mob. It'll be fun to see those wisenheimers squirm.

b. *Mil.* a military unit; outfit. [Common in BrE, though rarer in U.S.]

1894 in Dale *Songs of 7th* 91: The mob will shout "No Maud is out"/And yell till they get red. **1918** R. Casey *Cannoneers* [entry for Sept. 28]: I was just wandering along with this doughboy outfit and all their officers were knocked off so I inherited the mob. **1918** Griffin *Ballads of Reg't.* 24: Now he can take a soldier "mob"—can our "old man"…And…drill it with a vim and a smack. *Ibid.* 35: For I had served the colors there with all of that "old mob." **1941** in Whitehouse *Fighters in Sky* 43: They ran into the Lancer and his mob [*sc.,* squadron] one late afternoon. ca**1944** in Craven & Cate *AAF in WWII* VII 405: Several of our mob got in [the General Hospital]…when they got lost in the fog and crashed nearby. **1966** J. Lewis *Tell It to Marines* 30: And that jeep's a sort of status symbol to this outfit. If you lose it, the whole mob loses face. *a***1987** Coyle *Team Yankee* 187: Now tell your mob to ease up so the captain and I can get up. **1989** Leib *Fire Dream* 133: Hooper's mob is a lesser fate. **1989** Zumbro & Walker *Jungletracks* 221: You think we can get this mob on up there in time?

mob *v.* to go; travel; MOBILIZE, 2.

1993 "Snoop Doggy Dogg" *Gz Up, Hoes Down* (rap song): I mob to the beach.

mobbed up *adj. Police & Und.* connected with or dominated by organized crime. Cf. earlier MOB UP.

1973 Peterson *Sicilian Slaughter* 63: All [prize]fighting on the East Coast was totally "mobbed up." **1976** *Kojak* (CBS-TV): If that honcho is mobbed up,…we don't carry him on our books. **1988** Dietl & Gross *One Tough Cop* 47: He was…mobbed up and mean as shit. **1988** *Crossfire* (CNN-TV) (June 28): You've got individuals [who are] mobbed up all the way through. **1989** *Dream Street* (NBC-TV): Joni, he's mobbed up to the eyeballs.

mobby *n. Und.* a member of a criminal gang.
>**1888** in *Amer. Heritage* (Oct. 1979) 21: And the clever genteel mobby whose great and only hobby/ Was dipping in your fobby.

mobilize *v.* **1.** *N.Y.C.* to beat up; drub; vanquish.
>**1923** Ornitz *Haunch, Paunch & Jowl* 27: The Jewish boys cried, "Mopilize the Micks!" (A word, probably coming from the root of *mopel*, to abort. In any event it implied the direst punishment). **1934** H. Roth *Call It Sleep* 272 [ref. to *a*1918]: "Maybe you ain' gonna ged mobilized," Kushy answered ominously. **1934** Appel *Brain Guy* 218: They coulda mobilized him. **1936** Kingsley *Dead End* 683: Aw, I'll mobilize yuh! **1949** *Looney Tunes* (animation): You sappy swami—I'm gonna mobilize ya! **1956** G. Green *Last Angry Man* 150: My old man'll kill ya....My brother'll mobilize ya. **1963** Gant *Queen St.* 39: You just don't tangle with Frankie over his dame....Frankie'd mobilize him. **1967** G. Green *To Brooklyn* 21: I could mopilize you if I wanted, ya sissy! **1964–69** in Calt *Rather Be Devil* 102: They'd mobilize you, beat you right there. **1971** Sorrentino *Up from Never* 26: And I know one guy who lost on pernts to a guy he used to mobilize in the gym every time they sparred. **1977** Appel *Hell's Kitchen* 30 [ref. to *a*1918]: Bastids! We'll mobilize yuh!

2. to drive, motor.
>**1990** Rukuza *West Coast Turnaround* 205: Gunnysack, in his two-stack mack, mobilizin' eastbound.

mobsman *n. Police & Und.* a member of a gang of thieves or swindlers, esp. a pickpocket.
>***1851** H. Mayhew *London Labour* III 25: "Mobsmen," or those who plunder by manual dexterity—as the "light-fingered gentry." ***1859** Hotten *Slang Dict.:* Mobsmen, dressy swindlers. ***1889–90** Barrère & Leland *Dict. Slang* II 58: *Mobsman* (thieves), pickpocket. Getting obsolete. **1906** *Nat. Police Gaz.* (Oct. 6) 6: There were several mobs of pickpockets on hand. The liveliest work of such "mobsmen"...was witnessed on the trains. **1965** Carmichael & Longstreet *Sometimes I Wonder* 96: Mobsmen...with...submachine guns.

Mob Town *n.* Baltimore, Maryland. Also **Mob City.** See also MOBTOWNER.
>**1837** J. Greene *Glance at N.Y.* 97: Baltimore has been emphatically called the Mob-City. **1859** Bartlett *Amer.* (ed. 2) 274: *Mobtown.* A name given long ago to the city of Baltimore, and which the lawless character of a portion of its inhabitants renders a not unfitting appellation at the present day. **1888** Spear *Old Sailor's Story* 16 [ref. to 1820's]: We got under way for Mob Town, as the sailors call Baltimore.

Mobtowner *n. Naut.* a Baltimore-built vessel. Cf. MOB TOWN.
>**1837** *Everybody's Album* II 104: That 'are is a mobtowner, sir, as the levtenant says, and coming down with a big bone in her mouth, too.

mob up *v. Police & Und.* to go into illicit partnership (with); join a gang.
>**1924** in D. Hammett *Continental Op* 49: Where Ashcraft had lived...or who he had mobbed up with? **1929** in Hammett *Knockover* 38: Who's he mobbed up with? **1931** *Collier's* (Apr. 25) 7: He is mobbed up with some very good people in Philly. **1935** in R. Nelson *Dishonorable* 248: Those three fellas used to be mobbed up with the late Bill Ballard. **1938** in Partridge *Dict. Und.* 443: A couple of Harlem guys Joe the Joker is mobbed up with.

moby *adj.* [after *Moby-Dick,* great whale in Herman Melville's novel of the same name (1851)] *Stu.* huge. *Joc.*
>**1965** N.Y.C. high school student: What's big and purple and lives in the ocean? Moby Grape! [**1967** *Moby Grape* [name of rock band; self-titled album].] **1970** *Current Slang V* (Winter) 10: *Moby, adj.* Obese. **1981** D.E. Miller *Jargon* 187: *Moby.* A very large and seemingly malevolent group of devices, which threaten to come apart violently at any moment. **1982** in *Time* (Jan. 3, 1983) 39: Thus "moby," meaning large, is said to derive from Melville's *Moby Dick,* though some say from Moby Pickle. **1983** Naiman *Computer Dict.* 89: What a moby loss that idea was! *Ibid.* 96: So, moby wizard, how's hacking?

moc *n.* usu. *pl.* a moccasin.
>**1970** *Everett* (Wash.) *Herald* (Mar. 10) 12D: Smart oxfords and brogues, handsome demi-boots, mocs and other styles walk through a man's world this spring. **1976** *L.A. Times* (Sept. 12) ("Home") 24: Russet Brown patent leather moc slipon. **1967–79** in S. King *Bachman Bks.* 337: I'm saving the tennis shoes....But I think the mocs will finish it.

moccasin *n.* usu. *pl.* a shoe (of any kind); (*hence*) (*fig.*) someone's situation or "shoes."
>**1894** F.P. Dunne, in Schaaf *Dooley* 182: He's th' la-ad that have made th' Prince iv Wales thrimble in his moccasins. **1898** Brooks *Strong Hearts* 52: I wouldn't like to be in that boy's moccasins. **1903** A. Adams *Log of a Cowboy* 379: My little pattering feet...will require fifteen-dollar moccasins. **1925** W. James *Drifting Cowboy* 17: I'll be daggone if I didn't catch myself wishing I was in his warm moccasins. **1986** Colorado woman, age *ca*40: There's a saying: "Don't judge me till you've walked a mile in my mocassins."

¶ In phrase:

¶ **sun (someone's) moccasins** to knock (someone) to the ground.
>**1868** in G.W. Harris *High Times* 294: "Hoss" Lovingood openly avows his...ability to "maul the benzine out of Grant, *pere.*" "To sweat out his lard at his ears." "To sun his moccasins"—and to "snatch all sich, bald headed." **1873** J. Miller *Modocs* 162: Ef I ain't out o' this by dark...I'll sun somebody's moccasins, see if I don't.

moccasin telegraph *n. West.* (esp. among Native Americans) GRAPEVINE TELEGRAPH. Also **mocassin telegram.**
>**1908** in *OEDS:* Word of the white woman ran before the advancing traders by "moccasin telegram." **1912** Stringer *Shadow* 91: Like all yeggs, he was an upholder of the "moccasin telegraph." **1927** *Sat. Eve. Post* (July 23) 3: That agency known to white men as the Moccasin Telegraph, by which odd bits of news are flashed from one isolated native camp to another. **1931, 1956, 1958** in *DARE.* **1975** McCaig *Danger Trail* 89: He knew the...accuracy of...the moccasin telegraph. **1990** Crow Dog & Erdoes *Lakota Woman* 212: The "moccasin telegraph"...always spreads news among Indians in a mysterious way.

mocha *n.* coffee (of any kind); JAVA.
>**1929** L. Thomas *Woodfill* 25 [ref. to 1898]: So even if I did like my mocha, well I guess I kinda liked shootin' better. **1929** T. Wolfe *Look Homeward Angel,* in *DAS:* A couple cups of Mock-a. **1942** *ATS* 816: Coffee....*java, javvy, joe, mocha.*

mocha *adj.* racially black; African-American.
>**1943** Wolfert *Tucker's People* 274: A real, regular mocha tart. **1988** Barrow & Munder *Joe Louis* 11: A black boxer...called by American sportswriters "the mocha mauler."

mock *n.* a Jew; MOCKY[1].—used contemptuously.
>**1927** H. Miller *Moloch* 133: We've got a big mock for a landlord. **1963** in L. Bruce *Essential Bruce* 22: So anyway, I tell all these Mocks—Jewish people, you know. **1980** D. Hamill *Stomping Ground* 4: These mocks are sensitive sonsabitches.

mock[-out] *n.* an ironic turn of events.
>**1960** N.Y.C. high school students: What a mock-out! That'd be such a mock!

mock out *v.* [elab. of S.E. *mock*] to poke fun at, tease.
>**1960** N.Y.C. high school student: Don't mock him out. He can't help it if he's such a retard. **1971** N.Y.U. student: He wasn't mad or nothin' like that, he was just mockin' you out. **1994** *Parade* (Sept. 4) 19: You don't have the right to mock out that religion.

mocktail *n.* [blend *mock* + *cock*tail] a nonalcoholic drink.
>**1982** *Restaurant Business Magazine* (Jan. 1, 1983) (Nexis): The restaurants' "frozen fantasies from the garden" include a variety of "mocktails" and spirited blends. **1984** *N.Y. Times* (Jan. 18) B2: They traded recipes for "mocktails"—drinks with no alcohol. **1985** Source uncertain, in RH files (Nov. 1) 3: A recent survey...found wine coolers & spritzers replacing liquor. "Mocktails" are now challenging "cocktails." **1988** *S.F. Chronicle* (June 26) ("Punch") 7: Q. What's a 'mocktail lounge'? A. A hangout that serves soft drinks only.

mocky[1] *n.* [perh. Yiddish *makeh* 'a boil or sore'] a Jewish person.—used contemptuously. [See D.L. Gold, "The Etymology of the Derogatory American and Canadian English noun *maki* 'Jew'," *Jewish Linguistic Studies* II; "1937" date assigned by *OED2* and *DARE* to 1930 quot. below represents date of publication.]
>**1893** in F. Remington *Sel. Letters* 171: Dead right—make all the Moxies [*sic*] crazy and red in the face....You can't glorify a Jew. **1930** Conwell *Pro. Thief* 12: But a few days later I was over on the East Side and there saw this Jew who was pointed out to me as one of their best mocky cannons. **1933** Odets *Awake & Sing!* 43: What's that "mockie" bothering about? Who needs him? **1935** O'Hara *Butterfield 8* 101:

Gee, but that little Mocky could play that piano. **1936** Mencken *Amer. Lang.* (ed. 4) 295: For Jew: *kike, sheenie, arab, goose, mockie* and *yid.* **1937** Weidman *Can Get It Wholesale* 15: Let those mockies see that this thing was being run by people who mean business. **1939** N. West *Locust* 275: But how are you going to get rid of the illiterate mockies that run it? **1943** Wolfert *Tucker's People* 484: A dutchman or a square-head or a mockie or a slicked-up greaseball from the Argentine. **1951** Longstreet *Pedlocks* 409: Ike called him "a typical mockie—a Jewish sport." **1966** N.Y.C. woman, age *ca*30: My Uncle Bill called the Catskills the "Mocky Mountains" [in the 1940's]. **1967** Kornbluth *New Underground* 47: The spics/threaten the identity of the limeys/the mockies/threaten the identity of the square-heads. **1978** Kopp *Innocence* 19: Privately they referred to them as *Mockeys,* a Yiddish term referring to people who were "too Jewish." **1977–80** F.M. Stewart *Century* 92: Fights with the "Mockies"—Jews—in Williamsburg. **1981** *Film Comment* (May) 63: You got your mockies, your niggers, your slopes, your spics, your wops and your paddys. **1981–85** S. King *It* 40: Feeling like mockies, sheenies, kikes. *a***1994** H. Roth *Mercy of Rude Stream* 25 [ref. to *a*1920]: All the *goyim* jeering at Jews: "Mockies…*Makh geldt.*"

mocky[2] *n.* [orig. unkn.] *West.* a wild mare.
   1936 R. Adams *Cowboy Lingo* 81: A wild mare was sometimes called a "mockey." **1942** *ATS* 830: *Mockie,* a wild range mare.

mod *n.* Esp. *Journ.* (*cap.*) a member of a group of British youth of the 1960's who wore stylish, often Edwardian-style clothing (now *S.E.*); (*broadly*) a young person who wears extremely fashionable or (later) avant-garde clothing. Cf. ROCKER.
   ***1960** in *OED2:* Teds and Mods, Beatniks and Ravers. ***1964** in *OED2:* The Mods, neatly dressed and on scooters, the Rockers in studded leather jackets and on motor-bikes. **1965** *New Yorker* (Feb. 13) Juan Lejido, the most recent flamenco troubadour to reach this sunny Spanish shore, is a bit of a Mod. **1966** *Harper's* (July) 97: One dateless young girl danced with another, each an unmistakable Long Island Mod. **1967** *Look* (July 11) 2: The indomitable Katharine Hepburn, first of the mods, has come back. **1978** *New West* (Mar. 27) 59: They change costumes and musical styles (we see them as rockers, mods, psychedelic wizards and revolutionaries). **1982** *L.A. Times* (Sept. 20) VI 1: The club was filled with mods, a new breed of well-behaved young people whose trademarks are shiny Vespa scooters. **1993** P. Munro *U.C.L.A. Slang II* 59: *Mod n.* person who dresses in black and wears Dr. Martens, listens to alternative music, has a cynical attitude, and may have body piercings and colored hair. **1994** Danesi *Cool* 57: *Mods:* These teens listened to the new-wave music of the mid eighties and were generally sympathetic to the punk-rock movement.

mod *adj.* Esp. *Journ.* stylish; fashionable; avant-garde; (*also*) characteristic of a Mod (s.v. MOD, *n.*).
   ***1964** in *OED2:* Modgirl. **1965** *New Yorker* (Jan. 30) 103: Mod cotton dresses, several with That Ruffle at the bottom. **1965** *New Yorker* (Sept. 25) 44: Teen-agers here are clamoring for the Mod look….Short hair. Short skirts. Sculptured lines as opposed to froufrou. **1965** *N.Y. Times* (Oct. 24) III F11: The Mod look—Tom Jones ruffled shirts, corduroy jeans, high-heeled Chelsea boots and similar styles. **1967** *Harper's* (Aug.) 18: Others, especially among the young, think it is smarter to be mod than middlebrow. *Ibid.* (Sept.) 116: The mad, mod scene is about to witness the birth of a fantastic new magazine destined for greatness. Its name is *Avant-Garde.* **1975** Wambaugh *Choirboys* 319: Spencer's so mod he wears flared jockey shorts. **1967–80** Folb *Runnin' Lines* 247: *Mod* 1. Stylish/stylishly. 2. Up-to-date in dress. **1989** *It's Garry Shandling's Show* (Fox-TV): I envied you and your mod lifestyle. **1989** *Village Voice* (N.Y.C.) (Oct. 17) 6: She thinks she is so mod. But she isn't.

mode *adj.* [perh. alt. of MOD] *Stu.* fashionable; modish.
   1984 *Chicago Sun-Times* (Jan. 29) 20: A fraternity member, shopping with his mother, horrified her by saying a certain pair of shoes were not "mode."…He explained that mode meant stylish, fashionable, acceptable to the peer group. ***1990** T. Thorne *Dict. Contemp. Sl.* 342: *Mode* adj[.] British[.] affectedly fashionable, pretentious. A deliberate mispronunciation of *mod,* heard in the 1960s and used to express derision. "Oh yes, get a load of that gear, very mode."

Model-T *adj.* **1.** [alluding to the Ford *Model T* (last manufactured in 1927) as an inexpensive or old-fashioned automobile] cheap; outdated; obsolete.

1938 in Ruhm *Detective* 216: But you thought I was an innocent little kid who'd fall for this Model T line of yours. **1942** R. Chandler *High Window* 378: Now you take Model T jobs like this [old elevator]—it takes a man to run it. **1949** *N.Y. Times* (July 22) 7: We cannot afford Model T thinkers like Senator Taft. **1949** *Time* (Oct. 24) 26: The 1945 Hiroshima bomb, which scientists now consider a model-T bomb. **1950** *Harper's* (Mar.) 16: Our Model-T Congress. **1951** in *DAS:* A real Model-T speakeasy out of an early Warner Brothers movie. **1963** *Sat. Eve. Post* (June 1) 18: The Russians…could no longer afford "Model-T" liquid-fueled rockets with tedious countdowns. **1963** *Book Week* (Oct. 13) 8: We foolishly adhere to a Model-T concept of the atom.

2. *Army.* of technician grade. Also as *n.*
   1943 *Yank* (Jan. 13) 15: All Whammies rank as model-T corporals. *Ibid.* (Feb. 10) 14: A T/5 is a technician fifth grade, or a model T corporal. **1944** in *AS* XX 148: [Army:] *Model T.* Non-com technician. **1944** Kendall *Service Slang* 11: *Model T Sergeant….*soldier with a Technician 3rd Class Rating.

mo-dicker *n.* MOTHERFUCKER.—usu. considered vulgar. Hence **mo-dicking,** *adj.*
   1968–70 *Current Slang III & IV* 84: *Mo dicker,* n. A lazy, irresponsible person.—New Mexico State. *a***1987** Bunch & Cole *Reckoning for Kings* 326: Be nobody's mo-dickin' Christmas fucked up. **1989** D. Sherman *There I Was* 129: It started raining like a mo-dicker….I…said "mo-dicker"…'cause your momma don't like me saying "motherfucker," but it's really the same word.

modock *n.* [orig. unkn.] *Av.* a pilot given to boasting about flying experiences. [The sense 'an imaginary species of bird' sugg. as an orig. in 1942 quot. is not documented elsewhere.]
   1933 Stewart *Airman Speech* 78: *Modock.* One who talks about aviation but never flies. **1942** *Time* (June 1) 17: He was an early member of the Quiet Birdman, the group of flyers who set themselves apart from the kiwi…and from the "modock," legendary aviation term for a "bird that flies backwards to keep the dust out of its eyes." **1945** Hamann *Air Words: Modock.* A pilot who always tells others what he is going to do but never does it. His type first arose during the early barnstorming days….The true etymological origin of the word "modock" is missing from accepted records.

modock *v.* [orig. unkn.; cf. the *n.*] to run.
   1974 E. Thompson *Tattoo* 378: When he came down, he gave chase, modocking pretty good for a guy about seventy with bad pins. *Ibid.* 483: "Les cut!"…"Les mo-dock, mutha!"

modulate *v.* *CB.* to talk or converse over a two-way radio.
   1975 *Atlantic* (May) 44: You like to modulate with me a little bit? **1976** Bibb et al. *CB Bible* 62: But that doesn't mean I can't modulate with my friends between songs. **1976** Whelton *CB Baby* 20: The two of them modulated back and forth for a couple of minutes about the weather. **1977** Corder *Citizens Band* 33: You're walkin' all over a nice old man who's trying to modulate with a friend.

mofo *n.* [by reduction and alt.; cf. MOFUCK] (a partial euphem. for) MOTHERFUCKER.
   1965 in H.S. Thompson *Hell's Angels* 33: The "Mofo" club from San Francisco. **1966** Reynolds & McClure *Freewheelin Frank* 116: The Mofos (a motorcycle club that isn't in existence now). **1972** R. Wilson *Forbidden Words* 171: *Mother-jumper, mother-ferrier, mo'-fo', mammy-jammer,…futher-mucker.* **1973** *Oui* (Mar.) 69: And now you, too (you jive mofo) can control the minds of women! **1977** Univ. Tenn. student: I'm sincerely beginning to believe that mofo is a goddamn female impersonator. **1979** L. Blum et al. *Meatballs* (film): I will twist that mofo. **1982** Least Heat Moon *Blue Hwys.* 124: He's one useless black mofo. **1983** Leeson *Survivors* (film): Hey, you honky mofo, get the lead out of your ass! **1987** *Nat. Lampoon* (June) 79: It hurt like a mofo. **1989** *Daily Beacon* (Univ. Tenn.) (Apr. 28) 10: Intramural Team of the Week…Men's Team: Mofo's. **1989** W.E. Merritt *Rivers Ran Backward* 20: Get your white ass in the truck, mofo. **1993** P. Munro *U.C.L.A. Slang II* 59: The jerk was such a mofo!… What's up, mofo?

mofo *adj.* MOTHERFUCKING.
   1989 W.E. Merritt *Rivers Ran Backward* 20: You mofo lucky they sent me along.

mofuck *n.* [by reduction and alt.; cf. MOFO] MOTHERFUCKER.—usu. considered vulgar. Also **mo-fucker,** etc.
   1962 H. Simmons *On Eggshells* 143: Get out the way, moa-fugg.

1967–72 Weesner *Car Thief* 66: Muttering *mahfuck* often. **1982** Del Vecchio *13th Valley* 477: This mofuck division fucked up. **1983** R.C. Mason *Chickenhawk* 105: [The mongoose] was young and tame, and he named it Mo'fuck. *a***1987** Bunch & Cole *Reckoning for Kings* 70: You be thinkin' that, mo-fucker.

mog *v.* [orig. unkn.] to move slowly or aimlessly; trudge; go.
   1890 *JAF*, in *DARE*: Mogg—To move slowly. "He mogged along." **1894** *Harper's* (Feb.) 359: We could not get down to water, and as our horses were thirsty and foot-sore, we "mogged along." **1895** *DN* I 398: *Mog*...to walk. "We mogged along slowly." **1927** *AS* III 139: A neighbor often said "well, I must be mogging along," mog meaning to move slowly, to depart. **1950** *Time* (May 22) 24: Exhausted federal mediators who dutifully mogged back & forth trying to find a formula that would persuade Davey Robertson to order his men back to work. **1967–69, 1989** in *DARE*.

mo-gas *n.* [prob. *mo*tor + *gas* in contradistinction to *fougasse*, pop. understood as *foo-gas*] *Mil.* gasoline for vehicles. [Quots. ref. to Vietnam War.]
   1974–77 Heinemann *Close Quarters* 17: The gas truck...[had] two fuel tanks on the back marked "Mo-gas." **1978** Truscott *Dress Gray* 112: Flame throwers and mo-gas explosions all over the place. **1989** R. Miller *Profane Men* 88: Napalm,...mo-gas, body bags. **1990** Reinberg *In the Field* 142: Mogas short for motor gas.

moggy *n.* a promiscuous woman; prostitute.
   1726 in *William & Mary Qly.* (Ser. 3) XXXVIII (1981) 271: A scabby Offspring of a *Scotch* MOGGY, begot...by a...PEDLAR.

mojo *n.* [cf. Gullah *moco* 'witchcraft, magic', prob. akin to Fulani *moco'o* 'shaman'] Orig. *Black E.* **1.** magic; magical power; (*also*) a charm; (*broadly*) power or influence of any kind; in phr. **the mojo and the say-so** the ability to enforce one's wishes completely.
   1926 in Leadbitter & Slaven *Blues Records* 133: My Daddy's Got The Mojo, But I Got The Say-So. **1926** in *OEDS*: The term *mojo* is often used by the Mississippi Negroes to mean "charms, amulets, or tricks," as "to work mojo" on a person or "to carry a mojo." **1927** in Leadbitter & Slaven *Blues Records* 450: Mojoe Blues. **1928** in Garon *Blues* 142: I'm going to Louisiana, get me a mojo hand. **1928** "Blind Lemon" Jefferson *Mojo Woman Blues* [blues song title]. *ca***1950** in Garon *Blues* 141: My pistol may snap, my mojo may fail. **1953** *Sat. Eve. Post* (June 13) 110: I wonder what brand of mojo he's pumping at those Sunday meetings? **1954** Himes *Third Generation* 255: You the one got the most go and the mojo. **1956** in Leadbitter & Slaven *Blues Records* 250: Got My Mojo Working. **1961** in Himes *Black on Black* 18: You got the best go and the mojo. **1965** in Leadbitter & Slaven *Blues Records* 192: The Mojo Boogie. **1968** Gover *JC* 62: Well you catchin too much mojo at once, it's bound t'cross you up. *Ibid.* 154: They scared a you powers. Spears is the only kinda mojo they know. **1970** in D.C. Dance *Shuckin' & Jivin'* 231: Dolemite suddenly made a mojo turn. **1972** T.C. Bambara *Gorilla* 164: Love charms are temporary things if your mojo ain't total. **1973** in L. Bangs *Psychotic Reactions* 130: He works the audience with all the masterful puppeteer mojo of the Merlin he often poses as. **1975** New Brunswick, N.J., woman, age *ca*23 (July 12): Get your mojo workin' means "to get your act together, get it on." It's from a B.B. King song from about 1963. *ca***1975** in J.L. Gwaltney *Drylongso* 97: Then too, white people have the power. After all, they have the mojo and the sayso, as my father used to say [*ca*1900]. **1976–77** Kernochan *Dry Hustle* 191: My mobility is as important to me as my mojo. *a***1977** in S. King *Bachman* 100: I won't say I worshipped Joe McKennedy, but it was a close thing. He was my mojo. **1980** T. Jones *Adrift* 145: He's got his mo-jo workin'. **1981** T.C. Boyle *Water Music* 91: The man says he's got his *mojo* workin'....magic, black arts, hoodoo and voodoo. **1989** *Nat. Lampoon* (June) 12: In a Perfect World...Stephen Hawking would figure out a way to get his mojo working again. **1990** G. Lee *China Boy* 2: You bettah have some coin, and don be usin no oriental mo-jo on me. *a***1991** J. Phillips *You'll Never Eat Lunch* viii: Didn't want to put a mojo on it; didn't wanna tempt the evil eye. **1995** *New Yorker* (July 17) 57: "Before I perform, I cast a circle—a magic circle—around myself," she says. Its mojo is palpable.

   2. *Narc.* cocaine, morphine, or a similar drug.
   1935 Pollock *Und. Speaks*: *Mojo*, any of the poisonous habit-forming narcotics (dope). **1936** *AS* (Apr.) 124: *Mojo*. Dope of any kind, but especially morphine, heroin, or cocaine. **1946** *Amer. Mercury* (Feb.)

226: Usually, when an addict is *on the mojo* (well supplied with drugs) he feels too good to molest anyone. **1956** Nyswander *Drug Addict* 172: *Mojo*...Any kind of narcotic. **1973** N.Y.U. student: *Mojo* is dope. It may be restricted to cocaine, I'm not sure. But I've known that word for about as long as I can remember. **1974** N.Y.C. man, age *ca*28: *Mojo* means cocaine. I haven't heard that [word used] since I was a kid.

   3. *Black E.* a kind of dance.
   1970 in D.C. Dance *Shuckin' & Jivin'* 231: The popcorn, the mojo, the turkey, and the grind.

mojo *v.* to go; depart.
   1994 Knoxville, Tenn., attorney, age *ca*40: I gotta get mojoin'.

moke *n.* [orig. unkn.] **1.a.** a donkey or mule. *Rare* in U.S.
   *****1839** Brandon *Poverty, Mendacity, Crime* (gloss.): *Moak*—a donkey. *****1851** H. Mayhew, in *F & H* IV 329: I had a good moke, and a tidyish box of a cart. *****a***1871** in Hindley *Curios. Street Lit.* 146: He wack'd the moke till he made him start. **1899** Hamblen *Bucko Mate* 130: It was hardly necessary to kill the poor moke. *****1919** Downing *Digger Dialects* 34: *Moke* (n.)—A mule. **1920** *Field Arty. Jour.* (Mar.) 161: Sometimes one doubts very seriously, but on the whole I am inclined to believe that the "moke" has a distinct sense of humor.

   b. a horse.
   *****1879** in *OEDS*: For many a long time he tried a Derby to win, But I was the moke to carry him in. **1883** Keane *Blue-Water* 148: We were getting that short of fodder and grub we had to kill some of the poor old starvin' mokes and eat 'em. **1925** Bailey *Shanghaied* 63 [ref. to 1898]: Get up, ye moke. **1954–60** *DAS*: *Moke*...A horse, esp. an inferior race horse. *Not common in U.S. but fairly common in Australia.*

   2.a. a black person.—usu. used contemptuously.—usu. considered offensive.
   1847 Downey *Portsmouth* 121: Even the "mokes" in the "black sea" caught the infection, and laughed so long and strong at thee, as to raise thy Ebenezer. **1856** in *DA.* **1859** Matsell *Vocab.* 55: *Moke.* A negro. **1863** in Toll *Blacking Up* 125: A moke will be applying for a Senate seat. **1863** in S. Boyer *Naval Surgeon* I 51: Took a stroll over the island in the forenoon, but finding too many "mokes" about, I cut a bee line for the...ship. **1865** *Rogues & Rogueries of N.Y.* 14: "Dat's 44 last—ded sure."..."One up for a moke." **1867** Clark *Sailor's Life* 80: Say, old moke, what time does this train start for Bangor? **1867** in Utley *Custer's Cavalry* 85: But the "moaks" are now quarantined below here. **1869** *Overland Mo.* (Aug.) 131: "Moke," a negro. **1871** *Banka Pris. Life* 493: Negro....Make [sic]. **1878** Flipper *Colored Cadet* 173: Again, during my first year I many times overheard myself spoken of as "the nigger," "the moke," or "the thing." **1879** *Nat. Police Gaz.* (July 26) 5: Murderous Mokes Swung Off. **1882** Peck *Peck's Sunshine* 54: The moke struck an attitude...[resembling] Ole Bull. **1884** Carleton *Poker Club* 14: Dey's mo mokes dan wite pussons. **1890** E. Field *Sharps & Flats* I 211: A donkey is [in England] called a "moke"; in America a "moke" is a negro. **1894** J. Slocum *Liberdade* 133: The moke was rigged all ataunto for the occasion. **1895** Gore *Stu. Slang* 5: "Musical moke," a negro minstrel who plays a number of different instruments in succession. Cincinnati and elsewhere. **1897** *Harper's Wkly.* (Jan.) 90: The New York nickname for a negro is a "moke," and that name has been borrowed by the London costermongers and applied to their donkeys. **1901** in Robinson *Comics* 33: Dem shif'less lazy mokes. **1904** Hobart *Jim Hickey* 81: Dey's full of bad mokes. **1906** *Army & Navy Life* (Nov.): *Moke.* a Negro mess steward [at Annapolis]. **1919** White *Amer. Negro Folk-Songs* 207: My Daddy went out for to kill this black moke. **1928** *AS* III (Aug.) 453: *Moke.* Negro. **1965** Gallery *Eight Bells* 36 [ref. to 1917]: We had no Negroes at the [U.S. Naval] Academy when I was there except for what we called the Fifth Battalion—the colored mess "mokes."

   b. a dark-skinned person of any race.—usu. used contemptuously.—usu. considered offensive.
   1871 *Overland Mo.* (Feb.) 167: You oughter heard them mokes sing Hallelujah in Turkish. **1899** Young *Reminiscences* 531: Say, Aguinaldo, you little measly Malay moke. **1927** *AS* III 451: *Moke*...is the term for a Negro or Filipino. **1954–60** *DAS*: *Moke*...A Filipino. **1967** in *DARE*: *Moke*...a Hawaiian.

   3. a foolish or inconsequential fellow. Cf. MOOK.
   *****1855** in *OEDS*: He has an irreconcilable grudge against a poor moke of a fellow called Archer Gurney. **1871** Schele de Vere *Amer.*, in *F & H* IV 329: *Moke*, possibly a remnant of the obsolete *moky*, which is related to "murky," is used in New York to designate an old fogy or

any old person, disrespectfully spoken to. **1900** *DN* II 46: *Moke*, n. 1. An easy-going fellow; one in the habit of asking favors. 2. A moderate bore. **1915** *DN* IV 199: *Moke* about the same meaning and usage as *mutt*, or *boob*.

4. [fr. JAMOKE; cf. MOCHA] Esp. *Naut.* coffee.

1929 Bowen *Sea Slang* 91: *Moke*. Coffee in American ships. **1942–49** Goldin et al. *DAUL*: *Moke*. Coffee, usually of indifferent brew.

mokes *n.* MOKE, 3.

1985 J. Gleason, on *60 Minutes* (CBS-TV): He's just an ordinary mokes, trying to make it. **1989** *ALF* (NBC-TV): I'm such a mokes. **1989** *21 Jump St.* (Fox-TV): Boy, what a mokes I am!

mokus *n.* [orig. unkn.] **1.** a state of depression; the blues.—constr. with *the.*

1927 in Rust *Jazz Records* I 28: Mokus [title]. **1928** *AS* III (Aug.) 453: *Mokus.* Loneliness. **1941** Kendall *Army & Navy Slang* 22: I've got the moker's….the blues; depressed. **1947** *AS* XXII 304 [ref. to WWII]: *Mocus* (the). This [imaginary] disease, while usually general in application, has been definitely characterized as a morbid condition wherein "the gold in your teeth and the silver in your hair turn to lead in your tail." **1920–54** in Randolph & Legman *Bawdy Elements* 62: To say that a man has got the *mokus* (rhymes with *focus*) means that he is *"over-fucked and under-fed."* It usually applies to men, rarely to women.

2. a profoundly drunken state.

[**1954–60** *DAS: Mokus…Liquor…Not common.*] **1965–71** in *Qly. Jour. Studies on Alcohol* XXXII (1971) 734: *Mocus…*Sometimes refers to the stupor that wine drinkers are supposed to attain. **1974** N.Y.U. student: An old wino once told me on the street that the ultimate high is called "the holy mokus."

mokus *adj.* drunk; (*also*) needing a drink.

1954–60 *DAS: Mokus…Drunk….Not common.* **1970** Gattzden *Black Vendetta* 38: I'm mokus. Canned. Don't know nothing. *Ibid.* 109: "Lord have mercy," moaned a mostly mokus Marcus. **1965–71** in *Qly. Jour. Studies on Alcohol* XXXII (1971) 734: *Mocus* Intoxicated. **1971** D. Smith *Engine Co.* 62: Like a drunk without a drink, I feel a little "mokus," the need to get back to what I like.

mola var. MOOLA.

moldy¹ *adj.* worthless; unpleasant; outdated.

***1896** in *F & H* IV 362: *Mouldy….*Worthless: e.g., a mouldy offer. **1927** in Brookhouser *Our Years* 172: He turned out kind of moldy, and say! he was dumb….You've got moldy since I saw you last. **1955–57** Felder *Collegiate Slang* 3: *Moldy*—something repulsive. **1976** *L.A. Times* (May 12) IV 1: There is a country club party…calculated to reveal the upper crust at their moldiest. **1983** *Reader's Digest Success with Words* 87: Black English…*moldy* = "out of style."

moldy² *adj.* [sugg. by syn. SPOILING] uncontrollably eager.

*a***1907** R.H. Williams *Border Ruffians* 294 [ref. to Civil War]: Now these deserters…had riled the boys very much, and they were "blue mouldy" to get at them.

moldy fig *n.* **1.** *Jazz.* a person who admires older styles of jazz.—used derisively. Now *hist.*

1945 in *OEDS*: Why do aforementioned connoisseurs insist upon maintaining that the Chicago and New York (white) styles are the real Jazz, when it's perfectly obvious that New Orleans was—and is—the birthplace of the true "stuff?"…Sincerely, Moldy Fig, France. **1948** in R.S. Gold *Jazz Lexicon*: The moldy figs…are certain that the greatest jazz ever played…was played in New Orleans in 1915. **1948** in Botkin *Sidewalks* 405: All of jazz is divided today into two countries. One of these is the land of bebop, and the other is the land of moldy figs. **1950–52** Ulanov *Hist. Jazz* 352: *Moldy fig:* a modernist's name for an ardent admirer of Dixieland jazz. **1958** *PADS* (Nov.) 46: *Moldy fig:* one who likes or plays "traditional" jazz exclusively….(Refers mostly to fans, not musicians.). **1959** Zugsmith *Beat Generation* 54: They were moldy figs who vegetated while…Stan alone swung. **1959–60** R. Reisner *Jazz Titans* 161: *Moldy Fig:* a term applied by lovers of modern jazz to a person partial to the older forms. **1962** *N.Y. Times* (Sept. 9) II 24x: The historical view of jazz was held almost exclusively by supporters of earlier jazz forms who were sneeringly labeled "moldy figs" by the post-war be-boppers. **1992** *Nation* (Apr. 13) 497: These recurrent theological disputations about who is betraying the music's fundamental nature: 1940s moldy figs versus beboppers, 1960s beboppers versus free jazzers, 1980s neoboppers versus almost anybody else.

2. a person having outdated or conservative ideas.

1949 in W.S. Burroughs *Letters* 57: [He is] a mouldy fig with nuts.

1971 Cole *Rook* 78 [ref. to late 1940's]: They went away switching their hips…agreeing with each other that he was just a moldy fig. **1981** in Safire *Good Word* 108: I am a bit of what a jazz fan would have called, in the 1930's, a Moldy Fig—a person of possibly excessive conservatism.

mole *n.* [introduced into current vocab. by "John Le Carré" in *1974 novel; see quot.] a spy who works from within an enemy's government or spy agency; (*hence*) a person who spies on an organization from within.

[**1925** in *OED2*: I also have certain moles at my command.…When the Cirque Doré mobilizes itself it has many eyes and ears.] [***1960** in *OED2*: The latter displayed such a disconcerting knowledge of the innermost workings of the White military organizations that Fedossenko decided to join his network…in order to discover the source of his information. He was recruited under the alias of "The Mole."] ***1974** "J. Le Carré" *Tinker Tailor* 62: Ivlov's task was to service a mole. A mole is a deep penetration agent so called because he burrows deep into the fabric of Western imperialism. **1978** *N.Y. Post* (Mar. 17) 27: The suspicion that there was a Soviet "mole" high in the CIA who helped on this is the most disquieting part of the story. **1978** *L.A. Times* (Aug. 16) I 30: Agents who have no ostensible connections to official foreign delegations and who attempt to infiltrate quietly into positions from which they can obtain information. In the trade, they also are known as "moles." **1980** *Time* (Jan. 28) 40: This does not preclude the presence of a Soviet "mole," lurking within the [Yugoslav Communist] party and waiting to stir up trouble when Tito dies. **1983** *N.Y. Times* (June 9): Apparently a Reagan mole in the Carter camp had filched papers. **1984** *U.S. News & W.R.* (Oct. 29) 38: A KGB "mole" spent years working inside Britain's code-breaking center. **1992** G. Wolff *Day at the Beach* 83: I was a spook, a mole, a Company Man. **1994** *Newsweek* (May 9) 24: The KGB has always been in the market for moles, or "deep-penetration agents," as they are more properly known.

moleman *n.* [sugg. by the subterranean humanoid creatures in the film *Superman vs. the Molemen* (1956)] *USAF.* a member of a silo-based ICBM crew.

1961 Baar & Howard *Missileman* 150: It sure beats being a moleman down in the catacombs. **1975** Former USAF captain, age *ca*33: I used to be a moleman in North Dakota.

moley *n.* [pop. as a characteristic exclamation of "Captain Marvel," hero of a series of comic books begun 1940, first written by C.C. Beck; perh. reflecting *moly* 'magic herb in Greek mythology', in allusion to the invocation of mythological figures as a source of the character's powers; perh. euphem. and rhyming alt. of *holy Moses*] ¶ In phrase: **holy moley** (used as an exclamation of surprise).

1949 *Capt. Marvel Adventures,* in Barrier & Williams *Book of Comics* 87: Holey Moley! He got away. **1958** Reuss & Legman *Songs Mother Never Taught Me* (unp.): "Holy Moley," I cried out. **1960** MacCuish *Do Not Go Gentle* 315 [ref. to 1940's]: Holy Moley, four fifteen! **1965** Borowik *Lions* 132: Holy moly, a pool table. **1966** Dylan *Tarantula* 21: The kind of uncle that says "holy moly" in a mild whisper. **1972** Rossner *Any Minute* 224: "I think I'm getting ready to give up alcohol!" "Holy Moley!" **1973** Overgard *Hero* 164: HOLY MOLEY, it tastes like someone cured a huarachi in my mouth. **1977** Coover *Public Burning* 17: Holy Moley! This is terrible! **1988** *CBS Eve. News* (CBS-TV) (July 9): Holy moley, what'll I do? **1989** *It's Garry Shandling's Show* (Fox-TV): Holy moley—that's my actual brain! **1992** *Homefront* (ABC-TV): Holy moley! Look who just walked in.

moll *n.* [fr. *Molly,* hypocoristic form of female given name *Mary*] **1.** a prostitute. *Rare* in U.S.

***1604** in *OED*: None of these common Molls neither, but discontented and unfortunate gentlewomen. ***1785** Grose *Dict. Vulgar Tongue: Moll.* A whore. ***1877** in *F & H* 330: She went up to some of the swell streets at the West End to see another moll, a pal of hers. **1968** P. Roth *Portnoy* 236: This is somebody whom I picked up off the street!…Just look at her—a moll!

2.a. Orig. *Und.* a girl or woman; (*occ.*) one's wife or sweetheart; (now *specif.* esp. *Journ.* use, infl. by **(b),** below) a tough or rowdy young woman.

***1753** in *OEDS*: To nap the Slangs from the cull or moll; that is…to take the things from the man or woman. ***1839** Brandon *Poverty, Mendacity, Crime* (gloss.): *Moll*—a girl. **1859** Matsell *Vocab.* 55: *Moll.* A woman. ***1865** in *Comments on Ety.* (Oct. 1, 1987) 23: From what I've heard of her from my "moll." *ca*1866 in R.L. Wright *Irish Emigrant Ballads* 267: The English Molls are purty gals, to marriage they decline. **1866** *Nat. Police Gaz.* (Nov. 17) 3: As the chances are, if you "go through" a "moll" or a "bloke" in the market, you don't get…more than twenty "cases." **1867** *Galaxy* (Aug.) 429: Women are naturally shrewd at a bargain, and a pretty "moll" will wheedle out of the receiver a better price for goods. **1871** *Overland Mo.* (Feb.) 165: I'll go back into the country, and get a girl that's never seen blue water, and don't know a handspike from a hawser. None of your Molls that can box the compass for me. **1871** Banka *Prison Life* 493: Woman,…Moll. **1904** *Life in Sing Sing* 250: Moll. A woman. **1910** Hapgood *City Streets* 54: Well, I went, for it was a moll, yer know. She was a swell-looking lass. **1912** Stringer *Shadow* 93: His moll's aboard. **1913** *Sat. Eve. Post* (Mar. 15) 10: A young Moll of de green hills like you oughtn't to be runnin' round dis big town alone. **1927** H. Miller *Moloch* 146: You can never tell what a moll like that may be up to. *ca*1928 in Wilstach *Stage Slang* (unp.): "Mess moll" is the woman cook. **1928** *AS* III (Feb.) 219: *Haggy moll*—A thin, drooping, unattractive female. **1928** Coe *Swag* 115: Bill's gone to a show with that moll upstairs. **1931** *AS* (June) 333: *Moll, n.* A girl; does not necessarily have any unsavory connotation. **1963** in Wepman et al. *The Life* 80: She was a brown-skin moll like a Chinese doll. **1968** *Playboy* (June) 82: And a strong, acid-rock moll is used to going home with strange men. **1993** *TV Guide* (Sept. 25) 22: An over-the-top western sexpot moll. **1995** *N.Y. Observer* (May 22) 27: She's a shopping mall moll, the wickedest person in the Paramus Supercuts salon, maybe. **1996** *Simpsons Comics* (No. 17) (unp.): You're *my* moll now!

b. *Specif.*, a woman who is herself a criminal or the mistress or willing accomplice of a criminal. [Now the usu. sense; bracketed quot. may simply represent a proper name, but the context at the very least adumbrates later usage.]

[**a*1800 in Holloway & Black *Broadside Ballads* 104: From Newgate to St. Giles's pound,/Me and my Moll was carted;/But when we came to the gallows tree,/Me and my Moll were parted.] ***1823** "J. Bee" *Slang: Molls*—are the female companions of low thieves, at bed, board, and business. **1866** *Nat. Police Gaz.* (Nov. 3) 2: It seems that Annie and one of her "molls" made a raid on Jennie's domicile a few days ago. *Ibid.* 3: Maggie resented this insult, as all *honest* "molls" do when they are "jacketted." **1868** Williams *Black-Eyed Beauty* 30: How much will you put in my way to stop me going to tell your old man of your visits to such a veteran moll as Matty? **1869** "G. Ellington" *Women of N.Y.* 170: She generally becomes a thief's "moll," or partner. **1872** Burnham *Secret Service* vi: *Moll,* a female confederate, or mistress. *Ibid.* 96: Sixteen more of these same $50 notes were "shoved" in one day…by Tom Hale and his "moll." **1873** Sutton *N.Y. Tombs* 471: The police…have…become familiar with the members of the different gangs,…have learned their resorts, their "molls," their "pals," and their "fences." **1899** A.H. Lewis *Sandburrs* 153: He soaks his gazebo of a guard wit' a rubber billy his Moll sneaks in to him d' day before. **1932** L. Berg *Prison Doctor* 264: In these regions, every boy yearns to be a gang leader and every girl a "moll" who will work the streets, if necessary, for her man. **1935** Lorimer & Lorimer *Heart Specialist* 34: I'd much sooner be a bride than a gangster's moll. **1953** Nickerson *Ringside Jezebel* 76: There's the gangster's moll. **1964** in B. Jackson *Swim Like Me* 116: Now I did a hitch in San Quentin,/Just to keep an old moll out a the stir. **1978** *N.Y. Post* (Mar. 25) 3: Mobster's moll feared slain. **1987** *Ampersand's Entertainment Gde.* (Summer) 4: Dreyfuss falls for the con's moll. **1994** in *JAF* (Winter, 1995) 110: Female criminals are the focus of his chapter "Molls."

4. an effeminate male homosexual.

1923 (quot. at QUEER). **1942** *ATS* 373: Effeminate man.…*Moll, moll, Molly.*

moll *v.* to work as a prostitute.

1954 *Time* (June 28) 57: When a girl cannot get modeling dates in New York, there is nothing for her to do, it would appear, but to accept the $100 kind. She winds up molling for mobsters.

moll-buzzer *n. Und. & Police.* **1.a.** a pickpocket who preys upon women. Also **moll buzzard.**

1859 Matsell *Vocab.* 55: *Moll Buzzer.* A thief that devotes himself to picking the pockets of women. **1867** *Nat. Police Gaz.* (Jan. 26) 3/3: He "shook" the "mob" and commenced on his own hook as a "moll buzzer." *Ibid.* 3/4: She chose to be a "moll buzzer." **1899** A.H. Lewis *Sandburrs* 8: She hooks up wit' Billy, d' moll-buzzard; an' say! he's bad. **1902** Hapgood *Thief* 34 [ref. to *ca*1882]: We operated, at that time,

entirely upon women, and were consequently known technically as Moll-buzzers—or "flies" that "buzz" about women. **1904** *Life in Sing Sing* 250: *Moll-Buzzer.* Person who picks the pockets of women. **1905** *McClure's Mag.* (Sept.) 522: The "moll-buzzers" heard it; the "con" men caught it. *a*1909 Tillotson *Detective* 93: *Moll buzzer*—A man pickpocket who robs women. **1910** Hapgood *City Streets* 316: Moll-buzzers like me had a soft snap of it, for women kept their leathers on a big open pocket in the back of their dresses, and any door-mat thief could get all he wanted. **1914** Jackson & Hellyer *Vocab.* 21: *Buzzard,* Noun Current amongst pickpockets. A timid amateur or low life "gun" who operates on "molls," women. "The moll buzzards…glommed a batch of pokes." **1916** *Editor* (May 6) 487: Moll-buzzer. **1918** in *AS* (Oct. 1933) 29: *Moll-Buzzard.* Purse-snatcher or, by extension, other petty larcenist; usually opprobrious. **1919** *Our Navy* (May) 55: I've heard of clever crooks and moll-buzzers. **1930** Conwell *Pro. Thief* 149: The shopping districts are the spots where moll-buzzers do their best work. **1941** in Algren *Neon Wilderness* 56: 'R you one of them Chicago Av'noo moll-buzzers? **1955** Q. Reynolds *HQ* 235: I just collared a real live cannon and two moll buzzers. **1973** *Reader's Digest* (Oct.) 202: A pickpocket particularly dangerous to women is the "moll buzzer," a skilled operator who specializes in opening women's handbags. **1983** *N.Y. Times* (Sept. 6) B6: Bag openers, sometimes called "moll buzzers," are pickpockets who concentrate on women's handbags.

b. a panhandler who begs from women.

1925 Mullin *Scholar Tramp* 242 [ref. to *ca*1912]: While sitting there, I noticed at least a dozen panhandlers at work. One of the briskest of these…devoted himself exclusively to women; a Moll-buzzer, such a specialist is dubbed by his fellow cadgers. **1926** *AS* I (Jan.) 251: *Moll buzzer.* One who specializes in begging from women. **1944** (quot. at DUMMY-CHUCKER). **1982** *CBS Mystery Theater* (CBS radio series) (Jan. 21): As a rule, Joe wasn't usually a moll-buzzer. That's a [panhandler] who works on women.…Excuse me, ma'am. Could you spare fifty cents for a cup of coffee?

2. a female pickpocket or beggar.

[**1866** *Nat. Police Gaz.* (Nov. 24) 3: "Moll knucks" were…in the ascendant, among whom were Johanna Casey, Maggie Harzel, Lizzie Spencer, Hattie Morland, [etc.].] **1912** Berkman *Prison* 278 [ref. to 1894]: Moll buzzers*.…*Women thieves. **1925** in Partridge *Dict. Und.* 445: A moll buzzer…She worked wit' a gang o' dips, an' sported a little on the side. **1927** *DN* V 455: *Moll-buzzer…*A "lady beggar." **1935** Pollock *Und. Speaks: Moll buzzer,* a female pickpocket. **1937** Reitman *Box-Car Bertha* 144: There was Mary Ireland, a much photographed "moll-buzzer."

3. a ladies' man.

1913 Stringer *Shadow* 50: One of his most valuable assets…was his speaking acquaintance with the women of the underworld. He remained aloof from them even while he mixed with them. He never grew into a "moll buzzer." But in his rough way he cultivated them. [**1935** Pollock *Und. Speaks: Moll's buzzard,* a pimp.]

moll-buzzing *n. Und.* purse snatching.

*1900 in Partridge *Dict. Und.* 445: Her gift for mathematics made it clear that "moll buzzing" was much more remunerative than sleeping in cellars and peddling Park Row literature. **1902** Hapgood *Thief* 34 [ref. to *ca*1882]: In those days…Moll-buzzing, as well as picking pockets in general, was an easy and lucrative graft. **1942** *ATS* 454: *Moll buzzing,* snatching women's purses or picking their pockets. **1965–68** E.R. Johnson *Silver St.* 17: Lucky enough not to get caught stealing, or jack rolling, or moll buzzing.

moll crib *n. Und.* a brothel.

1866 *Night Side of N.Y.* 40: A midnight descent has just been made upon a "moll crib," as he calls the "boarding house" of the portly dame.

Molly *n.* **1.** an effeminate man or boy, esp. a homosexual; SISSY.—usu. used derisively. Also (*obs.*) **Miss Molly, molly boy.**

*1709 in *Social Problems* XVI (1968) 188: The Mollies' Club…adopt all the small vanities natural to the feminine [etc.]. ***1723** *Comical Pilgrim* 9: Speaking…effeminately, and *Molly* like. ***1754** in *OED2*: If he goes to school, he will be perpetually teized by the nick-name of Miss Molly. ***1785** Grose *Dict. Vulgar Tongue: Molly.* A Miss Molly; an effeminate fellow, a sodomite. **1811** in Howay *New Hazard* 52: The captain…called him a molly boy—a scoundrel—and threatening to flog him at the capstan. **1859** Matsell *Vocab.* 56: *Molley*…an effeminate fellow; sodomite. ***1889–90** Barrère & Leland *Dict. Slang* II 45: An effeminate youth or young man, [is] known in America as a Molly.

Ibid. 60: *Molly*…(London slang), a young sodomite. **1910** Solenberger *Homeless Men* 148: The true vagrants refer to him disrespectfully as a "Molly" for working at all. **1929** Bodenheim *60 Secs.* 43: Aw hell, only mollies got dreamy-eyed and made up things like that.

2. a prostitute; (*broadly*) a woman or girl.

   ***1719** T. D'Urfey, in *F & H* IV 331: Town follies and cullies, and. Molleys and Dolleys. **1881** Trumble *Man Traps* 21: "Packing mollies" is the term applied by the fraternity to designate a certain class of dishonest domestics. **1894** H.U. Johnson *Dixie to Canada* 95: I wonder if those two lasses can be the little Mollies I used to enjoy so much. **1904** *Life in Sing Sing* 250: *Molly.*—A prostitute. **1911** A.H. Lewis *Apaches of N.Y.* 169: Oodles of crazy Mollies'll fall for it. **1933** Duff & Sutherland *I've Got Your Number* (film): Out of a million skirts, you picked the itchy-fingered molly. **1935** *AS* (Feb.) 18 [ref. to *a*1910]: *Molly.* A prostitute.

3. *Narc.* BLACK MOLLY.

   1976 Lieberman & Rhodes *CB* 132: *Mollies*—Uppers or sleep-retarding pills.

mollycoddle *n.* a man or boy who is used to being coddled; SISSY. Now *colloq.* or *S.E.*

   ***1833** in *OED:* A "moll caudle" [*sic*] spirit that reigned supreme through all the acts of this government. ***1849** Thackeray, in *F & H* IV 331: You have been bred up as a molly-coddle, Pen, and spoilt by the women. ***1873** Hotten *Slang Dict.* (ed. 4): *Mollycoddle*, an effeminate man; one who "coddles" among the women, or does their work. **1906** in "O. Henry" *Works* 1141: A mollycoddle is…a monkey dressed up by its mother and sent out to pick daisies on the lawn. **1913** in Truman *Dear Bess* 117: There are getting to be too many moral mollycoddles in the family. **1914** U. Sinclair *K. Coal* 316: He spoke with contempt of "mollycoddles." **1922** Kyne *Pride of Palomar* 220: Nobody likes a mollycoddle. **1939** de Leon et al. *Union Pacific* (film): Get back to work, you mollycoddles. **1967** G. Green *To Brooklyn* 9: He can't go on being a mollycoddle all his life.

mollycoddle *v.* to coddle or treat with excessive kindness; pamper. Now *colloq.* or *S.E.*

   ***1863** in *OEDS:* It keeps up a wholesome protest against the molly-coddlers, to see a whole countryful of stout lasses devoted to field-labour only. **1925** *Sat. Eve. Post* (Aug. 29) 19: Some others…may endeavor to show that the new, more indulgent schools of thought are merely mollycoddlers. **1973** Breslin *World Without End* 93: All they ever do is mollycoddle criminals. **1988** T. Logan *Harder They Fall* 57: We mollycoddle young criminals. **1990** Crow Dog & Erdoes *Lakota Woman* 79: No use to mollycoddle those…irresponsible…women.

molly-dodger *n.* *Black E.* (see quot.). Cf. GRANNY-DODGER.

   1964–69 in Calt *Rather Be Devil* 64 [ref. to *ca*1920]: I say, "I don't want no mollydodger (motherfucker)…to ease me in [the "dozens"].

mollyfogging *adj.* MOTHERFUCKING.

   1978 T. Wolfe, in *Harper's* (Mar.) 117: The next one of you peckerwoods who…refers to me as "you mollyfoggin' lamehead" is gonna get a new hole in his nose.

Molotov breadbasket *n.* *Mil.* a cluster of incendiary bombs. Now *hist.*

   ***1940** in *OEDS:* The "Molotov Breadbasket"…appeared to consist of two types. **1942** in Morison *Naval Ops. in WWII* V 283: Between 0645 and 1530 about 17 "Big E" bombers worked over the helpless transports, dropped "Molotov breadbaskets" (incendiary clusters) on adjacent beaches with excellent results. **1956** Heflin *USAF Dict.* 332: *Molotoff breadbasket*, a particular adapter for holding 12 or more small incendiaries and for scattering them over an area.

Molotov cocktail *n.* Orig. *Journ.* a makeshift bomb typically consisting of a bottle of gasoline and a rag that serves as a wick and is ignited before throwing. Now *S.E.*

   1939 (cited in *W10*). ***1940** in *OEDS:* Used with success [against the Soviets] in the Finnish war, the so-called "Molotov cocktails" are considered an effective weapon against armoured divisions and have been adopted by the Home Guard. **1943** in *Best from Yank* 54: The…Jap Imperial Marines…"laughed at the tanks, ran up to them and threw grenades and Molotov cocktails on the backs to set them afire." **1944** *Word Study* (May) 5: *Molotov Cocktail*…a bottle of gasoline converted into a rough antitank bomb. **1948** A. Murphy *Hell & Back* 98: A Molotov cocktail…is simply a bottle of gasoline with an ignition fuse attached. **1949** McMillan *Old Breed* 38: The Japs…set it afire with Molotov cocktails. **1950** *Life* (July 31) 15: Molotov cocktail (gasoline

bottle) was conceived by Loyalists in Spain. **1950** *N.Y. Times* (Dec. 7) 40: A "Molotov cocktail" hurled from a speeding auto, started a fire in the big Gimbels department store warehouse tonight. **1956** Heflin *USAF Dict.* 332: ….*Molotoff cocktail*, a frangible bottle containing a flammable liquid. **1968** G. Edwards *Urban Frontier* 21: It takes some premeditation to make a Molotov cocktail. **1994** *NBC Nightly News* (NBC-TV) (July 17): Under a hail of Molotov cocktails the Israelis fired back.

Mom *n.* [acronym] *Hosp.* milk of magnesia. Also **Mom's.**

   1972 *Nat. Lampoon* (July) 77: *Mom's* milk of magnesia. **1988** MacHovec *Humor* 134: MOM, as any nurse can tell you, is Milk of Magnesia.

mom *n.* *Homosex.* a passive partner in a lesbian relationship; (*also*) a lesbian who is notably feminine in appearance and behavior.

   1957 Murtagh & Harris *First Stone* 30: She *was* the head pop and all the other moms thought I was hot stuff to get her. *Ibid.* 306: *Mom* The girl who takes the female role in a lesbian relationship. **1959–60** R. Reisner *Jazz Titans* 161: *Mom:* the girl who takes the female role in a lesbian affair. **1966** S. Harris *Hellhole* 84: And, at Hudson, I gained a lot because I was Jerry's mom. *a*1972 B. Rodgers *Queens' Vernacular* 137: *Mom* lesbian who plays up her femininity.

momma var. MAMA.

mommux *n.* a muddle; botch.

   1869 in G.W. Harris *High Times* 216: I always manages to make a momox ove the juty.

mommux *v.* to confuse; confound.—also constr. with *up.*

   1867 in G.W. Harris *Lovingood* 219: Mout a-lookt fur a gineral durn'd momoxin ove things, tho', when dad tuck the job. **1913** in Butterfield *Post Treasury* 152: The sign was all mummuxed up before we got there.

momo *n.* [perh. redup. of *moron;* perh. < dial. It *mammoccio* 'stupid rascal'] a stupid or useless person; blockhead.

   1954–60 *DAS:* Mo-mo…A moron. **1970** Sorrentino *Steelwork* 63 [ref. to *ca*1945]: Frank hit him in the head with a cueball, shrieking, Looka this fuckin momo! Looka this fuckin momo! **1978** R. Price *Ladies' Man* 85: La Donna would be sitting there with some big momo from Duluth front row center. **1987** *Miami Vice* (NBC-TV): I photograph beautiful girls—not meatballs! Those *momos!*

mon¹ /mʌn/ *n.* money. Also **mun.**

   1889 Trumble *Mott Street* 6: No playee polkel if you no havee mon. **1892** Crane *Maggie* 58: Put yer mon in yer pocket! **1895** Gore *Stu. Slang* 7: *Mun.*…Money. **1895** Wood *Yale Yarns* 274: It's all the mon I own at present. **1895** Townsend *Daughter* 17: He gone away; he take-a da mon; he no come back. **1898** *Amherst Portfolio* 51: Life Work: Making mon. **1904** *Independent* (Mar. 17) 620: The lady has the title and/The Nobleman has the "mon." *a*1904–11 D.G. Phillips *Susan Lenox* II 119: In little old New York…you've got to have the mon. **1917** Lardner *Gullible's Travels* 105: I don't have to work. I got the mon'. **1926** Trident Society *Navy Songs* 29: He stayed out nights and he spent all his mun', he did, he did. **1971** E. Sanders *Family* 187: This studio was owned by a gentleman…whose attitude was "Where's the mon?"

mon² /mɑn/ *n.* [imit. of a West Indian pron.; pop. through reggae music] MAN.

   1977 Eble *Campus Slang* (Apr.) 3: *Mon*…an alternate pronunciation of *man:* Hey, mon, what you doing? **1983** in G. Tate *Flyboy* 58: This juju music is wicked, mon. **1984** W. Gibson *Neuromancer* 165: Case, mon, big problem. **1992** J. Nichols *Elegy for September* 28: Oh, cut the bullshit, mon….You're so totally bogus. **1993** P. Munro *U.C.L.A. Slang II* 59: Hey, mon! What have you been up to?

Monday morning quarterback *n.* [fr. the criticism of football games, typically played on Sunday, the next morning] Esp. *Journ.* a person who offers hindsight criticisms of problems already faced by others; second-guesser.

   1932 (cited in *ODMS* 139). **1937** *Atlanta Constitution* (Oct. 1) 21: The Sophists used to…argue as to how many angels could stand on the point of a needle. The Monday morning quarterbacks were in just as fruitless an argument. **1950** *N.Y. Times* (Aug. 9) 28: A lot of "Monday-morning quarterbacks" are undertaking to blame Secretary of Defense Louis Johnson. **1957** *Time* (Jan. 14) 39: Like all Monday-morning quarterbacks, the committeemen wound up by blaming everything on the white-thatched, mild-mannered coach. **1958** R.

Chandler *Playback* 80: Common sense is the Monday morning quarterback who could have won the ball game if he had been on the team. **1969** Whittemore *Cop!* I 72: All these Monday morning quarterbacks, they'll never know about it, because the incident was killed right then and there! **1970** *Business Week* (June 6) 6: It satisfied the Monday morning quarterback in all of us with its details of how a handful of respected and knowledgeable companies missed the mark. **1988** *Supercarrier* (ABC-TV): Guys in the cheap seats don't play Monday morning quarterback—you follow? **1990** R. Herman, Jr. *Force of Eagles* 285: A bunch of congressional Monday-morning quarterbacks. **1992** *Garfield & Friends* (CBS-TV): Monday morning quarterbacks had nowhere to go.

Monday morning quarterback *v.* Esp. *Journ.* to criticize with the benefit of hindsight; second-guess. Hence **Monday morning quarterbacking,** *n.*

  1950 *N.Y. Times* (Oct. 22) VII 1: This Monday-morning quarterbacking is balanced by the fact that he knew the Allied course was wrong even in Italy. **1956** *N.Y. Times* (Nov. 25) I 34: This is a period of what Americans call "Monday morning quarterbacking" or post mortems. **1962** Tregaskis *Vietnam Diary* 43: It's easy to do Monday-morning quarterbacking. **1962** *Wash. Post* (Nov. 25) A2: Nothing he said should be taken as carping criticism or uninformed Monday-morning quarterbacking. **1964** H.S. Truman, in *L.A. Times* (Nov. 26) V 26: There will be no second guessing nor Monday morning quarterbacking, and where I have revised my opinions about an event of the past…I will state so frankly. **1971** *Seattle Times* (Jan. 17) A7: Shaw criticized "Monday-morning quarterbacking" of field operations from Washington. **1973** Droge *Patrolman* 144: Sure, it was easy to Monday morning quarterback. **1983** *Daily Beacon* (Univ. Tenn.) (Feb. 9) 3: That's why someone could say, "How could they be so foolish?" When you Monday morning quarterback, it looks very different. **1994** *N.Y. Times* (June 24) A24: Analyzing, second-guessing, prognosticating, handicapping, Monday morning quarterbacking.

mondo *adj.* [fr. *Mondo Cane* (lit. "A Dog's World") (1961), Italian film with bizarre scenes that became a cult favorite infl. other film titles, as below] great in size, amount, prominence, or degree; (*hence*) extraordinary. Rarely **mombo.**

  [**1968** (quot. at MONDO, *adv.*).] **1982** Pond *Valley Girl's Guide* 49: Last weekend Mom let me go visit her and stay in the dorm and everything. It was *mondo* party time….All these foxy dudes. *Ibid.* 60: Like we did a mondo mac-out. **1984** D. Jenkins *Life Its Ownself* 166: Money…mondo scratcho. **1984** Mason & Rheingold *Slanguage*: *Mombo*…big; huge. **1985** *Teenage Mutant Ninja Turtles* (CBS-TV): Mondo notion, dude! *Ibid.*: Whoa! Mondo nutsiness! **1987** *Prime News* (CNN-TV) (Apr. 15): This Easter….mondo eggs from Africa make ostriches better than bunnies. **1987** N.Y.C. man, age *ca*35: It's a mondo make-up job. **1989** *Daily Beacon* (Univ. Tenn.) (Jan. 12) 7: I can call you fat, or extra-pudgy, or mondo gut! **1990** *Teenage Mutant Ninja Turtles* (CBS-TV): Mondo disaster, dudes! **1991** *Oxf. Dict. New Words*: During the seventies such formations became more common outside the cinema, with the meaning "the weirder or seedier side of (a particular place, activity, etc.)": *mondo bizarro* began to be used attributively in the sense "extremely bizarre," and *mondo* began to be reinterpreted as an adverb (and the following word as an adjective). The connotations of seediness or grossness persisted for some time. **1991** A.J. Phillips *You'll Never Eat Lunch* xvi: President, or mondo-mondo rock 'n' roll star. **1993** *As World Turns* (CBS-TV): I forgot about this mondo portfolio. **1997** *New Yorker* (Feb. 10) 86: A very serious mondo metavacuum coming from some random black hellhole.

mondo *adv.* very; exceedingly; in phr. **mondo bizarro** exceedingly strange.

  [**1966** *Mondo Bizarro* [film title].] **1968** Guare *Cop-Out* 27: You're Mondo Perfecto….Mondo Studdo. [**1970** *Mondo Trasho* [film title].] **1980** *Wash. Post* (Apr. 19) C1: The news, particularly on ABC, went further and further into the realm of Mondo Bizarro. **1982** *Time* (Sept. 27) 56: Obsessed with fashion, crowding mondo cool stores. **1982** L. Glass *Deprogram Yr. Valley Girl* 32: "Very"…*fully, mega,…mondo.* **1984** D. Jenkins *Life Its Ownself* 28: Mondo craze-o leftist derelicts. **1985** *Knoxville* (Tenn.) *Journal* (Apr. 27) A2: "Way-sweet" and "mondo-choice." **1988** *Teenage Mutant Ninja Turtles* (CBS-TV): I'm like mondo confused! Where'd that humongous insect come from? **1989** *21 Jump St.* (Fox-TV): I feel mondo vicious. *a*1990 Poyer *Gulf* 288: Mondo bizarro. **1990** *Tiny Toon Adventures* (synd. TV series): Like, mondo bad karma, Plucky! **1992** Mowry *Way Past*

Cool 10: Mondo gross! **1994** *L.A. Times* (Jan. 12) B2: We're mondo relieved. **1994** in *Esquire* (Jan. 1995) 108: Men's fashion in America….It's always either Brit or Med. Here's an example of *mondo* Brit. **1995** *TV Guide* (Mar. 25) 33: This one's mondo bizarro. **1996** *Details* (Feb.) 60: Sitting on a salmon-colored, peanut-shaped couch in her mondo '50s living area.

monet *n.* [fr. Claude *Monet* (1840–1926), French impressionist painter; pop. by the movie *Clueless* (1995) (see 1994 quot., fr. the script), which app. borrowed the term fr. the 1993 glossary *infra cit.*] *Stu.* (see quots.). *Joc.*

  1993 P. Munro *U.C.L.A. Slang II* 59: *Monet* n. person who seems desirable from a distance, but isn't up close. **1994** A. Heckerling *Clueless* 83: She's a full[-]on monet….Like the paintings. O.K. from far away, but up close just a big mess. **1996** *UTSQ*: *Monet*…meaning that a person is attractive or sensible from far away, but not from a close perspective. "That girl is such a monet. She really isn't that great when you study her."

money *n.* **1.** a crucial element.

  1960 Krasna & Kanter *Let's Make Love* (film): You got to take that dip [when singing]. That's where the money is. **1993** P. Munro *U.C.L.A. Slang II* 59: *Money*…good shot! [said after a successful shot in basketball].

  2. *Rap Music.* a friend.—often used in direct address. Also **money dog, money grip.**

  1990 in A. Sexton *Rap on Rap* 119: Money Grip turns to his cadre. **1990** in A. Sexton *Rap on Rap* 123: Money can rap….he…can…rap. **1990** *TV Guide* (Oct. 20) 19: *Money*: a valued friend. **1990–91** *Street Talk!* 5: *Money (grip)* friend. "Yo, money grip." "Hey, my friend." **1993** P. Munro *U.C.L.A. Slang* II 59: Hey, money! Wanna go to a house party Saturday night? **1994** *Totally Unoffical Rap Dict.* (Internet): *Money* (n) See brother. **1994** *21st Cent. Dict. Sl.* 173: *Money*…one's best friend; also known as money grip. *Hey, money, what's happening?* **1995** Slavsky et al. *A 2 Z* 69: *Money, money dog, money grip*—friend: Yo, money dog, let's break out! **1996** N.Y.C. man, age *ca*40, on *Tempestt* (synd. TV series): Leave money [*i.e.*, him] alone, 'cause he's told off already.

¶ In phrases:

¶ **easy money** someone or something easily dealt with.

  1902 Remington *John Ermine* 174: He was easy money with his load, and then we packed him up here.

¶ **in the money** (of a horse or rider) finishing in one of the top three positions in a race; (*broadly*) finishing among the top winners; (*hence*) wealthy; successful.

  1902 in *OEDS*: It is true that when the Spurt is over I am generally in the Money. **1908** McGaffey *Show Girl* 20: Though we were not in the money we were still on the track. **1933** Seff & Seymour *Footlight Parade* (film): I see. You heard I was in the money. **1937** *Pic* (May) 13: Joe was in the big money. **1943** in *DAS*: I'm in the money at last. **1958** *N.Y. Times* (Aug. 3) I 1: All indications were that the critical test had run smoothly. "We were in the money all the way." **1960** *Time* (Nov. 7) 12: The New York *Daily News* poll, which has been in the money in every major election since 1948. **1961** *N.Y. Times* (Dec. 31) V 53: Forty-eight tournaments in which she was in the money.

¶ **money talks—bullshit walks** see s.v. BULLSHIT, *n.*, 1.a.

¶ **[right] on the money** precisely; perfectly; (*also*) perfect; on target. Now *colloq.*

  1944 Stiles *Big Bird* 28: I checked the oil pressure and tuned the RPM on the money. **1962** *New Yorker* (Nov. 10) 145: You've got to be right on the money when you [land the plane]. **1966** *Sat. Eve. Post* (July 2) 88: Some of them strong-armed guys can put the ball right on the money for one series but the next series they're liable to scatter it all over the field. **1974** R. Carter *16th Round* 116: Dog Company was on the money and looking good! *ca*1982 *Benson* (ABC-TV): Close? I thought I was right on the money. **1984** *L.A. Times* (July 21) III 3: Howard Cosell….His remark that to become a sportscaster you must first become "a gutteral illiterate and learn to catch a football" was right on the money. **1992** G. Wolff *Day at the Beach* 127: Karl Malden was on the money. **1995** *CBS This Morning* (CBS-TV) (Mar. 10): Our conclusions…were on the money.

¶ **smart money** see s.v. SMART.

money *adj.* [sugg. by *in the money* sv. MONEY] **1.** Orig. *Sports & Gamb.* highly successful or proficient in play; characterized by an unflagging intent on winning; (*hence*) decisive in

the outcome of a contest.—used prenominally. See also
MONEY PLAYER. [Bracketed quots. are prob. best considered
as colloq.]

[**1934** Weseen *Dict. Amer. Sl.* 260: *Money player*—A professional
athlete. *Money position*—The winner of a contest, especially a horse
race.] **1934** *Journalism Qly.* (Dec.) 353: *Money,* a[dj]. (general)—winning. A *money* player. **1942** *ATS* 572: Popular actor…*money star.* Ibid.
673: Boxing…Knockout blow.…*money punch.* **1949** Cummings
Dict. Sports 272: Money ball. **1949** *Daily News* (N.Y.) (Oct. 2): Pee
Wee Reese…Duke Snider…and…Luis Olmo…came through with
money hits to break the tie. **1950** *New Yorker* (Sept. 30) 48: Mr. Parker is one of those money actors who can pitch their way out of trouble. **1951** in *DAS:* The most spine-chilling event…was Robinson's
money smash. **1951** *Daily News* (N.Y.) (Sept. 30): He did it with as
self-punishing and spectacular a money play as the…fans…will ever
see. **1961** W. Mays, in *Sat. Eve. Post* (May 20) 68: It was a money
catch all right and helped win the series. *ca*1961 in T.L. Clark *Dict.
Gamb. & Gaming* 131: *Money rider* ["a jockey who is well-known for
riding winning horses."] **1963** *Time* (Oct. 11) 49: A reputation as a
"money" pitcher who is toughest under pressure. **1968** M.B. Scott
Racing Game 36: The "money jock"…is…concerned…with getting
the best mounts in the best races. *ca*1969 *Gunsmoke* (CBS-TV): The
money card's [*sc.,* a card needed to complete a winning poker hand]
on the way. I'll wait. **1974** *Everett* (Wash.) *Herald* (Oct. 16) 1C: We
are a money team. That's why we've been in the World Series for the
last three years.

2. *Film. & Journ.* crucial to financial success, usu. because
climactic and fulfilling expectation—used prenominally.—
usu. in phr. **money shot.**

1981 *N.Y. Times* (Mar. 22) (Nexis): Since special ability parts, silent
bits and, occasionally, stunts—all of which are known as "money
shots"—are usually given out spontaneously on the set as the scene
calls for them, a smart extra willl stay alert for opportunities. "I can
clear $300 to $400 in a three-day week with overtime, if I can get in a
money shot," says Gina Picerni. "If the timing seems right, I'll go up
to the A.D. (the assistant director) and ask if there will be any money
shots." **1989** *L.A. Times* (Nov. 26) (Nexis): These sexual numbers usually lead up to what is known as the "money shot"—a close-up of the
male orgasm, sometimes filmed in slow motion. In her book, Williams
quotes a 1977 porno film maker's guide as recommending the use of at
least 10 of these shots in a hard-core movie. **1990** *New Republic* (Feb.
19) 27: The conventions of pornography follow from efforts to capture what the trade calls a "money shot": proving visibly that the man
has satisfied himself. **1991** Kasdan & Kasdan *Grand Canyon* (film): You
took out the money shot!…The brains-on-the-visor shot! **1992** *L.A.
Times Mag.* (Aug. 23) 14: Tabloid-talk.…*money quote n.* the quote that
can sum up a whole story in one sentence. "What's the *money quote?*"
"'I killed John Belushi.'" **1995** *New Yorker* (Oct. 30) 69: The on-command male orgasm [in pornographic movies]…"the payoff shot," "the
cum shot"…"the money shot." **1996** *New Yorker* (July 15) 80: The
trailer…featured what they call in porno the "money shot": the White
House itself exploding.

money arm *n. Baseball.* a pitcher's throwing arm.
1971 (quot. at SOUP BONE).

moneybags *n.* a wealthy person. Now *S.E.* Also **moneybag.**
***1818** J. Keats, in *OED2:* How could these money-bags see east and
west? **1869** "G. Ellington" *Women of N.Y.* 334: He is invited to the
table of Mrs. Moneybags. [**1871** Crofutt *Tourist's Guide* 13: But Young
America did not live up to his theory or accept the dictum of moneybags.] **1883** *Life* (July 19) 47: There are no new engagements except
that of Col. Jack Nocash to Minnie Moneybags. ***1881–84** Davitt
Prison Diary I 67: A greasy well-thumbed book is diligently looked
through in search of the names "Fitzswell" and "Moneybags." **1888**
Pierson *Slave of Circumstances* 81: I hear he has pretty near as much as
old money-bags. **1893** Macdonald *Prison Secrets* 271: Money-bags
abused his starved and almost naked debtor. **1912** Siringo *Cowboy
Detective* 518: Every greedy old "Money-bag" in the land should be sat
down on hard. **1934** D. Runyon, in *Collier's* (Sept. 8) 8: Who is my
papa but an old money-bags, anyway. **1949** in *DAS:* They might
annoy some aged moneybags. **1978** Univ. Tenn. student: I think his
old lady is the real moneybags of the deal. **1980** W.C. Anderson *Bat-
21* 160: What say, moneybags? **1987** *Wkly. World News* (Sept. 15) 13:
The 28-year-old rock moneybags believes the story…is the perfect
part for him.

money bone *n. Baseball.* a pitcher's throwing arm.—constr.
with *the.*
1962 Houk & Dexter *Ballplayers* 55: When a pitcher's arm is troubling him, he doesn't have to hide it from me. He knows I understand
how it feels when the money-bone is out of ready cash.

money machine *n.* MONEY-MAKER, 1.—usu. considered offensive.
1961 Rubin *In the Life* 41: Well, hole, snatch. You know, my money
machine, that's what I thought of. *Ibid.* 158: *Money machine.* vagina.
1971 Rader *Govt. Inspected* 13: That's a money machine down
there.…I ain't no charity worker, dummy.

money-maker *n.* **1.** Orig. *Prost.* the vagina, usu. of a prostitute.—usu. considered offensive. [Bracketed quot. is conceivably a misprint for MONKEY, 6.]
[***1785** Grose *Dict. Vulgar Tongue:* Money. A girl's private parts,
commonly applied to little children: as, Take care Miss, or you will
show your money.] ***a*1890–96** *F & H* IV 333: *Money-box (Maker,* or
spinner). The female *pudendum.* **1968** Gover *JC* 85 [1]: Wash the jail
off my skin an the funk outa my moneymaker. **1971** Thigpen *Streets*
14: Black-ass whoe/stands on corners—sells her money-maker/ain't
no hope. **1973** Schulz *Pimp* 46: She won't be able to use her money-
maker no how for no one no more when I gets through with her.
1978 Sopher & McGregor *Up from Walking Dead* 59: I banged
away…as if it were my main squeeze's moneymaker.

2. the buttocks, usu. of a woman; BUTT, 1.a.—usu. considered offensive.
*a*1972 B. Rodgers *Queens' Vernacular* 24: Kick her on her money-
maker! **1979** C. Keel *Rituals* 11: Get your moneymaker in motion anyway, Dabney. **1979** Kunstler *Wampanaki Tales* 98: Françoise De Jour—
formerly of Her Majesty's London Troupay dee Ballay…(shake that
money-maker, honey). **1980** H. Gould *Ft. Apache* 94: She did a slow
walk down the hallway, hips swaying, heels clicking. She could still
shake that moneymaker. **1989** *Newsday Saturday* (CNN-TV) (July 15):
The right to shake one's moneymaker where there's money to be made.
1991 *Simpsons* (Fox-TV): Get out there and shake your money-maker.
1994 *Mystery Sci. Theater* (Comedy Central TV): That's it, baby!
Shake that money-maker! **1994** "G. Indiana" *Rent Boy* 49: Girls in tight
skirts who'd make about fifty trips to the coffee machine…shaking that
moneymaker for all the…studs in the room. **1996** Court TV (Feb. 19):
Shake Your Money-maker was a money-maker.

money out *v.* to pay up.
1868 Williams *Black-Eyed Beauty* 42: D— if I wouldn't look at him
all night if he'd money out for me!

money player *n. Gamb. & Sports.* one who performs well under
the pressure of intense competition. See also MONEY, *adj.*
1922 *Baseball Cyclopedia* 114, in Nichols *Baseball Term.* **1934** (quot.
at MONEY, *adj.,* 1). **1935** Pollock *Und. Speaks: Money player,* the tougher
the game, this particular gambler excels on account of having lots of
nerve. **1950** *Sat. Eve. Post* (Oct. 7) 111: One of those people who, in
professional sports circles, are known as money players: fellows who,
one way or another, deliver the goods when the chips are down. **1962**
Morris & Morris *Dict. Word & Phr. Orig.* 27: *Money player*—One who
can always be counted on to perform well when most is at stake. **1979**
Toronto Star (Nov. 17) D1: We have a lot of money players, who know
what it takes to win big games. **1996** *N.Y. Times* (May 22) B13: Then
Jordan reintroduced himself as the game's foremost money player.…
He outscored O'Neal by 25-10 in the second half.

money-puker *n.* (see quots.). *Joc.*
1993 W. Safire, in *N.Y. Times Mag.* (May 23) 14: *Moneypuker,* a vivid
word picture for "automatic teller machine." **1993** *Wkly. World News*
(July 13) 13: *Moneypuker*…Automatic teller machine. **1993** Pa. man,
age *ca*70 (coll. J. Sheidlower): I've heard *money-puker* for "A.T.M." in
Delaware County, Pennsylvania, recently.

money shot see s.v. MONEY, *adj.,* 2.

mongee *n. Hobo.* food. Rarely as v., to eat.
***1914** (cited in Partridge *DSUE* 528). **1926** *AS* I (Dec.) 652: *Mon-
gee.* Food. **1927** *DN* V 455: *Mongee,* n. Food. This word comes from
the French "manger" as it sounds to the tramp who has visited the
French-Canadian provinces. **1929** Milburn *Hobo's Hornbook* 79: I
learned about mongee from him. *Ibid.* 286: *Mongee,* food. **1930** G.
Irwin *Tramp & Und. Slang: Mongee.*—To eat. **1932–34** Minehan *Boy &
Girl Tramps* 217: I…talks him…into mongee.

-monger *comb. form.* a person who is enthusiastic or knowledgeable about (something specified in the initial element).
   *1674 in Duffett *Burlesque Plays* 15: For we the Parson must be
feasting....He's such an errant Mutton-monger. **1979** Alibrandi *Custody* 299: "Think of all the money I'll save." "Capitalist monger." **1988**
Rage (Univ. Tenn.) (Sept.) 34: The latest addition to Knoxville's hip
places to hang on a Saturday night. Especially if you're tired of being a
"Strip" monger. **1988** Univ. Tenn. student: You always were a party
monger. **1989** *Rage* (Univ. Tenn.) (Feb.) 14: Sex Mongers of U.T.—
Happy Valentine's Day! **1991** *Ultimate Challenge* (Fox-TV): I'm a
stress monger. I love challenge.

mongo¹ *n.* [prob. abbrev. of *mongoloid idiot*] an idiot; weirdo.
   1975 Univ. Tenn. student (Sept. 24): Look! A mongo! That's what
they call 'em in the trade. **1984** in "J.B. Briggs" *Drive-In* 247: The
mongo's died four times now.

mongo² *n.* [orig. unkn.] objects retrieved from trash; (*hence*) a
scavenger.
   1984 *New Yorker* (Sept. 24) 43: The walls sagged with what artists
call found objects, and what [sanitation men] call "mongo"; in fact,
this locker room contained a number of artifacts from the departmen-
tally famous "mongo wall" of Brooklyn's District 10. **1995** S. Moore
In the Cut 63: Mongo, n., scrap-metal scavenger (Brooklyn word).

mongo *adj.* [perh. infl by MONDO] **1.** HUMONGOUS. [The 1974
quot. is the name of a character of huge size in the film.]
   [**1974** M. Brooks *Blazing Saddles* (film): Mongo *like!*] **1985** Eble
Campus Slang (Oct.) 7: *Mongo*—huge. "I have a mongo mid-term
tomorrow." **1986** Univ. Tenn. student: The book gives a mongo number of cases. **1987** in F.P. Rice *Adolescent* (ed. 7) 420: *Mongo*—really
big, cool.
   2. very many.
   1986 Knoxville, Tenn., shoppers, age *ca*20: "How many [plums] do
you want?" "Mongo! Mongo!"

Mongoose *n. Mil. Av.* a McDonnell-Douglas A-4 Skyhawk
strike fighter, as modified for advanced combat training.
   1987 G. Hall *Top Gun* 37: The Top Gun Skyhawks are "Mongoose"
variants, stripped of all nonessential weight [etc.]. *Ibid.* 38: The Mongoose is determinedly subsonic. **1989** Joss *Strike* 92: Aggressor aircraft...are often (e.g., in the renowned A-4 "Mongoose") reengined
for extra go.

monicker or **moniker** *n.* [orig. unkn.] a name, esp. a nickname or alias. Occ. as v.
   *1851 H. Mayhew *London Labour* I 218: What is your 'monekeer'
[*sic*] (name)?"—Perhaps it turns out that one is "White-headed Bob,"
and the other "Plymouth Ned." **1859** Matsell *Vocab.* 56: *Moneker.* A
name. **1866** *Nat. Police Gaz.* (Apr. 21) 3: Hughey Price. The Buffalo
"knuck," who possesses the above well-known "moneker," arrived in
this city last week. *Ibid.*: Their "moneckers" are Caspar Karrel and
Stanislaus Hermanoe. *1882 in *OEDS: Monniker*, a person's name
(often assumed). *1881–84 Davitt *Prison Diary* I 151: The great
majority of convicts hide their real under assumed names, many of
them having a fresh "monicker" (name) each conviction, to be
dropped, for obvious reasons, upon release. **1895** *Harper's* (Oct.) 777:
That's the way she got her monkey*...*Nickname. **1895** in J. London
Tramp Diary 62: Wot's his monica? I mean wot's his name? Yer see, we
all travels by monicas on de road. *1896 *Gentleman's Mag.* (Oct.) 349:
"Moniker," a common coster word for "name." **1897** in J. London
Reports 320: Monica—cognomen—a distorted version, both in form
and meaning, of monogram. **1900** Willard & Hodler *Powers That Prey*
62: Mr. Renn [had] the descriptive "monikey" Shorty. **1907** London
Road 19 [ref. to 1892]: I had received my "monica." I was now "Sailor
Kid," later to be known as "Frisco Kid." **1911** Bronson-Howard
Enemy to Society 13: In adopting the "monaker," he made the necessary
alterations in vowels so that it might sound like a real name. **1911–12**
Ade *Knocking the Neighbors* 4: The other claimed the following brief
Monicker, to wit: Henry. **1912** Livingston *Curse* 83: Perhaps Jack had
left behind him his "monicker," the name-de-road left behind by every
tramp...upon the...water-tanks. **1921** Casey & Casey *Gay-Cat* 50:
What's your monaker, son? **1923** Ornitz *Haunch, Paunch & Jowl* 189:
Hunch, that's what I'll monicker you. **1925–26** J. Black *You Can't Win*
355: "You're from Chicago, eh? And your name is Brown? What do
they call you? What's your monger?"..."Chi Jimmy." **1926** Norwood
Other Side of Circus 58: Most everyone had a "moniker," as the men
termed nicknames. **1926** *AS* I (Dec.) 652: *Monicker*—Name, or pre-

tended name. **1928** Hammett *Harvest* 48: His real monacker is Al
Kennedy. **1929–31** (quot. at SQUARE, *adj.*). **1938** *AS* XIII 195: I
monikered him (gave him his moniker, or tramp name). **1944** C.B.
Davis *Leo McGuire* 167: This man's name or moniker was Cliff Emerson. **1948** J. Stevens *Jim Turner* 124: You're a team hand, now....And
you've earnt a moniker....*Big Jim.* **1949** in Daley *Sports of the Times* 7:
His honest monicker is Lawrence [Berra]. But everyone calls him
Yogi. **1950** Rackin *Enforcer* (film): Check the monicker file on some
guys named Big Babe, Philadelphia and Smiley. **1956** Neider *Hendry
Jones* 20: They had given him that monicker when he was just a boy.
1958 S.H. Adams *Tenderloin* 177: All the birds in the society headlines
have middle monickers. **1960** Jordan & Marberry *Fool's Gold* 10: But I
came right out in the open and had a double-barreled monicker. **1981**
Natural History (July) 10: A horse with the peculiar moniker of the
Asiatic half-ass (*E. hemionus*) has independently evolved a long, narrow
snout. **1988** *Ch. 7 Eyewitness News* (WABC-TV) (June 16): Word is
that Klaus [von Bulow] is dropping the "von" from his monicker.
1988 Norst *Colors* 15: One he knew by the moniker of Dog Bone.
1993 A. Lomax *Where Blues Began* 272: Every man is given a distinctive moniker that ticks him off in an apt and sometimes cruel way.
1994 Bak *Turkey Stearnes* 79: Thus was born the marvelous moniker
of...James "Cool Papa" Bell.

monish *n.* [app. alt. of *money*] money.—used in imitation of
Anglo-Yiddish speech.
   1804 Brackenridge *Mod. Chivalry* 442: It is all de love of de monish,
said a Jew. *1815 in Felsenstein *Anti-Semitic* 130: De Monish gives me
a relish for de Pork Chops. *1820–21 P. Egan *Life in London* 168:
Mordecai...don't care a single farthing about his "Monish." **1853** S.
Robinson *Hot Corn* 16: He can do no business—make no monish—
tonight.

monk¹ *n.* **1.** a monkey.
   1841 (quot. at MONKEY BAG). **1843** in *OEDS*: P. Fowler...is one and
identical with the celebrated jockey of Miss Foote, in stable parlance,
ycleped Monk....The word Monk in this case...is in fact an abbreviation of a noun substantive by which a certain animal is recognized, the
countenance of which is said strongly to resemble that of the very
jockey in question. **1894** in L. Levy *Flashes of Merriment* 178: The
"monk and parrot." **1896** in Outcault *Yellow Kid* [pl. 51]: It was de
monk dat scratched ye. **1901** Greenough & Kittredge *Words & Their
Ways* 61: Slang is fond of clipped words, as *monk* for *monkey*. **1912**
Siringo *Cowboy Detective* 451: But not all the monkeyshines were performed by the little "monks." **1938** Coldeway *When Were You Born?*
(film): Look! The monk's spotted it! **1949** *New Yorker* (Nov. 5) 88:
Whoever heard a monk demandin' more money? **1996** D. McCumber *Playing Off Rail* 67: They call him Monk because he looks like an
ape, man, check out his arms.
   2. a Chinese person.—used contemptuously. Cf. MONKEY, 4.
   1903 A.H. Lewis *Boss* 373: The munk who runs it...is cookin' the pill
for him when I shoves in. **1911** A.H. Lewis *Apaches of N.Y.* 226: Oh, a
couple of monks carries him to his bunk out back....I wish I could get a
job punchin' monks at a dollar a monk! **1925** *Sat. Eve. Post* (Dec. 19) 81
[ref. to *ca*1890]: A harrier of the Chinese—known to their Occidental
neighbors, the Irish especially, as monks. *Ibid.* 82: The monks was
always bad luck to me. **1931** Harlow *Old Bowery* 429 [ref. to 1880's]:
Like other boy neighbors of "the monks," as the East Side called the
Celestials, Chuck loved to pull Chinese pigtails. **1938** in A. Banks *First-
Person* 46: Monks—you know, Chinks....There was one man in Key
West who smuggled monks, but Hemingway didn't know about him.
   3. MONKEY-CHASER.—used contemptuously.
   1924 in Clarke *Amer. Negro Stories* 27: He'll hit the roof and fire
that monk.

monk² *n. Und.* a supreme court judge.
   1931 *AS* (Aug.) 440: Monk. A judge of the supreme court. **1942–49**
Goldin et al. *DAUL*: Monk. (Near South and scattered areas) A
Supreme court judge, especially of a State court.

monk *v.* MONKEY.
   1889–90 Barrère & Leland *Dict. Slang: Monk*...(American), abbreviation of *monkeying*, trifling with. **1897** *Cosmopolitan* (Mar.) 554: The
fust man I ketch a-munkin' in my waggin...I'm a-goin to kill right
then and there. *ca*1938 in *DARE*: She told me one day, "I am going to
get even with you." So I told 'er it was all right, that if she was to *monk*
with me I would shoot 'er. **1940** in *DARE*: I hope you don't expect me
just to set and sew all the time you're monking around in that swamp.
1954–60 *DAS: Monk*...v.t. To neck.

monkey *n.* **1.** a rascal; scamp.—used *Joc.*, esp. in reference to a woman or child. Now *S.E.*

*1602 Shakespeare *Othello* IV i: This is the monkey's own giving out; she is persuaded I will marry her. ***1606** in *F & H* IV 335: O she is a most sweet little monkey. **1855** S. Story *Caste* 51: Get off that, you monkey. **1861** in *Manuscripts* XXXVI (1984) 227: Kiss the little monkeys for me.

2.a. a man; fellow; character; "customer."—usu. used disparagingly.

[***1689** Shadwell *Bury-Fair* II: The activity of this Monky is as ridiculous as the Gravity of that Baboon.] **1815** Brackenridge *Mod. Chivalry* 652: I have heard even an accomplished lady, use the term monkey, speaking of an individual of the other sex. **1846** Codman *Sailors' Life* 30: And is't me for one, ye spalpeen, that ye're after calling a monkey?…You'll find that it's Abel Coffin, and not the monkey, that's captain here. **1846** *Crockett's Almanac* (unp.): In spite o' old Spain, an all the monkies called monarchs in creation. [**1847** Strong *Diary* I 297: A constitution-mongering monkey isn't a bad definition of a French philosopher of '89.] **1850** Melville *Moby-Dick* ch. xxv: Why, thou monkey,…thou hast not raised a whale yet. **1853** [G. Thompson] *Garter* 57: You milk-faced monkey! **1859** Avery *Comical Stories* 41: I'll not let that white-livered monkey think I'm afeerd. **1862** in C. Brewster *Cruel War* 157: I am afraid…they will send some Boston Monkey to command this Regt. **1893** M. Philips *Newspaper* 214: That monkey Babelton, on Hamlet, can't ride a goat. **1894** Bunner *More Short Sixes* 65: I'll do something to that Penrhyn monkey that won't be any young lady's dancing class, you bet your boots! **1895** F.P. Dunne, in Schaaf *Dooley* 166: I think that was what th' ol' munkey wanted. **1902** Corrothers *Black Cat Club* 22: He is…considered the peer of Burns, Milton, Shakespeare, and Tennyson, and, in levee vernacular, of, "any literary monkey dat evah push' a pen!" **1922** *Variety* (July 14) 8: We clipped a couple of monkeys for their whole roll. **1929** *AS* IV 342: *Monkey.* One of the general public. **1931** Walker *Music Box* (film): I don't want you. I want that other monkey. **1931** Hellinger *Moon* 66: Listen, you silly lookin' monkey…you'll come across with your moniker or you'll catch a sweet punch on the snoot. **1937** Parsons *Lafayette Escadrille* 25: I never had a chance. Eight of these monkeys all jumped on me at the same time. **1941** Cole & Wexley *Footsteps in Dark* (film): Get that straight, monkey! **1949** R. Chandler *Little Sister* 114: Some smart monkey tipped the cops he was Weepy Moyer. **1951–52** P. Frank *Hold Back Night* 28: Well, Beany Smith. He's a tough little monkey. **1953** R. Wright *Outsider* 111: Wish these white monkeys felt like you do. **1954** Schulberg *Waterfront* 9: He's a tough monkey, Joey Doyle. **1961** Steinbeck *Winter of Discontent* 7: A fascinating monkey. **1962** D. Tracy *Brass Ring* 425: They're pretty tough monkeys. **1970** Terkel *Hard Times* 71: Because we'd seen all these monkeys comin' in and out all the time. **1972** Buell *Shrewsdale* 141: Now the way those three monkeys tell it,…you started shooting, just like that. **1975** T. Berger *Sneaky People* 41: But I wanna do right by all concerned: that's the kind of monkey I am. **1983** De Vore *Heart of Steel* (film): What you got workin' for you is that tough bunch of old monkeys runnin' the union. **1991** B.E. Ellis *Amer. Psycho* 13: Courtney…finds this monkey attractive. **1992** *Middle Ages* (CBS-TV): You're so different from the other monkeys around here. *Ibid.*: This is the poor unfortunate soul whose job will be to put up with you monkeys. **1994** *Seinfeld* (NBC-TV): That is one tough monkey.

b. *Und.* a victim or intended victim of swindlers; SUCKER.

1922 *Variety* (Oct. 13) 7: The girls used the same tactics to loosen the "monkeys" from their "jack." **1930** *Variety* (Jan. 8) 123: Those honest guys…are the biggest monkeys of all.…Playing the duke is usually done in groups of three, with the "monkey" making the fourth. **1954–60** *DAS: Monkey*…A dupe; a victim. **1961** Scarne *Comp. Guide to Gambling* 288: Time is also important; another steerer may be on his way with another monkey.

3. *Naut.* MONKEY JACKET, 1.

*1838 Glascock *Land Sharks* II 37: The…"look-out men" had taken to their "monkies"*…*The sailor terms his great-coat or pea-jacket his "*monkey.*" **1889–90** Barrère & Leland *Dict. Slang: Monkey*…a short jacket.

4. a nonwhite or dark-complexioned person, esp. a person of African or Asian descent; (*specif.*) (in WWII) a Japanese person.—used contemptuously.—usu. considered offensive.

1839–40 Cobb *Green Hand* II 140: That niggur has done nothing but stare me in the face.…That ever the Lord should let monkeys grow to man's size, and learn them to talk. ***1849** "N. Buntline" *B'hoys*

of N.Y. 81: The bloody monkey 'ad hasked me hif I understood Spanish. **1851** Strong *Diary* II 62: A little whiskered monkey of a Spaniard. **1863** "E. Kirke" *So. Friends* 190: Yere, you yaller monkeys…tote dese 'mong 'em. *a*1870 *Coon-Hunt* 10: To be giggled and laughed at by a parcel of your town monkeys! **1884** Beard *Bristling with Thorns* 54: No 'count, triflin' monkey niggah. **1892** Norr *China Town* 34: You big, yellow-faced monkey…I've a good mind to smash this lamp on your ugly head.…You'd know something then, you monkey. **1898** F. Norris *Moran* 178–9: I'll tell you this, you filthy little monkey. *Ibid.* 190: Those dirty monkeys might have stood some show to the claim. **1899** F.P. Dunne *Countrymen* 5: Up gets this little monkey iv an' Aggynaldoo, an' says he, "Not for us," he says. **1904** "O. Henry" *Cabbages & Kings* 297: The monkeys were loading her up with big barges. **1911** A.H. Lewis *Apaches of N.Y.* 225: Did youse lobsters hear me handin' it to th' monkeys?…That chink, Low Foo, snakes two of me shirts. **1913–14** London *Elsinore* 278: I am Chink, monkey, damn fool—eh? **1918** Riesenberg *Under Sail* 297: Keep those black monkeys forward. ***1926** Walrond *Tropic Death* 64: Hey, Porto Rico, snap into it! Dis ain't no time to get foolin' wit' no monkey jane. **1928** Bodenheim *Georgie May* 9: Black monkeys, let them strain their bellies out. **1930** Lait *On the Spot* 207: *Monkey*…Chinaman (Var.: *Mustard*). **1930** Franklyn *Knights of Cockpit* 285: The only language these monkeys know is French and Creole. **1930** *Liberty* (Aug. 2) 40: *Monkey*…sometimes the mob term for a Jew. **1941** in Cannon *Nobody Asked* 316: I don't fear them monkeys at all.…Them Japs are little guys—they think they're tough. **1942** Hemingway *Men in War* xxi: All through the Pacific and the Far East in 1941 I heard about the general incapacity and worthlessness of, "those Little Monkeys." **1943** Horan & Frank *Boondocks* 24: Come on, you yellow monkeys, come and get it! **1943** Hubbard *Gung Ho* 99: We were just drawing the monkeys in, see? **1944** Chase & Mackenzie *Fighting Seabees* (film): If Tojo and his bug-eyed monkeys get in our way—. **1950** Blankfort *Halls of Montezuma* (film) [ref. to WWII]: Why don't we go out there and *get* those monkeys? **1952** Uris *Battle Cry* 254 [ref. to WWII]: What culture, Mary? They ain't nothing but a bunch of monkeys. **1957** E. Brown *Locust Fire* 116 [ref. to WWII]: Not the Japanese. The monkeys were nowhere near the strip. The snipers were slopies. **1958** Lederer & Burdick *Ugly American* 13: He suspected that the damned little monkeys always lied. **1962** Killens *Heard the Thunder* 128: Got one of them monkeys from the camp in here, Colonel. Thinks he's a soldier cause they let him wear a soldier suit. **1964** Gregory *Nigger* 171: Damn black monkey. **1967** *Time* (Aug. 4) 17: Those monkeys, those savages, all Negroes are rioters. To hell with them. **1968** *N.Y. Post* (Dec. 28) 33: Occasional taunts of "nigger" and "monkey." **1973** Droge *Patrolman* 99: We're down here keepin' these mother-fucking monkeys in line. **1984** Wallace & Gates *Close Encounters* 137: John Mitchell…let me know what he thought of America's black publishers. "Monkeys," he had called them.

5.a. a keg, flask, or other container for liquor; usu. in phr. **suck the monkey** to drink liquor surreptitiously and directly from the container, often an opened keg. Now *hist.*

*1785 Grose *Dict. Vulgar Tongue: To suck the monkey*; to suck or draw wine, or any other liquor, privately out of a cask, by means of a straw. ***1833** Marryat *Peter Simple* 241: "Mr. Simple, I am an old stager in the West Indies, and I'll let you into a secret. Do you know what '*sucking the monkey*' means?" "No, sir." "Well, then, I'll tell you; it is a term used among seamen for drinking *rum* out of *cocoa-nuts*, the milk having been poured out, and the liquor substituted." **1839–40** Cobb *Green Hand* I 147: He took a second pull at the monkey. *Ibid.* 189: We very well know that you have been taking,/As always, you rogue, a pull at the monkey. **1840** *Spirit of Times* (Sept. 12) 331: He…was expelled from the old grammar school, for sucking the monkey. ***1852** in *OED:* Having…filled his "monkey" full of sherry, our friend Jog slipped out the back way. **1865** Sala *Diary* I 357: These civic warriors…were taking "a suck at the monkey" (otherwise the whisky flask). *Ibid.* II 79: Nothing is more common in the cars than for soldiers to pass a can of spirits to a stranger, and ask him to take a "suck at the monkey." **1868** Macy *There She Blows!* 271: [Native liquor] is smuggled on board at almost every island where a white man has located himself; and it is well known that Jack will "suck the monkey" in whatever form or wherever he presents himself, as well in the Pacific as at the West Indies. **1980** Valle *Rocks & Shoals* 203 [ref. to 1840's]: This practice of drawing hidden liquor out of a cask or other container by means of a straw was known among the sailors as "sucking the monkey." **1991** Randolph & Legman *Roll Me in Your Arms* 427 [ref. to 1936]: When I asked what "sucking the monkey" meant, he told me cheerfully it was "an old Army word" for drinking whiskey straight, out of the bung-hole of a barrel.

b. *Naut.* a porous earthen vessel for the cooling of water or other beverages.

*1834 in *OED:* That claret, Brail—and the monkey of cool water—thank you. **1854** B. Mayer *Capt. Canot* 38 [ref. to 1820's]: We managed to cool the beverage by suspending it in a draft of air in porous vessels, which are known throughout the West Indies by the mischievous name of "monkeys." **1879** Shippen *30 Yrs.* 146: A monkey is a porous earthen jar, with two orifices. One is a funnel to fill it by, and the other a spout to drink from. The evaporation from the porous clay, especially when swinging in a draft, cools the water. **1903** *Our Naval Apprentice* (Aug.) 94: Why does water become cool and remain so when put in "water monkeys" such as we can buy over in Madeira and in some places in the West Indies?

6. the vulva or vagina.—usu. considered vulgar.

ca1888 *Stag Party* 139: In an instant I felt the head of his instrument inserted in my monkey. *Ibid.* 140: He played with and tickled my monkey. ***1889** (quot. at PUSSY, 1). **a1890–96** *F & H* IV 335: *Monkey*…(American).—The female *pudendum.* **1900** (quot. at PIECE). **1916** Cary *Venery* I 210: *Monkey*—The vagina. **1952** (quot. at SATCHEL). **1952** Randolph & Wilson *Down in the Holler* 105: Since the noun *monkey* refers to the female genitals, *monkeyin' around* suggests some kind of sexual approach or even a direct contact with the vulva. ***1970** in Wilkes *Dict. Austral. Colloq.* 221: 'E'd carry 'is bed any time a woman up an' showed 'im 'er monkey. **a1995** Radakovich *Wild Girls Club* 130: Nobody licks my monkey like you do!

7. a chorus girl; *(also)* a taxi dancer.

1928 *Amer. Mercury* (Aug.) 399: Several chorus girls from a Broadway show….One of the monkies, as they are called, sang and did an infinitely torrid dance. **1931** Cressey *Taxi-Dance Hall* 17 [ref. to ca1918]: The first efforts of its clientele to provide a satisfactory name for the taxi-dance hall resulted in such descriptive phrases as "dime-a-dance halls," "stag dance," and "monkey hops." *Ibid.* 35: *Monkeys.*—Dancing girls, either chorus girls or taxi-dancers…. *Monkey-chaser.*—A man interested in a taxi-dancer or chorus girl….*Monkey shows.*—Burlesque shows having chorus girls.

8. *Und.* a federal prohibition agent. Now *hist.*

1930 (cited in Partridge *Dict. Und.* 447). **1931** *AS* VI (Aug.) 440: *Monkey.* A prohibition officer. **1942–49** Goldin et al. *DAUL: Monkey.* 1. (Near South and Central U.S.; prohibition era) A prohibition agent.

9. *Narc.* an addiction, esp. to heroin.—also used fig. See also earlier *monkey on (one's) back,* below.

1949 in *DAS* 343: So hooked on morphine that there would be no getting the monkey off without another's help. **1953** W. Brown *Monkey on My Back* 11: And then there were those who fought the monkeys, each in his own way. **1954** E. Hunter *Jungle Kids* 60: The monkey was beginning to scratch, all right, the monkey was. **1959** W. Burroughs *Naked Lunch* xxxviii: The addict needs more and more junk to…buy off the Monkey. **1961** H. Ellison *Gentleman Junkie* 56: Cookie'd rather die than lose his monkey. **1964** in B. Jackson *Swim Like Me* 93: When you kick this monkey you'll live any type life—/Except the life of a junkie. **1966** in Wepman et al. *The Life* 70: Even the junkies gave up their monkeys. **1973** Childress *Hero* 61: Sometime I feel sorry for a guy who's carryin a monkey, but I don't feel sorry long. **1974** R. Carter *16th Round* 179: He was ignorant of the hungry monkey who had thumbed a ride home with him. **1985** *Miami Vice* (NBC-TV): When did you buy the monkey?…She would have said anything to feed that monkey. **1994** *Bon Appétit* (Mar.) 38: My father…was hooked on [Tabasco sauce] long before I was born, and by the time I was a teenager, I was carrying around a monkey bigger than a pro linebacker.

10. *Construction.* a pile driver.

1965 O'Neill *High Steel* 272: *Monkey.* a pile-driving hammer. **1974** R. Blount *3 Bricks Shy* 186: The monkey-man [is]…the one who sits up top…on a pile-driver rig.

11. the penis. See also *spank the monkey,* below.

1989 Univ. Tenn. student theme: "If you're gonna get funky, you better wrap your monkey"…means: Practice safe sex.

12. *Real Estate.* a mortgage.

1990 P. Dickson *Slang!* 191: *Monkey.* Mortgage, sometimes phrased as "monkey on the house," or "monkey with a long tail." **1993** *21st Cent. Dict. Sl.* 173: What's the monkey on that corner unit?

¶ In phrases:

¶ **barrel of monkeys** (used in prov. phrs. ref. to fun). Also vars.

1895 Gore *Stu. Slang* 15: *Barrel of monkeys,* or *bushel of monkeys, to have more fun than a.* To have an exceedingly jolly time. **1908** W.G. Davenport *Butte & Montana* 28: This is just more fun than a bag of monkeys. **1912** Siringo *Cowboy Detective* 323: I had more fun than a bushel of monkeys.

¶ **beat a monkey show** to be remarkably amusing, exasperating, or the like. Cf. *See the monkey show below!*

[**1792** in *DA:* Of all the foolish monkey-shows I ever was at, a Levee is the most so.] **1858** J.C. Reid *Tramp* 32: The "picters" would beat a monkey show.

¶ **brass monkey** see BRASS MONKEY.

¶ **cold enough to freeze the balls off a brass monkey** see s.v. BRASS MONKEY.

¶ **like a monkey trying to fuck** [or **bugger**] **a football** very clumsy; foolishly.—usu. considered vulgar. Also as adj.

1965 Braly *On theYard* 186: You look like a monkey trying to bugger a basketball. **1981** Hathaway *World of Hurt* 47: You look like a monkey fucking a football. **1988** Poyer *The Med* 422: You people cry like fifteen monkeys fuckin' a football.

¶ **make a monkey [out] of** to make a fool of; *(also)* to hold up to ridicule. Now *S.E.*

1895 F.P. Dunne, in Schaaf *Dooley* 167: Whin a rispected citizen…goes round makin' a pink monkey iv himself. **1896** (quot. at HOP[2]). **1900** G. Ade *Fables in Slang* 164, in *OEDS:* His friends would stand and watch him make monkeys of these anaemic Amateurs. **1904** Ade *True Bills* 129: He had made a Monkey of the Law. **1914** Lardner *You Know Me Al* 61: Anyway they didn't score and we made a monkey out of Dubuque, or whatever his name is. **1915** H.L. Wilson *Ruggles* 300: The woman's sole aim was to "make a monkey" of the Honourable George. **1938** J. Vogel *Man's Courage* 180: What are you trying to do, make a monkey out of us? **1946** E.S. Gardner *D.A. Breaks a Seal* 151: I'd just get up on the stand and some lawyer would make a monkey out of me. **1958** S.H. Adams *Tenderloin* 99: Doc, they made a ringtailed monkey outa you. **1984** *Tales from Darkside* (synd. TV series): I made a monkey out of that guy. **1993** B. Goldwater, on *Larry King Live* (CNN-TV) (June 9): If you send American troops in there [Bosnia-Herzegovina] they will make monkeys out of them. **1996** *Cigar Aficionado* (Summer) 291: Horses, being what they are, make a monkey out of you sooner or later.

¶ **monkey on (one's) back, 1.** *Narc.* an addiction to narcotics, esp. heroin.—also used fig. [No U.S. quots. of the sense defined in the bracketed quots. have come to light.]

[***1860** Hotten *Slang Dict.* (ed. 2): A man is said to have his monkey up, or the monkey on his back, when he is "riled," or out of temper.] [***a1889–90** Barrère & Leland *Dict. Slang: Monkey on one's back, to get a*…to get out of temper.] [***a1890–96** *F & H* IV 335: *He has a monkey on his back*…= he is angry.] **1936** Dai *Opium Addiction* 200: Habit. Addiction to drugs. Also called *monkey* as in "I have a monkey on my back," usually used when one is sick. **1939** in Leadbitter & Slaven *Blues Records* 370: You Can't Put That Monkey On My Back. **1946** Veiller *Killers* (film): "You're the guy with the monkey on your back, ain'tcha?" "Not any more." **1948** Lait & Mortimer *New York* 119: When one becomes so habituated that marijuana is an incurable obsession, "the monkey is riding on his (or her) back." **1952** "R. Marsten" *So Nude* 13: Leaving himself wide open for the monkey to hop on his back. **1953** W. Brown *Monkey on My Back* 7: To have a monkey on one's back describes, in the jargon of the drug user, the frightful sensations of the addict when he or she is unable to get a "fix." **1970** Knight *Black Voices* 87: 16 caps in my pocket and a monkey on my back. **1971** in Matthews & Amdur *My Race* 246: I've got to get this sugar monkey off my back. **1971** Goines *Dopefiend* 21: Just let her keep on chippin'. One of these days she would wake up with a little monkey on her back. **1987** *Newsweek* (Mar. 23) 72: He was carrying…a heroin monkey on his back. **1991** *Larry King Live* (CNN-TV) (July 9): These girls are drug addicts with a monkey on their back. **1995** *Donahue* (NBC-TV): [Nicotine] is one of the most monkey-on-your-back addictions out there.

2. a burden or great disadvantage; a source of emotional pressure. Now *colloq.*

1959 O'Connor *Talked to a Stranger* 103: The gang member's ego suffers a crushing blow when he hears the grave news that he is going to jail. The average teenage gang member is a realist and he knows that life will be more difficult from this point on; that he has a monkey on his back, one that he can't shake off; that it will be exceedingly hard now to make the transition from the bad life to the better. 1960 Duncan *If It Moves* 217: I can court-martial you on a dozen different counts. I can have you broken to private and dishonorably discharged for what you did. I can put a monkey on your back you'll never be able to shake. 1963 *Walt Disney's World of Color* (NBC-TV): When a bear has a monkey like this on his back, nothing can stop him. 1970 *Harper's* (Apr.) 41: He had never wanted to be President and had never sought out power; his every thought had been how to get the national monkey off his back and go home to Texas. 1974 Gober *Black Cop* 104: I ain't no slavin' fo' no honkie all my damn life! You ain't puttin' that kind of monkey on my back. 1975 Hynek & Vallee *Edge of Reality* 189: The Pentagon and the Wright Field people were relieved to have the scientists say that because it took the monkey off their backs. 1978 F. Messer on N.Y. Yankees vs. Detroit Tigers (WPIX-TV) (July 2): You don't want to put a monkey on anybody's back, but I feel that the key play of the ballgame was Mickey Stanley's two-base error on Rivers' fly ball. 1981 Centi *Positive/Negative* 36: Those who are brighter than others have a halo over their heads; those who are below or even average in intelligence carry a monkey on their backs. 1984–88 Hackworth & Sherman *About Face* 436: We had the monkey on our backs to clear the DZ. 1995 *CNN Sports Tonight* (CNN-TV) (June 18): It was my own monkey I put there on my own back....Now I've killed that dude. 1995 *CBS This Morning* (CBS-TV) (Dec. 22): They'll be carrying a monkey on their back called the House Freshman Class.

¶ **monkey's** see s.v. MONKEY, *n.* (used esp. in combs. to create often vulgar phrs. having the meaning 'a jot; a damn').

1893 Hampton *Maj. in Washington* 97: A poker I.O.U. that wasn't worth a monkey's snicker. *1960 in *OEDS*: The Old Man's door opened and the pair of them came out, Stillwell not seeming to give a monkey's, but too casual, and poor Jimmy Taylor with his hands clenched before him like the broken forelegs of a ginned rabbit. *1960 Partridge *DSUE* (ed. 5) 1188: *Monkey's f*ck, not to care a.* Not to care a rap: low (esp. Naval): since ca. 1920. [1976 in Bronner *Children's Folk.* 41: What time is it?...half past a monkey's ass, a quarter to his balls.] 1978 Alibrandi *Killshot* 71: I don't give a monkey's ass about your secretary's attendance record. 1979 T. Jones *Wayward Sailor* 186: I don't give a monkey's tit about that.

¶ **put it where the monkey put the nut** to stick it up one's anus.—used as a vulgar retort.

*1922 T.E. Lawrence *Mint* 168: "Put that where the monkey put the nuts," retorted Taffy. 1970 E. Thompson *Garden of Sand* 44: Tell em to do with it what the monkey did with the nut.

¶ **see the monkey show** [or **dance**] to see novel and entertaining things; *see the elephant* s.v. ELEPHANT.

1861 in W. Seale *Texas Riverman* 132: I've heard the thundering cannon sound,/I've seen the monkey show. 1862 in B. Wiley *Johnny Reb* 33: Martha...I can inform you that I have Seen the Monkey Show at last and I dont Waunt to see it no more I am satisfide with Ware Martha I Cant tell you how many ded men I did see. 1862 Malone *Whipt 'Em Everytime* 67: After nite I went to the show to see the Monkey. 1863 [Fitch] *Annals of Army* 649: A few who started in our crowd beheld "the *monkey* dance."

¶ **spank the monkey** (of a man or boy) to masturbate.—usu. considered vulgar. Also vars. Cf. MONKEY, 11.

1978 Raleigh, N.C., bartender, age 26: *Choking the monkey* is the same as beating your meat. 1989 Metcalfe *Jacknife* (film): Where you been, stud? Off spankin' the monkey in the men's room? 1993 *Beavis and Butt-head* (MTV): Spank your own monkey all you want, but keep your hands off mine. *Ibid.*: I've got to go spank my monkey. 1994 B. Maher *True Story* 132: Not that [he] was a big masturbator, but Jill had a look that could tempt a hardened homosexual to slap the monkey. 1994 D.O. Russell *Spanking the Monkey* [film title]. 1996 *Harper's* (June) 34: Jerking off....Jumping the monkey....playing with yourself.

¶ **suck the monkey** see s.v. **(5.a.)**, above.

¶ **your mother's monkey** yourself. *Joc.*

1882 *United Service* (June) 667: If you don't look out...your mother's monkey will get a lick in your nob. 1928 Harlow *Sailor* 37 [ref. to 1870's]: Don't talk back to me; if you do you'll get your mother's monkey into trouble.

monkey *v.* to tinker, trifle, or fool around (usu. *with*); involve oneself (with); (*also*) to tamper or interfere (with) surreptitiously; in phr. **monkey with the buzz saw** [or **bandwagon**] to meddle in a dangerous situation.

1877–78 *Cornelian* 86: *Monkey.* To fool around. 1881 in *DAE*: What with talking, running back and forth and general monkey-ing, Clara slipped and fell. 1884 in Lummis *Letters* 16: You can generally tell when a dog is monkeying just to hear himself bark. 1884 in *DA*: This reminds us of a sign in a Michigan planing mill, "Dont Munkey with the Buz Saw." 1887 [C. Mackenzie] *Jack Pots* 113: Come along and see I don't monkey with the cards. 1888 in F. Remington *Sel. Letters* 63: That wont give me much time [to] "monkey." 1890 in *DAE*: An ex-policeman in San Francisco who had monkeyed with that style of man...volunteered to make the arrest. 1891 in J.M. Carroll *Benteen-Goldin Lets.* 203: How much time we "monkeyed" away. 1891 in F. Remington *Sel. Letters* 117: Do you see how old Proctor has monkeyed this Indian soldier business,...it wont work. 1893 Hampton *Maj. in Washington* 57: No doubt the President is very busy but I am not here to monkey. 1895 Gore *Stu. Slang* 11: *Monkey...*To fool; to fritter away one's time. *monkey* with. To meddle with....*monkey* with the band wagon....Synonymous with "to monkey with the buzz-saw." 1896 in J.M. Carroll *Benteen-Goldin Lets.* 283: They are a bad lot of birds to monkey with. 1896 O. Wister, in *Harper's Mag.* (Mar.) 574: If you go to monkey with my Looloo girl,/I'll tell you what I'll do. 1899 Bangs *Type-Writer* 2: To "monkey" with a type-writing apparatus has always brought great joy into my heart. 1900 McManus *Soldier Life* 37: That's the stuff....Don't let them monkey with you. 1901 in Bierce *Letters* 47: Let me know how hard you hate me for monkeying with your sacred lines. 1901 Greenough & Kittredge *Words & Their Ways* 365: A vulgar but expressive American warning is "Don't monkey with the buzz-saw." 1903 in "O. Henry" *Works* 987: When a Marquis monkeys with the innocent affections of a cook-lady. 1906 Ford *Shorty McCabe* 98: I couldn't see the use of monkeyin' with that bughouse boarder. a1910 Veil *Memoirs* 170: I was "monkeying" with the machine. 1911 in Truman *Dear Bess* 60: If a man wants to get his name everlastingly before the public, he ought to monkey with the calendar. 1912 Siringo *Cowboy Detective* 78: I was regarded as a dangerous man to "monkey" with. 1916 in R. Lardner *Round Up* 114: You won't get nothin' but the worst of it, monkeying with me. 1920 S. Lewis, in *DAE*: I was brought up on a farm. And then monkeyin' round with silks! 1933 in Botkin *Treas. Amer. Folk.* 64: I'm a two-gun man and a very bad man and won't do to monkey with. 1949 *N.Y. Times* (Oct. 23) VII 39: Historical personages seem to me to have an integrity that we'd better not monkey with. 1952 Viereck *Men into Beasts* 34: Don't monkey with me or I'll put you in the Hole. 1966 "F. O'Brian" *Bugle & Spur* 32: You monkeying with fire, Boone. 1979 L.T. Carter *Eubie Blake* 53: Never monkey with a success. 1995 Coen & Coen *Fargo* (film): Didn't monkey with his car there, did ya?

-monkey *comb. form.* a person who provides, works with, or is responsible for (something specified in the initial element).—used chiefly in set colloc. Cf. AIR MONKEY; DECK MONKEY; GREASE MONKEY; POWDER MONKEY; ROAD MONKEY.

1959 *Sat. Eve. Post* (May 30) 41: He drove the machine at...a breakneck pace, the speeder pitching and rolling almost frighteningly....The speeder monkey rode it with a swaying, unconcerned detachment. 1968 *Pop. Science* (Aug.) 54: The gas monkey had filled the tanks of the wrong Bonanza. 1968 Adams *West. Words: Bridge monkey*—A logger's name for a bridge builder. 1980 in *DARE* [ref. to ca1900]: In a steam-driven threshing machine crew, the water monkey was the man who kept the machine supplied with water. 1984 in *DARE*: Chains required over most of the mountains....I put them on wrong, but found a "chain monkey," as they are called here, to do it right.

monkey around *v.* to act without purpose; play around. Now *colloq.*

1884 in Lummis *Letters* 164: Monkeying around with stock in a certain "Golden City Placer Mining Company." 1885 *Harper's Mo.* (July) 190: No time for "monkeying" round now. 1929–33 Farrell *Manhood of Lonigan* 203: Studs Lonigan was the wrong guy to monkey around with. 1950 *New Yorker* (June 24) 81: We go to open houses, eat, ride and sort of monkey around. 1947–51 Motley *We Fished* 10: He felt his need growing. "Let's monkey around," he said. 1963 Blechman *Camp Omongo* 29: Any of you guys think we're here to monkey around, get this straight: we mean business. **1995** *Calif. vs. Simpson* (Court TV) (Sept. 11): This isn't monkeying around! This is serious business!

monkey-assed *adj.* damned.—usu. considered vulgar.

　　1989 W.E. Merritt *Rivers Ran Backward* 218: Those mofo cameras and those monkey-assed earphones.

monkeyback *n. Black E.* a man who dresses in formal dinner clothes; dude.

　　1928 Fisher *Jericho* 147: Know where I seen 'im goin' to-night, dressed up like a monkey-back? *Ibid.* 302: *Monkey-Back* Dude.

monkey bag *n. Esp. Naut.* (see 1849 quot.). Also **monk bag.**

　　1841 [Mercier] *Man-of-War* 71: Each *monk-bag*, it was opened wide,/Purchasing you, *cologne*. **1847** in *OEDS*: A small leather wallet—a "monkey bag" (so called by sailors)—usually worn as a purse around the neck. **1849** Melville *White Jacket* 50 [ref. to 1843]: Such a fellow has three or four gold pieces in the monkey-bag, so called, or purse, which many tars wear round their necks, tucked out of sight.

monkey bite *n.* HICKEY, 2.b.

　　1942 *ATS* 337: *Kiss bite, monkey bite, hicky…*a red mark caused by sucking or biting. **1961** L.E. Young *Virgin Fleet* 68 [ref. to 1941]: Don't, Hank, don't. You'll give me monkey bites. *a*1970 Partridge *DSUE* (ed. 7) 1280: *Monkey(-)bite.* A mark left—often on the shoulder—by amorous biting: Canadian: since ca. 1930. **1970** Landy *Underground Dict.*: *Monkey bite…*Mark made on skin by sucking or biting. **1993** P. Munro *U.C.L.A. Slang II* 59: *Monkey bite* n. hickey.

monkey business *n.* foolishness; (*also*) underhanded actions or trickery; misbehavior. Now *colloq.* Occ. **monkey play.** Cf. earlier MONKEY CAPERS.

　　1883 G. Peck *Bad Boy* 109: There must be no monkey business going on. **1887** Francis *Saddle & Moccasin* 150: He always treated me well. But—! he didn't stand no monkey business, all the same. **1896** Lillard *Poker Stories* 52: Devoll comes back and begins his monkey business again. **1897** Siler & Houseman *Fight of the Century* 37: In case there is any monkey business, I shall not have the slightest hesitation in disqualifying the offender. **1901** Hapgood *Ghetto* 206: The "monkey business" of learning had ruined the child. **1912** Siringo *Cowboy Detective* 132: I had tired of her "monkey business." **1925** Dos Passos *Manhattan Transfer* 328: He's up to some kind of monkey business nine times out of ten. **1942** Garcia *Tough Trip* 426: Come out of there, you and them buck Injuns, and be sure you don't try any monkey work. **1946** in *DA*: Let's nip this political monkey business in the bud. **1953** M. Harris *Southpaw* 143: There will be no goddam monkeyplay afterwards. **1955** C. Berry *Monkey Business* (pop. song): It's too much monkey business/For me to get involved in! **1955** Paxton *Cobweb* (film): It's going to be bad enough without any monkey business. **1980** Whalen *Takes a Man* 217: Cut your monkey business. **1985** J. Hughes *Breakfast Club* (film): There's not supposed to be any monkey business. *Ibid.*: Any monkey business is ill-advised.

monkey cap *n. Army.* an overseas cap.

　　1919 Lovejoy *Story of 38th* 42 [ref. to 1918]: Officers in a funny looking "monkey cap" and those Sam Browne belts paid visits of official business to the vessel. **1930** in Faulkner *Coll. Stories* 414. **1973** Jackson *Fall Out* 134 [ref. to WWI]: Trucks loaded with servicemen wearing the "Go-to-hell" monkey caps affected by the A.E.F. shot past us.

monkey capers *n.pl.* MONKEY BUSINESS.

　　1846 *Crockett's Almanac* (unp.): Fashionable monkey capers…only fit for kittens an gentleman doll-babies.

monkey-chaser *n. Black E.* a black immigrant from the West Indies.—used contemptuously.

　　[**a*1889–90 Barrère & Leland *Dict. Slang: Monkey catcher* (West Indian). Amongst the Jamaican negroes this signifies a cute, shrewd, and level-headed individual.] **1924** in Clarke *Amer. Negro Stories* 27: Stealin's what that damn monkey-chaser tried to do to you. **1925** Van Vechten *Nigger Heaven* 60: Some black people from the British West Indies—monkey-chasers they called them on Lenox Avenue. **1926** *AS* (Dec.) 652: *Monkey chasers*—people from the West Indies. **1927** C. McKay *Home to Harlem* 20: Scotch! That's an ofay drink.…And I've seen the monkey-chasers order it when they want to put on style. **1947–52** R. Ellison *Invisible Man* 468: That monkey-chaser? **1958** *Life* (Apr. 14) 137: Monkey-chaser,…we gonna settle this here and now. **1988** in *DARE*: Your eyes got a little misty, and if you still thought of Jamaicans, Trinidadians, or Antiguans as "monkey chasers," you never said it aloud again.

monkey clothes *n.* a man's formal dress. Cf. MONKEY SUIT, 2.

　　1904 *DN* II 399: *Monkey clothes…*Dress clothes, evening clothes. **1926** *AS* (Oct.) 50: *Monkey clothes*—"Dress clothes." **1936** in R.E. Howard *Iron Man* 158: You done got me into these monkey clothes.

monkey dick *n.* **1.** a Vienna sausage; frankfurter.—usu. considered vulgar.

　　1965 IUFA *Folk Speech: Army Terms: Monkey dicks* (Hot dogs). **1983** Elting, Cragg & Deal *Dict. Soldier Talk* 363: *Monkey dicks* (Generally World War II; Marines)…Vienna sausage. **1985** *Maledicta* VIII 284: Nicknames for food used by college students at Michigan Technological University during the early 1970s:…*monkey dicks* for link sausages. **1995** Miss. woman, age *ca*30 (coll. J. Sheidlower): In Mississippi, *monkey dicks* refers to Vienna sausages.

2. a stupid or contemptible person.—usu. considered vulgar.

　　1988 Cogan & Ferguson *Presidio* 86: He's a monkey dick.

monkey drill *n.* **1.** *Esp. Navy & USMC.* calisthenics. Also as *v.*

　　1895 in Tisdale *Behind the Guns* 19: We had fifteen minutes at "monkey drill"—calesthenics. **1918** T. Smith *Biltmore* 19: The greatest disappointment awaited me at "Monkey Drill," or setting up exercises. **1919** *Our Navy* (May) 48: The feature of the day was the mugging of the crew and captain by the movie and account of this monkey drill was not had or held as all received the same effect by stretching the neck to be mugged for a close up ala William S. Hart. **1926** in *AS* I (Oct.): He may not care much for the "monkey drill," but give him good chow, a skipper who is no sundowner…and he is well content. **1929** *Our Army* (Jan.) 26: The Top called the roll and put us through the monkey drill. **1932** Pagano *Bluejackets* 21: We all expected the daily "monkey drill." **1935** F.H. Lea *Anchor Man* 2: Four years boning and monkey drill in this robot factory. **1948** Cozzens *Guard* 353: I came in to practice medicine, not do monkey drill, and have a lot of little twirps instruct me in my military duties. **1964** Stallings *Doughboys* 90: He secured some old sergeants of the Regular Line to monkey-drill them until they were acrobats. **1971** *U.S. Naval Inst. Proceedings* (June) 58 [ref. to WWII]: It required the crews of all ships to indulge in calesthenics for a quarter of an hour after morning quarters for muster.…This was called "spuds drill" or "monkey drill."

2. *Army.* **a.** mounted cavalry or artillery drill, often involving trick riding. Now *hist.*

　　1901 Oliver *Roughing It* 18 [ref. to 1898]: One trooper sung out: "Look at the soldiers' nice new trousers—I can see their finish after two-weeks of 'monkey drill.'" **1906** M'Govern *Sgt. Larry* 24: Larry was a little bit out of practice with the "monkey drill" we ust to have, but oncet a calvaryman, always a calvaryman, and the old calvary fever was now upon me. **1907** *Army & Navy Life* (Oct.) 432: No company from the city to the "monkey drill" today. **1919** *Btry. A.* 18: The drivers had a chance to practice their grooming on what horses we had and to take them out for "Monkey drills." **1919** McCarthy *Troop A* 4: Monkey drill taught the men the rudiments of trick riding and many of them became very well versed in handling their mounts. **1919** Witt *Riding to War* 160: Monkey drill. **1920** Baker *Co. History* 120: The "rookie" monkey drills at the armory. **1922** Jordan *Btry. B.* 10: On Thursday evenings it was "monkey drill" for the drivers—except for Mackie, he couldn't get on a horse, so became a cook. **1931** Rynning *Gun Notches* 48 [ref. to *ca*1880]: Dodd was the first officer to teach his men the famous monkey drill.

b. a scaling or climbing drill.

　　1982 F. Hailey *Soldier Talk* 41: *Monkey drill…*Ranger and Combat Engineer cliff-scaling drill (with the aid of grappling irons and scaling hooks)….Signal Corps lineman (pole climber) drill.

monkeyface *n.* a person with a monkey-like face.

　　1936 Sandburg *People, Yes* 130: Where did ja cop dat monkeyface. *Ibid.* 131: Gwan monkeyface peddle yer papers. **1949** Barker & Wright *Boy's Day* 60: Susan called out tauntingly, "Hey, monkey face, monkey face." [**1962** (quot. at ACE, *n.*, 6).]

monkey-fart *v.* to waste time; fool about.—constr. with *around.*—usu. considered vulgar.

　　*a*1970 Partridge *DSUE* (ed. 7) 1280: *Monkey-farting,* n. and adj. Applied to useless employment, waste of time, silly behaviour: Canadian (esp. soldiers'): C. 20. **1988** Willson *REMF* 40 [ref. to 1966]: Just a bunch of monkey-farting around and nonsense.

monkey hat *n. Mil.* MONKEY CAP; (*also*) (see 1944 quot.).

　　1917 in Grider *War Birds* 34: And we've got to wear these funny little monkey hats and R.F.C. belts. **1944** *N.Y. Times Mag.* (Sept. 17) 32:

Monkey Hat. Wac dress hat. **1950** Leland *Shell Hole* 31 [ref. to 1918]: The world famous "monkey hat" or fatigue cap of the U.S. Army made its appearance in Favieres and our good old campaign hats of memories went into the discard.

monkey house *n.* **1.** an insane asylum.

    [***1914** in *OEDS:* The rooms...were described by the agent and Timothy as "a lovely little bachelor suite" and a "self-contained monkey house" respectively.] **1958** "R. Traver" *Anatomy* 208: "A trip to the monkey house," I said morosely. **1964** "Doctor X" *Intern* 354: I still think she's schiz....I'm beginning to think that she's either going to end up starving to death or else going to the monkey house somewhere.

    2. *R.R.* a caboose.

    1945 Hubbard *R.R. Ave.* 352: *Monkey house* is caboose.

    3. *Mil.* a jail; prison stockade. [Quots. ref. to Vietnam War.]

    1982 "J. Cain" *Commandos* 93: A C.I.D. agent....Who had he come to take back to the Monkey House? **1986** "J. Cain" *Suicide Squad* 100: Trying to talk her way out of the monkeyhouse. **1990** Reinberg *In the Field* 143: *Monkey house* jail.

monkey hunt *n.* a wild goose chase.

    1848 J. Scott *Encarnation* 103: About the same time, five others went on a "monkey hunt" of the same character.

monkey island *n. Naut.* a small bridge set above a vessel's pilot house; monkey bridge.

    *1912 in *OEDS:* I was on Monkey Island (a pet name for the upper bridge) for hours. **1940** *AS* (Dec.) 451: *Monkey Island.* Exposed top side of wheelhouse. **1942** *ATS* 742: *Monkey island,* the top of the pilot house. ***1949** W. Granville *Sea Slang* 157: *Monkey island.* A ship's upper bridge. ***1963** in *OED2:* Up on the monkey island he had realized there would be no power for the lights.

monkey jacket *n.* [prob. in the ref. to the sometimes ornately decorated jackets, of various cuts and lengths, worn by performing monkeys] **1.** Orig. *Naut.* a short, close-fitting jacket; pea jacket; (*also*) a heavy thigh-length coat, esp. as worn by sailors. Now *S.E.*

    1822 (cited in Partridge *DSUE* (ed. 7) 1280). **1830** N. Ames *Mariner's Sks.* 187: My wardrobe consisted of a "monkey" jacket bought in Gravesend, [etc.]. **1833** N. Ames *Yarns* 44: Captain Kelson doffed his "monkey-jacket." **1834–40** R.H. Dana, Jr. *2 Yrs. Before Mast:* One of the party produced an old pack of Spanish cards from his monkey-jacket pocket. **1849** in R. Moody *Astor Pl. Riot* 132: He put on a short, light-colored "monkey-jacket" and Tom Hyer cap, ideal for action as well as disguise. **1849** Melville *Redburn* ch. iv: Another old tar in a shaggy monkey-jacket. **1850** G.G. Foster *Gas-Light* 108: A "monkey-jacket"...reaches half-way down the thigh. **1851** Melville *Moby-Dick* ch. iii: We were fain to button up our monkey jackets, and hold to our lips cups of scalding tea with our half frozen fingers. **1859** in C.A. Abbey *Before the Mast* 232: We shall have to resort to monkey jackets again. **1907** Lincoln *Cape Cod* 213: A [little] boy, wearing curls and a monkey-jacket. **1935** Whelan & Higgins *Murder Man* (film): Wearing a faun-colored monkey jacket. **1939** I. Baird *Waste Heritage* 89: Buttoning the monkey jacket and shivering suddenly. *a***1942** in Doerflinger *Shantymen* 123 (song learned *a*1900): But have a monkey pea jacket all ready. ***1949** W. Granville *Sea Slang* 157: *Monkey jacket.* A naval officer's "reefer" coat.

    2. a formal-dress jacket of any style; (*Mil.*) a full-dress coat or jacket.

    1851 *Harper's Mo.* (Mar.) 574 (caption): Do you make many of these monkey-jackets now? **1866** G.A. Townsend *Non-Combatant* 281: A certain youth, in a sort of legal monkey-jacket and with ponderously professional gold seals. **1928** *AS* III (Aug.) 453: *Monkey-jacket.* Full dress blouse [at U.S. Naval Academy]. **1940** *Life* (Nov. 18) 7: I can't tell you how much I appreciate your calling my "monkey-jacket" resplendent. **1941** in C.R. Bond & T. Anderson *Flying T. Diary* 32: George, Jim, and I dressed in our formal military "monkey jacket" outfits. **1950** *Sat. Eve. Post* (June 24) 45: Across the table sat another stranger, heavily mustached and wearing a double-breasted monkey jacket. **1978** R. Price *Ladies' Man* 17: An old-time waiter...wore a food-stained chest-high apron under a red monkey jacket.

monkey man *n.* **1.** *Black E.* a gullible or weak-willed man who is easily imposed upon by women; (*often*) such a man regarded as a woman's lover.

    1924 in Leadbitter & Slaven *Blues Records* 132: Get Yourself A Monkey Man, Make Him Strut His Stuff. **1924** in Calt *Rather Be Devil* 374: I'm goin' now, find my monkey man./I'll get all he's got now, then find my regular man. **1927** in Garon *Blues* 100: I think I'll fly to London, these monkey men make mama sore. **1928** R. Fisher *Jericho* 302: Monkey-Man "Cake-eater." **1929** in P. Oliver *Meaning of Blues* 141: Says my chief occupation—taking "monkey men's" women. **1937** R. Johnson "I'm a Steady Rollin' Man," in *Complete Recordings:* Well, boys, she get ramblin' in her brain/Hmm mmm mmm, some monkey man on her mind. **1964–69** in Calt *Rather Be Devil* 120: A monkey man grateful to touch the hem of a woman's garment. *a***1973–87** F.M. Davis *Livin' the Blues* 72 [ref. to *ca*1925]: Her monkey man comes home for lunch then goes back to work.

    2. *Mil.* a Japanese soldier or sailor.—used contemptuously.—usu. considered offensive. Cf. MONKEY, 4.

    1945 *Collier's* (Aug. 4) 55: He got the range and knocked the hell out of those standing, yelling monkey men. **1961** G. Forbes *Goodbye to Some* 138: What do you paint on your airplane if you get one of the monkeymen on the ground. **1974** L.D. Miller *Valiant* 178: This little monkey-man won't gut-shoot no more Marines!

    3. [perh. by confusion with **(1)**, above] *Black E.* a black man who is an immigrant from the West Indies; MONKEY-CHASER.—used contemptuously.

    1959 P. Oliver *Meaning of Blues* 141: The man...takes pleasure in ridiculing the "monkey men": the West Indians.

    4. see s.v. MONKEY, 10.

monkey march *n. USMC.* a close-order march.

    1952 Uris *Battle Cry* 50 [ref. to 1942]: We looked pretty sharp today on the monkey marches and the wind marches.

monkey meat *n.* Orig. *Army.* canned corned beef; (*hence*) poor-quality beef. [Early quots. ref. to WWI.]

    1918 Rendinell *One Man's War* 86: We had monkey meat for mess. After eating a can of it you are ready to climb a tree. Four cans, and you would grow a tail. The poor French people would not eat it. It was South American beef & carrots & tasted like coal oil. **1918** in Catlin *Few Marines* 224: They dig the "monkey meat" (South American canned beef) and bread from under the debris and earth deposited by the "whispering willies." **1918** in Cowing *Dear Folks at Home* 87: We gave him cigarettes and some of our monkey meat and hardtack. **1918–19** MacArthur *Bug's-Eye View* 19: Jim Weart and George Daugherty got four cans of monkey meat and a fit of apoplexy apiece. **1919** Catlin *Help of God and a Few Marines* 98: The men had to get along as best they could with bread, cold bacon, and "monkey" or tinned beef. **1927** Kyne *They Also Serve* 150: Hardtack, goldfish, canned beans and monkey meat. **1928** Havlin *Co. A* 101: Hard-tack and German "monkey-meat"...were the principal items of our menu. **1933** W. March *Company K* 89: Corporal Foster was opening cans of monkey meat with a bayonet. **1942** *Time* (Dec. 18): *Monkey meat*—tinned cornbeef. **1958** McCulloch *Woods Wds.* 118: *Monkey meat*—Prepared sandwich meat. **1983** *Daily Beacon* (Univ. Tenn.) (May 16) 2: The cafeteria....They use monkey meat for everything.

monkey model *n. Mil.* (see quot.).

    1991 Dunnigan & Bay *From Shield to Storm* 296: Russia does not export the best versions of its weapons. Instead, it exports what weapons experts call "monkey models," that lack many advanced features.

monkey money *n.* scrip or foreign paper money.

    1927 Kyne *They Also Serve* 200 [ref. to WWI]: Thirty-seven dollars and a handful of [French] monkey-money. **1930** G. Irwin *Tramp & Und. Slang: Monkey Money.*—Script or tokens issued in lieu of cash for use in a company store or commissary. Any foreign currency.

monkey-monk *n.* MUCKAMUCK.

    1918 R. Lardner *Treat 'Em Rough* 58: All the high monkey monks...will be paging Capt. Keefe.

monkey piss *n.* inferior beer or other liquor.—usu. considered vulgar.

    [**1929** V. Randolph, in *AS* IV 387: Monkey swill.] **1975** DeMille *Smack Man* 105: Bring three mugs of that monkey piss you call beer.

monkey rum *n.* Caribbean rum.

    1941 in *DA:* Corn liquor and monkey rum (which in North Carolina was the distilled sirup of sorghum cane), were concoctions taken stoically, with retching and running eyes, for the effect beyond the first fusel oil belch. **1972** Pearce *Pier Head Jump* 10: This little Porto

Rican guy named Chico who's in the…focsle…breaks out a bottle of monkey rum he's got stashed away in his locker.

monkey's see s.v. MONKEY, n.

monkey's allowance n. Naut. abuse and low pay.

*1785 Grose Vulgar Tongue: Monkey's allowance; more kicks than halfpence. *1829 (cited in Partridge DSUE 1280). *1833 Marryat Peter Simple 10: When you get on board, you'll find monkey's allowance—more kicks than half-pence. 1899 Boyd Shellback 236: I heard him call us the captain's pet monkeys, but he'd give us monkey's allowance the first chance he got.

monkey's ass n. MONKEY'S UNCLE.—usu. considered vulgar.

1978 Bobrick Flemming (play): Well, I'll be a monkey's ass!

monkeyshines n.pl. monkey-like antics; pranks or frivolous behavior; MONKEY BUSINESS.—rarely constr. in sing. Now colloq. or S.E.

1828 T. Rice, in Damon Old Amer. Songs (No. 15) (sheet music): I cut so many munky shines,/I dance de galloppade. 1847 Spirit of Times (Apr. 24) 105: Cutting "curlicues" and "monkey shines" till I was pretty tired. 1847 in DAE: Let me catch him cutting up any monkey shines in this house, and I'll beau him. 1852 Windeler Gold Rush Diary 138: Lots of men on a spree drinking & hallowing & kicking up monkey shines. 1872 in DAE: Their own mothers was a carousin' and a cuttin' up monkey shines all night. a1889–90 in Barrère & Leland Dict. Slang: How can human beings be guilty of such monkey shines. 1912 Siringo Cowboy Detective 123: Cutting all kinds of monkey-shines. 1932 R. Frost, in OED2: In a way it was a monkey-shine. 1937 J. Laughlin, in Witemeyer Williams-Laughlin 15: This is not just a monkeyshine. It's the way the thing works. ca1940 in Botkin Treas. Amer. Folk. 528: No time for monkeyshines! 1950 New Yorker (Mar. 11) 71: The plot in question has to do with some upper-echelon political monkeyshines in the French Republic. 1951 Time (Sept. 10) 30: The belief was growing that Communist monkeyshines in Korea were linked to the Japan treaty conference. 1964 in J. Campbell Myths to Live By 56: Monkeyshines of this kind still have an effect.

monkey's tail n. a short crowbar or hand spike.

1828 (cited in Partridge DSUE 1280). *1833 Marryat Peter Simple 31: "Youngster, hand me that monkey's tail." I saw nothing like a monkey's tail, but I was so frightened that I snatched up the first thing that I saw, which was a short bar of iron, and it so happened that it was the very article which he wanted. 1849 Melville White Jacket 168 [ref. to 1843]: This bright-work…is principally about the guns, embracing the "monkey-tails" of the carronades, the screws, prickers, little irons, and other things. 1851 Harper's Mo. (Sept.) 470: Hand me that monkey's tail…the short iron crowbar.

monkey strap n. Mil. a lifeline or safety strap. Also vars.

[*1933 in OEDS: Monkey, a handle made by putting a strap between two dees on a saddle and rolling it around itself. It is to hold on to when riding a bucking horse.] *1945 S.J. Baker Austral. Lang, in OED2: A monkey or monkey-strap, a looped strap on the offside of a saddle pommel, used by inferior "rough-riders." 1987 "J. Hawkins" Tunnel Warriors 19 [ref. to Vietnam War]: He tapped the monkeystrap attached to the back of his web belt. Ibid. 334: Monkeystrap…Lifeline. 1983–88 J.T. McLeod Crew Chief 38: Jim had Green strapped into his monkey harness.*…*Monkey harness—Restrainer straps that went around the waist and over the shoulders.…A long tail (thus the name) comes from the back of the harness and hooks onto a ring or secure part of the ship. Ibid. 319: The monkey belt had been unhooked. 1990 G.R. Clark Words of Viet. War 73: Monkey Strap…The gunner was tethered in the [helicopter gunship] by a safety strap (nicknamed a "monkey strap").

monkey style adv. West. riding (a horse) with one foot in a stirrup and the opposite leg thrown across the saddle.

1922 Rollins Cowboy 291 [ref. to 1890's]: The other method of riding the buck involved…pushing himself sideways out of the saddle standing in one stirrup…and his other leg…resting…across the saddle's seat.…This system [was] sometimes called "monkey style."

monkey suit n. 1. a man's formal dinner suit; a tailcoat or tuxedo.

1895 Townsend Fadden Explains 95: De next evenin' me and de Duchess, all rigged out in our monkey close, chases ourselves t' Mr. Paul's room. 1920 in OEDS: I and the Mrs. and Kate was the only ones there in evening clothes. The others had attended these functions before and knew that they wouldn't be enough suckers on hand to make any difference whether you wore a monkey suit or rompers. [1922 S.

Lewis Babbitt 12: Well, let me tell you that your revered paternal ancestor, Henry T., doesn't even call it a "Tux."! He calls it a "bobtail jacket for a ringtail monkey," and you couldn't get him into one unless you chloroformed him!] 1929 W.R. Burnett Iron Man 213: Do I have to wear a monkey-suit? 1931 Armour Little Caesar (film): I thought I better put on a monkey suit. 1932 Mason & Cockerell Age of Consent (film): My, but you look cute in that monkey suit. 1936 Mr. Deeds Goes to Town (film): Tails? Why, that's a monkey suit. Do you want to make me a laughing stock? I've never worn one of those things in my life. 1940 New Yorker (June 8) 16: I never can remember whether they wear black or white ties with their monkey suits. 1949 Sat. Eve. Post (Aug. 27) 87: "I will not be seen in public in a monkey suit!" "I didn't say a formal wedding, darling." 1961 J. Cheever, in New Yorker (Dec. 23) 30: His appearance in a tuxedo had not been forgotten. "My oldest daughter…was born two years after Barry Freeman wore his monkey suit to the Eastern Star Dance." 1969 Gonzales Paid My Dues 20: He also said I wouldn't have to wear the "monkey" suit. 1973 Oui (Apr.) 108: Guy Gourmet said the first night is always poor.…You don't have to put on your monkey suit that first night. 1977 Lieb Baseball 50: I ain't got a monkey suit and I ain't going to hire one. 1984 N.Y. Times ad. (WINS radio): A monkey suit…a top hat and tails.

2. a garish uniform thought to resemble one that might be worn by a trained monkey; (specif.) a bellboy's uniform; (also) a military dress uniform; (broadly) a uniform of any kind.

a1901 in OEDS: "Monkey suits," with jacket and waistcoat all in one, and trousers fastened over. 1926 AS (Oct.) 50: Monkey suit—A baseball uniform. 1929 N.Y. Times IX (June 2) 2: To the professional [baseball player], a uniform is "a monkey suit" or the "monkeys." 1933 Kingsley Men in White 417: I remember when I was a student in Berlin, one of my classmates came to an examination in military uniform.…Virchow looked at him, and said, "You! What are you doing here in that monkey suit?" 1933 Stewart Airman Speech 78: Monkey Suit. Any kind of uniform. 1934 Herbert & Erickson Fashions of '34 (film): I got tired being dressed up in this [chauffeur's] monkey suit. 1942 "D. Ormsbee" Sound of American 61: I didn't recognize you in that monkey suit. 1945 Hamann Air Words: Monkey clothes. Full dress uniform. 1948 Lowry Wolf That Fed Us 5: He put on his brown monkey suit and she laughed and laughed at him. 1949 Daves Task Force (film): This blasted monkey suit cost me two months' pay. 1952 Malamud Natural 38: Go on in the clubhouse and have Dizzy fit you up with a monkey suit [i.e., a baseball uniform]. 1954 Collans & Sterling House Detect. 9: He…got a job as a bellhop.…On…off-days Dev was allowed to swap his monkey suit for a blue serge. 1969 Whittemore Cop! 289: For some reason, when he's in uniform and makes an arrest, most of the time he doesn't get any trouble. The minute he gets out of the monkey suit, even showing 'em the badge, or the star, doesn't mean anything. 1970 Woods Killing Zone 30: I won't be worth a shit until the day I hang my monkey suit in mothballs. 1978 Diehl Sharky's Machine 242: You was wearin' a…monkey suit sittin' in the front seat of a…patrol car. 1984 J.R. Reeves Mekong 243: [We] put on our monkey suits—our dress uniforms. 1987 Santiago Undercover 9: I'll get rid of this monkey suit and make detective. 1988 Norst Colors 12: With two stripes…on the sleeve of his…monkey suit.

3. coveralls or a similar garment.

1928 in Pap. Mich. Acad.: Monkey suits, fur suits for high flying. 1929 Hemingway Farewell to Arms 190: Get me a monkey suit and I'll help you with the oil. 1930 in Faulkner Coll. Stories 557. 1942 ATS 716: Monkey suit…flying clothes. 1955 E. Bishop, in Nims Western Wind 73: Father wears a dirty,/oil-soaked monkey suit…/(it's a family filling station). 1961 L.G. Richards TAC 204: Jill just stared at that strange ape in the monkey suit, with his hands full of flight gear. 1962 Quirk Red Ribbons 173: His Skipper pulled on the flight gear, the green nylon monkey suit, and the orange Mae West. 1966 Kenney Caste 53: A…green hospital convalescent "monkey suit." 1983 Kaplan & Smith One Last Look 72 [ref. to WWII]: Keith Newhouse…never wore the electrically heated blue "monkey suit" because, "When I sweated I'd short the damn thing out."

monkey's uncle n. (used in mild oaths and expressions of surprise).

1926 Maines & Grant Wise-Crack Dict. 5: Be a monkey's uncle—Be surprised. 1934 Jevne & Purcell Palooka (film): Well, I'm a monkey's uncle! 1948 A. Murphy Hell & Back 98: If it works…I'm a blue-tailed monkey's uncle. 1957 Mayfield Hit 175: Well, I'll be a monkey's uncle! 1973 I. Reed La. Red 34: I'll be a monkey's uncle. 1974 E.

Thompson *Tattoo* 358: From Jack's point of view, if that milkmaid didn't have angry red bumps on her prat, he was a monkey's uncle. **1975** T. Berger *Sneaky People* 205: No lie?…Well, I'm a monkey's uncle.

Monkey Ward *n.* Montgomery Ward, Inc. *Joc.* Also **Monkey Ward's.**

1912 in Truman *Dear Bess* 106: Nor Monkey Ward's nor the ten-cent store. **1933** in G.G. Roberts *Cent a Story* 81: "Where'd you get that, sister?" "From Monkey Ward." **1936** Milburn *Catalogue* 12: "A whole truckload of Monkey Ward catalogues!" "Sears-Sawbuck catalogues, too!" **1947–51** Motley *We Fished* 57: She had worked at Monkey-Ward's and Spiegel's. *a*1956 Almirall *College to Cow Country* 106: The catalogues of Montgomery Ward, more familiarly known as "Monkey Ward." **1958** in Rosset *Evergreen Reader* 163: It's nothing against Monkey Ward. **1958** Bard & Spring *Horse Wrangler* 149: These Monkey Ward cowboys. **1962** T. Berger *Reinhart* 338: A catalogue of some Monkey Ward of the exotic. **1963–64** Kesey *Great Notion* 278: It ain't ordering from Monkey Ward. **1974** E. Thompson *Tattoo* 45: He was an open apple knocker from the West Side wearing plain Monkey Ward jeans rather than Levi's and high-top horsehide shit kickers. **1988** B.E. Wheeler *Outhouse Humor* 63: My wife sent off to Monkey Wards. **1992** J. Garry *This Ol' Drought* 121: The one thing you couldn't get from Sears, Roebuck, or "Monkey Ward's" was a mechanic.

monkey work *n.* MONKEY BUSINESS.

1898 in *DA*: Mind you, any monkey work'll get you into more trouble. **1911** Sinclair *Plays* 87: I've reason to believe there's some monkey-work being done with the court. **1958** Bard & Spring *Horse Wrangler* 96: All that monkey work didn't do any good. **1969** in *DARE.*

monkey wrench *n.* ¶ In phrase: **throw a monkey wrench into** to ruin or confuse (a plan or situation); sabotage. Now *S.E.*

1918–19 U. Sinclair *Jimmie Higgins* 60: That's why you've got to be good, and not throw monkey wrenches into the machinery. **1919** Darling *Jargon Book* 22: *Monkey Wrench*—Any act, deed or word that will injure or prevent the consummation of a plan or scheme. **1920** Colyer *323rd Field Arty.* 39: But he was still with us at Coetquidand just as busy as ever "throwing the monkey wrench into the machinery of the Regiment." **1927** S. Lewis *Elmer Gantry* 42 [ref. to 1903]: He would knock the block off any…bully who should dare come up to *him* in a meeting and try to throw a monkey-wrench into the machinery by dragging out a lot of…smart-aleck doubts! **1929** Hammett *Maltese Falcon* 77: My way of learning is to heave a…monkey-wrench into the machinery. **1936** J.T. Farrell *World I Never Made* 76: I've put a monkey wrench in Brophy's works now. **1937** in Goodstone *Pulps* 4: The S.P.C.A. and the Department of Health had thrown a monkey-wrench into Stade's program—stopped him cold. *ca*1938 in Rawick *Amer. Slave* II (Pt. 1) 35: Them red shirts was de monkey wrench in de cotton-gin of de carpet bag party. **1938** "E. Queen" *4 Hearts* 78: Now, listen, Queen.…Stop throwing monkey wrenches. **1950** *Time* (Sept. 4) 14: The union bosses who had thrown the latest monkey wrench into the act were two mild-looking men. **1950** Van Ronkel, Heinlein & O'Hanlon *Destination Moon* (film): Somebody's throwing a monkey wrench. **1960** Bannon *Journey* 115: You could louse up her whole life, throw a monkey wrench into her romance. **1983** *Green Arrow* (July) 9: You wouldn't want to see what a monkey wrench I could throw in the works if I wanted to. **1987** *N.Y. Times* (Mar. 17) I 16: Ribavirin throws a chemical monkey wrench into the genetic machinery. **1995** *CNN & Co.* (CNN-TV) (Mar. 14): Trying to throw a monkey wrench into the case [of *Calif.* vs. *Simpson*].

monkeywrench *v.* **1.** to *throw a monkey wrench into* s.v. MONKEY WRENCH, *n.*

1955 *Sat. Eve. Post* (Aug. 20) 62: "Every man I've got's out ——" "Monkey-wrenching the Strip. That's the beef Nick's getting." "That's right. I'll monkey-wrench 'em right out of ——." **1964** *Time* (Feb. 7) 23: Maggie claims that she is not out to monkey-wrench any other candidate. "I am going to run my own campaign on my own record." **1972** Carpentier *Flt. One* 103: He can monkey-wrench the whole thing.

2. [in allusion to Edward Abbey's novel *The Monkey Wrench Gang* (1975)] *Specif.*, to prevent or sabotage industrial development in wilderness areas, esp. through terrorism. —rarely used trans. Hence **monkeywrencher,** *n.*

1985 Foreman *Ecodefense: A Field Guide to Monkeywrenching* [book title]. **1985** *L.A. Times* (Sept. 19) V 21: Re "Earth First!: Radical Tactics Lead to Arrests"…The article about "monkeywrenching" was fas-

cinating. **1986** *Mother Jones* (Feb./Mar.) 8: The most controversial aspect of the EF! battle plan is *monkey-wrenching*—a term coined by author Edward Abbey to describe acts of sabotage in the name of environmentalism. **1989** *Nation* (July 17) 77: Tait also asked several of its Tucson people to put him in touch with monkeywrenchers in other states. **1990** *Whole Earth Review* (Winter): Staking out the position of unapologetic, uncompromising wilderness lovers with a bent for monkeywrenching and direct action. **1990** *N.Y. Times Mag.* (Nov. 4) 58: Acts of monkey wrenching have risen steadily.…There were at least 12 tree spikings in Northern California. **1995** *Nation* (Feb. 27) 269: The plot pits Arcology's security chief against ecoterrorists who will go to any lengths to monkey-wrench Todos Santos.

Monongahela *n.* rye whiskey distilled in the Monongahela Valley of Virginia and Pennsylvania.

[**1805** in *OEDS*: A Quantity of best Monongahela Whiskey for sale by the barrel.] [**1839** Briggs *Harry Franco* II 70: A glass of Monongahela whiskey.] **1851** in Derby *Phoenixiana* 144: Their Chairman…had informed them of the existence…of some specimens of a substance termed "Old Monongahela." **1859** Bartlett *Amer.* (ed. 2): *Monongahela.*…rye whiskey…and indeed American whiskey in general.

monster *n.* **1.** a formidable aircraft or automobile.

1955 Archibald *Aviation Cadet* 44: We're really throwing the iron monsters around now. *Ibid.* 90: We thought cockpit procedure on the monsters was confusing. **1959** in Loosbrock & Skinner *Wild Blue* 524: The B-36…was variously known as the Peacemaker, the Big Stick, or, sometimes, the "Monster." **1974** R. Carter *16th Round* 228: I pushed my monster off to the side of the road.…my black custom Eldorado.

2.a. a remarkable person or thing; a success.

1968 in *Rolling Stone Interviews* 52: Of course, man, she's a monster. She's like the best of that type of singer. **1973** R. Poole *Mack* (film): It's gonna be a monster, man! **1992** Strawberry & Rust *Darryl* 126: I had a monster of a season at Jackson.…home runs…and a whopping 97 RBIs.

b. Esp. *Entertainment Industry.* an extremely successful thing, as a music album or a movie.

1972 *New Yorker* (Dec. 23) 48: I give the smash L.P.'s, the Led Zeppelin, immediate monster. **1975** *DAS* (ed. 2): *Monster*…A big seller, esp. a recording. **1977** S. Gaines *Discotheque* 97: "I've got a monster here." Buckels tapped the white album jacket. **1980** *Pearl Pop. Slang* 101: *Monster*…(Business) an item which attains sudden and overwhelming popularity. **1984** Blumenthal *Hollywood* 111: This picture is gonna be a monster, kid. A monster! **1984** *Ratings Game* (film): *Wacked Out* will be a monster. It tested through the roof. **1989** S. Robinson & D. Ritz *Smokey* 168: This jam's a monster! **1994** *Bold and Beautiful* (CBS-TV): It's not going to be just a hit. It's going to be a monster.

3. *Narc.* amphetamines. Cf. METH MONSTER.

1971 *Amer. Scholar* (Autumn) 692: Users of scag and monster (drugs that stimulate the central nervous system). **1981** in *West. Folk.* XLIV (1985) 8: Methedrine is called "meth," "clang," "monster," and "speed."

4. *Baseball.* a powerfully hit ball.

1977 T. Seaver, on N.Y. Mets *Kiner's Korner* (WOR-TV) (Aug. 21): He doesn't hit the cheapies, he hits the monsters.…They go out there.

5. monster *n.* a person having formidable knowledge or skill (about something specified in the initial element).—used in combs. See also PARTY MONSTER.

1986 *Head of the Class* (ABC-TV): Darlene—a speech and debate monster. **1989** *Beachin' Times* 16: Anatomy of a Beach Monster. **1991** *Bill & Ted's Excellent Adventures* (Fox-TV): You're a total rock monster! **1991–95** Sack *Co. C* 50: "Stress monsters," one sang along with the Rolling Stones.

monster *adj.* **1.** extremely serious or significant; (*also*) (formerly *S.E.*) great in size, number, power, etc.—used prenominally. [Bracketed quots. reflect older *S.E.* usage, which is now uncommon.]

[****1837** in *OEDS*: The elements—earth, air, fire, water; or, The monster ballroom of 1837.] [**1882** in M. Calhoun *Med. Show* 91: Leavitt's Monster Minstrels.] **1975** V.B. Miller *Deadly Game* 48: I guess their career plans didn't include a monster foul-up. **1982** Hayano *Poker Faces* 55: They dream about making "monster" (huge) wins and winning for days and days without a loss. **1982** Trudeau *Dressed for Failure* (unp.): Last summer's monster vacation was a bust.

1985 *Cheers* (NBC-TV): We're talking monster laughs here. **1988** Dietl & Gross *One Tough Cop* 75: He is supposed to know if there is a break in a monster case. **1994** A. Heckerling *Clueless* 4: It's got four-wheel drive and a monster sound system.

2. Esp. *Entertainment Industry.* extraordinary, esp. in a positive way; hugely successful.

1968 *Rolling Stone Interviews* 44: When I was around fifteen I was a monster rock guitar player. **1973** TV ad (WNEW-TV) (Jan. 15): Yes, 20 fantastic monster hits…for $5.98. **1973** *Penthouse* (July) 41: Best cut: *Do Ya*, an all-time monster ass-shaker. *a***1980** in F. Hall *Dialogues in Swing* 123: They had a monster hit with Les Paul and Mary Ford. **1980** in *Penthouse* (Jan. 1981) 162: This stuff [cocaine] is *monster*.…This stuff is God, Jetty!…This stuff is really monster! **1989** S. Robinson & D. Ritz *Smokey* 118: Marv Tarplin is a monster musician. **1992** *Sports Close-up* (CNN-TV) (June 13): He was on his way to [having] a monster game. *a***1994** N. McCall *Wanna Holler* 121: This is *monster* herb!

monstro *adj.* huge.

1970 T. Southern *Blue Movie* 168: She's…blowing this monstro joint of hash.

monstrous *adv.* remarkable; IMMENSE.

1968 *Rolling Stone Interviews* 66: Great. Monstrous. Really talented cat.

Montezuma gold *n. Narc.* a kind of marijuana grown in Mexico.

1978 *N.Y. Times* (June 25) V 2: Montezuma gold, first-class weed, first-class weed, check it out, check it out.

Montezuma's revenge *n.* [alluding to *Montezuma* (now freq. *Moctezuma*) II (*ca*1470–1520), last Aztec emperor, defeated and killed by European invaders] traveler's diarrhea contracted by travelers esp. to Mexico. Cf. AZTEC TWO-STEP.

1961 T. Williams *Night of Iguana* 147 [ref. to 1940's]: Montezuma's Revenge! That's what we call it. **1962** *West. Folklore* XXI 28: The North American in Mexico has coined a number of names for the inevitable dysentary [*sic*] and diarrhea:…"Montezuma's revenge," the "Curse of Montezuma" and the "Aztec hop." **1970** *Pop. Science* (Mar.) 138: We were spared Montezuma's Revenge—a torment that makes a built-in toilet a necessity rather than a luxury. **1970** *Nat. Lampoon* (Aug.) 40: Human sacrifices Montezuma's Revenge poisonous snakes scorpions. *****1974** P. Beale, in Partridge *Concise Dict. Slang* 288: *Montezuma's revenge*…I heard it in Cyprus, late 1950s; later, more widespread. **1977** *S.F. Examiner* (Nov. 20) A11: An antibiotic is proving effective in preventing most episodes of "travelers' diarrhea," sometimes called "Montezuma's Revenge." **1988** F. Robinson & B. Stainback *Extra Innings* 32: Montezuma's revenge would literally knock the crap out of you. **1990** *Mystery Sci. Theater* (Comedy Central TV): She's got Montezuma's revenge like you wouldn't believe.

month and a month *n. Mil.* a month's confinement without pay.

1924 Farmer *Life with the Army* 25 [ref. to *ca*1859]: They were given a Garrison Court Martial, ordinar[il]y receiving as a sentence, one month's confinement with loss of pay. In Military Parlance "A month and a month." **1926** Nason *Sgt. Eadie* 54 [ref. to 1918]: They'd give you a month an' a month, sure, for losin' that rifle now.

monthly dues *n.pl.* [cf. earlier S.E. *month* and *monthlies*] menstruation. Also **monthly bill.**

1919 in Dreiser *Diaries* 289: Helen is sick—monthly dues. **1984** J. Hughes *16 Candles* (film): Her monthly bill came early.

moo[1] *n.* [by metonymy] **1.** beefsteak.

1916 in *DAS:* "An order of rump steak rare," says another [customer]. "Slab of moo—let him chew it!" **1919** S. Lewis *Free Air* 43: I guess he couldn't of, he'll be yodeling for friend soup and a couple slabs of moo. **1923** McKnight *English Words* 45: *Slab of moo* (beef).

2. milk or cream. Also **moo-moo.**

1942 *Sat. Eve. Post* (Nov. 28) 65: *Moo.* Cream. **1954–60** *DAS: Moo*…Milk; cream. **1964** Hill *Casualties* 246: We got any hommogized moo, or jus the blue john? *a***1967** Bombeck *Wit's End* 134: I had a fetish about the kids drinking their moo-moo from any cup that didn't have their name on it. **1991** *Get a Life* (Fox-TV): I think I'll have a little glass of moo.

moo[2] *n.* [short for MOOLA] money.

1941 Rossen *Blues in Night* (film): So maybe we got no moo. **1941** *Pittsburgh Courier* (Nov. 8) 7: Tossing 'round big gobs of MOO,/As if

the stuff on bushes grew. **1941** in D. Runyon *More Guys* 346: My goodness, this is important moo. **1945** Fay *Be Poor* 3: In the vernacular of those in the know, you have the "moola" (sometimes abbreviated "moo," meaning "money"). *Ibid.* 45: What Are We Gonna Do/To Get Rid of All Our "Moo?" **1949** W.R. Burnett *Asphalt Jungle* 57: Did you bring the moo? **1951** O'Hara *Farmers Hotel* 66: Don't they have enough moo to keep those pictures out of the papers.

moocah *n.* [app. var. of MOOTAH] *Narc.* marijuana.

1937 (quot. at MEZZ[1]). **1943** (quot. at MARY JANE). **1970** Landy *Underground Dict.: Moocah*.…Marijuana.

mooch *n.* **1.** a departure or expulsion.

1894 *Atlantic* (Sept.) 324: Boston! W'y, I'se got the mooch out o' Boston.…The bulls snared me, 'n' his Honor tole me to crawl. **1900** Willard & Hodler *Powers That Prey* 24: He had "to clear the deck" on the trolley with his razor to make good his "mooch."

2. a beggar or shiftless character; (*hence*) (used as a general term of disparagement).

1914 Jackson & Hellyer *Vocab.* 60: *Mooch*…A mendicant; an alms solicitor. **1943** *Sat. Eve. Post* (Sept. 25) 39: The type of idler who watches but does not buy is known to the [pitchmen] as a "mooch." **1954** in W.S. Burroughs *Letters* 217: I am really toughening up on mooches.…I've subsidized my last mooch. **1967** in Terkel *Great Divide* 118: These were the guys we need in our country. Who needs educated mooches? **1970** Terkel *Hard Times* 184: You can hire a mooch with muscle. But can you hire brains? **1978** Pilcer *Teen Angel* 83: You mooch! **1985** *Who's the Boss* (ABC-TV): Angela, the man is a mooch. **1995** Univ. Tenn. student: You such a mooch! **1996** D. McCumber *Playing Off Rail* 123: Instead of getting a game you get a mooch with a sad story.

3. *Gamb.* SUCKER.

1927 in Partridge *Dict. Und.* 447: The sucker or "Fall Guy"—any person who gives his money into the hands of these vampires of the financial underworld [the slick swindlers]—is known to the larcenous fraternity as a "mooch." **1935** Pollock *Und. Speaks: Mooch*, a sucker; chump; boob or easy mark for any stock sale or racket. **1944** *Time* (Mar. 13) 18: The prospect is [called] a sucker or a mooch. **1961** Scarne *Comp. Guide to Gambling* 459: *Mooch, Mark, or Chump:* Carnie slang for sucker. **1974** Stone *Dog Soldiers* 59: She had been so fucked up that night that she had been shortchanging herself instead of the mooches. **1996** D. McCumber *Playing Off Rail* 174: I'm going to pick out the worst mooch in the place and lose to him.

¶ In phrase:

¶ **on the mooch** Orig. *Und.* engaged in begging or (*hence*) sponging; looking for opportunities to get small sums of money, handouts, etc.

*****1864** Hotten *Slang Dict.* (ed. 3): *On the mooch*, on the look-out for any articles or circumstances which may be turned to profitable account. *****1867** in *F & H* IV 310: He would have said he was on the mouch, which being interpreted—French, *mouchard*, a spy; English *moucher*, to be on the look-out for something. *****a***1890–96** *F & H* IV 309: *Mouch*…To hang about: for alms, a job, or a chance to pilfer. Also *on the mouch.* **1902** "J. Flynt" *Little Bro.* 105: Blackie ain't much on the mooch himself, 'cept for clothes. **1955** in Kerouac *Letters* 494: I was on the mooch in my recent trip to NY. **1961** in Cannon *Nobody Asked* 358: The guys who gambled with him are long gone and busted, working as shills or on the mooch.

mooch *v.* **1.a.** to go; amble; MOSEY; (*also*) to sneak.

[*****149[?]** in *F & H* IV 309: The negons thai mowchid, and hadde no wile.] *****1851–61** H. Mayhew, in *F & H* IV 309: These hedge fellows are slow and dull; they go mouching along as if they were croaking themselves. **1894** *Century* (Feb.) 518: You've been up a tree, and you can't mooch out of it. **1895** *Harper's* (Oct.) 777: Ever since the kid mooched she's ben entertainin' 'em. **1899** Willard *Tramping* 384: Then I mooched. *Ibid.* 395: *Mooch*:…to "light out," "clear out." **1900** Willard & Hodler *Powers That Prey* 25: They're after you, you duffer…an' they'll have you if you don't mooch. **1906** London *Moon-Face* 44: We go mooching along the drag, with a sharp lamp out for John Law. **1910** T.A. Dorgan, in *N.Y. Eve. Jour.* (Jan. 3) 10: Jack Johnson mooched in to see Jeffreys fight Ruhlin in Frisco way back in 1901.…It was a cinch to beat your way into the pavilion if you could only make it to the Annex. **1911** *DN* III 545: *Mutch*…Move on; reported by one contributor. **1914** Jackson & Hellyer *Vocab.* 60: Mooch around the block and come back in ten minutes. **1918** *Sat. Eve. Post* (Aug. 24) 11: Shut up…and mooch along. Nothing's wrong here but you. **1918–19** MacArthur *Bug's-Eye View* 75: We roosted on the pieces, kidding the Kraut prisoners or mooching around the lately occupied positions. **1919** De Beck *Google* (July 29) 15: I'll mooch down in the first row before the mob gets in. *Ibid.* (Aug. 30) 23: I think I'll mooch over to the county jail. **1921** *Pirate Piece* (Aug.) 4: Let's mootch. Bo Soir. **1921** in Eckstrom & Smyth *Minstrelsy of Me.* 146: O'er the tote-road we'd mooch. **1924** Tully *Beggars of Life* 57: Maybe we'd better mooch on outta here. **1925** Mullin *Scholar Tramp* 299: Why, if I mooch around to that swell place o' his, he won't gimme nuthin' to eat. **1928** Bodenheim *Georgie May* 70: You all mooch out now fo' she busts out again. *Ibid.* 110: It's just about time for that dick Slattery to mooch along. **1930** Botkin *Folk-Say* 42: Whenever he'd get tired, he'd mooch over to the café and get a cup of coffee. **1936** Ferber & Kaufman *Stage Door* 858: Ah don't see how you tolerate that job of yours. Moochin' down there nine o'clock in the mawnin'. **1942** *ATS* 592: *Attend without a ticket*...mooch or mouch [*sic*] in. **1949** Cuppy *Decline & Fall* 142: Potemkin...would live for days on kvass and raw onions, mooching around the palace barefoot in a dirty old dressing gown, biting his nails. **1951** Herbert *Moon Is Blue* 629: I was just rehearsing a suitable gambit—when you mooched off. **1953** Peterson *Giant Step* 47: You mooched down all those stairs without batting an eye. **1964** Whitehouse *Fledgling* 21: I decided to mooch about. **1978** *Atlantic* (Nov.) 65: Narcisse [a donkey] mooched along as before. The road to Goudet was all uphill. **1987–89** M.H. Kingston *Tripmaster Monkey* 13: Mooch to your left, then you mooch to your right.

2. to obtain, as by begging; beg; FREELOAD; SPONGE; (*also*) to steal.

1857 "Ducange Anglicus" *Vulgar Tongue* 13: *Mouch, v.* to go about sponging on your friends. *Gen[eral usage]. *1888* in *F & H* IV 309: They never mouched a penny from anybody. *a1889–90* in Barrère & Leland *Dict. Slang:* Mooching is the art of getting what things you want to eat at different houses. **1891** Maitland *Slang Dict.* 179: *Mooch,* to play the truant....To sponge, to loaf about. *On the mooch,* on the lookout for odd jobs. **1895** *Harper's Wkly.* (Aug. 10) 756: Moochin' spiles workin' jes ez workin' spiles moochin'. **1903** *Enquirer* (Cincinnati) (May 9) 13: *Mooch*—To beg. **1906** Beyer *Amer. Battleship* 244: She mooched your whole pay-day. *a1909* Tillotson *Detective* 93: *Mouch*—To beg. **1910** Livingston *Life* 97: I began "mooching" among the padres (priests). **1911** *DN* III 545: *Mootch, v.* Take, sneak, sponge. "Some one mootched my handkerchief." "He mootched offn his roommate." **1914** Jackson & Hellyer *Vocab.* 60: *Mooch*...to beg. **1914** Kemp *Cry of Youth* 60: We'd have to mooch again. **1914** *Sat. Eve. Post* (Apr. 4) 10: And State Street, Chicago, bo. He sure mooched that stem. **1916** Thompson *Round the Levee* 45: To "mooch" is to beg. **1917** *Editor* (Feb. 24) 152: *Mooch*...the main drag—to beg or bum along the main street. **1918** Casey *Cannoneers* 203: Dozens of these lads come to our kitchen to mooch some hot coffee and a handful of Willy. **1918** in *AS* (Oct. 1933) 29: [Ft. Leavenworth:] *Mooch.* 1. Steal. 2. Less often: Beg. *ca1920* *Hobo Songs* (unp.): They had mooched the stem and threw their feet. **1929** Milburn *Hobo's Hornbook* 223: Oh, I know it's not conventional/To mooch a cop in blue,/But I thought you were a fireman—/I apologize to you. **1930** "D. Stiff" *Milk & Honey* 33: A bum...will mooch you for half your [razor] blades. **1929–33** Farrell *Manhood* 269: Give these mooching bastards a quarter. **1938** Macaulay & Wald *Brother Rat* (film): I'll set her itinerary. Stop mooching. **1947** Motley *Knock on Any Door* 85: But most of the time I give them a sob story about my mother and mooch enough for something to eat with—sometimes—a little left over for a drink or a girl. **1948** Seward & Ryan *Angel's Alley* (film): Furdermore, dere ain't gonna be no more moochin'. You pay as you go. **1954** G. Kersh, in Pohl *Star of Stars* 29: I came across a student, mooching drinks. **1965** Wallace *Skid Row* 205: *Mooch*—to beg. Also, to walk along. **1970** Thackrey *Thief* 191: Listen—cut it out. I'm not trying to mooch you. **1970** Boatright & Owens *Derrick* 139: Old Toledo Jack was...always mooching everybody. **1977** *L.A. Times* (June 7) III 1: I have been quoted as misquoted, lied to and lied about, cheated, squeezed, walked on and mooched.

moocher *n.* Orig. *Und.* an unskilled beggar or petty thief; no-account; (*hence*) a sponger; FREELOADER.

1857 "Ducange Anglicus" *Vulgar Tongue* 13: *Moucher,* n. Beggar. *Th[ieves' slang].* *1867* (quot. at *on the mooch* s.v. MOOCH, *n.*) *1888* in *F & H* IV 310: The mouchers or cadgers. *a1889–90* in Barrère & Leland *Dict. Slang:* A successful moocher must be a man of some imagination who can not only lie, but lie in a logical and plausible manner. **1894** *Century* (Mar.) 706: I's been a crook, I's been a moocher,

an' now I's shatin' [*sic*] on me uppers. **1895** *Harper's* (Oct.) 780: They think I'm a purty good moocher. *a1890–96* *F & H* IV 310: *Moucher,* or *Moocher*...(common).—A skulker; a petty thief; a beggar. **1903** *Enquirer* (Cincinnati) (May 9) 13: *Moocher*—A beggar; one who bums. **1908** W.G. Davenport *Butte & Montana* 10: Tea was poured by Miss Moocher. *a1909* Tillotson *Detective* 93: *Moucher*—A beggar. **1911** *DN* III 545: You're a mootcher. **1913** Brown *Broke* 68: Men are compelled to...seek shelter in a vermin-infested jail, or else become a common "Moocher." **1922** N. Anderson *Hobo* 50: The "panhandler" is a beggar who knows how to beg without loss of dignity. He is not docile and fawning. He appeals in a frank, open manner and usually "comes away with the goods." The "moocher" begs for nickels and dimes. He is an amateur. **1924** Tully *Beggars of Life* 58: You kids're dern good moochers. *ca1928* in Wilstach *Stage Slang* (unp.): A "moocher" is a cigarette borrower. **1929** Bodenheim *60 Secs.* 182: It was lessening his health...and making a third-rate moocher out of him. **1929** M. Gill *Und. Slang* (unp.): *Moocher*—Begger [*sic*]. **1930** Graham & Graham *Queer People* 89: The rest are a lot of moochers. A Hollywood party to them means a riot, at which someone else supplies the riotous materials. **1930** Lait *On the Spot* 207: *Moocher*...single-handed thief, usually of low-caste. Also a snooper or spy. **1935** Pollock *Und. Speaks:* *Moocher,* one who constantly borrows small sums of money from acquaintances. **1992** *Knoxville* (Tenn.) *News-Sentinel* (Oct. 24) A8: We cannot become a nation of moochers. **1993** *Sally Jessy Raphaël* (synd. TV series): "What's a *moocher?*" "She borrows everything...anything."

mooey-mooey *n.* lovemaking.
[*1860* cited in Partridge *Dict. Und.* 448]. **1942** in *ATS* 782: Lovemaking; courting....*flossing, jobbing, mooey-mooey, mousing.* **1959** Hecht *Sensualists* 115: "No," she said, "he was interested in mooey-mooey with Ann. He didn't even know I was around."

moofky-poofky, moofty-poofty vars. MIFKY-PIFKY.

moo juice *n.* milk or cream; COW JUICE; MOO, 2.
1942 *ATS* 105: Milk or cream....*cow, cow* or *moo juice.* **1945** *Calif. Folk. Qly.* IV 52: Occasionally a waggish hasher demands "Moo juice!" or "Cat beer!" **1946** Mezzrow & Wolfe *Really Blues* 109: Leave the milkman a note telling him to nix out the moo-juice. **1970** E. Thompson *Garden of Sand* 299: Get the kid a horsecock and cheese sandwich and some moo juice. **1976** *N.Y. Folklore* II 239: Milk is called *moo juice* by many. **1991** *Simpsons* (Fox-TV): Pass the moo juice.

mook /muk/ *n.* [prob alter. MOKE] an ineffectual, foolish, or contemptible person.
1930 in Perelman *Old Gang* 94: Even ordinary mooks like you and me. **1973** Scorsese & Martin *Mean Streets* (film): "This guy's a fuckin' mook!" "Mook? What's a mook?" **1976** R. Price *Bloodbrothers* 84: We're all sittin' there an' some mook puts "High Noon" on the juke. **1979** *Rolling Stone* (Feb. 8) 11: Their enemies are legion, many dismissing the four as hopeless mooks. **1980** Gould *Ft. Apache* 232: No, we're runnin' to collar some mooks with bricks. **1980** Algren *Dev. Stocking* 188: The bar mooks looked dully at the [TV] screen. **1984** B. Singer *Meatballs II* (film): Hey, I ain't seen you since we whipped them mooks on East Side. **1984** Opper *City Limits* (film): You're a mook! **1984** P.A. Robinson *All of Me* (film): You're a honkie *mook!* **1987** *21 Jump St.* (Fox-TV): What a mook! You think if I killed him there's a jury in the world that'd convict me? **1995** in *N.Y. Press* (Jan. 3, 1996) 12: Mooks spend money and can keep you in the black, but they don't make for a very attractive social environment....By Mooks I mean not only outer-borough types and out-and-out greaseballs, but Wall Streeters, unattractive and socially useless Eurotrash, advertising execs and Upper East Siders. **1996** *Village Voice* (N.Y.C.) (Aug. 27) 13: The clutch of Little Italy's mooks and mobsters.

mooky *adj.* being or resembling a MOOK.
1967 Ragni & Rado *Hair* 100: Excuse me, sir did you see a mooky-lookin' blond guy *cruisin'* around here?

moola or **moolah** *n.* [orig. unkn.] money. Also **mola**.
1939 C.R. Cooper *In Scarlet* 16: What about it, baby, is it my fault I forgot my wallet? I got plenty of mullah. **1939** D. Runyon, in *Collier's* (June 17) 9: He is very desperate for a little moolah. **1940** O'Hara *Pal Joey* 97: I never saw the day wherein no matter how much moola I had I could not use some more. **1941** Brackett & Wilder *Ball of Fire* (film): That's what I need the moola for. **1941** Rossen *Blues in Night* (film): You got any moola on you?...You were just gonna divvy up the moola. **1942** Bowers & Spence *7 Days Leave* (film): If we don't take the moola back to the boys, we'll be facing a firing squad. **1943** Darling *Jitterbugs* (film): Kale, mazuma, moola! **1943** in W.C. Fields

By Himself 249: I have plenty of mola [*sic*]—meaning spondulix—as we college boys say. **1947** S.J. Perelman *Westward Ha!* 122: I hear *el moola* (the moola) jingling in their pockets. **1947** H.T. Webster *Best of H.T.W.* 215: Why ain't *you* smart like them quiz kids? Ya could be earnin' a lot of moolah instead of me workin' my fingers to the bone. **1947** Beloin & Rose *Favorite Brunette* (film): Five grand is a lot of moola. **1953** J.M. Cain *Galatea* 53: Oh—moola. Grift. **1955** Kurtzman *Inside Mad* 48: I want to be where the *cash* is...the *green stuff...moolah...pound notes!* **1956** Longstreet *Real Jazz* 74: And last, not least, moola, the money to be had for playing it was up-river along the lake front. **1965** Pei *Story of Lang.* (rev. ed.) 179: It was Chuck Green, a close friend of Damon Runyon, who invented "moolah." **1968** Swarthout *Loveland* 141: Too much moolah and too many people after it. **1979** Charyn *7th Babe* 210: Did anybody see the moolah change hands? **1981** *Time* (Dec. 14) 58: $10 Billion by 1985...Big Mylar and big moola. **1986** Heinemann *Paco's Story* 80: The cashbox...was just brimming with moolah. **1992** *Martin* (Fox-TV): See, the moola is a down payment. **1995** Spot ad (Comedy Central TV): One heckuva lot of moolah [inscribed on face of large novelty check]. **1996** LaManna & Eliason *Titanic* (CBS-TV): The men get all the moola out of the safe.

moon[1] *n.* **1.a.** the buttocks; BUTT, 1.a.; (*hence*) the anus or rectum.
   ***1756** in *OEDS*: But his moon shall never be covered by me or Buck...till they put down the Ready—and no Brummagums. **1912** Berkman *Prison* 169 [ref. to 1893]: Well, d'ye know a moon when you see it? **1916** Cary *Venery* I 212: Moon—The posteriors. French, la lune. *Blood on the face of the moon*—A woman's monthlies. **1927** C. McKay *Harlem* 26: They done jumped on me soon as I turned mah black moon on that li'l saloon tha's catering to us niggers. *Ibid.*: "Decent mah black moon!" shouted Zeddy. **1927** *Immortalia* 170: She sits in her room / With her bare little moon. **1928** C. McKay *Banjo* 168: All we get outa him is "damned dirty nigger" and his red moon in our face. **1968** Radano *Walking the Beat* 30: That's sticking it up a guy's moon and breaking it off. **1972** *Nat. Lampoon* (Apr.) 35: Up my moon with a gravy spoon! **1977** in *Comments on Ety.* (Jan. 1989) 7: We cover every moon under the sun. **1979** Gram *Foxes* 214: He bent over and treated the punks to a view of his private moon.

   b. *Stu.* the act of exposing the bare buttocks as a prank to shock or insult an onlooker.—usu. constr. with a word like *throw* or *shoot*.
   1965 *Sex & College Student* 65: The exposure of buttocks or genitals to innocent bystanders as a kind of ribald prank or vulgar insult has provided many a lusty joke in the annals of literature....College students today identify this activity as "shooting the moon," and a favored arena is public highways. One teenager protrudes the anatomical part in question from the car window to the hilarious gratification of his companions and the presumed shock of the unwary onlooker. **1965** in *Esquire* (Jan. 1966) 60: There are even some girls who enjoy throwing a moon now and then, just for the hell of it or maybe to strike a blow for academic freedom. *a*1968 in Haines & Taggart *Ft. Lauderdale* 11: A "moon" is when you're a guy and you want to gross out a girl, so you drop your pants down part way and stick your ass out at her, like from a car window or a dorm window or any kind of window. **1968** Lockridge *Hartspring* 159: A...girl...had been arrested for...giving the Moon to passing drivers. **1970** *Nat. Lampoon* (Nov.) 4: The average *National Lampoon* subscriber...is twenty-four years of age—too old to flash moons from speeding convertibles. **1970** Zindel *Your Mind* 27: Whenever we got loaded, he insisted on throwing moons at the police station. **1972** N.Y.U. student: Ever hear of *to chuck a moon?* A girl can do it just by lifting her skirt and showing her ass, but it's tougher for a guy. He has to take his pants down. **1977** Olsen *Fire Five* 249: Buncha schoolkids, hanging moons in the boys' room. **1979** Gutcheon *New Girls* 65: He leaped on a table...and he pulls down his pants and throws a moon right in her face. **1979–82** Gwin *Overboard* 104: Shoot us a moon, women. **1982** *N.Y. Post* (Sept. 4) 40: There was the time he "shot a moon" during a tournament and was disqualified. **1988** *TV Guide* (Mar. 19) 17: People would go around all the time shooting moons and goosing each other.

   2.a. a month, esp. as a term of imprisonment. Cf. S.E. usage.
   ***1823** in *F & H* IV 346: If you wait, sir, till the land-breeze fills your sails, you will wait another moon, I believe. ***1830** in *DSUE* 530:

They've lumbered him for a few moons, that's all. **1859** Matsell *Vocab.* 56: *Moon.* One month; thirty days' imprisonment. "The poor cove was done for two stretches and six moons," the poor fellow was sentenced for two years and six months. **1866** (quot. at JUG GRAFTER). **1867** *Nat. Police Gaz.* (Oct. 26) 2: Dougherty ... got four "moons" on the Island last week. **1896** Ade *Artie* 94: In a couple o' moons they go back home. **1904** *Life in Sing Sing* 263: Plant me for a few moons till the smoke rolls away. ... Hide me for a few months until the affair is forgotten. **1935** Pollock *Und. Speaks*: One moon, thirty days in jail.

   b. *Hobo.* a night.
   1884 Peck *Boss Book* 111: After a few moons the plaster...got its work. **1899** "J. Flynt" *Tramping* 384: I was batterin'...one moon (night) on the Dope (Baltimore and Ohio Railroad).

   3. a dollar coin; dollar.
   1919 *Amer. Legion Wkly.* (July 11) 24: I've got a job waiting for me that pays thirty moons a week instead of thirty a month.

¶ In phrases:

¶ **many moons** a long time.
   1896 Ade *Artie* 50: This is the first time I've had a day-after head in many moons. **1905** Hobart *Get Next!* 97: We lived in Baltimore many moons ago. **1956** E. Hunter *Second Ending* 22: Well, he's been with Fredericks for many moons now, and he told me they're getting ready to bounce the cat they got blowing second. **1963** W.C. Anderson *Penelope* 85: Ah've been talkin' to you fo' many moons. **1972** P. Thomas *Savior* 83: Concho, man, I ain't seen you for many moons.

¶ **see two moons** to be drunk.
   1722 B. Franklin, in *AS* XV (Feb.) 103: [Drunkards]...See two moons. **1900** *Puck* (Feb. 14) (unp.): Mr. Gaylush.—Officer! I can—hic!—see two moons up zhere and—hic!—hear 'em talking to each other! Officer.—Ye can, eh? Well, ye don't want to believe nawthing that ye hear, and only half what ye see!

moon[2] *n.* MOONSHINE, 1.
   1928 *Collier's* (Dec. 29). **1928** York *Sgt. York* 7: Tennessee "moon" is potent, overproof, and so clear, they say, that one can read the Constitution of the United States right through it. **1929** *AS* IV (June) 386: Some of the common names for whisky—*moonshine, moon, mooney, shine, blockade, brush whiskey, swamproot, squirrel* and *mountain dew*—seem to refer to its alleged origin, suggesting that it is manufactured by moonlight in the wilderness. **1929–33** Farrell *Young Manhood* 379: The supply of moon goes on forever. **1937** Reitman *Box-Car Bertha* 73: After Earl Ford downed a pint of "moon," he recited part of *The Ballad of Reading Gaol*. **1941** H.A. Smith *Low Man* 29: I...bought two bottles of sugar moon from a bootlegger named Nowatney. **1950, 1962, 1965–70** in *DARE*.

moon *v.* **1.** to have anal intercourse with.—usu. considered vulgar.
   1912 Berkman *Prison* 169 [ref. to 1893]: "You know what 'moon' is, don't you?" he asks, abruptly, with an evident effort to suppress a smile....."I'll bet my corn dodger you don't....Moonology...is the truly Christian science of loving your neighbor, provided he be a nice little boy. Understand now?" **1929–30** Farrell *Young Lonigan* 78: Then he looked at Danny O'Neil, who was his own size, and said he'd like to start mooning punks. He said he was fed up on the dago chickens around State Street anyway. **1933** Farrell *Gas-House McGinty* 30: A hobo passed, holding the arm of a punk in dirty clothes. That wolf, mooning a punk, might once have been a clean, decent kid.

   2. *Wrestling.* to be defeated in a wrestling exhibition. *Joc.*
   1955 *TV Guide* (Jan. 15) 19: "You moon tonight at 55 with a flying-tackle blowoff."..."You lose (looking at the moon, on your back) in 55 minutes after a flying tackle finish."

   3. *Stu.* to expose the buttocks as a coarse prank; shock or insult by exposing the naked buttocks to.
   [**1958** Frees *Beatniks* (film): [Spoken by a character named *Moon:*] "One more word...and I'm gonna *moon* you." "You're going to what?" "*Moon* you!"] **1963** *Look* (Aug. 27) 18: A game called mooning. Three or four boys will...lower their trousers and, at a signal, push their bare bottoms out of every available window. This pastime originated about two years ago in southern California and has crossed the country: it has now turned up in Florida. **1965** Walnut Ridge, Ark., teenager (coll. J. Ball): Everybody in the back of the band bus was mooning. **1968** Lockridge *Hartspring* 158: And as an automobile passed mine, I was initiated into the quaint custom known here in Indiana as "Mooning." **1971** Jacobs & Casey *Grease* 29: I'm king of the mooners....I'm the mooning champ of

Rydell High. *Ibid.* 30: I even mooned Old Lady Lynch once. **1971** *Nat. Lampoon* (Nov.) 21: Have a few "brews," gross out some chicks, "moon" a townie. **1986** *ALF* (NBC-TV): I guess I'll just moon some state troopers. **1989** *Murphy Brown* (CBS-TV): Have you ever mooned anyone? **1993** *New Yorker* (June 7) 63: He had "taken pictures of kids...mooning." **1995** *Reader's Digest* (Mar.) 76: Though it would be funny if he "mooned" friends from a...dormitory window. **1996** *CNN Saturday Morning* (CNN-TV) (May 4): The boy...was mooning the driver.

moonball *n.* **1.** *Tennis.* a high lob or defensive shot; any high, soft shot. Also as v.

   1976 *AS* 51: 293. **1977** Bredes *Hard Feelings* 314: I...blooped it back at him, fucking moonball. **1982** *Chicago Sun-Times* (Sept. 7): Jaeger held at love in her first service game, which featured an interminable rally of moon balls. **1991** *N.Y. Times* (June 30) ("Sports") 10: How about the endless baseline rallies by the women? Moonballs? Poor net performance? **1991** *Harper's* (Dec.) 72: I...could play just forever, sending back moon balls baroque with ornate spins. **1993** *New Yorker* (Oct. 4) 178: He cramped, he moonballed, he served underhand. **1994** *New Yorker* (July 25) 40: Yesterday...she hit nothing but moon balls....Then she plays Maggie and boom, boom, *bang!*

   2. *Basketball.* a slowly rising shot.

   1976 Rosen *Above Rim* 180: Reed...forced up a moonball that plopped on the front rim and crawled through.

mooner *n.* *Police.* a person whose wrongdoing is supposedly caused by the influence of the full moon. Cf. S.E. *lunatic.*

   1958 *N.Y. Times Mag.* (Mar. 16) 88: *Mooner.*—One of a number of people who keep policemen busy during full moons (when, according to police lore, categories of crime show an increase).

mooney *n.* MOONSHINE, 1.

   1929 (quot. at MOON²). **1942** *ATS* 99: Illicit liquor....*hootch, moon, mooney, moonlight, moonshine.*

moon-eyed *adj.* drunk.

   1737 in *OEDS*: He sees two Moons, Merry, Middling, Moon-Ey'd, Muddled, [etc.]. **1940** *AS* (Dec.) 447]: *Moon-Eyed.* Intoxicated. "Sid gits moon-eyed every Saturday night."

moon-face *n.* an East Asian person.—used contemptuously.—usu. considered offensive.

   1870 Greey *Blue Jackets* 78: "Most illustrious sir!" exclaimed the foremost moon-face. **1876** Dixon *White Conquest* II 235: Moon-face picked himself up. *Ibid.* 239: The two moon-faces...could hardly overtake their work. **1970** *Nat. Lampoon* (Nov.) 22: "Die, moon-face!" I growled as the spitting lead ripped into one of them. **1985** Yeager & Janos *Yeager* 34: This moon-face I don't trust.

Moonie *n.* [after Rev. Sun Myung *Moon,* founder of the church, with pun on S.E. *moony* 'dreamy; listless'] a member of the Unification Church.—usu. used derisively.

   1974 in *OED2*: The Moonies...are extremely media-conscious. **1976** *L.A. Times* (Feb. 25) I 1: Those critical of Creative Initiative refer to its members as upper-class "moonies," alluding to the followers of the Rev. Sun Yung [*sic*] Moon. **1976** *Harper's* (Dec.) 61: The Lockheed Corporation's indirectly subsidizing the Moonies' spread from Seoul to Savannah. **1977** *Atlantic* (Nov.) 103: Sontag visited three continents to interview zealous "Moonies," disillusioned dropouts, bitter parents, and professional deprogrammers. **1978** *L.A. Times* (Mar. 30) II 8: The Rev. Sun Myung Moon and leaders of his controversial Unification Church have been sued for $150 million by a man who claims his son is a psychological prisoner of the "Moonies." **1979** *U.S. News & W.R.* (Oct. 1) 75: Young cultists—the "Moonies" and others—have generated complaints from alarmed parents and politicians. **1980** *Atlantic* (Feb.) 94: He was willing to listen, however; he was no Moonie. **1980** D. Hamill *Stomping Ground* 14: Gotta be a Moonie. **1984** J. McNamara *First Directive* 6: Why his daughter just couldn't have run away to be a Moonie. **1994** *New York* (Mar. 7) 43: Washington *Times:* Many find the quirky conservative point of view in this Moonie-owned paper provocative.

moon juice *n.* (see 1973 quot.).

   1973 R. Roth *Sand in Wind* 226: A Vietnamese...tried to sell them what he called "moon juice."...Cough syrup with speed in it. **1977** Natkin & Furie *Boys in Co. C* (film): Hey buddy! Moon juice!

moonlight *v.* **1.** *Und.* to operate as a MOONLIGHTER; steal under cover of night.

   *1888 in *F & H* IV 349: The prisoners...were arrested on a charge of moonlighting in county Clare. **1942** *ATS* 455: Moonlight...*to rob at night.* **1971** Heckelmann *Durango* 55: You been doin' any rustlin' or moonlightin' with that crowd up in Rincon? *a1985* in K. Walker *Piece of My Heart* 353 [ref. to 1967]: That was kind of what everybody did, you know, moonlighting, scrounging.

   2. to work at an additional job, esp. at night, as well as one's regular job.—rarely used trans. Now *S.E.*

   1957 *Time* (July 22) 70: MOONLIGHTING A Problem Born of Prosperity...One of the paradoxes—and problems—of the U.S. full-employment prosperity is moonlighting, *i.e.,* holding two jobs at once....The amount a man makes on his regular job does not necessarily determine whether he moonlights. **1957** in *OEDS* (Aug. 8): He takes two or three hours off and then departs for a second job....The practice is known as "moonlighting." **1959** *N.Y. Times* (Oct. 4) 86: The Bureau of the Census has reported a sharp increase in "moonlighting"—holding two or more jobs—during the current decade. **1963** E. Hunter *Ten Plus One* 123: The commissioner had issued his edict against moonlighting. **1966** I. Reed *Pall-Bearers* 146: I drive this truck for SAM. Doing a little moonlightin'. **1969** Leyden & Snyder *Diff. Game* 49: But being a coach did open some doors to what they now call moonlighting. **1970** Terkel *Hard Times* 391: Just here in the last month, they have allowed policemen to moonlight by driving taxi cabs. **1976** *L.A. Times* ("Home") (May 16) 27: A struggling young songwriter who had begun moonlighting an offbeat specialty. **1981** G. Wolf *Roger Rabbit* 177: He used to moonlight as a gymnasium punching bag. **1982** WINS radio report (Aug. 19): Are you moonlighting to make ends meet as are so many Americans these days? **1983** Helprin *Winter's Tale* 315: Do you moonlight in a shooting gallery? **1983** *Daily Beacon* (Univ. Tenn.) (Feb. 9) 8: If you need to moonlight, we have the jobs. **1983** Flaherty *Tin Wife* 188: Even Jackie O has to moonlight to afford her pad. **1985** E. Leonard *Glitz* 88: Which doesn't mean she couldn't have been moonlighting. **1989** *CampusUSA* (Spring) 16: Anthony Thistlethwaite plays a mean sax when he's not moonlighting on mandolin. **1993** *Donahue* (NBC-TV): You have a regular normal job and you moonlight.

moonlighter *n.* *Und.* a burglar or other criminal who operates at night.

   *1882 in *F & H* IV 349: Taking moonlighters under his direct protection. **1889–90* Barrère & Leland *Dict. Slang: Moonlighters*...men in Ireland who carry out sentences of secret societies against individuals and perform their work of violence by night. **1908** Sullivan *Criminal Slang* 15: *Moonlighter*—A midnight prowler (Irish). **1935** *AS* (Feb.) 18: [Underworld, 1910:] *Moonlighter.* A burglar.

moonlight express *n.* *Trucking.* driving back roads at night to avoid notice.

   1976 (quot. at BOONDOCK, *v.,* 3). **1976** Lieberman & Rhodes *CB* 140: *Working for the Moonlight Express*—Running back roads at night to avoid weigh stations.

moonlight requisition *n.* *Mil.* the act of pilfering supplies or equipment under cover of darkness; (*hence,* in 1951 Leveridge quot.) an item or items so obtained. *Joc.*

   1944–46 in *AS* XXII 55: [Army:] *Moonlight Requisition.* Illegal requisition, unauthorized trade, or downright thievery of supplies. **1951** Leveridge *Walk on Water* 176: Yeah?...Moonlight requisition? **1951** Sheldon *Troubling Star* 119: Maybe we can make a moonlight requisition some night. **1955** Heflin *USAF Dict.: Moonlight requisition.* The surreptitious appropriation of equipment or supplies during hours of darkness. **1956** Heflin *USAF Dict.* 332: *Moonlight requisition.* The surreptitious appropriation of equipment or supplies during hours of darkness. Slang. **1962** Mahurin *Honest John* 78: This looked like a parts bonanza, so we set up a special moonlight requisition unit under my group maintenance officer. **1967** Lockwood *Subs* 42 [ref. to 1914]: We had to prove to Mr. Carr's satisfaction that our "moonlight requisitions were justified." *Ibid.* 63 [ref. to 1915]: Lastly, there was a decided drop in the exciting but dangerous game of "borrowing" materials in the course of *moonlight requisitioning,* a 23-letter term for clandestine operations which, in World War II, became known as scrounging.

moonlight requisition *v.* *Mil.* to steal at night. *Joc.* Hence **moonlight requisitioning.**

   1943 in *Best from Yank* 139: This was known as "moonlight requisitioning." **1944** *Yank* (Feb. 25) 9: When it can't wait for equipment replacements from the States, and when ingenuity fails, a service squadron must sometimes resort to what is politely called "moonlight requisitioning." **1945** Stetson *573rd AAA* 46: Units for miles around sent "Moonlight Requisitioning Parties" for supplies. **1952** Vonnegut *Player Piano* 242: Up comes Mergenthaler with a truck and generator he's moonlight-requisitioned from the 57th. **1953** *Sat. Eve. Post* (Apr. 11) 99: The soldiers…enjoy very few of the fancy items they unload unless they moonlight-requisition them. **1963** *Texana* (Summer) 258: Much of this foraging by the Texans…was accomplished by the comparatively safe "moonlight requisitioning" route.

moon pie *n.* [MOON[1] + *pie*, sugg. by *Moon Pie*, trademark for a brand of snack food; Cf. FUR PIE, HAIR PIE] anal copulation; *(hence)* coitus.—usu. considered vulgar. *Joc.*

    1978 Price *Ladies' Man* 214: There was no way I wasn't going upstairs for a slice of moon pie. **1979** Charyn *7th Babe* 71: Their bench jockeys…crowed at Rags. "How's the babe? Don't you see the hair on his lip? The kid's been eatin' moon pie."

moonrock *n. Narc.* (see quots.).

    1989 *PrimeNews* (CNN-TV) (Aug. 31): A new [smokable] combination [of heroin and cocaine] called *moonrock* or *speedball*. **1990* T. Thorne *Dict. Contemp. Slang: Moonrock*…crack laced with heroin. A preparation which appeared…in 1989. **1992** N. Cohn *Heart of World* 229: Smack and crack, angel dust, delaudids [*sic*], moonrock. **1994** *Street Terms: Moonrock*—crack and heroin.

moonsail *n. Naut.* an imaginary sail set above a skysail. *Joc.* Also **moon-raker.**

    *1805 J. Davis *Post-Captain* 25: She had royals set; sky-scrapers, moon-rakers, and a cursed god above all. **1841** R.H. Dana, in *OED2: Moon-sail*, a small sail sometimes carried in light winds, above a skysail. **1883** (quot. at ANGEL's FOOTSTOOL). **1884** Symondson *Abaft the Mast* 303: Above her main-royal she carried a skysail, moonsail, cloud-cleaner, star-gazer, sky-scraper, and an angels' footstool.

moonshine *n.* **1.** bootleg liquor; *(broadly)* liquor. Now *S.E.*

    *1782 in *N & Q* CCXXXI (1986) 21: In that being a house of call for smugglers, one is sure of meeting always with genuine Moonshine…whereby is splendidly signified run Hollands. **1796* Grose *Dict. Vulgar Tongue* (ed. 3): The white brandy smuggled on the coasts of Kent and Sussex, and the gin in the north of Yorkshire, are also called moonshine. **1875** in *OEDS:* Producing from his pocket a flask of "moonshine" whiskey, [he] invited us to drink. **1906** *Army & Navy Life* (Oct.) 393: The judge, who was a witty fellow, asked the prisoner what was his Christian name. The prisoner replied, "Joshua," and the judge answered, "Are you the man that made the sun shine?" and the prisoner replied, "No, sir, your Honor, I'm the one that made the moonshine."

    2. *West.* rice.

    1933 *AS* (Feb.) 27: [W. Tx.:] *Moonshine.* Rice. **1936** R. Adams *Cowboy Lingo* 149: Rice is called "moonshine."

    ¶ In phrase:

    ¶ **keep out of (one's) moonshine** (see quot.).

    1919 *DN* V 34: *Moonshine, to keep out of one's,* v. phr. Not to meddle with one's business. "You get out o' my *moonshine,* and keep out."

moonshine hunter *n.* a poacher who operates under cover of night.

    1976 Adcock *Not Truckers Only* 37: "Poachers" or "moonshine hunters," as they're sometimes known, aren't bothering to hunt game on animal reserves under cover of darkness.

moontan *n.* [pun on *suntan*] an act of lovemaking or petting outdoors at night. *Joc.* Also as *v.*

    1947 *ATS* (Supp.) 8: "Necking."…*moon-tanning, mousing, mugging, smooching.* **1975** Univ. Tenn. grad. student: In high school [in Memphis, 1960's] we called it "getting a moontan." **1984** N. Bell *Raw Youth* 22: You getting a moon-tan? **1987** Forsyth *Housekeeping* (film): Getting a moontan.

moorings *n.* In phrase: ¶ **slip (one's) moorings, 1.** to die.

    1901 J. London *God of His Fathers* 95: "Slipped her moorings?"…"Ay. Childbirth."

    2. to become irrational or insane.

    1968 "R. Hooker" *M*A*S*H* 35: "We're serious, Red," Hawkeye said. "Painless has parted his mooring." **1971** WINS radio news (Nov. 26): Harry Truman cheerfully predicted he would win the election of 1948 while everybody else thought he'd slipped his moorings.

moose[1] *n.* **1.** a large, powerful, or clumsy person.—sometimes used as a nickname.

1910 *N.Y. Eve. Jour.* (Mar. 15) 12: F. Mitchell has been christened "Moose." **1911** Van Loan *Big League* 53: "Moose" McGuigan…was preparing for the fray. **1919** De Beck *Google* 5: I wanna show you how Jack is gonna rattle the big moose. **1931** in D.O. Smith *Cradle* 175: I couldn't knock the big moose out. **1932** Gates & Boylan *Hell Divers* (film): The poor moose is in the hoosegow. **1935** Coburn *Law Rides Range* 58: He can't trade punches with that moose. **1939** *They Made Me a Criminal* (film): I wouldn't get in the ring with that big ugly moose for $5000 a round. **1943** Trumbo *Guy Named Joe* (film): Give me another kiss, you big moose. **1944** Paxton *Murder, My Sweet* (film): The name is Moose—Moose, 'count of I'm large. **1962** Kesey *Cuckoo's Nest* 186: You must of had a real moose of an old lady. How big was she? **1968** Baker et al. *CUSS* 158: *Moose.* a strong, often offensive male. **1974** Clifton, N.J., nurse (Mar. 21): Get off, you moose! **1991** Bak *Cobb Would Have Caught It* 42 [ref. to 1929]: "Moose" [Alexander], a six-foot three, 210-pound offensive machine from Greenville, Tennessee,…batted .343.

    2. something that is large and difficult to manage.

    1973 M. Collins *Carrying the Fire* 248: John can start steering this moose toward our landing area. **1976** Univ. Tenn. student: This one's [a tune] a real moose to play. **1989** *CBS This Morning* (CBS-TV) (Apr. 25): The oil [spill] has become a big "moose," as they call it.

    ¶ In phrase:

    ¶ **like a moose needs a hat rack** not at all. *Joc.*

    1966 *Batman* (ABC-TV): He needs that like a moose needs a hat rack. **1978** Selby *Requiem* 5: She's needing you like a moose needs a hat rack.

moose[2] *n.* [< Japn *musume* 'girl; daughter'] **1.** *Mil.* in Far East. a Japanese or Korean prostitute; *(hence)* any Asian woman who cohabits with a serviceman.

    [**1868** in Boyer *Naval Surgeon* II 31: I am a young bachelor doing business in the place [a brothel] and wish a "moosmie."] **1951** Sheldon *Troubling Star* 36: First she trotted out three stock model mooses and tried to pass 'em off on me. *Ibid.* 51: These Japanese moose…know their stuff all right. (Or is it *meese?*). **1954** *AS* XXIX 302: The spelling *moose*…is most encountered in semiformal Army poop sheets; in signs urging Americans to a Japanese tavern to meet the best mooses in Kyoto; [etc.]. **1962** Butterworth *Court-Martial* 53: But we enlisted men had something these gentlemen do not apparently have….What we referred to in our quaint Korean cant as "loose moose." **1962** G. Ross *Last Campaign* 75 [ref. to 1950]: That could be the very one's shacking with your moose. **1963** *Sat. Eve. Post* (July 27) 25: A [Korean] girl is still a "moose" (from the Japanese *musume,* girl). **1965** C.D.B. Bryan *P.S. Wilkinson* 10: In other words, they were expected to move in a prostitute from the village—a *moose,* a curious slang word derived from the Japanese musame, meaning "little wife" or "sister." **1971** Glasser *365 Days* 193: Even his moose was beginning to annoy him. **1976** Atlee *Domino* 36: When we fought the police action in Korea, you remembered your shackup "moose" by the knockdown odor of *kimchi.* **1982** Cox & Frazier *Buck* 67: Maybe he got one of them moose 'fore they all got rounded up. **1985** Roskey *Muffled Shots* 82: If a man could not afford…a "moose," he joined the bachelor party excursion trips.

    2. a girl.

    [**1954–60** *DAS: Moose*…A younger sister. *Some c1940 child use.*] **1974** E. Thompson *Tattoo* 191: Don'ta make me look bad to my moose. **1984** A. Davis, D. Gilbert & P. Golding *Beat Street* (film): I never stole no moose from you.

moose cat *n. Logging.* (see quot.).

    1956 Sorden & Ebert *Logger's* 23 [ref. to *a*1925]: *Moose-cat,*…Anything unusually large or an unusually good lumber-jacket.

mooseface *n.* an ugly person.

    1859 Matsell *Vocab.* 56: *Moose-Face.* A rich, ugly-faced man; a poor but handsome young girl who marries an old, wrinkle-faced, ill-looking rich man, is said to have married a moose-face. **1942** *ATS* 385: Unattractive person….*lemon, mess, mooseface.*

moose milk *n.* any of various usu. improvised alcoholic drinks. Also **moose juice.**

    1957 in *Dict. Canad.:* A man who had drunk too freely of the native "moose milk" homebrew and started fighting. **1958** McCulloch *Woods Words* 119: *Moose milk*—A stiff drink made of coffee, milk, and rum, mostly rum. **1954–60** *DAS: Moose milk*…Whisky. **1983** C. Hanson et al. *Never Cry Wolf* (film): Moose juice…consisted of equal parts of Moose brand beer and ethyl alcohol. **1994** Kernan *Crossing Line* 23 [ref. to 1941]: Happily drunk on "moosemilk," a mixture of coffee and bombsight alcohol, of 99 percent purity, used for cleaning the Norden bombsights. *Ibid.* 50: Murphy [was] sipping moosemilk.

moose shit *interj.* (used as an oath); NUTS.—usu. considered vulgar. Also **moose fuck.**

　1967 Dibner *Admiral* 19: "He told us about your broken hand and how you went on to win the Olympic crown." "Moose shit," Paige said and turned away. **1973** Yount *Last Shot* 95: "Moose shit!" Beau Jim said and sat down again. **1977** Univ. Tenn. student: Moose shit! **1990** Westcott *Half a Klick* 34: Gawl damn moose-fuck!

moosey *n.* the vagina.—usu. considered vulgar.

　1920–54 (quot. at HOG-EYE). **1952** (quot. at SATCHEL).

mootah *n.* Esp. *Jazz.* marijuana; (*also*) a marijuana cigarette. Also **muta.**

　1933 in *OEDS:* This drug…looked like chopped hay, or dried clover….In short, a "muggles," "weed," or "mootie," cannabis indica. **1943** (quot. at MARY JANE). **1946** Mezzrow & Wolfe *Really Blues* 61, in R.S. Gold *Jazz Lexicon:* He kept waiting for a big train to pull in with a carload of muta. **1948** *Neurotica* (Summer) 37: The guy was married to the muta and the jazz. **1954** E. Hunter *Jungle Kids* 54: Mootah ain't habit forming. **1956** E. Hunter *Second Ending* 21: Like what they said about marijuana, hell, Buddy, mootah never hurt a fly. **1965** Carmichael & Longstreet *Sometimes I Wonder* 90 [ref. to *ca*1930]: They hit the weed….Marijuana, tea, muggles, muta, reefer. They call it lots of things. **1993** Rebennack & Rummel *Under Hoodoo Moon* 33: My partners and I would sit around…smoking mootahs.

Mop *n. Hobo.* the Missouri Pacific Railroad.

　1925 *Writer's Mo.* (June) 487: MOP—Missouri Pacific Railroad. **1929** *AS* (June) 342: The Vocabulary of Bums…*Mop*—The Missouri Pacific Railroad. **1930** Irwin *Tramp & Und. Sl.: Mop*—The Missouri Pacific Railway,…another of the abbreviations and diminutives the tramp is fond of coining.

mop *n.* **1.** the hair of the head.

　*1820–21 P. Egan *Life in London* 273: His *black mug* and *white mop.* **1911** A.H. Lewis *Apaches of N.Y.* 129: You'll take May out of number Nineteen be th' mop. **1957** H. Simmons *Corner Boy* 146: Dig the crazy mop, man. **1972** Claerbaut *Black Jargon* 73: *Mop*…the processed hair of a black person. **1981** Graziano & Corsel *Somebody Down Here* 21: I even go see my barber…and get 'im to fix my mop like Raft's. **1989** *California Raisins* (CBS-TV): She's still foolin' with her face and teasin' her mop.

　2. a drinking bout; binge; (*also*) a drunkard.

　*ca1860 in *F & H* IV 351: "It was all along of Bill Jones, the printer, as keeps company with me," she muttered. "He'd been having a mop, as he called it, because he was on piecework, and the author…hadn't sent the copy; whatever that may mean." **1873* Hotten *Slang Dict.* (ed. 4): *Mop*, an habitual drunkard. Also a period of intoxication. "To be on the *mop*" is to be on the drink from day to day—to be perpetually "stale drunk." **1891** Maitland *Slang Dict.* 179: *Mop*, an habitual drunkard. **1908** McGaffey *Show Girl* 14: They rush into a shop for their early morning "thought mop" and have to cling to the bar.

mop *v.* **1.** to defeat utterly.—often constr. in passive. Cf. MOP UP, 3.

　*1892 in *F & H* IV 352: They say he's mopped out; I dunnow. **1910* in *DSUE* 531: This is pretty rocky….We shall get mopped. **1971** L. Cameron *First Blood* 93: And you figure to get mopped if you make your stand out here in the open like this!

　2. *Homosex.* to shoplift; filch.

　a1972 B. Rodgers *Queens' Vernacular* 36: *Boost*…to shoplift….broadly, to steal anything.. Syn: *liberate; mop* (…SF hustler sl, late '60s: "I mop only the *prime* cuts from Safeway."). **1991** *Donahue* (NBC-TV): Mopping is the [homosexual] slang expression for stealing….I shop, not mop.

¶ In phrase:

¶ **mop [up] the floor with** to beat severely; thrash; drub; trounce. Also vars.

　1880 Nye *Boomerang* 38: He knows…I can mop the North American continent with his remains, and don't you forget it. **1887* in *F & H* IV 352: I'll mop the floor up with him any day. **1888** in *F & H:* I told him that I could mop the earth with him, but had been careful not to use provoking language! **1889–90** Barrère & Leland *Dict. Slang: Mopped the floor* (American), a common slang phrase, signifying that one man has thrashed another so completely [etc.]. **1896** F.H. Smith *Tom Grogan* 65: He "mopped up the floor" with one after another of the ring-leaders. **1897** Hamblen *General Mgr.* 101:

I'll…yank that d—d hound out from behind his desk, and mop up the floor with him. **1920** De Beck *Google* 96: He'll mop the floor with me if he spots me. **1928** Bodenheim *Georgie May* 71: He'd mop the floah with Emmy if he evah caught them at it. **1967** *AS* XLII 24: Other Marines…proceeded to *mop up the deck* with them.

mope[1] *n.* **1.** a slow-witted or inept person; JERK. Orig. *colloq.*

　*1540 in *OED:* Nor thou shalt not thereof be reckoned the more moope and foole but the more wise. **1638* R. Burton *Anat. Melancholy* (ed. 3), in *OED:* A mope or a noddy. **1726* Pope *Dunciad*, in *F & H:* No meagre, Muse-rid mope, adust and thin. **1919** *Wadsworth Gas Attack* 36: Then they shipped us all the dope/That they had to teach a mope/For to fit him fer this complicated fight. **1919** T. Kelly *What Outfit?* 146: Let those two mopes *cushay.* **1929** Bodenheim *60 Secs.* 33: Those who excelled in [studies] were most always sissies, or mopes, or teachers' pets. **1929** E. Booth *Stealing* 66 [ref. to *ca*1916]: Mope! Screw! G'wan—I'll bust you in the mouth! **1929–30** J.T. Farrell *Young Lonigan* 103: Hell, they're all mopes. **1930** *AS* V (Feb.) 238: *A mope:* a person who is not clever. "Charles is a mope when it comes to books." **1929–33** J.T. Farrell *Young Manhood* 314: He was different from all the mopes at the poolroom. **1941** J.M. Cain *Mildred Pierce* 269: Who'd think the poor mope had it in her? **1949** Algren *Golden Arm* 117: Look at the mope—he's dreamin' he's marryin' a movie actress. **1951** S.J. Perelman, in *New Yorker* (Aug. 11) 23: You're so desperate for a son-in-law that a mope like Paul Latham is the best. **1956** *Honeymooners* (synd. TV series): I have got an explanation for that. I'm a mope. **1978** R. Price *Ladies' Man* 155: I was crying like a goddamn mope about loneliness. **1981** P. Sann *Trial* 200: That mope with the horn-rims. **1987** Taubman *Lady Cop* 117: I tried to remember what each one looked like, but they all looked like mopes. **1987** Norst & Black *Lethal Weapon* 71: A variety of subhuman…: worm, maggot, mope. *a1988* C. Adams *More Straight Dope* 123: Most historians believe the 1846 body was just some mope who had been dumped in…a common burial ground. **1996** *TV Guide* (Oct. 26) 18: How two miserable mopes…met and inexplicably fell in love.

　2. usu. *pl.* a feeling of sadness; blues.—usu. constr. with *the.*

　*1825 in *OED:* I have got the mopes. **1890–96* *F & H* IV 353: *Mope*…in *pl.*….Low spirits;…*The blues* (q.v.). **1928** J.M. March *Set-Up* 74: Snap outa yer mope! **1956** M. Wolff *Big Nick* 190: You're right, I have the mopes tonight.

mope[2] *n.* [fr. the v.] Esp. *Pris.* a usu. stealthy departure or escape; usu. in phr. **cop a mope.**

　1926 Maines & Grant *Wise-Crack Dict.* 6: *Cop a mope*—Take a walk. **1928** *New Yorker* (Dec. 8) 58: You got maybe a hundred seconds to work your keys, get in, unlock it, start the car, and cop a mope. **1931** *AS* VI (Aug.) 437: *Mope, cop a.* To make an escape. **1932** Lawes *Sing Sing* 53 [ref. to 1915]: I thought it over, expecting that Mike wanted to get away, "cop a mope" as they termed it in those days. **1935** Algren *Boots* 130: Mebbe I'll cop a mope on the very last night. **1935** Pollock *Und. Speaks: Cop a mope*, to escape. *Ibid.: Take a mope*, go away; scram; beat it. **1936** Duncan *Over the Wall* 329: How would you like to take a mope, or have you got that stuff out of your bean? *Ibid.:* 339: Yeah, that was a good mope we made. **1942–49** Goldin et al. *DAUL* 141: *Mope*…A stealthy departure, especially from custody….An escape from custody effected without the use of force. **1970** E. Thompson *Garden of Sand* 270: "Cop a mope," was his advice to Jack. **1974** *Time* (June 17) 59: *Cop a mope:* get away from me. **1974–75** Powledge *Mud Show* 37: These first of Mays you hire, first time it rains they take a mope.

mope *v.* **1.** to go away; make an escape.

　*1889–90 Barrère & Leland *Dict. Slang: Moper*…a deserter. **1914** Jackson & Hellyer *Vocab.* 60: *Mope*, Verb. General currency. To walk away; to remove one's presence. **1918** in *AS* (Oct. 1933) 29: [Ft. Leavenworth:] *Mope*….Escape: All I want's the least little show of a chanct, 'n' I'll mope. **1927–28** (quot. at BOTTLE AND STOPPER). **1929** *AS* (June) 342: *Mope.* To take a walk; to beat it. **1942–49** Goldin et al. *DAUL* 141: Some dude (fellow) moped with only two months to go (serve). **1961** A.J. Roth *Shame of Our Wounds* 13: He's moped out of here seven or eight times. *Ibid.* 18: Every week somebody mopes off. **1975** McKennon *Horse Dung Trail* 200: Several men have already "moped" as you know.

　2. to walk slowly; move along; MOSEY.

　1895 in J. London *Tramp Diary* 62: I wuz mopin' down de main drag, I mean de main street. **1918** in *AS* (Oct. 1933) 29: [Ft. Leavenworth:] *Mope*…To move along, to keep going: King, he's a good screw—'f yuh jus' keep mopin' along, he won't ride yuh. **1923** in

Kornbluh *Rebel Voices* 90: "Advance to the foot of my throne."...So I mopes up. **1925** *Amer. Leg. Wkly.* (Jan. 2) 12: The leadin' comedian...mopes onto the stage. **1935** Algren *Boots* 129: What d'ye say we mope along t'gether a while? *a***1994** H. Roth *Mercy of Rude Stream* 215 [ref. to 1920's]: So the two, inseparable pals,..."moped" about Farley's haunts..., palavered, kidded [etc.].

mopery *n. Police & Und.* stupidity or ineptitude; (*specif.*) a hypothetical absurd or trivial offense. Also vars. [Various specific, ironic definitions are current; 1918 quot. undoubtedly reflects one of these.]

    1907 *McClure's Mag.* (Feb.) 380: Come along, children, before the boogie man sloughs you in the skookum for mopery! **1918** in *AS* (Oct. 1933) 29: *Mopry.* Contraband [held by a prisoner]. **1927** *AS* (Mar.) 281: *Attempt to gog,* or *highway mopery.* **1929–33** J.T. Farrell *Young Manhood* 288: Come on, Vinc, for Christ sake, we don't want to get run in for mopery. **1933** Hammett *Thin Man* 238: All right...have me arrested for kidnapping...and mopery. *ca***1940** in Botkin *Treas. Amer. Folk.* 547: They ought to make it a penitentiary act for a helper "gapering, mopering, and attempting to gawk." **1941** H.A. Smith *Low Man* 64: The girls stop at nothing short of mopery to get in the papers, mopery being the old English misdemeanor of exposing one's self in front of a blind man on a public highway. **1941** "G.R. Lee" *G-String* 34: "What are you in for?"..."Mopery." **1946** in Partridge *Dict. Und.* 449: *Moprey* [*sic*]...is supposed to consist of exhibiting oneself in the nude to a blind woman. **1942–49** Goldin et al. *DAUL* 28: Everything from mopery on the high seas to spitting on the sidewalk. **1949** R. Chandler, in *DAS*: If he'd lived long enough you'd have had him up for mopery. **1953** Paley *Rumble* 64: Let's git out of here 'fore we git arrested for mopery! **1956** H. Gold *Not With It* 192: "What they pick you up for, Grack?"..."Mopery with intent to gog," he replied, chanting. "Spitting on hermits without a permit and stabbing a streetcar and stealing a transfer." **1974** *Police Woman* (NBC-TV): I'd say it was a clear case of blatant mopery. **1975** *Oui* (Mar.) 126: Do you know what mopery is? It's a jail term. It means exposing one's sexual parts to a blind woman on a highway. [**1977** Torres *Q & A* 121: Larry is a mopery next to Hank.] **1982** *Chicago Sun-Times* (Sept. 6) 72: The potpourri of mopery that wears the livery of Cleveland and Texas, both of whom are sixth in their divisions. **1988–89** in Safire *Quoth Maven* 173: From 1934 until 1942 I was a mounted state trooper in the Pennsylvania State Constabulary....I recall one proposed charge termed, "Mopery and Gapery with Intent to Gawk." **1988–89** in Safire *Quoth Maven* 173: The police instructor [in N.J.] jokingly...[said] "If push comes to shove you can arrest him for *mopery and dopery and intent to gawk* and sort it out later." **1994** *New Yorker* (Feb. 21) 82: Gotti apparently sanctioned guilty pleas only for what he called "malicious mopery"—minor offenses that had nothing to do with the existence of La Cosa Nostra. *Ibid.:* It's a malicious mopery, drunken-driving case, you'll get sixty days.

mop in *v.* to guzzle (liquor); MOP UP, 1.
    1892 F.P. Dunne, in Schaaf *Dooley* 43: They mopped in a few shills of beer. **1897** Ade *Horne* 173: I was moppin' in a scuttle o' beer.

moppy *adj.* drunk. Also (*later*) **mopped [up]**.
    ****1821** *Real Life in London* I 292: Frank [was] *moppy,* and all of them rather *muggy.* ****1889–90** Barrère & Leland *Dict. Slang: Moppy*...tipsy. **a***1890–96** *F & H* IV 353: *Moppy*...(common).—Drunk. **a***1890–1902** *F & H* V 129: *Screwed*...Drunk...ENGLISH SYNONYMS...*jagged,...mopped, moppy,* [etc.]. **1942** *New Yorker* (Oct. 17) 19: Gettin' theirself mopped up with your liquor,...good and soused. **1944** C.B. Davis *Leo McGuire* 173: I took a risk on a Mac who must have got moppy and given the office to a muff stool.

mop-squeezer *n.* [fr. earlier BrE slang sense 'housemaid', as in **1771 quot.] *Poker.* a queen.
    [****1771** in *OED*: She looks like a mop-squeezer.] **1949** G. Coffin *Winning Poker* 182: *Mop Squeezers* [*sic*]—Colloquial for queen. **1954–60** *DAS: Mop-squeezer*...In poker, the queen in a deck of cards.

mop stick *n.* (see 1915 quot.).
    1915 in *OEDS: Mopstick,* one who loafs around a cheap saloon or barrel house and cleans up the place for drinks. **1980** Bruns *Kts. of Road* 203: *Mop stick.* Barfly in cheap saloon.

mop-up *n.* **1.** *Mil.* the final stage in the defeat of an enemy; total defeat; rout.
    ****1917** in *OEDS*: The honour of the new attack was given to the "mop-up" battalions behind. **1949** in *DAS*: A complete mop-up of...a gang. **1950** *Time* (Nov. 27) 27: Division commanders had clamored incessantly for food and ammunition to keep the mop-up rolling. **1958**

Time (Mar. 24) 82: After the 27th move [in a chess game], Bobby's mop-up of his opponent's shattered forces was routine. **1962** E.J. Kahn, Jr., in *New Yorker* (Mar. 24) 53: Nobody on Guam doubted that some Japanese must have escaped Aguon's mopup. **1979** *L.A. Times* (Mar. 29) III 3: At tailback...he wouldn't play much at all except in mopups or emergencies. **1984–88** Hackworth & Sherman *About Face* 106: We were a little in shock by the time the "mop-up" was over. **1984–88** H. Berry *Where Ya Been?* 77: During the guerrilla mop-up in South Korea.
    2. *Army.* a Mills grenade.
    1919 Emmett *Give 'Way to Right* 106 [ref. to WWI]: I had a "mop-up" (another doughboy's name for a serrated grenade).

mop up *v.* **1.** to guzzle (liquor).
    ****1811** *Lex. Balatron.: To mop up.* To drink up. To empty a glass or pot. ****1851–61** H. Mayhew, in *F & H:* I have seen the youngest mop up his half-quartern as well as I did. ****1873** Hotten *Slang Dict.* (ed. 4): *Mop up,* to drink or empty a glass.—*Old Sea Term.* **1910** *N.Y. Eve. Jour.* (Mar. 26) 9: Bugs was...mopping up "suds" inside. **1911–12** J. London *Smoke Bellew* 11: It doesn't take a physical prodigy to mop up cocktails or pink tea. **1912** *Adventure* (June) 352: O'Hanlon...was too busy mopping up whisky to understand the purport of the last question.
    2. to gain or win (a significant amount of money); CLEAN UP, 1.
    ****1851–61** H. Mayhew, in *F & H* IV 352: If I gets inside, I'll mop up 1/- if it's good company, or perhaps 3d. or 4d., and always plenty to drink. **1932** Mankiewicz & Myer *Million Dollar Legs* (film): You'd mop up like the Baldwin brushes. **1936** Washburn *Parlor* 166: Frank A. P. (Apple Pie) Gazzolo, the enthusiastic sponsor,...had "mopped up." **1996** Poker player in N.Y.C. (coll. J. Sheidlower): You mopped up *again* this week? Man, that's some real luck you're having.
    3. *Esp. Mil.* to finish off, usu. by killing (usu. an adversary or the remnants of an enemy force); vanquish; (*hence*) to finish the remainder of (a task).—also constr. with *on.*—occ. used absol. Now *S.E.*
    ****1898** in *OEDS*: The birds...come over in one's and two's and are "mopped up." **1917** in Burton *Letters* 291: A German gentleman whom we failed to "mop up"...as his last act on this earth soaked me in the back with a small grenade and as near as I can make out, by all rights I should be pushing up the daisies, but "I ain't." **1918** *Everybody's Album* (Nov.) 38: You oughta seen me mop up that big Heinie, Doc. **1931** Grant *Gangdom's Doom* 66: Bring on your tough gorillas—I'll mop up all of them! **1934** Peters & Sklar *Stevedore* 121: Let's mop 'em up. **1938** H. Miller *Trop. Capricorn* 44: I was only hoping...he would go up to...wherever...the president and vice-presidents had their offices, and mop up the whole bloody gang. **1939** in Mencken *New Letters* 437: The Japs...have mopped up the Chinese. **1941** in Botkin *Treas. Amer. Folk.* 129: Come and get this bad man fore he mops up with us all. **1949** *Harper's* (Oct.) 94: Flying squads and patrol wagons went out to mop up. **1949** *N.Y. Times* (Oct. 16) I 73: He will return to the city tomorrow for "mopping up." **1949** *N.Y. Times* (Dec. 12) 35: Work was "virtually finished," with only a little "mopping up" left. **1954–60** *DAS: Mop up*...To exterminate; to finish a military or police campaign. *Mop up on* To beat up; to thrash severely. **1990** Bing *Do or Die* 31: I'd mop her up if she come to me...like that.

¶ In phrase:

¶ **mop [up] the floor with** see s.v. MOP, *v.*

mopus *n.* [orig. unkn.] a piece of money; coin.
    ****1698–99** "B.E." *Dict. Canting Crew: Mopus*...a half Penny or Farthing. ****1821** *Real Life in London* I 26: Finances were...low, and the *mopuses* ran taper. **1840** *Spirit of Times* (Jan. 11) 534. ****1841** in J. Farmer *Musa Pedestris* 131: And leave me not a mopus there. **1848** Baker *Glance at N.Y.* 13: I saw how willing he was to fork out the mopusses, so I came the Elephant dodge on him. **1857** in *AS* XXI 118: There he lost his every mopus:...All the rocks and all the mint drops...All his MONEY, in a word. ****1869** E. FitzGerald *Medley* 99: *Mopus.*—Money. "He'll come to his senses when all his Mopuses [*sic*] are gone."

moral *n.* [fr. phr. *a moral certainty*] *Esp. Horse Racing.* a horse that is virtually certain to win a race (*obs.*); (*hence*) a certainty. *Rare* in U.S.
    ****1861** in *OED*: A contingency which the dealer was pleased to observe amounted to what he called "a moral." ****1869** in *F & H* IV 354: Everything that is highly promising becomes, in the slang of the advertising tipster, a moral. **1880** *N.Y. Clipper Almanac* 45: *Moral*—"A moral" is a "sure thing." It is a contraction of "a moral certainty."

*1889–90 Barrère & Leland *Dict. Slang: Moral*…"That's a *moral*," equivalent to "that's a certainty." ***1986** in *ODMS* 141: The senior puisne judge…is an absolute moral for the Chief Justiceship come February next year.

more *adj. & adv. Jazz.* with greater skill. Cf. MOST.

   1959 in R.S. Gold *Jazz Lexicon:* I can still…play more tenor than them. **1962** in R.S. Gold *Jazz Lexicon:* Howard McGhee was quoted recently as saying that Davis used to play "more." **1963** in R.S. Gold *Jazz Lexicon:* Is drummer X…in New York playing more drums now than drummer Y in California?

Morgan Rattler *n.* [the title of a once popular dance tune, here perh. infl. by BrE slang *rattler* 'a sharp blow'] ¶ In phrase: **give Morgan Rattler** to assail vigorously; trounce.

   1807 J.R. Shaw *Autobiog.* 118: The young bucks of the town frequently making me groggy, for which I gave them Morgan Rattler in style. [***1902** in Partridge *DSUE: Morgan rattler*…A cane or stick with a knob of lead at one or both ends, and short enough to be carried up the sleeve.]

morgue *n.* **1.** a cheap eating or drinking place.

   1891 Riis *Other Half* 161: In the downtown "morgues" that make the lowest degradation of tramp-humanity pan out a paying interest…this sign is conspicuously displayed. **1899** Dunne *Countrymen* 4: An', whin ye're hungry, ye can go to th' morgue—we mane th' resth'rant—an' ate a good square meal iv ar-rmy beef. **1902** Hapgood *Thief* 216 [ref. to *ca*1890]: If one of them had five cents, he would go into a morgue (gin-mill where rot-gut whiskey could be obtained for that sum) and pour out almost a full tumbler of booze.

   2. a library of clippings and photographs maintained by a newspaper, orig. for aid in the compiling of obituaries. Now *S.E.*

   1903 in *OEDS:* This can be done with the aid of the "morgue" or cabinet of biographical and obituary materials that is maintained in every wide-awake newspaper office. **1918** in *OEDS:* To make sure that the details are true, a studio has filed away in its morgue photographs of the life it wishes to depict. **1939** "E. Queen" *Dragon's Teeth* 14: I buzzed Tom Creevich of the *Herald* and he dug some dope on Cole out of the morgue for me.

   3. Esp. *Theat.* a business with few patrons.

   1906 (quot. at DEADHOUSE). **1923** *N.Y. Times* VIII (Sept. 9) 2: *Morgue:* Theatre with poor patronage. **1924** *Sat. Eve. Post* (July 12) 15: *A Morgue*—a house that doesn't do business.

Mormon buckskin *n. West.* baling wire. *Joc.* Also **Mormon silk.**

   1977 Monaghan *Schoolboy, Cowboy* 90 [ref. to 1908]: I had to stop many times to patch the harness with "Mormon buckskin," the colloquial name for baling wire. **1979** Toelken *Dyn. of Folklore* 56: *Mormon silk* baling wire (based on the Mormons' high reputation for farming).

morning glory *n.* **1.** *Horse Racing.* a horse that runs well during a morning workout but poorly during the following race.

   1904 in *OEDS:* Didn't I tell you he was nothing but a morning glory—why that dog couldn't beat a ferry boat. **1926** J. Conway, in *Variety* (Dec. 29) 7: Racing with its "morning glories," "stoopers,"…"wind suckers,"…et al. **1935** Pollock *Und. Speaks: Morning glory,* race horse that works in fast time in the morning but fails to race well. **1949** Gresham *Limbo Tower* 179: I've held that watch on my last racehorse. How many of them are "morning glories," Don—fleet as the wind at dawn.…Then…when post time comes…they drag in half an hour late. **1963** *N.Y. Times* (Apr. 24): *Morning glory*—A horse that burns up the track in morning works but burns up bettors' money in afternoon races. **1968** M.B. Scott *Racing Game* 18: Two other terms used to designate the horse without heart are "quitter" and "morning glory." **1973** Haney *Jock* 177: *Morning glory:* A horse that works out brilliantly in the morning but performs poorly in a race in the afternoon.

   2. *Sports.* an initially promising but ultimately disappointing competitor.

   1909 in O. Johnson *Lawrenceville* 34: Here, Morning Glory,…show her how it's done. **1920** in Hemingway *Sel. Letters* (Sept. 16) 39: Geo. [Carpenter]…is no bloomer and no morning glory and don't think just because Dempsey is KOing all the tramps that he is going to make an ass out of Mr. Carp. **1922** *Variety* (July 14) 5: I get a flock of mornin' glories for coffee an' cakes. **1922** in S. Smith *Gumps* 28: I'll show these birds I'm no morning glory or daffodil. **1925** in Hammett *Big Knockover* 217: The ex-pug looked me up and down and spit at the

ground on my feet. "Ain't you a swell mornin'-glory?" **1929** in Paxton *Sport* 161: From the ranks of the morning-glories sometimes are produced the record-breakers—the sprinters whose names are remembered from generation to generation. **1948** Kaese *Braves* 19: The Boston Nationals discovered that unlovely flower of baseball now known as the "morning glory."

¶ In phrase:

¶ **what's your** [or **the**] **story, morning glory?** (used as a joc. form of greeting).

   1944 in Himes *Black on Black* 197: What's your story, morning glory? **1961** R. Russell *Sound* 15: I mean, what's your story, morning glory? **1968** [Beck] *Trick Baby* 161: What's your story, morning glory? **1972** N.Y.U. student: What's the story, morning glory? **1985** in Goss & Barnes *Talk That Talk* 480: Tell the truth, snaggle tooth,/What's your story, morning glory? **1987** Estes *Field of Innocence* 75: That's the story, morning glory.

morning wood *n.* an erection upon awakening.—usu. considered vulgar.

   1993 *Beavis and Butt-head* (MTV): "He has morning wood!" "Morning wood is cool!" "Sometimes I have morning wood in the afternoon."

moron *n.* a blockhead. Now *S.E.* [Orig. a colloq. extension of the early technical term in psychology, adopted in 1910; see *OED2*.]

   1921 *DN* V 142: *Moron,* n. A very stupid person. "A dim-wit! Why, she's positively a moron." **1922** D. Parker, in *Life* (Apr. 13) 24: Our little friend/Is something of a moron. **1925** S. Lewis *Arrowsmith* ch. xix: Sunday School superintendents and other morons. **1926** Hemingway *Sun Also Rises* 43: I was just telling Jake here that you're a moron. **1928** Segar *Thimble Theater* 19: Fool—sap—boob—dumb-bell—moron—fat head—half wit—fly-brained nincompoop! **1929** Borsodi *Ugly Civilization* 226: Manufacturers…have to write advertisements that will move these morons into action. **1934** Goldbeck *Murder on Blackboard* (film): The guy's a moron. **1942** in Cheever *Letters* 87: Maybe I can raise myself out of the moron class. **1947** Seaton *Shocking Miss Pilgrim* (film): Don't force me to believe that *all* men are morons. **1951** J. Reach *My Friend Irma* 29: She'll probably be one of the most famous morons in America. **1955** Fenwick *All Heaven Allows* (film): I've got to give a cocktail party this weekend for that moron Jo-Ann. **1961** Kohner *Gidget Goes Hawaiian* 116: "We behaved like morons!" my mother cried, beating her breast as if she were at a revival meeting. **1961** G. Forbes *Goodbye to Some* 116: I'm stupid. I'm a poor USN moron. **1965–70** T. Morrison *Bluest Eye* 21: "What am I supposed to do with these?" "Bury them, moron." **1978** J. Reynolds *Geniuses* 49: Shut up, Bart. The girl's a moron. **1978** Alibrandi *Killshot* 154: Settle down, you moron. *a***1982** in Berry *Semper Fi* 299: You know what college does to you morons; it makes you more stupider, that's what! **1987** Fine *With Boys* 175: The Iowan male subculture…uses "moron" rather than calling someone "sick." **1990** Alexander & Karaszewski *Problem Child* (film): "Moron?" I went to *Radcliffe!* **1991** Friedman & Levitt *Being from Another Planet* (film): What are you doing, you moron? **1993** *Sally Jessy Raphaël* (synd. TV series): You have a life and this moron doesn't.

morph *n. Narc. & Hosp.* morphine.

   1906 H. Green *Actors' Boarding House* 196: The old morph, y'know. **1914** (quot. at M). **1918** in *AS* (Oct. 1933) 30: *Morph.* Morphine. **1925–26** J. Black *You Can't Win* 160 [ref. to 1890's]: About a spoonful of water and some of their meager store of "morph" were put in the tin box. **1953** Gresham *Midway* 14: He's a drunk. Or he's on the morph. **1969** Sidney *Love of Dying* 36: Trade a little bit of morph now and then to the cooks to keep us in orange juice to mix with the alky. **1973** Peterson *Sicilian Slaughter* 151: Riarso had sneaked away from his post to give himself a jolt of morph. **1980** in Courtwright et al. *Addicts Who Survived* 298: She gets pills, morph. **1985** Bodey *F.N.G.* 113: They're bringing you some morph before long.

morphadite *n.* [alter. *hermaphrodite*] hermaphrodite; (*hence*) a homosexual person. Also **morphrodite, morphadike,** etc. Also fig.

   *ca1706 Vanbrugh *Provoked Wife* 181: I heard Mr. Constable say…she was little better than a morphrodite. ***1742** H. Fielding, in *OED:* You must…get a set of mophrodites [*sic*] to wait upon you. **1840** Olmsted *Whaling Voyage* 217: She is one of those vessels rigged in defiance of all symmetry, and very appropriately termed "Morferdites" (Hermaphrodites) by seamen. **1889–90** Barrère & Leland *Dict. Slang: Morfydite* (American), a maritime pronunciation for hermaphrodite, generally applied to the so-called hermaphrodite brig, a vessel between a brig and a schooner. **1929–30** J.T. Farrell *Young Lonigan* 75: "Listen! Wilson's a morphidite," Studs said. "What's that?" "A guy that's both a man and a women at the same time, like fat Leon," said Studs. **1934** W. Smith *Bessie Cotter* 171: Somebody who's built like a man and a woman at the same time…a "morphodike." **1942–49** Goldin et al. *DAUL* 141: *Morphodite*.…A hermaphrodite; (loosely in prison usage) a pederast; an oral sodomist. (Note: The word is often used in gross humor rather than literally. When said good-naturedly, inmates rarely take offense.). **1951** in *DAS:* You morphadite. **1956** H. Gold *Not With It* 174: I suppose morphodykes are likely to take it personally when people get married. **1962** T. Berger *Reinhart in Love* 180: "Raven is what you call a transvestite." "What's that?" …"Morphadike." **1971** Cole *Rook* 130: Now we will…listen to the music "Embraceable You" like a couple of morphadykes that can't get dates. **1974–75** Powledge *Mud Show* 45: The "morphodite" sat patiently waiting. *a*1973–87 F.M. Davis *Livin' the Blues* 36 [ref. to *ca*1920]: Anybody with both male and female characteristics was a morfydyke.

morris [sugg. by *morris* dance] (see *1725 quot.); *(also)* to depart immediately. *Rare* in U.S.
   *1725 *New Canting Dict.: Morris*, to hang dangling in the Air, to be executed. *1765 in *OED:* I think the Welshman must *morris.* *1773 O. Goldsmith, in *F & H* IV 356: Zounds, here they are! Morrice! Prance! *(Exit Hastings.).* 1791 [W. Smith] *Confess. T. Mount* 21: The tumbler shoves off, and I *morris.* *1796 Grose *Dict. Vulgar Tongue* (ed. 3): *Morris.* Come, morris off; dance off, or get you gone. *1838 Dickens *O. Twist,* in *F & H:* Up with you on your pins. There! Now then! Morrice!

mort *n.* [orig. unkn.] *Und.* a woman, esp. a harlot. *Rare* in U.S. See also explicitly r-less form MOT.
   *1567 Harman, in Partridge *Dict. Und.* 450: Their harlots, whiche they terme Mortes and Doxes. *1607 Dekker, in *F & H:* He is not worthy of the name of notable theefe among theeues, which is without his mort or punck. *1641 Brome *Jovial Crew* II ii: I think my mort is in drink. 1745 in C.H. Wilkinson *King of Beggars* 120: Hike Mort…and ogle him. *1796 Grose *Dict. Vulgar Tongue* (ed. 3): *Mort.* A woman or wench. *1874 G. Borrow, in Partridge *Dict. Vulgar Tongue* (ed. 3): *Mort*…woman, concubine; a cant word. **1954–60** *DAS: Mort*…A girl or woman.

mortal lock see s.v. LOCK.

'Mos *n.pl. Soccer.* the New York Cosmos professional soccer team.
   1983 *N.Y. Post* (Sept. 2) 55: 'Mos End Regular Season.…The Cosmos close out their regular season tonight…at Giants Stadium. **1984** *N.Y. Post* (Aug. 15) 70: He wants to restructure the 'Mos into a more "professional" image.

Mose *n.* [fr. *Mose,* hypocoristic or dial. form of *Moses,* a given name formerly regarded as common among blacks] *Black E.* a black man, often one who is subservient to whites.
   1944 Burley *Hndbk. Jive* 144: *Mose*—Negro. **1945** A.C. Powell *Marching Blacks* 98: Uncle Tom was dead—"Old man Mose had kicked the bucket." **1946** Mezzrow & Wolfe *Really Blues* 193: They were not the Old Mose's of the Southern plantations. **1954–60** *DAS: Mose* (derog.)…A Negro. Negro use. *ca*1974 in J.L. Gwaltney *Drylongso* 16: You give Mose half a chance and he will take over because he is just a better man than Chahlie ever dared to be.

Moses *interj.* (used as an element in var. mild oaths).
   *1855 in *F & H* IV 358: But, Holy Moses! what a rear? **1869** "M. Twain" *Innocents* I 38: The suffering Moses!—there ain't money enough in the ship to pay that bill! **1877** E. Wheeler *Deadwood Dick, Prince of the Road* 79: "Thunder 'n' Moses!" ejaculated the sharp. **1881** Small *Smith* 30: Mighty Moses!…I've got all I want. **1885** Siringo *Texas Cowboy* 39: He jumped ten feet in the air and roared out "Holy Moses!" **1919** Wilkins *Co. Fund* 17: Whistling Moses! **1920** *Amer. Leg. Wkly.* (June 11) 16: Great bull-rushin' Moses! **1920** E. O'Neill *Diff'rent* 217: Thunderin' Moses, that's the fust time evr I heerd good o' myself by listening! **1928** Nason *Sgt. Eadie* 52 [ref. to WWI]: Bellowin' Moses! **1932** M. Anderson *Rain* (film): Moses on the mountaintop! so this is the South Seas! **1932** V. Fisher *Tragic Life* 348: The Christ-killun Moses[!] *Ibid.* 352: Hey, the holy sneakun Moses! **1962** Hecht *Gaily, Gaily* 23: Moses on the Mountain! Look who's here! **1962** E. Stephens *Blow Negative* 205: Holy Moses! Look at that!

mosey *n.* an act of MOSEYING; a stroll.
   1960 *Sat. Eve. Post* (Dec. 24) 81: Go take a mosey around the place, Joe.

mosey *v.* to go away; *(also)* to amble.—often constr. with a prep.
   1829 in M. Mathews *Beginnings of Amer. English* 109: *Mosey.* "To move off." *Kentucky.* **1837** Neal *Charcoal Sketches* 13: I'd say you must mosey. **1847** R. Anderson *Arty. Officer* 173: He…"moseyed" off. **1849** Pennington *Blacksmith* 36: "I'll mosey* him down to —— before I eat or sleep."…*An expression which means to drive in a hurry. **1851** *Spirit of Times* (Nov. 8) 63: You know that I'm a grate feller for moseyin about in strange places and that, like Noey's dove, I can't find a spot of dry ground wharon to rest the heel of my boots. **1863** in J.W. Haley *Rebel Yell* 86: I moseyed along in the most agonizing manner, my heels galled to the bone. **1864** "E. Kirke" *Down in Tenn.* 161: I thort I'd better be a moseyin'. **1870** *Nation* (July 28) 56: "You'd better mosey" [used in E. Pa., *ca*1825]. **1871** Schele de Vere *Americanisms* 137: My friend, let me tell you, if you do not *mosey* this instant, and clear out for good, you will have to pay pretty dear. (Louisville *Journal,* October 9, 1857.). **1871** Hay *Pike Co. Ballads* 21: The nigger has to mosey. **1892** Bierce *Beetles* 246: Vanish—vamoose—mosy—Go! **1943** Farrell *Days of Anger* 149: Well, I got to mosey off now. **1956–60** J.A. Williams *Angry Ones* ch. vi: I began moseying up and down the streets after work. **1984** *Kate & Allie* (CBS-TV): We've done all we can here. Let's mosey. **1996** *Living Single* (Fox-TV): Let's mosey!

mosh *n.* a form of violent dancing similar to slam-dancing, typically performed to hardcore music; *(also)* a hardcore song.
   1987 "Anthrax" *Caught in a Mosh* [title of rock song]. **1987** *Village Voice* (N.Y.C.) (July 14) 27: By the guitar solos they are literally bouncing off the walls.…It's a mosh against whatever is left standing. **1987** *U.S. News & W.R.* (Sept. 7): The mosh: Male-only dancing in which people slam their bodies into each other. **1990** *Village Voice* (N.Y.C.) (Aug. 28) 96: Three simultaneous pits were active on the floor, giving those caught in the mosh a chance…[to] have some stupidass fun. **1992** *Village Voice* (N.Y.C.) (Feb. 28) 44: What's mosh? It's slam dancing several generations down the line, a human spin-cycle…in which people (young people) goose-walk and plow, bent at the waist, through dense packs of humans. **1994** *Phila. Inquirer* (Feb. 4) MD1: An old theater yields to the mosh.…The first 20 rows were ripped out last month to make room for moshing. **1995** Weisbard *Spin Record Guide* 332: It lets you hear Suicidal Tendencies' lurching mosh "Institutionalized," the greatest…underground smash in hardcore history.

mosh *v.* [prob. alter. *mash*] (in 1983 quot.) to shove against violently while slam-dancing; *(hence)* to dance violently in a manner similar to slam-dancing, usu. to hardcore music. Hence **mosher,** *n.*
   1983 *Village Voice* (N.Y.C.) (Jan. 18) 30: Slam dancers…agree that it is "violence within friendship."…Besides, "you're so into the music and dancing that you don't think about getting moshed." **1987** *Wash. Post* (June 4) (Nexis): To mosh: a verb meaning to fling every limb as far from the torso as possible while maintaining as little equilibrium as possible. *1987 in *Longman Register New Words* (1989 ed.): The hardcore fanatics thrashing, dive-bombing off the stage, writhing ("moshing") in an uninhibited physical mania. *1987 in *Ibid.:* Thrash metal fans…participate at concerts by "moshing": dirty-tackling each other in a mass body-slam dance. **1989** Huntsville, Ala., youth, age 16 (coll. J. Ball): A *mosher* is a mosh dancer. *Mosh dancing* is kind of like easy slam dancing—not as rough. **1990** *N.Y. Newsday* (Sept. 10) II 3: They were slamming like madmen at the Ritz.…Exodus singer Steve (Zetro) Souza egged the "moshers" on. **1987–91** D. Gaines *Teenage Wasteland:* Slamming (or moshing, dancing) was once a serious male-bonding ritual. **1992** *Closer Look* (NBC-TV) (July 14): The lead singer of the band Murphy's Law—he encourages kids to mosh during his performances.…Do you think moshing is dangerous at all?…Slam-dancing…it's basically the same thing. **1993** *Rolling Stone* (Mar. 18) 10: I am living proof that girls do mosh and understand what moshing is about. **1993** *Wash. Post* (July 21) D1: The people mosh. It is a cross between dancing and being crushed to death. **1994** *L.A. Times* (Mar. 3) E7: "My daughter's into moshing."…I sighed…and resigned myself to shadowing his daughter to various clubs while she jumped off the stage into a mass of writhing bodies.

mosh pit see s.v. PIT.

mosquito *n.* a musket. *Joc.*
   1845 *Recoll. of U.S. Army* 21: Och, holy Pope! It's tired I am of carryin' of this muskeether.

mosquito bite *n.* usu. *pl.* (see 1990 quot.).

1976 *UTSQ:* Breasts…*boobs, tits, mosquito bites.* **1990** P. Munro *Slang U.* 133: *Mosquito bites* small breasts.

mosquito boat *n. Navy.* a gunboat or torpedo boat.

1864 in E. Newsome *Experiences* 81: Two musquito boats (*tin-clads*)…were sent down there. **1864** Fosdick *Frank on a Gun-Boat* 130: Captain Wilson…commanded one of the musquito boats. **1943** Cave *Long Nights* vii: It is important that new men be trained for the mosquito boats, because the little PTs have proved their worth. **1971** Windchy *Tonkin* 114: Theoretically, one of these "mosquito boats" can pull alongside an aircraft carrier, order the ship to get moving, and sink her if she disobeys.

mosquito fleet *n. Navy.* **1.** a flotilla of small or secondary vessels. Now *hist.* [The 1918 O'Reilly quot. represents a joc. nonce usage.]

1804 in *OED:* Man and victual the Musquitoe Fleet (as Wit in its wantonness has described it). **1805 J. Davis *Post-Captain* 13: And dispersed their musquito fleet. **1847 in Peskin *Vols.* 39: The "Musquito Fleet"…of two or three very small vessels. **1862–64** Noel *Campaign* 51: Mr. Howell's description of the "Mosquito Fleet." **1873** Revere *Keel & Saddle* 2 [ref. to Seminole War]: I…was finally attached to what was called the "mosquito fleet,"—a flotilla of small vessels and boats co-operating with the army in Florida. **1880** *United Service* (Oct.) 590 [ref. to 1861]: Seven small merchant ships improvised into war ships, and commonly known under the derisive name of "mosquito fleet." **1880** *United Service* (June) 287: In the popular language during the Cuban troubles, "our mosquito fleet of torpedo craft would attack the ironclad dons in swarms." **1900** Reeves *Bamboo Tales* 31: This expedition was accompanied by two gunboats belonging to the "mosquito fleet." **1901** *Smoking Lamp* (Nov.) 145: Captain Bartlett praises the work and efficiency of the "mosquito fleet." [**1918** O'Reilly *Roving & Fighting* 151 [ref. to 1899]: It was the "mosquito fleet"—mounted infantrymen—of the Thirty-third commanded by General Luther R. Hare, brigade commander at Vigan.] **1918** Poague *Diary* (entry for Jan. 25): I have a title. I am "Admiral of the Mosquito Fleet" because I had the brilliant idea of using the ship's boats as lighters. The executive officer gave me four big boats and a steam launch. **1918** Kauffman *Our Navy at Work* 2. **1918** Abbot *Soldiers of Sea* 106: In close relation to the Florida war against the Indians stands the work done by the so-called "Mosquito Fleet" from June, 1838, to August, 1842. The fleet consisted of a varying number of United States boats, supplemented by a large number of canoes. **1929** Thomas *Woodfill* 234 [ref. to WWI]: A "mosquito fleet" of Yankee sub chasers and destroyers circled and buzzed around us as we zigzagged our way through the danger zone. **1943** Cave *Long Nights* vii: The commander is hard at work training new men for the mosquito fleet. **1963** Barrett *Civil War* 35: This North Carolina navy, popularly called the "mosquito fleet," was under instructions not only to act in defense of the sounds and rivers but to seize enemy shipping moving along the coast.

2. the U.S. naval reserve.

1917 Dos Passos *14th Chronicle* 71: I am trying to do three things at once—enlist in the mosquito fleet, [etc.] …I am still hesitating on the edge of—on the one hand—the Ambulance, and on the other the Naval Reserve.

3. the U.S. Asiatic fleet.

1918 Ruggles *Navy Explained* 10 [ref. to late 19th C.]: Gobbles was a very well known character in the "mosquito fleet," as the Asiatic Squadron was termed.

mosquito piss *n.* (see quot.).—usu. considered vulgar.

1983 K. Weaver *Texas Crude* 92: *Mosquito piss.* Any of a variety of light penetrating oils use for loosening pipe fittings.

mosquito wing *n.* usu. *pl. Army.* the single chevron formerly designating the rank of private first-class. Now *hist.*

1968 Tauber *Sunshine Soldiers* 77: "Oh, mercy," I protest, looking to CPA Stan for aid, "the man wants my mosquito wings." **1980** Cragg *Lex. Militaris* 305A: *Mosquito Wing.* This originally applied to the insignia of rank of a private first class, when it consisted of one chevron. **1982** "J. Cain" *Commandos* 175: The mosquito-wing private stripes on his uniform…labeled him…a newby in-country. **1983** "J. Cain" *Dinky-Dau* 11: How could a soldier…complete three tours in the 'Nam and still have mosquito wings for rank on his arms?

moss *n.* hair, esp. of the head.

1926 C.M. Russell *Trails* 65: He wears long moss on his chin which he's sure proud of. **1944** Burley *Hndbk. Jive:* And when the wind blows

the other way, Cholly Hoss, my moss gets in my eyes! **1958** Hughes & Bontemps *Negro Folklore* 485: *Moss:* Hair. She's got some mellow moss. **1961** Himes *Pinktoes* 142: It's all a matter of hair. If colored people had straight moss and white people had kinky moss, it would make everybody equal, I mean. **1969** Bouton *Ball Four* 272: *Moss* is hair. **1972** Hannah *Geronimo Rex* 35: You saw her totally nude and even her moss about five seconds before the strobe light went out.

mossback *n.* **1.** an elderly, old-fashioned, or extremely conservative person.—used derisively. Hence **mossbacked,** *adj.* [The 1878 quot. is presumably misdefined.]

[**1876** in *OEDS:* [In the cotton states] those too cowardly to fight…were known as "mossy-backed rangers" during the war.] **1878** in *OEDS: Mossback,* a settler; a homesteader; a pioneer farmer. (Western.). **1885** in *DA:* Everybody rejoices over the passage of the bill…except a few intense mossbacks, who were known during the war as copperheads. **1888** in *DA: Mossback*…seems to have originated in the swamps of North Carolina, where a particular class of the poor whites were said to have lived among the cypress until the moss had grown upon their backs. **1889** in *OEDS:* Still mouthing empty reverence for those moss-backed frauds. **1889–90** Barrère & Leland *Dict. Slang: Moss-backs* (American), old fogies, "fossils," men behind the times. **1897** Kipling *Capts. Courageous* 147: See 'em now, actin' to be genewine moss-backs. **1899** Robbins *Gam* 73: Then they set the old moss-back afire, beginning with his boots. **1933** Hemingway *Winner* 33: "Goddamned mossbacks," she said. **1935** J. Conroy *World to Win* 227: He wasn't one of those mossbacks who claim a woman's place is in the home and all that old-fashioned hooey. **1937** Mason & Heerman *Stella Dallas* (film): That bunch of mossbacks. **1938** Krims *Sisters* (film): Who cares what he says, the old mossback! **1947** Boyer *Dark Ship* 149: Listen, you little mossback,…I've a good mind to throw you out the window! **1950** *Harper's* (Mar.) 33: None of these men is very radical; on the other hand, the mossbacks are few. **1955** O'Connor *Last Hurrah* 202: There must be a few mossbacks in the electorate who don't bother to tape-record every political speech they hear. **1968** Johnson & Johnson *Count Me Gone* 121: The old mossbacks down at the court house. **ca1969** *Gunsmoke* (CBS-TV): You and that old mossback you're ridin' with. **1978** Maupin *Tales* 60: All the old mossbacks would stop us and say how nice it was to know there were still some decent, upstanding young men left in the world. **1979** Cassidy *Delta* 2: They're so moss-backed up there in Saigon. **1994** *New Republic* (Oct. 24) 39: Arch-conservatism in investment philosophy. I should disclose that I myself figure among the mossbacks.

2. *West.* an old steer; MOSSHORN.

1926 Branch *Cowboy* 94: A "maverick" steer, an old "mossback." **1942** *ATS* 828: Mossback, mosshead, mossy horn, wrinkle-horn, *an old steer whose horns have become wrinkled and scaly.*

mossbacker *n. Pol.* MOSSBACK, 1.

1884 in Lummis *Letters* 9: No doubt about their politics—all are moss-backers and hungry for spoils.

mosshorn *n. West.* an old steer; (*hence*) a veteran cowboy. Also **mossy horn.**

1885 in *OEDS:* They were all old mossy horn fellows from seven to twenty-seven years old. **1920–23** in J.M. Hunter *Trail Drivers* II 981 [ref. to 1870's]: We went to work gathering a mixed herd for Nebraska and one of wild old "moss-horns" for the Indian reservation. *Ibid.* 1022: We held our "old mossy heads" all right till about one o'clock. **1931** Rynning *Gun Notches* 4: What I'm driving at, none of them was mossy horns; not ornery yet to speak of. **1936** McCarthy *Mosshorn* (unp.): *Mosshorn* [*sic*], n. Old cowboys and old cattle. **a1940** in Lanning & Lanning *Texas Cowboys* 38: That was the old mossyhorns, of course. **1942** (quot. at MOSSBACK).

mossy doughnut *n.* (see quot.).—usu. considered vulgar. *Joc.*

1988 Hynes *Flights of Passage* 35 [ref. to WWII]: The female organ was "the bearded clam" or "the mossy doughnut."

most *n.* Orig. *Jazz.* that which is splendid or remarkable; the best or most extraordinary person or thing.—constr. with *the.*—usu. used predicatively. Occ. as quasi-adj. or adv. Cf. LEAST.

1953 in S. Allen *Bop Fables* 44: "And Grandma," said Red, "your ears are the most, to say the least." **1954** in R.S. Gold *Jazz Lexicon:* That's the most horn in the world. **1954** in R.S. Gold *Jazz Lexicon:* I'm feeling the most today. **1955** *Science Digest* (Aug.) 33: What was…"real gone" last year…is now "the greatest" or "the most." **1955** McGovern *Fräulein* 194: It's the most.…It's the greatest. All the cats are havin' a ball. **1955** G.D. Adams *3 Bad Sisters* (film): As a back scratcher, Jim is simply the most. **1956** Reach *Teachers* 9: [He's a] dreamboat—I mean the most to say the least! **1957** Gutwillig *Long Silence* 51: He's the most. I mean the most to say the least. **1957** Blumgarten *Mr. Rock & Roll* (film): Baby, that's the most. **1957** H. Simmons *Corner Boy* 37: Dig him the most to say the least. **1958** J. Davis *College Vocab.* 1: "It's the most to say the least"—Description of something extraordinarily good or pleasing. **1959** Zugsmith *Beat Generation* 23: You're the most, Meg. **1959** L. Hughes *Simply Heavenly* 131: Melon, this is the most. **1962** Killens *Heard the Thunder* 15: You shoulda stayed in law school. Sam's Army is just about the most [*i.e.,* extraordinarily bad]. *Ibid.* 412: You're absolutely hysterically the ever-loving most. **1966** *New Yorker* (Sept. 10) 20: New fabrics that mothers think are adorable and boys think are the most. **1968** Heard *Howard St.* 68: This is the most, baby. I mean abso-goddamn-lute most! **1976** Rosten *To Anywhere* 27: You're the *most*, doll-face. **1991** McDonald's restaurants TV ad: Hey, man, this is the most!

mostest *n.* the most; (*hence*) the best. [Orig. dial.]
   1885 in *OEDS:* We set around the kitchen fire an' has the mostest fun. *ca***1939** in *DAS: The Hostess with the Mostest on the Ball* [song title]. **1952** *Topper* (NBC-TV): Marian Kirby, the ghostess with the mostest. **1953** *I Love Lucy* (CBS-TV): We're the mostest! **1956** T. Betts *Across Board*, in *DAS:* Man o' War...described for all time by his Kentucky groom...as "de mostest horse." *a***1991** J. Phillips *You'll Never Eat Lunch* 157: There I am, hostess with the mostess.

mot *n.* [orig. r-less var. of MORT] *Hiberno-E. & Und.* a woman. Now *rare* in U.S. Also **mott, mat.** [Later quots. are from Irish sources; quots. with spelling *mat* may reflect an independent word fr. a fig. application of S.E. *mat.*]
   ****1773** in Partridge *Dict. Und.* 451: The first time I saw the flaming mot,/Was at the sign of the Porter Pot. ****1785** Grose *Vulgar Tongue: Mot.* A girl, or wench. ****1821** *Real Life in London* I 145: Tom...was in close conversation with his *mott.* ****1822** D. Carey *Life in Paris* I 186: Mot; i.e. courtezan. ****1839** Brandon *Poverty* (gloss.): *Mott*—a woman. **1848** *Ladies' Repository* VIII (Oct.) 315: *Mott*, Any decent female, generally a mother, a sister, or wife. **1932** in *AS* VIII (1933) 27: Prison Parlance...*Mat...Maud.* A woman. **1942–49** Goldin et al. *DAUL* 137: *Mat.* A prostitute or a very promiscuous woman. ****1959** B. Behan *Borstal Boy* 346: *Mot:* Dublin slang for *wife* or *girl.* **1954–60** *DAS: Mat...*A woman; one's wife. *Some Negro use.* ****1963** B. Behan *N.Y.* 56: McSorley would not sell hard liquor and he would not allow a woman in the place....You will get no malt and no mots. ****1994** R. Doyle *Snapper* (film): He must have a mot hidden away somewhere.

mota *n.* [orig. unkn.] marijuana. Also vars. Cf. MOOTAH.
   1933 in *OEDS:* This drug looked like chopped hay, or dried clover....In short, a "muggles," "weed," or "mootie," cannabis indica. **1946** Mezzrow & Wolfe *Really Blues* 53: Rapp smoked his muta while he played the new guitar. **1942–49** Goldin et al. *DAUL* 141: Some Spik all charged up on mota chivved (knifed) Johnny the Mugg. **1967** Rosevear *Pot* 159: *Mota, Muta:* Mexican slang for marihuana. *a***1979** Pepper & Pepper *Straight Life* 41 [ref. to 1940's]: We had Mota, which is moist and black. **1988** Norst *Colors* 45: A laugh made free and easy by the pungent *mota.*

motate *v.* to go; MOTIVATE.
   1967–68 von Hoffman *Parents Warned Us* 61: I needed to motate out of there.

mote *v.* [back formation fr. *motor*] Esp. *Naut.* to move quickly, esp. by means of motors or engines.
   1926 *AS* (Oct.): But the majority of Navy men like a ship that, once the "mud-hook" is up, will make knots. He yearns to have her "mote." In fact, "mote" is a ubiquitous term. **1932** Ellsberg *S-54* 225 [ref. to WWI]: What ails this tub, anyway? The other pigs've managed to keep on moting. ****1937** in *Austral. Nat. Dict.: To mote* is defined by Mr Partridge as "to drive or ride in a motor car", but for many years now Australian schoolboys have been using it in the more general sense of "move quickly", so that often they say in praise of an athlete "There is no doubt he can mote."

motel *n.* see NO-TELL MOTEL.

mothball *n.* **1.** *pl.* a condition of long storage, as of decommissioned naval vessels.—constr. with *in* or *out of.* Now *S.E.*
   1916 R. Lardner, in *Sat. Eve. Post* (Feb. 19) 36: They put him in moth balls and they ask Joss to join their tong. **1949** *N.Y. Times* (Nov.

19) 2: Many of the four-engined bombers were "taken out of mothballs" and readied for strategic and reconnaissance use. **1951** *N.Y. Times* (Jan. 3) 3: To modernize a number of B-29 Superfortresses now in "moth balls." **1956** in Asimov et al. *Sci. Fi. Short Shorts* 174: Spaceships were a drug on the market. They put them in mothballs. **1962** *N.Y. Times* (Sept. 23) I 42: Some 40 destroyers...were taken out of mothballs last year. *a***1966** Barth *Giles Goat-Boy* 276: I guess you wonder why/we took you out of mothballs, huh? **1974** *U.S. News & W.R.* (Apr. 1) 58: 80 elevated cars are in "mothballs," awaiting recall if warranted by business. **1980** S. Fuller *Big Red* 141: Your cock's been in mothballs. **1988** *TV Guide* (Mar. 12) A-3: MCA plans to put "E.T." back in mothballs after four months of selling cassettes.

2 *Stu.* an obnoxious person; (*also*) an overdiligent student.
   1944 *Slanguage Dict.* 60: *Mothball*—a teenage jerk. **1944** Kendall *Service Slang* 11: *Mothballs....*recruits. **1945** *Amer. N & Q* (Aug.) 70: A prude—touch-me-not, moth ball, mona lizard. **1947** *ATS* (Supp.) 2: *Mothball,* a girl who never "dates." **1954–60** *DAS: Mothball...*A serious student; a grind; a student who never dates a girl.

mothball *v. Mil.* to put (ships, equipment, etc.) into long-term storage; (*hence*) to inactivate; decommission, etc. Now *colloq.* or *S.E.*
   1949 *N.Y. Times* (Oct. 31) 1: A fleet that comprised 268 combat vessels, when the "mothballing" began in September. **1949** *Time* (Nov. 7) 20: They were asked to mothball most of the great and glorious fleet. **1950** *Time* (Oct. 2) 18: The Navy was able to mothball 2,027 ships, for the small cost of $173 million. *Ibid.* (Oct. 9) 20: He would be able to revive some reluctantly mothballed plans for windmilling personally into the 1950 congressional elections. **1951** *Sat. Eve. Post* (Oct. 6) 143: He inspected twenty-seven moth-balled amphibians at the Philadelphia Navy Yard. *Ibid.* (Nov. 17) 70: The moth-balling process had been widely praised as the all-inclusive answer for maintenance of a battle fleet without impossible peacetime costs. **1957** *Sat. Eve. Post* (Dec. 7) 6: Our sick bay had been mothballed, but the corpsmen really turned to and had it ready. **1959** *N.Y. Times* (May 17) 44: The best service a retired general can perform is to turn in his tongue along with his suit and mothball his opinions. **1962** E. Stephens *Blow Negative* 340: Men working on better ways to moth-ball decommissioned ships. **1974** *U.S. News & W.R.* (Apr. 1) 59: Mr. Cusick had ordered new buses in advance and "mothballed" older vehicles. **1980** *Business Week* (Dec. 8) 24: Imperial Oil...said it would mothball its Cold Lake tar sands project. **1984** Trotti *Phantom* 177: We needed to get [the airplane] to Da Nang, where it could be mothballed and embarked. **1984** *Chicago Sun-Times* (Sept. 2) 1: The mothballing of Commonwealth Edison Co.'s...nuclear reactor will cost the utility $71.5 million.

mothball fleet *n. Navy.* a reserve fleet of decommissioned vessels. Now *colloq.*
   1946 in *OEDS:* "*Mothball fleet*": inactive U.S. Navy ships to be preserved for long periods by newly-developed techniques. **1949** *Sat. Eve. Post* (Oct. 29) 37: Why scuttle our present investment in the active and mothball fleets...? **1950** *N.Y. Times* (Mar. 19) VI 69: The reserve, or "mothball" fleet, the inactive ships laid up since the war. **1957** *N.Y. Times* (Feb. 7) 20: Along with similarly converted freighters, all from the mothball fleet, [etc.]. **1961** *Time* (July 28) 15: From the Navy's huge mothball fleet, landing craft and (possibly) troopships will be activated. **1966** Noel & Bush *Naval Terms* 224: *Mothball fleet...*Same as Reserve Fleet.

mother[1] *n.* **1.** *Prost.* a madam (of a brothel).
   ****1698–99** "B.E." *Dict. Canting Crew: Mother,* a bawd. ****1785** Grose *Dict. Vulgar Tongue: Mother* or *the Mother,* a bawd. **1842** in R.H. Dana *Journal* I 79: In the middle of the room...sat the old harridan, the "mother" of the house. **1913** Kneeland *Commercialized Prostitution* 92: It is not uncommon for the girls as well as the customers to call her "mother." **1980** E. Jong, in *OEDAS* I 106: I enter'd Mother Coxtart's House once more.

2. *Homosex.* an effeminate homosexual man who befriends a younger person.
   1946 J.H. Burns *Gallery* 154: Your mother's awfully late tonight, but she'll try and make it up to you! **1949** De Forrest *Gay Years* 37: Listen to Mother like a good girl. **1954–60** *DAS: Mother...*An effeminate male. **1967** *DAS* (Supp.): *Mother...*The social leader, spokesman, or most attractive member of a group of homosexuals....Any homosexual or effeminate man. **1967** Humphreys *Tearoom Trade* 47: Don't knock (criticize) a trick (sex partner)—he may be somebody's mother (homosexual mentor). **1971–74** in *West. Folk.* XXXIII (1974) 214: Another

common female reference is "Your mother" when the [male homosexual] speaker refers to himself as an authority figure. "You're talkin' to your mother now." **1981** in Goodwin *More Man* 55: I consider my mother, it would be Sonja Moritz.

3. *pl. Black E.* DOZENS.—constr. with *the.*

   1962 Killens *Heard the Thunder* 54 [ref. to 1940's]: I have too much love and respect for women to play the mothers or the dozens or whatever you call it.

¶ In phrase:

¶ **does your mother know you're out?** (used to deride the childishness or stupidity of the addressee).

   *1836 in *F & H* IV 360: He smiled and said, "Sir, does your mother know, that you are out?" **1838* in Partridge *DSUE* 534: How's your mother? Does she know that you are out? **1840** *Spirit of Times* (Nov. 21) 446: "Does your mother know you're out?" The whole room burst out a-larfin' at me. **1842** in Damon *Old Amer. Songs* No. 31 (sheet music): Good morning, Mister Phisick!/Does your mother know you're out. **1843** [W.T. Thompson] *Scenes in Ga.* 31: Maybe his ma don't know he's out. **1846** Codman *Sailors' Life* 39: Johnny Raw…does your mother know you are out? **1848** in *AS* X (1935): 42: *Does your mother know you are out?* A rebuke. *ca*1849 in Jackson *Early Songs of Uncle Sam* 59: We're rugged and tough and that's enough,/Our mammys know we're out. **1886** Abbot *Blue Jackets of '61* 270: You look as if your mothers didn't know you were out. **1887** Hinman *Si Klegg* 63 [ref. to Civil War]: Hello, sonny, does yer mother know ye're out?

mother[2] *n.* (a partial euphem. for) MOTHERFUCKER (in any sense). Also in pron.-sp. vars. [The appositeness here of 1939 quot. is dubious; though the author was an American, his use of the word almost surely represents "A [British] Western Front nickname for various big howitzers (9.2's)" (Partridge *DSUE* 534). The form *mother for you* should be compared with *motherferyer* s.v. MOTHER-FUCKER, from the same period and milieu.]

   1935 in Leadbitter & Slaven *Blues Records* 513: Dirty Mother For You. **1936** in Leadbitter & Slaven *Blues Records* 297: She's A Mellow Mother For You. [**1939** Hartney *Up and at 'Em* 231 [ref. to WWI]: He and his plane spent the hours of darkness parked under one of the big "Mothers"—the 16-inch American naval railroad guns.] **1944** in Himes *Black on Black* 209: That old mother, cotton, is gonna kill me yet. **1955** in R.S. Gold *Jazz Lexicon*: Hell, this mother never could blow. **1958** Gilbert *Vice Trap* 110: Jive and lush don't use together, you mother. **1960** in T.C. Bambara *Gorilla* 49: Now this jive mother who is my boss thinks he can make some bread by recording some of the old-timers. **1961** G. Forbes *Goodbye to Some* 82 [ref. to WWII]: That mother Stevens dropped a crab in the beer. **1961** Brosnan *Pennant Race* 74: Malone pulls that ball on a line and Willie is a dead mother. **1961** L.G. Richards *TAC* 138: Boy, was I glad to see that mother. **1961** H. Ellison *Gentleman Junkie* 144: He just grabbed that muthuh by the neck and…beat the crap outta him. **1962** Kesey *Cuckoo's Nest* 175: Drive, you puny mothers, *drive!*…Practice, you mothers, get that ball and let's get a little sweat rollin'! **1961–64** Barthelme *Dr. Caligari* 142: You brought the darkness, you black mother. **1964** Newhafer *Last Tallyho* 182: If ever…I get out of this mother of a thunderstorm. *Ibid.* 302: There's nothing wrong with these mothers at all. **1965** Herlihy *Midnight Cowboy* 101: It's a powerful mothah, ain't it? **1966–67** P. Thomas *Mean Streets* 47: I hadn't ratted.…I was in like a mother. **1967** Moorse *Duck* 139: Jeez, Doc,…you're about the smartest muther in the whole world. **1971** Sloan *War Games* 125: There sits a man who is going to go home and tell his wife a mother of a story. **1972** Jenkins *Semi-Tough* 188: Some wives is gonna read that mother you writin', you dig what I'm sayin'? **1972** C. Gaines *Stay Hungry* 34: He had worked [his calves] so hard he thought they would pop off, but the mothers wouldn't grow. **1973** Karlin et al. *Free Fire Zone* 164: I can take work!…I can work like a mother! **1974** Loken *Come Monday Mornin'* 135: Be colder'n a mother out there. **1974** in Mamet *Sexual Perversity* 15: This little…clock radio. So I pick the mother up and heave it at her. **1976** C.R. Anderson *Grunts* 47: You mean it's that hill over there, the bald mother? **1978** Selby *Requiem* 247: Yeah, he be a cool mutha jim. **1980** Hillstrom *Coal* 427: Burn the mother. **1984** Holland *Let Soldier* 156: Deal those mothers! **1985** Killerman *Hellrider* 9: You muvva. **1986** B. Breathed *Bloom Co.* (synd. comic strip) (Dec. 3): Just wing that mother. **1987** *N.Y. Daily News* (July 2) M3: Here comes that evil mother; we can't win now. **1988** *Living Dangerously*

(A&E-TV): The river is one tough mother [to cross]. **1991** "Tribe Called Quest" *8 Million Stories* (rap song): Smiling like a mother. **1992** *New York* (Mar. 30) 61: He's a tough little mother with a ten-pound chip on his shoulder. **1996** *To Sir with Love II* (CBS-TV): You are one mean mother, Mr. Thackeray.

¶ In phrases:

¶ **ham and mothers** *Mil.* ham and motherfuckers [or *mothers*] s.v. MOTHERFUCKER. [Quots. ref. to Vietnam War.]

   1973 (quot. at *ham and motherfuckers* s.v. MOTHERFUCKER). **1978** Hasford *Short-Timers* 86 [ref. to Vietnam War]: Ham and mothers.…I hate…ham and lima beans.

¶ **your mother!** Esp. *Juve.* (used as a derisive retort, often postpositively).—usu. considered vulgar. Also in elab. vars. [The phr. is widely perceived to suggest *go fuck your mother*, and for many speakers is therefore equally provoking; it is also reminiscent of the DOZENS, as reflected in 1891 quot.]

   [**1891** in Dobie *Rainbow in Morning* 172: Talk about one thing, talk about another;/But ef you talk about me, I'm gwain to talk about your mother.] [**1929** in Hemingway *Sel. Letters* 298: In a purely conversational way in a latin language in an argument one man says to another "Cogar su madre!"] **1934** H. Roth *Call It Sleep* 356 [ref. to *ca*1915]: Yuh mudduh's ass! **1937** Odets *Golden Boy* 243: [On telephone] I'll bring him right over…you can take my word—the kid's a cock-eyed wonder…*your* mother too! **1939** in Dundes *Mother Wit* 288: An upper-class Negro woman [in a northern city] said…[that] in her high school group…a simple reference to "your ma" or "your mother" was a fighting challenge. The woman herself did not know why one had to fight when she heard this but did know that fight one must. **1953** Paley *Rumble* 86: "Your mother!" Pooch murmured. **1956** Ross *Hustlers* 44: Some day, I'd kill him. "In your mother's — " he heard me say, but he didn't let me finish.…I saw a million white dots in front of my eye from…his back hand swing. **1957** H. Simmons *Corner Boy* 79: *Your mother, your mother.* **1968** K. Hunter *Soul Bros.* 39: If a Southside boy wanted to start a fight, all he had to say…was, "Your mother —." He didn't even have to finish the sentence. The other boy would tear into him…in a blind fury. **1971** D. Smith *Engine Co.* 49: Ahh, ahh, your mother's ass. **1972** in W. King *Black Anthol.* 145: "Your motha'!" she yelled. **1973** Lucas, Katz & Huyck *Amer. Graffiti* 23: "What happened to your flathead?" "Ah, your mother!" **1974** Strasburger *Rounding Third* 159: Carter turned around. "Your mother," he said to the guy who had just finished talking. **1977** Bunker *Animal Factory* 29: "I'm gonna bust you someday." "You'll bust your mother." **1978** Schrader *Hardcore* 65: "You're thinking about your father."…"Keep him out of this or I'll break your balls." "Who?" "Your mother, smart-ass." **1985** *Cheers* (NBC-TV): Ya mother! **1991–95** K. Burns, in A. Sexton *Rap on Rap* 35: According to brother Morgan Dalphinis, author of *Caribbean and African Languages*, this is the ultimate pan-African insult. The Hausa say *uwarka* ("your mother"), which is really short for *ka ci uwarka* (unprintable).

¶ **your mother wears army shoes** (used as a derisive taunt). Also vars. [S. Bronner, *Amer. Children's Folklore* (1988), pp. 43–44, lists more than forty variants, collected 1976–82.]

   1956 Seaton *Proud & Profane* (film) [ref. to WWII]: Hey, your mother wears army shoes! **1954–60** *DAS* s.v. *Your: Your mother wears Army boots!* Orig. a strong W.W.II term of derision; now mainly jocular. **1963** Clarke & Clarke *Intro. Folklore* 91: Yer ma wears army shoes. **1965** Cassavetes *Faces* 45: Your mother wears Army shoes. **1971** *Mad* (June) 42: Ahh, Your Sister Wears Army Shoes! **1974** *Odd Couple* (ABC-TV): He says, "Your mother wears combat boots!" **1978** in Lyle & Golenbock *Bronx Zoo* 100: There's the normal crap you have to listen to every night: "Your mother wears Army boots," that kind of stuff. **1985** *Night Court* (NBC-TV): Aah, ya mother wears combat boots. **1990** *Tenn. Ling.* X (Winter) 39: Your mother wears combat boots. **1987–91** D. Gaines *Teenage Wasteland* 107: This was a tradition. Accusing someone of being a narc was like saying your mother wore combat boots.

mother *adj. & adv.* (a partial euphem. for) MOTHERFUCKING.

   1958 Meltzer & Blees *H.S. Confidential* (film): You're the swingin'est chick in the whole mother kingdom. **1960** in R.S. Gold *Jazz Lexicon*: The Gasser…made himself a connection that shook the whole Mother Peninsula! **1961** in R.S. Gold *Jazz Lexicon*: That's just too mother much! **1962** Reiter *Night in Sodom* 134: You a fool, Chollie. A rotten muvva fool. **1966–67** P. Thomas *Mean Streets* 201: What a sick mudder scene! **1968** Vidal *Breckinridge* 98: I am going to sell the whole mother score. *ca***1969** Rabe *Hummel* 23: Jesus God Almighty I hate this mother army stickin' me in with weird people! **1970** La Motta, Carter & Savage *Raging Bull* 25: Everybody down on his knees, you mothers, down on your fuckin' mother knees! **1971** *Go Ask Alice* 102: The fuzz has clamped down till the town is mother dry. **1972** Carpentier *Flight One* 75: This mother lead sled better be ready to go! **1976** J.W. Thomas *Heavy Number* 44: Wait a mother-minute! *Ibid.* 115: I…can't use them…in the middle of the mother desert!

mother *interj.* (used to express surprise or pain).
    [**1869** "M. Twain," in *OEDS:* Twenty-five cigars, at 100 reis, 2500 reis! Oh, my sainted mother!] *****1898** Whiteing *John St.* 217: Oh, mother! Don't the paint make you feel good? **1952** B. Wilder & E. Blum *Stalag 17* (film): And, oh mother! You've got yourself a situation. **1965** Hardman *Chaplains* 6: Oh, mother! Will I be glad when you leave! **1972** Ponicsan *Cinderella Liberty* 25: Mother, does it ever hurt! **1976** Hayden *Voyage* 227: Oh, Mother, dear Mother, would you clowns jest take a look at that!

Mother Carey's chicken *n.* a stormy petrel.
    1767 (cited in *W10*). **1808** in Nevins & Weitenkampf *Cartoons* 25: Here's a flock of Mother Cary's chickens. *****1853** Chesterton *Peace, War & Adv.* I 16: Stormy petrels, by sailors profanely yclept "Mother Carey's Chickens." **1856** in C.A. Abbey *Before Mast* 42: There are also plenty of *"Gulls" "Boobys" "Stormy Petrels"* or as the sailors call them *"Mother Carys Chickens."* **1893** Barra *Two Oceans* 81: "Mother Carey's chickens"…very much resemble…swallows. **1909** in *Calif. Hist. Soc. Qly.* VI (1927) 269: Stormy petrel[s], or Mother Carey's chickens as the sailors called them [in 1849].

motheree *n.* (a partial euphem. for) MOTHERFUCKER. Also **motheroo.**
    1948 Manone & Vandervoort *Trumpet* 70: I'll be a motheree if I'll wear any damn bedpan intern's suit. **1972** D. Pearce *Pier Head Jump* 82: Like that motheroo Phillips, you mean?

motheren *n.* (a partial euphem. for) MOTHERFUCKER.
    1959 W. Miller *Cool World* 26: Motheren Wolves. Motheren Wolves. Come at me you Motherens. **1966** S. Harris *Hellhole* 112: You son of a bitch, taking all the jobs from all the rest of us. You motheren. You come back and we going to kill you.

motheren *adj.* see s.v. MOTHERING.

motherferyer see s.v. MOTHERFUCKER, 1.a.

mother five-fingers see MARY FIVE-FINGERS.

motherfouler *n. Black E.* (a partial euphem. for) MOTHER-FUCKER.
    1947–52 R. Ellison *Invisible Man* 422: Coolcrack the motherfouler! **1962** L. Hughes *Tambourines to Glory* 238: Sister Laura's going to crack-up and all over Buddy Lomax—who everybody knows is a motherfouler.

motherfuck *n.* **1.** MOTHERFUCKER (in any sense).—usu. considered vulgar.
    1964 in Gover *Trilogy* 341: That puts this…lily-white mothahfug on like mad. **1967** Mailer *Vietnam* 54: Don't come near, motherfuck. *Ibid.* 82: How'd you get this motherfuck? **1972** *N.Y.U. Cold Duck* (Apr. 17): Fuck you, motherfuck, you're trying to censor my work! **1970** Landy *Underground Dict.* 135: *Mother fuck*….Greeting to another person. It has a positive connotation. **1978** Schrader *Hardcore* 99: You muthafuck! **1982** Del Vecchio *13th Valley* 271: How they gonna get a bird inta the middle a dis mothafuck? *a***1986** D. Tate *Bravo Burning* 96: Hey, motherfucks, you don't have to treat him like that. **1989** R. Miller *Profane Men* 62: This big ugly motherfuck of a war. *a***1990** E. Currie *Dope & Trouble* 14: She a grown motherfuck.

    2.a. a damn; FUCK, 2.—usu. considered vulgar.
    1967 [R. Beck] *Pimp* 277: I wouldn't give a mother-fuck. **1972** Pelfrey *Big V* 106: And I don't *give* a motherfuck. **1985** Knoxville, Tenn., attorney, age 32: Who gives a motherfuck anyway?

    b. (used as an emphatic expletive); HELL; *the fuck* s.v. FUCK.—constr. with *the.*—usu. considered vulgar.
    1975 De Mille *Smack Man* 70: How the motherfuck do a pimp's girl get jealous, man? **1973–76** J. Allen *Assault* 188: You better get the motherfuck out of my place. **1982** Del Vecchio *13th Valley* 309: Where the motherfuck is the C-4? **1986** Philbin *Under Cover* 120:

Who the motherfuck are you? **1988** Norst *Colors* 22: What the motherfuck was that you just did.

motherfuck *v.* **1.** goddamn; FUCK; curse.—usu. considered vulgar.
    1942 (implied at M.F., v.). *a***1961** Peacock *Valhalla* 323: Motherfuck the OD! **1965** in *Social Problems* XIII 351: Mother Fuck the Police! **1969** *Black Panther* (Oakland, Calif.): Well, motherfuck the police. **1971** *Who Took Weight?* 10: Mothafuck you. **1972** Davidson *Cut Off* 29 [ref. to WWII]: Mother-fuck this fuckin' war. **1968–73** Agar *Ripping & Running* 137: Aw man, motherfuck it. **1975** S.P. Smith *Amer. Boys* 37: "Three tears in the bucket," he yelled. "They don't flow, mother fuck it!" **1977** Torres *Q & A* 16: Motha fuck you, ain't tellin' you shit. Who the hell're *you!* **1994** Berendt *Midnight in Garden* 114: If I offended anyone, two tears in a bucket, honey. Motherfuck it. **1995** *Jerry Springer Show* (synd. TV series): Mother—k [electronically deleted] her!

    2. to destroy; confuse; FUCK UP, 1.—usu. considered vulgar.
    1975 in *Urban Life* IV (1976) 489: We'll motherfuck the bastard's mind!

motherfuck *adv.* (used as an intensive).—usu. considered vulgar.
    1970 E. Sanders, in Padgett & Shapiro *N.Y. Poets* 386: And don't you motherfuck forget it!!!

motherfuck *interj.* var. MOTHERFUCKER, *interj.*

motherfucker *n.* **1.a.** (literally) a man who commits incest with his mother (*rare*); (*hence*, usu.) a despicable or contemptible man or woman. Also partially euphem. nonce vars. not presented as main entries.—usu. considered vulgar. [In part an intensification of FUCKER. Perh. from his interviews with elderly musicians, R.S. Gold, *Jazz Lexicon* (1964), asserts the term's existence as early as "c[irca] 1900"; though lacking documentation, some currency at such a date is entirely likely. Notable discussions are P. Tamony, "Mother Fucker" (unpub. MS., *ca*1966, Tamony Collection), and H. Rawson, *Wicked Words* (1989), pp. 257–58. Forms such as *motherferyer, -fuyer* are euphem.]
    1928 C. McKay *Banjo* 229: I've been made a fool of by many a skirt, but it's the first time a mother-plugger done got me like this. [**1935** G.W. Henderson *Ollie Miss* 82: The man from Swanson had passed the ugly word then, and the Hannon boy had flung it back…neatly compounded, with the word "mother" preceding it. The Swanson boy…whipped out his razor.] **1935** in P. Oliver *Blues Tradition* 232: He's a dirty mother fuyer, he don't mean no good. *ca***1935** in Logsdon *Whorehouse Bells* 95: Motherfucker, I'll slice off your prick. [**1936** Little *Harlem to Rhine* 5 [ref. to 1917]: And so I saiz ter him, Cap'n Suh, "Ever-ting you saiz Ah am—yoo is double—even de part against yoo mudder….Ef yoo saiz anyt'ing mo' ter me Ah'll cut yoo heart out."] **1938** "Justinian" *Amer. Sexualis* 29: Mother-Fucker. n. An incestuous male. The most intense term of opprobrium among the U.S. lower classes. Probable Sicilian origin, C. 20. Urban communities only. No sexual connotation; used merely as an epithet. **1939** in A. Banks *First-Person* 255: Why you poor Brooklyn motherfrigger, I'll wreck this goddamn place with you. **1941** G. Legman, in G. Henry *Sex Vars.* II 1172: Incestuous love directed toward a mother, one of the most powerful tabus of our civilization, with which is connected the superlatively derogatory colloquial epithet, *mother-fucker.* **1946** Mezzrow & Wolfe *Really Blues* 14: A motherferyer that would cut your throat for looking. **1946** in Del Torto TS.: Susie is a mother fucker. **1947** in Leadbitter & Slaven *Blues Records* 65: Mother Fuyer. **1947** Mailer *Naked & Dead* 152 [ref. to WWII]: I was gonna shoot the mother-fugger but you were in the way. **1950** *Commentary* X 62: When asked what his chief duties were in a Negro settlement house for boys, a social worker answered, "Teaching them euphemisms for mother—— (unprintable word)." **1954** Lindner *50-Minute Hour* 152 [ref. to *ca*1940]: During my years in prison work I had observed that one expletive, that referring to intercourse between son and mother (m-f-), was at once the most dangerous and the most frequent on the lips of the psychopath. I had actually seen men killed for using it. **1954** in Wepman et al. *The Life* 110: Cocksuckers by the dozens, motherfuckers and their cousins. **1956** in P. Oliver *Blues Tradition* 240: Your mama…she's a runnin' motherfucker, cheap cocksucker. **1958** *Stack A Lee* 5: I'm that bad motherfucker they call Stack A Lee. **1959** W. Burroughs *Naked Lunch* 40: I'll cut your throat you white mother fucker. **1958–60** I. Freeman *Out of Burning* 93: Ya did that on purpose, ya mother-fucker! **1962** R. McDavid, in *Mencken's Amer. Lang.* 354: The agentive noun of this verb [*fuck*], with *mother*-prefixed…is a survival of rural Southern white usage; I first encountered it in 1928, at…Fort Oglethorpe, Ga., patronized chiefly by Southern

uplanders. **1962** Killens *Heard the Thunder* 284 [ref. to WWII]: Every time I walk up the company street I hear somebody calling somebody else a mother-fucker or a sonofabitch. **1963–64** Kesey *Great Notion* 71: My brother is a motherfucker. **1965** C. Brown *Manchild* 137: Don't explain yourself to that mother-fucker. **1965** Conot *Rivers of Blood* 222: Even the word *motherfucker* takes on different connotation. For the white it is the image of incest; for the Negro it is the picture of a white man lying with a black woman who is his, the Negro's, mother. *ca*1966 Tamony *Mother Fucker* 9: An ex-con…told me in the 1930's that he had heard the vocable in Dirty Dozen displays through the 1920's [in San Quentin prison]. **1968** A. Montagu, letter to P. Tamony (June 24) (Tamony Coll.): *Motherfucker*…Mr. Donald C. Greason has written to me that he heard the epithet often from a friend of his at the front during late 1917. **1968** Van Dyke *Strawberries* 177: If you even touch it, motherfucker, you die. **1968** Gover *JC* 34: Sonny you nacheral sack a twenty diffrent mothahfuggahs. **1971** Guffy & Ledner *Ossie* 46 [ref. to *ca*1940]: "You're a motherfucker." "Your mama's one." **1974** V. Smith *Jones Men* 18: Look at that bitch. Nasty motherfucker. **a*1984 Partridge *DSUE* (ed. 8): *Mother-fucker.* A very low term of abuse: adopted, ex US, earlyish 1970s. **1985** in G. Tate *Flyboy* 146: A mother-fer-ya. *a*1973–87 F.M. Davis *Livin' the Blues* 66 [ref. to Kans., *ca*1925]: You ungrateful motherfucker! *a*1991 J. Phillips *You'll Never Eat Lunch* vii: Supercilious motherfucker. **1992** Hosansky & Sparling *Working Vice* 197: People called her motherfucker…[and] bitch. *a*1994 Smitherman *Black Talk* 164: Muthafucka *never* refers to a person who has sex with his/her mother. **1994** Bak *Turkey Stearnes* 138 [ref. to 1920's]: "What the hell are you looking at?"…"At you, motherfucker." **1995** *Jerry Springer Show* (synd. TV series): Come on, motherf—er [electronically deleted]!

b. Esp. *Black E & Mil.* (with reduced force) fellow; person; (*hence*) a close friend or admirable person; (*often*) an extraordinary or formidable person.—usu. considered vulgar. Cf. identical sense development of BASTARD, FUCKER, SON OF A BITCH, etc.

1958 *Stack A Lee* 1: He…said who put the hole in this motherfucker's head?/ Who could the murderer of this poor man be? **1967** *DAS* (ed. 2): *Mother fucker*…A familiar, jocular, even affectionate term of address between males. **1969** *Atlantic* (Sept.) 50: The emergence of the word "motherfucker"…The word might well have originated with the black American subculture, and certainly has been given fullest expression there and used with great nuance to express not only contempt but also awe or even admiration. **1970** Landy *Underground Dict.* 135: *Mother fucker*….Positive, complimentary name for a friend—eg., *Hey, mother fucker, what's happening?* **1971** in Horwitt *Call Me Rebel* 4 [ref. to 1930's]: Pretty soon word of the incident spread throughout the gang. "That Alinsky, he's an all-right motherfucker," the kids would say, and…they began to trust me. **1971** in Cheever *Letters* 284: A puertorican drug-pusher…exclaimed: "Oh what a cool motherfucker was that Machiavelli." **1972** in W. King *Black Anthol.* 101: Joe was a motherfucker. A revolutionary motherfucker. A black man made of steel iron. **1973** J.R. Coleman *Blue-Collar* 62: A word like "motherfucker" here is often just a synonym for man, no more and no less. ("Who's that new motherfucker over there?" or "I told the motherfucker we'd pick up him and his bitch at eight.") **1973** R. Roth *Sand in Wind* 154: Hey, motherfuckers, look at this. *Ibid.* 438: I've met some of the best motherfuckers I've ever known in the [Marine Corps]. **1972–74** Hawes & Asher *Raise Up* 98 [ref. to 1930's]: We…talked about Debussy and Bach and what bad motherfuckers those cats were hundreds of years ago. **1974** Lacy *Native Daughter* 108: Fine…nice legs…tall…—would be a motherfucker if she didn't talk so much. **1974** V.E. Smith *Jones Men* 156: I'm just as cool as the next motherfucker. **1977** L. Jordan *Hype* 44: "C'mere, you little motherfucker," he said tenderly, reaching for her. **1978** B. Johnson *What's Happenin'?* 57: Once I figured out that a "bad mother-fucker" was an all-right dude, I at least had a shot at communicating. **1978** Strieber *Wolfen* 127: You the scaredest motherfucker I've seen in a good long while. **1980** Knoxville, Tenn., high school teacher, age 27: Man, I *love* that motherfucker! *a*1983 Baugh *Black Street Speech* 24: See, like if a brother gets on my case I can tell blood, "Hey motherfucker, you can kiss my ass," and the brother can…take it in stride—cause he know where I'm comin from. But you can't be tellin no white dude that. **1987** D. Sherman *Main Force* 96 [ref. to Vietnam War]: "That bad out there, huh?" "Worse, except we're the baddest mother-fuckers in the valley." **1984–88** Hackworth & Sherman *About Face* 510 [ref. to Vietnam War]: In the Airborne, the term "motherfucker," unless spoken harsh-

ly, was among the highest terms of endearment. **1993** K. Burns, in A. Sexton *Rap on Rap* 36: *Motherfucker*…has been used by black women as an endearment to their men. **1991–95** Sack *Co. C* 45: The lieutenant…often said *fuck, fucker, fuckin'* and *motherfucker* as though these words [merely] meant space, next word.

2.a. an infuriating, formidable, difficult, or oppressive thing, situation, task, place, etc.; (with reduced force) a thing, etc.—usu. considered vulgar.

1947 Mailer *Naked & Dead* 345 [ref. to WWII]: You know what the mother-fugger'll be like?…We'll be lucky to get out of there with our goddam heads on. **1960** Peacock *Valhalla* ch. iv: I'll get the motherfuckers [*sc.*, beer cans]. **1952** in Kerouac *Letters* 336: Hear that you goddamn motherfucker Frisco. **1962** B. Jackson *In the Life* 156: Oh, life's a motherfucker, Bruce. **1962** T. Berger *Reinhart* 386: Let me run that big motherfu——. **1967–68** von Hoffman *Parents Warned Us* 98: The street is a rough motherfucker. **1968** in B. Edelman *Dear Amer.* 81: Sometimes it gets pretty hairy in this motherfucker. **1969** *Playboy* (Dec.) 290: Let's burn this motherfucker down. **1970** Landy *Underground Dict.* 135: *Mother fucker*…Hard-to-solve problem; rough situation. **1973** Jong *Fear of Flying* 4: So I keep concentrating very hard, helping the pilot…fly the 250-passenger motherfucker. **1975** De Mille *Smack Man* 108: What a motherfucker that's going to be, given the rules of evidence in this state. **1978** S. King *Stand* 84: Eight milkshakes (why…had he bought eight of the mother-fuckers?) **1981** L. Heinemann, in *Harper's* (Aug.) 58: The whole company…caught some mean kind of shit and every swinging dick *but* him bought the motherfucker. **1981** Hathaway *World of Hurt* 14: This is the dumbest motherfucker I ever been in. **1981** *Penthouse* (Mar.) 174: Heroin is…an insidious motherfucker. **1982** Downey *Losing the War* 23 [ref. to WWII]: Some of them…cussed their native state for being a "prejudiced motherfucker." **1989** Chafets *Devil's Night* 44: We'll probably never solve the motherfucker. **1989** S. Robinson & D. Ritz *Smokey* 78: We're going to remember this motherfucker…'cause I don't intend to let it happen again. **1991** J. Lamar *Bourgeois Blues* 32: I knew how to make those motherfuckers gleam. **1991** Lott & Lieber *Total Impact* 6: We've got to win this motherfucker [*sc.*, a game]. **1988–93** Wilcock & Guy *Damn Right* 42: Sign the motherfucker, man. *a*1994 Hallas *Devil's Anvil* 59 [ref. to WWII]: Get this motherfucker off the rocks, or I'll blow your head off and I'll drive it in!

b. Esp. *Black E.* a large or outstanding example; HUMDINGER.—usu. considered vulgar.

1972–74 Hawes & Asher *Raise Up* 3 [ref. to 1930's]: Anybody who *looked* good was automatically a motherfucker. **1977** *Nat. Lampoon* (Aug.) 33: Have I got a motherfucker of a stunt for you! **1981** C.M. Brown, in C. Major *Calling Wind* 414: They got some skies in Africa that are a motherfucker, man!

3. Esp. *Black E.* (used as an indefinite standard of comparison).—usu. considered vulgar.

1962 Riccio & Slocum *All the Way Down* 149: Something new has been added…the letters LAMF under a personal name or a gang name.…It means "Like A Mother Fucker," and it's supposed to suggest to all who read it that the person or the gang…is rough and tough and hell-bent for war or what may come. **1962** in Wepman et al. *The Life* 139: I just come back.…Mad as a motherfucker. **1966–67** P. Thomas *Mean Streets* 160 [ref. to *ca*1950]: He went limper'n a motherfucker. **1973** Wideman *Lynchers* 39: It be dark as a muthafucka. **1975** S.P. Smith *Amer. Boys* 100: LaMont was [running] like fifty motherfuckers. **1978–79** in Jankowski *Islands in Street* 156: He was…scared as a motherfucker. **1985** in G. Tate *Flyboy* 33: Tripping out of our minds like a motherfucker. *Ibid.* 34: The record was selling like a motherfucker.…Faster than a motherfucker. **1990** Rukuza *West Coast Turnaround* 39: It was raining like six motherfuckers. **1994** in C. Long *Love Awaits* 11: Now in his mind she's obligated like a muthafucka to fuck him.

¶ In phrases:

¶ **beans and motherfuckers** *Mil.* a C-ration portion of lima beans and ham.—usu. considered vulgar. [This quot. ref. to Vietnam War, is an antedating of the main entry found at BEANS AND MOTHERFUCKERS.]

1980 M. Baker *Nam* 11: I'm not going to say he had cold beans and motherfuckers for breakfast. *Ibid.* 320: *Beans and motherfuckers*—C-ration delicacy composed of lima beans and ham.

¶ **bends and motherfuckers** *Mil.* calisthenic squats and

thrusts.—usu. considered vulgar. [Quots. ref. to Vietnam War.]

1980 M. Baker *Nam* 39 [ref. to *ca*1970]: You look like shit, so we're going to do a little PT now. Bends and motherfuckers. Many, many, many of them. *Ibid.* 320: *Bends and motherfuckers*: the squat-thrust exercise. **1990** G.R. Clark *Words of Vietnam War* 55: Bends-and-Motherfuckers…squat-thrust exercises.

¶ **ham and motherfuckers** [or **mothers**] *Mil.* a C-ration portion of ham and lima beans.—usu. considered vulgar. [Most quots. ref. to Vietnam War.]

1973 Layne *Murphy* (unp.): Packaged into the 1942 C-ration case….Ham & little muther fahckers,/Affectionately called,/Ham /&/ Mutha's. **1980** DiFusco et al. *Tracers* 41: I haven't got anything left except some ham and motherfuckers, man. **1982** E. Leonard *Cat Chaser* 76: Ham and lima beans: ham and motherfuckers. **1987** "J. Hawkins" *Tunnel Warriors* 332: Ham & Motherfuckers. C-rations serving of ham and lima beans. **1988** Clodfelter *Mad Minutes* 258: Cans of "ham and mother fuckers" (ham and lima beans). *a*1989 C.S. Crawford *Four Deuces* 107 [ref. to Korean War]: Ham and lima beans…was considered to be one of the good rations even though we called them "ham and motherfuckers." **1990** G.R. Clark *Words of Vietnam War* 52: Ham and lima beans…"ham-and-mothers."

motherfucker *interj.* (used to express astonishment, anger, etc.).—usu. considered vulgar. Also **motherfuck.**

1968 *Nation* (Dec. 2) 595: Motherfucker!…You a bunch of jive motherfuckers. **1970** Landy *Underground Dict.*: Mother fucker…Exclamation of anger. **1970** Woods *Killing Zone* 143: Mother*fuck*—what happened to you? **1972** R. Barrett *Lovomaniacs* 366: I stepped back, to get a better view of the watch…."*Motherfucker!*" I said. **1974** L.D. Miller *Valiant* 21 [ref. to WWII]: Mudderfucker!…I'm hit! **1976** Price *Bloodbrothers* 20: Mother-*fuck!* **1979** Gutcheon *New Girls* 249: Motherfuck, guess who that is? **1985** Bodey *F.N.G.* 144: Muthafucker, *can this be?* **1990** G. Lee *China Boy* 272 [ref. to 1950's]: "Motherfuck!" he says in pain.

motherfucking *adj. & adv.* **1.** goddamned; FUCKING.—usu. considered vulgar. Also euphem. vars.

[**1933** J. Conroy *Disinherited* 30: Scab! Scab! O, you bloody mother-killin' bastards! O, you lowdown sons of bitches!] **1933** O'Hara *Samarra* 154: Why, you small-time chiseling bastard, you. You dirty mother——— bastard. **1936** Levin *Old Bunch* 122: Listen, you mother-f——— little runt, if you don't—. **1947** Mailer *Naked & Dead* 12 [ref. to WWII]: Of all the mother-fuggin' luck, that sonofabitch takes it all. *Ibid.* 400: That's the mother-fuggin' truth. [**1948** Manone & Vandervoort *Trumpet* 131: If I hurt your beat-out feelings, I beg your mother-robbin' pardon.] **1951** Jones *Face of War* 62: Mother fuggin' bastards. **1951** Kerouac *Cody* 119: I read every WORD of that motherfuckin thing. **1953–55** Kantor *Andersonville* 524: Mother-fucking old Yankee mudsills. [**1957** T.H. White *Mtn. Road* 21: The next guy doesn't know a mother-frigging thing about it.] **1958** T. Berger *Crazy in Berlin* 168: A Southerner or a Negro, passing on the sidewalk out front, described to a mute companion a succession of events that were invariably *mothafuhn.* **1961** in Himes *Black on Black* 69: I'll cut your motherfucking throat. **1961** G. Forbes *Goodbye to Some* 128 [ref. to WWII]: You ain't home with your mother-fuckin' mother! [**1962–63** Kesey *Great Notion* 7: The whole motherkilling agreement.] **1962–65** Giallombardo *Soc. of Women* 49: She said…"I'm not showing you a mother———' thing." **1965** Linakis *In Spring* 75: He's a mother-fuckin' liar. **1965** C. Brown *Manchild* 140: I'm gon bust your mother-fuckin' ass. **1966–67** P. Thomas *Mean Streets* 129: They don't come no motherfuckin' better. **1964–69** in Calt *Rather Be Devil* 57 [ref. to *ca*1919]: The guys [at the Mississippi logging camp] wouldn't say, "Pass me such and such a thing," if they wanted a big pan of meat or biscuits or rice….They said, "Let such-and-such a thing *walk* up that motherfuckin' table." **1970** Neary *Julian Bond* 174: [During the Democratic National Convention of 1968] Mayor Richard J. Daley yelled "Get that motherfucking Jew out of here!" at United States Senator Abraham Ribicoff of Connecticut. **1977* T. Jones *Incred. Voyage* 284: That mother-fucking chief. **1986** N.Y.C. man, age *ca*35: You don't sound very motherfuckin' worried. **1986** P. Welsh *Tales Out of School* 64: [The pupils] lapse into street dialect, saying "be" for "are," "mines" for "mine" and of course the ubiquitous adjective "mother-f———." *a*1973–87 F.M. Davis *Livin' the Blues* 94 [ref. to Kans., *ca*1925]: I wouldn't give that motherfucking bastard a dollar. **1987** in Rawson *Wicked Words* 257 [ref. to N.Y.C., *ca*1930]: You motherfucking

cop, leave me alone. **1989** S. Robinson & D. Ritz *Smokey* 42: This is my motherfucking house and I'm gonna live here and no one's gonna stop me. **1993** *New Yorker* (Feb. 8) 35: Motherfucking cockroach. **1993** E. Richards *Cocaine True* 53: This guy's motherfuckin' free.

2. (used occ. to emphasize the positive qualities of a following noun).—usu. considered vulgar.

1954 in Wepman et al. *The Life* 42: I love him madly, he's my motherfucking man. **1961** Gover *$100 Misunderstanding* 95: Tee vee man talkin up a mothahfuggin storm! **1973** Flaherty *Fogarty* 157: What a motherfucking man he was, Shamus! **1991** Nelson & Gonzales *Bring Noise* 97: Dizzy Gillespie plays the trumpet, *not the mo'fugging sax.*

-motherfucking- *infix.* (used as an intensifier); -FUCKING-.—usu. considered vulgar.

[**1962–63** Kesey *Great Notion* 7: How do you expect *any-motherkilling-one* to know Hank Stamper's reasons?] **1967** Ragni & Rado *Hair* 154: Yeah! Emanci-motherfuckin'-pator of the slave. **1984–87** Ferrandino *Firefight* 124: Just hats up and dismotherfuckinappears. *a*1990 in Costello & Wallace *Sig. Rappers* 79: I shoulda kicked your ass/My-motherfuckin-self. **1988–92** in Ratner *Crack Pipe* 122: Who the fuck you think I am, your god-motherfuckin'-damn maid?

motherfucking-A *adv.* FUCKING-A.—usu. considered vulgar.

1977 Torres *Q & A* 54: Motherfuckin'-A right.

mothergrabber *n.* (a partial euphem. for) MOTHERFUCKER.

1963 in J. Blake *Joint* 357: You set me up, mother-grabber. **1966** I. Reed *Pall-Bearers* 34: Goofy mother-grabber!

mothergrabbing *adj.* (a partial euphem. for) MOTHERFUCKING.

1953–58 J.C. Holmes *Horn* 68: Those mother-grabbin' *slacks*…were full of *seeds!* **1961** J. Jones *Thin Red Line* 60: He's a jerkoff. A goddam mothergrabbing jerkoff. **1962** Serling *New Stories* 67: Are you out of your mothergrabbing mind? **1963** in *DAS* (Supp.): Serving…what he describes as "three hard mothergrabbin' years." **1971** *Playboy* (Mar.) 92: "Out of your mother-grabbing mind," Joanne said. **1974** Wilder & Brooks *Young Frankenstein* (film): You mothergrabbing bastard!

Mother Green *n.* *USMC.* the United States Marine Corps. [Quots. ref. to Vietnam War.]

1978 J. Webb *Fields of Fire* 222: So long, Mother Green. Hello, world. **1987** Kubrick et al. *Full Metal Jacket* (film): They call for Mother Green and her killing machines! **1990** G.R. Clark *Words of Vietnam War* 129: "Mother Green" was a nickname for the Marine Corps used by career soldiers.

motherhead *n.* (a partial euphem. for) MOTHERFUCKER.

1970 Quammen *Walk the Line* 85: You crazy-ass mother-head, what-choo doin'? **1982** Least Heat Moon *Blue Hwys.* 104: Those black motherheads'll manhandle you.

mother hubba *n.* *Black E.* (a partial euphem. for) MOTHERFUCKER. Also **Mother Hubbard, motherhugger, motherrubber.**

1959 A. Anderson *Lover Man* 52: There's a *bad* motherhubber/Down the road a way. **1973** "A.C. Clark" *Crime Partners* 73: Hey, my man, you got another one of those little mother hubba's? **1973** Overgard *Hero* 164: Motherrubber! My head! It feels like it's been drop-kicked. **1974** Goines *Eldorado* 137: We might just be able to blow the lid off this motherhubba before tomorrow night. **1974** "A.C. Clark" *Revenge* 8: I want to see some fuckin' sevens on these mothahuppas. *a*1986 D. Tate *Bravo Burning* 198: This poor…motherhugger. **1991** in *Rap Masters* (Jan. 1992) 54: He had to snatch that muthahubba off. *a*1994 Smitherman *Black Talk* 163: Mother Hubbard euphemism for *muthafucka.*

motherhumper *n.* (a partial euphem. for) MOTHERFUCKER.—usu. considered vulgar.

1963 Doulis *Path* 81: Death, I think, you mother-humper. **1967** Ford *Muc Wa* 133: "C'mon, you mother-humpers!" Ski yelled at his Raiders. **1970** Grissim *Country Music* 281: Anybody that can follow me is a motha-humper. And they ain't many that can do it….I'm a violent motha-humper today. Don't nobody fool with me or *I'll Kill!* **1972** *Nat. Lampoon* (Sept.) 6: There are fourteen *fuck you's*, nine *cocksucker's*, and six *motherhumper's* left over. **1977–81** S. King *Cujo* 73: I bet that motherhumper went two hundred pounds. **1986** Stinson & Carabatsos *Heartbreak* 77: Let's smoke this motherhumper's ass. *a*1990 Helms *Proud Bastards* 101: The battalion got its ass chewed up good around [Con Thien]….One bad motherhumper.

motherhumping *adj.* (a partial euphem. for) MOTHERFUCK-ING.—usu. considered vulgar. Also **motherhunching**.

　　1961 Gover *$100 Misunderstanding* 19: He kin hardly git his moth-ahhumpin hands roun that wad! **1963** Doulis *Path* 80: Why, that no-good, sneaky, mother-humpin' rebel. **1964** H. Rhodes *Chosen Few* 99 [ref. to *ca*1950]: That mother-humpin' fuckoff wanted *satisfaction!* **1964** in Gover *Trilogy* 215: Right inta this mothahhumpin lounge. **1967** W. Crawford *Gresham's War* 161: You motherhunching son of a hounddog whore. *Ibid.* 197: Motherhumping cowards. **1969** C. Brown *Mr. Jiveass* 20: Like, it's none of their motherhumping business, right? **1970** Quammen *Walk the Line* 86: I thought we been fittin' to make it to a gray jam, not do a suicide mission with some mother-humping cage-case. **1974** Loken *Come Monday Mornin'* 46: He scored every…motherhumpin' point!! **1986** Stinson & Carabatsos *Heartbreak* 163: Friggin' motherhumpin' Highway.

mothering *adj. & adv.* (a partial euphem. for) MOTHERFUCKING.

　　1951 in J. Blake *Joint* 27: He said if the motherin' screw ever caught up to us, he'd wish he hadn't. **1956** Algren *Wild Side* 160: His whole life he ain't worked one single mothering day! **1957** E. Brown *Locust Fire* 95 [ref. to 1944]: No more mothering flying. Well, hucklety buck. I don't give a one. **1959** Miller *Cool World* 15: Why shitman them Colts is the same motheren piece they was usen at Cussers Last Stan. *Ibid.* 37: Them headbreakers. Motheren headbreakers. **1959** in H. Ellison *Sex Misspelled* 103: You try my mutherin' patience. **1961** Russell *Sound* 31: You're too motherin' much, man. **1962** Riccio & Slocum *All the Way Down* 43: We'll show these mothern bastards. **1963–64** Kesey *Great Notion* 210: I feel…pretty motherin' good. **1965** Matthiessen *Fields of Lord* 37: Them poor mothering Indians. **1966–67** W. Stevens *Gunner* 56: They got some motherin big idea. **1968** *Sat. Eve. Post* (Sept. 16) 27: I hope you have four motherin' flat tires. *ca*1969 Rabe *Hummel* 26: You ain't no motherin' exception to that whistle! **1975** *Black World* (June) 75: Not that motherin day.

mother-in-law *n.* *Bowling.* the number 7 pin.

　　1976 *Webster's Sports Dict.* 276. **1980** Pearl *Pop. Slang* 102: *Mother-in-law n.* (Bowling) the left rear pin in the pin formation. **1982** Considine *Lang. Sport* 90.

mother-in-law seat *n.* *Av.* the back seat of a two-seat airplane. *Joc.*

　　1961 L.G. Richards *TAC* 64: Simple enough if you're riding the mother-in-law seat in the back end of an F-100F.

motherjumper *n.* (a partial euphem. for) MOTHERFUCKER.

　　1949 H. Ellson *Tomboy* 5: It was that no good mother-jumper that owns the store. **1952** H. Ellson *Golden Spike* 22: What mother-jumpers you been listening to? **1955** H. Ellson *Rock* 121: I hit for the candy store then, mad as a mother-jumper. **1957** Margulies *Punks* 43: But this motherjumper is a white stud. **1963–64** Kesey *Great Notion* 334: I thought…the motherjumper wasn't even gonna. **1965** Borowik *Lions* 155: Yessir, you motherjumper, you'll be laughing outa the other side of your mouth when the cops come for you. **1966** Fariña *Down So Long* 120: You old benevolent motherjumper, I love you! **1966–67** P. Thomas *Mean Streets* 91: I hate all you white motherjumps. **1970** Woods *Killing Zone* 88: He used to be a sad mother jumper. **1977** J. Wylie *Homestead Grays* 242: He was as quick as a motherjumper. **1977** Butler & Shryack *Gauntlet* 130: All right, you mother-jumpers. **1993** *Time* (June 14) 13: Among the…prime-time words acceptable to ABC [network programmers] are such bizarre semi-obscenities as mother jumper and humphead.

motherjumping *adj.* (a partial euphem. for) MOTHERFUCKING.

　　1952 H. Ellson *Golden Spike* 19: You mother-jumping thief! **1961** Gover *$100 Misunderstanding* 35: He sit up like a mothah jumpin jack-in-a-box. **1962** Crump *Killer* 163: You're a mother-jumping coward. **1963–64** Kesey *Great Notion* 209: And good motherjumpin' riddance. **1969** in Romm *Conspiracy* 138: Fucking sonofabitch Fascist mother jumping cops! **1980** McDowell *Our Honor* 156: Sanders, you seem to think you're running this mother-jumping platoon, only it's about time you learned differently.

motherless *adj. & adv.* (used as a term of abuse); goddamnd.

　　***1898** in *Dict. Austral. Eng.*: To these are prefixed the adjectives [*sic*] *motherless* and *dead*, thus *dead motherless broke*. **1899** Hamblen *Bucko Mate* 67: Sleep!…Sleep! You motherless lambs! Did you come aboard the Osceola to sleep? ***1911** O'Brien & Stephens *Australian Sl.* 86: *Motherless broke, motherless stiff,* i.e. very poor, very impecunious. **1933** Hemingway *Winner* 95: "You motherless bitch," I said to him. **1934** in

Lomax & Lomax *Our Singing Country* 203 [blues written 1918]: I went to Belgium, blowed my bugle horn,/Every time I blowed, motherless German gone. **1947** Carter *Devils* 261: That yellow-bellied obscenity! That motherless bastard! **1947** Motley *Knock on Any Door* 143: "Oh, you motherless bastard!" Vito yelled. **1949** Van Praag *Day Without End* 161: It's our own…a P-47…the no-good, motherless bastards! **1961** Gover *$100 Misunderstanding* 40: I hearin more tricks jes a-streamin in that mothahless front door downstairs. **1962** Ross *Last Campaign* 152: I give up. I quit. This is the motherless end! **1964** Brown *Brig* 61: Louder, you motherless maggots. **1971** in Sanchez *Word Sorcerers* 233: The dirty motherless bastards. **1973** Ace *Stand on It* 10: SLAM! I hit that motherless wall and came back off it. **1974** Radano *Cop Stories* 128: You lousy bunch of motherless bastards. **1972–76** Durden *No Bugles* 22: What motherless fuckin' child would bring bagpipes to a goddam war? **1976** R. Price *Bloodbrothers* 45: Do you know Mott, that motherless bastard, must got a prick like a dead twig?

motherlover *n.* (a partial euphem. for) MOTHERFUCKER.

　　1950 L. Brown *Iron City* 69: And as for *that* mother-lover——. **1954** E. Hunter *Runaway Black* 18: You broke the mother-lover. **1955** Graziano & Barber *Somebody Up There* 215: "Stand straight, you little mother-lover," he says. **1963** L. Cameron *Black Camp* 63 [ref. to WWII]: On your *feet,* motherlover!

motherloving *adj.* (a partial euphem. for) MOTHERFUCKING. [Several quots., incl. 1951, ref. to WWII.]

　　1951 "W. Williams" *Enemy* 149: Oh, those foggers. Those mother-loving foggers. **1954** Schulberg *Waterfront* 308: You're a cheap, lousy, dirty, stinkin', mother-lovin' bastard. **1955** Klaas *Maybe I'm Dead* 36: The dirty mother-loving bastards. **1955** E. Hunter *Jungle Kids* 103: He didn't get out of that mother-lovin' cellar. **1957** Laurents & Sondheim *West Side Story* 145: On the whole! Ever—! Mother—! Lovin'—! Street! **1959** Morrill *Dark Sea* 88: Don't be so mother-lovin' nosy. **1962** Killens *Heard the Thunder* 16: That's a smooth mother-loving curve you throwing. **1968** Spooner *War in General* 53: We got ourselves a mother lovin' home. **1972** *N.Y. Times* (Feb. 6) 19: His one indulgence: a St. Bernard weighing 260 mother-lovin' pounds. **1975** *Atlantic* (May) 43: I'm the Paul mother-lovin Bunyan of the Interstate system.

mother-raper *n.* (a partial euphem. for) MOTHERFUCKER.

　　1959 Himes *Crazy Kill* 33: Turn me loose, you mother-rapers! He's my brother and some mother-raper's going to pay—. *Ibid.* 57: I ain't given Dulcy any mother-raping knife. **1965** Himes *Imabelle* 92: Mother-raper, step on it! *Ibid.* 127: I bled that mother-raper like a boar hog. **1989** R. Miller *Profane Men* 62: I didn't even read that mother raper. **1989** M. Norman *These Good Men* 134: A caged assembly of thugs and cut-throats; "your basic murderers and mother-rapers."

mother-raping *adj.* (a partial euphem. for) MOTHERFUCKING.

　　1932 Halyburton & Goll *Shoot & Be Damned* 306 [ref. to WWI]: When I talked to you mother-raping sewer rats at roll call I thought you were Americans. **1960** MacCuish *Do Not Go Gentle* 191 [ref. to WWII]: An' that queer's *really* a first-class A-1 mother-rapin' gutless wonder of a horse's ass! **1965** Himes *Imabelle* 67: Leave me see that mother-rapin' roll. *Ibid.* 122: Let's take the mother-raping hearse, too. **1972** C. Gaines *Stay Hungry* 213: The last motharapin straw, Newton called it.

motherrubber var. MOTHER HUBBA.

mother's day *n.* a payday or day when welfare checks are issued.

　　1965 Conot *Rivers of Blood* 75: Mothers' day in the projects comes twice a month, the first and the fifteenth, when the checks from the county arrive, and the prices automatically go up a few cents in many stores. **1966** in *Trans-action* IV (Apr. 1967) 7: When the checks come in for child support, it's "mother's day." **1970** *Current Slang V* (Summer) 17: *Mother's Day,* n. Payday (from: You pay this mother, you pay that mother…). **1971** S. Stevens *Way Uptown* 250: It was Mother's Day in Harlem. Which is the day the welfare checks come in the mail. On Mother's Day and for a couple days after, all the food prices 'round here go up in the stores the whites own. **1973** Droge *Patrolman* 86: He told me that Mother's Days, the first and fifteenth of each month when the welfare checks came in the mail, were the busiest because everybody was high on booze or dope. **1979** *L.A. Times* (Nov. 18) II 1: Mother's Day comes twice a month—the 1st and 15th. That's when Social Security, veterans' pension and disability and welfare checks are delivered.

mother sucker *n.* **1.** (a partial euphem. for MOTHER-FUCKER).—usu. considered vulgar.

   1946–51 J. Jones *Here to Eternity* ch. iii: He's a good gambler all right. The mother sucker. **1981** in *West. Folklore* XLIV (1985) 18: A cool mother-sucker getting ready to rock,/I threw up my hands, punch him in the face.

2. a crybaby.

   1954 Arnow *Dollmaker* 246: Mother suckers, mother suckers; that's yer brothers, allus runnen home to yu old man....Mother suckers. Mother suckers....We made 'em run to their mama.

motion *n.* ¶ In phrase: **get a motion on** to get going, get a move on.

   1889 in F. Remington *Own West* 20: Come, boys, get a motion on.

motion lotion *n.* **1.** gasoline; fuel. *Joc.*

   1976 Dills *CB Slanguage* 49: I'm peeling off for some of that motion-lotion; see you on the boulevard in a short short. **1976** Lieberman & Rhodes *CB* 132: *Motion Lotion*—Gasoline. **1989** C. Bennett *Bitburg* 33: An Eagle is about to receive a top-up of "motion lotion."

2. alcoholic liquor. *Joc.*

   1978 UTSQ : (Strong liquor)...*booze, rot-gut, firewater, motion lotion.*

motivate *n.* to go, esp. in a motor vehicle; (*hence*) to go, travel, or depart, esp. hurriedly. See also MOTORVATE.

   1955 C. Berry, in Chipman *Hardening Rock* 43: As I was motivatin' over the hill,/I saw Mabelline in a Coup de Ville./...Nothin' will out-run my V-eight Ford. **1966** IUFA *Folk Speech* (Mar. 17): *Let's motivate*—To leave. **1985** Eble *Campus Slang* (Fall) 7: *Motivate*—to move, go, leave, bolt; usually in a hurried manner. "Let's motivate out of here!" **1993** *Nation* (Aug. 9) 165: "There's only a few crazy die-hard bastards like me around that still motivate," Blackie said, using a hobo term for traveling.

motor *n.* a motorcycle; (in 1967 quot.) a motorcyclist.

   1946–51 J. Jones *Eternity* ch. x [ref. to 1941]: "You pay your three bucks at the window now, Angelo," Private Sussman, whose motor was the dearest thing in his life, said testily. **1951** in Elliott *Among the Dangs* 161: "Glad to meet you," he said. "You have a nice motor." **1967** Hamma *Motorcycle Mommas* 44: That's why I joined the "motors." **1990** C.P. McDonald *Blue Truth* 192: When you rode motors you were spit-shined.

   ¶ In phrase:

   ¶ **race (one's) motor** to become overexcited.

   1947 Schulberg *Harder They Fall* 197: Quit racing your motor, Miniff. **1958** "R. Traver" *Anatomy of Murder* 142: "Don't race your motor," I said.

motor *v.* to go at great speed; (*also*) to get going; (*hence*) to get busy.

   1980 (quot. at HARD-CHARGING). **1984** *N.Y. Post* (Aug. 11) 34: Won his [*sc.,* a racehorse's] last three in Maryland; can motor. **1988** D. Waters *Heathers* (film): I gotta motor if I'm gonna be ready for that party tonight. **1989** P. Munro *U.C.L.A. Slang* 60: *Motor* to leave. **1989** P. Dickson *Baseball Dict.* 264: *Motor*...To run at top speed. **1990** UTSQ: *Motor*—to leave....."Hey dude, let's motor!" **1990* T. Thorne *Dict. Contemp. Slang: Motoring*...making good progress, performing well....Roughly the same as the American *cooking*. **1993** *New Yorker* (Oct. 6) 226: A few of these guys [*sc.,* hockey players] still have legs: they can *motor.* **1996** Lyday-Lee *Elon College Coll.* (Spring) 2: *To motor.* (verb) to leave quickly.

motor cop *n.* a motorcycle policeman.

   1942 *ATS* 418: *Motor cop,...speed cop*...a motorcycle policeman. **1949** W.R. Burnett *Asphalt Jungle* 197: None of them saw...the...motor cop behind him.

motorcycle *n.* (a joc. euphem. for) MOTHERFUCKER.—usu. constr. with *bad.*

   1938 in P. Oliver *Blues Tradition* 235: Ridin' Dirty Motorsickle...He's a dirty motor-cycle [*sic*]. **1967** Lit *Dict.* 2: *Bad Motorcycle*—One who is very sharp, cool, hip, and gets what he wants but, this type of cat is also a little sneaky tricky. **1973** *Oui* (Feb.) 38: She's a bad motorcycle. **1985** Heywood *Taxi Dancer* 92: We got us a bad *motor-cycle* this mornin', gents.

motor flicker *n. Black E.* (a partial euphem. for) MOTHER-FUCKER.

   1967 in *Trans-action* VI (Feb. 1969) 33: This black slick head motor flicker. **1974** S. Stevens *Rat Pack* 39: Lookit what says black, you funky motorflikker nigger.

motorhead *n.* **1.** a dolt.

   1973 N.Y.C. man, age 27: A *motorhead* is a real idiot. A guy [I know] up in Maine says it all the time. **1979** Kunstler *Wampanaki Tales* 111: She...told one of the motorheads to stick his nose in the perfumed slot between her breasts. **1980** Aykroyd & Landis *Blues Brothers* (film): So what do you say we do, motorhead? **1986** (quot. at WASTOID).

2. an automotive enthusiast.

   1974 Eble *Campus Slang* (Mar.) 4: *Motorhead*—someone who is over-enthusiastic about cars. **1978** *Adolescence* XIII 497: The motor-heads were...adolescent males who spent most of their time working on their cars and talking about car engines. **1984** *Hardcastle & McCormick* (ABC-TV): You motorhead! **1984** W.M. Henderson *Elvis* 63: They were scruffy, long-haired "motorheads"...tough kids,...bikers without bikes.

motorhuckle *n.* motorcycle. *Joc.*

   1983 S. King *Christine* 79: Get on your motorhuckle boots, boys. **1981–85** S. King *It* 340: All of them with their motorhuckle boots cocked up on the seats in front of them.

motor mac *n.* [alter. *motor mech*] *Navy.* a motor mechanic or machinist's mate. [Early quots. ref. to WWII.]

   1953 Dobson *All Boats* 48: The motor-mac sat in a drooping posture over the engine box. **1958** Plageman *Steel Cocoon* 155: McNulty usually had chow with men of his own stature, such as Kerensky, or Jensen, or motor-mac Tom Ward. **1973** Overgard *Hero* 83: A good old boy from Billings is engineer, an ex-Navy motor mac. **1988** Poyer *The Med* 266: This motormac I was with.

motormouth *n.* **1.** a person given to constant talking or chattering. Hence **motormouthed**, *adj.*

   1963 W.C. Anderson *Penelope* 103: Shut up, motormouth, and listen. **1971** (cited in *W10*). **1973** Roberts *Last American Hero* (film): Has that motormouth been givin' you that much trouble? **1974** WINS radio news (Jan. 25): Ali is boxing's motormouth. **1974** G.V. Higgins *Cogan's Trade* 136: I didn't know he was [a] motor-mouth. **1976** *Kojak* (CBS-TV): Motormouthed little termite! **1977** in G.A. Fine *With Boys* 169: *Motormouth,* n. Boy who talks constantly. **1977** Corder *Citizens Band* 36: I think the old motormouth's tellin' her life story! *a1979* Peers & Bennett *Logical Laws* 172: An energy crisis will never stop motor-mouths. **1982** in "J.B. Briggs" *Drive-In* 72: Wanda Bodine is a motor-mouth of the first order. **1984** "W.T. Tyler" *Shadow Cabinet* 195: He keeps on talking. A motor-mouth, this guy. **1985** *Los Angeles* (May) 62: His unsuspecting, motor-mouthed wife. **1987** J. Waters *Hairspray* (film): Miss Motormouth Maybelle herself! **1994** *New York* (Oct. 24) 73: The late great media motormouth Walter Winchell. **1997** *L.A. Times* (Jan. 24) F6: Michael Palin, no longer a stammerer, is a motor-mouthed zookeeper.

2. the mouth of a garrulous person; (*hence*) chatter.

   1976 P. Conroy *Santini* 370: He put the emergency brake on that motor mouth of his. **1977** J. Olsen *Fire Five* 4: Fat chance, with your motor mouth. **1980** D. Hamill *Stomping Ground* 25: Dr. Shipper's motor mouth was part of the anesthetic. **1983** Ehrhart *VN-Perkasie* 229: And in the middle of my motor-mouth, I noticed she was laughing. **1981–85** S. King *It* 472: You just keep talking, fatboy....You got the motormouth.

motormouth *v.* to talk without stopping; chatter.

   1985 Ark. man, age 35: She motormouths the whole time. **1996** J. Logan *Tornado* (film): Y'all gonna motormouth all day or are you gonna eat barbecue?

motor scooter *n.* (a joc. euphem. for) MOTHERFUCKER. Cf. MOTORCYCLE.

   1960 D. Frazier *Alley-Oop* (pop. song): A mean motor scooter and a bad go-getter. **1970** *Nat. Lampoon* (Aug.) 44: She's a mean motor scooter and a *Bad Go-Getter.* **1974** Carter *16th Round* 168: Some real bad motorscooters!...Some bad motherfuckers! **1978** J. Webb *Fields of Fire* 15: "Marines Retake Citadel at Hue"...There's some mean motorscooters for you. *a1986* D. Tate *Bravo Burning* 42: Called..."a bad motor scooter" by others—in admiration. Good dude to have with you in a firefight is what they meant.

motorvate *v.* MOTIVATE.

   1978 D. Marsh, in *Rolling Stone* (Aug. 10) 53: The exhilaration of motor-vating on the highway. **1979** *Rolling Stone* (Feb. 8) 33: Chuck reportedly took his $7500 fee for a two-set show and motor-vated to the airport after his first set. **1983** S. King *Christine* 407: I'm going to get in Christine and we're going to motorvate right the Christ out of this one-timetable town. **1986** F. Miller et al. *Batman* 24: Let's motorvate! **1986** Eble *Campus Slang* (Mar.) 7: He really motorvated to class when he thought he was late.

Motown *n.* [*motor* + *town*] Detroit, Michigan. [The sense 'pop-influenced style of rhythm and blues music' is S.E.]
  [**1970** in *OEDS*: Some of their songs are extremely unusual, for example "Jesus Buddha Moses Gauranga" which starts with a bit of 2001 string sound and contains one line which is pure Motown.] **1971** *Playboy* (May) 176: Detroit city—that's Motown city. **1980** *N.Y. Times* (July 20) IV 1: Motown Shuffle. **1988** *N.Y. Post* (June 7) 68: It's the…Lakers trying to uphold tradition against the Motown Maulers. **1988** Headline News network (Nov. 24): The New York Knicks haven't won in Motown in ten tries. **1989** W.E. Merritt *Rivers Ran Backward* 22: Down here from Motown. **1992** *TV Guide* (Oct. 31) 6: A trip to Detroit, a.k.a. Motown. **1992** Straight *In Sorrow's Kitchen* 63: I was eighteen when I left Motown.

mott var. MOT.

motzer *n.* a Jewish person.—used derisively. Also **motzie**.
  1894 in Outcault *Yellow Kid* 26: Remember dis, Issy Silberman may be a motzer. But de day will come when…[he is] a millionaire banker. **1894** *Harper's* (Oct.) 696: He was nothin' but Motser* Mose when we took him up and gave him his start.…*From the Hebrew *matzoth*…but here used as a nickname for a Hebrew. **1897** *Harper's Wkly* (Jan.) 90: "Motzer," the newest slang word for Jew, is a corruption of the Hebrew word *matzoth*, which signifies "unleavened bread." **1898** Thompson *Youth's Companion* (Apr. 14) 364: Across the street…the other "Motzes"—another slang word for East Side Jews—out on fire-escapes…crying "*ei wei, ei wei!*" **1900** *DN* II 46: *Motzy*, n. A Jew or Jewess.

moulenjam, moulonjam var. MULENYAM.

mounseer *n.* [spelling pron. of F *monsieur* 'mister'] a Frenchman or French vessel.
  1778 Connor *Songbag* (July 2) 56: Twas early in the morning we spied this proud Mounsear.…We…boarded this proud Mounsear. ***1803** in J. Ashton *Eng. Satires on Napoleon* 172: A Regiment of them French Mounseers. ***1822** D. Carey *Life in Paris* I 107: These Mounseers…are no great shakes. **1823** J.F. Cooper *Pioneers* 61: When we fell in with the mounsheers, under De Grasse, d' ye see, we had aboard of us a doctor—. **1846** in G.W. Harris *High Times* (Jan. 17) 54: As a "Mounseer" would say, "one gran, magnifique, pretty good Deer Hunt came off a few weeks since." **1849** *Crockett Almanac* (unp.): Half Yankee, half Mounseer, half Spanish.

mountain canary *n. West.* a burro. *Joc.*
  1921 *DN* V 114: *Mountain canary*…Burro. *a*1956 Almirall *College to Cow Country* 406 [ref. to *a*1918]: Mountain Canaries and the Rustler.

mountain dew *n.* whiskey, esp. if illicitly distilled. Now *colloq.*
  *1816 in *OED*: A pleasing liquor, which was vended…under the name of mountain dew. ***1821** in *F & H* IV 363: Bread, cheese, and mountain-dew were liberally provided. ***1826** in *OED*: Whiskey, or mountain dew. **1836** (quot. at CLAY[1]). **1839** *Spirit of Times* (Dec. 21) 498: A pleasant evening, seasoned with a glass of "mountain dew." **1843** in G.W. Harris *High Times* 20: The choice "mountain dew" circulated as free as water. **1843–45** T.J. Green *Tex. Exped.* 260: The nectar of the gods…they understood to be pure, unmixed, and unadulterated "mountain dew." **1848** Judson *Mysteries* 19: I was just thinking of brewing a bowl of "the real mountain dew." *Ibid.* 528: "Mountain-dew." Scotch whisky. **1850** Garrard *Wah-to-yah* 166: The first house we passed was a distillery, where the "mountain dew" of New Mexico—*aguardiente de Taos*—is made. **1861** in A.P. Hudson *Humor of Old So.* 335: So long as our "mountain dew" holds out. **1865** in *Kans. Hist. Qly.* VII (1938) 39: "Mountain dew" in the ascendant. **1870** Keim *Troopers* 16: Most of the passengers retired to an adjacent "rum mill" and "stowed away" a "slug" or two of "mountain dew" to keep up their spirits. **1888** Gordon & Page *Befo' De War* 105: Dis here is what de Cohees calls/De ray-ull Mount'in Jew—/It looks almos' as ole as me. **1888** Nye & Riley *Railway Guide* 65: You will find on the following day a large jug of mountain dew…that will make your hair grow. **1891** McCann & Jarrold *Odds & Ends* 37: That's the real mountain dew; now ain't it? **1955** Broonzy & Bruynoghe *Big Bill* 66: They called it "mountain dew" because they had to go to the mountain to get it. **1980** *Maclean's* (Mar. 3) 41: Although production of that good ol'

mountain dew has declined nationwide…output of the backwoodsmen's favorite brew has continued unabated in this corner of Virginia. **1991–95** Sack *Co. C* 127: To make mountain dew on his $975 pension.

mountain guinea *n.* [*mountain* + GUINEA, 2.a.] *Ital.-Amer.* a person of northern Italian descent.—used derisively or contemptuously. *Joc.*
  1967 N.Y.C. high school student: South Italians call people from North Italy "mountain guineas." **1984** H. Gould *Cocktail* 259: They think I'm a mountain guinea.

mountain muffin *n. N.W.* a piece of wild-animal excrement. *Joc.* Cf. MEADOW MUFFIN.
  *a*1979 Toelken *Dyn. of Folklore* 66: This big pile of fresh moose pellets. A real stack of mountain muffins, you know?

mountain oyster *n.* the testicle of a sheep or hog used as food. Cf. PRAIRIE OYSTER.
  1890 in *OEDS*: Mountain-oyster, a lamb's testicle. **1929** *AS* V (Oct.) 19: *Mountain oysters:* The testicles of sheep or hogs. Occasionally used as food, they are supposed to contain a powerful aphrodisiac, and must never be mentioned in polite conversation between the sexes. **1954–60** *DAS:* Mountain oysters Sheep or hog testicles used as food. **1977** *L.A. Times* (Sept. 4) ("Calendar") 84: There were beef and pork ribs, "mountain oysters" and, unexpectedly, sweetbreads.

mountie *n. Police.* a member of a local mounted police unit.
  1944 in P. Smith *Letter from Father* 438: We outwitted the "mounties" who were riding human herd. **1952** Lait & Mortimer *USA* 302: But mounties are dreams for this kind of work.

mourner's bench *n.* a bench on which prisoners sit while awaiting examination in a court or prison.
  1904 in *OEDS*: In the city police court a motley crowd of prisoners filled the mourners' benches. **1912** Lowrie *Prison* 358: The boy seated himself on the "mourner's bench," and the Captain went into his office. **1935** Pollock *Und. Speaks: Mourner's bench*, a convict [*sic*] seated on a bench outside of prison board room awaiting a hearing before parole board.

mournful Mary *n. Mil.* a warning siren. Now *hist.* Also **Mournful**.
  1918 *Independent* (June 29) 500: The sentry…sounds "Mournful Mary," a siren with a sob in her voice. **1918** in Grider *War Birds* 185: The Germans…send over the same number of shells at exactly the same hour. Everybody knows when to take shelter and Mournful Mary, the siren, goes off automatically ten minutes before. **1918** in Paine *1st Yale Unit* II 162: The French have installed about six new, loud "Mournful Marys." **1920** Clapp *17th Aero Squadron* 18: When the siren at Dunkirk, familiarly called "Mournful," bellowed…the dynamo in the workshop lorry came to a dead stop. **1931** Springs *Carol Banks* 4: Mournful Mary, the siren, had just advised the two citizens of Dunkirk.

mourning *n. & adj.* blackened by a blow, a bruise, or (in 1962 quot.) by dirt.—usu. in phr. **in mourning**. Also vars.
  *1708 in *F & H* IV 364: *Mar.* I would give ten guineas, I say, to be ranked in his acquaintance. But pr'ythee, introduce me. *Chas.* Well on condition you'll give us a true account of how you came by that mourning nose, I will. ***1814** in *OED*: Bolter had his eyes in mourning. **1846** Durivage & Burnham *Stray Subjects* 169: One of his eyes was in deep mourning, and his nose (none of the handsomest, by the way) was quite askew. **1848** Baker *Glance at N.Y.* 18: A black eye?…So it is! You're eye has gone into mourning, sure enough! **1871** in L.F. Browne *J.R. Browne* 384: I had, in the classic language of the Ring, a mourning circle round both eyes. ***1889–90** Barrère & Leland *Dict. Slang:* A full suit of *mourning*, two black eyes; half-*mourning*, one black eye. **1912** Furlong *Detective* 34: With my right eye and one side of my face discolored—as some of them said, "in mourning." **1920** *Inf. Jour.* XVII (July) 166: With their finger nails in "half mourning." **1920–21** Witwer *Leather Pushers* 28: The Kid sees his eyes in deep mournin'. **1929** T.A. Dorgan, in Zwilling *TAD Lexicon* 117: Listening to the guy with the mourning glim tell how he got it. *ca*1940 in Botkin *Treas. Amer. Folk.* 531: If a setter ain't watchful, he's liable to have his finger dressed in mournin'. **1962** T. Berger *Reinhart* 4: The vendor's fingernails were in severe mourning.

mouse *n.* **1.** a young woman. [No continuity can be shown between 18th- and 20th-C. usage.]
  *1781 in *OED*: The harlots or women taken up for assault or night-

brawls were there (in Wood Street Compter) called Mice. **1917** J. Kern, in *N.Y. World* (Feb. 4) ("Metro") 1: She's a cunning little mouse....It was a whale of a party. **1928** in E. Ferber *One Basket* 327: Whyn't the big stiff come along with'm, pay their fare and maybe a decent tip instead of a dime these kind of mice give a guy? **1938** in J. O'Hara *Sel. Letters* 140: The mouse and me give one another the office. **1941** Macaulay & Wald *Manpower* (film): I hate to disappoint a little mouse I had a date with tonight. *Ibid.*: I'd like to buy a birthday present for a mouse. **1942** in Bérubé *Coming Out* 71: Some of 'em shaped up as pretty good mice. **1943** in Ruhm *Detective* 361: She is a little frosty mouse, and looks like Daisy Gross. **1944** (quot. at MELLOW). **1946** J. Burns *Gallery* 240: A sharp mouse, a sharp mouse. **1949** *Set-Up* (film): You oughta see the mouse I got waiting outside. Built like a brick battleship. **1959** on *Golden Age of TV* (1988) (A&E-TV): That society mouse jilted him. **1962** D. Hamilton *Murderers' Row* 50: A mouse I've never seen before saves me from the cops and asks me to a conference in her motel. **1963–64** Kesey *Great Notion* 39: All them cute little college mice after you, you being such a big stud logger from the north woods? **1965** Spillane *Killer Mine* 31: I'm going to make a pass at this mouse here and try to snag her out of this place.

2. a swollen bruise; (now *specif.*) a black eye.

1842 *Spirit of Times* (Sept. 17) 346: Giving him the upper cut as he sank, and raising a "mouse" on his left cheek. **1854** "Youngster" *Swell Life* 326: Two servants rushed at Alfred, who gave the first of them what he subsequently described as a "mouse under the left eye." **1859** O.W. Holmes *Prof.* 280: Clap a slice o' raw beefsteak on to that mouse o' yours 'n' 't 'll take down the swellin'. (*Mouse* is a technical term for a bluish, oblong, rounded elevation occasioned by running one's forehead or eyebrow against another's knuckles.). **1891** Maitland *Slang Dict.* 181: *Mouse*...a black eye. **1903** Townsend *Sure* 66: Did you tink he needed a mouse under his eye to make Maggie see what a good looker he is? **1909* Ware *Passing Eng.* 91: *Cop a mouse*...Get a black eye. **1920–21** Witwer *Leather Pushers* 56: One of the Kid's eyes has a little mouse under it. **1948** in *DAS*: You'll see the beginning of a mouse on my left eye. **1951** *Time* (Nov. 5) 97: Sharp, probing Louis lefts started a mouse under Rocky's right eye. **1965** C.D.B. Bryan *P.S. Wilkinson* 266: "You're going to have a beautiful mouse." "I hope not. The guy didn't hit me in the eye, he hit me in the cheekbone." **1965** Hersey *Too Far to Walk* 6: The old mother-remedy, press a beefsteak on a mouse? **1969** *N.Y.P.D.* (ABC-TV): You got the makin's of a pretty good mouse there. **1980** *N.Y. Post* (June 20) 70: The 30-year-old pitcher had a mouse under his right eye. *a*1989 Berent *Rolling Thunder* 27: You're going to have quite a mouse.

3. Esp. *Und.* an informer; SQUEALER. Cf. WHITE MOUSE.

*1888 in *F & H* IV 365: He's turned mouse, has he? **1934** in North *New Masses* 154: To the epithet "Rat!" or "Mouse!" or "Weasel!" the scab finds his car doorless or even in flames. **1942–49** Goldin et al. *DAUL* 142: There's that mouse cutting it up with the bulls (detectives) again. I wonder who's buried (betrayed) now. **1981** Sann *Trial* 187: I don't want that mouse any deader than he was.

4. *Und.* an effeminate male homosexual; (*also*) (see quot.). Cf. MOUSER, 1.

1930 Conwell *Pro. Thief* 239: *Mouse*, n.—Extortion in connection with homosexual attempts; a homosexual person.

5. a child.

1974 *N.Y. Times* (July 14) II: 15: The children—or "mice" as network people refer to them—have been shipped off...to their grandparents in California.

6. *N.Y.P.D.* a New York City Police Department trainee. [Alluding to the gray uniform.]

1988 Dietl & Gross *One Tough Cop* 103 [ref. to 1970]: I show up in my grays—they called us mice—with my trainee manual.

¶ In phrase:

¶ **smell a mice** see s.v. MICE.

mouse *v.* **1.a.** Esp. *Stu.* to engage in amorous kissing or petting; NECK.

1942 *ATS* 782: Love-making; courting....*mousing*. *a*1961 Boroff *Campus U.S.A.* 46: "To mouse" is to neck. **1965** *AS* XL 77: Another student [at Univ. Nebraska] records the verb *mouse*...with the meaning "to make out on a date." **1969** *Current Slang I & II* 62: Mouse, v. To kiss.—College males, South Dakota. **1968–70** *Current Slang III & IV* 84: Mouse, v. To indulge in sexual intimacies short of intercourse. New Mexico State.

b. to copulate with.

1956 H. Gold *Not With It* 297: You been mousing Nancy's wife!

2. *Und.* to inform; RAT.

1942–49 Goldin et al. *DAUL* 142: *Mouse*...To inform against associates. **1956** Algren *Walk on Wild Side* 137: "He'll mouse on me and he'll mouse on you," she explained without heat. "He's a forty-faced pigeon straight from Rat Row, quack from head to toe."

3. to blacken (the eye) (of).

1950 *Sat. Eve. Post* (Apr. 1) 101: Gently he felt a moused eye. **1956** *Time* (June 18) 47: [He] took exception to Mickey's remarks and belabored Mr. Universe's face, mousing his left eye and dazing him.

mousebrain *n.* a fool; BIRDBRAIN.

1970 Thackrey *Thief* 259: The clout had done mouse-brain some good. **1989** Pini *Portrait of Love* (unp.): He'll be mad as hell if you do, mousebrain.

mouser *n.* **1.** a homosexual man.—usu. used derisively.

1914 Jackson & Hellyer *Vocab.* 60: *Mouser*. Noun. Current in cosmopolitan circles. A "fairy," a character obsessed by lewd passions. **1930** Irwin *Tramp & Und. Slang*: *Mouser.*—A degenerate; a lewd character.

2. a mustache.

1934 D. Runyon, in *Collier's* (Feb. 3) 7: This old guy has a big white mouser, and big white bristly eyebrows. **1937** in D. Runyon *More Guys* 213: He has a big mouser on his upper lip and no hair whatsoever on his head. **1942** *Yank* (Aug. 19) 14: He vows not to shave the mouser until...after Victory.

mousetrap *n.* the vulva or vagina.—usu. considered vulgar. [A reading of 'prostitute' for the 1973 quot., though seemingly clear and supported by similar semantic devel. of other terms for the female genitalia, may be factitious; the sense is otherwise unattested, and the song features many meaningless lyrics.]

a*1890–96 *F & H* IV 365: *Mousetrap*,...The female *pudendum*. **1942 H. Miller *Roofs of Paris* 12: Her mousetrap stretches when she puts one of her fingers in. [**1973** B. Springsteen *Blinded by the Light* (pop. song): Some kidnapped handicap was complaining that he caught the clap from some mousetrap he bought last night.]

mousing *n.* MOUSE, 2.

1854 Sleeper *Salt Water Bubbles* 265: His infuriated wife kept cracking away at my head with her broomstick, raising a *mousing* at every blow.

mouth *n.* **1.a.** an obnoxiously talkative person.

*1698–99 "B.E." *Dict. Canting Crew*: Mouth, a noisy Fellow. **1748* in *F & H* IV 366: *Mouth*...also a cant word for a noisy, silly, ignorant, prating, scolding fellow. **1812* Vaux *Vocab.*: *Mouth*: a foolish silly person; a man who does a very imprudent thing is said to be *a rank mouth*. **1942** *ATS* 381: Loquacious person...*mouth*. **1968** Baker et al. *CUSS* 159: *Mouth* An obnoxious person.

b. insolence; idle chatter; LIP.

a*1890–96 *F & H* II 83: *Cheek*,...Equivalents are *lip*,...*mouth, chin, chirrup,* and *nine shillings*. **1935 Z.N. Hurston *Mules & Men* 49: She got plenty hips, plenty mouf and no brains. **1942** *ATS* 332: Impudent talk....*lip, mouth*. **1947** *AS* (Apr.) 121: *Cut the mouth*. Shut up. Keep quiet. **1962** Blake *Heartbreak* 23: Then somebody...gives me a lot of mouth about why I haven't found...time. **1974** Goines *Eldorado* 160: If you give me some mouth, I'm going to kick the living shit out of you. **1985** *Children of the Night* (TV movie): You got enough mouth for five rows of teeth.

2. *Und.* a lawyer; MOUTHPIECE, 1.b.

1942 *ATS* 515: Criminal lawyer....*mouth, mouthpiece*. **1967** Lit *Dict.* 41: *The Man's Mouth*—Lawyer.

¶ In phrases:

¶ **put up a mouth** to whine or object with little justification.

1904 in A. Adams *Chisholm Trail* 91: The girl put up quite a mouth about it.

¶ **run (one's) mouth [off]** to speak volubly or indiscreetly.

[**1942** *ATS* 220: Be talkative....*run (off) at the mouth*.] **1952** E. Brown *Trespass* 64: You running your mouth off now, Big John. **1976** P. Conroy *Santini* 370: Well, he was in here the other day running his mouth about how good Peninsula was and how they were going to beat the stuffing out of Calhoun.

¶ **shoot (one's) mouth off** to talk critically, indiscreetly, boastfully, or obnoxiously. Also vars.

1864 in *DA:* A Dutch married woman...was taxed $17.80 for "shooting off her mouth" against the virtue and morality of a neighboring maiden. **1887** F. Francis *Saddle & Moccasin* 136: If he could kill Indians shooting off his mouth at them, he'd soon clean out all there is. **1892** S. Crane *Maggie* 37: Youse fellers er lookin' fer a scrap an' it's damn likely yeh'll fin' one if yeh keeps on shootin' off yer mout's. **1895** Townsend *Fadden* 142: We crowded up closer to de mug what was shootin' off his mouth. **1904** J. London *Sea Wolf* 92: "I understand you're not quite satisfied with those oilskins?" "No, I am not. They are no good sir." "And you've been shooting off your mouth about them." "I say what I think, sir." **1927** C. McKay *Harlem* 12: Don't go shooting off your mouth too free. Gov'ment still smoking out deserters and draft-dodgers. **1941** Hargrove *Pvt. Hargrove* 10: Soldiers, like Senators, "don't like for a new guy to shoot his mouth off." **1948** in *DA:* You would think that a psychiatrist would know better than to shoot off his mouth on a subject which he is evidently unqualified to discuss. **1959** Morrill *Dark Sea* 111: I told him to size up a party before he blew his mouth off. **1977** *Dallas Times Herald* (Mar. 27) 17: He was busy shooting off his mouth before the race about...how many lap records he had there.

mouth *v.* **1.** *Stu.* to bluff one's way through a recitation.

    1835 in *DAE:* Never shall you allow yourself to think of going into the recitation-room, and there trust to "skinning," as it is called in some colleges, or "phrasing" as in others, or "mouthing it," as in others. **1851** Hall *College Wds.* 211: *Mouth.* To recite in an affected manner, as if one knew the lesson, when in reality he does not.

2. to inform; RAT.

    1965 C. Brown *Manchild* 154: He got busted—and he mouthed on everybody he knew.

3. to insult or upbraid; speak insolently to.

    1975 Swarthout *Shootist* 128: These was loaded,...you wouldn't mouth me like that. **1977** Bredes *Hard Feelings* 154: Call him on the phone at like four o'clock in the morning, see, and you mouth him every way you know how. **1989** in *Harper's* (Mar. 1990) 75: Some kids mouthed him...and he...answered them back. **1992** *Donahue* (NBC-TV): The eldest daughter mouths her mother.

mouth-bet *n. Gamb.* (see quots.). Also as *v.*

    *a***1889** in Barrère & Leland *Dict. Slang:* "Then, governor, I see you ten dollars and raise you the whole State of Vermont." The game ceased. *Mouth-betting* was not a success. **1889–90** Barrère & Leland *Dict. Slang:* Mouth-bet (American), when a man in gambling gives only a verbal promise to pay it is called a *mouth-bet.*

mouthbreather *n.* stupid person. Hence **mouth-breathing,** *adj.*

    1986 *NDAS:* Mouth-breather...A stupid person; moron. **1992** *New Yorker* (July 13) 26: He also didn't seem to mind when we asked mouth-breather questions. **1994** *Time* (May 30) 70: Vaclav Havel was talking about the mouth-breathing heavies who ran Czechoslovakia during the communist years.

mouthfuck *v.* to fellate or irrumate.—usu. considered vulgar.—also used absol. Also as *n.*

    *ca***1866** *Romance of Lust* 447: Finishing off with a mouth fuck. **1976** "Studs" *Creative Head* 39: He mouthfucked her in earnest. **1981** *Penthouse* (Apr.) 196: She...began mouth-fucking me rapidly. **1996** "Anal Experiences of Submissive British Female," pornographic story on Usenet newsgroup alt.sex.stories: I...started to mouth fuck him, plunging his cock in and out of my mouth. **1996** "Later That Week," pornographic story on Usenet newsgroup alt.sex.stories: Watching these guys mouth fuck started to do weird things to my cunt.

mouthful *n.* a spoken remark of notable truth or relevance.—usu. constr. with *say,* etc. Now *colloq.*

    [****1790** in *OEDS:* I never said a *mouthful of ill against her* in my life.] **1916** Lait *Beef, Iron & Wine* 124: "These here is excitin' times." "Mouthful," said Luke. **1917** in Woods *Horse-Racing* 289: Ain't it the truth!...You surely spoke a mouthful then! **1918** *Chi. Sun. Tribune* V (Feb. 17) (unp.): Myrtle Crawford Spills a Mouthful. **1921** D. Parker, in *Life* (Feb. 3) 160: "You said a mouthful." I confess. **1922** *Sat. Eve. Post* (June 3) 10: You said a mouthful there, boy. **1923** in Kornbluh *Rebel Voices* 91: "Have you anything to say for yourself?" "I've got a mouthful." **1929** W.R. Burnett *Iron Man* 194: You said a mouthful. **1937** Weidman *Can Get It Wholesale* 29: Brother, you said a mouthful. **1944** F.G. Lieb *Cardinals* 164: You said more'n a mouthful, Frank.

mouth off *v.* to speak impertinently or out of turn; boast or complain loudly; *shoot (one's) mouth off* s.v. MOUTH. Hence (*rare*) **mouthoff,** *n.*

    1958 J. Davis *College Vocab.* 14: *Mouth off*—Talk about something which is none of your business. **1961** J. Flynn *Action Man* 95: You finished mouthing off? **1965** (quot. at BELGIQUE). **1964–66** R. Stone *Hall of Mirrors* 196: You're a drunk, you're cowardly, you're a mouthoff. **1966** H.S. Thompson *Hell's Angels* 64: Someone'd mouth off or try to move in on our chicks and then we'd fight. **1966** Derrig *Pride of Green Berets* 114: Then some dumb bastard there mouthed off about it to one of the Vietnamese high brass. **1968** Baker et al. *CUSS* 159: *Mouth off.* Make uncomplimentary remarks about someone. **1969** Linn & Pearl *Masque of Honor* 23: I'm sorry, pop....I'm always mouthing off, ask ma. **1969** *Playboy* (Dec.) 304: Don't go mouthing off, man. **1969** Whittemore *Cop!* I 93: You know, you go up on these family fights, and you hear this broad mouthing off: "He's beatin' on me, beatin' on me, and if you don't get that man outa here he's gonna be dead, blah, blah, blah." **1970** Woodfield *San Fran. International* (film): Stop mouthin' off. **1970** in *Rolling Stone Interviews* 398: I guess it didn't do a hell of a lot of good for me to mouth off. **1970** Rudensky & Riley *Gonif* 121: Hey, you Heebs wouldn't be mouthing off if Adolph were here! **1977** *Rolling Stone* (Dec. 27) 53: Mouthing off to a member of the Houston police force goes beyond macho. It's loco. **1990** *National Review* (Apr. 16) 26: Americans like to mouth off about the Japanese. **1995** *X-Files* (Fox-TV): At first...I just thought he was mouthing off.

mouth organ *n.* a spokesman; (*also*) the tongue. *Joc.*

    1881 Nye *Western Humor* 13: Secretary Spates, the silver-tongued orator and gilt-edged mouth organ of Wyoming. **1926** Maines & Grant *Wise-Crack Dict.* 11: *Mouth organ*—the tongue.

mouthpiece *n.* **1.a.** a spokesman. Orig. *S.E.*

    ****1805** R. Southey, in *OED2:* They look'd Toward their chief and mouth-piece, the High Priest Tezozomoc. ****1818** in *OED2.* **1865** *Nat. Police Gaz.* (Oct. 7). **1874** "A." *Sheaf of Papers* 88: Moses was but his representative and mouth-piece. **1880** in M. Lewis *Mining Frontier* 128: The boss mouthpiece of the heavenly will has gone done to Denver [*sic*], an' Bill is a goin' to stand in an' sling gospel for the boys as well as he can. **1904** (quot. at (b), below). **1930** Lavine *Third Degree* 98: Each tong has an official "mouthpiece" known as a secretary. **1949** *Time* (Dec. 5) 69: Dr. Morris Fishbein, long the big mouthpiece of the American Medical Association and self-appointed spokesman of organized U.S. medicine. **1978** *Vancouver* (Br. Columbia) *Sun* (July 22) A2: He is only fulfilling his elected union position as "mouthpiece"...for the rank and file in expressing their concerns. **1987** *Wkly. World News* (Sept. 15) 13: "I've heard the stories...," said the singer's mouthpiece.

    b. *Und.* a lawyer, esp. a criminal defense attorney.

    ****1857** "Ducange Anglicus" *Vulgar Tongue* 13: Mouthpiece, n. Counsel. Gen[eral use]. **1866** *Nat. Police Gaz.* (Apr. 21) 3: "Cops" have to be bought, and "mouth-pieces" paid. **1868** *Detective's Manual* 181: As soon as the two merchants were locked up, a "mouth piece," was put on them. **1871** Banka *Pris. Life* 493: Lawyer,...Mouth-piece. **1902** Hapgood *Thief* 38 [ref. to *ca*1880]: If a thief has not enough money to hire a "mouth-piece" (criminal lawyer) he is in a bad way. **1904** *Life in Sing Sing* 256: Mouthpiece. Spokesman; a lawyer. *a***1909** Tillotson *Detective* 93: Mouthpiece—A lawyer. **1913** *Sat. Eve. Post* (Jan. 4) 25: They...tell me to hire Gilbert Easterbrook as a mouthpiece. **1916** Scott *17 Yrs.* 74: The proceeds...were to go to procure a "mouthpiece" (a lawyer). **1927** (quot. at (2), below). **1928** *New Yorker* (Dec. 8) 58: I slip some mouthpiece a few grand to get out. **1929** E. Booth *Stealing* 216: I've give the "mouthpiece" all I could get for the "heaps"—and I've sent Dan's aunt about a thousand. **1936** Markey & Conselman *Private Number* (film): Sam Stapp, the mouthpiece. **1937** H. Gray *Arf* (unp.): But he ain't talkin' except to holler fer a mouthpiece, to git him out. **1942** "E. Queen" *Calamity Town* 174: Where's my mouthpiece? **1951** Yordan & Wyler *Detective Story* (film): There's a mouthpiece by the name of Simms outside. **1953** W. Brown *Monkey on My Back* 68: Who the hell are you? Another f—— mouthpiece? **1969** *Daredevil* (Dec.) 11: I hear he got himself a hotshot mouthpiece! **1977** Bunker *Animal Factory* 15: Fuckin' mouthpieces are lyin' bastards. **1986** Philbin *Under Cover* 178: My uncle, he a mouthpiece.

    2. an informer.

    1900 Willard & Hodler *Powers That Prey* 40: I'm a bad lot if you like, but I wouldn't turn mouthpiece for the whole five thousand. **1927** *DN* V 456: *Mouth piece*, n. (1) A stool pigeon. (2) a criminal lawyer.

    3. the mouth.

1919 in Horowitz *Campus Life* 122: Cultivate no hair on your mouth-pieces. **1949** Mende *Spit & Stars* 73: You have *some* mouthpiece, kid.

mouthy *adj.* voluble; impertinent; talkative. Now *colloq.*

1942 *ATS* 221: Talkative....*mouthy*. **1952** *Sat. Eve. Post* (July 5) 102: The kid was pretty mouthy. *****1963** in *OEDS*: Too free you have been...with your talk....Too mouthy all of you. **1971** Torres *Sting Like a Bee* 96: But that Cassius...was kinda mouthy. He was a wise know-it-all. **1977** "Dear Abby" (synd. column), in *L.A. Times* (May 4) II 2: At this point she got hot and mouthy. I calmly informed her that what she did was against the law. **1986** Heinemann *Paco's Story* 4: A distinct but mouthy minority.

move *n.* **1.a.** a trick; maneuver; stratagem; (*pl.*) *Sports.* ability to move quickly or skillfully. Also (*obs.*) in phr. **move on the board**. [*OED2* does not distinguish this sense from the S.E. sense 'an action toward an objective or goal; step'.]

*****1812** Vaux *Vocab.*: *Move*: any action or operation in life; the secret spring by which any project is conducted, as, There is a *move* in that business which you are not *down* to. To be *flash to every move upon the board*, is to have a general knowledge of the world, and all its numerous deceptions. **1840** *Crockett Almanac 1841* 10: Bill...was up to as many moves as a minnit watch. **1841** [Mercier] *Man-of-War* xvi: They wanted the *shore folks* to see a few of the *moves* on board a Yankee Frigate. Ibid. 168: There's a *move on the board*, I tell you. Joe has scented rum somewhere. *****1844** C. Dickens *Christmas Carol*, in *OED*: Gentlemen of the free-and-easy sort, who plume themselves upon being acquainted with a move or two. **1851** [G. Thompson] *Jack Harold* 60: I was down upon his move. *a***1868** N.H. Bishop *Across So. Amer.* 19: This Jim was the red-shirted sailor who had promised to instruct me in all the "moves" of an experienced salt. *****1889–90** Barrère & Leland *Dict. Slang*: *Move*...a cunning trick or device. **1970** Cassavetes *Husbands* (film): I was gonna be a basketball player. I had all the moves. **1976** "N. Ross" *Policeman* 168: I could feel things tightening up. So I decided to stop making the moves for a while. I became, for the moment, an honest cop. **1983** (quot. at **(c)**, below).

b. *pl.* knowledge or savoir-faire; ability to ingratiate oneself with or take advantage of others; cynical expertise; often in phr. **have [all] the moves.**

1966 *IUFA Folk Speech* (Dec. 13): He's got all the moves: a person who knows how to act. **1966** J. Hunt *Bobby Hull* 20: He was only fifteen then but he had the moves and savvy of an eighteen-year-old. **1974** G.V. Higgins *Cogan's Trade* 6: He's a prick but he's got all the moves. **1974** in Mamet *Sexual Perversity* 17: Danny. You think she was a pro? Bernie....She knew all the pro moves. **1982** in Horwitt *Call Me Rebel* 393: Mr. Charm, I mean Mr. Lovable, I mean he had all the moves, he was marvelous! **1982** Hayano *Poker Faces* 48: One [poker player] was said to have "more moves than a belly dancer." *a***1987** Bunch & Cole *Reckoning for Kings* 388: For a honkie, he ain't got no moves, but he's tryin' to get some.

c. usu. *pl.* a trick or method of the kind used by a seducer; esp. in phr. **put the moves on** to make sexual advances toward.

1968 Baker et al. *CUSS* 127: *Good moves*, a sexually expert male. **1969** *Current Slang I & II* 62: *Moves*, n. Dating maneuvers.—Air Force Academy cadets. **1970** Landy *Underground Dict.* 157: *Put the moves on*...Flirt with; try to have a sexual relation with. **1974** R. Price *Wanderers* 37 [ref. to 1960's]: I picked her up in Manny's last night. You know, just put the old moves on. **1976** P. Conroy *Santini* 296: We were parking at the old beach and I was puttin' my best moves on her. **1977** *Rolling Stone* (Aug. 25) 36: She claims that few men in the music business have ever seriously tried to put moves on her. **1980** *L.A. Times Book Rev.* (Dec. 7) 15: Clark...is putting moves on Whitmore's assistant Jenny. **1983** L. Frank *Hardball* 52: I've seen better moves [*i.e.,* baseball technique] in a drive-in! [or]...in a cheap hotel!; or "...in an orgy!" **1984** Ehrhart *Marking Time* 66: You're the one that put the moves on me, remember? You're the one wanted to get married! **1989** Ramis & Aykroyd *Ghostbusters II* (film): Don't put any of those cheap moves on me. **1992** *Donahue* (NBC-TV): I got romantic and put the moves on her. *a***1994** A. Radakovich *Wild Girls Club* 16: He continues his smooth moves by asking if we "want to take a look" at the bedroom. **1995** *Jenny Jones Show* (synd. TV series): "Did she put the moves on you?" "She asked me if I wanted oral sex." **1995** *Seinfeld* (NBC-TV): "I can't believe it! He stole my move!"... "Yeah, but I *like* the move."

d. the proper thing to do; something interesting or exciting.—constr. with *the*.

1986 N.Y.C. public service ad.: School's the Move! **1993** in Stavsky, Mozeson & Mozeson *A 2 Z*: Me and Evil was always doin' parties, that was always *the move* for us. **1995** Stavsky, Mozeson & Mozeson *A 2 Z*: *Move*...what's current, happening or the best thing to do.

3. a movie.

1912 in *Amer. Heritage* (Oct. 1976) 93: The moving picture show....It is commonly called "The Movies," or the "Moves." *****a***1970** Partridge *DSUE* (ed. 7) 1283: *Move*...A motion picture: since ca. 1935.

¶ In phrases:

¶ **bust a move** see s.v. BUST, *v.*

¶ **get a move on (one)** [or **(oneself)** or **it**] to bestir oneself; depart, esp. quickly; hasten. Now *colloq.*

1888 in *AS* XXXVII (1962) 76: Get a move on you. **1893** in *DAE*: Now is the time for the mover of dead animals to "get a move on himself." **1895** Foote *Coeur D'Alene* 234: Get a move on you! Shake it up, man! **1905** Sinclair *Jungle* 64: Get a move on you! **1896** in *DAE*: The political campaign seems...to be somewhat slower than usual in "getting a move on." **1906** in McCay *Little Nemo* 76: I've got to get a move on me or they'll get away. **1923** in *DAE*: With a further recommendation to get a move on! **1968** Baker et al. *CUSS* 159: *Move on it, get a.* Leave a place.

¶ **make a move** to act decisively, suddenly, or underhandedly.

1951 E. Arcaro, in Woods *Horse-Racing* 41: Any time, Eddie, you make a move on this colt, he'll give you an eighth of a mile in eleven seconds....As I was getting through at the top of the stretch, Dauber was making his move also. **1987** "J. Hawkins" *Tunnel Warriors* 223: Victor Charlie's makin' his move!

move *v.* **1.** to sell or dispose of for pay, esp. in quantity.

1938 in *OEDS*: A drastic tax on chain stores has been defeated in a referendum in California, where the function of the chains in "moving" citrus fruit surpluses is now more fully appreciated. **1954–60** *DAS*: *Move*...To sell merchandise; to dispose of a stock of merchandise by selling it....To transport or sell contraband or stolen goods. **1983** *Time* (July 18) 60: David Bowie's *Let's Dance* has moved 1 million in just three months. **1986** *Miami Vice* (NBC-TV): Any idea who's movin' [this heroin]?

2. (see quot.).

1988 *Newsday Mag.* (N.Y.) (Aug. 7) 21: Hell, I've had people moved (murdered) for less than this.

move back *v.* to cost; SET BACK.

1935 D. Runyon, in *DAS*: Fur coats, including a chinchilla flogger that moves [him] back thirty G's.

movement *n.* provocative movements of a woman's hips.—constr. with preceding modif., usu. alluding to the movement assembly of a timepiece.

1928 R. Fisher *Jericho* 150: It's that ball-bearin' movement, thass what. **1952** H. Grey *Hoods* 114: I was thinking of one of the redheads in Peggy's joint, the one with the wondrous Elgin movement. **1960** Carpenter *Youngest Harlot* 10: In bed you got Swiss movements.

mover *n.* **1.a.** one who is socially adept, esp. with women.

1959 Maier *College Terms* 3: *Mover*—a [socially] fast guy. **1961** Kohner *Gidget Goes Hawaiian* 29: They have a reputation of being...great *movers* with the ladies. **1968** *Everett* (Wash.) *Herald* (Mar. 27) 5: *Mover*...a swinger; as in "I was surprised he is such a mover." **1968** Baker et al. *CUSS* 159: *Mover.* A socially adept person. **1969** *Current Slang I & II* 62: *Mover*, n. Male reputed to be sexually aggressive.—College females, South Dakota, New York; Air Force Academy cadets. Ibid.: *Movers*, n. Cadets who make it with girls.—Air Force Academy cadets. *****1990** T. Thorne *Dict. Contemp. Slang*: *Mover*...a sexually enthusiastic person....anyone or anything considered dynamic, successful, extrovert or fast.

b. a successful person.

1977 Caron *Go-Boy* 263: *Mover*—somebody that is ambitious. **1983** Breathed *Bloom Co.* 82: You must be one smooth mover. Who else would own such a fine car? *****1990** (quot. at **(a)**, above).

2. *Mil.* a moving vehicle.

*a***1991** Kross *Splash One* 237 [ref. to Vietnam War]: All we got to do tonight is beat up on some hapless movers around Tchepone.

movie *n.* **1.** a moving picture. Now *S.E.*

1902 Jarrold *Mickey Finn* (ad on rev. title): After the Movies "Murine" Your Eyes. **1912** in *OEDS*: "Movies" and the law. **1934** Weseen *Dict. Sl.* 146: *Movie*—A motion picture.

2. a tedious, repetitive, or distasteful situation or succession of events.

    1969 Mitchell *Thumb Tripping* 190: Wait, haven't we seen this movie before? **1970** W.C. Woods *Killing Zone* 62: Anyway, haven't we been through this movie before? **1972** N.Y.U. student: But this is a whole new movie. **1981** P. Sann *Trial* 166: That had the smell of a frame because the cops didn't like him from another movie. **1985** *Miami Vice* (NBC-TV): Look, I'm sick of this whole *movie*. **1987** *Tour of Duty* (CBS-TV): I'm not gonna like this movie! **1989** R. Miller *Profane Men* 143: Shit, I hate this fucking movie. **1992** *Donahue* (NBC-TV): They've seen this movie too many times. **1996** *Good Morning America* (ABC-TV) (Aug. 13): Kemp was in that movie already.

3. *pl.* prison.—constr. with *the. Joc.*

    1974 Dubinsky & Standora *Decoy Cop* 66: "That little number is going to send you to the movies for a long time."...Movies is street talk for jail.

movie brat *n. Entertainment Industry.* a son or daughter of a film star, producer, director, etc. Cf. ARMY BRAT; BRAT, 1.

    1984 *Rod Serling's TZ Mag.* (Oct.) 40: Raffill enjoys taking an oblique swipe at the generation of directors often referred to as "movie brats."

mow *v.* to copulate with; copulate. [The 1859 def. is almost certainly in error, even for its time and place.]

    a*1554** Sir D. Lyndsay, in *F & H* IV 368: Quod scho, Will Leno mowit me. *****1669** *New Acad. of Complements* 245: Oh! *Jenny* daintily could mow,/But what's that to you? *Ibid.* 257: *Bonny Kate, Bonny Kate,* lay thy leg o'er me,/Thou bee'st a bonny Lass, fain would I mow thee. **1744** in *AS* (1967) XLII 217: Mr. Hogg...spoke a good neat bawdy before his wife who did not seem much surprised at it. He told me that a good mowing was a cure for such complaints....It is an inexcusable piece of rudeness and rusticity in the company of women to speak in this manner. *****1796** Grose *Dict. Vulgar Tongue* (ed. 3): *To Mow.* A Scotch word for the act of copulation. **1859** Matsell *Vocab.* 57: *Mow.* To kiss. "The man was mowing the molly," the man was kissing the girl.

moxie¹ *n.* [prob. alter. MOKE] a black person.—usu. considered offensive.

    1875 in Foner *U.S. Soldier* 135: I am thinking seriously of the 10th Cav. as my stopping place. You know they are all moxies which creates a great prejudice against them here.

moxie² *n.* [arbitrary application of *Moxie*, trademark name for a kind of soft drink marketed esp. in New England] **1.a.** competitive or courageous spirit; aggressiveness; tenacity; GUTS, 5.a.

    [**1908** *Atlantic* (Aug.) 222: [At a baseball game] Upon the ear fall raucous cries: "Hot roasted peanuts, five a bag," "Ice-cold moxie [*sic*]," "Fresh pop-corn"—uttered by savage brats in white coats and white caps.] **1930** D. Runyon, in *Collier's* (Jan. 20) 13: I always figure Louie is a petty-larceny kind of guy, with no more moxie than a canary bird. **1935** Saunders *Std. Equipment* 128: He's got a lot of moxie for a kid. I couldn't have handled him by myself. **1939** Appel *Power-House* 271: But then again, you never could tell who had the moxie. **1939–40** Tunis *Kid from Tomkinsville* 165: Has nothing but...a bucketful of moxie. **1942** Liebling *Telephone* 98: He had plenty of moxie, but...if the flesh is weak, the spirit don't mean a thing. **1943** M. Shulman *Barefoot Boy* 158: We knew you had the old moxie, the old get out and get. **1943** in Ruhm *Detective* 366: Then the moxie goes out of him. **1946** J.H. Burns *Gallery* 132: I know...how to hold my moxie. **1954** R. Davis *Marine at War* 10: See if you can get some moxie into your buddy there. He looks like he's ready to quit. **1960** Barber *Minsky's* 166: All it needed was a little more zip, pep and moxie. **1962** *Sat. Eve. Post* (Apr. 28) 30: Their job requires a great deal of courage, a lot of moxie. **1969** Pharr *Numbers* 201: But Jim didn't have the moxie or the brains. **1965–70** in *Qly. Jour. Studies on Alcohol* XXXII (1971) 734: *Moxie* Courage, usually obtained after a number of [alcoholic] drinks. **1971** H. Roberts *Third Ear: Moxey*...nerve; daring...e.g. He had the *moxey* to demand more money from the boss. **1966–80** McAleer & Dickson *Unit Pride* 196: Can you imagine the moxie that Audie Murphy must've had? **1993** *TV Guide* (June 26) 29: Ron has moxie. **1995** *Simpsons Comics* (No. 9) (unp.): I like you, pal. You've got *moxie*.

    b. impudence; effrontery; GUTS, 6.

1942 *ATS* 332: Impudence; audacity....*moxie*, nerve. **1942–49** Goldin et al. *DAUL* 142: *Moxie*...Effrontery; gall. "That crumb is got some moxie! After lousing Slim up (slandering him), now he's hanging out with the ghee (fellow)." **1984** D. Smith *Steely Blue* 41: Get out of here....you got a lot of moxie.

    2. know-how; SAVVY.

    1934 Weseen *Dict. Slang* 215: *Moxie*—Ability and skill as a baseball player. **1942** *ATS* 651: *Moxie*, skill as a baseball player. **1952** *Sat. Eve. Post* (Apr. 5) 21: Bill sneaked into the Navy when he was fifteen and never got beyond the ninth grade....He's not one of these spoiled-rich brats. He's got moxie. **1972** W.C. Anderson *Hurricane* 107: They're not infallible....But they've got about as much weather moxie as anybody in the business. **1975** in Thom *Letters to Ms.* 66: She proceeded to use her "moxie" to set standards for...the school system. **1995** *Early Prime* (CNN-TV) (May 13): Does Congress have the moxie to balance the budget?

    3. *Black E.* (see 1970 quot.).

    1966 I. Reed *Pall-Bearers* 84: How did a handicapped mind like yours ever get into judicial robes anyway, you weird-looking little moxy? **1970** Landy *Underground Dict.: Moxie*...Loud-mouth; "wise ass."

mox nix *interj.* [< G *machts nichts* 'it makes no difference'] *Army.* **1.** (used as an expression of indifference).

    1955 McGovern *Fräulein* 196 [ref. to ca.1947]: Mox nix....I'm a music lover. **1956** *AS* XXXI 142: *Mox nix*...means "I don't care" or "it doesn't matter." The expression's terse form and end alliteration make it an active tool in the hands of the GI. **1967** *DAS* (Supp.): *Mox nix* It doesn't matter; it doesn't make any difference; it's not important. **1970** Gattzden *Black Vendetta* 92: Mox nix, he's cleared. **1972** Ponicsan *Cinderella Liberty* 61: Mox nix to Baggs. **1975** S.P. Smith *Amer. Boys* 131: Mox nix to me. I'll go. What the fuck, sir. **1981–89** R. Atkinson *Long Gray Line* 373: The soldiers often expressed their indifference with the phrase "mox nix."

    2. inconsequential; of no interest or account. Also as adj.

    1967 Moorse *Duck* 74: He could not get over the insult of being "mox nix" in a dreary Bavarian Kaserne. **1976** Former lt., 11th ACR, age *ca*28: Then come all the mox nix bullshit organizations.

M.P. *n.* a member of a metropolitan police force.

    *ca*1849 in Jackson *Early Songs of Uncle Sam* 58: But I was bound to blaze, the M.P.'s were all amaze,/All owned up I was one of the boys. **1866** Williams *Gay Life in N.Y.* 14: As...there was no proof he was a going to steal it, the M.P. let him go. **1866** (quot. at OFFICE). **1899** Hamblen *Bucko Mate* 25: M.P.! M.P.! Look out for the M.P.'s!

Mr. [entries beginning with "Mr." are alphabetized under MISTER.]

M.R.S. degree *n.* [pun on *M.S.* ('Master of Science') degree and *Mrs.*] *Stu.* (see quots.). *Joc.* Also **M.R.S.**

    1974 Syracuse Univ. student: If a girl goes to college just to get married, she's *studying for her M.R.S.* **1979** Univ. Tenn. grad. student: Half the girls are just going for their M.R.S. **1983** *Los Angeles* (Dec.) 282: He was going to work in his father's law firm, and she dated him all through college. Graduated with her M.R.S. and they moved right into Hancock Park. **1984** Mason & Rheingold *Slanguage: M.r.s. degree*...Women who go to college to get married. **1996** M.I.T. student, age 20 (coll. J. Sheidlower): When women are obviously in school just to meet guys, you say they're there for an M.R.S. degree—like women majoring in humanities at M.I.T.

Mrs. Goff *n. Stu.* a woman.

    1819 Peirce *Rebelliad* 21: But cease the touching chords to sweep,/For Mrs. Goff has deign'd to weep. **1851** B. Hall *College Wds.* 211: *Mrs. Goff.* Formerly a cant phrase for any woman.

Mrs. Hobby's Wacs' Works *n.* Fort Des Moines, Iowa. *Joc.*

    1944 *N.Y. Times Mag.* (Sept. 17) 32: *Mrs. Hobby's Wacs Works.* Fort Des Moines (Iowa) Wac training center.

Mrs. Jones *n.* a privy.

    *****1855** in *DARE*: Johnny....A jakes....Also called Mrs Jones by country people. **1898** Green *Va. Folk-Speech* 205: *Jones, n.* Go to see *Mrs. Jones*, going to the privy. Used in the country. *****1936** Partridge *DSUE* 538: *Mrs. Jones.* A water closet. **1942** *ATS* 87: Toilet...Mrs. Jones. **1960, 1965–70** in *DARE*.

M.T. *n.* [pun on *empty*] empty; (*hence*) something that is empty of contents. *Joc.* Also as adj.

    1854 *Fourth* 8: Another M.T. [*sc.,* an empty bottle] overboard. **1859**

Matsell *Vocab.* 57: *MT.* Empty. "The bloke's leather was MT," the man's pocket-book had nothing in it—was empty. *1889–90 Barrère & Leland *Dict. Slang*: M.T. (railway), an empty carriage. *a1890–96 *F & H* IV 370: M.T....1. Empties, or empty [railway] carriages....2. (common).—an empty bottle. 1942 *ATS* 26: Empty. *Cold, full of emptiness, M.T.* 1996 Knoxville, Tenn., film electrician, age *ca*41: I label [floppy] disks I've erased and I can reuse "M.T."

much *interj.* not likely; certainly not.—used ironically.
    *1598 Shakespeare *2 Henry IV*, in *F & H* IV 370: What with two points on your shoulder? Much! *1599 B. Jonson, in *F & H* IV 370: To charge me bring my grain into the markets. Aye, much! when I have neither barn nor garner. 1848 *Life in Rochester* 67: Maybe he didn't take my advice, and take himself off, *much.* 1944 Johnston & Hoffman *Janie* (film): A quiet, peaceful little town where nothing ever happens—much! *1945 in Partridge *DSUE* (Supp.) 1284: He never goes out with Waafs—much! 1964 Whitehouse *Fledgling* 169: There's no mud—much—and we sleep in decent beds every night. 1990 L. Hampton *Fighting Strength* 19: Nurses don't panic...much! [1995 *My So-Called Life* (ABC-TV): "Try me at Katinsky's later." "Yeah, later. Much!"] 1997 *Good Morning America* (ABC-TV) (Mar. 7): The cat wasn't hurt, not at all. Much.

¶ In phrases:

¶ **not much** certainly not.
    1881 H.H. Kane *Opium* 11: "Do you think the [opium] habit will gradually die out...?" "Not much. It will rapidly increase." 1886 in *OEDS:* "Go home?—explain?" he began, more calmly. "Not much." 1970 N.Y.C. woman, age *ca*80: Do they call that "music"? Not much!

¶ **too much!** Esp. *Black E & Jazz.* (used as an exclamation of wonder or delight).
    1937 in *OEDS:* Man, if you didn't you really missed something. That man's too much! What great bass drum work he shows. 1944 C. Calloway *Hepster's Dictionary* : *Too much:* Term of highest praise. 1955 S. Allen *Bop Fables* 46: I just dug your nose and it's too much. 1964 E. Wilson *Wilson's N.Y.* 27: He's Too Much—He's so good he grabs you right here.

mucho *adj.* [< Sp 'much; many'; 'very'] many; a lot of; a great deal. Also as n.
    [1886 J.G. Bourke *Apache Campaign* II 47, in *OEDAS* I 109: Sing heap; sleep mucho to-night.] 1942 *ATS* 536: Large sum of money....*mucho dinero.* 1958 Frankel *Band of Bros.* 83: I got mucho troubles of my own. 1963 E.M. Miller *Exile* 265: That'll save mucho minutes each way. 1964 R. Kendall *Black School* 145: Gee, Teach, that's swell....Thanks mucho! 1967 in B. Edelman *Dear Amer.* 284: I got mucho goodies out of it. 1968 Baker et al. *CUSS* 160: *Mucho...Muchos* A great deal (of something). 1965–70 J. Carroll in *Paris Rev.* (No. 50) 110: Her old lady owns racehorses. 1984 *Calif. Business* (Sept.) 176: The continuing volatility of money, of [sic] which we have written mucho. *a*1989 R. Herman, Jr. *Warbirds* 55: Mucho thanks. *a*1995 M. Kelly *Proudly* 20: I was making *mucho* money.

mucho *adv.* very; extremely.
    1978 in *OEDAS* I 109: Your magazine is mucho enjoyable. 1992 Bubble Yum TV ad: Long-lastin', mucho blastin' Bubble Yum!

muck[1] *n.* [abbr. MUCKLE] *U.S. Mil. Acad.* muscle; strength. Also as v.
    1900 *Howitzer* (U.S. Mil. Acad.) (No. 1) 120: *Muck.*—Muscle, strength. 1908 *Howitzer* (U.S. Mil. Acad.) (No. 9) 325: *Muck,* n. Herculean strength. 1941 *AS* (Oct.) 167: *Muck.* Muscle (West Point). 1993 G. Lee *Honor & Duty* 85 [ref. to 1960's]: Think you can muck it through West Point? *Ibid.* 420: *Muck:* to strain by main effort at a task.

muck[2] *n.* MUCK-A-MUCK.—constr. with *high* or *big.*
    1906 *DN* III 140: He's the *high muck* of the concern. 1940 in *DAS:* DeWitt had handed him...a cigar. The way some of these big mucks do. 1953 *Sat. Eve. Post* (Apr. 18) 57: Will the high mucks not give you a helpful hint, Doris?

muck[3] *n.* **1.** *Circus.* greasepaint.
    1926 Norwood *Other Side of Circus* 163: In making up, the muck, as it's called, is smeared over the face, ears and neck. 1942 *ATS* 78: *Muck,* grease paint, esp. clown white.
    2. *Av.* heavy clouds; (also) *Mil.* hostile anti-aircraft fire.
    *1940 in *OEDS:* I climbed to 12,000 feet, circling along the outside of the searchlights and all the muck [gunfire] that was coming up. *1945 Partridge *RAF Slang:* Muck (Very) dirty weather. 1945 in *Calif.*

Folk. Qly. V (1946) 380: Anti-aircraft fire is *muck* or *ack-ack,* and *A.A.* batteries *sling muck.*

muck *v.* **1.** *Circus.* to apply greasepaint to.
    1926 Norwood *Other Side of Circus* 164: A student will muck his face clean into his hair.
    2. (euphem. for) FUCK (in fig. applications only). Cf. MUCK UP; FUCK UP. [In orig., prob. sugg. by *mess* (*about*), but the rhyme with FUCK has ultimately given the word the sound of euphem.; see Partridge's full note in *DSUE.* The 1984 ed. of R. Aldington's *Death of a Hero* (London: Hogarth) restores the author's ms. words that were euphemized in 1929 first ed., as cited below fr. *OEDS.*]
    [*a1890–96 *F & H* VI 372: To *muck about*...(coster[mongers' slang]). To fondle; to mess about.] [*1896 R. Kipling, in *OED:* Our Colonel...mucks about in 'orspital.] *1928 in *OEDS:* His art...[is] the one thing a genuine artist won't muck about with. *1929 R. Aldington, in *OEDS:* Spree be mucked—one of you * * fired his rifle and muckin' near copped me. *1936 Partridge *DSUE: Muck!, mucker, mucking,* have from ca. 1915 represented *f**k!*, etc. 1940 Hemingway *For Whom Bell Tolls* 369: You're just mucked....Muck this whole treacherous muck-faced mucking country. 1950 Hemingway *Across River* 58: Now muck off. 1950 in *DAS:* Too many bones mucking about. 1958 T. Capote *Breakfast at Tiffany's* 8: You got to be rich to go mucking around in Africa. 1961 *Time* (Jan. 27) 57: There is one in every outfit—the sniveling, creepy little muckup who not only fails to pull his weight but manages to add it to the load carried by others. 1982 *N.Y. Times* IV E19: Muck around with us and you'll reap the typhoon—unless you have H-bombs, rockets [etc.]. 1990 *Future Watch* (CNN-TV) (Aug. 18): I want to muck with real astrophysics.

muck-a-muck *n.* [Chinook Jargon] [**1.** Esp. *N.W.* food or drink; provisions. Also as v. [Not slang, but the source of (2), below.]
    1838 in *DA* s.v. *high-muck-a-muck:* Eat. mucamuc. 1847 in *DA:* Muck-a-muck, Provisions, eat. 1852 in *DA:* The aborigine "put" for the settlement...for his *muckamuck.* 1868 J.R. Browne *Apache Country* 454: Muck-a-muck, or food. 1880 in *DA:* We should have to come ashore and have some "muck-a-muck." 1915 in *OEDS:* He paid cash for his muckamuck. 1922 P.A. Rollins *Cowboy* 79 [ref. to late 19th C.]: "Muckamuck" (food, or to eat or drink).]
    2. [< Chinook Jargon *hiu muckamuck* 'plenty of food', infl. by *high;* see C.J. Lovell in *AS* (Apr. 1947), p. 91ff.] Orig. *N.W.* an important or self-important person; bigwig; chief.—usu. constr. with *high* or *big.* Also used attrib. Also vars., esp. **muckety-muck.**
    1856 in *DA:* The professors—the high "Muck-a-Mucks"—tried fusion, and produced confusion. 1866 in "M. Twain" *Letters from Hawaii* 32: If I was High-You-Muck-a-Muck and King of Wawhoo. 1869 "M. Twain" *Stories* 20: Noble Red Men, Braves, Grand Sachems, War Chiefs, Squaws, and High Muck-a-Mucks. 1877 in Miller & Snell *Why West Was Wild* 293: I, and only I, am high muck-i-muck. 1884 in Lummis *Letters* 120: Alonzo...must be a sort of High Muck-a-Muck among them. 1886 Lummis *Ft. Bowie* 54: Nachita being the hereditary high muck-a-muck of the Chiricahuas. 1888 in Farmer *Amer.:* A great high muck-a-muck United States senator. 1891 Kirkland *Capt. of Co. K* 259 [ref. to Civil War]: Ain't we pampered autocrats? Reg'lar high mukkemuks. 1892 H. Garland *Spoil of Office* 39: He's the high mucky-muck o' ther shebang. 1899 "J. Flynt" *Tramping* 368: We...went paradin' roun' the hang-out as if we was the high-monkey-monks of ev'rythin'. 1905 *DN* III 62: He was high mucky-muck in the show. 1914 *DN* IV 113: *Squeegee*...A person of importance; muckamuck. 1918 E.E. Rose *Cappy Ricks* 64: He's the hi-yu-muck-amuck who stood in my office...and told me he was going...[to] lick the Blue Star [Line] off the seas! 1927 C. McKay *Harlem* 36: You really spec's me to believe youse been associating with the mucty-mucks of the race? 1928 Hammett *Harvest* 6: Chief muckademuck of the I.W.W. in Personville. 1928 Bodenheim *Georgie May* 19: He's jake with some mighty high mucky-mucks roun' this town. 1932 L. Berg *Pris. Doctor* 105: Sammy has the "fix" in with a big mucky-muck in politics. 1935 *Esquire's Bedroom Companion* 191: I'm the high muckety mucks in Woodbury today. 1940 in *Amer. Jour. Sociol.* XLVIII (1943) 570: "Social Status"...The muck-ti-muck. 1942 Hurston *Dust Tracks* 153: Head muck-de-muck. 1954 L. Armstrong *Satchmo* 213: We all thought you had to be...some kind of a big muckity-muck to play the trumpet. 1956 Metalious *Peyton Place*

187: There's no man calls Lucas Cross a sonofabitch…. Not even a high mucky muck doctor like you. **1958** in C. Beaumont *Best* 68: All the high mucky-mucks from Mars were there. **1954–60** *DAS:* High-muckety-muck. **1966** "Petronius" *N.Y. Unexp.* 34: From interior decorators and midway designers to mucky-mucks. **1975** T. Berger *Sneaky People* 84: I figure all big muckety-mucks smoked El Ropos. **1977** Dunne *Confessions* 47: Though there was some that thought the poor man was in his dotage when he made a boy like yourself such a high monkey-monk. **1977** *Nat. Lampoon* (Aug.) 6: Jimmy Earl [Carter], he's the high muck-a-muck of the United States. *ca***1979** in J.L. Gwaltney *Drylongso* 28: We don't want to have anything to do with their big muckdemucks who are making all these little white people out there behave the way they do. **1980** R. Hogan *Lawman's Choice* 22: A couple of the big muckety-mucks…were in it clear up to their hatbands. **1982** Rucker *57th Kafka* 204: All the great high muck-a-mucks are downstairs hiding in the Situation Room. **1987** Gill & Israel *Mayflower Madam* (CBS-TV): You bust a mucky-muck, you get noticed. *a***1988** D. Smith *Firefighters* 37: Her dad was a big mucky-muck at the Chicago Bridge and Iron Company. **1988** *New Yorker* (Jan. 11) 76: An assistant director who's a shameless…groveller when the high-muck-a-mucks are in the vicinity. **1995** *Calif. vs. Simpson* (Court TV) (Sept. 27): Real muckety-mucks, real big shots in the field of science, forensic science.

mucker *n.* **1.** Esp. *Stu.* **a.** an offensive, dishonorable, or unrefined fellow. Now *rare* in U.S. [In vogue *ca*1895–*ca*1920; after WWI, freq. in BrE as a euphem. for BUGGER or FUCKER, as in 1961, 1968 U.S. quots. below, a nuance that has never been common in U.S. Cf. note in Partridge *DSUE* (ed. 1) p. 539.]

[*****1869** in FitzGerald *Medley* 99: [Suffolk, Eng.:] *Muck.*…"You little muck, you!" was a common call to a tiresome child. So *Mucker.*—Anything worthless—"Only a Mucker!"] *****1891** in *OED:* Don't I know the look on men's faces when they think me a—a "mucker," as they call it out here. **1893** W.K. Post *Harvard* 211: While a low-down mucker goes in to call on the…best girl. **1895** J.L. Williams *Princeton* 181: He wondered how he could have been such a mucker as to think it. **1899** A.H. Lewis *Sandburrs* 92: So I goes an' gets nex' to this mucker an' jollies his game. *Ibid.* 112: D' treat's on me, anyhow, bein' obliged to detain a respect'ble old mucker like you. **1899** Ade *Fables* 49: They were not Muckers; they were Nice Boys. **1905** D. Phillips *Plum Tree* 35: He liked to class himself and me together as "us gentlemen," in contrast to "them muckers." **1906** *Independent* (Nov. 22) 1224: After all it is only a football game and honor and manliness and fair play are better than a string of victories and a "mucker" reputation. **1910** in O. Johnson *Lawrenceville* 215: "Mucker trick!" "Put him out!" **1911** in Spectorsky *College Years* 146: His world of "muckers" and "grinds" and "cads" and "rotten sneaks." **1914** E.R. Burroughs *Mucker* 6: All were muckers, ready to insult the first woman who passed, or pick a quarrel with any stranger who did not appear too burly. **1916** M. Cowley, in Jay *Burke-Cowley Corres.* 32: Their male relatives are awful, true muckers. *a***1927** in F. Shay *Pious Friends* 54: You're a gang of muckers all—/Damn your eyes! **1935** S. Lewis *Can't Happen* 216: A gentleman's blackjack hurts just as much as a mucker's. **1938** H. Miller *Trop. Capricorn* 275: You're a son of a bitch of a mucker if I know what I'm talking about. **1947–48** J.H. Burns *Lucifer* 66: Their speech was the argot of refined muckers. **1952** *N.Y. Times* (Mar. 2) VII 24: Why Fraser, a mucker at some points, should acquire the conscience of a well-fed beadle at another. **1961** Granat *Important Thing* 157: There was just about two squads of the muckers. **1968** C. Victor *Sky Burned* 26: All right, you muckers, now listen to me. **1970** R. Lynes, in *Harper's* (Apr.) 32: Some whose speech was slangy were fiercely correct when it came to opinions about the written word, which suggested that their slang was an affectation, not a natural manner of speech…an example of what has been called "the mucker pose." **1995** in *Reader's Digest* (May 1996) 86 [ref. to 1935]: As a 17-year-old senior at the exclusive Choate School, John [F.] Kennedy organized the "Muckers" club after the…headmaster had railed against some troublemaking students.…He called them "muckers," slang for the local Irish-American ditchdiggers who were a familiar sight around campus.

b. a street urchin; (*also*) a young man of a college town who does not attend college.

1893 W.K. Post *Harvard* 75: Four small boys (the occasionally useful Harvard muckers). **1895** Wood *Yale Yarns* 273: Paige…advised Little Jack not to monkey with the townies down on Church Street or the muckers would "push in his little mug." **1895** *DN* I 399: *Muckers,* street

Arabs…in Harvard slang. **1895** J.L. Williams *Princeton* 8: So did the sporting gentlemen of the town, and even the little muckers cheered shrilly for their favorite class. **1915** [Swartwood] *Choice Slang* 88: *Mucker*…A youthful inhabitant of the vicinity not belonging to the college.

2. Esp. *Mining.* a manual laborer, esp. a shoveler; (*hence*) *Stu.* a mining student. (*obs.*).

1899 in *OEDS:* [The] Company…paid $3 for miners and $2.50 for "muckers" or underground laborers. **1902** K. Harriman *Ann Arbor Tales* 227: They're muckers; farm-hands; easiest sort o' pickin'! **1907** *Army & Navy Life* (Aug.) 169: I remember one man who, in civil life, had worked for years as a "mucker" in a mine. **1908** W.G. Davenport *Butte & Montana* 137: A "mucker" in the mines. **1912** Siringo *Cowboy Detective* 191 [ref. to 1890's]: They made a demand…that "muckers" and common roustabouts receive $3.50 per day. **1918** *DN* V 26: *Mucker,* n. 1. A student of mining. 2. A man with a shovel in the mines. **1922** N. Anderson *Hobo* 93: A "mucker" or a "shovel stiff" is a man who does manual labor on construction jobs. **1927** *DN* V 456: *Mucker,* n. A shovel man. **1929** *AS* IV (June) 342: *Mucker.* A shoveler. **1960** MacCuish *Do Not Go Gentle* 60: I'm head nipper and mucker on the thirty-six hundred. **1969** J. Hunter *Death in Mtn.* 22: What are you? Drill master? Powder man? Mucker? **1995** (quot. at **(1.a.)**, above).

mucket *n.* [orig. unkn.] a hairpiece.

1953 *Sat. Eve. Post* (Mar. 14) 41: It's generally known that for screen purposes I wear a device the trade calls a "scalp doily," "a mucket" or "a divot.".…Donning a mucket. Not that it's such a chore to put on, but the glue in it makes my forehead itch. **1954–60** *DAS: Mucket*…A toupee. [**1975** Legman *No Laughing Matter* 459: In modern times, the terms "merkin" or "mugget" refer usually to artificial vulvas for masturbation by men.]

muckety-muck var. MUCK-A-MUCK.

muckhole *n.* the anus; (*also*) a detestable place; SHITHOLE.—usu. considered vulgar.

1929–30 Dos Passos *42d Parallel* 146: I might have known there wouldn't be a woman in this muckhole with a human spark in her. **1934** "J.M. Hall" *Anecdota* 23: Now you wants to fuck up me muck hole.

muckle *n.* muscle.

1862 (cited in P. Dickson *Baseball Dict.*). **1883–84** Whittaker *L. Locke* 184: Well, I hear tell how you're some on the muckle.

mucklehead *n.* MUSCLEHEAD.

1936 Kromer *Waiting* 168: That…mucklehead Johnson.

muck out *v.* to clear manure from (a barn or stall). Now *colloq.* or *S.E.*

1851 in *OED:* He would not half muck his stables out, for he said he wanted his horses to lay warm. **1973** Haney *Jock* 28: I can muck out a stall, but I don't know how to clean house. **1978** T. Berger *Arthur Rex* 96: He ordered…the churls…to muck out the great cage. **1979** Gutcheon *New Girls* 231: You'd have to muck out all the stalls in the lower barn every day. **1988** Shoemaker & Nagler *Shoemaker* 23: Somebody to muck out a stall.

muck stick *n.* Esp. *West.* a shovel.

1908 in Butterfield *Post Treasury* 92: Get me another "muck stick." **1918** *DN* V 26: *Muck-stick,* n. A shovel. **1919** Wilkins *Co. Fund* 15: When they handed you that muck-stick they tell us you were pretty anxious to end the war. **1926** *AS* (Dec.) 652: *Muck-stick.* Longhandled shovel. **1937** in J.P. Cannon *Notebook* 116: Like a natural-born muck-stick artist. **1938** Steinbeck *Grapes of Wrath* 327: We got here a first-grade muckstick man. **1942** *Calif. Folk. Qly.* I 228: He contemptuously reminds "Okies," "Native Sons," and "farmers" of their inferior position behind the "muck stick." **1978** L'Amour *Proving Trail* 74: Folks who…swing a muck stick…don't have much use for late hours.

mucksuck *v.* to act in a disgusting manner. Hence **mucksucker,** *n.*

1960–69 Runkel *Law* 140: All the mucksuckin' goin' on in my house for as long as I can remember. **1984** Glick *Winters Coming* 327: Every mucksucker but *us* made a buck off it.

muck up *v.* to botch; spoil; ruin. [In 20th C., often taken as euphem. for FUCK UP; cf. MUCK.]

*****1886** (cited in Partridge *DSUE*). *****1922** in *OEDS:* You seem to have pretty well mucked it up. **1938** (quot. at PUSS). **1949** *Sat. Eve. Post* (Oct. 8) 125: That does make it bad, doesn't it? Makes a pair of us mucking things up. **1951** *N.Y. Times* (July 22) I 11: The Iranians had always done something to "muck things up." **1954–60** *DAS: Muck* *up…* = *fuck up*, a euphem. **1967–68** von Hoffman *Parents Warned Us* 91: We need the tourists even if they may have mucked up the Haight. **1968** C. Victor *Sky Burned* 44: The squad would probably muck up the mission on top of it. **1982** *N.Y. Times* (Mar. 25) D2: You mucked it all up, gang. **1984** Ehrhart *Marking Time* 3: We're certainly managing to muck things up in a hurry. **1987** Mamet *House of Games* (film): You're mucking up my timing. **1988** *Newsday* (N.Y.) (June 20) II 6: By the mid-70's, Thompson…had already mucked things up nicely. **1994** *New Republic* (Nov. 28) 56: Francis Ford Coppola…has been mucking up his own career lately. **1996** *Dr. Katz* (Comedy Central TV): Dad, please. Don't muck it up with conversation!

mud *n.* **1.a.** coffee.
   1875 Sheppard *Love Afloat* 209: He…was bearing a cup of "Navy mud," *alias* coffee, according to the custom of the service in morning watches. **1900** Wister *Jimmyjohn* 40: "What's that mud?" he demanded. "Coffee," said Sam politely. **1918** in *Pirate Piece* (Sept. 1925) 4: Two slices bread, two pieces (small) bacon and weak coffee (mud) for a he-man breakfast. **1919** Jacobsen *Blue & Gray* 16 [ref. to WWI]: After a delicious "canned willie" supper with a cup of "mud" on the side. **1920** Simmons *20th Engrs.* (unp.) [ref. to WWI]: A hunk of punk, and, steaming to tell,/A mug of mud. **1922** *Leatherneck* (Apr. 29) 5: *Mud*—Coffee. **1925** Mullin *Scholar Tramp* 34 [ref. to ca1912]: I received punk (bread) and a cup of mud (black coffee). **1926** Finerty *Criminalese* 12: *Cup o' mud*—Coffee. **1927** (quot. at SINKER). **1948** Maresca *My Flag* 127: Leave that cup of mud…and come right out. **1954** *I Love Lucy* (CBS-TV): Cup a mud, comin' up. **1961** L.E. Young *Virgin Fleet* 21: You'll have to come into the casemates to drink your mud. **1974** Miami Univ. student: How 'bout a cup of mud? **1977** M. Franklin *Last of Cowboys* 90: Kelly, you want some more mud? **1978** Diehl *Sharky's Machine* 69: You want some mud? It's strong enough to play fullback for the Falcons. **1986** S. Bauer *Amazing Stories* 223: Gimme a cup of that mud, will ya? **1989** *Dream Street* (NBC-TV): Throw me a cup a mud, Andy!

   b. cocoa.
   1944 (quot. at BLOOD, 4).

   2. opium, esp. raw opium.
   1915 Howard *God's Man* 355: I was showing the sucker here what would happen if any…guy got it into his head to try an' stop us from landing our black mud from our little ship-ahoy! **1922** Murphy *Black Candle* 113: Opium ready for smoking is usually about the consistency of black molasses or tar. Pedlars call it "mud" but the Chinese name for the mixture is *pen yang*. **1922** *DN* V 182: Opium…*Mud*—Obviously so-named from the color and consistency of the drug. Very common [in Calif.]. **1924** Henderson *Keys to Crookdom* 411: *Mud*. Smoking opium. **1924** in D. Hammett *Continental Op* 56: He went up against his mud pipe regularly. **1925** *Collier's* (Aug. 8) 39: Opium is "mud." **1936** Dai *Opium Add.* 197: Brick gum. Raw opium. Also called *leaf gum* or *mud*. **1936** (quot. at TAR). **1936** *AS* (Apr.) 124: *Mud*. Opium before it is rolled into pills for smoking. **1949** *Sat. Eve. Post* (June 18) 70: Raw opium…Brown lumps of it, wrapped in the leaf of the poppy. I've handled a deal of the stuff. Mud, it's called in the trade. **1968–70** *Current Slang III & IV* 85: *Mud*, n. Opium. (Drug users' jargon)—Watts. **1980** in Courtwright et al. *Addicts Who Survived* 87 [ref. to 1930's]: You take your *yen-hok* and dip down into the mud.

   3. chocolate pudding.
   1918 in *AS* (Oct. 1933) 30: [Ft. Leavenworth:] *Mud*. Chocolate pudding.

   4. *Constr.* cement or mortar.
   1918 in Acker *Thru the War* 63: He had his coat off and was slinging "mud" in great shape. **1956** in *DAS*: Bricklayers…call for *mud*—mortar or cement. *a*1981 H.A. Applebaum *Royal Blue* 24: Masons refer to the mortar used to hold their bricks and blocks as "mud." **1946–92** Westheimer *Sitting It Out* 172: We called cement "mud."

   5. anti-inflammatory salve.
   1923 McKnight *Eng. Words* 45: The drug store contributes:…*mud* for antiphlogistine. The bricklayers…harassed us constantly with cries for mud.

   6. plaster or cheap plaster figurines.
   1935 *Amer. Mercury* (June) 230: *Mud*: plaster figurines. **1942** *ATS* 552: *Mud*, plaster, plaster figurines. **1976** "N. Ross" *Policeman* 33: My brother's a plaster man…whacking that mud all damn day.

   7. *R.R.* coal.
   1942 *Sat. Eve. Post* (June 13) 27: Coal?…"Mud," "slack," or, preferably, "diamonds" is what you mean.

¶ In phrases:

¶ **as mud** *adv.* exceedingly.
   1825 in *JAF* LXXVI (1963) 279: Hee'l git as rich as mud if he keeps on. **1928 in Partridge *DSUE* 503: Joan will be mad as mud with me for telling.

¶ **bring mud** *Black E.* to cause trouble.
   1928 R. Fisher *Jericho* 144: Shine [is]…Bringin' me mud. *Ibid.* 297: *Bring Mud* To fall below expectations, disappoint. He who escorts a homely sheba to a dicty shout brings mud.

¶ **clear as mud** entirely unclear.
   1839 *Spirit of Times* (Mar. 16) 24: It must be as clear as mud to everybody. **1837–40 in *F & H* IV 374: Well, I get her to set down and go over it all ever so slow, and explain it all as clear as mud, and then she says,—Now do you see, Sam, ain't it horrid pretty? **1911** Howard *Enemy to Society* 106: "As clear as mud," commented Kernahan. **1992** G. Wolff *Day at the Beach* 186: All that remained was to follow the *Yachtsman's Guide*.…Clear as mud.

¶ **here's mud in your eye** (used as a joc. toast). Also in elliptical vars.
   1927 Nicholson *Barker* 39: Well, here's mud in your eye. **1929** McEvoy *Hollywood Girl* 148: Mud in your eye! **1929** Paramore & Estabrook *Virginian* (film): Here's mud. **1933** Young & Wylie *Island of Lost Souls* (film): Here's mud in your eye, Doc. **1936** in R.E. Howard *Iron Man* 159: "Well, here's mud in your eye!" I tossed it up with one gulp. **1938–40** W. Clark *Ox-Bow* 11: Here's mud in your eye. *Ibid.* 19: Then he'd toss the drink off in one gulp without looking at anybody or saying a "mud." **1941** J.M. Cain *Mildred Pierce* 130: He took his glass, waited for her to take hers, said "Mud in your eye," and sipped. **1952** Brossard *Darkness* 100: "Here's mud," he said. We drank. **1953** Wicker *Kingpin* 45: Mud in your eye, Fred. **1958** "R. Traver" *Anatomy of a Murder* 26: Here's mud in your eye! **1967** "M.T. Knight" *Terrible Ten* 64: Here's mud in yer eye. **1971** Knopf *Bravos* (film): Here's mud! **1996** *As World Turns* (CBS-TV): And here's mud in your eye!

¶ **hold (one's) mud** Esp. *Black E.* to bear up, keep (one's) composure under adversity; (specif.) *Und.* to refuse to give information under questioning.—used in negative constrs. only.
   1966 Braly *Cold* 93: And the old man here—he'd never hold his mud if anyone came around leaning on him. **1966** in *Trans-action* IV (Apr. 1967) 8: Providing that he can "hold his mud," keep cool, and out of trouble. **1968** Cleaver *Soul on Ice* 152: And when Clay…the Body…becomes Muhammad Ali, the Brain, whitey can't hold his mud! **1968–70** *Current Slang III & IV* 69: Hold your mud, v. To show courage. (Drug users' jargon)—Watts. **1970** *Current Slang V* (Winter) 8: Hold…mud, v. To remain composed; to stay "cool."—College students, both sexes, Minnesota. [**1973** W. Crawford *Stryker* 16: Drop your mud, man. Don't be a fool.…Tell us and get it off your back.] **1980** *Oui* (Aug.) 135: Nobody really gives a shit what you do or how you look, as long as you hold your own mud. **1980** *Easyriders* (May) 48: Try to hold your mud and hang in there. **1985** Ponicsan *Vision Quest* (film): You got problems. You can't hold your mud.

¶ **kick mud** *Prost.* to be a streetwalker. Cf. MUDKICKER.
   1961 C. Cooper *Weed* 122: Baby, I been kickin mud for five years. **1962** in B. Jackson *Swim Like Me* 115: The whores…went back on their own just a steady kickin' mud. **1968** [R. Beck] *Trick Baby* 178: He had a stable of whores kicking mud for him.

¶ **move mud** *Mil. Av.* to crater the ground with bombs or rockets from aircraft. Cf. MUD-MOVER.
   *a*1989 R. Herman, Jr. *Warbirds* 132: He was an expert at "mud moving,"…dropping bombs. **1989** Joss *Strike* 31: Just strapping on an airplane and driving off to move mud, drop bombs on the bad guys.

¶ **mud for (one's) turtle** sexual intercourse (from the man's perspective). *Joc.*
   1983 LaBarge & Holt *Sweetwater Gunslinger* 65: Getting some mud for your turtle…Get laid. **1991** Marcinko & Weisman *Rogue Warrior* 126: I'd like some wine for my men, some hay for my horses, and some mud for my turtle.

¶ **pull** [or **cut**] **mud** to go on foot; plod; march; run. [Early cites ref. to Civil War.]
   1884 in *DAE*: We took up our line of march, or, as Wad Rider expressed it, "began to pull mud." **1887** Johnson & Buel *Battles & Leaders* II 158: With intervals of rest, we "pulled mud" until about 4

o'clock in the afternoon, when we halted near Manassas Junction. **1952** Randolph & Wilson *Down in the Holler* 238: *Cut mud: phr.* To make haste. One of your neighbors said to his small son, "You just *cut mud* for home, afore I take a hickory to you!"

mudcat *n.* **1.** a stupid or contemptible person.
> **1865** in S. Clemens *Twain's Letters* I 323: A scheming, groveling, mud-cat of a *lawyer.* **1882** "M. Twain" *Life on Miss.* 128 [ref. to *ca*1860]: Snatch her! Snatch her! Derndest mud-cat I ever saw! **1948** McIlwaine *Memphis* 203: That damned mud cat, dumb as an ox!

2. a Mississippian.
> **1871** Schele De Vere *Amer.* 660: Mississippi is occasionally spoken of humorously as the *Mudcat State,* the inhabitants being quite generally known as Mud-cats. *a*1890–96 *F & H* IV 374: *Mud-cat…*A Mississippi man. **1983** Whiteford *How to Talk Baseball* 138: *Jim (Mudcat) Grant* A teammate, mistakenly thinking Grant hailed from Mississippi, the Mudcat State, began calling him "Mudcat."

mud chicken *n. R.R.* a surveyor.
> **1940** *Railroad Mag.* (Apr.) 48: *Mud Chickens*—Surveyor [*sic*].

mud clerk *n.* a second clerk aboard a river steamboat. Now *hist.*
> **1872** in *OEDS*: It was natural enough that the "mud-clerk" on the old steamboat Iatan should have taken a fancy to the "striker," as the engineer's apprentice was called. **1875** "M. Twain" *Old Times* 40 [ref. to *ca*1860]: The doctor's and the postmaster's sons became "mud clerks." **1881** "M. Twain" *Stories* 185: His constant comrade…had been a Yankee youth…who had served for a couple of years as "mud clerk" (that is subordinate purser) on certain of the packet-boats plying…the Mississippi. **1912** in *DA*: Even her two mud clerks…wore uniforms. **1983** Curry *River's in My Blood* 274: *Mud clerk.* Second clerk, whose duties included going out in all weather on unpaved levees to receive or deliver freight.

mud-cruncher *n. Army.* an infantryman. Hence **mud-crunching,** *adj.*
> **1917** Empey *Over the Top* 71: I don't hanker to ship in with a damned mud-crunching outfit, but the cavalry's full. **1918** in *Pap. Mich. Acad.* (1928): Mud-crunchers. **1941** *Sat. Review* (Oct. 4): *Mud-crunchers:* The infantry.

mud-crusher *n. Army.* an infantryman; GRAVEL CRUSHER.
> **1864** in Horrocks *Dear Parents* 84: The mud-crushers (or infantry) must be quite envious to see such as me and other mounted gentlemen gallop past them. **1888** *Jour. of U.S. Cav. Assn.* (Nov.) 10 [ref. to 1865]: "Oh, we've got a feller that can fight all around you mud crushers," was the reply of a Michigan trooper. "Come out of your rat holes and we'll learn ye how." **1889** C. King *Marion's Faith* 94: Come, join us, ye gallants of mud-crushers. **1924** *Inf. Jour.* (June): When I joined an infantry regiment more than 50 years ago, the Eighth…I often heard the term "mud-crushers," but do not recall "doughboys" as being used at that time. **1930** Nason *Corporal* 263 [ref. to WWI]: Well, that's a doughboy's job.…That's what a mud-crusher gets paid for! I ain't a doughboy, I'm a cavalryman! *Ibid.* 277: You mean I got to hike all day on foot like a god-damned mud-crusher?

mudder *n. Sports.* an athlete, as a runner or football player (or, in 1950 quot., a team), who performs well in muddy conditions. [Applied to racehorses, the term is S.E.]
> [**1889–90 Barrère & Leland *Dict. Slang: Mud player* (cricketers), one who plays best when the ground is soft.] **1942** *ATS* 661: *Mudder…*a player for whom a wet field is no great handicap. **1950** *New Yorker* (Nov. 11) 121: Cornell's last one [*sc.,* a fumble] gave Columbia, a remarkably good mudder, the chance to tie the score. **1952** *Time,* in *AS* XVIII 1 (Feb. 1953): Gehrmann and Druetzler proved no mudders, and…Johansson, 23, splashed past the leaders on the last lap. **1976** *Dallas Morning News* (Oct. 31) 5B: Gary Semics is considered one of the better "mudders" in the field [of motocross racers]. **1981** Univ. Tenn. instructor, age 40: In the fall of 1957, up in Wisconsin, our football coach referred to our fullback as, "He's a real mudder," meaning he ran well in the mud.

mud-eater *n. Army.* an infantryman.
> **1942** *Sat. Eve. Post* (May 30) 67: *Mud-eater*—infantryman. **1942–45** Caniff *Male Call* (unp.): Fall back…mud-eater! **1977** T. McCoy *Remembers* 128 [ref. to 1917]: The cavalry [called] the infantry "mud-eaters."

mudfoot *n. Army.* an infantryman.
> ***1918** *Independent* (Jan. 26) 143: The boys…invent nicknames for each other—names as vile as the muck they tramp in, but full of good nature. They are tokens of affection. Flea-face, horse's neck, bull-beef, mud-foot, are some of them. **1970** Former U.S. Army sergeant, N.Y.C. [ref. to 1966]: I think it's a navy word; my buddy was in the navy and he always called me "mudfoot."

mudfucker *n.* MOTHERFUCKER.—usu. considered vulgar. Also **mudfuck.**
> **1978** Corder *Deer Hunter* 85: Move it out, mudfuckers! Move it out! **1980** Kotzwinkle *Jack* 142: You mudfucks comin'?

mud-grappler *n.* a hand.
> **1844** "J. Slick" *High Life in N.Y.* 118: I wish my mudgrappler had been cut off close up to the wrist.

mudguard *n. Football.* a fictitious position or player on a football team. *Joc.*
> **1929–33** J.T. Farrell *Manhood of Lonigan* 247: Haggerty! The other team needs a couple of mudguards. Go on over there.

mudhead *n.* a blockhead. [No clearly independent confirmation of the specific sense asserted in 1838 quot. is known.]
> **1838** [Haliburton] *Clockmaker* (Ser. 2) 181: There's the hoosiers of Indiana, the suckers of Illanoy, the pukes of Missouri, the buckeyes of Ohio, the red horses of Kentucky, the mudheads of Tennessee, the wolverines of Michigan, the eels of New England and the corn-crackers of Virginia. **1892** *Outing* (Aug.) 408: Now, see here, you dog-killing mudheads; no shooting of this spaniel by accident. **1905** in "O. Henry" *Works* 1436: Which barrel, ye mudhead? **1907** J.C. Lincoln *Cape Cod* 157: Turn out, you mud'ead. **1958** R. Chandler *Playback* 35: Mudheads always bore me.

mud hen *n. Stock Market.* a naive stock speculator.
> **1876** in *F & H* IV 375: The average mud-hen is middle-aged, rather stout in person, as voluble in conversation as a stump-speaker, and possessed of an inordinate desire to become a "stock-sharp." **1890** Quinn *Fools of Fortune* 448: If a stock touches $10 a share, there is a decided flurry among the "chippers" and "mud hens" as the men and women are respectively termed who persist on hanging around the board rooms and losing what little money they have.

mud hog *n.* **1.** *Army.* a field artilleryman.
> **1918** O'Brien *Wine, Women & War* 39: Their captaincies and plush jobs in Paris, by contrast with humble lieutenancy in mud-hogs, further confirmation of suspicion that I'm a damned fool.

2. *Petroleum Industry.* (see 1972 quot.).
> **1932** in *OEDS*: Mud-hog. **1942** *ATS* 488: *Mud hog,…*a high-pressure pump used for circulating rotary mud. **1944** Boatright & Day *Hell to Breakfast* 144: The bottom of the standpipe connects to reciprocating "slush pumps" or "mud hogs" and drilling fluid or "mud" is pumped through the drill pipe and bit all the time it is rotating on bottom. **1972** Haslam *Oil Fields* 107: *Mud Hog,* n. A pump for circulating the mud in rotary drilling.

mudhole *n. Black E.* ¶ In phrase: **kick a mudhole in** to thrash. Also vars. Cf. *tear someone a new asshole* s.v. ASSHOLE, *n.,* 6.
> **1973** Goines *Players* 58: They would gladly kick a mudhole in his white ass for him. **1974** R. Carter *16th Round* 251: I lay in my cell watching a squad of bedbugs stomp mudholes in a team of roaches.

mud hook *n.* **1.** *Naut.* a ship's anchor.
> **1827** J.F. Cooper *Rover* 37: He would…fasten her to the spot with good hempen cables and iron mud-hooks. **1847** Downey *Portsmouth* 106: After a deal of humbugging, we at last down Mudhook. **1853** *Harper's Mo.* (Feb.) 423: See that 'are mud-hook all clear for lettin' go. **1856** in C.A. Abbey *Before the Mast* 63: Let go a mudhook but it did not hold. **1867** Clark *Sailor's Life* 41: Down went the mud-hook. **1877** Bartlett *Amer.* (ed. 4) 789: "Drap *mud-hook,*" i.e. cast anchor. **1898** Doubleday *Gunner* 77: The mud-hook was dropped…May 26th. **1906** Beyer *Battleship* 84: "Mud hook"—the ship's anchor. **1907** J.H. Williams, in *Independent* (May 23) 1189: We dropped our mudhook abreast the tall lighthouse at Aujer Point. **1918** "Commander" *Clear the Decks!* 125: Each powerful anchor engine wrestled its heavy "mud-hook" from the harbor bottom. **1925** in J. Thomason *Stories* 484: Her mud-hook rumbled down off Puerto Dios just after midnight some twenty hours later. **1926** *AS* (Oct.): But the majority of Navy men like a ship that, once the "mud-hook" is up, will make knots. **1930** F. Shay *Here's Audacity* 18: Stormie, the bosun, gives the order to h'ist the mudhook. **1933** Witherspoon *Jarge* (unp.): We dropped the mud hook a mile off shore. **1958–70** Mjelde *Glory of Seas* 148: Attached a 3-inch manila line from the ship to the mud hook.

2. usu. *pl.* a big or clumsy foot.

   1850 Garrard *Wah-to-yah* 238: This "mudhook," holding out his foot, "hasn't a moccasin on for nothin', an' that's a fact!" **1890** Goss *Recollections* 23 [ref. to Civil War]: The boys called their feet "pontoons," "mud-hooks," "soil-excavators," and other names not quite so polite…."Keep your mud-hooks out of my way!" "Save your pontoons for another bridge." **1915** *DN* IV 244: Get your big mud hooks out of the way. **1952** in *DAS*: C'mon, lift them mud hooks!

3. usu. *pl.* a finger or hand. Cf. earlier MUD-GRAPPLER.

   1926 Norwood *Other Side of Circus* 176: Blime me if he hadn't kept a piece of my mud hook! **1975** McCaig *Danger Trail* 109: Now, Cris, if that spalpeen could get his mudhooks on this shipment…A pretty profit he'd turn.

4. a tire chain or other device used to gain traction in mud.

   1938 *AS* (Dec.) 308: Mudhooks. Chains or lugs.

mud hop *n. R.R.* a yard clerk.

   1929 *Bookman* (July) 524: I recognized him as the young punk who was a mud hop in the yard where I once made up trains. **1945** Hubbard *R.R. Ave.* 353: *Mudhop* is yard clerk, *mudshop* his office. **1972** *Urban Life & Culture* I 372: "Mudhops"…car clerks who work outside.

mudkicker *n. Prost.* a streetwalker. Hence **mudkicking**, *adj.* engaged in streetwalking. [Def. in 1932 quot. is prob. erroneously overspecific.]

   1932 in *AS* (Feb. 1934) 27: *Mud-kicker.* A woman who with promise of her body lures a man somewhere and instead of giving herself robs the man. **1940** Zinberg *Walk-Hard* 89: Lay off the chorus girls and the high-priced mudkickers. **1955** in Wepman et al. *The Life* 147: She was a stomp-down mud-kicker with kelsey hair. **1962** in B. Jackson *Swim Like Me* 114: About this time come along this mudkickin' whore. **1964** in B. Jackson *Swim Like Me* 106: She was a stompdown mudkicker and her mug was fair. **1968** Heard *Howard St.* 40: That bitch is a real mudkicker. *a***1971** in *West. Folk.* XXXIII (1974) 292: She was a stomp down mud kicker, Jim, and her mug was fair. **1974** Angelou *Gather Together* 137 [ref. to *ca*1950]: I'm a mud kicker. In the streets I make more money by accident than most bitches make on purpose.

mud lark *n.* **1.** a hog.

   *****1785** Grose *Dict. Vulgar Tongue*: Mud lark. A hog. **1833** J. Neal *Down-Easters* I 46: An' mud-larks that's made into Virginny-ham. **1869** *Overland Mo.* (Aug.) 129 [ref. to Civil War]: "Mud-lark" signified the same thing [sc., a hog].

2. a waterfront thief or scavenger; (*hence*) one who scavenges in gutters; guttersnipe.

   *****1796** in Partridge *Dict. Und.* 454: Men and boys, known [as] *mudlarks*, who prowl about, and watch under the ship when the tide will permit, and to whom they [sc., dishonest stevedores] throw *small parcels of sugar, coffee*, and other articles of plunder, which are conveyed to the receivers by these *mud-larks*, who generally have a certain share of the booty. *****1821** *Real Life in London* II 98: 'Twas low water, and the *mud-larks*…engaged the eye of the Squire….Peggy Jones, the well-known Mud-lark at Black Friars…carried in her…calling [until] 1805. **1855** Wise *Tales for Marines* 120: We've sculled in the same boat, as mud larks and ship thieves, and we've done many a bit of work. **a***1889–90** Barrère & Leland *Dict. Slang*: He…became what is called a *mud-lark*; that is, a plunderer of the ships' cargoes that unload in the Thames. **1907** in "O. Henry" *Works* 938: Such gin-swilling, scurvy, unbecoming mud larks as you.

3. *Horse Racing.* a mudder.

   1909 *Cent. Dict. Supp.*, cited in *OEDS*. **1935** Pollock *Und. Speaks*: *Mud lark*, a race horse that excels in mud….a burglar or safecracker who tunnels to gain entrance. **1968** Ainslie *Racing Guide* 471: Horse that prefers muddy going; "mudlark."

mud marine *n. USMC.* a Marine combat infantryman. Cf. MUD SOLDIER. [Quots. ref. to WWII.]

   1946 De Chant *Devilbirds* 57: Making like "Mud Marines" was not a well-loved chore for the birdmen at first. **1951** Grant *Flying Leathernecks* (film): We'd have clobbered that Nip position and the mud marines'd be off an' running.

mud-masher *n. Army.* an infantryman.

   1880 *United Service* (Dec.) 691: Our prairie Indians do not stand in any great awe of our regular troopers, while they pay every respect to our "mud-mashers," the foot-men. **1882** *United Service* (Apr.) 440: Such derogatory epithets applied to the infantry by the cavalry,—as "mud-mashers," "foot-wobblers," etc.

mud-mover *n. Mil. Av.* a ground-attack aircraft; (*also*) the pilot or crew of such an aircraft.

   1979 (cited in Partridge *Concise Dict. Sl.* 292). **1987** G. Hall *Top Gun* 35: Phantom-era mud-movers. *a***1989** R. Herman, Jr. *Warbirds* 180: You mud movers, come…and meet the latest addition to the wing. **1989** G. Hall *Air Guard* 2: Mud movers from Navy and Marine attack outfits. **1991** Dorr & Benson *TAC Fighters* 85: The attack guys, the mud-movers.

mud scow *n.* **1.** usu. *pl.* a large, cheap, or clumsy shoe; (*also*) a large foot.

   1860 Sleeper *In Forecastle* 386 [ref. to *ca*1820]: *Tread water* lustily with those mud scows (pointing to his feet). **1863** in *DA*: Expensive shoes…are frequently thrown away unused, for despised Government "mudscows." These "mudscows" or "gunboats"…are low-cut, stitched, very light, and very cheap. **1865** in J.W. Haley *Rebel Yell* 235: Had my brogans been anything but mudscows, they would have been condemned as unseaworthy. [**1875** *Minstrel Gags* 92: De feet was like two mud scows.] **1886** in Herdegan & Beaudot *At Gettysburg* 79 [ref. to 1861]: Gunboats…and mud scows [were derisive names for shoes]. **1909** *DN* III 413: *Mud scows*, n. Large shoes. **1919** *Co. D* 50: He was tryin' to extricate his mud scows out from under the corner of the tent and cussin' the guy that used the strings for tent stays. **1928** Nason *Eadie* 365 [ref. to 1918]: Keep those big mudscows of yours out of my messkit!

2. MUD WAGON. Now *hist.*

   1866 in Hilleary *Webfoot* 194: Six fine black horses were attached to our "mud scow."

mud show *n. Circus.* a small, second-rate traveling circus or other outdoor show. Also **mud opera.**

   1909 in *OEDS*: *Mud show*, an agricultural, or other out-door show. **1926** *AS* I (Feb.) 282: *Mud Show.* The old time wagon show. Sometimes called a "mud op'ry." **1931** in *OEDS*: *Mud show*, the old-time horse-and-wagon circus; now derisive. **1935** *Amer. Mercury* (June) 230: *Mud show*: one which moves by truck. **1942** *ATS* 621: *Mud show, mud opera*…a small circus or carnival that travels by wagon. **1943** J. Mitchell *McSorley's* 88: She started out with a tramp circus or "mud show," whose rickety, louse-infested wagons were pulled by oxen. **1971** *Playboy* (May) 145: The carnival was a bummer. One of those little mud shows, traveling by truck. **1974–75** Powledge *Mud Show* 19: This mud show has one run-through before hitting the road. *Ibid.* 99: Anything on trucks they call it a mud show.

mud-slogger *n. Mil.* an infantryman.

   *ca***1915** in Wiley & Milhollen *They Who Fought* 14 [ref. to Civil War]: Out of the way, mud-sloggers, and give the real fighters a chance. **1936** Reddan *Other Men's Lives* ix [ref. to 1918]: Definitions of Army Expressions…."Mud Sloggers" The Infantry. **1954** B. Wiley, in Fletcher *Rebel Private* v [ref. to 1865]: The retorts from the mounted men, if they ran true to form, were equally disrespectful, bristling with such epithets as "wagon dogs," "web feet," and "mud sloggers." **1971** Faust *Willy* 192: I got Frank into the Signal Corps, where at least he would not be a mud slogger.

mud-smeller *n. Petroleum Industry.* a geologist employed to seek out likely petroleum deposits.

   1926 *Writer's Mo.* (July) 42: *Mud Smeller*—Geologist of the oil fields. **1972** Haslam *Oil Fields* 107: *Mud Smeller*, n. A geologist.

mud soldier *n. Mil.* a combat soldier, esp. an infantryman. Cf. MUD MARINE.

   1982 *Newsweek* (Mar. 15) 26: As a "mud soldier" in World War II, he earned a battlefield commission at the Anzio beachhead. *a***1989** C.S. Crawford *Four Deuces* 163: They were just rear-echelon pogues, not mud soldiers. **1989** G.C. Wilson *Mud Soldiers* 5: General John W. Vesey Jr., Chairman of the Joint Chiefs of Staff under President Reagan, took pride in calling himself a Mud Soldier.

mud-stomping *adj. Prost.* mudkicking s.v. MUDKICKER.

   1968 Heard *Howard Street* 11: But long months of mud-stomping prostitution caused her to hesitate. **1974** R. Carter *16th Round* 157: How much bread they pulled in off the streets every day from their mud-stomping prostitutes.

mud-sucker *n. R.R.* (see 1940 quot.).

   1939 *Sat. Eve. Post* (Apr. 13) 26: The guns went off under the mud-suckers. **1940** in *AS* XVIII 167: *Mud Sucker.* A nonlifting injector.

mud-thumper *n.* **1.** *Mil. Av.* a high-explosive aerial bomb.

   1984 Trotti *Phantom* 170 [ref. to Vietnam War]: If I had punched the pickle, a stick of…500-pound mud-thumpers would have fanned out to flatten the town. **1989** Joss *Strike* 35: A-7 carries quartet of 500-pound mudthumpers.

2. usu. *pl. Mil.* a combat boot.

　1987 D. Sherman *Main Force* 181 [ref. to Vietnam War]: When we get back *I'm* gonna put my mud thumpers up their asses.

mud turtle *n.* **1.** *Mil.* an ironclad gunboat. Now *hist.*

　[**1862** in Heartsill *1491 Days* 89: One of those black mud-turtle looking Gunboats passed.] **1939** D. Beard *Hardly a Man* 237 [ref. to 1865]: Witnessed the sinking of one of Uncle Sam's iron "mud turtles," known as monitors.

2. a worthless or obnoxious person.

　1873 in *OEDS*: He's in that pilot-house now, showing those mud-turtles how to hunt for easy water. **1883** Sweet & Knox *Mustang* 24: There is an amount of jealousy exhibited…by the inhabitants of both cities [Houston and Galveston]; and the calling of each other names, such as "sand-crabs" and "mud-turtles," is one of the harmless ways in which they ventilate their spleen. **1930** J.T. Farrell *Calico Shoes* 50: "Sa-ay, don't be a mud turtle," she said.

mud wagon *n.* a stagecoach. Now *hist.*

　1835 in *DA*: We had to put up with an open "mud-waggon" with spring seats. **1866** in Hilleary *Webfoot* 194: Our baggage and ourselves was stowed on a mud wagon. **1868** in *DAE*: The inferior coaches, commonly known on the plains as "mud wagons." **1969** C. Adams *Tragg's Choice* 61: Don't anybody ever travel this road, except the mud wagon?

muff1 *n.* **1.a.** the pubic hair, esp. of a woman; *(hence)* the vulva or vagina.—usu. considered vulgar.

　1698–99 "B.E." *Dict. Cant. Crew: Muff*.…a Woman's Secrets. To the well-wearing of your Muff Mort.…to the happy Consummation of your Marriage Madam, a Health. **ca*1700 in Pinto & Rodway *Common Muse* 396: She told me 'twould pleasure an Earl,/For she had a delicate Muff. ***1707 in Farmer *Merry Songs* IV 110: The Muff between her Haunches,/Resembl'd…a *Mag-Pye's* Nest. **ca*1795 in Barke & Smith *Merry Muses* 149: Meg had a muff and it was rough/'Twas black without and red within. **1934** H. Miller *Trop. Cancer* 109: He buried his head in her muff. **1941** in Legman *Limerick* 37: Alas for the Countess d'Isère,/Whose muff wasn't furnished with hair. **1967** W. Murray *Sweet Ride* 154: She's got nothing on under them, man, and she goes right on dancing, bouncing that little muff of hers at them. **1968** Cuomo *Thieves* 42: He cupped his hand right over her muff. **1969–71** Kahn *Boys of Summer* 148: I liked it when he screwed that brunette and they describe her muff. **1979–81** C. Buckley *To Bamboola* 139: No muff too tough,/No thigh too high. **1984** S. Zacharias & J. Buhai *Nerds* (film): Step aside, mamma, I wanna see some of that muff. **1986** M. Howard *Expensive Tastes* 192: This perky muff…this dusky pubic pelt. **1990** Rukuza *West Coast Turnaround* 50: Her muff…was trimmed into a heart and dyed bright red! **1994** *UTSQ: Muff* female pubic hair.

b. copulation.—usu. considered vulgar.

　1976 Conroy *Santini* 297: Philip turns down more muff than you ever dream about. **1979** Univ. Tenn grad. student: I'll be getting lots of muff this summer.

c. a woman or women, esp. if promiscuous.—usu. considered vulgar.

　1914 Jackson & Hellyer *Vocab.* 30: "The muffs are cruising on the drag tonight" i.e. soliciting on the street. **1918** *DN* V 26: *Muff,* n. A girl. South Idaho and University of Idaho. **1944** C.B. Davis *Leo McGuire* 175: A guy that drinks with a muff is simple. Keep 'em separate. Muffs are fine in their place. But take 'em and love 'em and leave 'em. **1942–49** Goldin et al. *DAUL* 142: *Muff.* (South) A prostitute or very loose woman. **1958** Gilbert *Vice Trap* 73: They won't be able to find you with all the muff hanging on you. **1969–70** *Current Slang I & II* 63: *Muff,* n. A girl.—Air Force Academy cadets. **1974** Lahr *Trot* 217: You mangy muff! Twat! Cunt! You forgot my birthday!

2. a beard.

　1942 in *ATS* 148: Beard; whiskers…*muff, shrubbery, spinach.* **1959** Vittes & Girard *Rebel Set* (film): You even sprouted a muff.

3. a toupee.

　1949 R. Chandler, in *DAS:* Hicks…wasn't wearing his muff.

¶ In phrase:

¶ **dive a muff** to perform cunnilingus.—usu. considered vulgar. Cf. MUFF-DIVE, MUFF-DIVER, 1.

1972 *Anthro. Linguistics* (Mar.) 101: *Dive A Muff* (v): To perform cunnilingus.

muff2 *n.* [orig. unkn.; see *OED2*] **1.** a dolt or bungler; oaf; silly fool; weakling; *(specif.) Sports. (obs.)* a weak or inferior player, esp. a fielder in baseball.

　***1812 Vaux *Vocab.: Muff* …a foolish silly person. ***1837 Dickens *Pickwick Papers* 97: "Ah, ah!—stupid"—"Now, butterfingers"—"Muff"—"Humbug"—and so forth. ***1837 in *F & H* VI 377: My friends, that young man's a muff! ***1845 in *F & H* VI 377: Why you're a regular muff! ***1849 Thackeray, in *F & H* VI 377: Another called me a *muff* (which means, in the slang language, a very silly fellow). ***1850 in *F & H* VI 377: Put on the gloves!…Oh, you muff! don't you understand?—of course I mean the boxing-gloves! **1854** "Youngster" *Swell Life* 248: What a muff you are, to be sure. ***1855 in T. Taylor *Plays* 42: Those muffs at the Home Office. **1864** F.C. Adams *Story of Trooper* 162: You can't cuss a muff like this Major, without having the guard-house shook in your face. ***1866 in *F & H* VI 377: I must now proceed to football, a game I like…far more than cricket.…I was a tolerably good hand at the former, and rather a *muff* at the latter. **ca*1866 *Romance of Lust* 124: She told me that her husband was a *muff*, who had no idea of enjoying a woman but in one way. **1867** in *DA*: Every player who makes a miss is regarded as a muff. **1867** in Leitner *Diamond in Rough* 79: Chicago…the greatest muffs in the country. **1868** Williams *Black-Eyed Beauty* 13: He's that muff that wanted to wear one of our hats in the last Triennial Turn out! **1869** Logan *Foot Lights* 270: Either a "prig" or a "muff;" in other words, a pedant or an ignoramus. ***1873 Hotten *Slang Dict.* (ed. 4): *Muff*, a silly or weak-minded person, a duffer; *muff* has been defined to be "a soft thing that holds a lady's hand without squeezing it." **1886** P.D. Haywood *Cruise* 39: He didn't care a snap for the muffs that couldn't pull their pound. ***1888 in *F & H* VI 378: What a muff Sir Ferdinand must be. **1891** Campbell, Knox & Byrnes *Darkness & Daylight* 626: The city's full of muffs.…Talk about the hayseeds from the country! **1892** Gunter *Miss Dividends* 14: That muff, Oliver, actually giggled. **1893** Palmer *Question of Honor* 51: Oh, don't be a muff! You might know he didn't. **1907** R.W. Chambers *Younger Set* 307: Oh, what a muff! to let Eileen beat you six–five, six–three! **1910** in O. Johnson *Lawrenceville* 221: You're a muff, a low-down muff, in every sense of the word!

2. Esp. *Sports.* a fielding error or fumble; mistake.

　1868 in *DAE*: In the…score sheet…to the left the initials represent the words Runs, Outs, Times, Bases, Muffs, Balks, Left, Home. **1874** *Chi. Inter Ocean* (July 1) (cited in Nichols *Baseball Term.*) **1880** in *DAE*: Captain Sam…inwardly groaned "he'll make a muff!" **1884** in Fountain *Sportswriter* 60: On the latter's muff of Orr's ball a life was given. **1886** in *DAE*: General Garfield…was constantly exclaiming: "Good catch!" "Fine hit!" "Oh! what a muff!" **1893** in *DAE*: As a punt may traverse a distance of fifty yards, a muff may mean a loss of that distance. **1942** *ATS* 631: Bungling play.…*muff.* **1952** in *DAS*: [A player] had dropped the ball, "the $75,000 muff," as it was called.

muff1 *v.* to make an error; *(trans.)* to lose (an opportunity), spoil (an attempt); bungle; *(specif.) Baseball. (obs.)* to fail to field (a ball) effectively. Now *colloq.*

　1827 (cited in *W10*). ***1846 in *OEDS*: All the best of our players completely muffed their batting. ***1857 in *F & H* IV 178: *I don't* see why you should have muffed that shot. **1867** in *DAE*: Balls were muffed, picked up clumsily, and allowed to run through legs. **1867** in *DA* s.v. *hot:* Abrams reached…2d by the muffing. **1872** Chadwick *Dime Base-Ball* 27: *Muffed Balls.*—A ball is "muffed" when the fielder fails to stop it as it comes within his reach, or to pick it up and hold it so as to throw it in promptly, or to hold it when it is thrown to him accurately. **1880** in *DAE*: Pat Adams muffed the ball. **1889** in Kaese *Braves* 45: The catcher muff'd, and to the ground it fell. **1889** in S. White *Colored Base Ball* 136: I have seen him muff balls intentionally. **1912** C. Mathewson *Pitching in Pinch* 162: I muffed fly after fly. **1928** Dahlberg *Bottom Dogs* 91: He was always muffing the ball when his side was about to win. **1930** *AS* V (Feb.) 239: *Muff.*…misunderstand. "That professor knows his stuff and don't you muff it!" **1936** Kenyon & Daves *Petrified Forest* (film): I had my chance and I muffed it. **1965** Spillane *Killer Mine* 23: Nobody knew he had left Chi until he muffed this operation here. **1966** in T.C. Bambara *Gorilla* 39: I muffed the goddamn shot. Ball bounced off the rim. **1977** Lieb *Baseball* 18: Lieb muffs a line drive. **1984** A. Pincus *How to Talk Football* 50: *Muff*…to touch a loose ball (usually after a kick) in an unsuccessful attempt to gain possession. **1994** Bak *Turkey Stearnes* 45: Purposely muffing throws to avoid the flashing spikes.

muff[2] *v.* to perform cunnilingus on; MUFF-DIVE.—usu. considered vulgar.

> **1965** Linakis *In Spring* 19 [ref. to WWII]: I mean, can you see me muffin' some redheaded, sonofabitchin' broad? *a*1972 B. Rodgers *Queens' Vernacular* 139: *Muff*…To tongue the clitoris and vulva. **1977** T. Berger *Villanova* 234: Whatinhell they *really* do, Rome? Muff one another?

muff-dive *v.* to perform cunnilingus.—usu. considered vulgar. Also as *n.*

> [**1927** (quot. at CANYON, *n.*).]. **1948** in Legman *Limerick* 86: When you muff-dive on/The living-room divan,/Please use an anti-macassar. **1969** Girodias *New Olympia Reader* 629: Let's go on to "muff-diving," shall we? **1970** Peters *Sex Newspapers* 27: I remember one expression from high school that I always dug. We called [cunnilingus] "muff-diving." **1981** *Penthouse* (Apr.) 31: David had removed her pants and was doing the biggest muff dive I've ever seen. **1990** *Nat. Lampoon* (Apr.) 99: So, does she muff-dive or what? *a*1994 A. Radakovich *Wild Girls Club* 131: The sport of muff-diving is not practiced more often…[because] some men don't know how to do it.

muff-diver *n.* **1.** a performer of cunnilingus.—usu. considered vulgar.

> **1930** *AS* V (June) 391: *Muff-diver.* A pervert of either sex who is addicted to cunnilinctus. *ca*1936 in Holt *Dirty Comics* 146: I'm no muffdiver…because my tongue is tied! **1938** "Justinian" *Amer. Sexualis* 29: *Muff-diver*, a male cunnilinguist. C. 19–20. **1942–49** Goldin et al. *DAUL* 143: *Muff-diver*…See *Bumper*…*Bumper*…A male oral copulator whose degeneracy extends only to women. **1961** Granat *Important Thing* 264: You never told me nothin' about bein' a muff-diver. **1965** Schmitt *All Hands Aloft!* 282 [ref. to 1918]: "The fur? Oh, they make it into earmuffs—big demand in California." "Yeah, for muff divers, no doubt," chuckled Laurence as he left to relieve the wheel. **1972** Hannah *Geronimo Rex* 250: Let me get on my muff-diver goggles. **1985** "J. Blowdryer" *Mod. Eng.* 74: Homosexual women…*Muff Divers.*

2. a contemptible fellow.—usu. considered vulgar.

> **1945** Bowman *Beach Red* 38: The little muffdiver…took the middle of the vine up with him. **1958** T. Berger *Crazy in Berlin* 288: How I used to ache to get that dirty muff diver in an alley and slam the poison outen him. **1968** Myrer *Eagle* 761: The dirty little muff-divers are going to drink it all up.

muff-diving *adj.* (of persons) despicable.—usu. considered vulgar.

> **1952** H. Grey *Hoods* 341: You muff divin', stinkin' bitch. **1968** P. Roth *Portnoy* 118: You muff-diving, mother-fucking son of a bitch! **1977–81** S. King *Cujo* 34: A bunch of long-haired muff-diving…pinko fucksticks.

muffer[1] *n. Baseball.* an unskilled player.

> **1867** *Harper's Wkly.* (Sept. 14) 91: The President said he was not much on the catch; they would probably term him a "muffer." **1867** in *DA*: The "muffers" are probably a much-abused class. The "champion" muffer's experience is varied—always the last to be chosen on a side. **1874** *Chi. Inter Ocean* (July 25) (cited in Nichols *Baseball Term.*).

muffer[2] *n.* MUFF-DIVER.

> **1960** Hoagland *Circle Home* 191: I'm going to sleep you in with Maud. She has this streak of muffer in her and I'm trying to broaden her out. *a*1972 B. Rodgers *Queens' Vernacular* 139: Cunnilinctrice … *muffer.*

muffin *n.* **1.** [pun on MUFF[2], *n.*] **a.** Esp. *Baseball.* a weak or inferior player; MUFF[2].—also used attrib. Now *hist.*

> **1860** in W. Goldstein *Playing for Keeps* 56: Veterans…[vs.] muffins. **1864** in Leitner *Diamond in Rough* 54: This afternoon the "muffin" match between the Mutuals will take place at Elysian Fields, Hoboken. **1867** in *DAE*: Balls were…allowed to run through legs, in real muffin style. **1866–71** Bagg *Yale* 45: *Muffin*, an unskilful player at base-ball. *Ibid.* 317: "Muffins," or clubs which make no pretence to good playing. **1872** Chadwick *Dime Base-Ball* 28: *Muffins.*—This is the term applied to the poorest class of fielders. A player may be able to hit long balls, and to make home runs, and yet for all that be a veritable muffin from the simple fact that he can not field, catch, or throw a ball decently. **1973** H. Peterson *Man Who Invented Baseball* 77 [ref. to 1846]: The Knick "muffins"—as the second string was called—put at least eight men on base in the first inning alone.

b. a dolt; fool. [No continuity of usage can be shown between quots.]

> **1837* in *F & H* VI 377: A visitor? hurrah: some muffin, I daresay. **1984** *N.Y. Times* (Aug. 6) B2: It was hard to understand what they were saying, because they talk different.…They call stupid people "muffins." We couldn't understand that.

2. a male chaperone or companion.

> **1865** Sala *Diary* II 159: You commit her solemnly to his charge.…Throughout the voyage that male person is the lady's "muffin." If she be sea-sick he worries the stewardess out of her life. **1936* Partridge *DSUE* 541: *Muffin.*…A man that chaperones or acts as a companion to women.

3. a female friend or sweetheart.

> **1870** in *F & H* IV 378: When a man, availing himself of the custom of the country, has secured a young lady for the season, to share with him his sleigh-driving and other of the national amusements, in Canadian phrase she is called his muffin. **1870** Rivington *Remin.* 60: As a consequence of this peculiar form of Platonic friendship, it is said that a man never marries his own, but often his friend's "muffin," as it is supposed that he knows less of his friend's than of his own "muffin!" *a*1889–90 in Barrère & Leland *Dict. Slang*: If any young lady, not previously engaged, of course, found favour in your sight, you were at liberty then and there to constitute her your *muffin*. **1954–60** *DAS*: *Muffin*…A girl. **1976** Whelton *CB Baby* 15: "Don't worry about me, muffin," she said.

muffler *n.* **1.** usu. *pl. Boxing.* a boxing glove.

> **1747* in Barrère & Leland *Dict. Slang*: *Mufflers* are provided that will effectually secure them from the inconvenience of black eyes, broken jaws, and bloody noses. **1755* in *F & H* IV 379: He has the shape and constitution of a porter, and is sturdy enough to encounter Broughton without mufflers. **1849** *Nat. Police Gaz.* (Jan. 20) 1: On gaining his feet, Williams pulled off one of his gloves meaningly and Boyle followed suit, as if they would fight it out, but being called to order by the audience, they resumed the "mufflers" and went at it again. **1859** Matsell *Vocab.* 57: *Mufflers.* Boxing-gloves. **1866** *Night Side of N.Y.* 83: The combatants have their "mawleys" encased in the "mufflers."

2. *Army.* a gas mask.

> **1917** Imbrie *War Ambulance* 115: A helmet was a "trench derby," a gas mask "a muffler."

Mug *n. Pol.* MUGWUMP, 2.

> **1894** Bangs *Three Weeks in Politics* 12: *Diss* is what comes o' puttin' up a Mugwump. Dere ain't no life in de Mugs!

mug *n.* **1.a.** the face or mouth; an ugly face; *(rare) (obs.)* the nose.

> **1708* in *OED*: My Lawyer has a Desk, nine Law-books without Covers, two with Covers, a Temple-Mug, and the hopes of being a Judge. **1791** [W. Smith] *Confess. T. Mount* 18: Nose, *mug.* **1812* Vaux *Vocab.*: *Mug*: the face; a queer *mug* is an ugly face. **1821* *Real Life in Ireland* 31: Curse your ugly mug! **1821–26* Stewart *Man-of-War's-Man* I 169: Haul out your beautiful mugs to their full stretch. **1826* in J. Farmer *Musa Pedestris* 98: Why is thy mug so wan and blue? **1832** *Spirit of Times* (Mar. 3) 3: Both came up with ugly *mugs*, neither appeared to be pleased with their punishment. **1835* Marryat *Midshipman Easy* 163: All you have to answer for is the boatswain's mug,—I think you've stopped his jaw for the future. **1836** *Every Body's Album* I 79: Why, my sakes, mamma, said Miss Arabella, with a toss of her pretty little saucy mug. *Ibid.* 134: Three Ugly Mugs Disputing Their Beauty. All three are beauties; but the old fellow with his ears swathed has it, in our minds, against all odds. **1838** [Haliburton] *Clockmaker* (Ser. 2) 100: He turned up his ugly cantin' mug. **1842** *Spirit of Times* (Oct. 29) 416: Your ugly mug won't bear much further spoiling. **1847** "N. Buntline" *Curse* 35: Some foreigner, by the cut of his mug. *ca*1849 in G. Jackson *Early Songs of Uncle Sam* 57: Another one grabs at your cap, or, if you wear a plug,/'Tis jammed down, by no gentle hand, on your unresisting mug. **1849** Mackay *Western World* I 154: They think because they have got a little whitewash on their ugly mugs, that they're the real china. **1858** [S. Hammett] *Piney Woods* 65: Yer ugly consated mug. **1858** O.W. Holmes *Autocrat* 54: The smile…such as the Champion of the Heavy Weights…wears upon what he…calls his "mug." **1863** "E. Kirke" *So. Friends* 57: Hit 'im agin! Smash his mug! **1863** in T. Whitman *Dear Walt* 23: I would like to get a fair chance at his ugly mug. *ca*1865 O.W. Holmes, Jr., in M.D. Howe *Shaping Yrs.* 104: The victim contemplated the operation with a very grievous mug. **1866** (quot. at PIPE, *n.*). **1870** *Putnam's Mag.* (Mar.) 301: The combatants struck each

other…upon the head, the nut, the cone, the conk, the canister, the noddle, the mug, the knowledge box. **1871** Willis *Forecastle Echoes* 20: With anxious "mugs" we were debating/How best to act. **1880** Small *Mother-in-Law* 15: I buried my mug in the mysteries of that affair. **1891** Kirkland *Capt. of Co. K* 88 [ref. to Civil War]: If I had such a mug as yours I'd lie on it all the time. **1891** Riis *Other Half* 168: The homeliest ruffian of the lot…insisted on being taken [*i.e.*, photographed] with the growler to his "mug." **1895** Townsend *Fadden* 74: Hold yer mug, ye onreasonable ole hag. **1904** *Life in Sing Sing* 250: *Mug.*—The face. **1914** Z. Grey *West. Stars* 43: With his red mug turnin' green he went for his gun. **1932** Fisher *Tragic Life* 454: Get that crazy look off your mug! **1933–34** "Max Brand" *Mt. Riders* 7: In fact, he had what is generally called a "mug," but his eyes were so bright and good-humored and active…that people always put him down as a harmless sort. **1946** Boulware *Jive & Slang* 6: *Plug the Mug*…Be quiet. **1950** Calmer *Strange Land* 131: That Achelis never changes his mug so you can tell one thing or another. **1951** J. Reach *My Friend Irma* 26: Every time I look at a society page, there's one of your muggs splashed over it. **1954** Gordon & Wood *Jail Bait* (film): So you closed his mug. So what? **1984** J. McNamara *First Directive* 194: I had needed a few stitches on my mug. **1989** *Tracey Ullman Show* (Fox-TV): All the papers had my mug on the front page. **1989** *Life Goes On* (ABC-TV): Who wants to see Lester's ugly mug on a campaign poster? **1994** *TV Guide* (June 18) 35: Lauer's handsome mug is clearly an asset.

b. a grimace.

   *1821 in *DSUE* 1285: *Mug*, a grimace. **1837** (quot. at AGONY, 1). **1878** *Funny Fatherland* 56: The child makes a Mug at him. **1930** Irwin *Tramp & Und. Slang*: *Mug*….A grimace.

c. *Und. & Police.* a chokehold placed on a victim's throat during the course of a robbery.—constr. with *the*.

   *1862 in Partridge *Dict. Und.* 454: I apprehended Roberts…he said, "you want me for putting the mug on, do you? I will put the b—y mug on you,"…mug is slang used by thieves; it means garrotting. **1902** Hapgood *Thief* 271: I explained how I would "put the mug on her" while my husky pal went through her. **1902** Townsend *Sure* 46: "Daddy, please show me de back and front mug, again." Before a "mug" meant a man, it meant de kind of strangle holt dat footpads give from behind, or de elbow in de neck, from in front. **1962** Perry *Young Man* 69: I put the mug on him and started feeling around for his wallet.

d. *Esp. Und. & Police.* a photograph taken for the future identification of a suspect or prisoner; (*broadly*) any portrait photograph.

   1866 (quot. at JACKET, *v.*). **1887** *Lantern* (N.O.) (July 9) 2: He had his mug taken in fireman's clothes. **1889* in Partridge *Dict. Und.* 454: Circulating thieves' photos…Pushing the mugs around. **1890** Roe *Police* 379: Rogues Object To Having Their "Mugs" Placed On File. **1899** A.H. Lewis *Sandburrs* 46: It would be safe for d' chief to take me mug out of d' gallery now, an' rub d' name off Mollie Matches off d' books. **1911** A.H. Lewis *Apaches of N.Y.* 32: It pleased Spanish vastly when his mug came out of the gallery. **1912** Field *Watch Yourself Go By* 320: Send for the Bertillon officers. I think you'll find their mugs in the Hall of Fame. **1913** J. London *Valley of Moon* 175: I got to go to a picture garage an' get my mug taken.…And I cough up another dollar for the mug. **1928** Callahan *Man's Grim Justice* 187: I knew that my "record," my "mug" (picture) and Bertillon measurements were in the gallery. **1931** *AS* (June) 333: *Mug snapper*, n. an itinerant photographer. **1940** *AS* (Dec.) 359: *Mug*. A portrait photograph. *To mug* is to take a portrait picture. **1950** Duffy *S. Quentin* 112: The boy was good-looking, even in the harsh prison mug pasted on the card. **1958** *N.Y. Times Mag.* (Mar. 16) 88: *Mug*—A police photograph; also—almost exclusively in New York—robbery by use of physical force. **1966** Braly *On Yard* 10: But even the first of his numerous mugs…had shown him the face of a born wrongdoer. **1973** J.E. Martin *95 File* 26: Think you can make them from their mugs? **1989** Hiaasen *Skin Tight* 16: They got the mugs back from the FBI.

2.a. *Orig. Und. & Carnival.* a dupe; fool; SUCKER.

   *1857 "Ducange Anglicus" *Vulgar Tongue* 13: *Mug*, n. Dupe. "Who is the *mug*?" **1859** Matsell *Vocab.* 57: *Mug*. A simple fellow. **1851–61* H. Mayhew *London Labour* IV 237: The woman looks out for a "mug," that is, a drunken fellow, or a stupid, foolish sort of fellow. **1889–90** Barrère & Leland *Dict. Slang* II 73: *Mug*, a simpleton, a person easily imposed upon. **1893** in Dreiser *Jour.* I 90: Did you ever see a mug?…He don't know a good thing when he sees it. **1899* Whiteing

John St. 220: Let's chuck it; they must think us mugs. *ca*1921 in W.C. Fields *By Himself* 107: Don't be a mug. **1928** Guerin *Crime* 31 [ref. to *a*1880]: There were always plenty of "mugs" to be found in the big towns visited by the circus. **1928** Delmar *Bad Girl* 75: Don't be a mug, Dot. **1929** *Variety* (Oct. 30) 70: What muggs these mortals be! **1938** Lennon et al. *Crowd Roars* (film): I still say McCoy is…a mug. **1964** Whitehouse *Fledgling* 51: The public…assumed that anyone who rushed in [to volunteer for WWI] was something of a mug. **1980* Leland *Kiwi-Yankee Dict.: Mug:* sucker. **1983–89** K. Dunn *Geek Love* 5: I stood in the front to lead in the mugs.

b. a low, crude fellow; hoodlum; lout; (now *rare*) thug; (with weakened force) (now *rare*) fellow or man; a commonplace individual.

   1865 Williams *Joaquin* 130: Anyway, those three ugly mugs with him are of the band, I'll bet. **1867** *Nat. Police Gaz.* (Oct. 26) 2: Each "ugly mug" [secured] a sailor, regardless of choice, for a partner. *a*1890 in Barrère & Leland *Dict. Slang* II 73: "See 'em.…There's mugs for you—look at 'em." "Mugs?…What are mugs?" "Hard characters…the fellows that rob immigrants, steal cotton from the bales, go through trunks…and empty pockets on the ferries." **1892** S. Crane *Maggie* 18: Dere was a mug come in deh place deh odder day wid an idear he wus goin' teh own deh place! **1892** Norr *China Town* 13: Harrison's shook "Chuck," and he's a dead sore mug. See? **1893** Frye *Field & Staff* 174: Are youse mugs wid me, or agin me? **1894** *Harper's* (Oct.) 696: Is dat mug been around? Dat mug dat chucked us der slack las' Sunday? **1895** Townsend *Fadden Explains* 25: What mug has de dead cinch on bein de dandiest dresser on de avnoo? **1895** in Remington *Wister* 118: Behold you d—— ignorant gold besodden rum bloated mugs. **1897** Townsend *City Full* 136: I'd tell her…about the mugs—the folks, I mean—what were in the book. **1903** *Enquirer* (Cincinnati) (May 9) 13: *Mug*…tough character. **1903** A.H. Lewis *Boss* 272: This Billy Van Flange is a tough mug to handle. **1904** *Life in Sing Sing* 250: *Mug*.…a fellow. **1913** W. Wilson *Hell in Nebr.* 110: Did you see some of them tough mugs sit up and take notice? **1933** Boehn & Gelsey *Jimmy Dolan* (film): Look at that mug! He's doin' sixty! **1934** in Fountain *Sportswriter* 60: Unlettered chroniclers (muggs) writing for an audience of their own kind. **1934** Schary & Waggoner *He Couldn't Take It* (film): So I'm a mug and he's respectable, huh? **1938** "E. Queen" *4 Hearts* 17: I could really care for a mugg like you; you're an honest man. **1941** J.V. Kern *Look Who's Laughing* (film): Them ugly mugs. **1942** Algren *Morning* 16: I spend it all on myself. I guess I'm just a mug. **1945** Kanin *Born Yesterday* 188: Go ahead! Pan me! Tell me how I'm a mugg and a roughneck. **1950** F. Brown *Space* 88: What are these mugs? **1951** G. Fowler *Schnozzola* 67: The Durante band members looked like mugs and dressed that way. **1954** Schulberg *Waterfront* (film): You're a dirty lousy cheap stinkin' mug. **1973** D. Morrow *Maurie* 12: The four mugs are not impressed. **1981** R. Baker, in *N.Y. Times Mag.* (June 27) 10: Everybody started wearing sunglasses, including the mug who lifted your wallet while his knife tickled your rib cage. **1985** C. Busch *Times Sq. Angel* 43: That mug is on every wanted list from coast to coast. **1986** R. Walker *AF Wives* 99: Why would a girl like Shelley marry a mug like him?

c. *Und.* a police officer or detective.

   1902 Hapgood *Thief* 268 [ref. to 1898]: I'm only stealin' for certain mugs (policemen)…so they can buy real estate. **1903** *Enquirer* (Cincinnati) (May 9) 13: *Mug*…a detective. **1904** *Life in Sing Sing* 250: *Mug*.…policeman. **1911** Roe *Prodigal* 36: He told me that he was in a little trouble with the "mugs," that is with the policemen, that is what he called them, "mugs." **1925** (quot. at ELBOW). **1934** in North *New Masses* 152: Three ruddy faced cops—"mugs"—pretended to ignore the hackies picketing the Parmelee garage.

d. *Black E.* (as in (b), above, but regarded as a euphem. for MOTHERFUCKER).

   1984 in G. Tate *Flyboy* 169: I had to laugh like a mug. **1985** in G. Tate *Flyboy* 35: Just thinking about a mug doing that many. *Ibid.* 36: Y'all were rag-ged-y as a mug on that tour. **1990** in G. Tate *Flyboy* 118: I went to the…cut-out bin and copped the mug for like, a $1.99. **1993** P. Munro *U.C.L.A. Slang* II 60: *Mug*…identified by some people as a euphemism for *mother fucker*. *a*1994 Smitherman *Black Talk* 163: *Mug* Euphemism for *muthafucka*.

3.a. a chamber pot.

   1863 in Beer *Civil War Letters* 42: He died very easy, as nearly all do that dies with the Diarhea. He died while on the mug and so easy that they hardly knew that he was gone. **1942** *ATS* 87: Chamber pot .... *mug.*

b. *Sports.* a trophy cup.

1893 (quot. at MUG-HUNTER). **1942** *ATS* 637: *Mug,*...a trophy cup. **1949** Cummings *Dict. Sports* 274.

¶ In phrase:

¶ **on (one's) mug** solely on the basis of (one's) appearance.

1907 in "O. Henry" *Works* 1511: Some joint where he can get cash on his mug.

mug[1] *v.* **1.** Esp. *Theat.* to assume exaggerated facial expressions; grimace. Now *colloq.* or *S.E.*

*1762 in *F & H* IV 381: Ev'n Humour seem'd to mourn, And silently sat mugging o'er his urn. **1855* Dickens, in Partridge *DSUE* 541: The low comedian had "mugged" at him...fifty nights for a wager. **1881** *Wash. Post* (Mar. 13) 3: A comedian who depends on unnatural grimaces to evoke the laughter of the multitude is said to "mug." **1903** McCardell *Conversations of Chorus Girl* 147: I want a good mugger and musician. **1925** *AS* I (Oct.) 37: A gentleman given to pulling funny faces to draw a laugh is called a "mugger." **1935** Lorimer & Lorimer *Heart Specialist* 36: Mugging at the camera instead of acting. **1938** "E. Queen" *4 Hearts* 41: Oh, stop mugging. You're not doing the big scene now. **1939** O'Hara *Pal Joey,* in *DAS:* One of the mice...is mugging even in rehearsal. **1951** *New Yorker* (Nov. 24) 143: He signified his pleasure on opening night by yelling and mugging his way through an old-style, rabble-rousing performance. **1952** *N.Y. Times* (Oct. 5) II X3: Abbott should turn and "mug" at the audience, which is to say, he must make a grotesque face. **1970** A. Young *Snakes* 3: He and Flo...are posed together, mugging for the camera. **1975** C.W. Smith *Country Music* 139: One corner held a strip of photos from a five-for-25¢ booth showing Ginger and a girlfriend mugging in various poses. **1979** Gram *Foxes* 21: Deirdre mugged a how-stupid-can-you-get face. **1980** Teichmann *Fonda* 104: The director said, "Hank, you're mugging a bit."...To any actor...mugging smacks of scene stealing, of upstaging, of hamming it up, of unprofessionalism. **1987** *Daily News* (N.Y.) (July 2) 7: The guys mugged it up for the cameramen. **1997** *As World Turns* (CBS-TV): I mug for cameras.

2.a. Orig. *Boxing.* to punch in the face.

*1818 in *OED:* The latter got away, and in return mugged him. **1821* in *F & H* IV 380: Madgbury showed game, drove Abbot in a corner, but got well mugg'd. **1846* in *OED2:* She felt inclined to mug her rival, only she thought it would be no bottle [*sic*]. **1857* "Ducange Anglicus" *Vulgar Tongue* 42: And if you come to *fibbery,*/You must *mug* one or two. **1865** Woodruff *Union Soldier* 56: *Dad*...takes too much of the O-be-Joyful, sidewalk flies up & strikes him in the face spoiling his "phiz" for him. Swore some one had "mugged" him. **1889–90* Barrère & Leland *Dict. Slang:* II: *Mug, to*...to strike in the face, to thrash.

b. to assault (a victim) with intent to rob, often by seizing in a chokehold from behind; (*hence*) (now *S.E.*) to rob someone, usu. by using or brandishing a weapon.—also used fig.

*1864 Hotten *Slang Dict.* (ed. 3): *Mug*...to rob by the garrote. **1865** Woodruff *Union Soldier* 48: One of Co. "G" comes in after retreat & tatoo is over, minus his coat & Boots. was *Mugged* by the Regulars in the Suburbs & lost them. **1865** J.H. Browne *Secessia* 339: Mugging is the argot expression for robbing, and one of the most popular words in the Southern-Prison lexicon. *Ibid.* 344: Men were frequently mugged in the Prison-yard. Several of the band would gather round the intended victim, who on a sudden would be thrown to the ground; his pockets turned inside out, [etc.]. *Ibid.* 345: No attempt was ever made to mug either my *confrère* or myself. **1890–96* *F & H* IV 381: *Mug*...(common.)—To rob. **1904** *Life in Sing Sing* 250: *Mug*...to strangle. [**1936** in Leadbitter & Slaven *Blues Records* 219: Let's Go Muggin'.] **1939** in *OEDS:* The vicious art of "mugging" by which a Negro thug grabs the wayfarer around the neck, from behind, while two others with knives clean out his pockets. **1943** Ottley *New World* 158: [Some streetwalkers] are a pretty vicious lot, and it was they who introduced that violent crime called "mugging," a form of assault with intent to rob. The woman's role is to lure a man into a tenement hallway, where he is set upon by three, four, or five accomplices—called "muggers"—usually armed with switchblades. *Ibid.* 162: They waylaid Joseph Keelan,...mugged him, rifled his pockets of seventeen cents, stole his suit, and left him dying...in Morningside Park. **1945** *Reader's Digest* (June) 110: The victim is trailed, mugged, robbed....Mugging is common....By the time the police arrive the muggers have vanished.

1942–49 Goldin et al. *DAUL* 142: *Mugg*...To assault by crushing the victim's head or throat in an armlock; (by loose extension in New York City) to rob with any degree of force, with or without weapons. **1950** Salt *Lonely Place* (film): "She was...strangled by the vise-like grip of an arm." "You know—mugged." **1951** H. Robbins *Danny Fisher* 134: That guy there got mugged. **1952** Bellow *Augie March* 485: She said she was mugged in Central Park while walking the dog in the evening. **1953** W. Brown *Monkey on My Back* 196: All they'd done was mug a few guys and an old woman. **1955** Q. Reynolds *HQ* 311: "They tried to mug me," the man gasped. **1956** E. Hunter *Second Ending* 315: You will steal, and you will mug, and you will roll...you will do anything to feed that gorilla. **1961** Parkhurst *Undertow* 50: We used to go out lookin' for 'em; mug 'em, take money off 'em, stab 'em, beat 'em. **1966** Farrar *N.Y. Times Crosswords #14* 19: Assault from behind: Slang: MUGG. **1967** Sankey *Golden Screw* 64: Don't get mugged while out in the park. **1970** S. Ross *Fortune Machine* 12: Guys are mugged and robbed every day. **1979** in Terkel *Amer. Dreams* 126: One time I got mugged in the South Bronx....One guy stops me for a cigarette and...two guys grab me from behind. **1980** *N.Y. Post* (June 20) 74: The Angels mugged Ed Figueroa and Mike Griffin for 13 hits by the fifth inning. **1980** M. Harris *Why Nothing Works* 7: It's about old ladies getting mugged and raped. **1980** L. Fleischer & C. Gore *Fame* 226: Don't go mugging or raping anyone.

c. to steal (something) in a mugging.

1976–77 C. McFadden *Serial* 237: Who mugged your watch?

3.a. Esp. *Stu.* to kiss; (*hence*) to caress; NECK (in 1927 quot., in contrast to engaging in greater intimacies).—in recent use also constr. with *up.*

*1820–21 P. Egan *Life in London* 230: But while you both *mug* me together,/You'll make me a *spooney,*...I say. **1890* in *Dict. Austral. Eng.:* The mugging and kissing which M.E....bestowed so freely upon certain young ladies. **1916* C.J. Dennis, in *OEDS: Mug, to,* to kiss. **1924** P. Marks *Plastic Age* 271: I hate mugging and petting and that sort of thing. **1927** C. Aiken *Blue Voyage* 238: She's just a teaser. What they call a "mugger." **1929** Bodenheim *60 Secs.* 198: Cripes, another guy mugged her a few weeks after she left, for all I know. **1933** J.T. Farrell *Guillotine Party* 202: She was swell muggings, too. **1934** Weseen *Dict. Amer. Sl.* 189: *Mug*—To kiss. **1937** *AS* (Feb.) 74: *Mugging*—necking. **1942** *Yank* (Sept. 23) 14: He mugged her lightly. **1946** Boulware *Jive & Slang* 5: *Mugging Up*...Making love....*Mugging*...kissing. **1953** Eyster *Customary Skies* 49: A real blowout, not a mugging party with a chocolate. **1968** Baker et al. *CUSS* 160: *Mug.* To neck. **1971** Dahlskog *Dict.* 41: *Mugging up*....Making love; petting. **1970–72** in *AS* L (1976) 63: Razorback [Univ. Ark.] Slang...*mug* vt To kiss. **1996** La. woman, age 31 (coll. J. Sheidlower): We used *mugging* for kissing all the time in Louisiana—I would have heard it around 1986 or 1987.

b. (see quot.).

1954–60 *DAS: Mug*...To have sexual intercourse with. *Negro use.*

4.a. *Police.* to photograph (someone's) face for purposes of identification.

1899 "J. Flynt" *Tramping* 389: In some cities suspicious characters are arrested on general principles and immediately photographed by police authorities. Such towns are called "muggin' joints," and the police authorities "muggin' fiends." *Ibid.* 395: Mug...*verb,* to photograph. **1899–1900** Cullen *Tales* 332: He'd often been mugged for the picture papers. **1900** Willard & Hodler *Powers That Prey* 182: Good job for us 't we wasn't mugged that time that old Freckleton got 'is glims on us. **1912** *N.Y. Tribune Magazine* (Apr. 21) 11: Just tryin' to mug him? **1918** Livingston *Delcassee* 29: I was led to the "rogues' gallery" to be "mugged." **1918** in Sandburg *Letters* 131: And he has to get mugged and hand in three pictures of what kind of pickpocket he looks like. **1925** *Collier's* (Aug. 8) 30: When crooks are photographed, they are "mugged." **1928** Sharpe *Chicago May* 46: I got mugged and a place in the rogues' gallery. **1929** E. Booth *Stealing* 213: If he's been "mugged" before, we'd've had the return on him from Leavenworth by now. **1931** Post & Gatty *Around World* 160: Murderers and around-the-world flyers...have to get "mugged" in their working clothes. **1936** Benton & Ballou *Where Do I Go?* 116: Every new prisoner entering the walls was "mugged." **1940** *AS* (Dec.) 359: *Mugger.* One who specializes in portrait photographs. **1941** D'Usseau & Collins *Lady Scarface* (film): Slade's never even been mugged or finger-printed. **1944** C.B. Davis *Leo McGuire* 169: The Bertillon business and the fingerprinting and mugging. **1942–49** Goldin et al. *DAUL* 142: *Mugg*...To photograph, especially for the Criminal Bureau of

Identification. **1960** Himes *Gold Dream* 104: She was mugged and fingerprinted and her Bertillon measurements were taken. **1980** Gould *Ft. Apache* 53: Get the prisoners printed, mugged, and locked up.

b. *Und.* to apprehend (a criminal suspect), esp. for the purpose of identification.

1906 H. Green *Actors' Boarding House* 62: Holler out he's mugged an' sent you for the bankroll to spring him. **1929** Hotstetter & Beesley *Racket* 232: *Mug*—To take a suspect or a known criminal to the detective bureau for purposes of identification.

5. [extended fr. **(2)**, above] *West.* to throw (a steer); BULL-DOG, 1. Hence **mugger,** *n.*

1942 *ATS* 834: *Bulldog, mug him,* to throw a steer by a grip on his horns and nose and twisting his neck. **1968–70** *Current Slang III & IV* 85: *Mugger,* n. One who holds a cow's head down.—New Mexico State.

6. *Horse Racing.* to commit a foul.

1984 *N.Y. Post* (Sept. 3) 28: *Dorset* [was] DQd from second for mugging *Floating Rate* deep stretch. **1990** *N.Y. Post* (Jan. 2) 35: Oh How We Danced [was] DQd for mugging Cyclops Woman midstretch.

mug² *v.* to treat to a drink of liquor; (*hence*) to drink liquor; become intoxicated. *Rare* in U.S.

***1830** in *OED:* Having...mugged, as we say in England, our pilot. ***1854** in *OEDS:* Come! mug the girls, and they'll get on with their work. **1855** Brougham *Chips* 369: The private soakers...locks themselves up with the grog, and mugs themselves, alone. ***1889–90** Barrère & Leland *Dict. Slang* II 74: *To mug* oneself, to get tipsy. **1954–60** *DAS: Mug*...To drink an alcoholic beverage, esp. beer. ***1966** F. Shaw et al. *Scouse* 42: *Ile mug yer*—Allow me to treat you.

mug book *n.* **1.** *Police.* an album containing photographs of criminals and suspects.

1902 (quot. at MUSH, 3). **1950** Breen & Duff *Appt. with Danger* (film): "I picked it out of their mug book." "Mug book?" "It's a phrase she picked up." **1959** Zugsmith *Beat Generation* 61: Dave concentrated on the mug book. **1965** Spillane *Killer Mine* 142: There are police photos in the mug books and some newspaper full-length shots taken when he was arrested in a barroom brawl over there. **1981** R.B. Parker *Savage Place* 111: I'll want both of you downtown tomorrow to go through the mug books.

2. a collection of photographs of prominent people.

1935 Pollock *Und. Speaks: Mug book,* a book published for prominent business and professional men who are induced by high pressure solicitors to vividly write about themselves with youthful photographs. They pay well for this blue book privilege. **1989** Emmons *Butte Irish* 195: A hagiographic "mugbook" commemorating the members' contributions to the prosperity of the city.

mugger *n.* **1.** *Boxing.* a heavy blow to the face or mouth.

***1821** (cited in Partridge *DSUE* 1285). **1832** *Spirit of Times* (Mar. 31) 2: Larkins made play, hit short and received two muggers, bang, bang, which brought forth lots of claret.

2. one who assaults a person with intent to rob; a felon who MUGS people. Now *S.E.* [Early U.S. quots. ref. to Civil War.]

1863 (cited in *W10*). **1865** J.H. Browne *Secessia* 340: The Muggers, like most bullies and ruffians, manifested a fine discrimination respecting the party they attacked, selecting those they thought they could rob with little resistance and entire impunity. Every place in Secessia where miscellaneous captives are held contains its Muggers in abundance. [***1873** Hotten *Slang Dict: Maceman* or *macer*...a...general swindler; a "street-mugger."] **1888** Hawes *Cahaba* 221 [ref. to Castle Morgan Prison, Ala., 1864]: The N'Yaarkers...had been enlisted in the slums of the Empire City....The average robber assaults his victim from behind; the mugger assailed the one he would rob when standing almost face to face with him. Accepting this explanation for the origin of his cognomen, mugger would be synonymous with "facer" (mug, slang for face), one who faced his victim at the moment of assault. **1895** in *War Papers* I 304 [ref. to Salisbury, N.C., 1864]: This coterie of villains soon took the name of "Muggers," a synonym for thieves and murderers. *a***1910** A. Small *Rd. to Richmond* 165: Among them were desperadoes called "Muggers," who seemed to have the white card to beat, rob, and kill the weaker of their fellow prisoners....A "Mugger"...attempted to force his way in. **1943** Ottley *New World* 162: The case history of a mugger. **1944** D. Runyon, in *Collier's* (Jan. 15) 12: He is called Mike the Mugger because it seems his occupation is reaching out of doorways on dark nights and taking passers-by by

the neck...and examining their pockets. **1945** Crow & Crow *Teen-age* 256: The carrying of knives to school, and his boasts that he is a "mugger." *a***1946** W.G. Stevens *Chip on Shoulder* 155: Such are the conditions from which petty thieves, muggers, and potential murderers are moulded. **1948** *Neurotica* (Spring) 32: A mugger...stuck a knife in Jake's gizzard. **1955** Ellson *Rock* 43: That's what I'm most scared of,...a mugger or a guy needing moolah for dope. **1957** H. Danforth & J. Horan *D.A.'s Man* 223: Blackjack just grunted "Muggers." **1970–71** J. Rubinstein *City Police* 357: With fewer people on the street, muggers are encouraged to act. **1972** A. Kemp *Savior* 171: If the police don't get you the muggers will. **1974** Dubinsky & Standora *Decoy Cop* 172: Sneakers—what we in Anti-Crime refer to as "muggers' work shoes." **1977** Stinnett *Pleasures* 196: I am told I must always have $10 in my wallet for a possible mugger because without that I will surely be stabbed. **1978** Strieber *Wolfen* 40: Why don't you get the muggers off the street? **1980** in Courtwright et al. *Addicts Who Survived* 149: I wasn't a mugger or a stick-up man. *a***1982** Medved *Hospital* 254: Some muggers can't wait for you to take your rings off, so they take a knife and cut off your finger.

3. see MUG¹, *v.*, 5.

mugging *n.* [MUG¹, *v.*, 2.b.] a robbery of a person by any means on the street or in an isolated spot. Now *S.E.*

1943 *Yank* (Apr. 9) 19: A "mugging" wave hit uptown New York City residents. **1943** Halper *Inch from Glory* 102: What was it, Miss Lynch? A mugging?...Huh, they got dames mugging now, too? **1948** Lait & Mortimer *New York* 114: The result of these disclosures and the hundreds of muggings has been to drive the New York white element...out of the area. **1951** Yordan & Wyler *Detective Story* (film): Three muggings, one rape. **1953** W. Brown *Monkey on My Back* 17: Get...out of here before you get rolled. There's a dozen or more muggings around here every night.

muggins *n.* **1.** a fool; blockhead. *Obs.* in U.S.

1855 in *OEDS:* You are a veritable "Muggins" in [choosing] cigars. **1859** in C.A. Abbey *Before Mast* 208: We denominated him a "*Muggins.*" *a***1860** Hundley *So. States* 235: Suited only to gratify the taste and the financial credit of a Muggins. **1873** in *OED.* **1884** "M. Twain" *Huck. Finn* 191: Why, you talk like a muggins. ***1889–90** Barrère & Leland *Dict. Slang: Muggins*...one easily taken in, a simpleton. ***1990** T. Thorne *Dict. Contemp. Slang: Muggins*...British a victim, dupe or "loser."...It is now so common as to be an innocent colloquialism rather than true slang.

2. a kind of card game.

***1855** in *OEDS:* We returned to the hotel, to engage in the intellectual game of Muggins. Ladies and gentlemen were all decided to be Muggins ere the game had closed. **1864** Cheadle *Journal* 295: Played Old Maid & "Muggins," a kind of complicated Patience. **1865** C. Barney *Field Service* 173: "Whiskey Poker," "California Jack," and "Old Sledge," alternating with "Poker," "Muggins" and "Euchre."

3. (see quot.).

1862 in Babcock *Letters & Diaries* 94: A "muggins" is a bottle of whisky, and a "big muggins" is a gallon jug full.

4. *Und.* food.

1933 Ersine *Pris. Slang* 54: *Muggins,* n. Food.

muggled up *adj. Narc.* high on marijuana.

1933 (cited in Partridge *Dict. Und.* 455). **1941** S.J. Perelman, in *New Yorker* (Mar. 8) 14: Drunk? Possibly. Muggled up, more than likely. **1947** Boyer *Dark Ship* 153: An addict is "muggled up." **1959** in J. Cannon *Nobody Asked* 147: It doesn't need horns or a muggled-up drummer busting out with a solo until his sticks bust.

mugglehead *n. Narc.* a habitual smoker of marijuana.

1926 Maines & Grant *Wise-Crack Dict.* 11: *Mugglehead*—Smoker of Mexican loco weed. **1938** in La Guardia Comm. *Marihuana* 6: Youngsters known to be "muggle-heads" fortified themselves with the narcotic and proceeded to shoot down police. **1970** Landy *Underground Dict.: Muggle head*...User of marijuana.

muggles *n.* [orig. unkn.] *Narc.* **1.** marijuana.

1928 in *OEDS:* Muggles [title of gramophone record]. **1929** Tully *Shadows* 214: The Mexican convicts called it "Greefo." Hypo called it "muggles." **1929** Connelly *Green Pastures* 210: Used to peddle muggles. Said it had a kick like reg'lar snow. **1933** (quot. at MOTA). **1933** in Partridge *Dict. Und.* 455: I found myself on the Mexican border with a bad "yin" and nothing to relieve me but...marijuana. In New Orleans and other Southern American towns...this is known as "muggles," being sold in the form of cigarettes. **1936** D.W. Maurer, in *AS* (Apr.) 124: *Muggles*. Marijuana leaves before they are made into cigarettes, or *reefers*. **1937** Reitman *Box-Car Bertha* 119: Marajuana is called among the users, "muggles." **1938** in La Guardia Comm. *Marihuana* 6: They couldn't get their "muggles" at the Bureau. **1956** Ross *Hustlers* 91: It's just the muggles in the blood. **1958** R. Chandler *Playback* 104: How in hell do you get away with it? The muggles, I mean.

2. a marijuana cigarette or cigarettes. Also **muggle.**

    1933 *Fortune* (Aug.) 90: *Muggles* (named for the Mexican cigarettes drugged with marijuana which have inspired perfectly incredible solos). **1933** Ersine *Prison Slang* 54: *Muggles*, n. Cigarettes containing dope. **1933** *Newsweek* (Aug. 5) 26: One of the greatest problems now confronting Federal agents is the upswing in the use of marihuana cigarettes, better known to users as "reefers," "muggles," or "Mary Warners." **1939** R. Bradford *John Henry* 68: I done smoked…muggles. **1946** Mezzrow & Wolfe *Really Blues* 68: You got to hold that muggle so that it barely touches your lips. *Ibid.* 117: Do nothing but roll muggles all day long, each one five foot long. **1948** Lait & Mortimer *New York* 117: Hashish…is commonly called "tea," and the cigarettes made therefrom are called "reefers" or "muggles." **1949** R. MacDonald *Moving Target* 151: Douse the muggles, Marcie. **1950** Riesenberg *Reporter* 118: The underworld calls the cigarettes "reefers," "sticks," "muggles," and sometimes "Mary Warners." **1956** Resko *Reprieve* 237 [ref. to 1940's]: A reefer or muggle. **1958** Motley *Epitaph* 109: The muggles were going around like crazy, loose lip to loose lip. **1958–59** Lipton *Barbarians* 77: Muggles we called the marijuana cigarettes, and tea. **1959–60** R. Reisner *Jazz Titans* 162: *Pigfoot:* obsolete expression for marijuana; also *muggles*. **1962** *New Yorker* (Aug. 25) 36: "Do you handle muggles?" "Them marijuana cigarettes? No." **1965** H. Carmichael & S. Longstreet *Sometimes I Wonder* 101 [ref. to 1920's]: I lit my first muggle as Louis and King Oliver broke into…*Bugle Call Rag*. **1970** Landy *Underground Dict.: Muggle*…Marijuana cigarette.

mug-hunter *n. Tennis.* a player who enters many inferior competitions for the sake of collecting trophies.

    [***1889–90** Barrère & Leland *Dict. Slang: Mug-hunter*…one of a wretched horde…who infest the streets at night to pick up and rob those who are made foolish (mugs) by their drunkenness.] **1893** W.K. Post *Harvard* 170: He is simply a mug hunter. **1942** *ATS* 627: Contestant for a prize. *Mug hunter*. **1949** Cummings *Dict. Sports* 274. **1976** *AS* 51: 293.

mug joint *n. Circus & Carnival.* a photography concession.

    1931 *Amer. Mercury* (Nov.) 353: *Mug joint*…a while-you-wait photographer's tent. **1935** *Amer. Mercury* (June) 230: *Mug joint*: photograph gallery. **1939** *Life* (July 31) 24: Mug-joint in Sun Valley was almost a flop until gate was upped to 40¢. **1970** A. Lewis *Carnival* 302: Mrs. Lee Hos, an attractive blonde mugg-joint operator.

mugman *n. Carnival.* a portrait photographer.

    1931 *AS* (June) 333: *Mugman*, n. An itinerant photographer. **1942** *ATS* 624: *Mugger, mug man, mugman, mugsnapper*, the photographer in a picture concession.

mug room *n. Police.* (see quots.).

    1931 *AS* VI (Aug.) 440: *Mug Room.* The room where prisoners are photographed. **1934** (cited in Partridge *Dict. Und.* 455).

mug's game *n.* an enterprise known to be foolish, useless, or unprofitable.

    ***1910** H. Belloc, in *OED2*: One cannot arrest millionaires with impunity.…Even in a wild democracy to arrest them is Mug's [*sic*] game. ***1918** in *OED2*: Flying is a mug's game, mater, A fact I know full well. ***1930** G.B. Shaw, in *OED2*: Politics is a mug's game. ***1960** A. Sillitoe (cited in J. Green *Dict. Contemp. Sl.* 185). **1965–70** in *Qly. Jour. Studies on Alcohol* XXXII (1971) 734: *Mug's game* A useless, continually painful endeavor; e.g., alcoholism. **1970** La Motta, Carter & Savage *Raging Bull* 83: It's a sucker game. A mug's game. **1992** *Sonya Live* (CNN-TV) (Mar. 31): I'm not in the business of picking [winners]. That's, as they say, a mug's game. **1996** *Skeptical Inquirer* (Sept.) 24: Made a conscious decision that science fiction was a mug's game, and that the real money was in starting a religion.

mug-shoot *v.* to take a MUG SHOT of. Hence **mug-shooter,** *n.*

    1939 Howsley *Argot* 34: *Mug Shooter*—Photographer. **1979** in Terkel *Amer. Dreams* 246: They did fingerprint me and mug-shot me. **1996** *News Day* (CNN-TV) (Oct. 14): They…fingerprinted us and mug-shotted me.

mug shot *n. Esp. Police.* MUG, *n.,* 1.d. Now *S.E.*

1950 in *DAS*: Police passed around a mug shot of Willie. **1955** Q. Reynolds *HQ* 80: Go to the B. of I. and look at their mug shots. **1973** J.E. Martin *95 File* 9: A wall papered with sullen-faced mug shots. **1974** Millard *Thunderbolt* 12: The intruder's features were cloaked in shadow, but he needed no mug shot to identify the gangling figure. **1976** Hoffman & Pecznick *Drop a Dime* 24: The policeman punched Pecznick in the face—the mug shots show him with a black eye. **1980** D. Hamill *Stomping Ground* 166: Mug shots of notorious bank robbers. **1983** WINS radio news (N.Y.C.) (Aug. 24): They have asked the parishioners to come down and try to identify some mug shots. **1984** J. McNamara *First Directive* 225: I got some mug shots of him. **1988** De Lillo *Libra* 327: Seeing himself as he would appear in the mug shots, dignified and balding. **1989** Hiaasen *Skin Tight* 16: It didn't match the mug shot. **1992** M. Gelman *Crime Scene* 82: The only sign of Richardson was his mug shot. **1994** *Daybreak Saturday* (CNN-TV) (June 18): Was fingerprinted and his mug shot was taken.

mug-up *n. Esp. Naut.* a snack or drink of coffee; (*hence*) a short respite, as for such a snack.

    1933 in *OEDS*: Back at the tent we had a mug-up, lashed up and said good-bye to the Indians. **1942** *Amer. Neptune* (July) 236 [ref. to Pensacola, Fla., 1915–19]: The crew…pile down into the forecastle for their sunrise "mug-up." *Ibid.* 239: There is another break around ten-thirty o'clock for the mid-morning "mug-up." **1949** *Sat. Eve. Post* (May 21) 40: "I make coffee?" he asked, knowing the Finn was always a sucker for a mug-up. **1957** *Sat. Eve. Post* (Mar. 16) 139: At our noon mug-up at the cabin I heard a piece of news. **1972** Cleaves *Sea Fever* 246: I went…to get a mug-up of coffee.

mug up[1] *v. Stu.* to study hard; BONE, 4.a. Also (*obs.*) **mug.**

    ***1848** in *OED*: Please to write about your Prizes at College, and about coming here to mug. ***1866** in *F & H* IV 381: The praefects would…set to work mugging. **1942** *ATS* 778: *Load, mug, mug up (on),*…to engage in an intense period of study or memorizing, as for an examination. ***1952** *Harper's* (Aug.) 75: One had feverishly mugged up spot subjects just before an examination. **1962** *N.Y. Times* (Feb. 4) VII 36: "Mugging up" science, technology, or anything else for the purpose of getting "material" is worse than useless; the writer's basic lack of insight will stick out like a sore thumb. **1962** *New Yorker* (Nov. 16) 118: All very nice, but dull, too—dull and conscientious, mugged up from picture books. **1977** *N.Y. Times Book Review* (Aug. 7) 18: Here is the place to mug up on Gerard Manley Hopkins's influential revival of sprung rhythm.

mug up[2] *v.* to drink, esp. one's fill of coffee; (*also*) to eat, esp. a snack.

    1917** in *OEDS*: Coats and mufflers were donned and a bottle of sloe-gin uncorked. "Mug-up!" cried the Sub. "Mug-up, and let's get 'appy and chatty." **1923** Southgate *Rusty Door* 116: Do we eat reg'lar or just mug up to-night? *a1930** in Tomlinson *Sea Stories* 578: Well, we mugged up about seven o'clock. **1933** Ersine *Prison Slang* 54: *Mug up.* To eat. **1945** in *Calif. Folk. Qly.* V (1946) 380: *Mug up.* Drink one or more cups of coffee. Drink one's fill. **1958** McCulloch *Woods Wds.* 119: *Mug up*—To have a cup of coffee around a campfire, or other than at regular meal times. **1962** *Sat. Eve. Post* (Sept. 8) 40: Dorymen coming off watch could "mug up" on tea and cookies.

mugwump *n.* **1.** Orig. *N.E.* a person in authority, as an official of a fraternal society (*obs.*); (*hence*) a self-important person; (*broadly*) an obnoxious person.

    1832 in *DAE*: The secret bulletin…has extensively circulated among the Knights of Kadosh and the Most Worshipful Mug-Wumps of the Cabletow. **1835** in *DA*: The significant appellation of *Mugwump*…[is] used at the present day vulgarly and masonically, as synonymous with greatness and strength. **1840** in *F & H* IV 383: Then the great mugwump was delivered of a speech which the faithful loudly applauded. **1865** in *DAE*: One other political bruiser we like to have forgotten…is "Uncle Nat Eaton," formerly of Calais, but now "Mugwump" No. 2, of Middlesex. **1877** in *DAE*: John A. Logan is the…King Pin, the Main Spring, Mogul, and Mugwump of the final plot. **1884** in *Century Dict.*: We have yet to see a Blaine organ which speaks of the Independent Republicans otherwise than as Pharisees, hypocrites, dudes, mugwumps, transcendentalists, or something of that sort. **1890** *DN* I 22: *Mugwump*…I spent my boyhood in Franklin County, Vt. My wife spent her early life in a village which was both in Vermont and Canada. She was likewise familiar with the same word…current with the meaning, "a person who makes great pretensions and whose character or ability or resources are not equal to his pretensions." [Our memories certify] that the word goes back to the early fifties. **1899** Boyd *Shellback* 98: You infernal mugwump! **1950** in M. Daly *Profile of Youth* 241: What makes a boy a "scrounger" or a "slob," a girl a…"mugwump"? Here is what high-school fellows and girls reveal as their pet personality dislikes.

2. (often *cap.*) *Pol.* a person, esp. a politician, who withdraws support from his own party; a bolter; (*hence*) one who refuses to take a strong stand on an issue when expected by colleagues to do so.—also used attrib. Now *colloq.* [Applied, orig. as a mere extension of **(1),** above, to Republicans who would not support the party's presidential candidate, James G. Blaine, in the election of 1884; cf. 1884 quot. at **(1),** above.]

    1884 in *DA:* It may be that in a few years…a little group of British Mugwumps…will arise in their might [etc.]. **1885** in M. Keller *T. Nast* (plate 238): Democratic and Republican Mugwumps. **1886** Nye *Remarks* 37: To the President.—I write this letter…on behalf of a personal friend of mine who is known as a mugwump. **1887** in *F & H* IV 383: *Mugwump*…is now generally applied to those who profess to study the interests of their country before those of their party. **1887** F. Francis *Saddle & Moccasin* 188: I am uncertain what the *burro's* politics were; some of the boys asserted that he was a Mugwump. **1894** in *DAE:* I'd have believed anything but that you [a Democrat] would be a dashed Mugwump! **1902** Mead *Word-Coinage* 179: "Mugwump"…will be in every dictionary in the year 1950, just as the good slang of fifty years ago is in the lexicons of to-day. **1905** Riordan *Plunkitt* 12: Fifty-five Republicans and mugwumps…! **1909** in O. Johnson *Lawrenceville* 151: Crazy Opdyke had organized a Mugwump party. **1919** Fiske *Midshipman* 86: Mr. Cleveland was elected [in 1884] with the assistance of the so-called "mugwumps," who were Republicans who revolted against Blaine. **1950** *N.Y. Times* (Oct. 4) 21: This suggestion pleases that small group of political mugwumps in Washington. **1952** C. Sandburg *Young Strangers* 163 [ref. to 1884]: I heard a Blaine Republican say, "A mugwump is a man who sits with his mug on one side of the fence and his wump on the other." **1989** Rawson *Wicked Words* 260: The classic definition of a *mugwump* is "a man with his mug on one side of the fence and his wump on the other" (attr. [to] Harold Willis Dodds, president of Princeton University, 1933–37). **1992** *Capital Gang* (CNN-TV) (May 16): The problem with George Bush is he's a mugwump.

mugwump *v. Journ.* to behave in the manner of a political MUGWUMP.

    1889 in *DAE:* E. D. Graves…"Mugwumped to Cleveland," in 1884 because he "could not conscientiously support James G. Blaine." **1958** *Time* (Mar. 3) 12: Brossard mugwumped, but the other five members all said no.

muhfuh *n.* [repr. a strongly elided pronun. of MOTHERFUCKER] Esp. *Black E.* MOTHERFUCKER; MOFO.—usu. considered vulgar. Also **muhfuhkuh.**

    1969 B. Beckham *Main Mother* 148: Where you muh fuhs from? **1972** B. Beckham *Runner Mack* 186: We're taking over, muhfuh. **1974** *Village Voice* (N.Y.C.), in *DAS* (ed. 3): I had a .22 in my bag because I was headed for the New Lots and them muh-fuhs are superbad. **1974** in *Black World* (Jan. 1975) 57: Get *out* of here, you muh-fuh! **1980** Gould *Ft. Apache* 81: Hey, muh fuh, I ain't no junkie. **1983** in G. Tate *Flyboy* 91: What was you gonna do, marry the muhfuh? **1993** in A. Sexton *Rap on Rap* 20: A muhfuhkuh.

Muldoon *n.* ¶ In phrase: **the solid Muldoon** [pop. by "Muldoon the Solid Man," a vaudeville song by Harrigan and Hart (1874)] the real thing, esp. the truth.

    1879 in E. West *Saloon* 162: Solid Muldoon [name of newspaper of Ouray, Colo.]. [**1882** Peck *Peck's Sunshine* 72: They…were playing a selection from the opera of "Solid Muldoon."] **1958** S.H. Adams *Tenderloin* 170 [ref. to 1890's]: The cops ain't givin' us the solid Muldoon on this thing.

mule *n.* **1.** Esp. *Mil.* tough or stringy beef, esp. corned beef.

    1862 in J.M. Williams *That Terrible Field* 67: Salt Beef…which our boys always call "mule meet" [*sic*]. *Ibid.* 100: Old pickled beef (better known in camp as "mule meat". **1887** Peck *Pvt. Peck* 58 [ref. to Civil War]: There was no man that could boil corned mule so as to take the taste of the saltpetre out, as he could. **1899** Elderkin *Sketches* 168 [ref. to Civil War]: Our rations were pretty good except the corn beef; it was very bad and of coarse grain, and the boys called it "Salt horse, or

mule meat." **1919** *Lit. Digest* (June 1) 78: You make no mention of corned beef, affectionately (???) called canned Bill, embalmed mule, etc. **1919** (quot. at EMBALMED BEEF). **1937** *Our Army* (Jan.) 20: Right after lunch, consisting of the lousiest G.I. mule ever foisted upon defenseless doggies, I'm picking the harness out of my teeth as I walk into the orderly room.

2. any of various small powered vehicles used for dragging, towing, conveying, etc. Now *colloq.* or *S.E.*

    1903 in *OEDS:* The "mule" has two large hooks for the towropes. **1941** Attaway *Blood on the Forge* 61: A few would stoke the "mules," small engines that hauled steel along the river front. **1942** *AS* (Dec.) 222: *Iron Mule.* A small dumpcart with caterpillar drive [used in logging operations]. **1959** *Harper's* (June) 64: Small powered wagons called mules. **1964** *N.Y. Times* (Feb. 2) I 30: Ships…are towed by electric mules, small locomotives running on rails. **1985** M. Brennan *War* 18 [ref. to 1965]: The graves registration team had to meet each chopper with its load of carrion and transport the bodies on their bouncing "mules," little four-wheel-drive vehicles that looked like platforms on wheels, back to the processing tent. *a*1990 Helms *Proud Bastards* 179: A couple of balloon-tired "mules" sporting 106mm recoilless rifles.

3. raw alcohol or illicitly distilled whiskey; WHITE MULE.

    1922 *Harper's* (Mar.) 530: They found some of the pill peddlers drinking mule and aqua. **1926** *AS* I (Dec.) 652: *Mule.* corn alcohol. **1929** Milburn *Hobo's Hornbook* 150: Justice Grimes…called the constabule,/ Who tossed us in the booby, and took away our mule. **1929** *AS* IV (June) 385: It appears that the ordinary liquor of the region is a white distillate of corn or rye, variously known as *corn, corn-mule, rye-sap, corn-juice, roasting-ear wine, mule, rye, booze* and *hootch.* **1929** Barr *Let Tomorrow Come* 40: I'm rummy from a lot o' mule I drank farther up the line. *Ibid.* 267: *Mule*—Raw alcohol. **1938** in Oliver *Meaning of Blues* 193: An' if we can't get decent whisky, we will take a drink of mule. **1942** *ATS* 114: Mule,…raw corn whiskey, esp. illicit. **1948** *Sat. Eve. Post* (June 26) 86: A drink compared to which Kentucky mule is soda pop. **1952** Viereck *Men into Beasts* 123: A woman is only a woman, but a good shot of mule is a drink.

4. *Und. & Police.* a person who smuggles or delivers contraband, esp. illicit drugs, usu. as a low-level member of a criminal organization.

    1922 E. Murphy *Black Candle* 128: The "mules" and "joy shots" are among the most vicious elements in the [morphine] plague. **1935** Pollock *Und. Speaks: Mule,* person who carries dope for a drug trafficker and passes drug to buyer after a sale has been made. **1952** *Sat. Eve. Post* (Aug. 23) 30: Heroin is smuggled into this country by "mules," who are professional carriers. **1955** Q. Reynolds *HQ* 276: My boys have spotted…a couple of mules." …Mules…are young drug peddlers who make a specialty of selling narcotics to high school students. **1958** *N.Y. Times Mag.* (Mar. 16) 88: *Mule*—One—usually a minor—who delivers or sells narcotics within his own age group. **1972** *Newsweek* (Jan. 24) 25: Customs officials arrested a sickly looking 24-year-old Panamanian named Rafael Gonzalez Richard—a "mule" or heroin courier—and his "shotgun," who accompanied him to report back on the success of the deal. **1975** V.B. Miller *Deadly Game* 96: We got a million in heroin, three of his mules in the joint, and we lost him! **1977** Bunker *Animal Factory* 124: And he's a mule. He won't bring dope or anything hot, but he'll pack out letters and bring in money. **1981** Jenkins *Baja Okla.* 14: Dove's "mule" had used the method in returning from a buying trip to Bolivia. **1984** *L.A. Daily Journal* (May 18) I 1: [He] described himself in bankruptcy papers as a "smuggler and mule of legal tangible goods." **1990** G.R. Clark *Words of Viet. War* 337: *Mule* GI nickname for a Viet civilian who transported arms, ammunition, and supplies for the NVA/VC. **1994** *Newsweek* (Apr. 18) 22: Thailand may incarcerate loads of small-fry mules smuggling dope, but it leaves untouched the drug kingpins. **1994** *N.Y. Times* (Aug. 15) D5: "Mules" pass the checks in return for 20 percent of the take. Typically, cells of six or seven mules travel to a city with one or two controllers, who buy their tickets and provide the checks to forge.

5. *R.R.* a fourth cook or waiter.

    1927 C. McKay *Harlem* 66: The fourth waiter on the railroad is nicknamed "mule" because he works under the orders of the pantry-man. **1942** *Pittsburgh Courier* (Sept. 19) 15: *Mule*—Fourth cook on the railroad.

6. *R.R.* a brakeman.

    1929 *Bookman* (July) 526: There is no danger of being struck down if you call either [head or hind brakeman] a Mule. **1942** *ATS* 723: Brakeman.…*juggler, mule.*

7. the penis.—usu. considered vulgar. See also *lope (one's) mule, water (one's) mule,* below.

1947–53 W. Guthrie *Seeds* 68: I'm a cravin' to slip my big slick mule, Honey Gal, into your little stable so's he won't feel so big an' so hot all the time. **1968** Lockridge *Hartspring* 65: Hartspring…leaps his desk, whips out his tired old mule. **1991** Marcinko & Weisberg *Rogue Warrior* 101: Sitting…stroking our mules.

8. *Auto Racing.* a backup or practice car.

1976 *Webster's Sports Dict.* 277. **1980** Pearl *Pop. Slang* 103: *Mule*…(Auto Racing) a car used for practice.

¶ In phrases:

¶ **here's your mule** (used as a soldier's catch phrase during the Civil War).

1865 in Dolph *Sound Off!* 304: When a horseman passes, the soldiers have a rule,/To cry out at their loudest, "Mister here's your mule." **1882** S. Watkin *Co. Aytch* 33 [ref. to 1862]: I felt Schwartz grab me, and give me a shake, and at the same time raised his gun and fired, and yelled out at the top of his voice, "Here is your mule."

¶ **lope (one's) mule, 1.** Esp. *So. & West.* (of a man) to masturbate.—usu. considered vulgar. Also **lope (one's) pony.**

1961 L.E. Young *Virgin Fleet* 27 [ref. to 1941]: It keeps you swab jockeys from finding corners in which to lope your mules. **1965** Trimble *Sex Words* 123: *Lope The Mule*…To Masturbate the Penis. **1966** Braly *On Yard* 13: He sniffs it while he lopes his mule. **1968** J.P. Miller *Race for Home* 284 [ref. to ca1930]: You cain't even get a hard on to lope yer mule, nohow. **1972** *Nat. Lampoon* (Apr.) 30: Harry P. Ness, Lope DeMule, Claude Balls, Stella Virgin, Hugo Jerkov. **1973** Gwaltney *Destiny's Chickens* 9: Man like old Orval's particular where he hides his pickup when he's loping his mule. **1975** Wambaugh *Choirboys* 99: I'm tellin you she was lopin my mule under the table. **1979** Crews *Blood & Grits* 50: I loped my pony in the tiled, sterile bathroom and brought the little cup of come to the nurse. **1985** Dye *Between Raindrops* 221: You can't go loping your fucking mule up there. We got a job to do. **1985** Heywood *Taxi Dancer* 145: Where you been, babes?…Lopin' your mule? **1989** *Nat. Lampoon* (June) 67: Lope the mule? Why the hell not?

2. to copulate.—usu. considered vulgar.

1961 Peacock *Valhalla* 11: And they ain't gonna let us run wild lopin our mules in Yokohama.

¶ **ride Morgan's mule** [alluding to General John Hunt Morgan, Confederate cavalry commander noted for an 1863 raid into Indiana and Ohio to secure horses and mules] *Confederate Army.* (see 1867 quot.).

1867 B. Duke *Morgan's Cavalry* 499 [ref. to 1863]: Others, again, were made to "ride Morgan's mule" (as a scantling frame, of ten or twelve feet in height, was called), the peculiar and beautiful feature of this method of torture, was the very sharp back of "the mule." Sometimes, heavy blocks, humorously styled spurs, were attached to the feet of the rider. *ca*1890 in H.W. Williams *Civil War* 87: Riding Morgan's mule. **1900** *Confed. Veteran* VIII 351 [ref. to 1863]: Reb was threatened with a ride on "Morgan's mule" if he did not inform on the others. **1914** Giles *Rags & Hope* 227 [ref. to 1864]: I…thereby escaped a ride on "Morgan's Mule."

¶ **suck-egg mule** see SUCK-EGG MULE.

¶ **water (one's) mule** (of a male) to urinate. *Joc.*

1990 *UTSQ: Water your mule*—Means to urinate. "Don't leave yet, I have to water my mule."

mule *v. Und. & Police.* to act as a courier of contraband, esp. illicit drugs; *(trans.)* to convey (contraband).

1965 *Sat. Eve. Post* (Dec. 4) 26: A favorite technique is "muling," a term which stems from the days when Mexican peons smuggled marijuana, hidden under heads of lettuce and other produce, on the backs of mules. Today old trucks and cars are used. **1978** Nolan & Mann *Jericho Mile* (film): I'm gonna be Dr. D's junk mule?…I'm gonna mule in his smack? **1980** *Magnum P.I.* (ABC-TV): He wasn't mulin' for anybody. **1986** *Miami Vice* (NBC-TV): He wanted me to mule fifty keys over to Baton Rouge for him. **1990** *Twin Peaks* (ABC-TV): You and your brother mule it across the border.

mule breakfast *n.* a straw hat. *Joc.*

1929 E. Booth *Stealing* 306 [ref. to ca1922]: The large and grotesquely shaped "mule breakfasts" covering our heads gave no pro-

tection from the forge heat welling up about us. **1942** *ATS* 90: Straw hat.… *mule's breakfast.*

mule cavalry *n. Army.* mounted infantry. *Joc.*

1862 F. Moore *Rebellion Rec.* V 599: The mounted infantry, or "mule cavalry," proved an entire success.…They move with the celerity of cavalry, yet fight as infantry.

mulenyam *n.* [var. of It *melanzana* 'eggplant'] *Ital.-Amer.* a black person.—used contemptuously. Also vars. [Perh. see also MULLION, which may be a var. of this.]

1967 Riessman & Dawkins *Play It Cool* 68: *Moulenjam n.* a Negro: Her old man's no moulenjam. **1972** Grogan *Ringolevio* 222: He spent so many…hours hanging out with his black buddies that the…apple-knockers…formed the opinion that Kenny was probably a "moulon-jam" himself. **1988** R. Menllo & R. Rubin *Tougher Than Leather* (film): This business with these fuckin mulenyahns [pronunciation *sic*], it's tearin' my heart out. **1989** in *Harper's* (Mar. 1990) 71: Blacks are called *mulenyam*, a corruption of *melanzane*, eggplants. **1994** Kriegel *Bless Me, Father* 45: Those *moolinyans* at the park.

mule's earful *n.* (see quot.).

1876 J.M. Reid *Old Settlers* 156: Luke always took what he termed a "snort" or a "mules ear full" at a drink.

mule shit *interj.* (used to express disbelief, astonishment, or the like).—usu. considered vulgar.

1928 in Read *Lexical Evidence* 75: Mule shit. **1968** J.P. Miller *Race for Home* 237 [ref. to 1930s]: Did I say horse shit? I meant pig shit! Mule shit! Percheron piss! Now git outa here, you little limbertwig, and leave us alone! **1977** Sayles *Union Dues* 14: Muleshit.…We pulled one apiece.

mule skinner *n. Esp. West.* a mule driver. Now *S.E.*

1870 in *DAE*: I took to the plains…in the capacity of a "mule-skinner." **1879** (quot. at COWPUNCHER). **1881** Crofutt *Gde. to Colo.* 178: On the plains…mule drivers [are called] "mule-skinners." **1888** in *DAE*: Teamsters, known either as "bull-whackers" or as "mule-skinners." **1906** M'Govern *Sarjint Larry* 72: These "mule-skinners" (so the soldiers call the packers in sour-grapish moments) are high priced civilian employees of the army who look upon ordinary soldiers as being socially too small fry for them to talk to. **1909** J. Moss *Officer's Manual* 283: *Mule-Skinner.* A teamster. **1915** H. Young *Hard Knocks* 43: The term used for mule drivers in those days [1868] was "mule-skinners." *Ibid.* 174: The traces…were made of chain, covered with leather, which…would become worn and…the bare chain would skin the mule up awfully, and I believe that this why they termed teamsters "mule-skinners." **1937** *AS* (Feb.) 75: *Mule-skinner*—driver of mules. *a*1956 Almirall *College to Cow Country* 212 [ref. to *a*1918]: I had heard mule skinners in New Mexico display an amazing vocabulary [of expletives and invective].

mule-skinning *adj.* COTTON-PICKING; damned.

1963 E.M. Miller *Exile* 23: Tell him to call you sir and keep his mule-skinning hands to himself. *Ibid.* 116: Mule-skinnin'est weather I ever did see. Blows hot, blows cold.

mule whacker *n.* a mule driver.

1873 Beadle *Undeveloped West* 97: The Author as A "Mulewhacker." **1887** Hinman *Si Klegg* 250 [ref. to Civil War]: All the soljers does, from the major-gin'rals down to the tail-end o' the mule-whackers. **1896** T.C.S. Brown et al. *Behind Guns* 127 [ref. to Civil War]: A fine six-mule team, driven by a sturdy "mule whacker." **1926** *AS* II (Nov.) 88: The *mule whacker,* who formerly drove the mule cars to the *level station,* has become an electric motorman.

muley *n. West.* a hornless saddle. *Joc.*

1909 Fletcher *Up the Trail* 108 [ref. to 1879]: The soldiers…were bouncing up and down in their "muley" saddles in hot pursuit of the bandits. **1936** R. Adams *Cowboy Lingo* 47: A saddle…without a horn or pommel was a "muley."

mullarkey var. MALARKEY.

mulled *adj.* drunk.—sometimes constr. with *up.*

1930 D. Runyon, in *Collier's* (Feb. 1) 7: But being mulled up like I tell you, things look very different to Wilbur Willard. *Ibid.* 8: He is only a little bit mulled. **1954–60** *DAS: Mulled*[,] *mulled up*…Drunk. Never common. **1965–70** in *Qly. Jour. Studies on Alcohol* XXXII (1971) 734: *Mulled up* Intoxicated. Also, *half-mulled up. Well-mulled* = pleasant state of intoxication.

mullet *n.* a fool; MULLETHEAD.

1955 in J. Blake *Joint* 103: If I don't have bread, I may look around for a likely prospect (locally, "mullet") to buy it for me. **1959** *AS* (May) 154: The opposite of a B.M.O.C. is a...*mullet*. **1976** Eble *Campus Slang* (Nov.) 4: *Mullet*...a person who is gullible or easily persuaded. **1981–89** R. Atkinson *Long Gray Line* 155: Gimme twenty-five right now, mullet!

mullethead *n.* a blockhead; numskull. Hence **mullet-headed**, *adj.*

    1857 in *DA:* The men, for the most part sleepy, ignorant, mullet-headed looking wretches. [**1866** in *DA:* Dat fish is a mullet-head; it hain't got any brains.] **1884** "M. Twain" *Huck. Finn* ch. xxxix: They're so confiding and mullet-headed they don't take notice of nothing at all. **1934** Weseen *Dict. Sl.* 369: *Mullet head*—A stupid person. **1950** O'Brian & Evans *Chain Lightning* (film): That mullet-head from the 347th. **1963** E.M. Miller *Exile* 237: Someone who's just a damned mullet-head, whose stupidity could have killed me. **1970** M. Thomas *Total Beast* 247: Any time I can't beat this bunch of mullet heads, that'll be a day to remember.

mulligaloot *n.* [app. *mulli-* (orig. unkn., perh. abstracted fr. *mulligan*) + GALOOT] a crude or stupid person; oaf.

    1887 [C. Mackenzie] *Jack Pots* 101: "You're a liar!" "You're another, you dumbfounded old mulligaloot!"

mulligan *n.* [fr. *Mulligan*, common Irish family name] **1.a.** (cap.) an Irish person.—used derisively.—also used attrib.

    1874 in Alger *Julius* 11: We'll tell you what we know/Of marching in the Mulligan Guard,/From Sligo Ward below. **1898–1900** Cullen *Chances* 238: For a Mulligan that knows so little about business as you, Tim. **1899–1900** Cullen *Tales* 257: I don't know anything about you except that you've got a square jaw and a proper Mulligan look, but I guess you're worth taking a chance on. *Ibid.* 306: Just then a big bruiser of an Irish attendant sauntered by. "Hey, there, Hugo," said the man in the bunk on my right, calling after the Mulligan attendant. *Ibid.* 307: "Two days,"...said the Mulligan. **1939** Howsley *Argot* 34: *Mulligan*—a cop on the beat; an Irishman. **1939** Appel *Power House* 11: Whoever told you that's a cockeyed Mulligan.

b. Irish whiskey. [Perh. a nonce term.]

    1920 T.A. Dorgan, in Zwilling *TAD Lexicon* 117: (One of the guys...orders himself a shot) Say Al!! Pour me out a split of ale an' put a dash of mulligan in it.

2.a. a stew made of odds and ends of vegetables and meat. Now *S.E.*

    1904 in *OEDS:* All the roadhouses served big Christmas dinners and most of them made a mulligan. **1906** Beyer *Amer. Battleship* 83: "Mulligan"—a favorite dish [which] is an unknown quantity. **1907** J. London *Road* 27 [ref. to *ca*1894]: I...waited at water-tanks, "boiled-up," cooked "mulligan," "battered" the "drag" or "privates." *a*1909 Tillotson *Detective* 93: *Mulligan*—A stew. **1912** Lowrie *Prison* 106: We used to make "hash" or a "mulligan" each Sunday night. **1915** in Roy *Pvt. Fraser* 41: We dined on beef-steak instead of the everlasting mulligan and bully-beef. **1922** N. Anderson *Hobo* 18: "Mulligan," or "combination," is a "throw together" of vegetables and meat. **1928** M. Sharpe *Chicago May* 287: *Mulligan*—stew. **1942** *Yank* (Sept. 16) 20: McTurk makes a Mulligan. **1945** *Back to Bataan* (film): Without twenty years experience on that road, could I have made up a mulligan like that? **1948** B. Ives *Wayfaring Stranger* 133: Give him some mulligan. **1952** in *DAS:* You're just in time for hot mulligan! **1980** Bruns *Kts. of Road* 16: Here the 'boes could...share the mulligan. **1985** C. Busch *Times Sq. Angel* 10: My Mulligan stew.

b. *Logging.* a vehicle used to bring a work crew to meals.

    1958 McCulloch *Woods Wds.* 119: *Mulligan*—At one time hot noon meals were brought out to the men in the woods. A specially fitted railroad car was used for this purpose, known as a mulligan, from the mulligan or soup which it carried. Later the men were hauled to camp...[to eat] at noon, and mulligan became any crew carrier. Now it is applied to trucks and busses.

3. *Pris.* a police officer or prison guard.

    1939 (quot. at **(1)**, above). **1942–49** Goldin et al. *DAUL* 142: *Mulligan*...(La. and other Gulf State prisons) A prison guard. **1962–68** B. Jackson *In the Life* 283: They call 'em personnels now, call 'em officers. They used to call 'em guards, mulligans. **1970** M. Thomas *Total Beast* 10: A mulligan brought two slices of bread and a tin cup of water twice a day and slid them through a panel at the bottom of the steel plate.

4.a. *Golf.* a second chance to play a shot, granted to an opponent in an informal game.

    1949 Cummings *Dict. Sports* 275: *Mulligan*...a handicap of a free shot given after a player makes a bad one. **1952** in *OEDS:* It's just a friendly match....Wanna take a mulligan? **1960** in Davies *Hist. Dict. Golf.:* I don't even know if there *was* a Mulligan. But he gave his name to a wonderful gesture—letting you play a bad first drive over, and no penalty. **1970** Scharff *Encyc. of Golf* 419: *Mulligan.* A second shot, usually off the first tee, that is sometimes permitted in a casual game. Same as *Shapiro*. **1977** in Davies *Hist. Dict. Golf.:* Hope moans a lot about the way the fates treat him in golf....He will take six mulligans if you let him. **1996** *Weekend Edition* (Nat. Pub. Radio) (Nov. 16): "You mean he's taking mulligans?" "Yes. Extra shots."

b. any unexpected second chance.

    1996 *N.Y. Times* (Feb. 18) ("Wk. in Rev.") 13: You've got to call it quits and get a decent nominee. Take a mulligan. **1996** *Mystery Sci. Theater* (Comedy Central TV): I should destroy you, but I'll give you a mulligan on that one.

mulligrubs *n.* **1.** colic; diarrhea.

    ***1619** in *F & H* IV 384: Whose dog lies sick o' the mulligrubs. ***1698–1720** in D'Urfey *Pills* V 311: The Gout,...the Pox, the Mulli-grubs, [etc.]. ***1853** (cited in Partridge *DSUE* 542). **1973** N.Y.U. professor: I had the 24-hour mulligrubs last night.

2. sulkiness; depression; low spirits.

    [***1599** in *F & H* IV 384: Wherewith Peters successour was so in his mulliegrums that he had thought to have buffeted him, and cursed him with bell book and candle.] ***1796** Grose *Dict. Vulgar Tongue* (ed. 3): *Sick of the mulligrubs with eating chopped hay;* low-spirited, having an imaginary sickness. [**1804** Brackenridge *Mod. Chivalry* 343: He may call [his paper] the Mully-Grub.] ***1822** in *F & H* IV 384: Repeating as the rich cordial trickled forth in a smooth oily stream—"Right Rosa Solis, as ever washed the mulligrubs out of a moody brain." **1938** in *AS* (Apr. 1939) 91: [Tenn.:] In the *Mulligrubs.* Despondent or in low spirits. "He's in the mulligrubs." **1954–60** *DAS: Mulligrubs, the...= the blues.* **1960–61** Steinbeck *Discontent* 64: You seem to have got over your mullygrubs. *Ibid.* 260: It gives me a shiver of mullygrubs.

mullion *n.* [orig. uncert.; perh. related to MULENYAM] *Black E & Baseball.* an ugly person.

    1959 Brosnan *Long Season* 247: "Hey, Mullion-man!" Lawrence said to Daniels, and they both grinned...."I first heard it this spring over at St. Louis. Every colored player in the league seems to be using it this year....But what does it mean?" "...Like, not pretty. You know. Ugly, you might say." **1961** Brosnan *Pennant Race* 172: Real mullion....They're so bad they'd draw flies. *Ibid.* 207: Spider, your bambino looks like her momma. Pretty. Not like you, a mullion! **1969** Bouton *Ball Four* 354: They kept yelling that he was ugly and calling him "Mullion" and other nice things. **1969** Gordone *No Place* 413: Keep her in the dark, Gabe. Keep that mulyan in the black. *Ibid.* 418: Anybody'd think you was a wrinkled up ol' mulyan. **1972** Claerbaut *Black Jargon* 72: *Mullion*...a physically unattractive person. **1986** in P. Dickson *Baseball Dict.* 267: Ballplayers might sit around the dugout or bullpen and select their major-league all-mullion team. **1991** W. Chamberlain *View from Above* 62 [ref. to 1959]: An ugly girl was a "mullion."

mum *n.* a chrysanthemum. Now *colloq.* or *S.E.*

    ***1924** in *OEDS:* The gardeners call chrysanthemums "mums." **1947** in Paxton *Sport* 360: I wore the 'mum to the game, but I was too tired to go to the dance. **1950** *New Yorker* (Apr. 29) 23: Mums generally don't bloom until November. **1956–60** J.A. Williams *Angry Ones* ch. i: Their faces uplifted as wilting white mums seeking sun. **1963** *Wash. Post* (Nov. 27) A3: A woman...dropped a small cluster of mums inside the fence.

mumbly peg *n.* usu. *pl.* [rhyming slang] a leg. *Rare* in U.S.

    [***1890–96** *F & H: Mumblepeg*...The female *pudendum.*] **1920** T.A. Dorgan, in Zwilling *TAD Lexicon* 58: Mumbley pegs: that's the legs. **1928** M. Sharpe *Chicago May* 287: *Mumbly pegs*—legs. **1935** Pollock *Und. Speaks: Mumbly pegs*, the legs. **1944** (cited in Partridge *Dict. Und.* 456).

mummer *n.* *Und. & Boxing.* the mouth.

    ***1785** Grose *Dict. Vulgar Tongue: Mummer.* The mouth. **1791** [W. Smith] *Confess. T. Mount* 18: Mouth, *mumma.* ***1818** P. Egan, in *F & H* IV 387: Then he hit him on the mummer, and on the ropes he dropped. ***1822** D. Carey *Life in Paris* I 193: Darkening his *day-lights* for the advantage of his *mummer* (mouth).

mummick *v.* (see quot.).

1889–90 Barrère & Leland *Dict. Slang: Mummock, mummick* (American), to handle any object. To handle or feel the person. "Don't *mummick* me that-a-way, Billy, or I'll tell my ma!"

mumper *n.* [agential form of BrE *mump* 'to cheat', prob. < Du *mompen* 'to cheat'] *Und.* (see *1673 quot.); (*hence*) a beggar. *Obs.* in U.S.

*1665 R. Head, in *F & H* IV 388: *Mumpers* gentile [*sc.,* genteel] beggars. *1673 [R. Head] *Canting Academy* 41: *Mumpers* Gentile Beggars, Such as will not accept of Victuals, but money or cloaths, and these beg under the pretence of being decay'd Gentlemen, Tradesmen, or such who have been burn'd out or shipwrack'd. *1690 T. Durfey, in *F & H*: That even Vagabonds and mumpers, Have from my bounty had full Bumpers. *1745 in C.H. Wilkinson *King of Beggars* 40: That noted...Asylum for Mumpers. *1785 Grose *Dict. Vulgar Tongue: Mumpers.* Originally beggars of the genteel kind, but since used for beggars in general. **1807** W. Irving *Salmagundi* 177: Mumpers, ragamuffins, bravoes and beggars. *1839 Brandon *Poverty, Mendicity* (gloss.): *Mumper*—a beggar. **1859** Matsell *Vocab.* 57: *Mumpers.* Beggars. *1889–90 Barrère & Leland *Dict. Slang* II 76: *Mumper* (popular), a beggar. *1961 Partridge *Dict. Und.* (ed. 2) 848: *Mumper*...is, in mid C.19-20, predominantly a gypsies' word for a tramp. *1988 L. Rose *Rogues & Vagabonds* 212: *Mumper:* itinerant and beggar (especially in the West Country).

munch *v.* **1.** *Stu.* to eat, usu. heartily.—usu. constr. with *out* or *down*, occ. *up*.

*1923 (cited in Partridge *DSUE* 543). **1978** *UTSQ*: What time do we munch down? **1979** Gram *Foxes* 150: Why do we all the time have to munch out with grossly immature kids? **1980** in Safire *Good Word* 213: Munch down. **1980** Eble *Campus Slang* (Mar.) 4: *Munch out*—to eat: We munched out at the all-you-can-get buffet. *a*1986 in *NDAS*: You'll get together with your friends, right, and you'll be munching up or something. *a*1990 E. Currie *Dope & Trouble* 112: And I totally *munched* when I was at their house. **1993** Bahr & Small *Son-in-Law* (film): I'm gonna stay here and munch solo.

2. to perform oral copulation upon; EAT, 4.—usu. considered vulgar. *Joc.* See also RUG-MUNCHER.

*a*1970 Partridge *DSUE* (ed. 7) 1286: *Muncher boy.* A fellator: mostly Naval: since ca. 1950. **1981** (quot. at munch [or *chew*] *the carpet* s.v. CARPET). *1989 Partridge *Concise Dict. Sl.* 292: *Muncher boy*...Cf....a low, Army [catch phrase] current in the Far East, early 1960s, *munch my bunch!* **1994** *Details* (June) 67: These instruments of pleasure seemed to inspire a mass munching, because all the women...had their legs up in the air and a man's head in between.

3. [sugg. by syn. *eat (one's) lunch* s.v. LUNCH] to crash, esp. from a surfboard; WIPE OUT.

1977 Filosa *Surf. Almanac* 190. **1990** P. Munro *Slang U.* 134: *Munch* to crash, mess up, *mangle*....Johnny...munched his motorcycle.

munchie *n.* **1.** usu. *pl.* snack foods. [In 1917 quot., "a family name for a kind of chocolate" (*OEDS*).]

[*1917 in *OEDS*: All I really want is Cigarettes, Munchie, and plain Cadbury's.] *1959 in *OEDS*: Food in general is referred to as "bait"...."grub," or "grubber," "munchie," [etc.]. **1968** *Everett* (Wash.) *Herald* (Oct. 22) 7A: The munchies go by the name of ham wams, chicken pik'ns, beef bams and liver loves. **1971** Dahlskog *Dict.* 41: *Munchie, n.* a snack; food to nibble on. **1971** in L. Bangs *Psychotic Reactions* 7: Some imaginative souls started to call food "munchies." **1973** N.Y.U. flyer: Refreshments: Beer, Wine, Fruit and other Munchies. [**1976** Knapp & Knapp *One Potato* 46: To get a bite of someone else's candy bar, [a child] says, "Munchies!" "Bites!" or "Hey, kick down!"] **1977** *Bionic Woman* (ABC-TV): All these midnight walks were for...munchies? **1979** Hiler *Monkey Mt.* 337: At midnight...they invaded the storeroom in search of munchies to take back out. **1981** *Time* (Sept. 28) 77: The Chipwich scored in the munchie market. **1981** *L.A. Times* (Dec. 29) II 5: Some kinds of cocktail munchies. **1984** N. Stephenson *Big U.* 108: Cleverly made munchies on white linen napkins. **1989** *Rage* (Knoxville, Tenn.) (Mar.) 8: Get beer, munchies, real suntan oil.

2. *pl.* a craving for food, esp. sweets or snacks; (*specif.*) such a craving as an aftereffect of marijuana use. Occ. in elab. vars.

1959 (cited in *ODMS*). **1970** Landy *Underground Dict.* 136: *Munchies*...Hunger induced by marijuana. **1971** N.Y.U. student: The "blind munchies" or the "purple munchies" means you're really hungry,

especially after you've been smoking [marijuana]. **1970–72** in *AS* L (1976) 63: *Munchies*...Feelings of hunger. **1972** Smith & Gay *Don't Try It* 198: *Blind Munchies.* Overwhelming desire for something to eat, usually after smoking marijuana. **1972** *Playboy* (Apr.) 98: They eat cookies to satisfy the munchies. **1978** S. King *Stand* 89: When I get stoned, I get the munchies. **1980** Novak *High Culture* 41: Many smokers...will indulge in junk food after smoking marijuana. This phenomenon is commonly known as "getting the munchies." **1981** *N.Y. Times* (July 19) 38: I just smoked the smoke and I got the munchies and I got real fat. **1981** *Nat. Lampoon* (July) 77: "Oh, wow! Great grass!" "Yeah, an' dese li'l pastries is great fo' de munchies." **1985** Sawislak *Dwarf* 160: Hey, man....You getting the munchies too? **1988** T. Harris *Silence of Lambs* 108: I've got the munchies. **1988** *TV 101* (CBS-TV): Let's get out of here and scarf already. I got the munchies real bad. **1991** *Jenny Jones Show* (synd. TV series): You're sitting at home and you get the munchies. **1992** *Comedy on the Road* (A&E-TV): It'd be a drag to get high, get the munchies, and go stand on [a food] line for two hours. **1994** Harvest Crisps (brand of snacks) TV ad: "Can't sleep?" "I've got the munchies." **1996** in *Reader's Digest* (Jan. 1997) 87: [Marijuana]...causes bouts of the "munchies"—a craving for sugary food.

munchkin *n.* [fr. *munchkins* (prob. arbit. fr. *munch* + *-kin,* dimin. suff.), coined by L. Frank Baum to designate dwarflike characters in his children's book *The Wonderful Wizard of Oz* (1900), and prominent in 1939 filming of the book] **1.a.** a child; youngster.

1971 *Seattle Times* (May 16) A15: Munchkins (early teen-aged youth who have dropped out). **1984** L. Buscaglia, in *L.A. Times* (Aug. 12) IX 3: She had indeed changed from the cute little "munchkin" I remembered. But...she seemed typically teen-ager-ish.

b. a very short person.—also used attrib.

1975 Wambaugh *Choirboys* 311: Hey, munchkin!...You're the littlest guy around here. **1978** *L.A. Times* (Jan. 22) III 12: Overseeing a bunch of munchkin basketball players. **1979** *Omni* (June) 52: Munchkins. You know,...midgets. Little folk. **1980** Cragg *Lex. Militaris* 307: *Munchkin.* West Point slang for a short person. **1983** Wambaugh *Delta Star* 53: So I don't get tempted to do police work with...a split-tailed munchkin to back me up if I get in trouble. **1984** in "J.B. Briggs" *Drive-In* 285: The little munchkin pops her top. **1985** *Night Court* (NBC-TV): "Peewee," "munchkin," "dwarf,"...I've heard them all. **1991** W. Chamberlain *View from Above* 123: If I had to be a "munchkin" like that and still wanted to play basketball.

2. a menial employee or similarly inconsequential person.

1983 *L.A. Times* (Aug. 25) I 1: Justice Department spokesman Thomas P. DeCair described her as a "low-level munchkin." **1990** W. Safire, in *N.Y. Times Mag.* (Dec. 23) 10: Even today, *munchkins* is sometimes used to mock pretentious staff members. **1995** *CNN & Co.* (CNN-TV) (Mar. 27): He didn't make him into a munchkin where he had to do work around the house.

munch-out *n.* *Stu.* an occasion of a large repast.

1984 Eble *Campus Slang* (Mar.) 4: We had a real munch out at the all-you-can-eat buffet.

munch out see s.v. MUNCH.

mundane *n.* *Stu.* an unimaginative or uninteresting person.

*a*1990 P. Dickson *Slang!* 126: *Mundane.* A person with no knowledge of science fiction; nonfan. **1991** Univ. Tenn. student theme: *Mundanes*—Older, more "normal" people who don't wear black all the time or listen to strange music. Terribly derogatory. **1994** *21st Century Dict. Sl.* 176: Rich was the first mundane Sally had dated.

mung *n.* [orig. unkn.] Esp. *Stu.* filth; anything that is disgusting or offensive; muck; CRUD, 1.a. Occ. as interj. and in nonce compounds.

1948 J.H. Burns *Lucifer* 223: Mung. That was the Academy's name for the food they ate. **1962** (quot. (as interj.) at JEWEL). **1962** Quirk *Red Ribbons* 33 [ref. to 1940's]: "I gather her cup failed of running over." "Her cup was full of mung, if that's what you mean." *Ibid.* 70: You mung eaters haul your...asses out of the way. *Ibid.* 89: But you don't have to build things, either, like churches and all that mung. **1963** Fry TS.: Eat Mung. **1968** Baker et al. *CUSS* 160: *Mung* (mass noun) A pimple. **1968** Lockridge *Hartspring* 44: Hide your head beneath a pile of mung! **1969** *Current Slang I & II* 63: *Mung, n.* Anything distasteful or unsightly.—Air Force Academy cadets. **1969** *Zap Comix* (No. 4) (unp.): Mild-mannered reporter for the Muthalode Morning Mungpie. **1970** *Playboy* (Dec.) 330: I remember "mung" from Little Neck [L.I., *ca*1955]. It is what, when you hang a pregnant ape upside down by her toes and beat her in the stomach with a number-36 baseball bat, comes out of her nose. **1970** Peters *Sex Newspapers* 14: A surprising number of people have asked me what "Mung" is and how this column came to be called that....If you'll remember the old high school gross contests or rank-outs—back around 1960 or so—...Well, Mung was this stuff: "You take a pregnant lady gorilla...and you tie her by the heels upside-down from a branch, and you beat her on the belly with a board—and the stuff that comes out of her mouth, that's Mung." **1972** N.Y.U. student: *Mung* means "shit," like you say "Mung!" when you're surprised or mad. **1974** *Nat. Lampoon* (Nov.) 17: O'Dork redirected it more toward young mung. **1977** *Rolling Stone* (Oct. 20) 70: Jones noticed the mung on Lydon's never-brushed teeth. **1986** Huyck & Katz *Howard the Duck* (film): I'm tired of working in grungey mungholes. **1988** Poyer *The Med* 516: Goddammit, you mungbrains, *spread out!* **1988** H. Gould *Double Bang* 67: Vinnie's three daughters looked like him. "The Mung Sisters," he'd call them. "Six hundred pounds of shit in a wheelbarrow." **1991** *Saturday Night Live Halloween Special* (NBC-TV): "What's *mung*?" "Mung is the grossest thing there is." "Ooh! Mung is scary! I'm scared of mung!" **1994** *Esquire* (Dec.) 78: Don't allow the current level of censorious PC mung to rise above your zesty taste for fantasy! **1995** *CNN & Co.* (CNN-TV) (Aug. 3): You get the feeling there's mung and grunge all over the floor of the lab!

mung *adj.* [orig. unkn.] Orig. *Journ.* (of information) stale or untrue. [Relationship of 1968–70 quot. to this sense is uncertain; it may simply represent a predicative use of MUNG, *n.*]

   1844 in Thornton *Amer. Gloss.*: Mung News. **1849** in *F & H* IV 389: As many of our citizens who intend to go to California may base their arrangements on the mung news of some of the papers, we conceive it to be our duty to state that most of these letters are fictitious. **1856** "H. Hazel" *Jack Waid* 27: They were not endeavoring to sell the green ones with "mung" intelligence. **1859** in *DA: Mung*, sham, false, pretended. **1889–90** in Barrère & Leland *Dict. Slang: Mung news* (American), news which has been heard before. [**1968–70** *Current Slang III & IV* 85: *Mung*, adj. Spoiled, bad.—College females, New Hampshire.]

mung¹ *v. Und.* to beg.

   *1811 *Lex. Balatron.: Mung.* To beg. **1859** Matsell *Vocab.*, in *F & H* IV 389: *Mung.* To solicit; to beg. **1893** in *F & H*: Many's the time you've been waiting on me coming home to give you some of the grub I've munged.

mung² *v.* [fr. the n.] *Stu. & Computers.* to dirty; (*also*) to make a mess of, spoil, botch, ruin, etc.—usu. constr. with *up*.

   1968–70 *Current Slang III & IV* 85: *Mung*, v. To spoil; ruin.—He *mungs* up everything that he tries. **1981** D.E. Miller *Jargon* 187: [Computer] programs can mung up files if, due to some undiscovered bug, they run amok. **1983** Naiman *Computer Dict.* 99: I'm afraid I've munged this whole disk. **1986** *NDAS*: I munged up my shoes walking across the field. **1988** Willson *REMF* 141: The sergeant major chewed me out for munging up my boots so badly.

mungee *n.* [pidgin < F *manger*, It *mangiare*] *Naut.* food. *Rare* in U.S.

   [***1851–61** in *F & H* IV 390: We [strolling actors] call breakfast, dinner, tea, supper, all of them mungare.] **1904** J.H. Williams, in *Independent* (Mar. 24) 658: "Hm," said the Chinaman, "sailor-man too muchee bobbry; no likee mungee." ***1929** Bowen *Sea Slang* 93: *Mungy.* Food in the [Royal] Navy. ***a1950** W. Granville *Sea Slang* 160: *Mungy.* Food of any kind. (Lower-deck)....*Mungy* is less used than *scran* on the lower-deck. **1954–60** *DAS: Mung(e)y*...Food. *Some hobo and W.W.I Army use.* ***1982** in *ODMS* 144: There were odd complaints about the food...from mouths that nonetheless wrapped themselves gleefully around the free munga [*sic*] and booze.

muni *n.* **1.** *Hobo.* a municipal lodging house. Also **muny**.

   1930 "D. Stiff" *Milk & Honey* 46: Of munies I want to speak highly. I have seen many....The munie menu is never up to much. **1935** E. Anderson *Hungry Men* 174: You know where the Muny is around here? **1937** *Lit. Digest* (Apr. 10) 12: *Munies.* Municipal lodging-houses. **1981** Pietropinto & Congress *Clinic* 109: I'm not going to...put him in the Muny with a bunch of drunks.

   2. see s.v. MUNI, *adj.*

muni *adj.* municipal. Also **muny**. Also as n., a municipal bond.

   1973 *Newsweek*, in *OEDAS* I: Paragon...mounted an expensive advertising campaign aimed at peddling "munis" to the masses. **1975** *L.A. Times* (Nov. 16) I 3: When we got there, six or seven Muni drivers were standing around wondering what to do. **1979** in *OEDAS* I. **1980** *St. Louis Post-Dispatch* (Mar. 16) 8E: Auditions for the Muny Opera's singing and dancing choruses. **1983** WINS radio ad (Aug. 29): Merrill-Lynch....We know muni bonds. **1986** *L.A. Law* (NBC-TV): Just a simple little Muni Court dog-bite case. **1987** *Moneyline* (CNN-TV) (Oct. 13): It's going out of the muni business altogether.

muns *n.* [orig. unkn.] *Und.* the face or mouth. [The ref. to Virginia in *1726 quot. perh. suffices to establish some early usage in America; the speaker of *1745 quot. later traveled to N.C.]

   *1726 A. Smith *Mems. of J. Wild* 38: He had been *Glimm'd in the Muns*, that is to say, he had been Burnt in the Face...and *Transported*...[to] *Virginia*. ***1745** in C.H. Wilkinson *King of Beggars* 120: Ogle him in the Muns, sirs. ***1789** G. Parker *Life's Painter* 139: That all might smack his muns, sirs. ***1796** Grose *Dict. Vulgar Tongue: Muns.* The face, or rather the mouth. ***1821** *Real Life in Ireland* 16: Blarney...dabbed his right *flipper bones* in his *muns*. **1859** Matsell *Vocab.* 57: *Muns.* The mouth.

murdelize *n. Juve.* to trounce; drub.

   1960 Wohl *Cold Wind* 215: I'm gonna murdelize you! **1995** *Three Ninjas* (film): We'll murdelize 'em! **1996** N.Y.C. editor, age 48: I recall *murdelize* from grade-school days [1954–60]. But I haven't heard it since then.

murder *n.* **1.** something that is insufferable, unbearable, unmanageable, difficult, or blatantly unfair; (with weakened force) something that is very annoying. Also (in recent use, infl. by police jargon) **murder one, murder three.** Occ. (in very recent use) as quasi-adj.

   *1857 in *OEDS*: This cellar is perfectly abominable. It would be murder to put a bottle of wine into it till it has been roofed, walled, and floored....Goodenough never had a glass of wine that any man could drink. **1889** Reynolds *Kansas Hell* 42: To put me down in the mines and set me to digging coal was wicked. It was murder. Down in that dark pit how I suffered! **1919** in De Beck *Google* 18: It's murder! Nobuddy's givin' the pitcher any support. **1922** J. Conway, in *Variety* (Mar. 31) 8: There are only two punches in a fighter's catalogue—it's murder; watch for them. **1921–25** J. Gleason & R. Taber *Is Zat So?* 54: This ain't gonna be a race....It's gonna be a *murder*. **1935** Wolfson *Reckless* (film): Ain't that murder? Somebody picked my pocket. That's just awful. **1936** in D. Runyon *More Guys* 136: A pair of tight shoes is practically murder in the first degree. **1946** Kober *That Man Is Here Again* 94: Brother, it's murder, the service you get nowadays. **1949** Loos & Sales *Mother Is a Freshman* (film): Those entrance exams are mur–*der!* **1951** in Cannon *Nobody Asked* 257: Losing a broad is bad enough....Having a kid you loved like a son turn out to be a rat is murder. **1951** *Sat. Eve. Post* (Apr. 21) 10: It was murder at Hialeah. **1952** M. Chase *McThing* 65: A witch—that don't scare me none, but a dame that likes me—that is murder! **1958** P. O'Connor *At Le Mans* 36: The S-bends are pure murder. **1965** Gary *Ski Bum* 24: I'm sure you know about love, sir, as a policeman, I mean. It's murder. **1970** Della Femina *Wonderful Folks* 220: On the street it was murder. A hot, hot day in July. **1970–71** J. Rubinstein *City Police* 64: Man, when the sun comes up, it's murder. *a*1979 Pepper & Pepper *Straight Life* 284 [ref. to 1961]: That guy is murder three. Everybody's terrified of him. **1985** Donahue *Human Animal* 52: The change may be terrific for the individual peacock, but murder for peafowl as a species. **1990** P. Munro *Slang U.* 135: That exam was so murder! **1994** *Reliable Sources* (CNN-TV) (July 17): Some of us think our health care premiums *are* murder! **1995** N.Y.C. man, age *ca*45: God, this is gonna be murder one.

   2. *Esp. Theat. & Jazz.* something that is extraordinarily effective, pleasing, or impressive.

   [*a*1909 Tillotson *Detective* 93: *Murder*—A big gathering; excitement.] **1927** *N.Y. Times* (Oct. 30): It's Murder...There is a terrific amount of theatrical business. **1940** in *OEDS*: Murder, something excellent or terrific...."That's solid murder, gate!" **1941** in Ellington *Music Is My Mistress* 179: *Murder*...fine. **1942** Tugend *Star-Spangled Rhythm* (film): It's murder, Jack! **1942** Brackett & Wilder *Major & Minor* (film): Say, you're murder! **1943** M. Shulman *Barefoot Boy* 90: Benny Goodman....Man, he's murder, Jack! **1949** Shane & Cooper *City Across the River* (film): What a build! Murder! **1952** R. Alexander

Time Out 21: *Eddie.…*I'm murder on a [football] field. *Agnes.* I think you're murder off. **1980** Wielgus & Wolff *Basketball* 28: A good jump shooter can be murder in some knock-around shooting game. **1986** Ciardi *Good Words* 198: Indicates enthusiastic approval: *The new Stones album is pure murder!*

¶ In phrases:

¶ **get away with murder** to violate rules or limits with impunity. Now *colloq.*

1914 T.A. Dorgan, in Zwilling *TAD Lexicon* 58: He's been getting away with murder he has—it's a wonder they don't tumble to that fathead. **1921** *Amer. Leg. Wkly.* (Jan. 28) 7: Smoking the colonel's cigars…is considered "getting away with murder." **1929–33** J.T. Farrell *Young Manhood* 341: She eggs you into thinking you can get away with murder, and then pulls herself away. **1937** Barry *Here Come the Clowns* 554: The trouble with you is you never speak out. You let her get away with murder.

¶ **holler [bloody] murder** to raise a loud outcry.—also used fig. Also vars.

1847 Reid *McCulloch's Rangers* 76: A poor divil…was howlin' murther for a drink. **1864** Armstrong *Generals* 308: Good bye, Colonel; these brass bull-pups will roar bloody murder at Johnny Reb to-day. **1865** Woodruff *Union Soldier* (Oct. 19) 66: He hallows Bloody Murther, takes it back. **1881** Small *Farming* 16: So she howled, and danced and shouted bloody murder. **1882** Peck *Peck's Sunshine* 20: When the rat tried to run up her…leg she…screamed bloody murder. ***1887** in *F & H* I 260: The person…howled what the half-dozen officers…graphically described as *blue murder.* **1905** in A. Adams *Chisholm Trail* 136: But he beat me, bellowing bloody murder. **1916** D. Runyon, in Paxton *Sport USA* 94: A Boston guy or anybody else wuddah hollered murder for a week, and they 'dah nev' give up no thoity iron men neither. **1920–21** Witwer *Leather Pushers* 54: Carney is in New York yellin' murder about me havin' the Kid. **1921** J. Conway, in *Variety* (July 8) 5: But my ball club is shot to pieces and in last place. The wolves here are hollerin murder. **1941** E. Welty, in Baym et al. *Norton Anthol.* (ed. 2) II 1767: She yelled bloody murder, too. **1962** W. Robinson *Barbara* 145: They yell blue bloody murder for us to get up here, and where are they?

¶ **like murder** with great energy; like hell.

1862 in J.R. Lowell *Poetical Works* 220: An' yit she gin her sheer a jerk/…An' on her apples kep' to work,/Parin' away like murder.

murder *v.* **1.** Esp. *Theat.* to spoil through inept execution or performance; ruin. Orig. *S.E.,* now *colloq.*

*1644–47 in *OED:* As Hopkins and Sternhold murder the Psalmes. ***1830** F. Marryat, in *OED:* Don't kill Billy; it's bad enough to have murdered Shakespeare. ***1861** in *OED:* Murdering a duet. **1865** J. Miller *Va. City* (Apr. 30): Play was Macbeth by William Shakespeare and he was truly "murdered." It was decidedly void of merit. **1869** Logan *Foot Lights* 111: If it were a penal offense to "murder" a part, what a tumbling off of heads there would be. *a***1941** Schulberg *Sammy* 100: It's that goddam ham—he's murdering my line. **1942–49** Goldin et al. *DAUL* 143: *Murder…*To bungle; to ruin. "You sure murdered that trick (crime)."

2. *Baseball.* to hit (a pitched ball) hard.

1911 Van Loan *Big League* 64: He's going to put it over [the plate] for you, Biff. Murder it, boy! Laminate it! **1936** Monks & Finklehoffe *Brother Rat* 107: You give him a high one, he'll murder it. **1958** Abbott *Damn Yankees* (film): Don't try to murder it! Just slip one through the infield!

3. Esp. *Sports.* to defeat soundly; trounce.—also used fig.

1913–15 Van Loan *Taking the Count* 14: Doc, he used to *murder* fellows like this Brady. **1922** *Sat. Eve. Post* (June 3) 10: There isn't a pitcher in the league he hasn't murdered. **1921–25** J. Gleason & R. Taber *Is Zat So?* 82: I'll murder him if I get a crack at him. **1935** Mackenzie *Been Places* 46: I got Dot a ticket, so as she could see me murder this guy. **1940** Twist *Too Many Girls* (film): I saw them murder Princeton last year. **1941** *Sat. Eve. Post* (May 17) 86: The Cubs murdered the Phillies…16–2. **1952** in Marx *Groucho Letters* 199: To watch the Yankees murder the Brooklyn Dodgers. **1960** Aarons *Hell to Eternity* 24: He's too big. You'll get murdered! **1963** D. Tracy *Brass Ring* 3: They beat Choate and Kent and even Andover. They murdered 'em. **1972** J. Mills *Report* 104: He murdered the sergeant's test—one of the highest grades they've ever had, I hear. **1995** Headline News network (Apr. 11): She got creamed! She got murdered [in a women's boxing match]!

4. to cause unbearable annoyance to; exasperate thoroughly.

1921–25 J. Gleason & R. Taber *Is Zat So?* 55: He'll moider me yet. *a***1948** in Hodes & Hansen *Sel. from Gutter* 33: We'd be late, and that would murder the boss.

5. *Theat.* to impress or amuse (an audience) greatly.

1925 Cohan *Broadway* 41: Mother and you have all that sure-fire dialogue. You'll "murder" 'em with that. **1932** Hecht & Fowler *Great Magoo* 118: I got an idea for the orchestration that's gonna murder 'em. **1941** *Great Guns* (film): Ginger, you murder me. **1941** Schulberg *Sammy* 91: Jesus, I murdered them. The producer jumped up and kissed me. **1942** L.R. Foster *Mayor of 44th St.* (film): That band…murdered 'em! They laid 'em in the aisles! **1945** Bellah *Ward 20* 82: You murder me. You're funny. Ha. Ha. You're a wit—a half-wit. **1949** N. Johnson *Everybody Does It* (film): You murdered 'em, baby! **1953** Weidman et al. *Eddie Cantor Story* (film): Eddie could take this small part and do things with it and murder the people.

murder *interj.* (used trivially to express surprise, annoyance, pain, etc.). [*OED* cites nontrivial S.E. quots. fr. Henryson and Shakespeare.]

*1788 R. Burns, in *OED:* 'Twas laurelled Martial roaring murther! ***1837** in *OED:* Murdher! there's not a dhrop of wather in the pot! **1845** in Robb *Squatter Life* 90: Murder! boat's sinking!…help! **1847** in Dorson *Long Bow* 71: Oh! Murder!—Let go! **1848** in Blair & Meine *Half Horse* 202: Howly murther!…may be it's his captives. **1851** Ely *Wanderings* 25: Oh! Murder! How hot it is. **1895** F.P. Dunne, in Schaaf *Dooley* 199: Murther, but I was sick. **1897** R. Kipling *Capts. Courageous* 120: Murder!…Don't do that again, doctor. **1910** in O. Johnson *Lawrenceville* 274: Dink and Dennis protested. "Murder, no!"

murder board *n.* Orig. *Army.* a selection or examination board; (*hence*) a review board of any kind.

1944 *N.Y. Times Mag.* (Sept. 17): *Murder Board.* Selection board that passes on WAC officer candidates. **1976** in Safire *Coming to Terms* 211: "Program murder boards" have been established to insure that the concept is structured properly. **1980** in Safire *Coming to Terms* 211: [An] intervening scrub-down or murder board of the planning product. **1985** Westin *Love & Glory* 75 [ref. to WWII]: No wonder they called the OC Review Board the "murder board." **1987** W. Safire, in *N.Y. Times Mag.* (Oct. 11): *Murder board* is Pentagonese.…The original meaning was "rigorous examination of a proposed program" or…"a group charged with the responsibility to slam a candidate or proponent of an idea up against the wall with tough questioning." **1987** G. Hall *Top Gun* 7: When he feels he is ready, he will subject himself to a "murder board" [to review his qualifications].

murderer's row *n.* **1.** *Police.* a row of cells for condemned murderers.

1858 (cited in Nichols *Baseball Terminol.*). **1884** Triplett *American Crimes* 217: Walworth was committed to a cell in "Murderers' Row," in the Tombs. **1909** F. Harris *Bomb* 292: The so-called anarchists had been confined for the fifteen months in what was called "Murderers' Row" in the Cook County Jail. **1914** J. London *Jacket* 278: The Warden with a quart of champagne. I have dispatched it down Murderer's Row.

2. *Baseball.* a succession of powerful hitters. [Most notably associated with the 1927 New York Yankees, who included Babe Ruth and Lou Gehrig; see discussion in P. Dickson *Baseball Dict.* (1989), p. 267f.]

1858 (cited in Nichols *Baseball Terminol.*). **1935** *Sat. Eve. Post* (Apr. 24) 133 (Tamony Coll.): The first Murderers' Row—Home Run Baker, Babe Ruth, Bob Meusel and Wally Pipp—set a new style of offense. **1936** *S.F. Call-Bulletin* (June 30) 18 (Tamony Coll.): There was only one murderers' row…and Ruth, Gehrig, Meusel, that was it. **1942** *S.F. Examiner* (Aug. 7) 9 (Tamony Coll.): The original Murderers' Row was Cobb, Crawford and Veach of the Detroit Tigers. **1962** Houk & Dexter *Ballplayers* 188: But here's Johnny Blanchard of our 1961 Murderer's Row. **1963** *S.F. Call-Bulletin* (May 14) (Tamony Coll.): Giants Make Murderers' Row Look Like Hitless Wonders. **1982** *Sportstalk* (WKGN radio) (Oct. 5): Just look up and down the lineups of those teams. It's Murderer's Row. **1985** WINS radio news (Aug. 9): The Mets' murderer's row…went on a rampage in Canada yesterday. **1987** *N.Y. Times* (Aug. 13) A26: It wasn't murderer's row. **1989** P. Dickson *Baseball Dict.* 268: *Murderer's Row…*Baseball historian L. Robert David has found that the term was also used in describing the 1919 New York Yankees.

murder one *n.* [orig. police jargon] **1.** first-degree murder.

    1951 (cited in Partridge *Dict. Und.* 848). **1966** R.E. Alter *Carny Kill* 97: Haul her off on a Murder One rap. **1978** W. Brown *Tragic Magic* 125: If looks could kill, I'd be murder one! **1983** Sturz *Wid. Circles* 39: Don't give me that Murder One look, either. **1995** *Murder One* [ABC-TV series title].

    2. see s.v. MURDER, *n.*, 1.

murk *n.* coffee.

    1930 Irwin *Tramp & Und. Slang* 132: *Mug of Murk.*—A cup of coffee. **1936** *AS* (Feb.) 44: *Mug of murk.* Cup of coffee without cream. **1980** Mack & Connell *Naval Trads.* (ed. 5) 260: Others call coffee "java," "jamoke," [or] "murk."

murphy *n.* [fr. *Murphy*, common Irish family name] **1.** a potato. Cf. MICKEY, 5.

    *1811 Lex. Balatron: Murphies. Potatoes. **1813* Wheeler *Letters* 140: He ordered him to be released, saying "go to my servant and get your 'Murphys' I have only taken a few for my own dinner." **1815** Palmer *Diary* (entry for Mar. 4): Who'll buy some Murphys. all hot! all hot! **1821 Real Life in Ireland* 15: It were easier to bring murphys from Knock-lofty with a blind garran. **1846** Gibson *Soldier* 168: All we lack is *murphys*, which we will try to raise the coming season. **1865** in E. Stockwell *Pvt. Stockwell* 206: Raising murphys and sowbelly. **1877** *Puck* (July 11) 4: Mrs. Van Cott likes Murphies. **1884** in Lummis *Letters* 192: That'll beat sow-belly and murphies all hollow. **1891** Bourke *Border* 59: They have succeeded in raising the finest "Murphies" in the world. **1902** Jarrold *Mickey Finn* 88: Wid murphies boiled in their skins. **1906** in S.C. Wilson *Column South* 102: We got enough "murphies" to furnish a couple of meals. **1908** W. Davenport *Butte & Montana* 127: Undressin' de Murphys (peeling the potatoes). **1912** Berkman *Prison* 307: We should have had sweet "murphies" for Christmas. **1919** Kauffman *Victorious* 66: I went to the Ritz restaurant last night and asked for sweet potatoes and what do you think they brought me? Sugared murphies! **1920** Bissell *63rd Inf.* 183: The murphies I'm peeling have set my mind reeling. **1956** Sorden & Ebert *Logger's Wds.* 24 [ref. to *a*1925]: *Murphys*, Potatoes.

    2. (usu. *cap.*) **a.** an Irish person.—used derisively. Cf. MICKEY, 1.

    *a*1890–96 *F & H* IV 391: *Murphy*…(American).—An Irishman. **1929–30** Dos Passos *42d Parallel* 7: Scared cat…shanty Irish…Bow-legged Murphy…Running home to tell the cop.

    b. (usu. *cap.*) a police officer.

    1965 Hersey *Too Far to Walk* 123: Oh, man! They've got one of the Murphys' helmets! They're throwing it in the air!

    3. (*cap.*) *Und. & Police.* **a.** any of various simple confidence games practiced on victims who are seeking prostitutes, drugs, gambling, etc.—also used attrib., esp. in phr. **Murphy game.**

    1954 in Wepman et al. *The Life* 41: I'll play the Murphy to the point of death. **1959** L. Whitten, in Partridge *Dict. Und.* (ed. 2) 848: The "Murphy game" is…a confidence game.…The victim is lured by promises of a woman.…Old time detectives say the name comes from a long-gone New York bordello called Mrs. Murphy's. **1965** C. Brown *Manchild* 160 [ref. to N.Y.C., 1950's]: There were many different ways to play the Murphy. **1965** *Time* (Apr. 16) 16: "The Murphy Game" is underworld argot…named after an Irishman who was arrested many times for perpetrating such tricks. **1966** in *BDNE* 305: You can get it playing the Murphy. **1967** Hersey *Algiers Motel* 97: "The Murphy game…is a big crime in Detroit.…I think it came from Boston originally…where the fellow would say, 'I know a lovely woman, name of Mrs. Murphy, who's dyin' to give it to you. Just pay me. She's waitin' for you on the second floor.' The Murphy man collects. There's no woman there." All rolling of Johns by pimps, using their prostitutes as lures, is now loosely called Murphying; so even is stealing by gangs of prostitutes. **1970** Winick & Kinsie *Lively Commerce* 123: A version of the Murphy in which an accomplice is unnecessary involves a prostitute who carries a spare dress in her brassiere. She strips down to her underclothes and asks the client for the money in advance. When he pays, she goes to the bathroom, presumably to prepare herself, but actually puts on the dress and leaves either by the window or by running through the room. **1971** Woodley *Dealer* 39: Hey, have you ever heard of the Murphy game? You know what the Murphy is on the street? Somebody walks up and flashes a badge, and he is not the police, and he takes you off [*i.e.*, extorts money or drugs]. That's called

the Murphy. **1968–73** Agar *Ripping & Running* 46: [In] the *Murphy*, a man is sold the services of a prostitute who never shows up. **1980** in *Penthouse* (Jan. 1981) 174: That other customer…told me about them.…Is there something called a Murphy? *a*1987 Bunch & Cole *Reckoning for Kings* 234: The old Murphy gambit…"You give me money—she has apartment down this alley." **1990** *Night Court* (NBC-TV): [The charge is] Murphy solicitation. **1990** Steward *Bad Boys* 108 [ref. to Chicago, 1950's]: One of the more obnoxious scams practiced on the street was called the "Murphy gag," perhaps originated by a man of that name.

    b. a swindle (in general).

    1980 D. Hamill *Stomping Ground* 37: He was a first-rate Murphy artist.…he could sell a guy anything. *a*1994 N. McCall *Wanna Holler* 122: If…one person got away with running a Murphy, everybody would try it and I'd be out of business.

    4. *Stu.* WEDGIE.

    1990 P. Munro *Slang U.* 103: *Have a murphy* to have one's underwear hiked up. **1990** *AS* LXV 3: *Wedgy*…Connie Eble reports the synonyms *melvin* and *murphy*.

¶ In phrase:

¶ **Miss Murphy walker** *Und.* MURPHY MAN.

    1967 in Wepman et al. *The Life* 162: There are Miss Murphy walkers—oh, they're convincing talkers.

Murphy *v. Und. & Police.* to swindle by means of a MURPHY game.

    1964 *N.Y. Times,* in *DAS* (Supp.): Mayor Smitherman…and…a Selma lawyer…were "murphyed" by the Negro confidence man at 2:30 A.M. today. **1965** C. Brown *Manchild* 22: At times, older fellows would shake us down, con us, or Murphy us out of our loot. *Ibid.* 310: I taught him how to Murphy. **1967** (quot. at MURPHY, *n.*, 3). **1972** J. Mills *Report* 14: *Murphy.* To pose as a pimp, collect the money in advance, and disappear without providing a girl. *Ibid.* 56: I thought he was some school kid who had been Murphyed. **1990** T. Thorne *Dict. Contemp. Slang: Murphy…American* to subject (someone) to *the murphy* (a term denoting various forms of a simple confidence trick).

Murphyland *n.* Ireland. *Joc.*

    1838 *Crockett Almanac* (1839) 31: I felt as if all the Paddies in Murphy Land war dancing an Irish jig in my belly for three days arter. **1942** *ATS* 52: Ireland.…*Murphyland, Paddyland.*

Murphy man *n. Und. & Police.* a man who practices a MURPHY swindle.

    1963 in Wepman et al. *The Life* 80: A Murphy man. **1965** in J. Mills *On Edge* 2: Murphy men (confidence men who pose as pimps, then vanish when they have the money). **1966** "Petronius" *N.Y. Unexp.* 185: "Murphy Men" still operate freely…promising girls, collecting money in advance, giving you the key and hotel number…and fleeing. **1966** J. Mills *Needle Park* 42 [ref. to 1964]: He was a Murphy Man, which meant that he supported himself by posing as a pimp. He told Johns he found around the park that he could get them girls, but they'd have to come up with a little money "in front," before they saw the goods. **1970** Winick & Kinsie *Lively Commerce* 123: The "Murphy man," named after a legendary Tenderloin confidence man, appears to be a pander but takes money from a customer without producing a prostitute. **1974** in D.C. Dance *Shuckin' & Jivin'* 232: The Murphy man [is] a cat who cons men looking for whores. **1980** W. Sherman *Times Square* 11: The murphymen plied their trade. To any man who stopped to listen, they described the charms of a whore anxiously waiting in a bed at a nearby hotel.…The murphyman offered to steer him to the lady for ten dollars.…of course there was no whore waiting and when the angry mark came back…, the murphyman was gone.

Murphy money *n.* [app. after Robert *Murphy*, lawyer who tried to organize a baseball union in 1946] *Baseball.* (see quots.).

    1948 *S.F. Call-Bulletin* (Apr. 2) 18 (Tamony Coll.): We inquired what was meant by this here "Murphy money" and were told it was the $25 a week all major league players get during the training season. **1971** T.P. Coffin *Old Ball Game* 56: "Murphy money" (the spending money given in spring training). **1989** P. Dickson *Baseball Dict.: Murphy money*…Spring-training spending money and/or money given to players for meals while on the road.

Murphy's Law *n.* [see 1978 quot.] Orig. *USAF.* a now widely applied maxim having the general form "If anything can go wrong, it will."

1957 *S.F. Chronicle* (June 17) 21 (Tamony Coll.): "If anything can go wrong, it will."—Murphy's Law. **1958** *Nation* (June 7) 506: There is an old military maxim known as Murphy's Law which asserts that wherever there is a bolt to be turned, someday there will be someone to turn it the wrong way. **1961** *N.Y. Times* (Oct. 15) VII 48: Reader's Report of Oct. 8, apparently under the influence of Murphy's Law (If something can go wrong it will.) listed the wrong publisher. **1962** *New Yorker* (Nov. 10): As long as you have human beings, you're going to have Murphy's Law, which states that if there is a wrong way to do something, somebody will do it. **1962** *We Seven* 161: We [astronauts] blamed human errors like this on what aviation engineers call "Murphy's Law." Murphy was a fictitious character who appeared in a series of educational cartoons put out by the U.S. Navy to stress aviation safety among its maintenance crews. In the cartoons, Murphy was a careless, all-thumbs mechanic who was prone to making such mistakes as putting a propeller on backwards or forgetting to tighten a bolt. He finally became such an institution that someone thought up a principle of human error called Murphy's Law. It went like this: "Any part that can be installed wrong *will* be installed wrong at some point by someone." **1963** *Amer. N & Q* (Nov.) 40: The earliest report I have had of Murphy's Law, called as such, is from Los Angeles, 1955. **1964** Caidin *Everything But Flak* 112: Murphy's First Law of Physics: "What can go wrong—*will* go wrong." **1965** *N.Y. Times* (Nov. 14) IV 10E: Engineers sometimes speak wryly, though only semi-facetiously, of what they call Murphy's Second Law. This holds that if a mechanism or a process can possibly break down, then it will break down some time, somewhere, somehow. **1969** Cagle *Naval Av. Guide* 396: *Murphy's Law* If an aircraft part can be incorrectly installed, some one will install it that way. **1970** Lincke *No Lady* 230: Murphy's Law...states: "If something can be put together or operated improperly or otherwise screwed up, it eventually will be put together or operated improperly or screwed up." **1971** *N.Y. Post* (Mar. 25) 24: I would like to caution you about "Murphy's Law," which states: If something can go wrong, it will. **1971** *WCBS-TV News* (CBS-TV) (Feb. 23): Murphy's law...states that if anything can go wrong, it will, and it will go wrong when it is least expected. **1972** *N.Y. Post* (July 10) 51: Murphy's Law, of course, says that if anything can go wrong in a show-biz situation, it will. **1974** N.Y.U. student: Murphy's Law states that "wherever a necessary knob exists to be turned, a corresponding hand will eventually appear to turn it the wrong way." **1978** C. McCabe, in *S.F. Chronicle* (Mar. 16) 53 (Tamony Coll.): Nichols says the expression was first used in 1949 at Edwards Air Force Base. On the track at North Base there was Colonel J.P. Stapp's experimental crash research testing. The actual work was being done by Northrop Aircraft, and Nichols was Northrop's project manager. The Law's namesake was Captain Ed Murphy, a development engineer from Wright Field Aircraft Lab. Frustration with a strap transducer which was malfunctioning due to an error in wiring the strain gage bridges caused him to remark—"If there is any way to do things wrong, he will"—referring to the technician who had wired the bridges at the lab. A couple of weeks after the naming Colonel Stapp indicated at a press conference that our fine safety record during several years of simulated crash force testing was the result of a firm belief in Murphy's Law, and our consistent effort to deny the inevitable. The widespread references to the Law in manufacturers' ads within only a few months was fantastic—and Murphy's Law was off and running wild. **1982** *Business Week* (Sept. 13) 127: I want to know if they have factored Murphy (whose "law" is that anything that can go wrong, will) into it. **1993** T. Taylor *Lightning in Storm* 17: Where Murphy's Law did not apply.

murphy trap *n.* the mouth; POTATO TRAP.
    1853 *Mysteries & Miseries of S.F.* 55: Shut up your Murphy-trap.

muscadoodle *n.* muscatel. Also vars.
    1956 "R. Macdonald" *Barbarous Coast* 28: Lay off muscadoodle, lay off dames and reefers. **1965–70** in *Jour. of Studies on Alcohol* XXXII (1971) 734: Muscatel wine...*muskadoo, muskadoodle, muskydoodle.* **1989** *Verbatim* (Winter) 4: When he was on the skids...the favorite terms for...[muscatel] were *muscadoodle* and *Napa Valley smoke.*

muscle *n.* **1.a.** physical coercion or threats thereof. See also *put the muscle on,* below.
    1879 in J. Haskins *Pinchback* 243: They resort to the muscle employed on your Police Jury. **1936** Coe *G-Man* 50: Winky an' Palmy ain't hot for the muscle. **1942** Liebling *Telephone* 58: The hint is

enough ordinarily. When it is not, Jack uses the muscle. **1942–49** Goldin et al. *DAUL* 143: *Muscle*...Force, or the threat of force. **1958** *Sat. Eve. Post* (Oct. 11) 114: He would have applied the muscle to Clarke if Rummel hadn't convinced him that would be bad public relations. **1959** Lederer *Never Steal Anything Small* (film): Better lay off the muscle, Jake. **1980** McAleer & Dickson *Unit Pride* 2: Certainly it was hard to think of him applying muscle to deadbeats. **1978–89** in Jankowski *Islands in Street* 207: The order's been given to lay some muscle on him.

b. power of intimidation; political influence.
    1931 in Partridge *Dict. Und.* 457: He lets his "muscle" speak for him. When the police drag his name into every gang killing or big shot feud he makes no denial. This circumstance has given Madden that terrorizing thing known in the underworld as "muscle." **1963** D. Tracy *Brass Ring* 310: He had the muscle to back up what he said. **1972** J. Mills *Report* 48: He said that to get along in the world everyone has to have some kind of muscle, some kind of power. **1981** *Nat. Lampoon* (Mar.) 44: They got the best legal muscle in town.

c. a person or persons hired to use violence and threats to intimidate.
    1942 in Partridge *Dict. Und.* 457: You were the best muscle in the whole crowd, Julio. **1942–49** Goldin et al. *DAUL* 143: *Muscle*...The strong-arm man of a gang. **1949** in *DAS*: Send some gowed-up muscle to search my hotel room. **1950** *Sat. Eve. Post* (Mar. 18) 24: Bernie was the mob's muscle. **1966** McNeill *Moving Through Here* 51: He may finish by hiring some "muscle" to break the offender's arm. **1967** "M.T. Knight" *Terrible Ten* 140: Yeah, like I was sayin', he had a lotta muscle with him. **1969** L. Sanders *Anderson Tapes* 117: The plan was for Gino and two muscles....to break the warehouse. **1974** A. Bergman *Big Kiss-Off* 106: Joe, there's some muscle hanging around outside my house. **1977** *Kojak* (CBS-TV): They're the local muscle—the local hoods. **1977** Caron *Go-Boy* 33: Rocko, who was a muscle on the gang, grinned wolfishly and zapped Smokey with a rock. **1995** *N.Y. Observer* (June 19) 30: Wear a dark suit, ear microphone and a .44, and tell them you're the "muscle" for "Mr. Trump."

2. the penis.—usu. considered vulgar. See also LOVE MUSCLE.
    1965 Trimble *Sex Words* 136: *Muscle*...The Penis. **1972** R. Wilson *Playboy's Forbidden Words* 176: *Muscle* The penis; sometimes also called the *love muscle.*

¶ In phrases:

¶ **on the muscle, 1.a.** fit and ready, as for a fight or other competition; (*hence*) belligerent. Also **on (one's) muscle.**
    1859 Matsell *Vocab.* 61: *On the Muscle.* On the fight; a fighter; a pugilist. *Ibid.*: "The fellow travels on his muscle," he presumes on his abilities to fight. **1861** in *Civil War Times Illus.* (Nov. 1972) 25: There are but few very sick men in the regiment, but a good many kind of *run down,* but will soon be *on their muscle.* **1869** in Williams & Duffy *Chi. Wits* 50: The Devil is getting the upper hand, and you must go in on your muscle. **1874** Carter *Rollingpin* 43: Then we commenced our rounds and took in the saloons. If we were not on our muscle when we left the boat, we generally got on it by one or two o'clock in the morning, and a fight was pretty sure to result. *Ibid.*: He...dared him to come outside and fight....But all to no purpose. Wilks wasn't on his muscle. **1876** J.M. Reid *Old Settlers* 139: Tom White was a character, and was on his muscle....He gave Hearn...a terrible whipping. **1883** *Life* (Mar. 1) 108: The man who "walks off on his ear" has sometimes been known to return "on his muscle." **1883–84** (quot. at MUCKLE). **1884** Peck *Boss Book* 50: Learn him to keep his mouth shut about being a terror on the muscle. **1930** *Amer. Mercury* (Dec.) 456: *On the muscle:* Angry, quarrelsome. "He busts up to me strictly on the muscle. So I let him have it." **1948** J. Webb *Four Steps* 20: Dirteye's coming this way....He's on his muscle, too. **1952** Himes *Stone* 283: I got on my muscle. Why? Why have we got to watch ourselves? **1980** Manchester *Darkness* 155: Everybody was on the muscle. "Shape up or ship out" was the slogan heard most often. **1980** *N.Y. Times* (Mar. 23) II 21: The worst thing you can do is get on your muscle....Just...say, "I'm sure you don't realize it, but your talking is spoiling the movie for me." **1984** W. Murray *Dead Crab* 85: He was very much on the muscle, a phrase that simply indicates an animal is ready to run his best race.

b. nervous; jittery.
    1964 Mirvish *There You Are* 223: Well, she has all the other girls scared. Gives them a lot of crap about behaving or she'll tell their husbands. Has them all on the muscle. **1968** Hersey *Algiers Motel* 127: Maybe when you talk to him you'll think he's on the muscle....Maybe

sort of defensive. **1994** *L.A. Times* (Dec. 19) B8: Examples of "Copspeak"…*On the muscle*—said of a nervous suspect.

2. through the use or threat of violence.

1948 I. Shulman *Cry Tough!* 127: You know that this time it won't be on the muscle? **1942–49** Goldin et al. *DAUL* 143: *Muscle, on the*….1. By strong-arm methods; engaged in any criminal activity requiring strong-arm methods. 2. Acquired without paying as the result of a reputation for violence. **1952** H. Grey *Hoods* 284: They operated as we did, on the muscle. **1971** J. Brown & A. Groff *Monkey* 21 [ref. to 1930's]: In the cases where we didn't [succeed in bribing the police], we would be forced to operate "on the muscle."

¶ **put the muscle on** Orig. *Journ. & Und.* to coerce by violence or threats thereof.

1942 Liebling *Telephone* 57: Sometimes, when an act…fails to pay the agent his additional commission, Jack is engaged to put the muscle on the unethical performer. **1956** Resko *Reprieve* 206 [ref. to 1940's]: [His] racket was putting the muscle on cat joints. **1971** Horan *Blue Messiah* 235: They…put the muscle on Father John. **1976** *L.A. Times* (July 18) VI 8: Put a little muscle on the tour operator.

muscle *adj.* physically violent (as pertaining to the commission of criminal acts).—used prenominally.

1930 in Partridge *Dict. Und.* 457: "If you hire the bump-off…do it the right way." "I'm pretty fair at that muscle stuff myself." **1932–33** P. Cain *Fast One* 108: Rose has built up a muscle organization of his own. **1953** *N.Y. Times* (Apr. 5) I 16: He is under four indictments involving a variety of charges, including "muscle work" in connection with another New Jersey labor dispute. **1984** J. McNamara *First Directive* 227: I'd like to know a little more about why the kid suddenly goes in for muscle work.

muscle *v.* **1.a.** to coerce by means of threats or violence.

*ca***1830–50** in Holloway & Black *Broadsides* II 310: A rival he came in…And muscled me—don't grin. **1929** in *DA*: A certain gentleman in the illicit spirits business was accosted by two sinister characters, who "muscled" him…removing from his wallet the sum of $150. **1930** Irwin *Tramp & Und. Slang*: *Muscle*.—To use force or intimidation so as to secure a share in a "racket" or graft. **1936** Coe *G-Man* 142: If they're musclin' Rap, it won't be long before they're musclin' us too. **1950** *Time* (Nov. 27) 21: I ain't never muscled no one in my life. **1952** Holmes *Boots Malone* (film): He muscled me. **1961** J. Flynn *Action Man* 98: He's one of the boys trying to muscle me. **1968** Cuomo *Thieves* 217: Maybe a patsy to muscle tobacco and stuff out of. **1970** Cole *Street Kids* 19: He tried at first to muscle any of his boys who moved toward drugs but the lure was too strong and the numbers too many. **1975** *Barbary Coast* (ABC-TV): Don't muscle me, Ben. **1977** Caron *Go-Boy* 106: As I said no self-respecting con would risk his health and his reputation muscling a young prisoner to be his sweet kid, but there were other more subtle ways. **1983** *Agronsky & Co.* (Mutual Radio news): The purpose of those Marines in Lebanon is to muscle the Soviets and the Syrians. **1988** *Crossfire* (CNN-TV) (July 9): Are they trying to muscle Congress? **1995** *Talk Back Live* (CNN-TV) (May 23): They don't like being threatened and being muscled. **1996** McCumber *Playing Off Rail* 198: That's why they were muscling us: They didn't want anybody to…get out of there with his money.

b. to shift, carry, heave, shove, etc., with extreme muscular exertion. Now *colloq.* or *S.E.* Orig. dial.

1913 Kephart *So. Highlanders* 262: We can muscle this log up. **1952** *Sat. Eve. Post* (Mar. 15) 139: It was too heavy to be muscled overboard. **1978** in Lyle & Golenbock *Bronx Zoo* 108: He was trying to throw the ball too damn hard. He was trying to muscle the ball. **1979** *Pop. Science* (June) 122: No heavy metal panels have to be muscled into place. **1992–95** C.D.B. Bryan *Close Encounters* 216: Carol had to muscle the darkened, powerless car toward the shoulder of the road.

c. to push or elbow one's way (into something) or force one's attentions upon (someone); (*specif.*) *Journ., Police, & Und.* to force one's way (into) (usu. an illicit enterprise) by means of threats or violence; extort a share of; (*broadly*) to obtain unfairly.—usu. constr. with *in* (*on*) or *into*.

1928 T.A. Dorgan, in Zwilling *TAD Lexicon* 58: Panning the mugg who "muscles in" on the boss each day as he goes to chow. **1928** W.T. Burnett *Little Caesar* 157: I been watching you ever since you muscled in on Sam Vittori. **1929** E. Sullivan *Look at Chicago* 19: His rivals were out to get him the moment he "muscled into" the beer field. **1930** Pasley *Al Capone* 45: He…issued orders to his willing crew to start

muscling in and hijacking. **1930** *Amer. Mercury* (Dec.) 456: *Muscle in, v.:* To secure a share by force. "Broke? Go muscle in some beer joint." **1930** Lavine *3d Degree* 38: One of the lads will get ambitious and attempt to muscle in on some graft out of his own domain. **1930** J.T. Farrell *Guillotine Party* 234: I'm musclin' myself into the political racket. **1930** in S.J. Perelman *Old Gang* 94: Burning to muscle in on the big dough. **1931** Wilstach *Under Cover Man* 86: I'm going to…muscle in stronger than ever. **1931** C. Ford *Coconut Oil* 94: Somebody is trying to muscle in on our territory. **1931–34** Adamic *Dynamite* 340: Gangsters…began to "muscle" their way into…union…affairs. **1935** L. Hughes *Little Ham* 73: The Danny Jiggers gang's trying to muscle in against Manny Hudgins, and there's hell to pay. **1936** H. Gray *Arf* (unp.): How'd yuh ever muscle into such a swell joint? **1939** M. McCall *Maisie* (film): You told him the truth? That you muscled in on the [maid's] job? **1940** *New Yorker* (June 8) 16: And here you are trying to muscle in. **1946** I. Shulman *Amboy Dukes* 27: Nobody muscled in on another guy's date. **1947** Schulberg *Harder They Fall* 81: A mob that had muscled in on Nick's racket. **1953** Rodgers & Hammerstein *Me & Juliet* 482: It looks as if Charlie's trying to take your job away. Trying to muscle in on you. **1956** Ross *Hustlers* 18: I heard he was trying to muscle in on Lolita. **1958** Talsman *Gaudy Image* 228: O, that Titania! Don't muscle. She's currently engaged. **1960** Bannon *Journey* 128: I didn't know I was muscling in on anything. **1962** G. Olson *Roaring Road* 50: He had muscled his way from seventh to fourth [place in a sporting competition]. **1971** B.B. Johnson *Blues for Sister* 135: The syndicate boys…muscled her out. **1973** O'Neill & O'Neill *Shifting Gears* 153: There are some Americans who constantly try to muscle into lines. **1980** *N.Y. Times* (July 20) IV 4: Bolivian Military Muscles In Again….Last week, the fourth military takeover in 26 months.

2. to bluff. Also as *n.*

1929–32 in *AS* (Dec. 1934) 288: [Lincoln Univ.:] *Muscle.* Artificiality; bluff; wind. Derisive murmurs of Muscle are often shot at one who is obviously bluffing in a recitation. *Ibid.* 289: *Muscle.* To attempt to convince by bluffing; to discourse meaninglessly.

musclebound *adj.* ¶ In phrase: **musclebound between the ears** exceedingly stupid or slow-witted. Cf. MUSCLEHEAD.

1916 T.A. Dorgan, in Zwilling *TAD Lexicon* 58: Let 'im alone he's muscle bound between the ears. **1942** *ATS* 176: Stupid…*muscle-bound between the ears.*

muscle car *n. Auto.* a high-powered sports car.

1969 *Business Week* (Jan. 11) 98: A new "muscle" car, the Judge, will be unveiled this month by Pontiac. It's a pepped-up version of the jet-set GTO, with a 366-hp ram-air engine [etc.]. **1970** *Pop. Science* (Sept.) 33: Whether you're driving a muscle car or the family wagon. **1971** *Atlantic* (Sept.) 34: Laser stripes on musclecars. **1973** *Business Week* (July 14) 30: The reported demise of Detroit's "muscle cars," it turns out, was premature. **1973** *Playboy* (Sept.) 124: The megahorsepower "muscle cars" are gone. **1976** *U.S. News & W.R.* (Feb. 9) 48: The high-powered "muscle" cars with oversized engines and racing stripes. **1982** Abodaher *Iacocca* 177: [In 1967] American Motors produced two "muscle" cars, as Mustang types were being called, the Javelin and the AMX. **1983** Volvo ad (ABC-TV) (May 10): If you're still lamenting the loss of those muscle cars of the past. **1984** *U.S. News & W.R.* (Feb. 6) 56: Chevrolet's Corvette, Pontiac's Fiero, [etc.]…—these and other autos reminiscent of the "muscle" cars of the 1960s. **1986** *I'll Buy That!* 110: The 1969 Hurst/Oldsmobile, a popular "muscle car" of its day. **1988** *Wkly. World News* (Oct. 18) 3: Muscle cars are being produced at rates unrivaled since the 1960s. **1990** *World News Tonight* (ABC-TV) (July 30): The new economics of owning a muscle car—suddenly a hot investment. **1993** *Smithsonian* (July) 54: But by the 1970s, insurance problems and poor fuel mileage were phasing out the mass-produced muscle cars. **1994** *News Hour* (CNN-TV) (Mar. 7): Deadly muscle car showdowns have killed seven people. **1996** Oak Ridge, Tenn., graphics artist, age 42: And this *muscle car*—you know, these big red things with "turbo" and stripes and stuff printed on it—makes a quick 90-degree turn into the parking place…and nearly slams into us….Whenever Al sees someone doing crazy automobile things like that, he always says, "Sorry about your penis."…Not so they can hear!

muscle fuck *n.* (see quots.).—usu. considered vulgar.

1974 Univ. Tenn. grad. student: A…French fuck is when you rub your dick between her breasts. It's also called a *muscle fuck.* **1977** Univ. Tenn. grad. student: A muscle fuck is one where the Jane can contract the muscles in her vagina. It can drive you up the wall. I heard about muscle fucks in the Marines [*ca*1972].

musclehead *n.* a thickheaded fellow, esp. an athlete.

1923 Toomer *Cane* 111: Mussel-heads get along, Muriel. There is more to you than that—. **1937** Sturgess *Easy Living* (film): I waited twenty years to find out I was the father of a musclehead. **1940** Zinberg *Walk Hard* 77: I haven't anybody to talk to except the muscleheads at the gym. **1952** R. Alexander *Time Out* 20: Hya, muscle-head. **1961** McMurtry *Horseman, Pass By* 66: I was just part of it, just another muscle-head for you to boss around. **1969** R. Welch, in *Playboy* (Jan. 1970) 78: But I don't care for those muscleheads with the tremendously thick necks who can't even walk properly because their thighs are disproportionately developed. **1974** R. Price *Wanderers* 141: He's sleepin', the fuckin' musclehead. **1978** W. Wharton *Birdy* 178: Yeah, you, musclehead. **1993** J. Watson & K. Dockery *Point Man* 23: But I wasn't just a young musclehead jock-to-be.

muscleman *n.* **1.** a hired thug; strong-arm man; (*also*) a bodyguard. Also **muscle boy, muscle guy.**

1929 Hotstetter & Beesley *It's a Racket!* 232: "Muscle Men" are those who "muscle" their way. **1931** Wilstach *Under Cover Man* 25: My new muscle man. He takes it if I forget to dodge. **1931** C. Ford *Coconut Oil* 88: "We're wit' yuh, Jimmy boy!" replied his two musclemen. **1935** E. Levinson *Strikes* 66: Berghoff calls them the "musclemen." **1935** Mackenzie *Been Places* 28: She…was often overhauled by a faster boat armed with a mob of muscle-men and held up. **1937–40** in Whyte *Street Corner Soc.* 120: Then there's the muscle men. They muscle in to take over a business. **1940** in O'Hara *Pal Joey* 90: Dont let anybody tell you they got rid of the muscle boys in Chi. **1946** Mezzrow & Wolfe *Really Blues* 28: I got my kicks out of rubbing elbows with all those bigtime gamblers and muscle men. **1949** *Sat. Eve. Post* (Oct. 22) 102: A bookie loan shark had me for five hundred. He sent a muscle man around. **1950** *Time* (July 31) 13: Some of Harry's muscle boys broke up a second meeting with a well-timed fist fight. **1957** (quot. at HEAVY, *n.*). **1957** Ness & Fraley *Untouchables* 20: Nor would mere "muscle men" do because each had to have special investigative techniques at his command. **1960** Himes *Gold Dream* 147: Either Slick and his muscle boy, or Dummy alone, or all three together. **1960** Perry *Young Man Drowning* 144: There are a lot of muscle guys hanging around and hustling for us. **1962** in Cannon *Nobody Asked* 150: He was a fierce muscle guy for the syndicate bosses. **1966** *Time* (Dec. 9) 38: I am not a political muscleman…but I have a pretty strong and persistent will. **1981** D.E. Miller *Jargon* 22: The muscleman…had no appetite for further violence. **1985** *A-Team* (NBC-TV): When Kyle finds out what we did to his musclemen he won't be pleased.

2. a notably muscular man, as a wrestler, weightlifter, etc.; strongman. Now *S.E.*

1934 Weseen *Dict. Amer. Sl.* 261: Muscleman—A wrestler. **1942** *ATS* 386: Muscleman…a strong man. **1950** *Sat. Eve. Post* (Sept. 23) 141: Charley, my old Yankee side-kick, is a muscle man who can tear apart a game. **1949–51** M. Daly *Profile of Youth* 241: Girls say they dislike "musclemen" who show off biceps at every chance, like to strut on beaches and stand with arms folded to make muscles look more impressive. **1958** *Time* (Sept. 22) 44: One new quiz show…*Brains and Brawn*, in which intellectual quiz athletes team up with actual musclemen. (After the brains match memories in familiar fashion, the brawnier contestants match skills in athletic derring-do.). **1961** Kohner *Gidget Goes Hawaiian* 77: A group of bronzed musclemen sitting in a circle. **1977** *Texas Monthly* (Apr.) 150: In the strange world of muscle men Arnold's attitude is unique. **1982** *California* (June) 116: Yet another Hercules-type muscleman.

muscler *n.* a MUSCLEMAN, 1; (*also*) someone who uses force or fraud to achieve a goal.

1942 in *ATS* 423: Chisler, chiz, muscler, muscler-in.

muscle shirt *n.* a T-shirt with no sleeves or very short sleeves.

1972 *North Eastern Reporter, Second Series* 288:742: While on the bed Palmer removed a "muscle shirt" from his pocket. **1980** *Wash. Post* (Aug. 17) (Nexis): Gomez was always walking around in a muscle shirt, showing off. **1990** *Daily News Record* (July 27) 8: A contrasting collection of sheer muscle shirt styles in black and gold. **1994** *N.Y. Times* (Aug. 16) A10: In a black muscle shirt and jeans, skeleton tattoos on his arms. **1994** *N.Y. Times Mag.* (Sept. 25) 46: A muscle shirt adver-

tising the band Kreator. **1994** *New York* (Nov. 14) 53: [He] comes striding through the offices in a muscle shirt.

mush[1] *n.* [orig. unkn.] *Und.* (see quot.).

1791 [W. Smith] *Confess. T. Mount* 19: Thief's girl,…*mush. Ibid.* 21: Frank…to's mush did say,/With other prigs ne'er live, I pray.

mush[2] *n.* [prob. abbr. *mush*room] *Und. & Hobo.* an umbrella.

*****1821**, *****1851** (quots. at MUSHFAKER). *****1856** (quot. at MUSHROOM, 1). *****1857** "Ducange Anglicus" *Vulgar Tongue* 13: Mush, n. Umbrella. **1859** Matsell *Vocab.* 57: Mush. An umbrella. **1904** *Life in Sing Sing* 250: Mush.—An umbrella. **1914** *Wash. Post*, in *Comments on Ety.* (May 1995) 7: "Mush," which a few years ago meant to tramp…to-day is used by the thieves and hoboes for an umbrella. **1914** Jackson & Hellyer *Vocab.* 61: When you can't do anything else you can heel the hotels and depots for mushes and turkeys. **1923** *N.Y. Times* (Sept. 9) VIII 2: Mush: An umbrella. **1948** Mencken *Amer. Lang. Supp. II* 678: An umbrella is a *mush.* **1942–49** Goldin et al. *DAUL*: Mush…A stolen umbrella.

mush[3] *n.* [orig. unkn.] Esp. *Boxing.* the face or mouth. Also **moosh.** [The assertion by Farmer & Henley (IV, p. 391) that this word is entered in F. Grose, *Dict. of the Vulgar Tongue* (1785), as well as in *Lexicon Balatronicum* (1811), is false.]

1859 Matsell *Vocab.* 127: Mush. The mouth. **1902** Cullen *More Tales* 85: I'd often seen him in New York, and I'd seen his mush in Byrnes's mug book, too. **1905** (quot. at FRAP, *v.*). **1907** in H.C. Fisher *A. Mutt* 11: I've seen his mush in de paper. **1910** *N.Y. Eve. Jour.* (Mar. 16) 15: Welsh slapped him on the "mush" and messed his "phizog" all up. **1911** Van Loan *Big League* 54: Don't know that *mush* of his? **1914** Jackson & Hellyer *Vocab.* 60: Moosh, moush…The human face….Also the mouth…."He's got a harp moosh," i.e., Irish. **1915** in Grayson *New Stories* 550: You can wear a man out letting him hit you in the mush. Must be made of iron. **1917** E.R. Burroughs *Oakdale Affair* 18: I'm goin' to push his mush through the back of his bean. **1919** MacGill *Dough-Boys* 148: Well, the proper thing to do when there's a row on the Western Front is to put a fag in your moosh and smoke it! **1920** J. Conway, in *Variety* (Dec. 24) 5: We don't get the belts on the mush he does. **1921** Marquis *Carter* 91: Give him a wallop on his mush fer me. **1921–25** J. Gleason & R. Taber *Is Zat So?* 112: The egg here steps into a couple in the mush. **1925** Cohan *B'way* 70: "Soak him in the eye, Mickey!" "Upper-cut him in the mush, Red!" **1929–30** J.T. Farrell *Young Lonigan* 13: He…pasted Weary in the mush with an icy snowball. **1934** Loos *Red Headed Woman* (film): A little powder wouldn't do that gloomy mush of yours any harm. **1945** Wead *They Were Expendable* (film): For two bits I'd punch ya right in the mush! **1950** Bissell *Stretch on River* 91: Curly…pastes him a good one on the mush. **1952** Holmes *Boots Malone* (film): Scram or I'll bat ya in the mush! **1955** O'Connor *Last Hurrah* 98: He sticks his big mush in the public trough and says, "Stand back, nobody gets any o' this but me!" **1962** T. Berger *Reinhart* 42: You'll get punched right in the mush. **1963–64** Kesey *Great Notion* 34: A broken tooth I got from trying to field a bad hop with my mush. **1971** N.Y.U. student: I punched the guy right in the moosh. **1980** Feiffer *Popeye* (film): I oughta bust ya right in the mush.

mush[4] *n.* foolishness or nonsense; (*specif.*) (now usu.) silly or effusive sentiment. Now *S.E.*

[**1852** in *DAE*: Uncle Tom's Cabin has had a large sale, but the book is a perfect "mush."] **1884** in Lummis *Letters* 166: There wasn't any mush about it, either. *a***1889–90** in Barrère & Leland *Dict. Slang*: Just fancy her making him [go]…to a straight-backed pew to listen to Gospel *mush!* **1889–90** Barrère & Leland *Dict. Slang*: Mush…(American), stuff, nonsense, indifferent, uninteresting matter. **1904** in *DAE*: That sort of Bible defense is mere mush. **1908** H. Green *Maison de Shine* 118: You got too good a nut to fall for that mush he hands out. **1912** Lowrie *Prison* 288: This ain't no mush, it's good common sense. **1917–20** Dreiser *Newspaper Days* 219: Its grandest period of stage sentiment or mush. **1920** in Hemingway *By-Line* (Dec. 11) 13: It's mush to pull a job in that country but trust the boys to get theirs. **1922** (quot. at LIZZIE BOY). **1957** Bradbury *Dandelion Wine* 19: I spent…hours in the theater toilet waiting for the mush to be over so I could see…*The Bat.* **1983** *Green Lantern* (July) (unp.): Mush again! I should have known this would happen! **1987** *ALF* (NBC-TV): "Oh, Alf! That's so sweet!" "No mush!"

mush[5] *n.* [perh. abbr. MUSHHEAD; but cf. MUSH[3] with similar sense development of MUG] a fool; MUTT, 2. [Partridge's assertion, repeated by Thorne, that this represents a Romani word for 'man' is unsubstantiated.]

1906 *Nat. Police Gaz.* (Aug. 18) 6: The mush scratched checks...as he needed them. **1921** E. O'Neill *Anna Christie* 74: You're an old mush! *1968 in *OEDS*: So this mush is running a string of...houses of ill repute....So what? **1993** *Mystery Sci. Theater* (Comedy Central TV): I was just going with my feelings, you big mush!

mush[1] *v.* [fr. dogsledders' *mush* 'to cross snow with a dog sled', < F *marchons!* 'let's go!'] to go; depart; MOOCH.

[**1862** in *DA*: My dogs are *dogs!* and we will *mouche* very likely, after all.] **1906** H. Green *Actors' Boarding House* 26: Johnny McDuff's mushed. **1906** in *DA*: I never got off the train since I mushed out of Seattle, and I'm hungry. **1912** *Adventure* (May) 26: You mush on down the street and see if you can cop a boob. **1935** Faulkner *Pylon* 193.

mush[2] *v.* *Und.* MUSHFAKE.

1907 J. London *Road* [ref. to *ca*1894]: There were two more in their gang, who were across the river "mushing" in Harrisburg.

mush[3] *v.* to be foolishly affectionate (with); kiss and caress. Also **mush it up.**

1926 in J.M. March *Wild Party* 102: He's mushin' it up with your angel-face! **1927** H. Miller *Moloch* 163: Mushing it up in a corner. **1931** Lorimer & Lorimer *Streetcars* 22: I hate having men mush all over me. **1944** Burley *Hndbk. Jive* 144: Mush—Kiss. **1952** Bellow *Augie March* 86: The kind who'd never...let you stick around till one a.m. mushing with them on the steps. **1956** Metalious *Peyton Place* 61: After all I've done for her, she acts like a little tramp right under my nose, letting some pimply-faced boy paw her and mush her. **1972** P. Thomas *Savior* 9: Some kid was mushing it up with his girl.

mush[4] *v.* *Av.* to lose airspeed or altitude, as from a stalled or partially stalled engine; fly in this condition.

1935 Wead *Ceiling Zero* (film): I got the throttle wide open but she's mushing along at eighty-five. **1937** Lay *Wings* 325: Most modern airplanes will not spin from a stall, but will nose down (mush) and pick up flying speed again. **1942** in C.R. Bond & T. Anderson *Flying T. Diary* 160: We fear he may have mushed into the lake on a gunnery dive. **1944** E.H. Hunt *Limit* 36: The engine died and she mushed down the runway. **1948** La Farge *Eagle in Egg* 199: It still lost altitude, shaking violently, and "mushing" in the air. **1958** in F. Harvey *Air Force* 24: You're mushing. Drop your nose. **1966–67** W. Stevens *Gunner* 255: The chute had blown and the ship had mushed. *a*1989 Berent *Rolling Thunder* 49: Pilots...mushing through trees. **1992** *Duck Tales* (CBS-TV): You've mushed out of control!

mushbrain *n.* idiocy; (*also*) MUSHHEAD.

1982 *N.Y. Times* (July 18) (Nexis): Mush-brains are everywhere....If a person had a connection to training camp, he most certainly had a training camp mush-brain. [**1983** B. Breathed, in *Daily Beacon* (Univ. Tenn.) (Nov. 9) 2: This, mush-for-brains, has been a recording.] **1985** *L.A. Times* (Apr. 21) (Nexis): The left has no monopoly on mush brain. **1986** *L.A. Times* (May 17) (Nexis): This is a TV screen, and Daddy likes to watch it, and my Mommy thinks it gives you mush brain. **1988** *Wash. Post* (Jan. 16) (Nexis): Inexplicably, these sharpies turn into mush brains. **1996** *Scientific American* (TLC-TV): [They] call it the "mushbrain factor."

musher *n.* MUSHFAKER.

1907 J. London *Road* 81 [ref. to *ca*1894]: A "musher" is an itinerant fakir....The particular graft of the two mushers who had crossed the river was umbrella-mending.

mushfake *v.* *Hobo.* to be a MUSHFAKER. Also as quasi-adj.

1893 in *Independent* (Nov. 21, 1901) 2765: I have taken up Mush Faking or Umbrella mending since I left N. York. **1902** *Independent* (Feb. 6) 337: A long stretch of circus and "mush-fake" experience. **1930** "D. Stiff" *Milk & Honey* 41: In winter he goes south and spends his time mushfaking. **1952** Himes *Stone* 80: They...mush-faked. Mush-faking was the major industry within the prison. It was the manufacture of gadgets such as cigarette holders and lighters and jewel boxes and rings and pins and similar items from old bones, toothbrush handles, copper coins, and gold crowns [done in spare time].

mushfaker *n.* *Und. & Hobo.* an itinerant umbrella mender, tinker, or pitchman; a repairer or deviser of small, cheap contrivances; (*hence*) (used among tramps, etc., as a vague term of opprobrium); a no-account.

[*1821 in *OED*: Tommy Twenty, a mush toper feeker.] [*1839

Brandon *Poverty, Mendicity* (gloss.): *Mushroom fakers*—itinerant umbrella makers and repairers.] *1851 H. Mayhew, in *OED*: The term [Mushhead-fakers]...has become very generally condensed among those who carry on the trade—they are now mush-fakers. *1851 H. Mayhew, in Partridge *Dict. Und.* 458: In umbrellas and Parasols the second-hand traffic is large, but those vended in the streets are nearly all "done up" for street sale by the class known as "mush...Fakers." **1918** in *AS* (Oct. 1933) 30: *Mush-Faker.* Worker in light structural iron. Hence, also, an itinerant peddler and repairer of umbrellas. **1922** N. Anderson *Hobo* 99: The Mushfaker is a man who sells his services. He may be a tinker, a glazier, an umbrella mender, or he may repair sewing machines or typewriters. Some mushfakers even pose as piano tuners. **1927** *AS* 387: Wandering tinkers are called *mushfakirs.* **1927** *DN* V 456: *Mush-faker*...A low grade tramp. **1929** *AS* IV 342: *Mush-faker.* One who sits by another's fire and gathers no woods. **1930** "D. Stiff" *Milk & Honey* 101: Traditionally, a mushfaker is a man who goes about mending umbrellas, but the term may also include a man who goes to back doors soldering pots and kettles. Some mushfakers specialize in mending toys...[or] sharpening knives and scissors. **1931** J.T. Farrell *McGinty* 33: A crowd had gathered around a mush-faker who was selling Snake Oil. **1942–49** Goldin et al. *DAUL* 143: *Mush-faker.* An umbrella thief who solicits umbrellas for repair and fails to return them.

mushhead *n.* a fool; dolt. Hence **mush-headed**, *adj.*

1878 Hart *Sazerac* 161: Mushhead Smith. **1884** in Lummis *Letters* 73: You mush-headed idiots. **1889–90** Barrère & Leland *Dict. Slang*: *Mush-head* (American), a stupid, witless fellow. **1898** F. Norris *Moran* 39: I ain't a mush-head, like me dear friend Jim. **1903** *Pedagog. Sem.* X 379: Mushhead. **1919** in E. Wilson *Twenties* 57: John Reed's a mush-head. **1920** Ade *Hand-Made Fables* 47: All...regarded him as a Mush-Head because he stuck around Over-Time. **1924** Hecht & Bodenheim *Cutie* 65: He was a mush head. **1942** (quot. at MUTTHEAD). **1943** Twist *Bombardier* (film): Come on, ya mushhead! **1952** Bellow *Augie March* 94: Don't be a mushhead all your life. **1954–60** *DAS*: Mush-headed. **1962** Dougherty *Commissioner* 223: You're a mushhead that would only confuse the issues before us. **1990** *Oprah* (ABC-TV): She's become such a mushhead. **1993** *Simpsons* (Fox-TV): You're nothing but a pack of fickle mushheads!

mushmouth *n.* indistinct speech or a person who speaks indistinctly. Also (nonce) as *v.*

1930 *AS* V (Feb.) 239: *Mushmouth.* One who talks indistinctly. "The chapel-speaker was a mushmouth." **1942** *ATS* 218: *Mush-mouth*, poorly enunciated speech. **1971** E. Tidyman & J. Black *Shaft* (film): That's 'cause us black folk talk mushmouth. **1981** in *California* (Jan. 1982) 99: The distinguished cast mush-mouthed the gleaming Gertrude Stein text.

mush-rigger *n.* MUSHFAKER.

1918 (quot. at MUSHROOM, 1). **1925** Mullin *Scholar Tramp* 147 [ref. to *ca*1912]: A short distance out of New London, I fell in with a dishwasher, an old mush-faker or mush-rigger (umbrella-mender), and a third nondescript whom I failed to pigeonhole in any occupation.

mushroom *n.* **1.** an umbrella.

*1856 in *F & H* IV 391: Fanciful metaphors contribute largely to the formulation of slang. It is upon this principle that the mouth has come to be styled the "tater-trap";....umbrellas, "mushrooms" (or, briefly "mush"). **1918** Livingston *Delcassee* 82: Hoboes term umbrellas "mushrooms." Hence the itinerant umbrella mender came to his odd moniker "mush faker" or "mush rigger." **1942** *ATS* 78: Umbrella. ... *mush, mushroom.*

2. [alluding to the witticism reported in 1978 quot.] a person who is lied to or kept uninformed.

[**1978** in Partridge *Concise Slang Dict.*: I feel like a mushroom: everyone keeps me in the dark and is always feeding me bullshit.] *1979 A. Sullivan *Sully's Irish Music Bk.* 3: The Mushroom Treatment. **1979** *N.Y. Post* (Dec. 13) 6: Was the Marine hostage interviewed by NBC trying to send a secret message? Since Cpl. William Gallegos' appearance from Iran on Monday, analysts are trying to decipher what he meant by the cryptic word "mushroom."...No, it isn't a government code. But when things are confused, many military personnel apparently say: "I must be a mushroom, because they are keeping me in the dark and feeding me bull." **1988** C. Roberts & C. Sasser *Walking Dead* 13: The thinking behind keeping you in the dark—like a mushroom, ... and fed horseshit—was that if you were a grunt you didn't need to know the "Big Picture." **1995** Univ. Tenn. student: The "mushroom treatment" means keeping someone in the dark and feeding them shit.

3. an unwitting bystander caught in crossfire between criminals.

    1988 *Daily News* (N.Y.) (June 8) 7: Mushrooms. That's the street name for victims who get in the way of drug dealers. **1988** *N.Y. Times* (Aug. 1) A14: "Mushrooms"—that's the drug gunman's brutal slang for innocent bystanders who pop up unexpectedly in his line of fire. **1992** M. Gelman *Crime Scene* 49: The shootings gave rise to the stray bullet, a new and truly terrible addition to daily city living. Cops called these victims "mushrooms," because they popped up in the middle of gunfire.

mushroom-faker *n.* MUSHFAKER.

    *1839 Brandon *Poverty, Mendicity* (gloss.): *Mushroom fakers*—itinerant umbrella makers and repairers. **1859** Matsell *Vocab.* 57: *Mushroom-Fakers.* Umbrella hawkers.

mush worker *n.* [fr. MUSH[4], *n.*] *Und. & Police.* a criminal, usu. a woman, who swindles victims, usu. men, by playing upon their sympathies.

    1927 *DN* V 456: *Mush worker*…An attractive woman who fleeces unsuspecting men by telling them some pitiful *racket.* **1933–34** Lorimer & Lorimer *Stag Line* 145: These mush workers…tell you some sob story you catch wise it's phoney before they begin. **1949** *Harper's* (Aug.) 95: Mushworkers and lushworkers. **1970** Winick & Kinsie *Lively Commerce* 41: A prostitute who steals from her clients is called a "mush worker."

mushy *adj.* overly sentimental or romantic; soft. Orig. *colloq.* Also as *adv.* [Bracketed quots. clearly mean 'indistinctly formed or formulated', a S.E. usage.]

    [**1839** in *DAE:* I soon recognized old *Noth Calinur* in their nasal mushy pronunciation.] [**1870** in *DAE:* The death penalty is disappearing, like some better things, before a kind of mushy and unthinking doubt of its morality and expediency.] *1876 "G. Eliot," in *OED* 45: She's not mushy, but her heart is tender. **1896** Ade *Artie* 81: Nothin' mushy, eh? None o' this soft work? **1902–03** Ade *People You Know* 161: She chucked in a few mushy Extracts from the Oatmeal School of Thought and asked him the Name of his Favorite Poet. **1904** in "O. Henry" *Works* 1006: Do you think it is manly to use those mushy…forms of address? **1912** in Truman *Dear Bess* 68: That sounds awful mushy don't it? **1916** E.R. Burroughs *Return of Mucker* 97: I'd a-hated myself if I'd thought that I could ever talk mushy like I am now. **1918** Stringer *House of Intrigue* 298: Why that guy went mushy on you over two years ago.…That man's in love with you. **1921–25** J. Gleason & R. Taber *Is Zat So?* 116: Well, I don't want to be mushy. **1927** in Hammett *Knockover* 311: The Kid got mushy with the broad along the road and got knocked for a loop. **1932** Lorimer & Lorimer *Streetcars* 36: There's lots of ways to handle boys when they start to get mushy. **1938** Bellem *Blue Murder* 196: And then I thought: what the hell, I'm getting mushy. **1991** *Darkwing Duck* (ABC-TV): For a minute there I thought things was gonna get mushy.

music *n.* **1.** gunfire.

    1864 C.W. Wills *Army Life* 327: Have heard no "music" to-day. **1865** E.H. Rhodes *All for the Union* 215: The air is full of bursting shell. The Rebels are replying, and we have "Music in the air." **1865** H. Johnson *Talking Wire* 250: I would give the words of the "song," but I went to making music on my spencer and didn't get to hear it all. **1927** E. Stockwell *Pvt. Stockwell* 131: It settled down to picket firing with an occasional artillery bombardment. So we had the same old music we had had all summer. *a1940 in Lanning & Lanning *Texas Cowboys* 190 [ref. to Civil War]: We fought for three days and nights. There was plenty of music—it went…boom, and bang! **1992** J. Garry *This Ol' Drought* 141: Get up in the rocks and play some Winchester music for the locals.

2. talk; CHIN MUSIC, 1.

    1872 "W. Dexter" *Young Mustanger* 26: That's the music, cap'n.…I'll go out an' git Lasso Jack. **1889** "M. Twain" *Conn. Yankee* 193: Her tongue churned forth only railings and insult, whereas Sandy's music was of a kindlier sort. **1953** M. Harris *Southpaw* 202: I want to hear plenty of music.…I wish to hear plenty of chatter out there, and on the bench as well.

3. trouble; disturbance. Cf. *face the music,* below. [Bracketed quot. is almost certainly colloq.]

    [**1859** Bartlett *Amer.* (ed. 2): *Music.* Merriment, fun. "Jim is a right clever fellow; there is a great deal of music in him."] **1886** E.L.

Wheeler *N.Y. Nell* 18: I'm on the war-path now; so look out for music. **1894** *Harper's* (Oct.) 697: There'll be music if Yank gets on to Chop Miller being with her. **1922** in Ruhm *Detective* 24: John B. Combs cut a big figure and his son's arrest made some music. **1972** in *Playboy* (Jan. 1973) 250: Although I think now, I knew how much music it was gonna cost me, I would've paid the extra dough to take it out.

4. *Mil. Av.* electronic countermeasures against radar tracking or similar systems; (*also*) electronic equipment used for directing laser-guided weapons to a target. [Quots. ref. to Vietnam War.]

    1976 Lavalle *Airpower* 54 [ref. to 1972]: Within about 30 seconds he said "I've started the music" meaning the laser beam was on the target.…The LGB hit right on that [enemy tank].…Raccoon "started the music" again. **1982** Basel *Pak Six* 73: "Spread out, music on."…We turned on our jammers and spread into a wide…formation. **1987** Zeybel *Gunship* 172: I started my bomb pass.…My Sword heard the music. *a1989 Berent *Rolling Thunder* 320: "Music on."…All sixteen F-105 pilots…activated electronic countermeasure devices.

¶ In phrase:

¶ **face the music, 1.** to face danger or hardship.

    1850 in *DAE:* There should be no skulking or dodging…every man should "face the music." **1854** in G.W. Harris *High Times* 74: Now I will marry on *this spot* any lady in the crowd who has the nerve to face such music. (i.e., undertake such a thing). **1861** in W.R. Howell *Westward* 58: We conclude to "face the music" by staying in the open air all night. **1863** in Jackman *Diary* 95: Here we had to "face the music" without pits or breastworks. **1864** *Battle-Fields of So.* 284: One of the Ninth stepped from the ranks and told the captain, "he wasn't able to face the music." **1879** Pettit *Underground R.R.* 51: A marshal was brought from Rochester to make the arrest, for no citizen of Syracuse could be found who dared to "face the music." **1879** in Blockson *Und. Railroad* 252: A marshal was brought from Rochester to make the arrest, for no citizen of Syracuse could be found who dared to "face the music." **1904** J. London *Sea-Wolf* ch. xv: It's me and Johnson have to face the music.

2. to face the consequences. Now *S.E.*

    1862 "E. Kirke" *Among Pines* 88: Dat sort don't run; dey face de music! **1882** C. Morris *Shadow Sam* 5: But when a feller can't slip, he's got to face the music. **1908** in H.C. Fisher *A. Mutt* 154: I'm gonna face the music, tell her I'm sorry, and give her what's left of the dough. **1918** in *DAE:* I shall remain and face the music. **1925** B. Conners *Patsy* 54: I decided the sportsmanlike thing to do was to come back and face the music. **1948** J. Stevens *Jim Turner* 222: I'll go on to Idaho with you, boy, and help you face your music. **1950** P. Green *Peer Gynt* 155: Tighten your belt, Peer. Face the music. **1988** *Forerunner* (Mar.) 13: People use the concept of "separation of church and state" as a tool to carry out their own anti-Christian bias. It's a favorite war slogan to toss out to avoid facing the music. **1988** *N.Y. Post* (June 21) 2: Five In Pentagate Face Music. **1991** *Hammerman* (ABC-TV): It's time these jailbirds faced the music.

musical fruit *n.* beans. *Joc.* Also **music fruit.**

    1919 Small *Story of the 47th* 75 [ref. to WWI]: We played marbles on the deck with "music fruit" and rolled our eyes around like a dying calf when we lost our "stake." **1934** Halper *Foundry* 191: *Beans! That Musical Fruit!* **1935** J. Conroy *World to Win* 270: I made fer…the musical fruit and jerky. **1962** Mandel *Wax Boom* 125: Beans, beans, the music fruit, the more you eat the more you toot. **1974** *Sanford & Son* (NBC-TV): Beans, beans, the musical fruit.

music box *n.* a musical instrument, esp. a piano, fancied to resemble a box.

    *1863 in *F & H* IV 392: But just you hear her sing, that is all.…Just smiles and sits down to the music-box. *ca1895 in Fife & Fife *Ballads of West* 173: The fiddler tuned his music box. **1899** (quot. at *take a fall out of,* 2 s.v. FALL). **1924** in Lardner *Haircut* 175: Can certainly make old music box talk girlie and am always good for a $75 or $100 job. **1926** Dunning & Abbott *Broadway* 216: I ain't supposed to sit here and pound this music box. **1941** Rossen *Blues in Night* (film): This boy plays the music box [sc., piano] in the most terrific fashion.

Music City *n.* [alluding to Nashville as the "home of country music"] Nashville, Tennessee. Also **Music Town.**

    1976 Dills *CB Slanguage* 49: *Music City:* Nashville, Tennessee. **1976** Lieberman & Rhodes *CB* 132: *Music Town*—Nashville. **1989** *Rage*

(Knoxville, Tenn.) (Sept.) 26: I'm new to Knoxville. Just arrived from Music City.

musician *n. Horse Racing.* (see quot.).

    1880 *N.Y. Clipper Almanac* 45: *Musician.*—A horse that roars.

musket *n.* the penis.—usu. considered vulgar. *Joc.*

    1934 "J.M. Hall" *Anecdota* 107: Bonaparte's musket/Was well under four. *ca***1950** in Reisner *Graffiti* 108: Puritans with short muskets step up to the firing line. **1971** in Reisner *Graffiti* 108: Pilgrims with short muskets stand within firing range.

musky[1] *n. Angling.* a muskellunge.

    1894 in *DA:* We were then all ready for old musky to begin his real fight. **1928** in *OEDS:* The next most definite cult among anglers are those who devote themselves to muskies. **1936** in Pyle *Ernie's Amer.* 96: They drive the muskies all into a bay. **1949** in *Pop. Science* (Jan. 1950) 152: Large game fish such as muskies and pike. **1952** *New Yorker* (Apr. 5) 99: Fish for fighting bass, lake trout, musky, pike, wall-eyes. **1961** Forbes *Goodbye to Some* 101: But a musky now, there's a spark of divinity in him! **1969** in Cheever *Letters* 276: Muskies...weigh fifty pounds.

musky[2] *n.* muscatel wine.

    1968 *Provincetown Rev.* VII 85: Casks of t-bird, musky, even denatured alcohol. **1965–70** *Jour. Studies on Alcohol* XXXII (1971) 734: Muscatel wine...*musky.* **1975** S.P. Smith *Amer. Boys* 163: Where'd you get the musky?

muslin *n.* **1.** *Naut.* sails collectively; canvas.

    *1822 in *OED:* She shewed as little muslin as the weather required. **1841** [Mercier] *Man-of-War* 73: We'll have to take some of the old lady's *muslin* off before supper. **1894** in *OED:* When we got that fair wind we piled the muslin on her. **1929* Bowen *Sea Slang* 93: *Muslin.* The lighter sails.

    2. a girl; young woman.—usu. constr. with *bit, bundle,* or *piece.*

    *1823 in *F & H* IV 392: A bit of muslin on the sly. **1834* (cited in Partridge *DSUE* (ed. 7) 1287). **1843* in *F & H* IV 392: Leaving behind me as pretty a piece of muslin as you'd wish to see. **1849* W. Thackeray, in *F & H* IV 392: That was a pretty bit of muslin hanging on your arm—who was she? **1873* Hotten *Slang Dict.* (ed. 4): *Muslin,* a woman or girl. **1884* in *F & H* IV 392: Take my advice, and keep clear of muslin for the next six or seven years. **1901** "O. Henry" *Cabbages & Kings* 14: His Nibs skedaddled...with...the bundle of muslin he's spoony about. **1904** in "O. Henry" *Works* 556: His Nibs skedaddled yesterday per jack-rabbit line with all the coin in the kitty and the bundle of muslin he's spoony about. **1921** A. Jennings *Through Shadows* 202: A convict bundle of muslin.

muss *n.* a fight; altercation; commotion; row.

    1838 in *DAE:* The complainant testified that there was a "muss" in Chatham Street. **1841** [Mercier] *Man-of-War* 196: There appears to be considerable a *muss* around the cabin door. **1843** in L.F. Browne *J.R. Browne* 30: There was a "muss" between B. and the Captain. *ca***1845** in *DAE:* We'd have some of the awfulest musses that ever did take place. **1848** Judson *Mysteries of N.Y.* 65: Then I expect, you'll have to raise a muss. **1850** G.G. Foster *Gas-Light* 37: But they are savage, sullen, reckless dogs, and are continually promoting some "muss" or other, which not unfrequently leads to absolute riot. **1851** Doten *Journals* I 93: They had quite a "muss" with some Frenchmen. **1851** in Harlow *Old Bowery* 198: I told them I would not have any muss in my house, and requested them to go out. **1857** in *OED:* I got into a "muss" down at the store last night, and was whipped. **1859** Matsell *Vocab.* 57: *Muss.* A quarrel; a row. **1863** in F. Moore *Rebel. Rec.* VI p11: Oh! when we meet again, my boys,/There'll be a pretty *muss.* **1864** in Rowell *Artillerymen* 164: The old 18th is...ready for another muss. **1878** Beadle *West. Wilds* 303: They've been kicking up such a muss about polygamy. **1883–84** Whittaker *L. Locke* 156: But what was the muss?

    ¶ In phrase:

    ¶ **on the muss** *on the muscle,* 1, s.v. MUSCLE; looking for a fight.

    1863 in O.J. Hopkins *Under the Flag* 60: Go ahead, boys. It all belongs to the Rebels; go in on your "mus"! **1865** in H. Johnson *Talking Wire* 250: They saw us going for our arms...they thought we were "on the muss."

muss *v.* to fight. Hence **musser,** *n.*

    1851 in Harlow *Old Bowery* 198: The prisoner, with two other men, came into my place and began to muss with each other by pushing each other about. **1904** *Life in Sing Sing* 251: *Musser*—A fighter; a bully. **1924** in Partridge *Dict. Und.* 459: *Musser*—one who picks fights.

mussel-digger *n. Whaling.* a California gray whale.

    1860 in *DA:* It being difficult to capture them, they have a variety of names among whalemen, as..."muscle digger" [*sic*]. **1873** Scammon *Marine Mammals* 24: When returning to the surface, they have been seen with head and lips besmeared with dark ooze from the depths below; hence the name of "Mussel-digger."

muss up *v.* to manhandle or treat violently; ROUGH UP.

    1922 *Variety* (Aug. 4) 9: He mussed Benny up the first round and Benny couldn't do a thing about it. **1924** (cited in Partridge *Dict. Und.* 459).

mustache *n.* **1.a.** a man having a mustache.

    1898 in Felleman *Best Loved Poems* 435: For some fierce "mustache" to eat. **1962** Serling *New Stories* 51: They were a motley collection of tough mustaches who galloped and gunned their way across the then new West. **1981** Sann *Trial* 162: The mustache...agreed to answer some questions by mail.

    b. *Und. & Police.* MUSTACHE PETE.

    1973 Toma & Brett *Toma* 123: Like some of the old-time Italians occasionally referred to as Mustaches. **1985** E. Leonard *Glitz* 107: It started out the young guys hitting the old guys, the mustaches. **1986** R. Campbell *In La-La Land* 17: The old struggle between the mustaches and the young turks came over pushing hard drugs...to the school kids.

    2. oral copulation; cunnilingus.—usu. considered vulgar. Cf. MUSTACHE RIDE.

    1935 Pollock *Und. Speaks: Mustache,* sodomy.

Mustache Pete *n.* a man having a large mustache; (*specif.*) a mustached Italian immigrant, esp. a mafioso.

    1938 in D. Runyon *More Guys* 195: Mustache Petes...are old-time Italians with large black mustaches. **1959** in Tyler *Org. Crime* 304: Various reporters have written that...the old "mustache Petes" have disappeared. **1965** Horan *Seat of Power* 16: The wops on the East Side....All Moustache Petes. After the war the young Turks started to take over. **1973** W. Crawford *Stryker* 49: Actually, Sam had never even *seen* a real old Moustache Pete. **1978** Bequai *White-Collar Crime* 130: [In the 1930's] the old "mustache Petes" who had dominated the Mafia groups in this country gave way to new and aggressive leadership. **1981** Sann *Trial* 40: Them Mustache Petes ain't...happy. **1985** Sawislak *Dwarf* 207: To the new young guys he was just another Mustache Pete...out of date and in the way. **1996** *Leeza* (synd. TV series): I saw this man. Mustache Pete. He was in the Wild West.

mustache ride *n.* an act of cunnilingus (from the woman's perspective).—usu. considered vulgar.

    1981 *Nat. Lampoon* (Aug.) 91: [Ad for T-shirts:] The Most Rudest Sayings On Hats And T-Shirts....Free Mustache Rides....Champion Mustache Rider...I Rode the Mustache. **1981** *Easyriders* (Oct.) 100: "Ride On" T-Shirts. His: Mustache Rides, 25¢. Hers: Champion Mustache Rider. **1985** *Nat. Lampoon* (Sept.) 38: Friedrich Nietzsche Memorial Mustache Riding Championship. *a***1990** P. Dickson *Slang!* 198: *Mustache ride.* Oral sex. **1996** *Trial Story* (Court-TV) (June 2): He asked [female coworkers] if they wanted a mustache ride.

mustang *n. Mil.* **1.** an officer or enlisted man of a volunteer regiment.

    1847 McClellan *Mexican War Diary* 23: "Mind, Mr. Smith," said the old Mustang the night before, "mind and appear as early as possible, so that you may not delay us"—all this with that air of dignity and importance so peculiarly characteristic of Mustangs. *Ibid.* 43: This is but one instance of the many that occurred when these Mustang Generals were actually *afraid* to exert their authority upon the Volunteers....I have repeatedly seen a Second Lieutenant of the regular army exercise more authority over the Volunteers—*officers and privates*—than a Mustang General. **1847** Furber *Volunteer* 376: Any one that could raise the means to buy a long-eared *burro* (jackass), or a mule, or old Mexican horse, or any such conveyance, immediately entered the mustang cavalry. **1866** Marcy *Army Life* 396 [ref. to Texas, 1840's]: Colonel McLeod thought he would like to witness the general's method of enforcing discipline among the "*Mustangs.*" **1874** in *OEDS* [ref. to Civil War]: Le surnom dérisoire de *mustang*...qu'il appliquait aux volontaires inexpérimentés avant l'épreuve commune.

    2. an officer who is not a graduate of a military or naval academy and who has received a commission for meritorious prior service, esp. in an enlisted grade.

    1878 Shippen *30 Yrs.* 267 [ref. to 1861]: He cusses...the new ones, the "mustang" officers. **1890–96** *F & H* IV 393: *Mustang....*An officer entering the U.S. navy from the merchant service, after serving through the Civil War. **1900** *Howitzer* (U.S. Mil. Acad.) (No. 1) 120: *Mustang.*—An officer of the regular army who was appointed from the volunteers after the Civil War. **1910** *Everybody's Album* (May) 591: Mustangs are rare in the Navy. The merchant officers who received commissions during the Rebellion first owned the name....To-day any enlisted man who rates himself upward...and finally passes his examinations for ensign, is called a mustang. **1931** *Leatherneck* (Feb.) 13: We have three golden-haired mustangs, two of whom are on the verge of completing their probationary periods. **1936** Denlinger & Gary *War in Pacific* 166: There are also a number of officers in the navy (known colloquially as "mustangs") who have risen through the ratings to commissioned rank. **1938** Connolly *Navy Men* 172 [ref. to 1918]: What set me up a bit quickly perhaps against that bright one of the station ship staff was that he was a "mustang"—up from the enlisted ranks—and already he was kowtowing servilely to high official rank. **1940** *Time* (Jan. 29) 14: [During 1917–18 a naval officer] promoted from the ranks was stigmatized as a "mustang." **1942** *Leatherneck* (Nov.) 148: *Mustang*—Officer who came up through the ranks. **1950** *N.Y. Times* (Feb. 5) 19: "Mustangs" are Naval officers up from the ranks. **1951** Morris *China Station* 30: The third man...was a lieutenant (junior grade), a roguish mustang. **1957** R. O'Connor *Co. Q* 3: He was a mustang, up through the ranks from the Old Army. **1967** Dibner *Admiral* 230: Joe's a mustang. Went from seaman second to lieutenant commander. **1967** Lockwood *Subs* 79 [ref. to 1917]: Now that the Navy had a school at New London, which was to become the Annapolis of the Submarine Service, we undersea skippers of the preschool days would be more used of the name *mustangs*. This meant, in Navy terms, that we did not have a formal submarine education but had—as the barnaclebacks called it—"come up through the hawsepipe." **1968** in Hayes *Apocalypse* 782: And one of his aides, a tough mustang of a first lieutenant, would pitch a hard, ironic smile above the Major's stare. **1971** *N.Y. Times Mag.* (Sept. 5) 11: The general recommended to the Pentagon that the most decorated enlisted man in the Korean war—the mustang everybody thought was the perfect combat commander—never be allowed to command in the U.S. Army again. **1976** C.R. Anderson *Grunts* 39: A "mustang," an enlisted man...offered a commission because of his demonstrated leadership and military knowledge. **1992** O. Kelly *Brave Men* 185: A number of the officers were...mustangs who had entered the navy as enlisted men and later earned their commissions. **1996** *New Yorker* (Sept. 16) 70: To this day, up-from-the-ranks American Navy officers...are called "mustangs," as distinct from creatures of pure breeding.

3. a Mexican.—now usu. considered offensive.
    *a***1899** B.F. Sands *Reefer* 181 [ref. to 1847]: We were elated at the prospect of a "brush" with the *Greasers* or *Mustangs* as they were euphoniously called.

mustard *n*. **1.a.** keen spirit, esp. in opposition; courage; (*hence*) an individual or individuals of keen spirit or courage.
    1903 A. Adams *Log of Cowboy* 237: For fear they [*sc.*, a pair of dogs] were not the proper mustard. **1903** in F. Remington *Sel. Letters* 345: The public is a funny old cat and won't stand for the mustard. **1908** "O. Henry" *Strictly Business* 1486: Bob Hart, "All the Mustard and a Whole Show in Himself." ***1931** in *OEDS: To be mustard,* to be excellent at anything. It must never be used of the female sex. **1941** *AS* (Oct.) 167: *Mustard.* A smart pilot. **1943** W. Simmons *Joe Foss* 61: A little fellow, full of mustard. **1943** D. Hertz *Pilot No. 5* (film): He's a mustard of a pilot. That means hot, Major. **1966–67** W. Stevens *Gunner* 76: They won't say I had to jump out of a bottle every morning to get the mustard to go up.

b. daylights; stuffing.
    1929–31 J.T. Farrell *Young Lonigan* 94: He could kick a lot of mustard out of the whole bunch of 'em.

c. Esp. *Baseball.* force or speed (applied to a pitched or batted ball).
    1971 T. Coffin *Old Ball Game* 55: "Mustard" (speed on a fast ball). **1977** Eble *Campus Slang* (Apr.) 3: *Mustard*—power, speed: Put some mustard on it! (from football). **1978** H. Cosell, on *ABC-TV Monday Night Baseball* (ABC-TV) (July 3): He had some mustard on that pitch. **1980** Lorenz *Guys Like Us* 69: Buddy hit the glove with mustard, low and away. **1982** E. Johnson, on *Atlanta Braves Baseball* (WKGN radio) (July 24): Plenty of mustard on that fastball. **1983** Whiteford *How to Talk Baseball* 113: A good fastball has a lot of mustard on it.

2. *Constr.* cement; in phr. **pack mustard** to carry hods of cement.
    1926 *AS* I 652: *Mustard, packing.* Carrying the hod. **1927** *DN* V 457: *Pack mustard,* v. To carry a hod. **1965** O'Neill *High Steel* 272: *Mustard.* Cement.

3. *Und.* an Asian person or persons.—used contemptuously.
    1930 (quot. at MONKEY). **1933** Ersine *Pris. Slang* 54: *Mustard, n.* A Chinaman. **1935** Pollock *Und. Speaks: Cargo of mustards,* smuggled Chinese or Japanese.

¶ In phrases:

¶ **[all] to the mustard** sharp-witted; keen; (*also*) excellent; perfect; sharp.
    1905 [Hobart] *Search Me* 17: He's all to the mustard....He can pull off some of the best tricks I ever blinked at. **1905** in "O. Henry" *Works* 1464: Why don't you invite him then, if he's so much to the mustard. *ca***1921** Sandburg *Sunburnt West* 7: Kid each other, you cheap skates/Tell each other you're all to the mustard—/You're the gravy. **1926** Wood & Goddard *Amer. Slang* 3: All to the...mustard. Excellent. **1927** *AS* II 275: *Mustard, all to the.* excellent. **1928** Bodenheim *Georgie May* 47: Youah all to the mustahd, Dago, ol' boy.

¶ **by mustard** (used as a mild oath).
    1885 Carleton *City Ballads* 157: But my man he says, "By mustard!"

¶ **cut [the] mustard** see s.v. CUT, *v.*

mustard pot *n.* **1.a.** the vagina or (usu. *Homosex.*) anus.—usu. considered vulgar. Also **mustard box, mustard jar.**
    a*1890–96** *F & H* IV 393: *Mustard-pot...*The female *pudendum.* **1928** J. Carpenter *Chanties* 488 [song learned *a*1900]: Once I had a wife,/And she was doublejointed;/I thought she had two mustard pots,/But I was disappointed. **1960–69** Runkel *Law* 280: She didn't like me t' put my tongue in 'er mustard box....I'd feel my hand up 'er mustard jar. *a***1972** B. Rodgers *Queens' Vernacular* 19: Anus...*mustard pot* ('40s–'50s).

2. *Pris.* a homosexual pedicant.
    1932 (quot. at MUZZLER, 5).

mustard road *n.* ¶ In phrase: **go up the mustard road** (see quots.).—usu. considered vulgar.
    1972 R. Wilson *Playboy's Forbidden Words* 39: Analingus...*going up the mustard road* or *going up the Hershey Bar road. Ibid.* 182: To go...*up the mustard road* is to have anal intercourse.

muta var. MOOTAH, MOTA.

mutant *n.* a loathsome or sociopathic person.
    1984 D. Jenkins *Life Its Ownself* 52: I'm a person too, you selfish mutant! **1986** Sliwa *Attitude* 97: These guys are mutants! They should be hurt! **1987** *Magical World of Disney* (NBC-TV): I'm *not* a mutant. **1989** *Rage* (Knoxville, Tenn.) (Oct.) 8: These people gotta be mutants! **1989** *Village Voice* (N.Y.C.) (May 9) 10: Mob psychology...has branded these kids "mutants." **1989** *Reporters* (Fox-TV): He gets locked up with the rest of the mutants, the scum, the slime. **1990** *In Living Color* (Fox-TV): Take a good look at these mutants. These are the ugliest kids in this school. **1991** *Owl* (NBC-TV): You mutant. **1996** *America's Funniest Home Videos* (ABC-TV): They're a bunch of mutants.

mute *n. Horse Racing.* a parimutuel machine.
    1942 *ATS* 692: Pari-mutuel machine...*mute.* **1949** Cummings *Dict. Sports* 275. *a***1951** D. Maurer *Lang. Und.* 223: *Play the...mutes....*To bet on horses through the pari-mutuel machines.

mutt *n.* [orig. unkn.] **1.a.** a worthless dog; mongrel. Now *colloq.* or *S.E.* [Always the prevailing sense; there appears to be no sound semantic basis for assuming derivation fr. MUTTONHEAD, as asserted by var. authorities.]
    1898–1900 Cullen *Chances* 179: He's no trick mutt, anyhow. **1902** Cullen *More Tales* 16: The mutt [*sc.*, a fox terrier] ran along the inside of the fence and handed me a bunch of barks that joggled my spine. **1908** McGaffey *Show Girl* 190: Run over the mutt. **1911** in *DA:* And 'round and 'round the little mutts all run. **1943** Panama et al. *Thank Lucky Stars* (film): Go home, you mutts! **1949** in *DA:* That cat! That mutt! they fight it out And back and forth they shuffle. **1951** H. Robbins *Danny Fisher* 10: That dopey mutt ain't got enough sense to get outta there. **1958** H. Gardner *Piece of the Action* 15: Sometimes...I'd spot a dog, and even the mutts in midtown seem to have appointments. **1969** B. Beckham *Main Mother* 178: A grown dog in a hammock....nothing but a spoiled mutt. **1972–79** C. Major *Emergency Exit* 112: Little ugly mut!

b. *Horse Racing.* a slow or worthless racehorse; DOG, 8.a.

> **1899** Cullen *Tales* 80: I was going…to bet $100 on Long Bridge at 20 to 1 and take a chance on being crunched to a pulp if the mutt lost the race. **1898–1900** Cullen *Tales* 35: He took the mutt away with the show. **1905** *Nat. Police Gaz.* (Nov. 18) 3: What are you betting on? Orinoco; too bad; he's a stiff.…That mut's feet won't last him the mile out. **1907** *McClure's Mag.* (Feb.) 380: They commenced picking out the worst mutts they could. **1956** "T. Betts" *Across the Board* 101: Hold the mutts. **1967** Schaefer *Mavericks* 56: We'll run that jug-headed mutt of yours off its legs tomorrow.

2. Now esp. *Police.* a stupid or contemptible person; dolt; no-account.

> **1899** A.H. Lewis *Sandburrs* 26: On d' square! at d' end of a week in d' dark, a mut don't know he's livin'. **1901** [Hobart] *Line* 79: I knew that Clara Jane would at once cancel the contract with the mutt. **1903** Ade *Society* 29: If these Mutts come and lean over the Fence and start to get off their Colored-Weekly Jokes we'll fan the Hill-side with them. **1905** *Nat. Police Gaz.* (Dec. 23) 3: I'd like to see the mutt what shot him get the electric chair. **1906** H. Green *Boarding House* 21: She's a mut. **1908** W. Davenport *Butte & Montana* 35: The pirates who…lure the mutts from the ranches up into their rooms [for poker games]. **1913** *Chi. Defender* (May 10) 3: She doesn't want to talk to a mutt. **1914** Ellis *Billy Sunday* 149: You're afraid and God despises a coward—a mutt. **1915** [Swartwood] *Choice Slang* 54: *Mutt*…A person who is below ordinary standards of intelligence, perception or good manners. **1950** Bissell *Stretch on the River* 10: You…spend your time with Schwartz and the rest of them mutts. **1952** Wildman *Zorba* 95: Why go looking for mines, you poor mutt? **1955** Deutsch *Cops* 172: You'll all land in prison, you mutts. **1963** D. Tracy *Brass Ring* 11: No it's not, you poor little mutt. **1969** L. Sanders *Anderson Tapes* 172: A mutt? Yeah, he's that all right. Not too much brains. **1974** Dubinsky & Standora *Decoy Cop* 178: All it takes is a guy with a gun and a hatred for cops and nowadays there seem to be more and more of these mutts roaming the streets. **1974** Charyn *Blue Eyes* 27: Brodsky, you were a mutt before Isaac took you in. **1985** Briskin *Too Much* 132: You poor ignorant mutt. **1987** Taubman *Lady Cop* 105: Geri knew if the mutt they were after tried to run, she would be chasing him alone. *Ibid.* 269: *Mutt*: Derogatory term used by police to describe people with records, usually for violent crimes. **1989** Hynes & Drury *Howard Beach* 230: So here you have one of the main mutts in the [racist] attack. **1995** *Harper's* (Dec.) 50: We ended up with Ivankov and essentially a bunch of mutts [*sc.*, small-time mobsters]. **1996** *New Yorker* (May 13) 74: Brandishing the back of her hand, "You fresh mutt."

3. an unattractive person of the opposite sex; DOG, 16.

> **1977** in G.A. Fine *With Boys* 169: *Mutt*, n. Disliked or ugly girl. **1983** in Rawson *Wicked Words* 262: The consultant, testifying for the defense in Miss Craft's $1.2-million sex-discrimination trial, was heard on tapes…to say: "Is she a mutt?" **1987** Univ. Tenn. student theme: A "mutt" is a female who resembles a canine. **1996** Philbin *Cop Speak* 156: *Mutt*…traditional…term to describe an ugly woman.

4. an unsatisfactory device, piece of equipment, etc.; DOG, 15.b.

> **1990** Verier *Ft. Bragg* 115: Replacing the M-151 "Mutt"…the "Humm Vee" is truly ubiquitous.

Mutt and Jeff *n.* [sugg. by *Mutt & Jeff*, cartoon characters introduced (1907) by Harry C. "Bud" Fisher (1885–1954)]
1. Esp. *Police & Journ.* a pair of associates, one of whom is much taller than the other.—often used attrib.

> **1914** in Truman *Dear Bess* 157: Together they look like Mutt and Jeff. **1949** in *OEDS*: Richard—, identified as the taller man in the recent series of "Mutt and Jeff" robberies here, yesterday pleaded guilty to armed robbery. **1959** Horan *Mob's Man* 22: The circulars warned…to be on the lookout for a man about six feet three inches and a smaller companion, five feet five.…"The Mutt and Jeff Holdup Team." **1981** Ballenger *Terror* 19: Mutt and Jeff, people called them, because of their disparity in size. **1983** WKGN news (Feb. 17): Knoxville police think they have the Mutt and Jeff robbery team in jail. **1985** Sawislak *Dwarf* 2: He…waved the Mutt and Jeff team…into Fargo's cubicle office. **1988** Dietl & Gross *One Tough Cop* 37: A two-man Mutt-and-Jeff burglary team.

2. *Police.* a pair of interrogators, one of whom adopts a violent or threatening mien, while the other pretends to be conciliatory.—often used attrib. Also as v.

> **1971** *Playboy* (Dec.) 341: So here, then, were those two familiars of the station house, Jeff ravening on one side of the detainee and Mutt conciliating on the other. **1974** R. Stone *Dog Soldiers* 193: A one-man Mutt and Jeff routine, Hicks thought. **1976** "N. Ross" *Policeman* 177: The G-men…don't come down with the Mutt and Jeff routine. It's just the facts man. **1981** R.O. Butler *Alleys* 37: I'll play it tough. You'll be the good guy. We'll Mutt and Jeff him. **1984** J. McNamara *First Directive* 108: It was a variation on the Mutt-and-Jeff interrogation: nice guy-bad guy. **1988** T. Logan *Harder They Fall* 14: They did a good Mutt and Jeff during interrogations.

mutthead *n.* MUTT, 2; MUTTONHEAD.

> **1941** F. Ryan & W. Hamilton *Call Out Marines* (film): It's over there, you mutthead. **1942** *ATS* 368: Terms of disparagement.…*mush head, mutt, mutt-head.*

mutton *n.* **1.a.** a woman or women regarded as a source of sexual gratification; a prostitute or prostitutes; (*hence*) the vulva and vagina; copulation.—usu. considered vulgar. Now *rare* in U.S. Cf. MEAT. [The comparative lateness of Amer. evidence is perh. owing to the strongly sexual connotations of the term.]

> ***a1518** J. Skelton, in *OED*: Why, is there any store of rawe motton? ***1538** in *OED*: What wylt thu fall to mutton?…Ranke loue is full of heate. [***1569** in *F & H* 393: Courtisans…*oves.*] ***ca1590** R. Greene, in *OED*: The old leacher hath gotten holy mutton to him, a Nunne, my Lord. ***ca1590** C. Marlowe, in *OED*: I am one that loues an inch of raw Mutton…and the first letter of my name beginnes with leachery. ***1606** in *F & H* IV 393: But there's no pleasure always to be tied to a piece of mutton.…For mine own part…I am well-provided with three bouncing wenches. ***1624** B. Jonson, in *F & H* IV 394: A fine lac'd mutton Or two; and either has her frisking husband. ***1633** in *F & H* IV 394: Say she be young.…young mutton. ***1675** in Duffet *Burlesque Plays* 82: The pox will take him, for he is a Termagant at laced Mutton. ***1698–99** "B.E." *Dict. Canting Crew*: Mutton-monger, a Lover of Women.…*Mutton-in-long-coats*, Women. ***1726** A. Smith *Mems. J. Wild* 120: He has fed himself a long Time upon lac'd Mutton, and will to his dying Day, if he can have it *Gratis.* ***1811** *Lex. Balatron.*: Mutton. In her mutton, i.e. having carnal knowledge of a woman. ***1841** in J. Atkins *Sex in Lit.* III 216: Here's mutton, Scotch fashion, with the hair on it. **1859** Matsell *Vocab.* 49: Laced mutton. A common woman. ***1864** Hotten *Slang Dict.* (ed. 3): In that class of English society which does not lay claim to refinement, a fond lover is often spoken of as being "fond of his mutton," which, by the way, in this place does not mean the woman so much as something else. **1889–90** Barrère & Leland *Dict. Slang: Mutton*…used in the phrase "a bit of *mutton*," a woman. The term is used also in America. ***1973** in *OEDS*: They're aw cows hawkin' their mutton. **1981** Sann *Trial* 187: You cut off his mutton.

2.a. one's person or self. Cf. *save (one's) bacon* s.v. BACON.

> **1789** in Meserve & Reardon *Satiric Comedies* 110: Some may think I meant to save my mutton. **1887** DeVol *Gambler* 243: I could see he was sizing me up, and I knew he wanted some of my mutton.

b. human flesh or weight.

> **1863** in J. Crawford *Dear Lizzie* 86: The fact is I have been gaining mutton very fast since I got well and weigh about 137 lbs.

3. something that is ideally suited to one; one's meat.—also constr. in pl. *Obs.* in U.S.

> **1875** *Minstrel Gags* 6: "You're my mutton," says he. "Any one dat can sling folks around in dat way can beat Forrist in Damon." ***1940** in *OEDS*: Milk, however, is small Charlie's muttons.

4. cowardice.

> **1969** P. Hamill *Doc* 121: I knew you had a streak of mutton in you, and I found it. **1972** *N.Y. Post* (Dec. 20) 39: Only people with a lot of mutton in them beat up midgets.

¶ In phrases:

¶ **fix (someone's) mutton** to settle or do for (someone).

> *a***1846** in *DA*: The time had come for him to walk into one on 'em [bears] at last, and fix his mutton for him right. **1888** Gordon & Page *Befo' De War* 103: Take holt de axe;/Six or eight cracks/'ull fix de critter's mutton.

¶ **to (one's) muttons** [or **mutton**] to (one's) subject, as in conversation. Now *rare* in U.S.

> ***1821** in *OEDS*: I think he is winning…the heart of Lady Caroline—But to return to my muttons. **1887** J.W. Nichols *Hear My Horn*

20: But again to my mutton....I hollowed for Asa but could not raise him. ***1889** in *F & H* IV 395: Now to return to our muttons. Here is a drawer full of M.P.'s, Liberals, Radicals, Conservatives. **1933** in *OEDS*: Let's stick to our muttons, old man radio, and make it music alone. ***1974** in *OEDS*: I digress....Shall we return to our muttons?

mutton v. to thrash or mangle.
  1775 in Trumbull *Satiric Poems* 124: Kept off that Satan of a Putnam,/From breaking in to maul and mutt'n him.

muttonhead n. [back formation fr. MUTTON-HEADED; cf. earlier BrE *sheepshead*] a blockhead. [*DAE* dates "1803" quot. to "1804" with the name "B—" spelled out and "thou" in conventional orthography; the *OEDS* version app. represents an earlier printing.]
  1803 in *OEDS*: And couldst thow, pertinacious B—, But maul these mutton heads, most sadly. **1825** in *DAE*: Peace, mutton-head! **1862** C.F. Browne *A. Ward* 196: The Sonny South is makin a egrejus mutton-hed of herself! **1873** Badger *L. Thunderbolt* 66: Ye pesky muttonhead, you. **a1877** in Bartlett *Amer.* (ed. 4) 417: A parcel of *muttonheads*. **1899** in J. London *Short Stories* 30: He...held his mutton-head companion responsible. **1908** W.G. Davenport *Butte & Montana* 145: Such a gang of brainless muttonheads. **a1904–11** D.G. Phillips *Susan Lenox* I 354: And ain't they muttonheads? Do you ever find any of 'em saying or doing a sensible thing? **1912** W.M. Raine *Brand Blotters* 238: You'd *savez* it now, if you weren't a muttonhead. ***1928** D.H. Lawrence, in *OEDS*: That *fool*, Joe, standing there like a mutton-head. **1936** Gaddis *Courtesan* 53: Don't be a mutton-head, Beulah. **1960** Serling *Stories from Twilight Zone* 6: Did this muttonhead put you up to it? **1993** *Mystery Sci. Theater* (Comedy Central TV): Knock it off, you muttonheads.

mutton-headed adj. stupid.
  *1768 in *OED*: A poor "mutton-headed" flock, ready to follow any bell-weather. ***1788** Grose *Dict. Vulgar Tongue* (ed. 2): Mutton-headed. Stupid. **1821** Waln *Hermit in Phila.* 27: A mutton-headed Aminadab. **1897** in *OEDS*: He were such a mutton-headed fool theer were no valley in ootwittin' him. **1954–60** *DAS*. **a1991** in Clayton & Davis *Horsing Around* 30: That mutton-headed idiot went plumb crazy.

mutt up v. Und. to guard with a dog or to acquire a dog for use as a guard.
  1933 Ersine *Prison Slang* 54: Mutted up. Guarded by a dog. "Every joint in town is mutted up." **1942–49** Goldin et al. *DAUL* 143: Mutt up. To keep a dog as burglary protection.

mux n. [app. fr. the v.] Esp. N. Eng. a muddle; (*also*) a botched piece of work.
  1848 in *AS* X (1935) 41: "In a mux." Confused, disarranged. **1865** in *OEDS*: Now we are in a mux. **1873** Scammon *Marine Mammals* 311: He made a mux of it and missed the whale. **1890** *Century Dict.*: Mux...work performed in an awkward or improper manner; a botch; a mess; as, he made a mux of it. **1910** *DN* III 454: All in a mux.

mux v. [orig. unkn.; cf. 17th-C. N. Eng. *mux* 'any sharp-pointed metal instrument that may be used, according to its design, for boring holes, spearing fish, etc.' (*DA*), prob. of BrE dial. orig.] Esp. N. Eng. to tangle up or muddle; botch.—also constr. with *up*.
  1806 in *DAE*: Wink lovingly, mux chastity away. **1859** Bartlett *Amer.* (ed. 2): To mux is much used in New England for *muss*; as, "Don't *mux* my crinoline." ***1869** Blackmore *Lorna Doone*, in *F & H* IV 397: Nicholas...had thoroughly muxed up everything. **1872** in *F & H*: Stop muxin' that bread! one would think you were a drove of young hogs....I shan't have you *muxing* and *gauming* up the victuals.

muzzle n. a person's face, nose, or mouth. Orig. *S.E.*
  *1426 Lydgate, in *OED*: Hit semyth...By lyfftynge vp off thy mosel, That thow pleyest the ape wel. ***a1586** Sir P. Sidney, in *OED*: Her muzzell...might well haue giuen a surfet to any weake louers stomacke. ***1664** in Dryden *Dramatic Wks.* IV 473: And off at once the *Rumkin* goes;/No Drops beside her Muzzle falling. ***1803** in J. Ashton *Eng. Satires on Napoleon* 161: I will shave him with razor so notch'd,/As shall leave his black muzzle most famously scotch'd. ***1821** in *F & H* IV 396: He [a prizefighter]...got hit anywhere and everywhere, about the muzzle particularly. ***1821–26** Stewart *Man-of-War's-Man* I 53: I'll be d—d if you'd speak that way did you not expect to get a few of those same spoonfulls, as you call 'em, whistled into your own muzzle. *Ibid.* 168: Will you clap a stopper on that old muz-

zle of yours, and make less noise, if you please? ***1836** in *F & H* IV 396: The worthy lady painted our friend's face and muzzle in a most ludicrous manner. **1841, 1849** (quots. at MUZZLE-LASHINGS). ***1873** Hotten *Slang Dict.* (ed. 4): *Muzzle*, the mouth. **1889** in Kaese *Braves* 45: The second one that came in, broke my muzzle, nose and all. **1930** Nason *Corporal* 130: How! [A drinking toast.] Down the muzzle! **a1976** in Georges & Jones *Folkloristics* 246: Lift the nozzle/To your muzzle./And let it swizzle/Down the guzzle.

¶ In phrases:

¶ **take the wrong dog by the muzzle** to blunder; make the wrong choice.
  1885 Byrn *Greenhorn* 48: His honor now became confused and took the wrong dog by the muzzle.

¶ **up to the muzzle** completely.
  1880 (quot. at KNOWLEDGE BOX). **1907** S.E. White *Arizona Nights* 130: Why, an hour after filling myself up to the muzzle, I'd be hungry again.

muzzle v. **1.** to kiss, esp. roughly; (*hence*) to kiss and fondle roughly.—occ. constr. with *up*.
  *1697 Vanbrugh, in *OED*: Ah, you young, hot, lusty Thief, let me muzzle you—*Kissing*. ***1708** in *OED*: I will, Chargee, so muzle, and tuzle, and hug thee. **1942** *ATS* 337: Kiss....*mug, muzzle, nuzzle*. **1944** Johnston & Hoffman *Janie* (film): "Spooning, muzzling, bunny-hugging, I don't know." "You mean you and mother never spooned? ... Muzzled? ... Bunny-hugged?" **a1955** in D.W. Maurer *Lang. Und.* 247: *Muzzlers*...molest women sexually in a crowd. **1959** Horan *Mob's Man* 38: We were muzzling the dames and having a ball. **1973** Hirschfeld *Victors* 123: I was even going to let you fool around a little, muzzle me up. **1974** Radano *Cop Stories* 131: So what if each week I don't get to muzzle a new broad! I'm satisfied to go home and kiss my tired and sometimes nagging wife.

2. to steal; seize.
  1841 [Mercier] *Man-of-War* 154: Dick...*muzzles* two belonging to some of the cooks. ***1889–90** Barrère & Leland *Dict. Slang*: Muzzle, to...to get, to take.

muzzle-lashings n.pl. Navy. whiskers.
  1841 [Mercier] *Man-of-War* 145: Ere the drum beat to evening quarters, every one throughout the ship (to use an old sea phrase) "had their muzzle lashings taken off." **1849** Melville *White Jacket* 343: Sir, our *muzzle-lashings* are cast off!

muzzle-loader n. **1.** Esp. *Logging*. (see 1908, 1958 quots.).
  1908 Whittles *Lumberjack* 75: The...double-decked bunks are built with the ends toward the center of the room, "muzzle-loaders," the boys call them. **1942** *AS* (Dec.) 223: *Muzzle Loaders*. Old fashion bunks into which men had to crawl over the foot of the bed. **1944** V.H. Jensen *Lumber & Labor* 37: In most early camps bunks were built in tiers in such a fashion that the men slept with their feet to the stove—"muzzle-loaders." **1958** McCulloch *Woods Wds.* 120: *Muzzle loader*—Anything loaded or entered from the head end.

2. R.R. (see 1937 quot.).
  1937 *AS* (Apr.) 154: *Muzzle-loader*. Hand-fired locomotive. **1939** *Sat. Eve. Post* (Apr. 15) 26: In those days the hogs weren't jerkers, and besides, this one was a muzzle-loader. **1945** Hubbard *R.R. Ave.* 353: *Muzzle Loader*—Hand-fired locomotive.

muzzle-loading adj. absolute; thoroughgoing.
  1903 A. Adams *Log of a Cowboy* 133 [ref. to 1880's]: Isn't he a muzzle-loading daisy? If I loved a liar, I'd hug that man to death.

muzzler n. **1.a.** *Boxing*. a hard blow to the mouth or face.
  *1811 *Lex. Balatron.*: Muzzler. A violent blow on the mouth. *The milling cove tipped the cull a muzzler*; the boxer gave the fellow a blow on the mouth. ***1821** *Real Life in London* I 228: The Porter...re-saluted poor Pat with a *muzzler*...A blow on the mouth. **1832** *Spirit of Times* (Mar. 3) 3: O'Hegan made a straight forward hit at Mc's *phiz*, but missed and received a *muzzler* from McDonnell's right. **1844** in Robb *Squatter Life* 180: With a "muzzler" he floored the Dutchman and his pipe.

b. *Naut.* a strong headwind.
  1857 in C.E. Stedman *Sketchbk.* 32: A reg'lar muzzler. ***1878** in *OED*: *Muzzler*, a wind that blows directly down a vessel's intended course. **1929** Bowen *Sea Slang* 94: *Muzzler*. A strong head wind.

2. [sugg. by BrE dial. *muzzle* 'to befuddle'] a drink of liquor. [The 1942 quot. may be misdefined.]

*1821–26 Stewart *Man-of-War's-Man* I 125: On these cursed unhappy occasions, a muzzler of Teneriffe, or a sparkler of Madeira, is all in my eye. ***1873** Hotten *Slang Dict.* (ed. 4): *Muzzler*...a dram of spirits. [**1942** *ATS* 111: Liquor....*muzzler*.]

3. *Und.* a strong-arm robber.

1865 *Rogues & Rogueries of N.Y.* 112: "Muzzling"—A New Dodge...."Muzzlers" stand on corners, apparently skylarking among themselves. Suddenly one of them falls down and rolls himself against the pedestrian, who also must tumble. The man...is soon on top of the [pedestrian]...and...places his hand upon his face, presses his nostrils together...and covers his mouth with his hand....While this is done by one, the others go through the man's pockets.

4. a worthless or contemptible fellow. [The 1928 quot. is presumably an overspecific definition.]

1927–28 Tasker *Grimhaven* 109: Why, you big muzzler!...What do you think you are? An officer of the law or Jesus Christ? **1928** *New Yorker* (Nov. 3) 94: Taxicab Words...*Muzzler*—A driver who crosses over from one traffic lane to another and faster lane, in front of you. **1928** in R.W. Snyder *Voice of City* 99 [ref. to 1908]: Take the muzzler off!...Go to work, you bum! **1930** *Amer. Mercury* (Oct.) 159: Hang out de flag, yuh muzzler! **1934** L. Berg *Prison Nurse* 49: Pay no attention to that muzzler. The only way these cheap grifters can get by is by trying to put someone on the pan. **1934** Duff & Sauber *20 Million Sweethearts* (film): Hey, muzzler! Let those gentlemen through! **1940** in W.C. Fields *By Himself* 463: The muzzlers and politicians who were instrumental in causing your discomfort are sure to come a cropper sooner than they imagine. **1940** Meehan & Tugend *Seven Sinners* (film): You muzzler! **1941** Macaulay & Wald *Manpower* (film): Freeze, muzzler! **1942** Liebling *Telephone* 6: So you're the muzzler who's going to rob me! **1942** B. Morgan & B. Orkow *Wings for Eagle* (film): Why don't you give that muzzler the breeze and step out with a real guy? **1944** *AS* XIX 104: A *muzzler*, meaning an obnoxious type [of sailor]. **1995** N.Y.C woman, age *ca*60 [ref. to 1940's]: My father [a Manhattan teamster] always called people he didn't like, "That muzzler!" or "That bunch of muzzlers!"

5. Esp. *Pris.* a fellator.

1928 Panzram *Killer* 157: And last but not least muzzlers and guzzlers. **1932** V. Nelson *Pris. Days & Nights* 149: The oral copulators are variously referred to as "muzzlers," "fairies," "fags," "pansies," and the like; the passive participants in sodomy are called "punks," "gonsils," "mustard pots," or even more direct physical terms are used. **1941** G. Legman, in G. Henry *Sex Vars.* II 1172: *Muzzler* A homosexual, a derogatory term used by male prostitutes, and usually denoting a fellator. **1942–49** Goldin et al. *DAUL* 314: Sodomist, oral....*fag; faggot; fairy;...muzzler.*

muzzy *adj.* drunk; tipsy. Orig. *S.E.*

*1730 in *F & H* IV 398: Your fellows of colleges are a parcel of sad, muzzy, humdrum, lazy, ignorant old caterpillars. ***1775** in *OED*: All [were] muzzy. ***1789** G. Parker *Life's Painter* 138: With whom came muzzy Tom. ***1803** in J. Ashton *Eng. Satires on Napoleon* 138: Why, bless your heart, my fine fellow, you must be Muzzy. **1837** in G. Jackson *Early Songs of Uncle Sam* 34: Cries Giles, half muzzy, "Ned, I vow/I never more will drive the plough." **1839–40** Cobb *Green Hand* I 147:

Oh, the old fellow was muzzy, and has forgotten before this, that any prisoners are on board. **1863** in J.H. Gooding *Altar of Freedom* 10: They were inclined to be "muzzy." **1931** Lubbock *Bully Hayes* 58: And the sheriff's that muzzy he don' know whether he's ashore or afloat.

my eye see s.v. EYE.

myob *interj.* (see quots.).

1915 in *DN* IV 246: *M.y.o.b.* Mind your own business. **1984** Mason & Rheingold *Slanguage: Myob*...Mind your own business. (Pronounced as one word, not as separate letters).

mystery *n.* meat of dubious origin served as hash, sausages, meat loaf, hamburgers, etc., esp. in institutional dining facilities. Now usu. **mystery meat.** [The 1877–78 quot. is in a pseudo-Latin form.]

1877–78 *Cornelian* 86: *Mystericum.* Hash. **1882** Miller & Harlow *9'-51"* 280: Suppose, for example, he thinks of some common, fleshly thing like "hash." Now you all know what hash is but behold the result. My machine weaves off something like this: Ye mystery, that makes the whole world kin! **1885** (quot. at SLEEVE BUTTONS). ***1887** in *F & H* IV 399: "O crikey Bill!" she ses to me, she ses. "Look sharp," ses she, "with them there sossiges. Yea! sharp with them there bags of mysteree!" **1888** in *Amer. Heritage* (Oct. 1979) 20: Our hash is ever cold, our hash is ever cold....I'm sure you'll open wide your eyes and at the "mistery" start. ***1889–90** Barrère & Leland *Dict. Slang: Mysteries*...sausages; so called because no one is supposed to know what they are made of. [**1894** in S. Crane *Complete Stories* 145: There was a sign which read "No mystery about our hash!"] **1902** T.A. Dorgan, in Zwilling *TAD Lexicon* 58: Twice on the "mystery" and egg. **1906** M'Govern *Sgt. Larry* 52: "Will yez be afther havin' a wee bit of canned MYSTERY, sorr?" said Sergeant Tipprary, as he drew a half can of Armour corned beef hash from his haversack. **1918** Guttersen *Granville* 72: We had..."Mystery" steak for supper this evening, which is the new name that "Brownie" has given to the hamburger that we receive quite often. **1921** *15th Inf. Sentinel* (Mar. 25) 5: When "Mess call" sounds its welcome, you hurry to your seat/Of "beans" and "slum" and "mystery-hash" you get enough to eat. **1926** Maines & Grant *Wise-Crack Dict.* 11: *Mystery*—Hash. **1934** *Jour. Abnormal & Soc. Psychol.* XXX 363: *Mystery*—meat loaf. **1944** Kendall *Service Slang* 25: *Mystery balls*....meat balls. **1968** Baker et al. *CUSS* 160: *Mystery Meat.* Bad dining hall meat. **1969** Girodias *New Olympia Reader* 705: Hee hee hee. We...served them like mystery meat. **1969** *Current Slang I & II* 63: *Mystery meat.* n. Hamburger.—Air Force Academy cadets. **1971** *Winter Soldier* (film): Mystery meat or wop slop or whatever we had for chow. **1980** DiFusco et al. *Tracers* 60: And that fuckin' mystery meat they served for chow last night. **1984** Mason & Rheingold *Slanguage: Mystery Meat*...Entree at dining halls. **1986** WINS radio ad (July 4): Boar's Head hot dogs and hamburgers aren't the proverbial "mystery meat." **1988** Univ. Tenn. student theme: There will be *mystery meat* served at the *caf.* **1993** *Beavis and Butt-head* (MTV): Cool! Mystery meat! **1996** *N.Y. Times* (Apr. 30) B6: Things have become more sophisticated...with college chefs usually graduates of culinary schools. The old days of "mystery meat" and casseroles are gone.

my uncle see s.v. UNCLE.

N *n.* NIGGER, 1.

1971 F.J. Hodges *Black Wisdom* 25: What It Means to Be an "N." **1976** Whelton *CB Baby* 133: Those goddam N's! *Ibid.* 190: My wife got mugged...by a couple of N's.

nab *n.* **1.** *Und. & Black E.* a police officer or detective.

*1813 in *OED*: A nab stepp'd in and show'd his writ. **1848** Judson *Mysteries of N.Y.* 41: I don't know nothin' about no persuits, 'cept the nab's persuits. **1949** H. Ellson *Tomboy* 110: Chickie, the nabs! **1953** W. Brown *Monkey on My Back* 14: Then call the nabs. That'll settle things one way or another. *ca*1953 Hughes *Lodge* 118: Fran was stopped by the nabs. **1956** Ross *Hustlers* 53: The nabs get to you? **1956** Algren *Wild Side* 72: One noon an armed nab stuck his nose in a boxer door—"Come on out of there one by one!" **1961** H. Ellison *Gentleman Junkie* 42: I think you with the nabs, Tom. **1963** L. Jones, in Clarke *Amer. Negro Stories* 310: Then the Nabs came, and with them, the fire engines. **1967** Colebrook *Cross of Lassitude* 96: She has heard constant attacks made upon the police, the fuzz, the screws, the nabs. **1975** S.P. Smith *Amer. Boys* 100: One night the nab broke in on one of their fights. **1981** *Nat. Lampoon* (Mar.) 45: Undercover nabs sniffing around like hungry rats. **1983** *Reader's Digest Success with Words* 87: Black English...*nab* = "policeman."

2. the proceeds of a theft; HAUL.

1884 Hartranft *Sidesplitter* 130: It's the way I've picked up many a glorious nab; for when you stands guard, you know nobody is guard over you.

nab *v.* [perh. fr. Early ModE *nab* 'to bite'; cf. NAP] **1.** Esp. *Und.* to seize or steal.

*1665 R. Head *Eng. Rogue*, in Partridge *Dict. Und.* 460: Nab...To take; or cheat. ***1773** in Partridge *Dict. Und.* 460: To nab his rattle. ***1788** Grose *Dict. Vulgar Tongue* (ed. 2): *To nab the snow;* to steal linen left out to bleach. ***1789** G. Parker *Life's Painter* 135: They may all nab the rust [*i.e.*, money] since I have *got*/ The heart and hand of Moll. ***1821** *Real Life in London* I 118: Nabbing a lantern. **1847** in Peskin *Vols.* 49: Some hungry devil nabbed my supper. **1859** Bartlett *Dict. Amer.* (ed. 2): *Nabber*: In the city of New York, a thief. **1873** Perrie *Buckskin Mose* 230: The red skunks haven't nabbed 'em. **1883** Flagg *Versicles* 37: Ain't you nabbed the wrong goose,/ When you order round ladies from great Syracuse? **1894** Peirce *Man from Corpus Christi* 81: He's a black goat and there's no law in Texas against goat nabbing. **1921** Casey & Casey *Gay-Cat* 156: Yuh'll be on the spot when I nabs the pile. **1987** *Lame Monkey Manif.* (Univ. Tenn.) (Jan. 29) 5: UT Safety and Security has no idea just when they disappeared or any evidence that they really were nabbed.

2.a. *Orig. Und.* to catch or grasp (a person) usu. unawares, esp. to lay hold of or capture (a malefactor); (*specif.*, now *colloq.* or *S.E.*) to apprehend and place under arrest; (*obs.*) to capture (an enemy vessel) as a prize.

[***1673** R. Head *Canting Acad.* 11: But if the cully *nap* us, and the lurries from us take.] ***1686** in *OED*: Verselli was nabb'd playing at dice. ***1688** Shadwell *Squire of Alsatia* III i: Our *Suffolk* Heir is Nab-b'd...and I must find him some Sham-Bail. ***1698–99** "B.E." *Dict. Cant. Crew*: Nab'd...Apprehended, Taken, or Arrested. ***1728** in *F & H* V 4: Nab...to surprise, to take one napping. ***1733** H. Fielding, in *F & H* V 4: Were he a bully, a highwayman, or a prizefighter, I'd nab him. ***1755** S. Johnson *Dict.*: Nab....To catch unexpectedly; to seize without warning. A word seldom used but in low language. ***1768** O. Goldsmith, in *OED*: Ay, but if so be a man's nabbed, you know. **1797** Brackenridge *Mod. Chiv.* 286: Ah, have ye nabbed him. ***1803** in J. Ashton *Eng. Satires on Napoleon* 193: He had like to have been *nabbed* by Sir Sidney Smith. ***1821** *Real Life in London* I 82: They are sure to *nab* my gentleman before he gets much farther. ***1833** Marryat *Peter Simple* 127: Now, if they only wait a little longer, they are nabbed, as sure as fate. ***1835** *Mil. & Nav. Mag. of U.S.* (May) 218: By this, and other ways and means, we nabbed, now and then, a stray Yankee. **1837** *Spirit of Times* (Feb. 18) 7: Gallitt was..."nabbed" the day before and...bound over to keep the peace for twelve months. **1837** A.

Greene *Glance at N.Y.* 70: They venture forth more daringly, and are nabbed at last. **1837** Strong *Diary* I 60: I was in the room before I saw them and was fairly nabbed. ***1838** C. Dickens *Oliver Twist* ch. xliv: It...reminds you of being nabbed, does it? **1840** in *DAE* I 471: The Charlies...[are] the d—dest kind of fellows for nabbing chaps like you wot stay out late at night. **1845** in Cotton *Deck & Port* 76: You have gotten nabbed yourself—you old blood-sucker. **1845** *Nat. Police Gaz.* (Oct. 28) 78: Williams was "nabbed" at Memphis. **1848** *Rough & Ready Songster* 19: We "nab" their laggard vessels, but 'Connor lets them go. **1848** *Life in Rochester* 13: That was a grand idea to nab him and take him off to the city in the night. **1859** Matsell *Vocab.* 57: *Nabbed.* Arrested. *a*1860 [J. Jones] *Marie* 51: I helped you away when they would have nabbed you. **1864** in C.H. Moulton *Ft. Lyon* 215: There are 5 more...who will be "nabbed" as speedily as [possible]. **1865** Williams *Joaquin* 133: In a few minutes perhaps you will be nabbed. **1872** Burnham *Secret Service* 86: The result was the whole concern was nabbed, and two or three of the operators were "sent over." **1875** Sheppard *Love Afloat* 409: The cruiser'll nab the whole gang. **1880** J.C. Harris *Uncle Remus* 73: Dey wuz all time seein' one nudder, en 'bunnunce er times Brer Fox could er nab Brer Rabbit. **1882** D.J. Cook *Hands Up* 224: He had been "nabbed" with the assistance of Officer Hudson, and the two came marching up the street with the prisoner between them. **1887** DeVol *40 Yrs. a Gambler* 15: They nabbed and locked me up also. **1891** *Munsey's Mag.* (Nov.) 158: That's Tom Carlin...what escaped from jail. We just nabbed him a little while ago. *a*1893 W.K. Post *Harvard* 196: I'll nab him when he comes in. **1919** S. Anderson, in Woods *Horse-Racing* 31: We didn't want to put the folks on our trail and maybe be nabbed. **1955** Q. Reynolds *HQ* 11: He never pushed you around once he'd nabbed you. **1959** Kanin *Blow Up a Storm* 227: He was already in [the army] when they nabbed [*i.e.*, drafted] me. **1971** Sorrentino *Up from Never* 96: Tony nabbed him by the collar.

b. to kidnap.

1917 E.R. Burroughs *Oakdale Affair* 128: Blackie can knab [*sic*] The Kid an' I'll annex Miss Abigail Prim. **1981** *Magnum, P.I.* (CBS-TV): Just go back [and] pretend you really got nabbed.

3. to catch (in other senses). *Specif.*:

a. to catch unawares in deceit; catch out; (*Baseball*) to discover the significance of (a coach's or catcher's sign). [Though accepted by *OED* in this sense, the *1698–99 quot. clearly has a more specialized meaning; it has not been attested in America.]

[***1698–99** "B.E." *Dict. Cant. Crew*: *Nab*, c, a Hat, Cap, or Head; also a coxcomb. *I'll nab ye,* c. I'll have your hat or cap.] ***1742** in *OED*: Let's see, what have I said?—Ay, by my Soul, you have nabbed me cleverly. ***1796** Grose *Dict. Vulgar Tongue* (ed. 3): *To nab.* To...catch unawares. **1872** Burnham *Secret Service* 82: This notorious villain...on this occasion was fairly "nabbed in the hock." **1939–40** Tunis *Kid from Tomkinsville* 75: I can't be sure the runner on second will nab that sign.

b. *Baseball.* to field (a ball) successfully.

1920 Patten *Man on First* 127: You nabbed the ball and got Conroy at third. **1939–40** Tunis *Kid from Tomkinsville* 54: You go all out every time, whether you nab that old apple or not.

c. to obtain for oneself; secure; (*also*) *Hobo.* to steal a ride on (a train).—occ. constr. with *off.*

1925 S. Lewis *Arrowsmith* 652 [ref. to *ca*1910]: Uncle Clif has nabbed off a twenty-five-buck a week job *with* commissions, selling autos. **1933** D. Runyon, in *Collier's* (July 8) 8: A scheme...to nab the business on them. **1966** "Petronius" *N.Y. Unexp.* 8: New girls are detected, classified and nabbed by professional scouts. **1980** Bruns *Kts. of Road* 14: Still nabbing an occasional slow freight. **1994** *Reader's Digest* (Apr.) 186: She nabbed one of her early sponsors, a department store, by projecting good ratings by a certain deadline.

d. *Baseball.* to put out (a runner).

1939–40 Tunis *Kid from Tomkinsville* 96: He was too smart a catcher...and nabbed the runner on bases. **1989** Dickson *Baseball Dict.*: Nab...To throw or tag a runner out, especially when he is trying for extra bases.

nabber *n. Und.* a police officer.

    1837 Neal *Charcoal Sks.* 192: No—the nabbers must have you. **1949** Monteleone *Crim. Slang: Nabber*...A policeman. *ca***1953** Hughes *Lodge* 224: Nab, nabber policeman. **1956** Algren *Wild Side* 232: Another walked past a nabber with a bill in his hand, and the same nab said to another—"Uncle Charlie!" And let him pass. **1965** in B. Jackson *Swim Like Me* 141: A California nabber took me, white slavery was my charge.

nabe *n.* [clipping and resp. of *neighborhood*] **1.a.** usu. *pl. Entertainment Industry & Cinema.* a neighborhood theater.

    1935 in *OEDS*: On Sunday two powerful [box office pictures] were released to the nabes. **1936** *Esquire* (Sept.) 159: The nabes (neighborhood houses) are keeping the trade away from downtown. **1937** *AS* (Dec.) 317: Nabe. Neighborhood motion picture theatre. **1958** in Pohl *Star of Stars* 42: We...re-release them to the nabes. **1964** *New Yorker* (Sept. 26) 195: A Hollywood ending fit only for the nabes. **1972** M. Rodgers *Freaky Fri.* 24: "What's playing at the nabes?"..."Brucey and Betsy. I hear it's terrific." **1974** in *Mad Super Special* (No. 64) 39: Just wait until six more "Devil Flicks" hit the nabes! **1976** *N.Y. Times* (Oct. 28) 41: What's playing at the nabes? **1983** Flaherty *Tin Wife* 51: She loved the movies....The "nabes."

    b. a neighborhood tavern; LOCAL.

    1979 *N.Y. Times* (Mar. 8) B7: Every neighborhood has its "nabes"—humble, darkly reliable taverns that dress up a man's spirit like old clothes and let him stare Byronically into a glass.

    2. a neighborhood.

    1942 *ATS* 52: Nabe,...neighb, neighborhood. **1983** *U.S. News & W.R.* (Dec. 12) 71: Brooklyn...what its residents call "da nabes," the two dozen or so ethnic neighborhoods that distinguish it from Manhattan's concrete canyons. **1987** M.S. Bell *Year of Silence* 79: Went two years but never liked it. Missed my friends and my own nabe. **1988** *N.Y. Newsday* (July 22) 35: I wanted to start a real nabe place. **1994** *N.Y. Times* (Sept. 29) XIII 1: The floppy hat I never wear in the nabe. *Ibid.*: Cheap wine and vodka for the nabe's stumbling alcoholics.

Nab'em *n.* [punning NAB, *v.*, 2.a.] ¶ In phrase: **Squire** [or **Baron**] **Nabbem** a constable. *Joc.*

    1830 N. Ames *Mariner's Sketches* 116: Ships when coming to anchor near these islands commonly fire a gun by way of informing these refugees from the power of "Baron Nab'em" that they may calculate upon broken shins if they undertake any transactions in their vocation. **1834** *Mil. & Nav. Mag. of U.S.* (Apr.) 144: We clap on these borrowed outsides to puzzle Squire Nab'em.

nabs *n.* [of unkn. orig.] NIBS.

    ***1797** in Partridge *Dict. Und.* 461: Nabs. A person of either sex. ***1809** in Partridge *Dict. Und.* 461: How are you, my nabs? ***1812** Vaux *Vocab.*: His-Nabs: him, or himself; a term used by way of emphasis, when speaking of a third person....Mynabs: me, myself....Yournabs: yourself; an emphatical term used in speaking to another person. ***1873** Hotten *Slang Dict.* (ed. 4): My nabs, myself; his nabs, himself.—North Country Cant. **1889** Barrère & Leland *Dict. Slang* I 464: His nabs there (tailors), him, the individual referred to.

nad *n.* [fr. go*nad*] **1.** usu. *pl.* **a.** a testicle.—also used fig.—usu. considered vulgar.

    1964 Reuss *Field Collection* 146: Two sweaty nads. **1970** *Playboy* (Dec.) 282: He'd managed to kick a cop in the 'nads before they'd gotten to him. **1974** Lahr *Trot* 35: My balls have swollen to the size of oranges....I lift my throbbing nads carefully over the edge. **1980** Lorenz *Guys Like Us* 34: As though he hadn't sweated his nads off in the copper mill. **1984** N. Stephenson *Big U.* 222: Don't want blasted 'nads. **1984** Ark. man, age 35: I remember hearing *nads* in high school in 1966. A friend of mine was saying that where he came from—I think it was California—they talked about "getting kicked in the nads." **1985** J. Hughes *Breakfast Club* (film): "And Molay really pumps my nads." "Molière." **1993** *Beavis and Butt-head* (MTV): Remember the one with the big nads that hung way down? **1994** S. Johnson et al. *Ensucklopedia* (unp.): They hook up your weiner to your nads. **1996** *Dangerous Minds* (ABC-TV): They make your nads slide too close to your body.

    b. manly courage; BALLS, 4.a.

    1976 P. Conroy *Santini* 234: You just don't have the nads. You just

got a terminal case of the yellow spine. **1981** R.B. Parker *Savage Place* 103: You ain't got the 'nads to kill anything.

    2. *pl. Stu.* something wonderful; *the tits* s.v. TIT.—constr. with *the*.

    1983 *Nat. Lampoon* (Mar.) 30: College guys are the nads. They're cute as they come, and they've got the inside dope on Spinoza that makes a gal melt.

nada *n.* [< Sp] nothing.

    1914 (cited in *W10*). **1933** in E. Hemingway, *OEDS*: It was all a nothing and a man was nothing too....He knew it all was nada y pues nada y nada y pues nada. Our nada who art in nada, nada be thy name. **1972–76** Durden *No Bugles* 68: An' it's like nobody knows from nada. **1977** *Nat. Lampoon* (July) 18: And then—nadaville. Deneuve came along and cleaned up. **1986** Philbin *Under Cover* 159: She knew nada. **1989** Radford & Crowley *Drug Agent* 68: "Nada," the reports came back. **1991** B.E. Ellis *Amer. Psycho* 322: No incident. Nothing. The authorities have nada. **1994** G. Trudeau *Doonesbury* (synd. comic strip) (July 22): I'm an agent. 10% of nada means adios.

nade *n. Mil.* a grenade.

    1987 R. Miller *Slob* 265: The cans are just big enough to hold the 'nades in with the spoons depressed.

nag[1] *n.* **1.** a horse, esp. a racehorse. Now *S.E.* [Orig. (as now also) a standard term for 'a small riding horse', as in *1400 quot. Its recognition as slang probably occurred earlier than the present evidence indicates, but early quots. are difficult to identify.]

    1400** in *OED*: He neyt as a nagge, at his nose thrilles. **1840** *Spirit of Times* (Nov. 21) 450: She had decent claims as a race nag. **1841** *Spirit of Times* (Feb. 13) 595: I'll imagine your nag. **1843** in G.W. Harris *High Times* (Mar. 27) 19: I believe the Long Islanders brag mightily on their Quarter Nags. *a1860** Hundley *So. States* 260: A primitive-looking stall for his "nag." **1864** "E. Kirke" *Down in Tenn.* 21: I know'd thar wus more on 'em round, an' feared they'd be arter the nags. *ca***1870** in *Penn. Folklife* XVI (1966) 21: A pair of thoroughbred four thousand dollar nags. **1885** in Guerin *Mountain Charley* 97: I took this off'en a dead feller back yere, and I got his nag, too. **1887** E. Custer *Tenting* 244: That's not so bad a nag, after all. **1905** *Nat. Police Gaz.* (Nov. 18) 3: I ought to have put twenty on this nag. **1951** in *DAS*: To make dough on the nags. **1953** Paley *Rumble* 74: He was as good a judge of lawyers as he was of nags. **1956–60** J.A. Williams *Angry Ones* ch. v: Occasionally I'd have enough money to get horses and we'd select a couple of nags and jog through the deep, beautiful valleys. **1970** Terkel *Hard Times* 6: While lost blacks played the numbers, lost whites played the nags. **1981** *Time* (Aug. 17) 33: Gerard was convicted of substituting a champion horse for a nag. **1996** McCumber *Playing Off Rail* 214: He's tryin to get off the booze and the nags.

    2. a woman; (*hence*) *Gamb.* a queen in cards.

    ***1598** in *F & H* V 7: Gull with bombast lines the witless sense of these old nags. **1855** in Dwyer & Lingenfelter *Songs of Gold Rush* 125: Miss Ella is a gallus nag. **1987** T.L. Clark *Dict. Gamb. & Gaming* 133: Nag...in cards, a queen...[Heard in] 1983.

nag[2] *n.* a person who finds fault or complains habitually. Now *S.E.*

    1885 E. Custer *Boots & Saddles* 124 [ref. to 1870's]: To accept the position of "nag" and "torment" was far from desirable. **1942** *ATS* 374: Henpecker,...nag, a nagging wife.

nail *n.* **1.** a tough or dangerous fellow.—also (as a nickname) constr. in *pl.* See also NAILS, 2.

    ***1812** Vaux *Vocab.*: A person of an over-reaching, imposing disposition, is called a *nail*, a *dead nail*, a *nailing* rascal [etc.]. **1983** *Reader's Digest Success with Words* 87: Black English...nail = "a man." **1988** *Night Court* (NBC-TV): I'm gonna be tough! I'm gonna be hard! I'm gonna be a nail! **1989** P. Dickson *Baseball Dict.*: Nails...Generic nickname for a player who is tough.

    2. a cigarette; COFFIN NAIL.

    ***1925** Fraser & Gibbons *Soldier & Sailor Wds.* 163 [ref. to WWI]: *Nails*: Cigarettes. **1929** Bodenheim *60 Secs.* 235: A Spanish fellow was dancing and drawing at a nail....Ed...walked up and jerked the cig from his mouth and swore at him. **1942** *ATS* 127: Cigarette....lung duster, nail, nail in the coffin, [etc.]. **1953** Taradash *Eternity* (film): Gimme a nail, Prewitt. **1959** R. Smith *Girls Town* (film): "Got any nails?" "No smoking here." **1968** Baker et al. *CUSS* 161: *Nail* Cigarette. **1996** *Donahue* (NBC-TV): You still smokin' them nails?

3. *Narc.* a hypodermic needle.

    1936 *AS* (Apr.) 124: *Nail.* A hypodermic needle. **1966** Brunner *Face of Night* 234: *Nail*—the hypodermic needle used for injection.

4. a venereal infection.

    1940 E. O'Neill *Iceman* 162 [ref. to 1912]: You may be lucky for a long time, but you get nicked in the end. I picked up a nail from some tart in Altoona. **1972** Bertolucci *Last Tango* (film): I picked up a nail when I was in Cuba in '48, and now I've got a prostate the size of a potato.

5. *Army.* a fléchette; a shrapnel-producing projectile. Cf. NAILKEG, 1.

    1989 Halberstadt *Army Av.* 6: Four warheads with thousands of tiny steel arrows the crews call "nails." **1980–93** L. Heath *CW2* 282 [ref. to Vietnam War]: Be ready with nails.

¶ In phrases:

¶ **drive a nail** (see quot.).

    1889 Barrère & Leland *Dict. Slang* I 487: Invitations to drink (American)...*Let's drive another nail!*

¶ **drive nails** (see quot.).

    1987 Zeybel *Gunship* 58 [ref. to Vietnam War]: His rounds were concentrated on one spot and he "drove nails," or frequently scored multiple hits with one burst [of automatic fire].

¶ **get under (one's) nails** to annoy (one).

    1983 *TalkNet* (NBC radio network) (Oct. 28): Hold it! Hold it! You're gonna get under my nails in a minute.

¶ **keg of nails** see s.v. KEG, *n.*

¶ **nail in (one's) coffin** anything that may lead incrementally to ruin. Now *colloq.* See also COFFIN NAIL.

    *1820–21** P. Egan *Life in London* 183: A glass of spirits is termed, among the *wet* ones, adding "another nail to the coffin." **1853–54** in Burg *Amer. Seafarer* 28: Another nail in my coffin. **1867** Clark *Sailor's Life* 316: They will toss off the full glass and exclaim, "Here goes another nail in my coffin." *1874** in *F & H* V 9: Every dinner eaten under such conditions is another nail driven into one's coffin. *1884** in *F & H* V 9: It is one more nail in the coffin of slow acting. **1942** (quot. at (2), above). **1992** *Nation* (June 15) 807: This is the first nail in the coffin of public education. **1992** *New Yorker* (Oct. 26) 86: It was one more nail in the coffin of the self-image of Dallas as a city that can do anything. **1992** *N.Y. Times Mag.* (Nov. 8) 12: He cites the Houston Republican convention as one very big nail in Bush's re-election coffin.

¶ **on the nail** broke; destitute.

    1914 Graham *With Poor Immigrants* 173: He averred that he had not a dime now and was altogether "on the nail."

nail *v.* **1.a.** Orig. *Und.* to take or obtain for oneself; secure; make sure of.

    *1732** in Partridge *Dict. Und.:* *Nail* In general, to take possession of any Thing. *1760** in *OED:* Some bidders are shy, and only advance with a nod; but I nail them. *1796** Grose *Dict. Vulgar Tongue* (ed. 3): *Nailed.* Secured, fixed. *1805** in *OED:* I had learnt...to plume myself upon nailing a job. *1821–26** Stewart *Man-of-War's-Man* I 54: Here's to the Tottumfog and a' that's in her. May she soon nail a prize or twa. **1867** Williams *Brierly* 13: Down with her, Bill. I've nailed the swag! **1877–78** *Cornelian* 86: *Nail.* To secure. **1897** Ade *Pink* 182: 'En he flash 'at bundle o' papeh money....I s'pose she didn' nail him! **1903** Merriman *Letters* 159: I was nailing an order for 200 pails with Lige Higginbotham. **1914** J. London *Jacket* 144: The spirits couldn't tell her where the old man could nail a job or find a gold-mine. **1989** *Coach* (ABC-TV): That was the day...I nailed that C minus in Spanish.

b. Orig. *Und.* to steal; filch.

    *1732** in Partridge *Dict. Und.* 461: *Nail* To take away or steal Money or Goods. *1812** Vaux *Vocab.:* I nail'd the swell's montra in the push. *1851–61** H. Mayhew *London Labour* III 405: They used to go out nailing—that's thieving. **1891** Devere *Tramp Poems* 71: Although they ain't mine/I'd nail one [*sc.,* an apple] you bet, but I'm onto the sign. **1920** in DeBeck *Google* 79: That barber shop was where I nailed this swell hat. **1958** Rapp *High School Big Shot* (film): [It] doesn't give you cause to come in and nail my inventory.

c. *Und. & Police.* to catch (someone); apprehend; place under arrest. Now *colloq.*

    *1732** in Partridge *Dict. Und.* 461: He told me himself, that Peter [Buck] was nailed in his company. **1841** *Spirit of Times* (July 3) 211: But Sharptooth and Lion nailed him before he got to Dan. **1845** *Nat. Police Gaz.* (Dec. 6) 125: Jack Cherry Nailed at Last. **1846** Barbour *Journals*

105: They "nailed him" after a short chase. **1859** Matsell *Vocab.* 57: *Nailed....*arrested. *1851–61** H. Mayhew *London Labour* III 404: He was a shoplifter and a pickpocket: he has got two years now....I cried a good deal when he got nailed, sir. **1867** Williams *Brierly* 21: And how about lagging? If I'm nailed, it's a lifer! **1869** *Mysteries of Crime* 323: I was nailed very tight to-day; do you know who was the informer? **1889** Field *Western Verse* 97: At any rate we nailed him. **1892** Garland *Prairie Folks* 162: Grab 'im! Why don't ye nail 'im? **1893** W.K. Post *Harvard* 22: The Yale man..."nailed" him in the air. **1897** A.H. Lewis *Wolfville* 37: We-alls owes for his nailin' them hoss-thiefs. *a1906** Burke *Prison Gates* 9: I was then nailed for the trolley-car hold-up. *a1909** Tillotson *Detective* 93: *Nailed, Glued* or *Landed*—Arrested. **1912** Lowrie *Prison* 82: There ain't much dope here now, an' it's curtains t' get nailed with it. **1930** Conwell *Pro. Thief* 17: Where were you nailed? **1947** Motley *Any Door* 199: "Shall we nail him?" Lucky asked. **1976** G. Kirkham *Signal Zero* 38: Nail 'em and jail 'em. **1978** Diehl *Sharky's Machine* 100: She's been nailed so much she oughta be payin' rent down at the pound. **1967–80** Folb *Runnin' Lines* 247: *Nail-em-and-jail-em* Police. **1978–86** J.L. Burke *Lost Get Back Boogie* 209: Before I got nailed, I used to live with this mulatto girl.

d. to place in a finishing or inextricable position; defeat (an opponent); (*also*) *Baseball.* to put out (a runner).

    1888 *N.Y. Press* (Apr. 18) 4: He nailed every man who tried to steal a base. *1892** in *F & H* V 8: It nailed her. **1910** *N.Y. Eve. Jour.* (Mar. 15) 12: Let him walk....You kin nail him off first. **1950** *Daily News* (N.Y.) (Oct. 1): When you come right down to it, Abrams was nailed by a truly great peg. **1959** F. Astaire, in *OEDAS* I 114: A good horserace with...a close finish with Trip coming from pretty far back to nail...Honeymoon by a neck. *a1986** in *NDAS:* She nailed them with her last question. **1996** *Nat. Examiner* (Oct. 22) 1: New Evidence Nails OJ. **1996** *World Series* (Oct. 26) (Fox-TV): He was nailed at second base.

e. *Hobo.* to catch or steal a ride on (a freight train).

    1907 J. London *Road* 19 [ref. to 1892]: So, as soon as youse two nail a blind, deck her. **1929** L. Thomas *Woodfill* 65 [ref. to 1900]: So I nailed a rattler...and joined up for my second hitch. **1930** Irwin *Tramp & Und. Slang: Nail a Rattler.*—To board a fast train once it has got under way.

2.a. to hit hard or squarely.

    *1785** Grose *Vulgar Tongue:* He offered me a decus, and I nailed him; he offered me a crown and I struck or fixed him. *1785** R. Burns, in *OEDAS* I 113: I'll nail the self-conceited sot,/As dead's a herrin. **1842** *Spirit of Times* (May 28) 152: Broome nailed his man with his left. **1873** Bailey *Danbury Newsman* 185: The amateur Bergh...actually urged the youngster to "nail the old rip" [with a snowball]. *1886** in *OED:* To surround "Mad Shelly" and "nail" him with a ball...was a favourite pastime. **1895** in P. Dickson *Baseball Dict.:* He tried to nail the ball hard, but he only fanned and went back to the bench. **1898** Dunne *Peace & War* 167: Ye may talk iv th' immrality iv nailin' a man on th' jaw, but 'tis in this way on y'at th' wurruld increases in happiness an' th' race in strenth. **1911** Van Loan *Big League* 140: He nailed Dolan right on the chin. **1921** *Variety* (July 15) 7: Tomato nailed him right on the button with a right cross that would have dropped a sand bag. **1924** in Spectorsky *College Yrs.* 216: He was on his way to glory when Wilson, hurtling across the right of way, nailed him on the fifteen-yard line and threw him out of bounds. **1947** Schulberg *Harder They Fall* 4: Jackson...nails old Frank with a right that travels just this far. **1964** Brewer *Worser Days* 94: Dat [hurricane] Hazel sho did nail Wilmin'ton good—didn't take jes' one whop at de town—it took two, dat it did. **1969** Gardner *Fat City* 49: Don't drive too fast, Burgos. I'll nail you one. **1994** *Cops* (Fox-TV): He nails John with the ball bat. **1996** *N.Y. Times* (July 24) B6: I almost got nailed by a cab.

b. to shoot or kill; (*Mil.*) to destroy (a target).

    *1824** in *OEDAS* I 113: We say when we see a hare shot, that she's nail'd. **1844** Porter *Big Bear* 132: "Shall we nail him, Chunkey?" "*In course,*" says I. **1861** Wilkie *Iowa First* 76: Each...will "nail his man" at eight hundred yards. **1865** *Atlantic* (Mar.) 287: Show so much as your little finger outside of that, and the guard nails you with a bullet. **1865** in "M. Twain" *Sel. Shorter Writings* 16: He'd nail a fly every time as fur as he could see him. **1867** Macnamara *Irish Ninth* 44: When a pig passed them they seldom cried, "Who goes there?" but with malice *prepence* "nailed" the unfortunate porker without a word. **1876** J. Miller *First Fam'lies* 99: He's got the start just a little, if the Parson does nail him. **1892** F.P. Dunne, in Schaaf *Dooley* 45: Besides, McKenna never had fear of mortal man nailing him with a bomb. The worst he ever got was some friend of McElligott's soaking him with a brick. **1893** *McClure's Mag.* (June) 72: Then he shook down the breech of his rifle, and slipped a long cartridge into its place....“Why don't you nail him?” asked Farnbrough. *a***1907** R.H. Williams *Border Ruffians* 376: Lay your rifle on the spot he jumps to…and it's odds on your nailing him. **1913** [W. Dixon] *“Billy” Dixon* 102: Perkins…was sure Indians had nailed us. **1918** Grider *War Birds* 241: One of these new Fokkers came over after a balloon and A Flight nailed him after he got two and was trying to get back. **1929** L. Thomas *Woodfill* 270 [ref. to 1918]: My God,…I thought sure they nailed you. **1960** MacCuish *Do Not Go Gentle* 175: In the dome then. Nailed him in the head. **1962** T. Jones *Stairway* 56: Here he has it made with this dish Ophelia, and all he's thinking about is who nailed his old man. **1965** *In Harm's Way* (film): I know, but we might nail two or three of the escort vessels. **1977** Dunne *Confessions* 84: How about the guy who nailed her? What's he swimming in? **1989** Singerman *Amer. Hero* 43: “If you stop, they'll nail your ass, too.” “Course they may pick you off even if you don't stop.” **1993** *Mystery Sci. Theater* (Comedy Central TV): Oh, no! A Scud! It's gonna nail Santa!

c. to do (something) perfectly; master; (*also*) to affect strongly.

1989 P. Munro *U.C.L.A. Sl.*: *Nail*…to do well on, *ace*…I have to nail my math midterm. **1994** *New York* (Jan. 24) 18: These people were *nailed* by this script....The poetry crowd jumps and screams; I've never seen the café this quiet. **1995** *Opera News* (Mar. 4) 39: You can…nail the third act, and nobody cares if you had a sack over your head for the rest of the show. **1996** *N.Y. Observer* (Jan. 15) 7: The S.A.T....If you nail it, nothing will ever intimidate you again. **1996** *N.Y. Times* (June 19) C6: Did the chefs nail the lobster pot pie with version No. 4? **1996** Mutual of New York TV ad: And, when you've got the whole teenage thing nailed, [suddenly] you're an adult. **1996** *Good Morning America* (ABC-TV) (Dec. 12): I nailed [the pronunciation] for the first time in ten years.

3. to cheat or overcharge.

*****1812** in *OED:* To nail a person is to over-reach or take advantage of him in the course of trade or traffic. *****1821** in Partridge *DSUE* 1289: *Nail*…To charge extortionately. **1910** T.A. Dorgan, in *N.Y. Eve. Jour.* (Jan. 21) 16: He charged us only one buck for doing more than that U.S. guy nailed us four dollars for.

4. to identify or recognize.

1902 Cullen *More Tales* 39: I'd…try to dope it out where I'd stacked up against him before, but…I couldn't nail him. **1942** *ATS* 175: Recognize....*make, nail, peg.*

5. to copulate with (a woman).—usu. considered vulgar.

1957 in Legman *New Limerick* 3: He had to turn sideways to nail her. **1960** J. Updike *Rabbit* 45: It seems a great loss that it hadn't been him about to nail her. **1968** Standish *Non-Stand. Terms* 18: Did you hear about the lady who had a wooden baby? She got nailed by a carpenter! **1970** Southern *Blue Movie* 157: Little suspecting that…Junior was nailing her repeatedly. **1972** Jenkins *Semi-Tough* 59: Ever since Burt Danby thinks he discovered Barbara Jane he's been trying to nail her. **1976** R.B. Parker *Promised Land* 30: Man, she was eager. I thought I was gonna have to nail her right here in the bar. **1980** E. Sacks *Small Circle of Friends* (film): “Did…[he] sleep with her?”…“Jesus! This guy nails anything that walks within five feet of him.” **1980** *Penthouse* (Jan. 1981) 170: Men…never did anything for her except buy her drinks and nail her. *a***1994** A. Radakovich *Wild Girls Club* 115: Robert first nailed Mary in his car. **1995** *Esquire* (Jan. 1996) 62: Everyone knows that JFK was nailing her for years.

¶ In phrases:

¶ **nail (someone's) hide** [or (*vulgar*) **ass**] **to the wall** [or **barn door**] to punish or otherwise put a finish to (someone).

[**1937** Glidden *Brand of Empire* 88: Somebody is going to nail up his hide, Chris, and it won't be nice to see.] **1952** Sandburg *Young Strangers* 372 [ref. to 1890's]: Gersh Martin…liked nothing better than to hook a hypocrite and “nail his hide to the barn door.” **1957** O'Connor *Co. Q* 79: They're going to nail our hides to the barn door anyway. **1959** Cochrell *Barren Beaches* 362: I'd rather even up the score for Salty and Leeper, then they can nail my hide to the wall. **1971** Cole *Rook* 202: They'll nail your ass to the wall. **1975** *Railroad* (Mar.) 48: You'd better stay out of his way, or he'll nail your hide to the roundhouse wall. **1977** A. Patrick *Beyond Law* 118: Well, you God damn well better catch 'em, or I'll nail your ass to the wall!

¶ **nail (someone) to the cross** [or **mast**] to punish or

otherwise deal with (someone) in a final or decisive manner; (*often*) to castigate thoroughly.

1899 Garland *Eagle's Heart* 241: He pulled his gun and nailed me to the cross. **1907** Bush *Enlisted Man* 121: About a month after, when I thought it had all been forgotten, he called me in and “nailed me to the cross” “good and proper.” **1907** in “O. Henry” *Works* 1450: “What would you have done?” asked the Captain. “Nailed Pickering to the cross.” **1920** Colyer *323rd Field Arty.* 33: He introduced himself as “Spike,” explaining that “he nailed them to the cross.” **1921** Dienst *353rd Inf.* 3: He “nailed them to the cross” and at the same time strengthened their confidence in themselves. **1925** Nason *Three Lights* 42 [ref. to 1918]: Gee, they nailed young Bottle to the mast all right! He stopped about six bullets. **1927** in Hammett *Knockover* 321: So much for the arrest. Now for the conviction part. If you get him, are you sure you can nail him to the cross? **1958** Drury *Advise & Consent* 291: You tell him, Bob.…Nail the bastard to the mast.

nail-bender *n.* a carpenter or horseshoer.

1924 T.A. Dorgan, in Zwilling *TAD Lexicon* 118: Listening to a pair of nail benders as they pull off their daily razz…When I first seen you you used to show me a rule an say one of dese an' two of dese—You didn't know feet and inches. **1947** Grant *Angel & Badman* (film): You dimwitted nail-bender! Why don't you marry that girl?

nail-biter *n.* an anxiety-provoking situation, esp. a very close contest.

[**1941** in *OEDS*: But what was the symbolical meaning of all these…nail-biting figures?] **1971** (cited in *W10*). **1978** *Vancouver Sun* (July 15) A4: Here was a real nail-biter—the first major contract to be negotiated since wage controls were lifted. **1983** Kaplan & Smith *One Last Look* 85: It was, as one pilot said, “a real nail-biter.” **1989** *Daily Beacon* (Univ. Tenn.) (Jan. 30) 7: Vols lose nailbiter to Bulldogs. **1991** *CBS This Morning* (CBS-TV) (Oct. 28): The [World] Series was a seven-game nail-biter. **1994** *New York Times* (May 1) (“Business”) 11: While that 400 percent-plus gain …may sound like a giant “so what” to most people, it's been a nail-biter for brokerage executives.

nailed *adj.* drunk.—formerly constr. with *up*.

1836 *Spirit of Times* (July 16) 169: He was *nailed up, sewed up*, and swore…he would *leather* me. **1985** *UTSQ*: Sloshed, hammered, ripped,…*nailed.* **1987** Univ. Tenn. student theme: The students venture out with the goal of becoming heavily intoxicated, or *smashed, hammered, sloshed, wasted, nailed* [etc.].

nailer *n.* a police officer.

*****1863** in *OEDS*: Then there's the Nailer's been after me.…What, Hawkshaw, the 'cutest detective in the force? **1960** C. Cooper *Scene* 308: *Nailers:* police.

nailheaded *adj.* stupid; doltish. Hence **nailhead**, *n.*

1936 in *OEDS*: In my hand lies the same whispering, nail-headed dude, ever imploring the benefice of a hippograph. **1948** Miller & Rackin *Fighter Sq.* (film): Hey, nailhead! Where's that crack outfit of ours?

nailing *adv.* exceptionally. Also as *adj.*

1868 J. Chisholm *So. Pass* 184: It is not essential that she be *nailin'* good looking, but she must be cleanly and tidy. *****1883** in *OED*: He was a well-tried old dog, and we can have another nailing run out of him another day. *****1894** in *F & H* 11: A nailing good horse once.

nail keg *n.* **1.** *Mil.* an artillery shell.

[**1864** in E. Newsome *Experiences* 72: He…sent a shell about the size of a nail keg!] **1894** *Century* (Jan.) 478 [ref. to Civil War]: Dem nail-kegs* been flyin' 'roun hyah thick es bees 'bout er hive.…*Large shells. *Ibid.* 479: One er dem nail-kegs hit erbout seven foot f'om Jerry. **1918** Mills *War Letters* 343: You hear away off to the north a muffled roar and in a minute or so there comes a flock of Hun “nailkegs” shrieking through the air.

2. a top hat.

1866 W.W. Brown *Negro in Reb.* 275: Well, you had better notice it…or I'll blow half dat *nail-kag* off! **1867** Clark *Sailor's Life* 252: Well, you have got a hard cheek to wear a nail keg in sight of this vessel's crew.

Nails *n.* **1.** *Navy.* (see quots.).—used as a nickname. Cf. BOATS, CHIPS, etc.

1914 *DN* IV 150: *Nails*…Carpenter's mate. **1934** Weseen *Dict. Amer. Sl.* 128: *Nails*—A carpenter's mate. *a***1983** Elting, Cragg & Deal *Dict. Soldier Talk* 363: *Nails* (Old Sailing Navy) A ship's carpenter's mate.

2. see s.v. NAIL, 1.

naked *adj.* ¶ In phrase: **get naked** *Sports & Stu.* to get busy; (*also*) to enjoy oneself uninhibitedly.

[**1954** in Reuss *Field Collection* 178: Let's all get drunk and get naked,/Let's all get drunk and get naked,/Let's all get drunk and get naked....We'll have a naked good time.] **1961** Brosnan *Pennant Race* 36: "Tell Brosnan he's gonna finish up [the game as relief pitcher]."..."Get naked!" said Henry. I rushed up to the dugout...before I took the mound. *Ibid.* 58: "Hey, Nunn! Wake up and answer the phone!" "Get naked, Nunn." **1963** in Dickson *Baseball Dict.* 179: A coach might yell to a pitcher who seems to be losing his concentration: "Hey, get naked out there." **1965** Borowik *Lions* 129: Like pitchers say "get naked" for "warm up." **1982** *Time* (Nov. 8) 91: To *get naked* means to have a good time, whether or not sex is involved. **1984** Univ. Tenn student: At a party someone always yells "Get naked!" **1989** *Beachin' Times* 5: Wanna get naked? *a***1990** Dickson *Slang!* 218: Get naked...a way to say "let's go." **1995** *Esquire* (Sept.) 200: There's, like, a camera everywhere, even up in the windows. Be loud. Get naked. [**1996** *New Yorker* (Jan. 29) 33: He skis, he skates,...he gets naked with a lady.]

Naked Fanny *n. Mil. Av.* Nakhon Phanom, Thailand. Now *hist.* [Quots. ref. to Vietnam War.]

1966–67 Harvey *Air War* 142: Nakon Phanom [Thailand], called "Naked Fanny" by the pilots. **1981** Mersky & Polmar *Nav. Air War in Viet.* 171: Nakhon Phanom, known as "Naked Fanny" to the troops stationed there. **1985** Heywood *Taxi Dancer* 91: The Jolly Greens from Naked Fanny. **1986** Coonts *Intruder* 230: Nakhon Phanom in Thailand, a place referred to by the military as NKP, or "naked fanny." **1987** Zeybel *Gunship* 73: Nakhon Phanom Air Base (nicknamed Naked Fanny). **1990** G.R. Clark *Words of Viet. War* 339: *Naked Fanny*...Air Force...nickname for the Air Force control center at Nakhon Phanom [Royal Thai Air Force Base]...that collected and digested information gathered on the Ho Chi Minh [trail].

Nam *n. Mil.* Vietnam.—often constr. with *the.*

1962 in J.C. Pratt *Viet. Voices* 121: We're in the safest place. No one's going to nuke Nam. **1967** in Briscoe *Short-Timer* 14: Another day in "the Nam" has passed. **1967** in B. Edelman *Dear Amer.* 157: This is your "on the spot" correspondent in the *Big Nam* reporting. **1968** in Hayes *Smiling Through Apocalypse* 778: It is colder than the Nam ever gets. **1969** *Time* (Sept. 19) 23: Violence at home and in "the Nam." **1970** *CBS News* (CBS-TV): Just another day in the Nam. **1970** Hersh *My Lai 4* 155: There's this question—I think anyone who goes to Nam asks it. What's a civilian? Someone who works for us at day and puts on Viet Cong pajamas at night? **1970** *Playboy* (Apr.) 56: If you extend your tour of duty in the Nam, you can get out of the Army earlier. **1971** Glasser *365 Days* 45: A tour of Nam is twelve months. **1973** Karlin, Paquet & Rottmann *Free Fire Zone* 198: You're gonna want to have some souvenir of the 'Nam. **1974–75** Powledge *Mud Show* 17: How had the killings in Nam affected you? **1976** C.R. Anderson *Grunts* 24: Looks like this is your first tour in the Nam? **1984** *Harper's* (June) 69: He has nightmares, smashes up a few things, misses his buddies still in 'Nam. **1985** J.M.G. Brown *Rice Paddy Grunt* 139: Another stupid day in the stinkin' Nam. **1995** Donahue (NBC-TV): So he was in Nam? A soldier?

namas *v.* [orig. unkn.] *Und.* to abscond; run away.

***1841** in Partridge *Dict. Und.* 462: None of us knowed then...as Polly was the cause..., till it was blown...by some of the coves. Vell, she nammused, as you may guess. **1859** Matsell *Vocab.* 58: *Namased.* Run away; got out of sight; ran. **1866** *Nat. Police Gaz.* (Nov. 24) 3: Lizzie Spencer and Hattie Morland [pickpockets]...were on the lookout for a "trick" on the corner of Sixth street, immediately "piped" him, and Lizzie "beefed" to her "pal," "Let's 'namase;' [*sic*]. There's Billy, and he'll be sure to 'run us in.'" **1874** *Nat. Police Gaz.* (Dec. 5) 3: In the meanwhile the harlot had quietly "namased" away.

name *n.* ¶ In phrases:

¶ **name of that tune** [sugg. by the early TV quiz show *Name That Tune*, which challenged contestants to name popular tunes after hearing only the first few notes] the simple fact about a given state of affairs.—constr. with *the.*

1980 in *Nat. Lampoon* (Jan. 1981) 8: I come down hard on them—no ammo for a week. And that's the name of that tune. **1983** *Weekend Contact* (WKGN radio) (May 14): Israel is America's ally over there, and that's the name of *that* tune. **1990** *In Living Color* (Fox-TV): I'm from the hardcore streets—that's the name of *that* tune.

¶ **name of the game** [perh. alluding to the practice of announcing the name of the card game, e.g. "That's gin (rummy)," when claiming the winning hand] **1.** the end; the finish.

1957 Myrer *Big War* 13 [ref. to WWII]: Look at that. Name of the game [in cards]. *Ibid.* 203: Another one like this [war], it'll be the name of the game.

2. something of central or exclusive importance.—constr. with *the.*

1960 MacCuish *Do Not Go Gentle* 248 [ref. to WWII]: Yeah, Norman thought, the very last half. Hudge tossed it to him. "Name of the game." **1964** Howe *Valley of Fire* 48 [ref. to Korean War]: That's the name of the game, Joe....If I hadn't done it, somebody else would have. **1966–67** W. Stevens *Gunner* 17: That was the name of the game—Fifty. **1967** Ford *Muc Wa* 6: "Southeast Asia?" "That's the name of the game all right." **1968** Safire *New Language* 276: *Name of the game, the....*the goal; quintessence; the heart of the matter. **1972–75** W. Allen *Feathers* 86: Results is the name of the game. **1975** Bellak *Tenth Level* (film): The name of the game for you is self-sufficiency. **1979** WINS radio (N.Y.C.) (July 3): He had a fantastic instinct for the ball, which is the name of the game at his position. **1988** Poyer *The Med* 6: That's the name of the game. **1996** *CNN & Co.* (CNN-TV) (Oct. 22): Profit-taking is the name of the game on Wall Street [this morning].

¶ **(one's) name is mud** [or (*vulgar*) **shit**] (said of one who has been defeated, embarrassed, lost favor, etc.).

1823** in Partridge *DSUE* 539: "And his name is mud!" ejaculated upon the conclusion of a silly oration, or of a leader in the *Courier.* *a1890–1902** F & H IV 374: *His name is mud! phr.* (American political).—Said in cases of utter defeat. **1902** in *DA*: If there ever a man lived whose name ought to be Mud, it was Falk. **1926** Nason *Chevrons* 231 [ref. to 1918]: An' it wasn't long before their name was Excrement, neither. **1948** in *DA*: His name is mud in all classes—they feel toward him as Americans felt toward Herbert Hoover in 1933. **1973** N.Y.U. student: Your name'll be shit. *a***1994** in *21st Century Dict. Sl.*: When my parents see I haven't mowed the lawn yet my name will be mud.

¶ **(one's) name is on it** *Mil.* (said of a bullet or the like that is thought to be preordained to kill (one)). [Early quots. ref. to WWI.]

1917 Empey *Over the Top* 17: All I could think of was that there were a million German submarines with a torpedo on each, across the warhead of which was inscribed my name and address. **1918** Campbell *Diary-Letters* 116: Then came "the shell with his name on it." **1918** *Sat. Eve. Post* (Apr. 20) 3: The ole boche ain't got a shell in his whole dog-gone army with my name on it, Wally. ***1919** *Athenaeum* (July 18) 633: A soldier refers to a shell that kills him as "having his name and number on it," but perhaps that is poetry and not slang. ***1925** Fraser & Gibbons *Soldier & Sailor Wds.* 39 [ref. to WWI]: *Bullet With A Name On It:* A familiar phrase [in World War I] with reference to the chances of a man being killed in action, *e.g.* "I was all right; I knew there wasn't a bullet with my name on it." **1963** Cameron *Black Camp* 23: Remember that if there's a bullet with your name on it, there's nothing you can do about it, and the others won't get you. **1976** C.R. Anderson *Grunts* 45: Yeah, Lieutenant, don't worry about that round with your name on it. There's nothing you can do about that one. Just watch out for all those ones marked "To whom it may concern!" **1989** *Smithsonian* (Sept.) 82: The asteroid missed us by only six hours. We probably will not see the one with our name on it in any event.

nana *n. So.* a banana. *Joc.*

*ca***1929** in Sagendorf *Popeye* 17: [Names of cartoon characters:] Olive Oyl, Castor Oyl, Cole Oyl, Nana Oyl. **1974** E. Thompson *Tattoo* 86: And what on earth are you going to do with all them nanas?

nance *n.* [fr. NANCY[1]] a weak-willed or effeminate fellow; SISSY; (*specif.*) an effeminate male homosexual.—also used fig.—usu. used derisively.—usu. considered offensive. Also as quasi-adj.

1910 *Variety* (Aug. 6) 13: It is not good policy to have the Salvationist [played as] a "nance." **1921** *Variety* (Sept. 30) 12: Timmey's gag was based on a kiss which he receives from an impulsive Frenchman. Casey ruled it out under his "nance" regulation. **1924** G. Henderson *Keys to Crookdom* 412: *Nance.* Effeminate fellow, sissy man. *Nance walk*—walk like a woman. **1926** Maines & Grant *Wise-Crack Dict.* 11: *Nance*—Sissy. **1927** *Vanity Fair* (Nov.) 134: A "nance" is an effeminate man. **1928** Barry *Holiday* III 485: She doesn't sail until midnight. "She"—a boat that size, "she"—the big nance. **1930** Lait *On Spot* 207: *Nance...Effeminate man...Fairy, pansy, faggot.* **1931** C. Ford *Coconut Oil* 49: "Lookit the pansy!" exclaims Ego, as he and several other porters drop their labors for the nance. **1935** Odets *Paradise Lost* 169: I'll take the head off his shoulders! You heard him call you a nance! **1935** Pollock *Und. Speaks: Nance*, a fairy, a male sexual pervert. **1938** "Justinian" *Amer. Sexualis* 29: *Nance.* n. An effeminated or homosexual male....C. 20. **1939** in W.C. Fields *By Himself* 335: O.K., you big nance. **1941** Schulberg *Sammy* 211: A famous poet and an aesthetic nance. **1942** P. Wylie *Vipers* 61: America is still populated largely with male ignoramuses who stand ready to slug nances on sight and often do so. **1950** *N.Y. Times* (Dec. 31) VI 27: The classiest dumps in prohibition were two rooms knocked together, with a nance and six girls who wore nothing. **1954** Collans & Sterling *House Detect.* 149: Right away I spotted the nances, they were dolled up like Lady Astor's horses. **1956** Levin *Compulsion* 50 [ref. to 1920's]: And we did not even have, then, the common words that today denote the homosexual; *pansy* and *fairy* and *nance* were unknown because the whole subject was somewhat legendary. **1957** E. Lacy *Room to Swing* 144: Maybe he gave me a real tumble, that's why I wasn't content with your nance pawing. **1958** T. Berger *Crazy in Berlin* 72: God damn him that nance. **1965** Capote *In Cold Blood* 372: He was crying, too. Jimmy said, "Get a load of that nance." **1971** (quot. at FRUITCAKE, 2). **1974** *Coq* (Apr.) 44: The nance sits down at his table and takes up where he left off on his Singapore Sling. **1977** *Nat. Lampoon* (July) 39: I did, you little nance. **1986** S. Bauer *Amazing Stories* 191: Shut up, you little nance.

nance *v.* to behave or speak in an effeminate manner.
   1968 Brasselle *Cannibals* 283: "Good Lord," he nanced, "is nothing safe?" **1970** E. Thompson *Garden of Sand* 377: He...nanced around in front of the guys. **1974** E. Thompson *Tattoo* 264: Yet there was nothing prissy or nancing about him.

Nancy¹ *n.* [fr. the female given name *Nancy*] (often *cap.*) a weak-willed, priggish, or effeminate fellow; SISSY; (*specif.*) an effeminate male homosexual.—usu. used derisively.—usu. considered offensive. Cf. earlier MISS NANCY.
   1888 in F. Russell *Blooming Grove* 77: Jimmy telling Georgie...what an "old Nancy" he is. **1893** W.K. Post *Harvard* 142: "Nancy" Digges, the quiet, shy, little pale-faced student who looked as if he would blow away in a strong wind. **1899** in J. Katz *Gay Amer. Hist.* 45: Q. Who did you convict? A. All the Nancys and fairies that were there....Degenerates. **1899** Hamblen *Bucko Mate* 81: Though a perfect gentleman, he was no "Nancy," and would have made a first class officer. **1902** in F & H. **1904** *Life in Sing Sing* 251: *Nancy.* An effeminate man. **1916** H. Cary *Venery* II 2: *Nancy*—A cock sucker. **1927** Kyne *They Also Serve* 53: I decided to find out whether or not your half the Nancy you look. **1934** (quot. at DICKY-LICKER). **1940** *Tale of a Twist* 80: "Toby's a nancy," Ruth said. "What?" "A lily, a pansy. A cocksucker." **1951** Sheldon *Troubling Star* 165: "Anybody plays a guitar's a goddamned nancy," said Lensky. **1955–57** Felder *Collegiate Slang* 3: *Nancy-pants*—a sissy. **1960** Bannon *Journey* 145: He was gay—did that make him swishy, too? A nancy? **1966** C. Ross *N.Y.* 74: A...nancy out on the flesh prowl.

Nancy² *n. Av.* the Curtiss NC seaplane.
   1919 *N.Y. World* (May 7). **1919** *Our Navy* (July) 45: While the "Nancys" were getting ready to leave Canada for the flight across the Atlantic, the British aviators who were also preparing for a flight across the pond announced that mid-Atlantic weather conditions forbade a start.

Nancy boy *n.* a sissy; NANCY¹.—usu. used derisively.—usu. considered offensive.
   [*1691 in *F & H* V 12: The pipe and flute are the new Alamode for the nan-boys.] *1958 in *OEDS*: I can't stand that Toto fellow. He's an open nancy-boy. **1986** Kubicki *Breaker Boys* 288: At lunch they called him "nancy boy" and spilled coal dust on his food. **1990** *Swamp Thing* (USA-TV): This stuff is for Nancy boys. **1996** *Simpsons Comics* (No. 21) (unp.): That silk-wearin' Nancy boy Skinner.

nanny¹ *n.* [orig. unkn.] *Und.* the head.
   1791 [W. Smith] *Confessions T. Mount* 18: Head, *nanny.*

nanny² *n.* NANCY¹. Cf. Early ModE *nan-boy* s.v. NANCY BOY.
   1947 in Kerouac *Letters* 127: One night I pulled...[my gun] out on a fag and told him I was "Nanny-Beater Kelly" from Chicago. **1995** *Jerry Springer Show* (synd. TV series): He's a nanny....[He acts] feminine.

¶ In phrase:

¶ **get (someone's) nanny** to *get (someone's) goat* s.v. GOAT.
   1909 in *DARE:* Fedink's speed got Bunk's nanny something awful. **1911** *N.Y. Eve. Jour.* (Jan. 4) 14: I'm certain that Jeanette got that fellow's nanny. **1915** Braley *Songs of Workaday World* 44: And there's no one's got his nanny,/'Cause he's always on the job. **1918** in Cowing *Folks at Home* 239: Not a great deal is to be feared from these defeated divisions, for the Marines have their "Nanny." **1918** *Chi. Sun Trib.* (Apr. 7) ("Comics") (unp.): No dod-gasted goat can get my nanny. **1918** *Stars & Stripes* (July 12) 7: That naturally got my nanny. **1919** Cortelyou *Arizona* 35: The sheep got our goats...and the goats got our "Nannys." **1919** T. Kelly *What Outfit?* 116: They guys ain't lettin' no *guerre* get their nannies. **1919** *Our Navy* (June) 19: You girls back home are worried, and it's easy to be seen/That the thing that has your "Nanny," is not the submarine. **1926** Wood & Goddard *Amer. Slang* 35: *Nanny, get one's.* To get one's goat. **1929** J. Tully *Shadows* 247: Don't let him tease you, Dippy....He's jist tryin' to git your nanny. **1969, 1989** in *DARE.*

Nantucket sleigh ride *n. Whaling.* an instance of the towing of a whaling boat by a harpooned whale. *Joc.* Now *hist.*
   *ca*1873 in W. Williams *One Whaling Family* 302: Before we could get into action, the whale started to run and we were off on a "Nantucket sleigh ride," but it was not very fast. *a*1889–91 *Century Dict.: Nantucket sleigh-ride*, the towing of a whale boat by the whale. **1928** Tilton *Cap'n George Fred* 61: If the whale runs the line will be held by a turn around the loggerhead so that the boat will have to be towed along behind him. This is what they call a "Nantucket sleigh ride," although the Lord only knows what Nantucket has to do with it any more than any other place. **1932** Grant *Greasy Luck* 74: A Nantucket sleighride...often took the boat miles beyond the horizon. **1939** O.B. Miller *Heroes, Outlaws* 33: Our friends...are surely gettin' took off on a jolly little Nantucket sleigh ride. **1956** Lockwood & Adamson *Zoomies* 84: This twentieth-century version of the old-time Nantucket Sleigh Ride. **1973** P. Benchley *Jaws* 99: They said they planned to hook the shark with the gaff and go for a "Nantucket sleigh ride." **1989** *TV Guide* (July 22) (Knoxville-Chattanooga ed.) 73: Observed: a harpooned sperm whale taking a boat for a "Nantucket sleigh ride" during a 1916 hunt. **1996** *Sea Classics* (Oct.) 47: Their first...high-speed "Nantucket Sleigh Ride."

Nap var. NAPTOWN.

nap *n.* [fr. the earlier sense 'the tightly curled hair of a black person'] *Black E.* a black person.—sometimes used disparagingly.
   1944 Wheeler *Steamboatin' Days* 33 [ref. to *ca*1900]: I know the white folks don't b'lieve all the things the Naps* b'lieve in, but this worl' is full uv meanness....*The darkie's own word for those of his race. It refers to "nappy haired" or the thick woolly hair of the Negro. **1954–60** *DAS: Nap* [derog.] A Negro.

nap *v.* to seize, apprehend (*obs.*), or steal; NAB. Now *colloq.* or *S.E.* [The second element in *kidnap*, this long-obsolete word has been revived in semi-joc. journalistic prose, usu. as a suffix.]
   *1673 R. Head *Canting Acad.* 41: *Napper of Naps*, a Sheep-stealer. *Ibid.* 42: *Nap*, To take, or cheat with the Dice, that is, by securing one chance. *1698–99 "B.E." *Dict. Canting Crew: Nap the Wiper,...*to Steal the Handkerchief. *1698–1706 in D'Urfey *Pills* IV 320: Tally-men...napp'd them in the Streets,/By dozens. *1789 G. Parker *Life's Painter* 136: I only napt a couple of...wipes. **1791** [W. Smith] *Confessions T. Mount* 21: A clout he'll nap unseen. **1807** Tufts *Autobiog.* 293 [ref. to 1794]: *Prad napping...*horse stealing. **1963** *Time* (May 3) 98: They charge that Eastern boxcar-napping has produced a shortage of cars for moving grain and lumber. **1978** *Business Week* (Jan. 30) 6: The napped dog is Vicky—perhaps the first miniature schnauzer to win a place in American fiction. **1979** *Pop. Science* (Jan. 1980) 111: The visible alarm key is, in itself, a deterrent to carnapping. **1983** *South Central Bell Notes* (Aug.) (unp.): If you have a Calling Card, take these steps to protect it from number-nappers. **1993** *New Yorker* (Apr. 19) 74: The burlesque of the monkey-napping had its serious side. It was PETA's first flirtation with the notion of an animal-rights underground.

¶ In phrase:

¶ **nap the** [or **(one's)] bib** Esp. *Und.* to weep.
   *1781 G. Parker *View of Society* I 219: Last of all [I] napp'd my bib. *1789 G. Parker *Life's Painter* 138: [She] naps the bib. **1791** [W. Smith]

Confessions T. Mount 19: *I'm napping my bib*, I'm crying. **1807** Tufts *Autobiog.* 293 [ref. to 1794]: *Napping his bib...crying.* *1812 Vaux *Vocab.*: *Nap the bib:* to cry; as, the *mollisher nap'd* her *bib*, the woman fell a crying. *1864 Hotten *Slang Dict.* (ed. 3): *Nap one's bib*, to cry, shed tears.

nape *n. Mil. Av.* napalm; *(hence)* a napalm bomb. Now *hist.* [Quots. ref. to Vietnam War.]
> **1968** in Tuso *Vietnam Blues* 208: 9 nasty napes. **1974** W. Stevens *More There I Was* 89: Reload the napes! **1983** *L.A. Times Bk. Rev.* (May 15) 4: Get in here with an airplane loaded with nape, CBU, and 20 mike-mike. **1984** Trotti *Phantom* 235: *Nape.* Napalm. **1985** Dye *Between Raindrops* 217: Napalm is next. Nape on the walls. **1987** Robbins *Ravens* 196: You have got to go on the ground and see if nape is dropped. **1990** Yarborough *Da Nang Diary* 110: Give me a pass with the nape for starters.

nape *v. Mil. Av.* to bomb with napalm. Now *hist.* [Quots. ref. to Vietnam War.]
> **1984** Ehrhart *Marking Time* 19: Bomb 'em and nape 'em and blow 'em up. **1989** W. McDonald *Band of Bros.* 49: We'll make a rocket pass first and nape 'em the second time around. **1990** Yarborough *Da Nang Diary* 120: We naped and strafed the...field. **1994** E. Roth *Forrest Gump* (film): They're gonna nape the whole area.

naphead var. NAPPY-HEAD.

Napolis *n. Local.* Indianapolis, Indiana. Cf. NAPTOWN.
> **1980** in Safire *Good Word* 247: 'Napolis.

napoo *adj.* [< F *il n'y a plus* 'there is no more'] Esp. *Mil.* finished; done for; gone. *Rare* in U.S.
> *1915 (quot. at NAPOO, *v.*). *1917 W. Lewis, in Materer *Pound/Lewis* 75: That...photo is napoo. **1917** Cushing *Surgeon's Jour.* 202: The front line is "na poo." **1918** McBride *Emma Gees* 71: Needless to say, that rat was "na-poo," which is soldier-French meaning "finis." *1918 *Bodleian Qly. Rec.* II 124: *Napoo* (Il n'y a plus), 1. No more. 2. No. 3. "He's napoo," i.e. killed. **1920** Jacobson *107th Inf.* 368: If "Jerry" had succeeded in laying an egg in that field, the 54th Brigade would have been "na poo." **1940** E. Pound, in Ahearn *Pound/Zukofsky* 200: Its finish', na poo, its over, damn you.

napoo *v.* to finish off; kill. [The 1847–49 quot. at NEPO, though superficially similar, seems unlikely to be related to this term.]
> *1915 in *OEDS:* You say "Na pooh!" when you push your plate away after dinner....*"Poor Bill got na-poohed by a rifle-grenade yesterday."* **1918** McBride *Emma Gees* 129: After about a dozen direct hits they were pretty well satisfied that they have either driven us out or "na-pooed" us.

napper *n.* the head. *Rare* in U.S.
> *1724 (cited in Partridge *Dict. Und.* 463). *1785 Grose *Dict. Vulgar Tongue: Napper:* The head. **1859** *Spirit of Times* (Apr. 9) 104: Having lit...upon his "napper." *1959 in *ODMS* 147: If anyone ever asked for an orangeade bottle on his napper, Fruity did.

nappy *adj. Stu.* disgusting.
> [**1956** in *DAS:* To call a man *nappy* is to say his hair is kinky—a real insult.] **1983** *U.S. News & W.R.* (Aug. 1) 4: A new "teenspeak"...is beginning to be heard....In Atlanta, it's "nappy" for disgusting and "That's wicked" for cool or neat. **1990** P. Munro *Slang U.* 136: *Nappy...*Dirty, messy, neglected....Eeeewhh, Kelly's panties are nappy.

nappy-head *n. Black E.* an unsophisticated black person.—used derisively. Also **naphead.**
> **1943** in *DARE:* You sure a passel of nappy haids. **1959** A. Anderson *Lover Man* 101: You old nappy head. **1973** in *DARE:* All them ol' nappy-heads runnin' up there tryin' to pull his clothes off. **1974** S. Stevens *Rat Pack* 144: You funky naphead! I tell you I seen 'em.

Naps *n.pl. Baseball Journ.* the Cleveland Indians. Now *hist.*
> *a*1959 Danzig & Reichler *History of Baseball* 65 [ref. to *ca*1910]: Addie Joss of the Cleveland Naps. **1993** Fountain *Sportswriter* 78 [ref. to *a*1914]: When the writers felt a need to apply a nickname [to the Cleveland baseball club] they most commonly referred to the team as the "Naps," after player-manager Napoleon Lajoie.

Naptown *n. Local.* Indianapolis, Indiana; *(also)* Annapolis, Maryland. *Joc.* Also **Nap.**
> **1929** in Leadbitter & Slaven *Blues Records* 89: Naptown Stomp. **1961** in Leadbitter & Slaven *Blues Records* 106: Naptown Boogie. **1962–68** B. Jackson *In the Life* 180: They got lucky on a deal like that here in Naptown (Annapolis). **1971** Giovanni *Gemini* 137: I had spent the weekend in Nap. *Ibid.:* Indianapolis...was referred to by us as Naptown. **1982** P. Fussell, in *Harper's* (Aug.) 55: "Naptown" is what many locals call Indianapolis, and it does seem a somnolent place. **1987** WUOT radio (Knoxville, Tenn.) (Aug. 17): There were a lot of people who used to think Indianapolis was Naptown.

narc *n.* **1.** Orig. *Narc.* a narcotics detective. Also **nark.**
> **1967** *Zap Comix* (Oct.) 16: The narks were looking for Teen-Age Ric. **1967** *Everett* (Wash.) *Herald* (Nov. 28) 1D: The first buy I made, the peddler said "hey, man, are you a narc?" (federal agent). **1967** J.B. Williams *Narc. & Hallucin.* 114: *Narc*—Narcotics officer. **1967** in H.S. Thompson *Shark Hunt* 447: To refuse a proferred "joint" is to risk being labeled a "nark"—narcotics agent—a threat and a menace to practically everybody. **1968** Gover *JC* 137: Tole me he dream the narks come in an bust him for possessin [sic]. **1969** *Playboy* (Dec.) 289: The narcs are over there. **1970** *Evergreen Review* XIV (Apr.): Nothing would ever beat him, no cops, no narcs, and no jails. So he thought. **1976** *Harper's* (Jan. 1977) 75: All the odious army of narks has ever done is drive prices up, subsidize the world black market, and tighten the street pusher's cruel monopoly. **1981** O'Day & Eells *High Times* 176: The narcs nabbed him. **1988** *Newsweek* (Apr. 25) 65: Come to think of it, maybe I'd be a good narc.

2. *Police.* duty in a police narcotics division.
> **1976** "N. Ross" *Policeman* 46: Finally working narc, and I'm stuck with a square.

3. see NARK, 1 and 2.

narco *n.* **1.** narcotics.
> **1954** in J. Blake *Joint* 59: They brought him in...a wild-eyed savage hurling accusations of homosexual orgies spiced with all manner of narco. **1964** Harris *Junkie Priest* 29: The narco cops are on the street. **1976** "N. Ross" *Policeman* 46: John O'Banion could have been the greatest narco dick in the world. **1989** *This Week with D. Brinkley* (ABC-TV) (Mar. 19): The law enforcement and judiciary [in Colombia] has been neutralized by narco traffic and killings. **1995** L.A. policeman, on *Cops* (Fox-TV): A narco suspect.

2. *Police.* **a.** a narcotics detective. Cf. NARC.
> **1955** (cited in *W10*). **1960** J. Ciardi, in *DAS* (ed. 2): The Beat Generation has marijuana and the ritual of dodging the "narcos"—the narcotics squad. **1962** Larner & Tefferteller *Addict in Street* 241: Four narcos—four narcotic squad men from downtown. **1966** Goldstein *1 in 7* 117: The FBI is around—everyone knows it, and everyone knows how to spot a narco. **1966** J. Mills *Needle Park* 13: His adversaries in this continual quest are always the police: the "narcos," "The Man." **1967** *Esquire* (Sept.) 101: Just out of the clutches of the local narcos. **1971** Contini *Beast Within* 85: The narcos caught on. **1971** Woodley *Dealer* 86: They've got two hundred new narcos out there. **1976** C. Keane *Hunter* 130: The Federal narcos been working on the thing for months. **1976** Chinn *Dig Nigger Up* 212: These detectives weren't narcos. **1977** T. Berger *Villanova* 202: The limelight plays on the narcos. **1980** D. Hamill *Stomping Ground* 67: Friedman and Nelson, the two narcos. **1982–84** Chapple *Outlaws in Babylon* 22: These guys, these narcos.

b. a police narcotics division.
> **1961** in *OEDS:* Narco, the, federal narcotics agents. **1963** Braly *Shake Him* 24: He found himself remembering the last time the Narco had picked him up. **1971** B.B. Johnson *Blues for Sister* 24: Your boy...has asked to work with narco on this one. **1973** "A.C. Clark" *Crime Partners* 98: How about your buddy over in narco? **1980** Grosso & Rosenberg *Point Blank* 218: In all his years in Narco he had never flaked a guy.

3. *Und.* a narcotics addict; *(also)* a narcotics dealer.
> **1958** in *OEDS:* This informant is a thief, a narco, or a four-bottle bum. **1965** *N.Y. Times* (May 9) VI 93: Chuck has never been on drugs...but he came to believe that "narcos" probably knew more about their illness than the Establishment. **1978** Cleaver *Soul on Fire* 72: I definitely did not want the label of being a narco. **1988** *Fortune* (June 20) 29: The narcos are a small group here.

nard *n.* **1.** [perh. alter. NERD] *Stu.* an obnoxious person.
> **1962** in *AS* (Oct. 1963) 172: A male student who never engaged in social activities...gnard. **1964** *AS* (May) 117: *Nard* "a socially unacceptable person" (the term possibly is confined to the Midwest).

2. *Stu.* **a.** [var. of NAD] usu. *pl.* a testicle.
> **1968–70** *Current Slang III & IV* 85: *Nard*, n. Testicle.—New Mexico State. **1990** T. Thorne *Dict. Contemp. Slang: Nards...American* testicles. **1993** P. Munro *U.C.L.A. Slang II* 61: *Nards...*testicles.

b. usu. *pl.* (see quot.).

1993 P. Munro *U.C.L.A. Slang II* 61: *Nards…breasts.*

nark *n.* **1.** *Und.* a police informer; stool pigeon. Also **narc.** Cf. NARC, 1.

    *1859 "Ducange Anglicus" *Vulgar Tongue* (ed. 2): *Nark.* A person who obtains information under seal of confidence, and afterwards breaks faith. ***1860** Hotten *Slang Dict.* (ed. 2): *Nark…*A common informer. ***1879** *Macmillan's Mag.* (Oct.) 505: He had a nark (a policeman's spy) with him. ***1889–90** Barrère & Leland *Dict. Slang II* 82: *Nark…*a man or woman who is a police spy upon his comrades or class.…This seems to have some connection with the Dutch *narruken*, to follow about, spy. ***1898** in *F & H* V 16: The narks may light upon that swag even yet. **1924** Garahan *Stiffs* 13: *Nark.—*An informer. **1928** (quot. at SLIM). **1931–34** in Clemmer *Pris. Community* 334: *Nark,* n. A stool pigeon for the police. **1944** in *DAS:* Information about known gamblers, little bookmakers, and their narks. **1958** S.H. Adams *Tenderloin* 305 [ref. to 1890's]: The official thought uncomfortably of some of the regular police narks. **1971** *Everett* (Wash.) *Herald* (July 23) 1A: Students commonly call any person, paid or not, a Narc if he informs the police of narcotics sales and purchases. **1976** M. Calhoun *Med. Show* 50 [ref. to ca1900]: Calling police informers "narks" and referring to writing a letter as "flying a kite."

2. *Juve.* a tattletale. Also **narc.**

    1976 Knapp & Knapp *One Potato* 61: "Tattletale narc!"…"Nark" is venerable British slang for informer. American children once associated the term specifically with "narcotics agent" but have now generalized it to refer, once again, to any informer. **1978** *N.Y. Times Mag.* (July 23) 22: An old slang term, narc, has been revived for *tattletale.* **1987** Univ. Tenn. student theme: A *nark…*is always the one who tells on other students. **1993** P. Munro *U.C.L.A. Slang II* 61: *Narc…*person who exposes his or her peers' secrets or actions.

nark *v.* [ult. fr. NARK, *n.*, 1, but decisively infl. in AmE by NARC] to inform (upon); SNITCH.

    1969 L. Sanders *Anderson Tapes* 106: A peter keeps another peter on the string by saying he will nark on him.…Extortion. **1974** Eble *Campus Slang* (Oct.) 3: He narked on one of my roommate's friends. **1977** *L.A. Times Bk. Rev.* (Sept. 18) 12: He went to jail…because he would not nark to the House Un-American Activities Committee. **1979** Alibrandi *Custody* 289: "You'll have to call your probation officer and let him know you didn't keep your appointment.".…"Sure. Call the pig and narc on myself." **1980** Pearl *Pop. Slang* 105: *Narc…v.* to inform. **1980** *Residence Hall Companion* 3: I came up with a plan.…I narked to the strictest RA in the dorm.…The RA never told Tina who had narked, and she suspected it was this other woman down the hall who didn't like her. **1981** Univ. Tenn. student theme: Mike started with harassment at school and threats of beating me up if I "narked" on him. **1986** N. Jimenez *River's Edge* (film): Somebody fuckin' narked. **1987** *TV Guide* (Oct. 24) 22: Friends don't nark on friends—even when one commits murder in this controversial suspenser. **1989** *21 Jump St.* (Fox-TV): Somebody *narked!*

narly see s.v. GNARLY, 2.

narrow-assed *adj.* having slim hips; skinny.—usu. considered vulgar.

    1916–22 H. Cary *Sexual Vocab.* III s.v. *human body: Narrow-arsed.* Said of a thin woman. **1964** H. Rhodes *Chosen Few* 133: His narrow-ass deputy and a coupla white MP's. **1964–66** R. Stone *Hall of Mirrors* 24: He was slim and narrow-assed.

narrowback *n.* an Irish-American.—used contemptuously.

    1957 in *OEDS:* William Joseph Patrick (Pat) O'Brien, a Milwaukee-born Irishman or narrowback. **1963** B. Behan *N.Y.* 54: "What do you call us?" "You're an Irish-American." "Yeh, I know, but amongst yourselves, what do you call us?" "Narrowbacks." **1958–65** Alfred *Hogan's Goat* 114: You, you narrow-back plug. **1973** Flaherty *Chez Joey* xiv [ref. to 1940's]: Their Yankee-born sons ("narrowbacks" we were scornfully called) would follow in their fathers' steps. **1976** Berry *Kaiser* 309 [ref. to 1918]: The 69th, you see, was quite a thing to the Irish kids, narrow backs and greenhorns alike. **1983** Flaherty *Tin Wife* 43: Narrowback (Nellie loved the pejorative for Irish-Americans) blarney at that.

narrow gauge *n.* USMC. (see quot.).

    1922 *Leatherneck* (Apr. 29) 5: *Narrow Gauge—*A corporal.

nasty *n.* **1.** sexual intercourse. See also *do the nasty,* below.

    1934 "J.M. Hall" *Anecdota* 61: How about a bit of nasty, baby? **1967–80** Folb *Runnin' Lines* 247: *Nasty, the* Sexual intercourse. **1994**

Wild Oats (Fox-TV): Horny losers chummin' for nasty! **1997** *Mystery Sci. Theater* (Sci-Fi Channel): Go get yourself some nasty.

2. an unpleasant or dangerous person or thing; villain.

    1968 in *BDNE* 309: *Nasties…*persons with hateful, mean, offensive characters. **1978** *Runner's Almanac* 21: There are nasties out there, waiting to snare defenseless joggers. Bob Glover…offers these suggestions to runners who may be concerned about muggers and the like. **1980** W.C. Anderson *Bat-21* 161: The nastys decided on a quick, massive attack to crush the South Vietnamese. **1981** *L.A. Times Bk. Rev.* (Feb. 22) 8: Such basic nasties as looted luggage, cheating cabin attendants, pirate cab drivers. **1983** *Mother Jones* (Apr.) 15 (ad): No sugars of any kind are added, no hydrogenated fats, no preservatives or "nasties" disguised under other names. **1984** *N.Y. Post* (Aug. 16) 29: Now here she is…racing through the jungle being menaced by modern nasties. *a***1990** Poyer *Gulf* 205: The list of nasties here was longer than in Lake Champlain. Sea snakes, scorpion fish, sharks. *a***1990** R. Herman, Jr. *Force of Eagles* 125: Any more nasties up your sleeve?

¶ In phrases:

¶ **do nasty** *Black E.* to treat badly or unfairly.

    1969 in I. Reed *Conjure* 79: Dese are d reasons u did me nasty.

¶ **do the nasty** Esp. *Black E.* to copulate.

    [**1929–31** J.T. Farrell *Young Lonigan* 63: Don't do anything naughty-nasty…like tickling the girlies.] **1977** *Nat. Lampoon* (July) 27: I'd like to make her do a [*sic*] nasty on the White House lawn. *a***1982** Naylor *Women of Brewster Place* 109: Cora Lee had been doing nasty with the Murphy boy behind the basement steps. **1983** Eilert *Self & Country* 218 [ref. to 1968]: They were just about to do the *big nasty.* **1989** *Dream Street* (NBC-TV): You only do that when you've been up all night doin' the nasty. **1990** *In Living Color* (Fox-TV): My loins are ready to explode. I want to do the nasty! **1991** M. Rich *Straight Out of Bklyn.* (film): I know what you was doin'. You was doin' the nasty. **1992** *Donahue* (NBC-TV): Did you want to do the nasty, or what? **1993** *Martin* (Fox-TV): You won't be doin' the nasty until you get married, am I right? **1994** O'Leary *Univ. Delaware Sl.* 2: *Nasty, do the* 'have sex.' **1995** *Newsweek* (Dec. 25) 88: I ought to slap you silly for doin' the nasty with my wife's transvestite love slave!

nasty *adj.* first-class, esp. in respect of attractiveness or effectiveness; WICKED; MEAN.

    1834 in *DAE:* "Sling a nasty foot" means to dance exceedingly well.…"She is a nasty looking gal" implies she is a splendid woman. **1839** Marryatt *Diary* 267: In Kentucky…sometimes the word *nasty* is used for *nice.*…"That's my sister stranger; and I flatter myself that she shows the *nastiest* ankle in all Kentuck".…A good shot or a pretty shot is termed also a nasty shot, because it would make a *nasty* wound. **1896** Ade *Artie* 63: They've put up a new guy against him and he's makin' a nasty fight. **1911–12** J. London *Smoke Bellew* 96: We got it!…Look at it! A nasty mess of gold. Two hundred right there if it's a cent. **1920–21** Witwer *Leather Pushers* 37: That last baby…shook a nasty pair of dice! *Ibid.* 43: He swings a nasty right. **1940** in R.S. Gold *Jazz Talk* 187: Very fast semi-boogie blues…with nasty, heavy off-beat drumming. **1954–60** *DAS: Nasty…*Excellent, "wicked"; "mean."…*Jive use c*1935. **1955** Shapiro & Hentoff *Hear Me Talkin to Ya* 295: Listening to Lincoln's nasty beat. **1982** *N.Y. Post* (Sept. 4) 44: Ilie still swings a nasty racquet. **1985** Eble *Campus Slang* (Apr.) 6: *Nasty—*good. **1986** *Life* (Mar.) 46: "Nasty" (meaning wickedly good). **1986** Merkin *Zombie Jamboree* 16: Why don't you get yourself somethin' nasty in Italian shoes? **1990** P. Munro *Slang U.* 136: *Nasty…*gorgeous, sexually attractive. **1991** *Houston Chronicle* (Nov. 13) 5D: *Nasty:* sexy. **1996** M. Kearney *Southeastern La. Univ. Coll.* (May): *Nasty—*used to describe someone good looking. "That guy is nasty."

nastygram *n.* [*nasty* + tele*gram*] Esp. *Mil.* a written reprimand or record of misconduct; (*hence*) an unpleasant written notice.

    1966–67 F. Harvey *Air War* 6: If he has to send a "nastygram"—a curt reprimand—to anybody, on deck or aloft, he doesn't hesitate. **1971** Murphy & Gentry *Second in Command* 75: Bucher had a habit of writing "nastygrams," reminders of incidents that he wanted to recall when he made his next fitness reports. **1980** *New West* (July 28) 72: A nastygram from the Citadel's commandant to Fraser's father notifying the elder Fraser of his son's suspension for AWOL. **1988** Poyer *The Med* 167: They had to be filled out by the book or you got a nastygram from the computer. **1995** Univ. Tenn. librarian, age ca27: Did you get a nastygram [*i.e.,* overdue notice]?

natch *n.* ¶ In phrase: **on the natch** *Narc.* free of drugs.

   1969 Lingeman *Drugs A to Z* 181: *Natch, on the....*not using drugs; leading a natural life as opposed to a life centered around chemicals. **1973** *Drug Forum* II 139: An almost invariable return to "sex on the natch" (natural) is described. **1978** Selby *Requiem* 62: You have enough dexies to keep us goin? You know we aint about to make it on the natch. **1996** McCumber *Playing Off Rail* 46: His father [was] certain that he was on drugs. "Honest to God, I was on the natch the whole time—I wasn't even drinking."

natch *interj.* naturally! of course!

   1945 (cited in *OEDS*). **1946** Boulware *Jive & Slang* 5: *Nach...*Naturally. **1947** Spillane *I, the Jury* 21: Natch. What else? **1948** Mencken *Amer. Lang. Supp.* II 708: During the middle 1940s there was a rage for abbreviations, *e.g., natch* (naturally) and *def* (definitely), but...the trade journal of the publishers of Webster 1934...was reporting by March, 1947, that they were already "as passé as a yearling egg." **1949** Loos & Sales *Mother Is a Freshman* (film): Natch. You're scared spitless. **1950** *Sat. Eve. Post* (Apr. 22) 104: "Let me know, won't you?" She smiled. "Natch." **1951–52** P. Frank *Hold Back Night* 85: "It is an entirely different matter." "Natch." **1953** R. Chandler *Long Goodbye* 32: But we got to ask, natch. **1956** in Spectorsky *College Yrs.* 265: Natch, this is a d'mocracy. **1963** *New Yorker* (Nov. 16) 120: The program took a header into the race problem—natch—and came up with...a strong, angry piece. **1970** *Playboy* (Aug.) 160: Natch. **1976** Rosten *To Anywhere* 15: It's too goddamn hot....Natch! **1979** *St. Louis Post-Dispatch* (Nov. 4) 5C: A couple of monumental logos on the walls (the text in lower case, natch). **1984** *California* (Feb.) 145: "You have to go fast before you can do jumps." Natch. **1992** *N.Y. Observer* (Aug. 10) 5: She certainly didn't look homeless. She was tall and, natch, had salt-and-pepper hair. **1996** *Reader's Digest* (June) 155: A Montana stockbroker got a bear [tooled] on one boot and a bull on the other—in actual bearskin and bullhide, natch.

native dictionary see SLEEPING DICTIONARY.

native son *n.* **1.** Orig. *Calif.* a white man who is a native of California.

   1910 *N.Y. Eve. Jour.* (Feb. 8) 12: Many "native sons" remember what Choynski did to that other Pride of the Coast—"Big Joe" McAuliffe. **1918** (quot. at (2), below). **1942** (quot. at MUCKSTICK). *a***1968** in Longstreet *Wilder Shore* 48: The miners came in forty-nine,/The whores in fifty-one;/And when they got together/They produced the Native Son.

   2. *Army.* a prune. *Joc.*

   1918 F. Gibbons *Thought We Wouldn't Fight* 229: The simple prune, which the army used to call "native son" by reason of its California origin. **1923** McKnight *English Words* 55 [ref. to 1918]: *Native sons* for "prunes"; *spuds* for potatoes.

Nats *n.pl. Baseball. Journ.* the Washington Nationals or Senators. Now *hist.*

   1951 Jacobellis *Sports Photo Bk.* 46: Washington Senators. Irv Noren...[is] a great prospect for the Nats. **1971** *Black Scholar* (Nov.) 11: Just One of Nats Many Headaches. **1989** P. Dickson *Baseball Dict.*: *Nats* Nickname for the Washington Senators, especially during the years (1939–1957) when the team was known as the Nationals.

natty *adj.* [perh. var. of (poorly attested) 16th-C. *netty* in a similar sense] fashionable; spruce. Now *S.E.* Also as adv.

   1785 Grose *Dict. Vulgar Tongue: Natty lads.* Young thieves or pickpockets. *Cant.* **1789** G. Parker *Life's Painter* 136: Like *natty...kiddies. Ibid.* 158: Dresses smart, or what they term *natty.* **1806** in Partridge *DSUE*: A natty spark of eighteen. **1820–21** P. Egan *Life in London* 58: This expression is frequently made use of by *natty* coachmen. *Ibid.* 122: His *natty* gig and prime trotter. **1827** *Harvard Register* (Oct.) 247: Rattling in a *natty* gig. **1836** (quot. at HEAVY SWELL). **1859** Matsell *Vocab.* 59: *Natty kids.* Young thieves; smart, well-dressed youngsters. **1910** in *DAS*: A natty raincoat. **1942** in *DAS*: A natty convertible. **1969** B. Beckham *Main Mother* 29: A very natty dresser.

natural *n.* **1.a.** a person having natural talent; one especially well suited for or likely to succeed in a particular endeavor. Now *S.E.*

   1749 in Breslaw *Tues. Club* 141: We look upon the one to be a *Natural...*in vocal music, that is to Say...by nature furnished with those gifts that are requisite to form a good singer. **1930** Pasley *Capone* 231: He was rated "a natural" with a Thompson sub-machine-gun. **1935** A.G. Kennedy *Current Eng.* 557: A *natural* ("one who excels in some-

thing because of unusual native ability"). **1936** C. Mack, in Paxton *Sport U.S.A.* 7: Some of them—the "naturals"—couldn't be bothered. A natural hitter didn't care [what a pitcher threw]. **1949** Davies *Happens Every Spring* (film): But the boy's a natural, Jimmy. **1950** A. Lomax *Mr. Jelly Roll* 94: Jelly Roll, too, was such a "natural."

   b. *Gamb.* a winning combination in various gambling games, now esp. in craps. Now *S.E.*

   1762 in *OEDS*: He had something in his face gave me as much pleasure as a pair-royal of naturals in my own hand. **1912** T.A. Dorgan, in Zwilling *TAD Lexicon* 59: They were playing "twenty one"...The banker drew a "natural" and the mob signed their checks. **1931** (cited in Partridge *Dict. Und.* 464). **1926–35** Watters & Hopkins *Burlesque* 18: They's nothin' but naturals in that snap. **1952** *Sat. Eve. Post* (Sept. 20) 111: Mac mentioned four-letter words and throwing naturals in a tone of familiarity. That worries me. **1962** in *OEDS*: The dice bounced to a natural.

   c. something that is sure to succeed; winner.

   1920 in De Beck *Google* 93: Jim's a good scout. He's always there with a natural [*sc.,* a loan]. **1935** Pollock *Und. Speaks*: *A natural*, easy of accomplishment, a logical proposition. **1935** H. Gray *Arf!* (July 20) (unp.): Why, this is a natural—It's sure fire—It can't miss. **1942** Schnitzer *Bowery at Midnight* (film): We cover Frankie's getaway from here. It's a natural. **1949** in *DAS*: A novel which looks like a natural for Lassie. **1954** Lindner *50-Min. Hr.* 1: The case had made headlines for many days; it was composed of elements that were "naturals" for arousing public interest.

   2.a. [short for phr. *natural life*] one's life.

   1893 in *OEDS*: *In my natural*, phrase for "in my life", "at any time." **1894** in Ade *Chicago Stories* 38: You can bet y'r natural that's the size of it. **1898–1900** Cullen *Chances* 38: "Not on your natural," said he. **1903** Ade *Society* 6: All he had to do for the remainder of his Natural was to clip the Coupons every Six Months. **1910** *N.Y. Eve. Jour.* (Jan. 8): What? A pointer for President Lynch, did I hear someone remark? Not on your natural. **1951** Leveridge *Walk on Water* 168: KP for Koonce for the rest of his natural.

   b. [short for phr. *natural(-born) self*] *Black E.* one's self.

   1971 *Who Took Weight?* 33: He likes to see you being your natural?

   3. *Pris.* **a.** [sugg. by *natural* 'a throw of seven (in craps)'] a seven-year prison sentence.

   1930 Lait *On Spot* 207: Natural...A seven-year sentence. **1942** *N.Y. Times Mag.* (Jan. 25) 30: *Natural*—sentence of seven years in jail.

   b. a life sentence.

   1930 in Grayson *Stories for Men* 139: The Commonwealth sent him to Graymoor for a "natural"—for life.

natural-born *adj.* Esp. *Black E.* by nature; absolute; thoroughgoing; (occ. used for emphasis).

   1915 in N.I. White *Amer. Negro Folk-Songs* 137: It ain't no lie, it's a natural born fact. **1949** *N.Y. Times* (Nov. 27) I 106: A true, natural-born "night owl," he is unhappy if there is not a gay crowd dancing and drinking until the small hours every night. **1963** *Sat. Eve. Post* (Mar. 23) 35: "That's a natural-born fact," said Truman. **1965** C. Brown *Manchild* 42: I was gonna break his natural-born ass. **1972** C. Major *Dict. Afro-Amer. Sl.* 84: A natural-born freak. **1994** O. Stone *Natural Born Killers* [film title].

nature boy *n.* a naive, innocent man or boy.—used ironically.

   1948 E. Ahbez *Nature Boy* (pop. song title). **1949** Warner Bros. *Looney Tunes* (animation): Now look, nature boy, don't gimme no trouble. *Ibid.*: How naive nature boy can you get? **1954–60** *DAS*: *Nature Boy* 1. A virile man...2. A man or youth who needs a haircut....*From the title of the c1949 pop. song.* **1969** M. Richie, in *New Amer. Rev.* (No. 6) (Apr.) 64: Himself he called Nature Boy...since he decided he was right not to like Manhattan. **1992** *Vanity Fair* (Mar.) 114: He has brought along a plastic tub of guacamole and a bag of chips, which he is scooping into his mouth between brushstrokes. He wipes his hands on his jeans before he smears the pastels across the page. He is, at this moment, perfectly content. "Nature boy," Peter Eisenman calls him. **1992** *New Republic* (June 8) 36: This wilderness reflection is really McKibben's personal odyssey, his spiritual greening from boy wonder to barefoot nature boy. **1995** *Hercules* (synd. TV series): Go on, nature boy.

nautch *n.* a brothel. Hence **nautch broad** a prostitute working in a brothel. Also **nautch house, nautch joint, nautchery.** Cf. NOTCH, *n.,* 2 and NOTCH HOUSE.

   1872 in Miller & Snell *Why West Was Wild* 633: She...resumed her occupation as Madam of the "*nauch*." **1929** Hotstetter & Beesley *Racket* 232: *Nautch house*— Establishment, either apartment, home, or hotel, where professional or clandestine prostitutes or immoral women live or can be met. **1935** Pollock *Und. Speaks*: *Nautch joint*, a house of ill fame. **1939** N. West *Locust* 276: Nautch joints are depressing. **1940** in W.C. Fields *By Himself* 378: The staid "Los Angeles Times" [is] advertising asserted and purported nautch joints. **1942–49** Goldin et al. *DAUL: Nautch-broad*. A prostitute working in a brothel, not soliciting on streets. *Nautchery*. A brothel.

nav *n. Av.* a navigator; (*also*) navigation.—also used attrib. Also as quasi-adj.
    1956 *Pop. Science* (Jan. 1957) 101: Half a mile is usually nothing at all at the end of a nav run. **1972** Carpentier *Flt. One* 74: The mission, the weather, the nav poop. **1980** W.C. Anderson *Bat-21* 38: He's the nav who was shot down. **1987** Zeybel *Gunship* 21: Major Dick Kaulbach…was our table nav. *a*1991 Kross *Splash One* 130: You're the first "nav" I've seen here.

Navvy *n. SW.* a Navaho; (*hence*) a Navaho pony.
    1910 Z. Grey *Heritage of Desert* 8: Seen any Navvies? **1936** R. Adams *Cowboy Lingo* 86: The "navvy" was a Navajo Indian pony, said to be about the poorest specimen of horse-flesh on earth. **1957** Bean *Fancher Train* 28: The Navvies are damn smart when it comes to breedin'. **1971** Terrell *Bunkhouse Papers* 184: They're a no-good bunch of Navvies up around there. **1979–81** C. Buckley *To Bamboola* 112: She got used to the Navvies and they liked her.

navvy *n.* [*navigator* + *-y* dimin. suff.] an unskilled manual laborer. Now *S.E. Rare* in U.S.
    *1832–34 T. DeQuincey, in *OED*: If navvies had been wanted in those days. *1863 in *F & H* V 21: It was proved that one English navvy would do as much work as two French labourers. **1934** O'Hara *Appt. in Samarra* ch. ii: His father worked on a navvy gang. **1949** *Sat. Eve. Post* (June 4) 23: Foreign navvies don't know one foot from the other or their command of English is regrettably deficient. **1952** *Harper's* (June) 76: She…planted the child on the ground as a navvy might ram a pavement, with ferocity rather than indignation.

navy *n.* [*navy, navy plug*, a kind of tobacco associated with sailors] *Hobo.* scavenged cigarette or cigar butts. *Joc.*
    *ca*1905–26 in *AS* I (1926) 652: *Navy*. Cigar end [*sic*] or "butts" found on sidewalk. **1930** "D. Stiff" *Milk & Honey* 214: *Snipe* or *navy*— Butts of cigarettes and cigars.

Navy junior *n. Mil.* a naval officer's child.
    1934 *U.S. Naval Inst. Proc.* (Sept.) 1236: A "navy junior," he had entered the U.S. Navy as a midshipman in 1841. **1935** Lorimer & Lorimer *Heart Specialist* 175: Officers' children are Navy Juniors. **1956** Wier & Hickey *Navy Wife* 105: *Navy junior*. Child of a naval officer. **1967** Dibner *Admiral* 162: My heavens, I dated dozens of Navy juniors. **1971** Murphy & Gentry *2d in Command* 55: Although a Navy junior—he was the son of a chief petty officer—he seemed to know almost nothing about shipboard procedures.

navy sherry *n. Navy.* grog. *Joc.* Also **navy claret.**
    1863 S. Boyer *Naval Surgeon* I 164: He in return drank some "Navy claret" which we happened to bring with us. *a*1890–1902 *F & H* V 21: *Navy-Sherry*, subs. (American) Man-of-war grog.

naybo *interj.* [perh. *nay* + BO¹] *Black E.* no. Also **nayboo, nayo.**
    1938 *Variety* (June 22) 36: Hepster's Dictionary…*Neigho pops*— Nothing doing man! **1944** D. Burley *Hndbk. Jive* 144: *Neighbo Pops*— That's out, Chum, no chance. **1947** *Time* (Feb. 10) 12: *Nayo boss*— no, buddy, that's wrong. **1954–60** *DAS: Neighbo*… No; don't; I disagree. *Negro use.* **1986** *Cosby Show* (NBC-TV): Nayboo! Nayboo!

nay-nay *n.* usu. *pl.* [perh. imit. of baby talk] a woman's breast.
    1989 *Maledicta* X 52: Bazooms…nay-nays. **1994** *Married with Children* (Fox-TV): The Boston Bazooms and the St. Louis Nay-nays.

N.B.G. *adj. & interj. Mil.* "no bloody good."
    *1919 *Athenaeum* (Aug. 8) 729 [ref. to WWI]: "N.B.G."…in many units…was used for the opposite of "O.K."; the full form was, of course, "No b—y good." **1947** *AS* (Apr.) XXII 111 [ref. to WWII]: Though most [U.S.] personnel employ profanity freely, some prefer softer expressions like *N.B.G.*

N.C. *interj.* [abbr. joc. missp. *nuff ced*] enough said. Cf. N.S.
    1859 in Huntington *Songs Whalemen Sang* 8: Keep it furled N.C. nuff said. **1891** Maitland *Slang Dict.* 186: *N.C.*, "nuff ced," phonetic equivalent for "enough said." *a*1890–1902 *F & H* V 22: N.C. *phr.* (common)—"Enough said" (nuf ced).

near and far *n.* [rhyming slang] a bar.
    *1909 (cited in Partridge *DSUE* 554). **1920** T.A. Dorgan, in Zwilling *TAD Lexicon* 59: You pipe the cowboy at the near and far (bar) lifting his lip over a rye. **1928** Sharpe *Chicago May* 288: *Near and far*—bar.

neat *adj.* delightful; fine; (*hence*) (with heightened force) splendid; excellent; (*hence*) attractive. Also as interj. [Having generalized from *OED* defs. 5, 6, 7, and 8, pre-20th C. quots. appear to be primarily Hiberno-E and colloq.; the nuance "attractive" may not antedate the 1920's. The word has been notably associated with youthful speech since *ca*1930.]
    *1808 J.N. Barker *Indian Princess* I ii: "But arrah, take something for remembrance," said they; and then I dug up this neat jewel [*Shows a potato.*]. *1821 *Real Life in Ireland* 35: They are a nate pair of jockeys. *1827 in *OED*: So much for my new find! Is he not a neat one? **1833** J. Neal *Down-Easters* I 73: That's a plaguy neat lookin' watch o' yourn. **1834** Caruthers *Kentuck. in N.Y.* I 61: That's what I call a pretty neat job, to shirt a stranger the first night he comes to town. **1862** in F. Moore *Rebel. Rec.* V P37: Och! it is nate to be captain or colonel,/Divil a bit would I want to be higher. **1868** Macy *There She Blows!* 77: I wish the ould man would jist ask me to take a dhrop wid him.…Of course, I'd refuse; but then, 'twould be doin' the nate thing on his part. **1870** Medbery *Wall St.* 124: The stocks jumps up…thirty per cent.… "That is a neat figure for Northwest. You'd better sell." [**1882** Peck *Peck's Sunshine* 290: A Guinea pig…is quite a neat little plaything for children.] **1893** (quot. at JIG IN THE AIR). **1927** J. Yellen & M. Ager *Ain't She Sweet?* (sheet music): I repeat/Don't you think that's kind of neat?/And I ask you very confidentially,/Ain't she sweet? **1930** in J.T. Farrell *Calico Shoes* 53: There's something neat [*sc.*, a pretty girl] behind us. *Ibid.* 54: "Neat!" Jack appraised. "Keen!" **1933** Halper *Union Sq.* 184: In the window a neat jane was neatly flapping flapjacks. **1936** D. Taylor & A. Scott *Follow the Fleet* (film): Kinda neat, huh? **1941** *Pittsburgh Courier* (Nov. 15) 7: Hot chills ran through Dagwood—Gosh, she was neat. **1944** Stiles *Big Bird* 22: There was Dolly. What a neat gal she was. **1948** J.H. Burns *Lucifer* 123: Gee, Ben, you were neat today!…The way you carried that ball! **1959** Searls *Big X* 132: Isn't that neat? You're a goddamned hero. **1962** G. Olson *Roaring Road* 61: He's a neat guy, Mr. Flagg, but he's not polite. **1964** R. Kendall *Black School* 118: Television…I like them neat murder shows. **1966** "Petronius" *N.Y. Unexp.* 65: Real jazz, Dixieland, dancing, neat joint. **1979** Gutcheon *New Girls* 183: How *neat* all the clubs were, and how *neat* it would be to get in. **1980** J. Carroll *Land of Laughs* 46: You can't tell me that your life out there with all of those famous people wasn't neat. **1984** J. McCorkle *Cheer Leader* 164: There's this really neat bar where everybody goes! **1989** Univ. Tenn. student journal: I think it is a really neat and fun thing.…I met so many cute and neat girls. **1991** *Get a Life* (Fox-TV): Hey—neat! Neat! I can see the future! **1994** *Young & Restless* (CBS-TV): Thanks for tonight. It was really neat of you. **1995** *Early Editon* (CNN-TV) (May 1): It's a nice place and there are lots of neat people here.

neatnik *n.* [*neat* + -NIK, infl. by BEATNIK] an unusually tidy person.
    1959 *N.Y. Times* (Aug. 30) 67: The beatniks and the neatniks had at each other this week. **1960** in *AS* XXXVII 2 (May 1962): A neatnik is the opposite of a litterbug. **1970** *Everett* (Wash.) *Herald* (Apr. 14) 8B: Want your son to be a neatnik[?] Give him a room he can relate to. **1995** *Calif. vs. Simpson* (Court-TV) (July 20): This neatnik…would not have stood for any mess around the house. **1996** *New Yorker* (June 3) 82: Hypochondria or neatnik fixations.

neato *adj.* [NEAT + -O] Esp. *Juve.* wonderful; NEAT. Also joc. vars. Also as interj.
    1951 Longstreet *Pedlocks* 352: The meal was sure neato, sir! **1958** Meltzer & Blees *H.S. Confidential* (film): Man, this is el neato. **1966** N.Y.C. high school student: That'd be neato. **1968** in Giovanni *Gemini* 41: I have this really neato pink IBM. **1969** in T. Thorne *Dict. Contemp. Slang*: Wow, that's neato-keeno—I know I shouldn't say that! **1971** Dahlskog *Dict.* 42: *Neatojet*, *a.* Marvelous; great; outasite. **1978** De Christoforo *Grease* 150: He's neat-o. **1978** *UTSQ*: (Excellent)…unreal, neato-bandito. **1980** TV ad for *Blackstone* show: "Neato! Neato! A dazzling experience," raves WNBC-TV. **1985** B.E. Ellis *Less Than Zero* 76: No, did you? Neato. **1987** Lauro *Open Admissions* (film): Polonius and all those neato palace guys. **1989** Univ. Tenn.

student theme: "Neato mosquito"—*really* neat. **1995** *World News Tonight* (ABC-TV): Neato!

neb *n.* **1.** NEBBISH.

1922 in S. Smith *Gumps* 19: A lot of those guys had me pegged for a neb. **1941** Schulberg *Sammy* 119: I have seen too many of their lonely, frightened faces,...too many Jewish *nebs* and poets...and everyday little guys to consider the fascist answer to What Makes Sammy Run?

2. var. NEBBIE.

nebbie *n. Narc.* NEMBIE; Nembutal. Also **neb.**

1963 T.I. Rubin *Sweet Daddy* 61: Get him sec—neb or dex or something. **1969** Lingeman *Drugs A to Z* 182: *Nebbie.* Nembutal capsule. **1971** *Intern. Jour. of Add.* VI 364: *Nebbies* Nembutal capsules. *a*1972 Rodgers *Queens' Vernacular* 141: *Neb*...nembutal. **1980** (cited in Spears *Drugs & Drink*).

nebbish *n.* [< Yiddish *nebech!* '(you) poor thing!'] Orig. *Jewish.* a pitifully ineffectual person; (*broadly*) a nobody.—also used attrib. Also as quasi-adj.

*1892 in *OEDS:* "Achi nebbich, poor little thing!" cried Mrs. Kosminski, who was in a tender mood. **1936** Levin *Old Bunch* 505: Listen, Lou, you can't get rid of a *nebich* like that. **1941** Schulberg *Sammy* 102: A *nebbish* person is not exactly an incompetent, a dope or a weakling. He is simply the one in the crowd that you always forget to introduce. **1951** H. Robbins *Danny Fisher* 168: To go along with Sam...was...the only chance to escape being a nebuch like everybody else. **1951** in *DAS:* There was one poor little nebbish of a dame. **1966** E. Shepard *Doom Pussy* 219: No, not tycoon, you nebbish. **1969** *Atlantic* (Sept.) 57: Paranoid psychopaths who, after nebbish lives, suddenly feel themselves invulnerable in the certain wooing of sweet death. **1973** in L. Bangs *Psychotic Reactions* 116: The...fascist nebbishes who keep you from buying [liquor] in highschool. **1979** McGivern *Soldiers* 155: The dumb nebbish didn't want it. **1980** *Vegas* (NBC-TV): He's a nebbish. **1983** Flaherty *Tin Wife* 186: Sissy's self-deprecation was couched in nebbish humor. **1982–84** Safire *Take My Word* 332: A *wimp* is one who is both as weepy as a *drip* and as listless as a *nebbish.* **1990** Steward *Bad Boys* 128: A nebbish male and a...broken-down...B-girl. **1993** *TV Guide* (Mar. 6) 4: She and her nebbish boyfriend Neil. **1994** *TV Guide* (July 16) 8: A nice nebbish whose apartment is cluttered with '60s collectibles.

nebby *adj.* resembling a NEBBISH. Cf. earlier sense 'nosy; inquisitive' in *DARE.*

1995 *New Yorker* (June 19) 31: A clumsy writer played to nebby perfection.

necessary *n.* money; NEEDFUL, 1.—constr. with *the.*

*1897 in *OED:* A fund for the purpose of providing the "necessary" in order to bring test cases. **1954–60** *DAS: Necessary, the* Money. **1978** E. Thompson *Devil to Pay* 4: Willing to let his long-suffering wife get up the necessary.

neck *n.* **1.** the throat; in phr. **down (one's) neck.** Cf. NECK OIL.

1866 in Hilleary *Webfoot* 153: The [officers]...poured a number of draught[s] of rotten whiskey down their officious necks. **1972** Jenkins *Semi-Tough* 38: And his voice had a bit of a belligerent tone, seeing as how he had put a whole pile of gin down his neck. *Ibid.* 153: With a couple of bacon cheeseburgers down his neck. **1980** *Bosom Buddies* (ABC-TV): OK, go throw some groceries down your neck.

2. *Stu.* a partner in necking.

1942 A.C. Johnston *Courtship of A. Hardy* (film): She shouldn't be a free neck, but she has to have a good line. **1950** C.W. Gordon *High School* 126: All girls are labeled "good date," "hot neck," [or] "goody-goody." **1985** Briskin *Too Much* 68: Is Curt a good neck?

3. *N.Y.C. & L.I.* a littleneck clam.

1943 J. Mitchell *McSorley's* 197: Twelve beautiful clams...."I got four cherries, two necks, two chowders and four peanuts."

4. *Stu.* REDNECK.

1966 in *DARE.* **1969** *Current Slang I & II* 63: *Neck, n.* An extremely backward person, a rustic, a "square."—College students, both sexes, Mississippi. **1970–72** in *AS* L (1976) 63: Razorback Slang...*Neck*...Redneck, person regarded as socially unacceptable, usually because of rural ways. "Look at that neck wearing white socks." **1979** Graffito, Univ. Tenn.: [Gov.] Ray Blanton has already made this state look plenty bad why must you 'necks and bigots help him out. **1991** in *DARE:* In the mid eighties in Austin, Texas, I heard *neck* used by the locals as a short form for *redneck.*

¶ In phrases:

¶ **get it in the neck** to be thoroughly bested or victimized, as by overwhelming force, swindling, death, etc.

1881 in Earp & Boyer *Wyatt* 41: *Curly Bill.* This *Noted Desperado* Gets It in the Neck. **1883** *Life* (Aug. 30) 104: And some one shrieked: "He's got it in the neck!" **1893** W.K. Post *Harvard* 42: I got it in the neck twice in that round. **1893** in J.I. White *Git Along Dogies* 93: As soon as fall work's over,/We get it in the neck. **1895** in F. Remington *Sel. Letters* 269: I won the law suit...[Defense] gets it in the neck for $150. **1903** Adams *Log of a Cowboy* 175: Well, old Nat will get it in the neck this time, if that old girl dallies with him as she did with us. **1905** W.S. Kelly *Lariats* 85: If we "gets it in the neck," as you fellers say, we'll have a good excuse then. **1905** Phillips *Plum Tree* 26: You'll soon be used to getting it in the neck if you stay in politics. **1912** Siringo *Cowboy Detective* 274: Many freight conductors and engineers "got it in the neck." **1913** J. London *Valley of Moon* 154: Then, bang, right in the neck, a ten per cent [wage] cut. ***1925** *Englische Studien* LX 285 [ref. to WWI]: *Get it in the neck*...to be killed. **1926** Dunning & Abbott *Broadway* 221: If you fight with his mob—then I'll get it in the neck. **1932** C. McKay *Gingertown* 12: We black gals get it full in the neck all the time. **1978** Shem *House of God* 295: They'll get you, Roy....You'll get it in the neck. **1990** W. Savage *Comic Books* 59: They could watch the Nazis get it in the neck again.

¶ **it's (one's) neck** (one) is at risk or in jeopardy.

1945 *Nat. Geographic* (Mar.) 275: If we screw up it'll really be our necks. **1974** Millard *Thunderbolt* 102: If any of you want to take a chance and start spending it right away, it's your neck.

¶ **my neck**! indeed not!; like hell! Cf. *my eye* s.v. EYE; *my ass* s.v. ASS.

1918 Beston *Full Speed Ahead* 104: "Hatteras, my neck!" **1965** Spillane *Killer Mine* 85: "But you're still poison until after the investigation." "Investigation my neck!"

¶ **neck of the woods** area; neighborhood. Now *colloq.*

1839 *Spirit of Times* (June 15) 175: If yourself and Oliver don't make folks open their eyes in this neck of the woods (as we say in the Hoishier [*sic*] State). **1853** "P. Paxton" *In Texas* 47: He came to be considered as the "man of money" in his "neck-of-the-woods." [**1865** J. Pike *Scout & Ranger* 210: I will...show you one, before I leave this neck of timber.] **1903** McClallen *He Demons* 75: These Royal Rogues...will pass through your "Neck of the woods." **1948** Beath F. Feboldson 85: Down in my neck o' the woods...we gotta million of 'em. **1986** *Working Woman* (Feb.) 22: Talk to your employees about how things work in their neck of the woods. **1996** *Today* (NBC-TV): Here's what's happening in your neck of the woods.

¶ **neck or nothing** all or nothing.

*1715 in *OED:* Worth venturing Neck or Nothing for. **1844** in H. Nathan *D. Emmett* 346: Gwin de [whole] hog neck or nottin. **1942** *ATS* 273: *Neck or nothing*, success or failure at any cost.

¶ **pull in (one's) neck** to keep (one's) head down; (*hence*) (*obs.*) shut up! cut it out!

1921 (quot. at *on velvet* s.v. VELVET). **1926** in J.M. March *Wild Party* 110: "Pull in your neck!"—"/"Go soak your head!" **1927** in Hammett *Knockover* 304: "Lay off that."..."Pull in your neck." **1928** J.M. March *Set-Up* 92: "A-ah," said Louie:/"Pull in yer neck!" **1980** W.C. Anderson *Bat-21* 200: We're riding shotgun. Pull in your neck!

¶ **stick (one's) neck out** Orig. *Stu.* to expose (oneself) to criticism, risk, or jeopardy, usu. to a greater degree than others. Now *colloq.* or *S.E.*

1926 in *OEDS:* Absolutely original slang at the University of Virginia includes...*to stick one's neck out.* **1942** *ATS* 231: *Stick one's neck out,*...to expose oneself to criticism. **1978** Dabney *Across Years* 81: There was an almost pathological fear on the part of the students [at Univ. Va., *ca*1918] lest they do what was termed "sticking your neck out."...It was sticking your neck out if you spoke up in class and answered a professor's question to the group as a whole. It was likewise bad form to do reading for the course above and beyond the assignment and to let that be known.

¶ **stretch (someone's) neck** to execute (someone) by hanging.

1897 *Cosmopolitan* (Mar.) 562: They call hangin', "stretchin' a man's neck." **1942** *ATS* 468: Be hanged....*get one's neck...stretched.*

¶ **talk out of the side of (one's) neck** to talk nonsensically or insincerely.

    [***1899** in *OEDS*: "Don't talk through yer neck," snarled the convict. "Talk out straight, curse you!"] **1971** Goines *Dopefiend* 156: Don't worry....I ain't just talkin' out the side of my neck.

¶ **up to (one's) neck** deeply; beyond (one's) ability. Cf. *to the gills* s.v. GILLS.

    1903 A.H. Lewis *Boss* 174: You went in up to your neck on sparks an' voylets. ***1923** in *OEDS*: It's the very spot for hatching treacheries. One feels steeped in them up to the neck. **1942** *ATS* 182: Deeply involved or engrossed....*up to the neck,—the gills,—the eyes.*

neck *v.* **1.** Orig. *Stu.* to engage in amorous embracing and kissing; pet.—also used trans. Now *colloq.* Hence **necker, necking,** *n.* [Earlier in dial. BrE as 'to court'; see *EDD*.]

    *1825 in *OEDS*: Let's see nae mair o' Peter Wallett's neckin' an' touslin' here. **1922** *DN* V 148: *Necking,* dancing with cheeks together. **1923** H.L. Mencken *Amer. Lang.* (ed. 3) 373: *Necker,* one given to cheek-to-cheek dancing. **1923–24** in *DA*: Our main topic of discussion was "necking." **1924** P. Marks *Plastic Age* 149: Some of those janes certainly could neck, and they were ready for it any time. **1925** *Lit. Digest* (Mar. 14) 65: "Petting" now exists only in the college novels, the more forceful, if more obscure, "necking" having taken its place to describe amorous adventures. *a***1929** in Stratton *Pioneer Women* 139: We danced real dances—no "necking" set to jazz music. **1929** E. Wilson *Thought of Daisy* 139: He tries to neck other girls in the Jap's room. **1930** in S.J. Perelman *Old Gang* 119: Fred...tried to neck me going home in the subway. **1931** in D.O. Smith *Cradle* 141: There was no possibility of necking a girl anywhere. **1942** *Calif. Folk. Qly.* I 333: They parked and "necked" for a bit on the Pali road. **1944** Ruskin et al. *Andy Hardy's Blonde Trouble* (film): She's learning to neck. Oh boy! You said it! **1945** Fay *Be Poor* 128: Boy, if she's waited that long to be "necked," in some parts of the South they'd shoot her! **1951** Mannix *Sword-Swallower* 82: We'd...do some pretty heavy necking. **1952** R. Alexander *Time Out* 32: I caught two kids necking in the corridor. **1962** B. Davis *Lonely Life* 40: I...found the boys of my age delighted that I was interested in something besides necking. **1963** D. Tracy *Brass Ring* 48: You know. Neck. Pet. Kiss each other. **1963–64** Kesey *Great Notion* 104: Or whatever honey I might have been necking with. **1966** Goldstein *1 in 7* 98: The college maintains an amiable matron—known to the student body as the "necker checker"—to keep students at a respectable distance on lawns and in lounges. **1972** J. Mills *Report* 47: She wouldn't go out with him or neck with him or something. **1976** J. Harrison *Farmer* 35: Arlice was necking with her boyfriend. *a***1977** M. French *Women's Room* 36: Boys...wanted to "neck," but she despised it. **1982** Whissen *Way with Wds.* 21: She told him that it was all right to neck as long as he didn't mess up her [*coiffure*]. **1982** *Chicago Sun-Times* (June 27) 56: Drive-in operators continue to fight the theaters' reputation as being a necker's paradise. **1991** Rudnick *I Hate Hamlet* 27: Necking at the Cloisters Picnics on Amish quilts. **1994** Berendt *Midnight in Garden* 114: You two have been neckin' and carryin' on all through my number! **1996** *Simpsons Comics* (No. 21) (unp.): I can't remember the last time we sat through a movie without necking!

    2. *Und.* to seize by the neck; (*hence*) to apprehend or arrest; COLLAR.

    1850 "N. Buntline" *G'hals of N.Y.* 17: The poor fellers...are necked and kicked down stairs. **1899–1900** Cullen *Tales* 351: I hadn't any more 'n got out of the door...when I was necked. **1906** A.H. Lewis *Confessions* 24: He's so full that he won't remember about you necking him.

    3. to stare impertinently; RUBBERNECK.

    1914 Jackson & Hellyer *Vocab.* 61: *Necking,* Noun General circulation. A scrutiny: an impertinant staring....Example: "The guinea on the end is giving you a necking through the glass." Also used as a verb, to "neck," to peer, to watch. **1930** Irwin *Tramp & Und. Slang: Neck.—* To stare at or watch closely. The word came from the much older "rubber-neck."

necker *n.* **1.** a shirtfront.

    1916 T.A. Dorgan, in *N.Y. Eve. Jour.* (Feb. 28) 8: We'll have to go to the opera some night, eh? I'll put on the four-quart hat and the necker.

    2. see s.v. NECK, *v.*, 1.

necker's knob *n. Auto.* a knob-like device attached to a steer-

ing wheel that enables the driver to steer with one hand. *Joc.* Also **necker knob.**

    1954–60 *DAS: Necker's knob* A small knob attached to a car's steering wheel for easier maneuvering; it also makes it easier for the driver to drive with one hand, as when he has his arm around a girl. *Teenage use since c1950.* **1976** J.W. Thomas *Heavy Number* 103: He had a rubberized necker knob clamped between his toothless jaws. **1986** Heinemann *Paco's Story* 45: The kid [is] driving with one hand on the necker's knob and the other hand slapping the hollow of the door in 4/4 time.

necklace *n.* **1.** a hangman's noose; halter. Now *hist.*

    *1647 in *F & H* V 24: What's the crime committed That they wear necklaces? **1849** Melville *White Jacket* 281: Here am I, liable at any time to be run up at the yard-arm, with a necklace, made by no jeweller, round my neck! **1949** Monteleone *Crim. Slang: Necklace*...The hangman's noose.

    2. see s.v. NECKLACE, *v.*

necklace *v. Pol. Journ.* to kill by putting a gasoline-soaked tire around the victim's neck and setting it afire. Also as n. [Orig. South African E.]

    1986 *Time* (Apr. 28) 43: Brutal "necklacings," in which young radicals place gasoline-filled tires around the necks of suspected traitors to the antiapartheid cause and burn them alive. **1990** *Nation* (Sept. 10) 230: In South Africa, activists in the black townships have "necklaced" collaborators despite international condemnations. **1990** *Wash. Post* (Oct. 6): Firebombing a house or "necklacing" a person—an execution in which a gasoline-filled tire is secured around a person's neck or body and then ignited. **1991** *New Yorker* (Oct. 21) 30: The tools of the Père Lebrun, or "necklace," in which a flaming tire slung about the neck is used to burn an enemy alive. **1992** *New Republic* (Jan. 27) 17: Reporters are threatened with being necklaced as they try to cover a story. **1994** *New Republic* (May 16) 36: A black South African policeman who had been necklaced and was burning to death.

neck oil *n.* beer or strong liquor.

    *1860 Hotten *Slang Dict.* (ed. 2): *Neck,* to swallow. *Neck-oil,* drink of any kind. ***1880** in *OEDS: Neck-oil,* ale. A word I once heard at Walsall [Staffordshire]. **1883** Parker *Naval Officer* 87 [ref. to 1848]: We were treated to a small allowance of *pelos cochos*—two Greek words signifying *neck oil*—the midshipmen of my time said. **1927** Kyne *They Also Serve* 3: That there's certainly some neck oil. ***1970** in *ODMS* 148: A chance encounter...leads Barry to consume a lot of nice neck-oil.

necktie *n.* **1.** a hangman's noose; halter; NECKLACE. Now *hist.*

    1866 Dimsdale *Vigilantes* 207: What the state of a man's health has to do with the crime of the villain who shoots him will to us forever remain an enigma as difficult as the unravelling of the Gordian knot. The proper course, in such cases, seems to be, not the untying of the knot aforesaid, but the casting on of another, in the shape of a road agent's necktie. **1871** (quot. at NECKTIE SOCIABLE). **1878** *Nat. Police Gaz.* (May 4) 3: Neck-Ties for Three. **1889** *JAF* I 288: One man after another was supplied with a hempen neck-tie, and arrangements were made to send them to kingdom come at the same instant. **1928** W.R. Burnett *Little Caesar* 44: Well, they're gonna put a necktie on Gus he won't take off! **1936** Twist *We About to Die* (film): They're pressin' your necktie for ya, Barclay. **1947** in *Look* (Jan. 6, 1948) 26: Prison jargon...*Neck tie* —Hangman's noose. **1953** Fisher & Beauchamp *Man from Alamo* (film): We got a nice new necktie for you. **1975** (quot. at LEAD POISONING).

    2. *Logging.* a choker chain.

    1958 McCulloch *Woods Wds.* 121: *Necktie*—A choker.

necktie party *n.* Orig. *West.* a public hanging; lynching. Now *hist.*

    1882 D.J. Cook *Hands Up* 40: The results were numerous warnings to offenders to leave these places, and many "neck-tie parties" as well, at which no "duly elected" judge sat for days in weighing the evidence, but where justice was seldom, as in other courts, blind. **1882** in *DAE*: If Found within the Limits of this City after Ten O'Clock P.M. this Night, You will be Invited to attend a Grand Neck-tie Party. **1884** in H. Hutton *Vigilante Days* 88: We trust that there will be no necktie party in this instance but that the man will receive a fair trial. **1891** Maitland *Slang Dict.* 186: *Necktie party,* a lynching. **1903** in Porter & Dunn *Miami Riot* 3: Treat him to a necktie party. **1923** in *DAS:* That little necktie party we're giving. **1930** Sage *Last Rustler* 123: They wasn't any of us had a hankering for a necktie party. **1930** Evarts *Big Trail* (film): The captain promised me a necktie party. **1935** Coburn

Law Rides Range 73: When they catch up there'll be a necktie party. **1935** Mackenzie *Been Places* 82: Them Spicks were all set for a nice little necktie party. **1937** Reitman *Box-Car Bertha* 201: Invitations are already out for my "neck tie party." **1938–40** W.V. Clark *Ox-Bow* 37: The only thing would get me out faster, would be your necktie party, Moore. **1954** A. LeMay *Searchers* 196: This is an invite to a neck-tie party. **1959** *N.Y. Times* (May 31) II x33: Several members proposed direct action—vigilante necktie parties for the guilty. **1964** J. Thompson *Pop.* 1280 67: Howsoever, it sure looked like I was about to be the guest of honor at a necktie party. **1967** *Hondo* (ABC-TV): Bushwhackin' a padre's about the best way to wind up with a necktie party. **1968** I. Reed *Radio* 52: A necktie party…at best gives only a few epiphanous and titilating moments. **1970** Rudensky & Riley *Gonif* 21: While waiting for his special necktie party, President Woodrow Wilson commuted his death sentence. **1973** in J. Flaherty *Chez Joey* xxiii: The crowd sounded like those mobs that gather for lynchings or necktie parties in stock Westerns. **1975** W. Wright *Six-Guns & Soc.* 2: Gunfights, saloon brawls, schoolmarms, dance-hall girls, necktie parties, stampedes, [etc.]. **1976** Wren *Bury Me Not* 12: Pa and Alvin [are] ready to hold a neck-tie party for each other. *a*1973–87 F.M. Davis *Livin' the Blues* 13: A couple of third graders decided to stage their own junior [mock] necktie party.

necktie sociable *n. West.* NECKTIE PARTY. Also **necktie frolic.**

1871 in *DA*: Mr. Jim Clemenston, equine abductor, was…made the victim of a neck-tie sociable. **1876** in *DA*: It's hard to leave ye, old hills, but it's either the States or a neck-tie frolic for me. **1878** Beadle *Western Wilds* 46: He joined the Vigilantes, and had the pleasure of presiding at a "neck-tie sociable" where two of the men who had robbed him were hanged. **1908** W.G. Davenport *Butte & Montana* 51: His neighbors…were about to give him an impromptu necktie sociable.

ned *n.* **1.** money; (*specif.*) a ten-dollar gold piece.

[*1753 in Partridge *Dict. Und.* 465: Ringing of *Neds* and Sixes. Putting off bad Guineas and Thirty-six shilling Pieces. *Ibid.:* Tip him a *Nedd;* give him a Guinea.] **1838** [Haliburton] *Clockmaker* (Ser. 2) 62: Quacks…make their ned out of 'em. **1859** Matsell *Vocab.* 40: *Half-A-Ned.* A five-dollar gold piece. *Ibid.* 58: *Ned.* A ten-dollar gold piece. **1927** *DN* V 456: *Ned,* n. A ten dollar gold piece.

2. (*Cap.*) the devil; hell.—usu. constr. with *raise.* Also **by Ned!, holy Ned!** (used to indicate surprise, etc.). Cf. NICK.

1848 in J.R. Lowell *Works* 198: "An' your fact'ry gals…'ll go to work raisin' promiscoous Ned," sez John C. Calhoun. *a*1849 in C. Hill *Scenes* 173: They will raise Ned with you if they can, them city fellers. **1853** "P. Paxton" *Yankee in Texas* 227: "By Ned," says he, "if it ain't that owdacious critter of Miss Mash's." **1862** in R.B. Hayes *Diary* II 174: He got into the guard-house for raising Ned. *Ibid.* 232: Cold rain, deep mud, and "Ned to pay." **1864** in O.J. Hopkins *Under the Flag* 165: It comes in all the fury of a tornado, upsetting tents and tarpaulins,…and raising *ned* generally. **1882** *Judge* (Oct. 28) 7: By this Time We wus full-cocked, an begin too raze Ned. **1886** (quot at SNOOZER). **1899** in Davidson *Old West* 62: Of wild Montana steers we had about a thousand head,/Belonging to the "Circle C," and each one full of "Ned." **1906** in *DAE*: You've been raising merry Ned, Florian, in your Brassfield capacity. **1940** D. West, in C. Major *Calling Wind* 130: An investigator…woulda raised Ned. *a*1956 Almirall *College to Cow Country* 72: Raising Ned in general. **1956** Childress *Like One of Family* 122: Jim was walkin' around…raisin' merry Ned about votin'. **1959** Kellogg & Simms *Giant Gila Monster* (film): He's sure gonna raise Ned. **1962** Bonham *War Beneath Sea* 54: Holy Ned!…Get out of here, Rainey, you turn my stomach.

3.a. salt pork or bacon; (see also 1952 quot.).—usu. constr. with *old.*

1850 Garrard *Wah-to-yah* 246: They were entitled every day to three-fourths of a pound of mess pork or "Ned." *Ibid.* 278: Do they feed you on "Old Ned," as Hatcher called the pork? **1857** in Stacey & Beale *Uncle Sam's Camels* 83: Mr. Beale purchased at Corero two hundred sheep and we have mutton every day instead of "Old Ned," in other words, salt bacon. Our ration of salt provisions is very small. **1862** in W.R. Howell *Westward* 108: Meet a supply train and get some "old Ned" once more. **1952** Randolph & Wilson *Down in Holler* 97 [ref. to 19th C.]: The word *ned* means bacon in the Ozarks….Later on the father told me that *ned* is a very nasty word synonymous with boar, and that no son of his should use such language when girls were present. It appears that pioneer farmers farther west regarded *ned* as a general term for swine.

b. a soldier. Now *hist.*

1850 Garrard *Wah-to-yah* 137: Among many farmers, pork is familiarly called "Ned," and as pork forms a principal portion of the government rations, the United States employees were so termed by the mountain men, in derision. *Ibid.* 161: This hos is no b'ar to stick his nose under cover all the robe season, an' lay round camp, like a darned Ned. **1952** Randolph & Wilson *Down in Holler* 97 [ref. to 19th C.]: Soldiers were called *neds* also, because they fed largely upon pork.

¶ In phrase:

¶ **call (one) Ned** call (one) a fool.

1826 in *JAF* LXXVI (1963) 287: Iff yew evver kech me…in sich a darn hoal az this iz, yeu ma kall me Ned.

neddy *n.* [orig. unkn.] a bludgeon or billy; (*occ.*) a slingshot.

*1845 (cited in Partridge *Dict. Und.* 465). *1848 Carpenter *Juvenile Delinquents* 284: They would not have been the first we had settled with the neddy, (life-preserver). **1859** Matsell *Vocab.* 58: *Neddy.* A slung-shot. *1863 in T. Taylor *Plays* 202: A clip on the head with a neddy—a life-preserver. *1864 in *F & H* V 26: Pistols are rarely carried by them; the weapon is generally a neddy or life-preserver. **1867** Williams *Brierly* 20: I always said that that "neddy" of course would be doing somebody a mischief. **1878** Barry *Up & Down* 105 [ref. to 1850]: Men were knocked down with "neddys" and sling-shots in broad daylight and robbed.

Ned Ninety-Proof *n.* a bottle of whiskey. *Joc.*

1954 Collans & Sterling *House Detect.* 49: He lurks in a corridor waiting for some guest who has returned from a bout with Ned Ninety-Proof.

needful *n.* **1.** money, esp. ready money.—constr. with *the.* Cf. NECESSARY.

1750 (cited in *AS* (Oct. 1940) 231). *1820–21 P. Egan *Life in London* 279: The *needful*…*One of the numerous *cant* phrases for *money.* **1836** *Spirit of Times* (July 16) 170: They are prepared with the *needful.* **1836** Strong *Diary* I 38: Not more than one-third had brought the needful. **1841** [Mercier] *Man-of-War* 166: To replenish their pockets with the *needful.* **1843** in G.W. Harris *High Times* 23: The *needful* is so extremely scarce hereabouts, that the issues from *Big Lands,* though not particularly good (about one-eighth silver)…pass very currently. **1854** St. Clair *Metropolis* 65: Little of the "needful" ever reaches these poor creatures. **1854** Yellow Bird *Murieta* 43: He…had a purse amply filled with the *needful. ca*1855 [G. Thompson] *Outlaw* 95: We should endeavor to provide ourselves with the *needful*…even if we are obliged to rob our relatives. **1859** *Spirit of Times* (Apr. 2) 88: All the "brass" and all the "needful." **1862** *Iowa Jour. of Hist.* LVII (1959) 116: We have yet received no pay…[and are] much in need of some of the "needful." **1902** Spring *Arizona* 48: Lipowitz turned his pockets inside out, but in vain. "The needful" was not there.

2. whiskey.—constr. with *the.*

1854 Doten *Journals* I 191: Taking a bottle…of the "needful" along to keep up the excitement. **1890** E. Custer *Guidon* 211 [ref. to 1868]: A little flask was quietly brought forth…."Who produced the 'needful'?"

needle *n.* **1.** the penis.—usu. considered vulgar. [A var. of the *1638 quot. is dated "1632" in *F & H;* this date is considered inaccurate by mod. scholarship.]

*1638 in *OEDAS* I 120: Let my needle run in your Diall. *1707 in *OEDAS* I 120: The Seamans Needle nimbly points the Pole/But thine still turns to every craving Hole. *1720 T. D'Urfey, in *OEDAS* I 120: I straightway whip my Needle out. *1731 [J. Roberts] *Merry-Thought* II 19: In Revenge I will stitch/Up the Hole near her Breach/With a Needle as long as my Arm. **1936** in P. Oliver *Blues Trad.* 189: Take it easy now mama while I stick my needle in. **1936** R. Johnson "Phonograph Blues," in *Complete Recordings:* We played it on the sofa, now/We played it 'side the wall/My needles have got rusty, baby/They will not play at all. **1960–69** Runkel *Law* 272: Looks like I musta pissed with my needle pointed up toward twelve o'clock.

2. annoyance, nettling, or vexation, esp. in the form of a stinging or sarcastic remark; (*often pl.*) such a remark.—usu. constr. with *give the, get the, get the,* etc.

*1873 Hotten *Slang Dict.* (ed. 4): To "cop the *needle*" is to become vexed or annoyed. *1887 in *F & H* V 27: It give 'im the needle of course, being left in the lurch in this way. *a*1889–90 in Barrère & Leland *Dict. Slang* II 84: It gives a man the needle when he hasn't got a bob, To see his pals come round and wish him joy. *1891 Maitland *Slang Dict.* 186: *Needled* (Eng.), annoyed. "He gave me the needle," that is, vexed or annoyed me. **1929** Hammett *Maltese Falcon* 127: He did [time]...for pistol-whipping [a] twist that had given him the needle. **1933** Odets *Awake & Sing!* 70: Why give me the needles all the time? What'd I ever do to you? **1934** Halper *Foundry* 23: Duffy,...knowing that the big fellow had just received the "needles," grinned. **1942–49** Goldin et al. *DAUL: Needles*....Humorous or ill-natured criticism or ridicule....Statements or information prejudicial and detrimental to a criminal defendant. **1949** *Harper's* (Feb. 1950) 71: Marge...cannot resist throwing the needles to that catty Doris. **1959** on *Golden Age of TV* (A&E-TV) (1988): He doesn't make trouble for anybody. Why are you giving him the needle? **1962** G. Olson *Roaring Road* 18: So he gets snappish....When he gets his needle out, it's not you he's working on. **1963** *Wall St. Jour.*, in *OEDAS* I 120: It's much easier to take the needle from this crowd. **1969** Layden & Snyder *Diff. Game* 5: Rip Miller...is particularly good with this needle. **1976** Whelton *CB Baby* 24: She was putting the needle to me, trying to see what would leak out. **1985** Sawislak *Dwarf* 37: Anybody who stoops to a cheap needle job to make front page isn't worthy. **1984–88** in H. Berry *Where Ya Been?* 221: This other boot started giving me a needle over something.

3. [in ref. to a phonograph needle] repetitious nagging or complaining.—used allusively.

    1938 Baldwin & Schrank *Case of Murder* (film): Tell the old lady to change her needle, will ya? **1966** Elli *Riot* 84: "Get off the needle," Fletcher snapped. **1966–67** P. Thomas *Mean Streets* 49: Damn, Momma, you're wearin' the needle out.

¶ In phrase:

¶ **on the needle** *Narc.* addicted to injected narcotics.

    1942 *ATS* 478: Addicted to narcotics...*on the needle*...taking injections. **1942–49** Goldin et al. *DAUL* 144: Now she's back on the needle. **1953** R. Wright *Outsider* 99: Say, are you on the needle or something?

needle *v.* **1.** to annoy or tease; goad; (*occ.*) to react to teasing or provoking. Now *colloq.*

    1873 Hotten *Slang Dict.* (ed. 4): *Needle*, to annoy. **1881 in *OEDS*: There, he's off! the young warmint, he's needled; whenever I talks about work He puts on his cap and he hooks it. **1889–90 Barrère & Leland *Dict. Slang* II 84: *Needle, to* (common), to annoy. **1898 G.B. Shaw, in *OEDS*: Old Indian women get "fairly needled" at the spectacle of their houses and crops being burnt. **1930 Lait *On Spot* 207: *Needle*...to persecute or "ride." **1951** in *DAS*: She did what she gleefully called "needling him a little." **1953** Chandler *Goodbye* 37: He needled me into socking him....You must needle easy if this punk can do it. **1963** Serling *Twilight Zone* (CBS-TV): Stop needling, will ya? **1974** Radano *Cop Stories* 49: Or they would needle each other in the locker room with ethnic jokes. **1977** R.S. Parker *Effective Decisions* 62: He avoids transferring anger or needling people. **1982** Zicree *Twilight Zone Comp.* 422: Fenton, a bigot, enjoys needling him with racist slurs. **1995** *Calif. vs. Simpson* (Court TV) (July 19): Did you needle him? Did you challenge him?

2. to add alcohol, ether, etc., to (a nonalcoholic drink), as by injecting it through a cork. Hence **needle[d] beer**, *n.*

    1928 in *OED2*: You can get your needle beer—near beer shot with alki or ether. **1929** V. Randolph, in *AS* IV 387: Many Kansans...buy the ordinary non-alcoholic near-beer, and add a little alcohol to each bottle. The resulting mixture is called...*needled beer.* **1929** Hostetter & Beesley *Racket* 233: *Needle*, to inject alcohol or ether into any liquid, such as beer, to make it stimulating. **1930** Irwin *Tramp & Und. Slang*: *Needle*.—To treat a soft drink or "near beer" with some form of alcohol, ether, etc., to give it a "kick."...*Needle Beer*.—Beer treated as above. **1930–31** in Maurer *Lang. Underworld* 51: *Needle-beer*, n. Beer that has had alki or ether injected into it. **1931** D. Runyon *Guys & Dolls*, in *OED2*: Some of that needled beer he is feeding us. **1936** Dos Passos *Big Money* 81: Some glasses of needle beer.

3. to apply maximum power or acceleration.

    1955 R.L. Scott *Look of Eagle* 8: He was almost ready to pour the coal to her [sc., a jet plane]. Ready to "needle" her. [**1967** H.M. Mason *New Tigers* 222: *Give it the needle*: Use maximum power available.]

needle artist *n.* **1.** *Narc.* (see 1925 quot.).

    1925 *Writer's Mo.* (June) 487: *Needle-Artist*—A drug addict who uses a hypodermic needle with which to take his drug. **1990** G. Lee *China Boy* 219: Too early for the hookers, too late for the needle artists and just right for the Tokay crowd.

2. a person who deliberately teases or provokes others.

    1982 Hayano *Poker Face* 56: Targets for the barbs thrown by needlers, or "needle artists."

needle[d] beer see s.v. NEEDLE, *v.*, 2.

needledick *n.* a man having a small penis; (*hence*) a contemptible fellow.—usu. used as a vague term of abuse.—usu. considered vulgar. Cf. DICK, 2.a.

    1969 L. Woiwode, in *New Amer. Review* (No. 7) 90: He was...poorly endowed, and had picked up the nickname of "Needledick, the canary raper." **1972** *Nat. Lampoon* (Nov.) 34: Gee, you sure have a small cock, needle-dick daddy. **1973** (quot. at BUGFUCKER). **1975** *Nat. Lampoon Comical Funnies* (unp.): Just who are you callin' a horse's ass, needledick? **1977** (quot. at BUGFUCKER). **1980** *Nat. Lampoon* (June) 20: You and I, young man, shall get along very well. If you're not a goddamn needledick, that is. **1987** B. Helgeland & S. Pierce *Elm St. 4* (film): Hey you, needledick!

needle fiend *n. Narc.* (see 1938 quot.). Cf. FIEND, 1.

    1936 Dai *Opium Addiction* 199: *Gow heads.* Addicts who use hypodermic needles. Also called *junkies, needle fiends.* **1938** D.W. Maurer, in *AS* XIII: *Needle-fiend.* An addict who takes narcotics through the hypodermic. **1942** *ATS* 476: *Needle fiend*...one using hypodermic injections.

needle freak *n. Narc.* one who is addicted to hypodermic injections, as of heroin. Cf. FREAK, 5.

    1967 Wolf *Love Generation* 6: I finally found myself shooting a lot of speed...(and I'm not a needle-freak). I was shooting a hundred milligrams a day. **1967–68** von Hoffman *Parents Warned Us* 153: I'm a needle freak. I'm flashing on it right now, just...looking at it. **1972** Smith & Gay *Don't Try It* 204: *Needle Freak.* Someone who enjoys injecting almost anything; one who gets a sexual "flash" from the injection. **1972** Grogan *Ringolevio* 271: There were a few needle freaks crashing in the cellar and they had probably left behind their spikes. **1973** *Drug Forum* II 133: One needle freak regularly injects saline solution. **1975** *N.Y. Times Bk. Rev.* (June 15) 7: His spirit crumbled and he became a needlefreak along with the rest of them.

needle-jabber *n. Police.* an addict who injects narcotics.

    1929 Gill *Und. Slang*: *Needle Jabber*—Morphine addict. **1928–30** Fiaschetti *Gotta Be Rough* 91: Hop head, needle jabber, and snowbird.

needlenosed *adj.* having a sharply tapering nose.—used derisively. Hence **needlenose**, *n.*

    1943 in J. O'Hara *Sel. Letters* 177: Needle-Nose, as Buddy North calls Janet. **1963** Rifkin *K. Fisher's Rd.* 76: You little needle-nosed punk. **1974** Sann *Dead Heat* 81: No problem the way that needle-nosed handicapper is into us.

needle park *n. Journ.* [pop. by James Mills's 1966 *The Panic in Needle Park*, where "Needle Park" referred to a traffic island at Broadway and 74th Street in New York City] a small public area with benches, bushes, etc., where drug addicts are known to gather.

    1966 J. Mills *The Panic in Needle Park* [book title] [ref. to 1964]. **1974** Cull & Hardy *Drug Abusers* 197: *Needle Park*—To New York addicts, upper Broadway and Sherman Square. **1990** T. Thorne *Dict. Contemp. Slang: Needle park*...American a nickname given to a public place which narcotics users frequent in order to inject themselves. **1991** *N.Y. Times* (Aug. 11) 3: Drug addicts have turned the Platzspitz in Zurich, once elegant, into a needle park.

needle-pumper *n. Narc.* one who injects narcotics.

    1911 *Hampton's Mag.* (Mar.) 285: He uttered the one explanatory and self-sufficient word—Needle-pumper. **1928** Panzram *Killer* 157: *Snowbird*—cocaine sniffer; *needle pumper*—hypodermic user.

needle-pusher *n.* **1.** a tailor.

    1920 S. Lewis *Main Street* 243: But he used to be in a tailor shop in Minneapolis (they do say he's a smart needle-pusher, at that) and he tries to let on that he's a regular city fellow. **1942** *ATS* 458: Tailor or seamstress. *Needle pusher.*

2. *Narc.* NEEDLE-PUMPER.

    1929 Gill *Und. Slang: Needle Pusher*—Morphine addict.

needles *n.pl.* JITTERS.

    1922 Murphy *Black Candle* 226: I get "the needles"—that is to say, a mixture of nerves and muscles. **1927** *Vanity Fair* (Nov.) 132: "I've got the needles" is "My nerves are bad." "The Heebie-jeebies," ditto. **1931** Wilstach *Under Cover Man* 61: I got the needles....I see coppers everywhere.

Needless Markup *n.* a Neiman-Marcus department store. *Joc.*

 1995 Chicago man, age 29 (coll. J. Sheidlower): I'm dropping by Needless Markup this afternoon. **1996** S.F. woman, age *ca*55 (coll. J. Sheidlower): Do you know "Needless Markup" for Neiman-Marcus?

neg *interj.* Esp. *Mil.* NEGATIVE. Also **negs, negat.**

 1966 F. Elkins *Heart of Man* 49: "Eject! Eject!" "Negs." **1985** Eble *Campus Slang* (Apr.) 6: Neg—no. Clipping of *negative*...."Neg that." **1988** Poyer *Med* 442: Negat, flight leader, negat! We have firm word no combat aircraft over land.

negaholic *n.* a habitually negative person. Cf. -AHOLIC.

 1989 C. Carter-Scott *Negaholics* [title]. **1989** *Oprah* (synd. TV series): Carol Olson: Negaholic.

negat *var.* NEG.

negative *interj.* [orig. radiocommunications jargon] Esp. *Mil.* no. Also as quasi-n. Now *S.E.*

 1942 *ATS* 235: No....negative, nerts, nit. **1955** *AS* XXX (May) 118: *Negative...*, I refuse; I disagree; no (in answer to a question). **1966** *N.Y. Times Mag.* (Oct. 30) 104: It is fashionable to say "affirmative" and "negative" for "yes" and "no." **1991** LaBarge *Desert Voices* 187: I heard...that they weren't equipped properly. That's a big negative.

negative perspiration *interj.* no problem; *no sweat* s.v. SWEAT. *Joc.* Also as n.

 1970 N.Y.U. student: *Negative perspiration* means "No sweat!" I'm pretty sure it's from the '50s. **1983** S. King *Christine* 418: "Negative perspiration," Arnie said. He finished his beer and LeBay tossed it into a litter bag. "Another dead soldier." **1984** Hailey *Soldier Talk* 43: *No sweat.* Negative perspiration...no need to worry.

negatory *interj.* Orig. *USAF.* no; NEGATIVE. *Joc.* Also as adj.

 1955 *AS* XXX (May) 118: Negative; Negatory; Negatrix; Negatron. I refuse; I disagree; no. **1976** Lieberman & Rhodes *CB* 133: *Negatory*—No. **1976** Whelton *CB Baby* 22: Negatory, good buddy. **1977** Corder *Citizens Band* 14: Mercy. That's a negatory. **1992** *New Republic* (Nov. 16) 10: "Were you really going to ruin his daughter's wedding?"... "Negatory."

negatrix *interj.* *USAF.* NEGATORY. *Joc.* Also as adj.

 1955 (quot. at NEGATORY).

negatron *interj.* NEGATORY. *Joc.*

 1955 (quot. at NEGATORY). **1956** Heflin *USAF Dict.* **1980** D. Cragg *Lex. Militaris* 310: *Negatron*....Negative. **1986** "J. Cain" *Suicide Squad* 239: No! Negatron, and that's final.

nego *n.* [*negative* + -*o*] *Stu.* a person having a negative or objectionable attitude.

 1965 Hersey *Too Far to Walk* 37: Breed with his total nego outlook. **1979** G. Wolff *Duke of Deception* 188 [ref. to *ca*1952]: At Choate...the "negos"—carpers, corner-cutters, and wise-apples—bucked the system and had some fun.

negs *var.* NEG.

Nellie *n.* [fr. *Nellie*, regarded as a typically old-fashioned feminine pet name] Esp. *Homosex.* a prissy or effeminate fellow; sissy; (*specif.*) a male homosexual. [Orig. as a nickname.]

 1916 in Dunham *Long Carry* 10: My Company Officer was...known as "Nellie" to the troops, because of his girlish face and swanky ways. **1931 B. Niles *Strange Bro.* 196: Sometimes...the police would raid the place, and for a time the "Nellies" would vanish....And you would hear them calling each other "Nanette" and "Imogene" and speaking of themselves as girls. **1931** J.T. Farrell *McGinty* 79: Nellie in there spotted Mac right off the reel. **1946** J.H. Burns *Gallery* 162: So I told this Nellie to go peddle her fish somewhere else. **1968** Gover *JC* 14: Get on the horn to the meatwagon, tell those nellies where this garbage is at. **1973** *TULIPQ* (coll. B.K. Dumas): Male homosexuals...*gays, fairies, nellies.* **1987** E. White *Beautiful Room* 41: "But can't two nellies go to bed with each other?"..."And do what?" **1988** (quot. at MO).*

¶ In phrase:

¶ **nervous Nellie** see NERVOUS NELLIE.

nelly *adj.* *Homosex.* excessively effeminate.

 1966 "Petronius" *N.Y. Unexp.* 99: You're much too nelly for me. **1966** Herbert *Fortune* 61: Shut your nellie jaw, before I blind you, bitch. **1967** Crowley *Boys in Band* 880: I may be nellie, but I'm no coward. **1965–72** E. Newton *Mother Camp* 8: They tend to...flaunt an extremely "nellie" (effeminate) appearance and style of behavior. **1975**

Kangas & Solomon *Psych. of Strength* 46: It may not be possible merely to write him off as a "nellie fag." **1976** C. Keane *Hunter* 177: I ain't no nelly faggot. **1978** Price *Ladies' Man* 51: A real nelly faggot came to the door. **1981** in Bérubé *Coming Out* 185: He was what I'd call a real "Nellie Queen." **1982** *N.Y. Times* (May 17) C16: Mr. Miller has seen fit to portray him as what in the past, in preliberationist days, would have been described as a nelly queen. **1986–89** Norse *Memoirs* 169: Too nellie, or what? **1994** Berendt *Midnight in Garden* 104: I play with everybody, even the nelliest fags.

Nelson's blood *n.* *Naut.* rum.

 1925 Fraser & Gibbons *Soldier & Sailor Wds.* [ref. to WWI]: *Nelson's Blood:* Rum. Old Navy, and probably derived from the old story of the sailors on board the *Victory* tapping the cask in which Nelson's body was brought home and drinking the spirits. *1929 Bowen *Sea Slang* 94: *Nelson's Blood.* Navy dark rum. **1976 Hayden *Voyage* 129 [ref. to 1890's]: Black sweet rum. "Nelson's blood." *Ibid.* 655: A swig of Nelson's blood. *1992 Jernigan *Tin Can Man* 64 [ref. to WWII]: The Englishmen called it Nelson's blood.*

nembie *n.* *Narc.* a capsule of Nembutal, trademark name for a brand of pentobarbital.

 1950 *Neurotica* (Autumn) 41: Must have been cut with nembys. **1952** W.S. Burroughs *Junkie* 15: Nembies, Goof Balls, Yellow Jackets...Nembutal capsules. **1952** Mandel *Angry Strangers* 407: Nemby, too much. **1958** W.S. Burroughs *Naked Lunch* 13: A quart of P.G. and a hundred nembies. **1964** Harris *Junkie Priest* 47: Goofballs, nembies,...redbirds. **1971** *Intern. Jour. of Add.* VI 364: *Nembies* Nembutal.

nemmie *n.* *Narc.* NEMBIE.

 1950 *Time* (Aug. 28) 4: A goof ball is a nemmie (from Nembutal). **1968** Louria *Drug Scene* 209: *Nemmies.* Nembutal.

neo-maxi-zoom-dweebie *n.* NERD, 1. *Joc.* [Pop. by John Hughes's 1985 film *The Breakfast Club.*]

 1985 J. Hughes *Breakfast Club* (film): Face it, you're a neo-maxi-zoom-dweebie. **1986** Eble *Campus Slang* (Nov.) 6: *Neomaxumzumdweebie* [*sic*]—person with a personality that is wrong in every way, the extreme nerd: "That guy in my chemistry class with the slide rule is truly a *neomaxumzumdweebie.*" **1987** N.Y.C. child, age *ca*7: You're a neo-maxi-zoom-dweebie! **1990** *UTSQ: Neo-maxi-zoom-dweebie*—nerd.

Nep *n.* *Naut.* the sea god Neptune, esp. as portrayed in crossing-the-line rituals.—usu. constr. with *old*.

 1841 *So. Lit. Messenger* VII 54: But there being few reprisals now for tars,/[I] Have left old Nep for Venus and for Mars. **1858** in C.A. Abbey *Before the Mast* 132: If old Nep should get hold of this page. **1863** in Gibbons *Tales That Were Told* 77: How sadly times have changed/Since "Nep" first hailed me as a tenant. **1867** Clark *Sailor's Life* 25: A huge monster, clad like Old Nep, appeared over the knight heads.

nepo *v.* [orig. unkn.] *Und.* (see quot.). [See note at NAPOO, *v.*]

 1847–49 Bonney *Banditti* 226: They said Bonney would be "nepoed," which I understand to be their usual phrase for killed. They used the expression *nepo* seven or eight times.

nerd *n.* [prob. sugg. by the *nerd*, whimsical creature in *If I Ran the Zoo* (1950) by "Dr. Seuss" (Theodore Seuss Geisel (1904–91)), U.S. children's author, itself perh. infl. by *Mortimer Snerd*, name of dummy used by Edgar Bergen, U.S. ventriloquist] **1.** *Stu.* a dull, obnoxious, or unattractive person; DRIP, 2; JERK. Also **nurd.** Also as quasi-adj. [The 1957 quot., though from a Glasgow newspaper, seems likely to have been copied fr. a U.S. source.]

 [**1941** in C.R. Bond & T. Anderson *Flying T. Diary* 43: I discussed the P-40 flying characteristics with "Mortimer Snerd" Shilling.] [**1950** "Dr. Seuss" *If I Ran Zoo* 49: I'll sail to Ka-Troo/And Bring Back an It-Kutch, a Preep and a Proo, a Nerkle, a Nerd, and a Seersucker, too!] **1951** (cited in *W10*). **1957** in *OED2: Nerd*—a square. **1960** *Yale Record* (Oct.) 11: Ah, get outa here, nurd. **1960** Swarthout *Where Boys Are* 45: Malcolm was a real nurd. **1961** Kohner *Gidget Goes Hawaiian* 22: He was a real nurd. **1961** Sullivan *Shortest, Gladdest Years* 307: He was a whey-faced little nerd. **1963** *Princeton Tiger* (Mar.) 3: Are you guys all nuts in the head/To think that we'd go to bed/With you NURDS from Princeton U. **1963** in *IUFA Folk Speech*: A nerd is a person who isn't up to standards, a dope, etc. **1964** in *Time* (Jan. 1, 1965) 56: At the University of North Carolina, last year's *fink* is this year's *squid, cull, troll* or *nerd.* **1965** in *DAS* (ed. 2): *Nurd* a person who is not in the know, a square, not hip. **1968** Baker et al. *CUSS* 161: Nerd...*Gnurd,*

Knerd, Nurd, Nyrd. **1970** N.Y.U. grad. student: I first heard the word *nerd* in Texas about 1953. **1972** *Newsweek* (Feb. 14) 68: It shows the stereotyped liberal intellectual...as a cowardly, contemptible nerd who won't take a stand until the barbarians are inside his own house. **1976** W. Dyer *Erroneous Zones* 41: She doesn't like me, I must be a nerd. **1977** *L.A. Times* (Aug. 4) II 4: The My Lai massacre was used as "camp" and "chic" by the pampered nerds who could afford the luxury of college deferments. **1978** Pilcer *Teen Angel* 14: Why did she have to tell that nerd story? **1979** M. Lazarus *Momma*, synd. comic strip in *L.A. Times* (Mar. 27) IV: Why do you go out with that nerd, George? He's such a jerk! **1983** *Chi. Sun-Times* (Mar. 29) 8: Unnecessary subplots involving idiotic politicians who act like complete nerds. **1990** (quot. at DRAPE, *n.,* 2). **1991** *N.Y. Times* (nat. ed.) (Feb. 5) A12: I want to keep Dr. King's dream alive...[and] my friends...call me a nerd.

2. *Stu.* an overdiligent student; (*hence*) a person obsessively devoted to a (usu. specified) nonsocial activity.
 1974 Univ. Tenn. prof., age *ca*38: In the late 1950's, at St. Olaf College [in Northfield, Minn.] a "grind" was also referred to as a *nerd.* Because so many students were of Scandinavian ancestry the phrase *Nordic nerd* was also used. I had never heard *nerd* before that. **1980** (quot. at CEREB). **1982** *Time* (May 3) 52: The truly addicted—known half scornfully, half admiringly as computer nerds. **1984** *Personal Computing* (Apr.) 251: No literature nerds need write corrective letters. **1984** *Time* (Dec. 3) 76: The hackers looked more like backpackers or professional musicians than any stereotype image of computer nerds. **1984** N. Stephenson *Big U* 76: The brightest nerds and premeds. **1989** *Nat. Lampoon* (June) 29: A sixteen-year-old computer nerd. **1990** P. Munro *Slang U.* 136: *Nerd* person who studies a lot or is socially outdated. **1996** V-8 brand vegetable cocktail TV ad: I'm a wannabe computer nerd.

nerd around *v.* to fool about.
 1974 Univ. Pittsburgh student: To *nerd around* is kind of to goof off, loaf around. It was used in Pittsburgh by 1972.

nerdly *adj.* NERDY.
 1992 *World Today* (CNN-TV) (June 25): These nerdly researchers clip newspapers.

nerd pack *n.* a plastic envelope for one's shirt pocket, used to hold pens. *Joc.*
 1981 *Chicago Tribune* (Aug. 15): The stereotype of a man whose white undershirt shows at the neck and who holds pens in a plastic pocket protector "known to some as a nerd pack." *a*1989 Spears *NTC Dict. Sl.:* A lot of engineers have nerd packs. *1989 (cited in T. Thorne *Dict. Contemp. Slang*). **1990** T. Thorne *Dict. Contemp. Slang:* *Nerd pack*...a plastic shield worn on a shirt breastpocket to prevent ink stains from pens. **1996** *N.Y. Observer* (Apr. 8) 18: The computer software business, where anyone with a nerd pack in his shirt pocket...can sell stock on Wall Street at stratospheric price-earnings multiples.

nerdy *adj.* being, resembling, characteristic of, or suited to a NERD. Also **nurdy.**
 1960 *Yale Record* (Oct. 11): Of all the schleps...you are the nurdiest. **1971** Hyams *T.R. Baskin* (film): Most of the guys in accounting are pretty nerdy. **1972** *Nat. Lampoon* (Apr.) 31: I was sitting in the Hop Shoppe with some of my nerdy girl friends. **1981** (quot. at DISHY). **1982** *New York* (Aug. 16) 16: A nerdy, bespectacled ten-year-old. **1983** S. King *Christine* 142: The nerdy-looking freshman. **1985** *Time* (June 24) 60: The new drink...is nerdy and has none of the old Coke's snap. **1988** *Daily Beacon* (Univ. Tenn.) (Apr. 5) 6: Their New England home is thereafter occupied by a nerdy up-scale New York family. **1990** in *Texas Mo.* (Jan. 1991) 157: Guys who date...nerdy girls.

nerf *v. Drag Racing.* to strike the bumper of (another car).
 1952 *ATS* (ed. 2): *Nerfing,* bumping another car out of the way. **1953** Felsen *Street Rod* 129: "The crazy fool" Ricky exclaimed. "Nerfing me!" **1955** *Time* (Aug. 29) 82 (Scott-Foresman Coll.): *Nerf*—to push another car. **1957** *Life* (Apr. 29) 140: *Nerf*...to push another car. **1954–60** *DAS: Nerf*...To push one car with another. *Hot-rod use since c1955. From the nerfing bar that supports the bumper on most cars.* **1969** in *OEDS: Nerf,* to bump, shove, or push a car during a racing event with another racer. Nerfing is very popular on short tracks. **1969** *Esquire* (Aug.) 71: In the city, you could nerf a cab, i.e., bump it gently at a light.

nerf *comb. form.* [sugg. by *Nerf,* trademark name for a line of foam-rubber toys] (used in var. combs. to indicate foolishness or stupidity).

1984 Holland *Better Off Dead* (film): You're a spastic nerfbag all the time. **1986** Sliwa *Attitude* 29: Nerf-brained, pearly toothed, peroxide-haired [fashion models].

nerf bar *n. Drag Racing.* a resilient bumper fitted to a customized automobile. Also **nerfing bar.**
 1953 *New Yorker* (Mar. 7) 23: Almquist is showing chrome knerfing bars. **1955** in *OEDS:* The nerf bar itself is mounted in a "slip tube" that is welded permanently to the reworked bumper irons. **1957** *New Yorker* (Apr. 6) 87: The openwork bumpers (called nerf bars). **1954–60** (quot. at NERF). **1960** T. MacPherson *Dragging & Driving* 140: *Nerf bar:* Bumper. *1962 in *OEDS:* A custom-built nerfing bar (bumper).

nerts *n.* usu. *pl.* **1.** a testicle; NUT.—usu. considered vulgar.
 1930 Bodenheim *Roller Skates* 194: Twist his nerts then.

2. *pl.* something extraordinary; NUT, 1.b.—usu. constr. with *the.*
 1934 in *DAS:* Euologizing anything...as "the nerts."

3. *pl.* nothing.
 1989 *Tracey Ullman Show* (Fox-TV): There is nothing! Nada! Nerts!

nerts or **nertz** *interj.* [alter., orig. partially euphem., for NUTS] NUTS. Also as adj.
 1929 McEvoy *Hollywood Girl* 24: Just nerts. **1930** in D.O. Smith *Cradle* 28: If you *do* love her, if you are nerts about her,...then chuck this letter out the window. **1931** in Fitzgerald *Corres.* 270: Nurts. **1932** *AS* VII 329: Aw nertz—"It's absurd"; "nonsense"; an expression of disgust. **1932** Gates & Boylan *Hell Divers* (film): Aw, nerts! **1929–33** J. Lowell *Gal Reporter* 143: "What do you say to that?"..."Nertz." **1933** Ersine *Prison Slang* 40: *Gnerts, ex.* Pshaw, bunk! **1933** Halper *Union Square* 199: Aw nerts, Andre. The hell you are. **1932–34** Minehan *Boy & Girl Tramps* 39: He goes kinda nertz. **1934** Duff & Sauber *20 Million Sweethearts* (film): He sneered once again and said, "nerts"! **1934** Holm & Abbott *Three Men on a Horse* 522: Ertznay...you can sell that any place. **1934** *15th Inf. Sentinel* (Jan. 6) 10: Nerts to him. **1934** in Ruhm *Detective* 107: Nerts to you, you big turnip. **1937** Hemingway *To Have & Have Not* 129: "Oh, nerts to you," she was saying to the third tourist. **1942** *Time* (Feb. 16) 22: "Surrender, you bastards, we've got you surrounded!" The answer floated back in perfect English: "Nerts to you, Joe." **1943** Halper *Inch from Glory* 35: Aw, nerts to you, too. **1961** in Sagendorf *Popeye* 101: Granny is drivin' him nerts! **1964** B. Kaufman *Down Staircase* 109: Fuk. Screw. Crap. Goddam. Nerts to you. **1964** Faust *Steagle* 221: Nerts. **1969** Pharr *Numbers* 10: Nerts. **1970** *Playboy* (Aug.) 160: Nertz! I'll go absolutely nertz. **1972** Swarthout *Tin Lizzie* 119: Nerts. **1976** *N.Y. Times* (June 20) II 37: Movie: "The Terror"....Nerts. **1978** *M*A*S*H* (CBS-TV): Aw, nerts! **1987** Henzel *Doggerel* 105: Coddling them with euphemisms is nurtz. **1996** *Simpsons Comics* (No. 20) (unp.): Aw, nertz! I guess I *lost* more than I thought.

nerver *n.* a gate-crasher, one who gets into shows and sporting events without paying.
 1908 Sullivan *Criminal Slang* 1: *A nerver*—a fellow who gets by without paying at places of amusement, etc. **1935** D. Maurer, in *AS* (Feb.) 18 [ref. to *a*1910]: *Nerve Up* or *Nerver Up* [*sic*]. A gate-crasher; one who enters prizefights, etc., without a ticket.

nervous *adj.* Esp. *Jazz.* thrilling; great. Cf. CRAZY.
 1926 in R. Lardner *Best Stories* 87: But if the fans are looking for as "nervous" a finish as last year's, with a climax such as the Chicago and New York clubs staged on the memorable first day of October, they are doubtless in for a disappointment. **1953** *I Love Lucy* (CBS-TV): Dad, this cat's real nervous! **1954** Gottlieb *Susan Slept Here* (film): "Crazy!" "Real nervous!" **1959–60** R. Reisner *Jazz Titans* 161: *Nervous:* something that's so interesting it captures your attention.

¶ In phrase:

¶ **nervous in the service** *Mil.* jumpy; frightened; excitable.
 1944 Stiles *Serenade* 99: You nervous in the Service? **1945** *Sat. Rev. of Lit.* (Nov. 3) 7: "Are you nervous in the service?" (sometimes addressed to Mr. Jervis); and "Are you fed-up with the set-up?" **1946** G.C. Hall, Jr. *1000 Destroyed* 392: Dayhuff was a little "nervous in the service" as C.O. of the celebrated 4th. [**1946** Sherwood *Best Years* (film): Just nervous out of the service, I guess.] **1946** J.H. Burns *Gallery* 196: Nervous in the services? **1955** Goethals *Chains of Command* 32: No wonder they're getting nervous in the service. **1959** Knowles *Separate Peace* 131: I was what they call "nervous in the ser-

vice." **1944–61** D.K. Webster *Para. Inf.* 154: "Jesus Christ, tell the artillery to cease fire!..." "You're nervous in the service." **1962** Killens *Heard the Thunder* 103: I suppose I'm just *nervous* in the service. **1963** Keats *They Fought Alone* 325 [ref. to WWII]: What's the matter? You getting nervous in the service? **1969** M. Lynch *Amer. Soldier* 111 [ref. to Korean War]: What's the matter, baby? You getting a little nervous in the service? **1977** Caputo *Rumor of War* 72 [ref. to Vietnam War]: Hey,...P.J.'s getting nervous in the service.

nervous-jervis *adj.* extremely excitable; jittery. Cf. 1945 quot. at *nervous in the service* s.v. NERVOUS.
   1972 N.Y.U. student: *Nervous-jervis* mean like nervous, only worse. **1972** N.Y.U. student: *Nervous-jervis* is like when you have the heebie-jeebies. **1972** *Nat. Lampoon* (Apr.) 31: I don't...go home all nervous-jervis from holding back with a date.

nervous Nellie *n.* [orig. in derisive ref. to Frank B. Kellogg, Secretary of State 1925–29] Esp. *Pol.* a foolishly fearful or timid person. Also as quasi-adj.
   1926 (cited in *W10*). **1944** *S.F. News* (May 13) 7 (Tamony Coll.): Nervous Nellies who still fear a Japanese raid on Market Street. **1947** Blankfort *Big Yankee* 134 [ref. to Jan. 1927]: It was all "Nervous Nellie's" fault. That damned [Secretary of State Frank B.] Kellogg! He let the damned pacifists...talk him out of [further military action in Nicaragua]. **1953** *ATS* (ed. 2): *Nervous Nellie.* a jittery person. **1962** *Time* (Nov. 2): There were some Nervous Nelly reactions in the U.S. **1966** Gallery *Start Engines* 21: So he's a nervous Nellie whenever anything unusual happens. **1966** Pres. L.B. Johnson, in *Time* (May 27) 17: There will be some nervous Nellies and some who will become frustrated and bothered and break ranks under the strain. **1966** J. Daniels *Time Between Wars* 149 [ref. to 1927]: Kellogg, known in the Senate as "Nervous Nellie," had been...unenthusiastic. **1969** J. Abels *Silent Cal* 247: Secretary of State Frank B. Kellogg, a nervous man—Nervous Nellie he was called by former Senatorial colleagues—was described by associates as obstinate in the pursuit of a course of vacillation. **1971** Michelson *Very Simple Game* 71: We're a bunch of nervous Nellies.... I'm very high-strung. **1975** *Business Week* (Oct. 20) 102: Some nervous nellies might go to their banks and turn their deposits into currency. *a***1986** D. Tate *Bravo Burning* 103: If we let these Nervous Nellies run things, there's no telling who'll do us in first. **1987** da Cruz *Boot* 62: The shouting scares only the Nervous Nellies. **1988** P. Beck & P. Massman *Rich Men, Single Women* 5: What a nervous Nellie. **1995** *New Yorker* (Sept. 4) 63: Tell the Nervous Nellies it'll be their time before they know it.

nervous pudding *n.* a gelatin dessert. *Joc.* Also **nervous salad.**
   1936 *AS* (Feb.) 44: *Nervous Pudding.* Jello. **1942** *ATS* 98: *Nervous pudding*...gelatin. **1944** *PADS* (No. 2) 11: *Nervous salad*: n. Any gelatine salad. Alabama College slang. In use for at least ten years.

nervy *adj.* **1.** nervous.
   1891 in *OEDS*: I expect I be sort o' nervy, what with takin' a journey and the thought o' seein' Melindy. **1926** Hemingway *Sun Also Rises* 162: "I'm a little nervy about it," Brett said. "I'm worried whether I'll be able to go through with it all right." **1951** *Sat. Eve. Post* (Sept. 8) 123: He looked drawn and nervy.

2. impertinent. Now *S.E.*
   1896 G. Ade, in *DA*: I just received your nervy letter. **1899** in Davidson *Old West* 69: Say, Bill; you may think I'm nervy,/Wouldn't ask if I was flush.

nest *n.* the vulva or vagina.—usu. considered vulgar.
   *1782 in *F & H* V 29: Here's the nest in that bush, and the bird-nesting lover. **a1796* in J.S. Farmer *Merry Songs* IV 254: Ye still protest,/Ye never herried Maggie's nest. **1920–54** (quot. at HOG-EYE). **1940** Del Torto *TS*.: Her nest...was wet. **1971** Rader *Govt. Inspected* 68: He finger-fucked her nest.

nester *n. West.* a homesteader who settles on cattle-grazing land. Now *hist.*
   1880 in *DA*: [A sheep man is] a tramp, an ingrate, a "Nester," and a liar. **1913** Mulford *Coming of Cassidy* 356: He...hates sheep, barb' wire an' nesters as bad as I do. **1920–23** J.M. Hunter *Trail-Drivers* 860: In Kansas and Nebraska there were many nesters who had taken up claims of land under the laws of those states. *a***1940** in Lanning & Lanning *Texas Cowboys* 89: We ran into a bunch of settlers. The cowboys always called them "nesters." **1941** "L. Short" *Hard Men* 69: I'm only a nester over on Blue Crick! **1947** in *DA*: They did their best to

keep the nester...out of the West. **1950** Raine *Six* 63: Without pity he had harried nesters from the water holes they had homesteaded.

net *n.* ¶ In phrase: **drop a net on** to commit to an insane asylum.
   1942–49 Goldin et al. *DAUL* 144: The man in the white coat...will drop the net on you if you keep cabareting (indulging in erotic dreams) every night. **1956** *Phil Silvers Show* (CBS-TV): Someday they're gonna drop the net on me! **1958** *Phil Silvers Show* (CBS-TV): Someday they're going to drop a net over her.

neuro *n. Med.* neurosurgery; (*also*) a neurologist. Also as adj.
   1942 *ATS* 506: *Neuro*, a neurologist. **1982** Huttmann *Code Blue* 88: Ask a neuro doc. **1984** Holland *Let Soldier* 83: Well, there are six for the OR, counting the one for neuro.

neutral *adj.* stupid.
   1929 Botkin *Folk-Say I* 108: Well, looky what that *neutral* bastard has went and done!...*Neutral*...was a descriptive term applied to all brainless wonders....Well, when a car is not in gear, it's in *neutral*. And when a man's brain is out of gear, he's *neutral*. [**1975** Wambaugh *Choirboys* 142: Just put your mind in neutral with the car, partner.... We aren't going anywhere in this traffic.]

never happen see s.v. HAPPEN.

never hatchi see s.v. HATCHI.

never-mind *n.* ¶ In phrase: **make no never-mind** to make no difference.
   1924 Isman *Weber & Fields* 83 [ref. to 1880's]: Dot makes no nefer mind. **1924** *Sat. Eve. Post* (Jan. 3, 1925) 15: That should make a never mind....Pretty girls you could always put in [the movie]. **1937** *Esquire* (Feb.) 63: It don't make any never-mind to me. **1942** Pegler *Spelvin* 122: Makes no never mind about the Labor Board or the La Follette Committee. *Ibid.* 132: Makes no nevermind to me what the odds are. **1956** Evarts *Ambush Riders* 21: Back in Texas...we didn't pay much never mind to a horse thief's word. **1973** P. Benchley *Jaws* 276: Well, it don't make no never-mind.

never-sweat *n.* a person whose job requires or is thought to require little exertion. Cf. *no sweat* s.v. SWEAT.
   [**1863* Cheadle *Journal* 254: A large gold ring made on the Creek of "never sweat" gold worth some $50.] **1890** Erskine *Twenty Years* 18 [ref. to 1838]: I was one of the forties, that is, the "never-sweats,"—a mizzen-top man. **1928** Richie *Forty-Niners* 196: The lordly miners dubbed the farmers...Never Sweats. *ca***1950** in Logsdon *Whorehouse Bells* 112: Take the "never-sweat" from Nevada,/he's known as the "Son of the Sage." **1958** McCulloch *Woods Wds.* 120: *Never-sweat*—A lazy man or bum.

never-was *n.* [sugg. by *has-been*] Esp. *Sports.* an individual who has never succeeded in the pursuit of fame or popularity. Also (*obs.*) **never-waser.**
   1891 in *OEDS*: He is one of the "has beens" or else one of the "never wasers", as Dan Rice, the circus man, always called ambitious counterfeits. **1915** [Swartwood] *Choice Slang* 55: *Never wasser* [*sic*]...A person who has never amounted to anything and consequently can never be included within the category of "has beens." **1922** (quot. at NOT-YET). **1923** in *DA* s.v. *nope*: Nope, I'm a never-was. **1952** A. Cohn *Glory Alley* (film): Has-beens, would-have-beens, and never-wases. **1954–60** *DAS*: *Never-was*...A person who has never succeeded; one who has never had fame or fortune. **1995** *Morning Edition* (Nat. Pub. Radio) (Jan. 24): Bush league never-wases and washed-up old has-beens.

new *adj.* **1.** naive; gullible.
   1882 Peck *Peck's Sunshine* 227: They were awful "new" in regard to city ways. **1896** Ade *Artie* 83: When you see them fallin' into coal-holes and bein' snaked out by fake hotel-runners you think they're purty new. **1994** *As the World Turns* (CBS-TV): What are you, new? Don't ever touch a wire unless you know what it's connected to. **1996** Twohy *Arrival* (film): "You didn't tell anybody about our little club-house, did you?" "What am I, new?"

2. saucy; insolent; fresh.
   1896 Ade *Artie* 58: He was too new about it. **1900** *DN* II 47: *New,* adj. 1. Fresh....3. Forward. **1903** *Pedagog. Sem.* X 371: Don't get new. **1905** *Nat. Police Gaz.* (Dec. 2) 3: Just tell them that the Chinks are all right, see, and don't be so new. **1912** Ade *Babel* 170: Well, you'll be lookin' for another job if you get new with me.

¶ In phrase:

¶ **new one on (someone)** a complete novelty or surprise to (someone). Now *colloq.*

1887 *Lantern* (N.O.) (Dec. 17) 2: Isn't this a new one on you, Messrs. Police? **1905** Sinclair *Jungle* 194: That's a new one on me. **1911** A.H. Lewis *Apaches of N.Y.* 131: He's a new one on me. **1996** U.S. border patrol officer, age *ca*40, on *World News Tonight* (ABC-TV) (Oct. 7): That's a new one on me.

new bean *n. Mil.* NEWBIE.

1990 Yarborough *Da Nang Diary* 16 [ref. to Vietnam War]: According to the "new bean" pecking order…, I inherited the top bunk.

newbie *n. Esp. Mil. & Computers.* a newcomer, esp. a replacement in a combat unit or a new user of the Internet. Also **nubie.**

1970 in B. Edelman *Dear Amer.* 254: We got a lot of "Newbies" (replacements) in our company. **1970** *CBS Evening News* (CBS-TV) (July 12): "These guys were newbies and—" "What's a newby?" "A newby's a guy who hasn't been in the country long. They've just come over the border." **1971** *CBS Evening News* (CBS-TV) (Apr. 9): "Now let's all gather round while we welcome some of our newbies into our fellowship [of helicopter crewmen]. First let's have a song." "You're goin' home in a body-bag/Doodah, doodah!" **1974** (quot. at NEWFER). **1976** C.R. Anderson *Grunts* 40 [ref. to 1969]: [Lt.] Andrews…was the newest arrival—a "newby"—which meant he couldn't really lead or command anyone [without assistance]. **1983** Groen & Groen *Huey* 6: Made him feel like a newby, a new boy. **1985** (quot. at NEWK). **1987** Robbins *Ravens* 32: The new man was taken out on the town in a tradition known as "nubie night." **1990** R. Herman, Jr. *Force of Eagles* 11: He was flying like a newbee. **1991** K. Douglass *Viper Strike* 11: Dixon was a newbie. He'd come aboard…only three months earlier. **1993** *Reader's Digest* (May) 46: One rule calls for newbies to stand at rigid attention without moving. **1994** *Donahue* (NBC-TV): On the information highway we have people we call *newbies* who don't know what's going on. **1994** *N.Y. Times Mag.* (June 19) 14: He equates the use of all capital letters…with shouting, and finds it the sign of the *clueless newbie,* one new to the net. **1994** *Daily Beacon* (Univ. Tenn.) (July 22) 4: I'm an Internet idiot—a "newbie," as some would call me. **1995** *New Republic* (Apr. 10) 15: The influx of hundreds of thousands of newcomers via America Online, "newbies" who are stumbling around the net asking greenhorn questions. **1995** *Newsweek* (Dec. 25) 28: Perhaps the biggest short-term danger to the Net is the prospect of millions of newbies jumping on the boat.

New Cal *n. Mil.* New Caledonia, Canada. Now *hist.*

1944 in *Best from Yank* 23: There were times both in New Cal and later when he and the crew swore the whole shebang weighed a ton.

new cock *n. Pris.* a new inmate. [The 19th-C. quots. reflect different versions of the same ballad.]

ca*1870** in R. Palmer *Touch on Times* 250: Another new cock for Wakefield Gaol.…Each new cock must sing a song. *ca***1880** in Mackenzie *Ballads from Nova Scotia* 359: The kids [convicts] come out and did me hail,/"Here's another new cock for Kirtle Gaol!"…Till one old cock spoke up the rules:/That each new cock would sing a song,/Or tell a tale. **1957** in Algren *Lonesome Monsters* 130: Barton's my name. You're the new cock came in today. **1971** J. Blake *Joint* 65 [ref. to 1954]: These coveralls had a wide white stripe down the legs, and marked us as new-cocks.

Newf *n.* Newfoundland; *(also)* a Newfoundland dog.

1977 Langone *Life at Bottom* 74: "Right," says another, "bush leaguers all of 'em, the Coast Guard and the pipeliners and them pussy-stripers up in Newf." **1982** *Sunset* (May) 36: Newfs also retrieve underwater, tow boats, and leap off platforms to carry swimmers to safety. **1988** *Wkly. World News* (Apr. 5) 19: The handsome "Newf" is a breed well-known for its faithful devotion to people.

newfer *n. Mil.* NEWBIE. Also **newf.**

1971 *Army Reporter* (Feb. 1) 5: To better familiarize those newfers who have just arrived in Vietnam. **1974** Former 2Lt., 25th Inf. Div. [ref. to 1970–71]: A *newf* or a *newfer* was a new guy, a *newbie.* **1982** Del Vecchio *13th Valley* 24: Impatient disrespect for the newfers and for the army in general. **1990** G.R. Clark *Words of Viet. War* 345: *Newfer*…Any soldier new to the field lacking combat experience.

Newfie *n.* Newfoundland; *(also)* a Newfoundlander.—also used attrib.

1942 *ATS* 52: *Newfie,* New Foundland [*sic*]. **1943** *Yank* (May 7) 14: There're hobos in Newfie. **1944** *Yank* (Feb. 11) 9: The Yanks and the "Newfies"…have always hit it off well. **1945** Huie *Omaha to Oki.* 116: Newfie women. *Ibid.* 117: The International Fleet Canteen was Newfie's noisiest spot. **1948** *Newsweek* (Aug. 2): "Are we Newfies or Canadians?" the people of Newfoundland asked last week. **1949** *Time* (Nov. 14) 40: The hospitable Newfies and the free-spending Yanks. **1963** Hayden *Wanderer* 182: I'm a stupid goddam Newfie what's been haulin' his ass off on these Banks since he was thirteen years old. **1971** Waters *Smugglers* 38 [ref. to *ca*1930]: Newfie hijackers are always sneaking in here and raiding warehouses. **1974** Cherry *High Steel* xiv: The Newfies are often hockey freaks. **1976** *Dallas Morning News* (Nov. 14) 5C: I change my Polack stories to Newfie bits—about people from Newfoundland.

newie *n. Stu.* a new student; *(broadly)* a newcomer.

1834 *Mil. & Nav. Mag. of U.S.* (Oct.) 110: I was all unconscious that as yet I was but a "base plebe," an unexamined "newy." **1856** B. Hall *College Wds.* 334: *Newy.* At Princeton College, a fresh arrival. **1869** *Carmina Princetonia* 54: Greasing all the blackboards,/Going for the bell,/Getting some poor newie/On the latest sell. **1942** Breslow *Blondie Goes to College* (film): He's right over there with that newie.

new jack *n. Esp. Rap Music.* a newcomer or novice, esp. a raw or aggressive youngster. Cf. JACK.

1988 "Public Enemy" *Don't Believe the Hype* (rap song): They still consider me a new jack. **1988** T. Logan *Harder They Fall* 4: This new jack was actually coming after him. *Ibid.* 242: They're called "new jacks"—a generation of street toughs that grew up in…Detroit's inner city. **1988** *Spin* (Oct.) 47: *New jack n.* rapper who got started after whoever is speaking. *Ibid.* 58: The young new jacks [make] $2000 to $5000 a day selling…crack. **1989** "EPMD" *So What Ya Sayin'* (rap song): Don't need…a sucker new jack who needs a rappin' alignment. **1990** Vachss *Blossom* 29: A nujack…[with] a nine-millimeter automatic. **1990** *N.Y. Newsday* (June 14) II 8: Now, "new jacks" was a term in the rap world that I had heard around 1985, 1986, with a guy by the name of Grandmaster Caz.…He had a record dissing another rapper—and he said, "You're a new jack clown."…He said it was somebody who was green, a rookie, new to the game—and a sucker. **1991** Nelson & Gonzales *Bring Noise* 233: "Love and Marriage" (better known to new-jacks as the theme to shock TV's "Married With Children"). **1991** *Source* (Oct.) 28: All the new jacks [are] vying for props. **1992** *Melrose Place* (Fox-TV): Hey you guys! We got a new jack here. **1993** *Martin* (Fox-TV): Let the new jack handle it.

new-jack *adj. Esp. Rap Music.* new; recent; *(also)* of or pertaining to new-jack swing.—used prenominally. [The expression *new-jack swing* 'a style of rhythm-and-blues music influenced by rap music', coined in 1988, is S.E.]

1987 "EPMD," in B. Adler *Rap!* 67: Funky beat maker, new-jack exterminator. **1989** N. George, in *Village Voice* (N.Y.C.) (May 9) 28: The rap shows of DJ's Red Alert and Marley Marl, the supreme arbiters of new jack-speak. *Ibid.* (Aug. 15) 36: Old black tradition and new jack nihilism. **1991** N. George, in *Village Voice* (N.Y.C.) (May 28) 24: Was it less p.c. because today's new jack culture is often incorrect? **1992** *N.Y. Times* (Feb. 7) B11: The…New Jack drug dealers whose style informs the sport. **1992** *Rolling Stone* (Mar. 5) 4: The resultant New Jack harmony sound proved hard enough to get their breakthrough single "Motownphilly" over to rap fans, smooth enough for R&B radio and MTV.

New Jack City *n.* (see 1995 quot.).

1989 *Village Voice* (N.Y.C.) (July 11) 34: A new economic and psychic urban environment: New Jack City. New Jack City exists wherever there's a crack house, a back room stuffed with stolen VCRs and family jewelry, bleary-eyed young girls with bad breath willing to do the Unthinkable with the Anonymous.…New Jack City exists in Harlem, the Bronx, Baltimore, Philadelphia, Detroit, Los Angeles, [etc.]. **1991** Cooper & Wright *New Jack City* [film title]. **1995** Stavsky, Mozeson & Mozeson *A 2 Z: New Jack City*…New York City, or any large urban Black neighborhood like South-central L.A.

new jill *n. Rap Music.* a female performer of new-jack swing. Also as *adj.* Cf. JILL.

1990 *Village Voice* (N.Y.C.) (May 1) 91: The r&b, house, go-go, reggae, and new-jill swing on *Blacks' Magic*…have obvious cross over appeal…roots rap for black women. **1992** *N.Y. Newsday* (July 5) ("Fanfare") 7: New jills like TLC and Janet Jackson…have dominated the black charts.

newk *n.* [resp. *newc*omer] *Stu. & Mil.* a newcomer; NEWBIE.

1972 Eble *Campus Slang* (Oct.) 4: *Newk*—beginner, novice. **1985** Roskey *Muffled Shots* 45 [ref. to *ca*1965]: In the U.S. Army Pacific,...replacements were called variously "newks," "newbies," or "nugs."

new meat *n.* **1.** *Pris.* newly arrived prison inmates; a new inmate.

    1938 in A. Lomax *Mr. Jelly Roll* 118 [ref. to *ca*1905]: When the inmates on the gang saw us, they hollered "New meat in the market!" Then they jumped on us and took our money and cigarettes. **1968** Pearce & Pierson *Cool Hand Luke* (film): You new meats better shape up fast for this gang. **1993** *Mystery Sci. Theater* (Comedy Central TV): Buck up, new meat.

  2. *Stu.* a freshman.

    1962 in *AS* (Dec. 1963) 272: During a student's first year, he will be referred to as *new meat*.

  3. *Mil.* new replacements or a new replacement, esp. in a combat unit.—also used attrib.

    1971 *Newsweek* (Sept. 13) 40: A batch of twelve new replacements, "newmeats" in GI argot, for Bravo Company. **1973** Karlin, Paquet & Rottmann *Free Fire Zone* 80: I thought it was a pretty good trick, but I was just new meat and nothing bothered me. **1974** Former SP4, U.S. Army, age 24: New replacements are *new meats*. **1978** J. Webb *Fields of Fire* 79 [ref. to 1969]: Speedy!...Got some new meat for ya! **1983** N. Proffitt *Gardens of Stone* 150: He was a new meat, greased on his first day in the bush. **1983** Goldman & Fuller *Charlie Co.* 271: A fresh shipment of new-meat troopers. **1986** Dye *Platoon* 16: Let's try the other new meat. Get Gardner up here. **1988** Clodfelter *Mad Minutes* 75 [ref. to 1966]: The "new meat" replenishing our numbers suffered...the usual harassment. *Ibid.* 234: Who'd ya zap, new meat? **1988** C. Roberts & C. Sasser *Walking Dead* 126 [ref. to *ca*1966]: We actually got some new meat. **1989** Leib *Fire Dream* 82: They sang a cadence to welcome "new meat."

newshawk *n.* **1.** a journalist, esp. if zealous; NEWSHOUND.

    1931 in *OEDS*: *Newshawk*..., used for "reporter." **1934** in Ruhm *Detective* 100: Many times one or all of them had felt like socking the erstwhile newshawk. **1936** in M. Crane *Roosevelt* 242: He told newshawks of the sale of the...[magazine] to *Time*. **1941** Brecher & Kurnitz *Shadow of Thin Man* (film): Will you call these newshawks off? **1949** Wedlock et al. *Abbott & Costello Meet Killer* (film): All you newshawks hangin' around here. **1950** *N.Y. Times* (June 4) II 1: One of this newspaper's ever-vigilant newshawks happened by the Majestic Theatre at about 3:30 the A.M. of Memorial Day. **1959** Zugsmith *Beat Generation* 119: Some of those newshawks hate the Beats. **1966** H.S. Thompson *Hell's Angels* 37: The Attorney General...handed it out in a neat white package, one to each news hawk. **1972** W.C. Anderson *Hurricane* 114: He...seems to be a spanking good newshawk.

  2. a newsdealer.

    1957 H. Simmons *Corner Boy* 82: "How you expect to keep up with what's going on in the world, mister?" the news hawk said. **1971–73** Sheehy *Hustling* 21: All-night counter men, hotel staffers, newshawks.

news hen *n. Journ.* a female news reporter.

    1946 G.C. Hall, Jr. *1000 Destroyed* 308: Leaving me bereft of all save my memories of Lee Carson, Hearst news-hen. **1949** *Time* (Aug. 29) 9: To impress Newshen Florabel Muir he even let one of his retainers...win a couple of hands. **1954** *Time* (Jan. 11) 3: [Letter to ed. from a female reader:] Newshen is one of the cleverest coined words. Short, flattering....Why the profound research into the feminine of newshawk? Female! A hideous word. Let the girls remember the feminine of newshound. **1978** *Mary Worth*, synd. comic strip, in *L.A. Times* (May 19): News*men* are usually unbiased! But newshens tend to reflect the station manager's opinions!

news hole *n. Journ.* the amount of space or air time available for news stories.

    1973, 1974, 1975, 1976 in *AS* 51 (1976) 217.

newshound *n. Journ.* a news reporter.

    1918 in *OEDS*: "Got what all figured out," queried the news hound eagerly. **1931** Rouverol *Dance, Fools, Dance* (film): Hello, kid. How's the little newshound? **1949** Bartlett & Lay *Twelve O'Clock High!* (film): Don't let that kraut newshound throw you too much. **1953** F. Gibbons *Floyd Gibbons* 137: Fortunately, there were available a new crop of energetic "news hounds" to fill the vacancies. **1970** *Playboy* (Feb.) 32: A town overrun by boozy old newshounds. **1975** Stanley *WWIII* 234: I was drunk when one of your newshounds saw me in that bar. **1978**

Strieber *Wolfen* 229: There ain't any other newshounds hangin' around. **1981** R. Baker, in *N.Y. Times Mag.* (June 27) 10: The newshounds found another door to bay at. **1981** *Rod Serling's Mag.* (Sept.) 53: Darren McGavin as the slightly threadbare news-hound Carl Kolchak, alias The Night Stalker. **1982** Braun *Judas Tree* 24: A seasoned newshound, he employed flattery with the subtle touch of a diplomat.

newsie *n.* **1.** a newsboy or newsdealer.

    1875 in *OEDS*: A newsboy on the M. and C. road was cruelly beating a dog which had jumped on the train, when its owner suddenly appeared at the car door, knocked "newsy" off and commenced to pay him in his own coin. **1885** *Nat. Police Gaz.* (Oct. 10) 3: This rule bears rather hard on the "newsies" and bootblacks. **1903** Kildare *Mamie Rose* 52 [ref. to 1880's]: Then began the usual existence of the "newsies." **1904** McCardell *Show Girl* 62: So I tipped Moxie, the newsy. **1915** Poole *Harbor* 157: Another boy, a little New York "newsie," with a pack of evening papers, came loitering along the pier. **1928** Dahlberg *Bottom Dogs* 134: At least that's what the 8th street newsies said. *Ibid.* 250: He could blah with a newsie. **1930** Shaw *Jack-Roller* 141: The alley was usually filled with a large number of "newsies" and truck chauffeurs. **1933** Mahin & Furthman *Bombshell* (film): Newsies start selling it to the man on the street. [**1969** Geller & Boas *Drug Beat* 135: Once the marijuana arrives in the United States, it is distributed through dealers (called at various levels "pushers," "connections," "score boys," "newsies," and so on).] **1974** *Atlantic* (Dec.) 29: Volume is everything; the newsie is indifferent to your particular presence, and don't waste his time. **1975** *Harper's* (June) 29: Checking out your corner drugstore and newsie. **1992** Tzudiker & White *Newsies* [film title].

  2. *Journ.* a journalist or broadcast news announcer.

    1951 Twist *Ft. Worth* (film): Outside papers'll start diggin', and them newsies stick together like sorghum. **1954–60** *DAS*: Newsie...A newscaster, a radio news announcer. *Not common.* **1967** "M.T. Knight" *Terrible Ten* 58: You ain't a cop and you ain't a newsie, so what's your angle? **1970–71** Rubinstein *City Police* 382: Maybe you can tell me about a few other newsies in the area. **1973** *Atlantic* (Feb.) 58: You were too damn stiff with the newsies, Paul....That made the difference. The *Time* cover, all that horseshit. **1980** *L.A. Times* (Oct. 6) VI 7: If TV newsies can't get a little tax break on wardrobes and beautification, then they'll be less inclined to keep up appearances. **1984** (quot. at RIP-'N'-READER). **1985** Sawislak *Dwarf* 11: It made him the unchallenged king of the newsies. **1991** *Capital Gang* (CNN-TV) (June 29): Could this be a vendetta of the newsies? **1993** *All Things Considered* (Nat. Pub. Radio) (Mar. 2): Old [network] newsies, skilled in production. **1996** *Time* (Mar. 18) 24: Establishment Republicans, Democrats, and newsies from left and right.

newspaper *n. Pris.* a thirty-day jail sentence.

    1926 Maines & Grant *Wise-Crack Dict.* 11: Newspaper—Crook's term for thirty days in jail. **1929** *AS* IV (June) 343: Newspaper. Thirty days in jail. **1935** Pollock *Und. Speaks*: Newspaper, sentenced to jail for thirty days.

newsroom *n.* a galley or kitchen where gossip circulates. Also **news office.**

    1841 [Mercier] *Man-of-War* 96: This is the frigate's *news room*, where you hear/Of all events transpired both far and near. **1917** Lord *Boyd's Btry.* 24: News Office—the kitchen, where the rumors come from.

newt *n. Stu.* a foolish person.

    1929 Botkin *Folk-Say I* 109: From the adjective [*neutral*] is derived the noun *newt*. A *newt* is a *dumb-bell*, a *blockhead*. **1954–60** *DAS*: Newt...A stupid person. **1990** P. Munro *Slang U.* 137: Newt inept or inexperienced person....Adrian can't get girls 'cause he's such a newt.

New York minute *n.* a moment; instant.

    1967 in *DARE*: It won't take any longer than...[a] New York minute. **1980** in Safire *Coming to Terms* 155: They'd be on us in a New York minute. **1985** *Miami Vice* (NBC-TV): I don't believe that for a New York minute. **1984–87** Ferrandino *Firefight* 88: Some of the motherfuckers will rat you out in a New York minute. **1988** Launer & Henning *Dirty Rotten Scoundrels* (film): I could kick your ass off this hill in a New York minute. [*a*1989 in Safire *Coming to Terms* 156: My father died in 1930 at the age of sixty-nine, when I was twenty-seven....[He] would often say, "I can do that in a York minute."] **1989** *Donahue* (NBC-TV): If he was pregnant, he'd have an abortion in a New York minute. **1992** G. Wolff *Day at the Beach* 37: Hang on just a New York minute. **1993** *New Yorker* (Mar. 22) 41: It took a New York minute before the dashing

CBS newcomers got crossways with Roslyn. **1996** *Montel Williams Show* (synd. TV series): A "New York minute" is like *that* fast.

next *adj.* **1.a.** informed; aware; in the know; (*hence*) sophisticated; WISE.—often constr. with *to*. Cf. *get next to*, below.

 1896 Ade *Artie* 14: I said I was dead sore about not bein' next to the point. *Ibid.* 16: I never put you next to how I come to meet her, did I? *Ibid.* 68: Get next to the walk, Miller; get on, get on! *Ibid.* 83: They can't spring none o' that happy-childhood-days-down-on-the-farm business on me. I've been next, I'll tell you those. **1900** Willard & Hodler *Powers That Prey* 131: Ain't no one put you next? **1902** Bell *Worth of Words* 206: *Getting next* means getting inside information. **1902** K. Harriman *Ann Arbor Tales* 228: I'm goin' to get next to-night. **1903** in *DA*: Be dead certain not to let anybody, even pikers, get next, so that none of the fellows in the ring will get hit with that 30 to 1 I chalked up. **1903** Ade *Society* 152: You seem to be Next. Did they teach all this at Boarding-School? **1904** *Life in Sing Sing* 258: *Are you next?* Do you understand? **1905** *DN* III 77: I'm *dead next to* what he's up to. **1906** M'Govern *Sarjint Larry* 59: One of de cavalrymen put us next. **1908** McGaffey *Show Girl* 200: Some gabby girl put wifey next. *a*1909 Tillotson *Detective* 93: *Next*—To be informed. **1912** Lowrie *Prison* 152: Th' play was too good t' keep t' myself, an' I put most of th' gang next. **1914** E.R. Burroughs *Mucker* 31: "You'll understand that it's to avert any possible suspicion later." "I'm next." **1928** C. McKay *Banjo* 148: Why didn't you put me next, too? **1936** Tully *Bruiser* 41: She took me for a hundred before I got next. **1971** in H.S. Thompson *Shark Hunt* 138: The Hotel Ashmun is a good place to stay if you want to get next to whatever's happening on Whittier Boulevard. **1972** Grogan *Ringolevio* 266: The heavy dopers stone-refused to get next to anything nutritional—so they died. **1973** *N.Y. Times* (Sept. 16) II 3: It takes a lot of historical sympathy to get next to that one.

 b. impudent.

 1896 Ade *Artie* 102: I must be gettin' purty far along when that guy gets next and tries to play horse with me.

 2. close; friendly.—usu. constr. with *to*.

 1896 Ade *Artie* 19: As soon as I see her...I swore I'd get next no matter what kind of a brash play I had to make. **1897** Ade *Pink* 133: I figgah out what I got to do to get nex' to 'at lady. **1899–1900** Cullen *Tales* 227: You dig out the old geezers, get next to them, interview 'em about their early experiences. *a*1904–11 D.G. Phillips *Susan Lenox* II 148: Nobody amounts to anything...unless he's got a pull or is next to somebody else that has. **1928** Dahlberg *Bottom Dogs* 50: If a kid could get next to Ahnie in the laundry, he could come out with some biscuits with raisins every Wednesday nite. **1929–30** Dos Passos *42d Parallel* 63: He liked...Olive, better, but Ike got next to her first. **1930** Sage *Last Rustler* 22: If you don't git next to that horse with kindness, you won't git next at all. **1978** Maggin *Superman* 35: I figure'd the chicks'd be climbing the walls like King Kong to get next to me. **1979–82** Gwin *Overboard* 112: I decided, sure, I'll go ahead and get next to Willy.

¶ In phrases:

¶ **get next to, 1.** to get for oneself.

 1896 Ade *Artie* 43: I wonder he got next to that fancy pass about severin' relationships. **1908** McGaffey *Show Girl* 28: Some hussy got next to my toothpicks and I had to use a hairpin for a liner.

 2. Esp. *Black E.* **a.** strongly affect, appeal to.

 1939 Bontemps *Drums* 30: This'll get next to *you*....You'll feel new-made. It's a real aphrodisiac to the females. **1965** C. Brown *Manchild* 271: Then the manhood thing started getting next to cats through drugs. *Ibid.* 354: She had so much self-confidence that it just got next to me.

 b. to succeed in annoying.

 1972 in W. King *Black Anthol.* 373: Damn, she musta' really got nex' to you, man. What she do? **1978** W. Brown *Tragic Magic* 52: Paula had really gotten next to me. I didn't want to believe that my only reason for not going into the army was to get attention.

 3. to become sexually intimate with; seduce.

 1944 Micheaux *Mrs. Wingate* 31: Wonder if any has ever got next to her? **1950** A. Lomax *Mr. Jelly Roll* 19: I'm telling you we're liable to get next to that broad. She liked that very much. **1952** Viereck *Men into Beasts* 65: Not a feather on him. What I wouldn't give to get next to that. **1965** Trimble *Sex Words* 89: *Get Next To*...To accomplish Copulation or other Sex Relations with someone. **1965** C. Brown *Manchild* 208: Lord, when I saw her, I wanted to get next to her so badly. **1978** W. Brown *Tragic Magic* 43: Growing up, I never thought seriously

about getting next to her. **1993** *Class of '96* (Fox-TV): You tellin' me she had to lie to get next to you?

¶ **put next to** to introduce or direct to.

 1903 A.H. Lewis *Boss* 273: I could put you next to a hundred blokes...who'd do him up for half th' price. *a*1904–11 D.G. Phillips *Susan Lenox* I 265: I'm sure I can put her next to something. **1913** J. London *Valley of Moon* 58: I'll put you next to some of the good dancers. **1988** *Miami Vice* (NBC-TV): So you put him next to Stiles.

next-of-kin button *n. Mil. Av.* a control switch that operates an automatic ejection seat. *Joc.* Also **next-of-kin trigger.**

 1959 R.L. Scott *Tiger in Sky* 43: A T-bar located on the floor of the cockpit...was dubbed by the inventors of the new pilot vocabulary as the "next-of-kin" button; the clumsy one would be shot out of the cockpit like a cannonball. **1961** L.G. Richards *TAC* 52: If you happen to hit the "next-of-kin" triggers or ejection controls. *Ibid.* 56: When we quit climbing and the airspeed starts dying off, hit the next-of-kin button.

N.F.G. *adj.* **1.** [elab. of N.G.] no fucking good.—usu. considered vulgar. Also as *interj.* Cf. N.B.G.

 1977 Torres *Q & A* 162: He's...N.F.G., with the oak leaf clusters. **1988** T. Logan *Harder They Fall* 106: N.F.G.! Start grouping your shots....Like this. **1990** G.R. Clark *Words of Viet. War* 356: NFG...no-fuckin'-good.

 2. *Army.* FNG.

 1992 Rodrique *Heading Home* 152 [ref. to Viet. War]: "You're just one more N.F.G." "An N.F.G." "New Fucking Guy; a cherry."

N.F.W. *interj.* no fucking way.—usu. considered vulgar.

 1974 J. Mills *One Just Man* 125: Just NFW. No fuckin' *way.* **1987** in Rawson *Wicked Words* 165: A rude rejoinder: "N.F.W." Loosely translated: "No Feasible Way."

N.G. *n.* **1.** a no-good.

 1879 *Tribe of Tammany* 5: He...became a brawler and an N.G. **1898–1900** Cullen *Chances* 15: This nag...was sold as an N.G. last year for $25.

 2. [back formation fr. FNG] *Army.* new guy; a newly arrived replacement. [Quot. ref. to Vietnam War.]

 1974 Former sgt., 11th Armored Cav. Regt.: In Vietnam we called a new guy an N.G. or an F.N.G. You'd say, "We got a new N.G."

N.G. *adj.* **1.** no go; unsuccessful.

 1839 *Spirit of Times* (May 25) 139: And though his grey-headed rival tried hard to win, it was n.g. (no go!). *Ibid.* (June 15) 174: Fordham marked "N.G."—*no go.* **1886** Nye *Remarks* 345: We tried "snubbing" and everything we could think of, but it was N.G.

 2. no good.

 1876 Grover *Boarding House* 204: His Anti-bilious-what-you-call-it is N.G. Why don't he cure himself? **1877** *Puck* (Mar.) 10: Chicago is N.G. **1877–78** *Cornelian* 86: N.G. No good. **1879** *Tribe of Tammany* 8: He was ignominiously ejected from the Wigwam as N.G. **1885** in Lummis *Letters* 234: And then find it n.g. **1897** Paramore *Klondike* 9: As a river pilot he is "N.G." **1909** Klein & Hornblow *3rd Degree* 7: I'm N.G.—that's a cinch! *a*1904–11 D.G. Phillips *Susan Lenox* II 270: Susie, at bottom I'm N.G. **1934** Appel *Brain Guy* 7: The numbers'd been n.g. **1934** H.L. Mencken *Amer. Lang.* (ed. 4) 92: Such highly typical Americanisms as *O.K., N.G.,* and *P.D.Q.* **1940** in A. Lomax *Mr. Jelly Roll* 254: She is N.G. and I don't owe her anything. **1962** Perry *Young Man Drowning* 124: "How'd it go?" "N.G. Somebody made us." **1970** Thackrey *Thief* 362: It's got to be n.g....They don't know what the fuck they're talking about. **1970** Gattzden *Black Vendetta* 45: They were three anti-social hoodlums—strictly N.G.

nib *n.* [dial. var. of ME *neb* 'a beak'] the mouth or face. *Rare* in U.S.

 [***1698–99** "B.E." *Dict. Canting Crew:* She holds up her *neb:* she turns up her mouth to be kissed.] ***1796** Grose *Dict. Vulgar Tongue* (ed. 3): *Neb,* or *nib.* The bill of a bird....Figuratively, the face and mouth of a woman. **1800** *Amorous Songster* 64: Pray how do you like my nib,/My trowses wide my trampler on,/My nab and flowing jib? **1859** Matsell *Vocab.* 58: *Nib.* The mouth.

nibs *n.* [perh. synechdochically fr. NIB; cf. NABS] a person readily identifiable from context; (*ironically*) an important or self-important person.—usu. constr. with *his, her,* or *your* [royal].

 [***1812** Vaux *Vocab.* Nib: a gentleman or person of the higher order.] ***1821** (cited in *OED*). ***1846** in *OEDS:* She flokessed his nibs, and hooked it off to his crib. **1848** Baker *Glance at N.Y.* 15: I say, Mike, do you know his knibbs? **1862** in J.W. Haley *Rebel Yell* 32: Had his Royal ~~Nibs lived in these days of steam~~ [etc.]. **1867** (quot. at CULLY, 2). *__1870__ Greey *Blue Jackets* 52: My nibs ain't vardi for that. **1874** (quot. at STAG, *v.*). **1879** *Nat. Police Gaz.* (Mar. 15) 11: Say, Mike, d'ye hear his nibs? **1880** Small *Mother-in-Law* 30: "See the cove as is a gadderin' up dogs for a sassage mill. Hey!" "Twig his nibs!" **1882** A.W. Aiken *Joe Buck* 8: And what handle will suit your royal nibs? **1882** Field *Tribune Verse* 210: I have his royal nibs in tow. **1883** Field *Sharps & Flats* I 64: Hail monarch!.../And bless thy fate that foes should fail/To slay a nibs so nobby. **1887** Peck *Pvt. Peck* 48 [ref. to 1864]: I went up to the general's tent...and I said I wanted to see "his nibs," and I walked right by the guard, who seemed stunned by my cheek. **1889** Barrère & Leland *Dict. Slang* I 464: *His nibs* (theatrical), himself; his person. **1891** Munroe *Campmates* 71: How's her royal nibs today? **1892** Bierce *Beetles* 100: His nibs the popular John S. Gray. *__1892__ in J. Farmer *Musa Pedestris* 188: Out of his nibs I had taken a rise. **1901** in "O. Henry" *Cabbages & Kings* 14: His Nibs skedaddled. **1903** A. Adams *Log of Cowboy* 333: Just to show his royal nibs that he's been thoughtless. **1905** in "O. Henry" *Works* 1574: Well, good-night Your Nibs. **1907** Corbin *Cave Man* 324: Her nibs wanted to know...if I was a gentleman. **1908** in H.C. Fisher *A. Mutt* 22: The single blessedness didn't make a hit with his nibs. **1912** Siringo *Cowboy Detective* 24: So as to find out how much money his Royal Nibs was blowing in. **1926** *AS* I 651: *His Nibs.* Police Magistrate. **1927** H. Miller *Moloch* 103: Her nibs, perched on a high stool. **1932–33** P. Cain *Fast One* 45: You'd better get a doctor for his nibs. **1934** Burns *Female Convict* 100: The nibs is as mad as a hatter this morning. **1935** Whelan & Higgins *Murder Man* (film): You heard me tell his nibs I wasn't going to work here anymore. **1935** C.J. Daly *Murder* 290: And His Nibs. **1937** *AS* XII 46: *Hisnibs* [*sic*]. The leader of the [jazz] band. **1942** Horman & Corley *Capts. of Clouds* (film): I doubt if his nibs will. **1950** F. Brown *Space on Hands* 192: The freckled copy boy said, "His Nibs wants to see ya." **1958** S.H. Adams *Tenderloin* 41: Are you gonna put Georgiana wise to his Nibs? **1973** "J. Godey" *Pelham* 54: Tell his nibs supervision is on the way. **1978** Strieber *Wolfen* 38: His nibs is awaiting us. **1987** Blankenship *Blood Stripe* 44: I could see that, and so could his nibs. **1994** *Mystery Sci. Theater* (Comedy Central TV): We'd better check on his nibs.

¶ In phrase:

¶ **sherry (one's) nibs** to leave in a hurry.
    1890 Quinn *Fools of Fortune* 373: I says: "Swipe the swag and sherry your nibs." That's slang you know. **1899** A.H. Lewis *Sandburrs* 80: At last she's seen enough an' sherries her nibs to d' cat'edral. **1903** C.B. Loomis *Cheerful Amer.* 238: Ah, git a move on....sherry yer nibs, now. **1921** Conklin & Root *Circus* 173 [ref. to ca1880]: They had just begun to do a good business [swindling] when they got the word "sherry your nibs."

nibshit *n.* [*nib* (of unkn. orig.) + SHIT] **1.** a useless or meddlesome person; a nobody.—usu. considered vulgar. Cf. DIP-SHIT.
    *ca*1960 IUFA *Folk Speech*: Denotes someone who is overly curious. adj: nibby noun: nib or nib-shit. **1979** G. Wolff *Duke of Deception* 235 [ref. to *ca*1960]: The banker was a "nibshit."
    2. emphatically nothing.—usu. considered vulgar.
    1979 G. Wolff *Duke of Deception* 38 [ref. to 1940's]: I'm finished....What's the point....nibshit, kid...nibshit.

nibshit *v.* to meddle or fool around.—usu. considered vulgar.
    1972 Andrews & Dickens *Big House* 73: Now, I knew where Virginia was and I also knew what happened to niggers who went down there nibshitting.

Nic *n.* Nicaragua. Also as adj.
    1933 *Leatherneck* (Jan.) 31: My old razor-blade buddies were being entertained by Sandino down in "Nic." **1984** *N.Y. Post* (Aug. 3) 4: GOP plank backs Nic rebels.

nice *adj.* ¶ In phrase: **make nice** see s.v. MAKE, *v.*

nice guy see s.v. MISTER NICE GUY.

nice Nellie *n.* a prissy or overly fastidious person.—used derisively. Also (*nonce*) as v. and adj.
    1936 in *OEDS*: Perhaps, it is true, as charged that the British press is displaying a brand of Nice Nellyism in refusing to mention the subject [*sc.*, the divorce of Mrs. Wallis Simpson, later Duchess of Windsor]. **1942** *ATS* 391: Respectable girl.... *nice Nellie.* **1947** *Tomorrow* (Aug.) 31: Pedants and Nice Nellies. **1952** in *DAS*: I've got to use "heck" [instead of "hell"] because practically all my editors are...being

more rabidly nice Nellie than usual. **1954** Collans & Sterling *House Detect.* 127: The lecherous couple...will be "surprised" *in flagrante delicto*, as the legal bigwigs nice-nelly it. **1975** Boatner et al *Dict. Amer. Idioms* 232: We took him for a nice Nelly when he wouldn't fight.

Nick *n.* the devil.—usu. constr. with *old.* Cf. NED, 3.
    *__1643__ in *OED:* For Roundheads Old Nick stand up now. *__1668__ (cited in Partridge *DSUE* 585). *__a1720__ in D'Urfey *Pills* I 264: The God of Love, or else old Nick. **1851** M. Reid *Scalp-Hunters* 105: Warm his collops wi' the bull-rope,...Nick syrup him! **1866** in Hilleary *Webfoot* 174: Every fellow for himself and old nick for the hindmost. *a***1904–11** D.G. Phillips *Susan Lenox* II 157: I get full every night and raise old Nick.

nick *n.* **1.** a hybrid.
    *__1824__ in *OEDS:* Some rearers of game fowls...are favourable to breeding from the third remove, which they call a nick. **1973** Walkup & Otis *Race* 42: You might get one hell of a nick—fantastic speed and staying power—if you crossed Sparky's bloodlines with that new Australian mare of yours.
    2.a. a nickel coin; (*hence*) the value of a nickel coin. [The name *nickel* was applied initially to the one-cent piece issued 1857–64; a three-cent nickel was minted 1866–83; the five-cent nickel, since 1883.]
    1857 in *DA:* The bags containing the "Nicks"...each...held five hundred [of the new coins]. **1859** Bartlett *Amer.* (ed. 2) 292: *Nick.* The name already given to the new cent, from the material (nickel) of which it is composed. **1865** Sala *Diary* II 54: Two sticks of lollipops are to be had for two "nicks." **1894** in S. Crane *N.Y.C. Sks.* 106: Say, Jimmie, gimme change for a nick! **1899** Cullen *Tales* 89: I was shy on the price of them. Didn't have a nick. **1910** Ade *I Knew Him When* 17: At the age of 7 he paid a Nick for three Cheroots. **1912–14** in E. O'Neill *Lost Plays* 38: I ain't got a nick. **1932** *AS* VII 402: *Nick,* n. A nickle [*sic*]. **1976** Knapp & Knapp *One Potato* 21: They can draw straws or flip a "nick" (nickel). **1976** Mamet *Amer. Buffalo* 46: He goes ninety [dollars] on the [collector's rare] nick. **1983** *Publishers Wkly.* (Apr. 15) 52: We stocked up on this paper a while ago...so now it's only a nick more expensive than our regular stock.
    b. five dollars; five dollars' worth.
    *ca*1961 (cited in T.L. Clark *Dict. Gamb. & Gaming* in sense 'a five-dollar chip'). **1994** *N.Y. Times* (Feb. 6) IV 18: $5 "nickel bag" A nick.
    3. *Und.* (see 1942–49 quot.).
    1928 in Partridge *Dict. Und.* 468: "How much do you figure the first nick?" "Oh, about ten grand." **1935** *AS* (Feb.) 18 [ref. to *a*1910]: *Nick.* n. A successful job. Modern *score.* **1942–49** Goldin et al. *DAUL: Nick*...(Heard rarely but over widely scattered areas) A successful criminal coup; the proceeds of a crime; anything borrowed or begged; the act of obtaining anything by begging or borrowing.
    4. a nickname.
    1985 Bodey *F.N.G.* 195: "Gabriel Sauers." "No nick?" "Nope."

nick *v.* **1.** Esp. *Und.* **a.** to rob.
    *__1617__ in *F & H* V 37: You men of wares, the men of wars will nick ye: For starve nor beg they must not. *__1727–28__ J. Gay, in *F & H* V 37: He was nick'd of three pieces of cambric before he could look off. *__1829__ in Partridge *Dict. Und.* 468: That oil-shop the corner of Cannon-street, i went in a [*i.e.,* to] nick the *lob* of 7 *peg.* **1849** "N. Buntline" *B'hoys of N.Y.* 41: Nicked, sure as gospel!...pickpockets about. **1902** Hapgood *Thief* 210: She stopped; and at that moment the Kid nicked her. **1907** in H.C. Fisher *A. Mutt* 20: Just one word, sir, before you nick me. **1911** Howard *Enemy to Society* 302: We had tuh...swear th' guy he was gonna nick had stole from th' poor. **1925** in Hammett *Knockover* 68: She was stuck-up a couple of months back and nicked for eight hundred dollars. **1927** in Hammett *Knockover* 277: All I got was that the Seaman's [bank] is gonna be nicked. **1928** Sharpe *Chicago May* 37: The first of those years we nicked the builders, the second the visitors. **1935** in Galewitz *Great Comics* 256: Wot th'!—so you was gonna nick me for my gun! Yah little tramp!
    b. to cheat; defraud.
    *__1676__ Wycherley *Plain Dealer* III: I ventured my last stake upon the squire to nick him of his mother. *__1746__ in Dugaw *Warrior Women* 53: Slap then we're nick'd of 20,000 Spouses. *__1817__ Sir W. Scott, in *F & H* V 37: The polite and accomplished adventurer, who nicked you out of your money at White's. *__1823__ "J. Bee" *Slang:* To nick...means "to cheat"—of money, of chattels, or of life. **1827** in *JAF* LXXVI (1963) 291: *Joe,*...yuve nik't the hol boodle ov um. **1929** McEvoy *Hollywood*

Girl 120: Krunch is nicking the lady. **1939** in W.C. Fields *By Himself* 364: We were going to nick him for a hunk for the writing. **1977** Coover *Public Burning* 204: After nicking gullible old Peter Minuit...for twenty-four dollars. **1981** G. Wolf *Roger Rabbit* 144: For how much did you nick Rocco? **1988** *ALF* (NBC-TV): You got took...nicked...hornswoggled.

c. *Orig. Und.* to steal; pilfer.

   *1869 in Partridge *DSUE* 559: I bolted in and nicked a nice silver teapot. ***1873** Hotten *Slang Dict.* (ed. 4): *Nick,...*Also to steal. To be "out on the *nick*" is to be out thieving. **1908** in Blackbeard & Williams *Smithsonian Comics* 58: She must have nicked my bankroll. **1911** Howard *Enemy to Society* 237: Don't ever think I'd 'a' taught you to "nick" anythin'. **1916** E.R. Burroughs *Return of Mucker* 115: That money was the enemy's resources, an' I just nicked their resources. **1927** *DN* V 456: *Nick, v.* To steal. **1928** Guerin *Crime* 21 [ref. to *a*1880]: I said I was in for "nicking" a box of cutlery. **1986–89** Norse *Memoirs* 266: God knows where he nicked them.

d. to ask or demand (of); exact (something) from; (*Baseball*) to get hits from (a pitcher).—often constr. with *from.*

   1878 Pinkerton *Strikers Communists* 54: He will then immediately edge around the boys and "nick the office." "Nicking" the office consists in begging among the printers for nickels, or any other loose change they may have to bestow; and the tramp under these circumstances will not despise even coppers. **1912** in P. Dickson *Baseball Dict.:* Nick a [baseball] pitcher [for hits or runs]. **1925** Cohan *Broadway* 206: They were the only guys left we hadn't "nicked" for the eighty. **1930** in *DAS:* A chap in Chicago who nicks the racketeers one grand a year. **1934** Weseen *Dict. Amer. Sl.* 215: Baseball...*Nick a pitcher*—To get hits off a pitcher. **1944** Busch *Dream of Home* 143: Figure I'd nick you for a bottle of beer. **1942–49** Goldin et al. *DAUL: Nick...*To beg, borrow, or steal from; to obtain something for nothing. **1950** Jacoby & Brady *Champagne* (film): For the first time...a contestant has nicked us for $320.

2. *Esp. Police.* to catch (a person), esp. to place under arrest; apprehend.

   *1622 Fletcher & Massinger, in *OED:* We must be sometimes witty, To knick a knave. ***1700** in *F & H* V 38: Well madam, you see I'm punctual—you've nicked your man, faith. ***1706** in *OED:* If he gets him dead drunk, then is the critical Minute to nick him. ***1806** in *OED:* He...stands a chance of getting nicked, because he was found in bad company. ***1830** in Partridge *Dict. Und.* 468: He beat us on Friday—but I will nick him on Monday. ***1836** F. Marryat, in *OED:* He has come to get off his accomplice, and now we've just nicked them both. **1908** McGaffey *Show Girl* 188: I'll have you know that I am only nicked by the best cops on Broadway. **1909** C. Chrysler *White Slavery* 70: And if you get nicked, you can...get "sprung." **1913** in Fountain *Sportswriter* 128: Who can get away with it and not be nicked with the goods. **1914** E.R. Burroughs *Mucker* 13: You've always been too slick to get nicked before. **1970** Landy *Underground Dict.* 139: *Nicked...*Arrested.

3. to shoot with a firearm.

   1924 (quot. at SAP, *v.*). **1928** Wharton *Squad* 186 [ref. to 1918]: Got nicked—through the neck—lucky devil. **1953** Paley *Rumble* 279: But we were afraid it might be you who was nicked!

nickel *n.* **1.** *USAF.* a propaganda leaflet dropped from an airplane. Also as *v.*

   1945 Hamann *Air Words: Nickels.* Propaganda newspapers dropped behind enemy lines. The name is derived from the fact that a metropolitan newspaper is usually sold for a nickel. **1946** *N.Y. Times Mag.* (Aug. 11) 24. **1956** Heflin *USAF Dict.* 344: *Nickel, n.* A propaganda leaflet. *Slang. nickeling mission.* In Europe in WW II, an air mission for the purpose of dropping leaflets. *Slang.* "Nickeling" was adopted as a code word by the British.

2.a. five dollars; (*Narc.*) five dollars' worth, esp. of heroin, marijuana, or crack cocaine; (*broadly*) (see 1996 quot.). Cf. earlier NICKEL NOTE.

   1946 in R.S. Gold *Jazz Talk* 188: *Nickel:* $5. **1959** Trocchi *Cain's Book* 171: First there's that nickel you owe me from last week. **1966** McNeill *Moving Through Here* 51: The teeny-bopper on MacDougal Street who buys a "nickel" ($5.00 worth) of marijuana and gets a nickel's (Five cents') worth of oregano has little recourse. **1966** J. Mills *Needle Park* 20 [ref. to 1964]: Often the junkie pusher will deal "nickel bags" at $5 each, as well as $3 "treys." **1967** *DAS* (Supp.): *Nickel...*

nickel note. **1967** Colebrook *Lassitude* 313: He could only promise her a "nickel" cap. **1967** *Esquire* (Sept.) 191: We always get seven nickels to one ounce, or three dimes. **1968** Carey *College Drug Scene* 35: "Nickel bags" or one-fifth—one-sixth of an ounce selling for $5 are seldom sold in and around the Colony because the work and risk is too great for all parties to the sale considering the small amount of marijuana and money involved. **1970** N.Y.U. student: I bought a nickel of hash over the weekend. It's the nicest stuff. **1970–71** Rubinstein *City Police* 413: Nobody gives him a lot, a "nickel" or a "dime" ($5 or $10) is considered a quite decent tip. **1968–73** Agar *Ripping & Running* 61: Well, you can cop seven nickels, man. **1973** E. Knight *Belly Song* 18: White/America wants you to be/a lame crawling from nickel bag to nickel bag. **1975** V. Miller *Trade-Off* 6: A street dealer comes in and buys enough to bundle "nickel bags" after hitting it one and one. **1977** B. Davidson *Collura* 58: Two nickels, bro. **1979** Feldman et al. *Angel Dust* 76: Most snort a $5 dose,...aptly called a "nickel," at least twice a week. **1983** *Time* (May 30) 23: Five parcels, half a gram of heroin in each "nickel bag," were exchanged for $150. **1990** Steward *Bad Boys* 143 [ref. to 1950's]: When he got started on marijuana he was always bringing me a "nickel's worth." *ca*1990 in Ratner *Crack Pipe* 42: You...buy a nickel and then you smoke that. **1993** E. Richards *Cocaine True* 15: A nickel? Five dollars of cocaine. **1994** *New Yorker* (Jan. 31) 63: I wanted to do a nickel of coke. **1996** N.Y.C. woman, age 28 (coll. J. Sheidlower): A nickel bag doesn't cost five dollars any more. It's always a standardized amount, but the cost varies.

b. *Esp. Gamb.* five hundred dollars.

   1974 Mayer *Bookie* 256: *Nickel:* $500. **1982** R. Sutton *Don't Get Taken* 368: *A Nickel:* Five hundred dollars [among used-car dealers]. **1983** A. Alvarez *Biggest Game* 3: "Raise it up a nickel."...In gambling parlance, a nickel is $500. **1996** Alson *Ivy League Bookie* 22: In the language of gamblers...a nickel was $500.

3. *Pris.* a five-year prison sentence.

   1962 Maurer & Vogel *Narc. & Narc. Add.* (ed. 2) 314: *Nickel.* A five-year sentence. **1962–63** in Giallombardo *Soc. of Women* 206: *Nickle* [*sic*]. A five-year prison sentence. **1966** Braly *On Yard* 72: It's only a nickel....you can...see the end of it. **1966** C. Cooper *Farm* 85: And they probably got nickels and dimes, and you got an "Under Pressure" 6 month cure. **1970** Cain *Blueschild* 9: I just got out of the joint myself, Monday. Did a nickel at Attica. Five calendars, it was a bitch. **1971** J. Brown & A. Groff *Monkey* 39: My very first conviction cost me a "nickel"—five years in...Leavenworth. **1978** W. Brown *Tragic Magic* 101: They gave me a nickel. I've already done two years. **1980** H. Gould *Ft. Apache* 206: I did a nickel at Lewisburg. **1989** Hiaasen *Skin Tight* 17: Did a nickel for extortion. **1989** *Nat. Lampoon* (June) 34: Mr. Woods...pulls a nickel in Soledad for heisting a 7-Eleven. **1994** *Mystery Sci. Theater* (Comedy Central TV): "What's he doing in Attica?" "A nickel."

4. *USAF.* a Republic F-105 Thunderchief fighter-bomber.

   *ca*1966 in Tuso *Vietnam Blues* 22: I have seen them in their Nickels when their eyes were dancing flame. *Ibid.* 196: Then he stops by a Nickel that's tied up in twine.

5. the number five.—also used attrib.

   1975 Dills *CB Slanguage* 29: *Double Nickel:* 55 miles per hour. *Double Nickel Highway:* Interstate 55. **1979** D.K. Schneider *AF Heroes* 20 [ref. to Vietnam War]: We are in the vicinity of Triple Nickel (Highway 555) and 602. **1980** Pearl *Pop. Slang* 106: *Nickel defense n.* (Football) a defensive play using five defensive backs. **1983–86** G.C. Wilson *Supercarrier* 134: To find their assigned bomber, triple nickel, or number 555. **1987** T. Clark *Dict. Gamb. & Gaming: Nickles* [*sic*]...In craps, a roll of two 5s on the dice...[Heard in] 1983. *a*1991 Reinberg *In Field* 151 [ref. to Vietnam War]: *Nickel* slang for the number five.

6. a dent or nick, as on the body of an automobile.

   1982 R. Sutton *Don't Get Taken* 71: There were a lot of "nickels," small dents from rocks.

¶ In phrases:

¶ **it's your nickel** [sugg. by the former cost of a local telephone call] (see quot.).

   1943 *AS* XVIII 154: *It's your nickel, go ahead....*"start talking, I'm waiting."

¶ **on (one's) nickel** [sugg. by the former cost of a local telephone call] at (one's) expense; on (one's) time.

   1992 *Atlantic* (Oct.) 20: Too many people...get care only when it's too late and too expensive and at the emergency room, on somebody else's nickel. **1994** *Esquire* (May) 72: Hicks and Sims went home, on their own nickel, to their own miseries. **1996** *JAG* (NBC-TV): This mission's on the Navy's nickel, sir.

¶ **plugged nickel** (used as a symbol of minimal value). Cf. RED CENT.

[**1864** *Battle-Fields of So.* 283: Can't shoot worth a bad five-cent piece!] **1912** Berkman *Prison* 186 [ref. to 1893]: Old Sandy didn' have a plugged nickel to his name when he come 'ere. **1918** Raine *Four-Square* 76: You make him look like a plugged nickel. **1931** Grant *Gangdom's Doom* 40: I wouldn't give a plugged nickel for all the gangs in New York. **1955** L. Shapiro *Sixth of June* 186: It don't look worth a plugged nickel to me. *a***1984** in Terry *Bloods* 124: On a little piece of land that's not worth a plug nickel to me.

¶ **to the nickel** precisely.

1978 Wharton *Birdy* 55: He's got the psychiatrist grin down to the nickel.

¶ **wooden nickel** see WOODEN NICKEL.

nickel *adj.* second-rate; inferior.

1932 (quot. at NICKEL CURVE). **1964** in B. Jackson *Swim Like Me* 87: Wilson, I'm gettin' tired a you fellas…doin' these nickel-assed crimes. **1979** D. Thoreau *City at Bay* 23: Fuckin' nickel pimps. **1983** N. Proffitt *Gardens of Stone* 54: I'm supposed to give you the nickel briefing on the Old Guard.

nickel-and-dime *adj.* insignificant; contemptible; unprofitable; PENNY-ANTE. Hence **nickel-and-dimer,** *n.* a contemptible or insignificant person. Also **nickel-dime.** Now *colloq.*

[**1936** Cormack & Lang *Fury* (film): That's five-and-ten-cent store talk.] **1941** Macaulay & Wald *Manpower* (film): A nickel-and-dime dame. **1959** Horan *Mob's Man* 103: That nickel and dime game? **1960** *Twilight Zone* (CBS-TV): You're nickel-and-dime and everybody knows it. **1963** *Twilight Zone* (CBS-TV): That nickel-and-dimer! I could buy and sell him a year ago! **1966** Westlake *Busy Body* 145: He's got a nickel-dime delivery outfit over by the piers on the West Side. **1966–67** P. Thomas *Mean Streets* 80: But the lemonade syndicate…was nickel and dime. **1974** *Business Week* (Aug. 10) 21: One gets a sense of revulsion in reading how some of the "nickel-and-dimers"…treat patients. **1967–80** Folb *Runnin' Lines* 118: He nothin' but a fonky nickel-dime nigger. **1983** *Business Week* (Aug. 22) 140: The smorgasbord of nickel-and-dime perks. **1985** Grave *Florida Burn* 54: Who gives a damn about that nickel-and-dime jive? **1985** *Newsweek* (Dec. 23) 32: "These are nickel-and-dime operations," says a U.S. official.

nickel-and-dime *v.* **1.** to work for or get along on small amounts of money.—often constr. with *it.*

1942 *ATS* 451: Nickel-and-dime…To beg on the streets. **1963** *Time* (Nov. 15) 103: By 1929 they had "nickeled-and-dimed" their way to their first million, then lost it all in the crash. **1975** Lichtenstein *Long Way* 48: Bobby Riggs, nickel-and-diming in men's seniors, had decided to get himself a piece of that increasingly rich action in the women's game. **1977** *L.A. Times* (July 31) V 1: Appeal to the parishes, think up fund-raising schemes. In short, try to nickel and dime their way to $55,000.

2. to treat in a stingy, niggardly fashion; (*hence*) to hinder, annoy, or harass with trivialities; eat away at. Now *colloq.*

1961 (cited in *W10*). **1967** R. Morris *Modern Millie* (film): Rich people can nickel-and-dime you to death. **1969** *U.S. News & W.R.* (Apr. 21) 59: We are being nickeled and dimed on funds for equipment. **1973** J. Ehrlichman, in *U.S. News & W.R.* (Feb. 26) 41: Once you begin to nickel and dime the issue on these individual programmatic questions, you jeopardize the success of the over-all objective. **1976** D. Halberstam, in *Atlantic* (Feb.) 90: Watergate needed above all to be summed up, not nickel-and-dimed. **1977** *L.A. Times* (Feb. 6) IV 4: Ever hear of being nickel-and-dimed to death? That's what is happening to America as a result of federal regulation. **1984** *L.A. Times* (Sept. 26) III 6: The Raiders would have played more aggressively on defense. "We would have let them nickel and dime us for a while, then we'd have to pressure him." **1984–88** Hackworth & Sherman *About Face* 184: We'd be nickeled and dimed to death by [grenades]. **1989** *Rolling Stone* (Oct. 19) 47: I don't mind nickel-and-diming everyone else, but not him.

nickel bag see s.v. NICKEL, *n.*, 2.a.

Nickel City *n.* [sugg. by phr. *buffalo nickel*] *Local.* Buffalo, New York.

1978 Dills *CB Slanguage* 72: Nickel City: Buffalo, New York. **1980**

in Safire *Good Word* 234: He picked them up from a friend here in Nickel City.

nickel curve *n. Baseball.* a slider pitch. Now *hist.*

1932 *Baseball Mag.* (Oct.) 496 (cited in Nichols *Baseball Dict.*). **1975** Durocher & Linn *Nice Guys* 149 [ref. to 1940's]: He had a slider (called a nickel-curve in those days).

nickel-hopper *n.* a taxi dancer.

1931 Cressey *Taxi-Dance Hall* 17: At the same time [*ca*1918] the taxi-dancer in Chicago, because her revenue from each separate dance had been fixed at five cents, was awarded the apt title "nickel-hopper"—a nickname that has remained with her until the present time. **1935** Pollock *Und. Speaks*: Nickel hopper; a female who dances with all races in the lowest type of dance hall.

nickelnose *n.* a Jewish person.—usu. used contemptuously.—usu. considered offensive.

1975 in *Nat. Lampoon* (Jan. 1976) 24: UN Resolution Says Nickelnoses [Jews] Discriminate Against Tentheads [Arabs]. **1983** Beckwith & Knox *Delta Force* 151 [ref. to 1978]: He then advised me I was a nickel nose. Other miserly expletives, many of which I'd never heard before, filled the room. [*a*1973–87 F.M. Davis *Livin' the Blues* 44 [ref. to Kans., *ca*1920]: If I had your nose fulla nickels, I'd be rich.]

nickel note *n.* a five-dollar bill.

*ca***1905–26** in *AS* I (1926) 652: Nickel note—five dollar paper bill. **1930** "D. Stiff" *Milk & Honey* 210: Nickel note—Five dollar bill. **1944** D. Burley *Hndbk. Jive* 144: Nickel note—A five-dollar bill. **1971** in R.S. Gold *Jazz Talk* 188: I only hit him for a nickel note, man! **1978** T. Sanchez *Zoot-Suit* 68: Here's a nickel note, that's all I'll bet.

nickel-nurser *n.* [sugg. by PENNY-PINCHER] a miser; TIGHTWAD. Hence **nickel-nursing,** *n. & adj.*

1916 T.A. Dorgan, in Zwilling *TAD Lexicon* 59: Nickel nursers with hand cuffs, fishhooks and boxing gloves waiting for someone to buy. **1918** T.A. Dorgan, in *N.Y. Eve. Jour.* (Aug. 28) 12: Sticking a nickel nurser for the carfare two nights in succession. **1922–24** McIntyre *White Light Nights* 189: Famed for nickel-nursing. **1925** Bailey *Shanghaied* 58: Guess the old nickel-nurser is playing hee-fee-fi-fo-fum himself on his bone harp (the skeleton's ribs!). **1926** Maines & Grant *Wise-Crack Dict.* 11: Nickel nurser—One who has a passion for seeing that his nickels don't stray. **1928** Hammett *Harvest* 61: She called me a damned nickel-nurser and reached for the gin. **1928** J.V. Weaver *Poems* 207: Those hard-bitten, nickel-nursing farmers. **1928** in Blackbeard & Williams *Smithsonian Comics* 154: Savin' that old nickel-nurser from a watery grave. **1941** in Galewitz *Great Comics* 123: What! And pay that nickel nurser's cabfare? **1941** Rossen *Blues in Night* (film): We'll draw the money guys instead of the nickel-nursers. **1946** Gresham *Nightmare Alley* 268: McGraw's a hard cookie, but he ain't a nickel-nurser once you got him sold. **1975** Schott *No Left Turns* 29: Collins was a…nickel-nursing tightwad.

Nickel Plate *n. R.R.* the New York, St. Louis, and Chicago Railroad.

1910 Ade *I Knew Him When* 9: Bill was born in a Hamlet that came very near being on the Nickel Plate. **1922** *In the Clutch of Circumstance* 68: The Nickel Plate road was easier to beat. **1942** *ATS* 727: Nickel Plate, the New York, Chicago, and St. Louis R.R.

nickel-plated *adj.* first-class; thoroughgoing.

1885 *Puck* (Apr. 22) 115: "You are a nickel-plated prophet with a silver tip." "You bet your burnoose I am." *Ibid.* (May 27) 197: Oh, my nickel-plated daisy,/In her airy little gown. **1976–77** C. McFadden *Serial* 61: She was still confusing being a liberated woman with being a nickel-plated bitch.

nickel-snatcher *n.* a streetcar conductor. Also vars.

1919 Piesbergen *Aero Squadron* 66: He was a nickel-chaser on the street cars of Toledo. **1931** J.T. Farrell *McGinty* 81: Why the hell were all these nickel-snatchers on the street-cars so dumb! **1945** Hubbard *R.R. Ave.* 353: Nickel Grabber—Streetcar conductor.

nickel sport *n.* TINHORN SPORT.

1917 in Rossano *Price of Honor* 13: A…cheap outfit….a bunch of nickel sports.

nickel-squeezer *n.* NICKEL-NURSER.

1922 *Amer. Leg. Wkly.* (July 14) 5: The "nickel-squeezer" who *thinks* he can't afford it. **1935** Pollock *Und. Speaks*: Nickel squeezer; a miserly person.

nicknack *n. Pris.* a homosexual man; (see also 1973 quot.).

1966 Elli *Riot* 228: Every nicknack in the joint must be over there, man. They're holdin' a regular dance. *a***1972** B. Rodgers *Queens' Vernacular* 161: Punk...prison sl...*jailhouse pussy; nick-nack.* **1973** in D.W. Maurer *Lang. of Und.* 323: *Nic nac* or *nick nack* or *knick knack* 1. A homosexual....2. A disgusting person.

nickumpoop var. NINCOMPOOP.

niftik *adj.* [alter. *nifty*] NIFTY.
   1919 Law *Air Svc.* (unp.): I sleep on a little bunk made fer some sawedoff dutchman about five feet long and Al the wire slattin made some awful niftick designs on my back and hips. **1929** Milburn *Hobo's Hornbook* 152: I've done some niftik moochin' with the best bums on the road. **1934** Weseen *Dict. Amer. Sl.* 190: *Niftic*—stylish; neat; attractive.

nifty *n.* **1.a.** a clever or facetious remark; (*also*) a prank.
   1918 *Chi. Sunday Trib.* (Feb. 10) V (unp.): I am not given to re-recital of my own utterances which might be classed as "nifties" or bon mots. **1923** *N.Y. Times* (Sept. 9) VIII 2: *Nifty:* The tag of a joke. **1923** Ornitz *Haunch, Paunch & Jowl* 81: Over and over again we do the choruses, solos, gags, nifties. **1924** Isman *Weber & Fields* 231: The best nifties of 1924 will be sad and wall-eyed in 1951. **1925** *Sat. Eve. Post* (Feb. 14) 44: The Palace, Chicago, will howl at...a nifty, that Duluth audiences won't [understand]. **1926** Finerty *Criminalese* 41: *Nifties*—Witticisms. **1927** *Vanity Fair* (Nov.) 132: M—...likes to pull a nifty now and then. **1940** Chandler *Farewell, My Lovely* 14: Poor old Nulty. Let's go on up and throw a couple of nifties at him. **1942** "D. Ormsbee" *Sound of American* 227: Town wits afraid to tell each other their new nifties. **1950** S.J. Perelman, in *New Yorker* (Aug. 5) 21: I can use a nifty or two in that Folwell yarn to lighten it up.
   b. a clever plan.
   1927 in *DAS:* Another nifty is the circularization of telephone subscribers. **1937** in H. Gray *Arf* (unp.): Ha! Ha! That's a nifty all right. *Ibid.* (Feb. 20): Who else would ever have thought of a nifty like that?
   2. a NIFTY person; (*specif.*) a pretty girl.
   1923 in *AS* LXI (1986) 192: Bernard and Collier's "Nifties" comes to a halt at the Fulton this Saturday. **1932** *AS* VII 334: *A nifty*—n.—an attractive girl. **1937** Weidman *Wholesale* 130: Ast with his six blonde nifties, and me with Ruthie Rivkin of the Bronx! **1949** *N.Y. Times* (July 2) 8: As played by Susan Hayward, she is a nifty to look at. **1970** Southern *Blue Movie* 23: By now the two nifties had gotten it slightly together. **1973** *Oui* (Apr.) 112: One nubile nifty squinted over her sunglasses at me.

nifty *adj.* [orig. unkn.] **1.** splendid; stylish; attractive; fine. Now *colloq.*
   1865 B. Harte *Poems* 103: Here comes Rosey's new turn-out! Smart! You bet your life 'twas that. Nifty! (short for *magnificat*). **1869** Carleton *Kaleidoscope* 19: No gentleman but will allow my tile is the kniftiest. **1871** "M. Twain" *Roughing It* 251: He was always nifty himself, and so you bet you his funeral ain't going to be no slouch. **1897** A.H. Lewis *Wolfville* 88: He's a nifty-lookin' savage. **1900** Ade *More Fables* 170: Lutie was just about as Nifty as the Next One. **1926** Tully *Jarnegan* 142: Beautiful girl, isn't she?—I never saw a niftier. **1936** in H. Gray *Arf* (unp.): Dis is swell—th' niftiest penthouse in town. **1944** Kapelner *Lonely Boys Blues* 19: I remember...how nifty you looked in your orange and white bathing suit. **1950** in *DAS:* Everything's going to be nifty in 1950. **1963** Grant *McClintock* (film): Junior's not a dude. He's nifty. **1982** *Time* (Apr. 12) 23: A group of high-rolling local businessmen started thinking that a Knoxville World's Fair would be a nifty thing to whip up.
   2. clever; skillful; handy; (*hence*) (of wind) unpredictable. Now *colloq.*
   1895 *Harper's* (Apr.) 786: Hully gee, fellers! look at Nifty gittin' out der window widout payin'! **1908** J. London *M. Eden* 358: He's nifty with his mits. **1908** McGaffey *Show Girl* 120: I [am]...pretty nifty with my fins. **1915–16** Lait *Beef, Iron & Wine* 263: He was pretty nifty with his mitts. **1917** *Camp Meade Herald* (Oct. 12) 3: It would take a pretty nifty enemy to get at me. *****1926** Walrond *Tropic Death* 60: The chef [*sic*] cook, a nifty, freckle-faced Carolina "cracker." **1928** MacArthur *War Bugs* 24: One barracks invaded another, which called for sly plans and nifty strategy. **1958** J. King *Pro Football* 125: Eddie LeBaron has been nifty on the rollout. **1963** G. Abbott *Mr. Abbott* 36: I wasn't very nifty with the pasteboards. **1969** Ruben *N.Y.P.D.* (ABC-TV): Nifty racket, huh? **1971** N.Y.U. student: That's pretty nifty. **1974** J. Rubin *Barking Deer* 193: That's a mighty nifty wind....Nifty, sir. Real quick

and full of surprises. **1996** *World Series* (Fox-TV) (Oct. 26): Nifty base running by the Atlanta catcher.
   3. insolent.
   1904 Ade *True Bills* 101: I shall cut out the apologetic and try being Nifty. **1904** *Life in Sing Sing* 251: *Nifty.*—Too familiar. **1935** D.W. Maurer, in *AS* (Feb.) 18 [ref. to *ca*1910]: *Nifty*...insolent; cocky; without proper respect for those in authority.

nifty-keen *adj. Juve.* absolutely splendid.—often used ironically. Also (*joc.*) **nifty beans.**
   1971 Dahlskog *Dict.* 42: *Niftykeen, a.* Great; wonderful; admirable. **1982** R.M. Brown *So. Discomfort* 66: "Nifty beans," Athena said. "No slang in this house, miss." Ada frowned.

nig *n.* NIGGER, 1.a., b.—also (as in 1994 quot.) used fig.—usu. used contemptuously.—usu. considered offensive.
   1828 T. Rice *Jim Crow*, in Damon *Old Amer. Songs* (No. 15) (sheet music): But Nigs in ole Virginny,/Be so black dey shine. **1838** *Crockett Almanac* (1839) 18: It's no use, Mr. Nig, or whatever your name is. **1840** in H. Nathan *D. Emmett* 473: He...saw dat nig. **1842** *Ben Hardin's Crockett* (unp.): Whar's the traps, Mr. Nig? *ca***1844** in H. Nathan *D. Emmett* 324: Hansome niggs are boun to shine. **1853** W.W. Brown *Clotel* 125: He gets up early in the morn, like all the other nigs. **1855** S. Story *Caste* 61: Dat ar little nig come mighty nigh losin' he supper. **1863** J. Dooley *Confed. Soldier* 140: And I may as well remark upon the word "nig" and "nigger," that I never heard this epithet applied to slaves in the South by any person of refinement and education. **1864** in Lyman *Meade's HQ* 159: Nobody was there, save a lot of nigs. **1864** "E. Kirke" *Down in Tenn.* 21: A ole nig thet war passin' 'long the road heerd the ole Squire's cries. **1868–71** C.G. Leland *Breitmann's Ballads* 60: De nigs...takes de *Tribune.* **1879** R. Wheeler *In Leadville* 3: This nig's all level. **1883** R. Cowden *Brief Sketch* 45: A dozen of the *little* "nigs"...did not, together, have enough clothing...to wad a shot-gun. **1887** E. Custer *Tenting* 121: The possums are accepted with many a scrape and flourish by the "nigs." **1891** Wawn *South Sea Islanders* 17: The raw, untravelled "nig" is a very pliable article in their hands. **1953–55** Kantor *Andersonville* 418: You nigs step lively. **1959** Griffin *Black Like Me* [entry for Nov. 24]: I recalled it was considered sport among some elements in Alabama to hunt "nigs" and I backed away. **1970** Hatch *Cedarhurst* 185: There must be 300 nigs out there picketing! **1971** Hilaire *Thanatos* 291: You with that nig? **1968–77** Herr *Dispatches* 40: You ever catch one of them li'l nigs just pinch 'em. **1982** in S. King *Bachman* 902: You're going to be chopping cotton when this is over, nig! **1987** *Tour of Duty* (CBS-TV): If I wanted that nig dead I'd shot him straight out. *a***1994** D. Frey *Last Shot* 226: How come this shit only happens to us Coney Island niggers?...It's about time there was a little something for the niggs. **1994** Bak *Turkey Stearnes* 112 [ref. to 1920's]: White ballplayers with Negroid features—full lips, say, or dark skin—were routinely dubbed "Nig," including...Babe Ruth.

nig *v. Cards.* to renege.
   1829 in *DA:* If you hadn't a nig'd...you might have had better luck. **1859** *Harper's Mag.* (Mar.) 568: If you have got any trumps you had better play them and not undertake to nig any more! **1949** Monteleone *Crim. Slang: Nig*...to renege.

nigger *n.* [prob. Early ModE (later dial.) *Niger, niger* /nɪgr/ < L *niger* 'black in color'; a commonly asserted orig. in Early ModE (and later dial.) *neger, neager,* etc. /negr/ or /nɛgr/ (< F *negre, nègre*) is phonologically unlikely; nor is it in orig. a "mispronunciation of *Negro.*" See additional note at **(1.a.),** below]
   I. Senses referring to people. [For further U.S. data, see esp. the extended treatment in *DARE.*]
   1. a black African person or person of black African descent; Negro; (now *hist.*) a Negro slave.—also used attrib. *Specif.:*
   a. Now *Black E.* (used formerly in Early ModE and later in nonstandard speech as a racial designation apparently without rancorous intent, and now surviving among black speakers as an affectionate, ironic, jocular, or occ. complimentary epithet).
   [The historical record epitomized here and at **(b),** below, suggests that the high degree of offensiveness attached to

this term *per se*, particularly in the discourse of whites, has increased markedly over time, perh. esp. during the 20th C. To illustrate: Both 16th-C. quots. below appear in learned discourse. The Hampshire-born judge Samuel Sewall's 1700 exx. of *Niger* occur in a denunciation of slavery that is anchored in Scripture and exhibits throughout the character of dignified argumentation. By way of contrast, the 1788 quot. from American playwright Samuel Low occurs in a comedic portrayal of provincial New York speech (significantly, Low's own stage directions at Act V sc. i have *Negro*).

By 1700 both the Latinate *Niger* and the more freq., French-derived *Neger* had nearly been supplanted by *Negro* in S.E. writings; they rarely appear in such writings thereafter. The retention of the outmoded forms *Niger* and *Neger* in the freq. opprobrious usage of uncultivated speakers must have hastened their decline into disrepute.

Consistent with the pronuns. clearly indicated in the 1766, *1786, and 1818 quots., the learned 16th-C. English pronun. of Renaissance Latin *Niger* presumably required [i] in the initial syllable, but a coexisting, usu. allophonic [ɪ] may reasonably be surmised as well. Indeed, a shift from [i] to [ɪ] in words such as *been, creek, sheep,* and *sleep* is occ. noted in rural BrE dials. prior to 1600, and the first two instances later became widespread in America. (See esp. Helge Kökeritz, *Shakespeare's Pronunciation* (New Haven: Yale Univ. Press, 1953), p. 191).

The *1786 Burns quot. appears inaccurately spelled as "nigger" in *OED*, as well as in Henley & Henderson's 1896–97 ed. of *The Poetry of Robert Burns* (I, p. 211); however, James O. Kinsley's authoritative modern ed. of *Poems and Songs of Robert Burns* (Oxford: Clarendon Press, 1968) shows Burns's spelling to have been "niger," the [i] of which may be inferred from the required rhyme with "rigour," "vigour," and "tiger," all pron. as [i] in 18th-C. Scots.

The existence *ca*1400 of a form *nigger,* represented by a lone quot. in *MED* as a dial. var. of *niggard,* is coincidental. *DARE* records the form once or twice in the U.S. as well; see also *1792 quot. at **(3),** below. It remains unknown whether this is the etymological inspiration behind the obscure oaths *niggers!, 'sniggers!* (presumably for **God's niggers!*), and *nigger-noggers!,* all reported by *OED* solely from the playwright Samuel Rowley (1637).]

*1574 in *OED*: The Massgets bordering upon the Indians, and the Nigers of Aethiop, bearing witnes. *1584 R. Scot *Discoverie of Witchcraft* 139: An ouglie divell hauing hornes on his head,...a tail in his breech,...fanges like a dog, a skin like a Niger, and a voice roring like a lion. 1676 S. Sewall *Diary* I 18: Jethro, his Niger, was then taken: retaken by Capt. Bradford the Thorsday following. 1689 in *AS* (1967) 160: One niggor Boy [inventoried as estate property in Gravesend, N.Y.]. *1698–99 in *OED*: John Langley a Niger of Jameca...was baptized. 1700 S. Sewall *Selling of Joseph* 14: Obj[ection]....The Nigers *are brought out of a Pagan Country, into places where the Gospel is Preached. Answ.* Evil must not be done, that good may come of it. *Ibid.* 15: And yet, 'tis to be feared, we have no other kind of Title to our *Nigers.* 1721 S. Sewall *Diary* II 984: We met a Niger Funeral. 1766 in *Harper's Mo.* LXXXVIII (1894) 535: I, Governor Cuff of the Niegro's [*sic*] in the province of Connecticut, do resign my Governmentship to John Anderson Niegor man to Governor Skene....And I hope that you will obey him as you have Done me for this ten years' past when Colonel Willis' niegor Dayed I [*sic*] was the next....I John Anderson Governor...will do my utmost endevere to serve you....[signed] JOHN ANDERSON Governor over the niegors in Connecticut. *1786 R. Burns *Poems & Songs* (1968 ed.) I 214: The Ordination [title]...How graceless *Ham* leughed [*sic*] at his Dad,/Which made *Canaan* a niger. 1788 S. Low *Politician Out-witted* III i: HUMPHRY. He talks as crooked [*i.e.,* unintelligibly] as a Guinea niger. 1816–17 Torrey *Domestic Slavery* 33: [In Washington, D.C., in 1815 I heard] a stammering boy...[say] "There goes the Ge-Ge-Ge-orgy men with a drove o' nig-

gers chain'd together two and two." 1818 in *DARE*: [Among New Eng. words regarded as inelegant:] *Neeger* for negro. 1819 in Mencken *Amer. Lang. Supp. I* 47: Other words...peculiar to the United States...*Nigger.* Negro. *Lengthy.* Long. *Boss.* Master [etc.]. 1836 in *DAE*: I have toiled night and day, I've worked like a nigger, and more than any nigger. 1836–37 Bird *Nick of the Woods* ch. viii: I'm your slave jist as much as that niggur. *1840 F. Sheridan *Galveston* I. 92: An Elderly Nigger at work...lighting his toils with a cheerful song. 1842 in U.B. Phillips *Life & Labour in Old So.* 214: I may say with Abram, "I love a nigger, they are better than we." So they are: grateful, devoted, self-sacrificing for their masters. 1843 in *DAE*: Right hard to get gals here, mam—folks has to be their own niggurs, mam. 1843 in J. Hollander *Amer. Poetry: 19th C.* II 785: De nigger-trader got me. 1845 Mowatt *Fashion* II i: Sir, you've a handsome house—fine carriage—nigger in livery—...everything first-rate. *Ibid.* IV ii: Dis here's de stuff to make a nigger feel like a gemman! 1846 Corbin *Mneomi* 14: I guess he no call de nigger. 1857 *Autobiog. Female Slave* 212: I 'gin to talk jist as dough dey was niggers same as I. 1857 in M. Moses *Rep. Amer. Plays* II 723: I was a right cute little nigga, too. *a*1880 *Year of Wreck* 137: The niggers are...fond of 'em. 1880 "M. Twain" *Tramp Abroad* ch. iii: He laid into his work like a nigger. 1884 in J.L. Dillard *Perspectives on Black E.* 176: [Exx. of "Negro English":] De soones' nigger on de plantation. *Ibid.* 181: *To tu'n er nigger right loose* "to give a man free play." *Ibid.* 194: *Er milerterry nigger-chap* "a negro soldier." 1885 W.G. Eliot *A. Alexander* 47: He went..."to ask the good Lord what this pore forsaken nigger should do." *Ibid.* 81: Two niggers, a woman and a gal. 1899 C. Chesnutt *Conjure-Woman* 12: Ef you...doan' min' lis'nin' ter a ole nigger run on a minute er two. 1904 in "O. Henry" *Works* 911: The nigger man's head that was used by the old patrons to throw baseballs at is now illegal. 1904 *DN* II 419: *Nigger*...Negro. The universal word in Arkansas, whether respect is intended or not. 1925 Van Vechten *Nigger Heaven* 26: I'm...tired to death of all these Niggers downstairs....[footnote:] While this informal epithet is freely used by Negroes among themselves, not only as a term of opprobrium, but also as a term of endearment, its employment by a white person is always fiercely resented. *a*1932 in Kephart et al. *Smoky Mountain Voices* 116: I b'lieve in treatin' niggers squar'. 1932 C. McKay *Gingertown* 63: A black person may be called "nigger" as a joke in Aframerica, but never "black," which is considered a term of reproach in the mouths of colored people. *a*1937 Dollard *Southern Town* 47: Evidently southern white men say "nigger" as standard practice, "nigruh," a slightly more respectful form, when talking to a northerner (from whom they expect criticism on the score of treatment of Negroes), but never Negro; that is the hallmark of a northerner and a caste-enemy. 1939 *Chi. Defender,* in *AS* XIX (1944) 166: Nigger...is a common expression among the ordinary Negroes and is used frequently in conversation between them. It carries no...sting when used by themselves, but they object keenly to whites using it. 1941 in Samuelson *Love, War* 10: "Poor nigger," I said. "He could have beat his case, too." 1943 Ottley *New World* 279: However, the term "nigger" is used by Negroes quite freely when out of the earshot of whites, sometimes having a good deal of affectionate meaning to them. 1949 Botkin *Treasury So. Folk.* xxiii: The Negro has taken over the objectionable word "nigger"...and made it a term of praise or blame, depending on the context. 1955 Broonzy & Bruynoghe *Big Bill* 107: In Mississippi [*ca*1900] we didn't mind being called nigger, because we called one another nigger and all the people called us that way. 1956–60 J.A. Williams *Angry Ones* ch. xviii: They're black—and, baby, they're not going to make any headway if I [a black man] give up, if a hundred qualified niggers give up and call it quits. *1961 Hugill *Shanties from Seven Seas* xiv [ref. to 1920's]: Many readers may object to the appearance of the word "nigger" in the shanties. But many of the shanties in which this word is found were products of the Negro himself and *he* sang "nigger" in those far-off days. 1962 B. Atwood *Vocab. of Texas* 73: Negro...is felt by most to be polite rather than neutral. *Nigger*...is sometimes said to be neutral, but more often to be derogatory. 1965 in Bontemps *Old South* 9: He was horrified by Buddy's casual and frequent use of the word *nigger.* Buddy even forgot and used it in the presence of white people once or twice that year, and was soundly criticized for it. 1970 C. Major *Dict. Afro-Amer. Sl.*: *Nigger*...when used by a white person when addressing a black person usually it is offensive and disparaging; used by black people among themselves, it is a racial term with undertones of warmth and good will. 1973 Andrews & Owens *Black Lang.* 60: *Act Like a Nigga*...has taken on a positive connotation when black people use it.

1977 G. Smitherman *Talkin & Testifyin* 62: *Nigguh*....the term may simply identify black folks—period. In this sense, the word has neutral value. **1981** *L.A. Times* (June 12) V 3: The word "nigger" when used by blacks is often seen as an affectionate phrase. **1989** in Rawson *Wicked Words* 268: Today Borrego Springs [Calif.] residents have forgotten—or have never known—that...this place was...[named] Nigger Springs...in the 1870s after a black man named Jim Green who lived and explored in the valley. **1993** *N.Y. Times* (Jan. 24) B1: "Nigger," of course, has long been an element of black vernacular, almost an honorific of the streets. **1993** in *DARE* [ref. to 1930's]: I've heard [white] livestock men speak in admiration of a black cowboy and noted rider...simply as "Nigger Bill." Around New Plymouth there was another respected rider...called "Nigger Abe." And there was a black settler...who raised and sold good horses. His name was simply "Nigger Ned." All of this is hard to accommodate, so sensitive have we become to the negative aspects of such language. *a***1994** N. McCall *Wanna Holler* 40: Aw, niggah, you fallin' in love! *Ibid.* 63: Like I was the baaddest nigger on the East Coast. **1995** *New York* (Sept. 18) 72: Blacks [sometimes] use "nigger" as...a compliment.

b. (used, esp. by whites, with dismissive, abusive, or contemptuous force).—usu. considered offensive.—also (as in 1871 quot.) used fig. [See note at **(a)**, above. The 1775 quot. occurs in a Tory lampoon of the Continental Army and may reasonably be regarded as derisive in intent.]

    1775 in F. Moore *Songs of Amer. Revolution* 101: And here and there a nigger. *****1811** Lord Byron, in *OED:* The rest of the world—niggers and what not. **1817** in Fearon *Sks. of Amer.* 46: When social converse [in New York City] has been exhausted upon the bad conduct and inferior nature of *niggars* (negroes). *Ibid.* 240: I always serve my b[laste]d *niggars* that way [in Kentucky]. **1819** in *OED:* Contempt of the poor blacks, or niggers, as they are there called, seems the national sin of America. **1834** in *DAE:* A negro boy under my window [in Philadelphia] calls a lad of the same race, by way of reproach, "*nigger.*" **1836** Hildreth *Slave* 36: A damned nigger's insolence. **1836** Cather *Voyage* 85: Keep the horse steady, you nigger. **1836** L. Child *Appeal* 204: Yet if a person of refinement from Hayti, or Brazil, or other countries, which we deem less enlightened than our own, should visit us, the very boys in the street would dog his footsteps with the vulgar outcry of "Nigger! Nigger!" I have known this to be done, from no other provocation than the sight of a colored man with the dress and deportment of a gentleman. *Ibid.* 205: Your wife a'n't a lady; she is a nigger. **1837** in C.P. Ripley *Black Abolitionist Papers* III 209: A colored man preach? Did you ever hear of a nigger's preaching? **1849** Melville *White Jacket* 264: He [a black sailor] considered him a "*nigger,*" which, among some blacks, is held a great term of reproach. **1852** Stowe *Uncle Tom's Cabin* ch. xiv: Them high forrads always shows calculatin niggers. **1853** in S. Clemens *Twain's Letters* I 4: I reckon I had better black my face, for in these Eastern States niggers are considerably better than white people. **1855** in C.G. Woodson *Negro Letters* 635: Was struck a severe blow by a man who rebuked him for upholding Abolitionists and "niggers." **1857** J.D. Long *Pict. of Slavery* 381: They have no objection to being called African. They do not like the word Negro, because of the resemblance of the word to "Nigger." **1857** *Autobiog. Female Slave* 212: Dey...say dey was not niggers, but colored pussons, and dey called one anoder Mr. *a***1860** Hundley *So. States* 170: A Southern gentleman rarely, if ever, says *nigger.* **1862** Union Army court-martial record of Lieut. W. Young, 11th Mass. Inf. Vols., in Nat. Archives: Half-fucked bastard...nigger-fucked whore. **1864** P.H. Clark *Black Brigade* 11: Some sleep in that pit where Robert Gould Shaw lies "buried with his niggers." **1865** in *Jour. So. History* XLIV (1978) 222: You are the cause that respectable colored people are slandered, are called lazy, thieving niggers. **1869** Ossoli *Life Without* 317: My little son, scarce able to speak, will cry out, "Nigger! Nigger!" whenever he sees one, and try to throw things at them. **1871** in *DA* s.v. *white Negro:* "Ole Miss Meanses' white nigger," as some of them called her, in allusion to her slavish life. **1877** Wheeler *Deadwood Dick, Prince of Road* 83: Shoot the accursed nigger! **1877** in Bergen & Papanikolas *Looking Far West* 291: It was the City vs. Monroe Henderson, all being "n—s" except the City Attorney and Mr. Murphy. **1899** DuBois *Phila. Negro* 328: I wouldn't have a darky to clean out my store....What do you suppose we'd want of a nigger? *Ibid.* 333: A large section of the public...applaud the stamina of a man who refuses to work with a "Nigger." **1907** in Brandon *Houdini* 18: In Bohemia and Austria they think as much of a nigger as a jew. **1911** Ovington *Half a*

Man 72: My mother tells me to smack anyone who calls me "nigger." **1925** (quot. at **(a)**, above). **1927** H. Miller *Moloch* 39: We've got to fire the niggers. **1936** H.L. Mencken *Amer. Lang.* (ed. 4) 305: *Kike, yid, dago,* and *nigger* are prohibited altogether [from use in motion pictures]. **1936** in *AS* XIX (1944) 167: [A publication should be barred from schools because it used] the opprobrious term *N——* . **1944** in P. McGuire *Jim Crow Army* 88: You n———s keep quiet or we will beat the h—l out of you. **1950** in M. Daly *Profile of Youth* 184: One teacher, talking about the Civil War, kept using the word "nigger" instead of "Negro." **1954** Arnow *Dollmaker* 192: We don't have to go to school with niggers an Jews an hillbillies. **1958** Smith & Douglas *Defiant Ones* (film): You call me "nigger" again...and I'll kill you! **1958** T. Capote *Breakfast at Tiffany's* 59: I read that story twice. Brats and niggers. **1965** C. Brown *Manchild* 67 [ref. to *ca*1950]: Mama got mad and said, "You little dumb nigger..."...Mama looked at the floor for a little while and I knew she was ashamed that the white man had heard her call me a nigger. **1965–70** T. Morrison *Bluest Eye* 8: Well, that old crazy nigger she married up with didn't help her head none. *Ibid.* 67: Colored people were neat and quiet; niggers were dirty and loud. She belonged to the former group. **1970** (quot. at **(a)**, above). **1971** Geismar *Fanon* 41: He despaired of these islands where the blacks treated each other as "dirty niggers." *a***1975** Ali & Durham *Greatest* 414: Nigger, you one of them loud-mouthed Martin Luther King niggers?...One of them smart-alecky civil-rights niggers. **1975** Karon *Black Scars* 19: Although southern whites knew that blacks found the terms "nigger" and "darkie" insulting, they habitually used these terms in the presence of blacks, thus reinforcing the latter's ritualized degradation. **1976** R. Rosenthal et al. *Different Strokes* 55: She never allowed the word "nigger" to be used in her home...."We're proud to be black." *a***1977** M. French *Women's Room* 386: Lazy lying niggers. **1979** in L. Bangs *Psychotic Reactions* 277: Whenever he hears the word "nigger," no matter who says it, black and white, he wants to kill. **1979** in Terkel *Amer. Dreams* 144: We were told that up north niggers run everything. **1979** in J.L. Gwaltney *Drylongso* 4: You can call me anything but nigger, nigra or gal, and get along with me. **1979–81** C. Buckley *To Bamboola* 165: I'm gonna fuck him up *bad*....He called me a nigger. **1982** *Psychology Today* (Aug.) 64: Hank Stram began drafting all these niggers, picking them up from Grambling and Southern while the NFL was bidding for the talent from Notre Dame and Michigan State. **1982** D. Williams *Hit Hard* [ref. to WWII] 15: There is one word that I [a white officer] do not tolerate, and that word is *nigger.* **1986** J.J. Maloney *Chain* 76: They worked me like a nigger, paid me like a nigger, and treated me like a nigger. **1995** *N.Y. Times* (Sept. 6) A16: Mr. Darden...called "nigger" "the most vile word in the English language" and begged Judge Ito to preclude the defense from offering any more testimony about it....Another witness recalled Mr. Fuhrman declaring, "The only good nigger is a dead nigger." **1996** *Dangerous Minds* (ABC-TV): "These other niggers....Lady, black kids can call each other that." "Not in this class they can't."

2. a dark-skinned person of any race or origin.—used contemptuously.—usu. considered offensive.

    [*****1707** in Donnan *Docs. of Slave Trade* II 17: For each negro of India.] **1836** (quot. fr. Child at **(1.b.)**, above). **1843** in *DARE:* Heathen Indgean niggers. **1847** Ruxton *Far West* 166: What does the niggur [*sc.*, a Native American] say? **1851** M. Reid *Scalp-Hunters* 90: Injuns....Watch for the niggurs a-goin' south. **1896** in F. Remington *Sel. Letters* 216: Cuba...a lot of d—— niggers who are better off under the yoke. **1899** in J. Merrill *Uncommon Valor* 251: We came here [to the Philippines] to lick the niggers and...we came very near doing it. **1901** Greenough & Kittredge *Words & Ways* 66: Witness the contemptuous use of *nigger* for many dark-skinned races who have no similarity to the negro. **1901** Sonnichsen *Among Filipinos* 385: The heaps of dead and dying natives are then photographed by our people, and exhibited with such mottoes: "Can the —d Regiment boys shoot? You bet they can. Count the dead niggers." This is meant to be humor. **1902** M.W. Gibbs *Shadow & Light* 366: Look here, Mr. Harris; don't you think that $5,000...[is] too much to give them d—n nigger Indians? *****1950** W. Granville *Sea Slang* 164: *Nigger.* Nickname for any dark-featured or dark-haired [Caucasian] man. **1985** A. Naff *Becoming Amer.* 250: By the 1920s, the epithet "niggers" was particularly used by...children because the Syrians were "poor and some were dark-skinned." *a***1991** Bak *Cobb Would Have Caught It* 31: [Ty] Cobb's taunting of [Babe] Ruth over the years was systematic and vicious. On the field he regularly called him "nigger"—a dig at Ruth's broad nose and dark complexion. **1992** N. Morris *Brothel Boy* 9: He's trying to suck up to Veraswami for some reason....He must know we can't let niggers in. **1994** Bak *Turkey Stearnes* 113: The Tigers fielded a pair of [white] southern outfielders in the early '30s, Joyner "Jo-Jo" White and Gerald "Gee" Walker, whose pet name for each other was "nigger." **1994** *Donahue* (NBC-TV): The kids called me [a Samoan-American] "nigger." **1995** *Newsweek* (Mar. 6) 50: He also recounts how schoolmates called him "nigger" because of his dark skin.

3. Now esp. *Black E.* a reprehensible person (of any race); lout; (used as a coarse term of contempt).—usu. considered offensive. [Though conveying this sense in context, the bracketed **1792 Scots quot.—apparently unique—prob. represents the etymologically unrelated dial. *niggar* 'a niggard; miser'.]

[***1792** in *SND*: An illiterate kintra niggar/Blest wi' a smart external figure.] **1836–37** Bird *Nick of Woods* ch. viii: The negro cried aloud..."Hanging too good for him, white niggah t'ief, hah!" **1839–40** Simms *Border Beagles* ch. xxv: They [*sc.,* white officers of justice]'re afraid of me [a white man], the niggers, and you see I ain't afraid of them. D—n 'em, I don't mind half a dozen of them. **1845** in H.C. Lewis *Works* 98: The imperdent nigger turned his ugly pictur and said he'd be cussed if he warn't goin' to play his hand out. **1861** in H. Holzer *Dear Mr. Lincoln* 361: Abe Lincoln...goddam you...you are nothing but a goddam Black nigger. **1866** in H.W. Williams *Civil War* 115: They would kill every "white nigger" of us, before we could reach the other depot. **1922** in *OEDAS* I 129: Without this safeguard he [*sc.,* the missionary] is soon in danger of becoming a nigger, as it is called here. **1942** Z.N. Hurston *Dust Tracks* 25: He called me Snidlits, explaining that Zora was a hell of a name...."Snidlits, don't be a nigger*," he would say...."Niggers lie and lie."...*The word "nigger" used in this sense does not mean race. It means a weak, contemptible person of any race. **1971** in *DARE:* "You're a nigger."...A nigger is just a slander word. Anybody, it don't make no difference what nationality and color you is, anybody can be a nigger. We have a lot of Negroes and we have some niggers. **1973** Reader letter in *RHD* files: *Nigger*...a slang word given to any person of no particular race who are [*sic*] uneducated, stupid, ignorant, filthy, [etc.]. **1977** G. Smitherman *Talkin & Testifyin* 62: *Nigguh* may also be a way of expressing disapproval of a person's actions. In this sense, even white folk, when they are acting inappropriately, are called *nigguhs.* **1978** *Maledicta* II 164: *Nigger!* may also be screamed by blacks at whites, on the theory that the last thing any white would want to be is a black person. **1981** Reader letter in *RHD* files: A nigger could be any race as long as a person carried himself in a negative manner....a lazy, shiftless, no good, low, run-down person of any race. **1981** Reader letter in *RHD* files: The word *nigger*...means any low down person, someone who has no regard for others; the very lowest of the human race not simply the "dark-skinned race." *a1982 *Dict. Bahamian Eng.* 142: *Nigger*...a person (of any race) who acts the opposite of a gentleman. **1982** Reader letter in *RHD* files: A nigger is one of any race who is ignorant. That means whites too. **1983** White Knoxville, Tenn., student, to white sorority member: Oh yeah? Well, you're a *nigger!* **1994** *Jerry Springer Show* (synd. TV series): A *nigger* can be a white person *or* a black person. We are *Negroes!* **1995** Reader letter in *RHD* files: Anyone can be a nigger!! White, Spanish etc. Even you! You should...delete the definition "a black person." **1995** White woman, age *ca25*, on *Jerry Springer Show* (synd. TV series): Nn—I won't say the word—it doesn't mean white, it doesn't mean black, it means *trash!* **1997** C. Rock, black comedian, on *Fresh Air* (Nat. Public Radio) (Feb. 6): There's a civil war going on between black people and niggers....You can't go to the movies because there's niggers shooting at the screen.

4. Now *Black E.* (with diminished force) fellow; a person (of any race).—also (as in 1993 quot.) used fig. [The early quots. represent the speech of white fur trappers in the Rocky Mountains; continuity of usage with recent quots. is not demonstrable.]

1847 Ruxton *Life in Far West* 80: "This niggur [*sc.,* the speaker]," answered Rube solemnly, "has been dorn'd upon a sight too often to be skeared by what can come out of them waters. *Ibid.* 166: What does the niggur say? **1850** Garrard *Wah-to-yah* 161: They...pick up a beaver trap to ask what it is—just shows whar the niggurs had their bringin' up. **1851** M. Reid *Scalp-Hunters* 108: Oncet on a time, this niggur [*sc.,* the speaker] chawed a varmint that wasn't much sweeter. **1978** *Maledicta* II 164: Moreover, in all-black company, "Nigger" has become a generic synonym for "human being"; the author was once

warned by a black gang-leader that "them Chinese niggers is the worst kind." **1986** in Bak *Cobb Would Have Caught It* 229 [ref. to 1930's]: Gee Walker...was great friends with Jo-Jo White. They were both [whites] from down south. They called each other "nig-gah." They'd gamble on any goddamn thing. **1993** N.Y.C. man, age *ca*18 (coll. J. Sheidlower): Hey, check out that fat nigger [*sc.,* a gray pigeon] over there! *a1994* in C. Major *Juba to Jive* 320: Those niggers [*sc.,* the U.S. government] don't know what the fuck they doing. **1994** in Stavsky, Mozeson & Mozeson *A 2 Z* 98: *Nigga, nigger*...any guy. **1994** C. Major *Juba to Jive* 320: In the nineties members of the black youth culture say that "nigger" is no longer derogatory, that it's used to mean friend, brother, man, person, girl, woman. Even white people can be niggers. **1995** *Harper's* (Nov.) 21: Primo would casually describe me to others as "the white nigga who always be hangin' with me." *Ibid.:* [To a white man:] You're a good nigga. **1995** White N.Y.C. man, age *ca*29 (coll. J. Sheidlower): I live in [a largely black neighborhood] and people occasionally call *me* nigger. I go to the store and a guy will say, "Hey, nigger, you're next in line." [Q.: Do you ever get the sense that you could use the word to them? A.:] Absolutely *not.* But it is kind of like "dude!" There's no racial sentiment behind it at all.

5. Esp. *Black E.* a close (usu. black) friend; companion; BROTHER, 3.—usu. constr. with possessive pronoun, freq. with MAIN.—also used fig.

1956–60 J.A. Williams *Angry Ones* ch. xxi: Obie, you can't go nowhere but up, man, and you know I'm with you all the way. Obie, I *got* to be with you, you know that. You know you're my nigger, man. **1965** C. Brown *Manchild* 140 [ref. to *ca*1951]: Look, this is my main nigger, my number one nigger, and anybody who fucks wit him, it's just as well as if they'd came and fucked wit me. **1970** in *DARE: Joking names that a woman may use to refer to her husband:* "It's time to go and get supper for my...Nigger.["] **1970** in *DARE: A close friend...* "He's my...Nigger.["] **1973** Andrews & Owens *Black Lang.* 60: "Nigga, give me a call when you make it to the pad, hear?"...*Nigga*...boyfriend. **1977** G. Smitherman *Talkin & Testifyin* 62: It may be a term of personal affection or endearment, as in *He my main nigguh* (He's my best friend). *a1982 *Dict. Bahamian Eng.* 142: *Nigger*...a male friend or boyfriend (youth slang; not derogatory). **1984** in G. Cohen *Studies in Slang* I 69: A [Cajun] woman may refer to her sweetheart as "Mon Nègre" (my Nigger), perhaps indicating Slave....Once I was bowling in New Orleans, and at getting a strike at a particularly important time, I was shocked to hear my team sponsor shout happily, "That's MY Nigger!" (I am [a] white [male]). **1993** *N.Y. Times* (Jan. 24) B31: In rap and hip-hop music,..."nigger" is virtually interchangeable with words like "guy," "man," or "brother." *a1994* G. Smitherman *Black Talk* 167: "She my main nigga," that is, She is my close friend. **1994** in C. Long *Love Awaits* 106: Yeah, I'm layin' down tracks for my nigga. *a1996* "Mobb Deep" (rap group), in *Esquire* (Mar. 1996) 132: Tommy Hil [*i.e.,* Tommy Hilfiger, a white fashion designer] was my nigga/And others couldn't figure/How me and Hilfiger used to move through with vigor.

6. *Black E.* a nonblack person behaving in an admirable manner associated with African-Americans; any person identifying with aspects of black popular culture.

[**1965** C. Brown *Manchild* 137 [ref. to *ca*1951]: As far as I'm concerned, that paddy boy is twice the nigger any of you cats might think you are or might ever try to be.] **1977** G. Smitherman *Talkin & Testifyin* 62: *Nigguh*....Sometimes it means culturally black, identifying with and sharing the values and experiences of black people. **1978** Patti Smith, in *Rolling Stone* (July 27) 53: He's a really great guy. I mean, he's really a nigger. If anyone qualifies to be a nigger, it's Mick Jagger. [Interviewer: How is Mick Jagger qualified to be a nigger?] On our liner notes I redefined the word nigger as being an artist-mutant that was going beyond gender [*sic*]. **1995** Message on Usenet newsgroup rec.music.hip-hop: I'm white, pale white, and people call me a nigga. It isn't my skin, it's the way I dress and the way I act.

7. usu. *pl. Pol. & Journ.* a victim of racial or other prejudice; (now *specif.*) a person who is disfranchised economically, politically, or socially.—also used fig. Now *S.E.* [The 1922 quot. in *OEDAS* I, though placed with that book's version of this sense, seems more properly to belong at (**3**), above.]

1963 in H.S. Thompson *Proud Highway* 411: My earlier concept of The Nigger. [Editor's note: "After reading Norman Mailer's *The White Negro,* Thompson developed a theory that all working-class people were niggers. **1969** in *L.A. Times* (July 20, 1979) I 10: I didn't stop being the white man's nigger to become a black man's nigger. **1971** *Harper's* (July)

27: French-Canadian workers….They are the White Niggers of America, which is the title of their literary testament by Pierre Vallières. **1972** *Harper's* (Aug.) 78: We're the niggers now, that's what's happened….It just is who's on top. The group that's second's gonna catch shit—they're gonna be niggers. **1972** Y. Ono *Woman Is the Nigger of the World* [pop. song title]. **1972** *Atlantic* (Dec.) 91: The Jewish, the Italian, and the Irish people were the niggers of the white world. **1974** *Everett* (Wash.) *Herald* (Dec. 31) 9A: What with blacks having won their civil rights, and women working hard for similar victory, kids are said to be "the last niggers." **1976** *L.A. Times* (July 29) II 5: Not long ago we antiwarniks were ourselves social and political pariahs….To the orthodox political majority we were, you might say, foreign-policy "niggers." **1977** *L.A. Times* (Feb. 21) II 8: The public must come to understand that the term "nigger" is not restricted to blacks. "A 'nigger' is anyone whose role and circumstances are defined by others," [Congressman Ron] Dellums said. In that sense, he told a cheering audience, there are "yellow niggers, white niggers, brown niggers, gay niggers, leftist niggers, environmentalist niggers, hard-hat niggers, silent majority niggers, and blue-collar niggers." **1978** *Rolling Stone* (Nov. 2) 41: Ron once told us ceramic sculpture was "the nigger of the art world." **1979** *L.A. Times* (Apr. 27) I 7: The official [of a company resisting federal affirmative-action enforcement]…characterized the government's equal opportunity programs as "the nigger of all government programs." **1979** *U.S. News & W.R.* (Oct. 15) 41: Palestinian Arabs, homeless and dispossessed of land. A black clergyman in New York said, "Palestinians are the 'niggers' of the Middle East." **1987* R. Doyle *Commitments* 9: The Irish are the niggers of Europe, lads….An' Dubliners are the niggers of Ireland. The culchies [*sc.*, rural residents] have fuckin' everythin'. An' the northside Dubliners are the niggers o' Dublin. *a1991* J. Phillips *You'll Never Eat Lunch* 88: Writers and women are the niggers of Hollywood. **1995** *Newsweek* (Aug. 28) 40: He's especially surprised that black cadets, who faced similar isolation when they integrated the corps in 1966, didn't offer to help….[Pat] Conroy says…"They've made Shannon Faulkner the 'nigger' of the '90s."

II. Other senses.—all now usu. considered offensive.

8. Esp. *Riverboating.* a steam capstan or auxiliary steam-driven engine.—also used attrib. In full, **nigger engine.**

    1867 in *OEDS:* The boat…struck the bar; they then began to work with the spars and nigger, and at two o'clock we got off. **1875** in *DA: Nigger,*…a steam-engine employed in hoisting; especially on shipboard and on the Western and Southern rivers. **1878** Beadle *Western Wilds* 378: Then oaths, spars, "nigger engine" and all the other available machinery were set in operation. **1952** Bissell *Monongahela* 90: The steam capstan, or "nigger." **1978** in Curry *River's in My Blood* 86: And then we'd get our nigger line in these steam caps, and then just kinda pull her up a little bit. *Ibid.* 93: A "nigger" is a steam capstan, and that was out on the forecastle, as a capstan.

9. [prob. sugg. by *nigger in the woodpile,* 1, below] a fault or defect.—usu. considered offensive.

    1886 *Sci. Amer.* LIV 308: The consequence of neglect might be what the workmen call "a nigger" would get into the armature, and burn it so as to destroy its service.

10. ire or annoyance (of a black person).—usu. constr. with *up.*—usu. used contemptuously. Cf. earlier ᴀꜰʀɪᴄᴀ or ᴀꜰʀɪᴄᴀɴ and comparable use of *get (someone's) Dutch up* s.v. Dᴜᴛᴄʜ, Iʀɪsʜ.

    1902 Corrothers *Black Cat Club* 212: I got mad. Yes, indeed, got ma niggah up! **1961** Himes *Pinktoes* 31: It goes without saying that this allusion to her weakest charm would get Mamie's nigger up, too, as they say in that part of the world, and she would retort with sweet acid bile. [**1983** Note in RHD files (Oct.): User asks redefinition—"a nigger refers to a nasty attitude"? As in "He's had a nigger ever since he started to work here"?]

11. *Logging.* (see 1956 quot.).

    1910 in *DA:* The "nigger" rose…to turn the log half-way round. **1938** Holbrook *Mackinaw* 97: A Mr. Rodgers of Muskegon invented the friction nigger, a device for automatically handling logs on the headrig carriage, and a Mr. Hill of Kalamazoo improved the nigger by adding direct steam. **1956** Sorden & Ebert *Logger's* 24 [ref. to *a*1925]: *Nigger,* A fast moving device on the log carriage in a saw mill that turned the log for sawing.

12. *Photography & Cinema.* a black, opaque screen or similar surface used to conceal studio lights, prevent reflections, etc.

1927 *AS* III 366: "Nigger" (a black frame covered with black cloth to guard the camera lens from lamps' light). **1934* in *OEDS:* The film world has a colourful compilation of expressions unlike those in other walks of life. "Niggers" are not men of colour, but blackboards used to "kill" unwanted reflections from the powerful lights. **1940** *AS* (Dec.) 359: *Nigger.* A large opaque screen, used to screen lights which would otherwise enter the [camera] lens directly and cause flare.

¶ In phrases:

¶ **nigger in the woodpile** [or **fence** or **woodshed**] [app. sugg. by the title of the blackface minstrel song alluded to in bracketed quots.] **1.** a trick or drawback, esp. if deliberately concealed; something inconsistent or out of place.—usu. considered offensive.

    [**1843** in H. Nathan *D. Emmett* 315: Nigger on [*sic*] de wood-pile barkin like a dog.] [**1845** in H. Nathan *D. Emmett* 292: Nigger on de Wood Pile.] **1847** in *DARE:* A Nigger in De Fence. This phrase was never so perfectly illustrated as by the law of Pennsylvania respecting the recovery of fugitive slaves. **1850** in *DA:* A majority of the papers…think that there "is a nigger in the fence" somewhere. **1852** in *Kans. Hist. Qly.* XI (1942) 235: No "nigger in the wood pile" here…; white men are at the bottom of this speculation. **1862** in *OEDS:* [These gentlemen] spoke two whole hours…in showing—to borrow an elegant phrase, the paternity of which belongs, I think, to their side of the House,—that there was "a nigger in the wood-pile." **1876** in *DA:* Someone "has blundered," or else there is a "nigger in the fence" somewhere. *a1890–1902* F & H V 40: *Nigger in the fence…*(American).—An underhand design, motive, or purpose. **1913–15** Van Loan *Taking the Count* 313: When your friend here began to bet, I thought there was a nigger in the woodpile somewhere. **1918** E.E. Rose *Cappy Ricks* 70: Ricks isn't the man to let anything slip through his fingers at a loss, unless there's a nigger in the woodpile somewhere. *a1922* in Kephart et al. *Smoky Mountain Voices* 116: I suspected a nigger in the woodpile. **1925** in Grayson *Stories for Men* 11: A nigger in the woodpile!…You see, our most dangerous rival…also wants this trail. **1925** in W.A. Graham *Custer Myth* 316: There has always been a "nigger in the woodpile" all through that Custer battle riddle. **1930** Sage *Last Rustler* 7: Sure enough, if that's…Headlight there's a nigger in the woodshed. **1932** T. Wolfe *Death to Morning* 227: There's a nigger in the woodpile somewheres: that story *just won't wash.* **1955** O'Connor *Last Hurrah* 45: I gained the impression that he'd just as soon be our next mayor, but apparently there's a nigger in the woodpile in the form of the gracious Mrs. Collins. **1981** C. Nelson *Picked Bullets Up* 147: There's always a nigger in the woodpile.

2. an unacknowledged black forebear of a white person.—usu. considered offensive.

    1953 Brossard *Saboteurs* 10: I feared she was unconsciously beginning to sniff a nigger in the woodpile. **1972–73** in M.J. Bell *Brown's Lounge* 11: It was said jokingly that there was a "nigger in my woodpile." **1977** Blockson & Fry *Black Genealogy* 109: One of the stories…was that the child was really killed because its father was black. From this incident emerged the term "nigger in the woodpile."

¶ (used in various, usu. racist similes and prov. phrases).—usu. considered offensive.

    1845 in H.C. Lewis *Works* 98: He had to stay still, doubled up like a long nigger in a short bed. **1848** in Botkin *Treas. Amer. Folklore* 275: Dumb as a dead nigger in a mud hole….Travel like a nigger in a thunder-storm. **1853** "P. Paxton" *In Texas* 411: I wouldn't be in your boots for a hogshead of niggers. **1868** in S. Boyer *Naval Surgeon* II 21: Mr. Poulterer sticks to Miss Oglesbey like grim death to a dead nigger—no chance thus for a young bachelor like myself. **1896** in L. Levy *Flashes of Merriment* 135: Nigger's eyeball, like a diamond sure to shine. **1906** *DN* III 160: *Sweat worse than a nigger at election…*To sweat copiously. **1912** Siringo *Cowboy Detective* 218: Hubbard was sweating like a "Nigger" at election. **1918** Paine *Fighting Fleets* 8: Not a light showing on a cussed one of 'em! Every destroyer as dark as the inside of a nigger's pocket. **1919** McKenna *Btty. A* 156: All shined up like a nigger's eyeball. **1925** Mullin *Scholar Tramp* 300 [ref. to *ca*1912]: He gets the back of 'is neck shaved at a barber's every week, and lilac-grease put on 'is hair, so he comes out shinin' like a nigger's heel. **1925** Nason *Three Lights* 70: This night's so black it'd made a nigger look like a snowman. **1926** Siringo *Riata & Spurs* 17: I hung on like grim death to a dead "nigger." **1926** Boatright *Texas Folk* 218: Sweating like a nigger at election. **1926** C.M. Russell *Trails* 204: It's black as a nigger's pocket; you couldn't find your nose with both hands. **1929** E.

Caldwell *Bastard* 75: And I'm a son of a gun if it wasn't licked off the deck before you could have said "Jump nigger!" **1929** Tully *Shadows* 81: Nobody gives a cockeyed nigger for what you was. **1930** E. Caldwell *Poor Fool* 188: She's working like a nigger full of turpentine tonight. **1933** J. Conroy *Disinherited* 102: Trouble is, the dad-blamed sojers keep the gals busy as a nigger at election most o' the time. **1936** Raine *Run of Brush* 161: You keep me sweating like a nigger on election day. **1956** N.Y.C. woman, age *ca*40: Who was your nigger-waiter last year? **1958** Frankel *Band of Bros.* 8: All mornin' he's been fidgety as a nigger in new shoes. **1962** T. Berger *Reinhart* 352: There was an old schoolboy retort that you made to the over-officious fellow: Who was your nigger last year? **1965** Capote *In Cold Blood* 115: Which to his partner seemed a ploy so feeble that it couldn't possibly "fool a day-old nigger." **1970** Sample *Dirty Ballplayer* 223: I'll guarantee that if you close down on this end, they won't get through. If they do, I'll kiss a nigger's ass. **1972** Swarthout *Tin Lizzie* 64: Boots shining like a nigger's heel. **1980** D. Smith *Glitter & Ash* 126: Spend it like a nigger before the bastards find ya got it.

nigger *adj.* (used variously to describe contemptible, disreputable, odd, or inferior things supposed to be used by, characteristic of, or suitable for black persons).—usu. used contemptuously.—usu. considered offensive. See also assorted following entries using NIGGER as first element.

    1901 (quot. at NIGGER GIN). **1930** Faulkner *As I Lay Dying* 190, in *OEDAS* I 129: She would maybe buy a cheap comb or a bottle of nigger toilet water. **1942** *ATS* 733: *Nigger tip*, any tip of an odd amount between fifteen and fifty cents. **1953** in *OEDAS* I 129: He…received a nigger offer from the Ottawa Rough Riders, and accepted it. **1965** "Malcolm X" & Haley *Autobiog.* ch. vi: The numbers game was referred to by the white racketeers as "nigger pool." **1967** in *DARE*: *Nigger fixings*—careless or hasty work. Common. **1968** F. Wallace *Poker* 219: *Nigger Bet*—An unusual bet such as a nine-dollar bet instead of the normal ten-dollar bet. **1972** in *DARE*: In some parts of the deep South, whites call some forbidden foods "nigger foods," meaning that these substances are fit only for blacks. **1978** *Maledicta* II 165: *Nigger logic*, any inferior, erroneous, overly simplistic or absurdly convoluted form of reasoning. **1988** in *DARE* [ref. to *ca*1980]: I heard the phrase "nigger brick" from a Houston heart surgeon who was showing me an old post office, the exterior of which was finished in tin painted to look like brick.

nigger *v.* **1.** *Logging.* to divide (a log) into desired lengths by burning it where necessary.—usu. constr. with *off*.—usu. considered offensive.

    1833 S. Smith *Maj. Jack Downing* 22: He laid sticks across the large logs…, and *niggered* them off with fire, and then rolled them up in piles. **1843** in *DA*: Niggering pertains to very large timber. **1887** in *DA*: This method of severing logs is called in the vernacular "niggering them off," either because of the laziness or of the blackness of the resulting heads. **1888** in *DARE*: It was easier to lay them on the fire and "nigger" them in two. **1891** Maitland *Slang Dict.* 187: *Nigger*, to burn in two, as a log is burned. **1942** *ATS* 34: *Nigger off*, to burn a log in two by building a fire on it. **1948** Dick *Dixie Frontier* 126: Morning and evening dry limbs were laid in the widening gap until the log was burnt into its length. After about a week the fires had done their work. This was called "niggering off."

    2. to do menial or subservient work; (*hence*) to idle or play about; mess around.—also constr. with *around*.—usu. considered offensive.

    1899 *Sat. Eve. Post* (Sept. 2) 147: I've been "niggerin'" for some cooks of a volunteer regiment, just for a chance to get near the front. **1903** in *Chrons. of Okla.* XLVI (1968) 39: A poker player that was stood pat on two duces [*sic*] and nothing to nigger with. **1912** Siringo *Cowboy Detective* 504: I had been told that the railroad company would furnish…sawed-off shotguns…; but a Winchester rifle, and a Colts 45 pistol to "nigger" with, are good enough for Yours Truly. **1977** J. Wylie *Homestead Grays* 278: I ain't gonna nigger around, so what else is there for me?

¶ In phrase:

¶ **nigger it** (of a nonblack person) to labor or endure privation in the manner of a black slave.—usu. considered offensive.

    1857 in *DA*: Many of the people express satisfaction in seeing these "better-dressed fellers" obliged to "nigger it" as well as themselves.

    1860–61 R.F. Burton *City of Saints* 482: They look with horror at the position of the "slavey" of a pauper mechanic, at being required to "nigger it" up on love and starvation.

nigger baby *n.* **1.** *Confed. Army.* a large artillery projectile.—usu. considered offensive.

    1871 De Vere *Americanisms* 117: Among the cant words produced by the late Civil War, *nigger babies* also became very popular; the term originated with the Veterans serving under the Confederate General Hardee, who gave that name to the enormous projectiles thrown into the city of Charleston by the *Swamp Angel* of General Gilmore, as his monster-gun in the swamps was ironically called.

    2. a small piece of licorice or chocolate candy cast in the stylized shape of a baby.—usu. considered offensive.

    1940 H.L. Mencken, in *DARE*: He much preferred the black licorice nigger-babies sold by Old Man Kunker in Baltimore street. **1948** H.L. Mencken *Amer. Lang. Supp.* II 163 [ref. to *ca*1890]: The sweetmeats…had names that are now forgotten. A *nigger-baby* was a small, hard, black licorice candy cast in the image of a colored baby. It sold at four or five for a cent. **1948** in *DA*: Candies with birds and flowers in the centers, nigger-babies, gumdrops, an' lickorish whips. **1957** in *DARE* [ref. to *ca*1895]: Nigger babies—licorice dolls about 3/4" long. **1960** N.Y.C. woman, age 78 [ref. to *ca*1900]: We used to call those [chewy chocolate candies] "nigger babies." **1965–70** in *DARE*.

    ¶ In phrase:

    ¶ **rain pitchforks and nigger babies** to rain heavily.—usu. considered offensive.

    1940 W.R. Burnett *High Sierra* 59: It rained pitchforks and nigger babies. *a*1955 Kantor *Andersonville* 261: It's raining pitchforks and nigger-babies. **1965–70** in *DARE*: Raining pitchforks and nigger babies.

nigger bankroll var. NIGGER ROLL.

nigger bean *n.* a black bean.—usu. considered offensive.

    1864 in Mattocks *Unspoiled Heart* 157: 1/4 [gill] Beans ("Nigger").

nigger boy *n.* *Riverboating.* (see quot.).—usu. considered offensive.

    1944 Boatright & Day *Hell to Breakfast* 145: The boilers are the "pots" and the automatic firing control on the boilers is the "nigger boy."

nigger brand *n.* *West.* a saddle sore.—usu. considered offensive. Also as *v.*

    1927 P.A. Rollins *Jinglebob* 180 [ref. to 1880's]: Selectin' the live stock for the pilgrims to "nigger brand." **1936** R. Adams *Cowboy Lingo* 87: To ride a horse until his back became sore was to "beefsteak"… him, and such sores were called "nigger brands." **1942** *ATS* 840: Nigger brand, set fast, *a saddle sore on a horse.*

nigger-chaser *n.* a small, squib-like firecracker that shoots off in several directions just above the ground.—usu. considered offensive.

    1882 Miller & Harlow *9'-51"* 263: "Nigger-chasers," pin-wheels, small torpedoes, sky-rockets, etc. **1882** Peck *Peck's Sunshine* 167: One of these nigger chasers, that run all over the ground. **1933** J. Conroy *Disinherited* 48: The squibs were like Fourth of July nigger-chasers. **1943** Wendt & Kogan *Bosses* 132: Skyrockets, roman candles, blue fire and nigger chasers.

nigger egg *n.* a black bowling ball.—usu. considered offensive. *Joc.*

    1976 in H.S. Thompson *Shark Hunt* 528: Bowling balls…"He thought they were nigger eggs."

niggereye *n.* a kind of candy.—usu. considered offensive.

    1955 O'Connor *Last Hurrah* 307: An assortment of niggereyes, gumdrops and jellybeans.

nigger gin *n.* inferior gin.—usu. considered offensive.

    [**1890** in *DA*: A "jigger" of negro gin.] **1901** in S. Dennison *Scandalize My Name* 408: But I saw when you came in you was blin' from niggah gin. *a*1915 in *JAF* XXVIII 299: That niggah gin…makes me grin. **1921** in H. Cannon *Cowboy Poetry* 19: I was suckled by a grizzly and was weaned on nigger gin. **1926** Tully *Jarnegan* 164: I could make a better [world] myself on nigger gin. **1929** *AS* IV 386: *Nigger gin*…means any sort of inferior synthetic gin. **1929** (quot. at JUNIPER JUICE). **1934** Peters & Sklar *Stevedore* 93: How many shots of nigger gin you got in you?

nigger golf *n.* the game of craps.—usu. considered offensive. *Joc.* Cf. AFRICAN GOLF.

1918 *Camp Pike Carry-On* (Dec. 19) 11: Cigarettes, "nigger golf," and passes to town. *Ibid.* (Dec. 26) 9: The snapping of fingers in "nigger golf."

nigger ham *n. Black E.* watermelon.—usu. considered offensive. *Joc.*

1974 Angelou *Gather Together* 36 [ref. to 1945]: *Nigger ham.* A watermelon.

niggerhead *n.* **1.** a kind of strong, dark-colored tobacco.—usu. considered offensive. [Many additional, chiefly local, senses, referring mainly to species of plants, appear in *DARE*.]

[**1809** W. Irving, in *DA*: He...thrust a prodigious quid of negro head tobacco into his left cheek.] **1843** in *DA*: My next communication will probably contain full details of the methods adopted by the Virginian planters in the manufacturing of the nigger-head, ladies'-twist, [etc.]. **1885** S.S. Hall *Gold Buttons* 18: The other chipped off tobacco from a plug of "niggerhead." *ca*1925 in Fife & Fife *Ballads of West* 185: We all sat smoking niggerhead. **1945** Mencken *Amer. Lang. Supp. I* 528: In 1943 there was another [scandal] over the discovery that the American Tobacco Company was making a brand of tobacco called *Nigger Head.*

2.a. a dark, rounded, often rough or knobby stone; (*also*) a boulder usu. of small or medium size; (see also 1886–89 quot.).

1847 in *DAE*: It was a saw mill, with a small pair of stones attached, made of boulders, or "nigger heads," as they are commonly called. *a*1877 Bartlett *Amer.* (ed. 4) 425: *Niggerhead stone.* The hard, heavy, black rock with which the country about Baltimore is filled, and which is so useful in making turnpike roads. **1886–89** *Smithsonian Inst. Annual Report 1886* II 523: *Nigger head.* (1) The black concretionary nodules found in granite; (2) Any hard, dark, colored rock weathering out into rounded nodules or bowlders; (3) Slaty rock associated with sandstone. A quarryman's term. **1916** C. Sandburg *Chicago Poems* 41: A boy...throws a niggerhead. **1927** *AS* (June) 408: Dark, rounded rocks..."niggerheads." **1958** McCulloch *Woods Wds.* 121: *Niggerhead*—a. A rock in a stream bed which interferes with driving or splashing. b. A knotted-up clump of rocks uncovered on a grading job; or a boulder the size of a man's head. **1976** Arble *Long Tunnel* 201: They worked on that niggerhead [in the roof of a mining tunnel] with wedges, rock bars, every damn thing, but they couldn't pull it down. **1985** Bodey *F.N.G.* 241: The dark gray...[rocks] he calls niggerheads.

b. a rain cloud.—usu. considered offensive.

1893 in J. London *Short Stories* 3: A few light, fleecy "niggerheads"...seemed abashed [by the sun]...and soon disappeared. **1914** *DN* IV 110: *Nigger-head*...Dark cumulous clouds [*sic*] close to the horizon. **1967** in *DARE: Big clouds that roll up high before a rainstorm*...Niggerheads—my grandmother said that.

c. *Naut.* a large, knobby or mushroom-shaped coral formation.—usu. considered offensive.

*1931 Lubbock *Bully Hayes* 170: Coral mushrooms, nigger-heads, and reefs to navigate through. **1944** Huie *Can Do!* 100: "Niggerheads"...are mushroom-like coral deposits on the ocean floor, and they have to be blown out so they won't obstruct [sea]planes. They are anywhere from ten to twenty feet high. **1947** Heavey *Down Ramp!* 106: One LCVP did get hung up on a coral "niggerhead." **1953** *New Yorker* (Aug. 15) 34: All around us, breaking the surface of the water, were large chunks of coral, called niggerheads.

d. (among jewelers) a flawed diamond.—usu. considered offensive.

1937 in Botkin *Sidewalks* 88 [ref. to 1870's]: Subsequently some of the "jewels" reached London, where they were recognized as South African "niggerheads." **1955** in D.W. Maurer *Lang. Und.* 247: *Nigger head*...A flawed diamond (jeweler's term).

e. *Steel Industry.* (see quot.).—usu. considered offensive.

1948 H.L. Mencken *Amer. Lang. Supp. II* 773: *Niggerhead.* A piece of scrap sticking above the surface of molten steel in a furnace.

3. a raised clump of thick vegetation; tussock.—usu. considered offensive.

1859 Bartlett *Amer.* (ed. 2) 292: *Nigger heads.* The tussocks or knotted masses of the roots of sedges and ferns projecting above the wet surface of a swamp. *South.* **1892** in *DAE*: Hummocks, called in the borough dialect "nigger-heads," formed by tufts of swamp grass. **1894** *DN* I 342: *Nigger-head:* clump of fern-roots in swamps. When the land

is reclaimed they remain for years undecayed, showing as black lumps in the plowed field. **1903** J. London *Call of Wild* ch. vii: Through the forest aisles and across the open spaces where the niggerheads bunched. **1930** Sage *Last Rustler* 284: Then we climbed a sidehill covered with niggerheads and boulders. **1944** H.F. Gregory *Helicopter* 132: "Niggerheads," as the rough grass hummocks are called in Alaska. **1947** in *DA*: The ptarmigan cackled in the manner of a Bronx cheer as it flew to a nearby niggerhead. **1963–64** Kesey *Great Notion* 84: Place is jus' *overrun* with Canada thistle an' niggerheads. **1976** in *DARE:* A niggerhead flat....great big hummocks of matted grass that looked like giant mops.

4. Esp. *Naut.* a bollard; mooring post; (*also*) a drum or cylinder that is part of a capstan or winch.—usu. considered offensive.

1911 in *DARE: Niggerhead*...A spool or capstan for lifting or hauling, formed on the end of a shaft which is turned by power: so called because it is usually black. **1927** Bradford *Gloss. Sea Terms* 119: *Niggerheads,* a name for bollards, and sometimes applied to winch heads. **1942** *ATS* 740: *Niggerheads,* the drums of a steam capstan. **1948** Mencken *Amer. Lang. Supp. II* 770: *Niggerhead*...a cylinder on a power winch. **1949** Cummings *Dict. Sports* 43: *Bollard*...Sometimes called "nigger head." **1958** McCulloch *Woods Words* 121: *Niggerhead*...The outside spool on the shaft of a donkey drum. **1977** Bartlett *Finest Kind* 65: Santo takes a double turn on the niggerhead, puts pressure on the line, and draws the net up.

5. very dark rum.—usu. considered offensive. In full, **niggerhead rum.**

*ca*1930 in Fife & Fife *Ballads of West* 227: Too much nigger-head rum.

6. *R.R.* (see 1948 quot.).—usu. considered offensive.

1932 *R.R. Mag.* (Oct.) 369: *Niggerhead*—Steam exit on top of boiler from which pipes to injector, etc., issue. **1939** *Sat. Eve. Post* (Apr. 15) 26: When she hit the first high-daddy she was carrying the white feather and fogging from the niggerhead. **1948** Mencken *Amer. Lang. Supp. II* 716: *Niggerhead.* The steam dome atop a locomotive boiler.

7. *Und.* a small cylindrical wall safe.—usu. considered offensive.

1937 E. Anderson *Thieves Like Us* 17: Chicamaw was talking now about a bank he robbed in Kansas. "I knew I hadn't sacked up no more than two thousand out of that nigger-head and I just happened to pick up that cash slip." **1962–68** B. Jackson *In the Life* 107: Those keysters, niggerheads (round wall safes), they're punch-proof.

8. a kink in a rope, hose, or line.—usu. considered offensive.

1978 Univ. Tenn. student: "Shake them niggerheads out of the line." That's a construction term.

9. (in various other specific senses) (see quots.).—usu. considered offensive.

1939 in A. Banks *First-Person* 131 [ref. to *ca*1900]: The old niggerhead* did prove practical....*A shoe nailing machine, so named "because a man from Brazil invented it." **1948** McIlwaine *Memphis* 218: The captain explained that a "niggerhead" was a long pole with a block on the end used in guiding a line of rolling barrels down the stage. **1942–49** Goldin et al. *DAUL: Nigger heads*....Prunes.

nigger heaven *n.* **1.** *Theat.* the topmost balcony in a theater.—usu. considered offensive.

1866 in W.H. Jackson *Diaries* 85: Went to the theatre....Went away up into "Nigger heaven," 25 ct. place. **1878** in *DA*: There is a "Nigger Heaven" (as the third tier is called in Troy) here. **1900** *DN* II 47: *Nigger-heaven,* n. Topmost gallery of a theatre. **1908** J. London *M. Eden* 73: A seat in nigger heaven. **1912** Thornton *Amer. Glossary* 608: *Nigger heaven.* The gallery of a theatre or place of entertainment. Common in Boston in 1888–91. **1913** Light *Hobo* 59: This is the Nigger heaven. **1929** T. Gordon *Born to Be* 153: They sat up on a little Nigger Heaven in the back of the small house. **1932** Harvey *Me and Bad Eye* 25: My seat...was in nigger heaven and the girls on the stage looked so small I couldent see their shapes. **1932** C. McKay, in C. Major *Calling Wind* 39: The show finished. Barclay Oram and his wife...descended from Nigger Heaven. **1952** C. Sandburg *Strangers* 272 [ref. to *ca*1890]: It was an up-to-date theater with a main floor, a balcony, and a gallery that nearly everybody called "Nigger Heaven." **1961** Ernst *Trouping* 80: In the spacious nigger heaven, gamins had bored many auger holes, the better to see and hear what went on below. **1964** W. Beech *Article 92* 140: I can't fix it for us to sit in nigger heaven. **1976** S. Hayden *Voyage* 368: Having misplaced his tickets,

[he] found himself and his companions in..."Nigger Heaven." **1982** T.C. Mason *Battleship* 144: I sat in the seventy-five cent seats, in the highest level of what was then called nigger heaven. *a*1973–87 F.M. Davis *Livin' the Blues* 6: The second balcony "for colored only"...was dubbed "nigger heaven."

2. (see quot.).—usu. considered offensive.

　　1906 *DN* III 148: "*To be in nigger heaven,*" i.e., to enjoy one's self cheaply and vulgarly. "He's in *nigger-heaven* now."

3. a place where blacks congregate; a black neighborhood.—usu. considered offensive.

　　1925 Van Vechten *Nigger Heaven* 15: Dis Place, where Ah met you—Harlem. Ah calls et, specherly tonight, Ah calls et Nigger Heaven! **1932** L. Berg *Prison Doctor* 135: Jesus, it's getting so a white man can't sleep with all this stink from nigger heaven. **1954–60** *DAS: Nigger heaven*...The Harlem section of New York City; any heavily populated Negro neighborhood.

nigger-heeled *adj. West.* (see 1936 quot.).—usu. considered offensive.

　　[**1847** J.S. Robb, in Botkin *Treas. Amer. Folklore* 44: Why, you couldn't hit the hinder part of that nigger's heel up thar on the bluff...and that ain't no shot to crow about. *Ibid.* 46: I want you to pay me fur trimmin' the heel of one of your town niggers! I've jest altered his breed, and arter this his posterity kin warr the neatest kind of a boot!] [**1927** in *DARE: Nigger heel*—an unusually long heel (of a person); a rearward projection of the heel beyond average.] **1936** R. Adams *Cowboy Lingo* 86: A horse...was said to be "nigger-heeled" when his front toes pointed out and his heels in.

nigger-heel molasses *n. West.* blackstrap molasses.—usu. considered offensive.

　　1942 Garcia *Tough Trip* 110 [ref. to 1880's]: We had a quart bottle filled with black-strap or nigger-heel molasses, which was as black as tar.

nigger in a blanket *n.* a dessert consisting of raisins, blackberries, or other dark fruit, rolled in dough and steamed in a sack.—usu. considered offensive.

　　1936 R. Adams *Cowboy Lingo* 149: "Nigger in a blanket" was a form of dessert. **1941** in *DARE*: Blackberries cooked in pastry turnovers are known [in Louisiana] as "niggers in a blanket." **1944** R. Adams *Western Words* 104: *Nigger-in-a-blanket* A cowboy dessert, usually made of raisins in dough.

niggerish *adj.* shiftless; no-account.—used contemptuously.—usu. considered offensive.

　　1825 J. Neal *Bro. Jonathan* 67: Ye great, niggerish, wap-sided, haw. **1866** in *DAE*: When I say "colored," I mean one thing, respectfully; and when I say "niggerish," I mean another, disgustedly. **1970** in P. Heller *In This Corner* 95: But I got niggerish and I just let [my career] go.

niggerize *v. Pol.* to relegate to a position of marginal power or opportunity.—usu. considered offensive. Hence **niggerization,** *n.*

　　1972 *Harper's* (Oct.) 57: There's a whole lotta people out there who are afraid to win because they don't think of themselves as running the show. They've been *niggerized,* the only way they know is suckin'. **1973** F. Kennedy, in *Bartlett's Quots.* (16th ed.) 739: Niggerization is the result of oppression—and it doesn't just apply to black people. Old people, poor people, and students can also get niggerized. **1976** *Harper's* (Nov.) 66: Women can afford the kind of political action they [*sc.,* blacks] now shrink from. But it's easier to cringe and talk about being "niggerized." **1982** *Harper's* (July) 68: Life in these here United States is a series of niggerizations. The schools, she said, "niggerize" us, the churches "niggerize" us, the police and the federal government "niggerize" us.

nigger jockey *n.* (see quot.).—usu. considered offensive.

　　1838 [Haliburton] *Clockmaker* (Ser. 2) 30: A nigger-jockey, sir, says I, is a gentleman that trades in niggers,—buys them in one state, and sells them in another, where they ar'n't known....He fixes on a spot in the next state for meetin' ag'in, and Sambo...is sold a second time ag'in.

nigger-kickers *n.pl.* heavy boots.—usu. considered offensive. Also **nigger-stompers.**

　　1974 Univ. Tenn grad. student: Nigger-stompers are any kind of big boots, like with pointed toes. I heard it in New York City in the early '60's. **1988** Terkel *Great Divide* 281 [ref. to 1969]: I had just bought these big boots for mountain climbing....This student who was friendly to me...said, "Oh, you got your nigger-kickers on."

nigger-killer *n.* **1.** a slingshot; NIGGER-SHOOTER.—usu. considered offensive.

　　1940 in *DA*: It is barefoot boys on country roads, with nigger-killers dangling from the pockets of their overalls and strings of "yeller catfish" slung over their shoulders. **1961** in *DARE*: Boys' weapon made of rubber strips on a forked stick...nigger killer. **1970** in *DARE*: The majority of informants [in N.E. Texas] call this weapon a *nigger-shooter....*Another name is *nigger-killer.*

2. a pistol.—usu. considered offensive.

　　1944 in *DA*: This gun was popularly known to the trade as a "nigger killer," and it was said that it fired a standard short thirty-two caliber bullet sideways [*sic*]. **1976–77** Kernochan *Dry Hustle* 45: His favorite gun was a World War I snubnose, the "nigger killer."

nigger-knocker *n.* a club or length of wood to be used as a weapon, esp. against blacks.—usu. considered offensive. [The bracketed quot. is incorrectly dated "1859" in Thornton *Amer. Glossary;* the error is repeated in *DA.*]

　　[*a*1883 in *DARE*: Another name for the nigger-knocker is hogfish....Catfish are sweet and pretty compared to nigger-knockers.] **1965** Conot *Rivers of Blood* 41: Two weeks later he had been able to shrug at such expressions as "nigger knockers." **1968** *Sat. Eve. Post* (Sept. 16) 27: Marres tenses, grabs his nightstick—some of his colleagues call it a "nigger-knocker"—and jumps from the car. **1974** Pi4pt. *Short Eyes* 79: Now Joey got the nigger knocker wrapped around his hand. **1985** Univ. Tenn. grad. student: A big piece of wood that you could swing on somebody is called a *nigger-knocker.*

niggerlip *v.* to moisten the end of a cigarette with saliva while smoking it.—usu. considered offensive.—also used trans.

　　1940 *AS* (Oct.) 335: To moisten the tip of one's cigaret is to *niggerlip.* **1958** Capote *Breakfast at Tiffany's* 32: You're such a slob. You always niggar-lip [*sic*]. **1976** *N.Y. Times Mag.* (Mar. 28) 39: I hadn't heard anything like that since I'd left the children of the white bourgeoisie nigger-lippin' their cigarettes in Baltimore in 1954. **1983** Flaherty *Tin Wife* 213: She had grown up hearing her friends say, "Don't nigger-lip it," to sloppy cigarette smokers who asked for a drag. **1991** *UTSQ: Nigger-lip it*—get saliva all over cigarette or cigar by putting your lips over it...Don't nigger-lip that cigarette!

nigger local *n. R.R.* (see quots.).—usu. considered offensive.

　　1916 *DN* IV 356: *Nigger local.* A local freight train involving very hard work. **1969** *AS* XLIV 250: On the Rock Island the nigger local is a slow train that runs...from Chicago to Peoria on Saturday nights only. In the days when riding the rails was more common, blacks frequently traveled on weekend freight trains to Peoria.

nigger-lover *n.* a white or other nonblack person who shows favor to blacks or other dark-skinned persons.—used contemptuously.—usu. considered offensive.

　　1856 in Fornell *Galveston Era* 173: A wiseacre and a nigger lover. **1864** in O.J. Hopkins *Under the Flag* 113: Death to Abolition nigger-lovers! **1896** T.C.S. Brown et al. *Behind Guns* 26: Breathing out curses against the "Yankee nigger lovers." **1906** M'Govern *Sarjint Larry* 135: Oi, messilf...am not wot we calls in de States "a nigger-lover," an Oi don't be believing dat "a nigger is a white soul in a black man's body," although Oi've seen mannie's de American black face in de Philypeens wot's a honor to de States. **1912** in Truman *Dear Bess* 78: John Greenleaf Whittier, the old nigger lover, also went into spasms over snow. **1919** Sandburg *Race Riot* 5: A mayor whose opponents failed to defeat him with the covert circulation of the epithet of "nigger lover." **1929–30** Dos Passos *42d Parallel* 122: "Niggerlover," yelled Joe in her ear. **1931** Cressey *Taxi-Dance* 35: *Nigger lover.*—A girl who "dates" Filipinos. **1933** J. Conroy *Disinherited* 249: I ain't no nigger lover. **1936** N. West *Cool Million* 244: He ain't no nigger-lover. *a*1937 Dollard *Southern Town* 47: "Nigger-lover" is a phrase used in Southerntown and not infrequently applied to northerners....to call a southerner this...would lead to physical violence in most cases. **1944** R. Brooks *Brick Foxhole* 12: But you're a nigger-lover....You like niggers. **1946** K. Archibald *Shipyard* 64: I found signs red-lettered with the damning caption, "Nigger-lover," attached to my desk and chair. **1952** Uris *Battle Cry* 312: "What the hell are you guys. A bunch of nigger-lovers?" Speedy fumed. "He ain't nothing but a kike draftee." **1954** Killens *Youngblood* 119: You talk like a nigger-lover. **1960** H. Lee *Mockingbird* 117: "Scout," said Atticus, "nigger-lover is just one of those terms that don't mean anything....It's hard to explain—ignorant, trashy people use it when they think somebody's favoring Negroes over and above themselves. It's slipped into usage with some people like ourselves, when they want a common, ugly term to label somebody." **1960** *Time* (Dec. 12), in *Time* (Dec. 11, 1995): Nigger lover, nigger lover, nigger lover, Jew: we hate niggers, we hate you. **1967** in A.K. Johnson *Urban Ghetto Riots* 80: And they said to them white women, called them nigger lovers and like they was a dog. **1980** King & Riley *Daddy King* 63: If the woman saw him doing a favor for a "nigger"...she might tell others that he was a nigger-lover....and he'd find a stone crashing through his window. **1979–82** Gwin *Overboard* 180: You're such a damned bleeding-heart niggerlover. **1983** in Bak *Cobb Would Have Caught It* 249 [ref. to 1930's]: Shit, these bench jockeys, they'd call their friends from down south "nigger lovers." Tried to get them stirred up. **1984** D. Smith *Steely Blue* 264: Anyone who thought that was not right, or unfair, was called a nigger lover. **1991** D'Souza *Illiberal Education* 134: Assailants yelled "Pinko,"...and "nigger lover." **1992** N. Russell *Suicide Charlie* 20: It serves the nigger-lover right. **1993** A. Lomax *Where Blues Began* x: Whites who protested were stigmatized as "nigger lovers" and faced social exclusion or worse. **1996** *Jerry Springer Show* (synd. TV series): I get called a "nigger-lover" at least once a day....[My] brother is a member of the KKK.

nigger-loving *adj.* Esp. *So.* **1.** (of a white or other nonblack person) showing favor to black or other dark-skinned persons.—used contemptuously.—usu. considered offensive.

    1879 [Tourgée] *Fool's Errand* 177: They took him out and whipped him, because they said he was a "nigger-loving Radical." **1914** S. Lewis *Our Mr. Wrenn* 3: A nigger-lovin' Yankee...couldn't appreciate the subtle sorrows of a Zapp of Zapp's Bog. **1929–34** Farrell *Judgment Day* 471: Dirty nigger-loving Reds. **1953** H. Carter *Main Street* 183: Nigger-loving Yankeefied communists. **1954** Arrow *Dollmaker* 223: No nigger-loven, Jew-loven communist's gonna...tell me wot I gotta do. **1956** in Rowan *Go South* 167: Nigger lovin' sonofabitch....Hit the nigger lovin' whore. **1964** *Newsweek* (July 13) 19: A carload of whites pulled up and hooted: "Goddam you nigger-lovin' bastards!" **1985** Boyne & Thompson *Wild Blue* 218: Or I'm going to shove this nightstick up your nigger-loving ass.

    2. [infl. by EVER-LOVING] damned.—usu. considered offensive.

    1985 M. Brennan *War* 219 [ref. to 1969]: He threw up his arms in a helpless gesture. "Not a thing, Sarge. Not a nigger lovin' thing."

nigger luck *n.* unexpected or undeserved good fortune.—usu. considered offensive.

    1851 Glisan *Army Life* 90: I occasionally made him a little envious by my nigger-luck, as he is pleased to term it. **1869** B. Harte, in *DAE:* When a man gets a streak of luck,—nigger luck,—he don't get tired. **1875** B. Harte *Argonauts* 136: "He will sink it all in the next hole" was the prevailing belief, predicated upon the usual manner in which the possessor of "nigger luck" disposed of his fortune. **1888** in Farmer *Amer.:* I am cussed...if any darned rebel can have such nigger luck and enjoy it while I live. **1896** Lillard *Poker Stories* 74: Simultaneously the son began to play in "nigger luck." He held surprising hands, and made his bets with a blundering shrewdness that landed him winner or saved him from loss. **1898** B. Harte *Light & Shadow* 213: You're in nigger luck, Mad! **1899** in Thompson *Youth's Companion* 359: This was called "nigger luck"—that is, the inexplicable good fortune of the inferior and incompetent. **1914** *Collier's* (Aug. 1) 6: Just nigger luck!...That busher won't get another hit off me all season. **1950** Raine *Six* 27: I had nigger luck.

niggerly *adj.* [infl. by *niggardly*] despicable.—usu. considered offensive.

    1846 N.J.T. Dana *Monterrey* 61: Highly incensed at the idea of a surrender to those "niggerly rascals." [**1909** *DN* III 352: *Niggerly...Niggardly.*]

nigger navel *n.* a black-eyed susan.—usu. considered offensive.

    1942 in *DARE.* **1966** in IUFA *Folk Speech:* Black-eyed Susans are called in Alabama by whites and coloureds [*sic*], "Nigger Navels." Used in my father's youth, 1920's and '30's. **1968** in *DARE: A kind of daisy, bright yellow with a dark center, that grows along roadsides in late summer....Nigger nabel* [*sic*].

nigger news *n. So.* gossip.—usu. considered offensive.

    1857 J.D. Long *Pict. of Slavery* 75: It is considered dishonorable for persons to break friendship on what is called "nigger news." *Ibid.* 78: Well, it's "nigger news"; yet I believe niggers can tell the truth sometimes. **1859** in Eliason *Tarheel Talk* 152: The family depend upon Is to supply me with the latest *nigger news.* ca**1960** in *DARE: Nigger*

news...Gossip, scuttlebutt, just such news as a servant might hint to her employer.

nigger out *v.* to back out.—usu. considered offensive.

    1898–1900 Cullen *Chances* 240: Of all the niggering out I ever saw...this is the worst. **1977** Univ. Tenn. student: We were supposed to go, but she niggered out on me. Called me up at seven o'clock and said there was some emergency and she couldn't make it.

nigger-rich *adj.* vulgarly extravagant, esp. while having little cash; newly flush and eager to spend money.—usu. used derisively.—usu. considered offensive.

    1930 Gowen *Racketeers and Their Methods* 81 (Tamony Coll.): In those sections of the South where the old traditions of gentle birth and culture still assert their ancient authority and draw the lines of social demarcation, there is commonly in use a vivid, brutal phrase to describe ostentatious display by the merely vulgar wealthy. The phrase is "nigger rich." ca**1930** in *DARE: Nigger rich:* One who spends money foolishly. **1931** Bontemps *Sends Sunday* 96: Everybody had money; everybody was nigger-rich. **1945** in Hemingway *Sel. Letters* 584: Don't tell him so he won't get nigger rich. **1965** D.G. Moore *20th C. Cowboy* 121: Yaqui Ordunus felt nigger rich after his winnings. **1968–70** in *DARE: Nigger rich*—somebody who's just made a lot and is flashing it around—common word [in California]. *Ibid.: A woman who overdresses or...spends too much on clothes...Nigger rich. Ibid.:—Nigger rich*—acting like she just got rich but it's only a few bucks. **1971** B.B. Johnson *Blues for Sister* 86: He would be a little high, nigger-rich, and...never [see] a dime further. **1979** J.L. Gwaltney *Drylongso* xvi: *Nigger-rich*—pseudo-rich. **1980** D. Smith *Glitter & Ash* 78: Like I say, when Petey Ahearn is nigger rich, everyone gets a drink. **1986** L. Pederson, in *DARE: Nigger rich*—making money, spending it immediately.

    2. (see quots.).—usu. considered offensive.

    1942 *ATS* 378: *Nigger rich*, with only enough money for a bare existence. **1968–72** Milner & Milner *Black Players* 273: *Nigger-Rich* deeply in debt, in order to maintain symbols of affluence, such as an expensive car.

nigger-rig *v.* Esp. *So.* to assemble or repair hastily or poorly, usu. from whatever materials are at hand; jury-rig.—usu. considered offensive. Also as *n.*

    1965 in *DARE: Nigger-rigged*—rigging, etc., put together or repaired quickly and poorly Inf[ormant] says term is not used much anymore [in Oklahoma]. **1977** Univ. Tenn. grad. student: If the engine breaks down you have to nigger-rig another one. It's an Arkansas expression. **1977** Univ. Tenn. grad. student: A nigger-rig is anything makeshift, any kind of contraption set up without the proper equipment or components. I first heard it as a Mississippi river term [ca1970]. **1983** V. McDavid, in RHD files: In northern Indiana, to do a makeshift repair job is to "nigger rig." I would use jury rig, but among men, it is to nigger rig. **1992** Mowry *Way Past Cool* 119: The nigger-rigged plumbing was a leaky...joke. **1993** Mowry *Six Out Seven* 29: It was a nigger-rig, and full of splinters, but it worked. **1994** in *DARE* [ref. to 1950's]: To nigger-rig was to improvise...as in "I had to nigger-rig that exhaust system, Cletus." **1994** Univ. Tenn. prof., age ca62: To *nigger-rig* is to throw something together temporarily or hastily. I just heard it [for the first time] within the past week.

nigger roll *n. Gamb.* MICHIGAN ROLL.—usu. considered offensive. Also **nigger bankroll.**

    1929 Gill *Und. Slang: Nigger bank roll*—Roll of one dollar bills. **1942** *ATS* 536: *Nigger roll*, a roll of dollar bills. **1967–80** Folb *Runnin' Lines* 112: A phony bankroll—a wad of money with maybe a large bill on top and a few singles in the middle (and sometimes paper on the bottom) is variously called *a California bankroll, a nigger's bankroll,* or *a Chicago bankroll.*

nigger-shooter *n.* a slingshot.—usu. considered offensive.

    1876 in *PADS* (No. 52) 41: I had a job on hand making Nigger shooters for Dr's children. **1879** in Sweet *Sweet's Texas* 76: One live boy with a nigger-shooter...can be looked up to with awe. **1903** in "O. Henry" *Cabbages & Kings* 110: Like a bean out of a little boy's nigger shooter. **1908** W.G. Davenport *Butte & Montana* 326: David putting a kibosh on Goliath with a nigger shooter. **1915** *DN* IV 227: *Nigger-shooter...*A sort of slingshot, composed of wooden handle and two rubber bands ending in a leather "pocket" from which stones are shot. Every boy in Texas is proficient in its use. **1931** Bontemps *Sends Sunday* 72: Rubber bands to make "nigger-shooters." **1970** (quot. at NIGGER-KILLER). **1982** D.A. Harper *Good Company* 130: A lot of the tramps carry "nigger shooters," that's a slingshot. **1984** Sample *Raceboss* 71: I carried…rocks and steel ball ammunition for my "nigger shooter."

nigger steak *n.* liver.—usu. considered offensive. *Joc.*

    1940 *AS* (Apr.) 211: Wieners, *pups*; liver, *nigger steak*. **1942** *ATS* 762: *Nigger steak and a bad breath*, liver and onions. **1944** *Papers Mich. Acad.* XXX 599: Prison Jargon…*nigger steak*, liver. *a*1983 Elting, Cragg & Deal *Dict. Soldier Talk* 363: *Nigger steak* (1940s–1950s; Marines)…Fried liver.

nigger stick *n.* a club to be used as a weapon against blacks; NIGGER-KNOCKER.—usu. considered offensive.

    1971 *N.Y. Post* (Sept. 15) 36: Nigger sticks. **1977** *New Times* (May 27) 26: They also carried…billy clubs nicknamed "nigger sticks."

nigger-sticker *n.* a knife carried as a weapon, usu. against blacks.—usu. considered offensive.

    1969 in *DARE*: A large pocket knife with blades that fold in and out…*Nigger sticker.* **1985** Ark. man, age 35: I've heard knives referred to as *nigger-stickers* frequently [esp. in 1960's], both in Arkansas and later in the service.

nigger-stompers var. NIGGER-KICKERS.

nigger toe *n.* **1.** a variety of potato.—usu. considered offensive.

    1853 in *DAE*: Some of the more approved [kinds of potatoes] are…the Niggertoe, the Meshannock, the Cumberland Kempt.

    2. a Brazil nut; (see also 1985 quot.).—usu. considered offensive.

    1896 *DN* I 421: *Niggertoes:* for Brazil nuts. **1915** *Confed. Vet.* XXIII 494 [ref. to Civil War]: "Nigger toes" and English walnuts. **1951** *PADS* (No. 15) 58 [ref. to 1890's]: Nigger-toe. **1953–57** Ruark *Old Man & Boy* 79: The greasy, plump white Brazil nuts we called nigger-toes. **1975** in C. Major *Calling Wind* 378: A nigger-toe nut is black. **1980** Lorenz *Guys Like Us* 94: Almonds, pecans, pistachios, nigger toes. **1985** Univ. Tenn. grad. student: A *nigger toe* is a [kind of] chocolate bon-bon. **1989** Rawson *Wicked Words* 270: The taboo has grown so strong that…no one of any refinement eats *nigger toes* (Brazil nuts)…any more.

niggertown *n.* a black neighborhood or district.—usu. considered offensive. Also **niggerville.** Cf. DARKTOWN.

    1857 in *DARE*: Like all other *niggervilles* in our disreputable part of the confederacy, the commercial emporium of South Carolina is sick and impoverished. **1904** Dunbar *Happy Hollow* 225: Whites from every section, and blacks from "nigger town," as the west portion of the place was called. **1942** *ATS* 49: Negro District…*Darktown,…Niggertown.* **1945** Saxon *Gumbo Ya-Ya* 240: Every big plantation was like a little ole nigger town, there was so many of us. **1965** "Malcolm X" & Haley *Autobiog. Malcolm X* 147: He…suddenly suggested going over to the black ghetto. Every Negro that lives in a city has seen…the Northern cracker who will go to visit "niggertown," to be amused at "the coons." **1968** in *DARE*: Niggerville. **1978** E. Thompson *Devil to Pay* 3: A nameless niggertown alley in Wichita. **1979** in *Mother Jones* (Jan. 1980) 55: He's probably down there.…In niggertown. **1979–82** Gwin *Overboard* 122: Niggertown's got a Laundromat.

nigger work *n.* menial or degrading employment.—usu. considered offensive.

    1939 M. Levin *Citizens* 140: First Will would yell the niggers had all the jobs, then he would spit at a job because it was nigger work. **1978** J. Updike, in *OEDAS* I 129: In my student need across the seas I had held a variety of lowly jobs—"nigger work," in the friendly phrase of the lily-white elite of Franchise. **1979–82** Gwin *Overboard* 67: You're welcome to all the nigger work on the boat.

niggie *n.* NIG.

    1854 in White *Amer. Negro Folk-Songs* 443: Hoe cotton, dig corn,/Den we feed de niggies.

night bomber *n. Mil. Av.* an airman who goes carousing at night. Hence **night bombing,** *n.*

    1928 *Pop. Sci. Mo.* (May) 72: A "night bomber" is a pilot who likes to sleep in daytime and visit night clubs and festive gatherings at night. **1933** Stewart *Airman Speech* 37: A "night bomber" is sometimes that low fellow who patronizes night clubs. **1937** Codman *Contact* 69 [ref. to 1918]: "Where have *you* been?" "Practicing night-bombing. Know all about it, now. Be very careful of husbands, though." **1941** Kendall *Army & Navy Sl.*: He's a night bomber…playboy.

night bounce *n. Naval Av.* training in night landings.

1945 in Rea *Wings of Gold* 300: We are here for night bounce. *Ibid.* 301: We finished night bounce out at Holtville very satisfactorily.

nightcap *n.* **1.** the final alcoholic drink of the evening; a drink taken shortly before bedtime. Now *S.E.*

    1818 in *OED*: A pint of table beer, (or Ale, if you make it for a "Night-Cap"). **1841 (quot. at SNORTER). **1842** *Spirit of Times* (July 23) 243: We, after a nightcap, soon retired. **1887** "Zor" *Breaking Chains* 132: Let us take a "night cap" and send for a cab.

    2.a. *Baseball.* the evening game of a doubleheader. Now *colloq.*

    1917 *N.Y. Times* (Oct. 5) (cited in Nicholls *Baseball Dict.*). **1948** (quot. at LID-LIFTER).

    b. *Horse Racing.* the final race of the day.

    1939 in *OEDS*: *Nightcap*, the final race or contest of a day's sports. **1984** W. Murray *Dead Crab* 35: It happened just before the nightcap.

night crawler *n.* a person who stays out or works late at night. Hence **night crawl** an instance of staying out late at night.

    1951 (quot. at CREEP, *n.,* 2). **1973** Kingry *Monk & Marines* 48: We called ourselves the "night crawlers." **1976** Adcock *Not for Truckers Only* 47: Maybe never even shoot an eyeball at a…nightcrawler, a boogie man, or blue jeans. **1981** *N.Y. Daily News* (July 7) 20: For night-crawlers in L.A., there's nowhere to go. Until now. During our recent stay on the Coast, we were thrilled to see the Beverly Hills Hotel has started serving "Midnight Supper," with live music. **1992** *Middle Ages* (CBS-TV): Just till the night crawlers come out. **1993** A. Adams & W. Stadiem *Madam* 11: Very-early-morning calls precluded night crawls.

night eye *n.* a callosity on a horse's leg.

    *ca*1938, 1943 in *DARE*. **1956** "T. Betts" *Across the Board* 155: Photographs included the pictures of night eyes or chestnuts on a horse's leg. Under microscopic examination, these horny calluses are as individual as fingerprints. **1984** W. Murray *Dead Crab* 144: "Night eyes," Lewis said, leaning over and pointing to two little knobs high up inside the young colt's front legs. "Them little buttons is like fingerprints, no two alike." *Ibid.* 178: The one thing they couldn't fix would be the night eyes, but they're not using those for routine identification yet and probably never will. **1991** in *DARE*.

night fighter *n.* **1.** Esp. *Mil.* a black or dark-skinned person.—often used derisively. *Joc.* Hence **night-fighting,** *adj.* [Early quots. ref. to WWII.]

    1945 *AS* (Oct.) 227: *Night fighters.* Maori girls (Night fighter planes are painted black.). **1946** *Amer. N & Q* (Feb.) 176: "Night fighter" in Washington, D.C. (and possibly elsewhere) is a synonym for *Negro.* [**1946** J.H. Burns *Gallery* 289: There were Negroes who told their shack-jobs that they weren't really black, just stained that way for camouflage and night-fighting.] **1948** White *Man Called White* 279: Stones, empty beer bottles, and other missiles were thrown from the trucks into the Negro camp accompanied by such epithets as "niggers," "night-fighters," and "black sons-of-bitches." **1977** Torres *Q & A* 30: Fuck you, night fighter. **1980** W.C. Anderson *Bat-21* 216: "You're *black!*"…"You got something against night fighters?" **1982** in S. King *Bachman* 902: You…night-fighting sonofabitch. **1985** Boyne & Thompson *Wild Blue* 143: You don't have to make those awful jokes about "nightfighters."

    2. a homely young woman.—used derisively. *Joc.*

    1974 Univ. Tenn student: A night-fighter is a girl who looks OK in the dark but in the daylight she's a real hog.

night hack *n. Und.* a watchman or policeman on duty at night.

    1929 in Partridge *Dict. Und.* 469: "We've got to tab the 'night hack' (watchman)," he said; "get a line on his movements." *Ibid.:* There's only one nighthack (cop) in the town, and he goes home at one in the morning and doesn't come out again until five. **1930** *Liberty* (July 5) 24: When we flash on the lights we see a night hack asleep on a cot.

nighthawk *n.* **1.a.** a person who is active at night, esp. for a nefarious purpose.

    1818 in *OEDS*: There are night-hawks abroad, so that I cannot give you…the meeting…whilk was my purpose. **1856 Olmstead *Slave States* 399: "I left Wilmington night before last, about ten o'clock. I have been ever since on the road." "Reckon yer a night-bird." "What?" "Reckon you are a night-bird—what we calls a night-hawk, keeps a goin' at night, you know." **1864** in S.C. Wilson *Column South* 151: They go by the name of the "Night Hawks" because they were out…night and day, harassing the enemy. **1886** Harbaugh *Coldgrip in*

N.Y. 2: Can't I hold this night-hawk [*sc.*, a burglar] at bay till they come? **1916** Cary *Venery* II 8: *Night Hawk*—A street walker. **1925** (cited in Partridge *Dict. Und.* 469).

b. *Specif.*, (*Labor*). a worker on a night shift, as a cab driver, reporter, watchman, herder, etc.

1868 S. Clemens, in *Twain's Letters* II 144: Charlie Langdon, Jack Van Nostrand, & Dan & I, (all Quaker City night-hawks,) had a blow-out. **1884** Costello *Police Protectors* 481: McGowan…sprang into the carriage, telling the driver, a "nighthawk," to go on. **1891** Maitland *Slang Dict.* 186: *Night hawk*, a term sometimes applied to a night police reporter. **1899** in Davidson *Old West* 75: Cotton-Eye, the night hawk,/Was then a top cow hand. **1910** in Botkin *Treas. Amer. Folk.* 364: He told me about "day wranglers" and "night hawks." **1916** *Editor* (May 20) 533: "Nighthawk," the night herder of the cavey. **1926** W. James *Smoky* 148: The "nighthawk" (rider who herds the remuda at night) drives the wood wagon. **1928** Dobie *Vaquero* 91 [ref. to *ca*1880]: With some outfits a *remudero*, or wrangler—"nighthawk," he was often called—herded the horses; other outfits had no night-herder for the horses but simply hobbled them. **1931** Steffens *Autobiog.* 271 [ref. to 1890's]: When Schmittberger had "the night-hawks on his string," his captain switched him to…the panel-houses. **1935** *AS* (Feb.) 76: *Night hawk*. Night watchman. **1952** Lait & Mortimer *USA* 62: But the wise nighthawk pulled up before a police station and ran in. **1958** Bard & Spring *Horse Wrangler* 31: That spring of 1891…I hired out as night-hawk or night herder to a large survey party. **1977** Monaghan *Schoolboy, Cowboy* 42: A good nighthawk must know each group and keep track of it in the dark. **1981** Ryerson *Rattlers* 52: They were short-handed.…Thorne would have to act as night-hawk.

2. a taxicab or other vehicle that operates at night.—also used attrib.

[**1884** (quot. at (**1.b.**), above)]. **1891** R.H. Davis *Gallegher* 3: He knew several drivers of "night hawks"—those cabs that prowl the streets at night looking for belated passengers. **1897** Norris *Vandover* 461: The drivers of the nighthawks recognized his figure by the street lamps, paling in the light of many an early dawn. *Ibid.* 530: Occasionally a belated coupé, a nighthawk, rattled over the cobbles. **1931** Wilstach *Under Cover Man* 131: He…[stopped] another night hawk to be driven home. **1963** D. Tracy *Brass Ring* 256: They flagged down a nighthawk truck and hitched a ride to Danbury.

3. *Naut.* (see quot.).

1956 H. Beck *Folklore of Maine* 196: A vessel hoisted the night hawk (a long black pennant, sometimes called a homeward bound pennant to signify to all ships she was going home).

4. Esp. *West.* a late-night work shift.

1966 T.V. Olsen *Hard Men* 112: "Where's Soderstrom, Mac?" "Out on nighthawk."

nighthawk *v.* to work or carouse at night.

1887 Walling *N.Y. Chief of Police* 409: Mr. Gutermuth…had a *penchant* for "nighthawking." He was not a depraved or vicious man, but he loved good fellowship. **1930** Sage *Last Rustler* 142: I'll do the nighthawkin', if there's enough money in it. **1949** W.R. Burnett *Asphalt Jungle* 190: I'm getting ready to quit my job if they don't give me another beat. Nighthawking's bad enough any place. **1981** Ryerson *Rattlers* 53: After another round of night-hawking, Thorne had just got into bed.

nightingale *n.* **1.** a singer.

[*1796 Grose *Dict. Vulgar Tongue* (ed. 3): *Nightingale*. A soldier who, as the term is, sings out at the halberts.] **1891** Townsend *Negro Minstrels* 37: Mose am a reg'lar *nightingale*. **1900** Ade *More Fables* 174: She had herself billed as a Nightingale. **1911** Ovington *Half a Man* 126: A boy "nightingale" will earn the needed money for rent while learning, all too quickly, the ways of viciousness.

2. [ref. to Florence *Nightingale* (1820–1910), English nurse during Crimean War] *Army.* a woman who is a battlefield nurse.

1862 Lauderdale *Wounded River* 73: Our "*Nightingales*," as Dr. Hoff playfully calls our female nurses. *Ibid.* 81: Where we landed one of our "Nightingales."

Nightmare Alley *n.* [sugg. by *Nightmare Alley*, title of 1947 film] *Mil.* (see quots.). Now *hist.* [Quots. ref. to Korean War.]

1951 *Sat. Eve. Post* (Jan. 27) 31: The bloody trail out of what the leathernecks dubbed "Nightmare Alley." **1951** *Reader's Digest* (May)

43 [ref. to Dec. 1950]: Nightmare Alley.…the canyon that led down from the Changjin plateau.

night owl *n.* a person who is active at night. Now *colloq.* or *S.E.*

1847 in *OEDS:* You no-souled, shad-bellied, squash-headed, old night-owl you! **1891** Maitland *Slang Dict.* 186: *Night owl*, a term applied indifferently to night-workers of the predatory character and to the morning newspaper men who are compelled to labor at night. **1906** in A. Adams *Chisholm Trail* 237: He was a night owl. **1942** *ATS* 785: Forest ranger…*Night owls*, the night fire-suppression crew. **1948** in F. Brown *Homicide San.* 19: He's a night-owl. Goes to bed at dawn and sleeps till after noon. **1949** *N.Y. Times* (Nov. 27) I 106: A true, natural-born "night-owl," he is unhappy if there is not a gay crowd dancing and drinking until the small hours every night. **1963** Gant *Queen St.* 14: A couple of night owls, eh? **1972–75** W. Allen *Feathers* 52: Apparently there's a killer on the loose—it can't wait for the morning. He's a night owl.

night-owl *adj.* operating or occurring at night; nighttime. Now *colloq.*

1955 Morison *Naval Ops. in WWII* 282: He dove, surfaced once before midnight, and was promptly pounced on by two "night owl" Avengers. **1977** L. Jordan *Hype* 83: The Night Owl edition of the *Daily News.* **1980** in McCauley *Dark Forces* 139: Something about the people who work night-owl shifts anywhere. **1982** *N.Y. Post* (Aug. 27) 57: Night owl [bus] departures 7 days a week. **1983** Goldman & Fuller *Charlie Co.* 302: At the local Post Office, working a night-owl watch from four to eight in the mornings.

night rider *n.* **1.** *Av.* a night-flying aircraft.

1918 Palmer *Americans in France* 284: The [German] aeroplanes, whose hum the men of the Thirtieth [Div.] heard overhead in the darkness, they named "night riders." **1979** L. Heinemann, in *TriQuarterly* (Spring) 184: Washing Machine Charlie, the legendary nightrider of Guadalcanal.

2. a man who keeps late hours in carousing or fornicating.

[**1946–51** J. Jones *From Here to Eternity:* We're Captain Billy's troopers,/We are riders of the night,/We're dirty sons of bitches,/And we'd rather fuck than fight.] **1975** Durocher & Linn *Nice Guys* 165: We had our share of oddballs, night riders and drinkers.

nightside *n. Labor.* a night shift; workers on a night shift.

1954 Collans & Sterling *House Detect.* 108: B was careful to check in after four o'clock, when the night-side goes on duty. **1964–66** R. Stone *Hall of Mirrors* 176: You folks on the nightside…in the all-night laundries. **1978** Hamill *Dirty Laundry* 40: It was like being back on the nightside…interviewing the father of the slain gang leader.

night stick *n.* Esp. *Police.* the penis.—usu. considered vulgar. *Joc.*

1916 Cary *Venery* II 9: *Night Stick*—The penis. From the practice of American police in carrying a large club on the night watch. *ca*1930 G. Legman, in *F & H* (rev. ed.) (1966 ed.) ix: One plied his Nightstick up a girl's Dark Alley. **1960–69** Runkel *Law* 240: Everyone of 'em's got a bigger nightstick than me. **1979** *Penthouse* (Dec.) 48: She sucked my "nightstick." **1990** C.P. McDonald *Blue Truth* 90: They'd like to see you twirl that nightstick of yours, dig it?

niglet *n.* [NIG + -*let* dimin. suff.] a black child.—used contemptuously.—usu. considered offensive.

1990 C.P. McDonald *Blue Truth* 67: Here's this little niglet standing there in his bare feet.

nig-nog *n.* [fr. BrE slang *nigmenog* 'an oaf', infl. by NIGGER] a black person; (*broadly*) a dark-skinned person of any race or origin.—also used attrib.—used contemptuously.—usu. considered offensive.

*****1959** in *OEDS:* First lot, and look lively. Lot of nig-nogs off the trees. *****1965** *N.Y. Times* (Nov. 14) VI 64: You're an American. I could tell right off. The American colored are different from the nig-nogs we get here from the West Indies. *****1967** in Partridge *Concise Sl. Dict.:* A younger generation has begun referring to coloured immigrants as "nig-nogs." **1971** W. Just, in *Atlantic* (Dec.) 76: The 1950s was a bleak period, for the wars were small and of little account. Nig-nog wars, the columnist called them; gratuitous insurgencies in the Middle East and the Orient. **1975** *Nat. Lampoon* (Sept.) 39: Once you've established yourself as a legal nig-nog, the scholastic advantages are overwhelming. *****1984** *Time* (Feb. 6) 40: Suddenly the Turks, Pakistanis and Algerians are no longer individuals: they are *Kanaken*, nig-nogs and *bougnouls*.

-nik *suffix.* [< Yiddish; later cites infl. by *Sputnik*] (used to create nonce coinages designating persons who espouse a cause, represent a particular attitude, or are ardent enthusiasts of the thing or indicated by the initial element).—usu. used derisively. See also ALLRIGHTNIK, BEATNIK, NEATNIK, NO-GOODNIK, PEACENIK.

 1929 M. Gold *Jews Without Money* 212 [ref. to ca1905]: He is also a *real estatnik!* He says he will sell me a good lot! **1965** *N.Y. Times* (Dec. 5) V 90: They were "OOB-niks," Off Off Broadway regulars, attending plays on the pass-the-hat circuit at least once a week. **1966** G. Samuels *People vs. Baby* 222: No contributions…without consent of the sickniks. **1967** *Time* (Jan. 6) 89: The Jeep appeals to the outdoors-minded (notable Jeepniks: Lyndon Johnson, Hubert Humphrey and Sargent Shriver). **1974** *Business Week* (June 22) 104: The computerniks come around to make you fill out IBM cards. **1981** *L.A. Times Bk. Rev.* (June 7) 8: *SoHo: The Artist in the City*…would be of little more than passing interest to Los Angeles artniks. **1983** J. Falwell, in *L.A. Times* (Apr. 20) I-A 1: I believe the nuclear freezeniks are attempting to put the United States in a position where there will be no peace and the Gospel cannot be preached. **1983** *Harper's* (July) 16: Video-game lotteries.…Affluent arcadeniks constitute a vast unexploited resource. *a***1991** J. Phillips *You'll Never Eat Lunch* 19: A wealthy Jewish middle classnik.

nimby *n.* [alt. *Nemb*utal + *-y*] *Narc.* a capsule containing Nembutal or a similar drug. Also **nimbie.**

 1962 Maurer & Vogel *Narc. & Narc. Add.* (ed. 2) 315: *Nimby* or *Nimbie.* A Nembutal capsule. **1967** J.B. Williams *Narc. & Hallucin.* 114: *Nimby*— "Nembutal" (brand of pentobarbital, Abbott Laboratories) capsules [*sic*]. **1969** Lingeman *Drugs A to Z* 183: *Nimby* Nembutal, a barbiturate.

NIMBY or **Nimby** *adj.* [acronym for "*not in my b*ackyard," cliché response to such projects] vehemently opposed to any project or institution perceived as injurious to a residential or other local neighborhood. Also as n.

 1980 (cited in *BDNE3*). **1982** in *Atlantic* (Aug. 1987) 88: A few years ago ANS [American Nuclear Society] stalwart Walton Rodger coined the acronym NIMBY…to describe the…syndrome that urges the immediate rejection of almost any large construction project in any local area. **1987** *Atlantic* (Aug.) 88: The *Nimbys*…those who want no construction that might disturb the character and real estate value of their neighborhoods. **1988** *Ch. 2 News at Five* (WCBS-TV) (June 29): Neighbors got caught up in the NIMBY syndrome—"Not in my back yard." **1988** *Time* (Dec. 26) 29: Playing Atomic NIMBY…Pileup of radioactive waste may close a bomb plant. **1989** "Capt. X" & Dodson *Unfriendly Skies* 65: We're in the well-known "Nimby" (Not in my backyard) Syndrome. **1991** *Nation* (June 17) 805: Services and other institutions that no organized community wants in its backyard—prisons, sanitation works and other "NIMBYs"—have followed. **1992** *N.Y. Observer* (Dec. 7) 12: Some Nimbys learned that a methadone clinic was planned for West 110th Street. **1994** *N.Y. Times* (July 17) ("Arts & Leisure") 1: All politics is local, and the local perspective is a recipe for disaster: ignorance, Nimby selfishness, isolationism, tribal and racial strife.

nimrod *n.* [app. a fanciful application of the literary sense 'a hunter', fr. a tyrant and hunter in Genesis 10:8–10; currency of the term owes much to its appearance in a 1940's Warner Bros. cartoon in which Bugs Bunny mockingly refers to the hunter Elmer Fudd as "poor little Nimrod"] a stupid or obnoxious person; JERK.—also used attrib.

 1932 Hecht & Fowler *Great Magoo* 183: He's in love with her. That makes about the tenth. The same old Nimrod. Won't let her alone for a second. **1934** de Leon & Jones *You're Telling Me* (film): Little too much whip in that club, nimrod. **1963** *Newsweek* (Apr. 1) 6: The advertisers' use of the masculine, ear-ringed scrubwoman Mr. Clean.…If [Aunt Jemima's] image slights the Negroes, what does the aforementioned nimrod do for whites? **1988** D. Waters *Heathers* (film): What…if every nimrod followed her cue? **1989** WLUP radio (Chicago) (Dec. 17): Maybe the person stringing the lights is a *nimrod!* **1990** *Guys Next Door* (NBC-TV): Gimme your lunch, nimrod! **1995** *TV Guide* (Apr. 1) 4: Asked me to come in and read a part, and it turned out to be this nimrod, dim-witted duck. **1996** *Harper's* (July) 31: Nat is serving breakfast to Steve and Steve's two nimrod half-brothers. **1996** *Territory Ahead* (catalog) 11: Until some nimrod swiped it from your locker during gym.

nimshi *n.* [cf. dial. BrE *nimshie* 'a flighty girl', of unkn. orig.] *N.E.* a fool; simpleton.

 1848 Bartlett *Amer.* 233: *Nimshi.* A foolish fellow…Connecticut. **1853** in *DN* IV 203: Why any nimshi can jump across that little creek. **1944** in *DA:* There were "Nimshies"…village nitwits. **1952** in *DARE.*

nimwad *n.* [prob. alter. NIMROD] a fool.

 1983 *Nat. Lampoon* (Mar.) 69: I've been treated like such a nimwad all of my married life that now I can barely read. **1984** Univ. Tenn. student: Don't be a nimwad!

Nina *n.* [sugg. by *niner*] *Craps.* the point nine.—used in var. usu. joc. compounds.

 [**1932** *AS* VII (June) 331: 9—Carolina Nine.] **1939** Hart *135th Aero Squadron* 30 [ref. to 1918]: Neena, the blind-eyed girl from Neufchateau—please nine, dice. **1950** (cited in T.L. Clark *Dict. Gamb. & Gaming*). **1986** F. Walton *Once Were Eagles* 72: Come Nina Ross, the Winnin' Hoss. **1986** Ciardi *Good Words* 103: Nina with the golden boobies, come home to love you big-titted slut! **1987** T.L. Clark *Dict. Gamb. & Gaming: Nina from Argentina, nina from Carolina, nina ross (the stable hoss)*, and *nina, nina, ocean liner.*

nincom *n.* NINCOMPOOP.

 1807 W. Irving *Salmagundi* 61: D—d the Professors for nincoms. *****1887** in Partridge *DSUE* 562: Nincum.

nincompoop *n.* [app. of fanciful orig.] a fool; simpleton. Now *S.E.* Also (*obs.*) **nickumpoop.**

 *****1673** T. Shadwell, in *F & H* V 45: Yes, you nicompoop [*sic*]! you are a pretty fellow to please a woman indeed! *****1676** Wycherley *Plain-Dealer* II i: Thou senseless, impertinent, quibbling, drivelling, feeble, paralytic, impotent, fumbling, frigid nincompoop. *****1698–99** "B.E." *Dict. Cant. Crew:* Nickum-poop, a Fool, also a silly soft, Uxorious Fellow. *****1706** in *OED:* Nincumpoop or Nickumpoop, a meer Blockhead, Sot or Dolt. **1749** in Breslaw *Tues. Club* 141: We look upon the one to be a *Natural* the other to be a mere Nincompoop in vocal music. *****1796** Grose *Dict. Vulgar Tongue* (ed. 3): *Nickumpoop* , or *nincumpoop.* A foolish fellow; also one who never saw his wife's ****. **1831** Seabury *Moneygripe* 66: Being called a nincompoop for my ignorance. *****1890** in *OED:* I know how to behave without making too great a nincumpoop of myself. **1982** in Rawson *Wicked Words* 270: We are fools, dolts, and nincompoops. **1991** McCarthy & Mallowe *Vice Cop* 308: It could have belonged to some nincompoop. **1991** D. Jenkins *Gotta Play Hurt* 11: Glad-handing nincompoops.

nine *n.* ¶ In phrases:

¶ **to the nines** [orig. unkn.] to the limit; to perfection. Now *colloq.* and usu. constr. with *dressed.*

 [*****1787** R. Burns, in *OED2:* 'Twad please me to the nine.] *a***1793** R. Burns, in *OED2:* Thou paints auld Nature to the nines. *****1820** in *F & H* V 46: He was always togged out to the nines. **1836** in Haliburton *Sam Slick* 48: A-praisin' a man's farm to the nines. **1838** [Haliburton] *Clockmaker* (Ser. 2) 22: If I didn't touch it off to the nines it's a pity. **1857** Wilcox *Faca* 59: You are either a scamp to the nines, or a tiptop good sailor. *****1859** Hotten *Slang Dict.:* "Dressed up to the *nines*," in a showy or *recherché* manner. *****1891** in *F & H* V 46: You do things up to the nines here. *****1892** Jacobs *Celtic Fairy Tales* 119: Oh…we believe you to the nines. **1950** *New Yorker* (Sept. 15) 10 (ad): The conquering hero comes—dressed to the nines in a Viyella robe. **1979** *Texas Monthly* (Nov.) 123: Pevsner, who manages an Yves St. Laurent boutique in Dallas, dresses to the nines for her job. **1990** L.I., N.Y., editor, age ca35: She was dressed to the *nines.* **1995** *Wash. Post* (Nov. 10) F1: The play is ferocious yet oddly, almost delicately, pure. And the production…is being acted to the nines.

¶ **the whole nine yards** [the orig. ref. of the phr. remains obscure; var. hypotheses relating to e.g. football yardage, cloth length in suit manufacture, or capacity of cement mixers have been shown to be unfounded. The fact that nine yards is a customary length for a burial shroud, as shown in the 1958 quot. ref. to Appalachian folklore, is provocative, but this suggestion cannot be shown to be related] everything possible; the WORKS. Also (*later*) **the whole nine.**

 [**1958** M.W. Wellman *Nine Yards of Other Cloth*, in *Mag. Fantasy & S.F.* (Nov.): I'll weave nine yards of other cloth/For John to have and keep,/He'll need it where he's going to lie,/To warm him in his sleep.] **1966** E. Shepard *Doom Pussy* 173: The first thing in the early pearly morning and the last thing at night. Beds all over the gahdam house. The whole nine yards. **1970** in *OED2: Whole nine yards*, the entire thing. **1972** J. Morris *Strawberry Soldier* 18: The Combat Infantryman's Badge, a senior parachutist's badge, Vietnamese parachutist's wings, the whole nine yards of his Freddy Fascist suit. **1978** Wheeler & Kerby *Steel Cowboy* (film): Hijacked Russian tank parts, mari-ju-ana, the whole nine yards. **1981** in *OED2*: A Japanese disaster film, *Virus*, goes the whole nine yards, showing the city as a deserted freeway underpass. **1983** *Wash. Post* (Oct. 12) E22: A 1983 Lincoln....It had "smoked windows, antennas, the whole nine yards." **1985** *New Yorker* (Apr. 1): Everybody in the United States...can see what's going on. Floods. Fires. The whole nine yards. **1988** *Christian Science Monitor* (Mar. 17) ("Home") 31: They come in saying, "I just want a dress to be married in," and then they leave with the whole nine yards—the veil, the beads, the lace. **1991** Nelson & Gonzales *Bring Noise* xiii: I was living a relatively exciting life—travelling, the whole nine. **1991** in N. George *Buppies, B-Boys* 65: These kids are baaaaaaad little dudes with beepers and the whole nine. **1994** in C. Long *Love Awaits* 11: Dinners, movies, the whole nine.

nine-dollar bill *n.* a homosexual; in phr. **three times as queer as a three-dollar bill** notably homosexual. Also (*BrE*) **nine-bob note.** Cf. THREE-DOLLAR BILL.
　1965 Trimble *Sex Words* 138: *Nine-dollar Bill*...An Absolute Invert or Homosexual. From the inference that one is "Three times as queer as a three-dollar bill." **1968** Maule *Rub-A-Dub* 8: No one would take Curly for a homosexual, although he was actually as queer as a nine-dollar bill. *1990 T. Thorne *Dict. Contemp. Slang*: *Nine-bob note*...a homosexual....usually expressed in the phrase "*bent as a nine-bob note*."

nine miles *n.pl. Craps.* the point nine.
　1984 Sample *Racehoss* 30: Going for nine...."We ain' but *nine miles* frum home!"

Niners *n.pl. Sports Journ.* the San Francisco 49ers football team.
　1983 *N.Y. Post* (Sept. 2) 71: The Redskins...were last year's version of the Niners. **1984** *N.Y. Post* (Aug. 31) 81: Niners barely edged Detroit in '83 playoff at home.

nineteenth hole *n. Golf.* a bar located in a golfers' clubhouse. *Joc.*
　1901 in *OEDS*: The nineteenth hole, being tales of the fair green. **1915** in Davies *Hist. Dict. Golf.*: In the kingdom of the Nineteenth Hole he was "Philosopher Extraordinary and Authority Unquestioned." **1920** Ade *Hand-Made Fables* 11: Golf will make you forget everything except the 19th Hole. **1944** Botkin *Treas. Amer. Folklore* 212: Cf. the "nineteenth hole" of a golf course. **1960** L. Ellis *Kellogg* 8: There is...evidence...that he enjoyed the amenities connected with the so-called "nineteenth hole," despite the limiting factor of the Eighteenth Amendment. **1974** in Davies *Hist. Dict. Golf.*: Around every nineteenth hole, legends are recalled of astonishing shots.

ninety days *n.* [elab. of *nine*, in ref. to *ninety days*, standard sentence for var. petty crimes] *Craps.* the point nine.
　1909 (quot. at LITTLE JOE). **1911** *Howitzer* (U.S. Mil. Acad.) 177: *Ninety days*—seven come eleven! **1935** Pollock *Und. Speaks: Ninety days*, a 9 in craps. **1978** in T.L. Clark *Dict. Gamb. & Gaming*: You can hear any oldtimer use *ninety days* for the point nine....That was a standard [jail] sentence for getting caught running a game.

ninety-day wonder *n.* [cf. S.E. *nine days' wonder* 'something causing short-lived sensation', fr. 16th C.] **1.a.** *Mil.* an inexperienced junior officer who has completed a ninety-day officers' training course.—used derisively. [Early quots. to WWI.]
　1917 (quot. at WAR-BABY). **1919** Cortelyou *Arizona* 106: A "ninty day wonder" [*sic*] fresh from O.T.S. **1919** *Field Btry. Book* 15: The inexperience of officers was a circumstance of tremendous significance. The fact that we used to call them "ninety-day wonders" indicates our attitude toward them at the time. **1926** Nason *Chevrons* 136: You ninety-day wonder!...haven't you got brains enough to know this brook runs east and west? **1927** J. Stevens *Mattock* 50: Why can't you ninety-day wonders get next to yourselves? **1928** Havlin *Co. A* 7: As usual, they were dubbed "ninety-day wonders." **1959** Cochrell *Barren Beaches* 55: Those ninety-day wonders get better all the time. **1959** *Up Periscope!* (film) [ref. to 1942]: Now I got a ninety-day wonder on my back. **1961** Boyd *Lighter Than Air* 56: Reservists and 90-day wonders know vaguely that the Navy has an Academy in Annapolis. **1963** Boyle *Yanks Don't Cry* 245: It was our first look at a ninety-day wonder, our

Liberator. **1963** J. Ross *Dead Are Mine* 85: After all, we don't expect too much initiative from shavetails. And a ninety-day wonder at that. **1968** Smart *Long Watch* 52: In odd moments, I'd find myself on the fantail with two or three of these men, each of us with a mug of coffee in his hand, watching the clouds, the waves, and the wake, talking shop, bitching about the poor little ninety-day wonders...reminiscing about our homes and old jobs, and guessing about the future. **1968** Maule *Rub-A-Dub* 35: We get too many ninety-day wonders these days. **1970** Woods *Killing Zone* 5: A pale punk kid to run my company, another ninety day wonder. **1976** S. Lawrence *Northern Saga* 115: He wasn't taking anything from a navy ninety-day wonder. **1983–88** J.T. McLeod *Crew Chief* 110: The guys from West Point are usually...easier to get along with than...the "ninety day wonders." *a*1990 Helms *Proud Bastards* 88: Mr. Gung-Ho Ninety-Day Wonder.
　b. an inexperienced employee.—used derisively.
　1962 *Time* (Feb. 9) 50: Some of these 90-day wonders in Washington think mergers are the only way to save the airlines. **1975** C.W. Smith *Country Music* 25: Bobby Joe had grown up hearing the phrase "ninety-day wonder" applied not only to second lieutenants but likewise to anyone in the oil industry with a degree. **1984** [Source uncertain, in *RHD* files] (May 16) I 1: Business gets "90-day wonders" from "technical schools" to run expensive communications nets.

2. an employee, as a national park ranger, hired for a single season only.—used derisively.
　1954–60 *DAS: Ninety-day wonder*...A resort or park employee hired for the three-month summer vacation season only. **1988** Pres. G.R. Ford, in Barrow & Munder *Joe Louis* 68: I was a ranger in Yellowstone Park that summer [1936]—I was what they called a 90-day wonder.

ninety-nine *n.* [cf. SIXTY-NINE] anal intercourse.—usu. considered vulgar.
　1972 R. Wilson *Playboy's Forbidden Words* 181: The "99" (anal intercourse).

ninety-six *n.* [sugg. by SIXTY-NINE] *Homosex.* homosexual anal intercourse.—usu. considered vulgar.
　1925 (quot. at SUZIE STOOP-AND-TAKE-IT). **1949** *Gay Girl's Guide* 13: *Ninety-six:* California term for reciprocal anal intercourse. **1947–51** (quot. at OLD-FASHIONED).

Ninja car *n. Mil.* a Fast Attack Vehicle.
　1991 *Weapons at War* (A&E-TV): Fast Attack Vehicles (FAVs)...earned...the nickname "Ninja cars" [during the Gulf War].

ninny[1] *n.* [cf. NINNYHAMMER] a fool. Now *S.E.*
　*1593 in *OED*: I should be quickly rid of a mere mishap, in being prevented of matching with a nice ninnie. *1698–99 "B.E." *Dict. Canting Crew: Ninny*...a Fool. *1796 (quot. at NINNYHAMMER). *1598 in *F & H* V 46: An idle loytring gull, a ninnie. **1824** in Nevins & Weitenkampf *Cartoons* 33: It serves you right, you stupid *ninny*, an' so it does.

ninny[2] *n.* usu. *pl.* Esp. *So.* a woman's breast. Also **ninny jug.**
　1909 *DN* III 352: *Ninny*....one of the breasts. **1942** *ATS* 145: Breasts....*ninnies.* **1965–70** in *DARE.* **1970** Landy *Underground Dict.* 139: *Ninny jug*...Female's breast. **1971** Sorrentino *Up from Never* 46: I teetered on the brink of squeezing her "ninnies."

ninny[3] *n.* [fr. PICKANINNY] a black person.—used contemptuously.—usu. considered offensive.
　1993 G. Lee *Honor & Duty* 191: You're not a kike or a ninny. *Ibid.* 292: Ninnies and Jews.

ninnyhammer *n.* [prob. of fanciful orig.] a dolt; fool. Hence **ninnyhammered,** *adj.*
　*1592 T. Nashe, in *OED*: Whoreson Ninihammer, that wilt assault a man and haue no stronger weapons. *1622 in *OED*: I might haue been a scholler, learn'd my Grammar, But I haue lost all like a Ninniehammer. *1698–99 "B.E." *Dict. Canting Crew: Ninny-hammer*, a silly senseless fellow. *1712 (quot. at NUMBSKULL). *1796 Grose *Dict. Vulgar Tongue* (ed. 3): *Ninny,* or *ninnyhammer*. A simpleton. **1839** *Spirit of Times* (Dec. 28) 509: A starched up nincompoop? a witless ninnyhammer? a soft pawed squirt? **1840** *Spirit of Times* (June 27) 200: *You* ninnyhammer! That buffalo will get up when she's done saying her prayers. *a*1870 *Coon-Hunt* 10: You know cussed well, you weazel-faced ninnyhammer! **1923** *N.Y. Times* (Sept. 9) VIII 2: *Ninnyhammer*: Almost any critic. **1968** Myrer *Eagle* 70: The Germans, you ninnyhammered idiot! **1985** *Los Angeles* (Apr.) 34: A sort of goony ninnyhammer with a weird smile.

Nip *n.* [fr. *Nip*pon] **1.** Orig. *Mil.* a Japanese.—used contemptuously.—usu. considered offensive. Also as adj.

 1942 *Time* (Jan. 5) 20: Chief Tomas picked up three Nip pilots forced down in his territory. **1942** Tregaskis *Guadalcanal Diary* [entry for Aug. 12]: The Japanese casualties were about 400. Not a single Nip gave up. **1942** in Tapert *Lines of Battle* 41: This battalion…rode roughshod over the Nips. **1944** in R. Kennard *Letters* 15: The Nips had taken off. *1945 S.J. Baker *Austral. Lang.* 153: Nip, a Japanese soldier. **1962** Blake *Heartbreak* 32: A…smiling Nip girl. **1968** W. Crawford *Gresham's War* 77: He said something to the Nip bartender in Japanese. **1970** Grissim *Country Music* 176: Now you take the Beatles.…It's like this nude picture of this kid, the Nip, this Jap, whatever she was, with him on the front of a record cover with him. **1977** *Rolling Stone* (Aug. 25) 11: Tell them Nips I've never read anything about me from Japan that wasn't disgusting bullshit. **1967–80** Folb *Runnin' Lines* 248: Nip…Japanese person. **1980** Manchester *Darkness* 16: Every moment lengthened my odds against the Nip sharpshooter. **1981** C. Nelson *Picked Bullets Up* 167: What pleasure the Nips find in playing the game lies without my understanding. *a*1982 in H. Berry *Semper Fi* 310: The Nip army. **1986** C. Freeman *Seasons of Heart* 99: You're going to get a chance to kill some Nips. **1987** *Nat. Lampoon* (Dec.) 33: "Smaller is better," say the Nips. **1992** G. Wolff *Day at the Beach* 23: He…escaped the evil, dread Nips by wooden raft.

2. an East Asian person (of any nationality).—used contemptuously.—usu. considered offensive.

 1993 *Newsweek* (July 26) 57: I was the only ticket hustler to get jailed at the Seoul Olympics.…[The] Nips made me an example.

nip¹ *n.* [prob. abbr. of *nip*perkin] a little drink (usu. of spirits); SWIG; in phr. (*obs.*) *Naut.* **nip at the cable.** Now *colloq.*

 1736 (cited in *AS* (Oct. 1940) 231). **1752** in Breslaw *Tues. Club* 381: And thought a Cool pipe and a Nip' still was good. *1796 Grose *Dict. Vulgar Tongue* (ed. 3): Nyp, or nip. A half pint, a nip of ale. *1808 Jamieson *Scot. Dict.*: Nip. A small quantity of spirits; as a *nip* of whiskey,—generally half a glass. *1815 in Wetherell *Adventures* 342: I…took a bottle and tumblers.…We took a nip. *1821 *Real Life in London* I 275: So finish your nip, and let us be off. **1847** "N. Buntline" *Curse* 17: A nip might cheer you up a bit. **1849** Melville *White Jacket* 173: He craves a more vigorous *nip at the cable*, a more sturdy *swig at the halyards.* **1859** L. Barney *Auraria* 28: A groggery, dealing out whisky at from 10 to 20 cents a "nip." **1861** in F. Moore *Rebel. Rec.* I P38: Buchanan…took another "nip" of "rye." **1866** in Hilleary *Webfoot* 170: Frequent halts were made to take a "nip" from bottles that had been provided for the occasion. *a*1880 *Year of Wreck* 31: Some called it "a morning nip," others "an eye-opener." **1881** Crofutt *Gde. to Colo.* 101: It is tough on the "old soakers" who now have to "pack in" their "nips" on the sly. **1884** Blanding *Sailor Boy* 189: Go with me first and get a nip. *1888 in R. Kipling *Under the Deodars* 106: Strengthened by a four-finger "nip," which he swallowed without a wink. **1905** E. Wharton *Mirth* 227: I'll give you a nip of brandy. **1917** in Hammerstein *Kern Song Bk.* 19: A little nip of brandy. *a*1924 A. Hunter *Yr. on Monitor* 41: An early "nip" of hot coffee. **1963** Gann *Of Good & Evil* 52: "Her uncle likes his little nip." "You mean he's a drunkard?" **1973** Ellington *Music Is My Mistress* 47: The other would be backstage taking a nip. *a*1973–87 F.M. Davis *Livin' the Blues* 9: I was soon insisting on a nightly nip. **1987** in T. McMillan *Breaking Ice* 23: "And a nip, man," he added in slightly slurred afterthought.

¶ In phrase:

¶ **freshen the nip** [cf. standard nautical sense in *OED2* s.v. *freshen*, def. 3] *Naut.* to refresh oneself, esp. by taking a drink of spirits. Now *hist.*

 1827 J.F. Cooper *Red Rover* ch. iii: Profiting by the occasion "to freshen his nip," as he quaintly called swallowing a pint of rum and water, he continued his narrative. **1834** *Mil. & Nav. Mag. of U.S.* 116: So, go below and freshen the nip. **1839–40** Cobb *Green Hand* II 38: You freshened your nip with a new chaw…just before the last scene. **1840** *Spirit of Times* (May 2) 103: "Freshening your nip" each time you freshened your bait. **1841** [Mercier] *Man-of-War* 6: A few poor sailors…perhaps…a little elated from…their last *extra* glass of whiskey, were somewhat anxious to *freshen the nip*. **1841** *So. Lit. Messenger* VII 764: After going into the saloon (grog-shop) to "freshen the nip"—as they professionally called taking a glass of brandy and water. **1854** Sleeper *Salt Water Bubbles* 338: Captain Grampus had just been below, "freshening the nip." **1963** Hoole *Confed. Navy* 73: Crewmen enjoyed shore leave…"freshening the nip" with the local ladies of leisure.

nip² *n.* usu. *pl.* a human nipple.

 *a*1972 B. Rodgers *Queens' Vernacular* 142: Nips breast nipples. **1972** D. Jenkins *Semi-Tough* 222: Barbara Jane's lungs…have the good nips. **1980** L. Fleischer & C. Gore *Fame* 118: Little nips like raisins. **1980** Lorenz *Guys Like Us* 216: With her legs in the air and her nips sticking out. **1980** *Nat. Lampoon* (June) 60: I do custom nips, say, with extra-large auries. **1985** Univ. Tenn. student theme: "A nip tease" ([a girl] wearing a shirt without a bra.). **1987** "J. Hawkins" *Tunnel Warriors* 144: Nips as big as silver dollars. *a*1990 Westcott *Half a Klick* 97: Nice firm little boobies with nips that follow ya around the room.

nip *v.* **1.** [specialized development of earlier sense 'to snatch, catch, seize, or take smartly' (*OED*)] to pilfer; steal.

 *1566 in Partridge *Dict. Und.* 470: To nyp a boung, to cut a purse. *1698–99 "B.E." *Dict. Canting Crew*: Nip…also to *pinch* or *sharp* any thing. Nip a bung…to cut a Purse. **1821** Martin & Waldo *Lightfoot* 46: Here…it is possible we may *nip* something. **1867** "M. Twain," in A.L. Scott *Twain's Poetry* 57: They'd a way of nipping cash. **1867** in Davidson *Old West* 187: Indians…have nipped his cattle. **1876** "M. Twain" *Tom Sawyer* 203 [ref. to *ca*1845]: Whoever nipped the whiskey in No. 2, nipped the money, too, I reckon. **1887** *Lantern* (N.O.) (Apr. 16) 2: The car drivers on the Magazine line nip more fares. **1899** (quot. at READER). **1903** A.H. Lewis *Boss* 96: He's a pickpocket…an' as fly a dip as ever nipped a watch or copped a leather. **1929** Milburn *Hornbook* 152: I've kipped in Ritzy Hotels, and nipped some doozy rocks. **1971** Dahlskog *Dict.* 42: Nip, v. To quickly and slyly take something, as: to nip a candy bar from the store when no one is looking.

2. Orig. *Und.* to apprehend or place under arrest; NAB, 2.a.

 *1566 in *OED.* *1851–61 H. Mayhew, in *F & H* V 49: They'd follow you about, and keep on nipping a fellow. **1887** Flinn *Chicago Police* 386: Palmer nipped him one day stealing diamonds at Giles Bros. **1891** in Hoppenstand *Dime Novel Detective* 159: The next moment…he is nipped. **1899** A.H. Lewis *Sandburrs* 231: Every gent for himself! an' if youse is nipped, don't knock! **1904** *Life in Sing Sing* 251: Nipped, Nabbed.—Arrested. **1922** F.L. Packard *Doors of Night* 88: If we nip him…that'll be…fair. **1930** Lait *On Spot* 34: I'll go out and nip her myself—in person.

3. to shoot (someone).

 1865 *Harper's Mo.* (June) 11: If I'd a had a six-shooter…they'd a carried away the fellow that nipped Jack! **1871** in Caughey *Mob* 79: One and another exchanged the belief that this sort of thing was more sensible than "'nipping' [Mexicans] on sight."

4. *Baseball.* to put out (an opposing runner); NAB, *v.*, 3.d.

 1868 (cited in Nicholls *Baseball Dict.*). **1869** *N.Y. Herald* (July 13), cited in Nicholls *Baseball Dict.* **1891** in Leitner *Diamond in Rough* 155: Sometimes…we get nipped by old Nick at the plate. **1914** in R. Lardner *Round Up* 254: Clarke…pegs down to second to nip him.

5. to take a drink of liquor. Now *colloq.*

 *1888 in *F & H* V 49: You never saw a man look so scared as the passenger on the box-seat, a stout, jolly commercial, who'd been giving the coachman Havana cigars, and yarning and nipping with him at every house they passed. *1896 in *F & H* V 49: Women have learned the fatal habit of *nipping* , and slowly but surely become confirmed dipsomaniacs. **1975** R.P. Davis *Pilot* 49: That's a long way from nipping on the job. **1996** *Cigar Aficionado* (Summer) 418: The more he nipped, the more he talked.

6.a. Now *Sports Journ.* to defeat, usu. by a narrow margin.

 1893 Hampton *Maj. in Washington* 67: I got nipped at poker agin yesterday evenin'. **1942** *ATS* 634: Defeat…nick, nip, outbeat. **1944** Warner Bros. *Merrie Melodies* (animation [cartoon title]): Bugs Bunny Nips the Nips. **1970** *Everett* (Wash.) *Herald* (May 12) 3B: Atlanta nipped Chicago 7–6 in 10 innings.

b. to take advantage of; cheat.

 1930 *Variety* (Jan. 8) 123: Suckers wouldn't be nipped…if they weren't trying to beat some game themselves. **1942** *ATS* 312: Cheat; defraud…nip.

nipcheese *n.* **1.** *Naut.* a purser or purser's steward. Now *hist.*

 *1785 Grose *Dict. Vulgar Tongue*: Nip Cheese. A nick name for the purser of a ship; from those gentlemen being supposed sometimes to nip, or diminish, the allowance of seamen, in that and every other article. It is also applied to stingy persons in general. *1805 J. Davis *Post-Captain* 5: Mr. Nipcheese the purser. **1835** *Mil. & Nav. Mag. of U.S.* (May) 224: Mr. Nipcheese, you had better go look out for your iron chest. **1849** Melville *White Jacket* 201: Among sailors…pursers go by the name of *nipcheeses.* **1863** in S. Boyer *Nav. Surgeon* I 68: Took a stroll…with the "nipcheese" of the ship. *Ibid.:* 243: Here comes the "sawbones," "nipcheese," and in fact all the officers except the captain. **1929* Bowen *Sea Slang* 95: *Nipcheese.* The Purser's steward. **1980** Valle *Rocks & Shoals* 229 [ref. to *a*1860]: It is no wonder that pursers were often distrusted by the line officers and referred to as "nipcheeses" among the crew.

2. a miser.

  *1785 (quot. at (1), above). **1898** Green *Va. Folk-Speech* 255: *Nipcheese, n.*…a skinflint.

Nipper *n. Mil.* a NIP.—used contemptuously.—usu. considered offensive.

  1942 R. Casey *Torpedo Junction* 20: A weird surprise for the little nippers, eh wot? **1957** Campbell *Happy* 2: It had been a bank before it was taken over from the Nippers.

nipper *n.* **1.** a thief or swindler. [No continuity of usage is apparent between 17th- and 19th-C. quots.]

  *1585 in *OED*: He that could take a piece of sylver out of the purse without the noyse of any of the bells, he was adjudged a judiciall Nypper. **1592* R. Greene, in Partridge *Dict. Und.* 471: This fellow he had heard to be one of the finest Nippers about the towne. **1659* in *F & H* V 50: Your nipper, your foyst, your rogue, your cheat, your pander. **1886** P.D. Haywood *Cruise* 68: All trade in Kingston is in the hands of these people, and nippers they are. **1899** A.H. Lewis *Sandburrs* 108: He's a nipper, but a dead queer one see! He always woiks alone, an' his lay is diamonds.

2. *pl. Und. & Police.* handcuffs.

  *1821 in *OEDS*: That's one of the bulkies from Dumfries, wanting to clap the nippers on me. **1892** Norr *China Town* 51: The flatties closed in on me to put on the nippers. **1894** in A. Charters *Ragtime Songbk.* 49: Cops slipped the nippers on his hands. **1904** *Life in Sing Sing* 251: *Nippers.* Handcuffs. **1905** in "O. Henry" *Works* 1419: You can take dose nippers off. **1912** Lowrie *Prison* 10: It is always the right wrist that feels the nippers. **1918** *N.Y. Age* (Sept. 28) 1: They hit him over the head, although the nippers had been put on him. **1928** Callahan *Man's Grim Justice* 261: He pulled out a pair of "nippers" and proceeded to slip them around the wrist of my right hand. **1929** "E. Queen" *Roman Hat* 60: Put the nippers on him, officer. **1931** Wilstach *Under Cover Man* 43: It cost me ten grand to get a pair of nippers. **1938** Bellem *Blue Murder* 58: They put nippers on my wrists and…took me to the clink. **1953** Paley *Rumble* 297: Fitz whirled the nippers as easily as a zoot chain. **1955** Q. Reynolds *HQ* 35 [ref. to 1920's]: He had to buy a set of nippers (he had learned never to call them handcuffs).

3. *pl.* fingers or hands.

  *1821–26 Stewart *Man-Of-War's-Man* II 219: The first fellow that lays his nippers on me, I'll fell him like a bullock. **1842** *Ben Hardin's Crockett* (unp.): The long one aimed her nippers right for the short one's peepers.

4. a policeman.

  *1843 (cited in Partridge *Dict. Und.* 471). **1875** in L. Hearn *Occid. Gleanings* I 85: He first feigned sleep and drunken insensibility to the "nippers," and a wholesome tapping with a club. **a1890* in Barrère & Leland *Dict. Slang* II 87: "Dowse the glim! here come the *nippers.*" That a *nipper* was a policeman, I well knew.

5. a small child, usu. a boy. Now *colloq.* [The bracketed quot., a nickname, strongly suggests earlier currency.]

  [**1847* C. Dickens *Dombey & Son* ch. xxiii: The Nipper…shook her head in resolute denial.] **1859* Hotten *Slang Dict.: Nipper,* a small boy. **1851–61* H. Mayhew in *F & H* V 50: Such lads, however, are the smallest class of costermongering youths; and are sometimes called…*nippers.* **1889–90* Barrère & Leland *Dict. Slang* II 87: *Nipper* (popular), a baby, a child. **1901* in *OEDS*: By George, you're a wonderful looking girl!…You are such a little nipper. **1940** M. West & W.C. Fields *My Little Chickadee* (film): This reminds me of the old swimming hole when I was a nipper. **1950** *Sat. Eve. Post* (Nov. 11) 22: Just thought there might be a nipper who ——. **1983** *Magnum, P.I.* (CBS-TV): Have Simm give the little nipper a sawbuck on me. **1986** Kubicki *Breaker Boys* 13: He hated to be called nipper, an errand boy, the most lowly job underground. **1993** *Natural History* (Sept.) 26: Show the little nippers that science ain't always pretty. **1995** Turner Classic Movies TV network: There's Elizabeth Taylor, when she was just a nipper.

6. a drink of liquor; NIP[1].

  1848 in J.R. Lowell *Works*: Step up and take a nipper, sir. *ca*1855

[G. Thompson] *Outlaw* 33: Three cent nippers was the cause of my ruin. **1889** Bailey *Ups & Downs* 13: "It is quite fresh," said I, "and I don't mind if I do take a nipper." **1889–90* Barrère & Leland *Dict. Slang* II 87: *Nipper*…a small draught.

¶ In phrase: [perh. sugg. by S.E. *nippers* 'a pince-nez']

¶ **clap a nipper on** to take a look at.

  1839–40 J. Cobb *Green Hand* I 37: Clap a nipper…upon yon hawk bill who is admiring the beauties of the joint of beef.

nipping jig *n. Und.* a gallows; (*hence*) a hanging.

  1807 Tufts *Autobiog.* 292 [ref. to 1794]: *Nipping jig*…a gallows. *Ibid.* 293: He's going to the nipping jig to be topt…He is going to the gallows to be hanged. **a1890–1902* *F & H* V 51: *Nipping jig.*…Hanging.

nipple-chaser *n. Petroleum Industry.* an oil-field foreman.

  1934 Weseen *Dict. Amer. Sl.* 90: *Nipple*—A short piece of pipe used as a connection or a reducing joint. *Nipple chaser*—A foreman in charge of oil-drilling operations. **1972** Haslam *Oil Fields* 107: *Nipples, n.* Handle-like connections that can be screwed into bits and tools for manual lifting. *Nipple Chaser, n.* A foreman.

Nippo *n. Mil.* NIP.—used contemptuously.—usu. considered offensive.

  1942 Gamet & Trivers *Flying Tigers* (film): He got another Nippo today. **1943** in M. Curtiss *Letters Home* 258: "Ole Nippo" doesn't like us. **1945** in Galewitz *Great Comics* 273: She…turned her cunning on the Nippos. **1960** Aarons *Hell to Eternity* 86: Three Nippos just scooted into a cave over there.

nisket *n.* [orig. unkn.] *Whaling.* (see quots.).

  *1725 in *OED*: The Whale…got the Fluke into her Nisket, or the orifice of the Uterus. **1873** Scammon *Marine Mammals* 311: *Nisket*—the anus of a whale.

nit *n.* an inconsequential or obnoxious person; (*hence*) NITWIT.

  1902–03 Ade *People You Know* 77: I don't read Books.…I am an Intellectual Nit. Clear Out! **1919** in Horowitz *Campus Life* 122: We are the Its. You are the Nits. **1935** Wead *Ceiling Zero* (film): Why don't those nits in New York do something about it? **1954** Collans & Sterling *House Detect.* 219: *Nit.* A nuisance; also, sometimes a poor tipper. **1962** Dougherty *Commissioner* 278: The prick is very much alive, you friggin' nit. **1965** in H. Ellison *Sex Misspelled* 325: Man, you are such a nit. **1968** Vidal *Breckinridge* 99: Ten men and ten girls, you nit. **1975** *Nat. Lampoon* (Apr.) 4: The poor nit is inevitably driven…into composing something shrill. **1981** G. Wolf *Roger Rabbit* 103: I'm such a nit when it comes to keeping records. **1987** *Kate & Allie* (CBS-TV): We like nits. **1996** McCumber *Playing Off Rail* 77: Watching a couple of nits play pool.

nit *interj.* [< dial. G] no; not. Cf. ABER NIT; NOT. [The 1896 Crane quot. represents a nominalization of this interj.]

  1894 in S. Crane *Stories* 206: And as he glowered at the little Cuban, he ended his oration with one eloquent word, "Nit!" **1895** *DN* I 421: *Nit:* a decided negative, much stronger than *no.* Also added to positive assertions to give a negative meaning (equivalent to "I don't think")….In O[hio] also "*aber nit.*" **1896** in Outcault *Yellow Kid* 137: But I sez nit! **1896** Ade *Artie* 9: Well, I should say nit! **1896** in S. Crane *N.Y.C. Sks.* 164: "Leggo me loidy." "A couple a nits." **1897** in Outcault *Yellow Kid* 127: Kin yiz beat it? Nit! **1897** in J. London *Reports* 320: Nit! **1898** Kountz *Baxter's Letters* 5: I let go with the first barrel, right into the center of the [flight of ducks]. Nit duck. **1899** F.E. Daniel *Rebel Surgeon* 126: He would…follow in the footsteps of his pa (nit). **1905** in "O. Henry" *Works* 1315: The old man says "nit"—but that don't go. **1908** W.G. Davenport *Butte & Montana* 15: Heaven forbid! Nit! **1927** *AS* II 475: Nit. **1942** *Life* (Jan. 5) 57: A fine bunch of statesmen they got in this town—nit. **1960** in *DARE: Nit,* a term of very short duration some years ago. Generally it meant "No." **1968** in *DARE.*

nitery *n. Journ.* a nightclub. Now *colloq.* or *S.E.*

  1934 Weseen *Dict. Amer. Slang* 147: *Nitery*—A night club. **1936** *Esquire* (Sept.) 159: Some hot nitery (night club). **1954** *New Yorker* (May 8) 100: A man feels the need to step out into the bright world of the niteries. **1960** *Time* (Aug. 22) 46: San Francisco's six banjo bars are respectable, all-beer niteries with red-checked tablecloths. **1965** *L.A. Times* (Mar. 5) I 18: Youngsters commandeered the Sunset Strip for their rock 'n' roll antics, so several nitery operators catering to adults decided to "move out." **1973** *Business Week* (Nov. 24) 82: The best niteries in town are small and filled with modern jazz, folk, and rock music.

nitro *n.* nitroglycerin. Now *S.E.*

1903 *St. Louis Post-Dispatch* (May 3) II 2: *Nito* [*sic*]—Explosive to blow open a safe. **1906** *Nat. Police Gaz.* (Aug. 11) 7: It was easy for experts with the nitro. **1911** *Hampton's Mag.* (Mar.) 285: It...broke his nerve for nitro work. **1919** *Amer. Leg. Wkly.* (Sept. 12) 9: I blew it open with nitro. **1921** Casey & Casey *Gay-Cat* 71: We'll distribute a little of our nitro among them. **1953** *Looney Tunes* (animation): Careful with the nitro, Bugsy. **1967** "M.T. Knight" *Terrible Ten* 99: Forgetting all about the nitro, he left it too near a steam pipe. **1975** Julien *Cogburn* 24: Any fool can blow nitro. **1992** G. Wolff *Day at the Beach* 145: Because angina wasn't my problem, the "nitro"...was no remedy.

nitro *adj.* excellent; DYNAMITE, 2.

　　1989 *Yo! MTV Raps* (MTV): I'm nitro and I'm hype! *a*1990 P. Dickson *Slang!* 222: *Nitro.* Very good.

nitshit *n.* petty nonsense; CHICKENSHIT, 1.b.—usu. considered vulgar.—often used attrib. Also as *v.*

　　1966 Braly *On the Yard* 236: I got to listen to you nitshitting about that punk. **1970** M. Thomas *Total Beast* 83: That's all nit-shit stuff, see, like if you drop something in the messhall or don't jump quick enough to suit one of these fucking mulligans or back-talk one of them, they sign an order on you and you have to stand at attention over there in that bullring for two hours after evening rack-up, three or four nights is all but it's kid stuff, see. **1972** Bunker *No Beast* 232: This ain't a nit-shit game or a B movie. **1976** Braly *False Starts* 355: They don't violate for that sort of nitshit.

nitski [NIT + -SKI] *interj.* NIT.

　　1904 McCardell *Show Girl* 133: Well, I guess nitski. **1906** M'Govern *Sarjint Larry* 13: Of course you would! *Auber nitski!* **1910** T.A. Dorgan, in *N.Y. Eve. Jour.* (May 2) 18: Not us—nitsky. **1913** J. London *Valley of Moon* 53: An' beyond that—nitsky.

nitty *n.* NITTY-GRITTY.

　　1973 *Oui* (Apr.) 12: A preposterously cheery voice will give you the up-to-the-minute nitty on who walked out where and for how long. **1982** in "J.B. Briggs" *Drive-In* 41: I'd just as soon...get right down to the nitty.

nitty-gritty *n.* [prob. rhyming elab. of *grit(ty)*] **1.** Orig. *Black E.* the fundamental issues; stark realities; essential facts; (*also*) a difficult situation; usu. in phr. **down to the nitty-gritty.**—also used attrib. Now *colloq.* or *S.E.*

　　1956 Childress *Like One of Family* 83: You'll find nobody comes down to the nitty-gritty when it calls for namin' things for what they are. *Ibid.* 157: Every minute of grandma's life was a struggle....Sometimes she'd get down to the "nitty gritty" and have her back to the wall. **1961** J.A. Williams *Night Song* 85: This crap is gettin' down to the knitty-gritty here now, and there are two or three cats I wants to burn when the shit hits the fan. **1963** in *DAS* (ed. 2): Negroes...know perfectly well that the nitty-gritty of a situation is the essentials of it. **1964** Gregory *Nigger* 35: When it came down to the nitty-gritty you could always go to Mr. Ben. **1965** Hentoff *Jazz Country* 62: Now, let's get down to the nitty-gritty. **1968** Kirkwood *Good Times/Bad Times* 150: Now we get down to the nitty-gritty. **1968** *N.Y.P.D.* (ABC-TV): Now let's get down to the real nitty-gritty. **1970** Segal *Love Story* 56: Ah, here we come. The goddamn nitty gritty. **1970** *Harper's* (Mar.) 87: Many meetings, finally at the nitty-gritty, are interrupted by your secretary. **1975** V. Miller *Trade-Off* 13: All right then, let's get down to the nitty-gritty. **1979** Hurling *Boomers* 55: If you get down to the nitty-gritty, you stole that money. **1992** *CBS This Morning* (CBS-TV) (Apr. 29): Parents who wanted the real nitty-gritty for their children. **1992** Strawberry & Rust *Darryl* 57: Gets right down to the nitty gritty of life. **1996** *Evans & Novak* (CNN-TV) (June 23): Let's get down to the nitty-gritty.

　　2. something that is impressive or attractive.

　　1965 Caillou *Village of Giants* (film): Dig that nitty gritty!

nitty-gritty *adj.* Orig. *Black E.* gritty; fundamental.—used prenominally.—also used fig. Now *colloq.* or *S.E.* Hence **nitty-grittily,** *adv.*

　　1964 Gregory *Nigger* 61: While I watched, the boys on the football team, who had played against those hoods, been down in the nitty-gritty dirt with them, stepped out with their dates. **1966** *L.A. Times* (Feb. 9) I 3: We want the white to understand the nitty-gritty Negro off the streets as well as the educated Negro. **1967** *L.A. Times* (Apr. 22) III 1: A local firm that makes superb commercials, truly nitty-gritty quickies that plumb the unconscious. **1968** *Business Week* (Mar. 23) 87: To transmit what it calls "this nitty-gritty technical dope." **1976** Kahone *Logic & Rhet.* 90: He doesn't want to get down to the nitty-gritty details or read the fine print. *1978** Gribbin *Timewarps* 63:

A very good nitty-gritty guide to the theories of relativity. **1980** *New West* (Sept. 22) 50: At its most nitty-grittily basic, it is the standard San Jose two-tone-avocado-with-racing-stripe tile-up...that can currently be seen going up all over the valley.

nitwit *n.* [NIT, *interj.* + *wit*] a foolish or stupid person.

　　1921 *DN* V 142: *Nit-wit, n.* See *dim-wit.* **1926** Nason *Chevrons* 170 [ref. to 1918]: Listen, nit-wit. **1928–29** Nason *White Slicker* 78: What of it, yuh nitwit? **1935** Wolfson *Reckless* (film): You nitwit! **1928** W.C. Williams *Pagany* 163: Just the buffoonery of nitwits. **1933** Duff & Sutherland *I've Got Yr. Number* (film): Listen, nitwit, will you stop annoying me? **1935** Wolfson *Reckless* (film): I don't want it ruined! You nitwit! **1937** Kalmar et al. *Life of Party* (film): No more singing. Nitwit! **1938** "E. Queen" *4 Hearts* 12: Why, you incomparable nitwit. **1948** Mareska *My Flag* 116: Why, you nitwit. **1949** O. Atkinson *Big Eyes* 53: Who'd marry such a nitwit as that? **1958** P. O'Connor *At Le Mans* 15: What kind of a nitwit...thinks I could put twenty complete sets of racing gears in that old Dodge of mine. **1981** Gilliland *Rosinante* 130: But they aren't twittering nitwits either. **1989** Guare *Six Degrees* 31: The nitwit—Chapman—who shot John Lennon.

nitzy *adj.* [perh. alter. NIFTY] stylish; attractive.

　　1973 *Playboy* (Mar.) EA2: The nitziest brushed sateens, seersuckers, and blue denims.

nix *n.* [< G *nichts*] nothing; none.

　　*1789** G. Parker *Life's Painter* 134: It won't do I say, to stand here for *nicks*—all heavers and no buyers. *Ibid.* 151: How they have brought a German word into cant I know not, but *nicks* means *nothing* in the cant language. *1811** *Lex. Balatron.*: *Nix.* Nothing. **1837** Neal *Charc. Sks.* 134: For what? Why, for nix. **1853** in Darby *Phoenixiana* 173: Batten...shakes his head sadly...[and] utters the significant monosyllable "Nix." **1855** in *DA*: You will soon be..."good for nix." **1859** Matsell *Vocab.* 59: *Nix.* Nothing. **1862** in Bensill *Yamhill* 60: Nix [doing]. Taps. **1863** in Bensill *Yamhill* 88: Apr. 29, 1863. Clear. Nix. **1864** in Bensill *Yamhill* 171: A general search resulted in "nix." **1864** in C.W. Wills *Army Life* 208: His nix-Grahamite diet of army rations. **1868–71** C.G. Leland *Breitmann's Ballads* 60: I don't know nix. **1884** *Life* (June 19) 347: My boom'll be nix in the coming July. **1887** M. Roberts *W. Avernus* 40: "He's got as much as I have and that's nix" (corrupt German for "nichts."). **1889** in L. Levy *Flashes of Merriment* 354: His board would cost him nix. **1891** Maitland *Slang Dict.* 188: *Nix* (German *nichts*), nothing. *1899** Whiteing *John St.* 268: There's a whole tanner's worth for nix. **1909** in *DA*: "What are our chances?" "Nix." **1925** *Sat. Eve. Post* (Oct. 31) 62: The score [is] nix to nix. **1930–31** Farrell *Grandeur* 149: He probably wasn't taking her out here in the park for nix. **1934** Appel *Brain Guy* 32: You'll be nix carrying a rod. **1948** Cozzen *Guard* 174: "Brains he has nix," Nathaniel Hicks said. *1988** Cleese *Fish Called Wanda* (film): Nix! Zip! Diddly! Bupkis!

　　2. *Post Office.* NIXIE.

　　1879 in *DAE*: Misdirected second-class matter ("nixes"). **1883** in *DAE:* "Nixes" is a term used in the railway mail service to denote matter of domestic origin, chiefly of the first and second class, which is unmailable because addressed to places which are not post offices, or to States, etc., in which there is no such post office as that indicated in the address.

　　3. a refusal or rejection.—usu. constr. with *on*.

　　1948 *Variety*, in *DAS*: Yanks' Nix on Coupling U.S., British Pix Seen as Johnston's Trump Card....If the Petrillo nix stands [etc.]. **1974** A. Bergman *Big Kiss-Off* 5: Last month's [lack of] business...put the nix on [taking] cabs for a couple of weeks. **1989** *CBS This Morning* (CBS-TV) (Oct. 11): They...put the nix on that.

　　¶ In phrase:

　　¶ **nix my doll** [the orig. of the element *my doll* is unkn.] *Und.* nothing; NIX.

　　*1797** in Partridge *Dict. Und.* 472: Nix my doll. *1812** Vaux *Vocab.*: *Nix,* or *Nix my doll:* nothing. **1840** *Spirit of Times* (Nov. 21) 454: Says he to me..."What's the matter?" Why, says I, "Nix my doll."...So I cut my lucky.

nix *adj.* spoiled; worthless.

　　1859 *Spirit of Times* (Feb. 19) 17: The foam is all "nix" on the goblet of life,/So I takes to the foam on mine beer. **1954–60** *DAS: Nix*...Worthless; no good. *Not common.*

nix *prep.* without.

　　1898–1900 Cullen *Chances* 107: Winter'll be coming on soon, and you'll be nix the price of a doss.

nix *v.* **1.** to reject; prohibit; cancel; eliminate; discard; avoid.—occ. constr. with *out* or *off.*

    1902–03 Ade *People You Know* 156: Nix the Orphan Asylum....They would bring a million witnesses to prove that I had been out of my Head for 20 years. **1934** Weseen *Dict. Amer. Slang* 371: *Nix*—To refuse an offer...to deny a request. **1935** *Variety* (July 17) 1: Sticks Nix Hick Pix. **1936** *Esquire* (Sept.) 159: A broadside goes out on what phrases to nix. **1938** *Variety* (June 22) 36: Hepster's Dictionary...*Nix out*—to eliminate. **1940** in *OEDS: Nix out*, to eliminate, get rid of. Ex. "I nixed that chick out last week." "I nixed my garments" (undressed). **1944** D. Burley *Hndbk. Jive* 97: Nix out the play. **1945** W. Winchell, in *DAS:* The blue-penciler nixed the story. **1950** G. Kelly, in *Sat. Eve. Post* (July 8) 69: If I had a worst [sic] foot, I wanted it to stick out right in their faces so I'd be nixed then, instead of rehearsing and being canned later. **1954** L. Armstrong *Satchmo* 116: We kids nixed the joint [because there were too many fights there]. **1958** Hughes & Bontemps *Negro Folklore* 486: *Nix out:* To freeze, eliminate. Two in love nix out all others. **1960** Himes *Gold Dream* 152: They've been trying to proposition me into helping them rob some women, but I nixed them off. **1935–62** Ragen & Finston *Toughest Pris.* 810: *Nix out*—Same as "nix." **1971** Sorrentino *Up from Never* 82: "Here, nix these." I handed him the price tags. **1976** Selby *Demon* 51: He quickly nixed that idea. **1977** A. Patrick *Beyond Law* 148: The higher-ups nixed it. **1982** *N.Y. Post* (Sept. 2) 1: Israel Nixes Reagan's Peace Plan. **1986** E. Weiner *Howard the Duck* 5: But his boss had nixed it and chosen a different one.

    2. to ruin; spoil.

    1993 *Cool Like that Christmas* (Fox-TV): Jervis better not nix my boom box, man! **1995** *Dr. Katz* (Comedy Central TV): I had an opportunity and you nixed it.

nix *interj.* no.

    1862 E.S. Ellis *Hunter's Cabin* 34: "Have you asked her yet?" "Nix; I'm going to ask her next time." **1862** in R.B. Hayes *Diary* II 344: I said "nix" either way. **1877** Wheeler *Deadwood Dick, Prince of the Road* 82: They never hed it in their hearts to say Nix to an offer uv a good feed or a decoction o' brandy. **1886** E.L. Wheeler *N.Y. Nell* 4: Nix! it's what suits me. **1896** Ade *Artie* 10: "Nix," I says. **1908** McGaffey *Show Girl* 108: That ain't little Sabrina's graft. Nix. **1912** Mathewson *Pitching* 254: Nix, Mac....be reasonable. **1912–14** in E. O'Neill *Lost Plays* 40: Nix! Yuh heard what I said, didn't yuh? **1942** R. Chandler, in *DAS:* "The guy's heeled."..."Under that suit? Nix." **1948** Mareska *My Flag* 17: Nix....I don't get this and I don't like this. **1963** D. Tracy *Brass Ring* 4: "How about letting me drive a little ways?" "Nix." **1988** Cronenberger & Snider *Dead Ringers* (film): Unh-unh. Nix. No. **1994** *My So-Called Life* (ABC-TV): "You need a place to crash, I know a place." "Nix."

    ¶ In phrases:

    ¶ **nix come-arouse** [< G *nichts kommt heraus* 'nothing will come of this'] it doesn't matter; never; no indeed. Also vars.

    1844 in *DA:* Clay must rest contented; For he's "nics cum arous" at the old White House. **1865–67** De Forest *Miss Ravenel* 322: In ole, ole times, after fought a big battle, used to stop....But now nix cum rouse the stop. **1877** Wheeler *Deadwood Dick, Prince of Road* 81: "Nix cum-a-rouse!" disagreed the old prospector. **1898** in *DARE:* As fur 's the bus'nis itself 's concerned, the hull thing's all nix-cum-rouse to me. **1919** in *DARE:* All hands is doomed, because two of the pumps is nix comarous. **1936** Mencken *Amer. Lang.* (ed. 4) 157: Nix come erous. **1970** in *DARE* [ref. to ca1920]: *Nix-com-erouse*—It doesn't matter, nothing will come of it. (Fairly current in popular speech.).

    ¶ **nix on** no more of; stop! away with!

    *1753** in Partridge *Dict. Und.* 472: Nix in [sic] masoning!...Nix in [sic] whideling! **1902** in *OEDS:* We decided before we stepped on the Pullman that it would be nix on the sweetheart talk. **1907** in H.C. Fisher *A. Mutt* 7: Aw, nix on that old talk. **1908** in McCay *Little Nemo* 157: "Take me right home." "Nix on any home. Remember, kid, you're with me. Take it easy!" **1912–14** in E. O'Neill *Lost Plays* 43: Nix on that stuff about your not bein' worth it! **1919** S. Lewis *Free Air* 273: Nix on clippers over the ears. **1925** Cobb *Many Laughs* 88: "Nix on any box seat for me," he stated firmly. **1929** in Oliver *Blues Tradition* 51: Nix on standing out there holdin' his hand. **1929** Kaufman *Cocoanuts* (film): Hey, nix on that stuff. **1945** in *DAS:* Nix on swiping anything. **1966, 1969–70** in *DARE*.

nixie *n. Post Office.* an undeliverable piece of mail; an incorrect address; (*also*) (see 1966 and 1977 quots.).

    1890 in *OEDS:* These poor "nixie" clerks in the postoffices of this country. **1901** in *DAE:* Mailing clerks,...directory and nixie clerks. **1905** in *DAE:* What the railway postal clerks most dread is the class of mail matter they know as "nixies." **1949** *Sat. Eve. Post* (Dec. 17) 84: Between 60,000 and 80,000 third-class cards became "nixies"—post-office slang for mail that can be neither delivered nor returned. **1958** *New Yorker* (Feb. 8) 24: Within ten days the "nixies"—the magazine's word for returned letters—started coming. **1966** *L.A. Times* (Dec. 22) II 1: Nixies are postal clerks with special deciphering talents. They're magicians at reading scribble....Nixies are...expediting hundreds of thousands of carelessly addressed Christmas messages and packages. **1972** *N.Y. Times Mag.* (Oct. 22) 30: Crossing off "nixies"—nondeliverable addresses—and adding new customers. **1977** *L.A. Times* (Dec. 19) II 1: A Nixie is...a specialized postal worker whose full-time job is to somehow figure out what destination the sender had in mind. **1978** in *RHD* files [note from collector commenting on 1977 quot., above]: *Nixie*...My dear ma used to work this kind of mail...but she and her co-workers used the term for the letters, not the people working them.

nixie *interj.* [NIX + -*ie* dimin. suff.] NIX.

    1877 *Puck* (No. 3) 2: He was heard to mutter "Nixie Culley" and other mysterious phrases. **1887** [C. Mackenzie] *Jack Pots* 148: "Has he fasted 40 days?"..."Nixey." **1887** in Barrère & Leland *Dict. Slang.* I 141: MacClarty objected; giving the young man a warning look, he said, "Nixey, Toohey, get out flash—*blow it*, man, *blow it!*" which mean that Mr. MacClarty thought that Mr. Toohey ought not to talk so much. **1891** Maitland *Slang Dict.* 188: *Nixey*, no. **1893** in Dreiser *Jour.* I 111: "Nixy," replied the tramp...."I will not steal their coin." **1903** *Pedagog. Sem.* X 373: Ah, go on. Nixy. **1904** in "O. Henry" *Works* 51: One day she says he will; the same evenin' she says nixy. **1908** *DN* III 352: *Nit, nix(y)*, adv. Variants of *no.* Slang. **1908** in McCay *Little Nemo* 141: I'm no kid! Nixey! **1909** in McCay *Little Nemo* 188: Not for me! Nixie on this place! **1910** Livingston *Life* 64: "Nixie, kid," he retorted. **1912** Berkman *Prison* 163: Refuse? Me? Nixie. **1914** Atherton *Perch* 108: They're all right to marry,...but to sacrifice your life for, nixie. **1919** Darling *Jargon Book* 23: *Nixie*—Means and stands for, No, Sir.

nixo *interj.* [NIX + -O] NIX.

    1980 *Nat. Lampoon* (Sept.) 29: Good question, Rich, but nixo, nixo.

no- *prefix.* conspicuously lacking in (something).—recently also used in nominal constrs. Usu. *joc.* [The semantic basis for the application reported in 1956 quot. is unclear. For phrs. beginning with *no*, see s.v. the next word of the phr.; e.g., for *no sweat* see s.v. SWEAT, *n.*]

    1908 *Atlantic* (Oct.) 497: The great army of No-Taste theatre-goers. **1931** J.T. Farrell *McGinty* 168: You dirty lousy no-dough redhead. **1944** M. Shulman *Feather Merchants* 144: Say, Gimpy, No-Nose, T.B., Sterno, Dehorn, come over here. **1956** *AS* XXXI (Oct.) 191: A buddy manifestly selfish about possessions...may have his surname prefixed by *no-nose*, occasionally a term of endearment. **1983** K. Miller *Lurp Dog* 44: Trying to keep that no-pride Tiger from running off. **1988** Clodfelter *Mad Minutes* 286: You no-balls mother fucker. **1989** *Married with Children* (Fox-TV): You'd have to be a real no-life to be home on a gorgeous day like this! **1990** Linklater *Slacker* (film): Jeez, you're a no-fun. **1992** *Business Week* (Sept. 25) 126: Customers are paying for the no-brain nature of the machine. **1994** *N.Y. Times* (Apr. 29) C15: You think it's easy to make a no-brain action movie. **1994** N. McCall *Wanna Holler* 27: Without revealing myself as a no-name lame.

nob¹ var. KNOB, *n.*, 1.

nob² *n.* a person of wealth or social importance; a preeminent person. Now *S.E.* Cf. NOBS.

    *1703** in *F & H* V 54: Be unto him ever ready to promote his wishes, whether for spree or sport, in term and out of term...against dun or don—nob or big-wig—so may you never want a bumper of bishop. *1755** in *OED:* Doughty geer That either knabbs or lairds may weer. *1811** *Lex. Balatron.:* Nob. A king. A man of rank. *1831** B. Hall *Voyages* I 142: Many were the execrations hurled upwards at the offending "knobs." **1832** *Spirit of Times* (Mar. 3) 3: As I said before, the match was made between the *nobs* and *swells.* **1841** *Spirit of Times* (Feb. 13) 589: It's the west end nobs. **1849** "N. Buntline" *B'hoys of N.Y.* 39: We can make a raise out of these western nobs. **1849** Melville *White Jacket* 228: He's been blackguarding the young nob in the green coat, there. **1890** McBallastir *Society* 11: There was no Society, and there were no Nobs and Swells. **1898** W. Payne *Money Capt.* 71: That's the way the nobs do it. **1899** A.H. Lewis *Sandburrs* 24: Of all d' crooks he was d' nob. **1931** Harlow *Old Bowery* 231 [ref. to 1850's]: He adds that the "nobs" of upper Broadway and Union Square…would go around through the Bowery. **1959** *N.Y. Times* (Feb. 8) IV E5: Literary nobs are fairly well acquainted with American prose writers.

nobble *v.* [orig. unkn.] **1.a.** to swindle; influence underhandedly; corrupt. *Rare* in U.S. Hence **nobbler**, *n.*

    1839** in Partridge *Dict. Und.* 473: *Nobblers*—confederates of the thimblemen, who appear to play to induce others to do the same. **1852** *Harper's Mo.* (Dec.) 90: He…fancied that he could descry something in my face that would be sure to attract the sympathies of the benevolent, and loosen their purse-strings, or, as he phrased it, "nobble the Flats." ***1855** Thackeray, in *F & H* V 56: I don't know out of how much the reverend party has nobbled his poor old sister at Brighton. **a1889–90** Barrère & Leland *Dict. Slang*: Don't you fancy the hunemployed bunkum has *nobbled* me: not such a mug!

b. to obtain for oneself undeservedly; FINAGLE.

    1995 *Nation* (Oct. 30) 500: Keyes became a protégé of Allan Bloom as a Cornell undergraduate before following Bloom to Harvard, where he nobbled a Ph.D.

2. *Horse Racing.* to lame or drug a horse (or dog) before a race; (*broadly*) to interfere with a race in any manner. Hence **nobbler**, *n.*

    1847** in *OED*: A shadowy vision of creditors "done," horses "nobbled." ***1873** Hotten *Slang Dict.* (ed. 4): *Nobble*…In the racing world, to "*nobble*" a horse is to "get at," and lame or poison him. **1880** *N.Y. Clipper Almanac* 45: *Nobble.*—To poison a horse on the eve of a race, or otherwise unfit him. *a1890** in Barrère & Leland *Dict. Slang*: The horse was *nobbled*—by whom it does not concern us to conjecture. **1946** in *DAS*: Superior chemistry and some luck on the part of the nobblers who drugged dogs in a race. ***1952** *Time* (May 19) 66: In the past, nobblers (English version of U.S. fixers) have been known to ambush a favorite, or give a longshot an autoborne boost along the trail. ***1990** T. Thorne *Dict. Contemp. Slang: Nobble*…to incapacitate or subvert. The term applies specifically to drugging or otherwise distressing a racehorse.

nobbler *n.* **1.** see s.v. NOBBLE.

2. *Steel Industry.* (see quot.).

    1979 in Terkel *Amer. Dreams* 289: My father's father was a nobbler. He shaped steel with long tongs. He earned sixty dollars a week when ordinary workers were earning six. After the Bessemer process came in, he never got another job.

nobby *adj.* **1.** fashionable; high-class; fancy. Also **knobby.**

    1808** in *F & H* V 57: *Nobby.* Neat, trim, well dressed; hence applied to a person who dresses above his position. **ca1810** in *F & H* V 57: A werry nobby dog's meat man. **1846** in H.L. Gates, Jr. *Sig. Monkey* 95: Nalagy treats ob de head and is derfor a *nobby* study. **1855** Brougham *Chips* 177: You don't suppose I'd try a knobby crib like this, without the persuaders. **1858** *Harvard Mag.*, in *DAS*: His summer hat also is as good as new, quite nobby when compared with his old cap. **1864** in "M. Twain" *Sketches* 37: Mr. Papilius Lena remarked to George W. Cassius (commonly known as the "Nobby Boy of the Third Ward"), a bruiser in the pay of the Opposition, that he hoped his enterprise today might thrive. **1867** in Utley *Custer's Cavalry* 101: We *are* quite dressy—or as Lieut. Commagere says "Knobby"—I don't know where he picked up that word! **1867** Alger *Ragged Dick* 167: "What's a swell?" "Oh, a feller that wears nobby clothes like you." **1869** Carleton *Kaleidoscope* 19: Nobby hat, that of yours, Steve! Where did you raise it? **1866–71** Bagg *Yale* 46: *Nobby*, stylish, fashionable, well-dressed. Applied to young men only. **1871** "M. Twain" *Roughing It* 244: I mean to have the nobbiest rig that's going. **1879** Maitland *Sensations* 181: This is a very nobby hat. **1887** Peck *Pvt. Peck* 179: A stiff, cheap, shoddy hat…was to take the place of my nobby, soft felt hat. *a***1893** W.K. Post *Harvard* 201: Just watch me do the nobby [thing]. **1897** Biddle *Shantytown Sketches* 60: How fine und nobby you do look in dem pants. ***1899** Whiteing *John St.* 48: She do look nobby, don't she now? **1899** Ade *Fables* 28: He was a Nobby and Boss Minister. **1900** Dreiser *Carrie* 12: Genteel business men in "nobby suits." **1910** *Harper's* (Jan.) 178: That top is sure the nobbiest thing that ever came over these roads. **1918** in T. Lewis *H. Crane's Letters* 102: It is very plain but elegant & nobby. **1920** J.V. Weaver *In American* 13: The swellest dresser, with them nifty shirts/That fold down, and them lovely nobby shoes. **1922** P.A. Rollins *Cowboy* 189: Nobby clothing for city use. **1930** J.T. Farrell, in *DAS*: Polo shirts, nobby ties. **1965** in De Turk & Poulin *Amer. Folk Scene* 208: The Rainbow Room, the nobby night club atop a skyscraper in Rockefeller Center.

2. wonderful. Also **knobby.**

    1876 "M. Twain" *T. Sawyer* 161 [ref. to *ca*1845]: But we'll play Robin Hood—it's nobby fun. **1879** Burt *Prof. Smith* 13: Its a "knobby" dance, you bet.

noble *n.* **1.** *Labor & Und.* one who guards and directs a group of strikebreakers. Now *hist.*

    1930 *Amer. Mercury* (Dec.) 456: *Noble, n.*: A guard for strike breakers. "Me work? Don't be foolish. I'm a noble, I am." **1934** E. Levinson *Strikes* 53: The guards, armed and unarmed,…are known as "nobles." Between the finks and the nobles are the "boots" who constitute the personnel of the Strike Prevention and Undercover departments. *Ibid.* 55: So eminent a strikebreaker as Val O'Farrell designated the guards as "nobles" back in 1913. **1939** Appel *Power-House* 386: What I wanna know is who the hell the nobles of this load of finks is gonna be?…Nobles're the guys they pick out from the finks to boss the finks. **1952** H. Grey *Hoods* 254: "What the hell is a noble?" "…We're like the bosses over the finks." **1956** in *DAS*: *Noble*—Captain of a strike-breaking team.

2. *Pris.* an influential convict.

    1966 in Wepman, Newman & Binderman *The Life* 61: Those real boss meals are eaten by wheels,/Nobles and all of that jazz.

noble *adj. Black E.* fine; excellent; satisfying.

    1902 Corrothors *Black Cat Club* 158: Preachah's son wuz a noble dancah, too! **1921** Wiley *Lady Luck* 95: Sho's noble when de train stops; boy can sleep peaceful.…Boy sure can sleep noble.…Sho is noble water. **1926** Thomason *Red Pants* 19: Cap'n, is you ever tried dat coon-yac? It sho is noble booze!

nobody *n.* ¶ In phrases:

    ¶ **nobody home** see s.v. HOME, *n.*

    ¶ **the lights are on but nobody's home** see s.v. LIGHT, *n.*, 3.

Nobody's Land *n. Mil.* no man's land. [Quots. ref. to WWI.]

    1918 Lardner *Treat 'Em Rough* 69: It floats across Nobodys land and comes to the other trenches. **1919** *Our Navy* (Sept.) 60: One night I was out on patrol on listening duty in Nobody's Land. **1919** Sanborn *131st Inf.* 203: At 5:30 a.m. we climbed over, found the paths which our working party had cut through our wire and advanced in the bright moon-light across "Nobody-land" until we reached the swamp. **1919** Streeter *Same Old Bill* 52: The Lootenant showed me where Nobodies Land was.

no-brainer *n.* **1.a.** something requiring very little intelligence.—also used attrib.

    1973 (cited in *W10*). **1974** Univ. Tenn. grad. student: We used to call a real easy exam a damn no-brainer [at Chilhowee College, N.C., in 1973]. **1982** *Santa Barbara* (Calif.) *News-Press* (June 30) C9: "No-brainers"…are cakes that begin with a package cake mix plus, usually, a packaged pudding mix or gelatin mix. **1988** (June 17) in *AS* LXIV(1989) 157: On two occasions, last year, I overheard students referring to a certain course as being a "no-brainer." **1988** *N.Y. Post* (June 22) 23: You know how easy it is to make dumb no-brainer action movies. **1991** *Time* (Apr. 8) 29: As issues go, infant mortality should be a no-brainer for a politician. Find a catchy slogan, throw money at the problem and ride the quick results. **1992** Strawberry & Rust *Darryl* 99: Basketball…was a real "no brainer."…It took more intelligence to figure out baseball situations. **1994** *New Yorker* (Mar. 21) 152: The manufacture of the VKF sprocket is a "no-brainer"…compared to making the Maltese cross, where serious flaws are measured in millionths of an inch.

b. *Specif.*, an easily made decision; something obvious.

    1980 in *AS* LXIV (1989) 157: Sometimes the decision is a real no-brainer. If Iran releases the hostages we don't have to think twice about the lead [*sc.*, the lead broadcast in a news report]. **1987** in *AS* LXIV (1989) 157: The business decision in that is what we call a no-brainer. **1991** *Wash. Post* (Oct. 3) B1: The rich guy is willing.…This is a no-brainer. Let him build it. **1994** *Wash. Post* (Feb. 14) C10: The league's most valuable player—and this is a no-brainer—is Scottie Pippen. **1995** *N.Y. Times Mag.* (Aug. 27) 36: Voting for Clinton in 1992 was a no-brainer. **1996** *All Things Considered* (Nat. Pub. Radio) (June 18): When you think about it, it's a no-brainer.

2. something or someone foolish.

    1978 Alibrandi *Killshot* 69: I'll unanimously be voted the no-brainer-of-the-month award. **1987** in *AS* LXIV (Summer 1989) 157: If a no-brainer wants to talk on the radio—even if the message makes no sense whatsoever—he or she can do it. **1989** *TV Guide* (Jan. 14) 23: The sitcom…pulled a real no-brainer with its popular 1988 wall calendar. December began a day late. **1990** *Teenage Mutant Ninja Turtles* (CBS-TV): Using the personality alternator ray on Leonardo was a real no-brainer. **1992** *New Yorker* (Oct. 12) 45: Jerk…Fool…Asshole.…No brainer.

nobrow *adj.* [pun on LOWBROW] exceptionally crude or tasteless.
　　1995 *Time* (Mar. 27) 62: A pair of funny, nobrow epics in which…he co-starred with an orangutan named Clyde.

nobs *n.* a person of importance; NIBS.—usu. constr. with poss. pronoun. Cf. NOB².
　　1877 in Asbury *Gem of Prairie* (opp. 144): His nobs has changed socks. **1896** Ade *Artie* 43: Let *me* write to his nobs and *I'll* fix him. *Ibid.* 66: W'y, t'e four-eyed nobs dat sent me out on t'e Sout' Side. **1897** Siler & Houseman *Fight of the Century* 27: So is his nobs. **1903** C.E. Stewart *Uncle Josh* 154: I'm engaged to his nobs for this set. **1904** in "O. Henry" *Works* 1264: Did you make a hit with his nobs, Masie? **1912** Lowrie *Prison* 110: A kind o' credit from his Nobs down below. *a*1950 R. Spence *Gorilla* 29: Keep your eye on his nobs.

nockandro *n.* [Early ModE *nock* 'the cleft of the buttocks' + *-andro*, of unkn. orig.] the buttocks.
　　*1611 Cotgrave *Dict.: Cul.* An arse, bumme, tayle, nockandro, fundament. ***1653** in *F & H* V 58: My foul nockandrow all bemerded. **1751** in Breslaw *Tues. Club* 297: It were to be wished, that valiant John had only Shown that merciless Scoundrell his *Nockandroe* or posteriors thro' the port hole.

no-class *adj.* showing no refinement in behavior.
　　[**1897** Hayne *Klondyke* 8: Some of our "first class sailors" suddenly and very ignobly…proved themselves, so to speak, "no class at all."] **1965** Pollini *Glover* 354: That low-down, no-good, no-class *dirty bum!* **1966** Braly *Cold* 67: No-class slobs. **1973** Haney *Jock* 54: That dumb no class broad that Johnny married. **1996** Juhl et al. *Muppet Treasure Island* (film): Of all the backwater, no-class piles of sand in the ocean!

nod *n.* **1.** *Narc.* a drug-induced stupor; esp. in phr. **on the nod** in such a stupor; (*hence*) falling asleep; asleep.
　　1936 Dai *Opium Addiction* 202: *Playing the nod.* To go to sleep from overindulgence. **1951** *Life* (June 11) 126: He…becomes comatose and lethargic (goes on the nod in junkie parlance). **1951** *New Yorker* (Nov. 10) 48: They had taken a shot…and were on the nod—sitting there with their eyes open, but hardly able to talk and practically asleep, and their heads bobbing like mechanical dolls. **1952** in W.S. Burroughs *Letters* 139: He is on the nod a good part of the time. **1953** W. Brown *Monkey on My Back* 39: They kept hitting it until Terry went on the nod. **1954–55** in *Social Problems* VII (1959) 245: Go on the nod [from taking heroin]. **1955** Q. Reynolds *HQ* 274: There were ten men and one woman "on the nod" when we broke in. **1959–60** R. Reisner *Jazz Titans* 162: *On The Nod:* sleeping, usually in a standing or sitting position. **1960** C.L. Cooper *Scene* 267: I did about ten [capsules of heroin] before I got some nod. **1963** *Sat. Eve. Post* (July 27) 76: After the first shock it sends the user into a "nod," a sort of semiconscious daydream. **1965** in *DAS* (ed. 2): When the heroin addict…gets a sufficiently powerful shot he goes on a "nod"—his head drooping, eyelids heavy. **1966** H.S. Thompson *Hell's Angels* 198: But crashing means nothing more sinister than going on the nod, either from booze or simple fatigue. **1966–67** P. Thomas *Mean Streets* 195: You're in a nod of your own special dimension. **1968** Algren *Chicago* 138: Some on the nod and some on the hunt. **1965–70** J. Carroll, in *Paris Rev.* (No. 50) 108: Codeine cough medicine…for a nice long Saturday afternoon nod. **1971** (quot. at NOD OUT). **1971** *Who Took Weight?* 194: The whole black nation's in a motherfucken *nod!* **1975** Wambaugh *Choirboys* 222: When he's geezing and on the nod, he'll burn himself half to death when he's smoking cigarettes. **1995** *Donahue* (NBC-TV): There's what you call a nod where your head falls loose and your eyes roll back.
　　2. Esp. *Black. E.* a nap.—usu. constr. with *cop.* [The main entry for the phr. **cop a nod** is found at *cop a nod* s.v. COP, *v.*; the following two quots. antedate the evidence found there.]
　　1938 C. Calloway, in R.S. Gold *Jazz Lexicon: Nod:* sleep. Example: "I then I'll cop a nod." **1944** Kendall *Service Slang* 58: *Lay on a pad and cop a nod.…*retire to the bunk bed.

nod *v. Narc.* to fall asleep or into a daze, esp. under the influence of a drug.
　　1958 *So. Folk. Qly.* (Sept.) 132: *Nodding:* succumbing to a drug. **1965** C. Brown *Manchild* 206: It was a hip thing to do, to know about—to be nodding. **1976–77** Kernochan *Dry Hustle* 267: Shit, I got to *nod. a*1979 in P. Goldstein *Prost. & Drugs* 107: And when you

nod, you can't work. **1997** *N.Y. Times Bk. Rev.* (May 4) 16: Shooting up in empty lots, nodding on the hulks of abandoned cars.

noddle *n.* [ME *nodel* 'the back of the head', of unkn. orig.] the head; (*hence*) the mind. Cf. NOODLE. Orig. *S.E.*
　　*1579 in *OED:* The divell…puteth into their braines and foolishe noddles to make great shewes. ***1593** Shakespeare *Taming Shrew* I i, in *F & H* V 59: Doubt not her cares should be to comb your noddle with a three-legg'd stool, and paint your face. ***1611** in *F & H* V 59: I have 't in my noddle, i' faith. ***1664** in Partridge *DSUE* 567: My Head's not made of brass/As Friar Bacon's noddle was. ***1698–99** "B.E." *Dict. Canting Crew: Noddle,* a Head. ******a*1720 in D'Urfey *Pills* I 149: Why…plague your Noddles? **1793** in St. G. Tucker *Poems* 91: Like Colossus, you stride/O'er our noddles so wide. **1800** *Amorous Songster* 62: Shaking noddle, widdle, waddle. **1813–18** Weems *Drunkard's Looking Glass* 63: *Idle* with their noddles full of whiskey. **1829** in Blair & Meine *Half Horse* 261: Hold your noddle steady, Carpenter, and don't spill the whiskey. **1850** in A. Pratt *Journals* 50: [A sperm whale's head] is called his noddle end. **1864** in J.W. Haley *Rebel Yell* 179: With this silly notion in their noddle. **1870** (quot. at NUT, 2). **1905** in *DAS:* I suppose the axle grease gave him wheels in the noddle. **1914** Patten *Lefty o' the Bush* 153: Why did you go and put such a notion in the noddles of the Bancrofters? **1968–70** in *DARE.*

nod out *v.* Orig. *Narc.* to fall asleep, esp. under the influence of a drug. Now *colloq.* Also **nod off.**
　　*ca*1953 Hughes *Lodge* 103: I didn't dig nodding out. **1965** in Waldman *World Anthol.* 14: Slapstick told us to take a shower and nod off. *Ibid.* 15: I get a great urge to nod out. **1971** N.Y.U. student: Twenty pages of *Walden* and I started to nod out. **1971** Dahlskog *Dict.* 42: *Nodding out, on the nod,* in a drug-induced stupor. **1982** *N.Y. Times* (Apr. 28) A24: He was a narcotics user. He proves it later by nodding out in front of the judge. **1985** D. Steel *Secrets* 43: She doesn't even go to auditions anymore.…She nodded out at the last one. **1996** *Newsweek* (Aug. 26) 50: He finally did use it [*sc.,* heroin] around me.…He nodded out on my couch midway through a sentence; he threw up in my bathroom.

noggin *n.* [prob. *noggin* 'a small mug'] the head; (*hence*) the mind; consciousness; in phr. **off (one's) noggin** insane. Now *colloq.*
　　1859 "Skitt" *Fisher's River* 35 [ref. to 1820's]: The first idea that entered his "noggin" was that he was in a general "still-house" fight. *Ibid.* 53: I…turned my noggin round to look fur the critter. **1865** Byrn *Fudge Fumble* 205: Down I brought it over Paddy's noggin. **1880** in S. Dennison *Scandalize My Name* 274: He hit me 'cross my noggen wid a great big chunk of wood. **1880** Pilgrim *Old Nick's Camp-Meetin'* 66: Dern'd if it aint good enough to git away with your long-eared noggin. **1893** M.A. Owen *Voodoo Tales* 23: Lemme scratch dis hyeah ole noggin. *a*1890–1902 *F & H* V 61: *Noggin*…(old)—The head. **1906** R. Casey *Parson's Boys* 143 [ref. to *ca*1860]: Be careful not to blow their noggins off. **1931** *PMLA* XLVI 1304: Samp's Bob got hisself cracked on the noggin (head) in the fray yistidday. **1942** Davis & Wolsey *Call House Madam* 46: The guy who said he wanted a woman with common sense was off his noggin. **1943** in *DAS:* The psychiatrist after diagnosing his noggin. **1951** *Sat. Eve. Post* (Apr. 21) 165: Players…occasionally throw one that bounces off the noggin. **1959** *N.Y. Times* (Mar. 8) II 1: [They] cannot seem to get it through their noggins that there are other sorts of people in this world. **1961** Himes *Pinktoes* 204: Mamie bopped him on the noggin with her shoe heel. "That's your due," she raved. **1963** G. Parks *Learning Tree* 10: You…busted the ground with that noggin of yours. **1975** Mahl *Beating Bookie* 47: That's where you have to use your noggin! **1978** R. Price *Ladies' Man* 114: His almost bald noggin was topped with a wispy gray fuzz. **1982** *Morning Line* (WKGN radio) (July 9): You've got a lot of knowledge up there in that noggin of yours. **1983–89** K. Dunn *Geek Love* 82: Don't worry your…noggin about it. **1992** *In Living Color* (Fox-TV): A giant meteor…is…gonna knock you on the noggin.

no go *n.* no success; no use; no good.—also used allusively. Now *colloq.* Also as interj.
　　*1824 (cited in Partridge *DSUE* 1297). ***1825** in *OED:* It won't do, *no go* Dick. **1826** in McCall *Letters from Frontier* 162: But it was "*no go.*" ***1829** in *OEDS:* According to the Earl and myself, Fanny Kemble is no go. **1833** Hoffman *Winter in West* I 118: It was "no go," however, as the sturdy yeoman said. ***1833** Marryat *Peter Simple* ch. xxxi: That's *no go.* **1837** *Spirit of Times* (Apr. 1) 52: Linnet…challenged Fanny, but it was "no go." **1844** Carleton *Logbooks* 81: So far as they were con-

cerned 'twas "no go." **1847** in *West. Penna. Hist. Mag.* LII (1969) 401: A private is no go there. **1848** in *AS* X (1935) 42: *No go.* Not successful. [**1851** Strong *Diary* II 63: Plenty of voice and little music—lots of action and no go, as sporting people say.] **1852–55** C.G. Parsons *Inside View* 73: "All ready now! Roll it up!" But "*no go!*" **1856** in *Calif. Hist. Soc. Qly.* IX (1930) 58: Trying to raise some money…but no go. ***1857–58** Trollope *Dr. Thorne* II 121: It "was no go," as he graphically described it to his mother. **1864** in Mattocks *Unspoiled Heart* 252: Have tried to be sent to Columbia but it is "no go." ***1871** in *F & H* V 53: It is a case of *no go.* **1952** Bonham *Snaketrack* 55: It's no-go on the money for a while. **1969** Searls *Hero Ship* 19: The Nevada had a nickname too: *No-Go Maru,* from her rickety engines. **1976** Dillard *American Talk* xviii: No go…[is] certainly pidgin in structure. **1989** Strieber *Majestic* 90: We considered that possibility.…It's a no-go. **1991** *New Yorker* (July 8) 54: There's a blanket no-go on new…pilots.

no-good *n.* a worthless individual. Now *colloq.* or *S.E.* [The 1908 quot. in *OED2* is clearly adjectival.]
　　1924 in *OED2*: I'll learn you half-suckled no-goods what it means. ***1931** in *OED2*: A pack of crazy no-goods. **1949** *New Yorker* (June 18) 78: This amusing and opportunistic no-good…presently starts blackmailing him. **1950** *Sat. Eve. Post* (Aug. 19) 134: Ed Barrow…periodically offered to lick any no-good who got out of line. **1952** *Time* (Mar. 3) 33: A street corner no-good until he joined Hitler's brownshirts. **1961** *N.Y. Times* (Aug. 20) VII 4: A really ugly mob of Saturnine no-goods. **1965** *New Yorker* (Jan. 23) 2: A musical about a no-good who makes it big in Hollywood.

no-gooder *n.* a NO-GOOD.
　　1936 in *OEDS*: Oh you dirty no-gooder, you don't mean me no good. **1956** *Time* (Mar. 19) 8: Not the part that says I am an old codger, a boozer, and no-gooder, all of which is doubtless true. **1965** *N.Y. Times* (Mar. 28) I 79: The affluent, the self-supporting of Appalachia, have become increasingly bitter in recent years over those they call the "no-gooders up the hollows." **1968** *Business Week* (Mar. 9) 4: Treat them like third-class citizens and eventually we'll wind up with misfits and no-gooders. **1974–77** A. Hoffman *Property Of* 148: He's a no-gooder, that one. *a***1988** C. Adams *More Straight Dope* 22: Some apparently evil-minded no-gooders.

no-goodnik *n.* [NO-GOOD + -NIK, perh. partially based on Russ *negódnik* 'good-for-nothing'] NO-GOOD. Usu. *joc.*
　　1936 S.J. Perelman, in M. Crane *Roosevelt* 71: Altogether a five-star no goodnick! **1949** A. Capp *Li'l Abner* (synd. cartoon strip) (June 5): Nogoodnik. **1951** *Sat. Eve. Post* (Nov. 10) 131: Obviously he was a creep, a nogoodnik and a reprehensible spirit. **1958** *Time* (May 5) 13: The service has to use force sometimes to get rid of "nogoodniks." **1960** *Rocky & His Friends* (ABC-TV): The world's biggest no-goodnik, Boris Badenov. **1960** Barber *Minsky's* 10: Their business, they complained, was in a sorry state thanks to moochers, no-goodniks, and schnorrers. **1961** *Bullwinkle* (NBC-TV): And the two no-goodniks ducked behind a nearby rock. **1967–68** von Hoffman *Parents Warned Us* 205: Then the kid who dropped out was a failure or poor or a no-good-nik. **1972** M. Rodgers *Freaky Friday* 42: Well *I* call 'em no-goodniks. **1978** *Nat. Lampoon* (Oct.) 10: So we killed a million people.…They were nogoodniks, all of them. **1981** Sann *Trial* 45: They put him in Sing Sing, that nogoodnik. **1982** *World's Finest Comics* (Oct.) (unp.): I thought I heard some no-goodniks in there! **1987** *New Yorker* (July 13) 26: A no-goodnik.…A blot on the family name. **1988** in MacHovec *Humor* 149: You no-goodniks.

no-go pill *n. Mil.* a sedative; (*also*) an antidiarrheal pill.
　　1961 L.G. Richards *TAC* 51: "No-go" pills, or "stop" pills, as some docs call them—seco barbitol. They…put a man to sleep. **1962** Tregaskis *Vietnam Diary* 77: "No go" pills [are] handy for the emergency of drippy tummy.

no-hoper *n.* a hopeless case.
　　***1943** in *OEDS*: No-hoper, an outsider [in horse racing]. ***1944** in Partridge *DSUE* 1297: "Is he bad?" I asked.—"A no-hoper, Mick. Copped two in the guts." **1956** *Sat. Eve. Post* (July 7) 75: Bush boys without shoes or shirts…no-hopers getting away from their pasts, [etc.]. **1978** E. Thompson *Devil to Pay* 322: The no-hopers and idiot aspirants. **1979** *Toronto Star* (Dec. 8) G1: "Reform school" has connotations of locked doors and no-hopers doomed to a life of crime.

noise *n.* **1.** nonsensical talk; (*hence*) foolishness; often in phr. (*vulgar*) **to hell with** [or **fuck**] **that noise!**
　　1871 Thomes *Whaleman* 379: Stop your noise, you fool.…You

don't know what you is talkin' about. **1902** T.A. Dorgan, in Zwilling *TAD Lexicon* 118: Get away from that noise. What would I do with a dog. **1909** T.A. Dorgan, in Zwilling *TAD Lexicon* 118: "An Silkie Hattie Harry's duckey wuckey doan likeum whiskers on um sweetie facie." "Oh take that noise outside." **1920** Haslett *Luck on the Wing* 105 [ref. to 1918]: Where do you get the noise of firing at a friendly plane. **1929** Brecht *Downfall* 142: The hell with that noise. *ca***1935** in Barkley *Sex Cartoons* 64: So I said to hell with that noise. **1936** Moffitt & Solkow *Murder with Pictures* (film): You can can that virtuous noise, Gerard. **1956** Ross *Hustlers* 26: To hell with this noise. **1957** Myrer *Big War* 11: Shake…what should I shake for?…Frig that noise. **1959** Cochrell *Barren Beaches* 29: They'd rather look at the boys than ask if you got it. To hell with that noise. **1963** T.I. Rubin *Sweet Daddy* 21: What a bird brain—went in for all this horoscope noise and all. **1974** in Mamet *Sexual Perversity* 65: I can see her fucking snatch.…Where does she get off with that noise? **1988** *CBS This Morning* (CBS-TV) (July 6): Look at that bull [in Pamplona, Spain]. Forget *that* noise! **1990** R. Herman, Jr. *Force of Eagles* 346: Fuck that noise.

2. a self-important person.
　　***1908** in *OEDS*: A lot of people are beginning to think that Teddy's a mere noise. **1930** Lait *On the Spot* 75: Stools an' lice crawl to a noise like Kinky King.

3. *Narc.* heroin.
　　1928 *AS* III (Feb.) 254: *Noise.* Heroin. **1942–49** Goldin et al. *DAUL: Noise.* The narcotic heroin.

4. information, news.
　　1942 *ATS* 445: Information.…*inside dope, the know, noise.* **1975** Univ. Tenn. student: [Referring to newspaper item:] Hey, get this noise. This old lady was having trouble starting her car and this cop was driving by.…

¶ In phrases:

¶ **bring the noise** *Rap Music.* to have a wild party or a good time; play music.
　　[**1972–73** in M.J. Bell *Brown's Lounge* 32: [Troublesome patrons] brought noise with them [and] heated up the bar.] **1988** "Public Enemy" *Bring the Noise* [rap song title]. *a***1994** Smitherman *Black Talk* 70: Bring/Brang the noise! Turn on and/or up the music.…Let's par-tay! **1996** *Bring In 'da Noise, Bring In 'da Funk* [title of musical].

¶ **make a noise like a ——** (used in var. usu. joc. phrs.). Cf. *make like a——* s.v. MAKE, *v.*
　　1902 Townsend *Fadden & Mr. Paul* 274: "Climb a tree, and make a noise like a nut," I says. **1908** McGaffey *Show Girl* 11: If you make a noise like a dollar bill…you're liable to be the center of a raging mob. **1917** Oemler *Slippy McGee* 27: And if some people knew how to be obliging they'd make a noise like a hoop and roll away, so's other people could pound their ear in peace. **1921** Dos Passos *Three Soldiers* 366 [ref. to 1918]: Couldn't you just make a noise like a hoop an' roll away. **1959** Sterling *Wake of the Wahoo* 88: Why don't you make a noise like a depth charge and go off?

¶ **red noise** tomato soup.
　　1936 *AS* (Feb.) 45: [Soda fountain N.Y.C.:] *Splash of Red Noise.* Bowl of tomato soup. **1942** *ATS* 103: Red noise, splash of red noise, *tomato soup.*

noise tool *n. West.* a firearm. *Joc.*
　　1922 P.A. Rollins *Cowboy* 49 [ref. to *a*1900]: The average puncher…had better use for his money than the purchase of ammunition to be fired through a "noise tool" at a tree or can.

no joy see s.v. JOY, *n.*

no-knock *n. Police.* a no-knock search warrant.
　　1970 in *OEDS*: John Mitchell puts on a happy face and suggests that the name of the "no-knock" law be changed to something more felicitous, like "quick-entry." **1984** Caunitz *Police Plaza* 249: Why the request for the "No Knock"?

nola *n.* [perh. fr. *Nola,* female given name] an effeminate homosexual man.—usu. used derisively.
　　1931 *AS* VI (Aug.) 440: *Nola.* A homosexual. **1942–49** Goldin et al. *DAUL: Nola.* (South) A passive pederast. **1965** *Time* (Mar. 26) 23B: Homosexual…nola…queer…faggot [etc.].

nolly *n. Law.* an entry of nolle prosequi.
　　1871 in *DA*: I now enter a *nolle* in his case. **1981** *Texas Monthly* (Jan. 1982) 148: A "nolly"—prosecutorese for a dismissal.

no-load *n.* a gloomy or lazy individual.

1929 Botkin *Folk-Say I* 111: A *no-load* or a *no-load guy* is any [taxi] driver with pessimistic tendencies. **1983–86** G.C. Wilson *Supercarrier* 220: A "no load" [is] navalese for someone who does not carry his share of the work load on the ship.

no-man's land *n. Mil.* servicewomen's quarters. *Joc.*

    1942–47 *ATS* (Supp.) 19: Servicewomen's quarters. *No man's land.* **1961** L.E. Young *Virgin Fleet* 66 [ref. to WWII]: You're getting awful close to no-man's-land….That's enough of that.

nomenclature *n. Mil.* a name or the like. *Joc.*

    1941 *New Yorker* (Feb. 22) 45: Andy was the corporal of a squad that numbered some real museum pieces in nomenclature….Matiejus Kristinavicius, Joseph Wszolek, William Bazilianskas, and Stanley Zjumnjmnt. **1956** *AS* XXXI 193: *Nomenclature.* Used facetiously to denote an individual's name, rank and serial number. **1994** *Metropulse* (Knoxville, Tenn.) (June 3) 11: Pigeon Forge's nomenclature is…more exotic.

nominate *v.* ¶ In phrase: **nominate your poison** see s.v. POISON.

noncom *n. Mil.* a noncommissioned officer. Now *colloq.* or *S.E.*

    1834 *Mil. & Nav. Mag. of U.S.* (Apr.) 122: But although I am only a *non com*…I would ask, is it *republican?* **1845** *Recollections of the U.S. Army* 137: My name is Stanley—Sergeant Stanley,—or as my brother "Non Coms" call me, "Long Ned." **1847** in Smith & Judah *Gringos* 428: At the report of the pistol the non-com officer in charge of the guard ordered them to my assistance. **1848** "Corporal of the Guard" *Private* 3: A "plain, unvarnished tale" of facts, mysteries, miseries & c., of "non com.'s" and "high privates" during the Mexican War. *Ibid.* 21: Noncom's. **1862** in Bensill *Yambill* 37: We are drilled almost entirely by the "Non Coms." **1862** in S.C. Wilson *Column South* 7: Our non-coms are in the mounted drill to-day. **1863** in A.A. Siegel *For Glory of Union* 170: Several other "non-coms." and privates. **1865** in H. Johnson *Talking Wire* 238: It is not often that non-coms are reduced at their own request. **1878** B. Benson *Civil War Book* 57: It may be the non-com officer wasn't always as well pleased as he might be. **1878** Mulford *Indians* 43: He was the best *non-com* in the 7th. **1884** Johnson & Buel *Civil War* I 158 [ref. to 1861]: Mingled with these gaudy, useless officers were citizens in search of fat contracts, privates, "non-com's" and officers whose uniforms were well worn and faded, showing that they were from encampments and active service. **1899** Creager *14th Ohio* 89: Many a good "non-com" received his chevrons. **1900** Reeves *Bamboo Tales* 19: The "non-coms" resigned in a body. **1906** M'Govern *Bolo & Krag* 63: Only a few nights before the non com in charge…had erected a tent for his guard on such night. **1907** Bush *Enlisted Man* 22: The non-coms paid no attention to them and hustled them up a little more. **1915** Braley *Workaday World* 149: I was sick of young Lieutenants an' of non-coms too. **1917** Morse *Letters* 13: Bruno gives the non-coms no end of trouble.

non-con *n.* a religious nonconformist.

    ***1698–99** "B.E." *Dict. Canting Crew: Non-con,* one that don't conform to the church of *England.* ***1717** in D'Urfey *Pills* I 258: And Toleration has each *Non Con.* ***a1720** in D'Urfey *Pills* I 21: A Canting Bleer-Ey'd *Non Con.* **1786** *N.H. Spy* (Portsmouth, N.H.) (Nov. 17) 2: A formal non-con. ***1796** Grose *Dict. Vulgar Tongue* (ed. 3): *Non-con.* A nonconformist, presbyterian, or any other dissenter.

no-neck *n.* a usu. thickset person having a very short neck (regarded as a sign of oafishness).—also used attrib.

    1955 T. Williams *Cat on Hot Tin Roof* I: One of those no-neck monsters hit me with a hot buttered biscuit so I have t' change! **1961** H. Ellison *Memos* 119: You program them to be no-necks; to be nerds. **1988** Dye *Outrage* 22: Someday they'll be studying that little no-neck maggot in the War College. [***1995** *Absolutely Fabulous* (BBC-TV): In No-Neck, Virginia.]

non est *adj. Stu.* [< L 'it is not'] absent; nonexistent.

    ***1870** (cited in *OED*). **1903** Ade *Society* 82: He never interfered with any of her Arrangements, for the Reason that when the Arrangements were being made he was Non Est. **1909** (quot. at NOSE POKER). ***1945** in *OEDS*: Eggs are practically *non est,* unless one has hens.

nonhacker *n. Mil.* a lazy or incompetent trainee or other person. Cf. HACK², *v.,* 3.b. [Quots. generally ref. to Vietnam War.]

    1978 Hasford *Short-Timers* 5: My orders are to weed out all nonhackers. **1978** (quot. at *pack the gear* s.v. GEAR, *n.*). **1984–85** Schneider & Schneider *Sound Off!* 27: You're a nonhacker and you're not going to make it. *a***1986** K.W. Nolan *Into Laos* 194: A unit…beefed up with heads and nonhackers…shirkers. *a***1990** Helms *Proud Bastards* 32: A true fuckup.…A nonhacker.

no-no *n.* **1.** *Joc.* [orig. baby talk; pop. as a catch phr. by NBC-TV's *Rowan & Martin's Laugh-In* (1968)] something that is forbidden or prohibited. Now *colloq.*

    1942 *ATS* 309: *No-no, very bad no-no,* something that should not be done. **1968** *Rowan & Martin's Laugh-In* (NBC-TV): That's a no-no! **1970** in *DAS* (ed. 3): The company says mustaches are a no-no. **1971** Dahlskog *Dict.* 42: No-no, *n.* Something forbidden or taboo. **1978** Maupin *Tales* 98: I was honest with a client. The Ultimate No-No. **1978** Rascoe & Stone *Who'll Stop Rain?* (film): What you've got to sell is a no-no around here. **1978** *N.Y. Times Mag.* (June 25) 19: Einstein had divided by zero at one point in his calculations. This is a no-no in mathematics. **1980** L. Fleischer & C. Gore *Fame* 57: All the jeans Doris owned were full-cut and faded—two no-no's this year. **1982** *N.Y. Post* (Aug. 27) 5: A no-no by the Marines. **1982** Basel *Pak Six* 14: The worst thing a new pilot can do is lose his leader. It's a no-no. **1985** M. Baker *Cops* 226: That's a no-no. You don't hit prisoners in court. **1987** *Time* (June 8) 36: [In] Rumania…reform is a no-no. **1988** *Mad* (Oct.) 7: Wrath is strictly a no-no. **1991** D. Anderson *In Corner* 59: Putting professional input into an amateur is a no-no.

2. *Baseball.* a no-hitter.

    1988 *N.Y. Post* (June 6) 61: "I thought he was pretty awesome.…I thought today was the day for the no-no." Gooden had taken a no-hitter into the eighth inning one other time. **1991** *N.Y. Times Mag.* (June 2) 56: The no-hitter talk takes on new earnestness.…Dreams of a no-no bounce up the middle.

non-reg *adj. Mil.* nonregulation; unauthorized.

    1918 Grider *War Birds* 148: He saw these three disreputable looking Americans with non-reg uniforms and slacks. **1918** in Rossano *Price of Honor* 95: Strictly non-reg in the navy. **1986** R. Zumbro *Tank Sgt.* 111 [ref. to 1967–68]: The "wheels" in Headquarters were always in need of a detail NCO…who can be depended on…and not get caught if his methods have to be a little "nonreg."

noodge var. NUDGE.

noodle *n.* [var. or alter. NODDLE] **1.a.** the head; (*hence*) the intelligence; mind; in phr. **off (one's) noodle** insane. [Despite the spelling *noddle,* *1664 quot. appears to require a rhyme already tending toward that of the present form; the spelling in 1790 quot. is perh. of questionable accuracy, as Tucker elsewhere employs *noddle* (see 1793 quot. s.v. NODDLE). The form *noodle* is poorly attested before the 20th C.]

    [***1664** S. Butler *Hudibras,* in *OED* s.v. *fop-doodle:* Where sturdy Butchers broke your Noddle,/And handl'd you like a Fop-doodle.] [**1790** in St. G. Tucker *Poems* 139: Destruction in each noodle brewing.] ***1803** in Wetherell *Adventures* 87: Drawing my Pistol from my belt [I] gave him the contents thro his noodle and laid him in the water. **1806** in Tyler *Verse* 139: The sacred laurel must not be debas'd,/Nor on a zany actor's noodle plac'd. ***1821** *Real Life in Ireland* 80: Morrison's port now began to work in the noodle of Captain Gramachree. [**1850** Butler *Barnum's Parnassus* 49: O what fancies through my noodle [*sic*]/Jump Jim Crow!/Hail Columbia! Yankee Doodle!/Round about we go!] **1904** T.A. Dorgan, in Zwilling *TAD Lexicon* 60: Others are there with the wise noodles and will cop the green. **1906** M'Govern *Bolo & Krag* 23: The idea of me taking on again in the Army never once entered into my noodle. **1908** in H.C. Fisher *A. Mutt* 40: Dr. Day…was called in to examine the state of Mutt's noodle. **1908** W.G. Davenport *Butte & Montana* 135: The boy…has his noodle sharpened. **1910** T.A. Dorgan, in *N.Y. Eve. Jour.* (Apr. 7) 16: Wow!!! Right on his noodle. **1912** Lowrie *Prison* 55: I'd do ten years…t' git at pipe dream outer dese judges' solid ivory noodles. **1914** Kreymborg *Edna* 24: Can't you get that through your thick little noodle? **1918** *N.Y. Eve. Jour.* (Aug. 2) 14: Even the most illiterate fan bows low before what he terms "the old noodle." **1918** *Chi. Sunday Tribune* (Feb. 10) V (unp.): I got a lot more back in my noodle. **1925** in Hammett *Knockover* 30: I knocked him on the noodle with my borrowed crutch. **1926** Norwood *Other Side of Circus* 143: That's the way Nellie's noodle used to work. **1927** in Dundes *Mother Wit* 200: Get that stuff out of your noodle. **1928–30** Fiaschetti *Gotta Be Rough* 39: Sherlock Holmes kept his sources of information deep inside of his noodle. **1929–30** in *DAS:* I've been as near off my noodle…as a sane man can get. **1934** H. Miller *Tropic of Cancer* 36: I'm going to put down everything that goes on in my noodle. **1943** Wolfert *Tucker's*

People 69: Only a man…has to…use his noodle. **1945** in *OEDS:* She's off her noodle. **1947** Schulberg *Harder They Fall* 160: I feel like I'm going off my noodle. **1952** Black *Critical Thinking* (ed. 2) 171: A friend is "understandably confused," an enemy "has gone a bit off his noodle." **1953** Brossard *Bold Saboteurs* 7: He was a wee bit off his noodle, you see. **1964** Persky & Denoff *Dick Van Dyke Show* (CBS-TV): I think there's something wrong with *your* noodle. **1967** Talbot *Chatty Jones* 91: As soon as that goop back there starts usin' his noodle. **1992** G. Wolff *Day at the Beach* 119: I use the old noodle…remember to bring the tickets.

b. thinking; cogitation.

    1930 Lait *On Spot* 5: This calls for some noodle.

2. a simpleton (now *S.E.*); (*hence*) (*obs.*) a lunatic.

    *1753 in *OED:* The words ninnyhammer, noodle, and numscull, are frequently bandied to and fro betwixt them. **1775** in F. Moore *Songs & Ballads of Revolution* 93: And to look on the ground like a parcel of noodles,/And sing, how the Yankees have beaten the Doodles. **1782** in Trumbull *Satiric Poems* 134: Out went they not each native Noodle. *1785 (quot. at DOODLE, 1.a.). **1838** [Haliburton] *Clockmaker* (Ser. 2) 200: The shaller-pated noodles that it belongs to. **1860** Sleeper *In Forecastle* 11: Ridiculous! You are a noodle for thinking of such a thing. **1903** in "O. Henry" *Works* 221: You tell me they pinched old Redruth for the noodle villa [*i.e.,* lunatic asylum] just because he said he was King Solomon? **1925** Mullin *Scholar Tramp* 97 [ref. to *ca*1912]: There wasn't an insane asylum in all New England in which he hadn't at some time or other been an orderly. He could stand taking care of the noodles just so long, he said, and then, to keep himself from going cuckoo, he would hit the Road for a while. **1951** *New Yorker* (Apr. 28) 62: The most misguided and sadistic group of noodles in the entire history of show business. **1951** *New Yorker* (May 12) 106: The reality slides away and Sarah becomes any noodle who can't decide which of two brothers to have. **1973** *Harper's* (Apr.) 43: It didn't matter at all if an officer thought I was hard core or a noodle.

3. the penis; DOODLE, 2.—usu. considered vulgar. *Joc.*

    1975 Wambaugh *Choirboys* 225: Too much booze makes a limp noodle. **1978** Schrader *Hardcore* 63: All you've got is a limp noodle. **1978** in *Maledicta* VI (1982) 23: Penis…noodle. **1992** *Good Morning, America* (ABC-TV) (Oct. 12): "Just use your noodle!" "I do. Whenever I have sex." [Laughter].

¶ In phrase:

¶ **flip (one's) noodle** see *flip (one's) lid* s.v. FLIP, *v.*

noodle *v.* **1.a.** *Music,* esp. *Jazz.* to play usu. improvised turns, runs, etc., founded on a particular note or notes; (*also*) to play a sequence of notes in an casual manner, esp. in rehearsal; improvise or play around with a musical passage.

    1937 in *OEDS: Noodling,* the tuning up of musical instruments with practice runs, trills, scales, etc. **1940** in R.S. Gold *Jazz Lexicon: Noodlin'* [song title]. **1952** *Sat. Eve. Post* (May 10) 131: A few musicians…were noodling half-heartedly with a tune. **1958** *Time* (Aug. 4) 34: She can swing upbeat ballads in a light-textured voice or noodle a bit of the blues in tones as soft as velvet. **1959** Kanin *Blow Up a Storm* 6: Woody rode the main line, and I noodled around: filling in or playing rhythm figures, and sometimes locking in harmonically with him for a phrase or a break. **1960** Brunn *Orig. Dixieland Jazz Band* 164: Larry Shields will go down in history as the father of the "noodling" style [on the clarinet]. **1964** *New Yorker* (Feb. 15) 125: Since all the instrumentalists were noodling irresponsibly, the result was pure chaos. **1985** Sawislak *Dwarf* 164: They noodled a few minutes with their instruments and launched into their opening number. **1989** S. Robinson & D. Ritz *Smokey* 117: He noodled some more, and the shit sounded even better. **1993** *Wilson Qly.* (Summer) 24: Arty organ noodling. **1994** N.Y.C. book editor, age 25: Sitting at the piano and just noodling along.

b. to play (around); fiddle.

    1973 *Harper's* (Aug.) 86: Noodling about in the foreground, then retreating again an inch or two above the horizon. **1982** *California* (Oct.) 117: All this dizzy noodling with film history is to no real effect.

2.a. *Intrans.* to think; brainstorm; (now usu., with diminished force) to muse.

    1942 *ATS* 185: *Nobby noodling,* clever thinking. **1945** *AS* (Oct.) 233: I finally got down to work and really noodled for about an hour. **1949** *Sat. Eve. Post* (Dec. 17) 44: Noodling around, Gould decided the hero ought to be a modernized Sherlock Holmes. **1960** Matheson *Beardless*

Warriors 168: Let me do the noodling, right? **1964** *Time* (Jan. 31) 69: The President and his top brass are noodling around a vast baize table at the Pentagon. **1969** *Business Week* (Feb. 1) 72: Some of his staff…are back in the chrome-plated Fifth Avenue offices… "noodling" with numbers. **1975** *Pop. Science* (Sept.) 105: Filling the…space under the flat roof at the rear required some careful noodling. **1978** *New West* (Sept. 25) 68: Hill assembled a scale model of what he wanted to do, noodled around with it for a while, and in 1936 began working. **1982** *N.Y. Times* (Oct. 7) A27: Noodling around about politics that was was fun. **1996** *Morning Edition* (Nat. Pub. Radio) (July 5): President Reagan was noodling about how the nations would unite if they were threatened by an alien force.

b. *Trans.* to plan or consider thoughtfully; mull over; explore (an idea); (*also*) to think up.—usu. constr. with *out* or *up.*

    1950 *Pop. Science* (Sept.) 252: When a piece of equipment doesn't do the job as they think it should be done, American farmers traditionally noodle up their own version. **1952** *Sat. Eve. Post* (Sept. 20) 95: "I already thought of something." "Think some more. I'll noodle it around too." **1953** *Pop. Science* (Feb.) 156: Friends who saw and admired his work asked him to noodle up their own cars. **1961** H. Ellison *Memos* 192: The Captain said something short and brusque, and Tooley noodled it out and said something else. **1971** Dahlskog *Dict.* 42: *Noodle*…To think about (something); to mull (something) over, as: to *noodle* an idea before acting upon it. **1981** *TV Guide* (May 9) 1: I'll brief you on the subject and we can noodle it together. **1983** *Business Week* (Nov.) 78: We haven't really noodled out what we're going to do.

noodlehead *n.* a blockhead; NOODLE, 2. Hence **noodle-headed,** *adj.* Also **noodlebrain.**

    1919 *DN* V 61: *Noodle-head,* a dull person. "That old lady has always been a *noodle-head.*" New Mexico. **1976** Univ. Tenn. grad. student: I've got some real noodlebrains in that class. **1982** *Harper's* (Aug.) 63: "Gawps" is the perfect word to catch the flavor of Jimmy Stewart's noodleheaded awe. **1984** *Psychol. Today* (Apr.) 74: This is not, however, another noodle-headed plea for more "self-actualization." **1992** *Simpsons* (Fox-TV): Noodleheads!

noodnik var. NUDNIK.

noogie *n.* [orig. unkn.] **1.** *Juve.* an act of rubbing or striking a person's head with the knuckles, esp. as a penalty. Also as *v.*

    1972 N.Y.U. student: A *noogie* is a kind of a punch or a jab you give someone with your third and middle finger. You do it on the forehead or the shoulder. **1978** C. Miller *Animal House* 14: Furious, Larry gave Kent a hard noogie punch on the arm. **1978** *Saturday Night Live* (NBC-TV): Ha! Noogies for that! **1979** *L.A. Times* (June 27) IV 1: Deliver a noogie to his head. **1983** S. King *Christine* 162: I kept poking my fingers at him, giving him what we used to call "side-noogies" when we were little kids. *Ibid.* 163: He poked me in the stomach. "Gut-noogies, Dennis!" *Ibid.* 228: Want some head-noogies. **1988** *Geraldo!* (NBC-TV) (July 7): He'd get me on the top of the head and give me *one* noogie—I mean! **1990** *Saved by the Bell* (NBC-TV): It keeps the football team from giving me noogies. **1993** P. Munro *U.C.L.A. Slang II: Noogie v.* to rub one's knuckles on the top of (someone's) head: to give noogies to. **1995** *Phoenix* (Univ. Tenn.) (Spring) 25: After every tear-filled noogie and groin crunching wedgy my brother would say, "Don't ever think I'm going to let you win." **1996** *L.A. Times* (Apr. 18) E15: Usually I give him a noogie. **1996** *CNN Saturday Morning* (CNN-TV) (Apr. 27): Who's noogieing whom?

2. usu. *pl.* a testicle. *Joc.*

    1985 Northport, N.Y., woman, age 33: It's better than freezing your noogies off.

¶ In phrase:

¶ **tough noogies!** hard luck! too bad!

    1972 N.Y.U. student: *Tough noogies!* is something we used to say [*ca*1959] for *tough shit!* **1979** Kunstler *Wampanaki Tales* 19: Tough noogies, then. **1984** *L.A. Times* (Jan. 30) II 5: Tough noogies, sis. **1995** in *DARE.* **1997** *CNN & Co.* (CNN-TV) (Jan. 7): Tough noogies!

nook *n.* NOOKIE, 1. [The otherwise unexplained *nook-dah* in 1984–87 quot. app. represents Anglo-Vietnamese pidgin.]

    1979 G. Wolff *Duke of Deception* 181 [ref. to 1950's]: Plenty of nook up here in Maine. Went the distance with that babe from Walker's. **1984–87** Ferrandino *Firefight* 54 [ref. to Vietnam War]: Got any good nook? *Ibid.* 74: Number one *nook-dah.*

nookie *n.* [orig. uncert.] **1.** sexual intercourse or a sexual partner. Also **nookey, nooky, nucky.**

1928 Bodenheim *Georgie May* 11: He had a weakness fo' slim nooky with real blonde hair. **1928** Hecht & MacArthur *Front Page* I i: *Mollie Malloy enters. She is a North Clark Street [Chicago] tart...* Well, well! Nookie! **1929–30** Dos Passos *42d Parallel* 345: He was getting his nookie every night. **1929–31** J.T. Farrell *Young Lonigan* 124: Schreiber...liked his nooky, and he was always mixed up with some woman or other. **1931** J.T. Farrell *McGinty* 163: A guy can't have a decent piece of nooky for fun. **1934** "J.M. Hall" *Anecdota* 109: N stands for Nooky,/The tired workman's joy. *Ibid.* 180: A lady likes her nooky. **1936** Kingsley *Dead End* 725: Boy, some nice nooky, huh? **1938** in Randolph *Pissing in Snow* 11: But poor nooky is better than none. **1938** "Justinian" *Americana Sexualis* 29: *Nookie.* n. Sexual intercourse. C. 19, Br. mostly. Literary and facetious euphemism in C. 20, Br. & U.S. Generally, *make nookie* or *do nookie.* **1941** *Chippie Wagon* 33: We know when a dame is nookie or not. **1941** Schulberg *Sammy* 240: Hey, fellers, lookit Sammy tryin' to get his first nookey! **1943** in P. Smith *Letter from Father* 321: She loved her "nookey." **1944** Bellow *Dangling Man* 85: One nice thing about the coast, though,...the nooky situation is awfully good where there aren't too many soldiers. **1948** Wolfert *Act of Love* 158: Maybe he's got some nucky lined up for himself. **1956** G. Green *Last Angry Man* 77: Too much money, too much good booze, too much nooky. **1960** in J. O'Hara *Sel. Letters* 343: I hope you will go to bat on the word nooky. **1965** W. Crawford *Bronc Rider* 170: Looky, here's nooky! Which one's mine, Del? **1965** Friedman *Totempole* 274: "Nooky-nooky!" Melody shouted at a young woman. **1968** Heard *Howard St.* 70: She sure got hot nookie, huh, Sy? **1968** Yglesias *Orderly Life* 39: I got to get some nookey too. **1965–70** T. Morrison *Bluest Eye* 64: They do not drink, smoke, or swear, and they still call sex "nookey." **1970** Sorrentino *Steelwork* 83: Kill some barbarians, get some good nookie. **1971** Terrell *Bunkhouse Papers* 105: A man should have his nooky before he goes out herdin' sheep. **1973** N.Y.U. student: *Nooky-nooky* means sex. **1974** Strasburger *Rounding Third* 18: Carter, let's pull over right now and make nooky. **1988** Poyer *The Med* 142: I wasn't the only one scarfing up a little nookie at Lily's. **1991** K. Douglass *Viper Strike* 61: Deprived of nookie. **1996** M. Kearney *Southeastern La. Coll.* (May): *Nookie*—intercourse—They went to Lover's Lane for a little nookie.

2. the vagina.—usu. considered vulgar.

1968 R. Beck *Trick Baby* 218: To make the top of the nookie love it, you must shove the collar back to your balls on your putz. **1970** Landy *Underground Dict.*: *Nookie...*Vagina. **1972** C. Major *Dict. Afro-Amer Sl.*: *Nookie*: Vagina.

nookie bookie *n.* a person who provides prostitutes for customers; pimp or madam. *Joc.*

1942 Davis & Wolsey *Call House Madam* 266: Why wasn't I someone else—anybody but a nookie-bookie. **1945** in R.A. Freeman *Mighty Eighth* 310: Nooky Booky IV [name on P-51K Mustang]. **1953** in Dundes & Pagter *Alligators* 24: *Pimp.* A crack salesman, a nookie bookie. **1962** Crump *Killer* 111: All you nookie bookies has got dyin' mothers. *a***1982** Berry *Semper Fi* 272 [ref. to 1945]: He...dealt in real good-looking young things. To top it off, his name actually sounded like "nukie bookie," which went over great with the men. We had a special armband made for him with the big letters "nukie bookie" on it.

nookie house *n.* a brothel.

1982 "W.T. Tyler" *Rogue's March* 217: "That raises an interesting point."..."You birds couldn't raise a bamboo dildo in a Bangkok nooky house."

nooner *n.* **1.** an alcoholic drink taken at midday.

1836 in McCall *Ltrs. from Frontiers* 313: I took up the black bottle from which we had taken our *noon-er,* still half full of whisky. *****1949** Granville *Sea Slang* 165: *Nooner.* A midday drink in the wardroom. **1980** Mack & Connell *Naval Trads.* (ed. 5) 291: The first drink, a "nooner." **1980** (quot. at (2), below).

2. an act of copulation engaged in at midday, as during a lunch hour. Cf. MATINEE.

1973 Gwaltney *Destiny's Chickens* 59: He liked to come home...and...pull off a nooner. **1974** Loken *Come Monday Morning* 186: She...wants to meet you somewhere for a little nooner. **1980** Ciardi *Browser's Dict.* 274: *Nooner* labels any midday habit, as a drink or a sex act. **1981** R.O. Butler *Alleys* 154: Bring back the nooner. Take a hooker to lunch. **1986** R. Walker *AF Wives* 184: Tad...pulled her into the bedroom for what he called a "nooner." **1990** *Night Court*

(NBC-TV): So your girlfriend's getting married. She'll still be available for nooners. **1993** *Mystery Sci. Theater* (Comedy Central TV): "Nooner. Come on."..."No time." **1996** *Melrose Place* (Fox-TV): Let's not make *nooners* a habit!

3. any activity engaged in at midday.

1980 (quot. at (2), above). **1988** Poyer *The Med* 101: He kept a Florida tan current with nooners on the flight deck.

noosed *adj.* married. *Joc.*

*****1617** in *F & H* V 64: I'll take the freedom of sending for our noble commodore and his lady too, who are by this time noozed. *****1698–99** "B.E." *Dict. Canting Crew*: *Nooz'd,* or caught in a *Nooze,* married. **1859** Matsell *Vocab.* 59: *Noosed.* Married.

nope *interj.* [*no* + excrescent *-p*] no. Cf. YUP. Now *colloq.*

1888 in J. Farmer *Amer.*: "I suppose you will be a literary man, when you grow up." "Nope," said the little boy..."Literary nuthin'! I'm goin' to be a ten-thousand-dollar cook." **1895** *Harper's* (June) 152: Did you see Billy Wilkins?...Nope. **1897** *Chi. Tribune* (July 25) 15: *Nope*—No—Purely Kansas. "The Legislature said nope to Peffer." **1902** *N.Y. Eve. Jour.* (Dec. 4) 1: "Got a warrant?" "Nope!" **1902** Harriman *Ann Arbor* 89: "Nope," was the dogged reply. **1913** A. Palmer *Salvage* 145: Nope...Don't care much whether I ever start at all. **1924** P. Marks *Plastic Age* 28: Nope, I can't go walking. **1949** *Sat. Eve. Post* (June 4) 55: "Does Steve know I'm coming?" "Nope."

nord *n.* usu. *pl.* [var. NARD] a testicle.

1966 Manus *Mott the Hoople* 28: Well, goddammit, I'll let you have it in the nords with this bottle.

nork *n.* usu. *pl.* [perh. fr. *Norco,* an Austral. butter manufacturer whose label once featured a cow's udder] a woman's breast. Esp. Austral. E; *rare* in U.S.

*****1962** in Wilkes *Dict. Austral. Colloq.*: Honey, that sweater—one deep breath and your norks will be in my soup. *****1966**, *****1970** in Wilkes *Dict. Austral. Colloq.* *****1973** in Wilkes *Dict. Austral. Colloq.*: Hits herself in the eye with an independent nork. **1989** *Maledicta* X 52: Knockers...*jugs...norks* [etc.]. *****1990** T. Thorne *Dict. Contemp. Slang*: *Norks...*breasts....The word was introduced to British speakers by the *Barry McKenzie* cartoon series, running in *Private Eye* magazine in the 1960s.

norm *n.* a person who is normal (in some specific sense); (*hence*) *Stu.* a dull or conventional individual. Also **normal.**

1983 *Maclean's* (Nov. 28) 68: A female giantess whose great size affords her no protection from the problems of "normals." **1983–89** K. Dunn *Geek Love* 46: These are written by norms for norms. **1991** *L.A. Times Mag.* (Dec. 22) 42: I think there's a bias against any of these drugs being used in normals. **1994** Danesi *Cool* 57: *Normals* (or *Norms*): Any teen [*sic*] who did not belong to a clique with specific musical, clothing, and grooming standards was a Norm [*ca*1988]. **1995** *Mutant League* (synd. TV series): Mutant League. No Norms Allowed.

Norskie *n.* [< Norw *Norsk,* infl. by *Nor*wegian + -SKI] a Norwegian. Also vars.

1901 *Chi. Tribune* (Aug. 25) 19: "Norskie" Larson will be back. **1920** S. Lewis *Main Street* 31: Lots of Swedes and Norskes there. **1926** B. Traven *Death Ship* ch. XLV: Let's go over to that Norske and have a little talk with them. **1965** LeMay & Kantor *Mission with LeMay* 237: I remember being thrilled by an anecdote of the Great War: about a Minnesota brigade, big Swedes and Nordskis from the wheat farms and lakes and forests up there. **1983** *Prairie Home Companion* (WUOT radio) (Oct. 22): Did you hear the joke about the Norwegian?...He was out getting drunk with all the other Norskies.

north *adj.* ¶ In phrase: **north end of a southbound horse** [or **mule**] HORSE'S ASS. *Joc.* Also vars.

1965 N.Y.C. high school teacher: You look like the north end of a horse going south. **1971** N.Y.U. student: "The north end of a southbound horse" is one I've heard a few times in Washington State. **1987** Univ. Tenn. student: He reminds me of the north end of a southbound mule.

north *adv.* Esp. *Business.* upward in value; in or to a favorable position or situation; in phr. **north of** higher than. Cf. SOUTH.

1983 *Business Week* (June 13) 37: The company has unfunded medical and pension liabilities that are "north of $300 million." **1989** *Time* (Jan. 30) 52: Buy when the market heads north,...sell the instant it flounders. **1993** *N.Y. Times* (Aug. 15) ("Business") 12: Last week, it was about $20 and heading north. **1996** *New Republic* (Apr. 29) 25: A short-term capital gain north of $80,000. **1996** N.Y.C. man, age 27 (coll. J. Sheidlower): Looks like the Knicks' chances are goin' north this year.

north and south *n.* **1.** [rhyming slang] the mouth.
  *****1857** (cited in Partridge *DSUE* 1298.) *****1858** in *OEDS:* "I'll smash your 'glass case,' and damage your 'north and south,'" roared Bill, referring to the *face* and *mouth* of his opponent. **1928** Sharpe *Chicago May* 287: *North and South*—mouth. **1943** Holmes & Scott *Mr. Lucky* (film): He kissed me right on the north and south. *****1960** in T. Thorne *Dict. Contemp. Slang:* What a mouth, what a mouth/What a north and south. **1966** Braly *On the Yard* 175: Now give your north-and-south a rest.

2. a quick visual inspection; UP AND DOWN.
  1916 T.A. Dorgan, in Zwilling *TAD Lexicon* 60: Get out the old slippers, clean off the cheaters and give these the North and South.

northwester *n. Naut.* a strong drink of liquor. Also **nor'wester.**
  *****1830** in *OED:* Pouring him out a northwester. *****1831** B. Hall *Voyages* I 97 [ref. to *ca*1805]: A Northwester...one half of each glass shall consist of rum, and the other half of rum and water. *****1838** Glascock *Land Sharks* II 44: The master-at-arms....swallow[ed] a stiff "norwester." **1899** Boyd *Shellback* 40: Then he filled out a regular nor'wester, and took it down in a couple of gulps.

Norwegian steam *n. Naut.* muscular power, usu. as a method of operating a ship's machinery. *Joc.* Cf. ARMSTRONG, *n. & adj.*
  1944 *AS* XIX 106: Norwegian steam is brute manpower. **1947** R. Boyer *Dark Ship* 53: We got there by Norwegian steam....By rowing. **1950** *N.Y. Times* (Aug. 29) 43: Youthful seafarers,...their biceps and forearms reflecting the degree to which they had appplied "Norwegian steam" in their daily tasks. **1952** H.P. Beck, Jr. *Down-East Songs* 277: Long before sail was abolished the use of the old fashioned "Norwegian steam" was replaced by the steam boiler. **1971** Water *Smugglers* 6 [ref. to 1920]: He's crazy about "Norwegian steam."*...*Any heavy shipboard task involving manual work. **1972** Kaplan & Hunt *Coast Guard* 234: Knowledge, skill and that raw strength which seafarers call "Norwegian steam."

nose *n.* **1.** *Und. & Pris.* **a.** an informer; stool pigeon. [The *****1789 quot. could as well represent the verb.]
  *****1789** G. Parker *Life's Painter* 167: Nose. Snitch. *****1811** *Lex. Balatron.:* Nose. A man who informs or turns king's evidence. *****1812** Vaux *Vocab.:* Nose: A thief who becomes an evidence against his accomplices; also a person who seeing one or more suspicious characters in the streets, makes a point of watching them in order to frustrate any attempt they may make, or to cause their apprehension; also a spy or informer of any description. **1859** Matsell *Vocab.* 59: Nose. A spy; one who informs. "His pal nosed, and the bene cove was pulled for a crack," his partner informed against him, and the good fellow was arrested for burglary. *****1851–61** H. Mayhew, in *F & H* V 66: I'd rather not tell you where....People might think I was a nose. **1930** *Amer. Mercury* (Dec.) 456: Nose, n.: A police spy. "On the Erie it's a nose." **1931–34** Clemmer *Pris. Community* 334: Nose, n. A stool pigeon for the police. **1938** R. Chandler, in *Dime Detective* (Jan.): Some nose puts the bulls on me tomorrow,...what the hell? **1959** Duffy & Lane *Warden's Wife* 233: Extra guards had to be posted in the mess hall when a "nose" warned of an impending riot.

b. *Und.* a detective.
  *****1860** (cited in Partridge *Dict. Und.* 474). *****1877** (cited in Partridge *DSUE* 569). **1925** (cited in Partridge *Dict. Und.* 474). **1933** Ersine *Pris. Slang* 54: Nose, n. A dick.

2. Esp. *Horse Racing.* a very narrow margin of defeat, literally that measurable by the length of a horse's nose (now *S.E.*); (hence, as quasi-adv.) by or as if by a nose.
  1908 in *OEDS:* Flying Cloud slipped by the pair and won on the post by a nose in one forty nine! **1918** (quot. at BENZINE BOARD). **1928** Havlin *Co. A* 29: Jimmie...won the race by a "nose." **1931** D. Runyon, in *Collier's* (May 16) 12: He gets beat three dirty noses the day before at Belmont....In all the years I know Regret he must get beat ten thousand noses, and always they are dirty noses...but of course this is only the way horse racing guys talk. **1973** Walkup & Otis *Race* 241: I always talk about how "we" won a race or "we" got beat a nose.

3. *Winetasting.* distinctive bouquet. Now *S.E.*
  1936 in *OEDS:* The bouquet, or "nose" to use a more technical word, is very important and serves to reveal the characteristics of wines to a connoisseur. **1981** D.E. Miller *Jargon* 300: An interesting molasses and raisin nose with a hint of cantaloupe. *Ibid.* 301: This is

done to appreciate the wine's nose. **1984** Eisen & Farley *Powertalk!* 36: This wine has a good nose. **1985** B. Griffith *Having Fun Yet* 56: I like th' label. It has a fine nose.

4. *Narc.* cocaine. Cf. NOSE CANDY.
  1980 in *Penthouse* (Jan. 1981) 127: For one g of nose and a source of Percodan. *Ibid.* 162: Is the nose really worth Miami prices? **1986** *Miami Vice* (NBC-TV): So you think...[he's] rock-and-rollin' with the nose crowd.

¶ In phrases:

¶ **have (one's) nose full** to be drunk. Cf. SNOOTFULL.
  1917–20 Dreiser *Newspaper Days* 86 [ref. to 1892]: Much drinking...having, as one of the members of the staff used to express it, "his nose full" so often.

¶ **have** [or **get**] **(one's) nose open** *Black E.* to be intensely attracted or cause (someone) to be so attracted; (*Narc.*) to be addicted. Also vars.
  1957 in Leadbitter & Slaven *Blues Records* 110: You Got My Nose Wide Open. **1962** D. Maurer, in McDavid *Mencken's Amer. Lang* 745: A *cat* in hot pursuit of a *chick* or *fox* is said to *have his nose wide open.* **1965** in W. King *Black Anthol.* 302: Making meaningless chit-chat, you know, like she had both our noses open. **1967** in T.C. Bambara *Gorilla* 72: She opened his nose, is how she did it. **1968** I. Reed *Yellow Back Radio* 11: I let her open my nose, Zozo. **1971** Goines *Dopefiend* 135: You still got your nose open for that young bitch, ain't you? **1971** Hilaire *Thanatos* 170: But he's got my nose opened. **1972** *Tuesday Mag.* (synd. TV series): In the idiom, there is the phrase, "to have one's nose open," which means that you are helplessly involved in someone or thing. **1972** A. Kemp *Savior* 14: Them pink devils will hook you on anything to make some bread and get your nose opened. **1972** P. Fenty *Superfly* (film): It's about enough to keep your nose open for about a year. **1973** Wideman *Lynchers* 239: Like maybe he was curious about what kept his brother's nose open so long. **1974** Matthews & Amdur *My Race* 76 [ref. to 1960's]: "Ain't no way you're gonna get Cheryl's nose."..."Getting a nose" was slang for winning a girl's heart. *Ibid.* 80: Before too long, some Southern girl is going to open your nose. **1974** Gober *Black Cop* 151: Yeah, that nigger has got his nose wide behind Sue. **1981** *Psychol. Today* (Feb.) 54: In Tennessee, the vernacular for falling in love is "She really opened my nose." **1985** Eble *Campus Slang* (Oct.) 7: *Nose is wide open*—madly in love...."Your nose is wide open." **1990** Vachss *Blossom* 192: Get his nose open. Make him a deal. *a*1994 N. McCall *Wanna Holler* 106: The fellas said she had my nose open.

¶ **keep (one's) nose clean** to keep out of trouble. Now *colloq.*
  1887 *Lantern* (N.O.) (Oct. 13) 5: There's worse fellows than you looking for it, and if you only keep your nose clean, we'll let you have it. **1904** in F. Remington *Sel. Letters* 351: Keep your nose clean. *****1909** Ware *Passing Eng.* 162: Keep your nose clean (Army). Avoid drink. **1919** Wilkins *Co. Fund* 45: Company Expressions: Keep your nose clean. **1930** Fredenburgh *Soldiers March!* 5: Well, keep your nose clean. **1930** G. Schuyler *Black No More* 118: It'll be hell for you if these babies find you out; so keep your nose clean. **1933** O'Hara *Samarra* ch. ii: I gave you the sawbuck because you just got outa the can. Keep your nose clean. **1953** Roman *Vice Squad* (film): Well, you should've kept your nose clean. **1969** Whittemore *Cop!* 50: Well, as long as you keep your nose clean, right? **1981** "K. Rollins" *Fighter Pilots* 49: Meanwhile keep your nose clean. **1983** *U.S. News & W.R.* (Aug. 22) 45: He was a straight kid who kept his nose clean. He wasn't much for parties. **1984–85** in Schneider & Schneider *Sound Off!* 86: Keep your nose clean.

¶ **on the nose, 1.** on the lookout, esp. as a police informer.
  *****1821** in *F & H* 67: Their ogles were on the roll, under an apprehension that the beaks were "on the nose." **1891** Maitland *Slang Dict.* 189: Nose, "on the," giving information to the police.

2. directly; squarely; exactly.
  1883 *Sporting Life* (May 20) 1 (cited in Nichols *Baseball Term.*). **1885** in Lummis *Letters* 196: Virgil...hit it on the nose...when he made Pious Aeneas say [etc.]. **1907** S. White *Colored Base Ball* 108: He caught the [baseball] on the nose. **1908** in Fleming *Unforget. Season* 109: The ball shook its way across the plate without meeting a bat on the nose more than three times. **1915** in Lardner *Round Up* 44: He'd hit three [pitches] on the nose that afternoon. **1918** Cobb *Glory of the Coming* 36: Say, what'll them Detroits do without old Ty in there bustin' the fast ones on the nose, huh? **1928** C. MacArthur *War Bugs* 71: *Bam!!!!*—right on the nose, not fifty feet from the first gun. **1937**

AS (Apr.) 101: *On the Nose* means that a program is running exactly on schedule. **1957** Bradbury *Dandelion Wine* 19: Two hundred fifty-six on the nose! **1960** Bannon *Journey* 41: "How old are you, Beth, my dear?" "Thirty." "On the nose?" **1974** A. Bergman *Big Kiss-Off* 57: "The other guy was Fenton." "On the nose, Jack. Duke Fenton."

3. *Horse Racing & Gamb.* (of a wager) placed decisively to win.

1923 in Hemingway *Dateline* 436: "Ten on the Dictator in the sixth at Juarez."…"On the nose?" **1930** Pasley *Capone* 56: He seldom played them across the board. He liked to "slap it on the nose." **1931** Wilstach *Under Cover Man* 215: If you play my tips on the nose, and to place, you can't lose. **1935** D.H. Clarke *Regards to Broadway* 141 [ref. to *ca*1918]: I got ten grand on the nose on Hot Stuff in the third this afternoon. **1935** Sistrom *Hot Tip* (film): I hocked my restaurant and put it right on her nose. **1938** Macaulay & Wald *Brother Rat* (film): Bet that on VMI. Right on the nose. **1939** Saroyan *Time of Your Life* I: Ten dollars? Across the board?…No. On the nose. **1944** Breslow & Turcell *Follow the Boys* (film): Alabama in the fifth! Yeah, ten on the nose! **1952** B. Wilder & E. Blum *Stalag 17* (film): Gimme Equipoise—ten on the nose. **1952** A. Sheekman *Young Man with Ideas* (film): He wants me to put two dollars on Mother Machree's nose. **1984** W. Murray *Dead Crab* 10: So we're going to put a thousand on the Flyer's nose.

¶ **pay through the nose** to pay an exorbitant amount. Now *colloq.*

*1672 in *OED:* Made them pay for it most unconscionably and through the nose. *1870 in *F & H* V 69: The Prussians, to whom an immediate supply of these is necessary, have to pay what is vulgarly called through the nose. **1920–21** Witwer *Leather Pushers* 59: Payment Through the Nose. **1946** K. Archibald *Shipyard* 198: Let the suckers do the…paying through the nose. **1982** Whissen *Way with Wds.* 13: A lot of people eat with their eyes—and pay through their noses. **1984** J.R. Reeves *Mekong* 91: Taxpayers [are] payin' through the nose for that! **1988** F. Robinson & B. Stainback *Extra Innings* 49: And you'll pay through the nose.

¶ **put (someone's) nose out of joint** to frustrate; anger; annoy.

*1581 in *F & H* V 68: Who…was verie well assured that it could bee no other than his owne manne that had thrust his nose so farre out of joynte. **1962** G. Olson *Roaring Road* 57: You know, let his nose get back in joint. **1980** Lorenz *Guys Like Us* 8: Besides, you're getting your nose out of joint pointlessly. **1988** Dietl & Gross *One Tough Cop* 17: I have put a few of their noses out of joint.

¶ **show (one's) nose** to make an appearance.

1843 Field *Pokerville* 20: He had been rather nervous about his *debut*, poor fellow, but he had *shown his nose*, and all was right, and he was happy! *1922 in *OEDS:* In Shangolden where he daren't show his nose.

¶ **up (one's) nose** annoying (one); *up (someone's) ass* s.v. ASS.

1967 Wolf *Love Generation* 35: Here I was with that hysterical trial and reporters up my nose, and there I was with a bundle of wet laundry, too, because that had to be done. *1975 in *ODMS* 152: The implication that granny was a little whining knockout with a system that couldn't be bettered…does, I'm afraid, get rather up my nose. **1993** *Nation* (July 26) 127: It's…not so O.K. to get up the noses of the Muslim fanatics. **1993** *New Yorker* (Sept. 20) 88: There is something about Dr. Archer that gets up people's noses.

¶ **[shove it] up your nose** (used as a disparaging and dismissive retort).

1922 in O'Brien *Best Stories of 1922* 15: You can stick your colleges up your nose for all of me. [**1946** Heggen *Mr. Roberts* 84: "Screw you, you silly bastard," he said coldly. "Right through the nose," Billings replied and went out.] **1949** in Bradbury *Illus. Man* 25: Up your nose, you bastard! **1964** Hill *Casualties* 68: F'ya information, smart ass, ol Jerr's got a virus. Shove at up yer nose an try sneezin. **1971** Cole *Rook* 327: Shove it up your nose. **1971** N.Y.U. student: Up your nose, sweetheart! **1974** Cherry *High Steel* xv: Shove it up your nose. I've done the best I could. **1974** U.C.L.A. student: Up your nose with a rubber hose. Up your ass with broken glass. **1976–77** Kernochan *Dry Hustle* 66: Shove your lousy twenty-five bucks up your nose, mister. **1981** *Hill St. Blues* (NBC-TV): In your nose, grandpa! Your mama swims after troop ships! **1989** *Oprah* (ABC-TV): I says, "Up your nose with a rubber *hose!*" **1993** *Donahue* (NBC-TV): Up your nose, buddy!

nose *v.* **1.** *Und.* (see quot.)

1791 [W. Smith] *Confess. T. Mount* 19: *Nose the Cove*, watch the man and see where he goes.

2. *Und.* to inform.—also used trans. Cf. *1789 quot. and note at NOSE, *n.*, 1.a.

*1811 *Lex. Balatron.*: To Nose. To give evidence. To inform. *His pall nosed and he was twisted for a crack*; his confederate turned king's evidence, and he was hanged for burglary. *1820–21 P. Egan *Life in London* 277: No *nosing*, Jerry. *1838 Glascock *Land Sharks* I 194: I tells ye…he's on the prying lay…."Twon't do to be *nosed*, you know." **1859** Matsell *Vocab.* 59: "His pal *nosed*"…His partner informed against him. **1867** *Nat. Police Gaz.* (Mar. 23) 2: The "bursters" were afraid to dispose of the stolen "wedge" to any of the "fences"…in case they should "nose" on them. **1886** (quot. at PUSH).

3. BROWN-NOSE.

1968 Baker, Ladd & Robb *CUSS* 163: *Nose.* Curry favor with a professor. **1972** C. Gaines *Stay Hungry* 113: Look at that bastad now. Nosing Joe.

nosebag *n. Labor.* a lunch bag, lunchbox, or dinner pail.

*1873 (implied at *put* [or *tie*] *on the nosebag*, below). [*a1889–90 Barrère & Leland *Dict. Slang: Nose-bag*…a visitor at a house of refreshment who carries his own victuals.] **1907** "O. Henry" *Heart of West* 149: We want the nosebags crammed with all the Chief Deveries de cuisine. **1908** McGaffey *Show Girl* 32: So I climb into the nosebag without a peep. **1926** *AS* I (Dec.) 652: *Nosebag:* Lunch handed out in paper bag. **1942** *AS* (Dec.) 223: *Nosebag.* Dinner pail. **1942** Sonnichsen *Billy King* 170 [ref. to *a*1900]: He used to "pack his nose bag" with a miner's lunch every day. **1945** Hubbard *R.R. Ave.* 353: *Nosebag*—Lunch carried to work. **1956** Sorden & Ebert *Logger's* 24 [ref. to *a*1925]: *Nose-bag*,…Lunch bucket carried by river drivers. **1958** McCulloch *Woods Wds.* 122: *Nosebag show*—a. A job where it is necessary to pack a lunch every day. b. A piece of work which will take all day away from camp. *a*1979 Toelken *Dyn. of Folklore* 56: *Nosebag* usually a lunch box, but applied to any container used for bringing food into the woods. *Ibid.* 61: Heading down the road to get his nosebag.

¶ In phrase:

¶ **put** [or **tie**] **on the nosebag** to eat a meal. Cf. *put* [or *tie*] *on the feedbag* s.v. FEEDBAG.

*1873 Hotten *Slang Dict.* (ed. 4) s.v. *nose in the manger*: To "put on the nose-bag" is to eat hurriedly, or to eat while continuing at work. *1919 in *Austral. Nat. Dict.:* What's wrong with us putting on our nose-bags? I ain't had a feed all day. **1920** in De Beck *Google* 53: If you're lookin' for Barney, he's in there puttin' on the nose bag. **1922** E. Rice *Adding Machine* 106: Walk in, hang up your hat, an' put on the nose-bag. **1925** *AS* I 139: The use of the term "nose-bag" for lunch has also come down from the old teaming days. The logger "puts on a nose-bag" at the lunch hour, even when he is "over the hump" and "calking cement" in the towns. **1937** Mason & Heerman *Stella Dallas* (film): I'll come back and tie on the nosebag with ya.

nosebleed *adj.* (used allusively in var. constrs. ref. actually or figuratively to great heights). Also as *n.*

1978 *Wash. Post* (Jan. 17) D1 (Nexis): From the nose-bleed altitude of Section 209, the Red Coats marveled at an NHL game. **1981** *N.Y. Times* (Sept. 15) C14 (Nexis): The official…has the best vantage point in the stadium—far better than the people whistling in disagreement from Row XX in the nosebleed section. **1984** N.Y. high school student (coll. J. Sheidlower): I got tickets, but they're way up in the nosebleeds. **1991** *N.Y. Times* (Dec. 18) C24: Every seat in the house is a good seat and even the nose-bleed sections way up high are good. **1993** *New Republic* (Mar. 8) 6: I passed the evening of January 1 in the nosebleed section of the Louisiana Superdome. **1995** *Wired* (Sept.) 80: Raising the level of Congressional hypocrisy to nosebleed heights. **1996** *Entertainment Weekly* (June 14): Whoopi Goldberg is Eddie, a die-hard New York Knicks fan plucked out of the nosebleed bleachers to be the basketball team's head coach. **1996** *Time* (Nov. 4): The business of making loans to people with damaged credit at interest rates that start at high and extend to very high and nosebleed.

nosebleeder *n. Basketball.* (see quot.). *Joc.*

1983 Goldaper & Pincus *How to Talk Basketball* 102: *Nose bleeder*…a player who jumps so high that he can suffer nose bleeds. **1990** P. Dickson *Slang!* 206: *Nose bleeder.* (Basketball) Player who can go high in the air for rebounds.

nose candy *n. Narc.* a crystalline narcotic, as heroin, morphine, or cocaine, to be taken by inhalation.

1925 in Hammett *Big Knockover* 156: Since then Dummy had become an errand boy for whoever would stake him to the price of his necessary nose candy....The Dummy's yellowish eyes should have shown the pinpoint pupils of the heroin addict. **1934** W. Smith *Bessie Cotter* 46: I think she's got a sniff of that nose candy in her, too. **1939** in *DAS:* A deck of nose candy for sale. **1940** Longstreet *Decade* 357: No use knocking against a scut loaded with nose candy. **1941** *Amer. N & Q* (Nov.) 123: "Nose candy" is slang for cocaine. *a***1946** in W.C. Fields *By Himself* 70: I saved Chick from becoming a nose candy addict. **1949** "J. Evans" *Halo in Brass* 33: No slim-waisted junker with a snapbrim hat and a deck of nose candy for sale to the right guy. **1954** Schulberg *Waterfront* 40: Not to mention the pay-off on the ship jumpers and the nose candy from the Italian mob. **1977** *Daily Beacon* (Univ. Tenn.) (Apr. 1) 3: Reed...will speak on the evils of alcohol between hits on his favorite "nose candy." **1977** Schrader *Blue Collar* 46: Let me have some of that nose candy. **1977–81** S. King *Cujo* 280: A lot heavier than a little nose candy stashed in the wheel well. **1982** in G. Trudeau *Doonesbury Dossier* (unp.): All that nose candy for me? **1984** W.M. Henderson *Elvis* 66: Coke....The final ingredient, a little nose candy. **1992** *UTSQ: Nose candy*—cocaine. **1995** *N.Y. Press* (Oct. 18) 8: Availing themselves of some of the unknown dancers-for-hire and more than a little nose candy.

nosedive *n.* **1.** *Hobo.* the act of suddenly professing religion at a religious mission. Also as *v.*

    1935 E. Anderson *Hungry Men* 4: You got to do a nose dive....Go up in front while they're singing and kneel down and let 'em pray over you. **1936** Mackenzie *Living Rough* 207: To get anything from them they want you to nose-dive. I wasn't going to get on my knees and nose-dive with a bunch of mission stiffs. **1952** in *Qly. Jour. Studies on Alcoholism* XIV (1953) 476: Exploiting the mission...entails too many "ear bangings" (sermons) and "nose dives" (prayers). **1961** Bendcher *Bowery Man* 39: Some claim that they were raised on prayer, but they resent being required to "nose-dive" at this late stage. **1968** Spradley *Owe Yourself a Drunk* 42: Says you don't have to take a "nose dive" my place. **1970** Terkel *Hard Times* 38: Once in a while somebody would take a nose dive, profess religion. They'd stick around a while, just to have a roof.

2. a loss of control over one's emotions, usu. a fit of depression.

    1936 Gaddis *Courtesan* 80: The same dame the colonel did a nose-dive about. **1944** *Slanguage Dict.* 53: *Nose-dive*—intoxication; temperamental tail spin. **1976** Univ. Tenn. student: I really went into a nosedive.

3. a fall or fainting spell.

    1942 *ATS* 61: *Nose-dive*...a fall on the nose. **1985** Ponicsan *Vision Quest* (film): The fellas told me you took a nosedive in the hallway.

nosediver *n. Hobo.* MISSION STIFF.

    1935 E. Anderson *Hungry Men* 8: He was not among the nose divers. **1968** Spradley *Owe Yourself a Drunk* 74: Nose diver [a type of] Mission Stiff.

no-see-um *n.* [orig. pidgin] **1.** any of various tiny biting flies.

    1842 in *DARE.* **1848** H.D. Thoreau, in *DA:* In the summer myriads of black flies, mosquitoes, and midges, or, as the Indians call them, "no-see-ums," make travelling in the woods almost impossible. **1886, 1905** in *DARE.* **1914** in *DA:* A No-seeum is a species of guerrilla gnat having two stingers in each foot and nine in the head. **1919** S. Lewis *Air* 296: Seattle is bad enough—it's so big that I feel like a no-see-um in a Norway pine reserve. **1920** in Hemingway *Dateline: Toronto* 44: Black flies, no-see-ums, deer flies, gnats, and mosquitoes. **1941** in Stageberg & Anderson *Poetry* 62: In order to shake off the moose-flies, the deer-flies, and the "no-see-ums." **1950** in *DARE.* **1957** *New Yorker* (Dec. 21) 28: The summers, too, with their mosquitoes, deer flies, and nosee-ums. **1972–79** T. Wolfe *Right Stuff* 134: Would have been devoured in midair by the No See'um bugs, as they were called. **1994** *CBS This Morning* (CBS-TV) (Apr. 21): With gnats and bugs and "no-see-ums," as you call them.

2. *Mil. Av.* a stealth-technology aircraft.

    1989 J. Weber *Defcon One* 31: They're already mad as hell about our "no-see-um" fighters.

nose gunner *n. Mil. Av.* (see *a*1989 quot.).

    1983 M. Skinner *USAFE* 14: The...term "Nosegunner" [is] hung on some F-4E pilots by their backseaters. *a***1989** R. Herman, Jr. *Warbirds* ix: *Nose gunner:* Nickname for pilot in two-place fighter aircraft. *Ibid.* 83: Jack, my nose gunner, lets me fly it all the time.

nose job *n.* **1.** a rhinoplasty, esp. when performed for a merely cosmetic purpose.

    1963 (cited in *W10*). **1966** *Dick Van Dyke Show* (CBS-TV): Take 'em all out, gimme a nose job, gimme a haircut. **1966** *Playboy* (Apr.)

25: The surgical aspects of a nose job. **1972–75** W. Allen *Feathers* 94: You ought to have a nose job. **1976** in Mack *Real Life* (unp.): I've got a confession...I've had a nose job. **1976** Conroy *Santini* 480: Why don't you die on the operating table while you're having a nose job? **1978** Pilcer *Teen Angel* 86: Why don't you get a nose job? *a***1982** Medved *Hospital* 218: Haggling over the price of a nose job. **1983** *Muppet Show* (CBS-TV) (Aug. 8): This is Pinocchio—he wants a nose job. **1985–87** Bogosian *Talk Radio* 23: Change the name, get a nose job.

2. [sugg. by *have* [or *get*] *(one's) nose open* s.v. NOSE, *n.*] *Black E.* an infatuation.

    1969 *Current Slang I & II* 64: *Nose job, n.* A planned assault on one's emotions; the act of falling in love.—High school students, both sexes, Negro, Maryland. **1968–70** *Current Slang III & IV* 87: *Nose job, n.* In love.—Watts—He's got a bad *nose job.* (He really is in love.).

nose out *v.* to defeat or deprive of winnings by a narrow margin.

    1907 in H.C. Fisher *A. Mutt* 6: Curses! Nosed out of $580. **1942** *ATS* 635: Barely defeat....*nose out.*

nose paint *n. West.* liquor. *Joc.*

    1881 A.A. Hayes *New Colo.* 158: We saw, not far from San José [Tex.], a sign, in which a name which I have never encountered elsewhere was given to stimulating beverages. This sign was *Nosepaint and Lunch.* **1899** A.H. Lewis *Sandburrs* 210: Set up the nosepaint ag'in barkeep! **1900** S.E. White *Westerners* 120: Frosty, trot out the nose paint. **1917** *Editor* (May 5) 309: "Nose paint" and "red eye" are affectionate names for whiskey. **1929** (quot. at THIRD RAIL). **1927** P.A. Rollins *Jinglebob* 75 [ref. to 1880's]: An', too, there won't be no nose paint at the ranch. **1940** [W.C. Fields] *Bank Dick* (film): He's evidently been on a bender. He's full of nose paint.

nose-picker *n.* a child or adult of offensive habits; gawker.

    1966 IUFA *Folk Speech* (Apr. 7): Term for children. *Nose pickers.* **1968–70** *Current Slang III & IV* 87: *Nose picker, n.* A rustic; a lout.—College males, South Dakota; Minnesota (from enlisted men's jargon, Viet Nam). **1981** *Easyriders* (Oct.) 10: It's a head-twister for nosepickers. **1987** *Tour of Duty* (CBS-TV): I ever catch that little nose-picker, I'll rip his arm off.

nose-picking speed *n. Av.* (see quot.).

    1988 *Proc. of Naval Inst.* (Oct.) 108: Aviation lexicon...*nose-picking speed* Aggravatingly and pointlessly slow.

nose poker *n.* (see 1909 quot.).

    1900 Reeves *Bamboo Tales* 69 [ref. to 1898]: Some playing "shuffle the brogan," others busy at "nosey poker." **1909** M'Govern *Krag Is Laid* 90: This is the game so popular in the army when real coin is *non est.* In nose-poker everything progresses in the usual manner until one of the members is "frozen out." Then the luckless one pays. He is allowed to shield his eyes with his five remaining cards. His nose must be left bare,...while every man in the game has the privilege of pelting the man's nose with his stack of pasteboards.

nose powder *n. Narc.* NOSE CANDY.

    1936 Chaplin *Modern Times* (film): Searching for hidden "nose powder." **1953** Anslinger & Tompkins *Traffic in Narc.* 313: *Nose powder.* Cocaine, heroin, or morphine, especially in a form for inhaling. **1979** Charyn *7th Babe* 265: He'll be too busy making dollars and sniffing nose powder.

nose trouble *n.* a propensity for prying; nosiness.

    1971 Dahlskog *Dict.* 42: To be a busy-body is to have *nose trouble.* **1966** Braly *On the Yard* 205: You got nose trouble? **1964** H. Rhodes *Chosen Few* 210: Anybody ever tell you you got a bad case of nose trouble?

nosh *n.* Orig. *Jewish-Amer.* **1.** a delicatessen; NOSHERY.

    1917 in *OEDS:* Come with me to Kettners' nosh at 8.0.

2. a snack; (*hence*) snacks. Now *colloq.*

    1951 *N.Y. Times* (July 29) II 16 (ad): Television—Snack and Nosch bar...All facilities for a better vacation in a friendly atmosphere. **1952** (cited in *W10*). **1953** *N.Y. Times* (Feb. 1) 6:2 76: People from uptown and out of town...enjoying a "nosh" at Yonah Shimmel's Knishery. **1965** in *BDNE* 322: A nosh is a snack. **1965** *N.Y. Times* (Feb. 28) VII 46: His leather-jacketed pals loot a friend's pantry. ("What a fabulous store of nosh!"). **1978** *L.A. Times* (June 7) I 17: Just perfect for a posh nosh at pool-side.

nosh *v.* [< Yid *nashn* 'to nibble'] Orig. *Jewish-Amer.* to nibble; eat as a snack. Now *colloq.* Hence **nosher**, *n.*

    1947 in *DARE:* Harold has always called me a "nascha." He too likes to "nasch." The expression...he told me it was Yiddish—or Jewish. ***1957** in *OEDS:* One eats breakfast or lunch, but one noshes in between. *Ibid.:* "Women don't know how to nosh," he continued, "except chocolate and sweets." **1972** *Harper's* (July) 22: The Armenian grandmaster would wear Bobby down, "noshing him like a herring." **1975** *L.A. Times* (Oct. 19) ("Calendar") 51: A vegetarian who noshes nuts and raisins during the day. **1978** *New West* (July 3) 38: He goes into this noshing behavior—he reaches down and takes a Triscuit. **1996** *Village Voice* (N.Y.C.) (Apr. 16) ("Educ. Supp.") 3: The rest sit around noshing junk food.

noshery *n.* a delicatessen; restaurant.
  1952 *N.Y. Times* (June 22) II X3: The guests are offered better accommodations, more food (a midnight "noshery" is the latest feature at some of these aspiring country clubs). **1962** McDavid *Mencken's Amer. Lang.* 261: *Nash*…has yielded *noshery* as a designation for a snack bar. **1971** Dahlskog *Dict.* 42: *Noshery, nashery, n.* A delicatessen or place where one obtains snacks. **1982** *Time* (Sept. 27) D3: A noshery whose menu features tongue on rye and chicken with walnuts.

no-shit *adj.* genuine.—used prenominally.—usu. considered vulgar. Cf. *no shit* s.v. SHIT, *n.*
  1979 L. Heinemann, in *TriQuarterly* (Spring) 186: A no-shit firefight with some…NVA. **1983** R. Thomas *Missionary* 77: You still think Baldy's got a real no-shit chance? *a***1992** T. Wilson *Termite Hill* 271: A real, no-shit virgin.

no-shitter *n.* an emphatically true statement.—usu. considered vulgar. *Joc.*
  1975 Ark. man, age 26: That's a no-shitter. **1987** Univ. Tenn. instructor, age *ca*35: "That's a no-shitter." I've heard that expression forever. **1991** Marcinko & Weisberg *Rogue Warrior* 70: This was a no-shitter. This was the real thing.

no-show *n.* **1.a.** a person, as a hotel guest or airline passenger, who fails to claim a reservation. Now *colloq.* or *S.E.*
  1941 in *OEDS:* He's what the airlines call a "no show." **1953** *Time* (Sept. 28) 41: Ten airlines…will crack down on "no-shows." **1954** Collans & Sterling *House Detect.* 219: No Show. Reservation which didn't claim room. **1958** *N.Y. Times* (Aug. 24) II X29: The airlines' plan to discourage costly "no-shows." **1962** *Time* (Feb. 2) 34: There were fewer no-shows than expected, and Flight 77 was in trouble. **1974** *CBS News* (CBS-TV) (Apr.): The airlines call them "no-shows," passengers who book on several airlines for insurance and then don't cancel the flights they don't use. **1981** *Time* (Dec. 14) 72: Some 25% of Delta's passengers at its hub airport in Atlanta were so-called no-shows.

b. a person who fails to appear on a given occasion. Now *colloq.* or *S.E.*
  1961 *Time* (July 14) 21: Faced by a no-show foe, the troopers concentrated on survival in the searing heat. **1964** Newhafer *Last Tallyho* 194: That no-show get a Betty? **1973** J.R. Coleman *Blue-Collar* 219: The deal with a no-show is that if the other men can clean up the route alone they split the missing man's base pay. **1975** *Oui* (Mar.) 30: The list of highly touted no-shows was impressive. Joan Baez wasn't there. **1980** Gould *Ft. Apache* 59: We already got eleven no-shows on the eight-to-four [shift]. **1981** *Daily News* (N.Y.) (July 21) 5: Draw up list of draft no-shows. 134 who didn't register may be prosecuted.

2. a failure to appear.
  1957 *N.Y. Times* (June 2) III 1: The traditional spring sales pick-up in new cars has been a "no-show." **1967** *Time* (Mar. 24) 16: Powell's no-show was prompted by prudence; there was a warrant out for his arrest. **1967** *L.A. Times* (Apr. 25) IV 1: The no-show of the press. **1976** C. Keane *Hunter* 36: Jumped bail the other day on a no-show. **1983** *Working Woman* (Jan. 1984) 82: Most professional public-relations people have had "no shows" when a major fire or political announcement diverted all media attention. **1984** *L.A. Times* (Feb. 16) VIII 33: Is a no-show for any item on such a limited menu inexcusable? Methinks so. **1985** WINS radio news (Sept. 2): She should have pulled a no-show.

3. a person who draws a salary for a job that requires no actual work or that does not truly exist.—often used attrib. Cf. GHOST, 2.c.
  1962 *Sat. Eve. Post* (Jan. 6) 82: A "no-show" job was the *crème de la crème* of the city's political bounty. *Ibid.:* [He] discovered 144 no-shows in a single city department. **1981** *L.A. Times* (June 13) I 3: The three allegedly tricked the movie companies into paying the salaries of persons who did not work, known as "no-shows." **1983** *Time* (Nov. 28) 28: Fictitious "no-shows" or "ghost" workers on the Schiavone payroll.

1984 *Atlantic* (Sept.) 30: Make-work, no-show projects run by poverty hustlers. **1985** *L.A. Times* (Mar. 30) II 3: It was a "no-show" job….All he would have to do is pick up his check every week. **1996** *Village Voice* (N.Y.C.) (Sept. 24) 14: Random House…will soon offer…lucrative book contracts or no-show editor jobs to get them to jump ship.

no-show *v.* to fail to appear (for).
  1953 *N.Y. Times* (Sept. 20) II 26X: A uniform penalty system for coach passengers who "no-show." **1961** *Time* (Jan. 6) 34: He no-showed his press conference.

not *interj.* **1.** (used jocularly to contradict one's own ironic assertion or another person's statement). [Repopularized by comedians Mike Myers and Dana Carvey on NBC-TV's *Saturday Night Live* series from 1989 and esp. by the movie *Wayne's World* (1992) based on this; discussed by J.T. Sheidlower and J.E. Lighter in *AS* LXVIII (1993), pp. 213–18.]
  1893 *Princeton Tiger* (Mar. 30) 103: An Historical Parallel—Not. **1900** Ade *More Fables* 126: Probably they preferred to go back in the Front Room and hear some more about Woman's Destiny not. **1905** E.P. Butler, in *Amer. Magazine* (Sept.) 499: Cert'nly, me dear frind Flannery. Delighted. *Not!* **1908** in Canemaker *W. McCay* 75: That confounded rarebit I ate…is making me sleep lovely. NOT!!! **1910** F.H. Webster *Comrades of Saddle* 145: He's a fine neighbor—not. **1918** *Bugler* (Mar. 9) 3: "Now he is talking about that doll again." "Sure she is a dream—not." **1920** F.S. Fitzgerald *Berniece Bobs Her Hair*, in *Stories* 47: "They were the models for our mothers." Marjorie laughed. "Yes they were—not!" **1926** E. Wilson *Twenties* [entry for July]: Held up by cyclone in South Amboy…"wicked little boy who kept jeering at us, 'You'll get there tonight—not!' " **1936** A. Moore *Wind over Range* 83: Is he real tickled, the way he lets on, that his dollars 'll come a-marchin' home in a few weeks? Yes, he is—not! **1955** R. Stout, in *Amer. Mag.* (Nov.): "A fine way to serve your country," I told him. "Not. In spite of a late start [etc.]." **1956** Ferrer & Morgan *Great Man* (film): I'll *bet* she did. *Not!* **1978** in *N.Y. Times Mag.* (Mar. 8, 1992) 20: That's a fabulous science fair project…Not! **1991** *Bill & Ted's Adventures* (CBS-TV): Smooth move, dude! Not! **1992** M. Myers et al. *Wayne's World* (film): Wayne'll understand that right away. Not! **1992** *N.Y. Times* (Mar. 8) II 15: Madonna is my girlfriend—NOT! **1992** *New Republic* (Oct. 5) 50: Survivors of Hurricane Andrew emerged…to spray-paint sound-bites on the wreckage…"Andrew thanks—NOT." **1994** *As the World Turns* (CBS-TV): You look like an Irish cream sort of guy—not! **1995** Playtex TV ad: A look that's flattering. Not! **1995** *Village Voice* (N.Y.C.) (Apr. 25) 85: Fabulous (Not) [headline of review of book about seamy side of modeling].

2. no indeed!
  1927 in *AS* LXVIII (1993) 216: Not!!

¶ In phrase:

¶ **not even!** *Stu.* emphatically not! that's absurd!
  1983 (cited in P. Munro *U.C.L.A. Slang II* 61). **1990** P. Munro *Slang U.: Not even!* No way! You're kidding! [example:] ["]That chick is way dyno.["]…["]Not even! I've seen her in a bikini.["] **1994** A. Heckerling *Clueless* 95: MURRAY Christian is [homosexual]…CHER Not even! How can that be? *Ibid.* 109: TAI…I'm sort of a mentally challenged airhead? CHER Not even! I didn't say that! **1995** *Jerry Springer Show* (synd. TV series): Not even!

no-talent *n.* a talentless person.—also used attrib.
  *a***1967** Bombeck *Wit's End* 39: Even my own children know I'm a no-talent. **1981** Centi *Positive/Negative* 16: I'm a no-talent who can never do anything right. **1984** Trotti *Phantom* 216: Lousy USO shows put on by no-talents with…guitars. **1985** Dillinger *Adrenaline* 21: Downtown Hollywood…the land of the losers and no-talents. **1986** *Wkly. World News* (July 22) 9: [He's] a weak no-talent. I don't even think he's funny. **1991** Jenkins *Gotta Play Hurt* 3: The phony little…no-talent…editor.

not bad *interj.* great; excellent.
  1942 *ATS* 295: Of approval and admiration.…*nifty!, not bad!* **1989** C. Matheson & E. Solomon *Excellent Adventure* (film): Whoa! Not bad!

notch *n.* [**1.** the vulva or vagina.—usu. considered vulgar. [Unattested in U.S., but the orig. of **(2)**, below.]
  ca*1720** in Burford *Bawdy Verse* 248: We'll scour off all their Notches. ***1796** Grose *Dict. Vulgar Tongue* (ed. 3): *Notch.* the private parts of a woman. **ca***1866** *Romance of Lust* 144: Her…tight little notch.]

2. a prostitute or promiscuous woman. Cf. NAUTCH.

    1935 D.W. Maurer, in *AS* (Feb.) 18 [ref. to *ca*1910]: *Notch* or *Notch Girl*. A prostitute. **1988** Univ. Tenn. student theme: Girls…involved in one-night stands are called…*notches* or *lay-babes*.

¶ In phrase:

¶ **up to the notch** up to a high standard.

    1838 [Haliburton] *Clockmaker* (Ser. 2) 23: Mind you're up to the notch, for I'm in earnest. **1840** [Haliburton] *Clockmaker* (ser. 3) 175: I like a man to be up to the notch, and stand to his lick-log; salt or no salt, say the word, or it's no offer. **1942** *ATS* 31: *Up to the notch*,…up to standard, hence excellent, perfect.

notch house *n.* a house of prostitution. Cf. NAUTCH. Also **notch joint, notchery [joint].**

    1926 Finerty *Criminalese* 40: *Notch house*—A house of ill-repute. **1928** O'Connor *B'way Racketeers* 65: That rat gets pinched in a notch joint raid. **1928** Carr *Rampant Age* 165: He…listened with interest to a discussion of "notch-house" etiquette. **1930** Lait *On the Spot* 207: *Notch-joint*…House of ill fame. **1930** "D. Stiff" *Milk & Honey* 202: A brothel…is sometimes called a *notch house*. **1931** *Amer. Mercury* (Nov.) 353: Circus Words…*Notch house*…A house of prostitution; also, *notcherie*. **1932** Nicholson & Robinson *Sailor Beware!* 57: Crucify me! And when I go busted and you end up…in a notchery joint, maybe you'll wisht you'd paid attention to me. You're hostesses ain't you? **1932** in Weinberg *Tough Guys* 46: I've got two notch-joints at the other end of town. **1934** W. Smith *B. Cotter* 238: I'd rather be in one of them two-bit notch-joints down by the river, no color and no holds barred. **1935** D.W. Maurer, in *AS* (Feb.) 18 [ref. to *ca*1910]: *Notch House*. A brothel. **1937** Reitman *Box-Car Bertha* 178: Kid, a notch house is a place of business and the customer must be satisfied. **1956** H. Gold *Not With It* 277: Nancy ran a notch-house. **1973** *AS* XLVI 77: Notch house. **1942** Algren *Morning* 44: I'd…start me up a notch-joint.

notch moll *n. Und.* a prostitute.

    1926 Finerty *Criminalese* 40: *Notch moll*—a female inmate of a house of ill-repute.

note *n.* **1.** (see quot.).

    1891 Maitland *Slang Dict.* 190: *Note*, a joke or a saying. "That's a good note."

2. a payment in the form of a currency note or notes.

    1970–71 Rubinstein *City Police* 383: Did the kid try and hit you for a note? **1990** T. Fahey *Joys of Jargon* 22: If the…investigators from Internal Affairs suspect you of *taking notes* (money)…a disciplinary hearing…[will] find out whether you were taking *good notes* (money for saving someone's life, for instance) or *bad notes* (a bribe). **1990** N.Y.C. beggar: Aw, man, can't you spare a note? Chump change don't make it!

¶ In phrase:

¶ **hell of a note** see s.v. HELL, *n.*

No-Tell Motel *n.* a cheap motel regarded as a place of rendezvous for illicit lovers. *Joc.*

    1974 Univ. Tenn. student: They went down to the no-tell motel. **1976** *Nat. Lampoon* (Sept.) 3: Miss Francis is currently suing the No Tell Motel. **1980** Ciardi *Browser's Dict.* 191: *Hot pillow joint.* A No-Tell Motel or Hotel which rents rooms by the hour for sexual assignations. **1986** *Smithsonian* (Mar.) 134: The motel as a locale for sin was a standard part of its image.…People joked about the "No-tell Motel," and John Margolies claims there really is one called that, on Division Street in Grand Rapids, Michigan. **1986** *Smithsonian* (May) 18: There was a "No-tel Motel" on U.S. 30 somewhere between Wooster and Canton, Ohio, when I was in school. It was a real thrill for some of the seniors to drive out and take one another's pictures underneath the sign. **1989** *Newsweek* (Oct. 2) 66: A room at the No-Tell Motel. **1992** *News Hour* (CNN-TV) (June 12): Rio's best no-tell motels. **1995** *Leeza* (synd. TV series): At the No-Tell Motel with Mary Lou. **1997** *N.Y. Times* (Mar. 9) ("Metro") 33: On this strip of garages and no-tell motels, The White Mana is like a breath of fresh air.

nothing *n.* ¶ In phrases:

¶ **[not] know from nothing** see s.v. KNOW, *v.*

¶ **nothing doing** (used as a refusal of a request); indeed not! no! no! Now *colloq.*

    1910 in *OEDS*: Spottford offered the porter a dime. The negro waved it aside and said: "Nothing doing; my price is a quarter at least." **1916** E.R. Burroughs *Return of Mucker* 54: Nothin' doin'…but t'anks just the same. **1922** F.L. Packard *Doors of Night* 53: "Kick it in,

Whitie!"…"Nothin' doin'." **1931** F. Marion *Champ* (film): Wash three or four times a day? All *over*? Nothin' doin'!

nothing *adj.* insipid; inconsequential; dull.

    1954–60 *DAS*: *Nothing*…Insipid, colorless, dull.…"He's a real nothing guy," or "That's a nothing book." **1959–60** Bloch *Dead Beat* 45: Larry pawed through the mess. A nothing bit. **1965** Bonham *Durango St.* 59: What makes you think I'd take a nothin' cat like you, anyway? **1966–67** P. Thomas *Mean Streets* 17: After all, a twelve-year old kid walking the streets at 3 a.m. was a nothing sight in Harlem. **1967** W. Murray *Sweet Ride* 46: It was a nothing place, just a few booths and a counter. **1969** M. Lynch *Amer. Soldier* 34 [ref. to 1953]: Two M.P.'s walked in step along the middle of the street.…All their clubs, Gerber shouted. All their pistols and their white gloves. Shit. What does it cover? Gerber called out. A pair of nothing balls? **1970** Rudensky & Riley *Gonif* 81: This was really a nothing burg and there wasn't a soul in sight. **1973** N.Y.U. student: She's a real nothing girl. You wouldn't like her. **1981** O'Day & Eells *High Times* 38: Earl and a lot of other people really dug a nothing song, "The Lady in Red."

nothing ball *n.* **1.a.** *Baseball.* a slow pitch.

    1937 *N.Y. Herald Tribune* (Oct. 3) (cited in Nichols *Baseball Term.*). **1964** Thompson & Rice *Every Diamond* 140: *Nothin' ball*…A slow pitch. **1989** P. Dickson *Baseball Dict.: Nuthin' ball*…Slowly pitched ball that is easy to hit because it does not move deceptively.

b. *Tennis.* a lob.

    1977 Bredes *Hard Feelings* 314: This Jeff character is a nothing-ball player, a very good lobber.

2. an insignificant person; a nobody.

    1968 Stahl *Hokey* 9: Clarence Hokey Horner, a nothingball with lots of ideas and no luck.

nothingburger *n.* something that is insignificant or worthless. Cf. NUTBURGER; -BURGER.

    1984 *U.S. News & W.R.* (Aug. 13) 9: Burford herself spread the jitters to Reagan's closest aides when she termed her job…"a joke" and "a nothingburger."

Novy *n. Naut.* a Nova Scotian; a Nova Scotian vessel.

    1885 in *OEDS*: The boats used in the ordinary fishing [along the Labrador coast] are of two kinds; those called "novies" or Nova Scotia boats, being long and narrow. **1897** Kipling *Capts. Courageous* 181: Git aout, you Novy! **1942** *ATS* 359: *Novy*, a Nova Scotian.

now *adj.* Esp. *Journ. & Fashion Industry.* extremely fashionable or up-to-date.

    [**1963** in *OEDS*: A black crepe dress…a now-and-future shaping of pebbly acetate-and-rayon crepe.] **1967** *Time* (Apr. 7) 20: The Now Generation. **1967** *L.A. Times* (May 28) I 7: An exciting pre-show display of "Now" jewelry, art and furniture. **1968** in *BDNE* 323: *Bullitt*…is completely typical of the "now" look in American movies. **1969** *Newsweek,* in *DAS* (ed. 3): It was a beautiful decade, a really weird time for tripping out on now words, on today's zonked-out speech patterns. **1970–72** Densen-Gerber *Drugs, Sex, Parents* 121: Oh, they're great. They're "now" people, Mom. **1977** *L.A. Times* (Feb. 22) You 9: A tasting search for the right wine to serve with that "now" food, peanut butter. **1982** *Harper's* (Mar.) 18: Too Marvelous!…It's so *Now*—that's why I like it. **1996** Ad for *Yush*, zine on the World Wide Web: YUSH is a globally-conscious, urban music, youth culture, fashion, arts, entertainment and lifestyle mag-e-zine. It covers now and emerging street trends, language and politics in an irreverent but accessible style.

no way see s.v. WAY, *interj.*

nowhere *adj.* **1.** without resources; beaten; at a loss. Now *colloq.*

    [***1755** in *OED*: His powerful deep rate, by which all the horses that ran against him were no-where at the end.] **1853** *Harper's Mag.* VII 323: My chances were small.…But it was no use; as the Western men say, I was "no whar." **1859** Bartlett *Dict. Amer.* (ed. 2): 207: To be nowhere is to be at sea; to be utterly at a loss; to be ignorant. **1868** in Schele de Vere *Amer.* 620: When he began to ask me questions about surgery, I was just nowhere. ***1869** in *F & H* V 72: The brave Panther…is, vulgarly speaking, nowhere. **1900** Dreiser *Carrie* 302: A poor man ain't nowhere. You could starve, by God, right in the streets, and there ain't most no one that would help you. **1946** Boulware *Jive & Slang* 4: *I Ain't Nowhere*…I'm not doing anything. **1947** *Time* (Oct. 6): "To be nowhere" (to be broke). **1958** Talsman *Gaudy Image* 169: Flat, man, flat. Broken, busted, cleaned, nowhere.

2.a. unimpressive, esp. by comparison; of no interest or importance; (*hence,* esp. in mod. use) foolish; tiresome; pointless.

    1843 Field *Pokerville* 14: A travelling *menagerie…*but *varmints* were "no whar," in comparison with…real live actors! **1847** Robb *Squatter Life* 22: Clay was no-where, Polk wasn't thought of, Webster was but a patching. *Ibid.* 132: I'm some in a *bar* fight,…but I warn't no *whar* in that fight with Jess. **1848** in Oehlschlaeger *Reveille* 221: They were both to be set down as "no whar." **1858** in Rosa *Wild Bill* 26: My mustache and goatee lays over hisen Considerable the fact of it is hisen ain't no Whare. **1858** [S. Hammett] *Piney Woods* 62: Yankees indeed! Yankees ain't no whar. *a***1867** in G.W. Harris *Lovingood* 79: A big craw-fish wit a hungry coon a-reachin fur him, wer jis' nowhar. **1870** *Overland Mo.* (Jan.) 89: A man who couldn't drink with the boys was nowhere. **1873** Revere *Keel & Saddle* 147: It was a fair test of the respective merits of…cavalry opposed to…infantry; and the former was, as sportsmen say, "nowhere." **1883** in Bunner *Letters* 77: As a professional performance it is simply nowhere. **1887** [C. Mackenzie] *Jack Pots* 80: Poke [*sic*] is de game I likes most of all; craps is nowhere. **1895** W.N. Woods *Big I* 3: Waterloo was nothing! Ten pins is nowhere! **1900** Hammond *Whaler* 257: Jiminy—*birds* wa' n't *nowhere* with *that* whale. **1942** *Yank* (Dec. 23) 18: They were so far hipped. St. Nick was no where. **1946** G.W. Henderson *Jule* 121: "That gal's got bitch in her."…"If she ain't got no bitch in her, she ain't nowhere." **1948** Manone & Vandervoort *Trumpet* 138: I didn't like the…job much. In fact, it was nowhere, as far as music kicks were concerned. **1947–52** R. Ellison *Invisible Man* 325: You are nowhere, mahn. Nowhere! [**1952** Bellow *Augie March* 501: Do you remember how the great Sherlock Holmes doped things out in his room on Baker Street? But compared to his brother Mycroft he was no place.] **1952** Kerouac *Cody* 120: I read that fuckin book.…The guy's just nowhere. **1953** Paxton *Wild One* (film): No man, that's nowhere. *ca***1953** Hughes *Fantastic Lodge* 71: My friends told me niggers were nowhere and that sort of thing. **1954** W.G. Smith *South St.* 166: Baby, you ain't *nowhere.* **1956** B. Holiday & Dufty *Lady Sings* 79: A Rolls is built for pleasure.…But it's nowhere for highballing a hundred and fifty miles to make a gig. **1956** E. Hunter *Second Ending* 21: Well, that road stuff is nowhere, man. **1958** in R. Russell *Perm. Playboy* 66: It was nowhere. Without Honker to keep us all on the ground, we were just making noise. **1958–59** Lipton *Barbarians* 317: *Nowhere*—If you're not with it, you're nowhere. **1959–60** R. Reisner *Jazz Titans* 161: *Nowhere:* the absolute of nothing. **1962** in Rosset *Evergreen Reader* 477: Jesus, that name ain't nowhere, dad. **1965** Hardman *Chaplains* 6: This is nowhere,…just nowhere! **1971** H. Roberts *Third Ear: Nowhere…*1. strange. 2. not acceptable. **1972** C. Major *Dict. Afro-Amer. Sl.* 85: *Nowhere:* Applied to a really dull or square person who is also undesirable; also, a place or thing of the same quality. *a***1986** D. Tate *Bravo Burning* 139: All that is so nowhere…now.

    b. (in recent use, often used prenominally).

    1953 W. Burroughs *Junkie* 93: The other patients were a square and sorry lot.…a beat, nowhere bunch of people. The type psychiatrists like. **1959** Tevis *Hustler* 30: And you let a nowhere bank hustler named Woody Fleming hit you for eight hundred dollars in Hot Springs. *****1965** J. Lennon & P. McCartney *Nowhere Man* (pop. song): He's a real nowhere man/sitting in his nowhere land/making all his nowhere plans for nobody. **1974** R. Campbell *Chasm* 176: There are a lot of nowhere teachers in the school system, right?

nowheresville see s.v. -SVILLE.

N.O.Y.B. *interj.* none of your business.

    1915 *DN* IV 246: *N.O.Y.B.* None of your business. **1942** *ATS* 266: None of your business!…*n.o.y.b!* **1976** Angelou *Singin' & Swingin'* 70: *N.O.Y.B.* None of Your Business.

nozzle *n.* **1.** a nose; (*also*) a nostril.

    ***1755** in *EDD: Nozle* [*sic*], the nose. ***1771** T. Smollett, in *OED:* His face was overshadowed by this tremendous nozzle. ***1785** Grose *Dict. Vulgar Tongue: Nozzle.* The nose of a man or woman. **1854** Sleeper *Salt Water Bubbles* 63: They very considerately put a muzzle on his nozzle. **1867** *Galaxy* (Jan. 1) 92: Fate had rid the elephant, and struck the critter when he put up his nozzle. **1870** *Putnam's Mag.* (Mar.) 301: The combatants struck each other…upon…the nose, the sneezer,…the nozzle. **1871** (quot. at GALOOT). **1876** *Harper's* (July) 196: Polly she jes grabbed de wheel an' held de nozzle ob de boat 'gin de sho'. **1934** Wagner *Old Neutriment* 149: Dandy was pantin' and all white with foam and his nozzles was a-quiverin'. **1974** Strasburger

Rounding Third 53: I figure once I get an answer, I'll know whether to swipe someone in the nozzle the next time they call *me* "bright-eyed and bushy-tailed."

    2. the penis.—usu. considered vulgar.

    1994 "G. Indiana" *Rent Boy* 8: A bulky Italian guy with a fat not very long nozzle. **1996** *THC: Bert Ellis,* story on Usenet newsgroup alt.sex.stories: The boy's whitewash blew out of his fleshy nozzle and painted the inside of Julia's cunt.

N.S. *interj.* enough said. Cf. N.C.

    1841 *Spirit of Times* (Oct. 30) 409: "N.S., *nuf sed,*" and up went *the soap.* **1845** Corcoran *Pickings* 64: *Verbum sat sapienti,* or as the vulgar translation has it, N.S.

nub *n.* an ugly or repulsive person.

    1942 *ATS* 771: Unattractive girl.…*mudhen, nub, oilcan.* **1971** Dahlskog *Dict.* 42: *Nub, n.* An ugly girl; an ugly or repulsive person. **1978** *UTSQ:* [Unattractive] male…*nird, nub, queer, dork.*

nubber *n. Baseball.* a weakly hit ball that glances off the end of the bat. Also **knubber.**

    1937 *Daily News* (N.Y.) (Jan. 17) (cited in Nichols *Baseball Term.*). **1984** *N.Y. Post* (Aug. 13) 28: Two [hits] were seeing-eye infield nubbers. **1989** P. Dickson *Baseball Dict.: Knubber…*A lucky hit that squirts through the infield; a scratch hit. Sometimes written as nubber.

nubbin *n.* Esp. *So.* the penis.—usu. considered vulgar.

    1968 J.P. Miller *Race for Home* 283 [ref. to *ca*1935]: Come on, boy, whup out yer nubbin and jazz 'er a little bit. Her name's Nellie. **1971** *Blushes & Bellylaffs* 158: The farmer's daughter had fingers too tender for shelling corn, but she was an expert at nubbin shuckin'! **1974** Univ. Tenn. grad. student, age 22 (Sept. 24): If a girl'll *shuck a nubbin* it means she'll give you some pussy.

nubie var. NEWBIE.

nuc var. NUKE, *n.*

nucky var. NOOKIE.

nuclear *adj. & adv.* enraged; BALLISTIC, 1.

    1989 *Newsweek* (Jan. 9), in *AS* LXV (1990) 144: Don't go nuclear. You can deal with things more rationally. **1995** *New Yorker* (Jan. 16) 49: The fraying of his friendship with Fuchs accelerated. As he recalls, "Michael was nuclear" about the promotion. **1995** *Donahue* (NBC-TV): "So it actually got to the point where it [*sc.,* a domestic argument] goes nuclear!"…"It's the little things that make us go ballistic."

    2. very impressive.

    1992 Mowry *Way Past Cool* 90: Nuthin nuclear, man, but it get me there.

nudge *n.* [< Yiddish; related to NUDNIK] a nag; pest. Also as *v.* Also **noodge, nudzh.**

    1970 *New Yorker* (June 20) 31: Rabbi Ben Kaddish…perhaps the greatest *noodge* of the medieval era. **1972** in *BDNE3:* He's not a writer, he's a nudge. On the phone twice a day asking how's it going! **1974** *Time* (Apr. 15) 92: Discharged from prison, Lou Jean Poplin—sometime beautician, full-time *nudzh*—must first spring her husband. **1977** *New West* (July 18) 69: The two women are at the living room piano, Mrs. Turner fingering an adequate "Frank Mills," *nudzhing* her daughter to sing forth boldly. **1980** W. Safire, in *N.Y. Times Mag.* (May 18) 18: It's a soupa dialect. If you don't like it, don't be a noodge. Lean off. **1983** *Time* (Feb. 14) 80: He stalks Jerry not as an assassin, but as a nudge and a nerd. **1993** *Publishers Wkly.* (Sept. 20): A literary editor and world-class nudge who spends half his time fretting about his deep personal isolation. **1994** *N.Y. Times Bk. Rev.* (Nov. 13) 39: God, who lives with his ailing, nudging mother, is surely one of Mr. Esterhazy's most audacious creations.

nudie *n.* **1.** Orig. *Carnival.* a show or motion picture that features nudity.

    1935 *Amer. Mercury* (June) 230: *Nudie:* nude show. **1954–60** *DAS: Nudie…*A show or performance in which a female nude or nudes appear. **1967** *L.A. Times* (Apr. 30) ("Calendar") 11: A rather dubious distinction between exploitation pictures and "nudies" per se, which he described as "typically having females posing as models with no sexual overtones involved." **1970** *Atlantic* (Nov.) 126: Director John G. Avildsen (who used to make nudies) did the location photography himself. **1973** *U.S. News & W.R.* (July 30) 25: Russ Meyer, a movie maker known as the "king of the nudies." **1982** in "J.B. Briggs" *Drive-In* 59: The first comedy nudie, made in Chicago in four days. **1984** *Daily News* (N.Y.) (Aug. 20) 11: Heavens! A nudie for Karen Black?

2. a nude performer or model; (*also*) a photograph of a nude person, esp. a woman.

    1951 in *DAS*: Some of the worried little nudies. **1977** Langone *Life at Bottom* 199: The chaplain comes in and looks at all these nudies on the walls and gets indignant and wants 'em all down. **1984** Tiburzi *Takeoff!* 106: I...found a view of a nudie in a *Playboy*-like pose.

nudie *adj.* nude; featuring nudity.

    1966 *Time* (Oct. 14) 118: Together they attend a nudie bacchanal. **1967** *L.A. Times* (Feb. 11) I 16: It has been badly dubbed and aimed at the nudie trade on the basis of some sexy scenes. **1967* in *OEDS*: He had...submitted Furd's photograph to several nudie magazines. **1973** *Washington Square Review* (May) 20: It was so hot, some people had tried some nudy dipping right there on the beach in broad daylight. **1974** Blount *3 Bricks Shy* 170: When I'm down there I go nudie. **1975** *Atlantic* (Dec.) 100: *Vogue* continues to run nudie photo layouts, shots of bra groping by males, and the like. **1995** *Married with Children* (Fox-TV): At the nudie bar!

nudnik *n.* [< Yiddish] Orig. *Jewish-Amer.* a pest; (*hence*) a dull, foolish, or inconsequential person. Also **noodnik.**

    1925 Yezierska *Bread-Givers* 126: Nag! *Noodnik!*...Stop making me miserable. **1944** M. Shulman *Feather Merchants* 56: Philomene Noodnik...for years had played the lead in the annual Sofia drama festival. **1947** A. Capp, in Tamony *Americanisms* (No. 24) 11: Go 'had, Little Noodnik, spik nice the pome. **1956** *Time* (Sept. 24) 6: A *nudnik* is a bothersome, querulous crank. *Ibid.*: A *nudnik* is a common pest. **1957** *AS* XXXII 155: "Nudnik"...I have known the word for some ten years, and always I have heard it used with the same meaning as *schnook.* **1972** D. Pearce *Pier Head Jump* 148: That noodnik. He wouldn't know the difference anyway. **1973** *TULIPQ* (coll. B.K. Dumas): A person who talks too much: *noodnik.* **1983** R. Salmaggi, on WINS radio (Sept. 1): Why do they always depict men as nudniks in the supermarket? **1995** *Donahue* (NBC-TV): A nudnik.

nudzh var. NUDGE.

nug /nəg/ *n.* [in current use perh. abbr. Austral. sl. *nugget,* as in 1967 quot.] *Stu.* **1.** a young woman. [Prominently employed by comedian Pauly Shore in the film *Son-in-Law* (1993).]

    [**1698–99* "B.E." *Dict. Canting Crew:* Nug, a Word of Love, as *my Dear Nug, my Dear Love.*] [**1967* Partridge *DSUE* (ed. 6) (Supp.): *Nugget...4.* A very attractive girl...Australian...1943.] **1993** Bahr & Small *Son-in-Law* (film): Where I come from, nugs stay active till they're senile! *Ibid.*: Grab a nug whose cones are busty! *Ibid.*: If you find a baby-fresh nug out there, send her my way. **1993** P. Munro *U.C.L.A. Slang II* 62: Nugs...women.

2. usu. *pl.* NUGGIE.

    1993 P. Munro *U.C.L.A. Slang II* 62: Nugs...2. breasts.

nugget *n.* **1.** usu. *pl.* a testicle.—usu. considered vulgar.

    1963 Doulis *Path* 234: "I'm freezing my nuggets off."..."You ain't got no nuggets to speak of." **1969** Corder *Slave Ship* 85: He-he, you almost lost your nuggets, Gabe. **1977** Sayles *Union Dues* 281: A...glare that would sizzle your average bleeding-heart radical's nuggets to a crisp. *Ibid.*: 379: I took a beatin, to tell you the truth. I got my nuggets handed to me.

2.a. Esp. *Naval Av.* a student pilot or inexperienced junior officer.—also used attrib.

    1966 F. Elkins *Heart of Man* 80: And that...SOB tried to make those green nuggets in-flight refuel at night, over water,...at *700 feet.* **1969** Cagle *Naval Av. Guide* 397: Nugget...A term used for a first tour pilot although it may be a student naval aviator. **1984** Cunningham & Ethell *Fox Two* 4 [ref. to Vietnam War]: The Navy normally placed an experienced pilot with a "nugget" backseater or vice-versa. *Ibid.* 148: *Nugget.* A new flight-crew member, denoting little experience. **1983–86** G.C. Wilson *Supercarrier* 3: A nugget pilot (the term for a pilot on his first cruise). **1986** Coonts *Intruder* 90: "I hope I don't get a nugget." A nugget was a new man on his first tour of duty. **1987** Nichols & Tillman *Yankee Sta.* 21: A blissfully ignorant "nugget"—a new aviator. **1989** T. Blackburn *Jolly Rogers* 8 [ref. to WWII]: What we knew our "nuggets" would need to know in combat. *Ibid.* xiv: *Nugget* a fledgling pilot. **1989** Joss *Strike* 110: A limited proportion of "nuggets," or inexperienced junior officers. **1991** K. Douglass *Viper Strike* 11: One of the nuggets flown into Japan to replace the men lost during the raid into North Korea. **1991** Linnekin *80 Knots* 100 [ref. to 1940's]: A number of us "nuggets" had missed carrier qualification.

1995 Cormier et al. *Wildcats* 11: It was heady stuff for nugget aviators. **1996** *JAG* (NBC-TV): We're not nuggets on our first mission!

b. *Stu.* (see quot.).

    1990 P. Munro *Slang U.*: Nugget fool, idiot.

nugget *adj. Stu.* first-class; genuine.

    1927 *AS* II 277: *Nugget.* excellent. **1993** *Real World* (MTV): The Dommer's in a nugget dilemma for sure.

nuggie *n.* usu. *pl.* [perh. *nug*get + *-ie*] a woman's breast.

    1974 Strasburger *Rounding Third* 40: Now, Amy, I'm going to reach up and grab your nuggies and play with them a while. **1974** Lahr *Trot* 218: "Nibble my nuggie," Sally whispers.

nuke *n.* **1.** *Mil.* a nuclear weapon.—also used fig. Now *colloq.*

    1958 *Time* (Jan. 27) 21: U.S. scientists have worked for years to build accident-proofing devices into Atomic Age bombs....A mid-air accident in which the accident-proofed "nuc" was jettisoned safely without explosion. **1959** *N.Y. Times* (Feb. 1) VI 46: Nuclear weapons are becoming even smaller and more portable; soon there may be 5-inch nuclear shells, and portable Davy Crockett "nukes" for the infantryman. **1961** *Time* (Oct. 13) 20: Ready to fight with gunpowder or tactical nukes. **1968** W.C. Anderson *Gooney Bird* 124: Without using nukes, I guess defoliation is the best way to clear the jungles. **1970** Just *Military Men* 29: One of them saw a possible tactical role for nuclear weapons, "small tac nukes," in places like Latin America. **1971** *New Yorker* (Jan. 9) 52: In the main...the experts proved cooperative, apprising me of many complexities that would necessarily attend the release of a "nuke," in the trade term. **1977** *New Times* (Aug. 5) 24: To approve what, to that moment, was the ultimate weapon....A nuke, after all, was a nuke. **1981** *L.A. Times* (Apr. 19) IV 3: His spots [*sc.,* political ads] were weaker and less focused...."It was going to be our nuke—to be held in abeyance," Jack McGrath...said of the Manson spot. **1992–95** C.D.B. Bryan *Close Encounters* 174: Nukes...exotic biology...high-tech weapons.

2. *Mil.* a nuclear-powered ship or submarine. Also **nukie.**

    1960 *Time* (July 4) 52: The nuclear submarines—called "nukes"—can cruise underwater for weeks at top speed. **1964** *USS Long Beach* 124: Today, Nukie "9" crosses the equator. **1964** Hunt *Ship with Flat Tire* 151: We have seven Nukes...then we have another half dozen conventional submersibles. **1971** Dibner *Trouble with Heroes* 32: Our nuke subs and ships are polluting their water with radioactivity.

3. *Navy.* an officer or crewman qualified to operate a nuclear-powered vessel. Also **nuc.**

    1964 *USS Long Beach* 33: Engineering Department personnel are known as "snipes" in the Navy, while those who have qualified in nuclear power are referred to as "Nucs." *a***1984** T. Clancy *Red October* 42: Captain Casimir...wore the wings of a naval aviator....He wasn't a "nuc." *Ibid.* 89: These guys are working sailors, nucs. *a***1995** Gallantin *Sub. Admiral:* I was past the point where I was eligible for consideration as a "nuke."

4. a nuclear power station.

    1969 *Business Week* (Sept. 20) 52: More than 100 nuclear plants are scheduled....Despite some picketing and...reprints of a Life magazine article questioning the safety of "nukes." **1971** in *BDNE* 324: According to the Hudson River Fishermen's Association, the nuke was directly responsible for the death of [fish]. **1975** *Business Week* (Jan. 20) 46: "Nukes" offer the cheapest electricity in the long run. **1982** *Mother Jones* (May) 2: Nukes aren't profitable. **1983** Breathed *Bloom Co.* 26: Welfare! Solar Power! No Nukes! *a***1988** C. Adams *More Straight Dope* 91: Sayonara OPEC, and toodaloo to nukes.

5. *Stu.* nuclear engineering.

    1978 Truscott *Dress Gray* 101: Helping you decipher yesterday's nuke problems.

nuke *v.* **1.** *Mil.* to destroy by means of nuclear attack; attack with a nuclear weapon. Now *colloq.*

    1962 in J.C. Pratt *Viet. Voices* 121: Even a big thing like the...Cuba missile standoff escapes our attention...."No one's going to nuke Nam." **1967** *Look* (July 11) 25: A group of American editors—whom he referred to as "superhawks"—who told him they favored "nuking" (A-bombing) China. **1968** J.K. Galbraith, in *Playboy* (June) 168: I'm always struck, when I go to the Pentagon, by how casually the Air Force generals talk about the possible use of nuclear weapons and how casually they have reduced such weapons to slang. The generals say, "Let's 'nuke' them." **1973** *N.Y. Times Mag.* (June 10) 65: I think we ought to nuke them all. **1976** Conroy *Santini* 370: Why don't we just go ahead and nuke the hell out of Moscow, Havana, and Peking. **1980** Univ. Tenn. student: Nuke 'em till they glow. **1981** *Daily Beacon* (Univ. Tenn.) 2: That's the movie that ends with New York being nuked. **1981** Gilliland *Rosinante* 172: A [science-fiction] terrorist [was] killed trying to nuke a prenatal care clinic. *a***1988** in Terkel *Great Divide* 62: When I turn on TV, I wanna see if Ron [Reagan] has nuked anybody today (laughs). **1990** *Daybreak* (CNN-TV) (Aug. 28): We hear everything from "Nuke 'em till they glow" to "Let's settle this diplomatically."

2. to punish severely; (*broadly*) to destroy; devastate; ruin; spoil.

1969 *Current Slang I & II* 64: *Nuke*, v. To get revenge in a big way.—Air Force Academy cadets. **1981** Stiehm *Bring Men & Women* 258: A cadet was either immune [from punishment] or "nuked." **1982** *Time* (Nov. 8) 91: That English test really *nuked* me. **1985** *N.Y. Times Higher Ed. Supp.* (Mar. 8): *Nuke*. To get rid of something. **1987** *Magical World of Disney* (NBC-TV): You nuked my brother. **1989** *Dream Street* (NBC-TV): You mean the Proust of postmodernism? Nuke 'im. **1989** *TV Guide* (Oct. 21) 41: Hannah...is tired of having Catherine..."nuke" her stories. **1990** *Days & Nights of Molly Dodd* (Lifetime TV): This storm is absolutely going to nuke my hairdo. **1991** *CBS This Morning* (CBS-TV) (Oct. 10): Rather than nuking your body with steroids. **1991** Nelson & Gonzales *Bring Noise* 156: Lyte...wants to nuke this chick. **1992** *Melrose Place* (Fox-TV): If I nuke him with the truth, he'll be devastated. **1992** *Time* (Aug. 10) 48: Mosquitos a problem? Just take some DDT and nuke 'em.

3.a. to cook or heat in a microwave oven. Hence **nuker**, *n.* a microwave oven.

1984 Eble *Campus Slang* (Sept.) 6: *Nuke*—cook something in a microwave oven: Nuke it—it'll only take a couple of minutes. **1986** Eble *Campus Slang* (Nov.) 6: *Nuke*—cook in a microwave: "How long should I *nuke* these leftovers?" **1988** Huntsville, Ala., electrical technician (coll. J. Ball): Have you heard *nuke*, meaning "to microwave"? My favorite [expression] is *nuke a dog*—"to cook a hot dog". **1988** Univ. Fla. student (coll. J. Ball) [ref. to 1987]: Yeah, *nuke*—you hear that all the time in Gainesville—"I'll nuke me up a jelly-roll." **1989** *Beachin' Times* 8: Any food you can nuke [vs.] dorm food. **1989** J. Weber *Defcon One* 120: There was a scramble for the...microwave as Hank Doherty "Nuked" the...doughnuts. **1990** P. Munro *Slang U.*: *Nuker* microwave oven. **1990** *Time* (Feb. 19) 86: Mastering new cooking techniques like zapping and nuking. With microwave ovens now installed in three-quarters of the nation's kitchens, [etc.]. **1991** *Sci. American* (Oct.) 134: To nuke a slab of pizza is a common task in the kitchen.

b. to cook thoroughly or overcook.

1989 *Married with Children* (Fox-TV): Give me four steaks. Nuke 'em.

4. to electrocute (a person); FRY, 2.b.

1992 Lavner *My Cousin Vinny* (film): They're gonna nuke this guy Norton this weekend. **1992** *Atlantic* (Feb. 1993) 20: A sentence that in exceptional circumstances my wife has been known to favor: "Nuke 'em till they glow."

Nuke Ridge *n.* Oak Ridge, Tennessee, center for early research on the atomic bomb.

1988 *Rage* (Univ. Tenn.) I (No. 11) 21: Nuke Ridge, Tn.

nukie var. NUKE, *n.*

numb *n.* NUMBSKULL.

1807 W. Irving *Salmagundi* 60: All the New Jersey lawyers [are] *nums*. **1973** N.Y.U. student: Hey, numb! **1983** Moranis et al. *Strange Brew* (film): You take off, you numb!

numb *adj.* **1.** drunk, esp. blind drunk.

1918 in *Wisc. Mag. of Hist.* 62: 240: I am not saying that the stuff is non-intoxicating, for one *can* get "numb" on it. **1949** Algren *Golden Arm* 53: But the customers come here to get numb off Schlitz; not off you.

2. stupid; inane. Cf. **numbheaded** s.v. NUMBHEAD.

1954–60 *DAS*: *Numb*...Stupid; inattentive. **1971** H. Roberts *Third Ear*: *Numb*...dumb; stupid. **1971** Dahlskog *Dict.* 43: *Numb*, *n.* stupid; brainless; vapid, as: a *numb* movie.

numbbrained *adj.* stupid. Hence **numbbrain**, *n.*

1930 Lavine *Third Degree* 30: To gain...recruits from the numb-brained hanger-ons. **1953** Dobson *Away All Boats* 470: Some numb brain will say..."When does the next plane for Eniwetok?" **1966** Braly *On the Yard* 136: How come he lets a batch of numb-brained fuzz catch him?

number *n.* **1.** one's name or identity. [In bracketed S.E. quot., '(of a vessel) to signal its number of identity'.]

[***1836** in *OED*: The Enterprise had made her number.] **1842** *Ben Hardin's Crockett* (unp.): "Darkey, mebby you don't belong to noboddy in this place. Jist give us your number."..."I ar gwoine to see the traps, massa, jest out hear in the forrest." **1883** Parker *Naval Officer* 23: We were surprised at seeing the *St. Louis* coming back alone, and my heart sank as we made out her "number." I could only think that the *Brandywine* had gone down with all hands.

2.a. an item, esp. of fashionable clothing. Now *colloq.*

*1894 in *OEDS*: The shop windows...had progressed...to straw hats, tennis shoes, and coloured Summer Numbers. **1946** Diamond & Kern *Never Say Goodbye* (film): Did you pick out these little numbers, Flip? **1948** in *DAS*: I found a number [*sc.* a suit] I liked pretty well.

b. *Broadly*, a thing, place, idea, etc., of a kind suggested by context.

1903 A.H. Lewis *Boss* 205: He tells me my light's goin' to flicker out inside a year. That's a nice number to hand a man! *Ibid.* 262: Me fadder kept a joint in Kelly's Alley; d' name of d' joint was d' Door of Death, see! It was a hot number, an' lots of trouble got pulled off inside. **1904** *Life in Sing Sing* 262: You missed the number. They hadn't the shot....But you missed the essential point—they lacked the means. **1928** in *DAS*: Picking up a number [*sc.*, an automobile to be stolen] on the street ain't like getting your shoes shined.

c. *Black E.* a pistol.

*a***1940** in Lomax & Lomax *Our Singing Country* 343: Well, he shot bad Laz'us, partner,/Shot him wid a great big number.

d. *Narc.* a marijuana cigarette; (in 1980 quot.) a dose of heroin.

1963 in Abel *Marihuana Dict.* 74: You smoke a number while I go and call John. **1967** J.B. Williams *Narc. & Hallucin.* 114: *Number*—Marijuana cigarette. **1969** "Holy Modal Rounders" *Roll Another Number for the Road* [song title]. **1970** A. Young *Snakes* 60: OK if we fall on in and do up a coupla numbers? **1971** *N.Y. Post* (May 24) 39: So we go down to the water point, swim a little, puff a few numbers (marijuana joints) and radio in. **1970–72** in *AS* L (1976) 63: Let's smoke a few numbers. **1972** N.Y.U. student: *Doing a number* means smoking grass. **1974** Hejinian *Extreme Remedies* 185: I thought you brought a number. **1978** J. Webb *Fields of Fire* 228: Hey, man. Wanna do a number? **1980** in Courtwright et al. *Addicts Who Survived* 106 [ref. to *ca*1940]: I'll keep snorting my number. **1992** N. Russell *Suicide Charlie* 75: Teamed up with Phil to...smoke a number.

3.a. a person, freq. an attractive member of the opposite sex. See also HOT NUMBER.

1896 in A. Charters *Ragtime Songbook* 55: Say gal, you' sure a red hot number. **1919** *DN* V 70: *Hot one, -number*, used as a term of disgust. "You're a *hot one* I must say." New Mexico. **1931** Rouverol *Dance, Fools, Dance* (film): So that's your new—number? **1931** in J.T. Farrell *Guillotine Party* 89: He had a date with a keen number....She was hot stuff. **1935** Sherwood *Idiot's Delight* 112: *Don.* What "dame"? *Harry.* That Russian number with Weber. **1935** in H. Gray *Arf* (unp.): He's a cold-blooded number. **1936** Ryskind & Hatch *My Man Godfrey* (film): She's a sweet-tempered little number. **1936** Monks & Finklehoffe *Brother Rat* 29: The smoothest fourteen-carat number that ever hit the Shenandoah Valley. **1938** O'Hara *Hope of Heaven* 106: Sure, I remember her. Nice little number. **1938** Miller & Totheroh *Dawn Patrol* (film): This little spotted number on my left goes by the name of Scotty. **1939** *New Directions* 131: She's not a day under forty but boy is she a number wow! **1939** I. Shaw *Sailor Off Bremen* 159: You were the prettiest number in Brooklyn. **1939** Trumbo *Sorority House* (film): See that lovely looking number sitting over there?...That's the dean's wife. **1939** Howsley *Argot* 6: *Bad Number*—dangerous; a desperate person; untrustworthy, unlucky. *a***1940** in Lanning & Lanning *Texas Cowboys* 103: We got one such number...and...poured sorghum molasses all over him. **1948** Lowry *Wolf That Fed Us* 91: There was a blonde in the bar—very neat number, well-dressed. **1952** A. Sheekman *Young Man with Ideas* (film): Quite a dish, isn't she? That Paris number. **1953** R. Chandler *Goodbye* 15: Down my street he's called a tough number. **1971** S. Stevens *Way Uptown* 162: That Sunny is one swift number. **1972** *Anthro. Linguistics* (Mar.) 105: Argot of the Homosexual Subculture...*Number* (n.): A male who is handsome or sexy. **1974** A. Bergman *Big Kiss-Off* 126: I...gave him a look. A sallow, black-haired number in his twenties. **1975** Schott *No Left Turns* 47: I picked up a couple of fast numbers in a blind pig. **1980** Algren *Devil's Stocking* 20: Most numbers talk out their fantasies in the joint. **1982** *Harper's* (Dec.) 52: Six muscular numbers wrestled him into a straitjacket.

b. *Specif.*, (*Prost.*) a customer of a (usu. male homosexual) prostitute; TRICK.

1967 Rechy *Numbers* 28: The number over there will drive you to the house when we have a carload. *a*1972 B. Rodgers *Queens' Vernacular* 142: *Number*...designation for all one's tricks past and present. **1975** *DAS* (ed. 3): *Number*...A casual homosexual lover. **1994** "G. Indiana" *Rent Boy* 24: Chip said he did the foot thing with this number once upon a time.

4. *pl.* an illegal lottery.—freq. constr. with *the*.

1897 in *OEDS*: She tell Belle 'at she heah I like gin an' roll'l bones an' play numbehs. **1930** Botkin *Folk-Say* 335: The horses and the numbers keeps most of them alive [in Harlem]. **1949** *New Yorker* (Nov. 12) 60: Any resemblance to the numbers racket is purely coincidental. **1950** *N.Y. Times* (Oct. 15) I 50: There was a large and open numbers racket operating in Philadelphia. **1960** *N.Y. Times* (Jan. 10) I 58: Mr. Powell's outburst last Sunday about numbers gambling—he said he opposed it. **1965** C. Brown *Manchild* 191: Numbers was like a community institution. Everybody accepted it and respected it. This was the way that the people got to the money.

5.a. Orig. *Theat.* a pattern of behavior or events, esp. if more or less predictable; (*broadly*) a situation or state of affairs; circumstance; ROUTINE.—freq. constr. with *do (one's)*.

1908 McGaffey *Show Girl* 31: I've got to roll my hoop and do a shopping number. *Ibid.* 46: After the hair dressing number I inhale about $4 worth of breakfast. **1941** *Pittsburgh Courier* (Dec. 20) 7: The only places that he "does his number" are in the walled confines of "inner cities." **1966–67** P. Thomas *Mean Streets* 243: God, if you're up there, I don't dig this number. **1971** *Mod Squad* (ABC-TV): Now captain, you're the man who started this whole number. **1971** S. Stevens *Way Uptown* 84: Then I seen the number. The only way I'd ever get a job with them was if I come in with a whitewash. **1971** *Interns* (CBS-TV): That would have blown his whole number. **1972** Kopp *Buddha* 220: I was...tempted to do my number of putting their whole thing down as superficial and without meaning. **1972** *Nat. Lampoon* (Dec.) 33: Cold cereal for breakfast, off-the-rack clothes, oleomargarine, I knew the whole depressing number. **1976** H. Ellison *Sex Misspelled* 33: If...one or the other of you took off and did your number and...the marriage dissolved, the career didn't materialize...forget it. **1977** Hamill *Flesh & Blood* 28: The blacks sit with the blacks at the movies. The whites do their number against the west wall. **1977** *New Yorker* (Oct. 17) 40: I did a bag-lady number on one of the platforms here...and I almost got arrested. They thought I was the real thing. **1979** Gram *Foxes* 73: I don't want you guys going through this big number just because of me.

b. a task; (*also*) a series of difficulties.

1970 Landy *Underground Dict.* 140: They really put me through a number....I can't do that number. *ca*1979 in J.L. Gwaltney *Drylongso* 121: Being an aunt is one of my biggest numbers.

6. a pair of sweethearts; couple; ITEM.

1976 Crews *Feast of Snakes* 5: Her sister and Joe Lon had been a number in Mystic, Georgia, in all of Lebeau County for that matter. **1980** L. Fleischer & C. Gore *Fame* 194: She and Leroy had been a heavy number for some time now. **1985** *Lady Blue* (ABC-TV): But you and he were a number.

7. *pl.* profit figures; wages. [The broader sense 'statistics' is not slang.]

1988 H. Gould *Double Bang* 62: You don't like your numbers, I'll get somebody else.

¶ In phrases:

¶ **by the numbers** *Mil.* as though according to standard procedures, esp. when such a procedure would be unnecessary or ludicrous; (*hence*) in a thoroughly blundering way.—now often constr. with *screw up* and vars. [Early quots. ref. to WWI.]

1918 in Peat *Legion Airs* 93: Give me a kiss by the numbers, I want to do things in a military way. **1919** *Amer. Leg. Wkly.* (Aug. 15) 9: What manner of person is this gold-striped (and incidentally gold-stripped) veteran who now walks "by the numbers." **1919** Langer *First Gas* 91: At dinner we now had a band, to the "jazz" of which we could chew our food by the numbers and digest it rhythmically. **1921** *Pirate Piece* (Nov.)

3: By the numbers, men, refill the glass on 4. **1925** van Vechten *Nigger Heaven* 59: They don't really stop playing numbers or dancing on Sunday. *Ibid.* 235: Everybody plays numbers, and yet it is just a lottery and consequently against the law. **1946** in Shibutani *Co. K* 391: As long as they can get away with it, they'll fuck off by the numbers. **1955** Goethals *Chains of Command* 165 [ref. to WWII]: I fucked up by the numbers, Major. **1955** Graziano & Barber *Somebody Up There* 231: Salute and yes-sir and shit by the numbers. **1967** G. Moore *Killing at Ngo Tho* 37: I guess he screwed up by the numbers during the short time, maybe three months, that he was there. **1970** in B. Edelman *Dear Amer.* 194: Good old [Smitty]. Still screw'n up by the numbers. **1987** Zeybel *Gunship* 98 [ref. to Vietnam War]: Sitting behind some numb-nuts and watching them fuck up by the numbers. *a*1987 Bunch & Cole *Reckoning for Kings* 151: He'd been fucking up by the numbers all along.

¶ **do a number, 1.** Esp. *Black E.* **a.** to act with surprising or devastating effect; ruin.—usu. constr. with *on*. Cf. **(5.a.)**, above.

1967 *Lit Dict.* 12: *Do a number*—To get mad; make a scene; to tell somebody off; blow your cool. *Ibid.* 42: *To Do A Number*—To fight for your rights....tell it like it is. **1968** Gover *JC* 20: Soon's somebody say *boo* at 'em, [the police] gonna be doin they main number [*i.e.*, shooting at people]. **1969** Crumb *Motor City Comics* (unp.): Let's split! We did a number here...Let's go do a number someplace else. **1970** in *Rolling Stone Interviews* 424: You can't really do any grandiose numbers with the ocean. It's a bit hard to bullshit the ocean. **1971** Adelman *Generations* 47: I'm going out to this underground radio station in California and do some heavy numbers on pig society. **1971** N.Y.U. philosophy prof.: If you *don't* believe in Him, and it turns out that God really *does* exist, you know He's gonna do a number on you. **1972** *N.Y. Times Mag.* (Sept. 24) 93: There were about four or five white cats doing a number on (beating hell out of) a Puerto Rican. **1974–77** Heinemann *Close Quarters* 28: I get about half a chance I'm gonna do a number square on his nappy fucken head. *a*1984 in Terry *Bloods* 115: The Phantoms were doing a number....The ground was just a-rumbling. **1991** LaBarge *Desert Voices* 189: A TOW missile...will definitely do a number on a tank. **1996** *Politically Incorrect* (Comedy Central TV): They've done a number on him, haven't they? His life is [ruined].

b. to trick; cheat; impose (upon); humiliate.—usu. constr. with *on*.

1971 S. Stevens *Way Uptown* 236: Somebody's doing a number on somebody awright. **1974** Mayes *Bank Shot* (film): Are you trying to do a number on me? **1978** in *BDNE3*: Johnny Carson...did a number on his new boss...with this line: "Freddy Silverman has just canceled his mother." **1985** Ferraro & Francke *Ferraro* 275: That's right, and you did a number on her [in a TV interview]. **1992** N. Cohn *Heart of World* 77: The numbers we did. The scams we pulled.

c. (with diminished force) to affect strongly.—usu. constr. with *on*.

1978 Selby *Requiem* 34: Thats some nice hash....Its really doin a number on my head. **1979** in *BDNE3*: Her big baby blues were too busy doing a number on my bloodshot brown ones.

2. to have sexual intercourse.

*a*1972 B. Rodgers *Queens' Vernacular* 219: *Do a zoo number* to turn to animals for sexual expression. **1978** Maupin *Tales* 18: "Him and me did a little number last month on his houseboat in Sausalito." "A little number?" "Fucked."

3. see **(2.d.)**, above.

¶ **good numbers** *CB.* best wishes; good luck.

1976 Whelton *CB Baby* 123: Good numbers on ya, sweetcakes. **1976** Lieberman & Rhodes *CB* 135: Put the Good Numbers On You—Best regards. **1977** Corder *Citizens Band* 193: Let me unload a bucketful of those good numbers on ya.

¶ **have (one's) number on it** *Mil.* (of a bullet, shell, etc.) to be fated to kill (one). Cf. *(one's) name is on it* s.v. NAME. [Early quots. ref. to WWI.]

1918 in Sullivan *Our Times* V 330: The phrase "It's got your number on it" suggests the fatalism of the soldier; a bullet or shell would not hit him unless it was intended especially for him, unless it was marked with "his number." *1921 N & Q* (Oct. 29) 344: *Number on (got your).* A bullet or shell intended for you. **1931** Dos Passos *Nineteen Nineteen* 411: The shell had his number on it. **1942** *Germans vs. Americans* 97: I heard about a thousand shells all around me, so I guess I heard the one that had my number. **1943** in *Best from Yank* 23: You thought every shell had your number on it.

¶ **have** [or **get**] **(someone's) number** to have precise, useful knowledge of (someone's) weaknesses; have (someone) in a critical position; (now *esp.*) to have correct, usu. insightful knowledge of (someone).

1853 in *OEDS:* Whenever a person proclaims to you "In worldly matters I am a child,"…that person is only a crying off from being held accountable, and…you have got that person's number, and it's Number One. **1908** in Fleming *Unforget. Season* 160: We have their number now…and they are due for a cleaning. **1909** in McCay *Little Nemo* 172: I'll make you suffer for this!…I've got your number, old pal! **1912** Stringer *Shadow* 257: I've got your number, Elsie Verriner, alias Chaddy Cravath. **1912** Mathewson *Pitching* 4: "I've got your number now, Matty!" he shouted at me as he drew up at second base. **1913** *Sat. Eve. Post* (May 31) 27: Patsy has had y'r number fr'm the first day.…'Tis plain…ye will never be a pitcher. **1913** J. London *Valley of Moon* 168: Well, I got his number. **1912–14** in E. O'Neill *Lost Plays* 173: Oh! I've got your number all right! **1914** E.R. Burroughs *Mucker* 54: I got your number, yeh big stiff. **1915** Poole *Harbor* 294: We've seen you in their meeting hall and we've all got your number. **1917** Oemler *Slippy McGee* 106: He's sure got your number in this burg. **1918** in *Chrons. of Okla.* LXV (1987) 32: Fritz dropped them [*sc.*, explosives] all around us last night but he didn't seem to have our number. **1918** in Gow *Lttrs. of Soldier* 426: Well, I expected to get it, but they haven't got my number yet. **1920** Ade *Hand-Made Fables* 55: Joe got his Number the first time he caught him hanging around. **1922** Colton & Randolph *Rain* 55: Ha, ha, the lady's got you're [*sic*] number, Tim, it's written all over your map! **1923** McAlmon *Comp. Volume* 4: We'll have to watch that Gammel guy. I got his number. **1928** W.R. Burnett *Little Caesar* 92: I got your number, Joe.…It's that damn skirt. She's making a softie of you, Joe. **1934** in *DAS:* She knew I had her number. **1968** Lockridge *Hartspring* 26: Deathwish, Hartspring. I've got your number. **1972** J. Mills *Report* 43: Then he goes back into his office to hide some more. Joey really has his number. **1979** *L.A. Times* (Jan. 20) II: Momma, you've got my number. **1995** Donahue (NBC-TV): I got your number now. **1996** *Jerry Springer Show* (synd. TV series): I got his *number!*

¶ **heavy number** a serious or difficult situation; sad story.

1971 Adelman *Generations* 91: And he puts down this very heavy number and his mind is so fucked up and I just get very uptight. **1976** R. Price *Bloodbrothers* 184: Look, there's this very heavy number goin' down with my father and uncle.

¶ **lose the number of (one's) mess** *Nav.* & *Mil.* to be killed. Also **lose (one's) number.**

1814 B. Palmer *Diary* [entry for Apr. 10]: I very much fear if they keep us here through the Summer that the majority of us will lose the number of our mess. ***1821–26*** Stewart *Man-of-War's Man* II 17: He's down, sir,…lost his number completely—lies in the outer trench yonder—…it was given him, slap through the head, sir. ***1833*** Marryat *Peter Simple* 420: I'm afraid there are many poor fellows who have lost the number of their mess. **1834** *Mil. & Naval Mag. of U.S.* (Oct.) 117: Why, as missing the number of one's mess sends us either below or aloft, where we shall be court-martialled 'cording as we carry sail here, them 'ere what minds the parson and steers in his wake is best off. **1838** *Crockett Almanac* (1839) 2: The Kurnel had lost the number of his mess amongst the Texicans. *ca***1840** Hawthorne *Privateer* 244 [ref. to 1814]: The man who informed was sent away by Capt. Shortland; for it would not have been good for his safety to have remained among the prisoners. In sailors' phrase, "he would have lost the number of his mess." **1871** *Overland Mo.* (Mar.) 277: Many a poor fellow…"lost the number of his mess," and was carried out from his "shebang" to his long home. **1893** Frye *Field & Staff* 178: Oh, Hickey, Hickey, you're in danger o' losin' de number o' y'r mess—den w'y worry 'bout a little t'ing like a pair o' miser'ble corp'ral's stripes. **1899** Robbins *Gam* 124: But you thought I'd lost the number of my mess, and in that you were all wrong. **1900** in Foner *Labor Songs* 186: They lost the number of their mess, but not much better we. **1907** *Independent* (May 23) 1184: Hundreds of able seamen "lost the number of their mess." **1918** Griffin *Reg't.* 28: You're too young to lose your number, and you don't know how to shoot. ***1931*** Tomlinson *Stories of the War* 387 [ref. to 1918]: It's the like o' them nine inchers can lose ye the number of yer mess, just by the blast of its passing.

¶ **make (one's) number** *Mil.* to make (oneself) known; curry favor.

1942 in Partridge *DSUE* (ed. 7) 1266: Make one's number. **1947**

Conarroe *Sea-Chest* 282: *Make numbers.* To curry favor with the top braid, hence get a good fitness report, hence retain or improve your seniority. (All Regular officers are listed by number according to seniority.).

¶ **(one's) number is up** *Esp. Mil.* (one) is about to die; (*hence*) (one's) fate is imminent, in the form of death or retribution.

1806 in *OEDS:* Though this is a lottery to which none but G. Barnett would choose to trust his all, there is no harm to call in at Despair's office for a friend, and see if his number is come up. **1894** Henderson *Sea Yarns* 52: I decided that my number were h'isted an' I were bound fur Davy Jones's locker. **1928** in O'Brien *Best Stories of 1928* 231: Your number's up, Smoothface. **1928** W.R. Burnett *Little Caesar* 110: Your number's up.…Take it like a man. **1939** H. Gray *Arf* (Dec. 4) (unp.): Yeah! Your number's up, Nick! **1939** L. Katz *Return of Dr. X* (film): The poor guy's number must have been up. **1943** J. Mitchell *McSorley's* 31: You can't live forever. When your number's up, rich or poor, you got to go. **1944** Huie *Can Do!* 52: Unless your number is up, all hell can't kill you. **1958** Camerer *Damned Wear Wings* 134: Jimmy knew his number was up. **1972** in *Playboy* (Jan. 1973) 180: My daughter is afraid to fly in an airplane because…it might be the pilot's number that's up. **1976** Whelton *CB Baby* 121: Tough guy!…Your…number is up, you hear me! **1977** M. Franklin *Last of Cowboys* 21: Your number's up. **1980** McAleer & Dickson *Unit Pride* 14: His number was up and nothin' he could do would've changed it. **1983** Nelkin & Brown *Workers* 105: Too damn bad. If my number's up, my number's up. **1986** S. Bauer *Amazing Stories* 20: I'm not going to die, Father. My number's not up. *a***1990** Helms *Proud Bastards* 185: When your number comes up, you're gone.

¶ **pull** [or **run**] **a number** to perpetrate a trick or deception.—usu. constr. with *on*. Cf. *do a number*, 1.b., above.

1973 in *DAS* (ed. 3): The first thing a good shrink teaches you is to stop fooling yourself.…When he's pulling one of his numbers, he knows what he's doing. **1977** *Rolling Stone* (Dec. 29) 65: She tolerated no emotional blackmail but was not unsympathetic to the lovers who tried to run their number on her. **1980** *Mother Jones* (Dec.) 50: I cannot be in control of the vulvas who happen to get my home phone and take it into their heads to run a number. **1983** Sturz *Wid. Circles* 9: He's running a number on us! **1988** *21 Jump St.* (Fox-TV): We're going to pull a little number on Four-Eyes. **1989** *Night Court* (NBC-TV): It sure sounds like Dan pulled a number on you last night. **1994** *My So-Called Life* (ABC-TV): You will not believe the number Sharon Cherski just tried to pull on me. **1995** *Young & Restless* (CBS-TV): I know that Jill has pulled a lot of numbers on you in the past.

number-chaser *n.* an accountant. Cf. NUMBER-CRUNCHER, 2.

1938 Haines *Tension* 61: But a big blond number chaser seen some of Beckett's time sheets and took to weeping red ink.…He come into my office, pencil in one hand and notebook in the other, chattering cost talk as bold as a bull chipmunk.

number-cruncher *n.* **1.** a computer designed to perform mathematical analyses. Hence **number-crunching,** *adj.* Now *colloq.*

1966 in *OEDS:* The Flowers report recommended the setting up of some "regional centres" each with a large "number-cruncher" to take the bulk-computing load off more local machines. [**1970–72** in *AS* L (1976) 63: *Number-cruncher course*…Course that involves much mathematics or many formulas "Second-semester physics is definitely a number-cruncher course."] **1974** Univ. Tenn. student: A *number-cruncher* is a large computer used for numerical analysis which can perform operations extremely rapidly. It's also called a *number-crunching machine.* It just sits there and crunches away. **1976** in *BDNE3:* A conventional giant number-cruncher like the CDC 7600. **1977** *Business Week* (Sept. 19) 138 (ad): One Prime computer can do it all: complex simulations…transaction processing, massive number crunching and more. **1979** Homer *Jargon* 149. **1982** *Time* (Jan. 3, 1983) 30: Today almost any home computer…can outperform poor old ENIAC as a "number cruncher."

2. an accountant or statistician, esp. one lacking imagination or creativity; BEAN-COUNTER. Now *colloq.*

1977 *Dallas Times-Herald* (May 22) B2: He acted only as a technical resource person, a "number-cruncher." **1980** Cragg *Lex. Militaris* 313: *Number Cruncher.* An analyst of any kind. **1982** *Chicago Sun-Times* (Nov. 18) 142: Despite the claims of the numbers crunchers [*sic*] in the NFL office, the plan was developed [etc.]. **1987** R.M. Brown *Starting*

185: Television networks are stocked with number-crunchers, people who desperately want guidelines and safe answers. **1987** *Campus Voice* (Winter) 45: We're not turning out number-crunchers....We turn out internationalists who can handle themselves in any country. **1993** *Young and Restless* (CBS-TV): He's turning this over to a roomful of thirty-year-old eagle-eyed number-crunchers.

number dummy *n.* Esp. *R.R.* a clerk.

    1931 *Writer's Dig.* (May) 42: *Number Dummy*—Yard clerk. **1931** *AS* VII 22: *Number dummy*—room clerk. **1945** Hubbard *R.R. Ave.* 353: *Number Dummy*—Yard clerk or car clerk; also called *number grabber.*

number-grabber *n.* **1.** *Army.* a draftee.

    1919 Ellington *Co. A* 113 [ref. to 1918]: *Number Grabbers*—Drafted men.

    2. *R.R.* a clerk.

    1926 *AS* I 250: Number-grabber. **1931** *Writer's Dig.* (May) 42: *Number Grabber*—Car clerk. **1945** (quot. at NUMBER DUMMY). **1972** *Urban Life & Culture* I 372: "Number grabbers," car clerks who work outside.

number one *n.* **1.** oneself, as the object of self-interest. Now *colloq.*

    *1704–05 in *OED:* The Knight I doubt not, but 'tis very careful of number one. **1829* Marryat *Mildmay* 283: As for that matter...we privateer's-men don't trouble our heads much about it; we always take care of Number One. **1833** A. Greene *Duckworth* I 146: Remember you're number one; and do to others as they do to you. **1838* C. Dickens, in *F & H* V 75: Ha! ha! cried Mr. Bolter. Number one for ever. *a*1860 Hundley *So. States* 236: And do you suppose...that the Southern horse-jockey...is yet any less shrewd...to...look after number One? **1862** in Hicken *Illinois in Civil War* 59: We found ourselves nearly surrounded and then we had to run to save No. 1....we got out but it was done by some of the tallest running that we ever done. **1873** Jewell *Among Our Sailors* 35: The law of self-preservation, to care for himself—to look out for "number one," as Jack styles it. **1873** Murdoch *Crockett* 142: Oh, he'll take care of Number One, I reckon. **1904** *Independent* (Mar. 24) 661: I always looked out for number one. **1962** *New Yorker* (July 7) 84: Grafting from municipal corporations, scheming for rich wives, and, in short, taking care of No. 1. **1976** *U.S. News & W.R.* (Nov. 1) 32: I'm for No. 1. I'm for the guy who is me.

    2. the act of urination; urine.—used euphem. Occ. as *v.* Cf. NUMBER TWO, 1.

    *1902 F & H V 75: *Number one....*Urination; also a chamber pot. **1934** H. Roth *Call It Sleep* 37: "You'd better go in and 'pee' first.... How does your mother say it?" "She says numbuh one." *Ibid.* 101: See if he wants to do number one or somethin'? **1935** *Bedroom Companion* 67: I've got to Number One. *Ibid.* 68: Making a Number One....Can you guess it, Agatha? *Ibid.* 69: Or doing Number One. **1936** Farrell *World I Never Made* 427: Papa has got something like you got to make number one with and he puts it in Mama. **1954–60** *DAS: Number One...*To urinate. **1962** T. Berger *Reinhart* 95: One raised finger,...the schoolroom signal for Number One. **1977** *L.A. Times* (Feb. 9) IV 1: In this time of drought and sun, We don't flush for No. 1. **1978** *Rolling Stone* (Dec. 28) 88: I'd love to talk to you about this, but I have to go visit the fire hydrant. I feel a number one coming one. **1990* T. Thorne *Dict. Contemp. Slang: Number one(s)...*urination.

    3. *Baseball.* a fastball. Cf. NUMBER TWO, 2.

    1932 *Baseball Mag.* (Oct.). **1989** P. Dickson *Baseball Dict.: Number 1...*Fastball, so-called because the catcher's traditional signal for the pitch is a single finger pointed down. **1996** *World Series* (Oct. 22) (Fox-TV): He's gonna rely on ol' number one.

number one *adj.* first-rate; splendid; excellent; great; (*hence*) favorite. Also as *adv.* [Hence recent S.E. *number one* 'best, preeminent'. Since 1960's, esp. assoc. with East Asian pidgins, though 1868 quot. shows the phr. to be at least a century older in such use.]

    1839 *Spirit of Times* (June 29) 195: He...will do all he can to make it "a number one" concern. **1848** in *DA:* I have some beautiful poems by me by Mrs. Barnes....They are No. 1, full of passionate feeling and eminently worthy of a place. **1854** in Bancroft *Slave-Trading* 82: This is truly a No. 1 woman. **1862** in C.W. Wills *Army Life* 74: George was a No. 1 soldier. **1866** Meline *On Horseback* 108: C. is a No. 1 doctor...a great surgeon. **1868** in Boyer *Naval Surgeon* II 126: The Mandarin spoke three or four words in English—"No. (number) one" and "Very good." **1877** in J.M. Carroll *Camp Talk* 85: Doane is a "No. 1" officer. **1882* in Partridge *DSUE:* Number one chow chow. **1885**

Siringo *Texas Cowboy* 103: A well-filled chuck wagon, a number one good cook. **1898** Bullen *Cachalot* 169: Samuela, the biggest of my two Kanakas, very earnestly informed me that he was no end of a "number one" whale slaughterer. **1917** *Editor* (July 25) 121: A Pidgin English vocabulary...Number one—very fine, first. **1933** *Leatherneck* (Nov.) 20: We ate Army chow—and take it from one who knows his chow—the fodder was number one. **1936** Twist *We About to Die* (film): You number-one good man; you make dying allee same like living. **1936** Dos Passos *Big Money* 299: Charley, you're number one. **1946** Dadswell *Hey, Sucker* 21: He has been affectionately called the world's Number One trainmaster. **1953** Russ *Last Parallel* 242: After the briefing I asked Cpl. Hanna what kind of an officer Guyol was. "Number fucking one," he replied. **1954** Voorhees *Show Me a Hero* 20: Dai Ichi. Means Number One in Jap. **1961** Barbeau *Ikon* 10: You want woman, GI? Nice woman—number one—four dollar. *Ibid.* 57: We've got a number one outfit. **1964** R. Moore *Green Berets* 292: She is a number-one woman. **1966** *N.Y. Times Mag.* (Oct. 30) 102: Hey, you. You No. 1 (the best). **1966** in Steinbrook *Allies* 22: You number one f--king GI. **1970–72** Densen-Gerber *Drugs, Sex, Parents* 67: This guy is number one and you're going to be his girlfriend—big deal. **1977** Caputo *Rumor of War* 36: With that and my retirement I figure old Wild Bill's gonna have it number fuckin' one. **1984–87** (quot. at NOOK). **1988** *Right On!* (June) 69: My No. 1 rappers are Salt 'n' Pepa and LL Cool J. **1991** LaBarge *Desert Voices* 96: Formations of people—saying, "George Bush number one."

number one-thousand *adj.* [pidgin] NUMBER TEN. [Quots. ref. to Vietnam War.]

    1978 J. Webb *Fields of Fire* 252: VC *bac-bac* Phony? Numbah fucking One Thousand. *a*1987 Bunch & Cole *Reckoning for Kings* 61: First Sergeant number fucking one thousand.

number sixty-nine *adj.* [sugg. by NUMBER TEN and SIXTY-NINE] *Mil.* exceptionally bad; worthless; terrible.

    1966–80 McAleer & Dickson *Unit Pride* 254 [ref. to Korean War]: American beer...number sixty-nine. Mean no good.

number ten *n.* a shoe or foot.

    1873 Small *Pythias* 27: I tore my hair and stamped my No. 10s. **1928** Panzram *Killer* 73: Then the ropes are pulled thru the eyeholes and a big burly screw slaps his No. 10 in the middle of your back and hauls with all his strength on the ropes until you're as tight as you can get. [**1970** Quammen *Walk the Line* 180: I still be fittin' to ram my foot up his ass...I'm gon' stick my size ten right up his crack.]

number ten *adj.* [pidgin, sugg. by NUMBER ONE] *Mil. in Far East.* very unsatisfactory; very bad. Also as *interj.* [Later quots. ref. to Vietnam War.]

    *1953 in Partridge *DSUE* (ed. 6) (Supp.): He's just "number one" to "number ten." **1961** Peacock *Valhalla* 117 [ref. to 1953]: Marine no good....No hucking good. Number hucking ten. *Ibid.* 138: Him *toxon* bad. Number hucking ten. **1966** *N.Y. Times Mag.* (Oct. 30) 102: She...tells him how mamasan (the woman in charge of the bargirls) is No. 10 (the worst). **1966** in Steinbrook *Allies* 22: You number one zero GI. **1969** M. Herr, in *New Amer. Rev.* (No. 7) (Aug.) 73: This grass is Number Ten. **1978** Hasford *Short-Timers* 43: That's number ten, the worst. **1983** N. Proffitt *Gardens of Stone* 342: "How'd it go?"..."Numbah Ten." **1985** Heywood *Taxi Dancer* 129: Then you're doin' a number-ten job, kiddo. **1985** Flowers *Mojo Blues* 17: Number ten, GI, don't bring Nam back with you.

number ten thou *adj.* [NUMBER TEN + *thou*sand] *Mil. in Far East.* as bad as can be; the worst. Usu. *joc.* Also **number ten thousand.** [Quots. ref. to Vietnam War.]

    *a*1983 Elting, Cragg & Deal *Dict. Soldier Talk* 212: *Number ten thousand* or *number ten thou* (very, very bad). **1984** Holland *Let Soldier* 142: *Number ten thou...the worst possible,* infinitely worse than *number ten.* **1988** Willson *REMF* 28: *Number 10 Thou* Unbelievably bad. **1994** Steinbrook *Allies* 71: You cheap Charlie, number 10 GI, number 10,000 GI.

number two *n.* **1.** an act of defecation; feces.—used euphem. Also as *v.* Cf. NUMBER ONE, 2.

    1936 J.T. Farrell *World I Never Made* 202: She doesn't like me to be in here with you when you're doing number two. **1949** Mende *Spit & Stars* 40: He fastened the leash to the collar. "Did he make anything, Tommy?" "Just number one on the pump, Mrs. Moscowitz." "Did he make number two?" "I don't think so," said Tommy. **1954–60** *DAS: Number two* To defecate. **1967** Mednick *Sand* 105: What if he has to do a No. 2 in the middle of the night? **1972** *Playboy* (Sept.) 20: A full-page fertilizer ad in the Newburgh (New York) *Evening News* reads, "We're Number One in the Number Two Business and That's No Bull." **1978** *Rolling Stone* (Nov. 2) 46: We don't go number two, we don't fart. **1981** C. Nelson *Picked Bullets Up* 112: [His] house smells like number two.

2. *Baseball.* a curve ball. Cf. DEUCE, *n.*, 9.

  1984 *N.Y. Post* (Aug. 13) 36: Heat and a scandalous Number Two—Koufax parlayed them into a ticket to Cooperstown. *a***1989** P. Dickson *Baseball Dict.*: Number 2...Curveball, so-called because the catcher's traditional signal for the pitch is two fingers pointed down.

numbhead *n.* NUMBSKULL. Hence **numbheaded,** *adj.*

  1856 in *DARE*: The old coot was so awful numbheaded I couldent [*sic*] beat anythin' into him. **1864** in Mattocks *Unspoiled Heart* 127: The *numheads* did not turn out the guard. **1941, 1975** in *DARE*.

numbnuts *n.* a stupid fellow; NUMBSKULL.—usu. considered vulgar.

  1960 MacCuish *Do Not Go Gentle* 115 [ref. to 1940's]: Makes a man weary, Al, havin' ta 'sociate with numbnuts like these. *Ibid.* 356: How 'bout that, numb nuts? **1967** W. Crawford *Gresham's War* 30: If numb-nuts up there spooks again he'll probably raise up to pitch his grenade. **1968** Mares *Marine Machine* 93: Numb nuts Harper was firing on BOTH targets during slow fire. **1970** N.Y.U. student: Numbnuts. I've heard that. **1972** N.Y.U. student: I used to call a friend of mine "numbnuts" whenever he did something really stupid. I thought I made it up. **1974** Cherry *High Steel* 60: About you, numbnuts. **1968–77** Herr *Dispatches* 21: Hey, numbnuts, you forgot something. **1977** Butler & Shryack *Gauntlet* 135: And this is *my* thirty-eight special, numb-nuts. **1978** J. Webb *Fields of Fire* 76: Did numbnuts here really do that? **1980** Syatt *Country Talk* 20: Ask old numbnuts over thar! **1982** Del Vecchio *13th Valley* 468: If Numbnuts is goin, I ain't. **1983–89** K. Dunn *Geek Love* 97: I say, like a numbnuts, "What other guys?" **1990** *Tracey Ullman Show* (Fox-TV): "Back off, buddy!" "Make me, numbnuts!" **1993** *New Yorker* (Aug. 9) 38: This numb-nuts just buried his pickup in the mud. **1995** *Newsweek* (Oct. 16) 82: That age-old practice of carping about the boss....A guy named "numbnuts," the nickname the women had for him.

numbskull *n.* a dolt. Now *S.E.* Also **numskull.**

  [***1712** in *F & H* V 76: Have you no more manners than to rail at my husband, that has saved that clodpated, numskulled, ninnyhammer of yours from ruin?] [***1712** in *F & H* V 76: D— this numbed skull of mine, quoth he, that I could not light on it sooner.] ***1742** in *F & H* V 76: Thou art a numskull I see already. **1793** in St. G. Tucker *Poems* 91: Democratical numbskulls. ***1796** Grose *Dict. Vulgar Tongue* (ed. 3): *Numbscull.* Stupid fellow. **1809** W. Irving *History of N.Y.* I 40: I called them jolter heads, numsculls, dunderpates, dom cops, botteticks, domme jordans and a thousand other equally indignant appellations. ***1832** B. Hall *Voyages* (Ser. 2) I 69: You numskull. **1839–40** Cobb *Green Hand* I 68: This ladder...must have been invented by a numbskull. **1861** in C. Brewster *Cruel War* 64: That he ought to know or any other "numbskull." **1862** Gilbert *Confed. Letters* 11: I...selected the biggest numb-skull I could find. **1880** Pinkerton *Prof. Thieves & Detective* 351: That numbskull of a sheriff had us arrested for killing him. **1882** "M. Twain" *Life on Miss.* 128: Derndest numskull I ever saw. **1892** Garland *Prairie Folks* 163: You numskull. **1919** *DN* V 69: *Numskull,* a dullard. She put all the *numskulls* to shame with her teasing. New Mexico. **1925** in Galewitz *Great Comics* 52: If I catch the numbskull...I'll wring his neck. **1926** Tully *Jarnegan* 227: He could always be found where the numbskulls gathered.

numero uno *n.* **1.** a most important or influential person; boss; (*also*) anything of leading importance.

  1960 (quot. at SHOWBOAT, *v.*). **1972** R. Barrett *Lovomaniacs* 209: Strauss...had to be *numero uno* on the Monarch shit list. **1974** Lahr *Hot to Trot* 63: Jeannie—Princess of the Palmer Method, my Numero Uno. **1976** *L.A. Times* (Apr. 20) IV 71: Los Angeles would overtake New York as numero uno in the apparel world. **1976** *Dallas Morning News* (Nov. 14) 5C: He will be "numero uno, a big man" in exactly two years. **1977** *Texas Monthly* (Aug.) 81: A prestigious company like Nikon—*número uno* in status and reputation in the 35mm camera business. **1981** *L.A. Times Bk. Rev.* (Mar. 29) 8: "Forever and Forever" is the Numero Uno that Hooker McNeal wrote back in his salad days. **1982** *L.A. Times* (Sept. 23) V 28: In the catnip business, he is Numero Uno—Mr. Big. **1986** *Tales from Darkside* (synd. TV series): Numero uno...thinks you're the cat's meow.

2. oneself; NUMBER ONE, 1.

  1973 in J. Flaherty *Chez Joey* 227: I learned a long time ago that you look out for *numero uno* on this planet. **1975** *Harper's* (Aug.) 82: The talk was primarily about the big me, numero uno. **1976** *L.A. Times* (Dec. 28) IV 14: She's out for numero uno and no one dares stand in the way of her steamroller tactics. **1979** *S.F. Chronicle* (Feb. 18): More good life for ol' *numero uno*!

numero uno *adj.* [< Sp or It 'number one'] first-rate; the best; NUMBER ONE. Occ. as *n.*

  1942–44 in Legman *Limerick* (no. 582): Now, women are fine,/And sheep are divine,/But llamas are *numero uno*. **1968** Kirk & Hanle *Surfer's Hndbk.* 15: Fiber-glassed foam is numero uno. **1974** S. Kaufman *Falling Bodies* 36: A "*numero uno* gourmet cook." **1975** Lichtenstein *Long Way* 151: I used to dream about being a great tennis player. Numero Uno. Wow! **1976–77** C. McFadden *Serial* 318: I still think he's *numero uno*. Commitmentwise. In the human journey.

numerous *adj.* superior; notable.

  1841 *Spirit of Times* (Mar. 27) 43: Stranger,...in bar hunts I am *numerous*. **1860** J.G. Holland *Miss Gilbert* 172: He *is* rather numerous, ain't he? **1876** J.M. Reid *Old Settlers* 80: But with tongue he's "numerous pumpkins,"/And with fist he's quite persuasive.

nummy *n.* NUMBSKULL.

  1902 Carrothers *Black Cat* 90: Chop down de tree! chop down de tree, you nummies! **1977** Caputo *Rumor of War* 39 [ref. to 1965]: What a day the nummies picked for a mount-out.

num-num *n.* **1.** NUMBSKULL.

  1986 *Head of the Class* (ABC-TV): I'm staying here with these num-nums till I'm mature.

2. usu. *pl.* a woman's breast.

  1989 *Tracey Ullman Show* (Fox-TV): Nice num-nums but she is a little old. **1990** Univ. Tenn. student: She's got enormous num-nums.

numskull var. NUMBSKULL.

nun *n.* ¶ In phrase: **a nun's tit[s]** [or (*euphem.*) **lips**] see s.v. TIT, *n.*

nurd, nurdy vars. NERD, NERDY.

nursery *n.* *Skiing.* a beginners' slope.

  1949 Cummings *Dict. Sports* 282.

nut *n.* **1.** *pl.* **a.** something that is pleasing, easy, or delightful; a treat.—usu. constr. with *for* or *to.*

  ***1617** in *OED*: But they are needful mischief, and such are Nuts to me. ***1678** in *F & H* 78: It will be nuts, if this my case is. ***1785** Grose *Dict. Vulgar Tongue*: *Nuts.* It was nuts for them; i.e. it was very agreeable to them. **1817** in Royall *Letters from Ala.* 112: This was nuts for me. **1821** Waln *Hermit in Phila.* 29: We're *nuts* for the bank. **1834–40** Dana *Before the Mast* 203: This was nuts to us, for we liked to have a Mexican wet with salt water. **1853** Downey *Filings* 116: These expeditions were "nuts" to the old rangers. **1853** Lippard *New York* 55: "He'll talk o' nothin' else...for months to come,—eh, Fetch? 'For years, for years....It will be nuts for Ghoul.'" **1876** "M. Twain" *Sawyer* 92 [ref. to *ca*1845]: "Ain't it gay?" said Joe. "It's *nuts!*" said Tom. "What would the boys say if they could see us?" **1882** D. Cook *Hands Up* 261: The telegraph quoted at the end of the last chapter was "nuts" for Cook. He knew his man. **1884** in "M. Twain" *Huck. Finn* 222: Tom had his store clothes on, and an audience—and that was always nuts for Tom Sawyer. ***1892** in *F & H* III 342: It's nuts to 'ook on to a swell. **1896** C.C. King *Garrison Tangle* 50: He gets huffy when they guy, and that's nuts for the crowd. **1890** Howells *Hazard* 457: I reckon this thing is nuts for Lindau, too. **1895** Wood *Yale Yarns* 226: It was nuts to me to rub it in! **1898** Green *Va. Folk-Speech* 258: *Nuts, n.pl.* Something especially agreeable or enjoyable. **1902** in "M. Twain" *Stories* 450: Say, wouldn't it a' been nuts if he'd a-been here last night? **1906** in S.C. Wilson *Column South* 159: All this was nuts to us, and we fully agreed with them. **1918** Lardner *Treat 'Em Rough* 67: It is going to be nuts to learn it because most of the words is just English. **1928** C. McKay *Banjo* 148: Youse one nuts of a black beggar, pardner.

b. something that is extraordinarily good or pleasing.—constr. with *the.*

  1917 in Niles *Singing Soldiers* 10: Oh, Jonah got a gas-bomb and said this is the nuts,/I'll polish off this monster, cause I surely hate his guts. **1930** Nason *Corporal* 53 [ref. to 1916]: "Ain't you the nuts!" said Stuffy enviously. **1930** in D.O. Smith *Cradle of Valor* 9: This school is certainly the nuts. All the buildings are old feudal castles covered with ivy. **1930** Farrell *Calico Shoes* 40: He started supposing that his father owned a car. It would be the nuts. **1930–31** Farrell *Grandeur* 139: "Wouldn't it be swell to be out in the country?"..."It would be the nuts." *Ibid.* 149: It was the nuts of a show. **1929–33** J.T. Farrell *Young Manhood* 347: She dressed up like the nuts. **1933** W. March *Co. K* 64 [ref. to 1918]: Christ knows how they do it, but they're the nuts when it comes to cooking. **1934** Holm & Abbott *Three Men* 526: *Charlie.* (*Pats him.*) That was the nuts. **1934** in Ruhm *Detective* 91: The wine's supposed to be the nuts. **1936** Kingsley *Dead End* 683: *Angel.* Howza wawda, Tommy? *Tommy.* Boy! Duh nuts! **1937** Di Donato *Christ in Concrete* 224: Yeah kiddo—big steel is *the* nuts. **1939** in A. Banks *First-Person* 54: They raised the wages...so the workers think Swift's is the nuts. **1939** Appel *Power House* 11: It was the nuts of a day, he thought. **1940** Lawes *Murderer!* 159: I never seen nuthin' like that before, an' I thought it was the nuts. **1942** Tugend *Star-Spangled Rhythm* (film): It's the nuts—here among the nuts and bolts...on the swing shift! **1944** in C. Gould *Tracy* 6: "Are you comfortable, Mr. Tracy?" "Perfectly—in fact, this is *the* nuts." **1949** Gresham *Limbo Tower* 92: Jees, this is the nuts. Eating at a table. **1956** Ross *Hustlers* 121: "Nice, huh?"..."The nuts." **1956** Margulies *Punks* 109: We think she's the nuts. **1956** Levin *Compulsion* 93: This is the nuts! **1963** D. Tracy *Brass Ring* 77: Gee...that's the nuts. **1965** Carmichael & Longstreet *Sometimes I Wonder* 156: ...is the unblemished nuts. **1968** Baker, Ladd & Robb *CUSS* 164: *Nuts, the* a socially adept person. Extraordinary, unusual, hard to believe. **1981** *Magnum, p.i.* (CBS-TV): Now she's getting married! Isn't it the nuts? **1984** Wallace & Gates *Close Encounters* 110: When Hewitt asked me what I thought of the pilot, I assured him emphatically that it was "the nuts."

c. something that is extraordinarily unpleasant or objectionable.—constr. with *the.*

1919 *Our Navy* (June) 21: This packet is all the nuts in a million fruitcakes and the ship is just as popular with me as a glass eye at a burlesque show. **1927** Stevens *Mattock* 281: The women were all the nuts except the ones who would be true to one guy....it was the nuts to rot in a mudhole like the Brest Camp, waiting to go home. **1931** Hellinger *Moon* 19: It's all the nuts, that's what it is. **1978** R. Price *Ladies' Man* 41: She sucked as a singer, she was putting herself through agony for nothing, and that was the dead nuts.

d. Esp. *Gamb.* an insuperable advantage (over someone), esp. in a game of cards; an unbeatable hand; streak of luck.—constr. with *the.*

1931 D.W. Maurer, in *AS* (June) 334: *Nuts*, n. Drop, in the sense of having someone covered with a gun. "He had the nuts on me, so I gave in." An assurance of victory; an unbeatable streak of luck. **1961** (cited in T.L. Clark *Dict. Gamb. & Gaming*). **1982** Hayano *Poker Faces* 68: He ain't seein' nothin' but the nuts from me from now on. *Ibid.* 186: *Nuts.* Strong or good hands. **1983** A. Alvarez *Biggest Game* 30: Throwing away hand after hand after hand, waiting for ironclad certainties—"the nuts." *Ibid.* 123: To sit in a...game and wait for the nuts. **1996** McCumber *Playing Off Rail* 315: I got the nuts now. He was shootin good but now he's in a losing funk.

2. the head; (*hence*) the mind. Cf. COCONUT, 1.a., b.

1841 Mercier *Man o' War* 185: Who ever thought you had so much poetry in that woolly nut of yours. ***1846** in *OEDS*: She'll go prat over nut (head over heels). ***1852** in J. Farmer *Musa Pedestris* 150: Which nearly split Dick's nut in two. ***1858** Mayhew *Paved with Gold* 189: The first round was soon terminated, for Jack got a "cracker on his nut." **1859** Matsell *Vocab.* 127: *Nut.* The head. **1870** *Putnam's Mag.* (Mar.) 301: The combatants struck each other...upon the head, the nut,...the noddle. ***1879** in *F & H* V 78: He rammed my nut against the wall. ***1888** in *F & H* V 78: If you've got a nut on you. **1892** L. Moore *Own Story* 447: Your nut is not screwed on right. **1893** F.P. Dunne, in Schaaf *Dooley* 75: I...got this here scar on me nut fr'm an unruly Clare man. **1895** Townsend *Fadden* 13: It hits some mug plunk on 'is nut. **1896** Ade *Artie* 84: They seemed to think I was wrong in my nut out there. **1899** A.H. Lewis *Sandburrs* 9: So when Billy sees Mary at Connorses spiel, like I says, she's such a bute he loses his nut. **1908** W.G. Davenport *Butte & Montana* 246: Jones could not get it through his nut. **1911** Bronson-Howard *Enemy to Society* 37: You've got a good nut on you. *a*1904–11 J. Phillips *Susan Lenox* I 330: You seem to have a nut on you. **1921** *Variety* (Aug. 19) 4: The umps loses his nut and takes a punch at him. **1930** D. Runyon, in *Collier's* (Sept. 13) 9: The minute Harry the Horse sees the coppers he loses his nut, and he outs with the old equalizer. **1949** H. Robbins *Dream Merchants* 90: You're beating your nut

against a stone wall, though. **1991** A. Sharp *Mission of Shark* (film): She just writes whatever comes into her nut.

3. a fellow; character.—often used derisively.—freq. (now usu.) constr. with *tough.*

1856 *Spirit of Times* (Apr. 5) 87: Zeb Beeswing was as hard lookin an old nut as you'd find on a twelve hours' travel. **1861** in H.L. Abbott *Fallen Leaves* 50: If he...doesn't get any absurd notions of being a tough nut. **1874** Pember *Metropolis* 339: Fact; the nut broke the bill at Newark; I saw him; he ain't drunk, and so can't be bust yet. ***1887** in *OED*: He is a close old nut. **1896** *Harper's Mo.* 150: "Who's the old nut walking out with your father-in-law?" "He's my clerk." **1916** *Sat. Eve. Post* (Feb. 12) 8: He's a tough old nut....He swore at me until he was black in the face. **1917** F. Hunt *Draft* 49: Let some of those nuts who are afraid to do any fighting come over here and take our jobs. **1917** in Truman *Letters Home* 34: I have written you a letter every night and gave it to a nut to mail and he failed to do it. **1918** in Truman *Letters Home* 50: Then if some inquisitive nut asks me a question, I'm up a creek. **1917–20** Dreiser *Newspaper Days* 386 [ref. to 1893]: When you're not here, [she's] dearie-ing up these other nuts. **1920** F.S. Fitzgerald, in *DAS*: Simple little nut. **1930** in R.E. Howard *Iron Man* 14: Mike is a queer nut....He ain't got a fighter's brain. **1948** McIlwaine *Memphis* 25: "I'm a tough nut," he says.

4.a. usu. *pl.* a testicle; BALL, 1.a.—usu. considered vulgar. Also in phrs. paralleling those at syn. BALL. [U.S. currency of BrE *nutmegs*, in bracketed quots., cannot be documented.]

[***a1697** in *F & H* V 80: My precious nutmegs doe not wound, For fear I should not live.] [***1785** Grose *Dict. Vulgar Tongue: Nutmegs.* Testicles.] [***a1832** in [Buchan] *Secret Songs* 57: I'll...whip off your nutmegs, he cried.] **1863** in McKee *Throb of Drums* 119: Such men...ought to be hung up by their n... till they starved to death. **1888** *Stag Party* 11: It's only a pet squirrel. He will come down when he finds out that there are no nuts up there [*i.e.*, under a woman's dress]. *Ibid.* 153: She'll offer to yank him right out of sin's ruts;/And she'll manage in some way to get at his —. **1898** Green *Va. Folk-Speech* 258: *Nuts, n.pl.* The testicles. ***a1890–1902** *F & H* V 78: *Nut...in pl....*The testes. **1916** Cary *Venery* II 13: *Nut...*In plural, the testes. Something a squirrel would not run up a woman's leg for. **1917** in Cochran *V. Randolph* 56: Mumps, by God!...Nuts look like these here Water-Wings. ***1914–21** Joyce *Ulysses* 476: How's the nuts?...Curiously they are on the right. **1924** Wilstach *Anecdota Erotica* 1: The most cheerful thing in the world. A peanut machine, that whistles while its nuts are being roasted. **1927** *Immortalia* 21: Arthur White had been castrated,/And had not a single nut. **1928** in Read *Lexical Evidence* 64: He bit the nuts off of a mule. **1928** Cowley, in *Jay Burke & Cowley Corres.* 181: He was either going to shoot off your nuts or blow out your brain. **1930** E. Pound, in Ahearn *Pound/Zukofsky* 32: Arter all, the bile weren't next to my nuts! **1933** Milburn *Trumpets* 312: "Ah, the little devil kicked me in the nuts," Claude breathed. **1932–34** Minehan *Boy & Girl Tramps* 172: I...kicked one cop in the nuts. **1935** Algren *Boots* 125: As soon as I smell 'em my left nut gets tight. **1938** Steinbeck *Grapes of Wrath* 89: Tom-cattin' hisself to death...an' his nuts is just a-eggin' him on. **1939** M. Levin *Citizens* 27: All he's gonna plant is his own dead nuts in...the cemetery. **1942** McAtee *Supp. Grant Co. Dial.* 7 [ref. to 1890's]: *Nuts, n.,* testicles. **1958** Camerer *Damned Wear Wings* 72: They'd simply tell the Big Brass to go roast their nuts. **1959** Morrill *Dark Sea* 70: He said, "I hope them mumps drop down to your nuts and you go soprano." **1960** MacCuish *Do Not Go Gentle* 16: He kicked Alvey in the nuts. 'At's dirty fightin', Normy. **1964** Peacock *Drill & Die* 264: A gravel pit! Well, drag my nuts through the gravy. A gravel pit! **1968** J.P. Miller *Race for Home* 250: No cracked nuts anyhow. **1969** Mitchell *Thumb Tripping* 116: Worked my nuts off eighty hours a week, and what for? **1970** T. Wolfe *Radical Chic* 118: You can get everything together once...to see people bury some gray cat's nuts and make him crawl and whine and sink in his own terrible grin. **1972** Singer *Boundaries* 310: Well, nuts are testicles. **1973** Goines *Black Girl* 30: If it doesn't bother you, it sure ain't no sweat off my nuts. **1974** Loken *Come Monday Morning* 116: Second mortgage, financed to the nuts. **1976** Conroy *Santini* 399: Besides, we'll just shoot it and run our nuts off. **1981** Raban *Old Glory* 27: It'd freeze your nuts off. **1994** N. McCall *Wanna Holler* 3: I kicked him in the...nuts. **1996** *Esquire* (Mar.) 96: Kick the other guy in the nuts.

b. *pl.* manly courage; BALLS, 4.a.—usu. considered vulgar.

1973 "A.C. Clark" *Crime Partners* 88: I wanted to see if you had any nuts. Now I see you ain't nothing but pure pussy, man. **1989** W. McDonald *Band of Bros.* 96: You gotta learn to turn it off....A man'll lose his nuts if he doesn't. **1993** *All Things Considered* (Nat. Pub. Radio) (Feb. 16): Black Men! It is time to get *wit'* it or *quit* it! Get some *guts* and *nuts!*...[signed] Queen Nzinga.

c. an orgasm; (*hence*) semen.—usu. considered vulgar. Cf. get (one's) nuts off, below.

*ca*1990 in Ratner *Crack Pipe* 83: He tries to get a nut. **1993** P. Munro *U.C.L.A. Slang II* 62: *Nut*...semen. *She had no idea that nut leaked out of the condom.*

5.a. a lunatic; fool.—also used attrib. Cf. 1906 quot. at NUTHOUSE, 1.a. [The 1903 quot. is perh. best interpreted as referring to the working of a shell game.]

[**a*1890–1902 F & H V 78: *Nut*...(provincial).—A harum-scarum ass.] [**1903** McCardell *Chorus Girl* 16: What with every bottle of Dogwood Essence sold, and..."Circus Joe," who worked the nuts on the edge of the crowd, they trimmed the towns.] **1908** in H.C. Fisher *A. Mutt* 156: They'll just think I'm some old nut. **1910** T.A. Dorgan, in *N.Y. Eve. Jour.* (Mar. 8) 14: Fight bugs and strong nuts are common around training quarters. **1914** Lardner *You Know Me Al* 152: But how would I feel if a boy of mine turned out like Allen and Joe Hill and some of them other nuts? **1918** (quot. at ACES-UP). **1919** *Amer. Legion Wkly.* (Aug. 22) 12: If you're crazy, they say it's safest to humor a nut. **1919** T. Kelly *What Outfit?* 63: The front, you nut! **1919** Piesbergen *Aero Squadron* 58: "Four Nuts"—A Quartette of Asylum Dodgers. **1925** in D. Hammett *Continental Op* 189: There was no profit in trying to find the reason behind any of her actions. She was a nut. **1930** *Scouting* (Jan.) 18: Say fellows, I was a nut....I didn't mean what I said. **1935** Lorimer & Lorimer *Heart Specialist* 278: Yes, I wear a brassière,...and any girl that doesn't is a nut. **1943** J. Mitchell *McSorley's* 13: You better keep your eyes on that long-haired nut. **1952** *Life* (Sept. 29) 111: Them nuts in the loony bin always cheered when they saw that. **1955** O'Connor *Last Hurrah* 50: I told you he was a nut kid. **1962** T. Berger *Reinhart* 2: He had at last got free of the nut ward. *a*1966 Barth *Giles Goat-Boy* 278: Your brother-in-law's a fool,/but you're a nut. **1969** Merrick *Lord Won't Mind* 206: What is all this? Are you a nut or something? **1980** *Daily News* (N.Y.) (Dec. 18) 50: Last week in New York, a nut shot John Lennon. **1993** *New Yorker* (May 17) 104: As the millennium draws near, every visionary nut seems to be running for God.

b. an enthusiast; buff; FREAK, 2.—usu. used in combs.

1915 in Lardner *Round Up* 185: He's a nut all right on the singin' stuff. **1921** *Amer. Leg. Wkly.* (Jan. 21) (cover): Have You a Little Movie Nut on Your Family Tree? **1927–28** Tasker *Grimhaven* 168: Don't you know that running around with them psychology nuts is the first step of insanity? **1928** *Amer. Mercury* (Aug.) 471: Daisy, to a dog nut like Chase, was royalty. **1936** in Pyle *Ernie's Amer.* 43: Duke is a nut on fires, too. He rides the engines on every alarm. **1942** Liebling *Telephone* 97: He is a "fishing nut." **1951** in *DAS*: When one football nut writes a book, another football nut should not be entrusted with the job of passing judgment on it. **1973** in *Playboy* (Jan. 1974) 71: She's a sports nut—an expert skier, swimmer and gymnast. **1987–89** M.H. Kingston *Tripmaster Monkey* 92: He's a health nut. **1989** T. Blackburn *Jolly Rogers* 4: Joe was a fitness nut. **1994** Bak *Turkey Stearnes* 138: An absolute nut about baseball.

c. *Vaudeville.* an eccentric comedian (*obs.*); (*hence, broadly*) a highly amusing person; card. Also attrib.

1917 *N.Y. Times* (Dec. 23) IV 6: A "nut comedian"...interpolates any made fancy that enters his mind...."Nut acts" are popular. **1919** *Variety* (Apr. 11) 9: Adler is a typical "nut" comedian. **1921** *Variety* (Jan. 28) 8: Kellam is a scream comic, part "nut" and part satirist. **1923** *N.Y. Times* (Oct. 7) VIII 2: *Nut Comic*—Comedian who says and does ridiculous things often impromptu...a daffy guy. **1929** Brecht *Downfall* 58: "Oh, Dick, you're such a nut," Kitty laughed. "Yes, I'm a nut from Nutville," Dick answered. **1931** in D.O. Smith *Cradle* 167: I went...to see Sweet and Low with Fanny Brice and a lot of other nuts in it. **1945** F. Baldwin *Ariz. Star* 110: Mona was a nut, he told himself, a charming, rather silly, yet far from stupid woman. **1978** Druck *Final Mission* 79: Virginia laughed. "You're priceless, you nut."

6.a. a sum of expenses that must be met; overhead; initial outlay.

1909 Irwin *Con Man* 81: First they took out the "nut." That is the general term, among gamblers for the expense account. *Ibid.* 88: A lit-

tle fine came out of the "nut." **1909** T.A. Dorgan, in Zwilling *TAD Lexicon* 60: We heard word last night that Jack Johnson and George Little, his manager, had a nut on moving pictures and that the champion would not exert himself in trying to knock Ketchel out so that the moving pictures would be a harvest. **1914** Jackson & Hellyer *Vocab.* 62: *Nut*...an expense incurred in connection with a venture. "The grift was punk; we were framed five strong and never got the nut off." "We went on the nut for two fifty." **1923** *N.Y. Times* (Sept. 9) VIII 2: *Nut:* The overhead charge; expense of operation. **1929** *Sat. Eve. Post* (Oct. 12) 29: *Nut.* Expenses. **1930** *Amer. Mercury* (Dec.) 456: *Nut, n.:* The cost of an operation; overhead. "I quit freightin'. Too much nut." **1930** Conwell *Pro. Thief* 35: A second rule is that the nut (expenses) must come off the top of every touch. **1933** Ersine *Pris. Slang* 55: *Nut*...Figuratively a place where losses are taken. "He put a grand on the geegaws and took it on the nut." **1935** *Amer. Mercury* (June) 230: *Nut:* concession charges for booking a joint; expenses. **1942** *Time* (Feb. 9) 75: The "nut" (overhead) is small. **1942** Liebling *Telephone* 10: All such refinements increase the "nut," or overhead. **1951** Mannix *Sword-Swallower* 33: The running expenses of the entire show—that's called the nut. **1953–58** J.C. Holmes *Horn* 39: How can you ever make the nut to pay all these cats? **1961** Clausen *Season's Over* 156: Going to be tough making the nut tonight. **1969** Gallery *Cap'n Fatso* 22: We wouldn't even clear the nut on the joint if we split right down the middle with you. **1970** Della Femina *Wonderful Folks* 100: The nut is very high for these folks. **1974–75** Powledge *Mud Show* 219: Always in excess of Hoxie's daily expenses, or "the nut." **1993** *CBS This Morning* (CBS-TV) (June 21): This [movie] is making its nut back. **1996** *Good Morning America* (ABC-TV) (June 5): Your total nut to cover is $154,000. **1996** McCumber *Playing Off Rail* 164: [A] hotel...that was still a third more than the Palmer House cost us. In a sense, the high daily nut fed our purpose, made us sharper, conveyed a sense of urgency.

b. *Und.* a payment or share, as of graft; payoff.

1929 M. Gill *Und. Slang: My nut*—My share. **1931–34** in Clemmer *Pris. Community* 334: *Nut*...protection money. **1942** *ATS* 436: Payment; gift....*nut*, a reward for an arrest. **1957** E. Lacy *Room to Swing* 36: The nut comes out to over nine hundred bucks—where's my pork chops? **1970** Cole *Street Kids* 149: I found out later from a friend who is a cop that a "nut" or payoff envelope of $2000 per month per man, in the middle echelons of the police, is pretty standard. **1972** *Nat. Lampoon* (Feb.) 72: He's out collecting "the nut," says Tracy. **1972** *N.Y. Times Mag.* (Dec. 17) 42: The "nut"...is the individual policeman's share of the "pad." **1973** Maas *Serpico* 156: And Serpico would still collect his "nut," or share, of the 7th Division pad. **1980** W. Sherman *Times Square* 42: To pay the shylock's weekly nut, Mack turned to...holdups. **1983** *Hardcastle & McCormick* (ABC-TV): You got a week for the first nut. After that we collect every Tuesday.

7. *Und.* (see quot.).

1933 Ersine *Pris. Slang* 55: *Nut*...The combination of a safe.

8. [perh. infl. by *nub*] the gist; NITTY-GRITTY, 1.—also constr. in pl.

1963–64 Kesey *Great Notion* 182: When it comes right down to the *nuts* of it. **1965** Horan *Seat of Power* 17: I told him to cut the carny and get down to the nuts of it. **1970** *N.Y. Times*, in *BDNE3:* Just the way it's always been, but without tackling the nut of the problem. **1989** *Joan Rivers Show* (synd. TV series): The nut of the show is just that you have to deal with your problems. **1991** *CNN News* (CNN-TV) (Dec. 5): Attorney Black did not get to the nut of her testimony.

9.a. a sexual orgasm; (*hence*) an act of copulation; copulation.—usu. considered vulgar.

1968 Heard *Howard St.* 12: You got a nut, didn't you? Ain't that what you paid for? *ca*1969 Rabe *Hummel* 76: You got that money stickin' outa your fly, you get laid. You get your nut! **1972** A. Kemp *Savior* 22: The crowd was so large that day it was going at a dollar a nut—and that was for it straight, no ad-libbing. **1974** Piñero *Short Eyes* 77: We're...tryin' to get this one last big nut together. **1978** *Penthouse* (Apr.) 129: Four girls...and four guys....They all come up together [to a singles resort], but I can tell no one's slipping the nut to no one. **1978** R. Price *Ladies' Man* 55: Finally...I was getting some nut....I sat back on the couch and waited, patting my banana. **1985** Dye *Between Raindrops* 195: Killed in mid-masturbation....Hope he got a final nut. His girlfriend won't be getting one for a long, long time. **1987** Eble *Campus Slang* (Apr.) 3: *Get a nut*—have sex: "Did you get a nut on your date last night?" **1987** E. Spencer *Macho Man* 92: This guy almost gets a nut brushing his teeth. *a*1994 Smitherman *Black Talk* 122: *Git a nut* To have an orgasm; used…[of] either a male or female.

b. a thrill of pleasure.

1974 Heard *Cold Fire* 82: It was an extra nut for me.

¶ In phrases:

¶ **beat (one's) nuts** *Black E.* (of a man) to have an orgasm.—usu. considered vulgar.

1967 Colebrook *Cross of Lassitude* 236: Ain't no need for your coming over this way again.…not going to beat your nuts here.

¶ **bust a nut** [or **(one's) nuts**] **1.** Esp. *Black E.* **a.** (of either sex) to have an orgasm.

1938 "R. Hallas" *You Play the Black* 74: Genter was so excited he like to bust a nut. **1963** in Wepman, Newman & Binderman *The Life* 83: Many a nut got busted in her butt. **1964** H. Rhodes *Chosen Few* 118: Jus' throw a rubber on, bust your nuts and git up. *Ibid.* 126: If you make her bust her nuts, you git your bread back. **1964** in B. Jackson *Swim Like Me* 103: Three whores.…They say, "Make me hot when a sucker get up on top a me and don't make me bust my nut." **1967** C. Cooper *Farm* 5: She lay with her arms spread like…a woman who has just busted her nuts. **1962–68** B. Jackson *In the Life* 433: You never busted your nuts with a man? Even if he goes down on you? **1968** Cleaver *Soul on Ice* 150: That's the only way I can bust my nuts with a black bitch, to close my eyes and pretend she is Jezebel. **1974** (quot. at ROUNDEYE). **1975** J.P. Smith *Amer. Boys* 49: He closed his eyes…while he was bustin' nut. **1977** Sayles *Union Dues* 189: At first she'd bust her nut with some of the tricks and she hated that. **1994** N. McCall *Wanna Holler* 40: They talked about…"beatin' your meat," "bustin' a nut," [etc.].

b. to become ecstatic.

1966 I. Reed *Pall-Bearers* 108: Why man, these rich kats are coming down here busting their nuts over you.

2. to strain or exert (oneself).—usu. considered vulgar.

1936 in P. Oliver *Blues Tradition* 224: Now I got a job, was paid to learn how to truck,/The boss tol' me this mornin' I like to busted one of my—/Nut-house is for crazy folks. **1967** Mailer *Vietnam* 17: You'll have to bust a nut to get it, Rottenbug. **1970** Thackrey *Thief* 147: There I was, busting a nut trying to do right and all that, and here I had to come home and listen to this kind of shit. **1979** in L. Bangs *Psychotic Reactions* 275: Busting their nuts trying to be decadent. **1984–88** Hackworth & Sherman *About Face* 437: Busting a nut with the rest of us as we hurriedly pushed…[equipment] out of the way.

¶ **bust (someone's) nuts** to pester (someone); *break* [or *bust*] *(one's) balls*, c, s.v. BALL.—usu. considered vulgar.

1956 E. Hunter *Second Ending* 37: I mean, this is getting like the comic bit where one guy's trying to figure out the atomic bomb, and the other guy keeps busting his nuts, isn't it?

¶ **crack (one's) nuts** to have an orgasm.—usu. considered vulgar.

1965 Trimble *Sex Words* 140: *Nuts cracked*…accomplishment of copulation or other intercourse in which ejaculation takes place in the male. **1966** King *Brave & Damned* 34 [ref. to WWII]: There's times a man has got to crack his nuts.

¶ **duck (one's) nut** to run away.

1912 Siringo *Cowboy Detective* 151: You had better duck your nut out of here, and do it quick.

¶ **for nuts** at all, for beans.—used in negative contexts.

1895 in *OEDS*: An' the eldest gal *she* thinks she can play, and, if you believe me, she can't play for nuts. **1899 in *OED*: They can't shoot for nuts. **1945** J. Bryan *Carrier* 7: Those crazy Japs can't fly for nuts.

¶ **get (one's) nuts off** (of either sex) to have an orgasm; *get (one's) balls off* s.v. ball.—usu. considered vulgar.

*ca*1932 in Holt *Dirty Comics* 54: I thought you might want to get your nuts off. *ca*1938 in Atkinson *Dirty Comics* 139: What other method do you use to get your nuts off? **1945–48** USMC *Marianas Coll.* (unp.): I wanted the thrill of the two of us getting our nuts off at the same time. The result was that I became pregnant. **1949** De Forrest *Gay Year* 54: Let's ditch this dump before that toothless old Queen over there gets off his nuts looking at us. **1958–59** Southern & Hoffenberg *Candy* 134: The guy's gittin' his *nuts* off fer chrissake! **1962** Killens *Heard the Thunder* 260 [ref. to WWII]: They get their nuts off whipping black heads. **1965** Friedman *Totempole* 290: Ain't he human?…Don't he have to get his nuts off? **1970** Peters *Sex Newspapers* 6: They are only interested in "getting their nuts off" and to hell with your satisfaction! **1975** C.W.

Smith *Country Music* 107: Tits and cunt and getting your nuts off and bragging about it. *ca*1990 in Ratner *Crack Pipe* 59: Stoney…was happy to have me get off his nut (make him climax).

¶ **get (one's) nuts rattled** (of a man) to copulate; experience orgasm.—usu. considered vulgar.

[**1914** in Cray *Erotic Muse* 193: Rattle your nuts against my guts,/I belong to an infantryman!] **1958** Cooley *Run for Home* 108 [ref. to *ca*1920]: You guys get yer nuts rattled?

¶ **give (one's) left nut** to want desperately.—usu. considered vulgar.

1958 Frankel *Band of Bros.* 234 [ref. to 1950]: I'd give my left nut to have a million-dollar wound like you got. **1966–67** W. Stevens *Gunner* 74 [ref. to WWII]: Would I ever give my left nut to get one. **1970** E. Thompson *Garden of Sand* 213: I'd give my left nut to have my vote back. **1975** De Mille *Smack Man* 144: I'd give my left nut [for your badge]. **1979** Hiler *Monkey Mt.* 51: There's a whole shitload of folks who'd give their left nut to trade places with you right now I'll bet. **1982** W.E.B. Griffin *Lieuts.* 165: When I was your age, I would have given my left nut for a commission. **1983** Flaherty *Tin Wife* 200: They'd give their left nut for what we got. **1985** Dye *Between Raindrops* 84: Goddamn guy is destroying a piece of gear I'd give my left nut to have. **1992** Mowry *Way Past Cool* 82: Lotta…kids give they left nuts to be your size.

¶ **have by the nuts** to have at one's mercy.—usu. considered vulgar. Cf. *by the balls* s.v. BALL[1].

1943 in Sherrod *Tarawa* 99: We got 'em by the nuts now! **1946–50** J. Jones *Here to Eternity* ch. iv: And they had you by the nuts. **1956** Resko *Reprieve* 184: The people…got us by the nuts. **1964** R. Moore *Green Berets* 84: If Minh talked, Chi would know you have him by the nuts, sir. **1968** Cameron *Dragon's Spine* 86: That way, the…bastard had you by the nuts. **1975** T. Berger *Sneaky People* 250: My old man's…in debt.…They got him by the nuts. **1978** Grosso & Rosenberg *Point Blank* 210: And before long they figure they've got him by the nuts.

¶ **Kelsey's nuts** see s.v. KELSEY.

¶ **make the nut** to be sufficient.

1966 H.S. Thompson *Hell's Angels* 184: Our eight cases [of beer] made the nut. **1970** in H.S. Thompson *Shark Hunt* 93: But with Killy in eclipse the Chevrolet team still made the nut with O.J. Simpson. **1971** in H.S. Thompson *Shark Hunt* 181: At that point it looked like 25 [phone calls] might make the nut…in a town with only 1623 registered voters. **1974** in H.S. Thompson *Shark Hunt* 511: After 72 hours, both the body and the brain are so depleted that only sleep will make the nut.

¶ **my nuts!** (used postpositively to express disgust or disbelief).—usu. considered vulgar. Cf. *my ass!* s.v. ASS; *my balls!* s.v. BALL[1].

1981 Wambaugh *Glitter Dome* 181: Me me me, my nuts! Siddown!

¶ **off** [or **out of**] **(one's) nut, 1.** crazy.

1860 Hotten *Slang Dict.* (ed. 2): To be "off one's nut," to be in liquor. [Corrected to "to be crazed or idiotic" in ed. 4 (1873).] **1876 in *F & H* V 79: Or to go off their nuts about ladies as dies for young fellers as fights. **1889–90 Barrère & Leland *Dict. Slang* II 92: To be off one's nut, *i.e.*, crazy. **1892 Norr *China Town* 13: Some one was givin' me that you were off your nut, but I see you're all right now. **1898** S. Crane, in *Complete Stories* 488: Kill you? Man, you're off your nut. **1909** "Clivette" *Café Cackle* 58: He was sure Pazazo was clean off his "nut." **1913–15** Van Loan *Taking the Count* 35: I'd go off my nut if I had to stay in this place another week. **1918** "M. Brand" *Harrigan* 26: He'll be broke before he goes off his nut. **1921** Casey & Casey *Gay-Cat* 181: Here I'm goin' off my nut 'bout a gun wot's safe in stir fur a stretch o' twenty year! **1926** Nason *Chevrons* 202: He's clean off his nut. **1928** MacArthur *War Bugs* 61: Mr. Secretary had an unusually low boiling point and went off his nut whenever it was sung. **1933** March Co. *K* 97: In September a fellow named Fallon out of the fourth platoon went off his nut. **1934** D.O. Stewart *Going Hollywood* (film): If you think you can give me the run-around, you're off your nut! **1935** Harris *Trapeze* (film): Aah, he's off his nut. He sent me on the same job. **1938** in W. Burnett *Best* 499: I cried like I was goin' outa my nut. **1939** Attaway *Breathe Thunder* 219: Maybe he was off his nut. **1940** R. Wright *Native Son* 318: He went off his nut from studying too much at the university. **1940** Meehan & Tugend *Seven Sinners* (film): Shut up! You're off your nut! **1947** Goodrich & Hackett *Wonderful Life* (film): Either I'm off my nut or he is. **1954** Krasna, Panama & Frank *White Christmas* (film): You're off your nut about a mile and a half.

1966 Neugeboren *Big Man* 72: You're off your nut, Rosen. **1966** Terkel *Division St.* 26: You heard of the guy who kicked the TV tube and took a pistol and shot into the—I mean, he was off his nut. **1968** Cuomo *Thieves* 128: This kid's a loony!—this kid's off his frigging nut! **1972** N.Y.U. student: I'm going off my nut with this stuff. **1973** Haring *Stranger* 11: Nearly drove me out of my nut. **1984–88** Hackworth & Sherman *About Face* 177: Temporarily off his nut. **1980–89** Chesire *Home Boy* 210: He was fucking off his nut.

2. wildly enthusiastic or infatutated.

*1873 in *OED*: There are the men who go off their nuts by the time they're worth a million or so. **1899** Garland *Eagle's Heart* 54: He considered them "a little off their nut"—that is to say, fanatic. **1913** in M. Gardner *Casey* 89: I'd like to know why any fan should be so off his nut/About the Mighty Casey who proved himself a mutt. **1928** E. Rice *Street Scene* 582: I tell you, I'm clean off my nut about you. **1941** Schulberg *Sammy* 178: I was just telling Chick Tyler my new story. He went off his nut about it.

¶ **off the nut** out of debt; showing a profit; in newly favorable circumstances.

1939 *Life* (July 31) 24: He expects to be *off the nut* (even) by the Fair's end. **1946** Dadswell *Hey, Sucker* 67: If we can reach the first of the season's fairs "off the nut"—without spending more than we earn—we are fortunate. *Ibid.* 77: Few such extravaganzas "get off the nut" in a season. **1966** Bogner *7th Ave.* 361: Well, how does it feel to get off the nut? **1975** Durocher & Linn *Nice Guys* 126: We'd be able to draw enough people in the two games at Ebbets Field to get us off the nut. **1978** *N.Y. Post* (July 31) 54: Billy has the job in the future, George is off the nut with a public which was really beginning to see the ugly side of him.

¶ **on the nut** on credit; (*hence*) in debt; without money; broke.

*a*1909 Tillotson *Detective* 93: *Nut*—Credit. **1911** A.H. Lewis *Apaches of N.Y.* 142: Th' trip was not only a waterhaul, but it leaves me on the nut for twelve hundred bones. **1922** *Variety* (July 7) 10: They…are put on the nut to the manager and forced into putting on crooked concessions of some kind to try and make up the nut and get even with the office. **1925** Gross *Nize Baby* 181: A fat chance I got gettin tree bucks around here when I'm on de nut. **1926** *Variety* (Mar. 24) 11: Many of the smaller rooms are heavily on the "nut" despite the recent splurge. **1929** in Hammett *Knockover* 57: They…were only waiting till Joe, who was on the nut, raised enough dough. **1935** Pollock *Und. Speaks*: On the nut, to obtain credit. **1938** J. O'Hara *Hope of Heaven* 173: If you're…badly on the nut…write me care of this guy, and I'll let you have some more. **1940** Zinberg *Walk Hard* 33: I'm on the nut for your gym expenses and for paying Happy and Pop to teach you. That will cost plenty. **1935–62** Ragen & Finston *Toughest Pris.* 810: *On the nut*—Out of funds. **1962** in Wepman, Newman & Binderman *The Life* 103: His luck was shattered,/For he was…"on the nut." **1970** Winick & Kinsie *Lively Commerce* 173: My old man is on the nut (out of work) and I can't get any other job except looking at the ceiling (prostitution) in a hook shop (brothel). **1965–71** in *Qly. Jour. Stud. on Alcohol* XXXII 734: *Nut, on the* On Skid Row. **1976** Wepman, Newman & Binderman *The Life* 186: *On the nut*…without money.

¶ **pop (one's) nuts** (of either sex) to have an orgasm.—usu. considered vulgar.—occ. used trans.—also used fig.

1956 Chamales *Never So Few* 20 [ref. to WWII]: How would you like to pop your nuts on a twenty-four hour basis. **1958** Cooley *Run for Home* 424 [ref. to *ca*1920]: We'll buy another bottle and get our nuts popped…just for old times' sake. **1963** T.I. Rubin *Sweet Daddy* 23: In the whole deal—if she pops her nuts once—be a lot. **1969** *Playboy* (Apr.) 221: While you're popping your nuts, you can't very well be thinking about whether Mayor Yorty is going to run again. **1974** H. Bennett *Wait Until Eve.* 238: I'd popped my nuts. **1978** R. Price *Ladies' Man* 253: I wanted to go back and have someone pop my nut…have an anonymous mouth suck my dick. **1966–80** McAleer & Dickson *Unit Pride* 496: He must've thought we'd pop our nuts to see he had so much on the ball. **1987** E. Spencer *Macho Man* 160: If you like watching ordnance go off…a B-52 strike can pop your nuts.

¶ **put (someone's) nuts in a vise** to put (someone) in a dangerous, nearly hopeless predicament.—usu. considered vulgar.

1980 W.C. Anderson *Bat 21* 178: How a stinking war can put a guy's nuts in a vise!

¶ **screw (one's) nut** to turn (one's) head around; (*hence*) to depart; go.

1900 Willard & Hodler *Powers That Prey* 21: I'll screw my nut down town an' rubber around. **1903** Sonnichsen *Deep Sea Vagabonds* 61: I 'id in the jungle all day, an' when night came I screwed my nut. **1906** *Nat. Police Gaz.* (Dec. 22) 3: When I got half way to the curb I happened to screw my nut, and there was Jack talking to her. **1923** *Atlanta Constitution* (Feb. 1) 12: Beat it—flag it—screw your nut.

¶ **with (one's) nuts in the sand** *Black E.* in a predicament; in trouble.—usu. considered vulgar.

1974 Goines *Eldorado* 33: When we fuck over Eldorado's shit, the dues are going to be mean for whatever nigger gets his nuts caught in the sand. **1974** R. Carter *16th Round* 254: That left the prosecutor with his nuts in the sand.

nut *v.* **1.** to castrate.—usu. considered vulgar.—also used fig.

1916 Cary *Venery* II 13: *Nut*—…to castrate. **1918** M. Cowley, in Jay *Burke-Cowley Corres.* 63: Tell Ellis to go nut himself on a briar bush. **1923** McAlmon *Village* 64: We ought to go and see if the old man is there tonight, and if he is, nut him. He…ought to cut out playing with the women. **1927** *Immortalia* 47: To the trusty lord of his English court/Who'd nut the King of France. **1952** Himes *Stone* 20: I felt ruptured and nutted. **1962** Crump *Killer* 126: "Hey, screw you!" "You do and I'll nut ya!" **1963** Braly *Shake Him* 72: Korin's liable to come out of that fog he's in long enough to see what's going on, and he'll probably try to nut you. **1963–64** Kesey *Great Notion* 77: Who's gonna learn him to shave with a ax blade? To nut a nigger?

2. to renege.

1963 J. Williamson *Hustler!* 122: He wanted to be with her in the respect of goin' to bed with her! She nutted on this. When I say nutted I mean she wouldn't go for this. **1966** Brunner *Face of Night* 234: *Nut*—to disappoint, to back out of a deal.

3.a. (of a man) to copulate with (a woman).—usu. considered vulgar. Cf. BALL, *v.*, 3.

1970 Landy *Underground Dict.* 140: Did you nut her?

b. to have an orgasm.—usu. considered vulgar.

1994 in C. Long *Love Awaits* 141: You nut from just the anticipation?

nutball *n.* SCREWBALL. Also as adj.

1973 *New York* (Oct. 1) 37: Maybe their nutball put-downs can be read as the handwriting on the wall for hyper-consumerism. **1974** *Nat. Lampoon* (Dec.) 57: Wouldn't you think that anyone who suggested that you worship a vicious criminal who had just robbed and stabbed you was a "nutball." **1979** *Quest* (May) 46: It is this quality that enables him to skip lightly from the most recondite subject to workaday matters to nutball comedy. **1984** Aykroyd & Ramis *Ghostbusters* (film): Just a nutball from off the street. *a*1988 C. Adams *More Straight Dope* 370: A collection of nutball questions. **1988** *21 Jump St.* (Fox-TV): This guy's a nutball. **1989** *Capital Gang* (CNN-TV) (Feb. 19): The guy's a nutball. He's a left-wing nutball. *Ibid.:* The nutball navy. **1991** *Simpsons* (Fox-TV): Thank you, Mr. Nutball. **1991** *CBS This Morning* (CBS-TV) (July 24): This [comedy] is just sort of nutball.

nutbar *n.* a crazy person; NUTCAKE.

1978 *Nat. Lampoon* (Oct.) 8: I thought the guy was a real nutbar until I followed his directions. **1979** *Edmonton* (Alberta) *Jour.* (June 30) I8: If you thought nutbars were restricted to California, read about the militant feminist agri-coops outside Eugene. **1984** Heath *A-Team* 157: Andre's a nut bar, pure and simple. **1988** *Nat. Lampoon* (Feb.) 39: Act like a nutbar, a loony.

nutbasket *n.* a lunatic; NUT. Also **nutbucket.**

1979–81 C. Buckley *To Bamboola* 167: Thought he'd lost it. Man, he was a nutbasket. **1993** E. Richards *Cocaine True* 127: She's a real nut. We call her Nutbucket.

nutbox *n.* a psychiatric hospital. Also **nutbin.**

1965 C. Brown *Manchild* 23: I had a lot of fun in the nutbox and learned a lot of new tricks. **1984** Heath *A-Team* 103: I called Triple A back at the nutbin.

nutburger *n.* a lunatic; NUT.—also used attrib.

1984 Heath *A-Team* 22: Counterculture nutburgers who'll do anything, anywhere if the price is right. **1992** *Mystery Sci. Theater* (Comedy Central TV): What a nutburger! **1994** *Esquire* (Oct.) 164: The Doctor's Thigh Cream, the Stimulator Pain Relief Device…here are the nutburger remedies.

nut-buster *n.* **1.** a mechanic or machinist.

1944 in *AS* XX 148: [Army:] *Nut Buster,* Mechanic. **1945** Hubbard *R.R. Ave.* 353: *Nut Splitter* or *Nut Buster*—Machinist.

2. BALLBUSTER.—usu. considered vulgar.

1976 Braly *False Starts* 158: And latent homosexuality is one of those impossible charges to defend against, like the nutbusters Joe McCarthy was beginning to invent. **1979** Crews *Blood & Grits* 62: The final nut buster is that there are men who have every reason to know about such things who think we did not need to go onto the North Slope to start with.

nutcake *n.* a lunatic; NUT, 5.a.—also used attrib.

1967 P. Welles *Babyhip* 177: She wasn't going to let a nut-cake bug her. **1968** Simoun *Madigan* (film): Till you guys collect that crazy piece of nutcake. **1974** Andrews & Dickens *Over the Wall* 80: The other cons kept looking over at me like I was a ding-a-ling, which is Q-talk for a nutcake. **1974** G.V. Higgins *Cogan's Trade* 158: I don't want no fuckin' nutcakes, either. **1988** *Daily News* (N.Y.) (June 17) 39: Come in, you nut cake! **1990** *21 Jump St.* (Fox-TV): They told my boss I was like a suicide nutcake. **1993** *CNN & Co.* (CNN-TV) (June 24): Some nutcake can always [commit acts of violence]. **1995** *New Republic* (July 10) 6: Russia is loaded with nuclear weapons and nutcake nationalists.

nut case *n.* an insane or very eccentric person; NUT, 5.a.

*1959 in *OEDS*: I couldn't get anyone to talk about it openly. The way they summed it up you'd have thought I was a spy or a nut-case. **1966* G.M. Williams *Camp* 135: God, he's a nut case. **1967* P. Cook *Bedazzled* (film): You're a bleedin' nut case. **1979** in Fierstein *Torch Song* 165: I figured him for a nut-case. **1980** *N.Y. Post* (July 2) 49: I don't know anything about crazy, emotional nut-cases! So I told her to wait till you came home! **1981** G. Wolf *Roger Rabbit* 35: He's a certified nut case. **1982** *Flash* (Dec.) 10: Get off me, you nut case! **1983** R. Thomas *Missionary* 211: My daughter, the nut case. **1985** *Daily Beacon* (Univ. Tenn.) (Feb. 7) 6: He must be a nut case! Use the hook! **1993** *Real World* (MTV): He's obviously a total nut case. **1996** *TV Guide* (Oct. 26) 85: The right-wing nutcases...despise the president.

nut college *n.* NUTHOUSE. Cf. BRAIN COLLEGE.

*a*1906 Burke *Prison Gates* 9 [ref. to 1880's]: I was sent to the "boobie hatch" (jail), played "daffy" (insane) and was landed in a "nut college" (insane asylum). It was the custom then to take the "bugs" (inmates) out to play ball every afternoon. *a*1909 Tillotson *Detective* 93: *Nut college*—An insane asylum. **1910** (quot. at KNOWLEDGE BOX). **1911–12** Ade *Knocking the Neighbors* 185: Liberate the present Inmates of all the Nut-Colleges. **1951** in *DAS*: He has been recalled by the nut college to join Napoleon...and Shakespeare, inventing paper dolls! **1967** *Lit Dict.* 51: *Nut College*—The funny farm.

nutcracker *n.* **1.** *Boxing.* (see quots.).

1859 Matsell *Vocab.* 127: *Nut-Cracker.* A severe blow on the head. **1889–90* Barrère & Leland *Dict. Slang* II 92: *Nut-cracker* (popular), sharp blow over the head. **1942** *ATS* 670: Blow to the head....*nutcracker.*

2. something that is difficult, threatening, or dangerous; BALLBREAKER, 1.a.—usu. considered vulgar. Also **nut-cruncher, nut-crusher.**

1948 in Hemingway *Sel. Letters* 656: Just because something was sold for a miserable price once when my nuts were in the nutcracker...is no reason to sell something else for a miserable price. **1959** E. Hunter *Killer's Wedge* 30: Four intelligent men with a nut cruncher of a problem. **1960** Carpenter *Youngest Harlot* 128: I was a ham-and-egger when I sailed on that nutcracker. **1968** Baker, Ladd & Robb *CUSS* 164: *Nut cracker* Difficult exam. **1973** *TULIPQ* (coll. B.K. Dumas): If a course is known to be very hard it might be called: [Ans.] a nutcrusher. **1978** T.H. White *In Search* 44: History I had the reputation of being a nut-cracker; no one ever got an A...except by luck.

3. a psychiatrist. Hence **nut-cracking,** *adj.*

1958 A. King *Mine Enemy* 200: But Mirko didn't seem to care too much for the "nutcrackers" around the place. **1963** T.I. Rubin *Sweet Daddy* 20: Screw it, enough of this nut cracking crap. **1966** Susann *Valley of Dolls* 360: He was a medical doctor, not a nutcracker. **1994** *N.Y. Observer* (Aug. 1) 5: My nutcracker is a 50ish blond with an accent....She's a little Jungian.

4. a martinet; BALLBREAKER, 1.b.—usu. considered vulgar.

1977 Sayles *Union Dues* 42: Now this Budka is notorious, worst accident record in the mine and pictures himself as a real nutcracker. Always on your back for chickenshit. **1981** Graziano & Corsel *Somebody Down Here* 38: There's all kinds of nutcrackers there....Everybody

is always ribbin everybody else. **1992** *Herman's Head* (Fox-TV): When Tchaikovsky wrote "The Nutcracker" he had her in mind.

nutcut *n.* NUT-CUTTING.—usu. considered vulgar. Also **nut-gut.**

1962 B. Jackson *In the Life* 155: If it comes down to the nutcut I'll sell a sonofabitch the Brooklyn Bridge....Nutcut: that's a southern expression. When they line up hogs to castrate them, it's what they call "coming up to the nutcut." You getting down to brass tacks. **1990** Berent *Steel Tiger* 328: In a nut-gut, I still want to make Ho's infiltration too costly....Tell me the nut-gut of the Igloo stuff.

nut-cutter *n.* BALLBREAKER, 1.a., b.; NUTCRACKER, 2, 4.—usu. considered vulgar.

1974 *TULIPQ* (coll. B.K. Dumas): That exam was a real nut-cutter. **1981** Ehrlichman *Witness* 106 [ref. to 1969]: "There's got to be one man in charge over there. Who will it be? Rehnquist?" "He's not a nut cutter."

nut-cutting *n.* repugnant but essential tasks or circumstances; NITTY-GRITTY, 1.—usu. considered vulgar.—also used attrib.

1968 Safire *New Language of Politics* 296: *Nut-cutting.* Dirty work; a slang allusion to castration, its political meaning is the denial of favors and the removal of power. To "get down to the nut-cutting" means to abandon broad policy discussion and deal with hard specifics of patronage and pecking order. Never used with ladies present, it has a second meaning of detail work or "brass tacks." **1972** Jenkins *Semi-Tough* 269: They're one thing you always do when you're down to the nut-cuttin'. **1974** in H.S. Thompson *Shark Hunt* 344: So Nixon is not without options, when it comes down to nut-cutting time. **1978** Diehl *Sharky's Machine* 77: Now let's get to the nut-cutting fast. **1978** in Lyle & Golenbock *Bronx Zoo* 125: "If they lose, they will get the blame." You know what that means—nut-cutting time. **1983** in D. Webster *Looka Yonder!* 137: I can't guarantee you anything except money and the fact that you're gonna be close to the nut-cuttin', if that's the kinda stuff you're interested in. **1987** Zeybel *Gunship* 20: Like all combat, the situation quickly evolved into what was quaintly called "nut cuttin' time." **1988** Dye *Outrage* 170: The nut-cutting cometh.

nut doctor *n.* a psychiatrist.

1931–34 in Clemmer *Pris. Community* 334: *Nut doctor*...A psychiatrist. **1937** Johnston *Pris. Life* 35: Say didja hear about the Warden gonna get all the screwy cons examined by the nut doctors? **1988** De Lillo *Libra* 10: Edward tried to get him to talk to the nut doctor.

nut factory *n.* NUTHOUSE, 1.a.; FUNNY FACTORY.

1899 Cullen *Tales* 129: I'm not speaking of...his failure to land the Melancholy Dane in a nut factory at the wind-up of the play (there must have been some kind of a Bloomingdale outfit in Denmark at that time for folks who had wheels). **1908** H. Green *Maison* 96: They ain't no place but the nut factory for her. **1915** *DN* IV 234. **1926** *AS* I (Dec.) 652: *Nut factory.* Hospital for insane. **1928** Bodenheim *Georgie May* 111: Ah'll wind up in the nut-fact'ry fo' ah know it. **1929** in Mencken *Amer. Lang. Supp. I* 441: A nut-factory, eh? **1933** Duff & Sutherland *I've Got Yr. Number* (film): Someplace in a nut factory! She's an imbecile! **1942** P. Wylie *Vipers* 92: It will very likely cause you to cork off screaming to the nut factory. **1956** Resko *Reprieve* 197: Maybe they shouldn't have let me out of the nut factory. **1960** Barber *Minsky's* 315: This is a regular Boob McNutt from the nut factory. **1966** Gallery *Start Engines* 45: "Don't call them mugs at the nut factory cops," said Napoleon Bonaparte indignantly. "Those bughouse keepers are all half-nuts themselves." **1981** Graziano & Corsel *Somebody Down Here* 79: I'm beginning to think this a real nut factory Marlon brung me to.

nut farm *n.* NUTHOUSE, 1.a.; FUNNY FARM.

1940 F.S. Fitzgerald *Last Tycoon* 12: Spouting tripe that'd land him on a nut-farm anywhere outside of California. **1954–60** *DAS*: *Nut farm = nut house. Not common.* **1966** Harris & Freeman *Lords of Hell* 55: You see them around...acting crazy before they go off somewhere else—to the House of Detention or the Bellevue nut farm. **1970** Siciliano *Unless They Kill Me First* 100: I might have made it across the wall into the nut farm that they keep up there with the prison.

nut foundry *n.* NUTHOUSE, 1.a.

1932 in Partridge *Dict. Und.* 80: We'll have the Marquis....Settled in the nut foundry. **1944** in Weinberg et al. *Tough Guys* 134: So now he's trying to sock me in the nut foundry!

nut-gut var. NUTCUT.

nut hatch *n.* **1.** NUTHOUSE, 1.a. Cf. BOOBY HATCH, 2.

1942 *ATS* 179: Insane asylum....*nut hatch.* **1962** Dougherty *Com-*

missioner 283: Is this a nuthatch or ain't it? **1966** K. Hunter *Landlord* 17: The Mental Health annex of the World Health Organization? The official U.N. nut-hatch? **1970** E. Thompson *Garden of Sand* 415: You're going to…find yourself in a nuthatch one day. **1971** Le Guin *Lathe of Heaven* 75: He…would be sent to jail or the nut hatch. **1971** E. Sanders *Family* 60: They shipped him to the Ascadero nut hatch. **1972** N.Y.U. student: An insane asylum is a *cuckoo house* or a *nut hatch*. **1978** E. Thompson *Devil to Pay* 75: If a man wasn't nuts, what was he doin' in a nut hatch? **1981–85** S. King *It* 412: Something that will land me in the nuthatch. **1987** A. Parker *Angel Heart* (film): About twelve years ago, you and your daughter snatched Favorite out of some nut hatch in Poughkeepsie. **1994** Univ. Tenn. instructor, age 42: He'd be bundled right off to the nut hatch.

2. a madman; fool.

    1972 *Nat. Lampoon* (Nov.) 87: My nuthatch of a commander in chief left the entire Pacific Fleet in Pearl Harbor with a "Bomb Me" sign on it.

nuthouse *n.* **1.a.** a hospital, ward, or other facility for the confinement or treatment of the mentally ill; insane asylum. Cf. BUGHOUSE, 2.

    1906 M'Govern *Sarjint Larry* [caption] (opp. 32): Nut house. **1921** in Inman *Diary* 196: Dead or in a nut house. **1929** *AS* IV (June) 343: *Nut-house.* An insane asylum. **1930** Dos Passos *Manhattan Transfer* 297: Oh Francie they'll be takin us to the nuthouse if we keep this up. **1936** West *Klondike Annie* (film): One more day like this and you'll end up in the nut house. **1936** Cormack & Lang *Fury* (film): You're on the way to the nuthouse or the pen! **1937** Osborn *On Borrowed Time* 324: In fact, this is the mornin' Demmie figured I'd be in the nut-house. **1965** in Wilner & Kassebaum *Narcotics* 202: You see,…the people that go to nut houses for help, these are the sniveling brats in my opinion. **1973** Toma & Brett *Toma* 62: You belong in a nuthouse under psychiatric care. **1978–79** in E.M. Miller *Street Woman* 101: They were puttin' me in the nut house. **1979–81** C. Buckley *To Bamboola* 41: He just got out of the nut house two or three months ago. **1987** Rugoff & Gottlieb *Mannequin* (film): Me? I'm gonna wind up in the nuthouse after this!

b. a place of noise and confusion; madhouse.

    1931 Farrell *McGinty* 355: You're gettin' the same pay, you ain't tied down in that nuthouse, and another guy gets all that grief. [**1929–33** Farrell *Manhood of Lonigan* 185: The Chicago loop was like a nuthouse on fire.] **1944** Solomon & Buchman *Snafu* 54: *Hiding?* This is a nut-house! **1955** Ellson *Rock* 83: It's a nuthouse inside. Men is cursing. Two women fighting over stuff. **1955** G.D. Adams *3 Bad Sisters* (film): I'm getting tired of being blamed for everything that happens in this nuthouse! **1971** *Go Ask Alice* 142: Today our area was a nut house with everyone running around preparing for tonight's annual "School Is Out" bash.

2. a fool.

    1926 Nichols & Tully *Twenty Below* 64: Go to sleep, you nut-house, there ain't nothing.

nuthouse *adj.* crazy; BUGHOUSE.

    1908 W.G. Davenport *Butte & Montana* 337: Going nuthouse over the crumbling ruins of ancient Rome.

nut job *n.* NUT CASE.

    1972 N.Y.U. student: He's a real nut job. **1975** S.P. Smith *Amer. Boys* 267 [ref. to 1960's]: He was led and followed by nut jobs, him the biggest of all for being here. **1977** Torres *Q & A* 91: We got a squeal that a nut job has got a knife. **1980** H. Gould *Ft. Apache* 270: Hey, nutjob.…What are you doing here? **1981** Pietropinto & Congress *Clinic* 100: She's too much of a nut-job to handle it. **1982** S.P. Smith *Officer & Gentleman* 119: Maybe someone would think he was a nut-job and call the men in the white coats. **1984** Caunitz *Police Plaza* 244: Terrorists are a tightly knit fraternity of nut jobs. **1987** *Beauty & Beast* (CBS-TV): He sounds like a major nut job. **1988** Northport, N.Y., writer, age *ca*35: Papa is such a nut job. **1994** Kriegel *Bless Me, Father* 44: There are no…freaks…and nut-jobs in his neighborhood. **1995** *Strange Luck* (Fox-TV): "On the word of a…" "Lunatic? Nut job?"

nut man *n. Carnival.* an operator of a shell game.

    1906 Wooldridge *Hands Up* 110: Shell men or "nut" men can be found occasionally about the depots. **1961** Scarne *Comp. Guide to Gambling* 686: *Nutman* a gambling hustler.

nutmeg *n.* a white New Englander, esp. of Connecticut, Massachusetts, or Rhode Island. Also **nutmeg-maker.**

    1821 Wetmore *Pedlar* 14: Your assurance is insufferable, Mr. Nutmeg. **1852** in *DA:* A real *nutmeg* came booming along, and in he comes with a heap of bundles in his fists. **1858** [S. Hammett] *Piney Woods* 110: I'll believe…that nutmegs is mighty onsartin. *a*1881 G.C. Harding *Misc. Writings* 306: Every cursed "Nutmeg," from the highest to the lowest, persisted in misrepresenting us. **1883** *United Svc.* (Feb.) 200: While I settle with this nutmeg-maker. **1896** in *DA:* Down Among the Nutmegs.…The printers of Hartford are alive to their own interests.

nut on *v.* to ignore.

    1966 Cooper *Farm* 97: I'm going to touch your arm, but nut on it, then turn a little to your left on a 3 quarter angle, so both matrons can see your hands in sight. **1970** Cain *Blueschild* 140: Should've known he'd nut on me. I don't even look like a junky.

nut out *v.* Esp. *Black E.* to become insane; abandon restraint.

    [**1919* Downing *Digger Dialects* 36: *Nut*—"Nut it out"—think it out.] **1966** C. Cooper *Farm* 170: A lotta guys starting looking at the tops of their shoes, nutting out completely. **1966** in R.S. Gold *Jazz Talk:* I just nutted out. **1972** Carr *Bad* 156: All the patients in the ward were…either nutting out or pretending to. **1974** "A.C. Clark" *Revenge* 93: Now don't you read into this. **1990* T. Thorne *Dict. Contemp. Slang: Nut out/up…*to go crazy, lose control of oneself, run amok.

nutpicker *n.* Esp. *Mil.* a psychiatrist. Also **nutpick.**

    1918 Cushing *Surgeon's Jour.* 386: [Capt.] Salmon…has been dubbed by the irrepressible Yates the "nut picker." *Ibid.* 451: Maj. Rhein has come in as C.O. with a new bunch of "nut pickers." **1918** *110th Field Arty. Mustard Roll* (Aug. 18) 1: Are you a soldier? Then You Need an Alienist. See Doc TANNSACK, Nutpicker. **1919** *Century* (Nov.) 2: You see, he was up against it, for if he was crazy, the nutpicks was laying for him up in the psychiatric ward; and if he was sane, the court martial was waiting for him. **1954–60** *DAS: Nutpick…*A psychiatrist. *Never common.*

nut role *n. Black E.* an instance of feigned insanity or stupidity. Also as *v.*

    1967 R. Beck *Pimp* 144: I'll "nut roll" [*sic*] on her. I'll stay outta the pimp role until I case her. *Ibid.* 316: *Nut Roll…*a pretense at stupidity or unawareness. **1983** *Reader's Digest Success with Words* 87: Black English…*nut role* = "stupidity or craziness pretended for a purpose": *I played the nut role on him and got my way.*

nut roll *n.* a lunatic; NUTCAKE.

    1995 *Time* (June 26) 60: Wake up, Ramon, this guy is a nut roll.

nuts *adj.* **1.** fond (of); infatuated, fascinated, or obsessed (with); very enthusiastic (about).—also (in **1846 quot.) used absol.—orig. constr. with *(up)on*, now usu. with *about* or *over.* [Later constrs. with *about* and *over* are strongly infl. by **(2)**, below, following colloq. *crazy about* (or *over*). Partridge *Dict. Und.* reasonably sugg. a semantic basis in "sweet on," infl. by cliché *sweet as a nut.*]

    *1785 Grose *Dict. Vulgar Tongue* s.v. *well-hung: The blowen was nutts upon the Kiddey because he is well-hung;* the girl is pleased with the youth because his genitals are large. **1811 Lex. Balatron.* s.v. *pound:* How the milling cove pounded the cull for being nuts on his blowen; how the boxer beat the fellow for taking liberties with his mistress. **1812* Vaux *Vocab.: Nuts upon it* to be very much pleased or gratified with any object, adventure, or overture; so a person who conceives a strong inclination for another of the opposite sex, is said to be quite *nutty,* or *nuts upon* him or her. **1846* in *OEDS:* Vhy, Owen…you knows it's no use of me being nuts, ven the donna [*sc.,* woman]'s only nut crackers [*sic*; sense not clear]. **1853* in *F & H* V 79: It's [*sic*] rich nutty flavour I'm nuts on no more. **1859** in C.A. Abbey *Before the Mast* 236: Whom the mate, to use a slang phrase, is "*dead nuts on.*" **1873* in *F & H* V 79: My aunt is awful nuts on Marcus Aurelius; I beg your pardon, you don't know the phrase; my aunt makes Marcus Aurelius her Bible. **1875–80** Kwong *Dict. Eng. Phr.* 405: The boy is *nuts on* the new teacher = The boy is fond of the new teacher. **1882* in *F & H* V 79: I am nuts upon Criminal Cases, Perlice News, you know, and all that. **1884 Randiana* 71: Our prim landlady…was nuts upon my brother-in-law. **1888** Bidwell *Forging His Chains* 130: As they all know me to be "dead nuts" on forgers, I should be the one called on to arrest Meigs. **1889–90* in Barrère & Leland *Dict. Slang* II 92: I ain't *nuts on* sweaters myself. **1891** Maitland *Slang Dict.* 90: To be "dead nuts" on one is to be in love with or fascinated with the person. **1914** Lardner *You Know Me Al* 38: She is nuts over me. **1914** in Lardner *Round Up* 335: This dame that's nuts about me. **1917** F. Hunt *Draft* 138: He isn't even

in our platoon, but everybody is nuts about him. **1920** in *OEDS:* Carrie's nuts about the Russian revolution. **1920** Ade *Hand-Made Fables* 30: The whole World that stays up after 9:30 went nuts over the New Dances. **1924** Garahan *Stiffs* 208: They're dead nuts on patent-leather. **1927** H. Miller *Moloch* 103: He was "nuts" on the Latin teacher. **1928** Bodenheim *Georgie May* 104: She's still nuts on Blackey Dunn. **1934** Boylan & Baldwin *Devil Dogs of the Air* (film): He's been nuts on aviation ever since. **1934** Jevne & Purcell *Palooka* (film): I'm nuts about ya, Nina! **1936** Dos Passos *Big Money* 43: Henry Ford had been nuts about machinery. **1953** Paul *Wayland* 48: I'm nuts about the way you sound. **1963** E.M. Miller *Exile* 80: She was nuts on the subject. **1965** Capote *In Cold Blood* 248: But I was nuts about Carol. **1989** S. Robinson & D. Ritz *Smokey* 214: I'm not always nuts about his lyrics.

2. insane; crazy; out of one's senses; (with diminished force, as in 1939–40 quot.) wild. *Occ. as adv.*

[*1846 (quot. at (1), above)]. **1908** in H.C. Fisher *A. Mutt* 23: What struck him? He must be nuts. **1908** Hopper & Bechdolt *9009* 85: What's got into me?…am I going nuts? **1908** W.G. Davenport *Butte & Montana* 209: An experience that almost drove him nuts. **1914** in Lardner *Round Up* 262: It's a wonder we didn't all go nuts. **1916** E.R. Burroughs *Return of Mucker* 48: W'en did youse go nuts? **1917** F. Hunt *Draft* 63: That guy was nuts. **1919** T. Kelly *What Outfit?* 14: They think we're nuts when we ask for water to drink. **1922** in Inman *Diary* 202: Driving me nuts. **1929** Botkin *Folk-Say I* 54: He'd just bash em up aside the jaw…an knock em nuts fer a while. **1930** *AS* VI 92: Gone Nuts. **1932** in Adamic *My America* 78: And life is just plain nuts. **1933** W. March *Co. K* 22: I'll be glad to get out of this place. Everybody here is nuts. *Ibid.* 43: Then Mamie, the galley mule, went nuts. *1936 Partridge *DSUE:* Nuts….Crazy: orig. (ca. 1905), U.S.; anglicized, thanks mainly to "the talkies," in 1929. **1939–40** Tunis *Kid from Tomkinsville* 137: Is this crowd nuts! They sure want to see the Dodgers get back into first place…and they're all out there pulling for that Kid in the box. **1949** in Elliot *Among the Dangs* 125: It's one way to keep from going nuts. **1949** *New Yorker* (Dec. 3) 158: The compulsion to get out a magazine every week or every month is one of the things that drive an editor nuts. **1956** Metalious *Peyton Place* 44: You're nuts. **1958** T. Capote *Breakfast at Tiffany's* 29: You'll read where she ends up at the bottom of a bottle of Seconals….She's nuts. **1960** H. Lee *Mockingbird* 89: Well, can't you just see his face when he gets a letter from me with nothing in it? It'll drive him nuts. **1968** R. Coles *Dead End School* 81: This is stupid. You're talking nuts. **1971** *Playboy* (Apr.) 24: To write effectively about insanity, you have to be a little nuts yourself. **1985** Meehan *One Magic Christmas* (film): Everybody thinks we're nuts for doin' this. **1994** Song intro., WNEW-FM radio (New York) (Feb. 16): He told us what a nuts time that was. **1996** *TV Guide* (Oct. 19): He's too nice and they're too nuts.

nuts *v.* to fool around.—*also constr. with around.*

1941 in Algren *Neon Wilderness* 58: "What's Benkowski doin' for a living these days, Lefty?" "Just nutsin' around." **1942** Algren *Morning* 23: They wouldn't have no good place to nuts around, like us guys. **1963** Williams *Sissie* 84: You nuts with that for a half hour or so and already it's four or four-thirty.

nuts *interj.* (used to express disgust, disbelief, rejection, anger, etc.).—*formerly considered vulgar. Cf. syn. BALLS, n., 2.a.*

1910 *Adventure* (Nov.) 47: "Nuts!" he said in deep scorn. "This regiment won the battle!" **1915** *DN* III 227: West Texas…*nuts,* interj….Expresses incredulity. **1916** E.R. Burroughs *Return of Mucker* 49: Oh, nuts!…Youse don't tink youse can put dat over on any wise guy…? **1918** Gutterson *Granville* 16: But forewarned is forearmed, so I said "Nuts! Let her ride!" **1918** in Buckley *Squadron 95* 147. **1921** O'Neill *Hairy Ape* 193: As for dis bein' hell—aw, nuts! **1927** Saunders *Wings* 172: Nuts. **1927–28** in R. Nelson *Dishonorable* 111: "For the good o'—" Nuts. **1932** Fowler & Brown *State's Attorney* (film): "You can't dictate to me!" "Nuts!" **1932** Hecht & Fowler *Great Magoo* 15: "I got some rights."…"Nuts! You got no rights whatsoever." **1935** D.H. Clarke *Broadway* 33 [ref. to ca1910]: "I don't want to be dependent on anybody." "Nuts!" Arthur said. **1936** *Esquire* (Jan. 1937) 88: Yes, mister. No, mister. Do this. Do that. Nuts! **1939** Fearing *Hospital* 115: So what? So nuts. I'm fed up, clean to the teeth. **1944** Gen. A. McAuliffe, in *N.Y. Times* (Dec. 28) 4: [Oral response to German army's demand for the surrender of Bastogne, Belgium:] Nuts! **1954** Matheson *Born of Man & Woman* 45: "Aah, nuts," he muttered and tossed his book on the bedside table. **1958** S.H. Adams *Tenderloin* 79 [ref. to 1890's]: "Oh, *nuts!*"…The word was a bombshell. It carried with it, in those days of verbal

innocence, all the force and shock of its worst modern four-letter congeners. **1956–60** J.A. Williams *Angry Ones* ch. xvi: "Consciences, Steve. Yours, mine, societies." "Nuts." **1960–61** Steinbeck *Discontent* 178: "I wouldn't ask you to break the law." "Nuts!" **1989** *Daily Beacon* (Univ. Tenn.) (Apr. 14) 7: Nuts. Could somebody get me an eraser? **1995** *Simpsons* (Fox-TV): Aw, nuts!

¶ In phrase:

¶ **nuts to** [or **on**] (used to express impatience, rejection, derision, etc.); to hell with.

1928 J.M. Marsh *Set-Up* 24: Aw, hell! Nuts to you! **1930** Fredenburgh *Soldiers March!* 205 [ref. to 1918]: Ah, nuts to you. **1932** L. Berg *Prison Dr.* 13: Nuts to you, Eddie. *Ibid.* 290: Aw, nuts on the wisecracks, see? **1934** O'Hara *Appt. in Samarra* ch. iv: Nuts to you, sister. **1934** Appel *Brain Guy* 55: "You're a skinny runt." "Nuts to you." **1935** H. McCoy *They Shoot Horses* 30: Nuts to you. **1936** Kingsley *Dead End* 732: Nuts tuh yew! **1936** in Pyle *Ernie's Amer.* 33: Nuts to sad people. **1938** Bezzerides *Long Haul* 70: Ah, nuts to him. We'll get back at him some other time. *Ibid.* 178: Nuts on that stuff, boy. **1939** Attaway *Breathe Thunder* 20: "Nuts to you," he growled back. **1940** W.C. Williams *In the Money* 37: Thought you could play us for a bunch of suckers, huh? Nuts to you. **1945** Baldwin *Arizona Star* 116: "Oh," said Mona, "nuts to that." **1948** Maresca *My Flag* 12: Nuts to that, wise guy. **1948** Lay & Bartlett *12 O'Clock High!* 28: I'm all for it. Nuts to the red tape. **1948** Cozzens *Guard of Honor* 331: Nuts to you, Captain. Hello, Mike. **1952** Pyles *Words & Ways* 151: The American co-ed, or even her maiden aunt, may unblushingly hiss "Nuts to you!" *1961 Loring & Hyatt *Gorgo* (film): Nuts to that! **1965** Matthiessen *Fields of Lord* 116: Well, nuts to that. **1971** *All in the Family* (CBS-TV): Nuts to you. **1980** *Time* (Feb. 11) 67: But the animals shouted "Nuts to you." And they kicked him out of the community. **1994** *Simpsons* (Fox-TV): Nuts to this! **1991–95** Sack *Co. C* 82: Nuts to Company C.

nutsack *n.* the scrotum.—*usu. considered vulgar.*

1971 Hilaire *Thanatos* 295: I'm drove to the nutsack. **1984** Sample *Racehoss* 85: Using her long fingernails, she ripped his nutsack.

nut sharp *n.* [NUT + SHARP] a psychiatrist.

1924 H.L. Wilson *Professor* 148: The poor fish…ought to be in some good booby-hatch…where the nut-sharps (alienists) could watch him.

nutso *n.* a crazy person.

1978 *L.A. Times* (Feb. 14) IV 6: Her husband was "a real nutso. I think he's going to drop out of society completely." **1979** Univ. Tenn. student: He's a real nutso.

nutso *adj.* [NUTS, 2 + -o] crazy. *Also as adv.*

1979 Gutcheon *New Girls* 185: You're getting nutso about food again. **1981** *Rod Serling's Mag.* (July) 31: Are you stark raving nutso, schmuck? **1981** Raban *Old Glory* 63: She'd go goddamn nutso. *a*1989 in T. O'Brien *Things They Carried* 76: Pretty nutso sometimes. **1989** Care *Viet. Spook Show* 233: He's nutso. **1991** B.E. Ellis *Amer. Psycho* 275: I think the guy went a little nutso. **1994** *TV Guide* (Dec. 31) 36: Kidnapped by a nutso fan.

nut-splitter *n. R.R.* a shopman or machinist.

1903 *St. Louis Post-Dispatch* (May 3) II 2: Nutsplitter—A machinest [*sic*]. **1931** *Writer's Digest* (May) 42: [Railroad slang:] Nut Splitter—Machinist. **1945** (quot. at NUT-BUSTER). **1945** *Amer. N & Q* (July) 55: Nut-splitter.

nutsy *n.* a crazy person.

1962 Serling *New Stories* 11: That old gleep with the Model A! Lemme tell ya, Irv—a real nutsy! **1964** Serling *Twilight Zone* (CBS-TV): This is where the men separate from the nutsies.

nutsy *adj.* [NUTS, 2 + -y] crazy; insane. *Occ. as nickname.*

1923 in Safire *Look It Up* 15: Nut-sey Fagan, Nut-sey Fagan,/He's the guy for me! **1931** Stevenson *St. Luke's* 28 [ref. to ca1910]: What was Nutsy saying to you? **1940** Baldwin *Brother Orchid* (film): That's a nutsy way to run an organization. **1953** M. Shulman *Affairs of Dobie Gillis* (film): So what if Dobie is a little nutsy? Who ain't? **1968** Kirkwood *Good Times/Bad Times* 86: You see, they had constant wracking headaches from figuring out how to say everything in iambic pentameter. No wonder they were all nutsy! **1970** R. Williams *New Exiles* 140: I was going a little nutsy. **1970** Della Femina *Wonderful Folks* 66: We get a great number of nutsy guys. **1975** T. Berger *Sneaky People* 143: Let's not start that nutsy stuff again, Leo. **1982** *Harper's* (Dec.) 55: The best poems of *Lord Weary's Castle*…won't stand long after all the nutsy hubbub in Lowell's life has cooled to ash.

nutter *n.* a crazy person. *Rare* in U.S.

*1958 in *OEDS:* The reason for this is to find out wether [*sic*] or not you are a nutter. ***1967** in T. Thorne *Dict. Contemp. Slang:* That boy of yours looks a nutter to me! **1981** *L.A. Times* (Jan. 1, 1980) VI 7: I had my wife and I had some friends. No psychiatrist—I wasn't a total nutter. **1987** M. Hastings *Korean War* 308: The drunks, the drug addicts, the nutters, the deadbeats.

nuttery *n.* NUTHOUSE, 1.a.

1915 in Botkin *Treas. Amer. Folk.* 471: A cozy corner in the nuttery for yours. **1931** in *OEDS:* Should the sociotechnic social worker be convinced that you are not normal she will have you bound for a nuttery before sunset.

nutty *n.* a crazy person.

1975 *L.A. Times* (Dec. 4) I 28: Teamsters Union President Frank E. Fitzsimmons…denounced as "nutties" and "would-be do-gooders" dissident groups in the union.

nutty *adj.* **1.a.** fond (of). infatuated, fascinated, or obsessed (with); NUTS, 1. [Bracketed quots. illustrate an earlier obs. sense of 'amorous', unattested in U.S.]

*1812 (quot. at NUTS, 1). ***1820–21** P. Egan *Life in London* 143: The *Mollishers* are all *nutty** upon him.…*Very fond. [***1821** *Real Life in London* I 145: Tom was getting… 'rather *nutty.*'*…**Nutty*—Amorous.] [***1823** "J. Bee" *Slang: Nutty*—sweet, amatory; bestowed by bucks upon buxom landladies, and spruce barmaids.] **1914** S. Lewis, in *DAS:* I'd be simply nutty about the quadrangles at Oxford. **1970** in *Rolling Stone Interviews* 360: I'm able to go really nutty for somebody. **1997** N.Y.C. man, age 48: I'm not really nutty about what's on TV these days.

b. crazy; eccentric; NUTS, 2. Also in joc. similes.

1892 Norr *China Town* 7: The boys guyed him…and volunteered the information that he was either "nutty" or "off his feed." **1893** Frye *Field & Staff* 175: Huh! w'at youse say cuts no ice wid me! It's clean nutty dat youse are. **1894** in Ade *Chicago Stories* 33: He always acted to me kind o' nutty. **1896** Ade *Artie* 88: Everybody's gone nutty on the proposition. **1897** (quot. at TROLLEY). **1898** in S. Crane *Dispatches* 254: "What's the matter with that feller?" asked Martin. "Nutty," said the man. **1899** A.H. Lewis *Sandburrs* 26: Say! if youse are out to make some poor mark nutty for fair, just give him d' dark hole for a week. There he is wit' nothin' in d' cell but himself, see! an' all as black as ink. *Ibid.* 92: Anyhow he's nutty to hold office. **1899** *Sat. Eve. Post* (Nov. 18) 396: I mus' be goin' nutty! **1900** S.E. White *Westerners* 313: "Nutty," they whispered to each other in undertones. **1901** *Smoking Lamp* (June) 48: Why, Choky,…are you nutty? **1906** Opper *Happy Hooligan* x: Nutty. Sure. **1908** W.G. Davenport *Butte & Montana* 137: Wearing themselves nutty over dead languages. **1913** *Chi. Defender* (Mar. 29) 7: Say,…you're nutty. **1912–14** in E. O'Neill *Lost Plays* 171: We sure are as nutty as a fruitcake or we wouldn't be here. **1926** Nichols & Tully *Twenty Below* 9: He's nutty as a walnut tree. [**1933** Milburn *Trumpets* 36: You think I'm as full of nuts as a peach-orchard boar, don't you? Crazy as hell, ain't I?] **1935** Lorimer & Lorimer *Heart Specialist* 163: You're nutty as a fruitcake. **1944** in C. Gould *Tracy* 3: Go *ahead*, driver, this guy's *nutty*. **1945** Hartman & Shavelson *Wonder Man* (film): You're nutty as a fruitcake! **1946–50** J. Jones *Here to Eternity* 644: Nuttier than a peach-orchard boar. *ca*1950 in Barkley *Sex Cartoons* 92: She's nutty as a pecan grove. **1958** "R. Traver" *Murder* 223: Nuttier than the proverbial fruitcake. **1959** in Asimov et al. *100 Fantasy Shorts* 5: A chance to make a good wedding present out of Aunt Hepsibah's nutty old bottle. **1965** D.G. Moore *20th C. Cowboy* 143: Boy! He was as nutty as a pinon tree. **1970** Grissim *Country Music* 283: He's as nutty as a fox squirrel. **1978** Groom *Better Times* 330: A weird nutty laughter, like that of a crazy person. **1983** Hofstadter & Dennett *Mind's I* 32: So we finally come to believe that the solipsistic view is nutty. **1992** Pres. G. Bush, campaign speech in Gainesville, Ga. (Oct. 19): Don't believe these nutty pollsters. **1996** Patchett & Fusco *Project: ALF* (film): They hauled her away. Nutty as a fruitcake.

2. [sugg. by CRAZY] Now *Jazz & Rap Music.* wonderful; excellent. [Bracketed quots. represent a similar but distinct nuance in obs. BrE slang 'pleasing or attractive', unattested in U.S.]

[******ca*1799** in Holloway & Black *Broadside Ballads* 81: She meets with a spoony that's nutty.] [***1823** Byron *Don Juan*, in *F & H* V 81: So prime, so gay, so nutty and so knowing.] [***1839** in *F & H* V 80: And the beak wore his nuttiest wig!] [***1893** in Partridge *DSUE* 575: Life goes on nutty and nice.] **1953** in S. Allen *Bop Fables* 42: "Nutty," said the wolf. **1955** *Science Digest* 33: "Nutty" has taken its place to mean good. **1953–58** J.C. Holmes *Horn* 219: Man, that's a real nutty tie, I dig that tie. **1959** *Swinging Syllables* s.v.: *Nutty*—Good, enjoyable, accomplished, anything pleasing. **1959–60** R. Reisner *Jazz Titans* 161: *Nutty:* great, exceptional. **1963** Braly *Shake Him* 87: The sound of Furg's horn was enough to scatter depression. Nutty! **1981** in G. Tate *Flyboy* 18: These nutty metropolitican [*sic*] nursery rhymes either stalk or they rumble.

nuts-and-bolts *adj.* crazy. *Joc.*

1929–31 J.T. Farrell *Young Lonigan* 78: Hello, Nuts and Bolts! **1931** J.T. Farrell *McGinty* 76: That punk is all nuts and bolts. Haw! Haw! **1931–34** Clemmer *Pris. Community* 334: *Nuts and bolts*, adj. Looney, feeble-minded. **1942** *ATS* 180: Insane; crazy.…*nuts, nuts and bolts, nutsy, nutty.*

nut up *v. Black E.* to go crazy or berserk.

1971–72 in *AS* L (1976) 63: *Nut up*…Go berserk "He's just going to nut up when he hears that." **1978** W. Brown *Tragic Magic* 96: I said later for all them Halls of Montezuma muthafuckas nuttin up behind bein in the Nam. ***1990** (quot. at NUT OUT).

nylon letdown *n. Mil. Av.* a parachute descent; a parachute. Also **nylon elevator.**

1983 M. Skinner *USAFE* 68: Avoiding a "nylon letdown"—or worse. **1984** *Call to Glory* (NBC-TV): And you've always got the nylon letdown. **1990** Yarborough *Da Nang Diary* 77 [ref. to Vietnam War]: There were no absolute guarantees on the "nylon elevator." **1990** Lightbody & Meyers *Complete Top Gun* 254: *Nylon letdown:* Slang for an ejection from an aircraft while in flight.

nymph *n.* **1.** a prostitute.

1833 in *OEDS:* Nymphs of the pave—numerous (in Honolulu). **1867** *Nat. Police Gaz.* (Apr. 13) 4: Sadé Montgomery is a *nymph* of the worst class, is well known to nearly all the *habitues* of houses of prostitution and assignation in this vicinity.

2. a nymphomaniac.

1916 Cary *Venery* II 14: *Nymph*—An abbreviation of nymphomaniac. A woman afflicted with insane sexual desires. **1952** Kerouac *Cody* 201: He claims she's a sex fiend nymph. **1963** in L. Bruce *Essent. Bruce* 142: She's a nymph, a nymphomaniac. **1966** Harris & Freeman *Lords of Hell* 61: It scary to be with a real nymph like Barbara, you know. **1969** Coppel *Little Time* 126: Am I turning into some kind of nymphomaniac? They say that real nymphs don't even like sex but they wallowed in it, trying to punish themselves for something.

nympho *n.* a nymphomaniac. Also as *adj.*

*ca*1910 (cited in *W10*). **1934** W. Smith *Bessie Cotter* 142: Jenny is a nympho. ***1935** in *OEDS:* Maniacs can't get far without cash…however dipso or nympho they may be. **1938** H. Miller *Trop. Capricorn* 107: Laura the nympho is doing the rhumba. **1946** Mezzrow & Wolfe *Really the Blues* 33: She seldom goes in for the nympho kick. **1946** H.A. Smith *Rhubarb* 33: That daffy nympho, Myra. **1954** in J. Jones *Reach* 212: They are always calling her (derogatorily) a nympho. **1959** E. Hunter *Conviction* 77: They're all nymphos. **1960** Carpenter *The Youngest Harlot* 39: Whats the matter with you? You a nympho? **1963** D. Tracy *Brass Ring* 170: A real, genuine, grade-A nympho. **1969** Susann *Love Machine* 69: Well, she was a good-natured nympho. **1971** C. Brown *Creative Murders* 136: "I guess she figures it's worth it," he said in a nonchalant voice. "Her being a nympho, and all." **1974** Fox & Puzo *Earthquake* (film): I'm not a nympho. **1985** Ferrell & Lichter *Vixens* (film): And that nympho stuff's just not my style. **1986** Bozzone *Buck Fever* 11: Not only a dyke, but a nympho dyke. **1992** *American Detective* (ABC-TV): She was a nympho—I'll tell you the truth. **1993** D. Lum, in J. Hagedorn *Chan Is Dead* 295: My Bosom Made Me a Nympho. *a*1994 A. Radakovich *Wild Girls Club* 15: The goal…is to put us in the mood, to get us turned on like crazed nymphos.

O *n.* **1.** *Narc.* opium. See also BIG O, 2.

 1933 D.W. Maurer, in *AS* (Apr.) 27: Opium is referred to specifically as *O, mud,* or *hop.* **1934** Weseen *Dict. Amer. Sl.* 28: *O*—Opium. **1951** in W.S. Burroughs *Letters* 83: Still smoke O once a week. **1952** in Kerouac *Letters* 347: Who'd just eaten some O after lush [*sic*]. **1963** Coon *Short End* 136: About the first time he finds some cat stoned on O.

2. *Narc.* an ounce of narcotic.

 1936 *AS* (Apr.) 124: *O.*...an "ounce" or *piece* of dope, especially of morphine.

3. *Sports.* offensive play; the offense. Cf. D, 3.

 1980 Wielgus & Wolff *Basketball* 137: Quick hands on D and triple pumps on O. **1996** *N.Y. Times* (Sept. 18) B1: Movable object (Giants "D") meets resistible force (Jets "O").

-o *suffix.* **1.** (a freq. derisive suffix used to form nouns or hypocoristic names). See also main entries, as DADDY-O, EL——O, FLOPPO, WEIRDO. [Perh. orig. partially in imit. of Spanish words ending with the letter; since *ca*1945 there has prob. been a contributing infl. from Japanese also, esp. in mil. speech in East Asia.]

 1905 T.A. Dorgan, in Zwilling *TAD Lexicon* 119: (TAD Shows How Fitz May Look After He Has Been "Made Ready" To Fight O'Brien) See that hump?..."Rubbo" did it. See that white spot. "Frecklo" did it. **1917** T.A. Dorgan, in Zwilling *TAD Lexicon* 119: Just as I'm ridin no hands he bucks an' off I go on me beano. **1920** *Hicoxy's Army* 11: Just as the hero is about to clout the villain on the beano, they both freeze stiff. **1925** *Adventure* (Dec. 10) 104: Blast your eyes, Greeko!...Stow them chains! *1930 J.M. Saunders *Dawn Patrol* (film) [ref. to 1918]: Give them hell, Scotto! **1936** S.I. Miller *Battling Bellhop* (film): He hit him with a right! What a socko! **1938** *AS* (Oct.) 239: A breezy comedy of young marriage, which takes a huge floppo. **1940** Wexley *City for Conquest* (film): Get wise to yourself...punko. **1952** Mandel *Angry Strangers* 241: If hashish don' put you on, lady, like—you better stick to lusho. **1952** in Kerouac *Letters* 360: Raymond-O, don't you think this romance has gone far enuf? **1953** K. Burke, in Jay *Burke-Cowley Corres.* 316: Wincing every time Truman did a botcho. **1955** B.J. Friedman, in *Antioch Rev.* XV 377: I got 150 bastardos waiting out there to be paid. **1956** H. Gold *Not With It* 247: What you mean, pal-o, is you don't want the life no more. **1958** *Life* (Apr. 28) 70 [ref. to *ca*1950]: Mr. Schultz...walked through the "dorm-o." **1958** Frankel *Band of Bros.* 217: C'mon, friendo, I've got a box of Tootsie Rolls fer you. **1958** Gilbert *Vice Trap* 74: Don't get any more ideas...buddy-o. **1963** E.M. Miller *Exile* 89: Not me, John-O. I got one gal to last me for life. **1965** Himes *Imabelle* 144: Baby-o, I got news for you. **1966** K. Hunter *Landlord* 192: Now what's the trouble this time, buddy-o? **1966–67** P. Thomas *Mean Streets* 82: You ain't playing fair, fuckos. **1968** S. Ross *Hang Up* 22: Give my buddy-o anything he wants. **1969** Sidney *Love of Dying* 84: You givin' me orders, buddy-o? **1972** *All in the Family* (CBS-TV): I won't have no creepos, weirdos, or sexos in my house! **1977** in G.A. Fine *With Boys* 169: Dork, dorko...Disliked boy. **1990** R. Herman, Jr. *Force of Eagles* 356: Except for klutzo here falling on his face. **1996** *Nick Freno* (Warner Bros. TV): Mr. Freno, you're using your bean-o! **1996** *Simpsons Comics* (No. 20) (unp.): Why don't you watch where you're going, klutzo!

2. (a usu. derisive suffix used to form adjectives fr. adjectives or nouns). See also main entries, as NUTSO.

 1904 J. London *Sea-Wolf* ch. vi: Killed 'im dead-oh. **1906** J. London *White Fang* ch. xix: He tried to take White Fang's meat, an' he's dead-O. **1917** Ford *Cheer-Up Letters* 128: I can't imagine an army brave enough to pull off an attack in this freezo weather. **1937** *AS* (Feb.) 18: H.G. Phillips's syndicated column, "The Once Over," August 29, 1936, remarks of pictures of women participating in the war in Spain, "Whatever the explanation may be, the effect on society is sure to be *punko.*" **1958** *Life* (Apr. 28) 69 [ref. to *ca*1950]: It griped me to have to put on "state-o" or official clothes. *Ibid.* 70: The elite of state-o society. **1966–67** P. Thomas *Mean Streets* 16: The bad-o feel-

ing came back. **1974** R. Price *Wanderers* 32: He had a...thick, hunko body. **1977** Stallone *Paradise Alley* 152: What if I ain't satisfied with this crap-o arrangement? **1986** N.Y.C. woman, age *ca*50: That comes from my Dutcho ancestors. **1985–87** Bogosian *Talk Radio* 59: Some fake-o story. **1991** C. Eddy *Stairway to Hell* 155: Ominoso...thumpola that anticipates a myriad mid-to-late-eighties gothic groovesters.

oakety-doakety *interj.* OKEY-DOKEY.

 1947 S. Boyer *Dark Ship* 176: He likes to indicate approval by saying "oakety doakety."

Oakie var. OKIE.

Oakley *n.* ANNIE OAKLEY, 1.

 1920 T.A. Dorgan, in Zwilling *TAD Lexicon* 60: Watching the office pass moocher as he gets ready to hit the sporting editor for a pair of oakleys to the big football game. **1927** (quot. at SKULL). **1938** in W.C. Fields *By Himself* 451: He said "O.K." and shot me eight Oakleys. **1960** Barber *Minsky's* 271: Morton left a sheaf of Oakleys.

oak towel *n.* a wooden club. Also (*obs.*) **oaken towel.** Cf. LOCUST.

 *1785 Grose *Dict. Vulgar Tongue:* An *oaken towel;* an oaken cudgel. To rub a man down with an oaken towel; to beat him. **1859** Matsell *Vocab.* 60: Oak Towel. An oaken cudgel. **1889** in *OEDS:* Oak towel...a stout oaken stick. There is an allusion here to "wiping" or "dressing one down." **1927** *DN* V 457: Oak towel, *n.* A club. The flatty give me a damn good rub down with his *oak towel.* **1946** Gresham *Nightmare Alley* 250: You got the bulls standing there with oak towels in their hands, all ready to rub you down.

Oaktown *n. Local & Rap Music.* Oakland, California.

 1990 *Puncture* (Summer) 45: They're keen to learn more about Oaktown. **1991** Nelson & Gonzales *Bring Noise* 255: Too Short is the real voice of Oaktown. **1991** N. Krulik *Hammer & Ice* 7: It was into that part of Oaktown that Stanley Kirk Burrell was born in 1963. **1991** in *RapPages* (Feb. 1992) 66: Oaktown (i.e. Oakland). **1995** Stavsky, Mozeson & Mozeson *A 2 Z: Oaktown*...Oakland, Calif.

O.A.O. *n.* [fr. one *and* only] *Stu.* one's sweetheart or fiancée.

 1928 *AS* III 453: *O.A.O.*—The "one and only" girl. **1935** Lorimer & Lorimer *Heart Specialist* 174: I want you for my O.A.O. **1939** *AS* XIV 29: *O.A.O.,* n. One and only, a [Citadel] cadet's true love. **1941** in J. Jones *Reach* 14: It seems her OAO got very jealous. **1947** *AS* XXII 111: A soldier's "one and only" girl is his *O.A.O.* **1968** Myrer *Eagle* 416: "No O-A-O?" She had picked up some of the slang from...West Point. "No One-And-Only." **1969** *Current Slang I & II* 64: *OAO,* n. One and only.—Air Force Academy cadets. **1993** G. Lee *Honor & Duty* 420: *OAO:* one and only—*the* girlfriend.

oar *n.* ¶ In phrases:

 ¶ **not have both oars in the water** to be stupid or mentally unbalanced.

 1982 *N.Y. Times* (May 9): Let me assure you that our Secretary of State has both oars in the water. **1982** *Harper's* (June) 34: Not Bugsy, a nickname Siegel detested. It had been hung on him in New York with the suggestion that he did not quite have both oars in the water. **1982** Randi *Flim-Flam!* 227: It seems that Dr. Eisenbud is not rowing with both oars in the water. *a*1984 in Safire *Stand Corrected* 51: You mention not having "both oars in the water" as a term for crazy. I first heard this in Waco 3 years ago. **1987** Kent *Phr. Book* 156: That guy doesn't have both oars in the water. **1996** *CNN & Co.* (CNN-TV) (Dec. 18): Maybe he was not playing with all his oars in the water.

 ¶ **put in (one's) oar** [sugg. by the proverb illustrated in bracketed quots.] to interfere; voice an unwanted opinion. Now *colloq.* Also vars.

 [*1596 in *F & H* V 83: A busie-body, medler in other's matters, one that hath an oare in other's boates.] [*1630 in *OEDS:* Youth...putting his oare in every mans boat.] **1821** Waln *Hermit in Phila.* 27: Always *putting in his oar.* **1846** in Lowell *Poetical Works* 181: The parson kind o' slicked off sum o' the last varses, but he told Hosee he did n't want to put his ore in to tetch to the Rest on 'em. **1847** Robb *Kaam* 10:

Thar's a young Ingin…goin' to put in his oar an' paddle out suthin' of that lingo. **1853** S. Robinson *Hot Corn* 76: Who axt you to put in your oar? **1887** Davis *Sea-Wanderer* 32: Who the h—l asked you to shove your oar in, Doctor. **1903** Harriman *Homebuilders* 70: Aw, g'wan.…What you got to stick your oar inteh everythin' fer? **1918** Ruggles *Navy Explained* 112: When an argument is in progress and some fellow butts in, one of those so engaged will always remark: "Well, stupid, who asked you to put in your oar?" **1932** *Collier's* (Jan. 30) 7: She seldom sticks in her oar, except maybe to ask a question. **1950** Calmer *Strange Land* 262: Cal puts his oar in. **1967** Talbot *Chatty Jones* 101: But what's he sticking his oar in for? **1971** Lavallee *Event 1000* 83: Commodore, can I stick my oar in?

¶ **stroke (one's) oar** (of a male) to masturbate.

    1971 *Nat. Lampoon* (Dec.) 37: It is perfectly natural that at your age you may become preoccupied with banging your whang. Stroking your oar. You know, whipping your lizard. **1975** in *West. Folk.* XXXVI (1977) 359: Stroke my oar.

oary-eyed var. ORY-EYED.

oatburner *n.* a horse esp. a worthless horse. Also vars.

    1916 *DN* IV 341: *Oatsmobile*…A horse. **1941** in *OEDS:* There isn't a galloper in the lot who can say "I'm the boss," so your milkman's oat burner might do just as well as any of 'em. **1942** *ATS* 140: Horse…*hay-burner…oats consumer, -destroyer, -grinder* or *-muncher, oatsmobile* [etc.]. **1951** *PADS* XVI 45: *Oat muncher (burner)*…Any worthless horse. **1952** in *DAS:* Even an oat-burner must sport a tax stamp on its stem or stern. **1955** in *DARE.* **1968** (quot. at HAY-BURNER). **1973** Haney *Jock* 177: *Oat muncher:* A horse that does not pay for its feed with its winnings.

oater *n. Entertainment Industry.* a movie, television show, radio show, or book about cowboys; a Western.

    1946 (cited in *W10*). **1950** *Sat. Eve. Post* (Jan. 14) 68: Cooper should be cast in Westerns, and for a while he appeared only in such "they-went-thataway" oaters as Arizona Bound and Nevada. **1950** *N.Y. Times* (Sept. 24) VI 20: The first Hopalong "oaters," as Western stories are known among film, radio and television people, appeared on TV in August, 1948. **1958** *Time* (Nov. 3) 80: The fact that he owns 15% of *Wells Fargo* does not keep him from writing scripts for other oaters (*e.g.,* Desilu's *The Texan*). **1968** Vidal *Breckinridge* 49: I did make eighteen feature-length oaters. **1977** *Kansas City Star* (Dec. 4) 50A: "Shane" emerged as the finest oater of them all. **1980** *L.A. Times Bk. Rev.* (Jan. 20) 3: Gone, then, from the new-books shelf is the folksy oater of Zane Grey and Ernest Haycox. **1981** *Time* (Sept. 7) E5: Hollywood has virtually stopped manufacturing oaters. **1986** *Time* (Mar. 10) 79: Roy Rogers and Dale Evans, both 73, introduce one of the oaters they made from 1938 to 1948.

oath *n.* ¶ In phrase: **take the oath** to take a drink of liquor.

    1859 (cited in *F & H*). **1864** in H. Johnson *Talking Wire* 192: The Lieut got to talking with the guard and "*administered the oath*" a second time. **1865** Sala *Diary* II 314: No other mystery is there in the grand ceremony of "taking the oath," "putting oneself outside suthin'," or "liquoring up." **1868** J. Chisholm *So. Pass* 119: So we stopped and took the oath.

oat muncher var. OATBURNER.

oats *n.pl.* spirit; (*hence*) power or strength. Orig. and usu. in phr. **feel (one's) oats** (orig. of horses) to be high-spirited; (*hence, broadly*) to be aware of or call attention to (one's) own power or strength. Now *colloq.*

    1831 in *DA:* Whether the pony felt his oats,…He took a frightful canter. **1856** *Harper's Mag.* (Feb.) 427: They begin to feel their oats. **1900** in "O. Henry" *Works* 1216: When the pony was "feeling his oats," he might step a little higher and farther. **1908** W.G. Davenport *Butte & Montana* 94: The wily senator began to feel his oats. *Ibid.* 164: "Everything I have, I owe to my wife." "Not quite everything—you must be full of oats rolled." **1941–42** Kennerly & Berry *Eagles Roar* 97: And the Hurricane had several hundred horse-power more "oats" than the Master. **1950** *N.Y. Times* (June 18) IV E3: Western Germany has gone ahead on an industrial recovery which is impressive and…some Germans have felt their oats. **1965** Carmichael & Longstreet *Sometimes I Wonder* 76: A young man feeling his oats. **1979** Stallone *Rocky II* 91: Maybe he'd been eatin' better lately, or feelin' his oats, or maybe he had a girlfriend on the side. **1995** W.J. Taylor *Elvis* 127: The Soviets are feeling their oats.

oats opera *n.* OATER. Also **oat opera.**

1937 *AS* (Dec.) 318: *Oats Opera.* A western film. **1947** in *OEDS:* Roy Rodgers, Gene Autry and other oat opera stars.

O.B. *n.* **1.** organized baseball.

    1915 *Baseball Mag.* (Dec.) 89 (cited in Nichols *Baseball Term.*). **1969** Bouton *Ball Four* 272: Organized baseball is *O.B.,* and a stupid player has the *worst head in O.B.*

2. see s.v. OBIE.

o-be-joyful var. OH-BE-JOYFUL.

obey var. OBIE.

obflisticate *v.* to vanquish; obliterate.

    1832 J. Hall *Legends* 38: These Mingoes…ought to be…tee-totally obflisticated off of the face of the whole yearth. **1839** *Crockett Almanac 1840* 10: He looked obflisticated.

obfuscate *v.* to intoxicate; make drunk. Hence **obfuscation,** *n.* a state of drunkenness.

    [*1729 in *OED2:* Curb…every passion, each whereof inebriates and obfuscates no less than drink.] *1861 in *F & H* V 85: In a general state of obfuscation, in consequence of being plied with strange liquors by their patrons. **1866** (quot. at *have a brick in (one's) hat* s.v. BRICK). **1911–12** (quot. at SNOOTED). **1979** Univ. Tenn. student theme: Drunk—stoned…obfuscated…soused.

obfusticated *adj.* confounded or confused.

    1834 in *DA:* [Crockett] swore "he'd be tee-to-natiously obfusticated if he would take office on any condition." *ca*1844 in *DA:* I see, Doctor, you are a little obfusticated. **1871** in *DA:* Far fetched theories and other "obfusticated" nonsense. **1909** *DN* III 353: *Obfusticated*…Excited, flustrated. **1966** in *DARE:* *Obfusticated*…bewildered, overshadowed, eclipsed.…The expression is obsolescent.

obie *n.* [orig. unkn.] *Und.* a post office. Also **O.B., obey.**

    1925 *Atlantic Mo.* (Dec.) 747: I had neither the intention nor the desire to learn the gentle art of "cracking boxes" in "obies" for my own enrichment and Uncle Sam's loss. **1927** *AS* (June) 385: An *obie,* or *O.B.,* was a post-office. O.B., I believe, is P.O. reversed with the P made into a B. The yegg pushes specialized in obies. **1927** *DN* V 457: *Obie,* n. A country post office. **1928** Callahan *Man's Grim Justice* 46: There's nobody sleeping over that obey (post office). **1942** *ATS* 466: Glue pot, O.B., obie, *a post office.* **1980** Bruns *Kts. of Road* 96: He would enlist a cadre of scouts to case obies and banks nationwide.

obit *n. Journ.* an obituary. [Orig. S.E., < MF; see *OED2.*]

    *1874 in *OEDS:* The sub-editor of a New York daily newspaper wrote to me begging me to send him the proper materials for the construction of an obit. He said it was the custom of his journal to keep obits in readiness. **1915–16** Lait *Beef, Iron & Wine* 258: I'll have the obit for you day after to-morrow. **1927** "S.S. Van Dine" "*Canary*" *Murder* ch. xxiv: The lad who manœuvred those two obits had real bean in him. **1940** Stout *Where There's a Will* 2: That was in his obit in the times. **1942** in E. O'Neill *Letters* 531: By Way Of Obit. **1943** K. Burke, in Jay *Burke-Cowley Corres.* 260: I think you should try for a year laying off the obits. **1948** D. West *Living Is Easy* 136: England was writing the obit of a Kaiser. **1950** F. Brown *Space on Hands* 161: We were reading some old copies of *Interplanetary Variety* and came across his obit. **1963** E.M. Miller *Exile* 47: He had covered every beat from obits to police blotter for more than twenty years. **1966** in L. Williams *City of Angels* 29: A bold face notice in the obits. **1974** in *Atlantic* (Jan. 1975) 52: He had prepared his own obit. **1984** H. Gould *Cocktail* 14: My obit was due the next evening. **1985** Dye *Between Raindrops* 249: Don't think I'll be writing anything at all for a while. No obits. Nothing. **1992** G. Wolff *Day at the Beach* 9: Have we got art with the Makepeace obit?

obliterated *adj.* extremely intoxicated.

    1988 Univ. Chicago student (coll. J. Sheidlower): I was totally obliterated last night. **1990** P. Munro *Slang U.:* Obliterated drunk, intoxicated.

oblong *n.* a banknote.

    *a*1794 in *DA:* It was a common expression among the troops to call the bank bills *oblongs.* This was more especially the case at the gaming tables.

obno *n. & adj.* an obnoxious person; (as adj.) obnoxious.

    1979 Eble *Campus Slang* (Mar.) 5: *Obno*—an obnoxious, loud, crude person. **1979** Univ. Tenn. student theme: [Drunk:] Smashed, Bombed, Blitzed,…fried, obno (obnoxious). **1990** P. Munro *Slang U.: Obno* obnoxious.

O'Brien *n.* ¶ In phrase: **John O'Brien** *Hobo.* a boxcar; (*also*) a freight train.

    1914 Jackson & Hellyer *Vocab.* 51: John O'Brien…A freight train, used in contradistinction to a "rattler," a passenger train. **1917** *Editor* (Feb. 24) 153: *John O'Brien*…a box-car. **1921** Casey & Casey *Gay-Cat* 61: I've bin wanderin'…on the rods and blinds and in John O'Briens. **1925–26** J. Black *You Can't Win* 127 [ref. to 1890's]: The "John O'Brien"—the bums' term for hand car, so called because every other section boss in those days was named O'Brien. **1928** Callahan *Man's Grim Justice* 76: I was huddled up in the corner of the John O'Brien (box car).

obsquatulate var. ABSQUATULATE.

ocean wave *n.* [rhyming slang] a shave. *Rare* in U.S.

    1927–28 (quot. at SYDNEY HARBOR). **1928** Sharpe *Chicago May* 287: *Ocean waves* [*sic*]—shave. **1934* in *OED2*: I 'as my ocean wave.

octane *n.* verve; zest.

    1994 *Bon Appétit* (Oct.) 34: Chunks of it [*sc.*, chocolate]…add octane to Hershey's traditional chocolate cream pie. **1996** *N.Y. Times* (Mar. 27) B3: Entering with low odds and high octane.

octopus *n.* (among women) a man who makes excessive attempts to fondle a woman, as on a date.

    1932 Lorimer *Streetcars* 217: Come on, don't be an octopus, Davy. **1932–33** Nicholson & Robinson *Sailor, Beware!* 149: On your way, octopus! **1941** Macaulay & Wald *Manpower* (film): The nurses are all afraid to come near this octopus. **1955–57** Felder *Collegiate Slang* 4: *Octopus*—a boy who pawed on a date. **1962** in *AS* (Dec. 1963) 273: Girls call an aggressive boy who is *all hands…an octopus.* **1965** *N.Y. Times* (Dec. 27) 20: A difficult date is an "octopus." **1974** *Police Woman* (NBC-TV): "I'm not a fighter—I'm a lover." "And a pretty good singer—for an octopus." **1988** Kienzle *Marked for Murder* 117: He…did not appear to be your run-of-the-mill octopus when it came to women. **1989** *Life* (July) 27: At parties he'd…become a real *octopus*, just couldn't keep his hands off girls.

OD[1] *n.* [fr. *olive drab*, after the color of the pill] *Army.* a greenish compound cathartic pill, routinely given to soldiers reporting for sick call. In full, **OD pill.**

    1916 *Rio Grande Rattler* (Sept. 6) 3: They feed you O.D. pills you see—/On the Texas border line. **1918** Rowse *Doughboy Dope* 21: The Medical Corps orderly sees to it that you get the other fellow's throat gargle and he gets your O.D. pills. **1919** Piesbergen *Aero Squadron* 58: Thanks to the enormous supply of iodine and O.D. pills we were always healthy. **1919** Shryer *Co. C* 3 [ref. to 1918]: O.D. pills and mark him duty. **1919** Slosser *212th Engrs.* 23: They greet you with the selfsame cure—a little O.D. pill. **1919** Wilson *364th Inf.* 9 [ref. to 1918]: The panacea for all was the inevitable "O.D.'s" or "Camp Lewis Special." **1920** *Amer. Leg. Wkly.* (Feb. 13) 13: Sergeant, the doc gave me some O.D.s last night. **1921** Dienst *353rd Inf.* 252: Take these O.D.'s. **1923** S. Whitney *Squad. A* 22: Medical supplies (chiefly O.D. pills). **1928** Richardson *Here Comes the Band!* 79 [ref. to 1918]: Lampe's chest was decorated with iodine and the regulation number of O.D. pills administered. **1936** Reilly *Americans All* 164 [ref. to 1918]: We finally got to our destination and turned the wounded man over to a pair of O.D. Pill Dispensers.

OD[2] *n.* [abbr. *overdose*] *Esp. Narc.* an overdose of a narcotic or other medication.

    1958–59 Lipton *Barbarians* 186: It was an OD…of horse that led him back to marijuana. **1959–60** R. Reisner *Jazz Titans* 162: *O.D.:* an overdose of narcotics. **1965** C. Brown *Manchild* 188: The cat took an O.D. **1967** J.B. Williams *Narc. & Hallucin.* 114: *O.D.*—overdose of narcotics, usu. heroin. **1968** *Seattle Times* (Mar. 17) ("Magazine") 5: Some day it's an O.D. (overdose) and I'll be D.O.A. **1978** *Harper's* (July) 88: She enjoys watching Reed risk an o.d. every time he shoots up. *a***1996** D.F. Wallace *Infinite Jest* 70: This latest [suicide] attempt [is] a straightforward meds O.D.

OD *adj.* [*olive drab*] *Army.* rigidly or typically military.

    [**1915** in *OEDS:* Two O.D. shirts you next slip in, A pair of shoes goes in between.] **1916** *Rio Grande Rattler* (Sept. 6) 4: My shoes are full of O.D. dirt/My hair of O.D. glue. **1917** *Wadsworth Gas Attack* 5: This is the second year that the 27th Division has received 18 ounces of O.D. turkey in a mess kit. *Ibid.:* He hereby applies for one large O.D. horse. **1919** Duffy *G.P.F. Book* 301 [ref. to 1918]: That O.D. haircut he got at the cootie mill must have brought back the days of the mother and the bowl. **1919** T. Kelly *What Outfit?* 11: Now, you see, we call anything that is regulation, red tape, and all that kind of

stuff, O.D.—just sort of a nickname. When I first saw you I thought you was a soldier out of the drill regulation-book. You're O.D.-lookin', that's all. You're the first of that kind I've seen in a mighty long time. **1919** Kuhn *Co. A* 54: The pile of forage was soon transformed into the most delicious stew ever served at an O.D. banquet. **1919** H. Law *Army Air Service* (unp.): Our Supply of O.D. Bull is always complete and we are always glad to have the ahviators drop in for a little chat. **1919** in Fletcher *113th Field Arty.* (opp. 148): They fed us big and they ain't mentioned mutton nor O.D. gravy yet. **1919** Duffy *G.P.F. Book* 87: For the first time we met O.D. hash,/Entirely new to us,/But we tackled the stuff as soldiers should/To clean it up, or bust. *Ibid.* 309: He was a victim of stomach trouble, but the way he went after seconds of O.D. and other varieties at meal time would put anybody under. **1982** Del Vecchio *13th Valley* 201: Theys lifers and it don't matter what color a lifer is. They all OD.

OD *v.* **1.** *Esp. Narc.* to overdose, esp. on an illicit drug; (*also*) to cause to overdose.

    1966 Braly *On Yard* 30: Some little junior flip bitch oh-deed. **1966** J. Mills *Needle Park* 45 [ref. to 1964]: Frankie's OD'ing up in Marcie's room in the Reynolds. He needs help bad honey. You gotta come right now. **1966** *L.A. Free Press* (July 15) 6: Ragged girls would stumble across the room, OD'd on pills. **1971** *Atlantic* (Feb.) 104: The drummer OD'd and had to be replaced. **1975** *Bronk* (CBS-TV): Somebody else O.D.'d her. **1978** *L.A. Times* (Feb. 4) II 4: Other kids get pregnant, OD, smash up their cars. **1978** D. Marsh, in *Rolling Stone* (Oct. 5) 46: Instead of ODing, those boys just drank themselves to death. **1980** D. Hamill *Stomping Ground* 68: Enough goofballs…to OD Godzilla. **1980** L. Fleischer & C. Gore *Fame* 157: OD-ing in some motel room. **1985** B.E. Ellis *Less Than Zero* 29: I thought he O.D.'d. **1985** J. Dillinger *Adrenaline* 65: End up accidentally OD'ing. **1993** E. Richards *Cocaine True* 72: I had OD'd from it.

2. to get too much of or become surfeited with; overindulge in; (*also*) to cause to be surfeited.—constr. with *on.*

    1974 in H.S. Thompson *Shark Hunt* 513: Yeah…just a couple of good ole boys O.D.'d on booze. **1974** *Atlantic* (Dec.) 98: Hey, Brother, haven't you found Jesus yet? You'll never o.d. on him. **1972–76** Durden *No Bugles* 234: He's gonna OD on visitors. **1976** Univ. Tenn. student: I used to collect recruiting literature as a hobby. But I O.D.'d on that when I got out of the Army. **1976–77** C. McFadden *Serial* 22: Leonard was "enchilada'd out" and had also "O.D.'d on tostadas compuestas." **1978** Maupin *Tales* 68: He was…OD'ing on Tiffany lamplight. **1986** C. Horrall & C. Vincent *Wimps* (film): Don't you think we've O.D.'d on Charles for the evening? **1986** Gilmour *Pretty in Pink* 116: You're going to OD on nostalgia. **1987** B. Raskin *Hot Flashes* 295: Another *kvetch* novel.…I think we've OD'd on those. **1987–89** M.H. Kingston *Tripmaster Monkey* 267: O.d. your listener, give her plenty to choose from. **1994** *Mystery Sci. Theater* (Comedy Central TV): I'm ODing on slang here! **1996** *TV Guide* (Feb. 11) 39: Some of us have OD'ed [*sic*] on O.J.

o-dark-hundred *n. Mil.* O-DARK-THIRTY.

    1982 Basel *Pak Six* 67 [ref. to 1967]: It was O-dark-hundred hours when we waddled out to our airplanes. **1991** Marcinko & Weisman *Rogue Warrior* 194: At oh dark hundred I'd head north again.

o-dark-thirty *n.* [sugg. by mil. time *0130, 0230,* etc.] *Mil.* the wee hours of the morning; before or roughly at dawn.—also used attrib. Also **zero-dark-thirty.** Cf. DARK-THIRTY. *Joc.* [Several quots. ref. to Vietnam War.]

    1980 Cragg *Lex. Militaris* 316: O-Dark-Thirty. Very early in the morning.…O may be pronounced "oh" or "zero." **1984** Trotti *Phantom* 112: No more "zero-dark-thirty" briefs. **1984–85** in Schneider & Schneider *Sound Off!* 212: You have to work from zero dark thirty until whenever. **1985** (quot. at DARK-THIRTY). **1986** *DayWatch* (CNN-TV) (Dec. 22): *O-dark-thirty*…is a phrase he likes to use. It means from any time before dawn to about half an hour after. **1981–89** R. Atkinson *Long Gray Line* 153: The next morning at O-dark-thirty. **1989** "Capt. X" & Dodson *Unfriendly Skies* 156: "Red-eyes"…are the o'pitchdark-thirty flights. **1990** Berent *Steel Tiger* 201: I've got an oh-dark-thirty get up and go. **1990** Yarborough *Da Nang Diary* 7: A little over three hours after our "oh-dark-thirty" departure from Clark Air Base. **1993** Watson & Dockery *Point Man* 73: We were able to…sleep just as it hit O-dark-30.

oday *n.* [pron.-sp. of pig Latin form of DOUGH] money; DOUGH, 1.

1929 *AS* IV (June) 343: *Oday*—Money. **1929** Hotstetter & Beesley *Racket* 233: *Oday*—Money. **1932** *Writer's Digest* (Aug.) 47: Money [is] "oday," which is "pig latin" and of circus derivation. **1933** Guest *Limey* 162: You don't have to worry about a little O-day. **1936** Steel *College* 318: You got that oday? **1942–49** Goldin et al. *DAUL* 148: This rap…would be a cinch to beat if I had the oday to get a good mouthpiece. **1981** O'Day & Eells *High Times* 34: I'd decided [the name] O'Day was groovy because in pig Latin it meant dough which was what I hoped to make.

OD coffee *n. Army.* Army coffee. [Quots. ref. to WWI.]
    1919 Whittemore *B Co.'s Book* 33: O.D. coffee or salt-water tea. **1920** Hart *Co. Log* 29: Slum, bread, and O.D. coffee. **1921** *Ohio Doughboys* 17: A scant cup of O.D. coffee was given each man, nothing more. **1925** *Amer. Leg. Wkly.* (Sept. 4) 6: Oatmeal, of course, and O.D. coffee.

oddball *n.* a peculiar or eccentric person.
    1948 in *AS* XXXII 221: *Odd Ball*…connoted that the individual's strangeness was not the result of prison camp experiences. **1952** Malamud *Natural* 59: The place often resembled a zoo full of oddballs, including gamblers, bums, drunks, and some ugly crackpots. **1953** *Sat. Eve. Post* (June 13) 48: A real odd-ball, that one. Clever as Satan in some ways, very dumb in others. **1956** Hess *Battle Hymn* 45: My desire to make them see that a minister was not different or an "odd ball" was stronger than my distaste for liquor. **1958** J. Davis *College Vocab.* 6: *Odd ball*—…A different type person. **1958–59** Lipton *Barbarians* 45: Sooner or later they'd get hip to the fact that I'm an oddball. **1960** Swarthout *Where Boys Are* 18: We right away asked them if they had heard of an oddball named TV Thompson. **1962** Simeon *Ring of Terror* (film): You've been acting like an oddball. **1962** L'Engle *Wrinkle in Time* 12: I *hate* being an oddball. **1963** *Harper's* (Feb.) 90: Hamlet would be an oddball in the Air Force. **1963** Hayden *Wanderer* 336: They were the odd-balls. **1966** Braly *Cold* 98: We'll have this oddball picked up and your phone number changed. **1968** Hawley *Hurricane Yrs.* 219: Unquestionably he was an oddball. **1977** Kleinberg *Live with Computers* 12: The people…did include a higher than average percentage of oddballs. **1980** Messman *Jogger's Moon* 23: No one remembered ever seeing her with any oddballs. **1983** *Good Morning America* (ABC-TV) (Apr. 22): I was sort of a unique oddball. **1989** Dorsett & Frommer *Running Tough* 106: The crazies, the oddballs, the guys past their prime. **1996** *Everybody Loves Raymond* (CBS-TV): Is he some kind of an oddball here? He's an oddball, that guy.

oddball *adj.* markedly peculiar or eccentric.
    1957 *Sat. Eve. Post* (Jan. 26) 27: "The most happy fellahs," said an odd-ball correspondent. **1958** *N.Y. Times* (Feb. 16) VI 28: Wilson is accused of fomenting every odd-ball name around. **1958** *Sat. Eve. Post* (Mar. 8) 19: Chaplin is that rare kind of oddball genius. **1959** *Twilight Zone* (CBS-TV): It's a real oddball thing. **1959–60** Bloch *Dead Beat* 65: A few oddball characters thrown in for comedy relief. **1961** J.A. Williams *Night Song* 80: I don't have any oddball sickness. **1962** Serling *New Stories* 9: It was the screwiest odd-ball feeling he'd ever felt. **1962** G. Olson *Roaring Road* 58: You had some oddball carburetors on the bench years ago. **1963** Braly *Shake Him* 7: Little oddball art galleries. **1964** Hunt *Ship with Flat Tire* 43: You don't expect me to cook up all these oddball recipes you get, do you, sir? **1964–66** R. Stone *Hall of Mirrors* 230: He was the oddballest son of a bitch of all o' them. **1968** *Rolling Stone Interviews* 74: They figured we were *odd-ball*. **1970** W.M. Hudson *Hunters & Healers* 117: Things…get done in a quirky, oddball fashion. **1974** V.B. Miller *Girl in River* 36: I don't care how oddball you think the idea is. **1980** L.N. Smith *Venus Belt* 146: The other two were military-issue .38 Special, one an oddball bastard with a cannelure, or crimping-groove, around the middle of the slug to hold it in the case. **1980** Garrison *Snakedoctor* 106: The main oddball thing to me is the razor blade. **1987** *N.Y. Times Bk. Rev.* (June 21) 15: Forsaking the Oddball Life. *a***1990** E. Currie *Dope & Trouble* 222: Just oddball people. **1993** *Science News* (Jan. 9) 20: Some oddball [galactic] group.

oddball *v.* to act strangely.
    1972 Hannah *Geronimo Rex* 281: I'm not going to oddball on you any more.

ods *pron.* (used in var. mild imprecations as a euphem. for *God's*). [*OED2* has a number of examples of different constructions.]
    *****1601** Shakespeare *Twelfth Night* V. i. 187: Odd's lifelings, heere he is. *****1695** Congreve, in *OED2*: Odso, my son Ben come? Odd, I'm glad on't: Where is he? **1776** in Meserve & Reardon *Satiric Comedies*

85: Odss, almost twelve o'clock. *****1812** in *F & H* V 89: O! were she in coal-pit bottom, And all such jades, 'Od rot 'em! My cares would then be over, And I should live in clover. *****1844** in *F & H* V 89: Ods fish, why this interest in poor Lady Lucy. **1873** *Slang & Vulgar Forms* 17: *Odd's boddikins* either refers to the nails under the name of bodkins, or to God's body.…*Odd splutter her nails* signifies *God's blood* and the *nails* which fastened Him to the cross. **1937** Partridge *DSUE* 579: Ods, od's; odds.…God's.

O.D.V. *n.* [punning English resp. of F *eau-de-vie*] brandy.
    1836 *Every Body's Album* I 143: There you'll see *nature's* charms!— "O.D.V." too. **1839** in *OEDS*: Why, that in French, is nothing but O.D.V.

ofaginzy *n. & adj.* [alter. OFAY] *Black E.* OFAY.
    1946 Mezzrow & Wolfe *Really Blues* 175: Don't nobody fault you for makin' out you's ofaginzy. **1956** Longstreet *Real Jazz* 147: The white visitor is called an "ofay" by Negroes.…He is also known as an "ofaginzy," just to make it harder.

ofay *n.* [orig. unkn.; the proposed derivation fr. a pig Latin form of *foe*, while superficially appealing, seems unlikely owing to the primarily literary distribution of the word; proposed African etyma remain dubious; nor is there convincing evidence for an origin in French *au fait* 'experienced; expert'; discussed by F. Cassidy in *AS* 50 (1975) 87–89] *Black E.* a white person.—usu. used contemptuously.
    1925 *Inter-State Tatler* (Mar. 6), in *DARE*: We hear that "Booker Red" had three ofays on his staff. **1925** Van Vechten *Nigger Heaven* 11: Ah met an ofay wanted to change his luck. He gimme a tenner. **1928** R. Fisher *Jericho* 299: *Ofay*. A person who, so far as is known, is white. *Fay* is said to be the original term and *ofay* a contraction of "old" and "fay." **1928** C. McKay *Home to Harlem* 22: I ain't told no nigger but you, boh. Nor ofay neither. **1932** in *DARE*: The root of the word appears to come from the Ibibio *Afia*, white or light-coloured. Hence in Harlem *Offay* means any light-coloured person and therefore a European. **1935** Michaux *Murder in Harlem* (film): Negro or ofay [pron. /ou'fei/]—get him outta here! **1937** *Writer* L 239, in *DARE*: *Ofay*—a white person. **1946** Mezzrow & Wolfe *Really Blues* 192: Take the word "ofay." Ninety million white Americans right now probably don't know that that means "a white," but Negroes know it. **1954** L. Armstrong *Satchmo* 189: The ofays were not used to seeing colored boys blowing horns and making fine music for them to dance by. **1956** Holiday & Dufty *Lady Sings* 52: Most of the ofays, the white people, who came to Harlem those nights were looking for atmosphere. **1957** E. Lacy *Room to Swing* 15: This is my town as much as the ofays'—why give it to them? **1959–60** R. Reisner *Jazz Titans* 162: *Ofay:* a white person. **1962** Crump *Killer* 312: That Dipper is one straight ofay. **1966** S. Harris *Hellhole* 159: And she is an old woman and an ofay besides! **1969** H.R. Brown *Die Nigger Die* 42: My father was away fighting for the land of the Ofay. **1978** L. Bangs, in *Rolling Stone* (June 1) 59: Marijuana should only be legalized for Third World peoples, since ofays in general just can't handle it. **1979** Hiler *Monkey Mt.* 155: All them offays feelin' guilty, so now's the time, you dig? *a***1981** D. Travis *Black Chicago* 85: Bandleaders to those "ofays." **1988** Poyer *The Med* 53: Oreo, you fucked-up ofay-lover, you can't even pass power right. **1992** N. Cohn *Heart of World* 296: There was a band called the O'Fays, white boys who wished they were black. *a***1994** N. McCall *Wanna Holler* 283: Some Deep South ofay.

ofay *adj. Black E.* characteristic of whites; ethnically white. Also as adv.
    1911 *Adventure* (Jan.) 446: I saw a mardi-gras suit of clothes that might have been "ofay" on a negro minstrel.…They were made of wonderfully figured stuff and had red lapels. *****1926** Walrond *Tropic Death* 61: The Latin was the nearest thing to a white man the *ofay* men aboard had yet met. **1927** McKay *Harlem* 21: "Scotch! That's an ofay drink," Rose remarked. **1954** L. Armstrong *Satchmo* 147: Ofay (white) business men and planters. **1961** Gover *$100 Misunderstanding* 96: He's all dress up o'fay. **1964** *Sat. Eve. Post* (Sept. 12) 65: You're all just waiting to see me die, you ofay finks. **1967** Gonzales *Paid My Dues* 15: In six weeks myself and two of the other musicians had scored with "ofay chicks." *a***1979** A. Rose *Eubie Blake* 152: Eubie calls Terry Waldo "my ofay son"—my white son.

ofer *n.* [fr. *oh* 'zero' + *fer*, var. *for*, in such phrs. as *0-for-4* 'no hits in four times at bat'] *Baseball.* an instance of a pitcher holding a batter hitless throughout a ballgame; (*also*) a second-rate player. Also vars.

1966 *S.F. Examiner* (Aug. 1), in Dickson *Baseball Dict.*: The players…didn't look like Yankees. They looked like…a bunch of oh-fers. **1983** Whiteford *How to Talk Baseball* 114: *Ohfer*…a hitless day for a hitter, as in "oh for three." **1984** *N.Y. Post* (Aug. 15) 76: Langston…became the first pitcher to hang a combined o-fer on Dave Winfield (0-for-3) and Don Mattingly (0-for-4) in 27 games. **1991** *Nation* (Aug. 26) 225: Two occasions when he was hitless in his last five. But in each case these "oh-fors" spanned two games instead of being confined to one.

off *adv.* to the point of orgasm. See also JERK OFF, 1.a.; SUCK OFF.

*1675 in Duffet *Burlesque Plays* 86: My Lord *Bacchus* leads 'em on; my Lady *Venus* brings 'em off. *1909 in J. Joyce *Sel. Letters* 191: Do you frig yourself off first? **1916** H. Cary *Venery* I 122: *To bring down* (or *off*) *by hand*—To masturbate. **1919** in T. Dreiser *Diaries* 293: Sensual play follows—Helen finally working me off. *ca*1938 in D.W. Maurer *Lang. Und.* 116: To *blow* (you) *off*. To hold intercourse through the mouth. **1947** in G. Legman *Limerick* 264: There was a young man of Kutki/Who could blink himself off with one eye. **1969** Crumb *Motor City Comics* (unp.): Now it's my turn to bring *you* off. **1971** N.Y.U. student: This kid would have four or five others blow him off. It made him feel he had power over them. **1972** J. Wells *Come Fly with Us* 156: He told me to masturbate in the phone booth, to…bring myself off. **1974** N.Y.C. man, age *ca*27: To hum somebody off is to give them a *hum job*. **1974** Millard *Thunderbolt* 108: Oh my God, don't bring me off before I even get in. **1977** Dittographed list of slang terms from Univ. Tenn. instructor: Feeling-off, jack-off, beatin' your meat.

off *prep.* **1.** no longer interested in; avoiding.

*1889 in *OEDS*: You are perhaps right in being "off" Gortsachoff's though the cooking is less deleterious than Pinolis. **1915** *N.Y. Eve. Jour.* (Aug. 2) 13: I am offa you for life. **1931** Rouverol *Dance, Fools, Dance* (film): Bonnie's sort of off the bunch. She…thinks they let her down.

2. by means of; at the expense of.

1963 Parks *Learning Tree* 17: Lucy stays drunk offa canned heat and Chappie's likker. **1965** in W. King *Black Anthol.* 309: We were eating off him. **1985** "Blowdryer" *Mod. Eng.* 32: So here I am, groovin' off some of my favorite tunes.

off *v.* **1.** Esp. *Black E.* to discharge; reject; (*hence*) to eliminate; stop. [U.S. usage is much later and apparently independent of British.]

*1908 in Partridge *DSUE*: I haven't offed that yet—haven't refused it, I mean. **1971** *Who Took Weight?* 153: I only worked five weeks before they offed me. **1972** *Tuesday Mag.* (May) 24: History will either off you or make you valid. **1974** Piñero *Short Eyes* 5: Off the fucking noise. **1976–77** C. McFadden *Serial* 119: I've gotta go tell Joan to off that goddamn rock [music]. **1984** W.M. Henderson *Elvis* 58: No movies, man. We're going to off movies in that theater for good. **1995** *Newsweek* (June 12) 69: Judge Ito…offed a juror.

2. *Und.* to dispose of, as by selling.

1960 C.L. Cooper *Scene* 180: This guy is supposed to have stuff unlimited, says he was gonna off it and get it right out. **1963** Braly *Shake Him* 51: It's a lawn mower.…Do you know where we could off it? **1967** Rosevear *Pot* 159: *Off, To*: To sell marihuana. **1974** V.E. Smith *Jones Men* 166: You gettin' a damn good buy.…My man wants to off a big hunk pretty quick. **1977** B. Davidson *Collura* 74: He…probably bought a "bundle" of fifteen $5 "nickel bags" of heroin, which he would cut up into many more "treys," or $3 bags, which he would "off" (sell). **1978** Selby *Requiem* 119: Harry went back to the pad and picked up another load [of heroin] and offd that too before going to Marions.

3. to copulate with (a woman).

1966 Braly *On Yard* 173: Blake would rather boot a convict in the ass than off his old lady. **1968** E. Cleaver *Soul on Ice* 150: You may not believe this…when I off a nigger bitch, I close my eyes and concentrate real hard, and pretty soon I get to believe that I'm riding one of them bucking blondes.

4.a. Orig. *Und.* to kill or murder; KNOCK OFF.

[**1930** Brophy & Partridge *Songs* 143 [ref. to WWI]: *Off it*, to die.] **1966–67** P. Thomas *Mean Streets* 193 [ref. to 1950's]: If he lays a hand on me again, I'm gonna off him. **1968** in Giovanni *Gemini* 43: We can only justify offing a brother if we have already offed twenty whiteys. **1968** *N.Y. Post* (June 7) 12: It was no nut offed Kennedy. **1969** *Atlantic* (Dec.) 38: Bang, bang,/Off the pig. **1971** D. Smith *Engine Co.* 171:

Some one tried to off 'im, man. **1976** *Deadly Game* (ABC-TV): In case he decides to off me you'll get to hear it. **1976** *Kojak* (CBS-TV): I say he was offed by a rival outfit. **1981** *Rod Serling's TZ Mag.* (June) 28: Out you walk, free to…off a few more old folks playing bridge in their yellow pants and white shoes. **1983** *Green Arrow* (July) 6: A sniper tried to off me. **1987** *Sable* (ABC-TV): Why do people off themselves? **1990** Linklater *Slacker* (film): Offed himself, man. Blew himself away right there. *a*1994 N. McCall *Wanna Holler* 64: If I offed Jimmy, it would be talked about…for years. **1997** *TV Guide* (Mar. 8) 13: His partner…is offed too.

b. *Black E.* to knock senseless; beat up.

1970 Cain *Blueschild Baby* 86: We drink awhile and the lame hits to cop my joint and while he's on his knees I off him. He's still out. **1983** *Reader's Digest Success with Words* 87: Black English…*off* = (1) "to beat up (someone)."

5. *Und.* to rob, esp. by violence.

1968 Heard *Howard St.* 16: He'd be too weak to off that big trick. **1974** *Village Voice* (N.Y.C.) (Feb. 7) 32: He wanted to "off" an old couple who were probably living off social security.

6. *Police.* to place under arrest.

1975 Sepe & Telano *Cop Team* 178: We can *off* him when he gets back.

off and on *interj. Army.* get up and get going!—used as a command.

1942 in *Best from Yank* 64: Okay, boys! Off and on! Hit the deck! **1943** *Yank* (Aug. 20) 16: Come on, you goldbricks. Off and on! **1944** Brown *Walk in the Sun* 36: He went back to the platoon. "All right, off and on," he said. "We're going over in the woods. Squad columns. Hop to it, for Christ's sake." **1944** Kendall *Service Slang* 12: *Off and On!*.…unofficial command meaning off your bed and on your feet. **1944–48** A. Lyon *Unknown Station* 99: You gotta turn your bedroll in and get some chow, so off and on. **1953** W. Fisher *Waiters* 44: Off and on.…Off your ass and on your feet. **1957** Leckie *Helmet for My Pillow* 25 [ref. to 1942]: Then came the command: "Off and on!" It means off your behind and on your feet. **1967** Coon *First to Fight* (film): All right, you people, off and on. Let's go. **1973** Hirschfeld *Victors* 17: Off and on. Let's get back to work. **1984** Jackson & Lupica *Reggie* 14: That comes from Dad always saying, "Off and on," meaning, "Off your ass and on the deck."

off-angle *adj.* OFFBEAT, 1.

1962 Houk & Dexter *Ballplayers* 117: Mickey, Roger and the Moose broke one of those off-angle records—two homers in the same game, six in all.

off artist see s.v. TAKE-OFF ARTIST.

offbeat *adj.* **1.** Orig. *Jazz.* unusual; unconventional; strange. Now *S.E.* Also as adv., occ. as n.

1938 in *OEDS*: He tried…to teach him to sweep with a utilitarian slant, all the strokes going in the same direction in such a way that…you inevitably have a pile of whatever it is, right there in front of your broom.…But…Smoke would go right back into his off-beat swishing. **1944** Burley *Hndbk. Jive* 56: Nix the offbeat, Jack, play the game. [**1946** De Chant *Devilbirds* 70: Everybody strained his ear for the off-beat motors of Washing Machine Charlie or Louie the Louse.] **1948** Kingsley *Detective Story* 327: There is something "off-beat," something disturbing about both these men. **1949** *N.Y. Times* (Oct. 23) II 5: An off-beat company with some distinctive ideas about the what and the how of motion pictures. **1952** *N.Y. Times* (Feb. 3) II x5: We are trying to do something off beat.…We may blaze a trail or burn our pants. **1953** in T. Williams *Letters* 282: There are two kinds of writing, on beat and off beat. Some very good writers are always on beat, such as Irwin Shaw and most of Steinbeck. **1954** Collans & Sterling *House Detect.* 145: In hotels these off-beat she-males don't get together in groups, wearing mannish clothes. **1955** Abbey *Brave Cowboy* 185: I mean, that he's kind of…eccentric? Offbeat? Queer? **1959** *Time* (Nov. 2) 38: [He] prodded them to "think off-beat." **1977** Kleinberg *Live with Computers* 33: Boole's…off-beat algebra was an important ingredient in the history of the computer.

2. mistaken; in error.

1958 S.H. Adams *Tenderloin* 170: That's where you're off beat, Dominic. You could learn a lot of things…by reading the *P.G.*

3. *Black E.* worthless.

1962 Crump *Killer* 306: She starts making you over into the image of what she thinks you should be. Later for that off-beat jazz!

off-brand *adj.* odd or unusual; (*hence*) second-rate. Occ. as n.

1960 in *DARE:* There was a sprinkling of Cumberland Presbyterians and Campbellites; but these off-brand folk attended our Sunday-school meetings and church services. **1965** in *DARE: Off-brand*—unconventional, strange. **1967** in *DARE: Off-brand* = non-standard. Used, among other things, of grammatical uses. **1967–70** in *DARE: Off-brand*—any different or strange one, e.g., Jehovah's Witnesses....Off-brand churches. **1967–80** Folb *Runnin' Lines* 248: *Off-brand* adj. 1.Weird, strange. 2.Inferior (in quality). 3.Different. **1991** in *UTNE Reader* (Mar. 1992) 129: It's amazing how well even an off-brand Kennedy like William Smith sells in this country. **1992** *New Yorker* (Feb. 10) 72: It made him [*sc.*, Jesse Jackson]..."sort of a misfit, an off-brand, yeah."

office *n.* **1.** a toilet, esp. one outdoors; privy.

   ***1727** in *OED2:* Proposals for erecting 500 Publick Offices of Ease in London. ***1871** in *OED2:* The forty-five big and little lodgers...were provided with a single office in the corner of the yard. **1941** *Ling. Atlas N.E.,* in *DARE:* Jocular euphemisms...for the terms *privy* [etc.]....*The office.* **1942** *ATS* 87: Toilet....*crapper...john...office.* **1950, 1968, 1973** in *DARE.*

2.a. information.

   ***1803** in *OED:* Giving the office—is when you suffer any person, who may stand behind your chair, to look over your hand. **1880** *N.Y. Clipper Almanac* 45: *Office.*—The same thing as the "tip," which is secret information as to the condition of a horse or the purpose in the race of those who have him in charge. **1921** Casey & Casey *Gay-Cat* 101: The Portugee Kid gave the road-kids the "office" to lay off the rough stuff. **1944** C.B. Davis *Leo McGuire* 173: I took a risk on a Mac who must have got moppy and given the office to a muff stool.

b. a surreptitious signal, esp. as a warning.

   1818** in *F & H* V 90: Reynolds observed to his seconds that if he could but see his man he certainly must win. The office was immediately given, when a farmer jumped into the ring, and lanced his eyes. ***1820–21** P. Egan *Life in London* 147: The *office* has been given to shove the poor *flue-faker.* *ca1830** in Holloway & Black *Broadsides* II 61: He tipt me the office to give him a leg. **1837** *Spirit of Times* (Feb. 17) 7: The "trap" was not sufficiently awake, and the "office" being given, the men were "non est inventus" when sought. **1838** Glascock *Land Sharks* I 198: I thinks half a crown won't be too much for keeping the coast clear outside, and tipping *the office,* if any busy-body's on the prowl. **1859** Matsell *Vocab.* 60: *Office.* Information conveyed by a look, word, or in any way by which the person receiving it is intelligibly impressed. "The cove tipped the office, and I was fly to the cop," the fellow gave me the hint, and then I knew it was a policeman. **1865** (quot. at BABY, 2). **1866** *Nat. Police Gaz.* (Nov. 24) 3: Curly..."slung the office" to an "M.P."...across the street. **1867** *Nat. Police Gaz.* (Oct. 19) 3: The tallest of the three "slung the office," and they closed on a very reverend looking "bloke." **1887** DeVol *Gambler* 195: I gave Bill the office to raise him about $4000. **1894** Gardner *Doctor & Devil* 48: I gave Dr. Parkhurst "the office" (that's Bowery for a hint). *Ibid.* 66: I...can give the fellow the usual "office" (slang for warning him), so that he can lay low. **1899** A.H. Lewis *Sandburrs* 135: Just before dey makes d' corner, d' Face gives d' office to Spot to be stampin' onct...on d' sidewalk. **1908** McGaffey *Show Girl* 203: If you need any change give me the office and I will slip it to you. **1920–21** Witwer *Leather Pushers* 171: When I give you the office I want you to knock Hamilton stiff. **1925–26** Black *You Can't Win* 177: Sanc snapped his fingers, which was the "office" to me that he was going in. **1931** Perelman & Johnstone *Monkey Business* (film): Stay that way until I give you the office. **1985** Milicevic et al. *Runaway Train* (film): Wait till I give you the office!

3. *Av.* a cockpit or bombardier's compartment.

   ***1917** in *OEDS:* I strapped our baggage, some new gramophone records, and myself into the observer's office. **1918** Roberts *Flying Fighter* 337: The Office. The pilot's cockpit. **1919** Rickenbacker *Flying Circus* 1: *Office.* The cockpit of an airplane, where the pilot sits. **1939** Hart *135th Aero Squadron* 43: *Hart* was on his hands and knees in the "office," looking through the little glass plate in the floor. **1940** Hartney *Up & At 'Em* 59: Stanley signalled me that both his guns were jammed and his head disappeared in the front cockpit, which he called his office, as he bent over to fix them. **1941–42** Kennerly & Berry *Eagles Roar* 206: I swing into the "office." **1970** Corrington *Bombardier* 204: You're locked into a kind of special world, almost like being up front in the office of a 17. **1989** Joss *Strike* 128: It's time to look around the "office."

office *v.* to notify; signal; alert.

   ***1812** in *OED:* The letter was to office Trist about laying bets on

thick. ***1819** [T. Moore] *Tom Crib* 19: To *office*...To signify by letter. ***1841** in *OEDS: Office,* giving warning. **1859** Matsell *Vocab.* 60: *Officing.* Signalizing; a preconcerted signal by a confederate. **1866** *Nat. Police Gaz.* (Apr. 21) 3: He waited until his "pals" came out of the store, and then he "officed" them over to him. **1915** Howard *God's Man* 128: Joe...offices me to pull some rough stuff. **1920** *Variety* (Dec. 31) 8: The Brooklyn guy..."officed" both upstairs and downstairs guards and they're inside. **1925–26** Black *You Can't Win* 182: Sanc "officed" me to follow him out. **1928** W.R. Burnett *Little Caesar* 56: Will you let her out when I office you? **1929** E. Booth *Stealing* 297 [ref. to *ca*1920]: Turn this heap around, and we'll office them to follow us again. **1930** Conwell *Pro. Thief* 19: The police were watching us carefully, and I could not office (warn) my partner by moving my eyes toward them. **1937** *Chicago Tribune* ("Graphic Sec.") 9: Hijackers' Argot...*Office*—to warn, tip off. **1967** [R. Beck] *Pimp* 37: He "officed" my "flash" cue.

office hours *n. Mil.* a time devoted to reprimand or evaluation of subordinates.

   1898 Parker *Gatling Gun* 23: I don't want to hear anything about it. I don't believe in it, and I don't feel like hearing it. If you want to see me about this subject, come to me in office hours. **1922** *Marine Corps Gaz.* (June) 212 [ref. to 1906]: Well, one morning after *Office Hours* the C.O. was sitting at his desk grumbling to himself and holding his head in his hands. **1933** *Leatherneck* (Apr.) 14: Again a month has passed with a clean slate. No "office hours" were held during the month of January for any "A" Company Marines. **1956** *AS* XXXI (Oct.) 193: *Office Hours,* n. A scheduled appearance before the commanding officer for punishment; usually preceded by *up for.* **1966** Noel *Naval Terms: Office Hours*...Process by which the commanding officer awards punishment, listens to requests (Request Mast) or commends men for special services (Meritorious or Commendatory Mast). **1967** Dubus *Lt.* 41: He committed an offense, he was brought in to office hours. **1971** Jeffers & Levitan *See Parris* 148: A man awaiting disposition of his case at the Brooklyn brig is first interviewed by the brig commander...during his "office hours."

officer material *n. Mil.* (see quots.). *Joc.*

   1945 in *AS* (Oct. 1946) 238: *Officer Material.* An enlisted man short in mentality. **1980** Cragg *Lex. Militaris* 317: *Officer Material.* A person who is patently *not* of the material the Army wants in its officers.

officers' country *n. Navy.* officers' quarters.

   1942–47 *ATS* (Supp.) 37: *Officers' country,* officers' quarters ashore or aboard ship. **1992** Jernigan *Tin Can Man* 37 [ref. to 1941]: "Officers' Country" consisted of the wardroom and officers' state-rooms.

off the wall *adj.* odd or eccentric; crazy; (*broadly*) obnoxious, offensive, pointless, etc. Also as adv. [The sense of the bracketed 1937 quot. is unclear; perh. it implies "only a wallflower." Current meanings are not attested before 1953.]

   [**1937** in Starks *Cocaine Fiends* 103: "Oh, Jimmy—you don't love me. I'm off the wall."... "I know Sally, but I don't mind." "In the old days, parents knew what their kids were doing evenings."] **1953** in Leadbitter & Slaven *Blues Records* 201: Off the Wall. **1959** F.L. Brown *Trumbull Pk.* 354: We all said thanks in our own off-the-wall ways. *Ibid.* 223: Not that off-the-wall holyroller kind of clapping. **1962** Tregaskis *Viet. Diary* 129: Some had dirty green uniforms, or some off-the-wall color. **1962–63** in Giallombardo *Soc. of Women* 206: *Off the Wall Jive....*anything untrue. **1964** H. Rhodes *Chosen Few* 179: He blew his cool, called me some off th' wall names. **1966** H.S. Thompson *Hell's Angels* 192: The "off-the-wall broad...rolled up to the El Adobe...in a taxicab." **1966** I. Reed *Pall-Bearers* 114: Land! Country!...Are you off the wall? **1967** Baraka *Tales* 19: I mean, talkin' some off the wall shit, too, baby. **1968** *English Jour.* (Mar.) 363: This guy Ramsay is really *off-the-wall about the age for owning a motor vehicle....*off-the-wall, means: could you picture someone bouncing himself off a wall. **1969** H. Brown *Die Nigger Die* 44: One night he said something off-the-wall to one of the brothers and I told the brother to whup his ass. **1970** A. Young *Snakes:* I felt about as off the wall as they came—half-drunk, half-scared. **1972** N.Y.U. student: *Off the wall* means crazy. Like you say, "Man, you're off the wall!" Or *off the ceiling,* which means the same thing. Or "He's off the wall with a spatula!" "Off the wall for extra bases" is even worse. **1972** Claerbaut *Black Jargon* 74: An off the wall place. **1976** Humez & Humez *Latin* 72: For all but a very few utterly off the wall irregular verbs, you form the present subjunctive in the following way. **1967–80** Folb *Runnin' Lines* 248: *Off-the-wall* 1.Irrelevant. 2.Nonsensical. 3.Inappropriate. 4.Childish. **1983** *Hour Magazine* (ABC-TV) (Apr. 20): They make a lot of remarks off the wall.…But other than that there's not much heckling. **1988** P. Beck & P. Massman *Rich Men, Single Women* 8: Paige was kind of off-the-wall, dramatic, a bit of a sex kitten. **1993** *CNN & Co.* (CNN-TV) (Mar. 9): All you need is somebody who is off the wall.

off-time *adj. Jazz.* unsatisfactory; unacceptable.

    1938 *Variety* (June 22) 36: *Off-time jive*—sorry excuse. **1946** Mezzrow & Wolfe *Really Blues* 187 [ref. to 1930's]: Dig that vine all offtime. *Ibid.* 308: *Offtime:* out of harmony, old-fashioned, corny, offensive.

O.G.[1] *n.* [*old girl*] a woman, esp. OLD LADY. *Joc.*

    1878 *Nat. Police Gaz.* (May 4) 2: The old girl.…"Ha, ha, ha! Here's to the o.g.!" **1928** *AS* III (June) 375: *O.G.*—Old girl. A woman who comes to the sale only to spend the afternoon. **1972** Claerbaut *Black Jargon* 73: *O.G.* n. Old Girl; mother: *My O.G. won't dig it.*

O.G.[2] *n.* [*original gangster*] **1.a.** *Und.* a veteran male member of a street gang, esp. one who commands much respect.

    1988 Norst *Colors* 16: He was an OG, an original gangster. **1989** *21 Jump St.* (Fox-TV): Gon' talk to the O.G.'s. **1993** K. Scott *Monster* 80 [ref. to 1980]: Sidewinder, in effect, won liberation of the set, which was then simply called Original Gangster Crips (OGC). This is where the term "O.G." originated. **1994** *N.Y. Times Mag.* (Nov. 13) 47: "I care about my O.G.'s"—original gangsters—"and they care about me." *Ibid.:* He thinks what he might accomplish if he could employ Fred and his other O.G.'s full time.

    b. Esp. *Rap Music.* a veteran (in some other specified context); original.—also used attrib.

    [**1991** *Source* (Dec.) 34: O.G. gang bangers.] **1991** in P. Munro *U.C.L.A. Slang II:* O.G.…something old and good. **1993** P. Munro *U.C.L.A. Slang II:* Sony's the O.G. of walkmans. **1993** *Source* (July) 76: A collection interesting enough to keep their O.G. fans satisfied.

    2. a close male friend.—used in direct address. Cf. G, 4.a.

    [**1994** (quot. at (1.a.), above).] **1996** *Dangerous Minds* (ABC-TV): O.G., you gonna let her dis your homegirl?

ogle *n.* Esp. *Boxing.* an eye.

    *1676 (cited in Partridge *DSUE* 580). **1698–99* "B.E." *Dict. Cant. Crew: The Gentry mort has rum Ogles,* c. that Lady has charming black Eyes. **1705* in *OED:* He rowl'd his Ogles with a Grace Becoming so a zealous Face. **1748* in *F & H* V 90: *Ogles,* in the *Cant language,* are the eyes. **1819* [T. Moore] *Tom Crib* 22: *Ogles…Eyes.* **1820–21* P. Egan *Life in London* 21: Carrotty Poll…got her *ogles* [blackened]. **1836* *Spirit of Times* (Feb. 20) 7: Now, keep your ogles on me, and see as I don't deceive you. **1842** *Spirit of Times* (Oct. 29) 416: Nor ogles clothed in black, nor bleeding snouts. **1859** Matsell *Vocab.* 127: *Ogles.* The eyes. **1866** (quot. at SOFT, *n.*). **1870** *Putnam's Mag.* (Mar.) 301: The combatants struck each other…upon…the eyes, the ogles, the optics, the peepers. **1906** A.H. Lewis *Confessions* 206: Bang! right before your ogles.

ogle *v.* to stare at, esp. with amorous interest; look at squarely or intently; watch. Now *S.E.* Cf. OOGLE.

    *1682 in Partridge *DSUE* 580: They say their Wives learn ogling in the Pit. **1688* Shadwell *Squire of Alsatia* I i: What *Ogling* there will be between thee and the *Blowings:* Old staring at thy *Equipage. Ibid.* IV i: I warrant they came to *Ogle.* **1697* Vanbrugh *Provoked Wife* 63: A crowd of young fellows ogling and glancing and watching all occasions. **a1720* in D'Urfey *Pills* I 20: She'd Oagle and Wheedle. **1745* in C.H. Wilkinson *King of Beggars* 120: Ogle him in the Muns. **1806** in R. Tyler *Verse* 154: She…ogles rakes and beaux. **1820–21* P. Egan *Life in London* 73: All the *peepers* of the *Fancy* were on the stretch to *ogle* his beau-ideal form. *Ibid.* 121: The Debauchee…*ogling* all the girls. **1848** *Ladies' Repository* VIII (Oct.) 316: *Ogle,* Watch, keep your eye on. **1848** [G. Thompson] *House Breaker* 6: "Let us…*ogle the boodle* and *reg up.*"…*"Let us*…examine the booty, and divide the spoils." **1853** "Tally Rhand" *Guttle* 14: He's oglin' the turtle!

ogler *n.* an eye.

    *1821 *Real Life in London* I 89: A little boy…kept his oglers upon 'em. **1821* in Partridge *Dict. Und.* 479: Oglers. **1883** Flagg *Versicles* 42: This 'ere one long shaggy eyebrow…and this one ogler.

oh-be-joyful *n.* whiskey; liquor. Also **oh-be-cheerful, o-be-joyful.**

    *1815 in Wetherell *Adventures* 328: Took a little taste of Obejoyful. **1823* P. Egan *Vulgar Tongue: O be joyful.* Good liquor; brandy. *Sea term.* **1830** N. Ames *Mariner's Sketches* 153: They frying pan and coffee kettle were got under way; and some "O! be joyful" was "being making"…into a hot sling. **1830** in *DA:* The old woman…poured some o be joy full down their throats. **1837** *Every Body's Album* II 139: They are sucking o-be-joyful from a cask, with a straw. **1840** *Spirit of Times* (Apr. 4) 49: Dealers in "O, be Joyful." **1845** in *DA* s.v. *Black Betts:* There I was loaded…with a plenty of what some call "Black Betts," or "O be joyful." **1847** Hartman *Own Journal* 10: Of course took a little of the "O be Cheerful." Returned…quite merry. **1853** Doten *Journals* I 165: We had plenty of the "oh be joyful." **1861** in B. Wiley *Johnny Reb* 167: I invited my companions to assist me in Emptying 3 canteens of "Oh! be Joyful." [**1862** Gilbert *Confed. Letters* 24: In New Orleans there is a whiskey shop run by "O.B. Joyful."] **1863** in A.W. Petty *3d Mo. Cav.* 31: The boys found a quantity of the "O be joyful," and…got drunk. **1863** Bensill *Yamhill* 95: Had an excellent dinner and plenty of "O, be joyful." **1864** in S. Boyer *Nav. Surgeon* I 304: An obliging chum…had the extreme kindness to give me a dose of the "Oh! be joyful," which was rather a pleasant beverage [in] this warm weather. **1865** in Woodruff *Union Soldier* 56: Dad…takes too much of the O-be-Joyful, sidewalk flies up and strikes him in the face. **1865** in *PADS* (No. 70) 44: A little too much of the *o be joyful.* **1874** *History of Mulligan Guard* 24: Widow Mahoney no longer put a price on her liquid oh-be-joyful. **1901** *Chi. Tribune* (Aug. 18) 33: Under the influence of our old acquaintance, "O.B. Joyful." **1905** W.S. Kelly *Lariats* 322: That is one of the mysterious differences between tears of joy and "Oh be joyful." **1968** Myrer *Eagle* 314: I'm a trifle low on the oh-be-joyful at present. **1968–70** in *DARE.* **1972** R. Barrett *Lovomaniacs* 352: Maybe it was a little bit of the Old [*sic*] Bejoyful talking.

oh-be-joyful *adj.* drunk.

    1839 Strong *Diary* I 100: Seemed to favor the idea that the great Dan Webster was slightly "O be joyful" when he made his war speech in the Senate.

OHIO *n. Mil.* "*Over the Hill In October,*" an exhortation to desert. Now *hist.* [Quots. ref. to 1941.]

    1941 *Daily News* (N.Y.) (Aug. 28) 2. **1945** *Yank* (Sept. 21) 3: After the draft was extended and the men started talking of O-H-I-O, they weren't referring to the state. **1946** Sevareid *Wild Dream* 202: OHIO was furtively printed on barrack walls—it meant: "Over the hill in October." **1946** Bowker *Out of Uniform* 107: One manifestation was the Ohio "Over-the-Hill-in-October" movement in Second Army units—contemplating large-scale desertions only a few weeks before the Japanese carriers sailed for Hawaii. **1948** Cozzens *Guard of Honor* 317: "Writing things up on walls that way is a kind of sounding-out—to get to know who else feels the same. You remember all that 'OHIO' stuff back in '41?" "Colonel Ross stirred and says: 'How many of them *did* go over the hill in October?'" **1969** Hicken *Amer. Fighting Man* 118: Their favorite phrase was OHIO (over the hill in October). **1971** Tuchman *Stilwell* 213: This was reflected in the OHIO movement—Over the Hill in October—which infected the one-year men. **1995** *N.Y. Review of Books* (Oct. 19) 47: How was General Marshall to keep his forces together when OHIO (Over the Hill In October) was scrawled on the walls of every camp?

-oholic *suffix.* -AHOLIC. [The main entry for this is found at -AHOLIC; the first cite below provides evidence antedating that entry.]

    1963 E.M. Miller *Exile* 105: The advertising, the songs, the movies, everything is oriented to sex. We are all—even poor Cam—sexoholics, and not very anonymous. **1978** *N.Y. Times Mag.* (June 28) 23: The -aholic suffix, from "alcoholic," [is] now used in *workaholic, chocoholic* and *bookaholic.*

O-H-ten *n.* Ohio. *Joc.*

    1946 Sawyer *Gunboats* 147 [ref. to ca1900]: The officer of the deck of the British man-of-war hailed his quartermaster asking the *Ohio's* name. "I cawn't quite make it out, sir. It looks like a ho, a haitch, and a bloody ten." **1964** H. Rhodes *Chosen Few* 16: One a' your homeboys.…Straight from O-H ten.

oh-zee var. O.Z.

-oid *suffix.* (used to create various nominal or adjectival jocular, usu. derisive, nonce forms).

    1978 C. Miller *Animal House* 51: The wimpoid was feeling indignant. **1978** Shem *House of God* 202: In the Siberianoid Provinces of upper New York State. The tundra. **1981** *Film Comment* (May) 26: *The Sleazoid Express.* a**1982** in Safire *Good Word* 152: Patients have been known to turn "gomeroid." a**1986** *NDAS:* flakoid/fusionoid/ Grouchoid/klutzoid.…technoid/zomboid. **1987** *Wkly. World News*

(Sept. 1) 36: That's why he's such a runtoid. **1989** *Time* (Nov. 20) 95: Snippets of old TV series, excerpts from stand-up performances and other laughtoids [*sic*]. **1995** *New Republic* (Oct. 9) 9: The sentimentalization of the Unabomber's acts and ideas that some Leftoids have fallen into. **1996** *N.Y Observer* (Oct. 21) 42: Attention Harvoids: Pack up the station wagon picnic and head up to Cambridge for the Head of the Charles Regatta.

oids *n.pl. Med.* corticosteroids.
    1981 in Safire *Good Word* 152: "What are you giving this lady?" "Oids."

oil *n.* **1.a.** money.
    1885 *Uncle Daniel's Story* 111: They care much less for their lives than for their "oil." **1954–60** *DAS: Oil...Money, esp. graft.*

    b. bribe money; a bribe; GREASE, 2.
    1903 A.H. Lewis *Boss* 121: The sooner we get th' oil, th' sooner we'll begin to light up. **1935** in *OED2*: She didn't take care of her protection directly, that is, she didn't slip the oil to the cops herself. **1954–60** (quot. at **(a)**, above). **1969** Pendleton *Death Squad* 118: Promotion, you know, a bit of oil to the deejays here and there. **1970** Winick & Kinsie *Lively Commerce* 214: There are only a few recent situations in which police have been apprehended taking "oil" or payoff money from a prostitute. **1970** C. Major *Dict. Afro-Amer. Sl.: Oil:* graft, pay-off to authorities.

    2. *Esp. Und.* nitroglycerin; GREASE, 6.
    1902 in "O. Henry" *Works* 978: The nitroglycerine—"the oil," as his brethren of the brace and bit term it. *a***1909** Tillotson *Detective* 93: *Oil*—Nitro-glycerine. **1926** Clark & Eubank *Lockstep* 36: Dynamite is placed in warm water and the oil (nitro) collected. Then you have soup.

    3. an alcoholic beverage, esp. whiskey.
    1917 (quot. at RUM HOUND). **1918** Ruggles *Navy Explained* 106: It is sometimes said that a man has had a little too much oil, meaning, of course, that he has had his cargo well filled with booze and is sailing two points to the wind. **1923** Ornitz *Haunch, Paunch & Jowl* 92: The barkeep comes in carrying a glass of whiskey. "A little oil for the music box." **1968** Radano *Walking the Beat* 67: You know he likes his oil. **1974** Radano *Cop Stories* 24: His clothes are dirty and he's got a load of oil in him. That's his problem—oil. **1967–80** Folb *Runnin' Lines* 248: *Oil* Liquor, wine. **1983** Whiteford *How to Talk Baseball* 52: *Oil* (liquor). **1983** *Reader's Digest Success with Words* 87: Black English...*oil* = ..."whiskey." **1996** J. Logan *Tornado* (film): Nothing a little oil won't fix.

    4. unctuous flattery; suavity; BANANA OIL.
    1917 in *OEDS*: "Why dearie!" I remarks, kissin' her; "You know I—". "Easy with the oil!" she cuts me off. **1919** Witwer *Alex the Great* 133: "I'm so glad to meet you, Mister Sells," she says, givin' Hector the old oil. **1926** Maines & Grant *Wise-Crack Dict.* 14: *Throwing the oil*—Telling glib falsehoods. **1930** Graham & Graham *Queer People* 82: That's the old oil. **1932** *AS* VII (June) 334: *Oil*—flattery; "hokum." **1937** Weidman *Wholesale* 274: Aah, stop the oil, will you? **1941** Schulberg *Sammy* 81: So Dotty goes out to save George's soul and he starts feeding her the old oil. **1942** "D. Ormsbee" *Sound of American* 32: Save the oil. **1944–48** A. Lyon *Unknown Station* 53: "Save your oil for your M-1," Ben said dryly. **1948** Maresca *My Flag* 91: His voice was mellow and sweet,...and he keeps giving me the oil. **1963** in Woods *Horse-Racing* 173: That...is the old, old oil.

    5. *Navy.* chewing tobacco; in phr. **burn oil** to chew tobacco.
    1922 Taylor *Naval Acad. Song Book* 15: Someone was skagging and some burning oil. **1928** *AS* III (Aug.) 454: *Oil*—Chewing tobacco. **1931** Ellsberg *Pigboats* 61 [ref. to 1918]: "Mebbe you'd better lay off the cigarettes fer a while though 'n stick to burnin' oil." "Burnin' oil? What's that?" asked the puzzled seaman. "Chewin' tobacco. Ye don't make no smoke, so we call it 'burnin' oil.'"

    6. trouble; HOT WATER.
    1934 Appel *Brain Guy* 83: He'll be havin' you in oil with Duffy.

    7. coffee.
    1942 *ATS* 764: *Coffee*....murk, pot of oil, scuttle of java. **1975** Greer *Slammer* 12: Better get you a hot cup of oil, huh?

    ¶ In phrases:

    ¶ **check (someone's) oil** (of a man) to copulate with (someone). *Joc.*
    1936 in P. Oliver *Blues Trad.* 189: I'm goin' h'ist your hood mama, I'm boun' to check your oil. **1961** in Oster *Country Blues* 353: Come

out here, little baby, you know I'm boun' to check yo' oil. **1970** D. Long *Nia* 16: Hey bitch can i check your oil. **1977** Sayles *Union Dues* 20: Hey Needledick, checked anybody's oil lately? **1980** Kotzwinkle *Jack* 157: I'd like to check *her*...oil. **1982** in Rucker *57th Kafka* 37: And what have you been doing down there, Simon...checking Helen's oil?

    ¶ **oil of birch** a thrashing with a birch rod. Also vars. with other woods. Cf. HICKORY OIL.
    1833 A. Greene *Duckworth* II 36: I suppose you hav 'nt any notion of using the oil of birch, have you? **1837** *Every Body's Album* II 125: The oil of hickory is his sovereign *panacea*. **1880** *United Service* (Sept.) 369: There seems to be no better way to correct them than by applying a little of the "oil of birch." **1907** *DN* III 195: That young one needs *oil of* birch the worst way. **1930** in *DARE: Oil of hazel*—A sound whipping. **1939** in *DARE* [ref. to 1860's]: She had a long birch switch in her hand...If oil of birch could do it, the baby would take his place and tend to business. **1941** in *DARE*: A little oil of walnut....A little oil of birch. **1942** *ATS* 317: Beating, thrashing...*oil of birch, -hazel, -hickory &c.*

    ¶ **strike oil** to succeed.
    1863 in Hoole *Confed. Navy* 84: Our skipper was...impatient to learn if Low had "struck ile." **1942** *ATS* 273: Succeed....*stack up points, strike oil.*

oil burner *n.* **1.** a tobacco chewer.
    1928 *AS* III (Aug.) 454: *Oil burner.* One who chews tobacco. **1942** *ATS* 395: *Oil burner,* a gum or tobacco chewer.

    2. *Narc.* a severe and expensive drug addiction.—also used attrib. Also **oil-burning habit.**
    1938 D.W. Maurer, in *AS* (Oct.) 185: *Oil-burning habit.* A ravenous appetite for drugs; probably a metaphorical variant of [synonymous] *lamp habit.* **1962** in J. Blake *Joint* 298: He'll go back to her, they'll both start using shit again, and then he'll come back to Ma to kick the oil-burner. **1963** Braly *Shake Him* 139: I'm not studying no oil-burner of a habit. **1964** Harris *Junkie Priest* 1: A forty-dollar a day heroin habit, a real oil-burner. **1962–68** B. Jackson *In the Life* 86: I had this habit, a real bad oil-burning habit. **1970** L. Johnson *Devil's Front Porch* 197 [ref. to *ca*1922]: I was older than most of these kids and was already a drug addict with an "oil-burning" habit. **1972** Grogan *Ringolevio* 50: Long enough to give the three of them oil burner habits. **1993** Rebennack & Rummel *Under Hoodoo Moon* 34: His habit was an oil-burner. *Ibid.* 87: He had an oil-burning dope habit.

    3. *Mil. Av.* a jet plane that uses kerosene-based fuel.
    1955 Archibald *Aviation Cadet* 117: He wanted to know how they were doing with the oil-burners, and said that it took real he-men to fly the heavy stuff. **1956** Heflin *USAF Dict.* 356: *Oil burner. Specif.* A jet engine or jet airplane using kerosene or other like fuel, as distinguished from an engine that uses gasoline.

    4. *R.R.* a smoking car.
    1976 Lieberman & Rhodes *CB* 133: *Oil Burner*—Smoking car.

oil-butt *n. Whaling.* a whale likely to yield much oil.
    1823 J.F. Cooper *Pilot* 142: "No sir, 'tis a right whale," answered Tom...."He's a raal oil-butt, that fellow!"

oil can *n.* **1.** a worthless person or thing.
    1920 *Amer. Leg. Wkly.* (June 11) 27: *Are You An Oil-Can?*...the Dumb-Bell Handicap....If you cannot answer the questions in a certain definite time—say forty-five minutes or a couple of days for each one—you are a certified oil can. **1922** J. Conway, in *Variety* (May 5) 12: She's a female oil can and no mistake. **1923** *N.Y. Times* (Sept. 9) VIII 2: *Oil Can:* See *all wet.* **1923** *N.Y. Times* (Oct. 7) VIII 4: *Oil Can*— A bad act or actor. **1926** Maines & Grant *Wise-Crack Dict.* 12: *Oil can*—One who cannot grease the slides to popularity. **1926** Dunning & Abbott *Broadway* 232: Hey oilcan, what is this? **1926** Lardner *Haircut* 60: Poor sis! She married a terrible oil can! **1926** MacIssac *Tin Hats* 72 [ref. to 1917]: What an oil can Boulogny turned out to be! **1926** Thomason *Red Pants* 159: The poor oil-can got it from a bootlegger in the Black Belt. **1927** *AS* II (Mar.) 277: *Oil Can.* a good-fornothing. **1927** in E. Wilson *Twenties* 354: What an oilcan *you* turned out to be! **1928** *AS* III (Feb.) 220: *Oil Can.* One who backs out, or crums the deal, or spoils the party. **1931** *AS* VII (Oct.) 22: *Oil can*— "wild" girl.

    2. a liquor bottle.
    1929 Springs *Carol Banks* 85: He...began applying the oil-can liberally.

oiled *adj.* drunk.—occ. constr. with *up.*
    1737 *Penn. Gazette*: He's Oil'd. ***1899** in *OED2*: He was certainly well "oiled." **1908** *Sat. Eve. Post* (Dec. 5) 16: Can't they ever drink

enough to get oiled happy? *1916 in Dunham *Long Carry* 15: Phillips…was "well oiled," and it did not take long for him to fall asleep. 1917 in Grider *War Birds* 38: By the time Springs got there they were well oiled. 1920 E. Hemingway, in *N.Y. Times Mag.* (Aug. 18, 1985) 61: The stools are going to try and get him oiled tonight. 1924 P. Marks *Plastic Age* 251: Cynthia had assured him that she would dance until doomsday if he kept her "well oiled with hooch." *Ibid.* 252: Some of the couples had got at least half "oiled" before the dance began. 1924 in D. Hammett *Continental Op:* You ought to stay oiled all the time. 1925 *Writer's Mo.* (June) 487: *Oiled.* Drunk. 1927 *Vanity Fair* (Aug.) 48: The "good fellow" whose mind works better when "oiled." 1928 Shay *More Pious Friends* 111: The Chief bartender is concert-meister and when the Board of Examination and Eligibility is completely and properly oiled he will give the word to the First Ivory Thumper. 1928 *AS* (Feb.) 220: *Oiled.* Intoxicated. "Dutch certainly was oiled Wednesday—Thursday too." 1931 J.T. Farrell *McGinty* 272: Pat Molloy got his whole wagon stoled when he was oiled. *1934 Yeates *Winged Victory* 334: He was a bit oiled, major. 1938 "R. Hallas" *You Play the Black* 35: I had three or four Scotch and sodas and was feeling pretty well oiled. 1940 Baldwin *Brother Orchid* (film): You sound like you're oiled. Have you been drinkin'? 1954 Overholser *Violent Land* 108: He got oiled up pretty well. 1963–64 Kesey *Great Notion* 219: Oiled to the gills again. 1970 in Thigpen *Streets* 18: My Grandmother is/so oiled she don't know shit. 1967–72 Weesner *Car Thief* 196: They were both so oiled they could barely walk straight. 1975 S.P. Smith *Amer. Boys* 209: We'll really get oiled tomorrow night. 1982 Least Heat Moon *Blue Hwys.* 210: He came in a little oiled and then got tighter than Dick's hatband.

oiler *n.* **1.** *West.* GREASER, 1.a.—used contemptuously.
   1907 S.E. White *Arizona* 49: A few oilers livin' near had water holes in the foothills. 1935 *Bedroom Companion* 129: If he doesn't find/The oiler hugging the gal! 1954–60 *DAS: Oiler*…A Mexican; a greaser.
   2. a heavy drinker.
   *1916 (cited in Partridge *DSUE* (ed. 8)). *a*1994 N. McCall *Wanna Holler* 83: Heavy drinkers.…The fellas and I called them "oilers."

oil king *n. Naut.* a petty officer responsible for fuel levels, records, etc. [Quots. chiefly ref. to WWII.]
   1947 *ATS* (Supp.) 35: *Oil king*, the man detailed to check oil aboard ship. 1949 Morison *Naval Ops. in WWII* V 132. 1958 Cope & Dyer *Petty Officer's Guide* (ed. 2) 360: *Oil King.* Petty officer who keeps fuel records. 1961 L.E. Young *Virgin Fleet* 123: The Oil King and his Petty Officers checked the fuel tanks' dip sticks. 1969 Searls *Hero Ship* 122: The oil king on the cruiser *Biloxi* was a Martian. 1981 Ballenger *Terror* 100: Kramer…had been oil king on the *Indianapolis.* 1992 Jernigan *Tin Can Man* 36: At sea, the fuel oil king had to keep pumping oil from one compartment to another as we used it to keep the ship's trim right.…The fuel oil king was also in charge of refueling at sea.

oil merchant *n.* a flatterer; (*also*) a swindler.
   1935 (cited in Partridge *Dict. Und.* 479). 1942–49 Goldin et al. *DAUL* 148: *Oil merchant*…A confidence man; a clever swindler. 1959 Morrill *Dark Sea Running* 104: You're quite an oil merchant, kiddo.

oil of disturbance *n.* liquor.
   1897 Ade *Pink Marsh* 124: 'At's what made me dange'ous—wuz 'at oil o' distuhb'ance.

oil of joy *n.* liquor.
   1919 *DN* V 57: *Oil of joy.* Strong drink. Not quite as happy (in jail) as when packing a full cargo of *oil of joy.* 1931 (cited in Partridge *Dict. Und.* 480).

oil patch *n. Petroleum Industry.* the petroleum industry or a petroleum-producing area.
   1980 *Texas Monthly* (Oct.) 134: They say in the oil patch that wildcatters have a sixth sense about where to find oil and gas. 1981 *Business Week* (Feb. 16) 61: Texas Instruments Inc. made a brilliant leap from the oil patch into the semiconductor business. 1985 *N.Y. Times* (Aug. 12) A16: What's bad for the oil patch is not necessarily bad for America. 1986 *Time* (Mar. 24) 58: The U.S. has its own depressed oil patch.…Texas, Oklahoma and Louisiana have been plagued by bankruptcies and layoffs. 1987 *Prime News* (CNN-TV) (Mar. 2): Hard times in the oil patch. 1988 *CBS This Morning* (CBS-TV) (June 22): It's not just in the oil patch; as you've suggested it's also in California. 1991 *CBS Morning News* (CBS-TV) (July 18): Help is desperately

needed in the Soviet oil patch. 1992 J. Garry *This Ol' Drought* 137: I…had gotten a job surveying sites in the oilpatch.

oilskin jacket *n. Naut.* (see quot.).
   1973 H. Beck *Folklore & Sea* 83: Small puffy clouds, called "oilskin jackets," portend rain.

oil up *v.* **1.** to take a drink of liquor; get drunk.
   1870 *Overland Mo.* (Jan.) 86: "I guess I'll ile up a little…" said he, as he filled himself another glass. 1886 Harbaugh *Coldgrip in N.Y.* 14: I'll have to oil up to get the kinks out of me. I'll drop into Simon Peter's place and…do so. 1902 Cullen *More Tales* 44: We cut a quart into equal parts and oiled up on that. 1921 Floyd *Co. F* 86 [ref. to 1918]: Everybody proceeded to oil up. 1932 Hecht & Fowler *Great Magoo* 141: Time for oiling up.
   2. to bribe; GREASE, 1.a.
   1894 Bangs *In Politics* 12: I tell you the thing can't be done without oiling up the machine.

oink *n.* a police officer; PIG.—used contemptuously.
   1970 C. Major *Dict. Afro-Amer. Slang: Oink:*…a cop; policeman; law-enforcement officer. 1972 Grogan *Ringolevio* 447: When you goin' blow one o' them oinks away? 1975 *DAS* (ed. 3): *Oink*…A law-enforcement office; policeman. *Not common.* 1979 Alibrandi *Custody* 102: Let go of me, oink. 1980 D. Hamill *Stomping Ground* 183: You and the rest of your oink friends. 1980 *AS* (Fall) 197: Cop, copper,…hog…oink…pig.

oinker *n.* **1.** an ugly young woman; PIG.
   1981 *Nat. Lampoon* (Nov.) 18: If that doesn't send her diving for the compact mirror, you're hooked up with an oinker! 1987 *Wkly. World News* (May 26) 45: I'm sure they wouldn't give that oinker a second look.
   2. a policeman; PIG.—used contemptuously.
   1982 in S. King *Bachman* 791: I hate them…oinkers. 1991 *Get a Life* (Fox-TV): Listen up, oinkers! Here are my demands!
   3. a pig.
   1988 Cogan & Ferguson *Presidio* 96: An oinker rooting…in…slops.
   4. a glutton.
   1992 D. Burke *Street Talk* I 133: *Oinker*…one who eats like a pig.

oink out *v.* to be a glutton; overeat.
   1988 *Right On!* (June) 60: Speaking of oinking out,…they served bagels for breakfast. 1990 *Newsweek Special Issue: New Teens* 60: His weight shot up—"I oinked out," he says.

OJ *n.* **1.** orange juice. Now *colloq.*
   1942 *ATS* 765: *Fruit juice*….O.J., sunkissed, orange juice. 1945 *Calif. Folk. Qly.* IV 55: *O.J.:* Orange juice. 1954–60 *DAS: O.j.*…A glass of orange juice. 1975 *Black World* (June) 67: Another drink of…port and o.j. 1978 *Penthouse* (Apr.) 124: Fill a brandy snifter with a triple rum and a squirt of OJ. 1978 B. Johnson *What's Happenin'* 109: I've been drinking OJ and 7-Up since high school, great for hangovers. 1983 Harris & Weingrod *Trading Places* (film): We want you to buy as much OJ as you can. 1992 N. Cohn *Heart of World* 224: She wolfed down her OJ.
   2. [opium J(OINT)] *Narc.* a marijuana cigarette laced with opium.
   1970 *Look* (June 16) 72: They [*sc.* U.S. soldiers in Vietnam] would begin with marijuana, or "J"s, as the joints were nicknamed. They would move on to "OJ's," for "opium joints"—before smoking a marijuana joint they would dip it in liquid opium. 1971 *Seattle Times* (May 23) D5: Everybody conked out on O.J.s (opium joints). 1971 *N.Y. Times Mag.* (Dec. 5) 37: He lit up, took a deep puff and passed the O.J. (opium joint) around. 1972 Smith & Gay *Don't Try It* 67: Smoking a marijuana joint dipped in opium has created…the OJ or "opium joint." 1980 Novak *High Culture* 169: They would indulge in "o-jays," marijuana cigarettes treated with opium. 1982 Del Vecchio *13th Valley* 28: The O-Js were…marijuana cigarettes soaked in an opium solution. 1983 S. Wright *Meditations* 317: He sucked steadily on the OJ.

O.K. *n.* an indication of approval. Now *colloq.* or *S.E.* In 20th C. also **okeh** (*obs.*), **okay**.
   1841 in *AS* XXXIX (1964) 84: Fortitude…infuses new life into his soul, while Hope adds an O.K. to his condition. 1896 in *OEDS:* The deputy marshall…would send word to the prosecuting attorney asking for an "O.K." 1909 H.L. Mencken, in Riggio *Dreiser-Mencken Letters* I 40: If this program wins your O.K./we shall proceed. *a*1904–11 D.G. Phillips *Susan Lenox* II 29: I feel as if we had it with his O.K. on it.

1925 G. Ade, in *OEDS:* He was putting his okeh on this material. **1928** J. O'Connor *B'way Racketeers* 156: A doorman would question his right to enter until given the O.K. by the steerer. **1961** Scarne *Comp. Guide to Gambling* 686: Okay Protection furnished by politicians and police enabling illegal gambling schemes to operate. "We got the okay."

O.K. *adj.* [for *oll korrect*, facetious alt. of *all correct*] **1.a.** in order; quite satisfactory or acceptable; very good; all right; (occ. with heightened force) splendid. Now *colloq.* or *S.E.* Also as adv. In 20th C. also **okeh** (*obs.*), **okay**.

[Allen Walker Read, "The First Stage in the History of 'O.K.'" *AS* XXXVIII (1963), p. 27: "In a frolicsome group called the Anti-Bell-Ringing Society in Boston in the spring of 1839, *O.K.* became current as standing for 'oll korrect,' in a slang application...and from there it became widespread over the country." Read adduces abundant documentation for this conclusion in the form of the earliest known citations as well as the extensive sociolinguistic context that brought the term into being. The casual occurrence of the term in the first 1850 quot. below, unreliably implying recognized usage in 1837, is by itself insufficient to refute Read's findings.

Early in 1840, Democratic party supporters of the presidential candidacy of Martin Van Buren began publicly to reinterpret the initials as abbreviating the name of his birthplace at Old Kinderhook, N.Y., but the earlier quots. discovered by Read and Woodford Heflin prove that this usage represented a transmutation of the expression and not its origin; nevertheless, the association of the initials with Van Buren in 1840 clearly played a role in popularizing *O.K.* nationwide.

Without concrete evidence of a prior and established English borrowing from Choctaw-Chickasaw *okah*, *okeh* 'it is indeed', 'amen'; from Liberian Djabo *O-ke* 'yes, of course!'; from Mandingo *O ke*, 'certainly', 'do it'; etc., such derivational claims must remain gratuitous, as is the notion that *O.K.* resulted from an American misanalysis of Scots *Och, aye!* or corresponding Ulster Scots *Ough, aye!* 'oh, yes (indeed)!' Still less plausible origins have been proffered, generally in letters-to-the-editor columns.

For references to further research articles, which together afford an indispensible case history of the turns and pitfalls awaiting etymologizers of nonstandard terms, see p. xxxi and footnotes 37 and 38 of Vol. I of the present work.]

1839 *Morning Post* (Boston) (Mar. 23) 2, in *AS* XXXVIII (1963) 12: He of the Journal...would have the "contribution box," et ceteras, *o.k.*—all correct—and cause the corks to fly, like *sparks*, upward. **1839** *Evening Transcript* (Boston) (Oct. 11) 2, in *AS* XXXVIII (1963) 13: The suspension of the U.S. Bank and its dependencies...is o.k. (*all correct*) in this quarter. **1839** *Phila. Gazette* (Nov. 12) 2, in *AS* XXXVI (1962) 246: "Yes—that's good—O.K...." ...O.K., all correct. **1840** in *AS* XXXVII (1962) 246: We hope this will satisfy him, and that he will give us an acknowledgment that it is o. k. (all correct). **1840** in *DA:* The band rode in a stage, which had a barrel of hard cider on the baggage rack, marked with large letters "O.K."—oll korrect. **1840** in *DAE:* Old Tip is O.K. in Pennsylvania. **1841** *Spirit of Times* (Feb. 13) 595: The banking-house is most conveniently situated opposite the rooms—of course it's O.K. **1847** Robb *Squatter Life* 72: His express reported himself after his night ride, assured Allen that all was O.K., and received his dollar for delivering the message. **1848** Judson *Mysteries* 39: 'Tis one of us, it's OK. **1848** *Life in Rochester* 68: "This is good brandy."..."O.K." **1848** G.G. Foster *N.Y. in Slices* 11: If you can touch your hat to fifty people in Broadway, your character is "O.K."—you are an established man. **1848** "Corporal of the Guard" *Private* 37: If they were "friends," and all things "O.K.", they would most certainly have been happy and willing to vindicate Col. Burnett's character. *a***1849** in C. Hill *Scenes* 193: Rather reserved and suspicious when appearances are not marked *O.K.* **1850** J. Greene *Tombs* 144 [ref. to 1837]: "Oh, all is O.K.," replied the sucker Captain. **1850** in Cleveland *Letters* 3: I get along very well as everything else was O.K. **1855**

in Barnum *Letters* 85: Yours is recd. O.K. **1863** in H. Nathan *D. Emmett* 398: High Daddy won't come nigh....'Tis all "OK,"...and right upon the goose. **1864** Berkeley *Confed. Arty.* 67: I told him it was "O.K." **1864** Armstrong *Generals* 218: Tom played it just as well there, and yesterday his discharge came down, all O.K. **1873** in *DAE:* So we had an O.K. time till we went to bed. ***1873** Hotten *Slang Dict.* (ed. 4): *O.K.*, a matter to be *o.k.* (OLL KORRECT, *i.e.* all correct) must be on the "square," and perfectly in order. This is an Americanism. **1876** in W.A. Graham *Custer Myth* 178: I...had him see that the aparejos were "O.K." ropes, bridles, &c., all right. **1879** in Sweet *Sweet's Texas* 34: The face of the father of his country is all O.K., having evidently been taken from a three-cent postage stamp. **1879** in S. Dennison *Scandalize My Name* 284: For skillful Revolutions,/...De Skids are all O.K. **1886** *Lantern* (N.O.) (Sept. 29) 3: Favetto umpired the game all O.K. **1888** Gunter *Mr. Potter* 262: "Yes, these are O.K.!" returns the Texan, pocketing the documents. **1891** in F. Harris *Conklin* 21: 'Twar a high old fight!...Oh, 'twas O.K., you bet! **1895** *Harper's* (Nov.) 964: Then where's your wrench? Screw up your bar,...elevate your saddle, and you're O.K. **1896** in J.M. Carroll *Benteen-Goldin Letters* 300: Now I really am only guessing...but...[I bet] I'm O.K. **1904** in "O. Henry" *Works* 633: Your proposition is O.K. You're a good fellow, Goodwin. **1909** T. Dreiser, in Riggio *Dreiser-Mencken Letters* I 35: The Artist is ok. It is very clever. **1915** in Charters & Kunstadt *Jazz* 55: Lots of bows, an encore, more bows and another encore stamped this offering O.K. **1918** Mencken *Amer. Lang.* 161: Dr. [Woodrow] Wilson is said to support this [Choctaw] theory [of the origin of *O.K.*] and to use *okeh* in endorsing government papers. **1938** Smitter *Detroit* 81: Six dollars o-keh? **1943** Holmes & Scott *Mr. Lucky* (film): "Need any dough?" "Naa, I'm O.K." **1952** *N.Y. Times* (Feb. 17) II 3: It's an okay play—okay for children—but not for us. **1964** *AS* XXXIX 16: *Okeh*...was the name given to a new style of Arrow collars, advertised in New York streetcars in January, 1919, and the Okeh phonograph records were very popular in the 1920s. **1979** *St. Louis Post-Dispatch* (Oct. 14) 3G: After an OK season at .531,...the St. Louis Cardinals have managed to pull 14 games ahead of the Chicago Cubs. **1990** Stuck *Adolescent Worlds* 41: Both...found school to be basically "OK" (i.e., neither particularly outstanding nor particularly bothersome). **1994** *Bold & Beautiful* (CBS-TV): Sure this place is O.K.?

b. well; safe; unharmed; undamaged.

1839 *Morning Post* (Boston) (Mar. 26) 2, in *AS* XXXVIII (1963) 13: Had the pleasure of taking these "interesting strangers" by the hand, and wishing them a speedy passage to the Commercial Emporium, They were o.k. **1840** in *DAE:* The Locos having gone into Masonic Hall O.K., and come out K.O (Kicked out). **1840** Strong *Diary* I 137: But we'll be O.K. by and by. *Ibid.* 155: Went to Erben's...and found Goliath O.K. **1840** Strong, in *AS* XXXIX (1964) 83: Feel reasonably O.K. to day, the [smallpox] eruption is beginning to disappear. **1848** "N. Buntline" *Mysteries of N.Y.* 39: He said: " 'Tis one of us, it's O K," and proceeded to unbolt the door. **1856** in *DA:* Here is your dog; all O.K., only a little out of breath. **1861** in Heartsill *1491 Days* 5: Well after a roll down and a scramble up, I am all OK again. *Ibid.* 27: I am sick this morning. Late in the day I am all "O.K." **1862** in Byrne & Soman *Marcus* 58: If I could only now see you and the children...I would feel O.K. **1862** in Mohr *Cormany Diaries* 211: James W.A. and I settled O.K. *Ibid.* 236: We moved him to the Hospital—Were he not so awfully homesick he'd soon be O.K. **1863** in Heartsill *1491 Days* 159: At 12 o'clk Alvin comes in all "O.K." **1863** S. Boyer *Nav. Surgeon* I 99: Mr. Henderson sent up a rocket in the vicinity of Wolf Island so as to inform us that all was O.K. *Ibid.* 150: Keep him on the list until his ankle is O.K. **1863** in R.G. Carter *4 Bros.* 266: Let him get his "bureau" and other numerous straps, etc., off, lie down a little while, or pitch a poncho, if he has time, and he is "O.K." **1864** in D. Chisholm *Civil War Notebook* 7: I have a good fire in my tent and feel O.K. **1864** in W. Wilkinson *Mother* 300: I hasten to inform you that I am *still* O.K. **1864** in *Ala. Review* X (1957) 217: I have been in a few skirmishes...and so far have come out O.K. as the boys say. **1865** in O.J. Hopkins *Under the Flag* 267: I reached here O.K. this evening. **1869** Logan *Foot Lights* 178: He replied that he felt O.K. **1884** in Lummis *Letters* 107: "The folks" got through to Los Angeles O.K. **1887** [C. Mackenzie] *Jack Pots* 88: Have two men frozen, and six others out. Cattle all O.K. **1891** Kirkland *Co. K.* 103: I guess Clint will come out all O.K. **1896** J.M. Jones *Hearts of Gold* 197: "How is my fair cousin?" "All O.K. **1940** in A. Lomax *Mr. Jelly Roll* 253: Then I know you will be okeh. **1943** O. Garrett & S. Lauren *Flight for Freedom* (film): We don't *know* she ain't OK. **1954** Coen & O'Callaghan *This

Island Earth (film): "Are you OK?" "OK." **1965–70** T. Morrison *Bluest Eye* 26: Looka here, buddy. It was O.K. when I put it on the truck. **1973** D. Morrow *Maurie* 15: You okay?...You sure? **1975** in Applegate & O'Donnell *Talking on Paper* 295: Is everyone OK?

c. (esp. of persons) of good or estimable character; decent; "regular." [Allen Walker Read, "The Second Stage in the History of 'O.K.'" *AS* XXXVIII (1963), pp. 89–92, observes that the politically partisan 1840 quot. below, attempting to link *O.K.* with a supposedly illiterate President Jackson, has no discoverable basis in either probability or fact. Another ex. of *O.K.*, ascribed to Jackson and purportedly written on a court document in 1790, has been shown by Woodford Heflin to be an obvious misreading of the legal abbr. *O.R.* for "Ordered Recorded"; see Heflin's "'O.K.'—But What Do We Know About It?" *AS* XVI (1941), pp. 89–95.]

1839 *Morning Post* (Boston) (Apr. 10) 2, in *AS* XXXVIII (1963) 13: It is hardly necessary to say to those who know Mr. Hughes, that his establishment will be found to be "A. No. One"—that is, O.K.—all correct. [**1840** in *AS* XXXVIII (1963) 89: A few years ago, some person accused Amos Kendall to General Jackson of being no better than he should be. "Let me examine the papers," said the old hero....The General did so and found everything right. "Tie up them papers," said the General...."Mark on them, O.K.," continued the General. O.K. was marked upon them. "By the eternal," said the good old General..., "Amos is *Ole Kurrek* (all correct) and no mistake."] **1871** Banka *Prison Life* 61: I say, boys, let up on that feller. I had a chat with him to-day, and he's all O.K. **1878** Flipper *Cadet* 281: He is O.K. towards me, and the others are afraid of him. **1885** S.S. Hall *Gold Buttons* 2: I...set you down in my mental memorandum as O.K. **1938** *New Directions* 12: You're, you're an O.K. guy. *a*1956 Almirall *College to Cow Country* 144: That kid's O.K., and so is his family. **1967** Hinton *Outsiders* 11: You're an okay kid, Pony. **1972** in Trudeau *Chronicles* (unp.): Unlike other Commies, he happens to be an O.K. guy.

2. very fashionable or stylish; socially correct.

*1869 in *OEDS:* The Stilton, sir, the cheese, the O.K. thing to do, On Sunday afternoon, is to toddle in the Zoo. *ca*1869 in L. Levy *Grace Notes* 79: "The Roman Fall"...The Roman Fall's O.K. to do/ For me a dashing beau. **1870** *Comic Songster* 34: The *O.K.* thing for you and I is walking in the Park. *ca*1890 in Spaeth *Read 'Em* 49: The O.K. thing on Saturday is walking down Broadway. *1899 Whiteing *John St.* 218: She objected to the parting of the ass's mane as "too O.K. for a moke."

3. comfortable; not upset.—constr. with *with* or *about*.

[**1969** T. Harris *I'm OK, You're OK* [book title].] **1991** *Blossom* (NBC-TV): Are you O.K. with that? **1993** *Donahue* (NBC-TV): Is she O.K. with your haircut? **1994** *Bold & Beautiful* (CBS-TV): If you did, was she O.K. about it? **1994** *Sally Jessy Raphaël* (synd. TV series): When you're O.K. with yourself you're not gonna have this neurotic need for attention.

O.K. *v.* to grant approval to. Now *S.E.* In 20th C. also **okeh** (*obs.*), **okay.**

1888 in *AS* XXXIX (1964) 94: The expression, "Please O.K. and hurry return of my account," is grammatically correct. The noun account is governed by the preposition of, and is also the object of the active transitive verb O.K. **1891** Maitland *Slang Dict.* 193: To "O.K." an account, is to initial it in evidence of its correctness, and as the two letters are easily written, the practice has become common in business circles. **1892** in F. Remington *Sel. Letters* 135: So just O.K. this letter. **1893** Frye *Field & Staff* 57: O.K. that last message, Millar, and add, "*Explain.*" **1896** Ade *Artie* 65: I didn't think you'd O.K. the scheme. **1896** Lillard *Poker Stories* 22: The...order was...OK'd by Colonel Hill. **1899** in J. London *Letters* 58: Same Ms. had been O.K.'d. **1914** S. Lewis *Mr. Wrenn* 154: That same afternoon the manager enthusiastically O.K.'d the plan. **1919** Truman *Dear Bess* 293: It's my opinion that we'll stay there until Woodie gets his pet peace plans refused or okayed. **1919** Witwer *Alex the Great* 58: Get your bill and I'll O.K. it. **1923** Sennett *Extra Girl* (film): Well, your father has O.K.'d our marriage. **1930** *AS* VI 119: Parachute company stock okehed. **1934** Smith & Cohn *Harold Teen* (film): Would you mind okaying this?

O.K. *interj.* all right; very well; go ahead! etc.; (*hence*, interrogatively) is that all right?; do you agree?; (after a request)

will you, please?; won't you? Now *colloq.* or *S.E.* In 20th C. also **okeh** (*obs.*), **okay.** See also KAY, *interj.*

1839 *Evening Tattler* (N.Y.C.) (July 27) 2, in *AS* XXXVIII (1963) 15: These "wise men from the East"...are right...to play at bowls with us as long as we are willing to set ourselves up, like skittles, to be knocked down for their amusement and emolument. OK ! all correct! **1845** Mowatt *Fashion* III. i: Ex-actly—very obliging of her—so I will....*O.K.*, all correct. **1846** in *DAE:* That's it. O.K. Now I have got you. Go ahead. **1859** Matsell *Vocab.* 60: *O.K.* All right; "Oll kerect." **1863** in Harwell *Confed. Reader* 84: "Now, let me test the line to Nashville and Louisville."..."O.K.," said Ellsworth; "what is your earliest office hour?" **1874** Pinkerton *Expressman* 237: The way-bill checked off all right; Chase said "O.K.," so I locked the pouch. **1891** in F. Harris *Conklin* 9: You ain't afraid? O.K. then. **1929** McEvoy *Hollywood Girl* 147: Okay, big boy. **1929** in E. Wilson *Twenties* 514: *Slang*...O.K. (K.O.)—All right? **1932** L. Berg *Prison Doctor* 224: This is an age of speed, ain't it? O.K. We travel. **1932–33** Nicholson & Robinson *Sailor, Beware!* 136: O.K., Mattie...I'll take all you got. *Ibid.* 142: That's eighty bucks altogether...O.K.? **1933** D.O. Stewart *Going Hollywood* (film): O.K., then it's all set. **1936** Steel *College* 39: OK. Where'll we find a phone that won't be likely to be tapped? **1937** Weidman *Wholesale* 49: "Remember....Okay?" "Okay." **1938** in Kober *That Man* 129: "O.K., go ahead," I says to them. **1943** *New Yorker* (Apr. 17) 20: So I figger O.K., I'm gonna stand around and boss a lotta privates. **1944** F. Butler & F. Cavett *Going My Way* (film): Will you go down there? Okay? **1949** *N.Y. Times* (Apr. 24) I 41: Okay, girls, start dancing. **1951–52** (quot. at GONG, *v.*). *a*1956 Almirall *College to Cow Country* 206: O.K. I didn't recognize Adolph. **1965** Carmichael & Longstreet *Sometimes I Wonder* 39: Hokay—you gotta the job. **1976–85** Zinsser *On Writing Well* (ed. 3) 42 [ref. to mid-1960's]: One of our [usage] panelists, Katherine Anne Porter [1890–1980], called "O.K." a "detestable vulgarity" and claimed that she had never spoken the word in her life. **1994** in C. Long *Love Awaits* 20: I had to say, OK, [it was] fiction. **1995** *National Review* (Feb. 6) 20: In my day lusty agnostics would on the least invitation happily engage in trench warfare against Christianity. Okay. But it is worse now. **1996** *As World Turns* (CBS-TV): Just get lost, okay? **1996** in *Reader's Digest* (Jan. 1997) 84: "Okay," she conceded. "Just one puff."

oke /ouk/ *adj.* O.K. Also as *interj.*

1929 Hammett *Dain Curse* 168: Everything will probably be oke. **1931** *AS* VI 205: *Oke:* all right, abbreviation for the abbreviation O.K. **1932–33** P. Cain *Fast One* 4: Everything was oke for a couple of weeks. *Ibid.* 229: Kells...said, "Oke," sat down. **1933** Hammett *Thin Man* 224: Oke. There's plenty of time. **1933** Ersine *Pris. Slang* 55: Joe says that the layout is oke. *1933 in *AS* XXXIX (1964) 95: Everything is O.K., or "Oke," as they say in England. **1935** in *AS* XXXIX (1964) 95: A child replied "oke" to something I said. After a shudder of dismay, I reflected that this telescoped version of "O.K."...will ultimately appear in the textbooks as a legitimate word. **1936** Dos Passos *Big Money* 334: Everythin's goin' to be oke, Margo. **1949** *Sat. Eve. Post* (June 4) 68: Macey's house. Oke. **1951** Elgart *Over Sexteen* 102: "Oke, I'll take you up on that," agreed the friend. **1958** T. Berger *Crazy in Berlin* 109: I know you're oke, but you'll do okay by us if you crap out easy.

okey-doke *n.* Esp. *Black E.* **1.** a swindle; trick or deception.

1967 [R. Beck] *Pimp* 43: I went for the "okey-doke." I took a bootlegging rap for a pal. **1970** C. Major *Dict. Afro-Amer. Sl.* 87: *Okeydoke*...a "con game." **1972** Grogan *Ringolevio* 2: They just bit for the old USA oakey-doke and remained oblivious to the realities of what life is actually about. **1973** E. Knight *Belly Song* 22: White/america will whip out her boss okie doke. **1974** Gober *Black Cop* 34: Now, if you're trying to find somebody to take the pressure off your own ass, you'd best better look elsewhere, you dig. I ain't going for the okeydoke. **1974** Angelou *Gather Together* 49: Johnnie Mae wasn't bright, but she'd always be too clever to just go for the okey-doke. **1975** R. Hill *O.J. Simpson* 13: I put the "okey-doke" on them, bounce around them, and look for daylight. *a*1994 N. McCall *Wanna Holler* 272: Got hip and figured out ways to pull the okeydoke.

2. foolishness; pretense.

1969 Whittemore *Cop!* 157: "What's happening man?" "Same ol' okeydoke." **1970** C. Major *Dict. Afro-Amer. Sl.* 87: *Okey-doke*...stupid talk. **1976** Braly *False Starts* 230: This time, I told myself, I wasn't going for the okie-doke. **1982** in G. Tate *Flyboy* 21: I took the brouhaha for okey-doke. **1989** *Village Voice* (N.Y.C.) (May 9) 29: I...had seen the "okie-doke" and that shit didn't work anymore.

okey-doke *adj.* **1.** OKEY-DOKEY.

> **1963–64** Kesey *Great Notion* 39: But it's okeedoke.

2. [fr. OKEY-DOKE, *n.*] absurd; ridiculous.

> **1988** S. Lee *School Daze* (film): These okey-doke Negroes.

okey-doke *v.* [fr. OKEY-DOKE, *n.*, 1] to swindle; deceive.

> **1996** Alson *Ivy League Bookie* 133: Bob wasn't especially sympathetic when I told him about the unreturned phone calls. "You got okey-doked. The guy okeydoked you."

okey-doke *interj.* OKEY-DOKEY.

> **1934** Faulkner *Pylon* 36: "Okey doke," Jiggs said. **1935** *N.Y. Times* (Feb. 7) 5. **1935** Sherwood *Idiot's Delight* 118: Okey-doke. Give us a fanfare, professor. **1935** L. Hughes *Little Ham* 59 [ref. to *ca*1927]: Okeydoke! Sweetheart, I'll see you tonight. **1938** Riskind *Room Service* (film): Okey-doke. I'll be right over. **1938** O'Hara *Hope of Heaven* 47: If I get it, okey-doke. **1938** in *DAS*: The modern "O.K." with its babyfied "okey-doke." **1939** Willoughby *Sondra* 199: Okey-doke then. Let's get going. **1941** J.M. Cain *Mildred Pierce* 156: He said gee that was swell of her, and if she really meant it, it was okey-doke by him. **1950** *Sat. Eve. Post* (Sept. 23) 83: Okey-doke....But if I was you two, I don't know as I'd tell everybody. **1955** O'Connor *Last Hurrah* 120: Okey-doke, Sambo. **1961** *Newsweek* (July 31) 19: "Okey doke," replied Grissom. **1967** Mailer *Vietnam* 37: Okey-doke, Henry. **1970** Harington *Lightning Bug* 12: "Okey-doke," says Earl Coe. **1973** P. Benchley *Jaws* 142: "Okeydoke," said Brody. **1987** *21 Jump St.* (Fox-TV): "Yeah. Okey-dokey." "Okey-doke." **1996** *Simpsons Comics* (No. 20) (unp.): Okey-doke! It was gettin' kinda dull anyway.

okey-dokey *adj.* **1.** (see 1942 quot.).

> **1942** *ATS* 286: Satisfactory, correct, good....*okey-dokey, okie-dokie.* **1987** *Wkly. World News* (Feb. 3) 13: Things are not okeydokey with Dale Robertson.

2. OKEY-DOKE, *adj.*, 2.

> **1993** *Source* (July) 11: How many okeydokey brothers you see every day frontin' they hip-hop?

okey-dokey *interj.* O.K. In recent use also (*joc.*) **okle-dokle; okely-dokely; okey-dokey, artichokey.** [The joc. *okely-dokely* has been widely popularized through association with the cartoon character Ned Flanders on the Fox-TV program *The Simpsons*.]

> **1932** *AS* VII 334: *Okey-dokey*—O.K. **1935** Odets *Paradise Lost* 226: Okey-dokey. **1936** in *Esquire* (Jan. 1937) 74: Hokie dokie, Paulie. **1940** Hartman & Butler *Rd. to Singapore* (film): Okey-dokey. One for Monday. **1943** *Yank* (June 18) 9: Okey-dokey, 10 *piasters*. **1955** Nabokov *Lolita* 248: "Okey-dokey," big Frank sang out. **1954–60** *DAS*: Okle-dokle = O.K. *Fairly common jocular use.* **1964** A.W. Read, in *AS* XXXIX 96: Solid citizens abominated the form *okie-dokie*....Another stretch form was *okle-dokle*, memorialized in a popular song of 1947...: Ok'l Baby Dok'l I kilekel [*sic*] baby you [etc.]. **1974** Angelou *Gather Together* 37: Okee dokee. See you then. **1983** Breathed *Bloom Co.* 76: Right! Check! Okey-dokey! **1990** *Simpsons* (Fox-TV): Okely-dokely, neighbor! **1992** L. Johnson *My Posse* 18: Okie dokie, artichokie. **1995** in *Esquire* (Jan. 1996) 50: According to *The Washington Post*, Hillary Clinton often ends conversations with staff members by saying, "Okey-dokey, artichokey." **1995** Coen & Coen *Fargo* (film): Okey-dokey. Thanks a bunch. **1996** TV ad for AT&T (July 9): Okey-dokey. I'll tell her.

Oki var. OKIE, 3.

Okie *n.* **1.a.** a native or resident of Oklahoma; (*specif.*, now *hist.*) an Oklahoman made homeless during the Great Depression and seeking employment, esp. in California; (*broadly*, now *hist.*) any Southwestern migrant worker during the Great Depression.—often used contemptuously. [The 1983 quot. is fig.]

> **1918** P. Crowe *Pat Crowe, Aviator* 132: That is why, no doubt, they call him "Oklahoma," or "Oakey" for short. **1938** *Forum* (Jan. 12), in *DARE*: About a fifth of them [*sc.*, migrant workers in California] are Okies. **1938** Steinbeck *Grapes of Wrath* 225: Well, Okie use' ta mean you was from Oklahoma. Now it means you're a dirty son-of-a-bitch. **1941** Lomax & Lomax *Our Singing Country* xii: Woody Guthrie, proud of being an Okie. **1947** in Kerouac *Letters* 311: Not that there's anything wrong with Okies. **1949** *AS* XIV 26: In a little while *Okie* began to be used to designate any bankrupt and mendicant farmer. **1949** Bradbury *Illus. Man* 154: What have I got here?...A planet full

of Okies? **1950** *Sat. Eve. Post* (June 24) 32: It's like I'm an Okie—a guy from Oklahoma. **1950** *N.Y. Times* (Sept. 3) I 28: 50,000 migrant workers—most of them Negroes—are gathering in the crops. These are the "Okies" of the East, itinerant, rootless and frequently hopeless. **1953** A. Kahn *Brownstone* 62: Cynthia would have her hands full with her "Okie" in-laws. **1958** McCulloch *Woods Wds.* 125: *Oakie*—A native of Oklahoma or nearby regions. **1968** Merle Haggard *Okie from Muskogee* (country song): I'm proud to be an Okie from Muskogee. **1965–70** in *DARE*: *Nicknames for a rustic or countrified person*...Okie. *a*1982 Medved *Hospital* 23: This rawboned Jewish Okie. **1983** *U.S. News & W.R.* (Jan. 17) 23: Today's "Okies" are abandoning economically downtrodden hometowns in the North to chase dreams of a fresh start, mainly in the sun belt. **1988** Terkel *Great Divide* 32: All of a sudden us dumb Okies were not dumb Okies any more. **1996** McCumber *Playing Off Rail* 348: Irish by heritage, Okie by birth.

b. *Army in Germany.* a slave laborer of the Nazis. Now *hist.*

> **1945** *AS* (Apr.) 151: *Oakies.* The name applied by American soldiers to the Russian, French, Italian, Polish and even Mongolian men and women who had been brought to Germany as slave labor and, now liberated, are wandering on the roads.

2.a. Oklahoma.

> **1967** Zimmer *Ribs of Death* 49: Charlie's here with blues from Bismark/And the Okie cities.

b. *Navy.* the battleship USS *Oklahoma*. Now *hist.*

> **1933** *Leatherneck* (Aug.) 30: Now when I was on the Okie. **1982** T.C. Mason *Battleship* 180 [ref. to 1941]: They were often sent to the "Okie," which had no admiral on board.

3.a. *Mil.* a native or resident of Okinawa.

> **1945** *AS* (Apr.) 150: *Okies.* The name adopted by Marines and soldiers for the Okinawans. **1955** Reifer *New Words* 146: Okie *n.*....*Mil. Slang.* An inhabitant of Okinawa. **1967** G. Moore *Ngo Tho* 10: Boyd came through the door as if he were charging the Navy line, leaving time for only a glimpse of a group waiting behind him, including at least two Oki; houseboys bearing breakfast trays. **1970** R. Sylvester *Guilty Bystander* 284 [ref. to 1945]: The Okinawa Japs...were the Okies.

b. *Mil.* Okinawa.

> **1945** *Yank* (Nov. 16) 22: "Where you guys from? Okie?" the Air Evacuation sergeant was asking. **1955** R.L. Scott *Look of Eagle* 39: They weren't going to stay on Oky while more fortunate brothers went with Doug to Tokyo. **1964** R. Moore *Green Berets* 23: Okie—Okinawa. **1969** Searls *Hero Ship* 55: There were fifty on Okie ready for use on the first day of the invasion. **1970** Whitmore *Memphis-Nam-Sweden* 114: I'll see you on Oki tomorrow. **1976** C.R. Anderson *Grunts* 24: Believe me! I just think about that first steam bath I'm going to get on Oki. *a*1982 in Berry *Semper Fi* 205: Hell, even the generals could get killed on Okie.

Okie-land *n.* Oklahoma. *Joc.*

> **1971** Keith *Long Line Rider* 79: I'm a displaced wild Indian from Okie-land.

Oklahoma credit card *n. West.* a siphon tube used for stealing gasoline. *Joc.*

> **1966** E. Shepard *Doom Pussy* 137: "Perhaps you could siphon gas out of the Associated Press jeep when we get there...." "Can't do that without an Oklahoma credit card." **1974** *Seattle Times* (Mar. 17) A23: Since many gas stations won't fill containers, patrons would use the siphons to keep their cars topped off. "Of course, there is always the possibility that some will use them for—what do you call them?—Oklahoma credit cards." *a*1989 in Safire *Coming to Terms* 157: I have heard since childhood of Oklahoma (or Okie) credit cards [in California].

Oklahoma rain *n. Oklahoma & Kansas.* a sand storm or dust storm. *Joc.*

> **1919** *DN* V 37: *Oklahoma rain*, n. phr. A sand storm, common in that state. **1936** R. Adams *Cowboy Lingo* 203: A sandstorm was an "Oklahoma rain." **1941** S. Vestal, in Botkin *Treas. Amer. Folk.* 313: Everyone jestingly referred to a dust storm as an "Oklahoma rain."

okole *n.* [< Hawaiian] *Hawaii.* the buttocks; ASS, 1.a.; (*hence*) the rearmost part (of anything).

> **1938** in *DARE*: Okole...Arse, in the sense of either anus or buttocks, or both....Of inanimate things, the rear or bottom end. **1954–60** in *DARE*. *a*1965 Shirota *Lucky Come Hawaii* 242: A-w-w, kiss my okole. **1991** W. Chamberlain *View from Above* 4: I am a leg and, as the Hawaiians say, an 'ōkole man....."She's got an awfully nice 'ōkole." **1991**

in *DARE:* Maybe [there will be] somethin in the paper if the cops aren't sitting on their *okoles.*

O.K. sign *n.* a hand gesture indicating perfection, approval, agreement, or safety made by touching the tips of the thumb and forefinger while raising and usu. separating the remaining three fingers. Now *S.E.*

[**1947** *Time* (Mar. 17) 52 (Tamony Coll.) [ad for Penzoil motor oil]: OK! [over picture of hand making the O.K. sign].] [**1949** *West. Folk.* VIII 263: A common sign to indicate "everything is all right" is made by joining the thumb and the forefinger to form a circle. This is exposed to the questioner and given a little shake. This sign may be used by the gesturer to indicate he enjoyed a meal.] [**1961** *Life* (Mar. 17) 30 (Tamony Coll.) [ad for Chevrolet OK used cars]: The OK sign means Used Car variety and value....For the best Used Car buy, go where you see the OK sign.] **1979** Stallone *Rocky II* 60: They give me back the okay sign like everythin' was gonna be hunky-dory. **1995** *Living Single* (Fox-TV): When you pass the window, flash the O.K. sign. **1996** N.Y.C. editor, age *ca*60: I've known the gesture since I was a kid, but I don't think I heard it called "the O.K. sign" until I was an adult, like my thirties or forties. I don't think we called it anything [before that]. **OKVS** *n.* see s.v. HOKUS-POCUS.

-ola *suffix.* [sugg. by use in trade names, e.g. *Victrola*] (used freely esp. after nouns and adjectives to create joc. forms). Cf. BOFFOLA, CRAPOLA, DRUGOLA, PAYOLA.

1919 A.M. Kendall & J.R. Robinson *Jazzola* [musical composition] (N.Y.: Leo. Feist, Inc., 1919). **1933** Mahin & Furthman *Bombshell* (film): Maybe the folks would like a little dramola. **1935** Fowler & Praskins *Call of Wild* (film): Thanks very much for the snortola [*sc.,* a SNORT of whiskey]. **1939** N. West *Locust* 266: That dame thinks she can give me the fingeroo, but she's got another thinkola coming. **1941** Brackett & Wilder *Ball of Fire* (film): This quizola they got on the radio. **1955** Kurtzman *Inside Mad* 16: Any time I'm on the good old waterola, kid.... **1958** Capote *Breakfast at Tiffany's* 79: They're not so hideola that I gulp Seconal. **1961** Wolfe *Magic of Their Singing* 128: Are you a fagola, sir? **1966** Longstreet & Godoff *Wm. Kite* 283: I'd ruther have a Sorrock supercharger in thar instead of that injector crapola. **1966** Samuels *People vs. Baby* 157: The biggest boffola...was...the crack about selecting your friends. **1968** W.C. Anderson *Gooney Bird* 110: Crapola! **1973** *TULIPQ* (coll. B.K. Dumas): Cash, bills, cashola. **1980** D. Hamill *Stomping Ground* 50: He had a real wopola face. **1982** in "J.B. Briggs" *Drive-In* 41: A bunch of wimpola surfers. **1986–89** Norse *Memoirs* 57 [ref. to 1939]: We attached the suffix *-ola* to words for comic effect. **1991** C. Eddy *Stairway to Hell* 129: An enchantingly hypnosymphonic groovola. *Ibid.* 155: Bodies-rolling-down-the-stairs thumpola [*sc.* thumping music]. **1996** *TV Guide* (Oct. 26) 32: I've done a lot of junkola along the way.

old *adj.* **1.** [fr. S.E. sense 'experienced; practiced'] sly; crafty.

*1722 D. DeFoe, in *OED:* The Germans were too old for us there. **1847–49** Bonney *Banditti* 157: I never should have thought of that plan to prevent deception. *Bonney!* you are an *old one! *a1890–1902 in *F & H* V 93: Old...crafty; cunning.

2. tiresome.—usu. constr. with *get.* Now *colloq.*

1864 in C.W. Wills *Army Life* 255: [Campaigning] occasionally gets a little *old,* but so does everything in this life. **1865** in C.W. Wills *Army Life* 365: Too much of a good thing gets *old.* **1865** in H. Johnson *Talking Wire* 267: Blue is getting old to me. I am getting tired of [it]. **1866** in Hilleary *Webfoot* 210: [The excuse of] "Scurvy" is getting old. **1951** W. Stegner, in *Harper's* (Feb. 1952) 43: That old strawboss keep eyeballin' me and givin' me that old hurry-up, hurry-up, that gets *old.* **1996** Univ. Tenn. prof., age 48: This waiting around for a decision is getting *old.*

old army game see s.v. ARMY GAME.

old boy *n.* **1.a.** the devil.—constr. with *the.*

1782 in *DARE.* **1802** in Thornton *Amer. Gloss.:* The devil has been nicknamed the old boy. **1853** *Harper's Mag.* VII 326: The "Old Boy" himself...the "Evil One." **1865** J. Pike *Scout & Ranger* 163: Yer kin get ter go to de ole boy, I guess. **1865** *Harper's Mag.* (Feb.) 427: He is doubtless in league with the "Old Boy." **1871, 1887** in *DARE.* **1899** Green *Va. Folk-Sp.* 304: *Old boy...*The devil. **1953** A. Miller, in *OEDS* I 343: The Church's enemies relied no less upon the Old Boy to keep the human mind enthralled. **1965–70** in *DARE.*

b. (*fig.*) hell; (*esp.*) daylights, stuffing.—constr. with *the.*

1840 *Crockett's Comic Alm.* (unp.): He'll play the old boy with you,

and no mistake. **1858** [S. Hammett] *Piney Woods* 84: Keep shady,...and you'll see the old boy riz *directly.* **1864** Hill *Our Boys* 40: J-j-just you try reportin' me, and I'll kn-kn-knock the old b-b-boy out o' you.

2. the penis.—usu. constr. with *the.* Cf. OLD FELLOW.

1943 in P. Smith *Letter from Father* 240: A final dose of cold water on the old "boy" himself. **1959** [*41st Ftr. Sq. Songbk.*] 29: I rammed the old boy up her. **1974** Blount *3 Bricks Shy* 263: Someone back home whose old boy was so big "the *veins* in it are like your little finger."

old clo *n.* old clothes. Often attrib.

*1881–84 Davitt *Prison Diary* I 75: An "old clo' man" would not have speculated upon two and six pence upon his entire outfit. **1895** Coup *Sawdust* 29: These old rascals are as sharp at a trade as the shreweest "old clo" merchant in Chatham Street.

Old Davy *n. Naut.* DAVY JONES; DAVY JONES'S LOCKER.

*1790 in *F & H* II 258: And if to old Davy I should go, friend Poll,/Why you will ne'er hear of me more. **1806** in Whiting *Early Amer. Provs.* 94: Give a quick passport to old Davy. **1807** in Whiting *Early Amer. Provs.:* His...navy,/Which thousands of Frenchmen has sent to old Davy. **1809, 1813, 1815** in Whiting *Early Amer. Provs. ca*1816 (quot. at *stop (someone's) grog* s.v. GROG). **1833** *Mil. & Nav. Mag. of U.S.* (Oct.) 118: I am just off to sea, and if I should go to Old Davy, why, you see, I had rather you should have it than any body I know.

old dog *n.* syphilis; DOG, 19.—constr. with *the.*

1935 Pollock *Und. Speaks: Old dog,* syphilis. **1942–49** Goldin et al. *DAUL* 60: Getting a bite of the old dog (syphilis). **1956** Resko *Reprieve* 84 [ref. to *ca*1940]: I guess I'll be pushin the ol dog line myself nex week....Never could pass up a chippy.

Old Ephraim *n.* (see quot.). *Joc.*

1860–61 R.F. Burton *City of Saints* 212: "Old Ephraim" is the mountain-man's *soubriquet* for the grizzly bear.

old-fashioned *adj.* denoting heterosexual genital intercourse with the couple face to face and the man on top; the missionary position. Also as *n.*

*ca1866 *Romance of Lust* 395: Aunt and I coupled in the old-fashioned way. **1947–51** Motley *We Fished* 246: The madam would be up there—"Old-fashioned, half and half, 96, around-the-world"—. **1965** Trimble *Sex Words* 142: *Old-fashioned way...*The Man-above Position, or Copulation performed Heterosexually in the position of Venus Observa.

old fellow *n.* the penis.—constr. with *the.*

*ca1888 *Stag Party* 225: She...takes the old fellow/Again by the throat. [*a1890–1902 F & H* V 99: *Old man...*The penis.]

old fiddle *adj.* passé; OLD HAT.

1979 in Curry *River's in My Blood* 10: The thing had got old fiddle.

old flag *n. Navy.* a flag officer.

1862 in Keeler *U.S.S. Monitor* 87: Capt. Jeffers gets almost frantic at times & goes down to see the Old Flag (as the Commodore is called) but it does no good. *Ibid.* 101: The "Old Flag" (the Commodore) is anticipating an attack tonight.

old gentleman *n. Gambl.* (see 1935 quot.). Also **old gent.**

*1828 in *F & H* V 97: An old gentleman (a card somewhat larger and thicker than the rest of the pack, and now in considerable use amongst the "legs"). *1828 in Partridge *Dict. Und.* 480: A well-known macer, who is celebrated for slipping an "old gentleman" (a long card) into the pack. **1935** Pollock *Und. Speaks: Old gent,* a playing card slightly longer than others of the pack, which cheaters deal when desired.

Old Hannah *n. Black E.* the sun.

1933 in Leadbitter & Slaven *Blues Records* 54: Go Down Old Hannah. **1933** Lomax & Lomax *Amer. Ballads & Folk Songs* 59: Go down, Ol' Hannah, doncha rise no mo',/Ef you rise any mo' bring judgment day. **1934** Hurston *Jonah's Gourd Vine* 152: When Lucy woke up, old Hannah was riding high. The light was strong in her face. **1970** in *DARE.*

Old Harry *n.* the devil; (*also*) hell. Cf. *by the Lord Harry* s.v. HARRY.

[*1698–99 "B.E." *Dict. Cant. Crew: Old Harry,* a Composition used by Vintners, when they bedevil their Wines.] *1785 in Grose *Dict. Vulgar Tongue: Old Harry....*the nick-name for the Devil. **1838, 1843** in *DARE. ca*1855 in L. Levy *Flashes of Merriment* 36: It...rained...like the old Harry. **1872** in Aswell *Humor* 316: Who the Old Harry is she?...And where the Old Harry did you get it? **1880** Pinkerton *Prof. Thieves & Detective* 30: And everything is going to the Old Harry while I am playing detective. **1907** J.C. Lincoln *Cape Cod* 270: We need him more than the old Harry needs a conscience. **1912** Siringo *Cowboy*

Detective 256: He bucked like the old Harry. **1928** Dahlberg *Bottom Dogs* 43: Seventh graders fooled around…and…raised old harry. **1939, 1941, 1965–70** in *DARE*.

old hat *n.* the vulva or vagina; (*also*) sexual intercourse.—usu. considered vulgar.

    *1754 in *F & H* V 98: I shall conclude this learned note with remarking that the term old hat is used by the vulgar in no very honorable sense. ***ca1775** *Frisky Songster* 83: He should never touch her old hat. ***1785** Grose *Dict. Vulgar Tongue: Old Hat.* A woman's privities; because frequently felt. **1888** *Stag Party* 45: On the edge of a piss-pot a maiden once sat,/…And she sighed and she cried for a little "old hat."…"I wish some bold lover would end my suspense,"/"Would I were possessed of a penis immense." *Ibid.* 144: The girls grow fat/On the lunches they've taken of Little Old Hat. **a1900** in H.P. Beck, Jr. *Down-East Ballads* 395: The night that I went away I had a bit of old hat.

old hat *adj.* trite or outdated.—usu. used predicatively. Now *S.E.*

    *1911 in *OED2*: Men have…put it, with like doctrines, silently aside in disgust. So it has happened with Satan and his fork: they have become "old hat." ***1916** D.H. Lawrence, in *OED2*: The whole of the consciousness and the conscious content is old hat. **1928** in E. O'Neill *Letters* 284: But that is all "old hat." **1935** S. Lewis *Can't Happen* 9: I guess some of the things I said in my former speech were kind of a little bit obvious and what we used to call "old hat" when my brigade was quartered in England. **1949** *New Yorker* (Oct. 15) 60: Tubular stuff [*sc.,* furniture] is now old hat, and the best modern designers are using plastics, molded or laminated wood, [etc.]. **1949** *N.Y. Times* (Dec. 11) VI 15: A good many operas have suffered from an accretion of old-hat acting and staging traditions. **1961** *N.Y. Times* (Oct. 22) II 1: One cannot rule out the validity of even the old-hat way so long as it has a flair. **1971** *Playboy* (June) 36: The plot of *A New Leaf* is surprisingly old hat. **1971** in J. Flaherty *Chez Joey* 88: One has to be terribly old hat to believe it. **1980** Druffel & Rogo *Tujunga Contacts* 57: What Moody recalled will probably strike the seasoned UFO student as pretty old hat. **1983** Flaherty *Tin Wife* 185: You're so old hat that everybody's eyes cloud over when you open your mouth.

old head *n. Esp. So.* a veteran; old-timer.

    [**1891** in *DARE*: Some of the older heads predicted that he would come to the gallows.] **1899** Green *Va. Folk-Sp.* 305: *Old-heads.*…The old people of the neighborhood. **1919** Amerine *Alabama's Own* 25: The second, an "oldhead" in things military, then nearly split his sides laughing. **1926** Norwood *Other Side of Circus* 191: The boss told about the "old-heads," as he and Blackie Diller called the horses that had been with the show for many years. **1942** (quot. at PEDDLER). **1956** Heflin *USAF Dict.* 356: *Old head.* A person who has been around a long time. *Slang.* **1958** McCulloch *Woods Wds.* 126: *Old head*—An old timer. **1959–60** R. Reisner *Jazz Titans* 162: *Old Head:* a long-time user of marijuana. **1987** Robbins *Ravens* 5: Through the gradual process where an FNG…developed into an "old head." **a1994** N. McCall *Wanna Holler* 40: The old-heads said there was no place for love in a *real* man's life. **1994** *N.Y. Times* (July 3) ("Week in Rev.") 9: A generation of city teen-agers is turning…away from counsel from the old heads in their community.

Old Hickory *n.* [fr. the picture of Andrew Jackson, whose nickname was *Old Hickory*, on the bill] a twenty-dollar bill.

    1966 in *DARE*.

Old Horny *n.* OLD HARRY.

    1853 in *DARE*: The old Horny swore it should be so, and I told him! **1855** W.G. Simms *Forayers* 52: Open to the devil and all his imps!…Hurrah for old Horny! **1950, 1967** in *DARE*.

old horse see s.v. HORSE, 3.

oldie *n.* **1.** an old person.

    *1874 in Troubridge *Among Troubridges* 97: I am now in my seventeenth year, isn't it sad? I shall soon be an "oldy." **1973** Overgard *Hero* 31: Oh well, if the oldies had their Sun Cities, why not buildings for singles, young marrieds, middle-aged discontents and so on? **1973** M. Van Duyn, in J.P. Hunter *Norton Intro. Poetry* (ed. 2) 176: It's Nowsville, man. Passed Oldies, Uglies,/Straighties, Honkies. **1974** Fair *New Nonsense* 68: Young people form a faction whose hate object is parents or "oldies" in general. **1976** *Dallas Morning News* (Oct. 31) E1: 10 per cent taken off their bill because the desk clerk gave them a senior-citizen ID.…"freebies and cheapies for oldies." **1992** *N.Y. Times* (Oct. 18) ("Sports") 4: There's a golden patch of oldies coming through who can still play great tennis.

2. an old saying, story, object, etc.

    1934 W. Winchell, in *DAS*: Our pet oldie [*sc.,* an old joke] concerns the India rubber skin man. **1949** *N.Y. Times* (Mar. 13) II 1: The story, of course, is the same oldie, having been filmed two previous times. **1951** in *OEDS*: If your old jalopy is cranky and has been acting up under the stress of urban life, maybe you ought to retire it to Prudence Island.…Real oldies are just the thing on Prudence Island. **1952** Lait & Mortimer *USA* 396: Then you don't believe that oldie about honor among thieves? **1973** *Seattle Times* (Feb. 25) C8: A 1916 Pierce-Arrow chauffeur-driven limousine.…He has more of the oldies in mint condition. **1983** *Business Week* (Apr. 18) 30: New cars, holdovers, and venerable oldies that together total almost 300 models.

3. *Entertainment Industry.* an old and familiar popular song, motion picture, etc. See also GOLDEN OLDIE; *oldie but goodie,* 1, below.

    1939–40 O'Hara *Pal Joey,* in *DAS:* The other song was an oldy like "My Buddy." **1940** *AS* (Apr.) 205: *Oldies.* Old tunes or films. **1945** Fay *Be Poor* 125: Here's a chorus of an "oldie" I've done many times. **1950** *Time* (Oct. 9) 44: Younger singers could take pointers from the confident way she wrapped her voice around such oldies as *Get Happy, Embraceable You,* [etc.]. **1952** Vonnegut *Player Piano* 100: And lots of 'em [are] steals from oldies. **1961** F. Brown *Geezenstacks* 116: Happier because I found an oldie on your juke box and it fits. **1976** *L.A. Times* (Oct. 19) "You" 21: An excellent selection of songbooks and singles (especially oldies). **1977** *Rolling Stone* (Apr. 7) 36: I don't want to give the oldies more significance than they're worth, just because people want to hear them.

  ¶ In phrase:

  ¶ **oldie but goodie, 1.** an old song that is still popular or is being revived.—occ. used attrib.

    1957 Wallrich *Air Force Airs* 75: An oldie and a goodie sung to the tune of the same name. **1963** J. Berry & B. Wilson *Surf City* [pop. song]. **1966** I. Reed *Pall-Bearers* 27: Dere's some oldie but goodie records on da victrola. **1966** Samuels *People vs. Baby* 72: They sat…listening to Louis Armstrong and Sammy Davis records, to "Oldies but Goodies" and cha-cha. **1971** *Essence* (Oct.) 46: The "oldies but goodies." **1971** *Playboy* (Mar.) 48: I would hate to see my collection of oldies but goodies reduced to nothing but needle scratches.

2. any person or thing that is old but still desirable.—occ. used attrib.

    1968 Hudson *Case of Need* 186: You got an oldie but goodie here to see you. **1971** Sonzski *Punch Goes Judy* 1: That…is another of Baxter's oldie but goodie expressions from the fifties. **1974** *Harper's* (Mar.) 91: An oldie but goodie (first printing, 1968) is…*BASIC and the Personal Computer.* **1976** H. Ellison *Sex Misspelled* 28: Now *none* of those oldies but goodies is being spoken by a man or woman on a first date. **1992** *Time* (July 13) 27: Another oldie but goodie destined for recycling is the man-in-the-street commercial, in which residents of Arkansas will trash Clinton's governance.

Old Issue *n. Army.* (see quot.).

    1909 J. Moss *Officer's Manual* 284: *Old Issue.* an old soldier.

Old Joe *n.* [orig. unkn.] **1.** (see quot.).

    1923 McKnight *Eng. Words* 45: The drug store contributes:…*Old Joe* for U.S. Dispensary book of formulae.

2. *Esp. Navy.* syphilis; (*rarely*) gonorrhea.—also constr. with *the.*

    1942 T. Williams *Letters* (Feb. 24) 24: Suddenly broke out with a dreadful itching rash. I thought sure I finally had the old Joe so I rushed to the family doctor. **1942** E.H. Hunt *East of Farewell* 160: "Make sure it's not the old Joe."…"I don't want to have anything like that in my old age." **1942** *ATS* 158: Syphilis…*Old Joe, pox, ral.* **1940–46** McPeak MS. [Indiana Univ.]: When it came to venereal diseases the sailors use a euphemism, as syphilis is the "old Joe"; gonorrhea was "clapp." **1952** Steinbeck *E. of Eden* 468: I come out of that and I got the old Joe. **1962** Quirk *Red Ribbons* 30 [ref. to 1940's]: The incidence of Old Joe was remarkably low, considering the exposure. *Ibid.* 200: She's as popular as a whore with the Old Joe. **1963** T.I. Rubin *Sweet Daddy* 110: Twice I got old Joe, you know a dose, little one. **1965** Schmitt *All Hands Aloft!* 281 [ref. to 1918]: In addition to our other miseries an epidemic of boils had broken out.…Remembering our escapades ashore, our worries were not lessened by our cadaverous Slim with, "Oh, oh! Just what I expected. Old Joe! I told you to stay away from them damn Jap girls." **1973** Lott *Bluejackets Manual*

23: There are five general types of VD: *syphilis* (syph, pox, old Joe); *gonorrhea* (clap, dose, the drip, GC); *chancroid* (bubo, hair cut); *granulema inguinale*; and *lymphogranuloma venereum*.

old lady *n.* **1.** a mother (regardless of age).

[***1722** Defoe *Moll Flanders*: His elder brother was married and we, being then removed to London, were written to by the old lady to come and be at the wedding.] **1877** (quot. at GRASS, *v.*, 1). **1891** *Outing* (Oct.) 88: On their return Charlie met the "old lady" [*sc.*, a bear] almost face to face. **1907** in Robinson *Comics* 44: I ought to get that hundred the old lady save [*sic*] up and run it into a couple-o-million easy. **1924** P. Marks *Plastic Age* 49: Carl had written his nightly letter to the "old lady." **1956** Algren *Wild Side* 67 [ref. to ca1930]: The only bedtime story my old lady ever told me began and ended with "You leave me cold," Kitty Twist recalled. **1962** N.Y.C. high school student: His old lady's mad about something. **1963** E. Hunter *Ten Plus One* 7: Oedipus....He was this Greek king. He slept with his old lady. **1972** Kopp *Buddha* 180: Sure, you're just like the old lady. **1978** Wharton *Birdy* 4: Birdy's old lady'd keep any baseballs that went over the fence. **1981** Carpi *Escape 2000* (film): What about my old man and my old lady? **1988** *Wonder Years* (ABC-TV): Yeah. My old lady's the same way.

2.a. a wife (regardless of age).

1836 in Haliburton *Sam Slick* 48: Inquirin' how the old lady is to home and the little boy that made such a wonderful smart answer. **1871** in *DAE*: Here's the old lady and Shocky. **1874** Carter *Rollingpin* 102: Yes, the old lady likes my pieces. **1880** Bailey *Danbury Boom* 190: It's the old lady. **1884** Nye *Baled Hay* 88: It would kinda harden me and the old lady. **1885** E. Custer *Boots & Saddles* 184: My soubriquet of "the old lady" dated back to the first days of my married life. **1890** in F. Remington *Sel. Letters* 97: I had the old lady packed over the mountains on a "cayuse." **1895** Remington *Wister* 66: Old lady has grip and we have detained here. **1907** in H.C. Fisher *A. Mutt* 6: Here I am into the old lady's hundred again. **1950** L. Brown *Iron City* 106: I'll be right back...to that sweet little woman. You got an old lady? **1952** E. Brown *Trespass* 17: "She your old lady." "She my *wife*. You call her that." **1959–60** R. Reisner *Jazz Titans* 162: *Old Lady*: Wife or sweetheart; girl with whom one sleeps. **1963** J. Williamson *Hustler!* 51: He had paid his ol' lady's* rent....*Common law or legal wife. **1969** Whittemore *Cop!* I 92: Husbands are always beating up their old ladies here. **1972** Claerbaut *Black Jargon* 74: *Old lady*...wife. **1989** Singerman *Amer. Hero* 181: I'll bet you a night in the sack with my ol' lady against that Lincoln you're drivin'. **1997** *Drew Carey Show* (ABC-TV): His old lady just had a baby.

b. a mistress or steady girlfriend (regardless of age).

1918 Ruggles *Navy Explained* 82: The best girl is...the old lady,...broad, [etc.]. **1946** Mezzrow & Wolfe *Really Blues* 30: I know you're Capone's old lady. **1952** H. Ellson *Golden Spike* 152: I'll cop some stuff, see my old lady, stay with her all day, go to the movies. **1953** W. Fisher *Waiters* 34: She was just like my old lady out in Chi. **1957** (quot. at BULLSKATE). **1958** Plagemann *Steel Cocoon* 65 [ref. to WWII]: Here a man came to shack up with a woman, and if he had shacked up with her before, he recognized the durability of the relationship by referring to her as his "old lady." A man's wife was his old lady, but so was a shack-up job whose charms brought a man back more than once. **1959–60** (quot. at (**a**), above). **1966** H. Thompson *Hell's Angels* 119: Many who would ordinarily take their "old ladies" had left the girls behind. **1967** W. Murray *Sweet Ride* 97: "You his Old Lady?" "Old Lady?" Yeah. You make it with him only? **1967–68** von Hoffman *Parents Warned Us* 176: His new old lady, Little Bit, was squawish and submissive. **1969** Gustaitis *Turning On* 115: Nico [is] Bill's "old lady." **1971** Freeman *Catcher* (film): I was up in Alberta searching for a sixteen-year-old girl. When I found her she was with her boyfriend, who wasn't much older....When I said I had to take her back, he kept sobbing, "Don't take my old lady. Don't take my old lady." **1971** E. Sanders *Family* 23 [ref. to ca1957]: We'd rap a lot about whores, especially how to control them. We talked about Main Old Ladies—a pimp's number one girl who controlled all the others. **1972** J. Mills *Report* 103: Then she said he wanted her to move in with him, to be his old lady. **1974** *Socio. Symposium* XI 76: I can't ever really be his old lady because I doubt that I could not talk back. **1983** De Lello *Bad Boys* (film): Your old lady's got a bad mouth. **a1988** M. Atwood *Cat's Eye* 298: They refer to their girlfriends, some of whom live with them; these are called "my old lady." **1990** Crow Dog & Erdoes *Lakota Woman* 78: Usually a boy would say to a girl, "Be my old lady." **1995** *Jerry Springer Show* (synd. TV series): I looked at her, I seen my old lady's sister.

c. *Stu.* a roommate (of the same sex). *Joc.*

1929–32 in *AS* (Dec. 1934) 288: [Lincoln Univ.:] *Ole Miss* (also *Ole Lady*). Roommate. **1942–44** in *AS* (Feb. 1946) 34: *Old Lady*, n. Roommate. **1954** Killens *Youngblood* 135: Some of the students called Richie's "old lady" Randy the Radical. **1959** A. Anderson *Lover Man* 82: Down here we don't say room-mate, we say "old gal" or "old lady."

d. Esp. *Pris.* the passive partner, regardless of sex, in a homosexual relationship.

1937 Herndon *Let Me Live* 210: The principal victims of these sexual orgies were mere children of twelve or thirteen years, boys who had been convicted of petty thievery. The prisoners...called them "Old Ladies." **1952** Himes *Stone* 140: "I want you for my woman—my old lady."...His eyes looked sick. **1953** *Collier's* (Oct. 30) 76: A vot...wears no lipstick and acts like a boy. She can have an "old lady." **1962** Perry *Young Man Drowning* 176: He becomes some con's old lady. **1965** Ward & Kassebaum *Women's Pris.* 107: She often interrupted her "old lady" and continued the conversation for her. **a1979** Pepper & Pepper *Straight Life* [ref. to 1961] 286: "That's your old lady, man."..."No he's not."

e. a young woman.

1979 D. Milne *Second Chance* 129: Hey, look at that nice-lookin' old lady out there.

3. *Naut.* a ship.—used affectionately.

1841 [Mercier] *Man o' War* 73: I would'nt be afraid to bet...we'll have to take some of the old lady's *muslin* off before supper. **1856** Olmstead *Slave States* 614: De ole lady too heavy...I could pitch a few ton of dat freight off her bow. **1932** Riesenberg *Log* 55: The old lady...was...driven almost beyond the power of endurance. **1962** Farago *10th Fleet* 152: Henke...fired his first torpedo into the old lady. **1965** Harvey *Hudasky's Raiders* 7: "Is it rough?" "Not too bad in this old lady." **1967** Lord *Victory* 33: They certainly didn't wish the "Old Lady" ill, but the damage from that bomb should keep her in dry dock for a long time. **1973** Greenberg *Pueblo* (ABC-TV): This old lady gets a hole in her, ten–twelve inches, she's gonna go down like a whore.

4. *West.* a male cook, as on a ranch or in camp.

1892 *Outing* (Feb.) 359: The cook..."the old lady," as the herders usually term him. **1922** P.A. Rollins *Cowboy* 165 [ref. to 1890's]: The cook...if...white,...behind his back was spoken of as the "old woman" or "old lady." **1926** Branch *Cowboy* 31: The [camp] cook...the "old lady." **1972** Bercovici & Prentiss *Culpepper Cattle Co.* (film): Hey, old lady, you got some coffee here?

old maid *n.* **1.** a kernel of popcorn that has failed to pop.

1947 in *DARE*. **1949** *Sat. Eve. Post* (May 21) 36: All hands kept right on pitching in, and munching, until there was nothing left but a few unpopped kernels derisively known as old maids. **1967, 1970** in *DARE*. **1978** Univ. Tenn. student: When I was a kid in the '50's I seem to recall the other kids used to call unpopped kernels of popcorn "old maids." **1983** S. King *Christine* 412: The bowl of popcorn was down to the old maids and the burny-bottoms when I took myself in hand and asked one of the questions I had been avoiding.

2. [fr. the dial. sense 'the last piece of food left on a plate'; see *DARE* def. 4] a leftover item.

1982 R. Sutton *Don't Get Taken* 182: The...cars were all "old maids."

old maid's hall *n.* [sugg. by BACHELOR'S HALL] ¶ In phrase: **keep old maid's hall** to live or keep house without the presence of a man.

1858 in Eliason *Tarheel Talk* 151: Mary and I are keeping old Maid's Hall. Your Pa and Frank started this morning for Portsmouth.

old man *n.* **1.a.** a husband (regardless of age).

[***1768** in *OED*: His wife join'd her old man again, as their children and grandchildren danced before them.] **1839** *American Joe Miller* 68: In three weeks Jonathan and Prudence were "my old man," and "my old woman." **ca1851** in J.Q. Anderson *With Bark on* 136: The old Parson is going over to see Aunt Sally Wilden's old man. **1851** in J. Levy *Saw the Elephant* 106: She earnt her *old man* (said individual twenty-one years of age, perhaps) "nine hundred dollars in nine weeks." **1864** in O.J. Hopkins *Under the Flag* 176: My brother-in-law is here from Indianapolis, Eliza and her "old man." **1868** in Huckaby & Simpson *Tulip* 101: "A happy New Year" to you and your "old man." **1874** "M. Twain" in *Stories* 95: Well, sah, my ole man—dat's my husban'—he was lovin' an' kind to me. **1906** Buffum *Bear City* 22: Well, one thing my old man has learned,—he can shoot himself if he can't hit anything else. **1908** in H.C. Fisher *A. Mutt* 160: My old man has to get to the track. **1954** L. Armstrong *Satchmo* 152 [ref. to 1918]: She had an "Old Man"—the name we used to have for a common law husband. **1990** K. Friedman *Cadillac Man* (film): It's Donna's old man. Her husband.

b. *Pros.* a prostitute's pimp or lover (regardless of age).

    1891 in Dobie *Rainbow* 169: My old man's a railroad man, he works on Number Four;/He's a rustlin' son of a —, and I'm his dirty —. **1957** Greenwald *Call Girl* 18: Her status is based on her attractiveness, financial standing, political connections, dress, apartment, manners and the state in which she keeps her "old man" or pimp. **1959** Hunter *Conviction* 126: This person serves as part-time pimp and part-time lover. He is referred to as "my old man." **1963** Hunter *Ten Plus One* 41: Harry Wallach…lived with or was habitually in the company of the prostitute named Blanche Lettiger.…Everybody knew who Blanche's "old man" was. **1968** Gover *JC* 22: He needs that shit worse'n my ole man needs his. **1974** *Socio. Symposium* XI 75: Ann teaches each girl the racket's Four Rules governing her behavior toward her "old man." **1978** (quot. at HOT-SHIT). **1980** Gould *Ft. Apache* 49: There were the hookers, who were afraid to go home because they knew they'd catch a beating from their old men for not earning enough. **1983** Wambaugh *Delta Star* 170: "Did she have an old man?" "A pimp? I don't think."

c. a boyfriend or lover (regardless of age). [The 1966 quot. is in a homosexual context in prison.]

    1966 Herbert *Fortune & Men's Eyes* 33: You're sittin' duck for a gang splash if y'ain't got a old man. **1970** Ebert *Beyond Valley of Dolls* (film): I got a real nice old man. He's studying for a law exam. **1973** N.Y.U. female student: I've still got my old man, so everything's cool. **1973** in *Playboy* (Jan. 1974) 47: For the past few years, I've been living with a gentle, slightly withdrawn longhair. I dig our relationship.…I have gone out with several [other men]…and…they are a different breed of cat from my old man. **1974** Hejinian *Extreme Remedies* 27: Cute chick. Does she have an old man? **1976–77** C. McFadden *Serial* 41: It's Michael's.…Anita's new old man. **1983** W. Walker *Dime to Dance* 52: Suppose I was to tell you I've gotten myself an old man?

2. a father (regardless of age).

    1811 in Eliason *Tarheel Talk* (Mar. 28) 167: There is one thing above all others that the old man enjoins upon you. **1839** Briggs *Harry Franco* I 116: I say, Nick…how much does your old man allow you per week? **1845** in Oehlschlaeger *Reveille* 243: The old man has set me up in a store here. **1845** (quot. at BARK, *n.*). **1847** Neal *Charcoal Sketches* 178: You can tell your old man that you fell down, and spilt the whiskey. **1855** (quot. at GOVERNOR). **1868** Williams *Black-Eyed Beauty* 9: 'Fraid of the old man. And you said because it would ruin you if it got around that you were in company with what you call "bad girls." *Ibid.* 30: How much will you put in my way to stop me going to tell your old man of your visits to…Matty? **1870** *Overland Mo.* (Jan.) 84: The old man said I shouldn't go. **1871** in Brownmiller *Against Our Will* 129: They came back…after my old man again. **1873** Lening *N.Y. Life* 381: The "old man" at home…will now learn how his son spends his evenings. **1880** in Chesnutt *Journals* 145: Finally they decide to leave it to the "old man." **1880** (quot. at COIN). **1880** Merriman *Letters* 73: He's vulgar enough to call you the "ould man." **1924** P. Marks *Plastic Age* 12: My old man never went to college. **1942** Root & Fortune *Mokey* (film): If your old man's gone, that's perfect. **1949** Quigley *Corsica* 14: The Banker's an old man now!…Mother and son doing well. **1954** G. Kersh, in Pohl *Star of Stars* 25: He looked after me like a son—a hell of a lot better than my old man ever looked after me. **1954** Cassill *Writing Fiction* 163: Sit around and talk, I guess; drink beer with Gracie's old man or somethin'. **1955** L. Shapiro *6th of June* 67: The geezer on the end stands just like my old man when he's got a skinful. **1960** Bluestone *Cully* 5: Don' shove, don' shove. Look what your old man got for shovin'! [*i.e.*, you]. **1969** in Dundes *Interp. Folklore* 80: The moment a man becomes a father, he becomes his child's "old man." **1994** *Donahue* (NBC-TV): It's gotta be no picnic to tell your old man about this. **1995** *Strange Luck* (Fox-TV): Your old man. He's cool?

3.a. *Naut.* the master of a vessel (regardless of age).—constr. with *the*.

    1823 J.F. Cooper *Pilot* 5: "Is the old man mad?" exclaimed the young officer in the whale-boat. **1833** N. Ames *Yarns* 50: The commander of a merchantman, although perhaps under twenty years of age, is invariably called the "old man," by all hands on board. **1840** *New Yorker* (Mar. 28) 19: "Whom do you mean by the old man?"

"Why, in course, who should I mean—Admiral Lord Nelson. We always called him the old man." **1847** Downey *Portsmouth* 9: The Old Man determined to crack on for Rio, where we arrived on the 27th. **1849** Melville *Redburn* ch. vi: Don't let the "old man" see the snuff-box;…pitch it overboard. **1855** [S. Hammett] *Capt. Priest* 28: The keen eyes of the "old man" are certain to detect the end of some rope that needs whipping or knotting. **1864** Hotten *Slang Dict.* (ed. 3): *Old man*, in American merchant ships, the master. The phrase is becoming common in English ships. *a*1868 N.H. Bishop *Across So. Amer.* 14: From the old man (the captain) in the cabin. **1893** Barra *Two Oceans* 59 [ref. to 1849]: The captain is always called the old man, though he be a boy. **1918** O'Neill *Caribbees* 34: That's right—tell the Old Man about ut, an' the Mate too.

b. *Mil.* a commanding officer.—constr. with *the*.

    1830 J. Martin *Revolutionary Soldier* 263 [ref. to 1782]: One day, two or three of our young hotheads told me that they and some others of the men, whom they mentioned, were about to have some fun with "the old man," as they generally called the captain. *Ibid.* 280: Our "old man" had a number of these last-mentioned symbols of honor and affection presented him. **1845** *Recollections of Army* 167: So when I got back to the fort, I tells the old man all about my escape. **1864** in Gould *Maine Regt.* 485: The "old man" turned us out very early this morning. **1885** Whitman *Slang in America:* Always among soldiers during the Succession War, one heard of "Little Mac" (Gen. McClellan), or of "Uncle Billy" (Gen. Sherman.) "The old man" was, of course, very common. **1887** W. Watson *Life in Confed. Army* 156: The "old man" (as we called the captain) might…refuse him. **1890** C.C. King *Portia* 41: The "old man," as the soldiers called the colonel, ordered out his blockaders. **1890** Finerty *War-Path* 202 [ref. to 1876]: Neither of the officers named was very venerable, but when a soldier speaks of his superior as "the old man" you may be sure he is in good humor with him. **1890** E. Custer *Guidon* 153: See here, cap'n, where's the old man? **1892** Cox *5 Yrs. in Army* 94: We all felt like asking the same question, when the "old man" General C., came from his quarters. **1900** Remington *Bark on* 26: The "old man" had been captain of L for years and years. **1907** Bush *Enlisted Man* 55: The way the "old man" worked that regiment was a sin. *ca*1910 (quot. at CINCH, *n.*, 2.a.). **1917** Hunt *Draft* 204: But the "Old Man" up on Headquarters Hill did both yesterday. **1920** Bissell *63rd Inf.* 49: The Old Man can see more with one eye than I can with two. **1928** Wharton *Squad* 190 [ref. to 1918]: Good fer th' Old Man. Dam' nonsense to try to go agenst those machine-guns. **1930** Weaver *Poems* 234: I took it to the Old Man. He went to college. **1948** Lay & Bartlett *12 O'Clock High!* 56: Henderson…wondered if the Old Man was satisfied with the briefing they had attended. **1950** *Sat. Eve. Post* (Oct. 14): "We couldn't believe it at first," one officer said. "The Old Man had told us when we started the drive that we would not surrender and we would not retreat." **1958** Cooley *Run for Home* 26 [ref. to *ca*1925]: He said the Old Man was sick too. **1983** *Daily Beacon* (Univ. Tenn.) (May 16) 2: I was invited to…make the floor shine so well that the "old man," a lieutenant aged 22, wouldn't mind eating from it. **1983–88** J.T. McLeod *Crew Chief* 118: The old man wants all the doors put back on. **1988** Clodfelter *Mad Minutes* 132: Until the "old man" (battalion commander) was satisfied.

c. a man in charge; boss.

    1837 in *OEDS:* I say, darkie, the old man keeps good liquor, and plenty of belly timber, don't he? **1878** Bardeen *Home* 239: Our…firm hires a boy…to cut all notices of the "Spheroid" out o' the noospapers befor the ol' man sees 'em. **1891** Lummis *David* 80: He galloped down towards "the old man"—as the manager of a ranch is always familiarly called by his men. **1897** (quot. at BRICK, 1). **1902** "J. Flynt" *Little Bro.* 142: At last the day came when the court prisoners were to meet the "old man"—the judge. *Ibid.* 143: It is the anxiety as to what the "old man" will do. **1902** Hapgood *Thief* 77 [ref. to *ca*1885]: The old man (the [police] chief) won't stand for it much longer. **1904** in "O. Henry" *Works* 932: I don't blame the "old man" for cutting it out. **1904** *Life in Sing Sing* 256: *Old man.*—Head person. **1906** Kildare *Old Bailiwick* 255: The police captain—the Old Man. **1916** *Editor* XLIII (Mar. 25) 343. **1926–35** Watters & Hopkins *Burlesque* 21: Lefty knows the old man has been usin' you. **1935** *AS* (Feb.) 18: [Underworld—1910:] *Old Man.* 1. The chief or head of a gang. Modern wheels, big shot. 2. The warden of a prison. **1936** Fellows & Freeman *Big Show* 116: The Old Man (circus owner) and I were…settling up the day's business. **1967** J. Kramer *Instant Replay* 113: He saw Lombardi coming…and here I am hiding an ice cream cone from the old man.

d. (*caps.*) God.—constr. with *the.*

1902 *DN* II 240: *Old man.…*The very ignorant thus commonly designate the deity. 1906 *DN* III 122: *Old Man.…*Used commonly for the deity. 1942 in *DARE.* 1953 Randolph & Wilson *Down in Holler* 268: The *Old Man,* or the *Good Man,* or the *Old Gentleman*—these names for God are used even by deeply religious hillfolk.

4. (see 1926, 1944 quots.).

1925 (cited in Partridge *Dict. Und.* 481). 1926 in *AS* LVII (1982) 262: *Old man.* Long-handled tool used to secure leverage in safecracking. 1944 Boatright & Day *Hell to Breakfast* 147: A hand-operated brace for drilling holes in steel by hand is "the old man."

¶ In phrase:

¶ **so's your old man** (used as a derisive retort).

1925 Kearney *Man's Man* 51: So's your old man. 1925 E. Wilson *Twenties* 232: They wanted to paint "So's your old man!" under it. 1925 van Vechten *Nigger Heaven* 244: So's your old man. 1926 in J.M. March *Wild Party* 68: So's your old man. 1926 in Leadbitter & Slaven *Blues Records* 89: So's Your Old Man. 1926 Maines & Grant *Wise-Crack Dict.* 14: *So's your old man*—impudent comeback. 1928 Sharpe *Chicago May* 122: Our present American slang, "So's your old man." *1945 S.J. Baker *Austral. Lang.* 288: A group of Americanisms that has wide currency in Australia.…*says you…so's your old man…corny…jive.* 1987 *Kate & Allie* (CBS-TV): "Low! Lower! Lowest!" "So's your old man!"

Old Muddy *n.* the Mississippi or Missouri river. Cf. Big Muddy.

1846 *Crockett's Almanac* (unp.): The Great Mississippi Snag Alligator…I war goin down old muddy one day…when [etc.]. 1942 *ATS* 71: *Old Muddy,* the Missouri River.

Old Ned *n.* **1.** *So. & S.W.* salt pork or bacon.

1833 in *DARE:* Bacon, or 'Old Ned,' as it is called in Tennessee. 1869 *Overland Mo.* (Aug.) 129 [ref. to Civil War]: Southern smoke-cured pork…in allusion to the famous negro song, was termed "Old Ned" from its sable appearance. 1870 Duval *Big Foot* 313: I don't want to give up old "Ned," of which I am remarkably fond. 1931 *PMLA* XLVI 1304: This old ned (bacon) orter last a good span. 1936 *AS* XI 316: *Old Ned…*Home-cured bacon.

2. Old Nick.

1939 *AS* XIV 268: Euphemisms…referring to the Devil:…"old Ned." 1943 McAtee *Supp. Dial. Grant Co. Ind.* 11 [ref. to 1890's]: *Old Ned…*the devil. 1949 *JAF* LXII 63: The devil was referred to as "Old Ned" or "Old Scratch." 1967–69 in *DARE.*

Old Nick *n.* **1.** the devil; (*hence,* as in 1941 quot.) (used as a vague standard of comparison).—constr. with *like;* (*also,* as in 1868 quot.) (used as an expletive); "the hell".

*1662 in *F & H* V 99: In this prodigal trick They have outdone Old Nick For what he did give he did show. *1668 (cited in Partridge *DSUE* 585). *1731 [J. Roberts] *Merry-Thought* IV 26: But *Old Nick* has got them all. *1744 in Baring-Gould *Mother Goose* 39: Old Nick was glad to see them so mad. 1764 in *DARE:* By which, they with a Magic Trick/Could shew white Folks as black's Oldnick [*sic*]. 1777 in St. G. Tucker *Poems* 42: But, as soon as I grew wonderous sick,/I wished my carcass at Old Nick. 1809 in *DARE:* Tom is a negro, and as black as Old Nick. 1854 *Fourth* 7: Supposed that crew, at any rate, were going to the port known as "Old Nick's." 1855 *Crockett Almanac* (unp.): A boat's crew of witches, with old Nick for a pilot. 1864 in Cate *Two Soldiers* 138: Old Nick must have welcomed about one hundred new visitors into the lower regions. 1868 M. Reid *Helpless Hand* 85: What the ole Nick are ye whisperin' 'bout? 1891 in Leitner *Diamond in Rough* 155: Sometimes…we get nipped by old Nick at the plate. 1914 *DN* IV 123: *Nick.…*The devil. Usually *Old Nick.* 1941 in *DARE:* He ran like…Old Nick. 1943, 1965–70 in *DARE.*

2.a. devilishness; mischief.

1817 in J. Gallatin *Diary* 105: Mamma was a Miss Nicholson; I must have some of the "Old Nick" in me from that side of the family. 1940 Zinberg *Walk Hard* 190: Full of free love and the old nick. 1956 in Harvey *Air Force* 50: Ruth [had] the Old Nick peeking out of her eyes.

b. daylights; stuffing.

1948 J. Stevens *Jim Turner* 9 [ref. to *ca*1910]: When he took a boy in hand to scare the Old Nick out of him, he did an almighty job.

old pie *n.* an admirable or adept fellow.

1882 (quot. at FEATHERBED, 1).

Old Prob *n.* a meteorologist.

*ca*1900 *Buffalo Bill* 95: But on nights when "Old Prob" goes on a spree, leaves the bung out of his water barrel above, prowls around with his flash-box, raising a breeze…the cowboy's voice, like the rest of the outfit, is drowned out. 1942 *ATS* 389: *Old Probabilities, Old Prob,* the chief of the U.S. Weather Bureau.

old rail *n.* a veteran railroader.

1930 *Danger Lights* (film): An old rail like you. 1942 *ATS* 722: Old hand. *Broken-, old or rusty rail.*

old rale *n.* syphilis. Also **old ral.**

1899 J.M. Harrell *Hot Springs Dr.* 77. 1908 W.G. Davenport *Butte & Montana* 17: "Whiskey Bill"…lay dying with…the old ral…in the heart of Butte's underworld district. 1928 W.G. Clugston *Facts You Should Know About Arkansas* (Girard, Kans.: Haldeman-Julius) 23: The *Old Ral* hole, where syphilitic paupers could bathe in the curative waters without charge, is gone forever. 1942 (quot. at OLD JOE). 1956 Longstreet *Real Jazz* 73: It was a tough row, and it got you. The old rale, the sauce, the reefers, or you froze to death on doorways, too stewed to move. 1954–60 *DAS: Old Rale, the.* Syphilis. 1965 Longstreet *Sportin' House* 43: Most likely the innocent nun didn't know the patches were often used to hide the sores of the old rale, as the disease of Venus was called on the frontier.

old red *n. West.* whiskey; REDEYE.

1905 W.S. Kelly *Lariats* 250: "Give me a little 'old red,'" said Jack, as the bartender looked at him.

old salt see s.v. SALT, *n.*

Olds *n.* an Oldsmobile automobile.

1932 in *OEDAS* I: An oil-tempered regulator, automatic choke and thermostatic manifold heat control are refinements destined to play a part in Olds popularity for 1932. 1942 *ATS* 82: Makes of automobiles…*Olds,* an Oldsmobile. 1955 (quot. at OOMPHY). 1959, 1976, 1987 in *OEDAS* I.

Old Sam *n. Black E.* the devil.

1979 J.L. Gwaltney *Drylongso* 227: When I was a girl in the country [*ca*1930], the Negroes used to speak of the devil as Old Sam.

old-school *adj.* Esp. *Rap Music.* old-fashioned; behind the times.

1989 *Village Voice* (N.Y.C.) (June 20) 39: Perez feels the clothes that accompany it juice old-school slickness with youngblood freshness. 1991 in P. Munro *U.C.L.A. Slang* II: *Old school…*of or characterized by a previous time period. 1993 P. Munro *U.C.L.A. Slang* II: That skateboard is old school—you should buy one of the newer models. 1996 *Village Voice* (N.Y.C.) (June 11) 30: [He] bought his girlfriend a pair of old-school Nikes. 1996 *Wayans Bros.* (Warner Bros. TV): Oh, Pop, you're just old-school.

Old Scratch *n.* the devil.

*1740 (cited in Partridge *DSUE* 585). *1762 in *F & H* V 101: He must have sold himself to Old Scratch; and, being a servant of the devil, how could he be a good subject to his Majesty. 1824 W. Irving, in *DARE:* If I mistake not,…you are he commonly called old Scratch. 1838 [Haliburton] *Clockmaker* (Ser. 2) 24: Looking so like Old Scratch. 1849 W. Irving, in Botkin *Treas. Amer. Folk.* 736: Old Scratch must have had a tough time of it. 1862 in C. Brewster *Cruel War* 84: I believe the men would volunteer to go to the "old scratch" himself if they could only have a change. 1862 in Dannett *Civil War Humor* 145: Raisin' the old scratch generally for ten years. 1865 J.H. Browne *Secessia* 34: If we were not all in Tophet, no one could deny we had gone to the old Scratch. 1941 in Botkin *Treas. Amer. Folk.* 123: He had sold his soul to old Scratch. 1949 (quot. at OLD NED). 1949 Gresham *Limbo Tower* 68: The Old Scratch won it! 1965–70 in *DARE.*

old shoe see s.v. SHOE.

old smoky *n.* **1.** *Pris.* an electric chair.

1929 (cited in Partridge *Dict. Und.* 566). 1954–60 *DAS: Old smoky* The electric chair. 1961 Peacock *Valhalla* 111: Being strapped into an electric chair to ride old Smoky.

2. the penis.

1953 in Cray *Erotic Muse* 133: The doc was dumbfounded; Old Smoky was blue.

3. a pistol.

1959 F.L. Brown *Trumbull Pk.* 188: One brick just misses my face, and that's when I jerks out ol' smoky.

old sock *n.* (used as a form of direct address to a man). Also (*obs.*) **old stockings.**

1879 Dacus *Frank & Jesse* 198: That's all, old sock. **1908** W.G. Davenport *Butte & Montana* 18: All right, old stockings, we will fix you out. **1914** S. Lewis, in *DAS:* Yuh—sure, old socks. **1930** Botkin *Folk-Say* 78 [ref. to Indiana, 1860's]: All the boys had names...but they were just called *Socks—Old Socks* (there wasn't any reason for it at all). **1934** in H. Miller *Letters to Emil* 148: Dear old Sock! **1972** M. Rodgers *Freaky Fri.* 73: Annabel, old sock,...I certainly hope you're being careful with yourself! **1989** Hynes & Drury *Howard Beach* 217: Miller issued his standard greeting—"What's up, old sock?"

old soldier *n.* **1.** *Mil.* a malingerer.
   *1805 (cited in Partridge *DSUE* 586). **1858** Viele *Drum* 221: Then came "sick call," especially agreeable to "Old Soldiers."
   2. the stub of a cigar or a plug of tobacco.
   1834 Caruthers *Kentuckian in N.Y.* I i: I smokes the old sodgers what the gentlemen throws on the bar-room floor. **1843–45** T.J. Green *Tex. Exped.* 272: The most usual bet was an *old soldier.* An "old soldier"...is a chew of tobacco....These "old soldiers," after losing all the virtues of the "weed" from long grinding, are dried and smoked in a pipe. **1853** "P. Paxton" *In Texas* 143: I suppose they gave them a certain length of "old soldier" to define the exact quantity of a "labore" (eighty acres). **1853** in Derby *Phoenixiana* 172: With the exception of two or three contributions of "old soldiers" and a half-dollar...nothing has come of it. **1869** in "M. Twain" *Stories* 27: There was a wooden box of sand, sprinkled with cigar stubs and "old soldiers," and a stove with a door hanging by its upper hinge. **1891** Maitland *Slang Dict.* 194: *Old soldiers,* stubs of cigars or empty bottles. **1898** Green *Va. Folk-Speech* 260: *Old soldiers, n.pl.* Ends of cigars and quids of tobacco that have been used.
   3. the penis.—constr. with *the.*
   1977 T. Berger *Villanova* 234: The old soldier stood right up at attention.
   ¶ In phrase:
   ¶ **play the old soldier** *Mil.* to malinger; feign illness; practice deception.
   *1713 in *F & H* V 162: The Devil a Farthing he owes me—but however, I'll put the old soldier upon him. **1809** W. Wheeler *Ltrs.* 7: We all thought he was acting the old soldier, whether it is the case or no, it would be improper for me to judge. **1834** *Mil. & Nav. Mag. of U.S.* (May) 203: If you are not unwell, you must play the old soldier, and bribe Dr. Scott not to insist on your taking the dose. **1862** in M. Lane *Dear Mother* 165: Some perhaps [are] playing the *old soldier.* **1870** Duval *Big-Foot* 240: Thompson...had played "old soldier" upon the Mexicans the whole time.

old-soldier *v. Mil.* to hoodwink, as by feigning illness.
   *1892 (cited in Partridge *DSUE* 586). **1902** *Papers M.I. Hist. Soc. Mass.* XIII 240 [ref. to Civil War]: I...then saw that they were "old-soldiering the surgeon."

old son *n.* (used as a form of direct address to a man).
   1887 in F. Remington *Sel. Letters* 43: Clark Old Son—As the Cornish miners say. **1959** in H. Ellison *Sex Misspelled* 105: Pull out of it, old son.

Old Sparky *n. Pris.* an electric chair.
   1971 J. Brown & A. Groff *Monkey* 84: I was next door to "Old Sparky"—the electric chair. **1981** S. King, in *Rod Serling's TZ Mag.* 28: Foggia['s]...lawyer had told him that he would in all probability be the next to ride Old Sparky. **1986** *Atlanta Constitution* (Apr. 16) 14: Clearing the way for the scheduled 12:01 p.m. electrocution in Florida's "Old Sparky" electric chair. **1994** La. coroner, on *CBS This Morning* (CBS-TV) (Nov. 22): Now he's facing what we call down there [in Louisiana] "Old Sparky"—the electric chair. **1994** *N.Y. Times* (Nov. 27) ("Metro") 49: References to the expected return of "Old Sparky," New York State's electric chair.

old stockings var. OLD SOCK.

Old Tom *n.* strong gin.
   *1821 *Real Life in London* I 122: It is customary in public-houses and gin shops in London and its vicinity to exhibit a cask inscribed with large letters—OLD TOM, intended to indicate the best gin in the house. ***1823** (cited in Partridge *DSUE* 586). **1851** Ely *Wanderings* 163: I think I have a little "Old Tom" on board and you must be thirsty after your dusty tramp. **1867** Clark *Sailor's Life* 113: Tobacco fumes, old tom, and curses are plenty. ***1873** Hotten *Slang Dict.* (ed. 4): *Old Tom,* extra strong gin...Various reasons are given for the use of the words *Old Tom.* The distillers have the sign of a tom cat on their

illuminated placards. **1939** in W.C. Fields *By Himself* 337: That's Old Tom—a very famous name—they named a gin after him.

old top *n.* (used as a form of direct address to a man).
   1887 in F. Remington *Sel. Letters* 42: Well so long old top. *ca*1894 McCloskey *Across Continent* 79: Well, there is the Old Top....my father, of course. **1928** in E. O'Neill *Letters* 310: Sorry, old top!

old vet *n.* OLD SOLDIER.
   1862 in W. Whitman *Civil War* 79: Old vet's (i.e. veterans)—Skedaddlers—some would skulk, of course, on their way to the fight—but not many.

old woman *n.* **1.** a wife; OLD LADY, 2.a.
   a*1775** in *OEDS:* Could my *old woman,* whilst I labour'd thus, At night reward me with a *smouch,* or buss. **1835** in Eliason *Tarheel Talk* 286: Well Old Woman [beginning of letter to wife]. **1843** Oliver *Illinois* 34: The *old woman,* as a wife, of whatever age, is familiarly termed. **1853** "P. Paxton" *In Texas* 113: Thar's his old woman, she'll tell you. **1860–61** R.F. Burton *City of Saints* 212: He had set the "ole woman" to her work. ***1881–84** Davitt *Prison Diary* I 126: His chief support, however, is his "old woman," as he always terms the unfortunate creature who cohabits with him, and whom he frequently ill-uses in the most brutal and cowardly manner. **1905** in "O. Henry" *Works* 1271: The old woman...wants a peach. **1931** Farrell *Young Lonigan* ch. vi: Lee here said his old woman asked him to come to supper.
   2. *Navy.* a swivel-mounted deck gun.
   1823 J.F. Cooper *Pilot* 66: "Why have you thrown the midship gun without the pale of your baptism?" asked the pilot; "or do you know it by the usual title of the 'old woman'?"
   3. a mother; OLD LADY, 1.
   *1834 (cited in Partridge *DSUE* 587). **1931** Farrell *Young Lonigan* ch. vi: She had to help her old woman clean house. She cursed her mother, glibly.
   4. *Cards.* a queen.
   1878 Pinkerton *Crim. Reminiscences* 143: I'll bet you ten dollars you can't tell me which one is the "old woman."
   5. *West.* a male cook, as on a ranch; OLD LADY, 4.
   1922 (quot. at OLD LADY, 4). **1927–30** P.A. Rollins *Jinglebob* 2 [ref. to 1880's]: Did the Old Woman die last night? 'Pears like he did.

olive oil *interj.* [intentional malapropism] au revoir. *Joc.*
   1906 *DN* III 148: *Olive oil*...Au revoir. Facetious. **1911** *DN* III 546: *Olive oil*...Facetious for *au revoir.* **1915** [Swartwood] *Choice Slang* 55: *Olive oil*—Used as a humorous take off on "Au revoir." ***1917** *Living Age* (Nov. 10) 380: Thus one will hear a Cockney saying "Olive oil!" to his friend instead of "Au-revoir." **1918** Streeter *Dere Mable* 2: Olive Oil. Yours Faithfully, Bill. **1920** *DN* V 79: *Olive oil,* au revoir. "I'll see you on Tuesday. *Olive oil.*" **1932** J.T. Farrell *Guillotine Party* 179: Olive Oil, Lil. **1953** Brackett, Reisch & Breen *Niagara* (film): Olive oil, as the French say. **1975** W. Salt *Day of Locust* (film): I'm late! Olive oil!

Oliver *n. Und.* the moon.
   *1753 in Partridge *Dict. Und.* 481: Tis a rum Darky, and Oliver shows; 'tis a good Night, and the Moon shines. ***1781** G. Parker *View of Soc.* II 133: *Oliver don't widdle**...*The Moon [is] not up. **1807** Tufts *Autobiog.* 292 [ref. to 1794]: Oliver...the moon. ***1834** Ainsworth *Rookwood* 19: "Dost see 'em?" "Ay, thanks to old Oliver—yonder they are." **1848** *Ladies' Repository* VIII (Oct.) 315: Oliver, The moon. *Ibid.: Oliver's Night-Cap,* The hour the moon goes down. **1859** Matsell *Vocab.* 61: *Oliver.* The moon. ***1860** Hotten *Slang Dict.* (ed. 2): *Oliver,* the moon....*Nearly obsolete. a*1909 Tillotson *Detective* 93: Oliver—The moon. **1923** *N.Y. Times* (Sept. 9) VIII 2: *Oliver:* The moon. **1928** in Wilstach *Stage Slang* (unp.): "Oliver" may be shining outside the circus.

Omahog *n.* a resident of Omaha, Nebraska. *Joc.*
   1876 in *DA:* A party of eight...Omahogs, or, in other words, citizens of Omaha, left Cheyenne Wednesday for the Black Hills. **1889** in *DA.* **1933** *AS* VIII 4:80: Out-state newspapers often call the inhabitants of Omaha, Nebraska, *Omahogs.* **1949** *AS* XIV 25: *Omahog* for a citizen of Omaha.

on *adj.* **1.a.** drunk.
   *1802 in *OED:* The *Amelia*'s men being a little *on,* could not bear being thwarted. ***1860** Hotten *Slang Dict.* (ed. 2): "To be *on,*" in public-house or vulgar parlance, is synonymous with with getting "tight" or tipsy. **1883** Keane *Blue-Water* 189: Now you may believe that those who came aboard "a bit on" had done so much work by this time, that the liquor they had aboard was pretty well dead in them. **1891** Maitland

Slang Dict. 194: "To be on" is to be drunk or getting that way. *1894 in *OED*: Pimlico, who was now slightly "on"…was shouted down.

b. *Narc.* intoxicated by an illicit drug; HIGH. See also GET ON, *v.*

   1946 Mezzrow & Wolfe *Really Blues* 186 [ref. to 1930's]: I know I'm gonna get straight now, I know you're gonna put me on. **1947** Lindesmith *Opiate Addiction* 217: On, to be: To be using drugs. **1952** Brossard *Darkness* 11: He laughed again. He was really on. **1952** Mandel *Angry Strangers* 30: You wanna get on? I got some pot stashed by the subway. *a*1953 in *Amer. Jour. Socio.* LIX 238: I got on a big laughing kick.…Then I really knew I was on. **1954** in *Social Problems* III (1955) 42: I was already getting on (using marihuana). **1956** Holiday & Dufty *Lady Sings* 114: When I was on, I was on and nobody gave me any trouble. **1959** *Social Problems* VII 244: Musicians playing while "on" (having taken marijuana). **1964** Wepman et al. *The Life* 56: They went to his pad to get on. **1965** N. Hentoff, in *New Yorker* (July 3) 34: There were women who showed up here in the office—women I never knew were on. **1966** Braly *On Yard* 77: If I could just score enough to really get on. **1966–67** P. Thomas *Mean Streets* 117: You on, man?…I got some H.

2. making a wager; IN.

   *1812 in *OED:* They declared themselves off, a thing unknown in sporting; after they had been on. *1873 Hotten *Slang Dict.* (ed. 4): "I'm ON" also expresses a person's acceptance of an offered bet. **1880** (quot. at (4), below). **1891** Maitland *Slang Dict.* 194: To "get on" to a bet is to accept or a man may be "put on" to a "good thing." **1909** Irwin *Con Man* 58: I'm on for a five.

3. Orig. *Entertainment Industry.* behaving as though on stage or on camera; attempting to be the center of attention; (*hence*) performing or functioning at one's best. [Though approximating current usage, the *1869 quot. means literally 'appearing on stage'.]

   [*1869 Logan *Foot Lights* 108: I was not always what I am now. Time was when these eyes, now dim with tears, were—no, hang it I'm not "on" now. My father kept a large public house in Kent, and he had a pretty barmaid.] **1960** Kirkwood *Pony* 247: Merwin was pretty much "on" all evening. **1964** E. Wilson *Wilson's N.Y.* 27: He's Always On— He's always giving a performance. **1973** Haney *Jock* 100: Robyn Smith is both a jockey and an actress, and she always plays both roles simultaneously. She is "on" all the time. **1980** *Daily News* (N.Y.) (Manhattan ed.) (Sept. 10) 9: Her workaholic needs enable me to relax. I don't have to be "on" with Helen. **1983** Van Riper *Glenn* 144: It was Glenn who was always "on," anxious to go into his patriotic act whenever he was stopped in public or asked to speak. **1988** *Newsweek* (Mar. 28) 33: Presidential candidates have to be "on" nearly every waking minute. **1988** Beck & Massman *Rich Men, Single Women* 332: It saved her from having to be "on" with people who didn't make her feel "on." **1994** *Seinfeld* (NBC-TV): You always have to be *on.* **1997** *N.Y. Times Mag.* (Apr. 20) 55: We are only passively, not actively, wholeheartedly, specializing in our emotional ties. We aren't "on."

4. WISE; well aware (of); fully comprehending the nature (of).—freq. constr. with *to* (someone or something).

   1876 in F. Remington *Sel. Letters* 12: I've got a black-eye, playing football. It's a nice thing to have, why don't you get on. **1877** in Asbury *Gem of Prairie* 135: Very nearly all of the boys are on to you. **1878** *Nat. Police Gaz.* (May 18) 3: The lawful spouse "was on" to her coming. **1880** *N.Y. Clipper Almanac* 45: On.—To be "on" is to back a horse. A person is also "on" who fancies he knows what will be the outcome of a race that other persons believe is to be conducted squarely. **1882** Peck *Peck's Sunshine* 95: The livery men have "got onto the racket." **1883** Peck *Bad Boy* 138: I am on to you bigger than an elevator. **1885** in *OEDS:* He hoped to sell the cavalry a large lot of supplies, but Major Van Horn was "on." **1885** *Puck* (Apr. 22) 115: That's all right. I got on to that long ago. **1887** Peck *Pvt. Peck* 176: The officer was "on" all right enough. **1887** Walling *N.Y. Chief of Police* 316: O, I'm right onto *you* with all four feet. **1887** Flinn *Chicago Police* 386: They must get him out and away before the police could "get onto" him. **1889** Pierson *Vagabond's Honor* 90: Ah, it tuk us a long, long time to git onto the change in his cranium. **1889** Meriwether *Tramp at Home* 216: I say, mate, you ain't onto this 'ere boardin'-house racket, air ye? **1891** Maitland *Slang Dict.* 195: To "be on to" a thing is to understand it. **1891** Clurman *Nick Carter* 21: We're "onto" you, my man. River pirates don't go around with wigs and false mustaches. **1893** in Philips *Newspaper* 62: As to how the newspapers "got on to her." **1896** Ade *Artie* 25: I'm on to you bigger'n

a house. *Ibid.* 102: Everybody must be on. **1899** Ade *Fables* 30: The Preacher didn't know what all This meant, and he didn't care, but you can rest easy that the Pew-Holders were On in a minute. **1904** in "O. Henry" *Works* 1134: They ain't on, at all. **1904** in "O. Henry" *Works* 481: I thought he was on. **1905** *McClure's Mag.* (Sept.) 516: I'll make the collar. Are you on? **1907** "O. Henry" *Works* 1418: The lady can wear 'em along with us and nobody'll be on. **1908** Beach *Barrier* 107: Cut that out, Lee. We're on. **1913** Jocknick *Early Days* 123 [ref. to 1870's]: Thus his dogs soon got "onto" their jobs (to use his expression). **1916–17** in McManus *Bringing Up Father* 8: By Golly—I'm on! It's nearly Christmas! **1929** W.R. Burnett *Iron Man* 28: "I'm on," said Coke. **1967** IUFA *Folk Speech* (Jan. 2): "Ring the bell, conductor, I'm on, I'm on"—I get your meaning.

5. planned; (*hence*) in progress. Now *colloq.*

   *a*1881 G.C. Harding *Misc. Writings* 108: When a fresh revolution is "on." **1930** Biggers *Chan Carries On* 49: We went to a show.…We didn't have nothing else on, so we stuck it out.

6. correct.—often constr. with *dead.*

   1888 Pinkerton *Scaffold* 11: I was "dead on." **1895** Townsend *Fadden* 5: "Is dis Chimmie Fadden?" says 'e. "Ye're dead on," says I. **1976** Braly *False Starts* 20: But for me, he was dead on. I was much better off.

7. ready or eager, esp. to take part.

   1899 Boyd *Shellback* 236: I'm not on for a cold bath to-night, and I don't suppose either of us wants to leave our carcass in the Pacific. **1899–1900** (quot. at DITCH, *v.,* 1). **1923** McAlmon *Companion Volume* 34: I'm on. Let's go. **1916** in Lardner *Round Up* 113: "Take it or leave it."… "All right. I'm on." **1938** in Conklin *Sci. Fi. Omnibus* 11: Well, I need an asseestant. We're going to find out about this hair beezness. Are you on?

¶ In phrases:

¶ **get on to** to look at; notice; observe appreciatively or critically.

   1882 in *N.Y. Folk. Qly.* XXIV 169 (1968): Oh, get on to our nobby style,/We are happy all the while. **1885** *Puck* (Apr. 22) 118: Hi, git on to Shorty. **1885** in Saunders *Parodies of Whitman* 59: Get on to my red shirt. **1887** Walling *N.Y. Chief of Police* 311: Hi, fellers! Git onto de Sheenys! **1889** Pierson *Vagabond's Honor* 90: Ah, it tuk us a long, long time to git onto the change in his cranium. **1890** in F. Remington *Sel. Letters* 93: There aint any little boys to say "git on to his waist band." **1891** in Outcault *Yellow Kid* 129: Git on to de dude. **1892** Bierce *Beetles* 150: Get onto the…Joo! **1892** Crane *Maggie* 36: Git onto deh mug on deh blokie. Dat's enough to make a feller turn hand-springs in 'is sleep. **1893** W.K. Post *Harvard* 153: Get on to de legs! **1896** (quot. at *get next* s.v. NEXT). **1897** Norris *Vandover* 358: Ah, get on to the red hat! **1899** Norris *McTeague* 17: Get on to the size of him, anyhow. **1918** O'Reilly *Roving & Fighting* 7: Get on to the guy with the high-water pants!

¶ **get on to (oneself)** to stop (one's) foolishness; realize the truth about (one's) own actions.

   1897 Norris *Vandover* 570: "Ah, get on to yourself!" shouted Geary, now thoroughly disgusted. **1926** Thompson *Youth's Companion* (Nov. 11) 46: "Get on to yourself," added Patrick. "If you don't register for the draft, you will be arrested." **1942** Horman & Corley *Capts. of Clouds* (film): I thought you'd get on to yourself, sucker.

¶ **have it on (someone)** to have an advantage over (someone); excel.

   1908 in H.C. Fisher *A. Mutt* 47: The young man…has your goat. In other words he has it on you. *Ibid.* 66: Nobody has anything on Mutt when it comes to doing things in grand style. **1919** in Gelman *Photoplay* 32: The girl of today, as compared with her sister of preceding generations has it "on" the latter…when it comes to having something for which to wish and dream and work. **1930** Farrell *Calico Shoes* 6: "If I was as goofy as you, I'd do something about it."…"Yeh. Well, I ain't got nothing on you."

¶ **put (someone) on** to tell; introduce; familiarize.

   *a*1893 W.K. Post *Harvard* 201: Put me on to de young one. **1895** in J. London *Tramp Diary* 61: If I spots'm I'll put yer on. **1898** L.J. Beck *Chinatown* 318: I'm goin' to pull off anoder in a few days, and I'll put yer on, see. **1901** A.H. Lewis *Croker* 59: I'll put you onto what's the matter with the theaters. **1906** in Bierce *Letters* 124: I'm not familiar with the poetry of William Vaughan Moody. Can you "put me on?"

¶ **you're on** "I accept your offer, challenge, or bet."

   1899 Cullen *Tales* 77: "Give you forty cents for every bunch of 'em you sell for a dollar." "You're on," said I. **1902** Cullen *More Tales* 18: "Come on in and have some breakfast."..."Not giving you a short answer," said I, "you're on." **1902–03** Ade *People You Know* 44: You're on! Get your License to-morrow morning. **1905** in "O. Henry" *Works* 1442: You're on!...Fifty dollars to $25 I take Annie to the dance. **1907** in H.C. Fisher *A. Mutt* 19: "Even money he hits the ground in 3 seconds." "You're on." **1911** Van Loan *Big League* 52: Thursday night, eh? You're on! **1911** *Hampton's Mag.* (Jan.) 122: Damn you! You're on! **1913** in Blackbeard & Williams *Smithsonian Comics* 26: "Harken Boy, dost wish to purchase *punkins*?"..."You're on, Bo!" **1917** *Forum* (Dec.) 688: A sign slowly comes up behind the enemy's sand bags...."Americans, Exchange With Us Cigars for Good German Beer. We Send Out One Soldier With Beer, You Send Out One Soldier With Cigars. Nobody Shoot."...Then you see a sign come up from over the American trenches: "You're On." **1987** *My Sister Sam* (NBC-TV): "Let's take a coffee break." "You're on."

on *prep.* **1.** (of a joke or prank) at the expense of. Now *colloq.*

1866 in *OEDS:* There may be a joke about it; but if there is, it is on the Colonel, for he told me so. **1866** in B. Harte *Harte's Calif.* 31: The conventional expression of a joke is "to have a good thing *on* such and such a one."

2. (of a treat or bill) to be paid for by; charged to. Now *colloq.*

1871 in *OEDS:* After the first round they said it was "on me." **1893** W.K. Post *Harvard* 58: The return trip would be "on Mr. Holworthy." **1914** S. Lewis *Mr. Wrenn* 12: This lunch is on me. Let me pay for it, Charley. **1943** in P. Smith *Letter from Father* 246: The "dicks" had something to eat on me. **1968** *Saturday Review* (Mar. 16) 10: "Waiter, may I have the check, please?" "No, no, this is on me, boy."

3. *Gamb.* having placed a wager upon.

1902 T.A. Dorgan, in Zwilling *TAD Lexicon* 120: The wise guinea from Chicago is "on" Root.

4. *Narc.* addicted to (a usu. specified drug). Now *S.E.*

1925 *Amer. Mercury* (Feb.) 196: They are "on the stuff." **1926** Finerty *Criminalese* 41: On junk—Dope user. **1954** *Time* (Nov. 8) 70: *On*, prep. Addicted to a drug. **1955** in *Tenn. Folk. Soc. Bull.* XXII (1956) 26: "What's he on?" means "What drug is he high on?" **1996** Penningroth *Chasing Dragon* (film): I'm *asking* you! What are you *on*?

¶ **In phrases:**

¶ **have (something) on (someone)** *Police & Und.* to have (incriminating evidence) against (someone). Now *colloq.*

1909 C. Chrysler *White Slavery* 70: "No dick has anything on you."...No detective can make a case against you. **1911** E. Howe *Sayings* 191: Haven't you heard something "on" everyone in town? **1922** Ruhm *Detective* 23: I'm not a murderer....I didn't see where they had a thing on me. **1923** in D. Hammett *Continental Op* 35: What have you got on him? **1929** "E. Queen" *Roman Hat* 74: Cronin, an assistant D.A. at the time, couldn't get a thing on him. *Ibid.* 120: Field had something on you, and he thought that that was a good time to tell you about it. **1938** Chandler *Big Sleep* 57: You ain't got nothing on me.

¶ **on it, 1.** in favor (of something); (*hence*) ready or eager (for something, esp. a fight).

1862 C.F. Browne *Artemus Ward* 96: "Do you bleeve in...the immaculateness of the Mormin Church and the Latter-day Revelashuns?" Sez I, "I'm on it!" I make it a pint to git along plesunt. **1865** J.R. Browne, in *Harper's Mo.* (July) 158: He was "on it" or I greatly misjudged his countenance...."I see you're on it." "You bet," was the answer. "When do you expect the fight to come off?" **1867** in A.K. McClure *Rocky Mtns.* 211: When a Western man declines any proposition, he "ain't on it." **1868** J. Chisholm *So. Pass* 108: It isn't safe to meddle with a Buffalo, unless you mean to finish him at one shot. Don't fool with him 'cause he aint on it. **1870** "M. Twain," in A.L. Scott *Twain's Poetry* 80: Them three smooth chaps was on it, and wasn't skeered at danger. **1871** "M. Twain" *Roughing It* 245: I'm *on* it, old man! Let 'em out! *Ibid.* 251: Pard, he was *on* it! He was on it bigger than an Injun! **1871** Schele de Vere *Americanisms* 513: *To be on it*, is a recent slang term, meaning to be ready for a fight. **1873** J. Miller *Modocs* 116: I hope the Indians are "on it"—hope to God they are "heeled." **1877** in Stallard *Glittering Misery* 113: I deny seducing the girl. I have proof that the girl has been on it before, that she has made solicitations of the soldiers at the garrison. **1882** in Sweet *Texas* 31: You don't know who I am. I'm *on* it, I want you to know....when it comes to fightin' Indians. **1916** *DN* IV 326: On it....Lustful, esp. at the immediate time of desire.

2. (*broadly*) shrewd; cunning.

1865 in *DA:* She's tolerable peert—the old 'oman is. Oh, she's on it, you bet. **1868–71** Leland *Breitmann's Ballads* 101: Dese vitches...are *on* id, I see.

¶ **on the ——** **1.** (used before nominalized verbs) engaged in or eager to engage in —*ing*. See also *on the shoot* s.v. SHOOT, *n.*

1851 [G. Thompson] *Jack Harold* 60: I caught them on the snooze*....*Snooze*, asleep. **1866** Dimsdale *Vigilantes* 122: Marshland said he did not wish to go, as he could make money without murder. He was, he said, "on the rob, but not on the kill." **1880** *Harper's* (Nov.) 838: Mate,...I ain't on the marry no more. **1883** Peck *Bad Boy* 160: There are brave men, I know, that are on the marry, but none of them would want to be brevet father to a cherubim like me, except he got pretty good wages. **1883** *Life* (Jan. 11) 22: I ain't much on the write, but I haven't been 'round the streets of New York ten years for nothing, and what I don't know about [Penal] Codes ain't worth knowing. **1884** in Lummis *Letters* 167: The men were on the sell. **1906** in A. Adams *Chisholm Trail* 212: There was a number of the...gang...still on the rustle. **1968** S.O. Barker *Rawhide* 7: They sometimes talk as serious as a preacher on the pray. **1972** D. Pendleton *Boston Blitz* 55: There was everything to lose and nothing—absolutely nothing—to gain out there in that darkness with Bolan on the blitz.

2. (used before adjs. and advs.) (used as an intensive).

1901 Irwin *Sonnets* (unp.): Gunboat shoes and half-hose on the gay. *Ibid.*: Say, will she.../Shovel me dirt, or treat me on the grand. **1904** *Life in Sing Sing* 263: Everything was on the good, when we got a blow. **1933** Ersine *Prison Slang* 19: Blackie's been on the blue for a month [*i.e.*, blue, sad].

once-over *n.* **1.** a visual inspection; appraising glance. Now *colloq.*

1913 T.A. Dorgan, in Zwilling *TAD Lexicon* 61: I jes gave it "de once ovah." *Ibid.*: Think I'll go in and give the jury the once over. **1912–14** in E. O'Neill *Lost Plays* 174: Phew! Talk about the icy once-over! She looked at me as if I was a wet dog. **1914** in E. O'Neill *Letters* 23: I give your script the "once-over." **1913–15** Van Loan *Taking the Count* 127: I see her givin' me the once-over a while ago. **1918** Wagar *Spotter* 9: I'm going to have a once-over at the inside of your room. **1920** Colyer *323rd Field Arty.* 29: Every one busied himself giving, from a distance, our first European city the "once-over." **1920** J. Weaver *In American* 19: One day I hands her quite a piece o' work/To give it the once-over. **1922** E. Rice *Adding Machine* 110: Give me the once-over, you guys. Do I look like a murderer. **1924** Marks *Plastic Age* 161: We'd all be pulled up to heaven where Christ would give us the once-over. **1951** *Sat. Eve. Post* (May 19) 92: He wasn't the first one to give her the once-over. **1958** Drury *Advise and Consent* 131: "And I," Vasily Tashikov murmured, his little shrewd eyes...giving the entire gathering a split-second once-over. **1978** W. Brown *Tragic Magic* 7: He...immediately began giving Tonya the once-over. **1978** Pilcer *Teen Angel* 115: The rest of the class gave her the once-over. **1981** Raban *Old Glory* 28: I got a brief once-over from behind a pair of clip-on dark glasses. **1988** P. Beck & P. Massman *Rich Men, Single Women* 202: He gave her a flirtatious once-over. **1987–89** M.H. Kingston *Tripmaster Monkey* 59: He and she gave each other the old once-over. **1995** *New Yorker* (Oct. 9) 33: The machine gave you the once-over, like a night-club bouncer, before granting passage.

2. a quick or superficial treatment.

[**1908** T.A. Dorgan, in Zwilling *TAD Lexicon* 61: I want a shave Tony. Once over and let it be fast.] **1931** Perelman & Johnstone *Monkey Business* (film): "How 'bout a shave?" "Sure, give me a once-over." **1942** *ATS* 255: *Once-over*, a hasty preparation. **1950** *Time* (Oct. 2) 83: With 20 years of hard riding, most of the political animals on the original *Merry-Go-Round* have worn out or fallen off. *The Truman Merry-Go-Round* gives the once-over, not very lightly, to their replacements. **1952** in *DAS:* One of this brothers gave him a...shirt and a razor for a hasty once-over.

once-over *v.* to inspect.

1920 Ade *Hand-Made Fables* 245: Clara once-overed the whole Layout through the Specs that she carried on a Mother-of-Pearl Handle.

one *n.* **1.** a blow, as with the fist. Cf. similar senses at *OED* def. 1.d.

1853 Lippard *New York* 97: I'll tell you what I'll give you....I'll give you *one* under yer, if you don't keep quiet. **1877** (quot. at PASTE). **1880** Small *Mother-in-Law* 21: I was sending out my "awful right" for the purpose of giving that imaginary mother-in-law one right on her "bugle." **1882** Field *Tribune Primer* 105: His Mother complimented him on his Truthfulness, but gave him One in the Neck for using Bad Grammar. **1903** T.W. Jackson *Slow Train* 56: He gave me one right across the head and knocked me through the window. **1941** Schulberg *Sammy* 230: Sheik would run in and lay one on him.

2. an extraordinary person. Cf. *one of 'em*, below.

1880 in *OEDS*: Tittering, and now and then, "O Miss Annie, don't, pray!" "O Miss Annie, you are a one!" *ca*1940 in Botkin *Treas. Amer. Folk.* 526: He was a one, that Big Frank!

3. a drink, as of an alcoholic beverage. See also COLD ONE, 2; COOL ONE; TALL ONE.

1899 Cullen *Tales* 57: I had the man bring me three high ones.

4. any; a single.—used postnominally. See also *day one*, below.

1941 in Botkin *Treas. Amer. Folk.* 125: He didn't have penny one on him but he had a fist full of tricks. **1946** Mezzrow & Wolfe *Really Blues* 149: Not penny one did I have. **1949** Quigley *Corsica* 109: I ain't seen Thing One of this war! **1951** in W.S. Burroughs *Letters* 103: There is not factory 1 in Ecuador. **1960** Leckie *Marines!* 4 [ref. to WWII]: Pistol Pete [a certain Japanese gun] ain't let out fart one all day. **1986** *Hunter* (NBC-TV): Nobody thinks you had thing one to do with it. **1991** *N.Y. Times* (Nov. 3) ("Arts & Leisure") 1: Looked at from a business sense, it doesn't deserve dollar one.

¶ In phrases:

¶ **day one** the beginning; long ago. Cf. earlier **(4)**, above.

1984 Hindle *Dragon Fall* 79: Real pals from day one. **1987** Univ. Tenn. instructor, age 38: She hasn't done a lick of work since day one. **1994** B. Maher *True Story* 175: Buck had caught on from day one that The Club...followed no logical system. **1996** *N.Y. Times* (May 29) B6: He sent negative vibrations about the strength of the case since Day One and it filters down to the grand jury.

¶ **good one** a joke. Now *colloq.*

*1813 in *OEDS*: Now this was a good one, for everybody knew [etc.]. **1842** Mogridge *Soldiers & Sailors* 32: I'm came here to be spliced, and spliced I'll be. Wait a fortnight! that's a good un! **1879** Rooney *Quaint Conundrums* 4: A good one happened at a camp meeting. **1896** Ade *Artie* 108: That's a good one on you.

¶ **have one on** to be intoxicated.

1894 F.P. Dunne, in Schaaf *Dooley* 110: An' oh! but he had a good wan on, Jawn, a good wan.

¶ **one of 'em** a remarkable or estimable person.

1846 Durivage & Burnham *Stray Subjects* 95: HAM was one of 'em—*he* was! He "knew sufficient to get out of the rain," albeit he wasn't thought *very* witty! *Ibid.* 145: Catch "No. 3" napping, if you can! He's *one* of 'em, and has been there! **1847** in G.W. Harris *High Times* 68: He was "one of 'em," as sure as you live. **1848** J. Scott *Encarnation* 112: When questioned about it, he answered that, "if he was to die,...he might as well die happy." He was "one of them." **1848** Baker *Glance at N.Y.* 22: Did you ever see George Christy play de bones? ain't he one of 'em? *Ibid.* 28: I'll show you my prize lamb [girlfriend]—she's one of 'em. **1849** [G. Thompson] *Countess* 21: The sporting boys...'bet high" that she was "one of 'em." *Ibid.* 50: Kate was exquisitely beautiful, and decidedly "one of 'em." **1850** "N. Buntline" *G'hals of N.Y.* 41: That feller's one of 'em. **1850** G.G. Foster *Gas-Light* 39: The widow is one of 'em—she can travel, *she* can! **1865** Derby *Squibob Papers* 22: Isabella...had a srong [*sic*] conviction that Columbus was "one of them." *a*1867 in G.W. Harris *Lovingood* 40: She outbreeds enything frum thar tu the river, takin in the minks....Oh! she's wun ove 'em, an' sumtimes she's two ur three, she is.

one arm *n.* **1.** see s.v. ONE-ARM, *adj.*

2. a post or operation that can be handled by one person.

1958 *N.Y. Times Mag.* (Mar. 16) 88: *One-arm*—A [policeman's] post covering only one side of the street. **1974** Radano *Cop Stories* 59: I was on a late tour, a one-arm post about a half a block long. There I was twelve years on the job...and I'm all alone. **1961** H. Ellison *Gentleman Junkie* 46: He walked into the little one-arm grocery.

one-arm *adj.* being a cheap eating place. Usu. in phr. **one-arm joint.** Also used absol.

1912 in *OEDS*: Everybody's saying "Stop, Look, Listen!"...the white aprons in the one-arm lunch rooms say it now when you kick on the size of the buns. **1915** in *OEDS*: One arm joint, a chair dairy lunch.

1919 *Our Navy* (June) 12: I'da made that guy's puss look like a week old cream puff in a one-arm joint. **1923** T. Dreiser, in Riggio *Dreiser-Mencken Letters* II 485: I know a one-arm lunch stand around the corner. **1927** [Fliesler] *Anecdota* 108: The waitress in a one-armed beanery determined to have some fun. **1928** Hecht & MacArthur *Front Page* 462: When you're crawling up fire escapes, and eating Christmas dinner in a one-armed joint, don't forget your old pal, Hildy Johnson! **1929** in Galewitz *Great Comics* 110: I'd rather go out and eat in a one arm joint. **1939–40** O'Hara *Pal Joey* 56: She went with me to this one-arm where I eat. **1942–43** C. Jackson *Lost Weekend* 92: The bars;...the bowling alleys;...the one-arm joints. **1948** Erskine *All My Sons* (film): This isn't a one-arm joint you're running here any more. **1948** Manone & Vandervoort *Trumpet* 238: So we went to a one-arm joint over on Seventh Avenue to buy some dessert. **1957** Murtagh & Harris *First Stone* 4: They hang around the one-arm joints where people eat standing up, a fifteen-cent slice of pizza pie that drips tomato sauce, a frankfurter or a burger (also fifteen cents) washed down by a soft drink that costs only a dime. **1959** Goffman *Presentation of Self* 129: [Cheap] restaurants...called "one-arm joints." **1963** in H. Ellison *Sex Misspelled* 58: We pulled in at a one-arm joint on 101. **1970** Gattzden *Black Vendetta* 78: Kippy's was a short-order, one-armed joint. **1971** Cole *Rook* 141: The place he chose was a smoky one-arm where a lot of men in leather coats were sitting around drinking coffee and talking about strikes.

one-armed bandit *n.* *Gamb.* an automatic slot machine for gambling. Now *S.E.*

1938 in *OEDS*: The Court of Appeals at Annapolis yesterday declared...that the so-called "one-arm bandit" type of slot machine is illegal. **1940** Thompson & Raymond *Gang Rule in N.Y.* 379: In relation to sums put into them the machines paid off so little that Westbrook Pegler once called them the "one armed bandits." **1943** in Truman *Dear Bess* 501: There's roulette, blackjack, one-armed bandits (slot machines). *1945 S.J. Baker *Austral. Lang.* 88: *Ned Kelly* is displacing *one-armed bandit* for a poker machine. **1950** *N.Y. Times* (Mar. 12) VI 59: In Idaho racing handbooks are out, legally; one-armed bandits (slot machines) in. **1956** Lennart *Meet Me in Las Vegas* (film): There's a one-armed bandit—a slot machine—in the lobby.

one-armed Johnnie *n.* *Petroleum Industry.* a hand pump.

1937 *AS* (Apr.) 154: One Armed Johnnie. Hand pump. **1944** Boatright & Day *Hell to Breakfast* 147: A hand-operated pump used to lift water out of a "cellar" (the hole around a well head while it is being drilled) is a "one-armed Johnnie."

one-armed paper-hanger *n.* (used in various similes).—usu. constr. with *busy as a.*

1908 in "O. Henry" *Works* 353: And then I got as busy as a one-armed man with the nettle-rash pasting on wall-paper. **1918** R.J. Casey *Cannoneers* 224: Still working like a one-armed paper-hanger for one division or another. **1924** Lardner *Haircut* 180: I...have been busier than a one-armed paper hanger the last week. **1932** Ford *Worst Taste* 184: This business packs more funny kinks than a one-armed paper-hanger! **1936** C. Sandburg *People, Yes* 64: He was quiet as a wooden-legged man on a tin/roof and as busy as a one-armed paper-hanger/with the hives. **1949** Van Praag *Day Without End* 206: We've been busy as a one-armed paper-hanger with the crabs back here. [**1952** C. Sandburg *Young Strangers* 165 [ref. to *ca*1880]: We tried to picture the man we heard of, "busy as a paper-hanger with the hives."]

one-digit midget *n.* *Army.* SINGLE-DIGIT MIDGET.

1986 Thacker *Pawn* 142 [ref. to 1970]: Pretty bummed out for a One-Digit Midget.

one-eighty *n.* [fr. *one-hundred-and-eighty degree turn*] Orig. *Mil. Av.* a complete reversal in thinking or behavior.

[**1942** *ATS* 714: One-eighty, a 180-degree turn when coming in for a landing, requirement for license tests.] **1956** Heflin *USAF Dict.* 357: One-eighty, *n.*....A reversal of stand, policy, or the like, as in "he did a one-eighty and agreed with the commander." *Colloq.* **1969** *Current Slang I & II* 27: Do a 180, *v.* To change one's mind or actions completely.—Air Force Academy cadets. **1984** *Hardcastle & McCormick* (ABC-TV): Thirty years later he shows up doing a total one-eighty. **1984** Nettles & Golenbock *Balls* 9: I wonder if George will do a 180 and make a trade to get Reggie back. **1985** T. Wells *444 Days* 9: The driver did a quick 180 to get out of there. **1996** *N.Y. Observer* (Oct. 28) 1: It's a done deal....Assuming Tina doesn't do a 180...all that remains is getting some signatures on paper.

one-eye *n.* the penis.—usu. considered vulgar. *Joc.*

   1961 Gover *$100 Misunderstanding* 136: I can' stand t'think o' all them mothahless Joe College one-eyes I'm gonna haff t'work on, I go t'work.

one-eyed *adj.* **1.** (used in var. joc. metaphors designating the penis).—usu. considered vulgar.

   *ca***1775** *Frisky Songster* 92: Toasts and Sentiments....Adam's dagger....The one-eyed stag. **1972** R. Wilson *Playboy's Forbidden Words* 183: *One-Eyed Monster* The penis. **1974** Rhinebeck, N.Y., man, age 24: When I was working on construction last year there was one guy who called his penis *the one-eyed monster.* Like he'd say, "Then I gave her a look at the one-eyed monster." **1976** *UTSQ:* Penis...*One-eyed trouser snake.* **1976** Hayden *Voyage* 196: Outa th' slot in th' one-eyed worm. **1978** in *Maledicta* VI (1982) 23: Penis...*one-eyed worm.* **1986** Eble *Campus Slang* (Nov.) 6: *One-eyed wonder worm*—penis. **1987** Frumkes *Street Trash* (film): Yeah, you just want my one-eyed wonder worm, aye? **1988** Dye *Outrage* 185: He'd like to...cut loose the terrible one-eyed trouser worm. **1990** in *AS* (1992) 380: One-eyed trouser snake. **1993** P. Munro *U.C.L.A. Slang II:* One-eyed rocket...penis.

   2. tiny; ONE-HORSE.

   1871 D.G. Rossetti, in *OEDS:* A little hamlet called Kelmscott, the nearest town to which is Lechlade,—that being however but a "one-eyed" town as the Yankees say. **1935** Mackenzie *Been Places* 67: Who the hell would stow away to get into a lousy one-eyed hole like this town?

   3. *Auto.* having only one working headlight.

   *a***1937** Dollard *Southern Town* 103: All too frequently at night one comes on "one-eyed" cars on the road, or cars without tail lights. **1972** Buell *Shrewsdale* 10: It was a car, a one-eyed car. *a***1979** Toelken *Dyn. of Folklore* 252: I'll be down to get you in my one-eyed Ford.

   4. *Poker.* (of face cards of modern conventional design, esp. when used as wild cards) depicted in profile.

   1962 Olmsted *Heads I Win* 45: Deuces often are used as wild cards, and other common ones are "one-eyed jacks." **1963** in T.L. Clark *Dict. Gamb.* 141: One-eyed jack...one-eyed king. **1978** Diehl *Sharky's Machine* 81: You remind me of a one-eyed jack. **1983** P. Brickman *Risky Business* (film): Deuces, aces, one-eyed faces wild. **1986** S. Bauer *Amazing Stories* 222: Deuces, queens, and one-eyed kings wild.

one-eyed hash *n.* a serving of hash with a fried egg on top.

   1966 Braly *On Yard* 127: It was one-eyed hash, a scoop of hash...hidden under a...fried egg.

one-eyed monster *n.* **1.** a television set. *Joc.*

   1967 Tamony *Americanisms* (No. 16) 7: Plick McGill, the one-armed juggler on the one-eyed monster. **1968** Baker et al. *CUSS* 165: *One-Eyed Monster.* Television.

   2. see s.v. ONE-EYED, 1.

one-finger salute *n.* **1.** FINGER, 4.a. *Joc.*

   1966 (quot. at BIRD, 9.d.). **1982** *Maclean's* (Nov. 1) 18: Trudeau's charismatic coinage has been devalued after 14 years in office—particularly after his one-finger salute during his western train ride this summer.

   2. *Med.* a digital examination of the prostate. *Joc.*

   1984 Knoxville, Tenn., physician, age *ca*40: Army doctors call a prostate exam a *one-finger salute.*

one-horse *adj.* small and inconsequential; undersized; extremely limited; second-rate. Now *colloq.*, esp. in phr. **one-horse town.**

   1853 in *OEDS:* These *one-horse* meetings are got up by men whose capital consists in *brass.* **1854** Yellow Bird *Murieta* 44: A careless spree at a little "one-horse" grocery. **1858** [S. Hammett] *Piney Woods* 41: I...found a little one-horse boat a going to the island. **1858** in G.W. Harris *High Times* 137: I speck that wer sorter prayin' in his durn'd one horse way. **1859** Avery *Comical Stories* 52: I'm done with *one-horse bedsteads,* I am. **1860–61** R.F. Burton *City of Saints* 276: They have been served with "small fry" politicians and "one-horse" officials. **1861** in Lowell *Works* 225: A one-hoss, starn-wheel chaplin. **1861** Wilkie *Iowa First* 76: It was none of the ordinary, "one-horse" processions usually gotten up in country towns like Dubuque. **1861** in Hough *Soldier in W.* 50: I believe I have told you all that would interest in this monotonous place, for it is emphatically a *one-horse* town. **1862** C.F. Browne *A. Ward* 153: If these one-horse offishuls cood know how I see threw all their moves...thayd stop kissin my hands & fawnin over me. **1863** in G. Whitman *Letters* 155: Went to the Theater (a one-horse affair). *a***1865** in J.I. Robertson *Blue & Gray* 111: My

girl is none of your one-horse girls. **1865** in H. Johnson *Talking Wire* 295: Editors of some of those little one-horse papers. **1865** M.S. White *Pris. Life* 83: The *Celt* [a ship] was a mean...half painted one horse affair. **1866** in Hilleary *Webfoot* 148: The one-horse Theatre...is in full blast now. *a***1867** in G.W. Harris *Lovingood* 128: Ef a wun-hoss preacher sits intu the pulpit while a two-hoss one preaches, don't they print hit that he 'sisted? *Ibid.* 193: Thar lay Doltin on a low one-hoss bedstid. **1887** *Lantern* (N.O.) (Oct. 29) 3: He keeps a one-horse grocery. **1896** Anderson *Camp Fire Stories* 93: Yew Feds is a mean, sneakin', ornery set anyhow; jest one-hoss. Yew-uns steal, and hook, and lie, and play the divil right smart. **1907** J.C. Lincoln *Cape Cod* 158: A little one-horse coral island. **1912** *Hampton's Mag.* (Jan.) 842: There used to be a little one horse county jail on the main line of the Santa Fe. **1915** C. Peters *Autobiog.* 103: A lot of one-horse Politicians. **1928** Dahlberg *Bottom Dogs* 3: A one-horse town like St. Joseph or Joplin. **1933** in R.E. Howard *Iron Man* 53: There's a sort of one-horse fight club here. **1973** B. Joel *Captain Jack* (pop. song): Tired of living in your one-horse town. **1994** *Time Trax* (synd. TV series): You stranded me in this one-horse town.

one-lunger *n.* **1.** a single-cylinder motor; (*hence*) a machine, esp. an automobile, having such a motor.

   1908 in *OEDS:* Then me and Sadie in her bubble, towin' the busted one-lunger behind. **1911–12** Ade *Knocking the Neighbors* 52: It was a One-Lunger with a Wheel Base of nearly 28 inches. **1918** *Nat. Geographic* (Jan.) 99: It is to the latest speedster war-plane what the "one-lunger" automobile of fifteen years ago is to the 12 cylinder racer of today. **1918** Kauffman *Our Navy at Work* 14: We had seen into safety the "one-lunger"—the single-funneled tramp. **1932** Pagano *Bluejackets* 37: How 'n hell are ya gonna speed this one lunger up? **1951** in *DAS:* A simple old one-lunger. **1960–61** Steinbeck *Discontent* 49: I heard the slow puttering of a boat engine, a one-lunger, a fishing craft. **1964** Selby *Last Exit* 85: He had this Indian—you know, one of those small jobs. Not a onelunger. None a the boys would have one a those. They can really move and all that, but theyre small. **1975** *Pop. Science* (Oct.) 134: He'd incur the wrath of neighbors if he yanked a howling one-lunger to life.

   2. a small or inferior device, business, etc.

   1942 *ATS* 610: *One-lunger,* a small broadcasting station. **1980** Pearl *Pop. Slang* 110: *One-lunger, n.* (Crime) a wristwatch or other mechanical device shoddily made but usually bearing the counterfeit label of some reputable firm.

one-man band *n.* a person, esp. a show-off, who attempts to do the work of several people.

   *****1938** Partridge *DSUE* (Supp.) 1018: *One-man band.* A person that takes rather too much on himself. **1977** *U.S. News & W.R.* (Feb. 21) 27: Who, if anyone, is really in charge of U.S. foreign policy now? Is Kissinger's one-man band being replaced by a kind of administrative anarchy? **1977** *L.A. Times* (May 16) I 8: He disputes the notion that he is trying to be too much of a one-man band. **1981** *U.S. News & W.R.* (June 1) 32: [Pope] John Paul insists on being a one-man band. **1986** *Heart of the City* (ABC-TV): You really think I was too much of a one-man band?

one-nighter *n.* **1.** *Jazz & Entertainment Industry.* a single performance in one locale.

   1937 *AS* XII 184: *One nighter,* an engagement to play for a single night. **1939** Goodman & Kolodin *Swing* 156: Playing one-nighters from Boston to Galveston. **1942** *ATS* 576: *One-nighter, one-night stand,* a place at which but one night's performance is given. **1959** *N.Y. Times* (Apr. 19) II 1: Using highly mobile production methods, National Phoenix would play one-nighters as well as standard city bookings. **1963** *Harper's* (Apr.) 57: I was playing a one-nighter at the William Penn Hotel...when I first heard Tommy Dorsey. **1975** *Atlantic* (May) 79: Ellington at fifty-seven had survived the collapse of the rest of the bands by being willing to accept low prices, by accepting all one-nighters. **1978** D. Marsh, in *Rolling Stone* (May 4) 24: Her incalculable ability to be at the center of any significant rock event, whether it's a one-nighter at CBGB's...or a national tour by the Rolling Stones. **1980** *Texas Monthly* (Oct.) 210: We played every little village and hamlet, mostly one-nighters. **1982** *L.A. Times* (Nov. 24) VI 1: It was designed for one-nighters...not for a reprise in a key city.

   2. ONE-NIGHT STAND, 2.

   1969 *Atlantic* (Apr.) 60: He saw many girls: curious students, unexpected bus-stop pickups, and assorted other one-nighters. **1980** *Maclean's* (Mar. 17) 59: Out-of-town one-nighters with a married man.

1980 *New West* (July 28) 37: It was not that he wanted that seemingly endless and tasteless…string of one-nighters that seemed the alternative to a deeper relationship. **1994** *New York* (Oct. 10) 43: He really loved Amy…but he still had his one-nighters.

one-night stand *n.* **1.** *Theat.* a small rural town. [The sense 'a single performance in one locale', as in *1880 quot., is S.E.]

[***1880** in *OED2*: This coming week…is to be what they call "one-night stands."] **1883** in *OEDS*: One night stands are not going to be subject, if they can help it, to the experiments of one troupe of queer fakirs after another. **1899** Ade *Fables* 4: The Primitive Yokels of a One-Night Stand could not Attune Themselves to the Views of one who was troubled with Ideals. **1908** McGaffey *Show Girl* 21: Those one-night stand dumps. **1915–16** Lait *Beef, Iron & Wine* 168: I drinks a toast to the guy what was clever enough to think up a game like that…in a Reub one-night stand.

2. a sexual relationship lasting only one night; (*hence*) a person with whom one has such a relationship.

*1937 in Partridge *Dict. Und.* 681. **1940** W.R. Burnett *High Sierra* 224: She was…strictly a one-night stand type. **1945** J.H. Burns *Gallery* 306: I was wondering…whether you got it from a one-night stand or from love. Because you seem so bitter. **1946** G.W. Henderson *Jule* 130: On a one-night stand! **1955** Lindner *Must You Conform?* 48: He has held…[homosexual partners] briefly for "one-night stands," or has participated in longer affairs. **1962** T. Jones *Stairway* 10: Jennie has a bedroom all to herself, except for a one-night stand every week or two. **1963** Blechman *Omongo* 142: He was just another one-night stand, not even a person. **1963** C. Wright *Messenger* 51: "Oh, him," Ruby said indifferently. "That was nothing. A one-night stand that went sour after a week." **1967** Mailer *Armies of Night* 98: A plump young waitress with a strong perfume, who looked nonetheless a goddess of a bucket for a one-night stand. **1970** *N.Y. Post* (Mar. 23) 36: I could forgive my husband if I caught him stepping out on me (I mean a one-night stand, not a serious affair of any duration). **1971** Simon *Sign of Fool* 68: I frequently held one-night stands with some far out chick or another. **1978** *New West* (Mar. 27) 70: A divorcée who refuses to be another of his one-night stands. **1983** Karr *K. Arthur Comp.* 58: The affair between Lancelot and Elaine would have been a one-night stand…if he had not been tricked again. **1989** *Murphy Brown* (CBS-TV): I had a meaningless one-night stand. **1995** *Jerry Springer Show* (synd. TV series): Scorned lovers confront the one-night stands that slept with them and then dumped them.

one-on-one *n.* **1.** a direct confrontation or fight.

1967 in *OEDS*: In the one-on-one, relatively "simple" intercepts run during the 1962–63 test series, the "old" *Nike-Zeus* scored on 10 of 14 attempted live ICBM intercepts. **1968–70** *Current Slang III & IV* 89: One on one, n. A fight.—College males, Kansas.—If you don't shut up, we're going to have a little one on one right here. **1976** Crews *Feast of Snakes* 59: It may be you can't go one-on-one with Joe Lon Mackey before you get out of Mystic, Georgia. **1978** Groom *Better Times* 228: Kahn shouldn't get into a one-on-one in something like this. **1984** Hammel *Root* 66: It was now time to have a one-on-one with his chief antagonist.

2. lovemaking.

1988 *Supercarrier* (ABC-TV): Gives us a little time for some one-on-one.

One-O-Worst *n. Army.* the 101st Airborne Division. *Joc.* [Quots. ref. to Vietnam War.]

1980 Cragg *Lex. Militaris* 320: One-Oh-Worst. The 101st Airborne Division. *a*1986 K.W. Nolan *Into Laos* 56: Sometimes the men sardonically referred to the division as the One-Oh-Worst. **1988** Clodfelter *Mad Minutes* 27 [ref. to 1965]: For the One O' Worst.

one-pound wonder *n. Army.* a 37-millimeter gun or shell. [Quots. ref. to WWI.]

[**1918** (quot. at DAISY-CLIPPER, 2 [for form "pound wonder"]).] **1925** *Amer. Leg. Wkly.* (Dec. 25) 8: Callin' cards was to be dropped by the field artillery, machine guns, trench mortars and one-pound wonders.

one's *pron.* (used, usu. in form *mine*, as a pron. in objective case).—usu. constr. with *for. Cf. in (one's)* s.v. IN, *prep.* [The original entry for this construction is found at *for (one's)* s.v. FOR *prep.*; the following citations provide additional evidence.]

1901 *Our Naval Apprentice* (Oct.) 12: The only thing for mine was to conclude that I'd been buzzed for the roll by some San Francisco

leatherworker. **1906** *DN* III 136: For mine…Good enough for me. "Arkansas *for mine*." **1907** "O. Henry" *Trimmed Lamp* 1369: "Him?" said Nancy, with her coolest, sweetest, most impersonal, Van Alstyne smile; "not for mine. I saw him drive up outside." **1919** Darling *Jargon Book* 45: *Not for Mine*—I do not want anything to do with it. **1922** Colton & Randolph *Rain* 75: Well, Apia my foot—it's Sidney for mine! **1925** Faulkner *N.O. Sketches* 96: And one more yap outa you, and the street for yours. **1929** A.C. Doyle *Maricot* ch. ii: Say, Doc, it's mine for the surface.…Ring up the elevator and get her going.

ones-and-twos *n.pl.* [rhyming slang] shoes.

1928 Sharpe *Chicago May* 288: Ones and twos—shoes. **1943** Holmes & Scott *Mr. Lucky* (film): Hat: *tit for tat*. Shoes: *ones and twos*.…You're a girl: *twist and twirl*. **1966** Braly *Cold* 131: A new suit…, a pair of sharp-toed ones and twos that hurt his feet. **1970** Landy *Underground Dict.* 142: Ones and twos…Shoes.

one-shot *n.* something that occurs only once.—often used attrib.

1929–33 J. Lowell *Gal Reporter* 12: A one-shot creative accomplishment. *Ibid.* 15: I am not a one-shot success. **1938** in *DAS*: He put her in a one-shot whodunit. **1943** in *DAS*: The softest affairs [sc., plays] to knock over are the one-shots. **1952** *Sat. Eve. Post* (Sept. 20) 9: Maybe it was a one-shot shakedown. **1968** *Business Week* (June 15) 39: The phenomenon of instant magazine publishing—called "one-shots" in the trade. *Ibid.*: There have been one-shots on the Beatles, Jacqueline Kennedy, [etc.]. **1970** *Pop. Science* (Nov.) 72: If you're recording a one-shot—an event or interview that won't be repeated—don't take a chance. **1973** *U.S. News & W.R.* (Feb. 26) 86: The hijacking pact is a one-shot deal. **1977** *Rolling Stone* (Aug. 25) 43: Yeah, it was a one-shot and I was really lucky. **1978** *L.A. Times* (May 10) I 10: The late Sunday-early Monday rioting had been a "one-shot deal." **1981** *Time* (Aug. 3) 81: We are basically geared to take care of one-shot problems. **1982** A. Shaw *Dict. Pop/Rock* 266: "One-shots."…artists and groups…who achieved only a single hit record. **1982** *Flash* (Dec.) 14: Let's just call it a one-shot, Mick. A sort of special return engagement for a noble cause.

one-spot *n.* a one-dollar bill.

1899 Cullen *Tales* 81: I was slowly stripping bills from that little bundle of one-spots. **1903** McCardell *Chorus Girl* 133: He never flashes anything higher than a one-spot. **1928** Bodenheim *Georgie May* 6: Yez was so koind to me, lendin' me that one-spot the other day. *a*1973–87 F.M. Davis *Livin' the Blues* 71: She…only sets you back a one-spot.

one-star *n.* [from the insigne of rank] *Army & USMC.* a brigadier general.

1942 *Yank* (July 8) 12: One-star W.C. Lee. **1982** "J. Cain" *Commandos* 367: Aw, give old one-star a break.

one-step *n. Mil. in S.E. Asia.* a krait or other poisonous snake. *Cf.* ASIAN TWO-STEP.

1972 Rottman *Hearts & Minds* 27: There are two kinds of snakes in Vietnam/Mr. One Step/And Mr. Two Step/Named for how far you go after being bitten.

one-story *adj.* puny.

1865 in G.W. Harris *High Times* 158: That ar cussed one story varmint…stole my breetches. **1897** *Cosmopolitan* (Mar.) 564: He was one o' these yer fellers with a three-storied eddicashun and a one-storey brain.

one-striper *n.* [fr. the insignia] *Army.* a private first-class; (*Navy*) an ensign.

1941 *AS* (Oct.) 167: One-Striper. Private 1st class. **1958** Camerer *Damned Wear Wings* 94: He recalled the wild look on the one-striper's homesick face. **1954–60** *DAS*: One-striper…In the USN, an ensign.…In the Army a private first class.

one-time *n.* [orig. unkn.] *Rap Music.* a police officer; the police.

1991 "Ice-T" *Midnight* (rap song): Fuckin' police on a gang sweep/No time to deal with one-time. **1992** *L.A. Times* (Aug. 18) E1: Gaffled up [arrested] by a one time. *Ibid.* E5: *Five Os* and *one times* refer to police officers. **1993** "Dr. Dre" *Bitches Ain't Shit* (rap song): Got daffled [sic] by one-time/I'm back to the motherfuckin' county jail. **1996** N.Y.C. youth, age 16 (coll. J. Sheidlower): *One-time* means the police. Like, you be standin' around with your friends and a cop comes by, you say, "One-time!" and everybody runs away. It's a California word, but it's in all those movies.

one-two *n. Boxing.* two quick punches with alternate hands; (*hence, broadly*) any combination of two people or things having a rapid or powerful effect.—also used attrib. Now *S.E.* except in phr. **the old one-two.**

*1811 in *OEDS*: He…had no difficulty in getting at his man when he chose with a *one, two.* **1902** *N.Y. Eve. Jour.* (Dec. 2) 12: Then Choynski put Childs down with a "one-two" on the jaw. **1922** Tully *Emmett Lawler* 287: By laying him out with a one-two punch, Emmett had sent his name across the country. **1923** Witwer *Fighting Blood* 195: I dropped him to his knees with a one-two punch to the jaw. **1932** H. Mankiewicz et al. *Girl Crazy* (film): Give him the old one-two! **1932** Hecht & Fowler *Great Magoo* 83: The old one-two….Bing! Bing! **1933** D. Boehm & E. Gelsey *Jimmy Dolan* (film): Jack'll give him the old one-two, just like he showed us! **1936** "M. Brand," in M.H. Greenberg *In Ring* 177: The old one-two, kid! **1936** Tully *Bruiser* 70: He was knocked to the canvas with zipping "one-twos" to the jaw. **1937** Steinbeck *Mice & Men* 85: Jus' the ol' one-two an' he'll go down. **1946** Mezzrow & Wolfe *Really Blues* 116: Inspiration's old lady…conked me with a one-two. **1949** *N.Y. Times* (July 30) 13: Now how are you going to give the old one-two punch of yes-but-things-could-be-better to people who talk like that? **1951** *Sat. Eve. Post* (Jan. 6) 74: Mick came forward in two swift bounds, his front paws upraised, ready to give me the old one-two. **1951** *Time* (Mar. 19) 104: An old-fashioned Joe Louis one-two would have finished the fight. **1959** *Time* (Dec. 14) 15: The French subjected him to a diplomatic one-two. **1963** *New Yorker* (Jan. 19) 31: I…threw a wild right hand at him, but he ducked under it neatly and countered…with a classic one-two. **1972** *All in the Family* (CBS-TV): They okayed busin', too, till President Nixon give 'em the old one-two. **1978** *Houston Chronicle* (Feb. 19) III 19: The nation's largest manufacturer of electric cars has gone bankrupt, downed by the one-two punch of energy unawareness and safety worries. **1981** *Life* (Oct.) 132: Nematodes…can attack pests in fields that have been sprayed with insecticides, giving farmers a one-two punch. **1984** *L.A. Times* (Aug. 7) VI 1: A one-two punch: a kidney stone and then an inner-ear infection.

one-way *adj.* **1.** honest; legitimate.

1930 Lait *On Spot* 208: *One-way-guy*…Honest man. (A crook is a "Two-way-guy."). **1933** Ersine *Prison Slang* 55: *One-Way, adj.* Honest. **1935** Pollock *Und. Speaks*: *One-way moniker*, true name of a person. **1936** *Our Army* (July) 42: One-Way Guy. **1942–49** Goldin et al *DAUL* 149: *One-way ghee*….(Rare) A forthright, dependable person.

2.a. completely close-minded.

[***1938** in *OEDS*: Endurance of one-way thinking.] [**1956** (quot. at (b), below).] **1961** L.E. Young *Virgin Fleet* 10 [ref. to 1941]: Chicken-shit regulations and one-way officers. **1965** E. Franklin *Cold in Pongo-ni* 17 [ref. to Korean War]: If the Chinese are so one-way they won't recognize this as a genuine offer. *a*1979 Pepper & Pepper *Straight Life* 24: Moses was very one-way about his thinking.

b. Esp. *USMC.* selfish or self-seeking.

[**1926** Maines & Grant *Wise-Crack Dict.* 11: *One-way pockets*, pockets of tightwad.] **1947** Carter *Devils* 97: These goddamned, half-witted, dirty, one-way…sonuva bitches, sitting in their goddamned big tents drinking ice water, while we beat out our brains in this hellhole of sand and cactus! **1942–49** Goldin et al. *DAUL* 149: *One-way ghee*…A thoroughly selfish person. **1949** (quot. at SEMPER FI). **1952** Uris *Battle Cry* 104: The most one-way bastard in creation. **1956** *AS* XXXI (Oct.) 191: A buddy manifestly selfish about possessions is considered *one-way*, which may broaden to include any demonstration of a disagreeable aspect of behavior. **1957** Myrer *Big War* 271: You lousy one-way son of a bitch. **1958** Plagemann *Steel Cocoon* 44: We had put you down as a sort of one-way guy. **1960** Leckie *Marines!* 74: "C'mon, you one-way bastard," I screeched. "Gimme back my glasses." **1964** Gallant *Friendly Dead* 134: It takes a worthless, selfish, one-way son-of-a-bitch with ingrowin' hairs to do somethin' like that, this bein' an emergency an' all. **1966** Elli *Riot* 235: He wasn't being one-way, he kept telling himself. **1985** Dye *Between Raindrops* 84: You assholes are a bunch of one-way motherfuckers. **1995** Leuci *Fence Jumpers* 301: You're a sneaky, one-way bastard, always have been.

3. *Homosex.* heterosexual. Also as n.

1965 Trimble *Sex Words* 143: *One-way* or *one-way baby* or *one-way cat*…A Heterosexual.

one-way ride *n. Und.* a murder perpetrated by gangsters who transport their victim in an automobile.

1942 *ATS* 135: *One way ride*,…murder by gangsters. **1957** Ness & Fraley *Untouchables* 5: Mobsters…made a national institution of the "one-way ride."

onion *n.* **1.** the head; in phr. **off (one's) onion** crazy.

a*1889–90** in Barrère & Leland *Dict. Slang*: I've a chap on the book now for a hundred and twenty who's gone clean off his onion betting. ***1889–90** Barrère & Leland *Dict. Slang*: Off his onion…imbecile, cracked. *Ibid.*: Onion (popular), the head. **1933** D. Runyon, in *Collier's* (Oct. 28) 7: He…taps Cecil on the onion. **1936** in D. Runyon *More Guys* 150: Benny…is practically off his onion about her. **1950** *Merrie Melodies* (animated cartoon): This cluck's off her onion.

2. a stupid or obnoxious fellow.

1903 Ade *Society* 21: Wilbur was 18 and an Onion. He had outgrown his last year's Tunic, and his Smalls were hardly on speaking terms with his Uppers. **1904** Hobart *Jim Hickey* 21: The lobster!…Oh, oh! what an onion that slob is! **1921** *Variety* (Mar. 25) 4: My onion is back on his pins before ten [is counted]. **1921** *Variety* (Oct. 28) 7: I made a coupla matches for Tomato…and I didn't pick no onions either. **1928** Hammett *Harvest*: What kind of a dumb onion do you take me for? **1934** Ruhm *Detective* 103: I'm going to hate to prosecute that onion for murder. **1941** Kendall *Army & Navy Sl.* 10: *Onion*….a dope or a wet blanket.

3. *Naut.* a fraction of a nautical mile per hour.—constr. with *and an.*

1916 in *OEDS*: We got about six and an onion out of the old bus,…and reached there about noon. **1919** *Our Navy* (July) 15: Some ships made thirty-three knots an hour and burnt up the sea. Others made two and an onion and had a steering wheel and a jury sail and a prayer.

4. *Mil. Av.* a kind of incendiary antiaircraft projectile. See also FLAMING ONION, 1. [Quots. ref. to WWI.]

*1917 in *OEDS*: A line of fiery rectangles shot up….These were "onions," the flaming rockets which the Boche keeps…for hostile aircraft. **1918** *Wadsworth Gas Attack* 26: The airmen's pest is the "onion," or large flaming anti-aircraft shell. **1918** Bishop *Winged Warfare* 67: I have never had an "onion" nearer than 200 feet of me, but the effect of these balls of fire reaching for you is most terrifying. **1918** in Loosbrock & Skinner *Wild Blue* 54: Sometimes they shoot up a bunch of "onions," burning balls of chemicals strung together on a wire. **1927** Cushing *Doughboy Ditties* 57: "Onions" and "archies" are hurled through space.

5. *Baseball.* a baseball.

1917 *Amer. Mag.* (July) 42. **1919** Wilkins *Co. Fund* 30: He sure was some pitcher and he had a real team goofing the onion in the pasture. **1928** Ruth *Baseball* 24: Go up there and lay on that onion. Knock it a mile.

6. *Und.* a watch or clock. Cf. TURNIP.

1924 *N.Y. Times* (Aug. 3) viii16: Watch—thimble, kettle, turnip, souper, onion, a red or a white, according to its metal. **1935** Pollock *Und. Speaks*: *Onion*, the clock (prison). **1949** Monteleone *Criminal Slang* 168: *Onion*…a watch.

7. *Und.* a failure.

1933 Ersine *Prison Slang* 55: *Onion*…A failure. "That last job was an onion." **1949** Partridge *Dict. Und.* 485: *Onion*….Of, e.g. an enterprise, a crime: a failure.

8. a dollar.

1936 Farrell *World I Never Made* 118: "Has he got plenty of onions in the bank?" "He's a millionaire." **1951** in *DAS*: Any of the patients in this institution got a few onions I could take till payday?

¶ In phrases:

¶ **big onion** an important person or thing.

1942 Davis & Wolsey *Call House Madam* 220: A parade in which he was the biggest onion, the highest paid attraction. **1970** Newman & Benton *Crooked Man* (film): He seemed to think it was pretty big onions that you built it yourself.

¶ **the whole onion** everything.

1979 Gram *Blvd. Nights* 78: They gotta deal with all of us….Like, the whole onion, man!

onionhead *n.* **1.** a foolish or offensive person. Cf. earlier ONION.

1928 Nason *Sgt. Eadie* 46 [ref. to 1918]: You and that big onion head been layin' up somewhere! **1954** Day & Lay *SAC* (film): Take over, onionhead.

2.a. a bald person. Hence **onionheaded,** *adj.* bald.

[**1854** in Harris *Lovingood* 37: Thar wer dad's bald hed fur all the yeath like a peeled inyin.] **1938** in *AS* (Apr. 1939) 91: *Onion Headed.* Bald

headed. "Pa's been onion headed since I was a baby." **1973** N.Y.C. woman, age *ca*25: An *onionhead* is a bald guy with a shiny head, a *skinhead*.
b. (see quot.).
   1990 G.R. Clark *Words of Viet. War* 362: Onion Heads...the close, shaved haircuts of the U.S. Marines.

onion-peeler *n.* a knife; APPLE-PEELER.
   1958 Meltzer & Blees *H.S. Confidential* (film): You think you're tall with that onion-peeler.

onions *n.pl.* business, affairs.
   1954 W.G. Smith *South St.* 297: You just sit here, tend your onions, let me handle the people what cross me.

only *n. Mil.* an Asian mistress of a serviceman. Cf. O.A.O.
   1952 *Sat. Eve. Post* (Aug. 23) 96: Rows of shedlike little houses which...were the homes of "onlies," Japanese girls who remain faithful companions for one soldier, and are supported by him. **1964** Crane *Sgt. & Queen* 54 [ref. to Korean War]: Then there are the "onlys"— girls who are living with just one soldier, and wholly supported by him. **1969** Moskos *Enlisted Man* 92 [ref. to Korean War]: These mistresses (variously called "onlies," "steadies," "shack-jobs," or even putative fiances) are given a mutually agreed upon monthly sum by the serviceman which pays for a domicile as well as the girl's (presumed) exclusive favors. **1971** Cole *Rook* 305: "We rove you." "We be your onlies."

on to see s.v. ON, *adj.*, 4.

o.o. *n.* ONCE-OVER. Cf. DOUBLE-O, 1.
   1913 T.A. Dorgan, in Zwilling *TAD Lexicon* 61: Think I'll go in and give the jury the once over. Think I'll give them the o.o. myself. **1920** *Hicoxy's Army* 60: Pop...gives his shoes the o.o. **1923** Wilstach *Stage Slang* 16: *Given the O.O.*—The once over. **1924** Hecht & Bodenheim *Cutie* 20: "Say, bozo," Cutie said, handing him an o.o. **1930** Deitrick *Parade Ground* 51: They certainly do give you the o.o. different. **1934** in Partridge *Dict. Und.* 201: Scrutinize sharply...to give the double O; give the OO. **1939** Hart *135th Aero Squadron* 96: While we were sitting down eating, two huge rats...came walking across the floor and gave us the o.o. **1942–45** Caniff *Male Call* (unp.): I give you the o.o., see that you're not convoyed [etc.].

o.o. *v.* to give the ONCE-OVER.
   1936 *Esquire* (Sept.) 162: To "gander at the gams" (o.o. the legs).

ooch *v.* to slide quickly, as along a bench; scoot.—usu. constr. with *over*. Also **ootch**.
   1930 in *DAS*: He lay down on the lounge with Rose. "Ooch over," he said. **1950** *Time* (Mar. 6) 19: The Communists diplomatically ooched over on the seat. **1992** *Wash. Post* (Sept. 14) D10: What Kim saw was a human being ootching the dog closer to the fountain.

oodles *n.pl.* [orig. unkn.] a great many; a great amount; lots. Now *colloq.* Occ. as adv.
   *a*1867 in G.W. Harris *High Times* 176: The brilein chickins an' coffee an' the oodils ove flour. **1869** *Overland Mo.* (Aug.) 131: A Texan never has a great quantity of any thing, but he has "scads" of it, or "oodles," or "dead oodles." **1883** Sweet & Knox *Mustang* 100: When I kem here in '46 thar was dead-oodles of game all around here. **1886** in *F & H* V 107: We've got oodles of 'em right here. **1888** *Scribner's Mag.* (Aug.) 157: Thar's Dake doin' oodles er things fur Otter. **1911** (quot. at MOLLY²). **1913** J. London *Valley of Moon* 8: He's oodles better'n your bunch of hoodlums. **1918** Ruggles *Navy Explained* 106: *Oodles.* Another term that originated in the navy. It means plenty, to be well supplied with money or tobacco; to have had oodles of fun. Sometimes, instead of saying oodles, the men will use the word many. For example: "I have many tobacco" or "I had many liberty." Sounds silly, but one soon gets accustomed to it. **1928** Dahlberg *Bottom Dogs* 102: They were all making oodles of money. **1930** in Botkin *Treas. Amer. Folk.* 508: Dead oodles of buffalo grazed around us. **1938** *Sat. Review* (July 23) 22: Thanks oodles for your letter. **1979** E. Thompson *Golden Pond* 37: There are also oodles and oodles of mosquitoes. **1981** in G. Tate *Flyboy* 19: Oodles of cryptic licks. **1988** *Academe* (Jan.) 18: We have oodles to learn about how evolution happened. **1993** *Itchy & Scratchy Comics* (No. 1) (inside front cover): Oodles of dynamite.

oof *n.* [< F *oeuf*] *Mil. in France.* an egg. Also **uff.** [Quots. ref. to WWI.]
   1917 McArdle *Collier's* 195: After a sidewalk breakfast of "oofs" and so-called cafe in Bordeaux, I went to keep my engagements at court. **1918** Battey *Sub. Destroyer* 299: "Jennie" the French girl who keeps the place said she would cook us some "uffs" (eggs) and coffee. **1919**

Glock *316th Inf.* 93: Billets and vin shops and mayhap "oofs." **1925** J. Stevens *Mattock* 122: Oofs.

oofty-goofty *adj.* [of fanciful orig.] crazy. Cf. GOOFY.
   1890 in Sampson *Ghost Walks* 74: He's in the Asylum Now...Oofty Goofty [lunatic character]. **1938** (quot. at RINGY DINGY).

oogle *v.* [for the alt. in vowel quality, cf. earlier GONEY and GOONEY] OGLE. Hence, **oogley,** *adj.* worthy of ogling.
   1949 in *DAS*: It's Oogley, Also Bong. **1954–60** *DAS*: Oogle...To ogle. **1976** N.Y.C. man, age 34: She's oogling you...."Oogle" is the only pronunciation I've ever heard. **1982–84** Chapple *Outlaws in Babylon* 167: Ace is being oogled. **1997** *Fresh Air* (Jan. 21) (Nat. Pub. Radio): And he *oogles* me—*oogles* me—as though I were a sexually desirable human being!

ooky *adj.* [alt. ICKY] unpleasant; ICKY.
   1964 in *OEDS*: He writes poems and reads them to Mama....He looks ooky when he says them. **1972** M. Rodgers *Freaky Fri.* 113: It's an ooky idea anyway. **1988** *Smithsonian* (Nov.) 48: Another customer has rejected a cake because the design is boring and the color red is "ooky." **1991** *Vanity Fair* (Oct.) 220: They're definitely mysterious and undoubtedly ooky; they do live in a museum. **1996** Knoxville, Tenn., graphic designer, age 43: It's ooky.

oomph *n.* [repr. a semiarticulate exclamation of surprise or a sound made during exertion] Esp. *Entertainment Industry.*
1. sex appeal; personal magnetism. [Esp. associated with Ann (nee Clara Lou) Sheridan (1915–67), U.S. film star designated "The Oomph Girl" in 1939 for publicity purposes; see 1939 quots.]
   [**1900** Dunbar *Gideon* 165: Dat Jim....Oomph, de debbil done got his stamp on dat boy.] [**1912** P.L. Dunbar, in *Chi. Defender* (Oct. 26) 7: Signs of the Time...Oomph! dat bird do' know what's comin'.] **1937** in *OEDS*: With actors, the "it" quality has to do with their visual personality—sex appeal, magnetism, or whatever you care to call it. Back of the camera, we refer to the ingredient as "umphh." **1939** *Life* (July 24) 64: The word "Oomph," long current in U.S. slang, had rarely appeared in print before being used to describe the peculiar attractions of Ann Sheridan....The Earl of Warwick [explained], "Oomph is a feminine desirability which can be observed with pleasure but cannot be discussed with respectability." *Ibid.*: AMERICA'S OOMPH GIRL. Ann Sheridan...is the movie find of the year. Clara Lou Sheridan became the Oomph Girl of America on March 16, 1939, when Lucius Beebe, Busby Berkeley,...David Niven, [et al.]...awarded her the title. **1940** Slesinger & Davis *Dance, Girl, Dance* (film): You don't learn *oomph.* You are born with it. **1941** H.A. Smith *Low Man* 83: Georgie Hale doesn't think corsets give a girl the old oomph. **1941** Macaulay & Wald *Manpower* (film): Is she an *oomph* girl or an *it* girl? **1942** A.C. Johnston *Courtship of A. Hardy* (film): He has to have oomph. **1944** D. Hartman et al. *Princess & Pirate* (film): This dame of mine has so much oomph—. **1952** *N.Y. Times* (Feb. 17) II x5: Ann Sheridan. The titian-haired star, whose particular kind of beauty became synonymous with "oomph," [etc.]. **1962** *Time* (Jan. 12) 48: That dame has plenty of oomph in her voice. **1976** Eble *Campus Slang* (Nov.) 4: Oomph—n. Irrepressible enthusiasm; sex appeal: That blond sure has oomph. **1981** *N.Y. Post* (Aug. 17) 30: Dressing Sexy...Opening a few buttons on the top of your blouse is a great way to give your wardrobe some oomph and catch a man's eye. **1984** J. McNamara *First Directive* 263: Sexy pictures...wouldn't have provided enough umph to pull a rip-off like that. **1996** *CNN Today* (CNN TV) (Apr. 15): She says she likes her men with a little more oomph.

2. vitality; effectiveness; zip; energy; enthusiasm. Occ. as *v.*
   1937 in *OEDS*: Jolson's energy gave the show most of its umph too, that gave the Gershwin memorial program its pace. **1937** M. Mooney *You Can't Buy Luck* (film): Something like "Frankie and Johnny" but it's got more *mmff!* **1942** Chase & Mackenzie *Fighting Seabees* (film): No oomph, sir? **1951** *New Yorker* (Oct. 6) 34: Q—What else does it lack? A—Substance, drive, authority, emotional power, and oomph. **1955** S. Wilson *Gray Flannel Suit* 122: Give it a fresh approach. Put some *oomph* into it. **1961** *New Yorker* (Sept. 9) 34: We've used muted colors...but we've added some oomph, don't you think? **1972** Ad on WINS radio (Oct. 28): The octane rating—the oomph you worry about—is what's really important. **1974** in Mamet *Sexual Perversity* 24: The extra added oomph of involuntary continence. **1975** Lichtenstein *Long Way* 38: All three meant getting more oomph on the ball. **1976** (quot. at (1), above). **1980** E. Morgan *Surgeon* 159: Put some oomph

into it. **1979–82** Gwin *Overboard* 170: I poured on the oomph, inched even farther ahead. **1983** *Hour Magazine* (ABC-TV) (Feb. 3): The rutabaga adds oomph to the soup. **1985** *Discover* (May) 20: There's simply not enough gravitational oomph for galaxies to grow from such small seeds. **1989** Post Grape-Nuts TV ad (Jan. 2): Oomph up your oatmeal with Post Grape-Nuts cereal! **1990** *New Yorker* (Sept. 17) 69: The Catholic Church was very boring....Bible Gospel got more *oomph*. **1995** *Space Ghost* (TV Cartoon Network): This show needs oomph! Pizazz!

oomphy *adj.* lively; powerful; (*also*) sexy.
   1955 *Pop. Science* (Aug.) 89: Olds will have that spectacular new transmission, a more sophisticaed version of the automatic that for years has been the oomphiest in existence. **1980** *N.Y. Post* (Mar. 13) 6: Past...spots had her looking oomphy in skimpy garb.

oops *n.* an oversight; error.
   1979 in Fierstein *Torch Song* 151: That was an "Oops." **1981** Fontana wine ad on WINS radio (June): That's an oops. I forgot. **1988** *48 Hours* (CBS-TV): It was just a big oops. **1989** *Garfield & Friends* (CBS-TV): That's a major oopsie. **1990** *Top Cops* (CBS-TV): You're only allowed one oops. **1993** *Jerry Springer Show* (synd. TV series): Now this is not just an oops. **1995** *Jerry Springer Show* (synd. TV series): Suddenly there's an oops and she's pregnant.

oops *v.* to vomit.
   1965 Hersey *Too Far to Walk* 69: It makes me really oops, that kind of image.

ootch var. OOCH.

ootchimagootchi *n.* [perh. cf. HOOTCHY-KOOTCHY] lovemaking. Also **ouchimagooga.**
   1942 *Time* (Mar. 2) 80: The Hollywood section fails to include "ootchimagootchi" (hot talk as an obbligato to Latin love-making.). [**1947** Riskin *Magic Town* (film): Ouchimagouch!] **1978** T. Sanchez *Zoot-Suit* 195: You been making some *hotcha ouchimagooga?*

ootz /uts/ *v.* [orig. unkn.] to cheat; (*hence*) to treat in a treacherous manner.
   1947 Schulberg *Harder They Fall* 237: But you're not gonna ootz us out of that extra dough? You and Nick together? **1962** Serling *New Stories* 2: It was not the extra sixty-five bucks he ootzed out of a hapless customer. **1994** Attanasio *Quiz Show* (film): They have to ootz me with a question any child knows.

ooze *v.* to move listlessly or stealthily; ease.
   1929 in *OEDS:* Whenever I came oozing along the street, he sort of edged away. **1931** in *DAS:* [He] oozed forward, like a seal. **1944** C.B. Davis *Leo McGuire* 82: That afternoon we oozed out casually to look over the hotel. **1950** in *DAS:* I did my best, oozing along Front Street furtively.

O.P. *n.* other people's (liquor or money). *Joc.* Cf. O.P.M., O.P.'s.
   1886 McAfee *Kentucky Politicians* 224: The opportunity is generally sought by him when he has diagnosed the hour for the party upon whom he thrust himself to be about going for some "O.P."—which means other people's whisky—a brand which the most fastidious drinker rarely fails to take. [**1905** in J.I. Robertson *Blue & Gray* 94 [ref. to Civil War]: When out of money, a man stayed in the game by resorting to the use of "O.P."'s (order on the paymaster).] **1956** "T. Betts" *Across the Board* 294: Touts work with other people's money. O.P. That's what they call it at the track.

op *n.* **1.** *Mil.* a military operation.
   *1916 in *OED2*. **1918** in *Papers of Mich. Acad.* (1928) 310: *Night ops,* night operations or maneuvers. **1944** *Yank* (Jan. 21) 7: My pilot just finished his ops and he's off combat now. **1951** Sheldon *Troubling Star* 3: Take him out of Wing ops and give him a squadron command. **1962** E. Stephens *Blow Negative* 31: That misprint in the op order for Operation Wind—. **1966** F. Elkins *Heart of Man* 21: Flight ops and a fast-pace day. **1968** in Neary *J. Bond* 100: I got a package of kool aid...Dad sent out on the op. **1976** C.R. Anderson *Grunts* 39: Bravo Company had someone else at the start of this new op too. **1978** Hasford *Short-Timers* 84: I was on an op with them down by Hoi An. **1985** Dye *Between Raindrops* 281: Got hit before the op was over.
   2.a. *Und.* an undercover operator or operative; private investigator.
   1924 in D. Hammett *Continental Op* 67: I wired your office for another op. **1926** in *AS* LVII (1982) 262: *Op.* Private detective agency operator. **1928** D. Hammett *Red Harvest* 35: I'm the Continental op

who tipped Dinah Brand off that Noonan was framing you. **1936** in Weinberg et al. *Tough Guys* 21: I guess this private op is the head of something called Marine Investigations. **1939** M. Levin *Citizens* 308: That op we caught in Warren, he was a financial sec. **1939** Appel *Power-House* 297: "First, we want to hook a union man to tip us off about the union—" "Hook?" "We're hookers and the union man we're going to hook, we called a hooked man...or an op. Op is short for operative....Stoolie is what the workers call an op." **1947** Spillane *I, the Jury* 11: Not only that, but she had a private op's ticket and on occasions when she went out with me on a case, packed a flat .32 automatic. **1951** A. Boucher, in *N.Y. Times* (Nov. 18) VII 50: The best of the modern private op stories. **1993** L. Barnes *Snapshot* 256: How does a guy who employs squirrelly ops like Sanchez rate a plush office in the Pru?
   b. operator (in any sense).
   1930 G. Irwin *Tramp & Und. Sl.: Op.*—A telegraph operator. **1951** *Sat. Eve. Post* (Sept. 1) 88: On the flight deck, Bill Altoff, our radio op, was putting the pieces of the receiver together. **1961** Granat *Important Thing* 15: I thought your Dad was a big op in Valley Glenn. **1966** R.E. Alter *Carny Kill* 7: I handed the rifle back to the op. *Ibid.* 8: The shooting gallery op. **1989** Care *Viet. Spook Show* 115: Thank God SAM ops aren't...prima donnas.
   3. a surgical operation.
   *1925 in *OEDS:* Motor-bus ran over her...pretty hopeless. Winter has seen her,—but thought she wouldn't stand an op. **1939** Fearing *Hospital* 37: You can make it up. Post-op. **1946** W.C. Williams, in Witemeyer *Williams-Laughlin* 131: It was thirteen days after the op. **1952** *New Yorker* (Oct. 4) 27: All the surgeons use it for pre and post op. **1953** Hughes *Fantastic Lodge* 68: You're...enclosed in a little, warm world with separate and individual ops. And each operation...gasses you more. *Ibid.:* You forget about it, as soon as the op is over.
   4. *Journ.* an opportunity; usu. in phr. **photo op.**
   1988 *Newsday* (N.Y.C.) (Dec. 7) 18: For the press it is headlines and photo ops. For some denizens of Times Square it's a "getting-over op." **1988–89** Safire *Quoth Maven* 136: *Op*...has come to mean *opportunity.* **1989** *CBS This Morning* (CBS-TV) (Feb. 23): Leaders dance from meeting to meeting, photo op to photo op.

op *v.* **1.** to operate; get along; function.
   *ca*1953 Hughes *Fantastic Lodge* 68: I start feeling real tired...like I can hardly op. *Ibid.* 117: Spade junkers can op in Spade Town. **1954** in *Social Problems* III (1955) 40: I was afraid that I would get high and not be able to op (operate), you dig?
   2. to do; accomplish.
   *ca*1953 Hughes *Fantastic Lodge* 94: And I started to op everything. **1961** in Partridge *Dict. Und.* 850: This was the way we opped it.

ope *n. Narc.* opium.
   *1929 (cited in Partridge *Dict. Und.* 486). **1930** *AS* IV 133. **1954–60** *DAS: Ope*...Opium. *Never used by narcotic addicts.* **1961** C. Cooper *Weed* 23: The charge of sweet tasting ope.

open *n. Hobo.* (see quot.).
   1978 *Texas Monthly* (May) 206: We begin looking for "opens." An "open" is an empty boxcar with both doors open, not just one. Leonard says tramps will not hop onto boxcars with only one door open—"What happens if that one open door goes shut on you?"

opener *n.* (see quots.). *Joc.*
   1909 J. Moss *Officers' Manual* 284: *Openers.* Cathartic pills. **1930** G. Irwin *Tramp & Und. Sl.: Openers.*—Cathartic pills.

opera house *n. West.* the top rail of a corral, as a perch for spectators. *Joc.*
   1922 P.A. Rollins *Cowboy* 167: That top rail was the point from which gratuitous and unwelcome advice was hurled at round-up time to the cowboys toiling...amid the milling animals within the corral. In some localities it bore the name of "opera-house." **1936** R. Adams *Cowboy Lingo* 96: From the "op'ra house," the top rail of the corral, or the side lines, perhaps, came the unwelcome advice to "stay with 'er."

operator *n.* **1.a.** a swindler or thief; sharper.
   *1820–21 P. Egan *Life in London* 123: The real Sportsman and the *Black Leg*—the Heavy Toddlers and the *Operators*. ***1848** (cited in Partridge *Dict. Und.* 486). **1873** Lening *N.Y. Life* 126: The "operator" who stole a pocket-book...is promised a suitable reward. **1879** *Snares of N.Y.* 1: The railroad and steamboat "operators" generally "work" in parties. **1882** "M. Twain" *Life on Miss.* 179: Here is a paragraph or two

concerning this big operator. *a1890–1902 *F & H* V 108: *Operator*...(old).—A pickpocket. **1908** in H.C. Fisher *A. Mutt* 33: The police are leaving no stone unturned in their efforts to locate that daring operator A. Mutt. **1909** Irwin *Con Man* 18: Pat...wasn't a very smooth operator. *Ibid.* 23: The operator takes...anilin dye...and marks over all the white figures in the scroll work except one. **1933** in S. Smith *Gumps* 84: He's one of the slickest operators in the country— but we've got the goods on him this time. **1943** Pyle *Brave Men* 132: Some smart operator had simply gathered up a batch of empty cans and lids, put sand in the cans, and then neatly crimped the lids back on. **1947** Schulberg *Harder They Fall* 6: Grifters, chiselers, two-bit gamblers, big-time operators with small-time minds. **1961** *N.Y. Times* (July 23) II x5: He is a scrounger, a cheat, an operator throughout. **1969** Crumley *One to Count Cadence* 52: He was an operator, a big man in the black-market.

b. a person who pursues success cynically or ruthlessly.

1872 McCabe *New York Life* 287: Daniel Drew is a great operator. His gains are immense, as are also his losses. He is not popular in the street, and the brokers are fond of abusing him. He has handled too many of them mercilessly to have many friends. They say that he does not hesitate to sacrifice a friend to gain his ends, and that he is utterly without sympathy for those who go down before his heavy blows. **1927** Hemingway *Men Without Women* 130: That Happy Steinfelt's a big operator....He's a pretty smooth boy. **1942** in *Best from Yank* 104: Know thou the Big Operator, but trust him not: he *worketh* always upon a deal and he speaketh confidentially. **1944** Stiles *Big Bird* 2: Ross was some sort of clerk in the daytime...and a big-time operator at night. **1945** M. Shulman *Dobie Gillis* 120: I took one look at her and knew what a patriot he must be to run out on a smooth operator like that. **1951** Elgart *Over Sixteen* 154: A certain Big Time Operator came home one evening and raved about his new secretary. **1956** Holiday & Dufty *Lady Sings* 149: He was a big-time operator taking an interest in a chick fresh out of jail. **1956** Heflin *USAF Dict.* 361: *Operator*...A person with a knack for getting things done, or, opprobriously, a person who works assiduously at advancing himself. **1959** *Phil Silvers Show* (CBS-TV): Bilko, you're a conniver, a sharpster and an operator. **1961** *Time* (June 16) 53: A smart operator could have made a million. **1966** J. Sutton *River* 48: In Mason's world there were two kinds of people—operators and pigeons.

2. a man who successfully pursues many women; a wily seducer.

1944 *Slanguage Dict.* 59: *Big-time operator*—a slick chick's smooth fellow. **1946** Sherwood *Best Years of Our Lives* (film): You think a kiss from a smooth operator like him—you think that means anything? **1956** J. Brown *Kings Go Forth* 101: He's a smooth operator, I said. **1956** *Sat. Eve. Post* (May 19) 77: Sorry I blew up....The thought of that smooth operator working on you was more than I could take. **1957** E. Brown *Locust Fire* 61 [ref. to 1942]: Are you trying to tell me you're an operator, mister? **1962** *Leave It to Beaver* (ABC-TV): It's kind of hard figuring your own mother thinking of you as an operator. **1964** Faust *Steagle* 183: She's turned down three operators, Harold. Real make-out artists. **1977** C.A. Owen *Canterb. Tales* 102: Expert in astrology and "deerne love," "sleigh and ful privee," he is the operator par excellence. **1982** T.C. Mason *Battleship Sailor* 3: One of the great "operators" of the radio gang, he knew at least two girls on the beach who would lend him small amounts of money.

O.P.H. *adj.* [supposedly illiterate resp. of *off*] on one's way; gone.—constr. with *be.*—used proleptically. *Joc.* Occ. as v. Also **oph.**

1838 *Morning Post* (Boston) (Mar. 14) 1, in *AS* XXXVIII (1963) 16: I'm o-p-h. **1838** in *AS* XXXVIII (1963) 16: Come, bucks, let's o.p.h. **1839** in *AS* XXXVIII (1963) 16: While Mr. L. was getting ready, the man was o-p-h. **1839** in *Essex Inst. Hist. Coll.* LXXXIV (1948) 215: He got frightened, and was oph. **1840** *Spirit of Times* (Apr. 18) 77: "My name is Haines" enjoys a popularity which no other slang or cant phrase has ever attained. "I'm o-p-h," "I must mizzle," "I must make myself scarce," are frequently used, but the expression which heads this article leaves them all out of sight. **1850** "N. Buntline" *G'hals of N.Y.* 40: Then I'm o-p-h!

O.P.M. *n.* other people's money. Cf. O.P., O.P.'s.

1901 in Partridge *Dict. Und.* 478: It cost me nothing to play the game, because I played it with O.P.M. (other people's money). **1935** Pollock *Und. Speaks*: O.P.M., using other people's money in any ven-

ture. **1983** in P. Heller *Bad Intentions* 216: King is essentially a brilliant con man who uses what he calls "OPM"—other people's money—to make deals as a broker. **1984** Blumenthal *Hollywood* 159: *OPM. Other people's money.* **1984** *Santa Barbara* [Calif.] *News-Press* (July 24) B3: Free drinks and food supplied by Brown with OPM—other people's money. **1996** *L.A. Times* (Dec. 11) D6: A big equity stake—as opposed to 95% OPM (other peoples' money)—means today's LBO financiers have much greater incentive to structure deals that work.

O.P.P. *n.* [*other people's property* or (*vulgar*) P(USSY) or *penis* cf. O.P., O.P.M., O.P.'s] *Rap Music.* another person's steady sexual partner or sweetheart; (*hence*) sexual or romantic involvement with another person's steady sweetheart or sexual partner.—also used collectively. Also as v. [Coined or popularized by the rap group "Naughty by Nature" as in initial quot. below.]

1991 "Naughty by Nature," in L.A. Stanley *Rap* 227: O.P.P. [title]...O.P.P. how can I explain it?...O is for "other," P is for "People [*sic*],".../The last P.../It's...like...another way to call a cat a kitten....Now for the ladies.../It's another five-letter word rhymin' with cleanes'..../I'll say the last P hmmmm, stands for Property....Ya down wit O.P.P. *Ibid.* 229: A scab tried to O.P.P. me....You knew I was O.P.P. **1991** in Slavsky, Mozeson & Mozeson *A 2 Z* 75: I don't care who you sleep with. I'm down wit' *O.P.P.*, but we live in the age of AIDS, and you have to be careful. **1992** Eble *Campus Slang* (Spring) 7: OPP— someone else's boyfriend or girlfriend. From Other People's Property.... "John wants to go with Jack's woman. John is down with OPP." **1993** P. Munro *U.C.L.A. Slang II* 23: Did you know she's O.P.P.? *Ibid.* 62: I think O.P.P. is wrong. **1994** *Totally Unofficial Rap Dictionary* (Internet): *O.P.P....Other people's pussy....Other people's penis....Other people's property.*

O.P.'s *n.* other people's (liquor or cigarettes). Cf. O.P., O.P.M. *Joc.*

1929 Brecht *Downfall* 146: He smokes O.P.'s. **1929–33** Farrell *Manhood of Lonigan* 194: "Kilarney, don't you ever smoke your own?" "O.P.'s satisfy me." **1939** Bessie *Men in Battle* 58: Each man carried a cigarette case in which he collected butts; his own or o.p.'s. **1956** E. Hunter *Second Ending* 398: Why do *you* smoke? I smoke O.P.'s. **1984** Caunitz *Police Plaza* 81: Now I only smoke O.P.'s...other people's. **1991** *New Yorker* (Sept. 2) 27: We asked Chris what brand of cigarette she smoked. "O.P.'s,...Other People's. When I buy my own, I get one of the cheapies."

ops *n. Mil.* an operations officer; (*also*) an operations headquarters. Also attrib.

1941–42 Kennerly & Berry *Eagles Roar* 172: "Ops'" voice was fainter. **1966** *N.Y. Times Mag.* (Oct. 30) 102: He will tell her about his vital job at base ops (the office where flight plans are filed), the zoomies (pilots) he deals with and the three-quarter (small truck) he drives around the base. *ca*1966 in Tuso *Vietnam Blues* 195: I was hangin' round Ops. **1977** J. Wylie *Homestead Grays* 150 [ref. to WWII]: Keep in touch with the Red Cross, Ops. **1989** W. McDonald *Band of Bros.* 5: Colonel Tydings was halfway to base ops. **1989** Zumbro & Walker *Jungletracks* 47 [ref. to Vietnam War]: Come on into the op-shop and meet the rest of the staff. *a*1991 Ethell & Sand *Ftr. Command* 12 [ref. to WWII]: We...strode back to squadron ops. **1993** Carhart *Iron Soldiers* 311: You're the ops guy who got taught that Arabic phrase book.

optic *n.* an eye. Now *joc.*

*1600 in *F & H* V 108: Whose optiques have drunke the spirit of beautie. *1891 in *DSUE* 590: A deep cut under the dexter optic. **1901** Irwin *Sonnets* (unp.): Love has put your optics on the bum. **1928** Guerin *Crime* 62: We've had our optics on you for a long while.

-orama *suffix.* (applied for joc. emphasis to nouns and, later, adjectives). [Modern U.S. usage may be directly traceable to the promotional use of the suffix in the creation of nonce coinages designating panoramic exhibitions, trade shows, special merchandising sales, etc., a practice especially common in the 1950's and 1960's; see bracketed 1936 quot. for a very early ex. The bracketed *1896 quot. translates Balzac's account of independent French usage.]

[*1896 in *OEDS*: The diorama, a recent invention,...had given rise to a mania among art students for ending every word with *rama*...."Well Monsieur-r-r Poiret,...how is your health-orama?" *Ibid.*:

"There is an uncommon *frozerama* outside!"..."Why do you say *frozerama*?...it should be *frozenrama*."] [**1936** *Scouting* (Apr.) 4: The Greater New York Boy Scout-O-Rama March 27th and 28th. The first city-wide Boy Scout-O-Rama in which Boy Scouts of the Greater City should present a living panorama of Scouting activities, with...almost 15,000 Scouts participating in the Arena of Madison Square Garden.] **1963** Gidding *Haunting* (film): What would you call this house—*Funorama?* **1981** *Harper's* (Apr.) 27: A form of encounter therapy they practiced on each other—the Gestalt-O-Rama. **1983** J. Hughes *Nat. Lampoon's Vacation* (film): Weird-orama! **1984** *Miami Vice* (NBC-TV): You're not goin' on the word of a known sleaze-orama who'd testify against his own grandmother. **1987** Boulder, Colo., anti-nuclear activist, age 23: There's a guy at work who's from California who says everything is -*orama*. Like, "It'll be fun-*orama*," or "We've got signatures-*orama*." We told him to quit saying it. **1988** J.S. Young *China Beach* (film): It means fame, fortune, and men-*orama!* **1989** *Married with Children* (Fox-TV): Look at them, Kel. Old-orama. **1989** *Rage* (Knoxville, Tenn.) (Oct.) 8: Right, Mr. Red-Neck-O-Rama. **1990** *Daily Beacon* (Univ. Tenn.) (Feb. 14) 8: Hey, Babe O Rama! **1991** *Mystery Sci. Theater* (Comedy Central TV): That was bad. Bad-o-rama!

orbit *n.* **1.** a state of extreme delight or anger.—constr. with *in* or *into*.
    1961 Kohner *Gidget Goes Hawaiian* 3: With him I'm in orbit. **1961** Terry *Old Liberty* 49: Pretty soon he is in orbit again over some old hack of a Russky textbook writer. **1965** Gallery *Eight Bells* 23: Even now I can paint better pictures with either foot than most of the phonies who pose as "modern" artists and palm off stuff on the public which insults normal intelligence but which sends screwball longhairs into orbit. **1967** G. Moore *Ngo Tho* 18: For Christ's sake, let's not go into orbit, Boyd. **1986** Univ. Tenn. grad. student: Tony'll go into *orbit* when he hears about this. **1991** *Sally Jessy Raphaël* (synd. TV series): My mother heard this and of course she went into orbit. She got very upset. **1993** Headline News Network (Apr. 17): That just sends some people into orbit. **1995** *World Today* (CNN-TV) (Apr. 27): That last point sent several political groups into orbit.
    2. a state of intoxication produced by drugs or alcohol; HIGH.—constr. with *in* or *into*.
    1973 (cited in Spears *Dict. Drugs & Drink*). **1972–76** Durden *No Bugles* 181: I went into orbit after three hits.
    ¶ In phrase:
    ¶ **in orbit, 1.** doing well; performing at a high level.
    1961 Brosnan *Pennant Race* 124: My E.R.A. is in orbit now. **1966** IUFA *Folk Speech* (Mar. 31): *In orbit*—A person who is on the ball.
    2. see s.v. **(1),** above.

orch var. ORK.

orchard *n.* *Baseball.* the outfield; (*also*) a baseball park or stadium.
    1922 *Variety* (July 21) 4: He is all set to stay in the big orchard until his bones rattle. **1938** in *DAS:* He clouted the pellet out of the orchard.

ord *n.* *Mil.* ordnance. [Quots. ref. to Vietnam War.]
    1986 Zeybel *First Ace* 276: No ord hanging. **1990** G.R. Clark *Words of Viet. War* 384: Ord...ordnance.

orderly bucker *n.* *Army.* an enlisted soldier who strives to be appointed an orderly; (*hence*) one who attempts to impress officers with his seemingly military deportment.
    1901 Freeman *Soldier in Philippines* 101: Some soldiers would keep their guns polished and oiled, and set them away, and borrow guns and belts from other soldiers to do guard duty with. These received the appellation of "orderly buckers" by their comrades, and were too lazy to walk post and perform a soldier's duty. **1907** J. Moss *Officers' Manual* 244: *Orderly Bucker*—a soldier who competes for orderly. **1909** J. Moss *Officers' Manual* (ed. 2) 284: *Orderly Buckle* [*sic*]—a soldier, when going on guard, strives by extra neatness of appearance to be designated as orderly by the commanding officer. **1925** Williams *15th Inf. Annual* 15: Pvt. 1cl. A.J. Bedard...Orderly bucker.

orderly dog *n.* *Army.* an orderly corporal. *Rare* in U.S. [Early quots. ref. to WWI.]
    *1925 Fraser & Gibbons *Soldier & Sailor Wds.* 216: *Orderly dog,* orderly corporal. *1934 Yeates *Winged Victory* 61: Taylor...was orderly dog for the day. **1946–92** Westheimer *Sitting It Out* 169 [ref. to WWII]: Other daily chores were done according to roster. The man who did it was called the dog, for orderly dog.

ordie *n.* [*ord*nance + -*ie* (dimin. personalizing suff.)] *Navy.* an ordnance handler.
    1983–86 G.C. Wilson *Supercarrier* 148: He and fellow red-shirted ordies struggled with a fresh load of bombs. **1989** T. Holmes *Fallon* 70: Ask these..."ordies." **1989** T. Clancy *Clear & Pres. Danger* 316: I'll make sure the ordies put the weapons in a convenient place. **1990** *NewsDay* (CNN-TV) (Dec. 28): Ordies of the [USS.] *America.*

Oregon boot *n.* *Pris.* (see 1901–11 quot.).
    1909 T.A. Dorgan, in Zwilling *TAD Lexicon* 61: Why Hal could wear an "Oregon boot" and beat Tenny at first. **1901–11** in Partridge *Dict. Und.* 486: Before leaving Memphis the officer had locked an "Oregon boot" on the prisoner's leg....An "Oregon boot" consists of a lead collar that fits about the ankle. It weighs, I should judge, between twenty and thirty pounds....It is either riveted or locked about the ankle....He can only walk by dragging the weighted leg behind him. **1921** *DN* V 109: *Oregon boot,* n. A device to hobble criminals in the open, somewhat like the ball and chain but less cumbersome. Said to have been devised in Oregon. **1941** Hargrove *Pvt. Hargrove* 17: With these Oregon boots and this burden of misery...I couldn't even walk over to the thing.

Oregon wrench *n.* *N.W.* (see quot.). *Joc.*
    1958 McCulloch *Woods Words* 127: *Oregon wrench*—Cold chisel and hammer.

Oreo *n.* [fr. *Oreo,* a trademark for a chocolate cookie containing a layer of vanilla filling in the middle] *Black E.* a black person who inappropriately adopts white attitudes, fashions, or the like.—used derisively. Also **Oreo cookie.** Cf. APPLE, 12; BANANA, 10; COCONUT, 5.
    [**1968** Tauber *Sunshine Soldiers* 44: He has become Oreolized—black on the outside, white on the inside.] **1969** *Harper's* (Mar.) 61: Negroes been programmed by white folks to believe their products are inferior. We've developed into a generation of Oreos—black on the outside, white on the inside. **1969** *Fortune* (Apr.), in *DAS* (ed. 3): Successful black businessmen who were regarded as "Oreos" after the cookie that is black on the outside and white within. **1969** *Time* (Sept. 19) 22: Senator Edward Brooke is [called] an "Oreo" cookie—black on the outside, white on the inside. **1969** in Willie *Oreo* 17: Dr. Willie is an Oreo cookie. **1970** *N.Y. Times Mag.* (Sept. 20) 74: Young is frequently derogated as "Uncle Whitney" or "*Whitey* Young" or "the Oreo cookie"—that is, black on the outside but white inside. **1970** *Black Scholar* (Nov.) 14: Black sailors refer to him as an "Oreo." **1969–71** Kahn *Boys of Summer* 365: I began to talk and some shouted "Oreo." You know. The cookie that's black outside and white underneath. **1971** *Playboy* (Aug.) 207: Black militants...were charging whites and "Oreos"—black on the outside, white on the inside—a toll to go to the latrine without being beaten up. **1972** *Ramparts* (May) 18: The black cop: an Oreo cookie. **1974** *Nat. Lampoon* (Aug.) 74: Scotch...is just plain jive-ass oreo booshwah bullshit! **1977** Schrader *Blue Collar* 31: Goddamn skinny Oreo...with all his goddamn honky friends. **1977** *Indiana Folklore* X 98: We are Oreos!...We have black covers with white images within us because we have been brainwashed to think the way the honkey wants us to think. **1982** Del Vecchio *13th Valley* 289: Dat man a Oreo. Yo got whut I mean. **1982** Least Heat Moon *Blue Hwys.* 104: Nothin' but Oreos—black out, white in. **1983** Rovin *Pryor* 54: In those days, if he hadn't done what we would consider not white-washed material, "Oreo" material, he never would have gotten to square one. **1988** (quot. at OFAY). **1991** *Village Voice* (N.Y.C.) (Sept. 10) 22: It is absurd to characterize him [*sc.,* Clarence Thomas] as someone who has discarded his roots, who has no interest in blacks at the bottom, and is the very model of an Oreo. **1992** *Donahue* (NBC-TV): He appointed the biggest Oreo in the country to the Supreme Court, you filthy pig! **1994** *704 Hauser* (CBS-TV): I am *not* an Oreo, Pop—and *you* are a bigot!

Oreo *adj.* *Police.* consisting of a black person and a white person. *Joc.*
    1981 Wambaugh *Glitter Dome* 67: The Oreo bandit teams were popular for a while.

Oreo queen *n.* *Homosex.* a black homosexual man who prefers to engage in homosexual activity with whites.
    1961 H. Ellison *Purgatory* 23: Then I want to take you inside a New York jail, and let you sit on the metal benches with the junkies and the Oreo queens and the mixed-up kids who don't know their backside from their belly-button.

org *n.* an organization.

    1936 *Esquire* (Sept.) 160: The…Hays org influence on pix. **1974** *Coq* (Apr.) 43: A prominent gay lib org. *a***1991** J. Phillips *You'll Never Eat Lunch* 50: The first really legitimate right-wing org.

ork *n. Music.* an orchestra or orchestration. Also **orch.**

    1936 Levin *Old Bunch* 97: He began to worry would the orch come on time? **1941** *Pittsburgh Courier* (Nov. 1) 20: The Erskine Hawkins ork. **1948** in *DAS:* Orch leader. **1959** Bechet *Treat It Gentle* 88 [ref. to *ca*1910]: There I was, working in the Eagle Orch. **1982** A. Shaw *Dict. Pop/Rock* 268: "Ork." Abbreviated form of "orchestration" and "orchestra."

ornery *adj.* [orig. dial. contr. *ordinary*] mean or poor; (hence) (*now usu.*) bad-tempered; stubborn; crotchety. Now *S.E.*

    1816 in *OEDS:* The Land is old, completely worn out, the farming extremely ornary in general. **1878** E. Wheeler *Deadwood Dick on Deck* 12: I'll show ye, directly, ye ornery cuss! **1902** Wister *Virginian* 151: He could take just little o'rn'ry frawgs and dandy 'em up to suit the bloods. **1904** B. Bower *Chip of Flying U* 21: We'll…catch up the orneriest cayuses in our strings. **1913** Mulford *Coming of Cassidy* 24: He is too ornery an' downright cussed for any human bein' to worry about. **1920** E.M. Rhodes *Stepsons of Light* 33: Mr. Hales is thinkin' some of buying that ornery…horse of mine. **1930** "M. Brand" *Destry* 152: You ornery, low-lifed son of misery. **1936** N. Nye *No-Gun Fighter* 28: They do run pretty ornery hereabouts. **1953** L'Amour *Hondo* 74: Ornery cuss. **1978** T. Evans *Longarm* 17: Ornery pissant, ain't he? **1985** McMurtry *Lonesome Dove* 378: It's too bad Call's ornery about women. **1993** *Bold & Beautiful* (CBS-TV): Stop being so ornery.

orph *n.* an orphan.

    1928 Dahlberg *Bottom Dogs* 110: He said "ta ta to all the orphs."

orphan *n. Printing.* a first line of a paragraph that appears as the last line on a page. Now *S.E.* Cf. WIDOW.

    1983 Naiman *Computer Dict.* 103. **1983** Kleper *Dict. Typog. Commun.* 123: *Orphan.* A make-up error in which the last line on a page is indented or otherwise excessively short.

orthopod *n.* [pun on *arthropod*] *Med.* an orthopedic surgeon. *Joc.*

    ***1960** in *OEDS:* We were interrupted by the surgeon himself, a big red-faced, jolly Irishman. Most orthopods are, when you come to think of it. **1980** E. Morgan *Surgeon* 138 [ref. to 1971]: You're thinking of being an orthopod, aren't you?

ory-eyed *adj.* [orig. uncert.; perh. var. of *awry*; perh. cf. *SND oorie* 'having a debauched or dissipated look'] **1.** quite drunk. Also **oary-eyed.**

    1895 (quot. at WHITE LINE). **1908** J. London *M. Eden* 398: No gettin' oryide for me. **1908** W.G. Davenport *Butte & Montana* 144: Orry-eyed beastly drunk. **1911–12** (quot. at SNOOTED). **1926** Nason *Chevrons* 107: He's the man that brought you home the night you got orey-eyed at Cokeydown. **1938** Holbrook *Holy Old Mackinaw* 18: The loggers…got ory-eyed on free champagne. **1948** J. Stevens *Jim Turner* 233: I was oary-eyed from rye whisky.

    2. angry.

    1921 Z. Grey *Mysterious Rider* 16: Didn't Wils always get ory-eyed when any of the other boys shined up to you?

O's *n.pl. Baseball.* the Baltimore Orioles baseball club.

    *ca***1983** *N.Y. Post* (Sept. 2) 65: Yanks have seven games with the Brewers, eight with the O's. **1989** P. Dickson *Baseball Dict.:* O's Common nickname for the Baltimore Orioles.

Oscar *n.* **1.** a foolish or unpleasant man; fellow.

    1905 Hobart *Get Next!* 77: Despair would grab him and he'd be Oscar with the souse thing for sure. **1918** in "M. Brand" *Coll. Stories* 22: He asks her to show off her skill, but she says, "Nothing stirring, Oscar." **1924** in Clarke *Amer. Negro Stories* 30: Dumb Oscar! Wonder how much we can make before the cops nab him? **1928** R. Fisher *Jericho* 90: You listen, Oscar. *Ibid.* 181: If a tight Oscar held out on 'em, they could jes' let him out on the wrong side o' the wall. *Ibid.* 201: There now, you dumb Oscar. *Ibid.* 303: *Oscar* Dumbbell. **1929** T. Gordon *Born to Be* 220: I could have killed that dumb Oscar. **1933** Ersine *Pris. Slang* 55: *Oscar, n.* Any hoosier. Like *John*, this name is applied to any person who is disliked by the speaker. **1946** Mezzrow & Wolfe *Really Blues* 43: They were a hard lot of oscars in the Bridewell. **1957** E. Lacy *Room to Swing* 35: He's a rough oscar.

    2. [rhyming slang *Oscar Asche* 'cash', after an Austral. actor] money; cash. *Rare* in U.S.

***1919** Downing *Digger Dial.* 36: *Oscar,* money. ***1942, ***1945 in *OED2.* **1949** in *DAS:* He would have been glad to buy me a pail of suds if he'd had any Oscar.

    3. the penis.—usu. considered vulgar. *Joc.*

    1935 in Atkinson *Dirty Comics* 141: So hold your oscar in your hand and open your eyes and you will soon be satisfied. **1978** Shem *House of God* 227: That…thing…who could squeeze Oscar as only twenty percent of vaginal vaults can. **1979** *Penthouse* (Mar.) 177: She…placed her fingers inside my shorts on my swelling Oscar.

    4. *Parachuting.* a dummy pushed out of the plane to determine wind speed and direction. [Quots. ref. to WWII.]

    1941 *Nat. Geo.* (July) 12: Before jumping, men throw out "Oscar," a dummy; its chute, opening, shows wind speed and direction. **1945** Hamann *Air Words: Oscar* the dummy. The parachute-equipped dummy that is pushed from an airplane prior to the descent of paratroops. The fall of the dummy indicates the direction of the wind.

oscar *v.* [orig. unkn.] to move hurriedly.

    1927 Coe *Me—Gangster* 172: It shot over the heads of people and just sent them oscaring for a safe place. *Ibid.* 253: You better oscar outa here, kid. **1933–34** Lorimer & Lorimer *Stag Line* 165: Let's oscar over to the other end.

Oscar-Deuce *n.* [*Oscar* (mil. communications alphabet for *O*) + DEUCE, 6.c.] *Mil. Av.* a Cessna O-2 Super Skymaster light observation airplane. Also **Oscar Douche, Oscar Pig.** [Quots. ref. to Vietnam War.]

    1971 in Yarborough *Da Nang Diary* 217: I love to fly the Oscar Deuce from channel one-oh-three. **1975** in Higham & Siddall *Combat Aircraft* 119: Known affectionately and unofficially as the "Oscar Deuce,"…Forward Air Controllers…labeled it "Oscar Pig" and "Oscar Douche"…[for] its sluggish performance, poor visibility, and lack of power. **1983–90** L. Heath *CW2* 135: Out in an Oscar-Deuce trying to find them. **1990** Berent *Steel Tiger* 159: Even something as small as the Oscar Pig, as the underpowered, prop-driven Cessna O-2A was nicknamed. *Ibid.* 311: Our little Oscar Deuce…is a bit underpowered for the mission.

Oscar Hock *n.* usu. *pl.* [rhyming slang] a sock.

    1928 Sharpe *Chicago May* 288: *Oscar Hocks*—socks. **1966** Braly *Cold* 38: They take off a few touches, get a little gold in the oscar hock, and right off they start studying a Cadillac automobile. *Ibid.* 64: "Oscar Hocks. Oscar Hocks." Clean socks every night.

O sign *n. Hosp.* a relaxation of a patient's jaw muscles indicative of a coma. Cf. Q SIGN.

    1980 E. Morgan *Surgeon* 137 [ref. to 1971]: "The 'O' sign means you lie with your mouth open so wide that a fly can buzz in and out and never get wet. After the 'O' sign comes the 'Q' sign." The resident sprawled back in the chair, his mouth sagged open and he stuck his tongue limply out at the side. "That's the 'Q,'" he said.…"Your patient isn't far from it." *a***1982** Medved *Hospital* 215: "This morning he showed a positive O sign." An O sign is where the patient is just lying there comatose with his mouth open in the shape of an O. **1987** N. Bell *Cold Sweat* 20: That's not the Q-sign. That's an O.…The O is…like a coma.

ossifer *n.* [intentional metathesis] officer. *Joc.*

    1819 Noah *She Wd. Be a Soldier* I i: Then I'm…a *brevet* ossifer in the militia besides. *Ibid.*: Mr. Lenox, the infantry ossifer. **1839** *Spirit of Times* (June 1) 153: I tink a milishy ossifer, when he's sober, is jis as good as any nigger. *Ibid.* (Nov. 14) 484: Some malicious ossifer. **1859** "Skitt" *Fisher's R.* 21: The "capting," "leftenant," "sargint"—all the "ossifers." **1861** in C.W. Wills *Army Life* 23: Our "ossifers" we think are really scared. **1864** "E. Kirke" *Down in Tenn.* 170: Nine ossifers.…a cunnel, two majors, a sargeon, two cap'ns, an the rest leftenants. **1864** in *PADS* (No. 70) 45: There would be two or three "ossifers," that I was acquainted with. **1894** Henderson *Sea-Yarns* 33: The ossifer o' the deck says he to me, says he, "W'ere away?" **1917** in Rossano *Price of Honor* 44: Haw haw, I'm an ossifer. **1918** in Hemingway *Sel. Letters* 20: I left…to visit some pals. Ossifers in the R.G.A. British outside of Padova. **1980** McDowell *Our Honor* 142: "I don't want to be an ossifer," he said, deliberately mispronouncing the word. *a***1987** Bunch & Cole *Reckoning for Kings* 6: You're supposed to be back at the Ossifer's Club. **1989** Care *Viet. Spook Show* 62: Better than me trying to pass as an ossifer.

ossified *adj.* highly intoxicated. *Joc.* Cf. later STONED.

    1901 in *OEDS:* "Did you hear about the row over in Peabody

Museum?" "What was the trouble?" "A lot of the exhibits got ossified." **1904** Hobart *Missouri* 55: I wasn't anybody's ossified man myself. **1908** in "O. Henry" *Works* 751: Ossified!…I knew what would happen if you kept it up. **1911–12** (quot. at SNOOTED). **1927** (quot. at STIFF). **1962** Butterworth *Court-Martial* 55: I think I had best say good-night to our host before I become physically as well as mentally ossified. **1967–80** Folb *Runnin' Some Lines* 248: *Ossifed* Excessively *high.*

OTD *adj.* [*out the door*] gone.
   1989 S. Hunter *Mother Wears Boots* (film): In three weeks we're gonna be OTD. Out the door.

OTL *adj. Stu. out to lunch* s.v. LUNCH.
   1958 J. Davis *College Vocab.* 8: *O.T.L.*—Out to Lunch—Not conforming to the social standards of the group; not exactly knowing what is going on. **1976** Eble *Campus Slang* (Nov.) 4: *Out to Lunch*—adj. distracted, detached from the real world: Don't talk to Becky now—she's out to lunch. *OTL* same as above.

OTR *adj.* **1.** [*on the rag* s.v. RAG] *Stu.* menstruating; (*hence*) in a bad mood.
   1968 Baker et al. *CUSS* 164: *OTR.* Be menstruating. *Ibid*: *OTR.* Constantly complaining and irritable. **1970** Landy *Und. Dict.* 143: *O.T.R.*…on the menstrual cycle. **1974** Univ. Tenn. grad. student, age 22: Maybe she's o.t.r. **1981** Eble *Campus Slang* (Mar.) 5: *OTR*—acronym of On the Rag. Snappish, testy, in a bad mood: "Lynn stayed up all night and is really OTR today." **1985** Eble *Campus Slang* (Oct.) 8: *OTR*—on the rag; in a bad mood. "I think he's OTR today because he had three exams." **1990** P. Munro *Slang U.:* Stay away from her today, she's O.T.R.
   2. (of liquor) on the rocks.
   1975 De Mille *Smack Man* 118: He picked up an o.t.r. glass.

otter-slide *n. Logging.* (see quot.).
   1956 Sorden & Ebert *Logger's* 24 [ref. to *a*1925]: *Otter-slide,* A saloon in the basement of a building.

ouchimagooga var. OOTCHIMAGOOTCHI.

Ouija board *n. Naval Av.* (see 1989 quot.).
   1966 Gallery *Start Engines* 153: They watched a grizzled chief respot the deck for the next flight, using miniature scale models on the "ouija board" in his office at the base of the island. **1989** T. Blackburn *Jolly Rogers* 67 [ref. to WWII]: The "Ouija board" [was] a scaled diagram of the hangar or flight deck on which are positioned flat cutouts of the various aircraft aboard the ship, one set…modeling planes with wings folded and the other with wings extended.

oui-oui *n.* a French person.—used derisively. Also **wiwi.** [Asterisked quots. represent New Zealand usage.]
   *1845 in *F & H* VII 361: If I had sold the land to the white missionaries, might they not have sold it again to the Wiwi [*sic*] (Frenchmen) or Americans? **1848** in Leyda *Melville Log* I 281: There was also a diminutive young "oui oui" tumbling about the floor. ***1859** in *F & H* VII·361: Before the Wewis, as the French are now called, departed. **1897** Kelley *Ship's Company* 137: The "oui-ouis," as the French were contemptuously called.

ounce man *n. Narc.* a mid-level dealer of illicit drugs.
   1966 Samuels *People vs. Baby* 105: Half-Pint bought directly from the "ounce man," the "bag man," the Man himself. **1969** Smith & Gay *Don't Try It* 105: The customer of the kilo connection is known as…an *ounce man.* **1987** *21 Jump St.* (Fox-TV): He became an ounce man. Moved up on his own.

out *n.* **1.** a way of evading responsibility, blame, or the like; a way out of difficulty; (*hence*) an excuse.
   1910 T.A. Dorgan, in Zwilling *TAD Lexicon* 62: Walcott slipped the Dixie one of the grandest trimmings ever witnessed by man, and Duck was looking for an "out" all the way through. **1913–15** Van Loan *Taking the Count* 165: They ain't leaving me a single out! **1922** J. Conway, in *Variety* (Jan. 27) 11: I will have to figure an out some way else. **1927** Coe *Gangster* 262: What have you given us? Just a sweet out for yourself! **1928** Levin *Reporter* 30: What do you care if we don't make it? We got a good out, haven't we? **1930** Conwell *Pro. Thief* 92: If the testimony of the witness and the coppers cannot be fixed so as to justify dismissal, the prosecuting attorney may need to twist the testimony or else the judge may need to find an out (a way out of the difficulty). **1934** L. Berg *Prison Nurse* 28: You declared yourself in because you wanted the dough and now you're trying to find an "out." **1933–35** D. Lamson *About to Die* 188: This was a [*sic*] easy out for him, an' would

put him solid with the wife. **1942** in E. O'Neill *Letters* 528: We left the Germans at the close of the last war with too many "outs." **1949** W.R. Burnett *Asphalt Jungle* 132: It's too easy an out for him. **1965** R.H. Dillon *J.R. Browne* 49: Their "out" was that the late Deputy Collector had declared the animals duty exempt. **1994** *N.Y. Times* (Nov. 27) I 28: She complained of unending pain and said, "I would like an out."
   2. *Specif., Gamb.* (see quot.).
   1996 Alson *Ivy League Bookie* 16: "Outs," I learned, were bookies who took other bookies' layoff bets. *Ibid.* 74: Our outs in the Dominican Republic…had been busted.

¶ In phrase:

¶ **on the outs, 1.** in disfavor; on unfriendly terms. Now *colloq.*
   *1824 in *OEDS:* "To be at outs," is to be at variance. **1887** *Lantern* (N.O.) (Dec. 10) 2: The young people are on the outs now. **1896** in Outcault *Yellow Kid* 141: Liz an' me wuz on de outs yestiddy. **1904** in W.C. Fields *By Himself* 29: I…didn't want to be on the outs with any of them. **1925** in Hammett *Big Knockover* 236: Are you and the girl still on the outs? **1954** Matheson *Born of Man & Woman* 91: "Still on the outs with Ramsay?" Chris shrugged.
   2. *Pris.* outside of prison.
   1967 Salas *Tattoo* 315 [ref. to *ca*1951]: And when we make probation, we'll continue on the outs, we'll shake down bookmakers and that for protection. **1970** Landy *Underground Dict.* 141: When I get on the outs, I'm going to get me a big steak. *a*1990 E. Currie *Dope & Trouble* 190: I never went to school on the outs, either. **1990** Bing *Do or Die* 19: On the outs, this pig was sayin', "You shouldn't steal."

out *adj.* **1.** unfashionable.
   *1660 in *F & H* V 112: Calling at my father's to change my long black cloake for a short one (long cloakes being now quite out). **1936** in *OEDS:* He had seen no pantalets on the streets, so he imagined they were "out." **1959** on *Golden Age of TV* (A&E-TV) (1987): "I got it out of town." "Yeah, it's very out." **1965** R. Baker, in *N.Y. Times* (May 2) IV 10E: Now Mailer is out. The tastemakers threw his body over the Kremlin wall last month when he published "An American Dream."
   2. in existence.
   1859 in *OED:* Fanny was the worst causist out. ***1872** in *OEDS:* The ginger-beer merchant…gesticulating and pattering one sultry morning.…"The Best Drink Out!" **1882** Peck *Peck's Sunshine* 87: The animal kicked for all that was out. **1891** (quot. at DAISY). **1900** Fisher *Job* 16: It's the biggest thing out—beats a horse-race!
   3. in error; (*hence*) demented; "off."
   1874 Pinkerton *Expressman* 35 [ref. to 1859]: "Bin sellin' niggers, eh?" "You're out thar.…I've bin sellin' cotton." **1904** in *AS* XLI (1961) 24: We people…kind o' thought he was out.
   4. [sugg. by *knock out*] unconscious. Now *colloq.*
   1898 in *OEDS:* A competitor stopped by a blow on the mark is as much "out" as though rendered helpless by a hit on the point. **1901** Ade *Modern Fables* 51: Whereupon his Wife Shrieked and flounced over into an Arm-Chair, completely Out. **1913** J. London *J. Barleycorn* 120: My reeling brain told me I would go down and out. **1956–60** J.A. Williams *Angry Ones* ch. iv: He seemed out or dead—I couldn't tell.
   5. unacceptable; impossible; prohibited. Now *colloq.*
   1921–25 J. Gleason & R. Taber *Is Zat So?* 29: Dat's out! **1936** in *OEDS:* Any form of hell raising is completely out.
   6. Orig. *Homosex.* admittedly or openly a homosexual. Cf. *come out of the closet* s.v. CLOSET.
   *1979 in *OEDAS* I: If you publish this letter, I would be grateful if you would withhold my full name, because I am not yet fully "out." ***1983** in *OEDAS* I: Only forty-three per cent of homosexuals were "out" at work. **1990** *Newsday* (N.Y.) (Oct. 2) II 5: A lot of people have just bought the equation that to be an out-lesbian [*sic*] is an obscenity. **1992** *Crier & Co.* (CNN-TV) (Apr. 9): I'm an out lesbian. **1993** *Donahue* (NBC-TV): I'm very out in Chicago.…I'm not out with my mother. **1993** *Nation* (May 10) 590: Suddenly, "out" gays inhabit high and midlevel positions in journalism and publishing. **1995** *Ricki Lake Show* (synd. TV series): You guys are both out, and you're comfortable with being out. **1996** Detroit man, age *ca*30, on *Rolanda* (synd. TV series): At the age of seventeen I was already out.

¶ In phrases:

¶ **go out** to die. [The following citation represents an

antedating of the U.S. evidence for this entry, found in full s.v. GO OUT.]

1932 L. Berg *Prison Doctor* 54: A young fellow…begged for dope to make his last moments easy. The warden refused. He said it wasn't fair that a man should not be in full possession of his senses when he went "out."

¶ **out like a light** having lost consciousness immediately or completely.

1929–33 Farrell *Young Manhood* 455: She's out like a light. **1933** in D. Runyon *More Guys* 17: John Withington White III went out like a light. **1934** in *OEDS*: When it came time to come out for the third curtain call I said, "Bobby, I just can't make it no further," and I passed out like a light. **1933–35** D. Lamson *About to Die* 193: So Mike goes out like a light. **1942–43** C. Jackson *Lost Weekend* 109: You were out like a lamp. **1954** Collans & Sterling *House Detect.* 212: She went out like a light.

out *v.* **1.** to discharge; oust.

*1902 in Partridge *DSUE* 1312: Yes I shall be outed. *1927 in *OEDS*: I'll out 'em both, even if it breaks the contract. **1946** Mezzrow & Wolfe *Really Blues* 59: We outed that nickelodeon piano player. *Ibid.* 308: *Out*: oust, get rid of, destroy. **1952** in *DARE*: Out that wet dog before he shakes hisself.

2. *Jazz.* to overwhelm; daze.

1946 Mezzrow & Wolfe *Really Blues* 21: The music we heard like to outed all of us.

3.a. Orig. *Homosex.* to publicly expose the homosexuality of (esp. a public figure).

1990 *Time* (Jan. 29): The spread of a phenomenon known as "outing," the intentional exposure of secret gays by other gays. **1990** *L.A. Times* (Mar. 22) E1: Forbes has become the latest target of "outing," a growing practice in which undeclared gay men, lesbians or bisexuals are involuntarily yanked from the sexual closet. **1990** R. Shilts, in *N.Y. Times* (Apr. 12) A23: Gay newspapers and militant AIDS activists have launched a campaign of "outing": publicly revealing the sexual orientation of people who'd rather keep it quiet. **1990** *48 Hours* (CBS-TV): If outing catches on, do you think we'll see the outing not just of celebrities but of ordinary people too? **1990** *New Republic* (Dec. 17) 22: Many pastors in Harlem are themselves closeted gay men….Yet ACT-UP has not "outed" these men. **1991** *Village Voice* (N.Y.C.) (July 30) 40: Outing celebrities catalyzes the gay movement's growth because it demonstrates the ubiquity of queers. **1991** *Geraldo* (synd. TV series): She outs her brother, saying her brother is gay, and that's never been [publicized]. **1992** *Newsweek* (June 1) 44: The Advocate, a gay magazine, outed a senior civilian DOD official who had access to classified materials. **1993** *New Yorker* (May 17) 46: He wouldn't out a homosexual. **1997** *Geraldo* (CBS-TV): We don't out anyone on this program.

b. to publicly expose private and usu. damaging facts about (a person or group).

1990 *N.Y. Newsday* (Aug. 3) II 3: Gays have been promoting a growing boycott of Philip Morris products….The Oral Majority is outing [Sen. Jesse] Helms' other corporate contributors. **1991** *Economist* (Feb. 16) 22: At Brown, women began "outing" their alleged rapists by writing their names on a lavatory wall. **1991** *Village Voice* (N.Y.C.) (July 30) 43: The series outs Tinseltown's profit motive with great flourish. **1991** *Village Voice* (N.Y.C.) (Aug. 20) 5: "Outing" someone as HIV-positive can be a death sentence. **1991** *Nation* (Aug. 26) 221: J. Edgar Hoover used the gossip columnist Walter Winchell to out Commies. **1993** *L.A. Times* (Oct. 11) E1: She would be "outed"—a tactic that involves publishing names of doctors who allegedly perform abortions. **1994** *Publishers Weekly* (Oct. 17) 70: She traces the history of public response to the "outing" of incest. **1996** *UTNE Reader* (Mar.) 26: Hoff…"outs" celebrity wannabe thrifters who just try to *look* like they shop at Goodwill.

out *prep.* ¶ In phrase: **be out of here** to be in the act of departing rapidly; be gone.—used proleptically.

1980 L. Birnbach et al. *Preppy Handbk.* 223: 8 Exit Lines…"Let's cruise."…"We're out of here." **1982–84** Safire *Take My Word* 109: The youth…cries, "I'm outta here." **1985** Eble *Campus Slang* (Oct.) 8: *Outta here*—finished. "After this semester, I am outta here." **1990** *Guiding Light* (CBS-TV): It's getting late so I'm out of here. **1994** *Vanity Fair* (Aug.) 147: The people were leaving with their mattress, saying, "We're outta here." **1995** *N.Y. Times* (July 2) ("Week in Rev.") 11: Remember that really liberal guy who thought that good govern-

ment meant more government? He's outta here. **1996** "Sapphire" *Push* 38: I'm outta here!

-out *comb. form.* (esp. in adjectival nonce coinages) thoroughly; to the limit. [A recent development of *out* 'to the conclusion or finish; to an end, and so either to completion or exhaustion' (*OED* def. 7). *Stressed out* and *drugged out* are now perh. the most frequent collocations.]

1954 in D. McKay *Wild Wheels* 95: Compared to the old guy's junked-out jalopy. **1968–70** *Current Slang III & IV* 95: Pot-out v. To smoke marijuana,—College males, Wisconsin. **1970** Quammen *Walk the Line* 105: The doped-out expression of one who has been swallowing money and enjoying it. **1974** N.Y.C. barmaid, age 22: *Panicked out* means really upset. *Hippied out* means into a real hippy scene. **1981** *Penthouse* (Mar.) 172: The image of the drugged-out poet. **1982** Huttmann *Code Blue* 171: Boy, was I out in left field…totally stressed out! **1982** Eble *Campus Slang* (Nov.) 3: *Jam-out*—to listen to music, to play music, to sing: I just got a new album. Let's jam-out. **1984** *Tri-Quarterly* (Spring) 143: At left: Nude man drugged-out at rock concert. **1985** Eble *Campus Slang* (Apr.) 8: *Stress out*—to buckle under pressure: "I refuse to stress out over my six exams." **1985** O'Neil *Lady Blue* (film): They know you're a good cop. Just a little stressed out. **1988** *Right On!* (June) 14: Jaded, drugged-out preppies in Los Angeles. **1994** *New Yorker* (Sept. 5) 98: He was cracked out. **1996** *Dr. Katz* (Comedy Central TV): You need a makeover, honey. That's why you're crabbin' out.

out-and-outer *n.* a brawl; fistfight. Also **out-and-out.**

1874 in Krause & Olson *Prelude to Glory* 102: He showed fight. The boys encouraged them until they got into a good square out-and-outer. **1973** Knopf *Emperor of North Pole* (film): A regular out-and-out.

outer space *n.* ¶ In phrase: **from** [or **in**] **outer space** crazy; demented; ludicrously eccentric.

1958 Feiffer *Sick Sick Sick* (unp.): What does she think I am?—From outer space? **1960** Thom *Subterraneans* (film): He's from outer space—thinks we're *real* people! [**1968** K. Hunter *Soul Bros.* 15: You squares…think everything has to sound like it came from outer space, or it isn't music.] **1970** Thackrey *Thief* 342: And he was a real honest-to-Christ ding. A nut. Outer space. Should have been out of there and into a laughing academy. **1974** Radano *Cop Stories* 67: And, believe me, one or two were really in outer space. They'd be a menace on the street. **1988** *Newsday* (N.Y.) (July 29) 38: He was the weirdest….Thomas was from outer space. **1995** Court TV (Feb. 27): I talked to her, and she was from outer space.

outfit *n.* **1.** *West.* an object, item, device, etc.; (*also*) a person.

1867 A.D. Richardson *Beyond Miss.* 239 [ref. to W. Texas, 1859]: "Outfit"…might mean one's…watch, his horse, or even his mistress. **1867** in A.K. McClure *Rocky Mtns.* 211: Everything is an "outfit," from a train on the plains to a pocket-knife….a wife, a horse, a dog, a cat, or a row of pins. **1870** Ludlow *Heart of Continent* 121: The use of that word "outfit," is curiously broad upon the Plains,…applied to a suit of clothes, or even…[a] ranch….But it is rather amusing to hear a Durham bull referred to as having rather a short outfit of horns; a mother threatening a refractory child with the worst outfit he ever got in his life….A man in Colorado…[told] me of a friend…who had come home "with just the prettiest outfit of small-pox that he ever see." [**1879** Cody *Life* 66 [ref. to 1857]: The whole train was denominated a "bull-outfit." Everything at that time was called an "outfit."] **1882** Baillie-Grohman *Rockies* 1: "Outfit"…is an expressive Western term, covering every imaginable human, animate, and inanimate being or article. The Plainsman calls a funeral or a wedding, his domestic kitchen utensils or his rifle, "that yer outfit."…An old trapper—who, happening to observe that the woman…was riding her horse in man's fashion—asked me whether "them outfits as I heerd called lady's maids *always* straddle their horses?" **1903** in "O. Henry" *Works* 1198: Mexico Sam…was a tough outfit. **1924** in *DAE*: You ain't believin' everythin' *this* outfit [*sc.*, person] tells you, are you? **1941** Ryan & Granet *Girl, Guy, & Gob* (film): If I had a little outfit like this [motorcycle] we wouldn't need a taxi! **1963–64** Kesey *Great Notion* 265: I should think this outfit snuggling her little tail against me here would make a qualification like that pretty damned unnecessary. *Ibid.* 539: The Indians eat an outfit called a wapatoo, a tuber-like affair.

2. Orig. *West.* **a.** a group of individuals, esp. of men traveling together.

1869 in *DA:* With a mounted escort of about twenty gallant young miners...we made up a grand "outfit." 1870 Ludlow *Heart of Continent* 121: A stage-driver saying he has a big outfit of passengers. 1882 Baillie-Grohman *Rockies* 1:The Missourian speaks of his wife and little ones as the outfit he left behind when he came West. 1883 "M. Twain" *Life on Mississippi* ch. ii: All [early] explorers traveled with an outfit of priests. 1899 (quot. at TALKFEST). 1931 in *DA:* The whole outfit acted like a lot of college boys after winning a big football game.

b. *Mil.* a military unit. Now *S.E.*

1869 in *Montana* XXXV (Summer 1985) 64: I want $1000 when I get out of this outfit. 1876 in Steckmesser *Western Hero* 186: The whole outfit would support me. *ca*1890 in J.M. Carroll *Benteen-Goldin Letters* 170: Custer...[informed] him that he would support him with the whole "Outfit." 1891 Bourke *On the Border* 15: There hain't ennuther man 'n th' hull dog-goned outfit 's got ez menny toes's me. 1895 King *Signal Butte* 193: They passed a wagon-train—a quartermaster's "outfit" westward bound. 1901 Oliver *Roughing It* 163: Some volunteer doughboy outfit. 1906 Stewart *N'th Foot* 170: It was the 71st New York that he sought....."Say, do you know of any such outfit?" 1910 *Everybody's Mag.* (May) 592: He had run away from home and "shipped in the outfit." 1914 Paine *Wall Between* 266: The tip was out that unless we came frolicking right along in a hurry your outfit of marines would be bilged entirely.

c. *Und.* a criminal organization; gang.

1933 in Partridge *Dict. Und.* 488: Outfit....Any gang. 1939 de Leon et al. *Union Pacific* (film): My job is to clear him and his outfit out of here. 1950 *Sat. Eve. Post* (Mar. 18) 64: The Syndicate, called by hoodlums the Outfit, is the racketeering organization that has been constructed on the foundation laid by Al Capone. 1953 Weidman et al. *Eddie Cantor Story* (film): I could use a kid like you in my outfit. 1963 Westlake *Getaway Face* 38: The syndicate....They call it the Outfit. 1991 M. Berle, on *Class of 20th Century* (A&E-TV): If it hadn't been for the outfits [in the 1920's] there would be no nightclubs.

3. *Narc.* **a.** equipment for the preparation and smoking of opium or for the injection of other drugs.

1881 H.H. Kane *Opium* 12: Men who could easily buy their own outfit and the purest opium. *Ibid.* 70: I have never seen a smoker who found pleasure in using the drug at home and alone, no matter how complete his outfit, or how excellent his opium. 1937 Dai *Opium Add.*, cited in Spears *Drugs & Drink.* 1970 C. Major *Dict. Afro-Amer. Sl.: Outfit:* the various artifacts used by an addict.

b. *Specif.*, a hypodermic needle and syringe for the injection of narcotics.

1951 *N.Y. Times* (June 14) 22: "John" went into a drugstore on upper Park Avenue, asked for an "outfit," and...got an envelope containing a medicinal dropper and a hypodermic needle. 1967 [R. Beck] *Pimp* 100: Cook it for me and load my outfit. 1973 W. Burroughs, Jr. *Ky. Ham* 77: I pick up an outfit (syringe). 1978 *L.A. Times* (Mar. 2) I 1: Often they are dissolved and injected into the bloodstream with hypodermic needle and syringe, known as "outfits."

out front *adj.* frank; straightforward; unabashed.

1968 T. Wolfe *Kool-Aid* 47: A community of intelligent, very open, out-front people who cared deeply for one another. 1977 in *OEDS:* Powell himself was said to be deeply bothered by that, and to have realized that he had been too "out front" on the issue. 1981–85 S. King *It* 23: That's why you want to get out front with us. 1988 *Knoxville* [Tenn.] *News-Sentinel* (Feb. 21) A10: If we couldn't convict this guy, as out-front, as brash, as arrogant as he was...what could we do?

outfuck *v.* to outfox.—usu. considered vulgar.

1980 in *Penthouse* (Jan. 1981) 200: Today marks the thirtieth year that old Albert T. Weatherfield has out-fucked the Internal Revenue Service.

outie *n.* a convex navel or a person with that characteristic. Cf. INNIE.

*1973 *Playboy* (June) 64: I have an intense interest in female navels—especially the type that protrudes, usually called an outie. 1973 (quot. at INNIE). 1974 (quot. at INNIE). 1981 *N.Y. Post* (July 28) 34: In response to Funny Navel, I am a 22-year-old woman who also has an "outie" (a belly button that sticks out). 1984 J. McCorkle *Cheer Leader* 38: Her navel (an outie). 1987 *UTSQ: Navel.* Innie, outie. 1992 *Murphy Brown* (CBS-TV): He's an outie just like me! 1997 7th on

Sixth (NY-1 TV) (Apr. 21): The [dresses] were cut so tight you could practically tell if the models had innies or outies.

outlaw *n.* **1.a.** *West.* a dangerous or refractory horse or steer, usu. an unmanageable horse not broken to the saddle despite the efforts of previous riders.

1885 in *DARE:* Many a fine, spirited animal is ruined, made an "outlaw" that no man can ride, just by the fiendish way in which they are first ridden. 1903 in *OEDS:* The whole Western country was scoured for the wildest and most vicious "outlaw" bronchos [*sic*] that could be found. 1908 J. Thorp *Songs of Cowboys:* An old black steer, kind of an old outlaw. 1912 in J.I. White *Git Along Dogies* 149: Old Dun he was a rocky outlaw. 1915 C. Fletcher, in J.I. White *Git Along Dogies* 144: I steps out tuh see if that outlaw can buck. 1915 D. Collins *Indians' Last Fight* 62 [ref. to 1880's]: He is nothing like those outlaw horses on the 81 ranch. 1915 in *Calif. Folk. Qly.* I (1942) 280: Got no fear of an outlaw steer. 1917–20 in J.M. Hunter *Trail Drivers* I 142: We...received twenty-eight head of outlaw horses....the worst horses we ever handled. 1922 P.A. Rollins *Cowboy* 281 [ref. to 1890's]: One horse in...five hundred was an "outlaw," a brute that never could be broken and that would buck almost in its sleep. 1922 Knibbs *Saddle Songs* 23: An outlaw horse. 1930 Sage *Last Rustler* 236: All the saddle horses that's left is broncs and old outlaws. 1939 Appel *People Talk* 205: Them outlaws from Nebraska and the Dakotas! Take you all day to shoe one of them. 1940 F. Hunt *Trail fr. Tex.* 123 [ref. to 1870's]: In a half-hour the dozen or more outlaws [*sc.*, steers] had been necked to gentle critters. 1965–70 in *DARE.*

b. *West.* an unreliable pistol.

1917–20 in J.M. Hunter *Trail Drivers* I 341 [ref. to 1870's]: We used...the old cap and ball sixshooter, sometimes called "outlaws." At times they would behave and fire one shot, and again they would fire two, three or possibly all six chambers at one time.

c. *Logging.* (see quot.).

1958 McCulloch *Woods Words* 128: Outlaw—...b. A machine which has killed a man. c. A tree which is dangerous to fall.

2. *Und. & Prost.* a prostitute who does not support a pimp.

1935 Pollock *Und. Speaks: Outlaw,* a prostitute who doesn't give her income to a pimp. 1957 Murtagh & Harris *First Stone* 129: A girl without a man might's well be without an arm or a leg....She'd be called an *outlaw* in the houses I used to work. 1966 Jarrett *Private Affair* 11: I know that house dicks and bellhops don't like "outlaws"— their name for interlopers who don't cut them in on the profits. 1962–68 B. Jackson *In the Life* 206: She's probably an outlaw whore. An outlaw whore is one that has turned herself out. 1968 Gover *JC* 62: Being a lone outlaw in this life, with the johnlaws up one side and the pimps down the other. 1973 Schulz *Pimp* 39: I met her when she was an outlaw. You know, trying to work a stroll all by herself. 1988 Kienzle *Marked for Murder* 4: For years now she had been pimpless— in the language of her profession, an outlaw.

3. a usu. fractious person who operates outside an established organization or regulations.

1956 "T. Betts" *Across the Board* 156: Tinhorns who tried to make book or tout without getting an okay. These are known...as "outlaws." 1956 in *DAS:* Outlaw strike—A walkout not approved by union officials. 1974 Scalzo *Stand on Gas* 73: Years ago...the mighty American Automobile Association...adjudged any [racing] driver who wasn't an AAA member as an "outlaw." It was most derogatory. 1990 *Marshall Chronicles* (ABC-TV): You're a real outlaw, ain't ya?

outlaw *v. Prost.* to practice prostitution without supporting a pimp.

1968 Gover *JC* 62: Odessa you such a strong-*strong* broad, outlawin like that. 1988 N. Stone *Tricks of Trade* (film): I don't have a pimp. I outlaw.

out of it *adj.* **1.** in error.

1835 *Mil. & Nav. Mag. of U.S.* (Aug.) 423: "I was in daily expectation of a quantity of letters from—" "Your sweet Lizzy," said Hobbs, with a wink. "No, Hobbs, you're out of it—from home."

2. excluded or excluding oneself from one's customary company or activities.

1897 Ade *Pink* 164: Oh, I think you're prejudiced in favor of Peter....He's out of it now. 1910 Hapgood *City Streets* 48: He has developed himself highly, but in the wrong direction. He is consequently side-tracked, "out of it."...His old pals seem stupid to him;

and yet he is poorly adapted to live in the world of acceptability. **1916** S. Lewis *Job* 34: It's just as bad as parties at Panama. Never really enjoyed 'em. I'm out of it. I'll stick to my work. Oh, drat it!

3.a. out of touch with current social fashions or interests; behind the times; (*also*) stupid.

    1945 E. Rice *Dream Girl* 374: No, what I really want is *Always Opal*. You see, all my friends are reading it, and I feel so out of it. **1955** *Science Digest* (Aug.) 33: Slang…denotes immediately whether the speaker is "on the ball" or "out of it." **1957** Gutwillig *Long Silence* 191: It would have been impossible to find two people who were more "out of it" in 1951. **1959** in H. Ellison *Sex Misspelled* 101: This guy was really out of it. But *nowhere!* **1960** Swarthout *Where Boys Are* 6: If you never go [to Florida for spring break] you are really out of it. *a***1961** Boroff *Campus U.S.A.* 177: "They're just out of it," a flip woman undergraduate said dismissively. **1962** T. Jones *Stairway* 55: Man, he is really out of it. **1968** Sebald *Adolescence* 251: Out-of-it—behind the times, stupid, as a parent may be "out-of-it." **1970** C. Major *Dict. Afro-Amer. Slang: Out of it:* (1950's) unfashionable; unpopular idea, etc. **1971** H. Roberts *Third Ear* (unp.): *Out of it*…unaware; not "hip." **1971** S. Stevens *Way Uptown* 120: She was so out of it she musta been from some other world. She was seventeen and she loved everybody. **1971** *Night Gallery* (NBC-TV): You've got to be out of it. **1972** Kopp *Buddha* 27: As a child, I was often lonely and out of it. **1993** Bahr & Small *Son-in-Law* (film): You are so *out* of it, Connie!

b. muddled or oblivious, as from drink, drugs, or boredom. [The 1959 quot. seems to be wrongly defined, though it would clearly belong here if the usage applied to intoxication.]

    [**1959** *AS* (May) 155: One who is extremely happy is on *cloud 88* or *out of it.*] **1963** Braly *Shake Him* 138: Anything he does, he does without even knowing he's doing it. Believe me, he's out of it. **1966** IUFA *Folk Speech* (Apr. 30): *Out of it*—Drunk. **1970** Segal *Love Story* 28: I had been so out of it, I hadn't heard her question. **1973** in P. Dickson *Slang!* 95: *Out of it*…To be out of touch with reality when under the influence of a drug, especially hallucinogens. **1974** Cull & Hardy *Types of Drug Abusers* 197: *Out-of-it*—Confused, disoriented. **1967–80** Folb *Runnin' Lines* 248: *Out of it* Excessively *high.* ***1986** in Thorne *Dict. Contemp. Slang:* Her main hobby these days seems to be getting out of it as often as possible.

c. fatigued or unconscious; (*also*) ill or disabled.

    1970 Landy *Underground Dict.* 143: *Out of it*…Unable to function. **1972** N.Y.U. student: *Out of it* means completely worn out, *pooped. a***1984** in Terry *Bloods* 9: This [wounded] guy was really out of it. He was like moanin'. **1996** Univ. Tenn. student: You do look kind of out of it.

out of sight *adj.* **1.** unsurpassable; of extraordinary excellence; wonderfully good or impressive; very fine. Also as *interj.*

    1876 in *Buffalo Bill* 205: For ye see our beans an' crackers an' our pork were outen sight,/An' the boys expected rashuns when they struck our camp that night. [**1891** Maitland *Slang Dict.* 196: *Out of sight* (Am.), beyond reach, unattainable.] **1892** S. Crane *Maggie* 19: Say, Mag, I'm stuck on yer shape. It's outa sight. *Ibid.* 27: At the Museum, Maggie said, "Dis is outa sight." **1896** S. Crane *Maggie* (ed. 2) 32: Come ahn out wid me! We'll have a out-a-sight time. **1893** in F. Remington *Sel. Letters* 162: It is simply out of sight…too good to be true. **1895** Townsend *Fadden* 192: Say, if de boat had struck a whale dere couldn't been more fun in de cabin. It was out of sight. **1895** in Outcault *Yellow Kid* 138: Aw say! velveteen seats an' carpet on de floor—out o' sight. **1896** *Harper's Mag.* (Apr.) 781: That's out of sight!…It will please the old lady to the ground. **1896** in K. Chopin *Complete Works* II 532: "Oh! it's out of sight!" she told him after Mass. "You get to wear one of them gowns on the road and talk that language: the Egyptian ain't in it." **1896** Ade *Artie* 55: Oh, doctor! She looked out o' sight! **1896** F.H. Smith *Tom Grogan* 129: Carl had already dressed himself in his best clothes, producing so marked a change in the outward appearance of the young Swede that Cully in his admiration pronounced him "out o' sight." **1897** Norris *Vandover* 359: "Had a great feed: lettuce sandwiches with mayonnaise. Simply out of sight." **1899** Cook *Co. B* 106: He was an "out of sight" cook. **1899** Norris *Blix* 186: It's a corker! If it's rejected everywhere, it's an out-of-sight yarn just the same. **1899** Norris *McTeague* 147: The guests had shouted applause, "Outa sight." **1891–1900** in Hoyt *Five Plays* 130: It's out of sight, isn't it?…Great!…You have enjoyed yourselves?…Indeed we have! **1900** T. Dreiser *Carrie* 119: Good…fine; out o' sight! **1902** Corrothers *Black*

Cat Club 26: "Out o' sight!" yelled a dozen voices, as the poem was concluded. **1902** Mead *Word-Coinage* 170: An Englishman…said: "How do you feel old chap?" "Out of sight," replied the American. **1907** J. London *Road* 134: "And it *was* good bread," he often assured me; "and the meat was out of sight." **1908** in "O. Henry" *Works* 1588: That's out o' sight, Kid. **1909** T. Dreiser, in Riggio *Dreiser-Mencken Letters* I 31: "A Plea for Profanity" is all to the good…."A Plea for Hell" would be out of sight. **1911** *JAF* (Oct.) 360: You bet yo' life she's out o' sight,/She wore the Louisville curl. **1914** Dale *Songs of 7th* 93: The Captain says, "On public views you must look out of sight." **1917** in Kimball & Balcolm *Sissle & Blake* 33: What's the matter with Butler?/She's all right./What's the matter with Butler?/Out of sight. **1926** Pickens *American Aesop* 182: I'm out o' sight! I'm in the swim! **1927** *Immortalia* 96: The Judge had been up the previous night/At a game of draw that was *out of sight.* **1952** C. Sandburg *Strangers* 71 [ref. to *ca*1885]: With a big smile on his face Harry Smith broke in, "That's out of sight!" He was talking in the latest slang. Anything that hit you as new and wonderful was "out of sight." It was not polite and proper. **1962** Wepman et al. *The Life* 141: And your main man's loving was out of sight. **1966** J. Mills *Needle Park* 44: Man, that's outa sight, that's somethin' else. **1966** Samuels *Baby* 76: You're out of sight. **1967** *World of Acid* (film): Outasight, Derek, thank you! **1992** N. Cohn *Heart of World* 58: And the sex is out of sight.

2. at an extraordinary level; exceedingly high.

    1903 C.E. Stewart *Uncle Josh* 159: One day when the mercury wuz way out of sight.

3. extraordinary, esp. exceptionally bad; (*hence*) insane; deranged.

    1928 Carr *Rampant Age* 155: But she's clear outa sight as a date, Paul—"hands off" stuff, chaperones, maybe even corsets. **1959** F.L. Brown *Trumbull Pk.* 245: I called the group together right after that absolutely out-of-sight talk with Mr. O'Leary. **1962** H. Simmons *On Eggshells* 200: Man, some of our folks are out of sight. They want to integrate themselves into everything, even the white man's headaches. **1966** J. Mills *Needle Park* 74: And he was over at the house that night, and Helen had a toothache. And it was really—I mean, it was out of sight—it was too much. She was going crazy with it. **1969** *Playboy* (Dec.) 104: The race thing. It was really out of sight, man. **1970** J. Howard *Please Touch* 83: You act like some fuckin' latent sex queen. You're gettin' fuckin' out of sight. I'm gettin' fed up with your shit. **1978** W. Wharton *Birdy* 59: Birdy's deep into his creepy canaries….talking about…eggs.…He's out of sight. **1979** *N.Y. Post* (Sept. 11) 3: He can't be thinking straight….The last time I saw him he was really out of sight.

out of sight *adv.* **1.** to the limit of endurance; to an extraordinary degree; completely; to death.

    1839 Marryatt *Diary* 262: She'll talk you out of sight. **1840** *Spirit of Times* (Oct. 3) 366: One fellow has fattened up, *out of sight*, on the rare luxuries of the tide. **1890** Quinn *Fools of Fortune* 357: The tramp is beaten "out of sight." **1966** Reynolds & McClure *Freewheelin Frank* 5: I felt out of sight wonderful.

2. extremely; surpassingly.

    1896 *Pop. Sci. Mo.* (Dec.) 255: Tidy-holders were "an out-of-sight good graft."

3. extremely well.

    1894 (quot. at *up in* [or *to*] G s.v. G). **1894** in *Amer. Heritage* (Apr. 1985) 108: Have been in training, and feel as if I could play "out of sight." **1896** Ade *Artie* 4: Say, she treated me out o' sight. **1896** in Blackbeard & Williams *Smithsonian Comics* 22: Evans sings it out-o-sight. **1902** Dunbar *Sport* 76: There's a fellah in the house 'at plays "Rag-time" out o' sight.

¶ In phrase:

¶ **leave** [or **knock**] **out of sight** to surpass by far.

    1840 (quot. at HAINES). **1868–71** C.G. Leland *Breitmann's Ballads* 48: I'll 'stonish folk a-ridin' in de road [on a velocipede]…und knock dings out of sight.

out of state *adj.* [joc. alt. OUT OF SIGHT] *Stu.* splendid. *Joc.*

    1973 Eble *Campus Slang* (Nov.) 3: *Out of state!*—exclamation that something is great, fantastic: Hey baby, out of state! **1974** (quot. at RIGHT ARM). **1980** *Mork & Mindy* (ABC-TV): This America [is] really out of state!

out of this world *adj.* **1.** wonderful; extraordinary. Also as adv.

1928 R. Fisher *Jericho* 303: *Out (of) This World* Beyond mortal experience or belief. **1937** *New Yorker* (Apr. 17) 27: They are what a *sender*...gives when...he is...*out of the world*. **1938** Ward *Fog* 294: Lawd, chile; it's out of this world. **1941** Macaulay & Wald *Manpower* (film): Your singin' is sure out of this world. **1942** in C.R. Bond & T. Anderson *Flying T. Diary* 98: Both of us...decided to tell the RAF where to get off. George kept saying our comments were "out of this world." **1945** *Yank* (Dec. 28) 8: It's what's known on Broadway as "out of this world." **1946** Mezzrow & Wolfe *Really Blues* 47: Tony could play the blues out of this world. **1947** *Tomorrow* (Aug.) 28: *Out of this world*...has pretty well passed out of hip favor. **1950** *N.Y. Times* (Apr. 2) I 16 (adv.): A desire to have your room painted in some dreamy, out-of-this-world shade that you once saw in a magazine. **1988** M. Maloney *Thunder Alley* 159: Out of this world, isn't it?

2. extreme.

1942 A.C. Johnston *Courtship of Andy Hardy* (film): The color's all right, but it's out of this world....It takes things too seriously.

out of town *adv.* out of one's mind. Also as adj.

1942 *ATS* 180: Insane; crazy....*out of town*. **1963** Coon *Short End* 116: I dug the smell. Pot. T. Willie was stoned out of town.

out-psych *v.* to intimidate or confuse by psychological means; defeat by psychological maneuvering; PSYCH OUT, 2.

1974 in *OEDAS* I 148: Billy Jean King eventually outpsyched Riggs and beat him badly. **1980** *Forbes*, in *OEDAS* I 148: Old presidents...are supposed to have the ability to out-psych the vagaries of [the] market. **1987** *N.Y. Times* (Oct. 25) V 13: The more ferocious the fight,...the wearing-down, the out-psyching, the approach to the knockout and the knockout itself, the more spellbinding the event.

outrageous *adj.* extraordinary; amazing; *(hence)* marvelous; splendid.

1956 R. Ellison, in W. King *Black Anthol.* 266: Maybe he gave 'em to ole Aunt Mackie, man. I bet with them she could work up some outrageous spells! [*1968** T. Taylor *Cay* 98: [Bahamas:] I 'ave foun' an outrageous good 'ole on d' reef.] **1971** *Playboy* (Aug.) 32: Bo Diddley has been typed and hyped as..."the most outrageous, bad-assed guitar man alive," as the liner notes on his most recent disc have it. **1972** N.Y.U. student: Hey! This is outrageous stuff! **1972** Smith & Gay *Don't Try It* 205: *Outrageous*. Really good or really bad, exceptional; may be very amusing; highly unconventional. **1977** in Mack *Real Life* (unp.): Oh God!! Outrageous!! All right! **1980** L.I., N.Y., woman, age *ca*25: Here's [a photo] of the lake where we camped. It was so outrageous there. **1980** *N.Y. Times* (Dec. 14) IIA 21: The cobble-stone street is lined with little shops, lampposts, even trees...it really is outrageous. **1981** Hathaway *World of Hurt* 125: Hey, damn, that's great...outrageous. **1984** *Daily Beacon* (Univ. Tenn.) (July 31) 7: I think we've done an outrageous job of proving ourselves. **1989** *CBS This Morning* (CBS-TV) (Nov. 9): "The timing of your book is really outrageous." "Yes, we did rather well in that." **1990** *Good Morning America* (ABC-TV): This will bring music learning to the masses. It's really outrageous. And it's available now. **1992** *Middle Ages* (CBS-TV): The band is lame but you're outrageous! **1993** *CBS This Morning* (CBS-TV) (Dec. 13): What I am saying is something far more outrageous—that [patients] who were prayed for at a distance and didn't know they were being prayed for also improved dramatically. **1993** *I Witness Video* (NBC-TV): It was just outrageous that we lived through it!

outro *n.* [sugg. by *intro*] *Entertainment Industry*. (see 1983 quot.). Also as *v.*

1983 *USA Today* (Aug. 2) 1D: *Outro*—the part of a broadcast where the commentator signs off. **1986** E. Weiner *Howard the Duck* 3: Uncountable the S.F. movies intro'd or outro'd by facsimiles of me.

outsharp *v.* to outwit.

1976 "N. Ross" *Policeman* 26: His family will be proud when they listen to the story of how he outsharped or bribed a copper.

outside *n.* **1.** *Mil.* civilian life. Also as *adv.*

1898 Doubleday *Gunner* 243: The disgruntled members of the crew were...mainly the "outside" men—men not of the Naval Reserves. **1918** Rowse *Doughboy Dope* 9: A is the ARMY at that stage of your young life when you were on what the Army calls "the outside." **1920** *Am. Leg. Wkly.* (Mar. 26) 24: We stack up high with the outside here, and we're gonna keep it that way. **1923** Boyd *Wheat* 56: Lepere and Harriman were telling each other of what they used to do "on the outside," by which phrase they meant before they had enlisted. **1930** *Our Army*

(Feb.) 44: What did you do on the outside? **1933** March *Co. K* 19: I used to plan my first meal on the outside, but thinking about those things all the time made me so hungry. **1935** F.H. Lea *Anchor Man* 4: Just what career had you planned for yourself on the outside? **1940** Goodrich *Delilah* 107 [ref. to 1916]: Delilah's men referred to all the world and life beyond her decks as "the outside." **1941–42** Gach *In Army Now* 158: On the outside they would starve. **1946** Heggen *Mr. Roberts* 1: Captain Morton was a lieutenant-commander, and on the outside had been in the merchant marine. **1965** C.D.B. Bryan *P.S. Wilkinson* 369: You know, I never asked you what you were doing before this...I mean what you did on the outside, so to speak.

2. *Pris.* the world outside prison. Also as *adv.* Cf. INSIDE.

1871 Banka *Prison Life* 72: When I came here, I thought I should learn a trade at which I could earn an honest living "outside." **1900** Willard & Hodler *Powers That Prey* 131: He asked him for news of the outside. **1912** Lowrie *Prison* 381: He was given a towel by an acquaintance who had known him "outside." **1918** in *AS* (Oct. 1933) 30: [Ft. Leavenworth:] *Outside* (the), All the world beyond the walls. **1929** *AS* IV 343: *Outside*. Out of jail. **1965** C. Brown *Manchild* 163 [ref. to 1950's]: He'd been in jail for about four years....Reno wasn't on the outside, but cats kept coming up to [prison] for using horse.

¶ In phrases:

¶ **get outside of, 1.** (see quots.).

*****a*1890–1902** *F & H* V 115: *To get outside of*...to copulate: of women only. **1916** Cary *Venery* I 107: *Getting Outside Of*—To receive a prick. Said of women only.

2. see s.v. *get [oneself] [on the] outside of*, below.

¶ **get [oneself] [on the] outside of** to consume (food or drink); ingest. Also vars.

1864 in McKee *Throb of Drums* 155: We put ourselves on the outside of some of it at noon. **1865** (quot. at OATH). **1870** in C.G. Leland *Breitmann's Ballads* 224: "If I could see a glass of whisky,...I'd throw myself outside of it mighty quick."... "Each...would...get outside his own whisky." **1889** B. Harte *Dedlow Marsh* 61: You'd better hoist yourself outside some quinine. **1901** King *Dog-Watches* 35: On a table close by she placed a dish of cold potatoes and a glass of lager beer, saying, "Git on the outside of that, you d—d brat." *****a*1890–1902** *F & H* V 115: *To get outside of*...To eat or drink; as, to get outside of a pint of beer, or a chop. **1938** A.J. Liebling, in *DAS*: He got outside of a bowl of chili. **1970** in Brooks & Warren *Modern Rhetoric* 95: This one simply isn't himself until he gets outside of a little alcohol. **1972** Jenkins *Semi-Tough* 149: Let's...get on the outside of some bacon cheeseburgers. **1997** Knoxville, Tenn., man, age *ca*50: I need to get outside of some lunch.

outsider *n.* an act of copulation performed outdoors.

1985 Briskin *Too Much* 292: Since the afternoon of the outsider, they had made love only once.

outsiders *n.pl.* *Und.* a burglar's tool resembling a tiny pair of pliers used to open a door from the outside while the key is still in place.

1846 in Partridge *Dict. Und.* 488: Terrible instruments called *outsiders*—resemble pair of long pincers with end round and hollow. **1848** *Ladies' Repository* VIII (Oct.) 315: *Outsiders*, An instrument to unlock a door with its own key, one of the blessings of the congregate system of imprisonment, being first invented and made by a convict in state's prison, who was a blacksmith; made thus: [diagram].

outslick *v.* *Black E.* to outwit; prove craftier than.

1941 *Pittsburgh Courier* (May 24) 11: To outslick, out-figure, and outsmart the rest of the gambling playboys. **1943** in Boller *Not So!* 139: Whenever anyone is heard saying that the British are outslicking us or that we dare not trust Russia much,...this is Nazi propaganda. **1962** in Wepman et al. *The Life* 104: Now the young whores are trying to outslick me. **1972–74** Hawes & Asher *Raise Up* 111: Outslicking him and the cops all down the line.

outstanding *adj.* *Mil.* excellent.—used with more or less diminished force, often sarcastically. [Popularized during Vietnam War; largely founded on the use of the word as describing the highest level of proficiency or achievement on official personnel-evaluation forms.]

1964 *N.Y. Times* (Sept. 20) 4. **1965** *N.Y. Times* (Nov. 3) 2: Anything that is not grossly unsatisfactory is "outstanding!" **1974** Univ. Tenn.

student, served in Vietnam 1971–72: They used to say "outstanding" for anything good. Like, some bar girl would look "out*stand*ing!" Or a real disaster would be "out*stand*ing" the way you'd ordinarily say, "Oh, great!" You know, sarcastically? The first time I ever heard it was at Fort Campbell, Kentucky. And lots later. **1980** W.C. Anderson *Bat-21* 36: "We're having a farewell party." "Outstanding." **1988** Willson *REMF* 36: The key word of sarcasm over here [in Saigon] is *Outstanding* said with an accent on the "out" and the "standing" part sort of dragged out. Every other [vexing] thing is greeted with "Outstanding." **1989** P. Dickson *Slang!* 243: *Outstanding.* Term of mock enthusiasm for anything from the terrible to the barely passable. **1993** P. Dickson *War Slang* 283: Out-fucking-standing.

out to lunch see s.v. LUNCH.

oven *n.* [**1.** the vagina; (*hence*) the womb. [Although the following quots. are BrE, the sense survives in the U.S. in the phr. *have one in the oven* below.]

    ***1699** E. Ward *London-Spy* 140: 'Twas for picking a Countrymans Pocket of his Pouch, and hiding it in her Oven; but when she came to be search'd, the Fool having forgot to take up the Strings, was discovered in her Roguery, and sent here to be lashed; and does she not deserve it, sir, for trusting her Money in a box that has neither lid nor bottom to it? ***1698–1706** in D'Urfey *Pills* IV 117: A Lord, a Knight, a Gentleman,/Is welcome to my Oven. ***1720** D'Urfey *Pills* VI 92: But if my Oven be over-hot,/I dare not thrust in it Sir.]

2. the mouth.

    ***1785** Grose *Dict. Vulgar Tongue: Oven.* A great mouth. **1823** J.F. Cooper *Pioneers* 199: Shut your oven, you crow! **1859** Matsell *Vocab.* 62: *Oven.* A large mouth. "The bloke should be a baker—twig his oven," the man should be a baker—look at his big mouth.

¶ In phrase:

¶ **have one in the oven** to be pregnant. Also vars. Cf. *have a bun in the oven* s.v. BUN.

    1958 Frankel *Band of Bros.* 6 [ref. to 1950]: Bango! Six months later, I got one in the oven. **1962** Quirk *Red Ribbons* 328 [ref. to 1940's]: "Still got the muffin in the oven?" She patted her stomach and said, "Still there." **1967** R. Morris *Modern Millie* (film): I got seven kids and one in the oven. **1970** Wakefield *All the Way* 108 [ref. to ca1952]: Some guy...knocked her up. She had a pie in the oven, and the guy married her. **1977** Hamill *Flesh & Blood* 105: The last time I heard, you had a couple of kids and one in the oven. **1978** *N.Y. Times* (July 2) II 21 [ref. to 1955]: In telling that story, Bogie referred to the pregnancy as the time Betty "had one in the oven." I asked him later if he really wanted to use that phrase. He seemed astonished by my question. He went about asking everybody whether the phrase was offensive. **1966–80** McAleer & Dickson *Unit Pride* 271 [ref. to ca1952]: They've got a baby in the oven. **1984–88** in H. Berry *Where Ya Been?* 205: They won't count the one in the oven.

over *n. Mil.* a bullet or shell that overshoots its target.

    ***1915** in *OEDS:* He believes the Uhlans were North Irish Horse and the bullets "overs." **1984** Hammel *Root* 111: The first shells to strike...were "overs" intended for the Israelis.

over *adj.* no longer fashionable; HISTORY.

    1995 *Time Out N.Y.* (Oct. 18) 102: There are still a few people ogling one another downstairs but upstairs is over, as they say. **1997** *Off the Rack* [electronic magazine at www.offtherack.com] ("mediAnatomy") (Mar. 20): The press labors mightily to strike been-there-done-that poses. "That's so over" is the most commonly overheard response in insider conversations. **1997** *3rd Rock* (NBC-TV): Sally is *so* over.

over *adv. Police.* to prison. See also *send over* s.v. SEND. Cf. *over the road* s.v. ROAD.

    1941 Huston *Maltese Falcon* (film): You killed Miles and you're going over for it!

¶ In phrases:

¶ **put it all over** to outdo; excel; best.

    1899 Ade *Fables* 76: There was one Boy who could put it All Over the other Members. **1898–1900** Cullen *Chances* 31: The way that little filly Mazie V. put it all over her field was something ridiculous. **1905** *DN* III 91: *Put it all over*...To beat (literally or figuratively) thoroughly. "He put it all over him." Common. **1907** Hobart *Beat It!* 13: I met Fred and Henri Leoni at the Bingle Club not long ago, and they put it all over me [by speaking French]. **1920** S. Lewis *Main Street* 6: They

ought to of worked on the farm, the way I have. The workmen put it all over them.

¶ **put it over** to win.

    1914 Patten *Lefty o' the Bush* 12: Put it over by one measly run, that's all.

¶ **put** [or **slip**] **one over** [perh. of baseball origin, ref. to "putting one [*sc.*, a pitch] over" the plate for a (called) strike] to perpetrate a fraud or deception.—usu. constr. with *on*.

    1908 in Fleming *Unforget. Season* 242: "Muggsy" tried to be foxy and "put something over" on Chance. **1913** T.M. Osborne *Pris. Walls* 46: His attitude suggests that he has "slipped one over" on somebody. **1913** in J. Reed *Young Man* 28: I'd heard a lot of bogus counts, and so forth, putting one over on poor girls. **1917** in Truman *Dear Bess* 233: Captain Salisbury put a good one over on the officers yesterday. **1918** Stringer *House of Intrigue* 86: Say, Mister, my middle name is Jeremiah when it comes to putting one over on the penal code. **1929** "E. Queen" *Roman Hat* 49: What are you tryin' to put over on me? **1930** Gilman *Sob Sister* 15: She thinks I been slipping something over. **1997** Knoxville, Tenn., attorney, age 44: They'll put one over on you if they think they can get away with it.

overamp *v. Narc.* to overdose.

    1967 (cited in Spears *Dict. Drugs & Drink* s.v. *overamped* 'high on or overdosed on amphetamines'). **1967–68** von Hoffman *Parents Warned Us* 83: I make 'em overamp (overdose) till they scream. **1972** Smith & Gay *Don't Try It* 205: *Overamp.* Take too much of a stimulant.

overamped *adj.* overwrought; overexcited. Cf. AMPED and *overamped* 'high on or overdosed on amphetamines' s.v. OVERAMP.

    1988 *N.Y. Times Bk. Rev.* (Oct. 30) 28: Unlike Mr. Oster's earlier and more realistic procedural novels in this series, it is so overamped for effect that three chapters of explanation are needed to unscramble the plot. **1991** *Bill & Ted's Excellent Adv.* (Fox-TV): Mr. Keelson's totally overamped.

over-and-under *n. Mil.* a combination assault rifle and grenade launcher. [Later quots. ref. to Vietnam War. Bracketed 1930 quot. ref. to 'a kind of shotgun in which the barrels are mounted not side by side as usual, but one above the other'.]

    [**1930** in *OEDS:* I have ordered a pair of Over and Under guns as I prefer the grip on this type of gun.] **1972** J. Morris *Strawberry Soldier* 189: Cowboy slung his over-and-under M-16 over his shoulder. **1982** Del Vecchio *13th Valley* 462: The XM-203 was an over/under, an M-16 rifle on top mated to an M-79 grenade launcher on the bottom.

overcharged *adj. Narc.* (see quots.).

    1936 *AS* (Apr.) 124: [Drug addicts:] *Overcharged.* Having taken too much dope. See *gowed.* **1942** *ATS* 478: *Overcharged,* overdrugged.

overcoat *n.* **1.** a pie crust. *Joc.*

    1918 (quot. at SLUM). **1940** Simonsen *Soldier Bill* 11 [ref. to 1914]: "Hash with overcoats," meant meat balls with pie crust around them.

2. a condom. *Joc.*

    1938 "Justinian" *Amer. Sexualis* 30: *Overcoat.* n. A cundum....U.S. C.20. **1970** E. Knight *Black Voices* 101: Naw, man, I ain't got no overcoat. **1976** *AS* LI 12 [ref. to 1920's].

3. a parachute.

    1942 *ATS* 32: *Overcoat,* a parachute. **1944** *AAF* 369: *Overcoat.* parachute.

¶ In phrase:

¶ **wooden overcoat** see WOODEN OVERCOAT.

overhaul *v. Esp. Naut.* to look into; inspect. [Formerly S.E. (*OED:* 1705).]

    ***1830** T. DeQuincey, in *OED:* His own expressions of 'overhaul', for *investigate,* and 'attackable', are in the lowest style of colloquial slang. **1853** [J. Jones] *Jack Junk* 31: Ha!...a pedlar? Let's overhaul your cargo. **1942** *ATS* 164: Scrutinize; "give the once-over."...*overhaul.*

overjolt *n. Narc.* a drug overdose.

    1958–59 Lipton *Barbarians* 24: He took an overjolt and passed out. **1963** Braly *Shake Him* 149: You've seen overjolts. That was no overjolt. *a*1979 Pepper & Pepper *Straight Life* 211: There was nothing I could do except fix her....I was afraid she'd get an overjolt.

overland trout *n. West.* bacon. *Joc.*

    1906 in *Montana* (Winter 1974) 44: And every place you come you find bacon for breakfast-dinner-supper. They call it "Overland Trout," "North Dakota Beefsteak," etc. **1958** McCulloch *Woods Words* 128: *Overland trout*—Bacon.

Oversexed Weekly *n. Mil.* the *Overseas Weekly*, an independently published newspaper for servicemen. *Joc.*

    1969 Moskos *Enlisted Man* 102: The paper long ago acquired the nickname of the Oversexed Weekly by blending pinups with come-on headlines: "Torso Killer Lt. Mad, Headshrinkers Rule,"…"Raped Twice in BOQ, Army Nurse Charges," "Old Sarge Drops Dead on Gen's PT March." Yet along with its lurid tabloid qualities, the *Overseas Weekly*…is forthrightly concerned with GI rights. **1980** Cragg *Lex. Militaris* 325: Oversexed Weekly. *Overseas Weekly.*

owie *n. Juve.* a bruise or minor injury.

    1992 *CBS This Morning* (CBS-TV) (July 21): He's nursing a pretty bad owie this morning. **1997** *Santa Barbara* [Calif.] *News-Press* (Jan. 30) A9: Diaper duties, owies, and fascinations like gum on the ground make a shopping trip with children take FOREVER. **1997** *Mystery Sci. Theater* (Sci-Fi Channel): See the owie?

owl *n.* **1.** (used in various similes, usu. related to drunkenness, esp. involving phr. **boiled owl**).

    1857 in *DA*: I felt, to use a certain figurative expression, "like a boiled owl." **1861** in Matrau *Letters* 8: Smith is as tough as a boiled owl. **1862** C.F. Browne *Artemus Ward* 84: Iargo got Casheo drunk as a biled owl on corn whisky in order to karry out his sneekin desires. **1863** Hosmer *Color-Guard* 143: The cor-r-rpiral, shure, is tougher than a biled owl! **1881** B. Nye *Forty Liars* 73: She, too, is as drunk as a biled owl. **1881** Small *Farming* 54: He went off and got drunk as a boiled owl, returning home at about ten o'clock. **1890** C.C. King *Ranch* 20: He gets drunk as a boiled owl every pay-day. **1892 in OEDS: The expression, "Intoxicated as a boiled owl," is a gross libel upon a highly respectable teetotal bird. **1892** *JAF* V 60: To feel like a stewed owl….More idiomatically, like a biled owl. **1905** W.S. Kelly *Lariats* 297: I was as drunk as a biled owl. **1907** in "O. Henry" *Works* 1379: Babbitt was in last night as full as a boiled owl. *a*1910 in J. Lomax *Cowboy Songs* 227: I got drunk as a biled owl when I left for old Arkansaw. **1914–22 Joyce *Ulysses* 306: He brought him home drunk as a boiled owl. **1925** Mullin *Tramp* 39: They were as drunk as a couple of hoot-owls! **1928** Bradford *Ol' Man Adam* 23: He was layin' up in de pilot-house, drunker'n a b'iled owl. **1944** Pyle *Brave Men*: You look like a tree full of owls! [**1942–46** MSU GF2.1 Army: Jargon: 29: *Boiled owl*—Boiled chicken, which had been in cold storage too long.] **1948** in Bradbury *Golden Apples* 38: This is Billy-boy, drunk as an owl, Huxley, old pal, drunker than *two* owls! **1968** Styron *Nat Turner* 293: Drunker than a screech owl. *Ibid.* 375: Drunker than a hoot owl. **1971** S. Stevens *Uptown* 96: This crazy old woman was crazy as a hoot owl. **1976** Hayden *Voyage* 137: He's queer as a tree full of owls.

    2. *Prost.* a nocturnal streetwalker.

    1904 *F & H* VII 77: Tart,…owl. **1942 *ATS* 471: *Owl*, a night streetwalker. **1966** S. Harris *Hellhole* 161: Molly still designates [criminals] by the names with which she first learned to identify them [*ca*1910]: "cats" or "gooks"—the small-time madams she presently meets in the House of Detention; "bats" or "owls"—streetwalkers who work at night; "griffs"—young thieves, and "gips"—old ones.

¶ In phrase:

¶ **hear the owl** [or **owls**] **hoot** *West.* to travel by night, esp. as a fugitive; *(also)* (see 1936 quot.).

    1921–26 Santee *Men* 219: Whatever Jones was wanted for wouldn't bother the old man any, for he'd heard the owls hoot himself. **1936** R. Adams *Cowboy Lingo* 229: To have many and varied experiences was to "hear the owl hoot."

owl *adj.* operating, working, open, etc., at night.—used prenominally.

    1856 in *DA*: The "Owl Train," due at Jersey City at five o'clock yesterday morning, did not arrive until afternoon. **1880** Pinkerton *Thieves & Detective* 72: The night, or the "owl" train, as it was called, always being chosen. **1889** J. Farmer *Amer.* 405: Owl car. A tram-car plying late into the night. **1891** Rodenbough *Sabre* 192: There are men who [can] sleep soundly through the night on the "owl train." **1908** W.G. Davenport *Butte & Montana* 279: Never getting home

until the owl car arrives. **1915–16** Lait *Beef, Iron & Wine* 143: He…buzzes the night clerk in the owl drugstore. *Ibid.* 165: He passed the time of night with the owl clerk. **1918** Wagar *Spotter* 13: I would change again to the evening runs, or ride the "Owl" cars. **1918** *Variety* (Aug. 2) 18: It was easy to get an "owl cab" in that neighborhood. **1945** Hubbard *R.R. Ave.* 354: *Owl*—Street-car or train that runs late at night; almost anything having to do with night. **1951** (quot. at FLEABAG, 2.b.). **1953** *St. Louis Post-Dispatch* (July 5) 1 6A: Police continued to keep watch…, with officers riding some late "owl" runs to guard against possible violence. **1969** Gordone *No Place* 429: You gave it to me long time ago when I was a lookout for you when you was pullin' them owl jobs in Queens. **1986** R. Campbell *In La-La Land* 196: I work the owl shift in the all-night drugs.

owled *adj.* OWL-EYED.

    1922–24 McIntyre *White Light* 108: 'E was owled last night, 'e was….And comical! No end! **1927 (quot. at SQUIFFY).

owl-eyed *adj.* staring from drunkenness; very drunk. Also **owly-eyed.**

    1900 *DN* II 47: *Owly-eyed*, adj. Intoxicated. **1929** T. Gordon *Born to Be* 76: Once before in my life, I had had the experience of being drunk….I was owl-eyed. **1958–65** Alfred *Hogan's Goat* 131: You're owl-eyed drunk.

owlhead *n.* **1.** [perh. orig. a trade name; cf. 1944 quot.] a kind of usu. inexpensive revolver, esp. with an owl's head device featured on the stock. Also **owl's head.**

    1927 *DN* V 457: *Owl's head*, n. A short, heavy revolver, frequently having a finger hole in the grip allowing it to be used in addition as a *knuckle duster. a*1942 in S. Kennedy *Palmetto Country* 211: Capm [*sic*] got a owl-head, just like mine,/If he beats me to the trigger, I won't mind dyin'. **1944** in *DA*: The well-known Iver-Johnson "owl head"…was a double-acting piece of unreliable rubber-stocked artillery. **1967** [R. Beck] *Pimp* 203: I'd get Preston's owl-head and take her from Leroy at gun point.

    2. *West.* an intractable horse; OUTLAW, 1.a.

    1928 Santee *Cowboy* 70: There was always owlheads in the bunch that you had to haul around. **1937** *AS* (Apr.) 153: *Owl Head.* An animal that can not be trained either to work or ride.

owlheaded *adj. West.* (of horses) stubborn; intractable.

    1928 Santee *Cowboy* 61: Some owl-headed old bronc up in the lead would decide on some place else. **1990** *CBS This Morning* (CBS-TV) (Apr. 3): He [a horse] was an owlheaded galoot.

owlhoot *n. West.* a contemptible fellow, esp. a fugitive or outlaw.—often used attrib. [Though all are now freq. in Wild West fiction, no 19th-C. evidence appears to exist for this term, *owlhoot trail*, below, or OWLHOOTER.]

    1946 N. Nye *Breed* 135: The inevitable end of an owlhoot rider. **1958** P. Field *Devil's R.* 64: Them owlhoots are holdin' the steers at the river right now. **1961** *N.Y. Times* (July 23) VII 24: Ezra attempts to pay back his debt to an owlhoot gambler. **1968** N. Nye *Lost* 64: The big trouble with owlhoots was they generally played for keeps. **1971** Selby *Roan* 37: Shooting the dirty redskin or owl-hoot or sheriff or whoever else was chasing you. **1976** Whelton *CB Baby* 258: Bushwhackers and owlhoots lurking in every ravine. **1978** T. Evans *Longarm* 128: He said I was a wanted owlhoot who deserved a good hanging. **1980** R. Hogan *Lawman's Choice* 28: There's more owlhoots collected in this one place than anywhere else I've been—except for the pen. **1981** R. Hogan *D. Bullet* 29: Once that starts, the owl-hoots will take over the country.

¶ In phrase:

¶ **owlhoot trail** *West.* the life of a fugitive or outlaw.—constr. with *the.* Cf. *hear the owl hoot* s.v. OWL, *n.*

    1936 N. Nye *No-Gun Fighter* 160: He felt no longing for the Owlhoot Trail. **1967** W. Henry *Alias* v: The facts, the places, the personalities that first sent him along the owlhoot trail. **1969** L'Amour *Conagher* 72: You can ride the owl-hoot trail, or you can play it honest. **1982** Tippette *Texas* 94: I reckon we'll have enough money we could get off the owl hoot trail for a good little while.

owlhooter *n. West.* a fugitive or outlaw; OWLHOOT.

    1942 N. Nye *Trigger* 7: Galeyville was…a boom silver camp and owl-hooter hangout. **1954** LeMay *Searchers* 108: She meant owl-hooters of course—a term applied to hunted men, who liked to travel by night. **1968** N. Nye *Lost* 65: Arizona was largely an owlhooter's paradise. **1969** M. McCoy *Guns of Greed* 13: He knocked that owlhooter down from fifty yards.

owl's head var. OWLHEAD.

owl shit *n.* SHIT (in fig. senses).—often constr. with *sour*.—usu. considered vulgar. Also occ. in euphem. forms.

    1862 Brig. Gen. S.D. Sturgis, U.S. Army, in W. Garrison *Civil War Curiosities* 232: I don't care for John Pope one pinch of owl dung. **1928–29** Nason *White Slicker* 136 [ref. to WWI]: That old bird doesn't like me for sour owl feathers. **1932** Halyburton & Goll *Shoot & Be Damned* 206 [ref. to WWI]: That big tub of sour owl milk will jazz up the detail for all of us. You'd better dust off a court martial for him. **1947** Mailer *Naked & Dead* 69: "What's this stuff [*sc.*, food]?" "It's owl shit." **1966** Kazan *Arrangement* 34: I had a position, philosophically, a lover of humanity, profoundly optimistic, while Gwen was just owl shit, really. **1966** Purdum *Bro. John* 21: He don't push for sour owl crap. **1970** Thackrey *Thief* 422: So I was kind of short with them sometimes, and Birdie, she didn't dig that for sour owlshit. **1972** D. Jenkins *Semi-Tough* 147: He said that this didn't mean he didn't love Barbara Jane....I said "Owl shit." Or something. *Ibid.* 178: "No owl shit?" I said. "No owl shit," she said. **1972** R. Wilson *Forbidden Words* 185: The boss just dropped another load of owlshit on my desk. **1972** Swarthout *Tin Lizzie* 23: He...didn't give a pinch of dried owl dung. **1975** Swarthout *Shootist* 161: The West was filling up with women like her, and he would not give a pinch of dried owl shit for the lot of them. **1977** Caputo *Rumor of War* 74: Top, you're full of sour owlshit. **1982** D.J. Williams *Hit Hard* 43 [ref. to WWII]: Some folks, white folks,...think this whole colored tank unit is just political owl shit. *Ibid.* 68: He better stop stirring up owl shit in C Company. **1984** T. Kay *Dark Thirty* 240: They ain't worth a pinch of owl shit once they make up their minds. **1985** Ark. man, age 35: That's a lot of sour owl milk. *a***1987** Bunch & Cole *Reckoning for Kings* 35: Tanks don't float worth sour owl shit. **1987** Robbins *Ravens* 200: They can't take a picture for sour owl shit.

    ¶ In prov. similes:

    ¶ **slick as owl shit** very slick (in var. senses, esp. slang senses).—usu. considered vulgar.

    *a***1954–60** in *West. Folklore* XIX (1960) 255: Texas Folk Similes...Slick as greased owl s—. [Also known in] Calif. **1967** Mailer *Vietnam* 80: Slick as owl shit. **1967–68** in *DARE*: He's poor as...owl shit. **1974** Blount *3 Bricks Shy* 44: He was poor as owl dung. **1975** C.W. Smith *Country Music* 106: You could just slide through pre-law like greased owlshit! *a***1977** in S. King *Bachman* 100: You just look slicker than *owl shit!* **1979** Crews *Blood & Grits* 35: All you got to do is find that trough and ride it, slick as owl shit. **1978** F. Downs *Killing Zone* 18: They're ignorant as owl shit, you know? **1979** Decker *Holdouts* 91: They come through here like a streak of owl shit through the pines. **1982** D.J. Williams *Hit Hard* [ref. to WWII]: Gonna be ready to pass them tests slick as owl shit. **1983** N. Proffitt *Gardens of Stone* 294: The Old Man, slicker than owl shit, says "Rocks." **1982–84** Chapple *Outlaws in Babylon* 39: The...road...is as slick as owl shit. **1986** Thacker *Pawn* 14: Monsoon rain made the hillside owlshit slick.

owly-eyed var. OWL-EYED.

own up *v.* to admit truth or responsibility; confess. Now *S.E.*

    1853 in *OEDS*: However, you "own up," and confess. **1856** Smith *Among Convicts* 98: The Old Man refused to "own up." **1858** Hammett *Piney Woods* 28: I'm willin' to own up that I'm generally considered to rather have a gift that way myself. **1877** Bartlett *Amer.* (ed. 4) 446: *Own up.* To confess; to make a clean breast. *****1880** A. Trollope, in *OED*: If you own up in a genial sort of way the House will forgive anything. **1975** Boatner et al. *Dict. Amer. Idioms* 255: When Mr. Jones asked who broke the window, Johnny owned up.

Oxy *n. Stock Market.* Occidental Petroleum, Inc.

    1983 R. Thomas *Missionary* 166: Oxy, of course, was Occidental Petroleum.

O, you ——! *interj.* (used as an admiring exclamation).—also used ironically. See also *O, you kid!* s.v. KID¹, *n.*, 1.d.

    1848 Pry *Life in Baltimore* 7: Shouting forth his favorite war cry— "Oh, you Bloody Red!" *Ibid.* 8: Oh, you Hornet! **1898** in S. Crane *Stories* 425: Oh, you pair of peaches! **1908** in H.C. Fisher *A. Mutt* 88: Oh you Sooter Street! **1910** in O. Johnson *Lawrenceville* 306: "Oh,

you ribs!" "Oh, you wishbones!" **1922** E. Rice *Machine* 128: Say, she's some jane! Oh, you baby vamp! **1946** J.H. Burns *Gallery* 217: He... hooted paternally at the GI's. "Oooh you VD!"

oyster *n.* **1.** the vagina or vulva.—usu. considered vulgar. Cf. BEARDED CLAM.

    ca*1680–1707** in J. Atkins *Sex in Lit.* IV 48: Strait the Oyster shut...and clung so fast at ev'ry Stroke. *****1902** *F & H* V 119: Oyster,...The female *pudendum*. **1994** "G. Indiana" *Rent Boy* 61: She's got her legs crossed and keeps uncrossing them again and, I have to admit, I'm thinking the whole time about that oyster of hers.

    2. a gob of phlegm; CLAM, 7.

    *****1785** Grose *Dict. Vulgar Tongue*: Oyster. A gob of thick phlegm, spit by a consumptive man; in law Latin, *unum viridum gobbum*. *****1902** *F & H* V 119: Oyster...(common).—A gob of spittle. *****1914–21** Joyce *Ulysses* 331: He spat a Red bank oyster out of him right in the corner. **1931** Stevenson *St. Luke's* 31: He spat up a big oyster of spittle on Mac's trousers. **1967** Mailer *Vietnam* 170: Cough up an oyster, roll that phlegm. **1973** Schiano & Burton *Solo* 57: I spit the oyster...right in his face. **1977** Appel *Hell's Kitchen* 6 [ref. to ca1917]: The "oyster," as they called it, hit an inch off target. *a***1990** in *Maledicta* X 33: Oyster same as *Goober.*

    3.a. a person desired or sought for a particular purpose.—constr. with prec. possessive pronoun.

    1877 Burdette *Mustache* 242: Show me yer Treasury, avick; I'm yer oyster. **1952** H. Grey *Hoods* 65: The boss of this firm is a little, fat guy, with a very large nose. He's our oyster.

    b. a close-mouthed person; CLAM, 4.b.

    1888 Pierson *Slave of Circumstances* 133: I am a reg'lar oyster, I am, for knowin' how and when to shut up. **1905** in Cather *Short Fiction* 179: Yes, he was an oyster, since you put it so....He always gave one the impression of being detached....He distrusted men pretty thoroughly and women even more. **1954–60** *DAS*: Oyster...A person who talks little. [**1957–60** in *West. Folklore* XIX (1960) 255: Texas Folk Similes...Dumb as an oyster.]

    c. an odd or foolish person; CLAM, 2.

    [**1922** C. Sandburg, in *DA*: You ain't got the sense God Gave [*sic*] an oyster.] **1949** in Bradbury *Illus. Man* 154: Gallagher, you're a queer oyster, but I love you. [**1957–60** (quot. at **(b)**, above).] **1970** E. Thompson *Garden of Sand* 238: If he was but one-tenth the man Jack said he was, his old man made everybody else's old man an oyster.

    4. a pearl. *Joc.* Also **oysterberry.**

    1917 E.R. Burroughs *Oakdale Affair* 17: Didn't you lamp de oyster harness? To say nothin' of de mitful of rocks and kale. **1935** Pollock *Und. Speaks*: Real oysters, genuine pearls. **1939** Howsley *Argot* 35: Oysterberries—Pearls.

oysters *n.pl.* illicitly distilled liquor. Now *hist.*

    1903 *Independent* (July 16) 1681: In certain sections of New Jersey and Maryland the "wet goods" are shipped in the guise of oysters. **1972** N.Y.U. student: During Prohibition when they used to run booze in from ships outside the three-mile limit—this was out near Montauk—they used to call the booze *oysters*; like, "go out and get a load of oysters."

Oz *n.* [sugg. by pronun. of *Aus*tralia with voiced sibilant, with pun on *The Wonderful Wizard of Oz* (1900), internationally celebrated children's book by U.S. author L. Frank Baum] Australia. *Joc.*

    *****1908** in *OEDAS* I. *****1944**, *****1970** in *OEDAS* I. **1985** *N.Y. Post* (Aug. 2) 10: Yanks row, row...all the way to Oz. [Dateline] Cairns, Australia—An American couple rowed into the harbor here claiming to have crossed the Pacific in their 26-foot boat, officials said yesterday.

o.z. *n. Narc.* an ounce of narcotics. Also **oh-zee.**

    1933 Ersine *Pris. Slang* 55: Dave had ten o.z.'s stashed in his room when he got nabbed. **1942–49** Goldin et al. *DAUL* 150: O.Z. An ounce of any powdered narcotic. **1952** J.C. Holmes *Go* 83: He's gotten an o.z. from a passer up on One Hundred and Twenty-fifth Street. **1953–58** J.C. Holmes *Horn* 224: Two o.z.'s of...pot. **1966** Bogner *7th Ave.* 282: Vintage Chicago light green, a sawbuck an Oh-zee. **1967** Rosenthal *Sheeper* 83: Get me an O.Z. or even half an L.B. **1974** Matthews & Amdur *Race Be Won* 26: I need a yard to cop an O.Z., so I can break it down into nickel bags. *a***1994** N. McCall

Wanna Holler 99: A four-finger O.Z., an ounce of reefer…the height of four fingers.

ozone *n.* **1.** air.

   1907 in H.C. Fisher *A. Mutt* 20: This country ozone is the thing, Augustus. **1926** Dunning & Abbott *Broadway* 244: Better give it up, Dan, while you're able and take the ozone.

   2. a curt dismissal; AIR, 2.

   1942 *ATS* 67: Ousting; discharge; dismissal.…the *ozone*.

¶ In phrase:

¶ **in the ozone** in a dazed or drowsy state; (*specif.*) such a state induced by drugs or drink.

   1971 in L. Bangs *Psychotic Reactions* 81: She is in the *O-zone!* **1975** (cited in Spears *Drugs & Drink*). **1976** Eble *Campus Slang* (Nov.) 4: *Ozone* n a state of mind reached by drink or drugs: I was in the ozone at the party. **1981** *Easyriders* (Oct.) 17: I reckon the tape went awhile, puttin' me in the ozone. **1994** Court TV (Mar. 3): He's off in the ozone.…He doesn't seem to know what's going on.

ozone *v.* [sugg. by phr. *give* [or *get*] *the air* s.v. AIR] to dismiss curtly.

   1922 *Variety* (Aug. 4) 5: I ozoned him too.

ozoned *adj.* HIGH.

   *a*1979 in Feldman et al. *Angel Dust* 171: I really digged that, you know, getting ozoned to the max.

ozoner *n.* a drive-in movie theater.

   1948 in *OEDS:* This week, New York City will get its first "ozoner": a 600-car…affair on Staten Island. **1955** Reifer *New Words* 150: *Ozoner. n. Slang.* A drive-in theater.

Ozzie *n.* [repr. usu. Austral. pronun. of AUSSIE] Orig. *Mil.* an Australian. Also as adj. Cf. Oz.

   *1918 in *OEDAS* I. **1919** *N.Y. Times* (Feb. 23): There was nothing an Ozzie liked so much as fighting with a Yankee company. **a*1980 in Partridge *Concise Dict. Sl.* 320: *Ozzy* …. I [Partridge] first noticed it, in England, in *The Times*, 24 Mar. 1977. **1993** *Early Prime* (CNN-TV) (June 16): An adventurous Ozzie lifeguard. **1995** *Simpsons* (Fox-TV): The Ozzies thought this would be a permanent thing.